KT-574-157

Stanley Gibbons
Simplified Catalogue

Stamps of the World

000000735341

Stanley Gibbons Simplified Catalogue

Stamps of the World 6

2015 Edition

Countries **Sirmoor – Zululand**

Stanley Gibbons Ltd
London and Ringwood

BY APPOINTMENT TO
HER MAJESTY THE QUEEN
PHILATELISTS
STANLEY GIBBONS LTD
LONDON

1914 - 2014

80th Edition
Published in Great Britain by
Stanley Gibbons Ltd
Publications Editorial, Sales Offices and Distribution Centre
7, Parkside, Christchurch Road,
Ringwood, Hampshire BH24 3SH
Telephone +44 (0) 1425 472363

British Library Cataloguing in
Publication Data.
A catalogue record for this book is available
from the British Library.

Volume 6
ISBN 10: 0-85259-934-X
ISBN 13: 978-0-85259-934-1

Boxed Set
ISBN 10: 0-85259-936-6
ISBN 13: 978-0-85259-936-5

Published as Stanley Gibbons Simplified Catalogue from 1934 to 1970,
renamed Stamps of the World in 1971, and produced in two (1982-88),
three (1989-2001), four (2002-2005) five (2006-2010) and six from
2011 volumes as Stanley Gibbons Simplified Catalogue of Stamps of
the World.

© Stanley Gibbons Ltd 2014

DUDLEY
LIBRARIES

000000735341

Askews & Holts	27-Oct-2014
	£275.00 per set
SED	

The contents of this catalogue, including the numbering system and
illustrations, are fully protected by copyright. No part of this publication may be reproduced, stored in a retrieval system, or transmitted,
in any form or by any means, electronic, mechanical, photocopying,
recording or otherwise, without the prior permission of Stanley Gibbons Limited. Requests for such permission should be addressed to
the Catalogue Editor at Ringwood.

This catalogue is sold on condition that it is not, by way of trade
or otherwise lent, re-sold, hired out, circulated or otherwise
disposed of other than in its complete, original and unaltered form and
without a similar condition including this condition being imposed on the
subsequent purchaser.

Errors and omissions excepted. The colour reproduction of stamps in
this catalogue is only as accurate as the printing process allows.

Item No. 2881– Set15

Printed and bound in Wales by Stephens & George

Contents – Volume 6

Gibbons Stamp Monthly

The first choice for stamp collectors since 1890

Subscribe TODAY!

"The premier philatelic magazine available anywhere – it's difficult to improve on perfection"

– Everett L. Parker, Global Stamp News

Gibbons Stamp Monthly offers you:

- Great value, usually 20-30% more pages than other stamp magazines
- More news
- More articles
- More on Great Britain and Commonwealth
- A magazine written by stamp collectors for stamp collectors
- Comprehensive catalogue supplement every month

By subscribing you will also receive:

- Monthly subscriber letters offering big discounts off Stanley Gibbons products
- Savings on the latest Stanley Gibbons catalogues
- Free access to GSM online with postal subscription

The UK's No.1 stamp magazine

3 easy ways to subscribe

 Subscription Hotline **0800 611 622** (UK)
+44 1425 472 363 (Overseas)

 subscriptions@stanleygibbons.com

 Complete the form facing this page and return to:
Gibbons Stamp Monthly, Stanley Gibbons Publications, FREEPOST (BH252), Ringwood, Hampshire, BH24 3BR, UK

www.stanleygibbons.com

Est 1856
STANLEY GIBBONS
A Stanley Gibbons Publication

Introduction

The ultimate reference work for all stamps issued around the world since the very first Penny Black of 1840, now with an improved layout.

Stamps of the World provides a comprehensive, illustrated, priced guide to postage stamps, and is the standard reference tool for every collector. It will help you to identify those elusive stamps, to value your collection, and to learn more about the background to issues. *Stamps of the World* was first published in 1934 and has been updated every year since 1950.

Included is a guide to stamp identification so that you can easily discover which country issued your stamp.

Re-designed to provide more colourful, clearer, and easy-to-navigate listings, these volumes continue to present you with a wealth of information to enhance your enjoyment of stamp collecting.

Features:

► Current values for every stamp in the world

► Easy-to-use simplified listings

► World-recognised Stanley Gibbons catalogue numbers

► A wealth of historical, geographical and currency information

► Indexing and cross-referencing throughout the volumes

► Worldwide miniature sheets listed and priced

► Thousands of new issues since the last edition

For this edition, prices have been thoroughly reviewed for Great Britain and the Channel Islands up to date, and all Commonwealth countries up to 1970, with further updates for Commonwealth countries which have appeared in our recently-published or forthcoming comprehensive catalogues under the titles *Brunei, Malaysia and Singapore, Falkland Islands, Western Pacific, St Helena and Dependencies, New Zealand and Canada*. Other countries with complete price updates from the following comprehensive catalogues are: *Italy and Switzerland, Russia* and *China*. New issues received from all other countries have been listed and priced. The first *Gibbons Stamp Monthly* Catalogue Supplement to this edition is September 2014.

Information for users

Scope of the Catalogue

Stamps of the World contains listings of postage stamps only. Apart from the ordinary definitive, commemorative and air-mail stamps of each country there are sections for the following, where appropriate. Noted below are the Prefixes used for each section (see Guide to Entries for further information):

▶ postage due stamps –	Prefix in listing D
▶ parcel post or postcard stamps –	Prefix P
▶ official stamps –	Prefix O
▶ express and special delivery stamps -	Prefix E
▶ frank stamps –	Prefix F
▶ charity tax stamps –	Prefix J
▶ newspaper and journal stamps –	Prefix N
▶ printed matter stamps –	Prefix P
▶ registration stamps -	Prefix R
▶ acknowledgement of receipt stamps –	Prefix AR
▶ late fee and too late stamps –	Prefix L
▶ military post stamps-	Prefix M
▶ recorded message stamps –	Prefix RM
▶ personal delivery stamps –	Prefix P
▶ concessional letter post –	Prefix CL
▶ concessional parcel post –	Prefix CP
▶ pneumatic post stamps –	Prefix PE
▶ publicity envelope stamps –	Prefix B
▶ bulk mail stamps –	Prefix BP
▶ telegraph stamps used for postage –	Prefix PT
▶ telegraph stamps (Commonwealth Countries) –	Prefix T
▶ obligatory tax –	Prefix T

As this is a simplified listing, the following are NOT included:

Fiscal or revenue stamps: stamps used solely in collecting taxes or fees for non-postal purposes. For example, stamps which pay a tax on a receipt, represent the stamp duty on a contract, or frank a customs document. Common inscriptions found include: Documentary, Proprietary, Internal Revenue and Contract Note.

Local stamps: postage stamps whose validity and use are limited in area to a prescribed district, town or country, or on certain routes where there is no government postal service. They may be issued by private carriers and freight companies, municipal authorities or private individuals.

Local carriage labels and Private local issues: many labels exist ostensibly to cover the cost of ferrying mail from one of Great Britain's offshore islands to the nearest mainland post office. They are not recognised as valid for national or international mail. Examples: Calf of Man, Davaar, Herm, Lundy, Pabay, Stroma.

Telegraph stamps: stamps intended solely for the prepayment of telegraphic communication.

Bogus or "phantom" stamps: labels from mythical places or non-existent administrations. Examples in the classical period were Sedang, Counani, Clipperton Island and in modern times Thomond and Monte Bello Islands. Numerous labels have also appeared since the War from dissident groups as propaganda for their claims and without authority from the home governments. Common examples are the numerous issues for Nagaland.

Railway letter fee stamps: special stamps issued by railway companies for the conveyance of letters by rail. Example: Talyllyn Railway. Similar services are now offered by some bus companies and the labels they issue likewise do not qualify for inclusion in the catalogue.

Perfins ("perforated initials"): stamps perforated with the initials or emblems of firms as a security measure to prevent pilferage by office staff.

Labels: Slips of paper with an adhesive backing. Collectors tend to make a distinction between stamps, which have postal validity and anything else, which has not.

Cut-outs: Embossed or impressed stamps found on postal stationery, which are cut out if the stationery has been ruined and re-used as adhesives.

Further information on a wealth of terms is in *Philatelic Terms Illustrated*, published by Stanley Gibbons, details are listed under Stanley Gibbons Publications. There is also a priced listing of the postal fiscals of Great Britain in our *Commonwealth & British Empire Stamps 1840-1970* Catalogue and in Volume 1 of the *Great Britain Specialised Catalogue* (5th and later editions). A full list of our current publications is given on page xiv

Organisation of the Catalogue

The catalogue lists countries in alphabetical order with country headers on each page and extra introductory information such as philatelic historical background at the beginning of each section. The Contents list provides a detailed guide to each volume, and the Index has full cross-referencing to locate each country in each volume.

Each country lists postage stamps in order of date of issue, from earliest to most recent, followed by separate sections for categories such as postage due stamps, express stamps, official stamps, and so on (see above for a complete listing).

"Appendix" Countries

Since 1968 Stanley Gibbons has listed in an appendix stamps which are judged to be in excess of true postal needs. The appendix also contains stamps which have not fulfilled all the

normal conditions for full catalogue listing. Full catalogue listing requires a stamp to be:

▶ issued by a legitimate postal authority

▶ recognised by the government concerned

▶ adhesive

▶ valid for proper postal use in the class of service for which they are inscribed

▶ available to the general public at face value with no artificial restrictions being imposed on their distribution (with the exception of categories such as postage dues and officials)

Only stamps issued from component parts of otherwise united territories which represent a genuine political, historical or postal division within the country concerned have a full catalogue listing. Any such issues which do not fulfil this stipulation will be recorded in the Catalogue Appendix only.

Stamps listed in the Appendix are constantly under review in light of newly acquired information about them. If we are satisfied that a stamp qualifies for proper listing in the body of the catalogue it will be moved in the next edition.

"Undesirable Issues"

The rules governing many competitive exhibitions are set by the Federation Internationale de Philatelie and stipulate a downgrading of marks for stamps classed as "undesirable issues".

This catalogue can be taken as a guide to status. All stamps in the main listings are acceptable. Stamps in the Appendix are considered, "undesirable issues" and should not be entered for competition.

Correspondence

We welcome information and suggestions but we must ask correspondents to include the cost of postage for the return of any materials, plus registration where appropriate. Letters and emails should be addressed to Lorraine Holcombe, 7 Parkside, Christchurch Road, Ringwood, Hampshire BH24 3SH, UK. lholcombe@stanleygibbons.co.uk. Where information is

solicited purely for the benefit of the enquirer we regret we are seldom able to reply.

Identification of Stamps

We regret we do not give opinion on the authenticity of stamps, nor do we identify stamps or number them by our Catalogue.

Thematic Collectors

Stanley Gibbons publishes a range of thematic catalogues (see page xiv for details) and *Stamps of the World* is ideal to use with these titles, as it supplements those listings with extra information.

Type numbers

Type numbers (in bold) refer to illustrations, and are not the Stanley Gibbons Catalogue numbers.

A brief description of the stamp design subject is given below or beside the Illustrations, or close by in the entry, where needed. Where a design is not illustrated, it is usually the same shape and size as a related design, unless otherwise indicated.

Watermarks

Watermarks are not covered in this catalogue. Stamps of the same issue with differing watermarks are not listed separately.

Perforations

Perforations – all stamps are perforated unless otherwise stated. No distinction is made between the various gauges of perforation but early stamp issues which exist both imperforate and perforated are usually listed separately. Where a heading states, "Imperf or perf"or "Perf. or rouletted" this does not necessarily mean that all values of the issue are found in both conditions

Se-tenant Pairs

Se-tenant Pairs – Many modern issues are printed in sheets containing different designs or face values. Such pairs, blocks, strips or sheets are described as being "*se-tenant*" and they are outside the scope of this catalogue, although reference to them may occur in instances where they form a composite design.

Miniature Sheets are now fully listed.

Guide to Entries

Ⓐ Country of Issue

Ⓑ Part Number – shows where to find more detailed listings in the Stanley Gibbons Comprehensive Catalogue. Part 6 refers to France and so on – see p. li for further information on the breakdown of the Catalogue.

Ⓒ Country Information – Brief geographical and historical details for the issuing country.

Ⓓ Currency – Details of the currency, and dates of earliest use where applicable, on the face value of the stamps. Where a Colony has the same currency as the Mother Country, see the details given in that country.

Ⓔ Year Date – When a set of definitive stamps has been issued over several years the Year Date given is for the earliest issue, commeorative sets are listed in chronological order. As stamps of the same design or issue are usually grouped together, a list of King George VI stamps, for example, headed "1938" may include stamps issued from 1938 to the end of the reign.

Ⓕ Stanley Gibbons Catalogue number – This is a unique number for each stamp to help the collector identify stamps in the listing. The Stanley Gibbons numbering system is universally recognized as definitive. The majority of listings are in chronological order, but where a definitive set of stamps has been re-issued with a new watermark, perforation change or imprint date, the cheapest example is given; in such cases catalogue numbers may not be in numerical order.

Where insufficient numbers have been left to provide for additional stamps to a listing, some stamps will have a suffix letter after the catalogue number. If numbers have been left for additions to a set and not used they will be left vacant.

The separate type numbers (in bold) refer to illustrations (see M).

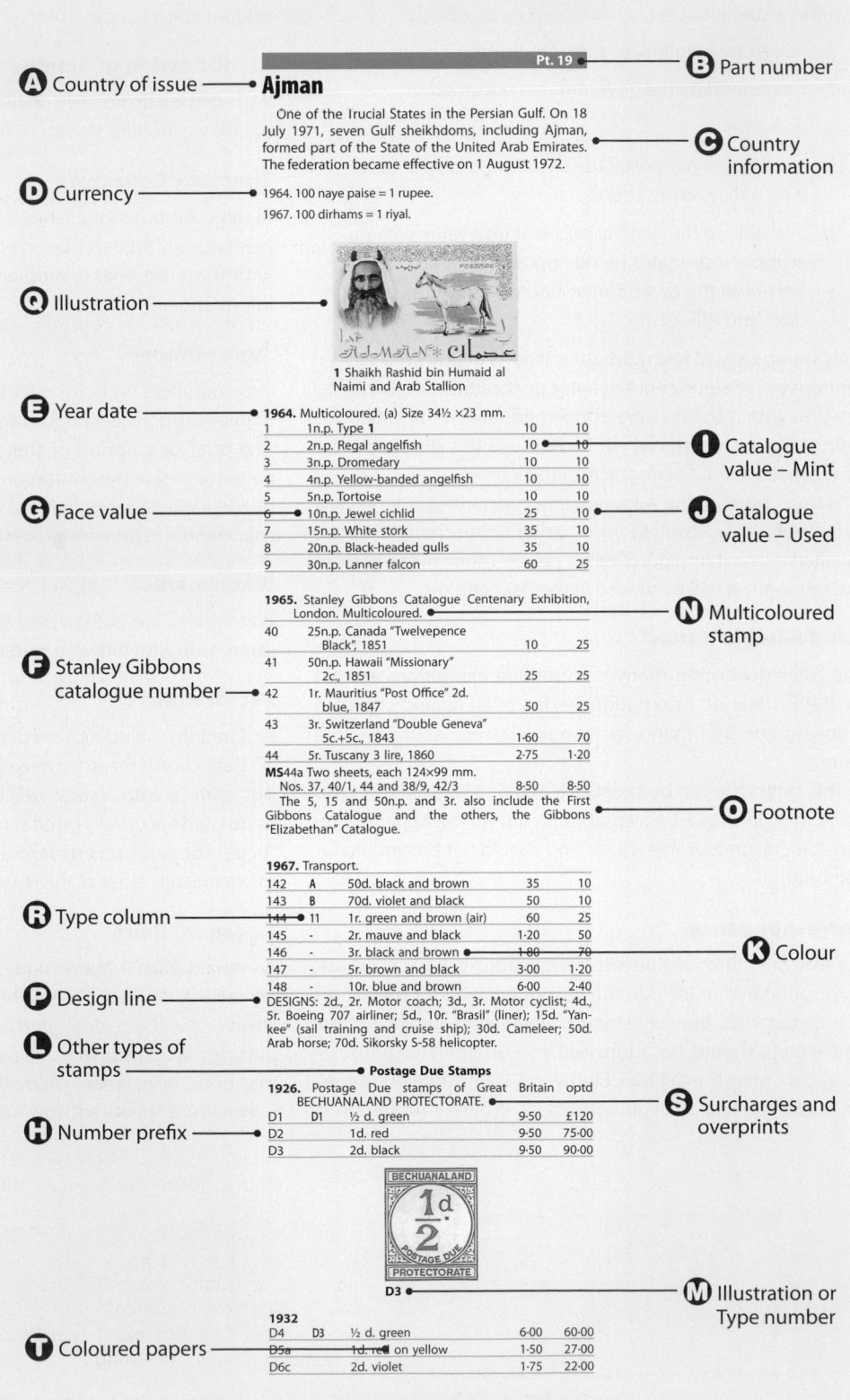

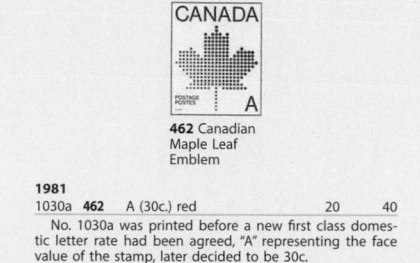

462 Canadian
Maple Leaf
Emblem

1981
1030a **462** A (30c.) red   20   40
No. 1030a was printed before a new first class domestic letter rate had been agreed, "A" representing the face value of the stamp, later decided to be 30c.

Ⓖ Face value – This refers to the value of each stamp and is the price it was sold for at the Post Office when issued. Some modern stamps do not have their values in figures but instead shown as a letter, see for example the entry above for Canada 1030a/Illustration 462.

Ⓗ Number Prefix – Stamps other than definitives and commemoratives have a prefix letter before the catalogue number. Such stamps may be found at the end of the normal listing for each country. (See Scope of the Catalogue p.viii for a list of other types of stamps covered, together with the list of the main abbreviations used in the Catalogue).

Other prefixes are also used in the Catalogue. Their use is explained in the text: some examples are A for airmail, E for East Germany or Express Delivery stamps.

Ⓘ Catalogue Value – Mint/Unused. Prices quoted for pre-1945 stamps are for lightly hinged examples. Prices quoted of unused King Edward VIII to Queen Elizabeth II issues are for unmounted mint.

Ⓙ Catalogue Value – Used. Prices generally refer to fine postally used examples. For certain issues they are for cancelled-to-order.

Prices

Prices are given in pence and pounds. Stamps worth £100 and over are shown in whole pounds:

Shown in Catalogue as	
10	10 pence
1.75	£1.75
15.00	£15
£150	£150
£2300	£2300

Prices assume stamps are in 'fine condition'; we may ask more for superb and less for those of lower quality. The minimum catalogue price quoted is 10p and is intended as a guide for catalogue users. The lowest price for individual stamps purchased from Stanley Gibbons is £1.

Prices quoted are for the cheapest variety of that particular stamp. Differences of watermark, perforation, or other details, outside the scope of this catalogue, often increase the value. Prices quoted for mint issues are for single examples. Those in *se-tenant* pairs, strips, blocks or sheets may be worth more. Where no prices are listed it is either because the stamps are not known to exist in that particular condition, or, more usually, because there is no reliable information on which to base their value.

All prices are subject to change without prior notice and we cannot guarantee to supply all stamps as priced. Prices quoted in advertisements are also subject to change without prior notice. Due to differing production schedules it is possible that new editions of Parts 2 to 22 will show revised prices which are not included in that year's Stamps of the World.

Ⓚ Colour – Colour of stamp (if fewer than four colours, otherwise noted as "multicoloured"– see N below). Colour descriptions are simple in this catalogue, and only expanded to aid identification – see other more comprehensive Stanley Gibbons catalogues for more detailed colour descriptions (see p.xxxix).

Where stamps are printed in two or more colours, the central portion of the design is the first colour given, unless otherwise stated.

Ⓛ Other Types of Stamps – See Scope of the Catalogue p.viii for a list of the types of stamps included.

Ⓜ Illustration or Type Number – These numbers are used to help identify stamps, either in the listing, type column, design line or footnote, usually the first value in a set. These type numbers are in a bold type face – **123**; when bracketed (**123**) an overprint or a surcharge is indicated. Some type numbers include a lower-case letter – **123a**, this indicates they have been added to an existing set. N   Multicoloured – Nearly all modern stamps are multicoloured; this is indicated in the heading, with a description of the stamp given in the listing.

Ⓞ Footnote – further information on background or key facts on issues

Ⓟ Design line – Further details on design variations

Ⓠ Illustration – Generally, the first stamp in the set. Stamp illustrations are reduced to 60%, with overprints and surcharges shown actual size.

Ⓡ Key Type – indicates a design type (see p. xii for further details) on which the stamp is based. These are the bold figures found below each illustration. The type numbers are also given in bold in the second column of figures alongside the stamp description to indicate the design of each stamp. Where an issue comprises stamps of similar design, the corresponding type number should be taken as indicating the general design. Where there are blanks in the type number column it means that the type of the corresponding stamp is that shown by the number in the type column of the same issue. A dash (–) in the type column means that the stamp is not illustrated. Where type numbers refer to stamps of another country, e.g. where stamps of one country are overprinted for use in another, this is always made clear in the text.

Ⓢ Surcharges and Overprints – usually described in the headings. Any actual wordings are shown in bold type. Descriptions clarify words and figures used in the overprint. Stamps with the same overprints in different colours are not listed separately. Numbers in brackets after the descriptions are the catalogue numbers of the non-overprinted stamps. The words "inscribed" or "inscription" refer to the wording incorporated in the design of a stamp and not surcharges or overprints.

Ⓣ Coloured Papers – stamps printed on coloured paper are shown – e.g. "brn on yell" indicates brown printed on yellow paper. No information on the texture of paper, e.g. laid or wove, is provided in this catalogue.

Key-Types

Standard designs frequently occuring on the stamps of the French, German, Portuguese and Spanish colonies are illustrated below together with the descriptive names and letters by which they are referred to in the lists to avoid repetition. Please see the Guide to Entries for further information.

French Group

A "Blanc" B "Mouchon" C "Merson" D "Tablet"

INTERNATIONAL COLONIAL EXHIBITION

E F " G H

I "Faidherbe" J "Palms" K "Balay" L "Natives" M "Figure"

German Group

N "Yacht" O "Yacht"

Spanish Group

X "Alfonso XII" Y "Baby" Z "Curly Head"

Portuguese Group

P "Crown" Q "Embossed" R "Figures" S "Carlos" T "Manoel" U Ceres V "Newspaper" W "Due"

PHILATELY UNDERSTOOD

Don't think we can pay you up to 36% more?

Collectors are right to be wary of lofty claims but there may be good reasons why you may find some of them to be true

The stamp market constantly fluctuates so that at any given moment **if there is too much of what you wish to sell on the market,** despite what anybody claims, no dealer can offer you **massively** more.

However, there may be good reasons why some stamp organisations can offer you **significantly more** and **pay you immediately** rather than waiting months for the unknown of what you may or may not sell at auction – and you will be waiting even longer for payment.

It all depends upon that stamp dealer's/ auction's business model. UPA buys and sells globally but if for example the nearest stamp dealer you approach only sells British stamps to a small market place then there is a strong possibility that he/she may be fully stocked already – so that if a price is proffered to you there is an increased likelihood of your receiving a lower offer as your collection, or part of your collection may be 'traded on' to a larger dealer. **Worse still,** other unrelated areas of your collection *may be neglected or not valued* in any offer you receive.

If you consign your collection to auction and it is unsuitable or too time-consuming for that auction to 'break' it into smaller lots – then there is a very strong probability that you will be paying an auction to sell your stamps to a stamp dealer **WHO could afford to pay you up to 36% more than you will receive.** Don't forget most auctions charge the **buyer of your collection up to twice the commission, or more, that they charge you.**

It **doesn't make sense** for you to pay an auction to sell your stamps to a stamp dealer, when – if you handle the transaction wisely – you can receive the up to 36% more for yourself.

What happens when you ask UPA to make you an offer?

First we ask you to tell us about your collection *and we listen.* Then we ask you how much you know about the market for your type of collection? At this stage we add to your knowledge, informing you of current conditions you may be unaware of. Then we discuss whether we may be well placed to assist you and how that may be achieved.

Providing your collection has sufficient potential we may offer to visit without charge or obligation, or we will offer to uplift your collection from your home at our expense, insured in transit (and whilst in our care) free of charge. If you are situated in mainland UK and your collection is too bulky for you to pack, provided your collection is valuable enough, we may even provide a

free packing service in addition to shipping to our office.

Now we assess your collection and offer you the choice of agreeing a price that will be paid immediately – or of our bidding against other dealers so that you know you are achieving the best possible price.

UNSOLICITED TESTIMONIAL:

Dear Folk at UPA,

I've dealt with the public for 37 + years, and as both a consumer, and a businessman, I have created huge numbers of orders from all over the world from a complete range of suppliers from all aspects of our daily lives.

But I don't believe I have ever encountered such sensitivity, such kind thought, such understanding as I have with you in our initial meeting, our subsequent successful transaction, and now this.

I recall well the item you highlight, and realise that this one item has such colossal personal value, I could never part with it.

It has been an absolute pleasure dealing with yourself, and I am more than willing for you to use this e-mail as commendation to others who may be thinking of disposing of their collection.

Many, many thanks for a memorable experience, and I will try to emulate your thought and care in my own business sphere.

Yours sincerely

D. E. B. Bath, UK

SCOTTISH & NORTH OFFICE – BUYER

COTSWOLD, MIDLANDS & SOUTH – BUYER

National number please contact: Andrew McGavin or John Cowell on 01451 861 111 number please contact: Andrew McGavin or John Cowell on 01451 861 111

Guarantee: We guarantee that you will never be under pressure at any stage of the process; you will always be in control. E mail or Contact UPA now: 01451 861 111

Why can UPA often pay considerably more?

We often buy at auction. That auction takes the **"up to 36% more" that we pay that you DO NOT RECEIVE.**

However – there is another equally important reason …. namely **The UPA Business Model.** Unlike most dealers we believe that if an item is not selling, then it must be too expensive. This is the reason why when you receive our quarterly catalogues of up to 20,671 different lots (you can request a sample one free) … you will find that if an item has been previously unsold **we actually tell you.** Furthermore each time an item is unsold we reduce the price and **we keep on reducing the price – until finally the lot sells** or it is given away. In practice good material sells quickly whilst other material finally finds its own price and sells. This is the reason

why there are always 1,000's of new offers at UPA …. and part of the reason why we are usually in a position to pay you more and pay you immediately.

Furthermore, unlike some, UPA has not one but **4 different selling systems** selling 95% of stamps to collectors, so that when a collection is purchased the most valuable/interesting stamps go into our Universal Philatelic Auctions (a NEW UPA UK record 1,750 different bidders in the last auction). Intermediate/lower-priced sets/ singles enter our Omniphil and Avon Approvals systems (established 56 years and over 1,350 regular collector clients), inexpensive stamps enter the Avon Mixtures system and eBay (universalphilatelic) for surplus material. All of which is why UPA can purchase and pay for almost literally anything.....

WHAT DOES UPA BUY?

UPA literally purchases almost any country collection worth £250 upwards from sets and singles to classics and entire British, British Empire, Europe and World collections. At the moment UPA has **exceptional demand for original collections and GB and British Empire** in particular.

What do I do next?

You contact UPA and talk to one of our friendly Team who will help to inform you so that you can decide how to progress matters …. there is no charge and no obligation …. please **CONTACT UPA NOW.**

Remember, if you are selling a collection …. collectors buy the stamps they are missing; this is why dealers exist. Most intact collections offered at auction sell to dealers. **Save commissions and uncertainty by contacting UPA today.** We guarantee that you will never be under pressure at any stage of the process, you will always be in control. **CONTACT our friendly UPA Team NOW:** 01451 861 111

To read the rest of this series 'SELLING YOUR STAMPS?' see the relevant pages in each volume:

Summary Tip 18 – Volume 1 (opposite Key Types)
Summary Tip 19 – Volume 2 (opposite Key Types)
Summary Tip 20 – Volume 3 (opposite Key Types)
Summary Tip 21 – Volume 4 (opposite Key Types)
Summary Tip 22 – Volume 5 (opposite Key Types)

STAMPS! WE LOVE THEM! Buying or selling your stamps? Collectors – we have four different departments that can help you find all the stamps you want. Our Auctions have up to 20,671 lots in our famous quarterly auctions.

Visit **www.upastampauctions.co.uk** when you want to buy or sell stamps.

If you'd like to receive the rest of the series, why not sign up for our **FREE** Stamp Tips of The Trade via our website

ANDREW PROMOTING PHILATELY ON THE ALAN TITCHMARSH SHOW ITV

TIPS OF THE TRADE
Your Expert Guide to Stamp Collecting

£53 OFF

REQUEST MY 'TIPS OF THE TRADE' FREE BOOKLET

If you'd like to discuss the sale of your collection

please contact Elaine or Andrew on 01451 861111

UNIVERSAL PHILATELIC AUCTIONS, 4 The Old Coalyard, West End Northleach, Glos. GL54 3HE UK

Tel: 01451 861111 • Fax: 01451 861297

www.upastampauctions.co.uk • sellSG@upastampauctions.co.uk

Stanley Gibbons
Stamp Catalogues

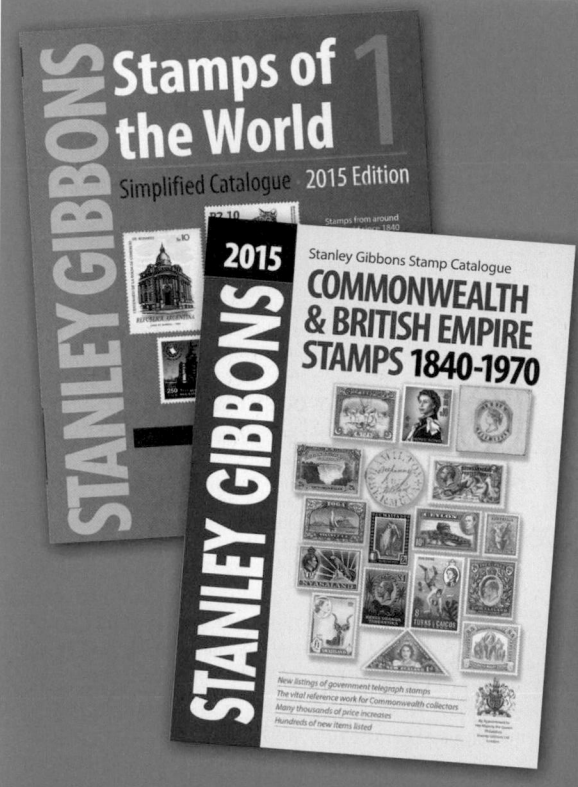

1 Commonwealth & British Empire Stamps 1840–1970 (117th edition, 2015)

Commonwealth Country Catalogues

Australia & Dependencies (9th Edition, 2014)
Bangladesh, Pakistan & Sri Lanka (2nd edition, 2010)
Belize, Guyana, Trinidad & Tobago (2nd edition, 2013)
Brunei, Malaysia & Singapore (4th edition, 2013)
Canada (5th edition, 2014)
Central Africa (2nd edition, 2008)
Cyprus, Gibraltar & Malta (3rd edition, 2011)
East Africa with Egypt & Sudan (3rd edition, 2014)
Eastern Pacific (2nd edition, 2011)
Falkland Islands (6th edition, 2013)
Hong Kong (4th edition, 2013)
India (including Convention & Feudatory States) (4th edition, 2013)
Indian Ocean (2nd edition, 2012)
Ireland (4th edition, 2011)
Leeward Islands (2nd edition, 2012)
New Zealand (5th edition, 2014)
Northern Caribbean, Bahamas & Bermuda (3rd edition, 2013)
St. Helena & Dependencies (5th edition, 2014)
Southern Africa (2nd edition, 2008)
Southern & Central Africa (1st edition, 2011)
West Africa (2nd edition, 2012)
Western Pacific (3rd edition, 2014)
Windward Islands & Barbados (2nd edition, 2012)

Stamps of the World 2015

Volume 1   Abu Dhabi – Charkhari
Volume 2   Chile – Georgia
Volume 3   German Commands – Jasdan
Volume 4   Jersey – New Republic
Volume 5   New South Wales – Singapore
Volume 6   Sirmoor – Zululand

We also produce a range of thematic catalogues for use with Stamps of the World.

Great Britain Catalogues

Collect British Stamps (65th edition, 2014)
Collect Channel Islands & Isle of Man (29th edition, 2014)
Great Britain Concise Stamp Catalogue (29th edition, 2014)

Great Britain Specialised

Volume 1   Queen Victoria (16th edition, 2012)
Volume 2   King Edward VII to King George VI (13th edition, 2009)
Volume 3   Queen Elizabeth II Pre-decimal issues (12th edition, 2011)
Volume 4   Queen Elizabeth II Decimal Definitive Issues – Part 1 (10th edition, 2008)
Queen Elizabeth II Decimal Definitive Issues – Part 2 (10th edition, 2010)

Foreign Countries

2   **Austria & Hungary** (7th edition, 2009)
3   **Balkans** (5th edition, 2009)
4   **Benelux** (6th edition, 2010)
5   **Czech Republic, Slovakia & Poland** (7th edition, 2012)
6   **France** (7th edition, 2010)
7   **Germany** (10th edition, 2012)
8   **Italy & Switzerland** (8th edition, 2013)
9   **Portugal & Spain** (6th edition, 2011)
10   **Russia** (7th edition, 2014)
11   **Scandinavia** (7th edition, 2013)
15   **Central America** (3rd edition, 2007)
16   **Central Asia** (4th edition, 2006)
17   **China** (10th edition, 2014)
18   **Japan & Korea** (5th edition, 2008)
19   **Middle East** (7th edition, 2009)
20   **South America** (4th edition, 2008)
21   **South-East Asia** (5th edition, 2012)
22   **United States of America** (7th edition, 2010)

We have catalogues to suit every aspect of stamp collecting

Our catalogues cover stamps issued from across the globe - from the Penny Black to the latest issues. Whether you're a specialist in a certain reign or a thematic collector, we should have something to suit your needs. All catalogues include the famous SG numbering system, making it as easy as possible to find the stamp you're looking for.

To order, call 01425 472 363 or for our full range of catalogues, visit www.stanleygibbons.com

Est 1856
STANLEY GIBBONS

Stanley Gibbons Limited
7 Parkside, Christchurch Road, Ringwood, Hants, BH24 3SH
+44 (0)1425 472 363
www.stanleygibbons.com

Stanley Gibbons
Ultra Violet Lamp

The only UV lamp that works in daylight

Ideal for detecting phosphor papers and inks for the majority of 20th century Machin stamps of Great Britain, plus Israel, USA, Finland and the early phosphors of Canada, Norway, Mexico, France, Hong Kong, People's Republic of China, Russia and later issues of Canada and Mexico.

£99.95

Prices correct as of August 2014 and are subject to change

- Shows fluorescent bands, papers and other devices
- Highlights cleaned pen cancellations and paper repairs
- Powerful bulb gives much stronger reaction than other lamps
- Effective in daylight/artificial light using special eye-piece

- Spectrum of 254 to 390 nm both 'short' and 'long' wavelengths
- Safe to use due to shielded UV light
- Lightweight pocket-size - ideal for fairs and exhibitions
- Long-life bulb will give 50,000 hours of use under normal viewing conditions

To order, call **0800 611 622** or visit **www.stanleygibbons.com**

Est 1856

STANLEY GIBBONS

Stanley Gibbons Limited
7 Parkside, Christchurch Road, Ringwood, Hants, BH24 3SH
+44 (0)1425 472 363
www.stanleygibbons.com

no penguins were harmed during the making of this advert

LOOKING
FOR SOMETHING DIFFERENT?

GREAT BRITAIN & COMMONWEALTH • CLASSIC TO MODERN • WWW.ZEBOOSE.COM

Stanley Gibbons
www.stanleygibbons.com

BY APPOINTMENT TO
HER MAJESTY THE QUEEN
PHILATELISTS
STANLEY GIBBONS LTD
LONDON

Stanley Gibbons - the home of stamp collecting since 1856 and today's market leader for all your philatelic needs.

For the best quality in stamps, catalogues, albums and all other accessories log on to our website today and explore our unrivalled range of products all available at the touch of a button.

visit **www.stanleygibbons.com**

Est 1856
STANLEY GIBBONS

Stanley Gibbons Limited
399 Strand, London, WC2R 0LX
+44 (0)20 7557 4444
www.stanleygibbons.com

Pt. 1

SIRMOOR

A state of the Punjab, India. Now uses Indian stamps.

12 pies = 1 anna; 16 annas = 1 rupee.

1 (1 pice)

1876

1	**1**	1pice green	28·00	£450
2	**1**	1pice blue	8·00	£225

2

1892

3*b*	**2**	1p. green	1·25	1·25
4	**2**	1pice blue	2·75	1·25

3 Raja Shamsher Parkash

1885

5*a*	**3**	3p. brown	40	50
6a	**3**	3p. orange	75	30
7*c*	**3**	6p. green	75	60
8*d*	**3**	1a. blue	50	3·00
9*a*	**3**	2a. red	3·50	3·00

4 Indian Elephant

1895

22	**4**	3p. orange	7·00	40
23	**4**	6p. green	3·00	75
24	**4**	1a. blue	11·00	3·00
25	**4**	2a. red	10·00	3·00
26	**4**	3a. green	35·00	60·00
27	**4**	4a. green	30·00	38·00
28	**4**	8a. blue	35·00	42·00
29	**4**	1r. red	55·00	£110

5 Raja Shamsher Parkash

1899

30	**5**	3a. green	8·50	22·00
31	**5**	4a. green	11·00	30·00
32	**5**	8a. blue	13·00	35·00
33	**5**	1r. red	20·00	75·00

OFFICIAL STAMPS

1890. Optd **On S. S. S.**

60	**3**	3p. orange	1·00	50
79	**3**	6p. green	1·75	60
80	**3**	1a. blue	35	70
63*a*	**3**	2a. red	9·00	7·00

Pt. 11

SLESVIG

Stamps issued during the plebiscite of 1920.

100 pfennig = 1 German mark. 100 ore = 1 Danish Krone.

1 Arms

3 Rural View

1920

1	**1**	2½pf. grey	25	1·00
2	**1**	5pf. green	25	1·00
3	**1**	7½pf. brown	25	1·00
4	**1**	10pf. red	25	1·00
5	**1**	15pf. purple	25	1·00
6	**1**	20pf. blue	25	1·00
7	**1**	25pf. orange	45	1·00
8	**1**	35pf. brown	55	1·20
9	**1**	40pf. violet	45	1·00
10	**1**	75pf. green	55	1·00
11	**3**	1m. brown	55	1·00
12	**3**	2m. blue	80	1·50
13	**3**	5m. green	1·70	2·00
14	**3**	10m. red	4·50	4·00

1920. Values in Danish currency and optd **1. ZONE**.

29	**1**	1ore grey	25	3·00
30	**1**	5ore green	25	1·50
31	**1**	7ore brown	25	2·00
32	**1**	10ore red	25	2·00
33	**1**	15ore purple	25	3·00
34	**1**	20ore blue	25	3·50
35	**1**	25ore orange	25	10·00
36	**1**	35ore brown	1·10	18·00
37	**1**	40ore violet	35	6·00
38	**1**	75ore green	55	10·00
39	**3**	1k. brown	80	16·00
40	**3**	2k. blue	9·00	60·00
41	**3**	5k. green	4·50	60·00
42	**3**	10k. red	10·50	£110

OFFICIAL STAMPS

1920. Nos. 1/14 optd **C.I.S.** (= "Comission Interalliee Slesvig").

O15	**1**	2½pf. grey	85·00	£130
O16	**1**	5pf. green	85·00	£150
O17	**1**	7½pf. brown	85·00	£130
O18	**1**	10pf. red	85·00	£160
O19	**1**	15pf. red	55·00	85·00
O20	**1**	20pf. blue	85·00	90·00
O21	**1**	25pf. orange	£170	£225
O22	**1**	35pf. brown	£170	£225
O23	**1**	40pf. violet	£150	£150
O24	**1**	75pf. green	£170	£350
O25	**3**	1m. brown	£170	£350
O26	**3**	2m. blue	£250	£375
O27	**3**	5m. green	£375	£550
O28	**3**	10m. red	£700	£850

Pt. 5

SLOVAKIA

Formerly part of Hungary, Slovakia joined with Bohemia and Moravia in 1918 to form Czechoslovakia. From 1939 to 1945 they were separate states.

In 1993 the federation of Czechoslovakia was dissolved and Slovakia became an independent republic.

100 haleru = 1 koruna.
2009 100c. = €1

A. REPUBLIC OF SLOVAKIA

1939. Stamps of Czechoslovakia optd **Slovensky stat 1939**.

2	**34**	5h. blue	1·30	1·70
3	**34**	10h. brown	15	10
4	**34**	20h. red	15	10
5	**34**	25h. green	4·25	5·00
6	**34**	30h. purple	15	10
7	**59**	40h. blue	15	35
8	**60a**	50h. green	15	10
9	**66**	50h. green	15	10
10	**60a**	60h. violet	15	10
11	**60a**	60h. blue	14·00	18·00
12	**61**	1k. purple	15	10
13	-	1k.20 purple (No. 354)	80	1·00
14	**64**	1k.50 red	80	1·00
15	-	1k.60 green (No. 355a)	2·20	3·50
16	-	2k. green (No. 356)	2·20	3·50
17	-	2k.50 blue (No. 357)	85	1·10
18	-	3k. brown (No. 358)	85	1·10
19	-	3k.50 violet (No. 359)	26·00	34·00
20	**65**	4k. violet	19·00	21·00
21	-	5k. green (No. 361)	25·00	29·00
22	-	10k. blue (No. 362)	£250	£225

4 Father Hlinka

1939. As T **4**, but inscr "CESKO-SLOVENSKO SLOVENSKA POSTA", optd **SLOVENSKY STAT**.

23	**4**	50h. green	1·40	85
24	**4**	1k. red	1·40	85

1939. Perf or imperf (20, 30h.), perf (others).

25	5h. blue	60	75
26	10h. green	1·00	1·20
27a	20h. red	85	95
28	30h. violet	1·00	1·20
29	50h. green	1·00	1·20
33	1k. red	1·00	85
31	2k.50 blue	1·50	50
35a	3k. sepia	1·90	1·20

See also No. 81.

7 Krivan

8 Chamois

9 Mgr. Tiso

10 Weaving

11 Sawyer

12 Presidential Palace, Bratislava

1939

40	-	5h. green	40	40
41	**7**	10h. brown	20	15
42	-	20h. grey	20	15
43	**8**	25h. brown	65	40
44	-	30h. brown	50	40
45	**9**	50h. green	50	65
46	**9**	70h. brown	35	25
47	**10**	2k. green	6·75	80
48	**11**	4k. brown	1·60	1·30
49	-	5k. red	1·20	65
50	**12**	10k. blue	1·10	1·30

DESIGNS—As Type **7**: 5h., Zelene Pleso; 20h. Kvety Satier (Edelweiss); 30h. Javorina. As Type **11**: 5k. Woman filling ewer at spring.

For 10 to 50h. values in larger size, see Nos. 125/9.

13 Rev. J. Murgas and Wireless Masts

1939. Tenth Death Anniv of Rev. J. Murgas.

52	**13**	1k.20 grey	[illegible]	[illegible]
53	**13**	60h. violet	[illegible]	40

1939. Child Welfare. As No. 45 but larger (24×30 mm) and inscr "+2.50 DETOM".

54	2k.50+2k.50 blue	4·25	5·25

14 Heinkel He 111C over Lake Csorba

15 Heinkel He 116A over Tatra Mountains

16 Eagle and Aero A-204

1939. Air.

55	**14**	30h. violet	50	65
56	**14**	50h. green	50	65
57	**14**	1k. red	50	65
58	**15**	2k. green	75	1·00
59	**15**	3k. brown	1·10	1·60
60	**15**	4k. blue	2·40	3·25
62	**16**	5k. purple	1·90	2·50
63	**16**	10k. grey	2·40	3·25
64	**16**	20k. green	2·75	4·00

17 Stiavnica Castle

1941

65	**17**	1k.20 purple	30	25
66	-	1k.50 red (Lietava)	30	25
67	-	1k.60 blue (Spissky Hrad)	30	25
68	-	2k. green (Bojnice)	30	25

18 S. M. Daxner and Bishop Moyses

1941. 80th Anniv of Presentation of Slovak Memorandum to Emperor Francis Joseph.

69	**18**	50h. green	2·40	2·40
70	**18**	1k. blue	9·50	11·00
71	**18**	2k. black	7·75	8·50

19 Wounded Soldier and Red Cross Orderly

1941. Red Cross Fund.

72	**19**	50h.+50h. green	55	75
73	**19**	1k.+1k. purple	75	95
74	**19**	2k.+1k. blue	2·40	3·00

20 Mother and Child

1941. Child Welfare Fund.

75	**20**	50h.+50h. green	1·00	1·20
76	**20**	1k.+1k. brown	1·00	1·20
77	**20**	2k.+1k. violet	1·00	1·20

21 Soldier with Hlinka Youth Member

1942. Hlinka Youth Fund.

78	**21**	70h.+1k. brown	45	60
79	**21**	1k.30+1k. blue	45	60
80	**21**	2k.+1k. red	1·70	1·80

1942. Father Hlinka. As T **4** but inscr "SLOVENSKO" (without "POSTA").

81	1k.30 violet	50	25

22 Boy Stamp Collector

1942. Philatelic Exhibition, Bratislava.

82	-	30h. green	1·40	1·70
83	**22**	70h. red	1·40	1·70
84	-	80h. violet	1·40	1·70
85	-	1k.30 brown	1·40	1·70

DESIGNS: 30h., 1k.30, Posthorn, round various arms, above Bratislava; 80h. Postmaster-General examining stamps.

23 Dove and St. Stephen's

1942. European Postal Congress.

86	**23**	70h. green	95	1·20
87	**23**	1k.30 green	1·90	2·40
88	**23**	2k. blue	2·75	3·75

24 Inaugural Ceremony

1942. 15th Anniv of Foundation of National Literacy Society.

89	**24**	70h. black	30	20
90	**24**	1k. red	40	25
91	**24**	1k.30 blue	40	25
92	**24**	2k. brown	50	35
93	**24**	3k. green	65	50
94	**24**	4k. violet	65	50

25 L. Stur

1943

95	**25**	80h. green	1·50	1·10
96	-	1k. red	45	35
97	-	1k.30 blue	55	45

PORTRAITS: 1k. M. Razus; 1k.30, Father Hlinka.

27 National Costumes

1943. Winter Relief Fund.

98	**27**	50h.+50h. green	45	35
99	-	70h.+1k. red	45	35
100	-	80h.+2k. blue	55	45

DESIGNS: 70h. Mother and child; 80h. Mother and two children.

29 Infantry

1943. Fighting Forces.

106	**29**	70h.+2k. red	1·00	1·10
107	-	1k.30+2k. blue	1·00	1·10
108	-	2k.+2k. green	1·00	1·10

DESIGNS—HORIZ. 2k. Artillery. VERT: 1k.30, Air Force.

30 Railway Tunnel

1943. Opening of the Strazke–Presov Railway.

109		70h. purple	1·10	1·00
110		80h. blue	1·10	1·00
111	**30**	1k.30 black	1·10	1·00
112	-	2k. brown	1·10	1·00

DESIGNS—HORIZ: 70h. Route map and Presov Church; 2k. Railway viaduct. VERT: 80h. Steam locomotive.

32 "The Slovak Language is our Life"

33 National Museum

1943. Culture Fund.

113	**32**	30h.+1k. brown	80	55
114	**33**	70h.+1k. green	80	55
115	-	80h.+2k. blue	80	55
116	-	1k.30+2k. brown	80	55

DESIGNS—HORIZ: 80h. Matica Slovenska College. VERT: 1k.30, Agricultural student.

34 Prince Pribina Okolo

1944. Fifth Anniv of Declaration of Independence.

117	**34**	50h. green	10	10
118	-	70h. mauve	15	10
119	-	80h. brown	25	15
120	-	1k.30 blue	40	25
121	-	2k. blue	45	30
122	-	3k. brown	55	35
123	-	5k. violet	1·20	90
124	-	10k. black	3·50	2·50

DESIGNS: 70h. Prince Mojmir; 80h. Prince Ratislav; 1k.30, King Svatopluk; 2k. Prince Kocel; 3k. Prince Mojmir II; 5k. Prince Svatopluk II; 10k. Prince Braslav.

1944. As 1939 issue but larger (18½×22½ mm).

125	**7**	10h. red	35	45
126	-	20h. blue	35	45
127	**8**	25h. purple	35	45
128	-	30h. purple	35	45
129	-	50h. green	35	45

DESIGN: 50h. Zelene Pleso (as No. 40).

35 Footballer

1944. Sports.

130	**35**	70h.+70h. green	1·10	1·50
131	-	1k.+1k. violet	1·10	1·50
132	-	1k.30+1k.30 green	1·10	1·50
133	-	2k.+2k. brown	1·10	1·50

DESIGNS—VERT: 1k. Skiing; 1k.30, Diving. HORIZ: 2k. Running.

36 Symbolic of "Protection"

1944. Protection Series.

134	**36**	70h.+4k. blue	1·50	1·70
135	**36**	1k.30+4k. brown	1·50	1·70
136	**36**	2k. green	80	90
137	**36**	3k.80 purple	80	90

37 Children Playing

1944. Child Welfare.

138	**37**	2k.+4k. blue	1·70	1·70

38 Mgr. Tiso

1945

139	**38**	1k. orange	85	55
140	**38**	1k.50 brown	35	25
141	**38**	2k. green	45	55
142	**38**	4k. red	1·40	80
143	**38**	5k. blue	1·10	55
144	**38**	10k. purple	90	45

B. SLOVAK REPUBLIC

39 State Arms

1993

145	**39**	3k. multicoloured	70	35
146	**39**	8k. mult (26×40 mm)	6·75	5·75

40 Ruzomberok

1993

146a	-	50h. lilac and blue	25	15
146b	-	2k. pink, black and blue	40	20
146c	-	3k. black, blue and red	50	25
146d	-	4k. black, green and blue	65	25
146e	-	4k. green, black and red	80	35
147	**40**	5k. blue and red	90	40
147a	-	5k. black, yellow and blue	90	45
147b	-	6k. blue, red and yellow	1·00	50
147c	-	7k. black and pink	1·20	60
147d	-	8k. black, blue and red	1·30	65
147e	-	9k. black, yellow and green	1·40	80
148	-	10k. lilac and orange	1·60	90
148a	-	10k. black, blue and red	1·30	65
148b	-	16k. black and blue	1·70	1·00
149	-	20k. blue and ochre	2·50	1·30
150	-	30k. black, blue and red	4·50	2·20
150a	-	40k. ochre and black	4·00	2·00
151	-	50k. black, orange & bl	6·50	4·00
152	-	50k. black, blue and red	5·25	2·50

DESIGNS—VERT: 50h. Bardejov; 2k. Nitra; 4k. (146c) Nova Bana; 4k. (146d) Presov; 5k. Trnava; 6k. Arms of Senica; 7k. St Martin's Church, Martin; 9k. Zilina; 10k. Kosice; 10k. (148a) Kezmarok; 20k. Roznava Watchtower; 50k. (151) Bratislava; 50k. (152) Komarno. HORIZ: 3k. Banska Bystrica; 8k. Trencin; 16k. Levoca; 30k. Suden Castle; 40k. Piestany.

41 Pres. Michal Kovac

1993

156	**41**	2k. black	25	15
157	**41**	3k. brown and mauve	40	20

42 St. John and Charles Bridge, Prague

1993. 600th Death Anniv of St. John of Nepomuk (patron saint of Bohemia).

158	**42**	8k. multicoloured	1·30	65

43 Pedunculate Oak

1993. Trees. Multicoloured.

159	3k. Type **43**	80	25
160	4k. Hornbeam	85	40
161	10k. Scots pine	1·10	80

44 Jan Levoslav Bella (composer)

1993. Anniversaries.

162	**44**	5k. cream, brown and blue	75	60
163	-	8k. brown, sepia and red	1·50	75
164	-	20k. buff, blue and orange	3·00	1·70

DESIGNS: 5k. Type **44** (150th birth anniv); 8k. Alexander Dubcek (statesman) (1st death anniv); 20k. Jan Kollar (poet and scholar) (birth bicent).

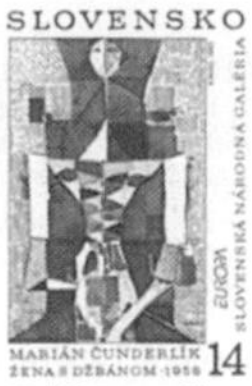

45 "Woman with Jug" (Marian Cunderlik)

1993. Europa. Contemporary Art.

165	**45**	14k. multicoloured	9·25	8·25

46 Sun

1993. Anniversaries. Multicoloured.

166	2k. Type **46** (150th anniv of Slovakian written language)	30	15
167	8k. Sts. Cyril and Methodius (1130th anniv of arrival in Moravia)	1·20	75

47 Arms of Dubnica nad Vahom

1993

168	**47**	1k. silver, black and blue	30	15

48 "The Big Pets" (Lane Smith)

1993. 14th Biennial Exhibition of Book Illustrations for Children, Bratislava.

169	**48**	5k. multicoloured	75	45

49 Canal Lock, Gabcikovo

1993. Rhine—Main—Danube Canal.

170	**49**	10k. multicoloured	1·80	1·10

50 Child's Face in Blood-drop

1993. Red Cross.

171	**50**	3k.+1k. red and blue	75	60

51 "Madonna and Child" (Jozef Klemens)

1993. Christmas.

172	**51**	2k. multicoloured	30	15

52 Milan Stefanik's Tomb, Bradlo

1993. Sheet 70×90 mm.

MS173	16k. multicoloured	3·00	2·75

53 "The Labourer's Spring" (Jozef Kostka)

1993. Art (1st series).

174	**53**	9k. multicoloured	3·75	3·50

See also Nos. 198/9, 227/8, 246/8, 271/3, 297, 300/1, 326/7, 351/2, 374/6, 400, 402, 412, 428/30, 449/50, 477/8 and 497/8 .

54 Ski Jumping

1994. Winter Olympic Games, Lillehammer, Norway.

175	**54**	2k. black, mauve and blue	45	15

55 Family

1994. International Year of the Family.

176	**55**	3k. multicoloured	55	25

56 Antoine de Saint-Exupery (writer and pilot) (50th death)

1994. Anniversaries.

177	-	8k. red and blue	1·40	70
178	**56**	9k. multicoloured	1·50	75

DESIGNS: 8k. Janos Andras Segner (mathematician and physicist) (290th birth).

57 Jozef Murgas
(radio-telegraphy
pioneer)

1994. Europa. Inventions.
179   **57**   28k. multicoloured   5·25   5·00

58 Cigarettes

1994. World No Smoking Day.
180   **58**   3k. multicoloured   45   15

59 Football Pitch
as Tie

1994. World Cup Football Championship, U.S.A.
181   **59**   2k. multicoloured   45   15

60 Ancient Greek Runner
passing Baton to Modern
Athlete

1994. Centenary of International Olympic Committee.
182   **60**   3k. multicoloured   75   45

61 Golden Eagle

1994. Birds. Multicoloured.
183   4k. Type **61**   1·40   30
184   5k. Peregrine falcon   1·50   45
185   7k. Eagle owl   2·30   75

62 Prince Svatopluk

1994. 1100th Death Anniv of Prince Svatopluk of
Moravia.
186   **62**   12k. brown, buff and
       black   2·75   2·50

63 Rowing Boat
with Stamp for
Sail

1994. 120th Anniv of Universal Postal Union.
187   **63**   8k. multicoloured   1·40   70

64 Generals Rudolf Viest and
Jan Golian

1994. 50th Anniv of Slovak Uprising.
188   **64**   6k. blue, pink and yellow   95   55
189   -   8k. multicoloured   95   55
DESIGNS: 8k. French volunteers and their Memorial.

65 Janko Matuska (lyricist
and Allegory of "As Well She
Dug" (melody)

1994. "Over The Tatras Lightning Breaks" (national
anthem). Sheet 66×79 mm.
MS190 34k. multicoloured   4·75   4·75

66 Medal (O.
Spaniel) and
Faculty Emblems

1994. 75th Anniv of Comenius University, Bratislava.
191   **66**   12k. gold, black and red   1·50   75

67 Tajar (winner of first race)

1994. 180th Anniv of Mojmirovce Horse Race.
192   **67**   2k. blue and yellow   60   25

68 St. George's Church,
Kostolany pod Tribecom

1994
193   **68**   20k. multicoloured   2·40   1·20

69 "Nativity" (early
19th- century glass
painting)

1994. Christmas.
194   **69**   2k. multicoloured   45   20

70 Chattam Sofer,
Rabbi of Bratislava

1994. Anniversaries. Multicoloured.
195   5k. Type **70** (165th death)   60   25
196   6k. Wolfgang Kempelen (con-
       ducted study into human
       speech) (190th death)   75   35
197   10k. Stefan Banic (inventor
       of parachute) (125th birth
       (1995))   1·20   60

1994. Art (2nd series). As T **53**. Multicoloured.
198   7k. "Girls" (Janko Alexy) (horiz)   1·20   1·20
199   14k. "Bulls" (Vincent Hloznik)   2·40   2·40

71 Container Ship

1994. Ships. Multicoloured.
200   5k. Type **71**   60   50
201   8k. "Ryn" (freighter)   1·20   95
202   10k. Passenger liner   1·30   1·10

72 Samuel Jurkovic
(founder)

1995. 150th Anniv of Landlords' Association.
203   **72**   9k. multicoloured   1·20   60

73 "Ciminalis clusii"

1995. European Nature Protection Year. Flowers.
Multicoloured.
204   2k. Type **73**   60   25
205   3k. "Pulsatilla slavica"   65   30
206   8k. "Onosoma tornense"   1·20   75

74 Theatre Masks

1995. 75th Anniv of Slovak National Theatre.
207   **74**   10k. pink, black and blue   1·30   60

75 Ice Hockey
Equipment

1995. World Cup Ice Hockey Championship Group B
Qualifying Round, Bratislava.
208   **75**   5k. yellow and blue   65   35

76 Bela Bartok (composer,
50th death)

1995. Anniversaries. Multicoloured.
209   3k. Type **76**   40   20
210   6k. Jan Bahyl (inventor, 80th
       death (1996)) and helicopter
       design   90   45
MS211 68×90 mm. 16k. Ludovit Stur
     (180th birth) (40×26 mm)   2·50   2·40

77 Allegory of Freedom

1995. Europa. Peace and Freedom.
212   **77**   8k. multicoloured   2·00   1·80

78 Concentration
Camp Victims

1995. 50th Anniv of Liberation of Concentration Camps.
213   **78**   12k. multicoloured   1·70   1·20

79 Scout

1995
214   **79**   5k. multicoloured   1·30   35

80 Pope John Paul II,
Map and Arms

1995. Papal Visit.
215   **80**   3k. red and pink   40   20

81 "Stamps"

1995. Centenary of Album Kremnica Philatelic
Association. Sheet 80×87 mm.
MS216 3k. ×2 grey, black and blue   2·50   2·40

82 Banska
Stiavnica

1995. UNESCO World Heritage Sites. Multicoloured.
217   7k. Type **82**   90   50
218   10k. Spis Castle (horiz)   1·70   75
219   15k. Vlkolinec (horiz)   2·00   1·20

83 Player

1995. Centenary of Volleyball.
220   **83**   9k. blue, black and
       yellow   1·30   75

84 Sad Clown
(Lorenzo
Mattotti)

1995. 15th Biennial Exhibition of Book Illustrations for
Children, Bratislava. Multicoloured.
221   2k. Type **84**   25   20
222   3k. Thin and fat men with long
       noses (Dusan Kallay)   40   30

85 Tree, Arch and
Association Emblem

1995. St. Adalbert Association.
223   **85**   4k. black, green and pink   50   35

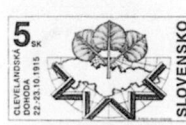

86 Map of Czechoslovakia,
Linden Leaves and National
Colours

1995. 80th Anniv of Cleveland Agreement.
224   **86**   5k. yellow, blue and red   65   45

87 Allegory of Celebration
and Peace

1995. 50th Anniv of United Nations Organization.
225   **87**   8k. multicoloured   1·60   1·20

88 Christmas Crib
(Peter Palka)

1995. Christmas.
226   **88**   2k. multicoloured   40   30

1995. Art (3rd series). As T **53**. Multicoloured.
227   8k. "Hlohovec Nativity"   1·30   1·20
228   16k. "Two Women" (Mikulas
          Galanda)   2·75   2·40

89 Jozef
Ciger-Hronsky (writer)

1996. Anniversaries. Multicoloured.
229   **89**   3k. Type **89** (death centenary)   55   25
230   4k. Jozef Ludovit Holuby (hota-
          nist, 160th birth anniv)   80   35

90 Alojz Szokol,
Athens, 1896

1996. Centenary of Modern Olympic Games.
231   **90**   9k. multicoloured   1·30   75

91 Dousing
Woman in Water

1996. Easter.
232   **91**   2k. multicoloured   40   25

92 Child replenishing
Desertland

1996. Year for the Eradication of Poverty. Sheet 74×90
mm.
MS233 7k. multicoloured   1·30   1·20

93 Izabela
Textorisova
(botanist)

1996. Europa. Famous Women. Multicoloured.
234   8k. Type **93**   1·10   85
235   8k. Botanist holding thistle   1·10   85

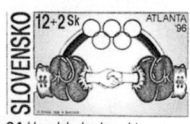
94 Handshake breaking
through Boxing Gloves

1996. Olympic Games, Atlanta. Sheet 70×79 mm.
MS236 12k.+2k. black, rose and
          ultramarine   2·00   1·80

95 Palo Bielik in
"Janosik"

1996. Centenary of Motion Pictures. Sheet 80×89 mm.
MS237 16k. indigo, orange and blue   2·75   2·40

96 Cyclist

1996. Round Slovakia Cycle Race.
238   **96**   3k. black, blue and red   65   35

97 Page and
Mountains

1996. 150th Anniv of "Slovenske Pohl'ady" ("Slovak
Perspectives" (review)).
239   **97**   18k. black, red and blue   2·75   1·50

98 European
Bison

1996. Mammals. Multicoloured.
240   4k. Type **98**   65   35
241   4k. Mouflon ("Ovis musimon")   65   35
242   4k. Chamois ("Rupicapra
          rupicapra")   65   35

99 Popradske

1996. Mountain Lakes. Multicoloured.
243   4k. Type **99**   65   25
244   8k. Skalnate   1·10   35
245   12k. Strbske   1·30   60

1996. Art (4th series). As T **53**.
246   7k. multicoloured   1·30   1·20
247   10k. deep blue, lilac and blue   1·60   1·50
248   14k. multicoloured   3·25   3·00
DESIGNS: 7k. "Queen Ntombi Twala" (Andy Warhol); 10k.
"Suppressed Laughter" (Franz Messerschmidt); 14k. Baroque chair (Endre Nemes).

100 Horse Tram and
Bratislava and Trnava
Stations

1996. Technological Monuments. Multicoloured.
249   4k. Type **100**   55   25
250   6k. Andrej Kvasz and his
          airplane   80   50

101
Snow-covered
Village, Kysuce

1996. Christmas.
251   **101** 2k. multicoloured   40   25

102 Unissued Stamp Design
and Benka

1996. Stamp Day. 25th Death Anniv of Martin Benka
(stamp designer).
252   **102** 3k. buff and blue   1·10   75

103 Michal Martikan

1996. Slovak Achievements at Olympic Games, Atlanta.
253   **103** 3k. brown and stone   65   35

104 Bishop
Stefan Moyses

1997. Birth Anniversaries of National Activists.
Multicoloured.
254   3k. Type **104** (first chairman
          of Matican Slovenska,
          bicentenary)   25   25
255   4k. Svetozar Vajansky (writer,
          150th)   55   30

105 Biathlon

1997. World Biathlon Championship, Osrblie.
256   **105** 6k. multicoloured   65   35

106 Collecting
Dew

1997. Folk Traditions.
257   **106** 3k. multicoloured   40   20

107 Church

1997. 700th Anniv of Franciscan Church, Bratislava.
258   **107** 16k. black, orange and
          blue   2·00   1·50

108 Guglielmo Marconi and
Radio Waves

1997. Centenary of Wireless Telegraphy.
259   **108** 10k. black, blue and
          yellow   1·30   1·20

109 Miraculous
Rain of Hron

1997. Europa. Tales and Legends.
260   **109** 9k. black, orange and
          blue   1·50   1·30

110 Domica Cave

1997. Caves. Multicoloured.
261   6k. Type **110**   75   50
262   8k. Argonite Cave, Ochtinska   1·20   80

111 Couple dancing

1997. Folklore Festival, Vychodna. Sheet 66×79 mm.
MS263 11k. multicoloured   1·50   1·30

112 "Dance" (Martin Jonas)

1997. Naive Art Triennale.
264   **112** 3k. multicoloured   45   25

113 Woman

1997. International Slovak Year.
265   **113** 9k. multicoloured   1·00   50

114 Cherubs blowing
Horns (J.
Kiselova-Sitekova)

1997. 16th Biennial Exhibition of Book Illustrations for
Children, Bratislava.
266   **114** 3k. multicoloured   45   25

115 Water Mill, Jelka

1997
267   **115** 4k. multicoloured   50   35

116 Flag, Arms
and Linden
Leaves

1997. Fifth Anniv of Constitution.
268   **116** 4k. multicoloured   50   35

117 Runners

1997. Sixth World Half-marathon Championship, Kosice.
269   **117** 9k. multicoloured   1·00   50

118 Bronze
Boletus ("Boletus
aereus")

1997. Endangered Fungi. Sheet 154×102 mm containing
T **118** and similar vert designs. Multicoloured.
MS270 9k. Type **118**; 9k. Common
morel ("Morchella esculenta"); 9k.
"Cathelasma Imperialie" 5·25 4·50

1997. Art (5th series). As T **53**.
271 9k. multicoloured 1·30 80
272 10k. multicoloured 1·60 1·00
273 12k. buff, black and red 2·10 1·30
DESIGNS—VERT: 9k. "Self-portrait with Wife" (Jan Ku-
pecky); 12k. "For Aim" (Koloman Sokol). HORIZ: 10k. "St.
Lucy and St. Peter" (detail of Bojnice altarpiece, Nardo di
Cione).

119 Weeping
Woman and
Church

1997. 90th Anniv of Cernova Massacre.
274 **119** 4k. lilac and green 50 35

120 Nativity

1997. Christmas.
275 **120** 3k. multicoloured 45 25

121 Nepela

1997. Ondrej Nepela (figure skater).
276 **121** 5k. black, mauve and
green 75 40

122 Risen Christ
amongst
Disciples

1997. Spiritual Regeneration.
277 **122** 4k. multicoloured 60 25

123 Burin as Posthorn

1997. Stamp Day.
278 **123** 4k. brown and blue 75 25

124 Bratislava and Arms of District
Towns

1998. Fifth Anniv of Independence.
279 **124** 4k. multicoloured 60 25

125 Martin Razus

1998. Writers' Anniversaries. Multicoloured.
280 4k. Type **125** (110th birth
anniv) 60 25
281 4k. Jozef Skultety and Slovak
Cultural Society building
(50th death anniv) 60 25
282 4k. Jan Smrek (birth centenary) 60 25

126 Ice Hockey

1998. Winter Olympic Games, Nagano, Japan.
283 **126** 19k. yellow, black and
blue 2·50 1·30

127 Banishing
of Moraine

1998. Folk Traditions.
284 **127** 3k. multicoloured 45 25

128 Budatin Castle

1998. Castles. Multicoloured.
285 6k. Type **128** 70 55
286 11k. Krasna Hoka castle 1·40 85
MS287 76×82 mm. 18k. Nitra castle 2·10 1·80

129 "Sending
Down of the
Holy Spirit"
(Vincent
Hloznik)

1998. Spiritual Renewal.
288 **129** 4k. multicoloured 55 30

130 Tekov
Wedding

1998. Europa. National Festivals.
289 **130** 12k. multicoloured 2·10 1·80

131 "Butterfly
and Rainbow"
(Livia
Merenicova)

1998. Children's Centre.
290 **131** 3k. multicoloured 40 20

132 Viktor
Kolibrik
(revolutionary)

1998. 80th Anniv of Kragujevac Uprising.
291 **132** 3k. multicoloured 40 20

133 Rebels

1998. 150th Anniv of Slovak Insurrection.
292 **133** 4k. black, blue and red 1·10 40

134 Steam
Locomotive

1998. 150th Anniv of Railway in Slovakia.
293 **134** 4k. black, red and blue 70 35
294 - 10k. black, yellow and
blue 1·10 65
295 - 15k. black, yellow and
brown 1·70 95
DESIGNS: 10k. Electric locomotive; 15k. Diesel locomotive.

135 European Mud minnow
("Umbra krameri") (B8)

1998. Fish. Sheet 109×165 mm containing T **135** and
similar horiz designs. Multicoloured.
MS296 4k. Type **135**; 11k. Zingel
("Zingel zingel"); 16k. Common carp
("Cyprinus carpio") 4·25 3·75

1998. Art (6th series). As T **53**. Multicoloured.
297 18k. "Pieta" (sculpture in Basilica
of Virgin Mary, Sastin) 2·75 2·50

136 Stone and
Butterfly

1998. Anti-drugs Campaign.
298 **136** 3k. multicoloured 40 20

137 Sunflower

1998. 25th Anniv of Ekotopfilm.
299 **137** 4k. orange, yellow and
blue 55 30

1998. Art (7th series). As T **53**. Multicoloured.
300 10k. "Countryside at Terchova"
(Martin Benka) 1·10 85
301 12k. "Fishermen" (Ludovit Fulla) 1·40 1·10

138 Adoration
of the Magi

1998. Christmas.
302 **138** 3k. multicoloured 40 20

139 Postman on Bicycle

1998. Stamp Day.
303 **139** 4k. multicoloured 70 35

140 Snowboarders

1999. 19th World University and Fourth EYOD Winter
Games, Poprad-Tatry.
304 **140** 12k. black, blue and red 1·40 1·10

141 Matej Bel
(historian, 250th
death)

1999. Anniversaries.
305 **141** 3k. black, yellow and
brown 40 20
306 - 4k. deep lilac, yellow
and lilac 55 30
307 - 11k. purple, orange
and blue 1·40 70
DESIGNS: 4k. Cardinal Juraj Haulik (130th death); 11k. Pavol Orszagh (pseudonym) Hviezdoslav (poet, 150th birth).

142 Automatic
Sorting Machine

1999. 125th Anniv of Universal Postal Union.
308 **142** 4k. multicoloured 55 30

143 Cajkov

1999. Women's Traditional Bonnets. Multicoloured.
309 4k. Type **143** 55 40
310 15k. Hel'pa 1·70 1·40
311 18k. Madunice 1·90 1·50

144 "Transfiguration"

1999. Spiritual Renewal.
312 **144** 5k. multicoloured 70 40

145 High Tatras National Park
(right hand detail)

1999. Europa. Parks and Gardens. Multicoloured.
313 9k. Type **145** 95 70
314 11k. High Tatras National Park
(left-hand detail) 1·30 95
Nos. 313/14 were issued together, *se-tenant*, forming a
composite design.

146 Face within Council
Emblem

1999. 50th Anniv of Council of Europe.
315 **146** 16k. ultramarine, blue
and yellow 2·00 1·20
MS316 66×85 mm. No. 315 2·50 2·20

147 Nightingale,
Score and Violin
Head

1999. 50th Anniv of Slovak Philharmonic Orchestra.
317 **147** 4k. multicoloured 50 25

148 Hands of Three Generations

1999. International Year of the Elderly.
318	**148**	5k. black, flesh and green	65	30

149 Ivan Bella and 'Mir' Space Station

1999. Space Flight of First Slovak Cosmonaut. Sheet 70×86 mm.
MS319	**149**	12k. multicoloured	1·60	1·20

150 Zilina University, Open Book and Keyboard

1999. 125th Anniv of Universal Postal Union. Multicoloured.
320		12k. Type **150**	1·30	60
321		16k. Globe and Slovak postal emblem	1·60	75

151 Spotlights on Theatre Stage

1999. 50th Anniv of University of Fine Arts, Bratislava.
322	**151**	4k. black, blue and pink	50	25

152 "Man's Head" (Martin Jarrie)

1999. 17th Biennial Exhibition of Book Illustrations for Children, Bratislava.
323	**152**	5k. multicoloured	65	35

153 Water Pillar Machine (J. K. Hell)

1999. Technical Monuments.
324	**153**	7k. yellow and brown	80	45

154 Bearded Reedling (*Panurus biarmicus*) (B8)

1999. Songbirds. Sheet 154×102 mm containing T **154** and similar horiz designs. Multicoloured.
MS325	14k. Type **154**; 15k. Red-backed shrike (*Lanius collurio*); 16k. Redstart (*Phoenicurus phoenicurus*)	5·25	4·75

1999. Art (8th series). As T **53**. Multicoloured.
326	13k. "Malatina" (Milos Alexander Bazovsky) (horiz)	1·40	1·20
327	14k. "Study of the Resting Blacksmith" (Dominik Skutecky)	1·60	1·30

155 Children playing in Snow (Stanislav Sekeres)

1999. Christmas.
328	**155**	4k. multicoloured	50	25

156 Woman's Head

1999. Tenth Anniv of Velvet Revolution.
329	**156**	5k. blue, red and black	65	35

157 18th-century Urn showing Visit to Sick Man

1999. Museum of Jewish Culture, Bratislava. Multicoloured.
330		12k. Type **157**	1·20	75
331		18k. 18th-century urn showing funeral procession	1·70	1·20

158 Albin Brunovsky (stamp designer) and "Czechoslovakia"

1999. Stamp Day.
332	**158**	5k. brown, stone and green	80	35

159 Dunajec Gap

2000. Valleys. Multicoloured.
333		10k. Type **159**	90	75
334		12k. Vah Gap	1·20	95

160 Hana Melickova (actress)

2000. Birth Anniversaries. Multicoloured.
335		4k. Type **160** (centenary)	50	25
336		5k. Stefan Anian Jedlik (scientist, bicentenary)	80	35

161 Christ's Head (detail of altar panel), St. Jacob's Church, Levoca

2000. Easter.
337	**161**	4k. brown	50	25

162 Globe as Basketball in Net

2000. Women's European Basketball Championship, Ruzomberok.
338	**162**	4k. multicoloured	50	25

163 Juraj Hronec and Stefan Schwarz (mathematicians)

2000. World Mathematics Year.
339	**163**	5k. multicoloured	65	35

164 Jan Holly (poet and priest)

2000.
340	**164**	5k.50 black, blue and red	70	45

165 "Building Europe"

2000. Europa.
341	**165**	12k. multicoloured	2·20	1·90

166 "Animals from Rainbow" (Alexandra Bankova)

2000. United Nations Children's Fund.
342	**166**	5k.50 multicoloured	80	50

167 Postman, Austria 1850 2k. Stamp

2000. First Stamps Used in Slovakia.
343	**167**	10k. multicoloured	1·90	70

168 Pres. Rudolf Schuster

2000.
344	**168**	5k.50 brown	80	50

169 Rifle Shooting

2000. Olympic Games, Sydney.
345	**169**	18k. multicoloured	3·00	2·75

170 Emblem

2000. 25th Anniv of Organization for Security and Co-operation in Europe.
346	**170**	4k. black and blue	70	35

171 Timber Bridge, Klukava

2000.
347	**171**	6k. multicoloured	85	50

172 Wild Raspberry (*Rubus idaeus*) (B26)

2000. Berries. Sheet 156×103 mm containing T **172** and similar vert designs. Multicoloured.
MS348	11k. Type **172**; 13k. Common strawberry (*Fragaria vesca*); 15k. Bilberry (*Vaccinium myrtillus*)	5·25	4·75

173 Mary and Jesus

2000. Holy Year 2000. Christmas.
349	**173**	4k. multicoloured	70	35

174 Emblem

2000. Agreement between the Postal Administration of the Slovak Republic and the Sovereign Order of the Knights of St. John.
350	**174**	10k. multicoloured	1·70	85

2000. Art (9th series). As T **53**. Multicoloured.
351	18k. Nativity (detail) (altar panel, Spisska-Stara Ves Church)	2·40	2·10
352	20k. "Descent from the Cross" (mural, Kocelovce Church) (horiz)	2·50	2·30

175 Apple on Newspaper

2000. Stamp Day.
353	**175**	5k.50 multicoloured	1·40	50

176 Maria Theresa

2000. History of Postal Law.
354	**176**	20k. multicoloured	4·25	4·00

177 Rococo Mantle Clock

2001.
355	**177**	13k. multicoloured	1·70	85

178 Blaho

2001. Birth Centenary of Janko Blaho (opera singer).
356 **178** 5k.50 multicoloured 85 60

179 Ice Skater

2001. European Figure Skating Championships, Bratislava.
357 **179** 16k. multicoloured 2·10 1·00

180 Male

2001. Traditional Costumes of Detva. Multicoloured.
358 5k.50 Type **180** 70 35
359 6k. Woman in costume, Detva 1·00 50

181 Woman with Apple

2001. 50th Anniv of Central Control and Check
Agricultural Institute, Bratislava.
360 **181** 12k. multicoloured 1·70 85

182 1st-century Gate and
Celtic Coins, Liptovska Mara,
Havranok

2001. Archaeological Sites. Multicoloured.
361 12k. Type **182** 1·60 1·20
362 15k. 9th-century courtyard, jewellery and button, Ducove,
Kostelec 1·90 1·60

183 Studenovodsky Waterfall

2001. Europa. Water Resources.
363 **183** 18k. multicoloured 2·50 2·30

184 Prince Pribina (800–861)

2001. Moravian Rulers. Sheet 110×165 mm containing T
184 and similar horiz designs. Each cinnamon and
sepia.
MS364 6k. Type **184**; 9k. Prince
Rastislav (820–870); 11k. Prince Kocel
(9th-century); 14k. Prince Svätopluk
(840–894) 5·75 5·25

185 Brown Bear
(*Ursus arctos*)

2001. Nature Protection. Carnivores. Sheet 118×165
mm containing T **185** and similar vert designs.
Multicoloured.
MS365 14k. Type **185**; 15k. Wolf (*Canis
lupus*); 16k. European lynx (*Lynx lynx*) 7·50 7·00

186 Guitar and Map of
United States

2001. Dobro Resonator Guitar.
366 **186** 19k. multicoloured 2·50 1·40

187 Man in Boat
(Peter Uchnar)

2001. 18th Biennial Exhibition of Book Illustrations for
Children, Bratislava.
367 **187** 7k. multicoloured 85 50

188 Face and Hand

2001. Memorial Day for Victims of the Holocaust.
368 **188** 14k. multicoloured 2·10 1·70

189 Dubcek

2001. Ninth Death Anniv of Alexander Dubcek
(statesman). Sheet 65×82 mm.
MS369 18k. multicoloured 2·75 2·50

190 Flowers

2001. Political Trials.
370 **190** 10k. multicoloured 1·70 85

191 Postman
and Posthorn

2001. Opening of Slovak Postal Museum, Banska Bystrica.
371 **191** 6k. multicoloured 85 50

192 Nativity

2001. Christmas.
372 **192** 5k.50 multicoloured 2·30 85

193 Sturovo–Ostrihom
Bridge

2001
373 **193** 10k. multicoloured 85 50

2001. Art (10th series). As T **53**.
374 16k. multicoloured 2·10 1·70
375 18k. green and brown 2·30 1·90
376 20k. multicoloured 2·50 2·30
DESIGNS: 16k. "Raftsman's Dream" (Imrich Weiner-Kral);
18k. "Light of the Soul" (Albin Brunovsky); 20k. "St.
Michael the Archangel with the Group of Saints" (icon).

194 Juraj Papanek

2002. Anniversaries. Multicoloured.
377 10k. Type **194** (historian, death
bicentenary) 1·40 70

378 14k. Bjornstjerne Bjornson
(writer and poet, 170th birth
anniv) 2·10 1·00

195 Skiers

2002. Winter Olympic Games, Salt Lake City, U.S.A.
379 **195** 18k. multicoloured 2·50 1·40

196 Dogs
pulling Sledge

2002. European Sled Dog Race Championship, Donovaly.
380 **196** 6k. multicoloured 95 50

197 Jesus and
Flowers (Karol
Ondreicka)

2002. Easter.
381 **197** 5k.50 multicoloured 85 50

198 Martin
Gymnasium and
Open Book

2002. Educational Anniversaries. Multicoloured.
382 12k. Type **198** (140th anniv) 1·60 70
383 13k. Revuca Gymnasium (140th
anniv) 1·70 85
384 15k. Klastor pod Znievom
Gymnasium (133rd anniv) 1·90 1·00

199 "Clown with
Trumpet" (Emil
Bacík)

2002. Europa. Circus.
385 **199** 18k. multicoloured 3·50 3·25

200 Beer Barrel and Kegs

2002. Industrial Technology. Multicoloured.
386 7k. Type **200** 1·00 70
387 9k. Wine press and grapes 1·20 1·00

201 Southern Festoon
(*Zerynthia polyxena*)

2002. Endangered Species. Butterflies. Sheet 109×165
mm containing T **201** and similar horiz designs.
Multicoloured.
MS388 10k. Type **201**; 16k. Peacock
(*Inachis io*); 25k. Swallowtail (*Papilio
machaon*) 7·00 6·50

202 Two Doves

2002. Greetings Stamp. "Congratulations".
389 **202** 6k. multicoloured 1·70 1·20

203 Player and Trophy

2002. Slovakia–Winners of World Ice Hockey
Championship, Sweden.
390 **203** 10k. multicoloured 1·70 1·00

204 Rudnay

2002. 171st Death Anniv of Alexander Rudnay
(Archbishop of Esztergom). Sheet 81×108 mm.
MS391 **204** 17k. multicoloured 2·75 2·50

205 Congtai
Pavilion, Handan

2002. Castles. Multicoloured.
392 6k. Type **205** 70 35
393 12k. Bojnice Castle 1·40 70
Stamps of a similar design were issued by China.

206 Emblem

2002. 50th Anniv of Kosice Technical College.
394 **206** 6k. multicoloured 85 50

207 Angel
(detail), Rajecka
Lesna Nativity
(sculpture) (Jozef
Pekara)

2002. Christmas.
395 **207** 5k.50 multicoloured 85 50

208 St. Michael's
Church, Klizske
Hradiste

2002. Churches. Multicoloured.
396 7k. Type **208** 85 65
397 14k. St. George's Church, Skalica 1·70 1·30
398 22k. St. Martin's Cathdral,
Spisska Kapitula 2·50 2·00

209 Moonwalk

2002. 30th Anniv of Flight of Apollo 17. Sheet 81×101
mm.
MS399 **209** 20k. multicoloured 65 65

2002. Art (11th series). As T **53**. Multicoloured.
400 23k. "In the Atelier" (Koloman
Sokol) 3·50 2·50

210 Kingfisher

2002. "NITRAFILA 2003" International Stamp Exhibition, Nitra.

| 401 | **210** | 10k. multicoloured | 1·70 | 1·30 |

2002. Art (12th series). As T **53**. Multicoloured.

| 402 | | 20k. "Decollation of St. James the Older" (Master Paul of Levoca) | 2·50 | 2·00 |

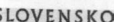

211 Family

2003. Tenth Anniv of Republic.

| 403 | **211** | 20k. multicoloured | 2·50 | 2·00 |

2003. As T **168** but with colour changed.

| 404 | **168** | 7k. blue | 85 | 65 |

212 Girl carrying the Lesola (decorated twigs) on Palm Sunday

2003. Easter.

| 405 | **212** | 7k. multicoloured | 85 | 65 |

213 Kremnica (town)

2003

| 406 | **213** | 18k. black and orange | 2·10 | 1·60 |

214 St. Cyril

2003. 25th Anniv of Slovak Ecclesiastical Province. Sheet 166×105 mm containing T **214** and similar vert design.

| MS407 | 17k. black, lemon and ochre; 22k. black, lemon and blue | 5·25 | 4·75 |

DESIGNS: 17k. Type **214**; 22k. St. Metod.

215 Ludwig van Beethoven (composer and musician)

2003

| 408 | **215** | 15k. multicoloured | 1·70 | 1·30 |

216 Bouquet

2003. Greetings Stamp.

| 409 | **216** | 7k. multicoloured | 85 | 65 |

217 Milan Stefanik

2003. Milan Rastislav Stefanik Commemoration (founder of Czechoslovakia).

| 410 | **217** | 14k. black, blue and red | 2·30 | 1·70 |

218 Don Juan Poster (Vladislav Rostoka)

2003. Europa. Poster Art.

| 411 | **218** | 14k. black, red and pink | 2·30 | 1·70 |

2003. Art (12th series). As T **53**. Multicoloured.

| 412 | | 18k. multicoloured | 2·50 | 2·00 |

DESIGN: 18k. "The Brook by the Barn" (Ladislav Mednansky) (horiz).

219 St. Benedict and St. Andrej Svorad

2003. St. Benedict and St. Andrej Svorad.

| 413 | **219** | 13k. black, yellow and orange | 1·70 | 1·30 |

220 Team Members

2003. Slovakia, World Ice Hockey Championship Bronze Medallists, Finland 2003.

| 414 | **220** | 20k. multicoloured | 3·50 | 2·50 |

221 Matko and Kubko (L. Capek)

2003. International Children's Day. Characters from book by Marianna Grznarova.

| 415 | **221** | 7k. multicoloured | 85 | 65 |

222 Wild Cat

2003. Endangered Species. Wild Cat (*Felis silvestris*). Sheet 158×103 mm containing T **222** and similar vert designs. Multicoloured.

| MS416 | 13k. Type **222**; 14k. Wild cat with bird; 16k. Two wild cats; 18k. Wild cat (different) | 8·75 | 8·50 |

223 Martina Moravcova (world champion swimmer)

2003. World Swimming Championships, Barcelona.

| 417 | **223** | 11k. multicoloured | 1·70 | 1·30 |

224 Lake Klinger

2003. UNESCO World Heritage Site. Banska Stiavnica. Multicoloured.

| 418 | | 9k. Type **224** | 1·40 | 1·00 |
| 419 | | 12k. Lake Rozgrund | 2·10 | 1·60 |

225 "Palculienka" (Jana Kiselova-Sitekova)

2003. 19th Biennial Exhibition of Book Illustrations for Children, Bratislava.

| 420 | **225** | 12k. multicoloured | 1·70 | 1·30 |

226 Pope John Paul II

2003. Third Visit of Pope John Paul II to Slovakia. Self-adhesive.

| 421 | **226** | 12k. violet | 1·70 | 1·30 |

227 Jan Magin

2003. Jan Baltazar Magin (writer) Commemoration.

| 422 | **227** | 8k. rose and black | 1·00 | 80 |

228 Pezinok (town)

2003

| 423 | **228** | 100k. black, blue and pink | 12·00 | 9·25 |

229 Sleigh

2003. Christmas.

| 424 | **229** | 7k. multicoloured | 85 | 65 |

230 Cross, Velka Maca, Sword Hilt, Krasna nad Hornadom and Bronze Buttons, Nitra

2003. Artefacts.

| 425 | **230** | 18k. multicoloured | 2·30 | 1·70 |

231 *Wright Flyer I*

2003. Centenary of Powered Flight.

| 426 | **231** | 18k. multicoloured | 2·30 | 1·70 |

232 Postal Delivery Symbols

2003. Stamp Day. 80th Birth Anniv of Jozef Balaz (stamp designer).

| 427 | **232** | 12k. multicoloured | 1·70 | 1·30 |

2003. Art (14th series). As T **53**. Multicoloured.

428		14k. "Holy Katarina" (Simon Vouet)	2·10	1·60
429		16k. "Bagpipes" (Rudolf Krivos) (horiz)	2·40	1·80
430		21k. "Annunciation of Our Lady" (Majster Jan)	3·25	2·30

233 Heart enclosing Rose

2004. St. Valentine's Day.

| 431 | **233** | 8k. multicoloured | 1·00 | 80 |

234 Liptovsky Mikulas

2004. Tourism.

| 432 | **234** | 9k. multicoloured | 1·20 | 90 |

235 Lily

2004. Flowers.

| 433 | **235** | 8k. multicoloured | 1·00 | 80 |

236 Tulips

2004. Greetings Stamp.

| 434 | **236** | 9k. multicoloured | 1·40 | 1·00 |

237 Decorated Egg

2004. Easter. Self adhesive.

| 435 | **237** | 8k. multicoloured | 1·20 | 90 |

238 Bridegroom, Pata

2004. Traditional Costumes. Multicoloured.

| 436 | | 15k. Type **238** | 2·10 | 1·60 |
| 437 | | 28k. Bride, Pata | 3·75 | 2·75 |

239 Flowers, Butterfly, Castle and Bird

2004. Europa. Holidays.

| 438 | **239** | 20k. multicoloured | 2·75 | 2·10 |

240 Flags of New Members

2004. Accession to the European Union.

| 439 | **240** | 18k. multicoloured | 3·50 | 2·50 |

241 NATO Emblem

2004. Accession to North Atlantic Treaty Organization (NATO).

| 440 | **241** | 60k. multicoloured | 11·50 | 9·25 |

242 Grandfather Vecernicek (Ladislav Capek)

2004. Vecernicek (character from children's television programme).
441 **242** 8k. multicoloured 1·00 80

243 Winged Athlete and Winged Torso

2004. Olympic Games, Athens (1st issue). Paralympics.
442 **243** 34k. multicoloured 5·25 4·00
See also Nos. 452/7.

244 Ivan Gasparovic

2004. Inauguration of President Ivan Gasparovic.
443 **244** 8k. multicoloured 1·00 80

245 Woodsman and Forest

2004. Dobrocsky Primeval Forest.
444 **245** 12k. multicoloured 1·60 1·20

246 Omnibus

2004. Centenary of Tatra Omnibus.
445 **246** 14k. multicoloured 1·90 1·40

247 Trees, Mountains and Mine Shaft

2004. Spania Valley Water Mining.
446 **247** 24k. multicoloured 3·25 2·50

248 Raft on River Dunajec

2004. Raft Men working on River Dunajec (bordering Slovakia and Poland). Phosphor.
447 **248** 21k. multicoloured 3·50 2·50
A stamp of the same design was issued by Poland.

249 Carved Tombstone

2004. Roman Occupation.
448 **249** 26k. multicoloured 3·75 2·75

2004. Art (15th series). As T **53**. Multicoloured.
449 33k. "Cockfight" (Jakub Bogdan) (horiz) 4·75 3·75
450 35k. "Don Qxiote" (Julius Jakoby) 5·50 4·25

250 The Nativity

2004. Christmas.
451 **250** 8k. multicoloured 1·20 90

251 Jozef Gonci

2004. Olympic Games, Athens (2nd issue). Medal Winners. Multicoloured. Self-adhesive.
452 8k. Type **251** (bronze medal, shooting) 1·20 90
453 8k. K4 canoe team (bronze medal) 1·20 90
454 14k. Josef Krnac (silver medal, Judo) 2·10 1·60
455 14k. Michael Martikan (silver medal, canoe slalom) 2·10 1·60
456 20k. Elena Kaliska (gold medal, women's K1 kayak slalom) 3·00 2·20
457 20k. Pavol and Peter Hochschornerovci (gold medal, K2 kayak slalom) 3·00 2·20

252 Post Woman and Transport Symbols

2004. Stamp Day.
458 **252** 9k. multicoloured 1·40 1·00

253 Cupid

2005. St. Valentine's Day.
459 **253** 9k. multicoloured 1·40 1·00

254 Family

2005. Family.
460 **254** 9k. multicoloured 1·40 1·00

255 Clock Tower

2005. 750th Anniv of Banska Bystrica.
461 **255** 16k. grey, vermilion and olive 2·30 1·70

256 Flags and Emblem

2005. Summit Meeting between Presidents George W. Bush and Vladimir Putin, Bratislava.
462 **256** 25k. ultramarine and vermilion 3·50 2·50

257 Lamb

2005. Easter.
463 **257** 9k. ultramarine and vermilion 1·40 1·00

258 Zdenka Schelingova

2005. Second Anniv of Beatification of Zdenka Schelingova. Sheet 82×108 mm.
MS464 **258** 34k. multicoloured 5·25 4·75

259 Radovan Kaufman

2005. Radovan Kaufman (Paralympics cycling gold medallist—Sydney 2000) Commemoration.
465 **259** 22k. multicoloured 3·25 2·30

260 "Poor Mother" (Frantisek Studeny)

2005. Solidarity with Asia (Tsunami disaster—2004).
466 **260** 25k. agate and green 3·50 2·50

261 Bread and Salt

2005. Europa. Gastronomy.
467 **261** 19k. multicoloured 3·00 2·20

262 Primate's Palace, Bratislava and Napoleon

2005. Bicentenary of Peace Treaty between Napoleon and Holy Roman Emperor Francis II.
468 **262** 23k. multicoloured 3·25 2·30

263 Lightning

2005. International Year of Physics.
469 **263** 18k. multicoloured 3·00 2·20

264 Fish (Juraj Kis)

2005. Children's Stamp. Winning Design in Children's Painting Competition.
470 **264** 9k. multicoloured 1·40 1·00

265 Fox as Magician (illustration by Iku Dekune)

2005. 20th Biennial Exhibition of Book Illustrations for Children, Bratislava.
471 **265** 30k. multicoloured 4·25 3·25

266 Roman Chapel, Holic

2005. Tourism.
472 **266** 22k. multicoloured 3·25 2·30

267 President Ivan Gasparovic

2005
473 **267** 9k. brown 1·40 1·00

268 Lipizzaner Horses and Carriage

2005. Horses. Sheet 165×108 mm containing T **268** and similar horiz design. Multicoloured.
MS474 29k. Type **268**; 31k. Slovak warm blood dressage horse and rider 8·75 8·50

269 Early Steam Locomotive (Cierny Balog)

2005. Forest Railways. Multicoloured.
475 21k. Type **269** 3·50 2·50
476 33k. U 34.901 (1909) (Vychylovka) 4·25 3·25

2005. Art (16th series). As T **53**.
477 28k. agate and buff 3·50 2·50
478 35k. multicoloured 5·25 4·00
DESIGNS: 28k. "Supper at Emmaus" (Rembrandt); 35k. "Magic of Still Life" (Karol Baron) (horiz).

270 Three Wise Men

2005. Christmas.
479 **270** 9k. multicoloured 1·20 90

271 Sword

2005. Stamp Day.
480 **271** 15k. multicoloured 2·10 1·60

272 Karol Kuzmany

2006. Birth Bicentenary of Karol Kuzmany (writer).
481 **272** 16k. multicoloured 1·90 1·40

273 Skier

2006. Winter Olympic Games, Turin.
482 **273** 21k. multicoloured 3·50 2·50

274 Towers, Poprad

2006. Tourism.
483   **274**   23k. multicoloured   3·25   2·30

275 Daffodil

2006. Greetings Stamp.
484   **275**   10k. multicoloured   1·70   1·30

276 Children

2006. Easter.
485   **276**   10k. multicoloured   1·20   90

277 *Flabelipecten solarium* and Rocks (Sandberg)

2006. Geology. Sheet 119×92 mm containing T **277** and similar vert design. Multicoloured.
MS486 32k. Type **277**; 35k. Basalt waterfall (Somoska)   8·75   8·50

278 Multicoloured Flower

2006. Europa. Integration.
487   **278**   18k. multicoloured   2·50   2·00

279 Kezmarok

2006. Renaissance Belfries. Multicoloured.
488   **279**   27k. Type **279**   3·25   2·50
489   29k. Podolinec   3·50   2·50

280 Flower

2006. Children's Stamp.
490   **280**   10k. multicoloured   1·40   1·00

281 Devin Castle

2006
491   **281**   10k. multicoloured   2·10   1·60

282 Fujara (shepherds' long pipe)

2006. Folk Crafts.
492   **282**   25k. multicoloured   3·25   2·30

283 Glass Goblet

2006. Museum Exhibits. Multicoloured.
493   28k. Type **283**   4·00   3·00
494   31k. Copper vase   4·25   3·25

284 Semar Puppet (Wayang Golek traditional theatre), Java

2006. Puppets. Multicoloured.
495   22k. Type **284**   3·25   2·50
496   25k. Gasparko puppet, Slovakia   3·50   2·50
Stamps of a similar design were issued by Indonesia.

2006. Art (17th series). As T **53**.
497   37k. multicoloured (horiz)   5·25   4·00
498   38k. black, brown and ochre   5·25   4·00
DESIGNS: 37k. "Krivy jarok" (Dezider Milly); 38k. Moravany Venus figurine.

285 Carollers

2006. Christmas.
499   **285**   10k. multicoloured   1·40   1·00

286 Josef Cincik (writer)

2006. Stamp Day.
500   **286**   19k. multicoloured   2·30   1·70

287 Modra

2007. Tourism.
501   **287**   14k. multicoloured   1·70   1·30

288 Terezia Vansova

2007. 150th Birth Anniv of Terezia Vansova (writer and promoter of women's cultural emancipation).
502   **288**   19k. multicoloured   2·30   1·70

289 Flowers

2007. Greetings Stamp. No value expressed.
503   **289**   (10k.) multicoloured   1·70   1·30

No. 503 was for use on internal second class up to 50g.

290 Crucifixion (V. Hložnik)

2007. Easter.
504   **290**   10k. multicoloured   1·40   1·00

291 Players

2007. Tennis.
505   **291**   16k. multicoloured   2·10   1·60

292 Cuvac

2007. Slovak Dogs. Sheet 118×91 mm containing T **292** and similar vert design. Multicoloured.
MS506 31k.×2, Type **292**; Kopov   8·75   8·50

293 Arms

2007. Centenary of Slovak League of America.
507   **293**   22k. multicoloured   2·50   2·00

294 Scouts

2007. Europa. Centenary of Scouting.
508   **294**   18k. multicoloured   2·10   1·60

295 Janko Hrasko (illustration by Stefan Cpin)

2007. Children's Stamp. Janko Hrasko (animated film).
509   **295**   10k. multicoloured   1·40   1·00

296 Jasov Monastery

2007. Tourism. Multicoloured.
510   30k. Type **296**   4·25   3·25
511   34k. Hrosky Benadik Monastery   4·75   3·50

297 Katze (illustration by Luboslav Palo)

2007. 21st Biennial Exhibition of Book Illustrations for Children, Bratislava.
512   **297**   25k. multicoloured   3·25   2·30

298 Bratislava Castle (detail from Vienna Illuminated Chronicles)

2007. 1100th Anniv of First Use of Name Bratislava. Sheet 118×164 mm.
MS513 37k. multicoloured   6·00   5·75

299 La Guaita (Rocca) Tower, San Marino

2007. The Oldest (San Marino–301) and Newest (Slovakia–1993) Republics of Europe. Multicoloured.
514   21k. Type **299**   3·25   2·30
515   21k. Orava Castle, Slovakia   3·25   2·30
Stamps of a similar design were issued by San Marino.

300 Jozef Hurban

2007. 190th Birth Anniv of Jozef Miloslav Hurban (writer and Nationalist leader).
516   **300**   31k. multicoloured   4·25   3·25

301 Bridge and Detail of Stonework

2007. Kralova Bridge over Cierna Voda River.
517   **301**   29k. multicoloured   4·00   3·25

302 Crucifixion, Madonna and St John (cover)

2007. Liturgical Gospel, Nitra (Slovakia's oldest preserved book).
518   **302**   15k. multicoloured   2·00   1·60

303 R. W. Seton Watson

2007. Robert William Seton Watson (nationalist) Commemoration.
519   **303**   24k. multicoloured   3·25   2·50

2007. Art (18th series). T **53**.
520   33k. *Saint Elizabeth* (Frantisek Palko)   5·50   4·50
521   33k. *Bouquet of Chrysanthemums* (Jan Zelibsky) (*horiz*)   5·50   4·50

304 Angel and Tree

2007. Christmas.
522 **304** 10k. multicoloured 1·40 1·10

305 20th-century Field Post

2007. Stamp Day.
523 **305** 28k. multicoloured 4·00 3·25

306 Map surrounded by National Tricolour.

2008. 15th Anniv of the Republic.
524 **306** T1 50g. multicoloured 2·40 1·90
No. 524 was for domestic 1st class mail weighing up to 50g.

307 Children carrying Lamb

2008. Easter.
525 **307** T2 50g. multicoloured 1·40 1·10
No. 525 was for domestic 2nd class mail weighing up to 50g.

308 Krupina

2008. Tourism.
526 **308** T2 100g. multicoloured 2·00 1·60
No. 526 was for domestic 2nd class mail weighing up to 100g.

309 Dahlia

2008. Personal Stamp.
527 **309** T2 50g. multicoloured 1·60 1·30

310 Roman Goddess of Justice (decoration, Old Town Hall, Bratislava)

2008. 15th Anniv of Constitutional Court.
528 **310** 25k. multicoloured 3·50 2·75

311 Eugen Suchon (composer)

2008. Birth Centenaries. Multicoloured.
529 **311** T2 500g. Type **311** 2·40 1·90
530 T1 100g. Masa Halʼamova (poet) (horiz) 3·00 2·30

No. 529 was for use on second class domestic mail up to 500 grams and 530 was for use on first class domestic mail up to 100 grams.

312 Seltenhofer Fire Appliance (1880)

2008. Early Fire-fighting Equipment. Multicoloured.
531 T2 1000g. Type **312** 3·00 2·30
532 T1 500g. Four-wheel hand-operated pumper, 1872 5·00 4·00
No. 531 was for use on second class domestic mail up to 1000 grams and 532 was for use on first class domestic mail up to 500 grams.

313 Cat using Mouse to Write Letter

2008. Europa. The Letter.
533 **313** 21k. multicoloured 3·25 2·50

314 Multi-headed Dragon

2008. Children's Stamp. 180th Birth Anniv of Pavol Dobsinsky (fairy tale collector and writer).
534 **314** T2 50g. multicoloured 1·60 1·30
No. 534 was for use on second class domestic mail up to 50 grams.

315 Long Jump

2008. Olympic Games, Beijing.
535 **315** 25k. multicoloured 3·50 2·75

316 Prosthetic Leg

2008. Paralympic Games, Beijing.
536 **316** 30k. multicoloured 5·00 4·00

317 Gilded Copper Plaque

2008. Archaeological Finds, Bojna.
537 **317** 33k. multicoloured 4·50 3·50

318 Karel Plicka

2008. Karel Plicka (photographer and film maker) Commemoration. Sheet 109×81 mm.
MS538 **318** 40k. multicoloured 5·50 4·25
A stamp of a similar design was issued by Czech Republic.

319 Matthias Corvinus (Matej Korvín)

2008. 550th Anniversary of Coronation of Matthias Corvinus, King of Hungary, 1458–1490.
539 **319** T1 50g. multicoloured 2·50 2·00
No. 539 was for use on first class domestic mail up to 50 grams.

320 Wooden Church, Hervartov

2008. Tourism. Churches. Multicoloured.
540 T1 100g. Type **320** 3·00 2·30
541 T1 100g. Church, Dobroslava 3·00 2·30
Nos. 540/1 were for use on first class domestic mail up to 100 grams.

321 *Cypripedium calceolus* (lady's slipper orchid)

2008. Nature Conservation. Orchids. Multicoloured.
542 T2 100g. Type **321** 2·00 1·60
543 T2 500g. *Ophrys apifera* (bee orchid) 2·40 1·90
Nos. 542/3 were for use on second class domestic mail up to 500 grams.

322 *The Holy Family* (detail)

2008. Christmas.
544 **322** T2 50g. multicoloured 1·60 1·30
No. 544 was for use on second class domestic mail up to 50 grams.

2008. Art (19th series). As T **53**.
545 T2 1000g. *A Girl in White with Factory Chimneys and Flowers* (Zoltan Palugyay) 4·50 3·50
546 T1 1000g. *Seven-coloured Flower* (Jozef Balaz) (book illustration) 5·25 4·00
No. 545 was for use on second class domestic mail up to 1000 grams.
No. 546 was for use on first class domestic mail up to 1000 grams.

323 Messenger

2008. Stamp Day. First Post Train, Bratislava–Ruzomberok–Kosice.
547 **323** T1 50g. multicoloured 2·40 1·90
No. 547 was for use on first class domestic mail up to 50 grams.

324 'ⅇ'

2009. First Euro Stamp.
548 **324** €1 multicoloured 4·25 3·50

325 Chapel of St. Margaret, Kopcany

2009. Cultural Heritage. Religious Architecture. Multicoloured.
549 1c. Type **325** 10 10
550 2c. Church of Mother of God, Boldog 20 15
551 5c. Round Church of St. Margaret, Sivetice 35 25
552 10c. Church of St. John the Baptist, Sedmerovec–Pominovce 45 35
553 20c. Church, Svatuse 85 70
554 33c. Church, Cierny Brod (34×26 mm) 1·50 1·20
555 50c. Church of St. Martin, Spisska Kapitula (26×22 mm) 2·20 1·70
556 66c. Church of St. Giles, Ilija (26×34 mm) 3·00 2·40
557 83c. Church of St. Stephen the King, Zilina-Zavodie (26×34 mm) 3·75 3·00
558 €1 Premonstratensian Monastery of Virgin Mary, Bina 4·25 3·50
559 €2 Church of St. Michael the Archangel, Drazovce 8·75 7·00
MS560 73×88 mm. €1.33 Church of St. Cross, Hamuliakovo 5·75 4·75

326 Decorated Egg

2009. Easter. Multicoloured. (a) Ordinary gum.
561 33c. Type **326** 2·20 1·70

(b) Self-adhesive.
562 33c. As Type **326** 1·80 1·30

327 Athlete

2009. Martial Arts.
563 **327** 60c. multicoloured 2·50 2·10

328 Aurel Stodola

2009. 150th Birth Anniv of Aurel Stodola (engineer, physicist, and inventor).
564 **328** 33c. multivcoloured 1·50 1·20

329 Magnifier and Map

2009. 40th Anniv of Foundation of Union of Slovak Philatelists (ZSF).
565 **329** T2 50g. multicoloured 1·70 1·40
No. 565 was for use on second class domestic mail up to 50 grams.

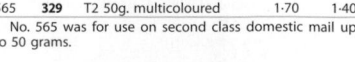

330 Arms

2009. 40th Anniv of Supreme Audit Office of Slovak Republic.
566 **330** 80c. silver and dull ultramarine 3·50 2·75

331 Vitruvian Man, Stars and Planets

2009. Europa. Astronomy.
567 **331** 90c. multicoloured 4·00 3·25

332 Zofia Bosniakova

2009. 400th Birth Anniv of Zofia Bosniaková (philanthropist) (oldest Slovak mummy). Sheet 79×103 mm.
MS568 **332** 80c. multicoloured 3·50 2·75

333 Ivan Gasparovic

2009. Ivan Gasparovic–President of the Slovak Republic. Sheet 102×69 mm.
MS569 **333** €1gold 4·50 3·75

334 It was dark and strangely quiet (illustration by Einar Turkowski (detail))

2009. 22nd Biennial Exhibition of Book Illustrations for Children, Bratislava.
570 **334** T2 50g. agate 1·80 1·50

335 Gateway and Soldier, Carnuntum

2009. Archaeology. Sheet 145×80 mm containing T **335** and similar horiz design. Multicoloured.
MS571 60c. Type **335**; 60c. Bas-relief
and mounted soldier, Gerulata 5·50 5·00
Stamps of a similar design were issued by Austria.

336 Salamandra salamandra

2009. Environmental Protection. Multicoloured.
572 €1.10 Type **336** 5·00 4·25
573 €1.10 Emys orbicularis 5·00 4·25

337 Skater

2009. Christmas. (a) Ordinary gum.
574 **337** 40c. multicoloured 1·80 1·50

(b) Self adhesive.
575 40c. multicoloured 2·30 1·90

2009. Art (20th series). As T **53**.
576 €1.20 Zena Klobukom (Jan Murdoch) 5·75 4·75
577 €1.20 Don Quijote (Cyprian Majernik) 5·75 4·75

338 Louis Braille

2009. Birth Bicentenary of Louis Braille (inventor of Braille writing for the blind).
578 **338** 70c. multicoloured 3·50 2·75

339 Cross

2010. Cultural Heritage. Church of the Assumption of the Virgin Mary in Spišska Nova Ves.
579 **339** 60c. multicoloured 2·75 2·30

340 Bobsleigh and Team

2010. Winter Olympic Games, Vancouver.
580 **340** €1 multicoloured 4·50 3·75

341 Ivan Gasparovic

2010. President of Slovakia.
581 **341** 40c. multicoloured 1·80 1·50

342 Suffering Christ (Mass-book of Bratislava)

2010. Easter. (a) Ordinary gum.
582 **342** 40c. multicoloured 1·80 1·50

(b) Self-adhesive.
583 40c. multicoloured 1·80 1·50

343 Matthew Czak

2010. Matthew Czak of Trencín (Matús Cák Trenciansky) (uncrowned king of Upper Hungary (Slovakia)) Commemoration.
584 **343** 70c. multicoloured 3·25 2·75

344 Central Panel of Altar (Speculum Justificationis (designed by Caspar Melissander for Count Juraj Thurzo))

2010. 400th Anniv of the Zilina Synod. Sheet 117×162 mm.
MS585 **344** €1.10 multicoloured 5·00 4·75

345 Milan Hodža

2010. Milan Hodža (politician and journalist) Commemoration
586 **345** 40c. multocoloured 1·75 1·75

346 Meluzína Jozefína (from Modrá kniha rozprávok (Blue Book of Fairy Tales) written by Lubomír Feldek and illustrated by Albín Brunovský)

2010. Europa
587 **346** 90c. multicoloured 4·00 4·00

347 Players

2010. World Cup Football Championships, South Africa. Multicoloured.
MS588 €2.30×2, Type **347** 21·00 21·00
No. **MS**588 has the flags of competing teams printed on the backing paper.

348 Castle of Topolcianky

2010. Castle of Topolčianky
589 **348** 40c. multicoloured 3·50 3·50

349 Castle Betliar

2010. Tourism
590 **349** 40c. multicoloured 1·75 1·75

350 St. Gorazd

2010. Saints. Multicoloured.
591 60c. Type **350** 6·50 6·50
592 60c. St. Clement 6·50 6·50

351 Topolcany Castle

2010. Personal Stamp
593 **351** 40c. multicoloured 1·75 1·75

352 Alabaster Canopic Jar

2010. Archaeology
594 **352** €1 multicoloured 4·50 4·50

353 Primula auricula

2010. Nature Protection. Multicoloured.
595 80c. Type **353** 3·75 3·75
596 80c. Daphne arbuscula 3·75 3·75

354 Initial 'P' containing Birth of Christ (Bratislava Missal)

2010. Christmas.

(a) Ordinary gum.
597 40c. Type **354** 2·00 2·00

(b) Booklet stamp. Self-adhesive.
598 40c. As Type **354** 2·00 2·00

355 Madonna, Church of the Assumption (Master Paul Levoca) (16th century)

2010. Gothic Mural Art, Spišská Kapitula. Multicoloured.
599 €1.20 Type **355** 2·20 2·20
600 €1.20 Coronation of Charles Robert of Anjou (detail) 2·20 2·20

No. 601 and Type **356** have been left for AIDS issued on 1 December 2010, not yet received.

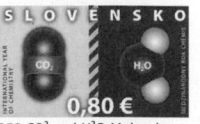

357 Karol Ondreička

2010. Stamp Day. Karol Ondreička Commemoration
602 **357** 70c. black and new blue 1·30 1·30

358 CO_2 and H_2O Molecules

2011. International Year of Chemistry
603 **358** 80c. multicoloured 1·50 1·50

359 St George

2011. Cultural Heritage. Church of St. George, Svätý Jur
604 **359** 70c. lavender, pale ochre and black 1·30 1·30

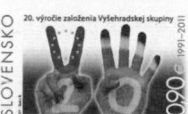

360 Hands inscribed '20'

2011. 20th Anniv of Visegrad Group (regional alliance of Czech Republic, Hungary, Poland and Slovakia)

| 605 | **360** | 90c. multicoloured | 1·60 | 1·60 |

361 Lamb

2011. Easter. Multicoloured.

(a) Sheet stamp. Ordinary gum

| 606 | **631** | 40c. multicoloured | 80 | 80 |

(b) Booklet stamp. Self-adhesive

| 607 | **631** | 40c. multicoloured | 80 | 80 |

No. 608 is left for stamp not yet received.

362 Players

2011. World Ice Hockey Championship 2011, Bratislava, Slovakia. Multicoloured.

| 609 | **362** | 50c. Type **362** | 90 | 90 |

363 Ice Cave in Dobšiná

2011. Tourism. Ice Cave in Dobšiná

| 610 | **363** | €1.10 multicoloured | 2·00 | 2·00 |

364 Pope John Paul II

2011. Beatification of Pope John Paul II

| 611 | **364** | 40c. multicoloured | 80 | 80 |

365 Dead Tree, National Park, Poloniny

2011. Europa. Forests

| 612 | **365** | 90c. multicoloured | 1·60 | 1·60 |

366 Flower

2011. Children's Stamp

| 613 | **366** | T2 50g. multicoloured | 1·60 | 1·60 |

367 Man in Chains, Angel and Members of Assembly

2011. 150th Anniv of Memorandum of Slovak Nation (adopted by Slovak National Assembly and laying down key requirements for recognition of national identity within Habsburg monarchy (Austria-Hungary)). Sheet 118×161 mm

| MS614 | **367** | €1.20 multicoloured | 2·40 | 2·40 |

368 Aero 30

2011. Vintage Cars. Multicoloured.

| 615 | 40c. Type **368** | 80 | 80 |
| 616 | 80c. Tatra 87 | 1·50 | 1·50 |

369 Ján Cikker

2011. Birth Centenary of Ján Cikker (composer)

| 617 | **369** | 50c. grey, scarlet-vermilion and black | 90 | 90 |

370 Tracy's Tiger (Martina Matlovičovej-Kralove)

2011. 23rd Biennial Exhibition of Book Illustrations for Children, Bratislava.

| 618 | **370** | 40c. multicoloured | 80 | 80 |

371 Michal Miloslav Hodža

2011. Birth Bicentenary of Michal Miloslav Hodža (national revivalist, Protestant priest, poet and linguist)

| 619 | **371** | 40c. greenish blue and black | 80 | 80 |

No. 620 is vacant.

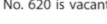

372 Otis tarda (Great Bustard)

2011. Nature Conservation. Great Bustard (Otis tarda)

| 621 | **372** | €1.10 multicoloured | 2·00 | 2·00 |

373 Embroidered Fish

2011. Christmas. Folk Art

| 622 | **373** | 40c. multicoloured | 80 | 80 |

374 Ján Sambucus

2011. Art. Johannes (Ján) Sambucus (poet and historian) Commemoration

| 623 | **374** | €1.20 yellow-ochre and black | 2·20 | 2·20 |

375 Mailbox

2011. Stamp Day. Mailboxes

| 624 | **375** | 50c. multicoloured | 90 | 90 |

376 Metercia from Rožňava

2011. Gothic Art. Painting of The Virgin and Child with St. Anne (Metercia from Rožňava). Sheet 100×140 mm

| MS625 | **376** | €1.60 multicoloured | 6·50 | 6·50 |

378 Jonáš Záborský

2012. Birth Bicentenary of Jonáš Záborský (writer and priest)

| 627 | **378** | 40c. multicoloured | 2·00 | 2·00 |

379 Samo Chalupka

2012. Birth Bicentenary of Samo Chalupka (poet)

| 628 | **379** | 50c. multicoloured | 2·20 | 2·20 |

380 Carrying the Cross (Hans von Aachen)

2012. Easter. Multicoloured.

(a) Sheet stamp. Ordinary gum

| 629 | **380** | 40c. multicoloured | 2·00 | 2·00 |

(b) Booklet stamp. Self-adhesive

| 630 | **380** | 40c. multicoloured | 2·00 | 2·00 |

381 John the Baptist

2012. 60th Death Anniv of Jan Koniarek (sculptor). Multicoloured.

| MS631 | €1.20×2, Type **381**×2 | 5·50 | 5·50 |

382 'Lanx Diskos' (2nd century BC from tomb of Germanic chief , Krakovany)

2012. Europa. Visit Slovakia

| 632 | **382** | 90c. multicoloured | 1·60 | 1·60 |

383 Team Members

2012. Slovakia, Silver Medallists, World Ice Hockey Championship 2012

| 633 | **383** | 40c. multicoloured | 2·00 | 2·00 |

384 Cake

2011. Children's Day. Multicoloured.

(a) Sheet stamp. Ordinary gum

| 634 | **384** | T2 50g. multicoloured | 1·60 | 1·60 |

(b) Booklet stamp. Self-adhesive

| 635 | **384** | T2 50g. multicoloured | 1·60 | 1·60 |

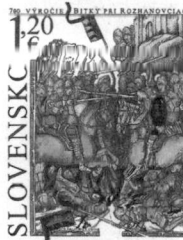

385 Battle Scene

2012. 700th Anniv of Battle of Rozhanovce. Sheet 99×139 mm

| MS636 | **385** | €1.20 multicoloured | 2·40 | 2·40 |

386 Wheelchair Racer

2012. Olympic and Paralympic Games, London. Multicoloured.

| 637 | 90c. Type **386** | 1·60 | 1·60 |
| 638 | 90c. Winged torch bearer and head of a 'Bronzi di Riace' | 1·60 | 1·60 |

387 Malá Skalka, Trenčín

2012. Tourism. Churches

| 639 | 40c. yellow and bistre-brown | 1·75 | 1·75 |
| 640 | 40c. azure and dull ultramarine | 1·75 | 1·75 |

Designs: 40c. Type **387**; Basilica of Our Lady of Sorrows, Šaštín (vert)

388 Anton Bernolák

2012. 250th Birth Anniv of Anton Bernolák (Roman Catholic priest, linguist and prominent in the Slovak National Revival) . Multicoloured.

| MS641 | **388** | €1.10 multicoloured | 5·50 | 5·50 |

389 *Loiseleuria procumbens*

2012. Nature Protection. Low Tatras National Park. Multicoloured.

MS642	70c.×2, Type **389**; *Saxifraga mutata*	7·00	7·00

390 Ľubovňany Castle

2012. Ľubovňany Castle

643	**390**	90c. multicoloured	4·00	4·00

391 *The Nativity* (attributed to Josef Ignaz Mildorfer)

2012. Christmas

(a) Ordinary gum

644	40c. Type **391**	1·75	1·75

(b) Booklet stamp. Self-adhesive

645	40c. As Type **391**	1·75	1·75

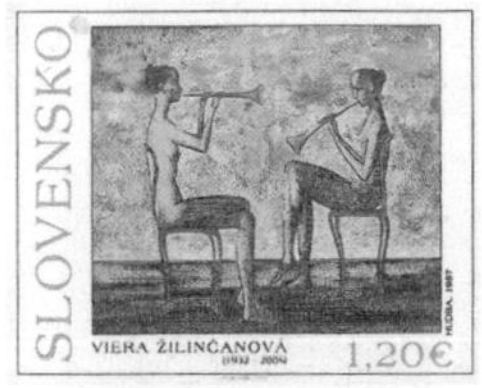

392 *Hudba* (Music) (Viera Žilinčanová)

2012. Art. Multicoloured.

646	€1.20 Type **392**	5·50	5·50
MS647	142×115 mm. €1.60 Dancers (Sala terrena in Červený Kameň Castle)	6·75	6·75

No. 623 and Type **374** are left for Art, issued on 25th November 2011, not yet received.

393 Pavol Socháň

2012. Stamp Day. 150th Birth Anniv of Pavol Socháň (ethnographer, photographer, journalist and dramatist)

648	**393**	50c. multicoloured	2·00	2·00

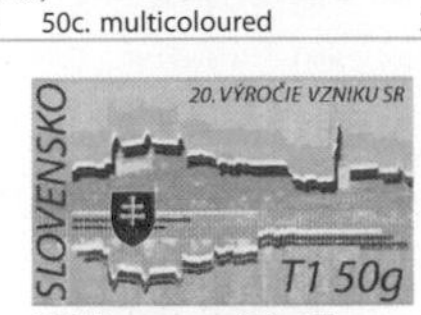

394 Panorama of Bratislava, Capital of Slovak Republic

2013. 20th Anniv of Slovak Republic. Košice - The European Capital of Culture 2013

649	**394**	T150g (65c.) multicoloured	2·75	2·30

395 Putti

2013. Cultural Heritage. Empire Theatre, Hlohovec

650	**395**	90c. multicoloured	4·00	4·00

396 Ján Popluhár

2013. Sport. Ján Popluhár (footballer) Commemoration

651	**396**	65c. multicoloured	2·80	2·40

397 Folk Themes

2012. Easter

(a) Sheet stamp. Ordinary gum

652	**397**	45c. multicoloured	2·00	2·00

(b) Booklet stamp. Self-adhesive

653	**397**	45c. multicoloured	2·00	2·00

398 Dominik Tatarka

2013. Birth Centenary of Dominik Tatarka (writer)

654	**398**	65c. multicoloured	2·75	2·30

399 Diana, The Huntress (As Type **2342** of USA)

2013. Breast Cancer Awareness Campaign

655	**399**	€1.10 multicoloured	5·00	4·50

No. 656 and Type **400** are left for Technical Monument, not yet received.

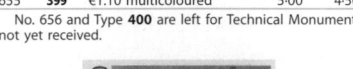

401 Early Mail Van

2013. Europa. Postal Transport

(a) Sheet stamp. Ordinary gum

657	**401**	90c. multicoloured	4·00	4·00

(b) Booklet stamp. Self-adhesive

658	**401**	90c. multicoloured	4·00	4·00

402 Dancers

2013. 65th Anniv of Lúčnica Art Ensemble. Tenth Anniv of Pansori designation as UNESCO 'Masterpiece of the Oral Tradition and Intangible Heritage of Humanity'. Multicoloured.

659	€1 Type **402**	4·50	3·75
660	€1 Pansori (musical storytelling performed by vocalist and drummer) (Korea)	4·50	3·75

403 Zodiac

2013. Personal Stamp. Zodiac

661	**403**	T2 50g. (45c.) multicoloured	1·75	1·75

No. 662 and Type **404** are left for 1150th Anniv of Arrival of St. Cyril and Methodius to Great Moravia, not yet received.

405 Gorazd Zvonický

2013. Birth Centenary of Gorazd Zvonický (Andrej Šándor) (priest and poet)

663	**405**	65c. multicoloured	2·75	2·30

NEWSPAPER STAMPS

1939. Nos. of Czechoslovakia optd **1939 SLOVENSKY STAT**.

N25	2h. brown	45	50
N26	5h. blue	45	50
N27	7h. red	45	50
N28	9h. green	45	50
N29	10h. red	45	50
N30	12h. blue	45	50
N31	20h. green	1·00	1·20
N32	50h. brown	2·50	3·00
N33	1k. green	9·50	12·00

N7

1939. Imperf.

N40	**N7**	2h. brown	25	25
N65	**N7**	5h. blue	1·70	1·50
N42	**N7**	7h. red	10	25
N43	**N7**	9h. green	10	25
N66	**N7**	10h. red	30	15
N45	**N7**	12h. blue	35	45
N67	**N7**	15h. purple	40	25
N68	**N7**	20h. green	75	90
N69	**N7**	25h. blue	75	90
N70	**N7**	40h. red	75	90
N71	**N7**	50h. brown	1·40	1·00
N72	**N7**	1k. green	1·40	1·00
N73	**N7**	2k. green	2·75	2·50

N29 Printer's Type

1943. Imperf.

N101	**N29**	10h. green	35	30
N102	**N29**	15h. brown	35	30
N103	**N29**	20h. blue	45	40
N104	**N29**	50h. red	45	40
N105	**N29**	1k. green	55	50
N106	**N29**	2k. blue	75	70

PERSONAL DELIVERY STAMPS

P17

1940. Imperf.

P65	**P17**	50h. blue	1·20	2·50
P66	**P17**	50h. red	1·20	2·50

POSTAGE DUE STAMPS

D13

1939

D51	**D13**	5h. blue	55	70
D52	**D13**	10h. blue	50	65
D53	**D13**	20h. blue	50	65
D54	**D13**	30h. blue	2·75	2·50
D55	**D13**	40h. blue	95	65
D56	**D13**	50h. blue	2·75	1·60
D57	**D13**	60h. blue	95	65
D58	**D13**	1k. red	95	65
D59	**D13**	2k. red	17·00	9·75
D60	**D13**	5k. red	3·75	3·25
D61	**D13**	10k. red	2·75	3·25
D62	**D13**	20k. red	19·00	13·00

D24

1942

D89	**D24**	10h. brown	20	10
D90	**D24**	20h. brown	20	10
D91	**D24**	40h. brown	20	10
D92	**D24**	50h. brown	95	95
D93	**D24**	60h. brown	50	25
D94	**D24**	80h. brown	50	25
D95	**D24**	1k. red	30	20
D96	**D24**	1k.10 red	65	85
D97	**D24**	1k.30 red	50	25
D98	**D24**	1k.60 red	50	25
D99	**D24**	2k. red	95	35
D100	**D24**	2k.60 red	1·40	1·50
D101	**D24**	3k.50 red	10·00	11·00
D102	**D24**	5k. red	3·50	2·75
D103	**D24**	10k. red	4·25	4·00

Pt. 3

SLOVENIA

Formerly part of Austria, in 1918 Slovenia was combined with other areas to form Yugoslavia. Separate stamps were issued during the Second World War whilst under Italian and German Occupation.

In 1991 Slovenia seceded and became an independent state.

1941. 100 paras = 1 dinar.
1991. 100 stotinas = 1 tolar.
2007. 100 cents = 1 euro.

ITALIAN OCCUPATION, 1941

1941. Nos. 330/1 and 414/26 of Yugoslavia optd **Co. Ci.**

1	**99**	25p. black	1·40	1·90
2	**99**	50p. orange	1·40	1·90
3	**99**	1d. green	1·40	1·90
4	**99**	1d.50 red	1·40	1·90
5	**99**	2d. red	1·40	1·90
6	**99**	3d. brown	1·40	1·90
7	**99**	4d. blue	1·40	1·90
8	**99**	5d. blue	1·40	1·90
9	**99**	5d.50 violet	1·40	1·90
10	**99**	6d. blue	1·90	2·30
11	**99**	8d. brown	2·30	2·75
12	**70**	10d. violet	2·30	2·75
13	**99**	12d. violet	4·75	4·25
14	**70**	15d. olive	£375	£400
15	**99**	16d. purple	4·75	4·75
16	**99**	20d. blue	11·00	17·00
17	**99**	30d. pink	70·00	80·00

1941. Nos. 330 and 414/26 of Yugoslavia optd **R.Commissariato Civile Territori Sloveni occupati LUBIANA**, with four lines of dots at foot.

23		25p. black	1·40	95
24		50p. orange	1·40	95
25		1d. green	1·40	95
26		1d.50 red	1·40	95
27		2d. red	1·40	95
28		3d. brown	1·40	95
29		4d. blue	1·40	95
30		5d. blue	1·60	1·10
31		5d.50 violet	1·40	95
32		6d. blue	1·40	95
33		8d. brown	1·40	95
34	**70**	10d. violet	3·25	1·90
35	**99**	12d. violet	1·60	1·10
36	**99**	16d. purple	3·25	1·90
37	**99**	20d. blue	11·00	9·25
38	**99**	30d. pink	£110	85·00

1941. Nos. 446/9 of Yugoslavia optd as Nos. 23/38 but with only three lines of dots at foot.

45	50p.+50p. on 5d. violet	14·00	17·00
46	1d.+1d. on 10d. lake	14·00	17·00
47	1d.50+1d.50 on 20d. green	14·00	17·00
48	2d.+2d. on 30d. blue	14·00	17·00

1941. Air. Nos. 360/7 and 443/4 of Yugoslavia optd as Nos. 23/38, with three or four (No. 57) lines of dots at foot.

49	50p. brown	3·75	4·75
50	1d. green	3·75	4·75
51	2d. blue	6·50	7·50
52	2d.50 red	6·50	7·50
53	5d. violet	9·25	11·00
54	10d. lake	9·25	11·00
55	20d. green	37·00	37·00
56	30d. blue	65·00	75·00
57	40d. green	£225	£250
58	50d. blue	£200	£200

1941. Nos. 26 and 29 surch.

59	0d.50 on 1d.50 red	95	1·40
60	0d.50 on 1d.50 red	£1400	£1800
61	1d. on 4d. blue	95	1·40

POSTAGE DUE STAMPS

1941. Postage Due stamps of Yugoslavia, Nos. D89/93 optd **Co. Ci.**

D18	**D56**	50p. violet	1·40	1·90
D19	**D56**	1d. mauve	1·40	1·90
D20	**D56**	2d. blue	1·40	1·90
D21	**D56**	5d. orange	17·00	14·00
D22	**D56**	10d. brown	17·00	14·00

Optd as Nos. 23/38, but with four lines of dots at top.

D40	50p. violet	95	1·40
D41	1d. mauve	95	1·40
D42	2d. blue	1·90	2·30
D43	5d. orange	55·00	70·00
D44	10d. brown	23·00	28·00

Optd as Nos. D40/44, but with narrower lettering.

D62	50p. violet	95	1·90
D63	1d. mauve	1·60	2·75
D64	2d. blue	47·00	55·00

GERMAN OCCUPATION, 1943–45

(3)

(4)

1944. Stamps of Italy optd with Type **3** or **4**. (a) On Postage stamps of 1929.

65	**4**	5c. brown	55	7·50
66	**3**	10c. brown	55	7·50
67	**4**	15c. green	55	7·50
68	**3**	20c. red	55	7·50
69	**4**	25c. green	55	7·50
70	**3**	30c. brown	55	7·50
71	**4**	35c. blue	55	7·50
72	**3**	50c. violet	55	9·50
73	**4**	75c. red	55	13·50
74	**3**	1l. violet	55	13·50
75	**4**	1l.25 blue	55	5·25
76	**3**	1l.75 orange	8·00	32·00
77	**4**	2l. red	55	9·50
78	**3**	10l. violet	13·00	75·00

Surch with new value.

79	-	2l.55 on 5c. brown	3·25	16·00
80	**4**	5l. on 25c. green	3·25	26·00
81	**4**	20l. on 20c. red	16·00	85·00
82	**3**	25l. on 2l. red	13·00	£170
83	**4**	50l. on 1l.75 orange	65·00	£275

In No. 79 the overprint inscriptions are at each side of the eagle.

(b) On Air stamps, Nos. 270, etc.

84		25c. green	13·00	55·00
85	**3**	50c. brown	13·00	£170
86	**4**	75c. brown	13·00	55·00
87	**3**	1l. violet	13·00	£170
88	**4**	2l. blue	13·00	£120
89	**3**	5l. green	13·00	£170
90	**4**	10l. red	13·00	£120

(c) On Air Express stamp.

E91	**3**	2l. black (No. E370)	13·00	£120

(d) On Express Letter stamp.

E92	1l.25 green (No. E350)	13·00	32·00

1944. Red Cross. Express Letter stamps of Italy surch as Type **3** or **4** with a red cross and new value alongside.

102	**E132**	1l.25+50l. green	48·00	£800
103	**E132**	2l.50+50l. orange	48·00	£800

1944. Homeless Relief Fund. Express Letter stamps of Italy surch as Type **3** and **4**, but in circular frame, and **BREZDOMCEM DEN OBDACHLOSEN** alongside with new value between.

104	1l.25+50l. green	48·00	£800
105	2l.50+50l. orange	48·00	£800

1944. Air. Orphans' Fund. Air stamps of Italy Nos. 270, etc., surch as Type **3** and **4**, but in circular frame between **DEN WAISEN SIROTAM** and new value.

106	-	25c.+10l. green	19·00	£550
107	**110**	50c.+10l. brown	19·00	£550
108	-	75c.+20l. brown	19·00	£550
109	-	1l.+20l. violet	19·00	£550
110	**113**	2l.+20l. blue	19·00	£550
111	**110**	5l.+20l. green	19·00	£550

1944. Air. Winter Relief Fund. Air stamps of Italy Nos. 270, etc., surch as Type **3** and **4**, but between **ZIMSKA POMOC WINTERHILFE** and new value.

112	-	25c.+10l. green	19·00	£550
113	**110**	50c.+10l. brown	19·00	£550
114	-	75c.+20l. brown	19·00	£550
115	-	1l.+20l. violet	19·00	£550
116	**113**	2l.+20l. blue	19·00	£550
117	**110**	5l.+20l. green	19·00	£550

9 Railway Viaduct, Borovnice

10 Church in Novo Mesto

1945. Inscr "PROVINZ LAIBACH".

118	-	5c. brown	55	5·25
119	-	10c. orange	55	5·25
120	**9**	20c. brown	55	5·25
121	-	25c. green	55	5·25
122	**10**	50c. violet	55	5·25
123	-	75c. red	55	5·25
124	-	1l. green	55	5·25
125	-	1l.25 blue	55	10·50
126	-	1l.50 green	55	10·50
127	-	2l. blue	80	12·50
128	-	2l.50 brown	80	12·50
129	-	3l. mauve	1·90	21·00
130	-	5l. brown	2·10	21·00
131	-	10l. green	4·25	95·00
132	-	20l. blue	26·00	£350
133	-	30l. red	£130	£1300

DESIGNS—VERT: 5c. Stalagmites, Krizna Jama; 1l.25, Kocevje; 1l.50, Borovnice Falls; 3l. Castle, Zuzemberg; 30l. View and Tabor Church. HORIZ: 10c. Zirknitz Lake; 25c. Farm near Ljubljana; 75c. View from Ribnica; 1l. Old Castle, Ljubljana; 2l. Castle, Kostanjevica; 2l.50, Castle, Turjak; 5l. View on River Krka; 10l. Castle, Otocec; 20l. Farm at Dolenjskom.

POSTAGE DUE STAMPS

(D5)

(D6)

1944. Postage Due stamps of Italy, Nos. D395, etc., optd as Type **D5**.

D93	**D141**	5c. brown	3·00	£110
D94	**D141**	10c. blue	3·00	£110
D95	**D141**	20c. red	1·10	7·50
D96	**D141**	25c. green	1·10	7·50
D97	**D141**	50c. violet	1·10	7·50
D98	**D 142**	1l. orange	1·10	7·50
D99	**D 142**	2l. green	1·10	7·50

Surch as Type D 6.

D100	**D 141**	30c. on 50c. violet	3·25	£110
D101	**D 141**	40c. on 5c. brown	3·25	£110

INDEPENDENT STATE

11 Parliament Building

1991. Declaration of Independence.

134	**11**	5d. multicoloured	1·00	95

12 Arms

1991

135	**12**	1t. multicoloured	10	10
136	**12**	4t. multicoloured	15	15
137	**12**	5t. multicoloured	20	20
138	**12**	11t. multicoloured	50	45

13 Ski Jumping

1992. Winter Olympic Games, Albertville. Multicoloured.

139	30t. Type **13**	3·00	2·75
140	50t. Slalom	4·00	3·75

14 Arms

1992. Multicoloured, background colours given.

141	**14**	1t. brown	10	10
142	**14**	2t. purple	15	15
143	**14**	4t. green	20	20
144	**14**	5t. red	25	25
145	**14**	6t. yellow	30	30
146	**14**	11t. orange	40	35
147	**14**	15t. blue	45	40
148	**14**	20t. violet	50	45
149	**14**	50t. green	1·40	1·30
150	**14**	100t. grey	2·75	2·50

15 Opera House

1992. Centenary of Ljubljana Opera House.

155	**15**	20t. multicoloured	1·60	1·50

16 Tartini and Violins

1992. 300th Birth Anniv of Giuseppe Tartini (violinist and composer).

156	**16**	27t. multicoloured	1·60	1·50

17 Map and Marko Anton Kappus preaching to Amerindians

1992. 500th Anniv of Discovery of America by Columbus. Multicoloured.

157	27t. Type **17**	3·25	3·00
158	47t. Map and "Santa Maria"	4·25	4·00

18

1992. Obligatory Tax. Red Cross.

159	**18**	3t. black, red and blue	85	80

19 Collapsible Chair by Niko Kralj and Map

1992. 17th World Industrial Design Congress, Ljubljana.

160	**19**	41t. multicoloured	1·00	95

20 Slomsek

1992. 130th Death Anniv of Anton Slomsek, Bishop of Maribor.

161	**20**	41t. multicoloured	1·00	95

21 Wreckage

1992. Obligatory Tax. Solidarity Week. Perf and imperf.

162	**21**	3t. brown, black and red	65	60

22 Rescuing Mountaineer

1992. 80th Anniv of Alpine Rescue Service.

164	**22**	41t. multicoloured	1·00	95

23 River Jousting

1992. 900th Anniv of River Jousting in Ljubljana.

165	**23**	6t. multicoloured	50	50

24 Linden Leaf and Flowers

1992. First Anniv of Independence.

166	**24**	41t. multicoloured	1·00	95

25 Leon Stukelj and Medals

1992. Olympic Games, Barcelona. Multicoloured.

167	40t. Type **25**	1·30	1·20
168	46t. Head of Apoxymenos repeated in three Slovene colours	1·40	1·30

26 Sheepdog

1992. "Psov '92" World Dog-training Championships, Ljubljana.

169	**26**	40t. multicoloured	1·00	95

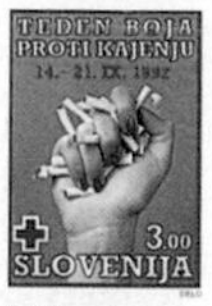

27 Hand crushing Cigarettes

1992. Obligatory Tax. Red Cross. Anti-smoking Week.

170	**27**	3t. multicoloured	50	50

28 Kogoj and scene from "Black Masks" (opera)

1992. Birth Centenary of Marij Kogoj (composer).

171	**28**	40t. multicoloured	1·00	95

29 Langus (self-portrait)

1992. Birth Bicentenary of Matevz Langus (painter).

172	**29**	40t. multicoloured	1·00	95

30 Nativity

1992. Christmas. Multicoloured.
173   6t. Type **30**   20   10
174   7t. Type **30**   50   50
175   41t. "Madonna and Child" (stained-glass window by V. Sorli-Puc in St. Mary's Church, Bovec) (vert)   1·00   95

31 Potocnik, View of Earth from Space and Satellite

1992. Birth Centenary of Herman Potocnik (space flight pioneer).
176   **31**   46t. multicoloured   1·00   95

32 Illustration from "Solzice"

1993. Birth Centenary of Prezihov Voranc (writer).
177   **32**   7t. multicoloured   50   50

33 "Underneath the Birches"

1993. 50th Death Anniv of Rihard Jakopic (painter).
178   **33**   44t. multicoloured   1·00   95

34 Bust of Stefan (J. Savinsek)

1993. Death Centenary of Jozef Stefan (physicist).
179   **34**   51t. multicoloured   1·00   95

35 Honey-cake from Skofja Loka

1993. Slovene Culture.

No.	Type	Description		
180	**35**	1t. brown, ochre & dp brn	20	10
181	-	2t. green and light green	20	10
182	-	5t. dp grey, grey & mauve	20	10
183	-	6t. lt green, green & yellow	20	10
184	-	7t. red, crimson and grey	20	10
185	-	8t. green, dp green & olive	20	10
186	-	9t. red, brown and grey	30	15
187	-	10t. brown and light brown	30	15
188	-	11t. green, lt green & yell	30	15
189	-	12t. red, orange and grey	30	15
189a	-	13t. green, black & dp grn	30	15
189b	-	14t. red, brown and grey	30	15
189c	-	15t. black, drab and red	30	15
189d	-	16t. brown, blue and orange	30	15
189e	-	17t. chocolate, yellow & brn	30	15
189f	-	18t. brown, black and blue	30	15
190	-	20t. green and grey	65	60
191	-	44t. blue, dp blue & blk	1·00	95
192	-	50t. purple and mauve	1·00	95
193	-	55t. black, grey & orge	75	70
194	-	65t. ochre, brown & pink	95	85
195	-	70t. grey, brown and green	1·00	95
196	-	75t. green, blue and lilac	1·00	95
197	-	80t. multicoloured	1·30	1·20
197a	-	90t. brown, red and grey	1·40	1·30
198	-	100t. brown, red & lt brn	2·20	1·90
198a	-	300t. chestnut and brown	5·00	4·25
198ab	-	200t. purple, green and blue	5·00	4·25
198b	-	400t. red and brown	7·00	6·25
198c	-	500t. violet, orge & grey	6·50	5·75

DESIGNS: 2t. Reed pipes; 5t. Double hay-drying frame; 6t. Shepherd's hut, Velika Planina; 7t. Zither; 8t. Mill on the Mur; 9t. Sledge; 10t. Earthenware double-bass; 11t. Hay basket; 12t. Boy on horse (statuette), Ribnica; 13t. Wind-operated bird-scarer, Prlekija; 14t. Hen-shaped wine jug, Sentjernej; 15t. Blast furnace, Zelezniki; 16t. Windmill, Stari, Gori; 17t. Maize store, Ptujskopolje; 18t. Accordion, Kranjska Gora; 20t. Farmhouse, Prekmurje; 44t. House, Karst; 50t. Wind-propelled pump, Secovlje salt-pans; 55t. Easter eggs, Bela Krajina; 65t. Lamp, Trzic; 70t. Ski; 75t. Wrought iron window lattice; 80t. Palm Sunday bundle, Ljubljana; 90t. Apiary; 100t. Nut cake; 200t. Bootjack in shape of stag beetle; 300t. Straw sculpture; 400t. Wine press; 500t. Decorated table.

36 Mountains and Founder Members

1993. Centenary of Alpine Association.
199   **36**   7t. multicoloured   35   35

37 Cop's Route up Triglav

1993. Birth Centenary of Joza Cop (climber and mountain rescuer).
200   **37**   44t. multicoloured   75   75

38 Chainbreaker (1919 stamp design)

1993. 75th Anniv of Slovenian Postal Service.
201   **38**   7t. multicoloured   20   20

39 "St. Nicholas" (altar painting, Tintoretto)

1993. 500th Anniv of College Chapter of Novo Mesto. Multicoloured.
202   7t. Type **39**   10   10
203   44t. Arms   1·10   1·10

40 "Table in Pompeii" (Marij Pregelj)

1993. Europa. Contemporary Art. Multicoloured.
204   44t. Type **40**   2·20   2·20
205   159t. "Girl with Toy" (Gabrijel Stupica)   5·50   5·50

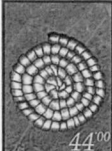

41 "Schwagerina carniolica"

1993. Fossils.
206   **41**   44t. multicoloured   1·10   1·10

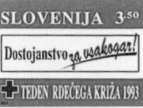

42

1993. Obligatory Tax. Red Cross.
207   **42**   3t.50 black, red and blue   35   35

43 6th-century B.C. Vase

1993. First Anniv of Admission to United Nations Organization.
208   **43**   62t. multicoloured   1·60   1·60

44 Red Cross Rescue Workers

1993. Obligatory Tax. Solidarity Week.
209   **44**   3t.50 multicoloured   35   35

45 Basketball, Johann and Swimming

1993. Mediterranean Games, Roussillon (Languedoc).
210   **45**   36t. multicoloured   85   85

46 "Battle of Sisak" (Johann Valvasor)

1993. 400th Anniv of Battle of Sisak.
211   **46**   49t. multicoloured   1·60   1·60

47 "Monolistra spinosissima"

1993. Cave Fauna. Multicoloured.
212   7t. Type **47**   20   20
213   40t. "Aphaenopidius kamnikensis" (insect)   1·10   1·10
214   55t. "Proteus anguinus"   1·20   1·20
215   65t. "Zospeum spelaeum" (mollusc)   1·40   1·40

48 Horse and Diagram of Movements

1993. European Dressage Championships, Lipica.
216   **48**   65t. multicoloured   1·60   1·60

49 Boy smoking and Emblem

1993. Obligatory Tax. Red Cross. Anti-smoking Week.
217   **49**   4t.50 multicoloured   35   35

50 Valvasor Arms

1993. 300th Anniversaries.
218   **50**   9t. black, lilac and gold   20   20
219   -   65t. black, stone and gold   1·40   1·40
DESIGN: 9t. Type **50** (death anniv of Johann Valvasor (historian)); 65t. Arms of Academia Operosorum.

51 "Slovenian Family at Christmas Crib" (M. Gaspari)

1993. Christmas. Multicoloured.
220   9t. Type **51**   20   20
221   65t. Dr. Joze Pogacnik (archbishop) (after B. Jakac) and seal   1·40   1·40

52 Illustration from "The Vagabond"

1994. 150th Anniversaries. Multicoloured.
222   8t. Type **52** (birth anniv of Josip Juncic (writer))   10   10
223   9t. Nightingale and bridge over river (birth anniv of Simon Gregorcic, poet)   25   25
224   55t. Book showing Slovenian vowels (birth anniv of Stanislav Skrabec, philologist)   1·20   1·20
225   65t. Cover of grammar book (death anniv of Jernei Kopitar, philologist)   1·40   1·40

53 Hearts

1994. Greetings Stamp.
226   **53**   9t. multicoloured   25   25

54 Cross-country Skiing

1994. Winter Olympic Games, Lillehammer, Norway. Multicoloured.
227   9t. Type **54**   25   25
228   65t. Slalom skiing   1·70   1·70

55 Ski Jumping

1994. 60th Anniv of Ski Jumping Championships, Planica.
| 229 | 55 | 70t. multicoloured | 1·70 | 1·70 |

56 Town Names

1994. 850th Anniv of First Official Record of Ljubljana.
| 230 | 56 | 9t. multicoloured | 25 | 25 |

57 Janez Puhar and Camera

1994. Europa. Discoveries and Inventions. Multicoloured.
| 231 | | 70t. Type **57** (invention of glass-plate photography) | 1·70 | 1·70 |
| 232 | | 215t. Moon, natural logarithm diagram and Jurij Vega (mathematician) | 5·75 | 5·75 |

58 Balloons

1994. Obligatory Tax. Red Cross.
| 233 | 58 | 4t.50 multicoloured | 35 | 35 |

59 "Primula carniolica"

1994. Flowers. Multicoloured.
234		9t. Type **59**	25	25
235		44t. "Hladnikia pastinacifolia"	95	95
236		60t. "Daphne blagayana"	1·30	1·30
237		70t. "Campanula zoysii"	1·50	1·50

60 Red Cross Worker with Child

1994. Obligatory Tax. Solidarity Week.
| 238 | 60 | 4t.50 multicoloured | 35 | 35 |

61 Inflating "Globe" Football

1994. World Cup Football Championship, U.S.A.
| 239 | 61 | 44t. multicoloured | 95 | 95 |

62 Globes in Olympic Colours and Flags

1994. Centenary of International Olympic Committee.
| 240 | 62 | 100t. multicoloured | 2·30 | 2·30 |

63 Mt. Ojstrica

1994
| 241 | 63 | 12t. multicoloured | 60 | 60 |

64 Maks Pletersnik (compiler) and University of Laibach Professors

1994. Centenary of First Slovenian–German Dictionary.
| 242 | 64 | 70t. multicoloured | 1·70 | 1·70 |

65 Roman Infantry

1994. 1600th Anniv of Battle of Frigidus.
| 243 | 65 | 60t. red, black and grey | 1·70 | 1·70 |

66 Post Office

1994. Centenary of Maribor Post Office.
| 244 | 66 | 70t. multicoloured | 1·70 | 1·70 |

67 Series kkStB Steam Locomotive No. 6777

1994. Centenary of Ljubljana Railway.
| 245 | 67 | 70t. multicoloured | 1·70 | 1·70 |

68 Orchestra Venue and Music

1994. Bicentenary of Ljubljana Philharmonic Society. Multicoloured.
| 246 | | 12t. Type **68** | 25 | 25 |
| 247 | | 70t. Ludwig van Beethoven, Johannes Brahms, Antonin Dvorak and Joseph Haydn (composers) and Niccolo Paganini (violinist) | 1·50 | 1·50 |

69 Christmas Tree, Window and Candles

1994. Christmas and International Year of the Family.
| 248 | 69 | 12t. multicoloured | 25 | 25 |
| 249 | | 70t. cream, black and blue | 1·50 | 1·50 |

DESIGN: 70t. "Children with Christmas Tree" (F. Kralj) and I.Y.F. emblem.

70 "Madonna and Child" (statue, Loreto Basilica)

1994. 700th Anniv of Loreto.
| 250 | 70 | 70t. multicoloured | 1·70 | 1·70 |

71 Ivan Hribar, Mihajlo Rostohar and Danilo Majaron (founders) and University

1994. 75th Anniv of Ljubljana University.
| 251 | 71 | 70t. multicoloured | 1·70 | 1·70 |

72 Postal Emblem

1995
| 252 | 72 | 13t. multicoloured | 60 | 60 |

73 Lili Novy (writer, 110th birth)

1995. Anniversaries.
253	73	20t. red, black and grey	60	60
254	-	70t. yellow, black and gold	1·70	1·70
255	-	70t. multicoloured	1·70	1·70

DESIGNS—HORIZ: No. 253, Silhouettes of figures and signature of Anton Tomasz Linhart (dramatist, death bicentenary). VERT: No. 255, Detail of facade of Zadruzna Co operative Bank, Ljubljana (110th birth anniv (1994) of Ivan Vurnik (architect)).

74 Cats and Hearts (Jure Kos)

1995. Greetings Stamp.
| 256 | 74 | 20t. multicoloured | 60 | 60 |

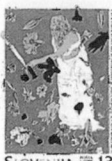

75 Allegory

1995. 50th Anniv of End of Second World War.
| 257 | 75 | 13t. multicoloured | 35 | 35 |

76 Skeleton and Woman

1995. Europa. Peace and Freedom. Multicoloured.
| 258 | | 60t. Type **76** (50th anniv of liberation of concentration camps) | 2·30 | 2·30 |
| 259 | | 70t. Woman running free | 2·40 | 2·40 |

77 "Karavankina schellwieni"

1995. Fossils.
| 260 | 77 | 70t. multicoloured | 1·70 | 1·70 |

78 Alpine Iris, Triglav National Park and Alpine Poppy

1995. European Nature Conservation Year.
| 261 | 78 | 70t. multicoloured | 1·70 | 1·70 |

79 Child painting Red Cross

1995. Obligatory Tax. Red Cross.
| 262 | 79 | 6t. multicoloured | 35 | 35 |

80 First Aiders tending Casualty

1995. Obligatory Tax. Solidarity Week.
| 263 | 80 | 6t.50 multicoloured | 35 | 35 |

81 Lesser Kestrel

1995. Birds. Multicoloured.
264		13t. Type **81**	25	25
265		60t. European roller	1·20	1·20
266		70t. Lesser grey shrike	1·40	1·40
267		215t. Black-headed bunting	4·25	1·25

82 Radovljica

1995. 500th Anniv of Radovljica.
| 268 | 82 | 44t. multicoloured | 95 | 95 |

83 Class KRB 37 Steam Locomotive "Podnart"

1995. 125th Anniv of Ljubljana–Jesenice Railway.
| 269 | 83 | 70t. black, red and yellow | 1·70 | 1·70 |

84 Mountain and Presbytery

1995. Centenary of Jakob Aljaz Presbytery, Mount Triglav.
| 270 | 84 | 100t. blue, black and red | 1·70 | 1·70 |

85 Scouts around Campfire

1995. Scouting.
| 271 | 85 | 70t. multicoloured | 1·70 | 1·70 |

86 "Death of a Genius"

1995. Birth Centenary of France Kralz (artist). Multicoloured.

| 272 | 60t. Type **86** | 1·20 | 1·20 |
| 273 | 70t. "Family of Horses" | 1·30 | 1·30 |

87 Handshake, Anniversary Emblem and Different Nationalities

1995. 50th Anniversaries of U.N.O. (274) and F.A.O. (275). Multicoloured.

| 274 | 70t. Type **87** | 1·20 | 1·20 |
| 275 | 70t. Foodstuffs, anniversary emblem and different nationalities | 1·20 | 1·20 |

88 "Winter" (Marlenka Stupica)

1995. Christmas. Paintings. Multicoloured.

| 276 | 13t. Type **88** | 25 | 25 |
| 277 | 70t. "Madonna and Child" (Leopold Layer) | 1·50 | 1·50 |

89 Birds and Heart (Karmen Podgornik)

1996. Greetings Stamp.

| 278 | **89** | 13t. multicoloured | 60 | 60 |

90 Swimming

1996. The European Pond Turtle. Multicoloured.

279	13t. Type **90**	35	35
280	50t. On bank	80	80
281	60t. In water	1·20	1·20
282	70t. Pair of turtles climbing up bank	1·40	1·40

91 Ptujsko Polje

1996. Masked Costumes. Multicoloured.

| 283 | 13t. Type **91** | 25 | 25 |
| 284 | 70t. Dravsko Polje | 1·50 | 1·50 |

92 Steam Locomotive "Aussee"

1996. 150th Anniv of Slovenian Railways.

| 285 | **92** | 70t. multicoloured | 1·40 | 1·40 |

93 Fran Finzgar (writer)

1996. Birth Anniversaries. Multicoloured.

| 286 | 13t. Type **93** (125th anniv) | 35 | 35 |
| 287 | 100t. Ita Rina (actress) (89th anniv) | 2·00 | 2·00 |

94 Child feeding Birds and Children of different Nationalities

1996. 50th Anniv of UNICEF.

| 288 | **94** | 65t. multicoloured | 1·20 | 1·20 |

95 "Vase of Dahlias"

1996. Europa. Famous Women. 70th Death Anniv of Ivana Koblica (painter). Multicoloured.

| 289 | 65t. "Children in the Grass" (detail) | 2·30 | 2·30 |
| 290 | 75t. Type **95** | 2·40 | 2·40 |

96 Pope John Paul II

1996. Papal Visit.

| 291 | **96** | 75t. multicoloured | 1·40 | 1·40 |
| MS292 | 60×90 mm. **96** 200t. multicoloured | | 3·50 | 3·50 |

97 Anniversary Emblem

1996. Obligatory Tax. 130th Anniv of Slovenian Red Cross.

| 293 | **97** | 7t. multicoloured | 35 | 35 |

98 Clasped Hands

1996. Obligatory Tax. Solidarity Week.

| 294 | **98** | 7t. multicoloured | 35 | 35 |

99 Gallenberg Castle

1996. 700th Anniv of Zagorje ob Savi.

| 295 | **99** | 24t. multicoloured | 60 | 60 |

100 Cyclists

1996. World Youth Cycling Championships, Novo Mesto.

| 296 | **100** | 55t. multicoloured | 95 | 95 |

101 Stars over Mountains

1996. Fifth Anniv of Independence.

| 297 | **101** | 75t. multicoloured | 1·70 | 1·70 |

102 Chanterelle (*Cantharellus cibarius*)

1996. Fungi. Sheet 114×80 mm containing T **102** and similar horiz designs. Multicoloured.

| MS298 | 65t. Type **102**; 75t. *Boletus aestivalis* | 4·00 | 4·00 |

103 Rowing and Canoeing

1996. Centenary of Modern Olympic Games and Olympic Games, Atlanta. Multicoloured.

| 299 | 75t. Type **103** | 1·40 | 1·40 |
| 300 | 100t. High jumping and hurdling | 2·10 | 2·10 |

104 Corner

1996. Traditional Lace Designs from Idria.

301	**104**	1t. brown	25	25
302	-	1t. brown	25	25
303	-	2t. red	25	25
304	-	2t. red	25	25
305	-	5t. blue	25	25
306	-	5t. blue	25	25
307	-	10t. mauve	25	25
308	-	10t. mauve	25	25
309	-	12t. green	30	30
310	-	12t. green	30	30
311	-	13t. red	30	30
312	-	13t. red	30	30
313	-	20t. violet	35	35
314	-	20t. violet	35	35
315	-	44t. blue	80	80
316	-	44t. blue	80	80
317	-	50t. purple	95	95
318	-	50t. purple	95	95
325	-	100t. brown	1·50	1·50
326	-	100t. brown	1·50	1·50

DESIGNS: No. 302, Corner (different); 303, Rounded collar incorporating scrolls; 304, Pointed collar with scalloped edging; 305, Flowers and leaves forming circular design; 306, Framed rose; 307, Oval with flower in centre; 308, "Q"-shaped with trefoil in centre; 309, Flower; 310, Diamond with flower in centre; 311, Square enclosing diamonds containing "flowers"; 312, Square containing circular motifs; 313, Butterfly; 314, Diamond; 315, Square; 316, Circle; 317, Heart-shaped edging; 318, Ornate edging; 325, Leaf; 326, Insect.

105 "Moscon Family"

1996. 130th Death Anniv of Jozef Tominc (painter).

| 331 | **105** | 65t. multicoloured | 1·30 | 1·30 |

106 Cave

1996. UNESCO World Heritage Sites. Skocjan Cave.

| 332 | **106** | 55t. multicoloured | 1·20 | 1·20 |

107 Gimbals

1996. 250th Anniv of Novo Mesto School.

| 333 | **107** | 55t. multicoloured | 1·20 | 1·20 |

108 Heart

1996. Centenary of Modern Cardiology.

| 334 | **108** | 12t. red, brown and cream | 60 | 60 |

109 Post Office Building, Ljubljana, and Doves carrying Letter

1996. Centenary of Post and Telecommunications Office.

| 335 | **109** | 100t. multicoloured | 1·70 | 1·70 |

110 Doves carrying Letter and Stylized Letter Sorting

1996. Introduction of Automatic Letter Sorting.

| 336 | **110** | 12t. black, red and orange | 60 | 60 |

111 Children and Christmas Tree on Sledge

1996. Christmas. Multicoloured.

| 337 | 12t. Type **111** | 25 | 25 |
| 338 | 65t. "Adoration of the Wise Men" (Stefan Subic) | 1·20 | 1·20 |

112 Cupids

1997. Greeting Stamp.

| 339 | **112** | 15t. multicoloured | 35 | 35 |

113 Mt. Sneznik

1997

| 340 | **113** | 20t. multicoloured | 95 | 95 |

114 "Ta Terjast"

1997. Masked Costumes. Multicoloured.

| 341 | 20r. Type **114** | 35 | 35 |
| 342 | 80r. "Pust" | 1·40 | 1·40 |

115 Marbled Trout

1997. Fish. Multicoloured.

343	12t. Type **115**	35	35
344	13t. Streber	60	60
345	80t. Zahrte	1·40	1·40
346	90t. European mudminnow	1·70	1·70
MS347	113×79 mm. As Nos. 343/6 but with inscriptions rearranged and fish enlarged (tails in margin)	4·00	4·00

116 The Golden Horns

1997. Europa. Tales and Legends.

| 348 | **116** | 80t. multicoloured | 1·50 | 1·50 |

117 Wulfenite

1997. Minerals.

| 349 | **117** | 80t. multicoloured | 1·50 | 1·50 |

118 Brick

1997. Red Cross.

| 350 | **118** | 7t. multicoloured | 35 | 35 |

119 Matija Cop (scholar)

1997. Birth Anniversaries. Multicoloured.

351	13t. Type **119** (bicentenary)	25	25
352	24t. Ziga Zois (naturalist, 250th)	35	35
353	80t. Skof Baraga (missionary, bicentenary)	1·20	1·20

120 Cockerel and Fireman's Helmet

1997. Fire Service.

| 354 | **120** | 70t. multicoloured | 1·20 | 1·20 |

121 Series SZ Steam Locomotive

1997. 140th Anniv of Ljubljana–Trieste Railway.

| 355 | **121** | 80t. black, yellow and red | 1·50 | 1·50 |

122 Red Cross

1997. Obligatory Tax. Solidarity Week.

| 356 | **122** | 7t. multicoloured | 35 | 35 |

123 Centre of Piran

1997. European Summit, Piran. Sheet 134×115 mm containing T 123 and similar vert designs. Multicoloured.

| MS357 | 100t. Type **123**; 200t. Arms of participating states | 5·25 | 5·25 |

124 Girl with Dog (Andrejka Cufer)

1997. Children's Week.

| 358 | **124** | 11t. multicoloured | 60 | 60 |

125 "The Shy Lover"

1997. Birth Centenary of France Gorse (sculptor). Multicoloured.

| 359 | 70t. Type **125** | 1·00 | 1·00 |
| 360 | 80t. "The Farmer's Wife" | 1·20 | 1·20 |

126 Judo Bout

1997. European Youth Judo Championships, Ljubljana.

| 361 | **126** | 90t. multicoloured | 1·70 | 1·70 |

127 Venezia Guilia and Istria 1945 Stamp, Anchor and Rose

1997. 50th Anniv of Incorporation of Istria and Slovene Coast into Yugoslavia.

| 362 | **127** | 50t. multicoloured | 95 | 95 |

128 Children watching Birds

1997. Christmas and New Year. Multicoloured.

| 363 | 14t. Type **128** | 25 | 25 |
| 364 | 90t. Crib (Liza Hribar), Church of the Blessed Virgin, Krope | 1·50 | 1·50 |

129 Globe, Golden Vixen and Skier

1997. World Cup Alpine Skiing Championships.

| 365 | **129** | 90t. multicoloured | 1·70 | 1·70 |

130 Dove, Envelope and Postal Centre

1997. Inauguration of New Postal Centre, Ljubljana.

| 366 | **130** | 30t. multicoloured | 60 | 60 |

131 Guests and Attendants

1998. Traditional Pine Brush Wedding. Multicoloured.

| 367 | 20t. Type **131** | 35 | 35 |
| 368 | 80t. Priest, accordionist and bride and groom | 1·20 | 1·20 |

Nos. 367/8 were issued together, *se-tenant*, forming a composite design.

132 Figure Skating

1998. Winter Olympic Games, Nagano, Japan. Multicoloured.

| 369 | 70t. Type **132** | 1·10 | 1·10 |
| 370 | 90t. Biathlon | 1·30 | 1·30 |

133 Airplane, Air Traffic Controllers and Flight Paths

1998. 35th Anniv of Eurocontrol Convention (on regional aviation safety co-operation).

| 371 | **133** | 90t. multicoloured | 1·70 | 1·70 |

134 Lakotnik eating Potato

1998. Cartoon Characters by Miki Muster. Multicoloured.

372	14t. Type **134**	35	35
373	105t. Trdonja (turtle) in sea	1·40	1·40
374	118t. Zvitorepec (fox) walking through meadow	1·70	1·70
MS375	172×100 mm. Nos. 372/4, each ×2	7·00	7·00

135 Louis Adamic and Maps highlighting Birthplace and American Residence

1998. Birth Anniversaries. Multicoloured.

| 376 | 26t. Type **135** (writer, centenary) | 45 | 45 |
| 377 | 90t. Altar figure from Zagreb Cathedral and fountain (300th anniv of Francesco Robba (sculptor)) | 1·30 | 1·30 |

136 St. George's Festival

1997. Europa. National Festivals.

| 378 | **136** | 90t. multicoloured | 1·30 | 1·30 |

137 Red Cross and Blood Drop

1998. Obligatory Tax. Red Cross.

| 379 | **137** | 7t. red and black | 45 | 45 |

138 Red Cross

1998. Obligatory Tax. Solidarity Week. Each red and black.

| 380 | 7t. Type **138** | 45 | 45 |
| 381 | 7t. Red cross (value at right) | 45 | 45 |

Nos. 380/1 were issued together, se-tenant, forming a composite design.

139 Mt. Boc

1998

| 382 | **139** | 14t. multicoloured | 60 | 60 |

140 Common Juniper (*Juniperus communis*)

1998. Conifers. Sheet 134×114 mm containing T 140 and similar vert designs. Multicoloured.

| MS383 | 14t. Type **140**; 15t. Norway spruce (*Picea abies*); 80t. Corsican pine (*Pinus nigra*); 90t. European larch (*Larix decdua*) | 4·00 | 4·00 |

141 Series SZ 06-018 Steam Locomotive

1998

| 384 | **141** | 80t. multicoloured | 1·70 | 1·70 |

142 Victory Sign

1998. Tenth Anniv of Committee for Protection of Human Rights.

| 385 | **142** | 15t. multicoloured | 60 | 60 |

143 Map of Slovenia

1998. 150th Anniv of Movement for the Independence of Slovenia.

| 386 | **143** | 80t. multicoloured | 1·70 | 1·70 |

144 St. Bernard of Clairvaux, Sticna Monastery Church and Foundation Document

1998. 900th Anniv of Cistercian Order and Centenary of Return of Cistercians to Sticna.

| 387 | **144** | 14t. multicoloured | 60 | 60 |

145 Sound Waves and European Cuckoo

1998. 70th Anniv of Cuckoo Emblem of Radio Ljubljana.

| 388 | **145** | 50t. multicoloured | 95 | 95 |

146 "The Banker" (watercolour and collage)

1998. Birth Centenary of August Cernigoj (artist). Multicoloured.

| 389 | **146** | 70t. Type **146** | 1·00 | 1·00 |
| 390 | | 80t. "El" (sculpture) | 1·20 | 1·20 |

147 Hands cradling Sleeping Infant

1998. 50th Anniv of Universal Declaration of Human Rights.

| 391 | **147** | 100t. multicoloured | 1·70 | 1·70 |

148 Children with Candle (Marjanca Bozic)

1998. Christmas and New Year. Multicoloured.

| 392 | **148** | 15t. Type **148** | 25 | 25 |
| 393 | | 90t. "Adoration of the Wise Men" (fresco, St. Nicholas's Church, Mace) | 1·50 | 1·50 |

149 Stukelj

1998. Birth Centenary of Leon Stukelj (gymnast). Sheet 135×115 mm containing T **149** and similar multicoloured designs.

MS394 100t. Type **149**; 100t. Floor exercise; 100t. With Juan Antonio Samaranch (president of International Olympic Committee) (57×40 mm)   4·75   4·75

150 Peter Kozler (cartographer)

1999. Anniversaries. Multicoloured.

395		14t. Type **150** (125th birth anniv)	25	25
396		15t. Bozidar Lavric (surgeon, birth centenary)	35	35
397		70t. General Rudolf Maister (125th birth anniv)	1·00	1·00
398		80t. France Preseren (writer, 150th death anniv)	1·30	1·30

151 White Horses, Planets and Hearts

1999. Greetings Stamp.

| 399 | **151** | 15t. multicoloured | 60 | 60 |

152 Carnival Procession

1999. Skoromati Carnival. Multicoloured.

| 400 | | 20t. Type **152** | 35 | 35 |
| 401 | | 80t. Horn-blower and procession | 1·30 | 1·30 |

Nos. 400/1 were issued together, *se-tenant*, forming a composite design.

153 Mt. Golica

1999

| 402 | **153** | 15t. multicoloured | 80 | 80 |

154 1919 20v. and 1997 14t. Stamps

1999. 50th Anniv of Slovenian Philatelic Society.

| 403 | **154** | 16t. multicoloured | 95 | 95 |

155 Cinnabarite

1999. Minerals.

| 404 | **155** | 80t. multicoloured | 1·40 | 1·40 |

156 "Co-operation"

1999. 50th Anniv of Council of Europe.

| 405 | **156** | 80t. multicoloured | 1·40 | 1·40 |

157 Triglav National Park

1999. Europa. Parks and Gardens.

| 406 | **157** | 90t. multicoloured | 1·50 | 1·50 |

158 Figures with Raised Arms

1999. Obligatory Tax. Red Cross.

| 407 | **158** | 8t. black and red | 45 | 45 |

159 Early Postman and Moon

1999. 125th Anniv of Universal Postal Union. Multicoloured.

| 408 | | 30t. Type **159** | 45 | 45 |
| 409 | | 90t. Astronaut on moon, posthorn and Earth | 1 30 | 1·30 |

160 Slovenian Coldblood

1999. Horses. Multicoloured.

410		60t. Type **160**	85	85
411		70t. Ljutomer trotting horse	1·00	1·00
412		120t. Slovenian warmblood (show jumping)	1·60	1·60
413		350t. Lipizzaner	4·75	4·75
MS414	113×80 mm. Nos. 410/13		8·25	8·25

161 Dogs and Handlers

1999. World Rescue Dogs Championship.

| 415 | **161** | 80t. multicoloured | 1·30 | 1·30 |

162 Children's Toys

1999. Year 2000. Multicoloured.

416		20t. Type **162**	35	35
417		70t. Forms of communication	85	85
418		80t. Symbols of science and culture	1·00	1·00
419		90t. Tree with symbols of education	1·10	1·10

163 "Self-portrait" and "Unravelling the Mysteries of Life"

1999. Birth Centenary of Bozidar Jakac (artist). Multicoloured.

| 420 | | 70t. Type **163** | 1·00 | 1·00 |
| 421 | | 80t. "Self-portrait" and "Novo Mesto" | 1·10 | 1·10 |

164 Terglou Locomotive

1999. 150th Anniv of Arrival of First Train in Ljubljana.

| 422 | **164** | 80t. multicoloured | 1·30 | 1·30 |

165 Slomsek

1999. Beatification of Bishop Anton Martin Slomsk.

| 423 | **165** | 90t. multicoloured | 1·60 | 1·60 |

1999. Obligatory Tax. Solidarity Week. As T **138**. Each orange, black and red.

| 424 | | 9t. Red cross (value at left) | 45 | 45 |
| 425 | | 9t. Red cross (value at right) | 45 | 45 |

Nos. 424/5 were issued together, *se-tenant*, each pair forming a composite design of a link in a chain.

166 Family watching Fireworks

1999. Christmas. Multicoloured.

426		17t. Type **166**	50	50
427		18t. Type **166**	55	55
428		80t. Letter "h" illuminated with Nativity scene (Kranj antiphonary)	1·30	1·30
429		90t. As No. 428	1·40	1·40

167 Teddy Bear and Baby's Bottle

2000. Greetings Stamp.

| 430 | **167** | 34t. multicoloured | 85 | 85 |

168 Masqueraders

2000. Pustovi Carnival Masks. Multicoloured.

| 431 | | 34t. Type **168** | 45 | 45 |
| 432 | | 80t. Four masqueraders | 1·20 | 1·20 |

169 Sailing Ship and Tone Seliskar (writer)

2000. Birth Centenaries. Multicoloured.

| 433 | | 64t. Type **169** | 1·10 | 1·10 |
| 434 | | 120t. Elvira Kralj (actress) and actors holding masks | 1·60 | 1·60 |

170 Stage Coach

2000. 500th Anniv of Postal Service in Slovenia.

| 435 | **170** | 500t. multicoloured | 7·00 | 7·00 |

171 Mt. Storzic

2000

| 436 | **171** | 18t. multicoloured | 55 | 55 |

172 Muri the Tom Cat

2000. Characters from Children's Books. Multicoloured. Ordinary or self-adhesive gum.

437		20t. Type **172**	1·10	1·10
438		20t. Mojca Pokrajculja	1·10	1·10
439		20t. Pedenjped	1·10	1·10

173 Swallows

2000. 55th Anniv of Return of Slovene Exiles.

| 443 | **173** | 25t. multicoloured | 65 | 65 |

174 Trilobite

2000. Fossil and Mineral. Multicoloured.

| 444 | | 80t. Type **174** | 1·30 | 1·30 |
| 445 | | 90t. Magnesium-tourmaliae | 1·60 | 1·60 |

175 Ljubljana Cathedral Doors

2000. Holy Year 2000. Sheet 60×90 mm.

| MS446 | **175** | 2000t. multicoloured | 33·00 | 33·00 |

176 Predjama Castle

2000. Castles.

447	**176**	1t. brown and bistre	10	10
448	-	1t. brown and bistre	10	10
449	-	100t. deep brown and brown	1·80	1·80
450	-	100t. deep brown and brown	1·80	1·80

DESIGNS: No. 448, Velenje Castle; 449, Podsreda Castle; 450, Bled Castle.

177 Apple Blossom Weevil on Flower Bed

2000. The Apple. Multicoloured.

451		10t. Type **177**	10	10
452		10t. Apple blossom	10	10
453		10t. Apple	10	10

2000. No. 189e surch 19.00.

| 454 | | 19t. on 17t. choc, yell & brn | 40 | 40 |

179 Red Cross

2000. OBLIGATORY TAX. Red Cross Week.

| 455 | **179** | 10t. red and black | 75 | 75 |

180 Globe and Radio Operator

2000. Third World Radiosport Team Championship and 50th Anniv of Amateur Radio in Slovenia.

| 456 | **180** | 20t. multicoloured | 55 | 55 |

181 Chicken and Football

2000. European Football Championship, Belgium and The Netherlands.

| 457 | **181** | 40t. multicoloured | 1·60 | 1·60 |

182 Racing Dinghies

2000. Olympic Games, Sydney. Multicoloured.

| 458 | | 80t. Type **182** | 2·10 | 2·10 |
| 459 | | 90t. Sydney Opera House | 2·20 | 2·20 |

Nos 458/9 were issued together, se-tenant forming a composite design.

183 "Building Europe"

2000. Europa.

| 460 | **183** | 90t. multicoloured | 4·25 | 4·25 |

184 Flowers, Frog, Dragonfly and Plants within Life Ring

2000. World Environment Day.

| 461 | **184** | 90t. multicoloured | 22·00 | 22·00 |

185 Lightning, Weather Vane and Carline Thistle

2000. World Meteorological Day. 150th Anniv of Meteorological Observation in Slovenia.

| 462 | **185** | 150t. multicoloured | 22·00 | 22·00 |

186 Cherry Blossom

2000. The Cherry. Multicoloured.

463		5t. Type **186**	10	10
464		5t. European cherry fruit fly	10	10
465		5t. Vigred sweet cherries	10	10

187 Ptuj Castle

2000. Castles and Manor Houses (1st series).

466	**187**	A (18t.) brown and yellow	65	65
467	-	A (18t.) brown and yellow	65	65
468	-	B (19t.) brown and green	75	75
469	-	B (19t.) brown and green	75	75

DESIGNS: No. 466, Type **187**; 467, Otocec Castle; 468, Zuzemberk Castle; 469, Turjak Castle. See also Nos. 520/3 and 646.

188 Zelen Grape

2000. Wine Grapes. Multicoloured.

470		20t. Type **188**	45	45
471		40t. Ranfol	65	65
472		80t. Zametovka	1·30	1·30
473		130t. Rumeni plavec	2·00	2·00
MS474		134×100 mm. Nos. 470/3	4·25	4·25

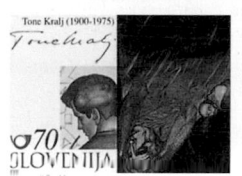

189 "Self-portrait" and "Storm"

2000. Birth Centenary of Tone Kralj (artist). Multicoloured.

| 475 | | 70t. Type **189** | 1·00 | 1·00 |
| 476 | | 80t. "Self-portrait" and "Judita" | 1·20 | 1·20 |

190 Iztok Cop and Luka Spik (coxless pairs)

2000. Olympic Gold Medal Winners. Multicoloured.

| 477 | | 21t. Type **190** | 55 | 55 |
| 478 | | 21t. Rajmond Debevec (rifle-shooting) | 55 | 55 |

2000. OBLIGATORY TAX. Solidarity Week. As T **138**. Each grey, black and red.

| 479 | | 10t. Type **191** (value at left) | 1·10 | 1·10 |
| 480 | | 10t. Red Cross (value at right) | 1·10 | 1·10 |

Nos. 479/80 were issued together, se-tenant, forming a composite design.

191 Healthy and Damaged Environments

2000. New Millennium. "EXPO 2000" World's Fair, Hanover, Germany.

| 481 | **191** | 40t. multicoloured | 55 | 55 |

192 Open Book and Tree

2000. 450th Anniv of First Printed Book in Slovenian Language.

| 482 | **192** | 50t. multicoloured | 75 | 75 |

193 Children

2000. Christmas. Multicoloured. Ordinary or self-adhesive gum.

| 483 | | B (21t.) Type **193** | 35 | 35 |
| 484 | | 90t. Baby Jesus | 1·30 | 1·30 |

194 Bucket (Dragotin Kette (poet))

2001. Birth Anniversaries. Multicoloured.

487		A(24t.) Type **194** (125th anniv)	55	55
488		95t. Jar of flowers (Ivan Tavcar (politician and writer)) (150th anniv)	1·50	1·50
489		107t. Cup of coffee (Ivan Cankar (writer)) (125th anniv)	1·60	1·60

195 Bride and Groom riding Bicycle

2001. Wedding Greetings Stamp.

| 490 | **195** | B (2t.) multicoloured | 55 | 55 |

196 Colourful Headdresses

2001. Dobrepolje Folk Masks. Multicoloured.

| 491 | | 50t. Type **196** | 55 | 55 |
| 492 | | 95t. Procession | 1·10 | 1·10 |

197 Mt. Jalovec

2001

| 493 | **197** | B (25t.) multicoloured | 85 | 85 |

198 Cowboy Pipec

2001. Cowboy Pipec (cartoon character) by Bozo Kos. Multicoloured. Ordinary or self-adhesive gum.

| 494 | | B (25t.) Type **198** | 1·10 | 1·10 |
| 495 | | B (25t.) Beetroot (Native American boy) | 1·10 | 1·10 |

199 Fluorite

2001

| 498 | **199** | 95t. multicoloured | 1·50 | 1·50 |

200 Fossilized Starfish

2001
| 499 | **200** | 107t. multicoloured | 1·60 | 1·60 |

201 Stars, Goddess Europa and Bull

2001. Europe Day (9 May).
| 500 | **201** | 221t. multicoloured | 2·50 | 2·50 |

202 Soca River and Bridge, Solkan

2001. Millenary of Solkan.
| 501 | **202** | 261t. multicoloured | 2·75 | 2·75 |

203 Dove with Lime Leaf

2001. 60th Anniv of Liberation Front.
| 502 | **203** | 24t. multicoloured | 85 | 85 |

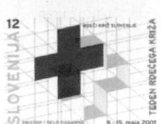

204 Red Cross

2001. OBLIGATORY TAX. Red Cross Week.
| 503 | **204** | 12t. red and grey | 75 | 75 |

205 Worker Bee gathering Nectar

2001. The Carniolan Honey Bee (Apis mellifera carnica). Sheet 113×80 mm containing T **205** and similar horiz designs. Multicoloured.
MS504 24t. Type **205**; 48t. Queen bee and drones; 95t. Queen, workers and drones on edge of honeycomb; 170t. Building and swarm .... 4·25 4·25

206 Flag

2001. Tenth Anniv of Independence.
| 505 | **206** | 100t. multicoloured | 2·75 | 2·75 |

207 Gospodicna Spring, Gorjanci

2001. Europa. Water Resources.
| 506 | **207** | 107t. multicoloured | 2·20 | 2·20 |

208 Tramcar No. 5

2001. Centenary of Introduction of Trams to Ljubljana.
| 507 | **208** | 113t. multicoloured | 2·20 | 2·20 |

209 Maxi-Ball and Ljubljana Skyline

2001. Sixth World Maxi-Basketball Championship, Ljubljana.
| 508 | **209** | 261t. multicoloured | 3·25 | 3·25 |

210 American and Russian Flags behind Bridge, Ljubljana

2001. First Summit Meeting between Pres. George W. Bush of America and Pres. Vladimir Putin of Russian Federation, Brdo Castle, Kranj.
| 509 | **210** | 107t. multicoloured | 1·60 | 1·60 |
| MS510 | 60×90 mm. No. 509 | | 1·60 | 1·60 |

211 Peach Blossom Dragon

2001. Peach Cultivation. Multicoloured.
511	50t. Type **211**		55	55
512	50t. Green peach aphid		55	55
513	50t. Redhaven peach		55	55

212 "Mohorjev koledar" 1920 Calendar Cover

2001. 150th Anniv of "Mohorjeva Druzba" Publishing House.
| 514 | **212** | B (31t.) multicoloured | 85 | 85 |

213 Logarithms, Building and Globe

2001. Centenary of Jurij Vega Grammar School, Idrija.
| 515 | **213** | A (26t.) multicoloured | 75 | 75 |

214 Score and Blaz Arnic

2001. Composers. Multicoloured.
| 516 | 95t. Type **214** | | 1·10 | 1·10 |
| 517 | 107t. Lucijan Marija Skerjanc and score | | 1·60 | 1·60 |

215 Cat

2001. World Animal Day (4th October).
| 518 | **215** | 107t. multicoloured | 1·60 | 1·60 |

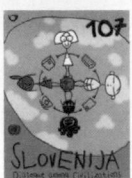

216 Children encircling Globe

2001. United Nations Year of Dialogue among Civilizations.
| 519 | **216** | 107t. multicoloured | 2·75 | 2·75 |

2001. Castles and Manor Houses (2nd series). As T **187**.
520	C (95t.) brown and vermilion	1·10	1·10
521	C (95t.) brown and red	1·10	1·10
522	D (107t.) deep blue and blue	1·30	1·30
523	D (107t.) indigo and blue	1·30	1·30
DESIGNS: No. 520, Dobrovo Manor; 521, Brezice Castle; 522, Olimje Manor; 523, Murska Sobota Manor.

217 Handprints

2001. OBLIGATORY TAX. Solidarity Week.
| 524 | **217** | 13t. multicoloured | 75 | 75 |

218 Christmas Tree

2001. Christmas. Multicoloured. Ordinary or self-adhesive gum.
| 525 | B (31t.) Type **218** | 35 | 35 |
| 526 | D (107t.) Nativity | 1·30 | 1·30 |

219 Wood Carving

2002. Greetings Stamp.
| 529 | **219** | B (31t.) multicoloured | 55 | 55 |

220 Rusa (animal) Mask

2002. Folk Masks. Multicoloured.
| 530 | 56t. Type **220** | 65 | 65 |
| 531 | 95t. Picek (cockerel) mask | 1·00 | 1·00 |

221 Joze Plecnik

2002. Birth Anniversaries. Multicoloured.
| 532 | 95t. Type **221** (architect) (130th) | 1·00 | 1·00 |
| 533 | 107t. Janko Kersnik (writer and politician) (150th) | 1·10 | 1·10 |

222 Toboggan

2002. Winter Olympic Games, Salt Lake City. Multicoloured.
| 534 | 95t. Type **222** | 1·10 | 1·10 |
| 535 | 107t. Skier | 1·30 | 1·30 |

223 Easter Eggs

2002. Easter (B) and Palm Sunday (D). Multicoloured.
| 536 | B (31t.) Type **223** | 35 | 35 |
| 537 | D (107t.) Butarice | 1·30 | 1·30 |

224 Alpine clematis (Clematis alpine) Martuljek Mountains, Triglav National Park

2002. Mountains. Multicoloured.
| 538 | A (30t.) Type **224** | 55 | 55 |
| 539 | D (107t.) Carniolan lily (Lilium carniolicum) and Mt. Spik | 1·10 | 1·10 |

225 Martin Krpan carrying his horse

2002. Martin Krpan (character from book by Fran Levstik). Multicoloured. Ordinary or self-adhesive gum.
540	B (31t.) Type **225**	1·50	1·50
541	B (31t.) Martin Krpan at forge	1·50	1·50
542	B (31t.) Martin Krpan in Ljubljana	1·50	1·50

226 Fossilized Fly

2002
| 546 | **226** | C (95t.) multicoloured | 1·80 | 1·80 |

227 Monastery and view of Kostanjevica

2002. 750th Anniv of First Written Record of Kostanjevica on the Krka.
| 547 | **227** | D (107t.) multicoloured | 1·90 | 1·90 |

228 Man
carrying Heart

2002. OBLIGATORY TAX. Red Cross Week.
548 **228** 15t. multicoloured   1·20 1·20

229 Dog Rose
(*Rosa canina*)

2002. Medicinal Plants. Multicoloured.
549 A (30t.) Type **229**   1·20 1·20
550 B (31t.) Camomile (*Chamomilla recutita*)   1·20 1·20
551 C (95t.) Valerian (*Valeriana officinalis*)   1·40 1·40
MS552 60×70 mm. D (107t.) Sweet violet (*Viola odorata*)   1·80 1·80

230 Mouse
supporting
Elephant

2002. Europa. Circus.
553 **230** D (107t.) multicoloured   22·00 22·00

231 Man with Painted Face
holding Binoculars

2002. World Cup Football Championship, Japan and South Korea.
554 **231** D (107t.) multicoloured   1·80 1·80

232 Lake Bled enclosed in
Map of Central Europe

2002. Ninth Central European States Presidential Conference, Bled. Sheet 65×87 mm containing T **232** and similar horiz design.
MS555 D (107t.) Type **232**; D (107t.)
Central Europe map and Brdo Castle
(conference venue)   3·00 3·00

233 Bilberry
Flowers

2002. The Bilberry (*Vaccinium myrtillus*). Multicoloured.
556 150t. Type **233**   1·70 1·70
557 150t. Winter moth (pest)   1·70 1·70
558 150t. Bilberry fruit   1·70 1·70

234 Horse and Competition
Emblem

2002. 35th Chess Olympiad, Bled. Sheet 70×70 mm containing T **234** and similar horiz design.
MS559 C (95t.) Type **234**; D (107t.)
Fields and emblem   3·00 3·00

235 "Kolo" (dance)

2002. Matija Jama (artist) Commemoration. Multicoloured.
560 95t. Type **235**   1·60 1·60
561 214t. "Village in Winter"   2·75 2·75

236 Profiles

2002. OBLIGATORY TAX. Solidarity Week.
562 **236** 15t. multicoloured   1·20 1·20

237 Snowman

2002. Christmas. Multicoloured. Ordinary or Self-adhesive gum.
563 B (31t.) Type **237**   50 50
564 D (107t.) Girl and house   1·30 1·30

238 Screw Propeller

2002. 175th Anniv of Patenting of the Screw Propeller by Josef Ressel.
567 **238** C (95t.) multicoloured   3·00 3·00

239 Couple

2003. National Costumes. Slovene Istria.
568 **239** A (30t.) multicoloured   95 95

240 Cover of
"Observationes Astromice"
and Chinese Sextant

2003. Birth Anniversaries. Multicoloured.
569 107t. Type **240** (Ferdinand Augustin Hellerstein, missionary and astronomer) (300th)   1·30 1·30
570 221t. Cover of "Flora Exiccata Carniocola" (Alfonz Paulin, botanist and writer) (150th)   3·00 3·00

241 Couple on Heart-shaped
Balloon

2003. Greetings Stamp.
571 **241** 180t. multicoloured   2·40 2·40

No. 571 was perforated in a heart-shape contained within an outer perforated square and impregnated with the scent of roses which is released when the stamp is rubbed.

242 Three Vixens

2003. Folk Tales. Multicoloured. Ordinary or Self-adhesive gum.
572 B (31t.) Type **242**   60 60
573 B (31t.) The Golden Bird (vert)   60 60

243 Avenue of
Stalactites

2003. Vilenica Cave, Lokev.
576 **243** D (107t.) multicoloured   1·20 1·20

244 Barite

2003.
577 **244** D (107t.) multicoloured   1·20 1·20

245 Kamen Castle, Begunje

2003
578 **245** 1000t. slate and blue   11·00 11·00

246 Red Droplet

2003. OBLIGATORY TAX. Red Cross Week.
579 **246** 19t. red and slate   85 85

247 Poster, Bucket
of Paste and Brush

2003. Europa. Poster Art.
580 **247** D (107t.) multicoloured   1·40 1·40

248 Kresnik (fire
spirit)

2003. Mythology.
581 **248** 110t. multicoloured   1·40 1·40

249 Goddess
Europa riding Bull
(Zeus)

2003. European Water Polo Championships, Kranj and Ljubljana.
582 **249** 180t. multicoloured   2·40 2·40

250 Vilko and Slavko
Avsenik

2003. 50th Anniv of Avsenik (music) Ensamble (founded by Slavko Avsenik). Sheet 60×70 mm.
MS583 **250** 180t. multicoloured   1·00 1·00

251 Painted Beehive Panel

2003. Bee Keeping.
584 **251** 218t. multicoloured   3·00 3·00

252 Letters showing
Franking Marks

2003. Pre-Stamp Postage.
585 **252** A (30t.) multicoloured   60 60

253 Olive
Flowers

2003. The Olive Tree. Multicoloured.
586 B (31t.) Type **253**   50 50
587 B (31t.) Olive fruit fly (pest)   50 50
588 B (31t.) Olives   50 50

254 Fallen Knight

2003. Illustrations from Gasper Lamberger's Tournament Book. Multicoloured.
589 76t. Type **254**   1·80 1·80
590 570t. Gasper Lamberger   6·00 6·00
Nos. 589/90 were issued together, *se-tenant*, forming a composite design of two pages from the book.

255 Black-belted (Krsko
polje) Pig

2003. Indigenous Farm Animals. Multicoloured.
591 95t. Type **255**   1·10 1·10
592 107t. Solcava sheep   1·20 1·20
593 107t. Cica cattle   2·40 2·40
MS594 60×70 mm. 368t. Styrian poultry (vert)   4·75 4·75

256 Emblem

2003. OBLIGATORY TAX. Solidarity Week.
595 **256** 19t. multicoloured   85 85

257 Automatic Sorting Machine and "www.posta.si"

2003. Mail Sorting and Logistics Centre, Maribor.
596 **257** 221t. multicoloured 2·40 2·40

258 Post Office Door, Zgormji Otok

2003. Cultural Heritage. Multicoloured.
597 A (38t.) Type **258** 35 35
598 R (44t.) Fishing boat, Piran 50 50
599 C (95t.) Scythe, Ljubno ob Savinji 95 95
600 D (107t.) Horse-collar comb 1·20 1·20

259 Parcel, Flowers, Bell, Bauble and Fir Twig

2003. Christmas. Multicoloured. Ordinary or self-adhesive gum.
601 B (44t.) Type **259** 85 85
602 D (107t.) The Nativity 1·40 1·40

260 Hospital

2003. 60th Anniv of Franja Partisan Hospital.
605 **260** 76t. sepia and bronze 1·40 1·40

261 Parizar (cart)

2003. Road Transport.
606 **261** 221t. multicoloured 3·50 3·50

262 Couple, Vipava Valley

2004. National Costumes.
607 **262** A (38t.) multicoloured 1·00 1·00

263 Soldiers marching through Snow

2004. 60th Anniv of 14th Division's March to Stajerska.
608 **263** B (44t.) multicoloured 1·00 1·00

264 Edvard Kocbek and Script

2004. Birth Centenary of Edvard Kocbek (writer and politician).
609 **264** D (107t.) multicoloured 2·00 2·00

265 Two Cats

2004. Greeting Stamp.
610 **265** 180t. multicoloured 3·00 3·00

266 Players

2004. Sixth European Men's Handball Championships, Slovenia.
611 **266** 221t. multicoloured 3·50 3·50

267 Stylized Portrait

2004. Birth Centenary of Srecko Kosovel (writer).
612 **267** 221t. vermilion and black 3·50 3·50

268 Keckec

2004. Keckec (character from children's stories created by Josip Vandot). Multicoloured. Ordinary or self-adhesive gum.
613 B (44t.) Type **268** 90 90
614 B (44t.) Pehta 90 90
615 B (44t.) Kosobrin 90 90

269 Gymnast

2004. European Men's Artistic Gymnastic Championship, Ljubljana.
616 **269** D (107t.) multicoloured 2·10 2·10

270 Fossilized Fish

2004
617 **270** D (107t.) multicoloured 2·10 2·10

271 Bled Castle

2004. Bled (town) Millenary.
618 **271** 218t. multicoloured 3·75 3·75

272 NATO Emblem

2004. Slovenia's Accession to North Atlantic Treaty Organization (NATO).
619 **272** D (107t.) blue and yellow 1·90 1·90

273 Stars and New Member's Flags

2004. Slovenia's Accession to European Union.
620 **273** 95t. multicoloured 1·80 1·80

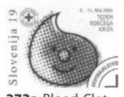

273a Blood Clot

2004. OBLIGATORY TAX. Red Cross Week.
620a 19t. Type **273a** 35 35
620b 19t. Girl 35 35
620c 19t. Bandaged head 35 35
620d 19t. Elderly woman 35 35

274 Iovrenc Kosir and Birthplace

2004. Birth Bicentenary of Iovrenc Kosir (postage stamp pioneer).
621 **274** B (48t.) multicoloured 1·00 1·00

275 Discus

2004. Olympic Games, Athens. Multicoloured.
622 C (95t.) Type **275** 1·60 1·60
623 D (107t.) Long jump 1·80 1·80

Nos. 622/3 were issued together, *se-tenant*, forming a composite design.

276 Fish with Umbrella

2004. Europa. Holidays.
624 **276** D (107t.) multicoloured 2·00 2·00

277 Bicycle Chain Wheel

2004. Puch Bicycles (bicycle manufacture pioneer).
625 **277** 110t. multicoloured 2·00 2·00

278 Miller and Wife (1869)

2004. Painted Beehive Panels.
626 **278** 218t. multicoloured 3·75 3·75

279 Town House, Trbovlje

2004
627 **279** B (48t.) multicoloured 1·00 1·00

280 Posthorn

2004
628 **280** B (48t.) blue and yellow 80 80

281 Crni Kal Viaduct

2004. Completion of Crni Kal Viaduct between Ljubljana and Klanec-Srmin. Sheet 70×60 mm.
MS629 **281** 95t. multicoloured 1·80 1·80

282 Pear Flowers

2004. William Pear (fruit tree). Multicoloured.
630 A (45t.) Type **282** 85 85
631 A (45t.) Fruit fly (pest) 85 85
632 A (45t.) Pear 85 85

2004. Cultural Heritage. As T **258**. Multicoloured.
633 D (107t.) Cupa (fishing boat) 2·00 2·00

283 Marsh Helleborine (Epipactis palustris)

2004. Orchids. Multicoloured.
634 B (52t.) Type **283** 1·00 1·00
MS635 70×60 mm. D (107t.) Spider orchid (*Ophrys holosericea*) 2·00 2·00

284 "750"

2004. 750th Anniversary of First Documentation of Maribor Town.
636 **284** C (95t.) multicoloured 1·80 1·80

285 Illuminated Writing

2004. Romanesque Art. Multicoloured.
637 107t. Type **285** 1·90 1·90
638 107t. Illuminated writing (different) 1·90 1·90

286 Map of
Southern Europe

2004. 50th Anniv of London Memorandum (Italy—
Slovenia border demarcation agreement). Sheet
60×70 mm.
MS639 **286** 221t. multicoloured   4·00   4·00

286a Air Drop and Roof

2004. OBLIGATORY TAX. Solidarity Week. Designs forming
burning house. Multicoloured.
639a	23t. Type **286a**	50	50
639b	23t. Burning roof	50	50
639c	23t. Red cross parcels and flower boxes	50	50
639d	23t. Damage to lower right of house	50	50

Nos. 639a/d were issued together, *se-tenant*, forming a
composite design of a house.

287 Children under
Umbrella

2004. Christmas. Multicoloured. Ordinary or self-adhesive
gum.
640	A (45t.) Type **287**	1·00	1·00
641	C (95t.) Baby Jesus enclosed in tree	1·80	1·80

288 Prekmurje Pie Cake

2004. Gastronomy. Multicoloured.
644	52t. Type **288**	85	85
645	52t. Bograc Goulash	85	85

2004. Castles and Manor Houses (3rd series). As T **187**.
646   C (95t.) brown and orange   1·80   1·80
DESIGN: No. 646, Gewerkenegg Castle.

289 Rojenice and
Sojenice (Fates)

2004. Mythology.
647   **289** 180t. multicoloured   3·25   3·25

290 Couple, Pohorje and
Kobansko

2005. National Costumes.
648   **290** A (45t.) multicoloured   1·00   1·00

2005. Posthorn. As T **280**.
649   **280** 83t. blue and yellow   1·50   1·50

291 Janez
Sigmund Valentin
Popovic (linguist
and scientist)
(birth
bicentenary)

2005. Anniversaries. Multicoloured.
650	107t. Type **291**	2·00	2·00
651	221t. Janez Trdina (writer) (death centenary)	4·00	4·00

292 Cupid

2005. Greeting Stamp.
652   **292** 180t. multicoloured   3·25   3·25

293 Refugees

2005. 60th Anniv of Return of Slovene Exiles.
653   **293** A (49t.) multicoloured   1·00   1·00

294 The Grateful
Bear

2005. Folk Tales. Multicoloured. (a) Ordinary gum.
654	A (49t.) Type **294**	95	95
655	A (49t.) The Golden Fish	95	95

              (b) Self-adhesive gum.
656	A (49t.) As No. 654	95	95
657	A (49t.) As No. 655	95	95

295 Soldiers

2005. 60th Anniv of End of World War II.
658   **295** B (57t.) multicoloured   1·00   1·00

296 Mountain, Waterside,
Farmland and Castle

2005. Centenary of National Tourist Association. Sheet
69×60 mm.
MS659 **296** 100t. multicoloured   1·80   1·80

297 Zoisite

2005
660   **297** D (107t.) multicoloured   1·90   1·90

298 Stylized
Figures

2005. OBLIGATORY TAX. Red Cross Week.
661   **298** 25t. scarlet and slate   1·00   1·00

299 Sunflower

2005. Greetings Stamp. Self-adhesive.
662   **299** A (49t.) multicoloured   1·00   1·00

300 No. 348 (detail),
Tweezers and Magnifier

2005. 50th Anniv of Europa Stamps. Designs showing
previous Europa stamps. Multicoloured.
663	60t. Type **300**	1·20	1·20
664	60t. No. 406 (detail)	1·20	1·20
665	60t. No. 553 (detail)	1·20	1·20
666	60t. No. 232 (detail)	1·20	1·20
MS667	135×85 mm. Nos. 663/6	4·25	4·25

301 Puch Motorbike
(1910)

2005. Janez Puh (Johann Puch) (cycle pioneer)
Commemoration.
668   **301** 98t. multicoloured   1·80   1·80

302 Potica (rolled cakes)

2005. Europa. Gastronomy.
669   **302** D (107t.) multicoloured   2·00   2·00

303 Horse-drawn Post
Van and Early Post Box

2005. Postal Museum Exhibits.
670   **303** 107t. multicoloured   2·00   2·00

304 Vesna

2005. Mythology.
671   **304** 180t. multicoloured   3·25   3·25

305 Shepherd shooting
Eagle

2005. Painted Beehive Panels.
672   **305** 221t. multicoloured   4·00   4·00

306 Institute Building and
Bishop Anton Jeglic
(founder)

2005. Centenary of St. Stanislav's Institute (educational
and cultural institution).
673   **306** 221t. multicoloured   4·00   4·00

307 Apricot
Flowers

2005. Apricot. Multicoloured.
674	D (107t.) Type **307**	1·80	1·80
675	D (107t.) Fruit	1·80	1·80
676	D (107t.) Pest	1·80	1·80

308 Posavec Hound

2005. Dogs. Multicoloured.
677	A (49t.) Type **308**	1·00	1·00
678	B (57t.) Istrian rough-coated hound	1·40	1·40
679	(95t.) Slovenian mountain hound	2·00	2·00
MS680	60×70 mm. D (107t.) Istrian smooth-coated hound (28×41 mm)	2·10	2·10

309 Dactylorhiza
sambucina

2005. Orchids.Multicoloured.
681	(57t.) Type **309**	1·10	1·10
MS682	70×60 mm D (107t.) *Platanthera biflora*	2·10	2·10

310 Priest, Skeleton and Bishop

2005. Art. "Dance of Death" (fresco by Janez of Kastav).
Multicoloured.
683	107t. Type **310**	2·00	2·00
684	107t. Two skeletons and cardinal	2·00	2·00

Nos. 683/4 were issued together, *se-tenant*, forming a
composite design.

310a Houses

2005. OBLIGATORY TAX. Solidarity Week. Multicoloured.
684a	25c. Type **310a**	55	55
684b	25c. Flood water	55	55

311 Child at Window

2005. Christmas. Multicoloured. (a) Ordinary gum.
685	A (49t.) Type **311**	85	85
686	C (95t.) Children carrying candles	1·70	1·70

              (b) Self-adhesive.
687	B (49t.) As No. 685	85	85
688	D (95t.) As No. 686	1·70	1·70

312 Prleska Gibanica and Ajdov Krapec (cakes)

2005. Gastronomy. Multicoloured.
689	107t. Type **312**		2·00	2·00
690	107t. Tunka (barrel), bread and meat		2·00	2·00

313 Umbrella and Jigsaw

2005. Slovenia's Chairmanship of Organization for Security and Co-operation in Europe (OSCE).
691	**313**	107t. multicoloured	1·40	1·40

2005. Vert designs as Nos. 197a; 536/7; 597/600; 627 and 633. Size 25×36 mm. Brown, red and grey (197a) or multicoloured (others).
691a	B (31t.) Type **223** (536)	1·00	1·00
691b	A (38t.) Type **258** (597)	1·10	1·10
691c	B (44t.) Fishing boat, Piran (598)	1·20	1·20
691d	B (48t.) Type **279** (627)	1·30	1·30
691e	90t. Apiary (197a)	1·70	1·70
691f	C (95t.) Scythe, Ljubno ob Savinji (599)	2·00	2·00
691g	D (107t.) Butarice (537)	2·20	2·20
691h	D (107t.) Horse collar comb (600)	2·20	2·20
691i	D (107t.) Cupa (fishing boat) (633)	2·20	2·20

2005. Vert designs as Nos. 447/50 and 520. Size 26×36 mm.
691j	1t. brown and bistre	20	20
691k	1t. olive-brown and bistre	20	20
691l	C (95t.) brown and vermilion	1·70	1·70
691m	100t. purple-brown and red-brown	2·00	2·00
691n	100t. purple-brown and red-brown	2·00	2·00

DESIGNS: 1t. Predjama Castle (447); 1t. Velenje Castle (448); C (95t.) Dobrovo Manor (520); 100t. Podsreda Castle (449); 100t. Bled Castle (450).

2005. Vert designs as Nos. 463/5; 511/13 and 630/2. Size 21×26 mm.
691o	5t. Type **186** (463)	20	20
691p	5t. European cherry fruit fly (464)	20	20
691q	5t. Vigred sweet cherries (465)	20	20
691r	10t. Type **177** (451)	45	45
691s	10t. Apple blossom (452)	45	45
691t	10t. Apple (453)	45	45
691u	A (49t.) Type **258** (630)	1·10	1·10
691v	A (49t.) Fruit fly (631)	1·10	1·10
691w	A (49t.) Pear (632)	1·10	1·10
691x	50t. Type **211** (511)	1·10	1·10
691y	50t. Green peach aphid (512)	1·10	1·10
691z	50t. Redhaven peach (513)	1·10	1·10
691za	B (57t.) Type **253** (586)	1·20	1·20
691zb	B (57t.) Olive fruit fly (587)	1·20	1·20
691zc	B (57t.) Olives (588)	1·20	1·20
691zd	150t. Type **233** (556)	2·75	2·75
691ze	150t. Winter moth (557)	2·75	2·75
691zf	150t. Bilberry fruit (558)	2·75	2·75

314 Couple, Carinthia

2006. National Costumes.
692	**314**	A (49t.) multicoloured	1·00	1·00

315 Anton Trstenjak

2006. Birth Centenary of Anton Trstenjak (theologian and anthropologist).
693	**315**	B (57t.) multicoloured	1·00	1·00

316 Couple

2006. Greetings Stamp.
694	**316**	B (57t.) multicoloured	1·00	1·00

317 Skier

2006. Winter Olympics, Turin. Multicoloured.
695		95t. Type **317**	1·70	1·70
696		107t. Snowboarder	1·80	1·80

318 The Cocks, Ponikeve

2006. Folk Masks.
697	**318**	420t. multicoloured	7·25	7·25

319 Twinkle Sleepyhead

2006. Children's Book Characters. Multicoloured. Ordinary or Self-adhesive gum.
698		A (49t.) Type **319**	1·00	1·00
699		A (49t.) Spotty the ball	1·00	1·00

320 Erannis ankeraria

2006. Butterflies. Multicoloured.
702		D (107t.) Type **320**	1·10	1·10
MS703	71×60 mm. D (107t.) *Erebia calcaria*		1·90	1·90

321 Pericnik Waterfall

2006
704	**321**	D (107t.) multicoloured	1·90	1·90

322 Fossil Shell

2006
705	**322**	D (107t.) multicoloured	1·90	1·90

323 Nurses

2006. OBLIGATORY TAX. Red Cross Week. 140th Anniv of Slovenia Red Cross.
706	**323**	25t. multicoloured	1·00	1·00

324 Bouquet

2006. Greetings Stamp. Self-adhesive.
707	**324**	C (95t.) multicoloured	1·60	1·60

325 Competitor

2006. Junior World White Water Slalom Kayak Competition, Solkan.
708	**325**	C (95t.) multicoloured	1·60	1·60

326 Cats (Sara Popovic)

2006. Europa. Integration. Winning Design in Children's Painting Competition.
709	**326**	C (107t.) multicoloured	1·90	1·90

327 Svarog

2006. Mythology.
710	**327**	D (107t.) multicoloured	1·90	1·90

328 Couple

2006. Painted Beehive Panels.
711	**328**	D (107t.) multicoloured	1·90	1·90

329 Radar Screen

2006. 15th Anniv of Independence, Stamp Issuing and Slovenia Air Traffic Control and Air Navigation Services. Sheet 90×60 mm.
MS712	**329**	C (95t.) multicoloured	1·70	1·70

330 Plant

2006. Salvinia natans. Multicoloured.
713		A (49t.) Type **330**	1·10	1·10
MS714	60×70 mm. D (107t.). Plant (different)		1·90	1·90

331 Rack Wagon

2006. Transport.
715	**331**	D (107t.) multicoloured	1·90	1·90

332 Ceiling

2006. 17th-century Painted Ceiling. Celje Mansion. Sheet 114×85 mm containing T **332** and similar horiz designs showing parts of the ceiling. Multicoloured.
MS716	D (107t.)×4, Type **332**; Top right; Bottom left; Bottom right		7·50	7·50

The stamps and margin of MS716 form a composite design of the ceiling and frescoes.

332a Fire-fighters

2006. OBLIGATORY TAX.
716a	**332a**	25t. multicoloured	1·00	1·00

332b Hands enclosing Globe

2006. OBLIGATORY TAX. Solidarity Week.
716b	**332b**	25t. multicoloured	1·00	1·00

333 Snowman

2006. Christmas. Multicoloured. Ordinary or Self-adhesive gum.
717		A (49t.) Type **333**	1·00	1·00
718		C (95t.) Carollers	1·80	1·80

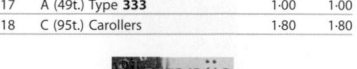

334 Soldiers

2006. Partisan Signallers and Couriers.
721	**334**	C (95t.) multicoloured	1·70	1·70

335 Father Asic

2006. Birth Centenary of Father Simon Asic (herbalist). Sheet 71×61 mm.
MS722 **335** D (107t.) multicoloured　　1·90　　1·90

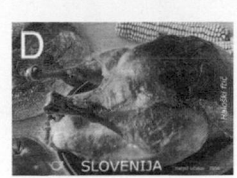

336 Turkey

2006. Gastronomy. Multicoloured.
723　D (107t.) Type **336**　　1·80　　1·80
724　D (107t.) Yeast cake　　1·80　　1·80

337
Persimmon
Flower

2006. Persimmon. Multicoloured.
725　D (107t.) Type **337**　　1·80　　1·80
726　D (107t.) Fruit　　1·80　　1·80
727　D (107t.) Pest　　1·80　　1·80

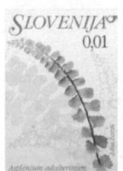

338 Asplenium
adulterinum

2007. Flora. Multicoloured.
728　1c. Type **338**　　20　　20
729　2c. Moebringia tommasinii　　20　　20
730　5c. Himantoglossum adriaticum　　20　　20
731　10c. Pulsatilis grandis　　45　　45
732　20c. Primula carniolica　　85　　85
733　26c. Goldiolur polurtis　　85　　85
734　55c. Ciratlum dharicum　　1·10　　1·10
735　48c. Adenophora liliifolia　　1·30　　1·30
736　A (49c.) Campanula zoysii　　1·30　　1·30
737　50c. Aqualegia bertolonii　　1·30　　1·30
738　B (57c.) Cypripedium calceolus　　1·60　　1·60
739　75c. Liparis loeslii　　1·80　　1·80
740　92c. Scilla litardierei　　2·20　　2·20
741　C (95c.) Serratula lycopifolia　　2·75　　2·75
742　100c. Eryngium alpinum　　3·00　　3·00
743　D (107c.) Genista bolopetala　　3·25　　3·25
744　200c. Rhododendron luteum　　6·50　　6·50

339 Coins

2007. Introduction of the Euro. Sheet 100×50 mm.
MS745 **339** 100c. multicoloured　　4·25　　4·25

340 Couple, Smlednik

2007. National Costumes.
746　**340**　20c. multicoloured　　1·00　　1·00

341 Newly Weds

2007. Greetings Stamp.
747　**341**　24c. multicoloured　　1·00　　1·00

342 Vasja Pirc

2007. Birth Centenary of Vasja Pirc (chess grand master).
748　**342**　48c. multicoloured　　2·00　　2·00

343 Bride and Groom

2007. Personal Stamps. Multicoloured. Self-adhesive.
749　A (49c.) Type **343**　　90　　90
750　A (49c.) Stork carrying babies
　　　(horiz)　　90　　90
751　A (49c.) Postman　　90　　90
752　A (49c.) Parcel (horiz)　　90　　90

344 Aragonite

2007
753　**344**　45c. multicoloured　　1·90　　1·90

345 Mangart Mountain and
Creeping Avens

2007. Tourism.
754　**345**　45c. multicoloured　　1·90　　1·90

346 Eurasian Red Squirrel

2007. Endangered Species. Eurasian Red Squirrel (Sciurus vulgaris). Multicoloured.
755　48c. Type **346**　　2·00　　2·00
756　48c. Eating　　2·00　　2·00
757　48c. Two squirrels　　2·00　　2·00
758　48c. Mother and babies　　2·00　　2·00

347 Animals as Scouts

2007. Europa. Centenary of Scouting.
759　**347**　50c. multicoloured　　2·10　　2·10

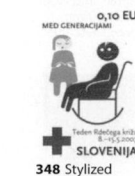

348 Stylized
Elderly Person
and Child

2007. OBLIGATORY TAX. Red Cross Week. Generations. Showing elderly person and child.
760　10c. Type **348**　　45　　45
761　10c. Walking contained in
　　　triangle　　45　　45
762　10c. On see-saw　　45　　45
763　10c. Listening using head-
　　　phones　　45　　45

349 Callimorpha
quadripunctaria (tiger moth)

2007. Butterfly and Moth. Multicoloured.
764　24c. Type **349**　　1·00　　1·00
MS765 61×71 mm. 45c. Colias myrmi-
　　done (Danube clouded yellow) (vert)　　1·90　　1·90

350 Perkmandeljc,
Taus, Catez (elves)

2007. Mythology.
766　**350**　45c. multicoloured　　1·90　　1·90

351 Windmill and
Stars

2007. 50th Anniv of Treaty of Rome.
767　**351**　45c. multicoloured　　1·90　　1·90

352 Bible

2007. Year of the Bible. Sheet 61×71 mm.
MS768 **352** 75c. multicoloured　　3·00　　3·00

353 Buggy

2007. Transport.
769　**353**　92c. multicoloured　　3·75　　3·75

354 Bridge, Moon, Sun and
Church

2007. Lent.
770　**354**　€1 multicoloured　　4·25　　4·25

355 Nuphar
luteum

2007. Flowering Aquatic Plants. Multicoloured.
771　20c. Type **355**　　85　　85
772　24c. Hydrocharis morsus-ranae　　1·10　　1·10
773　40c. Nyphoides peltata　　2·00　　2·00
MS774 60×70 mm. 45c. Nymphaea
　　alba (horiz)　　1·90　　1·90

356 Climber

2007. Sport. Rock Climbing.
775　**356**　48c. multicoloured　　2·00　　2·00

357 Ceiling Fresco,
Church of St. Nicholas
(Giulio Quaglio)

2007. Art.
776　**357**　92c. multicoloured　　3·75　　3·75

358 Fire Fighters

2007. OBLIGATORY TAX.
777　**358**　11c. multicoloured　　1·00　　1·00

358a Circles and
Figures

2007. OBLIGATORY TAX. Solidarity Week. Multicoloured.
777a　10t. Type **358a**　　45　　45
777b　10t. As Type **358a** but central
　　　circle blue　　45　　45
777c　10t. As Type **358a** but central
　　　circle green　　45　　45
777d　10t. As Type **358a** but central
　　　circle orange　　45　　45

359 Car passing through
Checkpoint

2007. Slovenia's Entry into Schengen Zone (European Union area without border controls).
778　**359**　45c. multicoloured　　1·90　　1·90

360 Stajerska Sour Soup and
Pohorski Pisker (stew)

2007. Gastronomy. Multicoloured.
779　45c. Type **360**　　1·80　　1·80
780　45c. Pohorje omelet　　1·80　　1·80

361 Symbols of Good
Luck

2007. New Year.
781　**361**　A (49c.) multicoloured　　1·00　　1·00

362 Sledge

2007. Personal Stamps. Multicoloured. Self-adhesive.
782　A (49c.) Type **362**　　90　　90
783　A (49c.) Nativity (vert)　　90　　90
784　C (95c.) Postman delivering
　　　deluxe telegram (vert)　　1·90　　1·90
785　C (95c.) Running shoe (Hitra
　　　Posta express mail)　　1·90　　1·90

363 Bone Flute, Divje Babe Cave

2007. Archaeological Finds. Sheet 72×62 mm.
MS786 **363** 92c. multicoloured   3·75   3·75

364 The Nativity (Christmas crib made by Janez Kosnik)

2007. Christmas.
787   **364**   C (92c.) multicoloured   1·60   1·60

365 Map of Slovenia and EU Members Flags

2008. Slovenia's Presidency of European Union. Sheet 70×60 mm.
788   **365**   €2.38 multicoloured   10·50   10·50

366 Couple, Scavnica and Pesnica

2008. National Costumes.
789   **366**   20c. multicoloured   1·00   1·00

367 Mouse Couple

2008. Greetings Stamp.
790   **367**   24c. multicoloured   1·10   1·10

368 Primoz Trubar and Frontispiece

2008. 500th Birth Anniv of Primoz Trubar (author of the first Slovenian book).
791   **368**   48c. multicoloured   2·10   2·10

369 Black and White Masks, Vrbica

2008. Folk Masks.
792   **369**   €1.75 multicoloured   7·75   7·75

370 Paeonia officinalis

2008. Flora. Multicoloured.
793   20c. Type **370**   1·00   1·00
794   24c. Pulsatilla montana   1·20   1·20
795   40c. Iris illyrica   2·00   2·00
MS796 60×70 mm. 45c. Gentiana tergestina (horiz)   2·00   2·00

371 Julius Kugy and Trenta Valley

2008. 150th Birth Anniv of Julius Kugy (mountaineer and writer).
797   **371**   45c. multicoloured   2·00   2·00

372 Boy

2008. OBLIGATORY TAX. Red Cross Week. Multicoloured.
798   10c. Type **372**   50   50
799   10c. Girl   50   50
      Nos. 798/9 were issued together, se-tenant, forming a composite design.

373 Academy of Sciences and Arts Building and Rajko Nahtigal

2008. 70th Anniv of Academy of Science and Arts. 50th Death Anniv of Rajko Nahtigal (linguist).
800   **373**   40c. multicoloured   1·80   1·80

374 Temple and Stylized Athletes (wrestling)

2008. Olympic Games, Beijing. Multicoloured.
801   40c. Type **374**   1·70   1·70
802   45c. Pagoda and stylized athlete (sailing)   1·80   1·80

375 Mokos (goddess of life)

2008. Mythology.
803   **375**   45c. multicoloured   2·00   2·00

376 Winged Mail

2008. Europa. The Letter. Multicoloured.
804   45c. Type **376**   2·00   2·00
805   92c. Mail van and envelopes as figures   4·00   4·00

377 School Philatelic Club Emblem

2008. Stamp Day.
806   **377**   23c. multicoloured   1·00   1·00

378 Rana latastei (Italian agile frog)

2008. Fauna. Multicoloured.
807   23c. Type **378**   1·20   1·20
808   27c. Bombina bombina (fire-bellied toad)   1·40   1·40
809   40c. Triturus carnifex (Italian crested newt)   2·10   2·10
MS810 70×60 mm. 45c. Elaphe quatuorlineata (Four-lined snake)   2·20   2·20

379 Alojzij Sustar

2008. Alojzij Sustar (Archbishop of Ljubljana) Commemoration.
811   **379**   45c. multicoloured   2·20   2·20

380 Stucco, Gruber Palace

2008. Rococo Decoration.
812   **380**   92c. multicoloured   4·50   4·50

381 Cargo Sledge

2008
813   **381**   92c. multicoloured   4·50   4·50

382 Boy and Flute

2008. 80th Anniv of Radio and 50th Anniv of Television in Slovenia. Sheet 70×60 mm.
MS814 **382** 92c. multicoloured   4·50   4·50

383 Children as Firefighters

2008. OBLIGATORY TAX.
815   **383**   12c. multicoloured   1·00   1·00

384 Primoz Kozmus

2008. Primoz Kozmus—2008 Hammer Throw Olympic Gold Medallist.
816   **384**   45c. multicoloured   2·10   2·10

385 Figures holding Jigsaw Puzzle Pieces

2008. OBLIGATORY TAX. Red Cross Solidarity Week.
817   **385**   12c. multicoloured   1·00   1·00

386 Rabbit under Tree

2008. Christmas and New Year. Multicoloured.
818   A (26c.) Type **386** (New Year)   1·40   1·40
819   C (40c.) Star and crib (Christmas) (horiz)   2·10   2·10

387 '10' and Euro Coin

2008. Tenth Anniv of Euro.
820   **387**   45c. multicoloured   2·20   2·20

388 Zgornjesavinjski zelodec

2008. Gastronomy. Multicoloured.
821   45c. Type **388**   2·20   2·20
822   45c. Ubrnenik and Solcavski sirnek   2·20   2·20

389 Trench Fortifications

2008. 90th Anniv of End of World War I.
823   **389**   92c. multicoloured   4·50   4·50

390 Wooden Wheel with Axle (c. 3200 BC) (found at Stare gmajne pri Verdu)

2008. National Heritage. Sheet 71×60 mm.
MS824 **390** 92c. multicoloured   4·50   4·50

391 Man and Women, Bela Kra (painting by F. K. Goldenstein)

2009. Traditional Costumes.
825   **391**   23c. multicoloured   1·00   1·00

392 Fishes kissing

2009. Greetings Stamp.
826 **392** 27c. multicoloured ..... 1·25 ..... 1·25

393 Alojz Knafelc

2009. 150th Birth Anniv of Alojz Knafelc (mountaineer).
827 **393** 45c. multicoloured ..... 2·00 ..... 2·00

394 Jozef Mrak

2009. 300th Birth Anniv of Jozcf Mrak (geodesist and builder).
828 **394** 92c. multicoloured ..... 4·00 ..... 4·00

395 Carnival Costumes, Selma

2009. Folk Traditions.
829 **395** €1.60 multicoloured ..... 7·00 ..... 7·00

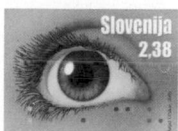

396 Eye

2009. Birth Bicentenary of Louis Braille (inventor of Braille writing for the blind). Sheet 70×63 mm.
MS830 **396** €2.38 multicoloured ..... 10·00 ..... 10·00
No. **MS**830 is embossed with Braille letters.

397 First Draft for Postage Due Stamp (Ivan Vavpotic)

2009. 90th Anniv of Chain Breaker Stamps.
831 **397** 23c. multicoloured ..... 1·00 ..... 1·00

398 *Centaurea cyanus*

2009. Flora. Multicoloured.
832 23c. Type **398** 90 90
833 27c. *Papaver rhoeas* ..... 1·20 ..... 1·20
834 40c. *Agrostemma githago* ..... 1·90 ..... 1·90
MS835 72×61 mm. 45c. *Ranunculus arvensis* ..... 2·40 ..... 2·40

399 Lovrenc Lakes

2009. Nature Reserve.
836 **399** 35c. multicoloured ..... 1·50 ..... 1·50

400 Puffins and Polar Bear

2009. Preserve Polar Regions and Glaciers. Sheet 121×81 mm containing T **400** and similar horiz design.
MS837 45c.×2, Type **400**; Killer whale and polar bears ..... 4·00 ..... 4·00
The stamps and margins of **MS**837 form a composite design.

401 Seiz Charterhouse

2009. Carthusian Monasteries. P 13×13½.
838 **401** 92c. multicoloured ..... 4·00 ..... 4·00

402 Battle

2009. OBLIGATORY TAX. 150th Anniv of Battle of Solferino (witnessed by Henry Dunant who instigated campaign resulting in establishment of Geneva Conventions and Red Cross).
839 **402** 13c. multicoloured ..... 1·00 ..... 1·00

403 '60 YEARS' and Emblem

2009. 60th Anniv of Council of Europe.
840 **403** 45c. multicoloured ..... 2·00 ..... 2·00

2009. Flora. As Type **338**. Self-adhesive.
841 1c. As Type **338** (*Asplenium adulterinum*) 15 15
842 10c. As No. 731 (*Pulsatilis grandis*) 30 30
843 20c. As No. 732 (*Primula carniolica*) 55 55
844 25c. As No. 733 (*Galdiolus palustis*) 70 70
845 A (26c.) As No. 736 (*Campanula zoysii*) 85 85
846 B (30c.) As No. 738 (*Cypripedium calceolus*) ..... 1·10 ..... 1·10
847 35c. As No. 734 (*Cerastium dinaricum*) ..... 1·50 ..... 1·50
848 C (40c.) As No. 740 (*Serratula lycopifolia*) ..... 1·90 ..... 1·90
849 D (45c.) As No. 743 (*Genista bolopetala*) ..... 2·50 ..... 2·50
850 75c. As No. 739 (*Liparis loeslii*) ..... 3·50 ..... 3·50
851 €1 As No. 742 (*Eryngium alpinum*) ..... 5·00 ..... 5·00

404 Heart-shaped Bread

2009. Slovenia as Brand. Self-adhesive.
852 **404** C (40c.) multicoloured ..... 1·75 ..... 1·75

405 Athletes

2009. World Athletics Championship, Berlin.
853 **405** 45c. multicoloured ..... 2·00 ..... 2·00

406 Ploughing

2009. World Ploughing Championship, Tesanorci, Slovenia.
854 **406** 45c. multicoloured ..... 2·00 ..... 2·00

407 Star gazing

2009. Europa. Astronomy. Multicoloured.
855 45c. Type **407** ..... 7·00 ..... 7·00
856 92c. Observatory ..... 14·00 ..... 14·00

408 Werewolf

2009. Legends.
857 **408** 70c. multicoloured ..... 5·00 ..... 5·00

409 'J50ZZ'

2009. 50th Anniv of Jazz Festival, Ljubljana.
858 **409** 92c. multicoloured ..... 4·00 ..... 4·00

410 *Lucanus cervus*

2009. Insects. Multicoloured.
859 26c. Type **410** ..... 1·50 ..... 1·50
860 30c. *Rosalia alpina* ..... 2·00 ..... 2·00
861 40c. *Osmoderma eremita* ..... 3·75 ..... 3·75
MS862 70×60 mm. 45c. *Carabus variolosus* ..... 2·00 ..... 2·00

411 Stoll Overhead Line Bus, Piran

2009. Centenary of Bus Line between Piran and Lucija.
863 **411** 92c. multicoloured ..... 4·00 ..... 4·00

412 Anton Martin Slomsek (bishop)

2009. 150th Anniv of Transference of Bishopric from Andra to Marburg.
864 **412** 92c. multicoloured ..... 4·00 ..... 4·00

413 Kazun, Pazin

2009. Kazun and Hiska (primitive dry stone buildings). Sheet 112×73 mm containing T **413** and similar horiz design. Multicoloured.
MS865 92c.×2, Type **413**; Hiska, Kopriva na Krasu ..... 8·00 ..... 8·00
Stamps of a similar design were issued by Croatia.

414 *Lake Bohinj* (Anton Karinger)

2009. Romantic Landscapes.
866 **414** €1.50 multicoloured ..... 5·75 ..... 5·75

415 Firefighters

2009. OBLIGATORY TAX.
867 **415** 14c. multicoloured 70 70

416 Family

2009. OBLIGATORY TAX. Solidarity.
867a **416** 13c. multicoloured 70 70

417 Tree ..... **418** Children and Crib

2009. Christmas. (a) Ordinary gum.
868 **417** A multicoloured ..... 1·50 ..... 1·50
869 **418** C multicoloured ..... 2·20 ..... 2·20

(b) Self adhesive.
870 A As Type **416** ..... 1·50 ..... 1·50
871 C As Type **417** ..... 2·20 ..... 2·20

419 Omelette and Pasta

2009. Gastronomy. Multicoloured.
872 45c. Type **419** ..... 2·00 ..... 2·00
873 45c. Liver sausage ..... 2·00 ..... 2·00

420 Bronze Dagger (found in Ljubljana Marshes)

2009. Museum Exhibit. Sheet 70×60 mm.
MS874 **420** 92c. multicoloured ..... 4·00 ..... 4·00

421 Couple (Prekmurje)

2010. Traditional Costumes.
875	**421**	26c. multicoloured	1·00	1·00

422 Squirrels

2010. Greetings Stamp.
876	**422**	30c. multicoloured	1·70	1·70

423 Giant Slalom Gate

2010. Winter Olympic Games, Vancouver. Multicoloured.
877	**423**	40c. Type **423**	1·70	1·70
878		45c. Hockey stick and putt	2·00	2·00

424 Arrow

2010. Priority Mail. Self-adhesive.
879	**424**	D+Priority multicoloured	2·75	2·75

425 Tiger

2010. Chinese New Year. Year of the Tiger.
880	**425**	92c. multicoloured	4·00	4·00

426 Stanko Vraz

2010. Birth Bicentenary of Jakob Frass (Stanko Vraz) (Croatian poet).
881	**426**	€1.10 multicoloured	4·25	4·25

427 Mozirski pustnaki Carnival

2010. Folk Masks and Tradtions.
882	**427**	€1.60 multicoloured	6·25	6·25

428 Palm Bundle

2010. Easter. Traditional Decorations from Ljubno Savinja. Multicoloured. Self-adhesive.
883		B Type **428**	2·30	2·30
884		D Heart shaped palm bundle	2·75	2·75

429 Ski Jumper

2010. Planica 2010. Sheet 100×50 mm.
MS885	**429**	€2.38 multicoloured	9·50	9·50

No. **MS**885 was additionally perforated 'PLANICA 2010'.

430 Dianthus sanguineus

2010. Flora. Multicoloured.
886		26c. Type **430**	1·00	1·00
887		30c. Dianthus sternbergii	1·70	2·00
888		40c. Dianthus deltoides	1·70	2·00
MS889		70×60 mm. 92c. Dianthus carthusianorum	4·25	4·25

431 Paeonia officinalis

2012. Flora. Multicoloured.
890		45c. Type **431**	2·20	2·20
891		92c. Paeonia rockii	4·00	4·00
MS892		120×80 mm. Nos. 890/1	6·25	6·25

432 Chartusian Monastery, Jurkloster

2010. Medieval Monasteries in Slovenia
893	**432**	92c. multicoloured	4·25	4·25

433 Harbour

2010. Tourism
894	**433**	92c. multicoloured	4·25	4·25

434 Butterflies

2010. OBLIGATORY TAX. Red Cross Week
895	**434**	13c. multicoloured	2·00	2·00

435 Carved Pigeon in Flight (symbolizing Holy Spirit) (Robert Perk)

2010. I Feel Slovenia
896	**435**	D (44c.) multicoloured	2·00	2·00

436 Boy reading

2010. Europa. Children's Books. Multicoloured.
897		D (44c.) Type **436**	2·10	2·10
898		92c. Girl reading, dog, fairy and toys	4·00	4·00

437 Kurent

2010. Mythology
899	**437**	70c. multicoloured	3·25	3·25

438 Foot and Football

2010. World Cup Football Championship, South Africa (900) or World Basketball Championship, Turkey. Multicoloured.
900		92c. Type **438**	4·00	4·00
901		92c. Hand and ball	4·00	4·00

439 Character from Tincek Petelincek (rod)

2010. Puppetry. Multicoloured.
902		92c. Type **439**	4·00	4·00
903		92c. Kaspar from Gaspercek (marionette)	4·00	4·00
904		92c. Character from Pavliho (hand puppet)	4·00	4·00
905		92c. Character from Desetnica (shadow)	4·00	4·00
906		92c. Krpan from Martin Krpan (bunraku)	4·00	4·00

440 Tina Maze (alpine skier)

2010. Winter Olympic Games, Vancouver Medallists. Multicoloured.
MS907		70c.×2, Type **440**; Petra Majdic (cross country skier)	6·25	6·25

441 First Greeting Card

2010. 60th (2009) Anniv of UNICEF Greeting Cards
908	**441**	A (27c) multicoloured	1·50	1·50

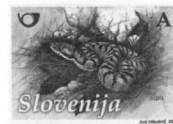

442 Vipera aspis

2010. Snakes. Multicoloured.
909		A (27c.) Type **442**	1·10	1·10
910		B (31c.) Coronella austriaca	1·70	1·70
911		C (40c.) Natrix natrix	2·20	2·20
MS912		60×70 mm. 92c. Vipera ammodytes (vert)	4·00	4·00

443 Trolleybus from Ljubljana

2010. Transport. Matjaž Učakar.
913	**443**	€1.50 multicoloured	6·75	6·75

444 The Letter (Janez Šubic)

2010. Art
914	**444**	€1.50 multicoloured	6·75	6·75

445 Teddy and Flames

2010. OBLIGATORY TAX. Fire Safety Week
915	**445**	14c. Multicoloured	1·00	1·00

446 Henry Dunant

2010. OBLIGATORY TAX. Birth Centenary of Henry Dunant (instigator of Red Cross)
916	**446**	13c. black and scarlet-vermilion	1·00	1·00

447 Molten Lead (used for divination)

2010. New Year. Multicoloured.

(a) Ordinary gum
917		A (27c.) Type **447**	1·40	1·40

(b) Booklet Stamps. Self-adhesive
918		A (27c.) As Type **447**	1·40	1·40

448 Advent Wreath

2010. Christmas. Multicoloured.

(a) Ordinary gum
919		C (40c.) Type **448**	3·50	3·50

(b) Booklet Stamps. Self-adhesive
920		C (40c.) Die-cut perf 13	3·50	3·50

449 Mežerli

2010. Traditional Dishes. Multicoloured.
921		49c. Type **449**	2·20	2·20
922		49c. Koroška curd cheese with pumpkin-seed oil	2·20	2·20

450 Iron Age Glass Bead Necklace

2010. Archaeological Finds, Novo Mesto. Sheet 70×60mm
MS923	**450**	92c. multicoloured	4·25	4·25

451 Couple (Notranjska)

2011. Traditional Costumes

924	451	A multicoloured	1·50	1·50

452 Kiss

2011. Love

925	452	B multicoloured	1·70	1·70

453 Matija Murko

2011. Matija Murko (philologist) Commemoration

926	453	41c. multicoloured	2·00	2·00

454 Church of the Holy Spirit, Javorca

2011. Tourism

927	454	44c. multicoloured	2·25	2·25

455 Rabbit

2011. Chinese New Year. Year of the Rabbit

928	455	77c. multicoloured	3·75	3·75

456 Franc Rozman

2011. Franc Rozman (Commander Stane of the Slovenian Partisan Brigade) Commemoration

929	456	92c. multicoloured	4·50	4·50

457 '60'

2011. 60th Anniv of Treaty of Paris

930	457	92c. multicoloured	4·50	4·50

457a Godlarji from Šenčur

2011. Folk Masks and Tradtions

930a	457a	€1.33 multicoloured	6·50	

458 Stična Monastery

2011. Medieval Monasteries

931	458	92c. multicoloured	4·50	4·50

459 Drosera rotundifolia

2011. Flora. Multicoloured.

932	A (27c.) Type **459**		1·10	1·10
933	B (31c.) Oxycoccus palustris		1·50	1·50
934	C (41c.) Eriophorum vaginatum		2·25	2·25
MS935	70×60 mm. 92c. Andromeda polifolia		4·50	4·50

460 Wind Orchestra

2011. 80th Anniv of KUD Mail Orchestra. Sheet 71×61 mm

MS936	460	B (31c.) multicoloured	1·50	1·50

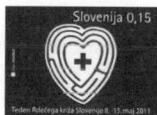

461 Vrhnika Easter Egg

2011. I Feel Slovenia

937	461	D (44c.) multicoloured	2·25	2·25

462 Heart-shaped Labyrinth containing Red Cross

2011. OBLIGATORY TAX. Red Cross Week

938	462	15c. scarlet-vermilion and black	1·00	1·00

463 Janko Ravnik filming first Slovenian Film and Herbert Drofenik (Gornik) ('actor') seated next to Camera, 1931

2011. 80th Anniv of First Slovene Films. *In the Realm of the Goldenhorn*

939	463	44c. multicoloured	2·10	2·10

464 Anniversary Emblem

2011. 50th Anniv of OECD (Organisation for Economic Co-operation and Development)

940	464	D multicoloured	2·10	2·10

465 River Man

2011. Mythology

941	465	77c. multicoloured	3·75	3·75

466 Rowers

2011. World Rowing Championships, 2011, Bled

942	466	92c. multicoloured	4·50	4·50

467 Pavli riding Bicycle

2011. Postman Pavli. Multicoloured.

943	A Type **467**		1·10	1·10
944	B Pavli delivering letter		1·90	1·90

468 Beech Tree, Kočevje

2011. Europa. Forests. Multicoloured.

945	D Type **468**		2·00	2·00
946	92c. Pine tree, Sgerm Farmhouse, Ribnica na Pohorju		4·50	4·50

469 Johann Gerstner

2011. 160th Birth Anniv of Johann Gerstner (violinist, teacher and conductor). Sheet 80×120 mm

MS947	469	€1.33 multicoloured	6·50	6·50

470 Bouquet

2011. 20th Anniv of Republic of Slovenia. Sheet 80×60 mm

MS948	470	€3.11 multicoloured	15·00	15·00

471 Stone Crayfish

2011. Endangered Species. Stone Crayfish (Austropotamobius torrentium). Multicoloured.

949	A Type **471**		90	90
950	B Brown crayfish		1·90	1·90
951	C Black crayfish		2·40	2·40
952	D Larger brown crayfish with enlarged claws		2·75	2·75

472 Numenius arquata (Eurasian Curlew)

2011. Birds. Multicoloured.

953	A Type **472**		90	90

954	B Dendrocopos leucotos (white-backed woodpecker)		1·90	1·90
955	C Emberiza hortulana (ortolan bunting)		2·40	2·40
MS956	60×70 mm. 92c. Ciconia ciconia (white stork)		4·50	4·50

473 Atrium of Old University Graz

2011. Bicentenary of Establishment of First Chair for Slovene Language

957	473	C multicoloured	1·90	1·90

474 Green Veil

2011. Art - Impressionism and Postimpressionism. Rihard Jakopič Commemoration

958	474	€1.33 multicoloured	6·50	6·50

475 Tomos Colibri T 12 Moped

2011. Motor Vehicles

959	475	€1.33 multicoloured	6·50	6·50

476 Children wearing Safety Helmets

2011. OBLIGATORY TAX. Fire Safety Week

960	476	15c. multicoloured	1·00	1·00

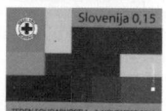

477 Red Cross

2011. OBLIGATORY TAX. Red Cross Week

961	477	15c. multicoloured	1·00	1·00

478 Snowman

2011. Greetings Stamps. Children's Drawings. Personal Stamps

962	A Type **478**		1·10	1·10
963	A Tree		1·10	1·10
964	A Snowy forest (horiz)		1·10	1·10
965	A Snowman and trees (horiz)		1·10	1·10
966	B Decorated tree and parcels		1·50	1·50
967	B Tree with star		1·50	1·50
968	B Wreath (horiz)		1·50	1·50
969	B Reindeer and Santa's sleigh (horiz)		1·50	1·50
970	C Tree and snow			
971	C Santa		1·90	1·90
972	C Multicoloured snowflakes (horiz)		1·90	1·90
973	C Santa's hat (horiz)		1·90	1·90
974	D Tree wth zigzag decorations		2·00	2·00
975	D Snowman, tree, parcels and falling snow		2·00	2·00
976	D Decorated tree and Santa (horiz)		2·00	2·00
977	D Jack in the box (horiz)		2·00	2·00

479 Poprtnik
(bread specially
baked for
Christmas)

2011. Christmas. Breads

		(a) Sheet stamps. Size 23×29 mm		
978	**479**	A multicoloured	1·10	1·10
979	**479**	C multicoloured	1·90	1·90

		(b) Booklet stamps. Size 25×34 mm		
980	**479**	A multicoloured	1·10	1·10
981	**479**	C multicoloured	1·90	1·90

480 Four Leaf
Clover

2011. New Year. Four Leaf Clover

		(a) Sheet stamps. Size 23×29 mm		
982	**480**	A multicoloured	1·10	1·10
983	**480**	C multicoloured	1·90	1·90

		(b) Booklet stamps. Size 25×34 mm		
984	**480**	A multicoloured	1·10	1·10
985	**480**	C multicoloured	1·90	1·90

481 Loška smojka (Turnip hot pot)

2011. Gastronomy. Multicoloured.

986	**D** Type **481**	2·00	2·00
987	**D** Bled cream slice	2·00	2·00

482 MKS-EXCLUSIVE
Microphone (Marko Turk)

2011. Slovenian Industrial Design.
988	**482**	58c. multicoloured	2·40	2·40

483 Salt Harvesters with
Gavero (traditional
salt-harvesting tool)

2011. Sečovlje Salina Nature Park. Sheet 70×60 mm
MS989 **483** 77c. multicoloured	3·25	3·25

484 Decorated Bronze Belt
Buckle

2011. Archaeological Finds, Novo Mesto. Sheet 70×60mm
MS990 **484** 92c. multicoloured	3·75	3·75

485 Couple from Bohinj

2012. Traditional Costumes
991	**485**	27c. multicoloured	1·10	1·10

486 Graffiti

2012. Love
992	**486**	31c. multicoloured	1·50	1·50

487 Dragon

2012. Chinese New Year. Year of the Dragon
993	**487**	92c. multicoloured	4·50	4·50

488 Mira Mihelič

2012. Birth Centenary of Mira Mihelič (writer and
translator)
994	**488**	€1.25 silver and black	6·00	6·00

489 Barbed Wire and Map
of Fence

2012. 70th Anniv of Barbed Wire Fence Blockade of
Ljubljana. Sheet 70×60 mm
MS995 **489** €1.33 multicoloured	7·00	7·00

490 Honey
Heart

2012. I Feel Slovenia
996	**490**	A multicoloured	1·10	1·10

491 Pavli
visiting School

2012. Postman Pavli. Multicoloured.
997	C Type **491**	2·25	2·25
998	D Pavli mending bicycle puncture	2·50	2·50

492 Primula×venusta

2012. Flora. Plants from Botanical Garden, Ljubljana.
Multicoloured.
999	77c. Scabiosa hladnikiana	3·50	3·50
1000	40c. Pastinaca sativa	2·25	2·25
1001	44c. Type **492**	2·50	2·50
MS1002 70×60 mm. 92c. Scopolia carniolica		5·00	5·00

493 Turning Point

2012. Europa. Visit Slovenia. Maribor - European Capital
of Culture 2012. Multicoloured.
1003	44c. Type **493**	2·50	2·50
1004	92c. Energy symbol	4·50	4·50

494 Three Valleys

2012. Tourism. Solčavsko
1005	**494**	€1.25 multicoloured	6·25	6·25

495 Minorite Monastery of
St. Peter and St. Paul, Ptuj

2012. Medieval Monasteries in Slovenia
1006	**495**	€1.33 multicoloured	6·50	6·50

496 'MLADI ZA BOLJŠI
SVET' (Youth for a Better
World)

2012. OBLIGATORY TAX. Red Cross Week
1007	**496**	15c. multicoloured	1·00	1·00

497 Emblem

2012. Maribofila 2012 International Stamp Exhibition.
Sheet 60×70 mm
MS1008 **497** D multicoloured	3·00	3·00

498 Taekwondo and Sailing

2012. Olympic Games, London. Multicoloured.
1009	77c. Type **498**	3·65	3·65
1010	92c. Swimming and handball	4·50	4·50

499 Decorated Pots

2012. Cultural Heritage. Filovci Pottery Village.
Multicoloured.
MS1011 92c.×2, Type **499**; Black jug	8·00	8·00

500 Woods and Valley

2012. Goričko Natural Park. Sheet 70×60 mm
MS1012 **500** €1.25 multicoloured	6·50	6·50

501 Bombus lapidaries

2012. Bees. Multicoloured.
1013	40c. Type **501**	2·25	2·25
1014	44c. Bombus pascuorum	3·00	3·00
1015	77c. Bombus humilis	3·65	3·65
MS1016 70×60 mm. 92c. Bombus lucorum		5·00	5·00

502 Urška Žolnir

2012. Urška Žolnir (Olympic Judo Gold Medal Winner)
1017	**502**	92k. multicoloured	4·50	4·50

503 Lacemaker

2012. Art - Expressionism. Veno Pilon Commemoration
1018	**503**	€1.33 multicoloured	7·00	7·00

504 Knight

2012. World Youth Chess Championship 2012, Maribor.
Sheet 70×60 mm
MS1019 **504** €1.33 multicoloured	7·50	7·50

2012. OBLIGATORY TAX. Fire Safety Week
1019a	**504a**	15c. multicoloured	1·00	1·00

504b Red Cross Workers
carrying Patient

2012. OBLIGATORY TAX. Red Cross Week
1019b	**504b**	15c. multicoloured	1·00	1·00

505 Nativity Crib

2012. Christmas. Multicoloured.
1020	A (27c.) Angel	1·10	1·10
1021	C (41c.) Type **505**	2·25	2·25

506 New Year
Fairy

2012. New Year. Multicoloured.
1022	A (27c.) Type **506**	1·10	1·10
1023	C (41c.) Piglet	2·25	2·25

507 ETA 80 Telephone

2012. Slovenian Industrial Design
1024	**507**	58c. multicoloured	3·25	3·25

508 Mountaineer

2012. 80th Anniv of First Slovene Films (2nd issue). *The Slopes of Triglav*

1025	**508**	58c. multicoloured	3·25	3·25

509 Kranjska Klobasa (Carniolan Sausage)

2012. Gastronomy. Multicoloured.

1026	77c. Type **509**		3·65	3·65
1027	77c. Sautéed potatoes		3·65	3·65

510 Couple, Ljubljana

2013. Traditional Costumes

1028	**510**	27c. multicoloured	1·10	1·10

511 Heart-shaped Lock

2013. Greetings Stamp

1029	**511**	31c. multicoloured	1·50	1·50

512 Snake

2013. Chinese New Year. Year of the Snake

1030	**512**	92c. multicoloured	4·50	4·50

513 Fran Miklošič

2013. Birth Bicentenary of Fran Miklošič (Franz Xaver Ritter von Miklosich) (philogist)

1031	**513**	€1.33 multicoloured	7·00	7·00

514 Pavli with Posthorn and Dog (Spring)

2013. Postman Pavli. Multicoloured.

1032	A Type **514**		1·10	1·10
1033	B Pavli eating watermelon (Summer)		1·50	1·50

514a Stylized Couple holding Blood Droplet

2013. OBLIGATORY TAX. 60th Anniv of Voluntary Blood Donation in Slovenia

1033a	**514a**	17c. multicoloured	1·25	1·25

515 Vase (Meta Šmalcelj)

2013. I Feel Slovenia

1034	**515**	D multicoloured	2·50	2·50

516 *Ziziphus jujube* (Jujube)

2013. Flora. Fruit Trees. Multicoloured.

1035	60c. Type **516**		3·30	3·30
1036	64c. *Ficus carica* (Fig)		3·40	3·40
1037	92c. *Eriobotrya japonica* (Loquat)		4·50	4·50
MS1038	70×60 mm. 97c. *Sorbus domestica* (Service Tree)		5·30	5·30

517 Post Office, Postojna Cave (world's first underground post office)

2013. Postojna Cave. Sheet 100×80 mm

MS1039	**517**	64c. multicoloured	3·50	3·50

518 Post Bicycle

2013. Europa. Postal Transport. Multicoloured.

1040	64c. Type **518**		3·40	3·40
1041	92c. Mail coach		4·50	4·50

519 Kolpa River

2013. Tourism

1042	**519**	€1.25 multicoloured	6·00	6·00

520 Capuchin Monastery, Vipavski Križ

2013. Medieval Monasteries

1043	**520**	€1.33 multicoloured	7·00	7·00

521 *Meeting between Count Coronini and Tolmin Rebels, Solkan* (Tone Kralj)

2013. 300th Anniv of Tolmin Peasant Revolt. Sheet 70×60 mm

MS1044	**521**	€2.18 multicoloured	9·00	9·00

522 Bridge over the Drava in Maribor

2013. Bridges. Multicoloured.

1045	27c. Type **522**		1·10	1·10
1046	31c. Rail Bridges at Zidani Most		1·50	1·50
1047	60c. Triple Bridge in Ljubljana		3·30	3·30
1048	64c. Kandija Bridge over the Krka in Novo Mesto		3·40	3·40
1049	97c. Bridge over the Soča in Kanal		5·30	5·30

523 Puppy

2013. Greetings Stamps. Pets. Personal Stamps. Multicoloured.

1050	A Type **523**		1·10	1·10
1051	A Sealyham Terrier		1·10	1·10
1052	A Wolfhound (horiz)		1·10	1·10
1053	A Bernese Mountain Dog (horiz)		1·10	1·10
1054	B YorkshireX Terrrier		1·50	1·50
1055	B White rat		1·50	1·50
1056	B Tabby and white cat (horiz)		1·50	1·50
1057	B Budgerigar (horiz)		1·50	1·50
1058	C Cairn Terrier		2·25	2·25
1059	C Lhasa Apso		2·25	2·25
1060	C Long-haired black cat (horiz)		2·25	2·25
1061	C Golden Retriever (horiz)		2·25	2·25
1062	D White cat		2·50	2·50
1063	D Goat kid		2·50	2·50
1064	D British Blue cat (horiz)		2·50	2·50
1065	D Long-haired tabby cat (horiz)		2·50	2·50

524 Emblem

2013. European Basketball Championship – EuroBasket 2013

1066	**524**	€1.33 multicoloured	7·00	7·00

525 Kozjansko Apples

2013. Kozjansko Regional Park. Sheet 70×60 mm

MS1067	**525**	€1.25 multicoloured	6·50	6·50

526 *Chromis chromis* (Damsel Fish)

2013. Marine Fauna. Multicoloured.

1068	60c. Type **526**		3·25	3·25
1069	64c. *Sepia officinalis* (Cuttlefish)		3·75	3·75
1070	92c. *Caretta caretta* (Loggerhead Sea Turtle)		4·50	4·50
MS1071	70×60 mm. 97c. *Liza aurata* (Golden Grey Mullet)		5·00	5·00

527 Fire Appliance

2013. OBLIGATORY TAX. Fire Safety Week

1072	**527**	15c. multicoloured	1·00	1·00

528 Community in Action

2013. OBLIGATORY TAX. Red Cross Week

1073	**528**	17c. multicoloured	1·00	1·00

529 Bean Štruklji with Sauerkraut

2013. Gastronomy. Multicoloured.

1074	92c. Type **529**		4·50	4·50
1075	92c. Roast Goose with Mlinci and Stewed Red Cabbage		4·50	4·50

530 K67 Kiosk (Saša J. Mächtig)

2013. Slovenian Industrial Design

1076	**530**	92c. multicoloured	4·50	4·50

531 Scene from *Vesna*

2013. Slovene Films - *Vesna* (Slovene film by Czech director Františsek Čáp)

1077	**531**	97c. multicoloured	4·50	4·50

532 Nativity   **533** Nativity

2013. Christmas. Multicoloured.

(a) Sheet stamps. Size 23×29 mm

1078	**532**	A multicoloured	1·10	1·10
1079	**533**	C multicoloured	1·90	1·90

(b) Booklet stamps. Size 25×34 mm

1080	A As T **432**		1·10	1·10
1081	C As T **433**		1·90	1·90

534 Young Girl

2013. New Year. Multicoloured.

(a) Sheet stamps. Size 23×29 mm

1082	A Type **534**		1·10	1·10
1083	C Gnome		1·90	1·90

(b) Booklet stamps. Size 25×34 mm

1084	A As Type **534**		1·10	1·10
1085	C As No. 1083		1·90	1·90

535 Mehdi Huseynzade

2013. Mehdi Huseynzade (Mikhailo) (Azerbaijan scout during World War II) Commemoration

1086	**535**	97c. multicoloured	4·50	4·50

Pt. 1

SOLOMON ISLANDS

A group of islands in the west Pacific, east of New Guinea.

1907. 12 pence = 1 shilling; 20 shillings = 1 pound.
1966. 100 cents = $1 Australian.

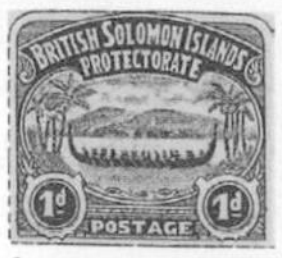

1

1907

1	1	½d. blue	9·00	14·00
2	1	1d. red	23·00	25·00
3	1	2d. blue	45·00	32·00
4	1	2½d. yellow	32·00	50·00
5	1	5d. green	60·00	70·00
6	1	6d. brown	55·00	70·00
7	1	1s. purple	80·00	85·00

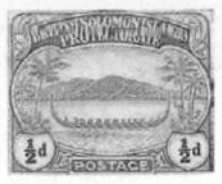

2

1908

8	2	½d. green	1·50	1·00
9	2	1d. red	1·25	1·25
10	2	2d. grey	1·25	1·00
11	2	2½d. blue	3·75	2·00
11a	2	4d. red on yellow	3·50	9·00
12	2	5d. olive	10·00	5·00
13	2	6d. red	10·00	5·50
14	2	1s. black on green	8·50	5·00
15	2	2s. purple on blue	50·00	55·00
16	2	2s.6d. red on blue	60·00	70·00
17	2	5s. green on yellow	90·00	£110

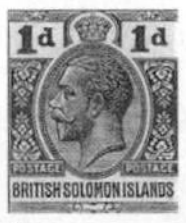

3

1913. Inscr "POSTAGE POSTAGE".

18	3	½d. green	1·00	3·50
19	3	1d. red	5·50	16·00
42	3	1½d. red	2·25	60
20	3	3d. purple on yellow	1·50	4·00
21	3	11d. purple and red	3·00	12·00

1914. Inscr "POSTAGE REVENUE".

39	½d. green	50	3·50
24	1d. red	1·50	1·25
41	1d. violet	1·00	7·50
26	2d. grey	4·25	9·00
27	2½d. blue	4·50	4·00
28	3d. purple on yellow	28·00	£140
44	3d. blue	70	4·50
29	4d. black and red on yellow	2·00	2·50
45a	4½d. brown	3·00	20·00
46	5d. purple and green	3·00	30·00
32	6d. purple	6·00	14·00
33	1s. black on green	4·75	7·00
34	2s. purple and blue on blue	7·00	10·00
35	2s.6d. black and red on blue	9·50	20·00
36	5s. green and red on yellow	48·00	48·00
37	10s. green and red on green	95·00	65·00
38	£1 purple and black on red	£250	£120

1935. Silver Jubilee. As T **32a** of St. Helena.

53	1½d. blue and red	1·00	1·00
54	3d. brown and blue	6·50	7·50
55	6d. blue and green	16·00	12·00
56	1s. grey and purple	7·50	22·00

1937. Coronation. As T **32b** of St. Helena.

57	1d. violet	30	1·25
58	1½d. red	30	60
59	3d. blue	50	50

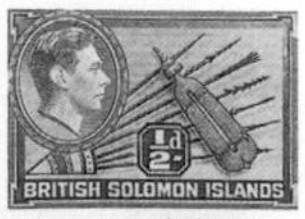

5 Spears and Shield

1939. Portrait of King George VI.

60	5	½d. blue and green	15	1·00
61	-	1d. brown and violet	30	1·50
62	-	1½d. green and red	1·75	1·75
63a	-	2d. brown and black	75	1·50
64	-	2½d. mauve and olive	3·75	2·25
65	-	3d. black and blue	3·00	2·00
66	-	4½d. green and brown	5·50	13·00
67	-	6d. violet and purple	2·50	1·00
68	-	1s. green and black	2·00	1·00
69	-	2s. black and orange	13·00	6·50
70	-	2s.6d. black and violet	30·00	4·50
71	-	5s. green and red	32·00	13·00
72	-	10s. green and mauve	4·00	8·50

DESIGNS—VERT: 1d. Native constable and chief; 4½d., 10s. Native house, Reef Islands; 6d. Coconut plantation. HORIZ: 1½d. Artificial 1sland., Malaita; 2½d. Roviana canoe; 1s. Breadfruit; 5s. Malaita canoe. LARGER (35½×22 mm): 2d. Canoe house; 3d. Roviana canoes; 2s. Tinakula volcano; 2s.6d. Bismarck scrub fowl.

1946. Victory. As T **33a** of St. Helena.

73	1½d. red	15	1·25
74	3d. blue	15	20

1949. Silver Wedding. As T **33b/c** of St. Helena.

75	2d. grey	50	50
76	10s. mauve	10·00	8·50

1949. 75th Anniv of U.P.U. As T **33d/g** of St. Helena.

77	2d. brown	50	1·00
78	3d. blue	2·25	1·50
79	5d. green	50	1·75
80	1s. black	50	1·75

1953. Coronation. As T **33h** of St. Helena.

81	2d. black and grey	1·50	1·25

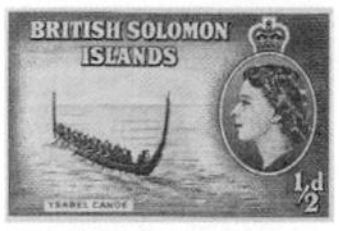

17 Ysabel Canoe

1956. Portrait of Queen Elizabeth II.

82	17	½d. orange and purple	15	50
83	-	1d. green & brn (as No. 65)	15	15
84	-	1½d. slate and red (No. 62)	15	1·00
105	-	2d. sepia and green (No. 63)	20	20
86	-	2½d. black and blue	1·50	60
106	-	3d. green and red (No. 71)	1·75	15
88	-	5d. black and blue	30	55
89	-	6d. black and green	60	25
90	-	8d. blue and black	25	30
108	-	9d. green and black	40	35
91	-	1s. slate and brown	3·00	50
109	-	1s.3d. black and blue	60	70
110	-	2s. black and red (No. 69)	1·00	5·50
93	-	2s.6d. green & pur (No. 66)	7·50	45
94	-	5s. brown	15·00	5·50
95	-	10s. sepia (No. 61)	25·00	9·00
96	-	£1 black and blue	32·00	35·00

DESIGNS—VERT: 2½d. Prow of Roviana canoe. 10s. Similar to No. 61, but constable in different uniform, without rifle; HORIZ: 5d., 1s.3d. Map; 6d. "Miena" (Schooner); 8d., 9d. Henderson Airfield, Guadalcanal; 1s. Chart showing voyage of H.M.S. "Swallow" in 1767; 5s. Mendana and "Todos los Santos"; £1 Arms of the Protectorate.

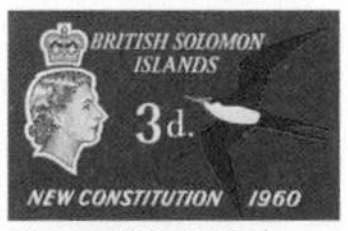

32 Great Frigate Bird

1961. New Constitution, 1960.

97	32	2d. black and turquoise	10	30
98	32	3d. black and red	10	10
99	32	9d. black and purple	15	30

1963. Freedom from Hunger. As T **63a** of St. Helena.

100	1s.3d. blue	75	35

1963. Cent of Red Cross. As T **63b** of St. Helena.

101	2d. red and black	25	20
102	9d. red and blue	50	90

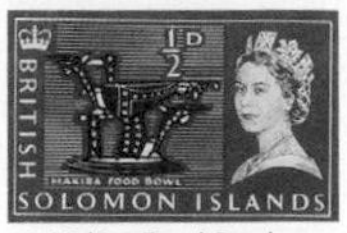

33 Makira Food Bowl

1965. Central design in black; background colours given.

112	33	½d. blue and light blue	10	1·40
113	-	1d. orange and yellow	70	60
114	-	1½d. blue and green	35	65
115	-	2d. ultramarine and blue	60	1·75
116	-	2½d. brown and light brown	10	1·25
117	-	3d. green and light green	10	10
118	-	6d. mauve and orange	35	80
119	-	9d. green and yellow	40	15
120	-	1s. brown and mauve	1·00	15
121	-	1s.3d. red	5·00	2·25
122	-	2s. purple and lilac	9·00	2·75
123	-	2s.6d. brown and light brown	1·00	70
124	-	5s. blue and violet	15·00	4·50
125	-	10s. green and yellow	18·00	3·00
126	-	£1 violet and pink	12·00	4·50

DESIGNS: 1d. "Dendrobium veratrifolium" (orchid); 1½d. Chiragra spider conch; 2d. Blyth's hornbill ("Hornbill"); 2½d. Ysabel shield; 3d. Rennellese club; 6d. Moorish idol (fish); 9d. Lesser frigate bird ("Frigate Bird"); 1s. "Dendrobium macrophyllum" (orchid); 1s.3d. "Dendrobium spectabilis" (orchid); 2s. Sanford's sea eagle ("Sanford's Eagle"); 2s.6d. Malaita belt; 5s. "Ornithoptera victoreae" (butterfly); 10s. Ducorp's cockatoo ("White Cockatoo"); £1 Western canoe figurehead.

1965. Cent of I.T.U. As T **64a** of St. Helena.

127	2d. red and turquoise	20	15
128	3d. turquoise and drab	20	15

1965. I.C.Y. As T **64b** of St. Helena.

129	1d. purple and turquoise	10	10
130	2s.6d. green and lavender	45	20

1966. Churchill Commemoration. As T **64c** of St. Helena.

131	2d. blue	15	10
132	9d. green	25	10
133	1s.3d. brown	35	10
134	2s.6d. violet	40	25

1966. Decimal Currency. Nos. 112/26 surch.

135A	1c. on ½d.	10	10
136A	2c. on 1d.	10	10
137A	3c. on 1½d.	10	10
138A	4c. on 2d.	15	10
139A	5c. on 6d.	15	10
140B	6c. on 2½d.	10	10
141B	7c. on 3d.	10	10
142B	8c. on 9d.	15	10
143A	10c. on 1s.	30	10
144B	12c. on 1s.3d.	65	10
145A	13c. on 1s.3d.	2·50	15
146B	14c. on 3d.	40	10
147A	20c. on 2s.	2·50	25
148A	25c. on 2s.6d.	60	40
149B	35c. on 2d.	2·00	25
150A	50c. on 5s.	4·50	1·50
151A	$1 on 10s.	3·00	1·50
152A	$2 on £1	2·25	3·00

1966. World Cup Football Championship. As T **64d** of St. Helena.

153	8c. multicoloured	15	15
154	35c. multicoloured	30	15

1966. Inauguration of W.H.O. Headquarters. Geneva. As T **64e** of St. Helena.

155	3c. black, green and blue	20	10
156	50c. black, purple and ochre	60	20

1966. 20th Anniv of UNESCO. As T **64f/h** of St. Helena.

157	3c. multicoloured	15	10
158	25c. yellow, violet and olive	30	15
159	$1 black, purple and orange	75	70

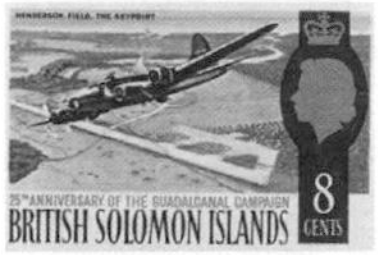

49 Henderson Field

1967. 25th Anniv of Guadalcanal Campaign (Pacific War). Multicoloured.

160	8c. Type **49**	15	15
161	35c. Red Beach landings	15	15

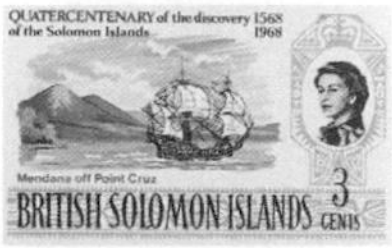

51 Mendana's "Todos los Santos" off Point Cruz

1968. 400th Anniv of Discovery of the Solomon Is. Multicoloured.

162	3c. Type **51**	20	10
163	8c. Arrival of missionaries	20	10
164	35c. Pacific Campaign, World War II	40	10
165	$1 Proclamation of the Protectorate	60	1·25

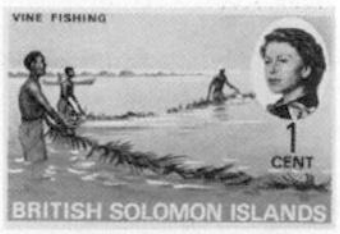

55 Vine Fishing

1968

166	55	1c. blue, black and brown	10	10
167	-	2c. green, black and brown	10	10
168	-	3c. green, myrtle and black	10	10
169	-	4c. purple, black and brown	15	10
170	-	6c. multicoloured	30	10
171	-	8c. multicoloured	25	10
172	-	12c. ochre, red and black	65	50
173	-	14c. red, brown and black	2·50	3·50
174	-	15c. multicoloured	80	80
175	-	20c. blue, red and black	4·50	3·00
176	-	24c. red, black and yellow	2·00	3·25
177	-	35c. multicoloured	2·00	30
178	-	45c. multicoloured	1·50	30
179	-	$1 blue, green and black	2·50	1·50
180	-	$2 multicoloured	8·50	3·50

DESIGNS: 2c. Kite fishing; 3c. Platform fishing; 4c. Net fishing; 6c. Gold lip shell diving; 8c. Night fishing; 12c. Boat building; 14c. Cocoa; 15c. Road building; 20c. Geological survey; 24c. Hauling timber; 35c. Copra; 45c. Harvesting rice; $1 Honiara Port; $2 Internal air service.

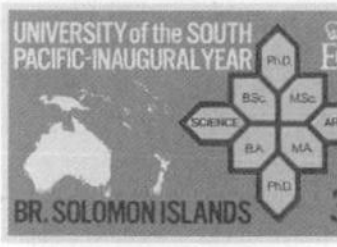

70 Map of Australasia and Diagram

1969. Inaugural Year of South Pacific University.

181	70	3c. multicoloured	10	10
182	70	12c. multicoloured	10	10
183	70	35c. multicoloured	15	10

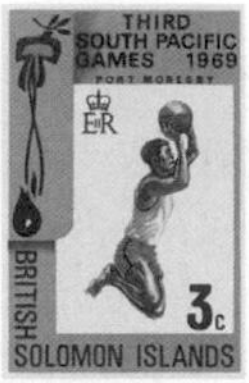

71 Basketball Player

1969. Third South Pacific Games, Port Moresby. Multicoloured.

184	3c. Type **71**	10	10
185	8c. Footballer	10	10
186	14c. Sprinter	10	10
187	45c. Rugby player	20	15
MS188	126×120 mm. Nos. 184/7	2·75	8·00

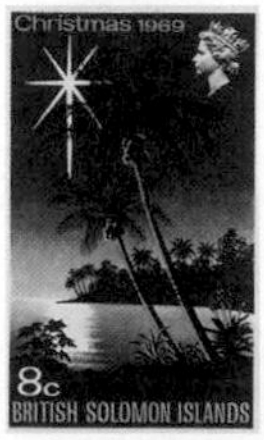

75 South Sea Island with Star of Bethlehem

1969. Christmas.

189	75	8c. black, violet and green	10	10
190	-	35c. multicoloured	20	20

DESIGN: 35c. Southern Cross, "PAX" and frigate bird (stained glass window).

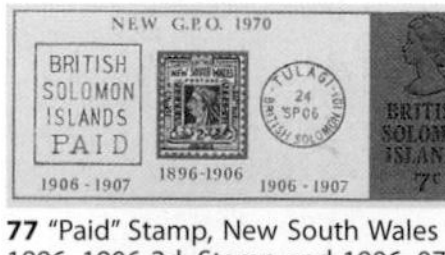

77 "Paid" Stamp, New South Wales 1896–1906 2d. Stamp and 1906–07 Tulagi Postmark

1970. New G.P.O., Honiara.

191	77	7c. mauve, blue and black	15	15
192	-	14c. green, blue and black	20	15
193	-	18c. multicoloured	20	15
194	-	23c. multicoloured	20	20

DESIGNS: 14c. 1906–07 2d. stamp and C. M. Woodford; 18c. 1910–14 5s. stamp and Tulagi postmark, 1913; 23c. New G.P.O., Honiara.

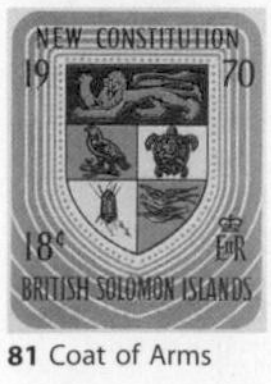

81 Coat of Arms

1970. New Constitution.

195	81	18c. multicoloured	15	10
196	-	35c. green, blue and ochre	35	20

DESIGN—HORIZ: 35c. Map.

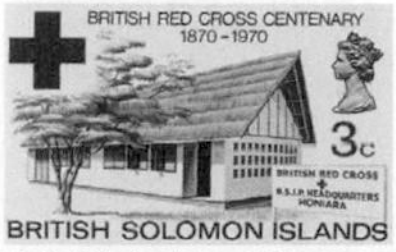

83 British Red Cross H.Q., Honiara

1970. Centenary of British Red Cross.

197	83	3c. multicoloured	10	10
198	-	35c. blue, red and black	25	20

DESIGN—VERT: 35c. Wheelchair and map.

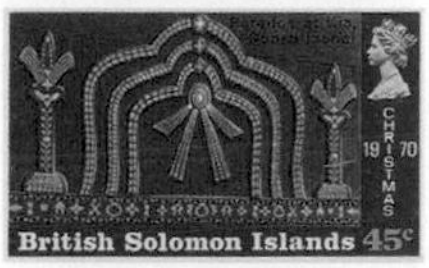

86 Reredos (Altar Screen)

1970. Christmas.

199		8c. ochre and violet	10	10
200	86	45c. chestnut, orange and brown	25	20

DESIGN—HORIZ: 8c. Carved angel.

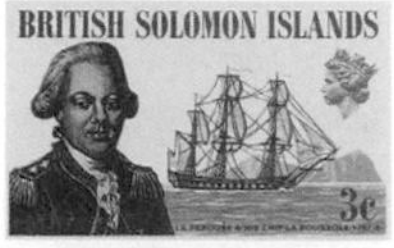

87 La Perouse and "La Boussole"

1971. Ships and Navigators (1st series). Multicoloured.

201	3c. Type **87**	45	20
202	4c. Astrolabe and Polynesian reed map	45	20
203	12c. Abel Tasman and "Heemskerk"	60	30
204	35c. Te puki canoe, Santa Cruz	70	50

See also Nos. 215/18, 236/9, 254/7 and 272/5.

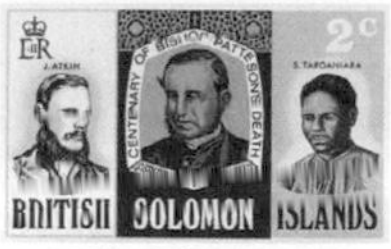

88 J. Atkin, Bishop Patteson and S. Taroaniara

1971. Death Cent of Bishop Patteson. Multicoloured.

205	2c. Type **88**	10	10
206	4c. Last landing at Nukapu	10	10
207	14c. Memorial Cross and Nukapu (vert)	10	10
208	45c. Knotted leaf and canoe (vert)	20	10

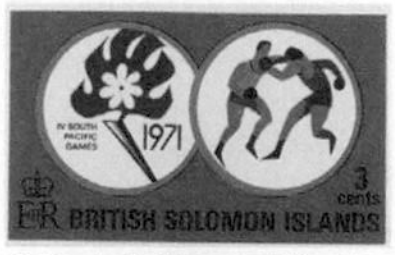

89 Torch Emblem and Boxers

1971. South Pacific Games, Tahiti. Multicoloured.

209	3c. Type **89**	10	25
210	8c. Emblem and footballers	10	25
211	12c. Emblem and runner	10	40
212	35c. Emblem and skin-diver	15	20

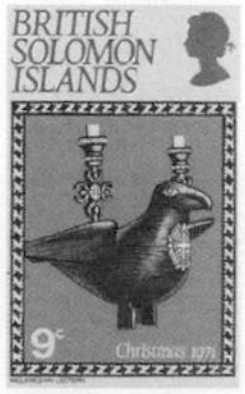

90 Melanesian Lectern

1971. Christmas. Multicoloured.

213	9c. Type **90**	10	10
214	45c. "United we Stand" (Margarita Bara)	20	20

1972. Ships and Navigators (2nd series). As T **87**. Multicoloured.

215	4c. Bougainville and "La Boudeuse"	30	10
216	9c. Horizontal planisphere and ivory backstaff	35	10
217	15c. Philip Carteret and H.M.S. "Swallow"	60	15
218	45c. Malaita canoe	70	90

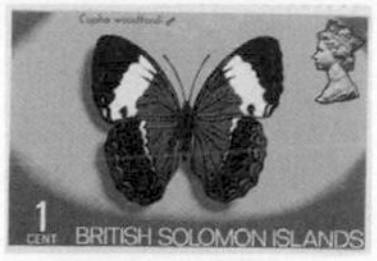

91 "Cupha woodfordi"

1972. Multicoloured.

219	1c. Type **91**	15	50
220	2c. "Ornithoptera priamus"	25	50
221	3c. "Vindula sapor"	25	60
222	4c. "Papilio ulysses"	25	60
223	5c. Big-eyed trevally	25	30
224	8c. Australian bonito	40	50
225	9c. Blue demoiselle	50	65
226	12c. "Costus speciosus"	1·25	90
227	15c. Clown anemonefish ("Orange anenome fish")	1·25	1·00
228	20c. "Spathoglottis plicata"	3·00	1·75
229	25c. "Ephemerantha comata"	3·00	1·50
230	35c. "Dendrobium cuthbertsonii"	3·00	2·25
231	45c. "Heliconia salomonica"	2·50	3·00
232	$1 Dotty triggerfish	3·00	4·50
233	$2 "Ornithoptera alottei"	9·00	15·00
233a	$5 Great frigate bird	14·00	16·00

The 2, 3, 4c. and $2 are butterflies; the 5, 8, 9, 15c. and $1 are fishes, and the 12, 20, 25, 35, 45c. are flowers.

1972. Royal Silver Wedding. As T **103** of St. Helena, but with Greetings and Message Drum in background.

234	8c. red	10	10
235	45c. green	20	20

1973. Ships and Navigators (3rd series). As T **87**. Multicoloured.

236	4c. D'Entrecasteaux and "La Recherche"	30	20
237	9c. Ship's hour-glass and chronometer	35	20
238	15c. Lt. Shortland and H.M.S. "Alexander"	70	30
239	35c. Tomoko (war canoe)	70	1·10

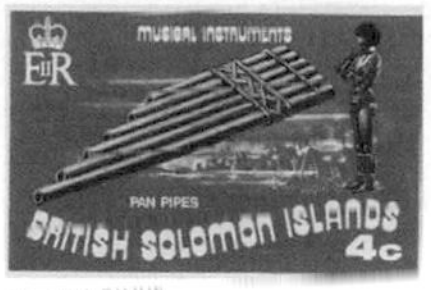

93 Pan Pipes

1973. Musical Instruments. Multicoloured.

240	4c. Type **93**	10	10
241	9c. Castanets	10	10
242	15c. Bamboo flute	15	10
243	35c. Bauro gongs	20	25
244	45c. Bamboo band	20	30

1973. Royal Wedding. As T **74a** of Pitcairn Islands.

245	4c. blue	10	10
246	35c. blue	15	10

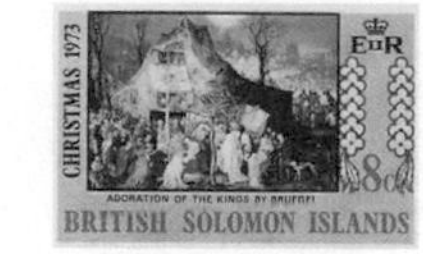

94 "Adoration of the Kings" (Jan Brueghel)

1973. Christmas. "Adoration of the Kings" by the artists listed. Multicoloured.

247	8c. Type **94**	10	10
248	22c. Pieter Brueghel (vert)	20	25
249	45c. Botticelli (48×35 mm)	50	50

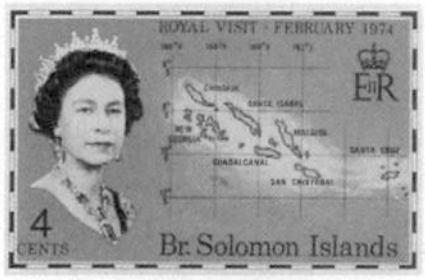

95 Queen Elizabeth II and Map

1974. Royal Visit.

250	95	4c. multicoloured	25	10
251	95	9c. multicoloured	25	10
252	95	15c. multicoloured	30	20
253	95	35c. multicoloured	50	1·25

1974. Ships and Navigators (4th series). As T **87**. Multicoloured.

254	4c. Commissioner landing from S.S. "Titus"	20	10
255	9c. Radar scanner	20	10
256	15c. Natives being transported to a "Blackbirder" brig	25	15
257	45c. Lieut. John F. Kennedy's "P.T. 109"	1·00	90

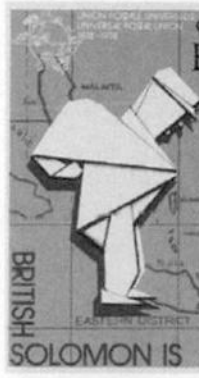

96 "Postman"

1974. Centenary of U.P.U.

258	96	4c. green, dp green & black	10	10
259	-	9c. lt brown, brown & black	10	10
260	-	15c. mauve, purple & black	15	10
261	-	45c. blue, deep blue & black	35	1·60

DESIGNS (Origami figures)—HORIZ: 9c. Carrier-pigeon; 45c. Pegasus. VERT: 15c. St. Gabriel.

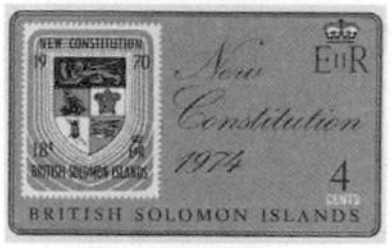

97 "New Constitution" Stamp of 1970

1974. New Constitution.

262	97	4c. multicoloured	10	10
263	-	9c. red, black and brown	10	10
264	-	15c. red, black and brown	15	10
265	97	35c. multicoloured	30	50
MS266		134×84 mm. Nos. 262/5	1·50	3·50

DESIGNS: 9c., 15c. "New Constitution" stamp of 1961 (inscr "1960").

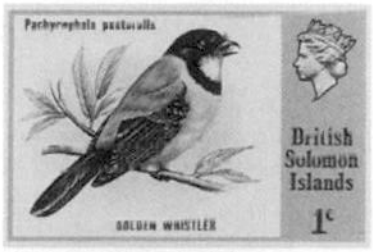

98 Mangrove Golden Whistler ("Golden Whistler")

1975. Birds. Multicoloured.

267	1c. Type **98**	45	[illegible]
268	2c. River kingfisher	60	1·00
269	3c. Red-bibbed fruit dove ("Red-throated Fruit Dove")	55	1·00
270	4c. Red-backed button quail ("Button Quail")	55	1·00
271	$2 Duchess lorikeet	4·00	10·50

See also Nos. 305/20.

1975. Ships and Navigators (5th series). As T **87**. Multicoloured.

272	4c. "Walande" (coaster)	30	10
273	9c. "Melanesian" (coaster)	35	10
274	15c. "Marsina" (container ship)	50	15
275	45c. "Himalaya" (liner)	75	1·50

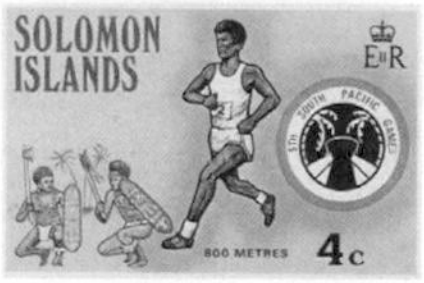

99 800 Metres Race

1975. Fifth South Pacific Games. Multicoloured.

276	4c. Type **99**	10	10
277	9c. Long jump	10	10
278	15c. Javelin-throwing	15	10
279	45c. Football	45	45
MS280	130×95 mm. Nos. 276/9	3·00	4·00

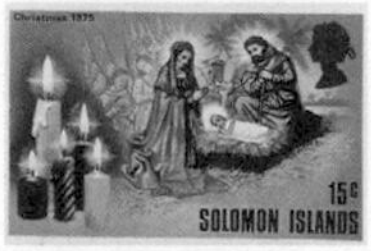

100 Nativity Scene and Candles

1975. Christmas. Multicoloured.

281	15c. Type **100**	15	10
282	35c. Shepherds, angels and candles	30	15
283	45c. The Magi and candles	40	40
MS284	140×130 mm. Nos. 281/3	3·00	5·00

1975. Nos. 267/70, 223/32, 271 and 233a with obliterating bar over "BRITISH". Multicoloured.

285	1c. Type **98**	60	55
286	2c. River kingfisher	1·00	55
287	3c. Red-bibbed fruit dove	70	55
288	4c. Red-backed button quail	1·00	55
289	5c. Big-eyed trevally	50	55
290	8c. Australian bonito	50	60
291	9c. Blue demoiselle	50	60
292	12c. "Costus speciosus"	1·50	1·00
293	15c. Clown anemonefish ("Orange anemone fish")	1·50	1·25
294	20c. "Spathoglottis plicata"	1·50	1·50
295	25c. "Ephemerantha comata"	1·50	1·75
296	35c. "Dendrobium cuthbertsonii"	1·50	1·25
297	45c. "Heliconia salomonica"	1·25	2·00
298	$1 Dotty triggerfish	1·00	1·25
299	$2 Duchess lorikeet	3·50	6·00
300	$5 Great frigate bird	3·25	8·00

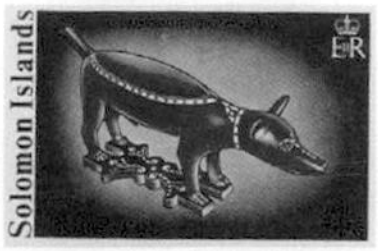

102 Ceremonial Food-bowl

1975. Artefacts (1st series). Multicoloured.

301	4c. Type **102**	10	10
302	15c. Chieftains' money	10	10
303	35c. Nguzu-nguzu (canoe protector spirit) (vert)	25	20
304	45c. Nguzu-nguzu canoe prow	30	25

See also Nos. 337/40, 353/6 and 376/9.

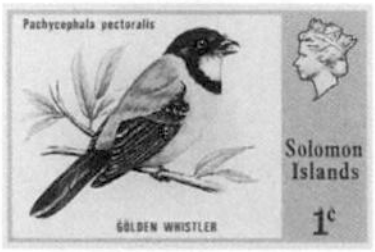

103 Mangrove Golden Whistler

1976. Multicoloured

305	1c. Type **103**	30	50
306	2c. River kingfisher	1·00	80
307	3c. Red-bibbed fruit dove	85	50
308	4c. Red-backed button quail	85	50
309	5c. Willie wagtail	1·00	80
310	6c. Golden cowrie	70	50
311	10c. Glory of the sea cone	70	60
312	12c. Rainbow lory	1·50	80
313	15c. Chambered or pearly nautilus	70	40
314	20c. Venus comb murex	1·00	45
315	25c. Commercial trochus	70	50
316	35c. Blood-red volute	80	50
317	45c. Orange spider conch	80	60
318	$1 Trumpet triton	1·00	1·75
319	$2 Duchess lorikeet	2·50	3·50
320	$5 Great frigate bird	1·75	3·75

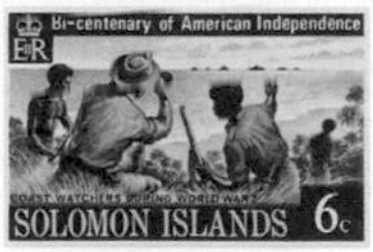

104 Coastwatchers, 1942

1976. Bicent of American Revolution. Multicoloured.

321	6c. Type **104**	20	10
322	20c. "Amagiri" (Japanese destroyer) ramming U.S.S. "PT109" and Lt. J. F. Kennedy	50	40
323	35c. Henderson Airfield	60	70
324	45c. Map of Guadalcanal	60	1·00
MS325	95×115 mm. Nos. 321/4	5·50	9·00

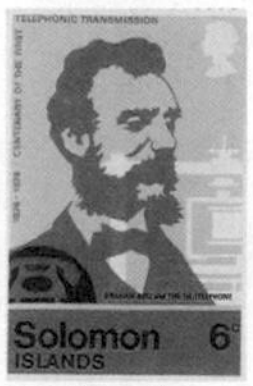

105 Alexander Graham Bell

1976. Centenary of Telephone.

326	105	6c. multicoloured	10	10
327	-	20c. multicoloured	15	10
328	-	35c. brown, orange and red	20	15
329	-	45c. multicoloured	25	35

DESIGNS: 20c. Radio telephone via satellite; 35c. Ericson's magneto telephone; 45c. Stick telephone and first telephone.

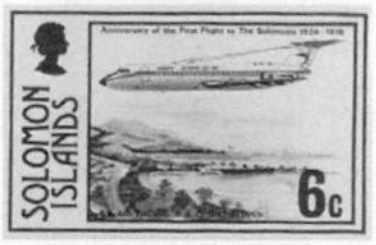

106 B.A.C. One Eleven 200/400

1976. 50th Anniv of First Flight to Solomon Is. Multicoloured.

330	6c. Type **106**	35	10
331	20c. Britten Norman Islander	65	25
332	35c. Douglas DC-3	90	45
333	45c. de Havilland D.H.50A Seaplane A8-1	95	1·00

107 The Communion Plate

1977. Silver Jubilee. Multicoloured.

334	6c. Queen's visit, 1974	10	10
335	35c. Type **107**	15	20
336	45c. The Communion	25	45

108 Carving from New Georgia

1977. Artefacts (2nd series). Carvings.

337	**108**	6c. multicoloured	10	10
338	-	20c. multicoloured	10	10
339	-	35c. black, grey and red	20	15
340	-	45c. multicoloured	25	30

DESIGNS: 20c. Sea adaro (spirit); 35c. Shark-headed man; 45c. Man from Ulawa or Malaita.

109 Spraying Roof and Mosquito

1977. Malaria Eradication. Multicoloured.

341	6c. Type **109**	10	10
342	20c. Taking blood samples	15	10
343	35c. Microscope and map	20	15
344	45c. Delivering drugs	30	40

110 The Shepherds

1977. Christmas. Multicoloured.

345	6c. Type **110**	10	10
346	20c. Mary and Jesus in stable	10	10
347	35c. The Three Kings	20	15
348	45c. "The Flight into Egypt"	25	25

111 Feather Money

1977. Introduction of Solomon Islands Coins and Banknotes. Multicoloured.

349	6c. Type **111**	10	10
350	6c. New currency coins	10	10
351	45c. New currency notes	25	25
352	45c. Shell money	25	25

112 Figure from Shortland Island

1977. Artefacts (3rd series).

353	**112**	6c. multicoloured	10	10
354	-	20c. multicoloured	10	10
355	-	35c. brown, black & orge	20	15
356	-	45c. multicoloured	25	30

DESIGNS: 20c. Ceremonial shield; 35c. Santa Cruz ritual figure; 45c. Decorative combs.

113 Sanford's Sea Eagle

1978. 25th Anniv of Coronation. Multicoloured.

357	45c. black, red and silver	15	25
358	45c. multicoloured	15	25
359	**113** 45c. black, red and silver	15	25

DESIGNS: No. 357, King's Dragon; 358, Queen Elizabeth II.

114 National Flag

1978. Independence. Multicoloured.

360	6c. Type **114**		15
361	15c. Governor-General's flag	35	15
362	35c. The Cenotaph, Honiara	35	30
363	45c. National coat of arms	40	50

115 John

1978. 450th Death Anniv of Durer. Detail's from "Four Apostles". Multicoloured.

364	6c. Type **115**	10	10
365	20c. Peter	15	10
366	35c. Paul	20	15
367	45c. Mark	30	30

116 Firelighting

1978. 50th Anniv of Scouting in Solomon Islands. Multicoloured.

368	6c. Type **116**	15	15
369	20c. Camping	20	25
370	35c. Solomon Islands scouts	40	45
371	45c. Canoeing	50	80

117 H.M.S. "Discovery"

1979. Bicentenary of Captain Cook's Voyages, 1768–79.

372	**117**	8c. multicoloured	25	15
373	-	18c. multicoloured	25	20
374	-	35c. black, green and grey	30	25
375	-	45c. multicoloured	30	50

DESIGNS: 18c. Portrait of Captain Cook by Nathaniel Dance; 35c. Sextant; 45c. Flaxman/Wedgwood medallion of Captain Cook.

118 Fish Net Float

1979. Artefacts (4th series).

376	**118**	8c. multicoloured	10	10
377	-	20c. multicoloured	10	10
378	-	35c. black, grey and red	15	15
379	-	45c. black, brown & green	20	30

DESIGNS—VERT: 20c. Armband of shell money; 45c. Forehead ornament. HORIZ: 35c. Ceremonial food bowl.

119 Running

1979. South Pacific Games, Fiji. Multicoloured.

380	8c. Type **119**	10	10
381	20c. Hurdling	10	10
382	35c. Football	15	15
383	45c. Swimming	20	30

120 1908 6d. Stamp

1979. Death Centenary of Sir Rowland Hill.

384	**120**	8c. red and pink	10	10
385	-	20c. mauve & pale mauve	15	30
386	-	35c. multicoloured	25	45
MS387	121×121 mm. 45c. red, green and pink		45	65

DESIGNS: 20c. Great Britain 1856 6d.; 35c. 1978 45c. Independence commemorative.

121 Sea Snake

1979. Reptiles. Multicoloured.

388A	1c. Type **121**	10	1·00
389A	3c. Red-banded tree snake	10	1·25
390A	4c. Whip snake	10	1·25
391A	6c. Pacific boa	10	1·25
392A	8c. Skink	10	80
393A	10c. Gecko	10	1·00
394Bw	12c. Monitor	30	1·00
395A	15c. Anglehead	30	1·25
396A	20c. Giant toad	30	60
397Bw	25c. Marsh frog	30	1·00
398A	30c. Horned frog	1·50	1·00
399A	35c. Tree frog	30	1·00
399cB	40c. Burrowing snake	45	1·75
400A	45c. Guppy's snake	30	1·25
400cB	50c. Tree gecko	50	1·25
401B	$1 Large skink	1·50	75
402A	$2 Guppy's frog	60	1·50
403A	$5 Estuarine crocodile	1·00	1·75
403cB	$10 Hawksbill turtle	3·50	4·50

122 "Madonna and Child" (Morando)

1979. International Year of the Child. *Madonna and Child* paintings by various artists. Multicoloured.

404	4c. Type **122**	10	10
405	20c. Luini	15	15
406	35c. Bellini	20	15
407	50c. Raphael	30	70
MS408	92×133 mm. Nos. 404/7	1·00	1·50

123 H.M.S. "Curacoa" (frigate), 1839

1980. Ships and Crests (1st series). Multicoloured.

409	8c. Type **123**	25	20
410	20c. H.M.S. "Herald" (survey ship), 1854	30	30
411	35c. H.M.S. "Royalist" (screw corvette), 1889	40	60
412	45c. H.M.S. "Beagle" (survey schooner), 1878	45	1·40

See also Nos. 430/3.

124 "Solomon Fisher" (fishery training vessel)

1980. Fishing. Ancillary Craft. Multicoloured.

413	8c. Type **124**	15	10
414	20c. "Solomon Hunter" (fishery training vessel)	20	20
415	45c. "Ufi Na Tasi" (refrigerated fish transport)	35	40
416	80c. Research vessel	60	1·75

125 "Comliebank" (cargo-liner) and 1935 Tulagi Registered Letter Postmark

1980. "London 1980" International Stamp Exhibition. Mail-carrying Transport. Multicoloured.

417	45c. Type **125**	30	45
418	45c. Douglas C-47 Skytrain (U.S. Army Postal Service, 1943)	30	45
419	45c. B.A.C. One Eleven airliner and 1979 Honiara postmark	30	45
420	45c. "Corabank" (container ship) and 1979 Auki postmark	30	45

126 Queen Elizabeth the Queen Mother

1980. 80th Birthday of The Queen Mother.

421	**126**	45c. multicoloured	30	35

127 Angel with Trumpet

1980. Christmas. Multicoloured.

422	8c. Type **127**	10	10
423	20c. Angel with fiddle	10	10
424	45c. Angel with trumpet (different)	25	25
425	80c. Angel with lute	40	45

128 "Parthenos sylvia"

1980. Butterflies (1st series). Multicoloured.

426	8c. Type **128**	30	10
427	20c. "Delias schoenbergi"	35	20
428	45c. "Jamides cephion"	55	30
429	80c. "Ornithoptera victoriae"	80	1·00

See also Nos. 456/9 and 610/13.

1981. Ships and Crests (2nd series). As T **123**. Multicoloured.

430	8c. H.M.S. "Mounts Bay" (frigate), 1959	15	10
431	20c. H.M.S. "Charybdis" (frigate), 1970	20	20

432	45c. H.M.S. "Hydra" (survey ship), 1972	30	30
433	$1 Royal Yacht "Britannia", 1974	75	1·90

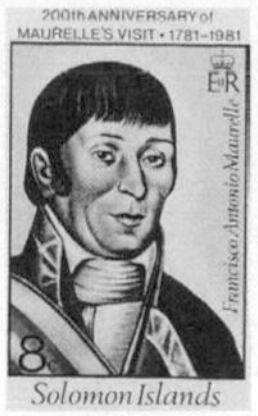

129 Francisco Antonio Maurelle

1981. Bicentenary of Maurelle's Visit and Production of Bauche's Chart, 1791.

434	**129**	8c. black, brown and yellow	15	10
435	-	10c. black, red and yellow	20	10
436	-	45c. multicoloured	50	50
437	-	$1 multicoloured	80	1·00
MS438		126×91 mm. 25c.×4, each black, red and stone	65	1·10

DESIGNS—HORIZ: 10c. Bellin's map of 1742 showing route of "La Princesa"; 45c. "La Princesa". VERT: $1 Spanish compass cards, 1745; **MS**438 "Chart of a part of the South Sea" (each stamp 44×28 mm).

The stamps in No. **MS**438 form a composite design.

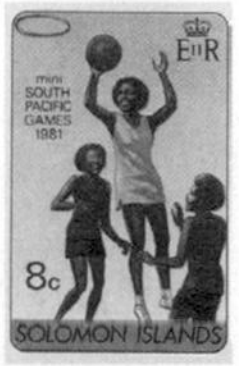

130 Netball

1981. Mini South Pacific Games. Multicoloured.

439	8c. Type **130**	10	10
440	10c. Tennis	15	15
441	25c. Running	25	25
442	30c. Football	25	25
443	45c. Boxing	40	40
MS444	102×67 mm. $1 Stylised athletes	70	75

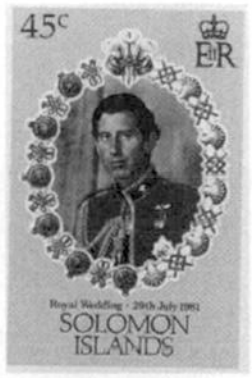

131 Prince Charles as Colonel-in-Chief, Royal Regiment of Wales

1981. Royal Wedding. Multicoloured.

445	8c. Wedding bouquet from Solomon Islands	10	10
446	45c. Type **131**	15	15
447	$1 Prince Charles and Lady Diana Spencer	45	70

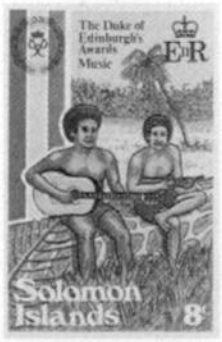

132 "Music"

1981. 25th Anniv of Duke of Edinburgh Award Scheme. Multicoloured.

448	8c. Type **132**	10	10
449	25c. "Handicrafts"	10	10
450	45c. "Canoeing"	15	10
451	$1 Duke of Edinburgh	35	60

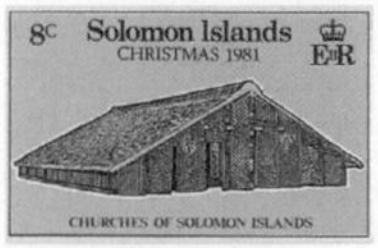

133 Primitive Church

1981. Christmas. Churches.

452	**133**	8c. black, buff and blue	10	10
453	-	10c. multicoloured	10	10
454	-	25c. black, buff and green	10	10
455	-	$2 multicoloured	45	1·25

DESIGNS: 10c. St. Barnabas Anglican Cathedral, Honiara; 25c. Early church; $2 Holy Cross Cathedral, Honiara.

1982. Butterflies (2nd series). As T **128**. Multicoloured.

456	10c. "Doleschallia bisaltide"	25	10
457	25c. "Papilio bridgei"	45	25
458	35c. "Taenaris phorcas"	50	30
459	$1 "Graphium sarpedon"	1·10	1·50

1982. Cyclone Relief Fund. No. 447 surch **50 CENTS SURCHARGE CYCLONE RELIEF FUND 1982**.

460	$1+50c. Prince Charles and Lady Diana Spencer	75	2·00

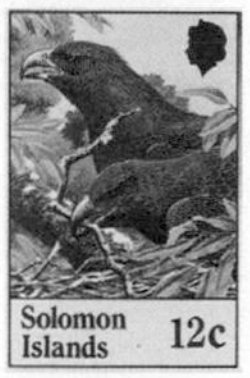

135 Pair of Sanford's Sea Eagles constructing Nest

1982. Sanford's Sea Eagle. Multicoloured.

461	12c. Type **135**	35	60
462	12c. Egg and chick	35	60
463	12c. Hen feeding chicks	35	60
464	12c. Fledgelings	35	60
465	12c. Young bird in flight	35	60
466	12c. Pair of birds and village dwellings	35	60

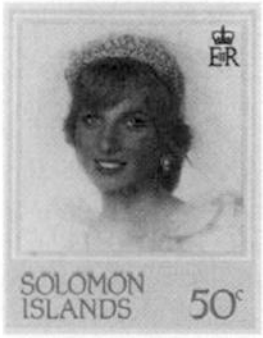

136 Wedding Portrait

1982. 21st Birthday of Princess of Wales. Multicoloured.

467	12c. Solomon Islands coat of arms	10	10
468	40c. Lady Diana Spencer at Broadlands, May 1981	25	25
469	50c. Type **136**	30	40
470	$1 Formal portrait	45	1·50

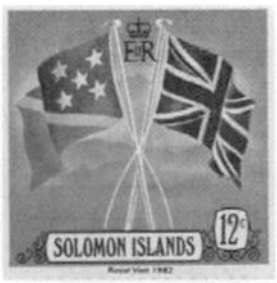

137 Flags of Solomon Islands and United Kingdom

1982. Royal Visit (Nos. 471/2) and Commonwealth Games, Brisbane (Nos. 473/4). Multicoloured.

471	12c. Type **137**	15	25
472	12c. Queen and Prince Philip	15	25
473	25c. Running	30	45
474	25c. Boxing	30	45
MS475	123×123 mm. Nos. 471/2 and $1 Royal Yacht "Britannia"	1·75	2·50
MS476	123×123 mm. Nos. 473/4 and $1 Royal Yacht "Britannia"	1·75	2·50

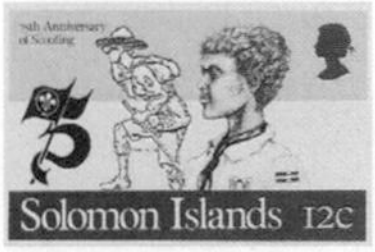

138 Boy Scouts

1982. 75th Anniv of Boy Scout Movement (Nos. 477, 479, 481, 483) and Centenary of Boys' Brigade (others). Multicoloured.

477	12c. Type **138**	10	15
478	12c. Boys' Brigade cadets	10	15
479	25c. Lord Baden-Powell	15	40
480	25c. Sir William Smith	15	40
481	35c. Type **138**	15	50
482	35c. As No. 478	15	50
483	50c. As No. 479	20	1·10
484	50c. As No. 480	20	1·10

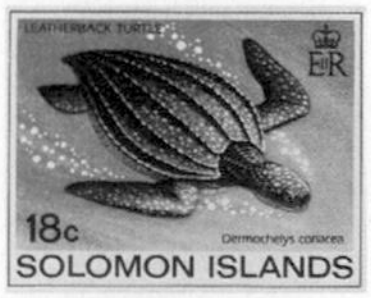

139 Leatherback Turtle

1983. Turtles. Multicoloured.

485	18c. Type **139**	20	25
486	35c. Loggerhead turtle	30	45
487	45c. Pacific ridley turtle	30	60
488	50c. Green turtle	30	65

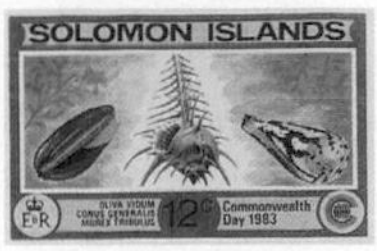

140 Black Olive, General Cone and Troschell's Murex

1983. Commonwealth Day. Shells. Multicoloured.

489	12c. Type **140**	15	15
490	35c. Romu, Kurila, Kakadu and money belt	35	40
491	45c. Shells from "Bride-price" necklaces	50	60
492	50c. Commercial trochus polished and in its natural state	55	65

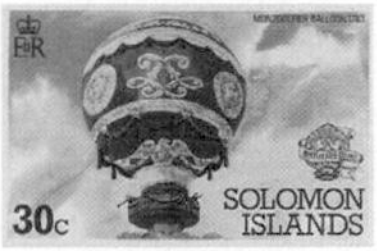

141 Montgolfier Balloon

1983. Bicentenary of Manned Flight. Multicoloured.

493	30c. Type **141**	25	40
494	35c. R.A.A.F. Lockheed Hercules	25	45
495	40c. Wright Brothers' Type A	30	55
496	45c. Space shuttle "Columbia"	30	60
497	50c. Beech C55 Baron	30	65

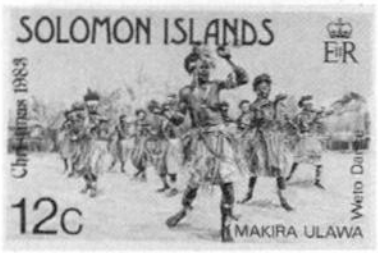

142 Weto Dancers

1983. Christmas. Multicoloured.

498	12c. Type **142**	10	10
499	15c. Custom wrestling	10	20
500	18c. Girl dancers	10	20
501	20c. Devil dancers	15	20
502	25c. Bamboo band	15	20
503	35c. Gilbertese dancers	20	25
504	40c. Pan pipers	20	35
505	45c. Girl dancers	20	40
506	50c. Cross surrounded by flowers	20	60
MS507	153×112 mm. Nos. 498/506	1·00	3·00

Stamps from No. **MS**507 are without the inscription, "Christmas 1983", on Nos. 498/506.

143 Earth Satellite Station

1983. World Communications Year. Multicoloured.

508	12c. Type **143**	15	15
509	18c. Ham radio operator	15	20
510	25c. 1908 2½d. Canoe stamp	15	30
511	$1 1908 6d. Canoe stamp	40	3·00
MS512	131×103 mm. No. 511	1·40	2·25

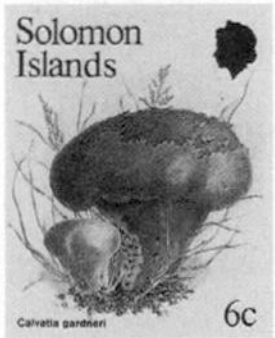

144 "Calvatia gardneri"

1984. Fungi. Multicoloured.

513	6c. Type **144**	15	10
514	18c. "Marasmiellus inoderma"	20	25
515	35c. "Pycnoporus sanguineus"	35	45
516	$2 "Filoboletus manipularis"	1·25	2·75

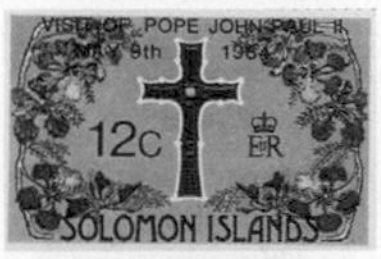

145 Cross surrounded by Flowers

1984. Visit of Pope John Paul II.

517	**145**	12c. multicoloured	40	20
518	**145**	50c. multicoloured	70	1·60

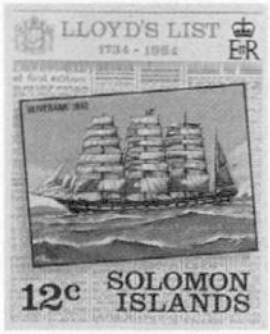

146 "Olivebank" (barque), 1882

1984. 250th Anniv of "Lloyds List" (newspaper). Multicoloured.

519	12c. Type **146**	70	15
520	15c. "Tinhow" (freighter), 1906	75	40
521	18c. "Oriana" (liner) at Point Cruz, Honiara	85	60
522	$1 "Silwyn Range" (container ship), Point Cruz, Honiara	1·40	3·25

1984. Universal Postal Union Congress, Hamburg. As No. **MS**512 but with changed sheet inscriptions and U.P.U. logo in margin. Multicoloured.

MS523	$1 1908 6d. Canoe stamp	1·75	1·60

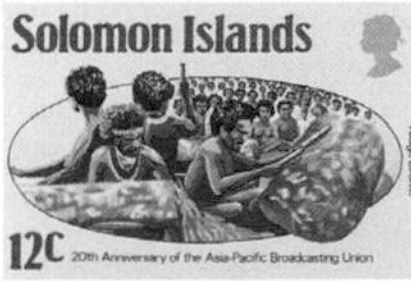

147 Village Drums

1984. 20th Anniv of Asia-Pacific Broadcasting Union. Multicoloured.

524	12c. Type **147**	15	15
525	45c. Radio City, Guadalcanal	35	60
526	60c. S.I.B.C. studios, Honiara	50	80
527	$1 S.I.B.C. Broadcasting House	60	1·50

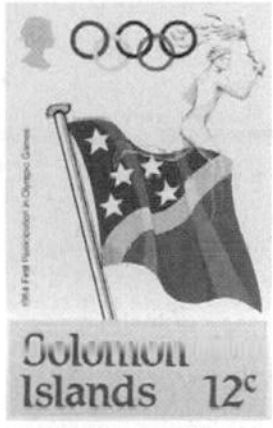

148 Solomon Islands Flag and Torch-bearer

1984. Olympic Games, Los Angeles. Multicoloured.

528	12c. Type **148**	15	10
529	25c. Lawson Tama Stadium, Honiara (horiz)	15	15
530	50c. Honiara Community Centre (horiz)	20	25
531	95c. Alick Wickham inventing crawl stroke, Bronte Baths, New South Wales, 1898 (horiz)	9·00	14·00
532	$1 Olympic Stadium, Los Angeles (horiz)	30	75

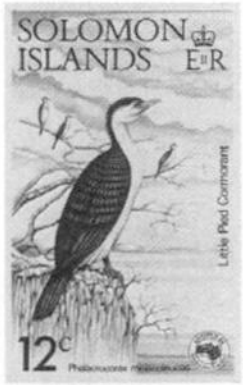

149 Little Pied Cormorant

1984. "Ausipex" International Stamp Exhibition, Melbourne. Birds. Multicoloured.

533	12c. Type **149**	50	50
534	18c. Pacific black duck ("Australian Grey Duck")	65	60
535	35c. Nankeen night heron	80	60
536	$1 Eastern broad-billed roller ("Dollar-bird")	1·25	4·25
MS537	130×96 mm. Nos. 533/6	2·50	4·50

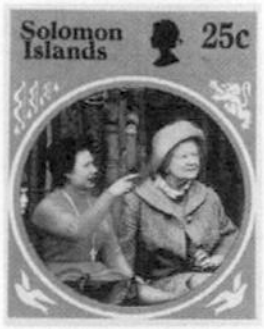

150 The Queen Mother with Princess Margaret at Badminton Horse Trials

1985. Life and Times of Queen Elizabeth the Queen Mother. Multicoloured.

538	12c. With Winston Churchill at Buckingham Palace, VE Day, 1945	50	10
539	25c. Type **150**	40	30
540	35c. At St. Patrick's Day parade	40	35
541	$1 With Prince Henry at his christening (from photo by Lord Snowdon)	80	1·25
MS542	91×73 mm. $1.50 In a gondola, Venice, 1985	1·10	1·50

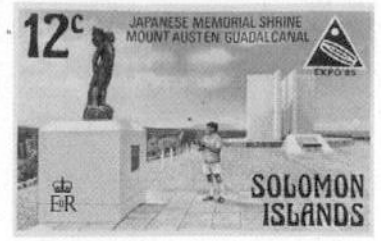

151 Japanese Memorial Shrine, Mount Austen, Guadalcanal

1985. "Expo '85" World Fair, Japan. Multicoloured.

543	12c. Type **151**	10	10
544	25c. Digital telephone exchange equipment	20	30
545	45c. Fishing vessel "Soltai No. 1"	50	55
546	85c. Coastal village scene	60	1·40

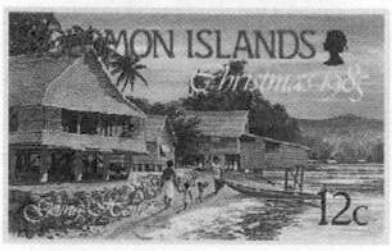

152 Titiana Village

1985. Christmas. "Going Home for the Holiday". Multicoloured.

547	12c. Type **152**	10	10
548	25c. Sigana, Santa Isabel	25	30
549	35c. Artificial Island and Langa Lagoon	30	35

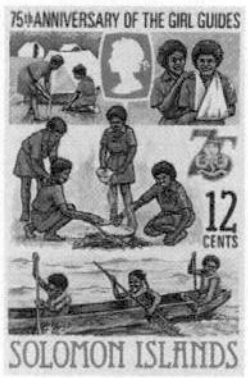

153 Girl Guide Activities

1985. 75th Anniv of Girl Guide Movement (12, 45c.) and International Youth Year (others). Multicoloured.

550	12c. Type **153**	60	15
551	15c. Boys playing and child in wheelchair (Stop Polio)	65	50
552	25c. Runners and Solomon Island scenes	90	85
553	35c. Runners and Australian scenes ("Run Round Australia")	1·10	90
554	45c. Guide colour party and badges	1·25	1·25
MS555	100×75 mm. Nos. 552/3	1·75	1·50

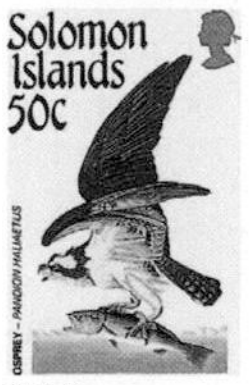

154 Osprey

1985. Birth Bicentenary of John J. Audobon (ornithologist). Sheet 121×107 mm containing T **154** and similar vert design.

MS556	45c. black, gold and blue; 50c. (×2) multicoloured	3·75	4·50

DESIGNS: 45c. John J. Audubon.

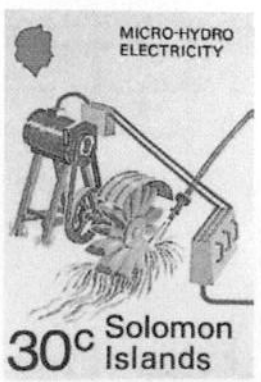

155 Water-powered Generator, Iriri

1986. Village Hydro-electric Schemes. Sheet 109×135 mm. containing T **155** and similar vert design. Multicoloured.

MS557	30c. Type **155**; 60c. Domestic lighting	1·00	1·25

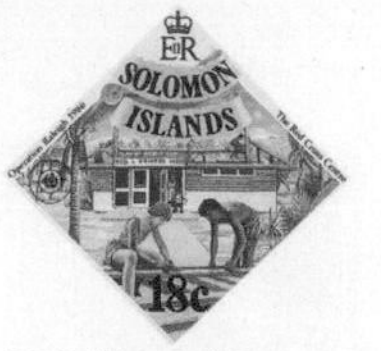

156 Building Red Cross Centre, Gizo

1986. Operation Raleigh (volunteer project). Multicoloured.

558	18c. Type **156**	80	25
559	30c. Exploring rainforest	1·50	50
560	60c. Observing Halley's Comet	2·25	1·60
561	$1 "Sir Walter Raleigh" (support ship) and "Zebu" (brigantine)	2·75	2·25

1986. 60th Birthday of Queen Elizabeth II. As T **145a** of St. Helena. Multicoloured.

562	5c. Princess Elizabeth and Duke of Edinburgh at Clydebank Town Hall, 1947	10	20
563	18c. At St. Paul's Cathedral for Queen Mother's 80th birthday service, 1980	15	20
564	22c. With children, Solomon Islands, 1982	20	25
565	55c. At Windsor Castle on her 50th birthday, 1976	35	45
566	$2 At Crown Agents Head Office, London, 1983	1·00	1·75

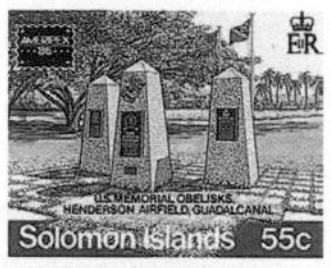

157 U.S. Memorial Obelisks, Henderson Airfield, Guadalcanal

1986. "Ameripex '86" International Stamp Exhibition, Chicago. International Peace Year. Sheet 100×75 mm containing T **157** and similar horiz design. Multicoloured.

MS567	55c. Type **157**; $1.65 Peace Corps emblem, President Kennedy and Statue of Liberty (25th anniv of Peace Corps)	1·10	1·25

1986. Royal Wedding. As T **146a** of St. Helena. Multicoloured.

568	55c. Prince Andrew and Miss Sarah Ferguson	40	55
569	60c. Prince Andrew at helm of yacht "Bluenose II" off Nova Scotia, 1985	45	1·10

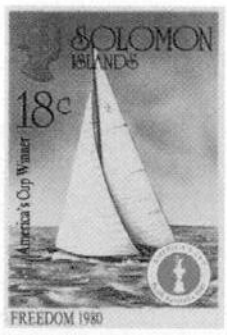

158 "Freedom" (winner, 1980)

1986. America's Cup Yachting Championship (1987).

570	**158**	18c. multicoloured	30	60
571	-	30c. multicoloured	1·00	3·00
572	-	$1 multicoloured	50	1·50

Nos. 570/2 were issued as a sheet of 50, each horizontal strip of 5 being separated by gutter margins. The sheet contains 20 different designs at 18c., 10 at 30c. and 20 at $1. Individual stamps depict yachts, charts, the America's Cup or the emblem of the Royal Perth Yacht Club.

See also No. **MS**575.

1986. Cyclone Relief Fund. No. 541 surch **+ 50c Cyclone Relief Fund 1986.**

573	$1+50c. Queen Mother with Prince Henry at his christening	75	1·25
MS574	100×75 mm. 55c.+25c. Type **157**; $1.65+75c. Peace Corps emblem, President Kennedy and Statue of Liberty (25th anniv of Peace Corps)	3·50	3·00

The surcharges on No. **MS**574 do not include "1986".

1987. America's Cup Yachting Championship (2nd issue). Sheet 111×75 mm, containing vert design as T **158**. Multicoloured.

MS575	$5 "Stars and Stripes" (1987 winner)	3·75	4·50

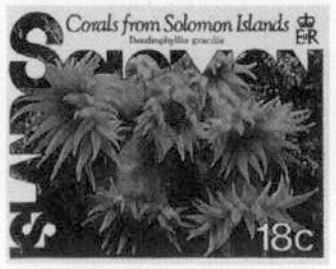

160 "Dendrophyllia gracilis"

1987. Corals. Multicoloured.

576	18c. Type **160**	20	15
577	45c. "Dendronephthya sp."	40	50
578	60c. "Clavularia sp."	45	1·40
579	$1.50 "Melithaea squamata"	75	3·50

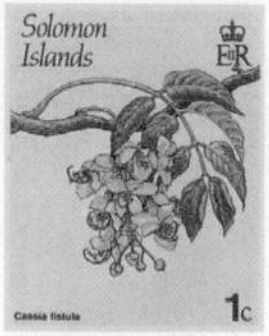

161 "Cassia fistula"

1987. Flowers. Multicoloured.

580	1c. Type **161**	10	1·00
581	5c. "Allamanda cathartica"	30	1·00
582	10c. "Catharanthus roseus"	40	1·00
583	18c. "Mimosa pudica"	60	15
584	20c. "Hibiscus rosa-sinensis"	60	15
585	22c. "Clerodendrum thomsonae"	60	15
586	25c. "Bauhinia variegata"	60	30
587	28c. "Gloriosa rothschildiana"	65	30
588	30c. "Heliconia solomonensis"	75	30
589	40c. "Episcia" hybrid	90	30
590	45c. "Bougainvillea" hybrid	90	30
591	50c. "Alpinia purpurata"	1·00	30
592	55c. "Plumeria rubra"	1·00	35
593	60c. "Acacia farnesiana"	1·25	60
594	$1 "Ipomea purpurea"	2·25	1·00
595	$2 "Dianella ensifolia"	3·25	5·00
596	$5 "Passiflora foetida"	4·75	9·00
597	$10 "Hemigraphis sp"	7·50	13·00

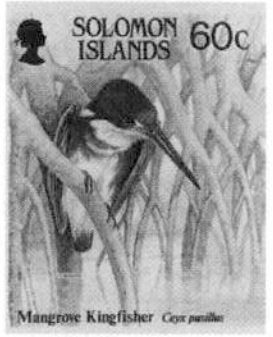

162 Mangrove Kingfisher on Branch

1987. Mangrove Kingfisher. Multicoloured.

598	60c. Type **162**	2·40	3·50
599	60c. Kingfisher diving	2·40	3·50
600	60c. Entering water	2·40	3·50
601	60c. Kingfisher with prey	2·40	3·50

Nos. 598/601 were printed together, *se-tenant*, forming a composite design.

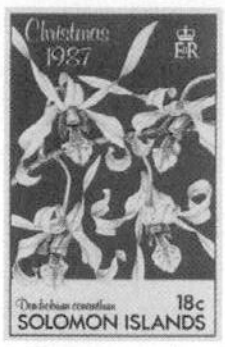

163 "Dendrobium conanthum"

1987. Christmas. Orchids (1st series). Multicoloured.

602	18c. Type **163**	85	10
603	30c. "Spathoglottis plicata"	1·50	30
604	55c. "Dendrobium gouldii"	1·75	50
605	$1.50 "Dendrobium goldfinchii"	3·75	6·00

See also Nos. 640/3 and 748/51.

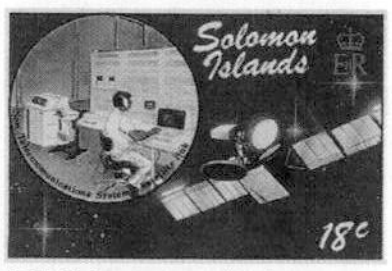

164 Telecommunications Control Room and Satellite

1987. Asia-Pacific Transport and Communications Decade. Multicoloured.

606	18c. Type **164**	20	15
607	30c. De Havilland Twin Otter 300 mail plane	45	20
608	60c. Guadalcanal road improvement project	50	60
609	$2 Beech 80 Queen Air and Henderson Control Tower	2·00	2·75

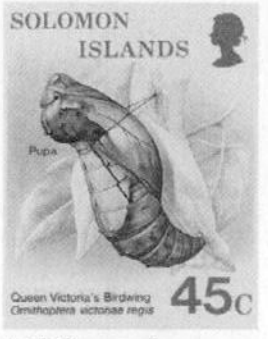

165 Pupa of "Ornithoptera victoriae"

1987. Butterflies (3rd series). "Ornithoptera victoriae" (Queen Victoria's Birdwing). Multicoloured.

610	45c. Type **165**	3·50	3·50
611	45c. Larva	3·50	3·50
612	45c. Female butterfly	3·50	3·50
613	45c. Male butterfly	3·50	3·50

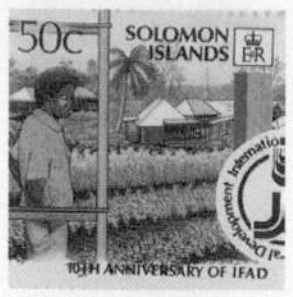

166 Student and National Agriculture Training Institute

1988. Tenth Anniv of International Fund for Agricultural Development. Multicoloured.

614	50c. Type **166**	40	55
615	50c. Students working in fields	40	55
616	$1 Transport by lorry	50	1·00
617	$1 Canoe transport	50	1·00

Nos. 614/15 and 616/17 were printed together, *se-tenant*, each pair forming a composite design.

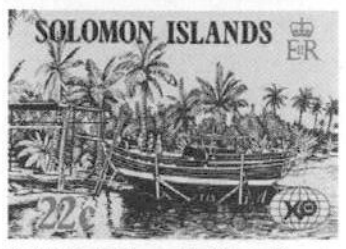

167 Building Fishing Boat

1988. "Expo '88" World Fair, Brisbane. Multicoloured.

618	22c. Type **167**	20	15
619	80c. War canoe	50	45
620	$1.50 Traditional village	95	85
MS621	130×53 mm. Nos. 618/20	1·50	1·40

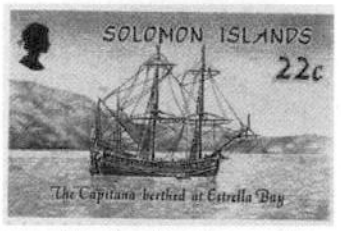

168 "Todos los Santos" in Estrella Bay, 1568

1988. Tenth Anniv of Independence. Multicoloured.

622	22c. Type **168**	1·25	25
623	55c. Raising the Union Jack, 1893	1·60	55
624	80c. High Court Building	1·25	1·25
625	$1 Dancers at traditional celebration	1·40	1·60

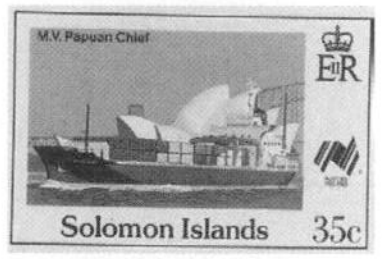

169 "Papuan Chief" (container ship)

1988. "Sydpex '88" National Stamp Exhibition, Sydney and Bicentenary of Australian Settlement. Multicoloured.

626	35c. Type **169**	1·00	25
627	60c. "Nimos" (container ship)	1·40	50
628	70c. "Malaita" (liner)	1·40	80
629	$1.30 "Makambo" (inter-island freighter)	1·75	2·00
MS630	140×76 mm. Nos. 626/9	2·50	2·00

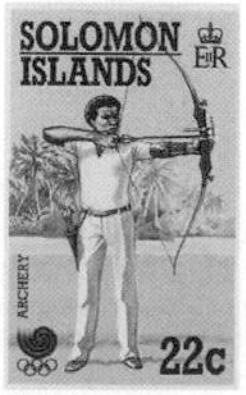

170 Archery

1988. Olympic Games, Seoul. Multicoloured.

631	22c. Type **170**	75	20
632	55c. Weightlifting	85	50
633	70c. Athletics	1·00	1·00
634	80c. Boxing	1·10	1·25
MS635	100×80 mm. $2 Olympic Stadium (horiz)	1·25	1·25

1988. 300th Anniv of Lloyd's of London. As T **152a** of St. Helena.

636	22c. black and brown	30	15
637	50c. multicoloured	1·10	30
638	65c. multicoloured	1·25	55
639	$2 multicoloured	2·75	1·75

DESIGNS—VERT: 22c. King George V and Queen Mary laying foundation stone of Leadenhall Street Building, 1925; $2 "Empress of China" (liner), 1911. HORIZ: 50c. "Forthbank" (container ship); 65c. Soltel satellite communications station.

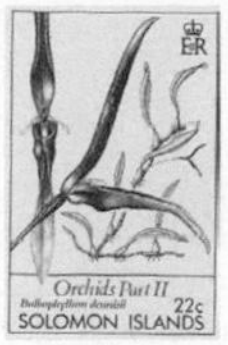

171 "Bulbophyllum dennisii"

1989. Orchids (2nd series). Multicoloured.

640	22c. Type **171**	1·00	20
641	35c. "Calanthe langei"	1·40	35
642	55c. "Bulbophyllum blumei"	1·75	55
643	$2 "Grammatophyllum speciosum"	3·25	7·00

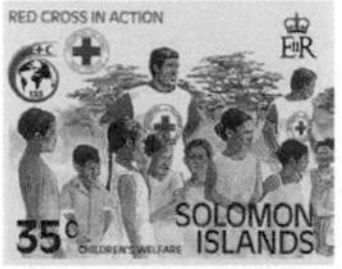

172 Red Cross Workers with Handicapped Children

1989. 125th Anniv of Int Red Cross. Multicoloured.

644	35c. Type **172**	1·00	1·00
645	35c. Handicapped Children Centre minibus	1·00	1·00
646	$1.50 Blood donor	1·50	2·00
647	$1.50 Balance test	1·50	2·00

Nos. 644/5 and 646/7 were each printed together, *se-tenant*, each pair forming a composite design.

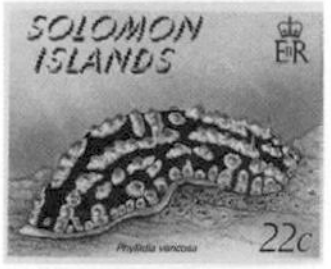

173 Varicose Nudibranch

1989. Nudibranchs (Sea Slugs). Multicoloured.

648	22c. Type **173**	80	20
649	70c. Bullock's nudibranch	2·00	1·50
650	80c. "Chromodoris leopardus"	[illegible]	1·00
651	$1.50 "Phidiana indica"	2·50	5·50

1989. 20th Anniv of First Manned Landing on Moon. As T **50a** of St. Kitts. Multicoloured.

652	22c. "Apollo 16" descending by parachute	55	25
653	35c. Launch of "Apollo 16" (30×30 mm)	80	45
654	70c. "Apollo 16" emblem (30×30 mm)	1·40	2·00
655	80c. Ultra-violet colour photograph of Earth	1·60	2·25
MS656	100×83 mm. $4 Moon's surface seen from Space	3·00	3·50

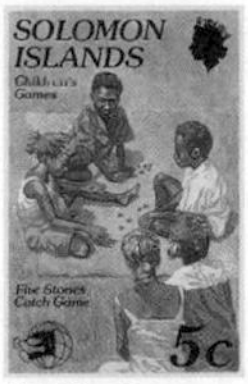

174 Five Stones Catch

1989. "World Stamp Expo '89". International Stamp Exhibition, Washington. Children's Games. Multicoloured.

657	5c. Type **174**	15	50
658	67c. Blowing soap bubbles (horiz)	1·25	1·50
659	73c. Coconut shell game (horiz)	1·25	1·50
660	$1 Seed wind sound	1·75	2·25
MS661	72×72 mm. $3 Softball	7·50	8·50

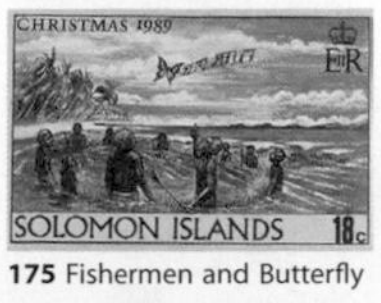

175 Fishermen and Butterfly

1989. Christmas. Multicoloured.

662	18c. Type **175**	40	10
663	25c. The Nativity	55	20
664	45c. Hospital ward at Christmas	1·00	30
665	$1.50 Village tug-of-war	2·50	5·50

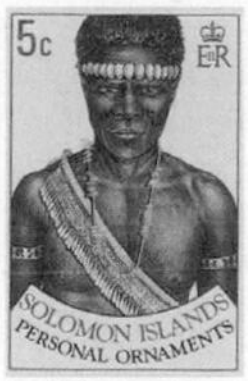

176 Man wearing Headband, Necklace and Sash

1990. Personal Ornaments. Multicoloured.

666	5c. Type **176**	40	1·00
667	12c. Pendant	60	30
668	18c. Man wearing medallion, nose ring and earrings	70	30
669	$2 Forehead ornament	4·50	7·50

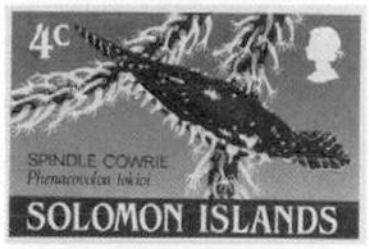

177 Spindle Cowrie or Tokio's Volva

1990. Cowrie Shells. Multicoloured.

670	4c. Type **177**	30	75
671	20c. All-red map cowrie	75	30
672	35c. Sieve cowrie	1·00	35
673	50c. Umbilical ovula or little egg cowrie	1·40	1·60
674	$1 Valentine or prince cowrie	2·25	3·25

1990. 90th Birthday of Queen Elizabeth the Queen Mother. As T **161a** of St. Helena.

675	25c. multicoloured	75	25
676	$5 black and red	3·75	4·75

DESIGNS—21×36 mm: 25c. Queen Mother, 1987. 29×37 mm: $5 King George VI and Queen Elizabeth inspecting bomb damage to Buckingham Palace, 1940.

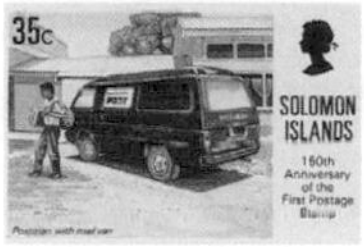

178 Postman with Mail Van

1990. 150th Anniv of the Penny Black. Multicoloured.

677	35c. Type **178**	1·75	40
678	45c. General Post Office	1·75	60
679	50c. 1907 ½d. stamp	1·90	1·75
680	55c. Child collecting stamps	2·00	2·50
681	60c. Penny Black and Solomon Islands 1913 1d. stamp	2·25	4·00

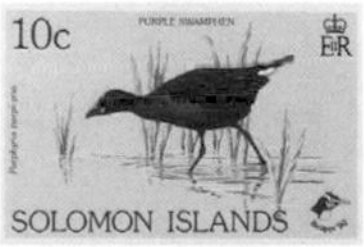

179 Purple Swamphen

1990. "Birdpex '90" Stamp Exhibition, Christchurch, New Zealand. Multicoloured.

682	10c. Type **179**	65	80
683	25c. Mackinlay's cuckoo dove ("Rufous Brown Pheasant Dove")	1·00	50
684	30c. Superb fruit dove	1·25	55
685	45c. Cardinal honeyeater	1·40	60
686	$2 Finsch's pygmy parrot ("Pigmy Parrot")	2·25	5·00

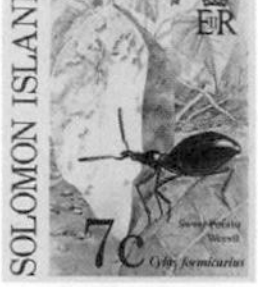

180 "Cylas formicarius" (weevil)

1991. Crop Pests. Multicoloured.

687	7c. Type **180**	60	55
688	25c. "Dacus cucurbitae" (fruit-fly)	90	30
689	40c. "Papuana uninodis" (beetle)	1·40	45
690	90c. "Pantorhytes biplagiastus" (weevil)	2·00	2·50
691	$1.50 "Scapanes australis" (beetle)	2·50	4·00

1991. 65th Birthday of Queen Elizabeth II and 70th Birthday of Prince Philip. As T **165a** of St. Helena. Multicoloured.

692	90c. Prince Philip in evening dress	1·00	1·25
693	$2 Queen Elizabeth II	1·40	1·75

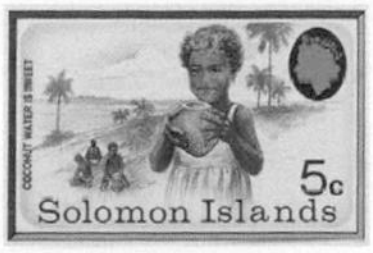

181 Child drinking from Coconut

1991. Health Campaign. Multicoloured.

694	5c. Type **181**	20	60
695	75c. Mother feeding child	1·25	1·25
696	80c. Breast feeding	1·40	1·60
697	90c. Local produce	1·60	1·75

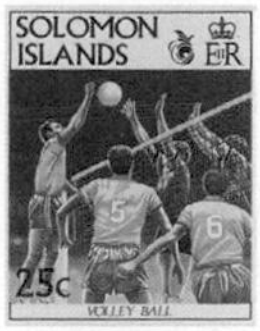

182 Volleyball

1991. Ninth South Pacific Games. Multicoloured.

698	25c. Type **182**	1·00	25
699	40c. Judo	1·40	55
700	65c. Squash	2·00	2·00
701	90c. Bowling	2·25	3·00
MS702	92×112 mm. $2 Games emblem	6·00	8·00

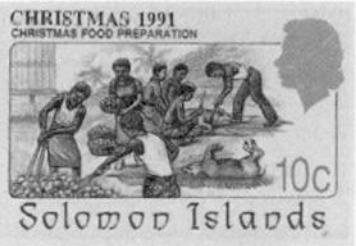

183 Preparing Food for Christmas

1991. Christmas. Multicoloured.

703	10c. Type **183**	30	10
704	25c. Christmas Day church service	60	15
705	65c. Christmas Day feast	1·50	85
706	$2 Cricket match	3·75	5·00
MS707	[illegible]×118 mm. Nos. 703/6	7·00	9·00

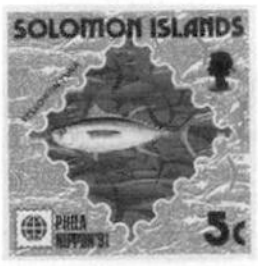

184 Yellow-finned Tuna

1991. "Phila Nippon '91" International Stamp Exhibition, Tokyo. Tuna Fishing. Multicoloured.

708	5c. Type **184**	10	20
709	30c. Pole and line tuna fishing boat	60	25
710	80c. Pole and line fishing	1·50	1·75
711	$2 Processing "arabushi" (smoked tuna)	2·75	4·00
MS712	101×80 mm. 80c. Plate of "tori nanban" (25×42 mm); 80c. Bowl of "aka miso" (25×42 mm)	2·00	2·50

1992. 40th Anniv of Queen Elizabeth II's Accession. As T **122c** of Pitcairn Islands. Multicoloured.

713	5c. Aerial view of Honiara	25	50
714	20c. Sunset across lagoon	40	20
715	40c. Honiara harbour	60	40
716	60c. Three portraits of Queen Elizabeth	65	1·00
717	$5 Queen Elizabeth II	2·75	4·50

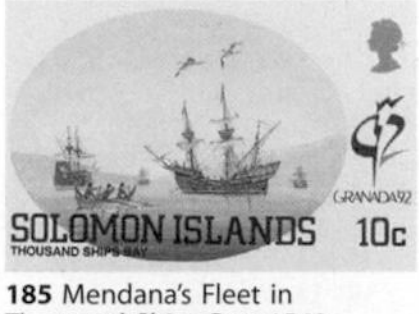

185 Mendana's Fleet in Thousand Ships Bay, 1568

1992. "Granada '92" International Stamp Exhibition, Spain. Mendana's Discovery of Solomon Islands. Multicoloured.

718	10c. Type **185**	75	40
719	65c. Map of voyage	1·40	60
720	80c. Alvaro Mendana de Niera	1·40	1·50
721	$1 Settlement at Graciosa Bay	1·75	2·00
722	$5 Mendana's fleet at sea	4·25	6·00

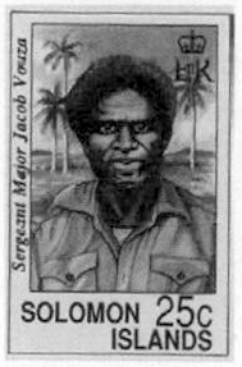

186 Sgt-major Jacob Vouza

1992. Birth Centenary of Sgt-major Jacob Vouza (war hero). Multicoloured.

723	25c. Type **186**	50	30
724	70c. Vouza in U.S. Marine Corps battle dress	1·00	1·25
725	90c. Vouza in U.S. Marine Corps uniform	1·00	1·40
726	$2 Statue of Vouza	1·25	2·25
MS727	113×76 mm. $4 Sgt-major Vouza in ceremonial uniform	7·00	7·00

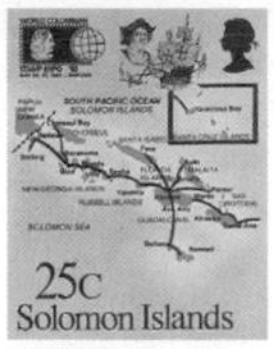

187 Solomon Airlines Domestic Routes

1992. 500th Anniv of Discovery of America by Columbus and "World Columbian Stamp Expo '92" Exhibition, Chicago. Multicoloured.

728	25c. Type **187**	60	20
729	80c. Solomon Airlines Boeing 737-400 "Guadalcanal"	1·40	1·25
730	$1.50 Solomon Airlines international routes	2·00	2·25
731	$5 Columbus and "Santa Maria"	4·75	6·00
MS732	120×94 mm. Nos. 728/31	8·50	9·00

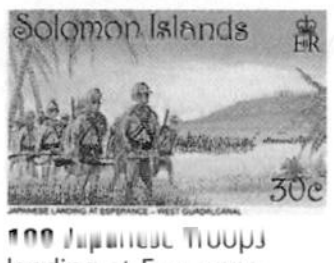

188 Japanese Troops landing at Esperance

1992. 50th Anniv of Battle of Guadalcanal. Multicoloured.

733	30c. Type **188**	80	80
734	30c. American troops in landing craft	80	80
735	30c. H.M.A.S. "Hobart" (cruiser)	80	80
736	30c. U.S. Navy post office	80	80
737	30c. R.N.Z.A.F. Consolidated PBY-5A Catalina flying boat	80	80
738	80c. U.S. Marine Corps Grumman F4F Wildcat fighters	1·10	1·10
739	80c. Henderson Field	1·10	1·10
740	80c. U.S.S. "Quincy" (heavy cruiser)	1·10	1·10
741	80c. H.M.A.S. "Canberra" (heavy cruiser)	1·10	1·10
742	80c. U.S. Marine Corps landing craft	1·10	1·10
743	80c. "Ryujo" (Japanese aircraft carrier)	1·10	1·10
744	80c. Japanese Mitsubishi A6M Zero-Sen fighters	1·10	1·10
745	80c. Japanese Mitsubishi G4M "Betty" bombers	1·10	1·10
746	80c. Japanese destroyer	1·10	1·10
747	80c. "Chockai" (Japanese heavy cruiser)	1·10	1·10

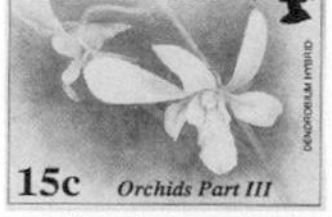

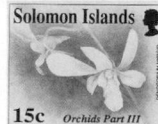

189 "Dendrobium" hybrid

1992. Orchids (3rd series). Multicoloured.

748	15c. Type **189**	65	20
749	70c. "Vanda Amy Laycock"	1·10	90
750	95c. "Dendrobium mirbelianum"	1·40	1·25
751	$2.50 "Dendrobium macrophyllum"	2·25	4·50

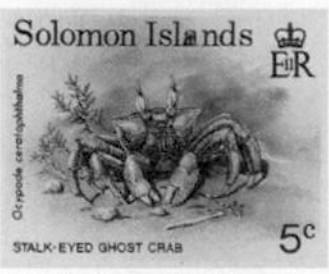

190 Stalk-eyed Ghost Crab

1993. Crabs. Multicoloured.

752	5c. Type **190**	20	60

753	10c. Red-spotted crab	20	60
754	25c. Flat crab	25	60
755	30c. Land hermit crab	25	20
756	40c. Grapsid crab	25	30
757	45c. Red and white painted crab	25	30
758	55c. Swift-footed crab	30	30
759	60c. Spanner crab	30	30
760	70c. Red hermit crab	40	40
761	80c. Red-eyed crab	40	40
762	90c. Rathbun red crab	40	50
763	$1 Coconut crab	50	50
764	$1.10 Red-spotted white crab	50	60
765	$4 Ghost crab	1·75	3·00
766	$10 Mangrove fiddler crab	3·25	5·50

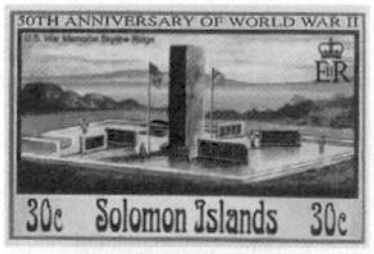

191 U.S. War Memorial, Skyline Ridge

1993. 50th Anniv of Second World War. Multicoloured.

767	30c. Type **191**	50	20
768	80c. National flags at half mast	1·50	1·10
769	95c. Major-general Alexander Vandegrift and map	1·60	1·25
770	$4 Aerial dogfight, U.S. carrier and Solomon Islands scouts	4·50	6·50

1993. 14th World Orchid Conference, Glasgow. As Nos. 748 and 751, but different face values, additionally inscr "World Orchid Conference". Multicoloured.

771	20c. Type **189**	40	25
772	$3 "Dendrobium macrophyllum"	2·00	2·75

1993. "Indopex '93" International Stamp Exhibition, Surabaya. As Nos. 749/50, but different face values, additionally inscr "Indopex '93" Exhibition". Multicoloured.

773	85c. "Vanda Amy Laycock"	90	1·00
774	$1.15 "Dendrobium mirbe-lianum"	1·00	1·25

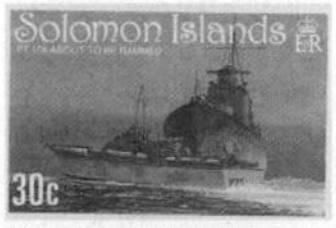

192 U.S.S. "PT 109" being rammed by "Amagiri" (Japanese destroyer)

1993. 50th Anniv of Sinking of U.S.S. "PT 109" (motor torpedo-boat commanded by John F. Kennedy). Multicoloured.

775	30c. Type **192**	45	25
776	50c. Kennedy thanking islander	60	50
777	95c. Message in coconut shell and islanders in canoe	80	1·10
778	$1.10 Pres. Kennedy and medal	1·00	2·00
MS779	77×43 mm. $5 U.S.S. "PT 109"	4·75	6·50

1993. "Taipei '93" Asian International Stamp Exhibition Taiwan. No. **MS**732 optd **"TAIPEI '93"** and emblem on sheet margin.

MS780	120×94 mm. Nos. 728/31	4·50	6·00

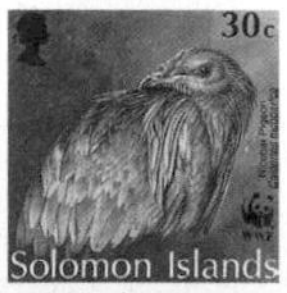

193 Nicobar Pigeon

1993. Endangered Species. Nicobar Pigeon. Multicoloured.

781	30c. Type **193**	35	20
782	50c. Pigeon on ground	50	35
783	65c. Pair of pigeons perched on branches	60	50
784	70c. Pigeon on branch looking left	65	60
785	$1.10 Pigeon on branch looking right	1·00	1·25
786	$3 Pigeons in flight	2·25	3·25

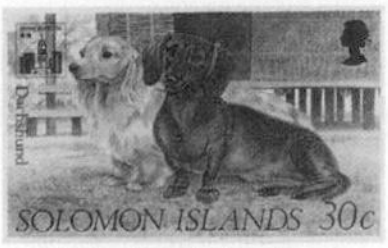

194 Pair of Dachshunds

1994. "Hong Kong '94" Int Stamp Exn. Chinese New Year ("Year of the Dog"). Mult.

787	30c. Type **194**	50	30
788	80c. German shepherd dog	80	1·10
789	95c. Pair of Dobermann pinschers	90	1·40
790	$1.10 Australian cattle dog	1·00	1·60
MS791	70×55 mm. $4 Boxer	6·50	8·50

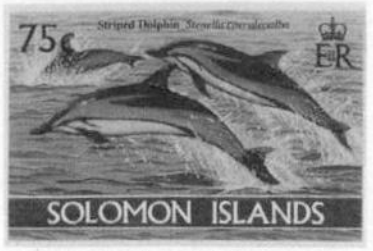

195 Striped Dolphin

1994. Dolphins. Multicoloured.

792	75c. Type **195**	70	65
793	85c. Risso's dolphin	80	80
794	$1.15 Common dolphin	1·10	1·40
795	$2.50 Spinner dolphin	2·25	3·25
796	$3 Bottlenose dolphin	2·50	3·50

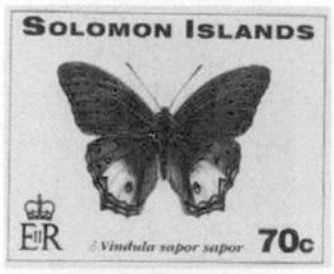

196 "Vindula sapor"

1994. "Philakorea '94" International Stamp Exhibition, Seoul. Butterflies. Multicoloured.

797	70c. Type **196**	50	70
798	70c. "Papilio aegeus"	50	70
799	70c. "Graphium hicetaon"	50	70
800	70c. "Graphium mendana"	50	70
801	70c. Exhibition logo	50	70
802	70c. "Graphium meeki"	50	70
803	70c. "Danaus schenkii"	50	70
804	70c. "Papilio ptolychus"	50	70
805	70c. "Phaedyma fissizonata vella"	50	70

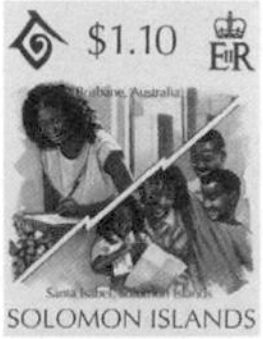

197 Girl in Brisbane writing letter to Family in Santa Islabel

1994. Int Year of the Family. Multicoloured.

806	$1.10 Type **197**	80	1·25
807	$1.10 Boeing 737-400 leaving Brisbane	80	1·25
808	$1.10 Boeing 737-400 at Henderson Airfield and De Havilland D.H.C.6 Twin Otter leaving for Santa Isabel	80	1·25
809	$1.10 De Havilland D.H.C.6 Twin Otter at Fera Airfield, Santa Isabe	80	1·25
810	$1.10 Family reunited	80	1·25
MS811	160×75 mm. Nos. 806/10	3·50	5·50

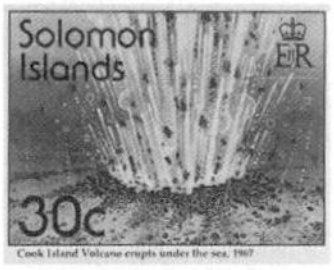

198 Cook Island Volcano, 1967

1994. Volcanoes. Multicoloured.

812	30c. Type **198**	65	30
813	70c. Kavachi underwater eruption, 1977	85	1·00
814	80c. Kavachi volcano forming temporary island, 1978	95	1·10
815	90c. Tinakula volcanic island	1·10	1·50
MS816	130×60 mm. $2 Map of Solomon Islands volcanoes; $2 Diagram showing formation of volcanic islands	3·50	4·25

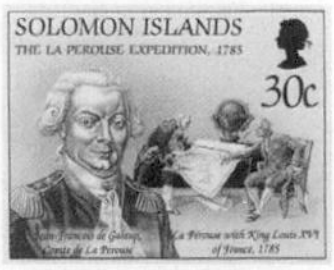

199 La Perouse with King Louis XVI and Map

1994. Loss of the La Perouse Expedition, Santa Cruz Islands, 1788. Multicoloured.

817	30c. Type **199**	55	20
818	80c. Map of Ile de La Perouse	1·25	80
819	95c. "L'Astrolabe"	1·40	1·00
820	$1.10 "La Boussole"	1·50	1·25
821	$3 "L'Astrolabe" foundering on reef	2·50	4·50

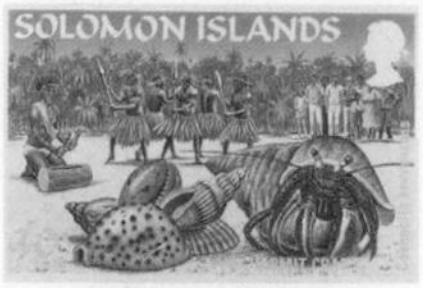

200 Hermit Crab, Shells and Dancers

1995. Visit South Pacific Year. Multicoloured.

822	30c. Type **200**	20	20
823	50c. "Dendrobium rennellii" (orchid) and "Danaus plexippus" (butterfly)	50	45
824	95c. Scuba diver and fish	60	1·10
825	$1.15 Grapsid crab, canoes, rusty Second World War gun and catamaran	65	1·25
MS826	98×81 mm. $4 Yellow-bibbed lory	6·50	7·50

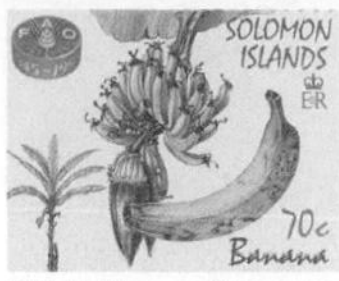

201 Emblem and Bananas

1995. 50th Anniv of F.A.O. Fruit. Multicoloured.

827	70c. Type **201**	1·00	90
828	75c. Paw paws	1·00	90
829	95c. Pomelos	1·40	1·25
830	$2 Star fruits	2·75	4·00
MS831	90×75 mm. $3 Mangos	1·90	3·00

1995. 50th Anniv of End of Second World War. As T **182a** of St. Helena. Multicoloured.

832	95c. Vice-Admiral Nagumo and "Akagi" (Japanese aircraft carrier)	1·00	1·00
833	$1 Rear-Admiral Fletcher and U.S.S. "Yorktown" (aircraft carrier)	1·00	1·00
834	$2 Vice-Admiral Ghormley and U.S.S. "Wasp" (aircraft carrier)	1·75	2·25
835	$3 Vice-Admiral Halsey and U.S.S. "Enterprise" (aircraft carrier)	2·50	3·50
MS836	75×85 mm. $5 Reverse of 1939-45 War Medal (vert)	2·25	2·75

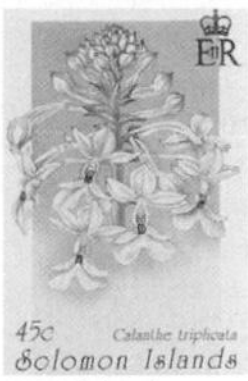

202 "Calanthe triplicata"

1995. Orchids. Multicoloured.

837	45c. Type **202**	1·50	30
838	75c. "Dendrobium mohlianum"	1·75	1·10
839	85c. "Flickingeria comata"	1·75	1·50
840	$1.15 "Dendrobium spectabile"	2·25	2·50
MS841	75×90 mm. $4 "Coelogyne asperata"	3·00	4·00

No. **MS**841 includes the "Singapore '95" International Stamp Exhibition emblem on the sheet margin.

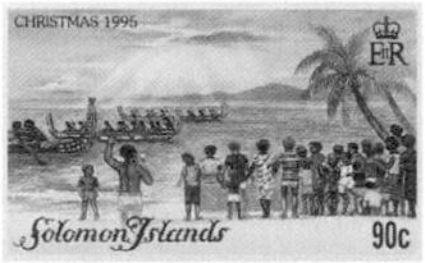

203 Start of Canoe Race

1995. Christmas. Local Festivities. Multicoloured.

842	90c. Type **203**	80	60
843	$1.05 Pan-pipe players and Christmas Tree	80	1·00
844	$1.25 Picnic on the beach	90	1·10
845	$1.45 Church service and infant Jesus	1·10	1·60

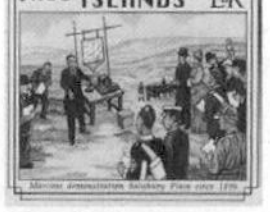

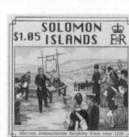

204 Marconi demonstrating Radio Transmitter, Salisbury Plain, 1896

1996. Centenary of Radio. Multicoloured.

846	$1.05 Type **204**	70	80
847	$1.20 Ship's radio room, 1900	80	1·00
848	$1.35 Wireless transmitter, Croydon Aerodrome, 1920	90	1·50
849	$1.45 Marconi in Japan, 1933	1·00	1·75

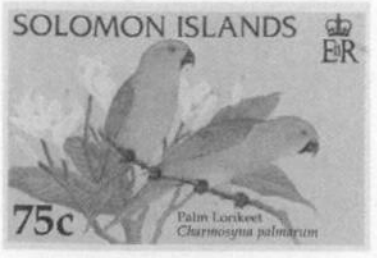

205 Palm Lorikeet

1996. Birds. Multicoloured.

850	75c. Type **205**	80	55
851	$1.05 Duchess lorikeet	95	90
852	$1.20 Yellow-bibbed lory	1·10	1·25
853	$1.35 Cardinal lory	1·50	2·00
854	$1.45 Meek's lorikeet	1·50	2·00
MS855	94×69 mm. $3 Rainbow lory ("Rainbow Lorikeet")	4·00	4·50

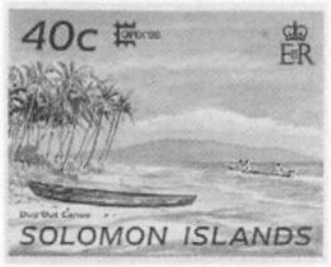

206 Dug-out Canoe on Beach and Canoe with Outboard Motor

1996. "CAPEX '96" International Stamp Exhibition, Toronto. Mail Transport. Multicoloured.

856	40c. Type **206**	35	20
857	90c. Postman with bicycle	1·25	80
858	$1.20 Post van	1·25	1·00
859	$1.45 "Tulagi Express" (cruise launch)	1·75	2·75
MS860	88×73 mm. $4 "Tepuke" (traditional canoe)	1·90	3·00

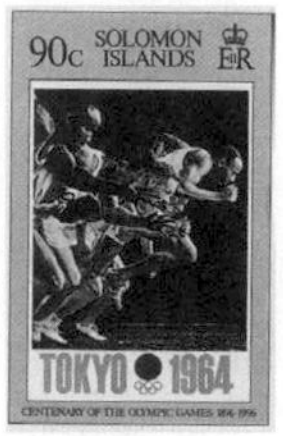

207 Tokyo 1964 Poster

1996. Centenary of Modern Olympic Games. Promotional Posters from Previous Games.

861	90c. Type **207**	50	40
862	$1.20 Los Angeles, 1932	60	70
863	$1.35 Paris, 1924	65	85
864	$2.50 London, 1908	1·10	2·25

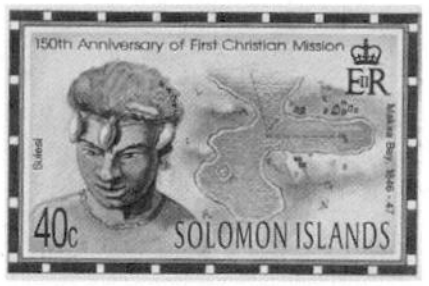

208 Suiesi and Map of Makira Bay

1996. 150th Anniv of First Christian Mission. Multicoloured.

865	40c. Type **208**	30	20
866	65c. Surimahe and sketches of artefacts by Revd. L. Verguet	45	45
867	$1.35 Bishop Espalle and grave, Isabel	60	1·25
868	$1.45 John Claude Colin and Makira Mission	65	1·40

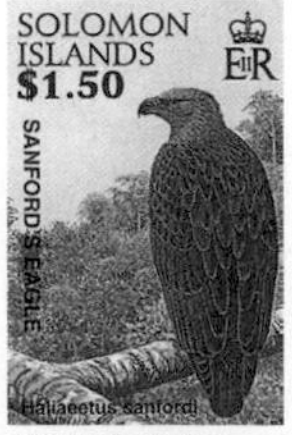

209 Sanford's Sea Eagle

1996. "Taipei '96" 10th Asian International Stamp Exhibition, Taiwan. Sheet 100×80 mm.

MS869	**209** $1.50, multicoloured	1·25	1·50

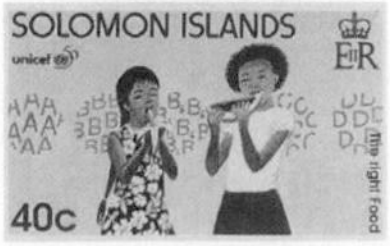

210 Children eating Fruit

1996. 50th Anniv of UNICEF. Multicoloured.

870	40c. Type **210**	25	20
871	$1.05 Children in canoes	50	50

872	$1.35 Doctor and child	60	75
873	$2.50 Teacher and child	1·00	2·50

1997. "HONG KONG '97" International Stamp Exhibition. Sheet 130×90 mm, containing design as No. 765. Multicoloured.

MS874	$4 Ghost crab	1·75	2·50

1997. "Singpex '97" International Stamp Exhibition. No. 797 optd **SINGPEX '97 FEBRUARY 21–23 SINGAPORE** and logo within "perforation" frame across the entire sheetlet.

875	70c. Type **196**	1·00	1·25
876	70c. "Papilio aegeus"	1·00	1·25
877	70c. "Graphium hicetaon"	1·00	1·25
878	70c. "Graphium mendana"	1·00	1·25
879	70c. "Exhibition logo"	1·00	1·25
880	70c. "Graphium meeki"	1·00	1·25
881	70c. "Danaus schenkii"	1·00	1·25
882	70c. "Papilio ptolychus"	1·00	1·25
883	70c. "Phaedyma fissizonata vella"	1·00	1·25

Individual stamps show parts of the overprint only.

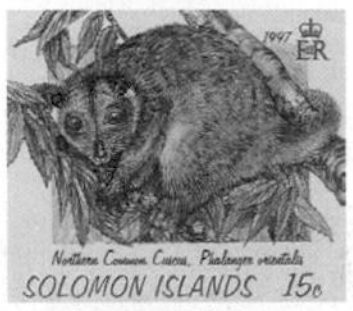

211 Common Phalanger

1997. Common Phalanger ("Northern Common Cuscus"). Multicoloured.

884	15c. Type **211**	20	15
885	60c. Common phalanger eating fruit	30	30
886	$2.50 Common phalanger hanging on branch	85	1·40
887	$3 Two common phalangers	95	1·60

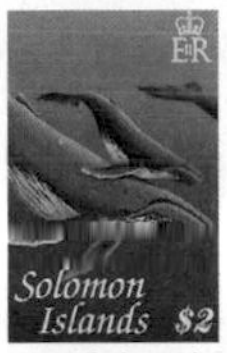

212 Whale and Calf

1997. "Pacific '97" International Stamp Exhibition, San Francisco. Sheet 96×74 mm, containnig T **212** and similar multicoloured design.

MS888	$2 Type **212**; $2 Whale breaking surface (horiz)	2·00	2·50

1997. Golden Wedding of Queen Elizabeth and Prince Philip. As T **192a** of St. Helena. Multicoloured.

889	$3 Prince Philip playing polo	2·50	2·75
890	$3 Queen Elizabeth	2·50	2·75
891	$3 Queen Elizabeth leading two horses	2·50	2·75
892	$3 Prince Philip	2·50	2·75
MS893	110×70 mm. $3 Queen Elizabeth and Prince Philip in landau (horiz)	2·00	2·50

Nos. 889/90 and 891/2 were printed together, *se-tenant*, with the backgrounds forming composite designs.

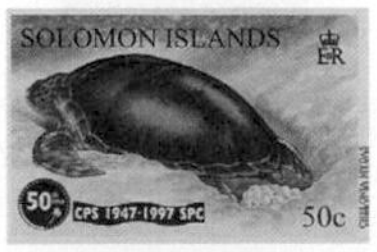

213 Turtle laying Eggs

1997. 50th Anniv of the South Pacific Commission. Common Green Turtle. Multicoloured.

894	50c. Type **213**	30	20
895	90c. Young turtles heading towards sea	50	50
896	$1.50 Four turtles swimming under water	70	1·25
897	$2 Pair of turtles swimming	85	1·60

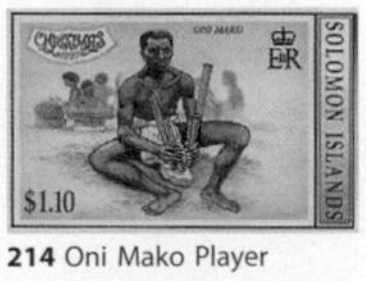

214 Oni Mako Player

1997. Christmas. Multicoloured.

898	$1.10 Type **214**	50	35
899	$1.40 Ysabel dancing women	60	70
900	$1.50 Pan pipers from Small Malaita	60	90
901	$1.70 Western bamboo band	75	1·50

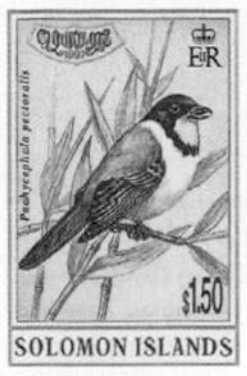

215 Golden Whistler

1997. "Bangkok '97" China Stamp Exhibition, Thailand. Christmas. Sheet 135×87 mm, containing T **215** and similar vert design. Multicoloured.

MS902	$1.50 Type **215**; $1.50 "Papilio aegeus" and "Graphium meeki" (butterflies)	3·00	4·50

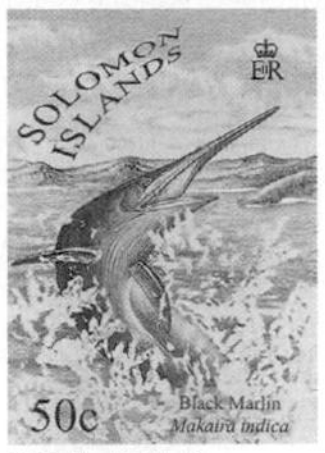

216 Black Marlin

1998. Billfish. Multicoloured.

903	50c. Type **216**	60	20
904	$1.20 Shortbill swordfish	95	75
905	$1.40 Swordfish	1·10	1·10
906	$2 Indo-Pacific sailfish	1·60	2·50

See also No. **MS**922.

1998. Diana, Princess of Wales Commemoration. As T **62a** of Tokelau. Multicoloured.

907	$2 Wearing pearl earrings	60	75
MS908	145×70 mm. $2.50 As No. 907; $2.50 Wearing white hat; $2.50 In evening dress; $2.50 Accepting flowers from children (sold at $10+50c. charity premium)	2·25	3·25

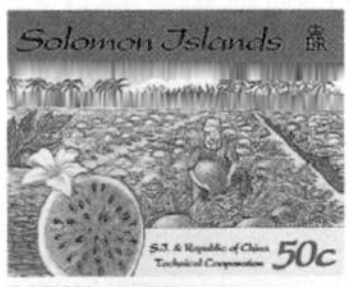

217 Water Melon Cultivation

1998. Technical Co-operation between Solomon Islands and Republic of China (Taiwan). Multicoloured.

909	50c. Type **217**	30	25
910	$1.50 Harvesting rice	70	1·00
MS911	105×60 mm. 80c. Growing cucumbers; $1.20 Inspecting tomato plants	1·00	1·50

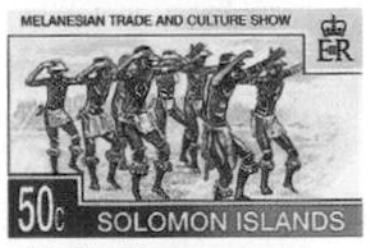

218 War Dance

1998. Melanesian Trade and Culture Show. Multicoloured.

912	50c. Type **218**	50	65
913	50c. Islanders with bows and arrows	50	65
914	50c. Man on beach	50	65
915	$1.20 War dance (different)	60	75
916	$1.20 Warrior in mask	60	75
917	$1.20 Woman wearing shell necklace and headband	60	75
918	$1.50 Dance with poles	65	80
919	$1.50 Hunter with spear, shield and axe	65	80
920	$1.50 Man with nose and ear ornaments	65	80

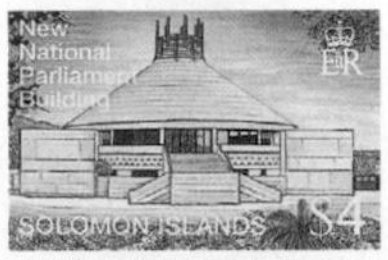

219 New National Parliament Building

1998. 20th Anniv of Independence. Sheet 110×79 mm.

MS921	**219** $4 multicoloured	1·50	2·50

1998. "Singpex 98" International Stamp Exhibition and International Year of the Ocean. Sheet 90×60 mm, containing No. 906. Multicoloured.

MS922	$2 Indo-pacific sailfish	1·25	1·75

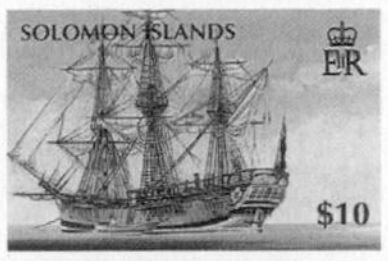

220 H.M.S. "Endeavour" (Cook), 1770

1999. "Australia '99" World Stamp Exhibition, Melbourne. Maritime History. Sheet, 96×55 mm, containing T **220** and similar horiz design. Multicoloured.

MS923	$10 Type **220**; $10 "Los Reyes" (Alvare Mendana) careened at Guadalcanal, 1568	6·50	8·00

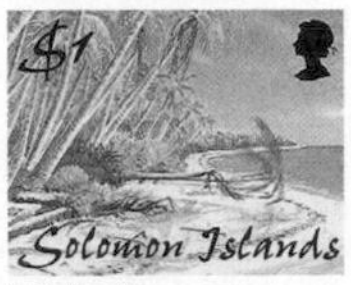

221 Beach

1999. "PhilexFrance '99" International Stamp Exhibition, Paris. Marine Life. Multicoloured.

924	$1 Type **221**	65	75
925	$1 Great frigate bird	65	75
926	$1 Coconut crab	65	75
927	$1 Green turtle	65	75
928	$1 Royal Spanish dancer nudibranch	65	75
929	$1 Sun noon and stars butterflyfish	65	75
930	$1 Striped sweetlips	65	75
931	$1 Saddle-back butterflyfish	65	75
932	$1 Cuttlefish	65	75
933	$1 Giant clam	65	75
934	$1 Lionfish	65	75
935	$1 Spiny lobster	65	75

Nos. 924/35 were printed together, *se-tenant*, with the backgrounds forming a composite design.

1999. 30th Anniv of First Manned Landing on Moon. As T **94a** of St. Kitts. Multicoloured.

936	50c. Lift-off	25	20
937	$1.50 Lunar module above Moon's surface	60	60
938	$2.50 Buzz Aldrin with American flag on Moon	90	1·40
939	$3.40 Command module [illegible]	1·75	1·90
MS940	90×80 mm. $4 Earth as seen from Moon (circular, 40 mm diam)	1·60	2·00

1999. "Queen Elizabeth the Queen Mother's Century". As T **199** of St. Helena. Multicoloured (except $5).

941	$1 Inspecting bomb damage at Portsmouth, 1941	50	30
942	$1.50 At the Derby, 1983	65	55
943	$2.30 Receiving birthday bouquets from children	80	1·10
944	$4.90 Inspecting Royal Army Medical Corps parade	1·50	2·50
MS945	145×70 mm. $5 Duchess of York, 1920s, and with King George VI and Prime Minister Winston Churchill, VE Day, 1945 (black)	2·00	3·00

1999. "China '99" International Stamp Exhibition, Beijing. No. 687 optd **SOLOMON ISLANDS: 21-30 NAUGUST CHINA 1999**.

946	7c. Type **180**	1·25	1·25

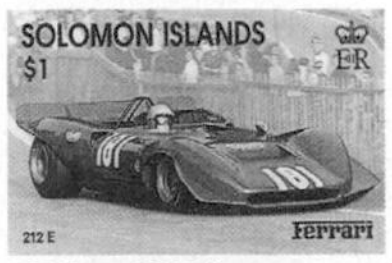

223 Ferrari 212 E

1999. Birth Centenary of Enzo Ferrari (car designer) (1998). Racing Cars. Multicoloured.

947	$1 Type **223**	55	35
948	$1.50 250 TR	65	50
949	$3.30 250 LM	1·25	2·00
950	$4.20 612 CAN-AM	1·40	2·25

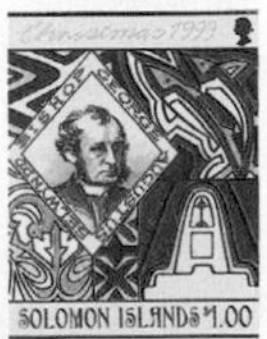

224 Bishop George Augustus Selwyn

1999. Christmas. 150th Anniv of Melanesian Mission. Multicoloured (except $3.30).

951	$1 Type **224**	50	70
952	$1 Bishop John Coleridge Patteson	50	70
953	$1.50 Stained glass windows	60	85
954	$1.50 "Southern Cross" (missionary ship) and religious symbols	60	85
955	$3.30 "150 YEARS MELANESIAN MISSION" (black)	1·00	1·50

Nos. 951/5 were printed together, *se-tenant*, with the $3.30 in the centre, throughout the sheet with the backgrounds forming a composite design.

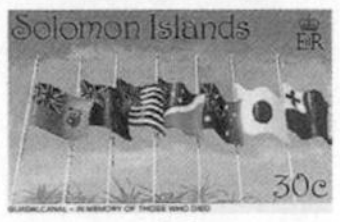

225 National Flags at Half Mast

1999. Second World War Veterans' Millennium Visit. Multicoloured.

956	30c. Type **225**	60	80
957	30c. The Cenotaph, Honiara	60	80
958	30c. Solomon Peace Memorial Park	60	80
959	30c. U.S. War Memorial, Skyline Ridge	60	80
960	30c. "Ocean Pearl" (cruise ship)	60	80

It was originally intended to issue Nos. 956/60 as part of the 1992 50th Anniv of Battle of Guadalcanal set, Nos. 733/47. This strip of 5 designs was removed from the sheet and was not placed on sale until late 1999.

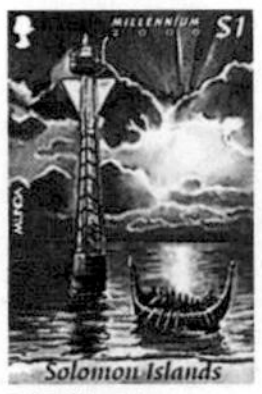

226 Munda Lighthouse and War Canoe

2000. New Millennium. Multicoloured.

961	$1 Type **226**	1·25	80
962	$4 Tulagi Lighthouse and launch	3·50	4·00
MS963	96×74 mm. Nos. 961/2	5·50	6·00

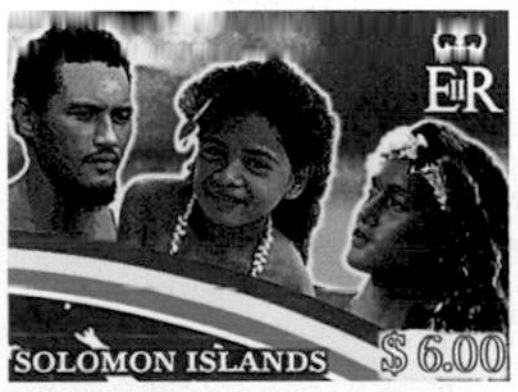

227 Islanders

2000. Commonwealth Youth Ministers' Meeting, Honiara. Sheet 130×90 mm.

MS964	**227** $6 multicoloured	6·50	7·50

2000. "EXPO 2000". International Stamp Exhibition, Anaheim, U.S.A. No. **MS**940 optd "**WORLD STAMP EXPO 2000 - USA VALUE $5.00**" on the sheet margin.

MS965	90×80 mm. $4 Earth as seen from Moon	1·75	2·50

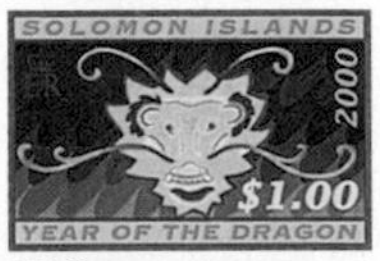

228 Dragon

2000. Chinese New Year ("Year of the Dragon"). Multicoloured.

966	$1 Type **228**	75	30
967	$3.90 Dragon roaring	2·25	2·75
MS968	131×85 mm. Nos. 966/7	3·00	3·25

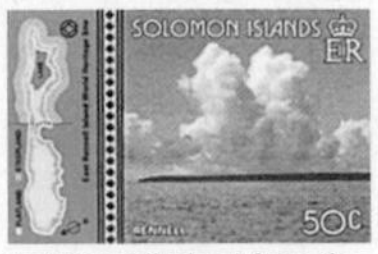

229 Rennell Island from the Sea

2000. Declaration of East Rennell Island as World Heritage Site. Multicoloured.

969	50c. Type **229**	50	60
970	$3.40 Canoe on Lake Tegano	1·40	1·60
971	$4 Rennell shrikebill	3·50	4·00
972	$4.90 Endemic orchid	4·00	4·50

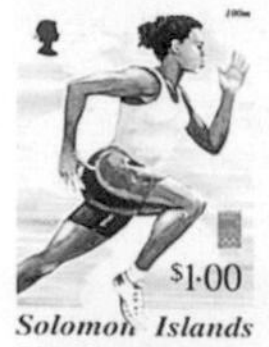

230 Woman running

2000. Olympic Games, Sydney. Multicoloured.

973	$1 Type **230**	1·00	50
974	$4.50 Man running	3·50	4·00
MS975	105×90 mm. Nos. 973/4	4·50	4·75

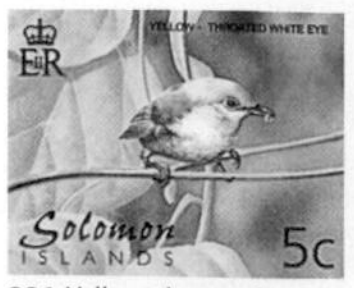

231 Yellow-throated White-Eye

2001. Birds. Multicoloured.

976	5c. Type **231**	30	1·00
977	20c. Purple swamphen	45	60
978	50c. Blyth's hornbill	65	30
979	80c. Yellow-faced myna	85	50
980	90c. Blue-faced parrot finch	90	60
981	$1 Greater crested tern ("Crested Tern")	90	60
982	$2 Rainbow lory ("Rainbow Lorikeet")	1·40	1·00
983	$3 Eclectus parrot	1·75	1·50
984	$4 Dwarf kingfisher	2·00	2·00
985	$10 Australian stone-curlew ("Beach Thick-knee")	4·00	5·00
986	$20 Brahminy kite (46×37 mm)	7·00	9·00
987	$50 Superb fruit-dove (46×37 mm)	12·00	16·00

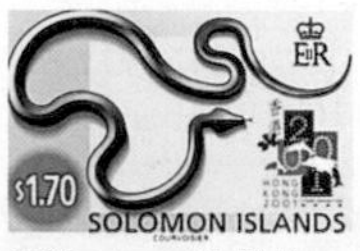

232 Snake and Exhibition Emblem

2001. "Hong Kong 2001" Stamp Exhibition.

988	**232** $1.70 multicoloured	1·00	1·00
989	**232** $2.30 multicoloured	1·10	1·25
MS990	115×85 mm. $5 multicoloured (as No. 972)	4·50	5·00

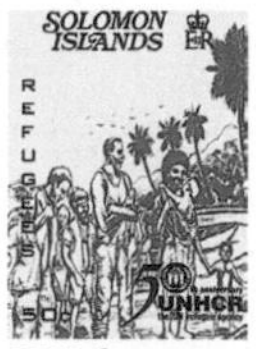

233 Refugees

2001. 50th Anniv of U.N. High Commission for Refugees.

991	**233** 50c. blue and black	35	25
992	- $1 red and black	75	40
993	- $1.90 green and black	1·25	1·40
994	- $2.30 brown and black	1·50	1·75

DESIGNS: $1 Red Cross volunteers distributing medical aid; $1.90 Temporary tent accommodation; $2.30 Refugee family.

2001. Chinese New Year ("Year of the Snake"). Sheet, 140×75 mm, containing designs as Nos. 389/91 and 400, each 24½×35 mm and inscr "YEAR OF THE SNAKE 2001". Multicoloured.

MS995	$1 Red-banded tree snake; $1 Whip snake; $1 Pacific boa; $1 Guppy's snake	2·50	3·25

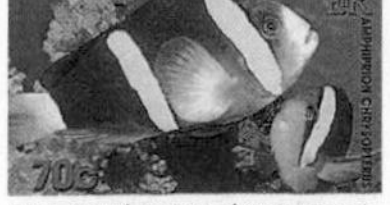

234 *Amphiprion chrysopterus* (fish)

2001. Reef Fish. Multicoloured.

996	70c. Type **234**	55	30
997	90c. *Amphiprion perideraion*	60	35
998	$1 *Premnas biaculeatus*	65	35
999	$1.50 *Amphiprion melanopus*	95	75
1000	$2.10 *Amphiprion clarkii*	1·25	1·40
1001	$4.50 *Dascyllus trimaculatus*	2·25	3·25
MS1002	160×85 mm. Nos. 996/1001	6·50	7·00

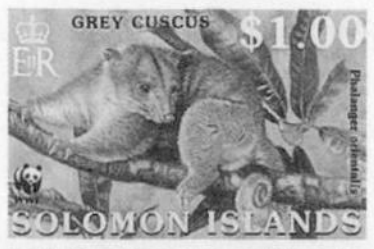

235 Grey Cuscus on Branch

2002. Endangered Species. Grey Cuscus. Multicoloured.

1003	$1 Type **235**	70	30
1004	$1.70 Grey Cuscus on branch	1·00	75
1005	$2.30 Grey Cuscus in leaves	1·25	1·25
1006	$5 Grey Cuscus in leaves	2·50	3·25

2002. Golden Jubilee. As T **211** of St. Helena.

1007	$1 black, red and gold	55	30
1008	$1.90 multicoloured	90	90
1009	$2.10 black, red and gold	95	1·00
1010	$2.30 multicoloured	1·00	1·10
MS1011	162×95 mm. Nos. 1002/5 and $10 multicoloured	6·00	7·00

DESIGNS—HORIZ (as Type **211** of St. Helena): $1 Princess Elizabeth with doll's pram, 1933; $1.90, Queen Elizabeth wearing sunglasses; $2.10, Queen Elizabeth in evening dress, 1955; $2.30, Queen Elizabeth in blue hat. VERT (38×51 mm): $10 Queen Elizabeth after Annigoni.

Designs as Nos. 1002/5 in No. **MS**1011 omit the gold frame around each stamp and the "Golden Jubilee 1952-2002" inscription.

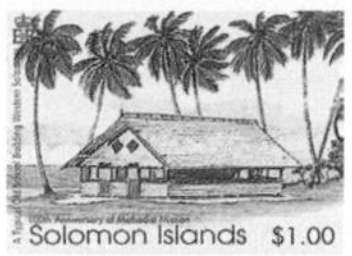

236 Old School Building, Western Solomons

2002. Centenary of Methodist Mission. Multicoloured.

1012	$1 Type **236**	60	35
1013	$1.70 Mrs. Goldie in canoe	95	95
1014	$2.10 Tandanya (missionary schooner)	1·25	1·40
1015	$2.30 Revd J Goldie with local chiefs	1·40	1·60
MS1016	140×80 mm. $5 Revd. J. Goldie with Sam Aqarao (vert)	2·00	2·50

2002. "United We Stand". Support for Victims of 11 September 2001 Terrorist Attacks. As T **445** of St. Vincent. Multicoloured.

1017	$2.10 US flag as Statue of Liberty and Solomon Islands flag	1·50	1·60

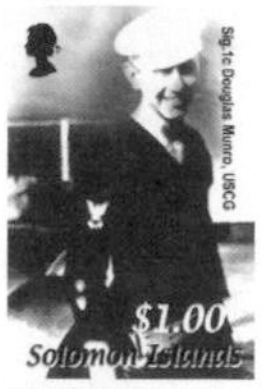

237 Signalman 1st Class Douglas Munro (USCG)

2002. 60th Anniv of Battle of Guadalcanal. Medal Recipients. Each green and black.

1018	$1 Type **237**	1·00	40
1019	$1.90 Captain Joe Foss (USMC)	1·50	1·25
1020	$2.10 Platoon Sergeant Mitchell Paige (USMC)	1·60	1·60
1021	$2.30 Rear Admiral Norman Scott (USN)	1·75	2·25
MS1022	127×181 mm. Nos. 1018/19, but each with a face value of $5	7·50	8·00

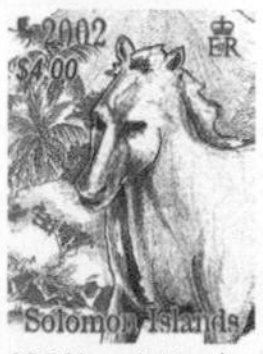

238 Horse's Head

2002. Chinese New Year ("Year of the Horse"). Sheet, 140×80 mm, containing T **238** and similar design, each brown and green.

MS1023	$4 Type **238**; $4 Horse (horiz)	4·50	4·50

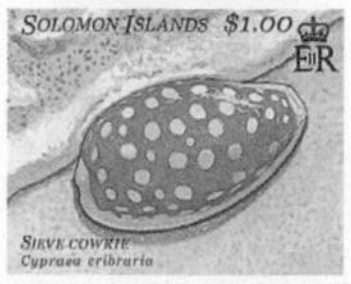

239 Sieve Cowrie Shell

2002. "Philakorea 2002" International Stamp Exhibition, Seoul. Cowrie Shells. Multicoloured.

1024	$1 Type **239**	80	90
1025	$1 Kitten cowrie	80	90
1026	$1 Eroded cowrie and stolid cowrie	80	90
1027	$1.90 Tapering cowrie	1·25	1·40
1028	$1.90 Tiger cowrie	1·25	1·40
1029	$1.90 Lynx cowrie	1·25	1·40
1030	$2.30 Map cowrie	1·40	1·50
1031	$2.30 Pacific deer cowrie	1·40	1·50
1032	$2.30 Tortoise cowrie	1·40	1·50
MS1033	88×58 mm. $10 Golden cowrie	5·50	7·00

2002. Queen Elizabeth the Queen Mother Commemoration. As T **215** of St. Helena.

1034	$1 brown, gold and purple	75	25
1035	$2.30 multicoloured	1·50	1·75
MS1036	145×70 mm. $5 black and gold; $5 multicoloured	4·00	4·50

DESIGNS: $1 Duchess of York, 1930; $2.30, Queen Mother at Royal Caledonian School, Bushey; $5 (black and gold) Queen Mother in evening dress, 1954; $5 (multicoloured) Queen Mother at St. Paul's Cathedral, 1997. Designs in No. **MS**1036 omit the "1900–2002" inscription and the coloured frame.

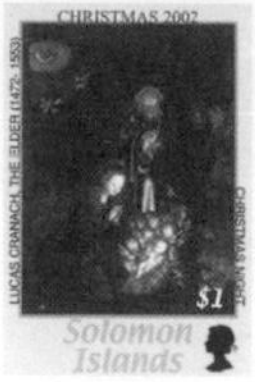

240 "Christmas Night"

2002. Christmas. Religious Paintings. Multicoloured.

1037	$1 Type **240**	65	25
1038	$2.10 "Madonna and Child" (Giovanni Bellini)	1·40	70
1039	$2.30 "Nativity" (Perugino) (horiz)	1·40	75
1040	$5 "Madonna and Child" (Simone Martini)	2·75	4·50

2003. World Aids Day. No. 872 surch **$1.35** and pink ribbon.

1041	$1.35+$3 Doctor and child	3·50	4·00

2003. Cyclones Zoe and Beni Relief Fund. No. 907 surch **Cyclones Zoe and Beni Relief Fund Surcharge - $5.00.**

1042	$5 on $2 Princess Diana wearing pearl earrings	2·25	3·00

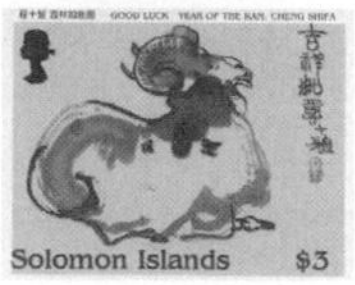

243 Ram (Lucas Cranach the Elder)

2003. Chinese New Year ("Year of the Ram").

MS1043	100×101 mm. **243** $3 ×4 multicoloured	8·00	9·00

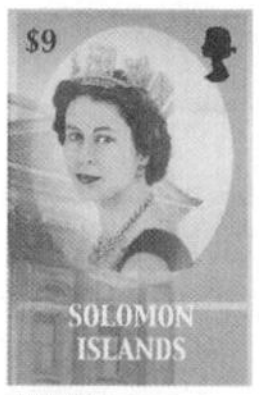

244 Queen Elizabeth II

2003. Golden Jubilee (2nd issue). Multicoloured.

MS1044	156×93 mm. $9 Type **244**; $9 Wearing green outfit; $9 Wearing blue outfit	11·00	12·00
MS1045	106×76 mm. $15 Queen Elizabeth II	9·00	10·00

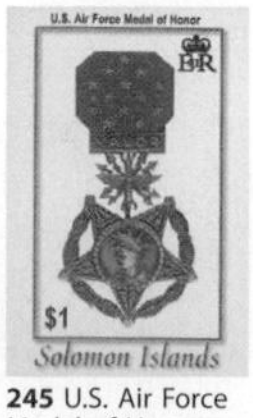

245 U.S. Air Force Medal of Honour

2003. Medals of Honour. Multicoloured.

1046	$1 Type **245**	80	35
1047	$1.90 U.S. Navy medal of Honour	1·40	1·00
1048	$2.10 U.S. Army medal of Honour	1·50	1·40
1049	$2.30 Medal of Honour ribbon	1·60	1·90

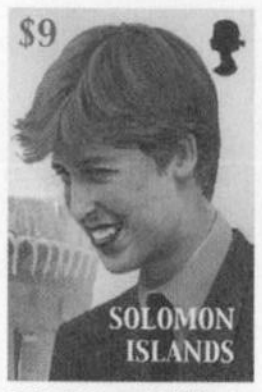

246 Prince William

2003. 21st Birthday of Prince William. Multicoloured.

MS1050	155×93 mm. $9 Type **246**; $9 Wearing red polo shirt; $9 Wearing suit and tie (different)	10·00	11·00
MS1051	75×105 mm. $15 Prince William	7·50	8·00

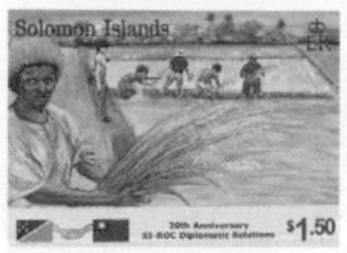

247 Harvesting Rice

2003. 20th Anniv of Diplomatic Relations with Republic of China. Multicoloured.

1052	$1.50 Type **247**	1·25	1·00
1053	$2.10 Hospital	2·00	2·00

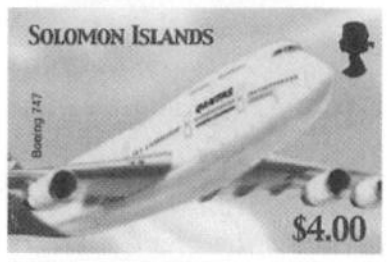

248 Boeing 747

2003. Centenary of Powered Flight. Multicoloured.

MS1054	108×178 mm. $4 Type **248**; $4 Boeing 707; $4 Lockheed Model 649; $4 Boeing Model 247D; $4 Fokker F.VII; $4 Orville and Wilbur Wright	10·00	11·00
MS1055	105×76 mm. $15 Mach 2 Concorde	7·00	7·00

The backgrounds of the stamps in No. **MS**1054 form a composite design.

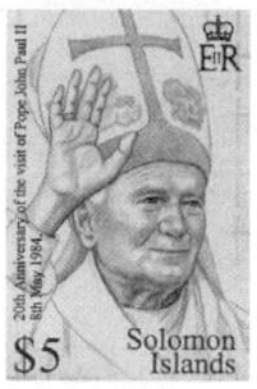

249 Pope John Paul II

2004. 20th Anniv of Papal Visit. Sheet 104×65 mm containing T **249** and similar vert design. Multicoloured.

MS1056	$5 Type **249**; $10 With head bowed	5·50	6·00

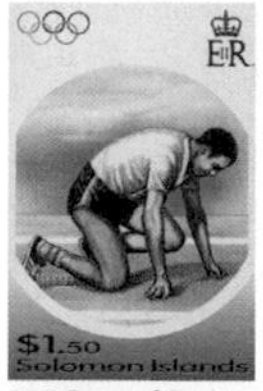

250 Start of Race

2004. Olympic Games, Athens. Multicoloured.

1057	$1.50 Type **250**	50	30
1058	$2 Running	70	70
1059	$2.20 Winning race	70	70
1060	$10 Solomon Islands flag and Olympic emblem	2·75	3·50

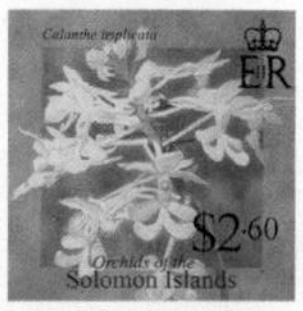

251 *Calanthe triplicate*

2004. Orchids. Multicoloured.

1061	$2.60 Type **251**	1·25	1·25
1062	$2.60 *Dendrobium johnsoniae*	1·25	1·25
1063	$2.60 *Dendrobium capituliflorum*	1·25	1·25
1064	$2.60 *Spathoglottis plicata*	1·25	1·25
1065	$2.60 *Dendrobium mirbelianum*	1·25	1·25
1066	$5 *Dendrobium polysema*	1·60	1·75
1067	$5 *Paphiopedilum bougainvilleanum*	1·60	1·75
1068	$5 *Coelogyne asperata*	1·60	1·75
1069	$5 *Dendrobium macrophyllum*	1·60	1·75
1070	$5 *Dendrobium spectabile*	1·60	1·75

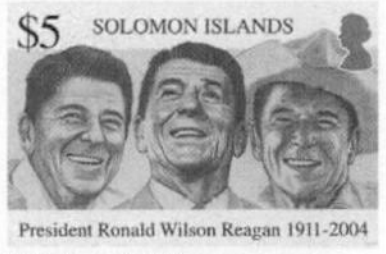
$5 SOLOMON ISLANDS
President Ronald Wilson Reagan 1911-2004
252 Ronald Reagan

2004. Ronald Reagan Commemoration.

MS1071	124×76 mm. **252** $5 ×4 blue, red and grey	4·50	6·00

2004. Merchant Ships. As T **227** of St. Helena. Multicoloured.

1072	$1.50 MV *Bilikiki*	1·00	50
1073	$2.20 MV *Spirit of Solomons*	1·40	75
1074	$3 SS *Oceana*	1·75	1·00
1075	$20 RMS *Queen Elizabeth II*	9·00	11·00

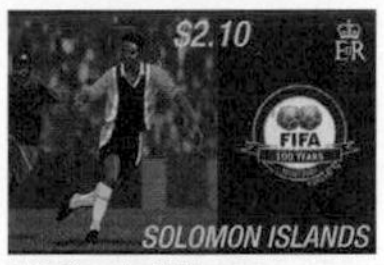
$2.10
SOLOMON ISLANDS
253 Football Player

2004. Centenary of FIFA (Federation Internationale de Football Association). Multicoloured.

1076	$2.10 Type **253**	75	80
1077	$2.10 Two players	75	80
1078	$10 Player No. 3 and opponent	2·50	3·50
1079	$10 Player No. 16 with ball	2·50	3·50

Nos. 1076/7 and 1078/9 were each printed together, *se-tenant*, with the backgrounds showing composite designs.

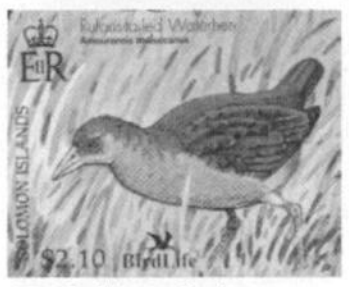
254 Rufous-tailed Waterhen

2004. Birds. Multicoloured.

MS1080 Three sheets, each 148×85 mm. (a) $2.10 Type **254**; $2.10 Buff-banded rail; $2.10 Purple swamphen; $2.10 Woodford's rail; $2.10 Roviana rail; $2.10 Makira moorhen. (b) $5 Solomon Islands hawk-owl from side; $5 Great ("White-Throated") eared nightjar in flight; $5 Solomon Islands hawk-owl from front; $5 Great ("White-throated") eared nightjar perched; $5 Marbled frogmouth; $5 Fearful owl. (c) $7.50 Beach kingfisher; $7.50 Collared kingfisher; $7.50 Ultramarine kingfisher; $7.50 Moustached kingfisher; $7.50 Mangrove ("Little") kingfisher; $7.50 Dwarf ("Variable") kingfisher Set of 3 sheets — 24·00 26·00

The backgrounds of Nos. **MS**1080a/c form composite designs.

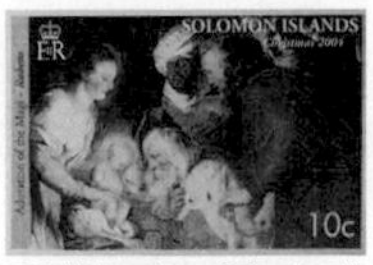
SOLOMON ISLANDS
10c
255 "Adoration of the Magi" (Rubens)

2004. Christmas. Religious Paintings. Multicoloured.

1081	10c. Type **255**	10	50
1082	50c. "Madonna della Tenda" (Raphael) (vert)	20	50
1083	$1.50 "Madonna and Child" (Titian) (vert)	60	40
1084	$2.60 "Madonna by the Arch" (Dürer) (vert)	80	50
1085	$3 "Holy Family" (Floris)	85	55
1086	$10 "Madonna and Child"	2·75	4·00

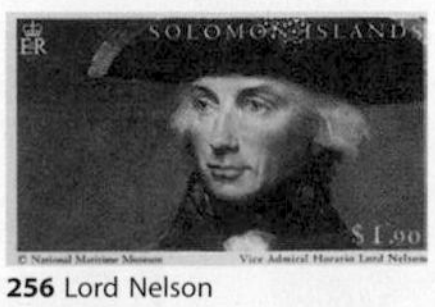
SOLOMON ISLANDS
$1.90
256 Lord Nelson

2005. Bicentenary of the Battle of Trafalgar (1st issue). Multicoloured.

1087-1092	$1.90×6 Type **256**; HMS *Victory*; Sir Thomas Masterman Hardy; The first engagement; Breaking the line; The death of Nelson	4·00	4·00
1093-1098	$2.60×6 Lord Cuthbert Collingwood; Napoleon Bonaparte; Destruction of the *Bucentaure*; Officers on deck; Nelson and officers at table; Ships from back	6·00	6·00
1099-1104	$5×6 Nelson and Hardy on deck; Nelson sending signal; Attempted siege of HMS *Victory*; *Neptune* towing *Victory*; Funeral procession on Thames; Nelson's Column	9·00	9·00
1105-1110	$10×6 Young Lord Nelson; Nelson's letters; Nelson loses eye at Siege of Calvi; Nelson loses arm at Santa Cruz de Tenerife; The Battle of Cape St. Vincent; The Battle of the Nile	17·00	17·00

See also No. 1159/61.

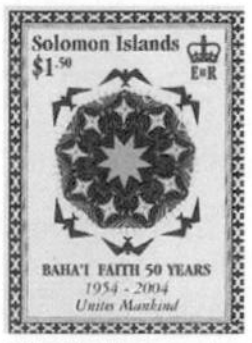
Solomon Islands $1.50
BAHA'I FAITH 50 YEARS
1954 - 2004
257 Emblem and Six Black Stylized Birds

2005. 50th Anniv of the Baha'I Faith.

1111	**257**	$1.50 multicoloured	50	40
1112	-	$3 multicoloured	90	1·00
1113	-	$5 olive, brown and black	1·40	1·75

DESIGNS: No. 1111, Type **257**; 1112, Globe held in hands; 1113, Alvin and Gertrude Blum (horiz).

2005. 60th Anniv of the End of World War II. Pacific Explorer World Stamp Exhibition (**MS**1121). As T **230** of St Helena. Multicoloured.

1114	$2.50 Japanese Forces land at Tulagi	1·25	1·25
1115	$2.50 USS *Lexington* during battle of the Coral Sea	1·25	1·25
1116	$2.50 Coastwatcher and British Solomon Islands Scouts, Guadalcanal	1·25	1·25
1117	$2.50 US Forces land at Tulagi and Guadalcanal	1·25	1·25
1118	$2.50 HMAS *Canberra* sinking at Iron Bottom Sound	1·25	1·25
1119	$2.50 Cactus Air Force over Henderson Airfield	1·25	1·25
1120	$2.50 Japanese warship	1·25	1·25
1121	$2.50 P-38 Lightning shoots down Admiral Yamamoto	1·25	1·25
1122	$2.50 Lt. John F. Kennedy and PT109	1·25	1·25
1123	$2.50 Sgt. Maj. Vouza, George Medal and US Silver Start Medal	1·25	1·25
MS1124	90×60 mm. $5 RAN Coast-watchers send enemy intelligence reports by Teleradio	2·25	2·75

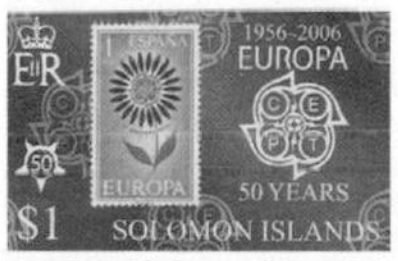
1956-2006
EUROPA
50 YEARS
$1 SOLOMON ISLANDS
258 Spanish Stamp (No. 1674)

2005. 50th Anniv of Europa Conference of Postal and Telecommunications Administrations. Designs showing worldwide stamps that have been issued to commemorate Europa. Multicoloured.

1125	$1 Type **258**	90	90
1126	$1 Netherlands stamp (No. 959)	90	90
1127	$2.10 Andorra stamp (No. F199)	1·25	1·25
1128	$2.10 Belgian stamp (No. 1794)	1·25	1·25
1129	$2.50 Belgian stamp (No. 1582)	1·40	1·40
1130	$2.50 Spanish stamp (No. 1979)	1·40	1·40
1131	$5 Austrian stamp (No. 1359)	2·25	2·25
1132	$5 San Marino stamp (No. 862)	2·25	2·25
1133	$10 Netherlands stamp (No. 1148)	4·00	4·50
1134	$10 Norwegian stamp (No. 935)	4·00	4·50
1135	$15 German stamp (No. 1168)	5·50	6·50
1136	$15 Italian stamp (No. 973)	5·50	6·50
MS1137	Six sheets, each 126×68 mm. (a) $1×2, Nos. 1125/6. (b) $2.10×2, Nos. 1127/8. (c) $2.50×2, Nos. 1129/30. (d) $5×2, Nos. 1131/2. (e) $10×2, Nos. 1133/34. (f) $15×2, Nos. 1135/6	23·00	27·00

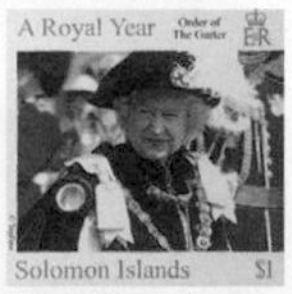
A Royal Year
Solomon Islands $1
259 Order of the Garter

2005. A Royal Year. Multicoloured.

1138	$1 Type **259**	90	90
1139	$1 Trooping the Colour	90	90
1140	$2.10 Royal Ascot	1·25	1·25
1141	$2.10 Garden Party	1·25	1·25
1142	$2.50 Royal visits	1·40	1·40
1143	$2.50 State visits	1·40	1·40
1144	$5 State Opening of Parliament	2·25	2·25
1145	$5 Remembrance Day	2·25	2·25
1146	$10 Investitures	4·00	4·50
1147	$10 Christmas broadcast	4·00	4·50
1148	$15 Maundy Service	5·50	6·50
1149	$15 Chelsea Flower Show	5·50	6·50

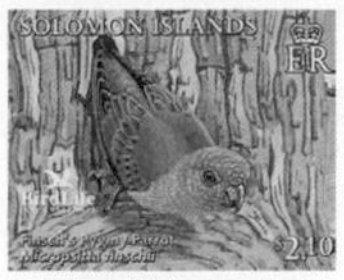
SOLOMON ISLANDS
2.10
260 Finsch's Pygmy Parrot

2005. Birdlife International (Part II). Multicoloured.

MS1150 Three sheets, each 170×85 mm. (a) $2.10×6, Type **260**; Cardinal lory; ducorps' ("Solomons") Cockatoo; Eclectus parrot; Rainbow lory; Singing ("Song") parrot. (b) $5×6, Red-knobbed imperial pigeon; Yellow-bibbed fruit dove; Red-bibbed ("Claret-breasted") fruit dove; Nicobar pigeon; Stephan's ("Ground") dove; Crested cuckoo dove. (c) $7.50×6, Pied goshawk; Imitator sparrowhawk; Buff-headed coucal; Black-faced pitta; Bismarck scrub fowl ("Melanesian Megapode"); Blyth's hornbill — 25·00 28·00

The backgrounds of Nos. **MS**1150a/c form composite designs.

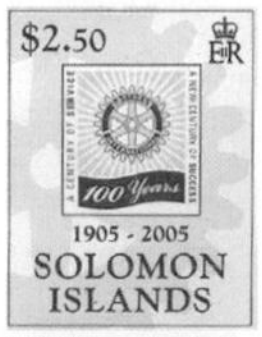
$2.50
100 Years
1905 - 2005
SOLOMON ISLANDS
261 Rotary Emblem

2005. Centenary of Rotary International.

1151	**261**	$2.50 multicoloured	1·00	1·00

2005. Pope John Paul II Commemoration. No. **MS**1056 optd **IN MEMORIAM (1920–2005).**

MS1152	$5; $10 With head bowed (ovpt against left edge of stamp)	5·50	6·00

2005. Christmas and Birth Bicentenary of Hans Christian Andersen (writer). As T **234** of St. Helena. Multicoloured.

1153	$1 *The Little Fir Tree*	35	20
1154	$2.10 *The Nightingale*	75	55
1155	$2.50 *The Emperor's New Clothes*	85	70
1156	$5 *The Phoenix*	1·50	1·50
1157	$10 *The Tinderbox*	2·75	3·50
1158	$15 *The Red Shoes*	4·00	6·00

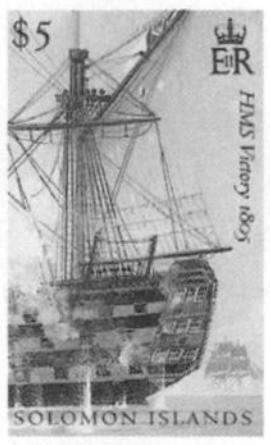
$5
HMS Victory 1805
SOLOMON ISLANDS
263 HMS *Victory*

2005. Bicentenary of the Battle of Trafalgar (2nd issue). Multicoloured.

1159	$5 Type **263**	2·25	1·60
1160	$10 Ships engaged in battle (horiz)	3·25	3·75
1161	$20 Admiral Lord Nelson	5·50	8·00

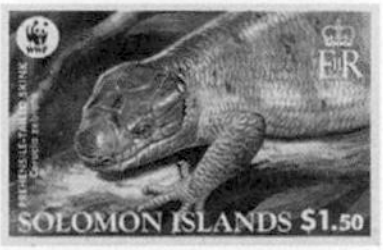
SOLOMON ISLANDS $1.50
264 Prehensile-tailed Skink

2005. Endangered Species. Prehensile-tailed Skink (Corucia zebrata). Multicoloured.

1162	$1.50 Type **264**	50	40
1163	$2.60 In foliage	90	75
1164	$3 Facing forwards	90	95
1165	$10 On branch	3·00	4·00

2006. 80th Birthday of Queen Elizabeth II. As T **237** of St. Helena. Multicoloured.

1166	$2.10 Princess Elizabeth	75	55
1167	$2.50 Queen Elizabeth II, c. 1952	85	70
1168	$5 Queen taking photograph	1·50	1·50
1169	$20 Wearing red hat	5·50	6·50
MS1170	144×75 mm. $10 As No. 1167; $15 As No. 1168	7·00	8·00

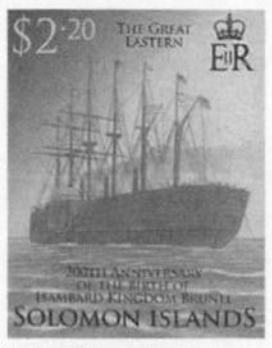
$2.20 The Great Eastern
SOLOMON ISLANDS
265 *Great Eastern* (paddle-steamer)

2006. Exploration and Innovation. Anniversaries. Multicoloured.

1171	$2.20 Type **265**	1·75	1·75
1172	$2.20 Isambard Kingdom Brunel (engineer) (birth bicentenary)	1·75	1·75
1173	$2.50 Charles Darwin (originator of "Theory of Evolution") (175th anniv of voyage on *Beagle*)	1·75	1·75
1174	$2.50 Green turtle	1·75	1·75
1175	$5 Diving bell	3·00	3·00
1176	$5 Edmund Halley (astronomer) (350th birth anniv)	3·00	3·00
1177	$10 G. and R. Stephenson's locomotive *Rocket*	6·00	6·00
1178	$10 George Stephenson (railway engineer) (225th birth anniv)	6·00	6·00

Nos. 1171/2, 1173/4, 1175/6 and 1177/8 were each printed together, *se-tenant*, forming a composite background design.

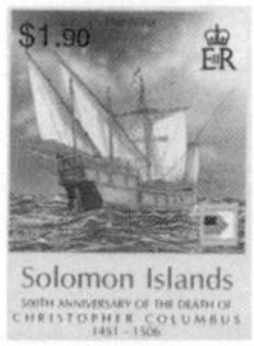
$1.90
Solomon Islands
266 *Nina*

2006. Washington 2006 International Stamp Exhibition. 500th Death Anniv of Christopher Columbus. Multicoloured.

1179	$1.90 Type **266**	1·00	70
1180	$2.20 *Pinta*	1·25	80
1181	$2.60 *Santa Maria*	1·40	90
1182	$10 Columbus's coat of arms	4·75	6·00
MS1183	55×67 mm. $20 Christopher Columbus	6·50	7·50

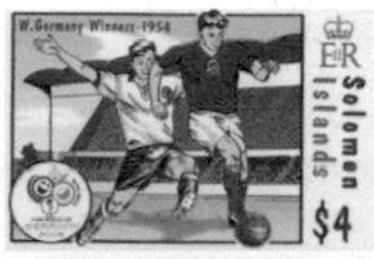
Solomon Islands
$4
267 West Germany (winners) v. Hungary Final, 1954

2006. World Cup Football Championship, Germany. Multicoloured.

1184	$4 Type **267**	1·25	1·00
1185	$5 England (winners) v. West Germany final, 1966	1·40	1·00
1186	$10 France (winners) v. Brazil final, 1998	2·75	2·75
1187	$20 Solomon Islands v. Australia (winners) qualifying match, 2005	4·75	5·50

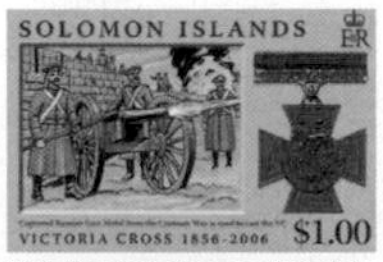
SOLOMON ISLANDS
VICTORIA CROSS 1856-2006
$1.00
268 Russian Gun captured in Crimean War (used to cast first V.C.s)

2006. 150th Anniv of the Victoria Cross. Each showing Victoria Cross at right. Multicoloured.

1188	$1 Type **268**	75	30
1189	$2.20 Midshipman Charles Lucas hurling live shell overboard, 1854	1·25	70
1190	$2.50 Queen Victoria awarding first Victoria Crosses, 1857	1·25	75
1191	$5 Corporal Sukanaivalu rescuing wounded soldier, Bougainville, 1944	2·00	2·00
1192	$10 Corporal Rattey attacking enemy bunker, Bougainville, 1945	3·75	4·25
1193	$15 Private Partridge attacking enemy bunker, Bougainville, 1945	6·00	7·00

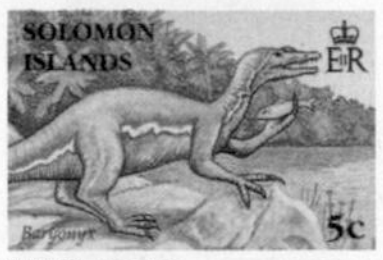
SOLOMON ISLANDS
5c
269 Baryonyx

2006. Dinosaurs. Multicoloured.

1194	5c. Type **269**	10	50
1195	10c. Diplodocus	10	50
1196	$1.50 Pteranodon	1·25	50
1197	$2.15 Argentinosaurus	1·40	75
1198	$2.40 Centrosaurus	1·60	1·10
1199	$3 Allosaurus	1·90	1·25
1200	$10 Ankylosaurus	4·75	5·00
1201	$20 Iguanodon	8·00	9·00

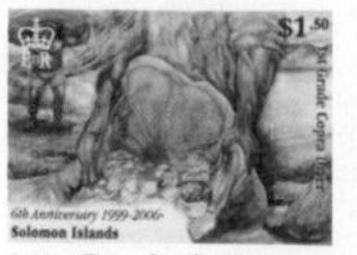

269a First Grade Copra Drier ('6th Anniversary 1999–2006')

2006. International Coconut Day. Multicoloured.

1201a	$1.50 Type **269a**	75	50
1201b	$2.40 Standard copra drier ('International Coconut Day')	1·25	1·00
1201c	$3 Coconut oil expeller ('Value Added Products')	1·50	1·50
1201d	$5 Coconut palm and cargo ship ('Economic Growth')	2·25	2·75

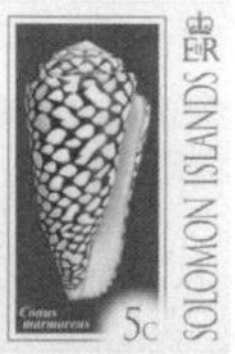

270 *Conus marmoreus*

2006. Cone Shells. Multicoloured.

1202	5c. Type **270**	10	60
1203	10c. *Conus auratinus*	15	60
1204	20c. *Conus ferrugineus*	20	60
1205	50c. *Conus consors*	45	30
1206	80c. *Conus magdalenae*	70	40
1207	90c. *Conus sulcatus brettinghami*	75	40
1208	$1 *Conus tmetus*	80	40
1209	$1.50 *Conus aureus*	1·25	40
1210	$2 *Conus corallinus*	1·50	90
1211	$3 *Conus floccatus*	1·75	1·00
1212	$4 *Conus panniculus*	1·90	1·50
1213	$10 *Conus pöhlianus*	3·75	3·75
1214	$20 *Conus proximus*	7·00	8·50
1215	$50 *Conus canonicus*	14·00	16·00

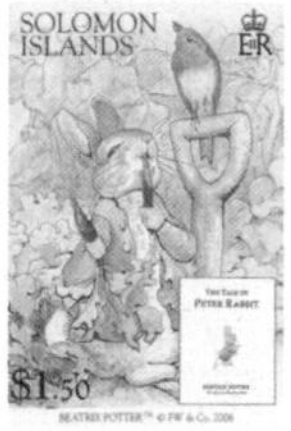

271 "The Tale of Peter Rabbit"

2006. The Tales of Beatrix Potter. Designs showing book cover and scene from book. Multicoloured.

1216	$1.50 Type **271**	1·00	55
1217	$1.90 "The Tale of Squirrel Nutkin"	1·25	80
1218	$2.15 "The Tailor of Gloucester"	1·40	1·00
1219	$2.40 "The Tale of Benjamin Bunny"	1·50	1·50
1220	$2.65 "The Tale of Two Bad Mice"	1·60	1·75
1221	$5 "The Tale of Mrs. Tiggy-Winkle"	2·75	3·25
MS1222	185×120 mm. Nos. 1216/21	8·50	8·50

2007. Diamond Wedding of Queen Elizabeth II and Duke of Edinburgh. As T **242** of St. Helena. Multicoloured.

1223	$2.10 Princess Elizabeth and Lt. Philip Mountbatten, c. 1947	1·10	90
1224	$2.50 Princess Elizabeth and Lt. Philip Mountbatten, c. 1947 (different)	1·25	1·00
1225	$5 Wedding ceremony, 1949	2·10	2·50
1226	$10 Princess Elizabeth and Duke of Edinburgh, c. 1950	4·00	5·00
MS1227	125×85 mm. $20 Wedding photograph, 1949 (42×56 mm)	7·50	8·50

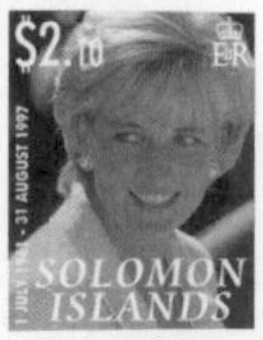

272 Diana, Princess of Wales

2007. Tenth Death Anniv of Diana, Princess of Wales (1st issue). No. **MS**908 optd **1997-2007** on the stamps and **'10th Anniversary in Memorium'** on left and right upper sheet margins.

MS1227a	145×70 mm. $2.50 Wearing pearl earrings; $2.50 Wearing white hat; $2.50 In evening dress; $2.50 Accepting flowers from children	2·50	2·50

2007. Tenth Death Anniv of Diana, Princess of Wales. Multicoloured.

1228	$2.10 Type **272**	1·50	1·00
1229	$2.50 Wearing turquoise-green jacket	1·75	1·25
1230	$5 Wearing white dress with narrow straps and drop earrings	3·00	3·00
1231	$20 Wearing white dress with narrow straps and pearl earrings	7·50	8·50

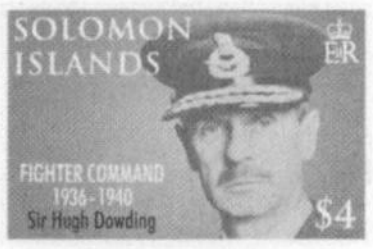

273 Sir Hugh Dowding (fighter command 1936–40)

2008. 90th Anniv of the Royal Air Force. Multicoloured.

1232	$4 Type **273**	3·25	3·25
1233	$4 Sir Hugh Trenchard ('father of the RAF')	3·25	3·25
1234	$4 Sir William Sholto Douglas (coastal command)	3·25	3·25
1235	$4 Sir Charles Portal (bomber command)	3·25	3·25
1236	$4 Wing Commander Guy Gibson	3·25	3·25
MS1237	110×70 mm. $20 Battle of Britain	14·00	14·00

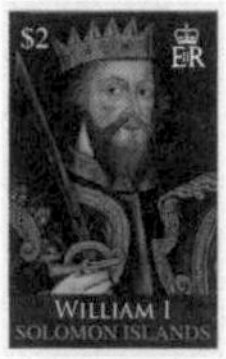

274 William I (1066–1087)

2008. Kings and Queens of England (1st series). Multicoloured.

1238	$2 Type **274**	2·00	2·00
1239	$2 Henry II (1154–1189)	2·00	2·00
1240	$2 Henry IV (1399–1413)	2·00	2·00
1241	$2 Henry VI (1422–1461, 1470–1471)	2·00	2·00
1242	$2 Richard III (1483–1485)	2·00	2·00
1243	$2 Elizabeth I (1558–1603)	2·00	2·00
1244	$2 James I (1603–1625)	2·00	2·00
1245	$2 Edward VII (1901–1910)	2·00	2·00

See also Nos. 1254/61.

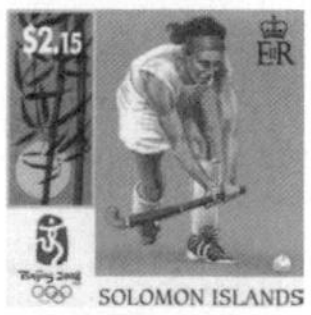

275 Hockey

2008. Olympic Games, Beijing. Multicoloured.

1246	$2.15 Type **275**	1·50	75
1247	$3 Pole vault	2·00	1·25
1248	$4 Table tennis	2·50	2·50
1249	$5 Running	2·75	3·00

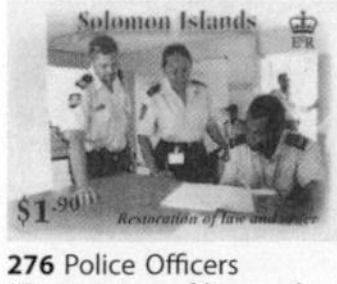

276 Police Officers ('Restoration of law and order')

2008. Fifth Anniv of Arrival of Regional Assistance Mission to Solomon Islands. Multicoloured.

1250	$1.90 Type **276**	1·50	1·25
1251	$2.15 'Freedom of movement'	1·50	1·25
1252	$2.40 Children relaxing	1·75	1·75
1253	$2.65 Ramsi officer with baby (vert) ('Community policing')	2·00	2·50

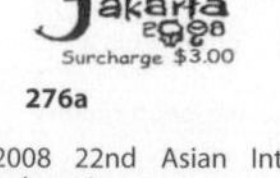

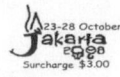

276a

2008. Jakarta 2008 22nd Asian International Stamp Exhibition, Indonesia

MS1253a	160×85 mm. Nos. 996/1001	6·50	7·00

2009. Kings and Queens of England (2nd series). As T **274**. Multicoloured.

1254	$2 William II (1087–1100)	2·00	2·00
1255	$2 Richard I (1189–1199)	2·00	2·00
1256	$2 Edward III (1327–77)	2·00	2·00
1257	$2 Edward IV (1461–70, 1471–83)	2·00	2·00
1258	$2 Henry VIII (1509–47)	2·00	2·00
1259	$2 Charles I (1625–49)	2·00	2·00
1260	$2 George I (1714–27)	2·00	2·00
1261	$2 George V (1910–36)	2·00	2·00

2009. Seafaring and Exploration. As T **209** of Seychelles. Multicoloured.

1262	$3 *Discovery* (Scott) (horiz)	2·50	1·50
1263	$4 HMS *Bounty* (Bligh) (horiz)	2·50	2·25
1264	$5 *Mayflower* (Pilgrim Fathers) (horiz)	2·50	2·25
1265	$6 USS *North Carolina* (battleship) (horiz)	2·75	2·75
1266	$10 *Boussole* and *Astrolabe* (La Perouse) (horiz)	5·00	5·50
1267	$20 USS *Saratoga* (aircraft carrier) (horiz)	9·00	10·00
MS1268	110×70 mm. $15 Alvaro de Mendana de Neira (vert). Wmk inverted	9·00	10·00

2009. Centenary of Naval Aviation. As T **255** of St. Helena. Multicoloured.

1269	$2 Grumman Hellcat	2·25	1·50
1270	$2.50 Blackburn Skua	2·25	1·75
1271	$3.50 Fairey Albacore	3·25	2·75
1272	$10 Gloster Sea Gladiator	6·50	7·50
MS1273	110×70 mm. $20 Short 184 Seaplane from HMS *Engadine*	15·00	15·00

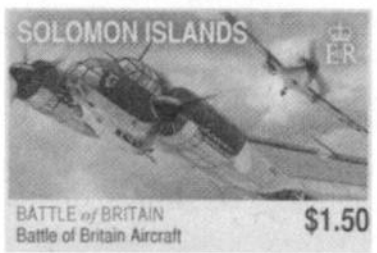

279 Supermarine Spitfire and Junkers Ju 88

2010. 70th Anniv of the Battle of Britain. Multicoloured.

1274	$1.50 Type **279**	1·50	1·25
1275	$1.90 Supermarine Spitfire and Messerschmitt Me 110	1·50	1·25
1276	$2.20 Hawker Hurricane and Heinkel He 111	1·50	1·25
1277	$2.65 Boulton Paul Defiant and Dornier Do 17	2·00	2·50
1278	$10 Supermarine Spitfire and Messerschmitt Me 109	5·00	5·50
1279	$15 Supermarine Spitfire and Junkers Ju 87	6·75	7·50
MS1280	110×70 mm. $20 Sir Douglas Bader (fighter pilot) (vert)	15·00	15·00

2010. Kings and Queens of England (3rd series). Multicoloured.

1281	$2 Henry I	2·00	2·00
1282	$2 John	2·00	2·00
1283	$2 Richard II	2·00	2·00
1284	$2 Edward V	2·00	2·00
1285	$2 Edward VI	2·00	2·00
1286	$2 Charles II	2·00	2·00
1287	$2 George III	2·00	2·00
1288	$2 George VI	2·00	2·00

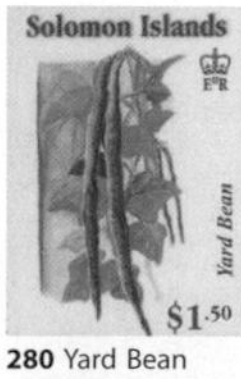

280 Yard Bean

2010. Vegetables. Multicoloured.

1289	$1.50 Type **280**	1·75	1·00
1290	$1.90 Tomato plant (35×35 mm)	1·50	1·25
1291	$2.20 Egg Plant	1·50	1·25
1292	$3 Pumpkin plant (35×35 mm)	2·50	1·50

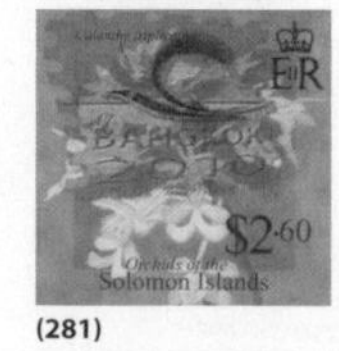

(281)

2010. Bangkok 2010 International Stamp Exhibition, Thailand. Multicoloured.

1293	$2.60 Type **251**	3·00	3·00
1294	$5 *Dendrobium spectabile*	5·75	5·75

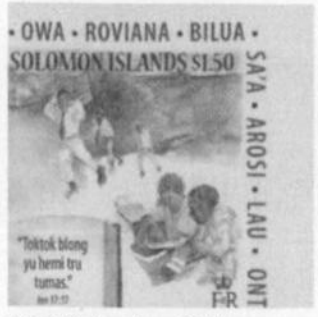

282 Bringing Bibles Ashore

2010. 'Celebrating Bible Translation in the Solomon Islands'. Multicoloured.

MS1295	$1.50 Type **282**; $2 Solomon Islanders reading Bibles; $2.20 Two men carrying model canoe with Cross and Bible; $2.60 Handing out and reading Bibles	8·50	8·50

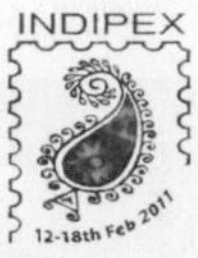

(283)

2011. Indipex 2011 International Stamp Exhibition, New Delhi

1296	$1.90 Tiger cowrie	1·50	1·25

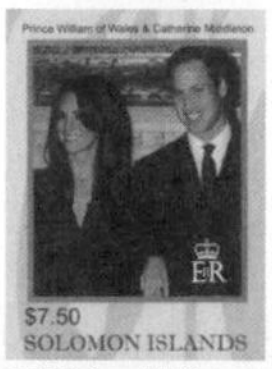

284 Prince William and Miss Catherine Middleton

2011. Royal Wedding. Multicoloured.

MS1297	160×110 mm. $7.50 Type **284**×2; $7.50 Prince William and Miss Catherine Middleton (head and shoulders photo of couple)×2	7·00	7·00
MS1298	101×141 mm. $15 Prince William; $15 Miss Catherine Middleton	14·00	14·00

POSTAGE DUE STAMPS

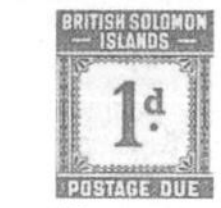

D1

1940

D1	**D 1**	1d. green	6·50	7·00
D2	**D 1**	2d. red	7·00	7·00
D3	**D 1**	3d. brown	7·00	11·00
D4	**D 1**	4d. blue	11·00	11·00
D5	**D 1**	5d. olive	12·00	21·00
D6	**D 1**	6d. purple	12·00	15·00
D7	**D 1**	1s. violet	14·00	29·00
D8	**D 1**	1s.6d. green	38·00	48·00

Pt. 8, Pt. 14

SOMALIA

A former Italian colony in East Africa on the Gulf of Aden, including Benadir (S. Somaliland), and Jubaland. Under British Administration 1943-50 (for stamps issued during this period see volume 1). Then under United Nations control with Italian Administration. Became independent on 1 July 1960. Following a revolution in October 1969, the country was designated "Somali Democratic Republic". See also British Post Office in Italian Colonies.

1903. 64 besa = 16 annas = 1 rupia.
1905. 100 centesimi = 1 lira.
1922. 100 besa = 1 rupia.
1926. 100 centesimi = 1 lira.
1950. 100 centesimi = 1 somalo.
1961. 100 cents = 1 Somali shilling.

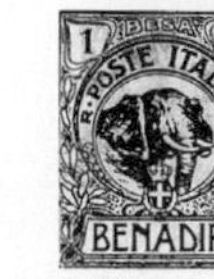

1 African Elephant

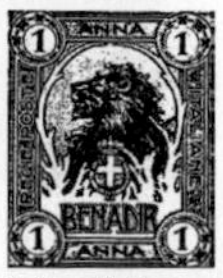

2 Somali Lion

1903

1	1	1b. brown	£100	23·00
2	1	2b. green	3·00	12·50
3	2	1a. red	3·00	15·00
4	2	2a. brown	5·75	29·00
5	2	2½a. blue	3·00	29·00
6	2	5a. yellow	5·75	60·00
7	2	10a. lilac	5·75	65·00

1905. Surch with new value without bars at top.

10	**1**	2c. on 1b. brown	14·50	23·00
11	**1**	5c. on 2b. green	14·50	17·00
12	**2**	10c. on 1a. red	14·50	17·00
13	**2**	15c. on 2a. brown	14·50	17·00
8		15c. on 5a. yellow	£3750	£1300
13a	**2**	20c. on 2a. brown	27·00	17·00
14	**2**	25c. on 2½a. blue	28·00	16·00
9		40c. on 10a. lilac	£1000	£350
15	**2**	50c. on 5a. yellow	41·00	35·00
16	**2**	1l. on 10a. lilac	38·00	49·00

For stamps with bars at top, see Nos. 68, etc.

1916. Nos. 15 and 16 re-surcharged and with bars cancelling original surcharge.

17		5c. on 50c. on 5a. yellow	60·00	60·00
18		20c. on 1l. on 10a. lilac	17·00	40·00

1916. Red Cross stamps of Italy optd **SOMALIA**.

19	**53**	10c.+5c. red	20·00	40·00
20	**54**	15c.+5c. grey	50·00	50·00
21	**54**	20c.+5c. orange	50·00	80·00
22	**54**	20 on 15c.+5c. grey	20·00	60·00

1922. Nos. 12, etc., again surch at top.

23	**1**	3b. on 5c. on 2b. green	20·00	29·00
24	**2**	6b. on 10c. on 1a. red	29·00	29·00
25	**2**	9b. on 15c. on 2a. brown	29·00	29·00
26	**2**	15b. on 25c. on 2½a. blue	37·00	29·00
27	**2**	30b. on 50c. on 5a. yellow	46·00	50·00
28	**2**	60b. on 1l. on 10a. lilac	46·00	90·00

1922. Victory stamps of Italy surch **SOMALIA ITALIANA** and new value.

29	**62**	3b. on 5c. green	3·00	9·25
30	**62**	6b. on 10c. red	3·00	9·25
31	**62**	9b. on 15c. grey	3·00	14·00
32	**62**	15b. on 25c. blue	3·00	14·00

1923. Nos. 11 to 16 re-surcharged with new values and bars (No. 33 is optd with bars only at bottom).

33	**1**	bars on 2c. on 1b. brown	17·00	40·00
34	**1**	2 on 2c. on 1b. brown	17·00	40·00
35	**1**	3 on 2c. on 1b. brown	17·00	27·00
36	**2**	5b. on 50c. on 5a. yellow	17·00	27·00
37	**1**	6 on 5c. on 2b. green	29·00	21·00
38	**2**	18b. on 10c. on 1a. red	29·00	21·00
39	**2**	20b. on 15c. on 2a. brown	29·00	21·00
40	**2**	25b. on 15c. on 2a. brown	38·00	21·00
41	**2**	30b. on 25c. on 2½a. blue	38·00	21·00
42	**2**	60b. on 1l. on 10a. lilac	38·00	70·00
43	**2**	1r. on 1l. on 10a. lilac	65·00	85·00

1923. Propaganda of Faith stamps of Italy surch **SOMALIA ITALIANA** and new value.

44	**66**	6b. on 20c. orange & green	8·75	40·00
45	**66**	13b. on 30c. orange and red	8·75	40·00
46	**66**	20b. on 50c. orange & violet	5·75	46·00
47	**66**	30b. on 1l. orange and blue	5·75	65·00

1923. Fascist March on Rome stamps of Italy surch **SOMALIA ITALIA** and new value.

48	**73**	3b. on 10c. green	11·50	17·00
49	**73**	13b. on 30c. violet	11·50	17·00
50	**73**	20b. on 50c. red	11·50	23·00
51	**74**	30b. on 1l. blue	11·50	46·00
52	**74**	1r. on 2l. brown	11·50	60·00
53	**75**	3l. on 5l. black and blue	11·50	90·00

1924. Manzoni stamps of Italy surch **SOMALIA ITALIANA** and new value.

54	**77**	6b. on 10c. black and purple	10·50	40·00
55	**77**	9b. on 15c. black and green	10·50	40·00
56	**77**	13b. on 30c. black	10·50	40·00
57	**77**	20b. on 50c. black & brown	10·50	40·00
58	**77**	30b. on 1l. black and blue	70·00	£300
59	**77**	3r. on 5l. black and purple	£850	£2750

1925. Holy Year stamps of Italy surch **SOMALIA ITALIANA** and new value.

60	-	6b.+3b. on 20c.+10c. brown and green	4·00	29·00
61	**81**	13b.+6b. on 30c.+15c. brown and chocolate	4·00	29·00
62	-	15b.+8b. on 50c.+25c. brown and violet	4·00	29·00
63	-	18b.+9b. on 60c.+30c. brown and red	4·00	35·00
64	-	30b.+15b. on 1l.+50c. purple and blue	4·50	40·00
65	-	1r.+50b. on 5l.+2l.50 purple and red	4·50	60·00

1925. Royal Jubilee stamps of Italy optd **SOMALIA ITALIANA.**

66A	**82**	60c. red	2·30	14·00
67B	**82**	1l. blue	4·00	16·00
67aA	**82**	1l.25 blue	2·30	25·00

1926. Nos. 10/13 and 13a/16 optd with bars at top.

68	**1**	2c. on 1b. brown	37·00	65·00
69	**1**	5c. on 2b. green	23·00	38·00
70	**2**	10c. on 1a. pink	15·00	16·00
71	**2**	15c. on 2a. brown	15·00	16·00
72	**2**	20c. on 2a. brown	17·00	16·00
73	**2**	25c. on 2½a. blue	17·00	23·00
74	**2**	50c. on 5a. yellow	27·00	35·00
75	**2**	1l. on 10a. lilac	37·00	60·00

1926. St. Francis of Assisi stamps of Italy optd **SOMALIA ITALIANA** (76/8) or **Somalia** (79/80).

76	**83**	20c. green	3·50	17·00
77	**83**	40c. violet	3·50	17·00
78	**83**	60c. red	3·50	23·00
79	**83**	1l.25 blue	3·50	35·00
80	**83**	5l.+2l.50 green	8·00	70·00

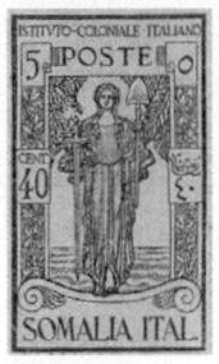

21

1926. Italian Colonial Institute.

81		5c.+5c. brown	1·20	8·00
82		10c.+5c. olive	1·20	8·00
83		20c.+5c. green	1·20	8·00
84	**21**	40c.+5c. red	1·20	8·00
85	**21**	60c.+5c. orange	1·20	8·00
86	**21**	1l.+5c. blue	1·20	14·00

1926. Italian stamps optd **SOMALIA ITALIANA**.

87	**31**	2c. brown	5·75	7·00
88	**37**	5c. green	5·75	7·00
89	**92**	7½c. brown	43·00	60·00
90	**37**	10c. pink	5·75	2·30
91	**39**	20c. purple	5·75	5·75
92	**34**	25c. green and light green	5·75	5·75
92a	**39**	30c. black	23·00	40·00
93	**91**	50c. grey and brown	43·00	17·00
94	**92**	50c. mauve	60·00	70·00
95	[illegible]	60c. orange	[illegible]	[illegible]
96	**34**	75c. red and carmine	£200	40·00
97	**34**	1l. brown and green	8·75	2·30
98	**34**	1l.25 blue & ultram	17·00	4·50
99	**91**	1l.75 brown	£130	29·00
100	**34**	2l. green and orange	43·00	21·00
101	**34**	2l.50 green and orange	43·00	31·00
102	**34**	5l. blue and pink	£120	60·00
103	**34**	10l. green and pink	£120	£120

1927. First National Defence issue of Italy (lira colours changed) optd **SOMALIA ITALIANA**.

104	**89**	40c.+20c. black & brown	3·50	35·00
105	-	60c.+30c. brown and red	3·50	35·00
106	-	1l.25+60c. black & blue	3·50	60·00
107	-	5l.+2l.50 black & green	7·00	80·00

1927. Centenary of Volta Stamps of Italy (colours changed) optd Somalia Italiana.

108	**90**	20c. violet	9·25	35·00
109	**90**	50c. orange	13·50	23·00
110	**90**	1l.25 blue	23·00	60·00

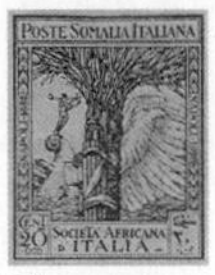

24

1928. 45th Anniv of Italian–African Society.

111	**24**	20c.+5c. green	3·50	11·50
112	**24**	30c.+5c. red	3·50	11·50
113	**24**	50c.+10c. violet	3·50	17·00
114	**24**	1l.25+20c. blue	3·50	23·00

1929. Second National Defence issue of Italy (colours changed) optd **SOMALIA ITALIANA**.

115	**89**	30c.+10c. black and red	5·75	23·00
116	-	50c.+20c. grey and lilac	5·75	23·00
117	-	1l.25+50c. blue & brown	8·75	46·00
118	-	5l.+2l. black and green	8·75	70·00

1929. Montecassino Abbey stamps of Italy (colours changed) optd **Somalia Italiana** (10l.) or **SOMALIA ITALIANA** (others).

119	**104**	20c. green	8·00	18·00
120	-	25c. red	8·00	18·00
121	-	50c.+10c. red	8·00	23·00
122	-	75c.+15c. brown	8·00	23·00
123	**104**	1l.25+25c. purple	16·00	40·00
124	-	5l.+1l. blue	16·00	46·00
125	-	10l.+2l. brown	16·00	70·00

1930. Royal Wedding stamps of Italy (colours changed) optd **SOMALIA ITALIANA**.

126	**109**	20c. green	2·30	5·75
127	**109**	50c.+10c. red	1·70	9·25
128	**109**	1l.25+25c. red	1·70	21·00

1930. Ferrucci stamps of Italy (colours changed) optd **SOMALIA ITALIANA.**

129	**114**	20c. violet	4·00	4·50
130	-	25c. green (No. 283)	4·00	4·50
131	-	50c. black (No. 284)	4·00	11·50
132	-	1l.25 blue (No. 285)	4·00	17·00
133	-	5l.+2l. red (No. 286)	11·50	32·00

1930. Third National Defence issue of Italy (colours changed) optd **SOMALIA ITALIANA**.

134	**89**	30c.+10c. green & dp grn	29·00	35·00
135	-	50c.+10c. purple & green	29·00	50·00
136	-	1l.25+30c. brown and deep brown	29·00	70·00
137	-	5l.+1l.50 green and blue	£100	£160

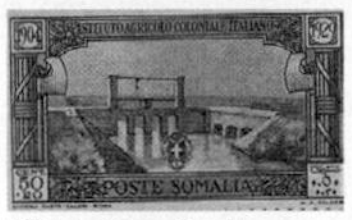

29 Irrigation Canal

1930. 25th Anniv (1929) of Colonial Agricultural Institute.

138	**29**	50c.+20c. brown	4·00	21·00
139	**29**	1l.25+20c. blue	4·00	21·00
140	**29**	1l.75+20c. green	4·00	23·00
141	**29**	2l.55+50c. violet	8·75	40·00
142	**29**	5l.+1l. red	8·75	60·00

1930. Bimillenary of Virgil stamps of Italy (colours changed) optd **SOMALIA**.

143		15c. grey	1·20	7·00
144		20c. brown	1·20	3·50
145		25c. green	1·20	3·50
146		30c. brown	1·20	3·50
147		50c. purple	1·20	3·50
148		75c. red	1·20	4·50
149		1l.25 blue	1·20	9·25
150		5l.+1l.50 purple	8·75	46·00
151		10l.+2l.50 brown	8·75	70·00

1931. Stamps of Italy optd **SOMALIA ITALIANA**.

152	-	25c. green (No. 244)	19·00	25·00
153	**103**	50c. violet	19·00	7·00

1931. St. Antony of Padua stamps of Italy optd **Somalia** (75c., 5l.) or **SOMALIA** (others).

154	**121**	20c. brown	3·00	16·00
155	-	25c. green	3·00	7·00
156	-	30c. brown	3·00	7·00
157	-	50c. purple	3·00	7·00
158	-	75c. grey	3·00	18·00
159	-	1l.25 blue	3·00	37·00
160	-	5l.+2l.50 brown	8·75	80·00

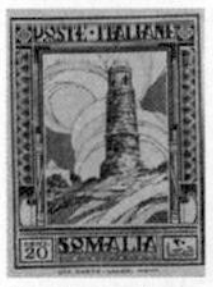

32 Tower at Mnara-Ciromo

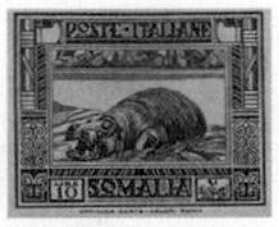

33 Hippopotamus

1932

161a		5c. brown	3·00	1·20
162a		7½c. violet	3·00	35·00
163a		10c. black	3·00	1·20
164		15c. green	8·75	2·30
165a	**32**	20c. red	3·00	1·20
166a	**32**	25c. green	3·00	1·20
167a	**32**	30c. brown	5·75	1·20
168	-	35c. blue	11·50	23·00
169a	-	50c. violet	29·00	1·20
170	-	75c. red	11·50	1·20
171	-	1l.25 blue	23·00	1·20
172	-	1l.75 red	17·00	1·20
173	-	2l. red	8·75	70
174	-	2l.55 blue	50·00	£100
175a	-	5l. red	23·00	5·75
176	**33**	10l. violet	46·00	35·00
177	-	20l. green	£140	£130
178	-	25l. blue	£140	£200

DESIGNS—HORIZ: 5, 7½, 10, 15c. Francesco Crispi Lighthouse, Cape Guardafui; 35, 50, 75c. Governor's Residence, Mogadishu; 25l. Lioness. VERT: 1l.25, 1l.75, 2l. Termitarium (ant-hill); 2l.55, 5l. Ostrich; 20l. Lesser kudu.

1934. Honouring the Duke of the Abruzzi. Stamps of 1932 (some colours changed) optd **ONORANZE AL DUCA DEGLI ABRUZZI.**

179		10c. brown	12·50	23·00
180	**32**	25c. green	12·50	23·00
181	-	50c. purple	12·50	23·00
182	-	1l.25 blue	12·50	23·00
183	-	5l. black	12·50	23·00
184	**33**	10l. red	12·50	40·00
185	-	20l. blue	12·50	40·00
186	-	25l. green	12·50	40·00

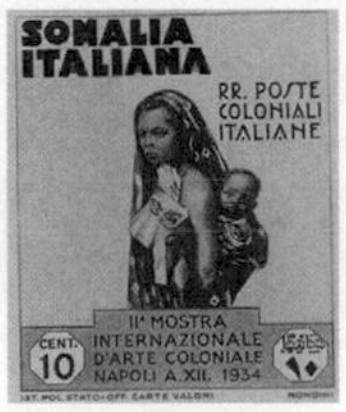

35 Woman and Child

1934. Second Int Colonial Exhibition, Naples.

187	**35**	5c. green & brown (postage)	7·00	18·00
188	**35**	10c. brown and black	7·00	18·00
189	**35**	20c. red and blue	7·00	18·00
190	**35**	50c. violet and brown	7·00	18·00
191	**35**	60c. brown and slate	7·00	25·00
192	**35**	1l.25 blue and green	7·00	38·00
193	-	25c. blue and orange (air)	7·00	18·00
194	-	50c. green and blue	7·00	18·00
195	-	75c. brown and orange	7·00	18·00
196	-	80c. brown and green	7·00	18·00
197	-	1l. red and green	7·00	25·00
198	-	2l. blue and brown	7·00	38·00

DESIGNS: 25c. to 75c. Caproni Ca 101 airplane over River Juba; 80c. to 2l. Cheetahs watching Caproni Ca 101 airplane.

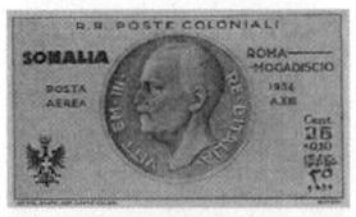

36

1934. Air. Rome–Mogadishu Flight.

199	**36**	25c.+10c. green	8·75	17·00
200	**36**	50c.+10c. brown	8·75	17·00
201	**36**	75c.+15c. red	8·75	17·00
202	**36**	80c.+15c. black	8·75	17·00
203	**36**	1l.+20c. brown	8·75	17·00
204	**36**	2l.+20c. blue	8·75	17·00
205	**36**	3l.+25c. violet	35·00	90·00
206	**36**	5l.+25c. red	35·00	90·00
207	**36**	10l.+30c. purple	35·00	90·00
208	**36**	25l.+2l. green	35·00	90·00

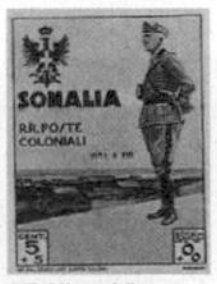

37 King Victor Emmanuel III

1934. King of Italy's Visit to Italian Somaliland.

209	**37**	5c.+5c. black	5·75	29·00
210	**37**	7½c.+7½c. purple	5·75	29·00
211	**37**	15c.+10c. green	5·75	29·00
212	**37**	20c.+10c. red	5·75	29·00
213	**37**	25c.+10c. green	5·75	29·00
214	**37**	30c.+10c. brown	5·75	29·00
215	**37**	50c.+10c. violet	5·75	29·00
216	**37**	75c.+15c. red	5·75	29·00
217	**37**	1l.25+15c. blue	5·75	29·00
218	**37**	1l.75+25c. orange	5·75	29·00
219	**37**	2l.75+25c. blue	40·00	£120
220	**37**	5l.+1l. purple	40·00	£120
221	**37**	10l.+1l.80 brown	40·00	£120
222	-	25l.+2l.75 sepia & brn	£275	£450

DESIGN—36×44 mm: 25l. King Victor Emmanuel III on horseback.

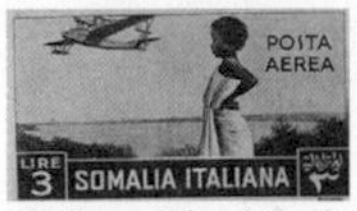

38a Native Girl and Macchi Castoldi MC-94 Flying Boat

1936. Air.

223		25c. green	3·50	11·50
224		50c. brown	1·20	30
225		60c. orange	5·75	14·00
226		75c. brown	3·50	3·50
227	**38a**	1l. blue	1·20	30
228	-	1l.50 violet	3·00	1·20
229	-	2l. blue	9·25	2·30
230	**38a**	3l. red	31·00	23·00
231	-	5l. green	35·00	23·00
232	-	10l. red	35·00	35·00

DESIGNS: 25c., 1l.50, Banana trees; 50c., 2l. Native woman in cotton plantation; 60c., 5l. Orchard; 75c., 10l. Native women harvesting.

ITALIAN TRUST TERRITORY

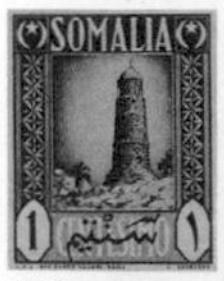
40 Tower at Mnara-Ciromo

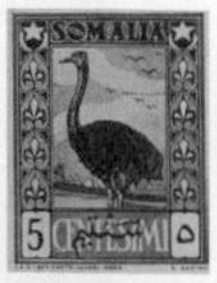
41 Ostrich

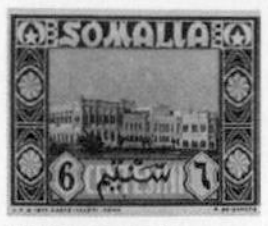
42 Governor's Residence, Mogadishu

1950

233	**40**	1c. black	5·75	9·25
234	**41**	5c. red	2·30	65
235	**42**	6c. violet	3·00	5·25
236	**40**	8c. green	3·00	5·25
237	**42**	10c. green	30	65
238	**41**	20c. green	30	65
239	**40**	35c. red	8·00	9·25
240	**42**	55c. blue	5·75	1·20
241	**41**	60c. violet	5·75	1·20
242	**40**	65c. brown	11·50	5·75
243	**42**	1s. orange	17·00	7·00

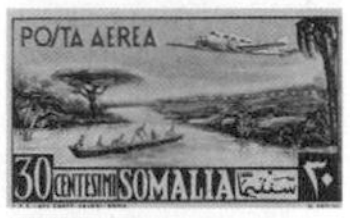
43 River Scene

1950. Air.

244	**43**	30c. brown	11·50	3·50
245	**43**	45c. red	11·50	3·50
246	**43**	65c. violet	11·50	3·50
247	**43**	70c. blue	11·50	3·50
248	**43**	90c. brown	11·50	4·50
249	**43**	1s. purple	11·50	7·00
250	**43**	1s.35 violet	17·00	7·00
251	**43**	1s.50 green	17·00	7·00
252	**43**	3s. blue	80·00	46·00
253	**43**	5s. brown	80·00	46·00
254	**43**	10s. orange	90·00	35·00

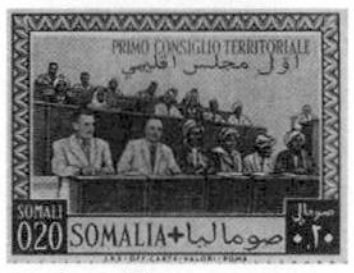
44 Councillors

1951. First Territorial Council.

255	**44**	20c. brown & grn (postage)	4·50	4·50
256	**44**	55c. violet and brown	12·50	12·50
257	-	1s. blue and violet (air)	4·50	4·50
258	-	1s.50 brown and green	12·50	12·50

DESIGN—VERT: 1s., 1s.50, Flags and Savoia Marchetti S.M.95C airliner over Mogadiscio.

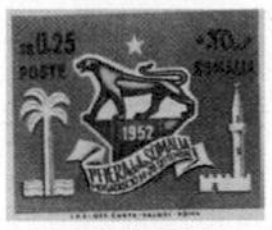
45 Symbol of Fair

1952. First Somali Fair, Mogadiscio.

259	**45**	25c. brown & red (postage)	3·00	3·50
260	**45**	55c. brown and blue	4·00	4·50
261	-	1s.20 blue and bistre (air)	4·50	7·00

DESIGN: 1s.20, Palm tree, Douglas DC-4 airliner and minaret.

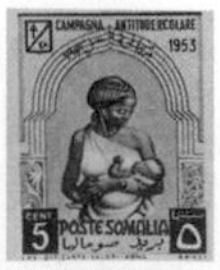
46 Mother and Baby

1953. Anti-tuberculosis Campaign.

262	**46**	5c. brown & violet (postage)	70	2·30
263	**46**	25c. brown and red	70	2·30
264	**46**	50c. brown and blue	1·50	3·50
265	**46**	1s.20 brown and green (air)	3·50	4·50

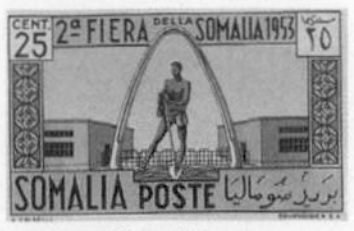
47 Somali and Entrance to Fair

1953. Second Somali Fair, Mogadiscio.

266	**47**	25c. green & grey (postage)	90	1·20
267	**47**	60c. blue and grey	1·70	2·30
268	-	1s.20 red and pink (air)	1·40	1·40
269	-	1s.50 brown and buff	1·70	2·20

DESIGN: 1s.20, 1s.50, Palm, airplane and entrance.

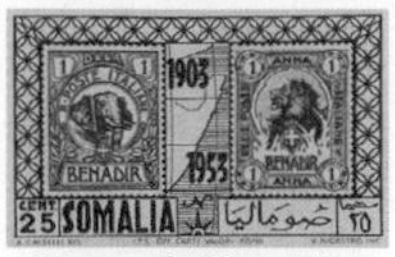
48 Stamps of 1903 and Map

1953. 50th Anniv of First Stamps of Italian Somaliland. (a) Postage.

270	**48**	25c. brown, red and lake	90	1·30
271	**48**	35c. brown, red and green	90	1·30
272	**48**	60c. brown, red and orange	1·50	3·25

(b) Air. Aeroplane on Map.

273		60c. brown, red & chestnut	1·40	1·70
274		1s. brown, red and black	4·00	4·50

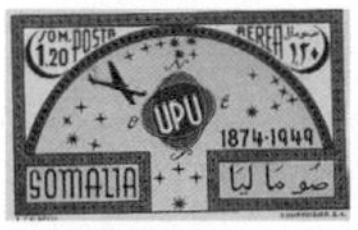
49 Airplane and Constellations

1953. Air. 75th Anniv of U.P.U.

275	**49**	1s.20 red and buff	1·50	3·50
276	**49**	1s.50 brown and buff	4·00	3·50
277	**49**	2s. green and blue	4·00	3·50

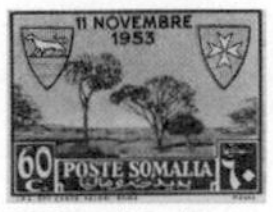
50 Somali Bush Country

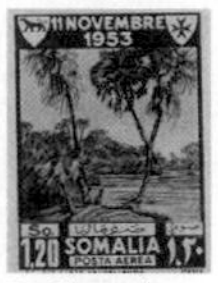
51 Alexander Island and River Juba

1954. Leprosy Relief Convention.

278	**50**	25c. green & blue (postage)	1·30	2·30
279	**50**	60c. sepia and brown	1·30	3·00
280	**51**	1s.20 brown & green (air)	1·70	2·30
281	**51**	2s. purple and red	3·00	3·00

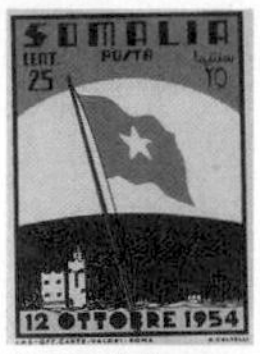
52 Somali Flag

1954. Institution of Somali Flag.

282	**52**	25c. multicoloured (postage)	65	70
283	**52**	1s.20 multicoloured (air)	1·40	1·50

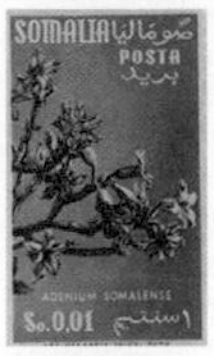
52a "Adenium somalense"

1955. Floral Designs.

284	**52a**	1c. red, black and blue	30	60
285	-	5c. mauve, green and blue	30	60
288	-	60c. red, green and black	30	65
289	-	1s. yellow, green & purple	65	1·30
290	-	1s.20 yellow, green & brn	65	2·40
290c	-	10c. yellow, green & lilac	35	35
290d	-	15c. multicoloured	40	40
290e	-	25c. yellow, green & brn	35	35
290f	-	50c. multicoloured	60	60

FLOWERS: 5c. Blood lily; 10c. "Grinum scabrum"; 15c. Baobab; 25c. "Poinciana elata"; 50c. Glory lily; 60c. "Calatropis procera"; 1s. Sea lily; 1s.20, "Sesamothamnus bussernus".

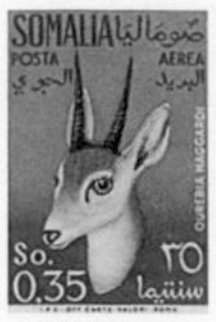
54 Oribi

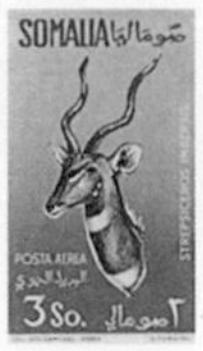
54a Lesser Kudu

1955. Air. Antelopes. (a) As T **54**. Heads in black and orange.

291	**54**	35c. green	30	1·20
292	-	45c. violet	5·75	2·30
293	-	50c. violet	1·20	1·70
294	-	75c. red	4·50	4·50
295	-	1s.20 green	4·50	7·00
296	-	1s.50 blue	9·25	9·25

ANTELOPES: 45c. Salt's dik-dik; 50c. Speke's gazelle; 75c. Gerenuk; 1s.20, Soemmering's gazelle; 1s.50, Waterbuck.

(b) As T **54a**.

296a	**54a**	3s. purple and brown	3·50	3·50
296b	-	5s. yellow and black	3·50	3·50

DESIGN: 5s. Hunter's hartebeest.

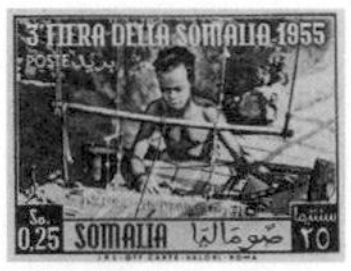
55 Native Weaver

1955. Third Somali Fair.

297	**55**	25c. brown (postage)	1·20	1·80
298	-	30c. green	1·20	1·80
299	-	45c. brown and orange (air)	1·00	1·80
300	-	1s.20 blue and pink	1·20	1·80

DESIGNS: 30c. Cattle fording river; 45c. Camels around well; 1s.20, Native woman at well.

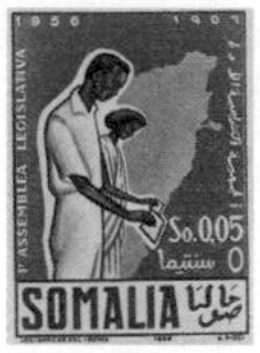
56 Voters and Map

1956. First Legislative Assembly.

301	**56**	5c. brown & green (postage)	30	45
302	**56**	10c. sepia and brown	30	45
303	**56**	25c. brown and red	30	45
304	**56**	60c. brown and blue (air)	1·40	1·00
305	**56**	1s.20 brown and orange	1·40	1·20

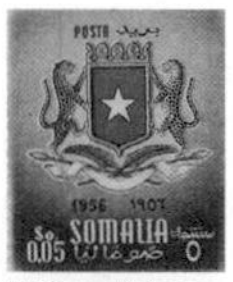
57 Somali Arms

1957. Inauguration of National Emblem. Arms in blue and brown.

306	**57**	5c. brown (postage)	30	1·20
307	**57**	25c. red	30	1·20
308	**57**	60c. violet	30	1·60
309	**57**	45c. blue (air)	1·40	1·50
310	**57**	1s.20 green	1·50	1·60

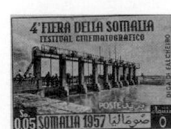

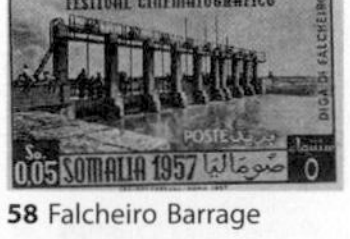
58 Falcheiro Barrage

1957. Fourth Somali Fair.

311	**58**	5c. lilac & brown (postage)	30	45
312	-	10c. green and bistre	30	50
313	-	25c. blue and red	30	1·20
314	-	60c. brown and blue (air)	1·60	1·40
315	-	1s.20 black and red	1·60	1·40

DESIGNS—HORIZ: 10c. Juba River bridge; 25c. Silos at Margherita; 60c. Irrigation canal. VERT: 1s.20, Oil well.

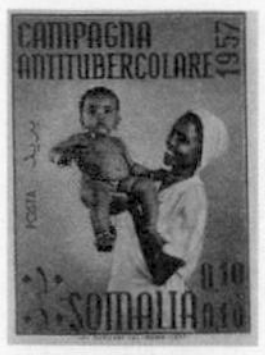
59 Somali Nurse with Baby

1957. Tuberculosis Relief Campaign.

316	**59**	10c.+10c. brown and red (postage)	90	90
317	**59**	25c.+10c. brown & green	90	90
318	**59**	55c.+20c. brown and blue (air)	1·50	1·50
319	**59**	1s.20c.+20c. brown and violet	1·50	1·50

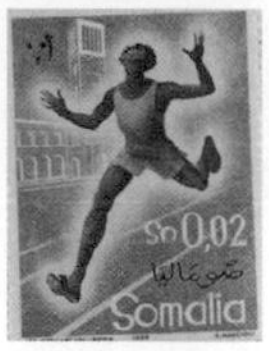
60 Track Running

1958. Sports.

320	**60**	2c. lilac (postage)	30	30
321	-	4c. green (Football)	30	30
322	-	5c. red (Discus)	30	30
323	-	6c. black (Motor-cycling)	30	30
324	-	8c. blue (Fencing)	30	30
325	-	10c. orange (Archery)	30	30
326	-	25c. green (Boxing)	30	30
327	-	60c. brown (Running) (air)	30	30
328	-	1s.20 blue (Cycling)	30	30
329	-	1s.50 red (Basketball)	30	30

The 4, 6, 10 and 25c. are horiz.

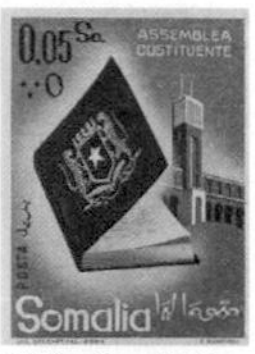
61 The Constitution and Assembly Building, Mogadishu

1959. Opening of Constituent Assembly. Inscr "ASSEMBLEA CONSTITUENTE".

330	**61**	5c. blue and green (postage)	45	45
331	**61**	25c. blue and brown	45	45
332	-	1s.20 blue and brown (air)	1·50	1·50
333	-	1s.50 blue and green	1·50	1·50
MS333a		150×200 mm. Nos. 330/3 (sold at 4s.50)	7·50	11·50

DESIGNS—HORIZ: 1s.20, 1s.50, Police bugler.

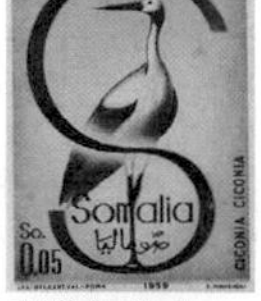
62 White Stork

1959. Somali Water Birds.

334	**62**	5c. black, red and yellow (postage)	70	30
335	-	10c. red, yellow and brown	70	30
336	-	15c. black and orange	70	30
337	-	25c. black, orange and red	70	30
338	-	1s.20 black, red and violet (air)	1·20	65
339	-	2s. red and blue	1·30	65

BIRDS—VERT: 10c. Saddle-bill stork; 15c. Sacred ibis; 25c. Pink-backed pelicans. HORIZ: 1s.20, Marabou stork; 2s. Great egret.

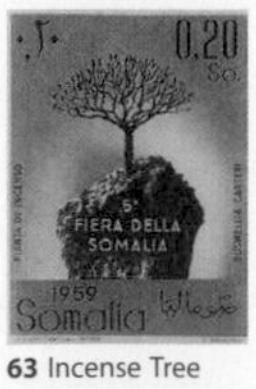
63 Incense Tree

1959. Fifth Somali Fair.

340	**63**	20c. black & orqe (postage)	35	35
341	-	60c. black, red and orange	45	45
342	-	1s.20 black and red (air)	1·50	1·50
343	-	2s. black, brown and blue	1·50	1·50

DESIGNS—VERT: 60c. Somali child with incense-burner. HORIZ: 1s.20, Ancient Egyptian transport of incense; 2s. Incense-burner and Mogadishu Harbour.

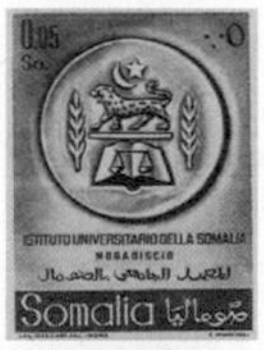

64 Institute Badge

1960. Opening of University Institute of Somalia, Mogadishu.

344	**64**	5c. red and brown (postage)	30	45
345	-	50c. brown and blue	30	45
346	-	80c. black and red	45	60
347	-	45c. brown, black and green (air)	40	45
348	-	1s.20 blue, black & lt blue	90	1·50

DESIGNS—HORIZ: 45c., 1s.20, Institute buildings; 50c. Map of Africa. VERT: 80c. Institute emblem.

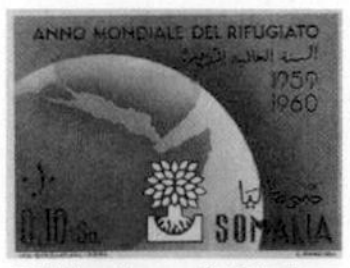

65 "The Horn of Africa"

1960. World Refugee Year.

349	**65**	10c. green, black and brown (postage)	45	45
350	-	60c. brown, ochre and black	45	45
351	-	80c. green, black and pink	60	60
352	-	1s.50 red, blue and green (air)	1·70	1·80

DESIGNS—HORIZ: 60c. Similar to Type **65**. VERT: 80c. Palm; 1s.50, White stork.

REPUBLIC

1960. Optd **Somaliland Independence 26 June 1960**.

353	10c. yellow, green and lilac (No. 290c) (postage)	30·00	26·00
354	50c. black, orange and violet (No. 293) (air)	65·00	55·00
355	1s.20 blk, orge & turq (No. 295)	45·00	40·00

Nos. 353/5 were only issued in the former British protectorate, which united with Somalia when the latter became independent on 1 July 1960.

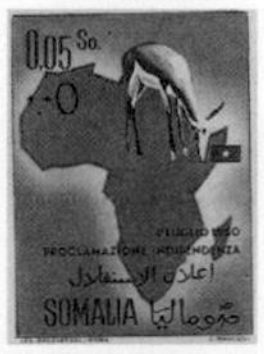

67 Gazelle and Map of Africa

1960. Proclamation of Independence.

356	**67**	5c. brn, bl & lilac (postage)	25	20
357	-	25c. blue	65	55
358	-	1s. brown, red & green (air)	1·30	1·10
359	-	1s.80 blue and orange	4·00	3·50

DESIGNS—VERT: 25c. U.N. Flag and Headquarters Building. HORIZ: 1s. Chamber of Deputies, Montecitorio Palace, Rome; 1s.80, Somali Flag.

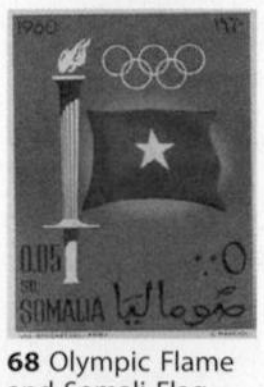

68 Olympic Flame and Somali Flag

1960. Olympic Games. Inscr "1960".

360	**68**	5c. blue and green (postage)	15	10
361	-	10c. blue and yellow	40	35
362	-	45c. blue and lilac (air)	1·40	1·20
363	-	1s.80 blue and red	2·75	2·40

DESIGNS: 10c. Relay race; 45c. Runner breasting tape; 1s.80, Runner.

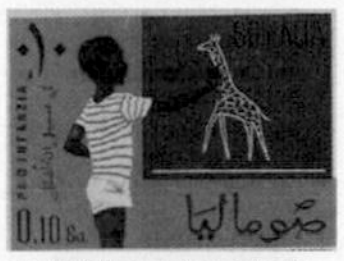
69 Child drawing Giraffe

1960. Child Welfare. Inscr "PRO INFANZIA".

364	**69**	10c. black, brown and green (postage)	50	45
365	-	15c. black, light green & red	65	55
366	-	25c. brown, black & yellow	75	65
367	-	3s. orange, black, blue and green (air)	5·00	4·50

ANIMALS: 15c. Common zebra; 25c. Black rhinoceros; 3s. Leopard.

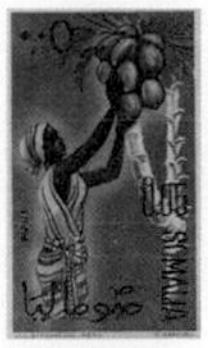

70 Girl harvesting Papaws

1961. Multicoloured. Designs each show a girl harvesting.

368	5c. Type **70**	10	10
369	10c. Girl harvesting durra	15	10
370	20c. Cotton	20	15
371	25c. Sesame	25	20
372	40c. Sugar cane	50	45
373	50c. Bananas	65	55
374	75c. Groundnuts (horiz)	1·30	1·10
375	80c. Grapefruit (horiz)	4·25	3·75

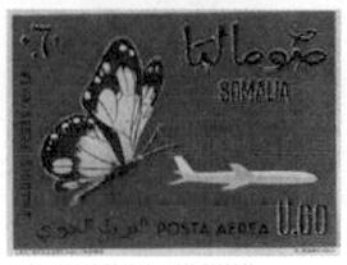

71 Amauris hyalites

1961. Air. Butterflies. Multicoloured.

376	60c. Type **71**	50	45
377	90c. "Euryphura chalcis"	65	55
378	1s. "Papilio lormieri"	3·25	55
379	1s.80 "Druryia antimachus"	1·80	1·50
380	3s. "Danaus formosa"	3·00	2·75
381	5s. "Papilio phorcas"	10·00	4·50
382	10s. "Charaxes cynthia"	16·00	7·25

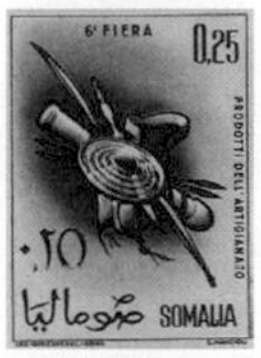

72 Shield, Bow and Arrow, Quiver and Dagger

1961. Sixth Somali Trade Fair.

383	**72**	25c. yellow, black and red (postage)	15	10
384	-	45c. yellow, black and green	40	35
385	-	1s. yellow, black & bl (air)	65	55
386	-	1s.80 brown, black & yell	3·50	3·00

DESIGNS—Handicrafts—VERT: 45c. "Tungi" wooden vase and pottery. HORIZ: 1s. National head-dress, support and comb; 1s.80, Statuettes of camel and man, and balancing novelty.

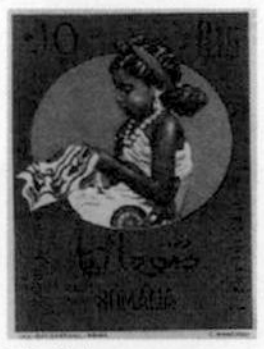

73 Girl embroidering

1962. Child Welfare. Tropical Fish. Inscr "PRO INFANZIA". Multicoloured.

387	15c. Type **73** (postage)	25	20
388	25c. Semicircle angelfish	50	45
389	40c. Dragon wrasse	1·00	90
390	2s.70 Emperor snapper (air)	5·00	4·50

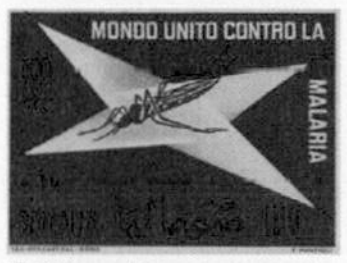

74 Mosquito

1962. Malaria Eradication. Inscr "MONDO UNITO CONTRO LA MALARIA".

391	**74**	10c. green and red (postage)	40	35
392	-	25c. brown and mauve	75	65
393	-	1s. brown and black (air)	1·40	1·20
394	-	1s.80 green and black	4·25	3·75

DESIGNS—VERT: 25c. Insecticide sprayer; 1s., 1s.80, Campaign emblem and mosquitoes.

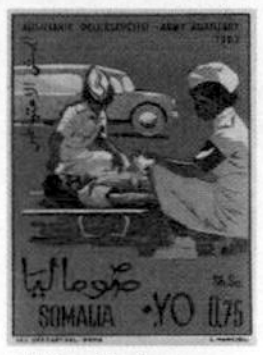

75 Auxiliaries tending Casualty

1963. Women's Auxiliary Forces Formation. Multicoloured.

395	5c. Policewoman (postage)	15	10
396	10c. Army auxiliary	25	20
397	25c. Policewomen with patrol car	40	35
398	75c. Type **75**	90	75
399	1s. Policewomen marching with flag (air)	1·40	1·20
400	1s.80 Army auxiliaries at attention with flag	4·25	3·75

The 5c., 10c. and 25c. are horiz.

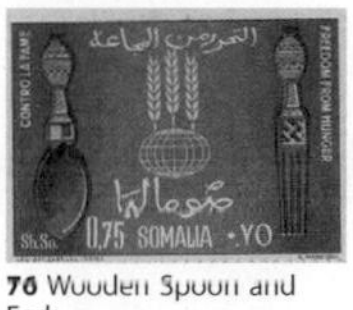

76 Wooden Spoon and Fork

1963. Freedom from Hunger.

401	**76**	75c. brown & grn (postage)	1·00	90
402	-	1s. multicoloured (air)	2·75	2·40

DESIGN: 1s. Sower.

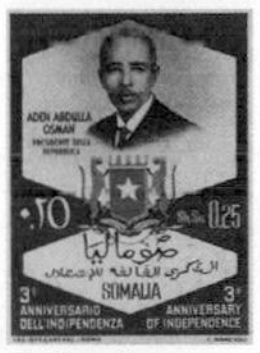

77 Pres. Osman and Arms

1963. Third Anniv of Independence. Arms in blue and yellow.

403	**77**	25c. sepia & blue (postage)	65	55
404	**77**	1s. sepia and red (air)	1·00	90
405	**77**	1s.80 sepia and green	2·00	1·80

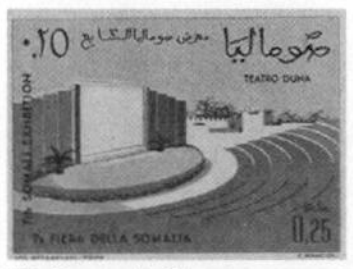

78 Open-air Theatre

1963. Seventh Somali Fair.

406	**78**	25c. green (postage)	65	55
407	-	55c. red	1·30	1·10
408	-	1s.80 blue (air)	3·25	2·75

DESIGNS: 55c. African Trade Building; 1s.80, Government Pavilion.

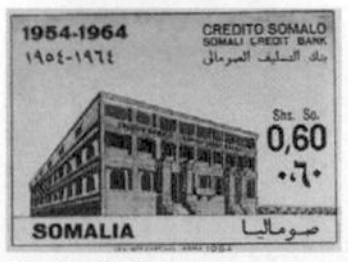

79 Credit Bank, Mogadishu

1964. Tenth Anniv of Somali Credit Bank. Multicoloured.

409	60c. Type **79** (postage)	1·40	1·20
410	1s. Map of Somalia and globe (air)	2·75	2·40
411	1s.80 Bank emblem	4·25	3·75

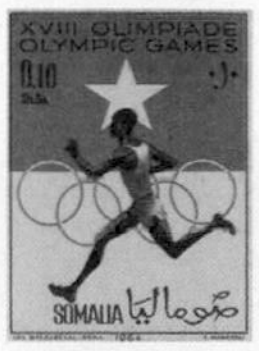

80 Running

1964. Olympic Games, Tokyo. Each sepia, brown and blue.

412	10c. Type **80** (postage)	15	10
413	25c. High-jumping	40	35
414	90c. Diving (air)	1·40	1·20
415	1s.80 Footballer	4·25	3·75
MS415a	170×138 mm. Nos. 412/15	50·00	44·00

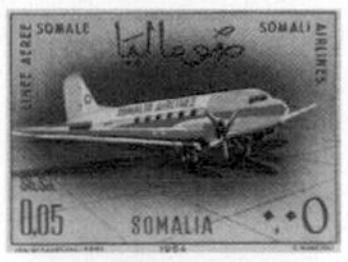

81 Douglas DC-3 Airliner

1964. Inauguration of Somali Airlines.

416	**81**	5c. blue and red (postage)	75	65
417	-	20c. blue and orange	1·50	1·30
418	-	1s. ochre and green (air)	4·50	4·00
419	-	1s.80 blue and black	8·25	7·25

DESIGNS: 20c. Passengers disembarking from DC-3; DC-3 in flight over: 1s. African elephants; 1s.80, Mogadishu.

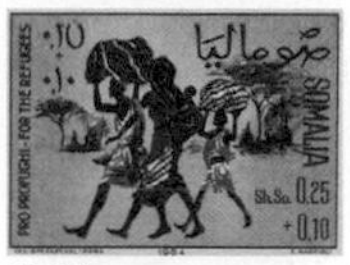

82 Refugees

1964. Somali Refugees Fund.

420	**82**	25c.+10c. red and blue (postage)	90	75
421	-	75c.+20c. purple, black and red (air)	1·40	1·20
422		1s.80+50c. green, black and bistre	4·00	3·50

DESIGNS—HORIZ: 75c. [illegible] VERT: 1s.80, [illegible] with child refugees.

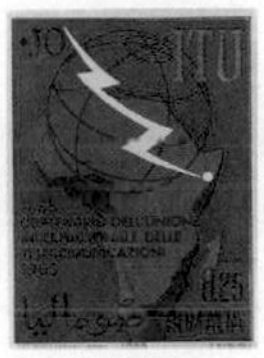

83 I.T.U. Emblem on Map of Africa

1965. I.T.U. Centenary.

423	**83**	25c. blue & orange (postage)	75	65
424	**83**	1s. black and green (air)	1·30	1·10
425	**83**	1s.80 brown and mauve	3·50	3·00

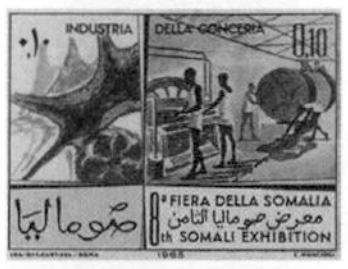

84 Tanning

1965. Somali Industries.

426	**84**	10c. sepia and buff (postage)	25	20
427	-	25c. sepia and pink	40	35
428	-	35c. sepia and blue	65	55
429	-	1s.50 sepia and green (air)	1·90	1·70
430	-	2s. sepia and mauve	4·00	3·50

DESIGNS: 25c. Meat processing and canning; 35c. Fish processing and canning; 1s.50, Sugar—cutting cane and refining; 2s. Dairying—milking and bottling.

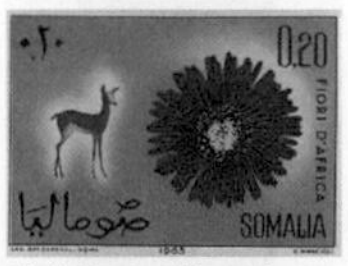

85 Hottentot Fig and Gazelle

1965. Somali Flora and Fauna. Multicoloured.

431	20c. Type **85**	15	10
432	60c. African tulips and giraffes	40	35
433	1s. White lotus and greater flamingoes	1·00	90
434	1s.30 Pervincia and ostriches	2·30	2·00

435		1s.80 Bignonia and common zebras	4·50	3·75

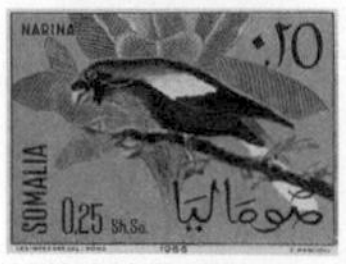

86 Narina's Trogon

1966. Somali Birds. Multicoloured.

436		25c. Type **86**	40	35
437		35c. Bateleur (vert)	50	45
438		50c. Ruppell's griffon	65	55
439		1s.30 European roller	3·00	2·75
440		2s. Vulturine guineafowl (vert)	5·00	4·50

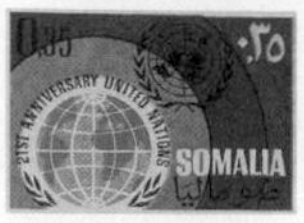

87 Globe and U.N. Emblem

1966. 21st Anniv of U.N.O. Multicoloured.

441		35c. Type **87**	65	55
442		1s. Map of Africa and U.N. emblem	90	75
443		1s.50 Map of Somalia and U.N. emblem	1·50	1·30

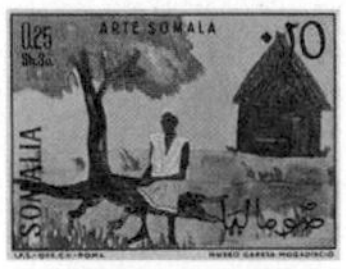

88 Woman sitting on Crocodile

1966. Somali Art. Showing Paintings from Garesa Museum, Mogadishu. Multicoloured.

444		25c. Type **88**	30	30
445		1s. Woman and warrior	50	45
446		1s.50 Boy leading camel	90	75
447		2s. Women pounding grain	2·40	2·10

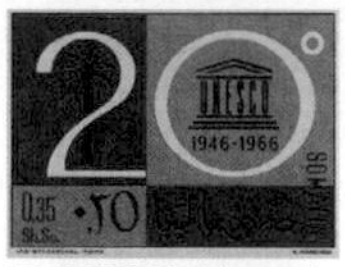

89 UNESCO Emblem and Palm

1966. 20th Anniv of UNESCO.

448	**89**	35c. black, red and grey	15	10
449	**89**	1s. black, green and yellow	40	35
450	**89**	1s.80 black, blue and red	2·75	2·40

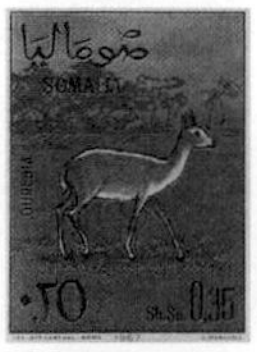

90 Oribi

1967. Antelopes.

451	**90**	35c. ochre, black and blue	20	15
452	-	60c. brown, black & orange	40	35
453	-	1s. bistre, black and red	65	55
454	-	1s.80 ochre, black & green	4·00	3·50

ANTELOPES: 60c. Kirk's dik-dik; 1s. Gerenuk gazelle; 1s.80, Soemmering's gazelle.

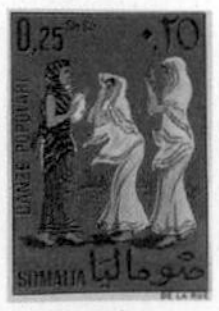

91 Somali Dancers

1967. "Popular Dances". Designs showing dancers.

455	**91**	25c. multicoloured	15	10
456	-	50c. multicoloured	25	20
457	-	1s.30 multicoloured	50	45
458	-	2s. multicoloured	3·25	2·75

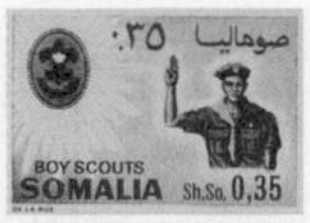

92 Badge and Scout Saluting

1967. World Scout Jamboree. Multicoloured.

459		35c. Type **92**	25	20
460		50c. Scouts and flags	40	35
461		1s. Camp scene	90	75
462		1s.80 Jamboree emblem	3·25	2·75

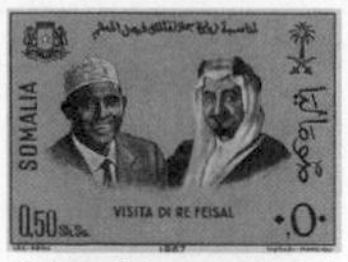

93 Pres. Schermarche and King Faisal

1967. Visit of King Faisal of Saudi Arabia.

463	**93**	50c. black & blue (postage)	40	35
464	-	1s. multicoloured	90	75
465	-	1s.80 multicoloured (air)	2·75	2·40

DESIGNS: 1s. Somali and Saudi Arabian flags; 1s.80, Kaaba, Mecca and portraits as Type **93**.

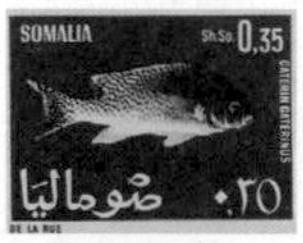

94 Black-spotted Sweetlips

1967. Fish. Multicoloured.

466		35c. Type **94**	40	35
467		50c. Blue-cheeked butterflyfish	65	55
468		1s. Catalufa	2·00	1·80
469		1s.80 Summana grouper	3·75	3·25

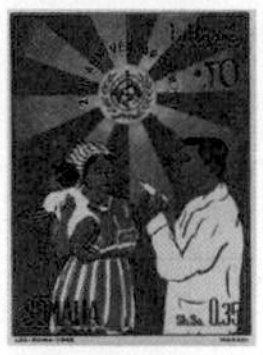

95 Inoculation

1968. 20th Anniv of W.H.O.

470	**95**	35c. multicoloured	15	10
471	-	1s. black, brown and green	50	45
472	-	1s.80 black brown & orge	2·30	2·00

DESIGNS: 1s. Chest examination; 1s.80, Heart examination.

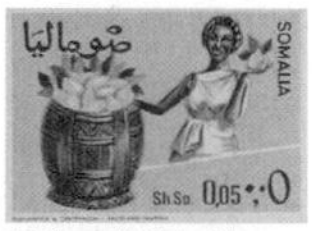

96 Somali Girl with Lemons

1968. Agricultural Produce. Multicoloured.

473		5c. Type **96**	15	10
474		10c. Oranges	20	15
475		25c. Coconuts	25	20
476		35c. Papaws	30	30
477		40c. Mangoes	40	35
478		50c. Grapefruit	45	40
479		1s. Bananas	1·40	1·20
480		1s.30 Cotton bolls	4·00	3·50

Each design includes a Somali girl.

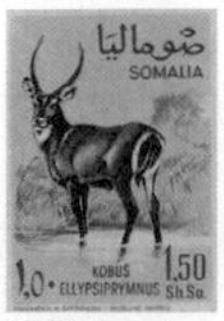

97 Waterbuck

1968. Somali Antelopes. Multicoloured.

481		1s.50 Type **97**	65	55
482		1s.80 Speke's gazelle	75	65
483		2s. Lesser kudu	2·10	1·90
484		5s. Hunter's hartebeest	4·25	3·75
485		10s. Dibatag gazelle	12·50	11·00

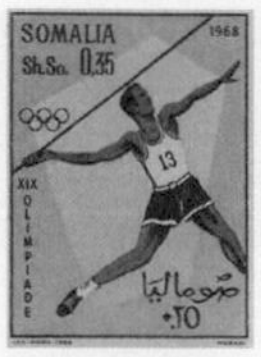

98 Throwing the Javelin

1968. Olympic Games, Mexico.

486	**98**	35c. black, brown & lemon	15	10
487	-	50c. black, brown and red	25	20
488	-	80c. black, brown & purple	40	35
489	-	1s.50 black, brown & green	3·00	2·50
MS490		163×182 mm. Nos. 486/9	10·50	9·25

DESIGNS: 50c. Running; 80c. Pole-vaulting; 1s.50, Basketball.

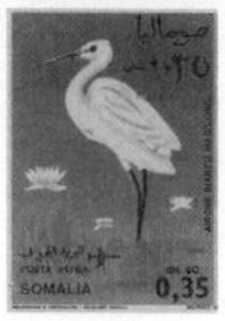

99 Great Egret

1968. Air. Birds. Multicoloured.

491		35c. Type **99**	50	45
492		1s. Carmine bee eater	75	65
493		1s.30 Yellow-bellied green pigeon	1·80	1·50
494		1s.80 Paradise whydah	4·50	3·75

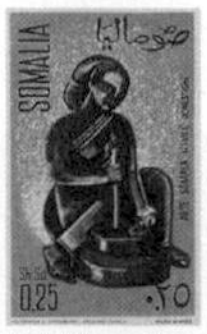

100 "Pounding Meal"

1968. Somali Art.

495	**100**	25c. brown, black and lilac	25	20
496	-	35c. brown, black and red	40	35
497	-	2s.80 brown, black & grn	3·00	2·75

DESIGNS (wood-carvings): 35c. "Preparing food"; 2s.80, "Rug-making".

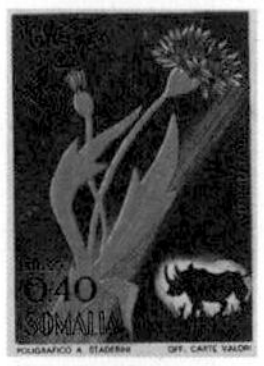

101 Cornflower

1969. Flowers. Multicoloured.

498		40c. Type **101**	15	10
499		80c. Sunflower	25	20
500		1s. Oleander	1·00	90
501		1s.80 Chrysanthemum	4·50	4·00

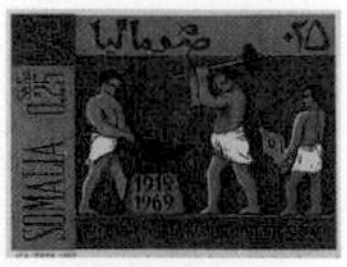

102 Workers at Anvil

1969. 50th Anniv of I.L.O. Multicoloured.

502		25c. Type **102**	25	20
503		1s. Ploughing with oxen	45	40
504		1s.80 Drawing water for irrigation	2·75	2·40

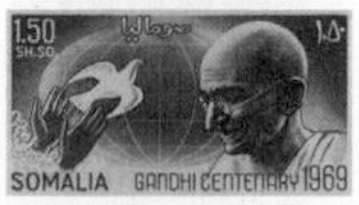

103 Gandhi, and Hands releasing Dove

1969. Birth Centenary of Mahatma Gandhi.

505	-	35c. purple	65	55
506	**103**	1s.50 orange	1·00	90
507	-	1s.80 brown	6·00	5·25

DESIGNS—VERT—(Size 25½×36 mm): 35c. Mahatma Gandhi; 1s.80, Gandhi seated.

SOMALI DEMOCRATIC REPUBLIC

An issue for the "Apollo 11" Moon Landing was prepared in 1970, but not issued.

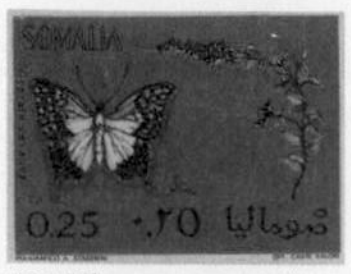

104 "Charaxes varanes"

1970. Butterflies. Multicoloured.

508		25c. Type **104**	25	20
509		50c. "Cethosia lamarcki"	45	40
510		1s.50 "Troides aeacus"	1·00	90
511		2s. "Chrysiridia ripheus"	3·75	3·25

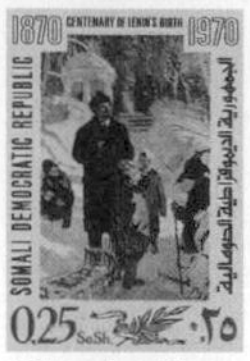

105 Lenin with Children

1970. Birth Centenary of Lenin.

512	**105**	25c. multicoloured	40	35
513	-	1s. multicoloured	75	65
514	-	1s.80 black, orange and brown	3·25	2·75

DESIGNS—VERT: 1s. Lenin making speech. HORIZ: 1s.80, Lenin at desk.

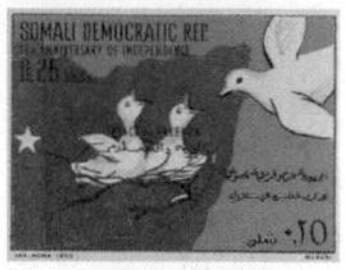

106 Dove feeding Young

1970. Tenth Anniv of Independence.

515		25c. Type **106**	15	10
516		35c. Dagahtur Memorial	25	20
517		1s. Somali arms (vert)	90	75
518		2s.80 Camel and star (vert)	3·25	2·75

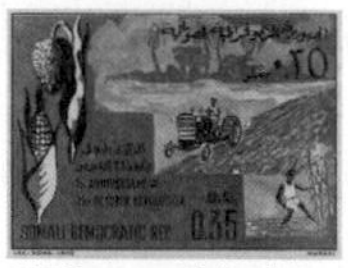

107 Tractor and Produce

1970. First Anniv of 21 October Revolution.

519	**107**	35c. multicoloured	25	20
520	-	40c. black and blue	65	55
521	-	1s. black and brown	90	75
522	-	1s.80 multicoloured	2·00	1·80

DESIGNS: 40c. Soldier and flag; 1s. Hand on open book; 1s.80, Emblems of Peace, Justice and Prosperity.

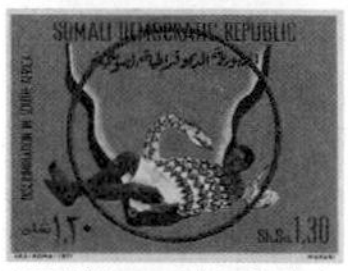

108 African within Snake's Coils

1971. Racial Equality Year.

523	**108**	1s.30 multicoloured	90	75
524	-	1s.80 black, red & brown	3·25	2·75

DESIGN: 1s.80, Human figures, chain and barbed wire.

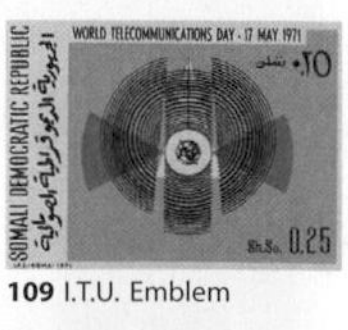

109 I.T.U. Emblem

1971. World Telecommunications Day.

525	**109**	25c. black, ultram & bl	65	55
526	-	2s.80 black, blue & green	3·25	2·75

DESIGN: 2s.80, Global emblem.

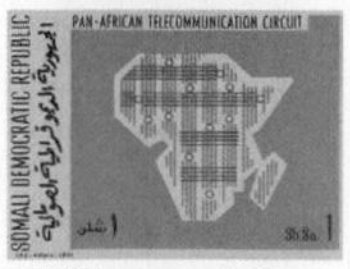

110 Telecommunications Map

1971. Pan-African Telecommunications Network.

527	**110**	1s. green, black and blue	90	75

528	-	1s.50 black, green & yell	2·30	2·00

DESIGN: 1s.50, similar to Type **110** but with different network pattern.

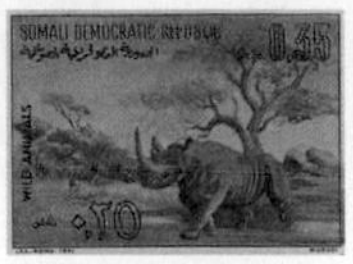
111 White Rhinoceros

1971. Wild Animals.

529	**111**	35c. multicoloured	65	55
530	-	1s. multicoloured	1·50	1·30
531	-	1s.30 black, yellow and violet	3·50	3·00
532	-	1s.80 multicoloured	7·00	6·00

DESIGNS: 1s. Cheetahs; 1s.30, Common zebras; 1s.80, Lion attacking dromedary.

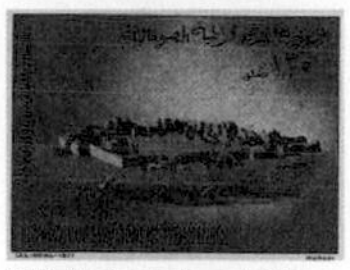
112 Ancient Desert City

1971. East and Central African Summit Conference, Mogadishu.

533	**112**	1s.30 brown, black & red	1·40	1·20
534	-	1s.50 multicoloured	2·75	2·40

DESIGN: 1s.50, Headquarters building, Mogadishu.

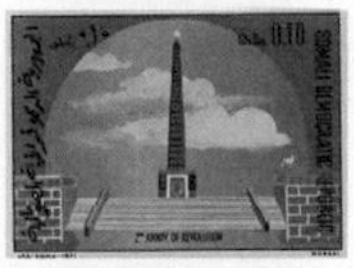
113 Memorial

1971. Second Anniv of Revolution.

535	**113**	10c. black, cobalt and blue	40	35
536	-	1s. multicoloured	90	75
537	-	1s.35 multicoloured	2·75	2·40

DESIGNS: 1s. Agricultural workers; 1s.35, Building workers.

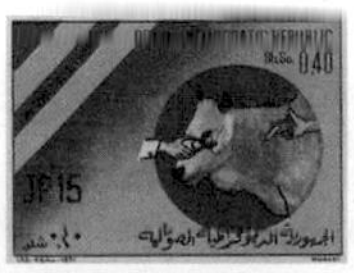
114 Inoculating Cattle

1971. Rinderpest Control Programme. Multicoloured.

538	40c. Type **114**	65	55
539	1s.80 Herdsmen with cattle	2·75	2·40

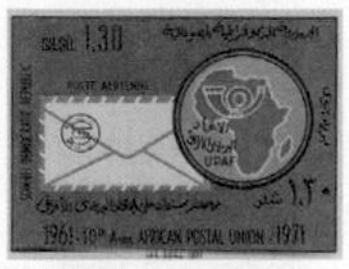
115 A.P.U. Emblem and Back of Airmail Envelope

1972. Tenth Anniv of African Postal Union.

540	1s.50 A.P.U. emblem and dove with letter (postage)	2·75	2·40
541	1s.30 Type **115** (air)	2·50	2·20

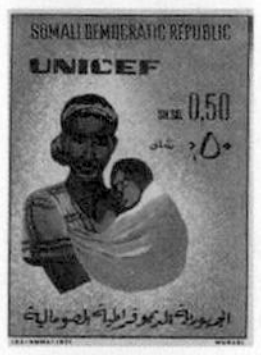

116 Mother and Child

1972. 25th Anniv of UNICEF.

542	**116**	50c. black, brown and light brown	40	35
543	-	2s.80 multicoloured	3·50	3·00

DESIGNS—HORIZ: 2s.80, UNICEF emblem and schoolchildren.

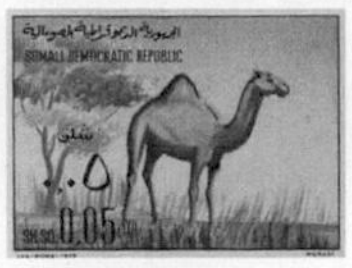
117 Dromedary

1972. Domestic Animals.

544	**117**	5c. multicoloured	15	10
545	-	10c. multicoloured	25	20
546	-	20c. multicoloured	40	35
547	-	40c. black, brown and red	65	55
548	-	1s.70 black, green & black	5·75	5·00

DESIGNS: 10c. Cattle on quayside; 20c. Bull; 40c. Black-headed sheep; 1s.70, Goat.

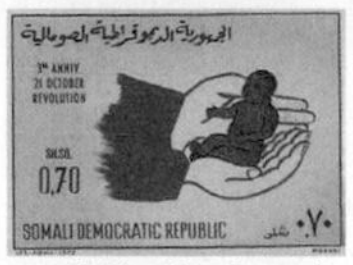

118 Child within Cupped Hands

1972. Third Anniv of 21 October Revolution. Multicoloured.

549	70c. Type **118**	25	20
550	1s. Parade of standards	65	55
551	1s.50 Youth Camps emblem	2·50	2·20

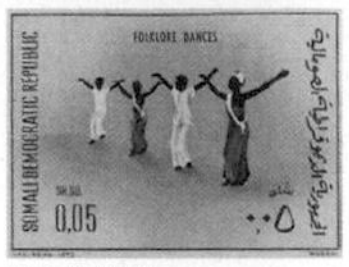
119 Folk Dancers

1973. Folk Dances. Multicoloured.

552	5c. Type **119**	15	10
553	40c. Pair of dancers (vert)	25	20
554	1s. Team of dancers (vert)	90	75
555	2s. Three dancers	3·00	2·75

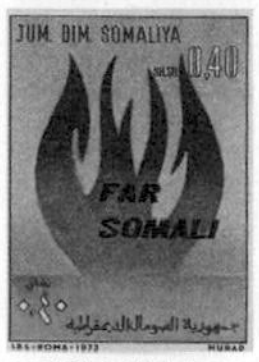

120 Old Alphabet in Flames

1973. Introduction of New Somali Script.

556	120	40c. multicoloured	25	20
557	-	1s. multicoloured	85	55
558	-	2s. black, stone and yellow	3·00	2·50

DESIGNS—HORIZ: 1s. Alphabet in sun's rays; 2s. Writing new script.

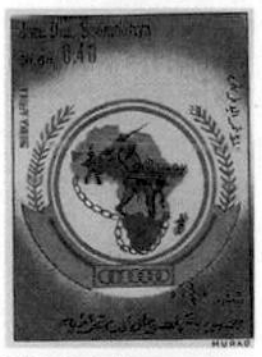
121 Soldiers and Chains within O.A.U. Emblem

1974. Tenth Anniv (1973) of Organization of African Unity. Multicoloured.

559	40c. Type **121**	65	55
560	2s. Spiral on map of Africa	3·25	2·75

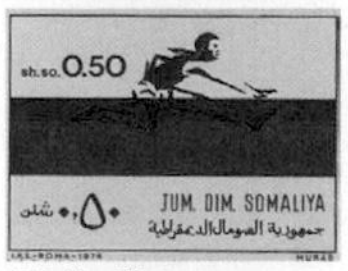

122 Hurdling

1974. Sports.

561	**122**	50c. black, red and orange	25	20
562	-	1s. black, grey and green	65	55
563	-	1s.40 black, grey and olive	3·25	2·75

DESIGNS—HORIZ: 1s. Running. VERT: 1s.40, Basketball.

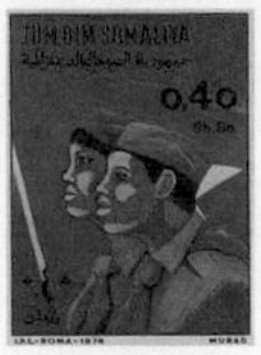

123 Somali Youth and Girl

1974. Guulwade Youth Movement. Multicoloured.

564	40c. Type **123**	25	20
565	2s. Guulwade members helping old woman	3·00	2·75

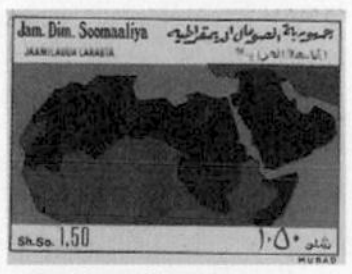
124 Map of League Members

1974. 30th Anniv (1975) of Arab League. Multicoloured.

566	1s.50 Type **124**	1·50	1·30
567	1s.70 Flags of Arab League countries	3·25	2·75

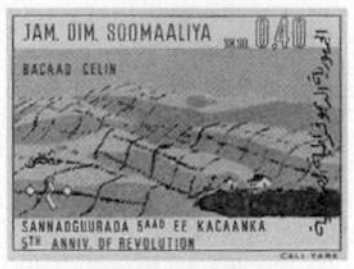

125 Desert Landscape

1975. Fifth Anniv of 21 October Revolution. Multicoloured.

568	40c. Type **125**	40	35
569	2s. Somali villagers reading books (vert)	2·75	2·40

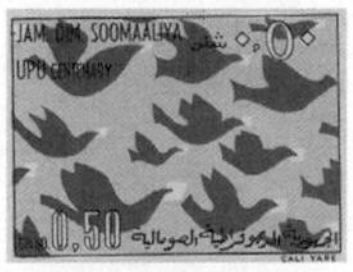
126 Doves

1975. Centenary of U.P.U. Multicoloured.

570	50c. Type **126**	40	35
571	3s. Mounted postman	2·75	2·40

1975. African Postal Union. As T **126**. Multicoloured.

572	1s. Maps of Africa (repetitive motif)	40	35
573	1s.50 Dove with letter	2·50	2·20

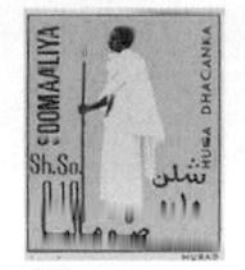
128

1975. Traditional Costumes.

574	**128**	10c. multicoloured	15	10
575	-	40c. multicoloured	25	20
576	-	50c. multicoloured	30	30
577	-	1s. multicoloured	40	35
578	-	5s. multicoloured	3·00	1·70
579	-	10s. multicoloured	8·25	3·25

DESIGNS: 40c. to 10s. Various costumes.

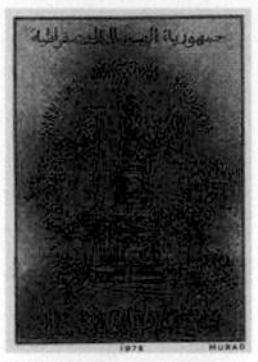
129 Independence Square, Mogadishu

1976. Int Women's Year. Multicoloured.

580	50c. Type **129**	40	35
581	2s.30 I.W.Y. emblem (horiz)	3·75	3·25

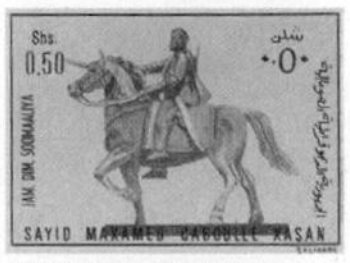
130 Hassan Statue

1976. Sayed M. A. Hassan Commemoration. Multicoloured.

582	50c. Type **130**	25	20
583	60c. Hassan directing warriors (vert)	40	35
584	1s.50 Hassan inspiring warriors (vert)	1·40	1·20
585	2s.30 Hassan leading attack	4·00	3·50

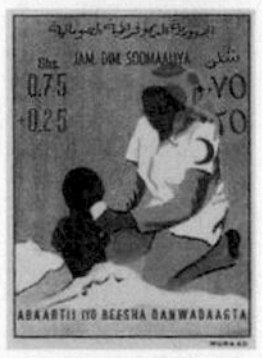
131 Nurse and Child

1976. Famine Relief. Multicoloured.

586	75c.+25c. Type **131**	75	65
587	80c.+20c. Devastated land (horiz)	90	75
588	2s.40+10c. Somali family with produce	2·75	2·40
589	2s.90+10c. Relief emblem and medical officer (horiz)	3·75	3·25

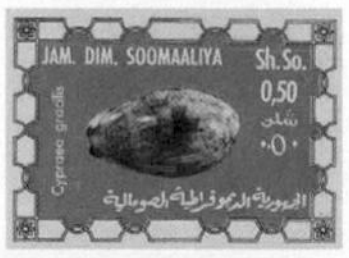

132 Noted Graceful Cowrie

1976. Somali Sea Shells. Multicoloured.

590	50c. Type **132**	40	35
591	75c. "Charonia bardayi"	50	45
592	1s. Townsend's scallop	75	65
593	2s. Ranzani's triton	3·25	2·75
594	2s.75 Clay cone	8·75	7·75
595	2s.90 Old's conch	12·50	11·00
MS596	199×217 mm. Nos. 590/5	48·00	44·00

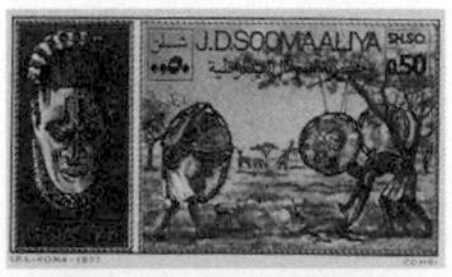
133 Benin Head and Hunters

1977. Second World Black and African Festival of Arts and Cultures, Lagos, Nigeria. Multicoloured.

597	50c. Type **133**	30	30
598	75c. Handicrafts	45	40
599	2s. Dancers	1·50	1·30
600	2s.90 Musicians	4·75	4·00

The Benin Head appears on all designs.

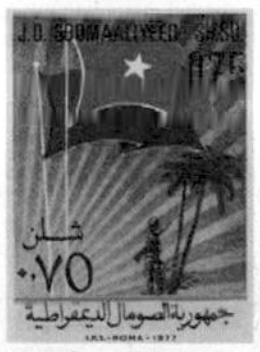
134 Somali Flags

1977. First Anniv of Somali Socialist Revolutionary Party. Multicoloured.

601	75c. Type **134**	40	35
602	1s. Somali Arms (horiz)	1·30	1·10
603	1s.50 Pres. Barre and globe (horiz)	1·60	1·40
604	2s. Arms over rising sun	3·25	2·75

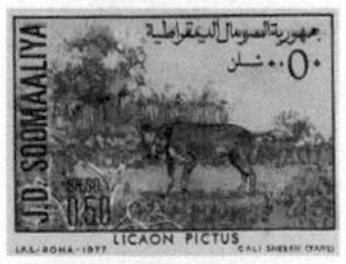

135 Hunting Dog

1977. Protected Animals. Multicoloured.

605	50c. Type **135**	40	35
606	75c. Lesser bushbaby	50	45
607	1s. African ass	1·60	1·40
608	1s.50 Aardwolf	2·50	2·20
609	2s. Greater kudu	3·75	3·25
610	3s. Giraffe	10·00	8·75
MS611	178×118 mm. Nos. 605/10	33·00	31·00

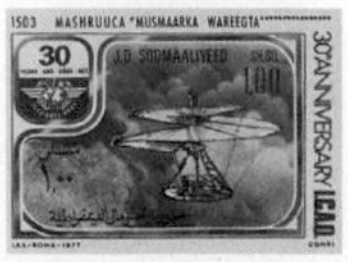
136 Leonardo da Vinci's Drawing of Helicopter

1977. 30th Anniv of I.C.A.O. Multicoloured.

612	1s. Type **136**	40	35
613	1s.50 Montgolfier Brothers' balloon	90	75
614	2s. Wright Flyer I	1·90	1·70
615	2s.90 Boeing 720B of Somali Airlines	3·75	3·25
MS616	169×100 mm. Nos. 612/15	19·00	18·00

137 Dome of the
Rock

1978. Palestine Freedom-Fighters.

617	**137**	75c. black, green and pink		40	35
618	**137**	2s. black, red and blue		2·75	2·40

138 Stadium and Footballer

1978. World Cup Football Championship, Argentina. Multicoloured.

619	1s.50 Type **138**		1·30	1·10
620	4s.90 Stadium and goalkeeper		3·75	3·25
621	5s.50 Stadium and footballer (different)		6·25	5·50
MS622	155×105 mm. Nos. 619/21		25·00	22·00

139 "Acacia tortilis"

1978. Trees. Multicoloured.

623	40c. Type **139**		15	10
624	50c. "Ficus sycomorus" (vert)		25	20
625	75c. "Terminalia catapa" (vert)		40	35
626	2s.90 "Adansonia digitata"		5·00	4·50

140 "Hibiscus
rosa-sinensis"

1978. Flowers. Multicoloured.

627	50c. Type **140**		40	35
628	1s. "Cassia baccarinii"		90	75
629	1s.50 "Kigelia somalensis"		2·50	2·20
630	2s.30 "Dichrostachys glomerata"		3·75	3·25
MS631	124×99 mm. Nos. 627/30		19·00	17·00

141 Fishing from Punt
and Marbled Rabbitfish

1979. Fishing. Multicoloured.

632	75c. Type **141**		75	65
633	80c. Fishing from felucca and black-spotted sweetlips		90	75
634	2s.30 Fishing fleet and leerfish		2·10	1·90
635	2s.50 Trawler and narrow-barred Spanish mackerel		5·00	4·50

142 "Child going to
School" (Ahmed
Dahir Mohamed)

1979. International Year of the Child. Children's Paintings. Multicoloured.

636	50c. Type **142**		25	20
637	75c. "Sailboat" (M. A. Mohamed)		50	45
638	1s.50 "House in the Country" (A. M. Ali)		1·00	90
639	3s. "Bird on Blossoming Branch" (A. A. Siyad)		3·25	2·75
MS640	138×92 mm. Nos. 636/9		15·00	15·00

143 University Students and
Open-air Class

1979. Tenth Anniv of Revolution. Multicoloured.

641	20c. Type **143**		20	15
642	50c. Housing construction		50	45
643	75c. Children at play		75	65
644	1s. Health and agriculture		1·00	90
645	2s.40 Hydro-electric power		3·00	2·75
646	3s. Telecommunications		3·75	3·25

144 Devecchi's Cave Barb

1979. Fish. Multicoloured.

647	50c. Type **144**		65	55
648	90c. Andruzzi's caveminnow		1·00	90
649	1s. Somali blind catfish		2·30	2·00
650	2s.50 Tarabini's catfish		2·75	2·40
MS651	139×92 mm. Nos. 647/50 (sold at 10s.)		15·00	15·00

145 Taleh Fortress

1980. First International Congress of Somali Studies.

652	**145**	2s.25 multicoloured	1·80	1·50
653	**145**	3s.50 multicoloured	2·75	2·40

146 Marka

1980. Landscapes (1st series). Multicoloured.

654	75c. Type **146**		40	35
655	1s. Gandershe		90	75
656	2s.30 Afgooye		1·30	1·10
657	3s.50 Mogadishu		5·00	4·50

See also Nos. 673/6.

147 Pygmy
Puff-back
Flycatcher

1980. Birds. Multicoloured.

658	1s. Type **147**		90	75
659	2s.25 Golden-winged grosbeak		2·30	2·00
660	5s. Red-crowned bush shrike		5·00	4·50
MS661	140×95 mm. Nos. 658/60 (sold at 10s.)		16·00	15·00

148 Parabolic
Antenna and
Shepherd

1981. World Telecommunications Day.

662	**148**	1s. multicoloured	1·30	1·10
663	-	3s. blue, black and red	2·50	2·20
664	-	4s.60 multicoloured	5·00	4·50

DESIGNS: 3s., 4s.60, Ribbons forming caduceus, I.T.U. and W.H.O. emblems.

149 F.A.O. Emblem
and Stylized Wheat

1981. World Food Day. Multicoloured.

665	75c. Type **149**		50	45
666	3s.25 F.A.O. emblem on stylized field (horiz)		2·40	2·10
667	5s.50 Type **149**		4·75	4·25

150 Refugee
Family

1981. Refugee Aid.

668	**150**	2s.+50c. multicoloured	1·40	1·20
669	**150**	6s.80+50c. multicoloured	6·25	5·50
MS670	92×137 mm. Nos. 668/9		12·50	12·00

151 Mosques,
Mecca and Medina

1981. 1500th Anniv of Hejira.

671	**151**	1s.50 multicoloured	90	75
672	**151**	3s.80 multicoloured	3·00	2·75

1982. Landscapes (2nd series). As T **146**. Multicoloured.

673	2s.25 Balcad		1·90	1·70
674	4s. Jowhar		2·50	2·20
675	5s.50 Golaleey		3·75	3·25
676	8s.30 Muqdisho		4·50	3·75

153 Footballer

1982. World Cup Football Championship, Spain. Multicoloured.

677	1s. Type **153**		90	75
678	1s.50 Footballer running to right		2·00	1·80
679	3s.25 Footballer running to left		4·75	4·25
MS680	137×93 mm. Nos. 677/9		19·00	18·00

154 I.T.U. Emblem

1982. I.T.U. Delegates' Conference, Nairobi.

681	**154**	75c. multicoloured	40	35
682	**154**	3s.25 multicoloured	2·30	2·00
683	**154**	5s.50 multicoloured	5·50	4·75

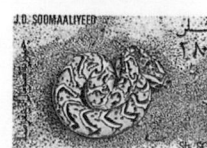

155 "Bitis arietans somalica"

1982. Snakes. Multicoloured.

684	2s.80 Type **155**		2·50	2·20
685	3s.20 "Psammophis punctulatus trivirgatus"		5·00	4·50
686	4s.60 "Rhamphiophis oxyrhynchis rostratus"		7·50	6·50
MS687	125×103 mm. 8s.60 "Sphalerosophis josephscorteccii galgala" (sold at 15s.)		28·00	25·00

156 Bacillus, Microscope and
Dr. Robert Koch

1982. Centenary of Discovery of Tubercle Bacillus.

688	**156**	4s.60+60c. mult	2·50	2·20
689	**156**	5s.80+60c. mult	3·75	3·25

157 Somali
Woman

1982

690	**157**	1s. multicoloured	50	45
691	**157**	5s.20 multicoloured	2·50	2·20
692	**157**	5s.80 multicoloured	2·75	2·40
693	**157**	6s.40 multicoloured	3·00	2·75
694	**157**	9s.40 multicoloured	4·50	3·75
695	**157**	25s. multicoloured	10·00	8·75

158 W.C.Y.
Emblem

1983. World Communications Year.

696	**158**	5s.20 multicoloured	2·30	2·00
697	**158**	6s.40 multicoloured	3·75	3·25

159 View of Hamburg

1983. Second International Congress of Somali Studies, Hamburg. Multicoloured.

698	5s.20 Type **159**		1·30	1·10
699	6s.40 View of Hamburg (different)		5·00	4·50

160 Air Force
Uniform

1983. Military Uniforms. Multicoloured.

700	3s.20 Type **160**		1·90	1·70
701	3s.20 Women's Auxiliary Corps		1·90	1·70
702	3s.20 Border Police		1·90	1·70
703	3s.20 People's Militia		1·90	1·70
704	3s.20 Infantry		1·90	1·70
705	3s.20 Custodial Corps		1·90	1·70
706	3s.20 Police Force		1·90	1·70
707	3s.20 Navy		1·90	1·70

161 Barawe

1983. Landscapes. Multicoloured.

708	2s.80 Type **161**		1·00	90
709	3s.20 Bur Hakaba		1·30	1·10
710	5s.50 Baydhabo		2·50	2·20
711	8s.60 Dooy Nuunaay		6·25	5·50

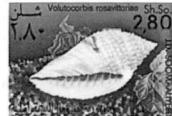

162 "Volutocorbis rosavittoriae"

1984. Shells. Multicoloured.
712	2s.80 Type **162**		1·00	90
713	3s.20 Valdiva bonnet		3·00	2·75
714	5s.50 Glory of India cone		7·50	6·50
MS715 133×95 mm. 15s. Broderip's cone			16·00	15·00

163 Running

1984. Olympic Games, Los Angeles. Multicoloured.
716	1s.50 Type **163**		90	75
717	3s. Throwing the discus		1·90	1·70
718	8s. High jumping		5·75	5·00
MS719 135×95 mm. Nos. 716/18 (sold at 15s.)			8·75	8·25

164 North African Crested Porcupine

1984. Mammals. Multicoloured.
720	1s. Type **164**		25	20
721	1s.50 White-tailed mongoose		50	45
722	2s. Banded mongoose		2·50	2·20
723	4s. Ratel		4·00	3·50
MS724 133×90 mm. Nos. 720/3 (sold at 15s.)			13·00	13·00

165 Girl holding Spider Conch to Ear

1984. 36th International Fair, Riccione.
725	**165**	5s.20 multicoloured	2·75	2·40
726	**165**	6s.40 multicoloured	5·75	5·00

166 Emblem within Winged Horse

1985. 40th Anniv of International Civil Aviation Organization.
727	**166**	3s. multicoloured	1·90	1·70
728	**166**	6s.40 multicoloured	3·75	3·25
MS729 134×94 mm. Nos. 727/8 (sold at 10s.)			12·50	11·50

167 Aquila

1985. Constellations. Illustrations from "The Book of Stars" by Abd al-Rahman al-Sufi. Multicoloured.
730	4s.30 Type **167**		1·90	1·70
731	11s. Taurus		3·25	2·75
732	12s.50 Aries		3·75	3·25
733	13s. Orion		4·50	4·00

168 Ras Kiambone

1985. Architecture (1st series). Multicoloured.
734	2s. Type **168**		40	35
735	6s.60 Hannassa		65	55
736	10s. Mnarani		1·90	1·70
737	18s.60 Ras Kiambone (different)		7·50	6·50
See also Nos. 758/61.				

169 Woman and Posthorn

1985. "Italia '85" Stamp Exhibition, Rome.
738	**169**	2s. multicoloured	1·50	1·30
739	**169**	20s. multicoloured	6·00	5·25
MS740 100×143 mm. Nos. 738/9 (sold at 30s.)			15·00	14·00

170 Persian Leaf-nosed Bat

1985. Bats. Multicoloured.
741	2s.50 Type **170**		1·60	1·40
742	4s.50 Heart-nosed false vampire bat		2·30	2·00
743	16s. Wrinkle-lipped bat		6·25	5·50
744	18s Mozambique sheath-tailed bat		8·25	7·25
MS745 144×104 mm. Nos. 741/4 (sold at 50s.)			25·00	24·00

171 Kenyan and Somali Presidents, Solar System and Industry

1986. Trade Agreement with Kenya.
746	**171**	9s. multicoloured	2·75	2·40
747	**171**	14s.50 multicoloured	4·25	3·75

172 Flower Arrangement

1986. "Euroflora" International Flower Exhibition, Genoa. Multicoloured.
748	10s. Type **172**		1·30	1·10
749	15s. Flower arrangement (different)		3·75	3·25
MS750 137×92 mm. Nos. 748/9 (sold at 30s.)			8·25	7·75

173 Seated Man holding Pottery Flask

1986. Third International Somali Studies Conference, Rome.
751	**173**	11s.35 multicoloured	1·30	1·10
752	**173**	20s. multicoloured	3·75	3·25

174 Footballers

1986. World Cup Football Championship, Mexico. Footballing Scenes.
753	**174**	3s.60 multicoloured	65	55
754	-	4s.80 multicoloured	90	75
755	-	6s.80 multicoloured	2·75	2·40
756	-	22s.60 multicoloured	3·75	3·25
MS757 138×93 mm. Nos. 753/6 (sold at 50s.)			16·00	15·00

1986. Architecture (2nd series). As T **168**. Multicoloured.
758	10s. Bulaxaar ruins		65	55
759	15s. Saylac mosque		90	75
760	20s. Saylac mosque (different)		1·30	1·10
761	31s. Jasiiradaha Jawaay tomb		7·50	6·50

175 Rehabilitation Centre, Mogadishu

1987. Norwegian Red Cross in Somalia.
762	**175**	56s. multicoloured	10·50	9·25
MS763 112×95 mm. 56s. Similar design to No. 762 (36×29 mm) (sold at 60s.)			11·50	10·50

176 Runner

1987. "Olymphilex '87" Olympic Stamps Exhibition, Rome. Multicoloured.
764	20s. Type **176**		3·25	2·75
765	48s. Javelin thrower		7·00	6·00
MS766 135×95 mm. Nos. 764/5 (sold at 75s.)			12·50	11·50

177 Modern and Shanty Towns

1987. International Year of Shelter for the Homeless.
767	**177**	53s. multicoloured	3·25	2·75
768	**177**	72s. multicoloured	5·75	5·00

178 Western Indian Ocean 160,000,000 Years Ago

1987. "Geosom 87" Geological Evolution of Western Indian Ocean Symposium. Multicoloured.
769	10s. Type **178**		2·00	1·80
770	20s. 60,000,000 years ago		3·75	3·25
771	40s. 15,000,000 years ago		7·50	6·50
772	50s. Today		10·00	8·75
MS773 134×94 mm. Nos. 770 and 772 (sold at 130s.)			55·00	50·00

179 Baby receiving Oral Vaccination (Italian inscr)

1988. 40th Anniv of W.H.O.
774	**179**	50s. multicoloured	1·30	1·10
775	**179**	168s. multicoloured (English inscr)	6·25	5·50

180 Somali Hare

1989. Animals. Multicoloured.
776	75s. Type **180**		90	75
777	198s. African buffalo		3·00	2·50
778	200s. Hamadryas baboon (horiz)		5·00	4·50
779	216s. Hippopotamus (horiz)		6·25	5·50
MS780 150×90 mm. Nos. 778/9 (sold at 700s.)			19·00	18·00

181 Water Lily and Boys playing Football

1989. 20th Anniv of 21 October Revolution. Multicoloured.
781	70s. Type **181**		1·30	1·10
782	100s. Boys playing on swing		2·50	2·20
783	150s. Girls on see-saw		3·75	3·25
784	300s. Girl skipping and boy rolling hoop		6·25	5·50

182 Dove and Broken Chain

1991. Liberation. (a) Type **182** (without opt).
785	**182**	150s. multicoloured	1·50	1·30
786	**182**	300s. multicoloured	3·00	2·75

(b) No. 785 additionally optd **"FREEDOM"**.
787	150s. multicoloured		65	55

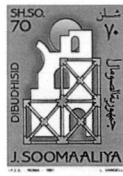

183 Sun, Building and Scaffolding

1991. Reconstruction.
788	**183**	70s. multicoloured	1·00	90
789	**183**	100s. multicoloured	1·50	1·30
790	**183**	150s. multicoloured	3·25	2·75
791	**183**	300s. multicoloured	5·00	4·50

EXPRESS LETTER STAMPS

1923. Express Letter stamps of Italy surch **Somalia Italiana** and value.
E44	**E12**	30b. on 60c. red	4·00	4·00
E45	**E 13**	60b. on 1l.20 blue & pink	4·00	4·00

E17

1924
E60	**E17**	30b. brown and red	17·00	21·00
E61	**E17**	60b. pink and blue	31·00	37·00
No. E61 is inscr "EXPRES".				

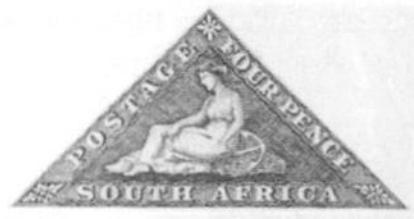

10 "Hope"

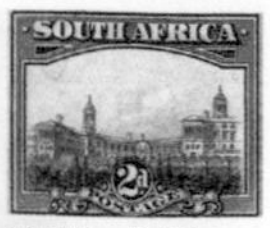

11 Union Buildings, Pretoria

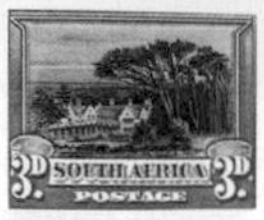

12 Groot Schuur

1926. Bilingual pairs ("SUIDAFRIKA" in one word on Afrikaans stamps). No. 33 is imperf.

42w	**6**	½d. black and green	5·50	10
31	**7**	1d. black and red	1·50	10
34	**11**	2d. grey and purple	14·00	60
44bw	**11**	2d. grey and lilac	22·00	20
44e	**11**	2d. blue and violet	£350	2·50
35	**12**	3d. black and red	16·00	60
45cw	**12**	3d. blue	6·00	10
33	**10**	4d. blue	1·75	1·25
46c	-	4d. brown	3·75	10
47	**8**	6d. green and orange	13·00	10
36	-	1s. brown and blue	30·00	1·00
49	-	2s.6d. green and brown	£120	3·25
49b	-	2s.6d. blue and brown	26·00	20
38	-	5s. black and green	£300	35·00
39	-	10s. blue and brown	£200	10·00

DESIGNS—As Type **11**: 4d. (No. 118) A native kraal; 1s. Black and blue wildebeest; 2s.6d. Ox-wagon inspanned; 5s. Ox-wagon outspanned; 10s. Cape Town and Table Bay.

On No. 33 the English and Afrikaans inscriptions are on separate sheets and our price is for a single stamp of either language.

For these designs with Afrikaans stamps inscr "SUID-AFRIKA", see Nos. 114 etc (issued 1933). For ½d., 1d., 2d., 3d. and 10s. in similar designs see Nos. 105/6, 107a, 116/17 and 64ba respectively.

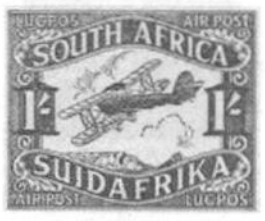

17 de Havilland DH.60 Cirrus Moth

1929. Air.

40	**17**	4d. green	6·00	1·75
41	**17**	1s. orange	10·00	14·00

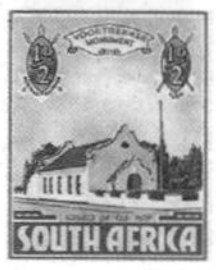

18 Church of the Vow

1933. Voortrekker Memorial Fund. Inscr as in T **18**. Bilingual pairs.

50	**18**	½d.+½d. green	4·50	1·00
51	-	1d.+½d. black and pink	3·25	25
52	-	2d.+1d. green and purple	4·50	55
53	-	3d.+1½d. green and blue	7·00	70

DESIGNS: 1d. The "Great Trek" (C. Michell); 2d. Voortrekker man; 3d. Voortrekker woman.

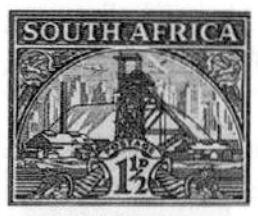

22 Gold Mine

1933. As Nos. 42 etc but with Afrikaans stamps inscr "SUID-AFRIKA" (with hyphen) and new design. Bilingual pairs.

114	**6**	½d. grey and green	3·00	10
56i	**7**	1d. grey and red	70	10
57dw	**22**	1½d. green and gold	1·75	10
58	**11**	2d. blue and violet	75·00	1·00
58a	**11**	2d. grey and purple	65·00	1·75
118	-	4d. brown	4·50	70
119a	**8**	6d. green and red	3·75	10
120	-	1s. brown and blue	11·00	10
121	-	2s.6d. green and brown	11·00	1·00
64b	-	5s. black and green	42·00	35

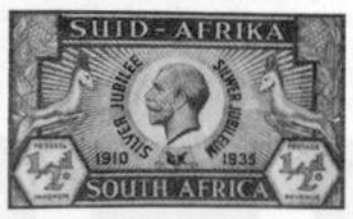

24

1935. Silver Jubilee. Bilingual pairs.

65	**24**	½d. black and green	3·00	20
66	**24**	1d. black and red	3·00	10
67	**24**	3d. blue	15·00	2·25
68	**24**	6d. green and orange	30·00	3·25

The positions of Afrikaans and English inscriptions are transposed on alternate stamps.

1936. Johannesburg International Philatelic Exhibition. Optd **JIPEX 1936**.

MS69	**6**	½d. grey and green (No. 114)	4·50	12·00
MS70	**7**	1d. grey and red (No. 56)	3·25	8·00

Issued each in miniature sheet of six stamps.

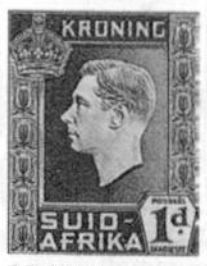

25 King George VI

1937. Coronation. Bilingual pairs.

71	**25**	½d. grey and green	1·00	10
72	**25**	1d. grey and red	1·00	10
73	**25**	1½d. orange and green	1·00	10
74	**25**	3d. blue	1·50	10
75	**25**	1s. brown and blue	3·25	15

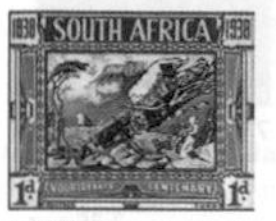

27 Wagon crossing Drakensberg

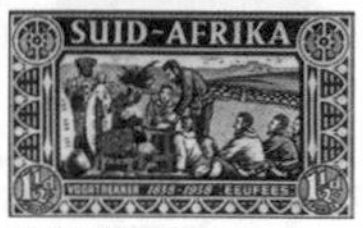

28 Signing of Dingaan-Retief Treaty

1938. Voortrekker Centenary Memorial Fund. Dated "1838 1938". Bilingual pairs.

76	-	½d.+½d. blue and green	18·00	50
77	**27**	1d.+1d. blue and red	22·00	40
78	**28**	1½d.+1½d. brown and green	24·00	1·00
79	-	3d.+3d. blue	26·00	1·00

DESIGNS—As T **27**: ½d. Voortrekker ploughing. As T **28**: 3d. Voortrekker Monument.

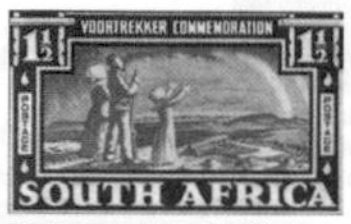

31 Voortrekker Family

1938. Voortrekker Commem. Bilingual pairs.

80		1d. blue and red	9·50	30
81	**31**	1½d. blue and brown	12·00	30

DESIGN: 1d. Wagon wheel.

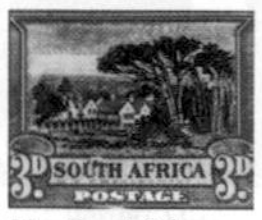

22a Groot Schuur

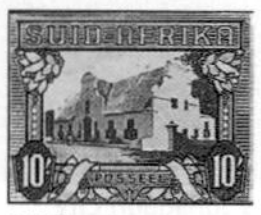

23 Groot Constantia

1939. Bilingual pairs.

117	**22a**	3d. blue	3·75	10
64ca	**23**	10s. blue and brown	45·00	30

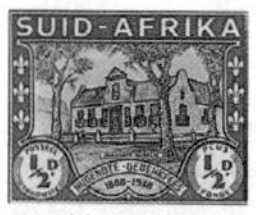

32 Old Vicarage, Paarl, now a Museum

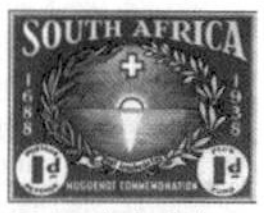

33 Symbol of the Reformation

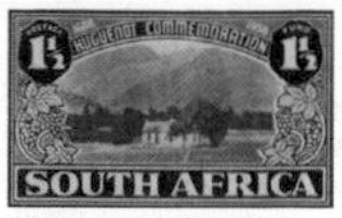

34 Huguenot Dwelling, Drakenstein Mountain Valley

1939. 250th Anniv of Landing of Huguenots in South Africa. Bilingual pairs.

82	**32**	½d.+½d. brown and green	9·00	40
83	**33**	1d.+1d. green and red	15·00	40
84	**34**	1½d.+1½d. green and purple	32·00	1·25

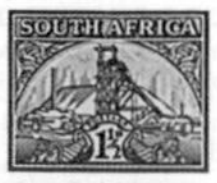

34a Gold Mine

1941. Bilingual pair.

87	**34a**	1½d. green and buff	3·50	10

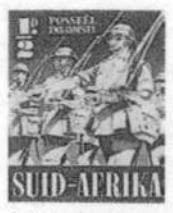

35 Infantry

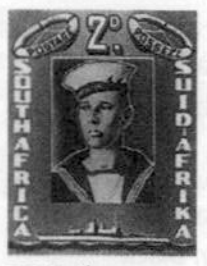

38 Sailor, Destroyer and Lifebelts

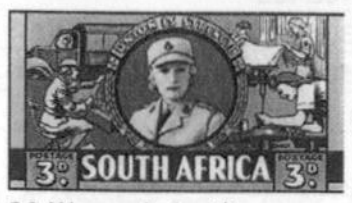

39 Women's Auxiliary Services

1941. War Effort. Bilingual pairs except the 2d. and 1s. which are inscr in both languages on each stamp.

88	**35**	½d. green	1·50	15
89	-	1d. red	2·00	15
90	-	1½d. green	1·50	15
95	**38**	2d. violet	1·00	75
91	**39**	3d. blue	23·00	80
92	-	4d. brown	27·00	25
93	-	6d. orange	12·00	20
96	-	1s. brown	3·75	1·00
94a	-	1s.3d. brown	7·00	20

DESIGNS—As Type **35**: 1d. Nurse and ambulance; 1½d. Airman; 1s.3d. Signaller. As Type **38**: 4d. Artillery; 6d. Welding. As Type **39**: 1s. Tank corps.

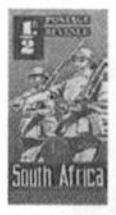

43 Infantry

1942. War Effort. Reduced size. Bilingual except 4d. and 1s. which are inscr in both languages on each stamp.

97	**43**	½d. green	2·00	10
98a	-	1d. red	1·00	10
99	-	1½d. brown	65	10
100	-	2d. violet	1·00	10
101	-	3d. blue	9·00	10
103	-	4d. green	19·00	10
102	-	6d. orange	2·00	10
104	-	1s. brown	19·00	10

DESIGNS—VERT: 1d. Nurse; 1½d. Airman; 2d. Sailor; 6d. Welder. HORIZ: 3d. Women's Auxiliary Services; 4d. Heavy gun in concrete turret; 6d. Heavy gun; 1s. Tanks.

Our unused prices for Nos. 97, 98, 101 and 103 are for units of three. The other stamps are in units of two.

1943. As 1926, but in single colours and with plain background to central oval. Bilingual pairs.

105	**6**	½d. green	3·75	25
106	**7**	1d. red	4·50	15

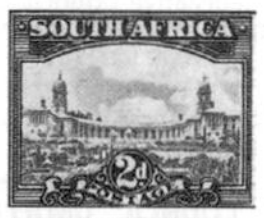

54 Union Buildings, Pretoria

1945. Type **11** redrawn. Bilingual pairs.

107b	**54**	2d. slate and violet	4·50	20
116	**54**	2d. blue and purple	5·50	80

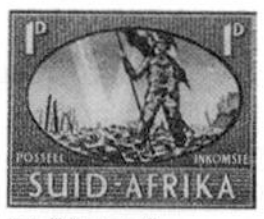

55 "Victory"

1945. Victory. Bilingual pairs.

108	**55**	1d. brown and red	20	10
109	-	2d. blue and violet	20	10
110	-	3d. blue	20	10

DESIGNS: 2d. Man and oxen ploughing ("Peace"); 3d. Man and woman gazing at a star ("Hope").

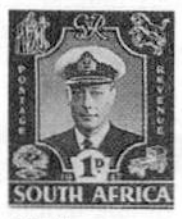

58 King George VI

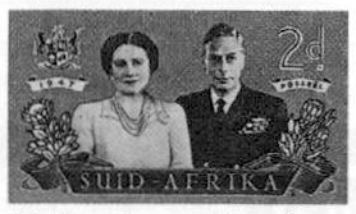

59 King George VI and Queen Elizabeth

1947. Royal Visit. Bilingual pairs.

111	**58**	1d. black and red	10	10
112	**59**	2d. violet	15	10
113	-	3d. blue	15	10

DESIGN—As Type **59**: 3d. Queen Elizabeth II when Princess and Princess Margaret.

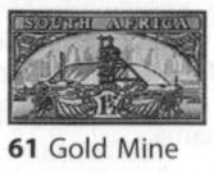

61 Gold Mine

1948. Bilingual.

124	**61**	1½d. green and buff	2·50	10

The price for No. 124 is for a unit of four stamps.

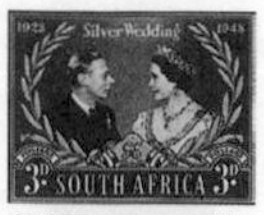

62 King George VI and Queen Elizabeth

1948. Royal Silver Wedding. Bilingual pair.

125	**62**	3d. blue and silver	1·00	10

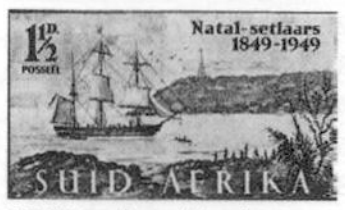

63 "Wanderer" (emigrant ship) entering Durban

1949. Centenary of Arrival of British Settlers in Natal. Bilingual pair.

127	**63**	1½d. brown	80	10

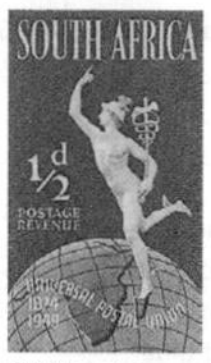

64 Hermes

1949. 75th Anniv of U.P.U. Bilingual pairs.

128	**64**	½d. green	50	10
129	**64**	1½d. red	50	10
130	**64**	3d. blue	60	10

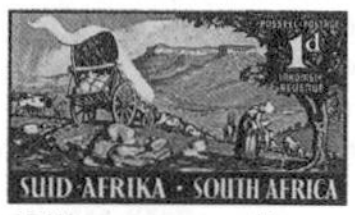

65 Wagons approaching Bingham's Berg

1949. Inauguration of Voortrekker Monument, Pretoria.

131	**65**	1d. mauve	10	10
132	-	1½d. green	10	10
133	-	3d. blue	15	15

DESIGNS: 1½d. Voortrekker Monument, Pretoria; 3d. Bible, candle and Voortrekkers.

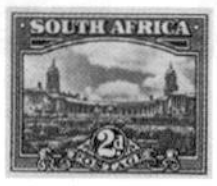

68 Union Buildings, Pretoria

1950. Bilingual pair.

134	**68**	2d. blue and violet	40	10

INSCRIPTIONS. In all later issues except Nos. 167 and 262/5, the stamps are inscribed in both Afrikaans and English. Our prices are for single examples, unused and used.

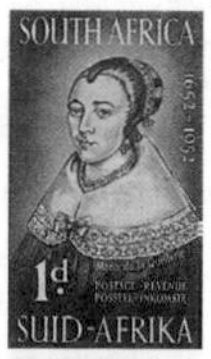

70 "Maria de la Quellerie" (D. Craey)

1952. Tercentenary of Landing of Van Riebeeck. Dated "1652–1952".

136	-	½d. purple and sepia	10	10
137	**70**	1d. green	10	10
138	-	2d. violet	50	10
139	-	4½d. blue	15	15
140	-	1s. brown	1·00	15

DESIGNS—HORIZ: ½d. Seal and monogram; 2d. Arrival of Van Riebeeck's ships; 1s. Landing at the Cape (D. Craey). VERT: 4½d. "Jan van Riebeeck" (D. Craey).

1952. South African Tercentenary Stamp Exn, Cape Town. No. 137 optd **SATISE** and No. 138 optd **SADIPU**.

141	**70**	1d. green	40	1·25
142	-	2d. violet	60	1·00

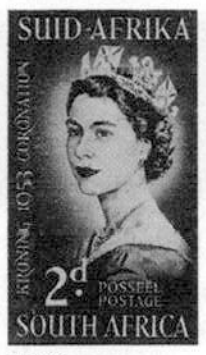

76 Queen Elizabeth II

1953. Coronation.

143	**76**	2d. blue	50	10

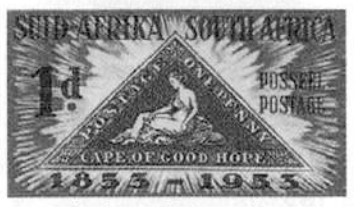

77 1d. Cape Triangular Stamp

1953. Stamp Cent of Cape of Good Hope.

144	**77**	1d. sepia and red	10	10
145	-	4d. indigo and blue	50	20

DESIGN: 4d. as Type **77** but reproducing 4d. "Triangular".

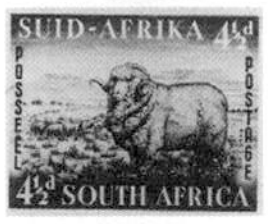

79 Merino Ram

1953

146	**79**	4½d. purple and yellow	20	10
147	-	1s.3d. brown	1·50	10
148	-	1s.6d. red and green	60	35

DESIGNS: 1s.3d. Springbok; 1s.6d. Aloes.

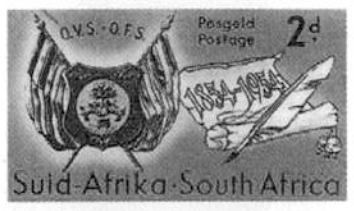

82 Arms of Orange Free State and Scroll

1954. Centenary of Orange Free State.

149	**82**	2d. sepia and red	10	10
150	**82**	4½d. purple and grey	20	50

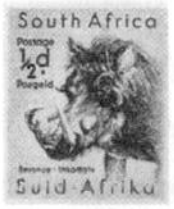

83 Warthog

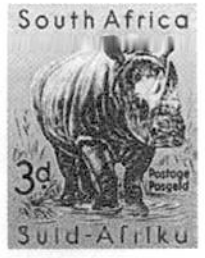

87 White Rhinoceros

1954. Wild Animals.

151	**83**	½d. green	10	10
152	-	1d. lake	10	10
153	-	1½d. sepia	10	10
154	-	2d. plum	10	10
155	**87**	3d. brown and blue	1·00	10
156	-	4d. blue and green	1·00	30
157	-	4½d. indigo and blue	60	1·00
158	-	6d. sepia and orange	50	10
159	-	1s. brown and light brown	1·25	10
160	-	1s.3d. brown and green	3·25	10
161	-	1s.6d. brown and pink	1·75	60
162	-	2s.6d. sepia and green	3·50	20
163	-	5s. sepia and buff	10·00	1·60
164	-	10s. black and blue	13·00	4·50

DESIGNS—VERT (as Type **83**): 1d. Black wildebeest; 1½d. Leopard; 2d. Mountain zebra. (As Type **87**): 4d. African elephant; 4½d. Hippopotamus; 1s. Greater kudu; 1s.6d. Gemsbok; 2s.6d. Nyala; 5s. Giraffe; 10s. Sable antelope. HORIZ (as Type **87**): 6d. Lion; 1s.3d. Springbok.

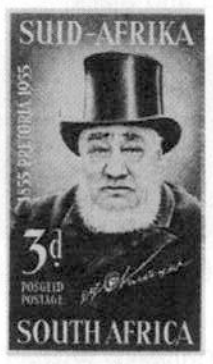

97 President Kruger

1955. Centenary of Pretoria.

165	**97**	3d. green	10	10
166	-	6d. purple (Pres. M. Pretorius)	10	30

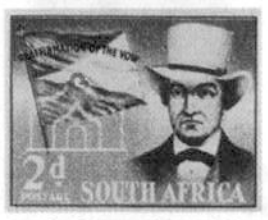

99 A. Pretorius, Church of the Vow and Flag

1955. Voortrekker Covenant Celebrations Pietermaritzburg. Bilingual pair.

167	**99**	2d. blue and red	45	10

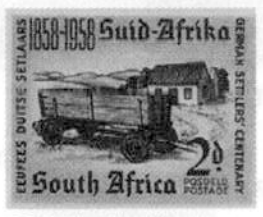

100 Settlers' Block- wagon and House

1958. Centenary of Arrival of German Settlers in South Africa.

168	**100**	2d. brown and purple	10	10

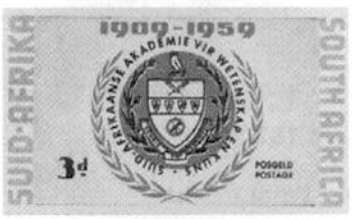

101 Arms of the Academy

1959. 50th Anniv of South African Academy of Science and Art, Pretoria.

169	**101**	3d. blue and turquoise	10	10

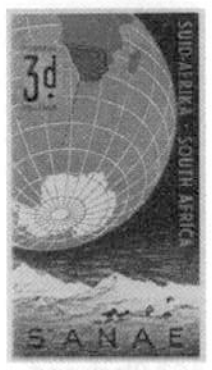

103 Globe and Antarctic Scene

1959. South African National Antarctic Expedition.

178	**103**	3d. turquoise and orange	20	10

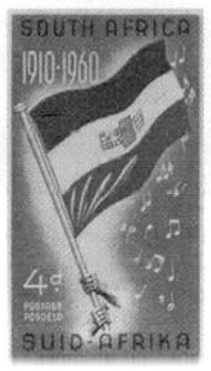

104 Union Flag

1960. 50th Anniv of Union of South Africa.

179	**104**	4d. orange and blue	30	10
180	-	6d. red, brown and green	30	10
181	-	1s. blue and yellow	30	10
182	-	1s.6d. black and blue	70	1·00

DESIGNS—VERT: 6d. Union arms. HORIZ: 1s. "Wheel of Progress"; 1s.6d. Union Festival emblem.

See also Nos. 190 and 192/3.

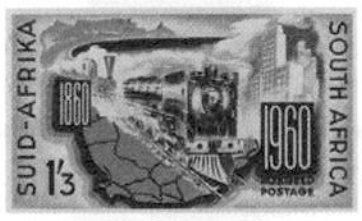

108 Steam Locomotives "Natal" (1860) and Class 25 (1950s)

1960. Centenary of South African Railways.

183	**108**	1s.3d. blue	1·10	30

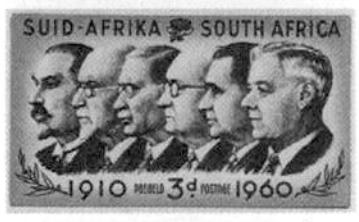

109 Prime Ministers Botha, Smuts, Hertzog, Malan, Strijdom and Verwoerd

1960. Union Day.

184	**109**	3d. brown and light brown	15	10

1961. Types as before but new currency.

185	**83**	½c. turquoise	10	10
186	-	1c. lake (as No. 152)	10	10
187	-	1½c. sepia (as No. 153)	10	10
188	-	2c. plum (as No. 154)	10	1·00
189	**109**	2½c. brown	20	10
190	**104**	3½c. orange and blue	15	2·50
191	-	5c. sepia & orge (as No. 158)	20	10
192	-	7½c. red, brown and green (as No. 180)	20	3·50
193	-	10c. bl & yell (as No. 181)	40	60
194	-	12½c. brown and green (as No. 160)	1·00	1·25
195	-	20c. brown and pink (as No. 161)	2·50	2·75
196	-	50c. sepia and buff (as No. 163)	4·50	10·00
197	-	1r. black & blue (as No. 164)	15·00	25·00

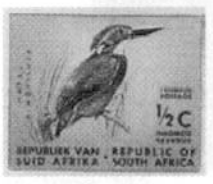

110 African Pygmy Kingfisher

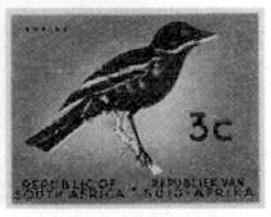

115 Burchell's Gonolek

1961. Republic Issue.

198	**110**	½c. blue, red and brown	10	10
199	-	1c. red and grey	10	10
200	-	1½c. lake and purple	10	10
241	-	2c. blue and yellow	20	10
230	-	2½c. violet and green	10	10
243	**115**	3c. red and blue	30	10
243b	-	4c. violet and green	75	30
204	-	5c. yellow and turquoise	30	10
290	-	6c. brown and green	70	1·25
205	-	7½c. brown and green	60	10
292	-	9c. red, yellow and green	2·00	1·50
233	-	10c. sepia and green	40	10
247	-	12½c. red, yellow and green	1·00	40
248	-	15c. black, olive & orange	85	25
234a	-	20c. turq, red & salmon	1·75	1·25
250	-	50c. black and blue	1·00	40
251	-	1r. orange, green and blue	1·00	1·00

Most values exist in two forms showing differences in the size of the inscriptions and figures of value.

See also Nos. 276/7.

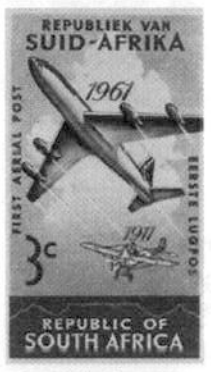

123 Bleriot XI Monoplane and Boeing 707 Airliner over Table Mountain

1962. 50th Anniv of First South African Aerial Post.

220	**123**	3c. blue and red	50	10

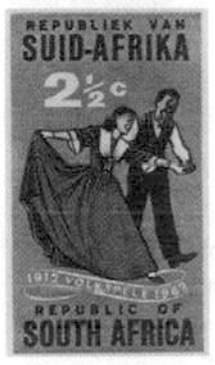

124 Folk-dancers

1962. 50th Anniv of Volkspele (folk-dancing) in South Africa.

221	**124**	2½c. red and brown	15	10

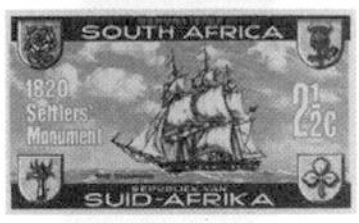

125 "The Chapman" (emigrant ship)

1962. Unveiling of Precinct Stone, British Settlers Monument, Grahamstown.

222	**125**	2½c. green and purple	50	10
223	**125**	12½c. blue and brown	1·75	1·25

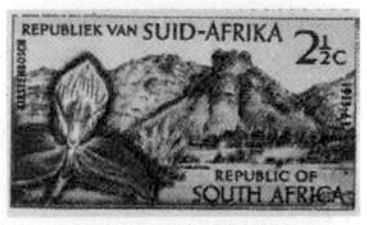

126 Red Disa (orchid), Castle Rock and Gardens

1963. 50th Anniv of Kirstenbosch Botanic Gardens, Cape Town.

224	**126**	2½c. multicoloured	20	10

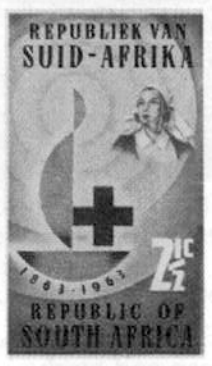

128 Centenary Emblem and Nurse

1963. Cent of Red Cross. Inscr "1863–1963".

225	**128**	2½c. red, black and purple	20	10
226	-	12½c. red and blue	1·75	1·00

DESIGN—HORIZ: 12½c. Centenary emblem and globe.

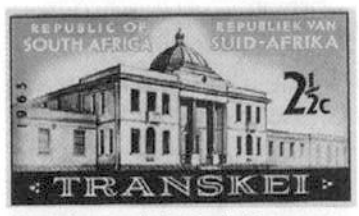

130 Assembly Building, Umtata

1963. First Meeting of Transkei Legislative Assembly.

237	**130**	2½c. sepia and green	10	10

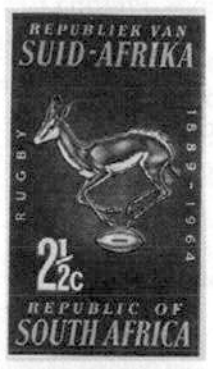

145 "Springbok" Badge of Rugby Board

1964. 75th Anniv of South African Rugby Board.

252	**145**	2½c. brown and green	15	10
253	-	12½c. black and green	2·00	2·25

DESIGN—HORIZ: 12½c. Rugby footballer.

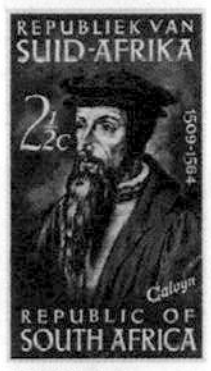

147 Calvin

1964. 400th Death Anniv of Calvin (Protestant reformer).

254	**147**	2½c. cerise, violet & brown	10	10

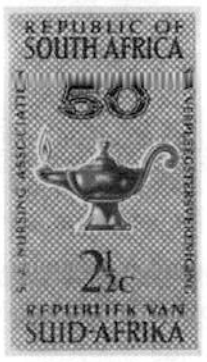

148 Nurse's Lamp

1964. 50th Anniv of South African Nursing Association.

255	**148**	2½c. blue and gold	10	10
257	-	12½c. blue and gold	1·75	1·25

DESIGN—HORIZ: 12½c. Nurse holding lamp.

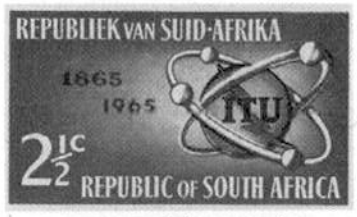

150 I.T.U. Emblem and Satellites

1965. Centenary of I.T.U.

258	**150**	2½c. orange and blue	25	10
259	-	12½c. purple and green	1·25	1·00

DESIGN: 12½c. I.T.U. emblem and symbols.

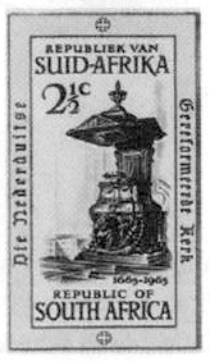

152 Pulpit in Groote Kerk, Cape Town

1965. Tercentenary of Nederduites Gereformeerde Kerk (Dutch Reformed Church) in South Africa.

260	**152**	2½c. brown and yellow	15	10
261	-	12½c. black, orange & blue	70	70

DESIGN—HORIZ: 12½c. Church emblem.

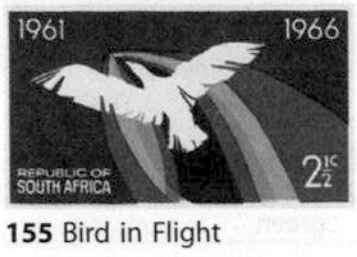

155 Bird in Flight

226 Richards Bay

1978. Harbours. Multicoloured.
442		15c. Type **226**	50	1·00
443		15c. Saldanhabaai	50	1·00

227 "Shepherd's Lonely Dwelling, Riversdale"

1978. 125th Birth Anniv of J. E. A. Volschenk (painter). Multicoloured.
444		10c. Type **227**	15	20
445		15c. "Clouds and Sunshine, Laneberg Range, Riversdale"	20	30
446		20c. "At the Foot of the Mountain"	30	75
447		25c. "Evening on the Veldt"	35	1·40
MS448		124×90 mm. Nos. 444/7	1·25	4·00

228 Pres. B. J. Vorster

1978. Inauguration of President Vorster.
449a	**228**	4c. brown and gold	10	10
450	**228**	15c. violet and gold	25	60

229 Golden Gate

1978. Tourism. Multicoloured.
451		10c. Type **229**	15	10
452		15c. Blyde River Canyon	25	35
453		20c. Amphitheatre, Drakensberg	40	1·10
454		25c. Cango Caves	55	1·50

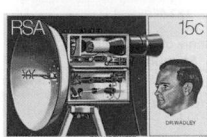

230 Dr. Wadley (inventor) and Tellurometer

1979. 25th Anniv of Tellurometer (radio distance measurer).
455	**230**	15c. multicoloured	20	20

231 1929 4d. Airmail Stamp

1979. 50th Anniv of Stamp Production in South Africa.
456	**231**	15c. green, cream and grey	30	20

232 "Save Fuel"

1979. Fuel Conservation.
457	**232**	4c. black and red	25	65
458	-	4c. black and red	25	65

No. 458 is as Type **232** but with face value and country initials in bottom left-hand corner, and Afrikaans inscription above English.

233 Isandlwana

1979. Centenary of Zulu War.
459	**233**	4c. black and red	20	10
460	-	15c. black and red	55	50
461	-	20c. black and red	70	1·25
MS462		125×90 mm. Nos. 459/61	1·75	3·50

DESIGNS: 15c. Ulundi; 20c. Rorke's Drift.

234 "Health Care"

1979. Health Year.
463	**234**	4c. multicoloured	10	10

235 Children looking at Candle

1979. 50th Anniv of Christmas Stamp Fund.
464	**235**	4c. multicoloured	10	10

236 University of Cape Town

1979. 50th Anniv of University of Cape Town.
465a	**236**	4c. multicoloured	15	15

237 "Gary Player"

1979. "Rosafari 1979" World Rose Convention, Pretoria. Multicoloured.
466		4c. Type **237**	15	10
467		15c. "Prof. Chris Barnard"	30	40
468		20c. "Southern Sun"	40	60
469		25c. "Soaring Wings"	40	85
MS470		100×125 mm. Nos. 466/9	1·10	2·50

238 University of Stellenbosch

1979. 300th Anniv of Stellenbosch (oldest town in South Africa). Multicoloured.
471		4c. Type **238**	10	10
472		15c. Rhenish Church on the Braak	20	40

239 F.A.K. Emblem

1979. 50th Anniv of F.A.K. (Federation of Afrikaans Cultural Societies).
473	**239**	4c. multicoloured	10	15

240 "Still-life with Sweet Peas"

1980. Paintings by Pieter Wenning. Multicoloured.
474		5c. Type **240**	10	10
475		25c. "House in the Suburbs, Cape Town" (44½×37 mm)	40	90
MS476		94×121 mm. Nos. 474/5	1·00	1·60

241 "Cullinan II"

1980. World Diamond Congresses, Johannesburg. Multicoloured.
477		15c. Type **241**	60	60
478		20c. "Cullinan I (Great Star of Africa)"	65	65

242 C. L. Leipoldt

1980. Birth Centenary of C. L. Leipoldt (poet).
479	**242**	5c. multicoloured	10	10

243 University of Pretoria

1980. 50th Anniv of University of Pretoria.
480	**243**	5c. multicoloured	10	10

244 "Marine with Shipping" (Willem van de Velde)

1980. Paintings from South African National Gallery, Cape Town. Multicoloured.
481		5c. Type **244**	15	10
482		10c. "Firetail and his Trainer" (George Stubbs)	20	25
483		15c. "Lavinia" (Thomas Gainsborough) (vert)	25	50
484		20c. "Classical Landscape" (Pieter Post)	30	80
MS485		126×90 mm. Nos. 481/4	1·00	1·75

245 Joubert, Kruger and M. Pretorius (Triumvirate Government)

1980. Centenary of Paardekraal Monument (cairn commemorating formation of Boer Triumvirate Government). Multicoloured.
486		5c. Type **245**	10	10
487		10c. Paardekraal Monument (vert)	20	90

246 Boers advancing up Amajuba Mountain

1981. Centenary of Battle of Amajuba. Multicoloured.
488		5c. Type **246**	20	10
489		15c. British troops defending hill (horiz)	40	90

247 Ballet "Raka"

1981. Opening of State Theatre, Pretoria. Multicoloured.
490		20c. Type **247**	25	30
491		25c. Opera "Aida"	40	35
MS492		110×90 mm. Nos. 490/1	65	70

248 Former Presidents C. R. Swart, J. J. Fouche, N. Diederichs and B. J. Vorster

1981. 20th Anniv of Republic.
493	**248**	5c. black, green and brown	15	10
494	-	15c. multicoloured	30	30

DESIGN—28×22 mm: 15c. President Marais Viljoen.

249 Girl with Hearing Aid

1981. Centenary of Institutes for Deaf and Blind, Worcester. Multicoloured.
495		5c. Type **249**	10	10
496		15c. Boy reading braille	20	90

250 Microscope

1981. 50th Anniv of National Cancer Association.
497	**250**	5c. multicoloured	10	10

251 "Calanthe natalensis"

1981. Tenth World Orchid Conference, Durban. Multicoloured.
498		5c. Type **251**	10	10
499		15c. "Eulophia speciosa"	20	35
500		20c. "Disperis fanniniae"	20	75
501		25c. "Disa uniflora"	25	1·10
MS502		120×91 mm. Nos. 498/501	2·25	2·00

252 Voortrekkers in
Uniform

1981. 50th Anniv of Voortrekker Movement (Afrikaans
cultural youth organization).
| 503 | **252** | 5c. multicoloured | 10 | 10 |

253 Lord
Baden- Powell

1982. 75th Anniv of Boy Scout Movement.
| 504 | **253** | 15c. multicoloured | 30 | 30 |

254 Dr. Robert
Koch

1982. Cent of Discovery of Tubercle Bacillus.
| 505 | **254** | 20c. multicoloured | 20 | 30 |

255 "Maria van Riebeck"
submarine

1982. 25th Anniv of Simonstown as South African Naval
Base. Multicoloured.
506		8c. Type **255**	15	10
507		15c. Missile patrol vessel	20	30
508		20c. *Mynveer* (minesweeper)	25	60
509		25c. Harbour patrol boats	30	85
MS510	125×90 mm. Nos. 506/9		2·00	2·00

256 Old Provost,
Grahamstown

1982. South African Architecture.
511	**256**	1c. brown	15	20
512b	-	2c. green	10	20
513	-	3c. violet	30	85
514	-	4c. green	20	80
515	-	5c. red	30	50
515a	-	5c. purple	10	25
516	-	6c. green	45	40
517	-	7c. green	30	1·50
518a	-	8c. blue	40	10
519	-	9c. mauve	40	20
520	-	10c. red	40	1·00
520a	-	10c. brown	40	1·00
520b	-	11c. mauve	40	1·00
520c	-	12c. blue	70	10
520d	-	14c. brown	2·25	10
521	-	15c. blue	30	15
521a	-	16c. red	1·00	1·75
522	-	20c. red	65	30
522a	-	20c. black	80	10
523	-	25c. brown	50	1·00
524	-	30c. brown	50	30
525	-	50c. blue	50	70
526	-	1r. violet	50	15
527	-	2r. red	65	80

DESIGNS—(28×20 mm): 2c. Tuynhuys, Cape Town; 3c.
Appelhof, Bloemfontein; 4c. Raadsaal, Pretoria; 5c. Cape
Town Castle; 6c. Goewermentsgebou, Bloemfontein; 7c.
Drostdy, Graaff-Reinet; 8c. Leeuwenhof, Cape Town; 9c.
Libertas, Pretoria; 10c. City Hall, Pietermaritzburg; 11c.
City Hall, Kimberley; 12c. City Hall, Port Elizabeth; 14c.
City Hall, Johannesburg; 15c. Matjesfontein; 16c. City Hall,
Durban; 20c. Post Office, Durban; 25c. Melrose House,
Pretoria. (45×28 mm): 30c. Old Legislative Asembly Build-
ing, Pietermaritzburg; 50c. Raadsaal, Bloemfontein; 1r.
Houses of Parliament, Cape Town; 2r. Uniegebou, Pretoria.

1982. Coil Stamps. As T **256**.
528	1c. brown	30	1·25
529	2c. green	30	1·25
530	5c. brown	30	1·25
531	10c. brown	30	1·25

DESIGNS: 1c. Drostdy, Swellendam; 2c. City Hall, East London; 5c. Head Post Office, Johannesburg; 10c. Morgen-
ster, Somerset West.

257 Bradysaurus

1982. Karoo Fossils. Multicoloured.
532		8c. Type **257**	30	10
533		15c. Lystrosaurus	35	60
534		20c. Euparkeria	40	75
535		25c. Thrinaxodon	45	90
MS536	107×95 mm. Nos. 532/5		1·50	3·25

258 Gough Island Base

1983. Weather Stations. Multicoloured.
537		8c. Type **258**	20	10
538		20c. Marion Island base	30	45
539		25c. Taking meteorological readings	30	50
540		40c. Launching weather bal-loon. Sanae	40	90

259 Class S2 Krupp
Locomotive, 1952

1983. Steam Railway Locomotives. Multicoloured.
541		10c. Type **259**	30	10
542		20c. Class 16E Henschel express locomotive, 1935	50	70
543		25c. Class 6H locomotive, 1901	55	80
544		40c. Class 15F locomotive, 1939	65	1·50

260 Rugby

1983. Sport in South Africa. Multicoloured.
545		10c. Type **260**	15	10
546		20c. Soccer (horiz)	20	30
547		25c. Yachting	25	50
548		40c. Horse-racing (horiz)	40	90

261 Plettenberg Bay

1983. Tourism Beaches. Multicoloured.
549		10c. Type **261**	10	10
550		20c. Durban	20	30
551		25c. West coast	20	35
552		40c. Clifton	35	65
MS553	128×90 mm. Nos. 549/52		1·10	2·50

262 Thomas
Pringle

1984. South African English Authors.
554	**262**	10c. brown, lt brn & grey	10	10
555	-	20c. brown, green and grey	20	40
556	-	25c. brown, pink and grey	20	50
557	-	40c. brown, lt brn & grey	35	85

DESIGNS: 20c. Pauline Smith; 25c. Olive Schreiner; 40c. Sir
Percy Fitzpatrick.

263 Manganese

1984. Strategic Minerals. Multicoloured.
558		11c. Type **263**	30	10
559		20c. Chromium	45	60
560		25c. Vanadium	50	80
561		30c. Titanium	60	90

264 Bloukrans River Bridge

1984. South African Bridges. Multicoloured.
562		11c. Type **264**	25	10
563		25c. Durban four-level inter-change	40	60
564		30c. Mfolozi railway bridge	45	75
565		45c. Gouritz River bridge	55	1·40

265 Preamble to
the Constitution in
Afrikaans

1984. New Constitution.
566	-	11c. stone, black and bistre	70	1·25
567	**265**	11c. stone, black and bistre	70	1·25
568	-	25c. stone, purple and bistre	45	50
569	-	30c. multicoloured	45	50

DESIGNS: No. 566, Preamble to the Constitution in English; 568, Last two lines of National Anthem; 569, South
African coat of arms.

266 Pres. P. W.
Botha

1984. Inauguration of President Botha.
| 570 | **266** | 11c. multicoloured | 30 | 10 |
| 571 | **266** | 25c. multicoloured | 55 | 40 |

267 Pro Patria
Medal

1984. Military Decorations. Multicoloured.
572		11c. Type **267**	20	10
573		25c. De Wet decoration	30	45
574		30c. John Chard decoration	30	65
575		45c. Honoris Crux (Diamond) decoration	35	1·00
MS576	71×116 mm. Nos. 572/5		1·00	3·00

268 "Reflections" (Frans
Oerder)

1985. Paintings by Frans Oerder. Multicoloured.
577		11c. Type **268**	20	15
578		25c. "Ladies in a Garden"	25	35
579		30c. "Still-life with Lobster"	25	45
580		50c. "Still-life with Marigolds"	40	70
MS581	129×74 mm. Nos. 577/80		1·25	3·00

269 Cape Parliament
Building

1985. Centenary of Cape Parliament Building.
Multicoloured.
582		12c. Type **269**	15	10
583		25c. Speaker's Chair	25	30
584		30c. "National Convention 1908–9" (Edward Roworth)	25	40
585		50c. Republic Parliamentary emblem	45	1·10

270 Freesia

1985. Floral Emigrants. Multicoloured.
586		12c. Type **270**	15	10
587		25c. Nerine	25	30
588		30c. Ixia	25	45
589		50c. Gladiolus	40	1·25

271 Sugar Bowl

1985. Cape Silverware. Multicoloured.
590		12c. Type **271**	20	10
591		25c. Teapot	30	30
592		30c. Loving cup (vert)	30	45
593		50c. Coffee pot (vert)	45	1·50

272 Blood Donor Session

1986. Blood Donor Campaign. Multicoloured.
594		12c. Type **272**	45	10
595		20c. Baby receiving blood transfusion	75	80
596		25c. Operation in progress	80	95
597		30c. Ambulanceman and ac-cident victim	95	1·60

273 National Flag

1986. 25th Anniv of Republic of South Africa.
| 598 | | 14c. Type **273** | 75 | 1·25 |
| 599 | | 14c. As Type **273**, but inscr "UNITY IS STRENGTH" | 75 | 1·25 |

274 Drostdyhof, Graaff-Reinet

1986. Restoration of Historic Buildings. Multicoloured.
600		14c. Type **274**	30	10
601		20c. Pilgrim's Rest mining village	55	70
602		25c. Strapp's Store, Bethlehem	60	90
603		30c. Palmdene, Pietermar-itzburg	75	1·40

275 Von Brandis Square, Johannesburg,
c. 1900

1986. Centenary of Johannesburg. Multicoloured.
604		14c. Type **275**	35	10
605		20c. Gold mine (26×20 mm)	1·25	1·25
606		25c. Johannesburg skyline, 1986	1·00	1·60
607		30c. Gold bars (26×20 mm)	1·75	2·50

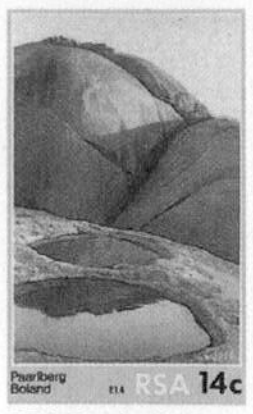

276 Gordon's Rock, Paarlberg

1986. Rock Formations. Multicoloured.

608	14c. Type **276**	45	10
609	20c. The Column, Drakensberg	70	80
610	25c. Maltese Cross, Sederberge	75	1·00
611	30c. Bourke's Luck Potholes, Blyde River Gorge	85	1·75

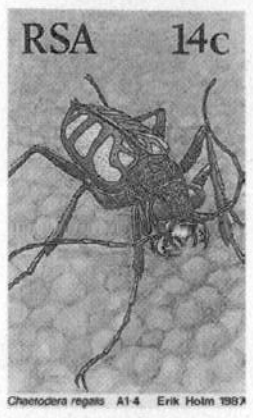

277 "Cicindela regalis"

1987. South African Beetles. Multicoloured.

612	14c. Type **277**	40	10
613	20c. "Trichostetha fascicularis"	55	60
614	25c. "Julodis viridipes"	65	90
615	30c. "Ceroplesis militaris"	75	2·00

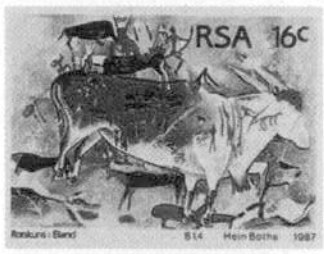

278 Eland, Sebaaieni Cave

1987. Rock Paintings. Multicoloured.

616	16c. Type **278**	40	10
617	20c. Leaping lion, Clocolan	60	65
618	25c. Black wildebeest, uMhlwazini Valley	75	90
619	30c. Bushman dance, Floukraal	80	1·75

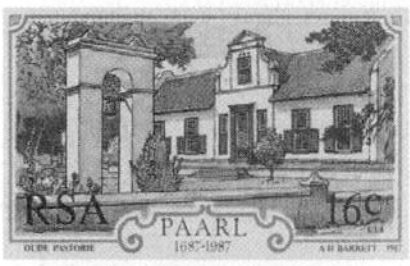

279 Oude Pastorie, Paarl

1987. 300th Anniv of Paarl. Multicoloured.

620	16c. Type **279**	20	10
621	20c. Grapevines	35	55
622	25c. Wagon-building	40	70
623	30c. KWV Cathedral Wine Cellar	45	1·50

1987. Natal Flood Relief Fund (1st issue). No. 521a surch.

624	16c.+10c. red (surch **VLOEDRAMP NATAL +10c**)	30	80
625	16c.+10c. (surch **NATAL FLOOD DISASTER +10c**)	30	80

See also Nos. 629/30 and 635/6.

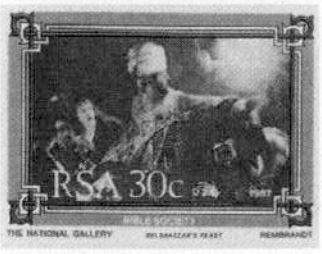

281 "Belshazzar's Feast" (Rembrandt)

1987. The Bible Society of South Africa. Multicoloured.

626	16c. "The Bible" in 75 languages (54×34 mm)	35	10
627	30c. Type **281**	55	70
628	50c. "St. Matthew and the Angel" (Rembrandt) (vert)	85	1·90

1987. Natal Flood Relief Fund (2nd issue). No. 626 surch.

629	16c.+10c. multicoloured (surch as No. 625)	50	80
630	16c.+10c. multicoloured (surch as No. 624)	50	80

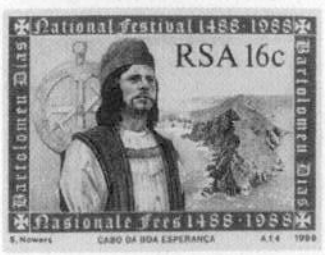

282 Bartolomeu Dias and Cape of Good Hope

1988. 500th Anniv of Discovery of Cape of Good Hope by Bartolomeu Dias. Multicoloured.

631	16c. Type **282**	60	10
632	30c. Kwaaihoek Monument	80	85
633	40c. Caravels	1·50	1·60
634	50c. Martellus map, c. 1489	1·90	2·50

1988. Natal Flood Relief Fund (3rd issue). No. 631 surch.

635	16c.+10c. multicoloured (surch as No. 624)	50	80
636	16c.+10c. multicoloured (surch as No. 625)	50	80

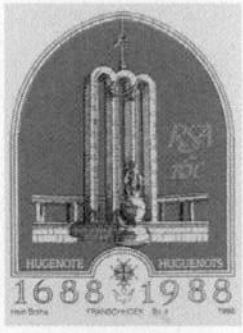

283 Huguenot Monument, Franschhoek

1988. 300th Anniv of Arrival of First French Huguenots at the Cape. Multicoloured.

637	16c. Type **283**	30	10
638	30c. Map of France showing Huguenot areas	85	80
639	40c. Title page of French/Dutch New Testament of 1672	85	1·25
640	50c. St. Bartholomew's Day Massacre, Paris, 1572	1·10	1·50

1988. National Flood Relief Fund Nos. 637/40 surch in English (**National Flood Disaster +10c**) (E) or in Afrikaans (**Nasionale Vloedramp +10c**) (A).

641	16c.+10c. multicoloured (E)	40	65
642	16c.+10c. multicoloured (A)	40	65
643	30c.+10c. multicoloured (A)	55	75
644	30c.+10c. multicoloured (E)	55	75
645	40c.+10c. multicoloured (A)	60	90
646	40c.+10c. multicoloured (E)	60	90
647	50c.+10c. multicoloured (E)	70	1·25
648	50c.+10c. multicoloured (A)	70	1·25

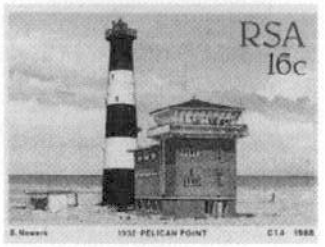

285 Pelican Point Lighthouse, Walvis Bay

1988. Lighthouses. Multicoloured.

649	16c. Type **285**	70	10
650	30c. Green Point, Cape Town	90	70
651	40c. Cape Agulhas	1·10	1·25
652	50c. Umhlanga Rocks, Durban	1·50	1·75
MS653	132×112 mm. Nos. 649/52	5·00	4·50

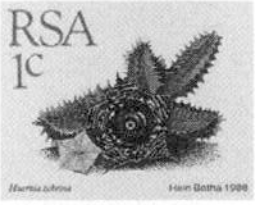

286 "Huernia zebrina"

1988. Succulents. Multicoloured.

654	1c. Type **286**	10	50
655	2c. "Euphorbia symmetrica"	10	50
656	5c. "Lithops dorotheae"	10	40
657	7c. "Gibbaeum nebrownii"	15	60
658	10c. "Didymaotus lapidiformis"	15	50
659	16c. "Vanheerdea divergens"	60	50
659a	18c. "Faucaria tigrina"	50	10
660	20c. "Conophytum mundum"	80	10
660a	21c. "Gasteria armstrongii"	40	10
661	25c. "Cheiridopsis peculiaris"	80	10
662	30c. "Tavaresia barklyi"	60	50
663	35c. "Dinteranthus wilmotianus"	1·00	20
664	40c. "Frithia pulchra"	1·00	25
665	50c. "Lapidaria margaretae"	1·00	25
666	90c. "Dioscorea elephantipes"	1·25	45
667	1r. "Trichocaulon cactiforme"	1·00	50
668	2r. "Crassula columnaris"	1·25	90
668a	5r. "Anacampseros albissima"	2·25	2·40

See also No. 778.

1988. Coil stamps. As T **286**. Multicoloured.

669	1c. "Adromischus marianiae"	1·00	1·75
670	2c. "Titanopsis calcarea"	60	1·25
671	5c. "Dactylopsis digitata"	65	1·25
672	10c. "Pleiospilos bolusii"	70	1·25

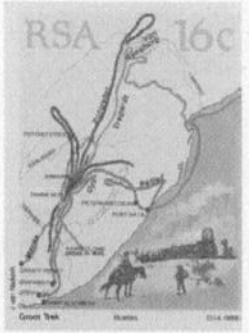

287 Map of Great Trek Routes

1988. 150th Anniv of Great Trek. Multicoloured.

673	16c. Type **287**	75	10
674	30c. "Exodus" (tapestry by W. Coetzer) (56×20 mm)	1·00	90
675	40c. "Crossing the Drakensberg" (tapestry by W. Coetzer) (77×20 mm)	1·25	1·10
676	50c. "After the Service, Church of the Vow" (J. H. Pierneef) (horiz)	1·50	1·75

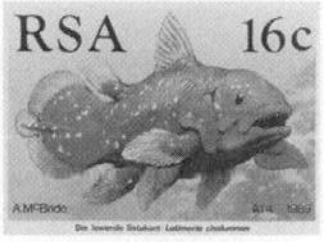

288 Coelacanth

1989. 50th Anniv of Discovery of Coelacanth. Multicoloured.

677	16c. Type **288**	75	15
678	30c. Prof. J. L. B. Smith and Dr. M. Courtenay-Latimer examining Coelacanth	1·10	1·25
679	40c. J. L. B. Smith Institute of Ichthyology, Grahamstown	1·40	1·60
680	50c. Coelacanth and "GEO" midget submarine	1·50	2·25

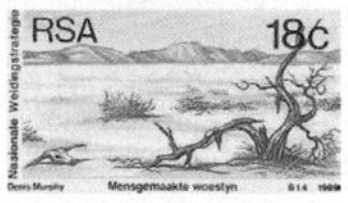

289 Man-made Desert

1989. National Grazing Strategy. Multicoloured.

681	18c. Type **289**	40	15
682	30c. Formation of erosion gully	65	75
683	40c. Concrete barrage in gully	70	1·00
684	50c. Reclaimed veldt	80	1·40

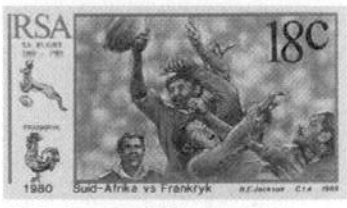

290 South Africa v. France Match, 1980

1989. Cent of South African Rugby Board. Multicoloured.

685	18c. Type **290**	80	15
686	30c. South Africa v. Australia, 1963	1·25	90
687	40c. South Africa v. New Zealand, 1937	1·50	1·60
688	50c. South Africa v. British Isles, 1896	1·50	2·00

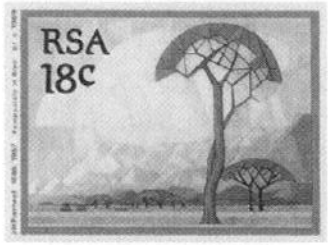

291 "Composition in Blue"

1989. Paintings by Jacob Hendrik Pierneef. Multicoloured.

689	18c. Type **291**	50	15
690	30c. "Zanzibar"	80	60
691	40c. "The Bushveld"	1·00	1·25
692	50c. "Cape Homestead"	1·10	1·75
MS693	114×86 mm. Nos. 689/92	2·25	2·75

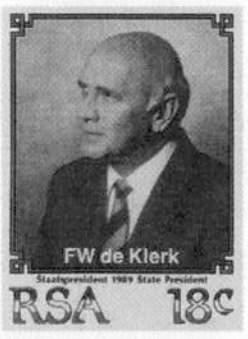

292 Pres. F. W. de Klerk

1989. Inaug of President F. W. de Klerk. Multicoloured.

694	18c. Type **292**	50	15
695	45c. F. W. de Klerk (different)	75	1·40

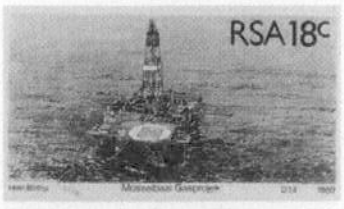

293 Gas-drilling Rig, Mossel Bay

1989. Energy Sources. Multicoloured.

696	18c. Type **293**	40	10
697	30c. Coal to oil conversion plant	70	70
698	40c. Nuclear power station	80	85
699	50c. Thermal electric power station	90	1·25

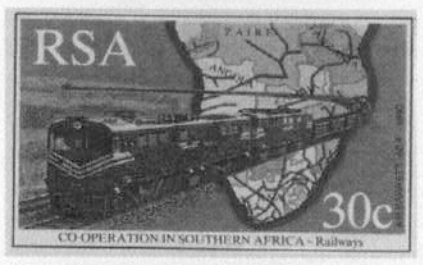

294 Electric Goods Train and Map of Railway Routes

1990. Co-operation in Southern Africa. Multicoloured.

700	18c. Cahora Bassa Hydro-electric Scheme, Mozambique, and map of transmission lines (68×26 mm)	70	25
701	30c. Type **294**	90	70
702	40c. Projected dam on upper Orange River, Lesotho, and map of Highlands Water Project (68×26 mm)	1·10	1·10
703	50c. Cow, syringe and outline map of Africa	1·40	1·25
MS704	136×78 mm. Nos. 700/3	3·25	2·75

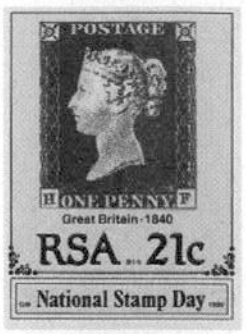

295 Great Britain 1840 Penny Black

1990. National Stamp Day. Multicoloured.

705	21c. Type **295**	40	55
706	21c. Cape of Good Hope 1853 4d. triangular pair	40	55
707	21c. Natal 1857 1s.	50	55
708	21c. Orange Free State 1868 1s.	50	55
709	21c. Transvaal 1869 1s.	50	55

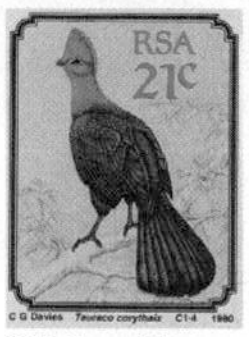

296 Green Turaco

1990. Birds. Multicoloured.

710	21c. Type **296**	85	20
711	35c. Red-capped robin chat	1·25	80
712	40c. Rufous-naped bush lark	1·25	1·50
713	50c. Bokmakierie shrike	1·50	2·00

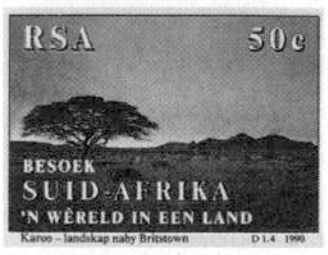

297 Karoo Landscape near Britstown

1990. Tourism. Multicoloured.

714	50c. Type **297**	1·25	1·75
715	50c. Camps Bay, Cape of Good Hope	1·25	1·75
716	50c. Giraffes in Kruger National Park	1·25	1·75
717	50c. Boschendal Vineyard, Drakenstein Mts	1·25	1·75

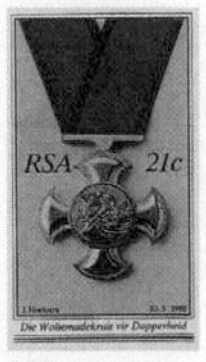

298 Woltemade Cross for Bravery

1990. National Orders. Multicoloured.

718	21c. Type **298**	50	60
719	21c. Order of the Southern Cross	50	60
720	21c. Order of the Star of South Africa	50	60
721	21c. Order for Meritorious Service	50	60
722	21c. Order of Good Hope	50	60
MS723	143×70 mm. Nos. 718/22	2·25	2·75

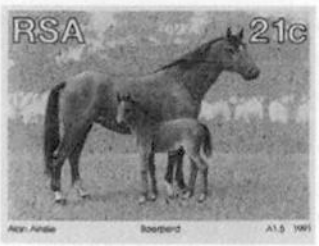

299 Boer Horses

1991. Animal Breeding in South Africa. Multicoloured.

724	21c. Type **299**	85	85
725	21c. Bonsmara bull	85	85
726	21c. Dorper sheep	85	85
727	21c. Ridgeback dogs	85	85
728	21c. Putterie racing pigeons	85	85

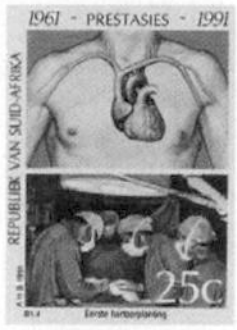

300 Diagram of Human Heart and Transplant Operation

1991. 30th Anniv of Republic. Scientific and Technological Achievements. Multicoloured.

729	25c. Type **300**	20	10
730	40c. Matimba Power Station (horiz)	35	35
731	50c. Dolos design breakwater (horiz)	45	45
732	60c. Western Deep Levels gold mine	60	60

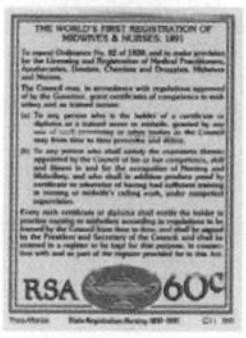

301 State Registration of Nurses Act, 1891

1991. Centenary of State Registration for Nurses and Midwives.

733	**301**	60c. multicoloured	60	60

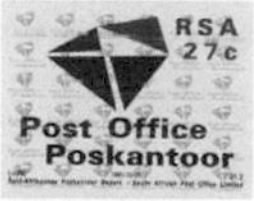

302 South Africa Post Office Ltd Emblem

1991. Establishment of Post Office Ltd and Telekom Ltd. Multicoloured.

734	27c. Type **302**	50	50
735	27c. Telekom SA Ltd emblem	50	50

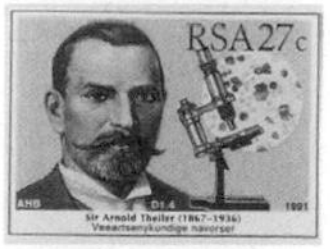

303 Sir Arnold Theiler (veterinarian)

1991. South African Scientists. Multicoloured.

736	27c. Type **303**	45	15
737	45c. Sir Basil Schonland (physicist)	65	60
738	65c. Dr. Robert Broom (palaeontologist)	1·25	1·40
739	85c. Dr. Alex du Toit (geologist)	1·50	2·25

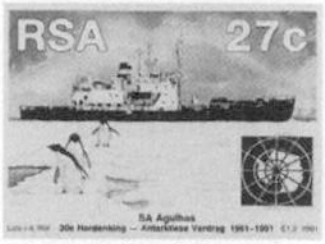

304 "Agulhas" (Antarctic research ship)

1991. 30th Anniv of Antarctic Treaty. Multicoloured.

740	27c. Type **304**	1·50	25
741	65c. Chart showing South African National Antarctic Expedition base	2·25	1·25

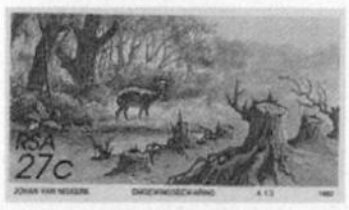

305 Soil Conservation

1992. Environmental Conservation. Multicoloured.

742	27c. Type **305**	50	15
743	65c. Water pollution	1·25	1·10
744	85c. Air pollution	1·50	1·50

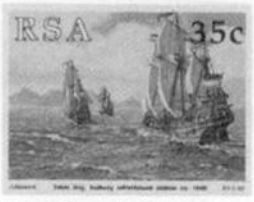

306 Dutch Fleet approaching Table Bay

1992. National Stamp Day. Cape of Good Hope Postal Stones. Multicoloured.

745	35c. Type **306**	65	65
746	35c. Landing for water and provisions	65	65
747	35c. Discovering a postal stone	65	65
748	35c. Leaving letters under a stone	65	65
749	35c. Reading letters	65	65

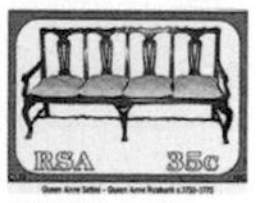

307 Queen Anne Settee, c. 1750

1992. Antique Cape Furniture. Multicoloured.

750	35c. Type **307**	55	60
751	35c. Stinkwood settee, c. 1800	55	60
752	35c. Canopy bed, c. 1800 (vert)	55	60
753	35c. 19th-century rocking cradle	55	60
754	35c. Water butt, c. 1800 (vert)	55	60
755	35c. Flemish style cabinet, c. 1700 (vert)	55	60
756	35c. Armoire, c. 1780 (vert)	55	60
757	35c. Late 17th-century church chair (vert)	55	60
758	35c. Tub chair, c. 1770 (vert)	55	60
759	35c. Bible desk, c. 1750 (vert)	55	60

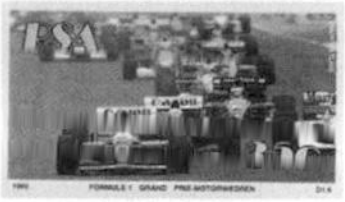

308 Grand Prix Motor Racing

1992. Sports. Multicoloured.

760	35c. Type **308**	30	25
761	35c. Football	30	25
762	55c. Total Paris–Cape Motor Rally	45	35
763	70c. Athletics	55	50
764	90c. Rugby	75	70
765	1r.05 Cricket	1·50	1·25
MS766	167×69 mm. Nos. 760/5	3·50	3·00

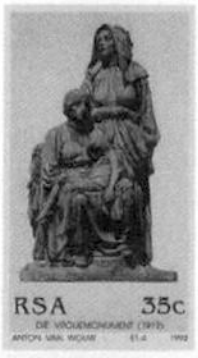

309 "Women's Monument" (Van Wouw)

1992. 130th Birth Anniv of Anton van Wouw (sculptor). Multicoloured.

767	35c. Type **309**	50	20
768	70c. "Sekupu Player"	90	60
769	90c. "The Hunter"	1·10	80
770	1r.05 "Postman Lehman"	1·25	1·00
MS771	96×149 mm. Nos. 767/70	2·75	2·40

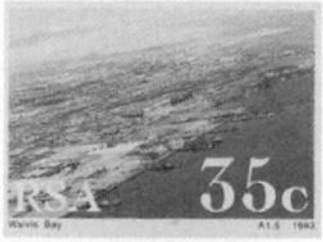

310 Walvis Bay Harbour

1993. South African Harbours. Multicoloured.

772	35c. Type **310**	40	20
773	55c. East London	50	35
774	70c. Port Elizabeth	75	50
775	90c. Cape Town	95	75
776	1r.05 Durban	1·00	95
MS777	147×112 mm. Nos. 772/6	2·75	2·50

1993. Succulents. As T **286**, but inscr "Standardised mail" in English and Afrikaans.

778	(–) "Stapelia grandiflora"	60	10

No. 778 was sold at 45c.

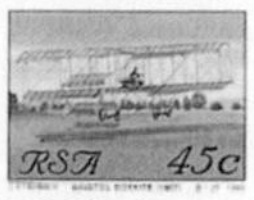

311 Bristol "Boxkite", 1907

1993. Aviation in South Africa. Multicoloured.

779	45c. Type **311**	70	70
780	45c. Voisin "Boxkite", 1909	70	70
781	45c. Bleriot XI, 1911	70	70
782	45c. Paterson No. 2 biplane, 1913	70	70
783	45c. Henri Farman H.F.27, 1915	70	70
784	45c. Royal Aircraft Factory B.E.2.E, 1918	70	70
785	45c. Vickers Vimy "Silver Queen II", 1920	70	70
786	45c. Royal Aircraft Factory S.E.5.A, 1921	70	70
787	45c. Avro 504k, 1921	70	70
788	45c. Armstrong Whitworth Atalanta, 1930	70	70
789	45c. de Havilland DH.66 Hercules, 1931	70	70
790	45c. Westland Wapiti, 1931	70	70
791	45c. Junkers F-13, 1932	70	70
792	45c. Handley Page H.P.42, 1933	70	70
793	45c. Junkers Ju 52/3m, 1934	70	70
794	45c. Junkers Ju 86, 1936	70	70
795	45c. Hawker Hartbees, 1936	70	70
796	45c. Short Empire "C" Class flying boat "Canopus", 1937	70	70
797	45c. Miles Master II and Airspeed A.S 10 Oxford, 1940	70	70
798	45c. North American Harvard Mk IIa, 1942	70	70
799	45c. Short Sunderland flying boat, 1945	70	70
800	45c. Avro Type 685 York, 1946	70	70
801	45c. Douglas DC-7B, 1955	70	70
802	45c. Sikorsky S-55c helicopter, 1956	70	70
803	45c. Boeing 707-344, 1959	70	70

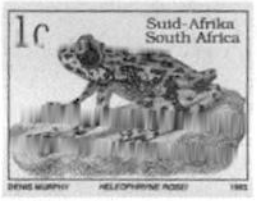

312 Table Mountain Ghost Frog

1993. Endangered Fauna. Multicoloured. (a) Face values as T **312**.

804	1c. Type **312** (I)	10	75
804c	1c. Type **312** (II)	20	1·00
805	2c. Smith's dwarf chameleon (I)	10	75
805c	2c. Smith's dwarf chameleon (II)	20	1·00
806	5c. Giant girdle-tailed lizard (I)	10	40
807	10c. Geometric tortoise (I)	10	30
807c	10c. Geometric tortoise (II)	45	70
808	20c. Southern African hedgehog (I)	20	30
913	20c. Southern African hedgehog (II)	20	40
809	40c. Riverine rabbit (I)	30	10
809c	40c. Riverine rabbit (II)	30	10
810	50c. Samango monkey (I)	30	20
914	50c. Samango monkey (II)	30	20
811	55c. Aardwolf (I)	30	10
811c	55c. Aardwolf (II)	45	60
812	60c. Cape hunting dog (I)	50	20
915	60c. Cape hunting dog (II)	40	15
813	70c. Roan antelope (I)	60	25
813c	70c. Roan antelope (II)	60	30
814	75c. African striped weasel (I)	50	20
815	80c. Kori bustard (I)	1·50	25
815a	85c. Lemon-breasted seed-eater (I)	1·50	25
816	90c. Jackass penguin (I)	1·40	30
816c	90c. Jackass penguin (II)	1·75	30
817	1r. Wattled crane (I)	1·50	30
916	1r. Wattled crane (II)	1·50	40
818	2r. Blue swallow (I)	1·75	55
818c	2r. Blue swallow (II)	1·75	55
819	5r. Martial eagle (I)	2·25	1·40
819c	5r. Martial eagle (II)	2·25	1·40
820	10r. Bateleur (I)	3·25	2·10
917	20r. African fish eagle (II)	6·50	5·00

(b) Inscr "Standardised mail" in Afrikaans and English (Nos. 821 and 918b) or "Airmail postcard rate" (others).

821	(–) Black rhinoceros (III)	60	25
821b	(–) Black rhinoceros (IV)	60	35
821c	(1r.) White rhinoceros (III)	65	30
821d	(1r.) Buffalo (II)	65	30
821e	(1r.) Lion (II)	65	30
821f	(1r.) Leopard (II)	65	30
821g	(1r.) African elephant (II)	65	30

I and III. Species name in Latin. II and IV. Species name in English, No. 821 has a small rhinoceros and No. 821b a larger rhinoceros; they were sold at 45c. at first but this was later increased to the prevailing rates.

For redrawn designs without frame and inscribed "South Africa" only, see Nos. 1029/44.

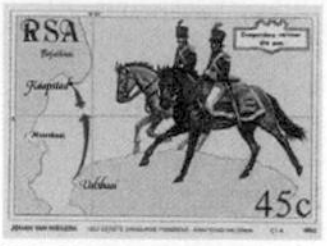

313 Dragoons carrying Mail between Cape Town and False Bay, 1803

1993. National Stamp Day. Early 19th-century Postal Services. Multicoloured.

822	45c. Type **313**	30	25
823	65c. Ox wagon carrying Stellenbosch to Cape Town mail, 1803	45	50
824	85c. Khoi-Khoin mail runners from Stellenbosch, 1803	65	70
825	1r.05 Mounted postmen, 1804	80	90

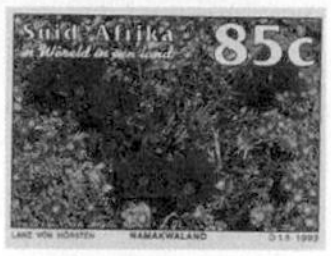

314 Flowers from Namaqualand

1993. Tourism. Multicoloured.

826	85c. Type **314** (Afrikaans inscr)	65	85
827	85c. North Beach, Durban (English inscr)	65	85
828	85c. Lion (German inscr)	65	85
829	85c. "Appel Express" on Van Staden's Bridge (Dutch inscr)	65	85
830	85c. Gemsbok (antelope) (French inscr)	65	85

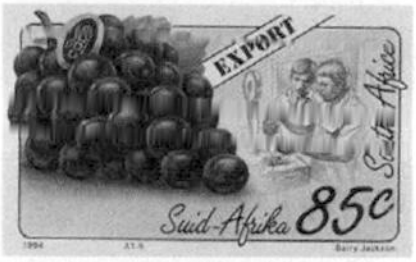

315 Grapes and Packing Bench

1994. Export Fruit. Multicoloured.

831	85c. Type **315**	55	50
832	90c. Apple and picker	55	50
833	1r.05 Plum and fork-lift truck	65	60
834	1r.25 Orange and tractor with trailer	75	70
835	1r.40 Avocado and loading freighter	85	80

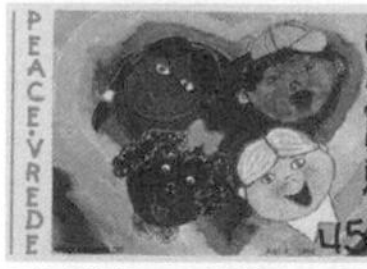

316 "Children of Different Races" (Nicole Davies)

1994. Peace Campaign. Children's Paintings. Multicoloured.

836	45c. Type **316**	25	20
837	70c. "Dove and Tree" (Robynne Lawrie)	40	40
838	95c. "Children and Dove" (Batami Nothmann)	55	55
839	1r.15 "Multi-racial Crowd" (Karen Uys)	75	80

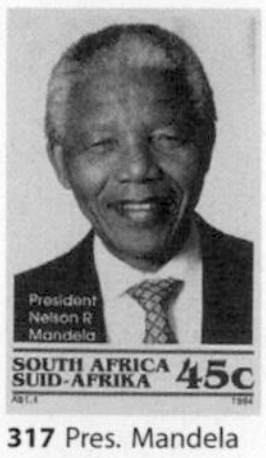

317 Pres. Mandela

1994. Inaug of President Nelson Mandela. Multicoloured.

840	45c. Type **317**	55	20
841	70c. South African national anthems	85	60
842	95c. New national flag	1·40	1·50
843	1r.15 Union Buildings, Pretoria	1·40	2·00

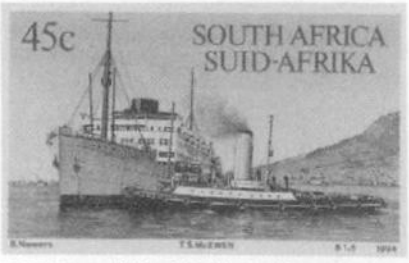

318 Tug "T.S. McEwen" towing "Winchester Castle" (liner), 1935

1994. Tugboats. Multicoloured.

844	45c. Type **318**	35	20
845	70c. "Sir William Hoy" with "Karanja" (liner), 1970	55	40
846	95c. "Sir Charles Elliott" and wreck of "Dunedin Star" (liner), 1942	70	55
847	1r.15 "Eland" and freighter at wharf, 1955	95	75
848	1r.35 "Pioneer" (paddle tug) and sailing ships, 1870	1·10	90
MS849	163×84 mm. Nos. 844/8	3·25	2·50

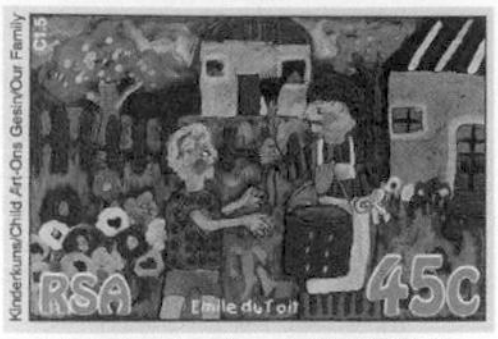

319 "Mother hands out Work" (Emile du Toit)

1994. International Year of the Family. Children's Paintings. Multicoloured.

850	45c. Type **319**	50	55
851	45c. "My Friends and I at Play" (Patrick Mackenzie)	50	55
852	45c. "Family Life" (Michelle du Pisani)	50	55
853	45c. "Sunday in Church" (Elizabeth Nel)	50	55
854	45c. "I visit my Brother in Hospital" (Zwelinzema Sam)	50	55

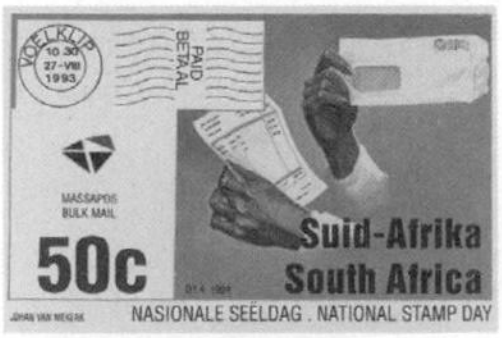

320 Hands holding Invoice and Bulk Mail Envelope

1994. National Stamp Day. Multicoloured.

855	50c. Type **320**	30	25
856	70c. Certified mail	40	40
857	95c. Registered mail	50	55
858	1r.15 Express Delivery mail	60	65

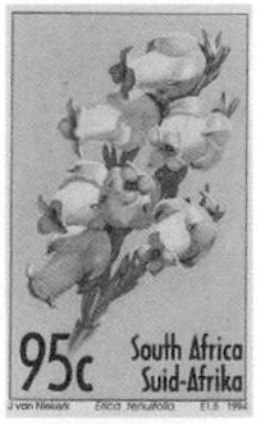

321 "Erica tenuifolia"

1994. Heathers. Multicoloured.

859	95c. Type **321**	65	70
860	95c. "Erica urna-viridis"	65	70
861	95c. "Erica decora"	65	70
862	95c. "Erica aristata"	65	70
863	95c. "Erica dichrus"	65	70

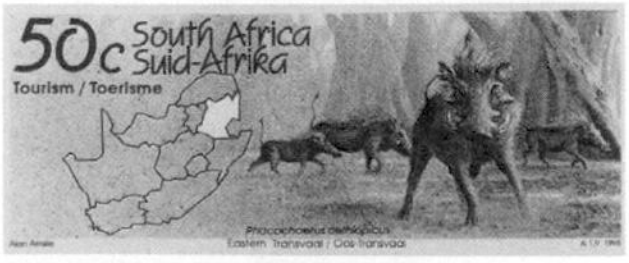

322 Warthogs (Eastern Transvaal) and Map

1995. Tourism. Multicoloured. (a) With face value.

864	50c. Type **322**	60	40
865	50c. Lost City resort (North-West Province)	60	40

(b) Inscr "Standardised mail" in English and Afrikaans.

866	(60c.) White rhinoceros and calf (KwaZulu/Natal)	60	60
867	(60c.) Cape Town waterfront (Western Cape)	60	40
868	(60c.) Baobab tree (Northern Transvaal)	80	80
869	(60c.) Highland Route (Free State)	80	80
870	(60c.) Augrabies Falls (Northern Cape)	80	80
871	(60c.) Herd of elephants, Addo National Park (Eastern Cape)	80	80
872	(60c.) Union Buildings, Pretoria (Gauteng)	80	80

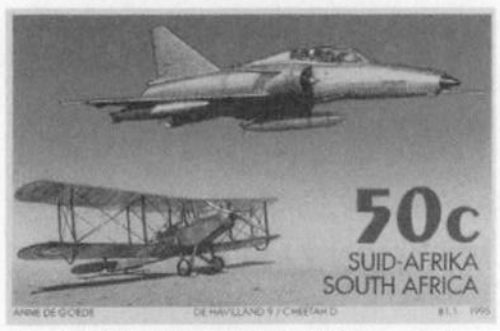

323 De Havilland D.H.9 Biplane and Cheetah D Jet Fighter

1995. Aviation Anniversaries. Multicoloured.

873	50c. Type **323** (75th anniv of South African Air Force)	1·00	40
874	95c. Vickers Vimy "Silver Queen II" (75th anniv of first Trans-African flight)	1·50	1·50

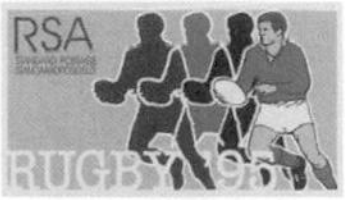

324 Player running with Ball and Silhouettes

1995. World Cup Rugby Championship, South Africa. Multicoloured.

875	(60c.) Type **324**	30	25
876	(60c.) Player running with ball and silhouettes (vert)	30	25
877	1r.15 Player taking ball from scrum (68×26½ mm)	75	85
MS878	109×61 mm. No. 876	75	75

Nos. 875/6 are inscribed "STANDARD POSTAGE" in English and Afrikaans.

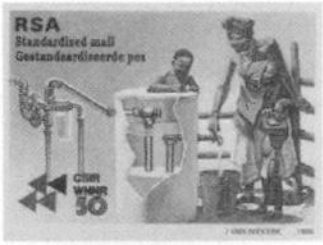

325 Rural Water Purification System

1995. 50th Anniv of C.S.I.R. (technological research organization).

879	**325** (60c.) multicoloured	45	45

No. 879 is inscribed "Standardised mail" in English and Afrikaans.

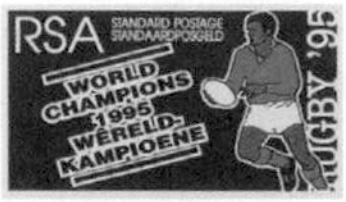

326 Player with Ball

1995. South Africa's Victory in Rugby World Cup. Multicoloured.

880	(60c.) Type **326**	40	50
881	(60c.) South African player holding trophy aloft (vert)	40	50

Nos. 880/1 are inscribed "STANDARD POSTAGE" in English and Afrikaans.

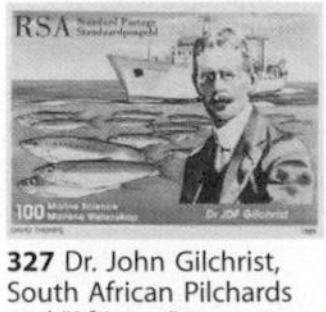

327 Dr. John Gilchrist, South African Pilchards and "Africana" (oceanographic research ship)

1995. Centenary of Marine Science in South Africa.

882	**327** (60c.) multicoloured	30	30

No. 882 is inscribed "Standard Postage" in English and Afrikaans.

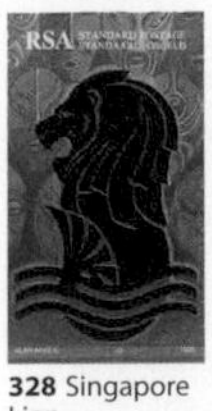

328 Singapore Lion

1995. "Singapore '95" International Stamp Exhibition. Sheet 71×55 mm.

MS883	**328** (60c.) multicoloured	1·25	1·75

No. **MS**883 is inscribed "STANDARD POSTAGE" in English and Afrikaans.

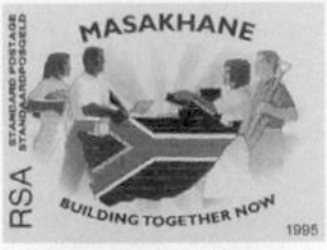

329 People building Flag Wall

1995. Masakhane Campaign.

884	**329** (60c.) multicoloured (34×24 mm)	20	20
884b	**329** (60c.) multicoloured (26×20 mm)	20	20

Nos. 884 and 884b are inscribed "STANDARD POSTAGE" in English and Afrikaans.

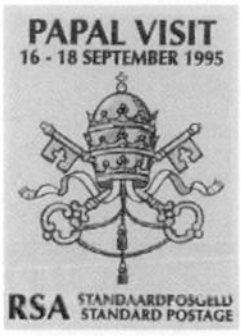

330 Papal Arms

1995. Visit of Pope John Paul II.

885	**330** (60c.) multicoloured	65	30

No. 885 is inscribed "STANDARD POSTAGE" in English and Afrikaans.

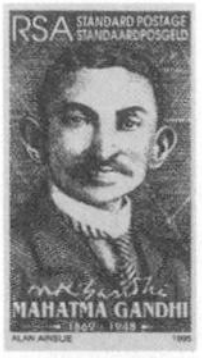

331 Gandhi wearing Suit

1995. 125th Birth Anniv (1994) of Mahatma Gandhi.

886	**331** (60c.) violet	1·00	40
887	- 1r.40 brown	1·50	1·60
MS888	71×71 mm. No. 887	1·40	1·60

No. 886 is inscribed "STANDARD POSTAGE" in English and Afrikaans.

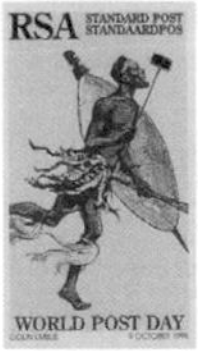

332 Traditional African Postman

1995. World Post Day.

889	**332** (60c.) multicoloured	30	30

No. 889 is inscribed "STANDARD POSTAGE" in English and Afrikaans.

1995. "Total Stampex '95" and "Ilsapex '98" Stamp Exhibitions. Sheet, 70×66 mm, containing T **332** and "ILSAPEX '98" logo. Imperf.

MS890	5r. multicoloured	2·00	2·50

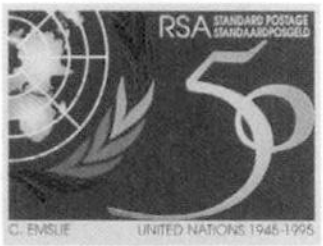

333 "50" and U.N. Emblem

1995. 50th Annivs of United Nations and UNESCO. Multicoloured.

891	**333** (60c.) multicoloured	30	30
MS892	101×78 mm. (60c.) Traditional village (30×47 mm)	30	45

No. 891 is inscribed "STANDARD POSTAGE" in English and Afrikaans.

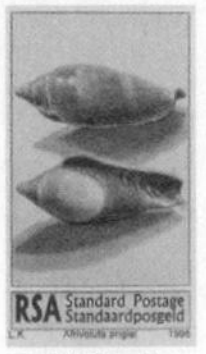

334 "Afrivoluta pringlei"

1995. Sea Shells. Multicoloured.

893	(60c.) Type **334**	40	40
894	(60c.) "Lyria africana"	40	40
895	(60c.) "Marginella mosaica"	40	40
896	(60c.) "Conus pictus"	40	40
897	(60c.) "Gypreaea fultoni"	40	40

Nos. 893/7 are inscribed "STANDARD POSTAGE" in English and Afrikaans.

No. 893 is inscribed "priglei" in error.

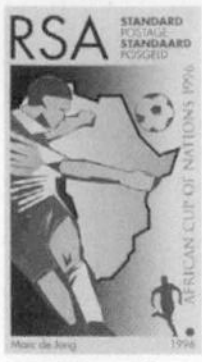

335 Map of Africa and Player

1996. African Nations Football Championship, South Africa. Map and Players.

898	**335**	(60c.) multicoloured ("RSA" in blue)	55	60
899	-	(60c.) multicoloured ("RSA" in brown)	55	60
900	-	(60c.) multicoloured ("RSA" in red)	55	60
901	-	(60c.) multicoloured ("RSA" in grey)	55	60
902	-	(60c.) multicoloured ("RSA" in green)	55	60
MS903		75×55 mm. (60c.) multicoloured (young player)	50	70

Nos. 898/903 are inscribed "STANDARD POSTAGE" in English and Afrikaans.

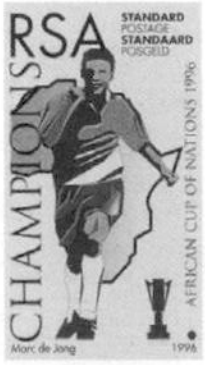

336 South African Player, Map and Trophy

1996. South Africa's Victory in African Nations Football Championship.

904	**336** (60c.) multicoloured	40	30

No. 904 is inscribed "STANDARD POSTAGE" in English and Afrikaans.

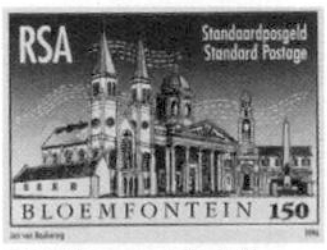

337 Historical Buildings, Bloemfontein

1996. 150th Anniv of City of Bloemfontein.

905	**337** (60c.) multicoloured	65	40

No. 905 is inscribed "Standard Postage" in English and Afrikaans.

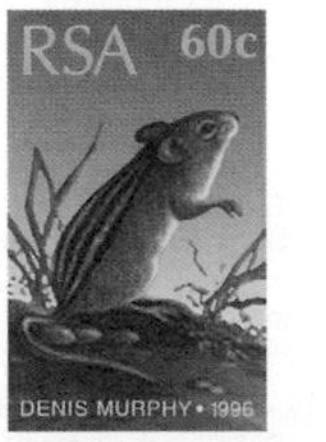

338 Rat

1996. "CHINA '96" 9th Asian International Stamp Exhibition, Peking. Sheet 109×85 mm.

MS906	**338** 60c. multicoloured	70	80

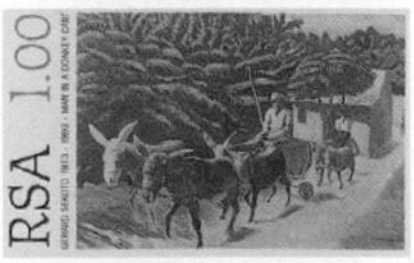

339 "Man in a Donkey Cart" (Gerard Sekoto)

1996. Gerard Sekoto (artist) Commemoration. Multicoloured.

907	1r. Type **339**	30	30
908	2r. "Song of the Pick"	80	80
MS909	108×70 mm. 2r. "Yellow Houses, Sophiatown" (detail) (vert)	1·00	1·10

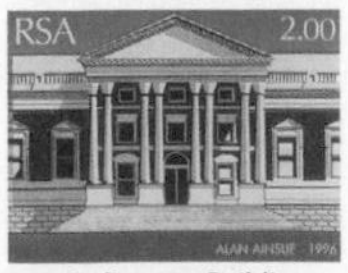

340 Parliament Building, Cape Town

1996. "CAPEX '96" International Stamp Exhibition, Toronto. Sheet 72×49 mm.
MS910 **340** 2r. multicoloured   1·00   1·10

341 Children playing

1996. Youth Day.
911 **341** (60c.) multicoloured   30   20

No. 911 is inscribed "STANDARD POSTAGE" in English and Afrikaans.

342 Marathon Runners

1996. 75th Anniv of Comrades Marathon.
912 **342** (60c.) multicoloured   30   20

No. 912 is inscribed "Standard postage" in English and Afrikaans.

343 Cycling

1996. Olympic Games, Atlanta. Multicoloured.
919 **343** (70c.) Type **343**   45   55
920   (70c.) Swimming   45   55
921   (70c.) Boxing   45   55
922   (70c.) Running   45   55
923   (70c.) Pole vaulting   45   55
924   1r.40 South African Olympic emblem   45   55

Nos. 919/24 are inscribed "STANDARD POSTAGE" in English and Afrikaans.

344 Constitutional Assembly Logo

1996. New Democratic Constitution.
925 **344** (70c.) green, red and black   30   30
926 **344** (70c.) blue, violet, and black   30   30
927 **344** (70c.) violet, yellow and black   30   30
928 **344** (70c.) blue, red and black   30   30
929 **344** (70c.) red, yellow and black   30   30

Nos. 925/9 are inscribed "Standard postage" in English and Afrikaans.

345 "Sea Pioneer" (bulk carrier)

1996. 50th Anniv of South African Merchant Marine. Multicoloured.
930 **345** (70c.) Type **345**   90   90
931   (70c.) "Winterberg" (container ship)   90   90
932   1r.40 "Langkloof" (freighter)   1·50   1·75
933   1r.40 "Vaal" (liner)   1·50   1·75
MS934 102×63 mm. 2r. "Constantia" (freighter) and tug (71×30 mm) (inscr "SOUTH AFRICAN MERCHANT MARINE 1946–1996" on top margin)   1·00   1·00

No. MS934 also comes with the top margin inscription replaced by "Safmarine" and logo.
Nos. 930/1 are inscribed "Standard Postage" in English and Afrikaans.

346 "Xhosa Woman" (G. Pemba)

1996. National Women's Day.
935 **346** 70c. multicoloured   30   25

347 Postman delivering Letters

1996. World Post Day.
936 **347** 70c. multicoloured   30   25

348 Candles and Holly

1996. Christmas.
937 **348** 70c. multicoloured   30   25

349 "Liner "Oranje" at Cape Town" (E. Wale)

1996. "Bloemfontein 150" National Stamp Show. Sheet 80×50 mm.
MS938 **349** 2r. multicoloured   1·50   1·50

350 Max Theiler (Medicine, 1951)

1996. South African Nobel Laureates.
939 **350** (70c.) violet and purple   50   55
940 –   (70c.) green, purple and violet   50   55
941 –   (70c.) purple and violet   50   55
942 –   (70c.) green, purple and violet   50   55
943 –   (70c.) violet and purple   50   55
944 –   (70c.) green, purple and violet   50   55
945 –   (70c.) green, purple and violet   50   55
946 –   (70c.) purple and violet   50   55
947 –   (70c.) green, purple and violet   50   55
948 –   (70c.) violet and purple   50   55

Nos. 939/48 are inscribed "Standard Postage" in English and Afrikaans.

351 Early Motor Car

1997. Centenary of Motoring in South Africa.
949 **351** (70c.) multicoloured   1·00   35

No. 949 is inscribed "STANDARD POSTAGE" in English and Afrikaans.

352 Lion

1997. "Hong Kong '97" International Stamp Exhibition. Sheet 82×68 mm.
MS950 **352** 3r. blue, gold and red   1·40   1·40

353 Vegetables and Water Pump

1997. National Water Conservation. Multicoloured.
951   (70c.) Type **353**   40   40
952   (70c.) Flowers and watering can   40   40
953   (70c.) Child in bath   40   40
954   (70c.) Building tools   40   40
955   (70c.) Water cart and stand pipe   40   40

Nos. 951/5 are inscribed "STANDARD POSTAGE".

354 S.A.S. "Umkomaas" (minesweeper)

1997. 75th Anniv of South African Navy. Multicoloured.
956   (70c.) Type **354**   75   75
957   (70c.) S.A.S. "Emily Hobhouse" (submarine) and S.A.S. "President Steyn" (frigate)   75   75
958   (70c.) S.A.S. "Kobie Coetsee" (fast attack craft)   75   75
959   (70c.) S.A.S. "Protea" (hydrographic survey ship)   75   75

Nos. 956/9 are inscribed "Standard Postage" in English and Afrikaans.

355 Election Day Poster

1997. Freedom Day. Each black and red.
960   (1r.) Type **355**   40   40
961   (1r.) People queueing   40   40
962   (1r.) People registering   40   40
963   (1r.) Voting booth   40   40
964   (1r.) Woman placing vote in ballot box   40   40

Nos. 960/4, which are inscribed "STANDARD POSTAGE", were printed together, se-tenant, forming a composite design.

356 Brahman Bull

1997. Chinese New Year ("Year of the Ox"). "SAPDA '97" Stamp Exhibition, Johannesburg. Sheet 107×61 mm.
MS965 **356** 4r.50 multicoloured   1·00   1·00

357 Zulu Baskets

1997. Year of Cultural Experiences. Multicoloured.
966   (1r.) Type **357**   40   40
967   (1r.) Southern Sotho figure   40   40
968   (1r.) South Ndebele figure   40   40
969   (1r.) Venda door   40   40
970   (1r.) Tsonga medicine gourd   40   40
971   (1r.) Wooden pot, Northern Cape   40   40
972   (1r.) Khoi walking stick   40   40
973   (1r.) Tswana knife handle   40   40
974   (1r.) Xhosa pipe   40   40
975   (1r.) Swazi vessel   40   40

Nos. 966/75 are inscribed "Standard Postage".

358 Grocott's, Muirhead and Gowie Buildings, Grahamstown

1997. "Pacific '97" International Stamp Exhibition, San Francisco. Sheet 94×49 mm.
MS976 **358** 5r. multicoloured   1·25   1·25

359 White-breasted Cormorant

1997. World Environment Day. Waterbirds. Multicoloured.
977   (1r.) Type **359**   40   40
978   (1r.) Hamerkop   40   40
979   (1r.) Lesser pied kingfisher ("Pied Kingfisher")   40   40
980   (1r.) Purple heron   40   40
981   (1r.) Black-headed heron   40   40
982   (1r.) African darter ("Darter")   40   40
983   (1r.) Green-backed heron   40   40
984   (1r.) White-face whistling duck ("White-faced Duck")   40   40
985   (1r.) Saddle-billed stork   40   40
986   (1r.) Water dikkop   40   40

Nos. 977/86 are inscribed "STANDARD POSTAGE" .

360 Double-headed Class 6E 1 Electric Locomotives

1997. Inauguration of Revived Blue Train Service. Multicoloured.
987   (1r.20) Type **360**   90   90
988   (1r.20) Double-headed Class 6E 1 electric locomotives (different)   90   90
989   (1r.20) Double-headed Class 25NC steam locomotives, 1960s   90   90
990   (1r.20) Double-headed Class 34,900 diesel locomotives on Modder River bridge   90   90
991   (1r.20) Double-headed Class 34 diesel locomotives and baobab tree   90   90

Nos. 987/91 are inscribed "AIRMAIL POSTAGE RATE".

361 Nguni Breed

1997. Cattle Breeds. Multicoloured.
992   (1r.) Type **361**   50   60
993   (1r.) Bonsmara   50   60
994   (1r.) Afrikander   50   60
995   (1r.) Drakensberger   50   60

Nos. 992/5 are inscribed "Standard Postage" in English and Afrikaans.

362 Leopard Seal

1997. Antarctic Fauna. Multicoloured.
996   (1r.) Type **362**   50   25
997   1r.20 Antarctic skua   90   50
998   1r.70 King penguin   1·40   90

No. 996 is inscribed "Standard Postage" in English and Afrikaans.

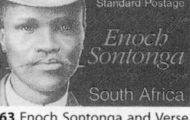

363 Enoch Sontonga and Verse from "Nkosi Sikele'i Afrika"

1997. Heritage Day. Centenary of "Nkosi Sikele'i Afrika" (National Anthem). Multicoloured.
999   (1r.) Type **363**   50   50
1000   (1r.) As Type **363** but portrait at right   50   50

Nos. 999/1000 are inscribed "Standard Postage".

364 Horse-drawn Postcart delivering Mail

1997. "Cape Town '97" National Stamp Show. Sheet 85×64 mm.

MS1001	**364** 4r.50 multicoloured	1·50	1·50

365 Modern Postbox

1997. World Post Day. Sheet, 108×69 mm.

MS1002	**365** (1 r.) multicoloured	70	70

No. **MS**1002 is inscribed "STANDARD POSTAGE".

366 Bethlehem

1997. Christmas. 50th Anniv of S.A.N.T.A. (South African National Tuberculosis Association). Charity Labels. Multicoloured.

1003	(1r.) Type **366**	35	35
1004	(1r.) Cross of Lorraine and candles	35	35
1005	(1r.) Cross of Lorraine, angels and candles	35	35
1006	(1r.) Angel kneeling before Cross of Lorraine	35	35
1007	(1r.) Father Christmas carrying sack	35	35
1008	(1r.) Mary and Jesus	35	35
1009	(1r.) Christmas trees	35	35
1010	(1r.) Wise men on camels	35	35
1011	(1r.) Christmas bell	35	35
1012	(1r.) Child kneeling	35	35

Nos. 1003/12 are inscribed "STANDARD POSTAGE".

367 Black Rhinoceros

1997. Endangered Fauna (3rd series). Redrawn values as 1993–97 issue and new designs (Nos. 1030/4), all without frame and inscr "South Africa" only as T **367**. Multicoloured. (a) Designs as Nos. 806/20, and some new values, redrawn.

1012a	5c. Giant girdle-tailed lizard	30	50
1013	10c. Geometric tortoise	10	50
1014	20c. Southern African hedgehog	15	60
1015	30c. Spotted hyena	20	60
1016	40c. Riverine rabbit	30	60
1017	50c. Samango monkey	30	40
1018	60c. Cape hunting dog	40	50
1019	70c. Roan antelope	40	50
1020	80c. Kori bustard	1·50	60
1021	90c. Jackass penguin	2·00	50
1022	1r. Wattled crane	1·50	45
1022a	1r.50 Tawny eagle (20×37 mm)	3·00	1·50
1027	2r. Blue swallow	1·50	45
1023a	2r.30 Cape vulture (20×37 mm)	3·00	2·00
1024	3r. Giraffe	2·50	1·00
1025	5r. Martial eagle	2·50	1·40
1026	10r. Bateleur (34×24 mm)	3·50	2·25
1028	20r. African fish eagle ("Fish Eagle") (34×24 mm)	6·50	5·00

(b) Inscr "Standard Postage" (No. 1029) or "standard postage" (others).

1029	(1r.) Type **367**	60	60
1030	(1r.) Eland (vert)	50	50
1031	(1r.10) Greater kudu (vert)	50	50
1032	(1r.10) Impala (vert)	50	50
1033	(1r.10) Waterbuck (vert)	50	50
1034	(1r.10) Blue wildebeest (vert)	50	50

(d) Inscr "Airmail Postcard".

1040	(1r.20) White rhinoceros	90	1·00
1041	(1r.20) Buffalo	90	1·00
1042	(1r.20) Lion	90	1·00
1043	(1r.20) Leopard	90	1·00
1044	(1r.20) African elephant	90	1·00

368 Tiger (woodcut)

1998. Chinese New Year ("Year of the Tiger"). Sheet 67×85 mm.

MS1051	**368** 5r. red, black and green	1·50	1·50

369 "Rescue 8" (lifeboat)

1998. 30th Anniv (1997) of National Sea Rescue Institute.

1052	**369** (1r.) multicoloured	65	30

370 Leopard

1998. "SAPDA '98" National Stamp Exhibition, Johannesburg. Sheet 64×84 mm.

MS1053	**370** 5r. multicoloured	1·50	1·50

371 Football Player

1998. World Cup Football Championship, France.

1054	**371** (1r.10) multicoloured	60	30

No. 1054 is inscribed "STANDARD POSTAGE".

372 Stone Age Hand Axe

1998. Early South African History. Multicoloured.

1055	(1r.10) Type **372**	50	40
1056	(1r.10) Musuku (altar)	50	40
1057	(1r.10) San rock engravings	50	40
1058	(1r.10) Early iron age pot	50	40
1059	(1r.10) Khoekhoe pot	50	40
1060	(1r.10) Florisbad skull	50	40
1061	(1r.10) San rock painting	50	40
1062	(1r.10) Mapungubwe gold rhinoceros and pot	50	40
1063	(1r.10) Lydenburg head (ceremonial mask)	50	40
1064	(1r.10) Taung skull	50	40

Nos. 1055/64 are inscribed "standard postage".

373 Pale Chanting Goshawk

1998. South African Raptors. Multicoloured.

1065	(1r.10) Type **373**	60	50
1066	(1r.10) Augur buzzard ("Jackal Buzzard")	60	50
1067	(1r.10) Lanner falcon	60	50
1068	(1r.10) Lammergeier ("Bearded Vulture")	60	50
1069	(1r.10) Black harrier	60	50
1070	(1r.10) Cape vulture	60	50
1071	(1r.10) Bateleur	60	50
1072	(1r.10) Spotted eagle owl	60	50
1073	(1r.10) White-headed vulture	60	50
1074	(1r.10) African fish eagle	60	50

Nos. 1065/74 are inscribed "standard postage".

1998. Endangered Fauna. Antelopes. Designs as Nos. 1030/4, but self-adhesive.

1075	(1r.10) Eland (vert)	50	50
1076	(1r.10) Greater kudu (vert)	50	50
1077	(1r.10) Impala (vert)	50	50
1078	(1r.10) Waterbuck (vert)	50	50
1079	(1r.10) Blue wildebeest (vert)	50	50

The above are inscribed "standard postage".

374 Shepherd's Tree

1998. Trees. Multicoloured.

1080	(1r.10) Type **374**	70	70
1081	(1r.10) Karee	70	70
1082	(1r.10) Baobab	70	70
1083	(1r.10) Umbrella thorn	70	70

Nos. 1080/3 are inscribed "Standard Postage".

375 Sandstone Cliffs, Cape Point

1998. "Explore South Africa" (1st series). Multicoloured. (a) Western Cape.

1084	(1r.30) Type **375**	90	70
1085	(1r.30) Robben Island	90	70
1086	(1r.30) Ostrich farming, Pinehurst Homestead	90	70
1087	(1r.30) Victoria and Alfred Waterfront, Capetown	90	70
1088	(1r.30) Homestead, Boschendal Wine Estate	90	70

(b) KwaZulu-Natal.

1089	(1r.30) Drakensberg waterfall	90	70
1090	(1r.30) Zulu women preparing food	90	70
1091	(1r.30) Eastern white pelicans and rhinoceros	90	70
1092	(1r.30) Rickshaw driver	90	70
1093	(1r.30) Indian dancers	90	70

Nos. 1084/8 and 1089/93 are inscribed "AIRMAIL POSTCARD".

See also Nos. 1338/42.

376 Angel

1998. Christmas. Multicoloured.

1094	(1r.10) Type **376**	75	75
1095	(1r.10) Christmas bell	75	75
1096	(1r.10) Present	75	75
1097	(1r.10) Christmas tree	75	75
1098	(1r.10) Star	75	75

Nos. 1094/8 are inscribed "STANDARD POSTAGE".

377 African Harrier Hawk

1998. World Post Day. Sheet 67×85 mm.

MS1099	**377** 5r. multicoloured	1·50	1·50

378 London Pictorial Essay, 1927

1998. "ILSAPEX '98" International Stamp Exhibition, Johannesburg. Sheet, 108×80 mm, containing T **378** and similar vert design.

MS1100	5r. green, red and cream (Type **378**); 5r. black, green and cream (as Type **378**, but "SOUTH AFRICA" at top)	2·25	2·50

379 Cuvier's Beaked Whale

1998. Endangered Species. Whales of the Southern Ocean. Multicoloured.

1101	(1r.30) Type **379**	1·10	75
1102	(1r.30) Minke whale	1·10	75
1103	(1r.30) Bryde's whale	1·10	75
1104	(1r.30) Pygmy right whale	1·10	75
MS1105	103×68 mm. 5r. Blue whale	1·75	1·75

Nos. 1101/4 are inscribed "airmail postcard".

No. **MS**1105 forms part of joint issue with Namibia and Norfolk Island.

380 Emblem and Building

1998. 50th Anniv of Universal Declaration of Human Rights.

1106	**380** (1r.10) multicoloured	1·00	35

No. 1106 is inscribed "Standard Postage".

381 Dennis Mail Van, 1913

1999. 125th Anniv of Universal Postal Union. Multicoloured.

1107	(1r.10) Type **381**	70	60
1108	(1r.10) Ford V8 post van, 1935	70	60
1109	(1r.10) Mobile Post Office, 1937	70	60
1110	(1r.10) Trojan Post Office van, 1927	70	60

Nos. 1107/10 are inscribed "Standard Postage".

382 Rabbit

1999. Chinese New Year ("Year of the Rabbit"). Sheet 85×67 mm.

MS1111	**382** 5r. multicoloured	1·50	1·50

383 "Discovery" (Scott)

1999. Famous Ships. Multicoloured.

1112	(1r.10) Type **383**	1·10	1·00
1113	(1r.10) "Heemskerk" (Tasman)	1·10	1·00
1114	(1r.10) H.M.S. "Endeavour" (Cook)	1·10	1·00
1115	(1r.10) H.M.S. "Beagle" (Darwin)	1·10	1·00

Nos. 1112/15 are inscribed "standard postage".

384 "Lawhill" (barque)

1999. "Australia '99" International Stamp Exhibition, Melbourne. Sheet 65×85 mm.

MS1116	**384** 5r. multicoloured	1·75	1·75

385
Traditional
Nguni Love
Token with
AIDS Ribbon

1999. AIDS Awareness Campaign.
1117	**385**	(1r.20) multicoloured (violet background)	65	65
1118	**385**	(1r.20) multicoloured (green background)	65	65

Nos. 1117/18 are inscribed "Standard Postage".

386 African Elephant

1999. "iBRA '99" International Stamp Exhibition, Nuremburg. Sheet 100×68 mm.
MS1119	**386**	5r. multicoloured	2·25	1·50

387 Class 19D Steam
Locomotive, South African
Railways

1999. "SAPDA '99" Stamp Show, Johannesburg. Sheet 100×75 mm.
MS1120	**387**	5r. multicoloured	2·25	1·50

388 Nurse

1999. Workers' Day. Multicoloured.
1121	(1r.20) Type **388**		60	60
1122	(1r.20) Cleaner with mop		60	60
1123	(1r.20) Forester with axe		60	60
1124	(1r.20) Farmer with spade		60	60
1125	(1r.20) Chef with sieve		60	60
1126	(1r.20) Fisherman with net		60	60
1127	(1r.20) Construction worker with scaffolding		60	60
1128	(1r.20) Miner with pick		60	60
1129	(1r.20) Postman with mail		60	60
1130	(1r.20) Road worker with pneumatic drill		60	60

389 President
Thabo Mbeki

1999. Inauguration of President Thabo Mbeki.
1131	**389**	(1r.20) multicoloured	1·00	45

No. 1131 is inscribed "standard postage".

390 Nelson Mandela
in Mantle of Order

1999. 900th Anniv of Order of St. John of Jerusalem. Sheet 108×68 mm.
MS1132	**390**	2r. multicoloured	1·25	1·25

391 Actress with
Drama Masks

1999. 25th Anniv of Standard Bank National Arts Festival. Multicoloured.
1133	(1r.20) Type **391**		70	70
1134	(1r.20) Woman with roll of film		70	70
1135	(1r.20) Woman playing guitar		70	70
1136	(1r.20) Woman dancing		70	70
1137	(1r.20) Painter		70	70

Nos. 1133// are inscribed "STANDARD POSTAGE".

1999. "Explore South Africa" (2nd series). Mpumalanga and Northern Province. As T 375. Multicoloured.
1138	(1r.70) Blyde River Canyon		1·10	1·10
1139	(1r.70) Lone Creek Falls, Sabie		1·10	1·10
1140	(1r.70) Ndebele women in traditional dress		1·10	1·10
1141	(1r.70) Pilgrim's Rest (historic town)		1·10	1·10
1142	(1r.70) Elephants, Kruger National Park		1·10	1·10

Nos. 1138/42 are inscribed "AIRMAIL POSTCARD".

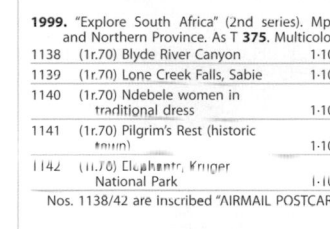

392 North Ndebele
Wall Pattern

1999. Traditional Wall Art. Designs showing sections of wall art. Multicoloured.
1143	(1r.20) Type **392**		60	60
1144	(1r.20) South Ndebele		60	60
1145	(1r.20) Swazi		60	60
1146	(1r.20) Venda		60	60
1147	(1r.20) South Sotho		60	60
1148	(1r.20) Xhosa		60	60
1149	(1r.20) North Sotho		60	60
1150	(1r.20) Tsonga		60	60
1151	(1r.20) Zulu		60	60
1152	(1r.20) Tswana		60	60

Nos. 1143/52 are inscribed "STANDARD POSTAGE".

393 South African
Rock Art Painting

1999. China '99 International Stamp Exhibition, Beijing. Sheet 154×85 mm.
MS1153	**393**	5r. multicoloured	1·75	1·75

394 Strelitzia reginae
(flower)

1999. "JOPEX '99" National Stamp Exhibition, Johannesburg. Sheet 65×85 mm.
MS1154	**394**	5r. multicoloured	1·75	1·75

395 Barn
Swallow

1999. Migratory Species of South Africa. Multicoloured.
1155	(1r.20) Type **395**		75	65
1156	(1r.20) Great white shark		75	65
1157	(1r.20) Lesser kestrel		75	65
1158	(1r.20) Common dolphin		75	65
1159	(1r.20) European bee-eater		75	65
1160	(1r.20) Loggerhead turtle		75	65
1161	(1r.20) Curlew sandpiper		75	65
1162	(1r.20) Wandering albatross		75	65
1163	(1r.20) Springbok		75	65
1164	(1r.20) Lesser flamingo		75	65

Nos. 1155/64 are inscribed "Standard Postage".

396 Boers leaving for
Commando

1999. Centenary of Anglo-Boer War (1st issue). Multicoloured.
1165	(1r.20) Type **396**		90	90
1166	(1r.20) British soldiers		90	90

See also Nos. 2003/4, 1343/4 and MS1384.

397 Landscape

2000. New Millennium.
1167	**397**	(1r.20) multicoloured	70	40

No. 1167 is inscribed "standard Postage".

398 National Lottery
Logo

2000. First National Lottery.
1168	**398**	(1r.20) multicoloured	65	30

No. 1168 is inscribed "STANDARD POSTAGE".

399 Family inside
Heart

2000. National Family Day.
1169	**399**	(1r.30) multicoloured	65	30

No. 1169 is inscribed "Standard Postage".

400 Green Turaco ("Knysna
Lourie")

2000. "The Stamp Show 2000" International Stamp Exhibition, London. Sheet 108×68 mm.
MS1170	**400**	4r.60 multicoloured	2·50	2·00

401 Banded Stream
Frog

2000. Frogs of South Africa. Multicoloured.
1171	1r.30 Type **401**		80	80
1172	1r.30 Yellow-striped reed frog		80	80
1173	1r.30 Natal leaf-folding frog		80	80
1174	1r.30 Paradise toad		80	80
1175	1r.30 Table Mountain ghost frog		80	80
1176	1r.30 Banded rubber frog		80	80
1177	1r.30 Dwarf grass frog		80	80
1178	1r.30 Long-toed tree frog		80	80
1179	1r.30 Namaqua rain frog		80	80
1180	1r.30 Bubbling kassina		80	80

402 Forest Tree Frog

2000. "JUNASS 2000" National Junior Stamp Show, Baksburg. Sheet 108×68 mm.
MS1181	**402**	4r.60 multicoloured	2·25	2·25

403 Stalked Bulbine

2000. Medicinal Plants. Multicoloured.
1182	1r.30 Type **403**		70	70
1183	1r.30 Wild dagga		70	70
1184	1r.30 Wild garlic		70	70
1185	1r.30 Pig's ear		70	70
1186	1r.30 Wild ginger		70	70
1187	2r.30 Red paintbrush		80	80
1188	2r.30 Cancer bush		80	80
1189	2r.30 Yellow star		80	80
1190	2r.30 Bitter aloe		80	80
1191	2r.30 Sour fig		80	80

404 Athlete
with South
African Flag

2000. Olympic Games, Sydney. Multicoloured.
1192	1r.30 Type **404**		60	25
1193	1r.50 Elana Meyer (medal winner, 1992)		60	35
1194	2r.20 Joshua Thugwane (medal winner, 1996)		80	75
1195	2r.30 Olympic rings and South African flag		95	80
1196	6r.30 Penny Heyns (medal winner, 1996)		1·75	2·75

405 Globe and Peace
Doves

2000. United Nations International Year of Peace.
1197	**405**	1r.30 multicoloured	65	30

406 Robben Island

2000. UNESCO World Heritage Sites. Multicoloured.
1198	1r.30 Type **406**		75	55
1199	1r.30 Greater St. Lucia Wetland Park		75	55
1200	1r.30 Early skull from Sterkfontein		75	55

407 Dragon

2000. Chinese New Year ("Year of the Dragon"). Sheet 85×65 mm.

MS1201	407	4r.60 multicoloured	1·50	1·50

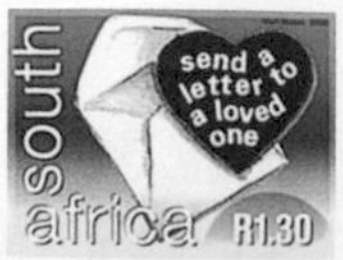

408 Heart and Envelope

2000. World Post Day.

1202	408	1r.30 multicoloured	70	40

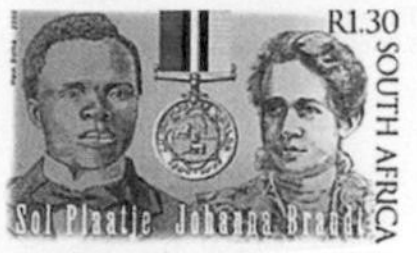

409 Sol Plaatje and Johanna Brandt

2000. Centenary of Anglo-Boer War (2nd issue). Authors. Multicoloured.

1203	1r.30 Type **409**	25	25
1204	4r.40 Arthur Conan Doyle and Winston Churchill	3·25	2·00

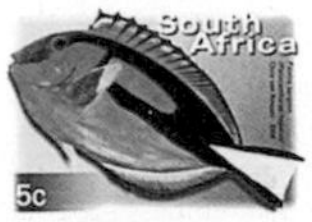

410 Palette Surgeonfish

2000. Flora and Fauna (1st issue). Multicoloured.

1205	5c. Type **410**	10	50
1206	10c. Clown surgeonfish ("Blue-banded Surgeon")	10	50
1207	20c. Regal angelfish	10	50
1208	30c. Emperor angelfish	10	50
1209	40c. Picasso triggerfish ("Black-bar triggerfish")	15	50
1210	50c. Coral hind ("Coral rockcod")	15	50
1211	60c. Powder-blue surgeonfish	20	60
1212	70c. Thread-finned butterflyfish	20	60
1213	80c. Long-horned cowfish	20	60
1214	90c. Forceps butterflyfish ("Longnose butterflyfish")	25	60
1215	1r. Two-spined angelfish ("Coral Beauty")	30	60
1216	1r.30 Botterblom (vert)	45	60
1217	1r.30 Blue marguerite (vert)	45	60
1218	1r.30 Karoo violet (vert)	45	60
1219	1r.30 Tree pelargonium (vert)	45	60
1220	1r.30 Black-eyed susy (vert)	45	60
1221	1r.40 Gold-banded forester	75	40
1222	1r.50 Brenton blue	85	50
1223	1r.90 Silver-barred charaxes	1·25	1·00
1224	2r. Lilac-breasted roller (vert)	1·50	1·00
1225	2r.30 Citrus butterfly	1·75	1·25
1226	3r. Woodland kingfisher (vert)	2·00	1·50
1227	5r. White-fronted bee eater (vert)	2·50	1·50
1228	6r.30 Narrow blue-banded swallowtail ("Green-banded swallowtail")	3·00	2·50
1229	10r. African green pigeon (vert)	4·50	4·00
1230	12r.60 False-dotted border	5·00	5·00
1231	20r. Violet-crested turaco ("Purplecrested lourie") (vert)	7·50	7·50

(b) Designs as Nos. 1216/20, but smaller (20×25 mm). Self-adhesive.

1232	1r.30 As No. 1216 (inscr "Afrika Borwa")	70	90
1233	1r.30 As No. 1216 (inscr "Afrika Dzonga")	70	90
1234	1r.30 As No. 1217 (inscr "Ningizimu Afrika")	70	90
1235	1r.30 As No. 1217 (inscr "Afrika Sewula")	70	90
1236	1r.30 As No. 1218 (inscr "Suid-Afrika")	70	90
1237	1r.30 As No. 1218 (inscr "Afrika Borwa")	70	90
1238	1r.30 As No. 1219 (inscr "Afrika Tshipembe")	70	90
1239	1r.30 As No. 1219 (inscr "Ningizimu Afrika")	70	90
1240	1r.30 As No. 1220 (inscr "Afrika Borwa")	70	90
1241	1r.30 As No. 1220 (inscr "Mzantsi Afrika")	70	90

DESIGNS from 5c. to 1r. show fish, 1r.30 flowers, 1r.40 to 1r.90, 2r.30, 6r.30 and 12r.60 butterflies and the 2, 3, 5, 10 and 20r. birds.

See also Nos. 1268/1314 and 1389/93.

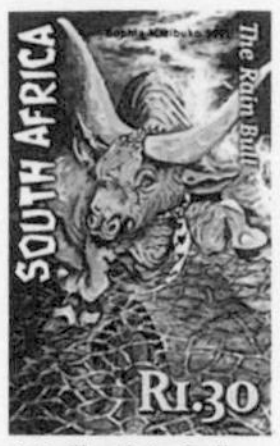

411 The Rain Bull

2001. South African Myths and Legends. Multicoloured.

1242	1r.30 Type **411**	50	25
1243	1r.50 The Grosvenor Treasure	55	30
1244	2r.20 Seven Magic Birds	70	45
1245	2r.30 The Hole in the Wall	75	55
1246	6r.30 Van Hunks and the Devil	1·60	2·25

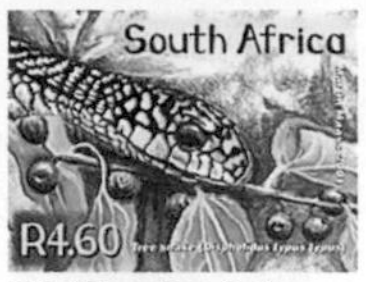

412 African Tree Snake

2001. Chinese New Year ("Year of the Snake") and "Hong Kong 2001" Stamp Exhibition. Sheet 65×85 mm.

MS1247	412	4r.60, multicoloured	1·75	1·75

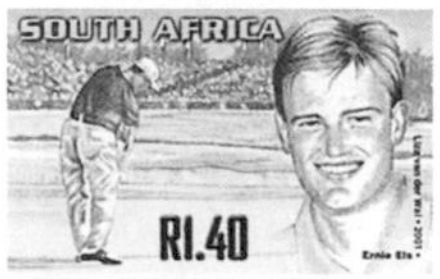

413 Ernie Els (golf)

2001. South African Sporting Heroes. Multicoloured.

1248	1r.40 Type **413**	80	65
1249	1r.40 Lucas Radebe (soccer)	80	65
1250	1r.40 Francois Pienaar (rugby)	80	65
1251	1r.40 Terrence Parkin (swimming)	80	65
1252	1r.40 Rosina Magola (netball)	80	65
1253	1r.40 Hestrie Cloete (high-jumping)	80	65
1254	1r.40 Hezekiel Sepeng (athletics)	80	65
1255	1r.40 Jonty Rhodes (cricket)	80	65
1256	1r.40 Zanele Situ (paralymic javelin)	80	65
1257	1r.40 Vuyani Bungu (boxing)	80	65

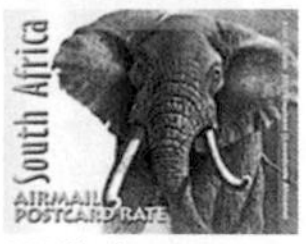

414 Elephant

2001. Wildlife. Multicoloured. (a) Designs 34×26 mm.

1258	(2r.10) Type **414**	1·10	1·10
1259	(2r.10) Lion	1·10	1·10
1260	(2r.10) Rhinoceros	1·10	1·10
1261	(2r.10) Leopard	1·10	1·10
1262	(2r.10) Buffalo	1·10	1·10

(b) Designs 29×24 mm. Self-adhesive.

1263	(2r.10) Buffalo	75	1·00
1264	(2r.10) Leopard	75	1·00
1265	(2r.10) Rhinoceros	75	1·00
1266	(2r.10) Lion	75	1·00
1267	(2r.10) Type **414**	75	1·00

Nos. 1258/67 are inscribed "AIRMAIL POSTCARD RATE" and were initially valid for 2r.10.

2001. Flora and Fauna (2nd issue). Multicoloured. (a) As T **410**.

1268	5c. Type **410**	10	50
1269	10c. Clown surgeonfish ("Blue-banded Surgeon")	15	50
1270	20c. Regal angelfish	25	50
1271	30c. Emperor angelfish	30	50
1272	40c. Picasso triggerfish	35	50
1273	50c. Coral hind ("Coral rockcod")	35	50
1274	60c. Powder-blue surgeonfish	40	40
1275	70c. Thread-finned butterflyfish	40	40
1276	80c. Long-horned cowfish	40	40
1277	90c. Forceps butterflyfish ("Longnose butterflyfish")	40	40
1278	1r. Two-spined angelfish ("Coral Beauty")	45	40
1279	1r.40 Botterblom (vert)	50	55
1280	1r.40 Blue marguerite (vert)	50	55
1281	1r.40 Karoo violet (vert)	50	55
1282	1r.40 Tree pelargonium (vert)	50	55
1283	1r.40 Black-eyed susy (vert)	50	55
1284	1r.60 Yellow pansy butterfly	1·00	55
1284a	(1r.65) Botterblom (vert)	60	65
1284b	(1r.65) Blue marguerite (vert)	60	65
1284c	(1r.65) Karoo violet (vert)	60	65
1284d	(1r.65) Tree pelargonium (vert)	60	65
1284e	(1r.65) Black-eyed Susy (vert)	60	65
1285	1r.90 Large-spotted acraea	1·40	50
1286	2r. Lilac-breasted roller (vert)	1·50	50
1287	2r.10 Kopje charaxes	1·50	70
1288	2r.50 Common grass-yellow	1·60	70
1289	3r. Woodland kingfisher (vert)	2·00	75
1290	5r. White-fronted bee-eater (vert)	2·50	1·00
1291	7r. Southern milkweed	3·00	1·75
1292	10r. African green pigeon (vert)	4·50	2·00
1293	14r. Lilac-tip	6·00	4·50
1294	20r. Purple-crested turacao ("Purplecrested lourie") (vert)	7·50	6·00

(b) Designs as Nos. 1279/83, but 20×25 mm and inscr "Standard Postage" instead of face value. Self-adhesive.

1295	(1r.40) As No. 1280 (inscr "Afrika Borwa")	45	55
1296	(1r.40) As No. 1280 (inscr "Afrika Dzonga")	45	55
1297	(1r.40) As No. 1281 (inscr "Ningizimu Afrika")	45	55
1298	(1r.40) As No. 1281 (inscr "Afrika Sewula")	45	55
1299	(1r.40) As No. 1282 (inscr "Suid-Afrika")	45	55
1300	(1r.40) As No. 1282 (inscr "Afrika Borwa")	45	55
1301	(1r.40) As No. 1283 (inscr "Afrika Tshipembe")	45	55
1302	(1r.40) As No. 1283 (inscr "Ningizimu Afrika")	45	55
1303	(1r.40) As No. 1284 (inscr "Afrika Borwa")	45	55
1304	(1r.40) As No. 1284 (inscr "Mzantsi Afrika")	45	55

Nos. 1284, 1285, 1287/8, 1291 and 1293 show butterflies.

Nos. 1284a/e and 1295/1304 are inscribed "Standard Postage" and were initially valid for 1r.65 and 1r.40 respectively.

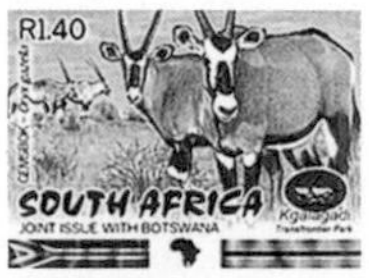

415 Gemsbok

2001. Kgalagadi Transfrontier Wildlife Park. Joint Issue with Botswana. Multicoloured.

1315	1r.40 Type **415**	40	25
1316	2r.50 Cheetah	75	55
1317	2r.90 Sociable weaver (bird)	1·25	1·25
1318	3r.60 Meercat	1·25	1·50
MS1319	114×78 mm. Nos. 1316/17	1·75	1·75

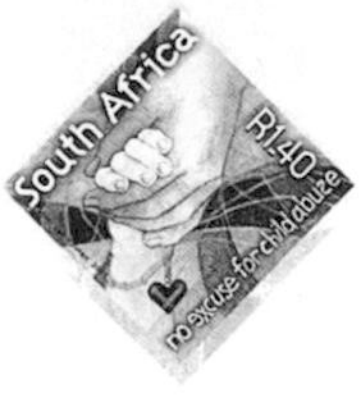

416 Adult holding Child's Hand

2001. "no excuse for child abuse" Campaign.

1320	416	1r.40 multicoloured	50	55

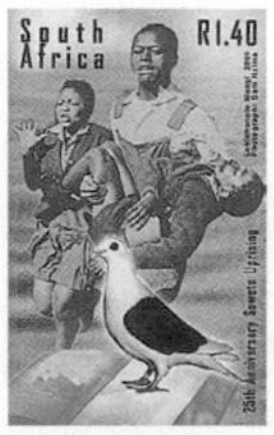

417 Victims of Soweto Uprising

2001. 25th Anniv of Soweto Uprising.

1321	417	1r.40 multicoloured	50	35

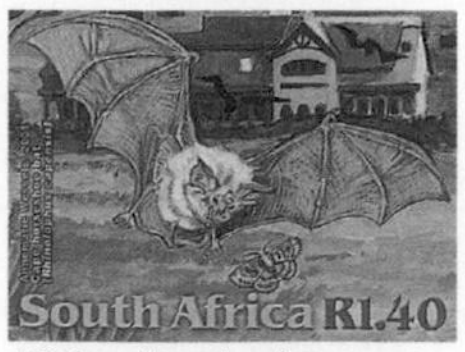

418 Cape Horseshoe Bat

2001. Bats of South Africa. Multicoloured. Self-adhesive.

1322	1r.40 Type **418**	35	45
1323	1r.40 Welwitsch's hairy bat	35	45
1324	1r.40 Schreiber's long-fingered bat	35	45
1325	1r.40 Wahlberg's epauletted fruit bat	35	45
1326	1r.40 Short-eared trident bat	35	45
1327	1r.40 Common slit-faced bat	35	45
1328	1r.40 Egyptian fruit bat	35	45
1329	1r.40 Egyptian free-tailed bat (vert)	35	45
1330	1r.40 De Winton's long-eared bat	35	45
1331	1r.40 Large-eared free-tailed bat	35	45

Nos. 1322/31 were printed in sheetlets of 10 with the background forming a composite design. Descriptions of the various species are printed on the reverse of the backing paper.

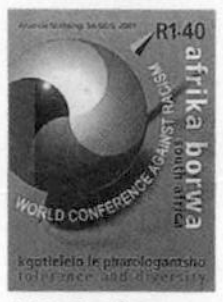

419 Conference Logo

2001. Third U.N. World Conference Against Racism, Durban.

1332	419	1r.40 mult (inscr as in T **419**)	30	40
1333	419	1r.40 mult (inscr "ningizimu afrika" and "kubeketelelana" at foot)	30	40
1334	419	1r.40 mult (inscr "suid-afrika")	30	40
1335	419	1r.40 mult (inscr "afrika tshipembe")	30	40
1336	419	1r.40 mult (inscr "afrika borwa" and "kutlwisiso" at foot)	30	40
1337	419	1r.40 mult (inscr "afrika dzonga")	30	40
1338	419	1r.40 mult (inscr "afrika sewula")	30	40
1339	419	1r.40 mult (inscr "afrika borwa" and "kgoth-lelelo" at foot)	30	40
1340	419	1r.40 mult (inscr "ningizimu afrika" and "ukubekezelelana" at foot)	30	40
1341	419	1r.40 mult (inscr "mzantsi afrika")	30	40
1342	-	2r.10 mult (logo and South Africans)	30	40

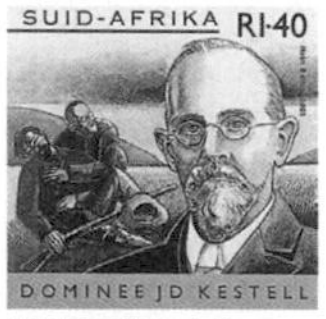

420 Dominee J. D. Kestell

2001. Centenary of Anglo-Boer War (3rd issue). Angels of Mercy. Multicoloured.

1343	1r.40 Type **420**	75	25
1344	3r. Captain Thomas Crean V.C., R.A.M.C.	1·25	1·25

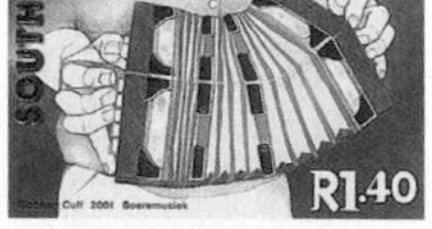

421 Boere Concertina

2001. Musical Instruments. Multicoloured.

1345	1r.40 Type **421**	40	25
1346	1r.90 Trumpet	50	45
1347	2r.50 Electric guitar	60	55
1348	3r. African drum	70	75
1349	7r. Cello	1·60	2·25

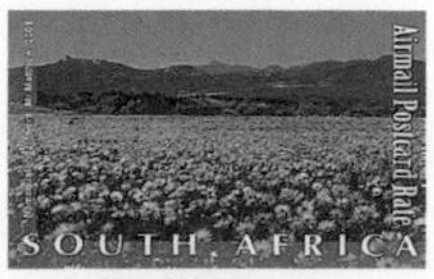

422 Fields of Flowers, Namaqualand

2001. Natural Wonders of South Africa. Multicoloured.

1350	(2r.10) Type **422**	70	70
1351	(2r.10) Cango Caves	70	70
1352	(2r.10) Richtersveld Desert	70	70
1353	(2r.10) Rocks on West Coast	70	70
1354	(2r.10) Snow covered mountains near Elliot	70	70
1355	(2r.10) Table Mountain	70	70
1356	(2r.10) Tsitsikamma Forest	70	70

1357	(2r.10) Augrabies Waterfall	70	70
1358	(2r.10) Cape Mountain Zebra	70	70
1359	(2r.10) Vineyards, Stellenbosch	70	70

Nos. 1350/9 are inscribed "Airmail Postcard Rate" and were initially valid at 2r.10 each.

423 Tree of Life decorated with Christmas Lights

2001. Christmas. Multicoloured.
| 1360 | 2r. Type **423** | 50 | 35 |
| 1361 | 3r. Angel | 60 | 50 |

424 Frame

2001. Greetings Stamps. Self-adhesive.
| 1362 | **424** | (1r.40) multicoloured | 60 | 40 |

No. 1362 is inscribed "Standard Postage" and was initially valid for 1r.40.

425 Class Volvo 60 Yacht

2001. Volvo Round the World Ocean Race. Multicoloured.
| 1363 | **425** | 1r.40 multicoloured | 1·00 | 45 |
| MS1364 55×85 mm. 6r. Volvo 60 yacht (horiz) | | | 1·25 | 1·25 |

426 International Cricket Council Logo

2001. Cricket World Cup (2003) (1st issue).
| 1365 | **426** | (1r.40) black, gold and silver | 1·50 | 65 |

No. 1365 is inscribed "Standard Postage" and was initially valid for 1r.40.
See also Nos. 1394/9 and **MS**1417.

427 Horse's Head

2001. Chinese New Year ("Year of the Horse").
| 1366 | **427** | 6r. multicoloured | 2·00 | 2·00 |

428 Scalloped Hammerhead Sharks

2001. Marine Life. Multicoloured. Self-adhesive.
1367	1r.40 Type **428**	55	55
1368	1r.40 Loggerhead turtle (vert)	55	55
1369	1r.40 Clown triggerfish (vert)	55	55
1370	1r.40 Cape fur seals (vert)	55	55
1371	1r.40 Bottlenosed dolphins	55	55
1372	1r.40 Crowned seahorses (vert)	55	55

1373	1r.40 Blue-spotted ribbontail ray (vert)	55	55
1374	1r.40 Moorish idols	55	55
1375	1r.40 Octopus	55	55
1376	1r.40 Coral rock cod	55	55

Nos. 1367/76 were printed together, se-tenant, with the background forming a composite design. Descriptions of the various species are printed on the reverse of the backing paper.

429 Child laughing

2002. World Summit for Sustainable Development, Johannesburg. Multicoloured. Ordinary gum.
1377	(1r.40) Type **429**	40	40
1378	(1r.40) Globe in rainforest	50	50
1379	(1r.40) Trees in sunset	50	50
1380	(3r.) Globe and South African landmarks (48×30 mm)	1·00	1·00

See also Nos. 1386/9.

2002. (b) Designs 20×25 mm. Self-adhesive.
1381	(1r.50) Type **429**	45	50
1382	(1r.50) As No. 1378	55	60
1383	(1r.50) As No. 1379	55	60

430 Earl Kitchener

2002. Centenary of Anglo-Boer War (4th issue). Treaty of Vereeniging. Sheet, 105×65 mm, containing T **430** and similar square design. Multicoloured.
| MS1384 1r.50 Type **430**; 3r.30 Boer representative signing Treaty | | 1·00 | 1·00 |

431 African Union Logo

2002. First African Union Summit, Durban.
| 1385 | **431** | 1r.50 multicoloured | 1·00 | 55 |

432 Water, Sanitation and Energy

2002. World Summit on Sustainable Development (2nd issue). Multicoloured.
1386	(1r.50) Type **432**	40	30
1387	(3r.) Child with hands raised to globe (Environment)	70	70
1388	(3r.30) Hands holding seedling (Food)	85	1·00

No. 1386 is inscribed "standard postage", No. 1387 "airmail postcard rate" and No. 1388 "international letter rate". The stamps were initially sold at the values quoted above.

2002. Flora and Fauna (3rd series). Moths. As T **410**. Multicoloured.
1389	1r.80 Emperor moth	60	35
1390	2r.20 Peach moth	70	50
1391	2r.80 Snouted tiger moth	80	65
1392	9r. False tiger moth	2·50	2·75
1393	16r. Moon moth	4·50	5·00

433 "Dazzler" Mascot as Batsman (running)

2002. Cricket World Cup (2003) (2nd issue). Designs showing "Dazzler" zebra mascot. Multicoloured.
| 1394 | (1r.50) Type **433** | 50 | 50 |
| 1395 | (1r.50) Bowler (after releasing ball) | 50 | 50 |

1396	(1r.50) Fielder	50	50
1397	(1r.50) Batsman (on one knee)	50	50
1398	(1r.50) Bowler (running with ball)	50	50
1399	(1r.50) Batsman (standing)	50	50

434 Postal Stone

2002. World Post Day. Sheet 105×65 mm.
| MS1400 **434** 4r.75 multicoloured | | 1·25 | 1·25 |

435 Steve Biko

2002. 25th Death Anniv of Steve Biko (anti-apartheid campaigner). Sheet 105×65 mm.
| MS1401 **435** 4r.75 black, red and cinnamon | | 1·25 | 1·25 |

436 Pristis microdon

2002. "Algoapex" (**MS**1402) and "JUNASS" (**MS**1403) National Stamp Show. Sawfish. Two sheets containing horiz designs as T **436**. Multicoloured.
| MS1402 104×65 mm. 7r. Type **436** | | 1·75 | 1·90 |
| MS1403 106×65 mm. 7r. *Pristis pectinata* | | 1·75 | 1·90 |

437 Stylised Goat

2002. Chinese New Year ("Year of the Goat"). Star-shaped sheet, 105×105 mm.
| MS1404 **437** 7r. multicoloured | | 1·75 | 2·00 |

438 "The Tree of Life"

2002. Christmas. Designs showing stained glass. Multicoloured.
| 1405 | 1r.50 Type **438** | 40 | 15 |
| 1406 | 3r. "The Totem" | 85 | 1·10 |

439 Man wearing Sunglasses

2002. AIDS Prevention. Self-adhesive.
1407	(1r.50) Type **439**	50	55
1408	(1r.50) Woman with AIDS ribbon on headband	50	55
1409	(1r.50) Woman wearing sunglasses and hat	50	55
1410	(1r.50) Hand holding purple candle and "STOP"	50	55
1411	(1r.50) Woman's face and "AiDS"	50	55
1412	(1r.50) Man holding purple candle and "Be safe"	50	55
1413	(1r.50) Hand touching AIDS ribbon and green candle	50	55
1414	(1r.50) Raised palm of hand and "AIDS"	50	55
1415	(1r.50) Woman's face in glass jar	50	55

| 1416 | (1r.50) Hand catching anti-HIV drugs and AIDS ribbon in heart | 50 | 55 |

Nos. 1407/16 are inscribed "Standard Postage" and were initially valid for 1r.50. They form a composite design.

440 Total Eclipse

2002. Total Solar Eclipse, 4 December 2002. Sheet 105×65 mm.
| MS1417 **440** 4r.75 black, orange and red | | 1·25 | 1·50 |

441 Traditional Thatched Huts

2003. Cricket World Cup (3rd issue). South African Scenes. Multicoloured.
| MS1418 174×90 mm. (1r.50) Type **441**; (1r.50) Man wearing brimmed hat on horse; (1r.50) Four cricketers and settlement houses; (1r.50) Passengers inside bus and on roof; (1r.50) Woman and baby; (1r.50) Double-decker bus | | 2·00 | 2·50 |

Stamps from **MS**1418 are inscribed "STANDARD POSTAGE" and were initially valid for 1r.50 each.

442 Chris Hani

2003. Tenth Death Anniv of Chris Hani (former Secretary-general of South African Communist Party). Sheet 105×65 mm.
| MS1419 **442** (1r.50) brown and red | | 60 | 75 |

No. **MS**1419 is inscribed "Standard Postage" and was initially valid for 1r.50.

443 Women carrying Water Drums

2003. Life in Informal Settlements. Multicoloured.
1420	(1r.65) Type **443**	40	50
1421	(1r.65) Boy playing musical instrument	40	50
1422	(1r.65) Workman laying road	40	50
1423	(1r.65) Seamstress	40	50
1424	(1r.65) Two schoolchildren	40	50
1425	(1r.65) Shopkeeper with customer	40	50
1426	(1r.65) Shoemakers	40	50
1427	(1r.65) Woman wearing green hat	40	50
1428	(1r.65) Teenager leaning on tyre	40	50
1429	(1r.65) Mother and child	40	50

Nos. 1420/9 are inscribed "STANDARD POSTAGE" and were initially valid for 1r.65 each.

444 Outline Map of Africa

2003. Africa Day. Sheet 105×65 mm.
| MS1430 **444** 11r.70 multicoloured | | 2·50 | 3·00 |

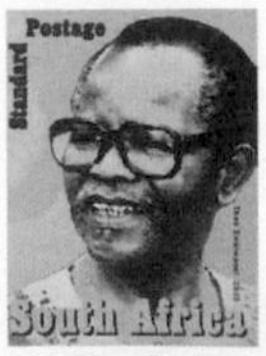

445 Oliver Tambo

2003. Tenth Death Anniv of Oliver Tambo. Sheet, 105×65 mm.

MS1431	**445** (1r.65) multicoloured	70	1·00

No. **MS**1431 is inscribed "Standard Postage" and was initially valid for 1r.65.

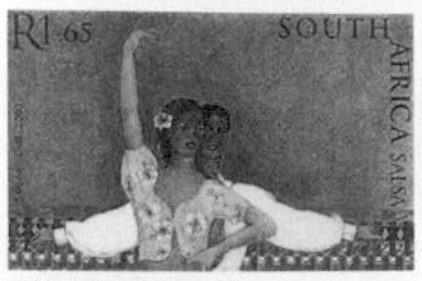

446 Salsa Dancers

2003. Dances. Multicoloured.

1432	1r.65 Type **446**	55	25
1433	2r.20 Rumba	70	45
1434	2r.80 Waltz	85	85
1435	3r.30 Foxtrot	1·00	1·40
1436	3r.80 Tango	1·40	1·75

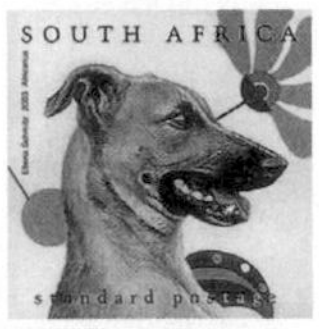

447 African Dog

2003. Dogs. Sheet 100×100 mm containing T **447** and similar square designs. Multicoloured.

MS1437	(1r.65) Type **447**; (1r.65) Rhodesian ridgeback; (1r.65) Boerboel; (1r.65) Basenji	2·50	2·50

The stamps of No. **MS**1437 are each inscribed "standard postage" and were sold for 1r.65.

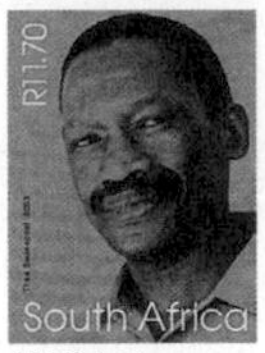

448 Robert Mangaliso Sobukwe

2003. 25th Death Anniv of Robert Mangaliso Sobukwe (nationalist leader and founder of the Pan-Africanist Congress). Sheet 105×65 mm.

MS1438	**448** 11r.70 multicoloured	3·25	3·50

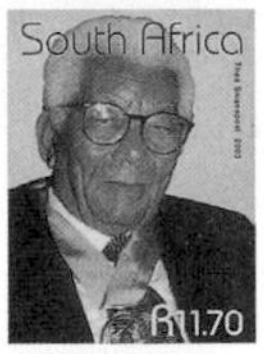

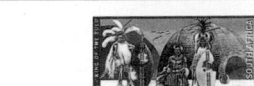

449 Walter Max Ulyate Sisulu

2003. Walter Max Ulyate Sisulu (political activist and member of the African National Congress) Commemoration. Sheet 105×65 mm.

MS1439	**449** 11r.70 multicoloured	3·25	3·50

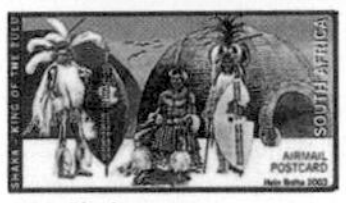
450 Shaka

2003. Shaka (Warrior King of the Zulu) Commemoration.

1440	**450**	(3r.) multicoloured	1·25	1·25

No. 1440 was inscribed "Airmail Postcard" and sold for 3r. each stamp.

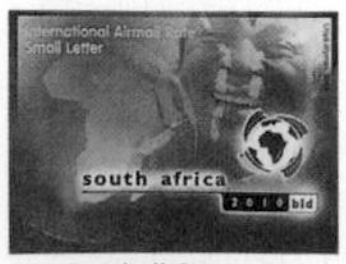

451 Football Supporter and Globe

2003. World Cup Football Bid. Multicoloured.

1441	(3r.80) Type **451**	1·00	1·00
1442	(4r.25) Supporter and children playing football	1·10	1·40

No. 1441 is inscribed "International Airmail Rate Small Letter" and was sold for 3r.80. No. 1442 is inscribed "B4 Domestic Large" and was sold for 4r.25.

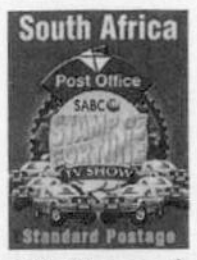

452 Stamp of Fortune and Post Office Logos and Cars

2003. Television and Post Office Joint Issue.

1443	**452**	(1r.65) multicoloured	50	35

No. 1443 is inscribed "Standard Postage" and was sold for 1r.65.

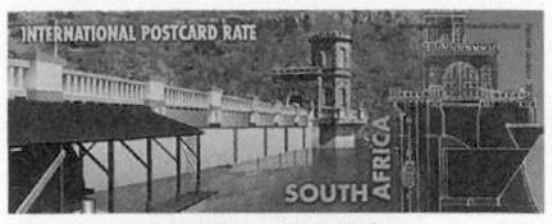

453 Shangweni Dam Kwa-Zulu

2003. Engineering and Postal Communication. Sheet 90×143 mm containing T **453** and similar multicoloured designs.

MS1444	(3r.30) Type **453**; (3r.30) Kimberly Microwave Tower (30×48 mm); (3r.30) Northern Cape Legislature (30×24 mm); (3r.30) Community Bridge, Limpopo (30×24 mm); (3r.30) Durban Westville Interchange (30×48 mm); (3r.30) Nelson Mandela Bridge, Gauteng (60×24 mm)	5·50	6·00

2003. 22nd PIARC World Road Congress. As No. **MS**1444 but inscr "XXIInd PIARC WORLD ROAD CONGRESS" on top margin, "CONNECTING THE WORLD" on bottom margin. Additional road agency logos are added to the left and right margins and the plate numbers, barcodes and SAICE logos are omitted. Sheet 90×143 mm containing T **453** and similar multicoloured designs.

MS1444a	(3r.30) Type **453**; (3r.30) Kimberly Microwave Tower (30×48 mm); (3r.30) Northern Cape Legislature (30×24 mm); (3r.30) Community Bridge, Limpopo (30×24 mm); (3r.30) Durban Westville Interchange (30×48 mm); (3r.30) Nelson Mandela Bridge, Gauteng (60×24 mm)	6·00	6·50

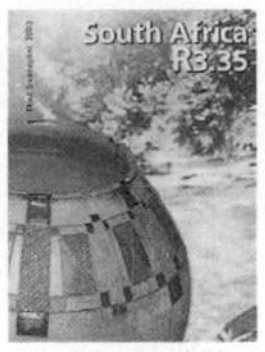

454 Pot created by Afrikania Job Creation Project

2003. Tenth Anniv of Diplomatic Relations with India. Sheet 105×65 mm.

MS1445	**454** 3r.35 multicoloured	1·50	1·75

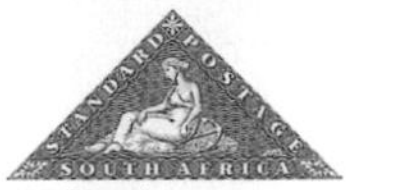

455 "Hope"

2003. 150th Anniv of the Cape Triangular Stamp. Design as T 10 but with face value as T 455.

1446	**455**	(1r.65) blue	1·00	1·00

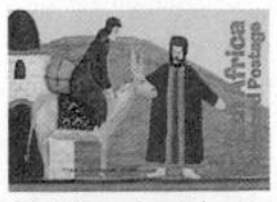

456 Joseph with Mary on Donkey

2003. Christmas. Multicoloured. (a) As T **456**.

1447	(1r.65) Type **456**	75	75
1448	(1r.65) Angels	75	75
1449	(1r.65) Three Wise Men	75	75
1450	(1r.65) Mary and Jesus	75	75
1451	(1r.65) Dove carrying holly	75	75

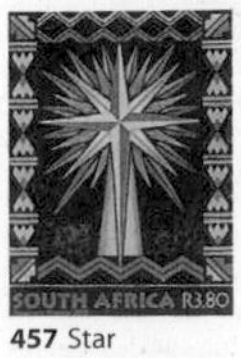

457 Star

(b) As T **457**.

1452	3r.80 Type **457**	1·50	1·50

Nos. 1447/51 are each inscribed "Standard Postage" and were sold for 1r.65.

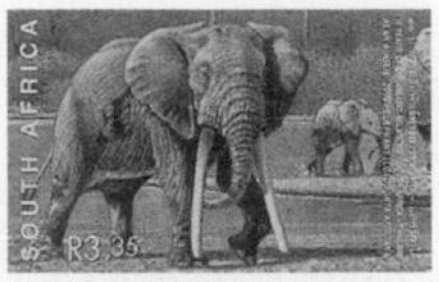

458 African Elephant

2003. Tenth Anniv of Diplomatic Relations with Thailand. Multicoloured.

1453	3r.35 Type **458**	2·50	2·00
1454	3r.35 Indian elephant	2·50	2·00

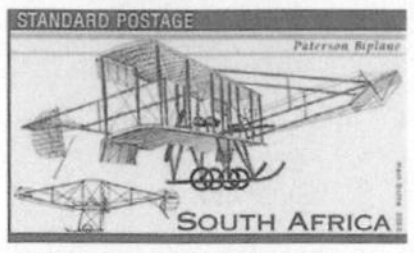

459 Paterson Biplane

2003. Centenary of Powered Flight. Multicoloured.

1455	(1r.65) Type **459**	70	70
1456	(1r.65) Silver Queen Vickers Vimy	70	70
1457	(1r.65) Wapiti	70	70
1458	(1r.65) De Havilland DH 9	70	70
1459	(1r.65) Junkers Ju52/53	70	70
1460	(1r.65) Sikorsky S-55	70	70
1461	(1r.65) Boeing 707	70	70
1462	(1r.65) Rooivalk	70	70
1463	(1r.65) SUNSAT Micro satellite	70	70
1464	(1r.65) Mark Shuttleworth (astronaut)	70	70

Nos. 1455/64 are inscribed "Standard Postage" and were sold for 1r.65 each.

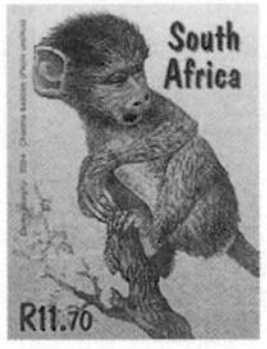

460 Monkey

2004. Chinese New Year ("Year of the Monkey"). Sheet 105×65 mm.

MS1465	**460** 11r.70 multicoloured	4·00	4·50

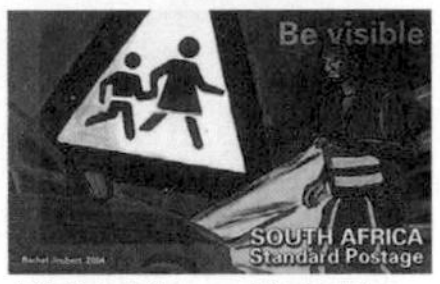

461 Patrol Sign and Pedestrian

2004. "Drive Alive" Road Safety Campaign. Multicoloured.

1466	(1r.65) Type **461**	1·50	1·10
1467	(1r.65) Slippery road sign and alcohol	1·50	1·10
1468	(1r.65) Service sign and car in disrepair	1·50	1·10
1469	(1r.65) Slow lorry sign and steering wheel	1·50	1·10
1470	(1r.65) Danger sign and sleeping driver	1·50	1·10

Nos. 1466/70 are inscribed "Standard Postage" and were initially sold for 1r.65 each.

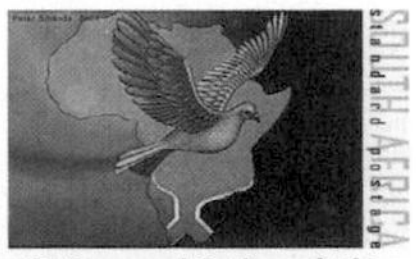

462 Dove and Outline of Africa

2004. Tenth Anniv of Democracy. Multicoloured.

1471	(1r.65) Type **462**	1·00	1·00
1472	(1r.65) Voters	1·00	1·00
1473	(1r.65) Accessing services (water, electricity)	1·00	1·00
1474	(1r.65) Sports supporters	1·00	1·00
1475	(1r.65) Traditional arts and crafts	1·00	1·00

Nos. 1471/5 are inscribed "Standard Postage" and were initially sold for 1r.65 each.

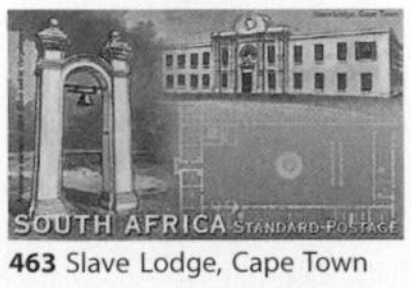

463 Slave Lodge, Cape Town

2004. The Legacy of Slaves. Multicoloured.

1476	(1r.70) Type **463**	70	70
1477	(1r.70) First book written in Arabic and Afrikaans	70	70
1478	(1r.70) Stinkwood Tulback chair and Jonkmans cupboard	70	70
1479	(1r.70) Traditional food	70	70
1480	(1r.70) Labourers on sugar cane farm	70	70
1481	(1r.70) Miners	70	70

Nos. 1476/81 are inscribed "Standard Postage" and were initially sold for 1r.70 each.

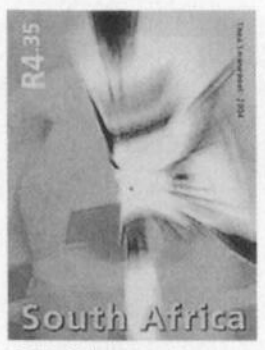

464 Abstract Footballer

2004. Centenary of FIFA (Federation Internationale de Football Association). Sheet 105×65 mm.

MS1482	**464** 4r.35 multicoloured	1·50	2·00

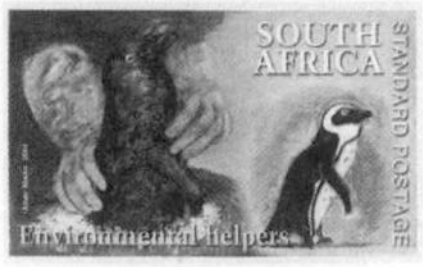

465 Penguins (Environmental Helpers)

2004. Volunteers. Multicoloured.

1483	(1r.70) Type **465**	90	90
1484	(1r.70) Volunteer assisting elderly person (Caring for the elderly)	90	90
1485	(1r.70) Child with building blocks (Education)	90	90
1486	(1r.70) Paramedics (Medical and ambulance services)	90	90
1487	(1r.70) Life guards (Surf life saving)	90	90
1488	(1r.70) Volunteer with dogs (Helping abandoned pets)	90	90
1489	(1r.70) Child in cot (Caring for orphans)	90	90
1490	(1r.70) Rescuing someone from fire (Fire fighters)	90	90
1491	(1r.70) Group gardening (Community gardens)	90	90
1492	(1r.70) Blind person and volunteer recording tape (Tape aids for the blind)	90	90

Nos. 1483/92 are inscribed "Standard Postage" and were sold for 1r.70 each.

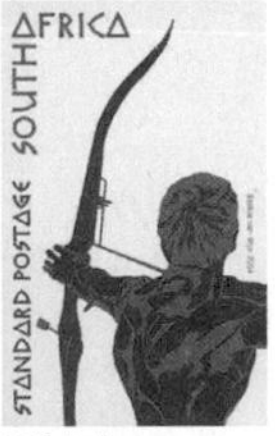

466 Archery

2004. Sport. Multicoloured.

1493	(1r.70) Type **466**	90	90
1494	(1r.70) Sprinting	90	90
1495	(1r.70) Show jumping	90	90
1496	(1r.70) Cycling	90	90
1497	(1r.70) Gymnastics	90	90
1498	(1r.70) Canoeing	90	90
1499	(1r.70) Football	90	90
1500	(1r.70) Swimming	90	90
1501	(1r.70) Boxing	90	90
1502	(1r.70) Tennis	90	90

Nos. 1493/1502 are inscribed "Standard Postage" and were sold for 1r.70 each.

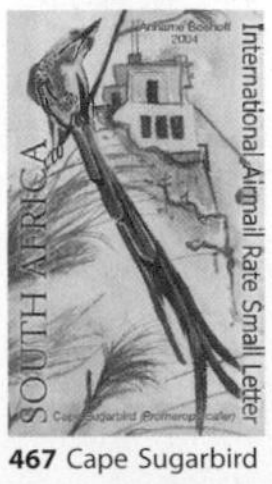

467 Cape Sugarbird

2004. Ecology of Table Mountain. Sheet 172×233 mm containing T **467** and similar multicoloured designs. Self-adhesive.

MS1503	(4r.) Type **467**; (4r.) Dark opal butterflies (horiz); (4r.) King protea (flower) (horiz); (4r.) Cape rock hyrax (horiz); (4r.) Cuckoo wasp (horiz); (4r.) Ghost frog (horiz); (4r.) Cockroaches (horiz); (4r.) *Staavia dodii* (flower); (4r.) Spotted skaapsteker (snake) (horiz); (4r.) *Duvalia immaculate* (horiz)	11·00	12·00

The stamps in No. **MS**1503 were each inscribed "International Airmail Rate Small Letter" and sold for 4r.

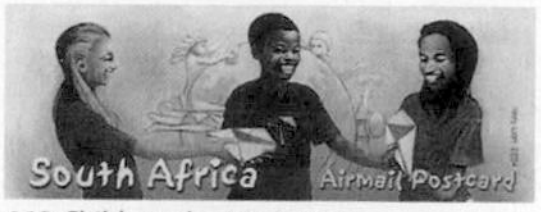

468 Children sharing Letters

2004. Universal Postal Union Congress, Romania.

1504	**468**	3r.45 multicoloured	1·00	1·25

No. 1504 was inscribed "Airmail Postcard" and sold for 3r.45.

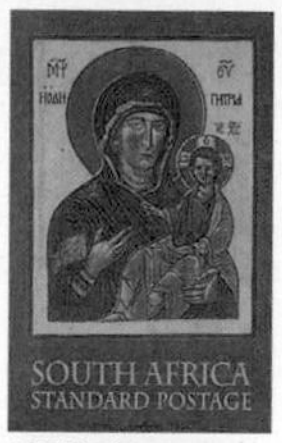

469 Virgin "Hodigitria"

2004. Christmas. Multicoloured.

1505	(1r.70) Type **469**	50	15
1506	(4r.) Christ Pantocrator (Almighty)	1·25	1·25

No. 1505 is inscribed "Standard Postage" and was initially sold for 1r.70. No. 1506 is inscribed "International Airmail Letter" and was initially sold for 4r.

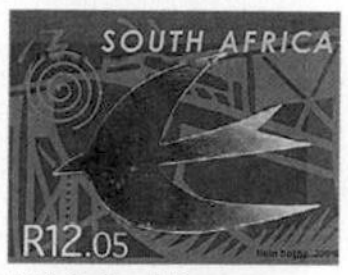

470 Stylized Dove

2004. World Post Day. Sheet 105×65 mm

MS1507	**470**	12r.50 multicoloured	3·25	3·75

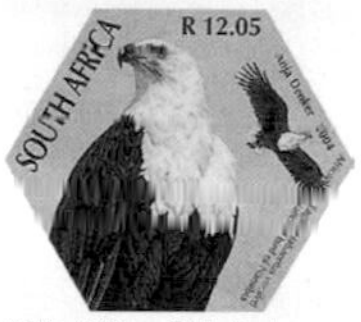

470a African Fish Eagle (Namibia)

2004. First Joint Issue of Southern Africa Postal Operators Association Members. Sheet 170×95 mm containing T **470a** and similar hexagonal designs showing national birds of Association members. Multicoloured.

MS1508 12r.50 Type **470a**; 12r.50 Two African fish eagles perched (Zimbabwe); 12r.50 Peregrine falcon (Angola); 12r.50 Cattle egret (Botswana); 12r.50 Purple-crested turaco ("Lourie") (Swaziland); 12r.50 Stanley ("Blue") crane (South Africa); 12r.50 Bar-tailed trogon (Malawi) (inscribed "apaloderma vittatum"); 12r.50 Two African fish eagles in flight (Zambia) 20·00 22·00

The stamp depicting the Bar-tailed trogon is not inscribed with the country of which the bird is a national symbol.

Miniature sheets of similar designs were also issued by Namibia, Zimbabwe, Angola, Botswana, Swaziland, Malawi and Zambia.

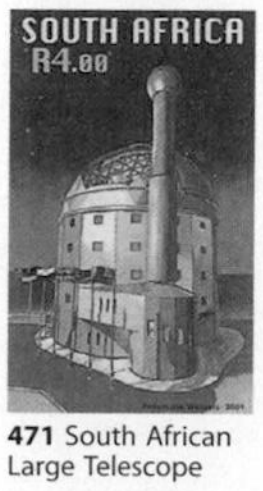

471 South African Large Telescope

2004. South African Large Telescope. Multicoloured.

1509	4r. Type **471**	95	1·00
1510	4r. Cross-section of observatory	95	1·00
1511	4r. View of the Southern Cross	95	1·00
1512	4r. Telescope	95	1·00
1513	4r. Telescope inside observatory	95	1·00

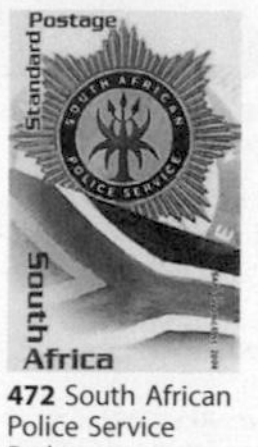

472 South African Police Service Badge

2004. South African Police Service (SAPS). Self-adhesive. Multicoloured.

1514	1r.70 Type **472**	90	90
1515	1r.70 Handcuffed hands and drugs (Fight Against Drugs)	90	90
1516	1r.70 Police helicopter (SAPS Air Wing)	90	90
1517	1r.70 Microscope (Fingerprint and Forensic Science Units)	90	90
1518	1r.70 Parachutists (Special Task Force)	90	90
1519	1r.70 Child and officer (Family Violence, Child Protection and Sexual Offences Unit)	90	90
1520	1r.70 Officers and map (Sector Policing)	90	90
1521	1r.70 Three police officers (The Dignified Blue)	90	90
1522	1r.70 Officer on horse (SAPS Mounted Unit)	90	90
1523	1r.70 Officer and police dog (SAPS Dog Unit)	90	90

Nos. 1514/23 are inscribed "Standard Postage" and were initially sold for 1r.70 each.

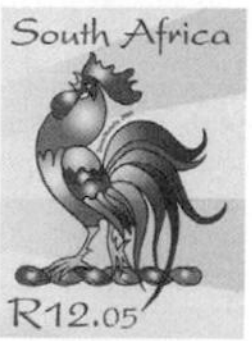

473 Rooster

2005. Chinese New Year ("Year of the Rooster"). Sheet 105×65 mm.

MS1524	**473**	12r.50 multicoloured	4·50	4·50

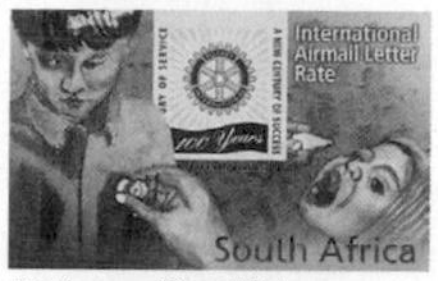

474 Immunising Children

2005. Centenary of Rotary International (humanitarian organisation).

1525	(4r.) Type **474**	1·25	1·25
1526	(4r.) Computer and metal work	1·25	1·25

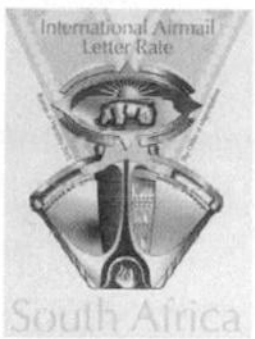

475 The Order of Mapungubwe

2005. National Orders of South Africa. Multicoloured.

1527	(4r.25) Type **475**	1·40	1·40
1528	(4r.25) The Order of Mendi for Bravery	1·40	1·40
1529	(4r.25) The Order of the Baobab	1·40	1·40
1530	(4r.25) The Order of Luthuli	1·40	1·40
1531	(4r.25) The Order of Ikhamanga	1·40	1·40
1532	(4r.25) The Order of the Companions of OR Tambo	1·40	1·40

Each was inscribed "International Airmail Letter Rate" and initially sold for 4r.25.

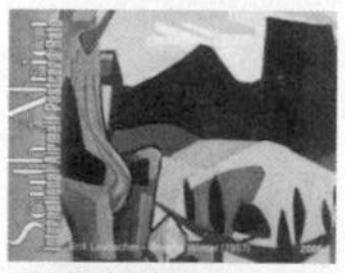

476 "Boland Winter" (Erik Laubscher)

2005. Landscape Paintings. Multicoloured.

1533	(3r.65) Type **476**	1·25	1·40
1534	(3r.65) "Table Mountain" (Maggie Laubser)	1·25	1·40
1535	(3r.65) "Fishermen Drawing Nets" (Walter Battiss)	1·25	1·40
1536	(3r.65) "Oh South Africa, you've turned my world completely upside down" (Lallitha Jawahirilal)	1·25	1·40
1537	(3r.65) "Untitled" (Lucky Sibiya)	1·25	1·40
1538	(3r.65) "Untitled" (Sophie Masiza)	1·25	1·40
1539	(3r.65) "Azibuye Emasisweni" (Trevor Makhoba)	1·25	1·40
1540	(3r.65) "Kontantwinkel Riebeeck-Wes" (John Kramer)	1·25	1·40
1541	(3r.65) "Houses in the Hills" (Gladys Mgudlandlu)	1·25	1·40
1542	(3r.65) "Sequence City" (Usha Seejarim)	1·25	1·40

Each was inscribed "International Airmail Postcard Rate" and initially sold for 3r.65.

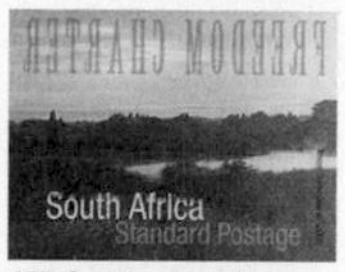

477 Sunrise over the Gariep and "Freedom Charter" Reversed

2005. 50th Anniv of the Freedom Charter. Sheet, 105×65 mm, containing T **477** and similar horiz design. Multicoloured.

MS1543 (1r.77) Type **477**; (1r.77) Sunrise over the Gariep, "Freedom Charter" and "50" 2·50 2·75

The stamps of **MS**1543 form a panoramic design. Both were inscribed "Standard Postage" and sold for 1r.77.

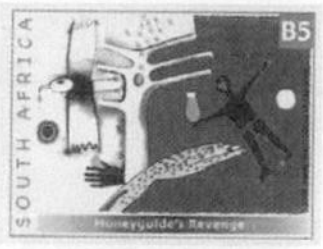

478 Honeyguide's Revenge (Isi Ndebele)

2005. Folklore and Legends. Multicoloured.

1544	(3r.75) Type **478**	1·25	1·40
1545	(3r.75) How Ostrich got his Long Neck (Sesotho)	1·25	1·40
1546	(3r.75) How Serval got his Spots (Setswana)	1·25	1·40
1547	(3r.75) How Zebra got his Stripes (Isi Zulu)	1·25	1·40
1548	(3r.75) Jackal the Tiger Eater (Cape Malay)	1·25	1·40
1549	(3r.75) Jackal and Wolf (Afrikaans)	1·25	1·40
1550	(3r.75) King Lion and King Eagle (Isi Xhosa)	1·25	1·40
1551	(3r.75) Mantis and the Moon (San)	1·25	1·40
1552	(3r.75) Words as Sweet as Honey (Tshi Venda)	1·25	1·40
1553	(3r.75) When Lion could Fly (Ancient Khoenkhoen languages)	1·25	1·40

Each was inscribed "B5" and sold initially for 3r.75.

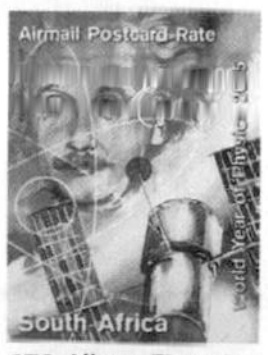

479 Albert Einstein and Satellite

2005. Year of Physics.

1554	**479**	(3r.65) multicoloured	1·00	1·00

No. 1554 was inscribed "Airmail Postcard Rate" and initially sold for 3r.65.

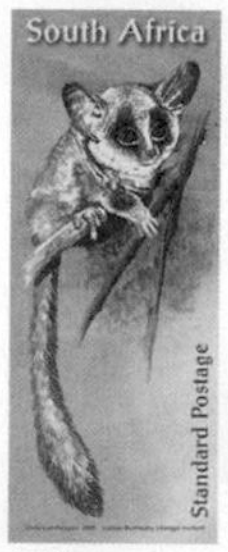

480 Lesser Bushbaby

2005. Small Indigenous Animals. Sheet, 145×90 mm, containing T **480** and similar multicoloured designs.

MS1555 (1r.77) Type **480**; (1r.77) Riverine Rabbit (24×30 mm); (1r.77) African wildcat (49×30 mm); (1r.77) Steenbok (49×30 mm); (1r.77) Cape fox (24×30 mm); (1r.77) Yellow mongoose 5·00 5·00

The stamps of No. **MS**1555 were each inscribed "Standard Postage" and initially sold for 1r.77.

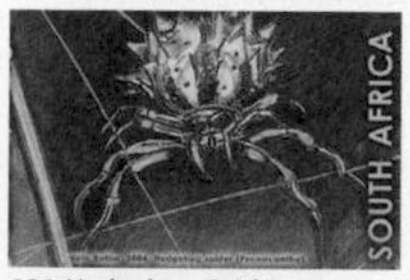

481 Hedgehog Spider

2005. Spiders. Sheet, 233×172 mm, containing T **481** and similar multicoloured designs. Self-adhesive.

MS1556 (1r.77)×10, Type **481**; Golden orb-web spider; Lynx spider; Black button spider; Ladybird spider; Flower crab spider; Rain spider; Horn Baboon spider; Trap door spider; Spotted crab spider 7·00 7·50

The backing paper of No. **MS**1556 is inscribed with details of all the species depicted on the stamps.

The stamps in No. **MS**1556 were each inscribed "Standard Postage" and sold for 1r.77.

No. **MS**1556 was originally due to be released 30 July 2004 and the stamps show "2004" imprint date.

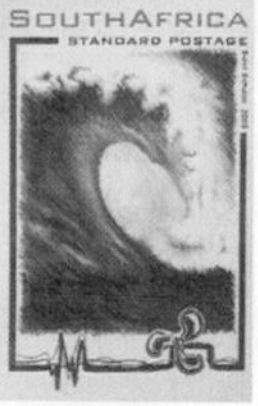

482 Wave

2005. Renewable Energy Sources. Multicoloured.

1557	(1r.77) Type **482**	60	60
1558	(3r.65) Wind	1·10	1·25
1559	(4r.25) Sun	1·25	1·50

Nos. 1557/9 were inscribed "Standard Postage", "International Airmail Postcard" and "International Airmail Letter" and sold for 1r.77, 3r.65 and 4r.25, respectively.

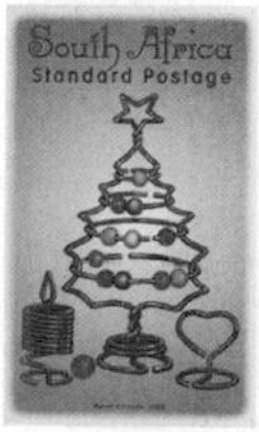

483 Christmas Tree, Candle and Heart

2005. Christmas. Showing wire and bead work decorations. Multicoloured.

1560	(1r.77) Type **483**	70	25
1561	(4r.25) Angel and dove	1·25	1·25

No. 1560 was inscribed "Standard Postage" and sold at 1r.77. No. 1561 was inscribed "International Airmail Letter" and sold at 4r.25.

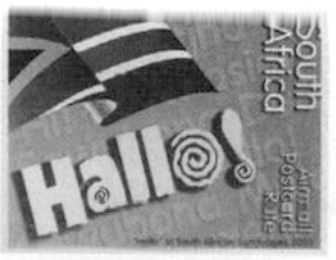

484 "Hallo!" (Afrikaans)

2005. World Post Day. Showing South African flag and "Hello" in South African languages. Multicoloured.

1562	(3r.65) Type **484**	1·10	1·25
1563	(3r.65) "Hi!" (English)	1·10	1·25
1564	(3r.65) "Sawubona" (IsiZulu and Siswati)	1·10	1·25
1565	(3r.65) "Ndi Masiari!" (Tshivenda)	1·10	1·25
1566	(3r.65) "Lotjha!" (IsiNdebele)	1·10	1·25
1567	(3r.65) "Avuxeni" (Xitsonga)	1·10	1·25
1568	(3r.65) "Dumela" (Northern Sotho)	1·10	1·25
1569	(3r.65) "Molo!" (IsiXhosa)	1·10	1·25

Each stamp was inscribed "Airmail Postcard Rate" and sold at 3r.65.

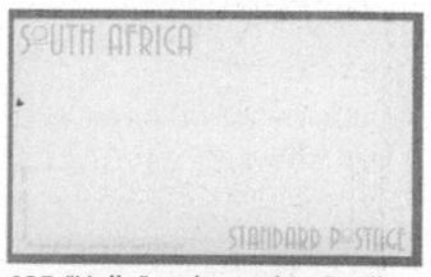

485 "Hello" embossed in Braille

2005. Prevention of Blindness.

1570	**485**	(1r.77) multicoloured	1·00	65

No. 1570 was inscribed "STANDARD POSTAGE" and sold at 1r.77.

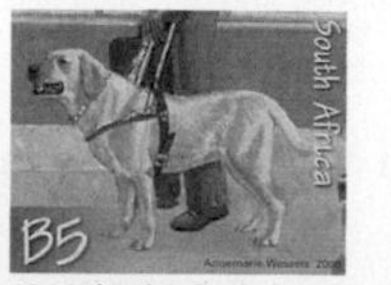

486 Labrador Guide Dog

2006. Chinese New Year ("Year of the Dog"). Sheet 125×65 mm. Multicoloured.

MS1571 (3r.75) Type **486**; (3r.75) Customs sniffer spaniel; (3r.75) Border collie chasing birds away from airport 4·75 4·75

The stamps within No. **MS**1571 were inscribed "B5" and the miniature sheet was sold for 11r.25.

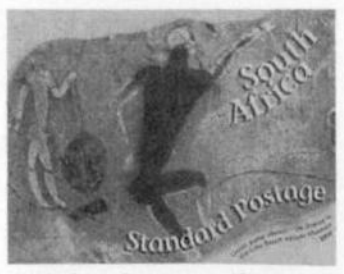

487 San Dancers (from Linton panel, Iziko South African Museum)

2006. Rock Art in South Africa. Multicoloured.

1572	(1r.77) Type **487**	1·10	1·10
1573	(1r.77) Mountain reedbuck (South African Museum of Rock Art)	1·10	1·10
1574	(1r.77) San ritual specialist (South African Museum of Rock Art)	1·10	1·10
1575	(1r.77) Rhinoceros (Wildebeest Kuil)	1·10	1·10
1576	(1r.77) Eland (Game Pass)	1·10	1·10

Nos. 1572/6 were inscribed "Standard Postage" and sold for 1r.77 each.

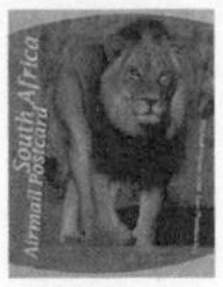

488 Lion

2006. Wildlife "The Big Five". Multicoloured. Self-adhesive.

1577	(3r.65) Type **488**	1·50	1·75
1578	(3r.65) Buffalo	1·50	1·75
1579	(3r.65) Elephant	1·50	1·75
1580	(3r.65) Black rhinoceros	1·50	1·75
1581	(3r.65) Leopard	1·50	1·75

Nos. 1577/81 are inscribed "Airmail Postcard" and were initially valid for 3r.65 each.

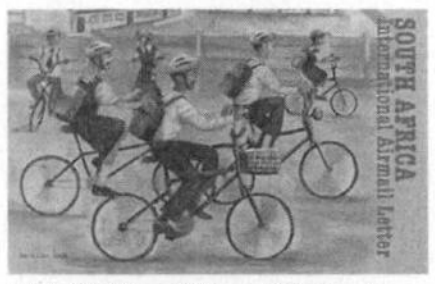

489 Children riding Bicycles to School

2006. Velo Mondial Conference, Cape Town.

1582	**489**	(4r.25) multicoloured	2·00	1·25

No. 1582 is inscribed "International Airmail Letter" and was sold for 4r.25.

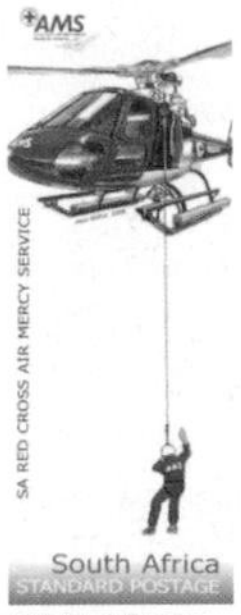

490 Red Cross MBB BO105 Helicopter

2006. Medical Outreach to Rural Areas. Multicoloured.

1583	(1r.85) Type **490**	1·75	1·75
1584	(1r.85) Clasped hands (24×30 mm)	1·75	1·75
1585	(1r.85) Red Cross Pilatus PC12 aircraft (48×30 mm)	1·75	1·75
1586	(1r.85) eRanger motorcycle ambulance (24×30 mm)	1·75	1·75
1587	(1r.85) Phelophepa Health Care Train (71×29 mm)	1·75	1·75
1588	(1r.85) St. John's ambulance (24×30 mm)	1·75	1·75

Nos. 1583/8 were inscribed "STANDARD POSTAGE" and sold for 1r.85 each.

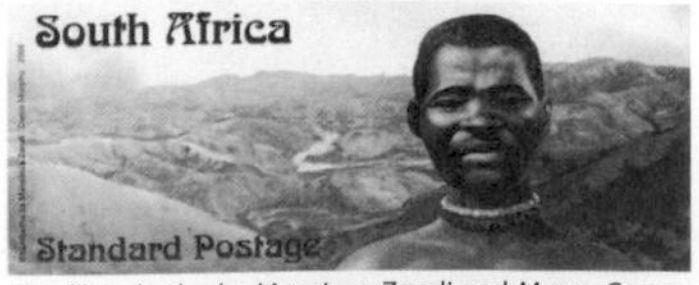

491 Bhambatha ka Mancinza Zondi and Mome Gorge

2006. Centenary of the Bhambatha Rebellion.

1589	**491**	(1r.85) multicoloured	65	40

No. 1589 is inscribed "Standard Postage" and was sold for 1r.85.

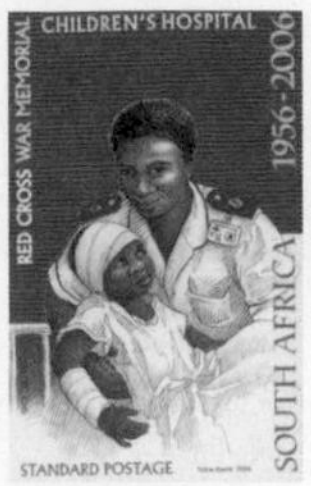

492 Nursing Sister with Child

2006. 50th Anniv of the Red Cross War Memorial Children's Hospital. Multicoloured.

1590	(1r.85) Type **492**	75	25
1591	(4r.40) Hospital building (horiz)	1·75	2·00

No. 1590 is inscribed "STANDARD POSTAGE" and was sold for 1r.85. No. 1591 is inscribed "INTERNATIONAL LETTER" and was sold for 4r.40.

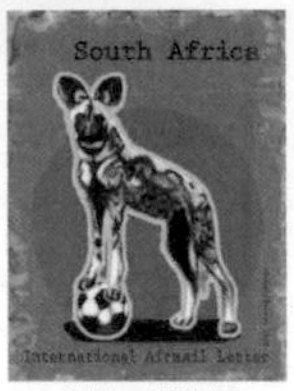

493 African Wild Dog standing on Football

2006. World Cup Football, South Africa, 2010. Sheet 105×65 mm.

MS1592	**493**	(4r.40) multicoloured	1·75	2·00

No. **MS**1592 is inscribed "International Airmail Letter" and was sold for 4r.40.

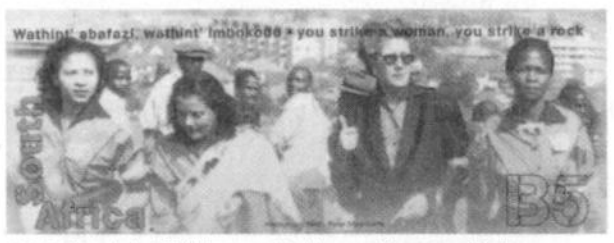

494 Sophia Williams, Rahima Moosa, Helen Joseph and Lillian Ngoyi leading March

2006. 50th Anniv of the Women's March to the Union Buildings, Pretoria. Sheet 105×65 mm.

MS1593	**494**	(3r.75) multicoloured	1·10	1·40

No. **MS**1593 is inscribed "B5" and was sold for 3r.75.

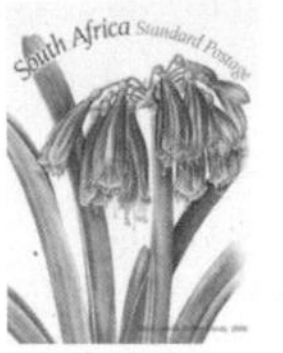

495 *Clivia nobilis*

2006. Clivias. Multicoloured.

1594	(1r.85) Type **495**	70	70
1595	(1r.85) *Clivia miniata*	70	70
1596	(1r.85) *Clivia gardenia*	70	70
1597	(1r.85) *Clivia caulescens*	70	70
1598	(1r.85) *Clivia mirabilis*	70	70
1599	(1r.85) *Clivia robusta*	70	70

Nos. 1594/9 were inscribed "Standard Postage" and sold for 1r.85 each.

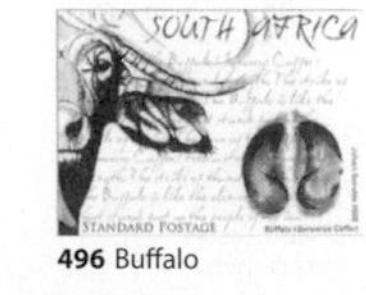

496 Buffalo

2006. Animal Tracks—"Stories in the Sand". Multicoloured.

1600	(1r.85) Type **496**	1·10	1·10
1601	(1r.85) Giraffe	1·10	1·10
1602	(1r.85) Elephant	1·10	1·10
1603	(1r.85) Spotted hyena	1·10	1·10
1604	(1r.85) Blue wildebeest	1·10	1·10
1605	(1r.85) Leopard	1·10	1·10
1606	(1r.85) Hippopotamus	1·10	1·10
1607	(1r.85) Warthog	1·10	1·10
1608	(1r.85) Black rhinoceros	1·10	1·10
1609	(1r.85) Burchell's zebra	1·10	1·10

Nos. 1600, 1602, 1604, 1606 and 1608 are inscribed "STANDARD POSTAGE", and Nos. 1601, 1603, 1605, 1607 and 1609 "standard postage". They were all sold for 1r.85.

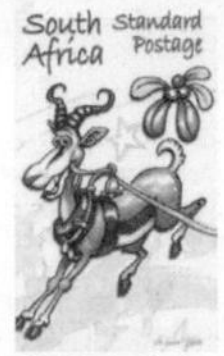

497 Springbok

2006. Christmas. "Jungle Bells". Multicoloured.

1610	(1r.85) Type **497**	75	75
1611	(1r.85) Warthog	75	75
1612	(1r.85) Zebra	75	75
1613	(1r.85) Hippopotamus	75	75
1614	(1r.85) King Lion as Father Christmas in donkey cart	75	75
1615	(4r.40) King Lion wearing Santa hat	1·75	1·75

Nos. 1610/14 were printed together, se-tenant, forming a composite design showing Springbok, Warthog, Zebra and Hippopotamus pulling Father Christmas in donkey cart. Nos. 1610/14 are inscribed "Standard Postage" and sold for 1r.85. No. 1615 is inscribed "International Airmail Letter" and sold for 4r.40.

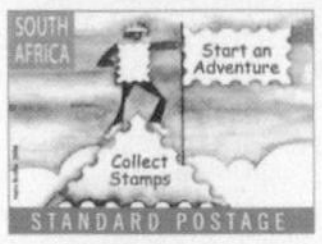

498 Climber ("Collect Stamps Start an Adventure")

2006. World Post Day. Multicoloured.

1616	(1r.85) Type **498**	75	80
1617	(1r.85) "Be Cool Collect Stamps"	75	80
1618	(1r.85) Reader ("Learn More Collect Stamps")	75	80
1619	(1r.85) "Have Fun Collect Stamps"	75	80
1620	(1r.85) Traveller with suitcase ("Travel the World Collect Stamps")	75	80

Nos. 1616/20 were inscribed "STANDARD POSTAGE" and sold for 1r.85 each.

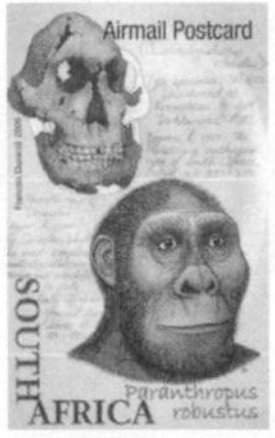

499 *Paranthropus robustus*

2006. Origin of Humankind. Sheet 182×126 mm containing T **499** and similar vert designs. Multicoloured. Self-adhesive.

MS1621	(3r.80)×4, Type **499**; *Australopithecus africanus*; *Homo heidelbergensis*; *Homo ergaster*	4·75	5·50

The stamps in **MS**1621 were each inscribed "Airmail Postcard" and sold for 3r.80 each.

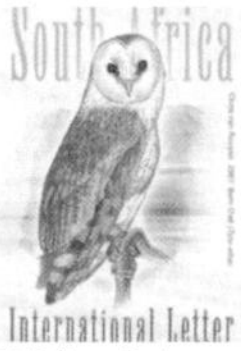

500 Barn Owl

2007. South African Owls. Multicoloured.

1622	(4r.64) Type **500**	2·25	2·25
1623	(4r.64) Cape eagle-owl	2·25	2·25
1624	(4r.64) African barred owlet	2·25	2·25
1625	(4r.64) Verreaux's eagle owl	2·25	2·25
1626	(4r.64) Pel's fishing owl	2·25	2·25

They were inscribed 'International Letter' and sold for 4r.64 each.

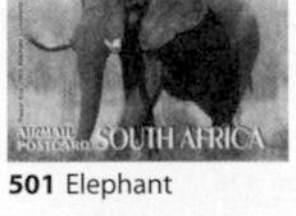

501 Elephant

2007. Wildlife 'The Big Five'. Multicoloured. Self-adhesive.

1627	(4r.01) Type **501**	1·40	1·60
1628	(4r.01) Leopard	1·40	1·60
1629	(4r.01) Buffalo	1·40	1·60
1630	(4r.01) Lion	1·40	1·60
1631	(4r.01) Black rhinoceros	1·40	1·60

Nos. 1627/31 are inscribed 'AIRMAIL POSTCARD' and sold for 4r.01 each.

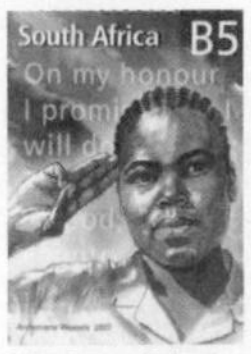

502 Scout Salute

2007. Centenary of World Scouting. Sheet 105×65 mm containing T **502** and similar vert design. Multicoloured.

MS1632	(3r.90) ×2 Type **502**; Scout emblem	1·90	2·25

The two stamps within **MS**1632 were each inscribed 'B5'. The miniature sheet was sold for 7r.80.

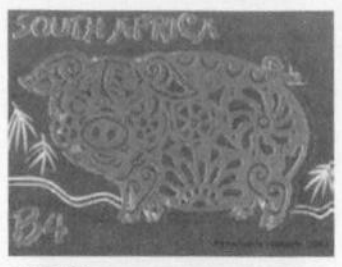

503 Pig

2007. Chinese New Year ('Year of the Pig'). Sheet 105×80 mm.

MS1633	**503**	(4r.70) multicoloured	2·25	2·25

No. **MS**1633 is inscr 'B4' and sold for 4r.70.

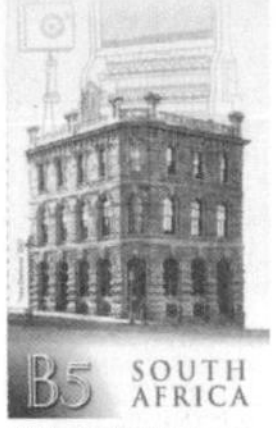

504 First Telephone Exchange in South Africa, Port Elizabeth, 1882

2007. World Post Day.

1634	**504**	(3r.90) multicoloured	1·50	1·00

No. 1634 is inscr 'B5' and sold for 3r.90.

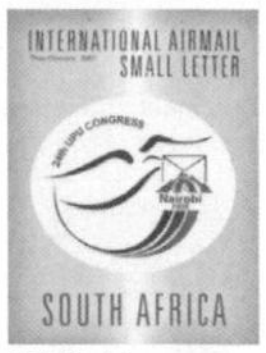

505 Emblem

2007. 24th UPU Congress, Nairobi, Kenya. Sheet 105×65 mm.

MS1635	**505**	(4r.64) multicoloured	1·10	1·40

No. **MS**1635 is inscr 'INTERNATIONAL AIRMAIL SMALL LETTER' and sold for 4r.64.

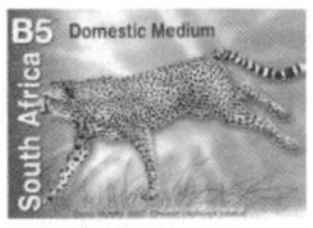

506 Cheetah

2007. Flora and Fauna (4th series). Multicoloured.

1636	(3r.90) Type **506**	1·25	1·25
1637	(4r.89) Ostrich	2·00	2·00

No. 1636 is inscr 'B5 Domestic Medium' and sold for 3r.90.

No. 1637 is inscr 'Domestic Large' and 'B4' and sold for 4r.89.

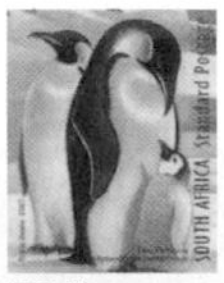

507 King Penguins

2007. International Polar and Heliophysical Year. Sheet 145×90 mm containing T **507** and similar multicoloured designs.

MS1638	(1r.93)×6 Type **507**; SANAE IV Base (72×30 mm); Wandering albatross (24×60 mm); Adélie penguins; Orca whale (48×30 mm); Weddell seal	4·75	4·75

The stamps within **MS**1638 form a composite design. They are all inscr 'Standard Postage' and were sold for 1r.93 each.

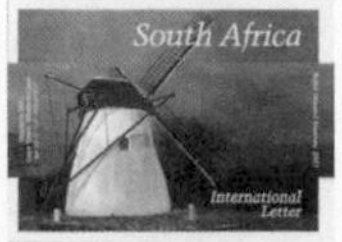

508 Mosterts Mill, Cape Town

2007. Mills of South Africa. Multicoloured.

1639	(2r.32) Type **508**	1·75	1·75
1640	(2r.32) La Cotte Watermill, Franschhoek, Western Cape	1·75	1·75
1641	(2r.32) Witpoort Watermill, Stoffberg, Mpumalanga	1·75	1·75
1642	(2r.32) Dwars River Watermill, Cederberg, Western Cape	1·75	1·75

1643	(2r.32) Colesberg Horse Mill, Colesberg, Northern Cape	1·75	1·75

Nos. 1639/43 are inscr 'International Letter' and sold for 4r.64 each.

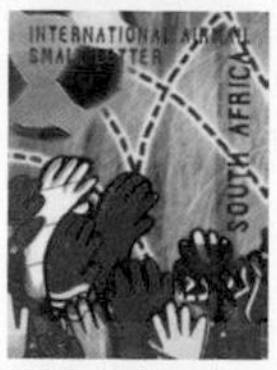

509 Raised Hands and Bouncing Football

2007. World Cup Football, South Africa, 2010 (2nd issue). Sheet 105×65 mm.

MS1644	**509** (4r.64) multicoloured	2·00	2·00

No. **MS**1644 is inscr 'INTERNATIONAL AIRMAIL SMALL LETTER' and sold for 4r.64.

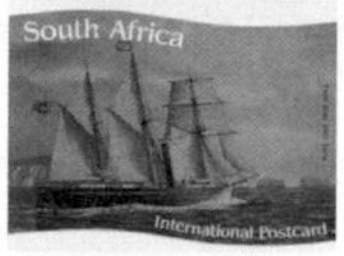

510 *Dane*

2007. Ships of the Union Castle Line. Multicoloured.

1645	(4r.01) Type **510**	1·75	1·75
1646	(4r.01) *Kildonan Castle*	1·75	1·75
1647	(4r.01) SA *Vaal*	1·75	1·75
1648	(4r.01) *Edinburgh Castle*	1·75	1·75
1649	(4r.01) *Windsor Castle*	1·75	1·75

Nos. 1645/9 are inscr 'International Postcard' and sold for 4r.01 each.

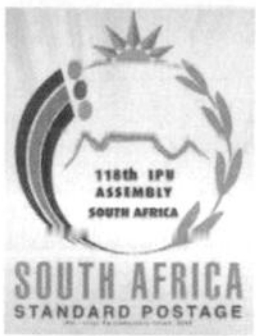

511 Assembly Logo

2008. 118th Inter-Parliamentary Union Assembly, Cape Town.

1650	**511** (2r.05) multicoloured	1·50	1·25

No. 1650 is inscr 'STANDARD POSTAGE' and was sold for 2r.05.

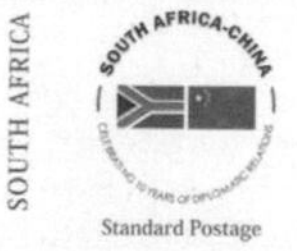

512 Flags of South Africa and China

2008. Tenth Anniv of Diplomatic Relations between South Africa and China. Sheet 105×65 mm. Multicolured.

MS1651	(2r.05) Type **512**; (4r.64) Flags of South Africa and China	1·25	1·75

The stamps within **MS**1651 are inscribed 'Standard Postage' (value 2r.05) and 'International Airmail Small Letter' (value 4r.64).

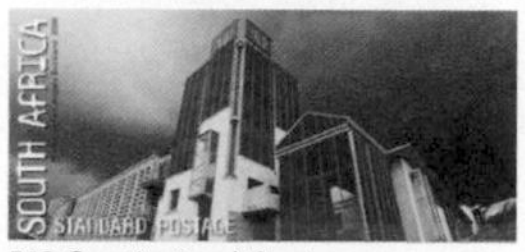

513 Constitutional Court

2008. Architecture of the Constitutional Court of South Africa, Johannesburg. Multicoloured.

1652	(2r.05) Type **513**	85	90
1653	(2r.05) Corner of building (30×30 mm)	85	90
1654	(2r.05) Courtyard	85	90
1655	(2r.05) Interior of building (30×30 mm)	85	90
1656	(2r.05) Glass tower (90×30 mm)	85	90
1657	(2r.05) Court buildings lit at dusk (30×30 mm)	85	90
1658	(2r.05) Column and spotlights (30×30 mm)	85	90
1659	(2r.05) Inscriptions on exterior wall (30×30 mm)	85	90
1660	(2r.05) Screen (30×30 mm)	85	90
1661	(2r.05) Court buildings on street corner	85	90

Nos. 1652/61 are inscr 'STANDARD POSTAGE' and sold for 2r.05 each.

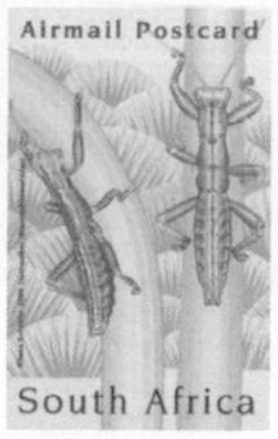

514 Heelwalkers (*Mantophasmatodea*) (discovered 2002)

2008. International Entomology Conference (ICE), Durban.

1662	**514**	(4r.20) multicoloured	1·75	1·50

No. 1662 is inscr 'Airmail Postcard' and was sold for 4r.20.

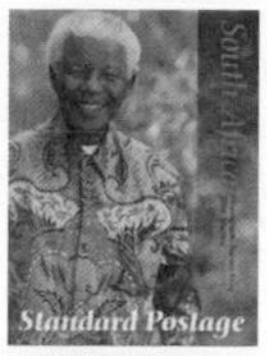

515 Nelson Mandela

2008. 90th Birthday of Nelson Mandela. Two sheets, each 77×105 mm, containing T **515** and similar vert design. Multicoloured.

MS1663	(a) (2r.05) Type **515**; (b) (4r.64) Nelson Mandela (seated in armchair, wearing blue shirt)	1·75	2·25

No. **MS**1663 (a) was inscr 'Standard Postage' and sold for 2r.05. No. **MS**1663 (b) was inscr 'International Airmail Small Letter' and sold for 4r.90.

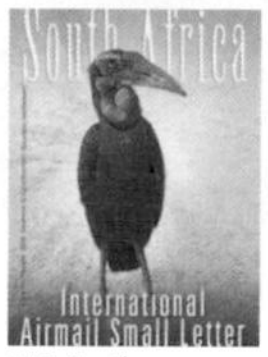

516 Southern Ground-Hornbill

2008. South African Big Five of Birds. Multicoloured.

1664	(4r.90) Type **516**	1·75	1·75
1665	(4r.90) Kori bustard	1·75	1·75
1666	(4r.90) Common ostrich	1·75	1·75
1667	(4r.90) Blue crane	1·75	1·75
1668	(4r.90) Bearded vulture	1·75	1·75

Nos. 1664/8 were inscr 'International Airmail Small Letter' and sold for 4r.90 each.

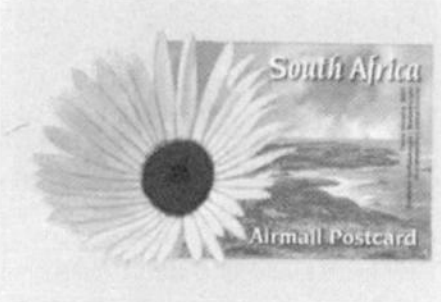

517 Common Bokbaaivygie (*Dorotheanthus bellidiformis*)

2008. Flowers of Namaqualand. Multicoloured. Self-adhesive.

1669	(4r.20) Type **517**	1·00	1·10
1670	(4r.20) Bokkeveld pride (*Geissorhiza splendidissima*)	1·00	1·10
1671	(4r.20) Springbok painted petals (*Lapeirousia silenoides*)	1·00	1·10
1672	(4r.20) White-eyed duiker-root (*Grielum humifusum*)	1·00	1·10
1673	(4r.20) Namaqualand daisy (*Dimorphotheca sinuata*)	1·00	1·10
1674	(4r.20) Satin boneseed (*Osteospermum pinnatum*)	1·00	1·10
1675	(4r.20) Karoo gazania (*Gazania rigida*)	1·00	1·10
1676	(4r.20) Harlequin hesperantha (*Hesperantha vaginata*)	1·00	1·10
1677	(4r.20) Showy sunflax (*Heliophila coronopifolia*)	1·00	1·10
1678	(4r.20) Red-eye sorrel (*Oxalis callosa*)	1·00	1·10

Nos. 1669/78 were all inscr 'Airmail Postcard' and sold for 4r.20 each. Nos. 1669/78 all have a wild flower scent contained in microscopic cells printed on the stamps using silkscreen.

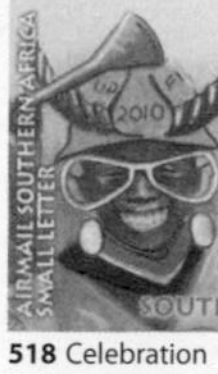

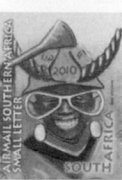

518 Celebration

2008. World Cup Football, South Africa, 2010 (3rd issue). Sheet 105×65 mm.

MS1679	**518** (3r.70) multicoloured	1·25	1·50

No. **MS**1679 is inscr 'AIRMAIL SOUTHERN AFRICA SMALL LETTER' and was sold for 3r.70.

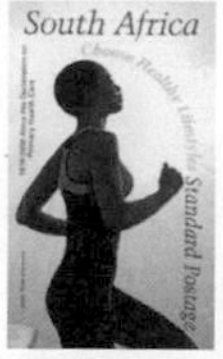

519 Young Woman running

2008. 30th Anniv of Alma Ata Declaration on Primary Health Care. Sheet 105×65 mm.

MS1680	**519** (2r.05) multicoloured	1·00	1·00

No **MS**1680 is inscr 'Standard Postage' and was sold for 2r.05.

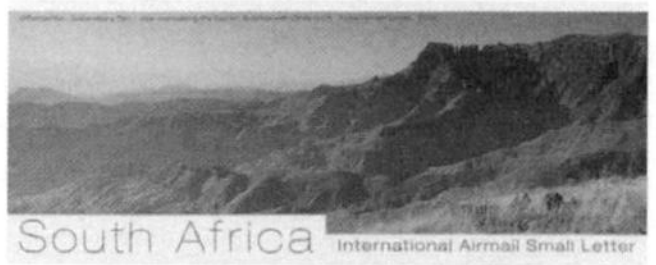

520 The Eastern Buttress and Devil's Tooth

2008. Drakensberg Park. Multicoloured.

1681	(4r.90) Type **520**	1·25	1·25
1682	(4r.90) The Eastern Buttress seen from the Sentinel	1·25	1·25
1683	(4r.90) Amphitheatre seen from the Royal Natal National Park	1·25	1·25
1684	(4r.90) The Sentinel and the Amphitheatre	1·25	1·25

Nos. 1681/4 were inscr 'International Airmail Small Letter' and valid for 4r.90 each.

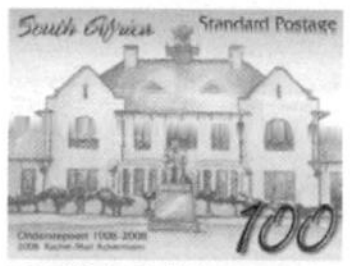

521 Main Building at Onderstepoort

2008. Centenary of Veterinary Research Laboratory, Onderstepoort. Sheet 105×65 mm.

MS1685	**521** (2r.) multicoloured	1·10	1·10

No. **MS**1685 was inscr 'Standard Postage' and sold for 2r.05.

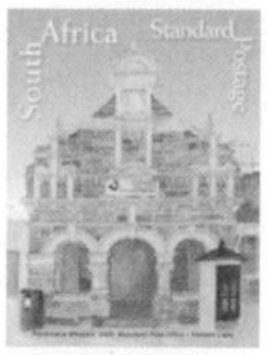

522 Aberdeen Post Office, Eastern Cape

2008. World Post Day. South African Post Office Buildings. Multicoloured.

1686	(2r.05) Type **522**	65	75
1687	(2r.05) West Bank Post Office, East London, Eastern Cape	65	75
1688	(2r.05) Main Post Office, Durban	65	75
1689	(2r.05) Church Square Post Office, Pretoria	65	75
1690	(2r.05) Frankfort Post Office, Free State	65	75

Nos. 1686/90 were inscr 'Standard Postage' and sold for 2r.05 each.

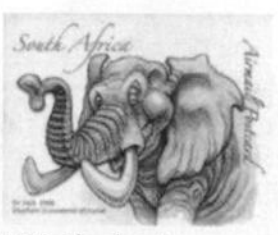

523 Elephant

2008. Wildlife. 'The Big Five' in Cartoons. Multicoloured. Self-adhesive.

1691	(4r.20) Type **523**	1·25	1·50
1692	(4r.20) Lion	1·25	1·50
1693	(4r.20) Leopard	1·25	1·50
1694	(4r.20) Buffalo	1·25	1·50
1695	(4r.20) Rhinoceros	1·25	1·50

Nos. 1691/5 were inscribed 'Airmail Postcard' and were valid for 4r.20 each.

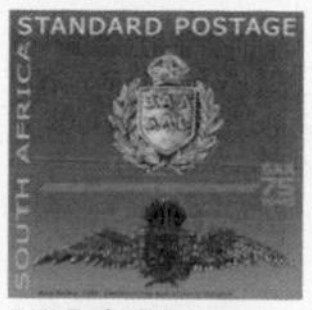

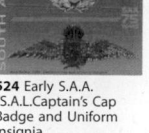

524 Early S.A.A. /S.A.L.Captain's Cap Badge and Uniform Insignia

2009. 75th Anniv of South African Airways. Designs showing Captain's cap badges and uniform insignia or aircraft tail fins. Multicoloured.

1696	(2r.05) Type **524**	75	75
1697	(2r.05) 'Flying springbok' and crown badge and pilot's wings, 1948	75	75
1698	(2r.05) 'Flying springbok' and arms of new South African Republic badge and arms wings, 1961	75	75
1699	(2r.05) 'Flying springbok' (facing right) badge and wings with shield, 1980s	75	75
1700	(2r.05) Flying springbok on blue shield badge and arms, 1991	75	75
1701	(2r.05) Flag emblem badge and arms, 1997	75	75
1702	(4r.90) Junkers Ju 53/3m, 1934–40	1·25	1·25
1703	(4r.90) Douglas DC-4, 1946–57	1·25	1·25
1704	(4r.90) Boeing 707, 1960–82	1·25	1·25
1705	(4r.90) Boeing 747, 1971–2008	1·25	1·25
1706	(4r.90) Airbus A300, 1976–2001	1·25	1·25
1707	(4r.90) Boeing 747, 1971–2008	1·25	1·25

Nos. 1696/1701 were each inscr 'STANDARD POSTAGE' and initially sold for 2r.05 each.

Nos. 1702/7 were each inscr 'INTERNATIONAL AIRMAIL SMALL LETTER' and initially sold for 5r.60 each.

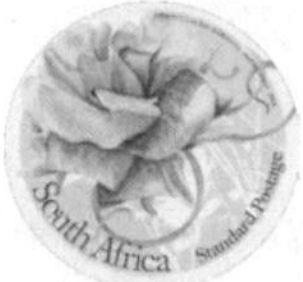

525 Rose 'Johannesburg Sun'

2009. 'All You Need is Love'. Sheet 167×187 mm containing T **525** and similar circular designs. Multicoloured. Self-adhesive.

MS1708	(2r.25)×10 Type **525**×2; 'Rina Hugo'×2; 'Beauty from Within'×2; 'Cotlands Rose'×2; 'Bewitched'×2	5·75	6·50

The stamps within **MS**1708 were all inscr 'Standard Postage'. The sheet was originally sold for 22r.50.

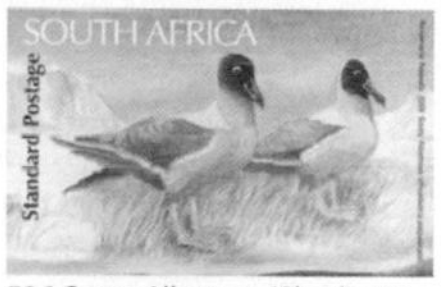

526 Sooty Albatross (*Phoebetria palpebrata*)

2009. Preserve the Polar Regions and Glaciers. Sheet 120×79 mm containing T **526** and similar horiz design. Multicoloured.

MS1709	(2r.25) Type **526**; (5r.40) Jellyfish (*Dipulmaris*)	3·00	3·00

The stamps within **MS**1709 were inscr 'Standard Postage' and 'International Small Letter'. The miniature sheet was sold for 7r.65.

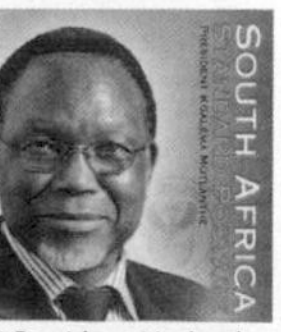

527 President Motlanthe

2009. President Kgalema Motlanthe.

1710	**527**	(2r.05) multicoloured	1·00	60

No. 1710 was inscr 'STANDARD POSTAGE' and initially sold for 2r.05.

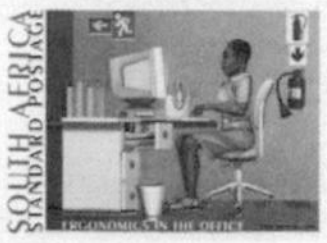

528 Ergonomics in the Office

2009. Occupational Health. Multicoloured.

1711	(2r.25) Type **528**	85	85
1712	(2r.25) Hearing test ('Medical surveillance')	85	85
1713	(2r.25) Firefighters ('Personal protective equipment')	85	85
1714	(2r.25) Inside a workshop ('Ensure a safe work place')	85	85

1715	(2r.25) Teaching safe method of lifting ('Training in the work place')	85	85

Nos. 1711/15 were inscr 'STANDARD POSTAGE' and originally sold for 2r.25 each.

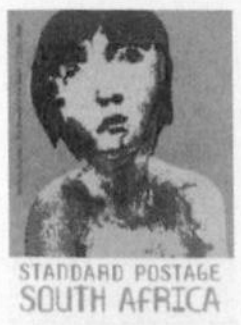

529 *The Benefit of the Doubt 2* (tapestry by Marlene Dumas), 2000

2009. Artwork in the Constitutional Court. Multicoloured.

1716	(2r.25) Type **529**	60	60
1717	(2r.25) *Forgotten Family 1* (Penny Siopis), 1996 (51×35 mm)	60	60
1718	(2r.25) *Bass Player* (Dumile Feni)	60	60
1719	(2r.25) *Head* (William Kentridge), 1993	60	60
1720	(2r.25) *Hotel with Landscape* (Robert Hodgins), 1996 (51×35 mm)	60	60
1721	(2r.25) *Hotlands 3* (Andrew Verster), 1993 (26×71 mm)	60	60
1722	(2r.25) *Discussion* (tapestry by Willie Bester), 1994 (51×35 mm)	60	60
1723	(2r.25) *The Smoker* (Gerard Sekoto), 1993 (51×35 mm)	60	60
1724	(2r.25) *Tethered Monkey* (Albert Adams)	60	60
1725	(2r.25) *The Man Who Sang and the Woman Who Kept Silent 3* (Judith Mason)	60	60

Nos. 1717/26, all inscr 'STANDARD POSTAGE', were sold for 22r.50 per sheetlet.

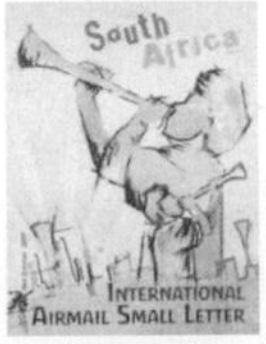

530 Football Fan blowing Vuvuzela

2009. World Cup Football, South Africa (2010) (4th issue). Sheet 105×65 mm.

MS1726	**530** (5r.40) multicoloured	2·75	2·75

No. **MS**1727 was inscr 'INTERNATIONAL AIRMAIL SMALL LETTER' and initially sold for 5r.40.

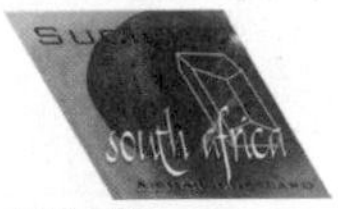

531 Sugilite

2009. South African Gemstones. Sheet 120×70 mm containing T **531** and similar diamond-shaped designs. Multicoloured.

MS1727	(4r.60)×4 Type **531**; Garnet; Jasper; Rodochrosite	7·00	7·00

The stamps within **MS**1727 were all inscr 'AIRMAIL POSTCARD' and were originally sold for 4r.60 each.

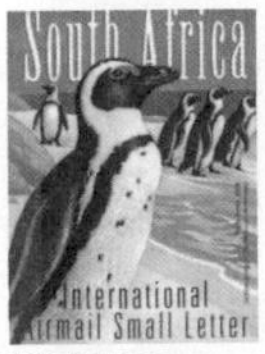

532 Jackass Penguin (*Spheniscus demersus*)

2009. Sea and Coastal Birds of South Africa. Multicoloured.

1728	(5r.40) Type **532**	2·25	2·25
1729	(5r.40) Black oystercatcher (*Haematopus bachmani*)	2·25	2·25
1730	(5r.40) Common cape gannet (*Morus capensis*)	2·25	2·25
1731	(5r.40) Cape cormorant (*Phalacrocorax capensis*)	2·25	2·25
1732	(5r.40) Black backed seagull (*Larus dominicanus*)	2·25	2·25

They were inscr 'International Airmail Small Letter' and originally sold for 5r.40 each.

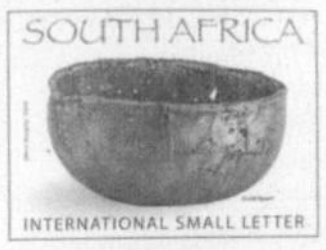

533 Gold Bowl

2009. Mapungubwe Cultural Landscape. Multicoloured.

1733	(5r.40) Type **533**	1·50	1·50
1734	(5r.40) Large and small bowls with spouts	1·50	1·50
1735	(5r.40) Gold rhinoceros	1·50	1·50
1736	(5r.40) Shallow terracotta bowl	1·50	1·50
1737	(5r.40) Gold sceptre	1·50	1·50

They were inscr 'INTERNATIONAL SMALL LETTER' and originally sold for 5r.40 each.

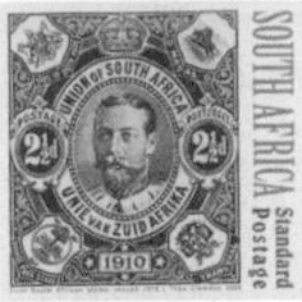

534 First South African Stamp (1910 Opening of Union Parliament 2½d.)

2009. Joburg 2010 International Stamp Show, Johannesburg. Two sheets, each 105×65 mm, containing T **534** and similar vert design. Multicoloured.

MS1738	(2r.25) Type **534**	1·10	1·10
MS1739	(5r.40) Exhibition logo (Nelson Mandela Bridge, Johannesburg)	2·50	2·50

No. **MS**1738 was inscr 'Standard Postage' and originally sold for 2r.25.

No. **MS**1739 was inscr 'INTERNATIONAL SMALL LETTER' and originally sold for 5r.40.

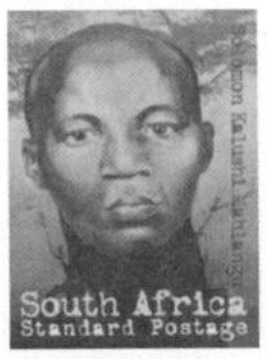

535 Solomon Kalushi Mahlangu

2009. 30th Death Anniv of Solomon Kalushi Mahlangu. Sheet 105×65 mm.

MS1740	**535** (2r.25) multicoloured	1·00	1·00

No. **MS**1740 was inscr 'Standard Postage' and originally sold for 2r.25.

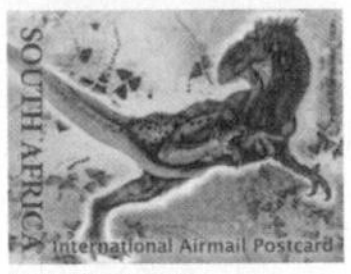

536 Afrovenator

2009. Dinosaurs. Sheet 234×172 mm containing T **536** and similar multicoloured designs.

MS1741	(4r.60)×10 Type **536**; Afrovenator skeleton; Heterodontosaurus (vert); Heterodontosaurus skeleton (vert); Ouranosaurus; Ouranosaurus skeleton; Jobaria (vert); Jobaria skeleton (vert); Suchomimus (vert); Suchomimus skeleton (vert)	13·00	13·00

The stamps within **MS**1741 were each inscr 'International Airmail Postcard' and sold for 4r.60 each.

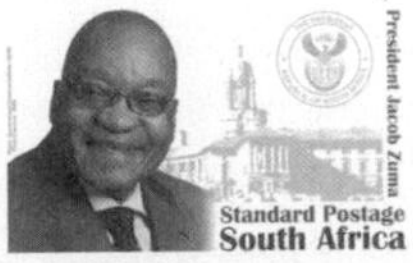

537 President Jacob Zuma

2009. Inauguration of President Jacob Zuma.

1742	**537** (2r.25) multicoloured	1·00	60

No. 1742 was inscr 'Standard Postage' and originally sold for 2r.25.

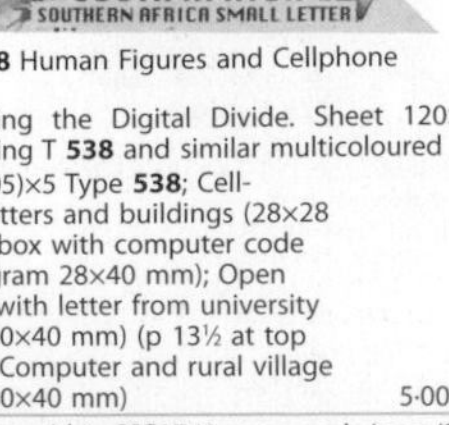

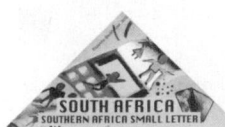

538 Human Figures and Cellphone

2010. Bridging the Digital Divide. Sheet 120×80 mm containing T **538** and similar multicoloured designs.

MS1743	(4r.05)×5 Type **538**; Cellphones, letters and buildings (28×28 mm); Postbox with computer code (parallelogram 28×40 mm); Open envelope with letter from university (triangle 80×40 mm) (p 13½ at top left only); Computer and rural village (triangle 80×40 mm)	5·00	6·00

The stamps within **MS**1743 were each inscr 'SOUHERN AFRICA SMALL LETTER' and sold for 4r.05 each.

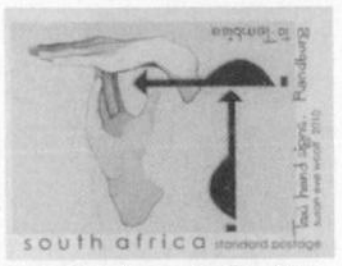

539 Randburg to Tembisa

2010. Taxi Hand Signs. Multicoloured.

1744	(2r.25) Type **539**	75	75
1745	(2r.25) Tembisa to Sebenza	75	75
1746	(2r.25) Turffontein to Mulbarton	75	75
1747	(2r.25) Gauteng to Johannesburg CBD	75	75
1748	(2r.25) Germiston to Katlehong	75	75
1749	(2r.25) Johannesburg to Sandton	75	75
1750	(2r.25) Alexandra to Randburg	75	75
1751	(2r.25) Emdeni to Highgate	75	75
1752	(2r.25) Local to the area	75	75
1753	(2r.25) Johannesburg to Phola Park	75	75

Nos. 1744/53 were all inscr 'standard postage' and sold for 2r.25 each.

They were printed with raised designs so that blind people could learn the signals, and contain traces of powdered limestone.

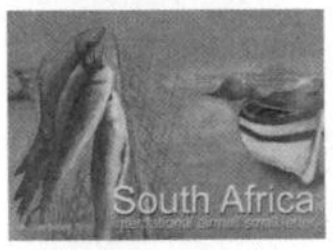

540 Fish in Net and Beached Boat

2010. The Life of Fisher Folk. Multicoloured.

1754	(5r.40) Type **540**	1·25	1·25
1755	(5r.40) Three fishermen launching boat	1·25	1·25
1756	(5r.40) Fisherman's cottage and setting sun	1·25	1·25
1757	(5r.40) Two fishermen sat on stern of beached boat	1·25	1·25
1758	(5r.40) Five fishermen walking away from beached boat	1·25	1·25
1759	(5r.40) Fishing village	1·25	1·25
1760	(5r.40) Cottage and two fishermen sat on stern of beached boat	1·25	1·25
1761	(5r.40) Angler and beached boat	1·25	1·25
1762	(5r.40) Fish, cottages and beached boat JEA 4JR	1·25	1·25
1763	(5r.40) Old man and rack of drying fish	1·25	1·25

Nos. 1754/63 were all inscr 'international airmail small letter' and sold for 5r.40 each.

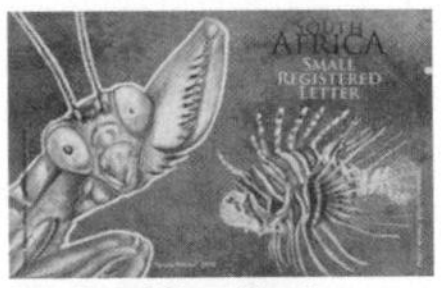

541 Giant African Mantis (*Sphodromantis viridis*) and Common Lionfish (*Pterois miles*)

2010. International Year of Biodiversity. Sheet 126×91 mm containing T **541** and similar horiz designs. Multicoloured.

MS1764	(15r.85)×4 Type **541**; Black rhinoceros (*Diceros bicornis*) and red-billed oxpecker (*Buphaguserythrorhynchus*); Common chameleon (*Chamaeleo chamaeleon*) and African reed frog (*Hyperolius argus*); Lilac-breasted roller (*Coracias caudatus*) and baobab tree (*Adansonia digitata*)	17·00	18·00

The stamps within **MS**1764 were all inscr 'SMALL REGISTERED LETTER' and originally sold for 15r.85 each.

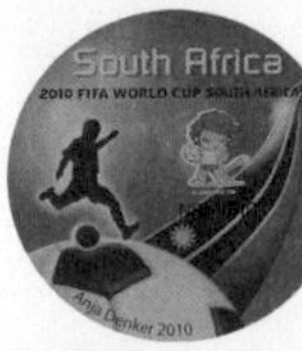

542 Player, Football, Namibian Flag and Zakumi Mascot

2010. Third Joint Issue of Southern Africa Postal Operators Association Members. World Cup Football Championship, South Africa (5th issue). Sheet 188×167 mm containing T **542** and similar circular designs, each showing Zakumi mascot, different silhouettes of players on football, and the national flag of a member country. Multicoloured.

MS1765	5r.75×9 Type **542**; South Africa; Zimbabwe; Malawi; Swaziland; Botswana; Mauritius; Lesotho; Zambia	17·00	17·00

Similar miniature sheets were issued by Botswana, Lesotho, Malawi, Mauritius, Namibia, Swaziland, Zambia and Zimbabwe.

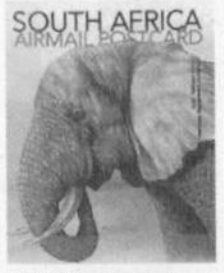

543 Elephant

2010. Wildlife. "The Big Five". Multicoloured.

1766	(4r.90) Type **543**	1·75	1·90
1767	(4r.90) Lion	1·75	1·90
1768	(4r.90) Buffalo	1·75	1·90
1769	(4r.90) Leopard	1·75	1·90
1770	(4r.90) Rhinoceros	1·75	1·90

Nos. 1766/70 were inscribed 'AIRMAIL POSTCARD' and originally sold for 4r.90 each.

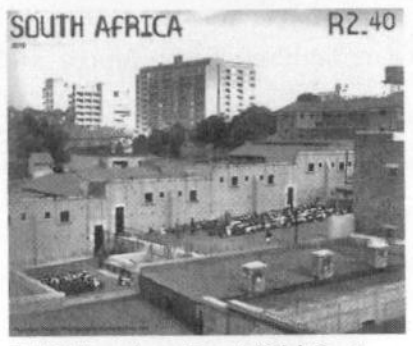

544 'Number Four' (Old Fort Prison Complex)

2010. History of Constitution Hill. Multicoloured.

1771	2r.40 Type **544**	80	80
1772	2r.40 Atrium of the women's jail (24×40 mm)	80	80
1773	2r.40 The Awaiting Trial Block, 1954	80	80
1774	2r.40 Flogging frame in cell no. 3	80	80
1775	2r.40 Remaining stairwells of the Awaiting Trial Block (24×40 mm)	80	80
1776	2r.40 Cells in the Fort (24×40 mm)	80	80
1777	2r.40 Isolation cells in Number Four (24×81 mm)	80	80
1778	2r.40 The Guard House in front of the isolation cells (24×40 mm)	80	80
1779	2r.40 Entrance to The Fort	80	80
1780	2r.40 The Ramparts (96×40 mm)	80	80

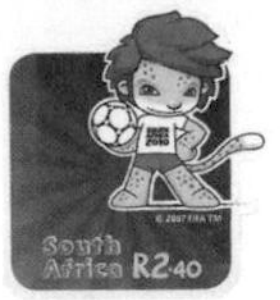

545 Zakumi Mascot holding Football

2010. World Cup Football Championship, South Africa (6th issue). Multicoloured.

1781	2r.40 Type **545**	90	90
1782	2r.40 Zakumi about to kick ball	90	90
1783	2r.40 Zakumi holding South African flag	90	90
1784	2r.40 Zakumi kicking ball	90	90
1785	2r.40 Zakumi with arms raised in triumph	90	90

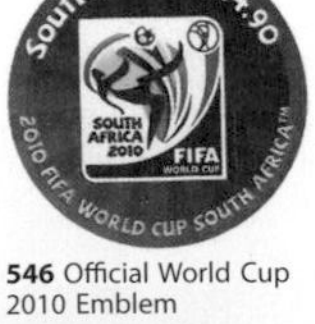

546 Official World Cup 2010 Emblem

2010. World Cup Football Championship, South Africa (7th issue). Multicoloured.

MS1786	Circular 125×125 mm. 4r.90×6 Type **546**×2; Jabulami (official match ball)×2; World Cup trophy×2	8·50	8·50

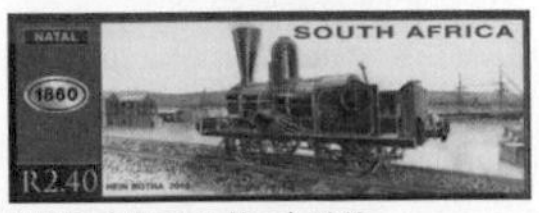

547 Tank Engine *Natal*, 1860

2010. 150th Anniv of South African Railways. Multicoloured.

1787	2r.40 Type **547**	95	95
1788	2r.40 Class NGG 16 Garratt steam locomotive, 1937	95	95
1789	2r.40 Class 24 steam locomotive pulling Outeniqua Choo-Tjoe train, 1948	95	95
1790	2r.40 Class 25 steam locomotive, 1953	95	95
1791	2r.40 Class GMA/M Garratt steam locomotive, 1954	95	95
1792	2r.40 Class 35 Co-Co diesel-electric locomotive, 1974	95	95

1793	2r.40 Class 9E Co-Co 50KV ac electric locomotive, 1978	95	95
1794	2r.40 Class 26 steam locomotive, No. 3450 *Red Devil*, 1981	95	95
1795	2r.40 Class 19E Bo-Bo dual voltage electric locomotive, 2009	95	95
1796	2r.40 Gautrain Electrostar Bo-bo, 2010	95	95

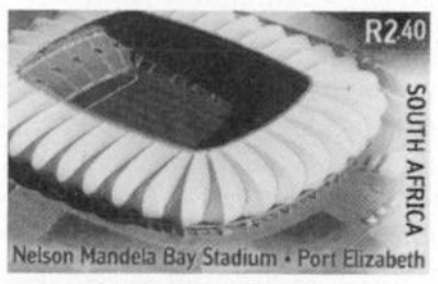

548 Nelson Mandela Bay Stadium, Port Elizabeth

2010. South African Sports Stadiums. Multicoloured.

1797	2r.40 Type **548**	80	80
1798	2r.40 Ellis Park Stadium, Johannesburg	80	80
1799	2r.40 Free State Stadium, Bloemfontein	80	80
1800	2r.40 Cape Town Stadium	80	80
1801	2r.40 Moses Mabhida Stadium, Durban	80	80
1802	2r.40 Loftus Versfeld Stadium, Tshwane/Pretoria	80	80
1803	2r.40 Peter Mokaba Stadium, Polokwane	80	80
1804	2r.40 Mbombela Stadium, Nelspruit	80	80
1805	2r.40 Soccer City Stadium, Johannesburg	80	80
1806	2r.40 Royal Bafokeng Stadium, Rustenburg	80	80

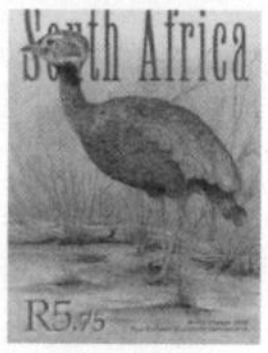

549 Blue Korhaan (*Eupodotis caerulescens*)

2010. Grassland Birds of South Africa. Multicoloured.

1807	5r.75 Type **549**	2·25	2·25
1808	5r.75 Buff-streaked chat (*Oenanthe bifasciata*)	2·25	2·25
1809	5r.75 White-bellied korhaan (*Eupodotis cafra*)	2·25	2·25
1810	5r.75 White winged flufftail (*Sarothrura ayresi*)	2·25	2·25
1811	5r.75 Yellow-breasted pipit (*Anthus chloris*)	2·25	2·25

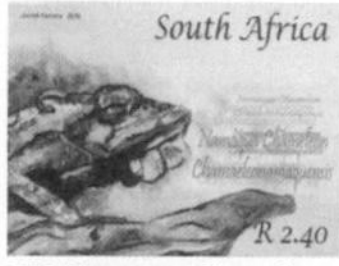

550 Namaqua Chameleon (*Chamaeleo namaquensis*)

2010. Richtersveld Cultural and Botanical Landscape. Multicoloured.

1812	2r.40 Type **550**	1·00	1·00
1813	2r.40 Namaqua sandgrouse (*Pterocles namaqua*)	1·00	1·00
1814	2r.40 Bastard quiver tree (*Aloe pilansii*)	1·00	1·00
1815	2r.40 Nama woman	1·00	1·00
1816	2r.40 Grey rhebok (*Pelea carpreolus*)	1·00	1·00

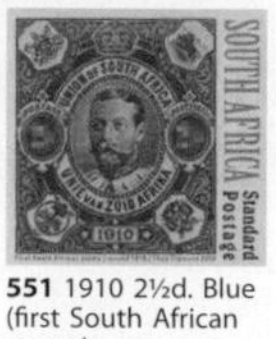

551 1910 2½d. Blue (first South African stamp)

2010. World Post Day. JOBURG 2010 International Stamp Show. 'Celebrating Printing Techniques on South African Stamps'. Multicoloured.

1817	(2r.40) Type **551**	80	80
1818	(2r.40) 1930 1s. Black and blue wildebeest stamp (first rotogravure stamp)	80	80
1819	(2r.40) 1929 4d. De Havilland DH60 Cirrus Moth airmail stamp (first letterpress stamp by Government Printing Works)	80	80
1820	(2r.40) 2009 75th anniv of South African Airways standard postage stamp (first stamp embossed and printed with gold foil)	80	80
1821	(2r.40) 1974 Centenary of the Burgerspond Coin 9c. stamp (first litho stamp) (30×60 mm)	80	80
1822	(2r.40) 1963 50th anniv of Kirstenbosch Botanic Gardens 2½c. stamp (first stamp produced using process colour) (60×30 mm)	80	80
1823	(2r.40) 1970 150th anniv of Bible Society 12½c. stamp (first stamp with gold foil) (60×30 mm)	80	80
1824	(2r.40) 2005 Prevention of blindness standard postage stamp (first Braille stamp) (60×30 mm)	80	80
1825	(2r.40) 2008 Karoo gazania airmail postcard stamp (Flowers of Namaqualand first stamps printed with fragrance) (60×30 mm)	80	80
1826	(2r.40) 1997 Tswana knife handle standard postage stamp (Year of Cultural Experiences first superlitho stamps in world) (30×60 mm)	80	80
1827	(2r.40) 2009 Suchomimus International airmail postcard stamp (Dinosaurs first 3D effect stamps)	80	80
1828	(2r.40) 1974 25th anniv of Voortrekker Monument 4c. stamp (first intaglio stamp) (90×30 mm)	80	80

Nos. 1817/28 were all inscr 'Standard Postage' and originally sold for 2r.40 each.

The face values on the original stamps have been digitally obscured.

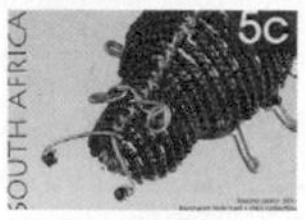

552 Ladybird

2010. South African Beadwork. Multicoloured.

(a) Ordinary gum

1829	5c. Type **552**	10	10
1830	10c. Dove	10	10
1831	20c. Llama	15	15
1832	30c. Cell phone	15	15
1833	40c. Hammerhead bird	15	15
1834	50c. Aeroplane	20	20
1835	60c. Angel	20	20
1836	70c. Nguni cow	25	25
1837	80c. Boxer	25	25
1838	90c. Zebra	30	30
1839	1r. Miner	30	30
1840	2r. Tsonga fertility figure	55	55
1841	(2r.40) Zulu neckpiece (vert)	60	60
1842	(2r.40) Ndebele neckpiece (vert)	60	60
1843	(2r.40) Xhosa neckpiece (vert)	60	60
1844	(2r.40) Swazi neckpiece (vert)	60	60
1845	(2r.40) Tsonga love token pin (vert)	60	60
1846	3r. Ndebele married woman's apron	60	60
1847	(4r.80) Tsonga neckpiece	1·25	1·25
1848	(4r.90) Zulu neckpieces	1·25	1·25
1849	5r. Mfengu tobacco bag	1·40	1·40
1850	(5r.40) Bhaca neckpiece (blue, white, green, yellow and black beads)	1·75	1·75
1851	(6r.) Bhaca neckpiece (blue, red and white beads)	2·25	2·25
1852	10r. South Sotho ceremonial whisk	2·75	2·75
1853	(Registered letter small) Bhaca neckpiece (yellow, red, blue and white beads)	3·25	3·25
1854	(Registered letter medium) Venda beadwork pin	3·25	3·25
1855	20r. Zulu neckpiece made of lion claws	5·50	5·50

(b) Self-adhesive booklet stamps

1856	(2r.40) As No. 1841	60	60
1857	(2r.40) As No. 1842	60	60
1858	(2r.40) As No. 1843	60	60
1859	(2r.40) As No. 1844	60	60
1860	(2r.40) As No. 1845	60	60
1861	(4r.80) As No. 1847 but vert	1·25	1·25
1862	(6r.) As No. 1851 but vert	2·25	2·25

Nos. 1841/5 and 1856/60 were inscr 'Standard Postage' and originally sold for 2r.40 each.

Nos. 1847 and 1861 were inscr 'B5' and originally sold for 4r.80.

No. 1848 was inscr 'Airmail Postcard' and originally sold for 4r.90.

No. 1850 was inscr 'International Small Letter' and originally sold for 5r.40.

Nos. 1851 and 1862 were inscr 'B4' and originally sold for 6r.

Nos. 1863/5 are left for possible additions to this definitive series.

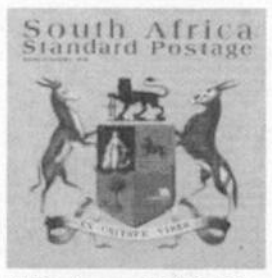

553 Arms, 1910–30

2010. Centenary of South Africa. Sheet 130×70 mm containing T **553** and similar square designs showing the coats of arms of South Africa from 1910 to 2010. Multicoloured.

MS1866	(2r.40)×4 Type **553**; Arms 1930–32 (on green base); Arms 1932–2000 (on green base, motto 'EX' 'UNITATE' 'VIRES' in three separate folds of scroll); Current coat of arms (shield with human figures, elephant tusks and secretary bird)	2·50	2·50

The stamps within **MS**1866 were all inscr 'Standard Postage' and were originally valid for 2r.40 each.

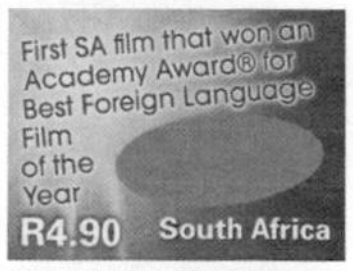

554 'First SA film that won an Academy Award® for Best Foreign Language Film of the Year'

2010. South African Quiz. Multicoloured.

1867	4r.90 Type **554**	1·00	1·00
1868	4r.90 'Number of UNESCO World Heritage Sites in SA'	1·00	1·00
1869	4r.90 'Which SA invention has been to the moon?'	1·00	1·00
1870	4r.90 'Which fish is known as a living fossil?'	1·00	1·00
1871	4r.90 'Indian spiritual and political leader whose career started in SA'	1·00	1·00
1872	4r.90 'When were SA's gold and diamond deposits formed?'	1·00	1·00
1873	4r.90 'Animal used by Dr Chris Barnard in trials preceding the first heart transplant'	1·00	1·00
1874	4r.90 'Telescope strong enough to see candle-light on the moon'	1·00	1·00
1875	4r.90 'The largest bird in the World occurring in SA'	1·00	1·00
1876	4r.90 'Where in SA was gold first mined?'	1·00	1·00

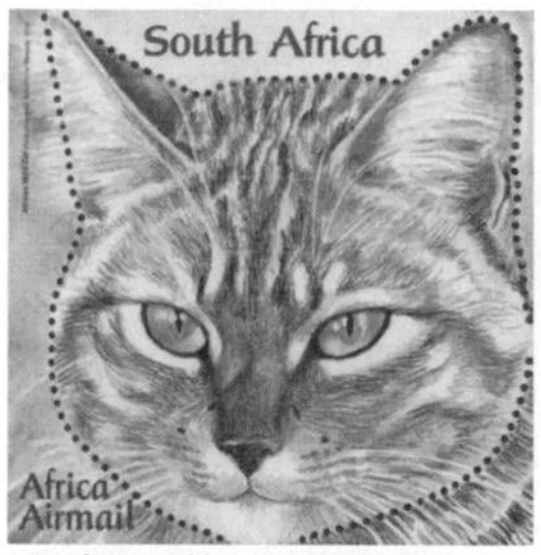

555 African Wild Cat (*Felis silvestris*)

2011. Small African Wild Cats. Multicoloured.

1877	(4r.30) Type **555**	1·25	1·25
1878	(4r.30) Serval (*Leptailarus serval*) (30×30 mm)	1·25	1·25
1879	(4r.30) Caracal (*Caracal caracal*) (30×30 mm)	1·25	1·25
1880	(4r.30) Black-footed cat (*Felis nigripes*) (30×30 mm)	1·25	1·25
1881	(4r.30) African golden cat (*Profelis aurata*) (30×30 mm)	1·25	1·25

Nos. 1877/81 were all inscr 'Africa Airmail' and were originally valid for 4r.30 each.

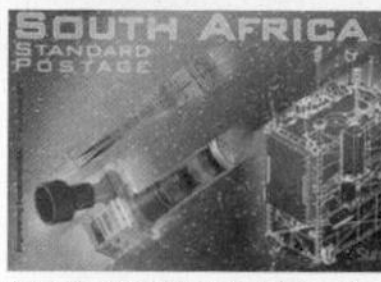

556 Engineering Sumbandilasat

2011. Sumbandilasat (South African micro-satellite). Multicoloured.

1882	(2r.50) Type **556** (University of Stellenbosch)	75	75
1883	(2r.50) Sumbandilasat in orbit	75	75
1884	(2r.50) 12m S-band antenna at Hartebeeshoek (satellite tracking)	75	75
1885	(2r.50) Soyuz 2.1b rocket on launch platform, Baikonur Cosmodrome, Kazakhstan (launch of Sumbandilasat), 2009	75	75
1886	(2r.50) Sumbandilasat (vert)	75	75

Nos. 1882/6 were inscr 'STANDARD POSTAGE' and were orignally valid for 2r.50.

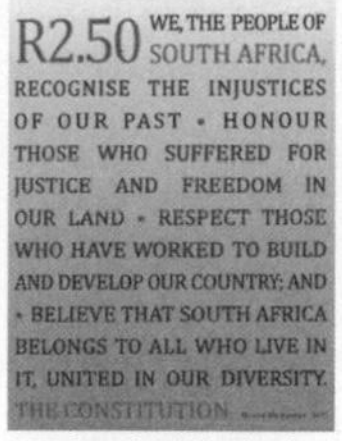

557 Opening Words of Preamble to the Constitution

2011. Honouring the Constitution. Sheet 105×75 mm

MS1887	**557** 2r.50 multicoloured	1·00	1·00

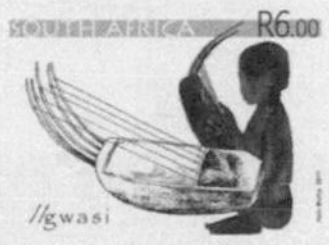

558 //gwasi

2011. Rare Musical Instruments. Multicoloured.

1888	6r. Type **558**	1·50	1·50
1889	6r. Ramkie	1·50	1·50
1890	6r. Sansa	1·50	1·50
1891	6r. Drums	1·50	1·50
1892	6r. Bullroarer	1·50	1·50
1893	6r. Horns	1·50	1·50
1894	6r. Flute	1·50	1·50
1895	6r. Xylophone	1·50	1·50
1896	6r. Rattles	1·50	1·50
1897	6r. Bows	1·50	1·50

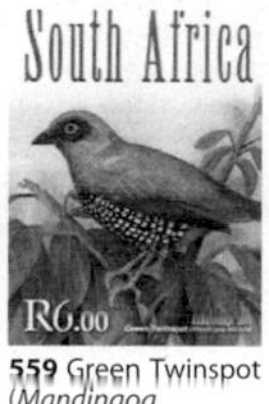

559 Green Twinspot (*Mandingoa nitidula*)

2011. Forest Birds of South Africa. Multicoloured.

1898	6r. Type **559**	1·50	1·50
1899	6r. Olive bush-shrike (*Telophorus olivaceus*)	1·50	1·50
1900	6r. Cape parrot (*Poicephalus robustus*)	1·50	1·50
1901	6r. Knysna turaco (*Tauraco corythaix*)	1·50	1·50
1902	6r. African crowned eagle (*Stephanoaetus coronatus*)	1·50	1·50

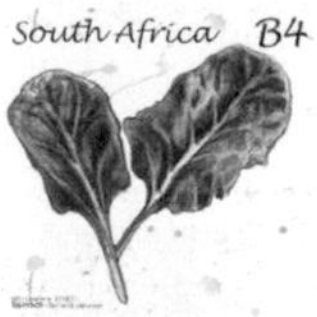

560 Spinach

2011. Green Earth Healthy Garden. Multicoloured.

MS1903	(6r.25)×6 Type **560**; Tomatoes; Beetroot; Carrots; Cabbage; Butternut squash	9·00	9·00

The stamps within **MS**1903 were all inscr 'B4' and were originally valid for 6r.25.

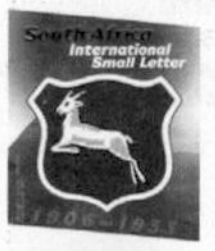

561 Springbok Emblem (1906-33)

2011. Evolution of the Springbok Emblem. Multicoloured.

1904	(6r.) Type **561**	1·50	1·50
1905	(6r.) South African Rugby Board badge, 193572	1·50	1·50
1906	(6r.) Springbok emblem, 193762	1·50	1·50
1907	(6r.) Springbok emblem, 19634	1·50	1·50
1908	(6r.) Springbok emblem, 196589	1·50	1·50
1909	(6r.) South African Rugby Union badge, 196691	1·50	1·50
1910	(6r.) Springbok emblem, 19925	1·50	1·50
1911	(6r.) Springbok emblem, 19962003	1·50	1·50
1912	(6r.) Springbok emblem, 20048	1·50	1·50
1913	(6r.) Springbok emblem, 200911	1·50	1·50

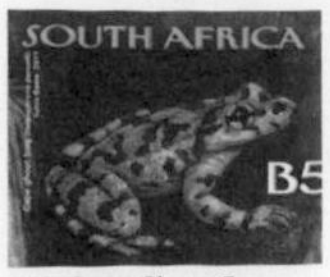

562 Cape Ghost Frog (*Heleophyrne purcelli*)

2011. South African Heritage Sites. Cape Floral Region. Multicoloured.

MS1914 (5r.)×10 Type **562**; Fish eagle (*Haliaeetus vocifer*) (vert); Cape vulture (*Gyps coprotheres*); Cape clawless otter (*Aonyx capensis*) (vert); Caracal (*Caracal caracal*); Strelitzia (*Strelitzia reginae*); Cape sugar bird (*Promerops cafer*) (vert); Cape aloe (*Aloe ferox*) (vert); Erica (*Erica patersonii*) (vert); King protea (*Protea cynaroides*)	15·00	15·00

The stamps within **MS**1914 were all inscr 'B5' and were originally valid for 5r. each.

The stamps and margins form a composite design.

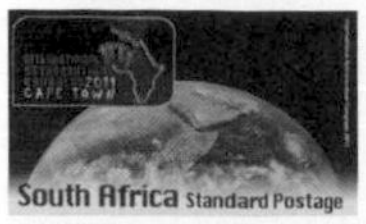

563 Globe

2011. 62nd International Astronautical Congress, Cape Town. Sheet 106×65 mm

MS1915 **563** (2r.50) multicoloured	70	70

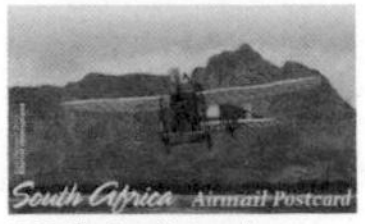

564 Bleriot Monoplane

2011. Centenary of the First South African Aerial Post Flight. Sheet 109×90 mm

MS1916 **564** (5r.10) multicoloured	1·40	1·40

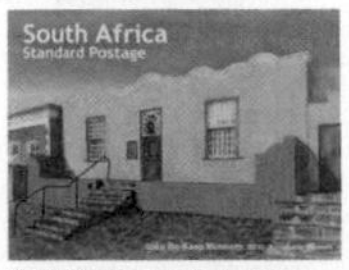

565 Bo-Kaap Museum, Cape Town

2011. 300 Years of Historic Link between South Africa and Indonesia. Multicoloured.

1917	(2r.50) Type **565**	70	70
1918	(2r.50) Ghoema drum-maker	70	70
1919	(2r.50) Toering hat and kaparang sandals	70	70
1920	(2r.50) Klopse playing Ghoema drum, trombone and trumpet at New Year	70	70
1921	(2r.50) Sheikh Yusuf of Macassar (scholar, Sufi mystic and founder of Cape Muslim community)	70	70

Nos. 1917/21 were inscr 'Standard Postage' and originally sold for 2r.50 each.

Similar designs were issued by Indonesia.

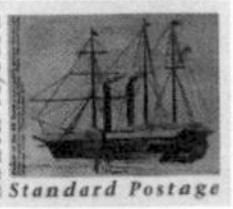

566 SS *Truro* (immigrant ship), 1860

2011. 150th Anniv of the Arrival of Indian Indentured Labourers (**MS**1922) and Indian Workers (**MS**1923) in South Africa. Multicoloured.

MS1922 (2r.50) Type **566**	70	70
MS1923 (2r.50) Labourers in sugar plantation; (2r.50) Indian indentured workers coming ashore at Durban harbour	1·40	1·40

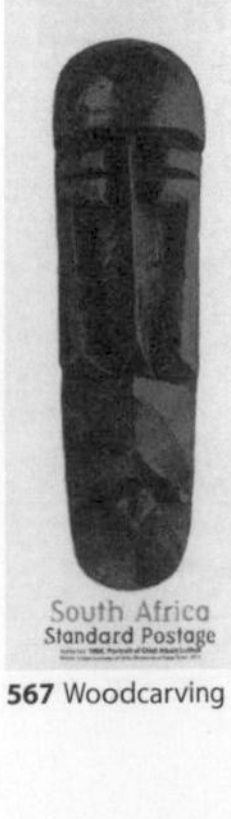

567 Woodcarving

2011. 50th Anniv of Chief Albert Luthuli's Nobel Peace Prize. Multicoloured.

1924	(2r.50) Type **567**	70	70
1925	(2r.50) Chief Albert Luthuli (with beard) (29×38 mm)	70	70
1926	(2r.50) Chief Albert Luthuli (without beard) (29×38 mm)	70	70

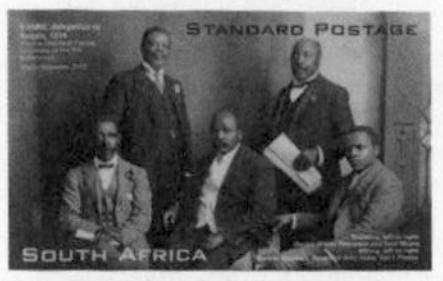

568 Dr. Walter Rabusana, Saul Msane, Thomas Mapikela, Revd John Dube and Sol Plaatje (SANNC delegation to Britain), 1914

2012. Centenary of the SANNC (South African Native National Congress, from 1923 African National Congress)

1927	**568**	(2r.50) multicoloured	70	70

No. 1927 was inscr 'STANDARD POSTAGE' and originally sold for 2r.50.

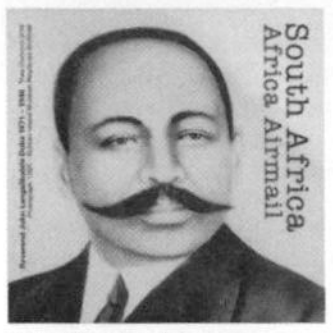

569 Revd John Langalibalele Dube

2012. John Dube (founding President of the SANNC, from 1923 ANC) Commemoration. Sheet 105×65 mm

MS1928 **569** (4r.80) multicoloured	1·25	1·25

The stamp within **MS**1928 was inscr 'Africa Airmail' and originally sold for 4r.80.

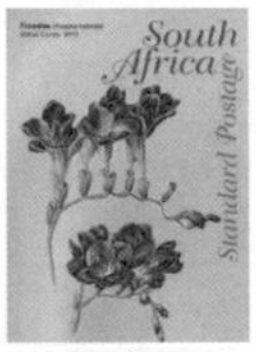

572 Freesias (*Freesia* hybrids)

2012. Commercial and Medicinal Plants. Multicoloured.

1947	(2r.65) Type **572**	70	70
1948	(2r.65) Rooibos tea (*Aspalathus linearis*)	70	70
1949	(2r.65) Barberton daisy (*Gerbera* hybrid) (inscr 'Baberton')	70	70
1950	(2r.65) Honeybush tea (*Cyclopia genistoides*)	70	70
1951	(2r.65) Cape aloe (*Aloe ferox*)	70	70
1952	(2r.65) Gladiolus (*Gladiolus* hybrid)	70	70
1953	(2r.65) African potato (*Hypoxis hemerocalllidea*)	70	70
1954	(2r.65) King protea (*Protea cynaroides*)	70	70
1955	(2r.65) Marula (*Sclerocarya birrea* subsp. *caffra*)	70	70
1956	(2r.65) Buchu (*Agathosma crenulata*)	70	70

Nos. 1947/56 were each inscr 'Standard Postage' and were originally valid for 2r.65.

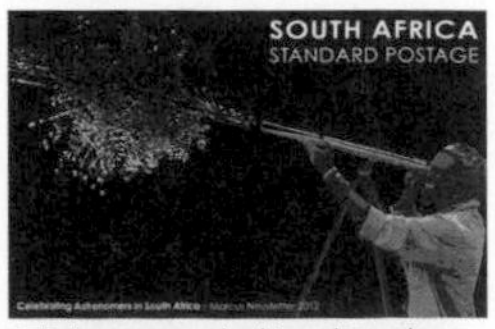

573 Astronomer looking through Telescope

2012. South Africa's Role in Astronomy

1957	(2r.65) Type **573**	70	70
1958	(2r.65) Karoo Array Telescope (KAT 7) receiving cosmic radio signals	70	70
1959	(2r.65) Ancestral South African hunter and drawing of night sky (28×74 mm)	70	70
1960	(2r.65) Starry sky (formation of South African National Space Agency SANSA) (28×37 mm)	70	70
1961	(2r.65) Two satellites orbiting Earth and digital traces of satellite imagery (SunSat1) (28×74 mm)	70	70
1962	(2r.65) Innes Telescope at Johannesburg Observatory and image of Proxima Centauri	70	70
1963	(2r.65) Sumbandila Satellite in front of satellite image (28×37 mm)	70	70
1964	(2r.65) Southern African Large Telescope (SALT) at Sutherland and hexagonal section of mirror surface (28×37 mm)	70	70
1965	(2r.65) Hartebeesthoek Radio Astronomy Observatory (HartRAO) near Johannesburg and sound waves (28×37 mm)	70	70
1966	(2r.65) South African Astronomical Observatory (SAAO) in Sutherland and diagrammatic data	70	70
1967	(2r.65) Royal Observatory, Cape Town, 1828, Milky Way, Magellan Clouds and stars	70	70

Nos. 1957/67 were all inscr 'STANDARD POSTAGE' and were originally valid for 2r.65 each.

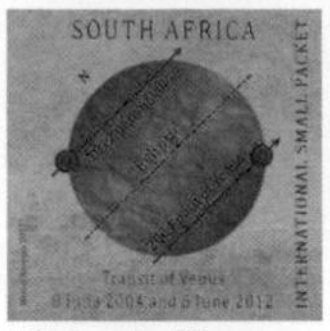

574 Transit of Venus across the Sun

2012. Transit of Venus. Sheet 106×65 mm

MS1968 **574** (27r.40) multicoloured	7·25	7·25

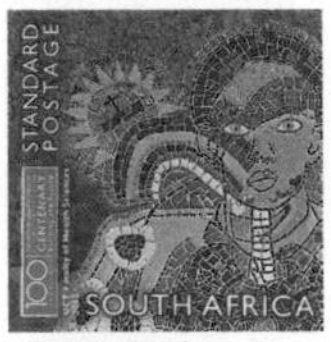

575 Mosaic of Nondumiso Hlwele (left portion)

2012. Centenary of Faculty of Health Sciences, University of Cape Town. Multicoloured.

MS1969 (2r.65) Type **575**; (2r.65) Mosaic (right portion, reaching hands)	1·40	1·40

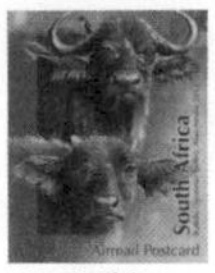

576 Buffalo Calves

2012. Wildlife. 'The Baby Big Five'. Multicoloured.

1970	(5r.40) Type **576**	1·40	1·40
1971	(5r.40) Elephant calves	1·40	1·40
1972	(5r.40) Leopard cubs	1·40	1·40
1973	(5r.40) Rhinoceros calves	1·40	1·40
1974	(5r.40) Lion cubs	1·40	1·40

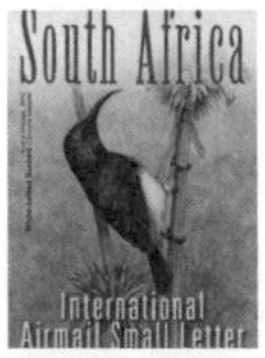

577 White-bellied Sunbird (*Cinnyris talatala*)

2012. Smallest Sunbirds of South Africa. Multicoloured.

1975	(5r.40) Type **577**	1·75	1·75
1976	(5r.40) Dusky Sunbird (*Cinnyris fuscus*)	1·75	1·75
1977	(5r.40) Neergaard's Sunbird (*Cinnyris neergaardi*)	1·75	1·75
1978	(5r.40) Plain-backed Sunbird (*Anthreptes reichenowi*)	1·75	1·75
1979	(5r.40) Collared Sunbird (*Hedydipna collaris*)	1·75	1·75

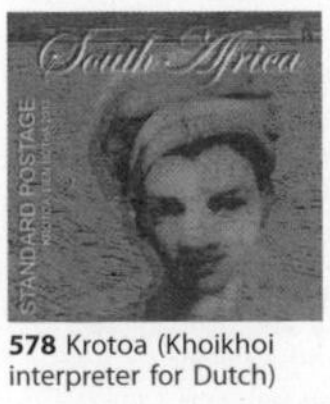

578 Krotoa (Khoikhoi interpreter for Dutch)

2012. 360th Anniv of the Arrival of the Dutch at the Cape. Sheet 105×65 mm

MS1980 **578** (2r.65) multicoloured	70	70

No. **MS**1980 was inscr 'STANDARD POSTAGE' and originally sold for 2r.65.

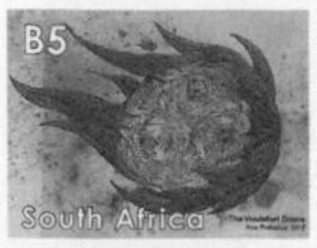

579 Meteorite

2012. South African Heritage Sites. The Vredefort Dome. Multicoloured.

1981	(5r.30) Type **579**	1·40	1·40
1982	(5r.30) Meteorite striking Earth	1·40	1·40
1983	(5r.30) Meteorite and crystals	1·40	1·40
1984	(5r.30) Meteorite and granophyre dyke	1·40	1·40
1985	(5r.30) Rock strata	1·40	1·40

Nos. 1981/5 were all inscribed 'B5' and were originally valid for 5r.30 each.

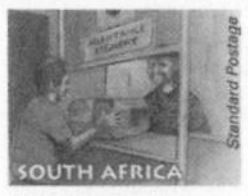

580 Accepting Parcel at Field Post Office 3

2012. South African 11 Field Post Unit. Multicoloured.

1986	(2r.65) Type **580**	70	70
1987	(2r.65) Scanning parcel before dispatch	70	70
1988	(2r.65) Loading mail into Hercules 130 aircraft at Field Post Office 3, Air Force Base Waterkloof	70	70
1989	(2r.65) Soldiers awaiting mail from home at field post office	70	70
1990	(2r.65) Soldier with parcel and letter outside field post office	70	70
1991	(2r.65) Parcels at field post office	70	70
1992	(2r.65) Packing parcels	70	70
1993	(2r.65) Soldier with letter and parcel	70	70
1994	(2r.65) Soldier reading letter	70	70
1995	(2r.65) Soldier posting letter	70	70

Nos. 1986/95 were all inscr 'Standard Postage' and were originally valid for 2r.65 each.

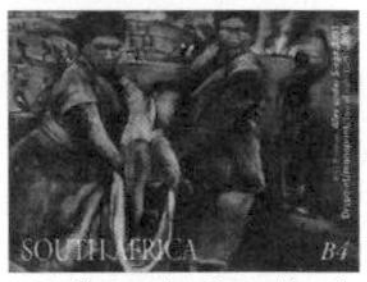

581 *Alex under Siege* (detail of dryprint/monoprint by Kim Berman), 1991

2012. Centenary of Alexandra Township, Johannesburg. Multicoloured.

1996	(6r.60) Type **581**	1·75	1·75
1997	(6r.60) *Alexandra Scene* (acrylic on paper, David Koloane), 2010	1·75	1·75
1998	(6r.60) *Alex from the Far East Bank*, 2002 (five circular paintings of Alexandra scenes by Joachim Schönfeldt) (80×73 mm)	1·75	1·75
1999	(6r.60) *Evening Township Scene* (oil on asbestos, Julian Motau), 1965	1·75	1·75
2000	(6r.60) *Alex Youth Collaborating* (pencil and pencil crayons, Sipho Gwala), 2011	1·75	1·75

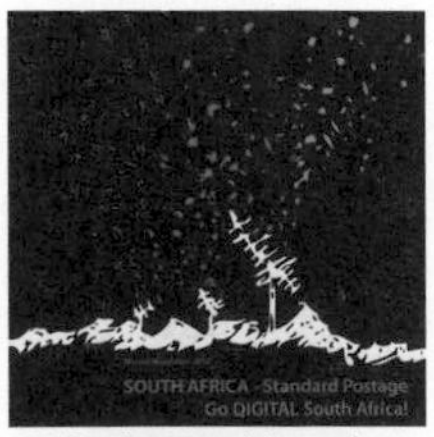

582 Receivers receiving and Translating Digital Data into Images

2012. Go DIGITAL South Africa! Campaign. Sheet 65×105 mm.

MS2001 **582** (2r.65) multicoloured	70	70

No. **MS**2001 was inscr 'Standard Postage' and originally sold for 2r.65.

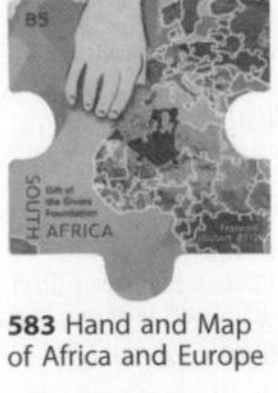

583 Hand and Map of Africa and Europe

2013. Gift of the Givers Foundation (humanitarian organisation). Multicoloured.

MS2002 (5r.30) Type **583**; (5r.30) Hand and map of Asia, Arabian Peninsula and Horn of Africa 2·75 2·75

The stamps within **MS**2002 were both inscr 'B5' and were originally valid for 5r.30 each. They both have 'jig-saw' perforations on all four sides.

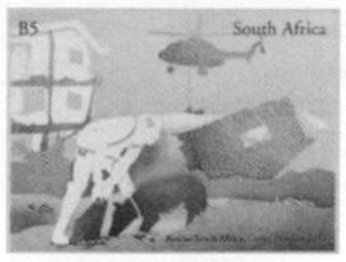

584 Rescuer and Helicopter

2013. Rescue South Africa (disaster response team). Multicoloured.

MS2003 (5r.30) Type **584**; (5r.30) Rescuers carrying casualty on stretcher 2·75 2·75

The stamps within **MS**2003 were both inscr 'B5' and were originally valid for 5r.30 each.

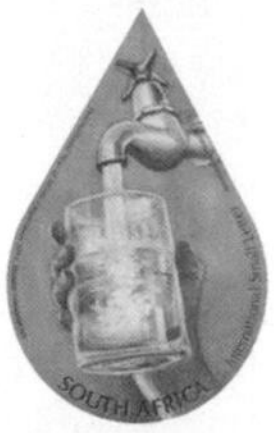

585 Clean Drinking Water ('Human Consumption')

2013. International Year of Water Co-operation. Multicoloured.

MS2004 (6r.30)×5 Type **585**; Irrigation at night to prevent evaporation ('Agriculture'); Worker removing alien trees from riverbank ('Working for Water Programme')); Clanwilliam Redfin and Mauve Bluet Damselfly ('Biodiversity'); Wind turbines ('Industry') 8·75 8·75

The stamps within **MS**2004 were all inscr 'International Small Letter' and were originally valid for 6r.30.

No. **MS**2004 consists of two discs. The top disc is die-cut with two apertures which can be rotated to reveal indvidual stamps and information about them on the bottom disc.

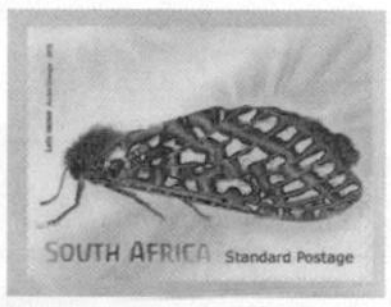

586 *Leto venus* (moth)

2013. Butterflies and Moths. Multicoloured.

2005	(2r.80) Type **586**	70	70
2006	(2r.80) *Alaena margaritacea* (Wolkberg Zulu)	70	70
2007	(2r.80) *Charaxes marieps* (Marieps Emperor)	70	70
2008	(2r.80) *Colotis erone* (Coast Purple Tip)	70	70
2009	(2r.80) *Chrysoritis dicksoni* (Dickson's Copper or Dickson's Strandveld Copper)	70	70
2010	(2r.80) *Lepidochrysops lotana* (Lotana Blue)	70	70
2011	(2r.80) *Kedestes barberae bunta* (Barber's Cape Flats Ranger)	70	70
2012	(2r.80) *Erikssonia edgei* (Waterberg Copper)	70	70
2013	(2r.80) *Trimenia malagrida maryae* (Scarce Mountain Copper)	70	70
2014	(2r.80) *Aeropetes tulbaghia* (Table Mountain Beauty)	70	70

Nos. 2005/14 were all inscr 'Standard Postage' and were originally valid for 2r.80.

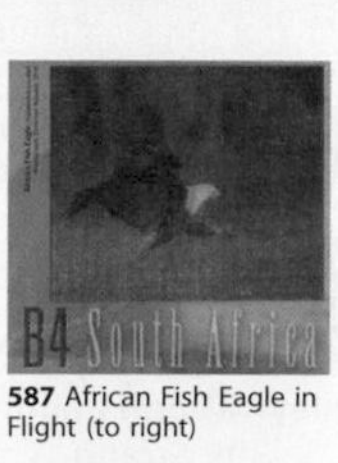

587 African Fish Eagle in Flight (to right)

2013. Flight of the African Fish Eagle (*Haliaeetus vocifer*). Multicoloured.

MS2015 (6r.90) Type **587**; (6r.90) African Fish Eagle in flight (to left) 3·50 3·50

The stamps within No. **MS**2015 were inscr 'B4' and were originally valid for 6r.90 each.

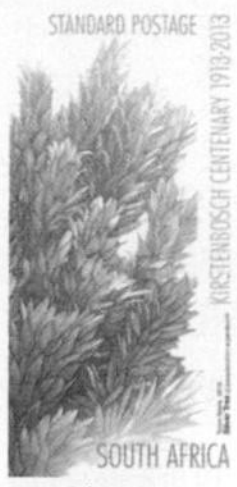

588 Silver Tree (*Leucadendron argenteum*)

2013. Centenary of Kirstenbosch National Botanical Garden. Sheet 233×172 mm containing T **588** and similar multicoloured designs

MS2016 (2r.80)×10 Type **588**; Natal Lily (*Crinum moorei*) (29×38 mm); Centenary Gold Strelitzia (*Strelitzia juncea* 'Centenary Gold') (triangle 40×40×56 mm); Krantz Aloe (*Aloe arborescens*); Ninepin Heath (*Erica mammosa*) (38×29 mm); Silver Restio (*Thamnochortus cinereus*) (triangle 40×40×56 mm); Albany Cycad (*Encephalartos latifrons*) (34×32 mm); Welwitschia (*Welwitschia mirabilis*) (Inverted triangle 56×40×40 mm); White Gardenia (*Gardenia thunbergia*) (horiz); King Protea (*Protea cynaroides*) (34×32 mm) 7·00 7·00

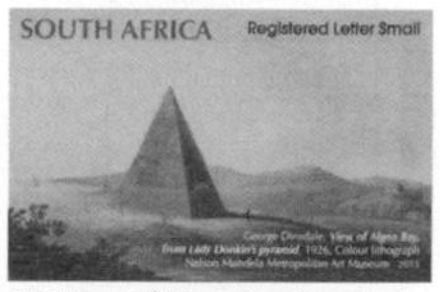

589 *View of Algoa Bay, from Lady Donkin's Pyramid* (colour lithograph, George Dinsdale), 1926

2013. Centenary of City of Port Elizabeth. Multicoloured.

2017	(19r.60) Type **589**	4·00	4·00
2018	(19r.60) The Donkin Reserve with sculpture of Nelson Mandela	4·00	4·00
2019	(19r.60) *Port Elizabeth* (oil on canvas, Ethel Sawyer), 1923	4·00	4·00
2020	(19r.60) Coega Harbour	4·00	4·00
2021	(19r.60) *Birth of Site and Service* (township) (watercolour, George Pemba), 1930	4·00	4·00
2022	(19r.60) Red Location Museum	4·00	4·00
2023	(19r.60) Old Doll House Railway Station, Uitenhage, 1910	4·00	4·00
2024	(19r.60) Old Court House, Uitenhage	4·00	4·00
2025	(19r.60) Queen Street and North End, 1880	4·00	4·00
2026	(19r.60) Nelson Mandela Bay Stadium	4·00	4·00

Nos. 2017/26 were all inscr 'Registered Letter Small' and were originally valid for 19r.60 each.

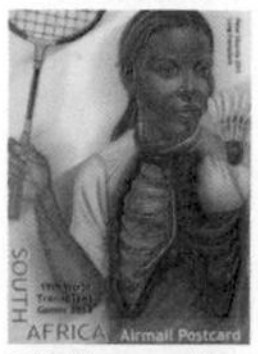

590 Woman with Lung Transplant playing Badminton

2013. 19th World Transplant Games, Durban. Multicoloured.

2027	(5r.70) Type **591**	1·40	1·40
2028	(5r.70) Man with heart transplant playing volleyball	1·40	1·40
2029	(5r.70) Cyclist with lung transplant	1·40	1·40
2030	(5r.70) Man with kidney transplant throwing javelin	1·40	1·40
2031	(5r.70) Girl with liver transplant running	1·40	1·40
2032	(5r.70) Man with heart transplant playing table tennis	1·40	1·40
2033	(5r.70) Woman with liver transplant in relay race	1·40	1·40
2034	(5r.70) Boy with kidney transplant playing tennis	1·40	1·40
2035	(5r.70) Man with lung transplant putting the shot	1·40	1·40
2036	(5r.70) Man with kidney and pancreas transplant hurdling	1·40	1·40

Nos. 2027/36 were all inscr 'Airmail Postcard' and originally sold for 5r.70 each.

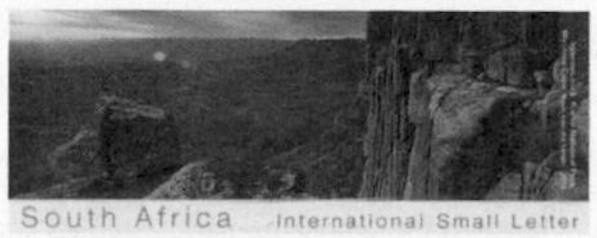

591 Igneous Dolerite, Karoo National Park, Western Cape

2013. Rock Formations and the Cederberg. Multicoloured.

2037	(6r.60) Type **591**	1·75	1·75
2038	(6r.60) Granite, Augrabies waterfalls, Northern Cape	1·75	1·75
2039	(6r.60) Basalt, Gray's Pass, Drakensberg, KwaZulu-Natal	1·75	1·75
2040	(6r.60) Metamorphic rock: Amphibolite in the Sand River Gneiss, Limpopo	1·75	1·75
2041	(6r.60) Metamorphic rock: Olifants River, Limpopo	1·75	1·75
2042	(6r.60) Metamorphic rock: \Ai-\Ais/Richtersveld National Park, Northern Cape	1·75	1·75
2043	(6r.60) Sedimentary rock: Golden Gate National Park, Free State	1·75	1·75
2044	(6r.60) Woody Cape Dunes (future sedimentary rocks), Addo Elephant National Park, Eastern Cape	1·75	1·75
2045	(6r.60) Sedimentary rock: Mapungubwe Hill, Greater Mapungubwe Transfrontier Conservation Area, Limpopo	1·75	1·75
2046	(6r.60) Table Mountain Sandstone: Cederberg Wilderness Area, Western Cape	1·75	1·75

Nos. 2037/46 were all inscr 'International Small Letter' and were originally valid for 6r.60 each.

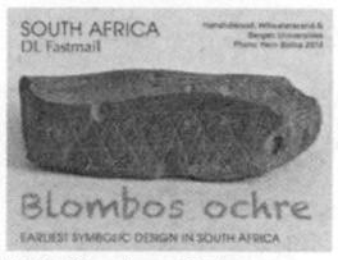

592 Blombos Ochre (engraving) (earliest symbolic design in South Africa)

2013. Symbols of South African Cultures. Multicoloured.

2047	(4r.50) Type **592**	1·10	1·10
2048	(4r.50) N'wana (child figure) (symbol of fertility)	1·10	1·10
2049	(4r.50) Zulu headrest with amasumpta patterns (symbol of wealth)	1·10	1·10
2050	(4r.50) Ukhamba (ceremonial beer container) (symbol of unity)	1·10	1·10
2051	(4r.50) Blombos shell beads (oldest symbolic ornaments in South Africa)	1·10	1·10
2052	(4r.50) Starburst rock engraving (symbol of womanhood)	1·10	1·10
2053	(4r.50) Rhino rock engraving (symbol of rain and abundance)	1·10	1·10
2054	(4r.50) Phalaphala (horn)	1·10	1·10
2055	(4r.50) Venda ndilo (divining bowl) with ngwenya (crocodile in his pool) design	1·10	1·10
2056	(4r.50) Litshoba mhlope (ritual whisk) (symbol of divine illumination)	1·10	1·10

Nos. 2047/56 were all inscr 'DL Fastmail' and were originally valid for 4r.50.

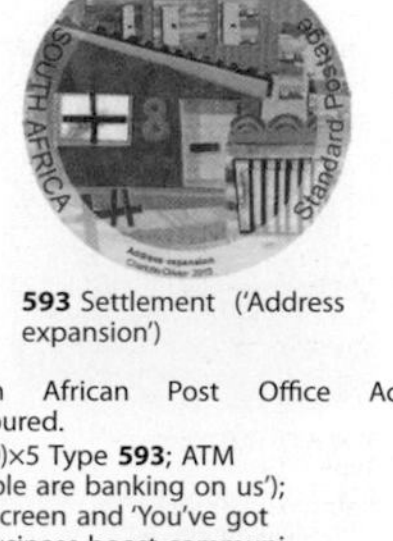

593 Settlement ('Address expansion')

2013. South African Post Office Achievements. Multicoloured.

MS2057 (2r.80)×5 Type **593**; ATM ('More people are banking on us'); Computer screen and 'You've got eMAIL!' (eBusiness boost communication'); Tree ('Steps to reduce our carbon footprint'); Smiling man ('Providing third-party services of other organisations to the people') 3·50 3·50

The stamps within **MS**2057 were all inscr 'Standard Postage' and were originally valid for 2r.80 each.

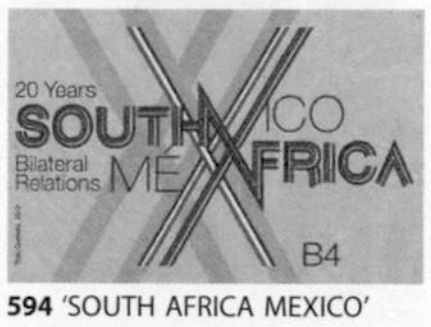

594 'SOUTH AFRICA MEXICO'

2013. 20th Anniv of Bilateral Relations between South Africa and Mexico. Sheet 115×85 mm

MS2058 **594** (6r.90) multicoloured 1·75 1·75

No. **MS**2058 is inscr 'B4' and was originally sold for 6r.90.

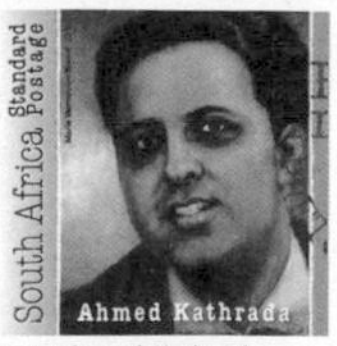

595 Ahmed Kathrada

2013. 50th Anniv of Rivonia Trial. Multicoloured.

2059	(2r.80) Type **595**	70	70
2060	(2r.80) Andrew Mlangeni	70	70
2061	(2r.80) Arthur Goldreich	70	70
2062	(2r.80) Denis Goldberg	70	70
2063	(2r.80) Elias Motsoaledi	70	70
2064	(2r.80) Govan Mbeki	70	70
2065	(2r.80) Harold Wolpe	70	70
2066	(2r.80) James Kantor	70	70
2067	(2r.80) Lionel Bernstein	70	70
2068	(2r.80) Nelson Mandela	70	70
2069	(2r.80) Raymond Mhlaba	70	70
2070	(2r.80) Walter Sisulu	70	70

Nos. 2059/70 were all inscr 'Standard Postage' and were originally valid for 2r.80 each.

OFFICIAL STAMPS

Prices for bilingual stamps are for mint pairs and used singles.

1926. Optd **OFFICIAL. OFFISIEEL.** (with full points). (a) On stamp of 1913.

O1	**3**	2d. purple	24·00	1·75

(b) On pictorial issues.

O2	**6**	½d. black and green	9·00	2·00
O3	**7**	1d. black and red	4·00	50
O4	**8**	6d. green and orange	£650	10·00

1928. Optd **OFFICIAL OFFISIEEL** (without full points).

O7	**6**	½d. black and green (No. 42)	2·75	35
O39	**6**	½d. black and green (No. 114)	70	15
O8	**7**	1d. black and red (No. 31)	3·00	45
O21b	**7**	1d. grey and red (No. 56)	4·00	30
O22aw	**22**	1½d. green and gold	32·00	1·00
O44	**34a**	1½d. green and buff	4·00	30
O5	**11**	2d. grey and purple (No. 34)	6·00	2·00
O14	**11**	2d. grey and lilac (No. 44)	6·50	1·50
O15	**11**	2d. blue and violet (No. 44d)	£160	9·00
O30	**11**	2d. grey and purple (No. 58a)	11·00	2·25
O36	**54**	2d. slate and violet	5·50	1·90
O45	**68**	2d. blue and violet	1·00	20
O16	**8**	6d. green and orange (No. 47)	6·50	85
O46	**8**	6d. green and red (No. 119a)	2·25	35
O10	-	1s. brown and blue (No. 36)	45·00	9·50
O47	-	1s. brown and blue (No. 120)	5·50	2·00
O18a	-	2s.6d. green and brown (No. 49)	60·00	8·50
O19	-	2s.6d. blue and brown (No. 49a)	55·00	6·50
O48	-	2s.6d. green and brown (No. 121)	8·50	3·50
O50	-	5s. black and green (No. 64a)	70·00	6·50
O51	-	10s. blue and brown (No. 39)	80·00	22·00

POSTAGE DUE STAMPS

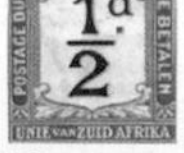

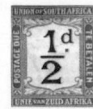

D1

1914. Perf or roul.

D11	**D1**	½d. black and green	80	1·75
D12	**D1**	1d. black and red	90	15
D13	**D1**	1½d. black and brown	1·00	1·25
D14	**D1**	2d. black and violet	1·00	70
D4	**D1**	3d. black and blue	2·25	60
D5	**D1**	5d. black and brown	4·00	35·00
D16	**D1**	6d. black and grey	12·00	2·00
D7	**D1**	1s. red and black	60·00	£170

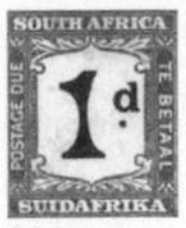

D2

1927

D17	D2	½d. black and green	1·00	3·25
D18	D2	1d. black and red	1·25	30
D19	D2	2d. black and mauve	1·25	30
D23	D2	2d. black and purple	21·00	2·50
D20	D2	3d. black and blue	8·50	24·00
D28	D2	3d. indigo and blue	7·00	30
D21	D2	6d. black and grey	21·00	3·50
D29	D2	6d. green and brown	25·00	3·50

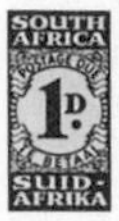
D3

1943

D30	D3	½d. green	19·00	40
D31	D3	1d. red	10·00	10
D32	D3	2d. violet	6·50	15
D33	D3	3d. blue	55·00	1·25

The above mint prices are for horiz units of three.

1948. Frame as Type **D2**, but with bolder figures of value and capital "D".

D34	½d. black and green	6·00	16·00
D39	1d. black and red	1·00	30
D40	2d. black and violet	50	20
D41	3d. indigo and blue	4·50	2·50
D42	4d. turquoise and green	12·00	15·00
D43	6d. green and orange	7·00	9·00
D44	1s. brown and purple	12·00	15·00

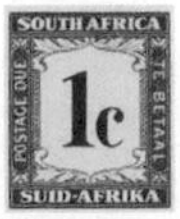

D5

1961

D45	D5	1c. black and red	20	3·75
D46	D5	2c. black and violet	35	3·75
D47	D5	4c. turquoise and green	80	8·50
D48	D5	5c. indigo and blue	1·75	8·50
D49	D5	6c. green and orange	5·00	8·50
D50	D5	10c. sepia and brown	6·00	10·00

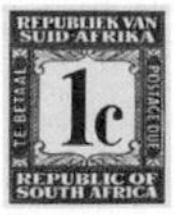

D6

1961. (A) Inscr as in Type **D6**; (B) English at top and left, Afrikans at bottom and right.

D59	D6	1c. black and red (A)	20	55
D60	D6	1c. black and red (B)	20	30
D53	D6	2c. black and violet (B)	40	55
D61	D6	2c. black and violet (A)	30	2·00
D54	D6	4c. myrtle and green (A)	2·25	2·25
D54a	D6	4c. myrtle and green (B)	12·00	26·00
D63	D6	4c. black and green (A)	32·00	42·00
D64	D6	4c. black and green (B)	32·00	42·00
D55	D6	5c. indigo and blue (B)	2·00	4·25
D65	D6	5c. black and blue (A)	50	1·50
D66	D6	5c. black and blue (B)	50	50
D57	D6	6c. green & salmon (A)	8·00	4·75
D68	D6	6c. green and salmon (B)	3·50	11·00
D58	D6	10c. sepia & brown (B)	2·25	1·40
D69a	D6	10c. black and brown (A)	1·00	3·00
D70a	D6	10c. black and brown (B)	1·00	3·00

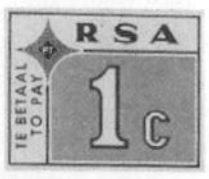

D8

1972

D75	D8	1c. green	50	2·25
D76	D8	2c. orange	70	3·00
D77	D8	4c. plum	1·75	3·50
D78	D8	6c. yellow	1·75	4·75
D79	D8	8c. blue	2·00	5·00
D80	D8	10c. red	6·00	7·50

Pt. 1

SOUTHERN ARABIAN FEDERATION

Comprising Aden and most of the territories of the former Western Aden Protectorate plus one from the Eastern Aden Protectorate. The South Arabian Federation became fully independent on 30 November 1967.

1963. 100 cents = 1 shilling.
1965. 1000 fils = 1 dinar.

1963. Cent of Red Cross. As T **63b** of St. Helena, but without portrait. Value in English and Arabic.

1	15c. red and black	30	30
2	1s.25 red and blue	70	95

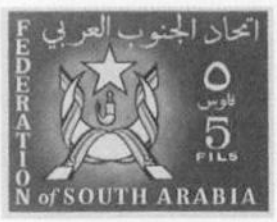

2 Federal Crest

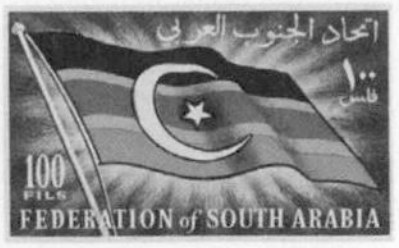

3 Federal Flag

1965

3	2	5f. blue	20	10
4	2	10f. lavender	20	10
5	2	15f. green	20	10
6	2	20f. green	20	10
7	2	25f. brown	20	10
8	2	30f. bistre	20	10
9	2	35f. brown	20	10
10	2	50f. red	20	10
11	2	65f. green	30	30
12	2	75f. red	30	10
13	3	100f. multicoloured	50	10
14	3	250f. multicoloured	5·00	1·50
15	3	500f. multicoloured	9·00	1·50
16	3	1d. multicoloured	16·00	19·00

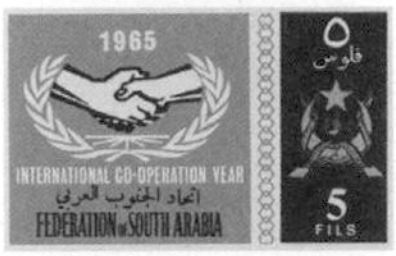

4 I.C.Y. Emblem

1965. International Co-operation Year.

17	4	5f. purple and turquoise	25	10
18	4	65f. green and lavender	1·00	30

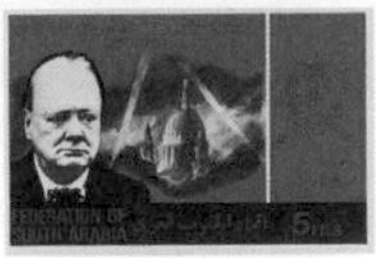
5 Sir Winston Churchill and St. Paul's Cathedral in Wartime

1966. Churchill Commem. Designs in black, cerise and gold with background in colours given.

19	5	5f. blue	15	10
20	5	10f. green	55	10
21	5	65f. brown	1·25	20
22	5	125f. violet	1·75	1·75

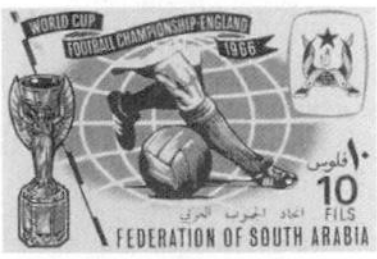

6 Footballer's Legs, Ball and Jules Rimet Cup

1966. World Cup Football Championship, England.

23	6	10f. multicoloured	50	10
24	6	50f. multicoloured	1·50	30

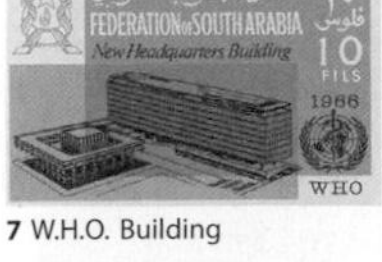

7 W.H.O. Building

1966. Inaug of W.H.O. Headquarters, Geneva.

25	7	10f. black, green and blue	50	10
26	7	75f. black, purple and brown	1·25	55

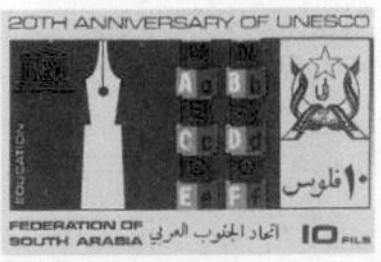

8 "Education"

1966. 20th Anniv of U.N.E.S.C.O.

27	8	10f. multicoloured	30	20
28	-	65f. yellow, violet and olive	1·25	1·40
29	-	125f. black, purple and orange	3·25	4·75

DESIGNS: 65f. "Science"; 125f. "Culture".

For later issues see **SOUTHERN YEMEN** and **YEMEN PEOPLE'S DEMOCRATIC REPUBLIC**.

Pt. 1

SOUTH AUSTRALIA

A state of the Australian Commonwealth whose stamps it now uses.

12 pence = 1 shilling; 20 shillings = 1 pound.

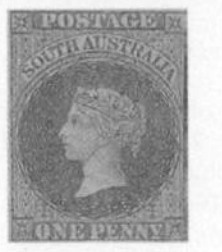

1

1855. Imperf.

1	1	1d. green	£8500	£475
2	1	2d. red	£750	80·00
3	1	6d. blue	£3750	£160
12	1	1s. orange	£10000	£450

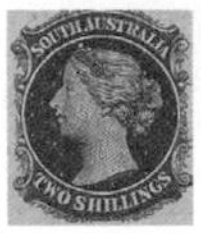

3

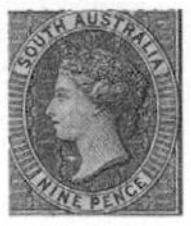

4

20		1d. green	£130	50·00
26		2d. red	£130	3·75
68	3	3d. on 4d. blue	£130	9·00
138	3	4d. purple	60·00	2·75
141	1	6d. blue	90·00	2·75
121	4	8d. on 9d. brown	£150	7·00
124	4	9d. purple	14·00	4·50
107	4	10d. on 9d. yellow	£250	55·00
38	1	1s. yellow	£1200	32·00
130	1	1s. brown	26·00	3·50
151	3	2s. red	26·00	11·00

The 3d., 8d. and 10d. are formed by surcharges: **3-PENCE**, **8 PENCE** and **TEN PENCE** (curved).

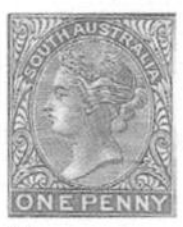

11

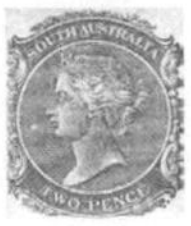

12

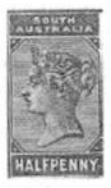

15

1868. Various frames.

191	15	½d. brown	4·75	30
175a	11	1d. green	10·00	20
176a	11	1d. red	7·50	1·25
177	12	2d. orange	14·00	10
178	12	2d. violet	5·50	10
229b	17	2½d. on 4d. green	8·00	1·75
192a	16	3d. green	5·50	3·00
193	17	4d. violet	6·00	1·00
230a	18	5d. on 6d. brown	19·00	6·00
194a	18	6d. blue	10·00	1·50

Nos. 230 and 231 are surch in figures over straight or curved line.

1882. No. 167 surch with T **14**

181	11	½d. on 1d. green	14·00	11·00

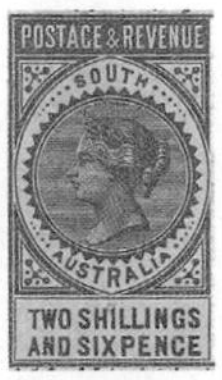

19

1886

195a	19	2s.6d. mauve	75·00	9·00
196a	19	5s. pink	90·00	18·00
197a	19	10s. green	£225	60.00
198a	19	15s. brown	£750	£200
199a	19	£1 blue	£450	£140

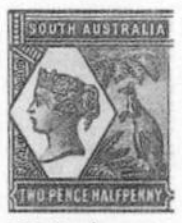

22 Red Kangaroo

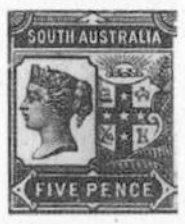

23

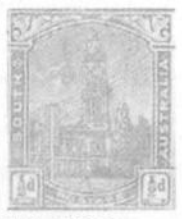
24 G.P.O., Adelaide

1894

241	24	½d. green	7·00	1·50
236	22	2½d. violet	27·00	1·25
237	22	2½d. blue	8·50	2·00
238a	23	5d. purple	9·50	1·50

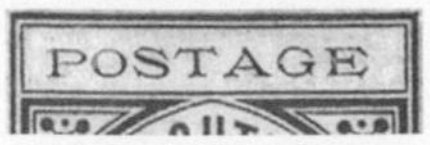

1902. As T **19**, but top tablet as T **25** (thin "POSTAGE").

268	19	3d. green	15·00	2·50
299	19	4d. orange	12·00	3·00
270	19	6d. green	10·00	2·50
271	19	8d. blue	8·50	15·00
273	19	9d. red	13·00	9·50
274	19	10d. orange	16·00	16·00
303	19	1s. brown	12·00	5·00
276a	19	2s.6d. violet	35·00	13·00
290	19	5s. red	70·00	45·00
278	19	10s. green	£180	85·00
292a	19	£1 blue	£200	£140

OFFICIAL STAMPS

1874. Various postage issues optd **O.S.** A. Issues of 1858.

O6	1	1d. green	£3000	£350
O7	3	3d. on 4d. blue	£7500	£2500
O17	3	4d. mauve	65·00	2·50
O19	1	6d. blue	£130	5·00
O26	4	8d. on 9d. brown	£5000	£2000
O11	4	9d. purple	£3750	£1500
O27	1	1s. brown	45·00	8·50
O35	3	2s. red	£120	10·00

B. General

1874. B. Issues of 1868- 82

O63	15	½d. brown	40·00	8·00
O48	11	½d. on 1d. green	£110	22·00
O56	11	1d. green	28·00	1·25
O81	11	1d. red	26·00	1·60
O44	12	2d. orange	12·00	1·00
O82	12	2d. violet	30·00	80
O71	-	2½d. on 4d. green	48·00	24·00
O61	-	4d. violet	65·00	4·75
O72	-	5d. on 6d. brown	48·00	18·00
O50	-	6d. blue	45·00	1·25

1874. C. Issues of 1886

O86	19	2s.6d. violet	£6500	£5000
O87	19	5s. pink	£7000	£5500

1874. D. Issues of 1894

O80	24	½d. green	20·00	7·00
O75	22	2½d. blue	80·00	7·50
O74	23	5d. purple	£100	18·00

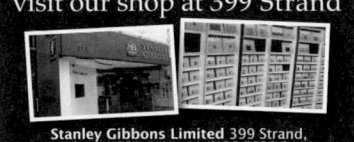

visit our shop at 399 Strand
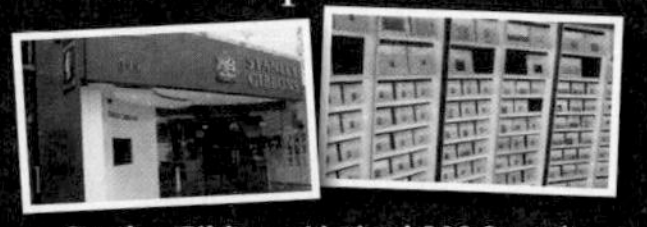
Stanley Gibbons Limited 399 Strand, London, WC2R 0LX +44 (0)20 7836 8444
www.stanleygibbons.com

Gibbons Stamp Monthly
Scan the QR code to get your FREE APP from Stanley Gibbons or visit stanley-gibbons.com/app
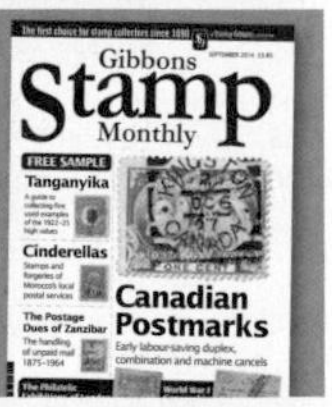

LOOKING FOR THAT ELUSIVE STAMP?
?
Send a copy of your wants list or call:
Andrew Mansi on 020 7557 4455
email amansi@stanleygibbons.com

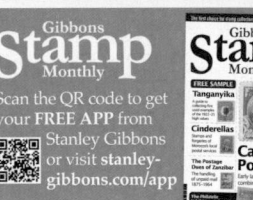

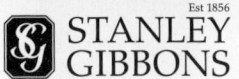

Est 1856
STANLEY GIBBONS
Stanley Gibbons Limited
399 Strand
London, WC2R 0LX
+44 (0)20 7836 8444
www.stanleygibbons.com

Pt. 1

SOUTH GEORGIA

An island in the Antarctic. From May 1980 to 1985 used stamps inscribed FALKLAND ISLANDS DEPENDENCIES and thereafter those of South Georgia and the South Sandwich Islands (q.v.).

1963. 12 pence = 1 shilling; 20 shillings = 1 pound.
1971. 100 pence = 1 pound.

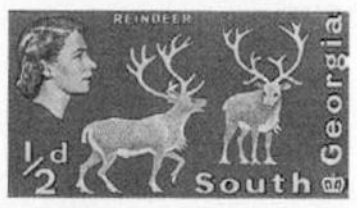

1 Reindeer

1963

1	1	½d. red	50	1·25
2	-	1d. blue	2·75	1·25
3	-	2d. blue	1·25	1·25
4	-	2½d. black	6·00	2·50
5	-	3d. bistre	2·75	30
6	-	4d. green	5·50	1·50
7	-	5½d. violet	2·50	30
8	-	6d. orange	75	50
9	-	9d. blue	7·50	2·00
10	-	1s. purple	75	30
11	-	2s. olive and blue	27·00	7·00
12	-	2s.6d. blue	25·00	4·00
13	-	5s. brown	22·00	4·00
14	-	10s. pink	48·00	13·00
15	-	£1 blue	90·00	48·00
16	-	£1 black	10·00	16·00

DESIGNS—HORIZ: 2½d. King penguins and Bearded penguin ("Chinstrap Penguin"); 4d. Fin whale; 5½d. Southern elephant-seal; 9d. Whale-catcher; 1s. Leopard seal; 2s. Shackleton's Cross; 2s.6d. Wandering albatross; 5s. Southern elephant seal and South American fur seal; £1 (No. 15) Blue whale. VERT: 1d. South Sandwich Islands map; 2d. Sperm whale; 3d. South American fur seal; 6d. Light-mantled sooty albatross ("Sooty Albatross"); 10s. Plankton and krill; £1 (No. 16) King penguins.

1971. Decimal Currency. Nos. 1/14 surch.

18a	½p. on 1/2d. red	1·00	1·00
19	1p. on 1d. blue	1·50	55
55	1½p. on 5½d. violet	1·00	1·75
21	2p. on 2d. blue	70	50
22	2½p. on 2½d. black	2·25	40
23	3p. on 3d. bistre	1·00	50
24	4p. on 4d. green	1·00	[illegible]
25	5p. on 6d. orange	2·00	30
26	6p. on 9d. blue	1·50	70
27	7½p. on 1s. purple	1·50	70
63w	10p. olive and blue	1·00	5·00
64w	15p. blue	1·50	5·50
65w	25p. brown	1·00	5·50
66	50p. on 10s. pink	1·00	3·00

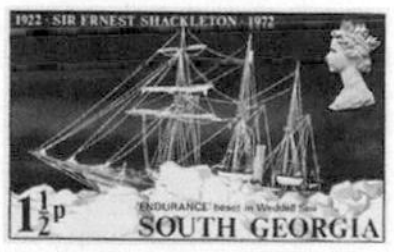

20 "Endurance" beset in Weddell Sea

1972. 50th Death Anniv of Sir Ernest Shackleton. Multicoloured.

32	1½p. Type **20**	1·00	1·50
33	5p. Launching of the longboat "James Caird"	1·00	1·75
34	10p. Route of the "James Caird"	1·25	2·00
35	20p. Sir Ernest Shackleton and the "Quest"	1·50	2·25

1972. Royal Silver Wedding. As T **103** of St. Helena, but with Elephant Seal and King Penguins in background.

36	5p. green	75	35
37	10p. violet	75	35

1973. Royal Wedding. As T **103a** of St. Helena. Background colours given. Multicoloured.

38	5p. brown	30	10
39	15p. lilac	40	20

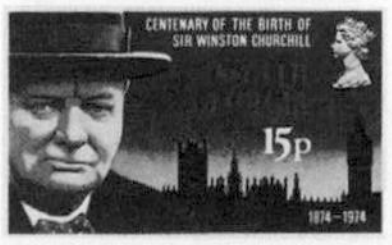

22 Churchill and Westminster Skyline

1974. Birth Cent of Sir Winston Churchill. Multicoloured.

40	15p. Type **22**	1·00	1·25
41	25p. Churchill and warship	1·25	1·25
MS42	122×98 mm. Nos. 40/1	6·00	6·00

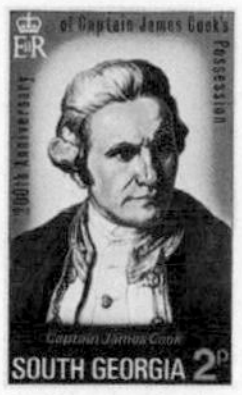

23 Captain Cook

1975. Bicentenary of Possession by Captain Cook.

43	2p. Type **23**	2·25	1·00
44	8p. H.M.S. "Resolution" (horiz)	3·50	1·50
45	16p. Possession Bay (horiz)	3·75	1·75

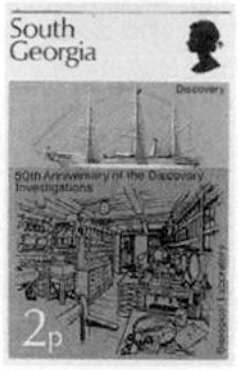

24 "Discovery" and Biological Laboratory

1976. 50th Anniv of "Discovery" Investigations. Multicoloured.

46	2p. Type **24**	1·50	1·00
47	8p. "William Scoresby" and water-sampling bottles	1·75	1·25
48	11p. "Discovery II" and plankton net	2·50	1·25
49	25p. Biological station and krill	2·50	1·50

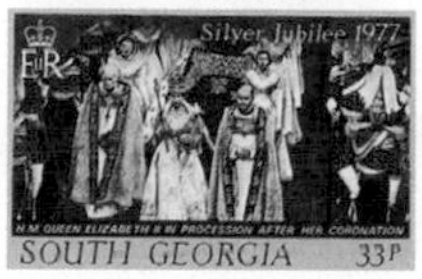

25 The Queen and Retinue after Coronation

1977. Silver Jubilee. Multicoloured.

50	6p. Visit by Prince Philip, 1957	50	30
51	11p. Queen Elizabeth and Westminster Abbey	70	35
52	33p. Type **25**	80	50

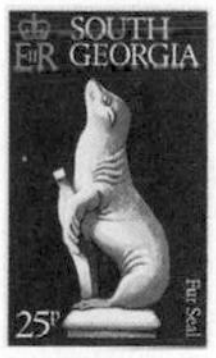

26 Fur Seal

1978. 25th Anniv of Coronation.

67	-	25p. deep blue, blue and silver	40	1·10
68	-	25p. multicoloured	40	1·10
69	26	25p. deep blue, blue and silver	40	1·10

DESIGNS: No. 67, Panther of Henry VI; No. 68, Queen Elizabeth II.

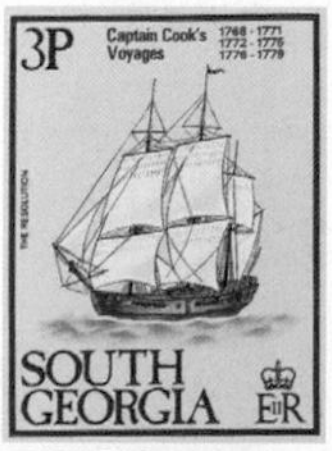

27 H.M.S. "Resolution"

1979. Bicentenary of Captain Cook's Voyages, 1768–79. Multicoloured.

70	3p. Type **27**	1·50	80
71	6p. "Resolution" and Map of South Georgia and S. Sandwich Isles showing route	1·50	70
72	11p. King penguin (from drawing by George Forster)	1·75	1·40
73	25p. Flaxman/Wedgwood medallion of Capt. Cook	2·00	1·75

Pt. 1

SOUTH GEORGIA AND THE SOUTH SANDWICH ISLANDS

Under the new constitution, effective 3 October 1985, South Georgia and the South Sandwich Islands ceased to be dependencies of the Falkland Islands.

100 pence = 1 pound.

1986. 60th Birthday of Queen Elizabeth II. As T **145a** of St. Helena. Multicoloured.

153	23	10p. Four generations of Royal Family at Prince Charles's christening, 1948	30	50
154	23	24p. With Prince Charles and Lady Diana Spencer, Buckingham Palace, 1981	40	75
155	23	29p. In robes of Order of the British Empire, St. Paul's Cathedral, London	40	80
156	23	45p. At banquet, Canada, 1976	60	1·00
157	23	58p. At Crown Agents Head Office London, 1983	65	1·25

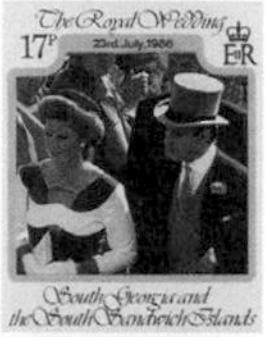

25a Prince Andrew and Miss Sarah Ferguson at Ascot

1986. Royal Wedding. Multicoloured.

158	17p. Type **25a**	75	1·25
159	22p. Wedding photograph	85	1·25
160	29p. Prince Andrew with Westland Lynx helicopter on board H.M.S. "Brazen"	1·75	1·75

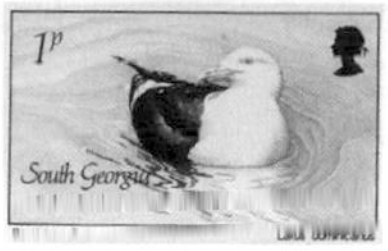

26 Southern Black-backed Gull ("Dominican Gull")

1987. Birds. Multicoloured.

161	1p. Type **26**	1·25	2·50
162	2p. South georgia cormorant ("Blue-eyed cormorant")	1·50	2·50
163	3p. Snowy sheathbill ("Wattled Sheatbill") (vert)	1·75	2·75
164	4p. Skua antarctic ("Brown Skua") (vert)	1·50	2·75
165	5p. Pintado petrel ("Coupe Pigeon")	1·50	2·75
166	6p. Georgian diving petrel ("South Georgia Diving Petrel")	1·50	2·75
167	7p. South Georgia pipit (vert)	1·75	2·75
168	8p. Georgian teal ("South Georgian Pintail") (vert)	1·75	2·75
169	9p. Fairy prion	1·75	2·75
170	10p. bearded penguin ("Chinstrap Penguin")	1·75	2·75
171	20p. Macaroni penguin (vert)	2·00	3·00
172	25p. Light-mantled sooty albatross (vert)	2·00	2·75
173	50p. Giant petrel ("Southern Giant Petrel") (vert)	2·25	3·00
174	£1 Wandering albatross	2·50	4·25
175	£3 King penguin (vert)	6·00	9·00

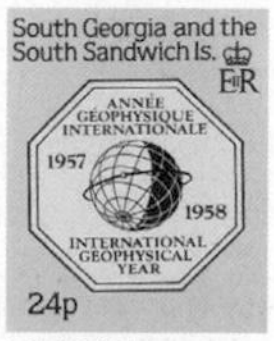

26a I.G.Y. Logo

1987. 30th Anniv of International Geophysical Year.

176	26a	24p. black and blue	70	55
177	-	29p. multicoloured	75	60
178	-	58p. multicoloured	1·40	1·25

DESIGNS: 29p. Grytviken; 58p. Glaciologist using hand-drill to take core sample.

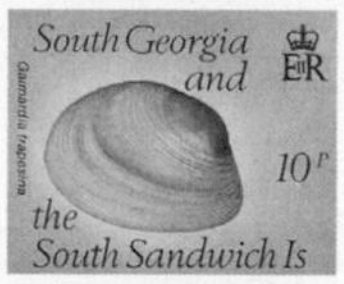

27 "Gaimardia trapesina"

1988. Sea Shells. Multicoloured.

179	10p. Type **27**	65	30
180	24p. "Margarella tropidophoroides"	1·00	60
181	29p. "Trophon geversianus"	1·10	65
182	58p. "Chlanidota densesculpta"	1·60	1·25

1988. 300th Anniv of Lloyd's of London. As T **192** of Samoa.

183	10p. black and brown	1·00	40
184	24p. multicoloured	1·50	75
185	29p. black and green	2·00	80
186	58p. black and red	2·25	1·60

DESIGNS—VERT: 10p. Queen Mother at opening of new Lloyd's building, 1957; 58p. "Horatio" (tanker) on fire, 1916. HORIZ: 24p. "Lindblad Explorer" (cruise liner); 29p. Whaling station, Leith Harbour.

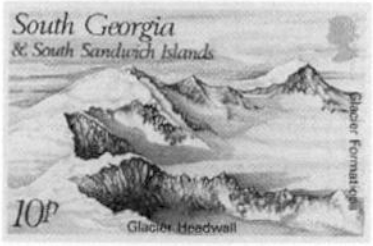

28 Glacier Headwall

1989. Glacier Formations. Multicoloured.

187	10p. Type **28**	50	35
188	24p. Accumulation area	90	70
189	29p. Ablation area	1·00	80
190	58p. Calving front	1·75	1·40

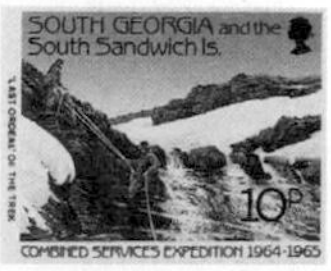

29 Retracing Shackleton's Trek

1989. 25th Anniv of Combined Services Expedition to South Georgia. Multicoloured.

191	10p. Type **29**	40	35
192	24p. Surveying at Royal Bay	90	70
193	29p. H.M.S. "Protector" (ice patrol ship)	1·00	80
194	58p. Raising Union Jack on Mount Paget	1·60	1·40

1990. 90th Birthday of Queen Elizabeth the Queen Mother. As T **161a** of St. Helena.

195	26p. multicoloured	1·00	1·75
196	£1 black and blue	2·75	3·75

DESIGNS—(21×36 mm): 26p. Queen Mother. (29×37 mm): King George VI and Queen Elizabeth with A.R.P. wardens, 1940.

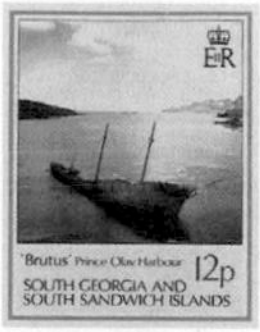

30 "Brutus", Prince Olav Harbour

1990. Wrecks and Hulks. Multicoloured.

197	12p. Type **30**	55	40
198	26p. "Bayard", Ocean Harbour	1·00	80
199	31p. "Karrakatta", Husvik	1·10	95
200	62p. "Louise", Grytviken	1·90	1·75

1991. 65th Birthday of Queen Elizabeth II and 70th Birthday of Prince Philip. As T **165a** of St. Helena. Multicoloured.

201	31p. Queen Elizabeth II	1·40	2·00
202	31p. Prince Philip in Grenadier Guards uniform	1·40	2·00

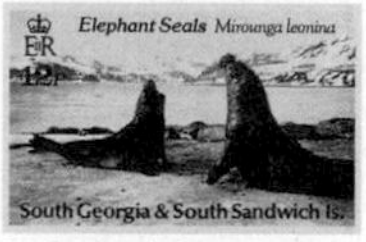

31 Contest between two Bull Elephant Seals

1991. Elephant Seals. Multicoloured.

203	12p. Type **31**	50	75
204	26p. Adult elephant seal	1·00	1·25
205	29p. Seal throwing sand	1·10	1·40
206	31p. Head of elephant seal	1·10	1·40
207	34p. Seals on beach	1·25	1·50
208	62p. Cow seal with pup	2·00	2·50

1992. 40th Anniv of Queen Elizabeth II's Accession. As T **168a** of St. Helena. Multicoloured.

209	7p. Ice-covered mountains	40	50
210	14p. Zavodovski Island	65	75
211	29p. Gulbrandsen Lake	1·00	1·00
212	34p. Three portraits of Queen Elizabeth	1·10	1·25
213	68p. Queen Elizabeth II	1·60	2·00

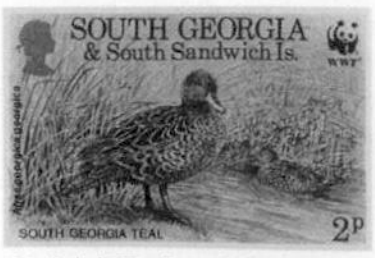

32 Adult Teal and Young Bird

1992. Endangered Species. Georgian Teal ("South Georgia Teal"). Multicoloured.

214	2p. Type **32**	50	50
215	6p. Adult with eggs	60	60
216	12p. Teals swimming	80	80
217	20p. Adult and two chicks	1·00	1·00

1992. Tenth Anniv of Liberation. As T **169** of St. Helena. Multicoloured.

218	14p.+6p. +6p. King Edward Point	70	70
219	29p.+11p. +11p. "Queen Elizabeth 2" (liner) in Cumberland Bay	1·50	1·25
220	34p.+16p. +16p. Royal Marines hoisting Union Jack on South Sandwich Islands	1·90	1·60
221	68p.+32p. +32p. H.M.S. "Endurance" (ice patrol ship) and Westland Wasp helicopter	3·50	3·00
MS222	116×116 mm. Nos. 218/21	9·00	7·50

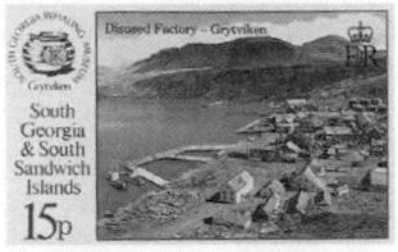

33 Disused Whale Factory, Grytviken

1993. Opening of South Georgia Whaling Museum. Multicoloured.

223	15p. Type **33**	75	60
224	31p. Whaler's lighter and whale bones	1·25	1·10
225	36p. Aerial view of King Edward Cove	1·60	1·40
226	72p. Museum building	2·75	2·75

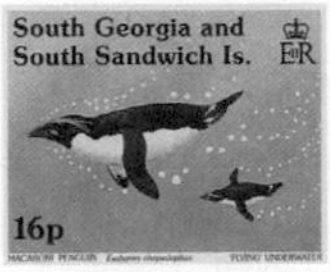

34 Pair of Swimming Penguins

1993. Macaroni Penguin. Multicoloured.

227	16p. Type **34**	70	45
228	34p. Group of penguins	1·40	1·00
229	39p. Two juvenile penguins	1·60	1·25
230	78p. Two adult penguins	2·50	2·25

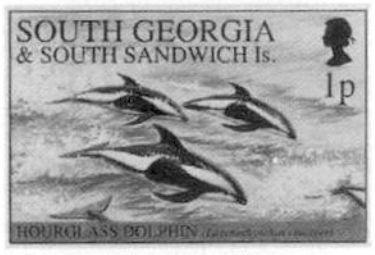

35 Hourglass Dolphin

1994. Whales and Dolphins. Multicoloured.

231	1p. Type **35**	1·10	1·00
232	2p. Southern right whale dolphin	1·50	1·25
233	5p. Long-finned pilot whale	2·25	1·40
234	8p. Southern bottlenose whale	2·50	1·40
235	9p. Killer whale	2·50	1·40
236	10p. Minke whale	2·50	1·40
237	20p. Sei whale	4·00	1·75
238	25p. Humpback whale	4·00	1·75
239	50p. Southern right whale	5·00	2·25
240	£1 Sperm whale	6·50	4·00
241	£3 Fin whale	10·00	8·00
242	£5 Blue whale	16·00	12·00

1994. "Hong Kong '94" International Stamp Exhibition. Nos. 227/30 optd **HONG KONG '94** and emblem.

243	16p. Type **34**	80	1·25
244	34p. Group of penguins	1·25	2·25
245	39p. Two juvenile penguins	1·40	2·50
246	78p. Two adult penguins	2·00	3·25

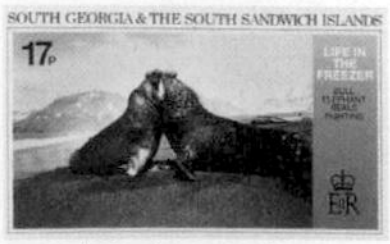

36 Bull Elephant Seals

1994. "Life in the Freezer". Scenes from the B.B.C. Natural History Unit series. Multicoloured.

247	17p. Type **36**	50	75
248	35p. Young fur seal (vert)	90	1·50
249	40p. Pair of grey-headed albatrosses	1·60	1·75
250	65p. King penguins in courtship display (vert)	2·50	2·75

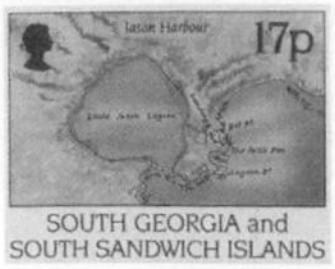

37 Map of Jason Harbour

1994. Centenary of C. A. Larsen's First Voyage to South Georgia. Multicoloured.

251	17p. Type **37**	60	75
252	35p. "Castor" (whaling ship), 1886	1·10	1·50
253	40p. "Hertha" (whaling ship), 1886	1·25	1·60
254	65p. "Jason" (whaling ship), 1881	2·25	2·75

1995. 50th Anniv of Second World War. As T **182a** of St. Helena. Multicoloured.

255	50p. H.M.S. "Queen of Bermuda" (armed merchant cruiser), Leith Harbour	3·50	4·00
256	50p. 4-inch coastal gun, Hansen Point	3·50	4·00
MS257	75×85 mm. £1 Reverse of 1939–45 war medal (vert)	3·00	3·25

Nos. 255/6 were printed together, *se-tenant*, forming a composite design.

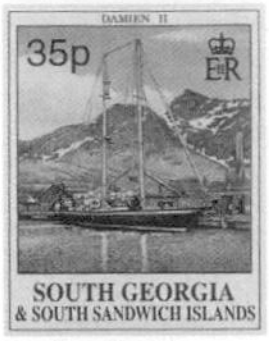

38 "Damien II" (research schooner)

1995. Sailing Ships. Multicoloured.

258	35p. Type **38**	1·25	1·75
259	40p. "Curlew" (cutter)	1·40	1·75
260	76p. "Mischief" (yacht)	2·25	2·75

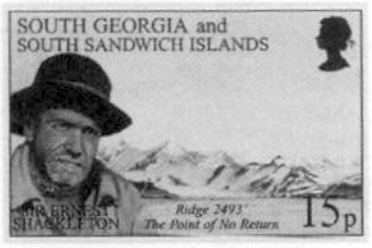

39 Sir Ernest Shackleton and Ridge 2493

1996. 80th Anniv of Sir Ernest Shackleton's Trek across South Georgia. Multicoloured.

261	15p. Type **39**	2·00	2·00
262	20p. Frank Worsley and King Haakon Bay	2·00	2·00
263	30p. Map of route	3·00	3·00
264	65p. Tom Crean and Manager's villa, Stromness whaling station	4·50	4·50

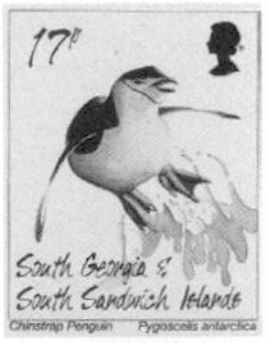

40 Bearded Penguin swimming

1996. Bearded Penguins ("Chinstrap Penguins"). Multicoloured.

265	17p. Type **40**	55	55
266	35p. Mutual display	90	90
267	40p. Adult feeding chicks	1·10	1·10
268	76p. Feeding on krill	1·90	1·90

1997. Return of Hong Kong to China Sheet 130×90 mm, containing No. 268.

MS269	76p. Feeding on krill	2·00	2·25

1997. Golden Wedding of Queen Elizabeth and Prince Philip. As T **192a** of St. Helena. Multicoloured.

270	15p. Queen Elizabeth wearing red hat, 1996	75	50
271	15p. Prince Philip in carriage-driving at Royal Windsor Horse Show	75	50
272	17p. Queen Elizabeth with show jumping team, 1993	80	55
273	17p. Prince Philip smiling	80	55
274	40p. Princess Anne on horse-back and Queen Elizabeth	1·75	1·40
275	40p. Zara Phillips horse riding and Prince Philip	1·75	1·40
MS276	110×70 mm. £1.50 Queen Elizabeth and Prince Philip in landau (horiz)	3·50	3·75

Nos. 270/1, 272/3 and 274/5 respectively were printed together, *se-tenant*, with the backgrounds forming composite designs.

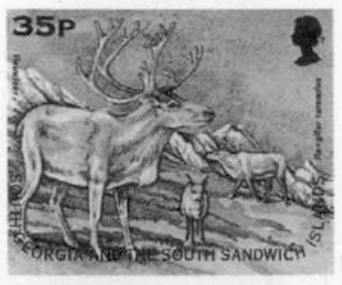

41 Reindeer

1998. Wildlife. Sheet, 138×84 mm, containing T **41** and similar horiz designs. Multicoloured.

MS277	35p. Type **41**; 35p. Antartic tern; 35p. Grey-headed albatross; 35p. King penguin; 35p. Prickly burr; 35p. Fur seal	6·50	5·00

1998. Diana, Princess of Wales Commemoration. Sheet, 145×70 mm, containing vert designs as T **194** of St. Helena. Multicoloured.

MS278	35p. Laughing, 1983; 35p. In evening dress, 1996; 35p. Wearing red jacket, 1991; 35p. Wearing white jacket, 1996 (sold at £1.40 + 20p. charity premium)	2·25	2·50

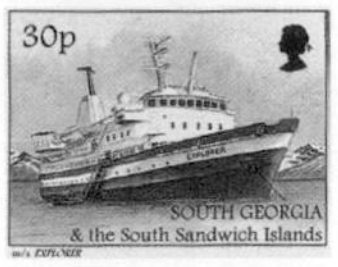

42 "Explorer" (cruise ship)

1998. Tourism. Multicoloured.

279	30p. Type **42**	1·50	1·10
280	35p. Wandering albatross	1·75	1·25
281	40p. Elephant seal	1·75	1·25
282	65p. Post Office at King Edward Point	2·00	1·75

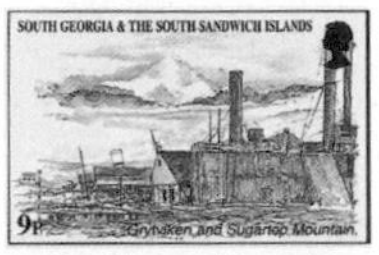

43 Grytviken and Sugartop Mountain

1999. Island Views. Multicoloured.

283	9p. Type **43**	1·60	65
284	17p. "Dias" and "Albatros" (abandoned sealing ships), Grytviken	2·25	95
285	35p. King Edward Point	2·75	1·40
286	40p. South Georgia from the sea	2·75	1·40
287	65p. Grytviken Church	3·75	1·75

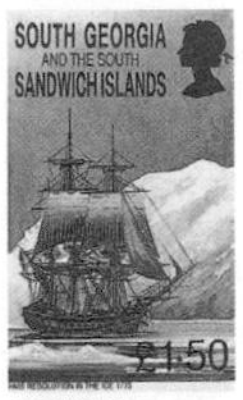

44 H.M.S. "Resolution" in Antarctic, 1773

1999. "Australia '99" World Stamp Exhibition, Melbourne. Sheet 120×83 mm.

MS288	**44** £1.50 multicoloured	18·00	13·00

1999. "Queen Elizabeth the Queen Mother's Century". As T **199** of St. Helena. Multicoloured. (except 30p., £1).

289	25p. Visiting air-raid shelter, 1940	2·25	2·50
290	30p. With grandchildren, 1970 (black)	2·50	2·75
291	35p. With Prince William, 1994	2·75	3·00
292	40p. Presenting colour to Royal Anglian Regt	3·00	3·25
MS293	145×70 mm. £1 Lady Elizabeth Boewes-Lyon, 1914, and funeral of Queen Victoria, 1901 (black)	13·00	13·00

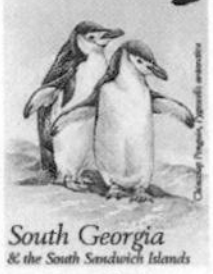

45 Bearded Penguins ("Chinstrap Penguins")

1999. Birds. Multicoloured.

294	1p. Type **45**	1·75	2·00
295	2p. White-chinned petrel (horiz)	2·00	2·25
296	5p. Grey-backed storm petrel	2·00	2·25
297	10p. South Georgia pipit	2·25	2·25
298	11p. Grey-headed albatross (horiz)	2·25	2·25
299	30p. Blue petrel	3·25	2·75
300	35p. Black-browed albatross (horiz)	3·25	2·75
301	40p. Georgian diving petrel ("South Georgia Diving Petrel") (horiz)	3·25	2·75
302	50p. Macaroni penguin	3·50	3·25
303	£1 Light-mantled sooty albatross (horiz)	6·50	6·50
304	£3 Georgian teal ("South Georgia Pintail") (horiz)	13·00	14·00
305	£5 King penguin	18·00	19·00

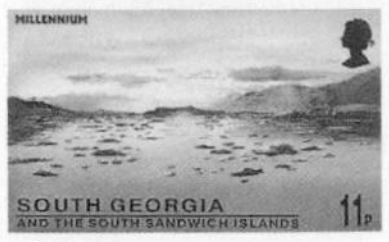

46 Sunrise

1999. New Millennium. Multicoloured.

306	11p. Type **46**	2·25	2·25
307	11p. Grytviken Church	2·25	2·25
308	11p. Nesting black-browed and grey-headed albatross	2·25	2·25
309	35p. Sunset	2·50	2·50
310	35p. Reindeer	2·50	2·50
311	35p. Macaroni penguins and chicks	2·50	2·50

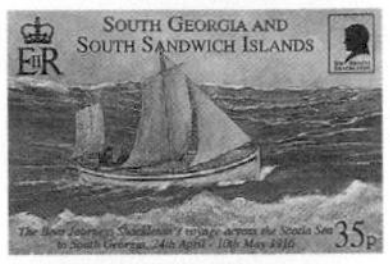

47 Shackleton in "James Caird" crossing Scotia Sea

2000. Shackleton's Trans-Antarctic Expedition, 1914–17, Commemoration. Multicoloured.

312	35p. Type **47**	6·50	4·00
313	40p. Shackleton and party approaching Stromness Whaling Station	7·00	4·50
314	65p. Shackleton's Cross at Hope Point	8·50	9·50

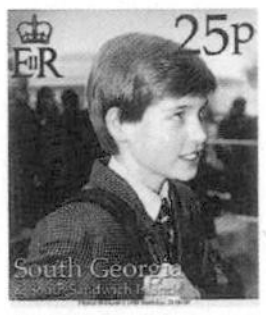

48 Prince William at Zurich Airport, 1994

2000. 18th Birthday of Prince William. Multicoloured.

315	25p. Type **48**	3·00	2·75
316	30p. Skiing in Klosters, Switzerland, 1994	3·25	3·00
317	35p. Prince William in 1997 (horiz)	3·50	3·25
318	40p. Prince William waving, 1999 (horiz)	3·75	3·50
MS319	175×95 mm. 50p. In Parachute Regiment uniform, 1986 (horiz) and Nos. 315/18	15·00	12·00

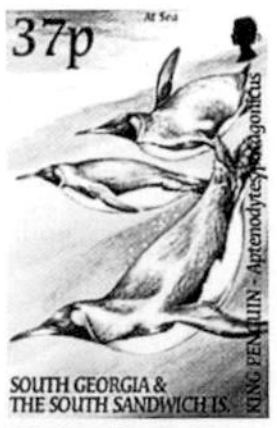

49 King Penguins swimming

2000. King Penguins. Multicoloured.

320	37p. Type **49**	4·75	4·50
321	37p. Adult penguin with chicks	4·75	4·50
322	43p. Penguins courting	5·50	5·00
323	43p. Penguins on nests	5·50	5·00

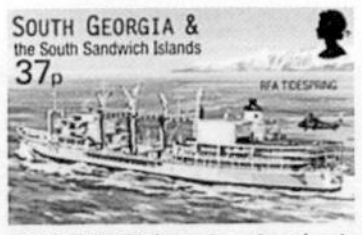

50 R.F.A. *Tidespring* (tanker)

2001. Royal Fleet Auxiliary Vessels. Multicoloured.

324	37p. Type **50**	4·25	4·00
325	37p. R.F.A. *Sir Percivale* (landing ship)	4·25	4·00
326	43p. R.F.A. *Diligence* (maintenance ship)	4·50	4·25
327	43p. R.F.A. *Gold Rover* (tanker)	4·50	4·25

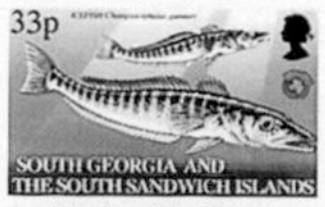

51 Mackerel Icefish

2001. 20th Anniv of Convention for the Conservation of Antarctic Marine Resources. Marine Life. Multicoloured.

328	33p. Type **51**	4·00	4·00
329	37p. Spiney back crab	4·50	4·50
330	37p. Krill (vert)	4·50	4·50
331	43p. Blenny rockcod ("Tooth-fish") (vert)	5·00	5·00

2002. Golden Jubilee. As T **211** of St. Helena.

332	20p. brown, turquoise and gold	1·75	1·75
333	37p. multicoloured	2·50	2·50
334	43p. black, turquoise and gold	3·00	3·00
335	50p. multicoloured	3·25	3·25
MS336 162×95 mm. Nos. 332/5 and 50p. multicoloured		11·00	12·00

DESIGNS—HORIZ (as Type **211** of St. Helena): 20p. Queen Elizabeth with corgi, 1952; 37p. Queen Elizabeth and Prince Philip in evening dress; 43p. Princess Elizabeth looking at stamp album, 1946; 50p. Queen Elizabeth at garden party, 1999. VERT (38×51 mm.): 50p. Queen Elizabeth after Annigoni.

Designs as Nos. 332/5 in No. **MS**336 omit the gold frame around each stamp and the "Golden Jubilee 1952-2002" inscription.

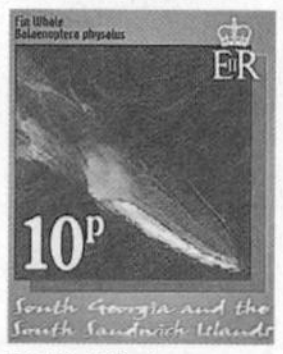

52 Fin Whale

2002. South Atlantic Sea Mammals. Multicoloured.

337	10p. Type **52**	2·25	2·50
338	10p. Blue whale	2·25	2·50
339	20p. Sperm whale	2·50	2·75
340	37p. Head of leopard seal	2·50	2·75
341	37p. Leopard seal on ice floe	2·50	2·75
342	43p. Elephant seal	2·75	3·00
MS343 90×67 mm. £1.50 Elephant seal		20·00	20·00

2002. Queen Elizabeth the Queen Mother Commemoration. As T **215** of St. Helena.

344	22p. brown, gold and purple	1·00	1·00
345	40p. multicoloured	1·40	1·40
346	45p. black, gold and purple	1·50	1·50
347	95p. multicoloured	2·50	2·50
MS348 145×70 mm. Nos. 346/7		5·50	6·50

DESIGNS: 22p. Queen Elizabeth at British Red Cross Society, London; 40p. Queen Mother at Birthday Variety Show, 1990; 45p. Duchess of York and corgi, 1936; 95p. Queen Mother at Royal College of Music, 1989.

Designs in No. **MS**348 omit the "1900–2002" inscription and the coloured frame.

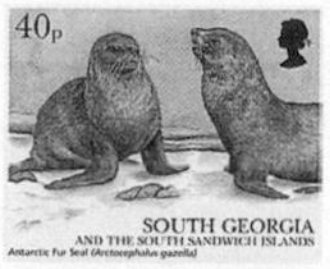

53 Antarctic Fur Seals on Ice

2002. Fur Seals. Multicoloured.

349	40p. Type **53**	5·00	5·00
350	40p. Fur seal underwater	5·00	5·00
351	45p. Fur seal in winter coat	5·00	5·00
352	45p. Competing males	5·00	5·00

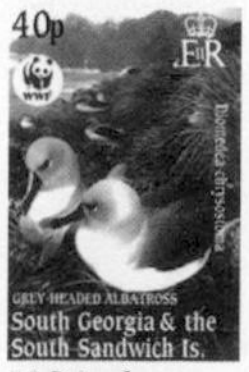

54 Pair of Grey-headed Albatrosses on Nest

2003. Endangered Species. Grey-headed Albatross. Multicoloured.

353	40p. Type **54**	1·40	1·40
354	45p. Adult with chick	1·50	1·50
355	45p. Two adults	1·50	1·50
356	70p. Grey-headed Albatross in flight	2·00	2·00

2003. As T **220** of St. Helena.

361	£2 black, yellow and brown	6·00	6·00

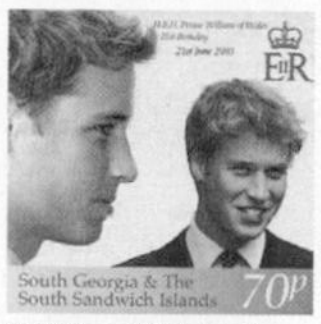

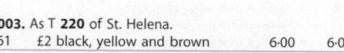

55 Prince William at Golden Jubilee Church Service and at Queen Mother's 101st Birthday

2003. 21st Birthday of Prince William of Wales. Multicoloured.

362	70p. Type **55**	2·75	2·50
363	70p. On Raleigh International Expedition and in Prefect's Common Room, Dr. Gailey's	2·75	2·50

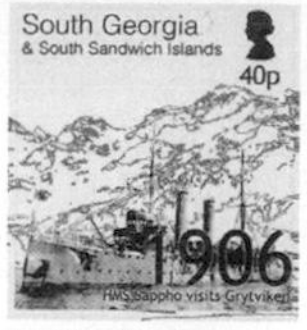

56 HMS *Sappho* (cruiser), Grytviken, 1906

2004. Aspects of South Georgia. Multicoloured.

364	40p. Type **56**	2·25	1·40
365	40p. Norwegian reindeer, introduced 1911	2·25	1·40
366	40p. Largest blue whale landed, 1912	2·25	1·40
367	40p. Shackleton's island crossing, 1916	2·25	1·40
368	40p. Shackleton's memorial cross, Grytviken, 1922	2·25	1·40
369	40p. *Discovery* I on expedition to study whale populations, 1925	2·25	1·40
370	40p. First powered flight over South Georgia, 1938	2·25	1·40
371	40p. Operation Tabarin, 1943	2·25	1·40
372	40p. Duke of Edinburgh (with penguins), 1957	2·25	1·40
373	40p. Bird Island Research Station, 1958	2·25	1·40
374	40p. Ascent of Mount Paget, 1964	2·25	1·40
375	40p. Royal Navy ship, Liberation of South Georgia, 1982	2·25	1·40
376	40p. Royal Charter and Crest, 1985	2·25	1·40
377	40p. Inauguration of South Georgia Musuem, Grytviken, 1992	2·25	1·40
378	40p. Applied fishery research, 2001	2·25	1·40
379	40p. Remedial work at old whaling station, Grytviken, 2003	2·25	1·40

Nos. 364/79 were printed together, *se-tenant*, each horizontal row of stamps forming a composite background design of Grytviken (Nos. 364/7), Bird Island (Nos. 368/71), Drygalski Fjord (Nos. 372/5) or King Haakon Bay (Nos. 376/9).

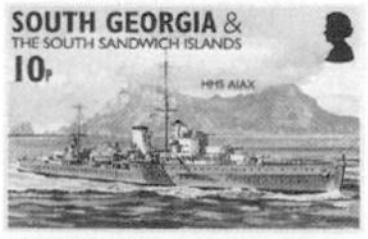

57 HMS *Ajax*

2004. Royal Navy Frigates and Cruisers. Multicoloured.

380	10p. Type **57**	1·50	1·25
381	25p. HMS *Amazon*	2·25	1·25
382	45p. HMS *Dartmouth*	3·50	2·25
383	50p. HMS *Penelope*	3·50	2·25
384	70p. HMS *St. Austell Bay*	4·50	3·50
385	£1 HMS *Plymouth*	6·00	4·50

2004. Merchant Ships. As T **227** of St. Helena. Multicoloured.

386	42p. MS *Endeavour*	3·00	3·00
387	42p. RMS *Queen Elizabeth II*	3·00	3·00
388	50p. MS *Lindblad Explorer*	3·50	3·00
389	75p. SS *Canberra*	4·50	4·00

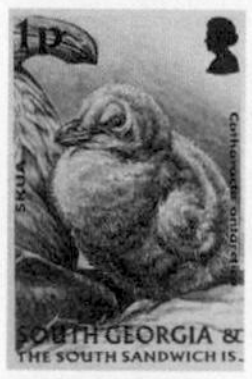

58 Antarctic Skua

2004. Juvenile Fauna. Multicoloured designs

(a) Ordinary gum

390	1p. Type **58**	1·25	1·75
391	2p. Reindeer	1·25	1·75
392	3p. Dove ("Antarctic") prion (horiz)	1·75	1·75
393	5p. Humpback whale (horiz)	2·25	1·75
394	10p. Gentoo penguin	2·25	1·75
395	25p. Antarctic fur seal	2·25	1·75
396	50p. South Georgia pintail (horiz)	4·00	3·25
397	75p. Light-mantled sooty albatross	5·50	5·50
398	£1 Weddell seal	6·00	7·00
399	£2 King penguin (horiz)	10·00	11·00
400	£3 Southern right whale (horiz)	13·00	14·00
401	£5 Wandering albatross	18·00	19·00

(b) Size 39×26 mm. Self-adhesive.

402	(42p.) Elephant seal pup	1·75	2·50

No. 402 is inscribed "Airmail Postcard" and was sold for 42p. each.

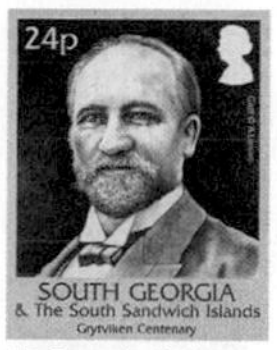

59 Captain C. A. Larsen

2004. Centenary of Grytviken (first settlement). Multicoloured.

403	24p. Type **59**	1·25	1·25
404	42p. View of Grytviken from Mount Hodges	1·75	1·75
405	50p. *Fortuna* (whaling ship)	3·00	3·00
406	£1 Ski jump	4·00	5·00

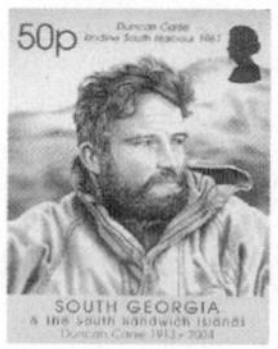

60 Duncan Carse

2005. Duncan Carse (broadcaster) Commemoration. Multicoloured.

407	30p. Type **60**	1·00	1·50
408	50p. Survey 1951–1957	2·00	2·50
409	75p. "Dick Barton (Special Agent)"	2·75	3·25
410	£1 "All My Own Work House" 1961	3·75	4·25

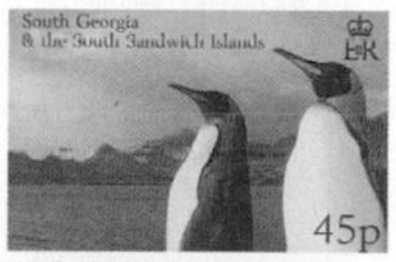

61 Emperor Penguins

2005. Penguins. King Penguins. Multicoloured.

411	45p. Type **61**	3·00	3·00
412	45p. Two penguins and third stooping	3·00	3·00
413	45p. Three penguins on shore	3·00	3·00
414	45p. Three penguins against sky	3·00	3·00
415	45p. Detail of breast	3·00	3·00
416	45p. Detail of neck	3·00	3·00

2006. 80th Birthday of Queen Elizabeth II. As T **237** of St. Helena. Multicoloured.

417	50p. Princess Elizabeth with corgi	1·25	1·25
418	50p. Princess Elizabeth, c. 1950	1·25	1·25
419	75p. Queen Elizabeth II, c. 1960	1·75	1·75
420	£1 Wearing pink hat	2·00	2·00
MS421 144×75 mm. As Nos. 418/19		5·50	5·50

Stamps from **MS**421 do not have white borders.

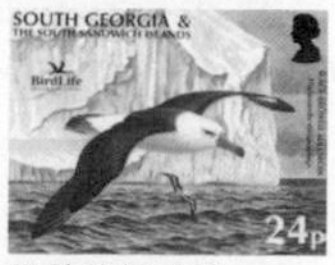

62 Black-browed Albatross and Iceberg

2006. BirdLife International. Save the Albatross Campaign. Multicoloured.

422	24p. Type **62**	1·75	1·75
423	45p. Southern giant petrel	2·25	2·25
424	50p. White-chinned petrel at sunset	2·25	2·25
425	75p. Wandering albatross	2·75	2·75
MS426 138×85 mm. £1 Black-browed albatross and South Georgia coast; £1 White-chinned petrel, coast and mountain		9·00	9·00

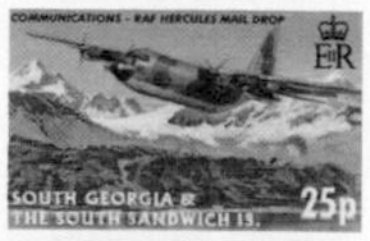

63 RAF Hercules Mail Drop (1982–2001)

2006. Communications. Multicoloured.

427	25p. Type **63**	2·00	2·00
428	50p. South Georgia radio room, c. 1980	2·75	2·75
429	60p. MV *Sigma* (fishery patrol vessel and current mail carrier)	3·25	3·25
430	£1.05 SS *Fleurus* (mail carrier 1924–33)	4·50	4·50

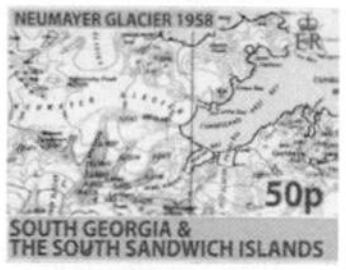

64 Map of Neumayer Glacier, 1958

2007. Mapping. Multicoloured.

431	50p. Type **64**	3·50	3·50
432	50p. Map of Neumayer Glacier, 2003	3·50	3·50
433	60p. Theodolite Kern DKM1 (used for 1951–2 survey)	3·50	3·50
434	60p. Landsat 7 satellite and curvature of Earth	3·50	3·50

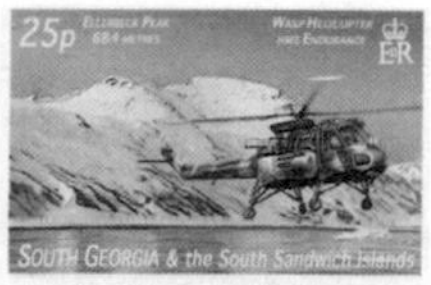

65 Wasp Helicopter from HMS *Endurance* and Ellerbeck Peak

2007. 25th Anniv of the Liberation of South Georgia and the South Sandwich Islands. Multicoloured.

435	25p. Type **65**	2·25	2·00
436	50p. Wessex 3 helicopter from HMS *Antrim* and Stanley Peak	3·50	3·25
437	60p. 42 Commando Royal Marines and Sheridan Peak	3·50	3·25
438	£1.05 Royal Marines Detachment from HMS *Endurance* and Mills Peak	4·50	5·00
MS439 126×84 mm. Nos. 435/8		12·00	12·00

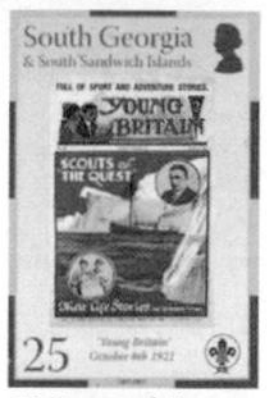

66 Cover of *Young Britain*, 1921

2007. Centenary of Scouting. Antarctic Voyage of Scout James Marr aboard the Quest, 1921–2. Multicoloured.

440	25p. Type **66**	1·25	1·25
441	50p. Scouts James Marr and Norman Mooney raising the King's Flag aboard the *Quest*	2·50	2·50
442	60p. Sir Ernest Shackleton and Scouts Mooney and Marr	3·00	3·00
443	85p. Autographed postcard of James Marr	3·25	3·50
444	£1.05 The *Quest* locked in ice	4·50	5·00

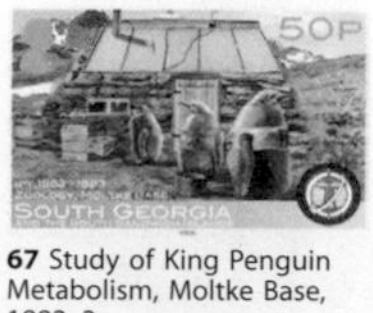

67 Study of King Penguin Metabolism, Moltke Base, 1882–3

2008. International Polar Year. Multicoloured.

445	50p. Type **67**	2·75	2·75
446	60p. Meteorological station, King Edward Point, 1932–3	2·75	2·75
447	85p. Zooplankton, 2007–9	3·50	3·75
448	£1.05 Leopard seal, 2007–9	4·25	4·75

68 Longliner, Patagonian Toothfish and Marine Stewardship Council Logo

2008. Fisheries. Multicoloured.

449	50p. Type **68**	2·50	2·50
450	60p. Trawler and mackerel icefish	2·50	2·50
451	85p. Krill trawler transhipping to larger reefer ship and krill	3·50	3·75
452	£1.05 Fishery patrol vessel *Pharos SG*	4·25	4·75

69 Chinstrap Penguins

2008. Endangered Species. Chinstrap Penguins (*Pygoscelis antarcticus*). Multicoloured.

453	55p. Type **69**	2·10	2·10
454	55p. Pair with chick	2·10	2·10
455	65p. Three penguins leaving the sea	2·25	2·25
456	90p. Head of penguin	2·75	2·75
MS457	140×198 mm. Nos. 453/6	8·50	9·50

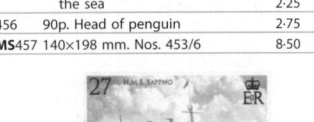

70 HMS *Sappho*, 1906

2008. Centenary of Letters Patent (setting out geographical extent of Falkland Islands Dependencies). Multicoloured.

458	27p. Type **70**	2·00	2·00
459	65p. Magistrate's Residence	3·00	3·00
460	90p. James Innes Wilson, Magistrate 1909–14	3·50	4·25
461	£1.10 SS *Coronda* delivering stores to Salveson whaling station, Leith Harbour, 1909–17	5·50	6·50

71 Ozone Map, September 2008

2009. 'Preserve the Polar Regions'. Sheet 88×119 mm containing T **71** and similar circular design. Multicoloured. Self-adhesive.

MS462	£1.10 Type **71**; £1.10 Ozone map, September 1979	8·00	10·00

72 Supermarine Walrus and HMS *Exeter*

2009. Centenary of Naval Aviation. Multicoloured.

463	27p. Type **72**	2·25	2·00
464	65p. Westland Wasp HAS1 helicopter and HMS *Plymouth*, 1982	4·00	3·25
465	90p. Westland Whirlwind HAR1 helicopter and HMS *Protector* (Antarctic patrol ship), 1955	5·50	6·00
466	£1.10 Agusta Westland AW101 Merlin helicopter and HMS *Lancaster* , 2002	6·00	6·50

73 Ernest Shackleton aged 11

2009. Ernest H. Shackleton (polar explorer) Commemoration. Multicoloured.

467	1p. Type **73**	20	30
468	2p. In White Star Line uniform, aged 16	25	30
469	5p. On Discovery Expedition, 1902	40	45
470	10p. Emily Shackleton and children Raymond, Cecily and Edward	50	60
471	27p. Wild, Shackleton, Marshall and Adams on British Antarctic Expedition, 1909	1·00	85
472	55p. *Endurance* trapped in ice, 1912	1·75	1·75
473	65p. Launching *James Caird* (*Endurance* lifeboat) (horiz)	2·00	2·00
474	90p. Tom Crean, Shackleton and Frank Worsley after crossing South Georgia (horiz)	2·75	2·75
475	£1 Major Shackleton, 1918	2·75	2·75
476	£2 *Quest*, 1922	5·25	5·25
477	£3 Shackleton's grave (horiz)	7·75	7·75
478	£5 Sir Ernest H. Shackleton (horiz)	13·00	13·00

74 *Thouarella* sp. 1

2009. Corals. Multicoloured.

479	55p. Type **74**	2·00	2·00
480	65p. *Paragorgia* sp.	2·25	2·25
481	90p. *Stylaster* sp.	3·00	3·25
482	£1.10 *Thouarella* sp. 2	3·25	3·50

75 SS *Cachalote* (first mail ship), 1909

2009. Centenary of South Georgia Post Office. Multicoloured.

483	65p. Type **75**	3·00	3·00
484	65p. Mail couriers outside Sörling Valley postal hut, c. 1912	3·00	3·00
485	90p. Post Office, King Edward Point, 2009	4·00	4·00
486	90p. Fishery patrol vessel *Pharos* (current mail ship)	4·00	4·00

Nos. 483/4 and 485/6 were each printed together, *se-tenant*, forming a composite background design.

76 *Galiteuthis glacialis*

2010. Cephalopods. Multicoloured.

487	27p. Type **76**	1·25	1·25
488	65p. *Psychroteuthis glacialis*	2·25	2·25
489	90p. *Thaumeledrone gunteri*	3·00	3·00
490	£1.10 *Stauroteuthis gilchristi*	3·50	3·50
MS491	80×80 mm. £2 Colossal Squid (*Mesonychoteuthis hamiltoni*) and sperm whale (*Physetermacrocephalus*) (51×51 mm)	7·00	7·00

77 Essay for South Georgia King George V 2½d. Stamp (never issued)

2010. London 2010 Festival of Stamps. Multicoloured. . Multicoloured.

492	65p. Type **77**	2·00	2·00
493	65p. Falkland Islands King George V 2d. maroon stamp overprinted 2½d. for use in South Georgia in 1928	18·00	18·00
494	65p. Falkland Islands 2d. King George V and penguin stamp bisected for use in South Georgia in 1930	2·00	2·00
495	65p. Falkland Islands 1s. stamp overprinted SOUTH GEORGIA DEPENDENCY OF in 1944	2·00	2·00
496	65p. Falkland Islands Dependencies 1953 1d. Coronation stamp	2·00	2·00
497	65p. South Georgia 1963 5s. elephant and fur seal stamp	2·00	2·00
498	65p. South Georgia 1975 8p. HMS *Resolution* (Captain Cook) stamp	2·00	2·00
499	65p. Falkland Islands Dependencies 1982 Rebuilding Fund £1+£1 surcharge	2·00	2·00
500	65p. South Georgia and South Sandwich Islands 1992 20p. Georgian teal stamp	2·00	2·00
501	65p. South Georgia and South Sandwich Islands 2009 £5 Shackleton stamp	2·00	2·00

78 *Bayard*

2010. Wrecks and Hulks. Multicoloured.

502	60p. Type **78**	2·25	2·25
503	70p. *Dias* and *Albatros*	2·25	2·25
504	95p. *Karrakatta*	3·00	3·00
505	£1.15 *Petrel*	3·50	3·50

79 *The Resolution in a Stream of Pack-Ice* (sketch)

2010. William Hodges: The Art of Discovery. Paintings and Sketches from Captain Cook's Second Voyage (1772–5). Multicoloured.

506	70p. Type **79**	2·25	2·25
507	70p. *A View of the Monuments of Easter Island* (horiz)	2·25	2·25
508	95p. *Captain James Cook*	3·00	3·00
509	£1.15 *Possession Bay in the Island of South Georgia* (horiz)	3·50	3·50

80 King Penguins

2010. South Georgia Penguins. Multicoloured.

510	(60p.) Type **80**	2·25	2·25
511	(60p.) Macaroni penguin	2·25	2·25
512	(60p.) Chinstrap penguin	2·25	2·25
513	(60p.) Gentoo penguin and chicks	2·25	2·25
MS514	160×170 mm. Nos. 510/13, each ×2	13·00	13·00

Nos. 510/14 were each inscr 'Airmail Postcard' and initially sold for 60p. each.

81 Small Fern (*Blechnum penna-marina*)

2010. Flora. Multicoloured.

515	27p. Type **81**	1·00	1·00
516	70p. Water blinks (*Montia fontana*)	2·50	2·50
517	95p. Antarctic pearlwort (*Colobanthus quitensis*)	3·00	3·00
518	£1.15 Adder's-tongue (*Ophioglossum crotalophoroides*)	3·50	3·50

82 Vervet Monkey (doctor's pet), 1914

2011. Pets. Multicoloured.

519	45p. Type **82**	1·50	1·50
520	60p. Anne-Marie Sorlle (daughter of Stromness whaling station manager) with puppies	2·25	2·25
521	70p. Whalers with dog and fox, Grytviken, c. 1925	2·25	2·25
522	95p. Nan Brown and gentoo penguin 'Stugie'	3·00	3·00
523	£1.15 Perce Blackborow and cat 'Mrs. Chippy'	3·50	3·50
524	£1.20 Ernest Shackleton bathing German shepherd puppy 'Query' aboard *Quest*, 1922	4·25	4·25

83 Sir Alister Hardy and Continuous Plankton Recorder Type II

2011. Sir Alister Clavering Hardy (marine biologist, inventor of continuous plankton recorder, artist and writer) Commemoration. Multicoloured.

525	60p. Type **83**	2·25	2·25
526	70p. Sir Alister Hardy at microscope, c. 1922	2·25	2·25
527	95p. *A Busy Day at the Whaling Station at Grytviken* (watercolour by Sir Alister Hardy, 1926)	3·00	3·00
528	£1.15 RRS *Discovery*, Antarctica, 1925–7	3·50	3·50

84 Prince William and Miss Catherine Middleton watching Rugby Union Match, Twickenham, 10 February 2007

2011. Royal Wedding. Multicoloured.

529	70p. Type **84**	2·25	2·25
530	95p. Prince William and Miss Catherine Middleton at St. James's Palace, November 2010	2·75	2·75
531	£1.15 Prince William and Miss Catherine Middleton during Wedding ceremony, 29 April 2011	3·25	3·25
MS532	94×64 mm. £2 Official Royal Wedding portrait, Buckingham Palace (vert)	7·00	7·00

85 Southern Giant Petrel

2011. South Georgia Petrels. Multicoloured.

533	60p. Type **85**	2·25	2·25
534	70p. Snow petrel	2·50	2·50
535	95p. Cape petrel	3·00	3·00
536	£1.15 South Georgia diving petrel	3·50	3·50

86 Elephant Seals (spring)

2011. BBC Frozen Planet. Multicoloured.

537	60p. Type **86**	2·25	2·25
538	70p. Wandering albatross (juvenile) (summer)	2·50	2·50
539	95p. Blonde fur seal pup (autumn)	3·00	3·00
540	£1.15 King penguin and chicks (winter)	3·50	3·50
MS541	94×64 mm. £2.50 Wandering albatross (adult in flight)	10·00	10·00

87 Frank Wild, *Discovery* and Polar Medal

2011. Frank Wild (John Robert Francis Wild) Commemoration. Multicoloured.

542	60p. Type **87** (*Discovery* Expedition, 1901-4)	2·25	2·25
543	60p. Robert Falcon Scott and *Discovery* locked in ice (*Discovery* Expedition, 1901-4)	2·25	2·25
544	70p. Frank Wild and Ernest Shackleton, Frank Wild, and Eric Marshall with Union flag at their furthest south latitude 97 miles from South Pole and Polar Medal (*Nimrod* Expedition, 1907-9)	2·50	2·50

545	70p. Ernest Shackleton and *Nimrod* (*Nimrod* Expedition, 1907-9)	2·50	2·50
546	95p. Frank Wild, Andrew Watson and another on *Aurora* Expedition (1911-14) and Polar Medal	2·75	2·75
547	95p. Douglas Mawson and *Aurora* (*Aurora* Expedition, 1911-14)	2·75	2·75
548	£1.15 Frank Wild, Ocean Camp and Polar Medal (*Endurance* Expedition, 1914-16)	3·25	3·25
549	£1.15 Ernest Shackleton and *Endurance* (*Endurance* Expedition, 1914-16)	3·25	3·25

88 Ten Legged Sea Spider (*Decolopoda australis*)

2012. Shallow Marine Life. Multicoloured.

550	70p. Type **88**	2·25	2·25
551	70p. Pink cushion seastar (*Odontaster validus*)	2·25	2·25
552	70p. White tipped nudibranch (*Flabellina falklandica*)	2·25	2·25
553	70p. Branching sea cucumber (*Heterocucumis steineni*)	2·25	2·25
554	70p. Giant Antarctic isopod (*Glyptonotis antarcticus*)	2·25	2·25
555	70p. South Georgia top shell (*Margarella tropidophoroides*)	2·25	2·25

89 Imperial Shag (*Phalacrocorax atriceps*)

2012. Endangered Species. Seabirds. Multicoloured.

556	60p. Type **89**	2·50	2·50
557	70p. Antarctic tern (*Sterna vittata*)	2·75	2·75
558	55p. Southern skua (*Catharacta antarctica*) (pair)	3·25	3·25
559	£1.15 Kelp gull (*Larus dominicanus*)	3·75	3·75
MS560	94×64 mm. £3.50 Southern skua (*Catharacta antarctica*) (adult and two chicks)	14·00	14·00

90 Queen Elizabeth II making her First Christmas Day Broadcast, Sandringham, 1952

2012. Diamond Jubilee. Multicoloured.

561	60p. Type **90**	1·60	1·60
562	70p. Queen Elizabeth II during walkabout, New Plymouth, New Zealand, 25 February 1977	1·75	1·75
563	95p. Queen Elizabeth II at Exeter on Golden Jubilee tour, 1 May 2002	2·25	2·25
564	£1.15 Queen Elizabeth II at Kings Lynn, 2012	3·25	3·25
MS565	70×100 mm. £3 Queen Elizabeth II arriving for reception at British Museum, 27 November 1957	9·50	9·50

91 Blue Whale

2012. Blue Whale (*Balaenoptera musculus*). Multicoloured.

566	65p. Type **91**	2·50	2·50
567	75p. Blue Whale at surface, rocky islets in background	3·00	3·00
568	£1 Blue Whale at surface, water droplets coming from blowhole	4·50	4·50
569	£1.20 Tail fin	5·50	5·50

92 Elephant Seals and Cruise Ship ('Tourism')

2012. Marine Protected Area. Multicoloured.

570	65p. Type **92**	2·50	2·50
571	65p. King Penguins and fisheries protection vessel *Pharos SG* ('Surveillance')	2·50	2·50
572	75p. Grey-headed Albatross and chick weighed on scales ('Scientific Monitoring')	3·00	3·00
573	75p. Longlining for Patagonian Toothfish ('Fisheries')	3·00	3·00
574	£1 Squid, Lantern Fish and Antarctic Krill ('Pelagic Abundance')	4·00	4·00
575	£1.20 Sponge, Starfish, Corals, Seaweed and diving Seal ('Benthic Diversity')	4·50	4·50

93 Stenhouse Peak (525m)

2012. Mountains. Multicoloured.

576	65p. Type **93**	2·50	2·50
577	65p. Cdr. Joseph R. Stenhouse (1887-1941, commander of *Aurora* in Shackleton Expedition 1914-16)	2·50	2·50
578	75p. Mt. Carse (2331m)	3·00	3·00
579	75p. Verner Duncan Carse (explorer and broadcaster, 1913-2004)	3·00	3·00
580	£1 Mt. Paget (2934m), Allardyce Range	4·00	4·00
581	£1 Sir William Lamond Allardyce (1861-1930, Governor of the Falkland Islands and its Dependencies 1904-15)	4·00	4·00

Nos. 576/7, 578/9 and 580/1 were each printed together, *se-tenant*, as horizontal pairs, each pair forming a composite design.

94 Star Trails over the Harker Glacier

2013. Star Trails. Multicoloured.

582	65p. Type **94**	2·25	2·25
583	75p. Star trails over Maiviken Hut	2·75	2·75
584	£1 Star trails over *Albatros* and *Dias* (wrecks of old whaling ships on shore at Grytviken)	3·75	3·75
585	£1.20 Shackleton Memorial Cross and star trails behind Hope Point	4·75	4·75

95 Sir Rex Hunt and Crashed Wasp Helicopter, St. Andrews Bay, South Georgia

2013. Sir Rex Hunt (1926-2012, Governor of the Falkland Islands 1980-5) Commemoration. Multicoloured.

586	65p. Type **95**	2·25	2·25
587	75p. Sir Rex Hunt outside Government House, Falkland Islands, December 1982	2·75	2·75
588	£1 At Pobjoy Mint holding 25th anniversary of Liberation of the Falkland Islands coin, May 2007	3·75	3·75
589	£1.20 Sir Rex Hunt in recent years	4·75	4·75

96 Queen Elizabeth II leaving Buckingham Palace for her Coronation

2013. 60th Anniv of the Coronation. Multicoloured.

590	65p. Type **96**	2·25	2·25
591	75p. Queen Elizabeth II riding in carriage after coronation	2·75	2·75
592	£1 Queen Elizabeth II on Buckingham Palace balcony after Coronation	3·75	3·75
593	£1.20 Queen Elizabeth II in Coronation chair, Westminster Abbey	4·75	4·75

97 Chiton (*Tonicina zschaui*)

2013. Shallow Marine Surveys Group. Multicoloured.

594	65p. Type **97**	2·25	2·25
595	75p. Anemone (*Edwardsia* sp.)	2·75	2·75
596	£1 Crocodile Fish (*Parachaenichthys georgianus*)	3·75	3·75
597	£1.20 Brittle Star (*Ophiomages cristatus*)	4·75	4·75
MS598	113×74 mm. Ascension Island £1 Anemone (*Isarachnanthus maderensis*); Falkland Islands £1 Painted Shrimp (*Campylonotus vagans*); £1 Starfish (*Henricia pagenstecheri*) (all vert)	9·00	9·00

98 RRS *Ernest Shackleton*

2013. Habitat Restoration. Multicoloured.

599	5p. Type **98**	15	15
600	30p. Bölkow BO-105 Helicopter	75	75
601	65p. Loading bait hopper	1·60	1·60
602	75p. Rat eating bait	1·90	1·90
603	£1 South Georgia Pintail	2·50	2·50
604	£1.20 South Georgia Pipit	3·00	3·00

99 Construction of Grytviken Church, December 1913

2013. Centenary of the Whaler's Church, Grytviken. Multicoloured.

605	30p. Type **99**	75	75
606	50p. Captain Carl Anton Larsen (founder of Grytviken whaling station and manager 1904-14)	1·25	1·25
607	65p. Church interior	1·60	1·60
608	75p. Grytviken Church	1·90	1·90
609	£1 Removal of steeple cross by helicopter for repainting	2·50	2·50
610	£1.20 Grytviken Church at night	3·00	3·00

Pt. 14

SOUTH KASAI

Region of Zaire around the town of Bakwanga. The area was declared autonomous in 1960, during the upheaval following independence, but returned to the control of the central government in October 1962.

Various stamps of Belgian Congo were overprinted "ETAT AUTONOME DU SUD-KASAI" and some surcharged in addition with new values. These were put on sale at the Philatelic Bureau in Brussels and were also valid for use in South Kasai but no supplies were sent out.

100 centimes = 1 franc.

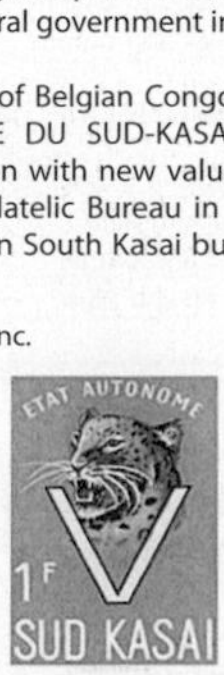

1 Leopard's Head and "V"

1961

1	1	1f. multicoloured	10	10
2	1	1f.50 multicoloured	10	10
3	1	3f.50 multicoloured	15	15
4	1	8f. multicoloured	25	25
5	1	10f. multicoloured	30	30

2 A. D. Kalonji

1961

6	**2**	6f.50 brown, blue and black	20	20
7	**2**	9f. light brown, brown & black	25	25
8	**2**	14f.50 brown, green and black	40	40
9	**2**	20f. multicoloured	45	1·45
MS10		95×135 mm. **2** 50f. (larger) multicoloured	6·00	

Pt. 10

SOUTH RUSSIA

Stamps of various anti-Bolshevist forces and temporary governments in S. Russia after the revolution.

100 kopeks = 1 rouble.

A. KUBAN TERRITORY: COSSACK GOVERNMENT

1918. Arms type of Russia surch. Imperf or perf.

8	**22**	25k. on 1k. orange	60	1·10
2	**22**	50k. on 2k. green	40	50
23	**22**	70k. on 1k. orange	1·00	1·50
10	**22**	70k. on 5k. red	1·30	2·50
11	**22**	1r. on 3k. red	1·40	2·00
13	**23**	3r. on 4k. red	16·00	21·00
14	**23**	10r. on 4k. red	9·00	10·50
15	**10**	10r. on 15k. blue and purple	2·00	2·20
16	**22**	25r. on 3k. red	9·00	7·75
17	**22**	25r. on 7k. blue	65·00	£130
18	**10**	25r. on 14k. red and blue	£140	£200
19	**10**	25r. on 25k. mauve & green	£100	£130

1919. Postal Savings Bank stamps of Russia surch.

20	10r. on 1k. red on buff	£100	£170
21	10r. on 5k. green on buff	£100	£170
22	10r. on 10k. brown on buff	£160	£450

B. DON TERRITORY: COSSACK GOVERNMENT

1919. Arms type of Russia surch in figures only. Imperf or perf.

25	**22**	25k. on 1k. orange	65	90
29	**22**	25k. on 2k. green	65	90
30	**22**	25k. on 3k. red	1·40	1·90
31	**23**	25k. on 4k. red	2·00	2·75
32	**22**	50k. on 7k. blue	5·25	6·50

10 T. Ermak (16th century Cossack Ataman)

1919. Currency stamp with arms and seven-line print on back used for postage.

33	**10**	20k. green	42·00	£110

C. CRIMEA: REGIONAL GOVERNMENT

1919. Arms type of Russia surch **35 Kon.** Imperf.

34	**22**	35k. on 1k. orange	40	1·00

13

1919. Currency and postage stamp. Arms and inscription on back. Imperf.

35	**13**	50k. brown on buff	90·00	£190

D. SOUTH RUSSIA: GOVERNMENT OF GENERAL DENIKIN

1919. Nos. G6 and G10 of Ukraine surch in figs.

36	**G 1**	35k. on 10s. brown	50·00	65·00
37	**G 5**	70k. on 50s. red	£100	£130

15

16

1919. Imperf or perf.

38	**15**	5k. yellow	20	25
39	**15**	10k. green	20	25
40	**15**	15k. red	20	30
41	**15**	35k. blue	20	25
42	**15**	70k. blue	20	25
43	**16**	1r. red and brown	65	80
44	**16**	2r. yellow and lilac	1·00	1·50
45	**16**	3r. green and brown	65	1·10
46	**16**	5r. violet and blue	1·10	1·50
47	**16**	7r. pink and green	1·80	3·50
48	**16**	10r. grey and red	2·00	2·20

Higher values similar to Type **16** are bogus.

E. SOUTH RUSSIA: GOVERNMENT OF GENERAL WRANGEL

5 пять рублей. (17)

Югъ Россіи. 100 рублей. (18)

1920. Crimea issue. Surch with T **17**. (a) On Arms types of Russia. Imperf or perf.

52	**22**	5r. on 5k. red	3·00	7·75
54	**14**	5r. on 20k. red and blue	3·00	7·75

(b) On No. 41 of South Russia.

55	**15**	5r. on 35k. blue	8·25	23·00

1920. Arms type of Russia surch with T **18**.

56	**22**	100r. on 1k. orange	4·00	6·50

Pt. 1

SOUTH WEST AFRICA

A territory in S.W. Africa formerly the German Colony of German South West Africa (q.v. in Volume 2). Administered by South Africa until 1990 when it became independent as Namibia.

1923. 12 pence = 1 shilling; 20 shillings = 1 pound.
1961. 100 cents = 1 rand.

NOTE. Stamps overprinted for South West Africa are always of South Africa, except where otherwise indicated. "Bilingual" in heading indicates that the stamps are inscribed alternately in English and Afrikaans throughout the sheet, "Bilingual" is not repeated in the heading where bilingual stamps of South Africa are overprinted. Our prices for surch issues are for mint bilingual pairs and used single stamps of either inscription.

1923. Optd **South West Africa.** or **Zuid-West Afrika.** alternately.

1	**2**	½d. green	4·00	1·00
2	**2**	1d. red	7·50	1·00
3	**2**	2d. purple	9·00	1·50
4	**2**	3d. blue	11·00	2·75
5	**2**	4d. orange and green	19·00	4·50
6	**2**	6d. black and violet	8·50	4·50
7	**2**	1s. yellow	18·00	5·00
8	**2**	1s.3d. violet	45·00	5·50
9	**2**	2s.6d. purple and green	70·00	18·00
13	**2**	5s. purple and blue	£160	45·00
14	**2**	10s. blue and green	£500	£140
12	**2**	£1 green and red	£750	£250

1923. Optd **Zuidwest Afrika.** or **South West Africa.*** alternately.

29	**2**	½d. green	7·00	5·50
30	**2**	1d. red	4·25	1·40
31	**2**	2d. purple	4·00	1·75
19	**2**	3d. blue	5·00	1·40
20	**2**	4d. yellow and green	6·00	2·75
34	**2**	6d. black and violet	10·00	5·00
35	**2**	1s. yellow	8·50	5·00
36	**2**	1s.3d. violet	11·00	5·00
37	**2**	2s.6d. purple and green	45·00	10·00
38	**2**	5s. purple and blue	60·00	14·00
39	**2**	10s. blue and green	95·00	20·00
40	**2**	£1 green and red	£300	55·00

*The English overprint is the same, for the purposes of this catalogue, as that on Nos. 1/12.

1926. Optd **South West Africa.** (on stamps inscr in English) or **Suidwes Afrika.** (on stamps inscr in Afrikaans) alternately.

41	**6**	½d. black and green	4·75	1·40
42	**7**	1d. black and red	4·00	90
49	**11**	2d. grey and purple	5·50	1·75
50	-	3d. black and red	4·75	2·50
43	**8**	6d. green and orange	25·00	7·00
51	-	1s. brown and blue	15·00	4·00
52	-	2s.6d. green and brown	38·00	13·00
53	-	5s. black and green	75·00	20·00
54	-	10s. blue and brown	65·00	20·00

1926. Optd **SOUTH WEST AFRICA** in two lines or **SUIDWES-AFRIKA** in one line. Imperf or perf.

44A	**10**	4d. blue	75	3·00

1927. Optd as Nos. 41/2 and 43 but with Afrikaans opt on stamp inscr in English and vice versa.

45	**6**	½d. black and green	2·00	1·40
46	**7**	1d. black and red	4·25	50
47	**8**	6d. green and orange	8·00	3·00

1927. Optd **SOUTH WEST AFRICA** in one line. Imperf.

48	**10**	4d. blue	7·00	19·00

1927. Optd **S.W.A.**

56	**2**	1s.3d. violet	1·25	6·50
57	**2**	£1 olive and red	95·00	£170

1927. Optd **S.W.A.**

58	**6**	½d. black and green	2·50	80
59	**7**	1d. black and red	1·25	55
60	**11**	2d. grey and purple	9·00	2·00
61	-	3d. black and red	5·00	3·25
62	-	4d. brown	12·00	7·00
63	**8**	6d. green and orange	6·00	2·75
64	-	1s. brown and blue	10·00	5·00
65	-	2s.6d. green and brown	42·00	12·00
66	-	5s black and green	65·00	18·00
67	-	10s. blue and brown	£110	28·00

1930. Air. Optd **S.W.A.**

72	**17**	4d. green	1·25	6·00
73	**17**	1s. orange	2·50	15·00

12 Kori Bustard

1931. Bilingual pairs.

74	**12**	½d. black and green	3·00	10
75	-	1d. blue and red	2·75	10
76	-	2d. blue and brown	1·50	15
77	-	3d. dull blue and blue	1·50	15
78	-	4d. green and purple	1·50	20
79	-	6d. blue and brown	1·50	20
80	-	1s. brown and blue	3·50	25
81	-	1s.3d. violet and yellow	6·00	50
82	-	2s.6d. red and grey	27·00	1·75
83	-	5s. green and brown	16·00	2·75
84	-	10s. brown and green	50·00	6·00
85	-	£1 lake and green	75·00	10·00

DESIGNS: 1d. Cape Cross; 2d. Bogenfels; 3d. Windhoek; 4d. Waterberg; 6d. Luderitz Bay; 1s. Bush scene; 1s.3d. Elands; 2s.6d. Mountain zebra and wildebeests; 5s. Herero huts; 10s. Welwitschia plant; £1 Okuwahaken Falls.

24 Fokker Monoplane over Windhoek

1931. Air. Bilingual pairs.

86	**24**	3d. brown and blue	29·00	2·50
87	-	10d. black and brown	55·00	7·00

DESIGN: 10d. Handley Page H.P.25 Hendon biplane over Windhoek.

26

1935. Silver Jubilee.

88	**26**	1d. black and red	1·00	25
89	**26**	2d. black and brown	1·50	25
90	**26**	3d. black and blue	7·50	25·00
91	**26**	6d. black and purple	3·00	15·00

1935. Voortrekker Memorial. Nos. 50/3 of South Africa optd **S.W.A.**

92		½d.+½d. black and green	1·75	75
93		1d.+½d. black and pink	2·25	40
94		2d.+1d. green and purple	7·00	80
95		3d.+1½d. green and blue	20·00	4·25

27 Mail Transport

1937. Bilingual pair.

96	**27**	1½d. brown	29·00	35

28

1937. Coronation. Bilingual pairs.

97	**28**	½d. black and green	40	10
98	**28**	1d. black and red	40	10
99	**28**	1½d. black and orange	40	10
100	**28**	2d. black and brown	40	10
101	**28**	3d. black and blue	50	10
102	**28**	4d. black and purple	50	10
103	**28**	6d. black and yellow	50	20
104	**28**	1s. black and grey	55	25

1938. Voortrekker Centenary Fund. Nos. 76/9 of South Africa optd **S.W.A.**

105	½d.+½d. blue and green	12·00	2·25
106	1d.+1d. blue and red	30·00	1·50
107	1½d.+1½d. brown and green	32·00	3·25
108	3d.+3d. blue	55·00	8·50

1938. Voortrekker Commem. Nos. 80/1 of South Africa optd **S.W.A.**

109	1d. blue and red	16·00	1·50
110	1½d. blue and brown	22·00	2·00

1939. 250th Anniv of Landing of Huguenots in South Africa. Nos. 82/4 of South Africa optd **S.W.A.**

111	½d.+½d. brown and green	14·00	1·25
112	1d.+1d. green and red	23·00	1·25
113	1½d.+1½d. green and purple	38·00	1·25

1941. War Effort. Nos. 88/94a of South Africa optd **SWA.**

114a	½d. green	1·50	15
115	1d. red	2·00	20
116	1½d. green	1·00	20
121	2d. violet	50	1·75
117	3d. blue	24·00	1·00
118	4d. brown	9·00	1·00
119	6d. orange	7·50	50
122	1s. brown	1·60	2·00
120	1s.3d. brown	13·00	1·25

1943. War Effort. Nos. 97/104 of South Africa optd **SWA.**

123	½d. green (T)	50	35
124a	1d. red (T)	3·50	30
125	1½d. brown (P)	50	15
126	2d. violet (P)	8·50	20
127	3d. blue (T)	3·25	1·00
129	4d. green (T)	2·00	75
128	6d. orange (P)	6·00	30
130b	1s. brown (P)	4·00	30

The units referred to above consist of pairs (P) or triplets (T).

1945. Victory. Nos. 108/10 of South Africa optd **SWA.**

131	1d. brown and red	25	10
132	2d. blue and violet	30	10
133	3d. blue	1·50	10

1947. Royal Visit. Nos. 111/13 of South Africa optd **SWA.**

134	1d. black and red	10	10
135	2d. violet	10	10
136	3d. blue	15	10

1948. Silver Wedding. No. 125 of South Africa optd **SWA.**

137	3d. blue and silver	1·00	10

1949. 75th Anniv of U.P.U. Nos 128/30 of South Africa optd **SWA.**

138	½d. green	75	25
139	1½d. red	75	15
140	3d. blue	1·25	25

1949. Inauguration of Voortrekker Monument Pretoria. Nos. 131/3 of South Africa optd **S W A.**

141	1d. mauve	10	10
142	1½d. green	10	10
143	3d. blue	15	60

1952. Tercentenary of Landing of Van Riebeeck. Nos. 136/40 of South Africa optd **SWA.**

144	½d. purple and sepia	10	50
145	1d. green	10	10
146	2d. violet	50	10
147	4½d. blue	30	2·25
148	1s. brown	75	20

33 Queen Elizabeth II and "Catophracties alexandri"

1953. Coronation. Native Flowers.

149	**33**	1d. red	40	10
150	-	2d. green ("Bauhinia macrantha")	40	10
151	-	4d. mauve ("Caralluma nebrownii")	50	30
152	-	6d. blue ("Gloriosa virescens")	50	70
153	-	1s. brown ("Rhigozum tricholotum")	65	20

34 "Two Bucks" (rock painting)

1954

154	**34**	1d. red	30	10
155	-	2d. brown	35	10
156	-	3d. purple	1·25	10
157	-	4d. black	1·50	10
158	-	4½d blue	70	40
159	-	6d. green	70	70
160	-	1s. mauve	70	50
161	-	1s.3d. red	2·00	1·25
162	-	1s.6d. purple	2·00	50
163	-	2s.6d. brown	4·50	70
164	-	5s. blue	6·00	2·75
165	-	10s. green	38·00	16·00

DESIGNS—VERT: 2d. "White Lady" (rock painting); 4½d. Karakul lamb; 6d. Ovambo woman blowing horn; 1s. Ovambo woman; 1s. 3d. Herero woman; 1s. 6d. Ovambo girl; 2s. 6d. Lioness; 5s. Gemsbok; 10s. African elephant. HORIZ: 3d. "Rhinoceros Hunt" (rock painting); 4d. "White Elephant and Giraffe" (rock painting).

46 G.P.O., Windhoek

1961

171	**46**	½c. brown and blue	60	10
172	-	1c. brown and lilac	15	10
173	-	1½c. violet and orange	20	10
174	-	2c. green and yellow	75	1·40
175	-	2½c. brown and blue	35	10
176	-	3c. blue and red	6·00	40
177	-	3½c. blue and green	1·00	15
209	-	4c. brown and blue	1·50	2·50
210	-	5c. red and blue	4·00	10
211	-	6c. sepia and yellow	10·00	11·00
179	-	7½c. brown and lemon	70	15
213	-	9c. blue and yellow	12·00	12·00
180	-	10c. blue and yellow	1·75	60
181	-	12½c. blue and yellow	60	40
182	-	15c. brown and blue	17·00	3·25
183	-	20c. brown and orange	4·00	30
184	-	50c. green and orange	4·50	1·50
185	-	1r. yellow, purple and blue	7·50	12·00

DESIGNS—VERT: 1c. Finger Rock; 1½c. Mounted Soldier Monument; 2c. Quivertree; 3c. Greater flamingoes and Swakopmund Lighthouse; 3½c. Fishing industry; 5c. Greater flamingo; 6c., 7½c. German Lutheran Church, Windhoek; 10c. Diamond; 20c. Topaz; 50c. Tourmaline; 1r. Heliodor. HORIZ: 2½c., 4c. S.W.A. House, Windhoek; 9c., 12½c. Fort Namutoni; 15c. Hardap Dam.

See also Nos. 224/26.

59 "Agricultural Development"

1963. Opening of Hardap Dam.

192	**59**	3c. brown and green	30	15

61 Centenary Emblem and part of Globe

1963. Centenary of Red Cross.

193	-	7½c. red, black and blue	4·50	5·00
194	**61**	15c. red, black and brown	6·50	8·00

DESIGN: 7½c. Centenary emblem and map.

62 Interior of Assembly Hall

1964. Opening of Legislative Assembly Hall, Windhoek.

195	**62**	3c. blue and orange	50	30

63 Calvin

1965. 400th Death Anniv of Calvin (Protestant reformer).

196	**63**	2½c. purple and gold	50	15
197	**63**	15c. green and gold	2·25	3·75

64 Mail Runner of 1890

1965. 75th Anniv of Windhoek.

198	**64**	3c. sepia and red	50	15
199	-	15c. brown and green	90	1·75

DESIGN: 15c. Kurt von Francois (founder).

66 Dr. H. Vedder

1966. 90th Birth Anniv of Dr. H. Vedder (philosopher and writer).

200	**66**	3c. green and orange	30	15
201	**66**	15c. brown and blue	70	40

67 Camelthorn Tree

1967. Verwoerd Commemoration.

217	**67**	2½c. black and green	15	10
218	-	3c. brown and blue	15	10
219	-	15c. brown and purple	55	45

DESIGNS—VERT: 3c. Waves breaking against rock; 15c. Dr. H. F. Verwoerd.

70 Pres. Swart

1968. Swart Commemoration. Inscr in German, Afrikaans or English.

220	**70**	3c. red, blue and black	35	20
221	-	15c. red, green and olive	1·50	1·75

DESIGN: 15c. Pres. and Mrs. Swart.

1970. Water 70 Campaign. As Nos. 299/300 of South Africa, but inscr "SWA".

222	2½c. green, blue and brown	50	30
223	3c. blue and buff	50	30

1970. As Nos. 171 etc, but with "POSGELD" "INKOMSTE" omitted and larger figure of value.

224	**46**	½c. brown and blue	1·00	30
225	-	1½c. violet and orange	16·00	20·00
226	-	2c. green and yellow	5·00	40

1970. 150th Anniv of Bible Society of South Africa. As Nos. 301/2 of South Africa. Inscr "SWA".

228	2½c. multicoloured	75	10
229	12½c. gold, black and blue	3·50	4·50

1971. "Interstex" Stamp Exhibition, Cape Town. As No. 303 of South Africa. Inscr "SWA".

230	5c. blue, black and yellow	3·25	1·50

1971. Tenth Anniv of Antarctic Treaty. As No. 304 of South Africa. Inscr "SWA".

231	12½c. black, blue and red	18·00	15·00

1971. Tenth Anniv of South African Republic. As Nos. 305/6 of South Africa. Inscr "SWA".

232	2c. flesh and red	3·25	75
233	4c. green and black	3·25	75

1972. Centenary of S.P.C.A. As No. 312 of South Africa. Inscr "SWA".

234	5c. multicoloured	3·00	1·25

73 "Red Sand-dunes, Eastern South-West Africa"

1973. Scenery. Paintings by Adolph Jentsch. Multicoloured.

235	2c. Type **73**	75	75
236	4c. "After the Rain"	85	1·00
237	5c. "Barren Country"	1·00	1·25
238	10c. "Schaap River" (vert)	1·25	1·75
239	15c. "Namib Desert" (vert)	2·25	3·25

74 "Sarcocaulon rigidum"

1973. Succulents. Multicoloured. (a) As T **74**.

241	1c. Type **74**	15	10
242a	2c. "Lapidaria margaretae"	20	10
243	3c. "Titanopsis schwantesii"	20	10
244	4c. "Lithops karasmontana"	25	10
245b	5c. "Caralluma lugardii"	50	20
246	6c. "Dinteranthus mircospermus"	2·50	3·50
247	7c. "Conophytum gratum"	1·50	2·75
248	9c. "Huernia oculata"	1·00	2·50
249b	10c. "Gasteria pillansii"	40	30
250	14c. "Stapelia pedunculata"	2·00	3·00
251	15c. "Fenestraria aurantiaca"	65	30
252	20c. "Decabelone grandiflora"	5·00	3·50
253	25c. "Hoodia bainii"	5·00	3·00

75 "Euphorbia virosa"

(b) As T **75**.

254	30c. Type **75**	75	1·00
255	1c. "Pachypodium namaquanum" (vert)	75	1·25
256	1r. "Welwitschia bainesii"	1·00	5·00

1973. As Nos. 241/2a and 245. Colours changed.

257	**18**	1c. black and mauve	70	75
258	-	2c. black and yellow	50	50
259a	-	5c. black and red	1·00	1·00

76 Chat-shrikes

1974. Rare Birds. Multicoloured.

260	4c. Type **76**	2·25	1·00
261	5c. Peach-faced lovebirds	2·75	1·50
262	10c. Damaraland rock jumper	5·00	5·50
263	15c. Ruppell's parrots	7·00	9·50

77 Giraffe, Antelope and Spoor

1974. Twyfelfontein Rock-engravings. Multicoloured.

264	4c. Type **77**	1·00	50
265	5c. Elephant, hyena, antelope and spoor	1·00	80
266	15c. Kudu cow (38 × 21 mm)	4·00	6·50

78 Cut Diamond

1974. Diamond Mining. Multicoloured.

267	10c. Type **78**	2·75	4·25
268	15c. Diagram of shore workings	2·75	4·25

79 Wagons and Map of the Trek

1974. Centenary of Thirstland Trek.

269	**79**	4c. multicoloured	75	1·00

80 Peregrine Falcon

1975. Protected Birds of Prey. Multicoloured.

270	4c. Type **80**	1·50	1·25
271	5c. Verreaux's eagle	1·50	1·75
272	10c. Martial eagle	2·50	4·00
273	15c. Egyptian vulture	3·50	6·00

81 Kolmannskop (ghost town)

1975. Historic Monuments. Multicoloured.

274	5c. Type **81**	15	15
275	9c. "Martin Luther" (steam tractor)	30	65
276	15c. Kurt von Francois and Old Fort, Windhoek	50	75

82 "View of Luderitz"

1975. Otto Schroder (painter). Multicoloured.

277	15c. Type **82**	30	60
278	15c. "View of Swakopmund"	30	60
279	15c. "Harbour Scene"	30	60
280	15c. "Quayside, Walvis Bay"	30	60
MS281	122×96 mm. Nos. 277/80	1·00	3·50

83 Elephants

1976. Prehistoric Rock Paintings. Multicoloured.

282	4c. Type **83**	30	15
283	10c. Rhinoceros	30	60
284	15c. Antelope	35	70
285	20c. Man with bow and arrow	40	1·00
MS286	121×95 mm. Nos. 282/5	1·25	3·50

84 Schwerinsburg

1976. Castles. Multicoloured.

287	10c. Type **84**	20	30
288	15c. Schloss Duwisib	30	50
289	20c. Heynitzburg	30	70

85 Large-toothed Rock Hyrax

1976. Fauna Conservation. Multicoloured.

290	4c. Type **85**	20	15
291	10c. Kirk's dik-dik	40	60
292	15c. Kuhl's tree squirrel	60	1·50

86 The Augustineum, Windhoek

1976. Modern Buildings.

293	**86**	15c. black and yellow	30	60
294	-	20c. black and yellow	40	80

DESIGN: 20c. Katutura Hospital, Windhoek.

87 Ovambo Water Canal System

1976. Water and Electricity Supply. Multicoloured.

295	15c. Type **87**	30	50
296	20c. Ruacana Falls Power Station	40	75

88 Coastline, near Pomona

1977. Namib Desert. Multicoloured.

297	4c. Type **88**	15	15
298	10c. Bush and dunes, Sossusvlei	20	20
299	15c. Plain near Brandberg	35	35
300	20c. Dunes, Sperr Gebiet	40	40

89 Kraal

1977. The Ovambo People.

301	**89**	4c. multicoloured	10	10
302	-	10c. black, orange & brown	20	15
303	-	15c. multicoloured	25	20
304	-	20c. multicoloured	25	35

DESIGNS: 10c. Grain baskets; 15c. Pounding grain; 20c. Women in tribal dress.

90 Terminal Buildings

1977. J. G. Strijdom Airport, Windhoek.

305	**90**	20c. multicoloured	40	30

91 Drostdy, Luderitz

1977. Historic Houses. Multicoloured.

306	5c. Type **91**	15	10
307	10c. Woermannhaus, Swakopmund	25	30
308	15c. Neu-Heusis, Windhoek	30	35
309	20c. Schmelenhaus, Bethanie	40	40
MS310	122×96 mm. Nos. 306/9	1·00	2·00

92 Side-winding Adder

1978. Small Animals. Multicoloured.

311	4c. Type **92**	15	10
312	10c. Grant's desert golden mole	25	20
313	15c. Palmato gecko	25	25
314	20c. Namaqua chameleon	25	25

93 Ostrich Hunting

1978. The Bushmen. Each brown, stone and black.

315	4c. Type **93**	25	10
316	10c. Woman carrying ostrich eggs	25	20
317	15c. Hunters kindling fire	30	20
318	20c. Woman with musical instrument	30	30

94 Lutheran Church, Windhoek

1978. Historic Churches.

319	**94**	4c. black and brown	10	10
320	-	10c. black and brown	15	20
321	-	15c. black and pink	20	25
322	-	20c. black and blue	30	35
MS323		125×90 mm. Nos. 319/22	75	1·75

DESIGNS: 10c. Lutheran Church, Swakopmund; 15c. Rhenish Mission Church, Otjimbingwe; 20c. Rhenish Missionary Church, Keetmanshoop.

1978. Universal Suffrage. Nos. 244/5, 249b and 251/3 optd **ALGEMENE STEMREG** (Afrikaans), **UNIVERSAL SUFFRAGE** (English) or **ALLGEMEINES WAHLRECHT** (German).

324	4c. "Lithops karasmontana"	10	10
325	5c. "Caralluma lugardii"	10	10
326	10c. "Gasteria pillansii"	10	10
327	15c. "Fenestraria aurantiaca"	10	15
328	20c. "Decabelone grandiflora"	10	15
329	25c. "Hoodia bainii"	15	15

Nos. 324/9 were issued in se-tenant strips of three, each stamp in the strip being optd in either Afrikaans, English or German. The same prices apply for any of the three languages.

96 Greater Flamingo

1979. Water Birds. Multicoloured.

330	4c. Type **96**	20	10
331	15c. White-breasted cormorant	35	25
332	20c. Chestnut-banded sand plover	35	35
333	25c. Eastern white pelican	35	40

97 Silver Topaz

1979. Gemstones. Multicoloured.

334	4c. Type **97**	30	10
335	15c. Aquamarine	65	35
336	20c. Malachite	70	45
337	25c. Amethyst	70	55

98 Killer Whale

1980. Whales. Multicoloured.

338	4c. Type **98**	20	15
339	5c. Humpback whale (38×22 mm)	20	20
340	10c. Black right whale (38×22 mm)	30	30
341	15c. Sperm whale (58×22 mm)	40	60
342	20c. Fin whale (58×22 mm)	45	70
343	25c. Blue whale (88×22 mm)	50	1·10
MS344	202×95 mm. Nos. 338/43	2·00	4·00

99 Impala

1980. 25th Anniv of Division of Nature Conservation and Tourism. Antelopes. Mult.

345	5c. Type **99**	15	10
346	10c. Topi	15	10
347	15c. Roan antelope	25	15
348	20c. Sable antelope	25	20

100 Black-backed Jackal

1980. Wildlife. Multicoloured.

349	1c. Type **100**	15	10
350	2c. Hunting dog	15	10
351	3c. Brown hyena	15	10
352	4c. Springbok	15	10
353	5c. Gemsbok	15	10
354	6c. Greater kudu	15	10
355	7c. Mountain zebra (horiz)	40	20
356	8c. Cape porcupine (horiz)	20	10
357	9c. Ratel (horiz)	20	10
358	10c. Cheetah (horiz)	30	10
358a	11c. Blue wildebeest	40	30
358b	12c. African buffalo (horiz)	70	1·75
358c	14c. Caracal (horiz)	3·50	2·25
359	15c. Hippopotamus (horiz)	30	10
359b	16c. Warthog (horiz)	2·25	1·75
360	20c. Eland (horiz)	30	10
361	25c. Black rhinoceros (horiz)	50	20
362	30c. Lion (horiz)	50	20
363	50c. Giraffe	50	30
364	1r. Leopard	50	55
365	2r. African elephant	50	90

101 Meerkat

1980. Wildlife.

366	**101**	1c. brown	20	20
367	-	2c. blue	20	20
368	-	5c. green	30	30

DESIGNS: 2c. Savanna monkey; 5c. Chacma baboon.

102 Von Bach

1980. Water Conservation. Dams. Multicoloured.

369	5c. Type **102**	10	10
370	10c. Swakoppoort	15	10
371	15c. Naute	15	20
372	20c. Hardap	15	25

103 View of Fish River Canyon

1981. Fish River Canyon.

373	-	5c. multicoloured	10	10
374	-	15c. multicoloured	15	20
375	-	20c. multicoloured	20	25
376	**103**	25c. multicoloured	20	30

DESIGNS: 5c. to 20c. Various views of Canyon.

104 "Aloe erinacea"

1981. Aloes. Multicoloured.

377	5c. Type **104**	15	10
378	15c. "Aloe viridiflora"	25	25
379	20c. "Aloe pearsonii"	35	25
380	25c. "Aloe littoralis"	35	30

105 Paul Weiss-Haus

1981. Historic Buildings of Luderitz.. Multicoloured.

381	5c. Type **105**	10	10
382	15c. Deutsche Afrika Bank	15	20
383	20c. Schroederhaus	20	30
384	25c. Altes Postamt	20	35
MS385	125×90 mm. Nos. 381/4	65	1·00

106 Salt Pan

1981. Salt Industry. Multicoloured.

386	5c. Type **106**	10	10
387	15c. Dumping and washing	20	20
388	20c. Loading by conveyor	25	30
389	25c. Dispatch to refinery	30	35

107 Kalahari Starred Tortoise ("Psammobates oculifer")

1982. Tortoises. Multicoloured.

390	5c. Type **107**	15	10
391	15c. Leopard tortoise ("Geochelone pardalis")	25	25
392	20c. Angulate tortoise ("Chersina angulata")	30	35
393	25c. Speckled padloper ("Homopus signatus")	40	45

108 Mythical Sea-monster

1982. Discoveries of South West Africa (1st series). Multicoloured.

394	15c. Type **108**	20	20
395	20c. Bartolomeu Dias and map of Africa showing voyage	40	30
396	25c. Dias' caravel	65	40
397	30c. Dias erecting commemorative cross, Angra das Voltas, 25 July 1488	70	1·10

See also Nos. 455/8.

109 Brandberg

1982. Mountains of South West Africa. Multicoloured.

398	6c. Type **109**	10	10
399	15c. Omatako	20	20
400	20c. Die Nadel	25	30
401	25c. Spitzkuppe	30	35

110 Otjikaeva Headdress of Herero Woman

1982. Traditional Headdresses of South West Africa (1st series). Multicoloured.

402	6c. Type **110**	10	10
403	15c. Ekori headdress of Himba	20	35
404	20c. Oshikoma hair-piece and iipanda plaits of Ngandjera	25	45
405	25c. Omhatela headdress of Kwanyama	25	60

See also Nos. 427/30.

111 Fort Vogelsang

1983. Centenary of Luderitz.

406	**111**	6c. black and red	10	10
407	-	20c. black and brown	15	20
408	-	25c. black and brown	20	25
409	-	30c. black and purple	20	30
410	-	40c. black and green	25	50

DESIGNS—VERT (23×29 mm): 20c. Chief Joseph Fredericks; 30c. Heinrich Vogelsang (founder); 40c. Adolf Luderitz (colonial promoter). HORIZ (as T **111**): 25c. Angra Pequena.

112 Searching for Diamonds, Kolmanskop, 1908

1983. 75th Anniv of Discovery of Diamonds.

411	**112**	10c. deep brown & brown	15	15
412	-	20c. red and brown	30	40
413	-	25c. blue and brown	35	45
414	-	40c. black and brown	55	85

DESIGNS—HORIZ (34×19 mm): 20c. Digging for diamonds, Kolmanskop, 1908. VERT (19×26 mm): 25c. Sir Ernest Oppenheimer (industrialist); 40c. August Stauch (prospector).

113 "Common Zebras drinking" (J. van Ellinckhuijzen)

1983. Painters of South West Africa. Multicoloured.

415	10c. Type **113**	15	15
416	20c. "Rossing Mountain" (H. Henckert)	20	30
417	25c. "Stampeding African Buffalo" (F. Krampe)	20	35
418	40c. "Erongo Mountains" (J. Blatt)	30	55

114 The Rock Lobster

1983. The Lobster Industry. Multicoloured.

419	10c. Type **114**	15	15
420	20c. Mother ship and fishing dinghies	20	30
421	25c. Netting lobsters from a dinghy	20	35
422	40c. Packing lobsters	30	55

115 Hohenzollern House

1984. Historic Buildings of Swakopmund.

423	**115**	10c. black and brown	15	15
424	-	20c. black and blue	20	25
425	-	25c. black and green	20	30
426	-	30c. black and brown	25	30

DESIGNS: 20c. Railway Station; 25c. Imperial District Bureau; 30c. Ritterburg.

1984. Traditional Headdresses of South West Africa (2nd series). As T **110**. Multicoloured.

427	11c. Eendjushi headdress of Kwambi	15	15
428	20c. Bushman woman	20	25
429	25c. Omulenda headdress of Kwaluudhi	20	35
430	30c. Mbukushu women	20	35

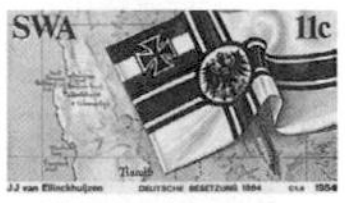

116 Map and German Flag

1984. Cent of German Colonization. Multicoloured.

431	11c. Type **116**	35	15
432	25c. Raising the German flag, 1884	65	50
433	30c. German Protectorate boundary marker	65	65
434	45c. "Elizabeth" and "Leipzig" (German corvettes)	1·40	2·00

117 Sweet Thorn

1984. Spring in South West Africa. Multicoloured.

435	11c. Type **117**	15	15
436	25c. Camel thorn	20	35
437	30c. Hook thorn	20	35
438	45c. Candle-pod acacia	25	50

118 Head of Ostrich

1985. Ostriches. Multicoloured.

439	11c. Type **118**	40	10
440	25c. Ostrich on eggs	60	30
441	30c. Newly-hatched chick and eggs	70	50
442	50c. Mating dance	90	75

119 Kaiserstrasse

1985. Historic Buildings of Windhoek.

443	119	12c. black and brown	15	10
444	-	25c. black and green	20	25
445	-	30c. black and brown	20	30
446	-	50c. black and brown	25	70

DESIGNS: 25c. Turnhalle; 30c. Old Supreme Court Building; 50c. Railway Station.

120 Zwilling Locomotive

1985. Narrow-gauge Railway Locomotives. Multicoloured.

447	12c. Type **120**	25	10
448	25c. Feldspur side-tank locomotive	45	25
449	30c. Jung and Henschel side-tank locomotive	40	35
450	50c. Henschel Hd locomotive	60	70

121 Lidumu-dumu (keyboard instrument)

1985. Traditional Musical Instruments. Multicoloured.

451	12c. Type **121**	10	10
452	25c. Ngoma (drum)	15	20
453	30c. Okambulumbumbwa (stringed instrument)	20	25
454	50c. //Gwashi (stringed instrument)	25	35

122 Erecting Commemorative Pillar at Cape Cross, 1486

1986. Discoverers of South West Africa (2nd series). Diogo Cao.

455	122	12c. black, grey and green	35	10
456	-	20c. black, grey and brown	55	35
457	-	25c. black, grey and blue	75	50
458	-	30c. black, grey and purple	80	85

DESIGNS: 20c. Diogo Cao's coat of arms; 25c. Caravel; 30c. Diogo Cao.

123 Ameib, Erongo Mountains

1986. Rock Formations. Multicoloured.

459	14c. Type **123**	35	15
460	20c. Vingerklip, near Outjo	40	25
461	25c. Petrified sand dunes, Kuiseb River	45	40
462	30c. Orgelpfeifen, Twyfelfontein	50	55

124 Model wearing Swakara Coat

1986. Karakul Industry. Multicoloured.

463	14c. Type **124**	15	15
464	20c. Weaving karakul wool carpet	25	30
465	25c. Flock of karakul ewes in veld	25	45
466	30c. Karakul rams	30	60

125 Pirogue, Lake Liambezi

1986. Life in the Caprivi Strip. Multicoloured.

467	14c. Type **125**	30	15
468	20c. Ploughing with oxen	50	80
469	25c. Settlement in Eastern Caprivi	60	1·25
470	30c. Map of Caprivi Strip	1·00	2·00

126 "Gobabis Mission Station", 1863

1987. Paintings by Thomas Baines. Multicoloured.

471	14c. Type **126**	30	15
472	20c. "Outspan at Koobie", 1861	55	80
473	25c. "Outspan under Oomahaama Tree", 1862	70	1·50
474	30c. "Swakop River", 1861	80	2·25

127 "Garreta nitens" (beetle)

1987. Useful Insects. Multicoloured.

475	16c. Type **127**	40	15
476	20c. "Alcimus stenurus" (fly)	60	80
477	25c. "Anthophora caerulea" (bee)	75	1·50
478	30c. "Hemiempusa capensis" (mantid)	1·10	2·00

128 Okaukuejo

1987. Tourist Camps. Multicoloured.

479	16c. Type **128**	25	15
480	20c. Daan Viljoen	40	55
481	25c. Al-Ais	45	1·25
482	30c. Hardap	50	1·40

129 Wreck of "Hope" (Dutch whaling schooner, 1804)

1987. Shipwrecks. Multicoloured.

483	16c. Type **129**	50	15
484	30c. "Tilly" (brig), 1885	75	80
485	40c. "Eduard Bohlen" (steamer), 1909	1·00	2·00
486	50c. "Dunedin Star" (liner), 1942	1·25	2·50

130 Bartolomeu Dias

1988. 500th Anniv of Discovery of Cape of Good Hope by Bartolomeu Dias. Multicoloured.

487	16c. Type **130**	35	15
488	30c. Caravel	70	55
489	40c. Map of South West Africa, c. 1502	80	70
490	50c. King Joao II of Portugal	80	75

131 Sossusvlei

1988. Landmarks of South West Africa. Multicoloured.

491	16c. Type **131**	30	15
492	30c. Sesriem Canyon	60	65
493	40c. Hoaruseb "clay castles"	70	1·25
494	50c. Hoba meteorite	80	1·50

132 First Postal Agency, Otyimbingue, 1888

1988. Centenary of Postal Service in South West Africa. Multicoloured.

495	16c. Type **132**	30	15
496	30c. Post Office, Windhoek, 1904	60	55
497	40c. Mail-runner and map	70	75
498	50c. Camel mail, 1904	80	1·00

133 Herero Chat

1988. Birds of South West Africa. Multicoloured.

499	16c. Type **133**	80	25
500	30c. Gray's lark	1·25	80
501	40c. Ruppell's bustard	1·40	1·25
502	50c. Monteiro's hornbill	1·40	1·40

134 Dr. C. H. Hahn and Gross-Barmen Mission

1989. Missionaries. Multicoloured.

503	16c. Type **134**	20	10
504	30c. Revd. J. G. Kronlein and Berseba Mission	35	60
505	40c. Revd. F. H. Kleinschmidt and Rehoboth Mission	40	70
506	50c. Revd. J. H. Schmelen and Bethanien Mission	40	85

135 Beech Commuter 1900

1989. 75th Anniv of Aviation in South West Africa. Multicoloured.

507	18c. Type **135**	55	20
508	30c. Ryan Navion	90	60
509	40c. Junkers F-13	1·00	65
510	50c. Pfalz Otto biplane	1·25	85

136 Barchan Dunes

1989. Namib Desert Sand Dunes. Multicoloured.

511	18c. Type **136**	20	15
512	30c. Star dunes (36×20 mm)	30	40
513	40c. Transverse dunes	35	60
514	50c. Crescentic dunes (36×20 mm)	40	80

137 Ballot Box and Outline Map of South West Africa

1989. South West Africa Constitutional Election.

515	137	18c. brown and orange	15	15
516	137	35c. blue and green	25	40
517	137	45c. purple and yellow	35	60
518	137	60c. green and ochre	45	80

138 Gypsum

139 Oranjemund Alluvial Diamond Field

1989. Minerals. Multicoloured.

519	1c. Type **138**	15	30
520	2c. Fluorite	20	30
521	5c. Mimetite	30	30
522	7c. Cuprite	45	45
523	10c. Azurite	50	20
524	18c. Boltwoodite	70	10
525	20c. Dioptase	75	15
526	25c. Type **139**	1·25	15
527	30c. Tsumeb lead and copper complex	1·00	20
528	35c. Rosh Pinah zinc mine	1·00	20
529	40c. Diamonds	1·25	30
530	45c. Wulfenite	1·00	30
531	50c. Uis tin mine	1·25	40
532	1r. Rossing uranium mine	1·75	1·00
533	2r. Gold	2·75	2·00

The 1, 2, 5, 7, 10, 18, 20, 40, 45c. and 2r. are vert as T **138**, and the remainder horiz as T **139**.

140 Arrow Poison

1990. Flora. Multicoloured.

534	18c. Type **140**	20	10
535	35c. Baobab flower	35	40
536	45c. Sausage tree flowers	40	50
537	60c. Devil's claw	45	1·25

OFFICIAL STAMPS

Prices are for pairs mint and for single stamps used.

1927. Pictorial and portrait (2d.) stamps alternately optd **OFFICIAL** South West Africa. or **OFFISIEEL** Suidwes Afrika.

O1	6	½d. black and green	£100	30·00
O2	7	1d. black and red	£110	30·00
O3	2	2d. purple	£275	45·00
O4	8	6d. green and orange	£140	30·00

1929. Pictorial stamps alternately optd **OFFICIAL S.W.A.** or **OFFISIEEL S.W.A.** horizontally or vertically.

O9	6	½d. black and green	75	2·75
O10	6	1d. black and red	1·00	2·75
O11	11	2d. grey and purple	1·00	3·25
O8	8	6d. green and orange	2·00	3·75

1931. Optd alternately **OFFICIAL** or **OFFISIEEL**.

O13	12	½d. black and green	10·00	3·75
O14	-	1d. blue and red (No. 75)	1·00	3·50
O25	27	1½d. brown	25·00	5·00
O15	-	2d. blue and brown (No. 76)	2·25	2·25
O16	-	6d. blue and brown (No. 79)	4·00	3·25

POSTAGE DUE STAMPS

Prices for Nos. D1/46 are for pairs mint and for single stamps used.

1923. Optd **South West Africa.** or **Zuid-West Afrika.** alternately. (i) On Postage Due stamps of Transvaal.

D1	D 1	5d. black and violet	4·00	11·00
D2	D 1	6d. black and brown	17·00	11·00

(ii) On Postage Due stamps of South Africa.

D6	D1	½d . black and green	6·00	5·50
D7	D1	1d. black and pink	7·00	6·00
D8	D1	1½d. black and brown	1·25	2·75
D9	D1	2d. black and violet	4·75	5·00
D12	D1	3d. black and blue	7·50	5·50
D5	D1	6d. black and grey	48·00	13·00

1923. Optd **South West Africa.*** or **Zuidwest Afrika.** (i) on Postage Due stamps of Transvaal.

D25	5d. black and violet	2·75	3·50
D14	6d. black and brown	21·00	20·00

(ii) On Postage Due stamps of South Africa.

D23	D20	½d. black and green	3·00	6·50
D28	D20	1d. black and pink	2·00	1·60
D29	D20	1½d. black and brown	4·50	7·50
D30	D20	2d. black and violet	2·50	3·50
D31	D20	3d. black and blue	4·50	3·75
D20	D1	6d. black and grey	2·25	9·00

*The English overprint is the same, for the purposes of this catalogue, as that on the previous set.

1927. Optd **South West Africa.*** or **Suidwes Afrika.** (a) On Postage Due stamps of Transvaal.

D33	5d. black and violet	24·00	23·00

(b) On Postage Due stamps of South Africa.

D34	D1	1½d. black and brown	1·00	3·50
D39	D 2	1d. black and red	1·00	2·25
D35	D1	2d. black and violet	4·75	3·25
D37	D1	3d. black and blue	16·00	11·00
D38	D1	6d. black and grey	14·00	8·50

*The English overprint is the same, for the purposes of this catalogue, as that on Nos. D33 and D34/8 of the previous sets.

1928. Postage Due stamps of South Africa optd **S.W.A.**
(a) On Nos. D4 and D16.

D40	**D 1**	3d. black and blue	1·50	17·00
D41	**D 1**	6d. black and grey	6·00	32·00

(b) On Nos. D 17 etc.

D42	**D 2**	½d. black and green	50	9·50
D43	**D 2**	1d. black and red	50	3·25
D44	**D 2**	2d. black and mauve	50	4·50
D45	**D 2**	3d. black and blue	2·25	26·00
D46	**D 2**	6d. black and grey	1·50	25·00

D3

1931. Size 19×23½ mm.

D47	**D3**	½d. black and green	1·00	7·50
D48	**D3**	1d. black and red	1·00	1·25
D49	**D3**	2d. black and violet	1·00	2·75
D50	**D3**	3d. black and blue	4·25	13·00
D51	**D3**	6d. black and slate	13·00	25·00

1959. As Type **D3** but smaller, 17½×21 mm.

D55	1d. black and red	1·50	3·00
D53	2d. black and violet	1·50	15·00
D56	3d. black and blue	1·50	3·75

1961. As Nos. D55, etc. but values in cents.

D57	1c. black and turquoise	70	3·75
D58	2c. black and red	70	3·75
D59	4c. black and violet	70	6·00
D60	5c. black and blue	1·00	4·25
D61	6c. black and green	1·25	6·50
D62	10c. black and yellow	4·00	9·00

1972. As Type **D8** of South Africa. Inscr "S.W.A.".

D63	1c. green	75	5·00
D64	8c. blue	3·00	8·50

For subsequent issues see **NAMIBIA**.

Pt. 1

SOUTHERN NIGERIA

A British possession on the west coast of Africa. In 1914 joined with Northern Nigeria to form Nigeria (q.v.).

12 pence = 1 shilling; 20 shillings = 1 pound.

1

1901

1	**1**	½d. black and green	1·75	3·00
2	**1**	1d. brown and red	2·00	2·50
3	**1**	2d. black and brown	3·25	6·00
4	**1**	4d. black and green	3·00	28·00
5	**1**	6d. black and purple	4·50	9·50
6	**1**	1s. green and black	8·50	28·00
7	**1**	2s.6d. black and brown	48·00	95·00
8	**1**	5s. black and yellow	65·00	£130
9	**1**	10s. black and purple on yellow	£150	£300

2

1903

21	**2**	½d. black and green	60	10
11	**2**	1d. black and red	1·25	70
23	**2**	2d. black and brown	2·75	45
24	**2**	2½d. black and blue	1·00	1·00
25	**2**	3d. brown and purple	9·50	1·25
14	**2**	4d. black and green	4·00	5·50
15	**2**	6d. black and purple	8·50	8·00
28	**2**	1s. green and black	3·25	3·50
29	**2**	2s.6d. black and brown	24·00	24·00
30	**2**	5s. black and yellow	55·00	90·00
19	**2**	10s. black & purple on yell	45·00	£150
32ab	**2**	£1 green and violet	£325	£400

1907

33b	**2**	½d. green	2·25	20
34ab	**2**	1d. red	1·00	10
35	**2**	2d. grey	2·75	70
36	**2**	2½d. blue	7·00	3·75
37	**2**	3d. purple on yellow	2·00	30
38	**2**	4d. black and red on yellow	2·25	80
39a	**2**	6d. purple	27·00	3·25
40	**2**	1s. black on green	7·00	40
41	**2**	2s.6d. black and red on blue	16·00	2·50
42	**2**	5s. green and red on yellow	40·00	48·00
43	**2**	10s. green and red on green	£100	£140
44	**2**	£1 purple and black on red	£250	£300

3

1912

45	**3**	½d. green	2·25	10
46	**3**	1d. red	2·25	10
47	**3**	2d. grey	75	85
48	**3**	2½d. blue	5·00	2·75
49	**3**	3d. purple on yellow	1·00	30
50	**3**	4d. black and red on yellow	1·25	2·00
51	**3**	6d. purple	3·00	1·25
52	**3**	1s. black on green	2·75	75
53	**3**	2s.6d. black and red on blue	8·00	50·00
54	**3**	5s. green and red on yellow	20·00	75·00
55	**3**	10s. green and red on green	48·00	95·00
56	**3**	£1 purple and black on red	£200	£275

Pt. 1

SOUTHERN RHODESIA

A Br. territory in the N. part of S. Africa, S. of the Zambesi. In 1954 became part of the Central African Federation which issued its own stamps inscribed "Rhodesia and Nyasaland" (q.v.), until 1964 when it resumed issuing after the break-up of the Federation. In October 1964, Southern Rhodesia was renamed Rhodesia.

12 pence = 1 shilling; 20 shillings = 1 pound.

1

1924

1	**1**	½d. green	4·25	60
2	**1**	1d. pink	3·25	10
3	**1**	1½d. brown	4·00	80
4	**1**	2d. black and grey	6·00	1·75
5	**1**	3d. blue	5·00	5·00
6	**1**	4d. black and red	5·00	2·75
7	**1**	6d. black and mauve	4·50	7·50
8	**1**	8d. purple and green	14·00	50·00
9	**1**	10d. blue and pink	19·00	55·00
10	**1**	1s. black and blue	8·00	11·00
11	**1**	1s.6d. black and yellow	22·00	40·00
12	**1**	2s. black and brown	17·00	19·00
13	**1**	2s.6d. black and brown	35·00	65·00
14	**1**	5s. blue and green	85·00	£170

2 King George V

3 Victoria Falls

1931

15a	**2**	½d. green	2·00	20
16b	**2**	1d. red	1·25	20
16d	**2**	1½d. brown	2·50	80
17	**3**	2d. black and brown	9·00	1·40
18	**3**	3d. blue	10·00	11·00
19	**2**	4d. black and red	1·50	1·50
20	**2**	6d. black and mauve	2·25	3·00
21	**2**	8d. violet and green	1·75	3·75
21b	**2**	9d. red and green	7·50	13·00
22	**2**	10d. blue and red	7·00	2·25
23	**2**	1s. black and blue	2·00	2·50
24	**2**	1s.6d. black and yellow	12·00	25·00
25	**2**	2s. black and brown	27·00	8·00
26a	**2**	2s.6d. blue and brown	30·00	48·00
27	**2**	5s. blue and green	50·00	50·00

4

1932

29	**4**	2d. green and brown	12·00	1·75
30	**4**	3d. blue	12·00	2·75

5 Victoria Falls

1935. Silver Jubilee.

31	**5**	1d. green and red	5·00	3·25
32	**5**	2d. green and brown	8·50	8·50
33	**5**	3d. violet and blue	6·50	11·00
34	**5**	6d. black and purple	11·00	23·00

1935. As Nos. 29/30, but inscr "POSTAGE AND REVENUE".

35a	**4**	2d. green and brown	3·00	10
35b	**4**	3d. blue	5·00	1·25

6 Victoria Falls and Railway Bridge

1937. Coronation.

36	**6**	1d. olive and red	60	1·25
37	**6**	2d. green and brown	60	1·75
38	**6**	3d. violet and blue	3·25	9·50
39	**6**	6d. black and purple	1·75	4·00

7 King George VI

1937

40	**7**	½d. green	50	10
41	**7**	1d. red	50	10
42	**7**	1½d. brown	1·00	30
43	**7**	4d. orange	1·50	10
44	**7**	6d. black	1·50	50
45	**7**	8d. green	2·00	4·25
46	**7**	9d. blue	1·50	1·00
47	**7**	10d. purple	3·00	3·50
48	**7**	1s. black and green	3·75	10
49	**7**	1s.6d. black and yellow	17·00	3·00
50	**7**	2s. black and brown	29·00	75
51	**7**	2s.6d. blue and purple	16·00	8·50
52	**7**	5s. blue and green	18·00	3·75

8 British South Africa Co's Arms

10 Cecil John Rhodes (after S. P. Kendrick)

1940. Golden Jubilee of British South Africa Company.

53	**8**	½d. violet and green	10	65
54	-	1d. blue and red	70	10
55	**10**	1½d. black and brown	15	80
56	-	2d. green and violet	30	70
57	-	3d. black and blue	1·00	1·50
58	-	4d. green and brown	2·50	3·75
59	-	6d. brown and green	2·50	4·00
60	-	1s. blue and green	3·75	3·25

DESIGNS—HORIZ: 1d. Fort Salisbury, 1890; 2d. Fort Victoria; 3d. Rhodes makes peace, 1896; 1s. Queen Victoria, King George VI, Lobengula's kraal and Govt. House, Salisbury. VERT: 4d. Victoria Falls Bridge; 6d. Statue of Sir Charles Coghlan.

16 Mounted Pioneer

1943. 50th Anniv of Occupation of Matabeleland.

61	**16**	2d. brown and green	25	2·00

17 Queen Elizabeth II when Princess, and Princess Margaret

1947. Royal Visit.

62	**17**	½d. black and green	30	60
63	-	1d. black and red	30	60

DESIGN: 1d. King George VI and Queen Elizabeth.

20 King George VI

1947. Victory.

64	-	1d. red	10	15
65	**20**	2d. slate	15	15
66	-	3d. blue	1·00	2·25
67	-	6d. orange	40	1·40

PORTRAITS: 1d. Queen Elizabeth; 3d. Queen Elizabeth II when Princess; 6d. Princess Margaret.

1949. 75th Anniv of U.P.U. As T **33d/g** of St. Helena.

68	2d. green	70	25
69	3d. blue	80	4·25

23 Queen Victoria, Arms and King George VI

1950. Diamond Jubilee of S. Rhodesia.

70	**23**	2d. green and brown	1·25	1·75

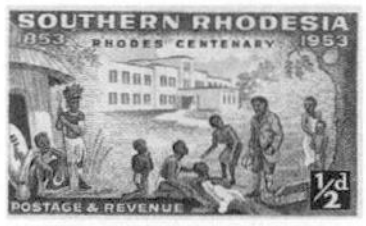
24 "Medical Services"

27 "Water Supplies"

1953. Birth Centenary of Cecil Rhodes. Inscr "RHODES CENTENARY".

71	**24**	½d. blue and sepia	15	2·50
72	-	1d. chestnut and green	75	10
73	-	2d. green and violet	20	10
74	**27**	4½d. green and blue	80	3·25
75	-	1s. black and brown	3·00	2·00

DESIGNS: 1d. "Agriculture"; 2d. "Building"; 4½d. "Water Supplies"; 1s. "Transport".

No. 74 also commemorates the Diamond Jubilee of Matabeleland.

1953. Rhodes Centenary Exhibition, Bulawayo. As No. 59 of Northern Rhodesia.

76	6d. violet	60	75

30 Queen Elizabeth II

1953. Coronation.

77	**30**	2s.6d. red	7·00	7·00

31 Sable Antelope

33 Rhodes's Grave

43 Balancing Rocks

1953

78	**31**	½d. grey and claret	30	50
79	-	1d. green and brown	30	10
80	**33**	2d. brown and violet	30	10
81	-	3d. brown and red	55	2·75
82	-	4d. red, green and blue	3·50	30
83	-	4½d. black and blue	2·50	4·25
84	-	6d. olive and turquoise	4·50	1·75
85	-	9d. blue and brown	4·50	4·25
86	-	1s. violet and blue	1·75	10
87	-	2s. purple and red	16·00	8·00
88	-	2s.6d. olive and brown	8·50	9·50
89	-	5s. brown and green	12·00	12·00
90	**43**	10s. brown and olive	21·00	30·00
91	-	£1 red and black	24·00	40·00

DESIGNS—VERT (as Type **31**): 1d Tobacco planter. (As Type **33**): 6d. Baobab tree; 5s. Basket maker. HORIZ (as Type **33**): 3d. Farm worker; 4d. Flame lily; 4½d. Victoria Falls; 9d. Lion; 1s. Zimbabwe ruins; 2s. Birchenough Bridge; 2s.6d. Kariba Gorge. (As Type **43**): £1 Coat of arms.

45 Maize

50 Flame Lily

56 Cattle

1964

92	**45**	½d. yellow, green and blue	20	2·75
93	-	1d. violet and ochre	15	10
94	-	2d. yellow and violet	60	10
95	-	3d. brown and blue	20	10
96	-	4d. orange and green	30	10
97	**50**	6d. red, yellow and green	40	10
98	-	9d. brown, yellow and green	2·75	1·50
99	-	1s. green and ochre	3·75	30
100	-	1s.3d. red, violet and green	3·00	10
101	-	2s. blue and ochre	2·50	3·50
102	-	2s.6d. blue and red	[illegible]	1·00
103	**56**	5s. multicoloured	3·50	2·75
104	-	10s. multicoloured	11·00	9·50
105	-	£1 multicoloured	9·00	22·00

DESIGNS—As Type **45**: 1d. African buffalo; 2d. Tobacco; 3d. Greater kudu; 4d. Citrus. As Type **50**: 9d. Ansellia orchid; 1s. Emeralds; 1s.3d. Aloe; 2s. Lake Kyle; 2s.6d. Tigerfish. As Type **56**: 10s. Helmeted guineafowl; £1 Coat of arms.

Similar designs inscribed "RHODESIA" are listed under that heading.

POSTAGE DUE STAMPS

1951. Postage due stamps of Great Britain optd **SOUTHERN RHODESIA.**

D1	**D 1**	½d. green	3·25	18·00
D2	**D 1**	1d. blue	3·00	2·00
D3	**D 1**	2d. black	2·50	1·75
D4	**D 1**	3d. violet	2·75	3·25
D5	**D 1**	4d. blue	1·75	4·00
D6	**D 1**	4d. green	£300	£700
D7	**D 1**	1s. blue	2·50	5·00

For later issues see **RHODESIA**.

Pt. 19

SOUTHERN YEMEN

Independent Republic comprising the areas formerly known as Aden, the Aden States and the South Arabian Federation.

From 30 November 1970 the country was renamed The People's Democratic Republic of Yemen.

1000 fils = 1 dinar.

PEOPLE'S REPUBLIC

1968. Stamps of South Arabian Federation optd **PEOPLE'S REPUBLIC OF SOUTHERN YEMEN** in English and Arabic.

1A	**2**	5f. blue	10	10
2A	**2**	10f. blue	10	10
3A	**2**	15f. green	20	10
4A	**2**	20f. green	20	20
5A	**2**	25f. brown	30	15
6B	**2**	30f. bistre	45	30
7A	**2**	35f. brown	55	45
8A	**2**	50f. red	65	55
9B	**2**	65f. green	75	65
10B	**2**	75f. red	1·10	75
11B	**3**	100f. multicoloured	1·60	1·30
12B	**3**	250f. multicoloured	3·25	2·75
13B	**3**	500f. multicoloured	6·00	5·25
14B	**3**	1d. multicoloured	14·00	12·00

3 National Flag across Globe

1968. Independence. Multicoloured.

15		10f. Type **3**	20	20
16		15f. Revolutionary (vert)	20	20
17		50f. Aden harbour	75	75
18		100f. Cotton-picking	2·10	2·10

4 Girl Guides

1968. Aden Girl Guides' Movement.

19	-	10f. brown and blue	75	75
20	-	25f. blue and brown	1·10	1·10
21	**4**	50f. multicoloured	2·00	2·00

DESIGNS—HORIZ: 10f. Guides around camp-fire. VERT: 25f. Brownies.

5 Revolutionary Soldier

1968. Revolution Day.

22	**5**	20f. brown and blue	30	30
23	-	30f. brown and green	65	65
24	-	100f. red and yellow	1·80	1·80

DESIGNS—HORIZ: 30f. Radfan Mountains ("where first martyr fell"). VERT: 100f. Open book and torch ("Freedom, Socialism and Unity").

6 Sculptured Plaque ("Assyrian influence")

1968. Antiquities.

25		5f. yellow and green	10	10
26		35f. blue and purple	65	65
27	**6**	50f. buff and blue	1·50	1·20
28	-	65f. green and purple	1·80	1·50

DESIGNS—VERT: 5f. King Yusdqil Far'am of Ausan (statue); 35f. Sculptured figure ("African-inspired"). HORIZ: 65f. Bull's head ("Moon God").

7 Martyrs' Monument, Aden

1969. Martyrs' Day.

29	**7**	15f. multicoloured	20	20
30	**7**	35f. multicoloured	65	65
31	**7**	100f. multicoloured	1·90	1·90

8 Albert Thomas Memorial, Geneva

1969. 50th Anniv of I.L.O.

32	**8**	10f. brown, black and green	20	20
33	**8**	25f. brown, black and mauve	85	65

9 Teacher and Class

1969. International Literacy Day.

34	**9**	35f. multicoloured	85	65
35	**9**	100f. multicoloured	2·10	1·90

10 Mahatma Gandhi

1969. Birth Centenary of Mahatma Gandhi.

36	**10**	35f. purple and blue	2·50	1·30

11 Yemeni Family

1969. Family Day.

37	**11**	25f. multicoloured	85	65
38	**11**	75f. multicoloured	2·10	1·60

12 U.N. Headquarters, New York

1969. United Nations Day.

39	**12**	20f. multicoloured	75	55
40	**12**	65f. multicoloured	2·00	1·30

13 Map and Flag

1969. Second Anniv of Independence. Multicoloured.

41		15f. Type **13**	30	30
42		35f. Type **13**	65	55
43		40f. Bulldozers (37×37 mm)	75	65
44		50f. As No. 43	1·30	85

14 Arab League Flag, Emblem and Map

1970. 25th Anniv of Arab League.

45	**14**	35f. multicoloured	1·10	65

15 Lenin

1970. Birth Centenary of Lenin.

46	**15**	75f. multicoloured	2·10	1·50

16 Palestinian Guerrilla

1970. Palestine Day. Multicoloured.

47		15f. Type **16**	20	20
48		35f. Guerrilla and attack on airliner	75	65
49		50f. Guerrillas and Palestinan flag (horiz)	1·50	1·10

17 New Headquarters Building, Berne

1970. Inauguration of New U.P.U. Headquarters Building, Berne.

50	**17**	15f. green and orange	1·10	30
51	**17**	65f. red and buff	1·80	1·10

18 Girl with Pitcher

1970. National Costumes. Multicoloured.

52		10f. Type **18**	55	20
53		15f. Woman in veil	65	55
54		20f. Girl in burnous	85	65
55		50f. Three Yemeni men	2·40	85

19 Dromedary and Calf

1970. Fauna. Multicoloured.

56		15f. Type **19**	55	30
57		25f. Goats	85	55
58		35f. Arabian oryx and kid	1·70	1·10
59		65f. Socotran dwarf cows	2·75	1·80

20 Torch and Flags

1970. Seventh Revolution Day. Multicoloured.

60		25f. Type **20**	65	30
61		35f. National Front Headquarters (57×27 mm)	1·10	85
62		50f. Farmer and soldier (42×25 mm)	3·00	2·10

21 U.N. H.Q., New York, and Emblem

1970. 25th Anniv of United Nations.

63	**21**	10f. orange and blue	75	20
64	**21**	65f. mauve and blue	2·40	1·50

For later issues see **YEMEN PEOPLE'S DEMOCRATIC REPUBLIC**.

Pt. 9

SPAIN

A kingdom in south-west Europe; a republic between 1873 and 1874, and from 1931 until 1939.

1850. 8½ (later 8) cuartos = 1 real.
1866. 80 cuartos = 100 centimos de escudo = 1 escudo.
1867. 1000 milesimas = 100 centimos de escudo = 80 cuartos = 1 escudo.
1872. 100 centimos = 1 peseta.
2002. 100 cents = 1 euro.

1 Queen Isabella II

2 Queen Isabella II

1850. Imperf.

2	**1**	6c. black	£475	18·00
3	**2**	12c. lilac	£2750	£325
4	**2**	5r. red	£2750	£325
5	**2**	6r. blue	£3750	£900
6	**2**	10r. green	£5000	£2500

3 Queen Isabella II

1851. Imperf.

9	**3**	6c. black	£300	3·50
10	**3**	12c. lilac	£4750	£200
11	**3**	2r. red	£22000	£13000
12	**3**	5r. pink	£2750	£300
13	**3**	6r. blue	£4250	£1200
14	**3**	10r. green	£3250	£550

4

1852. Imperf.

16	**4**	6c. pink	£425	3·00
17	**4**	12c. purple	£2250	£160
18	**4**	2r. red	£18000	£6000
19	**4**	5r. green	£2500	£140
20	**4**	6r. blue	£3750	£550

5

1853. Imperf.

22	**5**	6c. red	£550	2·75
23	**5**	12c. purple	£2250	£130
24	**5**	2r. red	£13000	£2250
25	**5**	5r. green	£2500	£130
26	**5**	6r. blue	£3500	£475

7 Arms of Castile and Leon

1854. Imperf.

32	**7**	2c. green	£2250	£550
33	**7**	4c. red	£450	2·50
34	**7**	6c. red	£375	1·80
35	**7**	1r. blue	£3750	£375
36	**7**	2r. red	£1700	£120
37	**7**	5r. green	£1700	£110
38	**7**	6r. blue	£2750	£350

9

1855. Imperf.

54	**9**	2c. green	£600	45·00
55a	**9**	4c. red	4·75	45
61	**9**	1r. blue	20·00	25·00
57	**9**	2r. purple	75·00	27·00

12

1860. Imperf.

63	**12**	2c. green on green	£375	22·00
64	**12**	4c. orange on green	44·00	80
65	**12**	12c. red on buff	£375	14·00
66	**12**	19c. brown on brown	£3000	£1600
67	**12**	1r. blue on green	£350	12·50
68	**12**	2r. lilac on lilac	£400	12·50

13

1862. Imperf.

69a	**13**	2c. blue on yellow	35·00	9·50
70	**13**	4c. brown on brown	5·75	65
70b	**13**	4c. brown on white	19·00	4·75
71	**13**	12c. blue on pink	49·00	9·25
72	**13**	19c. red on lilac	£200	£275
72a	**13**	19c. red on white	£275	£190
73a	**13**	1r. brown on yellow	75·00	25·00
74	**13**	2r. green on pink	41·00	14·00

14

1864. Imperf.

75	**14**	2c. blue on lilac	60·00	21·00
75b	**14**	2c. blue on white	60·00	28·00
76b	**14**	4c. red on red	2·50	1·00
76c	**14**	4c. pink on white	19·00	9·50
77a	**14**	12c. green on pink	42·00	12·00
78	**14**	19c. lilac on lilac	£225	£225
79	**14**	1r. brown on green	£200	95·00
80	**14**	2r. blue on pink	49·00	15·00
80b	**14**	2r. blue on white	65·00	24·00

15

1865. Imperf.

81a	**15**	2c. red	£375	41·00
82	**15**	12c. pink and blue	£450	22·00
83	**15**	19c. pink and brown	£1600	£850
84	**15**	1r. green	£450	75·00
85	**15**	2r. mauve	£450	37·00
85c	**15**	2r. red	£500	60·00
85e	**15**	2r. yellow	£500	75·00

1865. Perf.

86	2c. red	£500	£140
87	4c. blue	40·00	95
88	12c. pink and blue	£650	65·00
89	19c. pink and brown	£4000	£2750
90	1r. green	£1900	£550
91	2r. lilac	£1300	£275
91b	2r. orange	£1500	£350

16

1866. Perf.

92	**16**	2c. pink	£300	34·00
93a	**16**	4c. blue	37·00	65
94a	**16**	12c. orange	£275	13·50
95	**16**	19c. brown	£1200	£475
96	**16**	10c. de e. green	£325	30·00
97	**16**	20c. de e. lilac	£225	22·00

1866. As T **14**, but dated "1866", and perf.

98	20c. de e. lilac	£1200	80·00

19

1867. Inscr "CORREOS DE ESPANA". Various frames.

99a	**19**	2c. brown	£425	42·00
100	**19**	4c. blue	26·00	1·10
101a	**19**	12c. orange	£225	8·25
102	**19**	19c. pink	£1500	£450
150	**19**	19c. brown	£2500	£600
103	**19**	10c. de e. green	£275	25·00
104	**19**	20c. de e. lilac	£130	11·00

25

26

1867. Various frames.

105	**25**	5m. green	48·00	19·00
106	**25**	10m. brown	48·00	19·00
107	**26**	25m. pink and blue	£275	27·00
145	**26**	25m. blue	£300	17·00
108	**26**	50m. brown	22·00	80
146a	**19**	50m. purple	25·00	1·00
147	**19**	100m. brown	£600	80·00
148	**19**	200m. green	£200	13·50

1868. Various stamps optd **HABILITADO POR LA NACION**.

109	**25**	5m. green	19·00	5·75
110	**25**	10m. brown	14·00	4·75
111	**26**	25m. pink and blue	38·00	14·00
151	**26**	25m. blue	38·00	11·50
112	**26**	50m. brown	7·50	4·75
152	**19**	50m. purple	7·50	3·75
153	**19**	100m. brown	75·00	28·00
154	**19**	200m. green	26·00	9·50
115	**19**	12c. orange	38·00	9·50
116	**19**	19c. pink	£375	£140
156	**19**	19c. brown	£750	£190
113	**19**	10c. de e. green	28·00	14·00
114	**19**	20c. de e. lilac	24·00	9·50

36

1870

172	**36**	1m. brown on buff	8·50	8·25
173	**36**	2m. black on buff	11·00	10·00
174	**36**	4m. brown	22·00	17·00
175	**36**	10m. red	23·00	8·00
176a	**36**	25m. mauve	85·00	9·75
177a	**36**	50m. blue	13·50	45
178b	**36**	100m. brown	40·00	8·00
179	**36**	200m. brown	45·00	8·75
180	**36**	400m. green	£350	33·00
181	**36**	12c. red	£275	8·50
182	**36**	19c. green	£450	£275
183a	**36**	1e.60m. lilac	£1800	£1200
184	**36**	2e. blue	£1800	£750

38a

38

1872. Imperf.

185	**38a**	¼c. blue	2·50	2·50
186	**38**	¼c. green	2·10	1·60
187	**38a**	¼c. green	25	15

1872. As T **25**, but currency in centavos de peseta and bottom panel inscr "COMUNICS".

192	**25**	2c. lilac	26·00	19·00
193	**25**	5c. green	£190	90·00

40 King Amadeo

41

1872

194	**40**	5c. pink	26·00	8·25
195b	**40**	6c. blue	£180	70·00
196	**40**	10c. lilac	£375	£325
197	**40**	10c. blue	7·25	45
199	**40**	12c. lilac	17·00	2·20
200	**40**	20c. lilac	£160	85·00
201	**40**	25c. brown	60·00	10·00
202	**40**	40c. brown	85·00	11·00
203	**40**	50c. green	£110	10·00
204	**41**	1p. lilac	£110	55·00
205	**41**	4p. brown	£650	£600
206	**41**	10p. green	£2500	£2500

42 Allegorical Figure of Peace

1873

207	**42**	2c. orange	14·00	5·75
208	**42**	5c. pink	43·00	8·00
209	**42**	10c. green	9·00	45
210	**42**	20c. black	£120	38·00
211	**42**	25c. brown	42·00	8·00
212	**42**	40c. purple	45·00	8·00
213	**42**	50c. blue	17·00	8·00
214a	**42**	1p. lilac	60·00	42·00
215	**42**	4p. brown	£750	£600
216	**42**	10p. purple	£2500	£2500

43 Allegorical Figure of Justice

1874

217	**43**	2c. yellow	27·00	11·50
218a	**43**	5c. mauve	42·00	9·00
219	**43**	10c. blue	17·00	45
220	**43**	20c. green	£200	60·00
221	**43**	25c. brown	42·00	9·00
222a	**43**	40c. mauve	£475	11·00
223	**43**	50c. orange	£150	11·00
224	**43**	1p. green	£110	55·00
225	**43**	4p. red	£850	£600
226	**43**	10p. black	£3500	£2500

44

1874

227	**44**	10c. brown	27·00	85

45 King Alfonso XII

1875

228	**45**	2c. brown	22·00	11·00
229	**45**	5c. lilac	80·00	13·00
230	**45**	10c. blue	9·00	45
231	**45**	20c. brown	£325	£160
232	**45**	25c. pink	70·00	8·25
233	**45**	40c. brown	£130	43·00
234	**45**	50c. mauve	£200	38·00
235	**45**	1p. black	£225	95·00
236	**45**	4p. green	£550	£550
237	**45**	10p. blue	£1800	£1900

46 King Alfonso XII

1876

238	**46**	5c. brown	13·50	3·75
239	**46**	10c. blue	3·75	45
240	**46**	20c. green	23·00	17·00
241	**46**	25c. brown	8·75	5·50
242	**46**	40c. brown	90·00	£100
250	**46**	50c. green	15·50	8·75
244	**46**	1p. blue	23·00	10·50
245	**46**	4p. purple	65·00	75·00
246	**46**	10p. red	£150	£160

48

1878

253	**48**	2c. mauve	42·00	13·00
254a	**48**	5c. yellow	60·00	15·00
255	**48**	10c. brown	8·50	50
256	**48**	20c. black	£200	£150
257	**48**	25c. green	25·00	2·75
258	**48**	40c. brown	£190	£170
259	**48**	50c. green	£110	11·00
260	**48**	1p. grey	85·00	22·00
261	**48**	4p. violet	£250	£150
262a	**48**	10p. blue	£375	£375

49

1879

263	**49**	2c. black	9·25	4·25
264	**49**	5c. green	13·50	1·10
265	**49**	10c. pink	12·50	45
266	**49**	20c. brown	£130	17·00
267	**49**	25c. grey	17·00	45
268	**49**	40c. brown	31·00	5·50
269b	**49**	50c. yellow	£100	4·50
270	**49**	1p. red	£150	2·20
271	**49**	4p. grey	£800	42·00
272	**49**	10p. bistre	£2000	£275

50 King Alfonso XII

1882

273	**50**	15c. pink	10·50	20
273b	**50**	15c. yellow	65·00	1·50
274	**50**	30c. mauve	£375	6·00
275	**50**	75c. lilac	£325	6·00

51 King Alfonso XIII

1889

276	**51**	2c. green	5·50	45
289	**51**	2c. black	33·00	6·50
277	**51**	5c. blue	9·25	20
290	**51**	5c. green	£110	1·20
278	**51**	10c. brown	16·00	20
291	**51**	10c. red	£325	4·00
279	**51**	15c. brown	4·00	20
280	**51**	20c. green	42·00	4·00
281	**51**	25c. blue	16·00	20
282	**51**	30c. grey	65·00	3·75
283	**51**	40c. brown	65·00	2·50
284	**51**	50c. red	65·00	1·50
285	**51**	75c. orange	£225	4·00
286	**51**	1p. purple	49·00	40
287	**51**	4p. red	£700	46·00
288	**51**	10p. red	£1100	£120

For 15c. yellow see No. O289.

52

1900

292a	**52**	2c. brown	3·75	30
293b	**52**	5c. green	6·50	30
294	**52**	10c. red	10·50	25
295	**52**	15c. black	19·00	25
296	**52**	15c. mauve	12·50	25
297	**52**	15c. violet	7·00	25
298	**52**	20c. black	43·00	2·50
299	**52**	25c. blue	6·50	25
300	**52**	30c. green	43·00	50
301	**52**	40c. bistre	£150	4·75
302	**52**	40c. pink	£325	5·00
303	**52**	50c. blue	43·00	60
304	**52**	1p. purple	39·00	60
305	**52**	4p. purple	£325	22·00
306	**52**	10p. orange	£300	85·00

54 Quixote setting out

1905. Tercentenary of Publication of Cervantes' "Don Quixote".

307	**54**	5c. green	1·30	1·20
308	-	10c. red	3·00	2·00
309	-	15c. violet	3·00	2·00
310	-	25c. blue	10·00	3·75
311	-	30c. green	50·00	10·50
312	-	40c. red	£110	36·00
313	-	50c. grey	24·00	8·00
314	-	1p. red	£350	£100
315	-	4p. purple	£180	£100
316	-	10p. orange	£225	£190

DESIGNS: 10c. Quixote attacking windmill; 15c. Meeting country girls; 25c. Sancho Panza tossed in a blanket; 30c. Don Quixote knighted by innkeeper; 40c. Tilting at the flock of sheep; 50c. On the wooden horse; 1p. Adventure with lions; 4p. In the bullock-cart; 10p. The enchanted lady.

64

1909

344	**64**	2c. brown	65	65
330	**64**	5c. green	2·00	20
331	**64**	10c. red	2·50	20
332	**64**	15c. violet	12·50	20
343	**64**	15c. yellow	6·00	20
334	**64**	20c. green	65·00	75
335	**64**	20c. violet	49·00	20
336	**64**	25c. blue	4·75	20
337	**64**	30c. green	12·50	20
338	**64**	40c. pink	18·00	95
339a	**64**	50c. blue	17·00	45
340	**64**	1p. red	41·00	35
341	**64**	4p. purple	£110	13·50
342	**64**	10p. orange	£140	25·00

1920. Air. Optd **CORREO AEREO**.

353	5c. green	1·70	1·10
354	10c. red	2·75	1·60
355	25c. blue	4·25	3·00
356	50c. blue	18·00	9·00
357	1p. red	65·00	37·00

66

1920. Imperf.

358	**66**	1c. green	40	15

67 G.P.O., Madrid

1920. U.P.U. Congress, Madrid.

361	**67**	1c. black and green	60	25
362	**67**	2c. black and brown	60	20
363	**67**	5c. black and green	2·30	1·20
364	**67**	10c. black and red	2·30	1·10
365	**67**	15c. black and yellow	3·25	1·70
366	**67**	20c. black and violet	5·00	1·80
367	**67**	25c. black and blue	5·50	3·50
368	**67**	30c. black and green	18·00	6·75
369	**67**	40c. black and red	65·00	9·50
370	**67**	50c. black and blue	80·00	26·00
371	**67**	1p. black and pink	80·00	21·00
372	**67**	4p. black and brown	£225	£110
373	**67**	10p. black and orange	£500	£225

68

69

1922

374	**68**	2c. green	1·30	15
375	**68**	5c. purple	7·75	15
376	**68**	5c. red	3·50	15
377	**68**	10c. red	3·25	1·20
378a	**68**	10c. green	8·00	10
380	**68**	15c. blue	13·50	15
382	**68**	20c. violet	7·75	15
383a	**68**	25c. red	9·50	10
387	**68**	30c. brown	27·00	20
388	**68**	40c. blue	8·25	20
389	**68**	50c. orange	35·00	20
391	**69**	1p. grey	44·00	15
392	**69**	4p. red	£170	5·00
393	**69**	10p. brown	75·00	18·00

70 Princesses Maria Cristina and Beatriz

71 King Alfonso XIII

1926. Red Cross.

394	**70**	1c. black	3·25	2·40
395	-	2c. blue	3·25	2·40
396	-	5c. purple	8·00	5·25
397	-	10c. green	6·50	4·75
398	**70**	15c. blue	2·50	2·00
399	-	20c. violet	3·50	2·75
400	**71**	25c. red	1·10	50
401	**70**	30c. green	70·00	48·00
402	-	40c. blue	43·00	29·00
403	-	50c. red	42·00	28·00
404	-	1p. grey	2·50	1·70
405	-	4p. red	3·50	2·75
406	**71**	10p. brown	3·50	2·75

DESIGNS—VERT: 2, 50c. Queen Victoria Eugenie as nurse; 5, 40c., 4p. Queen Victoria Eugenie; 10, 20c., 1p. Prince of the Asturias.

75 CASA-built Dornier Do-J Wal Flying Boat M-MWAL "Plus Ultra"

76 Route Map and Gallarza and Loriga's Breguet 19A2 Biplane

1926. Air. Red Cross and Trans-Atlantic and Madrid-Manila Flights.

407	**75**	5c. violet and black	4·00	2·20
408	**75**	10c. black and blue	5·00	2·50
409	**76**	15c. blue and red	70	45
410	**76**	20c. red and green	70	45
411	**75**	25c. black and red	70	45
412	**76**	30c. brown and blue	70	45
413	**76**	40c. green and brown	70	45
414	**75**	50c. black and red	70	45
415	**75**	1p. green and black	4·75	3·25
416	**76**	4p. red and yellow	£170	£120

1927. 25th Anniv of Coronation. Red Cross stamps of 1926 variously optd or surch **17-V 1902 17-V 1927 A XIII** or **17-V-1902 17-V-1927 ALFONSO XIII** or **17 MAYO 17 1902 1927 ALFONSO XIII** with ornaments. (a) Postage stamps of Spain optd only.

417	**70**	1c. black	8·75	6·50
418	-	2c. blue	16·00	13·00
419	-	5c. purple	4·75	3·50
420	-	10c. green	£110	80·00
421	**70**	15c. blue	3·00	2·50
422	-	20c. violet	5·50	4·25
423	**71**	25c. red	95	80
424	**70**	30c. green	1·50	1·20
425	-	40c. blue	1·40	1·10
426	-	50c. red	1·40	1·10
427	-	1p. grey	3·25	2·20
428	-	4p. red	17·00	13·00
429	**71**	10p. brown	65·00	50·00

(b) Postage stamps of Spain also surch with new value.

430	-	3c. on 2c. blue	16·00	13·00
431	-	4c. on 2c. blue	15·00	12·00
432	**71**	10c. on 25c. red	80	55
433	**71**	25c. on 25c. red	80	55
434	-	55c. on 2c. blue	1·30	1·20
435	-	55c. on 10c. green	85·00	65·00
436	-	55c. on 20c. violet	85·00	65·00
437	**70**	75c. on 15c. blue	1·20	[illegible]
438	**70**	75c. on 30c. green	£300	£225
439	-	80c. on 5c. purple	80·00	60·00
440	-	2p. on 40c. blue	1·50	1·10
441	-	2p. on 1p. grey	1·50	1·10
442	-	5p. on 50c. red	3·25	2·10
443	-	5p. on 4p. red	5·00	3·25
444	**71**	10p. on 10p. brown	36·00	25·00

(c) Air stamps of Spain optd only.

445	**75**	5c. violet and black	3·50	1·90
446	**75**	10c. black and blue	7·75	3·75
447	**76**	15c. blue and red	70	45
448	**76**	20c. red and green	70	45
449	**75**	25c. black and red	70	45
450	**76**	30c. brown and blue	70	45
451	**76**	40c. green and brown	70	45
452	**75**	50c. black and red	70	45
453	**75**	1p. green and black	4·75	4·25
454	**76**	4p. red and yellow	£200	£140

(d) Air stamps of Spain also surch with new value.

455	**75**	75c. on 5c. violet and black	8·50	6·75
456	**75**	75c. on 10c. black and blue	46·00	29·00
457	**75**	75c. on 25c. black and red	85·00	60·00
458	**75**	75c. on 50c. black and red	33·00	25·00

(e) Nos. 24/5 of Spanish Post Offices in Tangier.

460	1p. on 10p. violet	£200	£200
461	4p. bistre	80·00	80·00

(f) Nos. 122/3 of Spanish Morocco.

462	55c. on 4p. bistre	40·00	40·00
463	80c. on 10p. violet	40·00	40·00

(g) Nos. 34 and 35 of Cape Juby.

464	5p. on 4p. bistre	£100	£100
465	10p. on 10p. violet	80·00	80·00

(h) Nos. 231/2 of Spanish Guinea.

466	1p. on 10p. violet	40·00	40·00
467	2p. on 4p. bistre	40·00	40·00

(i) Nos. 23/4 of Spanish Sahara.

468	80c. on 10p. violet	6·00	60·00
469	2p. on 4p. bistre	40·00	40·00

82 Pope Pius XI and King Alfonso XIII

1928. Rome Catacombs Restoration Fund.

470	**82**	2c. black and violet	55	30
471	**82**	2c. black and purple	60	50
486	**82**	2c. red and black	55	30
487	**82**	2c. red and blue	60	50
472	**82**	3c. violet and black	55	30
473	**82**	3c. violet and blue	60	50
488	**82**	3c. blue and bistre	55	30
489	**82**	3c. blue and green	60	50
474	**82**	5c. violet and green	1·10	80
490	**82**	5c. red and purple	1·10	80
475	**82**	10c. black and green	1·80	1·50
491	**82**	10c. blue and green	1·80	1·50
476	**82**	15c. violet and green	8·00	5·75
492	**82**	15c. red and blue	8·00	5·75
477	**82**	25c. violet and red	8·00	5·75
493	**82**	25c. blue and brown	8·00	5·75
478	**82**	40c. black and blue	55	30
494	**82**	40c. red and blue	55	30
479	**82**	55c. violet and brown	55	30
495	**82**	55c. blue and brown	55	30
480	**82**	80c. black and red	55	30
496	**82**	80c. red and black	55	30
481	**82**	1p. violet and grey	55	30
497	**82**	1p. red and yellow	55	30
482	**82**	2p. black and brown	9·50	7·25
498	**82**	2p. blue and grey	9·50	7·25
483	**82**	3p. violet and pink	9·50	7·25
499	**82**	3p. red and violet	9·50	7·25
484	**82**	4p. black and purple	9·50	7·25
500	**82**	4p. red and purple	9·50	7·25
485	**82**	5p. violet and black	9·50	7·25
501	**82**	5p. blue and yellow	9·50	7·25

83 A Spanish Caravel, Seville in background

84 Miniature of Exhibition Poster

1929. Seville and Barcelona Exhibitions. Inscr "EXPOSICION GENERAL (or GRAL.) ESPANOLA".

502	**83**	1c. green	2·50	2·10
503	**84**	2c. green	40	25
504	-	5c. red	65	45
505	-	10c. green	70	45
506	**83**	15c. blue	2·30	2·10
507	**84**	20c. violet	80	55
508	**83**	25c. red	80	45
509	-	30c. brown	7·50	5·00
510	-	40c. blue	12·50	9·25
511	**84**	50c. orange	7·50	5·00
512	-	1p. grey	17·00	10·00
513	-	4p. purple	46·00	37·00
514	-	10p. brown	£110	80·00

DESIGNS—VERT: 5, 30c., 1p. View of exhibition. HORIZ: 10, 40c., 4, 10p. Alfonso XIII and Barcelona.

87 Ryan NYP "Spirit of St. Louis" over Coast

1929. Air. Seville and Barcelona Exhibitions.

515	**87**	5c. brown	8·50	6·00
516	**87**	10c. red	9·00	6·50
517	**87**	25c. blue	17·00	13·50
518	**87**	50c. violet	13·00	9·00
519	**87**	1p. green	65·00	46·00
520	**87**	4p. black	44·00	32·00

1929. Meeting of Council of League of Nations at Madrid. Optd **Sociedad de las Naciones LV reunion del Consejo Madrid**.

521	**66**	1c. green	90	75
522	**68**	2c. green	90	75
523	**68**	5c. red	90	75
524	**68**	10c. green	90	75
525	**68**	15c. blue	90	75
526	**68**	20c. violet	90	75
527	**68**	25c. red	90	75
528	**68**	30c. brown	4·00	3·50

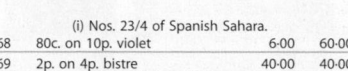

529	68	40c. blue	4·00	3·50
530	68	50c. orange	4·00	3·50
531	69	1p. grey	19·00	17·00
532	69	4p. red	19·00	17·00
533	69	10p. brown	70·00	60·00

89 Class 4601 Steam Locomotive, 1924

1930. 11th Int Railway Congress, Madrid.

534	89	1c. green (postage)	1·20	80
535	89	2c. green	1·20	80
536	89	5c. purple	1·20	80
537	89	10c. green	1·20	80
538	89	15c. blue	1·20	80
539	89	20c. violet	1·20	80
540	89	25c. red	1·20	75
541	89	30c. brown	3·50	2·75
542	89	40c. blue	3·50	2·50
543	89	50c. orange	10·50	5·75
544	-	1p. grey	10·50	6·25
545	-	4p. red	£200	£120
546	-	10p. brown	£800	£600

DESIGN: 1p. to 10p. Class 1301 steam locomotive (1914) at points.

90 Stinson Junior over Congress Emblem

547	90	5c. brown (air)	10·00	7·75
548	90	10c. red	10·00	7·75
549	90	25c. blue	10·00	7·75
550	90	50c. violet	29·00	19·00
551	90	1p. green	60·00	41·00
552	90	4p. black	65·00	43·00

91 Francisco Goya (after Lopez)

92

93 "The Naked Maja"

1930. Death Cent of Goya (painter). (a) Postage.

553	91	1c. yellow	20	15
554	91	2c. brown	20	15
555	92	2c. green	20	15
556	91	5c. mauve	20	15
557	92	5c. violet	20	15
558	91	10c. green	25	15
559	91	15c. blue	25	15
560	91	20c. purple	25	15
561	91	25c. red	25	15
562	92	25c. red	35	35
563	91	30c. brown	7·00	5·75
564	91	40c. blue	7·00	5·75
565	91	50c. red	7·00	5·75
566	91	1p. black	8·25	7·75
567	93	1p. purple	1·10	1·10
568	93	4p. black	80	75
569	93	10p. brown	17·00	17·00

94 "Flight"

(b) Air. Designs show works by Goya, all with curious flying figures.

570	94	5c. yellow and red	20	20
571	-	5c. blue and green	20	20
572	-	10c. green and turquoise	20	20
573	-	15c. red and black	55	40
574	-	20c. red and blue	20	20
575	94	25c. red and purple	25	25
576	-	30c. violet and brown	40	40
577	-	40c. blue and ultra-marine	75	60
578	-	50c. green and red	75	60
579	-	1p. violet and purple	1·90	1·20
580	-	4p. black and purple	2·50	2·30
581	-	4p. blue and light blue	3·75	3·00
582	-	10p. brown and sepia	16·00	13·00

DESIGNS—VERT: 5, 10, 20, 40c. Asmodeus and Cleofas; 1, 4 (581), 10p. Woman and dwarfs in flight. HORIZ: 30, 50c., 4p. (580), Weird flying methods.

97 King Alfonso XIII

1930

583	97	2c. brown	15	15
584	97	5c. brown	1·20	15
585	97	10c. green	6·25	15
586	97	15c. green	28·00	15
587	97	20c. violet	12·00	90
588	97	25c. red	1·20	15
589	97	30c. red	31·00	2·20
590	97	40c. blue	55·00	1·50
592	97	50c. orange	41·00	2·50

98 The *Santa Maria*

99

100 *Santa Maria, Pinta* and *Nina*

101 The Departure from Palos

1930. Columbus issue.

593	98	1c. brown	55	20
594	98	2c. green	55	20
595	99	2c. green	55	20
596	98	5c. purple	55	20
597	99	5c. purple	55	20
598	99	10c. green	1·60	1·00
599	98	15c. blue	1·60	1·00
600	99	20c. violet	2·20	1·50
601	100	25c. red	2·20	1·50
602	101	30c. brown, blue and sepia	12·00	8·00
603	100	40c. blue	11·00	7·50
604	101	50c. violet, blue and purple	13·50	11·00
605	100	1p. black	13·50	11·00
606	-	4p. black and blue	14·50	12·00
607	-	10p. brown and purple	60·00	55·00

DESIGNS—As Type **101**: 4, 10p. Arrival in America.

103 Monastery of La Rabida

104 Martin Pinzon

106 Columbus

1930. "Columbus" Air stamps (for Europe and Africa).

608	103	5c. red	25	15
609	103	5c. brown	25	15
610	103	10c. green	40	30
611	103	15c. violet	40	30
612	103	20c. blue	40	30
613	104	25c. red	40	30
614	-	30c. brown	2·75	2·40
615	104	40c. blue	2·75	2·40
616	-	50c. orange	2·75	2·40
617	104	1p. violet	2·75	2·40
618	106	4p. green	2·75	2·40
619	106	10p. brown	18·00	16·00

DESIGNS—As Type **104**: 30, 50c. Vincent Pinzon.

107 Monastery of La Rabida

108 Columbus

109 Columbus and the brothers Pinzon

1930. "Columbus" Air stamps (for America and Philippines).

620	107	5c. red	25	15
621	107	10c. green	25	15
622	108	25c. red	30	25
623	108	50c. grey	3·25	2·75
624	108	1p. brown	3·25	2·75
625	109	4p. blue	3·25	2·75
626	109	10p. purple	19·00	14·50

110 Arms of Bolivia and Paraguay

1930. Spanish-American Exhibition. Views of pavilions of various countries.

627	110	1c. green (postage)	30	15
628	-	2c. brown (C. America)	30	15
629	-	5c. brown (Venezuela)	30	15
630	-	10c. green (Colombia)	65	40
631	-	15c. blue (Dominican Republic)	65	40
632	-	20c. violet (Uruguay)	65	40
633	-	25c. red (Argentina)	65	40
634	-	25c. red (Chile)	65	40
635	-	30c. purple (Brazil)	3·50	2·30
636	-	40c. blue (Mexico)	1·80	1·30
637	-	40c. blue (Cuba)	1·80	1·30
638	-	50c. orange (Peru)	3·50	2·50
639	-	1p. blue (U.S.A.)	5·00	3·50
640	-	4p. purple (Portugal)	65·00	46·00
641	-	10p. brown	4·25	3·00

The 10p. shows King Alfonso and Queen Victoria, maps of S. America and Spain, and the Giralda, Seville. The 2, 5c., 4, 10p. are vert.

113 Sidar and Douglas 0-2-M Biplane

114 Breguet 19GR "Jesus del Gran Poder" over "Santa Maria"

643		5c. black (air)	1·80	95
644		10c. green	1·80	95
645		25c. blue	1·80	95
646		50c. blue	3·25	2·00
647	113	50c. black	3·25	2·00
648	-	1p. red	7·25	4·75
649	-	1p. purple	£160	85·00
650	-	1p. green	6·25	4·75
651	114	4p. blue	21·00	10·00

DESIGNS—HORIZ: 5c. Alberto Santos Dumont and Wright Flyer I over Rio de Janeiro; 10c. Teodoro Fels and Douglas 0-2-M biplane; 25c. Dagoberto Godoy and Nieuport 17 biplane; 50c. Admiral Gago Coutinha, Sacadura Cabral and Fairey IIID seaplane; 1p. (650) Charles Lindbergh and Ryan NYP Special "Spirirt of St. Louis". VERT: 1p. (648/9) Jimenez Iglesias and Breguet 19GR "Jesus de Gran Poder".

115

1930

652	115	5c. black	10·50	15

1931. Optd **REPUBLICA**. (a) Postage.

660	66	1c. green	20	20
673	97	2c. brown	30	30
662	97	5c. brown	20	20
671	115	5c. black	1·90	1·90
675	97	10c. green	30	30
664	97	15c. green	65	65
677	97	20c. violet	45	45
678	97	25c. red	45	45
667	97	30c. red	5·25	5·25
668	97	40c. blue	1·60	1·60
669	97	50c. orange	1·60	1·60
670	69	1p. grey	9·50	9·50

(b) Air. On Nos. 353/6.

683	64	5c. green	11·50	11·50
684	64	10c. red	11·50	11·50
685	64	25c. blue	16·00	16·00
686	64	50c. blue	33·00	33·00

1931. Optd **Republica Espanola** in two lines continuously.

687	97	2c. brown	15	15
688	97	5c. brown	45	15
689	97	10c. green	65	15
690	97	15c. green	6·25	20
691	97	20c. violet	2·20	1·40
692	97	25c. red	60	15
693	97	30c. red	10·00	1·60
694	97	40c. blue	8·25	80
695	97	50c. orange	16·00	95
696	69	1p. grey	£100	1·20

121 The Fountain of the Lions

1931. Third Pan-American Postal Union Congress. (a) Postage.

697	121	5c. purple	25	15
698	-	10c. green	75	55
699	-	15c. violet	75	55
700	-	25c. red	75	55
701	-	30c. green	75	55
702	121	40c. blue	2·00	1·30
703	-	50c. red	2·00	1·30
704	-	1p. black	4·00	2·75
705	-	4p. purple	21·00	14·50
706	-	10p. brown	65·00	46·00

DESIGNS—VERT: 10, 25, 50c. Cordoba Cathedral. HORIZ: 15c., 1p. Alcantara Bridge, Toledo; 30c. Dr. F. Garcia y Santos; 4, 10p. Revolutionaries hoisting Republican flag, 14 April, 1931.

123 Royal Palace and San Francisco el Grande

(b) Air.

707	123	5c. purple	20	15
708	123	10c. green	20	15
709	123	25c. red	20	15
710	-	50c. blue	60	60
711	-	1p. violet	1·10	90
712	-	4p. black	14·50	12·50

DESIGNS—HORIZ: 50c., 1p. G.P.O. and Cibeles Fountain; 4p. Calle de Alcala.

125a Montserrat Arms

1931. 900th Anniv of Montserrat Monastery.

713	**125a**	1c. green (postage)	2·20	1·90
714	**125a**	2c. brown	1·20	85
715	**125a**	5c. brown	1·50	1·00
716	**125a**	10c. green	1·50	1·00
717	-	15c. green	2·10	1·30
718	-	20c. purple	4·50	3·25
719	-	25c. purple	6·00	4·50
720	-	30c. red	70·00	50·00
721	-	40c. blue	40·00	22·00
722	-	50c. orange	95·00	60·00
723	-	1p. blue	95·00	60·00
724	-	4p. mauve	£850	£550
725	-	10p. brown	£700	£475

DESIGNS: 15, 50c. Monks planning Monastery; 20, 30c. "Black Virgin" (full length); 25c., 1, 10p. "Black Virgin" (profile); 40c., 4p. Monastery.

125b Airplane above Montserrat

726	**125b**	5c. brown (air)	70	60
727	**125b**	10c. green	3·75	3·50
728	**125b**	25c. purple	14·00	13·00
729	**125b**	50c. orange	49·00	43·00
730	**125b**	1p. blue	33·00	29·00

126 Blasco Ibanez

127 Pi y Margall

128 Joaquin Costa

129 Mariana Pineda

130 Nicolas Salmeron

131 Concepcion Arenal

132 Ruiz Zorilla

133 Pablo Iglesias

134 Ramon y Cajal

135 Azcarate

136 Jovellanos

137 Pablo Iglesias

138 Emilio Castelar

139 Pablo Iglesias

140 Velazquez

141 F. Salvoechea

142 Cuenca

1931

738	**126**	2c. brown	20	15
731	**127**	5c. brown	5·25	40
740	**126**	5c. brown	15	15
741	**128**	10c. green	8·75	15
742	**129**	10c. green	20	15
744	**130**	15c. green	1·30	15
745	**131**	15c. green	40	15
747	**131**	15c. black	40	10
748	**127**	20c. violet	50	15
734	**133**	25c. red	47·00	1·10
750	**132**	25c. red	1·00	15
751	**133**	30c. red	3·50	15
752	**134**	30c. brown	16·00	2·40
753	**135**	30c. red	17·00	30
755	**136**	30c. red	15	15
756	**137**	30c. red	20	10
757	**139**	30c. red	3·50	45
758	**138**	40c. blue	20	15
759	**138**	40c. red	3·25	45
760	**139**	45c. red	30	10
761	**130**	50c. orange	65·00	1·10
762	**130**	50c. blue	2·75	1·10
763	**140**	50c. blue	20	10
764	**138**	60c. green	20	15
765	**141**	60c. blue	1·90	1·20
766	**141**	60c. orange	17·00	11·50
767c	**142**	1p. black	30	20
768c	-	4p. mauve	95	30
769c	-	10p. brown	1·10	1·10

DESIGNS—As Type **142**: 4p. Castle of Segovia; 10p. Sun Gate, Toledo.

143

144

1933. Imperf (1c.), perf (others).

770	**143**	1c. green	20	20
771	**143**	2c. brown	55	10
772	**144**	2c. brown	†	†
773	**143**	5c. brown	†	†
774	**143**	10c. green	†	†
775	**143**	15c. green	20	20
776a	**143**	20c. violet	1·50	1·50
777a	**143**	25c. mauve	20	20
778	**143**	30c. red	†	†

145 Cierva C.30A Autogyro over Seville

1935

780	**145**	2p. blue	30	20

146 Lope De Vega's Book-plate

148 Scene from "Peribanez"

1935. 300th Death Anniv of Lope de Vega (author).

781	**146**	15c. green	12·00	30
782	-	30c. red	5·25	25
783	-	50c. blue	29·00	3·50
784	**148**	1p. black	47·00	2·30

DESIGN—As Type **146**: 30, 50c. Lope de Vega (after Tristan).

149 Old-time Map of the Amazon

1935. Iglesias' Amazon Expedition.

785	**149**	30c. red	4·75	1·20

150 M. Moya

151 House of Nazareth and Rotary Press

1936. 40th Anniv of Madrid Press Association.

786	**150**	1c. red (postage)	15	15
787	-	2c. brown	15	15
788	-	5c. brown	15	15
789	-	10c. green	15	15
790	**150**	15c. green	20	15
791	-	20c. violet	20	15
792	-	25c. mauve	20	15
793	-	30c. red	15	15
794	**150**	40c. orange	70	25
795	-	50c. blue	40	15
796	-	60c. green	90	30
797	-	1p. black	90	30
798	**151**	2p. blue	12·50	4·50
799	**151**	4p. purple	12·50	7·50
800	**151**	10p. red	29·00	18·00

SIZES: 1c. to 10c. 22×27 mm; 15c. to 30c. 24×30 mm; 40c. to 1p. 26×31½ mm.

152 Pyrenean Eagle and Newspapers

153 Airplane over Press Association Building

801	**152**	1c. red (air)	15	15
802	**153**	2c. brown	15	15
803	**152**	5c. brown	15	15
804	**153**	10c. green	15	15
805	-	15c. blue	35	15
806	**152**	20c. violet	35	15
807	**153**	25c. mauve	35	15
808	-	30c. red	15	15
809	**152**	40c. orange	75	35
810	**152**	50c. blue	50	35
811	**153**	60c. green	1·20	35
812	-	1p. black	1·20	35
813	-	2p. blue (45×34 mm)	7·50	4·25
814	-	4p. purple (45×34 mm)	8·25	6·75
815	-	10p. red (45×34 mm)	25·00	16·00

DESIGNS—VERT: 15, 30, 50c., 1p. Cierva C.30A autogyro over House of Nazareth. HORIZ: 2, 4, 10p. Don Quixote on wooden horse.

155 Gregorio Fernandez

1936. 300th Birth Anniv of Gregorio Fernandez (sculptor).

816	**155**	30c. red	2·20	1·00

156

1936. First National Philatelic Exhibition, Madrid. Imperf. (a) Postage.

817	**156**	10c. brown	65·00	55·00
818	**156**	15c. green	65·00	55·00

(b) Air. Optd **CORREO AEREO**.

819	10c. red	£225	£190
820	15c. blue	£225	£190

1936. Manila–Madrid Flight of Arnaiz and Calvo. Optd **VUELO MANILA MADRID 1936 ARNAIZ CALVO**.

821	**137**	30c. red	8·50	6·25

159

1937. Fiscal stamp of Austrias and Leon surch.

822	**159**	25c. on 5c. red	16·00	8·00
823	**159**	45c. on 5c. red	8·50	4·75
824	**159**	60c. on 5c. red	45	95
825	**159**	1p. on 5c. red	45	65

1938. Surch **45 centimos**.

826	**143**	45c. on 1c. green (imperf)	6·00	3·75
827	**143**	45c. on 1c. green (perf)	65	30
830	**143**	45c. on 2c. brown	47·00	45·00
831	**144**	45c. on 2c. brown	20	15
832	**126**	45c. on 2c. brown	36·00	16·00

160a Republican Symbol

1938

833	**160a**	40c. pink	15	15
834	**160a**	45c. red	15	15
835	**160a**	50c. blue	15	15
836	**160a**	60c. blue	80	40

1938. Seventh Anniv of Republic. Nos. 308/9 surch **14 ABRIL 1938 VII Aniversario de la Republica** and values. (a) Postage.

837	45c. on 15c. violet	19·00	18·00

(b) Air. Additionally optd **CORREO AEREO**.

838	2p.50 on 10c. red	£140	£130

163 Defence of Madrid

1938. Defence of Madrid Relief Fund. (a) Postage.

839	**163**	45c.+2p. blue & lt blue	95	85
MS840		120×105 mm. No. 839	40·00	48·00

(b) Air. Surch **AEREO + 5 Pts.**

841	45c.+2p.+5p. blue and light blue	£550	£425
MS842	120×105 mm. No. 841	£7500	£9500

1938. Labour Day. Surch **FIESTA DEL TRABAJO 1 MAYO 1938** and values.

843	**54**	45c. on 15c. violet	4·25	4·25
844	**54**	1p. on 15c. violet	7·75	7·25

167 Statue of Liberty and Flags

1938. 150th Anniv of U.S. Constitution. (a) Postage.

845	**167**	1p. multicoloured	29·00	26·00
MS846		120×105 mm. No. 845	45·00	41·00

(b) Air. Surch **AEREO + 5 Pts.**

847	1p.+5p. multicoloured	£450	£375
MS848	120×105 mm. No. 847	£1700	£1700

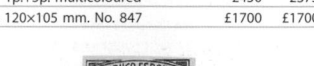

169

1938. Red Cross. (a) Postage.

849	**169**	45c.+5p. red	85	65

(b) Air. Surch **+3 Pts. Aereo.**

850	45c.+5p.+3p. red	17·00	13·00

1938. Air. No. 719 surch with two airplanes, **CORREO AEREO** twice and value.

851	50c. on 25c. purple	50·00	44·00
852	1p. on 25c. purple	1·90	1·40
853	1p.25 on 25c. purple	1·90	1·40
854	1p.50 on 25c. purple	2·00	1·50
855	2p. on 25c. purple	55·00	44·00

172 Steelworks

1938. Workers of Sagunto.

856	**172**	45c. black	20	15
857	-	1p.25 blue	20	15

DESIGN: 1p.25, Blast furnace and air raid victims.

173 "Isaac Peral"

1938. Submarine Service.

857a	**173**	1p. blue	6·75	6·75
857b	-	2p. brown	12·50	12·50
857c	-	4p. orange	14·50	14·50
857d	-	6p. blue	43·00	29·00
857e	-	10p. purple	55·00	50·00
857f	-	15p. green	£550	£500
MS857g 150×118 mm. 4p. black and red; 6p. black and blue; 15p. black and green			£650	£550

DESIGNS: 2, 6p. "Narciso Monturiol". 4, 10p. "B-2".

174 Troops on the Alert

1938. In Honour of 43rd Division. Perf or imperf.

858	**174**	25c. green	20·00	13·00
859	-	45c. brown	20·00	13·00

DESIGN—VERT: 45c. Two soldiers on guard.

1938. Second Anniv of Defence of Madrid. Optd **SEGUNDO ANIVERSARIO DE LA HEROICA DEFENSA DE MADRID 7 NOV. 1938**.

860	163	45c.+2p. blue and light blue	4·25	4·75

1938. No. 719 surch **2'50 PTAS.**, bars and ornaments.

861	2p.50 on 25c. purple	30	30

176a Man and Woman in Firing Position

1938. In Honour of the Militia.

861b	**176a**	5c. brown	4·75	4·25
861c	**176a**	10c. purple	4·75	4·25
861d	**176a**	25c. green	4·75	4·25
861e	-	45c. red	4·75	4·25
861f	-	60c. blue	10·00	7·25
861g	-	1p.20 black	£200	£160
861h	-	2p. orange	60·00	47·00
861i	-	5p. brown	£375	£300
861j	-	10p. green	65·00	55·00

DESIGNS—HORIZ: 45, 60c., 1p.20, Militia with machine gun. VERT: 2, 5, 10p. Grenade-thrower.

NATIONAL STATE

The Civil War began on 17 July 1936. Until it ended on 1 April 1939, the stamps listed below were current only in areas held by the forces of General Franco.

177 Seville Cathedral

178 Xavier Castle, Navarre

1936. Junta of National Defence.

862		5c. brown	95	80
863		15c. green	95	80
864	**177**	25c. red	95	80
865	**178**	30c. red	95	80
867	-	1p. black	8·25	5·25

DESIGNS—VERT: 5c. Burgos Cathedral. HORIZ: 15c. Zaragoza Cathedral; 1p. Alcantara Bridge and Alcazar, Toledo.

179

180 Cordoba Cathedral

1936

868	**179**	1c. green (imperf)	8·25	6·25
869	**179**	2c. brown	95	70
870	-	10c. green	95	70
871	-	50c. blue	24·00	13·50
872	**180**	60c. green	1·60	90
873	-	4p. lilac, red and yellow	95·00	41·00
874	-	10p. brown	85·00	41·00

DESIGNS (As T **180**)—HORIZ: 10c. Salamanca University; 50c. Court of Lions, Granada; 10p. Troops disembarking at Algeciras. VERT: 4p. National flag at Malaga.

181

182

183 "El Cid"

184 Isabella the Catholic

1937

875	**181**	1c. green (imperf)	20	15
876	**182**	2c. brown	20	15
902	**183**	5c. brown	25	15
879	**183**	10c. green	20	15
903	**183**	10c. red	20	15
880	**184**	15c. black	35	20
896	**183**	15c. green	25	15
881	**184**	20c. violet	75	20
882	**184**	25c. red	65	20
883	**184**	30c. red	1·00	20
885	**184**	40c. orange	3·75	20
886	**184**	50c. blue	3·75	20
887	**184**	60c. yellow	65	20
897	**184**	70c. blue	1·20	20
888	**184**	1p. blue	29·00	75
889	**184**	4p. mauve	35·00	7·25
891	**183**	10p. blue	70·00	20·00

See also No. 1113.

186 Santiago Cathedral

1937. Holy Year of Compostela.

905	-	15c. brown	3·50	80
906	**186**	30c. red	12·00	70
908	-	1p. orange and blue	41·00	4·25

DESIGNS—VERT: 15c. St. James of Compostela. HORIZ: 1p. Portico de la Gloria.

188 Alcazar, Toledo (before Siege)

1937. First Anniv of National Uprising. Sheets 140×110 mm containing T **188** and similar designs.

MS909 **188** 2p. (+2p.) orange	42·00	30·00
MS910 Imperf	£600	£500
MS911 – 2p. (+2p.) green	42·00	30·00
MS912 – Imperf	£600	£500

DESIGN: No. **MS**911/12 Alcazar in ruins.

189

1937. Anti-tuberculosis Fund. Cross in red.

913	**189**	10c. blue and black	15·00	6·00

189a Covadonga Monastery

1938. Historic Monuments. Sheet 140×100 mm containing T **189a** and similar designs.

MS914 20c. violet, 30c. red, 50c. blue, 1p. green (sold at 4p.)	75·00	65·00
MS915 Imperf	£130	£100

DESIGNS—VERT: 30c. Cathedral, Palma de Mallorca; 50c. Alcazar, Segovia. VERT 1p. Leon Cathedral.

190 Ferdinand the Catholic

1938

917	**190**	15c. green	4·00	15
918	**190**	20c. violet	17·00	2·50
919	**190**	25c. red	1·20	15
921	**190**	30c. red	11·50	15

1938. Air. Optd **correo aereo**.

922	50c. blue	1·70	80
923	1p. blue	4·75	80

191a Soldier with Flag

1938. Honouring Army and Navy. Sheet 175×132 mm containing designs as T **191a** (various frames).

MS924 2c. violet (Type **191a**), 2c. violet (a), 3c. blue (b), 3c. blue (c), 5c. sepia (a), 5c. sepia (Type **191a**), 10c. green (b), 10c. green (c), 30c. orange (b), 30c. orange (c). Two of each stamp (sold at 4p.)	50·00	48·00
MS925 Imperf	£250	£190

DESIGNS: (a) Cruiser *Almirante Cervera*; (b) Trenches near Teruel; (c) General Franco's Moorish bodyguard.

192

1938. Second Anniv of National Uprising.

926	**192**	15c. green and light green	7·25	5·50
927	**192**	25c. red and pink	7·25	5·50
928	**192**	30c. blue and light blue	3·75	3·00
929	**192**	1p. brown and yellow	£160	£110

193 Isabella the Catholic

1938

930	**193**	20c. violet	2·75	20
931	**193**	25c. red	14·50	80
932	**193**	30c. red	40	20
933	**193**	40c. mauve	40	15
934	**193**	50c. blue	55·00	3·25
935	**193**	1p. blue	19·00	1·30

193a Don Juan of Austria

1938. Battle of Lepanto. Sheets each 90×75 mm containing T **193a** and another design.

MS936 **193a** 30c. carmine (perf)	24·00	†
MS937 – 50c. blue	24·00	†
MS938 **193a** 30c. violet (imperf)	£500	†
MS939 – 50c. green	£500	†

DESIGN—(36½×23 mm): 50c. Naval Battle of Lepanto.

194

1938. Anti-tuberculosis Fund. Cross in red.

940	**194**	10c. blue and black	9·25	2·40

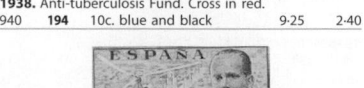

195 Juan de la Cierva and Cierva C.30A Autogyro

1939. Air.

1010	**195**	20c. orange	25	15
1011	**195**	25c. red	25	15
943	**195**	35c. mauve	80	40
1013	**195**	50c. brown	55	15
945	**195**	1p. blue	1·20	25
1015	**195**	2p. green	2·40	20
1016	**195**	4p. blue	8·25	30
1017	**195**	10p. violet	6·50	80

196 General Franco

1939

960	**196**	5c. brown	50	20
961	**196**	10c. red	2·50	1·00
962	**196**	15c. green	70	20
1114	**196**	20c. violet	25	15
1115	**196**	25c. purple	30	15
950	**196**	30c. red	40	20
1116	**196**	30c. blue	35	15
1117	**196**	35c. blue	55	20
951	**196**	40c. green	40	20
966	**196**	40c. grey	60	15
952	**196**	45c. red	3·25	2·50
1119	**196**	45c. blue	25	15
1120	**196**	50c. grey	45	15
1121	**196**	60c. orange	25	15
955	**196**	70c. blue	50	20
956	**196**	1Pts. black	19·00	20
974	**196**	1PTA. black	8·50	15
975	**196**	1PTS. grey	90·00	95
957	**196**	2Pts. brown	28·00	1·60
1124	**196**	2PTAS. brown	7·00	15
958	**196**	4Pts. purple	£170	19·00
1125	**196**	4PTAS. red	16·00	20
959	**196**	10Pts. brown	80·00	45·00
978	**196**	10PTS. brown	£250	4·75
1126	**196**	10PTAS. brown	3·75	60

For 10c. brown imperf, see No. 981.

197 "Spain" and Wreath of Peace

1939. Homage to the Army.

980	**197**	10c. blue	35	15

1939. Anti-tuberculosis Fund. Imperf.

981	**196**	10c. brown	35	15

198 Ruins of Belchite

1940. Zaragoza Cathedral Restoration Fund and 19th Centenary of Apparition of Virgin of El Pilar at Zaragoza. (a) Postage.

982	**198**	10c.+5c. brown and blue	20	15
983	-	15c.+10c. green and lilac	20	15
984	-	20c.+10c. blue & violet	20	15
985	-	25c.+10c. brown & red	20	15
986	-	40c.+10c. purple & grn	20	15
987	-	45c.+15c. red and blue	40	30
988	**198**	70c.+20c. black & brn	40	30
989	-	80c.+20c. violet and red	50	40
990	-	1p.+30c. purple & black	50	40
991	-	1p.40+40c. black & vio	60·00	48·00
992	-	1p.50+50c. purple & bl	70	60
993	-	2p.50+50c. blue & pur	70	60
994	-	4p.+1p. grey and lilac	21·00	16·00
995	-	10p.+4p. brown & blue	£300	£225

DESIGNS—HORIZ: 15, 80c. Procession of the Rosary; 20c., 1p.50, El Pilar; 25c., 1p. Mother Rafols praying; 40c., 2p.50, Sanctuary of the Virgin; 45c., 1p.40, Oath of the besieged; 4p. Miracle of Calanda; 10p. Virgin appearing to St. James.

(b) Air.

996	25c.+5c. grey and purple	30	30
997	50c.+5c. violet and red	30	30
998	65c.+15c. blue and violet	30	30
999	70c.+15c. violet and grey	30	30
1000	90c.+20c. red and brown	30	30
1001	1p.20+30c. purple & violet	30	30
1002	1p.40+40c. brown & blue	70	35
1003	2p.+50c. violet and purple	1·10	70
1004	4p.+1p. purple and green	16·00	11·00
1005	10p.+4p. blue and brown	£400	£300

DESIGNS—VERT: 25, 70c. Prayer during bombardment; 50c., 1p.40, Caravel and Image of the Virgin; 65, 90c. The Assumption; 1p.20, 2p. Coronation of the Virgin; 4p. "The Cave", after Goya; 10p. Bombing of Zaragoza Cathedral.

199 Gen. Franco

1940. Anti-tuberculosis Fund.

1006	**199**	10c. violet and red (post)	25	20
1007	**199**	20c.+5c. green and red	1·20	80
1008	**199**	40c.+10c. blue and red	1·90	50
1009	**199**	10c. pink and red (air)	1·80	1·10

200 Knight and Cross of Lorraine

1941. Anti-tuberculosis Fund.

1018	**200**	10c. black and red (post)	35	20
1019	**200**	20c.+5c. violet and red	90	40
1020	**200**	40c.+10c. grey and red	90	40
1021	**200**	10c. blue and red (air)	65	30

201 Gen. Franco

1942

1022	**201**	40c. brown	45	20
1023	**201**	75c. blue	5·25	70
1024a	**201**	90c. green	40	20
1025b	**201**	1p.35 violet	45	20

202 St. John of the Cross

1942. 400th Birth Anniv of St. John of the Cross.

1026	**202**	20c. violet	1·00	20
1027	**202**	40c. orange	2·40	40
1028	**202**	75c. blue	2·50	2·10

203 Arms and Lorraine Cross

1942. Anti-T.B. Fund. Inscr "1942–43".

1029	**203**	10c. orange and red (postage)	20	20
1030	**203**	20c.+5c. brown and red	2·10	1·90
1031	**203**	40c.+10c. green and red	1·70	30
1032	-	10c. orange and red (air)	1·40	65

DESIGN—HORIZ: No. 1032, Lorraine Cross and two doves in flight.

204 St. James of Compostela

205

1943. Holy Year. Inscr "ANO SANTO 1943".

1033	**204**	20c. blue	30	20
1034	-	20c. red	30	20
1035	-	20c. lilac	30	20
1036	-	40c. brown	85	20
1037	**205**	40c. green	70	20
1038	-	40c. brown	85	20
1039	-	75c. blue	4·00	2·30
1040	-	75c. blue	4·50	2·50
1041	-	75c. blue	65·00	47·00

DESIGNS—VERT: Nos. 1034 and 1040. Details of pillars in Santiago Cathedral; No. 1036, St. James enthroned; No. 1038, Portal of Santiago Cathedral; No. 1039, Censer; No. 1041, Santiago Cathedral. HORIZ: No. 1035, Tomb of St. James.

206

1943. Anti-Tuberculosis Fund. Inscr "1943–1944".

1042	**206**	10c. violet & red (postage)	45	30
1043	**206**	20c.+5c. green and red	6·00	1·90
1044	**206**	40c.+10c. blue and red	3·75	1·30
1045	-	10c. violet and red (air)	1·80	1·30

DESIGN: No. 1045. Lorraine Cross and outline of bird.

207 10th-cent Tower

208 Arms of Soria

1944. Millenary of Castile. Arms designs as T **208** inscr "MILENARIO DE CASTILLA".

1046	**207**	20c. lilac	40	25
1047	**208**	20c. lilac	30	25
1048	-	20c. lilac	30	25
1049	-	40c. brown	5·00	80
1050	-	40c. brown	5·00	80
1051	-	40c. brown	3·75	85
1052	-	75c. blue	5·25	4·50
1053	-	75c. blue	4·50	4·50
1054	-	75c. blue	6·25	5·00

DESIGNS: No. 1048, Avila (Shield at left); No. 1049, Castile (Arms in centre); No. 1050, Segovia (Shield at left); No. 1051, Burgos (Shield at right); No. 1052, Avila (Shield at left); No. 1053, Fernan Gonzalez, founder of Castile (Helmet, bow and arrows at left); No. 1054, Santander (Shield at right).

209 "Dr. Thebussem" (M. P. de Figueroa, author and postal historian) and Douglas DC-2

1944. Air. Stamp Day.

1055	**209**	5p. blue	27·00	20·00

210

1944. Anti-tuberculosis Fund. Inscr "1944 1945". (a) Postage.

1056	**210**	10c. orange and red	20	15
1057	**210**	20c.+5c. black and red	40	40
1058	**210**	40c.+10c. violet & red	90	70
1059	**210**	80c.+10c. blue and red	15·00	13·00

(b) Air. Inscr "CORRESPONDENCIA AEREA".

1060		25c. orange and red	7·00	5·75

DESIGN—HORIZ: No. 1060, Hospital.

211 Quevedo

1945. 300th Death Anniv of Francisco de Quevedo (author).

1061	**211**	40c. brown	1·20	80

212 Conde de San Luis, Mail Vehicle of 1850 and Airplane

1945. Air. Stamp Day.

1062	**212**	10p. green	35·00	21·00

213 Carlos de Haya Gonzalez

214 J. Garcia Morato and Fiat CR-32 biplane

1945. Air. Civil War Air Aces.

1063	**213**	4p. red	18·00	9·50
1064	**214**	10p. purple	48·00	9·75

215 St. George and Dragon

216 Lorraine Cross and Eagle

1945. Anti-T.B. Fund.

1065	**215**	10c. orge & red (postage)	25	15
1066	**215**	20c.+5c. green and red	40	35
1067	**215**	40c.+10c. violet and red	70	20
1068	**215**	80c.+10c. blue and red	17·00	11·50
1069	**216**	25c. red (air)	2·75	1·70

217 E. A. de Nebrija (compiler of first Spanish Grammar)

219 Statue of Fray Bartolome de las Casas and native Indian

1946. Stamp Day and Day of the Race.

1070	**217**	50c. red (postage)	85	25
1071	-	75c. blue	1·00	70
1072	**219**	5p.50 green (air)	5·50	3·50

DESIGN—As Type **217**: 75c. Salamanca University and signature of F. F. de Vitoria (founder of International Law).

220 Self-portrait of Goya

1946. Birth Bicentenary of Goya (painter).

1073	**220**	25c. red	20	15
1074	**220**	50c. green	25	15
1075	**220**	75c. blue	1·20	85

221 Woman and Child

1946. Anti-tuberculosis Fund. Dated "1946 1947".

1076	**221**	5c. violet and red (postage)	30	15
1077	**221**	10c. green and red	30	15
1078	-	25c. orange and red (air)	55	25

DESIGN—HORIZ: 25c. Eagle.

222 B. J. Feijoo y Montenegro

1947

1079	**222**	50c. green	1·40	70

223 Don Quixote in Library

224 Don Quixote

1947. Stamp Day and 400th Birth Anniv of Cervantes.

1080	**223**	50c. brown (postage)	50	20
1081	**224**	75c. blue	1·10	50
1082	-	5p.50 violet (air)	10·00	6·25

DESIGN—HORIZ: 5p.50, Quixote on Wooden Horse (after Gustav Dore).

226 Manuel de Falla (composer)

1947. Air.

1083	**226**	25p. purple	75·00	27·00
1084	-	50p. red	£275	60·00

PORTRAIT: 50p. Ignacio Zuloaga (painter).

228 Lorraine Cross

1947. Anti-tuberculosis Fund. Dated "1947 1948".

1085	**228**	5c. brown & red (postage)	25	15
1086	-	10c. blue and red	25	20
1087	-	25c. mauve and red (air)	55	25

DESIGNS—VERT: 10c. Deckchair in garden. HORIZ: 25c. Sanatorium.

229 General Franco

1948

1088	**229**	5c. brown	25	20
1088a	**229**	5c. green	20	20
1089	**229**	15c. green	25	20
1090	**229**	50c. brown	4·50	20
1091	**229**	80c. red	[illegible]	[illegible]

230 Hernando Cortes

1948

1092	**230**	35c. black	25	20
1093	-	70c. purple	4·25	2·50

PORTRAIT: 70c. M. Aleman (writer).

232 Gen. Franco and Castillo de la Mota

1948

1094	**232**	25c. orange	30	20
1095	**232**	30c. green	40	15
1096	**232**	35c. green	30	20
1097	**232**	40c. brown	1·70	20
1099	**232**	45c. red	1·20	20
1100	**232**	50c. purple	2·40	20
1101	**232**	70c. violet	3·50	20
1102	**232**	75c. blue	3·25	20
1103	**232**	1p. red	9·75	20

233 Ferdinand III of Castile

1948. 700th Anniv of Institution of Castilian Navy.

1104	**233**	25c. violet	55	20
1105	-	30c. red (Admiral R. de Bonifaz)	35	20

235 Marquis of Salamanca

236 Series ABJ Diesel Railcar (1936) and Lockheed Constellation Airliner

1948. Stamp Day and Spanish Railway Centenary Inscr "F.F.C.C. ESPANOLES 1848 1948".

1106	**235**	50c. brown (postage)	90	20
1107	-	5p. green	3·75	20
1108	**236**	2p. red (air)	4·25	2·20

DESIGN—HORIZ: 5p. Garganta de Pancorbo Viaduct.

238 Aesculapius

1948. Anti-tuberculosis Fund. Dated "1948 1949".

1109	**238**	5c. brown & red (postage)	25	15
1110	**238**	10c. green and red	25	20
1111	**238**	50c.+10c. brown & red	1·70	1·00
1112	-	25c. blue and red (air)	70	40

DESIGN: 25c. Lockheed Constellation airliner over sanatorium.

1949. Relief of War Victims. As T **183**, but larger and inscr "AUXILIO A LAS VICTIMAS DE LA GUERRA 1946".

1113	5c. violet	40	25

240 Globe and Buildings

1949. 75th Anniv of U.P.U.

1127	**240**	50c. brown (postage)	1·40	25
1128	**240**	75c. blue	1·00	50
1129	**240**	4p. green (air)	75	45

241 Galleon

1949. Anti-tuberculosis Fund. Inscr "1949 1950".

1130	**241**	5c. violet & red (postage)	15	15
1131	**241**	10c. green and red	15	15
1132	**241**	50c.+10c. brown & red	1·00	40
1133	-	25c. brown and red (air)	30	25

DESIGN: 25c. Bell.

242 San Juan de Dios and Leper

1950. 400th Death Anniv of San Juan de Dios.

1134	**242**	1p. violet	23·00	7·00

243 Calderon de la Barca (dramatist)

1950. Portraits.

1135	**243**	5c. brown	25	20
1136	-	10c. purple	25	25
1137	-	15c. green	50	20
1138	-	20c. violet	1·10	20
1139	-	2p. blue	35·00	35
1140	-	4p.50 purple	1·70	1·40

PORTRAITS—VERT: 10c. Lope de Vega (author); 15c. Tirso de Molina (poet); 20c. Ruiz de Alarcon (author); 2p. Dr. Ramon y Cajal (physician); 4p.50, Dr. Ferran y Clua (bacteriologist).

244 Isabella II

1950. Stamp Centenary. Imperf. (a) Postage. Reproduction of T 1.

1141	**244**	50c. violet	16·00	8·25
1142	**244**	75c. blue	16·00	8·25
1143	**244**	10p. green	£170	£120
1144	**244**	15p. red	£170	£120

(b) Air. Reproduction of T **2**.

1145	1p. purple	16·00	8·25
1146	2p.50 brown	16·00	8·25
1147	20p. blue	£170	£120
1148	25p. green	£170	£120

1950. Gen. Franco's Canary Is Visit. Nos. 1100 and 1103 surch **VISITA DEL CAUDILLO A CANARIAS OCTUBRE 1950 SOBRETASA: DIEZ CTS** and No. 1083 with **Correspondencia por avion** also.

1149B	**232**	10c. on 50c. purple (postage)	£100	60·00
1150B	**232**	10c. on 1p. red	£100	60·00
1151	**226**	10c. on 25p. purple (air)	£750	£350

246 Candle and Conifer

1950. Anti-T.B. Fund. Cross in red. Inscr "1950 1951".

1152	**246**	5c. violet (postage)	20	20
1153	**246**	10c. green	20	20
1154	**246**	50c.+10c. brown	3·00	1·40
1155	-	25c. blue (air)	90	40

DESIGN: 25c. Dove and flowers.

247 Map

1951. Air. Sixth Conference of Spanish-American Postal Union.

1156	**247**	1p. blue	9·50	3·50

248 Isabella the Catholic

1951. Fifth Centenary of Birth of Isabella.

1157	**248**	50c. brown	1·40	50
1158	**248**	75c. blue	1·80	45
1159	**248**	90c. purple	70	25
1160	**248**	1p.50 orange	19·00	10·00
1161	**248**	2p.80 olive	43·00	28·00

248a St. Antonio Claret

1951. Stamp Day.

1162	**248a**	50c. blue	6·50	4·25

249 Children on Beach

1951. Anti-tuberculosis Fund. Cross in red.

1163	**249**	5c. red (postage)	20	15
1164	**249**	10c. green	90	20
1165	-	25c. brown (air)	1·20	20

DESIGN: 25c. Nurse and child.

250 Isabella the Catholic

1951. Air. Stamp Day and 500th Birth Anniv of Isabella the Catholic.

1166	**250**	60c. green	10·00	55
1167	**250**	90c. yellow	1·30	70
1168	**250**	1p.30 red	13·50	6·25
1169	**250**	1p.90 sepia	10·00	7·75
1170	**250**	2p.30 blue	6·00	4·00

251 Ferdinand the Catholic

1952. 500th Birth Anniv of Ferdinand the Catholic.

1171	**251**	50c. green	1·10	25
1172	**251**	75c. blue	10·50	2·00
1173	**251**	90c. purple	75	25
1174	**251**	1p.50 orange	20·00	10·50
1175	**251**	2p.80 brown	32·00	22·00

252 St. Maria Micaela

1952. 35th International Eucharistic Congress, Barcelona.

1176	**252**	90c. red (postage)	35	20
1177	-	1p. green (air)	5·50	60

DESIGN: 1p. "The Eucharist" (Tiepolo).

252a St. Francis Xavier

1952. Air. 400th Death Anniv of St. Francis Xavier.

1178	**252a**	2p. blue	85·00	30·00

1952. Air. Stamp Day and 500th Anniv of Birth of Ferdinand the Catholic. As T **250** but interior scene and portrait of Ferdinand the Catholic.

1179	60c. green	25	20
1180	90c. orange	25	20
1181	1p.30 red	1·10	1·10
1182	1p.90 brown	4·00	2·75
1183	2p.30 blue	19·00	12·00

254 Nurse and Baby

1953. Anti-tuberculosis Fund. Cross in red.

1184	**254**	5c. lake (postage)	90	15
1185	**254**	10c. green	2·30	20
1186	-	25c. brown (air)	8·75	6·75

DESIGN: 25c. Girl and angel.

255 J. Sorolla (painter)

1953. Air.

1187	**255**	50p. violet	£850	31·00

256 Bas-relief

257 Fray Luis de Leon

1953. Stamp Day and 700th Anniv of Salamanca University. Inscr "UNIVDAD DE SALAMANCA".

1188	**256**	50c. red	55	25
1189	**257**	90c. green	3·25	3·00
1190	-	2p. brown	24·00	6·25

DESIGN—As Type **185**—HORIZ: 2p. Salamanca University.

258 M. L. de Legazpi (founder of Manila)

1953. Air. Signing of Filipino–Spanish Postal Convention.

1191	**258**	25p. black	£190	45·00

259 "St. Mary Magdalene"

1954. Death Tercentenary of Ribera (painter).

1192	**259**	1p.25 lake	35	20

260 St. James of Compostela

1954. Holy Year.

1193	**260**	50c. brown	65	25
1194	-	3p. blue	80·00	5·75

DESIGN: 3p. Santiago Cathedral.

261 "Purity" (after Cano)

1954. Marian Year.

1195	**261**	10c. red	35	15
1196	-	15c. green	35	15
1197	-	25c. violet	35	15
1198	-	30c. brown	35	15
1199	-	50c. green	1·20	15
1200	-	60c. black	35	15
1201	-	80c. green	4·75	15
1202	-	1p. violet	4·75	15
1203	-	2p. brown	1·40	20
1204	-	3p. blue	2·00	1·30

DESIGNS: 15c. Virgin of Begona, Bilbao; 25c. Virgin of the Abandoned, Valencia Cathedral; 30c. The "Black Virgin" of Montserrat; 50c. El Pilar Virgin, Zaragoza; 60c. Covadonga Virgin; 80c. Virgin of the Kings, Seville Cathedral; 1p. Almudena Virgin, Madrid; 2p. Virgin of Africa; 3p. Guadalupe Virgin.

262 M. Menendez Pelayo (historian)

1954. Stamp Day.

1205	**262**	80c. green	10·50	20

263 Gen. Franco

1955

1206	**263**	10c. red	15	15
1207	**263**	15c. ochre	15	15
1208	**263**	20c. green	15	15
1209	**263**	25c. violet	15	15
1210	**263**	30c. brown	15	15
1211	**263**	40c. purple	15	15
1212	**263**	50c. brown	15	15
1213	**263**	60c. purple	20	15
1214	**263**	70c. green	20	15
1215	**263**	80c. turquoise	20	15
1216	**263**	1p. orange	15	15
1217	**263**	1p.40 mauve	25	20
1218	**263**	1p.50 turquoise	25	20
1219	**263**	1p.80 green	25	20
1220	**263**	2p. red	23·00	1·00
1221	**263**	2p. mauve	25	20
1222	**263**	3p. blue	20	15
1222a	**263**	4p. red	15	15
1223	**263**	5p. brown	25	15
1224	**263**	6p. black	25	15
1224a	**263**	7p. blue	20	15
1225	**263**	8p. violet	25	20
1226	**263**	10p. green	25	15
1226a	**263**	12p. green	20	15
1226b	**263**	20p. red	20	15

264 Torres Quevedo (engineer and inventor)

1955. Air.

1229	-	25p. black	34·00	90
1230	**264**	50p. violet	13·00	2·20

PORTRAIT: 25p. Fortuny (painter).

265 St. Ignatius of Loyola

1955. Stamp Day and Fourth Centenary of Death of St. Ignatius of Loyola.

1231	**265**	25c. slate	20	20
1232	-	60c. ochre	1·00	45
1233	**265**	80c. green	4·50	45

DESIGN—HORIZ: 60c. St. Ignatius and Loyola Castle.

266 Lockheed L.1049 Super Constellation and Caravel

1955. Air.

1234	**266**	20c. green	20	20
1235	**266**	25c. violet	15	15
1236	**266**	50c. brown	20	20
1237	**266**	1p. red	15	15
1238	**266**	1p.10 green	35	20
1239	**266**	1p.40 mauve	20	15
1240	**266**	3p. blue	35	20
1241	**266**	4p.80 yellow	20	15
1242	**266**	5p. brown	2·00	15
1243	**266**	7p. mauve	1·00	20
1244	**266**	10p. green	90	35

267 "Telecommunications"

1955. Centenary of Telegraphs in Spain.

1245	**267**	15c. brown	55	25
1246	**267**	80c. green	13·00	25
1247	**267**	3p. blue	23·00	1·40

1955. 500th Anniv of Canonization of St. Vincent Ferrer. As T **259** but portrait of the Saint (after C. Vilar).

1248	15c. ochre	60	25

269 "The Holy Family" (after El Greco)

1955. Christmas.

1249	**269**	80c. myrtle	7·00	70

270

1956. 20th Anniv of Civil War.

1250	**270**	15c. brown and bistre	20	20
1251	**270**	50c. olive and green	90	50
1252	**270**	80c. grey and mauve	9·25	25
1253	**270**	3p. blue and ultramarine	13·00	2·50

271 "Ciudad de Toledo" (cargo liner)

1956. First Floating Exhibition of National Products.

1254	**271**	3p. blue	6·50	2·75

272 The "Black Virgin"

1956. 75th Anniv of "Black Virgin" of Montserrat.

1255	**272**	15c. brown	35	20
1256	-	60c. purple	40	25
1257	**272**	80c. green	45	45

DESIGN—VERT: 60c. Montserrat Monastery.

273 Archangel Gabriel

1956. Stamp Day.

1258	**273**	80c. green	70	40

274 "Statistics"

1956. Centenary of Statistics in Spain.

1259	**274**	15c. ochre	45	30
1260	**274**	80c. green	5·50	65
1261	**274**	1p. red	5·50	65

275 Hermitage and Monument

1956. 20th Anniv of Gen. Franco's Assumption of Office as Head of State.

1262	**275**	80c. green	6·50	40

276 Refugee Children

1956. Hungarian Children's Relief.

1263	**276**	10c. lake	20	20
1264	**276**	15c. brown	20	20
1265	**276**	50c. sepia	55	20
1266	**276**	80c. green	5·00	25
1267	**276**	1p. red	5·00	25
1268	**276**	3p. blue	19·00	2·75

277 Apparition of the Sacred Heart

1957. Stamp Day and Centenary Feast of the Sacred Heart.

1269	**277**	15c. brown	20	15
1270	**277**	60c. purple	25	20
1271	**277**	80c. green	25	20

278 "The Great Captain"

1958. Fifth Birth Cent of Gonzalves de Cordoba.

1272	**278**	1p.80 green	20	15

279 Francisco Goya after Lopez

1958. Stamp Day and Goya (painter) Commem. Frames in gold.

1273	-	15c. ochre	20	15
1274	-	40c. purple	20	15
1275	-	50c. green	20	15
1276	-	60c. purple	20	15
1277	-	70c. green	20	15
1278	**279**	80c. green	20	15
1279	-	1p. red	20	15
1280	-	1p.80 green	20	15
1281	-	2p. purple	45	25
1282	-	3p. blue	1·10	50

PAINTINGS—HORIZ: 15c. "The Sunshade"; 3p. "The Drinker". VERT: 40c. "The Bookseller's Wife"; 50c. "The Count of Fernan-Nunez"; 60c. "The Crockery Vendor"; 70c. "Dona Isabel Cobos de Porcel"; 1p. "The Carnival Doll"; 1p.80, "Marianito Goya"; 2p. "The Vintage".

For similar designs see Nos. 1301/10, 1333/42, 1391/1400, 1479/88, 1495/8, 1559/68, 1627/36, 1718/27, 1770/9, 1837/46, 1912/21, 1968/77, 2021/30, 2077/84, 2135/42 and 2204/11.

280 Exhibition Emblem

1958. Brussels International Exhibition.

1283	**280**	80c. brown, red and deep brown	20	15
1284	**280**	3p. blue, red and black	95	90

1958. Brussels Exhibition, Madrid. Sheets each 49×83 mm containing Nos. 1283/4 in new colours.

MS1285	80c. green, red and brown (sold at 2p.)	37·00	27·00
MS1286	3p. violet, orange and brown (sold at 5p.)	37·00	27·00

281 Emperor Charles V (after Strigell)

1958. Fourth Death Cent of Emperor Charles V.

1287	**281**	15c. brown and ochre	15	15
1288	-	50c. olive and green	15	15
1289	-	70c. green and drab	20	15
1290	-	80c. green and brown	20	15
1291	**281**	1p. red and buff	25	15
1292	-	1p.80 emerald and green	20	15
1293	-	2p. purple and grey	65	50
1294	-	3p. blue and brown	1·70	1·30

PORTRAITS of Charles V: 50c., 1p.80, At Battle of Muhlberg (after Titian); 70c., 2p. (after Leoni); 80c., 3p. (after Titian).

282 Talgo II Articulated Train and Escorial

1958. 17th Int Railway Congress, Madrid. Inscr "XVII CONGRESO", etc.

1295	**282**	15c. ochre	15	15
1296	-	60c. plum	15	15
1297	-	80c. green	20	15
1298	**282**	1p. orange	60	20
1299	-	2p. purple	60	25
1300		3p. blue	2·75	1·20

DESIGNS—VERT: 60c., 2p. Class 1600 diesel-electric loco- [illegible] Class 241F steam locomotive and Castillo de La Mota.

1959. Stamp Day and Velazquez Commem. Designs as T **279**. Frames in gold.

1301	15c. sepia	20	20
1302	40c. purple	20	20
1303	50c. olive	20	20
1304	60c. sepia	20	20
1305	70c. green	20	20
1306	80c. myrtle	20	20
1307	1p. brown	20	20
1308	1p.80 green	20	20
1309	2p. purple	50	30
1310	3p. blue	1·00	50

PAINTINGS—HORIZ: 15c. "The Drunkards". VERT: 40c. "The Spinners" (detail); 50c. "The Surrender of Breda"; 60c. "Las Meninas"; 70c. "Balthasar Don Carlos"; 80c. Self-portrait; 1p. "The Coronation of the Virgin"; 1p.80, "Aesop"; 2p. "The Forge of Vulcan"; 3p. "Menippus".

284 The Holy Cross of the Valley of the Fallen

1959. Completion of Monastery of the Holy Cross of the Valley of the Fallen.

1311	**284**	80c. green and brown	20	15

285 Mazarin and Luis de Haro (after tapestry by Lebrun)

1959. 300th Anniv of Treaty of the Pyrenees.

1312	**285**	1p. brown and gold	20	20

286 Monastery from Courtyard

1959. 50th Anniv of Entry of Franciscan Community into Guadeloupe Monastery.

1313	**286**	15c. brown	25	15
1314	-	80c. myrtle	30	15
1315	-	1p. red	30	20

DESIGNS: 80c. Exterior view of monastery; 1p. Entrance doors of church.

287 "The Holy Family" (after Goya)

1959. Christmas.

1316	**287**	1p. brown	35	15

288 Pass with Muleta

1960. Bullfighting.

1317	-	15c. brown and ochre (postage)	20	20
1318	-	20c. violet and blue	20	20
1319	-	25c. black	20	20
1320	-	30c. brown and bistre	20	20
1321	-	50c. brown and violet	20	20
1322	-	70c. green and brown	20	20
1323	**288**	80c. emerald and green	20	20
1324	-	1p. brown and red	25	20
1325	-	1p.40 purple and brown	20	20
1326	-	1p.50 green and blue	20	20
1327	-	1p.80 blue and green	20	20
1328	-	5p. red and brown	70	55
1329	-	25c. dp pur & pur (air)	20	20
1330	-	50c. blue and turquoise	20	20
1331	-	1p. red and vermilion	25	20
1332	-	5p. violet and purple	65	45

DESIGNS—HORIZ: No. 1317, Fighting bull; No. 1318, Rounding-up bull; No. 1327, Placing darts from horseback; No. 1330, Pass with cape; No. 1332, Bull-ring. VERT: No. 1319, Corralling bulls at Pamplona; No. 1320, Bull entering ring; No. 1321, As No. 1330 (different pass); No. 1322, Banderillero placing darts; No. 1323/6, As Type **288** (different passes with muleta); No. 1328, Old-time bullfighter; No. 1329, Village bull-ring; No. 1331, Dedicating the bull.

1960. Stamp Day and Murillo Commemoration. (painter). Designs as T **279**. Frames in gold.

1333	25c. violet	15	15
1334	40c. purple	15	15
1335	50c. olive	15	15
1336	70c. green	15	15
1337	80c. turquoise	15	15
1338	1p. brown	20	15
1339	1p.50 turquoise	20	15
1340	2p.50 red	20	15
1341	3p. blue	1·90	80
1342	5p. brown	45	25

PAINTINGS—VERT: 25c. "The Good Shepherd"; 40c. "Rebecca and Elizer"; 50c. "The Virgin of the Rosary"; 70c. "The Immaculate Conception"; 80c. "Children with Shells"; 1p. Self-portrait; 2p.50, "The Dice Game"; 3p. "Children Eating"; 5p. "Children with Coins". HORIZ: 1p.50, "The Holy Family with Bird".

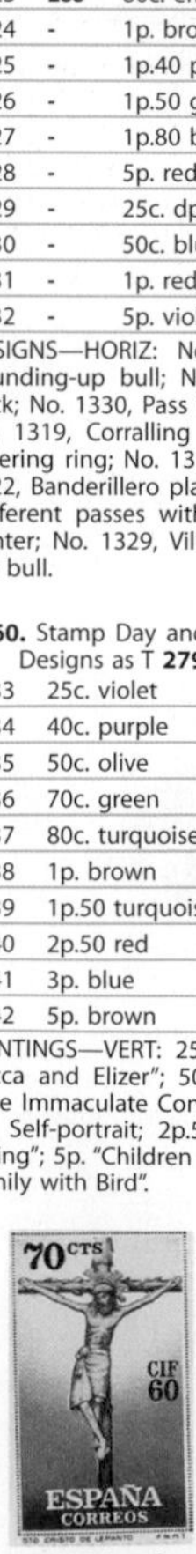

289 "Christ of Lepanto"

290 Pelota Player

1960. International Philatelic Congress and Exhibition, Barcelona. Inscr "CIF".

1343	**289**	70c. lake & green (postage)	1·80	1·50
1344	-	80c. black and sage	1·80	1·50
1345	**289**	1p. purple and red	1·80	1·50
1346	-	2p.50 slate and violet	1·80	1·50
1347	**289**	5p. sepia and bistre	1·80	1·50
1348	-	10p. sepia and ochre	1·80	1·50
1349	**290**	1p. black and red (air)	5·00	3·25
1350	**290**	5p. red and brown	5·00	3·25
1351	**290**	6p. red and purple	5·00	3·25
1352	**290**	10p. red and green	5·00	3·25

DESIGN—VERT: Nos. 1344, 1346, 1348, Church of the Holy Family, Barcelona.

291 St. John of Ribera

1960. Canonization of St. John of Ribera.

1353	**291**	1p. brown	20	15
1354	**291**	2p.50 mauve	25	20

1960. Europa. First Anniv of European Postal and Telecommunications Conference. As T **144a** of Switzerland but size 38½×22 mm.

1355	1p. drab and green	65	35
1356	5p. red and brown	1·20	1·10

292 St. Vincent de Paul

1960. 300th Death Anniv of St. Vincent de Paul.

1357	**292**	25c. violet	20	15
1358	**292**	1p. brown	25	15

293 Menendez de Aviles

1960. 400th Anniv of Discovery and Colonization of Florida.

1359	**293**	25c. blue and light blue	20	15
1360	-	70c. green and orange	20	15
1361	-	80c. green and stone	20	15
1362	-	1p. brown and yellow	20	15
1363	**293**	2p. red and pink	40	20
1364	-	2p.50 mauve and green	60	25
1365	-	3p. blue and green	4·00	85
1366	-	5p. brown and bistre	2·75	1·40

PORTRAITS: 70c., 2p.50, Hernando de Soto; 80c., 3p. Ponce de Leon; 1, 5p. Cabeza de Vaca.

294 Running

1960. Sports.

1367	**294**	25c. brn and bl (postage)	15	15
1368	-	40c. orange and violet	15	15
1369	-	70c. red and green	35	20
1370	-	80c. red and green	25	15
1371	-	1p. green and red	80	15
1372	**294**	1p.50 sepia and turquoise	35	20
1373	-	2p. green and purple	2·00	15
1374	-	2p.50 green and mauve	40	20
1375	-	3p. red and blue	90	40
1376	-	5p. blue and brown	75	70
1377	-	1p.25 red and brown (air)	20	20
1378	-	1p.50 brown and violet	35	25
1379	-	6p. red and violet	1·10	85
1380	-	10p. red and olive	1·70	1·10

DESIGNS—HORIZ: 40c., 2p. Cycling; 70c., 2p.50, Football; 1, 5p. Hockey; 1p.25, 6p. Horse-jumping. VERT: 80c., 3p. Gymnastics; 1p.50 (air), 10p. Pelota.

295 Albeniz

1960. Birth Cent of Isaac Albeniz (composer).

1381	**295**	25c. violet	15	15
1382	**295**	1p. brown	25	15

296 Cloisters

1960. Samos Monastery.

1383	**296**	80c. turquoise and green	20	15
1384	-	1p. lake and brown	1·30	20
1385	-	5p. sepia and bistre	1·50	1·10

DESIGNS—VERT: 1p. Fountain; 5p. Portico and facade.

297 "The Nativity" (Velazquez)

1960. Christmas.

1386	**297**	1p. brown	40	15

298 "The Flight to Egypt" (after Bayeu)

1961. World Refugee Year.

1387	**298**	1p. brown	25	20
1388	**298**	5p. brown	55	35

299 L. F. Moratin (after Goya)

1961. Birth Bicentenary of Moratin (poet and dramatist).

1389	**299**	1p. red	20	15
1390	**299**	1p.50 turquoise	20	15

1961. Stamp Day and El Greco (painter) Commem. Designs as T **279**. Frames in gold.

1391	25c. purple	20	15
1392	40c. purple	20	15
1393	70c. green	25	20
1394	80c. turquoise	25	15
1395	1p. purple	2·75	15
1396	1p.50 turquoise	25	15
1397	2p.50 lake	45	25
1398	3p. blue	2·10	1·20
1399	5p. sepia	4·50	2·50
1400	10p. violet	90	50

PAINTINGS: 25c. "St. Peter"; 40c. Madonna (detail, "The Holy Family" ("Madonna of the Good Milk")); 70c. Detail of "The Agony in the Garden"; 80c. "Man with Hand on Breast"; 1p. Self-portrait; 1p.50, "The Baptism of Christ"; 2p.50, "The Holy Trinity"; 3p. "Burial of the Count of Orgaz"; 5p. "The Spoliation"; 10p. "The Martyrdom of St. Maurice".

301 Velazquez (Prado Memorial)

1961. 300th Death Anniv of Velazquez.

1401	**301**	80c. green and blue	1·40	20
1402	-	1p. brown and red	6·75	20
1403	-	2p.50 violet and blue	1·00	55
1404	-	10p. green and light green	9·25	2·10

PAINTINGS—VERT: 1p. "The Duke of Olivares"; 2p.50, "Princess Margarita". HORIZ: Part of "The Spinners".

Sheets each 71×86 mm. Colours changed. Imperf.

MS1405	80c. slate and brown	8·50	8·75
MS1406	1p. violet and blue	8·50	8·75
MS1407	2p.50 blue and green	8·50	8·75
MS1408	10p. blue and slate	8·50	8·75

Sold at 1p.10, 1p.40, 3p.50 and 14p. respectively.

302 "Stamp" and "Postmark"

1961. World Stamp Day.

1409	**302**	25c. black and red	20	15
1410	**302**	1p. red and black	1·20	20
1411	**302**	10p. green and purple	1·30	65

303 Vazquez de Mella

1961. Birth Centenary of Juan Vazquez de Mella (politician and writer).

1412	**303**	1p. red	45	20
1413	**303**	2p.30 purple	20	20

304 Gen. Franco

1961. 25th Anniv of National Uprising. Multicoloured.

1414	70c. Angel and flag	15	15
1415	80c. Straits of Gibraltar	15	15
1416	1p. Knight and Alcazar, Toledo	20	15
1417	1p.50 Victory Arch	15	15
1418	2p. Knight crossing River Ebro	15	15
1419	2p.30 Soldier, flag and troops	25	15
1420	2p.50 Shipbuilding	25	15
1421	3p. Steelworks	30	25
1422	5p. Map of Spain showing electric power stations (horiz)	2·40	1·60
1423	6p. Irrigation (woman beside dam)	1·80	1·80
1424	8p. Mine	95	75
1425	10p. Type **304**	80	65

305 "Portico de la Gloria" (Cathedral of Santiago de Compostela)

1961. Council of Europe's Romanesque Art Exhibition. Inscr as in T **305**.

1426	**305**	25c. violet and gold	15	15
1427	-	1p. brown and gold	25	15
1428	-	2p. purple and gold	60	20
1429	-	3p. multicoloured	60	65

DESIGNS: 1p. Courtyard of Dominican Monastery, Santo Domingo de Silos; 2p. Madonna of Irache; 3p. "Christos Pantocrator" (from Tahull Church fresco).

306 L. de Gongora (after Velazquez)

1961. 400th Birth Anniv of De Gongora (poet).

1430	**306**	25c. violet	15	15
1431	**306**	1p. brown	30	15

307 Doves and C.E.P.T. Emblem

1961. Europa.

1432	**307**	1p. red	20	20
1433	**307**	5p. brown	50	45

308 Burgos Cathedral

1961. 25th Anniv of Gen. Franco as Head of State.

1434	**308**	1p. green and gold	20	20

309 S. de Belalcazar

1961. Explorers and Colonizers of America (1st series).

1435	**309**	25c. violet and green	15	15
1436	-	70c. green and buff	15	15
1437	-	80c. green and pink	15	15
1438	-	1p. blue and flesh	45	15
1439	**309**	2p. red and blue	3·75	40
1440	-	2p.50 purple and mauve	95	45
1441	-	3p. blue and grey	2·30	90
1442	-	5p. brown and yellow	2·30	1·30

PORTRAITS: 70c., 2p.50, B de Lezo; 80c., 3p. R. de Bastidas; 1, 5p. N. de Chaves.

See also Nos. 1515/22, 1587/94, 1683/90, 1738/45, 1810/17, 1877/84, 1947/51, 1997/2001 and 2054/8.

310 Courtyard

1961. Escorial.

1443		70c. green and turquoise	30	20
1444	**310**	80c. slate and green	25	15
1445	-	1p. red and brown	60	70
1446	-	2p.50 purple and violet	40	20
1447	-	5p. sepia and ochre	1·80	95
1448		6p. purple and blue	3·00	2·40

DESIGNS—VERT: 70c. Patio of the Kings; 2p.50, Grand Staircase; 6p. High Altar. HORIZ: 1p. Monks' Garden; 5p. View of Escorial.

311 King Alfonso XII Monument

1961. 400th Anniv of Madrid as Capital of Spain.

1449	**311**	25c. purple and green	20	15
1450	-	1p. brown and bistre	35	15
1451	-	2p. purple and grey	40	15
1452	-	2p.50 violet and red	25	15
1453	-	3p. black and blue	80	55
1454	-	5p. blue and brown	1·70	1·10

DESIGNS—VERT: 1p. King Philip II (after Pantoja); 5p. Plaza, Madrid. HORIZ: 2p. Town Hall, Madrid; 2p.50, Fountain of Cybele; 3p. Portals of Alcala Palace.

312 Santa Maria del Naranco Church

1961. 1200th Anniv of Oviedo.

1455	**312**	25c. violet and green	15	15
1456	-	1p. brown and bistre	45	15
1457	-	2p. sepia and purple	1·20	15
1458	-	2p.50 violet and purple	20	15
1459	-	3p. black and blue	95	55
1460	-	5p. brown and green	95	1·10

DESIGNS: 1p. Fruela (portrait); 2p. Cross of the Angels; 2p.50, Alfonso II; 3p. Alfonso III; 5p. Apostles of the Holy Hall, Oviedo Cathedral.

313 "The Nativity" (after Gines)

1961. Christmas.

1461	**313**	1p. plum	30	15

314 Cierva C.30A Autogyro

1961. 50th Anniv of Spanish Aviation.

1462	**314**	1p. violet and blue	20	15
1463	-	2p. green and lilac	40	15
1464	-	3p. black and green	1·40	70
1465	-	5p. purple and slate	3·75	1·60
1466	-	10p. brown and blue	1·50	60

DESIGNS—HORIZ: 2p. CASA-built Dornier Do-J Wal flying boat M-MWAL "Plus Ultra"; 3p. Breguet Bre. 19GR airplane "Jesus del Gran Poder" (Madrid-Manila Flight). VERT: 5p. Avro 504K biplane hunting great bustard; 10p. Madonna of Loreto (patron saint) and North American F-86F Sabre jet fighters.

315 Arms of Alava

1962. Arms of Provincial Capitals. Multicoloured.

1467	5p. Type **315**	20	20
1468	5p. Albacete	20	20
1469	5p. Alicante	25	25
1470	5p. Almeria	25	25
1471	5p. Avila	25	25
1472	5p. Badajoz	25	25
1473	5p. Baleares	25	20
1474	5p. Barcelona	25	20
1475	5p. Burgos	1·00	50
1476	5p. Caceres	70	45
1477	5p. Cadiz	75	45
1478	5p. Castellon de la Plana	5·00	2·30

See also Nos. 1542/53, 1612/23, 1692/1703 and 1756/64.

1962. Stamp Day and Zurbaran (painter) Commem. As T **279**. Frames in gold.

1479	25c. olive	20	15
1480	40c. purple	25	20
1481	70c. green	30	20
1482	80c. turquoise	25	20
1483	1p. sepia	8·00	35
1484	1p.50 turquoise	80	20
1485	2p.50 lake	80	30
1486	3p. blue	1·50	1·00
1487	5p. brown	3·50	1·90
1488	10p. olive	3·50	1·70

PAINTINGS—HORIZ: 25c. "Martyr". VERT: 40c. "Burial of St. Catalina"; 70c. "St. Casilda"; 80c. "Jesus crowning St. Joseph"; 1p. Self-portrait; 1p.50, "St. Hieronymus"; 2p.50, "Madonna of the Grace"; 3p. Detail from "Apotheosis of St. Thomas Aquinas"; 5p. "Madonna as a Child"; 10p. "The Immaculate Madonna".

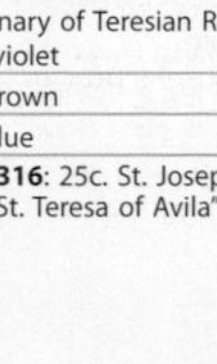

316 "Ecstasy of St. Teresa" (Bernini)

1962. Fourth Centenary of Teresian Reformation.

1489	-	25c. violet	15	15
1490	**316**	1p. brown	20	15
1491	-	3p. blue	1·40	60

DESIGNS—As Type **316**: 25c. St. Joseph's Monastery, Avila. (22×38½ mm): 3p. "St. Teresa of Avila" (Velazquez).

317 Mercury

1962. World Stamp Day.

1492	**317**	25c. pink, purple & violet	20	15
1493	**317**	1p. yellow, brown and bistre	25	20
1494	**317**	10p. green and turquoise	1·90	1·10

1962. Rubens Paintings. As T **279**. Frames in gold.

1495	25c. violet	25	20
1496	1p. brown	3·75	25
1497	3p. turquoise	5·75	2·50
1498	10p. green	7·00	2·40

PAINTINGS—As Type **279**: 25c. Ferdinand of Austria; 1p. Self-portrait; 3p. Philip II. (26×39 mm): 10p. Duke of Lerma.

318 St. Benedict

1962. 400th Death Anniv of Alonso Berruguete (sculptor). Sculptures by Berruguete.

1499	**318**	25c. mauve and blue	20	15
1500	-	80c. green and brown	20	15
1501	-	1p. red and stone	45	15
1502	-	2p. mauve and stone	4·00	15
1503	-	3p. blue and mauve	1·40	1·20
1504	-	10p. brown and pink	1·90	1·40

SCULPTURES: 80c. "The Apostle"; 1p. "St. Peter"; 2p. "St. Christopher and Child Jesus"; 3p. "Ecce Homo"; 10p. "St. Sebastian".

319 El Cid (R. Diaz de Vivar), after statue by J. Cristobal

1962. El Cid Campeador Commem. Inscr "EL CID".

1505	**319**	1p. drab and green	20	20
1506	-	2p. violet and sepia	1·70	20
1507	-	3p. green and blue	4·75	2·40
1508	-	10p. green and yellow	2·75	1·60

DESIGNS—VERT: 2p. El Cid (equestrian statue by A. Huntington). HORIZ: 3p. El Cid's treasure chest; 10p. Oath-taking ceremony of Santa Gadea.

320 Honey Bee and Honeycomb

1962. Europa.

1509	**320**	1p. red	35	20
1510	**320**	5p. green	1·30	70

321 Throwing the Discus

1962. Second Spanish-American Athletic Games, Madrid.

1511	**321**	25c. blue and pink	25	20
1512	-	80c. green and yellow	25	20
1513	-	1p. brown and pink	25	20
1514	-	3p. blue and light blue	30	25

DESIGNS: 80c. Running; 1p. Hurdling; 3p. Start of sprint.

1962. Explorers and Colonizers of America (2nd series). As T **309**.

1515	25c. mauve and grey	25	20
1516	70c. green and pink	80	20
1517	80c. green and yellow	55	20
1518	1p. brown and green	1·20	20
1519	2p. red and blue	3·25	40
1520	2p.50 violet and brown	75	25
1521	3p. blue and pink	8·00	1·90
1522	5p. brown and yellow	3·75	2·75

PORTRAITS: 25c., 2p. A. de Mendoza; 70c., 2p.50, J. de Quesada; 80c., 3p. J. de Garay; 1, 5p. P. de la Gasca.

322 U.P.A.E. Emblem

1962. 50th Anniv of Postal Union of the Americas and Spain.

1523	**322**	1p. brown, grn & dp grn	20	15

323 "The Annunciation" (after Murillo)

1962. Mysteries of the Rosary.

1524	**323**	25c. brn & vio (postage)	15	15
1525	-	70c. turquoise and green	15	15
1526	-	80c. turquoise and olive	15	15
1527	-	1p. sepia and green	5·75	75
1528	-	1p.50 blue and green	20	15
1529	-	2p. sepia and violet	1·30	55
1530	-	2p.50 red and purple	20	20
1531	-	3p. black and violet	20	20
1532	-	5p. lake and brown	90	85
1533	-	8p. black and purple	75	85
1534	-	10p. green and myrtle	75	45
1535	-	25c. violet and slate (air)	15	15
1536	-	1p. olive and purple	20	20
1537	-	5p. lake and purple	65	40
1538	-	10p. yellow, green & grey	1·70	1·00

PAINTINGS: "Joyful Mysteries": No. 1525, "Visit of Elizabeth" (Correa); 1526, "The Birth of Christ" (Murillo); 1527, "Christ shown to the Elders" (Campana); 1528, "Jesus lost and found in the Temple" (unknown artist). "Sorrowful Mysteries": 1529, "Prayer on the Mount of Olives" (Giaquinto); 1530, "Scourging" (Cano); 1531, "The Crown of Thorns" (Tiepolo); 1532, "Carrying the Cross" (El Greco); 1533, "The Crucifixion" (Murillo). "Glorious Mysteries": 1534, "The Resurrection" (Murillo); 1535, "The Ascension" (Bayeu); 1536, "The Sending-forth of the Holy Ghost" (El Greco); 1537, "The Assumption of the Virgin" (Cerezo); 1538, "The Coronation of the Virgin" (El Greco).

324 "The Nativity" (after Pedro de Mena)

1962. Christmas.

1539	**324**	1p. olive	40	20

325 Campaign Emblem and Swamp

1962. Malaria Eradication.

1540	**325**	1p. black, yellow & green	20	15

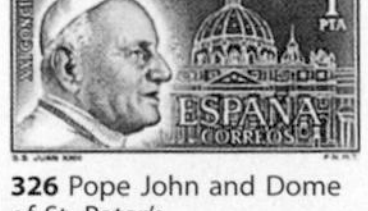

326 Pope John and Dome of St. Peter's

1962. Ecumenical Council. Vatican City (1st issue).

1541	**326**	1p. slate and purple	30	20

See also Nos. 1601 and 1755.

1963. Arms of Provincial Capitals. As T **315**. Multicoloured.

1542	5p. Ciudad Real	60	60
1543	5p. Cordoba	5·00	2·20
1544	5p. Coruna	70	65
1545	5p. Cuenca	75	60

1546	5p. Fernando Poo	1·10	1·30
1547	5p. Gerona	20	20
1548	5p. Gran Canaria	25	25
1549	5p. Granada	45	40
1550	5p. Guadalajara	75	40
1551	5p. Guipuzcoa	20	20
1552	5p. Huelva	20	20
1553	5p. Huesca	20	20

327 "St. Paul" (after El Greco)

1963. 1900th Anniv of Arrival of St. Paul in Spain.

1554	**327**	1p. sepia, olive and brown	30	20

328 Poblet Monastery

1963. Poblet Monastery.

1555	**328**	25c. purple, sepia & green	20	20
1556	-	1p. orange and red	45	20
1557	-	3p. blue and violet	1·20	35
1558	-	5p. ochre and brown	2·30	1·80

DESIGNS—VERT: 1p. Tomb; 5p. Arch. HORIZ: 3p. Aerial view of monastery.

1963. Stamp Day and Ribera (painter) Commem. As T **279**. Frames in gold.

1559	25c. violet	20	15
1560	40c. purple	20	15
1561	70c. green	45	20
1562	80c. turquoise	45	20
1563	1p. brown	55	15
1564	1p.50 turquoise	60	20
1565	2p.50 red	2·50	20
1566	3p. blue	4·50	1·10
1567	5p. brown	13·50	3·75
1568	10p. brown and purple	4·50	1·70

PAINTINGS: 25c. "Archimedes"; 40c. "Jacob's Flock"; 70c. "Triumph of Bacchus"; 80c. "St. Christopher"; 1p. Self-portrait; 1p.50, "St. Andrew"; 2p.50, "St. John the Baptist"; 3p. "St. Onofrius"; 5p. "St. Peter"; 10p. "The Madonna".

329 Mail Coach

1963. Centenary of Paris Postal Conference.

1569	**329**	1p. multicoloured	20	15

330 Globe

1963. World Stamp Day.

1570	**330**	25c. multicoloured	20	15
1571	**330**	1p. multicoloured	25	15
1572	**330**	10p. multicoloured	1·20	70

331 "Give us this day our daily bread"

1963. Freedom from Hunger.

1573	**331**	1p. multicoloured	20	15

332 Pillars and Globes

1963. Spanish Cultural Institutions Congress. Multicoloured.

1574	25c. Type **332**	20	15
1575	80c. "Santa Maria", "Pinta" and "Nina"	50	20
1576	1p. Columbus	50	20

333 Civic Seals

1963. 150th Anniv of San Sebastian.

1577	**333**	25c. blue and green	15	15
1578	-	80c. red and purple	20	15
1579	-	1p. green and bistre	20	15

DESIGNS: 80c. City aflame; 1p. View of San Sebastian, 1836.

334 "St. Maria of Europe"

1963. Europa.

1580	**334**	1p. brown and bistre	20	20
1581	**334**	5p. sepia and green	65	60

335 Arms of the Order of Mercy

1963. 75th Anniv of the Order of Mercy.

1582	**335**	25c. red, gold and black	20	15
1583	-	80c. sepia and green	20	15
1584	-	1p. purple and blue	20	15
1585	-	1p.50 brown and blue	20	15
1586	-	3p. black and violet	20	20

DESIGNS: 80c. King Jaime I; 1p. Our Lady of Mercy; 1p.50, St. Pedro Nolasco; 3p. St. Raimundo de Penafort.

1963. Explorers and Colonizers of America (3rd series). As T **309**.

1587	25c. deep blue and blue	20	15
1588	70c. green and salmon	20	15
1589	80c. green and cream	45	15
1590	1p. blue and salmon	60	15
1591	2p. red and blue	1·80	15
1592	2p.50 violet and flesh	1·40	15
1593	3p. blue and pink	2·75	1·60
1594	5p. brown and cream	3·75	3·00

PORTRAITS: 25c., 2p. Brother J. Serra; 70c., 2p.50, Vasco Nunez de Balboa; 80c., 3p. J. de Galvez; 1, 5p. D. Garcia de Paredes.

336 Scenes from Parable of the Good Samaritan

1963. Red Cross Centenary.

1595	**336**	1p. violet, red and gold	15	15

337 "The Nativity" (after sculpture by Berruguete)

1963. Christmas.

1596	**337**	1p. green	20	15

338 Fr. Raimundo Lulio

1963. Famous Spaniards (1st series).

1597	**338**	1p. black & vio (postage)	25	15
1598	-	1p.50 violet and sepia	20	15
1599	-	25p. purple and red (air)	1·40	35
1600	-	50p. black and green	1·80	55

PORTRAITS: 1p.50, Cardinal Belluga; 25p. King Recaredo; 50p. Cardinal Cisneros.

See also Nos. 1714/17.

339 Pope Paul and Dome of St. Peter's

1963. Ecumenical Council, Vatican City (2nd issue).

1601	**339**	1p. black and turquoise	15	15

340 Alcazar de Segovia

1964. Tourist Series.

1602	-	40c. brown, blue & green	25	20
1603	-	50c. sepia and blue	25	20
1604	-	70c. blue and green	25	20
1605	-	70c. brown and lilac	20	15
1606	-	80c. black and blue	25	20
1607	**340**	1p. lilac and violet	20	15
1608	-	1p. red and purple	20	15
1609	-	1p. black and green	20	15
1610	-	1p. red and purple	20	15
1611	-	1p.50 brown, green and blue	25	20

DESIGNS—HORIZ: No. 1602, Potes; 1604, Crypt of St. Isidore (Leon); 1608, Lion Court of the Alhambra (Granada); 1611, Gerona. VERT: 1603, Leon Cathedral; 1605, Costa Brava; 1606, "Christ of the Lanterns" (Cordoba); 1609, Drach Caves (Majorca); 1610, Mosque (Cordoba).

See also Nos. 1704/13, 1786/95, 1798/1805, 1860/6, 1867/74, 1933/42, 1985/9, 1993/6, 2035/9, 2040/5, 2311/6, 2379/84, 2466/7, 2575/8, 2696/2700, 2744/8, 2858/9, 2870/1 and 2915/18.

1964. Arms of Provincial Capitals. As T **315**. Multicoloured.

1612	5p. Ifni	20	20
1613	5p. Jaen	20	20
1614	5p. Leon	20	15
1615	5p. Lerida	20	15
1616	5p. Logrono	20	15
1617	5p. Lugo	20	15
1618	5p. Madrid	20	15
1619	5p. Malaga	20	15
1620	5p. Murcia	20	15
1621	5p. Navarra	20	15
1622	5p. Orense	20	15
1623	5p. Oviedo	20	15

341 Santa Maria Monastery

1964. Monastery of Santa Maria, Huerta.

1624	-	1p. bronze and green	20	15
1625	-	2p. sepia, black & turq	25	20
1626	**341**	5p. slate and violet	1·50	80

DESIGNS—VERT: 1p. Great Hall; 2p. Cloisters.

1964. Stamp Day and Sorolla (painter) Commem. As T **279**. Frames in gold.

1627	25c. violet	15	15
1628	40c. purple	15	15
1629	70c. green	15	15
1630	80c. turquoise	15	15
1631	1p. brown	15	15
1632	1p.50 turquoise	15	15
1633	2p.50 mauve	15	15
1634	3p. blue	45	40
1635	5p. brown	1·90	1·20
1636	10p. green	1·30	35

PAINTINGS—VERT: 25c. "The Earthen Jar"; 70c. "La Mancha Types"; 80c. "Valencian Fisherwoman"; 1p. Self-portrait; 5p. "Pulling the Boat"; 10p. "Valencian Couple on Horse". HORIZ: 40c. "Castillan Oxherd"; 1p.50, "The Catlepen"; 2p.50, "And people say fish is dear" (fish market); 3p. "Children on the Beach".

342 "25 Years of Peace"

1964. 25th Anniv of End of Spanish Civil War.

1637	**342**	25c. gold, green and black	15	15
1638	-	30c. red, blue and green	15	15
1639	-	40c. black and gold	15	15
1640	-	50c. multicoloured	15	15
1641	-	70c. multicoloured	15	15
1642	-	80c. multicoloured	15	15
1643	-	1p. multicoloured	30	15
1644	-	1p.50 olive, red and blue	20	15
1645	-	2p. multicoloured	20	15
1646	-	2p.50 multicoloured	20	15
1647	-	3p. multicoloured	1·10	1·20
1648	-	5p. red, green and gold	35	35
1649	-	6p. multicoloured	50	50
1650	-	10p. multicoloured	60	65

DESIGNS—VERT: 30c. Athletes ("Sport"); 50c. Apartment-houses ("National Housing Plan"); 1p. Graph and symbols ("Economic Development"); 1p.50, Rocks and tower ("Construction"); 2p.50, Wheatear and dam ("Irrigation"); 5p. "Tree of Learning" ("Scientific Research"); 10p. Gen. Franco. HORIZ: 40c. T.V. screen and symbols ("Radio and T.V."); 70c. Wheatears, tractor and landscape ("Agriculture"); 80c. Tree and forests ("Reafforestation"); 2p. Forms of transport ("Transport and Communications"); 3p. Pylon and part of dial ("Electrification"); 6p. Ancient buildings ("Tourism").

343 Spanish Pavilion at Fair

1964. New York World's Fair.

1651	**343**	1p. green and turquoise	20	15
1652	-	1p.50 brown and red	25	15
1653	-	2p.50 green and blue	25	15
1654	-	5p. red	25	35
1655	-	50p. blue and grey	1·10	40

DESIGNS—VERT: 1p.50, Bullfighting; 2p.50, Castillo de la Mota; 5p. Spanish dancing; 50p. Pelota.

344 6c. Stamp of 1850 and Globe

1964. World Stamp Day.

1656	**344**	25c. red and purple	20	15
1657	**344**	1p. green and blue	20	20
1658	**344**	10p. orange and red	35	30

345 Macarena Virgin

1964. Canonical Coronation of Macarena Virgin.

1659	**345**	1p. green and yellow	15	15

346 Medieval Ship

1964. Spanish Navy Commemoration.

1660	**346**	15c. slate and purple	15	15
1661	-	25c. green and orange	15	15
1662	-	40c. grey and blue	15	15
1663	-	50c. green and slate	15	15
1664	-	70c. violet and blue	15	15
1665	-	80c. blue and green	15	15
1666	-	1p. purple and brown	15	15
1667	-	1p.50 sepia and red	15	15
1668	-	2p. black and green	1·30	30
1669	-	2p.50 red and violet	15	15
1670	-	3p. blue and brown	15	15
1671	-	5p. blue and green	90	90
1672	-	6p. violet and turquoise	70	70
1673	-	10p. red and orange	25	25

SHIPS—VERT: 25c. Carrack; 1p. Ship of the line "Santissima Trinidad"; 1p.50, Corvette "Atrevida". HORIZ: 40c. "Santa Maria"; 50c. Galley; 70c. Galleon; 80c. Xebec; 2p. Steam frigate "Isabel II"; 2p.50, Frigate "Numancia"; 3p. Destroyer "Destructor"; 5p. Isaac Peral's submarine; 6p. Cruiser "Baleares"; 10p. Cadet schooner "Juan Sebastian de Elcano".

347 Europa "Flower"

1964. Europa.

1674	**347**	1p. ochre, red and green	40	30
1675	**347**	5p. blue, purple and green	95	90

348 "The Virgin of the Castle"

1964. 700th Anniv of Reconquest of Jerez.

1676	**348**	25c. brown and buff	15	15
1677	**348**	1p. blue and grey	20	15

349 Putting the Shot

1965. Olympic Games, Tokyo and Innsbruck. Olympic rings in gold.

1678	**349**	25c. blue and orange	15	15
1679	-	80c. blue and green	15	15
1680	-	1p. blue and light blue	15	15
1681	-	3p. blue and buff	20	20
1682	-	5p. blue and violet	20	20

DESIGNS: 80c. Long jumping; 1p. Skiing (slalom); 3p. Judo; 5p. Throwing the discus.

1964. Explorers and Colonizers of America (4th series). As T **309**. Inscr "1964" at foot.

1683	25c. violet and blue	15	15
1684	70c. olive and pink	15	15
1685	80c. green and buff	30	25
1686	1p. violet and buff	30	15
1687	2p. olive and blue	30	15
1688	2p.50 purple and turquoise	25	15
1689	3p. blue and grey	3·50	1·20
1690	5p. brown and cream	2·30	1·60

PORTRAITS: 25c., 2p. D. de Almagro; 70c., 2p.50, F. de Toledo; 80c., 3p. T. de Mogrovejo; 1, 5p. F. Pizarro.

350 "Adoration of the Shepherds" (after Zurbaran)

1964. Christmas.

1691	**350**	1p. brown	25	20

1965. Arms of Provincial Capitals. As T **315**. Multicoloured.

1692	5p. Palencia	20	15
1693	5p. Pontevedra	20	15
1694	5p. Rio Muni	20	15
1695	5p. Sahara	20	15
1696	5p. Salamanca	20	15
1697	5p. Santander	20	15
1698	5p. Segovia	20	15
1699	5p. Seville	20	15
1700	5p. Soria	20	15
1701	5p. Tarragona	20	15
1702	5p. Tenerife	20	15
1703	5p. Teruel	20	15

1965. Tourist Series. As T **340**.

1704	25c. black and blue	20	15
1705	30c. brown and turquoise	20	15
1706	50c. purple and red	20	15
1707	70c. indigo and blue	20	15
1708	80c. purple and mauve	20	15
1709	1p. mauve, red and sepia	20	15
1710	2p.50 purple and brown	20	15
1711	2p.50 olive and blue	20	15
1712	3p. purple and purple	20	15
1713	6p. violet and slate	20	15

DESIGNS—VERT: 25c. Columbus Monument, Barcelona; 30c. Santa Maria Church, Burgos; 50c. Synagogue, Toledo; 80c. Seville Cathedral; 1p. Cudillero Port; 2p.50, (No. 1710), Burgos Cathedral (interior); 3p. Bridge at Cambados (Pontevedra); 6p. Ceiling, Lonja (Valencia). HORIZ: 70c. Zamora; 2p.50, (No. 1711), Mogrovejo (Santander).

1965. Famous Spaniards (2nd series). As T **338**.

1714	25c. sepia and turquoise	15	15
1715	70c. deep blue and blue	20	20
1716	2p.50 sepia and bronze	20	20
1717	5p. bronze and green	35	35

PORTRAITS: 25c. Donoso Cortes; 70c. King Alfonso X (the Saint); 2p.50, G. M. de Jovellanos; 5p. St. Dominic de Guzman.

1965. Stamp Day and J. Romero de Torres Commem. As T **279**. Frames in gold.

1718	25c. purple	20	15
1719	40c. purple	20	15
1720	70c. green	20	15
1721	80c. turquoise	20	15
1722	1p. brown	20	15
1723	1p.50 turquoise	20	15
1724	2p.50 mauve	30	20
1725	3p. blue	40	35
1726	5p. brown	40	35
1727	10p. green	75	35

PAINTINGS (by J. Romero de Torres): 25c. "Girl with Jar"; 40c. "The Song"; 70c. "The Virgin of the Lanterns"; 80c. "Girl with Guitar"; 1p. Self-portrait; 1p.50, "Poem of Cordoba"; 2p.50, "Marta and Maria"; 3p. "Poem of Cordoba" (different); 5p. "A Little Charcoal-maker"; 10p. "Long Live the Hair!".

351 Bull and Stamps

1965. World Stamp Day.

1728	**351**	25c. multicoloured	15	15
1729	**351**	1p. multicoloured	15	15
1730	**351**	10p. multicoloured	45	40

352 I.T.U. Emblem and Symbols

1965. Centenary of I.T.U.

1731	**352**	1p. red, black and pink	15	15

353 Pilgrim

1965. Holy Year of Santiago de Compostela. Multicoloured.

1732	1p. Type **353**	15	15
1733	2p. Pilgrim (profile)	15	15

354 Spanish Knight and Banners

1965. 400th Anniv of Florida Settlement.

1734	**354**	3p. black, red and yellow	20	15

355 St. Benedict (after sculpture by Pereira)

1965. Europa.

1735	**355**	1p. green and emerald	25	25
1736	**355**	5p. violet and purple	55	35

356 Sports Palace, Madrid

1965. Int Olympic Committee Meeting, Madrid.

1737	**356**	1p. brown, gold and grey	15	15

1965. Explorers and Colonizers of America (5th series). As T **309**. Inscr "1965" at foot.

1738	25c. violet and green	15	15
1739	70c. brown and pink	15	15
1740	80c. green and cream	15	15
1741	1p. violet and buff	15	15
1742	2p. brown and blue	20	15
1743	2p.50 purple and turquoise	20	20
1744	3p. blue and grey	1·20	50
1745	5p. brown and yellow	1·20	45

PORTRAITS: 25c., 2p. Don Fadrique de Toledo; 70c., 2p.50, Padre Jose de Anchieta; 80c., 3p. Francisco de Orellana; 1p., 5p. St. Luis Beltran.

357 Cloisters

1965. Yuste Monastery.

1746	**357**	1p. blue and sepia	15	15
1747	-	2p. sepia and brown	20	15
1748	-	5p. green and blue	25	25

DESIGNS—VERT: 2p. Charles V room. HORIZ: 5p. Courtyard.

358 Spanish 1r. Stamp of 1865

1965. Centenary of Spanish Perforated Stamps.

1749	**358**	80c. green and bronze	15	15
1750	-	1p. brown and purple	15	15
1751	-	5p. brown and sepia	15	15

DESIGNS: 1p. 1865 19c. stamp; 5p. 1865 2r. stamp.

359 "The Nativity" (after Mayno)

1965. Christmas.

1752	**359**	1p. green and blue	15	15

360 Madonna of Antipolo

1965. 400th Anniv of Christianity in the Philippines.

1753	**360**	1p. brown, black and buff	20	15
1754	-	3p. blue and grey	20	20

DESIGN: 3p. Father Urdaneta.

361 Globe

1965. 21st Ecumenical Council, Vatican City (3rd issue).

1755	**361**	1p. multicoloured	15	15

1966. Arms of Provincial Capitals. As T **315**. Multicoloured.

1756	5p. Toledo	20	15
1757	5p. Valencia	20	15
1758	5p. Valladolid	20	15
1759	5p. Vizcaya	20	15
1760	5p. Zamora	20	15
1761	5p. Zaragoza	20	15
1762	5p. Ceuta	20	15
1763	5p. Melilla	20	15
1764	10p. Spain (26×38½ mm)	25	20

362 Admiral Alvaro de Bazan

1966. Celebrities (1st series).

1765	**362**	25c. black and blue (postage)	20	15
1766	-	2p. violet and purple	25	20
1767	-	25p. bronze & green (air)	1·30	25
1768	-	50p. grey and blue	2·00	75

PORTRAITS: 2p. Benito Daza de Valdes (doctor); 25p. Seneca; 50p. St. Damaso.

See also Nos. 1849/52.

363 Exhibition Emblem

1966. Graphic Arts Exn, "Graphispack", Barcelona.

1769	**363**	1p. green, blue and red	15	15

1966. Stamp Day and J. M. Sert Commem. Designs as T **279**. Frames in gold.

1770	25c. violet	20	15
1771	40c. purple	20	15
1772	70c. green	20	15
1773	80c. bronze	20	15
1774	1p. brown	20	15
1775	1p.50 blue	20	15
1776	2p.50 red	20	15
1777	3p. blue	20	15
1778	5p. sepia	20	15
1779	10p. green	20	15

1976. Bicentenary of American Revolution.

2367	**498**	1p. blue and brown	15	10
2368	-	3p. brown and green	95	10
2369	-	5p. green and brown	45	15
2370	-	12p. brown and green	45	25

DESIGNS: 3p. Bernardo de Galvez and emblem; 5p. Richmond $1 banknote of 1861; 12p. Battle of Pensacola.

499 Customs-house, Cadiz

1976. Spanish Customs Buildings.

2371	**499**	1p. brown and black	15	10
2372	-	3p. brown and green	65	15
2373	-	7p. purple and brown	1·10	35

BUILDINGS: 3p. Madrid; 7p. Barcelona.

500 Savings Jar and "Industry"

1976. Spanish Post Office. Multicoloured.

2374	1p. Type **500**	10	10
2375	3p. Railway mail-sorting van	35	10
2376	6p. Mounted postman (horiz)	15	15
2377	10p. Automatic letter sorting equipment (horiz)	25	15

501 King Juan Carlos I, Queen Sophia and Map of the Americas

1976. Royal Visit to America (1st issue).

2378	**501**	12p. multicoloured	25	15

See also No. 2434.

1976. Tourist Series. As T **340**.

2379	1p. brown and blue	15	10
2380	2p. green and blue	70	10
2381	3p. chocolate and brown	50	10
2382	4p. blue and brown	30	10
2383	7p. brown and blue	85	40
2384	12p. purple and red	1·30	25

DESIGNS—HORIZ: 1p. Cloisters, San Marcos, Leon; 2p. Las Canadas, Tenerife; 4p. Cruz de Tejeda, Las Palmas; 7p. Gredos, Avila; 12p. La Arruzafa, Cordoba. VERT: 3p. Hospice of the Catholic Kings, Santiago de Compostela.

502 Rowing

1976. Olympic Games, Montreal. Multicoloured.

2385	1p. Type **502**	15	10
2386	2p. Boxing	45	15
2387	3p. Wrestling (vert)	40	15
2388	12p. Basketball (vert)	25	15

503 King Juan Carlos I

1976

2389	**503**	10c. orange	10	10
2390	**503**	25c. yellow	10	10
2391	**503**	30c. blue	10	10
2392	**503**	50c. purple	10	10
2393	**503**	1p. green	10	10
2394	**503**	1p.50 red	10	10
2395	**503**	2p. blue	10	10
2396	**503**	3p. green	10	10
2397	**503**	4p. turquoise	10	10
2398	**503**	5p. red	10	10
2399	**503**	6p. turquoise	10	10
2400	**503**	7p. olive	15	10
2401	**503**	8p. blue	15	10
2402	**503**	10p. red	15	10
2403	**503**	12p. brown	20	10
2403a	**503**	13p. brown	25	10
2403b	**503**	14p. orange	20	10
2404	**503**	15p. violet	30	10
2405	**503**	16p. brown	25	10
2405a	**503**	17p. blue	35	10
2406	**503**	19p. orange	30	10
2407	**503**	20p. red	30	10
2408	**503**	30p. green	40	10
2409	**503**	50p. red	70	10
2409a	**503**	60p. blue	80	10
2409b	**503**	75p. green	1·00	25
2409c	**503**	85p. grey	1·20	40
2409d	-	100p. brown	1·40	10
2409e	-	200p. green	2·75	10
2409f	-	500p. blue	6·75	85

Nos. 2409d/f are as Type **503**, but larger, 25×30 mm.

1976. Spanish Military Uniforms (6th series). As T **448**. Multicoloured.

2410	1p. Alcantara Regiment, 1815	15	15
2411	2p. Regiment of the line, 1821	85	15
2412	3p. Gala Engineers, 1825	30	15
2413	7p. Artillery Regiment, 1828	25	25
2414	25p. Light Infantry Regiment, 1830	30	20

504 "Giving Blood"

1976. Blood Donors Publicity.

2415	**504**	3p. red and black	20	15

505 Batitales Mosaic

1976. Bimillenary of Lugo.

2416	**505**	1p. purple and black	15	15
2417	-	3p. brown and black	20	15
2418	-	7p. red and green	50	25

DESIGNS: 3p. Old City Wall; 7p. Roman coins.

506 Parliament House, Madrid

1976. 63rd Inter-Parliamentary Union Congress, Madrid.

2419	**506**	12p. brown and green	20	15

1976. Stamp Day and Luis Menendez Commemoration. Paintings as T **409**. Multicoloured.

2420	1p. "Jug, Cherries, Plums and Cheese"	10	10
2421	2p. "Jar, Melon, Oranges and Savouries"	10	10
2422	3p. "Barrel, Pears and Melon"	10	10
2423	4p. "Pigeons, Basket and Bowl"	15	10
2424	6p. "Fish and Oranges" (horiz)	20	10
2425	7p. "Melon and Bread" (horiz)	25	25
2426	10p. "Jug, Plums and Bread" (horiz)	25	15
2427	12p. "Pomegranates, Apples and Grapes" (horiz)	25	15

507 "The Nativity"

1976. Christmas. Statuettes. Multicoloured.

2428	3p. Type **507**	80	10
2429	12p. St. Christopher carrying Holy Child (vert)	1·50	55

508 Nicoya Church

1976. "Spain in the New World" (5th series). Costa Rica. Multicoloured.

2430	1p. Type **508**	15	10
2431	2p. Juan Vazquez de Coronado	25	15
2432	3p. Orosi Mission (horiz)	20	15
2433	12p. Tomas de Acosta	25	20

1976. Royal Visit to America (2nd issue). As T **501**. Multicoloured.

2434	12p. "Santa Maria" and South America	20	15

510 San Pedro de Alcantara Monastery

1976. Monastery of San Pedro de Alcantara.

2435	**510**	3p. brown and purple	35	15
2436	-	7p. purple and blue	15	15
2437	-	20p. chocolate. and brown	35	15

DESIGNS—VERT: 7p. High Altar; 20p. San Pedro de Alcantara.

511 Hand releasing Doves

1976. Civil War Invalids' Association Commem.

2438	**511**	3p. multicoloured	20	15

512 Pablo Casals and Cello

1976. Birth Centenaries.

2439	**512**	3p. black and blue	15	10
2440	-	5p. green and red	20	10

DESIGN: 5p. Manuel de Falla and "Fire Dance".

1977. Spanish Military Uniforms (7th series). Vert designs as T **448**. Multicoloured.

2441	1p. Calatrava Regiment of Lancers, 1844	15	10
2442	2p. Engineers' Regiment, 1850	35	10
2443	3p. Light Infantry Regiment, 1861	20	10
2444	4p. Infantry of the Line, 1861	20	15
2445	20p. Horse Artillery, 1862	25	15

513 King James I and Arms of Aragon

1977. 700th Death Anniv of King James I.

2446	**513**	4p. brown and violet	20	15

514 Jacinto Verdaguer (poet)

1977. Spanish Celebrities.

2447	**514**	5p. red and purple	25	10
2448	-	7p. green and brown	15	15
2449	-	12p. green and blue	20	15
2450	-	50p. brown and green	75	15

DESIGNS: 7p. Miguel Servet (theologian and physician); 12p. Pablo Sarasate (violinist); 50p. Francisco Tarrega (guitarist).

515 King Charles III

1977. Bicentenary of Economic Society of the Friends of the Land.

2451	**515**	4p. brown and green	20	15

516 Atlantic Salmon

1977. Spanish Fauna (6th series). Freshwater Fish. Multicoloured.

2452	1p. Type **516**	20	10
2453	2p. Brown trout (horiz)	20	10
2454	3p. European eel (horiz)	20	10
2455	4p. Common carp (horiz)	20	10
2456	6p. Barbel (horiz)	20	10

517 Skiing

1977. World Ski Championships, Granada.

2457	**517**	5p. multicoloured	20	15

518 La Cuadra, 1902

1977. Vintage Cars. Multicoloured.

2458	2p. Type **518**	10	10
2459	4p. Hispano Suiza, 1916	10	10
2460	5p. Elizade, 1915	15	15
2461	7p. Abadal, 1914	15	15

519 Donana

1977. Europa. Landscapes, National Parks. Multicoloured.

2462	3p. Type **519**	15	15
2463	12p. Ordesa	25	25

520 Plaza Mayor, Madrid and Stamps

1977. 50th Anniv of Philatelic Bourse on Plaza Mayor, Madrid.

2464	**520**	3p. green, red and violet	20	15

521 Enrique de Osso (founder)

1977. Centenary of Society of St. Theresa of Jesus.

2465	**521**	8p. multicoloured	20	15

1977. Tourist Series. As T **340**.

2466	1p. brown and orange	10	10
2467	2p. grey and brown	10	10
2468	3p. purple and blue	10	10

2469	4p. green and blue	10	10
2470	7p. grey and brown	10	10
2471	12p. brown and violet	15	10

DESIGNS—HORIZ: 1p. Toledo Gate, Ciudad Real; 2p. Roman Aqueduct, Almunecar; 7p. Ampudia Castle, Palencia; 12p. Bisagra Gate, Toledo. VERT: 3p. Jaen Cathedral; 4p. Bridge and Gate, Ronda Gorge, Malaga.

1977. Spanish Military Uniforms (8th series). As T **448**. Multicoloured.

2472	1p. Administration officer, 1875	20	10
2473	2p. Lancer, 1883	20	10
2474	3p. General Staff commander, 1884	20	10
2475	7p. Trumpeter, Divisional Artillery, 1887	20	15
2476	25p. Medical Corps officer, 1895	25	15

522 San Marino de la Cogalla (carving) and Early Castilian Manuscript

1977. Millenary of Castilian Language.

2477	**522**	5p. brown, green & pur	20	15

1977. Stamp Day and F. Madrazo (painter) Commemoration. Portraits. As T **409**. Multicoloured.

2478	1p. "The Youth of Florez"	10	10
2479	2p. "Duke of San Miguel"	10	10
2480	3p. "C. Coronado"	10	10
2481	4p. "Campoamor"	10	10
2482	6p. "Marquesa de Montelo"	10	10
2483	7p. "Rivadeneyra"	15	10
2484	10p. "Countess of Vilches"	15	10
2485	15p. "Gomez de Avellaneda"	20	10

523 West Indies Sailing Packet and Map of Mail Routes to America

1977. Bicentenary of Mail to the Indies, and "Espamer 77" Stamp Exhibition, Barcelona.

2486	**523**	15p. green and brown	25	25

524 St. Francis's Church

1977. Spanish–Guatemalan Relations. Guatemala City Buildings. Multicoloured.

2487	1p. Type **524**	10	10
2488	3p. High-rise flats	10	10
2489	7p. Government Palace	10	10
2490	12p. Monument, Columbus Square	15	15

525 Monastery Building

1977. St. Peter's Monastery, Cardena Commem.

2491	**525**	3p. grey and blue	10	10
2492	-	7p. red and brown	15	10
2493	-	20p. grey and green	25	15

DESIGNS: 7p. Cloisters; 20p. El Cid (effigy).

526 Adoration of the Kings

1977. Christmas. Miniatures from Manuscript "Romanico de Huesca". Multicoloured.

2494	5p. Type **526**	15	10
2495	12p. Flight into Egypt (vert)	20	10

527 Rohrbach RO.VII Roland M-CBBB, 1927, and Douglas DC-10 EC-CPN

1977. 50th Anniv of Iberia (State Airline).

2496	**527**	12p. multicoloured	20	15

528 Crown Prince Felipe

1977. Felipe de Borbon, Prince of Asturias.

2497	**528**	5p. multicoloured	20	15

529 Judo

1977. Tenth World Judo Championships.

2498	**529**	3p. black, red and brown	20	15

1977. Spanish Military Uniforms (9th series). Multicoloured. Vert designs as T **448**.

2499	1p. Standard bearer, Royal Infantry Regiment, 1908	10	10
2500	2p. Lieutenant-Colonel, Pavia Hussars, 1909	10	10
2501	3p. Lieutenant, Horse Artillery, 1912	10	10
2502	5p. Engineers' Captain, 1921	10	10
2503	12p. Captain-General of the Armed Forces, 1925	10	10

530 Hilarion Eslava (composer)

1977. Spanish Celebrities.

2504	**530**	5p. black and purple	10	10
2505	-	8p. black and green	15	10
2506	-	25p. black and green	30	10
2507	-	50p. purple and brown	65	20

DESIGNS: 8p. Jose Clara (sculptor); 25p. Pio Baroja (writer); 50p. Antonio Machado (writer).

531 "The Deposition of Christ" (detail Juan de Juni)

1978. Anniversaries of Artists.

2508	**531**	3p. multicoloured	10	10
2509	-	3p. multicoloured	10	10
2510	-	3p. mauve and violet	10	10
2511	-	5p. multicoloured	10	10
2512	-	5p. multicoloured	10	10
2513	-	5p. brown and black	10	10
2514	-	8p. multicoloured	10	10
2515	-	8p. multicoloured	10	10
2516	-	8p. pink and green	10	10

DESIGNS—As T **531**. No. 2510, Portrait of Juan de Juni (sculptor, 400th death anniv); No. 2511, Detail of "Rape of the Sabines" (Rubens); No. 2513, Artist's palette and Ruben's signature; No. 2514, Detail of "Bacchanal" (Titian); No. 2516, Artist's palette and Titian's initial. 46×25 mm: No. 2509, Different detail of "Deposition of Christ" and sculptor's tools; No. 2512, Different detail of "Rape of the Sabines" and portrait of Rubens (400th birth anniv); No. 2515, Different detail of "Bacchanal" and portrait of Titian (500th birth anniv).

532 Edelweiss in the Pyrenees

1978. Protection of the Environment. Multicoloured.

2517	3p. Type **532**	10	10
2518	5p. Brown trout and red-breasted merganser	10	10
2519	7p. Forest (fire prevention)	15	10
2520	12p. Tanker, oil rig and industrial complex (protection of the sea)	15	10
2521	20p. Audouin's gull and Mediterranean monk seal (vert)	25	10

533 Palace of Charles V, Granada

1978. Europa.

2522	**533**	5p. green and light green	20	15
2523	-	12p. red and green	30	20

DESIGN: 12p. Exchange building, Seville.

534 Council Emblem and Map of Spain

1978. Membership of the Council of Europe.

2524	**534**	12p. multicoloured	15	15

535 Columbus Hermitage

1978. 500th Anniv of Las Palmas, Gran Canaria. Multicoloured.

2525	3p. 16th-century plan of city (horiz)	10	10
2526	5p. Type **535**	15	10
2527	12p. View of Las Palmas (16th century) (horiz)	15	10

536 Post Box, Stamp, U.P.U. Emblem and Postal Transport

1978. World Stamp Day.

2528	**536**	5p. green and deep green	20	15

1978. Stamp Day and Picasso Commemoration. As T **409**. Multicoloured.

2529	3p. "Portrait of Senora Canals"	15	10
2530	5p. Self-portrait	15	10
2531	8p. "Portrait of Jaime Sabartes"	15	10
2532	10p. "The End of the Number"	15	10
2533	12p. "Science and Charity" (horiz)	15	10
2534	15p. "Las Meninas" (horiz)	15	10
2535	20p. "The Pigeons"	20	15
2536	25p. "The Painter and Model" (horiz)	25	15

537 Jose de San Martin

1978. Latin-American Heroes.

2537	**537**	7p. brown and red	10	10
2538	-	12p. violet and red	15	10

DESIGNS: 12p. Simon Bolivar.

538 Flight into Egypt

1978. Christmas. Capitals from Santa Maria de Nieva. Multicoloured.

2539	5p. Type **538**	10	10
2540	12p. The Annunciation	15	10

539 Aztec Calendar

1978. Royal Visits to Mexico, Peru and Argentina. Multicoloured.

2541	5p. Type **539**	10	10
2542	5p. Macchu Piccu, Peru	10	10
2543	5p. Pre-Columbian pots, Argentina	10	10

540 Philip V

1978. Spanish Kings and Queens of the House of Bourbon.

2544	**540**	5p. red and blue	10	10
2545	-	5p. deep green and green	10	10
2546	-	8p. lake and blue	20	15
2547	-	10p. black and green	20	15
2548	-	12p. lake and brown	20	15
2549	-	15p. blue and green	25	15
2550	-	20p. blue and olive	25	15
2551	-	25p. violet and blue	30	20
2552	-	50p. brown and red	55	25
2553	-	100p. violet and blue	1·40	55

DESIGNS: 5p. (No. 2545), Luis I; 8p. Ferdinand VI; 10p. Charles III; 12p. Charles IV; 15p. Ferdinand VII; 20p. Isabel II; 25p. Alfonso XII; 50p. Alfonso XIII; 100p. Juan Carlos I.

541 Miniatures from Bible

1978. Millenary of Consecration of Third Basilica of Santa Maria, Ripoll.

2554	**541**	5p. multicoloured	25	20

542 Flag, First Lines of Constitution and Cortes Building

1978. New Constitution.

2555	**542**	5p. multicoloured	25	20

543 Car and Oil Drop

1979. Energy Conservation. Multicoloured.

2556	5p. Type **543**	15	15
2557	8p. Insulated house and thermometer	20	15
2558	10p. Hand removing electric plug	20	15

544 St. Jean Baptiste de la Salle (founder)

1979. Centenary of Brothers of the Christian Schools in Spain.

| 2559 | **544** | 5p. brown, blue & mauve | 15 | 15 |

545 Jorge Manrique (poet)

1979. Spanish Celebrities.

2560	**545**	5p. brown and green	15	15
2561	-	8p. blue and red	15	15
2562	-	10p. violet and brown	15	15
2563	-	20p. green and bistre	30	15

DESIGNS: 8p. Fernan Caballero (novelist); 10p. Francisco Villaespesa (poet); 20p. Gregorio Maranon (writer).

546 Running and Jumping

1979. Sport for All.

2564	**546**	5p. red, green and black	15	15
2565	-	8p. blue, ochre and black	20	15
2566	-	10p. brown, blue & black	20	15

DESIGNS: 8p. Football, running, skipping and cycling; 10p. Running.

547 School Library (child's drawing)

1979. International Year of the Child.

| 2567 | **547** | 5p. multicoloured | 15 | 15 |

548 Cabinet Messenger and Postilion, 1761

1979. Europa.

| 2568 | **548** | 5p. deep brown and brown on yellow | 35 | 20 |
| 2569 | - | 12p. green and brown on yellow | 35 | 20 |

DESIGN—HORIZ: 12p. Manuel de Ysasi (postal reformer).

549 Wave Pattern and Television Screen

1979. World Telecommunications Day. Multicoloured.

| 2570 | 5p. Type **549** | 15 | 15 |
| 2571 | 8p. Satellite and receiving aerial (horiz) | 15 | 15 |

550 First Bulgarian Stamp and Exhibition Hall

1979. "Philaserdica 79" Stamp Exhibition, Sofia.

| 2572 | **550** | 12p. multicoloured | 15 | 10 |

551 Tank, "Roger de Lauria" (destroyer) and Hawker Siddeley Matador

1979. Armed Forces Day.

| 2573 | **551** | 5p. multicoloured | 10 | 10 |

1979. Stamp Day.

| 2574 | **552** | 5p. multicoloured | 10 | 10 |

552 King receiving Messenger

1979. Tourist Series. As T **340**.

2575	5p. lilac and blue	15	10
2576	8p. brown and blue	15	10
2577	10p. green and myrtle	15	15
2578	20p. sepia and brown	25	15

DESIGNS—VERT: 5p. Daroca Gate, Zaragoza; 8p. Gerona Cathedral; 10p. Interior of Carthusian Monastery Church, Granada; 20p. Portal of Marques de Dos Aguas Palace, Valencia.

553 Turkey Sponge

1979. Spanish Fauna (7th series). Invertebrates. Multicoloured.

2579	5p. Type **553**	10	10
2580	7p. Crayfish	15	10
2581	8p. Scorpion	15	10
2582	20p. Starfish	20	10
2583	25p. Sea anemone	25	15

554 Antonio Gutierrez

1979. Defence of Tenerife, 1797.

| 2584 | **554** | 5p. multicoloured | 15 | 10 |

1979. Stamp Day and J. de Juanes (painter) Commemoration. Religious Paintings as T **409**. Multicoloured.

2585	8p. "Immaculate Conception"	15	10
2586	10p. "Holy Family"	15	10
2587	15p. "Ecce Homo"	15	10
2588	20p. "St. Stephen in the Synagogue"	25	10
2589	30p. "The Last Supper" (horiz)	30	15
2590	50p. "Adoration of the Mystic Lamb" (horiz)	55	20

555 Cathedral and Statue of Virgin and Child, Zaragoza

1979. Eighth Mariological Congress, Zaragoza.

| 2591 | **555** | 5p. multicoloured | 10 | 10 |

556 St. Bartholomew's College, Bogota

1979. Latin-American Architecture.

| 2592 | **556** | 7p. green, blue and brown | 15 | 10 |
| 2593 | - | 12p. indigo, purple & brn | 15 | 15 |

DESIGN: 12p. University of San Marcos, Lima.

557 Hands and Governor's Palace, Barcelona

1979. Catalonian Autonomy.

| 2594 | **557** | 8p. multicoloured | 20 | 15 |

558 Autonomy Statute

1979. Basque Autonomy.

| 2595 | **558** | 8p. multicoloured | 20 | 15 |

559 Prince of Asturias and Hospital

1979. Centenary of Hospital of the Child Jesus, Madrid.

| 2596 | **559** | 5p. multicoloured | 20 | 15 |

560 Barcelona Tax Stamp, 1929

1979. 50th Anniv of Barcelona Exhibition Tax Stamps.

| 2597 | **560** | 5p. multicoloured | 20 | 15 |

561 The Nativity

1979. Christmas. Capitals from San Pedro el Viejo, Huesca. Multicoloured.

| 2598 | 8p. Type **561** | 10 | 10 |
| 2599 | 19p. Flight into Egypt | 25 | 10 |

562 Charles I

1979. Spanish Kings of the House of Hapsburg.

2600	**562**	15p. green and blue	30	10
2601	-	20p. blue and mauve	30	10
2602	-	25p. violet and brown	35	10
2603	-	50p. brown and green	65	15
2604	-	100p. mauve and brown	1·10	35

DESIGNS: 20p. Philip II; 25p. Philip III; 50p. Philip IV; 100p. Charles II.

563 Olive Plantation and Harvester

1979. International Olive Oil Year.

| 2605 | **563** | 8p. multicoloured | 20 | 15 |

564 Electric Train

1980. Public Transport.

2606	**564**	3p. lake and brown	10	10
2607	-	4p. blue and brown	10	10
2608	-	5p. green and brown	10	10

DESIGNS: 4p. Motorbus; 5p. Underground train.

565 Steel Products

1980. Spanish Exports (1st series). Multicoloured.

2609	5p. Type **565**	10	10
2610	8p. Tankers	15	10
2611	13p. Footwear	15	10
2612	19p. Industrial machinery	25	10
2613	25p. Factory buildings, bridge and symbols of technology	35	20

See also Nos. 2653/5.

566 Federico Garcia Lorca

1980. Europa. Writers.

| 2614 | **566** | 8p. violet and green | 20 | 15 |
| 2615 | - | 19p. brown and green | 25 | 20 |

DESIGN: 19p. J. Ortega y Gasset.

567 Footballers

1980. World Cup Football Championship, Spain (1982) (1st issue). Multicoloured.

| 2616 | 8p. Type **567** | 15 | 10 |
| 2617 | 19p. Football and flags | 25 | 10 |

See also Nos. 2640/1, 2668/9 and 2683/**MS**2685.

568 Armed Forces

1980. Armed Forces Day.

| 2618 | **568** | 8p. multicoloured | 15 | 10 |

569 Bourbon Arms, Ministry of Finance, Madrid

1980. Public Finances under the Bourbons.

| 2619 | **569** | 8p. deep brown & brown | 15 | 10 |

570 Helen Keller

1980. Birth Centenary of Helen Keller.

| 2620 | **570** | 19p. red and green | 25 | 10 |

571 Postal Courier (14th century)

1980. Stamp Day.

| 2621 | **571** | 8p. brown, stone and red | 15 | 10 |

572 King Alfonso XIII and Count of Maceda at Exhibition

1980. 50th Anniv of First National Stamp Exhibition.

| 2622 | **572** | 8p. multicoloured | 15 | 10 |

573 Altar of the
Virgin, La Palma
Cathedral

1980. 300th Anniv of Appearance of the Holy Virgin at
La Palma.

2623 **573** 8p. brown and black 15 10

574 Ramon Perez
de Ayala

1980. Birth Centenary of Ramon Perez de Ayala (writer).

2624 **574** 100p. green and brown 1·30 15

575 Manuel Falla, Ruins of Atlantis
and Bonampak Musicians

1980. "Espamer `80" International Stamp Exhibition,
Madrid. Sheet 150×100 mm containing T **575** and
similar horiz designs.
MS2625 25p. ×2, 50p., 100p. each
brown, green and blue (sold at
250p.) 2·30 2·10
DESIGNS: 25p. Type **575**; 25p. Sun Gate, Tiahuanaco and
Roman arch, Medinaceli; 50p. Alonos de Ercilla, Garcilaso
de la Vega and title pages from *La Araucana* and *Com-
mentarios Reales*; 100p. Virgin of Quito and Virgin of Sea-
farers.

576 Juan de Garay and Founding
of Buenos Aires (after Moreno
Carbonero)

1980. 400th Anniv of Buenos Aires.
2626 **576** 19p. blue, green and red 25 10

577 Tapestry Detail

1980. The Creation Tapestry, Gerona. Sheet 132×106
mm containing T **577** and similar designs showing
tapestry details.
MS2627 25p. ×3 (each 33×26 mm),
50p. ×3, multicoloured 2·40 2·30

578 Palace of
Congresses, Madrid

1980. European Security and Co-operation Conference,
Madrid.
2628 **578** 22p. multicoloured 25 15

579 "Nativity"
(mural from
Church of Santa
Maria de Cuina,
Oza de los Rios)

1980. Christmas. Multicoloured.
2629 10p. Type **579** 15 10
2630 22p. "Adoration of the Kings"
(doorway of Church of St.
Nicholas of Cines, Oza de los
Rios) (horiz) 25 10

580 Pedro Vives and
Farman M.F.7 Biplane

1980. Aviation Pioneers. Multicoloured.
2631 5p. Type **580** 15 10
2632 10p. Benito Loygorri and Farman H.F.20 type biplane 15 10
2633 15p. Alfonso de Orleans and
Caudron G-3 20 10
2634 22p. Alfredo Kindelan and
biplane 25 15

581 Games Emblem and
Skier

1981. Winter University Games.
2635 **581** 30p. multicoloured 30 15

582 "Homage to Picasso" (Joan Miro)

1981. Birth Centenary of Pablo Picasso (artist).
2636 **582** 100p. multicoloured 1·50 20

583 Newspaper, Camera,
Notepaper and Pen

1981. The Press.
2637 **583** 12p. multicoloured 15 10

584 Map of Galicia,
Arms and National
Anthem

1981. Galician Autonomy.
2638 **584** 12p. multicoloured 15 10

585 Mosaic
forming Human
Figure

1981. International Year of Disabled Persons.
2639 **585** 30p. multicoloured 35 10

586 Heading Ball

1981. World Cup Football Championship (1982) (2nd
issue). Multicoloured.
2640 12p. Type **586** 15 10
2641 30p. Kicking ball (horiz) 30 10

587 La Jota (folk dance)

1981. Europa.
2642 **587** 12p. black and brown 25 15
2643 - 30p. deep lilac and lilac 40 20
DESIGN: 30p. Procession of the Virgin of Rocio.

588 King Juan
Carlos reviewing
Army

1981. Armed Forces Day.
2644 **588** 12p. multicoloured 15 10

589 Gabriel Miro
(writer)

1981. Spanish Celebrities.
2645 **589** 6p. violet and green 15 15
2646 - 12p. brown and violet 15 15
2647 - 30p. green and brown 40 15
DESIGNS: 12p. Francisco de Quevedo (writer); 30p. St.
Benedict.

590 Messenger
(14th-century
woodcut)

1981. Stamp Day.
2648 **590** 12p. pink, brown &
green 15 10

591 Map of the Balearic Islands
(from Atlas of Diego Homem,
1563)

1981. Spanish Islands. Multicoloured.
2649 7p. Type **591** 15 10
2650 12p. Map of the Canary Islands
(from map of Mateo Prunes,
1563) 15 10

592 Alfonso XII, Juan Carlos
and Arms

1981. Century of Public Prosecutor's Office.
2651 **592** 50p. brown, green
& blue 55 10

593 King Sancho VI of
Navarre with
Foundation Charter

1981. 800th Anniv of Vitoria.
2652 **593** 12p. multicoloured 15 10

594 Citrus Fruit

1981. Spanish Exports (2nd series). Multicoloured.
2653 6p. Type **594** 10 10
2654 12p. Wine 15 10
2655 30p. CASA C-212 Aviocar
airplane, car and lorry 35 10

595 Foodstuffs

1981. World Food Day.
2656 **595** 30p. multicoloured 35 10

596 "Guernica" (image scaled to 60% of original size)

1981. Birth Centenary of Pablo Picasso (2nd issue) and
Return of "Guernica" to Spain. Sheet 163×105 mm.
MS2657 **596** 200p. black, grey and
green 2·40 2·40

597 Congress Palace,
Buenos Aires

1981. "Espamer 81" International Stamp Exhibition,
Buenos Aires.
2658 **597** 12p. red and blue 15 10

598 "Adoration of
the Kings" (from
Cervera de
Pisuerga)

1981. Christmas. Multicoloured.
2659 12p. Type **598** 15 10
2660 30p. "Nativity" (from Paredes
de Nava) 30 10

599 Plaza de Espana, Seville

1981. Air.
2661	**599**	13p. green and blue	15	10
2662	-	20p. blue and brown	25	10

DESIGN: 20p. Rande Bridge, Ria de Vigo.

600 Telegraph Operator

1981. Postal and Telecommunications Museum, Madrid.
2663	**600**	7p. green and brown	30	10
2664	-	12p. brown and violet	30	10
MS2665	135×100 mm. Nos. 2663/4; 50p. violet and green; 100p. green and brown		2·20	2·20

DESIGNS: 12p. Post wagon; 50p. Emblem of Spanish American and Philippines Postal Academy; 100p. Cap, pouch, posthorn, books and cancellation.

601 Royal Mint, Seville

1981. Financial Administration by the Bourbons in Spain and the Indies.
2666	**601**	12p. brown and grey	15	10

602 Iparraguirre

1981. Death Centenary of Jose Maria Iparraguirre.
2667	**602**	12p. blue and black	15	10

603 Publicity Poster by Joan Miro

1982. World Cup Football Championship, Spain (3rd issue). Multicoloured.
2668	**603**	14p. Type **603**	20	10
2669		33p. World Cup trophy and championship emblem	35	10

604 Andres Bello (author and philosopher) (birth bicent)

1982. Anniversaries (1981).
2670	**604**	30p. deep green and green	35	10
2671	-	30p. green and blue	35	15
2672	-	50p. violet and black	65	15

DESIGNS: No. 2671, J. R. Jimenez (author, birth centenary); 2672, P. Calderon (playwright, 300th death anniv).

605 St. James of Compostela (Codex illustration)

1982. Holy Year of Compostela.
2673	**605**	14p. multicoloured	15	10

606 Manuel Fernandez Caballero

1982. Masters of Operetta (1st series). As T **606** (2674, 2676, 2678) or T **625** (others). Multicoloured.
2674	3p. Type **606**	10	10
2675	3p. Scene from "Gigantes y Cabezudos" (horiz)	10	10
2676	6p. Amadeo Vives Roig	10	10
2677	6p. Scene from "Maruxa" (horiz)	10	10
2678	8p. Tomas Breton y Hernandez	10	10
2679	8p. Scene from "La Verbena de la Paloma" (horiz)	10	10

See also Nos. 2713/8 and 2772/7.

607 Arms, Seals and Signatures (Unification of Spain, 1479)

1982. Europa. Multicoloured.
2680	14p. Type **607**	25	20
2681	33p. Symbolic ship, Columbus map of "La Spanola" and signature (Discovery of America)	40	30

608 Swords, Arms and Flag

1982. Armed Forces Day and Centenary of General Military Academy.
2682	**608**	14p. multicoloured	15	10

609 Tackling

1982. World Cup Football Championship, Spain (4th issue). Multicoloured.
2683	14p. Type **609**	25	10
2684	33p. Goal	45	25
MS2685	163×105 mm. 9p. Handshake; 14p. Type **609**; 33p. As No. 2684; 100p. Players with cup	3·00	3·00

610 "St. Andrew and St. Francis"

1982. Air. Paintings by El Greco. Multicoloured.
2686	13p. Type **610**	15	10
2687	20p. "St. Thomas"	30	15

611 Map of Tenerife and Letter

1982. Stamp Day.
2688	**611**	14p. multicoloured	20	10

612 "Transplants"

1982. Organ Transplants.
2689	**612**	14p. multicoloured	20	10

613 White Storks and Diesel Locomotive

1982. 23rd International Railway Congress, Malaga. Multicoloured.
2690	9p. Type **613**	20	10
2691	14p. Steam locomotive "Antigua" (37×26 mm)	30	15
2692	33p. Steam locomotive "Montana" (wrongly inscr "Santa Fe") (37×26 mm)	45	15

614 La Fortaleza, San Juan

1982. "Espamer 82" Stamp Exhibition, San Juan, Puerto Rico.
2693	**614**	33p. blue and lilac	45	15

615 St. Theresa of Avila (sculpture by Gregorio Hernandez)

1982. 400th Death Anniv of St. Theresa of Avila.
2694	**615**	33p. brown, blue and green	45	15

616 Pope John Paul II

1982. Papal Visit.
2695	**616**	14p. blue and brown	20	15

1982. Tourist Series. As T **340**.
2696	4p. blue and grey	15	15
2697	6p. grey and blue	15	15
2698	9p. lilac and blue	15	15
2699	14p. lilac and blue	15	15
2700	33p. brown and red	35	15

DESIGNS—VERT: 4p. Arab water-wheel, Alcantarilla; 9p. Dying Christ, Seville; 14p. St. Martin's Tower, Teruel; 33p. St. Andrew's Gate, Villalpando. HORIZ: 6p. Bank of Spain, Madrid.

617 "Adoration of The Kings" (sculpture, Covarrubias Collegiate Church)

1982. Christmas. Multicoloured.
2701	14p. Type **617**	15	10
2702	33p. "The Flight into Egypt" (painting)	40	15

618 "The Prophet"

1982. Birth Centenary of Pablo Gargallo (sculptor).
2703	**618**	14p. green and blue	15	10

619 St. John Bosco (founder) and Children

1982. Centenary of Salesian Schools in Spain.
2704	**619**	14p. multicoloured	15	10

620 Arms of Spain

1983
2705	**620**	14p. multicoloured	20	10

621 Sunrise over Andalusia

1983. Andalusian Autonomy.
2706	**621**	14p. multicoloured	25	10

622 Arms of Cantabria, Mountains and Monuments

1983. Cantabrian Autonomy.
2707	**622**	14p. multicoloured	25	10

623 National Police

1983. State Security Forces. Multicoloured.
2708	9p. Type **623**	15	10
2709	14p. Civil Guard	20	15
2710	33p. Superior Police Corps	35	25

624 Cycling

1983. Air. Sports. Multicoloured.

| 2711 | 13p. Type **624** | 20 | 10 |
| 2712 | 20p. Bowling (horiz) | 30 | 10 |

625 Scene from "La Parranda"

1983. Masters of Operetta (2nd series). As T **625** (2714, 2716, 2718) or T **606** (others). Multicoloured.

2713	4p. Francisco Alonso (vert)	10	10
2714	4p. Type **625**	10	10
2715	6p. Jacinto Guerrero (vert)	10	10
2716	6p. Scene from "La Rosa del Azafran"	10	10
2717	9p. Jesus Guridi (vert)	15	15
2718	9p. Scene from "El Caserio"	15	15

626 Cervantes and Scene from "Don Quixote"

1983. Europa.

| 2719 | **626** | 16p. red and green | 30 | 20 |
| 2720 | - | 38p. sepia and brown | 60 | 35 |

DESIGN: 38p. Torres Quevedo and Niagara cable-car.

627 Francisco Salzillo (artist)

1983. Spanish Celebrities.

2721	**627**	16p. purple and green	20	15
2722	-	38p. blue and brown	50	25
2723	-	50p. blue and brown	65	25
2724	-	100p. brown and violet	1·30	50

DESIGNS: 38p. Antonio Soler (composer); 50p. Joaquin Turina (composer); 100p. St. Isidro Labrador (patron saint of Madrid).

628 W.C.Y. Emblem

1983. World Communications Year.

| 2725 | **628** | 38p. multicoloured | 45 | 15 |

629 Leaves

1983. Riojan Autonomy.

| 2726 | **629** | 16p. multicoloured | 25 | 15 |

630 Army Monument, Burgos

1983. Armed Forces Day.

| 2727 | **630** | 16p. multicoloured | 25 | 15 |

631 Burgos Setter

1983. Spanish Dogs.

2728	**631**	10p. blue, brown and red	20	15
2729	-	16p. multicoloured	30	15
2730	-	26p. multicoloured	45	25
2731	-	38p. multicoloured	65	20

DESIGNS: 16p. Spanish mastiff; 26p. Ibiza spaniel; 38p. Navarrese basset.

632 Juan-Jose and Fausto Elhuyar y de Suvisa

1983. Anniversaries. Multicoloured.

2732	16p. Type **632** (bicentenary of discovery of wolfram)	25	20
2733	38p. Scout camp (75th anniv of Boy Scout Movement)	60	20
2734	50p. University of Zaragoza (400th anniv)	80	20

633 Arms of Murcia

1983. Murcian Autonomy.

| 2735 | **633** | 16p. multicoloured | 25 | 15 |

634 Covadonga Basilica and Victory Cross

1983. Autonomy of Asturias.

| 2736 | **634** | 14p. multicoloured | 25 | 15 |

635 National Statistical Institute, Madrid

1983. 44th International Institute of Statistics Congress.

| 2737 | **635** | 38p. multicoloured | 50 | 20 |

636 Roman Horse-drawn Mail Cart

1983. Stamp Day.

| 2738 | **636** | 16p. pink and brown | 30 | 30 |

637 Palace and Arms of Valencia

1983. Valencian Autonomy.

| 2739 | **637** | 16p. multicoloured | 30 | 15 |

638 Seville (Illustration from "Floods of Guadalquivir" by Francisco Palomo)

1983. America–Spain.

| 2740 | **638** | 38p. violet and blue | 50 | 25 |

639 "Biblical King" (Leon Cathedral)

1983. Stained Glass Windows. Multicoloured.

2741	10p. Type **639**	20	15
2742	16p. "Epiphany" and Gerona Cathedral	30	20
2743	38p. "St. James" and Santiago de Compostela Hospital	55	20

1983. Tourist Series. As T **340**.

2744	3p. blue and green	20	15
2745	6p. indigo	20	15
2746	16p. violet and red	25	15
2747	38p. red and brown	45	25
2748	50p. red and brown	65	20

DESIGNS: 3p. Church and tower, Llivia, Gerona; 6p. Santa Maria del Mar, Barcelona; 16p. Ceuta Cathedral; 38p. Bridge gateway, Melilla; 50p. Charity Hospital, Seville.

640 "Nativity" (altarpiece, Tortosa)

1983. Christmas. Multicoloured.

| 2749 | 16p Type **640** | 25 | 15 |
| 2750 | 38p. "Adoration of the Kings" (altarpiece, Vich) | 55 | 20 |

641 Indalecio Prieto

1983. Birth Centenary of Indalecio Prieto (politician).

| 2751 | **641** | 16p. brown and black | 25 | 15 |

642 Worker falling from Scaffolding

1984. Safety at Work. Multicoloured.

2752	7p. Type **642**	10	10
2753	10p. Burning factory and extinguisher	15	10
2754	16p. Electric plug and wiring, cutters, gloved hands and warning sign	20	10

643 Tree

1984. Extremaduran Autonomy.

| 2755 | **643** | 16p. multicoloured | 25 | 10 |

644 Burgos Cathedral and Coat of Arms

1984. 1500th Anniv of Burgos City.

| 2756 | **644** | 16p. brown and blue | 20 | 10 |

645 Carnival Dancer, Santa Cruz, Tenerife

1984. Festivals. Multicoloured.

| 2757 | 16p. Type **645** | 25 | 10 |
| 2758 | 16p. Carnival figure and fireworks, Valencia | 25 | 10 |

646 "Man" (Leonardo da Vinci)

1984. Man and Biosphere.

| 2759 | **646** | 38p. multicoloured | 45 | 15 |

647 Map and Flag of Aragon and "Justice"

1984. Aragon Autonomy.

| 2760 | **647** | 16p. multicoloured | 25 | 10 |

648 King Juan Carlos I

1984. "Espana 84" International Stamp Exhibition, Madrid. Sheet 146×102 mm containing T **648** and similar vert designs, each maroon.

MS2761 38p. Type **648**; 38p. Queen Sophia; 38p. Princess Cristina; 38p. Prince of Asturias; 38p. Princess Elena 3·50 3·50

649 F.I.P. Emblem

1984. 53rd International Philatelic Federation Congress, Madrid.

| 2762 | **649** | 38p. red and violet | 45 | 15 |

650 Bridge

1984. Europa.

| 2763 | **650** | 16p. red | 50 | 15 |
| 2764 | **650** | 38p. blue | 60 | 45 |

651 Monument to the Alcantara Cazadores Regiment, Valladolid (Mariano Benlliure)

1984. Armed Forces Day.

| 2765 | **651** | 17p. multicoloured | 20 | 10 |

652 Arms of Canary Islands

1984. Autonomy of Canary Islands.

2766	652	16p. multicoloured	25	10

653 Arms of Castilla- La Mancha

1984. Autonomy of Castilla-La Mancha.

2767	653	17p. multicoloured	25	10

654 King Alfonso X, the Wise, of Castile and Leon (700th death anniv)

1984. Anniversaries.

2768	654	16p. red, blue and black	25	10
2769	-	38p. blue, red and black	50	25

DESIGN: 38p. Ignacio Barraquer (opthalmologist, birth centenary).

655 "James III confirming Grants"

1984. Autonomy of Balearic Islands.

2770	655	17p. multicoloured	25	10

656 Running before Bulls

1984. Pamplona Festival, San Fermin.

2771	656	17p. multicoloured	25	10

1984. Masters of Operetta (3rd series). Horiz designs as T **625** (2772, 2775/6) or vert designs as T **606** (others). Multicoloured.

2772		6p. Scene from "El Nino Judio"	15	10
2773		6p. Pablo Luna	15	10
2774		7p. Ruperto Chapi	15	10
2775		7p. Scene from "La Revoltosa"	15	10
2776		10p. Scene from "La Reina Mora"	15	10
2777		10p. Jose Serrano	15	10

657 Bronze of Swimmer ready to Dive

1984. Olympic Games, Los Angeles. Multicoloured.

2778		1p. Roman quadriga (horiz)	10	10
2779		2p. Type **657**	10	10
2780		5p. Bronze of two wrestlers (horiz)	10	10
2781		8p. "The Discus-thrower" (statue, Miron)	15	10

658 Arms and Map of Navarra

1984. Autonomy of Navarra.

2782	658	17p. multicoloured	25	10

659 Cyclist

1984. International Cycling Championship, Barcelona.

2783	659	17p. multicoloured	20	10

660 Arms (Levante Building Salamanca University)

1984. Autonomy of Castilla y Leon.

2784	660	17p. multicoloured	25	10

661 Women gathering Grapes

1984. Vintage Festival, Jerez.

2785	661	17p. multicoloured	25	10

662 Egeria on Donkey and Map of Middle East

1984. 1600th Anniv of Nun Egeria's Visit to Middle East.

2786	662	40p. multicoloured	45	25

663 Arab Courier

1984. Stamp Day.

2787	663	17p. multicoloured	20	10

664 Father Junipero Serra

1984. Death Bicentenary of Father Junipero Serra (missionary).

2788	664	40p. red and blue	45	20

665 "Adoration of the Kings" (Miguel Moguer) (Campos altarpiece)

1984. Christmas. Multicoloured.

2789		17p. "Nativity" (15th-century retable) (horiz)	20	10
2790		40p. Type **665**	55	25

666 Arms, Buildings and Trees

1984. Autonomy of Madrid.

2791	666	17p. multicoloured	25	10

667 Flags and Andean Condor

1985. 15th Anniv (1984) of Andes Pact.

2792	667	17p. multicoloured	20	10

668 "Virgin of Louvain" (attr Jan Gossaert)

1985. "Europalia 85 Espana" Festival.

2793	668	40p. multicoloured	55	30

669 College Porch and Tympanum

1985. 500th Anniv of Santa Cruz College, Valladolid University.

2794	669	17p. yellow, brown & red	20	10

670 Flames and "Olymphilex '85"

1985. "Olymphilex 85" International Olympic Stamps Exhibition, Lausanne.

2795	670	40p. red, yellow & black	55	20

671 Havana Cathedral

1985. "Espamer '85" International Stamp Exhibition, Havana, Cuba.

2796	671	40p. blue and purple	55	25

672 Couple in Traditional Dress on Horseback

1985. April Fair, Seville.

2797	672	17p. multicoloured	25	10

673 Heads as Holder for Flames

1985. International Youth Year.

2798	673	17p. green, black and red	20	10

674 Moors and Christians fighting

1985. Festival of Moors and Christians, Alcoy.

2799	674	17p. multicoloured	25	10

675 Don Antonio de Cabezon (organist)

1985. Europa.

2800	675	18p. red, black and blue on yellow	30	15
2801	-	45p. red, black and green on yellow	85	50

DESIGN: 45p. Musicians of National Youth Orchestra.

676 Capitania General Headquarters, La Coruna

1985. Armed Forces Day.

2802	676	18p. multicoloured	25	10

677 Carlos III's Arms, 1785 Decree and "Santissima Trinidad" (ship of the line)

1985. Bicentenary of National Flag. Multicoloured.

2803		18p. Type **677**	25	15
2804		18p. State arms, 1978 constitution and lion (detail from House of Deputies)	25	15

678 Sunflower and Bird

1985. World Environment Day.

2805	678	17p. multicoloured	20	15

679 Monstrance in Decorated Street

1985. Corpus Christi Festival, Toledo.

2806	679	18p. multicoloured	25	15

680 King Juan Carlos I

1985

2807	680	10c. blue	15	10
2808	680	50c. green	15	10
2809	680	1p. blue	15	15
2810	680	2p. green	10	10
2811	680	3p. brown	15	10
2812	680	4p. bistre	15	10
2813	680	5p. purple	2·50	90
2814	680	6p. brown	15	10
2815	680	7p. violet	15	10
2816	680	7p. green	10	10
2817	680	8p. grey	1·00	50
2818	680	10p. red	15	10
2819	680	12p. red	15	15
2820	680	13p. blue	20	10
2821	680	15p. green	20	10

2822	**680**	17p. orange	25	10
2823	**680**	18p. green	25	15
2824	**680**	19p. brown	30	10
2825	**680**	20p. mauve	30	10
2825a	**680**	25p. green	30	10
2825b	**680**	27p. mauve	30	10
2826	**680**	30p. blue	45	10
2827	**680**	45p. green	55	15
2828	**680**	50p. blue	65	10
2828a	**680**	55p. brown	70	15
2829	**680**	60p. red	90	15
2830	**680**	75p. mauve	1·00	15

681 Planetary System

1985. Inauguration of Astrophysical Observatories, Canary Islands.
2831	**681**	45p. multicoloured	55	20

682 Ataulfo Argenta (conductor)

1985. European Music Year. Multicoloured.
2832		12p. Type **682**	15	15
2833		17p. Tomas Luis de Victoria (composer)	25	15
2834		45p. Fernando Sor (guitarist and composer)	65	35

683 Bernal Diaz del Castillo (conquistador)

1985. Celebrities.
2835	**683**	7p. red, black and green on yellow	15	10
2836	-	12p. red, black and blue on yellow	20	10
2837	-	17p. green, red and black on yellow	30	15
2838	-	45p. green, black and brown on yellow	65	25

DESIGNS: 12p. Esteban Terradas (mathematician); 17p. Vicente Aleixandre (poet); 45p. Leon Felipe Camino (poet).

684 Canoeist

1985. "Descent down the Sella" Canoe Festival, Asturias.
2839	**684**	17p. multicoloured	25	10

685 Monk returning with Rotulet to Savigni Abbey, 1122

1985. Stamp Day.
2840	**685**	17p. multicoloured	25	10

686 Ribbon Exercise

1985. 12th World Rhythmic Gymnastics Championship, Valladolid. Multicoloured.
2841		17p. Type **686**	20	10
2842		45p. Hoop exercise	60	25

687 Prado Museum and "la Alcacofa" Fountain

1985. "Exfilna '85" National Stamp Exhibition, Madrid. Sheet 120×80 mm.
MS2843	**687**	17p. multicoloured	70	70

688 "Virgin and Child" (Escalas Chapel, Seville Cathedral)

1985. Stained Glass Windows. Multicoloured.
2844		7p. Type **688**	10	10
2845		12p. Monk (Toledo Cathedral)	15	10
2846		17p. King Enrique II of Castile and Leon (Alcazar of Segovia)	25	15

689 "Nativity" (detail of altarpiece by Ramon de Mur)

1985. Christmas. Multicoloured.
2847		17p. Type **689**	15	10
2848		45p. "Adoration of the Magi" (embroidered frontal, after Jaume Huguet)	60	25

690 Subalpine Warbler

1985. Birds. Multicoloured.
2849		6p. Type **690**	20	10
2850		7p. Rock thrush	20	10
2851		12p. Spotless starling	25	10
2852		17p. Bearded reedling	55	15

691 Count of Penaflorida

1985. Death Bicentenary of Count of Penaflorida (founder of Economic Society of Friends of the Land).
2853	**691**	17p. blue	20	10

692 Royal Palace, Madrid

1986. Admission of Spain and Portugal to European Economic Community. Multicoloured.
2854		12p. Type **692**	15	15
2855		17p. Map and flags of member countries	15	15
2856		30p. Hall of Columns, Royal Palace	35	15
2857		45p. Flags of Portugal and Spain uniting with flags of other members	65	35

1986. Tourist Series. As T **340**.
2858		12p. black and red	15	10
2859		35p. brown and blue	45	15

DESIGNS: 12p. Lupiana Monastery, Guadalajara; 35p. Balcony of Europe, Nerja.

693 Merino

1986. Second World Conference on Merinos.
2860	**693**	45p. multicoloured	45	15

694 "Revellers" (detail, F. Hohenleiter)

1986. Cadiz Carnival.
2861	**694**	17p. multicoloured	25	10

695 Helmets and Flower

1986. International Peace Year.
2862	**695**	45p. multicoloured	45	15

696 Organ Pipes

1986. Religious Music Week, Cuenca.
2863	**696**	17p. multicoloured	25	10

697 "Swearing in of Regent, Queen Maria Cristina" (detail, Joaquin Sorolla y Bastida)

1986. Centenary of Chambers of Commerce, Industry and Navigation.
2864	**697**	17p. black and green	20	10

698 Man with Suitcase

1986. Emigration.
2865	**698**	45p. multicoloured	45	15

699 Boy and Birds

1986. Europa. Multicoloured.
2866		17p. Type **699**	30	15
2867		45p. Woman watering young tree	65	45

700 Our Lady of the Dew

1986. Our Lady of the Dew Festival, Rocio, near Almonte.
2868	**700**	17p. multicoloured	25	10

701 Capitania General Building, Tenerife

1986. Armed Forces Day.
2869	**701**	17p. multicoloured	20	10

1986. Tourist Series. As T **340**. Multicoloured.
2870		12p. black and blue	15	15
2871		35p. brown and blue	45	15

DESIGNS: 12p. Ciudad Rodrigo Cathedral, Salamanca; 35p. Calella lighthouse, Barcelona.

702 Hands and Ball

1986. Tenth World Basketball Championship.
2872	**702**	45p. multicoloured	45	15

703 Francisco Loscos (botanist)

1986. Celebrities.
2873	**703**	7p. green and black	10	10
2874	-	11p. red and black	15	10
2875	-	17p. brown and black	20	10
2876	-	45p. purple, orange and black	70	35

DESIGNS: 11p. Salvador Espriu (writer); 17p. Azorin (José Martinez Ruiz) (writer); 45p. Juan Gris (artist).

704 Apostles awaiting Angels carrying Virgin's Soul

1986. Elche Mystery Play.
2877	**704**	17p. multicoloured	25	10

705 Swimmer

1986. Fifth World Swimming, Water Polo, Leap and Synchronous Swimming Championships.
2878	**705**	45p. multicoloured	45	15

706 Pelota Player

1986. Tenth World Pelota Championship.
2879	**706**	17p. multicoloured	25	10

707 King's Messenger with Letter summoning Nobleman to Court

1986. Stamp Day.
2880	**707**	17p. multicoloured	20	10

708 Man releasing Dove and Cordoba Mosque

1986. "Exfilna '86" National Stamp Exhibition, Corosba. Sheet 120×80 mm.
MS2881 **708** 17p. multicoloured .... 30 ... 30

709 Aristotle

1986. 500th Anniv (1992) of Discovery of America by Columbus (1st issue). Designs showing historic figures and prophecies of discovery of New World.

2882	**709**	7p. black and mauve	10	10
2883	-	12p. black and lilac	15	10
2884	-	17p. black and yellow	20	15
2885	-	30p. black and mauve	40	15
2886	-	35p. black and green	50	15
2887	-	45p. black and orange	65	15

DESIGNS: 12p. Seneca and quote from "Medea"; 17p. St. Isidoro of Seville and quote from "Etymologies"; 30p. Cardinal Pierre d'Ailly and quote from "Imago Mundi"; 35p. Mayan and quote from "Chilam Balam" books; 45p. Conquistador and quote from "Chilam Balam" books.
See also Nos. 2932/7, 2983/8, 3035/40, 3079/82, 3126/9, **MS**3147, 3175/6, **MS**3177 and 3190.

710 Gaspar de Portola

1986. Death Bicentenary of Gaspar de Portola (first Governor of California).
2888 **710** 22p. blue, red and black ... 30 ... 10

711 "Holy Family" (detail, Diego de Siloe)

1986. Christmas. Wood Carvings. Multicoloured.
2889 **711** 19p. Type **711** .... 25 ... 10
2890 48p. "Nativity" (detail, Toledo Cathedral altarpiece, Felipe de Borgona) (horiz) ..... 65 ... 15

712 Abd-er Rahman II and Cordoba Mosque

1986. Hispanic Islamic Culture.

2891	**712**	7p. brown and red	10	10
2892	-	12p. brown and red	15	10
2893	-	17p. blue and black	20	10
2894	-	45p. green and black	70	15

DESIGNS: 12p. Ibn Hazm (writer) and burning book; 17p. Al-Zarqali (astronomer) and azophea (astrolabe); 45p. King Alfonso VII of Castile and Leon and scholars of Toledo School of Translators.

713 "The Good Curate"

1986. Birth Centenary of Alfonso Castelao (artist and writer).
2895 **713** 32p. multicoloured .... 40 ... 15

714 Chateau de la Muette (headquarters)

1987. 25th Anniv of Organization for Economic Co-operation and Development.
2896 **714** 48p. multicoloured .... 55 ... 15

715 Abstract Shapes

1987. "Expo 92" World's Fair, Seville (1st issue). Multicoloured.
2897 **715** 19p. Type **715** .... 35 ... 10
2898 48p. Moon surface, Earth and symbol .... 90 ... 10
See also Nos. 2941/2, 2951/2, 3004/7, 3052/5, 3094/7, 3143 and 3148/**MS**3172.

716 Francisco de Vitoria

1987. 500th Birth Anniv of Francisco de Vitoria (jurist).
2899 **716** 48p. brown .... 55 ... 15

717 18th-century Warship and Standard Bearer

1987. 450th Anniv of Marine Corps.
2900 **717** 19p. multicoloured .... 25 ... 10

718 University

1987. Centenary of Deusto University.
2901 **718** 19p. red, green and black .... 25 ... 10

719 Breastfeeding Baby

1987. UNICEF Child Survival Campaign.
2902 **719** 19p. brown and deep brown .... 25 ... 10

720 Crowd

1987. 175th Anniv of Constitution of Cadiz. Multicoloured.

2903	**720**	25p. Type **720**	35	15
2904		25p. Crowd and herald on steps	35	15
2905		25p. Dignitaries on dais	35	15
2906		25p. Crown and Constitution	35	15

Nos. 2903/6 were printed together, se-tenant, the first three stamps forming a composite design showing "The Promulgation of the Constitution of 1812" by Salvador Viniegra.

721 15th-century Pharmacy Jar, Manises

1987. Ceramics. Multicoloured.

2907		7p. Type **721**	10	10
2908		14p. 20th-century glazed figure, Sargadelos	15	15
2909		19p. 18th-century vase, Buen Retiro	25	15
2910		32p. 20th-century pot, Salvatierra de los Barros	45	20
2911		40p. 18th-century jar, Talavera	55	20
2912		48p. 18–19th century jug, Granada	70	20

722 "Procession at Dawn, Zamora" (Gallego Marquina)

1987. Holy Week Festivals. Multicoloured.
2913 19p. Type **722** .... 30 ... 10
2914 48p. Gate of Pardon, Seville Cathedral and "Passion" (statue by Martinez Montanes) .... 65 ... 15

1987. Tourist Series. As T **340**.

2915		14p. green and blue	20	10
2916		19p. deep green and green	20	10
2917		40p. brown	50	15
2918		48p. black	90	15

DESIGNS—HORIZ: 14p. Ifach Rock, Calpe, Alicante; 19p. Ruins of Church of Santa Maria d'Ozo, Pontevedra; 40p. Palace of Sonanes, Villacarriedo, Santander. VERT: 48p. 11th-century monastery of Sant Joan de les Abadesses, Gerona.

723 Bilbao Bank, Madrid (Saenz de Oiza)

1987. Europa. Architecture.
2919 **723** 19p. multicoloured .... 60 ... 35
2920 - 48p. brown, bistre & grn .. 75 ... 35
DESIGN—HORIZ: 14p. National Museum of Roman Art, Merida (Rafael Moneo).

724 Horse's Head and Harnessed Pair

1987. Jerez Horse Fair.
2921 **724** 19p. multicoloured .... 35 ... 15

725 Carande

1987. Birth Centenary of Ramon Carande (historian and Honorary Postman).
2922 **725** 40p. black and brown .... 55 ... 20

726 Numbers on Pen Nib

1987. Postal Coding.
2923 **726** 19p. multicoloured .... 25 ... 15

727 Arms and School

1987. 75th Anniv of Eibar Armoury School.
2924 **727** 20p. multicoloured .... 25 ... 15

728 Batllo House Chimneys (Antonio Gaudi)

1987. Nomination of Barcelona as 1992 Olympic Games Host City. Multicoloured.
2925 **728** 32p. Type **728** .... 55 ... 20
2926 65p. Athletes .... 95 ... 20

729 Festival Poster (Fabri)

1987. 25th Pyrenees Folklore Festival, Jaca.
2927 **729** 50p. multicoloured .... 75 ... 15

730 Monturiol (after Marti Alsina) and Diagrams of Submarine "Ictineo"

1987. Death Cent of Narcis Monturiol (scientist).
2928 **730** 20p. black and brown .... 25 ... 15

731 Detail from Jaime II of Majorca's Law appointing Couriers

1987. Stamp Day.
2929 **731** 20p. multicoloured .... 25 ... 15

732 18th-century Pre-stamp Letter

1987. "Espamer '87" Stamp Exhibition, La Coruna. Maritime Post to America. Sheet 149×83 mm containing T **732** and similar horiz designs.
MS2930 8p. Type **732**; 12p. 19th-century engraving of La Coruna harbour; 20p. 18th-century view of Havana harbour; 50p. 18th-century sailing packets running between La Coruna and Havana (sold at 180p.) ... 4·50 ... 4·25
No. **MS**2930 included an entrance coupon divided from the sheet by a line of rouletting. Price quoted is for the sheet with coupon attached.

733 "Aesculapius" and Olympic Torch Bearer

1987. "Exfilna '87" National Stamp Exhibition, Gerona. Sheet 120×80 mm.
MS2931 **733** 20p. multicoloured .... 60 ... 35

734 Amerigo Vespucci

1987. 500th Anniv (1992) of Discovery of America by Columbus (2nd issue). Explorers. Multicoloured.

2932	14p. Type **734**		20	20
2933	20p. King Ferdinand and Queen Isabella the Catholic and arms on ships		25	20
2934	32p. Juan Perez and departing ships		40	20
2935	40p. Juan de la Cosa and ships		55	20
2936	50p. Map, ship and Christopher Columbus		65	30
2937	65p. Native on shore, approaching ships and Martin Alonzo and Vincente Yanez Pinzon		90	30

735 Star and Baubles

1987. Christmas. Multicoloured.

2938	20p. Type **735**		35	15
2939	50p. Zambomba and tambourine		75	30

736 Macho (self-sculpture)

1987. Birth Centenary of Victorio Macho (sculptor).

2940	**736**	50p. brown and black	65	20

1987. "Expo '92" World's Fair, Seville (2nd issue). As Nos. 2897/8 but values changed. Multicoloured.

2941	20p. Type **715**		35	15
2942	50p. As No. 2898		75	15

737 Queen Sofia

1988. 50th Birthdays of King Juan Carlos I and Queen Sofia. Each brown, yellow and violet.

2943	20p. Type **737**		20	15
2944	20p. King Juan Carlos I		20	15

738 Campoamor

1988. Birth Centenary of Clara Campoamor (politician and women's suffrage campaigner).

2945	**738**	20p. multicoloured	25	15

739 Speed Skating

1988. Winter Olympic Games, Calgary.

2946	**739**	45p. multicoloured	75	15

740 "Christ tied to the Pillar" (statue) and Valladolid Cathedral

1988. Holy Week Festivals. Multicoloured.

2947	20p. Type **740**		30	10
2948	50p. Float depicting Christ carrying the Cross, Malaga		65	15

741 Ingredients for and Dish of Paella

1988. Tourist Series. Multicoloured.

2949	18p. Type **741**		30	10
2950	45p. Covadonga National Park (70th anniv of National Parks)		65	15

742 Globe and Stylized Roads

1988. "Expo '92" World's Fair, Seville (3rd issue).

2951	8p. Type **742**		15	10
2952	45p. Compass rose and globe (horiz)		55	10

743 18th-Century Valencian Chalice

1988. Glassware. Multicoloured.

2953	20p. Type **743**		25	10
2954	20p. 18th-century pitcher, Cadalso de los Vidrios, Madrid		25	10
2955	20p. 18th-century crystal sweet jar, La Granja de San Ildefonso		25	10
2956	20p. 18th-century Andalusian two-handled jug, Castril		25	10
2957	20p. 17th-century Catalan four-spouted jug		25	10
2958	20p. 20th-century bottle, Balearic Islands		25	10

744 Francis of Taxis (organiser of European postal service, 1505)

1988. Stamp Day.

2959	**744**	20p. violet and brown	25	10

745 Pablo Iglesias (first President)

746 Steam Locomotive, 1837, Cuba

1988. Centenary of General Workers' Union.

2960	**745**	20p. multicoloured	20	10

1988. Europa. Transport and Communications.

2961	**746**	20p. red and black	30	30
2962	-	50p. green and black	95	50

DESIGN: 50p. Light telegraph, Philippines, 1818.

747 Monnet

1988. Birth Cent of Jean Monnet (statesman).

2963	**747**	45p. blue	65	30

748 Emblem

1988. Centenary of 1888 Universal Exhibition, Barcelona.

2964	**748**	50p. multicoloured	65	10

749 Couple in Granada

1988. International Festival of Music and Dance, Granada.

2965	**749**	50p. multicoloured	65	10

750 Bull

1988. "Expo 88" World's Fair, Brisbane.

2966	**750**	50p. multicoloured	65	10

751 "Virgin of Hope"

1988. Coronation of "Virgin of Hope", Malaga.

2967	**751**	20p. multicoloured	25	10

752 Plan of Pamplona Palace

1988. "Exfilna '87" National Stamp Exhibition, Pamplona. Sheet 120×81 mm.

MS2968	**752**	20p. multicoloured	30	25

753 Orreo (agricultural store), Cantabria

1988. Tourist Series.

2969	**753**	18p. green, brown & blue	25	10
2970	-	45p. black, brn & ochre	60	15

DESIGN: 45p. Dulzaina (wind instrument), Castilla y Leon.

754 Players

1988. 28th World Roller Skate Hockey Championship, La Coruna.

2971	**754**	20p. multicoloured	25	10

755 Congress Emblem

1988. First Spanish Regional Homes and Centres World Congress, Madrid.

2972	**755**	20p. multicoloured	25	10

756 "Olympic" Class Yacht

1988. Olympic Games, Seoul.

2973	**756**	50p. multicoloured	65	15

757 Borrell II, Count of Barcelona

1988. Millenary of Catalonia.

2974	**757**	20p. multicoloured	25	10

758 King Alfonso IX of Leon (detail of Codex of "Toxos Outos")

1988. 800th Anniv of 1st Leon Parliament.

2975	**758**	20p. multicoloured	25	10

759 Emblem on Band around Peace Year Stamps

1988. 25th Anniv of Spanish Philatelic Associations Federation.

2976	**759**	20p. multicoloured	25	10

760 Games Emblem

1988. Olympic Games, Barcelona (1992) (1st issue). Designs showing stylized representations of sports. Multicoloured.

2977	8p. Type **760**		10	10
2978	20p.+5p. Athletics		35	35
2979	45p.+5p. Badminton		70	70
2980	50p.+5p. Basketball		85	75

See also Nos. 3008/11, 3031/3, 3056/8, 3076/8, 3098/3100, 3123/5, 3144/6, 3180/2 and 3183/5.

761 Palace of the Generality, Valencia, and Seal of Jaime I

1988. 750th Anniv of Re-conquest of Valencia by King Jaime I of Aragon.

2981	**761**	20p. multicoloured	25	10

762 Manuel Alonso Martinez (statesman)

1988. Centenary of Civil Code.

2982	**762**	20p. multicoloured	25	10

763 Hernan Cortes and Quetzalcoatl Serpent

1988. 500th Anniv (1992) of Discovery of America by Columbus (3rd issue). Each red, blue and orange.

2983	10p. Type **763**		20	10
2984	10p. Vasco Nunez de Balboa and waves		20	10
2985	20p. Francisco Pizarro and guanaco		30	10
2986	20p. Ferdinand Magellan, Juan Sebastian del Cano and globe		30	10
2987	50p. Alvar Nunez Cabeza de Vaca and river		65	15
2988	50p. Andres de Urdaneta and maritime currents		65	15

764 Enrique III of Castile and Leon (first Prince of Asturias)

1988. 600th Anniv of Title of Prince of Asturias.

2989	**764**	20p. multicoloured	25	10

765 Snowflakes

1988. Christmas. Multicoloured.

2990	20p. Type **765**		30	10
2991	50p. Shepherd carrying sheep (vert)		65	25

766 Cordoba Mosque

1988. UNESCO World Heritage Sites.

2992	**766**	18p. brown	25	10

2993	-	20p. blue	30	15
2994	-	45p. brown	65	15
2995	-	50p. green	80	15

DESIGNS—VERT: 20p. Burgos Cathedral. HORIZ: 45p. San Lorenzo Monastery, El Escorial; 50p. Alhambra, Granada.

767 Representation of Political Parties

1988. Tenth Anniv of Constitution.

2996	**767**	20p. multicoloured	30	15

768 Courtiers in Palace Grounds

1988. Death Bicentenary of King Charles III. Sheet 100×80 mm.

MS2997	**768** 45p. green and black		65	35

769 Blind Person

1988. 50th Anniv of National Organization for the Blind.

2998	**769**	20p. multicoloured	30	15

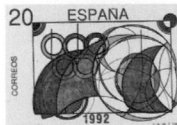

770 Luis de Granada

1988. 400th Death Anniv of Brother Luis de Granada (mystic).

2999	**770**	20p. multicoloured	30	15

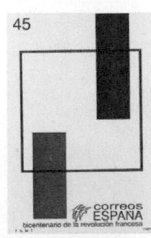

771 Olympic Rings and Sails (Natalia Barrio Fernandez)

1989. Children's Stamp Designs. Multicoloured.

3000	20p. Type **771**		30	10
3001	20p. Magnifying glass on stamp (Jose Luis Villegas Lopez) (vert)		30	10

772 Abstract

1989. Bicentenary of French Revolution.

3002	**772**	45p. red, blue and black	65	15

773 Maria de Maeztu

1989. 107th Birth Anniv of Maria de Maeztu (educationist).

3003	**773**	20p. multicoloured	25	10

774 London, 1851

1989. "Expo '92" World's Fair, Seville (4th issue). Great Exhibitions. Multicoloured.

3004	8p.+5p. Type **774**		15	15
3005	8p.+5p. Paris, 1889		15	15
3006	20p.+5p. Brussels, 1958		35	30
3007	20p.+5p. Osaka, 1970		35	30

1989. Olympic Games, Barcelona (1992) (2nd issue). As T **760**. Multicoloured.

3008	8p.+5p. Handball		30	15
3009	18p.+5p. Boxing		35	25
3010	20p.+5p. Cycling		35	35
3011	45p.+5p. Show jumping		90	70

775 Uniforms, 1889

1989. Centenary of Post Office.

3012	**775**	20p. multicoloured	25	10

776 International Postal Service Treaty, 1601

1989. Stamp Day.

3013	**776**	20p. black	25	10

777 Entrance Door

1989. Cordon House, Burgos.

3014	**777**	20p. black	25	10

778 Skittles

1989. Europa. Children's Toys. Multicoloured.

3015	40p. Type **778**		60	35
3016	50p. Spinning top		85	60

779 European Flag

1989. Spanish Presidency of European Economic Community.

3017	**779**	45p. multicoloured	65	35

780 "Holy Family with St. Anne" (El Greco)

1989. "Exfilna '89" National Stamp Exhibition, Toledo. Sheet 105×78 mm.

MS3018	**780** 20p. multicoloured		45	45

781 Manuscript and Portrait

1989. Birth Centenary of Gabriela Mistral (poet).

3019	**781**	50p. multicoloured	70	15

782 Flags forming Ballot Box

1989. European Parliament Elections.

3020	**782**	45p. multicoloured	65	35

783 Catalonia

1989. Lace. Typical designs from named region.

3021	**783**	20p. blue and brown	25	15
3022	-	20p. blue and brown	25	15
3023	-	20p. blue	25	15
3024	-	20p. blue	25	15
3025	-	20p. blue and brown	25	15
3026	-	20p. blue and brown	25	15

DESIGNS: No. 3022, Andalucia; 3023, Extremadura; 3024, Canary Islands; 3025, Castilla-La Mancha; 3026, Galicia.

784 Pope John Paul II and Youths

1989. Third Papal Visit.

3027	**784**	50p. green, brown & blk	65	15

785 Foot leaving Starting Block

1989. World Cup Athletics Championships, Barcelona.

3028	**785**	50p. multicoloured	55	15

786 Chaplin

1989. Birth Centenary of Charlie Chaplin (actor).

3029	**786**	50p. multicoloured	65	15

787 1p. Stamp

1989. Centenary of First King Alfonso XIII Stamps.
3030	**787**	50p. brown, grey and red	65	15

1989. Olympic Games, Barcelona (1992) (3rd issue). As T **760**.
3031	18p.+5p. Fencing	70	55
3032	20p.+5p. Football	70	60
3033	45p.+5p. Gymnastics	1·00	95

788 Fr. Andres Manjon (founder)

1989. Centenary of Ave Maria Schools.
3034	**788**	20p. multicoloured	25	10

789 Maize

1989. 500th Anniv (1992) of Discovery of America by Columbus (4th issue). Multicoloured.
3035	8p.+5p. Type **789**	15	15
3036	8p.+5p. Cacao nut	15	15
3037	20p.+5p. Tomato	30	25
3038	20p.+5p. Horse	30	25
3039	50p.+5p. Potato	70	55
3040	50p.+5p. Turkey	70	55

790 Inca irrigating Corn (from "New Chronicle" by Waman Puma)

1989. America. Pre-Columbian Life.
3041	**790**	50p. multicoloured	55	10

791 "Navidad 89"

1989. Christmas. Multicoloured.
3042	20p. Type **791**		25	10
3043	45p. Girl with Christmas present (horiz)		60	15

792 Altamira Caves

1989. World Heritage Sites. Multicoloured.
3044	20p. Type **792**		30	10
3045	20p. Segovia Aqueduct		30	10
3046	20p. Santiago de Compostela		30	10
3047	20p. Guell Park and Palace and Mila House		30	10

793 San Lorenzo Monastery, El Escorial

1989. National Heritage. Royal Palaces. Sheet 162×92 mm containing T **793** and similar horiz designs. Multicoloured.
MS3048	45p. Type **793**; 45p. Aranjuez; 45p. La Granja de San Ildefonso; 45p. Madrid	2·20	2·20

794 Olympic Rings, Compass Rose, Church of Holy Family, Barcelona, and Seville

1990. Children's Stamp Design.
3049	**794**	20p. multicoloured	25	10

795 Getxo City Hall and Competitor

1990. World Cyclo-cross Championship, Getxo.
3050	**795**	20p. multicoloured	25	10

796 Victoria Kent

1990. Third Death Anniv of Victoria Kent (prison reformer).
3051	**796**	20p. lilac	25	10

797 Curro (mascot) flying over Path of Discoveries

1990. "Expo '92" World's Fair, Seville (5th issue). Multicoloured.
3052	8p.+5p. Type **797**	15	15
3053	20p.+5p. Curro and Exhibition building	30	30
3054	45p.+5p. Curro and view of Project Cartuja '93	65	65
3055	50p.+5p. Curro crossing bridge in Project Cartuja '93	80	80

1990. Olympic Games, Barcelona (1992) (4th issue). As T **760**. Multicoloured.
3056	18p.+5p. Weightlifting	45	35
3057	20p.+5p. Hockey	45	35
3058	45p.+5p. Judo	90	60

798 Rafael Alvarez Sereix (Honorary Postman)

1990. Stamp Day.
3059	**798**	20p. flesh, brown & green	25	10

799 Vitoria Post Office

1990. Europa. Post Office Buildings.
3060	20p. Type **799**	55	30
3061	50p. Malaga Post Office (vert)	95	55

800 "Hispasat" Communications Satellite

1990. 125th Anniv of I.T.U.
3062	**800**	8p. multicoloured	20	10

801 Door Knocker, Aragon

1990. Wrought Ironwork. Each black, grey and red.
3063	20p. Type **801**	30	15
3064	20p. Door knocker, Andalucia	30	15
3065	20p. Pistol, Catalonia	30	15
3066	20p. Door knocker, Castilla-La Mancha	30	15
3067	20p. Mirror with lock, Galicia	30	15
3068	20p. Basque fireback	30	15

802 Infanta's Patio, Zaragoza

1990. "Exfilna '90" National Stamp Exhibition, Zaragoza. Sheet 105×78 mm.
MS3069	**802** 20p. chestnut	35	35

803 "Charity" (Lopez Alonso)

1990. Anniversaries.
3070	**803**	8p. multicoloured	15	10
3071	-	20p. multicoloured	25	10
3072	-	45p. orange and brown	60	15
3073	-	50p. red and blue	65	15

DESIGNS—VERT: 8p. Type **803** (bicent of arrival in Spain of Daughters of Charity); 50p. Page of book (500th anniv of publication of "Tirant lo Blanch" by Joanot Martorell and Marti Joan de Galba). HORIZ: 20p. Score of "Leilah" and Jose Padilla (composer, birth centenary (1989)); 45p. Palace of Kings of Navarre (900th anniv of grant of privileges to Estella).

804 St. Antolin's Crypt, Palencia Cathedral

1990. "Filatem '90" Third National Thematic Stamps Exhibition, Palencia. Sheet 105×77 mm.
MS3074	**804** 20p. brown	35	35

805 Poster

1990. 17th International Historical Sciences Congress, Madrid.
3075	**805**	50p. multicoloured	70	15

1990. Olympic Games, Barcelona (1992) (5th issue). As T **760**. Multicoloured.
3076	8p.+5p. Wrestling	20	15
3077	18p.+5p. Swimming	35	30
3078	20p.+5p. Baseball	45	35

806 Caravel and Compass Rose

1990. 500th Anniv of Discovery of America by Columbus (5th issue). Multicoloured.
3079	8p.+5p. Type **806**	20	15
3080	8p.+5p. Caravels	20	15
3081	20p.+5p. Caravel	35	30
3082	20p.+5p. Galleons	35	30

807 Puerto Rican Todys

1990. America. The Natural World.
3083	**807**	50p. multicoloured	70	15

808 Sun

1990. Christmas. Details of "Cosmic Poem" by Jose Antonio Sistiaga. Multicoloured.
3084	25p. Type **808**	35	10
3085	45p. Moon (horiz)	65	15

809 "Flemish Soldiers" (after Philips Wouvermans)

1990. Tapestries. Sheet 105×151 mm containing T **809** and similar vert designs. Multicoloured.
MS3086	20p. ×4: "Calvary" (Peter Pannemaker, after Jan van Roome and Bernard van Orley); Type **809**; "Wreck of the Telemach" (Urbano Leyniers after Miguel Houasse); "Flower Sellers" (Antonio Morena and Eusebio de Candano, after Goya)	1·40	1·20

810 Tourism Logo (Joan Miro)

1990. European Tourism Year.
3087	**810**	45p. multicoloured	65	40

811 Church of St. Miguel de Lillo, Oviedo

1990. World Heritage Sites. Multicoloured.

3088	20p.	Type **811**	25	10
3089	20p.	St. Peter's Tower, Teruel	25	10
3090	20p.	Bujaco Tower, Caceres (horiz)	25	10
3091	20p.	St. Vincent's Church, Avila (horiz)	25	10

812 Conductor and Orchestra

1990. Spanish National Orchestra.

3092	**812**	25p. green, turq & blk	35	10

813 Maria Moliner

1991. Tenth Death Anniv of Maria Moliner (philologist).

3093	**813**	25p. multicoloured	35	10

814 La Cartuja (Santa Maria de las Cuevas Monastery)

1991. "Expo 92" World's Fair, Seville (6th issue). Views of Seville. Multicoloured.

3094	15p.+5p.	Type **814**	25	25
3095	25p.+5p.	The Auditorium	45	35
3096	45p.+5p.	La Cartuja bridge	65	65
3097	55p.+5p.	La Barqueta bridge	80	75

1991. Olympic Games, Barcelona (1992) (6th series). As T **760**.

3098	15p.+5p.	grey, black and red	35	30
3099	25p.+5p.	multicoloured	40	40
3100	45p.+5p.	multicoloured	75	65

DESIGNS: 15p. Modern pentathlon; 25p. Canoeing; 45p. Rowing.

815 Olympic Rings and Yachts

1991. Children's Stamp Design.

3101	**815**	25p. multicoloured	35	10

816 Loja Gate

1991. "Granada '92" International Thematic Stamp Exhibition (1st issue) and 500th Anniv of Santa Fe. Sheet 106×78 mm.

MS3102	**816**	25p. purple and gold	40	40

See also No. MS3174.

817 Juan de Tassis y Peralta (Chief Courier to Kings Philip III and IV)

1991. Stamp Day.

3103	**817**	25p. black	35	15

818 Talavera Apothecary Jar

1991. Porcelain and Ceramics. Sheet 106×150 mm containing T **818** and similar vert designs. Multicoloured.

MS3104 25p. Type **818**; 25p. Buen Retiro figurine; 25p. Pickman bottle; 25p. La Moncloa plate	1·60	1·60

819 Dish Aerials, INTA-NASA Earth Station, Robledo de Chavela

1991. Europa. Europe in Space. Multicoloured.

3105	25p.	Type **819**	55	30
3106	45p.	"Olympus I" telecommunications satellite	1·10	55

820 Brother Luis Ponce de Leon (translator and poet, 400th death anniv)

1991. Anniversaries.

3107	-	15p. multicoloured	25	15
3108	**820**	15p. orange, red & black	25	15
3109	-	25p. multicoloured	40	15
3110	-	25p. multicoloured	40	15

DESIGNS—HORIZ: No. 3107, Table and chair (400th death anniv of St. John of the Cross). VERT: No. 3109, Banner and cap (500th birth anniv of St. Ignatius de Loyola (founder of Society of Jesus)); 3110, Abd-er Rahman III, Emir of Cordoba (1100th birth anniv).

821 Apollo Fountain

1991. Madrid. European City of Culture (1st issue). Multicoloured.

3111	15p.+5p.	Type **821**	45	45
3112	25p.+5p.	"Don Alvaro de Bazan" (statue, Mariano Benlliure)	50	50
3113	45p.+5p.	Bank of Spain	80	80
3114	55p.+5p.	Cloisters, St. Isidro Institute	90	90

See also Nos. 3195/8.

822 Choir (after mural mosaic, Palau de la Musica)

1991. Centenary of Orfeo Catala (Barcelona choral group).

3115	**822**	25p. multicoloured	30	10

823 Basque Drug Cupboard

1991. Furniture. Multicoloured.

3116	25p.	Type **823**	30	10
3117	25p.	Kitchen dresser, Castilla y Leon	30	10
3118	25p.	Chair, Murcia	30	10
3119	25p.	Cradle, Andalucia	30	10
3120	25p.	Travelling chest, Castilla-La Mancha	30	10
3121	25p.	Bridal chest, Catalonia	30	10

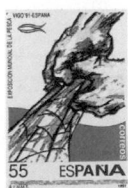

824 Hands holding Net

1991. World Fishing Exhibition, Vigo.

3122	**824**	55p. multicoloured	85	15

1991. Olympic Games, Barcelona (1992) (7th series). As T **760**. Multicoloured.

3123	15p.+5p.	Tennis	45	40
3124	25p.+5p.	Table tennis	65	60
3125	55p.+5p.	Shooting	1·30	1·20

825 Garcilaso de la Vega (Spanish-Inca poet)

1991. 500th Anniv of Discovery of America by Columbus (6th issue). Multicoloured.

3126	15p.+5p.	Type **825**	25	25
3127	25p.+5p.	Pope Alexander VI	45	40
3128	45p.+5p.	Luis de Santangel (banker)	70	70
3129	55p.+5p.	Brother Toribio Motolinia (missionary)	90	80

826 Nocturlabe

1991. America. Voyages of Discovery.

3130	**826**	55p. brown and purple	80	20

827 "Nativity" (from "New Chronicle" by Guaman Poma de Ayala)

1991. Christmas.

3131	**827**	25p. buff and brown	40	15
3132	-	45p. multicoloured	80	20

DESIGN: 45p. "Nativity" (16th-century Russian icon).

828 "The Meadow of San Isidro" (Francisco Goya)

1991. "Exfilna '91" National Stamp Exhibition, Madrid. Sheet 106×78 mm.

MS3133	**828**	25p. multicoloured	45	45

829 Alcantara Gate, Toledo

1991. World Heritage Sites.

3134	**829**	25p. agate and brown	45	15
3135	-	25p. black and brown	45	15
3136	-	25p. brown and blue	45	15
3137	-	25p. violet and green	45	15

DESIGNS—VERT: No. 3135, Casa de las Conchas, Salamanca. HORIZ: No. 3136, Seville Cathedral; 3137, Aeonio (flower) and Garajonay National Park, Gomera.

830 Gen. Carlos Ibanez de Ibero (cartographer)

1991. Anniversaries and Events. Multicoloured.

3138	25p.	Type **830** (death centenary)	50	15
3139	55p.	"Las Palmas" (Antarctic survey ship) (signing of Antarctic Treaty protocol of Madrid declaring the Antarctic a nature reserve)	95	20

831 Margarita Xirgu

1992. 23rd Death Anniv of Margarita Xirgu (actress).

3140	**831**	25p. brown and red	35	15

832 "Expo 92, Seville"

1992. Children's Stamp Design.

3141	**832**	25p. multicoloured	35	15

833 Pedro Rodriguez, Count of Campomanes (administrator and postal consultant)

1992. Stamp Day.
3142 **833** 27p. multicoloured 40 15

834 Spanish Pavilion

1992. "Expo '92" World's Fair, Seville (7th issue).
3143 **834** 27p. grey, black & brown 40 15

1992. Olympic Games, Barcelona (8th issue). As T **760**. Multicoloured.
3144 15p.+5p. Archery 50 50
3145 25p.+5p. Sailing 70 70
3146 55p.+5p. Volleyball 1·20 1·10

835 Columbus's Fleet

1992. 500th Anniv of Discovery of America by Columbus (7th issue). Sheet 164×94 mm reproducing 1930 Columbus design.
MS3147 **835** 17p.+5p. red; 17p.+5p. blue; 17p.+5p. black 1·50 1·50

836 Cable-cars

1992. "Expo '92" World's Fair, Seville (8th issue). Multicoloured.
3148 17p. Exhibition World Trade Centre 30 25
3149 17p. Type **836** 30 25
3150 17p. Fourth Avenue 30 25
3151 17p. Barqueta entrance 30 25
3152 17p. Nature pavilion 30 25
3153 17p. Bioclimatic sphere 30 25
3154 17p. Alamillo bridge 30 25
3155 17p. Press centre 30 25
3156 17p. Pavilion of the 15th century 30 25
3157 17p. Expo harbour 30 25
3158 17p. Tourist train 30 25
3159 17p. One-day entrance ticket showing bridge 30 25
3160 27p. Santa Maria de las Cuevas Carthusian monastery 50 40
3161 27p. Palisade 50 40
3162 27p. Monorail 50 40
3163 27p. Avenue of Europe 50 40
3164 27p. Pavilion of Discovery 50 40
3165 27p. Auditorium 50 40
3166 27p. First Avenue 50 40
3167 27p. Square of the Future 50 40
3168 27p. Italica entrance 50 40
3169 27p. Last avenue 50 40
3170 27p. Theatre 50 40
3171 27p. Curro (official mascot) 50 40
MS3172 105×77 mm. 17p.+5p. View of 16th-century Seville (after A. Sanchez Coello) 40 40

837 Wheelchair Sports

1992. Paralympic (Physically Handicapped) Games, Barcelona.
3173 **837** 27p. multicoloured 45 20

838 Arrival in America

1992. "Granada '92" International Thematic Stamp Exhibition (2nd issue). Sheet 114×105 mm reproducing 1930 Columbus stamps.
MS3174 **835** 250p. black; **838** 250p. brown 7·75 7·75

839 "Preparation before leaving Palos" (R. Espejo)

1992. Europa. 500th Anniv of Discovery of America by Columbus (7th issue).
3175 **839** 17p. multicoloured 65 45
3176 - 45p. grey and brown 70 45
DESIGN: 45p. Map of the Americas, Columbus's fleet and Monastery of Santa Maria de La Rabida.

840 Columbus soliciting Aid of Isabella

1992. 500th Anniv of Discovery of America by Columbus (9th issue). Six sheets, each 107×91 mm, containing horiz designs as T **840** reproducing scenes from United States 1893 Columbian Exposition issue.
MS3177 Six sheets. (a) 60p. brown (Type **840**); (b) 60p. blue (Columbus sighting land); (c) 60p. brown (Landing of Columbus); (d) 60p. violet (Columbus welcomed at Barcelona); (e) 60p. black (Columbus presenting natives); (f) 60p. black ("America", Columbus and "Liberty") Set of 6 sheets 7·75 7·75

841 "Water and the Environment"

1992. World Environment Day.
3178 **841** 27p. blue and yellow 40 15

842 "Albertville", Olympic Rings and "Barcelona"

1992. Winter Olympic Games, Albertville, and Summer Games, Barcelona.
3179 **842** 45p. multicoloured 65 20

843 Victorious Athlete

1992. Olympic Games, Barcelona (9th issue). Multicoloured.
3180 17p.+5p. Type **843** 40 40
3181 17p.+5p. Cobi (official mascot) 40 40
3182 17p.+5p. Olympic torch (horiz) 40 40

844 Olympic Stadium

1992. Olympic Games, Barcelona (10th issue). Multicoloured.
3183 27p.+5p. Type **844** 40 40
3184 27p.+5p. San Jordi sports arena 40 40

3185 27p.+5p. I.N.E.F. sports university 40 40

845 Cobi holding Magnifying Glass and Stamp Album

1992. "Olymphilex 92" International Stamp Exhibition, Barcelona. Multicoloured.
3186 17p.+5p. Type **845** 35 30
3187 17p.+5p. Church of the Holy Family, Barcelona, and exhibition emblem 35 30

846 Athletes

1992. Paralympic (Mentally Handicapped) Games, Madrid.
3188 **846** 27p. blue and red 40 20

847 St. Paul's Church

1992. "Exfilna '92" National Stamp Exhibition, Valladolid. Sheet 105×78 mm.
MS3189 **814** 27p. brown 45 45

848 Quarterdeck of "Santa Maria"

1992. America. 500th Anniv of Discovery of America by Columbus (8th issue).
3190 **848** 60p. brown, cinnamon and ochre 90 35

849 Luis Vives (philosopher)

1992. Anniversaries. Multicoloured.
3191 17p. Type **849** (500th birth anniv) 20 15
3192 27p. Pamplona Choir (centenary) (horiz) 45 20

850 Helmet of Mercury and European Community Emblem

1992. European Single Market.
3193 **850** 45p. blue and yellow 70 40

851 "Nativity" (Obdulia Acevedo)

1992. Christmas.
3194 **851** 27p. multicoloured 35 15

852 Municipal Museum

1992. Madrid, European City of Culture (2nd issue). Multicoloured.
3195 17p.+5p. Type **852** 40 30
3196 17p.+5p. Queen Sofia Art Museum 40 30
3197 17p.+5p. Prado Museum 40 30
3198 17p.+5p. Royal Theatre 40 30

853 Huitzilopochtli, Mexican God of War

1992. Codices. Sheet 106×151 mm containing T **853** and similar vert designs. Multicoloured.
MS3199 27p. Type **853** (Codex Veitia); 27p. "Mounted Spaniard" (Bishop Baltasar Jaime's *History of the Diocese of El Trujillo del Peru*); 27p. 13th-century miniature from King Alfonso X's *Book of Chess, Dice and Tablings*; 27p. "Of the Months and the Festivals" from Bernardino de Sahagun's *General History of the Matters of New Spain* 1·60 1·60

854 Bird, Sun, Leaves and Silhouettes

1993. Public Services. Protection of the Environment.
3200 **854** 28p. blue and green 40 15

855 Maria Zambrano

1993. Second Death Anniv of Maria Zambrano (writer).
3201 **855** 45p. multicoloured 70 25

856 Figures and Blue Cross

1993. Public Services. Health and Sanitation.
3202 **856** 65p. blue and green 95 25

857 Segovia

1993. Birth Centenary of Andres Segovia (guitarist).
3203 **857** 65p. black and brown 1·00 25

858 Post-box, Cadiz, 1908

1993. Stamp Day.
3204 **858** 28p. multicoloured 50 15

912 Lumiere Brothers

1995. Centenary of Motion Pictures.

3330	**912**	19p. brown	35	15

913 Typewriter, Pen and Camera

1995. Centenary of Madrid Press Association.

3331	**913**	30p. multicoloured	50	25

1995. Spanish Olympic Silver Medal Sports. As T **897**. Multicoloured.

3332	30p. Type **897**		45	40
3333	30p. Basketball		45	40
3334	30p. Boxing		45	40
3335	30p. As No. 3300		45	40
3336	30p. Gymnastics		45	40
3337	30p. As No. 3301		45	40
3338	30p. As No. 3302		45	40
3339	30p. Canoeing		45	40
3340	30p. Polo		45	40
3341	30p. Rowing		45	40
3342	30p. Tennis		45	40
3343	30p. Shooting		45	40
3344	30p. As No. 3306		45	40
3345	30p. Water polo		45	40

914 King Juan Carlos I at National Assembly, 1986

1995. Anniversaries. Multicoloured.

3346	60p. Type **914** (50th anniv of U.N.O.)		90	40
3347	60p. Anniversary emblem, globes and wheat ears (50th anniv of F.A.O.) (vert)		90	40
3348	60p. Emblem and coloured bands (20th anniv of World Tourism Organization)		90	40

915 Presidency Emblem

1995. Spanish Presidency of the European Union.

3349	**915**	60p. red, yellow and blue	1·20	65

916 Spotlight on Woman

1995. Fourth U.N. Conference on Women, Peking.

3350	**916**	60p. multicoloured	95	40

917 Cover Illustration of National Atlas of Spain

1995. 17th International Cartography Conference, Barcelona. Sheet 105×78 mm.

MS3351	**917**	130 p. multicoloured	2·00	2·00

918 Entrance to Hospital de la Azabacheria

1995. 500th Anniv of University of Santiago de Compostela.

3352	**918**	30p. multicoloured	50	25

919 Royal Monastery of Santa Maria, Guadalupe

1995. World Heritage Sites.

3353	**919**	60p. brown	90	40
3354	-	60p. multicoloured	90	40

DESIGN—HORIZ: No. 3354, Route map of Spanish section of road to Santiago de Compostela and statue of pilgrim.

920 The Peddler" (sculpture, Jamie Pimentel)

1994. "Exfilna '95" National Stamp Exhibition, Malaga. Sheet 105×78 mm.

MS3355	**920**	130p. green	2·00	2·00

921 Red-crested pochard, Mallard and Lagoon of La Mancha

1995. America. Environmental Protection.

3356	**921**	60p. multicoloured	85	40

922 La Cueva de Menga, Malaga (Bronze Age)

1995. Archaeology. Multicoloured.

3357	30p. Type **922**		45	25
3358	30p. La Taula de Torralba (c. 700 B.C.)		45	25

923 Reciation

1995. Art. Sheet 145×95 mm containing details of "The Contemporary Poets" by Antonio Wsquivel. As T **923**. Multicoloured.

MS3359	19p.; 30p.; 60p.; 60p. Composite design of painting		2·50	2·75

924 "Adoration of the Kings" (capital, Collegiate Church, San Martin de Elines)

1995. Christmas.

3360	**924**	30p. multicoloured	55	20

925 King Juan Carlos

1995. 20th Anniv of Accession of King Juan Carlos I.

3361	**925**	1000p. violet	47·00	8·25

See also Nos. 3408/11.

926 Cordoba Station, Plaza de Armas, Seville (venue)

1995. "Espamer" Spanish–Latin American and "Aviation and Space" Stamp Exhibitions, Seville. Multicoloured.

3362	60p. Type **926**		95	35
3363	60p. Dr. Lorenzo Galindez de Carvajal (Master Courier of the Indies and Terra Firma of the Ocean Sea, 1514)		95	35

See also **MS**3382.

927 "Leaving Mass at Pilar de Zaragoza" (first Spanish film, 1896)

1996. Centenary of Motion Pictures.

3364	**927**	30p. brown, mauve and black	40	20
3365	-	60p. multicoloured	65	40

DESIGN: 60p. "Bienvenido, Mister Marshall!" (poster).

928 Miner's Lamp

1996. Minerals (3rd series). Multicoloured.

3366	30p. Type **928**		60	20
3367	60p. Amber fluorite		1·00	40

929 Jose Mathe Aragua (General Director) and Telegraph Tower

1996. Stamp Day. 150th Anniv of Madrid–Irun Telegraph Signal Line.

3368	**929**	60p. green and red	80	40

930 Columbus (statue), "B" and Arch of Triumph

1996. Tenth Anniv (1995) of Start of Barcelona Urbanization Programme.

3369	**930**	30p. multicoloured	35	20

931 Brown Bear with Cubs

1996. Endangered Species.

3370	**931**	30p. multicoloured	4·00	20

932 Real Phelipe (ship of the line)

1996. 18th-century Ships. Two sheets each 87×165 mm containing vert designs as T **932**. Multicoloured.

MS3371	Two sheets. (a) 30p. ×4, Type **932**; (b) 60p. ×4, El Catalan (after Rafael Moleon)		5·50	5·50

933 Scales

1996. 400th Anniv of Madrid Bar Assocation.

3372	**933**	19p. multicoloured	30	20

1996. Spanish Olympic Bronze Medal Sports. As T **897**. Multicoloured. Dated "1996".

3373	30p. Type **897**		35	25
3374	30p. As No. 3334		35	25
3375	30p. As No. 3299		40	30
3376	30p. As No. 3302		40	30
3377	30p. As No. 3304		40	30
3378	30p. As No. 3339		40	30
3379	30p. As No. 3342		40	30
3380	30p. As No. 3343		40	30
3381	30p. As No. 3306		40	30

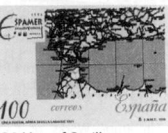

934 Map of Seville— Larache Postal Route

1996. "Espamer" Spanish-Latin American and "Aviation and Space" Stamp Exhibitions, Seville (2nd issue). Two sheets, each 164×87 mm containing T **934** and similar horiz designs (sheet a) or single stamp (b). Multicoloured.

MS3382	Two sheets. (a) 100p. Type **934**; 100p. Cover flown by airship LZ-127 Graf Zeppelin, 1930; 100p. Rocket launch, El Arenosillo, Huelva; 100 p. Hispano HA200 Saeta jet fighter. (b) 400p. The Royal Family (78×54 mm)		8·25	8·25

935 Carmen Amaya (flamenco dancer)

1996. Europa. Famous Women.

3383	**935**	60p. multicoloured	1·60	85

936 El Jabato (Victor Mora and Francisco Darnis)

1996. Comic Strip Characters. Multicoloured.

3384	19p. Type **936**		30	20
3385	30p. Reporter Tribulete (Guillermo Cifre) (horiz)		50	20

937 "General Don Antonio Ricardos"

1996. 250th Birth Anniv of Francisco de Goya (artist). Multicoloured.

3386	19p. Type **937**	40	20
3387	30p. "The Milkmaid of Bordeaux"	45	25
3388	60p. "Boys with Mastiffs" (horiz)	1·00	40
3389	130p. "3rd of May 1808 in Madrid" (horiz)	2·20	85

938 Magnifying Glass and Stamp Album

1996. 50th Anniv of Philatelic Service.

| 3390 | **938** 30p. multicoloured | 45 | 25 |

939 Jose Monge Cruz (Camaron de la Isla)

1996. Flamenco Artistes.

| 3391 | **939** 19p. multicoloured | 25 | 20 |
| 3392 | - 30p. purple and red | 40 | 25 |

DESIGN—HORIZ: 30p. Lola Flores.

940 Lanuza Market, Zaragoza (Felix Navarro Perez)

1996. 19th International Architects Congress, Barcelona. Metallic Buildings.

| 3393 | **940** 30p. multicoloured | 45 | 20 |

941 Gerardo Diego and Pen (poet, birth centenary)

1996. Anniversaries.

3394	**941** 19p. violet and red	25	20
3395	- 30p. multicoloured	40	25
3396	- 60p. black, red and blue	85	40

DESIGNS—HORIZ: 30p. Joaquin Costa and birthplace (politician and historian, 150th birth anniv). VERT: 60p. The five senses (50th anniv of UNICEF.).

942 Naveta (tomb) des Tudons, Minorca

1996. Archaeology. Multicoloured.

| 3397 | 30p. Type **942** | 50 | 20 |
| 3398 | 30p. Cabezo de Alcala de Azila, Teruel | 50 | 20 |

944 Salamancan Costumes

1996. America. Traditional Costumes.

| 3400 | **944** 60p. multicoloured | 80 | 40 |

945 Albaicin Quarter, Granada

1996. World Heritage Sites.

3401	**945** 19p. blue	30	20
3402	- 30p. purple	50	25
3403	- 60p. blue	1·00	40

DESIGNS—HORIZ: 30p. Tiberiades Square and statue of Maimonides (centre of Cordova). VERT: 60p. Deer, Donana National Park.

946 Oviedo Cathedral, Leopoldo Alas and Quotation from "La Regenta"

1996. Literature.

| 3404 | **946** 30p. blue and purple | 35 | 25 |
| 3405 | - 60p. blue and purple | 80 | 45 |

DESIGN—HORIZ: 60p. Scene from "Don Juan Tenorio" by Jose Zorrilla.

947 "Nativity" (Fernando Gallego)

1996. Christmas.

| 3406 | **947** 30p. multicoloured | 45 | 20 |

948 Map

1996. Autonomous Communities of Spain. Sheet 164×87 mm.

| MS3407 | **948** 130p. multicoloured | 1·90 | 1·90 |

1996. King Juan Carlos I.

3408	**925** 100p. brown	2·75	35
3409	**925** 200p. green	6·50	70
3410	**925** 300p. purple	13·50	2·40
3411	**925** 500p. blue	24·00	5·25

949 Genet

1997. Endangered Species.

| 3416 | **949** 32p. multicoloured | 40 | 20 |

950 Exhibition Poster (Jose Sanchez)

1997. "Juvenia '97" National Youth Stamp Exhibition, El Puerto de Santa Maria.

| 3417 | **950** 32p. multicoloured | 40 | 25 |

951 Stone Post Box, Madrid

1997. Stamp Day.

| 3418 | **951** 65p. blue and red | 85 | 45 |

952 "The Journey to Nowhere" (dir. Fernando Fernan)

1997. Spanish Cinema (3rd series). Posters. Multicoloured.

| 3419 | 21p. Type **952** | 25 | 20 |
| 3420 | 32p. "The South" (dir. Victor Erice) | 45 | 25 |

953 La Caprichosa and Bano de Diana Waterfalls, Monastery of Piedra Park

1997. World Water Day.

| 3421 | **953** 65p. multicoloured | 80 | 40 |

954 Asturias (frigate)

1997. 19th-century Ships. Two sheets each 87×164 mm containing similar vert designs as T **954**. Multicoloured.

MS3422 Two sheets (a) 21p. ×4, Type **954**; (b) 32p. ×4, 16-gun brigantine (after Rodriguez and Gasco) 3·75 3·75

955 Vizcaya Bridge

1997. Anniversaries. Metal Structures. Multicoloured.

| 3423 | 32p. Type **955** (centenary of Engineering School, Bilbao) | 40 | 20 |
| 3424 | 194p. Atocha railway station and AVE locomotive (fifth anniv of AVE high speed train) | 2·50 | 1·20 |

956 Joint and Trueta

1997. Birth Centenary of Josep Trueta i Raspall (orthopaedic surgeon).

| 3425 | **956** 32p. multicoloured | 40 | 25 |

957 Prince and Princess, Castle and Forest

1997. Europa. Tales and Legends.

| 3426 | **957** 65p. multicoloured | 1·60 | 90 |

958 Lazaro with Blind Beggar

1997. Spanish Literature.

| 3427 | **958** 21p. black and green | 25 | 15 |
| 3428 | - 32p. brown and blue | 45 | 25 |

DESIGNS—VERT: 21p. Type **958** ("Life of Lazarillo de Tormes and his Fortunes and Setbacks"). HORIZ: 32p. Jose Maria Peman and character El Seneca.

959 Anxel Fole (writer) (after Siro Lopez Lorenzo)

1997. Galician Literature Day.

| 3429 | **959** 65p. multicoloured | 85 | 40 |

960 The Ulysses Family (Mariano Benejam)

1997. Comic Strip Characters. Multicoloured.

| 3430 | 21p. Type **960** | 25 | 15 |
| 3431 | 32p. The Masked Warrior (Manuel Gago) | 45 | 25 |

961 Manolete (Manuel Rodriguez Sanchez) (matador)

1997. Anniversaries. Multicoloured.

| 3432 | 32p. Type **961** (50th death anniv) | 45 | 25 |
| 3433 | 65p. Charlie Rivel (Josep Andreu i Lasserre) (clown, birth centenary (1996)) | 90 | 40 |

962 "The Annunciation" (from Church of Our Lady of Sorrow, Agreda)

1997. Sixth "The Ages of Man" Exhibition. El Burgo de Osma. Sheet 92×148 mm containing T **962** and similar vert designs. Multicoloured.

MS3434 21p. Type **962**; 32p. El Burgo de Osma Cathedral; 65p. Illustration from Codex, 1086; 140p. Santo Domingo de Silos (17-century statue) 3·75 3·75

963 Championship Poster (Manel Esclusa)

1997. 30th Men's European Basketball Championship, Barcelona, Girona and Badalona.

| 3435 | **963** 65p. multicoloured | 1·10 | 40 |

964 Cibeles Fountain, Madrid

1997. North Atlantic Co-operation Council Summit, Madrid.

| 3436 | **964** | 65p. multicoloured | 1·10 | 40 |

965 Grape Harvest Monument (Jose Esteve Edo)

1997. 50th Anniv of Grape Harvest Festival, Requena.

| 3437 | **965** | 32p. multicoloured | 50 | 20 |

966 Antonio Canovas del Castillo (author of 1876 Constitution)

1997. Anniversaries. Multicoloured.

3438		21p. Type **966** (death centenary)	35	15
3439		32p. Roman coin and arrival of "Virgin of the Assumption" (statue) (2000th anniv of Elche)	55	25
3440		65p. Ships attacking city (after contemporary painting) (bicentenary of defence of Tenerife) (horiz)	95	40

967 Blue Ribbon

1997. Campaign for Peaceful Co-existence.

| 3441 | **967** | 32p. blue and black | 40 | 20 |

968 Mariano Benlliure and "Breath of Life"

1997. Spanish Art.

| 3442 | **968** | 32p. multicoloured | 45 | 20 |
| 3443 | - | 65p. black and stone | 90 | 40 |

DESIGNS: 32c. Type **968** (sculptor, 50th death anniv); 65c. "Basque Rower" (photograph by Jose Ortiz Echague).

969 Net and Boat

1997. Fourth World Fishing Fair, Vigo.

| 3444 | **969** | 32p. blue, deep blue and gold | 40 | 20 |

970 City

1997. Anniversaries.

3445	**970**	21p. multicoloured	25	15
3446	-	32p. multicoloured	45	25
3447	-	65p. violet and red	85	40

DESIGNS—VERT: 21p. Type **970** (500th anniv of Spanish administration of Melilla); 32p. St. Pascual Baylon (after Vincente Carducho) (centenary of proclamation as World Patron of Eucharistic Congresses). HORIZ: 65p. Ausias March (after Jacomart) (poet, 600th birth anniv).

971 San Julian de los Prados Church, Oviedo

1997. World Heritage Sites.

| 3448 | **971** | 21p. brown, blue and green | 40 | 15 |
| 3449 | - | 32p. brown, blue and green | 65 | 25 |

DESIGN: 32p. Santa Cristina de Lena.

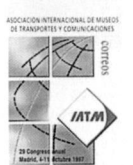

972 Emblem

1997. 29th Annual Congress of International Transport and Communications Museums Association, Madrid.

| 3450 | **972** | 140p. multicoloured | 1·80 | 85 |

973 Statue of Don Palayo (Jose Maria Lopez)

1997. "Exfilna '97" National Stamp Exhibition, Gijon. Sheet 105×78 mm.

| MS3451 | **973** | 140p. multicoloured | 2·00 | 2·00 |

974 Postman

1997. America. Postal Delivery.

| 3452 | **974** | 65p. multicoloured | 85 | 40 |

975 Miguel Fleta (tenor)

1997. Re-opening of Royal Theatre, Madrid.

| 3453 | **975** | 21p. brown | 25 | 15 |
| 3454 | - | 32p. brown | 45 | 25 |

DESIGNS: 21p. Type **975** (birth centenary); 32p. Theatre facade.

976 Town Arms

1997. 500th Anniv of San Cristobal de la Laguna, Tenerife.

| 3455 | **976** | 32p. multicoloured | 40 | 20 |

977 Emblem

1997. Sixth World Downs Syndrome Congress, Madrid.

| 3456 | **977** | 65p. blue and yellow | 85 | 40 |

978 School

1997. 150th Anniv of Cordoba Veterinary School.

| 3457 | **978** | 21p. green and blue | 30 | 15 |

979 "Adoration of the Kings" (detail, Pedro Berruguete)

1997. Christmas.

| 3458 | **979** | 32p. multicoloured | 40 | 20 |

980 New Gate, Ribadavia

1997. Jewish Quarters.

3459	**980**	21p. brown and black	25	25
3460	-	32p. violet and black	45	40
3461	-	32p. brown and black	45	40
3462	-	65p. violet and black	80	70

DESIGNS: No. 3460, Women's Gallery, Cordoba Synagogue; 3461, Facade of 15th-century building, St. Anthony's Quarter, Caceres; 3462, Street, El Call, Girona.

981 Ball in Net

1997. Spanish Sporting Success. Zarra's Winning Goal in Spain v England Match, World Cup Football Championship, Brazil, 1950.

| 3463 | **981** | 32p. multicoloured | 1·30 | 70 |

982 Emblem

1998. St. James's Holy Year (1999).

| 3464 | **982** | 35p. orange, grey and black | 40 | 20 |

983 Lynx

1998. Endangered Species.

| 3465 | **983** | 35p. multicoloured | 40 | 20 |

984 Club Flag and Emblem

1998. Centenary of Athletic Bilbao Football Club.

| 3466 | **984** | 35p. multicoloured | 40 | 20 |

985 Clever and Smart (Francisco Ibanez)

1998. Comic Strip Characters. Multicoloured.

| 3467 | | 35p. Type **985** | 45 | 20 |
| 3468 | | 70p. Zipi and Zape (Josep Escobar) (horiz) | 90 | 55 |

986 Gredos Parador

1998. 70th Anniv of Paradores (state hotels).

| 3469 | **986** | 35p. multicoloured | 40 | 20 |

987 St. Philip's Fort and Harbour, Ceuta

1998. Third Anniv of Autonomy of Ceuta and Melilla. Multicoloured.

| 3470 | | 150p. Type **987** | 1·90 | 90 |
| 3471 | | 150p. Plaza de Menendez Pelayo, Melilla (horiz) | 1·90 | 90 |

988 1898 Generation

1998. 1898 Generation of Spanish Writers.

| 3472 | **988** | 70p. multicoloured | 90 | 45 |

The writers depicted are Azorin, Pio Baroja, Miguel de Unamuno, Ramiro de Maeztu, Antonio Machado and Valle Inclan.

989 Pedro Abarca de Bolea, Count of Aranda

1998. Death Bicentenary of Pedro Abarca de Bolea, Count of Aranda (politician).

| 3473 | **989** | 35p. multicoloured | 40 | 20 |

990 "The Celestine" (Fernando de Rojas)

1998. Spanish Literature.

| 3474 | **990** | 35p. deep green and green | 45 | 20 |
| 3475 | - | 70p. green and red | 90 | 45 |

DESIGN: 70p. "Fortunata and Jacinta" (Benito Perez Galdos).

991 Royal Barge

1998. Ship Paintings by Carlos Broschi from "Royal Celebrations in Reign of Fernando VI". Multicoloured.
3476 35p. Type **991** 45 20
3477 70p. Tajo xebec (for court officials) 90 45

992 St. John's Bonfires, Alicante

1998. Europa. National Festivals.
3478 **992** 70p. multicoloured 1·60 90

993 Jimenez Diaz

1998. Centenary of Professional Institute of Doctors of Madrid and Birth Centenary of Carlos Jimenez Diaz (physician).
3479 **993** 35p. black and blue 40 20

994 Felix Rodriguez de la Fuente (naturalist, 70th anniv)

1998. Birth Anniversaries.
3480 **994** 35p. multicoloured 45 20
3481 - 70p. multicoloured 90 45
DESIGN—VERT: 70p. Fofo (Alfonso Aragon) (clown, 75th anniv).

995 Philip II (after Antonio Moro)

1998. 400th Death Anniv of King Philip II.
3482 **995** 35p. multicoloured 40 20

996 Lorca

1998. Birth Centenary of Federico Garcia Lorca (writer).
3483 **996** 35p. multicoloured 60 20

997 Antonio Manso Fernandez and 1978 Queen Isabel II Stamp

1998. Spanish Engravers.
3484 **997** 35p. brown, blue and deep blue 50 20
3485 - 70p. purple, blue and black 95 45
DESIGN: 70p. Jose Luis Sanchez Toda and 1935 Mariana Pineda stamp.

998 Spanish and Philippine Flags, Cebu Basilica (after M. Miguel) and "Holy Child" (statuette)

1998. Centenary of Philippine Independence.
3486 **998** 70p. multicoloured 85 45

999 "Foster Brothers" (sculpture, Aniceto Marinas)

1998. Spanish Art.
3487 **999** 35p. multicoloured 40 20

1000 "Union of the Oceans"

1998. "Expo '98" World's Fair, Lisbon.
3488 **1000** 70p. multicoloured 85 45

1001 Computer, Computer Disk and Letter

1998. 20th International Data Protection Conference, Santiago de Compostela.
3489 **1001** 70p. multicoloured 85 45

1002 Barcelona Cathedral

1998. "Exfilna '98" National Stamp Exhibition, Barcelona. Sheet 106×88 mm.
MS3490 **1002** 150p. black and blue 2·30 2·30

1003 Fortified City, Cuenca

1998. World Heritage Sites.
3491 **1003** 35p. brown and blue 55 20
3492 - 70p. brown and red 1·10 45
DESIGN: 70p. Silk Exchange, Valencia.

1004 Man writing with Quill

1998. School Correspondence Programme. Scenes from "Don Quixote" (novel by Cervantes). Multicoloured.
3493 20p. Type **1004** 35 25
3494 20p. Man reading book 35 25
3495 20p. Priest dubbing Quixote 35 25
3496 20p. Quixote riding off at dawn (angel blowing trumpet) 35 25
3497 20p. Man beating Quixote with stick 35 25
3498 20p. Investigator burning books 35 25
3499 20p. Quixote and Sancho on horseback 35 25
3500 20p. Quixote and horse on sail of windmill 35 25
3501 20p. Quixote watching Sancho fly through air 35 25
3502 20p. Quixote charging through flock of sheep 35 25
3503 20p. Quixote and galley slaves 35 25
3504 20p. Quixote piercing goat-skins of wine 35 25
3505 20p. Quixote in cage 35 25
3506 20p. Quixote and Sancho on knees and woman on donkey 35 25
3507 20p. Quixote on foot holding sword to Knight of the Mirrors 35 25
3508 20p. Lion escaping cage 35 25
3509 20p. Quixote attacking birds 35 25
3510 20p. Quixote on wooden horse 35 25
3511 20p. Sancho as governor at meal 35 25
3512 20p. Quixote surprised in bed by Dona Rodriguez 35 25
3513 20p. Sancho and donkey 35 25
3514 20p. Quixote and Sancho looking over lake 35 25
3515 20p. Quixote on horse holding sword to Knight of the White Moon 35 25
3516 20p. Quixote and Sancho returning home at night 35 25

1005 Angel Ganivet (writer, death centenary)

1998. Anniversaries.
3517 **1005** 35p. brown and violet 45 20
3518 - 70p. brown and blue 85 45
DESIGN—VERT: 70p. Giralda Tower, Seville (800th anniv).

1006 Ladies' Partal Gardens, Alhambra, Granada

1998. Aga Khan 1998 Architecture Award.
3519 **1006** 35p. brown and green 40 20

1007 U.P.U. Emblem

1998. World Stamp Day.
3520 **1007** 70p. blue and green 85 45

1008 Maria Guerrero (actress) and Scene from "The Lioness of Castille" by Francisco Villaespesa

1998. America. Famous Women.
3521 **1008** 70p. multicoloured 85 45

1009 Steam Locomotive "Mataro" (1848) and Euromed Electric Train (1998)

1998. 150th Anniv of Spanish Railways.
3522 **1009** 35p. blue and black 40 20

1010 Antarctic Base

1998. Tenth Anniv of Juan Carlos I Antarctic Base.
3523 **1010** 35p. multicoloured 40 20

1011 Altarpiece (detail)

1998. Restoration of San Salvador's Cathedral, Zaragoza. Details of Altarpiece by Hans of Swabia. Sheet 105×122 mm containing T **1011** and similar vert design. Multicoloured.
MS3524 35p. Type **1011**; 35p. Adoration of the Wise Men (detail) 1·40 1·40

1012 Chestnut Seller

1998. Christmas. Multicoloured.
3525 35p. Type **1012** 45 20
3526 70p. "Wedding of Virgin Mary and Joseph" (detail of capital from Oviedo Cathedral) 85 45

1013 Juan de Onate (expedition leader)

1998. 400th Anniv of Foundation of Spanish Province of New Mexico. Multicoloured.
3527 35p. Type **1013** 45 20
3528 70p. Map and arms of New Mexico 85 45

1014 House, Hervas

1998. Jewish Quarters.
3529 **1014** 35p. purple and blue 45 25
3530 - 35p. green and blue 45 25
3531 - 70p. purple and blue 65 40
3532 - 70p. green and blue 65 40
DESIGNS: No. 3530, Bust of Benjamin Tudela (travel writer); 3531, Corpus Christi Church (former synagogue), Segovia; 3532, Santa Maria la Blanca synagogue, Toledo.

1015 Alaior and Mt. Toro

1998. UNESCO Biosphere Reserve, Minorca.
3533 **1015** 35p. multicoloured 40 20

1016 Bust of Plato and Ancient Greek Amphora

1998. 30th Anniv of Spanish Olympic Academy.
3534 **1016** 70p. multicoloured 85 45

1017 Angel Sanz Briz (diplomat)

1998. 50th Anniv of Universal Declaration of Human Rights. Multicoloured.
3535 35p. Type **1017** 45 20
3536 70p. Fingerprints forming heart (painting, Javier Valmaseda Calvo) 85 45

1018 Mare and Foal

1998. "Espana 2000" International Stamp Exhibition (1st issue). La Cartuja-Hierro del Bocado Horses. Multicoloured.

3537	20p. Type **1018** (emblem bottom right)	55	55
3538	20p. Type **1018** (emblems top left and top right)	55	55
3539	35p. Brown horse (emblem top right)	90	90
3540	35p. As No. 3538 (emblem bottom left)	90	90
3541	70p. Horse's head (emblems bottom left and bottom right)	1·90	1·90
3542	70p. As No. 3541 (emblem top left)	1·90	1·90
3543	100p. Mare and foal (different) (emblems top left and top right)	3·00	3·00
3544	100p. As No. 3543 (emblem bottom right)	3·00	3·00
3545	150p. Grey (emblem bottom left)	4·00	4·00
3546	150p. As No. 3545 (emblem top right)	4·00	4·00
3547	185p. Two white horses (emblem top left)	5·00	5·00
3548	185p. As No. 3547 (emblems bottom left and bottom right)	5·00	5·00

See also Nos. 3612/23, 3662/73 and **MS**3701.

1019 Giant Lizard, El Hierro Island

1999. Endangered Species. Multicoloured.

3549	35p. Type **1019**	50	20
3550	70p. Osprey (vert)	1·00	30
3551	100p. Manx shearwater	1·50	55

1020 Stone Cross, Perelada, Galicia

1999. St. James's Holy Year. Multicoloured.

3552	35p. Type **1020**	40	20
3553	70p. Figure of St. James on tympanum, St. James's Church, Sanguesa, Navarra (horiz)	1·00	40
3554	100p. Stone cross and Cizur bridge, Pamplona, Navarra	1·30	55
3555	185p. Jurisdictional stone pillar, Boadilla del Camino, Palencia	2·50	55

1021 Poster (Antoni Tapies)

1999. Centenary of Barcelona Football Club.

3556	**1021** 35p. multicoloured	50	20

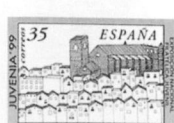

1022 "Alaior" (Aroa Vidal)

1999. "Juvenia'99" National Youth Stamp Exhibition, Alaior, Minorca.

3557	**1022** 35p. black, red and yellow	50	20

1023 Police Moped, Bolkow (MBB/Eurocopter) BO 105 and Men in Protective Suits

1999. 175th Anniv of Spanish Police Force.

3558	**1023** 35p. multicoloured	50	20

1024 Aljaferia Palace, Zaragoza

1999. "Exfilna '99" National Stamp Exhibition, Zaragoza. Sheet 106×79 mm.

MS3559	**1024** 185p. green and chestnut	2·75	2·75

1025 Radio Transmitter and Receiver

1999. 50th Anniv of Spanish Amateur Radio Union.

3560	**1025** 70p. multicoloured	90	40

1026 Emblem and Athletes

1999. Seventh World Athletics Championship, Seville.

3561	**1026** 70p. multicoloured	90	40

1027 Monfrague Nature Park, Caceres, and Wild Cat

1999. Europa. Parks and Gardens.

3562	**1027** 70p. multicoloured	1·50	90

1028 Underground Train

1999. 75th Anniv of Barcelona Metro.

3563	**1028** 70p. multicoloured	90	40

1029 "King Solomon" (detail of reredos from Becerril de Campos Church)

1999. "The Ages of Man" Exhibition, Palencia. Multicoloured.

3564	35p. Type **1029**	45	20
3565	70p. Detail of choir railing, Palencia Cathedral	90	40

1030 European Community Flag

1999. The Euro (European single currency). Showing maps of the participating countries and the appropriate exchange rate. Multicoloured.

3566	166p. Type **1030**	2·75	1·70
3567	166p. Germany	2·75	1·70
3568	166p. Austria	2·75	1·70
3569	166p. Belgium	2·75	1·70
3570	166p. Spain	2·75	1·70
3571	166p. Finland	2·75	1·70
3572	166p. France	2·75	1·70
3573	166p. Netherlands	2·75	1·70
3574	166p. Republic of Ireland	2·75	1·70
3575	166p. Italy	2·75	1·70
3576	166p. Luxembourg	2·75	1·70
3577	166p. Portugal	2·75	1·70

1031 Footballers and Club Badge

1999. Real Club Recreativo (Royal Recreation Club) of Huelva.

3578	**1031** 35p. multicoloured	50	20

1032 Dona Urraca (Jorge (Miguel Bernet Toledano))

1999. Comic Strip Characters. Multicoloured.

3579	35p. Type **1032**	45	20
3580	70p. El Coyote (Jose Mallorqui and Francisco Batet)	90	40

1033 Games Emblem

1999. World University Summer Games and Fifth National Thematic Stamps Exhibition, Palma de Mallorca. Sheet 105×78 mm.

MS3581	**1033** 185p. multicoloured	2·50	2·50

1034 Attack of Dutch Navy (after De Bry) and Arms of Las Palmas

1999. 400th Anniv of Defence of Las Palmas, Gran Canaria.

3582	**1034** 70p. black and yellow	90	40

1035 Cangas de Onis Parador (former Monastery of San Pedro de Villanueva)

1999. Paradores (state hotels).

3583	**1035** 35p. multicoloured	50	20

1036 Old Bridge

1999. 800th Anniv of Granting of Township Rights to Balmaseda.

3584	**1036** 35p. multicoloured	45	20

1037 Society and Anniversary Emblems

1999. Centenary of Society of Authors and Publishers.

3585	**1037** 70p. multicoloured	90	40

1038 Illuminated Fountain

1999. Birth Centenary of Carles Buigas (engineer).

3586	**1038** 70p. multicoloured	90	40

1039 Queen Isabel II, Geological Map of Spain and Founding Decree

1999. 150th Anniv of Spanish Technical Institute of Geology and Mining.

3587	**1039** 150p. multicoloured	2·10	90

1040 El Cid (after Vela Zanetti)

1999. 900th Death Anniv of El Cid (Rodrigo Diaz de Vivar).

3588	**1040** 35p. multicoloured	45	35

1041 "Winter"

1999. Spanish Art. Paintings by Vela Zanetti. Multicoloured.

3589	70p. Type **1041**	85	40
3590	150p. "The Harvest" (vert)	1·90	85

1042 "The Jester Don Sebastian de Morra"

1999. 400th Birth Anniv of Diego de Silva Velazquez (artist). Multicoloured.

3591	35p. Type **1042**	45	20
3592	70p. "A Sibyl"	90	40

1043 Emblem, Couple, Man and Baby

1999. International Year of the Elderly.

3593	**1043** 35p. multicoloured	50	20

1044 Oix Castle

1999. Catalan Lower Pyrenees Region.
3594 **1044** 70p. brown and blue 90 40

1045 St. Millan of Yuso
Monastery, La Rioja

1999. World Heritage Sites.
3595 **1045** 35p. brown, green and
blue 60 20
3596 – 70p. brown, green and
blue 1·30 40

DESIGN: 70p. St. Millan of Suso Monastery, La Rioja.

1046 U.P.U. Monument,
Berne

1999. Stamp Day. 125th Anniv of Universal Postal Union.
3597 **1046** 70p. multicoloured 90 40

1047 First Spanish Stamp,
1850

1999. School Correspondence Programme. Designs
showing a stamp performing various activities.
Multicoloured.
3598 **1047** 20p. Type **1047** 25 20
3599 20p. Watching Boeing 747 taking off over city 25 20
3600 20p. As postman delivering
letter 25 20
3601 20p. Writing letter 25 20
3602 20p. Reading book 25 20
3603 20p. With bird, butterfly and
fish (nature) 25 20
3604 20p. Viewing historical buildings (heritage) 25 20
3605 20p. Painting portrait 25 20
3606 20p. With football, tennis
racquet and sailboard 25 20
3607 20p. With baton, cello and
saxophone 25 20
3608 20p. Holding magnifying glass
over 40c. stamp 25 20
3609 20p. On horseback 25 20

1048 Dove on
Hand

1999. America. A New Millennium without Arms.
3610 **1048** 70p. multicoloured 90 40

1049 "The Money Changer and
his Wife" (Marinus Reymerswaele)

1999. National Money Museums Congress, Madrid.
3611 **1049** 70p. brown and blue 90 40

1050 Horse and Rider

1999. "Espana 2000" International Stamp Exhibition,
Madrid (2nd issue). La Cartuja-Hierro del Bocado
Horses. Paintings by Jose Manuel Gomez.
Multicoloured.
3612 20p. Type **1050** (emblem bottom right) 85 85
3613 20p. Type **1050** (emblem
top left) 85 85

3614 35p. Exhibition emblem and
horses (emblems top left
and right) 1·30 1·30
3615 35p. As No. 3614 (emblems
top left and right but
transposed) 1·30 1·30
3616 70p. Exhibition emblem (emblems bottom left and right) 2·20 2·20
3617 70p. As No. 3616 (emblems
bottom left and right but
transposed) 2·20 2·20
3618 100p. White horses (emblem
top right) 3·75 3·75
3619 100p. As No. 3618 (emblem
bottom left) 3·75 3·75
3620 150p. Heads of two white
horses (emblem bottom left) 5·00 5·00
3621 150p. As No. 3620 (emblem
top right) 5·00 5·00
3622 185p. Men inspecting horse
(emblem top left) 6·75 6·75
3623 185p. As No. 3622 (emblem
bottom right) 6·75 6·75

1051 "The
Epiphany"
(altarpiece,
Toledo Cathedral)

1999. Christmas. Multicoloured.
3624 35p. Type **1051** 45 20
3625 70p. "Christmas" (Isabel Guerra)
(horiz) 90 40

1052 King Juan Carlos and
1850 12c. Stamp

2000. 150th Anniv of First Spanish Stamp. Multicoloured.
3626 35p. Type **1052** 45 35
3627 35p. King Juan Carlos and 6c.
stamp 45 35
3628 35p. King Juan Carlos and 5r.
stamp 45 35
3629 35p. King Juan Carlos and 6r.
stamp 45 35
3630 35p. Anniversary emblem and
6c. stamp 45 35
3631 35p. King Juan Carlos and 10r.
stamp 45 35
3632 35p. King Juan Carlos and
State arms 45 35

1053 Apollo

2000. Endangered Butterflies. Multicoloured.
3633 35p. Type **1053** 45 20
3634 70p. *Agriades zullichi* 90 45

1054 Virgin Mary
and Baby Jesus
(xylographic
engraving, Juan
Luschner)

2000. 500th Anniv of the Monastery of Santa Maria of
Montserrat Printing House.
3635 **1054** 35p. multicoloured 45 20

1055 "Charles V as
Sovereign Master of
the Order of the
Golden Fleece" (anon)

2000. 500th Birth Anniv of King Charles V, Holy Roman
Emperor. Multicoloured.
3636 **1055** 35p. Type **1055** 45 25
3637 70p. "Charles V" (Corneille da
la Haye) 90 45
MS3638 126×91 mm. 150p. "Charles V
on Horseback" (40×49 mm) 2·10 2·10

1056 The Virgin
de al Majestad
(12th-century
statue), Astorga
Cathedral

2000. "The Age of Man" Exhibition, Astorga, Leon.
Multicoloured.
3639 **1056** 70p. Type **1056** 90 45
3640 100p. 12th-century Lignum
Crucis and 10th-century Arab
perfume bottle 1·40 75

1057 Pas del Rey Catolico,
Saragossa

2000. Paradores (state hotels).
3641 **1057** 35p. multicoloured 45 25

1058 Lleida University

2000. University Anniversaries.
3642 **1058** 35p. brown and mauve 45 25
3643 – 70p. brown and blue 90 45
DESIGNS: 35p. Type **1058** (700th anniv); 70p. Valencia
(500th anniv (1999)).

1059 Emblem

2000. Centenary of Reial Club Deportiu Espanyol Football
Club, Barcelona.
3644 **1059** 35p. multicoloured 45 25

1060 Maria de las
Mercedes
(painting, Ricardo
Macarron)

2000. Maria de las Mercedes de Borbon y Orleans
(mother of King Juan Carlos I) Commemoration.
3645 **1060** 35p. multicoloured 45 25

1061 "Building
Europe"

2000. Europa.
3646 **1061** 70p. multicoloured 1·60 1·20

1062 Emblem

2000. World Mathematics Year (3648) and Science
(others). Multicoloured.
3647 35p. Type **1062** (300th anniv of
Royal Academy of Medicine,
Seville) 45 25
3648 70p. Julio Rey Pastor (mathematician) (painting, Pedro
Piug Adam) and mathemati-
cal equation 90 45
3649 100p. School of Pharmacy, Granada (150th anniv) (vert) 1·30 75
3650 185p. Prince Felipe Science
Museum, Valencia 2·50 1·20

1063 Hermenegilda and
Leovigilda (Manuel
Vazquez Gallego)

2000. Comic Strip Characters. Multicoloured.
3651 35p. Type **1063** 45 25
3652 70p. Roberto Alcazar and
Pedrin (Eduardo Vano and
Juan Bautista Puerto Belda)
(vert) 90 45

1064 Guggenheim
Museum

2000. 700th Anniv of Bilbao.
3653 **1064** 70p. multicoloured 90 45

1065 "Prayer in
the Garden"
(detail, Francisco
Salzillo)

2000. Spanish Art.
3654 **1065** 70p. multicoloured 90 45

1066 Water
Fountain

2000. "Exfilna '2000" National Philatelic Exhibition, Aviles.
Sheet 105×78 mm.
MS3655 **1066** 185p. brown and blue 2·40 2·40

1067 Wild Pine (*Pinus silvestris*)

2001. 55th Birth Anniv of Carlos Cano (singer).

3794	**1114**	40p. black	50	30

1115 Woman and Flowers

2001. International Volunteers' Day.

3795	**1115**	120p. multicoloured	1·50	85

1116 12th-century Church of San Climent, Taull (Lleida)

2001. UNESCO. World Heritage Sites. Multicoloured.

3796	40p. Type **1116**	50	40
3797	40p. El Misteri d'Elx (religious festival at Elche cathedral)	50	40
3798	40p. Sant Pau Hospital, Barcelona	50	40
3799	40p. Map of St. Cristobal, La Laguna	50	40
3800	40p. Archeological excavations, Atapuerca	50	40
3801	40p. Protected palm trees, Elche	50	40
3802	40p. La Foncalada (medieval monument), Oviedo	50	40
3803	40p. Roman walls, Lugo	50	40
3804	40p. Cave painting, Cueva de los Caballos, Albocacer, Castellon	50	40
3805	40p. Dalt Villa, Eivissa, Ibiza	50	40
3806	40p. Roman amphitheatre, Tarraco	50	40
3807	40p. Renaissance university building, Alcala de Henares	50	40

1117 Map and Postal Emblem (Postal Service)

2001. 150th Anniv of Ministry of Public Works.

3808	**1117**	40p. multicoloured	50	50
3809	-	75p. lilac, black and blue	90	90
3810	-	120p. blue, green and black	1·50	1·50
3811	-	155p. multicoloured	1·90	1·90
3812	-	260p. multicoloured	3·25	3·25

DESIGNS: Maps showing—75p. Ports; 120p. Railways; 155p. Airports; 260p. Motorways.

1118 Crown Prince Felipe de Borbon

2001. Silver Jubilee of King Juan Carlos I. Sheet 125×80 mm. containing T **1118** and similar multicoloured designs.

MS3813 40p. Type **1118**; 40p. Infanta Elena; 40p. Arms; 40p. Infanta Cristina; 75p. King Juan Carlos; 75p. Queen Sofia; 260p. Palace (49×28 mm) 7·75 7·75

1119 King Juan Carlos I

2002. King Juan Carlos I

3814	**1119**	1c. black and silver	15	15
3815	**1119**	2c. magenta and silver	15	15
3818	**1119**	5c. blue and silver	15	15
3823	**1119**	10c. green and silver	20	20
3826	**1119**	25c. red and silver	35	20
3827	**1119**	27c. blue and silver	50	20
3827a	**1119**	28c. yellow	55	25
3827aa	**1119**	29c. sepia and silver	55	20
3827b	**1119**	35c. orange	65	25
3827c	**1119**	40c. blue	60	20
3828	**1119**	50c. green and silver	95	25
3829	**1119**	52c. cinnamon and silver	1·00	25
3829a	**1119**	53c. purple	1·00	25
3829b	**1119**	57c. orange and silver	1·10	25
3830	**1119**	75c. purple and silver	1·40	30
3831	**1119**	77c. green and silver	1·60	30
3831a	**1119**	78c. rosine	1·50	30
3832	**1119**	€1 green and silver	1·90	40
3832a	**1119**	€1.95 ochre	3·75	80
3833	**1119**	€2 red and silver	3·75	55
3833a	**1119**	€2.21 bistre	4·25	1·20
3833b	**1119**	€2.26 lilac and silver	4·00	1·00
3833c	**1119**	€2.33 carmine and silver	4·50	1·30
3833d	**1119**	€2.39 green and silver	4·50	1·50
MS3834		100×87 mm. No. 3827 ×4	2·40	2·40

1120 Emblem

2002. Spanish Presidency of European Union.

3835	**1120**	25c. red, black and yellow	55	30
3836	**1120**	50c. red, yellow and black	1·10	50

1121 Sabina

2002. Trees (3rd series). Multicoloured.

3837	50c. Type **1121**	1·00	50
3838	75c. Elm	1·50	85

1122 Orchids

2002. Flowers. Depicting paintings by Eduardo Naranjo. Multicoloured. Self-adhesive.

3839	25c. Type **1122**	50	30
3840	25c. Gardenia in vase	50	30
3841	25c. Hands holding white rose	50	30
3842	25c. Iris	50	30
3843	25c. Two white orchid blooms	50	30
3844	25c. Pink-tinged rose in vase	50	30
3845	25c. Two pink orchid blooms	50	30
3846	25c. Three pink orchid blooms on one stem	50	30

1123 Emblem

2002. "Espana 2002" International Youth Stamp Exhibition, Salamanca (1st issue). Multicoloured.

3847	50c. Type **1123**	1·00	45
MS3848	80×105 mm. £1.80 Salamanca Cathedral	4·25	3·75

See also Nos. 2913/22.

1124 Father Francisco Piquer (founder)

2002. 300th Anniv of Caja Madrid Savings Bank.

3849	**1124**	25c. multicoloured	50	30

1125 Anniversary Emblem

2002. Centenary of Real Madrid Football Club.

3850	**1125**	75c. yellow and grey	1·50	95

1126 Town Hall Portico, Tarazona

2002. "PHILAIBERIA '02" Spanish-Portuguese Stamp Exhibition, Tarazona. Sheet 106×80 mm.

MS3851 €2.10 multicoloured 4·50 4·50

1127 Mon

2002. Birth Centenary (2001) of Alejandro Mon (politician).

3852	**1127**	25c. multicoloured	50	30

1128 Stylized Coin

2002. "Homage to the Peseta".

3853	**1128**	25c. multicoloured	50	35

1129 Canon do Sil, Ribeira Sacra

2002. Nature. Multicoloured.

3854	75c. Type **1129**	1·50	95
3855	€2.10 Cabo de Gata, Nijer Park, Almeria (horiz)	4·25	2·40

1130 Cadets on Parade, 1886

2002. 75th Anniv of Military Academy, Zaragoza.

3856	**1130**	25c. multicoloured	50	30

1131 Emblem

2002. Centenary of Real Union Irun Football Club.

3857	**1131**	50c. multicoloured	1·00	45

1132 Tweezers, Stamp and Magnifying Glass

2002. Stamp Day.

3858	**1132**	25c. multicoloured	50	30

1133 Banyeres de Mariola Castle, Alicante

2002. Castles.

3859	**1133**	25c. brown and blue	50	35
3860	-	50c. black	1·00	55
3861	-	75c. black	1·50	95

DESIGNS: 50c. Soutomaior Castle, Pontevedra; 75c. Calatorao Castle, Zaragoza.

1134 View across River

2002. Anniversaries. Multlcoloured.

3862	75c. Type **1134** (1200th anniv of Tuleda)	1·50	95
3863	€1.80 View through pillars (millennium of St. Cugat Monastery)	3·75	1·90

1135 Luis Cernuda

2002. Birth Anniversaries. Multicoloured.

3864	50c. Type **1135** (poet, centenary)	1·00	50
3865	50c. Dr. Federico Rubio and nurses (175th anniv)	1·00	50

1136 Clown (Sara Blanco Quintas)

2002. Europa. The Circus.

3866	**1136**	50c. multicoloured	1·20	95

1137 Soldiers on Horseback

2002. Bicentenary of Inclusion of Menorca under Spanish Rule.

3867	**1137**	50c. multicoloured	1·00	50

1138 Driving

2002. World Equestrian Games, Jerez. Multicoloured.

3868	25c. Type **1138**	50	35
3869	25c. Hunting	50	35
3870	25c. Dressage	50	35
3871	25c. Reining	50	35
3872	25c. Acrobats	50	35
3873	75c. Racing	1·50	95
3874	€1.80 Show jumping	3·75	1·90

1139 Maria de las Dolores

2002. 108th Death Anniv of Maria "La Dolores" de las Dolores.

3875	**1139**	50c. multicoloured	1·00	50

1140 Plaza Mayor, Salamanca

2002. "EXFILNA 2002" National Stamp Exhibition, Salamanca. European City of Culture. Sheet 155×94 mm, containing T **1140** and similar horiz design. Multicoloured (€1.80) or orange and blue (others).

MS3876 25c. Type **1140**; 25c. Centre view of Plaza; 25c. Right side of Plaza; €1.80 Aerial view of Plaza ... 5·50 5·50

1141 Rohrbach R-VIII Aircraft, 1927

2002. 75th Anniv of IBERIA Airlines. Multicoloured.
3877 25c. Type **1141** ... 50 35
3878 50c. Boeing 747 ... 1·00 55

1142 Grapes (Rías Baixas)

2002. Wine Regions (1st series).
3879 **1142** 25c. multicoloured ... 50 35

1143 Grapes and glass of red wine (Rioja)

2002. Wine Regions (2nd series). Multicoloured.
3880 50c. Type **1143** ... 1·00 45
3881 75c. Grapes, wine bottle and glass of sherry (Manzanilla) ... 1·50 95

2002. School Correspondence Programme. Spanish History (3rd series). As T **1073** but with currency inscribed in euros. Multicoloured.
3882 10c. Man being knighted with pen (*Don Quixote* by Miguel de Cervantes) ... 25 20
3883 10c. Felipe IV and the Count-Duke of Olivares (accession, 1621) ... 25 20
3884 10c. Quevedo and Gongora pulling on rope of words (literary rivalry) ... 25 20
3885 10c. Velazquez (artist) sitting at easel ... 25 20
3886 10c. Carlos II and witch holding apple ... 25 20
3887 10c. Man rolling out carpet and Felipe V (start of War of the Spanish Succession) ... 25 20
3888 10c. Fernando VI (accession, 1746) ... 25 20
3889 10c. Carlos III holding architectural drawings (accession, 1759) ... 25 20
3890 10c. Bull and toreador (Riot of Esquilanche) ... 25 20
3891 10c. Book escaping from bird cage ... 25 20
3892 10c. Carlos IV (accession, 1788) and Napoleon ... 25 20
3893 10c. Manuel de Godoy (politician) and open door ... 25 20

1144 Temple Expiatori de la Sagrada Família, Barcelona

2002. 150th Birth Anniv of Antonio Gaudi (architect).
3894 **1144** 50c. blue and black ... 1·00 50

1145 Musicians

2002. Music. Designs depicting paintings by G. Dominguez. Multicoloured. Self-adhesive.
3895 25c. Type **1145** ... 50 30
3896 25c. Vase of flowers and lute ... 2·50 2·40
3897 25c. Woman holding lute ... 50 30
3898 25c. Flowers and open book of music ... 50 30
3899 25c. Vase of flowers, clock and violin ... 50 30
3900 25c. Man holding lute with woman ... 50 30
3901 25c. Flowers, violin, compass and sheet music ... 50 30
3902 25c. Woman wearing blue dress holding lute ... 50 30

1146 Alphabet Jigsaw Puzzle

2002. America. Education and Literacy Campaign.
3903 **1146** 75c. multicoloured ... 1·50 95

1147 Cordoba Mosque and Silhouette of Almanzor

2002. Death Millenary of Abu Amir Muhammad al-Ma'afiri (Almanzor) (Arab ruler).
3904 **1147** 75c. multicoloured ... 1·50 95

1148 Basket

2002. Dijous Bo Fair, Inca, Mallorca.
3905 **1148** 75c. multicoloured ... 1·50 95

1149 Cupola, Aranjuez

2002. UNESCO. World Heritage Sites. Multicoloured.
3906 25c. Type **1149** ... 50 35
3907 25c. Santa Maria church, Calatayud, Aragon ... 50 35
3908 50c. San Martin church, Teruel, Aragon ... 1·00 55
3909 75c. Santa Maria church, Tobed, Aragon ... 1·50 1·10
3910 €1.80 Santa Tecla church, Cervera de la Canada, Aragon ... 3·75 2·00
3911 €2.10 San Pablo church, Zaragoza, Aragon ... 4·25 2·50

1150 Alcaniz (former Monastery of Calatrava)

2002. Paradores (state hotels).
3912 **1150** 25c. multicoloured ... 50 35

1151 Capitan Alatriste (Arturo Perez-Reverte)

2002. "Espana 2002" International Youth Stamp Exhibition, Salamanca (2nd issue). Multicoloured. (a) Self-adhesive gum.
3913 50c. As No. 3847 ... 1·00 55
3914 75c. Type **1151** (comic strip character) ... 1·50 95
3915 75c. Television screen and emblem (television) ... 1·50 95
3916 75c. Hand and record (music) ... 1·50 95
3917 75c. Radio and music score (radio) ... 1·50 95
3918 75c. Cyclist, skier and football (sport) ... 1·50 95
3919 75c. Person holding camera (the press) ... 1·50 95
3920 75c. Film clapper board (film) ... 1·50 95
3921 €1.80 Salamanca Cathedral (vert) ... 3·75 2·30

(b) Ordinary gum.
MS3922 Seven sheets 79×106 mm (g) or 106×79 mm (others) (a) 75c. As No. 3920; (b) 75c. As 3915; (c) 75c. As 3919; (d) 75c. As 3917; (e) 75c. As 3918; (f) 75c. As 3916; (g) 75c. As 3914 Set of 7 sheets ... 12·50 12·50

1152 San Jorge Church, Alicante

2002
3923 **1152** 75c. multicoloured ... 1·50 95

1153 Cruceiro do Hio (crucifix) (Jose Cervino) Hio, Galicia

2002. Historical Monuments. Multicoloured.
3924 50c. Type **1153** ... 50 35
3925 50c. Herreria de Compludo (smithy), Leon (horiz) ... 1·00 50

1154 Mary (detail, stained glass window)

2002. 140th Anniv of St. Mary's Cathedral, Vitoria Gasteiz. Sheet 106×79 mm.
MS3926 50c. multicoloured ... 1·00 95

1155 "Adoration of Kings" (Carlos Munoz de Pablos) (alterpiece, Calzadilla de Barros Church)

2002. Christmas. Multicoloured.
3927 25c. Type **1155** ... 50 30
3928 50c. "Maternity" (Goyo Dominguez) ... 1·00 50

1156 Somport Tunnel Entrance

2003. Spain–France Tunnel through Pyrenees.
3929 **1156** 51c. multicoloured ... 1·00 50

1157 Costumes from Anso (Huesca)

2003. Traditional Costumes.
3930 **1157** 76c. multicoloured ... 1·60 95

1158 Fingerprints forming Flower

2003. 50th World Leprosy Awareness Day.
3931 **1158** 26c. multicoloured ... 55 30

1159 Pedro Campomanes

2003. Death Bicentenary of Pedro Rodriguez Campomanes (statesman and writer).
3932 **1159** 26c. multicoloured ... 55 30

1160 Benissa Cathedral

2003. Juvenia 2003 National Youth Stamp, Benissa, Alicante.
3933 **1160** 51c. Multicoloured ... 1·00 50

1161 Praxedes Sagasta

2003. Death Centenary of Praxedes Mateo Sagasta (politician).
3934 **1161** 26c. brown and blue ... 55 30

1162 "ABC"

2003. Centenary of "ABC" (newspaper).
3935 **1162** €2.15 multicoloured ... 4·50 2·20

1163 Santiago Ramon y Cajal (1906)

2003. Nobel Prize Winners for Medicine. Multicoloured.
3936 51c. Type **1163** ... 1·00 50
3937 76c. Severo Ochoa (1959) ... 1·50 95
Stamps of the same design were issued by Sweden.

1164 Tui Bridge to Valenca do Minho (Portugal)

2003. Bicentenary of School of Civil Engineers, Madrid. Multicoloured.
3938 **1164** 26c. Type **1164** ... 55 30

2004. Centenary (2001) of "Diario de Burgos" Newspaper.
4027   **1219**   27c. multicoloured   60   35

1220 Ribbon

2004. European Day (11 March) for Victims of Terrorism.
(a) Ordinary gum.
4028   **1220**   27c. black   60   35

(b) No value expressed. Self-adhesive gum.
4029   **1220**   A (27c.) black   60   30

1221 Eggs

2004. Painted Eggs Festival.
4030   **1221**   27c. multicoloured   60   35

1222 Floral Shawl and Shell

2004. Shawls. Sheet 80×105 mm containing T **1222** and similar vert designs showing details of paintings by Soledad Fernandez. Multicoloured.
MS4031 27c. Type **1222**; 52c. Hands across dark shawl; 77c. Gladioli and part of shawl; €1.90 Shawl draped over chair   7·00   7·00

1223 Saint Domingo de la Calzada

2004. 150th Anniv of Public Technical Engineering Works.
4032   **1223**   52c. multicoloured   1·00   50

1224 Cable Ingles Bridge, Almeria

2004. Centenary of Cable Ingles Bridge, Almeria.
4033   **1224**   52c. multicoloured   1·00   50

1225 Historical Buildings (Sagrada Familia, Barcelona, Antoni Gaudi's Church, Fuente de Cibeles, Madrid, Giralda and Torre del Oro, Seville) and Parasols on Beach

2004. Europa. Holidays.
4034   **1225**   77c. multicoloured   1·80   1·30

1226 "e" enclosing Figures

2004. Enlargement of European Union.
4035   **1226**   52c. multicoloured   1·10   60

1227 "Self Portrait with Neck of Raphael"

2004. Birth Centenary of Salvador Dali (artist).
4036   **1227**   77c. multicoloured   1·60   85

1228 "100" containing Football and FIFA Emblem

2004. Centenary of FIFA (Federation Internationale de Football Association).
4037   **1228**   77c. multicoloured   1·60   85

1229 Bourbon Royal Arms

2004. Wedding of Crown Prince Felipe de Bourbon and Letizia Ortiz.
4038   **1229**   27c. multicoloured   60   40

1230 Vincente Martin y Soler

2004. Espana 2004 International Stamp Exhibition, Madrid (1st issue). 350th Birth Anniv of Vincente Martin y Soler (musician). Multicoloured.
4039   27c. Type **1230**   60   35
4040   52c. Saxophone and drum   1·10   65
See also Nos. MS4041, 4042/3, MS4044 and 4045/6.

1231 Crown Prince Felipe and Princess Letizia

2004. Espana 2004 International Stamp Exhibition, Madrid (2nd issue). The Royal Family. Sheet 151×86 mm containing T **1231** and similar horiz designs.
MS4041 27c. multicoloured; 77c. multi-coloured; €6 blue and deep blue   14·00   14·00
DESIGNS: 27c. Type **1231**; 77c. Prince Felipe; €6 King Juan Carlos and Queen Sophia.

1232 Entry of the Bulls

2004. Espana 2004 International Stamp Exhibition, Madrid (3rd issue). Festivals. Multicoloured.
4042   27c. Type **1232**   60   35
4043   52c. Lance taurino (bullfighter's cape pass)   1·60   85

1233 Tennis Player (image scaled to 56% of original size)

2004. Espana 2004 International Stamp Exhibition, Madrid (4th issue). Sport. Sheet 232×86 mm containing T **1233** and similar horiz designs.. Multicoloured.
MS4044 35c. Type **1233**; 52c. Ricardo Tormo (motorcyclist) and Valencia circuit; €1.90 Golf course   5·75   5·75

1234 Bravo Espana (yacht)

2004. Espana 2004 International Stamp Exhibition (5th issue), Valencia. Multicoloured.
4045   27c. Type **1234**   1·00   55
4046   52c. Architectural heritage   1·60   95

1235 Newsboy and Masthead

2004. 214th Anniv of "Diario de Valencia" Newspaper.
4047   **1235**   27c. multicoloured   60   35

1236 Portico de la Gloria and Nave, Santiago Cathedral

2004. Xacobeo 2004 Holy Year (St. James jubilee year).
4048   **1236**   52c. multicoloured   1·00   50

1237 Lerma (former Ducal palace)

2004. Paradores (state hotels).
4049   **1237**   52c. multicoloured   1·00   50

1238 Aguas Mansas, Agoncillo

2004. Castles.
4050   -   27c. orange and red   60   30
4051   **1238**   52c. brown   1·10   45
4052   -   77c. green   1·60   1·10
4053   -   €1.90 black (vert)   4·00   1·90
DESIGNS: 27c. Granadilla Castle, Caceres; 52c. Type **1238**; 77c. Mota, Alcala la Real, Jaen; €1.90 Villafuerte de Esgueva, Valladolid.

1239 Danforth Anchor

2004. Salinas Anchor Museum, Castrillon, Asturias.
4054   **1239**   €1.90 multicoloured   3·75   2·10

1240 Pot with Handles and Lid

2004. Paintings. Designs depicting paintings of ceramics by Antonio Miguel Gonzalez. Multicoloured. Self-adhesive.
4055   A (27c.) Type **1240**   60   30
4056   A (27c.) Tall pot with handles, wide-necked pot and pot containing brushes   60   30
4057   A (27c.) Pot with central handle, bread and figs   60   30
4058   A (27c.) Pot with long neck and decorated body   60   30
4059   A (27c.) Broken bread, onions, tall pot and pentagon   60   30
4060   A (27c.) Decorated vase   60   30
4061   A (27c.) Fruit and jug   60   30
4062   A (27c.) Decorated storage jar   60   30

1241 Building Facade

2004. Centenary of the Circulo Oscense Building, Huesca.
4063   **1241**   52c. multicoloured   1·00   50

1242 Virgin and Celebrating Crowds

2004. White Virgin Festival, Vitoria-Gasteiz.
4064   **1242**   27c. multicoloured   60   35

1243 Grapes and Bottle (Ribeiro)

2004. Wine. Multicoloured.
4065   27c. Type **1243**   60   30
4066   52c. Glass and bottle (Malaga)   1·10   50

1244 1854 Philippine Stamp and Postmark

2004. 150th Anniv of First Philippine Stamp.
4067   **1244**   77c. multicoloured   1·60   85

1245 Mural (detail)

2004. 109th Anniv of "Heraldo de Aragon" Newspaper.
4068   **1245**   27c. multicoloured   60   35

1246 Jorge Juan (sailor and scientist)

2004. 250th Anniv of Nautical Astronomy.
4069   **1246**   €1.90 multicoloured   4·00   1·90

1247 Columbus Monument

2004. Exfilna 2004 National Stamp Exhibition, Valladolid. Sheet 78×106 mm.
MS4070 **1247** €1.90 brown and green   4·25   4·25

1248 Parc Guell,
Barcelona

2004. Urban Architecture. Multicoloured.
4071	52c. Type **1248**	1·10	50
4072	77c. Jinmao Tower, Shanghai	1·60	85

Stamps of the same design were issued by China.

1249 Rainbow, Torn Sky
and Fire (J. Carrero)

2004. America. Environmental Protection.
4073	**1249**	77c. multicoloured	1·60	85

1250 Accelerator

2004. 50th Anniv of European Organization for Nuclear
Research (CERN).
4074	**1250**	€1.90 multicoloured	4·00	1·90

1251 Cies
Archipelago

2004. Nature. Multicoloured.
4075	27c. Type **1251**	60	30
4076	52c. Ebro Delta National Park (horiz)	1·10	50
4077	77c. La Palm National Park (horiz)	1·60	85

1252 Letter

2004. Stamp Day. 400th Anniv of First Registered Letter.
4078	**1252**	77c. multicoloured	1·60	85

1253 Observatory

2004. Centenary of Erbe Observatory.
4079	**1253**	€1.90 multicoloured	3·75	1·90

1254 Alfonso I
(statue) (Jose
Bueno)

2004. 900th Anniv of Coronation of Alfonso I (king of
Aragon and Navarre).
4080	**1254**	€1.90 multicoloured	3·75	1·90

1255 The Nativity
(18th-century)

2004. Christmas. Multicoloured.
4081	27c. Type **1255**	60	30
4082	52c. The Nativity (Juan Manuel Cossio)	1·10	60

1256 Queen Isabel
and Castle

2004. 500th Death Anniv of Queen Isabel the Catholic.
4083	**1256**	€2.19 multicoloured	4·50	2·20

1257 Ship leaving Port

2004. 200th Anniv of Royal Expedition to take Anti-
Smallpox Vaccine to America and Asia.
4084	**1257**	77c. brown	1·60	85

1258 Santiago el
Mayor (stained
glass window)

2004. Toledo Cathedral. Sheet 105×79 mm.
MS4085	**1258**	€1.90 multicoloured	4·25	4·25

1259 Jugglers
at Rest

2005. Circus. Designs depicting paintings by Manola
Elices. Self-adhesive. Multicoloured.
4086	A (28c.) Type **1259**	55	35
4087	A (28c.) Performing dogs	55	35
4088	A (28c.) Unicyclist and juggler	55	35
4089	A (28c.) Balancing act	55	35
4090	A (28c.) Women with hoops	55	35
4091	A (28c.) Tightrope walker	55	35
4092	A (28c.) Two women and man balancing	55	35
4093	A (28c.) Fire-eating	55	35

Nos. 4086/93 were for standard mail within Spain
weighing up to 20grams.

1260 Emblem

2005. European Constitution.
4094	**1260**	28c. multicoloured	55	35

1261 Ahuehuete
Tree, Retiro Park,
Madrid

2005. Trees (6th series).
4095	**1261**	78c. multicoloured	1·50	85

1262 Stylized Car and
Pedestrians

2005. Civic Responsibility. Multicoloured.
4096	28c. Type **1262** (road safety campaign)	55	35
4097	53c. Stylized blood transfusion (blood donation campaign)	1·00	60

1263 Seville
University

2005. Anniversaries.
4098	**1263**	28c. brown and lake	55	35
4099	-	28c. ochre, lake and green	55	35

DESIGNS: Type **1263** (500th anniv); No. 4099 Frontispiece
Royal Pharmacopoeia (400th anniv of publication).

1264 Woman
watering Flowers
("Al levantar una
lancha")

2005. Children's Songs. Paintings by Raquel Farinas.
Sheet 144×124 mm containing T **1264** and similar
vert designs. Multicoloured.
MS4100	28c. Type **1264**; 28c. "Aqui tc espero"; 28c. "Estaba la pajara pinta"; 53c. "Cuatro esquinitas"; 53c. "El patio de mi casa"; 53c. "Pero mira como beben"; 78c. "Los pollitos cantan"; 78c. "Para entraer en clase"	7·75	7·75

1265 Belfry, Sant
Esteve Church,
Tordera

2005. Juvenia 2005 National Youth Stamp Exhibition,
Tordera.
4101	**1265**	28c. multicoloured	55	35

1266 Emblem

2005. Centenary of Seville Football Club.
4102	**1266**	35c. carmine	65	40

1267 Footballer

2005. Centenary of Real Sporting de Gijon Football Club.
4103	**1267**	40c. multicoloured	75	45

1268 Emblem

2005. 15th Mediterranean Games, Almería.
4104	**1268**	78c. multicoloured	1·50	85

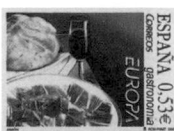

1269 Ham, Bread and Wine

2005. Europa. Gastronomy.
4105	**1269**	53c. multicoloured	1·10	55

1270 Juan Valera

2005. Death Centenary of Juan Valera (writer).
4106	**1270**	€2.21 chocolate and blue	4·25	2·50

1271 Don Quixote
and Sancho Panza

2005. 400th Anniv of Publication of "El Ingenioso Hidalgo
Don Quixote de la Mancha" (novel) by Miguel de
Cervantes. Sheet 80×107 mm containing T **1271**
and similar vert designs. Each black.
MS4107	28c. Type **1271**; 53c. Tilting at windmill; 78c. With sheep; €2.21 In cage	7·25	7·25

1272 Telegraph Machine

2005. 150th Anniv of Telegraph System.
4108	**1272**	28c. multicoloured	55	35

1273 Emblem and
"E=mc²"

2005. International Year of Physics. Self-adhesive.
4109	**1273**	28c. multicoloured	55	35

1328 Symbols of Energy
Use

2006. America. Energy Conservation.
4210	**1328**	78c. multicoloured	1·50	80

1329 Stylized Early and
Modern Postmen

2006. 250th Anniv of First Postman. Self-adhesive.
4211	**1329**	29c. multicoloured	55	35

1330 Ramon
Rubal

2006. Birth Centenary of Ramon Rubal (politician).
4212	**1330**	57c. black and vermilion	1·10	70

1331 "Adoracion de los
Pastores" (sculpture),
Cuenca Cathedral

2006. Christmas. Multicoloured.
4213		29c. Type **1331**	55	35
4214		57c. "Entranable Navidad" (painting) (Belén Elorrieta) (vert)	1·10	60

1332 Construction
(stained glass
window)

2006. Higher Architecture School of Madrid. Sheet
106×80 mm.
MS4215	**1332**	£2.39 multicoloured	4·50	4·50

1333 Francis Xavier

2006. 500th Birth Anniv of Saint Francis Xavier.
4216	**1333**	29c. multicoloured	55	35

1334 Symbols of Television

2006. 50th Anniv of Spanish Television.
4217	**1334**	29c. multicoloured	55	35

1335 Piles of
Newspaper

2006. 125th Anniv of *La Vanguardia* Newspaper.
4218	**1335**	29c. multicoloured	55	35

1336 Pio Baroja

2006. 50th Death Anniv of Pio Baroja (writer).
4219	**1336**	29c. multicoloured	55	35

1337 Arms

2006. 25th Anniv of Arms of Spain.
4220	**1337**	29c. multicoloured	55	35

1338 Dove and Flag

2006. International Year of Historical Memory.
4221	**1338**	29c. vermilion and lemon	55	35
4222	-	29c. multicoloured	55	35

DESIGNS: 4221, Type **1338**; 4222, Adult and child.

1339 Early Tricycle

2007. Toys. Multicoloured. Self-adhesive.
4223	A (30c.)	Type **1339**	55	45
4224	A (30c.)	Bus	55	45
4225	A (30c.)	Train	55	45
4226	A (30c.)	Skittles	55	45
4227	A (30c.)	Wooden pram	55	45
4228	A (30c.)	Aeroplane	55	45
4229	A (30c.)	Printing set	55	45
4230	A (30c.)	Fire truck	55	45

Nos. 4223/30 were for standard mail within Spain weighing up to 20 grams.

1340 Hoopoe

2007. Flora and Fauna. Multicoloured. Self-adhesive.
4231		30c. Type **1340**	55	45
4232		39c. Rose	75	60

1341 Teacher and Pupils

2007. Teacher Awareness. Self-adhesive.
4233	**1341**	58c. multicoloured	1·10	85

1342 Masthead

2007. 140th Anniv (2006) of *La Provincias* Newspaper.
4234	**1342**	42c. multicoloured	80	65

1343 Stylized Table of
Elements

2007. Science. Multicoloured. Self-adhesive.
4235		30c. Type **1343** (birth centenary of Dimtri Mendeleyiev (first classification))	55	45
4236		42c. Astrolabe (425th anniv of Gregorian calendar) (vert)	80	65

1344 Emblem and
Courtyard

2007. Centenary of Institut d'Estudis Catalans (Institute of Catalan Studies).
4237	**1344**	30c. multicoloured	55	45

1345 Yacht

2007. Desafio Español 2007 (Spanish entry in 32nd America's Cup Challenge Yacht Race, Valencia).
4238	**1345**	30c. multicoloured	55	45

1346 Map

2007. Earth and Universe Sciences. Multicoloured. Self-adhesive.
4239		30c. Type **1346** (basic cartography)	55	45
4240		78c. Radio telescope (Astronomy centre, Yebes)	1·50	1·20

See also Nos. 4193/4.

Nos. 4241 and Type **1347** have been left for 'Tree' issued on 5 March 2007, not yet received.

1348 Mosaic, Roman Villa,
La Olmeda

2007. Archaeology. Multicoloured.
4242		30c. Type **1348**	55	45
4243		30c. Roman baths, Campo Valdes	55	45

1349 Map of
Europe

2007. 50th Anniv of Treaty of Rome.
4244	**1349**	58c. multicoloured	1·30	85

1350 Canary

2007. Flora and Fauna. Multicoloured. Self-adhesive.
4245		30c. Type **1350**	55	45
4246		42c. Violet	80	65

1351 'Movida Madrilena'

2007. 25th Anniv of Movida Madrilena (Madrid movement). Sheet 79×106 mm.
MS4247	**1351**	30c. multicoloured	1·10	1·10

1352 Palma Cathedral

2007. EXFILNA 2007 National Philatelic Exhibition, Palma. Sheet 79×106 mm.
MS4248	**1352**	€2.43 blue	4·75	4·75

1353 Emblem and
Doves

2007. Europa. Centenary of Scouting.
4249	**1353**	58c. multicoloured	1·10	85

1354 Chapel of
Vallaceron,
Almadenejos

2007. Architecture.
4250	**1354**	30c. multicoloured	55	45
4251	-	39c. red	75	60
4252	-	42c. multicoloured	80	65
4253	-	58c. multicoloured	1·10	85
4254	-	78c. black	1·50	1·20
4255	-	€2.49 multicoloured	4·75	3·50

DESIGNS: 30c. Type **1354**; 39c. El Capricho, Comilla; 42c. Santa Caterina market; 58c. Vizcaya Bridge, Las Arenas (horiz); 78c. Terminal 4, Barajas Airport, Madrid; €2.49 Casa Lis Museum, Salamanca (horiz).

1355 Calahorra

2007. JUVENIA 2007 Youth Stamp Exhibition, Calahorra.
4256	**1355**	30c. multicoloured	55	45

1356 Stylized
Figures and Stamp

2007. Stamp Day. Spanish Philatelic Associations. Self-adhesive.
4257	**1356**	30c. multicoloured	55	45

1357 Script

2007. 800th Anniv of Cantar de Mio Cid (epic poem). Self-adhesive.
4258	**1357**	30c. multicoloured	55	45

1358 Court of
Auditors Building

2007. 25th Anniv of Court of Auditors.
4259	**1358**	30c. multicoloured	55	45

1359 'somos differntes somos iguales' (we are different we are the same)

2007. Civic Values. Multicoloured.
4260		30c. Type **1359**	55	45
4261		39c. Stylized students and open book (we are all classmates, against school violence)	75	60
4262		58c. Stylized couple (organ donation)	1·10	85
4263		78c. Multicoloured figure (sexual equality)	1·50	1·20

1360 Tricholoma equestre

2007. Fungi. Multicoloured.
| 4264 | | 30c. Type **1360** | 55 | 45 |
| 4265 | | 78c. Amanita muscaria | 1·50 | 1·20 |

1361 Carmen Conde (birth centenary)

2007. Women Writers.
| 4266 | **1361** | €2.49 black and vermillion | 4·75 | 3·50 |
| 4267 | – | €2.49 black and salmon | 4·75 | 3·50 |
DESIGNS: 4266, Type **1361**; 4267, Rosa Chacal (birth centenary) (1998)

1362 Emblem and Colours

2007. Centenary of Real Betis Balompie Football Club.
| 4268 | **1362** | 78c. multicoloured | 1·50 | 1·20 |

1363 Virgin Mary (wooden sculpture by Antonio Castillo Lastrucci)

2007. Coronation of Maria Santisima de la O, Triana, Seville.
| 4269 | **1363** | 30c. multicoloured | 55 | 45 |

1364 Nightingale

2007. Flora and Fauna. Multicoloured. Self-adhesive.
| 4270 | | 30c. Type **1364** | 55 | 45 |
| 4271 | | 30c. Hyacinth | 55 | 45 |

1365 Soldiers and Globe

2007. Armed Forces Peace Missions.
| 4272 | **1365** | 30c. multicoloured | 55 | 50 |

1366 Expo Emblem and Fluvi (Expo mascot)

2007. Expo 2008, Zaragoza. International Warter and Sustainable Development Exhibition (1st issue). Self-adhesive.
| 4273 | **1366** | 58c. multicoloured | 85 | 60 |
See also Nos. 4337, **MS**4370 and **MS** 4373.

2007. For the Young. Al filo de lo Imposible (On the edge of Impossible) (television programme) (3rd issue). Sheet 145×164 mm containing vert designs as T **1290**. Multicoloured.
MS4274 30c. Antarctic diving; 39c. Traversing mountain approach; 42c. Crossing snowfield with sleds; 58c. On board Le Sourire; 78c. Canoeing; €2.43 With dog sled during Iditarod race, Alaska ... 9·50 ... 7·50

The stamps of No. **MS**4274 are arranged amongst stamp size labels to construct composite designs of six scenes from the programme.

1367 Dehesa de Saler, L'Albufera Park

2007. Parks. Multicoloured.
| 4275 | | 30c. Type **1367** | 55 | 45 |
| 4276 | | 30c. Waterfall, Las Lagunas de Ruidera | 55 | 45 |

1368 Punta del Hidalgo Lighthouse, Tenerife

2007. Lighthouses. Sheet 116×106 mm containing T **1368** and similar vert designs showing lighthouses. Multicoloured.
MS4277 30c. Type **1368**; 39c. Cabo Mayor, Cantabria; 42c. Punta Almina, Ceuta; 58c. Melilla; 78c. Cabo de Palos, Murcia; €2.43 Gorliz, Vizcaya ... 9·25 ... 9·25

1369 Almenar Castle, Soria

2007. Castles.
| 4278 | **1369** | €2.49 agate and green | 4·75 | 3·50 |
| 4279 | – | €2.49 black and green | 4·75 | 3·50 |
DESIGNS: No. 4278, Type **1369**; No. 4279, Villena Castle, Alicante.

1370 Dupont's Lark

2007. Flora and Fauna. Multicoloured. Self-adhesive.
| 4280 | | 30c. Type **1370** | 55 | 45 |
| 4281 | | 30c. Daisy | 55 | 45 |

1371 Masthead

2007. Centenary (1901) of El Adelanto de Segovia.
| 4282 | **1371** | 78c. multicoloured | 1·50 | 1·20 |

1372 'education para todos'

2007. America. Education for All.
| 4283 | **1372** | 78c. multicoloured | 1·50 | 1·20 |

1373 Ivory Chantilly Lace over Taffeta, Empire Line Dress (1948–50)

2007. Fashion. Cristobal Balenciaga (designer). Sheet 105×150 mm containing T **1373** and similar vert designs showing his designs. Multicoloured.
MS4284 39c.Type **1373**; 42c. Red embroidered jacket and long dress (1960); 58c. Red coat and dress (c.1960); 78c.Yellow linen button through dress with belt ... 4·25 ... 4·25

1374 'The Nativity' (sculpture) (Damian Forment)

2007. Christmas. Multicoloured. Self-adhesive.
| 4285 | | 30c. Type **1374** | 55 | 45 |
| 4286 | | 58c. Children in envelope | 1·10 | 85 |

1375 Self Portrait (Pedro Berrugucte)

2007. Art. Multicoloured.
| 4287 | | 39c. Type **1375** | 75 | 60 |
| 4288 | | 42c. Self Portrait (Mariano Salvador Maella) | 80 | 65 |

1376 Construction (stained glass window)

2007. Operations Courtyard of the Bank of Spain. Sheet 106×80 mm.
MS4289 **1376** €2.43 multicoloured ... 4·75 ... 4·75

1377 King Juan Carlos

2008. King Juan Carlos I
4290	**1377**	1c. black and orange	15	15
4291	**1377**	2c. magenta and orange	15	15
4292	**1377**	5c. blue and orange	15	15
4293	**1377**	10c. green and orange	20	20
4293a	**1377**	30c. blue and pale orange (P 13×13½)	1·00	1·00
4294	**1377**	31c. brown and orange	60	40
4294a	**1377**	32c. scarlet and orange	65	40
4294b	**1377**	34c. blue and pale orange (P 13×13½)	2·00	2·00
4294ba		34c. violet and pale orange (P 13×13½)	2·00	2·00
4294c		45c. yellow-olive and pale orange (P 13×13½)	2·10	2·10
4294d		58c. dull yellow-green and pale orange (P 13×13½)		

4295	**1377**	60c. ultramarine and orange	1·10	70
4295a	**1377**	62c. slate and orange	1·20	80
4295b		64c. olive-bistre and pale orange (P 13×13½)	1·50	1·50
4296	**1377**	78c. carmine and orange (P 13×13½)	1·50	95
4296a		80c. emerald and pale orange (P 13×13½)	1·50	1·50
4296b		€2.43 Indian red and pale orange	3·75	3·75
4296c	**1377**	€2.47 yellow-olive and orange	4·75	3·00
4296d		€2.49 bright purple and pale orange (P 13×13½)	4·75	3·00
4297	**1377**	€2.60 deep dull green and pale orange	5·00	3·00
4298	**1377**	€2.70 ultramarine and pale orange	5·25	3·50
4299		€2.75 deep purple and pale orange (P 13×13½)	5·25	3·75
4300		€2.84 deep blue and pale orange (P 13×13½)	5·25	3·00
Numbers have been left for additions to this series.

1378 Ship

2008. Toys. Multicoloured. Self-adhesive.
4320	A	(30c.) Type **1378**	60	45
4321	A	(30c.) Clown shaped ball catcher	60	45
4322	A	(30c.) Buckets for bean bag catch	60	45
4323	A	(30c.) Stage coach	60	45
4324	A	(30c.) Barquillero (rolled wafer container)	60	45
4325	A	(30c.) Diablo	60	45
4326	A	(30c.) Architecture bricks	60	45
4327	A	(30c.) Submarine	60	45
Nos. 4320/7 were for use on standard mail within Spain weighing up to 20 grams.

1379 Green Woodpecker

2008. Flora and Fauna. Multicoloured. Self-adhesive.
| 4328 | **1379** | 31c. Type **1379** | 60 | 45 |
| 4329 | | 60c. Camellia | 1·10 | 85 |

1380 Symbols of Medicine

2008. Science. Multicoloured. Self-adhesive.
| 4330 | **1380** | 39c. Type **1380** | 75 | 60 |
| 4331 | | 43c. Symbols of meteorology | 85 | 65 |

1381 Masthead

2008. Centenary of La Voz de Aviles.
| 4332 | **1381** | 31c. multicoloured | 60 | 45 |

1382 Globe

2008. Science. Multicoloured. Self-adhesive.
| 4333 | **1382** | 78c. Type **1382** (International Polar Year) | 1·50 | 1·20 |
| 4334 | | €2.60 Leaves growing from rock (International Year of Planet Earth) | 5·00 | 3·75 |

1383 Hand and '016' (help line telephone number)

2008. Stop Violence against Women Campaign. Self-adhesive.

4335	**1383**	31c. multicoloured	60	45

1384 Black Poplar, Horcajjuelo (Alamo negro de Horajuelo)

2008. Trees (9th series).

4336	**1384**	€2.44 multcoloured	4·75	3·50

1385 Pabellon Puente and Torre del Agua (bridge pavillion and water tower), Zaragoza

2008. Zaragoza 2008 International Water and Sustainable Development Exhibition (2nd issue). Self- adhesive.

4337	**1385**	31c. multicoloured	60	45

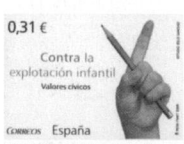

1386 'Contra la explocion infantil' (fight against child exploitation)

2008. Civic Values. Multicoloured.

4338		31c. Type **1386**	60	45
4339		39c. Two hands (intergenerational solidarity)	75	60
4340		43c. Multicoloured fingers (cultural diversity)	80	65

1387 Bicha of Balzote (6th century BC sculpture)

2008. Archaeology. Multicoloured.

4341		31c. Type **1387**	60	45
4342		31c. Apep I funerary vase ('Vaso cinerario Apofis I')	60	45

1388 Toledo Mountains

2008. Nature. Multicoloured.

4343		31c. Type **1388**	60	45
4344		31c. Hoces del Rio Duration park	60	45

1389 Helicopters and Boats

2008. Maritime Rescue.

4345	**1389**	31c. multicoloured	60	45

1390 University Building

2008. 400th Anniv of Oviedo University.

4346	**1390**	31c. multicoloured	60	45

1391 Emblem

2008. 50th Anniv of European Parliament.

4347	**1391**	60c. multicoloured	1·10	85

1392 Palacio de Longoria, Madrid (Josep Grases Riera)

2008. Architecture.

4348		31c. deep brown	60	45
4349		31c. reddish brown	60	45
4350		31c. multicoloured	60	45
4351		31c. multicoloured	60	45
4352		31c. multicoloured	60	45
4353		31c. multicoloured	60	45

DESIGNS: 4348 Type **1392**; 4349 Casa Vicens, Barcelona (Antoni Gaudi) (vert); 4350 Auditorio de Tenerife (Tenerife Auditorium) (Santiago Calatrava); 4351 Torre Agbar, Barcelona (Agbar Tower) (Jean Nouvel) (vert); 4352 Torrespana (television tower) (28×74 mm); 4353 Torre de Comunicaciones de Montjuic, Barcelona (Montjuic Comunications Tower) (Santiago Calatrava) (28×74 mm).

1393 Kestrel

2008. Flora and Fauna. Multicoloured. Self-adhesive.

4354		31c. Type **1393**	60	45
4355		43c. Tulip	85	65

1394 Pelota Valencia

2008. Traditional Sports. Multicoloured.

4356		43c. Type **1394**	85	65
4357		43c. Pelota Vasca (Basque) (vert)	85	65

1395 Envelopes

2008. Europa. The Letter. Sheet 80×105 mm.

MS4358	**1395**	60c. multicoloured	1·10	1·10

1396 Cross of Victory, Oviedo Cathedral

2008. Exfilna 2008 Philatelic Exhibition. Sheet 80×105 mm.

MS4359	**1396**	€2.44 multicoloured	4·75	4·75

1397 Arms from Maritime Post Royal Decree

2008. Stamp Day. Self-adhesive.

4360	**1397**	39c. brown, blue and black	75	60

1398 'El Progreso' and Tree (painting by Garcia Gesto)

2008. Centenary of El Progreso Newspaper.

4361	**1398**	31c. multicoloured	60	45

2008. Traditional Sports. Vert designs as T **1394**. Multicoloured.

4362		43c. Levantamiento de Piedras (stone lifting)	85	65
4363		43c. Tira con Honda (sling shot)	85	65
4364		43c. Lanzamiento de Barra (pitching the bar)	85	65

1399 Joan Oro

2008. Personalities.

4365		31c. black	55	45
4366		31c. black and vermilion	55	45
4367		31c. black and vermilion	55	45
4368		31c. black and vermilion	55	45

DESIGNS: 4365, Type **1399** (biochemist); 4366, Maria Lejarraga (Maria Martinez Sierra) (writer) (horiz); 4367, Carmen Martin Gaite (writer) (horiz); 4368, Zenobia Camprubi (writer and translator).

1400 Goya Monument, Zaragoza

2008. Zaragoza 2008 International Water and Sustainable Development Exhibition (3rd issue). Sheet 105×80 mm.

MS4370	**1400**	€2.60 green	5·00	5·00

1401 European Bee-eater

2008. Flora and Fauna. Multicoloured. Self-adhesive.

4371		31c. Type **1401**	60	45
4372		60c. Dahlia	1·10	80

1402 Water Plaza

2008. Zaragoza 2008 International Water and Sustainable Development Exhibition (4th issue). Sheet 106×80 mm containing T **1402** and similar horiz designs. Multicoloured.

MS4373		31c. Type **1402**; 78c. Exhibition compound; €2.60 Pabellon-Puente	7·00	7·00

The stamps and margins of **MS**4373 form a composite design of the exhibition site.

1403 Hurdler

2008. Olympic Games, Beijing.

4374	**1403**	31c. multicoloured	60	45

2008. Traditional Sports. As T **1394**. Multicoloured.

MS4376		144×115 mm. 43c.×2, Palo Canario (stick fighting); Lucha Leonesa (wrestling)	3·00	2·75

No. **MS**4376 includes six stamp size labels which, with the stamps, form composite designs of the sport.

1404 Ball and Foot

2008. Spain–Euro 2008 Championship Winners. Sheet 106×79 mm.

MS4377	**1404**	€1 multicoloured	1·90	1·90

1405 The Swing

2008. National Heritage. Tapestries. Two sheets containing T **1405** and similar vert design. Multicoloured.

MS4378		79×106 mm. 60c. Type **1405**	1·10	1·10
MS4379		106×79 mm. €2.60 The Blind Man and the Guitar	5·00	5·00

1406 Barbaria, Formentera

2008. Lighthouses. Multicoloured.

4380		60c. Type **1406**	1·10	1·10
4381		60c. Irta, Castellon	1·10	1·10
4382		60c. Pechiguera, Lanzarote	1·10	1·10
4383		60c. Silleiro, Pontevedra	1·10	1·10
4384		60c. Torredembarra, Tarragona	1·10	1·10
4385		60c. Punta Orchilla, El Hierro	1·10	1·10

1407 Self-Portrait (Antonio Maria Esquivel)

2008. Spanish Artists. Multicoloured.

4386		31c. Type **1407**	60	45
4387		43c. Self-Portrait (Darío de Regoyos)	85	65

1408 Emblem

2008. Centenary of Royal Spanish Tennis Federation.

4388	**1408**	31c. vermilion and yellow	60	45

1409 Jay

2008. Flora and Fauna. Multicoloured. Self-adhesive.

| 4389 | 31c. Type **1409** | 60 | 45 |
| 4390 | 31c. Narcissi | 60 | 45 |

2008. Traditional Sports. As T **1394**. Multicoloured.

| 4391 | 43c. Castillos humanos (human tower) | 85 | 65 |

1410 *Lepista nuda*

2008. Fungi. Multicoloured.

| 4392 | 31c. Type **1410** | 60 | 45 |
| 4393 | 31c. *Boletus regius* | 60 | 45 |

1411 Emblem

2008. America. Festivals. 12 October 1492 Festival (National Day).

| 4394 | **1411** | 78c. scarlet, yellow and black | 1·50 | 1·10 |

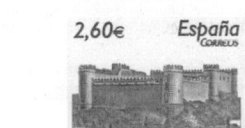

1412 Maqueda Castle, Toledo

2008. Castles.

| 4395 | €2.60 olive and magenta | 5·00 | 3·75 |
| 4396 | €2.60 black and violet | 5·00 | 3·75 |

DESIGNS: No. 4395, Type **1412**; No. 4396, La Calahorra Castle, Granada.

1413 Evening Dress

2008. Fashion. Pedro Rodriguez (designer). Multicoloured.

4397	31c. Type **1413**	60	60
4398	31c. Strapless embroidered evening gown	60	60
4399	31c. Multicoloured halter-neck dress	60	60
4400	31c. Pink evening coat	60	60

2008. Traditional Sports. As T **1394**. Multicoloured.

MS4401 106×115 mm. 43c.×3, Chito (throwing at wooden cylinder); Chave (throwing at post); La calva (throwing at curved piece of wood (morillo)) — 2·50 2·50

No. **MS**4401 includes three stamp size labels which, with the stamps, form composite designs of the sport.

1414 Belen del Príncipe (18th–century crib)

2008. Christmas. Multicoloured. Self-adhesive.

| 4402 | 31c. Type **1414** | 60 | 45 |
| 4403 | 60c. *Maternidad* (J. Carrero) (vert) | 1·10 | 85 |

1415 Flamenco Dancer

2008. Traditional Dances. Sheet 120×76 mm containing T **1415** and similar vert design. Multicoloured.

MS4404 60c. Type **1415**; 78c. Irish dancer — 2·75 2·75

Stamps of a similar design were issued by Ireland.

1416 *Elocuencia* (eloquence) (stained glass window)

2008. Real Academia Espanola (Royal Spanish Academy). Sheet 106×80 mm.

MS4405 **1416** €2.60 multicoloured — 3·75 5·00

1417 National Flag

2008. Autonomous Communities within Spain. Self-adhesive Booklet Stamps. Designs showing the community's flag and area outline. Multicoloured.

4406	A Type **1417**	65	50
4407	A Asturias	65	50
4408	A Galicia	65	50
4409	A Cantabria	65	50
4410	A National arms	65	50
4411	A Cataluna	65	50
4412	A Basque Country	65	50
4413	A Andalucia	65	50

Nos. 4402/13 were for use on mail within Spain up to 20g.

1418 Fan and Manila Shawl

2009. Cultural Heritage. Self-adhesive.

| 4414 | **1418** | B multicoloured | 1·20 | 90 |

No. 4414 was for use on mail within Europe up to 20g.

1419 Leaf

2009. Science. Multicoloured. Self-adhesive.

| 4415 | 39c. Type **1419** (Botany) | 75 | 60 |
| 4416 | €2.60 DNA strand (Genetics) | 85 | 65 |

1420 Emblems

2009. 120th Anniv of La Rioja.

| 4417 | **1420** | 32c. multicoloured | 65 | 50 |

1421 Great Tit

2009. Flora and Fauna. Multicoloured. Self-adhesive.

| 4418 | 32c. Type **1421** | 65 | 50 |
| 4419 | 62c. Hydrangea | 1·20 | 90 |

1422 Oceanus

2009. Archaeology. Mosaics, Casa sel Mitreo, Merida. Multicoloured.

| 4420 | €2.70 Type **1422** | 5·25 | 4·00 |
| 4421 | €2.70 Oriens | 5·25 | 4·00 |

1423 'Plantemos para el Planeta' (plant for the planet)

2009. Civic Values. Multicoloured.

4422	32c. Type **1423**	65	50
4423	62c. Key board (reconciliation of work and family life)	1·20	90
4424	78c. DESCO2ECTA	1·50	1·10

1424 Dam (hydro electricity)

2009. Renewable Energy. Multicoloured.

4425	32c. Type **1424**	65	50
4426	62c. Wind turbines	85	65
4427	62c. Solar energy	1·20	90
4428	78c. Geothermal energy	1·50	1·10

1425 Globe

2009. Millenium Development Goals.

| 4429 | **1425** | 32c. multicoloured | 65 | 50 |

1426 Izki Nature Park, Alava

2009. Nature. Multicoloured.

| 4430 | 43c. Type **1426** | 85 | 65 |
| 4431 | 43c. Canon del Río Lobos Nature Park, Segovia | 85 | 65 |

1427 Gladioli

2009. Flora and Fauna. Multicoloured. Self-adhesive.

| 4432 | 32c. Type **1427** | 65 | 50 |
| 4433 | 43c. Capercaillie | 85 | 65 |

1428 Emblem

2009. 60th Anniv of Council of Europe.

| 4434 | **1428** | 62c. multicoloured | 1·20 | 90 |

1429 Porto Colom, Mallorca

2009. Lighthouses. Multicoloured.

4435	62c. Type **1429**	1·20	90
4436	62c. La Higuera, Huelva	1·20	90
4437	62c. Igueldo, Guipuzcoa	1·20	90
4438	62c. Arinaga, Gran Canaria	1·20	90
4439	62c. Torre del Hercules, La Coruña	1·20	90
4440	62c. Torrox, Málaga	1·20	90

1430 Globe and Space

2009. Europa. Astronomy.

| 4441 | **1430** | 62c. multicoloured | 1·20 | 90 |

1431 La Isa

2009. Popular Dances (1st series). Multicoloured.

| 4442 | 43c. Type **1431** | 85 | 65 |

MS4443 106×79 mm. 43c. Las Sevillanas (vert) — 1·50 1·30

1432 King Alfonso VI of Leon and Castilla (Alfonso the Brave)

2009. 900th Death Anniversaries. Multicoloured.

| 4444 | 39c. Type **1432** | 75 | 55 |
| 4445 | 62c. Domingo García (Santo Domingo de La Calzada) (Bishop of Ostia) | 1·20 | 90 |

2009. Popular Dances (2nd series). As T **1431**. Multicoloured.

| 4446 | 43c. La Mateixa | 85 | 65 |
| 4447 | 43c. El Bolero | 85 | 65 |

No. 4447 was issued with a stamp size label, which with the stamp, forms a composite design of a dancer.

1433 Paper Making (stained glass window)

2009. Spanish National Mint (main stairway, Paper Factory). Sheet 80×106 mm.

MS4448 **1433** €2.70 multicoloured — 5·00 5·00

2009. Popular Dances (3rd series). As T **1431**. Multicoloured.

| 4449 | 43c. La Rueda (74×28 mm) | 85 | 65 |
| 4450 | 43c. El Aurresku (28×74 mm) | 85 | 65 |

1434 Sleeveless Top and Hat

2009. Fashion. Manuel Pina (designer). Sheet 106×150 mm containing T **1434** and similar vert designs. Multicoloured.

MS4451 32c.×4, Type **1434**; Dress and jacket; Multicoloured evening gown; White evening gown — 2·50 2·50

1435 *Graellsia isabelae*

2009. Flora and Fauna. Multicoloured. Self-adhesive.

| 4452 | 32c. Type **1435** | 65 | 50 |
| 4453 | 62c. Geranium | 1·20 | 90 |

1436 *El Juego de la pelota a pala* (Francisco de Goya)

2009. National Heritage. Tapestries. Sheet 144×115 mm containing T **1436** and similar horiz design. Multicoloured.

MS4454 78c. Type **1436**; €2.70 *Juego de bolos* (Antonio González Velazquez)   6·50   6·50

1437 Euro

2009. Tenth Anniv of Euro. Sheet 115×105 mm.
MS4455 **1437** €1 multicoloured   1·90   1·90

1438 Wine Bottle and Crashed Car

2009. Road Safety Campaign. Perils of Drink Driving.

| 4456 | **1438** | 32c. light bright carmine, black and grey | 65 | 17·00 |

1439 Charles Darwin (naturalist and evolutionary theorist)

2009. Birth Bicentenaries.

4457	32c. black and reddish lilac	60	35
4458	32c. black and carmine-vermilion	60	35
4459	32c. black and carmine	60	35

DESIGNS:Type **1439**; Claudio Moyano Samaniego (politician); Louis Braille (inventor of Braille writing for the blind).
No. 4459 has raised Braille letters on the surface of the stamp.

2009. Popular Dances (4th series). As T **1431**. Multicoloured.

| 4460 | 43c. La Muneira (33×50 mm) | 85 | 65 |
| 4461 | 43c. El Fandango (33×50 mm) | 85 | 65 |

Nos. 4460/1 each have a stamp size label attached at right, which with the stamp, creates a composite design.

1440 Bi-plane (designed by Gaspar Brunet)

2009. Centenary of First Spanish Powered Flight by Juan Olivert Serra.

| 4462 | **1440** | 32c. multicoloured | 65 | 50 |

1441 Footballer and Emblem

2009. Centenary of Real Sociedad de Futbol.

| 4463 | **1441** | 32c. multicoloured | 65 | 50 |

1442 Puente de los Tilos (built by Santiago Perez-Fadon Martinez and Jose Emilio Herrero Beneitez), Las Palmas

2009. Architecture. Multicoloured.

| 4464 | 32c. Type **1442** | 65 | 50 |
| 4465 | 32c. Canal de Castilla, Valldolid | 65 | 50 |

MS4466 150×105 mm. 32c.×4, Torre de Cristal (Cesar Pelli); Torre Espacio (Pei, Cobb Freed & Partners); Torre Sacyr Vallehermoso (Carlos Rubio Carvajal and Enrique Alvarez-Sala Walter); Torre Torre Caja Madrid (Norman Foster)   2·50   2·50

2009. Popular Dances (5th series). As T **1431**. Multicoloured.

| 4467 | 43c. El Candil (33×50 mm) | 85 | 65 |
| 4468 | 43c. Las Seguidillas (33×50 mm) | 85 | 65 |

Nos. 4467/8 each have a stamp size label attached at right, which with the stamp, creates a composite design.

1443 Javier Castle, Navarra

2009. Castles.

| 4469 | €2.70 black | 5·00 | 3·75 |
| 4470 | €2.70 black and orange-brown | 5·00 | 3·75 |

DESIGNS: No. 4469, Type **1443**; No. 4470, Arevalo Castle, Avila.

1444 *Hyphoraia dejeani*

2009. Flora and Fauna. Multicoloured. Self-adhesive.

| 4471 | 32c. Type **1444** | 65 | 65 |
| 4472 | 32c. Pansy (vert) | 65 | 65 |

1445 *Lisle de la Conference* (engraving by Adam Perelle) (showing Isla de los Faisanes, Bidosa river (neutral territory used in Royal marriages negotiations))

2009. EXFILNA 2009, the National Philatelic Exhibition, Irun. Sheet 106×80 mm.
MS4473 **1445** €2.47 multicoloured   4·75   4·75

1446 Spanish Baraja Cards

2009. America. Games.

| 4474 | **1446** | 78c. multicoloured | 1·50 | 1·50 |

1447 Player and Emblem

2009. Centenary of Royal Spanish Football Federation.

| 4475 | **1447** | 32c. multicoloured | 65 | 65 |

2009. Popular Dances (6th series). As T **1431**. Multicoloured.

| 4476 | 43c. La Sardana | 85 | 85 |

MS4477 106×80 mm. 43c. La Jota (29×41 mm)   85   85

No. 4476 has a stamp size label attached at left, which with the stamp, creates a composite design.

1448 *Cantharellus cibarius*

2009. Fungi. Multicoloured.

| 4478 | 32c. Type **1448** | 65 | 65 |
| 4479 | 32c. *Boletus pinophilus* | 65 | 65 |

1449 *Las Meninas (The Royal Family of Felipe IV)*

2009. Diego Rodriguez de Silva y Velazquez (artist) Commemoration. Sheet 106×151 mm containing T **1449** and similar horiz design. Multicoloured.
MS4480 62c. Type **1449**; 78c. *The Infanta Margarita Teresa in a Blue Dress*   2·75   2·75
Stamps of the same design were issued by Austria.

1450 Maternity

2009. Christmas. Multicoloured designs showing paintings by J. Carrero. (a) Self-adhesive.

| 4481 | 32c. Type **1450** | 65 | 65 |
| 4482 | 62c. *The arrival of the Magi* | 1·20 | 1·20 |

(b) Miniature sheet. Ordinary gum.
MS4483 115×105 mm. €2.47×2, *Adoracion al nino a y paisaje con mujer en rojo* (detail); *Adoracion al nino a y paisaje con mujer en rojo* (detail, different) (old wood carving from the Italian school and a painting by J.Carrero)   9·50   9·50

1451 Cartoon Airplane over Plaza de Requejo, Mieres

2009. Juvenia 2009–Youth Stamp Exhibition, Mieres

| 4484 | **1451** | 39c. multicoloured | 75 | 75 |

1452 Mujer con Manton de Manila (J. Carrero)

2010. Tourism

| 4485 | **1452** | B multicoloured | 1·20 | 1·20 |

1453 Congress Building

2010. Autonomous Communities. Multicoloured.

4486	A Type **1453**	65	50
4487	A La Rioja, map and flag	65	50
4488	A Castilla la Mancha, map and flag	65	50
4489	A Valencia, map and flag	65	50
4490	A Senate building	65	50
4491	A Canary Islands, map and flag	65	50
4492	A Murcia, map and flag	65	50
4493	A Aragon, map and flag	65	50

1454 *Artimelia latreillei*

2010. Fauna. Multicoloured.

| 4494 | 34c. Type **1454** | 65 | 65 |
| 4495 | 64c. *Zygaena rhadamanthus* | 1·20 | 1·20 |

1455 Hand holding Paper (recycling)

2010. Civic Values. Multicoloured.

| 4496 | €1 Type **1455** | 2·75 | 2·75 |
| 4497 | €2 Locked jar (responsible consumerism) | 5·75 | 5·75 |

1456 20th-Century Plate (right) and Amphora (left)

2010. Spanish Ceramics. Multicoloured.

4498	34c. Type **1456**	65	65
4499	34c. Amphora (right) and 18th-century inkwell (left)	65	65
4500	34c. Inkwell (right) and 18th-century Pitcher (left)	65	65
4501	34c. Pitcher (right) and plate (left)	65	65

Nos. 4498/501 were printed, *se-tenant*, in horizontal strips of four stamps within the sheet, each strip forming a composite design.

1457 'Presidencia de la Unión Europea'

2010. Spain's Presidency of European Union

| 4502 | **1457** | 34c. multicoloured | 65 | 65 |
| 4503 | **1457** | 64c. multicoloured | 1·20 | 1·20 |

1458 Saxaphone

2010. Musical Instruments

| 4504 | **1458** | 45c. multicoloured | 80 | 80 |

1459 Hand Print on Page

2010. Bicentenary of Constituent Assembly

| 4505 | **1459** | 34c. multicoloured | 65 | 65 |

1460 Old Chapter House (Sala Capitular), Plasencia Cathedral

2010. Cathedrals. Sheet 80×106 mm
MS4506 **1460** €2.75 chocolate and light blue   4·75   4·75

1461 Trophy and Poster for Celda 211

2010. Spanish Cinema (1st issue)
4507 **1461** 34c. multicoloured 65 65

1462 Zerynthia rumina

2010. Fauna. Multicoloured.
4508 34c. Type **1462** 65 65
4509 64c. Euphydryas aurinia 1·20 1·20

1463 Trophy and Film Poster

2010. Spanish Cinema (2nd issue)
4510 **1463** 34c. multicoloured 65 65

1464 Stylized figures

2010. Bicentenary of Independence of Latin American Republics
4511 **1464** €2.49 multicoloured 4·50 4·50

1466 Casa de las Torres, Ubeda

2010. World Heritage. Multicoloured.
4513 45c. Type **1466** 80 80
4514 45c. Jabalquinto Palace, Baeza 80 80

1467 Carlos María de Castro and Map of Expansion of Madrid

2010. Town Planning
4515 **1467** 34c. multicoloured 65 65

1468 Anniversary Emblem

2010. Centenary of Gran Via, Madrid
4516 **1468** 34c. multicoloured 65 65

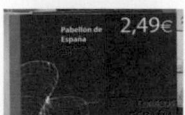

1469 Stylized Spain and Madrid Pavilllions

2010. Expo 2010, Shanghai. Sheet 106×80 mm
MS4517 **1469** €2.49 multicoloured 4·50 4·50

1470 Club and Anniversary Emblems

2010. Centenary of Levante U D Football Club
4518 **1470** 34c. multicoloured 65 65

1471 Newspapers

2010. Centenary of El Corro Newspaper
4519 **1471** 34c. multicoloured 65 65

1472 Infant with Book

2010. Europa. Children's Books
4520 **1472** 64c. multicoloured 1·10 1·10

1473 Early Banner of León with Lion Passant (image scaled to 52% of original size)

2010. 1100th Anniv of Kingdom of Leon
MS4521 **1473** €2.49 scarlet and gold 4·50 4·50

1474 Pilgrim and Cathedral of Santiago de Compostela

2010. Compostelian Jubilee Year (Ano Santo Xacobeo in Galician) (when St James's Day (July 25) falls on a Sunday)
4522 **1474** 34c. multicoloured 65 65

1475 Sierra de Cazorla, Segura y Las Villas Natural Park

2010. Nature Reserves. Multicoloured.
4523 45c. Type **1475** 1·10 1·10
4524 45c. Garajonay National Park 1·10 1·10
4525 45c. Doñana National Park 1·10 1·10

1476 Athlete (Ibero-American Athletics Championship, San Fernando, Cádiz)

2010. Sporting Events in 2010. Multicoloured.
4526 34c. Type **1476** 65 65
4527 64c. Barni (official mascot) (European Athletics Championships, Barcelona) 1·10 1·10
4528 78c. Championship emblem (World Cup Football Championships, South Africa) 1·25 1·25

1477 Gregorio Marañón and Microscope

2010. Personalities
4529 34c. black, deep ultramarine and dull orange 65 65
4530 34c. dull violet and dull orange (vert) 65 65
Designs:- 4529 Type **1477** (doctor and writer) (50th death anniv); 4530 Julián Gabino Arcas Lacal (Julián Arcas) (guitarist) Commemoration

1478 '25' and European 'Stars'

2010. 25th Anniv of Spain and Portugal's Accession to European Economic Community (EEC)
4531 **1478** 34c. multicoloured 65 65

1479 Oscar Niemeyer International Cultural Centre, Asturias

2010. FILATEM 2010 Thematic Philatelic Exhibition, Avilés
MS4532 **1479** €2.49 multicoloured 4·50 4·50

1480 Horn

2010. Musical Instruments
4532a **1480** 64c. multicoloured 1·10 1·10

1481 José Luis López Vázquez

2010. Spanish Cinema (3rd issue)
4533 **1481** 45c. multicoloured 80 80

1482 Julia Aurelia (Septimia Zenobia) captured by Emperor Aurelian

2010. Cultural Heritage
4534 **1482** 78c. multicoloured 1·25 1·25

1483 Cathedral Façade

2010. Cathedrals. Segovia Cathedral. Sheet 106×80 mm
MS4535 **1483** €2.75 reddish brown and deep turquoise-blue 5·00 5·00

1484 Cantabrian Brown Bear, Picos de Europa National Park

2010. Nature Reserves. Multicoloured.
4536 45c. Type **1484** 65 65
4537 45c. Egyptian vulture, Monfragüe National Park 65 65
4538 45c. Ibex, Sierra Nevada National Park 65 65

1485 Biomass

2010. Renewable Energy. Multicoloured.
4539 78c. Type **1485** 1·25 1·25
4540 78c. Wave energy ('undimotriz') 1·25 1·25
4541 78c. Tidal energy ('mareomotriz') 1·25 1·25

1486 Older Person

2010. Alzheimers Awareness Campaign
4542 **1486** 34c. multicoloured 65 65

1487 Football and Emblem

2010. Centenary of Cádiz Club de Futbol
4543 **1487** 34c. multicoloured 65 65

1488 Teide National Park

2010. Nature Reserves. Multicoloured.
4544 45c. Type **1488** 1·10 1·10
4545 45c. Chamois, Ordesa and Monteperdido National Park 1·10 1·10
4546 45c. Wolf, Sanabria Lake Nature Reserve 1·10 1·10

1489 Roman Walls of Lugo

2010. World Heritage Sites
4547 34c. Type **1489** 65 65
MS4548 105×150 mm. €2 Alhama Mosque, Cordoba (circular) 4·25 4·25

1490 Alviles

2010. Lighthouses. Multicoloured.
4549 64c. Type **1490** 1·10 1·10
4550 64c. Ciutadella de Menorca 1·10 1·10
4551 664c. Cabo de Huertas 1·10 1·10
4552 64c. Punta La Polacra 1·10 1·10
4553 64c. San Cibrao 1·10 1·10
4554 64c. Punta Cumplida 1·10 1·10

1491 Parque Natural de Gata

2010. Nature Reserves. Multicoloured.

4555	45c. Type **1491**	80	80
4556	45c. Archipiélago de Cabrera National Park	80	80
4557	45c. Aigüestortes y Lago de San Mauricio National Park	80	80

1492 Euphonium

2010. Musical Instruments

| 4558 | **1492** 34c. multicoloured | 65 | 65 |

1493 Gonzalo Torrente Ballester (writer and journalist)

2010. Personalities. Each black and new blue.

4559	34c. Type **1493**	65	65
4560	34c. Francisco Ayala (writer)	65	65
4561	34c. Vicente Ferrer (missionary and aid worker)	65	65

1494 Flag as Map Outline and Arms

2010. America

| 4562 | **1494** 78c. multicoloured | 1·25 | 1·25 |

1495 Outline Figures, Flags and Bicentennial Group Emblem

2010. Bicentenary of Latin-American Independence

| 4563 | **1495** 78c. multicoloured | 1·25 | 1·25 |

1496 Ildefonso Cerdá

2010. Town Planning

| 4564 | **1496** 34c. multicoloured | 65 | 65 |

1497 *La Prensa* (previous name) and *El Dia* Mast Heads

2010. Centenary of *El Dia* Newspaper

| 4565 | **1497** 34c. multicoloured | 65 | 65 |

1498 Evening Gown

2010. Spanish Fashion. Multicoloured.
MS4566 34c.×4, Type **1498**; Suit; Floral dress with frilled skirt; Strapless cocktail dress with black lace overlay   2·75   2·75

1499 Collegiate Church of Santa María la Mayor, Toro, Spain

2010. Alliance of Civilizations. Multicoloured.
MS4567 64c.×2, Type **1499**; Grand Imperial Mosque, Ortakoy, Turkey   2·25   2·25
Stamps of a similar design were issued by Turkey.

1500 Printing Plates

2010. EXFILNA 2009, the National Philatelic Exhibition, Madrid
MS4568 **1500** €2.49 multicoloured   4·50   4·50
The margins of **MS**4568 are inscribed for:140th anniversary of the Midwife; 80th anniversary of Goya's Naked Maja; 70th anniversary of El Cid and 35th anniversary of King Juan Carlos.

1501 Trophy

2010. Spain, World Cup Football Champions—2010
MS4569 **1501** €2 multicoloured   3·75   3·75

1502 Mother and Child

2010. Christmas. Multicoloured.

| 4570 | 34c. Type **1502** | 65 | 65 |
| 4571 | 64c. Arms cradling child | 1·10 | 1·10 |

1503 Holy Family (sculpture)

2010. Millenary of Monastery of San Salvador de Oña
MS4572 **1503** 78c. multicoloured   1·25   1·25

1504 Bilbao Cathedral

2010. Cathedrals. Sheet 80×106 mm
MS4573 **1504** €2.75 reddish brown and steel blue   5·50   5·50

1505 Constitutional Court

2011. Autonomous Communities. Booklet stamps. Multicoloured.

4574	A Type **1505**	65	50
4575	A Ciudad Autónoma de Ceuta, map and flag	65	50
4576	A Extremadura, map and flag	65	50
4577	A Ciudad Autónoma de Melilla, map and flag	65	50
4578	A Balearic Islands, map and flag	65	50
4579	A Comunidad de Madrid, map and flag	65	50
4580	A Comunidad de Castilla y León, map and flag	65	50
4581	A Comunidad Foral de Navarra, map and flag	65	50

1506 Symbols of Tourism (painting by J. Carrero)

2011. Spanish Tourism

| 4582 | **1506** B multicoloured | 1·20 | 1·20 |

1507 *Charaxes jasius*

2011. Fauna. Multicoloured.

4583	65c. Type **1507**	1·10	1·10
4584	65c. *Melanargia ines*	1·10	1·10
4585	65c. *Argynnis adippe*	1·10	1·10
4586	65c. *Papilio machaon*	1·10	1·10

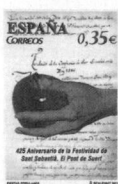

1508 Hand holding Apple (symbolizing hand-over to new priors)

2011. Festivals

| 4587 | **1508** 35c. multicoloured | 65 | 65 |

1509 *Hespérides* (research ship) with *Atrevida* (1st scientific expedition) as its Reflection and Specimen Jar

2011. International Year of Biodiversity

| 4588 | **1509** 50c. multicoloured | 90 | 90 |

1510 Guitar

2011. Musical Instruments. Multicoloured.

4589	35c. Type **1510**	65	65
4590	35c. Lute	65	65
4591	35c. Mandolin	65	65
4592	35c. Violin	65	65

1511 Almería Railway Station

2011. Architecture

| 4593 | **1511** 35c. multicoloured | 65 | 65 |

1512 Marie Curie (winner of Nobel Prize in Chemistry, 1903)

2011. International Year of Chemistry

| 4594 | **1512** 35c. multicoloured | 65 | 65 |

1513 Hands, Pen and Book

2011. 150th Anniv of Property Act

| 4595 | **1513** 65c. multicoloured | 1·10 | 1·10 |

1514 Safety Belt and Teddy (Use of Safety Belt)

2011. Civic Values. Multicoloured.

4596	35c. Type **1514**	65	65
4597	35c. Dog waste disposal (Keep your City Clean)	65	65
4598	35c. Disabled symbol and hand using computer mouse (Protection of Persons with Disabilities)	65	65
4599	35c. Stylized figures (Respect on the Net)	65	65

No. 4600 and Type **1515** are left for Cathedrals issued on 4 March 2011, not yet received.

1516 Emblem

2011. International Women's Day

| 4601 | **1516** 80c. multicoloured | 4·00 | 4·00 |

1517 Autumn in Hayedo de la Pedrosa (Juan A. González)

2011. Europa

| 4602 | **1517** 65c. multicoloured | 1·10 | 1·10 |

1518 Holy Cross
del Voto

2011. Jubilee Year to Mark 400th Anniv of Santa Cruz del Voto, Parish Church of Santa Cruz de Canjáyar

| 4603 | **1518** | 65c. multicoloured | 1·10 | 1·10 |

1519 Calella
(Barcelona)

2011. Lighthouses. Multicoloured.

4604	65c. Type **1519**	1·10	1·10
4605	65c. Chipiona (Cádiz)	1·10	1·10
4606	65c. La Entallada (Fuerteventura)	1·10	1·10
4607	65c. Cap de Sant Sebastiá (Girona)	1·10	1·10
4608	65c. Castell de Ferro (Granada)	1·10	1·10
4609	65c. Valencia lighthouse	1·10	1·10

1520 Centre of
Santa Fe and Boy
wearing
15th-century (1491,
year of the
Capitulations) Dress

2011. Juvenia 2011–National Youth Philatelic Exhibition, Posito Building, Granada

| 4610 | **1520** | 65c. multicoloured | 1·10 | 1·10 |

1521 Scene from Pa negre
(best film of 2010) (directed
by Agusti Villaronga)

2011. Spanish Cinema (4th issue). Multicoloured.

| 4611 | 35c. Type **1521** | 65 | 65 |
| **MS**4612 | 105×80 mm. €2.84 Trophy (bust of Francisco José de Goya y Lucientes) | 5·25 | 3·00 |

1522 €2 Coin
containing Image of
Patio de los Leones

2011. World Heritage Site. Alhambra. Sheet 104×150 mm

| **MS**4613 | **1522** €2 multicoloured | 9·50 | 9·50 |

1523 Dido bids farewell to Aeneas
(detail from Dido and Aeneas), Palacio
Real de Madrid

2011. Cultural Heritage. Sheet 144×115 mm

| **MS**4614 | **1523** €2.84 multicoloured | 13·50 | 13·50 |

1524 Super Puma
Aerospatiale SA-332

2011. Centenary of Military Aviation. Multicoloured.

MS4615 65c.×4, Type **1524**; CASA-101 Aviojet; C/KC-130 Lockheed Hercules; EF-2000 Eurofighter Typhoon (123×106 mm) — 13·50 13·50

1525 Hikers on Disused
Railway Line

2011. Vías Verdes (greenways from old disused railway lines)

| 4616 | **1525** | 35c. multicoloured | 1·90 | 1·90 |

1526 Sabatini Building,
Ministry of Economy and
Finance HQ, Alcala Street,
Madrid

2011. 105th Anniv of Corps of Architects of the Treasury

| 4617 | **1526** | 80c. multicoloured | 4·00 | 4·00 |

1527 Emblem

2011. World Youth Day, Madrid

| 4618 | **1527** | 80c. multicoloured | 4·00 | 4·00 |

1528 Salvador de
Albarracín

2011. Cathedrals. Sheet 80×106 mm

| **MS**4619 | **1528** €2.84 green | 13·25 | 13·25 |

1529 Luis García
Berlanga

2011. Spanish Cinema (5th issue). Multicoloured.

| 4620 | 80c. Type **1529** (director) | 3·75 | 3·75 |
| 4621 | 80c. Rafael Azcona (screenwriter) | 3·75 | 3·75 |

1530 Decorative
Water Jug

2011. Spanish Ceramics. Multicoloured.

4622	80c. Type **1530**	3·75	3·75
4623	80c. Vase decorated with gazelles	3·75	3·75
4624	80c. Plate showing traditional dress of Valencia bride	3·75	3·75
4625	80c. Modernist bottle showing woman in profile	3·75	3·75

Nos. 4622/5 were printed, se-tenant, in horizontal strips of four stamps within the sheet.

1531 Abstract

2011. Contemporary Art. Antoni Tàpies Commemoration. Multicoloured.

MS4626 80c.×4, Type **1531**; Palla i fusta; Cadira; 'Eye' — 15·00 15·00

1532 'PICHICHI' (Rafael
Moreno Aranzadi)

2011. Milestones of National Football Team. Multicoloured.

MS4627 80c.×5, Type **1532**; 'ZAMORA PARANDO' (Ricard Zamora i Martínez, goalkeeper); 'UNA EXCELENTE DELANTERA' (Miguel, Kubala, Di Stéfano, Suárez and Gento) (82×29 mm); 'EL GOL DE MARCELINO' (Marcelino Elena Sierra) (82×29 mm); 'EL GOL DE ZARRA' (Telmo Zarraonandia Montoya (Telmo Zarra)) — 18·50 18·50

MS4628 80c.×5, 'CELEBRACION DEL GOL CLASIFICATORIO PARA ARGENTINA 78' (Players celebrating); 'MUNDIAL ESPANA 82' (Ball and dove); 'VICTORIA DE LA SELECCIÓN EN LOS JUEGOS OLIMPICOS 92' (Four players celebrating) (82×29 mm); 'EL GOL DE INIESTA EN EL MUNDIAL 2010' (Iniesta's goal in World Cup 2010) (82×29 mm); 'EL GOL DE TORRES EN LA EUROCOPA 2008' (Torres's goal in European Cup 2008) — 18·50 18·50

1533 Cúpula del Milenio

2011. EXFILNA 2011 National Philatelic Exhibition. Sheet 106×80 mm

| **MS**4629 | **1533** €2.84 multicoloured | 13·25 | 13·25 |

1534 Luis Rosales

2011. Personalities. Multicoloured.

4630	80c. Type **1534** (poet)	3·75	3·75
4631	80c. Miguel Servet (Physician and theologian)	3·75	3·75
4632	80c. Gaspar Melchor de Jovellanos (judge and reformer)	3·75	3·75
4633	80c. Miguel Delibes (journalist and writer) (vert)	3·75	3·75
4633a	80c. 'Mario Vargas Llosa' (winner of Nobel Prize for Literature, 2010) (vert)	3·75	3·75

1535 White Marble
Lion's Head
Mailbox, Casa de
Postas, Puerta del
Sol, Madrid

2011. America. Mailboxes

| 4634 | **1535** | 80c. multicoloured | 4·00 | 4·00 |

1536 Evening
Dress

2011. Spanish Fashion. Elio Berhanyer (Elio Berenguer Ubeda). Multicoloured.

MS4635 80c.×4, Type **1536**; Green and white striped dress suit with small blue flowers; Knee length yellow coat with white and yellow dress; Long white cotton ball gown with small black polka dots on skirt and larger ones on bodice and black sash at waist — 1·75 1·75

1537 Holy Family (Luisa
Roldan)

2011. Christmas. Multicoloured.

| 4636 | 35c. Type **1537** | 2·00 | 2·00 |
| 4637 | 65c. Holy Family (J. Carrero) (vert) | 2·75 | 2·75 |

1538 Pediment and
Columns

2011. 300th Anniv of National Library

| 4638 | **1538** | 80c. multicoloured | 4·00 | 4·00 |

1539 Yacht

2011. 50th Anniv of Barcelona Boat Show

| 4639 | **1539** | 80c. multicoloured | 4·00 | 4·00 |

1540 Nuestra
Señora de la
Huerta de Tarazona

2011. Cathedrals. Sheet 80×106 mm

| **MS**4640 | **1540** €2.84 deep green and blue | 13·00 | 13·00 |

1541 Entwined Flags
(Lucinda Morrissey)

2011. 2011 - Year of Spain in Russia and Russia in Spain

| 4641 | **1541** | 80c. multicoloured | 4·00 | 4·00 |

1543 Shrine of La Virgen de
las Huertas

2012. Lorca. Multicoloured.

4643	36c. Type **1543**	2·10	2·10
4644	36c. Lorca Castle	2·10	2·10
4645	36c. Town Hall	2·10	2·10
4646	36c. Palacio de Guevara	2·10	2·10

4647	36c. Collegiate Church of Saint Patrick	2·10	2·10

1544 Macarena Gate, Seville

2012. Architecture. Monumental Arches and Gates. Booklet stamps. Multicoloured.

4648	A Type **1544**	2·10	2·10
4649	A Alcalá Gate, Madrid	2·10	2·10
4650	A Santa María Gate, Burgos	2·10	2·10
4651	A Serranos Tower, Valencia	2·10	2·10
4652	A Triumphal Arch, Barcelona	2·10	2·10
4653	A Palmas Gate, Badajoz	2·10	2·10
4654	A Bisagra Gate, Toledo	2·10	2·10
4655	A Bará Arch, Tarragona	2·10	2·10

1544a 'No Contamination'

2012. Civic Values. Multicoloured.

4656	36c. Type **1544a**	2·10	2·10
4657	51c. Speedometer ('Reduce Speed')	2·50	2·50
4658	70c. Mobile 'phone ('Dont' use 'Phone whilst Driving')	3·25	3·25

1545 King Juan Carlos I

2012. King Juan Carlos

4659	**1545**	36c. rosine and gold	1·90	1·90
4660	**1545**	37c. deep turquoise-green and gold (2.1.13)	1·90	1·90
4666	**1545**	51c. yellowish green and gold	2·50	2·50
4667	**1545**	52c. orange and gold (2.1.13)	2·50	2·50
4670	**1545**	75c. apple-green and gold (2.1.13)	13·00	13·00
4673	**1545**	85c. ultramarine and gold	13·00	13·00
4674	**1545**	90c. sepia and gold (2.1.13)	4·25	4·25
4675	**1545**	€2.90 brown-lake and gold	6·75	75·00

1546 Solar Panel, Wind Turbine and Lighted Cabin

2012. International Year of Sustainable Energy

4679	**1546**	70c. multicoloured	3·50	3·50

1547 Sun shining on Spain and Blue Sea

2012. Tourism

4680	**1547**	70c. multicoloured	3·50	3·50

1548 Battle of Navas de Tolosa (detail) (tapestry)

2012. Anniversaries. 800th Anniv of Battle of Navas de Tolosa (No. 4661) or 500th Anniv of Conquest of Navarre (No. 4662). Each brown-lake, scarlet-vermilion and black.

4681	85c. Type **1548**	4·00	4·00

4682	85c. Former territories of the Kingdom of Navarre (Conquest of Navarre)	4·00	4·00

1549 Woman reclining (Matron and Warrior in Boat manufactured in Brussels by Gerard Peemans)

2012. Cultural Heritage. Tapestry. Sheet 115×144 mm

MS4683	**1549** €2.90 multicoloured	13·00	13·00

1550 Laureate Cross of San Fernando

2012. 150th Anniv of Royal and Military Order of San Fernando

4684	**1550**	85c. multicoloured	4·00	4·00

1551 Cover of Deluxe Edition (engraved by José María de Santiago)

2012. Bicentenary of Constitution

4685	**1551**	36c. multicoloured	1·90	1·90

1552 €2 Euro Coin showing Burgos Cathedral

2012. Cathedrals. Cathedral of Burgos. Sheet 104×151 mm

MS4686	**1552** €2 multicoloured	8·50	8·50

1553 Harp

2012. Musical Instruments. Multicoloured.

4687	36c. Type **1553**	65	65
4688	36c. Balalaica	65	65
4689	36c. Banjo	65	65
4690	36c. Sitar	65	65
4691	36c. Rebec (Rabel)	65	65

1554 Tourism personified as Las Meninas by Diego Velazquez

2012. Europa. Visit Spain

4692	**1554**	70c. multicoloured	3·50	3·50

1555 Severiano Ballesteros

2012. Personalities. Multicoloured.

4693	70c. Type **1555**	3·50	3·50
4694	70c. José Hierro (writer)	3·50	3·50
4695	70c. Manuel Garcia Matos (musicologist)	3·50	3·50

1556 Cathedral Santa Maria de la Sede (Seville Cathedral)

2012. Cathedrals. Sheet 106×79 mm

MS4696	**1556** €2.90 multicoloured	13·00	13·00

1557 Fernando Rey

2012. Spanish Cinema (6th issue). Multicoloured.

4697	36c. Type **1557**	1·90	1·90
4698	36c. Francisco Rabal (actor)	1·90	1·90
4699	70c. *No habrá paz para los malvados* (written and directed by Enrique Urbizu) (winner of Goya Best Film) (horiz)	3·50	3·50

Nos. 4700 and Type **1558** are left for Cathedrals, issued on 21 May 2012, not yet received.

1559 'ANNIVERSARIO DF LA LEY NOTARIADO'

2012. 150th Anniv of Law of Notaries

4701	**1559**	85c. black, deep grey-blue and vermilion	4·25	4·25

1560 Antonio Mingote

2012. Angel Antonio Mingote Barrachina (Antonio Mingote) (cartoonist, writer, journalist and academician) Commemoration

4702	**1560**	36c. multicoloured	2·10	2·10

1561 Citroën C-11

2012. Vintage Cars. Multicoloured.

MS4703	85c.×4, Type **1561**; Renault Dauphine; Seat 600; Simca 1000	17·00	17·00

Nos. 4704/6 are now vacant.

1562 Emblem

2012. Centenary of Armory School

4707	**1562**	85c. multicoloured	4·25	4·25

1563 Flags of Leon

2012. Banners of Leon

4708	**1563**	85c. multicoloured	4·25	4·25

1564 St. James the Apostle (statue), Santiago de Compostela

2012. Cathedrals. Pilgrim Routes to Grave of Apostle James, Santiago de Compostela. Sheet 80×106 mm

MS4709	**1564** €2.90 multicoloured	8·00	8·00

1565 Arms

2012. 131st Anniv of Corps of Abogados del Estado (State Lawyers)

4710	**1565**	85c. multicoloured	4·25	4·25

1566 Lucius Minicius Natalis (best charioteer 227th Olympiad Hellenic Games)

2012. Centenary of Spanish Olympic Committee. Multicoloured.

4711	85c. Type **1566**	4·25	4·25
4712	85c. Gonzalo de Figueroa y Torres (creator of the Spanish Olympic Committee (COE))	4·25	4·25
4713	85c. Juan Antonio Samaranch (president 1980 - 2001)	4·25	4·25

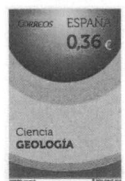

1567 Section of Earth's Crust (Geology)

2012. Science. Multicoloured.

4714	36c. Type **1567**	2·10	2·10
4715	36c. Sediment layer with trilobites (Palentology)	2·10	2·10

1568 Entrance, Oviedo Cathedral

2012. Cathedrals. Oviedo. Sheet 80×109 mm

MS4716	**1568** €2.90 orange-brown and slate-blue	8·00	8·00

1569 Episcopal Palace in Astorga (León)

2012. Cultural Heritage. Churches. Multicoloured.

| 4717 | **85c.** Type **1569** | 4·25 | 4·25 |
| 4718 | 85c. Church of the Saviour on Spilled Blood, St. Petersburg | 4·25 | 4·25 |

1570 Perfil con fondo azul

2012. Contemporary Art. Manolo Valdés. Multicoloured.
MS4719 51c.×4, Type **1570**; *La Infanta Margarita* (sculpture); *Reina Mariana XII* (sculpture); *Vivianne III* .... 10·00 ...... 10·00

1571 *Amanita Verna*

2012. Fungi. Multicoloured.

4720	51c. Type **1571**	2·50	2·50
4721	51c. *Entoloma lividum*	2·50	2·50
4722	51c. *Calocybe gambosa*	2·50	2·50

1572 Palma de Mallorca Cathedral

2012. Cathedrals. Palma de Mallorca. Sheet 80×109 mm
MS4723 **1572** €2.90 multicoloured .... 8·00 ...... 8·00

1573 Alcaudete Disused Railway Station, Oil Greenway, Jaen

2012. Vías Verdes (greenways from old disused railway lines)

| 4724 | **1573** 70c. multicoloured | 3·25 | 3·25 |

1574 Asymmetric Raspberry Shot Satin Evening Gown

2012. Spanish Fashion. Pedro del Hierro. Multicoloured.
MS4725 85c.×4, Type **1574**; Sleeveless, red and ivory coloured lace gown, with v-neckline, floral design and different coloured sequins; Hand pleated shot pink, tiered and ruffled evening gown with brown metal threading; Asymmetric, tulle gown with plunging v-neckline and full skirt cut on the bias, open from the hip down with appliqué flowers in ecru .... 17·00 ...... 17·00

1575 'Lady of Calahorra' (2nd-century Roman marble bust)

2012. EXFILNA 2012 National Philatelic Exhibition, Calahorra. 50th Anniv of EXFILNA. Sheet 80×106 mm
MS4726 **1575** €2.90 multicoloured ...... 8·00 ...... 8·00

1576 Entrance

2012. Cathedrals. Barcelona. Sheet 80×106 mm
MS4727 **1576** €2.90 multicoloured ...... 8·00 ...... 8·00

1577 Museum of Contemporary Art of Castilla and León (MUSAC)

2012. Architecture. Multicoloured.

4728	51c. Type **1577**	2·50	2·50
4729	51c. Centro de Arte Reina Sofia National Museum, Madrid	2·50	2·50
4730	51c. National Museum of Roman Art, Mérida (Badajoz)	2·50	2·50
4731	51c. Museum of Popular Arts of Seville,	2·50	2·50

1578 Paramillos Hut, Cordillera de los Andes

2012. Cultural Heritage. Colonial Postal Infrastructures in the Andes

| 4732 | **1578** 85c. multicoloured | 4·25 | 4·25 |

1579 Carpathian Red Deer

2012. Mountain Fauna. Multicoloured.

| 4733 | 85c. Type **1579** | 4·25 | 4·25 |
| 4734 | 85c. Spanish Ibex | 4·25 | 4·25 |

2012. Cathedrals. Toledo. Sheet 80×106 mm
MS4700 **1558** €2.90 reddish brown and steel blue .... 8·00 ...... 8·00

1580 Adoration of the Magi (mural, Chapel of St. Martin, Old Cathedral of Salamanca)

2012. Christmas. Multicoloured.

| 4735 | 36c. Type **1580** | 2·10 | 2·10 |
| 4736 | 70c. *Maternity* (J. Carrero) (vert) | 4·25 | 4·25 |

1581 UEFA Championship Trophy

2012. Football. Spain - Winner of EURO 2012 UEFA Championship. Sheet 150×105 mm
MS4737 **1581** €1 multicoloured .... 6·00

1582 Hands (Lovers of Teruel)

2012. America. Myths and Legends

| 4738 | **1582** 85c. multicoloured | 4·25 | 4·25 |

1583 Emblem of Higher Body of State Civil Administrators

2013. State Administrative Bodies. Multicoloured.

| 4739 | 85c. Type **1583** | 4·25 | 4·25 |
| 4740 | 85c. Arms of Higher Body of State Comptrollers and Auditors | 4·25 | 4·25 |

1584 White Virgin with Child

2012. Cathedrals. Leon. Sheet 100×134 mm
MS4741 **1584** €2.90 chestnut .... 8·00 ...... 8·00

1585 Emblem

2012. Ibero - American Summit, Cadiz

| 4742 | **1585** 36c. multicoloured | 2·10 | 2·10 |

1586 Puerta del Alcázar in Avila

2013. Architecture. Monumental Arches and Gates. Booklet stamps. Multicoloured.

4743	A Type **1586**	2·10	2·10
4744	A Roman Arch of Cáparra	2·10	2·10
4745	A Roman Arch of Medinaceli	2·10	2·10
4746	A Arch of the Capuchinos, Andújar (Jaén)	2·10	2·10
4747	A Arch of the Gigantes, Antequera (Málaga)	2·10	2·10
4748	A Puerta de Toledo, Madrid	2·10	2·10
4749	A Puerta de Castilla, Tolosa (Guipuzcoa)	2·10	2·10
4750	A Roman Arch of Cabanes	2·10	2·10

1587 'I need Spain'

2013. Tourism

| 4751 | **1587** 75c. multicoloured | 3·75 | 3·75 |

1588 Glass pouring into Tap

2013. Civic Values. International Year of Water Cooperation. Multicoloured.

| 4752 | **1588** 90c. multicoloured | 4·25 | |

1589 Clasped Hands

2013. 500th Anniv of Boundary Stones (Mugas) between Spain and France

| 4753 | **1589** 52c. multicoloured | 2·50 | 2·50 |

1591 America, Paragraph from Regulations and Christopher Columbus

2013. 500th Anniv of Laws of Burgos (governing the treatment of Native Americans)

| 4755 | **1591** 52c. multicoloured | 2·10 | 2·10 |

1590 Players

2013. Sport. Men's World Handball Championship, Spain

| 4754 | **1590** 90c. multicoloured | 4·75 | 4·75 |

1592 Drum

2013. Musical Instruments. Multicoloured.

4756	37c. Type **1592**	2·10	65
4757	37c. Tambourine	2·10	65
4758	37c. Castanets	2·10	65
4759	37c. Cymbals	2·10	65
4760	37c. Kettle drums (timpani)	2·10	65

No. 4761 and Type **1593** are left for Civic Values, not yet received.

1594 Bas Relief

2013. Milleniary of the Kingdom of Granada

| 4762 | **1594** 37c. multicoloured | 2·10 | 2·10 |

1595 Gran Via

2013. Contemporary Art. Antonio López. Multicoloured.
MS4763 52c.×4, Type **1595**; *Sink and Mirror; New Fridge; House of Antonio López Torres* .... 10·00 ...... 10·00

1596 Mereceds Benz 190

2013. Vintage Cars. Multicoloured.
MS4764 90c.×4, Type **1596**; Citroën
2CV; Volkswagen Beetle; Seat 1500   17·00   17·00

1597 Emblem

2013. World Heritage. 550th Anniv of Royal Monastery of
San Lorenzo del Escorial. Sheet 150×105 mm
MS4765 **1597** €3.10 multicoloured   9·50   9·50

1598 Rafael Gil

2013. Spanish Cinema (7th issue). Personalities.
Multicoloured.
MS4766 52c.×3, Type **1598** (film critic);
Fernando Fernáįn Gãmez (actor,
writer and film director); Tony Leb-
lanc (Ignacio Fernãįndez Sãįnchez)
(actor and comedian)   10·00   10·00

1599 Comarth Electric Post
Van

2013. Europa. Postal Transport
4767   **1599**   75c. multicoloured   3·75   3·75

1600 Wedding of Odotano and Zenobia

2013. Cultural Heritage. Tapestry. Sheet 144×115 mm
MS4768 **1600** €3.10 bright carmine   12·00   12·00

1601 FESOFI Emblem

2013. 50th Anniv of Spanish Federation of Philatelic
Societies (FESOFI)
4769   **1601**   37c. multicoloured   2·10   2·10

1602 Besalú Bridge

2013. Bridges of Spain. Multicoloured.
4770   €2 Type **1602**   7·50   7·50
MS4771 105×80 mm. €2 Los Santos
sobre la Ría de Ribadeo bridge
(70×28 mm)   8·00   8·00

1603 Bleriot XI flown by
Lãonce Garnier

2013. Centenaries. Multicoloured.
4772   52c. Type **1603** (centenary
of aviation in the Canary
Islands)   2·50   2·50

4773   52c. Centenary of the Baskonia
Sports Club and Baskonia
Mani Taldea of Basauri (vert)   2·50   2·50

1604 The Virgin
Adorned

2013. Marian Jubilee Year of the Virgin of El Rocío in
Almonte (Huelva)
4774   **1604**   90c. multicoloured   4·50   4·50

1605 North Atlantic Right
Whale

2013. Endangered Marine Species. Multicoloured.
MS4775 37c.×4, Type **1605**; Bluefin
Tuna; Mediterranean Monk Seal; Sea
Lamprey   8·00   8·00

1606 1881 Stamp used to
Validate Public
Administrative Documents

2013. Anniversaries. Multicoloured.
4776   52c. Type **1606** (Public Treasury
Inspection Services)   2·50   2·50
4777   52c. Locomotive No. 5 (150th
anniv of Barcelona -Sarriãį
TRailway)   2·50   2·50

1607 Miliki

2013. Personalities. Miliki (Emilio Aragon) (clown)
Commemoration
4778   **1607**   37c. multicoloured   2·10   2·10

1608 Sancho el Mayor Bridge, Navarra

2013. Bridges of Spain. Multicoloured.
4779   €1 Type **1608**   5·00   5·00
4780   €1 Puente de Piedra in Logroão   5·00   5·00
4781   €1 Puente del Tajo de Ronda
(28×74 mm)   5·00   5·00
4782   €2 Puente de Puentecillas,
Palencia (74×28 mm)   5·00   5·00

1609 Hands ('No to
Terrorism. Enough!')

2013. Day for Victims of Terrorism
4783   **1609**   37c. multicoloured   2·10   2·10

1610 Friar Rosendo Salvado
y Rotea

2013. Personalities. Multicoloured.
4784   70c. Type **1610** (first abbot
of diocese of New Norcia,
Western Australia)   3·50   3·50
4785   70c. St. Joseph of Cupertino
held by angels (Basilica of
Santa Maria de las Nieves
in Copertino) (350th death
anniv)   3·50   3·50
4786   70c. Saint Telmo (Pedro
Gonzãįlez Telmo) and Cathedral of Tui (vert)   3·50   3·50

1611 Hand holding Team
ball and ' XXIII World
Championship Men's
Handball'

2013. Sport. Spain - Men's World Handball Champions.
Sheet 80×107 mm
MS4787 **1611** €1 multicoloured   6·50   6·50

1612 Aranese
Galãn (equivalent
to about 20 litres
of wheat)

2013. Anniversaries. 700th Anniv of Era Querimonia
(awarding Aranese rights of tenure)
4788   **1612**   52c. multicoloured   2·50   2·50

1613 Long Dress
of Silver Plastic
Discs with Metal
Rings and Chains

2013. Spanish Fashion. Paco Rabanne. Multicoloured.
MS4789 52c.×4, Type **1613**; Short
dress of yellow and turquoise zips
of cotton and gold-plated metal laid
in checkerboard; Short red plastic
with diamond shaped cutouts; Short
dress with golden rhodoïd metallic
discs connected with metal rings   10·00   10·00

1614 Fellowship

2013. Civic Values. School Children. Multicoloured.
MS4790 37c.×4, Type **1614**; Respect;
Sport; Road safety (vert)   8·00   8·00

1615 Basilica of San Isidoro de León and
Ferdinand I, King of León

2013. EXFILNA 2013 National Philatelic Exhibition, Leon.
Sheet 105×80 mm
MS4791 **1615** €3.10 multicoloured   9·00   9·00

1616 Dragon Bridge, Alcalá de Guadaíra

2013. Bridges of Spain. Multicoloured.
4792   €1 Type **1616**   4·25   4·25
4793   €2 Puente Ingeniero Carlos
Fernández Casado (41×58
mm)   7·50   7·50
MS4794 105×80 mm. €2 Puente del
Pilar, Zaragoza (41×58 mm)   8·00   8·00

1617 Do Not Turn Away
('No des la Espalda')

2013. America. Fight Against Discrimination
4796   **1617**   37c. multicoloured   2·10   2·10

1618 Lottery Ball

2013. Anniversaries. 250th Anniversary of Creation of
State Lotteries and Bets
4797   **1618**   37c. multicoloured   2·10   2·10

1619 Agaricus xanthodermus

2013. Fungi. Multicoloured.
4798   37c. Type **1619**   2·10   2·10
4799   37c. Marasmius oreades   2·10   2·10
4800   37c. Amanita pantherina   2·10   2·10

1620 Puente de Frías,
Burgos

2013. Bridges of Spain. Multicoloured.
MS4801 105×80 mm. €3.10 Type **1620**   10·00   10·00
MS4802 150×105 mm. €3.10 Puente de
Toledo, Madrid   10·00   10·00

1621 Young Philatelists

2013. Juvenia 2013–National Youth Philatelic Exhibition,
Alicante
4803   **1621**   75c. multicoloured   3·75   3·75

1622 Red Cross

2013. 150th Anniv of Red Cross.. Scarlet-vermilion and
black.
MS4804 90c.×6, Type **1622**×6   22·00   22·00

1623 Queen Sofia and King
Juan Carlos

2013. 75th Birthdays of King Juan Carlos and Queen
Sofia. Sheet 151×105 mm
MS4805 **1623** €3 black   10·00   10·00

1624 Mary feeding Jesus (Alonso Cano)

2013. Christmas. Multicoloured.

| 4806 | A (37c.) Type **1624** | 2·10 | 2·10 |
| 4807 | B (75c.) Clock, Puerta del Sol, Madrid and traditional twelve grapes (eaten at each chime of New Year) | 3·25 | 3·25 |

1625 Long Distance Running

2013. Sport for All. Multicoloured.

4808	37c. Type **1625**	2·10	2·10
4809	37c. Cycle touring	2·10	2·10
4810	37c. Hiking	2·10	2·10

1626 Geranium (Spain)

2013. 400th Anniv of Spain - Japan Diplomatic Relations. Flowers of Spain and Japan. Multicoloured.

| 4811 | 90c. Type **1626** | 4·25 | 4·25 |
| 4812 | 90c. *Lespedeza Thunbergii* (Japan) | 4·25 | 4·25 |

1627 Adolfo Suárez González

2013. Personalities. Adolfo Suárez González (politician and president 1976 - 1981). Sheet 150×105 mm

| MS4814 **1627** €3.10 multicoloured | 8·00 | 8·00 |

1628 Arco de la Malena, Tarancón

2014. Architecture. Monumental Arches and Gates. Booklet stamps. Multicoloured.

4815	A Type **1628**	2·10	2·10
4816	A Puerta de la Finca Miralles gate, Barcelona	2·10	2·10
4817	A Puerta de San Ginés, Miranda del Castañar, Salamanca	2·10	2·10
4818	A Arco de Villalar, Baéza, Jaén	2·10	2·10
4819	A Arco de la Estrella, Cáceres	2·10	2·10
4820	A Arco de San Benito, Sahagún, León	2·10	2·10
4821	A Puerta del Puente, Córdoba	2·10	2·10
4822	A Puerta de San Lorenzo, Laredo, Cantabria	2·10	2·10

1629 Symbols of Spain

2014. Tourism

| 4823 | **1629** 76c. multicoloured | 3·25 | 3·25 |

1630 Symbols of Learning

2014. 300th Anniv of Spanish Royal Academy

| 4824 | **1630** 38c. multicoloured | 2·10 | 2·10 |

1631 Juan Ponce de León's and Ship

2014. Personalities. 500th Anniv of Juan Ponce de León's Arrival in Florida

| 4825 | **1631** 92c. multicoloured | 4·25 | 4·25 |

1632 Inside Particle Collider

2014. 60th Anniv of European Organisation for Nuclear Research (CERN)

| 4826 | **1632** 54c. multicoloured | 2·50 | 2·50 |

1633 Miquel Joseph Serra (Fray Junípero (missionary)) and Map of Baja California

2014. Personalities. 300th Birth Anniversaries. Multicoloured.

| 4827 | 92c. Type **1633** | 4·25 | 4·25 |
| 4828 | 92c. Pedro Cieza de León (explorer and chronicler of the Indies) | 4·25 | 4·25 |

1634 Black Pudding, Olla Podrida (made with pinto beans), Chorizo, Cheeses and Local Wine

2014. Burgos - Spanish Capital of Gastronomy, 2013

| 4829 | **1634** 54c. multicoloured | 2·50 | 2·50 |

1635 Royal Housing Patronage Foundation of Seville

2014. Centenaries

| 4830 | 54c. Type **1635** | 2·60 | 2·60 |
| 4831 | 54c. Royal Racing Club Santander | 2·60 | 2·60 |

1636 Lottery Tickets

2014. Collectables. Booklet stamps. Multicoloured.

4832	1c. Type **1636**	40	40
4833	2c. Postcards	50	50
4834	5c. Trading cards	75	75
4835	10c. Minerals	1·00	1·00
4836	25c. Watches	1·50	1·50
4837	50c. Toy (lead) soldiers	2·50	2·50
4838	€1 Coins	4·50	4·50
4839	€1 Stamps	4·50	4·50

1637 Windmills, La Mancha

2014. Rural Architecture. Multicoloured.

4840	54c. Type **1637**	2·60	2·60
4841	54c. Asturian Granary	2·60	2·60
4842	54c. Barraca, Valencia	2·60	2·60

1638 Early Student and Tickertape

2014. Centenary of Higher Education Technical School of Telecommunication Engineers (General School of Telegraphy)

| 4843 | **1638** 54c. multicoloured | 2·60 | 2·60 |

1639 Blas de Lezo and Ship

2014. Anniversaries. 325th Birth Anniv of Blas de Lezo y Olavarrieta (sailor) (No. 4884), 500th Anniv of Pilgrimage of Saint Francis of Assisi to Santiago de Compostela (No. 4885) or Millennary of the Kingdom of Badajoz. Multicoloured.

4844	54c. Type **1639**	2·60	2·60
4845	54c. St Francis	2·60	2·60
4846	54c. Badajoz in Arabic and monuments	2·60	2·60

1640 Isaac Peral y Caballero (inventor of first electric propulsion submarine)

2014. 125th Anniv of Launch of Isaac Peral y Caballero's Submarine

| 4847 | **1640** 54c. multicoloured | 2·60 | 2·60 |

1641 Torre de Pimentel

2014. EXFILNA 2014 National Philatelic Exhibition, Torremolinos. Sheet 105×80 mm

| MS4848 **1641** €3.16 multicoloured | 8·00 | 8·00 |

1642 Headquarters

2014. 50th Anniv of Sociedad Estatal de Participaciones Industriales (SEPI) (State Company for Industrial Shareholdings)

| 4849 | **1642** 38c. multicoloured | 2·60 | 2·60 |

1643 Plasterwork, Glass, Sculpture (Roman era (2nd century)) and Museum Façade

2014. Museums. Museo de Guadalajara (Museum of Guadalajara) and the Museo de Arte Abstracto Español (Museum of Spanish Abstract Art), Cuenca. Multicoloured.

| 4850 | 54c. Type **1643** | 2·60 | 2·60 |
| 4851 | 54c. Casas Colgadas, home of museum, and painting by Fernando Zóbel | 2·60 | 2·60 |

1644 QR Code and Emoticon

2014. Information and Communication Technologies (TIC)

| 4852 | **1644** A (37c.) multicoloured | 2·10 | 2·10 |

1645 Park Emblem

2014. World Heritage. Park Güell by Antoni Gaudí. Sheet 105×150 mm

| MS4853 **1645** €3.16 new blue and chrome yellow | 8·00 | 8·00 |

1646 Brand Spain Emblem

2014. Brand Spain

| 4854 | **1646** 92c. multicoloured | 4·40 | 4·40 |

1647 'E' Industry

2014. Brand Spain (2nd issue). 'E-Empresa' (Enterprise)

| 4855 | **1647** €1. multicoloured | 4·50 | 4·50 |

1648 Paco de Lucía

2014. Europa. Musical Instruments. Francisco Sánchez Gómez (Paco de Lucía) Commemoration

| 4856 | **1648** B (54c.) multicoloured | 2·60 | 2·60 |

1649 Ajoblanco (garlic and almond soup) (nouvelle cuisine by Ferran Adria)

2104. Spanish Gastronomy

| MS4857 €3.15×2,Type **1649**; Ajoblanco (traditional recipe) | 10·00 | 10·00 |
| MS4858 €3.15×2, Mandarin flower and fruit (41×29 mm.); Iberian ham (41×29 mm.) | 10·00 | 10·00 |

1650 Rocky Inlet

2014. Brand Spain (3rd issue). 'S-Sol' (Sun)

| 4859 | **1650** €1 multicoloured | 4·50 | 4·50 |

EXPRESS LETTER STAMPS

E53 Pegasus and Arms

1905

| E308 | **E53** | 20c. red | 42·00 | 1·10 |

E77 Spanish Royal Family

1926. Red Cross.

E417	**E77**	20c. purple and deep purple	15·00	9·00

1927. 25th Anniv of Coronation. No. E417 optd **17-V-1902 17-V-1927 ALFONSO XIII**.

E459	20c. purple and deep purple	14·50	8·25

E88 Gazelle

1929. Seville and Barcelona Exhibitions.

E521	**E88**	20c. brown	28·00	19·00

E89

1929

E522	**E89**	20c. red	28·00	4·00

1929. Optd **Sociedad de las Naciones LV reunion del Consejo Madrid.**

E534	20c. red	20·00	19·00

1930. Optd **URGENCIA**.

E535	20c. red	33·00	4·00

E91 Class 7201 Electric Locomotive

1930. 11th Int Railway Congress, Madrid.

E553	**E91**	20c. red	95·00	75·00

1930. "Goya" types optd **URGENTE**.

E570	**91**	20c. mauve (postage)	50	25
E583	-	20c. brown and blue (as No. 574) (air)	40	40

1930. "Columbus" type optd **URGENTE**.

E608	**99**	20c. purple	3·50	2·50

E113 Seville Exhibition

1930. Spanish–American Exhibition.

E643	**E113**	20c. orange	1·90	1·70

1931. Optd **REPUBLICA**.

E660	**E89**	20c. red (No. E535)	4·25	4·25
E672	**E89**	20c. red (No. E522)	4·75	4·75

1931. Optd **Republica Espanola** in two lines continuously.

E697	29c. red (No. E522)	19·00	3·00

E126

1931. 900th Anniv of Montserrat Monastery.

E731	**E126**	20c. red	38·00	33·00

E145

1934

E779	**E145**	20c. red	30	20

E152 Newspaper Boy

1936. 40th Anniv of Madrid Press Association.

E801	**E152**	20c. red	40	35

E185 Pegasus

1937

E906	**E185**	20c. brown	2·40	50

E198 Pegasus

1942

E1022	**E198**	25c. red	35	20

E199

1940. 19th Centenary of Apparition of Virgin of El Pilar at Zaragoza.

E1006	**E199**	25c.+5c. red & buff	40	30

E270 "Speed"

E271 Centaur

1956

E1250	**E270**	2p. red	20	15
E1251	**E270**	3p. red	20	15
E1252	**E 271**	4p. mauve and black	20	15
E1253	**E 270**	5p. red	15	15
E1254	**E 271**	6p.50 red and violet	20	15

E425 Roman Chariot

1971

E2099	**E425**	10p. green, blk & red	20	15
E2100	-	15p. blue, black & red	20	15

DESIGN—VERT: 15p. Letter encircling globe.

E862 Communications

1993. Public Services.

E3211	**E862**	180p. red and yellow	2·75	65

FRANK STAMPS

F36

1869. For use on "Cartilla Postal de Espana" (book) by Senor Castell.

F172	**F 36**	(-) blue	65·00	60·00

F50

1881. For use on book by A. F. Duro.

F273	**F 50**	(-) black on buff	47·00	21·00

F163

1938. For use by Agencia Filatelica Oficial, Barcelona.

F839	**F 163**	(-) blue	60·00	4·75
F840	**F 163**	(-) lilac	60·00	4·75
F841	**F 163**	(-) green	60·00	4·75
F842	**F 163**	(-) brown	60·00	4·75
F843	**F 163**	(-) black	60·00	4·75

OFFICIAL STAMPS

O9

1854. Imperf.

O46	**O 9**	½ onza black on orange	2·75	1·90
O47	**O 9**	1 onza black on pink	4·75	4·75
O48	**O 9**	4 onza black on green	11·50	9·50
O49	**O 9**	1 libra black on blue	70·00	65·00

The face values of Nos. O46/53 are expressed in onzas (ounces) and libra (pound) which refer to the maximum weight for which each value could prepay postage.

O10

1855. Imperf.

O50	**O10**	½ onza black on yellow	2·50	2·50
O52	**O10**	4 onza black on green	5·50	5·00
O53	**O10**	1 libra black on blue	18·00	25·00
O55	**O10**	1 onza black on pink	5·75	3·25

O52

1895. For use by Members of Chamber of Deputies.

O289	**51**	15c. yellow	11·00	4·25
O290	**O 52**	(-) pink	8·25	17·00
O291	**O 52**	(-) blue	27·00	8·50

O66 National Library

O67 Cervantes (from painting by J. de Jauregui)

O68 Statue of Cervantes by A. Sola

1916. Death Tercentenary of Cervantes. (a) For use by Members of the Chamber of Deputies.

O353	-	(-) black and violet	1·70	1·30
O354	**O 66**	(-) black and green	1·70	1·30
O355	**O 67**	(-) black and violet	1·70	1·30
O356	**O 68**	(-) black and red	1·70	1·30

(b) For use by Members of the Senate.

O357	-	(-) black and green	1·70	1·30
O358	**O 66**	(-) black and red	1·70	1·30
O359	**O 67**	(-) black and brown	1·70	1·30
O360	**O 68**	(-) black and brown	1·70	1·30

DESIGN—As Type **O 66**: Chamber of Deputies.

1931. Third Pan-American Postal Union Congress. T **121** etc optd **Oficial**.

O707	5c. purple	40	30
O708	10c. green	40	30
O709	15c. violet	40	30
O710	25c. red	40	30
O711	30c. green	40	30
O712	40c. blue	95	65
O713	50c. orange	95	65
O714	1p. grey	95	65
O715	4p. mauve	17·00	15·00
O716	10p. brown	43·00	34·00

Air. T **123** etc optd **OFICIAL**.

O717	5c. brown	20	15
O718	10c. green	20	15
O719	25c. red	20	15
O720	50c. blue	20	15
O721	1p. lilac	20	15
O722	4p. grey	7·75	5·75

WAR TAX STAMPS

W42

1874. The 5c. perf or imperf.

W217	**W42**	5c. de p. black	12·50	1·30
W218	**W42**	10c. de p. blue	16·00	2·50

1875. As Type **W42**, but large figures in bottom corners.

W228a	5c. de p. green	5·75	95
W229	10c. de p. mauve	17·00	4·25

W48

1876. Second Carlist War (1873–76) and Cuban War (1868–78).

W253	**W48**	5c. de p. green	5·50	85
W254	**W48**	10c. de p. blue	5·50	85
W255	**W48**	25c. de p. black	42·00	15·00
W256	**W48**	1p. lilac	£500	£110
W257	**W48**	5p. pink	£800	£325

W49

1877. Cuban War (1868–78).

W258	**W49**	15c. de p. purple	25·00	80
W259	**W49**	50c. de p. yellow	£850	£120

1897. Cuban War of Independence (1895–98). Inscr "1897–1898" (15c.) or "1897 A 1898" (others).

W289	5c. green	4·50	1·90
W290	10c. green	4·50	1·90
W291	15c. green	£550	£325
W292	20c. green	10·00	3·25

W52

1898. Cuban War of Independence (1895–98) and Spanish-American War (1898). Inscr "1898–99".

W293	**W 52**	5c. black	3·50	1·90
W294	**W 52**	10c. black	3·50	1·90
W295	**W 52**	15c. black	65·00	19·00
W296	**W 52**	20c. black	5·25	3·25

W53

1898. Cuban War of Independence (1895–98) and Spanish-American War (1898).

W297	**W 53**	5c. black	10·50	80

W163

1938

W839	**W 163**	10c. red	95	1·40
W840	**W 163**	20c. blue	95	95
W841	**W 163**	60c. pink	3·25	3·75
W842	**W 163**	1p. blue	95	1·10
W843	**W 163**	2p. green	95	1·10
W844	**W 163**	10p. blue	4·75	5·75

Nos. W842/3 have coloured figures of value on white backgrounds.

Pt. 9

SPANISH GUINEA

A Spanish colony consisting of the islands of Fernando Poo, Annobon and the Corisco Islands off the west coast of Africa and Rio Muni on the mainland. In 1959 it was divided into the two Spanish Overseas Provinces of Fernando Poo and Rio Muni.

100 centimos = 1 peseta.

1902. "Curly Head" key-type inscr "GUINEA ESPANOLA 1902".

1	**Z**	5c. green	17·00	10·50
2	**Z**	10c. grey	17·00	10·50
3	**Z**	25c. red	£120	80·00
4	**Z**	50c. brown	£120	80·00
5	**Z**	75c. lilac	£120	80·00
6	**Z**	1p. red	£190	80·00
7	**Z**	2p. green	£225	£180
8	**Z**	5p. red	£375	£325

1903. Fiscal stamps inscr "POSESIONES ESPANOLAS DE AFRICA OCCIDENTAL", surch **HABILITADO PARA CORREOS 10 cen de peseta**.

9	10c. on 25c. black	£600	£225
10	10c. on 50c. orange	£130	38·00
11	10c. on 1p.25 pink	£850	£375
12	10c. on 2p. red	£900	£550
13a	10c. on 2p.50 brown	£1900	£950
14a	10c. on 5p. black	£1900	£950
15	10c. on 10p. brown	£1200	£500
16	10c. on 15p. lilac	£950	£500
17	10c. on 25p. blue	£950	£750
18	10c. on 50p. brown	£1200	£850
19	10c. on 70p. violet	£1400	£750
20	10c. on 100p. green	£1900	£850

1903. "Curly Head" key-type inscr "GUINEA CONTIAL-ESPANOLA PARA 1903".

21	¼c. black	1·70	1·20
22	½c. green	1·70	1·20
23	1c. purple	1·70	1·00
24	2c. green	1·70	1·00
25	3c. brown	1·70	1·00
26	4c. red	1·70	1·00
27	5c. black	1·70	1·00
28	10c. brown	2·75	1·20
29	15c. blue	10·00	9·75
30	25c. orange	10·00	9·75
31	50c. red	18·00	22·00
32	75c. lilac	25·00	22·00
33	1p. green	41·00	33·00
34	2p. green	41·00	33·00
35	3p. red	£110	40·00
36	4p. blue	£140	75·00
37	5p. purple	£250	£110
38	10p. red	£425	£150

1905. "Curly Head" key-type inscr as above but dated "1905".

39	1c. black	30	20
40	2c. green	30	20
41	3c. red	30	20
42	4c. green	30	20
43	5c. brown	30	20
44	10c. red	1·70	95
45	15c. brown	5·25	3·25
46	25c. brown	5·25	3·25
47	50c. blue	13·00	7·50
48	75c. orange	14·00	7·50
49	1p. red	14·00	7·50
50	2p. lilac	30·00	17·00
51	3p. green	80·00	40·00
52	4p. green	80·00	49·00
53	5p. red	£130	60·00
54	10p. blue	£225	£160

1905. No. 19/34 of Elobey optd **CONTINENTAL GUINEA CORREOS ASSOBLA**.

55	1c. pink	7·00	5·00
56	2c. purple	7·00	5·00
57	3c. black	7·00	5·00
58	4c. red	7·00	5·00
59	5c. green	7·00	5·00
60	10c. green	14·00	10·00
61	15c. lilac	26·00	15·00
62	25c. red	26·00	15·00
63	50c. orange	34·00	18·00
64	75c. blue	41·00	21·00
65	1p. brown	80·00	37·00
66	2p. brown	£110	44·00
67	3p. red	£160	75·00
68	4p. brown	£600	£200
69	5p. green	£600	£200
70	10p. red	£2500	£1000

1907. As Nos. 18/33 of Rio de Oro, but inscr "GUINEA CONTIAL ESPANOLA".

71	1c. green	85	20
72	2c. blue	85	20
73	3c. lilac	85	20
74	4c. green	85	20
75	5c. red	85	20
76	10c. bistre	4·50	1·90
77	15c. brown	3·25	1·10
78	25c. blue	3·25	1·10
79	50c. brown	3·25	1·10
80	75c. green	3·25	1·10
81	1p. orange	15·00	2·00
82	2p. brown	19·00	9·25
83	3p. black	19·00	9·25
84	4p. red	24·00	19·00
85	5p. green	24·00	24·00
86	10p. purple	34·00	28·00

1908. Surch **HABILITADO PARA** and value in figures and **CTMS**.

87	**3**	05c. on 1c. green	5·50	3·00
88	**3**	05c. on 2c. blue	5·50	3·00
89	**3**	05c. on 3c. lilac	5·50	3·00
90	**3**	05c. on 4c. green	5·50	3·00
91	**3**	05c. on 10c. bistre	5·50	3·00
92	**3**	15c. on 10c. bistre	20·00	13·00

1909. Fiscal stamps inscr "TERRITORIOS ESPANOLES DEL AFRICA OCCIDENTAL", surch **HABILITADO PARA CORREOS 10 cen de peseta**.

93	10c. on 50c. green	£100	75·00
94	10c. on 1p.25 violet	£300	£180
95	10c. on 2p. brown	£750	£500
96	10c. on 5p. mauve	£750	£500
97	10c. on 25p. brown	£1100	£750
98	10c. on 50p. red	£3750	£1800
99	10c. on 75p. pink	£3750	£1800
100	10c. on 100p. orange	£3750	£1800

1909. As Nos. 47/59 of Rio de Oro, but inscr "TERRITORIOS ESPANOLES DEL GOLFO DE GUINEA".

101	1c. brown	20	20
102	2c. red	20	20
103	5c. green	1·50	20
104	10c. red	40	20
105	15c. brown	40	20
106	20c. mauve	70	40
107	25c. blue	70	40
108	30c. brown	95	20
109	40c. red	55	20
110	50c. lilac	55	20
111	1p. green	16·00	8·25
112	4p. orange	3·50	5·00
113	10p. orange	3·50	5·00

1911. Nos. 101/13 optd **GUINEA 1911** in oval.

114	1c. brown	40	40
115	2c. red	40	40
116	5c. green	1·70	55
117	10c. red	1·10	60
118	15c. brown	1·70	1·20
119	20c. mauve	2·30	1·80
120	25c. blue	2·75	3·50
121	30c. brown	3·50	4·50
122	40c. red	3·75	4·75
123	50c. lilac	6·75	7·75
124	1p. green	£100	39·00
125	4p. orange	28·00	29·00
126	10p. orange	38·00	48·00

1912. As Nos. 73/85 of Rio de Oro, but inscr "TERRS. ESPANOLES DEL GOLFO DE GUINEA".

127	1c. black	20	20
128	2c. brown	20	20
129	5c. green	20	20
130	10c. red	35	20
131	15c. red	35	20
132	20c. red	60	20
133	25c. blue	35	20
134	30c. red	5·75	3·00
135	40c. red	4·00	1·70
136	50c. orange	3·00	70
137	1p. lilac	4·00	2·10
138	4p. mauve	9·00	4·00
139	10p. green	20·00	16·00

1914. As Nos. 86/98 of Rio de Oro, but inscr as 1912 issue.

140	1c. violet	20	20
141	2c. red	20	20
142	5c. green	20	20
143	10c. red	20	20
144	15c. purple	20	20
145	20c. brown	1·40	55
146	25c. blue	35	35
147	30c. brown	1·70	60
148	40c. green	1·70	60
149	50c. red	65	40
150	1p. orange	1·70	2·30
151	4p. red	8·50	8·00
152	10p. brown	12·50	14·50

1917. Nos. 127/39 optd **1917**.

153	1c. black	£120	80·00
154	2c. brown	£120	80·00
155	5c. green	40	20
156	10c. orange	40	20
157	15c. purple	40	20
158	20c. red	40	20
159	25c. blue	20	20
160	30c. red	40	20
161	40c. pink	70	40
162	50c. orange	35	20
163	1p. brown	70	40
164	4p. violet	9·75	5·00
165	10p. green	9·75	5·00

1918. Stamps of 1912 surch **HTADO 1917** and value in figures and words.

166	**11**	5c. on 40c. pink	41·00	15·00
167	**11**	10c. on 4p. violet	41·00	15·00
168	**11**	15c. on 20c. red	80·00	26·00
169	**11**	25c. on 10p. green	80·00	26·00

12

1919

170	**12**	1c. violet	1·10	80
171	**12**	2c. red	1·10	80
172	**12**	5c. red	1·10	80
173	**12**	10c. purple	1·80	80
174	**12**	15c. brown	3·75	90
175	**12**	20c. blue	7·50	1·70
176	**12**	25c. green	3·75	1·70
177	**12**	30c. orange	1·70	1·70
178	**12**	40c. orange	4·75	1·70
179	**12**	50c. red	4·75	1·70
180	**12**	1p. green	4·75	5·00
181	**12**	4p. red	10·00	20·00
182	**12**	10p. brown	18·00	34·00

1920. As Nos. 125/37 of Rio de Oro, but inscr as T **12**.

183	1c. brown	20	20
184	2c. red	20	20
185	5c. green	20	20
186	10c. red	20	20
187	15c. orange	20	20
188	20c. yellow	20	20
189	25c. blue	70	40
190	30c. green	49·00	25·00
191	40c. brown	60	35
192	50c. purple	1·70	40
193	1p. brown	1·70	40
194	4p. red	5·50	6·25
195	10p. violet	11·00	13·00

13

1922

196	**13**	1c. brown	70	35
197	**13**	2c. red	70	35
198	**13**	5c. green	70	35
199	**13**	10c. red	4·75	1·60
200	**13**	15c. orange	70	35
201	**13**	20c. mauve	3·00	1·40
202	**13**	25c. blue	5·75	1·70
203	**13**	30c. violet	4·75	1·80
204	**13**	40c. blue	3·50	95
205	**13**	50c. red	3·50	95
206	**13**	1p. green	3·50	95
207	**13**	4p. brown	14·50	17·00
208	**13**	10p. yellow	28·00	33·00

14 Nipa House

1925

209	**14**	5c. blue and brown	20	20
210	**14**	10c. blue and green	20	20
211	**14**	15c. black and red	20	20
212	**14**	20c. black and violet	20	20
213	**14**	25c. black and red	50	20
214	**14**	30c. black and orange	50	20
215	**14**	40c. black and blue	50	20
216	**14**	50c. black and red	50	20
217	**14**	60c. black and brown	50	20
218	**14**	1p. black and violet	2·00	20
219	**14**	4p. black and blue	4·75	2·50
220	**14**	10p. black and green	10·50	5·00

1926. Red Cross stamps of Spain optd **GUINEA ESPANOLA**.

221	-	5c. brown	13·50	13·50
222	-	10c. green	13·50	13·50
223	**70**	15c. violet	3·00	3·00
224	-	20c. purple	3·00	3·00
225	**71**	25c. red	3·00	3·00
226	**70**	30c. green	3·00	3·00
227	-	40c. blue	65	65
228	-	50c. red	65	65
229	**71**	60c. green	65	65
230	-	1p. red	65	65
231	-	4p. bistre	2·50	2·50
232	**71**	10p. violet	9·00	9·00

1929. Seville and Barcelona Exhibition stamps of Spain (1929) optd **GUINEA**.

233	5c. red	40	40
234	10c. green	40	40
235	15c. blue	40	40
236	20c. violet	40	40
237	25c. red	40	40
238	30c. brown	40	40
239	40c. blue	70	70
240	50c. orange	70	70
241	1p. grey	13·00	13·00
242	4p. red	27·00	27·00
243	10p. brown	50·00	50·00

17 Porter

1931

244	**17**	1c. green	20	20
245	**17**	2c. brown	20	20
246	**17**	5c. black	20	20
318	**17**	5c. grey	3·00	20
247	**17**	10c. green	20	20
248	**17**	15c. black	20	20
290	**17**	15c. green	4·50	20
249	**17**	20c. lilac	20	20
250	-	25c. red	20	20
251	-	30c. red	35	20
252	-	40c. blue	1·00	70
320	-	40c. green	1·20	20
253	-	50c. orange	2·50	1·70
292	-	50c. blue	12·50	1·00
254	-	80c. blue	4·50	2·75
255	-	1p. black	7·75	6·25
256	-	4p. mauve	55·00	37·00
257	-	5p. brown	21·00	26·00

DESIGNS: 25c. to 50c. Native drummers; 80c. to 5p. King Alfonso XIII and Queen Victoria.

1931. Optd **REPUBLICA ESPANOLA** horiz.

258	**17**	1c. green	20	20
259	**17**	2c. brown	20	20
260	**17**	5c. grey	20	20
261	**17**	10c. green	20	20
262	**17**	15c. blue	20	20
263	**17**	20c. violet	20	20
264	-	25c. red	20	20
265	-	30c. red	65	30
266	-	40c. blue	4·75	65
267	-	50c. orange	18·00	8·50
268	-	80c. blue	4·75	2·50
269	-	1p. black	16·00	5·50
270	-	4p. red	36·00	36·00
271	-	5p. brown	28·00	17·00

1933. Optd **Republica Espanola**.

272	**17**	1c. green	20	20
273	**17**	2c. brown	20	20
274	**17**	5c. grey	20	20
275	**17**	10c. green	20	20
276	**17**	15c. blue	20	20
277	**17**	20c. violet	70	20
278	-	25c. red	60	35
279	-	30c. red	55	35
280	-	40c. blue	4·50	1·00
281	-	50c. orange	17·00	5·00
282	-	80c. blue	8·25	4·50
283	-	1p. black	17·00	4·50
284	-	4p. red	55·00	39·00
285	-	5p. brown	65·00	39·00

1937. Surch **HABILITADO 30 Cts.**

293	30c. on 40c. (No. 252)	5·50	3·25
294	30c. on 40c. (No. 266)	23·00	5·00
295	30c. on 40c. (No. 280)	85·00	26·00

1939. Stamps of Spain, 1937, optd **Territorios Espanoles del Golfo de Guinea** in script type.

296	**183**	10c. green	2·40	75
297	**184**	15c. black	2·40	75
298	**184**	20c. violet	5·00	2·50
299	**184**	25c. red	5·00	2·50

1939. Surch **Habilitado 40 cts.**

300	40c. on 80c. (No. 268)	24·00	11·50
301	40c. on 80c. (No. 282)	24·00	7·00

24

1940. Fiscal stamps as T **24** inscr "ESPECIAL MOVIL", "TIMBRE MOVIL" or "IMPUESTO SOBRE CONTRATOS" and surch or optd **Habilitado Correos**.

302	5c. red	5·75	1·70
304	5c. on 35c. green	6·75	2·40
307	10c. on 75c. brown	8·75	2·75
308	15c. on 1p.50 violet	6·75	2·75
305	25c. on 60c. brown	6·75	2·75
306	50c. on 75c. brown	8·75	2·75
310	1p. bistre	£100	39·00
303	1p. on 15c. green	21·00	6·75
316	1p. on 17p. red	50·00	16·00
315	1p. on 40p. green	15·00	4·75

26 Gen. Franco

1940

311	**26**	5c. brown	4·50	1·10
312	**26**	40c. blue	5·75	1·10
314	**26**	50c. green	8·00	1·10

1941. Air. Fiscal stamp as T **24** inscr "IMPUESTO SOBRE CONTRATOS" surch **Habilitado para Correo Aereo Intercolonial Una Peseta** and bar.

317a	1p. on 17p. red	45·00	25·00

1942. No. 249 surch **Habilitado 3 Pesetas**.

321	**17**	3p. on 20c. violet	14·50	2·30

1942. Stamps of Spain, 1939, optd **Golfo de Guinea**.

322	**196**	1PTA. black	60	20
323	**196**	4PTAS. pink	13·00	1·00

1942. Air. Air stamp of Spain optd **Golfo de Guinea**.

324	**195**	1p. blue	2·30	20

1943. Stamp of Spain, 1939, optd **Territorios espanoles del Golfo de Guinea.**

325	**196**	2PTAS. brown	1·20	20

1948. Air. Ministerial Visit. No. 323 optd **CORREO AEREO Viaje Ministerial 10-19 Enero 1948.**

326	4PTAS. pink	17·00	4·25

1949. Nos. 322 and 325 surch **Habilitado para** and value in words.

327	5c. on 1PTA. black	95	20
328	15c. on 2PTAS. brown	95	20

33 Natives in Pirogue

1949. 75th Anniv of U.P.U.

329	**33**	4p. violet	4·75	3·00

34 Count Argalejo and San Carlos Bay

1949. Air. Colonial Stamp Day.

330	**34**	5p. green	4·75	3·00

35 San Carlos Bay

1949

331	**35**	2c. brown	20	20
332	-	5c. violet	20	20
333	-	10c. blue	20	20
334	-	15c. green	20	20
335	**35**	25c. brown	20	20
336	-	30c. yellow	20	20
337	-	40c. green	20	20
338	-	45c. purple	20	20
339	**35**	50c. orange	20	20
340	-	75c. blue	20	20
341	-	90c. green	30	20
342	-	1p. black	1·90	20
343	**35**	1p.35 violet	7·50	2·40
344	-	2p. brown	21·00	5·75
345	-	5p. mauve	29·00	17·00
346	**35**	10p. brown	£120	70·00

DESIGNS: 5, 30, 75c., 2p. Benito River rapids; 10, 40, 90c., 5p. Coast scene and Clarence Peak, Fernando Poo; 15, 45, 1p. Niepan, Benito River.

36 Manuel Iradier y Bulfy

1950. Air. Colonial Stamp Day.

347	**36**	5p. brown	7·50	2·75

37 Hands and Natives

1951. Native Welfare.

348	**37**	50c.+10c. blue	45	45
349	**37**	1p.+25c. green	19·00	5·25
350	**37**	6p.50+1p.65 orange	4·25	2·40

38 Mt. Mioco

1951. Air.

351	-	25c. yellow	20	20
352	**38**	50c. mauve	20	20
353	-	1p. green	20	20
354	-	2p. blue	30	20
355	**38**	3p.25 violet	95	20
356	-	5p. sepia	8·25	4·00
357	-	10p. red	35·00	14·00

DESIGNS: 25c., 2, 10p. Benito Rapids; 1, 5p. Santa Isabel Bay.

1951. Air. 500th Birth Anniv of Isabella the Catholic. As T **9a** of Spanish Sahara.

358	5p. blue	24·00	14·00

39 Leopard

1951. Colonial Stamp Day.

359	**39**	5c.+5c. brown	55	45
360	**39**	10c.+5c. orange	60	45
361	**39**	60c.+15c. olive	1·20	95

40 Native and Map

1951. International West African Conference.

362	**40**	50c. orange	45	45
363	**40**	5p. blue	8·50	1·90

41 Native Man

1952

364	**41**	5c. brown	70	40
365	**41**	50c. olive	70	40
366	**41**	5p. violet	3·75	1·90

42 "Crinum giganteum"

1952. Native Welfare Fund.

367	**42**	5c.+5c. brown	60	40
368	**42**	50c.+10c. black	60	40
369	**42**	2p.+30c. blue	2·75	2·10

43 Ferdinand the Catholic

1952. Air. 500th Birth Anniv of Ferdinand the Catholic.

370	**43**	5p. brown	33·00	16·00

44 Brown-cheeked Hornbills

1952. Colonial Stamp Day.

371	**44**	5c.+5c. brown	50	50
372	**44**	10c.+5c. purple	50	50
373	**44**	60c.+15c. green	1·00	1·00

45 Native Musician

1953. Native Welfare Fund. Inscr "PRO INDIGENAS 1953".

374	**45**	5c.+5c. lake	50	50
375	-	10c.+5c. purple	50	50
376	**45**	15c. olive	50	50
377	-	60c. brown	55	55

DESIGN: 10, 60c. Musician facing right.

46 Native Woman and Dove

1953

378	**46**	5c. orange	50	20
379	**46**	10c. purple	50	20
380	**46**	60c. brown	50	25
381	-	1p. lilac	2·10	25
382	-	1p.90 green	4·75	1·20

DESIGN: 1, 1p.90, Native drummer.

47 "Tragocephala nobilis" (longhorn beetle)

1953. Colonial Stamp Day. Inscr "DIA DEL SELLO COLONIAL 1953".

383	**47**	5c.+5c. blue	50	50
384	-	10c.+5c. purple	50	50
385	**47**	15c. green	50	50
386	-	60c. brown	55	55

DESIGN: 10, 60c. African giant swallowtail (butterfly).

48 Hunting with Bow and Arrow

1954. Native Welfare Fund. Inscr "PRO-INDIGENAS 1954".

387	**48**	5c.+5c. lake	50	50
388	-	10c.+5c. lilac	50	50
389	**48**	15c. green	50	50
390	-	60c. brown	55	55

DESIGN: 10, 60c. Native hunting elephant with spear.

49 Turtle

1954. Colonial Stamp Day. Inscr "DIA DEL SELLO COLONIAL 1954".

391	**49**	5c.+5c. red	50	50
392	-	10c.+5c. purple	50	50
393	**49**	15c. green	50	50
394	-	60c. brown	55	55

DESIGN: 10, 60c. Barbelled houndshark (fish).

50 M. Iradier y Bulfy

1955. Birth Centenary of Iradier (explorer).

395	**50**	60c. brown	40	40
396	**50**	1p. violet	3·25	3·25

51 Native Priest

1955. Centenary of Apostolic Prefecture in Fernando Poo.

397	**51**	10c.+5c. purple	50	50
398	-	25c.+10c. violet	50	50
399	**51**	50c. olive	55	55

DESIGN: 25c. "Baptism".

52 Footballers

1955. Air.

400	**52**	25c. grey	35	25
401	**52**	50c. olive	35	25
402	**52**	1p.50 brown	1·40	35
403	**52**	4p. red	5·00	80
404	**52**	10p. green	2·75	1·20

53 El Pardo Palace, Madrid

1955. Treaty of Pardo, 1778.

405	**53**	5c. brown	50	50
406	**53**	15c. red	50	50
407	**53**	80c. green	55	55

54 Moustached Monkeys

1955. Colonial Stamp Day. Inscr "DIA DEL SELLO COLONIAL 1955".

408	**54**	5c.+5c. lake and brown	80	80
409	-	15c.+5c. sepia and lake	80	80
410	**54**	70c. blue and slate	1·10	1·10

DESIGN—HORIZ: 15c. Talapoin and young.

55 "Orquidea"

1956. Native Welfare Fund. Inscr "PRO INDIGENAS 1956".

411	**55**	5c.+5c. olive	50	50
412	-	15c.+5c. ochre	50	50
413	**55**	20c. turquoise	50	50
414	-	50c. brown	55	55

DESIGN: 15, 50c. "Strophantus kombe".

56 Arms of Santa Isabel

1956. Colonial Stamp Day. Inscr "DIA DEL SELLO 1956".

415	**56**	5c.+5c. brown	50	50
416	-	15c.+5c. violet	50	50
417	**56**	70c. green	55	55

DESIGN—HORIZ: 15c. Arms of Bata and natives.

57 Grey Parrot

1957. Native Welfare Fund. Inscr "PRO INDIGENAS 1957".

418	**57**	5c.+5c. purple	50	50
419	-	15c.+5c. ochre	50	50
420	**57**	70c. green	55	55

DESIGN—HORIZ: 15c. Grey parrot in flight.

58 "Flight"

1957. Air. 30th Anniv of Spain–Fernando Poo Flight by "Atlantida" Seaplane Squadron.

421	**58**	25p. sepia and bistre	16·00	3·25

59 African Elephant and Calf

1957. Colonial Stamp Day.

422	**59**	10c.+5c. mauve	50	50
423	-	15c.+5c. brown	50	50
424	**59**	20c. turquoise	50	50
425	-	70c. green	55	55

DESIGN—VERT: 15, 70c. African elephant trumpeting.

60 Doves and Arms of Valencia and Santa Isabel

1958. "Aid for Valencia".

426	**60**	10c.+5c. brown	50	50
427	**60**	15c.+10c. ochre	50	50
428	**60**	50c.+10c. brown	55	55

61 Boxing

1958. Sports.

429	**61**	5c. brown	25	25
430	-	10c. brown	25	25
431	-	15c. brown	25	25
432	-	80c. green	25	25
433	**61**	1p. red	25	25
434	-	2p. purple	40	25
435	-	2p.30 lilac	55	35
436	-	3p. blue	65	40

DESIGNS—VERT: 10c., 2p. Basketball; 80c., 3p. Running. HORIZ: 15c., 2p.30, Long jumping.

62 Missionary holding Cross

1958. Native Welfare Fund. Inscr "1883 PRO-INDIGENAS 1958".

437	**62**	10c.+5c. brown	50	50
438	-	15c.+5c. ochre	50	50
439	**62**	20c. turquoise	50	50
440	-	70c. green	55	55

DESIGN: 15, 70c. The Crucifixion.

63 African Monarchs

1958. Colonial Stamp Day. Inscr "1958".

441	**63**	10c.+5c. red	50	50
442	-	25c.+10c. violet	50	50
443	-	50c.+10c. olive	55	55

DESIGNS: 25, 50c. Different views of butterflies on plants.

64 Digitalis

1959. Child Welfare Fund. Floral designs as T **64**. Inscr "PRO-INFANCIA 1959".

444	**64**	10c.+5c. lake	50	50
445	-	15c.+5c. ochre	50	50
446	-	20c. myrtle	50	50
447	**64**	70c. green	55	55

DESIGN: 15, 20c. Castor bean.

65 Boy on "Penny-farthing" Cycle

1959. Colonial Stamp Day. Inscr "1959".

448	**65**	10c.+5c. lake	50	50
449	-	20c.+5c. myrtle	50	50
450	-	50c.+20c. olive	55	55

DESIGNS: 20c. Racing cyclists; 50c. Winning cyclist.

EXPRESS LETTER STAMP

E38 Fernando Poo

1951

E358	**E38**	25c. red	30	25

Pt. 9

SPANISH MOROCCO

100 centimos = 1 peseta.

I. SPANISH POST OFFICES IN MOROCCO

Nos. 2/150, except Nos. 93/8 and 124/37 are all stamps of Spain overprinted.

1903. Optd **CORREO ESPANOL MARRUECOS**.

2	**38a**	¼c. green	70	35

1903. Optd **CORREO ESPANOL MARRUECOS**.

3	**52**	2c. brown	1·70	1·70
4	**52**	5c. green	1·90	90
5	**52**	10c. red	2·50	35
6	**52**	15c. violet	3·25	95
7	**52**	20c. black	12·50	4·50
8	**52**	25c. blue	1·00	95
9	**52**	30c. green	7·50	4·50
10	**52**	40c. pink	13·50	7·50
11	**52**	50c. blue	7·50	7·25
12	**52**	1p. purple	28·00	10·50
13	**52**	4p. purple	65·00	18·00
14	**52**	10p. orange	38·00	45·00

1908. Stamps of Spain handstamped TETUAN.

15	**38a**	¼c. green	14·50	5·75
16	**52**	2c. brown	60·00	19·00
17	**52**	5c. green	75·00	33·00
18	**52**	10c. red	80·00	36·00
19	**52**	15c. violet	80·00	36·00
20	**52**	20c. black	£250	£200
21	**52**	25c. blue	£120	60·00
22	**52**	30c. green	£275	£110
23	**52**	40c. bistre	£375	£200

1908. Nos. 2/5 and 7/8 handstamped TETUAN.

24	**38a**	¼c. green	24·00	15·00
25	**52**	2c. brown	£200	£110
26	**52**	5c. green	£190	60·00
27	**52**	10c. red	£190	60·00
28	**52**	20c. grey	£425	£200
29	**52**	25c. blue	£160	60·00

1909. Optd **CORREO ESPANOL MARRUECOS**.

30	**64**	2c. brown	1·60	40
31	**64**	5c. green	6·25	40
32	**64**	10c. red	8·25	40
33	**64**	15c. violet	13·00	1·00
34	**64**	20c. green	25·00	1·60
35	**64**	25c. blue	£160	
36	**64**	30c. green	8·50	1·00
37	**64**	40c. pink	8·50	1·00
38	**64**	50c. blue	13·50	12·50
39	**64**	1p. lake	31·00	25·00
40	**64**	4p. purple	£140	
41	**64**	10p. orange	£140	

After the appearance of Nos. 42/54 for the Spanish Protectorate in 1914, the use of Nos. 30/41 was restricted to Tangier.

II. SPANISH PROTECTORATE (excluding Tangier)

1914. Optd **MARRUECOS**.

42	**38a**	¼c. green	20	20
43	**64**	2c. brown	20	20
44	**64**	5c. green	40	35
45	**64**	10c. red	40	35
46	**64**	15c. violet	1·90	1·30
47	**64**	20c. green	2·75	2·40
48	**64**	25c. blue	2·75	1·90
49	**64**	30c. green	3·75	3·25
50	**64**	40c. pink	11·50	4·75
51	**64**	50c. blue	7·50	2·40
52	**64**	1p. red	7·50	4·75
53	**64**	4p. purple	36·00	34·00
54	**64**	10p. orange	55·00	50·00

1915. Optd **PROTECTORADO ESPANOL EN MARRUECOS**.

55	**38a**	¼c. green	60	30
56	**64**	2c. brown	30	30
57	**64**	5c. green	70	30
58	**64**	10c. red	60	30
59	**64**	15c. violet	85	30
60	**64**	20c. green	2·20	30
61	**64**	25c. blue	2·40	45
62	**64**	30c. green	2·50	55
63	**64**	40c. pink	3·75	55
64	**64**	50c. blue	6·50	45
65	**64**	1p. red	8·50	55
66	**64**	4p. purple	50·00	34·00
67	**64**	10p. orange	65·00	50·00

1916. Optd **ZONA DE PROTECTORADO ESPANOL EN MARRUECOS**.

68	**38a**	¼c. green	1·80	40
69	**66**	1c. green	2·10	20
70	**64**	2c. brown	1·80	40
71	**64**	5c. green	7·50	40
72	**64**	10c. red	9·75	40
73	**64**	15c. orange	10·50	40
74	**64**	20c. violet	14·50	20
75	**64**	25c. blue	31·00	5·00
76	**64**	30c. green	41·00	33·00
77	**64**	40c. red	36·00	95
78	**64**	50c. blue	19·00	45
79	**64**	1p. red	44·00	3·50
80	**64**	4p. purple	65·00	19·00
81	**64**	10p. orange	£160	£140

1920. Optd **PROTECTORADO ESPANOL EN MARRUECOS** perf through centre and each half surch in figures and words.

82	10c.+10c. on 20c. green	5·75	2·75
83	15c.+15c. on 30c. green	17·00	12·50

1920. No. E68 perf through centre, and each half surch **10 centimos**.

84	**53**	10c.+10c. on 20c. red	20·00	10·00

1920. Fiscal stamps showing figure of Justice, bisected and surch **CORREOS** and value.

93	5c. on 5p. blue	11·50	2·30
94	5c. on 10p. green	65	20
95	10c. on 25p. green	30	20
96	10c. on 50p. grey	55	35
97	15c. on 100p. red	55	35
98	15c. on 500p. red	16·00	8·25

1923. Optd **ZONA DE PROTECTORADO ESPANOL EN MARRUECOS**.

101	**68**	2c. green	1·00	20
102	**68**	5c. purple	1·00	20
103	**68**	10c. green	4·50	20
105	**68**	15c. blue	4·50	20
106	**68**	20c. violet	10·00	20
107	**68**	25c. red	20·00	2·00
108	**68**	40c. blue	20·00	6·50
109	**68**	50c. orange	50·00	11·50
110	**69**	1p. grey	75·00	6·50

1926. Red Cross stamps optd **ZONA PROTECTORADO ESPANOL**.

111	**70**	1c. orange	11·00	11·00
112	-	2c. red	16·00	16·00
113	-	5c. brown	5·50	5·50
114	-	10c. green	5·50	5·50
115	**70**	15c. violet	1·00	1·00
116	-	20c. purple	1·00	1·00
117	**71**	25c. red	1·00	1·00
118	**70**	30c. green	1·00	1·00
119	-	40c. blue	20	20
120	-	50c. red	20	20
121	-	1p. red	20	20
122	-	4p. bistre	1·00	1·00
123	**71**	10p. violet	3·75	3·75

11 Mosque of Alcazarquivir

12 Moorish Gateway, Larache

1928

124	**11**	1c. red	20	20
126	**11**	2c. violet	20	20
127	**11**	3c. blue	20	20
128	**11**	10c. green	20	20
129	**11**	15c. brown	45	20
130	**12**	20c. olive	45	20
131	**12**	25c. red	45	20
132	**12**	30c. brown	1·80	20
133	**12**	40c. blue	2·50	20
134	**12**	50c. purple	4·75	20
135	-	1p. green	7·50	40
136	-	2p.50 purple	38·00	10·00
137	-	4p. blue	33·00	6·25

DESIGNS—HORIZ: 1p. Well at Alhucemas; 2p.50, Xauen; 4p. Tetuan.

1929. Seville–Barcelona Exhibition stamps, Nos. 502/14 optd **PROTECTORADO MARRUECOS**.

138	1c. blue	35	35
139	2c. green	35	35
140	5c. red	35	35
141	10c. green	35	35
142	15c. blue	35	35
143	20c. violet	35	35
144	25c. red	35	35
145	30c. brown	95	95
146	40c. blue	95	95
147	50c. orange	95	95
148	1p. grey	8·00	8·00
149	4p. red	19·00	19·00
150	10p. brown	41·00	41·00

14 Xauen

15 Market-place, Larache

1933

151	**14**	1c. red	20	20
152	-	2c. green	20	20
153	-	5c. mauve	20	20
154	-	10c. green	40	40
155	-	15c. yellow	2·30	45
156	**14**	20c. green	90	70
157	-	25c. red	25·00	70
165	-	25c. violet	1·30	35
158	-	30c. lake	9·25	50
166	-	30c. red	21·00	35
159	**15**	40c. blue	21·00	50
167	-	40c. red	10·50	45
160	-	50c. red	55·00	13·00

168	-	50c. blue	10·50	45
169	-	60c. green	10·50	45
161	-	1p. grey	23·00	50
170	-	2p. lake	75·00	16·00
162	-	2p.50 brown	38·00	13·00
163	-	4p. green	38·00	13·00
164	-	5p. black	50·00	13·00

DESIGNS—HORIZ: 2c., 1p. Xauen; 5c., 2p.50, Arcila; 25c. (No. 157), 5p. Sultan and bodyguard; 30c. (No. 166), 50c. (No. 168), 2p. Forest at Ketama. VERT: 10c., 30c. (No. 158), Tetuan; 15c., 4p. Alcazarquivir; 25c. (No. 165), 40c. (No. 167), Wayside scene at Arcila.

See also Nos. 177/83 and 213/6.

1936. Air. No. 157 surch with new value and **18-7-36**.

171	25c.+2p. on 25c. red	32·00	9·75

1936. Surch.

172	-	1c. on 4p. blue (137)	35	20
173	-	2c. on 2p.50 pur (136)	35	20
174	12	5c. on 25c. red (131)	20	20
175	-	10c. on 1p. green (135)	12·50	5·75
176	E 12	15c. on 20c. black	10·00	3·25

1937. Pictorials as T **14/15**.

177	1c. green	20	20
178	2c. mauve	20	20
179	5c. orange	20	20
180	15c. violet	20	70
181	30c. red	70	35
182	1p. blue	7·25	45
183	10p. brown	£120	44·00

DESIGNS—VERT: 1, 15c. Caliph and Viziers; 30c. Tetuan; 1p. Arcila; 10p. Caliph on horseback. HORIZ: 2c. Bokoia; 5c. Alcazarquivir.

Sheets each 105×95 mm comprising Nos. 177/83.

MS183a 1, 2, 5c., 1p.	21·00	21·00
MS183b 2, 5, 30c.	21·00	21·00

18 Legionaries

1937. First Anniv of Civil War.

184	-	1c. blue	20	20
185	18	2c. brown	20	20
186	-	5c. mauve	20	20
187	-	10c. green	20	20
188	-	15c. blue	20	20
189	-	20c. purple	20	20
190	-	25c. mauve	20	20
191	-	30c. red	20	20
192	-	40c. orange	20	20
193	-	50c. blue	20	20
194	-	60c. green	20	20
195	-	1p. violet	20	20
196	-	2p. blue	13·50	12·50
197	-	2p.50 black	13·50	12·50
198	-	4p. brown	13·50	12·50
199	-	10p. black	13·50	12·50

DESIGNS—VERT: 1c. Sentry; 5c. Trooper; 10c. Volunteers; 15c. Colour bearer; 20c. Desert halt; 25c. Ifni mounted riflemen; 30c. Trumpeters; 40c. Cape Juby Camel Corps; 50c. Infantryman; 60c., 1, 2, 4p. Sherifian Guards; 2p.50, Cavalryman. HORIZ: 10p. "Road to Victory".

19 General Franco

1937. Obligatory Tax. Disabled Soldiers in N. Africa.

200	19	10c. brown	60	20
201	19	10c. blue	60	20

Sheets each 120×100 mm containing blocks of four. Imperf.

MS202a **19** 10c. sepia	4·75	2·75
MS202b 10c. brown	4·75	2·75
MS202c 10c. blue	4·75	2·75

20 Yellow-billed Stork over Mosque

1938. Air.

203	-	5c. brown	20	20
204	20	10c. green	20	20
205	-	25c. red	20	20
206	-	40c. blue	3·00	90
207	-	50c. mauve	20	20
208	-	75c. blue	20	20
209	-	1p. brown	20	20
210	-	1p.50 violet	90	65
211	-	2p. red	65	20
212	-	3p. black	2·30	45

DESIGNS—VERT: 5c. Mosque de Baja, Tetuan; 25c. Straits of Gibraltar; 40c. Desert natives; 1p. Mounted postman; 1p.50, Farmers; 2p. Sunset; 3p. Shadow of airplane over city. HORIZ: 50c. Airplane over Tetuan; 75c. Airplane over Larache.

1939. Pictorials as T **14**.

213	5c. orange	20	20
214	10c. green	20	20
215	15c. brown	55	20
216	20c. blue	55	20

DESIGNS: 5c. "Carta de Espana"; 10c. "Carta de Marruecos"; 15c. Larache; 20c. Tetuan.

1940. Pictorials as T **14**, inscr "ZONA" on back.

217	1c. brown	20	20
218	2c. olive	20	20
219	5c. blue	20	20
220	10c. lilac	20	20
221	15c. green	20	20
222	20c. violet	20	20
223	25c. sepia	20	20
224	30c. green	20	20
225	40c. green	2·10	20
226	45c. orange	85	20
227	50c. brown	85	20
228	70c. blue	85	20
229	1p. brown and blue	2·75	20
230	2p.50 green and brown	32·00	5·50
231	5p. sepia and purple	2·75	35
232	10p. brown and olive	28·00	10·50

DESIGNS—VERT: 1c. Postman; 2c. Pillar-box; 5c. Winter landscape; 10c. Alcazar street; 15c. Castle wall, Xauen; 20c. Palace sentry, Tetuan; 25c. Caliph on horseback; 30c. Market-place, Larache; 40c. Gateway, Tetuan; 45c. Gateway, Xauen; 50c. Street, Alcazarquivir; 70c. Post Office; 1p. Spanish War veterans.

1940. Fourth Anniv of Civil War. Nos. 184/99 optd **17-VII-940 40 ANIVERSARIO**.

233	1c. blue	85	85
234	2c. brown	85	85
235	5c. mauve	85	85
236	10c. green	85	85
237	15c. blue	85	85
238	20c. purple	85	85
239	25c. mauve	85	85
240	30c. red	85	85
241	40c. orange	1·40	1·40
242	50c. blue	1·40	1·40
243	60c. green	1·40	1·40
244	1p. violet	1·40	1·40
245	2p. blue	60·00	60·00
246	2p.50 black	60·00	60·00
247	4p. brown	60·00	60·00
248	10p. black	60·00	60·00

22 Soldier on Horseback

1941. Obligatory Tax for Disabled Soldiers.

249	22	10c. green	5·00	20
250	22	10c. pink	5·00	20
251	22	10c. red	5·00	20
252	22	10c. blue	5·00	20

23 Larache

1941

253	23	5c. brown and deep brown	20	20
263	-	5c. blue	20	20
254	-	10c. deep red and red	20	20
255	-	15c. yellow and green	20	20
256	-	20c. blue and deep blue	60	20
257	-	40c. red and purple	1·70	20
264	-	40c. brown	75·00	40

DESIGNS: 5c. blue, 10c. Alcazarquivir; 15, 40c. brown, Larache market; 20c. Moorish house; 40c. purple, Gateway, Tangier.

1942. Air. New designs as T **14**, optd **Z**.

258	5c. blue	20	20
259	10c. brown	20	20
260	15c. green	20	20
261	90c. red	20	20
262	5p. black	1·10	60

DESIGNS—VERT: 5c. Atlas mountains; 10c. Mosque at Tangier; 15c. Velez fortress; 90c. Sanjurjo harbour; 5p. Straits of Gibraltar.

25 General Franco

1943. Obligatory Tax for Disabled Soldiers.

265	25	10c. grey	10·50	20
266	25	10c. blue	10·50	20
267	25	10c. brown	10·50	20
268	25	10c. violet	10·50	20
283	25	10c. brown and mauve	12·50	20
284	25	10c. green and orange	12·50	20
295	25	10c. brown and blue	12·50	20
296	25	10c. lilac and grey	12·50	20

26 Homeward Bound

1944. Agricultural Scenes.

269	-	1c. blue and brown	20	20
270	-	2c. green	20	20
271	26	5c. black and brown	20	20
272	-	10c. orange and blue	20	20
273	-	15c. green	20	20
274	-	20c. black and red	20	20
275	-	25c. brown and blue	20	20
276	-	30c. blue and green	20	20
277	-	40c. purple and brown	20	20
278	26	50c. brown and blue	55	20
279	-	75c. blue and green	75	20
280	-	1p. brown and blue	75	20
281	-	2p.50 blue and black	8·75	3·25
282	-	10p. black and orange	14·50	8·50

DESIGNS—HORIZ: 1, 30c. Ploughing; 2, 40c. Harvesting; 10, 75c. Threshing; 15c., 1p. Vegetable garden; 20c., 2p.50, Gathering oranges; 25c., 10p. Shepherd and flock.

27 Dyers

1946. Craftsmen.

285		1c. brown and purple	30	20
286	27	2c. violet and green	30	20
287	-	10c. blue and orange	30	20
288	27	15c. green and blue	30	20
289	-	25c. blue and green	30	20
290	-	40c. brown and blue	30	20
291	27	45c. red and black	75	20
292	27	1p. blue and green	1·00	20
293	-	2p.50 green and orange	2·75	70
294	-	10p. grey and blue	15·00	2·75

DESIGNS: 1, 10, 25c. Potters; 40c. Blacksmiths; 1p. Cobblers; 2p.50, Weavers; 10p. Metal workers.

28 Sanatorium

1946. Anti-T.B. Fund.

297		10c. green and red	30	20
298	28	25c. brown and red	30	20
299	-	25c.+5c. violet and red	30	20
300	-	50c.+10c. blue and red	40	20
301	-	90c.+10c. brown and red	95	55

DESIGNS: 10c. Emblem and arabesque ornamentation; 25c.+5c. Mountain roadway; 50c.+10c. Fountain; 90c.+10c. Wayfarers.

29 Sanatorium

1947. Anti-T.B. Fund.

302		10c. blue and red	30	20
303	29	25c. brown and red	30	20
304	-	25c.+5c. lilac and red	30	20
305	-	50c.+10c. blue and red	35	30
306	-	90c.+10c. brown and red	1·00	75

DESIGNS: 10c. Emblem, mosque and palm tree; 25c.+5c. Hospital ward; 50c.+10c. Nurse and children; 90c.+10c. Arab swordsman.

30 Steam Goods Train

1948. Transport and Commerce.

307	30	2c. brown and violet	30	20
308	-	5c. violet and red	30	20
309	-	15c. green and blue	30	20
310	-	25c. green and black	30	20
311	-	35c. black and blue	30	20
312	-	50c. violet and orange	30	20
313	-	70c. blue and green	30	20
314	-	90c. green and red	30	20
315	-	1p. violet and blue	80	45
316	30	2p.50 green and purple	2·20	45
317	-	10p. blue and black	4·75	1·80

DESIGNS: 5, 35c. Road transport; 15, 70c. Urban market; 25, 90c. Rural market; 50c., 1p. Camel caravan; 10p. "Arango" (freighter) at quay.

31 Emblem

32 Herald

1948. Anti-T.B. Fund.

318	31	10c. green and red	30	20
319	-	25c. green and red	2·20	1·10
320	32	50c.+10c. purple and red	30	20
321	-	90c.+10c. black and red	1·70	65
322	-	2p.50+50c. brown & red	13·00	4·50
323	-	5p.+1p. violet and red	19·00	8·75

DESIGNS: 25c. Airplane over sanatorium; 90c. Arab swordsman; 2p.50, Natives sitting in the sun; 5p. Airplane over Ben Karrich.

33 Market Day

1949. Air.

324		5c. green and purple	40	20
325	33	10c. mauve and black	40	20
326	-	30c. grey and blue	40	20
327	-	1p.75 blue and black	40	20
328	33	3p. black and blue	40	20
329	-	4p. red and black	85	20
330	-	6p.50 brown and green	2·50	30
331	-	8p. blue and mauve	4·25	75

DESIGNS—VERT: 5c., 1p.75, Straits of Gibraltar; 30c., 4p. Kebira Fortress; 6p.50, Arrival of mail plane; 8p. Galloping horseman.

34 Caliph on Horseback

1949. Caliph's Wedding Celebrations.

332	34	50c.+10c. red (postage)	40	20
333	-	1p.+10c. black (air)	1·10	40

DESIGN: 1p. Wedding crowds in palace grounds.

35 Emblem

1949. Anti-T.B. Fund.

334	35	5c. green and red	30	20
335	-	10c. blue and red	30	20
336	-	25c. black and red	75	30
337	-	50c.+10c. brown and red	45	20
338	-	90c.+10c. green and red	1·40	30

DESIGNS: 10c. Road to recovery; 25c. Palm tree and tower; 50c. Flag and followers; 90c. Moorish horseman.

36 Postman, 1890

1950. 75th Anniv of U.P.U.

339	**36**	5c. blue and brown	30	20
340	-	10c. black and blue	30	20
341	-	15c. green and black	30	20
342	-	35c. black and violet	30	20
343	-	45c. mauve and red	30	20
344	**36**	50c. black and green	30	20
345	-	75c. blue and deep blue	30	20
346	**36**	90c. red and black	30	20
347	-	1p. green and purple	30	20
348	-	1p.50 blue and red	75	20
349	-	5p. purple and black	1·50	20
350	-	10p. blue and violet	40·00	28·00

DESIGNS: 10, 45c., 1p. Mounted postman; 15c., 1p.50, Mail coach; 35, 75c., 5p. Mail van; 10p. Steam mail train.

37 Morabito

1950. Anti-T.B. Fund.

351		5c. black and red	30	20
352		10c. green and red	55	20
353		25c. blue and red	1·40	40
354		50c.+10c. brown and red	55	20
355	**37**	90c.+10c. green and red	1·40	40

DESIGNS: 5c. Arab horseman; 10c. Fort; 25c. Sanatorium; 50c. Crowd at Fountain of Life.

38 Hunting

1950

356	**38**	5c. mauve and brown	30	20
357	-	10c. grey and red	30	20
358	**38**	50c. sepia and green	30	20
359	-	1p. red and violet	85	20
360	-	5p. violet and red	1·30	20
361	-	10p. red and green	4·50	55

DESIGNS: 10c., 1p. Hunters and hounds; 5p. Fishermen; 10p. Carabo (fishing boat).

39 Emblem

1951. Anti-T.B. Fund.

362	**39**	5c. green and red	20	20
363	-	10c. blue and red	20	20
364	-	25c. black and red	75	50
365	-	50c.+10c. brown and red	20	20
366	-	90c.+10c. blue and red	35	20
367	-	1p.+5p. blue and red	10·00	4·00
368	-	1p.10+25c. sepia and red	3·75	2·30

DESIGNS: 10c. Natives and children; 25c. Airplane over Nubes; 50c. Moorish horsemen; 90c. Riverside fortress; 1p. Brig "Hernan Cortes"; 1p.10, Airplane over caravan.

40 Mounted Riflemen

1952

369	**40**	5c. brown and blue	20	20
370	-	10c. mauve and sepia	20	20
371	-	15c. green and black	20	20
372	-	20c. purple and green	20	20
373	-	25c. blue and red	20	20
374	-	35c. orange and olive	20	20
375	-	45c. red	20	20
376	-	50c. green and red	20	20
377	-	75c. blue and purple	20	20
378	-	90c. purple and blue	20	20
379	-	1p. brown and blue	20	20
380	-	5p. blue and red	1·70	35
381	-	10p. black and green	2·75	50

DESIGNS—HORIZ: 10c. Grooms leading horses; 15c. Parade of horsemen; 20c. Peasants; 25c. Monastic procession; 35c. Native band; 45c. Tribesmen; 50c. Natives overlooking roof tops; 75c. Inside a tea house; 90c. Wedding procession; 1p. Pilgrims on horseback; 5p. Storyteller and audience; 10p. Natives talking.

41 Road to Tetuan

1952. Air. Tetuan Postal Museum Fund.

382	**41**	2p. blue and black	40	20
383	-	4p. red and black	75	20
384	-	8p. green and black	1·20	25
385	-	16p. brown and black	7·25	1·40

DESIGNS: 4p. Moors watching airplane; 8p. Horseman and airplane; 16p. Shadow of airplane over Tetuan.

42 Natives at Prayer

1952. Anti-T.B. Fund. Frame in red.

386	**42**	5c. green	70	65
387	-	10c. brown	70	65
388	-	25c. blue	1·40	85
389	-	50c.+10c. black	70	65
390	-	60c.+25c. green	2·75	1·40
391	-	90c.+10c. purple	2·75	1·40
392	-	1p.10+25c. violet	9·00	3·50
393	-	5p.+2p. black	20·00	10·00

DESIGNS: 10c. Beggars outside doorway; 25c. Airplane over cactus; 50c. Natives on horseback; 60c. Airplane over palms; 90c. Hilltop fortress; 1p.10, Airplane over agaves; 5p. Mounted warrior.

43 Sidi Saidi

1953. Air.

394		35c. red and blue	20	20
395	**43**	60c. green and lake	20	20
396	-	1p.10 black and blue	25	20
397	-	4p.50 brown and lake	95	35

DESIGNS: 35c. Carabo (fishing boat); 1p.10, Le Yunta (ploughing); 4p.50, Fortress, Xauen.

1953. Air. No. 208 surch **50**.

398	50c. on 75c. blue	45	20

1953. Anti-T.B. Fund. As T **32** but inscr "PRO TUBERCULOSOS 1953". Frame in red.

400	5c. green	35	30
401	10c. purple	35	30
402	25c. green	1·60	85
403	50c.+10c. violet	35	30
404	60c.+25c. brown	3·75	1·60
405	90c.+10c. black	1·10	55
406	1p.10+25c. brown	6·25	2·75
407	5p.+2p. blue	25·00	12·50

DESIGNS: 5c. Herald; 10c. Moorish horseman; 25c. Airplane over Ben Karrich; 50c. Mounted warrior; 60c. Airplane over sanatorium; 90c. Moorish horseman; 1p.10, Airplane over sea; 5p. Arab swordsman.

46

1953

408	**46**	5c. red	20	20
409	**46**	10c. green	20	20

47 Water-carrier

1953. 25th Anniv of First Pictorial Stamps of Spanish Morocco.

410	-	25c. purple and green	45	20
411	**47**	50c. green and red	45	20
412	-	90c. orange and blue	45	20
413	-	1p. green and brown	45	20
414	-	1p.25 mauve and green	45	20
415	-	2p. blue and purple	70	25
416	**47**	2p.50 orange and grey	1·80	25
417	-	4p.50 green and mauve	9·50	60
418	-	10p. black and green	12·50	1·40

DESIGNS—VERT: 35c., 1p.25, Mountain women; 90c., 2p. Mountain tribesmen; 1, 4p.50, Veiled Moorish women; 10p. Arab dignitary.

1954. Anti-T.B. Fund. As T **32**, but inscr "PRO TUBERCULOSOS 1954". Frame in red.

419	5c. turquoise	25	25
420	5c.+5c. purple	25	25
421	10c. sepia	25	25
422	25c. blue	25	25
423	50c.+10c. green	95	70
424	5p.+2p. black	12·50	7·75

DESIGNS: 5c. Convent; 5c.+5c. White stork on a tower; 10c. Moroccan family; 25c. Airplane over Spanish coast; 50c. Father and child; 5p. Chapel.

48 Saida Gate

1955. Frames in black.

425	-	15c. green	20	20
426	**48**	25c. purple	20	20
427	-	80c. blue	20	20
428	**48**	1p. mauve	25	20
429	-	15p. turquoise	3·75	1·40

DESIGNS: 15c., 80c. Queen's Gate; 15p. Ceuta Gate.

49 Celebrations

1955. 30th Anniv of Caliph's Accession.

430	**49**	15c. olive and brown	40	40
431	-	25c. lake and purple	40	40
432	-	30c. green and sepia	40	40
433	**49**	70c. green and myrtle	40	40
434	-	80c. brown and olive	40	40
435	-	1p. brown and blue	40	40
436	**49**	1p.80 violet and black	40	40
437	-	3p. grey and blue	40	40
438	-	5p. brown and myrtle	3·25	1·50
439	-	15p. green and brown	8·00	5·00

DESIGNS: 25c., 80c., 3p. Caliph's portrait; 30c., 1, 5p. Procession; 15p. Coat of Arms.

EXPRESS LETTER STAMPS

Express Letter Stamps of Spain overprinted

1914. Optd **MARRUECOS.**

E55	**E53**	20c. red	6·25	3·00

1915. Optd **PROTECTORADO ESPANOL EN MARRUECOS.**

E68	20c. red	5·00	2·50

1923. Optd **ZONA DE PROTECTORADO ESPANOL EN MARRUECOS.**

E111	20c. red	17·00	13·50

1926. Red Cross. Optd **ZONA PROTECTORADO ESPANOL.**

E124	**E77**	20c. black and blue	3·75	3·75

E12 Moorish Courier

1928

E138	**E12**	20c. black	4·75	4·75

E16

1935

E171	**E16**	20c. red	2·30	50

E19 Moorish Courier

1937. First Anniv of Civil War.

E200	**E19**	20c. red	20	20

E21

1940

E233	**E21**	25c. red	45	35

1940. No. E200 optd as Nos. 233/48 and surch also.

E249	**E19**	25c. on 20c. red	17·00	17·00

E37 Air Mail 1935

1950. 75th Anniv of U.P.U.

E351	**E37**	25c. black and red	40·00	28·00

E41 Moorish Courier

1952

E382	**E41**	25c. red	20	20

E48 Moorish Courier

1953. 25th Anniv of First Pictorial Stamps of Spanish Morocco.

E419	**E48**	25c. mauve and blue	25	20

E49 Tangier Gate

1955

E430	**E49**	2p. violet and black	20	20

For later issues see **MORROCCO**.

Pt. 9

SPANISH POST OFFICES IN TANGIERS

See note below No. 41 of Spanish P.O.'s in Morocco, concerning the exclusive use of Nos. 30-41 in Tangier after 1941.

Postage stamps of Spain overprinted.

1921. Optd **CORREO ESPANOL MARRUECOS.**

1	**66**	1c. green	30	20
2	**64**	2c. brown	£500	
3	**64**	15c. yellow	2·00	20
4	**64**	20c. violet	3·25	20

1939. Optd as 1921.

5	**68**	2c. green	7·75	25

6	**68**	5c. purple	7·75	25
7	**68**	5c. red	7·75	25
8	**68**	10c. green	9·50	25
10	**68**	20c. violet	14·00	2·75
11	**68**	50c. orange	65·00	19·00
12	**69**	10p. brown	4·25	9·75

1926. Red Cross stamps optd **CORREO ESPANOL TANGER**.

13	**70**	1c. orange	10·50	10·50
14	-	2c. red	10·50	10·50
15	-	5c. grey	5·00	5·00
16	-	10c. green	5·00	5·00
17	**70**	15c. violet	1·90	1·90
18	-	20c. purple	1·90	1·90
19	**71**	25c. red	1·90	1·90
20	**70**	30c. olive	1·90	1·90
21	-	40c. blue	40	40
22	-	50c. brown	40	40
23	-	1p. red	95	95
24	-	4p. brown	95	95
25	**71**	10p. lilac	5·00	5·00

1929. Seville–Barcelona Exhibition stamps, Nos. 504/14 optd **TANGER**.

27	5c. red	40	40
28	10c. green	40	40
29	15c. blue	40	40
30	20c. violet	40	40
31	25c. red	40	40
32	30c. brown	40	40
33	40c. blue	1·10	1·10
34	50c. orange	1·10	1·10
35	1p. grey	11·50	11·50
36	4p. red	32·00	32·00
37	10p. brown	46·00	46·00

1930. Optd as 1921.

38	**97**	10c. green	3·75	55
39	**97**	15c. turquoise	£190	2·00
40	**97**	20c. violet	4·25	85
41	**97**	30c. red	4·50	2·00
42	**97**	40c. blue	17·00	11·00

1933. Optd **MARRUECOS**.

43	**143**	1c. green (imperf)	20	20
44	**143**	2c. brown	20	20
45	**127**	5c. brown	20	20
46	**128**	10c. green	20	20
47	**130**	15c. blue	20	20
48	**127**	20c. violet	20	20
49	**132**	25c. red	20	20
50	**133**	30c. red	75·00	9·25
51	**138**	40c. blue	40	20
52	**130**	50c. orange	1·00	20
53	**138**	60c. green	1·00	20
54	**142**	1p. black	1·00	40
55	-	4p. mauve	2·75	3·75
56	-	10p. brown	3·75	9·25

1937. Optd **TANGER**.

58	**143**	1c. green (imperf)	60	20
59	**143**	2c. brown	60	20
60	**127**	5c. brown	60	20
61	**128**	10c. green	60	20
62	**130**	15c. blue	70	20
63	**127**	20c. violet	70	65
64	**132**	25c. red	70	65
65	**136**	30c. red	70	20
66	**138**	40c. blue	1·90	90
67	**130**	50c. orange	5·50	90
68	**142**	1p. black	10·00	5·00
69	-	4p. mauve (No. 768c)	£375	
70	-	10p. brown (No. 769c)	£375	

1938. Optd **Correo Espanol Tanger**.

71	**143**	5c. brown	2·00	1·00
72	**143**	10c. green	2·00	1·00
73	**143**	15c. green	2·00	1·00
74	**143**	20c. violet	2·00	60
75	**143**	25c. mauve	2·00	60
76	**143**	30c. red	7·50	3·50
77	**160a**	40c. red	3·50	1·70
78	**160a**	45c. red	1·40	40
79	**160a**	50c. blue	1·40	40
80	**160a**	60c. blue	3·50	1·70
81	**145**	2p. blue	23·00	9·50
82	-	4p. mauve (No. 768c)	23·00	9·50

1938. Air. Optd **Correo Aereo TANGER**.

83	**143**	25c. mauve	1·10	55
84	**160a**	50c. blue	1·10	55

1938. Air. Optd **CORREO AEREO TANGER**.

85	**145**	2p. blue	9·00	3·25
86	**142**	1p. black	1·10	55
87	-	4p. mauve (No. 768c)	9·00	3·25
88	-	10p. brown (No. 769c)	65·00	41·00

1939. Optd **Tanger**.

89	**143**	5c. brown	70	40
90	**143**	10c. green	70	40
91	**143**	15c. green	70	40
92	**143**	20c. violet	70	40
93	**143**	25c. mauve	70	40
94	**143**	30c. red	70	40
95	**160a**	40c. red	70	40
96	**160a**	45c. red	70	40
97	**160a**	50c. blue	1·90	1·50
98	**160a**	60c. blue	1·10	40
99	**142**	1p. black	1·50	75
100	**145**	2p. blue	25·00	17·00
101	-	4p. mauve (No. 768c)	25·00	17·00
102	-	10p. brown (No. 769c)	25·00	17·00

1939. Air. Optd **Via Aerea Tanger**.

103	**143**	5c. brown	1·10	95
104	**143**	10c. green	1·10	95
105	**143**	15c. green	1·00	85
106	**143**	20c. violet	1·00	85
107	**143**	25c. mauve	1·00	85
108	**143**	30c. red	1·90	1·00
109	**160a**	40c. red	50·00	
110	**160a**	45c. red	45	35
111	**160a**	50c. blue	£100	
112	**160a**	60c. blue	13·00	10·50
113	**142**	1p. black	33·00	
114	-	4p. mauve (No. 768c)	55·00	30·00
115	-	10p. brown (No. 769c)	£160	

1939. Air. Express Letter stamp optd **Via Aerea Tanger**.

116	**E 145**	20c. red	3·50	1·70

1939. Various fiscal types inscr "DERECHOS CONSULARES ESPANOLES" optd **Correo Tanger.**

117	50c. pink	22·00	22·00
118	1p. pink	5·75	5·75
119	2p. pink	5·75	5·75
120	5p. red and green	6·25	6·25
121	10p. red and violet	29·00	29·00

1939. Air. Various fiscal types inscr "DERECHOS CONSULARES ESPANOLES" optd **Correo Aereo Tanger**.

122	1p. blue	75·00	75·00
123	2p. blue	75·00	75·00
124	5p. blue	10·50	10·50
125	10p. blue	10·50	10·50

15 Moroccan Woman

1948

126	-	1c. green	20	20
127	-	2c. orange	20	20
128	-	5c. purple	20	20
129	-	10c. blue	20	20
130	-	20c. sepia	20	20
131	-	25c. green	20	20
132	-	30c. grey	40	20
133	-	45c. red	40	20
134	**15**	50c. red	40	20
135	-	75c. blue	85	20
136	-	90c. green	65	20
137	-	1p.35 red	2·75	45
138	**15**	2p. violet	5·00	45
139	-	10p. green	6·25	95

DESIGNS: 1, 2c. Woman's head facing right; 5, 25c. Palm tree; 10, 20c. Woman's head facing left; 30c., 1p.35, Old map of Tangier; 45c., 10p. Street scene; 75, 90c. Head of Moor.

16 Douglas DC-3

1949. Air.

140		20c. brown	40	20
141	**16**	25c. red	40	20
142	-	35c. green	40	20
143	-	1p. violet	1·40	20
144	**16**	2p. green	2·30	40
145	-	10p. purple	4·25	1·70

DESIGNS: 20c., 1p. Lockheed Constellation and map; 35c., 10p. Boeing 377 Stratocruiser in clouds.

EXPRESS LETTER STAMPS

Express Letter Stamps of Spain overprinted.

1926. Red Cross. Optd **CORREO ESPANOL TANGER**.

E26	**E77**	20c. black and blue	5·00	5·00

1933. No. E17 optd **MARRUECOS**.

E57	**145**	20c. red	1·80	55

E17 Courier

1949

E146	**E17**	25c. red	90	45

Pt. 9

SPANISH SAHARA

Former Spanish territory on the north-west coast of Africa, previously called Rio de Oro. Later divided between Morocco and Mauritania.

100 centimos = 1 peseta.

1 Tuareg and Camel

1924

1	**1**	5c. green	3·00	1·10
2	**1**	10c. green	3·00	1·10
3	**1**	15c. blue	3·00	1·10
4	**1**	20c. violet	3·00	1·60
5	**1**	25c. red	3·00	1·60
6	**1**	30c. brown	3·00	1·60
7	**1**	40c. blue	3·00	1·60
8	**1**	50c. orange	3·00	1·60
9	**1**	60c. purple	3·00	1·60
10	**1**	1p. red	16·00	9·00
11	**1**	4p. brown	75·00	44·00
12	**1**	10p. purple	£170	£140

1926. Red Cross stamps of Spain optd **SAHARA ESPANOL**.

13	-	5c. grey	12·50	12·50
14	-	10c. green	12·50	12·50
15	**70**	15c. violet	3·50	3·50
16	-	20c. purple	3·50	3·50
17	**71**	25c. red	3·50	3·50
18	**70**	30c. olive	3·50	3·50
19	-	40c. blue	30	30
20	-	50c. brown	30	30
21	**71**	60c. green	30	30
22	-	1p. red	30	30
23	-	4p. brown	3·50	3·50
24	**71**	10p. lilac	8·75	8·75

1929. Seville and Barcelona Exn stamps of Spain. Nos. 504/14, optd **SAHARA**.

25	5c. red	30	30
26	10c. green	30	30
27	15c. blue	30	30
28	20c. violet	30	30
29	25c. red	30	30
30	30c. brown	30	30
31	40c. blue	75	75
32	50c. orange	75	75
33	1p. grey	4·25	4·25
34	4p. red	31·00	31·00
35	10p. brown	60·00	60·00

1931. Optd **Republica Espanola**.

36	**1**	5c. green	95	95
37	**1**	10c. green	95	95
38	**1**	15c. blue	95	95
39	**1**	20c. violet	95	95
40	**1**	25c. red	1·10	95
41	**1**	30c. brown	1·10	95
42	**1**	40c. blue	5·00	1·50
43	**1**	50c. orange	5·00	3·25
44	**1**	60c. purple	5·00	3·25
45	**1**	1p. red	5·00	3·25
46	**1**	4p. brown	65·00	38·00
47	**1**	10p. purple	£120	70·00

1941. Stamps of Spain optd **SAHARA ESPANOL**.

47a	**181**	1c. green	2·75	2·75
47b	**182**	2c. brown	2·75	2·75
48	**183**	5c. brown	75	75
49	**183**	10c. red	2·75	2·75
50	**183**	15c. green	75	75
51	**196**	20c. violet	75	75
52	**196**	25c. red	2·00	1·80
53	**196**	30c. blue	2·00	2·00
54	**196**	40c. green	75	75
55	**196**	50c. blue	9·75	2·75
56	**196**	70c. blue	6·75	4·00
57	**196**	1PTA. black	31·00	6·00
58	**196**	2PTAS. brown	£180	£140
59	**196**	4PTAS. red	£400	£325
60	**196**	10PTS. brown	£1200	£550

6 Dorcas Gazelles

1943

61	**6**	1c. mauve & brown (postage)	20	20
62	-	2c. blue and green	20	20
63	-	5c. blue and red	20	20
64	**6**	15c. green and myrtle	20	20
65	-	20c. brown and mauve	20	20
66	**6**	40c. mauve and purple	20	20
67	-	45c. red and purple	30	30
68	-	75c. blue and indigo	30	30
69	**6**	1p. brown and red	1·30	1·30
70	-	3p. green and violet	2·40	2·40
71	-	10p. black and sepia	41·00	41·00

DESIGNS—VERT: 2, 20, 45c., 3p. Camel caravan; 5, 75c., 10p. Camel troups.

7 Ostriches

72	**7**	5c. brown and red (air)	20	20
73	-	25c. olive and green	20	20
74	**7**	50c. turquoise and blue	20	20
75	-	1p. blue and mauve	20	20
76	**7**	1p.40 blue and green	20	20
77	-	2p. brown and purple	1·40	1·40
78	**7**	5p. mauve and brown	2·40	2·40
79	-	6p. green and blue	42·00	42·00

DESIGN: 25c., 1, 2, 6p. Airplane and camels.

8 Boy carrying Lamb

1950. Child Welfare.

80	**8**	50c.+10c. brown	35	35
81	**8**	1p.+25c. red	16·00	16·00
82	**8**	6p.50+1p.65 green	8·50	8·50

9 Diego de Herrera

1950. Air. Colonial Stamp Day.

83	**9**	5p. violet	4·50	4·50

9a Woman and Dove

1951. Air. 500th Birth Anniv of Isabella the Catholic.

84	**9a**	5p. green	37·00	18·00

9b General Franco

1951. Visit of General Franco.

85	**9b**	50c. orange	60	60
86	**9b**	1p. brown	75	75
87	**9b**	5p. turquoise	48·00	48·00

10 Dromedary and Calf

1951. Colonial Stamp Day.

88	10	5c.+5c. brown	55	55
89	10	10c.+5c. orange	60	60
90	10	60c.+15c. olive	1·20	1·20

11 Native Woman

1952. Child Welfare Fund.

91	11	5c.+5c. brown	65	65
92	11	50c.+10c. black	65	65
93	11	2p.+30c. blue	3·75	3·75

12 Morion, Sword and Banner

1952. Air. 500th Birth Anniv of Ferdinand the Catholic.

94	12	5p. brown	38·00	14·00

13 Head of Ostritch

1952. Colonial Stamp Day.

95	13	5c.+5c. brown	55	55
96	13	10c.+5c. red	60	60
97	13	60c.+15c. green	1·90	1·90

14 "Geography"

1953. 75th Anniv of Royal Geographical Society.

98	14	5c. red	55	55
99	14	35c. green	55	55
100	14	60c. brown	65	65

15 Woman Musician

1953. Child Welfare Fund. Inscr "PRO INFANCIA 1953".

101	15	5c.+5c. brown	55	55
102	-	10c.+5c. purple	55	55
103	15	15c. olive	55	55
104	-	60c. brown	65	65

DESIGN: 10, 60c. Native man musician.

16 Red Scorpionfish

1953. Colonial Stamp Day. Inscr "DIA DEL SELLO COLONIAL 1953".

105	16	5c.+5c. violet	55	55
106	-	10c.+5c. green	55	55
107	16	15c. olive	55	55
108	-	60c. orange	65	65

DESIGN—HORIZ: 10, 60c. Zebra seabreams.

17 Hurdlers

1954. Child Welfare Fund. Inscr "PRO INFANCIA 1954".

109	17	5c.+5c. brown	55	55
110	-	10c.+5c. violet	55	55
111	17	15c. green	55	55
112	-	60c. brown	65	65

DESIGN—VERT: 10, 60c. Native runner.

18 Atlantic Flyingfish

1954. Colonial Stamp Day. Inscr "DIA DEL SELLO COLONIAL 1954".

113	18	5c.+5c. red	55	55
114	-	10c.+5c. purple	55	55
115	18	15c. green	55	55
116	-	60c. brown	65	65

DESIGN—HORIZ: 10, 60c. Gilthead seabream.

19 F. Bonelli

1955. Birth Centenary of Bonelli (explorer).

117	19	10c.+5c. purple	55	55
118	-	25c.+10c. violet	55	55
119	19	50c. olive	65	65

DESIGN: 25c. Bonelli and felucca.

20 Scimitar Oryx

1955. Colonial Stamp Day. Inscr "DIA DEL SELLO COLONIAL 1955".

120	20	5c.+5c. brown	55	55
121	-	15c.+5c. bistre	55	55
122	20	70c. green	65	65

DESIGN: 15c. Scimitar oryx's head.

21 "Antirrhinum ramosissimum"

1956. Child Welfare Fund. Inscr "PRO INFANCIA 1956".

123	21	5c.+5c. olive	55	55
124	-	15c.+5c. ochre	55	55
125	21	20c. turquoise	55	55
126	-	60c. brown	65	65

DESIGN: 15, 50c. "Sesuvium portulacastrum" (wrongly inscr "Sesiviun").

22 Arms of Aaiun and Native on Camel

1956. Colonial Stamp Day. Inscr "DIA DEL SELLO 1956".

127	22	5c.+5c. black and violet	55	55
128	-	15c.+5c. green and ochre	55	55
129	22	70c. brown and green	65	65

DESIGN—VERT: 15c. Arms of Villa Cisneros and native chief.

23 Dromedaries

1957. Animals.

130	23	5c. violet	35	35
131	-	15c. ochre	35	35
132	-	50c. brown	40	35
133	23	70c. green	1·10	40
134	-	80c. turquoise	1·10	40
135	-	1p.80 mauve	1·40	75

DESIGNS: 15, 80c. Ostrich; 50c., 1p.80, Dorcas gazelle.

24 Golden Eagle

1957. Child Welfare Fund. Inscr "PRO-INFANCIA 1957".

136	24	5c.+5c. brown	55	55
137	-	15c.+5c. bistre	55	55
138	24	70c. green	65	65

DESIGN: 15c. Tawny eagle in flight.

25 Head of Striped Hyena

1957. Colonial Stamp Day. Inscr "DIA DEL SELLO 1957".

139	25	10c.+5c. purple	55	55
140	-	15c.+5c. ochre	55	55
141	25	20c. green	55	55
142	-	70c. myrtle	65	65

DESIGN: 15, 70c. Striped hyena.

26 White Stork and Arms of Valencia and Aaiun

1958. Aid for Valencia.

143	26	10c.+5c. brown	55	55
144	26	15c.+10c. ochre	55	55
145	26	50c.+10c. brown	65	65

27 Cervantes

1958. Child Welfare Fund. Inscr "1958".

146	27	10c.+5c. brown & chest	55	55
147	-	15c.+5c. myrtle & orange	55	55
148	-	20c. green and brown	55	55
149	27	70c. blue and green	65	65

DESIGNS—VERT: 15c. Don Quixote and Sancho Panza on horseback. HORIZ: 20c. Don Quixote and the lion.

28 Hoopoe Lark

1958. Colonial Stamp Day. Inscr "1958".

150	28	10c.+5c. red	55	55
151	-	25c.+10c. violet	55	55
152	-	50c.+10c. olive	65	65

DESIGNS—HORIZ: 25c. Hoopoe lark feeding young. VERT: 50c. Fulvous babbler.

29 Lope de Vega (author)

1959. Child Welfare Fund. Inscr "PRO INFANCIA 1959".

153	29	10c.+5c. olive and brown	55	55
154	-	15c.+5c. brown and bistre		55	55
155	29	20c. sepia and green	55	55
156	29	70c. myrtle and green	65	65

DESIGNS—Characters from the comedy "The Star of Seville": 15c. Spanish lady; 20c. Caballero.

30 Grey Heron

1959. Birds.

157	30	25c. violet	30	20
158	-	50c. green	30	20
159	-	75c. sepia	30	20
160	30	1p. red	30	20
161	-	1p.50 green	40	20
162	-	2p. purple	95	20
163	30	3p. blue	1·00	25
164	-	5p. brown	1·90	30
165	-	10p. olive	11·50	5·00

DESIGNS: 50c., 1p.50, 5p. Northern sparrow hawk; 75c., 2, 10p. Herring gull.

31 Sahara Postman

1959. Colonial Stamp Day. Inscr "1959".

166	31	10c.+5c. brown and red	55	55
167	-	20c.+5c. brown and green	55	55
168	-	50c.+20c. slate and olive	65	65

DESIGNS: 20c. Postman tendering letters; 50c. Camel postman.

32 F. de Quevedo (writer)

1960. Child Welfare Fund. Inscr "PRO-INFANCIA 1960".

169	32	10c.+5c. purple	55	55
170	-	15c.+5c. bistre	55	55
171	-	35c. green	55	55
172	32	80c. turquoise	65	65

DESIGNS—VERT: (representing Quevedo's works): 15c. Winged railway wheel and hour-glass; 25c. Man in plumed hat wearing cloak and sword.

33 Leopard

1960. Stamp Day. Inscr "1960".

173	33	10c.+5c. mauve	55	55
174	-	20c.+5c. myrtle	55	55
175	-	30c.+10c. brown	55	55
176	-	50c.+20c. brown	65	65

DESIGNS: 20c. Fennec fox; 30c. Golden eagle defying leopard; 50c. Red fox.

34 Houbara
Bustard

1961

177	**34**	25c. violet	20	20
178	-	50c. brown	20	20
179	**34**	75c. dull purple	20	20
180	-	1p. red	20	20
181	**34**	1p.50 green	20	20
182	-	2p. mauve	80	25
183	**34**	3p. blue	1·00	35
184	-	5p. brown	1·20	40
185	**34**	10p. olive	3·50	1·90

DESIGN: 50c., 1, 2, 5p. Feral rock doves.

35 Cameleer
and Airplane

1961. Air.

186	**35**	25p. sepia	3·75	1·90

36 Dorcas
Gazelle

1961. Child Welfare. Inscr "PRO-INFANCIA 1961".

187	**36**	10c.+5c. red	55	55
188	-	25c.+10c. violet	55	55
189	**36**	80c.+20c. green	65	65

DESIGN: 25c. One dorcas gazelle.

37

1961. 25th Anniv of Gen. Franco as Head of State.

190	-	25c. grey	55	55
191	**37**	50c. olive	55	55
192	-	70c. green	55	55
193	**37**	1p. orange	65	65

DESIGNS—VERT: 25c. Map; 70c. Aaiun Chapel.

38 A. Fernandez
de Lugo

1961. Stamp Day. Inscr "DIA DEL SELLO 1961".

194	**38**	10c.+5c. salmon	55	55
195	-	25c.+10c. plum	55	55
196	**38**	30c.+10c. brown	55	55
197	-	1p.+10c. orange	65	65

PORTRAIT: 25c., 1p. D. de Herrera.

39 "Neurada
procumbres
linn"

1962. Flowers.

198	**39**	25c. violet	20	20
199	-	50c. sepia	20	20
200	-	70c. green	20	20

201	**39**	1p. orange	20	20
202	-	1p.50 turquoise	40	20
203	-	2p. purple	1·20	25
204	**39**	3p. blue	2·20	40
205	-	10p. olive	5·00	1·90

FLOWERS: 50c., 1p.50, 10p. "Anabasis articulata moq"; 70c., 2p. "Euphorbia resinifera".

40 Hoefler's
Butterflyfish

1962. Child Welfare.

206	**40**	25c. violet	55	55
207	-	50c. green	55	55
208	**40**	1p. brown	65	65

DESIGN—HORIZ: 50c. Dungat groupers.

41 Goats

1962. Stamp Day.

209	**41**	15c. green	55	55
210	-	35c. purple	55	55
211	**41**	1p. brown	65	65

DESIGN: 35c. Sheep.

42 Seville
Cathedral

1963. Seville Flood Relief.

212	**42**	50c. olive	55	55
213	**42**	1p. brown	65	65

43 Cameleer
and Camel

1963. Child Welfare. Inscr "PRO-INFANCIA 1963".

214	-	25c. violet	55	55
215	**43**	50c. grey	55	55
216	-	1p. red	65	65

DESIGN: 25c., 1p. Three camels.

44 Dove in
Hands

1963. "For Barcelona".

217	**44**	50c. turquoise	55	55
218	**44**	1p. brown	65	65

45 John Dory

1964. Stamp Day. Inscr "DIA DEL SELLO 1963".

219	**45**	25c. violet	55	55
220	-	50c. olive	55	55
221	**45**	1p. brown	65	65

FISH—VERT: 50c. Plain bonito.

46 Striped Hawk Moth

1964. Child Welfare.

222	**46**	25c. violet	55	55
223	-	50c. olive	55	55
224	**46**	1p. red	65	65

DESIGN—VERT: 50c. Goat moths.

47 Mounted
Dromedary and
Microphone

1964

225	**47**	25c. purple	30	30
226	-	50c. olive	30	30
227	-	70c. green	30	30
228	**47**	1p. purple	30	30
229	-	1p.50 turquoise	30	30
230	-	2p. turquoise	30	30
231	-	3p. blue	30	30
232	-	10p. lake	1·80	95

DESIGNS: 50c., 1p.50, 3p. Flute-player; 70c., 2, 10p. Women drummer.

48 Barbary Ground Squirrel

1964. Stamp Day.

233	-	50c. olive	55	55
234	**48**	1p. lake	55	55
235	-	1p.50 green	65	65

DESIGN—VERT: 50c., 1p.50, Eurasian red squirrel eating.

49 Doctor tending Patient,
and Hospital

1965. 25th Anniv of End of Spanish Civil War.

236	-	50c. olive	55	55
237	**49**	1p. red	55	55
238	-	1p.50 blue	65	65

DESIGNS—VERT: 50c. Saharan woman; 1p.50, Desert installation and cameleer.

50 "Anthia sexmaculata"
(ground beetle)

1965. Child Welfare. Insects.

239	**50**	50c. blue	55	55
240	-	1p. green	55	55
241	**50**	1p.50 brown	55	55
242	-	3p. blue	65	65

INSECTS—VERT: 1, 3p. "Blepharopsis mendica" (praying mantis).

51 Handball

1965. Stamp Day.

243	**51**	50c. red	55	55
244	-	1p. green	55	55
245	**51**	1p.50 blue	65	65

DESIGN: 1p. Arms of Spanish Sahara.

52 Bows of "Rio de Oro"

1966. Child Welfare.

246	**52**	50c. olive	55	55
247	**52**	1p. brown	55	55
248	-	1p.50 green	65	65

DESIGN: 1p.50, Freighter "Fuerta Ventura".

53 Big-eyed Tuna

1966. Stamp Day.

249	**53**	10c. blue and yellow	55	55
250	-	40c. grey and salmon	55	55
251	**53**	1p.50 brown and green	55	55
252	-	4p. purple and green	65	65

DESIGN—VERT: 40c., 4p. Ocean sunfish.

54 Fig

1967. Child Welfare.

253	**54**	10c. yellow and blue	55	55
254	-	40c. purple and green	55	55
255	**54**	1p.50 yellow and green	55	55
256	-	4p. orange and blue	65	65

DESIGN: 40c., 4p. Lupin.

55 Quay, Aaiun

1967. Inauguration of Sahara Ports.

257	**55**	1p.50 brown and blue	55	55
258	-	4p. ochre and blue	85	85

DESIGN: 4p. Port of Villa Cisneros.

56 Ruddy Shelduck

1968. Stamp Day.

259	**56**	1p. brown and green	55	55
260	-	1p.50 mauve and black	55	55
261	-	3p.50 lake and brown	65	65

DESIGNS—VERT: 1p.50, Greater flamingo. HORIZ: 3p.50, Rufous scrub robin.

56a Scorpio (scorpion)

1968. Child Welfare. Signs of the Zodiac.

262	**56a**	1p. mauve on yellow	55	55
263	-	1p.50 brown on pink	55	55
264	-	2p.50 violet on yellow	65	65

DESIGNS: 1p.50, Capricorn (goat); 2p.50, Virgo (virgin).

57 Dove, and
Stamp within
Posthorn

1968. Stamp Day.

265	**57**	1p. blue and purple	55	55
266	-	1p.50 green and light green	55	55
267	-	2p.50 blue and orange	65	65

DESIGNS: 1p.50, Postal handstamp, stamps and letter; 2p.50, Saharan postman.

58 Head of Dorcas Gazelle

1969. Child Welfare.

268	**58**	1p. brown and black	45	45

269	-	1p.50 brown and black	45	45
270	-	2p.50 brown and black	70	70
271	-	6p. brown and black	1·20	1·20

DESIGNS: 1p.50, Dorcas gazelle tending young; 2p.50, Dorcas gazelle and camel; 6p. Dorcas gazelle leaping.

59 Woman beating Drum

1960. Stamp Day.

272	**59**	50c. brown and bistre	40	40
273	-	1p.50 turquoise and green	45	45
274	-	2p. blue and brown	55	55
275	-	25p. brown and green	2·40	2·40

DESIGNS—VERT: 1p.50, Man playing flute. HORIZ: 2p. Drum and mounted cameleer; 25p. Flute.

1970. Child Welfare. As T **58**.

276	-	50c. ochre and blue	45	45
277	-	2p. brown and blue	50	50
278	-	2p.50 ochre and blue	65	65
279	-	6p. ochre and blue	1·20	1·20

DESIGNS: 50c. Fennec fox; 2p. Fennec fox walking; 2p.50, Head of fennec fox; 6p. Fennec fox family.

60 "Grammodes boisdeffrei" (moth)

1970. Stamp Day. Butterflies. Multicoloured.

280	50c. Type **60**	45	45
281	1p. Type **60**	50	50
282	2p. African monarch	55	55
283	5p. As 2p.	80	80
284	8p. Spurge hawk moth	1·50	1·50

61 Dorcas Gazelle and Arms of El Aaiun

1971. Child Welfare.

285	**61**	1p. multicoloured	45	45
286	-	2p. green and olive	55	55
287	-	5p. blue, brown and grey	65	65
288	-	25p. green, grey and blue	2·20	2·20

DESIGNS—VERT: 25p. Smara Mosque. HORIZ: 2p. Tourist inn, Aaiun; 5p. Assembly House, Aaiun.

63 Trumpeter Finch

1971. Stamp Day. Multicoloured.

290	1p.50 Type **63**	45	45
291	2p. Type **63**	45	45
292	5p. Cream-coloured courser	85	85
293	24p. Lanner falcon	2·50	2·50

64 Seated Woman

1972. Saharan Nomads.

| 294 | **64** | 1p. black, pink and blue | 35 | 30 |

295	-	1p.50 slate, lilac and brown	35	30
296	-	2p. black, flesh and green	35	30
297	**64**	5p. purple, olive and green	35	30
298	-	8p. violet, green and black	70	30
299	-	10p. green, grey and black	70	30
300	-	12p. multicoloured	70	55
301	-	15p. multicoloured	80	55
302	-	24p. multicoloured	1·90	1·40

DESIGNS: 1p.50, 2p. Squatting nomad; 8, 10p. Head of nomad; 12p. Woman with bangles; 15p. Nomad with rifle; 24p. Woman displaying trinkets.

65 Tuareg Woman

1972. Child Welfare. Multicoloured.

| 303 | 8p. Type **65** | 1·00 | 1·00 |
| 304 | 12p. Tuareg elder | 1·20 | 1·20 |

66 Mother and Child

1972. Stamp Day. Multicoloured.

| 305 | 4p. Type **66** | 80 | 80 |
| 306 | 15p. Nomad | 1·30 | 1·30 |

67 Sahara Desert

1973. Child Welfare. Multicoloured.

| 307 | 2p. Type **67** | 70 | 70 |
| 308 | 7p. City Gate, El Aaiun | 1·20 | 1·20 |

68 Villa Cisneros

1973. Stamp Day. Multicoloured.

| 309 | 2p. Type **68** | 70 | 70 |
| 310 | 7p. Tuareg (vert) | 1·20 | 1·20 |

69 U.P.U. Monument, Berne

1974. Centenary of Universal Postal Union.

| 311 | **69** | 15p. multicoloured | 1·70 | 1·70 |

70 Archway, Smara Mosque

1974. Child Welfare. Multicoloured.

| 312 | 1p. Type **70** | 55 | 55 |
| 313 | 2p. Villa Cisneros Mosque | 85 | 85 |

71 Desert Eagle Owl

1974. Stamp Day. Multicoloured.

| 314 | 2p. Type **71** | 55 | 55 |
| 315 | 5p. Lappet-faced vulture | 85 | 85 |

72 "Espana" Emblem and Spanish Sahara Stamp

1975. "Espana 75" International Stamp Exhibition, Madrid.

| 316 | **72** | 8p. yellow, blue and black | 1·20 | 1·20 |

73 Desert Conference

1975. Child Welfare. Multicoloured.

| 317 | 1p.50 Type **73** | 55 | 55 |
| 318 | 3p. Desert oasis | 85 | 85 |

74 Tuareg Elder

1975

| 319 | **74** | 3p. purple, green and black | 70 | 70 |

EXPRESS LETTER STAMPS

1943. Design as No. 63, inscr "URGENTE".

| E80 | 25c. red and myrtle | 1·40 | 1·40 |

E62 Despatch-rider

1971

| E289 | **E62** | 10p. brown and red | 1·70 | 1·70 |

Pt. 9

SPANISH WEST AFRICA

Issues for use in Ifni and Spanish Sahara.

100 centimos = 1 peseta.

1 Native

1949. 75th Anniv of U.P.U.

| 1 | 1 | 4p. green | 3·75 | 3·75 |

2 Isabella the Catholic

1949. Air. Colonial Stamp Day.

| 2 | **2** | 5p. brown | 3·00 | 3·00 |

3 Tents

1950

3	**3**	2c. brown	20	20
4	-	5c. violet	20	20
5	-	10c. blue	20	20
6	-	15c. black	20	20
7	**3**	25c. brown	20	20
8	-	30c. yellow	20	20
9	-	40c. olive	20	20
10	-	45c. red	20	20
11	**3**	50c. orange	20	20
12	-	75c. blue	25	20
13	-	90c. green	25	20
14	-	1p. grey	25	20
15	**3**	1p.35 violet	70	55
16	-	2p. sepia	1·40	1·20
17	-	5p. mauve	21·00	4·75
18	-	10p. brown	45·00	30·00

DESIGNS: 5, 30, 75c., 2p. Palm trees, Lake Tinzgarrentz; 10, 40, 90c., 5p. Camels and irrigation; 15, 45c., 1p. Camel transport.

8 Camel Train

1951. Air.

19	-	25c. yellow	20	20
20	**8**	50c. mauve	20	20
21	-	1p. green	30	20
22	-	2p. blue	75	25
23	**8**	3p.25 violet	1·70	1·70
24	-	5p. sepia	22·00	5·75
25	-	10p. red	46·00	31·00

DESIGNS: 25c., 2, 10p. Desert camp; 1, 5p. Four camels.

EXPRESS LETTER STAMPS

E10 Port Tilimenzo

1951

| E26 | **E10** | 25c. red | 40 | 40 |

Pt. 1

SRI LANKA

Ceylon became a republic within the British Commonwealth on 22 May 1972 and changed its name to Sri Lanka (= "Resplendent Island").

100 cents = 1 rupee.

208 National Flower and Mountain of the Illustrious Foot

1972. Inaug of Republic of Sri Lanka.

| 591 | **208** | 15c. multicoloured | 30 | 30 |

209 Map of World with Buddhist Flag

1972. Tenth World Fellowship of Buddhists Conf.

| 592 | **209** | 5c. multicoloured | 30 | 60 |

210 Book Year Emblem

1972. International Book Year.
593 210 20c. orange and brown   20   50

211 Emperor Angelfish

1972. Fish. Multicoloured.
594   2c. Type **211**   10   1·25
595   5c. Green chromide   10   1·25
596   30c. Skipjack tuna   1·25   30
597   2r. Black ruby barb   3·50 5·25

212 Memorial Hall

1973. Opening of Bandaranaike Memorial Hall.
598 212 15c. cobalt and blue   30   30

213 King Vessantara giving
away his Children

1973. Rock and Temple Paintings. Multicoloured.
599   35c. Type **213**   35   10
600   50c. The Prince and the grave-
           digger   40   10
601   90c. Bearded old man   60   85
602   1r.55 Two female figures   70   2·00
MS603 115×141 mm. Nos. 599/602   3·25 3·50

214 Bandaranaike
Memorial Conference
Hall

1974. 20th Commonwealth Parliamentary Conf, Colombo.
604 214 85c. multicoloured   30   30

215 Prime
Minster
Bandaranaike

1974
605 215 15c. multicoloured   15   10

216 "U.P.U." and "100"

1974. Centenary of U.P.U.
606 216 50c. multicoloured   1·00   75

217 Sri Lanka
Parliament Building

1975. Inter-Parliamentary Meeting.
607 217 1r. multicoloured   30   50

218 Sir
Ponnambalam
Ramanathan
(politician)

1975. Ramanathan Commemoration.
608 218 75c. multicoloured   30   80

219 D. J.
Wimalasurendra
(engineer)

1975. Wimalasurendra Commemoration.
609 219 75c. black and blue   30   80

220 Mrs.
Bandaranaike, Map
and Dove

1975. International Women's Year.
610 220 1r.15 multicoloured   2·25 1·25

221 Ma-ratmal

1976. Indigenous Flora. Multicoloured.
611   25c. Type **221**   10   10
612   50c. Binara   10   10
613   75c. Daffodil orchid   15   15
614   10r. Diyapara   3·00   4·50
MS615 153×153 mm. Nos. 611/14   12·00 16·00

222 Mahaweli Dam

1976. Mahaweli River Diversion.
616 222   85c. turquoise, bl &
             azure   30   1·25

223 Dish Aerial

1976. Opening of Satellite Earth Station, Padukka.
617 223 1r. multicoloured   65   1·25

224 Conception of the Buddha

1976. Vesak. Multicoloured.
618   5c. Type **224**   10   90
619   10c. King Suddhodana and the
           astrologers   10   90
620   1r.50 The astrologers being
           entertained   90   95
621   2r. The Queen in a palanquin 1·00   95
622   2r.25 Royal procession   1·10 1·90
623   5r. Birth of the Buddha   1·60 3·25
MS624 161×95 mm. Nos 618/23   9·50 13·00
Nos. 618/23 show paintings from the Dambava Temple.

225 Blue Sapphire

1976. Gems of Sri Lanka. Multicoloured.
625   60c. Type **225**   4·75   30
626   1r.15 Cat's eye   7·50   1·50
627   2r. Star sapphire   9·00   3·25
628   5r. Ruby   11·00 11·00
MS629 152×152 mm. Nos. 625/8   42·00 27·00

226 Prime Minister
Mrs. S.
Bandaranaike

1976. Non-aligned Summit Conf, Colombo.
630 226 1r.15 multicoloured   25   50
631 226 2r. multicoloured   40   1·00

227 Statue of
Liberty

1976. Bicent of American Revolution.
632 227 2r.25 blue and indigo   65   1·50

228 Bell, Early
Telephone and
Telephone Lines

1976. Centenary of Telephone.
633 228 1r. multicoloured   60   20

229 Maitreya
(pre-carnate
Buddha)

1976. Centenary of Colombo Museum. Multicoloured.
634   50c. Type **229**   25   15
635   1r. Sundara Murti Swami (Tamil
           psalmist)   30   30
636   5r. Tara (goddess)   2·25 4·50

230 Kandyan Crown

1977. Regalia of the Kings of Kandy. Multicoloured.
637   1r. Type **230**   50   40
638   2r. Throne and footstool   1·10 3·25

231 Sri Rahula
Thero (poet)

1977. Sri Rahula Commemoration.
639 231 1r. multicoloured   75   1·00

232 Sir
Ponnambalam
Arunachalam

1977. Sir Ponnambalam Arunachalam (social reformer)
Commemoration.
640 232 1r. multicoloured   50   1·00

233 Brass Lamps

1977. Handicrafts. Multicoloured.
641   20c. Type **233**   20   15
642   25c. Jewellery box   20   15
643   50c. Caparisoned elephant   45   20
644   5r. Mask   1·60 3·25
MS645 205×89 mm. Nos. 641/4   3·75   4·50

234 Siddi Lebbe
(author and
educationist)

1977. Siddi Lebbe Commemoration.
646 234 1r. multicoloured   30   1·00

235 Girl Guide

1977. 60th Anniv of Sri Lanka Girl Guides Association.
647 235 75c. multicoloured   85   30

236 Parliament
Building and "Wheel
of Life"

1978. Election of New President.
648 236 15c. gold, green &
           emerald   20   10
For similar design in a smaller format, see Nos. 680/c.

237 Youths
Running

1978. National Youth Service Council.
649 237 15c. multicoloured   30   70

238 Prince Siddhartha's
Renunciation

1978. Vesak. Rock Carvings from Borobudur Temple.
650 238 15c. buff, brown and
           blue   75   30
651   -   50c. buff, brown and
           blue   1·00 1·50
DESIGN: 50c. Prince Siddhartha shaving his hair.

1978. Surch.
652   5c. on 90c. Bearded old man
           (No. 601)   2·00 4·00
653   10c. on 35c. Type **213**   50   50
654   25c. on 15c. Type **215**   4·25 4·25

655	25c. on 15c. Type **236**		4·25	4·25
656	25c. on 15c. Type **237**		4·25	4·25
657	1r. on 1r.55 Two female figures (No. 602)		1·25	45

240 Veera Puran Appu

1978. 130th Death Anniv of Veera Puran Appu (revolutionary).

658	**240**	15c. multicoloured	20	35

241 "Troides helena"

1978. Butterflies. Multicoloured.

659	25c. Type **241**		55	10
660	50c. "Cethosia nietneri"		1·00	10
661	5r. "Kallima horsfieldi"		1·75	1·25
662	10r. "Papilio polymnestor"		1·75	2·50
MS663	203×147 mm. Nos. 659/62		11·00	7·00

1979. No. 486 of Ceylon surch **SRI LANKA 15**.

664	15c. on 10c. green		2·75	1·75

243 Prince Danta and Princess Hema Mala bringing the Sacred Tooth Relic from Kalinga

1979. Vesak. Kelaniya Temple Paintings. Multicoloured.

665	25c. Type **243**		10	10
666	1r. Theri Sanghamitta bringing the Bodhi Tree branch to Sri Lanka		15	15
667	10r. King Kirti Sri Rajasinghe offering fan of authority to the Sangha Raja		1·50	2·75
MS668	120×80 mm. Nos. 665/7		2·75	3·75

244 Piyadasa Sirisena

1979. Piyadasa Sirisena (writer) Commem.

669	**244**	1r.25 multicoloured	40	40

245 Wrestlers

1979. Wood Carvings from Embekke Temple.

670	**245**	20r. brown, ochre & green	1·00	1·25
671	-	50r. agate, yellow & green	1·50	2·75

DESIGN: 50r. Dancer.

246 Dudley Senanayake

1979. Dudley Senanayake (former Prime Minister) Commemoration.

672	**246**	1r.25 green	15	20

247 Mother with Child

1979. International Year of the Child. Multicoloured.

673	5c. Type **247**		10	10
674	3r. Superimposed heads of children of different races		40	1·10
675	5r. Children playing		50	1·40

248 Ceylon 1857 6d. Stamp and Sir Rowland Hill

1979. Death Centenary of Sir Rowland Hill.

676	**248**	3r. multicoloured	30	1·25

249 Conference Emblem and Parliament Building

1979. International Conference of Parliamentarians on Population and Development, Colombo.

677	**249**	2r. multicoloured	70	1·50

250 Airline Emblem on Aircraft Tail-fin

1979. Inauguration of "Airlanka" Airline.

678	**250**	3r. black, blue and red	1·00	1·75

251 Coconut Tree

1979. Tenth Anniv of Asian and Pacific Coconut Community.

679	**251**	2r. multicoloured	1·25	1·75

1979. As No. 648, but 20×24 mm.

680	**236**	25c. gold, green and emerald	30	20
680d	**236**	50c. gold, green and emerald	2·75	10
680b	**236**	60c. gold, green and emerald	11·00	1·75
680c	**236**	75c. gold, green and emerald	15	10

252 Swami Vipulananda

1979. Swami Vipulananda (philosopher) Commem.

681	**252**	1r.25 multicoloured	30	60

253 Inscription and Crescent

1979. 1500th Anniv of Hegira (Mohammedan religion).

682	**253**	3r.75 black, deep green and green	35	2·00

254 "The Great Teacher" (Institute emblem)

1979. 50th Anniv of Institute of Ayurveda (school of medicine).

683	**254**	15c. multicoloured	30	70

255 Ceylon Blue Magpie

1979. Birds (1st series). Multicoloured.

684	10c. Type **255**		10	1·25
685	15c. Ceylon hanging parrot		1·00	10
686	75c. Ceylon whistling thrush		15	15
687	1r. Ceylon spurfowl		15	15
688	5r. Yellow-fronted barbet		75	1·75
689	10r. Yellow-tufted bulbul		75	1·75
MS690	151×151 mm. Nos. 684/9		5·50	7·00

See also Nos. 827/30, 985/8 and 1242/5.

256 Rotary International Emblem and Map of Sri Lanka

1980. 75th Anniv of Rotary International and 50th Anniv of Sri Lanka Rotary Movement.

691	**256**	1r.50 multicoloured	70	2·00

257 A. Ratnayake

1980. 80th Birth Anniv of A. Ratnayake (politician).

692	**257**	1r.25 green	20	30

1980. No. 680 surch **.35**.

693	**236**	35c. on 25c. gold, green and emerald	15	15

259 Tank and Stupa (symbols of Buddhist culture)

1980. 60th Anniv of All Ceylon Buddhist Congress. Multicoloured.

694	10c. Type **259**		25	1·50
695	35c. Bo-leaf wheel and fan		25	20

260 Colonel Olcott

1980. Centenary of Arrival of Colonel Olcott (campaigner for Buddhism).

696	**260**	2r. multicoloured	1·00	1·75

261 Patachara's Journey through Forest

1980. Vesak. Details from Temple Paintings, Purvaramaya, Kataluwa. Multicoloured.

697	35c. Type **261**		30	15
698	1r.60 Patachara crossing river		1·25	2·50

262 George E. de Silva

1980. George E. de Silva (politician) Commem.

699	**262**	1r.60 multicoloured	30	60

263 Dalada Maligawa

1980. UNESCO—Sri Lanka Cultural Triangle Project.

700	**263**	35c. claret	15	40
701	-	35c. grey	15	40
702	-	35c. red	15	40
703	-	1r.60 olive	45	1·10
704	-	1r.60 green	45	1·10
705	-	1r.60 brown	45	1·10
MS706	215×115 mm. Nos. 700/5		1·60	4·00

DESIGNS: No. 701, Dambulla; 702, Alahana Pirivena; 703, Jetavanarama; 704, Abhayagiri; 705, Sigiri.

264 Co-operation Symbols

1980. 50th Anniv of Co-operative Department.

707	**264**	20c. multicoloured	10	30

265 Lanka Mahila Samiti Emblem

1980. 50th Anniv of Lanka Mahila Samiti (Rural Women's Movement).

708	**265**	35c. violet, red and yellow	15	65

266 The Holy Family

1980. Christmas. Multicoloured.

709	35c. Type **266**		10	10
710	3r.75 The Three Wise Men		60	1·75
MS711	125×75 mm. Nos. 709/10		1·25	2·00

267 Colombo Public Library

1980. Opening of Colombo Public Library.

712	**267**	35c. multicoloured	10	10

268 Flag of Walapane Disawa

1980. Ancient Flags.

713	**268**	10c. black, green & purple	10	10
714	-	25c. black, yellow & purple	10	10
715	-	1r.60 black, yellow & purple	15	20

| 716 | - | 20r. black, yellow & purple | 85 | 2·50 |

MS717 215×140 mm. Nos. 713/16   1·50   3·00

DESIGNS: 25c. Flag of the Gajanayaka Huduhumpola, Kandy; 1r.60, Sinhala royal flag; 20r. Sinhala royal flag, Ratnapura.

No. **MS**717 was re-issued at a premium over face value on 22 November 2010 surch **National Stamp Fair, Colombo – 2010 Day 3 22-11-2010 Rs. 600.00**

269 Fishing Cat

1981. Animals. Multicoloured.

718		2r.50 on 1r.60 Type **269**	25	15
719		3r. on 1r.50 Golden palm civet	25	20
720		4r. on 2r. Indian-spotted chevrotain	25	30
721		5r. on 3r.75 Rusty-spotted cat	35	45
MS722 165×89 mm. Nos. 718/21			1·00	2·50

Nos. 718/21 are previously unissued stamps surcharged as in T **269**.

For stamps with revised face values see Nos. 780/3.

270 Heads and Houses on Map of Sri Lanka

1981. Population and Housing Census.

| 723 | **270** | 50c. multicoloured | 75 | 1·50 |

271 Sri Lanka Light Infantry Regimental Badge

1981. Centenary of Sri Lanka Light Infantry.

| 724 | **271** | 2r. multicoloured | 1·00 | 1·50 |

272 Panel from "The Great Stupa" in Honour of the Buddha, Sanci, India, 1st-century A.D.

1981. Vesak.

725	**272**	35c. black, dp green & green	10	10
726	-	50c. multicoloured	10	10
727	-	7r. black and pink	2·00	4·50
MS728 147×108 mm. Nos. 725/7			3·50	5·00

DESIGNS: 50c. Silk banner representing a Bodhisattva from "Thousand Buddhas", Tun-Huang, Central Asia; 7r. Bodhisattva from Fondukistan, Afghanistan.

273 St. John Baptist de la Salle

1981. 300th Anniv of De La Salle Brothers (Religious Order of the Brothers of the Christian Schools).

| 729 | **273** | 2r. pink, light blue & blue | 1·50 | 2·25 |

274 Rev. Polwatte Sri Buddadatta

1981. National Heroes.

730	**274**	50c. brown	60	1·25
731	-	50c. pink	60	1·25
732	-	50c. mauve	60	1·25

DESIGNS: No. 731, Rev. Mohottiwatte Gunananda; 732, Dr. Gnanaprakasar (each a scholar, writer and Buddhist campaigner).

275 Dr. Al-Haj T. B. Jayah

1981. Dr. Al-Haj T. B. Jayah (statesman) Commemoration.

| 733 | **275** | 50c. green | 70 | 1·25 |

276 Dr. N. M. Perera

1981. Dr. N. M. Perera (campaigner for social reform) Commemoration.

| 734 | **276** | 50c. red | 1·00 | 1·50 |

277 Stylized Disabled Person and Globe

1981. International Year for Disabled Persons.

| 735 | **277** | 2r. red, black and grey | 1·10 | 2·00 |

278 Hand placing Vote into Ballot Box

1981. 50th Anniv of Universal Franchise. Multicoloured.

| 736 | | 50c. Type **278** | 25 | 15 |
| 737 | | 7r. Ballot box and people forming map of Sri Lanka (vert) | 1·75 | 3·25 |

279 T. W. Rhys Davids (founder)

1981. Centenary of Pali Text Society.

| 738 | **279** | 35c. stone, dp brown & brown | 70 | 65 |

280 Federation Emblem and "25"

1981. 25th Anniv of All-Ceylon Buddhist Students' Federation.

| 739 | **280** | 2r. black, yellow and red | 1·00 | 1·50 |

281 "Plan for Happiness"

1981. Population and Family Planning.

| 740 | **281** | 50c. multicoloured | 1·25 | 1·75 |

282 Dove Symbol with Acupuncture Needle and "Yin-Yang" (Chinese universe duality emblem)

1981. World Acupuncture Congress.

| 741 | **282** | 2r. black, yellow & orange | 2·75 | 3·75 |

283 Union and Sri Lanka Flags

1981. Royal Visit.

/42	**283**	50c. multicoloured	50	25
743	**283**	5r. multicoloured	1·75	4·00
MS744 165×90 mm. Nos. 742/3			2·25	4·00

284 "Conserve our Forests"

1981. Forest Conservation.

745	**284**	35c. multicoloured	15	10
746	-	50c. brown and stone	20	20
747	-	5r. multicoloured	1·90	3·75
MS748 180×90 mm. Nos. 745/7			1·50	3·75

DESIGNS: 50c. "Plant a tree"; 5r. Jak (tree).

285 Sir James Peiris

1981. Birth Centenary of Sir James Peiris (politician).

| 749 | **285** | 50c. brown | 60 | 1·00 |

286 F. R. Senanayaka

1982. Birth Centenary of F. R. Senanayaka (national hero).

| 750 | **286** | 50c. brown | 1·00 | 1·25 |

287 Philip Gunawardhane

1982. Tenth Death Anniv of Philip Gunawardhane (politician).

| 751 | **287** | 50c. red | 70 | 1·25 |

288 Department of Inland Revenue Building, Colombo

1982. 50th Anniv of Department of Inland Revenue.

| 752 | **288** | 50c. black, blue & orange | 70 | 1·25 |

289 Rupavahini Emblem

1982. Inauguration of Rupavahini (national television service).

| 753 | **289** | 2r.50 yellow, brn & grey | 2·25 | 3·75 |

290 Cricketer and Ball

1982. First Sri Lanka–England Test Match, Colombo.

| 754 | **290** | 2r.50 multicoloured | 4·50 | 5·50 |

291 "Obsbeckia wightiana"

1982. Flowers. Multicoloured.

755		35c. Type **291**	10	10
756		2r. "Mesua nagassarium"	20	20
757		7r. "Rhodomyrtus tomentosa"	50	1·25
758		20r. "Phaius tancarvilleae"	1·40	4·50
MS759 180×110 mm. Nos. 755/8			6·00	7·50

No. **MS**759 was re-issued at a premium over face value on 24 November 2010 surch **National Stamp Fair, Colombo – 2010 Day 5 24-11-2010 Rs. 750.00**

292 Mother breast- feeding Child

1982. Food and Nutrition Policy Planning.

| 760 | **292** | 50c. multicoloured | 1·50 | 1·75 |

293 Conference Emblem

1982. World Hindu Conference.

| 761 | **293** | 50c. multicoloured | 1·00 | 1·50 |

294 King Vessantara giving away Magical, Rain-making White Elephant

1982. Vesak. Legend of Vessantara Jataka. Details of Cloth Painting from Arattana Rajamaha Vihara (temple), Hanguranketa, District of Nuwara Eliya. Multicoloured.

762		35c. Type **294**	45	10
763		50c. King Vessantara with family in Vankagiri Forest	55	15
764		2r.50 Vessantara giving away his children as slaves	2·00	2·25
765		5r. Vessantara and family returning to Jetuttara in royal chariot	2·75	3·50
MS766 160×115 mm. Nos. 762/5			7·00	7·00

295 Parliament Buildings, Sri Jayawardanapura

1982. Opening of Parliament Building Complex, Sri Jayawardanapura, Kotte.

| 767 | **295** | 50c. multicoloured | 1·00 | 1·50 |

296 Dr. C. W. W. Kannangara

1982. Dr. C. W. W. Kannangara ("Father of Free Education") Commemoration.

| 768 | **296** | 50c. green | 1·00 | 1·50 |

297 Lord Baden-Powell

1982. 125th Birth Anniv of Lord Baden-Powell.

| 769 | **297** | 50c. multicoloured | 1·75 | 1·75 |

298 Dr. G. P. Malalasekara

1982. Dr. G. P. Malalasekara (founder of World Fellowship of Buddhists) Commemoration.

| 770 | **298** | 50c. green | 1·00 | 1·50 |

299 Wheel encircling Globe

1982. World Buddhist Leaders Conference.

| 771 | **299** | 50c. multicoloured | 1·00 | 1·50 |

300 Wildlife

1982. World Environment Day.

| 772 | **300** | 50c. multicoloured | 1·90 | 1·75 |

301 Sir Waitialingam Duraiswamy

1982. Sir Waitialingam Duraiswamy (statesman and educationalist) Commemoration.

| 773 | **301** | 50c. deep brown and brown | 1·00 | 1·50 |

302 Y.M.C.A. Emblem

1982. Centenary of Colombo Y.M.C.A.

| 774 | **302** | 2r.50 multicoloured | 3·00 | 4·50 |

303 Rev. Weliwita Sri Saranankara Sangharaja

1982. Rev. Weliwita Sri Saranankara Sangharaja (Buddhist leader) Commemoration.

| 775 | **303** | 50c. brown and orange | 1·00 | 1·50 |

304 Maharagama Sasana Sevaka Samithiya Emblem

1982. 25th Anniv of Maharagama Sasana Sevaka Samithiya (Buddhist Social Reform Movement).

| 776 | **304** | 50c. multicoloured | 1·40 | 1·75 |

305 Dr. Robert Koch

1982. Centenary of Robert Koch's Discovery of Tubercle Bacillus.

| 777 | **305** | 50c. multicoloured | 2·00 | 1·75 |

306 Sir John Kotelawala

1982. Second Death Anniv of Sir John Kotelawala.

| 778 | **306** | 50c. green | 1·00 | 1·50 |

307 Eye Donation Society and Lions Club Emblems

1982. World-Wide Sight Conservation Project.

| 779 | **307** | 2r.50 multicoloured | 3·00 | 4·75 |

1982. As Nos. 718/21 but without surcharges and showing revised face values.

780	2r.50 Type **269**	50	20
781	3r. Golden palm civet*	6·25	5·50
782	4r. Indian-spotted chevrotain	50	40
783	5r. Rusty-spotted cat	50	50
1081	3r. Golden palm civet*	2·25	30

*No. 781 has the face value and inscriptions in brown, No. 1081 in black.

308 1859 4d. Rose and 1948 15c. Independence Commemorative

1982. 125th Anniv of First Postage Stamps. Multicoloured.

784	50c. Type **308**	50	50
785	2r.50 1859 1s.9d. green and 1981 50c. "Just Society" stamp	1·75	3·25
MS786	59×84 mm. Nos. 784/5 (sold at 5r.)	2·00	3·25

No. **MS**786 was re-issued at a premium over face value on 20 November 2010 surch **National Stamp Fair, Colombo – 2010 Day 1 20-11-2010 Rs. 350.00**

309 Goonetilleke

1983. Fourth Death Anniv of Sir Oliver Goonetilleke (statesman).

| 787 | **309** | 50c. grey, brown and black | 60 | 1·50 |

310 Sarvodaya Emblem

1983. 25th Anniv of Sarvodaya Movement.

| 788 | **310** | 50c. multicoloured | 1·00 | 1·50 |

311 Morse Key, Radio Aerial and Amateur Radio Society Emblem

1983. Amateur Radio Society.

| 789 | **311** | 2r.50 multicoloured | 2·75 | 4·75 |

312 Customs Co-operation Council Emblem and Sri Lanka Flag

1983. 30th Anniv of International Customs Day.

| 790 | **312** | 50c. multicoloured | 50 | 40 |
| 791 | **312** | 5r. multicoloured | 3·00 | 6·00 |

313 Bottle-nosed Dolphin

1983. Marine Mammals.

792	**313**	50c. black, blue and green	50	20
793	-	2r. multicoloured	1·00	1·00
794	-	2r.50 black, blue and grey	2·50	2·50
795	-	10r. multicoloured	6·00	7·50

DESIGNS: 2r. Dugongs; 2r.50, Humpback whale; 10r. Sperm whale.

314 "Lanka Athula" (container ship)

1983. Ships of the Ceylon Shipping Corporation. Multicoloured.

796	50c. Type **314**	25	15
797	2r.50 Map of routes	90	70
798	5r. "Lanka Kalyani" (freighter)	1·25	1·60
799	20r. "Tammanna" (tanker)	2·00	7·00

315 Woman with I.W.D. Emblem and Sri Lanka Flag

1983. International Women's Day. Multicoloured.

| 800 | 50c. Type **315** | 20 | 25 |
| 801 | 5r. Woman, emblem, map and symbols of progress | 80 | 2·75 |

316 Waterfall

1983. Commonwealth Day. Multicoloured.

802	50c. Type **316**	10	10
803	2r.50 Tea plucking	15	25
804	5r. Harvesting rice	25	40
805	20r. Decorated elephants	80	2·00

317 Lions Club International Badge

1983. 25th Anniv of Lions Club International in Sri Lanka.

| 806 | **317** | 2r.50 multicoloured | 2·50 | 2·50 |

318 "The Dream of Queen Mahamaya"

1983. Vesak. Life of Prince Siddhartha at Gotami Vihara. Multicoloured.

807	35c. Type **318**	15	10
808	50c. "Prince Siddhartha given to Maha Brahma"	15	10
809	5r. "Prince Siddhartha and the Sleeping Dancers"	85	1·50
810	10r. "The Meeting with Mara"	1·40	3·50
MS811	150×90 mm. Nos. 807/10	2·25	4·50

319 First Telegraph Transmission, Colombo to Galle, 1858

1983. 125th Anniv of Telecommunications in Sri Lanka (2r.) and World Communications Year (10r.). Multicoloured.

| 812 | 2r. Type **319** | 65 | 60 |
| 813 | 10r. World Communications Year emblem | 2·50 | 5·00 |

320 Henry Woodward Amarasuriya (philanthropist)

1983. National Heroes.

814	**320**	50c. green	30	1·00
815	-	50c. blue	30	1·00
816	-	50c. mauve	30	1·00
817	-	50c. green	30	1·00

DESIGNS: No. 815, Father Simon Perera (historian); 816, Charles Lorenz (lawyer and newspaper editor); 817, Noordeen Abdul Cader (first President of All-Ceylon Muslim League).

321 Family and Village

1983. Gam Udawa (Village Re-awakening Movement). Multicoloured.

| 818 | 50c. Type **321** | 10 | 25 |
| 819 | 5r. Village view | 55 | 2·25 |

322 Caravan of Bulls

1983. Transport. Multicoloured.

820	35c. Type **322**	10	10
821	2r. Steam train	2·00	1·75
822	2r.50 Ox and cart	1·00	2·25
823	5r. Ford motor car	2·25	4·25

323 Sir Tikiri Banda
Panabokke

1983. 20th Death Anniv of Adigar Sir Tikiri Banda Panabokke.

824	**323**	50c. red	1·00	1·50

324 C. W.
Thamotheram Pillai

1983. C. W. Thamotheram Pillai (Tamil scholar) Commemoration.

825	**324**	50c. brown	1·00	1·50

325 Arabi Pasha

1983. Centenary of Banishment of Arabi Pasha (Egyptian nationalist).

826	**325**	50c. green	1·00	1·50

326 Sri Lanka Wood
Pigeon

1983. Birds (2nd series). Multicoloured.

827	25c. Type **326**	1·00	1·75
828	35c. Large Sri Lanka white-eye	1·00	1·00
829	2r. Sri Lanka dusky blue flycatcher	1·00	40
829a	7r. As 35c.	50	30
830	20r. Ceylon coucal	1·50	4·00
MS831	183×93 mm. Nos. 827/9 and 830	2·75	6·50

No. **MS**831 was re-issued at a premium over face value on 23 November 2010 surch **National Stamp Fair, Colombo – 2010 Day 4 23-11.2010 Rs. 650.00**

327 Pelene Siri
Vajiragnana

1983. Pelene Siri Vajiragnana (scholar) Commem.

832	**327**	50c. brown	1·50	1·75

328 Mary
praying over
Jesus and St.
Joseph
welcoming
Shepherds

1983. Christmas.

833	**328**	50c. multicoloured	10	15
834	**328**	5r. multicoloured	30	2·00
MS835	85×141 mm. Nos. 833/4		65	2·50

1983. No. 680a surch **.60**.

836	**236**	60c. on 50c. gold, green and emerald	5·50	2·00

331 Paddy Field, Globe and
F.A.O. Emblem

1984. World Food Day.

838	**331**	3r. multicoloured	45	2·00

332 Modern Tea Factory

1984. Centenary of Colombo Tea Auctions. Multicoloured.

839	1r. Type **332**	20	15
840	2r. Logo	40	45
841	5r. Girl picking tea	90	2·00
842	10r. Auction in progress	1·60	4·00

333 Students and
University

1984. Fourth Anniv of Mahapola Scheme for Development and Education. Multicoloured.

843	60c. Type **333**	10	15
844	1r. Teacher with Gnana Darsana class	10	15
845	5r.50 Student with books and microscope	45	2·00
846	6r. Mahapola lamp symbol	50	2·00

334 King Daham Sonda
instructing Angels

1984. Vesak. The Story of King Daham Sonda from Ancient Casket Paintings. Multicoloured.

847	35c. Type **334**	30	10
848	60c. Elephant paraded with gift of gold	65	25
849	5r. King Daham Sonda leaps into mouth of God Sakra	1·50	3·00
850	10r. God Sakra carrying King Daham Sonda	1·90	5·00
MS851	154×109 mm. Nos. 847/50	4·00	7·00

335 Development
Programme Logo

1984. Sri Lanka Lions Clubs' Development Programme.

852	**335**	60c. multicoloured	1·40	1·00

336 Dodanduwe
Siri Piyaratana
Tissa Mahanayake
Thero (Buddhist
scholar)

1984. National Heroes.

853	**336**	60c. bistre	35	1·00
854	-	60c. green	35	1·00
855	-	60c. green	35	1·00
856	-	60c. red	35	1·00
857	-	60c. brown	35	1·00

DESIGNS: No. 854, G. P. Wickremarachchi (physician); 855, Sir Mohamed Macan Markar (politician); 856, Dr. W. Arthur de Silva (philanthropist); 857, K. Balasingham (lawyer).

337 Association Emblem

1984. Centenary of Public Service Mutual Provident Association.

858	**337**	4r.60 multicoloured	70	2·50

338 Sri Lanka
Village

1984. Sixth Anniv of "Gam Udawa" (Village Re-awakening Movement).

859	**338**	60c. multicoloured	30	1·00

339 World Map showing
A.P.B.U. Countries

1984. 20th Anniv of Asia-Pacific Broadcasting Union.

860	**339**	7r. multicoloured	2·25	3·75

340 Drummers and Elephant
carrying Royal Instructions

1984. Esala Perahera (Procession of the Tooth), Kandy. Multicoloured.

861	4r.60 Type **340**	1·25	2·10
862	4r.60 Dancers and elephants	1·25	2·10
863	4r.60 Elephant carrying Tooth Relic	1·25	2·10
864	4r.60 Custodian of the Sacred Tooth and attendants	1·25	2·10
MS865	223×108 mm. Nos. 861/4	4·50	7·50

Nos. 861/4 were printed together, se-tenant, forming a composite design.

341 "Vanda
memoria Ernest
Soysa" (orchid)

1984. 50th Anniv of Ceylon Orchid Circle. Multicoloured.

866a	60c. Type **341**	1·00	1·25
867a	4r.60 "Acanthephippium bicolor"	2·00	4·00
868a	5r. "Vanda tessellata var. rufescens"	1·25	4·00
869	10r. "Anoectochilus setaceus"	4·00	6·00
MS870	115×110 mm. Nos. 866/9	7·00	12·00

342 Symbolic
Athletes and
Stadium

1984. First National School Games.

871	**342**	60c. black, grey and blue	1·75	1·75

343 D. S. Senanayake,
Temple and Fields

1984. Birth Centenary of D. S. Senanayake (former Prime Minister). Multicoloured.

872	35c. Type **343**	10	10
873	60c. Senanayake and statue	10	10
874	4r.60 Senanayake and irrigation project	40	60
875	6r. Senanayake and House of Representatives	55	80

344 Lake House

1984. 150th Anniv of "Observer" Newspaper.

876	**344**	4r.60 multicoloured	2·75	4·00

345 Agricultural
Workers and Globe

1984. 20th Anniv of World Food Programme.

877	**345**	7r. multicoloured	2·25	1·50

346 College
Emblem

1984. Cent of Baari Arabic College, Weligama.

878	**346**	4r.60 green, turquoise & blue	1·25	3·25

347 Dove and
Stylized Figures

1985. International Youth Year. Multicoloured.

879	4r.60 Type **347**	75	75
880	20r. Dove, stylized figures and flower	2·25	4·00

348 Religious
Symbols

1985. World Religion Day.

881	**348**	4r.60 multicoloured	2·75	3·75

349 College
Crest

1985. 150th Anniv of Royal College, Colombo.

882	349	60c. yellow and blue	25	25
883	–	7r. multicoloured	2·75	4·50

DESIGN: 7r. Royal College.

350 Banknotes, Buildings, Ship and "Wheel of Life"

1985. Fifth Anniv of Mahapola Scheme.

884	350	60c. multicoloured	1·00	1·75

351 Wariyapola Sri Sumangala Thero

1985. Wariyapola Sri Sumangala Thero (Buddhist priest and patriot) Commemoration.

885	351	60c. brown, yellow & black	70	1·50

352 Victoria Dam

1985. Inaug of Victoria Hydro-electric Project. Multicoloured.

886	352	60c. Type **352**	1·00	50
887		7r. Map of Sri Lanka enclosing dam and power station (vert)	5·50	7·50

353 Cover of 50th Edition of International Buddhist Annual, "Vesak Sirisara"

1985. Centenary of Vesak Poya Holiday. Multicoloured.

888	353	35c. Type **353**	10	10
889		60c. Buddhists worshipping at temple	10	10
890		6r. Buddhist Theosophical Society Headquarters, Colombo	75	1·50
891		9r. Buddhist flag	2·00	3·00
MS892	180×110 mm. Nos. 888/91		4·00	6·50

354 Ven. Waskaduwe Sri Subhuthi (priest and scholar)

1985. Personalities.

893	354	60c. black, orange & brown	30	90
894	–	60c. black, orange & mauve	30	90
895	–	60c. black, orange & brown	30	90
896	–	60c. black, orange & green	30	90

DESIGNS: No. 894, Revd. Fr. Peter A. Pillai (educationist and social reformer); 895, Dr. Senarath Paranavitane (scholar); 896, A. M. Wapche Marikar (architect and educationist).

355 Stylized Village and People

1985. Gam Udawa '85 (Village Re-awakening Movement).

897	355	60c. multicoloured	1·00	1·50

356 Emblem

1985. 50th Anniv of Colombo Young Poets' Association.

898	356	60c. multicoloured	1·75	2·00

357 Kothmale Dam and Reservoir

1985. Inauguration of Kothmale Hydro-electric Project. Multicoloured.

899		60c. Type **357**	75	25
900		6r. Kothmale Power Station	3·75	5·00

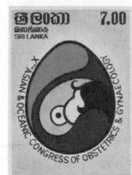

358 Federation Logo

1985. Tenth Asian and Oceanic Congress of Obstetrics and Gynaecology.

901	358	7r. multicoloured	3·25	4·50

359 Breast-feeding

1985. UNICEF Child Survival and Development Programme. Multicoloured.

902	359	35c. Type **359**	30	10
903		60c. Child and oral rehydration salts	45	30
904		6r. Weighing child (growth monitoring)	2·25	3·50
905		9r. Immunization	2·75	5·50
MS906	99×180 mm. Nos. 902/5		4·50	6·50

360 Blowing Indian Chank Shell

1985. Tenth Anniv of World Tourism Organization. Multicoloured.

907	360	1r. Type **360**	30	10
908		6r. Parliamentary Complex, Jayawardhanapura, Kotte	90	90
909		7r. Tea plantation	1·00	1·10
910		10r. Ruwanveliseya (Buddhist shrine), Anuradhapura	1·60	1·75
MS911	179×89 mm. Nos. 907/10		3·50	3·75

361 Casket containing Land Grant Deed

1985. 50th Anniv of Land Development Ordinance.

912	361	4r.60 multicoloured	2·00	3·75

362 Koran and Map of Sri Lanka

1985. Translation of The Koran into Sinhala.

913	362	60c. violet and gold	2·50	2·00

363 "Our Lady of Matara" Statue

1985. Christmas. Multicoloured.

914	363	60c. Type **363**	30	15
915		9r. "Our Lady of Madhu" Statue	1·50	3·00
MS916	180×100 mm. Nos. 914/15		7·00	8·50

1985. Nos. 680b, 780, 828, 860 and 879 surch.

917	236	75c. on 60c. gold, green and emerald	40	10
918	347	1r. on 4r.60 mult	9·00	4·50
919	339	1r. on 7r. multicoloured	12·00	4·50
920	269	5r.75 on 2r.50 mult	3·50	3·00
921	–	7r. on 35c. mult (No. 828)	8·00	1·50

365 Linked Arms and Map of S.A.A.R.C. Countries

1985. First Summit Meeting of South Asian Association for Regional Co-operation, Dhaka, Bangladesh. Multicoloured.

922	365	60c. Type **365**	5·00	7·50
923		3r.50 Logo and flags of member countries	5·00	5·00

366 "Viceroy Special" Train

1986. Inaugural Run of "Viceroy Special" Train from Colombo to Kandy.

924	366	1r. multicoloured	60	1·50

367 Girl and Boy Students

1986. Sixth Anniv of Mahapola Scheme.

925	367	75c. multicoloured	50	1·25

368 Wijewardena

1986. Birth Centenary of D. R. Wijewardena (newspaper publisher).

926	368	75c. brown and green	30	1·25

369 Ven. Welitara Gnanatillake Maha Nayake Thero

1986. Ven. Welitara Gnanatillake Maha Nayake Thero (scholar) Commemoration.

927	369	75c. multicoloured	70	1·00

370 Red Cross Flag and Personnel

1986. 50th Anniv of Sri Lanka Red Cross Society.

928	370	75c. multicoloured	2·00	1·75

371 Comet depicted as Goddess visiting Sun-god

1986. Appearance of Halley's Comet. Multicoloured.

929	371	50c. Type **371**	15	20
930		75c. Comet and constellations of Scorpius and Sagittarius	15	20
931		6r.50 Comet's orbit	30	1·50
932		8r.50 Edmond Halley	55	2·50
MS933	180×115 mm. Nos. 929/32		5·50	11·00

372 Woman lighting Lamp

1986. Sinhalese and Tamil New Year. Multicoloured.

934	372	50c. Type **372**	15	20
935		75c. Woman and festive foods	15	20
936		6r.50 Women playing drum	30	2·00
937		8r.50 Anointing and making offerings at temple	55	2·50
MS938	178×108 mm. Nos. 934/7		1·75	6·00

373 The King donating Elephant to the Brahmin

1986. Vesak. Wall paintings from Samudragiri Temple, Mirissa. Multicoloured.

939	373	50c. Type **373**	10	20
940		75c. The Bodhisattva in the Vasavarthi heaven	10	20
941		5r. The offering of milk rice by Sujatha	60	2·25
942		10r. The offering of parched corn and honey by Thapassu and Bhalluka	65	3·50

374 Ven. Kalukondayave Sri Prajnasekhara Maha Nayake Thero (Buddhist leader and social reformer)

1986. National Heroes. Multicoloured.

943	374	75c. Type **374**	15	80
944		75c. Brahmachari Walisinghe Harischandra (social reformer) (birth centenary)	15	80
945		75c. Martin Wickramasinghe (author and scholar)	15	80
946		75c. G. G. Ponnambalam (politician)	15	80
947		75c. A. M. A. Azeez (Islamic scholar) (75th birth anniv)	15	80

375 Stylized Village and People

1986. Gam Udawa '86 (Village Re-awakening Movement).
948 **375** 75c. multicoloured — 1·50 2·00

376 Co-op Flag and Emblem

1986. 75th Anniv of Sri Lanka Co-operative Movement.
949 **376** 1r. multicoloured — 1·00 2·00

377 Arthur V. Dias

1986. Birth Centenary of Arthur V. Dias (philanthropist).
950 **377** 1r. brown and blue — 1·50 2·25

378 Bull Elephant

1986. Sri Lanka Wild Elephant. Multicoloured.
951 5r. Type **378** — 11·00 8·00
952 5r. Cow elephant and calf — 11·00 8·00
953 5r. Cow elephant — 11·00 8·00
954 5r. Elephants bathing — 11·00 8·00

379 Congress Logo

1986. Second Indo-Pacific Congress on Legal Medicine and Forensic Sciences.
955 **379** 8r.50 multicoloured — 2·50 3·50

380 Map showing Route of Cable and Telephone Receiver

1986. SEA-ME-WE Submarine Cable Project.
956 **380** 5r.75 multicoloured — 6·00 3·00

381 Anniversary Logo

1986. 25th Anniv of Dag Hammarskjold Award.
957 **381** 2r. multicoloured — 1·40 1·50

382 Logo on Flag

1986. Second National School Games.
958 **382** 1r. multicoloured — 3·25 2·50

383 Logo

1986. 60th Anniv of Surveyors' Institute of Sri Lanka.
959 **383** 75c. brown & light brown — 60 1·50

384 College Building and Crest

1986. Centenary of Ananda College, Colombo.
960 **384** 75c. multicoloured — 10 10
961 – 5r. multicoloured — 30 1·00
962 – 5r.75 multicoloured — 35 1·00
963 – 6r. red, gold and lilac — 40 1·25
DESIGNS: 5r. Sports field and college crest; 5r.75, Col. H. S. Olcott (founder), Ven. Migettuwatte Gunananda, Ven. Hikkaduwe Sri Sumangala (Buddhist leaders) and Buddhist flag; 6r. College flag.

385 Mangrove Swamp

1986. Mangrove Conservation. Multicoloured.
964 35c. Type **385** — 1·00 20
965 50c. Mangrove tree — 1·10 30
966 75c. Germinating mangrove flower — 1·25 30
967 6r. Fiddler crab — 8·50 9·50

386 Family and Housing Estate

1987. International Year of Shelter for the Homeless.
968 **386** 75c. multicoloured — 1·75 70

387 Ven. Ambagahawatte Indasabhawaragnanasamy Thero

1987. Ven. Ambagahawatte Indasabhawaragnanasamy Thero (Buddhist monk) Commemoration.
969 **387** 5r.75 multicoloured — 2·50 1·25

388 Proctor John de Silva

1987. Proctor John de Silva (playwright) Commemoration.
970 **388** 5r.75 multicoloured — 1·00 1·00

389 Mahapola Logo and Aspects of Communication

1987. Seventh Anniv of Mahapola Scheme.
971 **389** 75c. multicoloured — 75 1·50

390 Dr. R. L. Brohier

1987. Dr. Richard L. Brohier (historian and surveyor) Commemoration.
972 **390** 5r.75 multicoloured — 2·00 1·40

391 Tyre Corporation Building, Kelaniya, and Logo

1987. 25th Anniv of Sri Lanka Tyre Corporation.
973 **391** 5r.75 black, red and orange — 50 70

392 Logo

1987. Centenary of Sri Lanka Medical Association.
974 **392** 5r.75 brown, yellow and black — 2·25 3·50

393 Clasped Hands, Farmer and Paddy Field

1987. Inauguration of Farmers' Pension and Social Security Benefit Scheme.
975 **393** 75c. multicoloured — 1·00 1·50

394 Exhibition Logo

1987. Mahaweli Maha Goviya Contest and Agro Mahaweli Exhibition.
976 **394** 75c. multicoloured — 30 30

395 Young Children with W.H.O. and Immunization Logos

1987. World Health Day.
977 **395** 1r. multicoloured — 2·50 1·50

396 Girls playing on Swing

1987. Sinhalese and Tamil New Year. Multicoloured.
978 75c. Type **396** — 10 10
979 5r. Girls with oil lamp and sun symbol — 50 50

397 Lotus Lanterns

1987. Vesak. Multicoloured.
980 50c. Type **397** — 10 10
981 75c. Octagonal lanterns — 10 10
982 5r. Star lanterns — 35 30
983 10r. Gok lanterns — 60 65
MS984 150×90 mm. Nos. 980/3 — 1·00 1·00

398 Emerald-collared Parakeet ("Layard's Parakeet")

1987. Birds (3rd series). Multicoloured.
985A 50c. Type **398** — 50 10
986A 1r. Legge's flowerpecker — 75 10
987A 5r. Ceylon white-headed starling ("Sri Lanka White-headed Starling") — 1·10 1·60
988A 10r. Ceylon jungle babbler ("Sri Lanka Rufous Babbler") — 1·40 2·75
MS989A 140×80 mm. Nos. 985/8 — 7·50 8·00

399 Ven. Heenatiyana Sri Dhammaloka Maha Nayake Thero (Buddhist monk)

1987. National Heroes. Multicoloured.
990 75c. Type **399** — 40 40
991 75c. P. de S. Kularatne (educationist) — 40 40
992 75c. M. C. Abdul Rahuman (legislator) — 40 40

400 Peasant Family and Village

1987. Gam Udawa '87 (Village Re-awakening Movement).
993 **400** 75c. multicoloured — 30 30

401 "Mesua nagassarium"

1987. Forest Conservation. Multicoloured.
994 75c. Type **401** — 10 10
995 5r. Elephants in forest — 1·50 1·25

402 Dharmaraja College, Crest and Col. Olcott (founder)

1987. Centenary of Dharmaraja College, Kandy.
996 **402** 75c. multicoloured — 2·25 30

403 Youth Sevices Logo

1987. 20th Anniv of National Youth Services.
997 **403** 75c. multicoloured — 20 20

404 Arm holding
Torch and Mahaweli
Logo

1987. Mahaweli Games.
998	**404**	75c. multicoloured	3·00	2·75

405 Open Bible and
Logo

1987. 175th Anniv of Ceylon Bible Society.
999	**405**	5r.75 multicoloured	40	40

406 Hurdler and Committee
Symbol

1987. 50th Anniv of National Olympic Committee.
1000	**406**	10r. multicoloured	2·50	1·25

407 Madonna and
Child, Flowers and
Oil Lamp

1987. Christmas. Multicoloured.
1001		75c. Type **407**	10	10
1002		10r. Christ Child in manger, star and dove	35	40
MS1003		145×82 mm. Nos. 1001/2	60	70

408 Sir Ernest de
Silva

1987. Birth Centenary of Sir Ernest de Silva (philanthropist and philatelist).
1004	**408**	75c. multicoloured	30	30

409 Society Logo

1987. 150th Anniv of Kandy Friend-in-Need Society.
1005	**409**	75c. multicoloured	30	30

410 University Flag
and Graduates

1987. First Convocation of Buddhist and Pali University.
1006	**410**	75c. multicoloured	30	30

411 Father Joseph
Vaz

1987. 300th Anniv of Arrival of Father Joseph Vaz in Kandy.
1007	**411**	75c. multicoloured	30	30

412 Wheel of
Dhamma, Dagaba
and Bo Leaf

1988. 30th Anniv of Buddhist Publication Society, Kandy.
1008	**412**	75c. multicoloured	30	30

413 Dharmayatra Lorry

1988. Fifth Anniv of Mahapola Dharmayatra Service.
1009	**413**	75c. multicoloured	30	30

414 Society Logo

1988. Centenary of Ceylon Society of Arts.
1010	**414**	75c. multicoloured	30	30

415 National Youth
Centre, Maharagama

1988. Opening of National Youth Centre, Maharagama.
1011	**415**	1r. multicoloured	3·50	30

416 Citizens with
National Flag and
Map of Sri Lanka

1988. 40th Anniv of Independence. Multicoloured.
1012		75c. Type **416**	10	10
1013		8r.50 "40" in figures and lion emblem	90	90

417 Graduates, Clay
Lamp and Open
Book

1988. Eighth Anniv of Mahapola Scheme.
1014	**417**	75c. multicoloured	20	20

418 Bus and Logo

1988. 30th Anniv of Sri Lanka Transport Board.
1015	**418**	5r.75 multicoloured	75	55

419 Ven. Weligama
Sri Sumangala
Maha Nayake Thero

1988. Ven. Weligama Sri Sumangala Maha Nayake Thero (Buddhist monk) Commemoration.
1016	**419**	75c. multicoloured	20	20

420 Regimental Colour

1988. Centenary of Regiment of Artillery.
1017	**420**	5r.75 multicoloured	2·50	80

421 Chevalier I. X.
Pereira

1988. Birth Centenary of Chevalier I. X. Pereira (politician).
1018	**421**	5r.75 multicoloured	50	50

422 Invitation to the Deities
and Brahmas

1988. Vesak. Paintings from Narendrarama Rajamaha Temple, Suriyagoda. Multicoloured.
1019		50c. Type **422**	15	15
1020		75c. Bodhisathva at the Seventh Step	15	15
MS1021		150×92 mm. Nos. 1019/20	1·75	1·75

423 Father
Ferdinand Bonnel
(educationist)

1988. National Heroes. Multicoloured.
1022		75c. Type **423**	15	20
1023		75c. Sir Razik Fareed (politician)	15	20
1024		75c. W. F. Gunawardhana (scholar)	15	20
1025		75c. Edward Nugawela (politician)	15	20
1026		75c. Chief Justice Sir Arthur Wijeyewardene	15	20

424 Stylized Figures and
Re-awakened Village

1988. Tenth Anniv of Gam Udawa (Village Re-awakening Movement).
1027	**424**	75c. multicoloured	20	20

425 Maliyadeva
College, Kurunegala,
and Crest

1988. Cent of Maliyadeva College, Kurunegala.
1028	**425**	75c. multicoloured	20	20

426 M. J. M. Lafir, Billiard
Game and Trophy

1988. Mohamed Junaid Mohamed Lafir (World Amateur Billiards Champion, 1973) Commem.
1029	**426**	5r.75 multicoloured	45	45

427 Flags of Australia and
Sri Lanka, Handclasp and
Map of Australia

1988. Bicentenary of Australian Settlement.
1030	**427**	8r.50 multicoloured	75	75

428 Ven. Kataluwe
Sri Gunaratana
Maha Nayake
Thero

1988. Ven. Kataluwe Sri Gunaratana Maha Nayake Thero (Buddhist monk) Commemoration.
1031	**428**	75c. multicoloured	20	20

429 Athlete, Rice
and Hydro-electric
Dam

1988. Mahaweli Games.
1032	**429**	75c. multicoloured	20	20

430 Athletics

1988. Olympic Games, Seoul. Multicoloured.
1033		75c. Type **430**	10	10
1034		1r. Swimming	10	10
1035		5r.75 Boxing	40	40
1036		8r.50 Map of Sri Lanka and logos of Olympic Committee and Seoul Games	70	70
MS1037		181×101 mm. Nos. 1033/6	1·10	1·40

431 Outline Map
of Sri Lanka and
Anniversary Logo

1988. 40th Anniv of W.H.O.
1038	**431**	75c. multicoloured	20	20

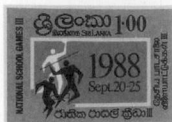

432 Games Logo

1988. Third National School Games.

1039	**432**	1r. black, gold and mauve	2·75	25

433 Mahatma Gandhi

1988. 40th Death Anniv of Mahatma Gandhi.

1040	**433**	75c. multicoloured	1·75	1·00

434 Globe with Forms of Transport and Communications

1988. Asia-Pacific Transport and Communications Decade.

1041	**434**	75c. multicoloured	75	10
1042	-	5r.75 mauve, blue & blk	2·75	1·60

DESIGN: 5r.75, Antenna tower with dish aerials and forms of transport.

435 Woman with Rice Sheaf and Hydro-electric Project

1988. Commissioning of Randenigala Project. Multicoloured.

1043		75c. Type **435**	10	10
1044		5r.75 Randenigala Dam and reservoir	90	90

436 Handicrafts and Centre Logo in Cupped Hands

1988. Opening of Gramodaya Folk Art Centre, Colombo.

1045	**436**	75c. multicoloured	20	20

437 Angel, Dove, Olive Branch and Globe

1988. Christmas. Multicoloured.

1046		75c. Type **437**	10	10
1047		8r.50 Shepherds and Star of Bethlehem	70	90
MS1048	175×100 mm. Nos. 1046/7		1·00	1·00

438 Dr. E. W. Adikaram

1988. Dr. E. W. Adikaram (educationist) Commemoration.

1049	**438**	75c. multicoloured	20	20

439 Open Book in Tree and Children reading

1989. Tenth Anniv of Free Distribution of School Text Books.

1050	**439**	75c. multicoloured	20	20

440 Wimalaratne Kumaragama

1989. Poets of Sri Lanka. Multicoloured.

1051		75c. Type **440**	15	20
1052		75c. G. H. Perera	15	20
1053		75c. Sagara Palansuriya	15	20
1054		75c. P. B. Alwis Perera	15	20

441 Logo and New Chamber of Commerce Building

1989. 150th Anniv of Ceylon Chamber of Commerce.

1055	**441**	75c. multicoloured	20	20

442 Bodhisatva at Lunch and Funeral Pyre

1989. Vesak. Wall Paintings from Medawala Monastery, Harispattuwa. Multicoloured.

1056		50c. Type **442**	10	10
1057		75c. Rescue of King Vessantara's childen by god Sakra	10	10
1058		5r. Bodhisatva ploughing and his son attacked by snake	30	40
1059		5r.75 King Vessantara giving away his children	30	55
MS1060	150×90 mm. Nos. 1056/9		1·00	1·00

443 Parawahera Vajiragnana Thero (Buddhist monk)

1989. National Heroes. Multicoloured.

1061		75c. Type **443**	25	25
1062		75c. Fr. Maurice Jacques Le Goc (educationist)	25	25
1063		75c. Hemapala Munidasa (author)	25	25
1064		75c. Ananda Samarakoon (composer)	25	25
1065		75c. Simon Casie Chitty (scholar) (horiz)	25	25

444 College Crest

1989. 150th Anniv of Harley College, Point-Pedro (1988).

1066	**444**	75c. multicoloured	20	20

445 Dramachakra, Lamp, Buddhist Flag and Map

1989. Establishment of Ministry of Buddha Sasana.

1067	**445**	75c. multicoloured	20	20

446 Hands holding Brick and Trowel, House and Family

1989. Gam Udawa '89 (Village Re-awakening Movement).

1068	**446**	75c. multicoloured	20	20

447 Two Families and Hand turning Cogwheel

1989. Janasaviya Development Programme.

1069	**447**	75c. multicoloured	20	20
1070	**447**	1r. multicoloured	30	20

448 Dunhinda Falls

1989. Waterfalls. Multicoloured.

1071		75c. Type **448**	10	10
1072		1r. Rawana Falls	10	10
1073		5r.75 Laxapana Falls	45	45
1074		8r.50 Diyaluma Falls	60	60

449 Rev. James Chater (missionary) and Baptist Church

1989. 177th Anniv of Baptist Church in Sri Lanka.

1075	**449**	5r.75 multicoloured	50	50

450 Bicentenary Logo

1989. Bicentenary of French Revolution.

1076	**450**	8r.50 black, blue and red	80	80

451 Old and New Bank Buildings and Logo

1989. 50th Anniv of Bank of Ceylon. Multicoloured.

1077		75c. Type **451**	10	10
1078		5r. "Bank of Ceylon orchid and logo"	50	50

452 Water Lily, Dharma Chakra and Books

453 Wilhelm Geiger

1989. State Literary Festival.

1079	**452**	75c. multicoloured	20	20

1989. Wilhelm Geiger (linguistic scholar) Commemoration.

1080	**453**	75c. multicoloured	20	20

454 H. V. Perera, Q.C.

1989. Constitutional Pioneers. Multicoloured.

1082		75c. Type **454**	20	20
1083		75c. Prof. Ivor Jennings	20	20

455 Sir Cyril de Zoysa

1989. Sir Cyril de Zoysa (Buddhist philanthropist) Commemoration.

1084	**455**	75c. multicoloured	20	20

456 Map of South-east Asia and Telecommunications Equipment

1989. Tenth Anniv of Asia-Pacific Telecommunity.

1085	**456**	5r.75 multicoloured	1·00	70

457 Members with Offerings and Water Lily on Map of Sri Lanka

1989. 50th Anniv of Sri Sucharitha Welfare Movement.

1086	**457**	75c. multicoloured	20	20

458 "Apollo 11" Blast- off and Astronauts

1989. 20th Anniv of First Manned Landing on Moon. Multicoloured.

1087		75c. Type **458**	15	10
1088		1r. Armstrong leaving lunar module "Eagle"	20	10
1089		2r. Astronaut on Moon	35	30
1090		5r.75 Lunar surface and Earth from Moon	60	70
MS1091	100×160 mm. Nos. 1087/90		2·00	1·75

459 Shepherds

1989. Christmas. Multicoloured.

1092	75c. Type **459**	10	10
1093	8r.50 Magi with gifts	60	2·25
MS1094	160×100 mm. Nos. 1092/3	1·25	2·50

460 Ven. Sri Devananda Nayake Thero

1989. Ven. Sri Devananda Nayake Thero (Buddhist monk) Commemoration.

1095	**460**	75c. multicoloured	30	20

461 College Building, Crest and Revd. William Ault (founder)

1989. 175th Anniv of Methodist Central College, Batticaloa.

1096	**461**	75c. multicoloured	20	20

462 Golf Ball, Clubs and Logo

1989. Cent of Nuwara Eliya Golf Club. Multicoloured.

1097	75c. Type **462**	2·00	25
1098	8r.50 Course and club house	9·00	7·50

463 "Raja"

1989. "Raja" Royal Ceremonial Elephant, Kandy Commemoration.

1099	**463**	75c. multicoloured	3·50	75

464 College Building and G. Wickremarachchi (founder)

1989. 60th Anniv of Gampaha Wickremarachchi Institute of Ayurveda Medicine.

1100	**464**	75c. multicoloured	25	25

465 Ven. Udunuwara Sri Sarananda Thero

1989. Ven. Udunuwara Sri Sarananda Thero (Buddhist monk) Commemoration.

1101	**465**	75c. multicoloured	25	25

466 Diesel Train on Viaduct, Ella–Demodara Line

1989. 125 Years of Sir Lanka Railways. Multicoloured.

1102	75c. Type **466**	1·00	25
1103	2r. Diesel train at Maradana Station	1·90	30
1104	3r. Steam train and semaphore signal	2·25	60
1105	7r. Steam train leaving station, 1864	3·00	2·00

467 Cardinal Thomas Cooray

1989. Cardinal Thomas Cooray Commemoration.

1106	**467**	75c. multicoloured	1·50	30

468 Farmer and Wife with Dagaba and Dam

1989. Agro Mahaweli Development Programme.

1107	**468**	75c. multicoloured	25	25

469 Justin Wijayawardena

1990. Justin Wijayawardena (scholar) Commemoration

1108	**469**	1r. multicoloured	2·25	25

1990. Surch.

1108a	25c. on 5r.75 King Vessantara giving away his children (No. 1059)	1·00	20
1109a	1r. on 75c. Type **447**	2·00	1·25

470 Ven. Induruwe Uttarananda Mahanayake Thero

1990. Fourth Death Anniv of Ven. Induruwe Uttarananda Mahanayake Thero (Buddhist theologian)

1109	**470**	1r. multicoloured	1·40	1·25

471 Two Graduates, Lamp and Open Book

1990. Ninth Anniv of Mahapola Scheme.

1110	**471**	75c. multicoloured	25	25

472 Traditional Drums

1990. 25th Anniv of Laksala Traditional Handicrafts Organization. Multicoloured.

1111	1r. Type **472**	30	10
1112	2r. Silverware	55	15
1113	3r. Lacquerware	75	30
1114	8r. Dumbara mats	2·25	2·75

473 King Maha Prathapa visiting Queen Chandra

1990. Vesak. Wall Paintings from Buduraja Maha Viharaya, Wewurukannala. Multicoloured.

1115	75c. Type **473**	10	10
1116	1r. Execution of Prince Dharmapala	15	10
1117	2r. Prince Mahinsasaka with the Water Demon	25	20
1118	8r. King Dahamsonda with the God Sakra disguised as a demon	1·00	1·00
MS1119	160×99 mm. Nos. 1115/18	1·40	1·25

474 Father T. Long (educationist)

1990. National Heroes. Multicoloured.

1120	1r. Type **474**	50	35
1121	1r. Prof. M. Ratnasuriya (37×25 mm)	50	35
1122	1r. D. Wijewardene (patriot) (37×25 mm)	50	35
1123	1r. L. Manjusri (artist) (37×25 mm)	50	35

475 Janasaviya Workers

1990. 12th Anniv of Gam Udawa and Opening of Janasaviya Centre, Pallekele.

1124	**475**	1r. multicoloured	2·00	30

476 Gold Reliquary

1990. Cent of Department of Archaeology.

1125	**476**	1r. black and yellow	35	10
1126	-	2r. black and grey	60	15
1127	-	3r. black, green & brown	80	35
1128	-	8r. black and brown	1·75	1·50

DESIGNS: 2r. Statuette of Ganesh; 3r. Terrace of the Bodhi-tree, Isurumuniya Vihara; 8r. Inscription of King Nissankamalla.

477 Male Tennis Player at Left

1990. 75th Anniv of Sri Lanka Tennis Association. Multicoloured.

1129	1r. Type **477**	75	75
1130	1r. Male tennis player at right	75	75
1131	8r. Male tennis players	2·50	2·50
1132	8r. Female tennis players	2·50	2·50

Nos. 1129/30 and 1131/2 were each printed together, se-tenant, each pair forming a composite design of a singles (1r.) or doubles (8r.) match.

478 Spotted Loach

1990. Endemic Fish. Multicoloured.

1133	25c. Type **478**	10	10
1134	2r. Spotted gourami ("Ornate paradise fish")	40	20
1135	8r. Mountain labeo	95	1·25
1136	20r. Cherry barb	1·75	3·50
MS1137	150×90 mm. Nos. 1133/6	2·75	4·50

479 Rukmani Devi

1990. 12th Death Anniv of Rukmani Devi (actress and singer).

1138	**479**	1r. multicoloured	2·75	1·25

480 Innkeeper turning away Mary and Joseph

1990. Christmas. Multicoloured.

1139	1r. Type **480**	50	10
1140	10r. Adoration of the Magi	4·50	5·00
MS1141	190×114 mm. Nos. 1139/40	5·50	6·00

481 Health Worker talking to Villagers

1990. World Aids Day. Multicoloured.

1142	1r. Type **481**	75	15
1143	8r. Emblem and Aids virus	4·00	4·50

482 Main College Building and Flag

1990. 50th Anniv of Dharmapala College, Pannipitiya.

1144	**482**	1r. multicoloured	3·00	1·25

483 Peri Sundaram

1990. Birth Centenary of Peri Sundaram (lawyer and politician).

1145	**483**	1r. brown and green	3·00	1·25

484 Letter Box, Galle, 1904

1990. 175th Anniv of Sri Lanka Postal Service. Multicoloured.

1146	1r. Type **484**	75	10
1147	2r. Mail runner, 1815	1·25	30
1148	5r. Mail coach, 1832	2·50	2·00
1149	10r. Nuwara-Eliya Post Office, 1894	3·25	4·50

485 Chemical Structure Diagram, Graduating Students and Emblem

1991. 50th Anniv of Institute of Chemistry.
1150   **485**   1r. multicoloured   3·00   1·25

486 Kastavahana on Royal Elephant

1991. Vesak. Temple Paintings from Karagampitiya Subodarama, Multicoloured.
1151   75c. Type **486**   40   20
1152   1r. Polo Janaka in prison   40   10
1153   2r. Two merchants offering food
           to Buddha   70   45
1154   11r. Escape of Queen   3·25   6·00
MS1155 150×90 mm. Nos. 1151/4   4·50   6·00

487 Narada Thero (Buddhist missionary)

1991. National Heroes. Multicoloured.
1156   1r. Type **487**   50   60
1157   1r. Wallewatta Silva (novelist)   50   60
1158   1r. Sir Muttu Coomaraswamy
           (lawyer and politician)   50   60
1159   1r. Dr. Andreas Nell (ophthalmic
           surgeon)   50   60

488 Society Building

1991. Centenary of Maha Bodhi Society.
1160   **488**   1r. multicoloured   1·25   1·00

489 Women working at Home

1991. 13th Anniv of Gam Udawa Movement.
1161   **489**   1r. multicoloured   2·00   80

490 Globe and Plan Symbol

1991. 40th Anniv of Colombo Plan.
1162   **490**   1r. violet and blue   2·25   80

491 17th-century Map and Modern Satellite Photo of Sri Lanka

1991. 190th Anniv of Sri Lanka Survey Department.
1163   **491**   1r. multicoloured   2·25   80

492 Ven. Henpitagedera Gnanaseeha Nayake Thero

1991. Tenth Death Anniv of Ven. Nayak Henpitagedera Gnanaseeha Nayake Thero (Buddhist theologian).
1164   **492**   1r. multicoloured   1·75   80

493 Police Officers of 1866 and 1991 with Badge

1991. 125th Anniv of Sri Lanka Police Force.
1165   **493**   1r. multicoloured   1·40   70

494 Kingswood College

1991. Centenary of Kingswood College, Kandy.
1166   **494**   1r. multicoloured   65   30

495 The Annunciation

1991. Christmas. Multicoloured.
1167   1r. Type **495**   20   20
1168   10r. The Presentation of Jesus
            in the Temple   1·10   2·25
MS1169 90×150 mm. Nos. 1167/8   1·50   2·50

496 Early Magneto Telephone

1991. Inauguration of Sri Lankan Telecom Corporation. Multicoloured.
1170   1r. Type **496**   20   10
1171   2r. Manual switchboard and
           telephonist   25   15
1172   8r. Satellite communications
           system   55   1·40
1173   10r. Fibre optics cable and
            mobile phone   70   1·40

497 S.A.A.R.C. Logo and Bandaranaike Memorial Hall

1991. Sixth South Asian Association for Regional Co-operation Summit, Colombo. Multicoloured.
1174   1r. Type **497**   15   10
1175   8r. Logo and hall surrounded
           by national flags   60   1·75

498 "Pancha" (Games mascot)

1991. Fifth South Asian Federation Games. Multicoloured.
1176   1r. Type **498**   25   10
1177   2r. Games logo   45   20

1178   4r. Sugathadasa Stadium   85   1·25
1179   11r. Asia map on globe and
            national flags   1·75   4·00

499 Crate, Boeing 747-300/400 Airliner and Container Ship

1992. Exports Year.
1180   **499**   1r. multicoloured   1·75   80

500 Plucking Tea

1992. 125th Anniv of Tea Industry. Multicoloured.
1181   1r. Type **500**   50   10
1102   2r. Healthy family, tea and
           tea estate   85   20
1183   5r. Ceylon tea symbol   2·25   2·25
1184   10r. James Taylor (founder)   3·00   4·25

501 General Ranjan Wijeratne

1992. First Death Anniv of General Ranjan Wijeratne.
1185   **501**   1r. multicoloured   50   20

502 Olcott Hall, Mahinda College

1992. Centenary of Mahinda College, Galle.
1186   **502**   1r. multicoloured   25   20

503 Newstead College and Logo

1992. 175th Anniv (1991) of Newstead Girls' College, Negombo.
1187   **503**   1r. multicoloured   25   20

504 Student and Oil Lamp

1992. 11th Anniv of Mahapola Scholarship Fund.
1188   **504**   1r. multicoloured   25   20

505 Sama's Parents leaving for Forest

1992. Vesak Festival. Sama Jataka Paintings from Kottimbulwala Cave Temple. Multicoloured.
1189   75c. Type **505**   20   10
1190   1r. Sama and parents in forest   20   10
1191   8r. Sama leading blind parents   1·40   1·75
1192   11r. Sama's parents grieving for
            wounded son   1·75   2·50
MS1193 151×91 mm. Nos. 1189/92   3·25   4·50

506 Ven. Devamottawe Amarawansa (Buddhist missionary)

1992. National Heroes. Multicoloured.
1194   1r. Type **506**   15   30
1195   1r. Richard Mirando (Buddhist
           philanthropist)   15   30
1196   1r. Gate Mudaliyar N. Canaga-
           nayagam (Buddhist social
           reformer)   15   30
1197   1r. Abdul Azeez (Moorish social
           reformer)   15   30

507 Map of Sri Lanka, Flag and Symbol

1992. 2300th Anniv of Arrival of Buddhism in Sri Lanka.
1198   **507**   1r. multicoloured   25   20

508 Family in House

1992. 14th Anniv of Gam Udawa Movement.
1199   **508**   1r. multicoloured   25   20

509 Postal Activities and Award

1992. Postal Service Awards. Multicoloured.
1200   1r. Type **509**   50   10
1201   10r. Medals and commemora-
            tive cachet   3·00   3·50

510 Narilata Mask

1992. Kolam Dance Masks. Multicoloured.
1202   1r. Type **510**   25   10
1203   2r. Mudali mask   35   20
1204   5r. Queen mask   75   75
1205   10r. King mask   1·25   2·25
MS1206 150×90 mm. Nos. 1202/5   3·00   3·50

511 19th and 20th-century Players and Match of 1838

1992. 160th Anniv of Cricket in Sri Lanka.
1207   **511**   5r. multicoloured   3·75   3·00

512 Running

1992. Olympic Games, Barcelona. Multicoloured.

1208	1r. Type **512**	30	10
1209	11r. Shooting	1·75	2·50
1210	13r. Swimming	2·00	3·00
1211	15r. Weightlifting	2·50	3·25
MS1212	91×151 mm. Nos. 1208/11	7·00	8·50

513 Vijaya
Kumaratunga

1992. Vijaya Kumaratunga (actor) Commemoration

1213	**513**	1r. multicoloured	40	20

514 College Building and
Crest

1992. Centenary of Al-Bahjathhul Ibraheemiyyah Arabic College.

1214	**514**	1r. multicoloured	40	20

515 Official Church
Seal

1992. 350th Anniv of Dutch Reformed Church in Sri Lanka.

1215	**515**	1r. black, green & yellow	1·50	60

516 Nativity

1992. Christmas. Multicoloured.

1216	1r. Type **516**	15	10
1217	9r. Family going to church	1·60	2·50
MS1218	150×90 mm. Nos. 1216/17	1·75	2·75

517 Fleet of Columbus

1992. 500th Anniv of Discovery of America by Columbus. Multicoloured.

1219	1r. Type **517**	50	10
1220	11r. Columbus landing in New World	1·25	1·50
1221	13r. Wreck of "Santa Maria"	1·50	2·25
1222	15r. Columbus reporting to Queen Isabella and King Ferdinand	1·50	2·25
MS1223	155×95 mm. Nos. 1219/22	4·25	6·50

1992. No. 684 surch **2.00**.

1224	**255**	2r. on 10c. multicoloured	5·50	1·00

519 Ven. Sumedhankara
Thero and Dagoba

1992. Birth Centenary of Ven. Dambagasare Sumedhankara Nayake Thero.

1225	**519**	1r. multicoloured	30	20

520 University Logo,
Students and Building

1992. 50th Anniv of University Education in Sri Lanka (1st issue).

1226	**520**	1r. multicoloured	30	20

See also No. 1227.

521 University of
Colombo Building and
Logo

1993. 50th Anniv of University Education in Sri Lanka (2nd issue).

1227	**521**	1r. multicoloured	75	20

522 College Building and
Crest

1993. Centenary of Zahira College, Colombo.

1228	**522**	1r. multicoloured	75	30

523 Mahamaya
being presented to
Buddha

1993. Vesak Festival. Verses from the "Dhammapada". Multicoloured.

1229	75c. Type **523**	20	10
1230	1r. Kisa Gotami carrying her dead baby	20	10
1231	3r. Patachara and her dying family	60	70
1232	10r. Angulimala praying	1·50	2·50
MS1233	180×101 mm. Nos. 1229/32	2·50	3·50

524 Girl Guide,
Badge and Camp

1993. 75th Anniv of Sri Lanka Girl Guides Association. Multicoloured.

1234	1r. Type **524**	50	10
1235	5r. Girl Guide activities	1·50	2·00

525 Ven. Yagirala
Pagnananda Maha
Nayaka Thero
(scholar)

1993. National Heroes. Multicoloured.

1236	1r. Type **525**	40	50
1237	1r. Charles de Silva (politician)	40	50
1238	1r. Wilmot A. Perera (politician)	40	50
1239	1r. Abdul Caffoor (philanthropist)	40	50

526 Family arriving at
New Home

1993. "Gam Udawa '93".

1240	**526**	1r. multicoloured	1·25	30

527 Consumer Movement
Flag and Logo

1993. 50th Anniv (1992) of Co-operative Consumer Movement.

1241	**527**	1r. multicoloured	1·50	30

528 Ashy-headed Laughing
Thrush

1993. Birds (4th series). Multicoloured.

1242	3r. Type **528**	40	20
1243	4r. Brown-capped jungle babbler ("Ceylon Brown-capped Babbler")	40	20
1244	5r. Red-faced malkoha	50	55
1245	10r. Ceylon grackle ("Ceylon Hill-Mynah")	95	1·40
MS1246	151×121 mm. Nos. 1242/5	3·25	4·00

529 Talawila Church

1993. 150th Anniv of Talawila Church.

1247	**529**	1r. multicoloured	1·00	30

530 Rosette and
Mail Delivery

1993. Sri Lanka Post Excellent Service Awards.

1248	**530**	1r. multicoloured	1·00	30

531 College and
Flag

1993. Centenary of Musaeus College.

1249	**531**	1r. multicoloured	1·75	30

532 Presentation of Jesus
in the Temple

1993. Christmas. Multicoloured.

1250	1r. Type **532**	10	10
1251	17r. Boy Jesus with the Jewish teachers	1·25	2·50
MS1252	180×102 mm. Nos. 1250/1	1·25	2·50

533 Healthy Youth and Drug
Addict

1993. Youth and Health Campaign.

1253	**533**	1r. multicoloured	70	30

534 Maradana Technical
College Building and
Emblems

1993. Centenary of Technical Education.

1254	**534**	1r. multicoloured	1·00	30

535 Trinity College
Logo

1994. Centenary of Trinity College, Kandy, Old Boys' Association.

1255	**535**	1r. multicoloured	30	20

536 College Flag

1994. 150th Anniv of St. Thomas' College, Matara.

1256	**536**	1r. brown and blue	30	20

537 Ven.
Siyambalangamuwe Sri
Gunaratana Thero

1994. Ven. Siyambalangamuwe Sri Gunaratana Thero (educationist) Commemoration.

1257	**537**	1r. multicoloured	2·00	40

538 College Building and
Arms

1994. 125th Anniv of St. Joseph's College, Trincomalee.

1258	**538**	1r. multicoloured	30	20

539 Man distributing Water

1994. Vesak Festival. Dasa Paramita (Ten Virtues). Multicoloured.

1259	1r. Type **539**	20	10
1260	2r. Man and elephant	1·25	40
1261	5r. Man surrounded by women	1·00	1·00
1262	17r. Ruler with snake charmer	2·75	4·50
MS1263	162/88 mm. Nos. 1259/62	4·25	6·50

540 I.L.O.
Monument, Geneva,
Logo and Workers

1994. 75th Anniv of I.L.O.
| 1264 | 540 | 1r. multicoloured | 1·25 | 40 |

541 Mahakavindra
Dhammaratana Thero
(Buddhist theologian)

1994. National Heroes. Multicoloured.
1265		1r. Type **541**	30	40
1266		1r. Ranasinghe Premadasa (former President)	30	40
1267		1r. Dr. Colvin de Silva (trade union leader)	30	40
1268		1r. E. Periyathambipillai (Tamil poet)	30	40

542 Conference Logo

1994. 13th International Federation of Social Workers World Conference, Colombo.
| 1269 | 542 | 8r. multicoloured | 3·00 | 3·00 |

543 Ven. Sri Somaratana Thero and Temple

1994. Tenth Death Anniv of Ven. Sri Somaratana Thero (Buddhist religious leader).
| 1270 | 543 | 1r. multicoloured | 2·25 | 50 |

544 Communication Technology and Logo

1994. "INFOTEL LANKA '94" International Computers and Telecommunications Exhibition.
| 1271 | 544 | 10r. multicoloured | 3·00 | 3·25 |

545 Veddah Tribesman stringing Bow

1994. Year of Indigenous People (1993). Multicoloured.
| 1272 | | 1r. Type **545** | 35 | 10 |
| 1273 | | 17r. Veddah artist and rock paintings | 4·50 | 5·00 |

546 Luca Pacioli (pioneer), Logo and Equipment inside "500"

1994. 500th Anniv of Accountancy.
| 1274 | 546 | 1r. multicoloured | 2·25 | 50 |

547 Society Emblem

1994. Centenary of Wildlife and Nature Society of Sri Lanka.
1275	547	1r. green and black	20	10
1276	-	2r. multicoloured	70	20
1277	-	10r. multicoloured	2·00	2·00
1278	-	17r. multicoloured	3·00	4·50
MS1279 130×96 mm. Nos. 1275/8			5·00	6·50
DESIGNS: 2r. Horned lizard; 10r. Giant squirrel; 17r. Sloth bear.

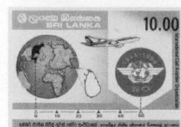

548 Airliner, I.C.A.O. Logo and Globe

1994. 50th Anniv of I.C.A.O.
| 1280 | 548 | 10r. multicoloured | 4·00 | 3·50 |

549 Christmas Crib

1994. Christmas. Multicoloured.
1281		1r. Type **549**	20	10
1282		17r. St. Joseph's carpentry workshop, Nazareth	3·25	4·00
MS1283 145×81 mm. Nos. 1281/2			3·00	4·00

550 Map of Sri Lanka and Aspects of Science

1994. 50th Anniv of Sri Lankan Association for the Advancement of Science.
| 1284 | 550 | 1r. multicoloured | 2·75 | 60 |

551 College Building and Arms

1994. Cent of Richmond College Old Boys' Assn.
| 1285 | 551 | 1r. black, red and blue | 25 | 20 |

552 "Dendrobium maccarthiae"

1994. 60th Anniv of Orchid Circle of Ceylon. Multicoloured.
1286		50c. Type **552**	30	10
1287		1r. "Cottonia peduncularis"	45	10
1288		5r. "Bulbophyllum wightii"	1·00	1·00
1289		17r. "Habenaria crinifera"	2·50	4·00
MS1290 127×95 mm. Nos. 1286/9			3·25	5·00

553 Father Joseph Vaz and Pope John Paul II

1995. Papal Visit and Beatification of Father Joseph Vaz.
| 1291 | 553 | 1r. multicoloured | 3·50 | 1·00 |

554 Blue Water Lily

1995
| 1292 | 554 | 1r. multicoloured | 1·00 | 10 |

555 College Building and Arms

1995. Centenary of St. Joseph's College, Colombo.
| 1293 | 555 | 1r. multicoloured | 1·50 | 50 |

556 Sirimavo Bandaranaike and National Flag

1995. Election of Sirimavo Banadaranaike as Prime Minister.
| 1294 | 556 | 2r. multicoloured | 2·25 | 1·25 |

557 Man offering Water to Crew of Outrigger Canoe

1995. Vesak Festival. Dasa Paramita (Ten Virtues). Multicoloured.
1295		1r. Type **557**	20	10
1296		2r. Catching falling man	35	15
1297		10r. Teacher with students	1·50	1·50
1298		17r. Stopping man digging	2·50	3·25
MS1299 170×90 mm. Nos. 1295/8			5·00	5·00

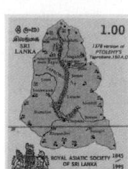

558 14th-century Map of Sri Lanka and Society Arms

1995. 150th Anniv of Royal Asiatic Society of Sri Lanka.
| 1300 | 558 | 1r. multicoloured | 2·50 | 75 |

559 Abdul Cader

1995. 120th Birth Anniv of Abdul Cader (lawyer).
| 1301 | 559 | 2r. multicoloured | 2·25 | 1·25 |

560 College Building

1995. Centenary of St. Aloysius's College, Galle.
| 1302 | 560 | 2r. multicoloured | 2·25 | 1·25 |

561 Tikiri Ilangaratna

1995. Tikiri Bandara Ilangaratna (politician and author) Commemoration.
| 1303 | 561 | 2r. multicoloured | 2·25 | 1·25 |

562 Lamps and Schools Flag

1995. Centenary of Dhamma Schools Movement.
| 1304 | 562 | 2r. multicoloured | 2·25 | 1·25 |

563 G.P.O. Building

1995. Centenary of General Post Office, Colombo.
| 1305 | 563 | 1r. multicoloured | 2·00 | 45 |

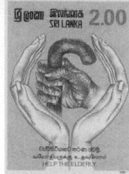

564 Young Hands surrounding Old Hand

1995. International Day for the Elderly.
| 1306 | 564 | 2r. multicoloured | 2·25 | 1·25 |

565 Sri Lankan Parliament Building and C.P.A. Logo

1995. 41st Commonwealth Parliamentary Conf, Colombo.
| 1307 | 565 | 2r. multicoloured | 2·25 | 1·25 |

566 Anniversary Emblem and Map of Sri Lanka

1995. 50th Anniv of United Nations.
| 1308 | 566 | 2r. multicoloured | 2·25 | 1·25 |

567 Money falling into Globe Money Box

1995. 71st Anniv of World Thrift Day and 110th Anniv of National Savings Bank.
| 1309 | 567 | 2r. multicoloured | 2·25 | 1·25 |

568 Diocesan Arms of Colombo and Kurunegala

1995. Christmas. 150th Anniv of Anglican Diocese of Colombo. Multicoloured.
1310		2r. Type **568**	25	10
1311		20r. Nativity scene and hands surrounding map	3·50	4·50
MS1312 150×90 mm. Nos. 1310/11			3·00	4·50

569 Flags of
Member Countries

1995. Tenth Anniv of South Asian Association for
Regional Co-operation.

1313	**569**	2r. multicoloured	2·75	1·25

570 School Emblem

1996. 175th Anniv of Vincent Girls' High School,
Batticaloa.

1314	**570**	2r. multicoloured	2·25	1·25

571 Little Basses
Lighthouse

1996. Lighthouses. Multicoloured.

1315	50c. Type **571**	60	25
1316	75c. Great Basses	70	25
1317	2r. Devinuwara	1·50	35
1317a	2r.50 As 2r.	5·00	1·50
1318	20r. Galle	3·25	4·25
MS1319	151×91 mm. Nos. 1315/17		
	and 1318	5·50	6·00

No. **MS**1319 was re-issued at a premium over face
value on 21 November 2010 surch **National Stamp Fair,
Colombo – 2010 Day 2 21-11.2010 Rs. 500.00**

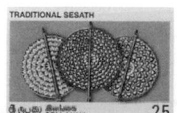

572 Traditional Sesath
(umbrellas)

1996. Traditional Handicrafts. Multicoloured.

1320	25c. Type **572**	10	10
1321	8r.50 Pottery	50	55
1322	10r.50 Mats	65	75
1323	17r. Lace	1·00	1·75
MS1324	150×90 mm. Nos. 1320/3	3·25	3·75

573 School Emblem
and Trees

1996. Centenary of Chundikuli Girls' College, Jaffna.

1325	**573**	2r. multicoloured	2·25	1·25

574 Upaka and
Capa

1996. Vesak Festival. Multicoloured.

1326	1r. Type **574**	15	10
1327	2r. Dantika and elephant	40	15
1328	5r. Subha removing her eye	60	70
1329	10r. Punna and the Brahmin	85	1·50
MS1330	170×90 mm. Nos. 1326/9	1·75	2·50

575 Diving

1996. Olympic Games, Atlanta. Multicoloured.

1331	1r. Type **575**	40	10
1332	2r. Tennis	90	20
1333	5r. Rifle shooting (horiz)	1·50	1·00
1334	17r. Running (horiz)	2·50	4·00

576 Bowler

1996. Sri Lanka's Victory in World Cup Cricket
Tournament. Multicoloured.

1335	2r. Type **576**	45	25
1336	10r.50 Wicket-keeper	80	90
1337	17r. Batsman	1·25	1·75
1338	20r. World Cup trophy	1·40	2·00
MS1339	150×90 mm. Nos. 1335/8	3·50	4·50

577 Main Building, Jaffna
Central College

1996. 180th Anniv of Jaffna Central College.

1340	**577**	2r. multicoloured	2·25	1·25

578 Globe in
Flowers and White
Dove

1996. 50th Anniv of UNESCO.

1341	**578**	2r. multicoloured	2·50	1·25

579 Jesus
washing the
Disciples' Feet

1996. Christmas. Murals by David Paynter from Trinity
College Chapel, Kandy. Multicoloured.

1342	2r. Type **579**	10	10
1343	17r. Parable of the Good		
	Samaritan	1·50	2·00
MS1344	150×90 mm. Nos. 1342/4	1·50	2·25

580 Cupped Hands
holding Child

1996. 50th Anniv of UNICEF.

1345	**580**	5r. multicoloured	70	1·00

581 Swami
Vivekananda and
Globe

1997. Centenary of Swami Vivekananda's Visit to Sri
Lanka.

1346	**581**	2r.50 multicoloured	1·50	1·00

1997. No. 1317 surch **2.50.**

1347	2r.50 on 2r. multicoloured	5·50	1·50

586 Venerable
Welivitiye Sorata
Thero (scholar)

1997. National Heroes (1st series). Multicoloured.

1351	2r. Type **586**	75	75
1352	2r. Mahagama Sekera (writer		
	and artist)	75	75
1353	2r. Dr. S. A. Wickremasinghe		
	(physician)	75	75
1354	2r. Lt. Gen. Denzil Kob-		
	bekaduwa	75	75

See also Nos. 1373/6.

1997. No. 1322 surch **11.00.**

1355	11r. on 10r.50 multicoloured	6·00	6·00

589 Thuparama
Stupa, 3rd-century
B.C.

1997. Vesak Festival. Anauradhapura Sites. Multicoloured.

1357	1r. Type **589**	15	10
1358	2r.50 Ruwanvalisaya stupa,		
	61–137 B.C.	25	10
1359	3r. Abhayagiri Dagaba, 103–102		
	B.C.	30	15
1360	17r. Jethavana Dagaba,		
	276–303 A.D.	1·50	2·25
MS1361	170×90 mm. Nos. 1357/60	1·75	2·25

590 Don Johannes
Kumarage

1997. Birth Centenary of D. J. Kumarage (Buddhist
teacher).

1362	**590**	2r.50 multicoloured	1·75	1·00

591 "Munronia
pinnata"

1997. Medicinal Herbs. Multicoloured.

1363	2r.50 Type **591**	25	10
1364	14r. "Rauvolfia serpentina"	1·00	1·75

592 Tourist Board Logo,
Airliner and Holiday
Resorts

1997. Visit Sri Lanka.

1365	**592**	20r. multicoloured	2·75	3·25

1997. No. 1321 surch **1.00.**

1366	1r. on 8r.50 Pottery	6·00	55

594 Lyre Head Lizard

1997. Reptiles. Multicoloured.

1367	2r.50 Type **594**	10	10
1368	5r. Boie's roughside (snake)	20	25
1369	7r. Common Lanka skink	75	1·40
1370	20r. Great forest gecko	1·00	1·75
MS1371	170×90 mm. Nos. 1367/70	1·75	3·00

595 St. Servatius' College,
Matara

1997. Centenary of St. Servatius' College, Matara.

1372	**595**	2r.50 multicoloured	60	30

1997. National Heroes (2nd series). As T **586.**
Multicoloured.

1373	2r.50 Sri Indasara Nayake Thero		
	(Buddhist leader)	30	40
1374	2r.50 Abdul Aziz (trade union		
	leader)	30	40
1375	2r.50 Prof. Subramaniam		
	Vithiananthan	30	40
1376	2r.50 Vivienne Goonewardene		
	(politician)	30	40

596 The Nativity

1997. Christmas. Multicoloured.

1377	2r.50 Type **596**	15	10
1378	20r. Visit of the Three Kings	1·25	1·75
MS1379	170×90 mm. Nos. 1377/8	1·40	2·00

597 Young Men's Buddhist
Association Building,
Colombo

1998. Centenary of Young Men's Buddhist Association,
Colombo.

1380	**597**	2r.50 multicoloured	40	30

598 Sri Jayawardenapura
Vidyalaya School

1998. 175th Anniv of Sri Jayawardenapura Vidyalaya
School, Kotte.

1381	**598**	2r.50 multicoloured	40	30

599 Children and
Mathematical Symbols

1998. 50th Anniv of Independence. Multicoloured.

1382	2r. Type **599**	40	10
1383	2r.50 Flag and 1949 4c.		
	Independence stamp (38×28		
	mm)	1·00	65
1384	2r.50 People with technological		
	and industrial symbols	60	65
1385	5r. Dancers with arts and music		
	symbols	80	80
1386	10r. Women with cultural and		
	historical symbols	1·00	1·50

600 Scouts raising
Flag and Jamboree
Logo

1998. Fifth National Scout Jamboree, Kandy. Multicoloured.

1387		2r.50 Type **600**	50	10
1388		17r. Scout saluting and Jamboree emblem	1·60	2·50

601 W.H.O. Emblem in "50" and Flag of Sri Lanka

1998. 50th Anniv of W.H.O.

1389	**601**	2r.50 multicoloured	50	20

602 Chunam Box

1998. Traditional Jewellery and Crafts. Multicoloured.

1390		2r.50 Type **602**	20	10
1391		5r. Agate necklace	30	20
1392		10r. Bangle and hairpin	50	60
1393		17r. Sigiri ear-ring	80	1·25
MS1394	151×91 mm. Nos. 1390/3		1·50	2·25

603 Kelani River and Stupa

1998. Vesak Festival. Wall Paintings from Kelaniya Temple. Multicoloured.

1395		1r. Type **603**	10	10
1396		2r.50 Crown Prince Mahanaga and his court on way to Magampura	20	10
1397		4r. Mahanaga and wife with baby Yatala Tissa	35	30
1398		17r. Prince Mahanaga with King's minister	80	1·10
MS1399	170×90 mm. Nos. 1395/8		1·25	2·00

604 School Building and Emblem

1998. 175th Anniv of St. John's College, Jaffna.

1400	**604**	2r.50 multicoloured	30	15

605 Elephants in River

1998. Elephants. Multicoloured.

1401		2r.50 Type **605**	45	15
1402		10r. Cow and calf	75	50
1403		17r. Family group	1·10	1·25
1404		50r. Bull elephant	1·75	4·00
MS1405	105×90 mm. Nos. 1401/4		3·50	5·50

606 S.A.A.R.C. Flags and Logo

1998. Tenth Anniv of South Asian Association for Regional Co-operation.

1406	**606**	2r.50 multicoloured	55	25

607 William Gopallawa

1998. William Gopallawa (first President of Sri Lanka) Commemoration.

1407	**607**	2r.50 multicoloured	30	15

608 Satellite and Computer

1998. Year of Information Technology.

1408	**608**	2r.50 multicoloured	30	15

609 Ven. Kotahene Pannakitti Nayaka Thero (Buddhist scholar)

1998. Distinguished Personalities. Multicoloured.

1409		2r.50 Type **609**	30	30
1410		2r.50 Prof. Ediriweera Sarachchandra (scholar)	30	30
1411		2r.50 Sir Nicholas Attygalle (medical pioneer)	30	30
1412		2r.50 Dr. Samuel Fisk Green (Tamil scholar)	30	30

610 Flag of Sri Lanka and Lions Club Emblem

1998. Lions Clubs International 26th South Asia, Africa and Middle East Forum, Colombo.

1413	**610**	2r.50 multicoloured	2·00	1·25

611 "50" and Meteorological Symbols

1998. 50th Anniv of Department of Meteorology.

1414	**611**	2r.50 multicoloured	1·00	55

612 Virgin Mary and the Infant Jesus

1998. Christmas. Multicoloured.

1415		2r.50 Type **612**	15	10
1416		20r. The Annunciation	1·25	1·75
MS1417	90 ×150 mm. Nos. 1415/16		1·40	2·00

613 S. W. Bandaranaike as a Young Man

1999. Birth Centenary of S. W. Bandaranaike. Multicoloured.

1418		3r.50 Type **613**	1·25	1·25
1419		3r.50 Bandaranaike as Prime Minister	1·25	1·25
MS1420	81×100 mm. Nos. 1418/19		2·25	2·50

614 Traditional Dancer

1999

1422	**614**	1r. brown	10	10
1423	**614**	2r. blue	10	10
1424	**614**	3r. purple	15	10
1425	**614**	3r.50 blue	20	10
1426	**614**	4r. red	20	10
1427	**614**	5r. green	20	10
1428	**614**	10r. violet	30	20
1429	**614**	13r.50 red	40	30
1430	**614**	17r. green	45	40
1431	**614**	20r. brown	55	50
1431a	-	50r. brown and orange	75	70
1431b	-	100r. brown and ochre	1·25	1·40
1431c	-	200r. lavender and blue	2·50	2·75

DESIGNS—(25×30 mm): 50, 100 and 200r. As T **614** but with background of scroll work.
The 5r. to 20r. are larger, 21×26 mm.

615 Sir Arthur C. Clarke (author) and Spacecraft

1999. 50 Years of Communication Improvement. Multicoloured.

1432		3r.50 Type **615**	1·00	1·00
1433		3r.50 Sir Arthur C. Clarke with spacecraft orbiting Earth	1·00	1·00

Nos. 1432/3 were printed together, se-tenant, forming a composite design.

616 Salvation Army Badge, Bible and Cross

1999. 116th Anniv of Salvation Army in Sri Lanka.

1434	**616**	3r.50 multicoloured	1·00	70

617 Activities of British Council

1999. 50th Anniv of British Council.

1435	**617**	3r.50 multicoloured	60	50

618 "Birth of Prince Siddhartha"

1999. Vesak Festival. Multicoloured.

1436		2r. Type **618**	10	10
1437		3r.50 "The Enlightenment"	15	15
1438		13r.50 "The Maha Parinirvana"	60	85
1439		17r. Celebrating Vesak	80	1·25
MS1440	151×90 mm. Nos. 1436/9		1·50	2·25

619 Dish Aerial and Transmitting Tower

1999. 20th Anniv of Independent Television.

1441	**619**	3r.50 multicoloured	80	40

620 Sumithrayo Logo

1999. 25th Anniv of Sumithrayo (humanitarian charity).

1442	**620**	3r.50 multicoloured	1·25	60

621 Scene from "Handaya" and Camera Crew

1999. 50 Years of Sri Lankan Cinema. Multicoloured.

1443		3r.50 Type **621**	20	10
1444		4r. Scene from "Nidhanaya" and film societies' emblems	20	10
1445		10r. Scene from "Gamperaliya" and camera crew	50	50
1446		17r. Two scenes from "Kadawunu Poronduwa"	90	1·60
MS1447	109×183 mm. Nos. 1443/6		1·60	2·25

622 Vidyodaya Pirivena

1999. 125th Anniv of Vidyodaya Pirivena (Buddhist education foundation).

1448	**622**	3r.50 multicoloured	45	30

623 Hector Kobbekaduwa

1999. Hector Kobbekaduwa (former Minister of Agriculture and Lands) Commemoration.

1449	**623**	3r.50 multicoloured	45	30

624 Hands holding Emblem, Fountain Pen and Magazine

1999. Centenary of Bhakthi Prabodanaya (religious magazine).

1450	**624**	3r.50 multicoloured	45	30

625 Army Emblem and Flags

1999. 50th Anniv of Sri Lankan Army.
1451 **625** 3r.50 multicoloured ... 65 ... 40

626 Emblem and Scenery within Segments of Circle

1999. 50th Anniv of Sri Lankan National Commission for UNESCO.
1452 **626** 13r.50 multicoloured ... 3·00 ... 3·00

627 Two Children on Globe within Hands

1999. Tenth Anniv of United Nations Rights of the Child Convention.
1453 **627** 3r.50 multicoloured ... 1·25 ... 80

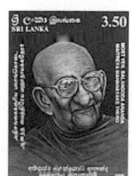

628 Ven. Balangoda Ananda Maitreya

1999. Ven. Balangoda Ananda Maitreya (Buddhist monk and teacher).
1454 **628** 3r.50 multicoloured ... 40 ... 30

629 The Nativity

1999. Christmas. Multicoloured.
1455 3r.50 Type **629** ... 40 ... 10
1456 20r. Visit of Three Wise Men ... 1·90 ... 2·50
MS1457 150×90 mm. Nos. 1455/6 ... 2·25 ... 2·75

630 Sunil Santha

1999. 85th Birth Anniv of Sunil Santha (musician and teacher).
1458 **630** 3r.50 multicoloured ... 1·75 ... 1·00

1999. No. 1317a surch **2.00**.
1459 2r. on 2r.50 Devinawara Lighthouse ... 6·00 ... 1·00

632 Dr. Pandithamani Kanapathipillai

1999. Birth Centenary of Dr. Pandithamani Kanapathipillai (Tamil scholar).
1460 **632** 3r.50 multicoloured ... 1·50 ... 80

633 Emblem, Figures and Inscriptions

1999. Bicentenary of State Audit Department.
1461 **633** 3r.50 multicoloured ... 1·00 ... 60

634 Dr. Badiudin Mahmud

1999. 95th Birth Anniv of Dr. Badiudin Mahmud (Islamic polititian).
1462 **634** 3r.50 multicoloured ... 1·75 ... 80

635 "Christian Family" (David Paynter)

1999. Sri Lankan Paintings. Multicoloured.
1463 3r.50 Type **635** ... 20 ... 10
1464 4r. "Sri Lankan Woman" (Justin Daraniyagala) ... 20 ... 10
1465 17r. "Waiting for the Fishermen" (Ivan Peries) ... 70 ... 1·10
1466 20r. "Composing the 'Tripitaka" (Soliyas Mendis) ... 80 ... 1·25
MS1467 150×91 mm. Nos. 1463/6 ... 1·50 ... 2·25

636 Kumar Anandan swimming Palk Strait

1999. Sporting Achievements. Multicoloured.
1468 1r. Type **636** ... 25 ... 10
1469 3r.50 Batsman and trophy (One Day Cricket World Champions, 1996) (vert) ... 70 ... 30
1470 13r.50 Athletics (vert) ... 1·25 ... 2·00

637 Striped Albatross (butterfly)

1999. Butterflies. Multicoloured.
1471 3r.50 Type **637** ... 55 ... 10
1472 13r.50 Ceylon tiger ... 1·25 ... 1·25
1473 17r. Three-spot grass yellow ... 1·60 ... 1·75
1474 20r. Great orange tip ... 1·75 ... 2·00
MS1475 90×148 mm. Nos. 1471/4 ... 4·50 ... 4·50

638 Doves at Nest and Religious Symbols

2000. New Millennium. Multicoloured.
1476 10r. Type **638** ... 75 ... 25
1477 100r. Girl reading within hands, Scales of Justice and Red Cross ... 3·25 ... 4·50
1478 100r. Man using computer, airliner and dish aerial ... 3·25 ... 4·50
1479 100r. People within open cupped hands ... 3·25 ... 4·50
MS1480 148×90 mm. Nos. 1476/9 ... 9·50 ... 12·00

639 Cathedral Church, Kurunagala

2000. 50th Anniv of Diocese of Kurunagala.
1481 **639** 13r.50 multicoloured ... 1·50 ... 2·00

640 College Logo and Figures around Globe

2000. 125th Anniv of Wesley College, Colombo.
1482 **640** 3r.50 multicoloured ... 45 ... 30

641 Buddhist Monk and Temple

2000. Centenary of Saddharmakara Pirivena (Buddhist college), Panadura.
1483 **641** 3r.50 multicoloured ... 45 ... 30

642 Boulder Coral

2000. Corals. Multicoloured.
1484 3r.50 Type **642** ... 55 ... 10
1485 13r.50 Blue-tipped coral ... 1·25 ... 1·50
1486 14r. Brain-boulder coral ... 1·25 ... 1·50
1487 22r. Elk-horn coral ... 1·75 ... 2·50
MS1488 148×90 mm. Nos. 1484/7 ... 4·25 ... 5·00

643 Arrival of Cutting from Jaya Sri Maha Bodhi (sacred tree)

2000. Vesak Festival. Multicoloured.
1489 2r. Type **643** ... 20 ... 10
1490 3r.50 King Devanampiyatissa carrying Jaya Sri Maha Bodhi ... 35 ... 20
1491 10r. Venerating the Java Sri Maha Bodhi ... 80 ... 90
1492 13r.50 Planting the cutting at Anuradhapura ... 1·10 ... 1·50
MS1493 98×166 mm. Nos 1489/92 ... 2·00 ... 2·50

644 Bar Association Logo and Courts

2000. 25th Anniv of Sri Lanka Bar Association.
1494 **644** 3r.50 multicoloured ... 45 ... 30

645 C.W.E. Emblem and People in Supermarket

2000. 50th Anniv of Co-operative Wholesale Establishment.
1495 **645** 3r.50 multicoloured ... 45 ... 30

2000. No. 1135 surch **.50**.
1496 50c. on 8r. Mountain labeo ... 6·00 ... 2·75

647 St. Patrick's College

2000. 150th Anniv of St. Patrick's College, Jaffna.
1497 **647** 3r.50 multicoloured ... 1·50 ... 80

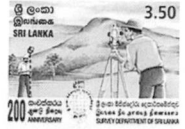

648 Surveyors at Work

2000. Bicentenary of Survey Department, Sri Lanka.
1498 **648** 3r.50 multicoloured ... 45 ... 30

649 Central Bank of Sri Lanka

2000. 50th Anniv of Central Bank of Sri Lanka.
1499 **649** 3r.50 multicoloured ... 45 ... 40

650 Dr. Maria Montessori

2000. 130th Birth Anniv of Dr. Maria Montessori (educator).
1500 **650** 3r.50 multicoloured ... 45 ... 30

651 "2" with Olympic Rings and Maps

2000. Olympic Games, Sydney. Multicoloured.
1501 10r. Type **651** ... 90 ... 1·00
1502 10r. Running ... 90 ... 1·00
1503 10r. Olympic flame ... 90 ... 1·00
1504 10r. Hurdling ... 90 ... 1·00
MS1505 172×96 mm. Nos. 1501/4 ... 3·00 ... 3·50

652 Association Flag and Conference Hall

2000. 50th Anniv of All Ceylon Young Men's Muslim Association Conference.
1506 **652** 3r.50 multicoloured ... 45 ... 30

653 Beach, Hotel and Bay-headed Bee Eaters

2000. 25th Anniv of Modern Hotel Industry.
1507   **653**   10r. multicoloured   2·50   2·00

654 Airliner, Ship and Globe

2000. 50th Anniv of Dept of Immigration and Emigration.
1508   **654**   3r.50 multicoloured   1·25   80

655 Saumiyamoorthy Thondaman

2000. Saumiyamoorthy Thondaman (politician) Commemoration.
1509   **655**   3r.50 multicoloured   75   50

656 Baddegama Siri Piyaratana Nayake Thero (Buddhist educator)

2000. Distinguished Personalities. Multicoloured.
1510   3r.50 Type **656**   40   50
1511   3r.50 Aluthgamage Simon de Silva (novelist)   40   50
1512   3r.50 Desigar Ramanujam (trade unionist)   40   50

657 Journey to Bethlehem

2000. Christmas. Multicoloured.
1513   2r. Type **657**   40   10
1514   17r. The Nativity   2·50   2·75
MS1515 150×91 mm. Nos. 1513/14   2·50   3·00

658 Lalith Athulathmudali

2000. Lalith Athulathmudali (politician) Commemoration.
1516   **658**   3r.50 multicoloured   45   30

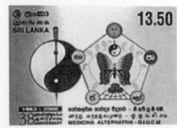

659 Five Elements and Butterfly

2000. 38th Anniv of Medicina Alternativa (alternative medicine society).
1517   **659**   13r.50 multicoloured   4·00   4·00

660 Chapel of Hope of the World

2000. Centenary of Ladies' College, Colombo.
1518   **660**   3r.50 multicoloured   45   30

661 Patrol Boat

2000. 50th Anniv of Sri Lanka Navy.
1519   **661**   3r.50 multicoloured   1·00   60

662 Peliyagoda Vidyalankara Pirivena Building

2000. 125th Anniv of Peliyagoda Vidyalankara Pirivena (Buddhist university).
1520   **662**   3r.50 multicoloured   45   30

663 Bishop's College

2001. 125th Anniv of Bishop's College, Colombo.
1521   **663**   3r.50 multicoloured   45   30

664 St. Thomas' College

2001. 150th Anniv of St. Thomas' College, Mount Lavinia.
1522   **664**   3r.50 multicoloured   45   30

665 Woman with Basket of Vegetables and Logo

2001. 70th Anniv of Lanka Mahili Samiti (rural women's society).
1523   **665**   3r.50 multicoloured   45   30

666 Air Force Crest and Aircraft

2001. 50th Anniv of Sri Lanka Air Force.
1524   **666**   3r.50 multicoloured   1·00   55

667 St. Lawrence's School

2001. Centenary (2000) of St. Lawrence's School, Wellawatta.
1525   **667**   3r.50 multicoloured   45   30

668 Bernard Soysa

2001. Bernard Soysa (politician) Commemoration.
1526   **668**   3r.50 multicoloured   45   30

669 Nagadeepa Stupa, Jaffna

2001. Vesak Festival. Buddhist shrines. Multicoloured.
1527   2r. Type **669**   10   10
1528   3r.50 Muthiyangana Chaithya, Badulla   20   10
1529   13r.50 Kirivehera Stupa, Kataragama   65   75
1530   17r. Temple of the Tooth, Kandy   90   1·25
MS1531 179×99 mm. Nos. 1527/30   1·60   2·25

670 "Hansa Jataka" (George Keyt)

2001. Birth Centenary of George Keyt (painter).
1532   **670**   13r.50 multicoloured   1·60   2·00

671 Gold Kahavanu Coin (9th century)

2001. Sri Lanka Coins. Multicoloured.
1533   3r.50 Type **671**   40   10
1534   13r.50 Silver coin of Vijayabahu I (11th-12th century)   1·00   1·00
1535   17r. Copper Sethu coin from Jaffna (13th-14th century)   1·40   1·60
1536   20r. Silver commemorative five rupee coin (1957)   1·60   1·75
MS1537 155×95 mm. Nos. 1533/6   4·00   4·25

672 Colombo Plan Emblem

2001. 50th Anniv of Colombo Plan.
1538   **672**   10r. multicoloured   85   1·00

673 Flags of Sri Lanka and U.S.A.

2001. 150th Anniv of Bi-lateral Relations with U.S.A.
1539   **673**   10r. multicoloured   85   1·00

674 Lance-Corporal Gamini Kularatne and Attack on Tank

2001. Tenth Death Anniv of Gamini Kularatne (war hero).
1540   **674**   3r.50 multicoloured   50   30

2001. No. 630 surch.
1541   **226**   5r. on 1r.15 multicoloured   4·00   1·75
1542   **226**   10r. on 1r.15 multicoloured   7·00   5·00

676 Prince and Princess of Wales Colleges, Moratuwa

2001. 125th Anniv of Prince and Princess of Wales Colleges, Moratuwa.
1543   **676**   3r.50 multicoloured   45   30

677 Congress Building

2001. All-Ceylon Buddhist Congress National Awards Ceremony.
1544   **677**   3r.50 multicoloured   1·50   80

678 Children encircling Globe

2001. U.N. Year of Dialogue among Civilizations.
1545   **678**   10r. multicoloured   85   1·00

679 Hand protecting Globe from Harmful Rays

2001. 13th Meeting of the Montreal Protocol Group (protection of Ozone Layer), Colombo.
1546   **679**   13r.50 multicoloured   1·25   1·50

680 Ramakrishna Mission Students' Home, Batticaloa

2001. 75th Anniv of Ramakrishna Mission Students' Home, Batticaloa.
1547   **680**   3r.50 multicoloured   45   30

681 Daul Drummer

2001. Drummers.
1548   1r. red   10   10
1549   -   2r. green   15   10
1550   -   3r. brown   25   10
1551   -   3r.50 blue   30   10
1552   -   4r. pink   30   10
1553   -   5r. orange   35   10
1554   -   10r. violet   65   20
1555   -   13r.50 violet   80   50
1555a   -   16r.50 violet   1·10   75
1556   -   17r. orange   1·10   55
1557   -   20r. blue   1·10   60
DESIGNS: (18×23 mm.)–1r. to 3r.50, Type **680**. (23×28 mm.)–4r. to 10r. Kandyan drummer; 13r.50 to 20r. Low Country drummer.

682 Bandaranaike Memorial International Conference Hall, Colombo

2001. 25th Anniv of S.W.R.D. Bandaranaike National Memorial Foundation.
1558   **682**   3r.50 multicoloured   50   25

683 Jesus with Children

2001. Christmas. Multicoloured.
1559   3r.50 Type **683**   15   10
1560   17r. Angel Gabriel appearing to Mary   85   1·25
MS1561 150×120 mm. Nos. 1559/60   1·00   1·40

684 Conical Wart Pygmy
Tree-frog

2001. Fourth World Congress of Herpetology. Frogs.
Multicoloured.

1562	3r.50 Type **684**	25	10
1563	13r.50 Sharp-snout saddle tree-frog	70	75
1564	17r. Round-snout pygmy tree-frog	85	1·00
1565	20r. Sri Lanka wood frog	95	1·25
MS1566	180×120 mm. Nos. 1562/5	2·50	3·25

685 St. Bridget's
Convent

2002. Centenary of St. Bridget's Convent, Colombo.

1567	**685**	3r.50 multicoloured	45	30

686 Front Page from First
Edition of Ceylon
Government Gazette, 1802

2002. Bicentenary of Ceylon Government Gazette.

1568	**686**	3r.50 multicoloured	45	30

687 Prime Minister
D. Senanayake

2002. 50th Death Anniv of D. Senanayake (first Sri
Lankan Prime Minister).

1569	**687**	3r.50 multicoloured	45	30

688 Gamini Dissanayake
and Victoria Dam

2002. 60th Birth Anniv of Gamini Dissanayake (former
government minister).

1570	**688**	3r.50 multicoloured	45	30

689 Lester James Peries
and Awards

2002. Lester James Peries (film director).

1571	**689**	3r.50 multicoloured	45	30

690 Sinharaja Forest Reserve

2002. Natural Beauty of Sri Lanka. Multicoloured.

1572	5r. Type **690**	20	15
1573	10r. Horton Plains National Park	35	30
1574	13r.50 Knuckles Range	45	60
1575	20r. Rumassala Cliff and Bon- avista Coral Reef	70	1·25

691 Mount Fuji
and Flags of Sri
Lanka and Japan

2002. 50th Anniv of Sri Lanka–Japan Diplomatic
Relations.

1576	**691**	16r.50 multicoloured	85	1·10

692 President Ranasinghe
Premadasa and Modern
Housing Development

2002. Ninth Death Anniv of Ranasinghe Premadasa
(President 1989–93).

1577	**692**	4r.50 multicoloured	30	25

693 Queen Mahamaya's
Dream

2002. Vesak. Dambulla Raja Maha Vihara Rock Paintings.
Multicoloured.

1578	3r. Type **693**	10	10
1579	4r.50 Birth of Prince Siddhartha	15	10
1580	16r.50 Prince Siddhartha dem- onstrating his archery skills	70	90
1581	23r. Ordination of Prince Sid- dhartha	80	1·25
MS1582	150×93 mm. Nos. 1578/81	1·60	2·00

694 Madihe
Pamasiha
Nayaka Thera

2002. 90th Birthday of Most Venerable Madihe Pamasiha
Maha Nayaka Thera (Supreme Patriarch of Sri Lanka
Amarapura Maha Nikaya).

1583	**694**	4r.50 multicoloured	40	25

695 Buddhist Monk with
Pen and Scroll and Society
Emblem

2002. Centenary of Sri Lanka Oriental Studies Society.

1584	**695**	4r.50 multicoloured	40	25

696 Anniversary Emblem
and Association
Headquarters

2002. 125th Anniv of Rifai Thareeq Association of Sri
Lanka.

1585	**696**	4r.50 multicoloured	40	25

697 Discus Thrower

2002. 14th Asian Athletic Championships, Colombo.
Multicoloured.

1586	4r.50 Type **697**	15	10
1587	16r.50 Sprinter	60	65
1588	23r. Hurdler	80	1·25
1589	26r. Long jumper	80	1·25

698 Carved Stone Lion of
12th Century (squatting)

2002. 125th Anniv of National Museum, Colombo.
Multicoloured.

1590	4r.50 Type **698**	75	90
1591	4r.50 Carved stone lion of 12th century (standing)	75	90

Nos. 1590/1 were printed together, *se-tenant*, forming
a composite design.

699 "Sapu Mudra"
Logo of Sri Lanka
Tourist Board

2002. Tourism. "Sri Lanka A land like no other".

1592	**699**	10r. multicoloured	70	75

700 Dr. A. C. S.
Hameed

2002. Third Death Anniv of Dr. A. C. S. Hameed (Foreign
Minister 1977–92).

1593	**700**	4r.50 multicoloured	40	25

701 Freemasons Hall,
Colombo

2002. Centenary of Freemasons Hall (Victoria Masonic
Temple), Colombo (2001).

1594	**701**	4r.50 multicoloured	75	60

702 Holy Cross College,
Kalutara

2002. Centenary of Holy Cross College, Kalutara.

1595	**702**	4r.50 multicoloured	40	25

703 Berlin Buddhist
Vihara (temple)

2002. 50th Anniv of German Dharmaduta Society.

1596	**703**	4r.50 multicoloured	40	25

704 Images from
Children's Paintings

2002. International Children's Day.

1597	**704**	4r.50 multicoloured	40	25

705 Dr. M. C. M.
Kaleel

2002. Al-Haj Dr. M. C. M. Kaleel Commemoration.

1598	**705**	4r.50 green	40	25

706 College Entrance,
Arms and Building

2002. 150th Anniv of Uduppiddy American Mission
College.

1599	**706**	4r.50 multicoloured	40	25

707 Dr.
Wijayananda
Dahanayake

2002. Birth Centenary of Dr. Wijayananda Dahanayake
(politician and educational reformer).

1600	**707**	4r.50 brown	40	25

708 Meeting of King of
Kandy and Admiral van
Spilbergen, 1602 (from
painting by C. L. Beling)

2002. 400th Anniv of Sri Lanka–Netherlands Relations.

1601	**708**	16r.50 multicoloured	85	1·00

709 Virgin and
Child

2002. Christmas. Design showing stained glass windows.
Multicoloured.

1602	4r.50 Type **709**	15	10
1603	26r. Holy Family	1·10	1·40
MS1604	190×130 mm. Nos. 1602/3	1·25	1·75

710 Woman harvesting
Rubber and Chinese Rice
Farmer

2002. 50th Anniv of Ceylon–China Rubber–Rice Pact.

1605	**710**	4r.50 multicoloured	40	25

711 Kopay Christian
College

2002. 150th Anniv of Kopay Christian College.

1606	**711**	4r.50 multicoloured	40	25

2002. No. 1075 surch **.25.**

1606a	25c. on 5r.75 multicoloured	50	25

2002. No. 1551 surch **4.25.**

1606b	4r.50 on 3r.50 blue	1·25	50

712 Teacher and Class

2003. Centenary of Teachers' College, Maharagama.
1607 **712** 4r.50 multicoloured 40 25

713 Stained Glass Window

2003. Centenary of Holy Family Convent, Bambalapitiya.
1608 **713** 4r.50 multicoloured 40 25

2003. No. 1556 surch **.50.**
1609 50c. on 17r. orange 50 40

715 M. D. Banda and Rice Fields

2003. 30th Death Anniv (2004) of M. D. Banda (politician).
1610 **715** 4r.50 multicoloured 40 25

716 Scholar and Buildings

2003. Centenary of Balagalle Saraswati Maha Pirivena.
1611 **716** 4r.50 multicoloured 40 25

717 D. B. Welagedara

2003. D. B. Welagedara (politician) Commemoration.
1612 **717** 4r.50 multicoloured 40 25

718 Children paying Obeisance to Parents

2003. Vesak. Multicoloured.
1613 2r.50 Type **718** 10 10
1614 3r. Dhamma school 15 15
1615 4r.50 Bhikku on alms round 20 15
1616 23r. Meditation 1·25 1·60
MS1617 93×152 mm. Nos. 1613/16 1·50 1·75

719 Stupa

2003. Features of Construction of Dagobas in Ancient Sri Lanka. Multicoloured.
1618 4r.50 Type **719** 15 10
1619 16r.50 Guard stones and flight of steps (57×28 mm) 70 70
1620 50r. Moonstone (horiz) 1·40 1·75
MS1621 155×116 mm. Nos. 1618/20 2·00 2·75

720 Emblem

2003. Second World Hindu Conference, Sri Lanka.
1622 **720** 4r.50 multicoloured 40 25

721 Nurses carrying Lamps and Florence Nightingale

2003. International Nursing Day.
1623 **721** 4r.50 multicoloured 40 25

722 Sirimavo Bandaranaike Memorial Exhibition Centre and Mrs. Bandaranaike (former Prime Minister)

2003. Opening of Sirimavo Bandaranaike Memorial Exhibition Centre. Joint issue with People's Republic of China.
1624 **722** 4r.50 multicoloured 40 25

723 Al-Haj H. S. Ismail

2003. Al-Haj H. S. Ismail (former Speaker of Parliament) Commemoration.
1625 **723** 4r.50 multicoloured 40 25

724 Plantation Workers, Port, Cogwheels and Computer

2003. 25th Anniv of Board of Investment of Sri Lanka.
1626 **724** 4r.50 multicoloured 40 25

725 Pidurutalagala Mountain Range

2003. World Bio-diversity Day. Multicoloured.
1627 4r. Type **725** 15 10
1628 4r.50 Seven Maidens Mountain Range 15 10
1629 16r.50 Kirigalpoththa Mountain 65 80
1630 23r. Ritigala Mountain 85 1·10

726 College Arms

2003. Centenary of G/Gonapinuwala Saralankara College.
1631 **726** 4r.50 multicoloured 40 25

727 Masjidul Abrar Jummah Mosque (central section)

2003. First Arab Settlement in Sri Lanka, Beruwala. Multicoloured.
1632 4r.50 Type **727** 15 10
1633 23r. Masjidul Abrar Jummah Mosque, Beruwala (57×22 mm) 85 1·25

728 Healthy People and Drug Addicts

2003. Anti Narcotic Week.
1634 **728** 4r.50 multicoloured 1·00 50

729 Malwathu Maha Viharaya

2003. 250th Anniv of Buddhist Higher Ordination in Sri Lanka. Multicoloured.
1635 4r.50 Type **729** 50 50
1636 4r.50 Asgiri Maha Viharaya 50 50

730 Two Cow Elephants with Calves

2003. Elephant Orphanage, Pinnawala. Multicoloured.
1637 4r.50 Type **730** 30 10
1638 16r.50 Keeper hand feeding milk to young elephant 75 75
1639 23r. Young elephant and calf 1·10 1·40
1640 26r. Tusker 1·10 1·40
MS1641 183×100 mm. Nos. 1637/40 3·00 3·75

731 Emblem and Mother with Children looking at Stamp Album

2003. "Lanka Philex 2003" Stamp Exhibition, Colombo. 25th Anniv of Philatelic Society of Sri Lanka.
1642 **731** 16r.50 multicoloured 1·00 1·25
MS1643 111×92 mm. **731** 16r.50 multicoloured 1·50 1·75

732 Dr. Ananda Tissa de Alwis

2003. Dr Ananda Tissa de Alwis (first Speaker of New Parliament, Kotte) Commemoration.
1644 **732** 4r.50 multicoloured 50 35

733 Ven Mohottiwatte Gunananda Thero, Wheel and Globe

2003. 130th Anniv of the Great Panadura Controversy (debate between Buddhists and Christians).
1645 **733** 4r.50 multicoloured 50 35

734 Ven Haldanduwana Dhammarakkitha Thero

2003. Ven Haldanduwana Dhammarakkitha Thero (Chief Sanganayake and Buddhist philosopher) Commemoration.
1646 **734** 4r.50 multicoloured 50 35

735 Shrine in Procession

2003. 75th Anniv of Poson Maha Perahara (cultural pageant).
1647 **735** 4r.50 multicoloured 1·00 50

736 M. H. M. Ashraff

2003. M. H. M. Ashraff (leader of National Unity Alliance) Commemoration.
1648 **736** 4r.50 multicoloured 70 40

737 Convent of Sisters of the Holy Angels

2003. Centenary of the Sisters of the Holy Angels.
1649 **737** 4r.50 multicoloured 35 35

738 Black-necked Stork

2003. Resident Birds of Sri Lanka. Multicoloured.
1650 4r.50 Type **738** 40 40
1651 4r.50 Purple swamphen 40 40
1652 4r.50 Grey heron 40 40
1653 4r.50 White-throated kingfisher 40 40
1654 4r.50 Black-crowned night heron 40 40
1655 4r.50 Scarlet minivet 40 40
1656 4r.50 White-rumped shama 40 40
1657 4r.50 Malabar trogon 40 40
1658 4r.50 Asiatic paradise flycatcher 40 40
1659 4r.50 Little green bee eater 40 40
1660 4r.50 Brown wood owl 40 40
1661 4r.50 Crested serpent eagle 40 40
1662 4r.50 Asian crested goshawk 40 40
1663 4r.50 Jungle owlet 40 40
1664 4r.50 Chestnut-bellied hawk eagle ("Rufous-bellied Eagle") 40 40
1665 4r.50 Chestnut mannikin ("Black-headed Munia") 40 40
1666 4r.50 Pompadour green pigeon 40 40
1667 4r.50 Plum-headed parakeet 40 40
1668 4r.50 Crimson-breasted barbet ("Coppersmith Barbet") 40 40
1669 4r.50 Emerald dove 40 40
1670 4r.50 Blue-faced Malkoha 40 40
1671 4r.50 Travancore scimitar babbler 40 40
1672 4r.50 Painted partridge ("Painted Francolin") 40 40
1673 4r.50 Lesser flame-backed woodpecker ("Red-backed Woodpecker") 40 40
1674 4r.50 Malabar pied hornbill 40 40

739 Globe and City

2003. World Habitat Day.
1675 **739** 4r.50 multicoloured 40 25

740 Globe, Post, Computer, Fax and Telephone

2003. World Post Day.
1676	**740**	23r. multicoloured	1·25	1·50

741 Blue Sapphire

2003. National Gem Stone of Sri Lanka (Blue Sapphire).
1677	**741**	4r.50 multicoloured	20	10
1677aa	**741**	5r. multicoloured	20	10

742 Pope John Paul II

2003. 25th Anniv of the Pontificate of Pope John Paul II.
1678	**742**	4r.50 multicoloured	75	45

743 Couple with Candle and Sacred Cow

2003. Deepavali Festival.
1679	**743**	4r.50 multicoloured	40	25

744 Ramboda Waterfall

2003. Waterfalls of Sri Lanka. Multicoloured.
1680	2r.50 Type **744**		10	10
1681	4r.50 Saint Clair Waterfall		20	10
1682	23r. Bopath Ella Waterfall		70	75
1683	50r. Devon Waterfall		1·40	2·00

745 Hon. U. B. Wanninayake

2003. Hon. U. B. Wanninayake (Minister of Finance, 1965–70) Commemoration.
1684	**745**	4r.50 multicoloured	40	25

746 St. Philipnery Church, Katukurunda, Kalutara

2003. Christmas. Multicoloured.
1685	4r.50 Type **746**		15	10
1686	16r.50 Angel and shepherds (vert)		60	80

747 Dr. Pandith Amaradeva

2003. Sri Lankan Artists' Day. Dr. Pandith W. D. Amaradeva (musician).
1687	**747**	4r.50 multicoloured	50	35

748 Gangarama Seemamalakaya

2003. Sri Jinaratana Vocational Training Centre.
1688	**748**	4r.50 multicoloured	40	25

749 Pushparamaya Temple, Malegoda

2003. Daham Pahana (Buddhist Religious Ceremony).
1689	**749**	4r.50 multicoloured	40	25

750 Jummah Mosque, Beruwala

2004. 140th Anniv of Shazuliyathul Fassiya Tharika.
1690	**750**	18r. multicoloured	70	90

751 Emblem of Chavakachcheri Hindu College

2004. Centenary of Chavakachcheri Hindu College.
1691	**751**	4r.50 multicoloured	30	25

752 Cricket Match

2004. 125th Cricket Match between The Royal and S. Thomas Colleges.
1692	**752**	4r.50 multicoloured	70	45

753 D. B. Wijetunga

2004. 82nd Birth Anniv of D. B. Wijetunga (President 1993–94).
1693	**753**	4r.50 multicoloured	30	25

754 Old and Young Trees

2004. 150th Anniv of Inauguration of the Planters Association.
1694	**754**	4r.50 multicoloured	75	50

755 Mapalagama Vipulasara Thero (artist)

2004. Distinguished Personalities. Multicoloured.
1695	3r.50 Type **755**		20	20
1696	3r.50 Cathiravelu Sittampalam (politician)		20	20
1697	3r.50 Maithripala Senanayeke (politician)		20	20
1698	3r.50 M. G. Mendis (politician)		20	20

756 Cricket Player, Ball and Emblems

2004. 75th Anniv of Ananda and Nalanda Cricket Matches. "Battle of the Maroons".
1699	**756**	4r.50 multicoloured	1·00	60

757 Anthony's College, Kandy

2004. 150th Anniv of St. Anthony's College, Kandy.
1700	**757**	4r.50 multicoloured	30	25

758 Sucharita going to Pandit Vidhura

2004. Vesak. Multicoloured.
1701	4r. Type **758**		15	10
1702	4r.50 Sucharita meeting with Pandit Vidhura		15	10
1703	16r.50 Sucharita introduced to Badraka by Pandit Vidhura		60	70
1704	20r. Sucharita going to Sanjaya, who advises meeting Prince Sambava		75	85
MS1705	122×81 mm. 26r. Sucharita meeting Badraka and Sanjaya		1·00	1·50

759 "Gongalegoda Banda"

2004. 155th Death Anniv of Wansapurna Deva David "Gongalegoda Banda" (leader of 1848 Rebellion).
1706	**759**	4r.50 multicoloured	30	25

760 Stylized Figure in Blood Droplet and Globe

2004. World Blood Donor Day (14th June).
1707	**760**	4r.50 multicoloured	50	25

761 Swimming

2004. Olympic Games, Athens. Multicoloured.
1708	4r.50 Type **761**		15	10
1709	16r.50 Woman sprinting		60	65
1710	17r. Shooting		60	65
1711	20r. Men's athletics		70	80

762 Sri Siddartha Buddharakkhita

2004. Most Venerable Sri Siddartha Buddharakkhita (the first Maha Nayaka of the Malwatta Chapter) Commemoration.
1712	**762**	4r.50 brown	30	20

763 Robert Gunawardena

2004. Robert Gunawardena (revolutionary politician) Commemoration.
1713	**763**	4r.50 multicoloured	30	20

764 Junius Richard Jayewardene

2004. 98th Birth Anniv of Junius Richard Jayewardene (first Executive President of Sri Lanka).
1714	**764**	4r.50 multicoloured	30	20

765 Dove

2004. International Day of Peace.
1715	**765**	4r.50 multicoloured	30	20

766 Sri Chandraratne Manawasinghe

2004. 40th Death Anniv of Sri Chandraratne Manawasinghe (writer).
1716	**766**	4r.50 multicoloured	30	25

767 Government Service Buddhist Association Headquarters

2004. 50th Anniv of the Government Service Buddhist Association.
1717 **767** 4r.50 multicoloured 30 20

768 Two Different Postal Workers

2004. World Post Day.
1718 **768** 4r.50 multicoloured 30 20

769 Raddelle Sri Pannaloka Anunayaka Thero

2004. 60th Death Anniv of Most Venerable Raddelle Sri Pannaloka Anunayaka Thero (priest).
1719 **769** 4r.50 multicoloured 30 20

770 Jesus with Parents and Dove

2004. Christmas. Multicoloured.
1720 5r. Type **770** 35 20
1721 20r. Rev. Fr. Jacome Gonsalves, Bolawatta Roman Catholic Church and Rt. Rev. Dr. Edmond Peiris (60×25 mm) 90 1·00

771 Stylized Buildings, Computer Terminals, Houses, Screen with Atlas and Satellite Dish

2004. Information and Communication Technology Week.
1722 **771** 5r. multicoloured 35 20

772 De Soysa Hospital for Women

2004. 125th Anniv of De Soysa Hospital for Women.
1723 **772** 5r. multicoloured 35 20

773 Thalalle Siri Dhammananda Maha Nayaka Thero

2005. Most Venerable Thalalle Siri Dhammananda Maha Nayaka Thero (academic) Commemoration.
1724 **773** 5r. multicoloured 35 20

2005. No. 684 surch **.50**.
1725 50c. on 10c. Type **255** 2·00 1·00

2005. No. 964 and No. 967 surch **.50**.
1726 50c. on 35c. Type **385** 2·00 1·00
1727 50c. on 6r. Fiddler crab 2·00 1·00

2005. No. 1090 surch **.50**.
1728 50c. on 5r.75 Lunar surface and Earth from Moon 2·00 1·00

778 Prof. Hammalawa Saddhatissa Nayaka Maha Thero

2005. 15th Death Anniv of Prof. Hammalawa Saddhatissa Nayaka Maha Thero (academic).
1729 **778** 5r. multicoloured 35 20

779 T. B. Tennakoon

2005. 25th Death Anniv of T. B. Tennakoon (poet and politician).
1730 **779** 5r. multicoloured 35 20

780 Don Alwin Rajapaksa

2005. Birth Centenary of Don Alwin Rajapaksa (politician).
1731 **780** 5r. multicoloured 35 20

781 Ambulatory Meditation

2005. Vesak (Buddha Day). Multicoloured.
1732 4r.50 Type **781** 30 20
1733 5r. Spiritual bliss through Buddhism 35 25
1734 10r. Meditation in standing posture 65 65
1735 50r. Sedentary meditation 3·00 3·50
MS1736 98×149 mm. Nos. 1732/5 3·75 4·50

782 Rev. Marcelline Jayakody

2005. Rev. Marcelline Jayakody (Catholic Priest, film personality and song writer) Commemoration.
1737 **782** 20r. multicoloured 1·50 1·75

783 Stylized Family under Helmet

2005. National Rana Viru Day.
1738 **783** 50r. multicoloured 2·50 3·00

785 Deshamanya M. A. Bakeer Markar

2005. Deshamanya M. A. Bakeer Markar (former Speaker of Parliament and Governor of Southern Province) Commemoration.
1740 **785** 5r. multicoloured 35 25

786 Most Ven. Matara Kithalagama Sri Seelalankara Nayaka Thero

2005. Most Ven. Matara Kithalagama Sri Seelalankara Nayaka Thero (Buddhist monk) Commemoration.
1741 **786** 25r. multicoloured 1·25 1·50

787 South Asian Scenes

2005. SAARC South Asia Tourism Year.
1742 **787** 100r. multicoloured 5·00 5·50

788 Kalutara Bodhi and Dagoba

2005. Kalutara Bodhi and Dagoba.
1743 **788** 5r. multicoloured 35 25

789 New Postal Headquarters, Colombo

2005. Opening of New Postal Headquarters, Colombo.
1744 **789** 5r. multicoloured 35 25

2005. No. 1549 surch **50c**.
1745 50c. on 2r. emerald 2·00 1·00

791 National Seminary, Ampitiya

2005. 50th Anniv of National Seminary of Our Lady of Sri Lanka, Ampitiya, Senkadagala.
1746 **791** 10r. multicoloured 60 60

792 Letter and Parcel encircling Globe

2005. World Post Day.
1747 **792** 5r. multicoloured 35 25

793 Emblem

2005. 25th Anniv of the General Sir John Kotelawala Defence Academy.
1748 **793** 5r. multicoloured 35 25

794 Mary, Baby Jesus and Angel

2005. Christmas. Multicoloured.
1749 5r. Type **794** 35 15
1750 30r. Nativity 1·75 2·00
MS1751 93×132 mm. Nos. 1749/50 2·10 2·10

795 UN Emblem and Sri Lanka Flag

2005. 50th Anniv of Sri Lanka's Admission to the United Nations.
1752 **795** 20r. multicoloured 1·40 1·60

796 Higher Ordination (Upasampada) Ceremony

2005. Bicentenary of Sri Lanka Amarapura Maha Nikaya.
1753 **796** 10r. multicoloured 60 60

797 Minihagalkanda Area and Stone Tools

2005. Ancient Sri Lanka (1st series). Prehistoric Era. Multicoloured.
1754 5r. Type **797** 40 30
1755 20r. Extinct elephant, hippo and rhinoceros and bone fragments 1·50 1·50
1756 25r. Kuruwita, Batadomba-lena and human skull 1·50 1·60
1757 30r. Horton Plains and fossilised barley pollen 1·60 1·75

798 Wrecked Vehicles and Post Office Ruins, Kalmunai

2005. First Anniv of Tsunami Disaster. Multicoloured.
1758 5r. Type **798** 45 15
1759 20r. Wreckage of train 1·50 1·50
1760 30r. Tsunami wave 1·60 1·75
1761 33r. Tsunami waves and lighthouse 2·00 2·25

799 *Muntiacusmuntjak* ("Barking Deer")

2006. National Parks of Sri Lanka (1st series). Wilpattu National Park. Multicoloured.
1762 5r. Type **799** 40 15
1763 10r. White-bellied sea eagle 1·25 75
1764 20r. Sloth bear 1·40 1·40
1765 50r. Leopard 2·75 3·25
MS1766 Four sheets, each 99×69 mm. (a) No. 1762. (b) No. 1763. (c) No. 1764. (d) No. 1765 5·25 5·50

800 Emblem

2006. Centenary of The Institution of Engineers, Sri Lanka.
1767 **800** 5r. blue and black 35 25

801 1957 First Ceylon Postage Stamp Centenary 35c. Stamp

2006. 50th Anniv of First Europa Stamp. Multicoloured.
1768	100r. Type **801**	2·50	2·75
1769	500r. Map of Europe and galleon	11·00	13·00
MS1770	100×72 mm. Nos. 1768/9	14·00	16·00

802 Most Ven. Madithiyawala Vijithasena Anunayaka Thero

2006. Most Ven. Madithiyawala Vijithasena Anunayaka Thero Commemoration.
| 1771 | **802** | 17r. multicoloured | 1·00 | 1·00 |

803 Cricket Balls and Match

2006. Centenary Cricket Match between Kingswood College and Dharmaraja College, Kandy.
| 1772 | **803** | 4r.50 multicoloured | 1·00 | 55 |

804 Anagarika Dharmapala (founder) and First *Sinhala Baudhhaya* Newspaper

2006. Centenary of Sinhala Baudhhaya (Buddhist newspaper).
| 1773 | **804** | 5r. multicoloured | 35 | 25 |

805 Emblem

2006. 125th Anniv of National Cadet Corps.
| 1774 | **805** | 2r. multicoloured | 20 | 20 |

806 "A Plea to the Master to descend from the Heaven" (wall painting) and Tivamka Image House, Polonnaruva

2006. 2550th Anniv of Buddha Jayanthi (Vesak). Multicoloured.
1775	2r.50 Type **806**	20	25
1776	2r.50 "Queen Mahamaya on her Way to Visit her Parents" (bas relief) and Jetavana Vihara, Anuradhapura	20	25
1777	2r.50 "The Great Birth of Prince Siddhartha" (wall painting) and Shailabimbarama Vihara, Dodanduwa	20	25
1778	2r.50 "Asita, the Royal Teacher visits Prince Siddhartha" (wall painting) and Purwarama Viharaya, Kataluva	20	25
1779	2r.50 "The Great reuncation" (bas relief) and Girihandu, Vihara Ambalantota	20	25
1780	2r.50 "Defeat of Maras (evils) by the Master" (rock painting) and Hindagala Vihara, Hindagala	20	25
1781	2r.50 "The First Sermon of Dhammachakka pavattana sutta" (rock painting) and Rangiri Dambulu Vihara, Dambulla	20	25
1782	2r.50 "The Conversion of Alavaka, a Demon" (wall painting) and Sapugoda Vihara, Beruvala	20	25
1783	2r.50 "The Great Funeral Pyre of the Master" (wall painting) and Veheragalla Samudragiri Vihara, Mirissa	20	25
1784	2r.50 "Tapassu and Bhalluka arriving in Sri Lanka with the Relics of the Master" and Girihandu seya, Tiriyaya	20	25
1785	4r.50 "Perfection of generosity; Vessantara Jataka" (wall painting) and Bodhirukkharama Vihara, Eluvapitiya	30	35
1786	4r.50 "Perfection of wisdom: Paduma Jataka" (rock painting) and Kaballelena Vihara, Wariyapola	30	35
1787	4r.50 "Perfection of renunciation: Sutasoma Jataka" (wall painting) and Degaldoruva Vihara, Kandy	30	35
1788	4r.50 "Perfection of Equanimity: Sivi Jataka" (wall painting) and Paramakanda Vihara, Anamaduwa	30	35
1789	4r.50 "Perfection of Loving-kindness: Sachchankira Jataka" (wall painting) and Sunandarama Vihara, Ambalangoda	30	35
1790	4r.50 "Recitation of Chullahastipadopama sutta by Arhat Mahinda" and the Stupa at Mihintale	30	35
1791	4r.50 Establishment of Buddhism in Sri Lanka and the Rajagiri lena, Mihintale	30	35
1792	4r.50 Sri Maha Bodhi entering the City and the Sri Maha Bodhi at Anuradhapura	30	35
1793	4r.50 Writing Dhamma on ola leafs and Alu Vihara, Matale	30	35
1794	4r.50 Arrival of the tooth relic of the Master and coast at Lankapattana in Trincomalee	30	35
1795	5r. "The practice of Aranyaka tradition" (drawing) and Situlpavuva Vihara	30	35
1796	5r. Lovamahapaya Abhayagiri vihara, Vajra symbol and lotus	30	35
1797	5r. Emergence of katikavatas (treaty) and Vatadage in Polonnaruwa	30	35
1798	5r. Buddhist discourse between Sri Lanka and south east Asia and Tooth Relic Temple, Kandy	30	35
1799	5r. Translation of the Tripitaka into Sinhala and the Buddhajayanti Vihara, Columbo	30	35
1800	5r. Vesak festival and Deepadut-tarama Vihara, Kotahena	30	35
1801	5r. Serving food to Buddhist clergy and the refectory at Abhayagiriya, Anuradhapura	30	35
1802	5r. Chanting Paritta and the Nishshanka Lata Mandapa in Polonnaruwa	30	35
1803	5r. Village, temple, tank and Tissamaharama Stupa	30	35
1804	5r. Veneration of the Bodhi tree and Bodhighara, Nillakgama	30	35
1805	10r. Hatthikuchchi Vihara in Galgamuva and a Padhanaghara in Anuradhapura	50	55
1806	10r. A ritual performance for the tooth relic and Atadage, Polonnaruva	50	55
1807	10r. "Perahara" (painting) and Subodharama Vihara, Karagampitiya	50	55
1808	10r. Street market (wall painting), Mulgirigala Vihara and ancient coin	50	55
1809	10r. Sanctity of the temple (painting) and Namal Uyana in Ranava	50	55
1810	10r. Great Stupas in Rajarata: Ruvanvalisaya and Thuparama in Anuradhapura	50	55
1811	10r. Great Stupas in Ruhuna: Kirivehera at Kataragama and Stupa at Seruvila	50	55
1812	10r. Great Stupas in Uva and the north: at Mahiyangana and Nagadipa, Jaffna	50	55
1813	10r. Stupa at Kelaniya and the Samantakuta	50	55
1814	10r. Mutiyangana Stupa at Badulla and Stupa at Deeghavapi	50	55
1815	17r. Painted Stupas: Hanguranketa Raja Maha Vihara and ancient stupas at Kandarodai	75	80
1816	17r. Facade of stupa at Mihintale and "Bahiravas" (bas-relief)	75	80
1817	17r. The Twin-pond at Anuradhapura and Punkalasa (lotus pond) at Polonnaruva	75	80
1818	17r. Ruins of Mangul Maha Vihara in Lahugala and moonstone	75	80
1819	17r. Ruins of Muhudumaha Vihara in Potuvil and Bodhisattva Avalokiteshvara (statue)	75	80
1820	17r. Nalanda Gedige at Naula and Satmahal Prasada at Polonnaruva	75	80
1821	17r. Ruins and drawing of Lankatilaka Vihara, Polonnaruva	75	80
1822	17r. Tampita Vihara, Menikkadawara and Thuparama Image House, Polonnaruva	75	80
1823	17r. "The Buddhist Cosmos" (wall painting) and Omalpe Vihara, Kolonne	75	80
1824	17r. Madanvala Vihara, Hanguranketa and Makara Torana motif	75	80

807 Kotte Sri Kalyani Samagridharma Maha Sanga Sabha

2006. 150th Anniv of First Higher Ordination Ceremony of Kotte Sri Kalyani Samagridharma Maha Sanga Sabha.
| 1825 | **807** | 4r.50 multicoloured | 30 | 20 |

808 Sri Lanka Ramanna Maha Nikaya

2006. 65th Upasampada (Higher Ordination) Ceremony of Sri Lanka Ramanna Maha Nikaya.
| 1826 | **808** | 4r.50 multicoloured | 30 | 20 |

809 Boys

2006. 125th Anniv of St. Vincent's Boys Home, Maggona.
| 1827 | **809** | 10r. multicoloured | 60 | 60 |

810 Lakshman Kadirgamar

2006. Lakshman Kadirgamar (Minister of Foreign Affairs 1994–2001, 2004–5) Commemoration.
| 1828 | **810** | 10r. multicoloured | 60 | 60 |

811 St. John Dal Bastone and St. John Dal Bastone Church

2006. 125th Anniv of St. John Dal Bastone Church, Talangama South.
| 1829 | **811** | 5r. multicoloured | 35 | 25 |

812 St. John Ambulance and Volunteers with Casualty

2006. Centenary of St. John Ambulance in Sri Lanka.
| 1830 | **812** | 5r. multicoloured | 60 | 30 |

813 High Jump

2006. Tenth South Asian Games, Colombo. Multicoloured.
| 1831 | 10r. Type **813** | 60 | 40 |
| 1832 | 100r. Cycling | 5·00 | 5·00 |

814 St. Joseph's Church, Wennappuwa

2006. 125th Anniv of St. Joseph's Church, Wennappuwa.
| 1833 | **814** | 2r. multicoloured | 15 | 15 |

815 Professor Senaka Bibile

2006. Professor Senaka Bibile (founder of State Pharmaceuticals Corporation) Commemoration.
| 1834 | **815** | 10r. multicoloured | 60 | 60 |

816 Children and Globe

2006. World Children's Day.
| 1835 | **816** | 5r. multicoloured | 35 | 25 |

817 *Nelumbo nucifera* (Sacred Lotus), Western Province

2006. Provincial Flowers of Sri Lanka. Multicoloured.
1836	4r.50 Type **817**	50	30
1837	4r.50 *Cassia fistula* (Indian laburnum), North-Central Province	50	30
1838	50r. *Murraya paniculata* (orange jessmine), North-Western Province	4·50	5·00
1839	50r. *Rhynchostylis retusa* (foxtail orchid), Uva-Province	4·50	5·00

818 "Post for All–For All Places" (Kanchana Imesha Gimhani)

2006. World Post Day. Winning Entry in Children's Art Competition.
| 1840 | **818** | 40r. multicoloured | 3·00 | 3·50 |

2006. No. 1550 surch.
| 1841 | 20r. on 3r. cinnamon | 3·00 | 3·00 |

820 "Birth of Holy Jesus" (Ann Ruchini Prasanika Fernando)

2006. Christmas. Multicoloured.
| 1842 | 5r. Type **820** | 35 | 25 |
| 1843 | 20r. St. Anthony's Shrine, Wahakotte (horiz) | 1·40 | 1·60 |

821 Rugby Players

2006. 125 Years (2004) of Rugby Football in Sri Lanka.
1844 **821** 4r.50 multicoloured   75   30

822 D. M.
Rajapaksa

2006. D. M. Rajapaksa (peasants leader, educationist and member of Hambantota District Council 1936–45) Commemoration.
1845 **822** 5r. multicoloured   35   25

823 Vee
Bissakara
Govijana
Chaityaya,
Ambuluwawa

2006. Biodiversity Complex and Religious Centre, Ambuluwawa. Multicoloured.
1846 5r. Type **823**   35   25
1847 25r. Biodiversity Complex, Ambuluwawa (40×30 mm)   1·40   1·60

2006. No. 1322 surch.
1848 10r. on 10r.50 Mats   3·00   2·50

825 Kande Viharaya,
Aluthgama

2007. Inauguration of New Giant Buddha Statue at Kande Vihara, Aluthgama.
1849 **825** 5r. multicoloured   35   25

2007. No. 715 surch.
1850 50r. on 1r.60 black, yellow and purple   6·00   6·00

2007. Nos. 459 and 518 of Ceylon and Nos. 610, 1042 and 1487 surch.
1851 4r.50 on 50c. indigo and slate-grey (No. 459 of Ceylon)   1·00   80
1852 4r.50 on 50c. Type **161**   1·00   80
1853 4r.50 on 1r.15 Type **220**   1·00   80
1854 4r.50 on 5r.75 magenta, blue and black (No. 1042)   1·00   80
1855 4r.50 on 22r. Elk-horn coral (No. 1487)   1·00   80

829 Sigiriya, Sri Lanka and Great Wall of China

2007. 50th Anniv of Sri Lanka–China Diplomatic Relations.
1856 **829** 50r. multicoloured   3·75   4·00

2007. Nos. 457 and 524 of Ceylon and Nos. 1085, 1321, 1552, 1322 and 1640 surch.
1857 50c. on 35c. red and green (No. 457)   75   75
1858 50c. on 60c. Adam's Peak (No. 524)   75   75
1859 50c. on 5r.75 Type **456** (No. 1085)   75   75

1860 50c. on 8r.50 Pottery (No. 1321)   75   75
1861 50c. on 26r. Tusker (No. 1640)   75   75
1862 5r. on 4r. rose (No. 1552)   2·25   2·25

831 Batsman and Ball

2007. World Cup Cricket, West Indies. Multicoloured.
1863 5r. Type **831**   70   40
1864 50r. Sri Lanka team and national flag   5·00   5·50

832 I. M. R. A.
Iriyagolle

2007. Birth Centenary of Imiya Mudiyanselage Raphiel Abayawansa Iriyagolle (Minister of Education and Culture, 1965–70).
1865 **832** 5r. multicoloured   35   25

833 Ceylon 1857 6d.
Stamp and Mail Steamship

2007. 150th Anniv of the First Sri Lanka (Ceylon) Stamps. Multicoloured.
1866 5r. Type **833**   35   25
1867 10r. Ceylon 1857 5d., 10d. and 1s. stamps and mail runner   75   85
1868 20r. Ceylon 1857 1d. and 2d. stamps and mail canoe   1·40   1·60
1869 45r. Ceylon 1857 ½d. stamp and mail coach   3·50   3·75
MS1870 130×112 mm. Nos. 1866/9   6·00   6·50

834 King and Queen
(kneeling), King with
Courtiers and House with
Sivavatuka (bird) Figure

2007. Vesak. T **834** and similar horiz designs showing Thelpattha Jathaka wall paintings from Sri Sudharshanaramaya Vihara. Multicoloured.
1871 5r. Type **834**   35   40
1872 5r. King with courtiers and house with woman levitating and unconscious man   35   40
1873 20r. King on throne and riding elephant in procession led by drummers   1·40   1·75
1874 20r. Couple in bedroom, people tempted and devoured by demons of sensual pleasure and King on throne and riding elephant   1·40   1·75
MS1875 100×170 mm. Nos. 1871/4   3·50   3·75

835 Sri Lanka Team and
Stadium

2007. Sri Lanka—Runner Up in World Cup Cricket, West Indies. Multicoloured.
1876 15r. Type **835**   1·75   2·00
1877 15r. Mahela Jayawardena (team captain) and cricketers in action   1·75   2·00

836 Textile Cone

2007. Seashells of Sri Lanka. Multicoloured.
1878 5r. Type **836**   35   25
1879 12r. Aquatile hairy triton   90   95
1880 15r. Rose branched murex   1·10   1·25
1881 45r. Trapezium horse-conch   3·50   3·75
MS1882 228×137 mm. Nos. 1878/81   5·75   6·25

837 Scout Leader, Rover Scout,
Senior Scout and Cub Scout

2007. Centenary of World Scouting.
1883 **837** 5r. multicoloured   35   25

838 Shield

2007. Centenary of Sri Sangamitta Balika Maha Vidyalaya (girls' school), Matale.
1884 **838** 5r. multicoloured   35   25

839 Flowers and Temples

2007. 50th Anniv (2006) of the Sri Lanka–Japan Friendship Society.
1885 **839** 15r. multicoloured   1·10   1·40

840 Emblem

2007. 50th Anniv of Ceylon Baithulmal Fund.
1886 **840** 5r. multicoloured   35   25

841 Bogambara
and Welikada
Prisons and
Rehabilitation
Emblem

2007. Sri Lanka Prisons Day.
1887 **841** 5r. multicoloured   35   25

842 Emblem

2007. 104th Anniv of K/Jabbar Central College, Galagedara.
1888 **842** 5r. multicoloured   35   25

843 Founding of
Buddhist Vihara
in Berlin

2007. 50th Anniv of First Buddhist Mission to Germany.
1889 **843** 5r. multicoloured   35   25

844 Queen Mahamaya Sculpture, Adam's Peak, Mount Everest and Mayadevi Sculpture

2007. 50th Anniv of Sri Lanka–Nepal Diplomatic Relations.
1890 **844** 15r. multicoloured   1·10   1·40

845 Statue and Shrine of
Our Lady of Matara

2007. Centenary of the Shrine of Our Lady of Matara.
1891 **845** 5r. multicoloured   35   25

846 Basket-maker,
Ayurvedic Medicine,
Dancer and Chef

2007. World Tourism Day. 'Tourism opens Doors for Women'.
1892 **846** 5r. multicoloured   35   25

847 Emblem

2007. 50th Anniv of Lions International in Sri Lanka.
1893 **847** 5r. multicoloured   35   25

848 IMS Ribbon connecting Letter
Recipients Worldwide

2007. World Post Day.
1894 **848** 5r. multicoloured   35   25

849 Aries

2007. Constellations. Multicoloured

(a) 19×24 mm

1895 50c. Type **849**   10   10
1896 1r. Taurus   10   10
1897 2r. Gemini   15   10
1898 3r. Cancer   20   15
1899 4r. Leo   30   20
1900 4r.50 Virgo   35   25
1901 5r. Libra   35   25
1902 10r. Scorpius   80   85
1903 12r. Sagittarius   90   95
1904 15r. Capricornus   1·10   1·25
1905 20r. Aquarius   1·50   1·75
1906 25r. Pisces   2·10   2·25

(b) Size 25×30 mm

1907 30r. Centaurus   2·25   2·50
1908 35r. Ursa major   2·50   2·75
1909 40r. Ophiuchus   2·75   3·00
1910 45r. Orion   3·50   3·75
MS1911 100×95 mm. Nos. 1895/906   16·00   17·00
MS1912 119×50 mm. Nos. 1907/10   27·00   28·00

850 Young Farmers
and Produce

2007. National Farmers Day.
1913 **850** 5r. multicoloured   35   25

851 Water Buffaloes

2007. National Parks of Sri Lanka (2nd series). Udawalawe National Park. Multicoloured.

1914	5r. Type **851**	35	25
1915	15r. Elephants	1·10	1·25
1916	40r. Ruddy mongoose	2·75	3·00
1917	45r. Common langur	3·50	3·75

MS1918 Two sheets, each 126×85 mm.
(a) As Type **851**; As No. 1917. (b) As
Nos. 1915/16   6·75   7·00

852 Leslie
Goonewardene

2007. Birth Centenary (2009) of Leslie Goonewardene (Minister of Transport and Communications 1970–5).

1919	**852**	5r. multicoloured	35	25

853 Emblem and
Traditional Musician

2007. Commonwealth Games Federation General Assembly, Colombo. Multicoloured.

1920	5r. Type **853**	35	25
1921	45r. Emblem and winged figures	3·50	3·75

854 St. Henry's College,
Ilavalei

2007. Centenary of St. Henry's College, Ilavalei.

1922	**854**	5r. multicoloured	35	25

855 Nativity (Minura Senal
Bandara Ranatunge)

2007. Christmas. Multicoloured.

1923	5r. Type **855**	35	25
1924	30r. St. James' Church, Mutwal	1·40	1·60

No. 1923 was the winning design in a children's Christmas stamp design competition on the theme of 'Christmas and Unity'.

856 Muttiah
Muralitharan

2007. Muttiah Muralitharan

1925	**856**	5r. multicoloured	50	30

857 Hare and
Tortoise at Start of
Race

2007. Children's Stories (1st series). International Children's Broadcasting Day. The Race between the Hare and the Tortoise. Multicoloured.

1926	5r. Type **857**	35	40
1927	5r. Tortoise passing sleeping Hare	35	40
1928	5r. Tortoise laughing at finish and running Hare	35	40

858 St. Mary's Church,
Maggona

2007. 150th Anniv of St. Mary's Church, Maggona.

1929	**858**	5r. multicoloured	35	25

859 Placard 'Say No to
Corruption'

2007. International Anti-Corruption Day.

1930	**859**	5r. black and blue	35	25

860 Rural Landscape, Map and Satellite

2008. 500th Nenasala Initiative (to provide Information and Communication Technology access to rural areas).

1931	**860**	5r. multicoloured	35	25

861 Most Ven.
Halgasthota Sri
Devananda
Mahanayaka Thero

2008. Most Ven. Halgasthota Sri Devananda Mahanayaka Thero Commemoration.

1932	**861**	5r. multicoloured	35	25

862 National Flag
and '60'

2008. 60th Independence Day.

1933	**862**	5r. multicoloured	35	25

863 Deshamanya N. U.
Jayawardena

2008. Birth Centenary of Deshamanya N. U. Jayawardena (first Sri Lankan Governor of Central Bank of Sri Lanka, businessman and financier).

1934	**863**	5r. multicoloured	35	25

864 Young Man and
Woman releasing
Peace Dove

2008. Seventh Commonwealth Youth Ministers Meeting, Colombo.

1935	**864**	5r. multicoloured	35	25

865 St. Mary's Convent
School, Matara

2008. Centenary of St. Mary's Convent School, Matara.

1936	**865**	5r. multicoloured	35	25

866 Megalithic Cist
Burial and Necklace
of Beads
(600–400BC)

2008. Ancient Sri Lanka (2nd series). Proto-historic and Early Anuradhapura Periods. Multicoloured.

1937	5r. Type **866**	35	25
1938	10r. Abhaya (Basawakkulama) Veva (earth bank for irrigation) (3BC)	80	85
1939	12r. Vallipuram gold plate (letters in Brahmi characters) (1AD)	90	95
1940	15r. Alakolaveva iron furnace (1–2AD)	1·10	1·25
1941	30r. Gajalakshmi coin (1BC–4AD) and punch mark coin (3BC–4AD)	1·40	1·60
1942	40r. Sigiri painting (5AD)	1·60	1·75

867 King Daham Sonda and
Courtiers

2008. Vesak. Designs showing wall paintings from Reswehera Raja Maha Vihara, Kudakatnoruwa, Meegalewa. Multicoloured.

1943	4r.50 Type **867**	35	25
1944	5r. Procession with elephant	35	25
1945	15r. Goddess and demon	1·10	1·25
1946	40r. King Daham Sonda	1·60	1·75

MS1947 143×110 mm. Nos. 1943/6   3·50   3·75

868 Pistol Shooting

2008. Olympic Games, Beijing. Multicoloured.

1948	5r. Type **868**	35	25
1949	15r. Javelin throwing	1·10	1·25
1950	40r. Boxing	1·60	1·75
1951	45r. Running	1·75	1·90

869 Sigiri Painting (5AD), Flags of
Member Countries and Emblem

2008. 15th SAARC (South Asian Association for Regional Co-operation) Summit, Colombo.

1952	**869**	15r. multicoloured	1·10	1·25

870 Takiko Yoshida

2008. Birth Centenary of Takiko Yoshida (educationist and philanthropist).

1953	**870**	5r. multicoloured	35	25

871 Clasped Hands

2008. 50th Anniv of Employees Provident Fund.

1954	**871**	5r. multicoloured	35	25

872 Middle Age Gold Coin, its Mould
and Gold Ingot (8–10th century AD)

2008. Ancient Sri Lanka (3rd series). Late Anuradhapura Era. Multicoloured.

1955	5r. Type **872**	35	25
1956	10r. Remnants of Medirigiriya Vatadage and conjectural drawing of it in 7th century	80	85
1957	15r. Urinal stone at Western Monasteries, Anuradhapura and cross-section of sanitary system (7th–9th century AD)	1·10	1·25
1958	20r. Bangle, pendant, anklet and necklace of terracotta beads (8th–9th century AD)	1·50	1·60
1959	30r. Bodhisattva Vajrapani and Avalokithesvara statues at Buduruvagala and carved tableau of King Dutugemunu and family at Isurumuniya Vihara Museum (8th–9th century AD)	1·60	1·75

873

2008. Multicoloured, background colour given.

1960	**873**	50r. magenta	3·75	4·00
1961	**873**	70r. blue	4·00	4·25
1962	**873**	100r. bistre	4·50	4·75
1963	**873**	500r. orange	7·00	7·25
1964	**873**	1000r. lavender	13·00	13·50
1965	**873**	2000r. green	21·00	22·00

874 Post Boxes

2008. World Post Day.

1966	**874**	5r. multicoloured	35	25

875 Dutch Burgher Union
Hall

2008. Centenary of the Dutch Burgher Union of Ceylon.

1967	**875**	5r. multicoloured	35	25

876 Anton
Jayasuriya

2008. Professor Anton Jayasuriya (founder of Medicine Alternativa and the Open International University for Complementary Medicine) Commemoration.

1968	**876**	5r. multicoloured	35	25

877 Pieter
Keuneman

2008. Pieter Keuneman (founder General Secretary of the Communist Party of Sri Lanka, MP 1947–77, Minister of Housing and Construction 1970–7) Commemoration.
1969 **877** 5r. multicoloured 35 25

878 Scenes from the Story

2008. Childrens' Stories (2nd series). Lanka Philex 2008 National Stamp Exhibition. The Story of Two Men and the Bear.
1970 **878** 5r. multicoloured 35 25

879 Most Ven. Weweldeniye Medhalankara Mahanayake Mahathero

2008. Birth Centenary of Most Ven. Weweldeniye Medhalankara Mahanayake Mahathero.
1971 **879** 5r. multicoloured 35 25

880 *Christmas is the Peace Bridge Join the North and South of Sri Lanka* (Isuri Dileka Tittagalle)

2008. Christmas. Multicoloured.
1972 5r. Type **880** 35 25
1973 30r. St. Mary's Cathedral, Kaluwella, Galle (vert) 1·60 1·75

881 People enclosed in Cupped Hands

2008. 60th Anniv of the Universal Declaration of Human Rights.
1974 **881** 5r. multicoloured 35 25

882 Emblem

2008. 50th Anniv of Sri Lanka Transport Board.
1975 **882** 5r. multicoloured 35 25

883 River Channel of Madu Ganga

2009. World Wetland Day. Madu Ganga RAMSAR Wetland. Multicoloured.
1976 5r. Type **883** 35 25
1977 25r. Mangroves of Madu Ganga 1·50 1·60

884 Students with English Books, using Computers and Standing on Top of Globe

2009. Year of English and Information Technology.
1978 **884** 5r. multicoloured 35 25

885 University of Sri Jayewardenepura

2009. 50th Anniv of University of Sri Jayewardenepura.
1979 **885** 5r. multicoloured 35 25

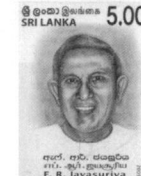

886 F. R. Jayasuriya

2009. Birth Centenary of Professor Felix Reginald Jayasuriya (former Professor of Economics at University of Kelaniya).
1980 **886** 5r. multicoloured 35 25

887 A. P. de Zoysa

2009. Agampodi Paulus de Zoysa (social reformer and Buddhist scholar) Commemoration.
1981 **887** 5r. multicolured 35 25

888 Pavilion, Moors Sports Club

2009. Centenary (2008) of Moors Sports Club, Colombo.
1982 **888** 5r. multicoloured 35 25

889 Steam Locomotive, Canadian Locomotive M-2/591 and Running Shed

2009. Centenary of Railway Running Shed, Dematagoda.
1983 **889** 5r. multicoloured 35 25

890 Mahmoud Shamsuddeen Kariapper

2009. Mahmoud Shamsuddeen Kariapper (politican and philanthropist) Commemoration.
1984 **890** 5r. multicoloured 35 25

891 Students and University Building

2009. Inauguration of University of Vocational Technology, Colombo.
1985 **891** 5r. multicoloured 35 25

892 Natural Rubber Research and Development

2009. Centenary of Natural Rubber Research and Development in Sri Lanka.
1986 **892** 5r. multicoloured 35 25

893 Jeyaraj Fernandopulle

2009. First Death Anniv of Jeyaraj Fernandopulle (Minister of Highways and Road Development).
1987 **893** 5r. multicoloured 35 25

894 Hand holding Flower and Plaque

2009. 300th Anniv (2008) of Leprosy Hospital, Hendala.
1988 **894** 5r. multicoloured 35 25

895 Sri Sumangala College, Panadura

2009. Centenary of Sri Sumangala College, Panadura.
1989 **895** 5r. multicoloured 35 25

896 Handupelpola Sri Punnaratana Nayaka Maha Thero

2009. Birth Centenary of Handupelpola Sri Punnaratana Nayaka Maha Thero (Professor of Archaeology and founder of Nalanda University College, Kudauduwa).
1990 **896** 5r. multicoloured 35 25

897 A Visit to the Temple

2009. Vesak. Multicoloured.
1991 4r. Type **897** 45 35
1992 5r. Meditation 55 45

898 Most Ven. Welithara Sri Gnanawimala Tissa Mahanayake Thero

2009. Most Ven. Welithara Sri Gnanawimala Tissa Mahanayake Thero Commemoration.
1993 **898** 5r. multicoloured 35 25

899 Hon. Nimal Siripala de Silva and Nurse with Baby

2009. Appointment of Hon. Nimal Siripala de Silva as President of World Health Assembly, 2009–10.
1994 **899** 5r. multicoloured 35 25

900 Galpotha Inscription of King Nissankamalla and Coin of Queen Leelawathi

2009. Ancient Sri Lanka (4th series). Polonnaruwa Era (1017–1235AD). Multicoloured.
1995 5r. Type **900** 20 20
1996 10r. Siva Temple and artefacts from temple 40 50
1997 15r. Parakrama Samudra reservoir and stone statue in Pothgul Vihara 60 70
1998 25r. Palace of King Parakrama-bahu and Audience Hall of King Nissankamalla 95 1·00
1999 30r. Ancient hospital with me-dicinal bath, surgical instru-ment and grinding stone 1·10 1·25
2000 40r. Hindu sculptures of Siva, Uma and Saint Karaikkal Ammaiyar 1·50 1·60

901 Mahmood Hasarath

2009. Mahmood Hasarath (Mahmood Abdul Majeed) (Principal of Cassimiyya Arabic College, 1944–85) Commemoration.
2001 **901** 5r. deep grey-green 35 25

902 Hameed Al Husseinie College, Colombo

2009. 125th Anniv of Hameed Al Husseinie College, Colombo.
2002 **902** 5r. multicoloured 35 25

903 Vidyalankara Pirivena and Modern Kelaniya University

2009. 50th Anniv of University of Kelaniya.
2003 **903** 5r. multicoloured 35 25

904 Bank of Ceylon

2009. 70th Anniv of the Bank of Ceylon.
2004 **904** 5r. multicoloured 35 25

905 Most Rev. Dr. Oswald Gomis

2009. Most Rev. Dr. Oswald Gomis, Archbishop of Colombo and Chancellor of the University of Colombo.

2005 **905** 15r. multicoloured 1·00 1·10

906 Globe, Ships, Airliner and Bullock Cart

2009. Bicentenary of Sri Lanka Customs.

2006 **906** 15r. multicoloured 1·00 1·10

907 Sree Narayana Gurudev

2009. 155th Birth Anniv of Sree Narayana Gurudev (Malayalee spiritual leader and social reformer).

2007 **907** 5r. chestnut and lake-brown 35 25

908 Sivali Central College, Ratnapura

2009. Centenary of Sivali Central College, Ratnapura.

2008 **908** 15r. multicoloured 1·00 1·10

909 Earth, Planets and Lines of Communication

2009. World Post Day.

2009 **909** 15r. multicoloured 1·00 1·10

910 Soldiers, Tanks and Arms and Flags of Sri Lanka

2009. 60th Anniv of Sri Lanka Army.

2010 **910** 15r. multicoloured 1·00 1·10

911 Community Dog

2009. Humane Eradication of Rabies.

2011 **911** 15r. multicoloured 1·00 1·10

912 Nativity (Isuru Sadara Miranda)

2009. Christmas. Multicoloured.

2012 5r. Type **912** 30 25
2013 15r. St. Mary's Cathedral, Badulla (horiz) 90 1·00

A miniature sheet containing No. 2012×2 was sold for 20r.
A miniature sheet containing No. 2013×2 was sold for 40r.

913 Mahogany Tree planted by Che Guevara at Horana

2009. 50th Anniv of Diplomatic Relations between Sri Lanka and Cuba.

2014 **913** 5r. multicoloured 35 25

914 Man in Wheelchair

2009. International Day of Persons with Disabilities.

2015 **914** 10r. multicoloured 50 60

915 Johannes Voet (Dutch jurist and Society founder)

2009. 110th Anniv of Voet Lights Society of Sri Lanka.

2016 **915** 15r. multicoloured 1·00 1·10

916 P. H. William De Silva

2009. Birth Centenary (2008) of Peduru Hewage William De Silva (Minister of Industries and Fisheries, 1956–9).

2017 **916** 10r. multicoloured 65 70

917 Dr. Hudson Silva

2009. 80th Birth Anniv of Dr. Hudson Silva (founder of Sri Lanka Eye Donation Society and Human Tissue Bank).

2018 **917** 10r. multicoloured 65 70

918 D. M. Dasanayake

2010. 2nd Death Anniv of Dasanayake Mudiyanselage Dasanayake (politician and Minister of Nation Building).

2019 **918** 10r. multicoloured 65 70

919 Thurstan College, Colombo

2010. 60th Anniv of Thurstan College, Colombo.

2020 **919** 10r. multicoloured 65 70

No. 2021, T **920** are left for Deyata Kirula personalised stamp, issued 4 February 2010, not yet received.

921 Trainees in Workshops and College Building

2010. 50th Anniv of Ceylon—German Technical Training Institute, Moratuwa.

2022 **921** 10r. multicoloured 65 70

922 Emblem and Government Officers

2010. Centenary of The Government Officers Benefits Association.

2023 **922** 5r. multicoloured 35 25

923 Rotary Emblem

2010. 80th Anniv of Rotary in Sri Lanka.

2024 **923** 10r. multicoloured 65 70

924 M. J. C. Fernando and Buddhist Hall, Moratuwa

2010. 125th Birth Anniv of M. J. C. Fernando (founder of Sri Lanka Bauddha Samitiya for Buddhist Education in Moratuwa)

2025 **924** 10r. multicoloured 70 70

925 Buddhist Flag and Globe

2010. 125th Anniv of the Buddhist Flag

2026 **925** 5r. multicoloured 50 50

926 Arrival of Lord Buddha to Mahiyanganaya

2010. Vesak. Multicoloured.

2027 4r. Type **926** 30 25
2028 5r. Mahiyangana Stupa 35 25
2029 10r. Mirisawetiya Stupa, Anuradhapura (horiz) 65 70
2030 30r. Jetawana Stupa, Anuradhapura (horiz) 1·75 2·00
MS2031 117×180 mm. Nos. 2027/30 3·00 3·00

927 St. Anthony's Shrine, Kochchikade, Colombo

2010. 175th Anniv of Consecration of St. Anthony's Shrine, Kochchikade, Colombo

2032 **927** 5r. multicoloured 35 25

928 Sri Kalyaniwansa Nikaya

2010. Bicentenary of Sri Kalyaniwansa Nikaya

2033 **928** 10r. multicoloured 70 70

929 Mahajana College, Tellippalai

2010. Centenary of Mahajana College, Tellippalai

2034 **929** 10r. multicoloured 70 70

930 Pepiliyana Sunethra Mahadevi Piriven Rajamaha Viharaya

2010. 600th Anniv of Pepiliyana Sunethra Mahadevi Piriven Rajamaha Viharaya

2035 **930** 5r. multicoloured 35 25

931 Dove with Olive Branch flying over Map of Sri Lanka (V. Jeyarajasinham)

2010. First Anniv of Victory and Peace

2036 **931** 5r. multicoloured 35 25

932 Postmen's Uniforms and Pillar Boxes, National Postal Museum

2010. Inauguration of National Postal Museum and Philatelic Exhibition Centre, Colombo. Multicoloured.

2037 5r. Type **932** 35 25
2038 5r. Early Ceylon stamps and stamp exhibits, Philatelic Exhibition Centre 35 25

933 Early and Modern Hospitals, Anuradhapura

2010. 50th Anniv of Teaching Hospital, Anuradhapura

2039 **933** 5r. multicoloured 35 25

934 Royal College, Colombo (Lahiru Anuradha Jayakody)

2010. 175th Anniv of Royal College, Colombo
2040 **934** 10r. multicoloured 70 70

935 Kokuvil Hindu College

2010. Centenary of Kokuvil Hindu College
2041 **935** 10r. multicoloured 70 70

936 M. P. De Zoysa

2010. Birth Centenary of M. P. De Zoysa (politician)
2042 **936** 10r. multicoloured 70 70

937 '1ST YOG', Mascots and Emblems

2010. First Youth Olympic Games, Singapore
2043 **937** 10r. multicoloured 70 70

938 Central Bank of Sri Lanka on Banknote

2010. 60th Anniv of Central Bank of Sri Lanka
2044 **938** 10r. multicoloured 70 70

939 Pasikudah Beach

2010. Beaches. Multicoloured.
2045 15r. Type **939** 1·00 1·10
2046 25r. Rocky headland, Trincomalee Beach 1·75 2·00
2047 40r. Surfer at Arugam Bay
Beach 2·75 3·00

940 Sri Lanka Whistling Thrush

2010. National Parks of Sri Lanka (3rd series). Multicoloured.
2048 5r. Type **940** 35 25
2049 15r. Sambur (horiz) 1·00 1·10
2050 25r. Rhinohorn lizard (horiz) 1·75 2·00
2051 40r. Purple-faced leaf monkey 2·75 3·00
MS2052 130×90 mm. No. 2049 1·10 1·25

941 Faculty of Engineering, University of Peradeniya

2010. 60th Anniv of Engineering Faculty, University of Peradeniya
2053 **941** 15r. multicoloured 1·00 1·10

942 Ozone Layer with Parasol

2010. 25th Anniv of Vienna Convention for Ozone Layer Protection
2054 **942** 5r. multicoloured 35 25

943 Indigenous People

2010. World Indigenous People's Day. Multicoloured.
2055 5r. Type **943** 35 25
2056 5r. Cave painting 35 25

944 St. Michael's Church, Koralawella

2010. 150th Anniv of St. Michael's Church, Koralawella
2057 **944** 5r. multicoloured 35 25

945 St. Michael's Church, Koralawella

2010. World Children's Day
2058 **945** 5r. multicoloured 35 25

946 Cranes carrying Tortoise

2010. Children's Stories (3rd series). *How the Tortoise Flew*
2059 **946** 5r. multicoloured 35 25

947 Globe and Letter

2010. World Post Day
2060 **947** 5r. multicoloured 35 25

948 Rankot Viharaya, Panadura

2010. Bicentenary of Rankot Viharaya, Panadura
2061 **948** 5r. multicoloured 35 25

949 Anglican Church

2010. 125th Anniv of Diocesan Council for Diocese of Colombo
2062 **949** 5r. multicoloured 35 25

950 Louis Braille

Birth Bicentenary of Louis Braille (inventor of Braille writing for the blind) and World White Cane Day
2063 **950** 5r. multicoloured 35 25

951 Buddhists praying

2010. World Fellowship of Buddhists
2064 **951** 5r. multicoloured 35 25

952 Magam Ruhunupura Port, Map of Southeast Asia and Pres. Rajapaksa

2010. Inauguration of Magam Ruhunupura Port
2065 **952** 5r. multicoloured 35 25

953 Family around Christmas Tree (R. P. G. Savinda Shyamal Karunathilake)

2010. Christmas. Multicoloured.
2066 5r. Type **953** 35 25
2067 15r. St. Mary's Church, Kegalle 90 80

954 Gunboat

2010. 60th Anniv of the Sri Lanka Navy
2068 **954** 5r. multicoloured 35 25

955 Holy Emmanuel Church, Moratuwa

2010. 150th Anniv of Holy Emmanuel Church, Moratuwa
2069 **955** 5r. multicoloured 35 25

956 Labugama Reservoir

2011. 125th Anniv of Labugama Reservoir
2070 **956** 5r. multicoloured 35 25

957 Dr. P. R. Anthonis

2011. Birth Centenary of Dr. Polwatte Arachchige Romeil Anthonis (surgeon)
2071 **957** 5r. multicoloured 35 25

958 Marie Curie, Prof. Sultanbawa and Structure of Aluminium Oxide

2011. International Year of Chemistry
2072 **958** 5r. multicoloured 35 25

959 'Viceroy Special' Steam Locomotive B8 240

2011. 25th Anniv of Viceroy Special Steam Train. Multicoloured.
2073 5r. Type **959** 35 25
2074 5r. 'Viceroy Special' locomotive
B2 213 35 25
2075 5r. Sentinel Camel steam rail
car V2 331 35 25
2076 5r. Narrow gauge steam locomotive J1 220 35 25

960 St. Mary's Church, Dehiwala

2011. 175th Anniv of St. Mary's Church, Dehiwala
2077 **960** 5r. multicoloured 35 25

961 Southlands College, Galle

2011. 125th Anniv of Southlands College, Galle
2078 **961** 5r. multicoloured 35 25

962 Fighter Aircraft

2011. 60th Anniv of Sri Lanka Air Force
2079 **962** 5r. multicoloured 35 25

15.00
(964)

2011. No. 1552b (Daul drummer) surch with T **963/4**
2080 15r. on 4r.50 bright blue (Type
963) 2·75 2·75
2081 15r. on 4r.50 bright blue (Type
964) 2·75 2·75

15.00
(963)

965 Yuri Gagarin

2011. 50th Anniv of First Manned Space Flight

2082	**965**	5r. multicoloured	1·00	90

966 'Buddhism is a universal doctrine'

2011. 2600th Sambuddhatva Jayantiya Vesak (1st issue). Multicoloured.

2083	5r. Type **966**		25	20
2084	5r. 'Let us practise Buddhist principles'		25	20
2085	5r. 'Let us take care of our parents and respect them'		25	20
2086	5r. 'Let us help the sick'		25	20
2087	5r. 'Person who practises Buddhism illuminates the entire world'		25	20
2088	5r. 'Let us build an antinarcotic society'		25	20

967 Rabindranath Tagore

2011. 150th Birth Anniv of Rabindranath Tagore (Bengali poet, writer and musician)

2089	**967**	5r. multicoloured	1·00	90

968 Lumbini

2011. 2600th Sambuddhatva Jayanthi Vesak (2nd issue). Multicoloured.

2090	5r. Type **968**		30	25
2091	5r. Temple at Buddhagaya		30	25
2092	5r. Baranesa Isipathanarama		30	25
2093	5r. Kusinara		30	25

969 Ancient Stone Bridge, Mahakanadarawa

2011. Bridges of Sri Lanka. Multicoloured.

2094	10r. Type **969**		45	40
2095	10r. Suspension bridge, Peradeniya		45	40
2096	15r. Wooden bridge, Bogoda		80	75
2097	15r. Steel arch bridge, Ruwanwella		80	75

970 Bank Building and Anniversary Emblem

2011. 50th Anniv of People's Bank

2098	**970**	5r. multicoloured	1·00	90

971 Radampala Sri Sumangala Central College

2011. Centenary of Radampala Sri Sumangala Central College, Matara

2099	**971**	5r. multicoloured	1·00	90

972 Emblem encircled by Flags of Member Countries

2011. 50th Anniv of the Non Aligned Movement

2100	**972**	5r. multicoloured	1·00	90

973 Buddhist Temple ('Heritage')

2011. World Tourism Day. Multicoloured.

2101	5r. Type **973**		20	25
2102	5r. Stone lion paws and staircase, Sigiriya Rock Fortress ('Heritage')		20	25
2103	5r. Kandyan dancers ('Festive')		20	25
2104	5r. Sinhala, Tamil, Muslim and Burgher girls ('Essence')		20	25
2105	15r. Woman in bath of flowers ('Bliss')		55	60
2106	15r. Waterfall ('Scenic')		55	60
2107	30r. Elephants ('Wild')		1·10	1·25
2108	35r. Leopard ('Wild')		1·40	1·50
2109	40r. Beach with boat offshore ('Pristine')		1·60	1·75
2110	45r. White water rafting ('Thrills')		1·75	1·90

974 Children and Sri Lanka Flag on Globe

2011. World Children's Day

2111	**974**	5r. multicoloured	1·00	90

975 Pillar Box and Postman delivering Letter

2011. World Post Day

2112	**975**	5r. multicoloured	1·00	90

976 Handball, Football and Volleyball Players on Beach (image scaled to 60% of original size)

2011. First South Asian Beach Games, Hambantota

2113	**976**	5r. multicoloured	1·00	90

977 Dudley Senanayake

2011. Birth Centenary of Hon. Dudley Senanayake (Prime Minister 1965-70)

2114	**977**	5r. light brown and black	1·00	90

978 '1919' (telephone number)

2011. Government Information Centre

2115	**978**	5r. multicoloured	1·00	90

979 Austin 12, 1928

2011. Vintage and Classic Cars of Sri Lanka. Black and grey.

2116	5r. Type **979**		25	20
2117	5r. Rolls-Royce 20/25, 1934		25	25
2118	5r. Jaguar SS 100, 1937		25	20
2119	5r. Morris Minor, 1949		25	20

980 Shrine of Our Lady of Lourdes, Kalaoya

2011. Christmas. Multicoloured.

2120	5r. Type **980**		25	20
2121	20r. Peace dove with Sri Lanka flag on wings enfolding nativity scene		1·40	1·50

981 Most Ven. Kotagama Wachissara Thero

2011. Most Ven, Kotagama Wachissara Thero (educationist) Commemoration

2122	**981**	5r. multicoloured	1·00	90

982 Emblem

2011. World AIDS Day

2123	**982**	5r. multicoloured	1·00	90

983 Eddy Jayamanna (actor, singer and director)

2012. Legends of Sinhala Cinema

2124	5r. deep claret, dull mauve and reddish-brown		25	20
2125	5r. deep rose-lilac, violet-grey and reddish-brown		25	20
2126	5r. deep turquoise-blue, slate-blue and reddish-brown		25	20
2127	10r. bottle-green, dull blue-green and reddish-brown		45	40
2128	15r. deep reddish-brown and grey-brown		60	55
2129	20r. brown-olive, grey-brown and reddish-brown		75	70
MS2130	109×160 mm. Nos. 2124/9		2·75	2·50

Designs: 2125, Sandaya Kumari (actress); 2126, Titus Thotawatta (director); 2127, Joe Abewickrama (actor) ; 2128, Malini Fonseka (actress); 2129, Gamini Fonseka (actor and director).

984 Sailing Ship, Liner and Container Ship (image scaled to 60% of original size)

2012. Centenary of Institute of Chartered Shipbrokers UK and 25th Anniv of Sri Lanka Branch

2131	**984**	5r. reddish-brown and black	1·00	90

985 '100', Tent and Backpack

2012. Centenary of Sri Lanka Scouting

2132	**985**	5r. multicoloured	1·00	90
MS2133	159×120 mm. As No. 2132 but imperf×4		1·00	90

986 Guardstone

2012. Guardstone of Chapter House of the Rathanaprasadaya, Abhayagiri Monastery Complex, Anuradhapura

2134	**986**	50r. multicoloured	3·50	2·50
2135	**986**	100r. multicoloured	7·00	5·00

987 Peony Flower

2012. Peony Flower. Multicoloured.
MS2136 125×185 mm. 30r. Type **987**×3; 30r. As Type **987** but inscriptions at right×3 ... 7·75 ... 6·75

988 Wind Turbines

2012. Sustainable Energy for All

2137	**988**	5r. multicoloured	1·00	90

989 Asian Pacific Postal Union

2012. 50th Anniv of the Asian-Pacific Postal Union

2138	**989**	5r. multicoloured	1·00	90

990 New Year Rituals

2012. Sinhala-Hindu New Year. Multicoloured.

2139	5r. Type **990**		25	20
2140	5r. Village temple and couple leaving for work at auspicious time		25	20
2141	5r. Woman giving sweetmeats to boy and women playing board game		25	20
2142	5r. Anointing with oil and and women playing board game		25	20

Nos. 2139/42 were printed together, *se-tenant*, as blocks of four stamps, each block forming a composite design.

991 Sapugaskanda Oil Refinery

2012. 50th Anniv of Ceylon Petroleum Corporation
| 2143 | 991 | 5r. multicoloured | 1·00 | 90 |

992 Sri Lanka on Globe Emblem

2012. 2600 Sambuddhatva Jayantiya
| 2144 | 992 | 5r. multicoloured | 1·00 | 90 |

993 Pandols depicting Jataka Stories

2012. Vesak. Multicoloured.
2145		5r. Type 993	25	20
2146		12r. Lanterns	45	40
MS2147	161×102 mm. Nos. 2145/6		70	60

994 Prof. Walpola Sri Rahula Thero

2012. Prof. Walpola Sri Rahula Thero (Buddhist scholar) Commemoration
| 2148 | 994 | 5r. multicoloured | 1·00 | 90 |

995 St. Philip Neri's Church

2012. 225th Anniv of St. Philip Neri's Church, Udammita South, Ja-ela
| 2149 | 995 | 5r. multicoloured | 1·00 | 90 |

996 Kusuma Gunawardena

2012. Birth Centenary of Mrs. Kusuma Gunawardena (MP 1947-59)
| 2150 | 996 | 5r. multicoloured | 1·00 | 90 |

997 Asgiri Gedige Rajamaha Viharaya

2012. 700th Anniv of Asgiri Maha Viharaya
| 2151 | 997 | 5r. multicoloured | 1·00 | 90 |

998 '100', Girl Signing and Blind Boy with Cane

2012. Centenary of Ceylon School for the Deaf and Blind, Ratmalana
| 2152 | 998 | 5r. multicoloured | 1·00 | 90 |

999 Terracotta Figure from Sigiriya

2012. National Archaeological Week
| 2153 | 999 | 5r. multicoloured | 1·00 | 90 |

1000 Farmer's Hands (gateway of Bata Atha Agriculture Technology Park) and Field Workers

2012. Centenary of the Department of Agriculture
| 2154 | 1000 | 5r. multicoloured | 1·00 | 90 |

1001 Athlete running and Big Ben

2012. Olympic Games, London. Multicoloured.
2155		5r. Type 1001	25	20
2156		15r. Swimmer	60	55
2157		25r. Shooting	1·10	1·25
2158		75r. Badminton player	5·25	4·50
MS2159	163×103 mm. As Nos. 2155/8		7·00	6·00

1002 Sri Lanka Parliament Building

2012. 58th Commonwealth Parliamentary Conference, Colombo
| 2160 | 1002 | 5r. multicoloured | 1·00 | 90 |

1003 Galle Face Hotel

2012. Colonial Buildings of Sri Lanka
2161	1003	15r. black and azure	60	55
2162	-	15r. black and dull mauve	60	55
2163	-	15r. black and pale green	60	55
2164	-	15r. black and buff	60	55
MS2165	174×84 mm. As Nos. 2161/2		1·25	1·10
MS2166	174×84 mm. As Nos. 2163/4		1·25	1·10

Designs: 2162, National Museum; 2163, Municipal Council, Colombo; 2164, Old Parliament.

1004 Children

2012. World Children's Day
| 2167 | 1004 | 5r. multicoloured | 1·00 | 90 |

1005 Emblems

2012. World Post Day
| 2168 | 1005 | 5r. multicoloured | 1·00 | 90 |

1006 Binara Flower (*Exacum trinervium*)

2012. Flowers of Sri Lanka. Multicoloured.
2169		5r. Type 1006	25	20
2170		5r. Frangipani (*Plumeria rubra*)	25	20
2171		5r. 'Shoe Flower' (*Hibiscus rosa-sinensis*)	25	20
2172		5r. Sun flower (*Helianthus annuus*)	25	20
MS2173	161×112 mm. Nos. 2169/72		1·00	80

No. MS2173 is inscr 'World Post Day Stamp Exhibition - 2012'.

1007 Woman with her Children

2012. 60th Anniv of World Health Organization in Sri Lanka
| 2174 | 1007 | 12r. multicoloured | 45 | 40 |

1008 Sri Lanka Insurance Building

2012. 50th Anniv of Sri Lanka Insurance
| 2175 | 1008 | 5r. multicoloured | 1·00 | 90 |

1009 Nativity Scene and Peace Doves flying to Family (Vojitha Heshan Herath)

2012. Christmas. Children's Paintings. Multicoloured.
2176		5r. Type 1009	25	20
2177		25r. Man pulling family in cart and nativity scene (K. G. Morini Anjela Thalis)	1·10	1·25
MS2178	170×93 mm. Nos. 2176/7		1·40	1·40

1010 Early Monoplane

2012. Centenary of Aviation. Multicoloured.
2179		5r. Type 1010	25	20
2180		12r. Air Ceylon (1947-78) plane	45	40
2181		15r. Sri Lankan Airlines airliner	60	55
2182		25r. Mihin Lanka airliner	1·10	1·25
MS2183	178×91 mm. Nos. 2179/82		2·40	2·40

1011 Moonstone, Vishnu Devale, Kandy

2012. Moonstones, Guardstones and Balustrades of Sri Lanka
2184		50c. Type 1011	10	10
2185		1r. Moonstone, Watadage, Polonnaruwa	10	10
2186		2r. Moonstone, Rajmaha Vihara, Beligala	10	10
2187		3r. Moonstone, Abayagiri Vihara, Anuradhapura	15	10
2188		4r. Guard stone, Jethawana Vihara, Anuradhapura (vert)	20	15
2189		4r. 50 Guard stone, Rajmaha Vihara, Arattana (vert)	25	20
2190		5r. Guard stone, Tissamahara-maya (vert)	25	20
2191		10r. Guard stone, Abayagiri Rathnaprasadaya, Anurad-hapura (vert)	45	40
2192		12r. Guard stone, Abayagiri Stupa, Anuradhapura (vert)	45	40
2193		15r. Guard stone, Dematamal Vihara, Buttala (vert)	60	55
2194		20r. Balustrade with dragon's tongue supported by dwarf carving, Mahavihara, An-uradhapura (bright carmine borders)	75	70
2195		25r. Balustrade, Lankathilaka Image House, Polonnaruwa	1·10	1·25
2196		30r. Balustrade, Jethawanarama Vihara, Anuradhapura	1·10	1·25
2197		40r. Balustrade, Mahavihara, Anuradhapura (orange-red borders)	1·60	1·75
2198		55r. Balustrade, Mahavihara, An-uradhapura (green borders)	3·75	2·75
2199		75r. Balustrade, Yapahuwa	5·25	4·50
MS2200	75×60 mm. Nos. 2184/7		45	40
MS2201	59×99 mm. Nos. 2188/93		2·25	1·90
MS2202	102×61 mm. Nos. 2194/9		13·00	12·00

1012 Lotus Flowers

2013. 60th Anniv of Sri Lanka - Japan Diplomatic Relations. Multicoloured.
2203		5r. Type 1012	25	20
2204		65r. Cherry blossom	4·50	3·00
MS2205	152×95 mm. Nos. 3203/4		4·75	3·25

1013 Scout Camp

2013. RISGO (Rajans International Scout Gathering) Centennial International Scout Jamboree, Kandy
| 2206 | 1013 | 25r. multicoloured | 1·10 | 1·25 |

1014 Airliner, Control Tower and Passenger Terminal

2013. Inauguration of Mattala Rajapaksa International Airport
| 2207 | 1014 | 5r. multicoloured | 25 | 20 |

1015 Pilgrims and Shrines

2013. Sixth Peace Pada Yatra, Sri Lanka
| 2208 | 1015 | 5r. multicoloured | 25 | 20 |

1016 Dharmasoka College, Ambalagoda

2013. Centenary of Dharmasoka College, Ambalagoda
| 2209 | 1016 | 5r. multicoloured | 25 | 20 |

1017 Prince Siddhartha encountered an Old Man

2013. Vesak. Sathera Pera Nimithi (Four Omens). Multicoloured.

2210	4r. Type **1017**	20	15
2211	5r. Prince Siddhartha encountered a diseased man	25	20
2212	15r. Prince Siddhartha encountered a corpse	60	55
2213	50r. Prince Siddhartha encountered an ascetic	3·50	2·50
MS2214	121×185 mm. As Nos. 2210/13	4·50	3·50

1018 Dambegoda Bodhisattva Statue

2013. Dambegoda Bodhisattva Statue

2215	**1018**	5r. multicoloured	25	20

1019 Swami Vivekananda

2013. 150th Birth Anniv of Swami Vivekananda (1863-1902, Hindu monk and spiritual leader, founder of Ramakrishna Mission)

2216	**1019**	25r. multicoloured	1·10	1·25

1020 Christ Church Girls' College

2013. 125th Anniv of Christ Church Girls' College, Baddegama

2217	**1020**	5r. multicoloured	25	20

1021 Hawksbill Turtle (*Eretmochelys imbricata*)

2013. National Parks of Sri Lanka (4th series). Yala National Park. Multicoloured.

2218	5r. Type **1021**	25	20
2219	15r. Swamp Crocodile (*Crocodylus palustris*)	60	55
2220	25r. Elephant (*Elephas maximus*) - tusker (vert)	1·10	1·25
2221	30r. Black-necked Stork (*Ephippiorhynchus asiaticus*) (vert)	1·10	1·25
2222	40r. Wild Boar (*Sus scrofa*)	1·60	1·75
2223	50r. Spotted Deer (*Axis axis*)	3·50	2·50
MS2224	144×97 mm. Nos. 2218 and 2223	3·75	2·75
MS2225	144×97 mm. Nos. 2219 and 2222	3·75	2·75
MS2226	145×96 mm. Nos. 2220/1	3·75	2·75

1022 Rev. Fr. Tissa Balasuriya

2013. Rev. Fr. Tissa Balasuriya (1924 - 2013, priest and founder of Centre for Society and Religion) Commemoration

2227	**1022**	5r. multicoloured	25	20

1023 Villagers using Leaves for Umbrellas and Kirimama buying Umbrella

2013. World Children's Day. *The Umbrella Thief* by Cybil Wettasinghe. Multicoloured.

2228	5r. Type **1023**	25	20
2229	5r. Kirimama searching for stolen umbrellas	25	20
2230	5r. Stolen umbrellas hanging from tree and Monkey curled up in umbrella	25	20

Nos. 2228/30 were printed together, *se-tenant*, as horizontal strips of three stamps, each horizontal strip forming a composite design.

1024 Letters, Parcels, Arrows and Globe

2013. World Post Day

2231	**1024**	5r. multicoloured	25	20

POSTAL FISCAL

1952. As T **57** but inscr "REVENUE" at sides.

F1	10r. green and orange	65·00	29·00

F1 Republic Crest

1979. As Type **F1** but with additional Sinhala and Tamil inscriptions on either side of crest.

F2	20r. green	5·00	2·75
F3	50r. violet	13·00	7·00
F4	100r. red	23·00	25·00

1984

F8	**F1**	100r. purple	2·00	3·00

1998

F9	**F1**	50r. orange	3·00	2·50
F10	**F1**	100r. brown	4·50	5·00

F4

2002

F11	**F4**	50r. blue and brown	2·50	2·00
F12	**F4**	100r. blue and green	3·50	4·00

F5

2007

F13	**F5**	50r. multicoloured	55	60
F14	**F5**	100r. multicoloured	1·10	1·25
F15	**F5**	200r. multicoloured	2·25	2·40

Stamps in this series with face values of 500 and 1000r. were not valid for postal purposes.

PARLIAMENT STAMPS

M1 Arms and Post Office

2005. Postal Facilities for the Members of Parliament.

M1	**M1**	5r. multicoloured	1·00	70

No. M1 was only issued to Members of Parliament.

M2 Arms and Parliament Building, Sri Jayawardenapura Kotte

2008. Postal Facilities for the Members of Parliament.

M2	**M2**	5r. multicoloured	35	40
M3	**M 2**	10r. multicoloured	70	80
M4	**M 2**	15r. multicoloured	1·10	1·25
M5	**M 2**	25r. multicoloured	1·75	2·00
M6	**M 2**	30r. multicoloured	2·10	2·40

Nos. M2/6 were only issued to Members of Parliament.

Pt. 1

STELLALAND

A temporary Boer republic annexed by the British in 1885 and later incorporated in Br. Bechuanaland.

12 pence = 1 shilling; 20 shillings = 1 pound.

1 Arms of the Republic

1884

1	1	1d. red	£190	£325
2	1	3d. orange	35·00	£375
3	1	4d. blue	30·00	£400
4	1	6d. mauve	35·00	£400
5	1	1s. green	80·00	£800

1885. Surch **Twee**.

6	2d. on 4d. blue	£3500	

Pt. 1

STRAITS SETTLEMENTS

A British Crown colony which included portions of the mainland of the Malay Peninsula and islands off its coasts, and the island of Labuan off the N. coast of Borneo.

100 cents = 1 dollar (Straits).

1867. Stamps of India surch with crown and value.

1	**11**	1½c. on ½a. blue	£120	£200
2	**11**	2c. on 1a. brown	£190	95·00
3	**11**	3c. on 1a. brown	£180	95·00
4	**11**	4c. on 1a. brown	£300	£275
5	**11**	6c. on 2a. orange	£800	£250
6	**11**	8c. on 2a. orange	£300	42·00
7	**11**	12c. on 4a. green	£1300	£325
8	**11**	24c. on 8a. red	£650	£100
9	**11**	32c. on 2a. orange	£450	£110

1869. No. 1 with "THREE HALF" deleted and "2" written above in manuscript.

10	2 on 1½c. on ½a. blue	£20000	£6500

5

8

9

1867

11	**5**	2c. brown	50·00	7·50
98	**5**	4c. red	14·00	1·25
66*a*	**5**	6c. lilac	2·50	14·00
52	**5**	8c. orange	5·50	1·00
15	**5**	12c. blue	£200	9·00
68*a*	**5**	24c. green	10·00	6·50
69	**8**	30c. red	21·00	22·00
70	**9**	32c. red	15·00	4·75
71	**9**	96c. grey	75·00	55·00

1879. Surch in words.

20		5c. on 8c. orange	£140	£190
21	**9**	7c. on 32c. red	£170	£200

1880. Surch in figures and words.

47	**5**	5c. on 4c. red	£375	£400
42	**5**	5c. on 8c. orange	£180	£225
44	**5**	10c. on 6c. lilac	85·00	6·00
45*a*	**5**	10c. on 12c. blue	70·00	9·00
23	**8**	10c. on 30c. red	£550	95·00

1880. Surch in figures only.

33	**8**	"10" on 30c.	£300	60·00

18

19

1882

63*a*	**5**	2c. red	13·00	85
64	**5**	4c. brown	55·00	4·75
65	**18**	5c. blue	19·00	1·00
99	**18**	5c. brown	15·00	1·00
100	**18**	5c. mauve	4·00	2·00
101	**5**	8c. blue	4·50	50
53	**19**	10c. grey	13·00	1·25
102	**5**	12c. purple	26·00	13·00

1883. Surch in words in one line horiz (No. 109) or vert.

57		2c. on 8c. orange	£180	90·00
59	**9**	2c. on 32c. orange	£900	£250
109	**18**	4c. on 5c. red	1·00	30

1883. Surch with figures over words in two lines.

61	**5**	2c. on 4c. red	95·00	£100
62	**5**	2c. on 12c. blue	£450	£170
82	**18**	3c. on 5c. blue	£160	£250
84	**18**	3c. on 5c. purple	£300	£325
73	**18**	4c. on 5c. blue (A)*	£170	£140
106	**18**	4c. on 5c. brown	2·75	4·75
107	**18**	4c. on 5c. blue (B)*	11·00	26·00
108*b*	**5**	4c. on 8c. blue	2·75	1·75
74	**5**	8c. on 12c. blue	£1000	£160
75	**5**	8c. on 12c. purple	£650	£170

*(A) "Cents" in italics. (B) "cents" (with small "c") in roman type.

1884. Surch **TWO CENTS** vert.

76	**18**	2c. on 5c. blue	£170	£180

1884. No. 75 additionally surch with large figure **8**.

80	**5**	8 on 8c. on 12c. purple	£500	£500

1885. Surch with words in one line and thick bar.

93	**5**	1c. on 8c. green	1·00	1·50
83*a*	**9**	3c. on 32c. purple	2·50	1·00
94	**9**	3c. on 32c. red	2·25	70

1887. Surch **2 Cents** in one line.

85	**18**	2c. on 5c. blue	45·00	95·00

1891. Surch **10 cents** in one line and thin bar

86	**5**	10c. on 24c. green	7·00	1·25

1891. Surch with words in two lines and thin bar.

88	**5**	1c. on 2c. red	2·00	4·25
89	**5**	1c. on 4c. brown	8·00	6·00
90	**5**	1c. on 6c. lilac	2·00	10·00
91	**5**	1c. on 8c. orange	1·00	3·50
92	**5**	1c. on 12c. purple	5·00	9·50
87	**9**	30c. on 32c. orange	14·00	3·50

33

1892

95	**33**	1c. green	8·00	70
96	**33**	3c. red	12·00	40
97*b*	**33**	3c. brown	14·00	1·25
103*c*	**33**	25c. purple and green	35·00	7·50
104	**33**	50c. olive and red	24·00	2·75
105	**33**	$5 orange and red	£400	£325

37

1902

110	**37**	1c. green	2·75	4·25
111	**37**	3c. purple and orange	3·50	20
112	**37**	4c. purple on red	4·75	30
113	**37**	5c. purple	5·50	2·00
157	**37**	5c. orange	2·75	2·50
114	**37**	8c. purple on blue	4·50	20
132	**37**	10c. purple & black on yellow	8·50	80
159	**37**	10c. purple on yellow	17·00	1·00
116	**37**	25c. purple and green	17·00	10·00
161	**37**	25c. purple	24·00	9·50
117	**37**	30c. grey and red	22·00	8·50
162	**37**	30c. purple and yellow	55·00	4·25
118	**37**	50c. green and red	22·00	22·00
164	**37**	50c. black on green	11·00	5·00
136*a*	**37**	$1 green and black	65·00	25·00
165	**37**	$1 black and red on blue	15·00	7·00
120	**37**	$2 purple and black	80·00	80·00
166	**37**	$2 green and red on yellow	28·00	24·00

138a	37	$5 green and orange	£325	£180
167	37	$5 green and red on green	£140	75·00
139	37	$25 green and black	£3250	£3250

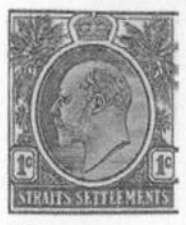
39
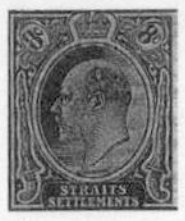
42
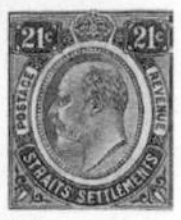
46
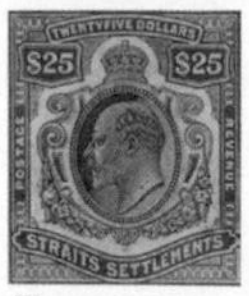
47

1903

127	39	1c. green	5·00	10
128	39	3c. purple	2·75	30
153	39	3c. red	7·50	10
125	39	4c. purple on red	13·00	30
154	39	4c. red	8·50	2·50
156	39	4c. purple	3·50	80
131	42	8c. purple on blue	55·00	1·50
158	42	8c. blue	4·25	60
160	46	21c. purple	6·50	38·00
163	46	45c. black on green	2·75	4·00
168	47	$25 purple and blue	£3500	£2250

1907. Stamps of Labuan (Crown type) optd **Straits Settlements.** (10c.) or **STRAITS SETTLEMENTS** (others) or surch in words also.

141	18	1c. black and purple	70·00	£180
142a	18	2c. black and green	£180	£325
143	18	3c. black and brown	24·00	95·00
144	18	4c. on 12c. black & yellow	3·25	11·00
145	18	4c. on 16c. green & brown	9·50	12·00
146	18	4c. on 18c. black & brown	2·75	11·00
147	18	8c. black and orange	6·00	11·00
148	18	10c. brown and blue	10·00	13·00
149	18	25c. green and blue	35·00	50·00
150	18	50c. purple and lilac	25·00	70·00
151	18	$1 red and orange	50·00	£120

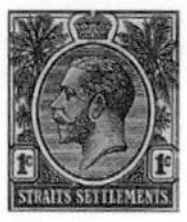
48
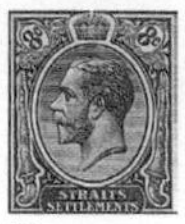
52
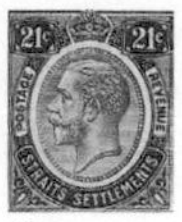
53
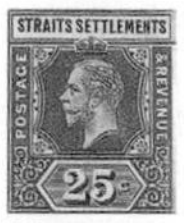
54

1912

193a	48	1c. green	13·00	1·50
196a	48	3c. red	2·75	10
197	48	4c. purple	3·50	60
225c	54	5c. orange	2·25	1·25
200	52	6c. purple	2·00	50
201	52	8c. blue	3·50	80
202	54	10c. purple on yellow	1·50	1·00
204	53	21c. purple	13·00	13·00
234b	54	25c. purple and mauve	5·00	1·75
235a	54	30c. purple and orange	2·00	1·25
208b	53	45c. black on green	5·50	13·00
238	54	50c. black on green	1·75	40
239	54	$1 black and red on blue	6·00	1·50
240	54	$2 green and red on yellow	10·00	8·00
240a	54	$5 green and red on green	£110	40·00
240b	-	$25 purple and blue on blue	£1400	£200

No. 240b is as Type **47** but with head of King George V.

1917. Surch **RED CROSS 2c.**

216	48	2c. on 3c. +2c. red	2·75	32·00
217	48	2c. on 4c. +2c. purple	3·75	32·00

1919

218		1c. black	60	10
219	52	2c. green	60	10
220	52	2c. brown	7·00	4·00
221	48	3c. green	1·50	80
198b		4c. red	1·75	20
223	48	4c. violet	60	10
224	48	4c. orange	1·00	10
226	54	5c. brown	3·00	10
227	52	6c. red	2·25	15
230	54	10c. blue	1·75	4·00
232	52	12c. blue	1·25	20
236a	53	35c. purple and orange	3·50	2·75
237	53	35c. red and purple	10·00	2·75

1922. Optd **MALAYA–BORNEO EXHIBITION.**

250	48	1c. black	3·00	23·00
251	52	2c. green	2·50	16·00
252	48	4c. red	4·00	50·00
243	54	5c. orange	9·50	19·00
244	52	8c. blue	2·00	11·00
254	54	10c. blue	2·25	26·00
245	54	25c. purple and mauve	4·50	50·00
246	53	45c. black on green	3·50	45·00
255	54	$1 black and red on blue	20·00	£160
248	54	$2 green and red on yellow	26·00	£160
249	54	$5 green and red on green	£425	£750

1935. Silver Jubilee. As T **32a** of St. Helena.

256	5c. blue and grey	3·00	30
257	8c. green and blue	3·00	3·25
258	12c. brown and blue	3·00	8·00
259	25c. grey and purple	4·25	12·00

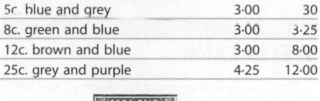

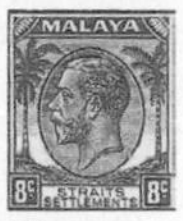
57

1936

260	57	1c. black	1·75	20
261	57	2c. green	2·00	70
262	57	4c. orange	2·25	70
263	57	5c. brown	1·00	30
264	57	6c. red	1·50	1·10
265	57	8c. grey	3·75	70
266	57	10c. purple	2·25	60
267	57	12c. blue	2·00	2·50
268	57	25c. purple and red	1·50	50
269	57	30c. purple and orange	1·50	3·25
270	57	40c. red and purple	1·50	2·50
271	57	50c. black on green	4·50	1·25
272	57	$1 black and red on blue	19·00	1·75
273	57	$2 green and red	55·00	10·00
274	57	$5 green and red on green	£130	10·00

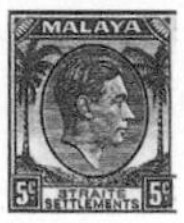
58

1937. Coronation. As T **32b** of St. Helena.

275	4c. orange	1·25	10
276	8c. grey	1·50	10
277	12c. blue	3·50	1·00

278	58	1c. black	14·00	10
279	58	2c. green	21·00	20
280	58	4c. orange	28·00	70
281	58	5c. brown	24·00	30
282	58	6c. red	11·00	60
283	58	8c. grey	38·00	10
284	58	10c. purple	14·00	10
285	58	12c. blue	14·00	50
286	58	25c. purple and red	48·00	1·10
287	58	30c. purple and orange	20·00	2·00
288	58	40c. red and purple	19·00	2·25
289	58	50c. black on green	15·00	10
290	58	$1 black and red on blue	18·00	20
291	58	$2 green and red	45·00	14·00
292	58	$5 green and red on green	28·00	8·00

294	58	2c. orange	2·00	19·00
295	58	3c. green	13·00	4·00
298	58	15c. blue	12·00	10·00

For Japanese issues see **JAPANESE OCCUPATION OF MALAYA** and for British military administration see **MALAYA.**

POSTAGE DUE STAMPS

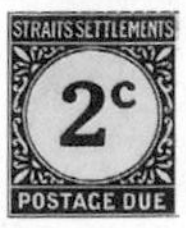
D1

1924

D1	D1	1c. violet	9·50	5·50
D2	D1	2c. black	3·25	1·00
D3	D1	4c. green	2·00	2·50
D4	D1	8c. red	4·50	55
D5	D1	10c. orange	6·00	85
D6	D1	12c. blue	7·00	65

For later issues see **MALAYAN POSTAL UNION.**

Pt. 1, Pt. 14

SUDAN

A territory in Africa, extending south from Egypt towards the Equator, jointly administered by Gt. Britain and Egypt until 1954 when the territory was granted a large measure of self-government. Became independent on 1 January 1956.

1897. 1000 milliemes = 100 piastres = £1 Sudanese.
1993. dinar.
2007. Sudanese pound

1897. Stamps of Egypt optd **SOUDAN** in English and Arabic.

1	18	1m. brown	4·25	2·00
3	18	2m. green	1·25	1·75
4	18	3m. yellow	1·40	1·50
5	18	5m. red	2·00	70
6	10	1p. blue	7·00	2·00
7	-	2p. orange	80·00	16·00
8	-	5p. grey	80·00	24·00
9	18	10p. mauve	50·00	60·00

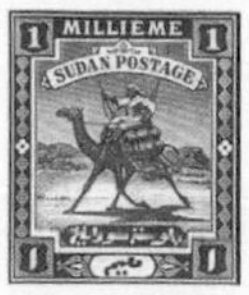
2 Arab Postman

1898

18	2	1m. brown and red	1·25	65
19	2	2m. green and brown	1·75	10
20	2	3m. mauve and green	2·25	25
21	2	4m. blue and brown	1·50	2·50
22	2	4m. red and brown	1·50	75
23	2	5m. red and black	2·00	10
24	2	1p. blue and brown	2·25	30
25	2	2p. black and blue	45·00	1·25
44	2	2p. purple and orange	4·50	10
44b	2	3p. brown and blue	10·00	10
44c	2	4p. blue and black	4·25	10
45	2	5p. brown and green	1·25	10
45b	2	6p. blue and black	15·00	3·00
45c	2	8p. green and black	15·00	5·00
46	2	10p. black and mauve	9·50	50
46b	2	20p. blue	15·00	60

1903. Surch **5 Milliemes.**

29	5m. on 5pi. brown and green	6·50	9·50

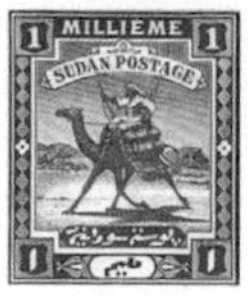
2 Arab Postman
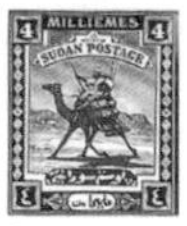
6

1921

37	6	1m. black and orange	70	10
38	6	2m. yellow and brown	75	10
39	6	3m. mauve and green	70	10
40	6	4m. green and brown	60	10
41	6	5m. brown and black	60	10
42	6	10m. red and black	1·50	10
43b	6	15m. blue and brown	4·50	10

For stamps as Type **2** and **6** with different Arabic inscriptions see issue of 1948.

1931. Air. Nos. 41/2 and 44 optd **AIR MAIL.**

47		5m. brown and black	35	70
48		10m. red and black	1·00	17·00
49	2	2p. purple and yellow	85	7·50

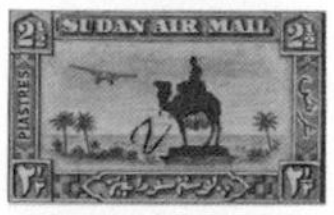
10 Statue of General Gordon

1931. Air.

49b	10	3m. green and brown	2·50	6·50
50	10	5m. black and green	1·00	10
51	10	10m. black and red	1·00	20
52	10	15m. brown	40	10
53	10	2p. black and orange	50	10
53cd	10	2½p. mauve and blue	5·00	10
54	10	3p. black and grey	60	15
55	10	3½p. black and violet	1·50	80
56	10	4½p. brown and grey	13·00	15·00
57	10	5p. black and blue	1·00	30
57d	10	10p. brown and blue	10·00	1·75

1932. Air. Surch **2½ 2½ AIR MAIL** and value in Arabic figures.

58	2	2½p. on 2p. purple and orange	1·40	3·75

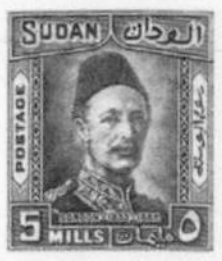
12 General Gordon (after C. Ouless)
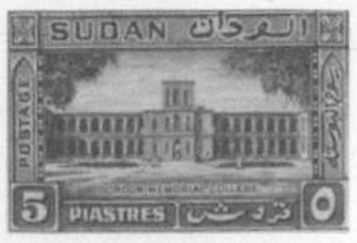
13 Gordon Memorial College, Khartoum

1935. 50th Death Anniv of Gen. Gordon.

59	12	5m. green	35	10
60	12	10m. brown	85	25
61	12	13m. blue	85	13·00
62	12	15m. red	1·75	25
63	13	2p. blue	1·75	20
64	13	5p. orange	1·75	40
65	13	10p. purple	9·00	9·00
66	-	20p. black	32·00	65·00
67	-	50p. brown	£100	£150

DESIGN—(44×20 mm): 20, 50p. Gordon Memorial Service, Khartoum.

1935. Air. Stamps of 1931 surch in English and Arabic.

74	10	5m. on 2½p. mauve and blue	3·50	10
68	10	15m. on 10m. black and red	40	10
69	10	2½p. on 3m. green & brown	85	3·25
70	10	2½p. on 5m. black and green	50	1·00
75	10	3p. on 3½p. black and violet	48·00	60·00
71	10	3p. on 4½p. brown and grey	1·75	21·00
76	10	3p. on 7½p. green	7·00	6·50
77	10	5p. on 10p. brown and blue	1·75	4·75
72	10	7½p. on 4½p. brown and grey	6·50	50·00
73	10	10p. on 4½p. brown and grey	6·50	50·00

1940. No. 42 surch **5 Mills.** and in Arabic.

78	6	5m. on 10m. red and black	2·00	2·00

1940. Nos. 41 surch **4½ PIASTRES** and No. 45c surch **4½ Piastres** in English and Arabic.

79		4½p. on 5m. brown and black	48·00	15·00
80	2	4½p. on 8p. green and black	42·00	9·00

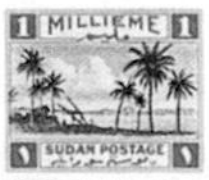
20 Tuti Island, R. Nile near Khartoum

1941

81	20	1m. black and orange	5·00	4·00
82	20	2m. orange and brown	5·00	5·50
83	20	3m. mauve and green	5·50	20
84	20	4m. green and brown	1·00	1·50
85	20	5m. brown and black	50	10
86	20	10m. red and black	29·00	5·50
87	20	15m. blue and brown	1·50	10
88	20	2p. purple and yellow	7·50	60
89	20	3p. brown and blue	1·25	10
90	20	4p. blue and black	6·50	10
91	20	5p. brown and green	11·00	13·00
92	20	6p. blue and black	27·00	2·00
93	20	8p. green and black	30·00	2·00
94	20	10p. slate and purple	£120	1·25
95	20	20p. blue	£100	50·00

The piastre values are larger, 30×25 mm.

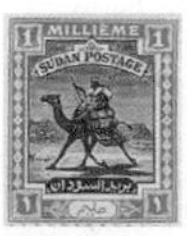
22 Arab Postman
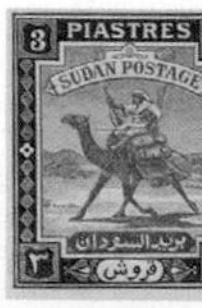
23 Arab Postman

1948

96	22	1m. black and orange	35	7·00
97	22	2m. orange and brown	80	5·50
98	22	3m. mauve and green	30	9·00
99	22	4m. green and brown	50	3·25
100	22	5m. brown and black	12·00	3·00
101	22	10m. red and black	5·50	10
102	22	15m. blue and brown	5·00	20
103	23	2p. purple and yellow	11·00	5·00
104	23	3p. brown and blue	7·50	30
105	23	4p. blue and black	4·00	1·75
106	23	5p. orange and green	4·00	7·00
107	23	6p. blue and black	4·50	3·50
108	23	8p. green and black	4·50	6·00
109	23	10p. black and mauve	16·00	10·00
110	23	20p. blue	4·50	50

111	23	50p. red and blue	6·50	2·75

In this issue the Arabic inscriptions below the camel differ from those in Types **2** and **6**.

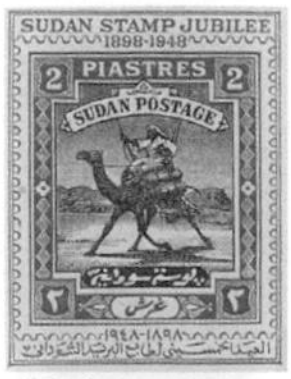

24 Arab Postman

1948. Golden Jubilee of "Camel Postman" design.

112	24	2p. black and blue	50	10

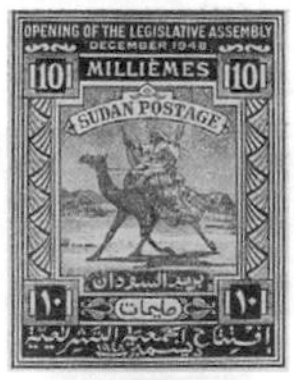

25 Arab Postman

1948. Opening of Legislative Assembly.

113	25	10m. red and black	1·25	10
114	25	5p. orange and green	1·75	2·75

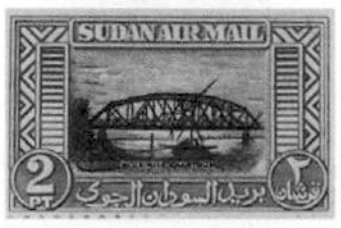

26 Blue Nile Bridge, Khartoum

1950. Air.

115	26	2p. black and green	6·00	1·50
116	-	2½p. blue and orange	1·25	1·75
117	-	3p. purple and blue	4·50	1·25
118	-	3½p. sepia and brown	6·00	6·00
119	-	4p. brown and blue	1·50	3·25
120	-	4½p. black and blue	3·00	6·50
121	-	6p. black and red	4·50	3·75
122	-	20p. black and purple	2·50	7·50

DESIGNS: 2½p. Kassala Jebel; 3p. Sagia (water wheel); 3½p. Port Sudan; 4p. Gordon Memorial College; 4½p. "Gordon Pasha" (Nile mail boat); 6p. Suakin; 20p. G.P.O. Khartoum.

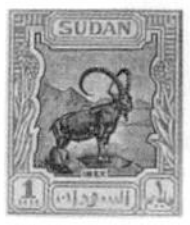

34 Ibex

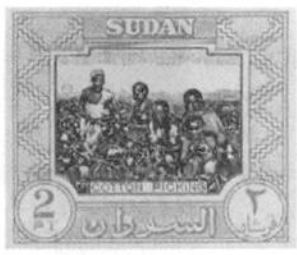

41 Cotton Picking

1951

123	34	1m. black and orange	4·00	1·50
124	-	2m. black and blue	3·50	1·50
125	-	3m. black and green	12·00	6·50
126	-	4m. black and green	3·50	6·50
127	-	5m. black and purple	2·25	10
128	-	10m. black and blue	30	10
129	-	15m. black and brown	10·00	10
130	41	2p. blue	30	10
131	-	3p. brown and blue	22·00	10
132	-	3½p. green and brown	2·75	10
133	-	4p. blue and black	6·50	25
134	-	5p. brown and green	3·00	10
135	-	6p. blue and black	8·50	2·75
136	-	8p. blue and brown	14·00	5·00
137	-	10p. black and green	1·50	1·50
138	-	20p. turquoise and black	12·00	3·75
139	-	50p. red and black	20·00	4·75

DESIGNS—VERT (As Type **34**): 2m. Whale-headed stork ("Shoebill");, 3m. Giraffe; 4m. Baggara girl; 5m. Shilluk warrior; 10m. Hadendowa; 15m. Policeman. (As Type **35**): 50p. Camel postman. HORIZ (As Type **35**): 3p. Ambatch reed canoe; 3½p. Nuba wrestlers; 4p. Weaving; 5p. Saluka farming; 6p. Gum tapping; 8p. Darfur chief; 10p. Stack Laboratory; 20p. Nile lechwe (antelope).

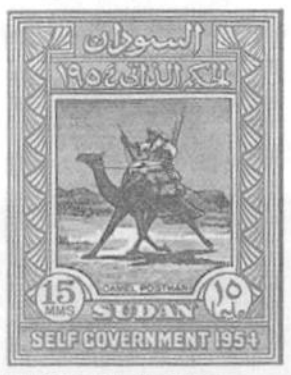

51 Camel Postman

1954. Self-Government.

140	51	15m. brown and green	50	1·25
141	51	3p. blue and indigo	75	5·00
142	51	5p. black and purple	50	2·50

Stamps as Type **51** but dated "1953" were released in error at the Sudan Agency in London. They had no postal validity.

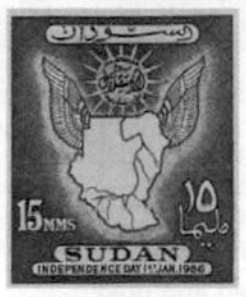

52 "Independent Sudan"

1956. Independence Commemoration.

143	52	15m. orange and purple	50	25
144	52	3p. orange and blue	65	50
145	52	5p. orange and green	75	65

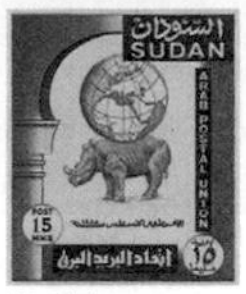

53 Globe on Rhinoceros (Badge of Sudan)

1958. Arab Postal Congress, Khartoum.

146	53	15m. orange and purple	50	25
147	53	3p. orange and blue	1·00	50
148	53	5p. orange and green	1·60	1·10

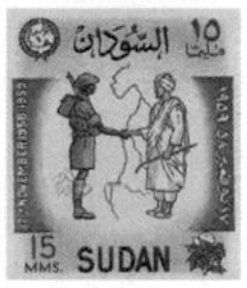

54 Sudanese Soldier and Farmer

1959. First Anniv of Army Revolution.

149	54	15m. yellow, blue & brown	40	25
150	54	3p. multicoloured	1·00	65
151	54	55m. multicoloured	1·30	90

1960. Inauguration of Arab League Centre, Cairo. As T **154a** of Syria.

152		15m. black and green	40	25

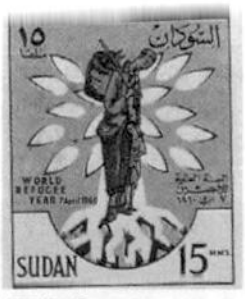

55 Refugees

1960. World Refugee Year.

153	55	15m. blue, black and brown	40	25
154	55	55m. red, black and sepia	1·00	75

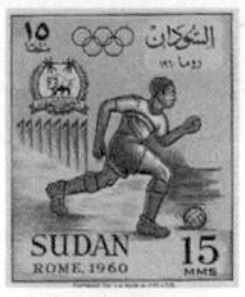

56 Football

1960. Olympic Games, Rome.

155	56	15m. multicoloured	40	15
156	56	3p. multicoloured	90	65
157	56	55m. multicoloured	1·30	75

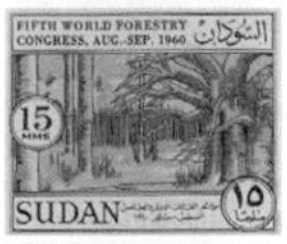

57 Forest

1960. Fifth World Forestry Congress, Seattle.

158	57	15m. green, brown and red	25	15
159	57	3p. green, brown and deep green	90	40
160	57	55m. multicoloured	1·00	75

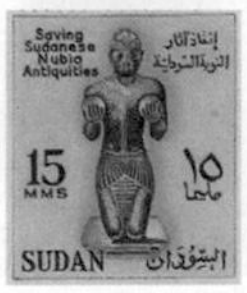

58 King Ta'rhaqa

1961. Sudanese Nubian Monuments Preservation Campaign.

161	58	15m. brown and green	40	25
162	58	3p. violet and orange	90	75
163	58	55m. brown and blue	1·30	1·00

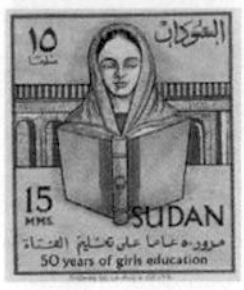

59 Girl with Book

1961. "50 Years of Girls' Education in the Sudan".

164	59	15m. mauve, purple & blue	40	15
165	59	3p. blue, orange and black	75	50
166	59	55m. brown, green & black	1·10	90

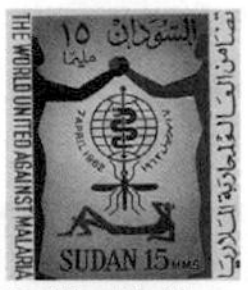

60 "The World United against Malaria"

1962. Malaria Eradication.

167	60	15m. violet, blue and black	40	25
168	60	55m. green, emerald & blk	1·00	75

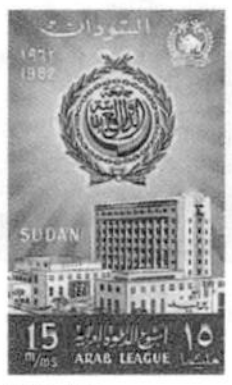

60a [illegible] Centre, Cairo and Emblem

1962. Arab League Week.

169	60a	15m. orange	25	15
170	60a	55m. turquoise	90	75

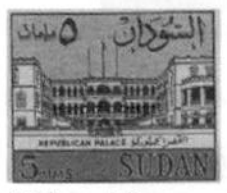

62 Republican Palace

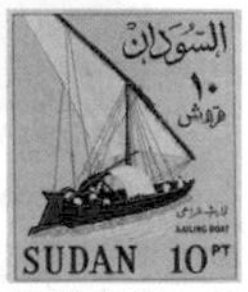

63 Nile Felucca

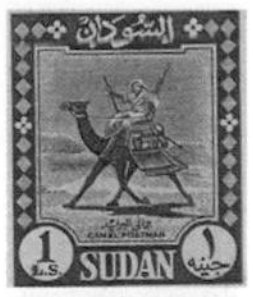

64 Camel Postman

1962

185	62	5m. blue	15	15
186	-	10m. purple and blue	15	15
187	-	15m. purple, orange & bistre	15	15
190	-	35m. brown, dp brown & green	1·00	30
192	-	55m. black and green	1·10	45
188	62	2p. purple	30	20
189	-	3p. brown and green	55	25
191	-	4p. mauve, red and blue	1·10	40
193	-	6p. brown and blue	1·40	50
194	-	8p. green	1·50	55
195	63	10p. brown, bistre and blue	1·70	65
196	-	20p. green and bronze	3·75	1·40
194a	-	25p. brown and green	†	†
197	-	50p. green, blue and black	9·75	2·10
469	64	£S1 brown and green	17·00	8·00
198	-	£S5 green and brown	25·00	12·50
199	63	£S10 orange and green	45·00	19·00

DESIGNS: As Type **62**—HORIZ: 15m. "Tabbaque" (food cover); 55m., 6, 25p. Cattle; 8p. Date palms. VERT: 10m., 3p. Cotton picking; 35m., 4p. Wild game. As Type **63**—HORIZ: 20p., £S5 Bohein Temple; 50p. Sennar Dam.

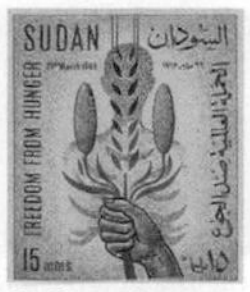

65 Campaign Emblem and "Millet" Cobs

1963. Freedom from Hunger.

226	65	15m. green and brown	30	20
227	65	55m. violet, lilac and blue	90	50

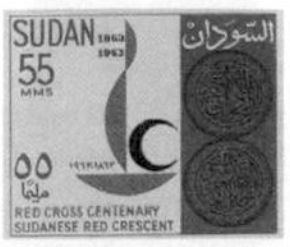

66 Centenary Emblem and Medallions

1963. Centenary of Red Cross.

228	66	15m. multicoloured	70	25
229	66	55m. multicoloured	1·40	65

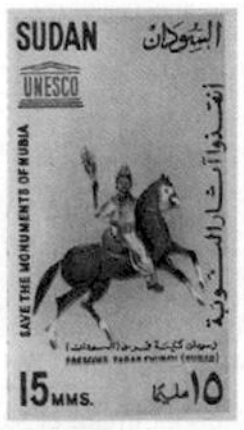

67 "Knight"

1964. Nubian Monuments Preservation. Frescoes from Faras Church, Nubia. Multicoloured.

230		15m. Type **67**	40	30
231		30m. "Saint" (horiz)	70	45
232		55m "Angel"	1·80	1·00

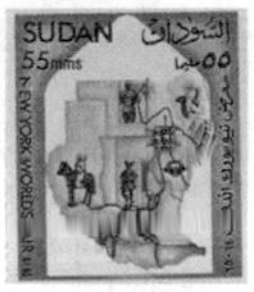

68 Sudan Map

1964. New York World's Fair. Multicoloured.

233		15m. Khashm el Girba Dam	15	10
234		3p. Sudan Pavilion	40	40
235		55m. Type **68**	1·10	50

Nos. 233/4 are horiz.

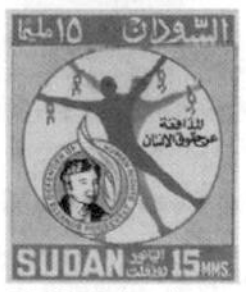

69 Chainbreakers and Mrs. E. Roosevelt

1964. 80th Birth Anniv of Mrs. Eleanor Roosevelt (Human Rights pioneer).

236	69	15m. blue and black	15	10
237	69	3p. violet and black	60	40
238	69	55m. brown and black	1·10	80

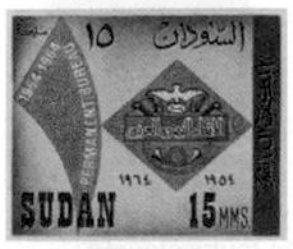

70 Postal Union Emblem

1964. Tenth Anniv of Arab Postal Unions' Permanent Bureau.

239	70	15m. black, gold and red	15	10
240	70	3p. black, gold and green	60	40
241	70	55m. black, gold and violet	1·10	80

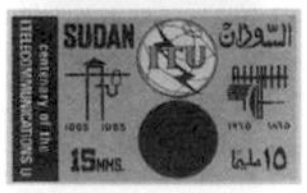

71 I.T.U. Symbol and Emblems

1965. Centenary of I.T.U.

242	71	15m. brown and gold	15	10
243	71	3p. black and gold	60	40
244	71	55m. green and gold	1·10	80

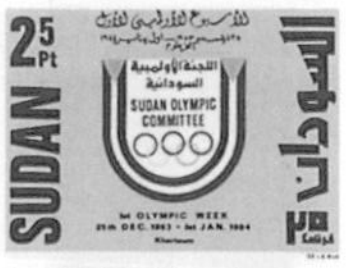

128 Sudan Olympic Committee Emblem

1984. First Olympic Week.

408	128	10p. multicoloured	60	25
409	128	25p. multicoloured	1·40	70
410	128	40p. multicoloured	2·30	1·10

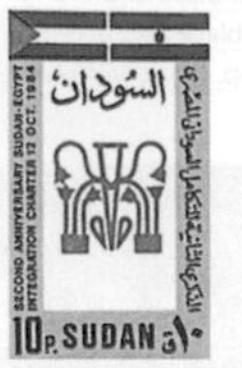

129 Emblem and Flags

1984. Second Anniv of Sudan–Egypt Co-operation Treaty.

411	129	10p. multicoloured	60	25
412	129	25p. multicoloured	1·40	80
413	129	40p. multicoloured	2·30	1·10

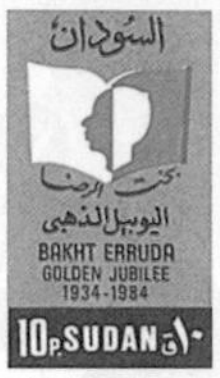

130 Institute Emblem

1985. 50th Anniv of Bakht Erruda Teacher Training Institute, Eddueim Town.

414	130	10p. multicoloured	45	25
415	130	25p. multicoloured	1·40	80
416	130	40p. multicoloured	2·10	1·10

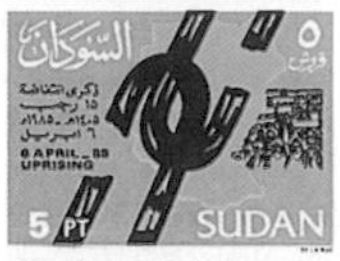

131 Map and Broken Chain

1986. First Anniv of 6 April Rising.

417	131	5p. black, green and brown	15	10
418	131	25p. black, green and blue	1·20	55
419	131	40p. black, green and brown	2·10	95

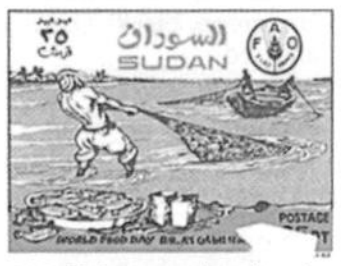

132 Fishermen hauling in Nets

1988. World Food Day (1986).

420	132	25p. black, silver and brown	45	15
421	-	30p. green and black	75	25
422	-	50p. multicoloured	1·20	70
423	-	75p. black, deep blue and blue	1·80	95
424	-	300p. blue, black and silver	7·50	3·00
MS425		100×70 mm. 75p. black, silver and ochre	3·00	2·75

DESIGNS—VERT: 30p. Two fishes. HORIZ: 50p. Plant and globe; 75p. Outline of fish and waves; 300p. Shoal of fish.

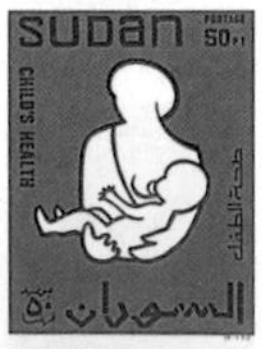

133 Mother breast-feeding Baby

1988. Child Health Campaign.

426	133	50p. black and mauve	1·20	40
427	-	75p. multicoloured	2·00	70
428	-	100p. multicoloured	2·50	95
429	-	150p. multicoloured	4·00	1·50
MS430		63×84 mm. 75p. black and mauve. No gum. Imperf	2·50	2·30

DESIGNS—HORIZ: No. 427, Mother spoon-feeding child; 428, Child being given oral vaccination; 429, Children on scales.

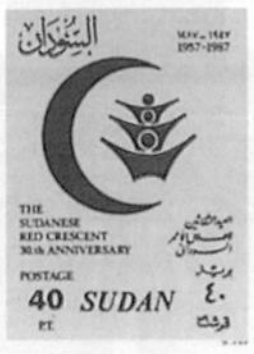

134 Emblem

1988. 30th Anniv of Sudan Red Crescent.

431	134	40p. black, yellow and red	90	40
432	-	100p. black, red and green	2·10	95
433	-	150p. black, red and blue	3·00	1·50

DESIGNS: 100p. Candle; 150p. Figure with crescent on head.

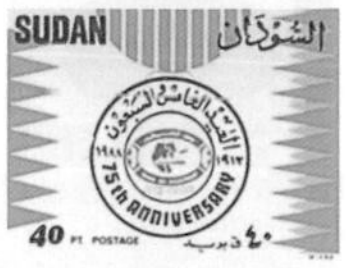

135 Anniversary Emblem

1988. 75th Anniv of Bank of Khartoum. Multicoloured.

434		40p. Type **135**	90	40
435		100p. Bubbles and medal	2·10	95
436		150p. Inscription and emblem	3·00	1·50

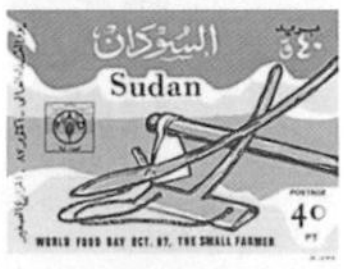

136 Plough

1988. World Food Day. The Small Farmer. Multicoloured.

437		40p. Type **136**	90	40
438		100p. Farmer ploughing	2·10	95
439		150p. Farmer drawing water from river	3·00	1·50

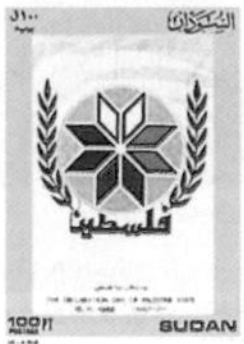

137 Emblem

1989. "Freedom of Palestine".

440	137	100p. multicoloured	1·10	40
441	137	150p. multicoloured	2·00	70
442	137	200p. multicoloured	3·00	1·10

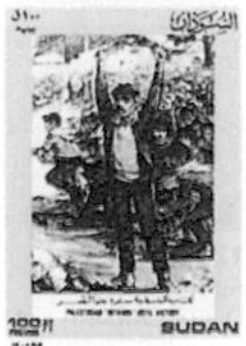

138 Crowd of Youths

1989. Palestinian "Intifada" Movement.

443	138	100p. multicoloured	1·10	40
444	138	150p. multicoloured	2·00	70
445	138	200p. multicoloured	3·00	1·10

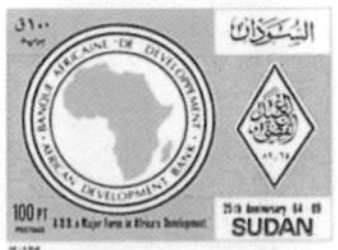

139 Emblem

1989. 25th Anniv of African Development Bank.

446	139	100p. green, black & silver	1·10	40
447	139	150p. blue, black and silver	2·00	70
448	139	200p. purple, black & sil	3·00	1·10

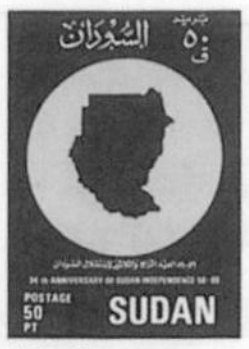

140 Map

1990. 34th Anniv of Independence.

449	140	50p. blue and yellow	45	15
450	140	100p. brown and yellow	1·10	40
451	140	150p. mauve and yellow	2·00	70
452	140	200p. mauve and yellow	2·50	95

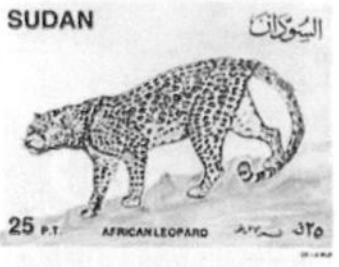

141 Leopard

1990. Mammals. Multicoloured.

453		25p. Type **141**	60	25
454		50p. African elephant	1·50	55
455		75p. Giraffe (vert)	2·30	1·10
456		100p. White rhinoceros	2·75	1·50
457		125p. Addax (vert)	3·00	2·00

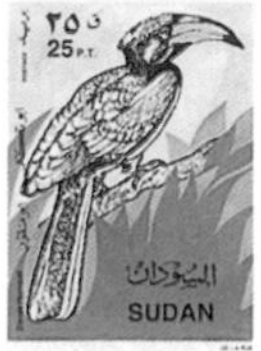

142 Pied Hornbill ("Zande Hornbill")

1990. Birds. Multicoloured.

458		25p. Type **142**	75	25
459		50p. Marabou stork	2·10	95
460		75p. Crested bustard ("Buff-crested Bustard")	3·00	1·40
461		100p. Saddle-bill stork ("Saddle-bill")	3·75	1·60
462		150p. Waldrapp ("Bald-headed Ibis")	4·75	2·00

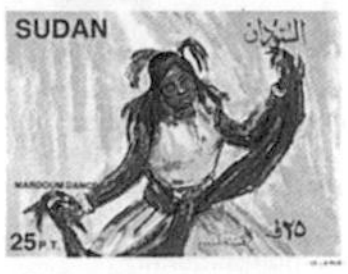

143 Mardoum Dance

1990. Traditional Dances. Multicoloured.

463		25p. Type **143**	30	15
464		50p. Zandi dance (vert)	90	40
465		75p. Kambala dance (vert)	1·40	80
466		100p. Nubian dance (vert)	1·70	1·10
467		125p. Sword dance	2·10	1·40

1990. No. 195 surch with new value in Arabic.

468	63	£S1 on 10p. brown, bistre & blue	£110	13·50

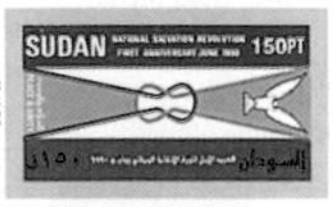

146 Flag

1991. First Anniv of "National Salvation Revolution".

470	146	150p. multicoloured	1·70	1·50
471	146	200p. multicoloured	2·30	2·00
472	146	250p. multicoloured	2·75	2·40
473	146	£S5 multicoloured	5·50	4·75
474	146	£S10 multicoloured	11·50	10·00

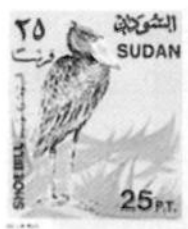

147 Whale-headed Stork ("Shoebill")

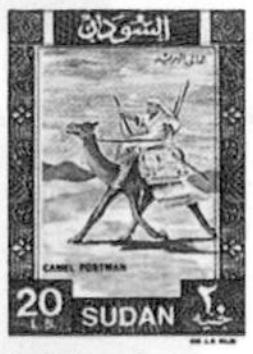

148 Camel Postman

1991. (a) As T **147**. Multicoloured.

475		25p. Type **147**	30	15
476		50p. Sunflower	45	25
477		75p. Collecting gum arabic	75	55
478		100p. Cotton	1·10	80
479		125p. South African crowned crane	1·40	1·10
480		150p. Kenana Sugar Co Ltd (29½×25 mm)	1·70	1·40
481		175p. Secretary bird (24×30½ mm)	1·80	1·50
482		£S2 Atbara Cement Factory (29½×25 mm)	5·25	4·75
483		250p. King Taharka (statue) (26×37 mm)	6·00	5·50
484		£S3 Republican Palace (26×37 mm)	2·10	1·80
485		£S4 Hug (scent container) (24×30½ mm)	2·75	2·40
486		£S5 Gabanah (coffee pot) (24×30½ mm)	3·00	2·75

(b) As T **148**. Multicoloured.

487		£S8 Lionfish (horiz)	9·75	8·75
488		£S10 Goat, ox and camel (horiz)	10·50	9·50
489		£S15 Nubian ibex	17·00	15·00
490		£S20 Type **148**	27·00	24·00

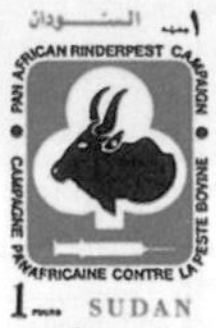

150 Campaign Emblem

1991. Pan-African Campaign against Rinderpest.

507	150	£S1 black and green	1·20	95
508	150	£S2 violet and green	2·30	1·90
509	150	£S5 orange and green	5·75	4·75

٢ر٥ دينار

(151)

1993. Various stamps handstamped as T **151**.

510	-	1d. on 100p. multicoloured (No. 478)	5·75	4·00
511	-	2d. on £S2 mult (No. 482)	11·00	8·00
512	147	2½d. on 25p. multicoloured (No. 475)	14·00	11·00
513	-	3d. on £S3 mult (No. 484)	17·00	13·00
514	-	4d. on £S4 mult (No. 485)	22·00	18·00

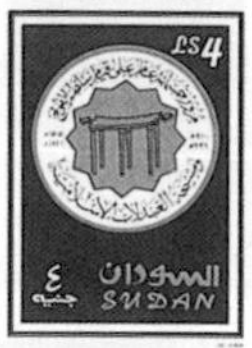

152 Emblem

1993. 500th Anniv of Fung Sultanate and Abdalab Islamic Shaikhdom. Multicoloured.

515		£S4 Type **152**	1·30	1·10
516		£S5 Arabic script on bottle	1·80	1·50
517		750p. Arabic script in cartouche and helmet (horiz)	2·75	2·20

Nos. 515/17 were sold at 4, 5 and 7½ dinars respectively.

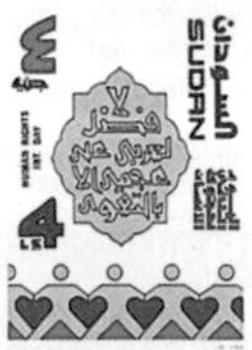

153 Arabic Script and Hearts

1993. International Human Rights Day.

518	153	£S4 multicoloured	1·30	1·10
519	-	£S5 multicoloured	1·80	1·50
520	-	750p. black, green and red	2·75	2·20

DESIGNS—HORIZ: £S5 Rainbow breaking through chains. VERT: 750p. Rose and Arabic script.

Nos. 518/20 were sold at 4, 5 and 7½ dinars respectively.

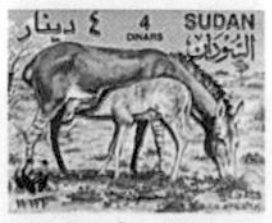

154 Feeding Young

1994. The Wild Ass. Multicoloured.

521		4d. Type **154**	65	55
522		8d. Adult	1·30	1·10
523		10d. Adult galloping	1·70	1·40
524		15d. Head of adult	2·75	2·20

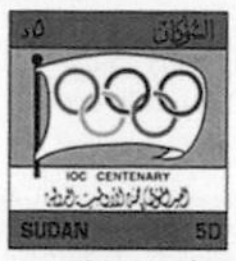
155 Olympic Flag

1994. Cent of International Olympic Committee.

525	**155**	5d. multicoloured	85	70
526	**155**	7d. multicoloured	1·70	1·40
527	**155**	15d. multicoloured	3·25	2·75

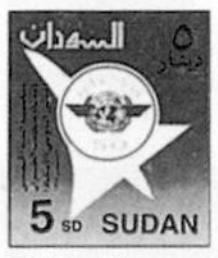
156 Anniversary Emblem

1994. 50th Anniv of I.C.A.O.

528	**156**	5d. purple, yellow & black	50	40
529	**156**	7d. brown, yellow & black	85	70
530	**156**	15d. blue, yellow and black	1·80	1·50

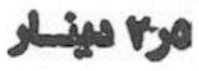
(157)

1995. Various stamps handstamped as T **157**.

531	2½d. on 25p. green and brown (No. 194a)	65	55
532	15d. on 150p. multicoloured (No. 480)	4·00	3·25
533	20d. on 75p. multicoloured (No. 477)	5·25	4·25

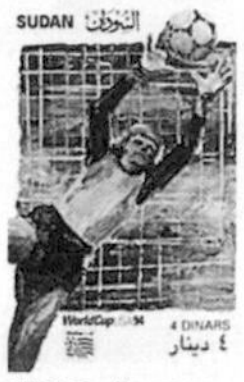
158 Goalkeeper

1995. World Cup Football Championship, U.S.A. (1994). Multicoloured.

534	4d. Type **158**	35	25
535	5d. Type **158**	50	40
536	7d. Player in green shirt	85	70
537	8d. As No. 536 but red shirt	1·00	80
538	10d. Player heading ball	1·20	95
539	15d. Brazilian player	1·80	1·50
540	20d. German player	2·50	2·00
541	25d. American player	2·75	2·30
542	35d. As No. 537	4·25	3·50
MS543	Two sheets each 100×70 mm. (a) 75d. Netherlands goalkeeper (horiz); (b) 100d. Kicking ball (horiz)	22·00	20·00

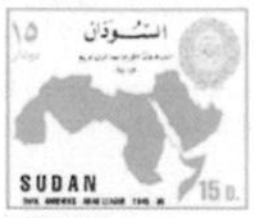
159 Map and Emblem

1995. 50th Anniv of Arab League.

544	**159**	15d. green and black	2·30	1·90
545	**159**	25d. blue and black	4·00	3·25
546	**159**	30d. violet and black	4·50	3·75

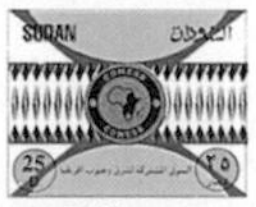
160 Emblem

1996. Common Market for Eastern and Southern Africa.

547	**160**	15d. multicoloured	2·30	1·90
548	**160**	25d. multicoloured	4·00	3·25
549	**160**	30d. multicoloured	4·50	3·75

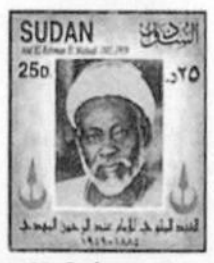
162 Rahman

1997. 42nd Death Anniv of Abdel Rahman al Mahadi.

557	**162**	25d. black and violet	4·25	3·50
558	**162**	35d. black and red	5·75	4·75
559	**162**	50d. black and brown	8·25	6·75

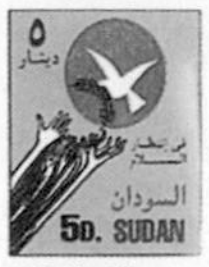
163 Hands reaching to Dove

1997. Peace.

560	**163**	5d. multicoloured	2·10	1·80

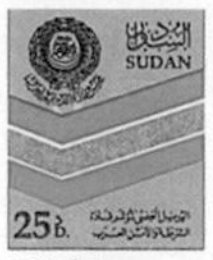
164 Stripes

1997. 25th Anniv of Police Force.

561	**164**	25d. multicoloured	3·25	2·75
562	**164**	35d. multicoloured	5·00	4·00
563	**164**	50d. silver, green and black	6·50	5·50

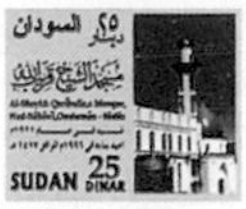
165 Mosque

1997. Fifth Anniv of Reconstruction of Sheikh Quribulla's Mosque, Omdurman. Multicoloured.

564	25d. Type **165**	2·75	2·30
565	35d. Close-up of facade	4·50	3·75
566	50d. Distant view of facade (vert)	6·00	4·75

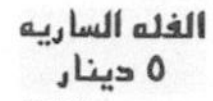
(166)

1997. Nos. 476, 483 and 487 surch as T **166**.

567	5d. on 50p. multicoloured	2·00	1·60
568	25d. on 250p. multicoloured	10·50	8·75
569	35d. on £S8 multicoloured	12·50	10·00

The size of surcharge differs for each value.

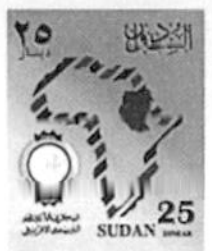
167 Emblem and Outline of Africa

1998. 18th Anniv of Pan-African Postal Union.

570	**167**	25d. multicoloured	3·00	2·40
571	**167**	35d. multicoloured	4·25	3·50
572	**167**	50d. multicoloured	6·00	4·75

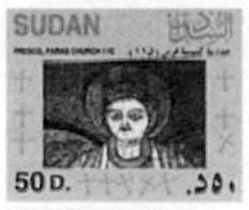
168 Faras Church Fresco (detail)

1998. Archaeological Finds. Multicoloured.

573	50d. Type **168**	3·75	3·00
574	50d. Drinking cup	3·75	3·00
575	50d. Faras Church fresco (different)	3·75	3·00
576	60d. Decorated dish (2000 B.C.)	4·25	3·50
577	75d. Statue of King Natakamani (vert)	5·50	4·50
578	75d. Meroe decorated pot (4000 B.C.)	5·50	4·50
579	100d. Bowl (2000 B.C.)	7·50	6·00

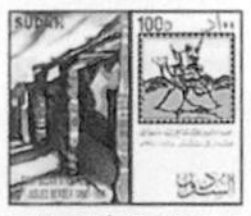
169 Arab Postman Design

1998. Centenary of First Sudanese Stamp.

580	**169**	100d. multicoloured	13·00	11·00

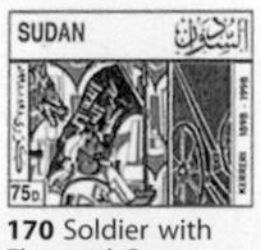
170 Soldier with Flag and Cannon

1999. Centenary of Battle of Kerreri.

581	**170**	75d. multicoloured	8·25	6·75
582	**170**	100d. multicoloured	11·50	9·50
583	**170**	150d. multicoloured	17·00	13·50

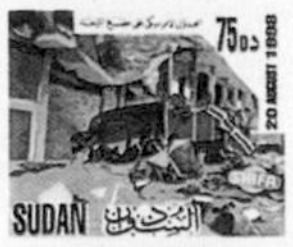
171 Factory Ruins

1999. First Anniv of Bombing of Shifa Pharmaceutical Factory. Multicoloured.

584	75d. Type **171**	8·25	6·75
585	100d. Shifa emblem (22×27 mm)	11·50	9·50
586	150d. Effects of bombing	17·00	13·50

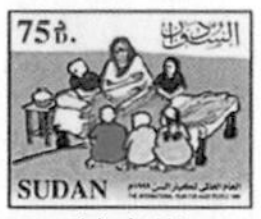
172 Elderly Women and Children

1999. International Year of the Elderly Person. Multicoloured.

587	75d. Type **172**	8·25	6·75
588	100d. Emblem (vert)	11·50	9·50
589	150d. Elderly man and children	17·00	13·50

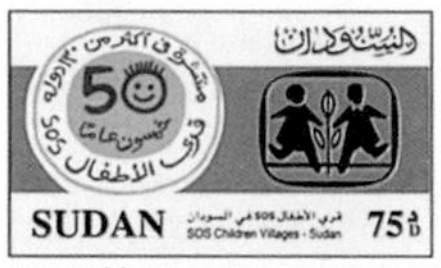
173 Emblems

1999. 50th Anniv of S.O.S. Children's Villages.

590	**173**	75d. multicoloured	8·25	6·75
591	**173**	100d. multicoloured	11·50	9·50
592	**173**	150d. multicoloured	17·00	13·50

(174)

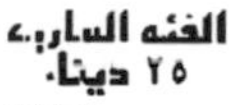
(174a)

2000. No. 480 (Kenana Sugar Co Ltd) overprinted as Type **174** and No. 483 (King Taharka (statue)) overprinted as Type **174a**.

593	150p. multicoloured	10·00	8·00
594	250p. multicoloured	21·00	18·00

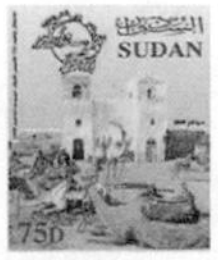
175 UPU Emblem, Fortified Gate and Camels

2000. 125th Anniv of Universal Postal Union (1999).

595	**175**	75d. multicoloured	8·25	6·75
596	**175**	100d. multicoloured	10·00	8·00
597	**175**	150d. multicoloured	17·00	13·50

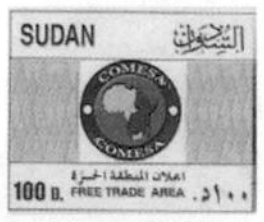
176 Map of Africa

2000. Seventh Anniv of Africa Free Trade Area (COMESA).

598	**176**	100d. multicoloured	10·00	8·00
599	**176**	150d. multicoloured	17·00	13·50
600	**176**	200d. multicoloured	20·00	16·00

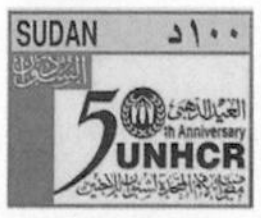
177 Anniversary Emblem

2001. 50th Anniv of United Nations High Commissioner for Refugees.

601	**177**	100d. black and light green	10·00	8·00
602	**177**	150d. black and red	17·00	13·50
603	**177**	200d. black and violet	20·00	16·00

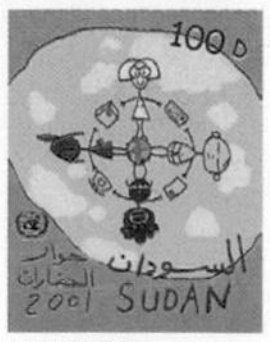
178 Children encircling Globe

2002. United Nations Year of Dialogue among Civilizations.

604	**178**	100d. multicoloured	10·00	8·00
605	**178**	150d. multicoloured	17·00	13·50
606	**178**	200d. multicoloured	20·00	16·00

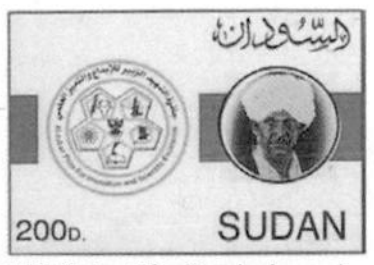
179 Scientific Symbols and Al-Zubair

2002. Al-Zubair Prize for Innovation and Scientific Excellence.

607	**179**	100d. multicoloured	10·00	8·00
608	**179**	150d. multicoloured	17·00	13·50
609	**179**	200d. multicoloured	20·00	16·00

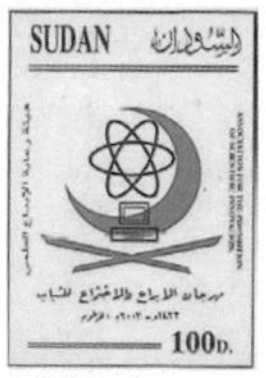
180 Atomic Symbol, Computer and Crescent

2002. Association for the Promotion of Scientific Innovation.

610	**180**	100d. black and blue	10·00	8·00
611	**180**	150d. black, red and blue	17·00	13·50
612	**180**	200d. black, green and blue	20·00	16·00

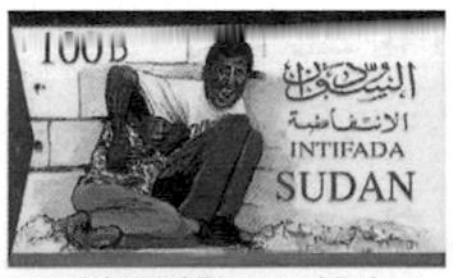
181 Mohamed Dorra and Father

2002. Mohamed Dorra Commemoration.

613	**181**	100d. multicoloured	10·00	8·00
614	**181**	150d. multicoloured	17·00	13·50
615	**181**	200d. multicoloured	20·00	16·00

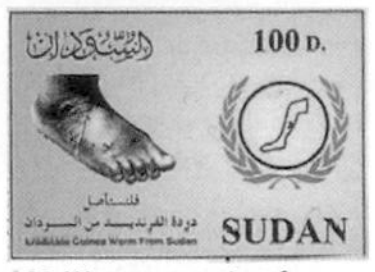
182 Worm emerging from Foot

2002. Guinea Worm Eradication Campaign. Multicoloured.

616	100d. Type **182**	10·00	8·00
617	150d. Emblem (Eradication programme managers meeting, Khartoum)	17·00	13·50
618	200d. Child	20·00	16·00

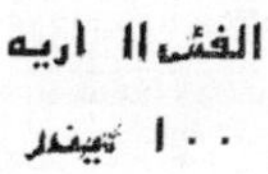
(183)

2003. No. 479 surch with T **183**.

619	100d. on 125p. multicoloured	12·50	10·00

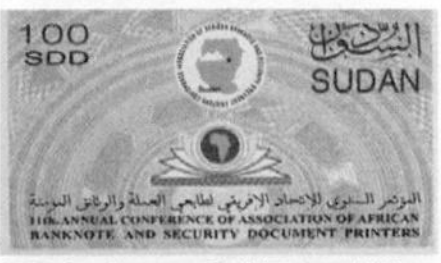
184 Conference Emblem and Map of Africa

2003. Annual Conference of Association of Banknote and Security Document Printers, Khartoum. Multicoloured.

620	100d. Type **184**	10·00	8·00
621	150d. Emblem and national arms	17·00	13·50
622	200d. Ruins	20·00	16·00

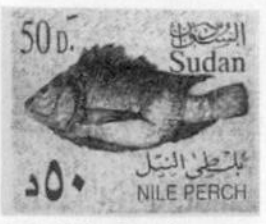

186 Nile Perch

2003. National Symbols. Multicoloured.

627	50d. Type **186**	1·20	95
628	50d. Mango (vert)	1·20	95
629	75d. Cattle	1·80	1·50
630	100d. Marchers carrying flags	2·30	1·90
631	100d. Al Imam El Mahadi	2·30	1·90
632	125d. Butterfly fish	3·00	2·40
633	150d. Amon Ra temple (vert)	3·75	3·00
634	150d. Leafless baobab tree (vert)	3·75	3·00
635	150d. Doum palm (vert)	3·75	3·00
636	150d. Sheep (vert)	3·75	3·00
637	200d. Wellhead (Sudan petrol) (vert)	5·00	4·00
638	200d. Grapefruit (vert)	5·00	4·00
639	300d. Tomb	7·25	6·00
640	500d. Camel postman (vert)	11·50	9·50

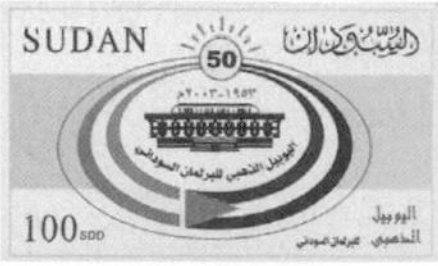

187 Anniversary Emblem

2004. 50th Anniv of National Parliament.

641	**187**	100d. multicoloured	2·30	1·90
642	**187**	200d. multicoloured	3·75	3·00
643	**187**	250d. multicoloured	5·00	4·00

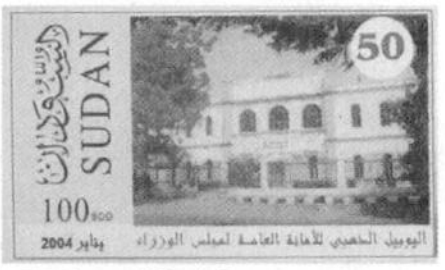

188 Council Building

2004. 50th Anniv of General Secretariat of Council of Ministers.

644	**188**	100d. multicoloured	2·30	1·90
645	**188**	200d. multicoloured	3·75	3·00
646	**188**	250d. multicoloured	5·00	4·00

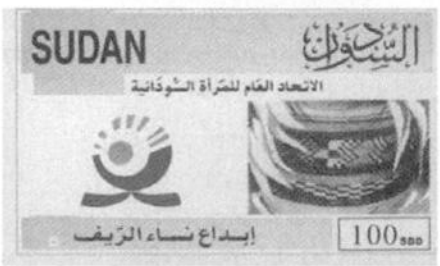

189 Veiled Woman

2004. Rural Women Innovation.

647	**189**	100d. multicoloured	2·30	1·90
648	**189**	200d. multicoloured	3·75	3·00
649	**189**	250d. multicoloured	5·00	4·00

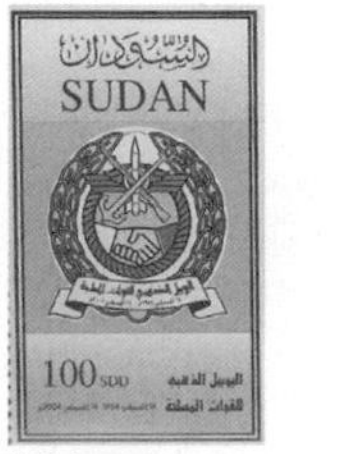

190 Arms

2004. 50th Anniv of Armed Forces.

650	**190**	100d. multicoloured	3·25	2·75
651	**190**	200d. multicoloured	6·50	5·50
652	**190**	250d. multicoloured	10·00	8·00

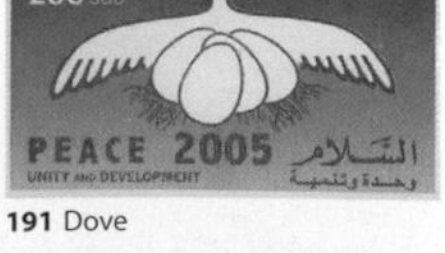

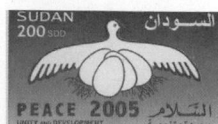

191 Dove

2005. Peace.

653	**191**	200d. blue, claret and black	4·50	3·75
654	**191**	300d. green, yellow and black	7·25	6·00
655	**191**	400d. blue and black	10·00	8·00

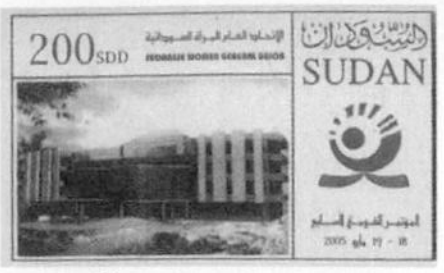

192 Building

2005. Women's General Union.

656	**192**	200d. multicoloured	4·50	3·75
657	**192**	300d. multicoloured	7·25	6·00
658	**192**	400d. multicoloured	10·00	8·00

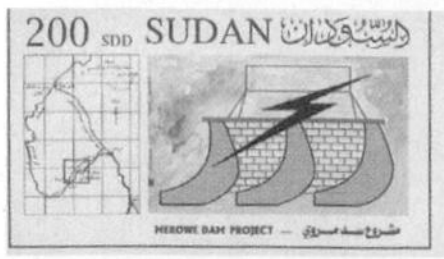

193 Map and Dam

2005. Merowe Dam Project.

659	**193**	200d. multicoloured	4·50	3·75
660	**193**	300d. multicoloured	7·25	6·00
661	**193**	400d. multicoloured	10·00	8·00

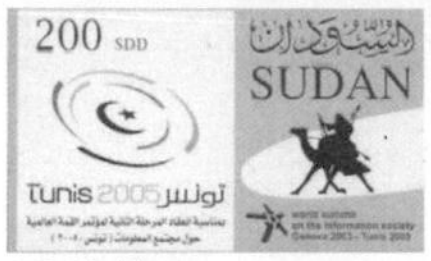

193a Emblem

2005. World Information Society Summit, Tunis.

662	**193a**	200d. multicoloured	4·50	3·75
663	**193a**	300d. multicoloured	7·25	6·00
664	**193a**	400d. multicoloured	10·00	8·00

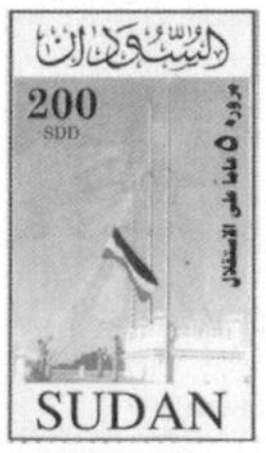

194 Raising Flag

2006. 50th Anniv of Independence. Multicoloured.

665	200d. Type **194**	4·50	3·75
666	300d. Building (horiz)	7·25	6·00
667	400d. Flag (horiz)	10·00	8·00

MS668 150×148 mm. Type **52**; Type **101**; Type **194**; No. 637; Nos. 665/6. Imperf 60·00 55·00

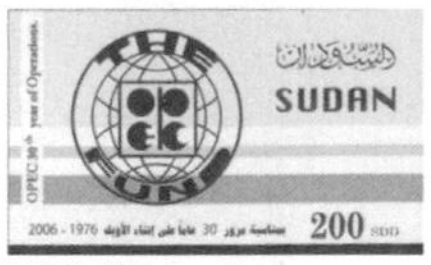

195 Emblem

2006. 50th Anniv of OPEC.

669	**195**	200d. red and black	4·50	3·75
670	**195**	300d. emerald and black	7·25	6·00
671	**195**	400d. ultramarine and black	10·00	8·00

NOTE: As part of the implementation of the Comprehensive Peace Agreement Sudan agreed to change its currency from dinars to pounds (100dinars £S1). This was due to take place at the end of 2006. However the currency did not actually change until 30 June 2007. The stamps below were inscribed in pounds. The equivalent value in dinars is shown in brackets

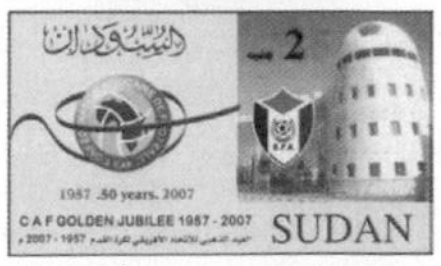

196 Emblems

2007. 50th Anniv of CAF (African Football Union).

672	**196**	2sdg. (200d.) multicoloured	4·50	3·75
673	**196**	3.50sdg (350d.) multicoloured	7·25	6·00
674	**196**	4.50sdg (450d.) multicoloured	10·00	8·00

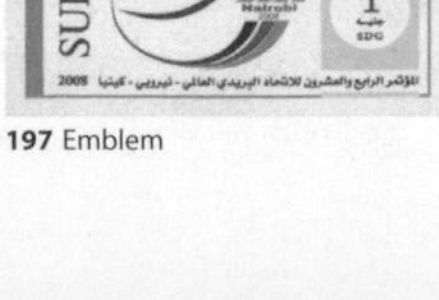

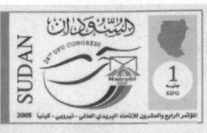

197 Emblem

2007. UPU Congress, Nairobi.

675	**197**	1sdg. multicoloured	2·50	2·10
676	**197**	2sdg. multicoloured	5·00	4·25
677	**197**	3.5sdg. multicoloured	8·75	7·25
678	**197**	4.5sdg. multicoloured	11·00	9·25

Note: Due to unrest the conference was moved to Geneva.

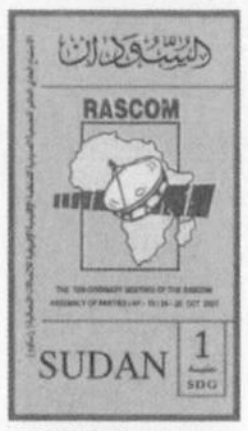

198 Emblem

2007. Tenth Ordinary Meeting of the General Assembly of the African Organization of Space Telecommunications (RASCOM).

679	**198**	1sdg. multicoloured	2·50	2·10
680	**198**	2sdg. multicoloured	5·00	4·25
681	**198**	3.5sdg. multicoloured	8·75	7·25
682	**198**	4.5sdg. multicoloured	11·00	9·25

2008. No. 487 ('Pterois volitans') surch **2 SDG**.

683	2sdg. on £S8 multicoloured	12·50	10·50

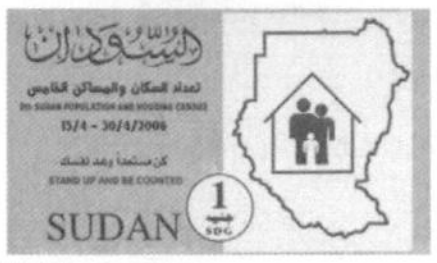

200 Emblem

2008. National Census.

684	**200**	1sdg. blue and black	2·50	2·10
685	**200**	2sdg. lemon and black	5·00	4·25
686	**200**	3.5sdg. lilac and black	8·75	7·25
687	**200**	4.5sdg. green and black	11·00	9·25

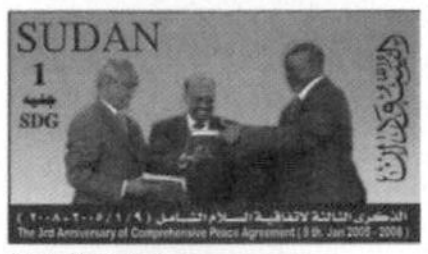

201 Signatories

2008. Third Anniv of Peace Agreement.

688	**201**	1sdg. multicoloured	2·50	2·10
689	**201**	2sdg. multicoloured	5·00	4·25
690	**201**	3.5sdg multicoloured	8·75	7·25
691	**201**	4.5sdg multicoloured	11·00	9·25

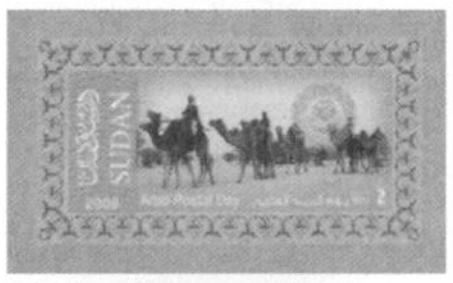

202 Camels

2008. Arab Post Day. Multicoloured.

692	2sdg. Type **202**	5·00	4·25
693	3.5sdg Pigeon	8·75	7·25

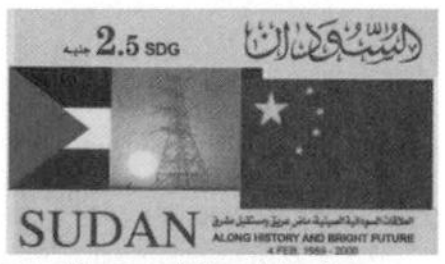

203 Flags and Electricity Pylon

2009. A Long History and a Bright Future. 50th Anniv of Sudan–China Diplomatic Relations.

694	**203**	2.5sdg. multicoloured	5·25	4·50
695	**203**	5sdg multicoloured	11·50	9·50
696	**203**	6sdg multicoloured	13·00	11·00

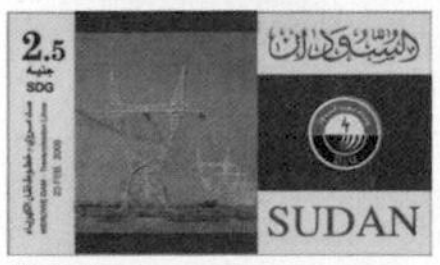

204 Pylons

2009. Merowe Dam–Transmission Lines.

697	**204**	2.5sdg. multicoloured	5·25	4·50
698	**204**	5sdg multicoloured	11·50	9·50
699	**204**	6sdg multicoloured	13·00	11·00

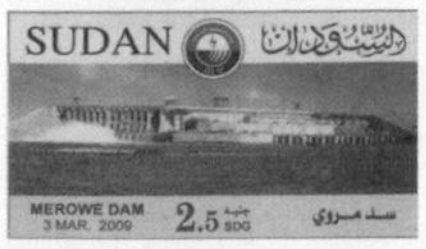

205 Merowe Dam

2009. Merowe Dam

700	**205**	2.5sdg. multicoloured	5·25	4·50
701	**205**	5sdg multicoloured	11·50	9·50
702	**205**	6sdg multicoloured	13·00	11·00

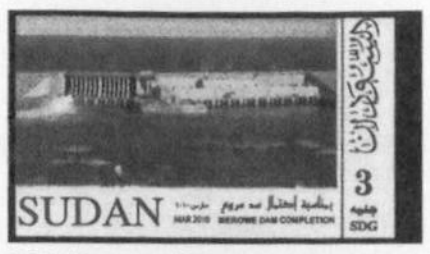

206 Merowe Dam

2010. Merowe Dam Completion

703	**206**	3sdg. multicoloured	5·50	4·50
704	**206**	5.5sdg. multicoloured	12·00	10·00
705	**206**	7sdg. multicoloured	14·00	11·50

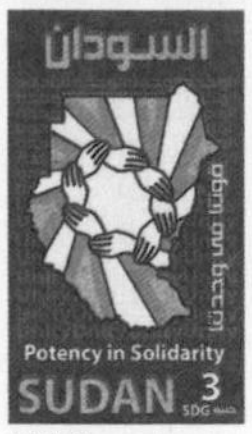

207 Clasped Hands

2010. National Unity

706	**207**	3sdg. multicoloured	5·50	4·50
707	**207**	5.5sdg. multicoloured	12·00	10·00
708	**207**	7sdg. multicoloured	14·00	11·50

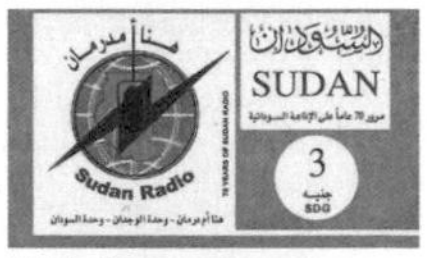

208 Emblem

2010. 70th Anniv of Sudan Radio

709	**208**	3sdg. multicoloured	5·50	4·50
710	**208**	5.5sdg. multicoloured	12·00	10·00
711	**208**	7sdg. multicoloured	14·00	11·50

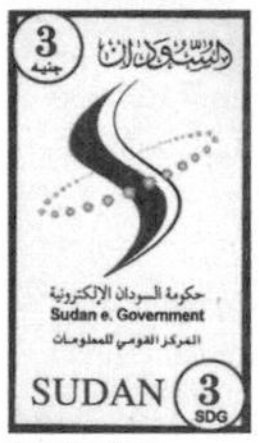

209 Emblem

2011. Sudan e. Government

712	**209**	3sdg. multicoloured	5·50	4·50
713	**209**	5.5sdg. multicoloured	12·00	10·00
714	**209**	7sdg. multicoloured	14·00	11·50

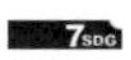

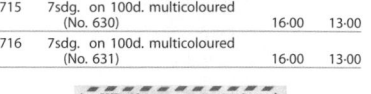

(210)

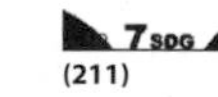

(211)

2012. Nos. 630 and 631 surch as T (**210**) or T (**211**)

715	7sdg. on 100d. multicoloured (No. 630)	16·00	13·00
716	7sdg. on 100d. multicoloured (No. 631)	16·00	13·00

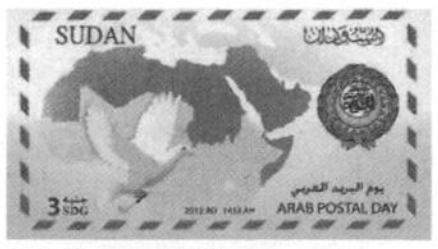

212 Dove and Map

2012. Arab Post Day

717	**212**	3sdg. multicoloured	5·50	4·50
718	**212**	5.5sdg. multicoloured	12·00	10·00
719	**212**	7sdg. multicoloured	14·00	11·50

ARMY OFFICIAL STAMPS

1905. Optd **ARMY OFFICIAL**.

A1	**2**	1m. brown and red	9·00	3·75

1906. Optd **ARMY SERVICE**.

A6	1m. brown and red	3·25	20
A7	2m. green and brown	27·00	1·00
A8	3m. mauve and green	25·00	40
A9	5m. red and black	4·75	10
A10	1p. blue and brown	28·00	15
A11	2p. black and blue	£100	13·00
A12	5p. brown and green	£180	65·00
A16	10p. black and mauve	£160	£425

OFFICIAL STAMPS

1902. Optd **O.S.G.S.**

O5	1m. brown and red	50	10

O6	3m. mauve and green	2·50	15
O7	5m. red and black	2·50	10
O8	1p. blue and brown	10·00	10
O9	2p. black and blue	38·00	20
O10	5p. brown and green	2·75	30
O4	10p. black and mauve	19·00	26·00

1936. Optd **S.G.**

O32	**6**	1m. black and orange	2·50	16·00
O33	**6**	2m. yellow and brown	5·50	9·00
O34	**6**	3m. mauve and green	5·00	10
O35	**6**	4m. green and brown	9·50	4·75
O36	**6**	5m. brown and black	8·00	10
O37	**6**	10m. red and black	1·75	10
O38	**6**	15m. blue and brown	14·00	30
O39	**6**	2p. purple and orange	18·00	10
O39b	**6**	3p. brown and blue	7·50	2·75
O39c	**6**	4p. blue and black	50·00	9·00
O40	**6**	5p. brown and green	17·00	10
O40b	**6**	6p. blue and black	14·00	12·00
O40c	**2**	8p. green and black	7·00	45·00
O41	**2**	10p. black and mauve	60·00	23·00
O42	**2**	20p. blue	38·00	35·00

1948. Optd **S.G.**

O43	**22**	1m. black and orange	30	6·50
O44	**22**	2m. orange and brown	2·25	1·25
O45	**22**	3m. mauve and green	5·00	12·00
O46	**22**	4m. green and brown	4·25	7·00
O47	**22**	5m. brown and black	3·75	10
O48	**22**	10m. red and black	3·75	3·00
O49	**22**	15m. blue and brown	4·50	10
O50	**23**	2p. purple and yellow	4·50	10
O51	**23**	3p. brown and blue	4·50	10
O52	**23**	4p. blue and black	4·00	10
O53	**23**	5p. orange and green	6·50	10
O54	**23**	6p. blue and black	3·50	10
O55	**23**	8p. green and black	3·50	8·00
O56	**23**	10p. black and mauve	8·00	20
O57	**23**	20p. blue	6·00	1·00
O58	**23**	50p. red and blue	70·00	60·00

1950. Air. Nos. 115/22 optd **S.G.**

O59	2p. black and green	16·00	4·00
O60	2½p. blue and orange	1·50	1·75
O61	3p. purple and blue	1·00	1·00
O62	3½p. sepia and brown	1·25	12·00
O63	4p. brown and blue	1·00	10·00
O64	4½p. black and blue	4·75	23·00
O65	6p. black and red	1·00	5·00
O66	20p. black and purple	4·50	12·00

1951. Nos. 123/39 optd **S.G.**

O67	1m. black and orange	50	6·50
O68	2m. black and blue	50	2·50
O69	3m. black and green	14·00	22·00
O70	4m. black and green	10	5·50
O71	5m. black and purple	10	10
O72	10m. black and blue	10	10
O73	15m. black and brown	1·00	10
O74	2p. blue	10	10
O75	3p. brown and blue	30·00	10
O76	3½p. green and brown	30	10
O77	4p. blue and black	8·00	10
O78	5p. brown and green	40	10
O79	6p. blue and black	70	4·00
O80	8p. blue and brown	1·00	30
O81	10p. black and green	70	10
O82	20p. turquoise and black	1·50	30
O83	50p. red and black	6·00	1·25

ح.س.

O65 "S.G."

1962. Nos. 171/84 optd with Type **O65** (larger on 10p. to £S10).

O185	**62**	5m. blue	15	15
O186	-	10m. purple and blue	15	15
O187	-	15m. purple, orge & bis	15	15
O188	**62**	2p. violet	15	15
O189	-	3p. brown and green	85	25
O190	-	35m. brown, deep brown and green	1·10	40
O191	-	4p. purple, red and blue	1·40	40
O192	-	55m. brown and green	2·00	50
O193	-	6p. brown and blue	2·10	65
O194	-	8p. green	2·40	1·00
O222	**63**	10p. brown, black & blue	2·75	1·30
O223	-	20p. green and olive	6·00	1·90
O223a	-	25p. brown and green	30	25
O224	-	50p. green, blue & black	9·75	4·00
O198	**64**	£S1 brown and green	35·00	18·00
O226	-	£S5 green and brown	14·00	12·50
O227	**63**	£S10 orange and blue	28·00	25·00

1991. Nos. 475/90 optd similarly to Type **O65**.

O491	25p. multicoloured	45	40
O492	50p. multicoloured	90	80
O493	75p. multicoloured	1·10	1·00
O494	100p. multicoloured	1·50	1·40
O495	125p. multicoloured	1·80	1·60
O496	150p. multicoloured	2·30	2·00
O497	175p. multicoloured	2·50	2·30
O498	£S2 multicoloured	3·00	2·75
O499	250p. multicoloured	3·75	3·50
O500	£S3 multicoloured	4·50	4·00
O501	£S4 multicoloured	6·00	5·50
O502	£S5 multicoloured	6·75	6·00
O503	£S8 multicoloured	11·50	10·00
O504	£S10 multicoloured	15·00	13·50
O505	£S15 multicoloured	23·00	20·00
O506	£S20 multicoloured	30·00	27·00

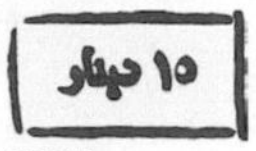

(O161)

1996. Nos. O494, O496, O498 and O500/2 handstamped.

(a) As Type **O161**.

O550	2d. on £S2 multicoloured	65	40
O551	3d. on £S3 multicoloured	1·00	70
O552	4d. on £S4 multicoloured	1·30	1·10
O553	5d. on £S5 multicoloured	1·80	1·50
O554	15d. on 100p. multicoloured	3·75	3·00
O555	15d. on 150p. multicoloured	5·25	4·25

(b) As T **151**.

O556	2d. on £S2 multicoloured	33·00	27·00

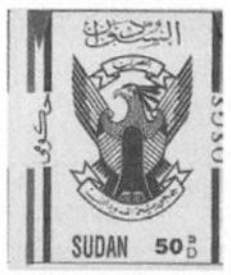

O185 National Arms

2003

O623	**O185**	50d. black, green and red	5·25	4·25
O624	**O185**	100d. black, green and red	10·50	8·75
O625	**O185**	200d. black, green and red	21·00	18·00
O626	**O185**	300d. black, green and red	31·00	26·00

POSTAGE DUE STAMPS

1897. Postage Due Stamps of Egypt optd **SOUDAN** in English and Arabic.

D1	**D23**	2m. green	1·75	5·00
D2	**D23**	4m. purple	[illegible]	5·00
D3	**D23**	1p. blue	10·00	3·50
D4	**D23**	2p. orange	10·00	7·00

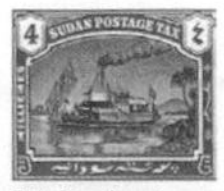

D1 Gunboat "Zafir"

1901

D5	**D1**	2m. black and brown	55	60
D10	**D1**	4m. brown and green	1·00	80
D11	**D1**	10m. green and mauve	1·75	1·60
D8	**D1**	20m. blue and red	3·25	3·25

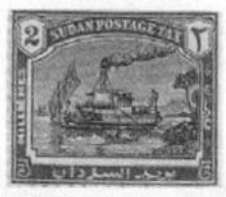

D2 Gunboat "Zafir"

1948

D12	**D 2**	2m. black and brown	4·75	50·00
D13	**D 2**	4m. brown and green	11·00	55·00
D14	**D 2**	10m. green and mauve	20·00	21·00
D15	**D 2**	20m. blue and red	20·00	40·00

The Arabic inscription in Type D **2** differs from that in Type D **1**.

Pt. 1

SUNGEI UJONG

A native state of the Malay Peninsula, later incorporated in Negri Sembilan.

100 cents = 1 dollar (Straits)

1878. Stamp of Straits Settlements optd with Crescent, Star and **SU** in an oval.

1	**5**	2c. brown	£4500	£4750

1881. Stamps of Straits Settlements optd **SUNGEI UJONG**.

28	**5**	2c. brown	65·00	£180
43	**5**	2c. red	16·00	18·00
22		4c. red	£1800	£1900
34	**5**	4c. brown	£300	£425
24		8c. orange	£1900	£1500
26	**19**	10c. grey	£600	£475

1882. Stamps of Straits Settlements optd **S.U.** (2c. with or without stops).

13	2c. brown	£275	£325
14	4c. red	£4500	£5000

1891. Stamp of Straits Settlements surch **SUNGEI UJONG Two CENTS**.

49	2c. on 24c. on 24c. green	£275	£275

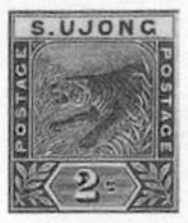

35 Tiger

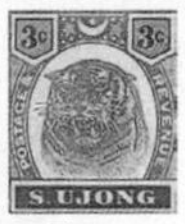

37 Tiger

1891

50	**35**	2c. red	35·00	27·00
51	**35**	2c. orange	1·75	4·25
55	**37**	3c. purple and red	22·00	6·50
52	**35**	5c. blue	9·50	6·50

1894. Surch in figures and words.

53	**35**	1c. on 5c. on 5c. green	1·00	70
54	**35**	3c. on 5c. on 5c. red	2·50	7·50

Pt. 4, Pt. 20

SURINAM

A Netherlands colony on the north-east coast of South America. In December 1954 Surinam became an autonomous state within the Kingdom of the Netherlands. Became an independent state in November 1975.

100 cents = 1 gulden.
2004. 100 cents = 1 dollar (SRD).

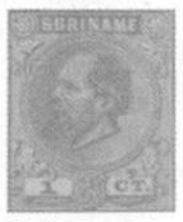

1 King William III

1873. No gum.

25	**1**	1c. grey	3·25	4·00
26	**1**	2c. yellow	2·20	2·20
14	**1**	2½c. red	2·20	2·20
15	**1**	3c. green	28·00	25·00
16	**1**	5c. lilac	28·00	7·75
17	**1**	10c. bistre	9·00	4·00
27	**1**	12½c. blue	28·00	11·00
18	**1**	15c. grey	33·00	11·00
19	**1**	20c. green	50·00	45·00
20	**1**	25c. blue	£110	13·50
22	**1**	30c. brown	50·00	55·00
23	**1**	40c. brown	47·00	45·00
12	**1**	50c. brown	45·00	28·00
28	**1**	1g. grey and brown	75·00	75·00
13	**1**	2½g. brown and green	£110	95·00

The gulden values are larger.

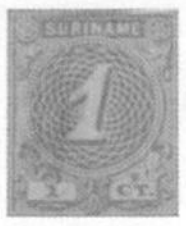

3

1890

44	**3**	1c. grey	2·75	1·70
45	**3**	2c. brown	3·25	2·75
46	**3**	2½c. red	4·00	2·75
47	**3**	3c. green	8·25	5·50
48	**3**	5c. blue	36·00	2·20

1892. Surch **2½ CENT**.

53	**1**	2½c. on 50c. brown	£400	17·00

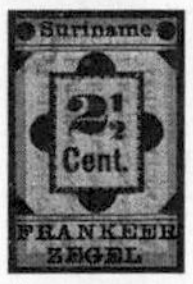

5

1892. No gum.

56	**5**	2½c. black and yellow	2·75	1·70

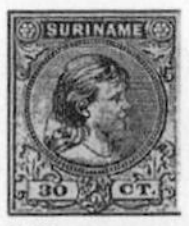

6 Queen Wilhelmina

1892

63	**6**	10c. bistre	55·00	4·50
64	**6**	12½c. mauve	65·00	8·00
65	**6**	15c. grey	5·50	3·75
66	**6**	20c. green	5·50	4·50
67	**6**	25c. blue	14·00	7·75
68	**6**	30c. brown	7·75	6·75

1898. Surch **10 CENT**.

69	**1**	10c. on 12½c. blue	36·00	5·50
70	**1**	10c. on 15c. grey	90·00	75·00
71	**1**	10c. on 20c. green	7·25	6·75
72	**1**	10c. on 25c. blue	17·00	9·00
74	**1**	10c. on 30c. brown	7·25	6·75

1900. Stamps of Netherlands surch **SURINAME** and value.

77	**13**	50c. on 50c. red and green	33·00	10·50
78	**11**	1g. on 1g. green	28·00	18·00
79	**11**	2½g. on 2½g. lilac	28·00	16·00

1900. Surch.

82	**1**	50c. on 2½g. brown and green	£190	£200
83	**1**	25c. on 40c. brown	5·50	4·00
84	**1**	25c. on 50c. brown	5·50	4·00
85	**1**	50c. on 1g. grey and brown	45·00	39·00

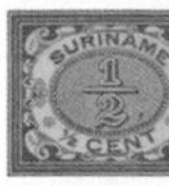

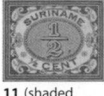

11 (shaded background)

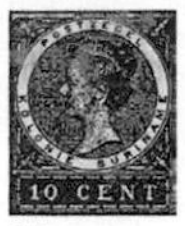

12

1902

87	**11**	½c. lilac	1·10	1·10
88	**11**	1c. green	2·75	1·70
89	**11**	2c. brown	14·00	5·50
90	**11**	2½c. green	6·25	55
91	**11**	3c. yellow	10·00	6·75
92	**11**	5c. red	10·50	55
93	**11**	7½c. grey	22·00	10·00
94	**12**	10c. slate	14·00	1·10
95	**12**	12½c. blue	5·00	55
96	**12**	15c. brown	39·00	13·00
97	**12**	20c. green	33·00	6·75
98	**12**	22½c. green and brown	28·00	16·00
99	**12**	25c. violet	26·00	1·70
100	**12**	30c. brown	55·00	18·00
101	**12**	50c. brown	45·00	11·00

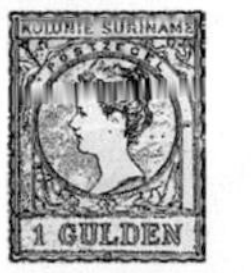

13

1907

102	**13**	1g. purple	75·00	22·00
103	**13**	2½g. slate	75·00	85·00

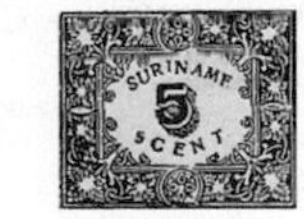

14

1909. Roul or perf. No gum.

104	**14**	5c. red	14·00	11·00

1911. Surch with crown and value.

106	**3**	½c. on 1c. grey	2·20	1·70
107	**3**	½c. on 2c. brown	13·00	10·00
108	**6**	15c. on 25c. blue	£100	80·00
109	**6**	20c. on 30c. brown	14·00	10·00
110	-	30c. on 2½g. on 2½g. purple (No. 79)	£170	£160

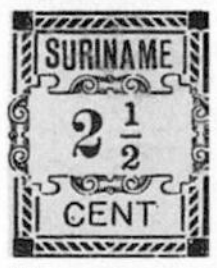

17

1912. No gum.

113	**17**	½c. lilac	1·30	1·30
114	**17**	2½c. green	1·30	1·30
115	**17**	5c. red	10·50	10·50
116	**17**	12½c. blue	14·50	14·50

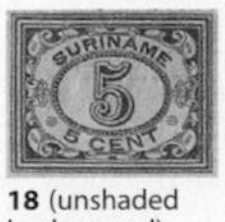

18 (unshaded background)

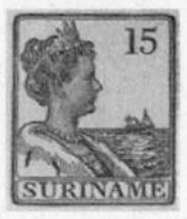

19

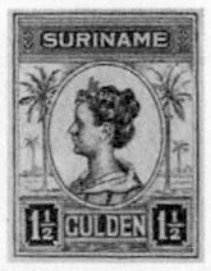

20

1913. With or without gum.

117	**18**	½c. lilac	55	45

118	18	1c. green	55	35
119	18	1½c. blue	55	35
120	18	2c. brown	2·20	1·70
121	18	2½c. green	1·10	35
122	18	3c. yellow	1·10	80
123	18	3c. green	4·00	3·25
125	18	4c. blue	10·00	6·25
126	18	5c. pink	2·20	35
127	18	5c. green	2·75	1·30
128	18	5c. violet	2·20	35
129	18	6c. buff	3·25	3·25
130	18	6c. red	2·75	80
131	18	7½c. brown	1·70	55
132	18	7½c. red	1·70	55
133	18	7½c. yellow	11·00	11·00
134	18	10c. lilac	6·25	6·25
135	18	10c. red	5·00	1·10
136	19	10c. red	1·70	65
137	19	12½c. blue	2·20	80
138	19	12½c. red	2·75	2·75
139	19	15c. green	1·10	90
140	19	15c. blue	9·50	5·75
142	19	20c. blue	3·25	2·75
143	19	20c. green	4·50	4·00
144	19	22½c. orange	3·25	3·25
145	19	25c. mauve	5·00	55
146	19	30c. grey	6·25	1·30
147	19	32½c. violet and orange	19·00	22·00
148	19	35c. blue and orange	6·25	6·25
149	20	50c. green	5·50	1·10
150	20	1g. brown	7·25	1·10
151	20	1½g. purple	45·00	45·00
152b	20	2½g. pink	36·00	33·00

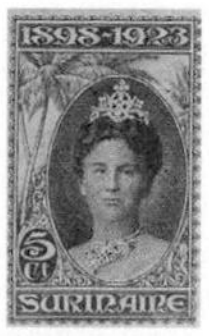
21

1923. Queen's Silver Jubilee.

169a	21	5c. green	1·10	90
170	21	10c. red	2·20	1·90
171	21	20c. blue	5·00	4·00
172a	21	50c. orange	25·00	27·00
173	21	1g. purple	33·00	22·00
174	21	2g.50 grey	£100	£275
175	21	5g. brown	£130	£325

1925. Surch.

176	18	3c. on 5c. green	1·10	1·10
177	19	10c. on 12½c. red	3·25	3·25
180	19	12½c. on 22½c. orange	31·00	33·00
178	19	15c. on 12½c. blue	1·70	1·70
179	19	15c. on 20c. blue	1·70	1·70

1926. Postage Due stamps surch **Frankeerzegel 12½ CENT SURINAME**. (a) In three lines with bars.

181	D6	12½c. on 40c. mve & blk	5·00	5·00

(b) In four lines without bars.

182	12½c. on 40c. lilac	37·00	37·00

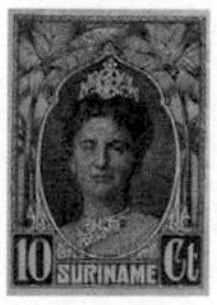
28

1927

183	28	10c. red	1·10	55
184	28	12½c. orange	2·20	2·20
185	28	15c. blue	2·75	90
186	28	20c. blue	2·75	1·10
187	28	21c. brown	26·00	26·00
188	28	22½c. brown	10·00	13·00
189	28	25c. purple	3·50	1·10
190	28	30c. green	3·50	1·30
191	28	35c. sepia	3·75	4·00

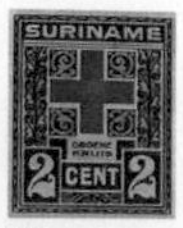
29

1927. Green Cross Fund. Various designs incorporating green cross.

192	29	2c.+2c. green and slate	1·30	1·30
193	-	5c.+3c. green and purple	1·30	1·30
194	-	10c.+3c. green and red	3·00	2·30

1927. Unissued Marine Insurance stamps (as Type **M22** of Netherlands but inscr "SURINAME") surch **FRANKEER ZEGEL** and value.

195	3c. on 15c. green	80	1·10
196	10c. on 60c. red	90	1·10
197	12½c. on 75c. brown	1·10	1·10
198	15c. on 1g.50 blue	3·25	3·25
199	25c. on 2g.25 brown	9·00	9·00
200	30c. on 4½g. black	11·00	8·50
201	50c. on 7½g. red	9·00	9·00

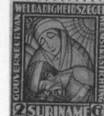

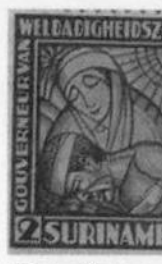
32 Indigenous Disease

1928. Governor Van Heemstrastichting Medical Foundation Fund.

202	32	1½c.+1½c. blue	6·75	6·75
203	32	2c.+2c. green	6·75	6·75
204	32	5c.+3c. violet	7·25	7·25
205	32	7½c.+2½c. red	7·25	7·25

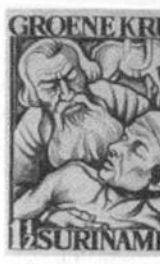
33 The Good Samaritan

1929. Green Cross Fund.

206	33	1½c.+1½c. green	7·75	7·75
207	33	2c.+2c. red	7·75	7·75
208	33	5c.+3c. blue	9·00	9·00
209	33	6c.+4c. black	9·00	9·00

1930. No. 132 surch **6**.

210	18	6c. on 7½c. red	2·50	1·30

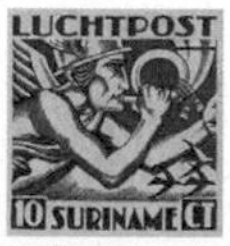
35 Mercury and Posthorn

1930. Air.

276	35	10c. red	4·75	95
212	35	15c. blue	4·50	90
213	35	20c. green	20	35
214	35	40c. red	35	55
215	35	60c. purple	1·00	55
216	35	1g. black	1·70	2·00
217	35	1½g. brown	2·20	2·20
281	35	2½g. yellow	21·00	17·00
282	35	5g. green	£475	£500
283	35	10g. bistre	75·00	80·00

1931. Air. "Dornier 10" Flight. Optd **Vlucht Do. X 1931**.

218	10c. red	26·00	20·00
219	15c. blue	26·00	22·00
220	20c. green	26·00	26·00
221	40c. red	39·00	32·00
222	60c. purple	80·00	80·00
223	1g. black	95·00	95·00
224	1½g. brown	£100	90·00

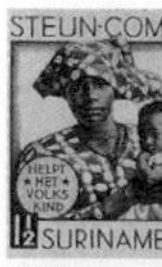
37 Mother and Child

1931. Child Welfare.

225	37	1½c.+1½c. black	6·25	6·25
226	37	2c.+2c. red	6·25	6·25
227	37	5c.+3c. blue	6·25	6·25
228	37	6c.+4c. green	6·25	6·25

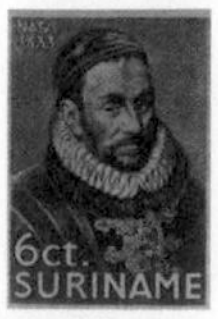
37a William I (after Key)

1933. 400th Birth Anniv of William I of Orange.

229	37a	6c. red	9·00	2·75

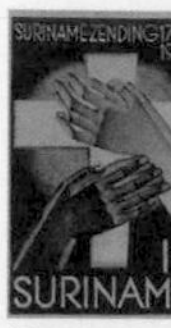
38 "Supplication"

1935. Bicent of Moravian Mission in Surinam.

230	38	1c.+½c. brown	3·00	3·00
231	38	2c.+1c. blue	3·50	3·50
232	-	3c.+1½c. green	3·50	3·50
233	-	4c.+2c. orange	4·00	4·00
234	-	5c.+2½c. black	4·75	4·75
235	38	10c.+5c. red	4·75	4·75

DESIGN: 3, 4, 5c. Cross and clasped hands.

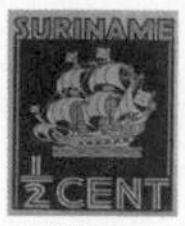
39 "Johannes van Walbeeck" (galleon)

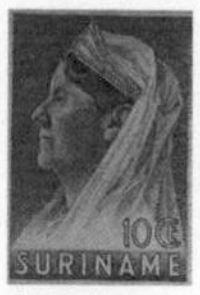
40 Queen Wilhelmina

1936

236	39	½c. brown	35	60
237	39	1c. green	45	35
238	39	1½c. blue	70	60
239	39	2c. brown	80	60
240	39	2½c. green	35	35
241	39	3c. blue	80	60
242	39	4c. orange	80	95
243	39	5c. grey	80	35
244	39	6c. red	3·25	2·30
245	39	7½c. purple	35	35
246	40	10c. red	1·20	35
247	40	12½c. green	4·00	1·60
248	40	15c. blue	1·70	80
249	40	20c. orange	3·00	95
250	40	21c. black	4·75	4·00
251	40	25c. red	3·00	1·70
252	40	30c. purple	4·75	1·40
253	40	35c. bistre	5·25	5·25
254	40	50c. green	5·25	2·30
255	40	1g. blue	9·25	3·00
256	40	1g.50 brown	28·00	21·00
257	40	2g.50 red	16·00	10·50

Nos. 254/7 are larger, 22×33 mm.

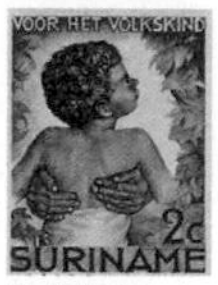
41 "Infant Support"

1936. Child Welfare.

258	41	2c.+1c. green	3·25	3·25
259	41	3c.+1½c. blue	3·25	3·25
260	41	5c.+2½c. black	4·25	4·25
261	41	10c.+5c. red	4·25	4·25

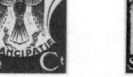

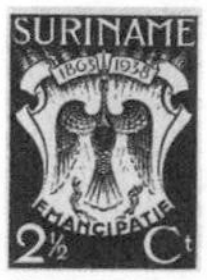
42 "Emancipation"

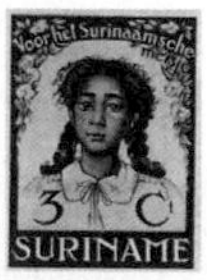
42a Surinam Girl

1938. 75th Anniv of Liberation of Slaves in Surinam and Paramaribo Girls' School Funds.

262	42	2½c.+2c. green	2·30	2·10
263	42a	3c.+2c. black	2·30	2·10
264	42a	5c.+3c. brown	3·00	2·50
265	42a	7½c.+5c. blue	3·00	2·50

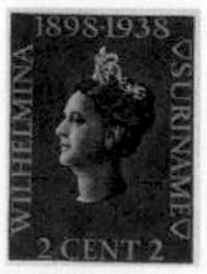
42b Queen Wilhelmina

1938. 40th Anniv of Coronation.

266	42b	2c. violet	60	60
267	42b	7½c. red	1·20	1·20
268	42b	15c. blue	3·50	3·50

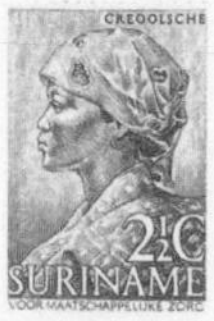
44 Creole

1940. Social Welfare Fund.

269	44	2½c.+2c. green	4·00	3·00
270	-	3c.+2c. red	4·00	3·00
271	-	5c.+3c. blue	4·75	3·00
272	-	7½c.+5c. red	4·75	3·00

DESIGNS: 3c. Javanese woman; 5c. Hindu woman; 7½c. Indian woman.

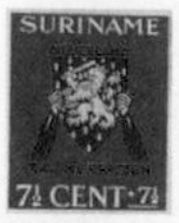
44a Netherlands Coat of Arms

1941. Prince Bernhard and "Spitfire" Funds.

273	44a	7½c.+7½c. blue & orge	8·25	8·25
274	44a	15c.+15c. blue and red	9·25	9·25
275	44a	1g.+1g. blue and grey	35·00	29·00

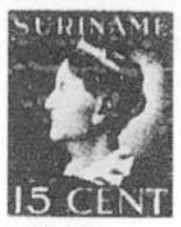
44b Queen Wilhelmina

1941

284	44b	15c. blue	35·00	14·50
342	44b	12½c. blue	1·70	35

1942. Red Cross. Surch with red cross and new values.

289	39	2c.+2c. brown (postage)	3·50	3·50
291	39	2½c.+2c. green	3·50	3·50
292	39	7½c.+5c. purple	3·50	3·50
293	35	10c.+5c. red (air)	9·25	9·25

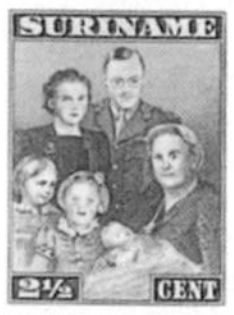
44d Dutch Royal Family

1943. Birth of Princess Margriet.

294	44d	2½c. orange	80	70
295	44d	7½c. red	80	45
296	44d	15c. black	3·50	2·75
297	44d	40c. blue	4·75	3·25

1945. Surch.

298	39	½c. on 1c. green	1·20	1·20
299	39	1½c. on 7½c. purple	60	60
300	39	2½c. on 7½c. purple	5·00	4·75
301	40	2½c. on 10c. red	1·70	45
302	40	5c. on 10c. red	1·20	1·20
303	40	7½c. on 10c. red	1·20	1·20

1945. Air. Surch.

304	35	22½c. on 60c. purple	4·75	4·75
305	35	1g. on 2½g. yellow	32·00	32·00
306	35	5g. on 10g. bistre	32·00	32·00

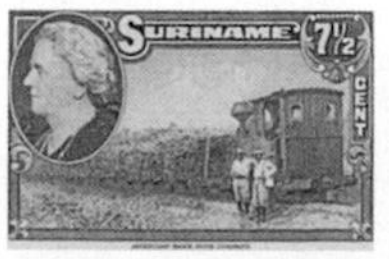
49 Sugar-cane Train

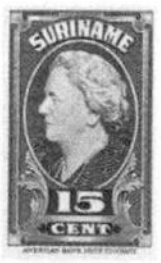
50 Queen Wilhelmina

1945. National Welfare Fund. Surch **CENT VOOR HET NATIONAAL STEUNFONDS** and premium.

307	49	7½c.+5c. orange	8·25	3·75
308	50	15c.+10c. brown	4·75	3·75
309	50	20c.+15c. green	4·75	3·75
310	50	22½c.+20c. grey	4·75	3·75
311	50	40c.+35c. red	4·75	3·75
312	50	60c.+50c. violet	4·75	3·75

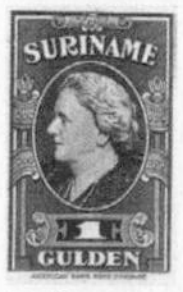
51 Queen Wilhelmina

1945

313	-	1c. red	1·20	45
314	-	1½c. red	3·00	1·60
315	-	2c. violet	1·40	45
316	-	2½c. brown	1·40	45
317	-	3c. green	3·00	1·20
318	-	4c. brown	3·00	1·20
319	-	5c. blue	3·00	45
320	-	6c. olive	5·75	1·90
321	49	7½c. orange	1·90	45
322	50	10c. blue	3·00	35
323	50	15c. brown	4·75	45
324	50	20c. green	5·75	35
325	50	22½c. grey	7·00	1·20
326	50	25c. red	14·50	5·75
327	50	30c. olive	14·50	2·30
328	50	35c. blue	23·00	9·25
329	50	40c. red	14·50	60
330	50	50c. red	14·50	60
331	50	60c. violet	14·50	1·20
332	51	1g. brown	17·00	60
333	51	1g.50 lilac	14·50	1·70
334	51	2g.50 brown	35·00	1·70
335	51	5g. red	65·00	20·00
336	51	10g. orange	£100	39·00

DESIGNS—As Type **49**: 1c. Bauxite mine, Moengo; 1½c. Natives in canoes; 2c. Native and stream; 2½c. Road in Coronie; 3c. River Surinam near Berg en Dal; 4c. Government Square, Paramaribo; 5c. Mining gold; 6c. Street in Paramaribo.

1946. Air. Anti-tuberculosis Fund. Surch **LUCHT POST** and premium.

340	50	10c.+40c. blue	3·50	3·00
341	50	15c.+60c. brown	3·50	3·00

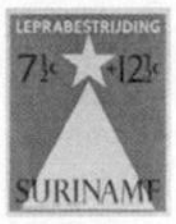

53 Star

1947. Anti-leprosy Fund.

343	53	7½c.+12½c. orange (postage)	5·75	4·75
344	53	12½c.+37½c. blue	5·75	4·75
345	53	22½c.+27½c. grey (air)	5·75	4·75
346	53	27½c.+47½c. green	5·75	4·75

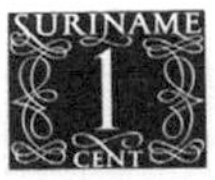

54

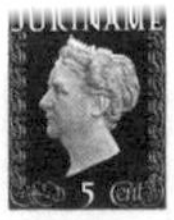

54a Queen Wilhelmina

1948

347	54	1c. red	45	35
348	54	1½c. purple	45	45
349	54	2c. violet	45	35
350	54	2½c. green	2·30	35
351	54	3c. green	45	35
352	54	4c. brown	45	35
353	54	5c. blue	2·30	35
355	54a	5c. blue	60	35
356	54a	6c. green	1·40	95
354	54	7½c. orange	4·75	1·60
357	54a	7½c. red	60	35
358	54a	10c. blue	80	35
359	54a	12½c. blue	1·50	1·40
360	54a	15c. brown	2·30	60
361	54a	17½c. purple	2·40	1·70
362	54a	20c. green	1·90	35
363	54a	22½c. blue	1·90	95
364	54a	25c. red	1·90	45
365	54a	27½c. red	1·90	35
366	54a	30c. green	2·75	35
367	54a	37½c. brown	3·75	2·50
368	54a	40c. purple	3·00	45
369	54a	50c. orange	3·25	45
370	54a	60c. violet	3·25	60
371	54a	70c. black	4·25	80

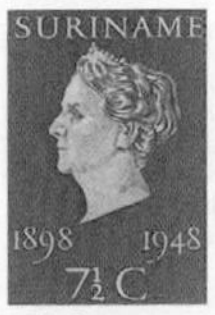

54b Queen Wilhelmina

1948. Queen Wilhelmina's Golden Jubilee.

372	54b	7½c. orange	1·70	1·20
373	54b	12½c. blue	1·70	1·20

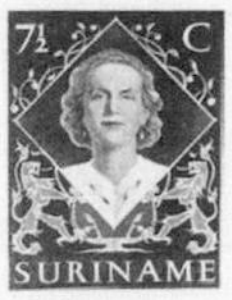

54c Queen Juliana

1948. Accession of Queen Juliana.

374	54c	7½c. orange	4·00	4·00
375	54c	12½c. blue	4·00	4·00

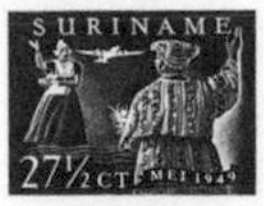

55 Women of Netherlands and Surinam

1949. Air. First K.L.M. Flight on Paramaribo–Amsterdam Service.

376	55	27½c. brown	9·25	4·75

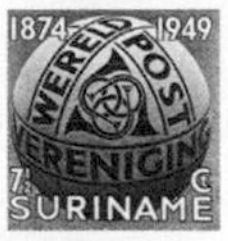

55a Posthorns and Globe

1949. 75th Anniv of U.P.U.

377	55a	7½c. red	8·75	4·00
378	55a	27½c. blue	8·75	3·00

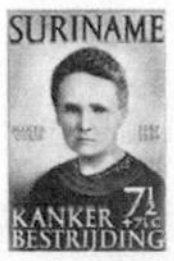

56 Marie Curie

1950. Cancer Research Fund.

379	56	7½c.+7½c. violet	26·00	14·50
380	-	7½c.+22½c. green	26·00	14·50
381	-	27½c.+12½c. blue	26·00	14·50
382	56	27½c.+97½c. brown	26·00	14·50

PORTRAIT: Nos. 380/1, Wilhelm Rontgen.

1950. Surch **1 Cent** and bars.

383	49	1c. on 7½c. orange	1·70	1·20

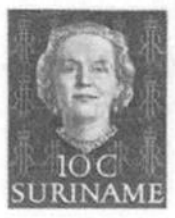

57a Queen Juliana

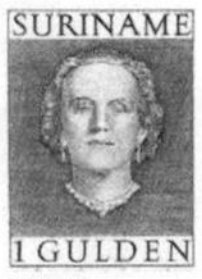

57b Queen Juliana

1951

395	57a	10c. blue	95	35
396	57a	15c. brown	2·10	45
397	57a	20c. turquoise	3·75	35
398	57a	25c. red	2·50	60
399	57a	27½c. lake	2·50	35
400	57a	30c. green	2·50	60
401	57a	35c. olive	3·25	1·50
402	57a	40c. mauve	3·75	60
403	57a	50c. orange	5·00	60
404	57b	1g. brown	38·00	70

1953. Netherlands Flood Relief Fund. Nos. 374/5 surch **STORMRAMP NEDERLAND 1953** and premium.

405		12½c.+7½c. on 7½c. orange	4·75	4·00
406		20c.+10c.on 12½c. blue	4·75	4·00

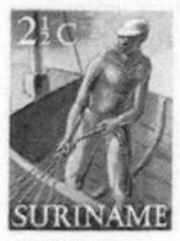

60 Fisherman

1953

407	-	2c. brown	35	35
408	60	2½c. green	45	35
409	-	5c. grey	45	35
410	-	6c. blue	2·30	1·60
411	-	7½c. violet	35	35
412	-	10c. red	35	35
413	-	12½c. blue	2·40	1·90
414	-	15c. red	80	45
415	-	17½c. brown	3·75	2·75
416	-	20c. green	70	35
417	-	25c. green	3·75	1·20

MS418 112×147 mm. Nos. 413/15 and 417 £120 65·00

DESIGNS—HORIZ: 2c. Native shooting fish; 10c. Woman gathering fruit. VERT: 5c. Bauxite mine; 6c. Log raft; 7½c. Ploughing with buffalo; 12½c. Brown hoplo (fish); 15c. Blue and yellow macaw; 17½c. Nine-banded armadillo; 20c. Poling pirogue; 25c. Iguana.

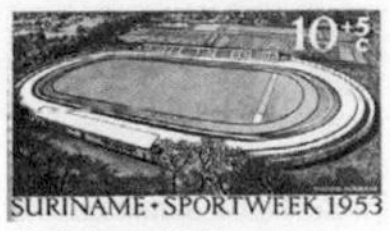

61 Surinam Stadium

1953. Sports Week.

419	61	10c.+5c. red	16·00	13·00
420	61	15c.+7½c. brown	16·00	13·00
421	61	30c.+15c. green	16·00	13·00

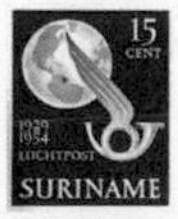

62 Posthorn and Globe

1954. Air. 25th Anniv of Surinam Airlines.

422	62	15c. blue	2·30	1·70

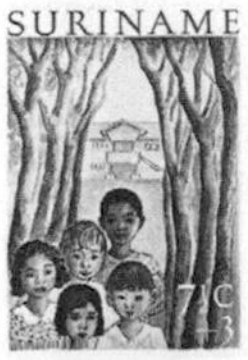

63 Native Children and Youth Centre

1954. Child Welfare Fund.

423	63	7½c.+3c. purple	8·25	6·50
424	63	10c.+5c. green	8·25	6·50
425	63	15c.+7½c. brown	8·25	6·50
426	63	30c.+15c. blue	8·25	6·50

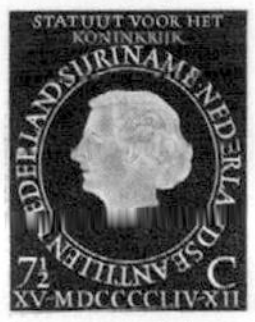

63a Queen Juliana

1954. Ratification of Statute for the Kingdom.

427	63a	7½c. purple	1·20	1·20

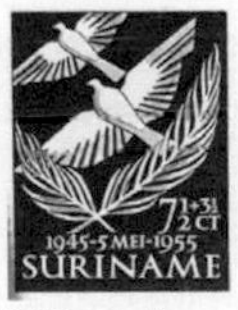

64 Doves of Peace

1955. Tenth Anniv of Liberation of Netherlands and War Victims Relief Fund.

428	64	7½c.+3½c. red	3·50	3·50
429	64	15c.+8c. blue	3·50	3·50

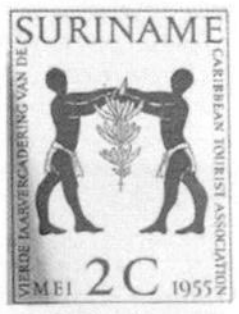

65 Gathering Bananas

1955. Fourth Caribbean Tourist Assn Meeting.

430	65	2c. green	2·30	1·60
431	-	7½c. yellow	3·75	2·75
432	-	10c. brown	3·75	2·75
433	-	15c. blue	4·00	2·75

DESIGNS: 7½c. Pounding rice; 10c. Preparing cassava; 15c. Fishing.

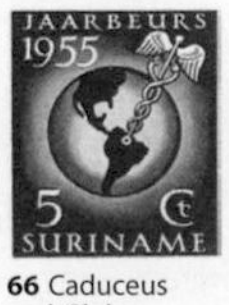

66 Caduceus and Globe

1955. Surinam Fair.

434	66	5c. blue	60	60

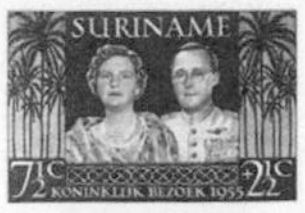

67 Queen Juliana and Prince Bernhard

1955. Royal Visit.

435	67	7½c.+2½c. olive	95	95

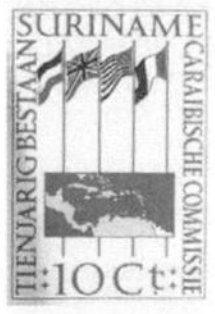

68 Flags and Caribbean Map

1956. Tenth Anniv of Caribbean Commission.

447	68	10c. blue and red	60	60

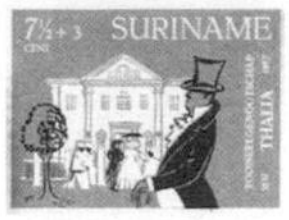

69 Facade of 19th-century Theatre

1958. 120th Anniv of "Thalia" Amateur Dramatic Society.

448	69	7½c.+3c. blue and black	70	70
449	-	10c.+5c. purple & black	70	70
450	-	15c.+7½c. green & black	70	70
451	-	20c.+10c. orange & black	70	70

DESIGNS: 10c. Early 20th-century theatre; 15c. Modern theatre; 20c. Performance on stage.

1959. No. 399 surch **8 C.**

452		8c. on 27½c. red	35	35

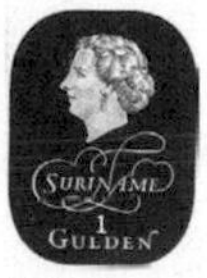

71 Queen Juliana

1959

453	71	1g. purple	2·30	35
454	71	1g.50 brown	3·25	70
455	71	2g.50 red	4·25	45
456	71	5g. blue	9·00	60

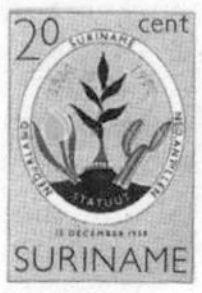

72 Symbolic Plants

1959. Fifth Anniv of Ratification of Statute for the Kingdom.

457	72	20c. multicoloured	4·00	2·30

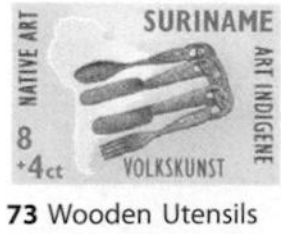

73 Wooden Utensils

1960. Surinam Handicrafts.

458	73	8c.+4c. multicoloured	1·50	1·50
459	-	10c.+5c. red, blue & brn	1·50	1·50
460	-	15c.+7c. green, brn & red	1·50	1·50
461	-	20c.+10c. multicoloured	1·50	1·50

DESIGNS: 10c. Indian chief's headgear; 15c. Clay pottery; 20c. Wooden stool.

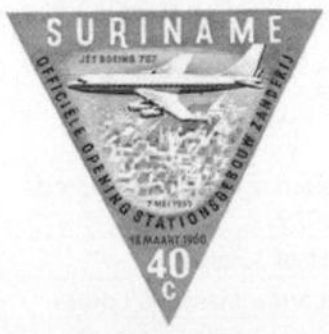

74 Boeing 707

1960. Opening of Zanderij Airport Building.

462		8c. blue	1·70	1·70
463		10c. green	2·75	2·75
464		15c. red	2·75	2·75
465		20c. lilac	3·00	3·00
466	74	40c. brown	4·25	3·25

DESIGNS: 8c. Charles Lindbergh's seaplane, 1929; 10c. Fokker "De Snip", 1934; 15c. Cessna 170A, 1954; 20c. Lockheed Super Constellation, 1957.

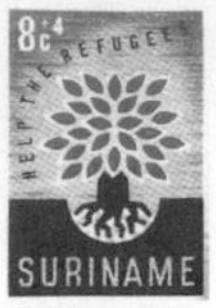

75 "Uprooted Tree"

1960. World Refugee Year.

467	**75**	8c.+4c. green and brown	35	35
468	**75**	10c.+5c. green and blue	35	35

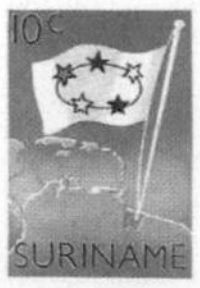

76 Surinam Flag

1960. Freedom Day. Multicoloured.

469	10c. Type **76**	95	95
470	15c. Coat-of-arms (30×26 mm)	95	95

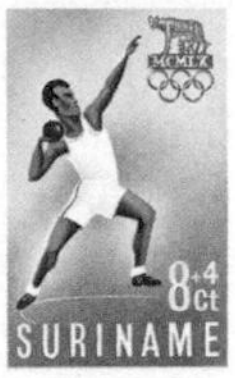

77 Putting the Shot

1960. Olympic Games, Rome.

471	**77**	8c.+4c. brown, blk & grey	1·20	1·20
472	-	10c.+5c. brown, blk & orge	1·20	1·20
473	-	15c.+7c. brown, blk & vio	1·50	1·50
474	-	20c.+10c. brown, blk & bl	1·50	1·50
475	-	40c.+20c. brown, blk & grn	1·60	1·60

DESIGNS: 10c. Basketball; 15c. Running; 20c. Swimming; 40c. Football.

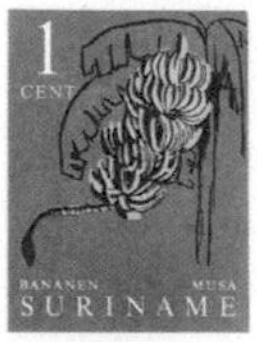

78 Bananas

1961. Local Produce.

476	**78**	1c. yellow, black and green	35	35
477	-	2c. green, black and yellow	35	35
478	-	3c. brown, black & choc	35	35
479	-	4c. yellow, black and blue	35	35
480	-	5c. red, black and brown	35	35
481	-	6c. yellow, black and green	35	35
482	-	8c. yellow, black and blue	35	35

DESIGNS: 2c. Citrus fruit; 3c. Cocoa; 4c. Sugar-cane; 5c. Coffee; 6c. Coconuts; 8c. Rice.

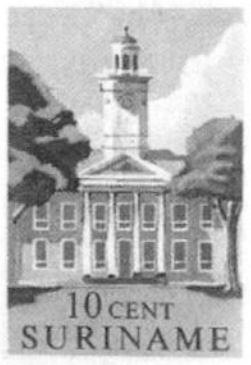

79 Treasury

1961. Surinam Buildings. Multicoloured.

483	10c. Type **79**	45	35
484	15c. Court of Justice	35	35
485	20c. Concordia Masonic Lodge	45	35
486	25c. Neve Shalom Synagogue	80	60
487	30c. Lock Gate, Nieuw Amsterdam	2·30	1·90
488	35c. Government Building	2·30	2·00
489	40c. Governor's House	1·20	95
490	50c. Legislative Assembly	1·20	45
491	60c. Old Dutch Reform Church	1·30	1·30
492	70c. Fort Zeelandia (1790)	1·40	1·50

The 10, 15, 20 and 30c. are vert and the rest horiz.

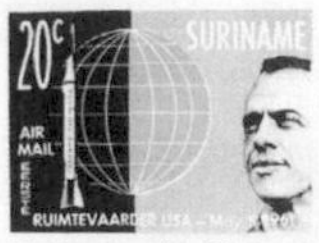

80 Commander Shepard, Rocket and Globe

1961. Air. "Man in Space". Multicoloured.

493	15c. Globe and astronaut in capsule	1·50	1·50
494	20c. Type **80**	1·50	1·50

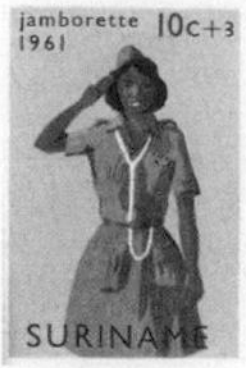

81 Girl Scout saluting

1961. Caribbean Girl Scout Jamborette. Multicoloured.

495	8c.+2c. Semaphoring (horiz)	80	60
496	10c.+3c. Type **81**	80	60
497	15c.+4c. Brownies around a "toadstool" (horiz)	80	60
498	20c.+5c. Campfire sing-song	95	95
499	25c.+6c. Lighting fire (horiz)	95	95

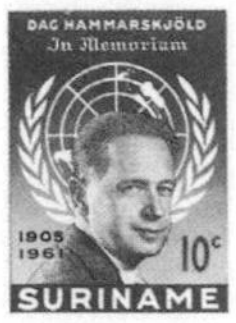

82 Dag Hammarskjold

1962. Dag Hammarskjold Memorial Issue.

500	**82**	10c. black and blue	35	35
501	**82**	20c. black and violet	35	35

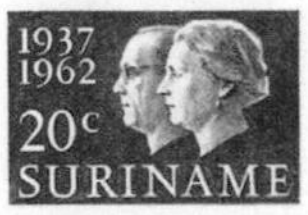

82a Queen Juliana and Prince Bernhard

1962. Royal Silver Wedding.

502	**82a**	20c. green	60	45

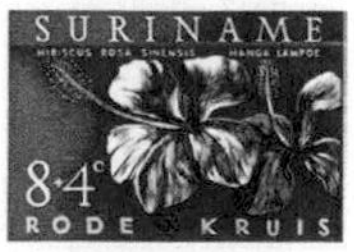

83 "Hibiscus rosa sinensis"

1962. Red Cross Fund. Flowers in natural colours. Background colours given.

503	**83**	8c.+4c. olive	80	45
504	-	10c.+5c. blue	80	45
505	-	15c.+6c. brown	80	45
506	-	20c.+10c. violet	80	45
507	-	25c.+12c. turquoise	80	45

FLOWERS: 10c. "Caesalpinia pulcherrima"; 15c. "Heliconia psittacorum"; 20c. "Lochnera rosea"; 25c. "Ixora macrothyrsa".

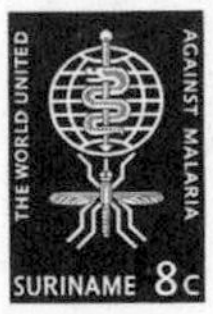

84 Campaign Emblem

1962. Malaria Eradication.

508	**84**	8c. red	35	35
509	**84**	10c. blue	35	35

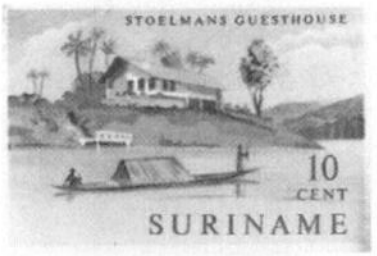

85 Stoelmans Guesthouse

1962. Opening of New Hotels. Multicoloured.

510	10c. Type **85**	60	60
511	15c. Torarica Hotel	60	60

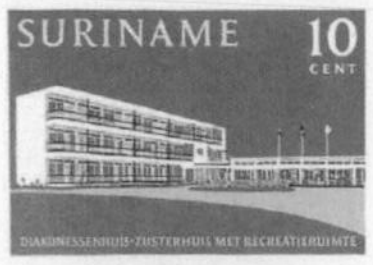

86 Sisters' Residence

1962. Nunnery and Hospital of the Deaconesses. Multicoloured.

512	10c. Type **86**	60	60
513	20c. Hospital building	60	60

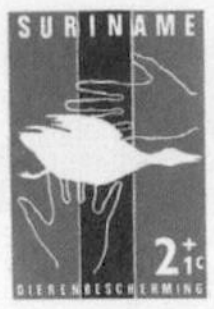

87 Wildfowl

1962. Animal Protection Fund.

514	**87**	2c.+1c. red and blue	60	35
515	-	8c.+2c. red and black	60	35
516	-	10c.+3c. black and green	60	35
517	-	15c.+4c. black and red	60	35

ANIMALS: 8c. Dog; 10c. Donkey; 15c. Horse.

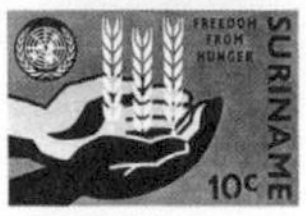

88 Emblem in Hands

1963. Freedom from Hunger.

518	**88**	10c. red	35	35
519	-	20c. blue	35	35

DESIGN—VERT: 20c. Tilling the land.

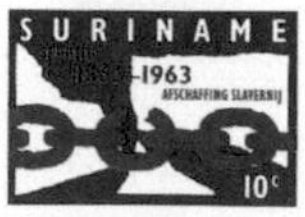

89 "Freedom"

1963. Centenary of Abolition of Slavery in Dutch West Indies.

520	**89**	10c. black and red	35	35
521	**89**	20c. black and green	35	35

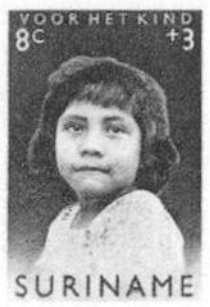

90 Indian Girl

1963. Child Welfare Fund.

522	**90**	8c.+3c. green	45	35
523	-	10c.+4c. brown	45	35
524	-	15c.+10c. blue	45	35
525	-	20c.+10c. red	45	35
526	-	40c.+20c. purple	45	35
MS527		95×131 mm. Nos. 522/3 (two of each)	3·00	3·00

PORTRAITS OF CHILDREN: 10c. Bush negro; 15c. Hindustani; 20c. Indonesian; 40c. Chinese.

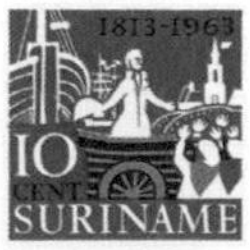

90a William of Orange at Scheveningen

1963. 150th Anniv of Kingdom of the Netherlands.

528	**90a**	10c. black, bistre and blue	35	35

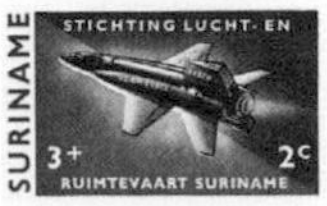

91 North American X-15

1964. Aeronautical and Astronomical Foundation, Surinam.

529	3c.+2c. sepia and lake	60	35
530	8c.+4c. sepia, indigo & blue	60	35
531	10c.+5c. sepia and green	60	35
532	15c.+7c. sepia and brown	60	35
533	20c.+10c. sepia and violet	60	35

DESIGNS: 3, 15c. Type **91**; 8c. Foundation flag; 10, 20c. Agena B-Ranger rocket.

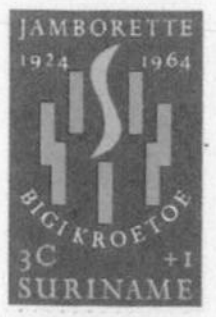

92 "Camp Fire"

1964. Scout Jamborette, Paramaribo, and 40th Anniv of Surinam Boy Scouts Association.

534	**92**	3c.+1c. lt yell, yell & bis	60	35
535	**92**	8c.+4c. brn, bl & dp bl	60	35
536	**92**	10c.+5c. brn, red & dp red	60	35
537	**92**	20c.+10c. brn, grn & bl	60	35

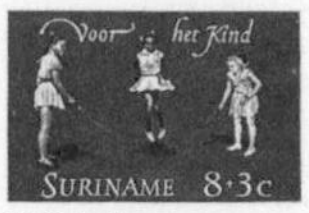

93 Skipping

1964. Child Welfare.

538	**93**	8c.+3c. blue	35	35
539	-	10c.+4c. red	35	35
540	-	15c.+9c. green	35	35
541	-	20c.+10c. purple	35	35
MS542		139×96 mm. Nos. 538/9 (two of each)	1·70	1·70

DESIGNS: 10c. Children swinging; 15c. Child on scooter; 20c. Child with hoop.

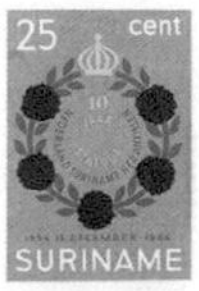

94 Crown and Wreath

1964. Tenth Anniv of Statute of the Kingdom.

543	**94**	25c. multicoloured	35	35

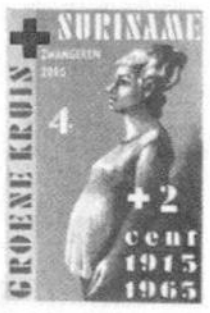

95 Expectant Mother ("Prenatal Care")

1965. 50th Anniv of "Het Groene Kruis" (The Green Cross).

544	**95**	4c.+2c. green	30	30
545	-	10c.+5c. brown and green	30	30
546	-	15c.+7c. blue and green	30	30
547	-	25c.+12c. violet and green	30	30

DESIGNS: 10c. Mother and baby ("Infant care"); 15c. Young girl ("Child care"); 25c. Old man ("Care in old age").

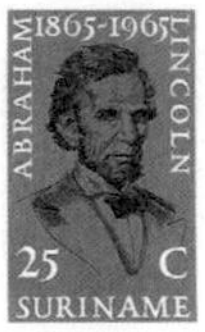

96 Abraham Lincoln

1965. Death Centenary of Abraham Lincoln.

548	**96**	25c. purple and bistre	35	35

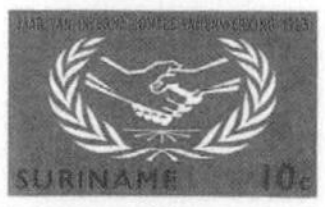

97 I.C.Y. Emblem

1965. International Co-operation Year.

549	**97**	10c. orange and blue	35	35
550	**97**	15c. red and blue	35	35

98 Surinam Waterworks

1965. Air. Size 25×18 mm.

551	**98**	10c. green	35	35
552	-	15c. ochre	35	35
553	-	20c. green	35	35
554	-	25c. indigo	35	35
555	-	30c. turquoise	35	35

556	-	35c. red	45	35
557	-	40c. orange	45	35
558	-	45c. red	45	45
559	-	50c. red	45	35
560	**98**	55c. green	45	45
561	-	65c. yellow	60	45
562	-	75c. blue	60	45

For same designs but size 22×18 mm, see Nos. 843a/h.

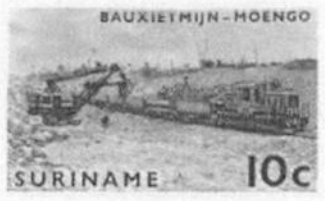

99 Bauxite Mine, Moengo

1965. Opening of Brokopondo Power Station.

563	**99**	10c. ochre	45	35
564	-	15c. green	45	35
565	-	20c. blue	45	35
566	-	25c. red	45	35

DESIGNS: 15c. Alum-earth works, Paranam; 20c. Power station and dam, Afobaka; 25c. Aluminium smeltery, Paranam.

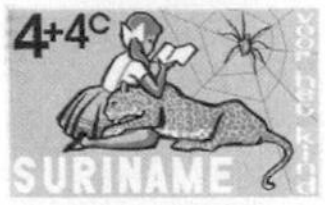

100 Girl with Leopard

1965. Child Welfare.

567	**100**	4c.+4c. black, turquoise and green	35	35
568	-	10c.+5c. black, brown and light brown	35	35
569	-	15c.+7c. black, orange and red	35	35
570	-	25c.+10c. black, blue and cobalt	35	35
MS571 140×96 mm. Nos. 567 and 569 (two of each)			1·70	1·70

DESIGNS: 10c. Boy with monkey; 15c. Girl with tortoise; 25c. Boy with rabbit.

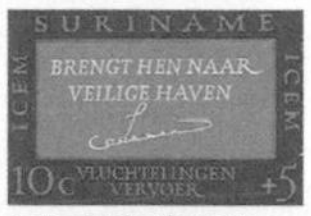

100a "Help them to a safe haven" (Queen Juliana)

1966. Intergovernmental Committee for European Migration (I.C.E.M.) Fund.

572	**100a**	10c.+5c. green & black	35	35
573	**100a**	25c.+10c. red and black	35	35
MS574 117½×43 mm. Nos. 572 (×2), 573			1·20	1·20

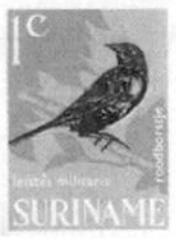

101 Red-breasted Blackbird

1966. Birds. Multicoloured.

575	1c. Type **101**	60	35
576	2c. Great kiskadee	60	35
577	3c. Silver-beaked tanager	60	35
578	4c. Ruddy ground dove	60	35
579	5c. Blue-grey tanager	60	35
580	6c. Straight-billed hermit	60	35
581	8c. Turquoise tanager	60	35
582	10c. Pale-breasted thrush	60	35

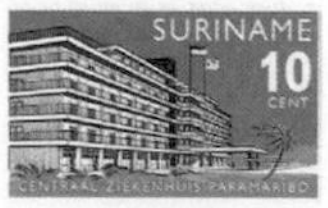

102 Hospital Building

1966. Opening of Central Hospital, Paramaribo. Multicoloured.

583	10c. Type **102**	35	35
584	15c. Different view	35	35

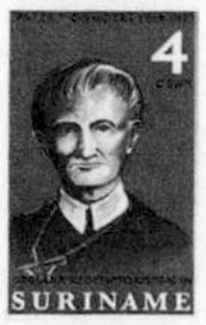

103 Father P. Donders

1966. Centenary of Redemptorists Mission.

585	**103**	4c. black and brown	35	35
586	-	10c. black, brown and red	35	35
587	-	15c. black and ochre	35	35
588	-	25c. black and lilac	35	35

DESIGNS: 10c. Batavia Church, Coppename; 15c. Mgr. J. B. Swinkels; 25c. Paramaribo Cathedral.

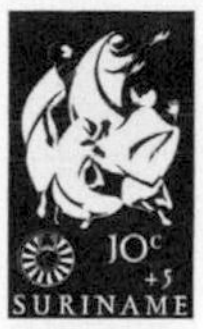

104 Mary Magdalene and Disciples

1966. Easter Charity.

589	**104**	10c.+5c. black, red and gold	35	35
590	**104**	15c.+8c. black, violet and blue	35	35
591	**104**	20c.+10c. black, yellow and blue	35	35
592	**104**	25c.+12c. black, green and gold	35	35
593	**104**	30c.+15c. black, blue and gold	35	35

On Nos. 590/3 the emblems at bottom left differ for each value. These represent various welfare organizations.

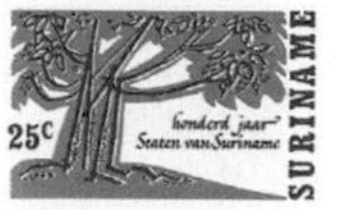

105 "Century Tree"

1966. Centenary of Surinam Parliament.

594	**105**	25c. black, green and red	35	35
595	**105**	30c. black, red and green	35	35

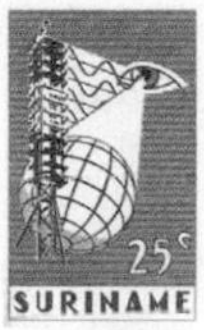

106 TV Mast, Eye and Globe

1966. Inauguration of Surinam Television Service.

596	**106**	25c. red and blue	35	35
597	**106**	30c. red and brown	35	35

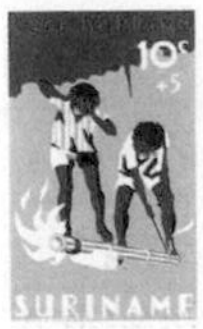

107 Boys with Bamboo Gun

1966. Child Welfare. Multicoloured.

598	10c.+5c. Type **107**	35	35
599	15c.+8c. Boy pouring liquid on another	35	35
600	20c.+10c. Children rejoicing	35	35
601	25c.+12c. Children on merry-go-round	35	35
602	30c.+15c. Children decorating room	35	35
MS603 96×76 mm. Nos. 598 (×2) and 600		1·40	1·20

The designs symbolize New Year's Eve, the End of Lent, Liberation Day, Queen's Birthday and Christmas respectively.

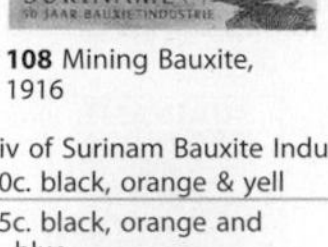

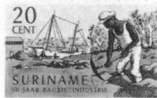

108 Mining Bauxite, 1916

1966. 50th Anniv of Surinam Bauxite Industry.

604	**108**	20c. black, orange & yell	35	35
605	-	25c. black, orange and blue	35	35

DESIGN: 25c. Modern bauxite plant.

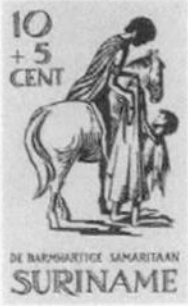

109 "The Good Samaritan"

1967. Easter Charity. Printed in black, background colours given.

606	**109**	10c.+5c. yellow	35	35
607	-	15c.+8c. blue	35	35
608	-	20c.+10c. ochre	35	35
609	-	25c.+12c. pink	35	35
610	-	30c.+15c. green	35	35

DESIGNS: 15 to 30c. Various episodes illustrating the parable of "The Good Samaritan".

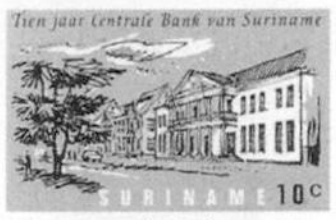

110 Central Bank

1967. Tenth Anniv of Surinam Central Bank.

611	**110**	10c. black and yellow	35	35
612	-	25c. black and lilac	35	35

DESIGN: 25c. Aerial view of Central Bank.

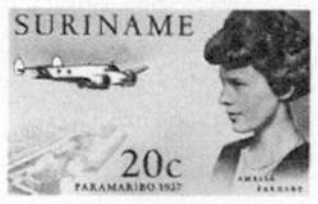

111 Amelia Earhart and Lockheed 10E Electra Airplane

1967. 30th Anniv of Visit of Amelia Earhart to Surinam.

613	**111**	20c. red and yellow	45	35
614	**111**	25c. green and yellow	45	35

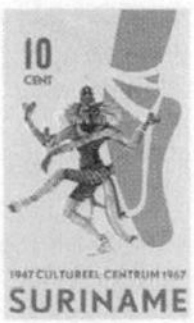

112 Siva Nataraja and Ballerina's Foot

1967. 20th Anniv of Surinam Cultural Centre. Multicoloured.

615	10c. Type **112**	35	35
616	25c. "Bashi-Lele" mask and violin scroll	35	35

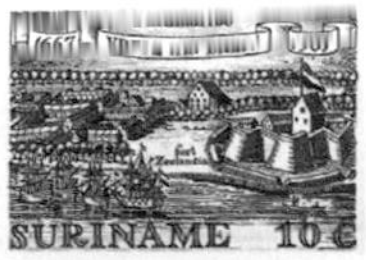

113 Fort Zeelandia, Paramaribo (c. 1670)

1967. 300th Anniv of Treaty of Breda. Multicoloured.

617	10c. Type **113**	45	35
618	20c. Nieuw Amsterdam (c. 1660)	45	35
619	25c. Breda Castle (c. 1667)	45	35

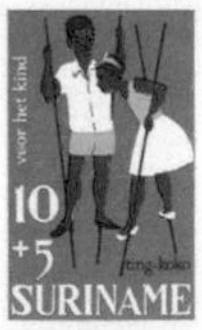

114 Stilt-walking

1967. Child Welfare. Multicoloured.

620	10c.+5c. Type **114**	45	35
621	15c.+8c. Playing marbles	45	35
622	20c.+10c. Playing dibs	45	35
623	25c.+12c. Kite-flying	45	35
624	30c.+15c. "Cooking" game	45	35
MS625 96×76 mm. Nos. 620 (×2) and 622		1·70	1·20

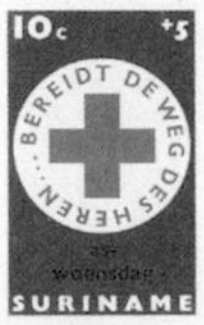

115 "Cross of Ashes"

1968. Easter Charity.

626	10c.+5c. grey and violet	45	35
627	15c.+8c. green and red	45	35
628	20c.+10c. green and yellow	45	35
629	25c.+12c. black and grey	45	35
630	30c.+15c. brown and yellow	45	35

DESIGNS: 10c. Type **115** (Ash Wednesday); 15c. Palm branches (Palm Sunday); 20c. Cup and wafer (Maundy Thursday); 25c. Cross (Good Friday); 30c. Symbol of Christ (Easter).

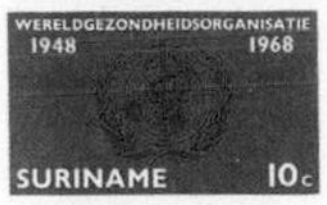

116 W.H.O. Emblem

1968. 20th Anniv of W.H.O.

631	**116**	10c. blue and purple	35	35
632	**116**	25c. violet and blue	35	35

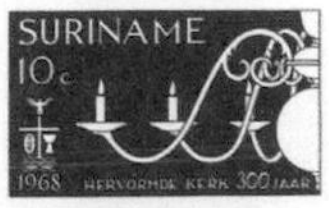

117 Chandelier, Reformed Church

1968. 300th Anniv of Reformed Church, Paramaribo.

633	**117**	10c. blue	35	35
634	-	25c. green	35	35

DESIGN: 25c. No. 633 reversed; chandelier on left.

118 Missionary Shop, 1768

1968. Bicentenary of Evangelist Brothers' Missionary Store, G. Kersten and Co.

635	**118**	10c. black and yellow	35	35
636	-	25c. black and blue	35	35
637	-	30c. black and mauve	35	35

DESIGNS: 25c. Paramaribo Church and Kersten's store, 1868; 30c. Kersten's modern store, Paramaribo.

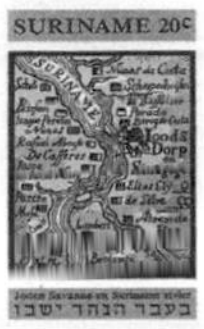

119 Map of Joden Savanne

1968. Restoration of Joden Savanne Synagogue. Multicoloured.

638	20c. Type **119**	60	60
639	25c. Synagogue, 1685	60	60
640	30c. Gravestone at Joden Savanne, dated 1733	60	60

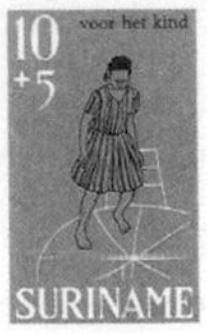

120 Playing Hopscotch

1968. Child Welfare.

641	**120**	10c.+5c. black & brown	45	35
642	-	15c.+8c. black and blue	45	35
643	-	20c.+10c. black & pink	45	35
644	-	25c.+12c. black & green	45	35
645	-	30c.+15c. black & lilac	45	35
MS646 98×76 mm. Nos. 641 (×2) and 643			1·70	1·20

DESIGNS: 15c. Forming "pyramids"; 20c. Playing ball; 25c. Handicrafts; 30c. Tug-of-war.

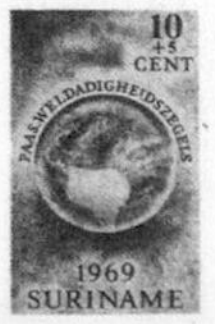

121 Western Hemisphere illuminated by Full Moon

1969. Easter Charity.

647	**121**	10c.+5c. blue & lt blue	45	45
648	**121**	15c.+8c. grey & yellow	45	45
649	**121**	20c.+10c. turq & green	45	45
650	**121**	25c.+12c. brown & buff	45	45
651	**121**	30c.+15c. violet & grey	45	45

122 Cayman

1969. Opening of Surinam Zoo, Paramaribo. Multicoloured.
652	10c. Type **122**	95	60
653	20c. Common squirrel-monkey (vert)	95	60
654	25c. Nine-banded armadillo	95	60

123 Mahatma Gandhi

1969. Birth Centenary of Mahatma Gandhi.
| 655 | **123** | 25c. black and red | 1·20 | 45 |

124 I.L.O. Emblem

1969. 50th Anniv of Int Labour Organization.
| 656 | **124** | 10c. green and black | 35 | 35 |
| 657 | **124** | 25c. red and black | 45 | 45 |

125 Pillow Fight

1969. Child Welfare.
658	10c.+5c. purple and blue	45	35
659	15c.+8c. brown and yellow	45	35
660	20c.+10c. blue and grey	45	35
661	25c.+12c. blue and pink	45	35
662	30c.+15c. brown and green	45	35
MS663 97×76 mm. Nos. 658 ×2 and 660		1·70	1·70

DESIGNS: 10c. Type **125**; 15c. Eating contest; 20c. Pole-climbing; 25c. Sack-race; 30c. Obstacle-race.

126 Queen Juliana and "Sunlit Road"

1969. 15th Anniv of Statute for the Kingdom.
| 664 | **126** | 25c. multicoloured | 45 | 45 |

127 "Flower"

1970. Easter Charity. "Wonderful Nature". Multicoloured.
665	10c.+5c. Type **127**	70	70
666	15c.+8c. "Butterfly"	70	70
667	20c.+10c. "Bird"	70	70
668	25c.+12c. "Sun"	70	70
669	30c.+15c. "Star"	70	70

128 "1950–1970"

1970. 20th Anniv of Secondary Education in Surinam.
| 670 | **128** | 10c. yellow, green and brown | 35 | 35 |
| 671 | **128** | 25c. yellow, blue and green | 35 | 35 |

129 New U.P.U. Headquarters Building

1970. New U.P.U. Headquarters Building.
| 672 | **129** | 10c. violet, blue & turq | 35 | 35 |
| 673 | - | 25c. black and red | 35 | 35 |

DESIGN: 25c. Aerial view of H.Q. Building.

130 U.N. "Diamond"

1970. 25th Anniv of United Nations.
| 674 | **130** | 10c. multicoloured | 35 | 35 |
| 675 | **130** | 25c. multicoloured | 35 | 35 |

131 Aircraft over Paramaribo Town Plan

1970. "40 Years of Inland Airmail Flights".
676	**131**	10c. grey, ultramarine & blue	60	45
677	-	20c. grey, red and yellow	60	45
678	-	25c. grey, red and pink	60	45

DESIGNS: As Type **131**, but showing different background maps—20c. Totness; 25c. Nieuw-Nickerie.

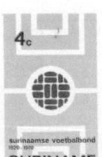

132 Football Pitch (ball in centre)

1970. 50th Anniv of Surinam Football Association.
679	**132**	4c. brown, yellow & black	45	35
680	-	10c. brown, olive and black	45	35
681	-	15c. brown, green & black	45	35
682	-	25c. brown, green & black	45	35

DESIGNS: As Type **132**, but with ball: 10c. in "corner"; 15c. at side ("throw-in"); 25c. at top ("goal").

133 Beethoven (1786)

1970. Child Welfare. Birth Bicentenary of Beethoven (composer).
683	**133**	10c.+5c. yellow, drab and green	80	70
684	-	15c.+8c. yellow, drab and red	80	70
685	-	20c.+10c. yellow, drab and blue	80	70
686	-	25c.+12c. yellow, drab and orange	80	70
687	-	30c.+15c. yellow, drab and violet	80	70
MS688 97×76 mm. Nos. 683 ×2 and 685		3·00	3·00

DESIGNS—Beethoven: 15c. 1804; 20c. 1812; 25c. 1814; 30c. 1827.

134 Grey Heron

1971. 25th Anniv of Netherlands–Surinam–Netherlands Antilles Air Service. Multicoloured.
689	15c. Type **134**	70	60
690	20c. Greater flamingo	70	60
691	25c. Scarlet macaw	70	60

135 Donkey and Palm

1971. Easter. The Bible Story. Multicoloured.
692	10c.+5c. Type **135**	70	70
693	15c.+8c. Cockerel	70	70
694	20c.+10c. Lamb	70	70
695	25c.+12c. Crown of Thorns	70	70
696	30c.+15c. Sun ("The Resurrection")	70	70

136 Morse Key

1971. World Telecommunications Day. Multicoloured.
697	15c. Type **136**	60	60
698	20c. Telephones	60	60
699	25c. Lunar module and telescope	60	60

EVENTS: 15c. First national telegraph, Washington–Baltimore, 1843; 20c. First international telephone communication, England–Sweden, 1926; 25c. First interplanetary television communication, Earth–Moon, 1969.

137 Prince Bernhard

1971. Prince Bernhard's 60th Birthday.
| 700 | **137** | 25c. multicoloured | 45 | 45 |

138 Population Map

1971. 50th Anniv of 1st Census and Introduction of Civil Registration.
| 701 | **138** | 15c. blue, black and red | 35 | 35 |
| 702 | **138** | 30c. red, black and blue | 45 | 45 |

DESIGN: 30c. "Individual" representing civil registration.

139 William Mogge's Map of Surinam

1971. 300th Anniv of First Surinam Map.
| 703 | **139** | 30c. brown on yellow | 80 | 70 |

140 Leap-frog

1971. Child Welfare. Details from Brueghel's "Children's Games". Multicoloured.
704	10c.+5c. Type **140**	70	70
705	15c.+8c. Strewing flowers	70	70
706	20c.+10c. Rolling hoop	70	70
707	25c.+12c. Playing ball	70	70

| 708 | 30c.+15c. Stilt-walking | 70 | 70 |
| **MS**709 121×84 mm. Nos. 704 ×2 and 706 | | 3·75 | 3·75 |

141 Plan of Albina

1971. 125th Anniv of Albina Settlement.
710	**141**	15c. black on blue	60	60
711	-	20c. black on green	60	60
712	-	25c. black on yellow	60	60

DESIGNS—HORIZ: 20c. Albina and River Marowijne. VERT: 25c. August Kappler (naturalist and founder).

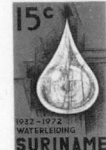

142 Drop of Water

1972. 40th Anniv of Surinam Waterworks.
| 713 | **142** | 15c. black and violet | 45 | 45 |
| 714 | - | 30c. black and blue | 60 | 60 |

DESIGN: 30c. Water tap.

143 Easter Candle

1972. Easter Charity. Multicoloured.
715	10c.+5c. Type **143**	70	70
716	15c.+8c. "Christ teaching the Apostles"	70	70
717	20c.+10c. Hands holding cup ("Christ in Gethsemane")	70	70
718	25c.+12c. Fishes in net ("Miracle of the Fishes")	70	70
719	30c.+15c. Pieces of silver ("Judas's Betrayal")	70	70

144 "Eucyane bicolor"

1972. Moths and Butterflies. Multicoloured.
720	15c. Type **144**	60	35
721	20c. Gold drop	60	35
722	25c. Orange swallowtail	60	35
723	30c. White tailed page	70	35
724	35c. "Stalachtis calliope"	70	35
725	40c. "Stalachtis phlegia"	70	35
726	45c. Malachite	70	35
727	50c. Spear-winged cattle heart	80	35
728	55c. Red anartia	1·00	35
729	60c. Five continent butterfly	1·00	1·00
730	65c. Doris	1·00	60
731	70c. "Nessaea obrinus"	1·20	80
732	75c. Cracker	1·20	60

145 Air-letter Motif

1972. 50th Anniv of First Airmail in Surinam.
| 733 | **145** | 15c. red and blue | 35 | 35 |
| 734 | **145** | 30c. blue and red | 45 | 45 |

146 Doll and Toys (kindergarten)

1972. Child Welfare. Multicoloured.
| 735 | 10c.+5c. Type **146** | 70 | 70 |
| 736 | 15c.+8c. Clock and abacus (primary education) | 70 | 70 |

737	20c.+10c. Blocks (primary education)	70	70
738	25c.+12c. Molecule complex (secondary education)	70	70
739	30c.+15c. Wrench and blueprint (technical education)	70	70
MS740 96×78 mm. Nos. 735 ×2 and 737		3·00	3·00

147 Giant Tree

1972. 25th Anniv of Surinam Forestry Commission.

741	147	15c. brown and yellow	35	35
742	-	20c. brown, black and blue	35	35
743	-	30c. chocolate, brn & grn	60	60

DESIGNS: 20c. Aerial transport of logs; 30c. Planting tree.

148 "The Storm on the Lake"

1973. Easter Charity. Jesus's Life and Death. Multicoloured.

744		10c.+5c. Type **148**	70	70
745		15c.+8c. "Washing the Disciples' Feet"	70	70
746		20c.+10c. "Jesus taken to Execution"	70	70
747		25c.+12c. The Cross	70	70
748		30c.+15c. "The Men of Emmaus"	70	70

149 Indian Immigrant Woman

1973. Centenary of Arrival of Indian Immigrants in Surinam.

749	149	15c. violet and yellow	45	45
750	-	25c. red and grey	45	45
751	-	30c. orange and blue	45	45

DESIGNS: 25c. J. F. A. Cateau van Rosevelt, Head of Department of Immigration, holding map; 30c. Symbols of immigration.

150 Queen Juliana

1973. Silver Jubilee of Queen Juliana's Reign.

| 752 | 150 | 30c. black, orange & silver | 95 | 60 |

151 Florence Nightingale and Red Cross

1973. 30th Anniv of Surinam Red Cross.

| 753 | 151 | 30c.+10c. multicoloured | 1·20 | 1·20 |

152 Interpol Emblem

1973. 50th Anniv of International Criminal Police Organization (Interpol). Multicoloured.

| 754 | | 15c. Type **152** | 35 | 35 |
| 755 | | 30c. Emblem within passport stamp | 45 | 45 |

153 Flower

1973. Child Welfare.

756	153	10c.+5c. multicoloured	80	70
757	-	15c.+8c. green, brown and emerald	80	70
758	-	20c.+10c. violet, blue and green	80	70
759	-	25c.+12c. multicoloured	80	70
760	-	30c.+15c. multicoloured	80	70
MS761 97×76 mm. Nos. 756 ×2 and 758			2·50	2·50

DESIGNS: 15c. Tree; 20c. Dog; 25c. House; 30c. Doll.

154 Carrier-pigeons

1973. Stamp Centenary.

762	154	15c. green and blue	35	35
763	-	25c. multicoloured	45	45
764	-	30c. multicoloured	70	70

DESIGNS: 25c. Postman; 30c. Map and postal routes.

155 "Quassia amara"

1974. Easter Charity Flowers. Multicoloured.

765		10c.+5c. Type **155**	80	70
766		15c.+8c. "Passiflora quadrangularis"	80	70
767		20c.+10c. "Combretum rotundifolium"	80	70
768		25c.+12c. "Cassia alata"	80	70
769		30c.+15c. "Asclepias curassavica"	80	70

156 Nurse and Blood Transfusion Equipment

1974. 75th Anniv of Surinam Medical School. Multicoloured.

| 770 | | 15c. Type **156** | 35 | 35 |
| 771 | | 30c. Microscope slide and oscilloscope scanner | 45 | 45 |

157 Aerial Crop-spraying

1974. 25th Anniv of Mechanized Agriculture. Multicoloured.

| 772 | | 15c. Type **157** | 35 | 35 |
| 773 | | 30c. Fertilizer plant | 45 | 45 |

158 Commemorative Text superimposed on Early Newspaper

1974. Bicentenary of Surinam's "Weekly Wednesday" Newspaper.

| 774 | 158 | 15c. multicoloured | 35 | 35 |
| 775 | 158 | 30c. multicoloured | 45 | 45 |

159 Scout and Tent

1974. "50 Years of Scouting in Surinam". Multicoloured.

776		10c.+5c. Type **159**	95	60
777		15c.+8c. Jamboree emblem	95	60
778		20c.+10c. Scouts and badge	95	60

160 G.P.O., Paramaribo

1974. Centenary of Universal Postal Union.

| 779 | 160 | 15c. black and brown | 35 | 35 |
| 780 | - | 30c. black and blue | 45 | 45 |

DESIGN: 30c. G.P.O., Paramaribo (different view).

161 Girl with Fruit

1974. Child Welfare.

781	161	10c.+5c. green, emerald and pink	70	70
782	-	15c.+8c. brown, mauve and green	70	70
783	-	20c.+10c. yellow, orange and mauve	70	70
784	-	25c.+12c. brown, lilac and yellow	70	70
785	-	30c.+15c. cobalt, blue and lilac	70	70
MS786 76×97 mm. Nos. 781 ×2 and 783			2·30	2·00

DESIGNS: 15c. Birds and nest; 20c. Mother and child with flower; 25c. Young boy in cornfield; 30c. Children at play.

162 Panning for Gold

1975. Centenary of Prospecting Concession Policy.

| 787 | 162 | 15c. brown and bistre | 60 | 35 |
| 788 | - | 30c. purple and red | 60 | 45 |

DESIGN: 30c. Claws of modern excavator.

163 "I am the Good Shepherd"

1975. Easter Charity.

789	163	15c.+5c. yellow and green	70	70
790	-	20c.+10c. yellow and blue	70	70
791	-	30c.+15c. yellow and red	70	70
792	-	35c.+20c. blue and violet	70	70

DESIGNS—Quotations from the New Testament: 20c. "I do not know the man"; 30c. "He is not here; He has been raised again"; 35c. "Because you have seen Me you have found faith. Happy are they who never saw Me and yet have found faith".

164 "Looking to Equality, Education and Peace"

1975. International Women's Year.

| 793 | 164 | 15c.+5c. blue and green | 70 | 70 |
| 794 | 164 | 30c.+15c. violet & mve | 70 | 70 |

165 "Weights and Measures"

1975. Centenary of Metre Convention.

795	165	15c. multicoloured	60	60
796	165	25c. multicoloured	60	60
796a	165	30c. multicoloured	60	60

166 Caribbean Water Jug

1975. Child Welfare. Multicoloured.

797		15c.+5c. Type **166**	70	70
798		20c.+10c. Indian arrowhead	70	70
799		30c.+15c. "Maluana" (protection against evil spirits)	70	70
800		35c.+20c. Indian arrowhead (different)	70	70
MS801 97×77 mm. Nos. 797 ×2 and 798			3·00	3·00

167 "Labour and Technology"

1975. Independence. "Nation in Development". Multicoloured.

802	167	25c. Type **167**	90	85
803		50c. Open book ("Education and Art")	1·70	1·60
804		75c. Hands with ball ("Physical Training")	2·40	2·30

168 Central Bank, Paramaribo

1975

805	168	1g. black, mauve & purple	2·20	20
806	168	1½g. black, orange & brn	3·25	20
807	168	2½g. black, red and brown	5·50	20
808	168	5g. black, emerald & green	11·00	20
808a	168	10g. black, blue & dp blue	24·00	75

169 "Oncidium lanceanum"

1976. Surinam Orchids. Multicoloured.

809	169	1c. Type **169**	45	10
810		2c. "Epidendrum stenopetalum"	45	10
811		3c. "Brassia lanceana"	45	10
812		4c. "Epidendrum ibaguense"	45	10
813		5c. "Epidendrum fragans"	45	10

170 Surinam Flag

1976. Multicoloured.

| 814 | | 25c. Type **170** | 75 | 75 |
| 815 | | 35c. Surinam arms | 1·10 | 1·10 |

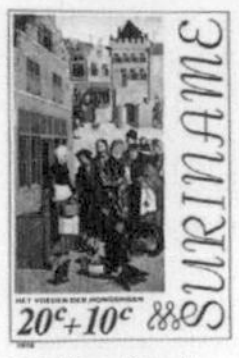

171 "Feeding the Hungry"

1976. Easter. Paintings in Alkmaar Church. Multicoloured.

816	20c.+10c. Type **171**	75	75
817	25c.+15c. "Visiting the Sick"	75	75
818	30c.+15c. "Clothing the Naked"	1·70	1·60
819	35c.+15c. "Burying the Dead"	1·70	1·60
820	50c.+25c. "Refreshing the Thirsty"	2·75	2·75
MS821	113×83 mm. Nos. 816 ×2 and 818	5·50	5·25

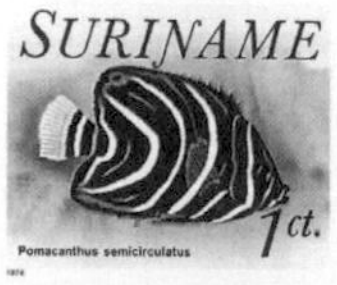

172 Semicircle Angelfish

1976. Fish. Multicoloured.

822	1c. Type **172** (postage)	10	10
823	2c. Diadem squirrelfish	10	10
824	3c. Zebra goby	10	10
825	4c. Queen triggerfish	10	10
826	5c. Black-barred soldierfish	20	10
827	35c. Teardrop butterflyfish (air)	1·00	75
828	60c. Flame angelfish	1·90	1·10
829	95c. Red-tailed butterflyfish	2·75	1·20

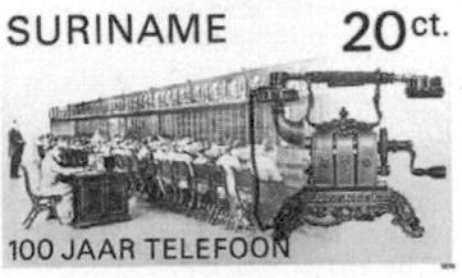

173 Early Telephone and Switchboard

1976. Telephone Centenary.

830	20c. Type **173**	75	45
831	35c. Globe, satellite and modern telephone	90	65

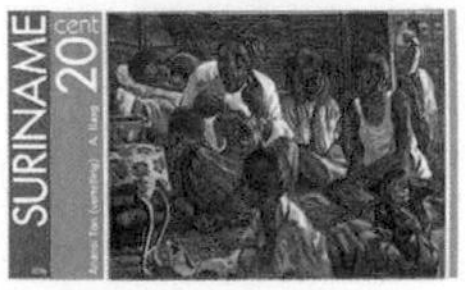

174 "Anansi Tori" (A. Baag)

1976. Paintings by Surinam Artists. Multicoloured.

832	20c. Type **174**	65	65
833	30c. "Surinam Now" (R. Chang)	90	85
834	35c. "Lamentation" (N. Hatterman) (vert)	1·10	1·10
835	50c. "Chess-players" (Q. Jan Telting)	1·50	1·50

175 "Join or Die" (Franklin's "Divided Snake" poster of 1754)

1976. Bicentenary of American Revolution.

836	**175**	20c. black, green & cream	75	55
837	**175**	60c. black, red and cream	2·75	1·90

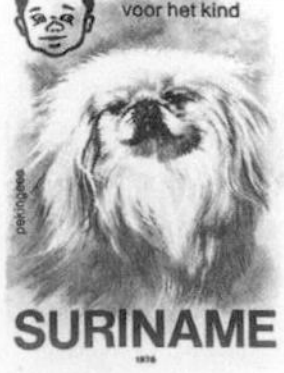

176 Pekinese

1976. Child Welfare. Pet Dogs.

838	20c.+10c. Type **176**	1·00	75
839	25c.+10c. Alsatian	1·30	85
840	30c.+10c. Dachshund	1·70	1·10
841	35c.+15c. Surinam breed	1·70	1·60
842	50c.+25c. Mongrel	2·75	2·10
MS843	140×100 mm. Nos. 838 ×2 and 840	10·00	9·50

1976. As Nos. 551/7 and new values but size 22×18 mm.

843a	-	5c. brown	10	10
843b	**98**	10c. green	1·00	95
843c	-	20c. green	20	10
843d	-	25c. blue	1·00	95
843e	-	30c. green	1·20	1·20
843f	-	35c. red	1·00	95
843g	-	40c. orange	1·70	1·60
843h	-	60c. red	1·30	1·30

NEW VALUES: 5c. Brewery; 60c. Jetty.

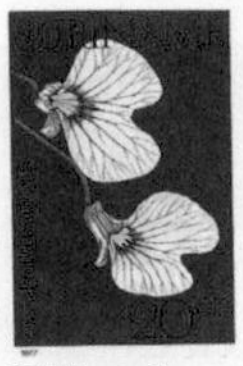

177 "Ionopsis utricularioides"

1977. Surinam Orchids. Multicoloured.

844	20c. Type **177**	65	45
845	30c. "Rodiguezia secunda"	90	65
846	35c. "Oncidium pusillum"	90	75
847	55c. "Sobralia sessulis"	1·40	1·20
848	60c. "Octomeria surinamensis"	1·40	1·30

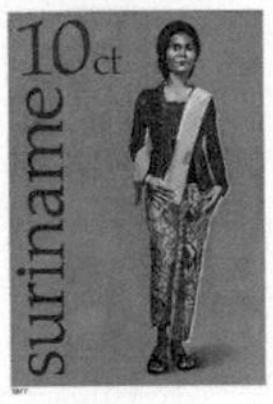

178 Javanese Costume

1977. Surinam Costumes (1st series). Multicoloured.

849	10c. Type **178**	20	20
850	15c. Forest Negro	35	30
851	35c. Chinese	75	75
852	60c. Creole	1·30	1·30
853	75c. Aborigine Indian	1·70	1·60
854	1g. Hindustani	2·20	2·10

DESIGNS: 15c. to 1g. Various women's festival costumes.

See also Nos. 906/11.

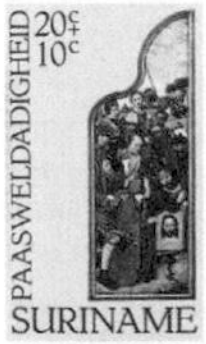

179 Triptych, left panel (Jan Mostaert)

1977. Easter. Multicoloured.

855	20c.+10c. Type **179**	65	65
856	25c.+15c. Right panel	75	75
857	30c.+15c. Right panel	75	75
858	35c.+15c. Centre panel (30×38 mm.)	90	85
859	50c.+25c. Left panel	1·30	1·30

The 20c. and 25c. show the triptych closed, the 30c. and 50c. show designs on the reverse of the doors, and the 35c. shows the centre panel.

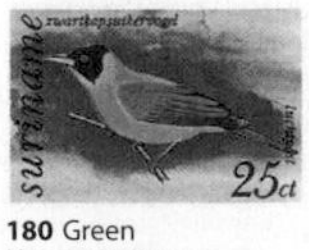

180 Green Honeycreeper

1977. Air. Birds. Multicoloured.

860	20c. Red-breasted blackbird	55	30
861	25c. Type **180**	55	30
862	30c. Paradise tanager	65	30
863	40c. Spot-tailed nightjar	1·00	55
864	45c. Yellow-backed tanager	1·10	55
865	50c. White-tailed goldenthroat	1·30	65
866	55c. Grey-breasted sabrewing	1·50	75
867	60c. Caica parrot (vert)	1·70	85
868	65c. Red-billed toucan (vert)	1·70	95
869	70c. Crimson-hooded manakin (vert)	1·90	95
870	75c. Hawk-headed parrot (vert)	2·00	1·20
871	80c. Spangled cotinga (vert)	2·00	1·20
872	85c. Black-tailed trogon (vert)	2·20	1·30
872a	90c. Orange-winged amazon (vert)	7·75	4·50
873	95c. Black-banded owl (vert)	2·75	1·60
MS874	109×76 mm. Nos. 861 ×2 and 862 ×2	6·00	5·75

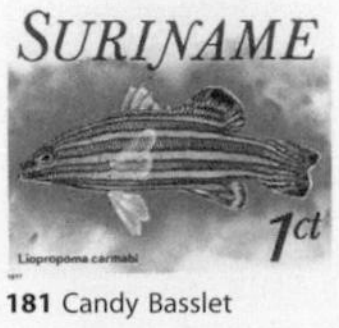

181 Candy Basslet

1977. Fish. Multicoloured.

875	1c. Type **181** (postage)	10	10
876	2c. Queen angelfish	10	10
877	3c. Yellow-headed jawfish	10	10
878	4c. Porkfish	10	10
879	5c. Royal gramma	10	10
880	60c. Banded butterflyfish (air)	1·40	1·10
881	90c. Spot-finned hogfish	2·20	1·60
882	120c. Cherub angelfish	3·25	2·30

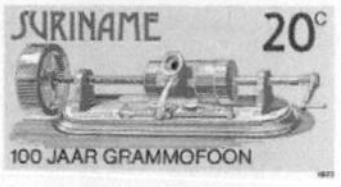

182 Edison's Phonograph, 1877

1977. Centenary of Sound Reproduction. Mult.

883	20c. Type **182**	20	20
883a	60c. Modern gramophone turntable	90	85

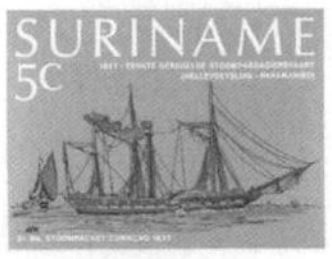

183 Paddle Steamer "Curacao"

1977. 150th Anniv of Regular Passenger Steam Service with Netherlands.

884	**183**	5c. blue and light blue	10	10
885	-	15c. red and orange	20	20
886	-	30c. black and ochre	20	20
887	-	35c. black and olive	35	30
888	-	60c. black and lilac	55	55
889	-	95c. green and light green	1·00	95

DESIGNS: 15c. Hellevoetsluis port; 30c. Chart of steamer route from Hellevoetsluis to Paramaribo; 35c. Log of "Curacao"; 60c. Chart of Paramaribo and 1852 postmark; 95c. Passenger liner "Stuyvesant".

1977. Surch.

890		1c. on 25c. mult (No. 722)	35	20
891	**144**	4c. on 15c. multicoloured	35	20
892	-	4c. on 30c. mult (No. 723)	35	20
893	-	5c. on 40c. mult (No. 725)	55	20
894	-	10c. on 75c. mult (No. 732)	65	30

The word "LUCHTPOST" ("AIR-MAIL") on the original stamp is obliterated by bars.

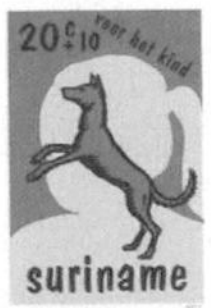

185 Dog

1977. Child Welfare. Multicoloured.

895	20c.+10c. Type **185**	70	60
896	25c.+15c. Monkey	1·00	90
897	30c.+15c. Rabbit	1·10	1·00
898	35c.+15c. Cat	1·30	1·10
899	50c.+25c. Parrot	1·90	1·70
MS900	101×73 mm. Nos. 852 ×2 and 897	2·75	2·75

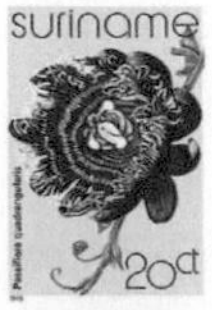

186 "Passiflora quadrangularis"

1978. Flowers. Multicoloured.

901	20c. Type **186**	45	40
902	30c. "Centropogon surinamensis"	70	60
903	55c. "Gloxinia perennis"	1·40	1·20
904	60c. "Hydrocleys nymphoides"	1·50	1·20
905	75c. "Clusia grandiflora"	1·90	1·70

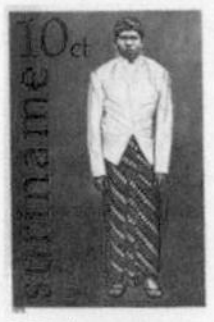

187 Javanese Costumes

1978. Surinam Costumes (2nd series). Multicoloured.

906	10c. Type **187**	25	20
907	20c. Forest Negro	25	20
908	35c. Chinese	45	40
909	60c. Creole	80	70
910	75c. Aborigine Indian	1·00	90
911	1g. Hindustani	1·60	1·40

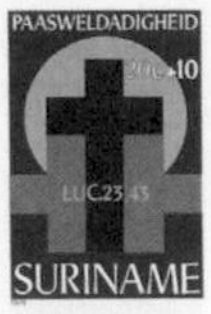

188 Cross and Halo

1978. Easter Charity.

912	**188**	20c.+10c. multicoloured	55	50
913	-	25c.+15c. brown, yellow and red	80	60
914	-	30c.+15c. brown, red and yellow	80	70
915	-	35c.+15c. brown, violet and red	90	80
916	-	60c.+30c. brown, yellow and green	1·70	1·40

DESIGNS: 25c. Serpent and cross; 30c. Blood and lamb; 35c. Passover dish and chalice; 60c. Eclipse and crucifix.

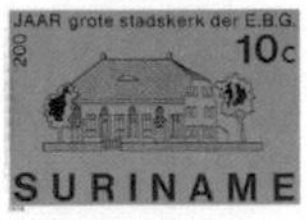

189 Municipal Church, 1783

1978. Bicentenary of Church of Evangelistic Brothers Community.

917	**189**	10c. brown, black and blue	25	20
918	-	20c. black and grey	25	20
919	-	55c. black and purple	70	60
920	-	60c. black and orange	80	70

DESIGNS: 20c. Brother Johannes King, 1830–1899; 55c. Modern Municipal Church; 60c. Brother Johannes Raillard, 1939–1954.

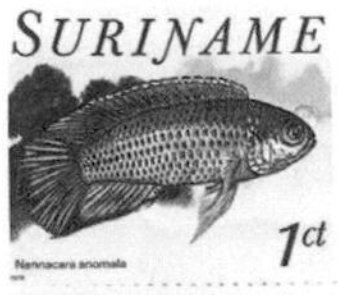

190 Golden-eyed Cichlid

1978. Tropical Fish. Multicoloured.

921	1c. Type **190** (postage)	10	10
922	2c. Banded leporinus	10	10
923	3c. X-ray tetra	10	10
924	4c. Golden pencilfish	10	10
925	5c. Agila rivulus	10	10
926	60c. Two-spotted astyanax (air)	1·50	1·00
927	90c. Blue-spotted corydoras	2·50	1·50
928	120c. River hatchetfish	2·75	2·00

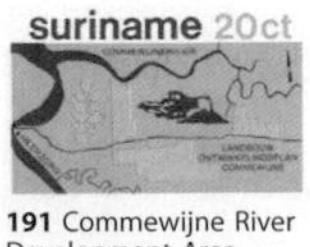

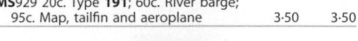

191 Commewijne River Development Area

1978. Surinam Development. Sheet 130×85 mm containing T **191** and similar horiz designs. Multicoloured.

MS929	20c. Type **191**; 60c. River barge; 95c. Map, tailfin and aeroplane	3·50	3·50

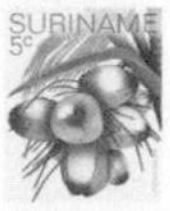

192 Coconuts

1978. Fruit. Multicoloured.

930	5c. Type **192**	10	10
931	10c. Citrus	10	10
932	15c. Papaya	10	10
933a	20c. Bananas	25	20
934	25c. Sour-sop	45	40

934b		30c. Cacao	45	40
935		35c. Water melons	55	50

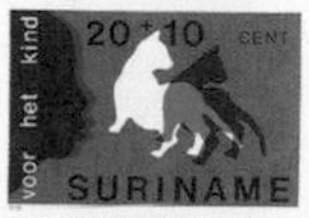
193 Children's Heads and Kittens

1978. Child Welfare.

936	**193**	20c.+10c. multicoloured	45	40
937	-	25c.+15c. multicoloured	80	60
938	-	30c.+15c. multicoloured	90	70
939	-	35c.+15c. multicoloured	90	80
940	-	60c.+30c. multicoloured	1·70	1·30
MS941 144×50 mm. Nos. 936 ×2 and 938			2·50	2·50

DESIGNS: 25c. to 60c. Different designs showing kittens at play.

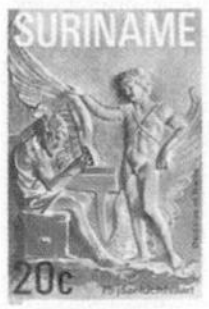
194 Daedalus and Icarus

1978. 75th Anniv of First Powered Flight. Multicoloured.

942	20c. Type **194**	55	50
943	60c. Wright Flyer I (horiz)	1·10	1·00
944	95c. Douglas DC-8-63 (horiz)	1·70	1·50
945	125c. Concorde (horiz)	2·30	2·00

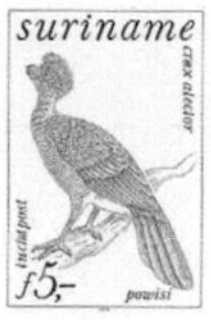
195 Black Curassow

1979. Air.

946	**195**	5g. purple	12·50	8·75

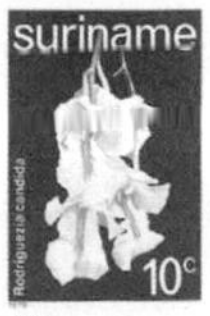
196 "Rodriguezia candida"

1979. Orchids. Multicoloured.

947	10c. Type **196**	25	20
948	20c. "Stanhopea grandiflora"	55	50
949	35c. "Scuticaria steelei"	1·10	1·00
950	60c. "Bollea violacea"	1·70	1·50

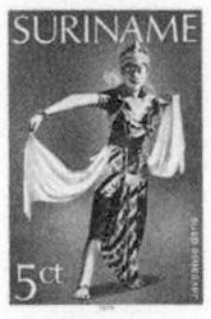
197 Javanese Dance

1979. Dancing Costumes. Multicoloured.

951	5c. Type **197**	25	20
952	10c. Forest Negro	35	30
953	15c. Chinese	35	30
954	20c. Creole	35	30
955	25c. Aborigine Indian	35	30
956	35c. Hindustani	55	1·70

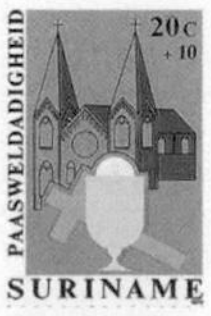
198 Church, Chalice and Cross

1979. Easter Charity.

957	**198**	20c.+10c. multicoloured	35	30
958	-	30c.+15c. multicoloured	70	65
959	-	35c.+15c. multicoloured	85	75
960	-	40c.+20c. multicoloured	95	85
961	-	60c.+30c. multicoloured	1·50	1·40

DESIGNS: 30c. to 60c. Different churches.

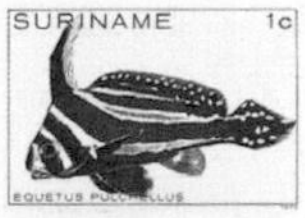
199 Spotted Drum

1979. Fish. Multicoloured.

962	1c. Type **199** (postage)	10	10
963	2c. Barred cardinalfish	10	10
964	3c. Porkfish	10	10
965	5c. Spanish hogfish	10	10
966	35c. Yellow-tailed damselfish	70	55
967	60c. White-spotted filefish (air)	1·20	1·10
968	90c. Long-spined squirrelfish	1·80	1·50
969	120c. Rock beauty	2·50	2·10

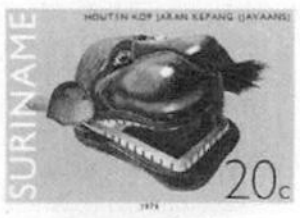
200 Javanese Wooden Head

1979. Art Objects. Multicoloured.

970	20c. Type **200**	45	45
971	35c. American Indian hair ornament	70	65
972	60c. Javanese horse's head	1·20	1·10

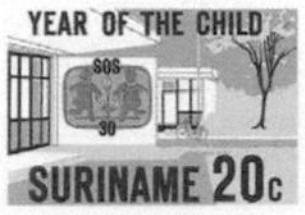
201 S.O.S. Children's Village and Emblem

1979. International Year of the Child. Multicoloured.

973	20c. Type **201**	35	20
974	60c. Different view of Village, and emblem	1·20	85

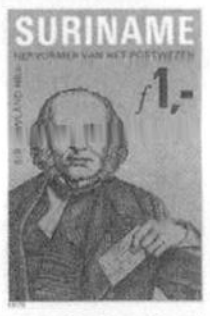
202 Sir Rowland Hill

1979. Death Centenary of Sir Rowland Hill.

975	**202**	1g. green and yellow	2·00	1·60

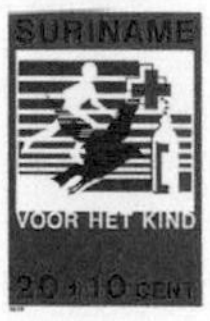
203 Bird, Running Youth and Blood Transfusion Bottle

1979. Child Welfare.

976	**203**	20c.+10c. blk, vio & red	45	45
977	**203**	30c.+15c. blk, red & vio	70	65
978	**203**	35c.+15c. multicoloured	70	65
979	**203**	40c.+20c. multicoloured	85	75
980	**203**	60c.+30c. multicoloured	1·40	1·30
MS981 99×72 mm. Nos. 976 ×2 and 978			2·50	2·50

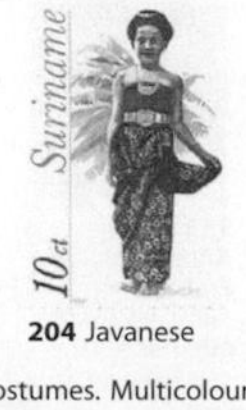
204 Javanese

1980. Children's Costumes. Multicoloured.

982	10c. Type **204**	25	20
983	15c. Forest Negro	25	20
984	25c. Chinese	45	30
985	60c. Creole	1·20	85
986	90c. Indian	1·80	1·30
987	1g. Hindustani	2·00	1·60

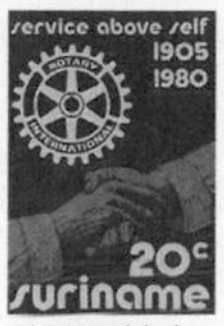
205 Handshake and Rotary Emblem

1980. 75th Anniv of Rotary International. Each blue and yellow.

988	20c. Type **205**	35	20
989	60c. Globe and Rotary emblem	1·20	85

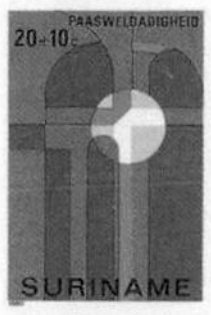
206 Church Interior

1980. Easter Charity. Various Easter symbols.

990	**206**	20c.+10c. multicoloured	60	55
991	-	30c.+15c. multicoloured	85	75
992	-	40c.+20c. multicoloured	1·30	1·20
993	-	50c.+25c. multicoloured	1·40	1·30
994	-	60c.+30c. multicoloured	1·80	1·60

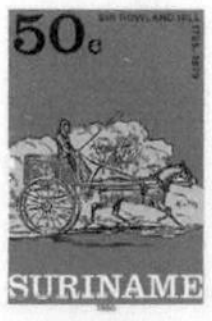
207 Mail Coach

1980. "London 1980" International Stamp Exhibition.

995	**207**	50c. yellow, black and blue	85	55
996	-	1g. yellow, black & purple	1·80	1·30
997	-	2g. pink, black & turq	3·50	2·75
MS998 140×90 mm. 1g. pink, black and green			1·80	1·80

DESIGNS: 1g. Sir Rowland Hill; 2g. [illegible] letters.

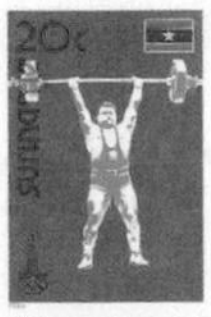
208 Weightlifting

1980. Olympic Games, Moscow.

999	**208**	20c. multicoloured	35	30
1000	-	30c. multicoloured	45	45
1001	-	50c. green, yellow and red	85	75
1002	-	75c. multicoloured	1·30	1·20
1003	-	150c. multicoloured	2·50	2·30
MS1004 100×72 mm. Nos. 1001/3			5·00	5·00

DESIGNS: 30c. Diving; 50c. Gymnastics; 75c. Basketball; 150c. Running.

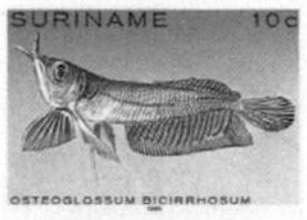
209 Arawana

1980. Tropical Fish. Multicoloured.

1005	10c. Type **209** (postage)	10	10
1006	15c. Colossoma	35	20
1007	25c. Garnet tetra	45	45
1008	30c. False rummy-nosed tetra	60	55
1009	45c. Red-spotted tetra	85	75
1010	60c. Red discus (air)	1·30	75
1011	75c. Flag acara	1·70	1·20
1012	90c. Wimple piranha	1·80	1·50

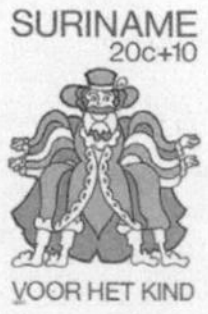
210 Anansi disguised as Spider

1980. Child Welfare. "The Story of Anansi and his Creditors".

1013	**210**	20c.+10c. bistre and yellow	60	55
1014	-	25c.+15c. yellow, brown and orange	60	55
1015	-	30c.+15c. brown, red and orange	85	75
1016	-	35c.+15c. green, light green and yellow	85	75
1017	-	60c.+30c. multicoloured	1·50	1·40
MS1018 100×72 mm. Nos. 1013 ×2 and 1017			3·00	3·00

DESIGNS—(Anansi in various disguises): 25c. Bear; 30c. Cockerel; 35c. Hunter; 60c. Beetle.

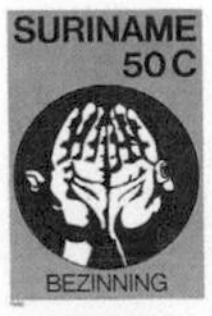
211 Open Hands (reflection)

1980. Fifth Anniv of Independence. Sheet 90×120 mm containing T **211** and similar vert designs.

MS1019 50c. black, vermilion and green; 1g. black, lake and blue; 2g. black, blue and brown	10·50	10·50

DESIGNS: 1g. Handshake (co-operation); 2g. "Victory" sign.

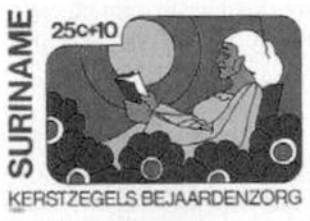
212 Old Woman reading

1980. Welfare of the Aged. Multicoloured.

1020	25c.+10c. Type **212**	60	55
1021	50c.+15c. Old man tending flowers	1·10	95
1022	75c.+20c. Grandfather and grandchildren	1·70	1·50

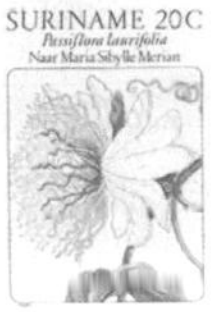
213 "Passiflora laurifolia"

1981. Flower Drawings by Maria Sibylle Merian. Multicoloured.

1023	20c. Type **213**	35	30
1024	30c. "Aphelandra pectinata"	60	55
1025	60c. "Caesalpinia pulcherrima"	1·20	1·10
1026	75c. "Hibiscus mutabilis"	1·40	1·30
1027	1g.25 "Hippeastrum puniceum"	2·40	2·10

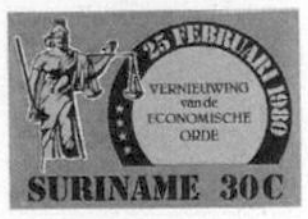
214 Justice and Text "Renewal of the Governmental and Political Order"

1981. The Four Renewals.

1028	-	30c. yellow, brown and deep yellow	25	20
1029	-	60c. orange, brown & red	70	65
1030	-	75c. green, deep green and olive	85	75
1031	**214**	1g. deep yellow, green and yellow	1·20	1·10
MS1032 108×50 mm. Nos. 1029 and 1031			4·25	4·25

DESIGNS: 30c. "Renewal of the Economic Order"; 60c. "Renewal of the Educational Order"; 75c. "Renewal of the Social Order".

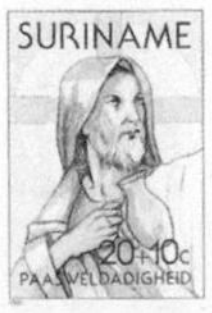
215 Christ with Jug

1981. Easter Charity. Multicoloured.

1033	20c.+10c. Type **215**	60	55
1034	30c.+15c. Christ and pointing hand	85	75
1035	50c.+25c. Christ and Roman soldier	1·30	1·20
1036	60c.+30c. Christ wearing crown of thorns	1·50	1·40
1037	75c.+35c. Christ and Mary	2·00	1·80

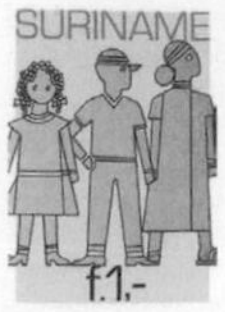

216 Young People

1981. Youth and its Future. Sheet 107×70 mm containing T **216** and similar vert design. Multicoloured.

MS1038	1g. Type **216**; 1g.50 Young people (different)	3·50	3·50

217 Surinam Independence Stamp and Hofburg Palace, Vienna

1981. WIPA 1981 International Stamp Exhibition, Vienna. Sheet 120×85 mm containing T **217** and similar horiz designs.

MS1039	50c. yellow, carmine and black; 1g. black, yellow and red; 2g. blue, black and light blue	6·50	6·50

DESIGNS: Hofburg Palace and—1g. Great Britain penny black; 2g. Austrian 9k. stamp of 1850.

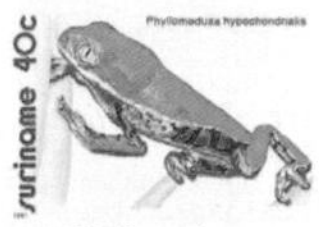

218 "Phyllomedusa hypochondrialis"

1981. Frogs. Multicoloured.

1040	40c. Type **218** (postage)	95	75
1041	50c. "Leptodactylus pentadactylus"	1·20	95
1042	60c. "Hyla boans"	1·40	1·10
1043	75c. "Phyllomedusa burmeisteri" (vert) (air)	1·80	1·30
1044	1g. "Dendrobates tinctorius" (vert)	3·00	1·80
1045	1g.25 "Bufo guttatus" (vert)	3·50	2·75

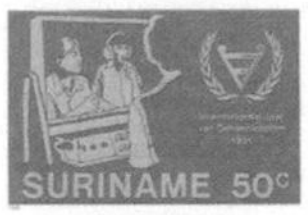

219 Deaf Child

1981. International Year of Disabled Persons.

1046	**219**	50c. yellow and green	95	85
1047	-	100c. yellow and green	2·00	1·80
1048	-	150c. yellow and red	3·00	2·75

DESIGNS: 100c. Child reading braille; 150c. Woman in wheelchair.

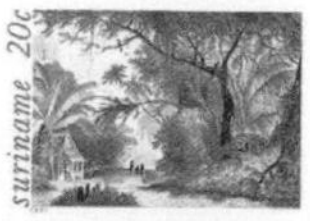

220 Planter's House on the Parakreek River

1981. Illustrations to "Journey to Surinam" by P. I. Benoit. Multicoloured.

1049	20c. Type **220**	35	30
1050	30c. Sarameca Street, Paramaribo	45	45
1051	75c. Negro hamlet, Paramaribo	1·40	1·30
1052	1g. Fish market, Paramaribo	1·90	1·70
1053	1g.25 Blaauwe Berg Cascade	2·40	2·10
MS1054	72×50 mm. No. 1052	2·40	2·40

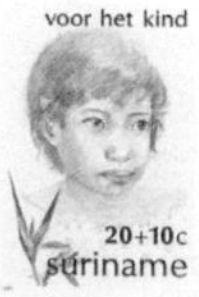

221 Indian Girl

1981. Child Welfare. Multicoloured.

1055	20c.+10c. Type **221**	70	65
1056	30c.+15c. Negro girl	95	85
1057	50c.+25c. Hindustani girl	1·40	1·30
1058	60c.+30c. Javanese girl	1·80	1·60
1059	75c.+35c. Chinese girl	2·00	1·80
MS1060	100×72 mm. Nos. 1056 ×2 and 1059	5·25	5·25

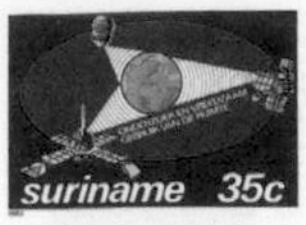

222 Satellites orbiting Earth

1982. Peaceful Uses of Outer Space. Multicoloured.

1061	35c. Type **222**	85	75
1062	65c. Space shuttle	1·40	1·30
1063	1g. U.S.–Russian space link	2·00	1·80

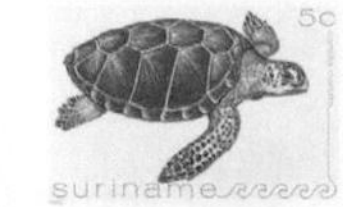

223 "Caretta caretta"

1982. Turtles. Multicoloured.

1064	5c. Type **223** (postage)	25	20
1065	10c. "Chelonia mydas"	25	20
1066	20c. "Dermochelys coriacea"	45	30
1067	25c. "Eretmochelys imbricata"	60	55
1068	35c. "Lepidochelys olivacea"	85	75
1069	65c. "Platemys platycephala" (air)	1·50	1·20
1070	75c. "Phrynops gibba"	1·90	1·60
1071	125c. "Rihnoclemys punctularia"	3·00	2·30

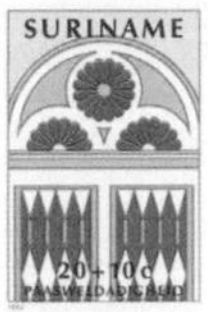

224 Pattern from Stained Glass Window

1982. Easter. Stained-glass Windows, Church of Saints Peter and Paul, Paramaribo.

1072	**224**	20c.+10c. multicoloured	85	75
1073	-	35c.+15c. multicoloured	1·20	1·10
1074	-	50c.+25c. multicoloured	1·80	1·60
1075	-	65c.+30c. multicoloured	2·10	2·10
1076	-	75c.+35c. multicoloured	2·40	2·10

DESIGNS: 35c. to 75c. Different patterns.

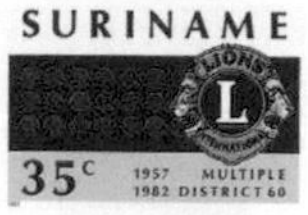

225 Lions Emblem

1982. 25th Anniv of Surinam Lions Club.

1077	**225**	35c. multicoloured	85	65
1078	**225**	70c. multicoloured	1·80	1·30

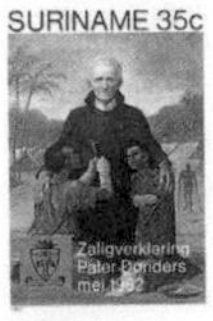

226 Father Donders with the Sick

1982. Beatification of Father Peter Donders.

1079	**226**	35c. multicoloured	1·20	1·10
1080	-	65c. silver, black and red	2·00	1·80
MS1081		50×72 mm. No. 1080	3·00	3·00

DESIGN: 65c. Portrait, birthplace, Tilburg, and map of South America.

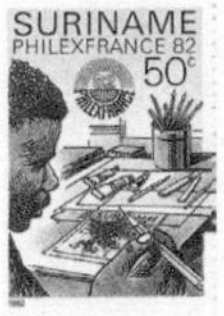

227 Stamp Designer

1982. "Philexfrance 82" International Stamp Exhibition, Paris. Multicoloured.

1082	50c. Type **227**	95	85
1083	100c. Stamp printing	2·00	1·80
1084	150c. Stamp collector	3·00	2·75
MS1085	100×72 mm. Nos. 1082/4	6·50	6·50

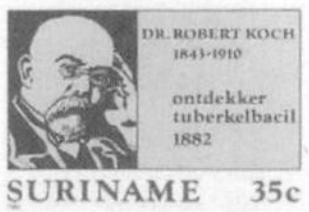

228 Dr. Robert Koch

1982. Cent of Discovery of Tubercle Bacillus.

1086	**228**	35c. yellow and green	70	65
1087	-	65c. orange and brown	1·40	1·30
1088	-	150c. light blue, blue and red	3·75	3·50

DESIGNS: 65c. Dr. Koch and microscope; 150c. Dr. Koch and Bacillus.

229 Sugar Mill

1982. Cent of Marienburg Sugar Company.

1089	**229**	35c. yellow, green and black	85	55
1090	-	65c. orange and brown	1·40	1·30
1091	-	100c. light blue, blue and black	2·00	1·80
1092	-	150c. lilac and purple	3·00	2·75

DESIGNS: 65c. Workers in cane fields; 100c. Sugar-cane railway; 150c. Mill machinery.

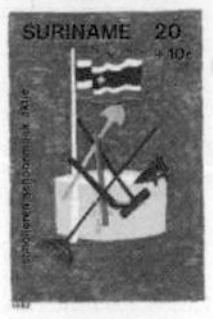

230 Cleaning Tools and Flag

1982. Child Welfare. "Keep Surinam Tidy" (children's paintings). Multicoloured.

1093	20c.+10c. Type **230**	60	55
1094	35c.+15c. Man with barrow	1·20	1·10
1095	50c.+25c. Litter bin and cleaning tools	1·80	1·60
1096	65c.+30c. Spraying weeds	2·10	1·90
1097	75c.+35c. Litter bin	2·50	2·30
MS1098	97×72 mm. Nos. 1094 ×2 and 1097	5·25	5·25

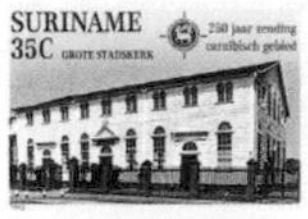

231 Municipal Church, Paramaribo

1982. 250th Anniv of Moravian Church Mission in the Caribbean.

1099	**231**	35c. multicoloured	85	75
1100	-	65c. light blue, black and blue	1·80	1·60
1101	-	150c. multicoloured	3·00	2·75

DESIGNS—HORIZ: 65c. Aerial view of St. Thomas Monastery. VERT: 150c. Johann Leonhardt Dober (missionary).

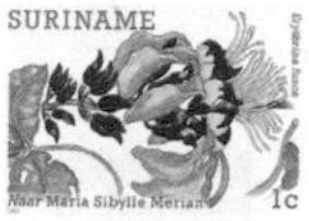

232 "Erythrina fusca"

1983. Flower Paintings by Maria Sibylle Merian. Multicoloured.

1102	1c. Type **232**	25	20
1103	2c. "Ipomoea acuminata"	25	20
1104	3c. "Heliconia psittacorum"	25	20
1105	5c. "Ipomoea"	25	20
1106	10c. "Herba non denominata"	35	30
1107	15c. "Anacardium occidentale"	60	55
1108	20c. "Inga edulis" (vert)	70	65
1109	25c. "Abelmoschus moschatus" (vert)	1·10	85
1110	30c. "Argemone mexicana" (vert)	1·40	1·20
1111	35c. "Costus arabicus" (vert)	1·40	1·30
1112	45c. "Muellera frutescens" (vert)	2·00	1·60
1113	65c. "Punica granatum" (vert)	3·00	2·30

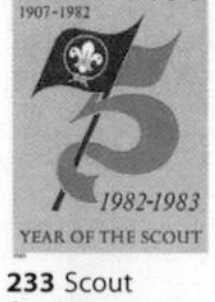

233 Scout Anniversary Emblem

1983. Year of the Scout.

1114	**233**	40c. mauve, violet & green	1·30	1·20
1115	-	65c. lt grey, blue & grey	2·00	1·80
1116	-	70c. multicoloured	2·10	1·90
1117	-	80c. blue, lt green & green	2·40	2·10

DESIGNS: 65c. Lord Baden-Powell; 70c. Tent and campfire; 80c. Axe in tree trunk.

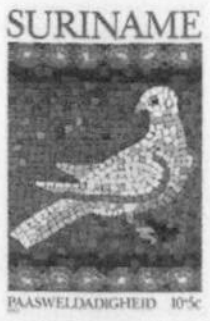

234 Dove of Peace

1983. Easter. Multicoloured.

1118	**234**	10c.+5c. Type	35	30
1119	**234**	15c.+5c. Bread	60	55
1120	**234**	25c.+10c. Fish	85	75
1121	**234**	50c.+25c. Eye	1·80	1·60
1122	**234**	65c.+30c. Chalice	2·40	2·10

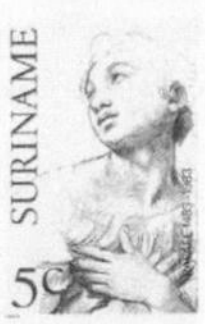

235 Drawing by Raphael

1983. 500th Birth Anniv of Raphael.

1123	**235**	5c. multicoloured	10	10
1124	-	10c. multicoloured	25	20
1125	-	40c. multicoloured	95	85
1126	-	65c. multicoloured	1·40	1·30
1127	-	70c. multicoloured	2·00	1·80
1128	-	80c. multicoloured	2·40	2·10

DESIGNS: 10c. to 80c. Drawings by Raphael.

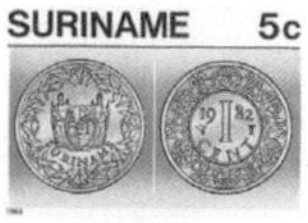

236 1c. Coin

1983. Coins and Banknotes. Multicoloured.

1129	5c. Type **236**	25	20
1130	10c. 5c. coin	25	20
1131	40c. 10c. coin	95	85
1132	65c. 25c. coin	1·40	1·30
1133	70c. 1g. note	1·80	1·60
1134	80c. 2½g. note	2·00	1·80

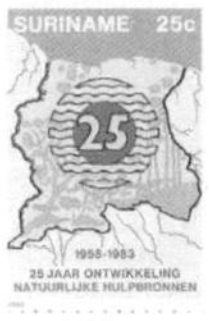

237 "25" on Map of Surinam

1983. 25th Anniv of Department of Construction. Multicoloured.

1135	25c. Type **237**	60	55
1136	50c. Construction vehicles on map	1·20	10

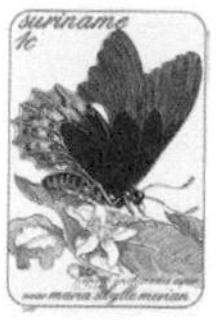

238 "Papilio anchisiades"

1983. Butterfly Paintings by Maria Sibylle Merian. Multicoloured.

1137	1c. Type **238**	25	20
1138	2c. "Urania leilus"	25	20
1139	3c. "Morpho deidamia"	25	20
1140	5c. "Thysania agrippina"	35	20
1141	10c. "Morpho sp."	45	20
1142	15c. "Philaethria dido"	70	45
1143	20c. "Morpho menelaus" (horiz)	85	55
1144	25c. "Protoparce rustica" (horiz)	1·30	65
1145	30c. "Rothschildia aurota" (horiz)	1·40	85
1146	35c. "Phoebis sennae" (horiz)	1·80	1·10
1147	45c. "Papilio androgeos" (horiz)	2·40	1·40
1148	65c. "Dupo vitis" (horiz)	3·50	2·10

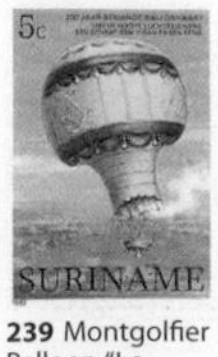

239 Montgolfier Balloon "Le Martial", 1783

1983. Bicentenary of Manned Flight. Multicoloured.

1149	5c. Type **239**	25	20
1150	10c. Montgolfier balloon (1st manned free flight by D'Arlandes and Pilatre de Rozier, 1783)	25	20
1151	40c. Charles's hydrogen balloon, 1783	1·30	1·20
1152	65c. Balloon "Armand Barbes", 1870	2·00	1·80
1153	70c. Balloon "Double Eagle II" (transatlantic flight, 1978)	2·10	1·90
1154	80c. Hot-air balloons at International Balloon Festival, Albuquerque, U.S.A.	2·40	2·10

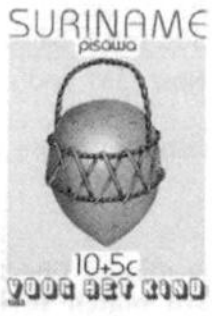

240 Calabash Pitcher

1983. Child Welfare. Caribbean Artifacts. Multicoloured.

1155	10c.+5c. Type **240**	35	30
1156	15c.+5c. Umari (headdress)	60	55
1157	25c.+10c. Maraka (medicine man's rattle)	85	75
1158	50c.+25c. Manari (sieve)	1·80	1·60
1159	65c.+30c. Pasuwa/pakara (basket)	2·40	2·10
MS1160	100×72 mm. Nos. 1156/7 and 1159	4·25	4·25

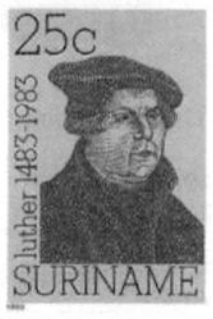

241 Martin Luther

1983. 500th Birth Anniv of Martin Luther (Protestant reformer).

1161	**241**	25c. yellow, brown and black	85	75
1162	-	50c. pink, purple & black	1·50	1·40

DESIGN: 50c. Selling of indulgences.

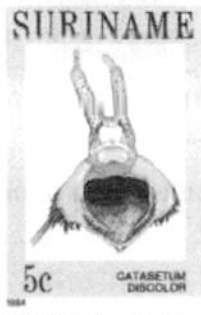

242 "Catasetum discolor"

1983. Orchids. Multicoloured.

1163	5c. Type **242**	25	20
1164	10c. "Menadenium labiosum"	25	20
1165	40c. "Comparettia falcata"	1·30	1·10
1166	50c. "Rodriguezia decora"	2·00	1·60
1167	70c. "Oncidium papilio"	2·10	1·80
1168	75c. "Epidendrum porpax"	2·40	1·80

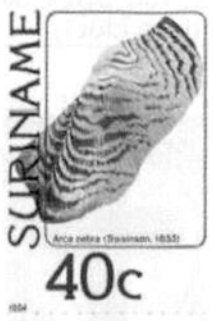

243 Atlantic Turkey Wing

1984. Sea Shells. Multicoloured.

1169	40c. Type **243**	1·10	95
1170	65c. American prickly cockle	1·80	1·50
1171	70c. Sunrise tellin	1·80	1·60
1172	80c. Knorr's worm shell	2·10	1·70

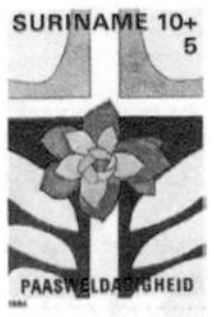

244 Cross and Flower

1984. Easter. Multicoloured.

1173	10c.+5c. Type **244**	35	30
1174	15c.+5c. Cross and gate of cemetery	60	55
1175	25c.+10c. Candle flames	1·00	85
1176	50c.+25c. Cross and crown of thorns	2·10	1·80
1177	65c.+30c. Lamp	2·40	2·10

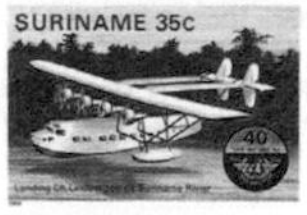

245 Sikorsky S-40 Flying Boat

1984. 40th Anniv of I.C.A.O. Multicoloured.

1178	35c. Type **245**	85	75
1179	65c. Surinam Airways De Havilland Twin Otter 200/300	2·20	1·90

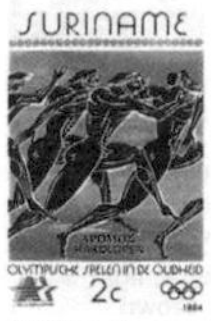

246 Running

1984. Olympic Games, Los Angeles. Multicoloured.

1180	2c. Type **246**	10	10
1181	3c. Javelin, discus and long jump	10	10
1182	5c. Massage	10	10
1183	10c. Rubbing with ointment	25	20
1184	15c. Wrestling	35	30
1185	20c. Boxing	60	55
1186	30c. Horse-racing	75	65
1187	35c. Chariot-racing	85	75
1188	45c. Temple of Olympia	1·20	1·10
1189	50c. Entrance to Stadium, Olympia	1·50	1·30
1190	65c. Stadium, Olympia	1·80	1·60
1191	75c. Zeus	2·40	2·10
MS1192	95×64 mm. Nos. 1180, 1187 and 1191	3·75	3·75

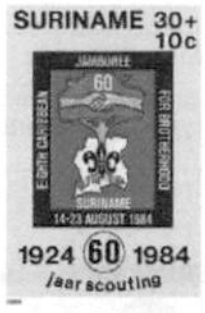

247 Emblem of 8th Caribbean Scout Jamboree

1984. 60th Anniv of Scouting in Surinam. Multicoloured.

1193	30c.+10c. Type **247**	1·60	1·40
1194	35c.+10c. Scout saluting	2·00	1·70
1195	50c.+10c. Scout camp	2·30	2·00
1196	90c.+10c. Campfire and map	4·00	3·50

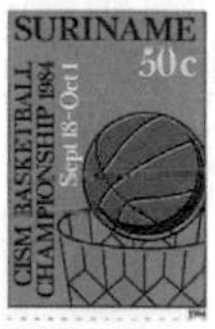

248 Ball entering Basket

1984. International Military Sports Council Basketball Championship. Multicoloured.

1197	50c. Type **248**	1·60	1·40
1198	90c. Ball leaving basket	2·75	2·30

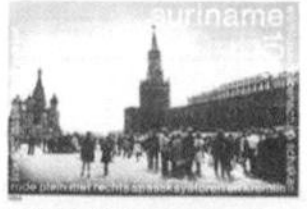

249 Red Square, Moscow

1984. World Chess Championship, Moscow.

1199	**249**	10c. brown	25	20
1200	-	15c. green and light green	60	55
1201	-	30c. light brown & brown	1·20	1·10
1202	-	50c. brown and purple	1·80	1·60
1203	-	75c. brown & light brown	2·40	2·10
1204	-	90c. green and blue	3·25	2·75
MS1205		144×50 mm. Nos. 1201/3	6·00	6·00

DESIGNS: 15c. Knight, king and pawn on board; 30c. Gary Kasparov; 50c. Start of game and clock; 75c. Anatoly Karpov; 90c. Position during Andersen–Kizeritski game.

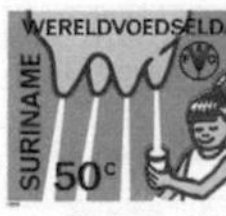

250 Children collecting Milk from Cow

1984. World Food Day. Multicoloured.

1206	50c. Type **250**	1·60	1·40
1207	90c. Platter of food	2·75	2·30

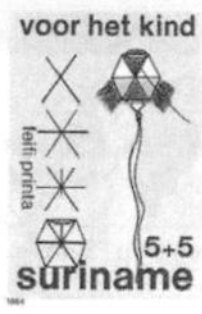

251 Kite

1984. Child Welfare. Multicoloured.

1208	5c.+5c. Type **251**	25	20
1209	10c.+5c. Kites	35	30
1210	30c.+10c. Pingi-pingi-kasi (game)	1·20	1·10
1211	50c.+25c. Cricket	2·40	2·10
1212	90c.+30c. Peroen, peroen (game)	3·75	3·25
MS1213	100×72 mm. Nos. 1209/11	4·25	4·25

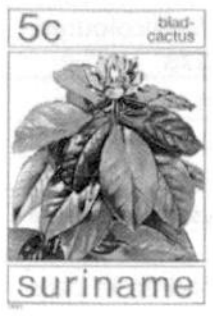

252 Leaf Cactus

1985. Cacti. Multicoloured.

1215	5c. Type **252**	10	10
1216	10c. Melocactus	35	30
1217	30c. Pillar cactus	1·30	1·20
1218	50c. Fig cactus	1·80	1·60
1219	75c. Night queen	3·00	2·75
1220	90c. Segment cactus	3·75	3·25

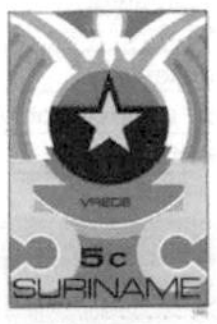

253 "Peace" and Star

1985. Fifth Anniv of Revolution. Multicoloured.

1221	5c. Type **253**	10	10
1222	30c. "Unity in labour" and manual workers	85	75
1223	50c. "5 years of Steadfastness" and flower	1·60	1·40
1224	75c. "Progress" and wheat as flower	2·30	2·00
1225	90c. "Unity", flower and dove	2·75	2·30
MS1226	100×72 mm. Nos. 1221 ×2 and 1223	2·00	2·00

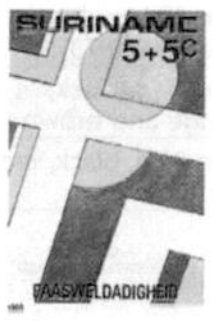

254 Crosses

1985. Easter. Multicoloured.

1227	5c.+5c. Type **254**	25	20
1228	10c.+5c. Crosses (different)	25	20
1229	30c.+15c. Sun's rays illuminating crosses	1·00	85
1230	50c.+25c. Crosses (different)	1·70	1·50
1231	90c.+30c. Crosses and leaves (Resurrection)	2·75	2·30

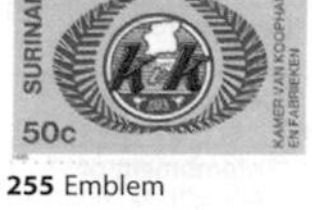

255 Emblem

1985. 75th Anniv of Chamber of Commerce and Industry.

1232	**255**	50c. yellow, green and red	1·10	95
1233	-	90c. green, blue & yellow	2·00	1·70

DESIGN: 90c. Chamber of Commerce building.

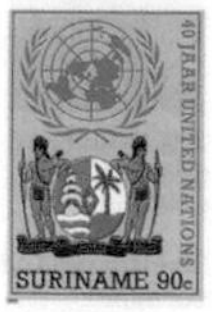

256 U.N. Emblem and State Arms

1985. 40th Anniv of U.N.O.

1234	**256**	50c. multicoloured	1·10	95
1235	**256**	90c. multicoloured	2·00	1·70

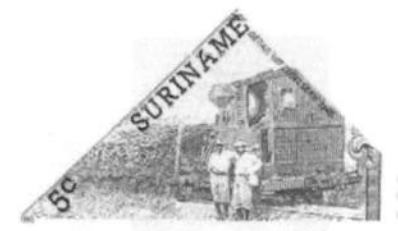

257 Sugar-cane Train (detail of 1945 stamp)

1985. Railway Locomotives.

1236	**257**	5c. orange and blue	10	10
1237	-	5c. green, red and blue	10	10
1238	-	10c. multicoloured	25	20
1239	-	10c. multicoloured	25	20
1240	-	20c. multicoloured	85	75
1241	-	20c. multicoloured	85	75
1242	-	30c. multicoloured	1·20	1·10
1243	-	30c. multicoloured	1·20	1·10
1244	-	50c. multicoloured	1·80	1·60
1245	-	50c. multicoloured	1·80	1·60
1246	-	75c. multicoloured	3·00	2·75
1247	-	75c. multicoloured	3·00	2·75

DESIGNS: No. 1237, Monaco 3f. Postage due train stamp; 1238, Steam locomotive "Dam"; 1239, Modern electric railcars; 1240, Steam locomotive No. 3737, Netherlands; 1241, Electric railcar Type IC-III, Netherlands; 1242, Stephenson's "Rocket"; 1243, TGV express train, France; 1244, Stephenson "Adler", Germany; 1245, Double-deck UB2N train, France; 1246, "General", U.S.A.; 1247, "Hikari" express train, Japan.

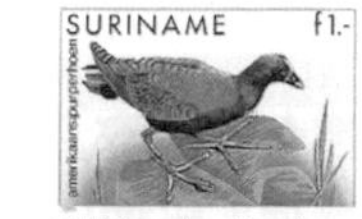

258 American Purple Gallinule

1985. Birds. Multicoloured.

1248	1g. Type **258**	3·00	85
1249	1g.50 Rufescent tiger heron	4·50	1·30
1250	2g.50 Scarlet ibis	8·00	2·10
1251	5g. Guianan cock of the rock	14·50	8·50
1252	10g. Harpy eagle	21·00	17·00
MS1253	70×50 mm. No. 1248	5·25	5·25

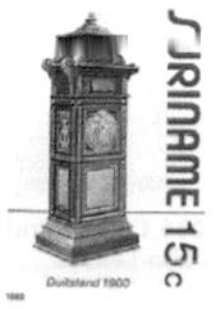

259 German Letterbox, 1900

1985. Old Letterboxes. Multicoloured.

1254	15c. Type **259**	35	30
1255	30c. French letterbox, 1900	85	75
1256	50c. English pillar box, 1932	1·50	1·30
1257	90c. Dutch letterbox, 1850	2·40	2·10

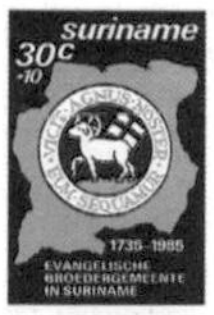

260 Emblem on Map

1985. 25th Anniv of Evangelical Brotherhood in Surinam.

1258	**260**	30c.+10c. multicoloured	1·20	1·10
1259	-	50c.+10c. red, yellow and brown	1·80	1·60
1260	-	90c.+20c. yellow, brown and red	3·75	3·25

DESIGNS: 50c. Different population groups around cross and clasped hands emblem; 90c. List of work undertaken by Brotherhood.

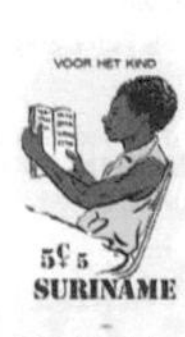

261 Studying

1985. Child Welfare. Multicoloured.

1261	5c.+5c. Type **261**	25	20
1262	10c.+5c. Writing alphabet on board	35	30
1263	30c.+10c. Writing	1·10	95
1264	50c.+25c. Reading	2·10	1·80
1265	90c.+30c. Thinking	3·25	2·75
MS1266	100×72 mm. Nos. 1262/4	4·25	4·25

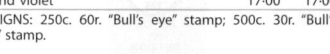

1991. Easter. Multicoloured.

1474	60c.+30c. Type **318**	2·30	2·00
1475	105c.+50c. Christ wearing crown of thorns	2·75	2·30
1476	110c.+55c. Woman cradling Christ's body	4·25	3·75
MS1477	75×72 mm. Nos. 1474 and 1476	6·75	6·75

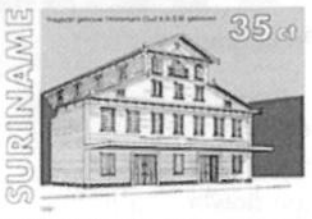

319 Shipping Company Store

1991. Buildings.

1478	**319**	35c. black, blue & lt blue	85	75
1479	-	60c. black, green and emerald	1·70	1·50
1480	-	75c. black, yell & lemon	2·10	1·80
1481	-	105c. black, orange and light orange	3·00	2·50
1482	-	110c. black, pink and red	3·00	2·75
1483	-	200c. black, deep mauve and mauve	5·50	5·00

DESIGNS: 60c. Upper class house; 75c. House converted into Labour Inspection offices; 105c. Plantation supervisor's house; 110c. Ministry of Labour building; 200c. Houses.

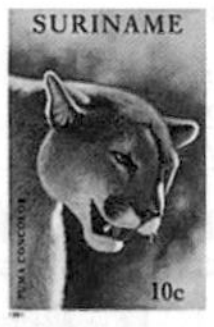

320 Puma

1991. The Puma. Multicoloured.

1484	10c. Type **320** (postage)	25	20
1485	20c. Stalking	35	30
1486	25c. Stretching	50	45
1487	30c. Licking nose	75	65
1488	125c. Lying down (horiz) (air)	2·75	2·30
1489	500c. Leaping (horiz)	9·75	8·50

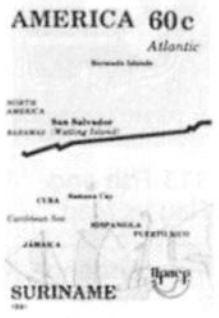

321 Route Map to Bahamas via San Salvador

1991. America. Voyages of Discovery. Each red, blue and black.

1490	60c. Type **321**	2·40	2·10
1491	110c. Route map from Canary Islands	4·25	3·75

Nos. 1490/1 were printed together, se-tenant, forming a composite design.

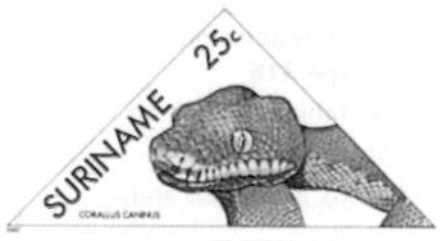

322 Green Tree Boa ("Corallus caninus")

1991. Snakes. Multicoloured.

1492	25c. Type **322**	60	55
1493	25c. Garden tree boa ("Corallus enydris")	60	55
1494	35c. Boa constrictor	75	65
1495	35c. Bushmaster ("Lachesis muta")	75	65
1496	60c. South American rattlesnake ("Crotalus durissus")	1·30	1·20
1497	60c. Surinam coral snake ("Micrurus surinamensis")	1·30	1·20
1498	75c. Mussurana ("Clelia cloelia")	1·70	1·50
1499	75c. Anaconda ("Eunectes murinus")	1·70	1·50
1500	110c. Rainbow boa ("Epicrutes cenchris")	2·40	2·10
1501	110c. Sipo ("Chrironius carinatus")	2·40	2·10
1502	200c. Black and yellow rat snake ("Spilotes pullatus")	4·25	3·75
1503	200c. Vine snake ("Oxybelis argenteus")	4·25	3·75

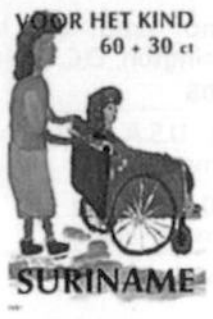

323 Child in Wheelchair

1991. Child Welfare. Multicoloured.

1504	60c.+30c. Type **323**	2·00	1·70
1505	105c.+50c. Trees and girl	3·25	2·75
1506	110c.+55c. Girls playing in yard	3·75	3·25
MS1507	75×80 mm. Nos. 1504 and 1506	5·50	5·50

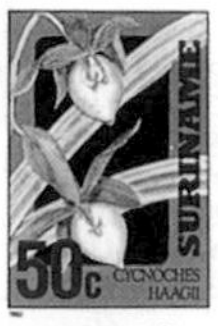

324 "Cycnoches haagii"

1992. Orchids. Multicoloured.

1508	50c. Type **324**	1·10	95
1509	60c. "Lycaste cristata"	1·30	1·20
1510	75c. "Galeandra dives" (horiz)	1·70	1·50
1511	125c. "Vanilla mexicana"	2·75	2·30
1512	150c. "Cyrtopodium glutiniferum"	3·25	2·75
1513	250c. "Gongora quinquenervis"	5·50	4·75

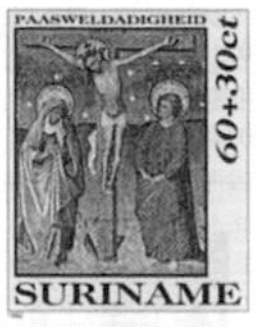

325 Crucifixion

1992. Easter. Multicoloured.

1514	60c.+30c. Type **325**	2·00	1·70
1515	105c.+50c. Women taking away Christ's body	3·25	2·75
1516	110c.+55c. The Resurrection	3·75	3·25

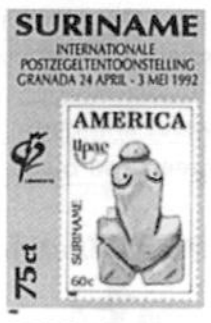

326 Surinam 1989 American Stamp

1992. Granada 92 International Stamp Exhibition. Sheet 125×75 mm containing T **326** and similar vert designs. Multicoloured.

MS1517	75c. Type **326**; 125c. 1989 America 110c. stamp; 150c. 1991 America 60c. stamp; 250c. 1991 America 110c. stamp	14·50	14·50

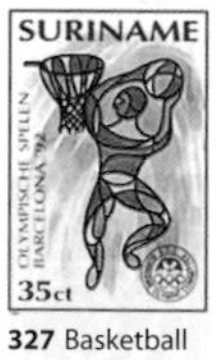

327 Basketball

1992. Olympic Games, Barcelona. Multicoloured.

1518	35c. Type **327**	75	65
1519	60c. Volleyball	1·30	1·20
1520	75c. Sprinting	1·70	1·50
1521	125c. Football	2·75	2·30
1522	150c. Cycling	3·25	2·75
1523	250c. Swimming	5·50	4·75
MS1524	100×72 mm. Nos. 1520/1	10·50	10·50

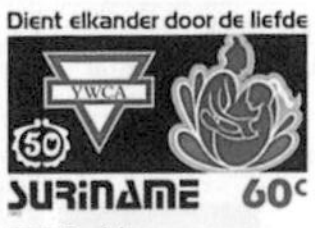

328 Emblems

1992. 50th Anniv of Young Women's Christian Association.

1525	**328**	60c. multicoloured	1·30	1·20
1526	**328**	250c. multicoloured	5·50	4·75

1992. Nos. 1236/7 surch **1 c.**

1527	1c. on 5c. orange and blue	60	55
1528	1c. on 5c. green, red and blue	60	55

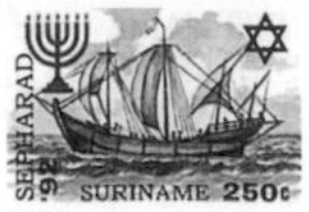

330 Nau

1992. 500th Anniv of Expulsion of Jews from Spain.

1529	**330**	250c. multicoloured	5·50	4·75

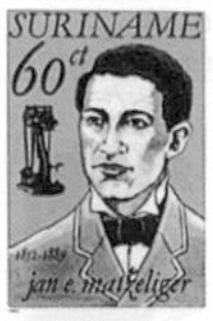

331 Matzeliger and Shoe-lasting Machine

1992. 140th Birth Anniv of Jan E. Matzeliger (inventor).

1530	**331**	60c. multicoloured	1·30	1·20
1531	**331**	250c. multicoloured	5·50	4·75

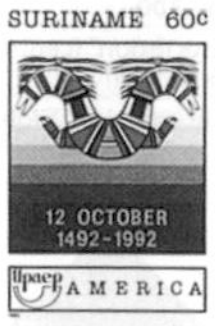

332 Amerindian Ornament

1992. America. 500th Anniv of Discovery of America by Columbus.

1532	**332**	60c. multicoloured	1·30	1·20
1533	**332**	250c. multicoloured	5·50	4·75

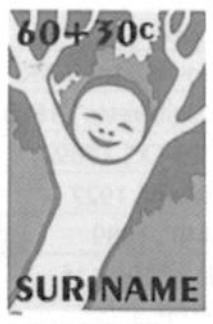

333 Tree with Child's Face

1992. Child Welfare. Multicoloured.

1534	60c.+30c. Type **333**	25	10
1535	105c.+50c. Tree with child's face beside flower	1·30	1·20
1536	110c.+55c. Children hanging from tree	5·50	4·75
MS1537	75×80 mm. Nos. 1534 and 1536	8·50	7·50

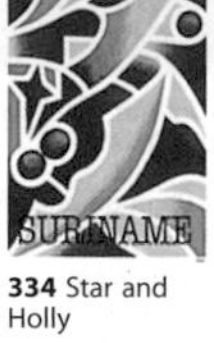

334 Star and Holly

1992. Christmas. Multicoloured.

1538	10c. Type **334**	2·00	1·70
1539	60c. Candle	3·25	2·75
1540	250c. Parcels	3·75	3·25
1541	400c. Crown	5·50	5·50

1993. Air. No. 865 surch **35 ct.**

1543	35c. on 50c. multicoloured	1·20	1·10

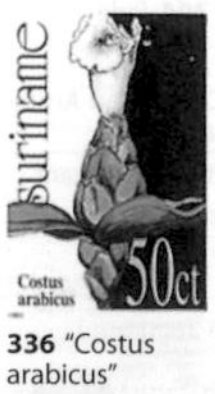

336 "Costus arabicus"

1993. Medicinal Plants. Multicoloured.

1544	50c. Type **336**	1·20	1·10
1545	75c. "Quassia amara"	1·80	1·60
1546	125c. "Combretum rotundifolium" (horiz)	3·00	2·75
1547	500c. "Bixa orellana" (horiz)	12·00	10·50

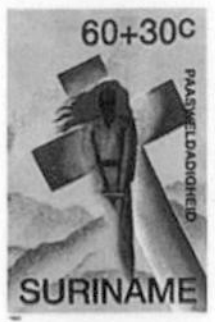

337 Christ and Cross

1993. Easter. Multicoloured.

1548	60c.+30c. Type **337**	2·20	1·90
1549	110c.+50c. Crucifixion	3·75	3·25
1550	125c.+60c. Resurrection	4·00	3·50

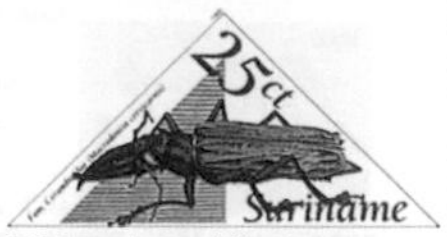

338 Long-horned Beetle ("Macrodontia cervicornis")

1993. Insects. Multicoloured.

1551	25c. Type **338**	50	45
1552	25c. Locust	50	45
1553	35c. Weevil ("Curculionidae")	75	65
1554	35c. Grasshopper ("Acrididae")	75	65
1555	50c. Goliath beetle ("Euchroma gigantea")	1·10	95
1556	50c. Bush cricket ("Tettigonidae")	1·10	95
1557	100c. "Tettigonidae"	2·10	1·80
1558	100c. Scarab beetle ("Phanaeus festivus")	2·10	1·80
1559	175c. Cricket ("Grylllidae")	4·00	3·50
1560	175c. Dung beetle ("Phanaeus lancifer")	4·00	3·50
1561	220c. "Tettigonidae" (different)	5·00	4·25
1562	220c. Longhorn beetle ("Batus barbicornis")	5·00	4·25

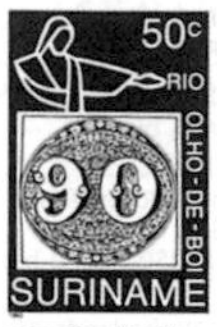

339 90r. "Bull's Eye" Stamp

1993. 150th Anniv of First Brazilian Stamps and "Brasiliana 93" International Stamp Exhibition, Rio de Janeiro.

1563	**339**	50c. black and violet	1·10	95
1564	-	250c. black and blue	5·50	4·75
1565	-	500c. black and green	11·00	9·50
MS1566		125×75 mm. 250c. black, blue and violet; 500c. black, green and violet	17·00	17·00

DESIGNS: 250c. 60r. "Bull's eye" stamp; 500c. 30r. "Bull's eye" stamp.

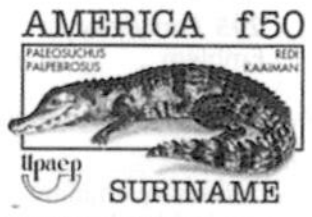

340 Dwarf Cayman

1993. America. Endangered Animals.

1567	**340**	50c. multicoloured	2·10	1·80
1568	**340**	100c. multicoloured	4·50	3·75

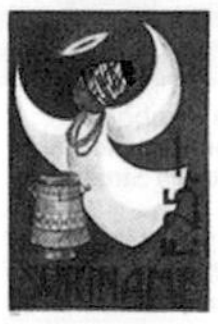
341 Afro-Caribbean Angel

1993. Christmas. Multicoloured.

1569	25c. Type **341**	1·20	1·10
1570	45c. Asian angel	2·40	2·10
1571	50c. Oriental angel	2·75	2·30
1572	150c. Amerindian angel	8·50	7·50

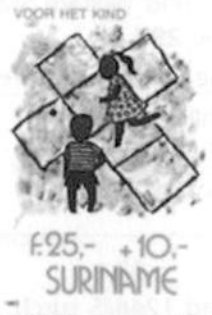

342 Hopscotch

1993. Child Welfare. Children's Games.

1573	**342**	25g.+10g. brown & grn	1·30	1·20
1574	-	35g.+10g. brown & blue	1·80	1·60

1575	- 50g.+25g. brown & grn	3·00	2·75
1576	- 75g.+25g. brown & blue	4·00	3·50
MS1577	75×72 mm. Nos. 1574/5	5·00	5·00

DESIGNS: 35g. Hopscotch (different); 50g. Djoel (variant of hopscotch); 75g. Djoel (different).

1993. Nos. 1252 and 1473 surch **f 5.-**.

1578	5g. on 10g. multicoloured	2·40	2·10
1579	5g. on 15g. multicoloured	2·40	2·10

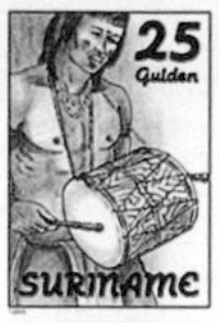

344 Sambura

1994. Traditional Drums. Multicoloured.

1580	25g. Type **344**	2·40	2·10
1581	50g. Apinti	4·25	3·75
1582	75g. Terbangan	6·75	5·75
1583	100g. Dhol	9·25	8·00

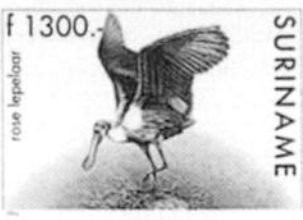

345 Roseate Spoonbill

1994

1584	**345**	1300g. multicoloured	49·00	43·00

1994. Air. No value expressed. Nos. 864 and 866/7 optd **Port Paye**.

1585	(-) on 45c. multicoloured	25	10
1586	(-) on 55c. multicoloured	1·50	1·30
1587	(-) on 60c. multicoloured	3·25	2·75

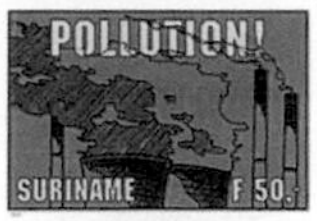

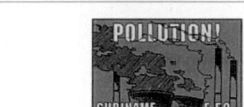

347 Smoking Chimneys

1994. Environmental Protection. Multicoloured.

1588	50g. Type **347**	2·20	1·90
1589	350g. Dead fish in polluted sea	16·00	14·00

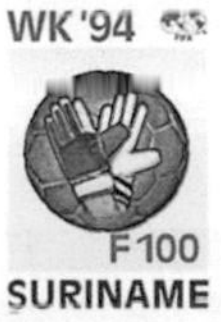

348 Goalkeeper's Gloves and Ball

1994. World Cup Football Championship, U.S.A. Multicoloured.

1590	100g. Type **348**	3·75	3·25
1591	250g. Boot on ball	9·75	8·50
1592	300g. Goal net on ball	11·00	9·50
MS1593	101×72 mm. Nos. 1591/2	22·00	22·00

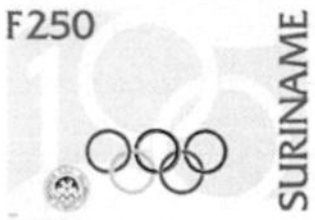

349 Anniversary Emblem

1994. Cent of International Olympic Committee.

1594	**349**	250g. multicoloured	9·75	8·50

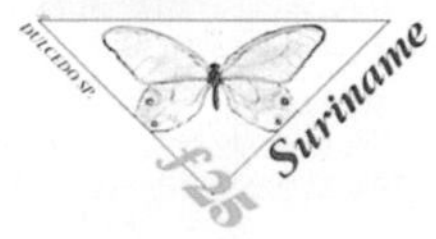

350 "Dulcedo sp."

1994. Butterflies. Multicoloured.

1595	25g. Type **350**	35	30
1596	25g. "Ithomia sp."	35	30
1597	30g. "Danaus sp." (brown wings)	50	45
1598	30g. "Danaus sp." (black and gold wings)	50	45
1599	45g. "Bithijs sp."	75	65
1600	45g. "Echenais sp."	75	65
1601	75g. White peacock ("Anartia jatrophae")	1·20	1·10
1602	75g. Caribbean buckeye ("Junonia evarete")	1·20	1·10
1603	250g. Small postman ("Heliconius erato")	4·25	3·75
1604	250g. "Heliconius sp."	4·25	3·75
1605	300g. "Parides sp."	5·00	4·25
1606	300g. "Eurytides sp."	5·00	4·25

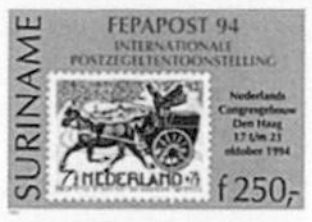

351 Netherlands 1943 Stamp Day Issue

1994. "Fepapost 94" European Stamp Exhibition, The Hague. Multicoloured.

1607	250g. Type **351**	9·75	8·50
1608	300g. Surinam 1936 1c. stamp	11·50	10·00
MS1609	108×60 mm. Nos. 1607/8	21·00	21·00

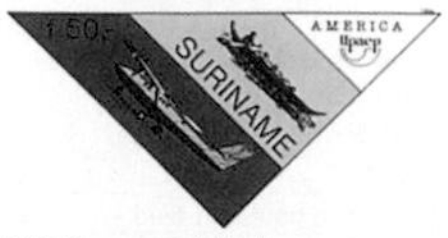

352 Canoe and Airplane

1994. America. Postal Transport. Multicoloured.

1610	50g. Type **352**	2·10	1·80
1611	400g. Donkey-cart and motor van	16·00	14·00

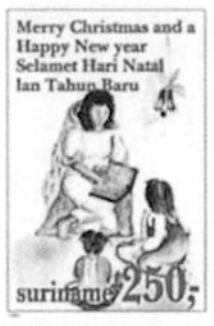

353 Mother reading to Children

1994. Christmas. Multicoloured. (a) Value indicated by letter "A".

1612	A Angel hovering over pine forest	1·00	85

(b) With face value.

1613	250g. Type **353**	2·75	2·30
1614	625g. Woman praying	6·75	5·75
MS1615	75×72 mm. Nos. 1613/14	18·00	18·00

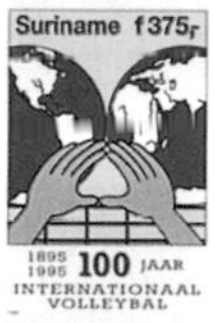

354 Hands and Globes

1995. Centenary of Volleyball. Multicoloured.

1616	375g. Type **354**	4·25	3·75
1617	650g. Balls	7·25	6·50

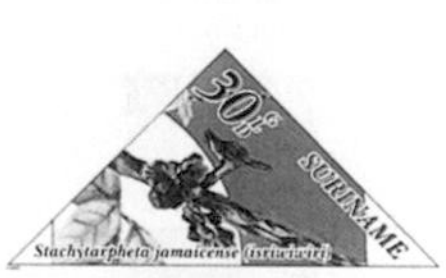

355 "Stachytarpheta Jamaicense"

1995. Medicinal Plants. Multicoloured.

1619	30g. Type **355**	35	30
1620	30g. "Ruellia tuberosa"	35	30
1621	50g. Sweet basil ("Ocimum sanctum")	60	55
1622	50g. "Peperomia pellucida"	60	55
1623	75g. "Phyllanthus amarus"	1·00	85
1624	75g. "Portulaca oleracea"	1·00	85
1625	250g. "Wulffia baccata"	3·25	2·75
1626	250g. Sesame ("Sesamum indicum")	3·25	2·75
1627	500g. Blood flower ("Asclepias curassavica")	6·75	5·75
1628	500g. "Heliotropium indicum"	6·75	5·75
1629	600g. "Wedelia tribolata"	8·00	7·00
1630	600g. "Lantana camara"	8·00	7·00

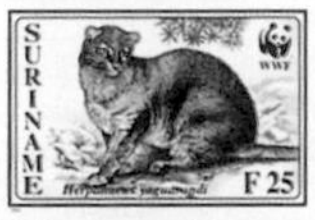

356 Jaguarundi

1995. Big Cats. Multicoloured.

1631	25g. Type **356** (postage)	1·00	85
1632	30g. Head of jaguarundi	1·10	90
1633	50g. Tiger cat	1·30	1·20
1634	100g. Head of tiger cat	3·00	2·50
1635	1000g. Tree ocelot (air)	8·50	7·50
1636	1200g. Head of tree ocelot	10·50	9·00

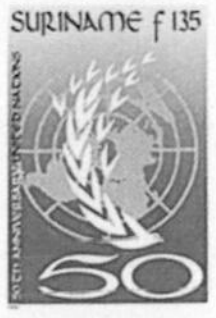

357 Emblem, Dove and "50"

1995. 50th Anniv of U.N.O. Multicoloured.

1637	135g. Type **357**	1·20	1·10
1638	740g. As T **357** but dove flying towards right	6·75	5·75

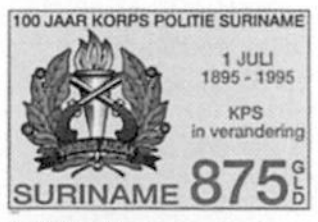

358 Emblem

1995. Centenary of Surinam Police Force.

1639	**358**	875g. multicoloured	12·00	10·50

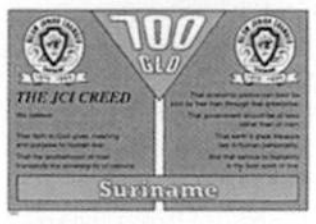

359 Emblem and Creed

1995. 25th Anniv of Nilom Junior Chamber.

1640	**359**	700g. orange, blue and deep blue	5·25	4·50

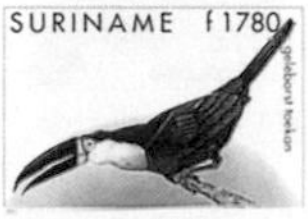

360 Channel-billed Toucan

1995. Birds. Multicoloured.

1641	1780g. Type **360**	13·50	11·50
1642	2225g. Rufous-throated sapphire	17·00	15·00
1643	2995g. Hoatzin	23·00	20·00

See also Nos. 1679/81, 1736/9, 1767/70 and 1826/7.

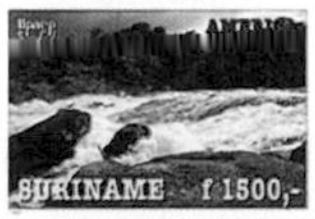

361 Waterfall

1995. America. Environmental Protection. Multicoloured.

1644	135g. Forest floor	1·50	1·30
1645	1500g. Type **361**	16·00	14·00

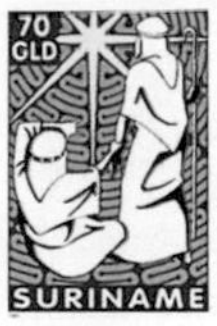

362 Shepherds and Star of Bethlehem

1995. Christmas. Multicoloured.

1646	70g. Type **362**	50	45
1647	135g. Joseph with Mary on donkey	1·10	95
1648	295g. Three wise men bearing gifts	2·40	2·10
1649	1000g. Wise men adoring child Jesus (horiz)	8·00	7·00
MS1650	70×48 mm. No. 1649	8·50	8·50

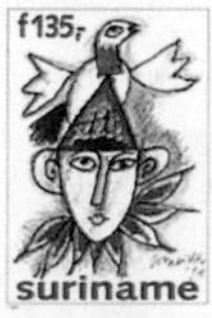

363 Jester and Bird

1995. Paintings by Corneille. Multicoloured.

1651	135g. Type **363**	1·50	1·30
1652	615g. Jester and cat	6·75	5·75

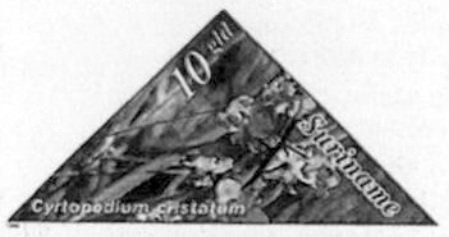

364 "Cyrtopodium cristatum"

1996. Flowers. Multicoloured.

1653	10g. Type **364**	25	20
1654	10g. "Epidendrum cristatum"	25	20
1655	75g. "Cochleanthes guianensis"	60	55
1656	75g. "Otostylis lepida"	60	55
1657	135g. "Catasetum longifolium"	1·20	1·10
1658	135g. "Rudolfiella aurantiaca"	1·20	1·10
1659	250g. "Encyclia granitica"	2·20	1·90
1660	250g. "Maxillaria splendens"	2·20	1·90
1661	300g. "Brassia caudata"	2·75	2·30
1662	300g. "Catasetum macrocarpum"	2·75	2·30
1663	750g. "Maxillaria rufescens"	6·75	5·75
1664	750g. "Vanilla grandiflora"	6·75	5·75

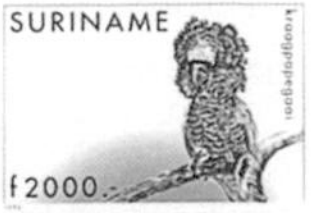

365 Hawk-headed Parrot

1996

1665	**365**	2000g. multicoloured	17·00	15·00

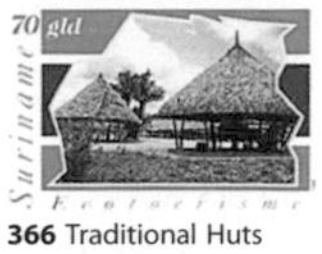

366 Traditional Huts

1996. Eco-tourism. Multicoloured.

1666	70g. Type **366**	60	55
1667	70g. Butterfly on leaf	60	55
1668	135g. Men in traditional costumes	1·20	1·10
1669	135g. Woman hand-spinning	1·20	1·10

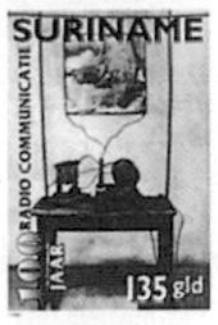

367 Radio Apparatus

1996. Centenary of Guglielmo Marconi's Wireless-telegraph. Multicoloured.

1670	135g. Type **367**	1·50	1·30
1671	615g. Marconi and world map (horiz)	6·75	5·75

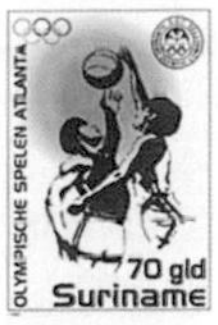

368 Basketball

1996. Olympic Games, Atlanta. Multicoloured.

1672	70g. Type **368**	75	65
1673	135g. Running	1·50	1·30
1674	195g. Badminton	2·10	1·80
1675	200g. Swimming	2·20	1·90
1676	900g. Cycling	9·75	8·50
1677	1000g. Hurdling	11·00	9·50

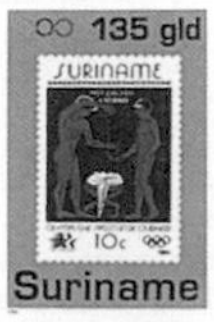

369 10c. Stamp

1996. Olymphilex 96 Sports Stamps Exhibition, Atlanta. Sheet 100×72 mm containing T **369** and similar vert design showing 1984 Olympic stamps. Multicoloured.

MS1678	135g. Type **369**; 865g. 45c. stamp	12·00	12·00

1996. Birds. As T **360**. Multicoloured.

1679	75g. Green kingfisher	60	55
1680	160g. Bat falcon	1·20	1·10
1681	1765g. Red-legged honeycreeper	13·50	11·50

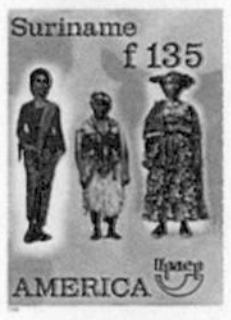

370 Women

1996. America. Traditional Costumes. Multicoloured.

1682	135g. Type **370**	1·50	1·30
1683	990g. Young women	11·00	9·50

Nos. 1682/3 were issued together, *se-tenant*, forming a composite design.

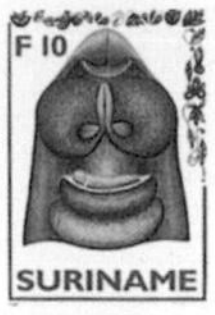

371 Mother praying over Child in Crib

1996. Christmas. Multicoloured.

1684	10g. Type **371**	25	20
1685	70g. Mother kneeling beside child	85	75
1686	135g. Mother with backpack kneeling beside "eye" on mouth/cushion	1·50	1·30
1687	285g. Mother playing with child on floor	3·25	2·75
1688	750g. Mother and child rocking on floor	8·50	7·50
MS1689	100×72 mm. No. 1688	8·50	8·50

1996. Nos. 1603/6 surch.

1690	50g. on 250g. mult (No. 1603)	1·10	95
1691	50g. on 250g. mult (No. 1604)	1·10	95
1692	100g. on 300g. mult (No. 1605)	1·80	1·60
1693	100g. on 300g. mult (No. 1606)	1·80	1·60

1996. No value expressed. Nos. 1648/9 optd **Port Paye**.

1694	(–) on 295g. multicoloured	2·40	2·10
1695	(–) on 1000g. multicoloured	2·40	2·10

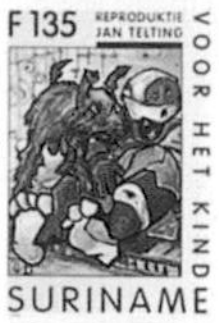

373 Brown Dog and Injured Boy

1996. Child Welfare. Paintings by Jan Telting. Multicoloured.

1696	135g. Type **373**	1·50	1·30
1697	865g. White dog and injured boy	9·75	8·50

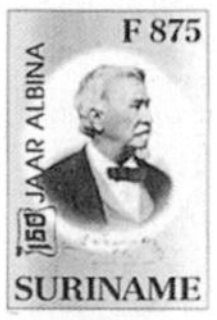

374 August Kappier (founder)

1996. 150th Anniv of Town of Albina.

1698	**374**	875g. multicoloured	9·75	8·50

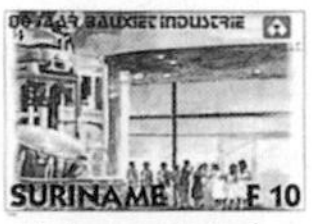

375 Inauguration of Aluminium Smelter, Paranam, 1965

1996. 80th Anniv of Bauxite Industry. Paintings by Michel Pawiroredjo. Multicoloured.

1699	10g. Type **375**	25	10
1700	70g. Drilling blasting holes, Moengo, 1947	85	75
1701	130g. Labourers' huts, Moengo, 1919	1·50	1·30
1702	150g. Loading "Tarpon" with alumina, Paranam, 1995	1·70	1·50
1703	160g. Construction of dam and power station, 1960	1·80	1·60
1704	730g. "Moengo" (schooner), 1922	8·00	7·00

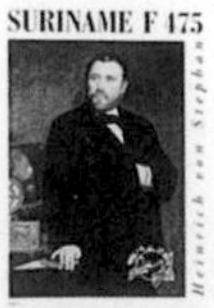

376 Von Stephan

1997. Death Centenary of Heinrich von Stephan (founder of U.P.U.).

1705	**376**	275g. multicoloured	3·00	2·75
1706	**376**	475g. multicoloured	5·50	4·75

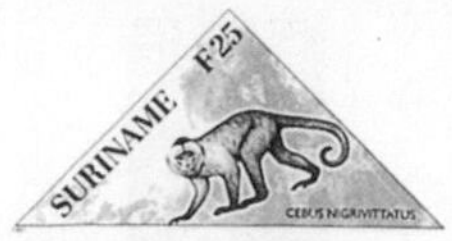

377 Weeper Capuchin ("Cebus nigrivittatus")

1997. Primates. Multicoloured.

1707	25g. Type **377**	25	20
1708	25g. Black-capped capuchin ("Cebus apella")	25	20
1709	75g. Yellow-handed marmoset ("Saguinus midas")	85	75
1710	75g. Black spider monkey ("Ateles paniscus")	85	75
1711	100g. Black-handed spider monkey ("Ateles geoffroyi panamensis")	1·10	95
1712	100g. Black-handed spider monkey ("Ateles geoffroyi frontatus")	1·10	95
1713	275g. Bald uakari ("Cacajao calvus")	3·00	2·75
1714	275g. Hendee's woolly monkey ("Lagothrix flavicauda")	3·00	2·75
1715	300g. Bare-faced tamarin ("Saguinus bicolor")	3·25	2·75
1716	300g. Cotton-headed tamarin ("Saguinus oedipus")	3·25	2·75
1717	725g. Red howler monkey ("Alouatta seniculus")	8·00	7·00
1718	725g. Common squirrel monkey ("Saimiri sciureus")	8·00	7·00

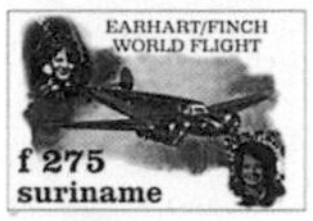

378 Earhart, Airplane and Finch

1997. Linda Finch's Reconstruction of Amelia Earhart's Last Flight.

1719	**378**	275g. multicoloured	3·25	2·75

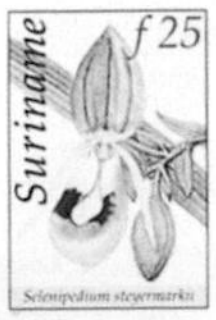

379 "Selenipedium steyermarkii"

1997. Orchids. Multicoloured.

1720	25g. Type **379**	25	10
1721	50g. "Phragmipedium schlimii"	50	45
1722	75g. "Criosanthes arietina"	85	75
1723	200g. "Cypripedium margaritaceum"	2·30	2·00
1724	775g. "Paphiopedilum gratrixianum"	8·50	7·50

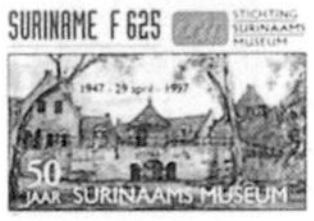

380 Museum

1997. 50th Anniv of Surinam Museum.

1725	**380**	625g. multicoloured	6·75	5·75

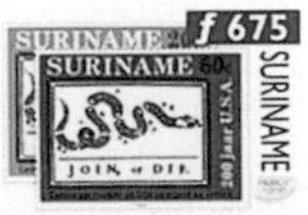

381 Surinam 1976 U.S. Bicentennial Stamps

1997. Pacific 97 International Stamp Exhibition, San Francisco. Sheet 72×55 mm.

MS1726	**381** 675g. multicoloured	7·25	7·25

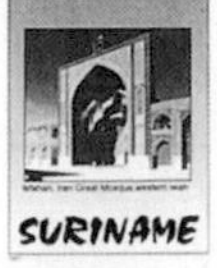

382 Great Mosque, Isfahan, Iran

1997. Mosques. Multicoloured.

1727	50g. Type **382**	50	45
1728	125g. Dome of the Rock, Jerusalem	1·30	1·20
1729	175g. Ulugh Beg's Mosque, Samarkand, Uzbekistan	1·80	1·60
1730	225g. Taj Mahal, Agra, India	2·40	2·10
1731	275g. Mosque on Keizerstraat, Paramaribo, Surinam	3·00	2·75
1732	325g. Suleiman Mosque, Istanbul, Turkey	3·75	3·25
MS1733	60×75 mm. No. 1730	4·00	4·00

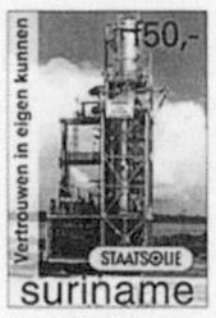

383 Tower

1997. 17th Anniv of State Oil Company. Multicoloured.

1734	50g. Type **383**	50	45
1735	125g. Oil derrick and butterfly	1·30	1·20
1736	275g. Tank	3·25	2·75
1737	275g. Pressure gauge in field	3·25	2·75

1997. Birds. As T **360**. Multicoloured.

1738	50g. Spectacled owl	50	45
1739	125g. Rufous pigeon	1·30	1·20
1740	275g. Blaack-crested antshrike	3·00	2·75
1741	3150g. Red-crested finch	37·00	32·00

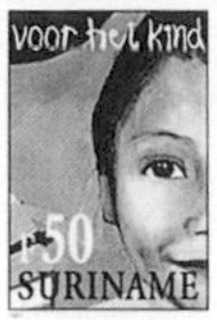

384 Child's Face (left side)

1997. Child Welfare. Multicoloured.

1742	50g. Type **384**	50	45
1743	100g. Child's face (right side)	1·10	95
1744	175g. Child with shoulder-length hair (left side)	1·80	1·60
1745	225g. Child with shoulder-length hair (right side)	2·40	2·10
1746	350g. Faces of the two children	4·00	3·50
MS1747	50×72 mm. 675g. Heads and shoulders of the two children	7·25	7·25

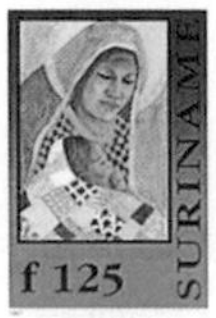

385 Madonna and Child

1997. Christmas. Multicoloured.

1748	125g. Type **385**	1·30	1·20
1749	225g. Children and baby	2·40	2·10
1750	450g. Angel and candle	5·00	4·25
MS1751	72×50 mm. 675g. Children carol singing (horiz)	7·25	7·25

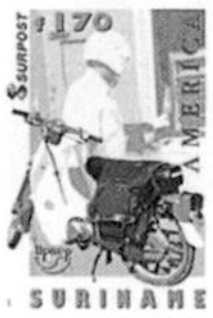

386 Motor Cycle Courier

1997. America. Postal Workers. Multicoloured.

1752	170g. Type **386**	1·60	1·40
1753	230g. Postal worker carrying parcel	2·10	1·80

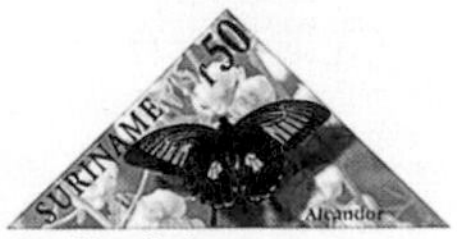

387 "Alcandor"

1998. Butterflies. Multicoloured.

1754	50g. Type **387**	50	45
1755	50g. "Achilles"	50	45
1756	75g. "Alphenor"	75	65
1757	75g. "Ceres"	75	65
1758	100g. "Cecropia"	1·10	95
1759	100g. "Helenor"	1·10	95
1760	175g. "Promothea"	1·80	1·60
1761	175g. "Cassiae"	1·80	1·60
1762	275g. "Ino"	3·00	2·75
1763	275g. "Phidippus"	3·00	2·75
1764	725g. "Palamedes"	8·00	7·00
1765	725g. "Helenor"	8·00	7·00

1998. Birds. As T **360**. Multicoloured.

1767	50g. Blue-headed parrot	50	45
1768	225g. Bicoloured sparrowhawk falcon	2·40	2·10
1769	2425g. Red-fronted woodpecker (vert)	24·00	21·00
1770	3800g. Green-backed heron	27·00	23·00

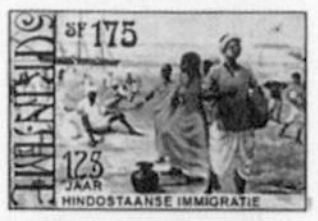

388 Immigrants and Lala Rooch (painting)

1998. 125th Anniv of Arrival of First Hindu Immigrants. Multicoloured.

1771	175g. Type **388**	1·80	1·60
1772	200g. "Baba and Mai" (statue) (first immigrants from India)	2·30	2·00

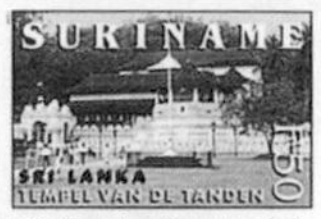

389 Tanden Temple, Sri Lanka

1998. Temples. Multicoloured.

1773	50g. Type **389**	50	45
1774	75g. Golden Pagoda, Myanmar (vert)	75	65
1775	275g. Swayambhunath, Nepal (vert)	3·00	2·50
1776	325g. Borobudur, Indonesia	3·25	2·75
1777	400g. Phra Kaew, Thailand (vert)	4·00	3·50
1778	450g. Peking, China (vert)	5·00	4·25
MS1779	50×72 mm. 675g. Head of Buddha, Borobudur (vert)	7·25	7·25

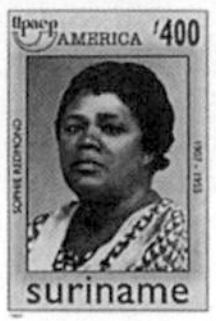

390 Sophie Redmond

1998. America. Famous Women. Multicoloured.

1780	400g. Type **390**	4·25	3·75
1781	1000g. Grace Ruth Schneiders-Howard	11·00	9·50

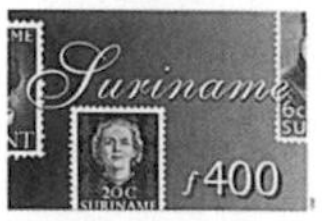

391 1951 20c. Queen Juliana Stamp

1998. International Stamp Exhibition, The Hague, Netherlands. Multicoloured.

1782	400g. Type **391**	4·25	3·75
1783	800g. 1946 12½c. Queen Wilhelmina stamp	8·50	7·50
MS1784	72×50 mm. 2400g. 1933 6c. William I of Orange stamp	27·00	27·00

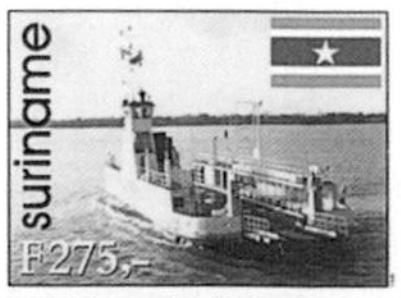

392 "Canawaima" (ferry)

1998. Surinam–Guyana Ferry.

1785	**392**	275g. multicoloured	3·00	2·50
1786	**392**	400g. multicoloured	4·50	3·75

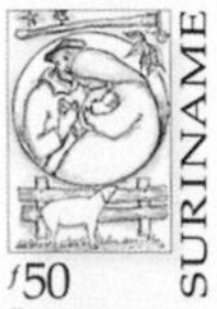

393 Holy Family

1998. Christmas. Multicoloured.

1787	50g. Type **393**	25	10
1788	325g. Angel with banner, Holy Family and stable of animals	2·40	2·10
1789	400g. Holy family and animals	3·00	2·75
1790	1225g. Nativity	9·25	8·00
MS1791	50×69 mm. 1400g. Close-up of central motif as Type **393**	11·00	11·00

394 Boy flying Kite

1998. Child Welfare. Multicoloured.
1792	375g. Type **394**	2·75	2·30
1793	400g. Girl flying kite	3·00	2·75
1794	1225g. Child holding kite	9·25	8·00

395 Mother and Child and Food

1998. 50th Anniv of W.H.O. "Mother and Child Care". Multicoloured.
| 1795 | 400g. Type **395** | 3·00 | 2·75 |
| 1796 | 1000g. Mother and baby | 8·00 | 7·00 |

396 "Heliconia pastazae"

1999. Flora. Multicoloured.
1797	50g. Type **396**	10	10
1798	50g. "Heliconia caribaea 'Kawauchi'"	10	10
1799	200g. "Heliconia rostrata"	85	75
1800	200g. "Heliconia 'Sexy Pink'"	85	75
1801	300g. "Heliconia collinsiana"	1·30	1·20
1802	300g. "Heliconia wagneriana"	1·30	1·20
1803	400g. "Heliconia 'Jaded Forest'"	1·80	1·60
1804	400g. "Heliconia 'Bihai-nappi'"	1·80	1·60
1805	750g. "Heliconia 'Golden Torch'"	3·25	2·75
1806	750g. "Heliconia latispatha 'Red Yellow Gyro'"	3·25	2·75
1807	1300g. "Heliconia 'Sexy Pink' (different)"	3·50	3·00
1808	1300g. "Heliconia Nappi Yellow"	5·50	5·00

397 Katwijk Plantation

1999. Plantation Houses.
1809	**397**	75g. black	25	10
1810	-	300g. purple and black	1·30	1·20
1811	-	400g. yellow and black	1·80	1·60
1812	-	2225g. blue and black	9·75	8·50
DESIGNS: 300g. Sorgvliet Plantation; 400g. Peperpot Plantation; 2225g. Speiringshoek Plantation.

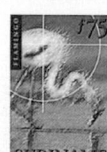

398 Greater Flamingo

1999. Endangered Species. Multicoloured.
1813	75g. Type **398**	20	10
1814	375g. Orang-utan	65	55
1815	450g. Elephant	90	75
1816	500g. Whale	1·00	90
1817	850g. Frog	1·50	1·30
1818	900g. Rhinoceros	1·80	1·50
1819	1600g. Giant panda	3·25	2·75
1820	7250g. Tiger	19·00	17·00

399 Coppename Bridge

1999. Coppename Bridge.
| 1821 | **399** | 850g. green, lt grn & blk | 1·50 | 1·30 |
| 1822 | **399** | 2250g. blue, dp bl & blk | 4·00 | 3·50 |

400 STINASU Emblem

1999. Conservation. Multicoloured.
1823	850g. Type **400** (30th anniv of Surinam Nature Protection Society)	1·50	1·30
1824	2650g. Map and rainforest (first anniv of Surinam Central Forest Nature Reserve)	4·50	3·75
MS1825 75×72 mm. Nos. 1823/4		6·25	6·25

1999. Birds. As T **360**. Multicoloured.
| 1826 | 1000g. Blue-grey tanager | 1·90 | 1·70 |
| 1827 | 5500g. Wattled jacana | 10·50 | 9·00 |

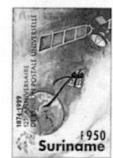

401 Earth, Letter and Satellite

1999. 125th Anniv of Universal Postal Union. Multicoloured.
| 1828 | 950g. Type **401** | 1·80 | 1·50 |
| 1829 | 1000g. Satellite, letter and ringed planet | 1·90 | 1·70 |

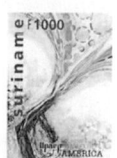

402 Gun firing Streamers and Flowers

1999. America. A Millennium without Arms. Multicoloured.
| 1830 | 1000g. Type **402** | 1·90 | 1·70 |
| 1831 | 2250g. Flowers | 4·00 | 3·50 |
Nos. 1830/1 were issued together, *se-tenant*, forming a composite design.

403 Star over Stable

1999. Christmas. Multicoloured.
1832	500g. Type **403**	1·00	90
1833	850g. Christmas tree	1·50	1·30
1834	900g. Angel	1·80	1·50
1835	1000g. Candle	1·90	1·70
MS1836 48×70 mm. 2275g. Nativity		4·25	4·25

404 Child's Painting

1999. Child Welfare.
1837	**404**	1100g. multicoloured	2·00	1·80
1838	-	1400g. multicoloured	2·50	2·20
1839	-	1600g. multicoloured	3·00	2·75
MS1840 76×54 mm. No. 1839		3·25	3·25
DESIGNS: 1400g. to 1600g. Different children's paintings.

405 Tennis Players, House and Car (Tahirih van Kanten)

2000. "Stampin' the Future". Children's Drawings. Multicoloured.
| 1841 | 1100g. Type **405** | 1·90 | 1·70 |
| 1842 | 2500g. Sunflower (Tirsa Braaf) (vert) | 5·00 | 4·50 |

406 One Way Sign

2000. Traffic Signs (1st series).
| 1843 | **406** | 2000g. multicoloured | 4·00 | 3·50 |
See also Nos. 1858, 1861, 1868, 1874, 1903, 1917, 1921, 1936, 1937, 1952, 1960, 1976, 1994, 2034, 2035 and MS2064.

407 Watermelon

2000. Tropical Fruit. Multicoloured.
1844	50g. Type **407** (postage)	15	10
1845	50g. Papaya (*Carica papaya*)	15	10
1846	175g. Mango (*Mangifera indica*)	40	35
1847	175g. Mangosteen (*Garcinia mangostana*)	40	35
1848	200g. Banana (*Musa nana*)	50	45
1849	200g. Grapefruit (*Citrus paradisi*)	50	45
1850	250g. *Punika granatum*	55	50
1851	250g. Pineapple (*Ananas comosus*)	55	50
1852	325g. Coconut (*Cocos nucifera*)	75	65
1853	325g. Giant granadilla (*Passiflora quadrangularis*)	75	65
1854	5000g. Sweet orange (*Citrus sinensis*) (air)	11·00	9·50
1855	5000g. Avocado (*Persea gratissima*)	11·00	9·50

408 Red-billed Whistling Duck

2000. Birds. Multicoloured.
| 1856 | 1100g. Type **408** | 2·40 | 2·10 |
| 1857 | 4425g. Ringed kingfisher | 9·50 | 8·50 |

409 Double Bend Sign

2000. Traffic Signs (2nd series).
| 1858 | **409** | 2000g. multicoloured | 4·50 | 3·75 |

410 Bridge over Suriname River

2000.
| 1859 | **410** | 1100g. multicoloured | 2·40 | 2·10 |
| 1860 | **410** | 1700g. multicoloured | 3·75 | 3·25 |

411 No Overtaking

2000. Traffic Signs (3rd series).
| 1861 | **411** | 2000g. multicoloured | 4·50 | 3·75 |

412 1000g. and 2500g. "Stampin the Future" Stamps

2000. World Stamp Expo 2000, Anaheim, California. Sheet 72×50 mm.
| MS1862 **412** 3575g. multicoloured | | 7·50 | 7·50 |

413 Running

2000. Olympic Games, Sydney. Multicoloured.
1863	1100g. Type **413**	2·40	2·10
1864	1100g. Football	2·40	2·10
1865	3900g. Swimming	8·50	7·50
1866	3900g. Tennis	8·50	7·50
MS1867 82×82 mm. 2500g. As No. 1865; 2500g. As No. 1864		10·00	10·00

414 Roundabout Ahead

2000. Traffic Signs (4th series).
| 1868 | **414** | 2000g. multicoloured | 4·50 | 3·75 |

415 Foot stamping on "AIDS"

2000. America. AIDS Awareness Campaign. Multicoloured.
| 1869 | 1100g. Type **415** | 2·50 | 2·20 |
| 1870 | 6400g. Stylized figures holding condoms (vert) | 12·50 | 11·00 |

416 Star of Bethelehem

2000. Christmas. Multicoloured.
1871	1100g. Type **416**	2·10	1·90
1872	3900g. Mary and Jesus	8·00	7·00
MS1873 72×51 mm. 3000g. Three Kings bearing gifts		6·00	6·00

417 No Parking

2000. Traffic (5th series).
| 1874 | **417** | 2000g. multicoloured | 4·50 | 3·75 |

418 Currency Notes

2000. 25th Anniv of International Philatelic Agency for Surinam Stamps. Multicoloured.
1875	125g. Type **418**	25	10
1876	5900g. Stamps	9·75	8·50
MS1877 75×73 mm. Nos. 1875/7		10·50	10·50

419 Emblem

2000. 25th Anniv of Independence.
| 1878 | **419** | 1100g. multicoloured | 1·90 | 1·70 |
| 1879 | **419** | 4900g. multicoloured | 8·25 | 7·25 |

420 Toddler

2000. Child Care. Multicoloured.
1880	1100g. Type **420**	1·90	1·70
1881	3900g. Baby at breast	7·00	6·00
MS1882	72×51 mm. 2000g. Baby	3·50	3·50

2000. Nos. 1551/2 surch **F 3100.**
| 1883 | 3100g. on 35c. multicoloured | 5·00 | 4·50 |
| 1884 | 3100g. on 35c. multicoloured | 5·00 | 4·50 |

2001. Nos. 1551/2 surch **F 1000.**
| 1885 | 1000g. on 25c. multicoloured | 1·90 | 1·70 |
| 1886 | 1000g. on 25c. multicoloured | 1·90 | 1·70 |

423 Silver-beaked
Tanager (*Ramphocelus
carbo*)

2001. Birds. Multicoloured.
1887	50g Type **423** (postage)	15	10
1888	50g Yellow-bellied elaenia (*Elaenia flavogaster*)	15	10
1889	175g Green-backed heron (*Butorides striatus*)	25	20
1890	175g Black-throated mango (*Athracothorax nigricollis*)	25	20
1891	200g Everglade kite (*Rostrha-mus sociabilis*)	30	30
1892	200g. *Veniliornis sanguineus*	30	30
1893	250g. Spangled cotinga (*Cot-inga cayana*)	40	35
1894	250g. *Bucco tamatia*	40	35
1895	825g. *Tapera naevia*	1·30	1·10
1896	825g. Green aracari (*Pteroglos-sus viridis*)	1·30	1·10
1897	7500g. Pompadour cotinga (*Xipholena punicea*) (air)	11·50	10·00
1898	7500g. *Caprimulgus nigrescens*	11·50	10·00

424 Male and
Female Symbols

2001. United Nations Women's Rights Campaign ("A life
free from violence"). Multicoloured.
| 1899 | 1400g. Type **424** | 1·90 | 1·70 |
| 1900 | 4600g. Woman | 7·00 | 6·00 |

425 Musician
(Bhoelai
Surender
Kumar)

2001. Youth Philately. Winning Entries in Children's
Design a Stamp Competition. Multicoloured.
| 1901 | 650g. Type **425** | 1·30 | 1·10 |
| 1902 | 5350g. Children (Sharon Cameron) | 7·50 | 6·50 |

426 Moveable
Bridge

2001. Traffic (6th series).
| 1903 | **426** | 4000g. multicoloured | 5·75 | 5·00 |

427 Collared Plover
(*Charadrius collaris*)

2001. Birds. Multicoloured.
| 1904 | 4500g. Type **427** | 6·25 | 5·50 |
| 1905 | 9000g. Great horned owl (*Bubo virginianus*) | 14·00 | 12·00 |

428 Sapodilla

2001. Fruit. Multicoloured.
1906	150g. Type **428**	25	10
1907	200g. Noni	40	35
1908	800g. Banana	1·30	1·10
1909	1200g. Mopé	1·90	1·70
1910	1700g. Pomerac	2·50	2·20

429 Bishop's House,
Paramaribo

2001. America. Cultural Heritage. Multicoloured.
1911	1700g. Type **429**	2·50	2·20
1912	7300g. Presidential Palace, Paramaribo	11·50	10·00
MS1913	72×75 mm. Nos. 1912/13	14·00	14·00

430 1983 15
cent Stamp

2001. Stamp Day. Multicoloured.
1914	3750g. Type **430**	7·00	6·00
1915	5250g. 1892 25 cent stamp	9·50	8·25
MS1916	75×72 mm. Nos. 1914/15	16·00	16·00

431 No Farm
Vehicles

2001. Traffic (7th series).
| 1917 | **431** | 4000g. multicoloured | 5·75 | 5·00 |

432 People

2001. Christmas (1700g.). Children and Sport (5000g.).
Multicoloured.
1918	1700g. Type **432**	2·50	2·20
1919	5000g. Judo (33×23 mm)	7·50	6·50
MS1920	72×80 mm. Nos. 1918/19	10·00	10·00

433 Pedestrian
Crossing

2001. Traffic (8th series).
| 1921 | **433** | 4000g. multicoloured | 5·75 | 5·00 |

2001. Nos. 1555/6 surch **SF 2500.**
| 1922 | 2500g. on 50c. multicoloured | 3·75 | 3·25 |
| 1923 | 2500g. on 50c. multicoloured | 3·75 | 3·25 |

435 Hawk-headed Parrot
(*Deroptyus accipitrinus*)

2002. Birds. Multicoloured.
1924	150g. Type **435** (postage)	25	10
1925	150g. *Amazona achrocephala*	25	10
1926	200g. Red-bellied macaw (*Ara manilata*)	30	10
1927	200g. *Amazona dufresniana*	30	10
1928	800g. Chestnut-fronted macaw (*Ara severa*)	1·30	1·10
1929	800g. Black-headed caique (*Pionites melanocaphaia*)	1·30	1·10
1930	1200g. Red-shouldered macaw (*Ara nobilis*)	1·90	1·70
1931	1200g. *Pionus fuscus* (inscr "fiscus")	1·90	1·70
1932	1700g. Green-winged macaw (*Ara chloroptera*)	2·75	2·40
1933	1700g. Caicca parrot (*Pionop-sitta caicca*)	2·75	2·40
1934	5325g. Scarlet macaw (*Ara macao*) (air)	7·50	6·50
1935	5325g. Mealy amazon (*Ama-zona farinose*)	7·50	6·50

436 Give Way

2002. Traffic (9th series).
| 1936 | **436** | 4000g. multicoloured | 5·75 | 5·00 |

437 No U-Turn

2002. Traffic (10th series).
| 1937 | **437** | 4000g. multicoloured | 5·75 | 5·00 |

438 Man
wearing Fez and
Shell Decoration

2002. Traditional Costumes. Multicoloured.
1938	150g. Type **438**	25	10
1939	150g. Woman wearing strap-less dress and elaborate headdress	25	10
1940	200g. Man holding stick	30	10
1941	200g. Woman wearing dress with straps	30	10
1942	800g. Man's Chinese costume	1·30	1·10
1943	800g. Women's Chinese costume	1·30	1·10
1944	1200g. Man wearing white trousers	1·90	1·70
1945	1200g. Woman wearing turban	1·90	1·70
1946	1700g. Man wearing beaded sash	2·75	2·40
1947	1700g. Woman wearing beaded dress	2·75	2·40
1948	4950g. Man wearing shirt and scarf	7·50	6·50
1949	4950g. Woman wearing sari	7·50	6·50

2002. Nos. 1561/2 surch as **SF 3750.**
| 1950 | 3750g. on 220c multicoloured | 3·75 | 3·25 |
| 1951 | 3750g. on 220c multicoloured | 3·75 | 3·25 |

440 Children
Crossing

2002. Traffic (11th series).
| 1952 | **440** | 4000g. multicoloured | 5·75 | 5·00 |

441 Royal Flycatcher
(*Onychorhynchus
coronatus*)

2002. Birds. Multicoloured.
| 1953 | 5000g. Type **441** | 7·50 | 6·50 |
| 1954 | 8500g. *Donacobius atricapillus* | 12·50 | 11·00 |

442 1942 2½ cent
Netherlands Stamp

2002. Amphilex 2002 International Stamp Exhibition,
Amsterdam. Multicoloured.
1955	1700g. Type **442**	2·50	2·20
1956	6800g. 1899 30 cent Nether-lands stamp	8·75	7·75
MS1957	72×75 mm. Nos. 1955/6 but with background colours reversed	11·50	11·50

443 Head and Question
Mark

2002. America. Literacy Campaign.
| 1958 | 1700g. black and red | 2·50 | 2·20 |
| 1959 | 7300g. blue, red and black | 10·00 | 8·75 |
DESIGNS: Type **443**; 7300g. Text and signature cross.

444 Trains
Crossing

2002. Traffic (12th series).
| 1960 | **444** | 4000g. multicoloured | 5·75 | 5·00 |

445 Father Christmas
and Cut-out Clothes

2002. Christmas. Multicoloured.
1961	1700g. Type **445**	2·50	2·20
1962	5000g. Tree, decorations and presents	7·00	6·00
MS1963	72×75 mm. Nos. 1959/60 but with background colours changed	9·75	9·75

2002. Nos. 1236/7 surch.
1963a	2500g. on 100c. multicoloured	3·75	3·25
1963b	2500g. on 100c. multicoloured	3·75	3·25
1963c	2750g. on 175c. multicoloured	4·50	3·75
1963d	2750g. on 175c. multicoloured	4·50	3·75

446 *Falco
deiroleucas*

2003. Birds (1st series). Multicoloured.
1964	150g. Type **446**	25	10
1965	150g. *Lophornis ornatus*	25	10
1966	200g. *Touit purpurata*	30	10
1967	200g. *Thalurania furcata*	30	10
1968	800g. *Myrmeciza ferruginea*	1·30	1·10
1969	800g. *Pteroglossus aracari*	1·30	1·10
1970	1200g. *Cotinga cotinga*	1·90	1·70
1971	1200g. *Granatellus pelzelni*	1·90	1·70
1972	1700g. *Euphonia musica*	2·75	2·40
1973	1700g. *Pitangus lector*	2·75	2·40
1974	4950g. *Cacicus haemorrhous*	7·50	6·50
1975	4950g. *Columba speciosa*	7·50	6·50
See also Nos. 1995/6, 2065/76, 2125/36, 2156/67, 2198
and 2239/7.

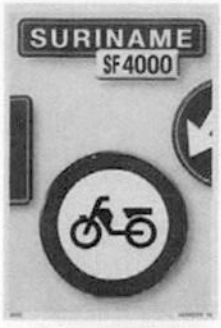

447 No Cycles

2003. Traffic (13th series).

1976	**447**	4000g. multicoloured	5·50	4·75

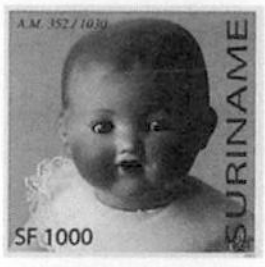

448 Doll (1930 (inscr "1030"))

2003. Dolls. Multicoloured.

1977	1000g. Type **448**	1·60	1·40
1978	1000g. Blonde dressed doll (1892)	1·60	1·40
1979	1000g. Dark haired doll with lace collar (1895)	1·60	1·40
1980	1000g. Dark haired doll with fringe and frilled collar (1895)	1·60	1·40
1981	1000g. Dark haired doll with mob cap (1900)	1·60	1·40
1982	1000g. Blonde doll (1900)	1·60	1·40
1983	1000g. Blonde boy doll (1905)	1·60	1·40
1984	1000g. Red haired doll (1905)	1·60	1·40
1985	1000g. Doll with white cap (1905)	1·60	1·40
1986	1000g. Doll with lace trimmed hood (1907)	1·60	1·40
1987	1000g. Dark haired boy doll (1920)	1·60	1·40
1988	1000g. Red haired doll with green and red clothes (1910)	1·60	1·40

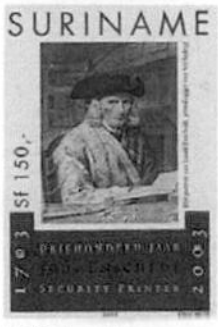

449 Izaak Enschedé

2003. 300th Anniv of Enschede Printing House. Multicoloured.

1989	150g. Type **449**	25	10
1990	800g. Original printing house (horiz)	1·00	90
1991	1700g. First Suriname stamp	2·50	2·20
1992	3850g. First banknote (horiz)	5·00	4·50
MS1993	57×40 mm. 7500g. As No. 1989	10·50	10·50

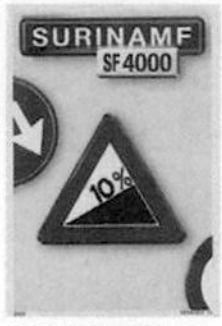

450 Hill 10% Incline

2003. Traffic (14th series).

1994	**450**	4000g. multicoloured	5·50	4·75

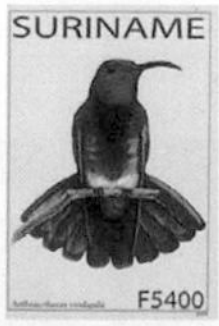

451 *Anthracothorax viridigula*

2003. Birds (2nd series). Multicoloured.

1995	5400g. Type **451**	7·50	6·50
1996	6600g. *Campephilus melanoleucos*	9·50	8·25

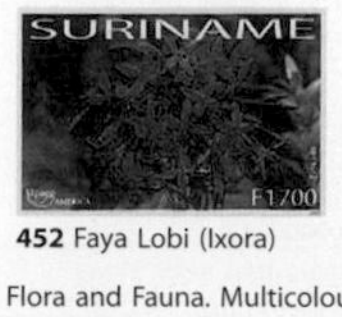

452 Faya Lobi (Ixora)

2003. America. Flora and Fauna. Multicoloured.

1997	1700g. Type **452**	2·50	2·20
1998	8500g. Puma	12·50	11·00
MS1999	97×50 mm. Nos. 1997/8	15·00	15·00

2003. Nos. 1236/7 surch **SF 3500**.

2000	3500g. on 1c. on 5c. orange and blue	3·75	3·25
2001	3500g. on 1c. on 5c. green, crimson and blue	3·75	3·25

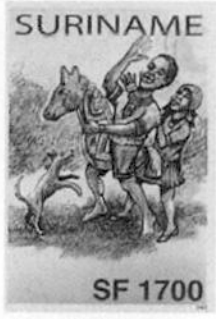

454 Children Playing

2003. Child Care. Christmas. Multicoloured.

2002	1700g. Type **454**	2·50	2·20
2003	5300g. Woman holding candle	8·25	7·25
MS2004	50×109 mm. Nos. 2002/3	11·00	11·00

2003. Nos. 1238/9 surch **SF 3500**.

2005	3500g. on 2c. on 10c. multicoloured	3·75	3·25
2006	3500g. on 2c. on 10c. multicoloured	3·75	3·25

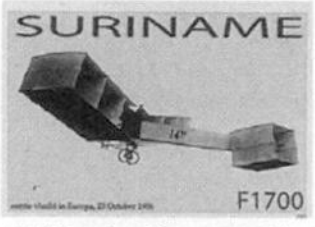

455 Santos Dumont *14 bis* Canard Biplane

2003. Centenary of Powered Flight. Multicoloured.

2007	1700g. Type **455**	2·50	2·20
2008	5300g. Replica of Richard Pearse's aircraft (first flight–31 March 1903)	8·25	7·25
MS2009	72×75 mm. Nos. 2007/8	11·00	11·00

Note: On 1 January 2004, the Surinam Dollar replaced the Surinam Guilder as the new monetary system. The new currency re-valued the previous gulden system to a ratio of 1000 guldens per 1 Surinam Dollar. Some stamps were issued after that date inscribed in the old currency and are listed as such.

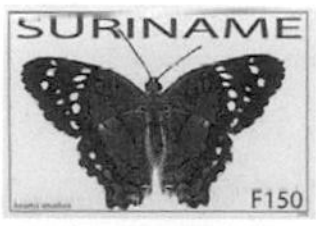

456 *Anartia amathea*

2004. Butterflies (1st series) (old currency). Multicoloured.

2010	150g. Type **456**	25	10
2011	150g. *Vanessa carye*	25	10
2012	200g. *Papilio Demetrius*	30	10
2013	200g. *Precis Octavia*	30	10
2014	800g. *Papilio blumei*	75	65
2015	800g. *Papilio aristodemus ponceanus* (inscr "aritodemus")	75	65
2016	1200g. *Zerynthia rumina*	1·30	1·10
2017	1200g. *Parides gundlachianus*	1·30	1·10
2018	1700g. *Ornithoptera priamus*	1·90	1·70
2019	1700g. *Lyropteryx apollonian*	1·90	1·70
2020	(L) *Agrias narcissus*	10·50	9·25
2021	(L) *Elzunia bonplandii*	10·50	9·25

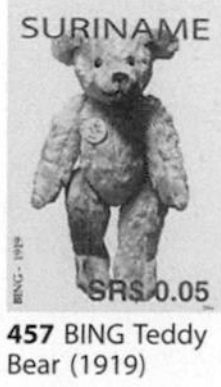

457 BING Teddy Bear (1919)

2004. Teddy Bears (1st series) (new currency). Multicoloured.

2022	5c. Type **457** (postage)	25	10
2023	5c. Steiff "Teddy Clown" (1926)	25	10
2024	15c. Steiff "Teddy Girl" (1905)	30	15
2025	15c. Steiff (1905)	30	15
2026	20c. Steiff "Elliot" (1907)	40	30
2027	20c. Ideal "Aloysius" (1907)	40	30
2028	45c. Steiff (1936)	55	45
2029	45c. Steiff "Zotty" (1951)	55	45
2030	80c. Steiff (1910)	95	85
2031	80c. Steiff "Titanic" (1912)	95	85
2032	(K) Steiff "Berlin" (1985) (air)	12·50	11·00
2033	(K) Aux Nations Mother and Baby (1993)	12·50	11·00

See also Nos. 2092/2103.

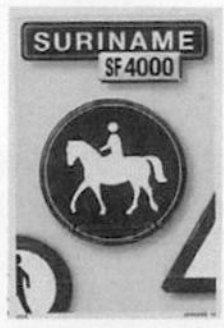

458 Horses Crossing

2004. Traffic (15 series) (old currency).

2034	**458**	4000g. multicoloured	5·50	4·75

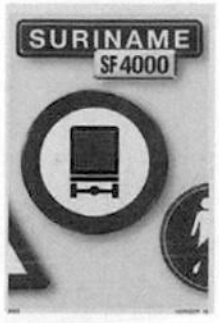

459 No Entry for Large Vehicles

2004. Traffic (16th series) (old currency).

2035	**459**	4000g. multicoloured	5·50	4·75

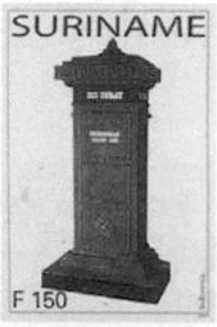

460 Indonesian Mail Box

2004. Mail Boxes (old currency). Designs showing mail boxes from around the world. Multicoloured.

2036	150g. Type **460**	25	10
2037	150g. Brazil	25	10
2038	200g. Macao	30	10
2039	200g. Germany	30	10
2040	800g. Uruguay	75	65
2041	800g. Republic of Korea	75	65
2042	1200g. Sultanate of Oman	1·30	1·10
2043	1200g. Mexico	1·30	1·10
2044	1700g. Australia	1·90	1·70
2045	1700g. Switzerland	1·90	1·70
2046	(K) Hong Kong	12·50	11·00
2047	(K) USA	12·50	11·00

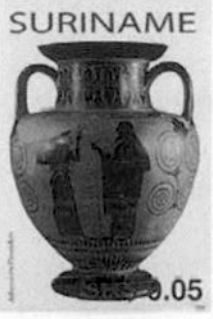

461 Athena and Poseidon on Vase (inscr "Athena en Poseidon")

2004. Olympic Games, Athens (new currency). Designs showing ancient Greek vases. Multicoloured.

2048	5c. Type **461** (postage)	25	10
2049	5c. Charioteer (inscr "Wedren")	25	10
2050	15c. Athena (inscr "Athena Promachus")	30	15
2051	15c. Chariot horses (inscr "Hippodamia ontvoerd door Pelops")	30	15
2052	20c. Musician (inscr "Winnaar Muziekconcours")	40	30
2053	20c. Riders and chariot (inscr "Wedren")	40	30
2054	45c. Gowned figure (inscr "Vaashals: speer-en discuswerpers")	55	45
2055	45c. Four horses (inscr "Wedren vier paarden")	55	45
2056	80c. Heracles fighting lion (inscr "Heracles met leeuw van Nemea")	95	85
2057	80c. Warrior (inscr "Amfoor")	95	85
2058	(M) Woman, deer, musician and seated man (inscr "Winnaar Muziekconcours") (air)	16·00	14·00
2059	(M) Musician on pedestal (inscr "Winnaar Muziekconcours")	16·00	14·00
MS2060	100×72 mm. 2srd. Horse and rider; 3srd. Rear of horse; 5srd. Rider, horse and bird	11·50	11·50

The stamps of **MS**2060 form a composite design of a vase showing horse riders.

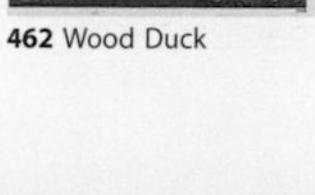

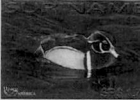

462 Wood Duck

2004. America. Fauna (new currency). Multicoloured.

2061	1srd.70 Type **462**	1·90	1·70
2062	12srd. Great green macaw	12·50	11·00
MS2063	72×75 mm. Nos. 2061/2	16·00	16·00

2004. Traffic (17th series) (old currency). As T **447**, **450** and **458/9**.

MS2064	125×61 mm. 4000g.×4. As Nos. 1976, 1994 and 2034/5	18·00	18·00

2004. Birds (3rd series) (new currency). As T **451**. Multicoloured.

2065	5c. *Chloroceryle India* (postage)	25	10
2066	5c. *Brotogeris chrysopterus* (inscr "chrysoperus")	25	10
2067	15c. *Buteo magnirostris*	30	15
2068	15c. *Buteo albicaudatus*	30	15
2069	20c. *Calliphlox amethystine*	40	30
2070	20c. Inscr "Calliphlox amethystine" (different)	40	30
2071	45c. *Harpagus diodon*	55	45
2072	45c. *Aratinga pertinax*	55	45
2073	80c. *Chloroceryle amazona* (inscr "Chlorocersyle")	95	85
2074	80c. *Galbula galbula*	95	85
2075	(M) *Buteogallus aequinoctialis* (air)	16·00	14·00
2076	(M) *Polyborus plancus*	16·00	14·00

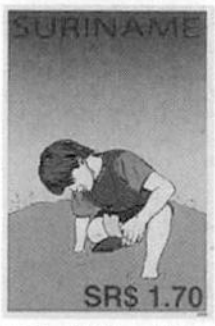

463 Child sailing Boat

2004. Child Care. Christmas (new currency). Multicoloured.

2077	1srd.70 Type **463**	1·90	1·70
2078	7srd.70 Angel and Nativity	8·75	7·75
MS2079	50×109 mm. Nos. 2077/8	11·00	11·00

2005. Teddy Bears (2nd series). As T **457**. Multicoloured.

2092	5c. Blue mohair (1938–52) (postage)	25	10
2093	5c. Musical bear (1937)	25	10
2094	15c. Red mohair (1908)	30	15
2095	15c. Shaggy beige mohair (1908)	30	15
2096	20c. Ally bear (1916)	40	30
2097	20c. The national bear (1917)	40	30
2098	45c. Cowboy (1940s)	55	45
2099	45c. Coronation bear (1953)	55	45
2100	80c. Tumbling bear (1920–30)	95	85
2101	80c. Messenger bear (1923)	95	85
2102	(N) Bear on tricycle (1958) (air)	17·00	15·00
2103	(N) Michi Takahashi (1999)	17·00	15·00

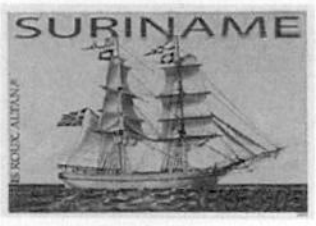

464 *Louis Roux*

2005. Sail Ships. Multicoloured.

2104	5c. Type **464** (postage)	25	10
2105	15c. *Fanerom Eni*	30	15
2106	20c. *Nafsika*	40	30
2107	80c. *Aristeidis Glykas*	95	85
2108	1srd.70 *G D'Esposito*	1·90	1·70
2109	(P) *G D'Esposito* (different) (air)	18·00	15·00

Nos. 2110/21 and Type **465** are vacant.

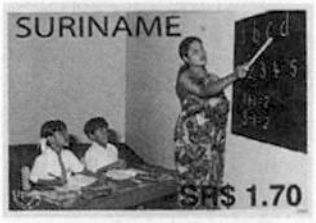

466 Teacher and Pupils

2005. America. Education and Agriculture. Multicoloured.

2122	1srd.70 Type **466**	1·90	1·70
2123	14srd.50 Ploughing with oxen (vert)	14·50	12·50
MS2124	50×72 mm. 14srd. Teacher and pupils at table (vert)	14·00	14·00

2005. Birds (4th series). As T **451**. Multicoloured.

2125	5c. *Porphyrula flavirostris* (postage)	25	10
2126	5c. *Asio clamator*	25	10
2127	15c. *Jacana jacana*	30	15
2128	15c. *Buteo albicaudatus*	30	15
2129	20c. *Touit batavica*	40	30
2130	20c. *Dendrocygna autumnalis*	40	30
2131	80c. *Coccyzus minor*	95	85
2132	80c. *Busarellus nigricollis*	95	85
2133	1srd.80 *Lophostrix cristata*	1·90	1·70
2134	1srd.80 *Otus choliba*	1·90	1·70
2135	(P) *Chrysolampis mosquitus* (air)	18·00	15·00
2136	(P) *Pyrrhura picta*	18·00	15·00

216 Surinam

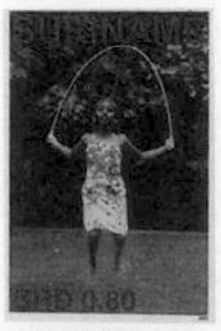
SURINAME
SRD 0,80

467 Girl Skipping

2005. Child Care. Christmas. Multicoloured.

2137	80c. Type **467**	95	85
2138	9srd.50 Boy swinging	11·00	9·75
MS2139	75×72 mm. 5srd.×2, As Nos. 2137/8 but with colour change	11·50	11·50

2005. Nos. 1244/5 surch.

2139a	3srd.50 on 3c. on 50c. multicoloured	3·50	3·00
2139b	3srd.50 on 3c. on 50c. multicoloured	3·50	3·00

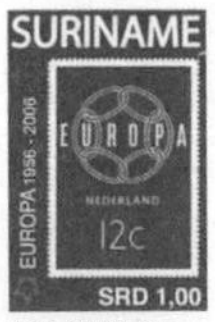
SURINAME
EUROPA 1956 - 2006
EUROPA
NEDERLAND
12c
SRD 1,00

468 1959 12c. Netherland Stamp (As. No. 882)

2006. 50th Anniv of Europa Stamps. Showing stamps of the Netherlands. Multicoloured.

2140	1srd. Type **468**	1·10	1·00
2141	2srd. 1956 25c. (As No. 835)	2·40	2·10
2142	9srd. 1958 12c. (As No. 868)	10·00	8·75
MS2143	125×82 mm. Nos. 2140/2	14·00	14·00

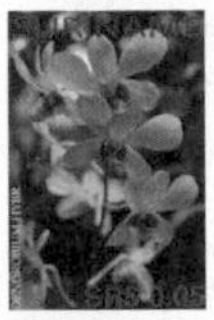

469 *Dendrobium*

2006. Orchids. Multicoloured.

2144	5c. Type **469** (postage)	25	10
2145	5c. *Dendrobium* (white)	25	10
2146	15c. *Phalaenopsis* (several blooms)	30	15
2147	15c. *Phalaenopsis* (two blooms)	30	15
2148	20c. *Vanda sandiana*	40	30
2149	20c. *Vanda* (purple)	40	30
2150	45c. *Dendrobium* (large blooms)	55	45
2151	45c. *Arachnis*	55	45
2152	80c. *Vanda* (small blooms)	95	85
2153	80c. *Vanda* (two spotted blooms)	95	85
2154	(Q) Inscr 'Complex' (air)	18·00	15·00
2155	(Q) *Vanda* (large spotted blooms)	18·00	15·00

2006. Birds (5th series). As T **451**. Multicoloured.

2156	5c. *Phaethornis ruber* (postage)	25	10
2157	5c. *Threnetes leucurus*	25	10
2158	15c. *Podager nacunda*	30	15
2159	15c. *Columbina passerine*	30	15
2160	20c. *Leptotila rufaxilla*	40	30
2161	20c. *Claravis pretiosa*	40	30
2162	45c. *Campylopterus largipennis*	55	45
2163	45c. *Otus choliba*	55	45
2164	80c. *Porzana albicollis*	95	85
2165	80c. *Amazilia fimbriata*	95	85
2166	(Q) *Ciccaba virgata* (air)	18·00	15·00
2167	(Q) *Nyctidromus albicollis*	18·00	15·00

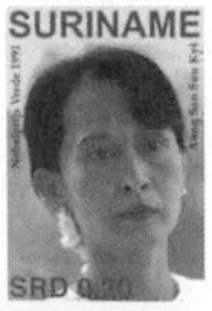
SURINAME

470 Aung San Suu Kyi (Peace prize winner, 1991)

2006. Nobel Prize Winners. Multicoloured.

2168	20c. Type **470**	40	30
2169	1srd.20 Milton Friedman (Economics, 1976)	1·30	1·10
2170	1srd.70 Marie Curie (Chemistry, 1911)	1·90	1·70
2171	2srd. Johannes Diderik van der Waals (Physics, 1910)	2·50	2·20
2172	3srd. Selma Ottilia Lovisa Lagerlöf (Literature, 1909)	3·25	2·75
2173	3srd.50 Gary S. Becker (Economics, 1992)	3·50	3·00

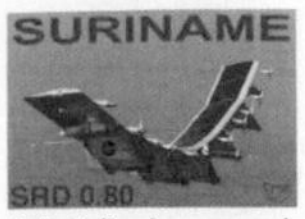
SURINAME
SRD 0,80

471 *Helios* (unmanned solar-powered aircraft)

2006. America. Energy Conservation. Multicoloured.

2174	80c. Type **471**	95	85
2175	16srd.20 Windmill	16·00	14·00
MS2176	72×78 mm. 3srd.50 Glider; 12srd.50 Four windmills	16·00	16·00

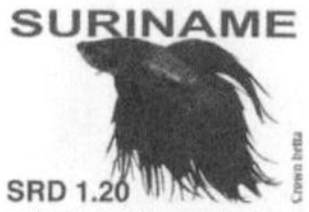
SURINAME
SRD 1,20

472 Inscr 'Crown betta'

2006. Fish. Multicoloured.

2177	1srd.20 Type **472**	1·30	1·10
2178	1srd.70 *Rarbus bariliodes*	1·90	1·70
2179	2srd. *Macropodus opercularis*	2·50	2·20
2180	3srd. *Xiphorus maculatus*1	3·25	2·75
2181	3srd.50 *Acanthuus lineatus*	3·50	3·00
2182	8srd.60 *Carassius auratus*	10·00	8·75

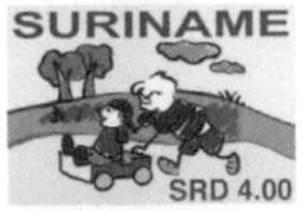
SURINAME
SRD 4,00

473 Children and Pushcart

2006. Child Care. Christmas. Multicoloured.

2183	4srd. Type **473**	4·00	3·50
2184	9srd.20 Angels (stained glass window)	10·50	9·25
MS2185	72×78 mm. 80c. Children playing football; 6srd. Christ and saints (stained glass window)	8·25	8·25

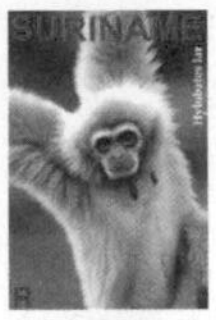
SURINAME
R

474 *Hylobates* (gibbon)

2006. Monkeys. Multicoloured.

2186	R Type **474**	30	15
2187	20c. *Leontopithecus rosalia* (golden lion tamarin)	40	30
2188	45c. *Saguinus imperator* (emperor tamarin)	55	45
2189	80c. *Callithrix geoffroyi* (Geoffroy's tufted-ear marmoset)	95	85
2190	1srd.20 *Callithrix argentata* (silvery marmoset)	1·30	1·10
2191	1srd.70 *Pygathrix nemaeus nemaeus* (Douc langur)	1·90	1·70
2192	2srd. *Saimiri sciureus* (South American squirrel monkey)	2·50	2·20
2193	3srd. *Pygathrix nemaeus nemaeus* (Douc langur)	3·25	2·75
2194	3srd.50 *Cercopithecus neglectus* (DeBrazza's monkey)	3·50	3·00
2195	4srd. *Alouatta caraya* (black howler monkey)	4·00	3·50
2196	5srd. *Verreaux's sifaka* (inscr 'Verreaux sitaka')	5·00	4·50
2197	10srd. *Pan troglodytes* (chimpanzee)	11·50	10·00

2006. Birds (6th series). As T **451**. Multicoloured.

2198	80c. *Phaethornis superciliousus* (inscr 'sutercilliosus')	11·50	10·00

2006. No. 822 surch.

2199	3srd.25 on 1c. multicoloured	3·25	2·75

2007. Orchids. As T **469**. Multicoloured.

2200	S *Cattleya* (insc 'Catteya') labiata	25	10
2201	20c. *Vuylstekeara*	40	30
2202	45c. *Cymbidium*	55	45
2203	80c. *Odontoglossum pestcatorei*	95	85
2204	1srd.20 *Odontocidium*	1·30	1·10
2205	1srd.70 *Odontioda*	1·90	1·70
2206	2srd. *Vanda*	2·50	2·20
2207	3srd. *Cattleya*	3·25	2·75
2208	3srd.50 *Paphiopedilum insigne*	3·50	3·00
2209	4srd. *Phalaenopsis*	4·00	3·50
2210	5srd. *Thunia*	5·00	4·50
2211	10srd. *Oncidium*	11·50	10·00

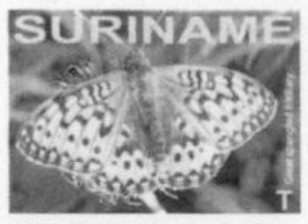
SURINAME
T

476 Great Spangled Fritillary

2007. Butterflies. Multicoloured.

2212	T Type **476**	25	10
2213	1srd.20 Peacock pansy	1·30	1·10
2214	1srd.70 Viceroy (Inscr 'Viceroyin daisy patch')	1·90	1·70
2215	2srd. Inscr 'Unidentified taxco'	2·50	2·20
2216	3srd. Tropical buckeye	3·25	2·75
2217	4srd. *Limenitis* (inscr 'popul') *populi*	4·00	3·50

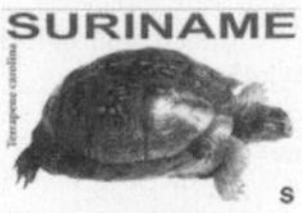
SURINAME
S

477 *Terrapine carolina*

2007. Reptiles. Multicoloured.

2218	S Type **477**	25	10
2219	20c. *Cuora flavomarginata*	40	30
2220	45c. *Chelonia mydas*	55	45
2221	80c. *Testudo hermanni*	95	85
2222	1srd.20 *Uromastyx acanthinura*	1·30	1·10
2223	1srd.70 *Physignathus cocincinus*	1·90	1·70
2224	2srd. *Iguana iguana*	2·50	2·20
2225	3srd. *Amblyrhynchus cristatus*	3·25	2·75
2226	3srd.50 *Chamaeleo jacksoni*	3·50	3·00
2227	4srd. *Crocodylus niloticus*	4·00	3·50
2228	5srd. *Caiman crocodiles*	5·00	4·50
2229	10srd. *Varanus komodoensis*	11·50	10·00

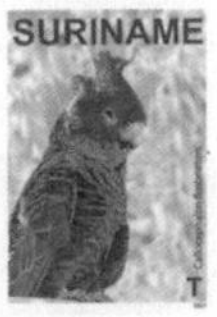
SURINAME
T

478 *Callocephalon fimbriatum*

2007. Parrots. Multicoloured.

2230	T Type **478**	30	15
2231	25c. *Cacatua ophthalmica*	45	30
2232	55c. *Cactua galleria*	65	50
2233	80c. Cockatoo (inscr 'Cacatua sulphure amazone')	95	85
2234	1srd.10 *Calyporhychus magunificus*	1·20	1·00
2235	1srd.20 Lesser Sulphur Crested Cockatoo (inscr 'Cacatua sulphure amazone')	1·30	1·10
2236	2srd. Lesser Sulphur Crested Cockatoo with crest raised (inscr 'Cacatua sulphure amazone')	2·50	2·20
2237	4srd. *Eolophus rosicapilus*	4·00	3·50
2238	5srd. Cockatoo (inscr 'Pan troglodytes')	5·00	4·50

2007. Birds (7th series). As T **451**. Multicoloured.

2239	T *Agamia agami*	30	15
2240	20c. *Botaurus pinnatus*	40	20
2241	45c. *Rallus maculates*	55	45
2242	80c. *Melanerpes cruentatus*	95	85
2243	1srd.20 *Piculus chrysochloros*	1·30	1·10
2244	2srd. *Paroaria gularis*	2·50	2·20
2245	4srd. *Cyanicterus cyanicterus*	4·00	3·50
2246	5srd. *Tersina viridis*	5·00	4·50
2247	10srd. *Sicalis flaveola* (inscr 'Sicalis floveola')	11·50	10·00

2007. Fish. As T **472**. Multicoloured.

2248	1srd.20 *Brachydanio rerio*	1·30	1·10
2249	1srd.70 *Pterois miles*	1·90	1·70
2250	2srd. *Pomacanthus annularis*	2·50	2·20
2251	3srd. *Balistoides conspicllum*	3·25	2·75
2252	3srd.50 *Plectorhynchus orientalis*	3·50	3·00
2253	8srd.60 *Chaetodon auriga*	10·00	8·75

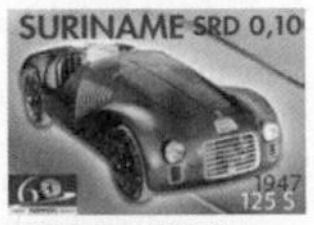
SURINAME SRD 0,10
1947
125 S

479 Ferrari 125 S (1947)

2007. Ferrari Motor Cars. Multicoloured.

2254	10c. Type **479**	25	10
2255	20c. 250 GTO (1962)	40	20
2256	50c. GTO (1984)	65	50
2257	1srd. F 399 (1999)	1·10	1·00
2258	1srd.60 Mondial Cabriolet (1983)	1·80	1·50
2259	1srd.75 F 33 SP (1994)	2·00	1·70
2260	3srd 365 GT4 BB (1971)	3·25	2·75
2261	5srd FXX (2006)	5·00	4·50

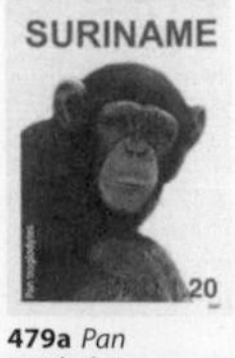
SURINAME

479a *Pan troglodytes* (chimpanzee)

2007. Apes. Multicoloured.

2662	1srd.20 Type **479a**	65	65
2663	1srd.70 *Cercopithecus neglectus* (DeBrazza's monkey)	90	90
2664	2srd. *Nasalis larvatus* (proboscis monkey)	1·10	1·10
2665	3srd. *Macaca fascicularis* (long-tailed macaque)	1·60	1·60
2666	3srd.50 *Mandrillus sphinx* (Mandrill)	1·90	1·90
2667	8srd.60 *Rhinopithecus roxellana* (golden snub-nosed monkey)	4·50	4·50

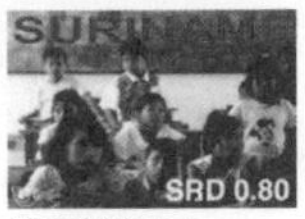
SRD 0,80

480 Children in Classroom

2007. America. Education for All. Multicoloured.

2268	80c. Type **480**	95	85
2269	16srd.20 Children making sheets	16·00	14·00
MS2270	72×78 mm. 7srd. Child writing on blackboard; 9srd. Two girls	16·00	16·00

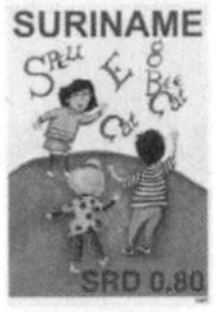
SURINAME
SRD 0,80

481 Children spelling

2007. Child Care. Christmas. Multicoloured. (a) Miniature Sheet.

MS2671	50×109 mm. 80c. Type **481**; 9srd.20 The Nativity	11·50	11·50

(b) Sheet Stamps.

2672	4srd. Children in classroom	4·00	3·50
2673	6srd. The Nativity (different)	6·25	5·50

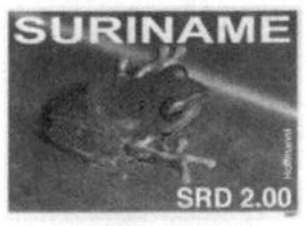
SURINAME
SRD 2,00

483 *Agalychnis callidryas*

2007. Frogs. Multicoloured.

2680	T Type **483**	30	15
2681	1srd.20 *Dendrobates pumilio*	1·30	1·10
2682	1srd.70 Inscr 'Phaeramia nematoptera'	1·90	1·70
2683	2srd. Inscr 'Hoffmanni'	2·50	2·20
2684	3srd. Inscr 'Phaeramia nematoptera'	3·25	2·75
2685	7srd. *Dendrobates histrionicus*	7·50	6·50

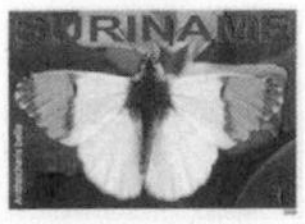

484 *Anthocharis belia* (Moroccan orange tip)

2008. Butterflies and Moths. Multicoloured.

2686	T Type **484**	30	15
2687	25c. Satyr anglewing	45	30
2688	45c. Red lacewing	55	45
2689	80c. *Inachis io* (peacock)	95	85
2690	1srd.20 Purple sapphire	1·30	1·10
2691	1srd.70 Pearly crescent spot	1·90	1·70
2692	2srd. Monarch	2·50	2·20
2693	3srd. Inscr 'Marpesia berania'	3·25	2·75
2694	3srd.50 Inscr 'Dark museum swallowtail'	3·50	3·00
2695	4srd. *Atticus atlas* Inscr 'Byasa alcinous'	4·00	3·50
2696	5srd. Inscr 'Brown peacock'	5·00	4·50
2697	10srd. Brown and orange Mexican	11·50	10·00

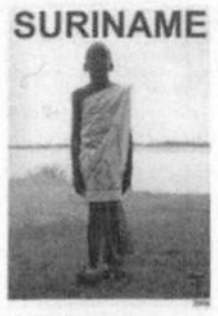

485 Boy

2008. Traditional Costumes. Multicoloured.

2698	T Type **485**	25	10
2699	25c. Woman wearing wrap skirt and bandeau top	45	30
2700	45c. Girl wearing red and white fringed dress	55	45
2701	80c. Boy wearing fringed cape and sarong	95	85
2702	1srd.20 Girl wearing pink hat, bolero and frilled skirt	1·30	1·10
2703	1srd.70 Boy wearing hat, white shirt and black trousers	2·30	2·00
2704	2srd. Man wearing cream trousers long tunic and red scarf	2·50	2·20
2705	3srd. Woman wearing pink sari	3·25	2·75
2706	3srd.50 Boy wearing red cap, tunic and trousers	3·50	3·00
2707	4srd. Woman wearing black print skirt, yellow jacket and holding fan	4·00	3·50
2708	5srd. Girl wearing pink cheong-sam and holding fan	5·00	4·50
2709	10srd. Boy wearing Mao suit with white cuffs	11·00	10·00

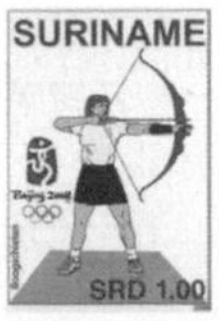

486 Archer

2008. Olympic Games, Beijing. Multicoloured.

2710	1srd. Type **486**	1·10	1·00
2711	1srd.50 Weight lifter	1·90	1·70
2712	2srd. Basketball players	2·50	2·20
2713	2srd.50 Runner	2·75	2·50

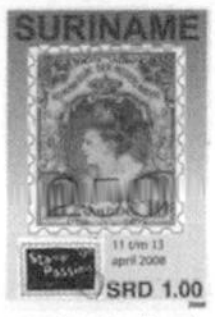

487 Netherlands 2g.50 on 10g. Stamp of 1920

2008. Stamp Passion 2008 International Stamp Exhibition. Multicoloured.

2714	1srd. Type **487**	1·10	1·00
2715	1srd.50 22½c. stamp of 1913	1·90	1·70
2716	2srd. Netherlands 10c. stamp of 1894	2·50	2·20
2717	2srd.50 Netherlands 60c. on 30c. (Zestig Cent) stamp of 1919	2·75	2·50
2718	3srd. Netherlands 12½c. stamp of 1935	3·25	2·75
2719	3srd.50 Netherlands 36c. AIR stamp of 1933	3·50	3·00
2720	4srd. Netherlands 50c. TE-BETALEN stamp of 1906	4·00	3·00
2721	5srd. Netherlands 2c. International Court of Justice stamp of 1950	5·00	4·50
2722	5srd.50 5c. stamp of 1929	5·75	5·00
2723	6srd. 1½g. stamp of 1931	6·25	5·50
2724	7srd. Netherlands 60c. stamp of 1925	7·00	6·00
2725	9srd. Netherlands 5c. stamp of 1913	10·00	8·75

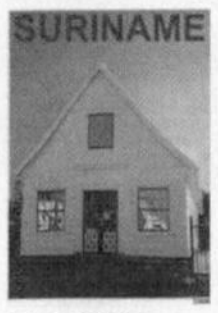

488 FHR Lim Postraat 34A

2008. Buildings. Multicoloured.

2726	V Type **488**	40	20
2727	40c. Combekerk	50	40
2728	50c. Waterkant 10	65	50
2729	80c. Waterkant 14	95	85
2730	1srd.20 Waterkant 12	1·30	1·10
2731	2srd. Officierswoning 6	2·50	2·20
2732	4srd. Grote Combeweg 33	4·00	3·50
2733	5srd. Officierswoning 5	5·00	4·50
2734	8srd. Officierswoning 9	9·50	8·25

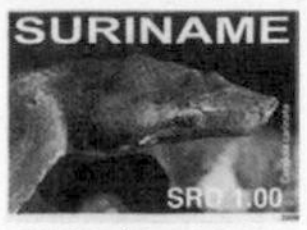

489 *Candoia carinata* (ground boa)

2008. Snakes. Multicoloured.

2735	1srd. Type **489**	1·10	1·00
2736	1srd.50 Viper	1·90	1·70
2737	2srd. *Chondropython viridis* (green python) (yellow)	2·50	2·20
2738	3srd. *Chondropython viridis* (green python) (red juvenile)	3·25	2·75
2739	5srd. Eyelash viper	5·00	4·50
2740	7srd.50 Green mamba	8·25	7·25
2741	10srd. Emerald tree boa	11·50	10·00
2742	15srd. Tiger rat snake	14·50	12·50

2008. Fish. As T **472**. Multicoloured.

2743	1srd. *Sphaeramia nematoptera*	1·10	1·00
2744	3srd. *Neophrynichthys latus*	3·25	2·75
2745	7srd.80 *Cheilodipterus quinquelineatus* (inscr 'isotigmus')	8·50	7·50

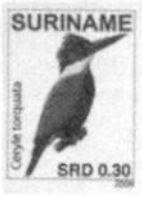

490 *Ceryle torquata* (ringed kingfisher)

2008. Birds. Multicoloured.

2746	30c. Type **490**	50	40
2747	45c. *Tangara velia* (opal-rumped tanager)	55	40
2748	50c. *Florisuga mellivora* (white-necked Jacobin)	65	50
2749	75c. *Psarocolius viridis* (green oropendola)	1·00	90
2750	90c. *Pionus fuscus* (dusky parrot)	1·10	90
2751	1srd.40 *Chloroceryle aenea* (American pygmy kingfisher)	1·60	1·40
2752	2srd.50 *Caryothraustes candensis* (yellow-green grosbeak)	2·75	2·50
2753	4srd. *Campephilius rubricollis* (red-necked woodpecker)	4·00	3·00
MS2753a	101×44 mm. 90c.×2, No. 2750×2; 1srd.40×2, No. 2751×2	5·00	5·50

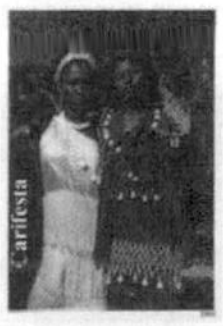

491 Two Girls

2008. America. Festivals. Multicoloured.

2754	9srd. Type **491**	10·00	8·75
2755	12srd.50 Banner	12·50	11·50
MS2756	78×72 mm. 7srd. Dancer; 15srd. Girl	22·50	22·50

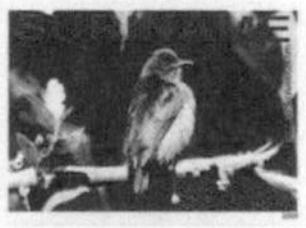

492 *Ceryle rudis* (pied kingfisher)

2008. Birds. Multicoloured.

2757	V Type **492**	45	25
2758	1srd.10 *Copsychus saularis* (Oriental magpie robin)	1·00	90
2759	1srd.80 *Dicaeum cruentatum* (scarlet-backed flower-pecker)	2·30	2·00
2760	3srd. *Garrulax perspicillatus* (masked laughingthrush)	3·25	2·75
2761	4srd. Insc 'Halcyonyanurus symrnensis'	4·00	3·50
2762	5srd. *Leiothrix lutea* (red-billed leiothrix)	5·00	5·50

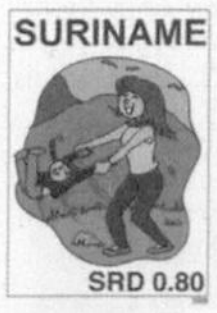

493 Mother and Daughter

2008. Child Care. Christmas. Multicoloured.

2763	80c. Type **493**	95	85
2764	11srd.20 Race car	12·00	12·00
MS2765	78×72 mm. 5srd. Girl giving flowers; 7srd. Girl painting pet home	13·00	13·00

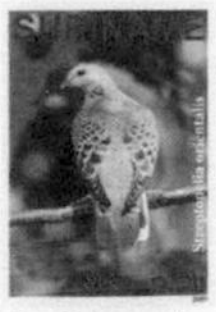

495 *Streptopelia orientalis* (Oriental turtle dove)

2009. Sheet 52×72 mm.

MS2772	**495** 9srd.50 multicoloured	10·50	10·50

Nos. 2766/71 and Type **494** have been left for Flora, issued on 20 December 2008, not yet received.

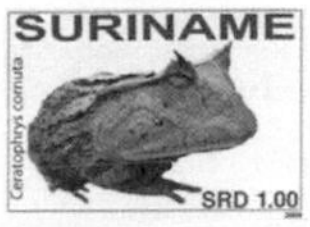

496 *Ceratophrys cornuta*

2009. Frogs. Multicoloured.

2773	1srd. Type **496**	1·20	1·10
2774	2srd. *Bufo marinus*	2·30	2·10
2775	2srd.50 *Eleutherodactylus counouspeus*	2·50	2·20
2776	3srd.50 *Gastrotheca monticola*	3·50	3·30
2777	5srd. *Leptodactylus pentadactylus*	5·00	4·50
2778	6srd. *Pipa pipa*	6·25	5·50
2779	7srd. *Pseudis paradoxa*	7·00	6·00

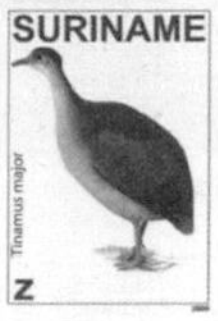

497 *Tinamus major* (great tinamou)

2009. Birds. Multicoloured.

2780	Z Type **497**	95	85
2781	1srd.50 *Crypturellus erythropus* (red-legged tinamou)	1·30	1·10
2782	2srd.50 *Crypturellus variegatus* (variegated tinamou)	[illegible]	[illegible]
2783	3srd. *Crypturellus cinereus* (cinereous tinamou)	3·25	2·75
2784	3srd.50 *Aburria pipile* (Trinidad piping-guan)	3·50	3·00
2785	4srd. *Bucco capensis* (collared puffbird)	4·00	3·50
2786	5srd. *Crypturellus soui* (little tinamou)	5·00	4·50
2787	5srd.50 *Ortalis motmot* (little chachalaca)	5·75	5·50
2788	7srd. *Penelope marail* (marail guan)	7·00	6·00
2789	12srd. *Chelidoptera tenebrosa* (swallow-winged puffbird)	12·50	12·00

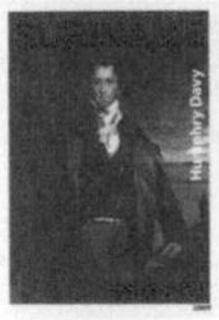

498 Humphry Davy

2009. Bicentenary of Electricity. Each black and scarlet-vermilion.

2790	2srd. Type **498**	2·50	2·20
2791	5srd. Light bulb	5·00	4·50
2792	8srd. Thomas Edison	8·75	8·00

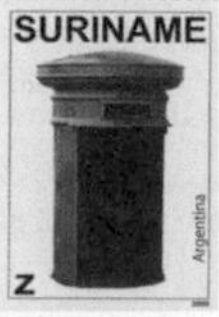

499 Argentina

2009. Post Boxes. Multicoloured.

2793	Z Type **499**	45	30
2794	2srd. Canada	2·20	1·00
2795	2srd.50 China	2·75	2·20
2796	3srd. India	3·50	3·00
2797	3srd.25 Ireland	3·50	3·00
2798	3srd.75 Russia	3·75	3·25
2799	5srd. Turkey	5·50	5·00
2800	5srd.50 Venezuela	5·50	5·00
2800a	6srd.50 Yemen	6·25	5·50
2800b	7srd. Great Britain	7·75	7·00

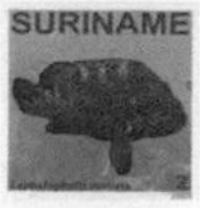

500 *Cephalopholis miniata*

2009. Fish. Multicoloured.

2801	Z Type **500**	95	85
2802	1srd.25 *Epinephelus fasciatus*	1·60	1·40
2803	1srd.50 Inscr 'Pomacanthus xanthocephalus'	1·90	1·70
2804	2srd. *Anampses meleagrides*	2·50	2·00
2805	2srd.50 *Chaetodon bennetti*	3·00	2·50
2806	3srd. *Cephalopholis argus*	3·25	2·75
2807	3srd.50 *Chaetodon xanthocephalus*	3·50	3·00
2808	4srd. *Scarus frenatus*	4·00	3·50
2809	5srd.75 *Priacanthus hamrur*	6·25	5·75
2810	6srd. *Cephalopholis polleni* (inscr 'Cephalopholis polieni')	6·50	5·00
2811	7srd. *Pomacanthus semicirculatus*	7·25	6·75
2812	7srd.50 *Ostracion cubicus*	8·25	8·75

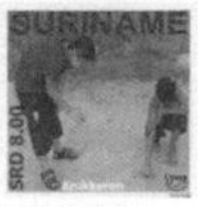

501 Knikkeren (marbles)

2009. America. Children's Games. Multicoloured.

2813	8srd. Type **501**	8·50	8·00
2814	15srd. Hoepelen (hoop rolling)	14·50	12·50
MS2815	46×79 mm. 10srd. Hoelahoep (hulahoop); 12srd. Vijfsteentje (five stones)	10·50	10·50

502 Black Rook

2009. Chess. Sheet 207×207 mm containing T **502** and similar square designs showing chess pieces. Each black and scarlet-vermilion.

MS2816	10c. Type **502**; 20c. Black bishop; 30c. Black queen; 40c. Bl[illegible] rook; 50c. Black king; 60c. Black pawn; 70c. Black pawn; 80c. Black pawn; 90c. Black pawn; 1srd. Black pawn; 1srd.10 Black knight; 1srd.20 Black pawn; 1srd.30 Black knight; 1srd.40 Black pawn; 1srd.50 White pawn; 1srd.60 White pawn; 1srd.70 White pawn; 1srd.80 White pawn; 1srd.90 White pawn; 2srd. White knight; 2srd.10 White bishop; 2srd.20 White bishop; 2srd.50 White pawn; 3srd. White pawn; 4srd.50 White rook; 4srd.80 white queen; 4srd.90 White rook; 5srd White king	55·00	55·00

No. **MS**2816 contains 28 stamps and 36 labels, which are laid out as a chess board with the game between Mikhail Botvinnik vs Paul Keres (1948) in progress.

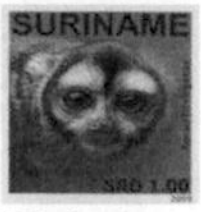

503 *Aotus trivirgatus* (northern owl monkey)

2009. Primates. Multicoloured.

2817	1srd. Type **503**	1·10	90
2818	1srd.50 *Alouatta palliata* (mantled howling monkey)	1·60	1·40
2819	2srd. *Cacajao calvus* (bald uakari)	2·20	1·00
2820	2srd.50 *Lagothrix lagotricha* (Humboldt's woolly monkey)	2·75	2·25
2821	3srd. *Pithecia pithecia* (white-faced saki)	3·50	3·00
2822	5srd. *Callithrix mauesi* (Rio Maues marmoset)	5·50	5·00
2823	7srd. *Alouatta seniculus* (red howler monkey)	7·75	7·75
2824	8srd. *Gorilla*	8·50	8·00
2825	9srd. *Cercopithecus diana* (Diana monkey)	9·75	9·25

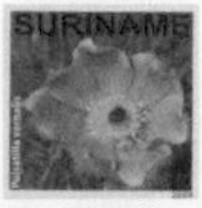

504 Pulsatilla vernalis

2009. Flowers. Multicoloured.

2826	Z Type **504**	45	35
2827	2srd. *Chrysanthemum maximum* (inscr 'Crisanthemum Maxima')	2·20	1·00

2828	2srd.50 *Abronia villosa*	2·75	2·20
2829	3srd *Aquilegia caerulea*	3·50	3·00
2830	3srd.25 *Zinnia elegans*	3·50	3·00
2831	3srd.75 *Bougainvillea glabra*	3·75	3·25
2832	5srd. *Narcissus* (inscr 'Daffodil')	5·50	5·00
2833	5srd.50 *Victoria cruziana*	5·50	5·00
2834	6srd.50 *Rosa palustris*	6·25	5·50
2835	7srd. *Nyphaea*	7·75	7·00

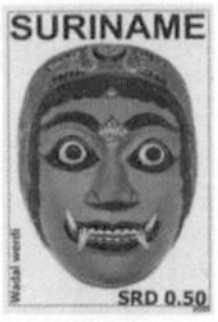

505 Wadal werdi

2009. Masks. Multicoloured.
MS2836 50c. Type **505**; 1srd. Bambang painem; 2srd. Demang mones; 3srd. Raden gunung sari; 8srd. Joyo rengangon; 15srd. Demang Tirtoyudo 18·00 18·00

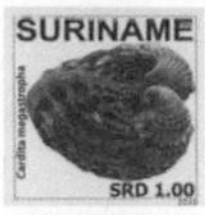

506 Cardita megastropha

2010. Shells. Multicoloured.

2837	Type **506**	1·20	1·10
2838	1srd.50 *Fragum unedo* (inscr 'Frangum unedo')	1·60	1·40
2839	2srd. *Galeodea echinophora*	2·20	1·50
2840	2srd.50 *Architectonica maxima*	2·75	2·20
2841	3srd. *Opeatostoma pseudodon*	3·50	3·00
2842	4srd. *Haliotis queketti*	3·50	3·00
2843	5srd. *Cymatium hepaticum*	5·50	5·00
2844	6srd. *Clanculus pharaonius*	5·75	5·25
2845	7srd. *Harpa harpa*	7·75	7·00
2846	8srd. *Hydatina nobilis*	8·25	75

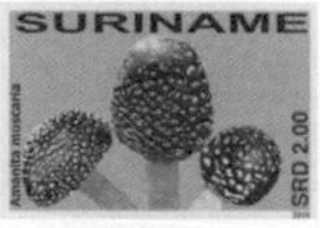

507 Amanita muscaria

2010. Fungi. Multicoloured.
MS2847 2srd. Type **507**; 5srd. *Boletus edulis*; 8srd. *Agaricus xanthoderma* 13·00 13·00

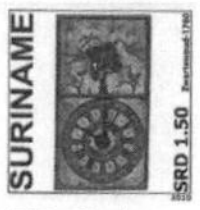

507a Cuckoo Clock, 1700

2010. Cuckoo Clocks of the Blackforest. Multicoloured.

2847a	1srd. 50 Type **507a**	1·60	1·40
2847b	2srd.50 With central deer and surmounted by bird, 1800	2·75	2·25
2847c	3srd.50 Light wood with crossed guns, hanging game and surmounted by antlered stag's head, 1900	3·50	3·00
2847d	4srd.50 Dark wood with crossed guns, horn and surmounted by stag's head, 1910	4·25	3·75
2847e	5srd. As chalet with trees, couple seated and three pendulums	5·50	5·00
2847f	8srd. As chalet with balcony and lower windows	8·25	7·74

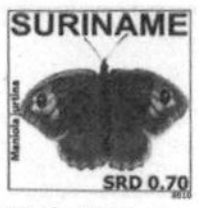

507b *Maniola jurtina*

2010. Butterflies. Multicoloured.

2847g	70c. Type **507b**	80	70
2847h	1srd.50 *Melanargia galathea*	1·40	1·20
2847i	1srd.75 *Argynnis adippe*	1·90	1·40
2847j	2srd.50 *Argynnis adippe*	2·75	2·25
2847k	2srd.75 *Lasiommata megera*	3·00	2·50
2847l	3srd. *Pararge aegeria*	3·50	3·00
2847m	3srd.75 *Argynnis paphia*	3·75	3·25
2847n	4srd.25 *Vanessa atalanta*	4·50	4·00
2847o	4srd.50 *Limenitis camilla*	4·50	4·00
2847p	5srd. *Polyommatus bellargus*	5·50	5·00
2847q	6srd. *Argynnis aglaja*	6·25	5·50
2847r	7srd. *Pyronia tithonus*	7·75	7·00
2847s	72×50 mm. 12srd. *Apatura ilia*		

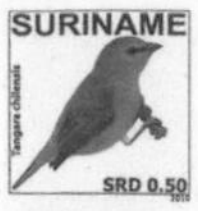

508 Dotted Tanager (inscr 'Tangara chilensis')

2010. Birds. Multicoloured.

2848	50c. Type **508**	45	35
2849	1srd. *Leptopogon amaurocephalus* (sepia-capped flycatcher)	1·20	1·10
2850	1srd.50 *Xolmis cinerea* (grey monjita)	1·60	1·40
2851	2srd. *Tangara cayana* (burnished-buff tanager)	2·20	1·50
2852	2srd.50 *Conopophaga aurita* (chestnut-belted gnateater)	2·75	2·20
2853	3srd. *Megarynchus pitangua* (boat-billed flycatcher)	3·50	3·00
2854	3srd.50 *Tangara mexicana* (turquoise tanager)	3·50	3·00
2856	5srd. *Hirundinea ferruginea* (cliff flycatcher)	5·50	5·00
2857	7srd. *Galbula albirostris* (yellow-billed jacamar)	5·50	5·00
2858	9srd. *Tyrannopsis sulphurea* (sulphury flycatcher)	9·00	8·25
2859	11srd. Paradise Tanager (insc 'Tangara varia')	10·00	9·50
2866	4srd. *Picumnus exilis* (golden-spangled piculet)	3·75	3·25

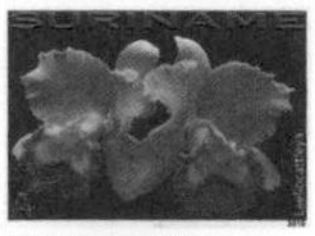
509 *Laeliocattleya*

2010. Orchids. Multicoloured.

2860	A Type **509**	20	10
2861	55c. *Coelogyne mooreana*	45	30
2862	1srd. *Phalaenopsis*	1·20	1·10
2863	1srd.50 *Calanthe*	1·60	1·40
2864	2srd. *Maxillaria fucata*	2·20	1·50
2865	2srd.50 *Cymbidium erythrostylum*	2·75	2·25
2866	3srd. (inscr 'Miltoniopsis portelet')	3·50	3·00
2867	4srd.50 *Cattleya portia*	4·00	3·25
2868	5srd. (inscr 'Miltoniopsis portelet')	5·50	5·00
2869	6srd.50	6·25	5·50
2870	7srd. *Dendrobium thwaitesii*	7·75	7·00
2871	11srd. *Ascocenda vernon*	10·00	9·50

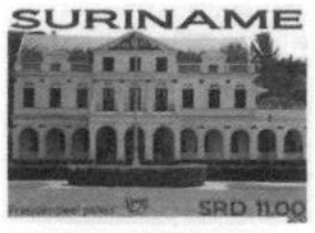

510 Presidential Palace

2010. America. Multicoloured.
MS2874 108×52 mm. 11srd. Type **510**; 13srd. National anthem 19·00 19·00

Nos. 2872/3 are left for single stamps not yet received.

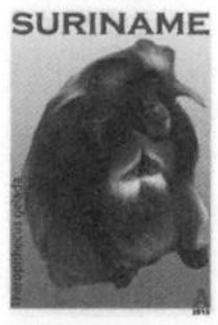

511 *Theropithecus gelada* (gelada)

2010. Primates. Multicoloured.

2875	A Type **511**	45	35
2876	55c. *Gorilla beringei* (eastern gorilla)	45	30
2877	1srd. *Cercopithecus nictitans* (greater spot-nosed monkey)	1·20	1·10
2878	1srd.50 *Microcebus myoxinus* (pygmy mouse lemur)	1·60	1·40
2879	2srd. *Macaca silenus* (lion-tailed macaque)	2·20	1·50
2880	2srd.50 *Lemur catta* (ring-tailed lemur)	2·50	2·00
2881	3srd. *Propithecus verreauxi* (Verreaux's sifaka)	3·50	3·00
2882	4srd. *Galago crassicaudatus* (greater galago)	4·25	3·75
2883	4srd.50 *Cacajao melanocephalus* (black-headed uakari)	4·25	3·75
2884	5srd. *Pan paniscus* (bonobo)	5·50	5·00
2885	6srd.50 *Lagothrix cana* (gray woolly monkey)	6·25	5·50
2886	9srd. Inscr 'Capucinus albifrons'	9·00	8·25

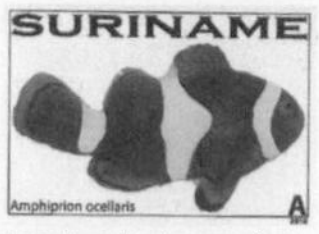

512 *Amphiprion ocellaris*

2010. Fish. Multicoloured.

2887	A (45c.) Type **512**	55	45
2888	1srd.55 *Pomacentrus caerleus*	1·60	1·40
2889	3srd. *Barbus tetrazona*	3·50	3·00
2890	5srd. *Betta smaragdina*	5·50	5·00
2891	7srd *Colisa lalia* (inscr 'Calisa lalia')	7·75	7·00
2892	8srd. *Geophagus brasiliensis*	8·25	7·75
2893	9srd. *Astronotus ocellatus*	9·00	8·25
2894	11srd. *Microgeophagus ramirezi*	10·00	9·50

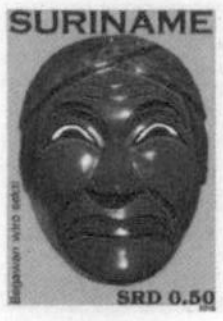

513 Begawan wiro sekti

2010. Masks. Multicoloured.

2895	50c. Type **513**	55	45
2896	1srd.50 Dewi kilisuci	1·60	1·40
2897	3srd.50 Kartolo	3·75	3·25
2898	6srd. Bilung	6·25	5·50
2899	8srd. Panji amerdadu	8·25	7·75
2900	10srd. Betara kalla	9·50	8·75

POSTAGE DUE STAMPS

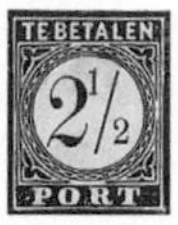

D2

1885

D36b	**D2**	2½c. mauve and black	3·25	3·25
D37b	**D2**	5c. mauve and black	11·00	11·00
D38b	**D2**	10c. mauve and black	£200	£170
D39b	**D2**	20c. mauve and black	17·00	17·00
D40b	**D2**	25c. mauve and black	22·00	22·00
D41b	**D2**	30c. mauve and black	5·50	5·50
D42b	**D2**	40c. mauve and black	9·00	9·00
D43b	**D2**	50c. mauve and black	5·50	5·50

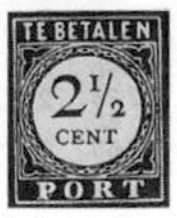

D6

1892

D57	**D6**	2½c. mauve and black	55	55
D58b	**D6**	5c. mauve and black	1·10	1·10
D59	**D6**	10c. mauve and black	32·00	28·00
D60b	**D6**	20c. mauve and black	2·75	2·20
D61b	**D6**	25c. mauve and black	10·00	9·00
D62	**D6**	40c. mauve and black	3·25	4·00

1911

D111b	**D2**	10c. on 30c. mve & blk	£130	£130
D112b	**D2**	10c. on 50c. mve & blk	£170	£170

1913

D153	**D6**	½c. lilac	35	35
D154	**D6**	1c. lilac	35	35
D155	**D6**	2c. lilac	35	35
D156	**D6**	2½c. lilac	35	35
D157	**D6**	5c. lilac	35	35
D158	**D6**	10c. lilac	35	35
D159a	**D6**	12c. lilac	35	35
D160a	**D6**	12½c. lilac	35	35
D161	**D6**	15c. lilac	45	35
D162a	**D6**	20c. lilac	90	65
D163	**D6**	25c. lilac	45	45
D164a	**D6**	30c. lilac	35	55
D165	**D6**	40c. lilac	13·50	13·50
D166a	**D6**	50c. lilac	1·30	1·10
D167a	**D6**	75c. lilac	1·30	1·30
D168a	**D6**	1g. lilac	1·70	1·50

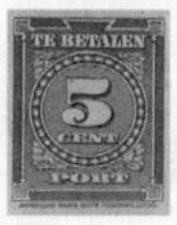

D52

1945

D337	**D52**	1c. purple	3·50	1·70
D338	**D52**	5c. purple	9·25	3·00
D339	**D52**	25c. purple	15·00	1·20

1950. As Type D **121** of Netherlands.

D384	1c. purple	17·00	9·25
D385	2c. purple	17·00	9·25
D386	2½c. purple	17·00	9·25
D387	5c. purple	11·50	2·30
D388	10c. purple	11·50	2·30
D389	15c. purple	17·00	9·25
D390	20c. purple	5·75	9·25
D391	25c. purple	35·00	2·30
D392	50c. purple	46·00	9·25
D393	75c. purple	65·00	46·00
D394	1g. purple	55·00	11·50

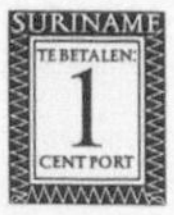

D68

1956

D436	**D68**	1c. purple	60	60
D437	**D68**	2c. purple	60	60
D438	**D68**	2½c. purple	60	60
D439	**D68**	5c. purple	60	60
D440	**D68**	10c. purple	60	60
D441	**D68**	15c. purple	1·20	1·20
D442	**D68**	20c. purple	1·20	1·20
D443	**D68**	25c. purple	1·20	60
D444	**D68**	50c. purple	3·00	60
D445	**D68**	75c. purple	3·50	1·70
D446	**D68**	1g. purple	4·75	1·20

1987. Various stamps optd **TE BETALEN**.

D1325	65c. mult (No. 868)	3·75	3·25
D1326	65c. mult (No. 1132)	3·75	3·25
D1327	80c. mult (No. 1134)	4·50	3·75
D1328	90c. mult (No. 872a)	5·25	4·50
D1329	95c. mult (No. 873)	5·50	4·75
D1330	1g. mult (No. 1248)	6·00	5·25

2007. Postage Due. Nos. D436, D439, D444 and D446 surch.

D2674	1srd. on 1c. lilac (436)	1·10	1·00
D2675	1srd.50 on 1g. lilac (446)	1·80	1·50
D2676	2srd. on 5c. lilac (439)	2·50	2·20
D2677	3srd. on 50c. lilac (444)	3·25	2·75
D2678	3srd.50 on 1g. lilac (446)	3·50	3·00
D2679	4srd. on 1g. lilac (446)	4·00	3·50

Stanley Gibbons
Ultra Violet Lamp

The only UV lamp that works in daylight

Ideal for detecting phosphor papers and inks for the majority of 20th century Machin stamps of Great Britain, plus Israel, USA, Finland and the early phosphors of Canada, Norway, Mexico, France, Hong Kong, People's Republic of China, Russia and later issues of Canada and Mexico.

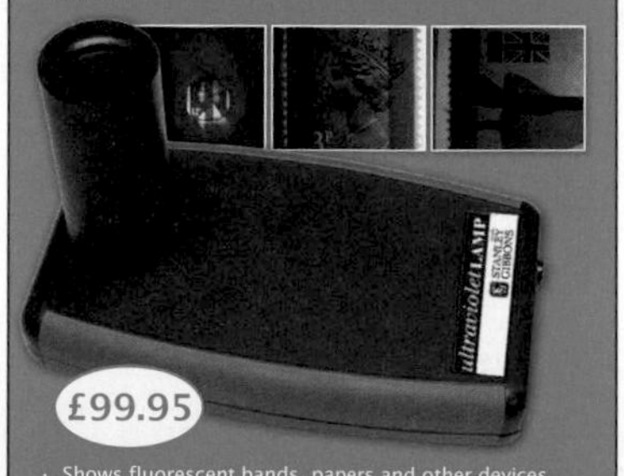

- Shows fluorescent bands, papers and other devices
- Highlights cleaned pen cancellations and paper repairs
- Powerful bulb gives much stronger reaction than other lamps
- Effective in daylight/artificial light using special eye-piece
- Spectrum of 254 to 390 nm both 'short' and 'long' wavelengths
- Safe to use due to shielded UV light
- Lightweight pocket-size - ideal for fairs and exhibitions
- Long-life bulb will give 50,000 hours of use under normal viewing conditions

Prices correct as of August 2014 and are subject to change

To order, call **0800 611 622** (UK only) or email **order@stanleygibbons.com**

Est 1856
STANLEY GIBBONS

Stanley Gibbons Limited
7 Parkside, Christchurch Road,
Ringwood, Hants, BH24 3SH
+44 (0)1425 472 363
www.stanleygibbons.com

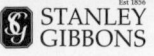

Pt. 1

SWAZILAND

A kingdom in the eastern part of S. Africa. Its early stamps were issued under joint control of Gt. Britain and the S. Africa Republic. Incorporated into the latter state in 1895 it was transferred in 1906 to the High Commissioner for S. Africa. Again issued stamps in 1933. Achieved independence in 1968.

1961. 100 cents = 1 rand.
1974. 100 cents = 1 lilangeni (plural: emalangeni).

1889. Stamps of Transvaal optd **Swazieland**.

10	**18**	½d. grey	7·50	16·00
1	**18**	1d. red	25·00	25·00
5	**18**	2d. bistre	32·00	18·00
6	**18**	6d. blue	42·00	60·00
3	**18**	1s. green	18·00	13·00
7	**18**	2s.6d. yellow	£325	£450
8	**18**	5s. blue	£170	£300
9	**18**	10s. brown	£6500	£4000

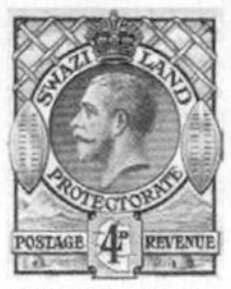

2 King George V

1933

11	**2**	½d. green	30	30
12	**2**	1d. red	30	20
13	**2**	2d. brown	30	45
14	**2**	3d. blue	45	3·50
15	**2**	4d. orange	3·25	3·50
16	**2**	6d. mauve	1·25	1·00
17	**2**	1s. olive	1·50	2·75
18	**2**	2s.6d. violet	15·00	22·00
19	**2**	5s. grey	38·00	55·00
20	**2**	10s. brown	£140	£180

1935. Silver Jubilee. As T **32a** of St. Helena.

21	1d. blue and red	50	1·50
22	2d. blue and black	2·50	4·00
23	3d. brown and blue	1·00	8·50
24	6d. grey and purple	4·25	6·00

1937. Coronation. As T **32b** of St. Helena.

25	1d. red	50	2·50
26	2d. brown	50	25
27	3d. blue	50	75

1938. As T **2** but with portrait of King George VI and inscr "SWAZILAND" only below portrait.

28a	½d. green	30	2·75
29a	1d. red	1·00	1·75
30b	1½d. blue	40	1·00
31a	2d. brown	40	50
32b	3d. blue	9·00	10·00
33a	4d. orange	1·25	1·40
34b	6d. purple	4·50	1·50
35a	1s. olive	1·25	65
36a	2s.6d. violet	29·00	6·00
37b	5s. grey	50·00	19·00
38a	10s. brown	10·00	7·00

1945. Victory stamps of South Africa (inscr alternately in English or Afrikaans) optd **Swaziland**.

39	**55**	1d. brown and red	65	10
40	-	2d. blue and violet (No. 109)	65	10
41	-	3d. blue (No. 110)	65	20

Unused prices are for bilingual pairs, used prices for single stamps in either language.

1947. Royal Visit. As Nos. 32/5 of Basutoland.

42	1d. red	10	10
43	2d. green	10	10
44	3d. blue	10	10
45	1s. mauve	10	10

1948. Silver Wedding. As T **33b/c** of St. Helena.

46	1½d. blue	50	1·00
47	10s. purple	40·00	45·00

1949. 75th Anniv of U.P.U. As T **33d/g** of St. Helena.

48	1½d. blue	15	20
49	3d. blue	2·00	3·75
50	6d. mauve	30	80
51	1s. olive	30	3·50

1953. Coronation. As T **33h** of St. Helena.

52	2d. black and brown	45	20

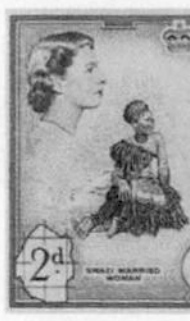

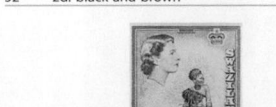

7 Swazi Married Woman

1956

53	-	½d. black and orange	40	10
54	-	1d. black and green	10	10
55	**7**	2d. black and brown	30	10
56	-	3d. black and red	20	10
57	-	4½d. black and blue	60	30
58	-	6d. black and mauve	3·00	10
59	-	1s. black and olive	55	10
60	-	1s.3d. black and sepia	5·00	6·00
61	-	2s.6d. green and red	3·50	3·50
62	-	5s. violet and grey	13·00	8·50
63	**7**	10s. black and violet	25·00	21·00
64	-	£1 black and turquoise	60·00	45·00

DESIGNS—HORIZ: ½d., 1s. Havelock asbestos mine; 1d., 2s.6d. Highveld view. VERT: 3d., 1s.3d. Swazi courting couple; 4½d., 5s. Swazi warrior in ceremonial dress; 6d., £1 Greater kudu.

1961. Stamps of 1956 surch in new currency.

65	½c. on ½d. black and orange	4·00	7·00
66	1c. on 1d. black and green	10	2·25
67	2c. on 2d. black and brown	10	2·75
68	2½c. on 2d. black and brown	10	1·25
69	2½c. on 3d. black and red	10	10
70	3½c. on 2d. black and brown	10	1·25
71	4c. on 4½d. black and blue	10	10
72	5c. on 6d. black and mauve	50	10
73	10c. on 1s. black and olive	42·00	9·00
74	25c. on 2s.6d. green and red	40	1·00
75	50c. on 5s. violet and grey	45	1·25
76	1r. on 10s. black and violet	1·50	1·25
77a	2r. on £1 black and turquoise	15·00	21·00

1961. As 1956 but values in new currency.

78	½c. black and orange (as ½d.)	10	1·25
79	1c. black and green (as 1d.)	10	10
80	2c. black and brown (as 2d.)	10	2·50
81	2½c. black and red (as 3d.)	15	10
82	4c. black and blue (as 4½d.)	20	1·50
83	5c. black and mauve (as 6d.)	1·25	15
84	10c. black and olive (as 1s.)	20	10
85	12½c. black and sepia (as 1s.3d.)	1·25	70
86	25c. green and red (as 2s.6d.)	4·50	7·00
87	50c. violet and grey (as 5s.)	5·50	3·25
88	1r. black and violet (as 10s.)	14·00	16·00
89	2r. black and turquoise (as £1)	22·00	13·00

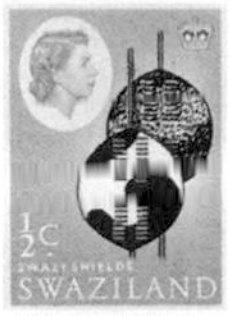

15 Swazi Shields

1962

90	**15**	½c. black, brown and buff	10	10
91	-	1c. orange and black	10	10
92	-	2c. green, black and olive	10	1·75
93	-	2½c. black and red	10	10
94	-	3½c. green and grey	10	40
95	-	4c. black and turquoise	10	10
96	-	5c. black, red and deep red	1·50	10
97	-	7½c. brown and buff	2·00	60
98	-	10c. black and blue	5·00	25
99	-	12½c. red and olive	2·25	3·50
100	-	15c. black and mauve	1·50	1·75
101	-	20c. black and green	40	1·00
102	-	25c. black and blue	50	1·00
103	-	50c. black and red	20·00	7·00
104	-	1r. green and ochre	2·75	2·50
105	-	2r. red and blue	24·00	15·00

DESIGNS—VERT: 1c. Battle axe; 2c. Forestry; 2½c. Ceremonial headdress; 3½c. Musical instrument; 4c. Irrigation; 5c. Long-tailed whydah ("Widowbird"); 7½c. Rock paintings; 10c. Secretary bird; 12½c. Pink arum; 15c. Swazi married woman; 20c. Malaria control; 25c. Swazi warrior; 1r. Aloes. HORIZ: 50c. Southern ground hornbill ("Ground Hornbill"); 2r. Msinsi in flower.

1963. Freedom from Hunger. As T **63a** of St. Helena.

106	15c. violet	50	15

1963. Cent of Red Cross. As T **63b** of St. Helena.

107	2½c. red and black	30	10
108	15c. red and blue	70	90

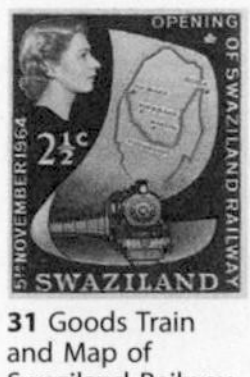

31 Goods Train and Map of Swaziland Railway

1964. Opening of Swaziland Railway.

109	**31**	2½c. green and purple	65	10
110	**31**	3½c. blue and olive	65	1·00
111	**31**	15c. orange and brown	1·00	70
112	**31**	25c. yellow and blue	1·10	80

1965. Cent of I.T.U. As T **64a** of St. Helena.

113	2½c. blue and bistre	15	10
114	15c. purple and red	35	20

1965. I.C.Y. As T **64b** of St. Helena.

115	½c. purple and turquoise	10	30
116	15c. green and lavender	40	20

1966. Churchill Commemoration. As T **64c** of St. Helena.

117	½c. blue	10	2·75
118	2½c. green	25	10
119	15c. brown	55	25
120	25c. violet	80	1·10

1966. 20th Anniv of UNESCO. As T **64f/h** of St. Helena.

121	2½c. multicoloured	20	10
122	7½c. yellow, violet and olive	60	60
123	15c. black, purple and orange	1·10	1·25

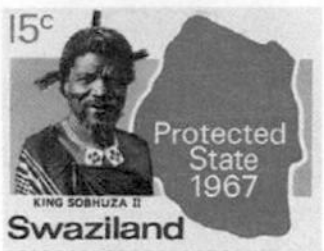

32 King Sobhuza II and Map

1967. Protected State.

124	**32**	2½c. multicoloured	10	10
125	-	7½c. multicoloured	15	15
126	**32**	15c. multicoloured	20	30
127	-	25c. multicoloured	25	40

DESIGN—VERT: 7½, 25c. King Sobhuza II.

1967. First Conferment of University Degrees. As Nos. 234/7 of Botswana.

128	2½c. sepia, blue and orange	10	10
129	7½c. sepia, blue and turquoise	15	15
130	15c. sepia, blue and red	25	30
131	25c. sepia, blue and violet	30	35

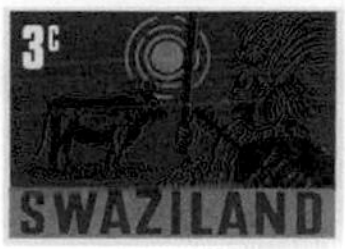

33 Incwala Ceremony

1968. Traditional Customs.

132	**35**	3c. silver, red and black	10	10
133	-	10c. multicoloured	10	10
134	**35**	15c. gold, red and black	15	20
135	-	25c. multicoloured	15	20

DESIGN—VERT: 10, 25c. Reed dance.

1968. No. 96 surch **3c**.

136	3c. on 5c. black, red & dp red	1·50	10

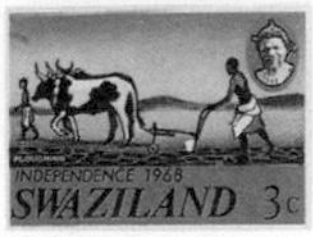

38 Cattle Ploughing

1968. Independence.

137	**38**	3c. multicoloured	10	10
138	-	4½c. multicoloured	10	45
139	-	17½c. multicoloured	15	70
140	-	25c. slate, black and gold	45	90

MS141 180×162 mm. Nos. 137/40 each × 5 — 14·00 23·00

DESIGNS: 4½c. Overhead cable carrying asbestos; 17½c. Cutting sugar cane; 25c. Iron ore mining and railway map.

1968. Nos. 90/105 optd **INDEPENDENCE 1968** and No. 93 additionally surch **3 c**.

142	**15**	½c. black, brown and buff	10	10
143	-	1c. orange and black	10	10
144	-	2c. green, black and olive	10	10
145	-	2½c. black and red	1·25	1·40
146	-	3c. on 2½c. black and red	10	10
147	-	3½c. green and grey	15	10
148	-	4c. black and turquoise	10	10
149	-	5c. black, red and deep red	4·25	10
150	-	7½c. brown and buff	60	10
151	-	10c. black and blue	4·50	10
152	-	12½c. red and olive	25	1·00
153	-	15c. black and mauve	25	1·25
154	-	20c. black and green	75	2·00
155	-	25c. black and blue	35	1·25
159	-	50c. black and red	3·50	11·00
157	-	1r. green and ochre	2·00	4·50
160	-	2r. red and blue	8·50	5·50

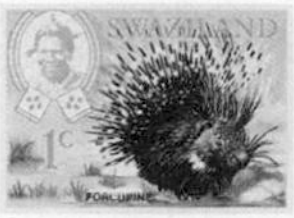

43 Porcupine

1969. Multicoloured.

161	½c. Caracal	10	10
162	1c. Type **43**	10	10
163	2c. Crocodile	20	10
164	3c. Lion	1·00	10
165	3½c. African elephant	1·00	10
166	5c. Bush pig	30	10
167	7½c. Impala	35	10
168	10c. Chacma baboon	45	10
169	12½c. Ratel	70	4·00
170	15c. Leopard	1·25	70
171	20c. Blue wildebeest	1·00	60
172	25c. White rhinoceros	1·75	1·75
173	50c. Common zebra	1·50	3·25
174	1r. Waterbuck (vert)	3·00	6·50
175	2r. Giraffe (vert)	8·00	11·00

Nos. 164/5 are larger, 35×24½ mm.

For designs as Nos. 174/5, but in new currency, see Nos. 219/20.

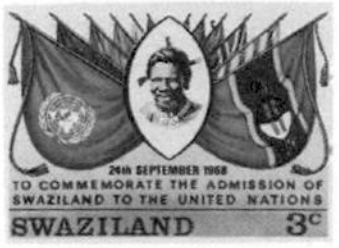

44 King Sobhuza II and Flags

1969. Swaziland's Admission to the U.N. Multicoloured.

176	3c. Type **44**	10	10
177	7½c. King Sobhuza II, U.N. Building and emblem	15	10
178	12½c. As Type **44**	25	10
179	25c. As 7½c.	40	40

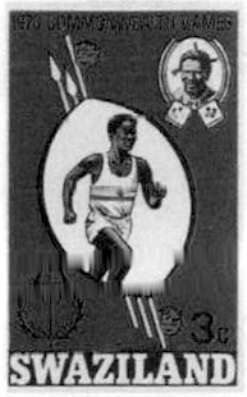

46 Athlete, Shield and Spears

1970. Ninth Commonwealth Games. Multicoloured.

180	3c. Type **46**	10	10
181	7½c. Runner	20	10
182	12½c. Hurdler	25	10
183	25c. Procession of Swaziland competitors	35	40

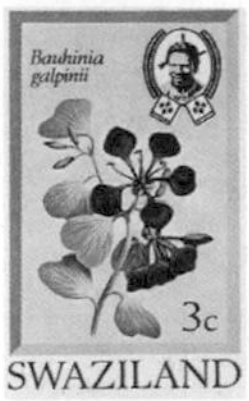

47 "Bauhinia galpinii"

1971. Flowers. Multicoloured.

184	3c. Type **47**	20	10
185	10c. "Crocosmia aurea"	20	10
186	15c. "Gloriosa superba"	30	25
187	25c. "Watsonia densiflora"	40	1·25

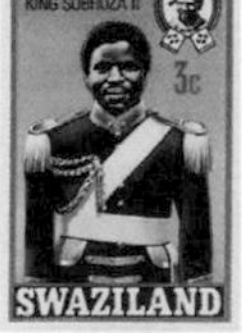

48 King Sobhuza II in Ceremonial Dress

1971. Golden Jubilee of King Sobhuza II's Accession. Multicoloured.

188	3c. Type **48**	10	10
189	3½c. Sobhuza II in medallion	10	10
190	7½c. Sobhuza II attending Incwala ceremony	15	10
191	25c. Sobhuza II and aides at opening of Parliament	30	35

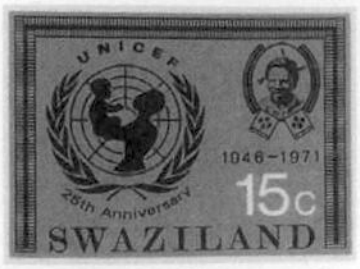

49 UNICEF Emblem

1972. 25th Anniv of UNICEF.

192	**49**	15c. black and lilac	15	20
193	-	25c. black and green	20	80

DESIGN: 25c. As Type **49**, but inscription rearranged.

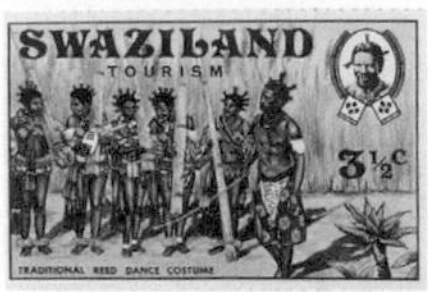

50 Local Dancers

1972. Tourism. Multicoloured.

194	3½c. Type **50**	10	10
195	7½c. Swazi beehive hut	15	15
196	15c. Ezulwini Valley	20	50
197	25c. Fishing, Usutu River	65	1·25

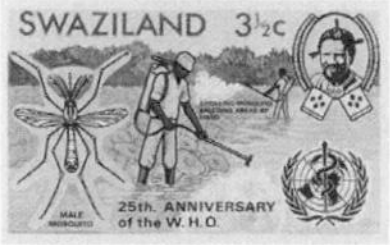

51 Spraying Mosquitoes

1973. 25th Anniv of W.H.O. Multicoloured.

198	3½c. Type **51**	20	10
199	7½c. Anti-malaria vaccination	40	80

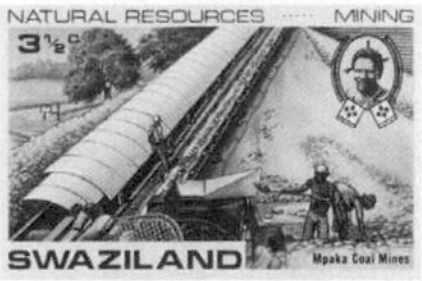

52 Mining

1973. Natural Resources. Multicoloured.

200	3½c. Type **52**	55	10
201	7½c. Cattle	25	15
202	15c. Water	30	20
203	25c. Rice	35	50

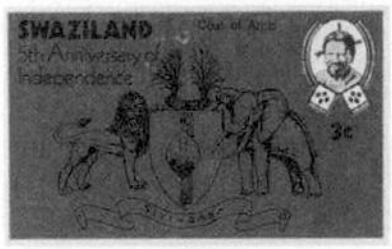

53 Coat of Arms

1973. Fifth Anniv of Independence.

204	**53**	3c. pink and black	10	10
205	-	10c. multicoloured	15	10
206	-	15c. multicoloured	30	75
207	-	25c. multicoloured	40	1·60

DESIGNS: 10c. King Sobhuza II saluting; 15c. Parliament buildings; 25c. National Somhlolo stadium.

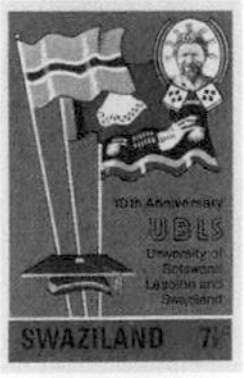

54 Flags and Mortar-board

1973. Tenth Anniv of University of Botswana, Lesotho and Swaziland. Multicoloured.

208	7½c. Type **54**	20	10
209	12½c. University campus	25	10
210	15c. Map of Southern Africa	30	20
211	25c. University badge	40	35

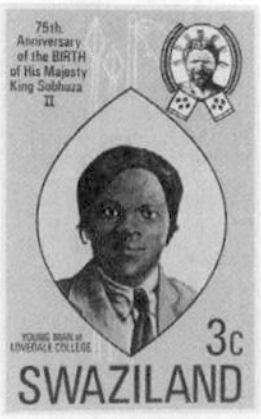

55 King Sobhuza as College Student

1974. 75th Birth Anniv of King Sobhuza II. Multicoloured.

212	3c. Type **55**	10	10
213	9c. King Sobhuza in middle-age	10	10
214	50c. King Sobhuza at 75 years of age	70	60

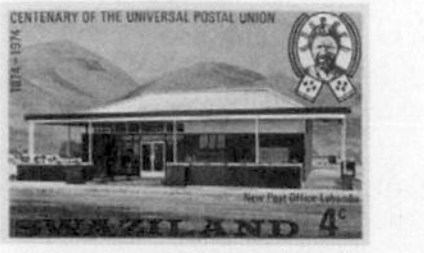

56 New Post Office, Lobamba

1974. Centenary of U.P.U. Multicoloured.

215	4c. Type **56**	10	10
216	10c. Mbabane Temporary Post Office, 1902	15	15
217	15c. Carrying mail by cableway	30	50
218	25c. Mule-drawn mail-coach	40	70

1975. As Nos. 174/5, but in new currency.

219	1e. Waterbuck	50	2·00
220	2e. Giraffe	1·10	4·00

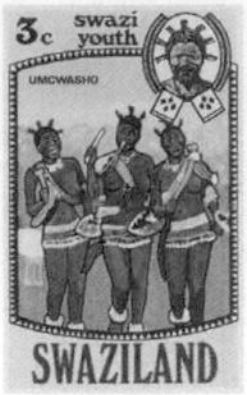

57 Umcwasho Ceremony

1975. Swazi Youth. Multicoloured.

221	3c. Type **57**	10	10
222	10c. Butimba (hunting party)	15	10
223	15c. Lusekwane (sacred shrub) (horiz)	40	40
224	25c. Goina Regiment	60	70

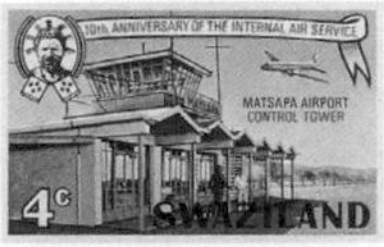

58 Control Tower, Matsapa Airport

1975. Tenth Anniv of Internal Air Service. Multicoloured.

225	4c. Type **58**	30	10
226	5c. Fire engine	70	20
227	15c. Douglas DC-3	1·25	1·40
228	25c. Hawker Siddeley H.S.748	2·00	2·00

1975. Nos. 167 and 169 surch.

230	3c. on 7½c. Impala	75	1·00
231	6c. on 12½c. Ratel	1·50	2·00

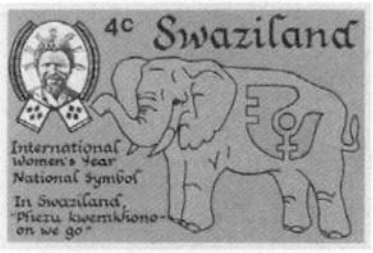

60 Elephant Symbol

1975. International Women's Year.

232	**60**	4c. grey, black and blue	10	10
233	-	5c. multicoloured	10	10
234	-	15c. multicoloured	30	60
235	-	25c. multicoloured	50	90

DESIGNS—HORIZ: 5c. Queen Labotsibeni. VERT: 15c. Craftswoman; 25c. "Women in Service".

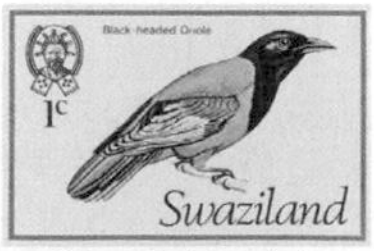

61 African Black-headed Oriole ("Black-headed Oriole")

1976. Birds. Multicoloured.

236	1c. Type **61**	75	2·50
237	2c. African green pigeon ("Green Pigeon") (vert)	80	2·50
238	3c. Green-winged pytilia ("Melba Finch")	1·00	1·00
239	4c. Violet starling ("Plum-coloured Starling") (vert)	80	15
240	5c. Black-headed heron (vert)	90	1·75
241	6c. Common stonechat ("Stone-chat") (vert)	1·50	2·50
242	7c. Chorister robin chat ("Chorister Robin") (vert)	1·40	2·75
243	10c. Four-coloured bush-shrike ("Gorgeous Bush Shrike") (vert)	1·50	1·75
244	15c. Black-collared barbet (vert)	2·25	55
245	20c. Grey heron (vert)	3·25	2·00
246	25c. Giant kingfisher (vert)	3·50	2·00
247	30c. Verreaux's eagle ("Black Eagle") (vert)	3·50	2·50
248a	50c. Red bishop (vert)	90	1·00
249a	1e. Pin-tailed whydah (vert)	1·40	2·50
250a	2e. Lilac-breasted roller	1·50	5·00

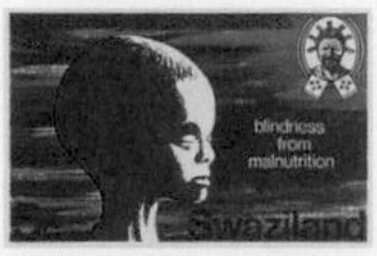

62 Blindness from Malnutrition

1976. Prevention of Blindness. Multicoloured.

251	5c. Type **62**	20	10
252	10c. Infected retina	25	20
253	20c. Blindness from trachoma	45	85
254	25c. Medicines	50	1·10

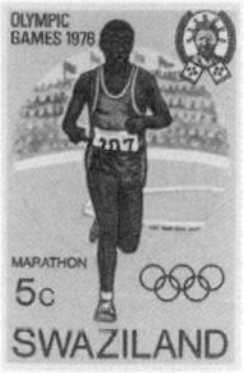

63 Marathon

1976. Olympic Games, Montreal. Multicoloured.

255	5c. Type **63**	15	10
256	6c. Boxing	20	10
257	20c. Football	45	45
258	25c. Olympic torch and flame	55	65

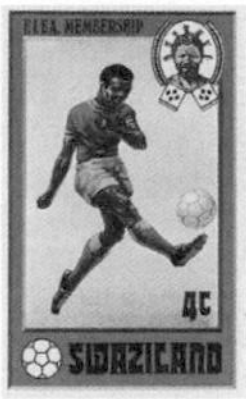

64 Footballer Shooting

1976. F.I.F.A. Membership. Multicoloured.

259	4c. Type **64**	20	10
260	6c. Heading	20	10
261	20c. Goalkeeping	50	25
262	25c. Player about to shoot	50	30

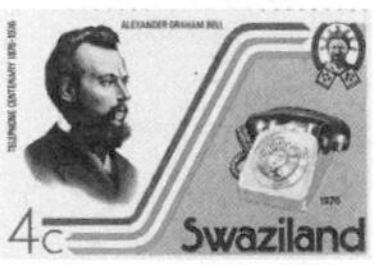

65 Alexander Graham Bell and Telephone

1976. Centenary of Telephone.

263	**65**	4c. multicoloured	10	10
264	-	5c. multicoloured	10	10
265	-	10c. multicoloured	10	10
266	-	15c. multicoloured	20	20
267	-	20c. multicoloured	25	30

Nos. 264/7 as Type **65**, but showing different telephones.

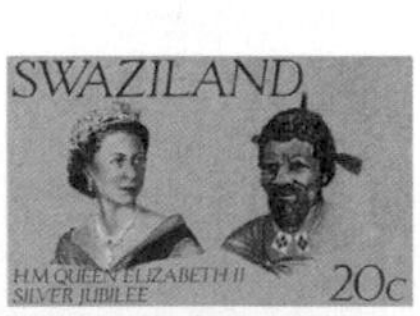

66 Queen Elizabeth II and King Sobhuza II

1977. Silver Jubilee. Multicoloured.

268	20c. Type **66**	15	15
269	25c. Coronation Coach at Admiralty Arch	15	15
270	50c. Queen in coach	20	40

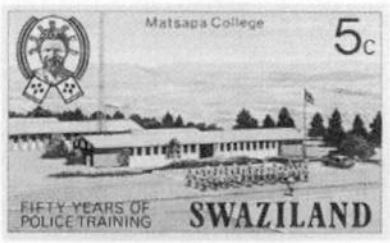

67 Matsapa College

1977. 50th Anniv of Police Training. Multicoloured.

271	5c. Type **67**	10	10
272	10c. Policemen and women on parade	50	30
273	20c. Royal Swaziland Police badge (vert)	70	1·10
274	25c. Dog handling	1·25	1·75

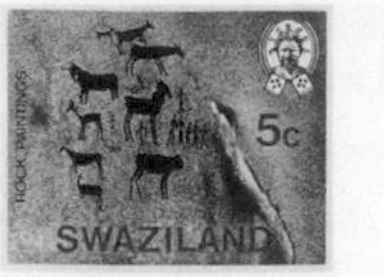

68 Animals and Hunters

1977. Rock Paintings. Multicoloured.

275	5c. Type **68**	30	10
276	10c. Four dancers in a procession	35	20
277	15c. Man with cattle	50	25
278	20c. Four dancers	55	35
MS279	103×124 mm. Nos. 275/8	2·00	2·75

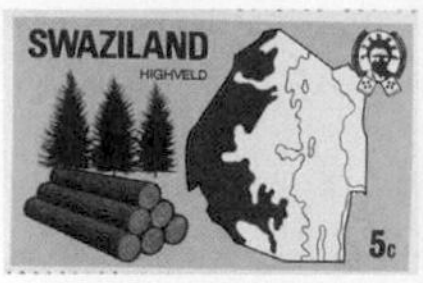

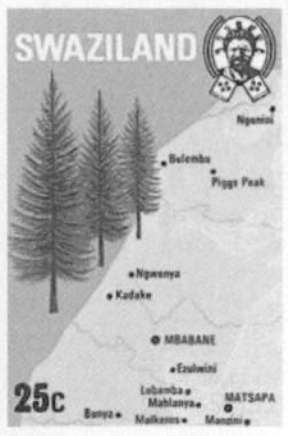

69 Timber, Highveld Region **70** Timber, Highveld Region

1977. Maps of the Regions. Multicoloured.

280	5c. Type **69**	50	10
281	10c. Pineapple, Middleveld	60	10
282	15c. Orange and lemon, Lowveld	80	65
283	20c. Cattle, Lubombo region	95	95
MS284	87×103 mm. Four 25c. designs as T **70**, together forming a composite map of Swaziland	1·40	1·60

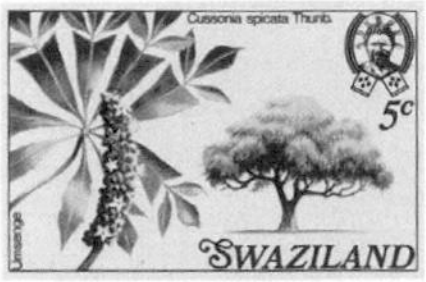

71 Cabbage Tree

1978. Trees of Swaziland.

285	**71**	5c. green, brown and black	15	15
286	-	10c. multicoloured	20	10
287	-	20c. multicoloured	45	1·25
288	-	25c. multicoloured	55	1·40

DESIGNS: 10c. Marula; 20c. Kiaat; 25c. Lucky bean-tree.

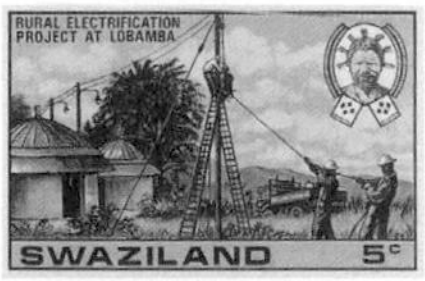

72 Rural Electrification at Lobamba

1978. Hydro-electric Power.

289	**72**	5c. black and brown	10	15
290	-	10c. black and green	15	15
291	-	20c. black and blue	25	40
292	-	25c. black and purple	30	50

DESIGNS: 10c. Edwaleni Power Station; 20c. Switch-gear, Magudza Power Station; 25c. Turbine Hall, Edwaleni.

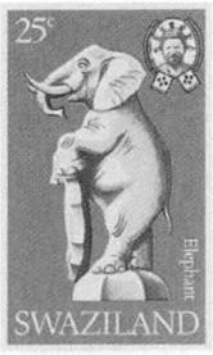

73 Elephant

1978. 25th Anniv of Coronation.

293	-	25c. blue, black and green	15	25
294	-	25c. multicoloured	15	25
295	**73**	25c. blue, black and green	15	25

DESIGNS: No. 293, Queen's Lion; No. 294, Queen Elizabeth II.

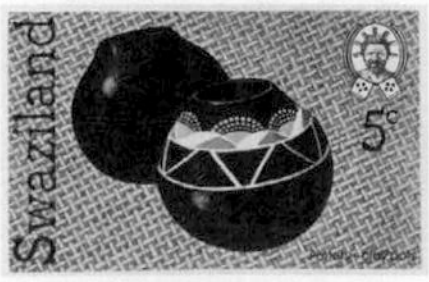

74 Clay Pots

1978. Handicrafts (1st series). Multicoloured.

296	5c. Type **74**	10	10
297	10c. Basketwork	10	10

298	20c. Wooden utensils	15	15
299	30c. Wooden pot	25	30

See also Nos. 310/13.

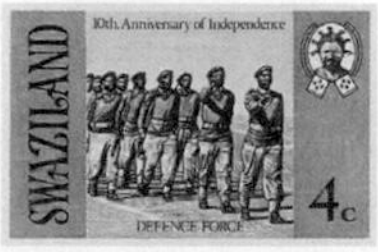

75 Defence Force

1978. Tenth Anniv of Independence. Multicoloured.

300	4c. Type **75**	15	10
301	6c. The King's Regiment	15	10
302	10c. Tinkabi tractor (agricultural development)	15	10
303	15c. Water-pipe laying (self-help scheme)	25	10
304	25c. Sebenta adult literacy scheme	30	25
305	50c. Fire emergency service	1·25	50

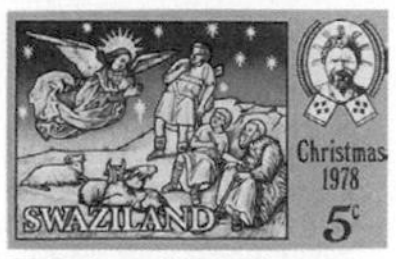

76 Archangel Gabriel appearing before Shepherds

1978. Christmas. Multicoloured.

306	5c. Type **76**	10	10
307	10c. Wise men paying homage to infant Jesus	15	10
308	15c. Archangel Gabriel warning Joseph	20	10
309	25c. Flight into Egypt	25	30

1979. Handicrafts (2nd series). As T **74**. Multicoloured.

310	5c. Sisal bowls	10	10
311	15c. Pottery	15	10
312	20c. Basket work	20	15
313	30c. Hide shield	30	20

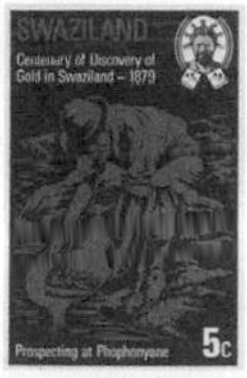

77 Prospecting at Phophonyane

1979. Centenary of Discovery of Gold in Swaziland.

314	**77**	5c. gold and blue	25	10
315	-	15c. gold and brown	45	20
316	-	25c. gold and green	65	35
317	-	50c. gold and red	90	2·00

DESIGNS: 15c. Early 3-stamp battery mill; 25c. Cyanide tanks at Piggs Peak; 50c. Pouring off molten gold.

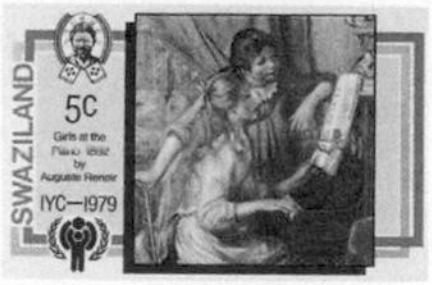

78 "Girls at the Piano"

1979. International Year of the Child. Paintings by Renoir. Multicoloured.

318	5c. Type **78**	10	10
319	15c. "Madame Charpentier and her Children"	25	10
320	25c. "Girls picking Flowers"	35	15
321	50c. "Girl with Watering Can"	70	55
MS322	123×135 mm. Nos. 318/21	1·25	1·75

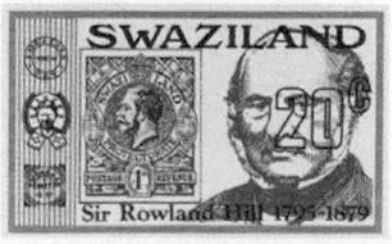

79 1933 1d. Carmine Stamp and Sir Rowland Hill

1979. Death Centenary of Sir Rowland Hill. Multicoloured.

323	10c. 1945 3d. Victory commemorative	15	10
324	20c. Type **79**	25	25
325	25c. 1968 25c. Independence commemorative	25	30
MS326	115×90 mm. 50c. 1956 6d. Great kudu antelope definitive	75	85

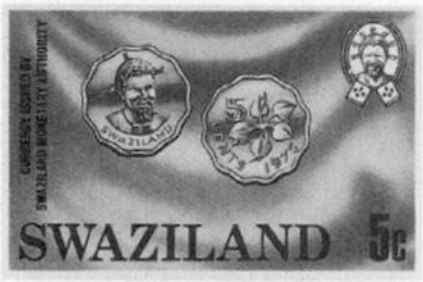

80 Obverse and Reverse of 5 Cents

1979. Coins.

327	**80**	5c. black and brown	15	10
328	-	10c. black and blue	20	10
329	-	20c. black and green	35	20
330	-	50c. black and orange	50	50
331	-	1e. black and cerise	75	1·00

DESIGNS: 10c. Obverse and reverse of 10 cents; 20c. Obverse and reverse of 20 cents; 50c. Reverse of 50 cents; 1e. Reverse of 1 lilangeni.

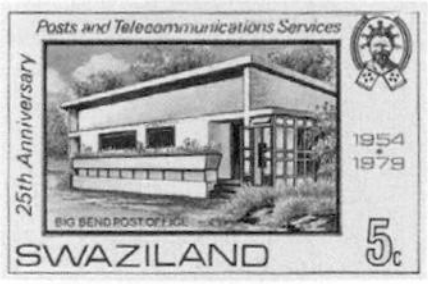

81 Big Bend Post Office

1979. Post Office Anniversaries.

332	**81**	5c. multicoloured	10	10
333	-	15c. multicoloured	15	10
334	-	20c. black, green and red	20	15
335	-	50c. multicoloured	40	60

DESIGNS AND COMMEMORATIONS—HORIZ: 5c. Type **81** (25th anniv of Posts and Tele- communications Services); 20c. 1949 75th anniv of U.P.U. 1s. stamp (10th anniv of U.P.U. membership); 50c. 1974 Centenary of U.P.U. 25c. stamp (10th anniv of U.P.U membership). VERT: 15c. Microwave antenna, Mount Ntondozi (25th anniv of Posts and Telecommunications Services).

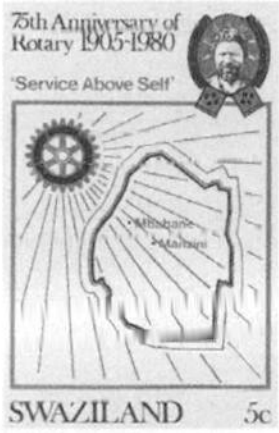

82 Map of Swaziland

1980. 75th Anniv of Rotary International.

336	**82**	5c. blue and gold	25	10
337	-	15c. blue and gold	45	10
338	-	50c. blue and gold	50	55
339	-	1e. blue and gold	85	1·25

DESIGNS: 15c. Vitreous cutter and optical illuminator; 50c. Scroll; 1e. Rotary Head quarters, Evanston, U.S.A.

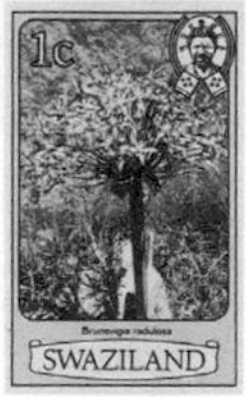

83 "Brunsvigia radulosa"

1980. Flowers. Multicoloured.

340A	1c. Type **83**	10	10
341A	2c. "Aloe suprafoliata"	10	10
342A	3c. "Haemanthus magnificus"	10	10
343A	4c. "Aloe marlothii"	10	10
344A	5c. "Dicoma zeyheri"	10	10
345A	6c. "Aloe kniphofioides"	15	30
346A	7c. "Cyrtanthus bicolor"	10	10
347A	10c. "Eucomis autumnalis" (horiz)	20	10
348A	15c. "Leucospermum gerrardii" (horiz)	15	10
349A	20c. "Haemanthus multiflorus" (horiz)	30	25
350A	30c. "Acridocarpus natalitius" (horiz)	20	20
351A	50c. "Adenium swazicum" (horiz)	20	30
352A	1e. "Protea simplex"	35	60
353A	2e. "Calodendrum capense"	80	1·25
354A	5e. "Gladiolus ecklonii"	1·10	3·00

Nos. 347A/51A are 42×45 mm and Nos. 352A/4A 28×38 mm.

Nos. 340A/1A, 343A, 345A, 347A and 349A come with and without date imprint.

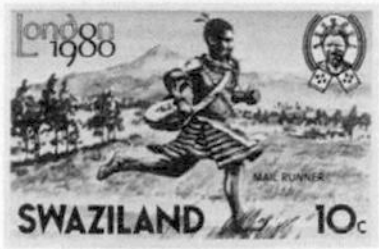

84 Mail Runner

1980. "London 1980" International Stamp Exhibition. Multicoloured.

355	10c. Type **84**	15	10
356	20c. Post Office mail truck	25	15
357	25c. Mail sorting office	30	20
358	50c. Ropeway conveying mail at Bulembu	70	70

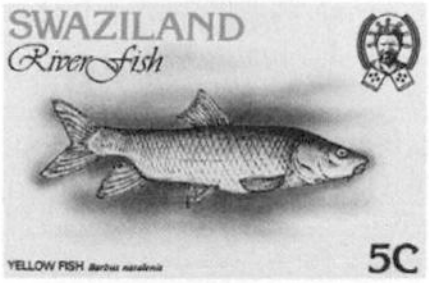

85 Scaly

1980. River Fish. Multicoloured.

359	5c. Type **85**	25	10
360	10c. Silver catfish ("Silver barbel")	25	10
361	15c. Tiger fish	40	15
362	30c. Brown squeaker	50	30
363	1e. Red-breasted tilapia ("Bream")	60	1·40

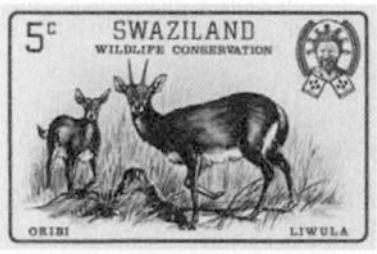

86 Oribi

1980. Wildlife Conservation. Multicoloured.

364	5c. Type **86**	15	10
365	10c. Nile crocodile (vert)	30	10
366	50c. Temminck's ground pangolin	50	70
367	1e. Leopard (vert)	1·25	1·50

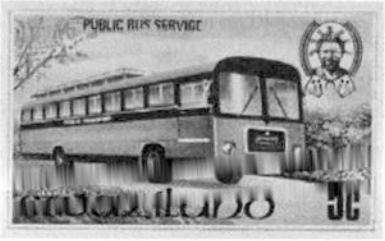

87 Public Bus Service

1981. Transport. Multicoloured.

368	5c. Type **87**	10	10
369	25c. Royal Swazi National Airways	25	15
370	30c. Swaziland United Transport	30	20
371	1e. Swaziland Railway	1·25	1·75

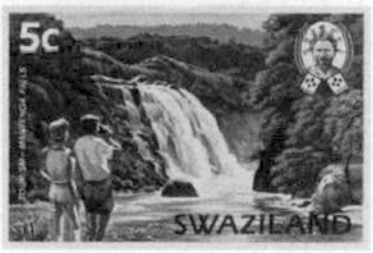

88 Mantenga Falls

1981. Tourism. Multicoloured.

372	5c. Type **88**	10	10
373	15c. Mananga Yacht Club	15	10
374	30c. White rhinoceros in Mlilwane Game Sanctuary	60	30
375	1e. Gambling equipment (casinos)	80	1·60

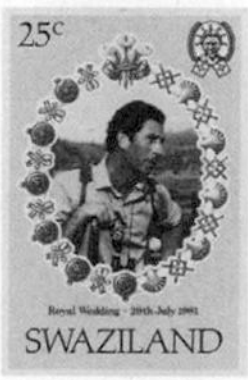

89 Prince Charles on Hike

1981. Royal Wedding. Multicoloured.

376	10c. Wedding bouquet from Swaziland	10	10
377	25c. Type **89**	15	10
378	1e. Prince Charles and Lady Diana Spencer	40	70

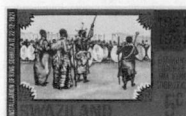

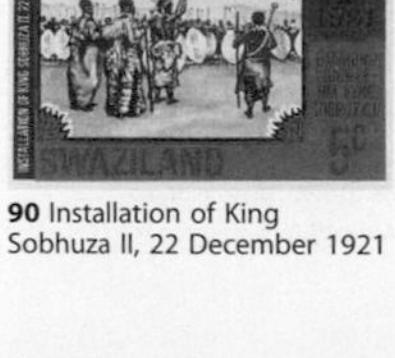
90 Installation of King Sobhuza II, 22 December 1921

1981. Diamond Jubilee of King Sobhuza II. Multicoloured.

379	5c. Type **90**	10	10
380	10c. Royal Visit, 1947	10	10
381	15c. King Sobhuza II and Coronation of Queen Elizabeth II, 1953	15	15
382	25c. King Sobhuza taking Royal Salute, Independence, 1968	15	15
383	30c. King Sobhuza in youth	20	20
384	1e. King Sobhuza and Parliament Buildings	50	90

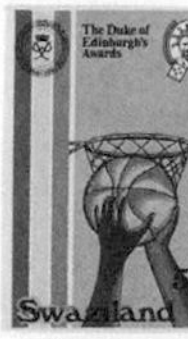

91 "Physical Recreation"

1981. 25th Anniv of Duke of Edinburgh Award Scheme. Multicoloured.

385	5c. Type **91**	10	10
386	20c. "Expeditions"	20	10
387	50c. "Skills"	35	25
388	1e. Duke of Edinburgh in ceremonial dress	50	80

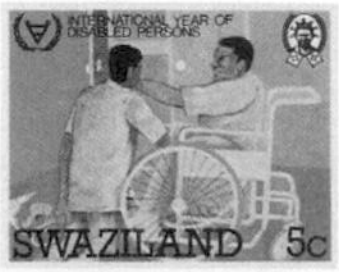

92 Disabled Person in Wheelchair

1981. International Year of Disabled Persons. Multicoloured.

389	5c. Type **92**	30	10
390	15c. Teacher with disabled child (vert)	50	15
391	25c. Disabled craftsman (vert)	75	20
392	1e. Disabled driver in invalid carriage	2·25	2·75

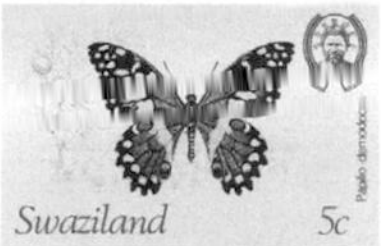

93 "Papilio demodocus"

1981. Butterflies. Multicoloured.

393	5c. Type **93**	50	10
394	10c. "Charaxes candiope"	50	10
395	50c. "Papilio nireus"	1·50	85
396	1e. "Terias desjardinsii"	2·00	2·00

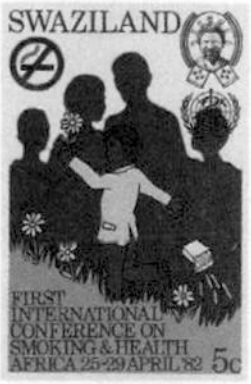

94 Man holding a Flower after discarding Cigarettes

1982. Pan-African Conference on Smoking and Health. Multicoloured.

397	5c. Type **94**	50	85
398	10c. Smoker and non-smoker	60	90

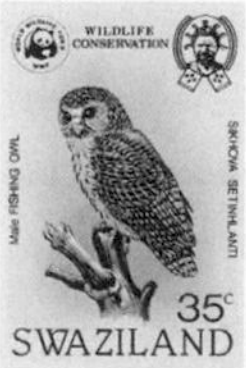

95 Male Pel's Fishing Owl

1982. Wildlife Conservation (1st series). Pel's Fishing Owl. Multicoloured.

399	35c. Type **95**	8·00	4·00
400	35c. Female Pel's fishing owl at nest	8·00	4·00
401	35c. Pair of Pel's fishing owls	8·00	4·00
402	35c. Pel's fishing owl, nest and eggs	8·00	4·00
403	35c. Adult Pel's fishing owl with youngster	8·00	4·00

See also Nos. 425/29 and 448/52.

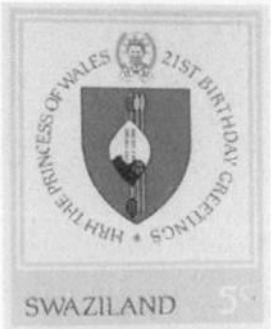

96 Swaziland Coat of Arms

1982. 21st Birthday of Princess of Wales. Multicoloured.

404	5c. Type **96**	10	10
405	20c. Princess leaving Eastleigh Airport, Southampton	80	10
406	50c. Bride at Buckingham Palace	60	30
407	1e. Formal portrait	1·50	85

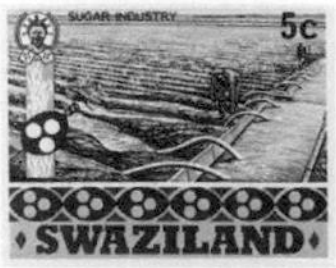

97 Irrigation

1982. Sugar Industry. Multicoloured.

408	5c. Type **97**	10	10
409	20c. Harvesting	25	15
410	30c. Mhlume mills	35	25
411	1e. Sugar transportation by train	1·00	2·00

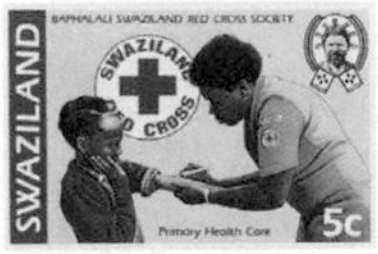

98 Doctor with Child

1982. Swaziland Red Cross Society (Baphaladi). Multicoloured.

412	5c. Type **98**	10	10
413	20c. Juniors carrying stretcher	25	15
414	50c. Disaster relief	55	75
415	1e. Henri Dunant (founder of Red Cross)	1·25	2·50

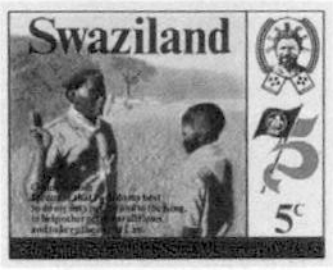

99 Taking the Oath

1982. 75th Anniv of Boy Scout Movement. Multicoloured.

416	5c. Type **99**	10	10
417	10c. Hiking and exploration	15	10
418	25c. Community development	30	30
419	75c. Lord Baden-Powell	1·00	1·25
MS420	107×109 mm. 1e. World Scout badge	1·00	1·40

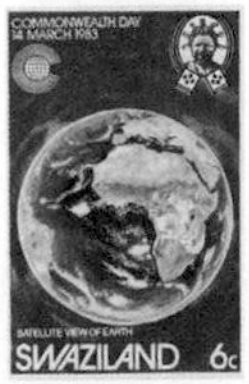

100 Satellite View of Earth

1982. Commonwealth Day. Multicoloured.

421	6c. Type **100**	10	10
422	10c. King Sobhuza II	10	10
423	50c. Swazi woman and beehive huts (horiz)	35	55
424	1e. Spraying sugar crops (horiz)	70	1·00

1983. Wildlife Conservation (2nd series). Lammergeier. As T **95**. Multicoloured.

425	35c. Adult male	2·50	2·50
426	35c. Pair	2·50	2·50
427	35c. Nest and egg	2·50	2·50
428	35c. Female at nest	2·50	2·50
429	35c. Adult bird with fledgling	2·50	2·50

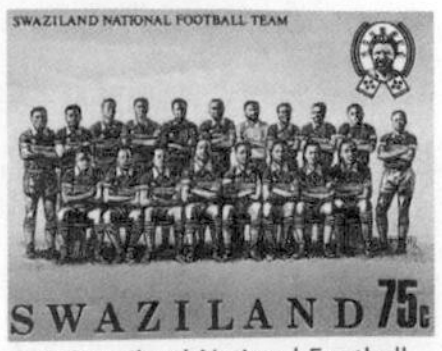

101 Swaziland National Football Team

1983. Tour of Swaziland by English Football Clubs. Three sheets, 101×72 mm, each containing one 75c. stamp as T **101**. Multicoloured.

MS430	75c. Type **101**; 75c. Tottenham Hotspur; 75c. Manchester United Set of 3 sheets	1·50	3·00

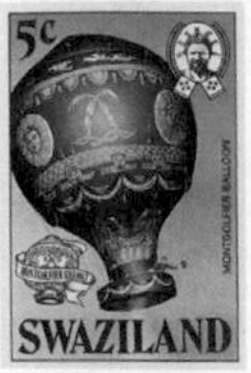

102 Montgolfier Balloon

1983. Bicentenary of Manned Flight. Multicoloured.

431	5c. Type **102**	10	10
432	10c. Wright brothers' Flyer I (horiz)	15	10
433	25c. Fokker Fellowship (horiz)	35	35
434	50c. Bell XS-1 (horiz)	85	65
MS435	73×73 mm. 1e. Space shuttle "Columbia"	1·00	1·40

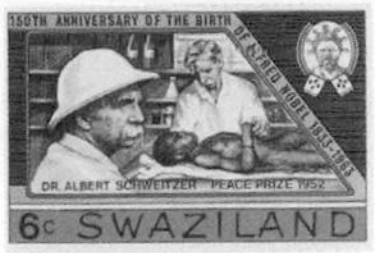

103 Dr. Albert Schweitzer (Peace Prize, 1952)

1983. 150th Birth Anniv of Alfred Nobel. Multicoloured.

436	6c. Type **103**	2·75	80
437	10c. Dag Hammarskjold (Peace Prize, 1961)	85	15
438	50c. Albert Einstein (Physics Prize, 1921)	3·75	2·25
439	1e. Alfred Nobel	3·75	4·50

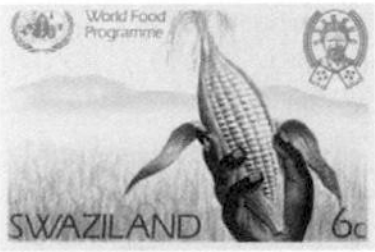

104 Maize

1983. World Food Day. Multicoloured.

440	6c. Type **104**	25	10
441	10c. Rice	25	10
442	50c. Cattle herding	1·00	1·00
443	1e. Ploughing	1·60	3·00

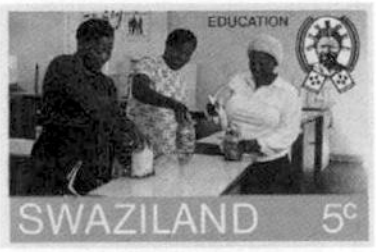

105 Women's College

1984. Education. Multicoloured.

444	5c. Type **105**	10	10
445	15c. Technical training school	15	15
446	50c. University	35	60
447	1e. Primary school	65	1·10

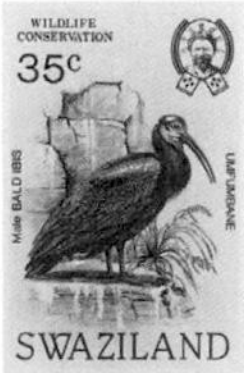

106 Male on Ledge

1984. Wildlife Conservation (3rd series). Bald Ibis. Multicoloured.

448	35c. Type **106**	3·00	3·00
449	35c. Male and female	3·00	3·00
450	35c. Bird and egg	3·00	3·00
451	35c. Female on nest of eggs	3·00	3·00
452	35c. Adult and fledgling	3·00	3·00

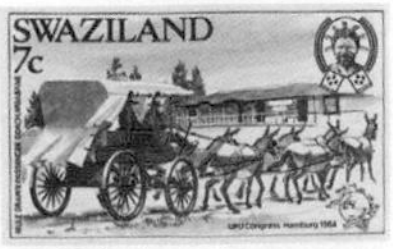

107 Mule-drawn Passenger Coach

1984. Universal Postal Union Congress, Hamburg. Multicoloured.

453	7c. Type **107**	30	15
454	15c. Ox-drawn post wagon	45	15
455	50c. Mule-drawn mail coach	90	1·00
456	1e. Bristol to London mail coach	1·40	2·00

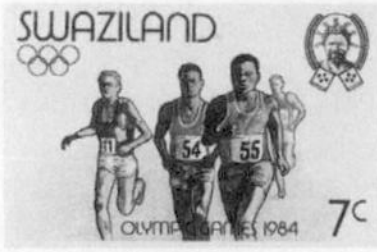

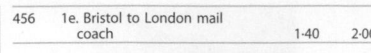

108 Running

1984. Olympic Games, Los Angeles. Multicoloured.

457	7c. Type **108**	15	15
458	10c. Swimming	15	15
459	50c. Shooting	60	1·00
460	1e. Boxing	1·10	2·00
MS461	100×70 mm. Nos. 457/60	3·25	5·50

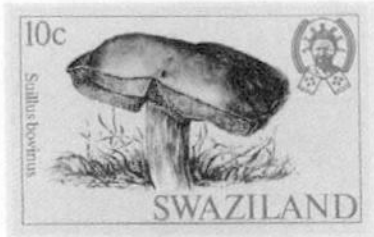

109 "Suillus bovinus"

1984. Fungi. Multicoloured.

462	10c. Type **109**	1·25	30
463	15c. "Langermannia gigantea" (vert)	2·00	55
464	50c. "Trametes versicolor" ("Coriolus versicolor") (vert)	2·25	2·75
465	1e. "Boletus edulis"	2·50	5·25

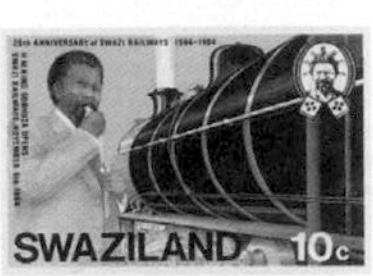

110 King Sobhuza opening Railway, 1964

1984. 20th Anniv of Swaziland Railways. Multicoloured.

466	10c. Type **110**	30	15
467	25c. Type 15A locomotive at Siweni Yard	55	40
468	30c. Container loading, Matsapha Station	55	40
469	1e. Locomotive No. 268 leaving Alto Tunnel	1·25	2·75
MS470	144×74 mm. Nos. 466/9	2·75	6·00

1985. Nos. 340, 342, 343, 345 and 346 surch.

471a	10c. on 4c. "Aloe marlothii"	35	10
472	15c. on 7c. "Cyrtanthus bicolor"	40	20
473	20c. on 3c. "Haemanthus magnificus"	35	15
474	25c. on 6c. "Aloe kniphofioides"	40	20
475	30c. on 1c. Type **83**	50	20
476	30c. on 2c. "Aloe suprafoliata"	2·75	4·25

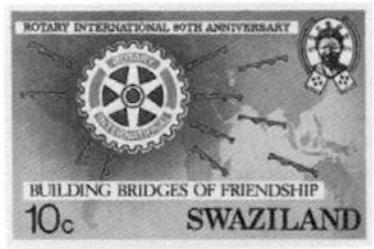

112 Rotary International Logo and Map of World

1985. 80th Anniv of Rotary International. Multicoloured.

477	10c. Type **112**	75	10
478	15c. Teacher and handicapped children	1·00	20
479	50c. Youth exchange	1·25	1·50
480	1e. Nurse and children	3·00	4·50

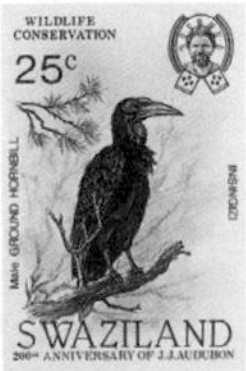

113 Male Southern Ground Hornbill

1985. Birth Bicentenary of John J. Audubon (ornithologist). Southern Ground Hornbills. Multicoloured.

481	25c. Type **113**	2·25	3·25
482	25c. Male and female ground hornbills	2·25	3·25
483	25c. Female at nest	2·25	3·25
484	25c. Ground hornbill in nest, and egg	2·25	3·25
485	25c. Adult and fledgling	2·25	3·25

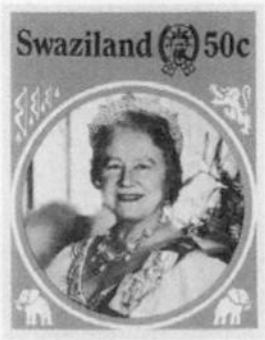

114 The Queen Mother in 1975

1985. Life and Times of Queen Elizabeth the Queen Mother. Multicoloured.

486	10c. The Queen Mother in South Africa, 1947	40	10
487	15c. With the Queen and Princess Margaret, 1985 (from photo by Norman Parkinson)	40	10
488	50c. Type **114**	1·10	1·10
489	1e. With Prince Henry at his christening (from photo by Lord Snowdon)	1·40	2·50
MS490	91×73 mm. 2e. Greeting Prince Andrew	3·00	1·75

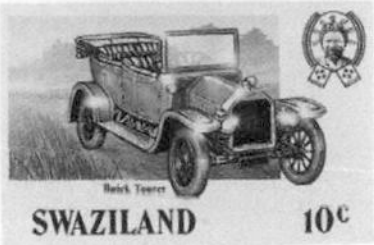

115 Buick "Tourer"

1985. Century of Motoring. Multicoloured.

491	10c. Type **115**	50	10
492	15c. Four cylinder Rover	70	25
493	50c. De Dion Bouton	1·75	2·00
494	1e. "Model T" Ford	2·25	4·00

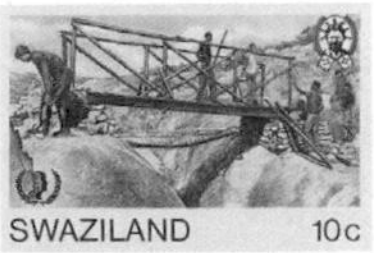

116 Youths building Bridge over Ravine

1985. International Youth Year (10, 50c.) and 75th Anniv of Girl Guide Movement (others). Multicoloured.

495	10c. Type **116**	25	10
496	20c. Girl Guides in camp	30	20
497	50c. Youth making model from sticks	60	1·25
498	1e. Guides collecting brushwood	80	2·25

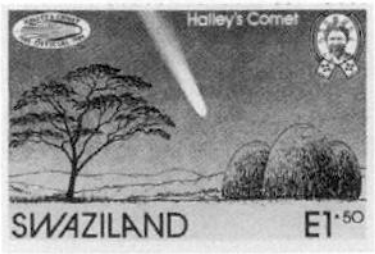

117 Halley's Comet over Swaziland

1986. Appearance of Halley's Comet.

499	**117**	1e.50 multicoloured	2·75	4·00

1986. 60th Birthday of Queen Elizabeth II. As T **145a** of St. Helena. Multicoloured.

500	10c. Christening of Princess Anne, 1950	10	10
501	30c. On Palace balcony after wedding of Prince and Princess of Wales, 1981	15	25
502	45c. Royal visit to Swaziland, 1947	15	30
503	1e. At Windsor Polo Ground, 1984	30	70
504	2e. At Crown Agents Head Office, London 1983	60	1·40

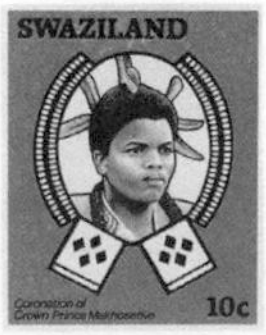

118 King Mswati III

1986. Coronation of King Mswati III.

505	**118**	10c. black and gold	35	25
506	-	20c. multicoloured	70	30
507	-	25c. multicoloured	80	35
508	-	30c. multicoloured	90	50
509	-	40c. multicoloured	3·25	2·00
510	-	2e. multicoloured	4·00	9·00

DESIGNS—HORIZ: 20c. Prince with King Sobhuza II at Incwala ceremony; 25c. At primary school; 30c. At school in England; 40c. Inspecting guard of honour at Matsapha Airport; 2e. Dancing the Simemo.

119 Emblems of Round Table and Project Orbis (eye disease campaign)

1986. 50th Anniv of Round Table Organization. Designs showing branch emblems. Multicoloured.

511	15c. Type **119**	30	10
512	25c. Ehlanzeni 51	40	20
513	55c. Mbabane 30	85	70
514	70c. Bulembu 54	1·10	1·75
515	2e. Manzini 44	2·00	4·50

120 "Precis hierta"

1987. Butterflies (1st series). Multicoloured.

516	10c. Type **120**	55	1·50
517	15c. "Hamanumida daedalus"	65	1·25
518	20c. "Charaxes boueti"	65	1·25
519	25c. "Abantis paradisea"	65	1·75
520	30c. "Acraea anemosa"	65	1·00
521	35c. "Graphium leonidas"	65	1·00
522	45c. "Graphium antheus"	70	2·00
523	50c. "Precis orithya"	70	1·25
524	55c. "Pinacopteryx eriphia"	70	1·25
525	70c. "Precis octavia"	80	1·40
526	1e. "Mylothris chloris"	1·00	3·00
527	5e. "Colotis regina"	85	1·50
528	10e. "Spindasis natalensis"	1·10	2·25

For these designs and similar 5c. with different portrait of King Mswati III, see Nos. 606/17.

121 Two White Rhinoceroses

1987. White Rhinoceros. Multicoloured.

529	15c. Type **121**	3·00	55
530	25c. Female and calf	3·50	1·00
531	45c. Rhinoceros charging	5·00	3·50
532	70c. Rhinoceros wallowing	7·25	8·50

122 Hybrid Tea Rose "Blue Moon"

1987. Garden Flowers. Multicoloured.

533	15c. Type **122**	1·25	20
534	35c. Rambler rose "Danse du feu"	2·25	80
535	55c. Pompon dahlia "Odin"	2·50	1·50
536	2e. "Lilium davidii var. willmottiae"	7·00	12·00

1987. Royal Ruby Wedding. Nos. 501/4 optd **40TH WEDDING ANNIVERSARY**.

537	30c. On Palace balcony after wedding of Prince and Princess of Wales, 1981	40	20
538	45c. Royal visit to Swaziland, 1947	50	30
539	1e. At Windsor Polo Ground, 1984	85	1·75
540	2e. At Crown Agents Head Office, London, 1983	1·25	3·25

123 "Zabalius aridus" (grasshopper)

1988. Insects. Multicoloured.

541	15c. Type **123**	1·40	15
542	55c. "Callidea bohemani" (shieldbug)	2·75	85
543	1e. "Phymateus viridipes" (grasshopper)	4·75	4·75
544	2e. "Nomadacris septemfasciata" (locust)	7·50	9·50

124 Athlete with Swazi Flag and Olympic Stadium

1988. Olympic Games, Seoul. Multicoloured.

545	15c. Type **124**	1·25	10
546	35c. Taekwondo	1·75	45
547	1e. Boxing	2·25	2·50
548	2e. Tennis	3·75	5·50

125 Savanna Monkey

1989. Small Mammals. Multicoloured.

549	35c. Type **125**	2·00	30
550	55c. Large-toothed rock hyrax	2·50	75
551	1e. Zorilla	4·25	4·50
552	2e. African wild cat	7·50	10·00

126 Dr. David Hynd (founder of Swazi Red Cross)

1989. 125th Anniv of Int Red Cross. Multicoloured.

553	15c. Type **126**	25	15
554	60c. First aid training	60	40
555	1e. Sigombeni Clinic	1·00	1·50
556	2e. Refugee camp	1·50	3·00

127 King Mswati III with Prince of Wales, 1987

1989. 21st Birthday of King Mswati III. Multicoloured.

557	15c. Type **127**	10	10
558	60c. King with Pope John Paul II, 1988	30	35
559	1e. Introduction of Crown Prince to people, 1983	50	55
560	2e. King Mswati III and Queen Mother	95	1·00

128 Manzini to Mahamba Road

1989. 25th Anniv of African Development Bank. Multicoloured.

561	15c. Type **128**	10	10
562	60c. Microwave Radio Receiver, Mbabane	30	40
563	1e. Mbabane Government Hospital	50	1·10
564	2e. Ezulwini Power Station switchyard	95	2·25

129 International Priority Mail Van

1990. "Stamp World London 90" International Stamp Exhibition. Multicoloured.

565	15c. Type **129**	15	10
566	60c. Facsimile service operators	40	40
567	1e. Rural post office	75	1·00
568	2e. Ezulwini Earth Station	1·40	2·50
MS569	105×85 mm. 2e. Mail runner	5·50	6·00

1990. 90th Birthday of Queen Elizabeth the Queen Mother. As T **161a** of St. Helena.

570	75c. multicoloured	50	50
571	4e. black and green	2·25	3·50

DESIGNS—21×36 mm: 75c. Queen Mother. 29×37 mm: 4e. King George VI and Queen Elizabeth visiting Civil Resettlement Unit, Hatfield House.

130 Pictorial Teaching

1990. International Literacy Year. Multicoloured.

572	15c. Type **130**	10	10
573	75c. Rural class	45	45
574	1e. Modern teaching methods	60	1·00
575	2e. Presentation of certificates	1·10	2·00

131 Rural Water Supply

1990. 40th Anniv of United Nations Development Programme. "Helping People to Help Themselves". Multicoloured.

576	60c. Type **131**	35	35
577	1e. Seed multiplication project	60	1·10
578	2e. Low-cost housing project	1·25	2·25

1990. Nos. 519/20, 522 and 524 surch.

579	10c. on 25c. "Abantis paradisea"	30	30
580	15c. on 30c. "Acraea anemosa"	40	40
580a	15c. on 45c. "Graphium antheus"	17·00	17·00
581	20c. on 45c. "Graphium antheus"	40	40
582	40c. on 55c. "Pinacopteryx eriphia"	55	55

133 Lobamba Hot Spring

1991. National Heritage. Multicoloured.

583	15c. Type **133**	40	10
584	60c. Sibebe Rock	1·50	45
585	1e. Jolobela Falls	2·00	2·00
586	2e. Mantjolo Sacred Pool	2·50	3·50
MS587	80×60 mm. 2e. Usushwana river	5·50	6·50

134 King Mswati III making Speech

1991. Fifth Anniv of King Mswati III's Coronation. Multicoloured.

588	15c. Type **134**	50	10
589	75c. Butimba Royal Hunt	1·40	60
590	1e. King and visiting school friends, 1986	1·75	2·00
591	2e. King opening Parliament	2·50	3·50

1991. 65th Birthday of Queen Elizabeth II and 70th Birthday of Prince Philip. As T **165a** of St. Helena. Multicoloured.

592	1e. Prince Philip	1·75	2·25
593	2e. Queen Elizabeth II	2·00	2·25

135 "Xerophyta retinervis"

1991. Indigenous Flowers. Multicoloured.

594	15c. Type **135**	50	10
595	75c. "Bauhinia galpinii"	1·25	80
596	1e. "Dombeya rotundifolia"	1·50	1·75
597	2e. "Kigelia africana"	2·25	3·50

136 Father Christmas arriving with Gifts

1991. Christmas. Multicoloured.

598	20c. Type **136**	15	10
599	70c. Singing carols	65	50
600	1e. Priest reading from Bible	80	1·25
601	2e. The Nativity	1·50	2·50

137 Lubombo Flat Lizard

1992. Reptiles (1st series). Multicoloured.

602	20c. Type **137**	90	20
603	70c. Natal hinged tortoise	2·25	1·50
604	1e. Swazi thick-toed gecko	2·75	2·75
605	2e. Nile monitor	3·75	5·50

See also Nos. 658/61.

138 "Precis hierta"

1992. Butterflies (2nd series). Nos. 516/26 and new value (5c.) showing different portrait of King Mswati III. Multicoloured.

606	5c. "Colotis antevippe"	10	50
607	10c. Type **138**	15	50
608	15c. "Hamanumida daedalus"	15	50
609	20c. "Charaxes boueti"	20	50
610	25c. "Abantis paradisea"	20	30
611	30c. "Acraea anemosa"	20	30
612	35c. "Graphium leonidas"	20	30
613	45c. "Graphium antheus"	25	30
614	50c. "Precis orithya"	25	30
615	55c. "Pinacopteryx eriphia"	25	30
616	70c. "Precis octavia"	60	40
617	1e. "Mylothris chloris"	70	90
618	5e. "Colotis regina"	15·00	5·00
619	10e. "Spindasis natalensis"	15·00	7·00

139 Missionaries visiting King Sobhuza II and Queen Lomawa

1992. Centenary of Evangelical Alliance Missions. Multicoloured.

620	20c. Type **139**	50	10
621	1e. Pioneer missionaries	2·50	3·25

140 Calabashes

1993. Archaeological and Contemporary Artifacts. Multicoloured.

622	20c. Type **140**	45	10
623	70c. Contemporary cooking pot	1·10	85
624	1e. Wooden bowl and containers	1·50	1·75
625	2e. Quern for grinding seeds	2·50	3·50

141 King Mswati
III as Baby

1993. 25th Birthday of King Mswati III and 25th Anniv of
Independence. Multicoloured.

626	25c. Type **141**	25	10
627	40c. King Mswati III addressing meeting	35	20
628	1e. King Sobhuza II receiving Instrument of Independence	90	1·50
629	2e. King Mswati III delivering Coronation speech	1·60	3·00

142 Male and
Female Common
Waxbills

1993. Common Waxbill. Multicoloured.

630	25c. Type **142**	40	20
631	40c. Waxbill and eggs in nest	55	25
632	1e. Waxbill on nest	1·25	1·50
633	2e. Waxbill feeding chicks	2·00	2·75

143 Classroom and
Practical Training

1994. 25th Anniv of U.S. Peace Corps in Swaziland.
Multicoloured.

634	25c. Type **143**	40	10
635	40c. Rural water supply	55	20
636	1e. Americans and Swazis in traditional costumes	2·00	2·00
637	2e. Swazi–American co-operation	2·25	3·25

144 "Agaricus
arvensis"

1994. Fungi. Multicoloured.

638	30c. Type **144**	1·25	50
639	40c. "Boletus edulis"	1·25	50
640	1e. "Russula virescens"	2·50	1·75
641	2e. "Armillaria mellea"	3·50	4·00

145 Emblem and Airliner on
Runway

1994. 50th Anniv of I.C.A.O. Multicoloured.

642	30c. Type **145**	50	10
643	40c. Control tower and dish aerial	55	20
644	1e. Crash tenders	1·25	1·50
645	2e. Air traffic controllers	1·75	2·75

146 Wooden
Bowls

1995. Handicrafts. Multicoloured.

646	35c. Type **146**	45	20
647	50c. Chicken nests	65	35
648	1e. Leather crafts	1·00	1·25
649	2e. Wood carvings	1·75	2·50

147 Harvesting
Maize

1995. 50th Anniv of F.A.O. Multicoloured.

650	35c. Type **147**	30	20
651	50c. Planting vegetables	45	35
652	1e. Herd of cattle	75	1·00
653	2e. Harvesting sorghum	1·25	2·00

148 Green Turaco

1995. Turacos ("Louries"). Multicoloured.

654	35c. Type **148**	40	30
655	50c. Green turaco in flight	55	45
656	1e. Violet-crested turaco	80	1·00
657	2e. Livingstone's turaco	1·25	2·00

1996. Reptiles (2nd series). As T **137** with King's portrait
at right. Multicoloured.

658	35c. Chameleon	70	20
659	50c. Rock monitor	80	35
660	1e. African python	1·40	1·60
661	2e. Tree agama	2·00	3·00

149 Waterberry

1996. Trees. Multicoloured.

662	40c. Type **149**	25	15
663	60c. Sycamore fig	30	20
664	1e. Stem fruit	50	80
665	2e. Wild medlar	90	1·60

150 Mahamba Methodist
Church

1996. Historic Monuments. Multicoloured.

666	40c. Type **150**	50	15
667	60c. Colonial Secretariat, Mbabane	65	20
668	1e. King Sobhuza II Monument, Lobamba	1·10	1·40
669	2e. First High Court Building, Hlatikulu	1·75	2·75

151 Children in Class

1996. 50th Anniv of UNICEF. Multicoloured.

670	40c. Type **151**	25	15
671	60c. Child being inoculated (vert)	35	20
672	1e. Child on crutches (vert)	60	90
673	2e. Mother and children (vert)	1·00	2·00

152 Klipspringer

1997. Mammals. Multicoloured.

674	50c. Type **152**	30	20
675	70c. Grey duiker	35	30
676	1e. Antbear (horiz)	50	70
677	2e. Cape clawless otter (horiz)	80	1·60

153 Umgaco
Costume

1997. Traditional Costumes. Multicoloured.

678	50c. Type **153**	25	15
679	70c. Sigeja cloak	35	25
680	1e. Umdada kilt	55	65
681	2e. Ligcebesha costume	90	1·40

154 Olive Toad

1998. Amphibians. Multicoloured.

682	55c. Type **154**	35	15
683	75c. African bullfrog	45	30
684	1e. Water lily frog	70	90
685	2e. Bushveld rain frog	1·25	1·90

155 Aerial View of King
Sobhuza II Memorial Park

1998. 30th Anniv of Independence and 30th Birthday of
King Mswati III. Multicoloured.

686	55c. Type **155**	40	15
687	75c. King Mswati III taking oath (vert)	50	25
688	1e. King Mswati delivering speech	75	90
689	2e. King Sobhuza II receiving Instrument of Independence	1·40	2·00

156 Grinding
Stone

1999. Local Culinary Utensils. Multicoloured.

690	60c. Type **156**	35	15
691	75c. Stirring sticks	40	20
692	80c. Clay pot	40	25
693	95c. Swazi spoons	55	45
694	1e.75 Beer cups	1·00	1·40
695	2e.40 Mortar and pestle	1·40	2·00

157 Internet
Service

1999. 125th Anniv of Universal Postal Union.
Multicoloured.

696	60c. Type **157**	35	15
697	80c. Cellular phone service	45	25
698	1e. Two post vans exchanging mail (horiz)	1·75	1·50
699	2e.40 Training school (horiz)	2·00	2·50

158 Lion and
Lioness

2000. Wildlife. Multicoloured.

700	65c. Type **158**	55	20
701	90c. Leopard (horiz)	75	35
702	1e.50 Rhinoceros (horiz)	3·00	1·75
703	2e.50 Buffalo	2·25	3·00

159 Oribi with Young

2001. Endangered Species. Antelopes. Multicoloured.

704	65c. Type **159**	45	25
705	90c. Oribi buck	70	40
706	1e.50 Young klipspringers	1·25	1·50
707	2e.50 Male and female klip-springers	1·75	2·25

160 Fighting Forest Fires

2001. Environment Protection. Multicoloured.

708	70c. Type **160**	50	20
709	95c. Tree planting	65	25
710	2e.05 Construction of Maguga Dam	1·40	1·75
711	2e.80 Building embankment	1·75	2·25

2002. Golden Jubilee. As T **211** of St. Helena.

712	70c. agate, violet and gold	65	10
713	95c. multicoloured	85	25
714	2e.05 agate, violet and gold	1·40	1·50
715	2e.80 multicoloured	1·75	2·00

MS716 162×95 mm. Nos. 715/15 and
22e.50 multicoloured | 6·00 | 7·00

DESIGNS—HORIZ (as T **211** of St. Helena): 70c. Princess
Elizabeth, Prince Philip, and children, 1951; 95c. Queen
Elizabeth in blue and white beret; 2e.05, Queen Elizabeth
in evening dress; 2e80, Queen Elizabeth on visit to Nor-
way, 2001. VERT (38×51 mm): 50p. Queen Elizabeth after
Annigoni.

Designs as Nos. 712/15 in No. **MS**716 omit the gold
frame around each stamp and the "Golden Jubilee 1952–
2002" inscription.

161 Swazi Village

2002. Tourism. Multicoloured.

717	75c. Type **161**	20	10
718	1e. King Mswati and lions (vert)	30	20
719	2e.05 Crocodile	1·25	1·50
720	2e.80 Ostrich with young	1·75	2·25

162 Sitolotolo
(mouth organ)

2003. Musical Instruments. Multicoloured.

721	80c. Type **162**	30	20
722	1e.05 Emafahlawane (rattles) (horiz)	40	25
723	2e.35 Impalampala (Kudu horn trumpet) (horiz)	85	1·25
724	2e.80 Makhoyane (chordphone)	1·10	1·60

163 Community Health
Worker with AIDS Patient

2004. AIDS Awareness Campaign. Multicoloured.

725	85c. Type **163**	50	20

726	1e.10 Care and Voluntary Counselling and Testing Centre	60	30
727	2e.45 Testing blood (vert)	1·40	1·40
728	3e.35 Nurse giving injection and sterilizer (vert)	1·75	2·25

164 King Mswati III and Outline of Africa

2004. Global 2003 Smart Partnership Movement. Multicoloured.

729	85c. Type **164**	35	20
730	1e.10 Outline of Africa and logos (horiz)	45	25
731	2e.45 Stylized people holding globe	95	1·25
732	3e.35 King Mswati III and speaker	1·10	1·60

2004. First Joint Issue of Southern Africa Postal Operators Association Members. Hexagonal designs as T **470a** of South Africa showing national birds of Association members. Multicoloured.

733	85c. Purple-crested turaco ("Lourie") (Swaziland)	70	50
734	1e.10 Stanley ("Blue") crane (South Africa)	70	50
735	1e.35 Cattle egret (Botswana)	75	60
736	1e.90 Two African fish eagles perched (Zimbabwe)	1·40	1·10
737	2e. African fish eagle (Namibia)	1·40	1·10
738	2e.45 Bar-tailed trogon (Malawi) (inscribed "apaloderma vittatum")	1·50	1·50
739	3e. Two African fish eagles in flight (Zambia)	1·75	2·00
740	3e.35 Peregrine falcon (Angola)	1·90	2·50
MS741	170x95 mm. Nos. 733/40	9·00	10·00

The stamp depicting the bar-tailed trogon is not inscribed with the country of which the bird is a national symbol.

Miniature sheets in similar designs were also issued by Namibia, Zimbabwe, Angola, Botswana, South Africa, Malawi and Zambia.

165 School Child under Car and Children by Road

2005. Road Safety Council. Multicoloured.

742	85c. Type **165**	50	35
743	1e.10 Fire rescue team pulling injured man from car	50	35
744	2e.45 Pedestrians and car approaching stop sign	80	1·10
745	3e.35 Bus and road safety officials	1·10	1·50

166 Black Mamba

2005. Snakes. Multicoloured.

746	85c. Type **166**	30	15
747	1e.10 Python	40	30
748	2e.45 Boomslang	80	1·10
749	3e.35 Puff adder	1·10	1·50

2005. Pope John Paul II Commemoration. As T **231** of St. Helena.

| 750 | 4e.50 multicoloured | 1·75 | 1·90 |

167 Schistocerca solitaria

2005. Locusts and Grasshoppers. Multicoloured.

751	85c. Type **167**	50	20
752	1e.10 Nomadacris septemfasciata (red locust)	60	35
753	2e.45 Schistocerca gregaria flaviventris (South African desert locust)	1·50	1·75
754	3e.35 Locusta migratoria migratoroides (African migratory locust)	2·00	2·50

168 Ntombi Tfwala (1983-)

2006. Queen Mothers of Swaziland. Multicoloured.

755	85c. Type **168**	50	20
756	1e.10 Dzeliwe Shongwe (1980–3)	60	35
757	2e. Lomawa Ndwandwe (1921–38)	1·25	1·00
758	2e.45 Labotsibeni Mdluli (1895–1921)	1·50	1·75
759	3e.35 Tibati Nkambule (1881–95)	2·00	2·50

169 Mgubudla Falls, Northern Hhohho

2006. Waterfalls. Multicoloured.

760	90c. Type **170**	60	25
761	1e.15 Phophonyane Falls, Phophonyane Nature Reserve	70	35
762	1e.40 Mantenga Falls, Mantenga Nature Reserve (horiz)	95	70
763	2e. Malolotja Falls, Malolotja Nature Reserve	1·40	1·10
764	2e.55 Mabhudlweni Falls, Mhlosheni, Shiselweni	2·25	2·75
765	3e.50 Manzamnyama Falls, Mdzimba Mountains (horiz)	2·50	2·75

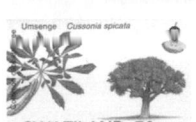

170 Cussonia spicata (common cabbage tree)

2007. Trees. Multicoloured.

766	70c. Type **171**	30	20
767	85c. Ficus sur (broom cluster fig)	30	35
768	90c. Acacia nilotica (scented thorn)	35	25
769	1e.05 Trichlia emetica (Natal mahogany)	40	25
770	1e.15 Sclerocarya birrea (marula)	45	30
771	1e.40 Bequaertiodendron megalismontanum (stem fruit)	50	35
772	2e. Acacia xanthophloea (fever tree)	65	50
773	2e.40 Erythrina latissima (large-leaved coral tree)	70	60
774	2e.55 Pterocarpus angolensis (African teak)	70	65
775	3e.50 Berchemia zeyheri (red ivory)	95	85
776	5e. Erythrina lysistemon (common coral tree)	1·40	1·50
777	10e. Pappea capensis (jacket-plum)	2·75	3·00
778	20e. Kigelia africana (sausage tree)	5·00	6·00

171 District Office/Post Office, Manzini, 1920s

2006. Postal History. Multicoloured.

779	90c. Type **169**	55	20
780	1e.15 Ox-wagon transferring post, 1880s–90s	65	35
781	2e. Bremersdorp Post Office, 1893	1·25	1·00
782	2e.55 Mail runner (vert)	1·60	1·75
783	3e.50 Temporary post office, Mbabane, 1902	2·25	2·75

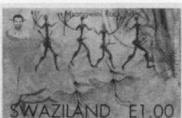

172 Nsangwini Rock Art

2008. Community Based Tourism. Multicoloured.

784	1e. Type **172**	60	20
785	1e.20 Mahamba Gorge Lodge	70	35
786	2e.70 Shewula Mountain Camp	1·50	1·75
787	3e.70 Khopho Camp, Ngwempisi trails	2·25	2·50

173 Inkhonyane

2008. Swazi Finery. Multicoloured.

788	1e. Type **173**	60	30
789	2e.70 Beaded necklace (horiz)	1·50	1·75
790	3e.70 Anklets (horiz)	2·25	2·50

174 Steam Locomotive and Airliner ('Transport Infrastructure')

2008. 40th Anniv of Independence and 40th Birthday of King Mswati III. Multicoloured.

791	1e. Type **174**	40	30
792	1e.05 King Mswati III receives new Swaziland constitution, 26 July 2005 (vert)	45	35
793	1e.30 Maguga Dam	50	40
794	1e.60 Maidens at reed dance (vert)	50	45
795	2e.15 One lilangeni note (First Lilangeni Currency, 1974)	60	55
796	2e.40 Nurse with boy ('Health and Social welfare')	70	80
797	2e.75 P j yimputi ('Information Communication Technology')	75	1·00
798	2e.90 King Mswati III's 40th birthday	1·25	1·50
799	3e.95 King Subhuza declaring independence, 1968 (vert)	1·90	2·50

2010. Third Joint Issue of Southern Africa Postal Operators Association Members. World Cup Football Championship, South Africa. Multicoloured.

800	1e. Zimbabwe	40	30
801	1e.25 South Africa	50	40
802	1e.50 Mauritius	55	50
803	1e.90 Namibia	55	45
804	2e.50 Zambia	70	80
805	3e.40 Swaziland	1·60	1·75
806	3e.80 Malawi	1·60	1·90
807	4e.60 Botswana	2·10	2·00
808	4e.90 Lesotho	2·25	2·10

2012. Locusts and Grasshoppers (2nd series). As Nos. 751/4 but inscr with A, B, C or D value indicator instead of face value and with '2011' imprint date

809	(1e.35) (A) Schistocerca gregaria flaviventris (Southern African desert locust)	55	50
810	(1e.70) (B) Schistocerca solitaria	55	50
811	(3e.30) (C) Locusta migratoria migratoriodes (African migratory locust)	1·60	1·75
812	4e.90 (D) Nomadacris septemfasciata (red locust)	2·25	2·10

Nos. 809/12 were inscr A, B, C or D and were originally sold for 1e.35, 1e.70, 3e.30 or 4e.90 respectively.

POSTAGE DUE STAMPS

D1

1933

| D1 | **D1** | 1d. red | 1·90 | 18·00 |
| D2 | **D1** | 2d. violet | 4·75 | 38·00 |

1961. Surch Postage Due **2d.**

| D3 | **7** | 2d. on 2d. black and brown | 1·25 | 2·75 |

These prices apply to stamps with large figure measuring 4½ mm high.

1961. As Type **D1** but with value in cents.

| D4 | 1c. red | 15 | 1·10 |

| D5 | 2c. violet | 15 | 1·10 |
| D6 | 5c. green | 20 | 1·10 |

1961. Surch Postage Due and value in cents.

D10	**7**	1c. on 2d. black and brown	70	4·00
D11	**7**	2c. on 2d. black and brown	50	2·75
D12	**7**	5c. on 2d. black and brown	90	2·25

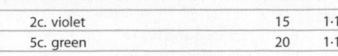

D6

1971

D19	**D6**	1c. red	30	1·75
D23	**D6**	2c. purple	10	35
D24	**D6**	5c. green	10	35
D25	**D6**	10c. blue	15	35
D26	**D6**	25c. brown	20	35

Pt. 11

SWEDEN

A kingdom of N. Europe, united to Norway till 1905.

1855. 48 skilling banco = 1 riksdaler.
1858. 100 ore = 1 riksdaler.
1875. 100 ore = 1 krona.

1

1855

1	1	3s. green	£11000	£4500
2	1	4s. blue	£1800	75·00
3	1	6s. grey	£11000	£1500
4	1	8s. orange	£5500	£800
5	1	24s. red	£8500	£2250

1858

6b	5ore green	£200	24·00
7a	9ore purple	£425	£275
8a	12ore blue	£250	7·50
9a	24ore orange	£830	65·00
10a	30ore brown	£600	55·00
11b	50ore red	£650	£110

2    **3**

1862

12bc	2	3ore brown	£275	16·00
13	3	17ore purple	£800	£160
14	3	17ore grey	£850	£800
15b	3	20ore red	£300	20·00

4   **5**   **6** King Oscar II

1872

29	4	2ore orange	2·50	8·75
30	4	3ore brown	16·00	25·00
31	4	4ore grey	39·00	2·00
32	4	5ore green	85·00	90
20	4	6ore green	£1100	£110
33	4	6ore mauve	39·00	65·00
34	6	10ore pink	90·00	50
21a	4	12ore blue	£250	5·00
35	4	20ore red	£130	1·00
23a	4	24ore yellow	£1000	44·00
36	4	30ore brown	£325	1·90
37	4	50ore red	£200	5·00
26	5	1r. blue and bistre	£1100	95·00
38	5	1k. blue and bistre	£120	4·50

No. 26 has the value expressed as one riksdaler and No. 38 one krona.

1889. Surch **10 10 TIO ORE** and Arms.

| 39 | 4 | 10ore on 12ore blue | 4·00 | 5·00 |
| 40 | 4 | 10ore on 24ore yellow | 10·50 | 50·00 |

9    **10** Oscar II    **11**

1891

41	9	1ore blue and brown	1·30	75
42a	9	2ore yellow and blue	4·00	50
43	9	3ore orange and brown	65	1·80
44	9	4ore blue and red	36·00	1·00
45c	10	5ore green	2·50	40
46	10	8ore purple	4·00	1·50
47	10	10ore red	4·50	40
48	10	15ore brown	29·00	50
49	10	20ore blue	29·00	50
56	10	25ore orange	30·00	4·50
51a	10	30ore brown	65·00	75
53	10	50ore grey	£100	90
54	11	1k. grey and red	£180	2·50

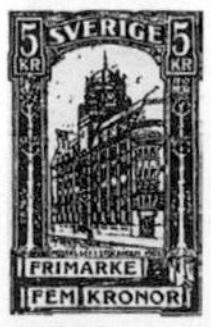

13 G.P.O., Stockholm

1903. Opening of new Post Office.

57	13	5k. blue	£250	28·00

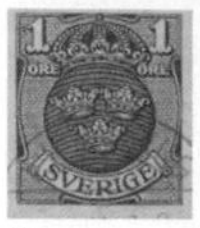

14

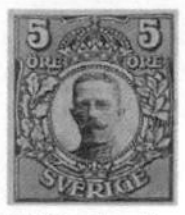

15 Gustav V

1910

65	14	1ore black	40	30
66	14	2ore orange	40	30
67	14	3ore brown	40	30
68	14	4ore mauve	40	30
69	15	5ore green	2·10	40
70	15	7ore green	40	25
71	15	8ore purple	40	25
72	15	10ore red	2·20	40
73	15	12ore purple	40	25
74	15	15ore brown	6·25	40
75	15	20ore blue	10·50	40
76	15	25ore orange	40	25
77	15	27ore blue	55	1·30
78	15	30ore brown	21·00	40
79	15	35ore violet	18·00	40
80	15	40ore green	28·00	40
81	15	50ore grey	70·00	40
82	15	55ore blue	£2500	£7000
83	15	65ore green	70	2·30
84	15	80ore black	£2500	£7000
85	15	90ore green	70	75
63	15	1k. black on yellow	£110	65
64	15	5k. purple on yellow	2·20	3·25

1916. Clothing Fund for Mobilized Reservists ("Landstorm"). (a) Postage stamps surch **FRIMARKE LANDSTORMEN** and value in figures and words round Arms.

86a	4	5+5 on 2ore orange	5·00	8·00
86b	4	5+5 on 3ore brown	5·00	8·00
86c	4	5+5 on 4ore grey	5·00	8·00
86d	4	5+5 on 5ore green	5·00	8·00
86e	4	5+5 on 6ore mauve	5·00	8·00
86f	4	10+10 on 12ore blue	5·00	8·00
86g	4	10+10 on 20ore red	5·00	8·00
86h	4	10+10 on 24ore yellow	5·00	8·00
86i	4	10+10 on 30ore brown	5·00	8·00
86j	4	10+10 on 50ore red	5·00	8·00

(b) Postage Due stamps surch **FRIMARKE SVERIGE** in frame round Arms, **LANDSTORMEN** and value in figures and words.

86k	D6	5+5 on 1ore black	31·00	10·50
86l	D6	5+5 on 3ore red	6·25	5·25
86m	D6	5+5 on 5ore brown	23·00	5·25
86n	D6	5+10 on 6ore orange	5·50	6·25
86o	D6	5+15 on 12ore red	55·00	27·00
86p	D6	10+20 on 20ore blue	19·00	21·00
86q	D6	10+40 on 24ore mauve	70·00	85·00
86r	D6	10+20 on 30ore green	8·50	6·25
86s	D6	10+40 on 50ore brown	25·00	37·00
86t	D6	10+90 on 1k. blue and brown	19·00	37·00

(c) No. 57 surch **FRIMARKE ORE 10 ORE FRIMARKE LANDSTORMEN KR. 4,90** and Arms.

86u	13	10 ore+4k.90 on 5k. blue	£190	£325

1917. Surch in figures only.

87	15	7 on 10ore red	45	40
88	15	12 on 25ore orange	2·30	40
89	15	12 on 65ore green	95	1·40
90	15	27 on 55ore blue	95	1·60
91	15	27 on 65ore green	1·90	3·75
92	15	27 on 80ore black	1·10	1·60
93	15	1.98k. on 5k. purple on yell	1·60	5·25
94	15	2.12k. on 5k. purple on yell	1·60	5·25

1918. Landstorm Fund. Nos. 86a/j surch.

94a	4	7+3 on 5ore on 2ore	9·25	8·75
94b	4	7+3 on 5ore on 3ore	3·00	1·20
94c	4	7+3 on 5ore on 4ore	3·00	1·20
94d	4	7+3 on 5ore on 5ore	3·00	1·20
94e	4	7+3 on 5ore on 6ore	3·00	1·20
94f	4	12+8 on 10ore on 12ore	3·00	1·20
94g	4	12+8 on 10ore on 20ore	3·00	1·20
94h	4	12+8 on 10ore on 24ore	3·00	1·20
94i	4	12+8 on 10ore on 30ore	3·00	1·20
94j	4	12+8 on 10ore on 50ore	3·00	1·20

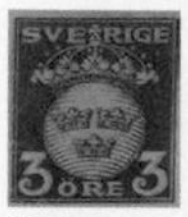

19 Arms

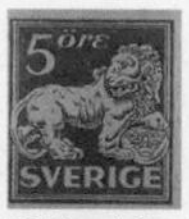

20 Lion (after sculpture by B. Foucquet)

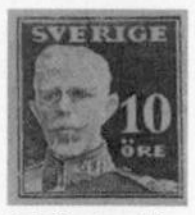

21 Gustav V

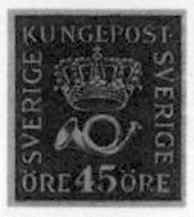

22 Emblem of Swedish Post

1920

95A	19	3ore red	45	60
96Bb	20	5ore green	1·60	7·50
97A	20	5ore brown	5·50	60
98B	20	10ore green	2·75	1·40
99A	20	10ore violet	6·25	60
102a	21	10ore red	14·00	7·00
103	21	15ore purple	45	60
104a	21	20ore blue	31·00	12·50
100A	20	25ore orange	14·00	60
101A	20	30ore brown	60	60
105A	22	35ore yellow	47·00	90
106A	22	40ore green	39·00	90
107A	22	45ore brown	1·60	60
108A	22	60ore purple	23·00	60
109A	22	70ore brown	80	3·50
110A	22	80ore green	60	60
111A	22	85ore green	5·50	60
112A	22	90ore blue	70·00	60
113A	22	1k. orange	7·75	60
114A	22	110ore blue	80	80
115A	22	115ore brown	11·50	60
116A	22	120ore black	70·00	60
117A	22	120ore mauve	19·00	60
118A	22	140ore black	1·10	60
119A	22	145ore green	9·25	60

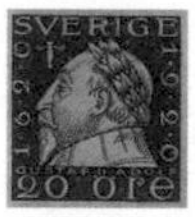

23 Gustavus II Adolphus

1920. Tercentenary of Swedish Post between Stockholm and Hamburg.

120A	23	20ore blue	3·25	60

1920. Air. Official stamps surch **LUFTPOST** and value.

120c	O 17	10 on 3ore brown	2·50	7·50
120d	O 17	20 on 2ore yellow	4·25	11·00
120e	O 17	50 on 4ore lilac	25·00	25·00

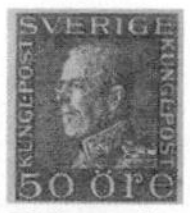

24 Gustav V (after portrait by E. Osterman)

1921

121	24	15ore violet	19·00	25
122	24	15ore red	5·50	70
123	24	15ore brown	5·50	60
124	24	20ore violet	45	35
125	24	20ore red	23·00	80
126	24	20ore orange	45	90
128	24	25ore red	60	1·70
129	24	25ore blue	19·00	60
131	24	25ore orange	35·00	60
133	24	30ore brown	23·00	60
134	24	30ore blue	7·75	90
135	24	35ore purple	20·00	60
136	24	40ore blue	60	70
137	24	40ore green	47·00	2·10
138	24	45ore brown	4·75	1·20
139a	24	50ore black	1·90	1·20
140	24	85ore green	22·00	2·30
141	24	115ore brown	14·00	2·30
142	24	145ore green	10·00	2·30

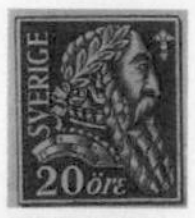

25 Gustavus Vasa

1921. 400th Anniv of Liberation of Sweden.

143	25	20ore violet	16·00	28·00
144	25	110ore blue	60·00	8·00
145	25	140ore black	39·00	8·00

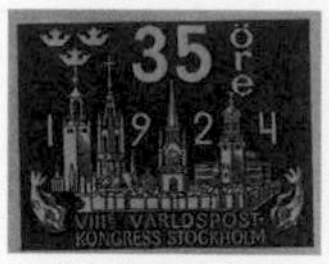

26 Old City, Stockholm

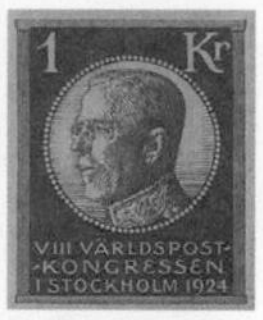

27 Gustav V

1924. Eighth Congress of U.P.U.

146	26	5ore brown	1·90	3·50
147	26	10ore green	1·90	4·00
148	26	15ore violet	2·30	3·00
149	26	20ore red	16·00	23·00
150	26	25ore orange	19·00	23·00
151	26	30ore blue	19·00	23·00
152	26	35ore black	22·00	29·00
153	26	40ore green	31·00	35·00
154	26	45ore brown	37·00	35·00
155	26	50ore grey	37·00	35·00
156	26	60ore purple	47·00	60·00
157	26	80ore green	43·00	40·00
158	27	1k. green	60·00	85·00
159	27	2k. red	£150	£250
160	27	5k. blue	£350	£450

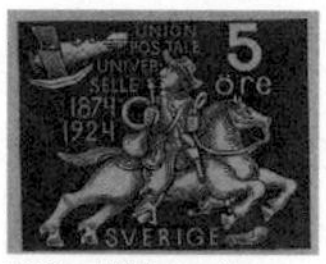

28 Post Rider and Friedrichsafen FF-49 Seaplane

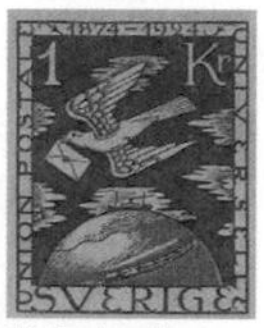

29 Carrier-pigeon

1924. 50th Anniv of U.P.U.

161	28	5ore brown	3·00	5·25
162	28	10ore green	3·00	6·25
163	28	15ore violet	4·00	3·50
164	28	20ore red	25·00	35·00
165	28	25ore orange	31·00	35·00
166	28	30ore blue	31·00	35·00
167	28	35ore black	37·00	50·00
168	28	40ore green	37·00	35·00
169	28	45ore brown	47·00	40·00
170	28	50ore grey	55·00	65·00
171	28	60ore purple	55·00	80·00
172	28	80ore green	43·00	40·00
173	29	1k. green	85·00	90·00
174	29	2k. red	£150	75·00
175	29	5k. blue	£300	£225

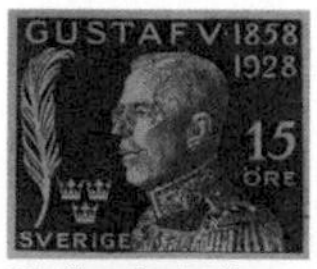

29a King Gustav V

1928. 70th Birthday of King Gustav V and Cancer Research Fund.

175a	29a	5(+5)ore green	2·30	5·75
175b	29a	10(+5)ore violet	2·30	5·75
175c	29a	15(+5)ore red	2·30	4·00
175d	29a	20(+5)ore orange	3·00	2·50
175e	29a	25(+5)ore blue	4·75	3·50

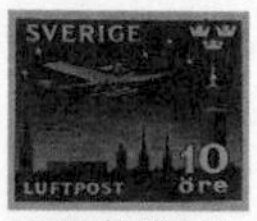

29c Night Flight by Junkers F-13 (with skis) over Stockholm

1930. Air.

175f	29c	10ore blue	45	60
175g	29c	50ore violet	80	1·70

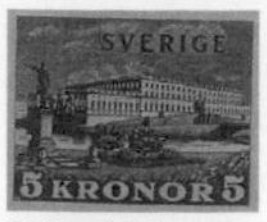

30 Royal Palace, Stockholm

1931

176	30	5k. green	£120	11·50

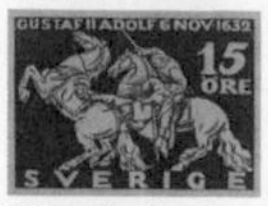

31 Death of Gustavus Adolphus at Lutzen

1932. Death Tercentenary of Gustavus Adolphus.

177	31	10ore violet	1·90	60
178	31	15ore red	2·30	60
179	31	25ore blue	5·50	1·20
180	31	90ore green	23·00	2·30

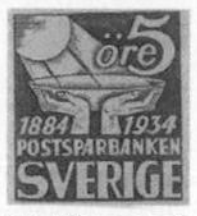

32 Allegory of Thrift

1933. 50th Anniv of Swedish Postal Savings Bank.

181a	32	5ore green	3·00	60

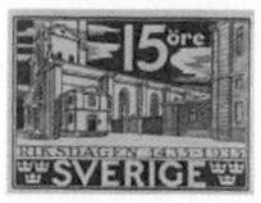

33 Stockholm Cathedral

1935. 500th Anniv of First Swedish Parliament. Stockholm Buildings.

182	-	5ore green	1·20	60
183	-	10ore violet	6·25	60
184	33	15ore red	2·50	60
185	-	25ore blue	6·25	60
186	-	35ore purple	12·50	2·50
187	-	60ore purple	19·00	1·70

DESIGNS: 5ore Old City Hall; 10ore Exchange; 25ore House of the Nobility; 35ore Houses of Parliament; 60ore Arms of Engelbrekt and representatives of the Four Estates.

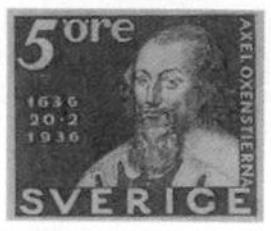

35 A. Oxenstierna (after D. Dumonstier)

1936. Tercentenary of Swedish Post.

188	35	5ore green	1·90	60
189	-	10ore violet	1·90	60
190	-	15ore red	4·00	60
191	-	20ore blue	9·25	5·75
192	-	25ore blue	6·25	60
193	-	30ore brown	19·00	3·50
194	-	35ore mauve	5·50	1·70
195	-	40ore green	6·25	3·00
196	-	45ore green	7·75	1·70
197	-	50ore grey	25·00	3·00
198	-	60ore purple	31·00	90
199	-	1k. blue	8·75	9·25

DESIGNS: 10ore Early courier; 15ore Post rider; 20ore Sailing packet "Hiorten"; 25ore Paddle-steamer "Constitutionen"; 30ore Mail coach; 35ore Arms; 40ore Class F steam locomotive and mail train; 45ore A. W. Roos (Postmaster General 1867–89); 50ore Motor bus and trailer; 60ore Liner "Gripsholm"; 1k. Junkers Ju 52/3m seaplane.

For similar designs, but dated "1972" at foot, see Nos. 700/4.

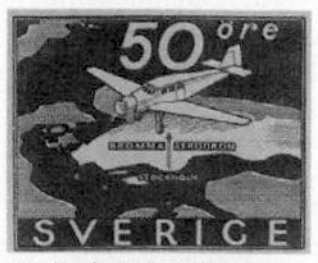

38 Junkers W.34 over Scandinavia

1936. Inauguration of Bromma Aerodrome.

200	38	50ore blue	5·50	9·25

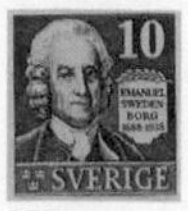

39 E. Swedenborg (after P. Krafft)

1938. 250th Birth Anniv of Swedenborg.

201	**39**	10ore violet	1·60	35
202	**39**	100ore green	5·50	1·40

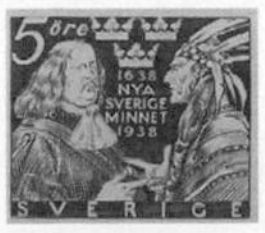

40 Governor Printz and Red Indian

1938. 300th Anniv of Founding of New Sweden, U.S.A.

203	**40**	5ore green	95	35
204	-	15ore brown	95	35
205	-	20ore red	2·30	80
206	-	30ore blue	5·50	80
207	-	60ore purple	9·25	45

DESIGNS: 15ore Emigrant ships "Calmare Nyckel" and "Fagel Grip"; 20ore Swedish landing in America; 30ore First Swedish church, Wilmington; 60ore Queen Christina (after S. Bourdon).

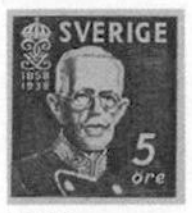

41 King Gustav V

1938. 80th Birthday of King Gustav V.

208	**41**	5ore green	1·90	35
209	**41**	15ore brown	1·90	35
210	**41**	30ore blue	17·00	80

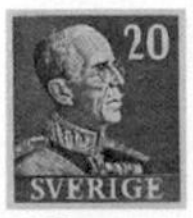

42 King Gustav V

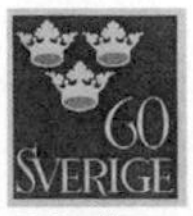

43 Small Arms of Sweden

1939

234	**42**	5ore green	30	25
299	**42**	5ore orange	30	30
235	**42**	10ore violet	30	25
300	**42**	10ore green	50	30
236b	**42**	15ore brown	30	45
237	**42**	20ore red	30	25
238	**42**	25ore orange	1·20	25
301	**42**	25ore violet	1·40	30
239	**42**	30ore blue	45	45
240	**42**	35ore purple	80	45
241	**42**	40ore green	60	25
242	**42**	45ore brown	70	25
243	**42**	50ore grey	3·00	25
301a	**43**	50ore grey	2·40	30
302	**43**	55ore brown	1·40	50
213	**43**	60ore red	60	35
302a	**43**	65ore green	70	30
302b	**43**	70ore blue	4·00	1·60
302c	**43**	75ore brown	3·00	90
303	**43**	80ore green	70	30
214	**43**	85ore green	30	35
303a	**43**	85ore brown	6·75	1·90
215	**43**	90ore blue	40	35
216	**43**	1k. orange	30	30
303b	**43**	1k.05 blue	1·50	40
304	**43**	1k.10 violet	6·00	30
217	**43**	1k.15 brown	40	35
218	**43**	1k.20 purple	1·90	35
304a	**43**	1k.20 blue	5·25	3·25
305	**43**	1k.40 green	95	30
219	**43**	1k.45 green	2·30	90
305a	**43**	1k.50 purple	1·80	1·40
305b	**43**	1k.50 brown	95	40
305c	**43**	1k.70 red	1·40	30
306	**43**	1k.75 blue	12·50	9·25
306a	**43**	1k.80 blue	2·40	65
306b	**43**	1k.85 blue	5·50	1·20
306c	**43**	2k. purple	95	30
306ca	**43**	2k. mauve	80	30
306d	**43**	2k.10 blue	8·75	30
306e	**43**	2k.15 green	5·25	65
306f	**43**	2k.30 brown	6·50	50
306g	**43**	2k.50 green	1·40	30
306h	**43**	2k.55 red	3·75	2·75
306i	**43**	2k.80 red	1·60	30
306j	**43**	2k.85 orange	3·75	4·00
306k	**43**	3k. blue	1·40	30

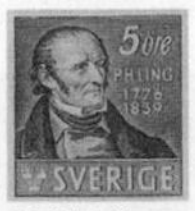

44 P. H. Ling (after J. G. Sandberg)

1939. Death Centenary of P. H. Ling (creator of "Swedish Drill").

228	**44**	5ore green	30	35
229	**44**	25ore brown	1·10	45

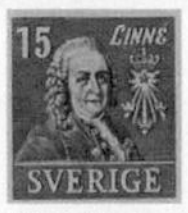

45 Carl von Linne (Linnaeus) (after A. Roslin)

1939. Bicent of Swedish Academy of Sciences.

230a	-	10ore violet	2·30	70
231	**45**	15ore brown	30	35
232	-	30ore blue	19·00	45
233	**45**	50ore grey	19·00	1·20

PORTRAIT: 10ore, 30ore J. J. Berzelius (after O. J. Sodermark).

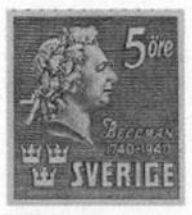

47 Carl Michael Bellman

1940. Birth Bicent of C. M. Bellman (poet).

244	**47**	5ore green	30	25
245	**47**	35ore red	80	45

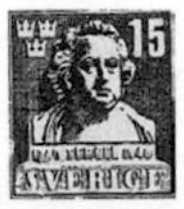

48 Johan Tobias Sergel (self-portrait bust)

1940. Birth Bicent of J. T. Sergel (sculptor).

246	**48**	15ore brown	4·75	45
247	**48**	50ore grey	22·00	1·40

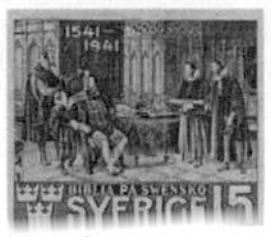

49 Reformers presenting Bible to Gustavus Vasa

1941. 400th Anniv of First Authorized Version of Bible in Swedish.

248	**49**	15ore brown	30	25
249	**49**	90ore blue	22·00	1·00

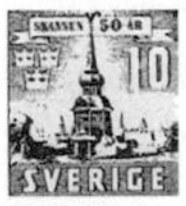

50 Hasjo Belfry

1941. 50th Anniv of Foundation of Skansen Open-air Museum.

250a	**50**	10ore violet	2·75	70
251	**50**	60ore purple	11·00	60

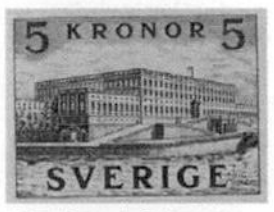

50a Royal Palace, Stockholm

1941

252	**50a**	5k. blue	1·90	3·00

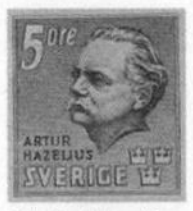

51 A. Hazelius

1941. Artur Hazelius (founder of Skansen Museum).

253	**51**	5ore green	30	25
254	**51**	1k. orange	8·50	4·50

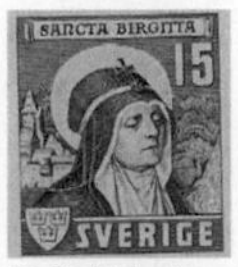

52 St. Bridget (from altar painting, Vasteras Cathedral)

1941. 550th Anniv of Canonization of St. Bridget (Foundress of Brigittine Order of Our Saviour).

255	**52**	15ore brown	30	45
256	**52**	120ore purple	31·00	11·50

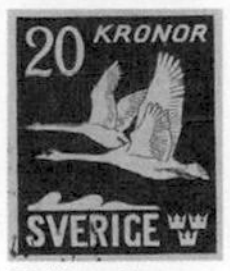

53 Mute Swans

1942

257a	**53**	20k. blue	16·00	35

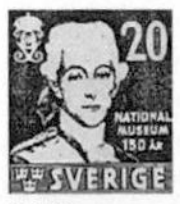

54 King Gustavus III (after A. Roslin)

1942. 150th Anniv of National Museum, Stockholm.

258	**54**	20ore red	70	35
259	-	40ore green	22·00	1·40

PORTRAIT: 40ore Carl Gustaf Tessin (architect and chancery president) (after Gustav Lundberg).

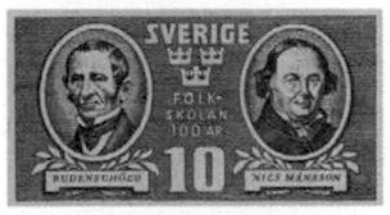

55 Count Rudenschold and Nils Mansson

1942. Centenary of Institution of National Elementary Education.

260	**55**	10ore red	30	45
261	**55**	90ore blue	2·75	7·00

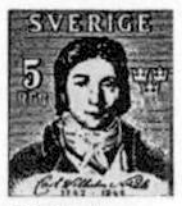

56 Carl Wilhelm Scheele

1942. Birth Bicent of C. W. Scheele (chemist).

262	**56**	5ore green	30	25
263	**56**	60ore red	9·00	60

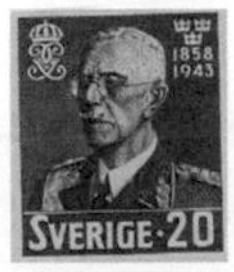

57 King Gustav V

1943. 85th Birthday of King Gustav V.

264	**57**	20ore red	95	45
265	**57**	30ore blue	95	3·00
266	**57**	60ore purple	1·60	3·50

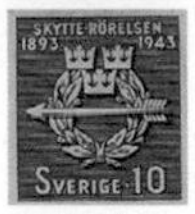

58 Rifle Assn Badge

1943. 50th Anniv of National Voluntary Rifle Association.

267	**58**	10ore purple	30	25
268	**58**	90ore blue	4·75	45

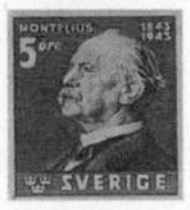

59 O. Montelius (after E. Stenberg)

1943. Birth Centenary of Oscar Montelius (archaeologist).

269	**59**	5ore green	30	25
270	**59**	120ore purple	7·00	2·75

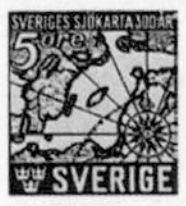

60 First Swedish Navigators' Chart

1944. Tercent of First Swedish Marine Chart.

271	**60**	5ore green	30	25
272	**60**	60ore red	5·50	80

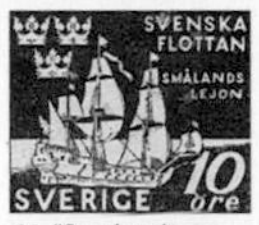

61 "Smalands Lejon" (ship of the line)

1944. Swedish Fleet (Tercentenary of Battle of Femern).

273	**61**	10ore violet	40	45
274	-	20ore red	40	25
275	-	30ore blue	60	90
276	-	40ore green	80	1·40
277	-	90ore grey	9·25	2·50

DESIGNS—27×22½ mm: 30ore "Kung Karl" (ship of the line); 40ore Stern of "Amphion" (royal yacht); 90ore "Gustav V" (cruiser). 18½×20½ mm: 20ore Admiral C. Fleming (after L. Pasch).

See also Nos. 517/22.

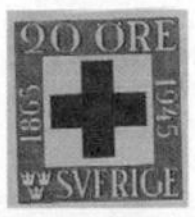

62 Red Cross

1945. 80th Anniv of Swedish Red Cross and Birthday of Prince Carl.

278	**62**	20ore red	45	25

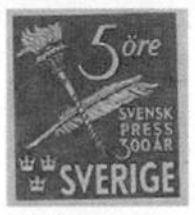

63 Press Symbols

1945. Tercentenary of Swedish Press.

279	**63**	5ore green	30	25
280	**63**	60ore red	4·75	45

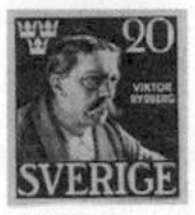

64 Viktor Rydberg (after A. Edelfelt)

1945. 50th Death Anniv of Viktor Rydberg (author).

281	**64**	20ore red	30	25
282	**64**	90ore blue	5·00	45

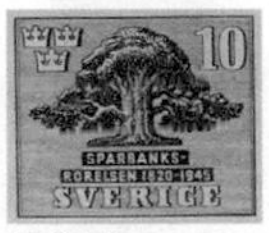

65 Oak Tree, Savings Banks' Symbol

1945. 125th Anniv of Swedish Savings Banks.

283	**65**	10ore violet	30	25
284	**65**	40ore green	1·20	1·40

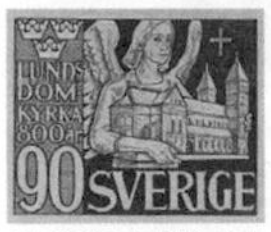

66 Cathedral Model

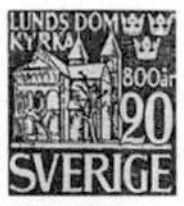

67 Lund Cathedral

1946. 800th Anniv of Lund Cathedral.

285	**66**	15ore brown	1·20	50
286	**67**	20ore red	50	25
287	**66**	90ore blue	11·00	95

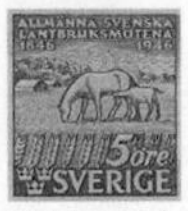

68 Mare and Foal

1946. Centenary of Swedish Agricultural Show.

288	**68**	5ore green	50	25
289	**68**	60ore red	6·50	55

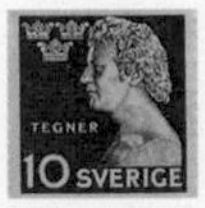

69 Tegner (after bust by J. N. Bystrom)

1946. Death Centenary of Esaias Tegner (poet).

290	**69**	10ore violet	50	25
291	**69**	40ore green	2·10	70

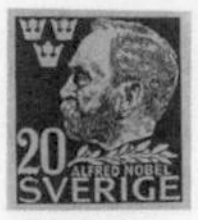

70 A. Nobel

1946. 50th Death Anniv of Alfred Nobel (scientist and creator of Nobel Foundation).

292	**70**	20ore red	1·00	25
293	**70**	30ore blue	3·50	55

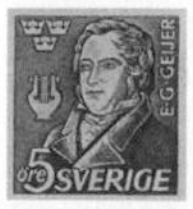

71 E. G. Geijer (after J. G. Sandberg)

1947. Death Centenary of Erik Gustav Geijer (historian, philosopher, poet and composer).

294	**71**	5ore green	40	25
295	**71**	90ore blue	5·25	50

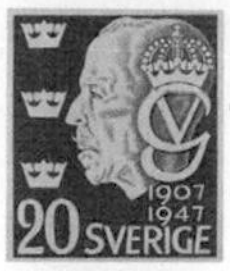

72 King Gustav V

1947. Forty Years Reign of King Gustav V.

296	**72**	10ore violet	40	30
297	**72**	20ore red	40	30
298	**72**	60ore purple	1·80	1·60

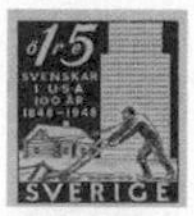

73 Ploughman and Skyscraper

1948. Centenary of Swedish Pioneers in U.S.A.

307	**73**	15ore brown	40	25
308	**73**	30ore blue	90	65
309	**73**	1k. orange	1·80	1·10

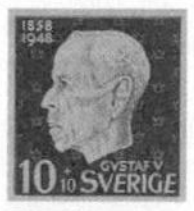

73a King Gustav V

1948. King Gustav V's 90th Birthday, and Youth Fund.

309a	**73a**	10ore+10ore green	70	80
309b	**73a**	20ore+10ore red	90	95
309c	**73a**	30ore+10ore blue	80	80

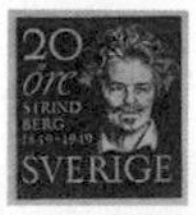

74 J. A. Strindberg (after R. Bergh)

1949. Birth Centenary of Strindberg (dramatist).

310	**74**	20ore red	55	30
311	**74**	30ore blue	1·10	90
312	**74**	80ore green	3·75	65

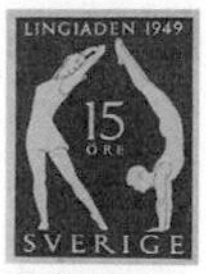

75 Gymnasts

1949. Second Lingiad, Stockholm.

313	**75**	5ore blue	40	50
314	**75**	15ore brown	40	30

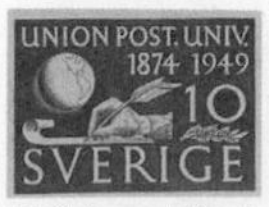

76 Globe and Hand Writing

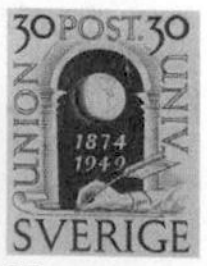

77

1949. 75th Anniv of U.P.U.

315	**76**	10ore green	40	30
316	**76**	20ore red	40	30
317	**77**	30ore blue	55	65

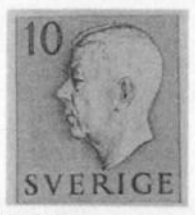

78 King Gustav VI Adolf

1951. (a) Coloured lettering and figures.

318	**78**	10ore green	25	25
318b	**78**	10ore brown	30	30
319	**78**	15ore brown	40	30
388	**78**	15ore red	35	35
320	**78**	20ore red	50	30
391	**78**	20ore black	45	35
322a	**78**	25ore black	65	50
323	**78**	25ore red	1·20	40
324a	**78**	25ore blue	25	25
392	**78**	25ore brown	1·30	35
326	**78**	30ore brown	55	50
326a	**78**	30ore red	8·50	30
393	**78**	30ore blue	50	25
327	**78**	40ore blue	90	30
328	**78**	40ore green	95	30

(b) White lettering and figures.

429	15ore red	25	25
430	20ore black	45	25
431	25ore brown	25	25
432a	30ore blue	95	35
433	30ore violet	70	35
433b	30ore red	1·20	1·00
434	35ore violet	85	25
435a	35ore blue	50	25
436	35ore black	85	35
437	40ore green	70	25
438a	40ore blue	50	25
439a	45ore orange	85	25
439b	45ore blue	85	25
440	50ore green	1·10	35
440a	50ore green	85	35
440c	55ore red	75	25
441	60ore red	1·10	95
441a	65ore blue	1·40	35
441c	70ore mauve	1·10	35
441d	85ore purple	1·20	60

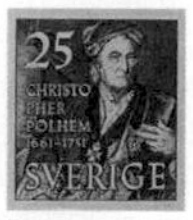

79 Christopher Polhem (after G. E. Schroder)

1951. Death Bicentenary of Polhem (engineer).

329a	**79**	25ore black	55	50
330	**79**	45ore brown	70	65

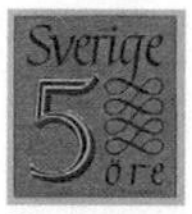

80

1951

383	**80**	5ore red	35	25
386	**80**	10ore blue	35	25
387a	**80**	10ore brown	35	35
389	**80**	15ore green	35	35
390a	**80**	15ore brown	75	70

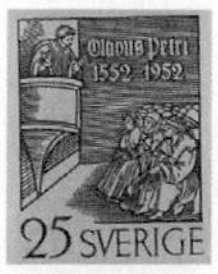

81 Olavus Petri Preaching

1952. 400th Death Anniv of Petri (reformer).

332	**81**	25ore black	50	30
333	**81**	1k.40 brown	5·25	1·00

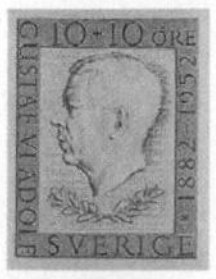

81a King Gustav VI Adolf

1952. 70th Birthday of King Gustav VI Adolf and Culture Fund.

333a	**81a**	10ore+10ore green	55	50
333bba	**81a**	25ore+10ore red	65	65
333c	**81a**	40ore+10ore blue	65	55

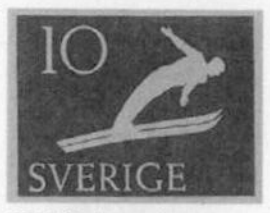

82 Ski Jumping

1953. 50th Anniv of Swedish Athletic Assn.

334	**82**	10ore green	65	30
335	-	15ore brown	90	80
336	-	40ore blue	1·80	2·10
337	-	1k.40 mauve	5·50	1·30

DESIGNS—HORIZ: 1k.40, Wrestling. VERT: 15ore Ice hockey; 40ore Slingball.

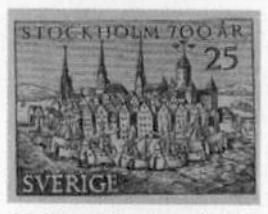

83 Stockholm, 1650

1953. 700th Anniv of Stockholm.

338	**83**	25ore blue	45	35
339	-	1k.70 red	3·75	85

DESIGN: 1k.70, Seal of Stockholm, 1296 (obverse and reverse).

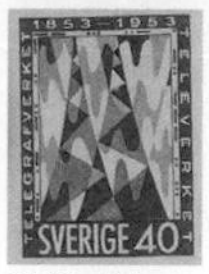

84 "Radio"

1953. Cent of Telecommunications in Sweden.

340		25ore blue ("Telephones")	45	35
341	**84**	40ore green	1·60	1·90
342	-	60ore red ("Telegraphs")	3·50	3·25

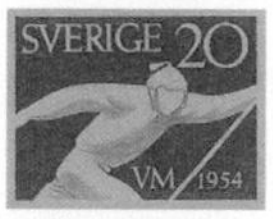

85 Skier

1954. World Skiing Championships.

343	**85**	20ore grey	60	45
344	-	1k. blue (Woman skier)	11·00	1·50

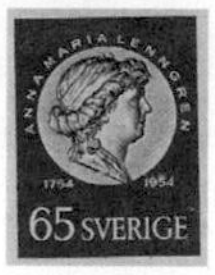

86 Anna Maria Lenngren (after medallion, J. T. Sergel)

1954. Birth Bicentenary of Anna Maria Lenngren (poetess).

345	**86**	20ore grey	45	35
346	**86**	65ore brown	5·50	4·00

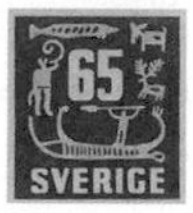

87 Rock-carvings

1954

347	**87**	50ore grey	45	35
348	**87**	55ore red	1·60	35
349	**87**	60ore red	70	35
350	**87**	65ore green	1·90	35
351	**87**	70ore orange	95	35
352	**87**	75ore brown	3·25	35
353	**87**	80ore green	75	35
355	**87**	90ore blue	75	35
356	**87**	95ore violet	4·25	4·25

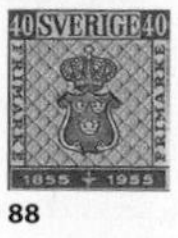

88

1955. Centenary of First Swedish Postage Stamps.

362	**88**	25ore blue	35	35
363	**88**	40ore green	1·40	50

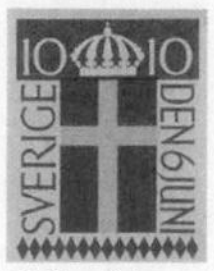

89 Swedish Flag

1955. National Flag Day.

364	**89**	10ore yellow, blue & green	35	35
365	**89**	15ore yellow, blue and red	50	35

1955. Cent of First Swedish Postage Stamps and "Stockholmia" Philatelic Exn. As T **1** but with two rules through bottom panel.

366	**1**	3ore green	3·00	6·00
367	**1**	4ore blue	3·00	6·00
368	**1**	6ore grey	3·00	6·00
369	**1**	8ore yellow	3·00	6·00
370	**1**	24ore orange	3·00	6·00

Nos. 366/70 were sold only at the exhibition in single sets, at 2k.45 (45ore face + 2k. entrance fee).

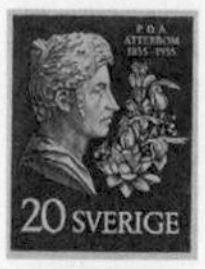

91 P. D. A. Atterbom (after Fogelberg)

1955. Death Centenary of Atterbom (poet).

371	**91**	20ore blue	35	35
372	**91**	1k.40 brown	5·50	75

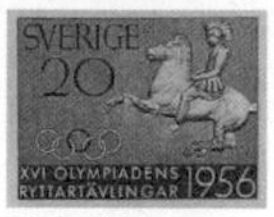

92 Greek Horseman, (from Parthenon frieze)

1956. 16th Olympic Games Equestrian Competitions, Stockholm.

373	**92**	20ore red	45	35
374	**92**	25ore blue	70	35
375	**92**	40ore green	3·00	2·50

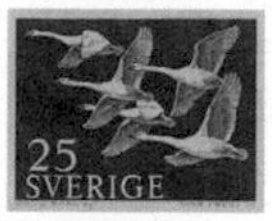

92a Whooper Swans

1956. Northern Countries' Day.

376	**92a**	25ore red	60	35
377	**92a**	40ore blue	1·40	95

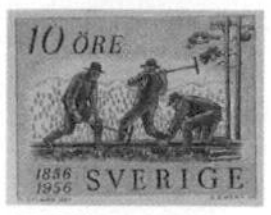

93 Railway Construction

1956. Centenary of Swedish Railways.

378	**93**	10ore green	60	35
379	-	25ore blue	50	35
380	-	40ore orange	4·25	4·00

DESIGNS: 25ore Steam locomotive, "Fryckstad" and passenger carriage; 40ore Type XOa5 electric train on Arsta Bridge, Stockholm.

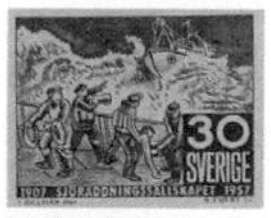

94 Trawler in Distress and Lifeboat

1957. 50th Anniv of Swedish Life Saving Service.

381	**94**	30ore blue	4·00	35
382	**94**	1k.40 red	7·25	1·70

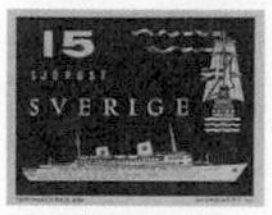

95 Galleon and "Gripsholm II"

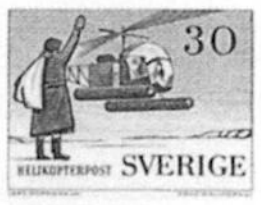

96 Bell 47G Helicopter with Floats

1958. Postal Services Commemoration.

395	**95**	15ore red	45	35
396	**96**	30ore blue	35	35
397	**95**	40ore green	5·50	4·00
398	**96**	1k.40 brown	6·00	1·20

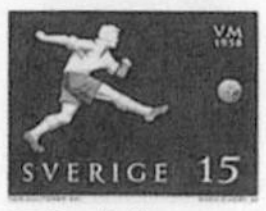

97 Footballer

1958. World Cup Football Championship.

399	**97**	15ore red	70	35
400	**97**	20ore green	70	35
401	**97**	1k.20 blue	2·00	1·00

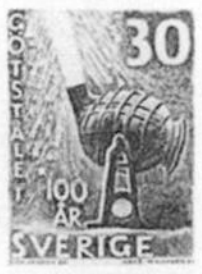

98 Bessemer Tilting-furnace

1958. Centenary of Swedish Steel Industry.

402	**98**	30ore blue	35	35
403	**98**	170ore brown	5·00	1·30

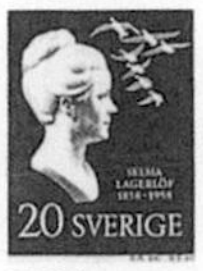

99 Selma Lagerlof (after bust by G. Malmquist)

1958. Birth Centenary of Selma Lagerlof (writer).

404	**99**	20ore red	35	35
405	**99**	30ore blue	35	35
406	**99**	80ore green	1·20	1·20

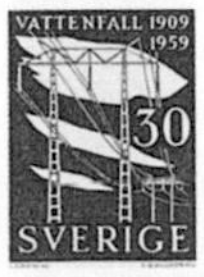

100 Overhead Power Lines

1959. 50th Anniv of Swedish State Power Board.

407	**100**	30ore blue	50	35
408	-	90ore red	4·75	3·00

DESIGN—HORIZ: 90ore Dam sluice-gates.

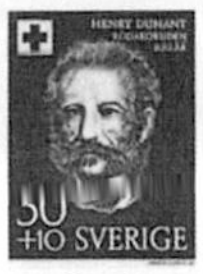

101 Henri Dunant (founder)

1959. Red Cross Centenary.

409	**101**	30ore+10ore red	75	75

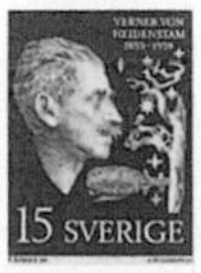

102 Heidenstam

1959. Birth Centenary of Verner von Heidenstam (poet).

410	**102**	15ore red	95	60
411	**102**	1k. black	4·25	1·20

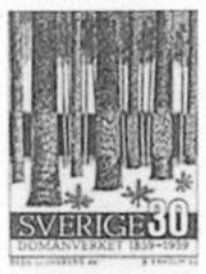

103 Forest Trees

1959. Centenary of Crown Lands and Forests Administration.

412	**103**	30ore green	1·60	35
413	-	1k.40 red	4·75	85

DESIGN: 1k.40, Forester felling tree.

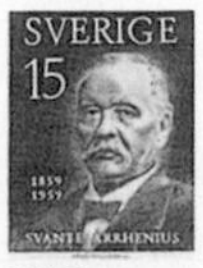

104 S. Arrhenius

1959. Birth Centenary of Arrhenius (chemist).

414	**104**	15ore brown	35	35
415	**104**	1k.70 blue	5·50	70

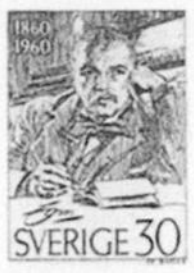

105 Anders Zorn (self portrait)

1960. Birth Cent of Zorn (painter and etcher).

416	**105**	30ore grey	35	35
417	**105**	80ore brown	4·25	2·00

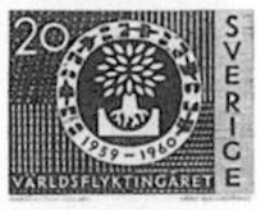

106 "Uprooted Tree"

1960. World Refugee Year.

418	**106**	20ore brown	35	35
419	-	40ore violet	60	45

DESIGN—VERT: 40ore Refugees.

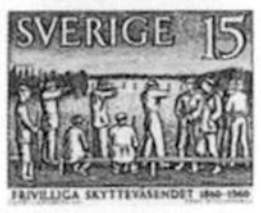

107 Target-shooting

1960. Centenary of Voluntary Shooting Organization.

420	**107**	15ore red	35	35
421	-	90ore blue	3·75	2·00

DESIGN: 90ore Organization members marching, 1860.

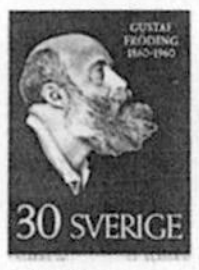

108 G. Froding

1960. Birth Centenary of Gustav Froding (poet).

422	**108**	30ore brown	35	35
423	**108**	1k.40 green	4·00	60

1960. Europa. As T **144a** of Switzerland.

424		40ore blue	60	50
425		[illegible]	1·10	70

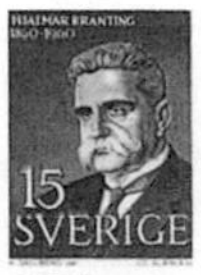

109 H. Branting

1960. Birth Centenary of Hjalmar Branting (statesman).

426	**109**	15ore red	35	35
427	**109**	1k.70 blue	4·25	75

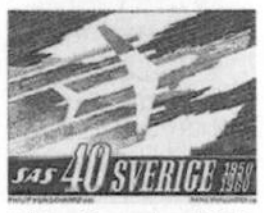

109a Douglas DC-8

1961. Tenth Anniv of Scandinavian Airlines System.

428	**109a**	40ore blue	60	35

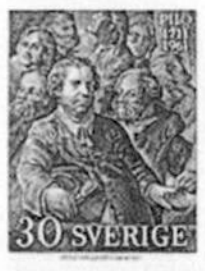

111 "Coronation of Gustav III" (after Pilo)

1961. 250th Birth Anniv of Carl Gustav Pilo (painter).

442	**111**	30ore brown	45	35
443	**111**	1k.40 blue	4·75	1·40

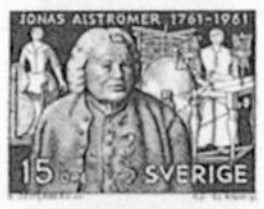

112 J. Alstromer (after bust by P. H. l'Archeveque)

1961. Death Bicentenary of Jonas Alstromer (industrial reformer).

444	**112**	15ore purple	35	35
445	**112**	90ore blue	1·70	2·00

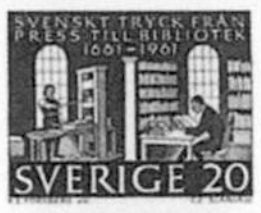

113 Printing Works and Library

1961. Tercentenary of Royal Library Regulation.

446	**113**	20ore red	35	35
447	**113**	1k. blue	7·25	1·20

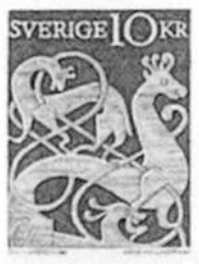

114 Motif on Runic Stone at Oland

1961

448	**114**	10k. purple	29·00	85

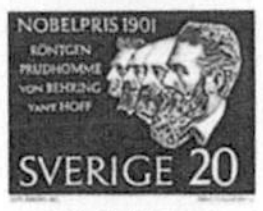

115 Nobel Prize Winners of 1901

1961. Nobel Prize Winners of 1901.

449	**115**	20ore red	35	35
450	**115**	40ore blue	35	35
451	**115**	50ore green	35	35

See also Nos. 458/9, 471/2, 477/8, 488/9, 523/4, 546/7 and 573/4.

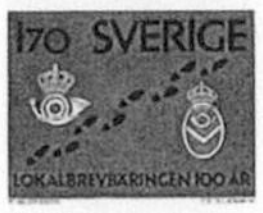

116 Postman's Footprints

1962. Cent of Swedish Local Mail Delivery Service.

452	**116**	30ore violet	35	35
453	**116**	1k.70 red	5·00	60

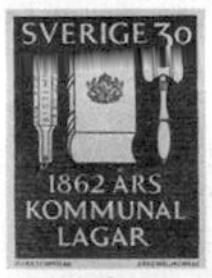

117 Code, Voting Instrument and Mallet

1962. Centenary of Municipal Laws.

454	**117**	30ore blue	45	35
455	**117**	2k. red	5·50	60

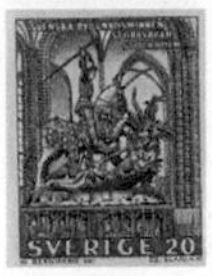

118 St. George and Dragon, Storkyrkan ("Great Church"), Stockholm

1962. Swedish Monuments (1st series).

456	**118**	20ore purple	35	35
457	-	50ore green	45	35

DESIGN—HORIZ: 50ore Skokloster Castle.

See also Nos. 469/70 and 479/80.

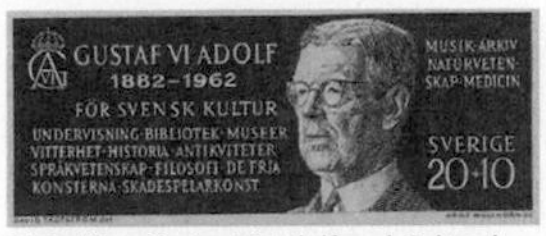

118a King Gustav VI Adolf and Cultural Themes

1962. King Gustav's 80th Birthday and Swedish Culture Fund.

457b	**118a**	20ore+10ore brown	35	35
457c	**118a**	35ore+10ore blue	35	35

1962. Nobel Prize Winners of 1902. As T **115** but inscr "NOBELPRIS 1902".

458	25ore red	35	35
459	50ore blue	60	35

PORTRAITS: 25ore Theodor Mommsen (literature) and Sir Ronald Ross (medicine); 50ore Emil Hermann Fischer (chemistry) and Pieter Zeeman and Hendrik Lorentz (physics).

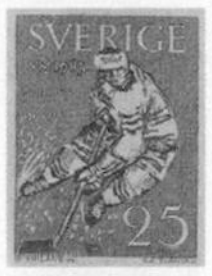

119 Ice Hockey Player

1963. World Ice Hockey Championships.

460	**119**	25ore green	35	35
461	**119**	1k.70 blue	4·75	50

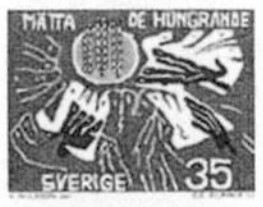

120 Hands reaching for Wheat

1963. Freedom from Hunger.

462	**120**	35ore mauve	35	35
463	**120**	50ore violet	35	35

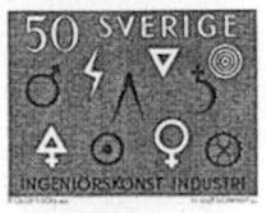

121 Engineering and Industrial Symbols

1963. "Engineering and Industry".

464	**121**	50ore black	35	35
465	**121**	1k.05 orange	4·00	3·75

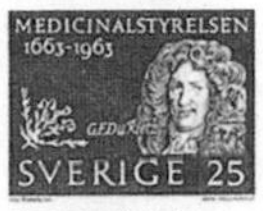

122 Dr. G. F. Du Rietz (after D. K. Ehrenstrahl)

1963. 300th Anniv of Swedish Board of Health.

466	**122**	25ore brown	45	45
467	**122**	35ore blue	45	35
468	**122**	2k. red	5·00	70

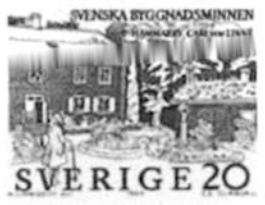

123 Linne's Hammarby (country house)

1963. Swedish Monuments (2nd series).

469	**123**	20ore red	35	35
470	**123**	50ore green	35	35

1963. Nobel Prize Winners of 1903. As T **115** but inscr "NOBELPRIS 1903".

471	25ore green	70	70
472	50ore brown	70	35

PORTRAITS: 25ore Svante Arrhenius (chemistry), Niels Ryberg Finsen (medicine) and Bjornstjerne Bjornson (literature); 50ore Antoine Henri Becquerel and Pierre and Marie Curie (physics).

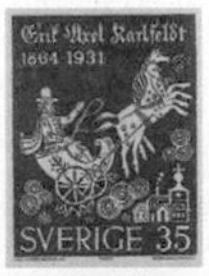

124 Motif from Poem "Elie Himmelsfard"

1964. Birth Centenary of E. A. Karlfeldt (poet).

473	**124**	35ore blue	75	35
474	**124**	1k.05 red	5·00	5·00

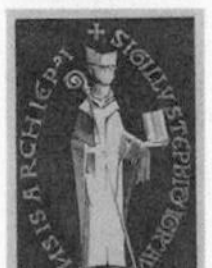

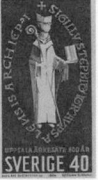

125 Seal of Archbishop Stefan

1964. 800th Anniv of Archbishopric of Uppsala.

475	**125**	40ore green	35	35
476	**125**	60ore brown	45	35

1964. Nobel Prize Winners of 1904. As T **115** but inscr "NOBELPRIS 1904".

477	30ore blue	50	70
478	40ore red	85	35

PORTRAITS: 30ore Jose Echegaray y Eizaguirre and Frederic Mistral (literature) and J. W. Strutt (Lord Rayleigh) (physics); 40ore Sir William Ramsay (chemistry) and Ivan Petrovich Pavlov (medicine).

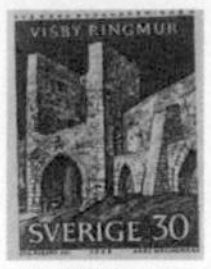

126 Visby Town Wall

1965. Swedish Monuments (3rd series).

479	**126**	30ore mauve	35	35
480	**126**	2k. blue	5·00	35

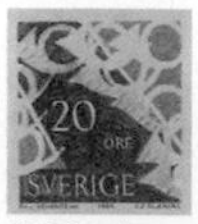

127 Posthorns

1965

481	**127**	20ore blue and yellow	35	35

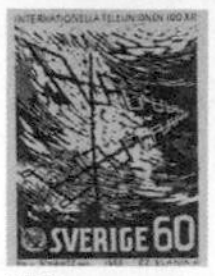

128 Telecommunications

1965. Centenary of I.T.U.

482	**128**	60ore violet	50	35
483	**128**	1k.40 blue	3·00	1·60

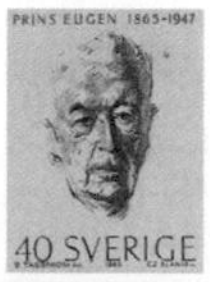

129 Prince Eugen (after D. Tagtstrom)

1965. Birth Centenary of Prince Fugen (painter).

484	**129**	40ore black	35	35
485	**129**	1k. brown	3·00	50

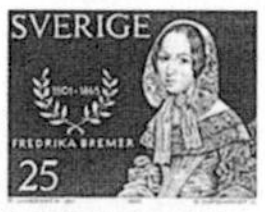

130 F. Bremer (after O. J. Sodermark)

1965. Death Centenary of Fredrika Bremer (novelist).

486	**130**	25ore violet	35	35
487	**130**	3k. green	6·50	60

1965. Nobel Prize Winners of 1905. As T **115** but inscr "NOBELPRIS 1905".

488	30ore blue	50	45
489	40ore red	50	35

PORTRAITS: 30ore Philipp von Lenard (physics) and Johann von Baeyer (chemistry); 40ore Robert Koch (medicine) and Henryk Sienkiewicz (literature).

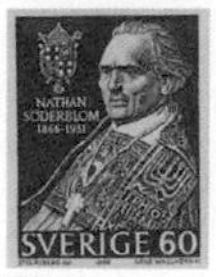

131 N. Soderblom

1966. Birth Centenary of Nathan Soderblom, Archbishop of Uppsala.

490	**131**	60ore brown	50	35
491	**131**	80ore green	1·40	35

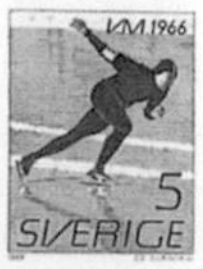

132 Skating

1966. World Men's Speed Skating Championships, Gothenburg.

492	**132**	5ore red	35	35
493	**132**	25ore green	35	35
494	**132**	40ore blue	75	70

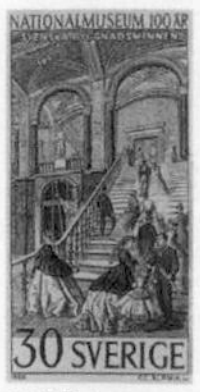

133 Entrance Hall, National Museum

1966. Centenary of Opening of National Museum Building.

495	**133**	30ore violet	35	35
496	**133**	2k.30 green	1·50	1·40

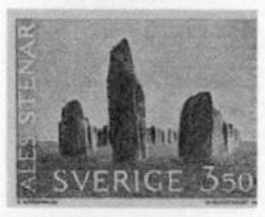

134 Ale's Stones, Ship Grave, Kaseberga

1966

498	-	35ore brown and blue	35	35
499	**134**	3k.50 grey	1·70	35
500	-	3k.70 violet	2·00	35
501	-	4k.50 red	2·50	35
502	-	7k. red and blue	3·50	70

DESIGNS—HORIZ: 35ore Fjeld (mountains); 7k. Gripsholm Castle. VERT: 3k.70, Lion Fortress, Gothenburg; 4k.50, Uppsala Cathedral (interior).

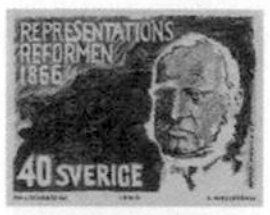

135 Louis de Geer (advocate of reform)

1966. Cent of Representative Assembly Reform.

510	**135**	40ore blue	45	35
511	**135**	3k. red	5·50	75

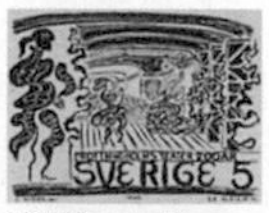

136 Theatre Stage

1966. Bicentenary of Drottningholm Theatre.

512	**136**	5ore red on pink	40	35
513	**136**	25ore bistre on pink	40	35
514	**136**	40ore purple on pink	85	80

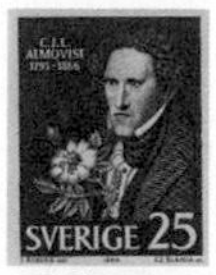

137 Almqvist (after C. P. Mazer)

1966. Death Centenary of Carl Almqvist (writer).

515	**137**	25ore mauve	40	35
516	**137**	1k. green	3·50	35

1966. National Cancer Fund. Swedish Ships. Designs as T **61**, but with imprint "1966" at foot.

517	10ore red	40	55
518	15ore red	40	55
519	20ore green	40	55
520	25ore blue	40	55
521	30ore red	40	55
522	40ore red	40	55

SHIPS—HORIZ: 10ore "Smalands Lejon"; 15ore "Calmare Nyckel" and "Fagel Grip"; 20ore "Hiorten"; 25ore "Constitutionen"; 30ore "Kung Karl"; 40ore Stern of "Amphion".

1966. Nobel Prize Winners of 1906. As T **115** but inscr "NOBELPRIS 1906".

523	30ore red	75	35
524	40ore green	65	35

PORTRAITS: 30ore Sir Joseph John Thomson (physics) and Giosue Carducci (literature); 40ore Henri Moissan (chemistry) and Camillo Golgi and Santiago Ramon y Cajal (medicine).

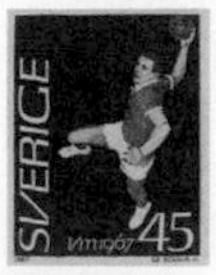

138 Handball

1967. World Handball Championships.

525	**138**	45ore blue	40	35
526	**138**	2k.70 mauve	4·75	1·90

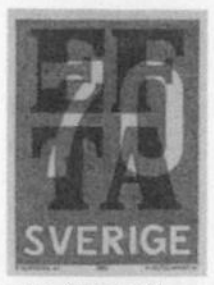

139 "E.F.T.A."

1967. European Free Trade Assn (E.F.T.A.).

527	**139**	70ore orange	65	35

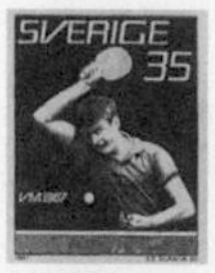

140 Table Tennis Player

1967. World Table Tennis Championships, Stockholm.

528	**140**	35ore mauve	40	35
529	**140**	90ore blue	1·80	70

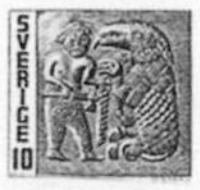

141 Axeman and Beast

1967. Iron Age Helmet Decorations, Oland.

530	**141**	10ore blue and brown	40	35
531	-	15ore brown and blue	40	35
532	-	30ore mauve and brown	40	35
533	-	35ore brown and mauve	40	35

DESIGNS: 15ore Man between two bears; 30ore "Lion man" putting enemy to flight; 35ore Two warriors.

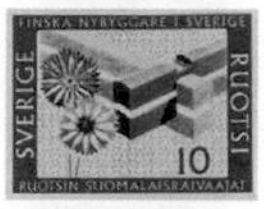

142 "Solidarity"

1967. Finnish Settlers in Sweden.

534	**142**	10ore multicoloured	40	35
535	**142**	35ore multicoloured	40	35

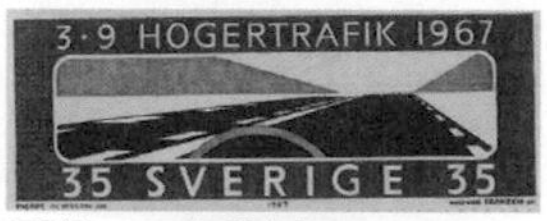

143 "Keep to the Right"

1967. Adoption of Changed Rule of the Road.

536	**143**	35ore black, yellow & blue	40	45
537	**143**	45ore black, yellow & grn	40	35

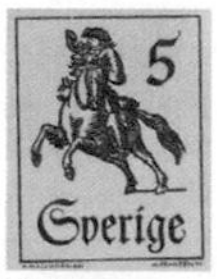

144 18th-century Post-rider

1967

538	**144**	5ore black and red	30	25
539	-	10ore black and blue	30	25
539b	-	20ore black on flesh	40	35
540	-	30ore red and blue	40	25
541	-	40ore blue, green & black	40	35
541b	-	45ore black and blue	40	35
542	-	90ore brown and blue	55	35
543	-	1k. green	65	35

DESIGNS—As T **144**. VERT: 10ore "Svent Skepp" (warship); 20ore "St. Stephen" (ceiling painting, Dadesjo Church, Smaland); 30ore Angelica plant on coast. HORIZ: 40ore Haverud Aqueduct, Dalsland Canal. 27½×22½ mm: 45ore Floating logs; 90ore Elk; 1k. Dancing cranes.

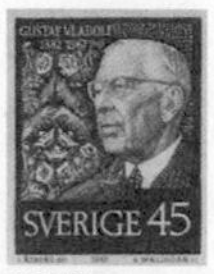

145 King Gustav VI Adolf

1967. 85th Birthday of King Gustav VI Adolf.

544	**145**	45ore blue	40	35
545	**145**	70ore green	50	35

1967. Nobel Prize Winners 1907. As T **115**, but inscr "NOBELPRIS 1907".

546	35ore red	1·00	60
547	45ore blue	50	35

PORTRAITS: 35ore Eduard Buchner (chemistry) and Albert Abraham Michelson (physics); 45ore Charles Louis Alphonse Laveran (medicine) and Rudyard Kipling (literature).

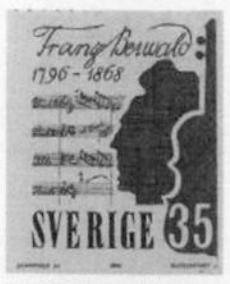

146 Berwald, Violin and Music

1968. Death Centenary of Franz Berwald (composer).

548	**146**	35ore black and red	40	35
549	**146**	2k. black, blue and yellow	4·75	90

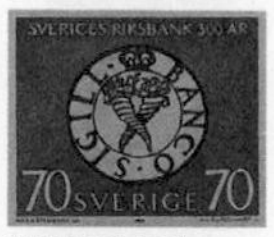

147 Bank Seal

1968. 300th Anniv of Bank of Sweden.

550	**147**	45ore blue	40	35
551	**147**	70ore black on orange	50	35

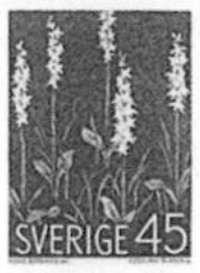

148 Butterfly Orchids

1968. Wild Flowers.

552	**148**	45ore green	1·50	55
553	-	45ore green	1·50	55
554	-	45ore red and green	1·50	55
555	-	45ore green	1·50	55
556	-	45ore green	1·50	55

DESIGNS: No. 553, Wood anemone; 554, Wild rose; 555, Wild cherry; 556, Lily of the valley.

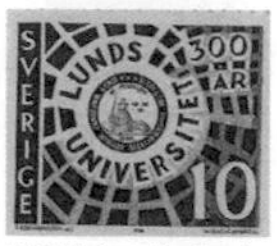

149 University Seal

1968. 300th Anniv of Lund University.

557	**149**	10ore blue	30	35
558	**149**	35ore red	55	60

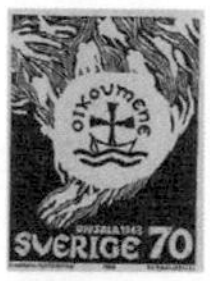

150 Ecumenical Emblem

1968. Fourth General Assembly of World Council of Churches, Uppsala.

559	**150**	70ore purple	55	45
560	**150**	90ore blue	1·40	55

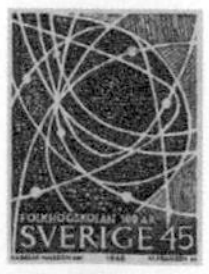

151 "The Universe"

1968. Centenary of the People's College.

561	**151**	45ore red	40	35
562	**151**	2k. blue	5·25	35

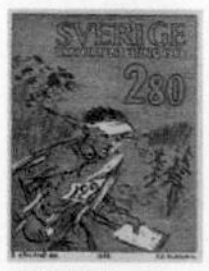

152 "Orienteer" crossing Forest

1968. World Orienteering Championships, Linkoping.

563	**152**	40ore red and violet	40	35
564	**152**	2k.80 violet and green	4·25	3·75

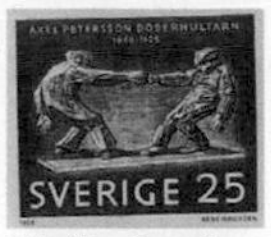

153 "The Tug of War" (wood-carving by Axel Petersson)

1968. Birth Centenary of Axel Petersson ("Doderhultarn").

565	**153**	5ore green	30	25
566	**153**	25ore brown	1·60	1·40
567	**153**	45ore brown and sepia	30	25

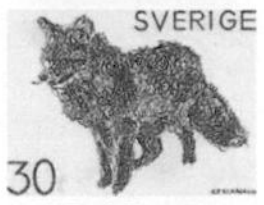

154 Red Fox

1968. Bruno Liljefors' Fauna Sketches.

568	-	30ore blue	1·20	95
569	-	30ore black	1·20	95
570	**154**	30ore brown	1·20	95
571	-	30ore brown	1·20	95
572	-	30ore blue	1·20	95

DESIGNS: No. 568, Arctic hare; 569, Greater black-backed gull; 571, Golden eagle and carrion crows; 572, Stoat.

1968. Nobel Prize Winner of 1908. As T **115**, but inscr "NOBELPRIS 1908".

573	35ore red	75	60
574	45ore green	75	35

PORTRAITS: 35ore Ilya Mechnikov and Paul Ehrlich (medicine) and Lord Rutherford (chemistry); 45ore Gabriel Lippman (physics) and Rudolf Eucken (literature).

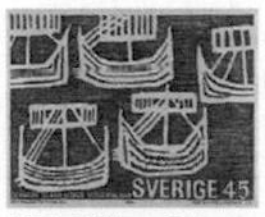

154a Viking Ships

1969. 50th Anniv of Northern Countries Union.

575	**154a**	45ore brown	55	35
576	**154a**	70ore blue	1·40	1·40

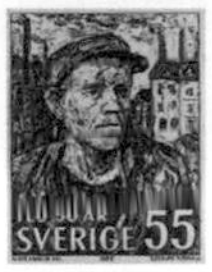

155 "The Worker" (A. Amelin)

1969. 50th Anniv of I.L.O.

577	**155**	55ore red	40	35
578	**155**	70ore blue	1·20	60

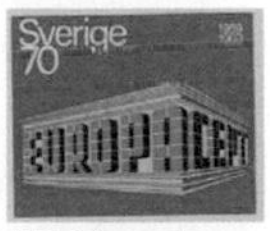

156 Colonnade

1969. Europa.

579	**156**	70ore multicoloured	3·50	80
580	**156**	1k. multicoloured	3·00	35

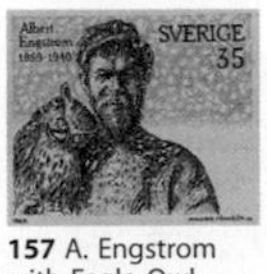

157 A. Engstrom with Eagle Owl (self-portrait)

1969. Birth Centenary of Albert Engstrom (painter and writer).

581	**157**	35ore black	50	35
582	**157**	55ore blue	50	35

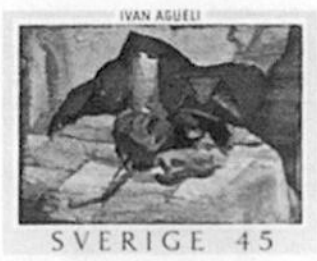

158 "Still Life"

1969. Birth Centenary of Ivan Agueli (painter) Sheet 135×90 mm containing multicoloured designs as T 158.

MS583 45ore "Landscape" (35×28 mm); 45ore Type **158**; 45ore "Arab town" (35×28 mm); 55ore "Egyptian Girl" (28×43 mm); 55ore "Street Scene" (48×43 mm); 55ore "Landscape" (28×43 mm) (sold at 3k.) 4·50 4·75

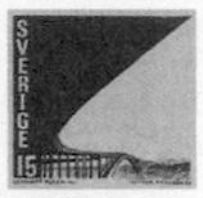

159 Tjorn Bridges

1969. Tjorn Bridges.

584	**159**	15ore blue on blue	1·90	70
585	-	30ore green and black on blue	1·90	70
586	-	55ore black and blue on blue	1·90	80

DESIGNS—As T **159**: 30ore Tjorn Bridges (different). 41×19 mm: 55ore Tjorn Bridges (different).

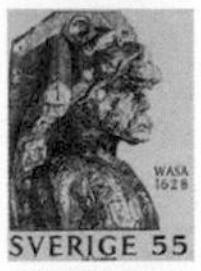

160 Helmeted Figure (carving)

1969. Warship "Wasa" Commemoration.

587	**160**	55ore red	65	35
588	-	55ore brown	65	35
589	-	55ore blue	65	35
590	-	55ore brown	65	35
591	-	55ore red	65	35
592	-	55ore blue	65	45

DESIGNS—As T **160**: No. 588, Crowned lion's head (carving); 590, Lion's head (carving); 591, Carved support. 46×28 mm: No. 589, Ship's coat-of-arms; 592, Ship of the line "Wasa", 1628.

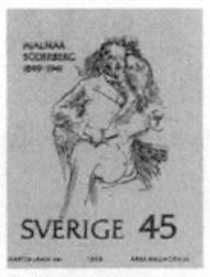

161 H. Soderberg (writer)

1969. Birth Centenaries of Hjalmar Soderberg and Bo Bergman.

593	**161**	45ore brown on cream	40	35
594	-	55ore green on green	50	35

DESIGN—HORIZ: 55ore Bo Bergman (poet).

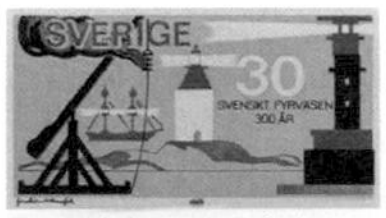

162 Lighthouses and Lightship "Cyklop"

1969. 300th Anniv of Swedish Lighthouse Service.

595	**162**	30ore black, red and grey	55	45
596	**162**	55ore black, orange & blue	55	35

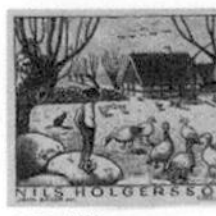

163 "The Adventures of Nils" by S. Lagerlof (illus by J. Bauer)

1969. Swedish Fairy Tales.

597	-	35ore brown, red & orange	2·75	2·10
598	**163**	35ore brown	2·75	2·10
599	-	35ore brown, red & orange	2·75	2·10
600	-	35ore brown	2·75	2·10
601	-	35ore red and orange	2·75	2·10

DESIGNS: No. 597, "Pelle's New Suit" written and illus by Elsa Beskow; 599, "Pippi Longstocking" by A. Lindgren (illus by I. Vang Nyman); 600, "Vill-Vallareman, the Shepherd" (from "With Pucks and Elves" illus by J. Bauer); 601, "The Cat's Journey" written and illus by I. Arosenius.

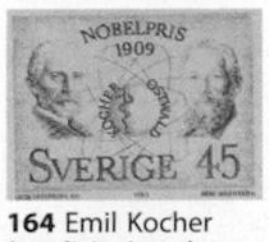

164 Emil Kocher (medicine) and Wilhelm Ostwald (chemistry)

1969. Nobel Prize Winners of 1909.

602a	**164**	45ore green	85	70
603	-	55ore black on flesh	85	35
604	-	70ore black	1·00	1·10

DESIGNS: 55ore Selma Lagerlof (literature); 70ore Guglielmo Marconi and Ferdinand Braun (physics).

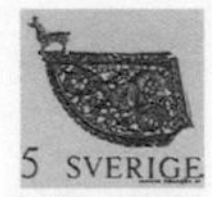

165 Weathervane, Soderala Church

1970. Swedish Forgings.

605	**165**	5ore green and brown	55	35
606	-	10 green and brown	55	35
607	-	30 ore black and green	65	35
608	-	55 ore brown and green	65	35

DESIGNS—As T **165**: 10ore As Type **165**, but design and country name/figures of value in reverse order; 30ore Memorial Cross, Eksharad Churchyard. 24×44 mm: 55ore 14th-century door, Bjorksta Church.

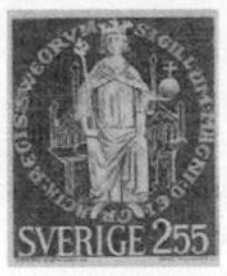

166 Seal of King Magnus Ladulas

1970

609	**166**	2k.55 blue on cream	1·20	70
610	-	3k. blue on cream	1·50	25
611	-	5k. green on cream	2·75	35

DESIGNS: 3k. Seal of Duke Erik Magnusson; 5k. Great Seal of Erik IX.

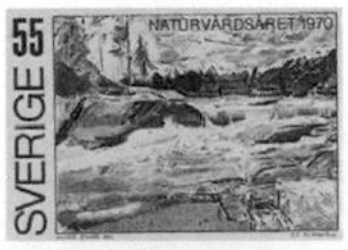

167 River Ljungan

1970. Nature Conservation Year.

612	**167**	55ore multicoloured	50	35
613	**167**	70ore multicoloured	1·10	70

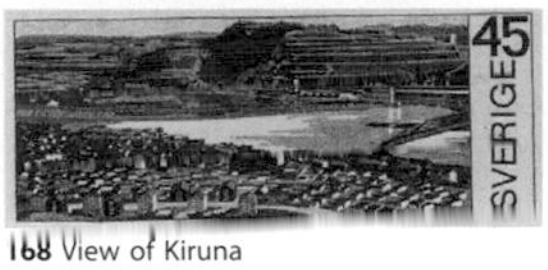

168 View of Kiruna

1970. Sweden within the Arctic Circle.

614	**168**	45ore brown	85	90
615	-	45ore blue	85	90
616	-	45ore green	85	90
617	-	45ore brown	85	90
618	-	45ore blue	85	90

DESIGNS: No. 615, Winter landscape and skiers; 616, Lake and Lapp hut, Stora National Park; 617, Reindeer herd; 618, Rocket-launching.

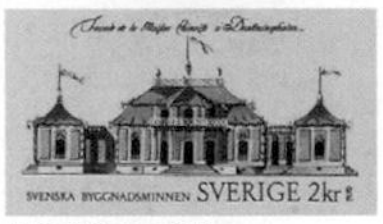

170 Chinese Palace, Drottningholm

1970. Historic Buildings.

619		55ore green	40	35
620	**170**	2k. multicoloured	2·30	35

DESIGN—21×27½ mm: 55ore Glimmingehus (15th-century castle).

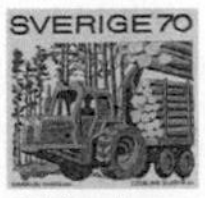

171 Lumber Trucks

1970. Swedish Trade and Industry.

621	**171**	70ore brown and blue	4·25	3·75
622	-	70ore blue, brown & pur	4·25	3·75
623	-	70ore purple and blue	4·25	3·75
624	-	70ore blue and purple	4·25	3·75
625	-	70ore blue and purple	4·25	3·75
626	-	70ore brown and purple	4·25	3·75
627a	-	1k. black on cream	65	35

DESIGNS—As Type **171**: No. 623, Ship's propeller; 624, Dam and Class Dm3 electric locomotive; 626, Technician and machinery. 44×20 mm: No. 622, Loading freighter at quayside; 625, Mine and electric ore train. 26×20 mm: No. 627a, Miners at coal face.

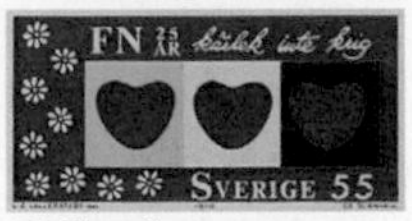

173 Three Hearts

1970. 25th Anniv of United Nations.

628	**173**	55ore red, yellow and black	50	35
629	-	70ore green, yellow & blk	85	35

DESIGN: 70ore Three four-leaved clovers.

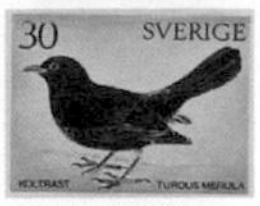

174 Blackbird

1970. Christmas. Birds. Multicoloured.

630	30ore Type **174**	1·30	1·10
631	30ore Great tit	1·30	1·10
632	30ore Northern bullfinch	1·30	1·10
633	30ore Western greenfinch	1·30	1·10
634	30ore Blue tit	1·30	1·10

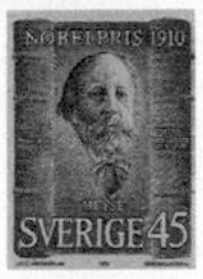

175 Paul Heyse (literature)

1970. Nobel Prize Winners of 1910.

635	**175**	45ore violet	1·50	70
636	-	55ore blue	1·00	35
637	-	70ore black	1·60	1·30

PORTRAITS: 55ore Otto Wallach (chemistry) and Johannes van der Waals (physics); 70ore Albrecht Kossel (medicine).

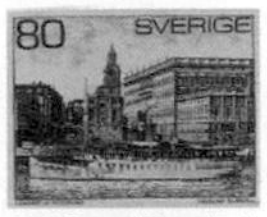

176 Ferry "Storskar" and Royal Palace, Stockholm

1971

638	**176**	80ore black and blue	65	35
639	-	4k. black	1·80	35
639a	-	6k. blue	3·00	35

DESIGN: 4k. 16th century "Blood Money" coins; 6k. Gustav Vasa's dollar.

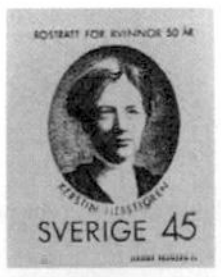

178 Kerstin Hesselgren (suffragette)

1971. 50th Anniv of Swedish Women's Suffrage.

640	**178**	45ore violet on green	50	35
641	**178**	1k. brown on yellow	85	35

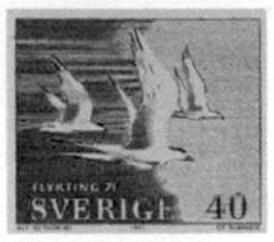

179 Arctic Terns

1971. Nordic Help for Refugees Campaign.

642	**179**	40ore red	50	55
643	**179**	55ore blue	1·10	35

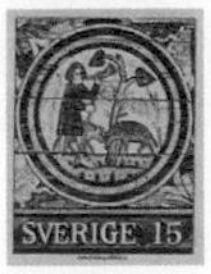

180 "The Prodigal Son" (painting, Sodra Rada Church)

1971

644	**180**	15ore green on green	40	35
645	-	25ore blue and brown	50	35
646	-	25ore blue and brown	50	35

DESIGNS—HORIZ (Panels from Grodinge Tapestry, Swedish Natural History Museum): No. 645, Griffin; 646, Lion.

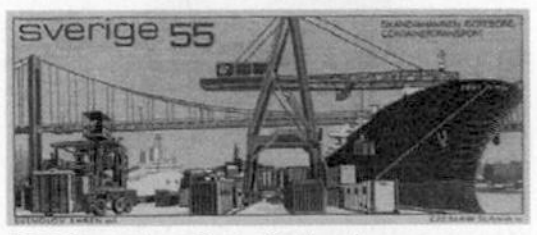

182 Container Port, Gothenburg

1971

647	**182**	55ore violet and blue	40	35
648	-	60ore brown on cream	40	35

649	-	75ore green on green	55	35

DESIGNS—28×23 mm: 60ore Timber-sledge; 75ore Windmills, Oland.

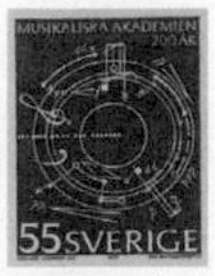

184 Musical Score

1971. Bicent of Swedish Royal Academy of Music.

650	184	55ore purple	40	35
651	184	85ore green	65	55

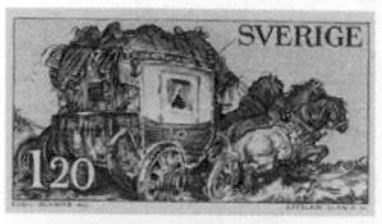

185 "The Mail Coach" (E. Schwab)

1971

652	185	1k.20 multicoloured	65	35

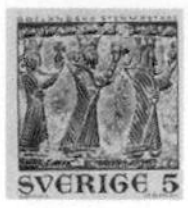

186 "The Three Wise Men"

1971. Gotland Stone-masons' Art.

653	186	5ore violet and brown	85	45
654	-	10ore violet and green	85	45
655	-	55ore green and brown	1·00	35
656	-	65ore brown and violet	75	35

DESIGNS—As T **186**: 10ore "Adam and Eve". 40×21 mm: 55ore "Winged Knight" and "Samson and the Lion"; 65ore "The Flight into Egypt".

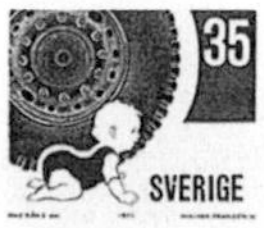

187 Child beside Lorry Wheel

1971. Road Safety.

657	187	35ore black and red	50	35
658	187	65ore blue and red	55	35

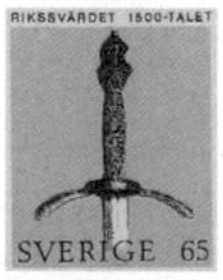

188 State Sword of Gustavus Vasa, c. 1500

1971. Swedish Crown Regalia. Multicoloured.

659	65ore Type **188**	85	55
660	65ore Sceptre of Erik XIV, 1561	85	55
661	65ore Crown of Erik XIV, 1561	85	55
662	65ore Orb of Erik XIV, 1561	85	55
663	65ore Anointing horn of Karl IX, 1606	85	55

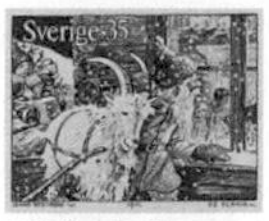
189 Santa Claus and Gifts

1971. Christmas. Traditional Prints.

664	189	35ore red	2·50	1·90
665	-	35ore blue	2·50	1·90
666	-	35ore purple	2·50	1·90
667	-	35ore blue	2·50	1·90
668	-	35ore green	2·50	1·90

DESIGNS: No. 665, Market scene; 666, Musical evening; 667, Skating; 668, Arriving for Christmas service.

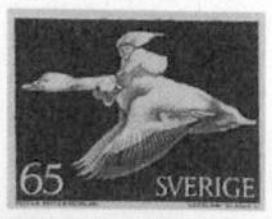

190 "Nils Holgersson on Goose" (from "The Wonderful Adventures of Nils" by Selma Lagerlof)

1971

669	190	65ore blue on cream	50	35

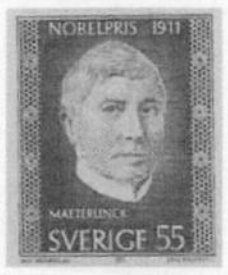

191 Maurice Maeterlinck (literature)

1971. Nobel Prize Winners of 1911.

670	191	55ore orange	95	55
671	-	65ore green	1·10	35
672	-	85ore red	1·20	90

DESIGNS: 65ore Allvar Gullstrand (medicine) and Wilhelm Wien (physics); 85ore Marie Curie (chemistry).

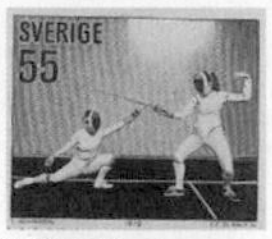

192 Fencing

1972. Sportswomen.

673	192	55ore purple	1·00	95
674	-	55ore blue	1·00	95
675	-	55ore green	1·00	95
676	-	55ore purple	1·00	95
677	-	55ore blue	1·00	95

DESIGNS: No. 674, Diving; 675, Gymnastics; 676, Tennis; 677, Figure-skating.

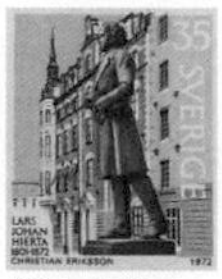

193 L. J. Hierta (newspaper editor, statue by C. Eriksson)

1972. Anniversaries of Swedish Cultural Celebrities.

678	193	35ore multicoloured	40	35
679	-	50ore violet	40	35
680	-	65ore blue	55	35
681	-	85ore multicoloured	75	55

DESIGNS AND ANNIVERSARIES—VERT: 35ore (death cent); 85ore G. Stiernhielm (poet 300th death anniv) (portrait by D. K. Ehrenstrahl). HORIZ: 50ore F. M. Franzen (poet and hymn-writer, birth bicent) (after K. Hultstrom); 65ore Hugo Alfven (composer, birth cent) (granite bust by C. Milles).

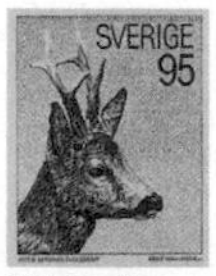

195 Roe Deer

1972

682	195	95ore brown on cream	55	35

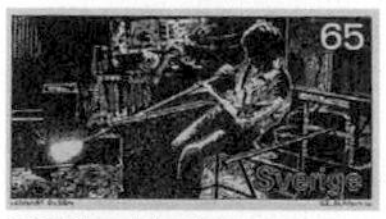

196 Glass-blowing

1972. Swedish Glass Industry.

683	196	65ore black	1·60	70
684	-	65ore blue	1·60	70
685	-	65ore red	1·60	70
686	-	65ore black	1·60	70
687	-	65ore blue	1·60	70

DESIGNS: No. 684, Glass-blowing (close-up); 685, Shaping glass; 686, Handling glass vase; 687, Bevelling glass vase.

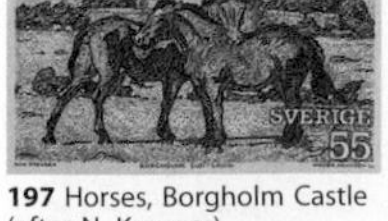

197 Horses, Borgholm Castle (after N. Kreuger)

1972. Tourism in South-east Sweden.

688	197	55ore brown on cream	75	70
689	-	55ore blue on cream	75	70
690	-	55ore brown on cream	75	70
691	-	55ore green on cream	75	70
692	-	55ore blue on cream	75	70

DESIGNS: No. 689, Oland Bridge and sailing barque "Meta"; 690, Kalmar Castle; 691, Salmon-fishing, Morrumsan; 692, Cadet schooner "Falken", Karlskrona Naval Base.

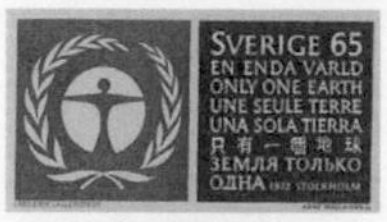

198 Conference Emblem and Motto, "Only One Earth"

1972. U.N. Environment Conservation Conference, Stockholm.

693	198	65ore blue and red on cream	55	35
694	-	85ore mult on cream	95	60

DESIGN—28×45 mm: 85ore "Spring" (wooden relief by B. Hjorth).

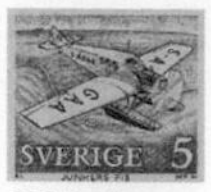

199 Junkers F-13 SA-GAA

1972. Swedish Mailplanes.

695	199	5ore lilac	40	35
696	-	15ore blue	55	35
697	-	25ore blue	55	35
698	-	75ore green	55	35

DESIGNS—45×19 mm: 15ore Junkers Ju 52/3m; 25ore Friedrichshafen FF-49 seaplane; 75ore Douglas DC-3 SE-BAB Hoken.

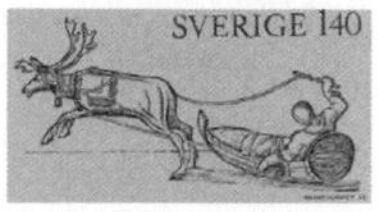

200 Reindeer and Sledge (woodcut from "Lapponia")

1972. Centenary of "Lapponia" (book by J. Schefferus).

699	200	1k.40 red and blue	75	35

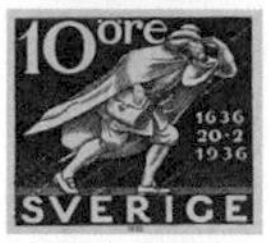

201 Early Courier

1972. "Stockholmia 74" Stamp Exhibition (1st issue) and Birth Centenary of Olle Hjortzberg (stamp designer).

700	201	10ore red	65	55
701	-	15ore green	65	55
702	-	40ore blue	65	55
703	-	50ore brown	65	55
704	-	60ore blue	65	55

DESIGNS: 15ore Post-rider; 40ore Steam train; 50ore Motor bus and trailer; 60ore Liner "Gripsholm".

See also Nos. 779/82.

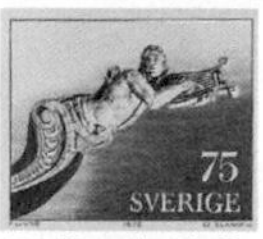

202 Figurehead of Royal Yacht "Amphion" (Per Ljung)

1972. Swedish 18th-century Art.

705		75ore green	65	35
706		75ore brown	65	35
707	202	75ore red	65	35
708	-	75ore red	65	35
709	-	75ore black, brown and red	65	35
710	-	75ore black, blue & purple	65	35

DESIGNS—59×24 mm: No. 705, "Stockholm" (F. Martin); 706, "The Forge" (P. Hillestrom). As T **202**: No. 708, "Quadriga" (Sergel). 28×37 mm: No. 709, "Lady with a Veil" (A. Roslin); 710, "Sophia Magdalena" (C. G. Pilo).

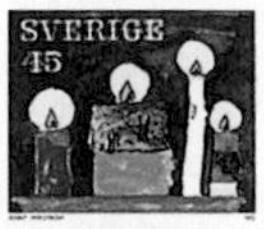

203 Christmas Candles (J. Wikstrom)

1972. Christmas. Multicoloured.

711	45ore Type **203**	50	35
712	45ore Father Christmas (E. Flygh)	50	35
713	75ore Carol singers (S. Hagg) (40×23 mm)	95	35

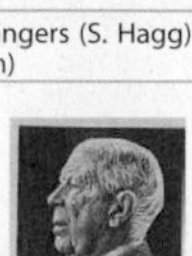

204 King Gustav VI Adolf

1972

714	204	75ore blue	50	25
715	204	1k. red	75	35

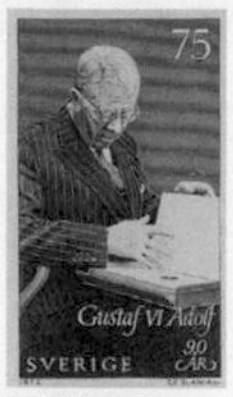

205 King Gustav with Book

1972. King Gustav VI Adolf's 90th Birthday.

716	205	75ore blue	3·00	3·50
717	-	75ore green	3·00	3·50
718	-	75ore red	3·00	3·50
719	-	75ore blue	3·00	3·50
720	-	75ore green	3·00	3·50

DESIGNS: No. 717, Chinese objets d'art; 718, Opening Parliament; 719, Greek objets d'art; 720, King Gustav tending flowers.

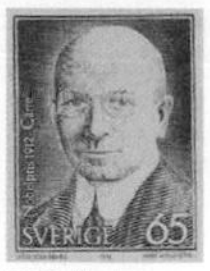

206 Alexis Carrel (medicine)

1972. Nobel Prize Winners of 1912.

721		60ore brown	85	55
722	206	65ore blue	1·00	55
723	-	75ore violet	1·60	35
724	-	1k. brown	1·60	35

DESIGNS—HORIZ: 60ore Paul Sabatier and Victor Grignard (chemistry). VERT: 75ore Nils Gustav Dalen (physics); 1k. Gerhart Hauptmann (literature).

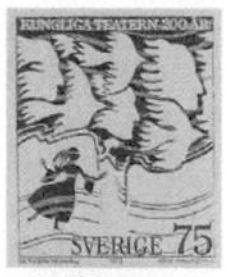

207 "Tintomara" Stage Set (B-R. Hedwall)

1973. Bicentenary of Swedish Royal Theatre.

725	207	75ore green	40	25
726	-	1k. purple	55	45

DESIGN—41×23 mm: 1k. "Orpheus" (P. Hillestrom).

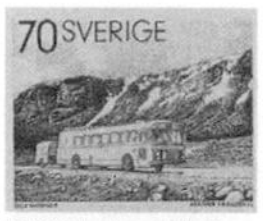

208 Modern Mail Coach, Vietas

1973

727		60ore black on yellow	40	35
728	208	70ore orange, blue & green	55	35

DESIGN: 60ore Mail bus, 1923.

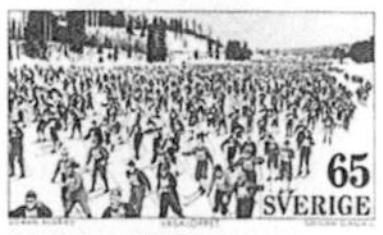

209 Vasa Ski Race

1973. Tourism in Dalecarlia.

729	209	65ore green	65	55
730	-	65ore green	65	55
731	-	65ore black	65	55
732	-	65ore green	65	55
733	-	65ore red	65	55

DESIGNS: No. 730, "Going to the Church in Mora" (A. Zorn); 731, Church stables in Rattvik; 732, "The Great Pit"; 733, "Mid-summer Dance" (B. Nordenberg).

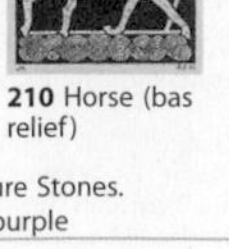

210 Horse (bas relief)

1973. Gottland Picture Stones.

734	210	5ore purple	30	25
735	-	10 blue	30	25

DESIGN: 10ore Viking longship (bas relief).

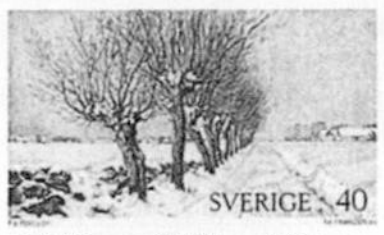

211 "Row of Willows" (P. Persson)

1973. Swedish Landscapes.

736	**211**	40ore brown	50	25
737	-	50ore black and brown	50	35
738	-	55ore green on cream	55	35

DESIGNS—20×28 mm: 50ore "View of Trosa" (R. Ljunggren). 27×23 mm: 55ore "Spring Birches" (O. Bergman).

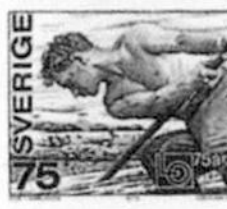

212 Lumberman

1973. 75th Anniv of Swedish Confederation of Trade Unions.

739	**212**	75ore red	40	35
740	**212**	1k.40 blue	65	35

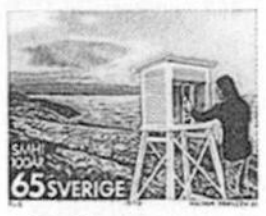

213 Observer reading Thermometer

1973. Centenary of I.M.O./W.M.O. and Swedish Meteorological Organizations.

741	**213**	65ore green	1·70	55
742	-	65ore blue and black	1·70	55

DESIGN: No. 742, U.S. satellite weather picture.

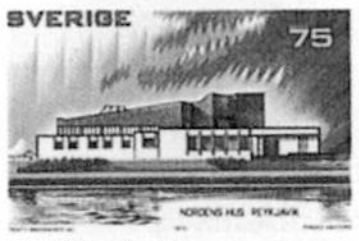

214 Nordic House, Reykjavik

1973. Nordic Countries' Postal Co-operation.

743	**214**	75ore multicoloured	75	35
744	**214**	1k. multicoloured	85	35

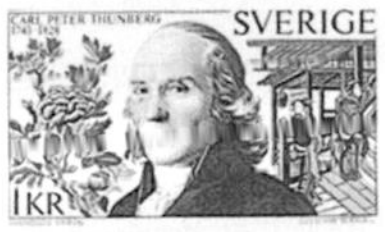

215 C. P. Thunberg, Japanese Flora and Scene

1973. Swedish Explorers.

745	**215**	1k. brown, green and blue	1·40	1·40
746	-	1k. multicoloured	1·40	1·40
747	-	1k. brown, green and blue	1·40	1·40
748	-	1k. multicoloured	1·40	1·40
749	-	1k. multicoloured	1·40	1·40

DESIGNS: No. 746, Anders Sparrman and Tahiti; 747, Adolf Erik Nordenskiold and the "Vega"; 748, Salomon Andree and wreckage of balloon "Ornen"; 749, Sven Hedin and camels.

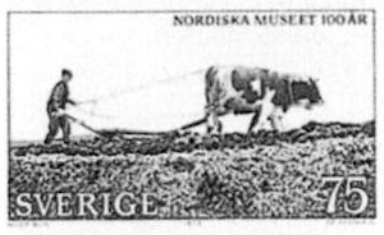

216 Team of Oxen

1973. Centenary of Nordic Museum.

750	**216**	75ore black	2·10	55
751	-	75ore brown	2·10	55
752	-	75ore black	2·10	55
753	-	75ore purple	2·10	55
754	-	75ore brown	2·10	55

DESIGNS: No. 751, Braking flax; 752, Potato-planting; 753, Baking bread; 754, Spring sowing.

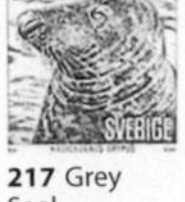

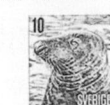

217 Grey Seal

1973. "Save Our Animals".

755	**217**	10ore green	40	35
756	-	20ore violet	40	35
757	-	25ore blue	40	35
758	-	55ore blue	50	35
759	-	65ore violet	50	35
760	-	75ore green	50	35

DESIGNS: 20ore Peregrine falcon; 25ore Lynx; 55ore European otter; 65ore Wolf; 75ore White-tailed sea eagle.

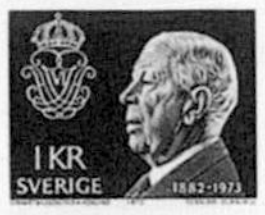

218 King Gustav VI Adolf

1973. King Gustav VI Adolf Memorial Issue.

761	**218**	75ore blue	40	35
762	**218**	1k. purple	55	35

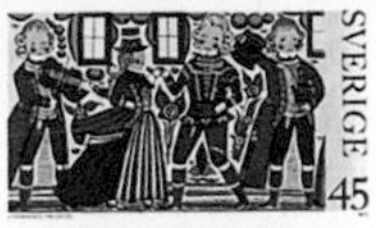

219 "Country Dance" (J. Nilsson)

1973. Christmas. Peasant Paintings. Multicoloured.

763	45ore Type **219**	85	45
764	45ore "The Three Wise Men" (A. Clemetson)	85	45
765	75ore "Gourd Plant" (B. A. Hansson) (23×28 mm)	2·50	35
766	75ore "The Rider" (K. E. Jonsson) (23×28 mm)	2·50	35

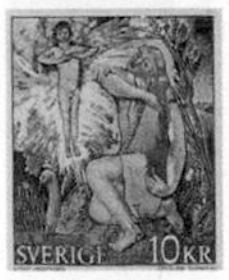

220 "Goosegirl" (E. Josephson)

1973. Ernst Josephson Commemoration.

767	**220**	10k multicoloured	5·25	35

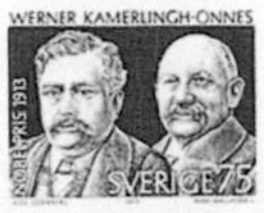

221 A. Werner (chemistry) and H. Kamerlingh-Onnes (physics)

1973. Nobel Prize Winners 1913.

768	**221**	75ore violet	75	35
769	-	1k. brown	85	35
770	-	1k.40 green	1·10	35

DESIGNS—VERT: 1k. Charles Robert Richet (medicine); 1k.40, Rabindranath Tagore (literature).

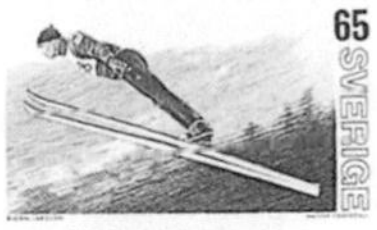

222 Ski Jumping

1974. "Winter Sports on Skis".

771	**222**	65ore green	85	70
772	-	65ore blue	85	70
773	-	65ore green	85	70
774	-	65ore red	85	70
775	-	65ore blue	85	70

DESIGNS: No 772, Cross-country (man); 773, Relay-racing; 774, Downhill-racing; 775, Cross-country (woman).

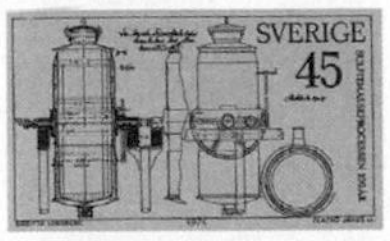

223 Ekman's Sulphite Pulping Machine

1974. Swedish Anniversaries.

776	**223**	45ore brown on grey	40	35
777	-	60ore green	40	55
778	-	75ore red	55	35

DESIGNS AND EVENTS: 45ore Type **223** (centenary of first sulphite pulp plant, Bergvik); 60ore Hans Jarta and part of Government Act (birth bicent); 75ore Samuel Owen and engineers (birth bicent).

224 U.P.U. Congress Stamp of 1924

1974. "Stockholmia '74" Stamp Exn (2nd issue).

779	**224**	20ore green	50	45
780	**224**	25ore blue	50	45
781	**224**	30ore brown	50	45
782	**224**	35ore red	50	45

MS783 Four sheets, 120×80 mm. containing stamps as Nos. 779/82, each in separate block of four. Colours changed. 20ore yellow; 25ore lilac; 30ore red; 35ore green. Set of 4 sheets	4·75	7·00

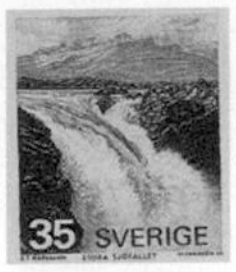

225 Great Falls

1974

784	**225**	35ore black and blue	40	35
785	-	75ore brown	40	35

DESIGN—HORIZ: 75ore Ystad (town).

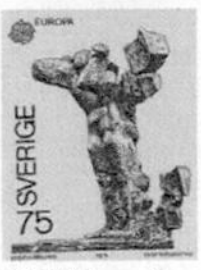

226 "Figure in a Storm" (B. Marklund)

1974. Europa. Sculptures.

786	**226**	75ore purple	1·70	45
787	-	1k. green	2·50	45

DESIGN: 1k. Picasso statue (from "Les Dames de Mougins"), Kristinehamn.

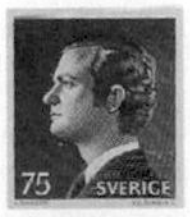

227 King Carl XVI Gustav

1974

788	**227**	75ore green	50	35
789	**227**	90ore blue	65	35
790	**227**	1k. purple	75	35
791	**227**	1k.10 red	65	35
792	**227**	1k.30 green	65	35
793	**227**	1k.40 blue	75	35
794	**227**	1k.50 mauve	85	35
795	**227**	1k.70 orange	85	35
796	**227**	2k. brown	95	35

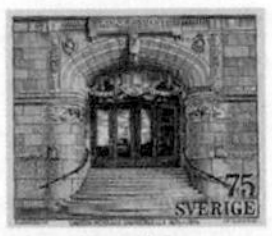

228 Central Post Office, Stockholm

1974. Centenary of Universal Postal Union.

800	**228**	75ore purple	1·50	35
801	-	75ore purple	1·50	35
802	-	1k. green	1·90	55

DESIGNS—As Type **228**: No. 801, Interior of Central Post Office, Stockholm. 40×24 mm: No. 802, Rural postman.

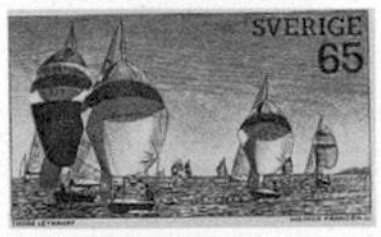

229 Regatta

1974. Tourism on Sweden's West Coast.

803	**229**	65ore red	75	55
804	-	65ore blue	75	55
805	-	65ore green	75	55
806	-	65ore green	75	55
807	-	65ore brown	75	55

DESIGNS: No. 804, Vinga Lighthouse; 805, Varberg Fortress; 806, Seine fishing; 807, Mollosund.

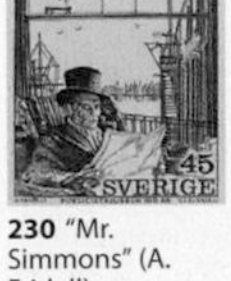

230 "Mr. Simmons" (A. Fridell)

1974. Centenary of Publicists' Club (Swedish press, radio and television association).

808	**230**	45ore black	40	35
809	**230**	1k.40 purple	55	35

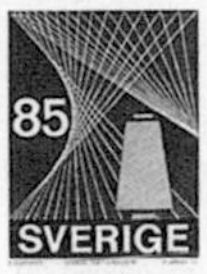

231 Thread and Spool

1974. Swedish Textile and Clothing Industry.

810	**231**	85ore violet	50	35
811	-	85ore black and orange	50	35

DESIGN: No. 811, Stylized sewing-machine.

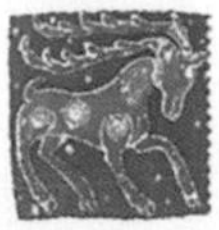
232 Deer

1974. Christmas. Mosaic Embroideries of Mythical Creatures. Each blue, red and green (45ore) or multicoloured (75ore).

812	45ore Type **232**	1·60	1·40
813	45ore Griffin	1·60	1·40
814	45ore Lion	1·60	1·40
815	45ore Griffin	1·60	1·40
816	45ore Unicorn	1·60	1·40
817	45ore Horse	1·60	1·40
818	45ore Lion	1·60	1·40
819	45ore Griffin	1·60	1·40
820	45ore Lion	1·60	1·40
821	45ore Lion-like creature	1·60	1·40
822	75ore Deer-like creature	50	35

No. 813 is facing right and has inscr at top, No. 815 faces left with similar inscr and No. 819 has inscr at bottom.

No. 814 has the inscr at top, No. 818 has it at the foot of the design, the lion having blue claws, No. 820 has similar inscr, but white claws.

Nos. 812/22 were issued together, *se-tenant*, forming a complete design.

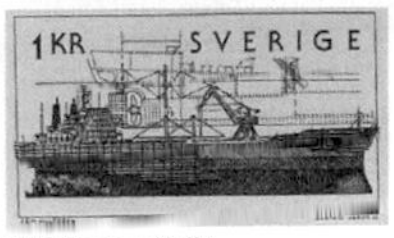

233 Tanker "Bill"

1974. Swedish Shipping. Each blue.

823	1k. Type **233**	1·10	90
824	1k. "Snow Storm" (liner)	1·10	90
825	1k. "Tor" and "Atle" (ice-breakers)	1·10	90
826	1k "Skanes" (train ferry)	1·10	90
827	1k. Tugs "Bill", "Bull" and "Starkodder"	1·10	90

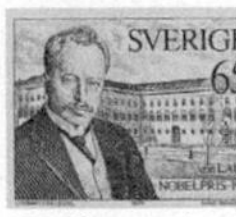

234 Max von Laue (physics)

1974. Nobel Prize Winners of 1914.

828	**234**	65ore red	65	35
829	-	70ore green	65	35
830	-	1k. blue	1·00	35

DESIGNS:—70ore Theodore William Richards (chemistry); 1k. Richard Barany (medicine).

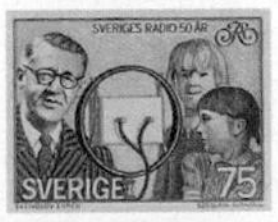

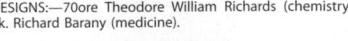

235 Sven Jerring (first announcer), Children and Microphone

1974. 50th Anniv of Swedish Broadcasting Corporation.

831	**235**	75ore blue and brown	1·20	35
832	-	75ore blue and brown	1·20	35

DESIGN: No. 832, Television camera at Parliamentary debate.

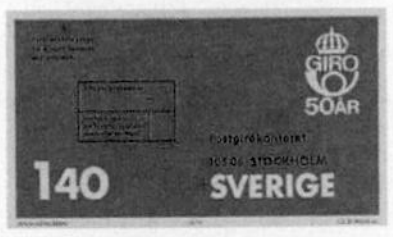

236 Giro Envelope

1975. 50th Anniv of Swedish Postal Giro Office.

833	**236**	1k.40 black and brown	65	35

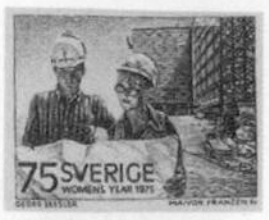

237 Male and Female Engineers

1975. International Women's Year.

834	**237**	75ore green	40	35
835	-	1k. purple	75	35

DESIGN—VERT: 1k. Jenny Lind (singer) (portrait by O. J. Sodermark).

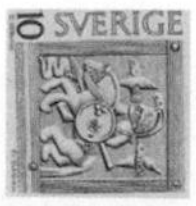

238 Bronze Helmet Decoration, Vendel

1975. Archaeological Discoveries.

836	**238**	10ore red	30	25
837	-	15ore green	30	25
838	-	20ore violet	30	25
839	-	25ore yellow	30	25
840	-	55ore brown	30	25

DESIGNS: 15ore Iron sword hilt and chapel, Vendel; 20ore Iron shield buckle, Vendel; 25ore Embossed gold plates (Gold Men), Eketorp Fortress, Oland; 55ore Iron helmet, Vendel.

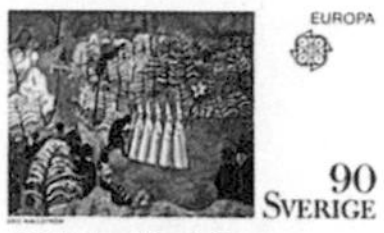

239 "New Year's Eve at Skansen" (Eric Hallstrom)

1975. Europa. Paintings. Multicoloured.

841	90ore Type **239**	1·60	45
842	1k.10 "Inferno" (August Strindberg) (vert)	1·90	55

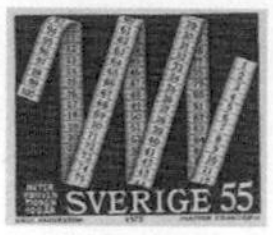

240 Metric Tape-measure (centenary of Metre Convention)

1975. Anniversaries.

843	**240**	55ore blue	50	35
844	-	70ore sepia and brown	50	45
845	-	75ore violet	55	45

DESIGNS AND EVENTS—44×27 mm: 70ore Peter Hernqvist (founder) and title-page of his book "Comprehensive Thesis on Glanders in Horses" (bicent of Swedish Veterinary Service). 24×31 mm: 75ore "Folke Filbyter" (birth centenary of Carl Milles (sculptor)).

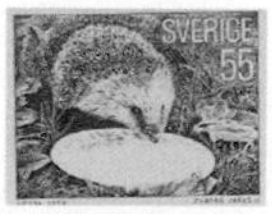

241 Western European Hedgehog

1975

846	**241**	55ore black	40	35
847	-	75ore red	50	35
848	-	1k.70 blue	75	35
849	-	2k. purple	1·10	35
850	-	7k. green	3·50	55

DESIGNS—HORIZ: 75ore Key-fiddler; 1k.70, Western capercaillie ("cock of the woods"). VERT: 2k. Rok stone (ancient inscribed rock), Ostergotland; 7k. Ballet dancers (from "Romeo and Juliet").

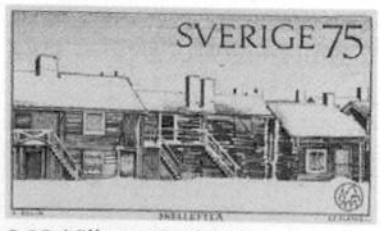

242 Village Buildings, Skelleftea

1975. European Architectural Heritage Year.

851	**242**	75ore black	55	45
852	-	75ore red	55	45
853	-	75ore black	55	45
854	-	75ore red	55	45
855	-	75ore blue	55	45

DESIGNS: No. 852, Engelsberg iron-works, Vastmanland; 853, Gunpowder tower, Visby, Gotland; 854, Iron-mine, Falun; 855, Rommehed military barracks, Dalecarlia.

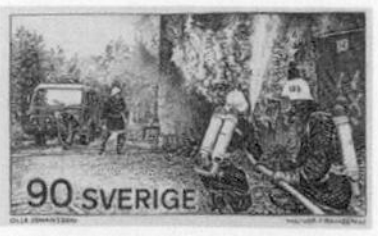

243 Fire Brigade

1975. "Watch, Guard and Help". Public Services.

856	**243**	90ore red	75	55
857	-	90ore blue	75	55
858	-	90ore red	75	55
859	-	90ore blue	75	55
860	-	90ore green	75	55

DESIGNS: No. 857, Customs service; 858, Police service; 859, Ambulance and hospital service; 860, Shipwreck of "Merkur" (Sea rescue service).

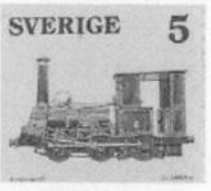

244 "Fryckstad"

1975. Swedish Steam Locomotives.

861	**244**	5ore green	40	25
862	-	5ore blue	40	25
863	-	90ore green	1·10	35

DESIGNS—As Type **244**: No. 862, "Gotland". 49×22 mm: 90ore "Prins August".

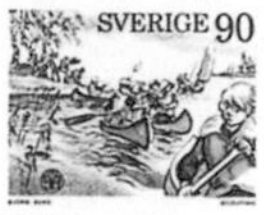

245 Canoeing

1975. Scouting. Multicoloured.

864	90ore Type **245**	1·10	35
865	90ore Camping	1·10	35

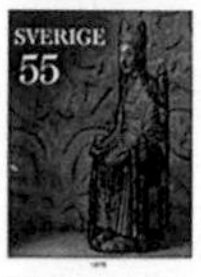

246 "Madonna" (sculpture), Vikiau church, Gotland

1975. Christmas. Religious Art.

866	**246**	55ore multicoloured	40	35
867	-	55ore multicoloured	65	45
868	-	55ore multicoloured	65	55
869	-	90ore brown	75	35
870	-	90ore red	1·00	35
871	-	90ore blue	1·00	35

DESIGNS—VERT: No. 867, "Birth of Christ" (embossed copper), Broddetorp church, Vastergotland; 868, "The Sun" (embossed copper), Broddetorp church, Vastergotland; 869, "Mourning Mary" (sculpture), Oja church, Gotland. HORIZ: Noore 870, 871, "Jesse at Foot of Christ's genealogical tree" (retable), Lofta church, Smaland.

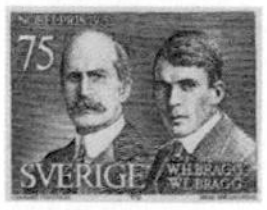

247 W. H. and W. L. Bragg (physics)

1975. Nobel Prize Winners of 1915.

872	**247**	75ore purple	40	35
873	-	90ore blue	65	35
874	-	1k.10 green	75	35

DESIGNS: 90ore Richard Willstatter (chemistry); 1k.10, Romain Rolland (literature).

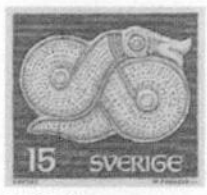

248 Bronze Coiled Snake Brooch, Vendel

1976

875	**248**	15ore bistre	30	25
876	-	20ore green	30	25
877	-	30ore purple	40	25
878	-	85ore blue	65	35
879	-	90ore blue	40	25
880	-	1k. purple	50	35
881	-	1k.90 green	95	35
882	-	9k. deep green and green	4·25	35

DESIGNS—21×19 mm: 20ore Pilgrim badge. 28×21 mm: 30ore Drinking horn; 85ore Common guillemot and razorbills. 28×23 mm: 1k.90, "Cave of the Winds" (sculpture) (Eric Grate). 21×28 mm: 90ore Chimney sweep; 1k. Bobbin lace-making; 9k. "Girl's Head" (wood-carving) (Bror Hjorth).

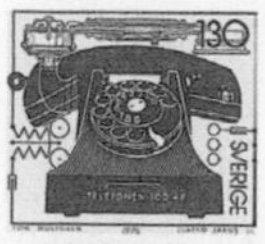

249 Early and Modern Telephones

1976. Telephone Centenary.

883	**249**	1k.30 mauve	65	35
884	**249**	3k.40 red	1·60	80

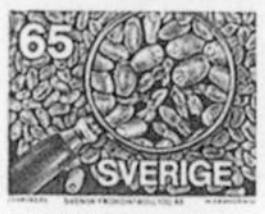

250 Wheat and Cornflower Seed

1976. Swedish Seed-testing Centenary.

885	**250**	65ore brown	50	35
886	-	65ore green and brown	50	35

DESIGN: No. 886, Viable and non-viable plants.

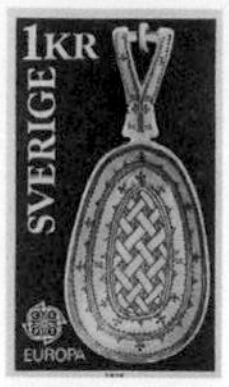

251 Lapp Spoon

1976. Europa. Handicrafts.

887	**251**	1k. black, pink and blue	1·40	45
888	-	1k.30 multicoloured	1·40	70

DESIGN: 1k.30, Tile stove (from aquarelle by C. Slania).

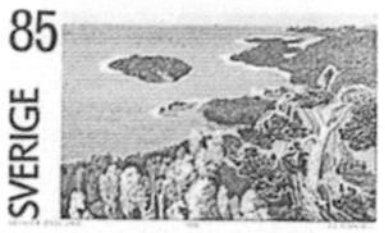

252 "View from Ringkallen" (H. Osslund)

1976. Tourism. Angermanland.

889	**252**	85ore green	55	55
890	-	85ore blue	55	55
891	-	85ore brown	55	55
892	-	85ore blue	55	55
893	-	85ore red	55	55

DESIGNS: No. 890, Tug towing timber; 891, Hay-drying racks; 892, Granvagsnipan; 893, Seine-net fishing.

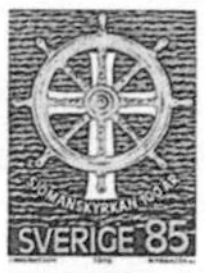

253 Ship's Wheel and Cross

1976. Centenary of Swedish Seamen's Church.

894	**253**	85ore blue	50	35

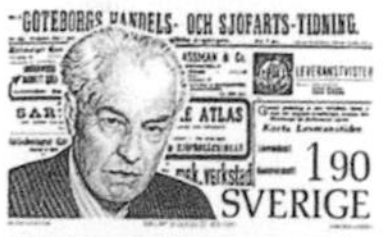

254 Torgny Segerstedt and "Goteborg Handels-och Sjofarts-tidning"

1976. Birth Centenary of Torgny Segerstedt (newspaper editor).

895	**254**	1k.90 black and brown	1·00	55

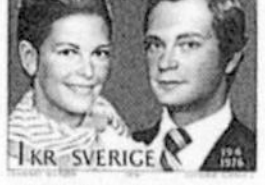

255 King Carl XVI Gustav and Queen Silvia

1976. Royal Wedding.

896	**255**	1k. red	55	35
897	**255**	1k.30 green	65	35

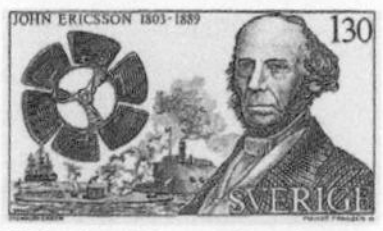

256 John Ericsson (marine propeller)

1976. Swedish Technological Pioneers. Multicoloured.

898	1k.30 Type **256**	95	90
899	1k.30 Helge Palmcrantz (hay maker)	95	90
900	1k.30 Lars Magnus Ericsson (telephone improvements)	95	90
901	1k.30 Sven Wingquist (ball bearing)	95	90
902	1k.30 Gustaf de Laval (milk separator and reaction turbine)	95	90

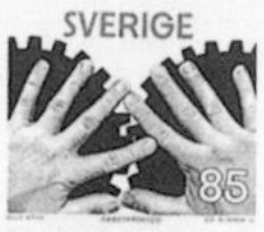

257 Hands and Cogwheels

1976. Industrial Safety.

903	**257**	85ore orange and violet	50	35
904	**257**	1k. green and brown	55	35

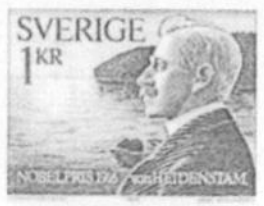

258 Verner von Heidenstam

1976. Literature Nobel Prize Winner of 1916.

905	**258**	1k. green	65	35
906	**258**	1k.30 blue	85	55

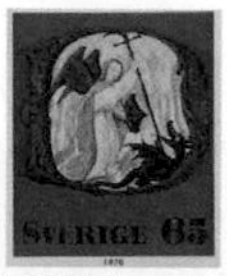

259 "Archangel Michael Destroying Lucifer" (Flemish prayer book)

1976. Christmas. Mediaeval Book Illustrations. Multicoloured.

907	65ore Type **259**	40	35
908	65ore "St. Nicholas awakening Children from Dead" (Flemish prayer book)	40	35
909	1k. "Mary visiting Elizabeth" (Austrian prayer book)	55	35
910	1k. "Prayer to the Virgin" (Austrian prayer book)	55	35

Nos. 909/10 are vert, 26×44 mm.

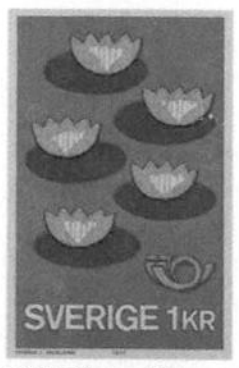

260 Water-lilies

1977. Nordic Countries Co-operation in Nature Conservation and Environment Protection.

911	**260**	1k. multicoloured	75	45
912	**260**	1k.30 multicoloured	65	60

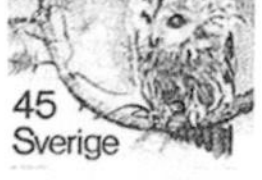

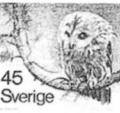

261 Tawny Owl

1977

913	**261**	45ore green	40	35
914	-	70ore blue	50	35
915	-	1k.40 brown	75	70
916	-	2k.10 brown	1·00	35

DESIGNS—23×29 mm: 70ore Norwegian cast-iron stove decoration. 41×21 mm: 1k.40, Gotland ponies. 28×22 mm: 2k.10, Tailor.

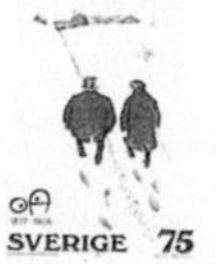

262 "Politeness"

1977. Birth Centenary of Oskar Andersson (cartoonist).

917	**262**	75ore black	40	35
918	**262**	3k.80 red	1·90	55

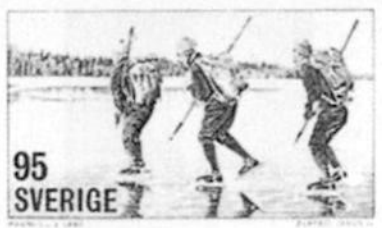

263 Skating

1977. Keep-fit Activities.

919	**263**	95ore blue	55	55
920	-	95ore green	55	55
921	-	95ore red	55	55
922	-	95ore green	55	55
923	-	95ore blue	55	55

DESIGNS: No. 920, Swimming; 921, Cycling; 922, Jogging; 923, Badminton.

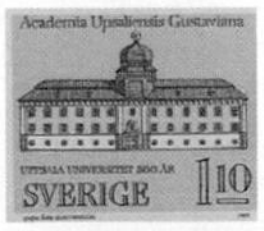

264 Gustavianum Building

1977. 500th Anniv of Uppsala University.

924	**264**	1k.10 black, yellow & blue	50	35

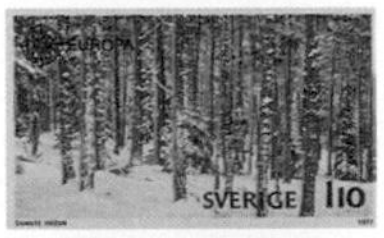

265 Winter Forest Scene

1977. Europa. Landscapes. Multicoloured.

925	1k.10 Type **265**	1·40	55
926	1k.40 Rapadalen valley, Sarek	1·50	90

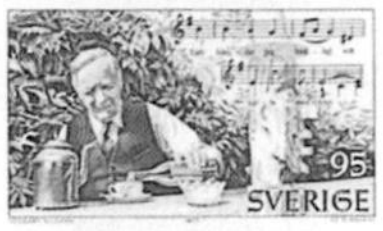

266 Calle Schewen at Breakfast

1977. Tourism. Roslagen. Poem "Calle Schewen Waltz" by E. Taube.

927	**266**	95ore green	60	55
928	-	95ore violet	60	55
929	-	95ore black and red	60	55
930	-	95ore blue	60	55
931	-	95ore red	60	55

DESIGNS: No. 928, Black-headed gull; 929, Calle Schewen dancing; 930, Fishing; 931, Sunset.

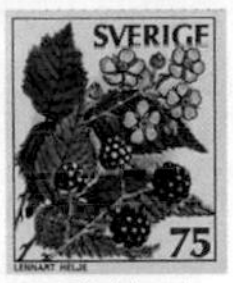

267 Blackberries

1977. Wild Berries. Multicoloured.

932	75ore Type **267**	40	35
933	75ore Cowberries	40	35
934	75ore Cloudberries	40	35
935	75ore Bilberries	40	35
936	75ore Strawberries	40	35

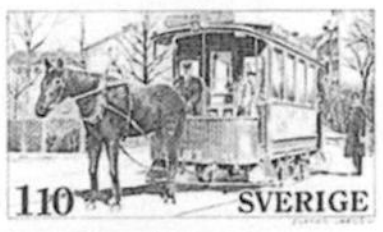

268 Horse-drawn Tram

1977. Public Transport.

937	**268**	1k.10 green	60	55
938	-	1k.10 blue	60	55
939	-	1k.10 blue	60	55
940	-	1k.10 blue	60	55
941	-	1k.10 green	60	55

DESIGN: No. 938, Electric tram; 939, Ferry "Djurgarden 6"; 940, Articulated bus; 941, Underground train, Stockholm.

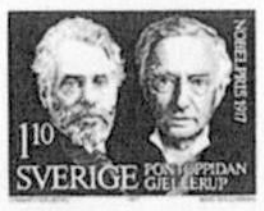

269 H. Pontoppidan and K. A. Gjellerup (literature)

1977. Nobel Prize Winners of 1917.

942	**269**	1k.10 brown	60	55
943	-	1k.40 green	90	80

DESIGN: 1k.40, Charles Glover Barkla (physics).

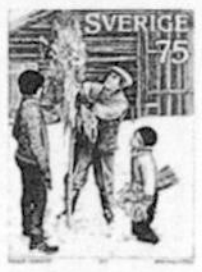

270 Erecting Sheaf for Birds

1977. Christmas. Seasonal Customs.

944	**270**	75ore violet	50	35
945	-	75ore orange	50	35
946	-	75ore green	50	35
947	-	1k.10 green	80	35
948	-	1k.10 red	80	35
949	-	1k.10 blue	80	35

DESIGNS: No. 945, Making gingersnaps; 946, Bringing in the Christmas tree; 947, Preparing the traditional fish dish; 948, Making straw goats for the pantomime; 949, Candle-making.

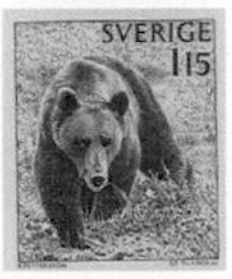

271 Brown Bear

1978

950	**271**	1k.15 brown	70	35
951	-	2k.50 blue	1·30	35

DESIGN: 2k.50, "Space without Affiliation" (sculpture by Arne Jones).

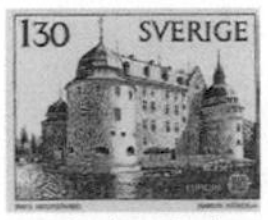

272 Orebro Castle

1978. Europa.

952	**272**	1k.30 green	1·60	45
953	-	1k.70 red	2·00	95

DESIGN—VERT: 1k.70, Doorway, Orebro Castle.

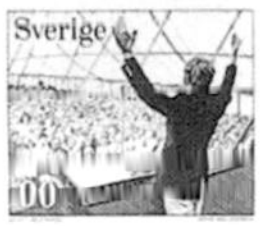

273 Pentecostal Meeting

1978. Independent Christian Associations.

954	**273**	90ore purple	60	55
955	-	90ore black	60	55
956	-	90ore violet	60	55
957	-	90ore green	60	55
958	-	90ore purple	60	55

DESIGNS: No. 955, Minister with children (Swedish Missionary Society); 956, Communion Service, Ethiopia (Evangelical National Missionary Society); 957, Baptism (Baptist Society); 958, Salvation Army band.

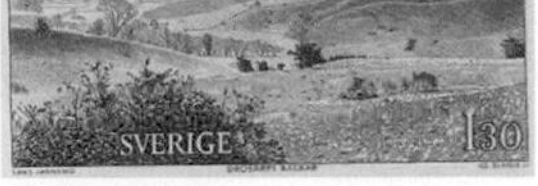

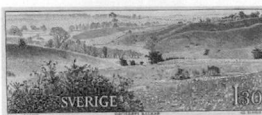

274 Brosarp Hills

1978. Travels of Carl Linne (botanist).

959	**274**	1k.30 black	80	55
960	-	1k.30 blue	80	55
961	-	1k.30 purple	80	55
962	-	1k.30 red	80	55
963	-	1k.30 blue	80	55
964	-	1k.30 purple	80	55

DESIGNS—58×23 mm: No. 960, Pied avocets. 27×23 mm: No. 961, Grindstone production (after J. W. Wallander); 962, "Linnaea borealis". 27×36 mm: No. 963, Red limestone cliff; 964, Linnaeus wearing Lapp dress and Dutch doctor's hat, and carrying Lapp drum (H. Kingsbury).

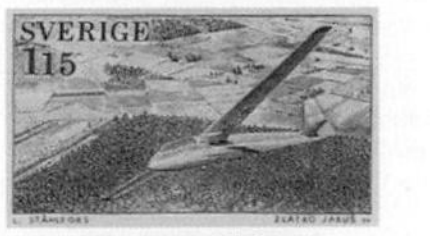

275 Glider over Alleberg Plateau

1978. Tourism. Vastergotland.

965	**275**	1k.15 green	70	55
966	-	1k.15 red	70	55
967	-	1k.15 blue	70	55
968	-	1k.15 grey	70	55
969	-	1k.15 black and purple	70	55

DESIGNS: No. 966, Common cranes; 967, Fortress on Lacko Island Skara; 968, Rock tomb, Luttra; 969, "Traders of South Vastergotland" (sculpture, N. Sjogren).

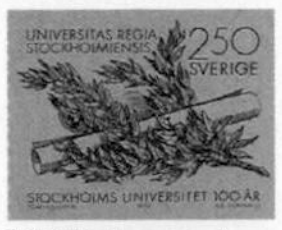

276 Diploma and Laurel Wreath

1978. Centenary of Stockholm University.

970	**276**	2k.50 green on brown	1·50	55

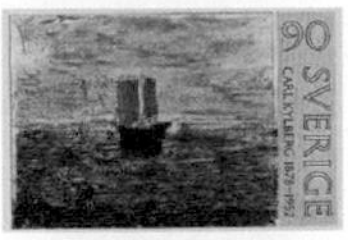

277 "The Homecoming" (Carl Kylberg)

1978. Paintings by Swedish Artists. Multicoloured.

971	90ore Type **277**	70	35
972	1k.15 "Standing Model seen from Behind" (Karl Isakson)	80	35
973	4k.50 "Self-portrait with a Floral Wreath" (Ivar Arosenius)	2·20	70

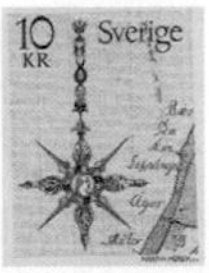

278 Northern Arrow

1978

974	**278**	10k. mauve	4·00	45

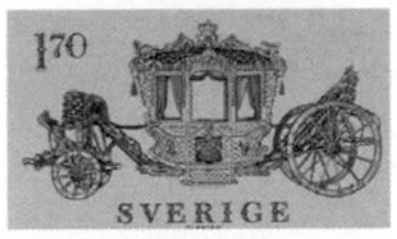

279 Coronation Carriage, 1699

1978

975	**279**	1k.70 red on buff	90	80

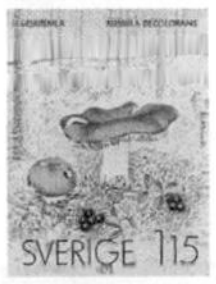

280 "Russula decolorans"

1978. Edible Mushrooms. Multicoloured.

976	1k.15 Type **280**	80	70
977	1k.15 Common puff-ball ("Lycoperdon perlatum")	80	70
978	1k.15 Parasol mushroom ("Macrolepiota procera")	80	70
979	1k.15 Chanterelle ("Cantharellus cibarius")	80	70
980	1k.15 Cep ("Boletus edulis")	80	70
981	1k.15 Cauliflower clavaria ("Ramaria botrytis")	80	70

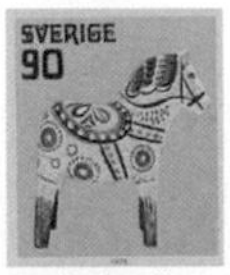

281 Dalecarlian Horse

1978. Christmas. Old Toys.

982	**281**	90ore multicoloured	60	35
983	-	90ore multicoloured	60	35
984	-	90ore green and red	60	35
985	-	1k.30 multicoloured	80	35
986	-	1k.30 multicoloured	80	35
987	-	1k.30 blue	80	35

DESIGNS—VERT: No. 983, Swedish Court doll; 984, Meccano; 987, Teddy bear. HORIZ: No. 985, Tops; 986, Equipage with water barrel (metal toy).

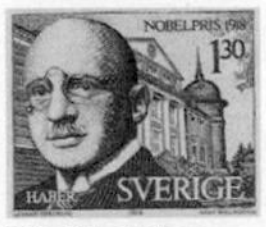

282 Fritz Haber (chemistry)

1978. Nobel Prize Winners of 1918.

988	**282**	1k.30 brown	90	35
989	-	1k.70 black	1·10	90

DESIGN: 1k.70, Max Planck (physics).

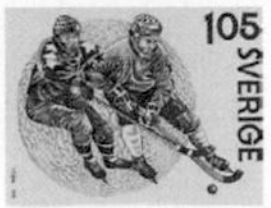

283 Bandy Players fighting for Ball

1979. Bandy.

990	**283**	1k.05 blue	80	35
991	**283**	2k.50 orange	1·10	35

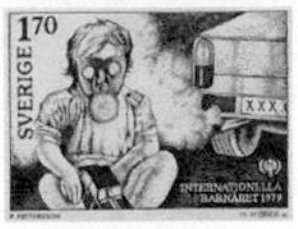

284 Child in Gas-mask

1979. International Year of the Child.

992	**284**	1k.70 blue	1·10	90

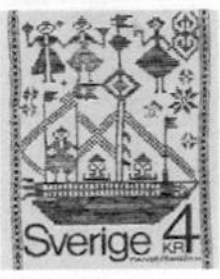

285 Wall Hanging

1979

993	**285**	4k. blue and red	1·90	35

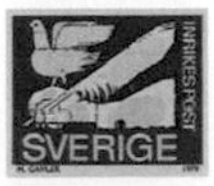

286 Carrier Pigeon and Hand with Quill

1979. Rebate Stamp.

994	**286**	(1k.) yellow, black and blue	1·90	35

No. 994 was only issued in booklets of 20 sold at 20k. in exchange for tokens distributed to all households in Sweden. Valid for inland postage only, they represented a rebate of 30ore on the normal rate of 1k.30.

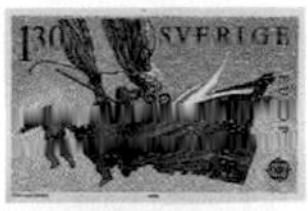

287 Sledge-boat

1979. Europa.

995	**287**	1k.30 black and green	3·50	55
996	-	1k.70 black and brown	3·75	1·10

DESIGN: 1k.70, Hand using telegraph key.

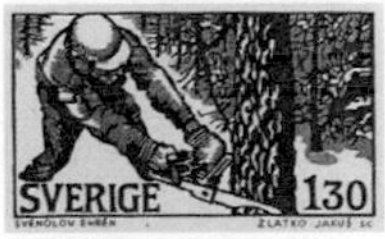

288 Felling Tree

1979. Farming.

997	**288**	1k.30 black, red & green	60	45
998	-	1k.30 green and black	60	45
999	-	1k.30 green and black	60	45
1000	-	1k.30 brown and green	60	45
1001	-	1k.30 red, black & green	60	45

DESIGNS: No. 998, Sowing; 999, Cows; 1000, Harvesting; 1001, Ploughing.

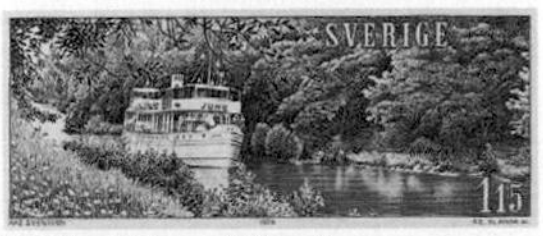

289 Tourist Launch "Juno"

1979. Tourism. Gota Canal.

1002	**289**	1k.15 violet	80	70
1003	-	1k.15 green	80	70
1004	-	1k.15 purple	80	70
1005	-	1k.15 red	80	70
1006	-	1k.15 violet	80	70
1007	-	1k.15 green	80	70

DESIGNS—As T **289**: No. 1003, Borenshult lock. 27×23½ mm: No. 1004, Hajstorp roller bridge; 1005, Opening lock gateore 27×36½ mm: No. 1006, Motor barge "Wilhelm Tham" in lock; 1007, Kayak in lock.

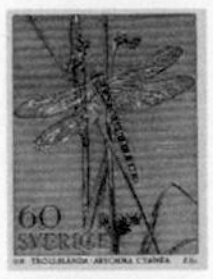

290 "Aeshna cyanea" (dragonfly)

1979. Wildlife.

1008	**290**	60ore violet	80	35
1009	-	65ore green	90	35
1010	-	80ore green	90	55

DESIGNS—41×21 mm: 65ore Northern pike. 27×22 mm: 80ore Green spotted toad.

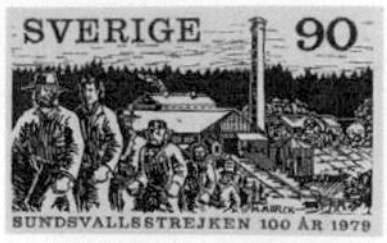

291 Workers leaving Sawmills

1979. Centenary of Sundsvall Strike.

1011	**291**	90ore brown and red	65	35

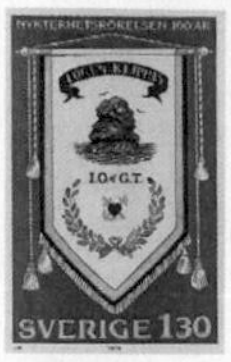

292 Banner

1979. Cent of Swedish Temperance Movement.

1012	**292**	1k.30 multicoloured	75	35

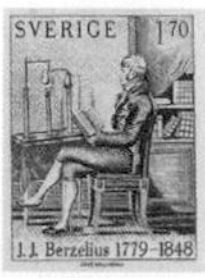

293 J. J. Berzelius

1979. Birth Bicentenaries of J. J. Berzelius (chemist) and J. O. Wallin (poet and hymn-writer).

1013	**293**	1k.70 brown and green	95	80
1014	-	4k.50 blue	3·00	70

DESIGN: 4k.50, J. O. Wallin and hymn numbers.

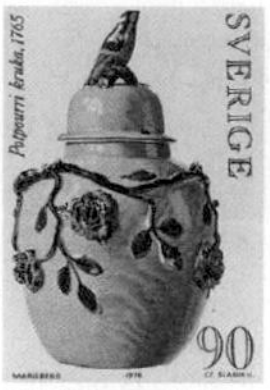

294 Pot-pourri Jar

1979. Swedish Rococo. Sheet 143×63 mm containing T **294** and similar vert designs.

MS1015 90ore multicoloured; 1k.15 multicoloured; 1k.30 blue, black and pink; 1k.15 multicoloured; 1k.30 blue, black and pink; 1k.70 buff and black (sold at 6k.)	4·25	3·25

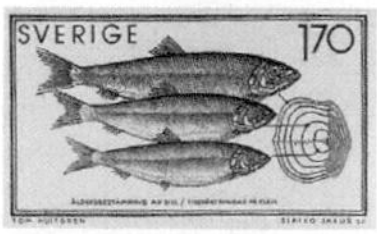

295 Atlantic Herrings and Growth Marks

1979. Marine Research.

1016	**295**	1k.70 green and blue	1·10	95
1017	-	1k.70 brown	1·10	95
1018	-	1k.70 green and blue	1·10	95
1019	-	1k.70 brown	1·10	95
1020	-	1k.70 green and blue	1·10	95

DESIGNS: No. 1017, Acoustic survey of sea-bed; 1018, Plankton bloom; 1019, Echo-sounding chart of Baltic Sea, October 1978; 1020, Fishery research ship "Argos".

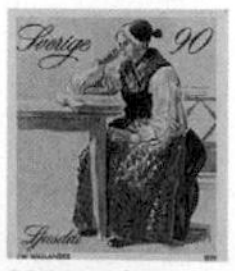

296 Ljusdal Costume

1979. Peasant Costumes and Jewellery.

1021	**296**	90ore multicoloured	65	35
1022	-	90ore multicoloured	65	35
1023	-	90ore blue	65	35
1024	-	1k.30 multicoloured	85	35
1025	-	1k.30 multicoloured	85	35
1026	-	1k.30 red	85	35

DESIGNS: As T **296**: No. 1022, Osteraker costume. 21×27 mm: No. 1023, Brooch from Jamtland; 1026, Brooch from Smaland. 23×40 mm: No. 1024, Goinge church dress; 1025, Mora church dress.

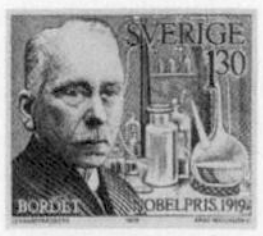

297 Jules Bordet (chemistry)

1979. Nobel Prize Winners of 1919.

1027	**297**	1k.30 mauve	75	35
1028	-	1k.70 blue	85	1·10
1029	-	2k.50 green	1·30	55

DESIGNS: 1k.70, Johannes Stark (physics); 2k.50, Carl Spitteler (literature).

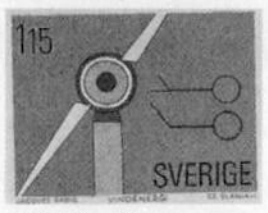

298 Wind Power

1980. Renewable Energy Sources.

1030	**298**	1k.15 blue	85	70
1031	-	1k.15 buff and green	85	70
1032	-	1k.15 orange	85	70
1033	-	1k.15 green	85	70
1034	-	1k.15 green and blue	85	70

DESIGNS: No. 1031, Biological energy; 1032, Solar energy; 1033, Geothermal energy; 1034, Wave energy.

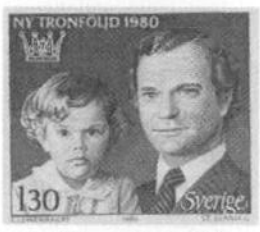

299 King Carl XVI Gustav and Crown Princess Victoria

1980. New Order of Succession to Throne.

1035	**299**	1k.30 blue	75	35
1036	**299**	1k.70 red	1·20	80

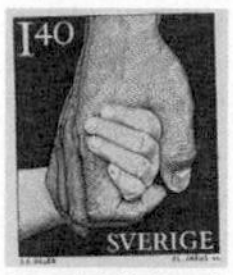

300 Child's Hand in Adult's

1980. Care.

1037	**300**	1k.40 brown	75	35
1038	-	1k.60 green	85	35

DESIGN: 1k.60, Aged hand clasping stick.

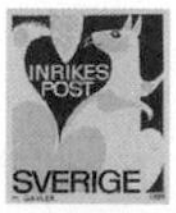

301 Squirrel

1980. Rebate Stamp.

1039	**301**	(1k.) yellow, blue & black	2·10	35

No. 1039 was only issued in booklets of 20 sold at 20k. on production of tokens distributed to all households in Sweden.

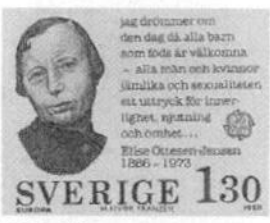

302 Elise Ottesen-Jensen (pioneer of birth control)

1980. Europa.

1040	**302**	1k.30 green	2·00	45
1041	-	1k.70 red	2·75	1·20

DESIGN: 1k.70, Joe Hill (member of workers' movement).

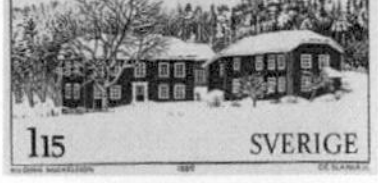

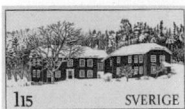

303 Tybling Farm, Tyby

1980. Tourism. Halsingland.

1042	**303**	1k.15 red	65	60
1043	-	1k.15 blue and purple	65	60
1044	-	1k.15 green	65	60
1045	-	1k.15 purple	65	60
1046	-	1k.15 blue	65	60

DESIGNS: No. 1043, Old iron works, Iggesund; 1044, Blaxas ridge, Forsa; 1045, Banga farm, Alfta; 1046, Sunds Canal, Hudiksvall.

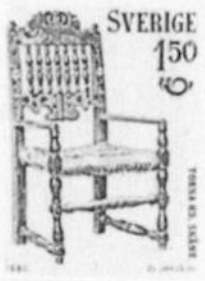

304 Chair from Scania (1831)

1980. Nordic Countries' Postal Co-operation.

1047	**304**	1k.50 green	95	35
1048	-	2k. brown	1·40	70

DESIGN: 2k. Cradle from North Bothnia (19th century).

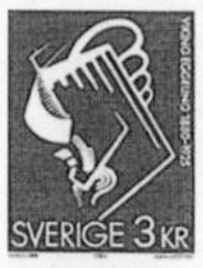

305 Motif from film "Diagonal Symphony"

1980. Birth Bicentenary of Viking Eggeling (film-maker).

1049	**305**	3k. blue	1·90	35

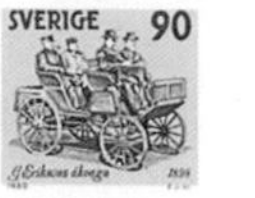

306 Gustaf Erikson's Paraffin-driven Car, 1898

1980. Swedish Motor Vehicles. Sheet 120×67 mm containing T **306** and similar horiz designs.

MS1050 90ore black and blue; 1k.15 black and ochre; 1k.30 black and blue; 1k.40 black and blue; 1k.50 black and ochre; 1k.70, black and blue (sold at 9k.)	5·25	4·75

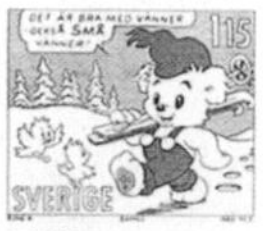

307 Bamse

1980. Christmas. Swedish Comic Strips.

1051	**307**	1k.15 blue and red	55	35
1052	-	1k.15 multicoloured	55	35
1053	-	1k.50 black	95	45
1054	-	1k.50 multicoloured	95	45

DESIGNS—As T **307** but VERT: No. 1052, Karlsson; 1053, Adamson. 40×23 mm: No. 1054, Kronblom.

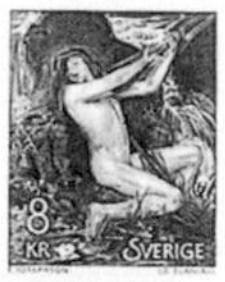

308 "Necken" (Ernst Josephson)

1980

1055	**308**	8k. brown, black and blue	4·50	35

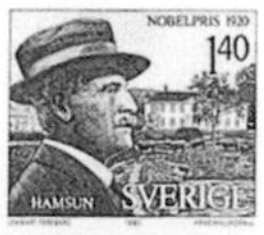

309 Knut Hamsun (literature)

1980. Nobel Prize Winners of 1920.

1056	**309**	1k.40 blue	85	55
1057	-	1k.40 red	85	55
1058	-	2k. green	1·10	70
1059	-	2k. brown	1·10	70

DESIGNS: No. 1057, August Krogh (medicine); 1058, Charles-Edouard Guillaume (physics); 1059, Walther Nernst (chemistry).

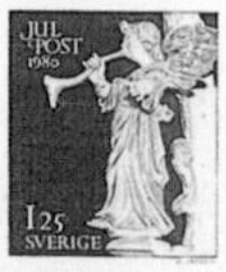

310 Angel blowing Horn

1980. Christmas.

1060	**310**	1k.25 brown and blue	75	35

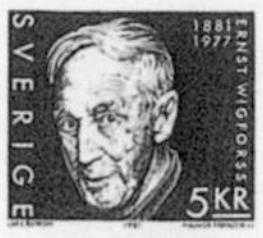

311 Ernst Wigforss

1981. Birth Centenary of Ernst Wigforss (politician).

1061	**311**	5k. red	2·50	60

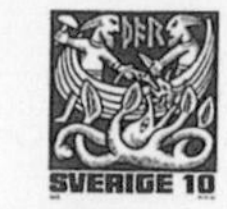

312 Thor catching Midgard Serpent

1981. Norse Mythology.

1062	**312**	10ore black	30	35
1063	-	15ore red	30	35
1064	-	50ore red	40	35
1065	-	75ore green	55	45
1066	-	1k. black	75	45

DESIGNS: 15ore Heimdall blowing horn; 50ore Freya riding boar; 75ore Freya in carriage drawn by cats; 1k. Odin on eight-footed steed.

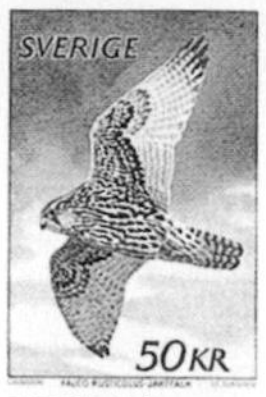

313 Gyr Falcon

1981

1067	**313**	50k. brown, black & blue	23·00	2·75

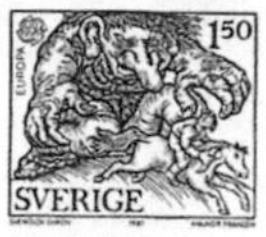

314 Troll

1981. Europa.

1068	**314**	1k.50 blue and red	2·30	45
1069	-	2k. red and green	2·75	55

DESIGN: 2k. The Lady of the Woods.

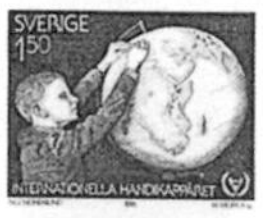

315 Blind Boy feeling Globe

1981. International Year of Disabled Persons.

1070	**315**	1k.50 green	75	35
1071	**315**	3k.50 violet	1·70	70

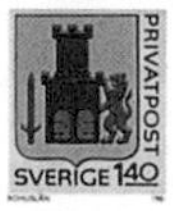

316 Arms of Bohuslan

1981. Rebate stamps. Arms of Swedish Provinces (1st series). Multicoloured.

1072	1k.40 Ostergotland	2·00	35
1073	1k.40 Jamtland	2·00	35
1074	1k.40 Dalarna	2·00	35
1075	1k.40 Type **316**	2·00	35

See also Nos. 1112/15, 1153/6, 1189/92, 1246/9 and 1302/5.

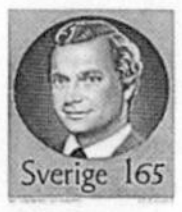

317 King Carl XVI Gustav

1981

1076	**317**	1k.65 green	75	35
1077	-	1k.75 blue	85	45
1077a	**317**	1k.80 blue	95	35
1077b	**317**	1k.90 red	1·10	35
1078	**317**	2k.40 purple	1·40	45
1078a	-	2k.40 green	1·70	80
1078b	**317**	2k.70 purple	1·40	55
1078c	-	3k.20 red	1·80	55

DESIGN: 1k.75, 2k.40 (1078a), 3k.20, Queen Silvia.

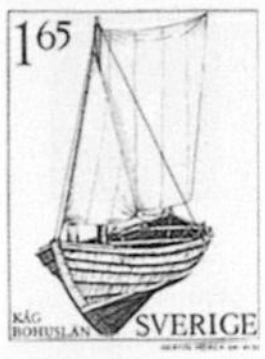

318 Boat from Bohuslan

1981. Provincial Sailing Boats.

1079	**318**	1k.65 blue	95	55
1080	-	1k.65 blue	95	55
1081	-	1k.65 blue	95	55
1082	-	1k.65 blue	95	55
1083	-	1k.65 blue	95	55
1084	-	1k.65 blue	95	55

DESIGNS: No. 1080, Boat from Blekinge; 1081, Boat from Norrbotten; 1082, Boat from Halsingland; 1083, Boat from Gotland; 1084, Boat from West Skane.

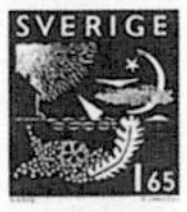

319 "Night and Day"

1981

1085	**319**	1k.65 violet	85	35

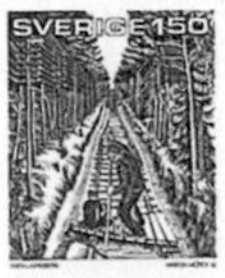

320 Par Lagerkvist riding Railway Trolley with Father (illustration from "Guest of Reality")

1981

1086	**320**	1k.50 green	85	35

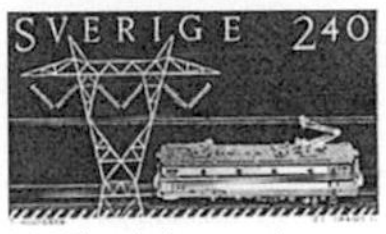

321 Electric Locom[illegible]

1981. "Sweden in the World".

1087	**321**	2k.40 red	1·20	90
1088	-	2k.40 red	1·20	90
1089	-	2k.40 purple	1·20	90
1090	-	2k.40 violet	1·20	90
1091	-	2k.40 blue	1·30	1·10
1092	-	2k.40 blue	1·30	1·10

DESIGNS—As T **321**: No. 1088, Scania trucks with rock drilling equipment; 1089, Birgit Nilsson (opera singer) and Sixten Ehrling (conductor); 1090, North Sea gas rig. 19×23 mm: No. 1091, Bjorn Borg (tennis player); 1092, Ingemar Stenmark (skier).

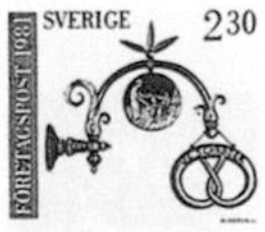

322 Baker's Sign

1981. Business Mail.

1093	**322**	2k.30 brown	1·80	45
1094	-	2k.30 brown	1·80	45

DESIGN: No. 1094, Pewterer's sign.

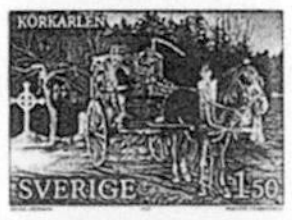

323 Olof As in *The Coachman*

1981. Swedish Film History. Sheet 135×69 mm containing T **323** and similar horiz designs.

MS1095	1k.50 black and yellow; 1k.50 black and blue; 1k.65 black and yellow; 1k.65 black and blue; 2k.40 multicoloured (sold at 10k.)	5·75	5·75

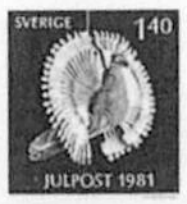

324 Wooden Bird

1981. Christmas.

1096	**324**	1k.40 red	75	35
1097	-	1k.40 green	75	35

DESIGN: No. 1097, Wooden bird (different).

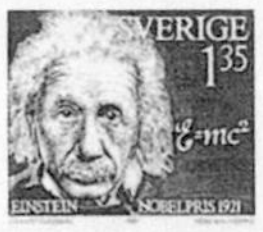

325 Albert Einstein (physics)

1981. Nobel Prize Winners of 1921.

1098	**325**	1k.35 red	75	60
1099	-	1k.65 green	85	35
1100	-	2k.70 blue	1·20	90

DESIGNS: 1k.65, Anatole France (literature); 2k.70, Frederick Soddy (chemistry).

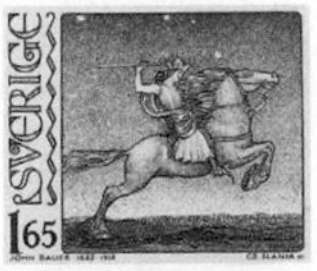

326 Knight on Horseback

1982. Birth Centenary of John Bauer (illustrator of fairy tales).

1101	**326**	1k.65 blue, yellow & lilac	85	55
1102	-	1k.65 multicoloured	85	55
1103	-	1k.65 black and yellow	85	55
1104	-	1k.65 yellow and lilac	85	55

DESIGNS: No. 1102, "What a wretched pale creature, said the Troll Woman"; 1103, "The Princess beside the Forest Lake"; 1104, "Now it is already twilight Night".

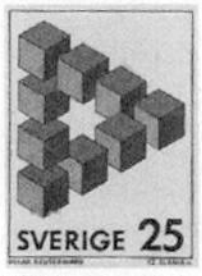

327 Impossible Triangle

1982

1105	**327**	25ore brown	30	25
1106	-	50ore brown	30	25
1107	-	75ore blue	40	35
1108	-	1k.35 blue	75	45
1109	-	5k. purple	2·75	35

DESIGNS: 50, 75ore, Impossible figures (different); 1k.35, Newspaper distributor; 5k. "Graziella wonders if she could be a Model" (etching, Carl Larsson).

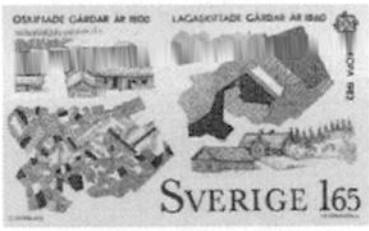

328 Villages before and after Land Reform

1982. Europa.

1110	**328**	1k.65 green and black	3·50	55
1111	-	2k.40 green	1·70	1·10

DESIGN—26×22 mm: 2k.40, Anders Celsius.

1982. Rebate Stamps. Arms of Swedish Provinces (2nd series). As T **316**. Multicoloured.

1112	1k.40 Dalsland	2·00	35
1113	1k.40 Oland	2·00	35
1114	1k.40 Vastmanland	2·00	35
1115	1k.40 Halsingland	2·00	35

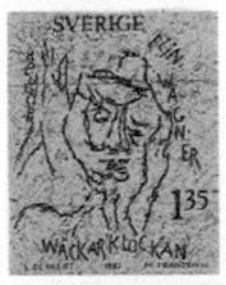

329 Elin Wagner

1982. Birth Centenary of Elin Wagner (novelist).

1116	**329**	1k.35 brown on grey	95	70

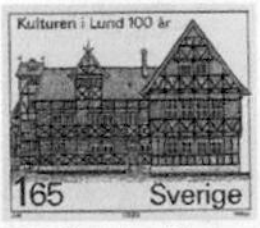

330 Burgher House

1982. Centenary of Museum of Cultural History, Lund.

1117	**330**	1k.65 brown	95	35
1118	-	2k.70 brown	1·40	80

DESIGN: 2k.70, Embroidered lace.

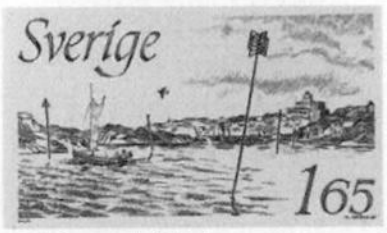

331 Lateral Mark

1982. New International Buoyage System.

1119	**331**	1k.65 blue and green	75	35
1120	-	1k.65 green and blue	75	35
1121	-	1k.65 deep blue and blue	75	35
1122	-	1k.65 blue and green	75	35
1123	-	1k.65 deep blue and blue	75	35

DESIGNS: No. 1120, Cardinal mark and Sweden–Finland ferry "Sally"; 1121, Racing yachts and special mark; 1122, Safe-water mark; 1123, Pilot boat, isolated danger mark and lighthouse.

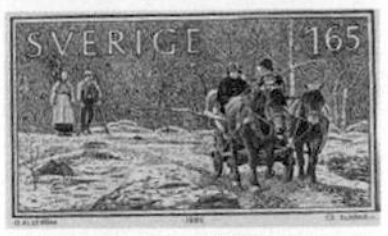

332 Scene from "The Emigrants" (film)

1982. Living Together.

1124	**332**	1k.65 green	95	45
1125	-	1k.65 purple	95	45
1126	-	1k.65 blue	95	45
1127	-	1k.65 red	95	45

DESIGNS: No. 1125, Vietnamese boat people in factory; 1126, Immigrants examining local election literature; 1127, Three girls arm-in-arm.

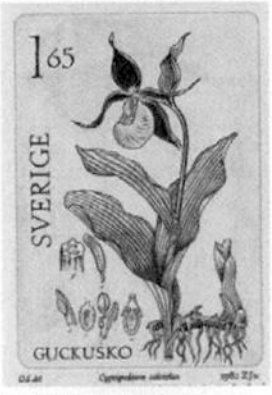

333 Lady's Slipper (*Cypropedium calceolus*)

1982. Wild Orchids. Sheet 144×63 mm containing T **333** and similar vert design.

MS1128	1k.65 Early purple orchid (*Orchis mascula*); 1k.65 Type **333**; 2 k.40 Marsh helleborine (*Epipactris*); 2k.70 Elderflowered orchid (*Dactylorhiza sambucia*) (sold at 10k.)	7·25	6·25

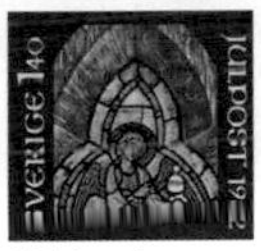

334 Angel

1982. Christmas. Medieval Glass Paintings from Lye Church. Multicoloured.

1129	1k.40 Type **334**	85	60
1130	1k.40 "The Child in the Temple"	85	60
1131	1k.40 "Adoration of the Magi"	85	60
1132	1k.40 "Tidings to the Shepherds"	85	60
1133	1k.40 "The Birth of Christ"	85	60

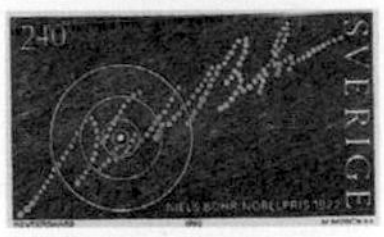

335 Quantum Mechanics (Niels Bohr, 1922)

1982. Nobel Prize Winners for Physics.

1134	**335**	2k.40 blue	1·30	95
1135	-	2k.40 red	1·30	95
1136	-	2k.40 green	1·30	95
1137	-	2k.40 lilac	1·30	95
1138	-	2k.40 red	1·30	95

DESIGNS: No. 1135, Fuse distribution (Erwin Schrodinger, 1933); 1136, Wave pattern (Louis de Broglie, 1929); 1137, Electrons (Paul Dirac, 1933); 1138, Atomic model (Werner Heisenberg, 1932).

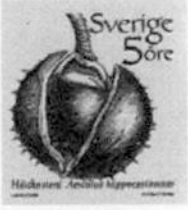

336 Horse Chestnut

1983. Fruit.

1139	**336**	5ore brown	30	25
1140	-	10ore green	30	25
1141	-	15ore red	30	25
1142	-	20ore blue	55	35

DESIGNS: 10ore Norway maple; 15ore Dog rose; 20ore Blackthorn.

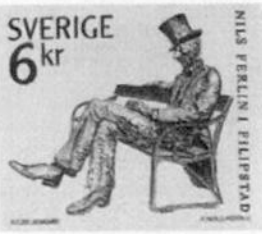

337 Ferlin (statue by K. Bejemark)

1983. 85th Birth Anniv of Nils Ferlin (poet).

1143	**337**	6k. green	3·00	45

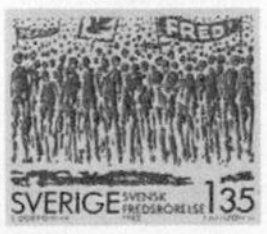

338 Peace March

1983. Centenary of Swedish Peace Movement.

1144	**338**	1k.35 blue	85	70

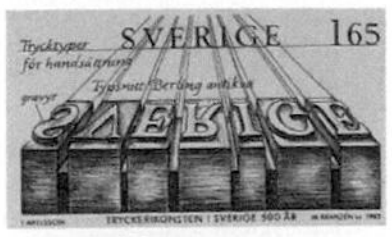

339 Lead Type

1983. 500th Anniv of Printing in Sweden.

1145	**339**	1k.65 black and brown on stone	85	35
1146	-	1k.65 black, green and red on stone	85	35
1147	-	1k.65 brown and black on stone	85	35
1148	**339**	1k.65 black and brown on stone	85	35
1149	-	1k.65 brown, green and black on stone	85	35

DESIGNS: No. 1146, Ox plough (illustration from "Dialogus creaturarum" by Johan Snell, 1483); 1147, Title page of Karl XII's Bible, 1703; 1148, 18th-century alphabet books; 1149, Laser photocomposition.

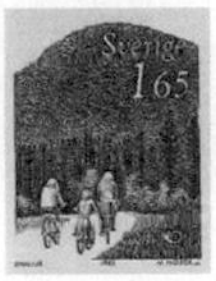

340 Family Cycling in Countryside

1983. Nordic Countries' Postal Co-operation. "Visit the North".

1150	**340**	1k.65 green	85	35
1151	-	2k.40 blue and brown	1·40	90

DESIGN: 2k.40, Yachts at Stockholm.

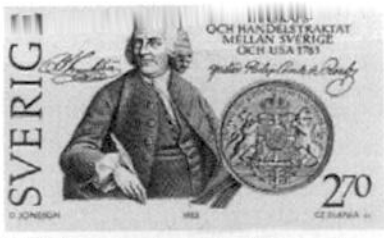

341 Benjamin Franklin and Great Seal of Sweden

1983. Bicentenary of Sweden–U.S.A. Treaty of Amity and Commerce.

1152	**341**	2k.70 blue, brown & blk	1·60	90

1983. Rebate Stamps. Arms of Swedish Provinces (3rd series). As T **316**. Multicoloured.

1153	1k.60 Vastergotland	2·00	35
1154	1k.60 Medelpad	2·00	35
1155	1k.60 Gotland	2·00	35
1156	1k.60 Gastrikland	2·00	35

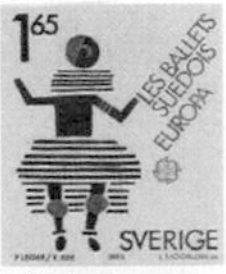

342 Costume Sketch by Fernand Leger for "Creation du Monde"

1983. Europa.

1157	1k.65 chocolate and brown	2·30	55
1158	2k.70 blue	3·50	1·60

DESIGNS: 1k.65, Type **342** (Swedish Ballet); 2k.70, J. P. Johansson's adjustable spanner.

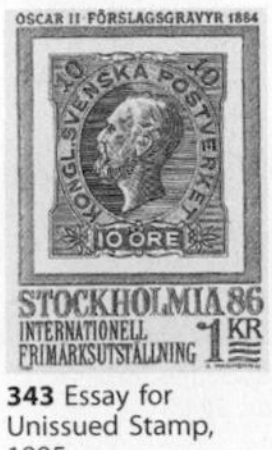

343 Essay for Unissued Stamp, 1885

1983. "Stockholmia 86" International Exhibition (1st issue). Oscar II stamp designs by Max Mirowsky.

1159	**343**	1k. blue	85	70
1160	-	2k. red	1·10	90
1161	-	3k. blue	1·40	1·10

1162	-	4k. green	1·60	1·20

DESIGNS: 2k. Issued stamp of 1885; 3k. Essay for unissued stamp, 1891; 4k. Issued stamp of 1891.

See also Nos. 1199/1202, 1252/5, 1285/8 and 1310/13.

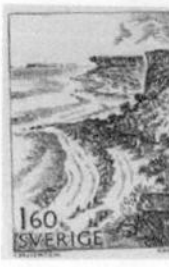

344 Greater Karlso

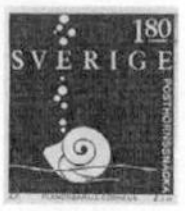

345 Freshwater Snail

1983

1163	**344**	1k.60 blue	95	35
1164	**345**	1k.80 green	1·10	35
1165	-	2k.10 green	1·20	35

DESIGN—22×27 mm: 2k.10, Arctic fox.

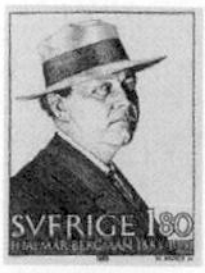

346 Bergman

1983. Birth Centenary of Hjalmar Bergman (novelist and dramatist).

1166	**346**	1k.80 blue	95	35
1167	-	1k.80 multicoloured	95	35

DESIGN: No. 1167, Jac the Clown (novel character).

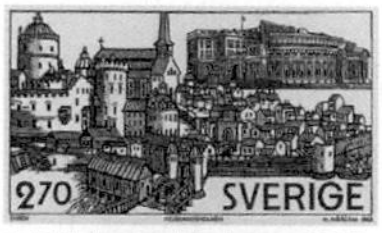

347 Helgeandsholmen, 1580 (after Franz Hogenberg) and Riksdag

1983. Return of Riksdag (Parliament) to Helgeandsholmen Island, Stockholm.

1168	**347**	2k.70 purple and blue	1·60	80

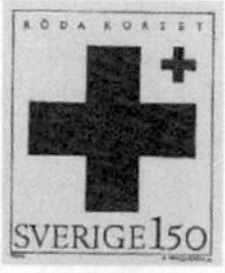

348 Red Cross

1983. Swedish Red Cross.

1169	**348**	1k.50 red	65	35

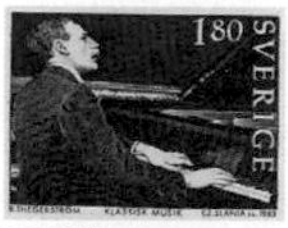

349 Wilhelm Stenhammer (after R. Thegerstrom) (classical music)

1983. Music in Sweden. Sheet 135×69 mm containing T **349** and similar designs.

MS1170 1k.80 green and black (Type **349**); 1k.80 yellow and black (*Aniara*) (opera)); 1k.80 pink and black (Abba (pop)); 2k.70, multicoloured ("Fiddler" (Anders Zorn) (folk music)) (44×48 mm) (sold at 11k. 50) 6·25 5·75

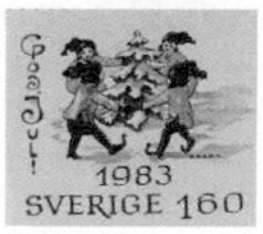

350 Dancing round the Christmas Tree

1983. Christmas. Early Christmas Cards. Multicoloured.

1171	1k.60 Type **350**	85	55
1172	1k.60 Straw goats	85	55
1173	1k.60 The Christmas table	85	55
1174	1k.60 Carrying Christmas presents on pole	85	55

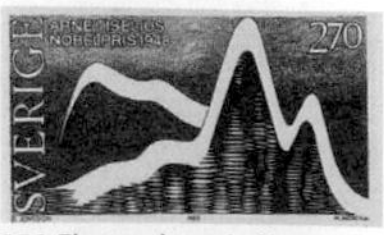

351 Electrophoresis (Arne Tiselius, 1948)

1983. Nobel Prize Winners for Chemistry.

1175	**351**	2k.70 black	1·40	1·10
1176	-	2k.70 violet	1·40	1·10
1177	-	2k.70 mauve	1·40	1·10
1178	-	2k.70 violet	1·40	1·10
1179	-	2k.70 black	1·40	1·10

DESIGNS: No. 1176, Radioactive isotopes (George de Hevesy, 1943); 1177, Electrolytic dissociation (Svante Arrhenius, 1903); 1178, Colloids (Theodor Svedberg, 1926); 1179, Fermentation of sugar (Hans von Euler-Chelpin, 1929).

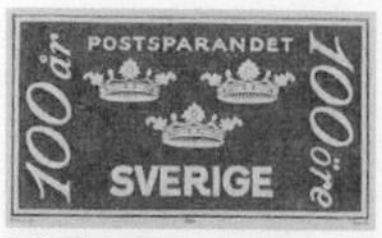

352 Three Crowns (detail from Postal Savings Receipt)

1984. Centenary of Postal Savings.

1180	**352**	100ore orange	65	25
1181	-	1k.60 violet	85	55
1182	-	1k.80 mauve	1·20	25

DESIGNS: 1k.60, 1k.80, Postal Savings badge.

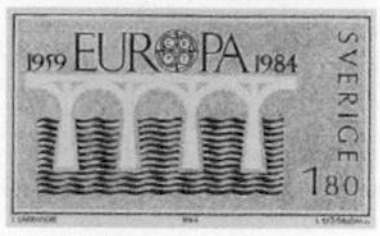

353 Bridge

1984. Europa. 25th Anniv of European Post and Telecommunications Conference.

1183	**353**	1k.80 red	1·30	35
1184	**353**	2k.70 blue	4·50	1·40

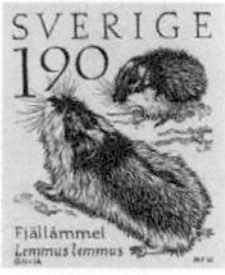

354 Norway Lemming

1984. Swedish Mountain World.

1185	**354**	1k.90 brown	95	35
1186	-	1k.90 blue	95	55
1187	-	2k. green	85	35
1188	-	2k.25 black	1·40	80

DESIGNS: No. 1186, Musk ox; 1187, Garden angelica; 1188, Tolpagorni mountain.

1984. Rebate Stamps. Arms of Swedish Provinces (4th series). As T **316**. Multicoloured.

1189	1k.60 Sodermanland	2·00	35
1190	1k.60 Blekinge	2·00	35
1191	1k.60 Vasterbotten	2·00	35
1192	1k.60 Skane	2·00	35

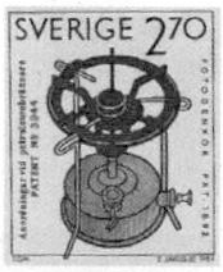

355 Paraffin Stove (F. W. Lindqvist)

1984. "Made in Sweden". Centenary of Patent Office. Patented Swedish Inventions.

1193	**355**	2k.70 red	1·50	1·10
1194	-	2k.70 lilac	1·50	1·10
1195	-	2k.70 green	1·50	1·10
1196	-	2k.70 green	1·50	1·10
1197	-	2k.70 lilac	1·50	1·10
1198	-	2k.70 blue	1·50	1·10

DESIGNS: No. 1194, "ASEA IRB 6" industrial robot for arc welding; 1195, Vacuum cleaner (Axel Wennergren); 1196, "AQ 200" inboard/outboard engine; 1197, Integrated circuit; 1198, Tetrahedron container.

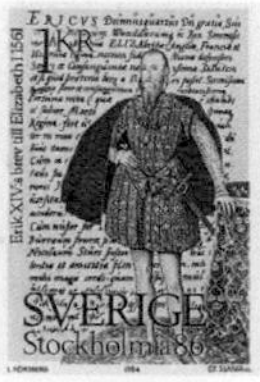

356 King Erik XIV (after S. van der Meulen) and Letter to Queen Elizabeth I of England

1984. "Stockholmia 86" International Stamp Exhibition (2nd issue).

1199	**356**	1k. brown, blue and ultramarine	85	60
1200	-	2k. multicoloured	1·20	80
1201	-	3k. multicoloured	1·50	95
1202	-	4k. multicoloured	1·90	1·10

DESIGNS: 2k. Erik Dahlbergh (architect) (after J. H. Stromer) and letter to Sten Bielke (Paymaster General), 1674; 3k. Feather letter, 1843; 4k. Harriet Bosse and letter from her husband, August Strindberg, 1905.

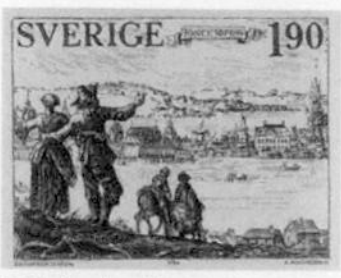

357 Jonkoping

1984. Old Towns. 17th-century views by M. Karl (1207) or Erik Dahlberg (others).

1203	**357**	1k.90 blue	1·10	80
1204	-	1k.90 brown	1·10	80
1205	-	1k.90 blue	1·10	80
1206	-	1k.90 brown	1·10	80
1207	-	1k.90 blue	1·10	80
1208	-	1k.90 brown	1·10	80

DESIGNS: No. 1204, Karlstad; 1205, Gavle; 1206, Sigtuna; 1207, Norrkoping; 1208, Vadstena.

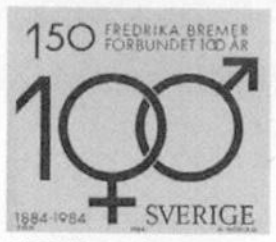

358 Genetic Symbols forming "100"

1984. Centenary of Fredrika Bremer Association (for promotion of male/female equal rights).

1209	**358**	1k.50 purple	85	35
1210	**358**	6k.50 red	3·75	80

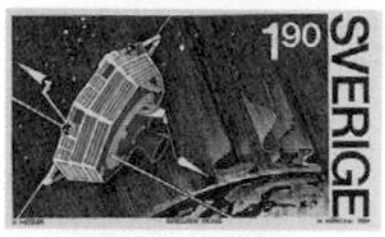

359 "Viking" in Orbit

1984. Launch of Swedish "Viking" Satellite.

1211	**359**	1k.90 ultramarine, blue and deep blue	85	35
1212	-	3k.20 green, yellow and black	1·80	1·10

DESIGN: 3k.20, Dish aerial and rocket pad at Esrange space station.

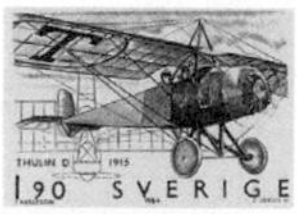

360 Thulin Type D Biplane, 1915

1984. Swedish Aviation History. Sheet 132×73 mm containing T **360** and similar designs.

MS1213 1k.90 ultramarine and red (Type **360**); 1k.90 ultramarine and orange (SAAB 90 Scandia, 1946); 1k.90 orange, ultramarine and red (Carl Gustaf Cedarstrom ("The Flying Baron") and Bleriot X1 monoplane, 1910); 1k.90 multicoloured (Ahrenberg's Junkers F-13 S-AAAB airplane *The Gnome* 1927); 2k.70 brown, red and dull ultramarine (Carl Nyberg and *The Tiny Fly*, 1900) (43×46 mm) (sold at 12k.) 6·75 5·25

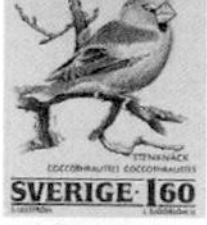

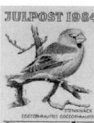

361 Hawfinch ("Coccothraustes coccothraustes")

1984. Christmas. Birds. Multicoloured.

1214	1k.60 Type **361**	95	60
1215	1k.60 Bohemian waxwing ("Bombycilla garrulus")	95	60
1216	1k.60 Great-spotted woodpecker ("Dendrocopos major")	95	60
1217	1k.60 Eurasian nuthatch ("Sitta europaea")	95	60

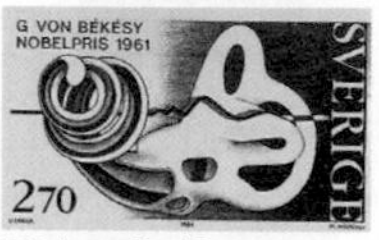

362 Inner Ear (Georg von Bekesy, 1961)

1984. Nobel Prize Winners for Medicine.

1218	**362**	2k.70 blue, black and red	1·50	1·10
1219	-	2k.70 blue and black	1·50	1·10
1220	-	2k.70 red, black and blue	1·50	1·10
1221	-	2k.70 blue and black	1·50	1·10
1222	-	2k.70 red, black and blue	1·50	1·10

DESIGNS: No. 1219, Nerve cell activation (John Eccles, Alan Hodgkin and Andrew Huxley, 1963); 1220, Nerve cell signals (Bernard Katz, Ulf von Euler and Julius Axelrod, 1970); 1221, Functions of the brain (Roger Sperry, 1981); 1222, Eye (David Hubel and Torsten Wiesel, 1981).

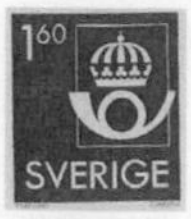

363 Post Office Emblem

1985

1223	**363**	1k.60 blue	95	35
1224	**363**	1k.70 violet	85	35
1326	**363**	1k.80 purple	95	35
1225	**363**	2k.50 yellow	1·30	35
1226	**363**	2k.80 green	1·60	80
1327	**363**	3k.20 brown	1·60	95
1227	**363**	4k. red	2·00	45
1328	**363**	6k. turquoise	3·00	80

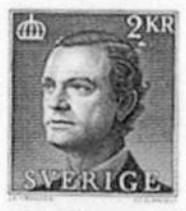

364 King Carl XVI Gustav

1985

1228	**364**	2k. black	85	35
1229	**364**	2k.10 blue	1·40	35
1230	**364**	2k.20 blue	1·30	35
1230a	**364**	2k.30 green	1·50	55
1230b	**364**	2k.50 purple	1·30	55
1231	**364**	2k.70 brown	1·40	80
1232	**364**	2k.90 green	1·70	70
1233	**364**	3k.10 brown	1·80	55
1234	-	3k.20 blue	1·70	1·10
1235	**364**	3k.30 purple	1·90	70
1236	-	3k.40 red	2·00	90
1237	-	3k.60 green	1·90	95
1238	-	3k.90 blue	2·30	1·10
1239	-	4k.60 orange	2·30	1·40

DESIGNS: 3k.20 and 3k.40 to 4k.60, Queen Silvia.

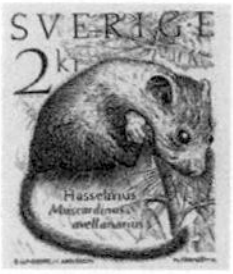

365 Hazel Dormouse ("Muscardinus avellanarius")

1985. Nature.

1240	**365**	2k. brown and black	95	35
1241	-	2k. orange and black	95	35
1242	-	2k.20 red	95	45
1243	-	3k.50 red and green	1·80	45

DESIGNS: No. 1241, Char ("Salvelinus salvelinus"); 1242, Black vanilla orchid ("Nigritella nigra"); 1243, White waterlily ("Nymphaea alba frosea").

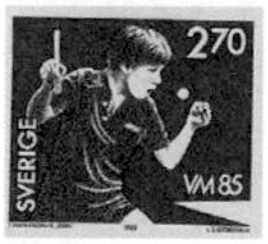

366 Jan-Ove Waldner

1985. World Table Tennis Championships, Gothenburg.

1244	**366**	2k.70 blue	1·90	90
1245	-	3k.20 mauve	2·00	1·10

DESIGN: 3k.20, Cai Zhenhua (Chinese player).

1985. Rebate Stamps. Arms of Swedish Provinces (5th series). As T **316**. Multicoloured.

1246	1k.80 Narke	2·00	35
1247	1k.80 Angermanland	2·00	35
1248	1k.80 Varmland	2·00	35
1249	1k.80 Smaland	2·00	35

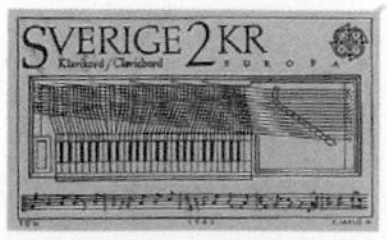

367 Clavichord

1985. Europa. Music Year.

1250	**367**	2k. purple on buff	7·25	35
1251	-	2k.70 brown on buff	1·90	1·30

DESIGN—28×24 mm: 2k.70, Keyed fiddle.

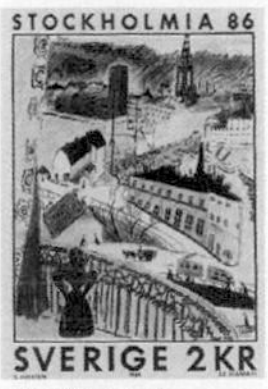

368 "View of Slussen" (Sigrid Hjerten)

1985. "Stockholmia 86" International Stamp Exhibition (3rd issue). Multicoloured.

1252	2k. Type **368**	1·20	90
1253	2k. "Skeppsholmen, Winter" (Gosta Adrian-Nilsson)	1·20	90
1254	3k. "A Summer's Night by Riddarholmen Canal" (Hilding Linnqvist)	1·80	1·20
1255	4k. "Klara Church Tower" (Otte Skold)	2·30	1·60

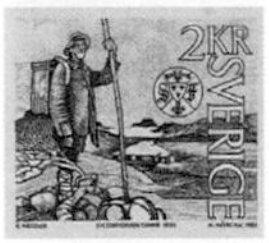

369 Syl Hostel, 1920

1985. Centenary of Swedish Touring Club.

1256	**369**	2k. blue and black	1·10	35
1257	-	2k. black and blue	1·10	35

DESIGN—58×24 mm: No. 1257, "Af Chapman" (youth hostel in Stockholm).

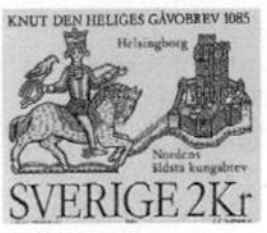

370 Canute and Helsingborg

1985. 900th Anniv of Saint Canute's Deed of Gift to Lund.

1258		2k. blue and black	1·10	35
1259	**370**	2k. red and black	1·10	35

DESIGN: No. 1258, Canute and Lund Cathedral.

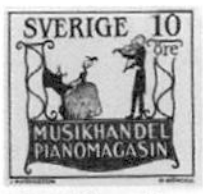

371 Nilsson's Music Shop Sign

1985. Trade Signs.

1260	**371**	10ore blue	30	25
1261	-	20ore brown	30	25
1262	-	20ore brown	30	25
1263	-	50ore blue	30	25
1264	-	2k. green	95	45

DESIGNS: No. 1261, Erik Johansson's furrier's sign; 1262, O. L. Sjowals's coppersmith's sign; 1263, Bodecker's hatter's sign; 1264, Berggren's shoemaker's sign.

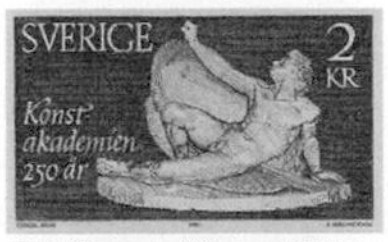

372 "Otryades" (Johan Tobias Sergel)

1985. 250th Anniv of Royal Academy of Fine Arts.

1265	**372**	2k. blue	95	45
1266	-	7k. brown	3·75	1·10

DESIGN—20×28 mm: 7k. "Baron Carl Fredrik Adelcrantz" (former Academy president) (Alexander Roslin).

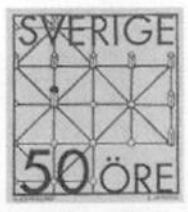

373 Fox and Geese

1985. Board Games.

1267	**373**	50ore blue	40	35
1268	-	60ore green	40	35
1269	-	70ore yellow	40	35
1270	-	80ore red	55	35
1271	-	90ore mauve	55	35
1272	-	3k. purple	1·30	35

DESIGNS—As T **373**: 60k. Dominoes; 70k. Ludo; 80k. Chinese checkers; 90k. Backgammon. 23×28 mm: 3k. Chess.

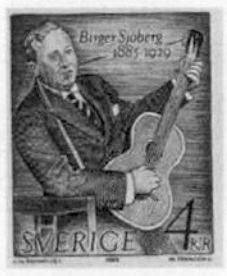

374 Birger Sjoberg (writer)

1985. Birth Centenaries.

1273		1k.60 red and black	85	60
1274	**374**	4k. green	2·30	45

DESIGN—40×24 mm: 1k.60, Per Albin Hansson (politician).

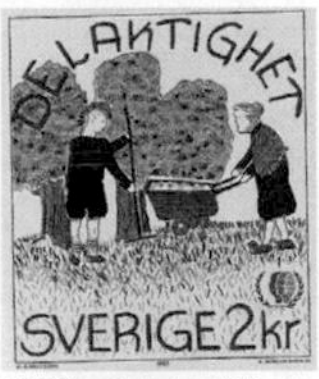

375 Boy helping Old Lady collect Leaves (Marina Karlsson)

1985. International Youth Year. Sheet 134×64 mm containing T **375** and similar vert designs showing children's drawings. Multicoloured.

MS1275	2k. Type **375**; 2k. Silhouettes and light (Madeleine Andersson); 3k.20 Children on swing (Charlotte Ankar) (sold at 10k)	5·75	5·75

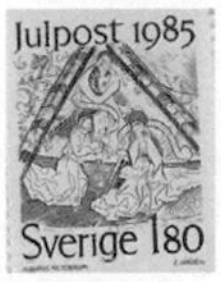

376 "Annunciation"

1985. Christmas. Medieval Church Frescoes by Albertus Pictor.

1276	**376**	1k.80 blue, brown and red	85	45
1277	-	1k.80 brown, blue and red	85	45
1278	-	1k.80 brown, blue and red	85	45
1279	-	1k.80 blue, brown and red	85	45

DESIGNS: No. 1277, "Birth of Christ"; 1278, "Adoration of the Magi", 1279, "Mary as the Apocalyptic Virgin".

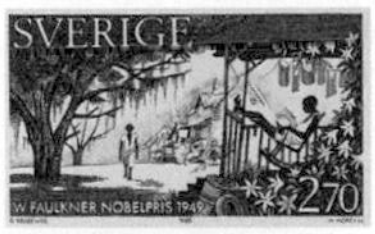

377 American Deep South Scene (William Faulkner, 1949)

1985. Nobel Prize Winners for Literature.

1280	**377**	2k.70 green	1·60	1·20
1281	-	2k.70 brown, blue and green	1·60	1·20
1282	-	2k.70 green and brown	1·60	1·20
1283	-	2k.70 green and blue	1·60	1·20
1284	-	2k.70 brown and blue	1·60	1·20

DESIGNS: No. 1281, Icelandic scene (Halldor Kiljan Laxness, 1955); 1282, Guatemalan scene (Miguel Angel Asturias, 1967); 1283, Japanese scene (Yasunari Kawabata, 1968); 1284, Australian scene (Patrick White, 1973).

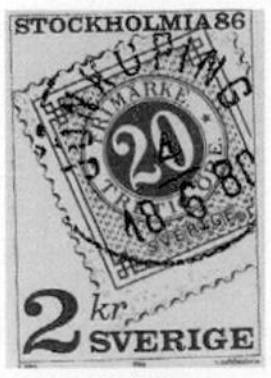

378 1879 "20 TRETIO" Error

1986. "Stockholmia 86" International Stamp Exhibition (4th issue).

1285	**378**	2k. orange, purple & grn	1·50	95
1286	-	2k. multicoloured	1·50	95
1287	-	3k. purple, blue and green	1·80	1·10
1288	-	4k. multicoloured	2·00	1·20

DESIGNS: No. 1286, Sven Ewert (engraver); 1287, Magnifying glass and United States 1938 Scandinavian Settlement 3c. stamp; 1288, Boy soaking stamps.

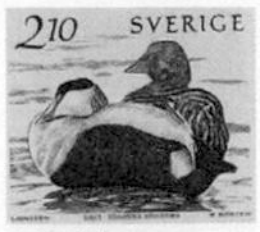

379 Eiders ("Somateria mollissima")

1986. Water Birds.

1289	**379**	2k.10 blue and brown	1·20	35
1290	-	2k.10 brown	1·20	35
1291	-	2k.30 blue	1·30	45

DESIGNS: No. 1290, Whimbrel ("Numenius phaeopus"); 1291, Black-throated diver ("Gavia arctica").

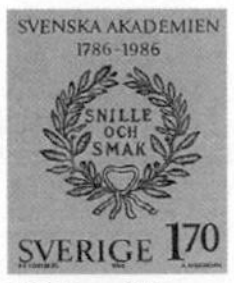

380 Swedish Academy Emblem

1986. Bicentenaries of Swedish Academy and Royal Swedish Academy of Letters, History and Antiquities.

1292	**380**	1k.70 green and red on grey	85	70
1293	-	1k.70 blue and purple on grey	85	70

DESIGN: No. 1293, Royal Swedish Academy emblem.

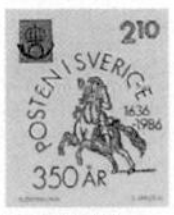

381 Jubilee Emblem

1986. 350th Anniv of Post Office.

1294	**381**	2k.10 blue and yellow	1·10	35

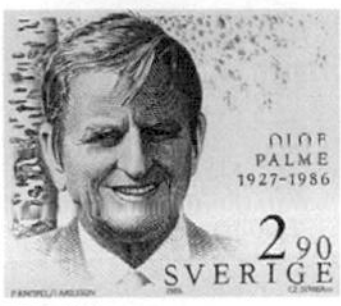

382 Palme

1986. Olof Palme (Prime Minister) Commemoration.

1295	**382**	2k.10 purple	1·80	1·40
1296	**382**	2k.90 black	1·80	1·40

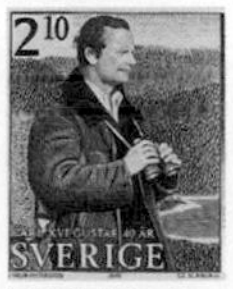

383 Carl Gustav Birdwatching

1986. 40th Birthday of King Carl XVI Gustav.

1297	**383**	2k.10 black and green	1·10	45
1298	-	2k.10 gold, mauve and blue	1·10	45
1299	-	2k.10 deep blue and blue	1·10	45
1300	-	2k.10 gold, blue and deep blue	1·10	45
1301	-	2k.10 black and mauve	1·10	45

DESIGNS: Nos. 1298, 1300, Crowned cypher; 1299, King presenting Nobel Prize for Literature to Czeslaw Milosz; 1301, King and family during summer holiday at Solliden Palace.

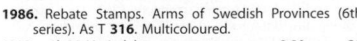

1986. Rebate Stamps. Arms of Swedish Provinces (6th series). As T **316**. Multicoloured.

1302	1k.90 Harjedalen	2·00	35
1303	1k.90 Uppland	2·00	35
1304	1k.90 Halland	2·00	35
1305	1k.90 Lappland	2·00	35

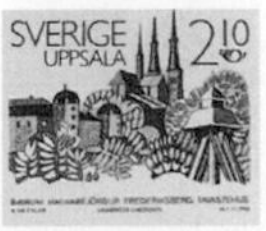

384 Uppsala

1986. Nordic Countries' Postal Co-operation. Twinned Towns.

1306	**384**	2k.10 green, chestnut and brown	95	35
1307	-	2k.90 green, red & brown	1·60	95

DESIGN: 2k.90, Eskilstuna.

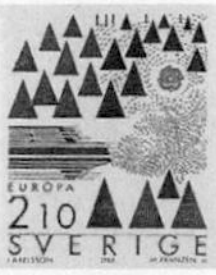

385 Forest and Car Fumes

1986. Europa. Each black, green and red.

1308	2k.10 Type **385**	3·25	55
1309	2k.90 Forest and industrial pollution	1·70	1·20

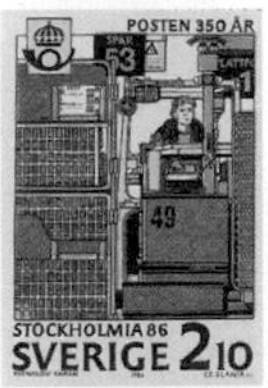

386 Tomteboda Sorting Office (20th-century)

1986. "Stockholmia 86" International Stamp Exhibition (5th issue). Multicoloured.

1310	2k.10 19th-century railway sorting carriage	6·75	6·25
1311	2k.10 Type **386**	6·75	6·25
1312	2k.90 17th-century farmhand postal messenger	6·75	6·25
1313	2k.90 18th-century post office	6·75	6·25

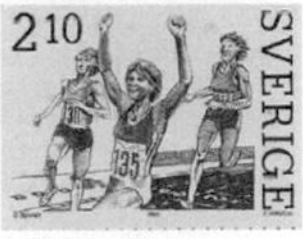

387 Ann-Louise Skoglund (400 m. hurdles European Champion, 1982)

1986. Athletics. Sheet 93×72 mm containing T **387** and similar horiz designs.

MS1314	2k.10 brown, blue and green (Type **387**); 2k.10 brown and green (Eric Lemming, early Olympic Medal winner, and Dag Wennlund (javelin throwers)); 2k.10 blue and brown (Patrik Sjoberg (high jumper)); 2k.10 green and brown (Anders Garderud, 3000 m. steeplechase world record holder) (sold at 11k.)	6·25	6·25

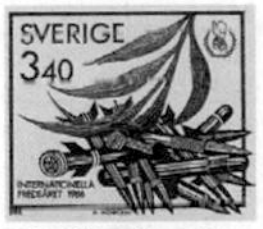

388 Olive Branch sweeping away Weapons

1986. International Peace Year (1315) and 25th Anniv of Amnesty International (1316).

1315	**388**	3k.40 green and black	1·90	1·50
1316	-	3k.40 red and black	1·90	1·50

DESIGN: No. 1316, Emblem above broken manacles.

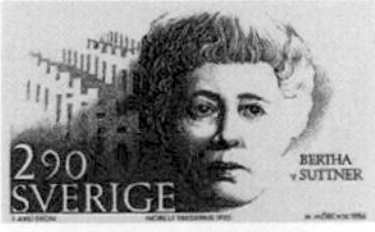

389 Bertha von Suttner (founder of Austrian Society of Peace Lovers, 1905)

1986. Nobel Prize Winners for Peace.

1317	**389**	2k.90 black, red and blue	1·70	1·30
1318	-	2k.90 black and red	1·70	1·30
1319	-	2k.90 black, brown and blue	1·70	1·30
1320	-	2k.90 brown and black	1·70	1·30
1321	-	2k.90 red, black and blue	1·70	1·30

DESIGNS: No. 1318, Carl von Ossietzky (anti-Nazi fighter and concentration camp victim, 1935); 1319, Albert Luthuli (South African anti-apartheid leader, 1960); 1320, Martin Luther King (American civil rights leader, 1964); 1321, Mother Teresa (worker amongst poor of Calcutta, 1979).

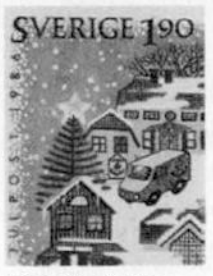

390 Mail Van

1986. Christmas. Designs showing a village at Christmas. Multicoloured.

1322	1k.90 Type **390**	85	45

1323		1k.90 Postman on cycle delivering mail	85	45
1324		1k.90 Children and sledge loaded with parcels	85	45
1325		1k.90 Christmas tree, man carrying parcel and child posting letter	85	45

Nos. 1322/5 were printed together, se-tenant, forming a composite design.

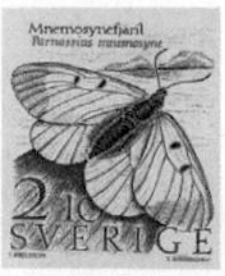

391 Clouded Apollo ("Parnassius mnemosyne")

1987. Threatened Species of Meadows and Pastures.

1331	**391**	2k.10 black, green and purple	95	35
1332	-	2k.10 black, green and purple	95	35
1333	-	2k.50 brown	1·20	35
1334	-	4k.20 green and yellow	1·90	35

DESIGNS: 2k.10 (1332), Field gentian ("Gentianella campestris"); 2k.50, Leather beetle ("Osmoderma eremita"); 4k.20, Arnica ("Arnica montana").

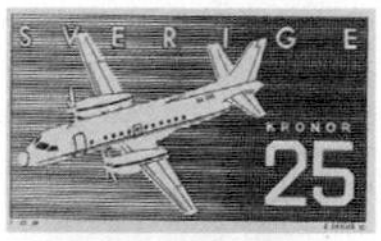

392 SAAB-Fairchild SF-340 SE-ISS

1987. Swedish Aircraft.

1335	**392**	25k. purple	12·00	1·10

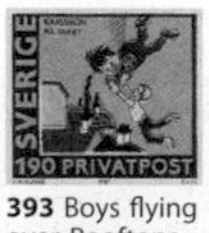

393 Boys flying over Rooftops ("Karlsson")

1987. Rebate Stamps. Characters from Children's Books by Astrid Lindgren. Multicoloured.

1336	1k.90 Type **393**	2·30	35
1337	1k.90 Girl holding doll ("Bullerby Children")	2·30	35
1338	1k.90 Girls dancing ("Madicken")	2·30	35
1339	1k.90 Boys on horse ("Mio, Min Mio")	2·30	35
1340	1k. Boy doing handstand ("Nils Karlsson-Pyssling")	2·30	35
1341	1k.90 Emil picking cherries ("Emil")	2·30	35
1342	1k.90 "Ronja the Robber's Daughter"	2·30	35
1343	1k.90 "Pippi Longstocking"	2·30	35
1344	1k.90 Dragon ("Brothers Lionheart")	2·30	35
1345	1k.90 "Lotta"	2·30	35

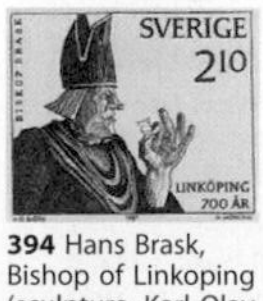

394 Hans Brask, Bishop of Linkoping (sculpture, Karl-Olav Bjork)

1987. Town Anniversaries. Each brown, blue and black.

1346	2k.10 Type **394** (700th anniv)	1·30	55
1347	2k.10 Nykoping Castle (800th anniv)	1·30	55

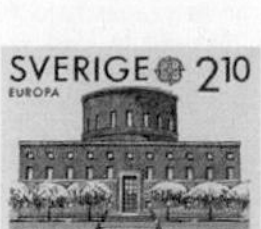

395 Stockholm City Library (Gunnar Asplund)

1987. Europa. Architecture.

1348	**395**	2k.10 brown and blue	4·50	60
1349	**395**	3k.10 brown and green	1·90	1·40
1350	-	3k.10 purple and green	1·90	1·40

DESIGN: No. 1350, Marcus Church (Sigurd Lewerentz).

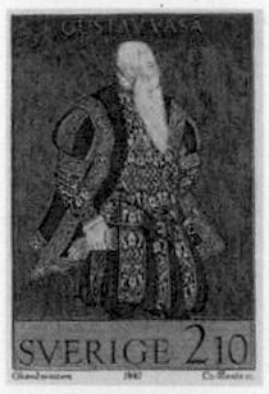

396 "King Gustavus Vasa" (anon)

1987. 450th Anniv of Gripsholm Castle.

1351	**396**	2k.10 multicoloured	1·20	55
1352	-	2k.10 multicoloured	1·20	55
1353	-	2k.10 multicoloured	1·20	55
1354	-	2k.10 brown, black and blue	1·20	55

DESIGNS: No. 1352, "Blue Tiger" (David Klocker Ehrenstrahl); 1353, "Hedvig Charlotta Nordenflycht" (after Johan Henrik Scheffel); 1354, "Gripsholm Castle" (lithograph, Carl Johan Billmark).

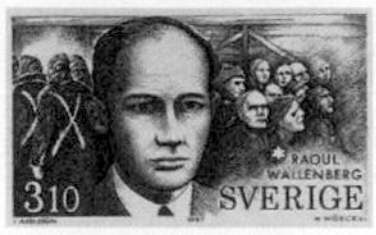

397 Raoul Wallenberg (rescuer of Hungarian Jews) and Prisoners

1987. "In the Service of Humanity".

1355	**397**	3k.10 blue	1·80	1·10
1356	-	3k.10 green	1·80	1·10
1357	-	3k.10 brown	1·80	1·10

DESIGNS: No. 1356, Dag Hammarskjold (U.N. Secretary-General, 1953–1961); 1357, Folke Bernadotte (leader of "white bus" relief action to rescue prisoners, 1945).

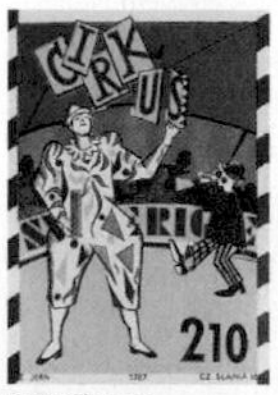

398 Clowns

1987. Stamp Day. Bicentenary of Circus in Sweden. Multicoloured.

1358	2k.10 Type **398**	1·30	1·10
1359	2k.10 Reino riding one-wheel cycle on wire	1·30	1·10
1360	2k.10 Acrobat on horseback	1·30	1·10

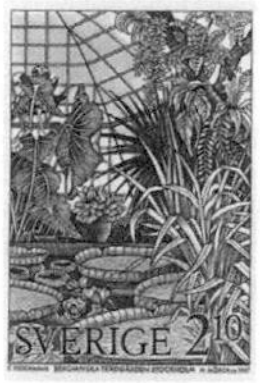

399 "Victoria cruziana" at Bergian Garden, Stockholm University

1987. Bicentenary of Swedish Botanical Gardens.

1361	**399**	2k.10 green, deep green and blue	95	45
1362	-	2k.10 green and brown	95	45
1363	-	2k.10 deep green, green and blue	95	45
1364	-	2k.10 yellow, brown and green	95	45

DESIGNS: No. 1362, Uppsala University Baroque Garden plan and Carl Harleman (architect); 1363, Rock garden, Gothenburg Botanical Garden; 1364, "Liriodendron tulipifera", Lund Botanical Garden.

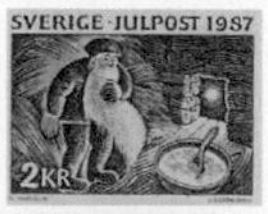

400 Porridge left for the Grey Christmas Elf

1987. Christmas. Folk Customs. Multicoloured.

1365	2k. Type **400**	95	55
1366	2k. Staffan ride (watering horses in North-running spring on Boxing Day)	95	55
1367	2k. Christmas Day sledge race home from church	95	55
1368	2k. Northern bullfinches on corn sheaf	95	55

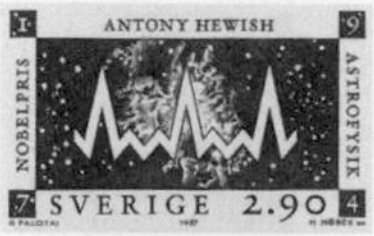

401 Pulsars (Antony Hewish, 1974)

1987. Nobel Prize Winners for Physics.

1369	**401**	2k.90 blue	1·40	1·10
1370	-	2k.90 black	1·40	1·10
1371	-	2k.90 blue	1·40	1·10
1372	-	2k.90 blue	1·40	1·10
1373	-	2k.90 black	1·40	1·10

DESIGNS: No. 1370, Formula of maximum white dwarf star mass (S. Chandrasekhar, 1983); 1371, Heavy atom nuclei construction (William Fowler, 1983); 1372, Temperature of cosmic background radiation (A. Penzias and R. Wilson, 1978); 1373, Radio telescopes receiving radio waves from galaxy (Martin Ryle, 1974).

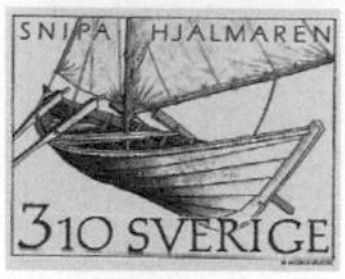

402 Lake Hjalmaren Fishing Skiff

1988. Inland Boats. Each purple on buff.

1374	3k.10 Type **402**	1·50	1·10
1375	3k.10 Lake Vattern market boat	1·50	1·10
1376	3k.10 River Byske logging boat	1·50	1·10
1377	3k.10 Lake Asnen rowing boat	1·50	1·10
1378	3k.10 Lake Vanern ice boat	1·50	1·10
1379	3k.10 Lake Lockne church longboat	1·50	1·10

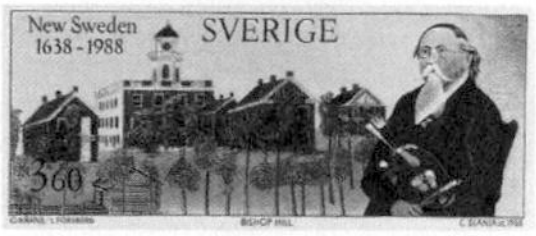

403 Bishop Hill and Erik Jansson (founder)

1988. 350th Anniv of New Sweden (settlement in America).

1380	-	3k.60 multicoloured	2·00	1·40
1381	**403**	3k.60 multicoloured	2·00	1·40
1382	-	3k.60 brown	2·00	1·40
1383	-	3k.60 blue and brown	2·00	1·40
1384	-	3k.60 blue, yellow and red	2·00	1·40
1385	-	3k.60 black, blue and red	2·00	1·40

DESIGNS—As T **403**: No. 1380, Map, settlers, Indians, "Calmare Nyckel" and "Fagel Grip". 27×23 mm: No. 1382, Carl Sandburg (American poet) and Jenny Lind (Swedish soprano); 1383, Charles Lindbergh (aviator) and Ryan NYP Special "Spirit of St. Louis". 27×37 mm: No. 1384, Alan Bean (astronaut) on Moon with Hasselblad camera; 1385, Ice hockey.

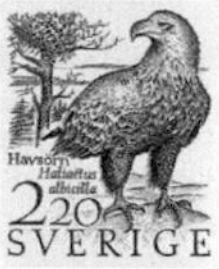

404 White-tailed Sea Eagle ("Haliaetus albicilla")

1988. Coastal Wildlife.

1386	**404**	2k.20 brown and red	1·20	45
1387	-	2k.20 brown and blue	1·20	45
1388	-	4k. black, brown and green	2·30	45

DESIGNS: No. 1387, Grey seal ("Halichoerus gryphus"); 1388, European eel ("Anguilla anguilla").

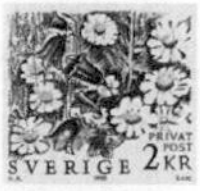

405 Daisies and Bluebells

1988. Rebate stamps. Midsummer Festival. Multicoloured.

1389	2k. Type **405**	2·30	35
1390	2k. Garlanded longboat	2·30	35
1391	2k. Children making garlands	2·30	35
1392	2k. Raising the maypole	2·30	35
1393	2k. Fiddlers	2·30	35
1394	2k. "Norrskar" (tourist launch)	2·30	35
1395	2k. Couples dancing	2·30	35
1396	2k. Accordianist	2·30	35
1397	2k. Archipelago with decorated landing stage	2·30	35
1398	2k. Bouquet of seven wild flowers	2·30	35

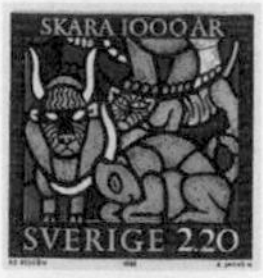

406 Detail of "Creation" Stained Glass Window (Bo Beskow), Skara Cathedral

1988. Anniversaries.

1399	**406**	2k.20 multicoloured	1·20	35
1400	-	4k.40 red on brown	2·00	55
1401	-	8k. red, green and black	4·00	1·50

DESIGNS: 2k.20, Type **406** (millenary of Skara). 23×41 mm: 4k.40, "Falun Copper Mine" (Pehr Hillestrom) (700th anniv of Stora Kopparberg (mining company)); 8k. Scene from play "The Queen's Diamond Ornament" (bicentenary of Royal Dramatic Theatre, Stockholm).

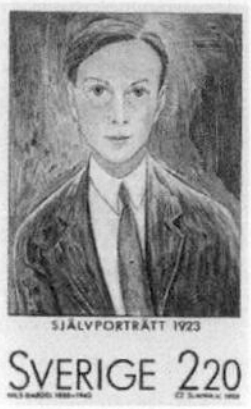

407 "Self-portrait" (Nils Dardel)

1988. Swedish Artists in Paris. Multicoloured.

1402	2k.20 Type **407**	1·20	90
1403	2k.20 "Autumn, Gubbhuset" (Vera Nilsson) (40×43 mm)	1·20	90
1404	2k.20 "Self-Portrait" (Isaac Grunewald)	1·20	90
1405	2k.20 "Visit to an Eccentric Lady" (Nils Dardel)	1·20	90
1406	2k.20 "Soap Bubbles" (Vera Nilsson) (40×43 mm)	1·20	90
1407	2k.20 "The Singing Tree" (Isaac Grunewald)	1·20	90

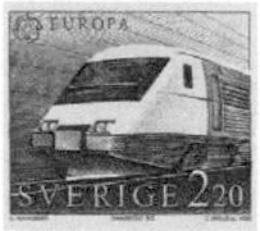

408 X2 High-speed Train

1988. Europa. Transport and Communications.

1408	**408**	2k.20 blue, orange and brown	4·00	70
1409	**408**	3k.10 blue, black and purple	1·80	1·30
1410	-	3k.10 black and purple	1·80	1·30

DESIGN: No. 1410, Narrow-gauge steam locomotive.

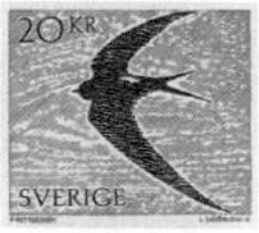

409 Common Swift

1988

1411	**409**	20k. purple and mauve	9·00	70

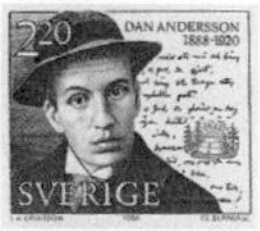

410 Andersson

1988. Birth Centenary of Dan Andersson (poet). Each violet, green and blue.

1412	2k.20 Type **410**	1·10	35
1413	2k.20 Lake, Finnmarken (58×24 mm)	1·10	35

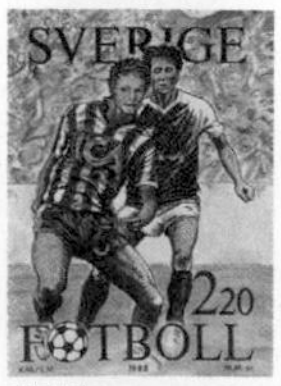

411 Players

1988. Swedish Football. Multicoloured.

1414	2k.20 Type **411**	1·50	1·10
1415	2k.20 Three players	1·50	1·10
1416	2k.20 Women players	1·50	1·10

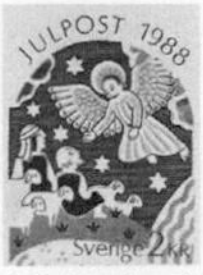

412 Angel and Shepherds

1988. Christmas. Multicoloured.

1417	2k. Type **412**	85	45
1418	2k. Horse and angel	85	45
1419	2k. Birds singing in trees	85	45
1420	2k. Three wise men	85	45
1421	2k. Holy Family	85	45
1422	2k. Shepherds and sheep	85	45

Nos. 1417/22 were printed together, se-tenant, forming a composite design.

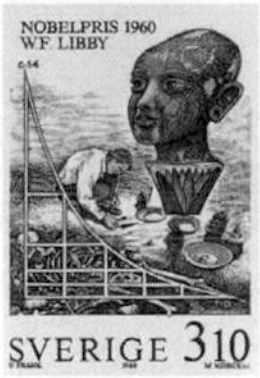

413 Archaeologist, Carbon 14 Dating Graph and Tutankhamun

1988. Nobel Prize Winners for Chemistry. Multicoloured.

1423	3k.10 Type **413** (Willard Frank Libby, 1960)	1·60	1·10
1424	3k.10 Plastics molecules (Karl Ziegler and Giulio Natta, 1963)	1·60	1·10
1425	3k.10 Electron microscope (Aaron Klug, 1982)	1·60	1·10
1426	3k.10 Landscape and symbols (Ilya Prigogine, 1977)	1·60	1·10

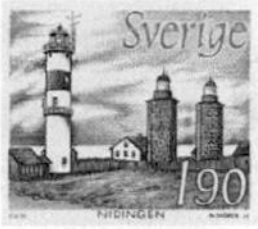

414 Nidingen 1946 Concrete and 1832 Twin lighthouses

1989. Lighthouses.

1427	**414**	1k.90 green, brown and black	85	35
1428	-	2k.70 blue, red and deep blue	1·30	90
1429	-	3k.80 brown, deep blue and blue	1·80	1·10
1430	-	3k.90 black, red & brown	1·80	1·10

DESIGNS: 2k.70, Soderarm stone lighthouse; 3k.80, Sydostbrotten caisson lighthouse; 3k.90, Sandhammaren iron lighthouse.

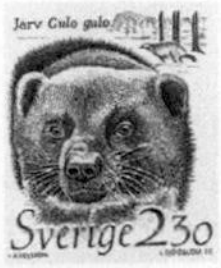

415 Wolverine ("Gulo gulo")

1989. Animals in Threatened Habitats.

1431	**415**	2k.30 brown, orange and green	1·10	35
1432	-	2k.30 brown, green and orange	1·10	35
1433	-	2k.40 brown, chocolate and red	1·10	35
1434	-	2k.60 agate, brown and orange	1·40	60
1435	-	3k.30 deep green, green and brown	1·70	80
1436	-	4k.60 black, green and orange	2·30	80

DESIGNS: 2k.30 (1432), Ural owl ("Strix uralensis"): 2k.40, Lesser spotted woodpecker ("Dendrocopos minor"); 2k.60, Dunlin ("Calidris alpina schinzii"); 3k.30, Common tree frog ("Hyla arborea"); 4k.60, Red-breasted flycatcher ("Ficedula parva").

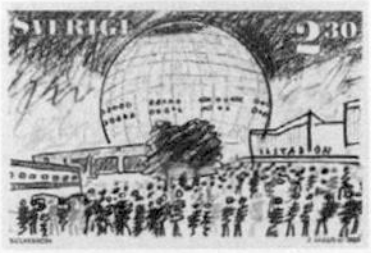

416 Globe Arena

1989. Opening of Globe Arena, Stockholm. Multicoloured.

1437	2k.30 Type **416**	1·20	45
1438	2k.30 Ice hockey	1·20	45
1439	2k.30 Gymnastics	1·20	45
1440	2k.30 Pop concert	1·20	45

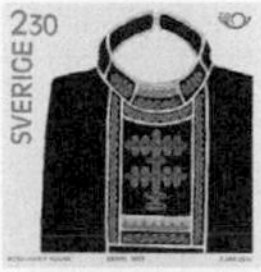

417 Woman's Woollen Bib Front

1989. Nordic Countries' Postal Co-operation. Traditional Lapp Costumes.

1441	2k.30 Type **417**	1·70	60
1442	3k.30 Man's belt pouch	2·30	1·30

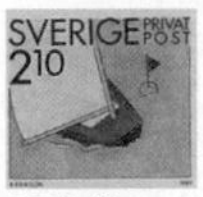

418 Sailing

1989. Rebate stamps. Summer Activities. Multicoloured.

1443	2k.10 Type **418**	2·30	45
1444	2k.10 Beach ball	2·30	45
1445	2k.10 Cycling	2·30	45
1446	2k.10 Canoeing	2·30	45
1447	2k.10 Fishing	2·30	45
1448	2k.10 Camping	2·30	45
1449	2k.10 Croquet	2·30	45
1450	2k.10 Badminton	2·30	45
1451	2k.10 Gardening	2·30	45
1452	2k.10 Sand castle, bucket and spade	2·30	45

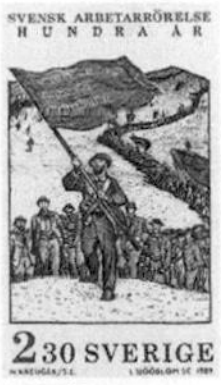

419 "Protest March" (Nils Kreuger)

1989. Centenary of Swedish Labour Movement.

1453	**419**	2k.30 black and red	1·40	45

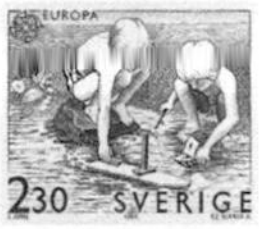

420 Playing with Boats

1989. Europa. Children's Games and Toys.

1454	**420**	2k.30 brown	4·50	90
1455	**420**	3k.30 mauve	1·70	1·40
1456	-	3k.30 green	1·70	1·40

DESIGN: No. 1456, Girl riding kick-sled.

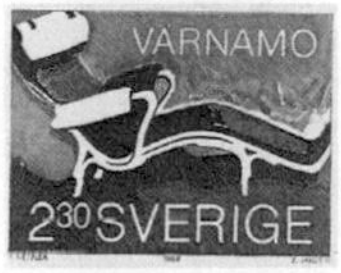

421 Lounger (Varnamo)

1989. Industries of Smaland Towns. Each mauve, orange and red.

1457	2k.30 Type **421**	1·20	90
1458	2k.30 Tools for self-assembly furniture (Almhult)	1·20	90
1459	2k.30 Sewing machine and embroidery (Huskvarna)	1·20	90
1460	2k.30 Blowing glass (Afors)	1·20	90
1461	2k.30 Coathanger hook and clothes-peg spring (Gnosjo)	1·20	90
1462	2k.30 Match (Jonkoping)	1·20	90

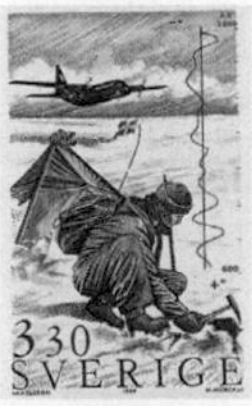

422 Researcher in Greenland, Lockheed C-130 Hercules and Temperature Curve

1989. 250th Anniv of Swedish Academy of Sciences. Polar Research. Multicoloured.

1463	3k.30 Type **422**	1·70	1·20
1464	3k.30 Abisko Natural Science Station, Lapland (40×43 mm)	1·70	1·20
1465	3k.30 "Oden" (ice research ship) and researchers	1·70	1·20
1466	3k.30 Otto Nordenskiold 1901–03 expedition's "Antarctic" and Emperor penguin with chick	1·70	1·20
1467	3k.30 1988 Antarctic expedition's vehicles and Hughes Model 500 helicopter (40×43 mm)	1·70	1·20
1468	3k.30 Geodimeter and South polar skua	1·70	1·20

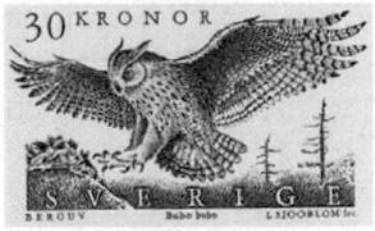

423 Eagle Owl

1989

1469	**423**	30k. brown, black & mve	13·00	1·70

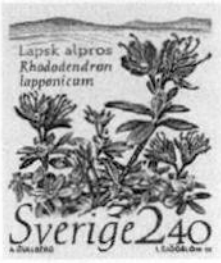

424 Arctic Rhododendron ("Rhododendron lapponicum")

1989. National Parks (1st series).

1470	**424**	2k.40 mauve, green & bl	1·20	45
1471	-	2k.40 mauve and green	1·20	45
1472	-	4k.30 red, black and blue	2·00	1·40

DESIGNS—HORIZ: No. 1471, Calypso ("Calypso bulbosa"). VERT: No. 1472, Black guillemots at Bla Jungfrun.

See also Nos. 1486/90.

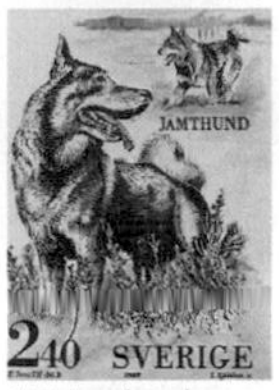

425 Jamthund

1989. Centenary of Swedish Kennel Club. Multicoloured.

1473	2k.40 Type **425**	1·60	1·30
1474	2k.40 Hamilton foxhound	1·60	1·30
1475	2k.40 Vastgota sheep dog	1·60	1·30

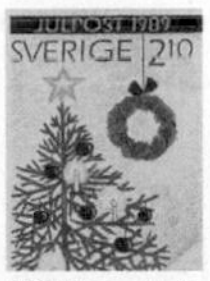

426 Decorated Tree

1989. Christmas. Multicoloured.

1476	2k.10 Type **426**	1·10	45
1477	2k.10 Candelabra and food	1·10	45
1478	2k.10 Star, poinsettia and tureen	1·10	45
1479	2k.10 Decorated tree and straw goat	1·10	45
1480	2k.10 Girl watching television	1·10	45
1481	2k.10 Family with present	1·10	45

Nos. 1476/81 were issued together, *se-tenant*, forming a composite design.

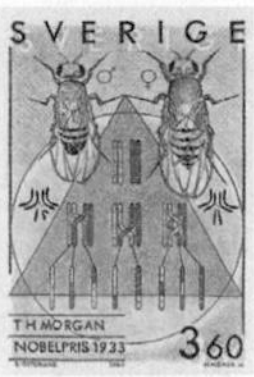

427 Vinegar Flies (T. H. Morgan, 1933)

1989. Nobel Prize Winners for Medicine.

1482	**427**	3k.60 brown, yellow & bl	1·90	1·30
1483	-	3k.60 yellow, blue & red	1·90	1·30
1484	-	3k.60 multicoloured	1·90	1·30
1485	-	3k.60 multicoloured	1·90	1·30

DESIGNS: No. 1483 X-ray diffractogram and D.N.A. molecule (Francis Crick, James Watson and Maurice Wilkins, 1962); 1484, D.N.A. molecule cut by restriction enzyme (W. Arber, D. Nathans and H. O. Smith, 1978); 1485, Maize kernels (Barbara McClintock, 1983).

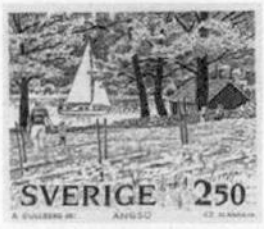

428 Angso

1990. National Parks (2nd series).

1486	**428**	2k.50 blue, green and red	1·10	65
1487	-	2k.50 red, green and blue	1·10	65
1488	-	3k.70 blue, brown & grn	2·00	1·10
1489	-	4k.10 blue, green & brn	2·30	1·40
1490	-	4k.80 green, brown & bl	2·50	1·40

DESIGNS: No. 1487, Pieljekaise; 1488, Muddus; 1489, Padjelanta; 1490, Sanfjallet.

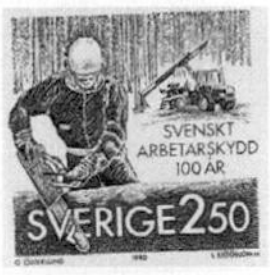

429 Lumberjack

1990. Centenary of Industrial Safety Inspectorate.

1491	**429**	2k.50 blue and brown	1·20	45

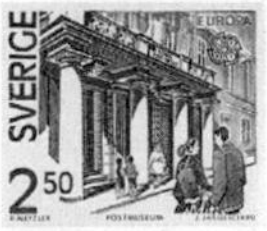

430 Postal Museum, Stockholm

1990. Europa. Post Office Buildings.

1492	**430**	2k.50 brown, orange & bl	5·00	1·00
1493	-	3k.80 blue, yellow and brown	2·30	1·50
1494	-	3k.80 brown, blue and yellow	2·30	1·50

DESIGNS: No. 1493, Sollebrunn Post Office; 1494, Vasteras Post Office.

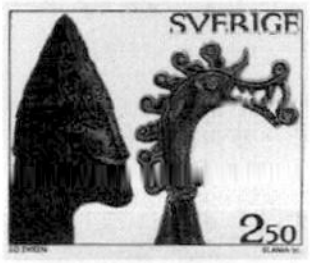

431 Carved Bone Head and Cast Dragon Head

1990. Vikings. Multicoloured.

1495	2k.50 Type **431**	1·20	80
1496	2k.50 Returning Viking long-ships (34×29 mm)	1·20	80
1497	2k.50 Wooden houses (34×29 mm)	1·20	80
1498	2k.50 Bronze figurine of God of Fertility and silver cross	1·20	80
1499	2k.50 Crosier and gold embroidered deer	1·20	80
1500	2k.50 Vikings in roundship (34×29 mm)	1·20	80
1501	2k.50 Viking disembarking (34×29 mm)	1·20	80
1502	2k.50 Viking swords	1·20	80

Nos. 1496/7 and 1500/1 form a composite design.

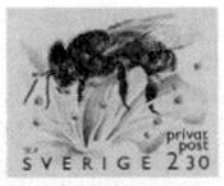

432 Worker collecting Pollen

1990. Rebate stamps. Honey Bees. Multicoloured.

1503	2k.30 Type **432**	2·30	45
1504	2k.30 Worker on bilberry	2·30	45
1505	2k.30 Worker flying back to hive	2·30	45
1506	2k.30 Beehive	2·30	45
1507	2k.30 Bees building honey-combs	2·30	45
1508	2k.30 Drone	2·30	45
1509	2k.30 Queen	2·30	45
1510	2k.30 Swarm on branch	2·30	45
1511	2k.30 Beekeeper collecting frame	2·30	45
1512	2k.30 Pot of honey	2·30	45

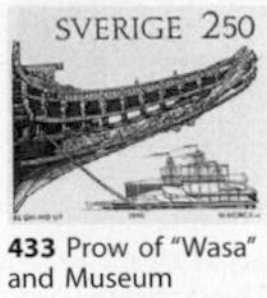

433 Prow of "Wasa" and Museum

1990. Opening of New "Wasa" (17th-century ship of the line) Museum.

1513	**433**	2k.50 black and red	1·80	55

| 1514 | - | 4k.60 blue and red | 3·00 | 1·60 |

DESIGNS: 4k.60, Stern of "Wasa" and museum.

434 Endurance Event

1990. World Equestrian Games, Stockholm. Multicoloured.

1515	3k.80 Type **434**	1·80	1·40
1516	3k.80 Mark Todd on Carisma jumping wall (3-day event)	1·80	1·40
1517	3k.80 John Whitaker on Next Milton jumping fence (show jumping)	1·80	1·40
1518	3k.80 Louise Nathorst (dressage)	1·80	1·40
1519	3k.80 Team vaulting	1·80	1·40
1520	3k.80 Pahlsson brothers driving four-in-hand	1·80	1·40

435 Papermaking, 1600

1990. Centenary of Swedish Pulp and Paper Industry. Multicoloured.

1521	2k.50 Type **435**	1·10	70
1522	2k.50 Crown watermark	1·10	70
1523	2k.50 Foreign newspapers using Swedish newsprint	1·10	70
1524	2k.50 Rolls of paper	1·10	70

436 "Dearest Brothers, Sisters and Friends"

1990. 250th Birth Anniv of Carl Michael Bellman (poet) (1525/7) and Birth Centenary of Evert Taube (poet) (1528/30). Designs showing illustrations of their poems.

1525	**436**	2k.50 brown and black	1·50	1·00
1526	-	2k.50 multicoloured	1·50	1·00
1527	-	2k.50 black, blue and red	1·50	1·00
1528	-	2k.50 multicoloured	1·50	1·00
1529	-	2k.50 multicoloured	1·50	1·00
1530	-	2k.50 multicoloured	1·50	1·00

DESIGNS—As Type **436**: No. 1527, "Fredman in the Gutter"; 1528, "Happy Baker of San Remo"; 1530, "Violava". 40×43 mm: 1526, "Proud City"; 1529, "At Sea".

437 Oved Castle

1990

| 1531 | **437** | 40k. brown, black and red | 17·00 | 3·50 |

439 Box Camera with Bellows

1990. Photography. Multicoloured.

1534	2k.50 Type **439**	1·60	1·40
1535	2k.50 August Strindberg (self-photograph)	1·60	1·40
1536	2k.50 Modern 35 mm camera	1·60	1·40

440 Cumulus Clouds

1990. Clouds.

1537	**440**	4k.50 multicoloured	2·30	45
1538	-	4k.70 black and blue	2·30	1·30
1539	-	4k.90 blue, green & brn	2·75	1·40
1540	-	5k.20 blue & ultramarine	3·00	1·50

DESIGNS: 4k.70, Cumulonimbus; 4k.90, Cirus uncinus; 5k.20, Altocumulus lenticularis.

441 Christmas Cactus ("Schlumbergera x buckleyi")

1990. Christmas. Flowers. Multicoloured.

1541	2k.30 Type **441**	1·30	55
1542	2k.30 Christmas rose ("Helleborus niger")	1·30	55
1543	2k.30 Azalea ("Rhododenron simsii")	1·30	55
1544	2k.30 Amaryllis ("Hippeastrum × hortorum")	1·30	55
1545	2k.30 Hyacinth ("Hyacinthus orientalis")	1·30	55
1546	2k.30 Poinsettia ("Euphorbia pulcherrima")	1·30	55

442 Par Lagerkvist (1951)

1990. Nobel Prize Winners for Literature.

1547	**442**	3k.80 blue	2·30	1·50
1548	-	3k.80 red	2·30	1·50
1549	-	3k.80 green	2·30	1·50
1550	-	3k.80 violet	2·30	1·50

DESIGNS: No. 1548, Ernest Hemingway (1954); 1549, Albert Camus (1957); 1550, Boris Pasternak (1958).

443 Heath of Wels ("Silurus glanis") and Young

1991. Freshwater Fish.

1551	**443**	2k.50 black, green & brn	1·30	45
1552	-	2k.50 black, green & brn	1·30	45
1553	-	5k. black, blue and brown	2·10	45
1554	-	5k.40 black, violet & red	2·75	1·70
1555	-	5k.50 brown and green	2·75	55
1556	-	5k.60 black, blue & orge	2·75	1·50

DESIGNS: No. 1552, Wels (different); 1553, Spined loach ("Cobitis taeina"); 1554, Gudgeon ("Gobio gobio"); 1555, Stone loach ("Noemacheilus barbataulus"); 1556, Sunbleak ("Leucaspius delineatus").
Nos. 1551/2 form a composite design of two catfish.

444 "Carta Marina", 1572 (Olaus Magnus)

1991. Maps. Multicoloured.

1557	5k. Type **444**	2·30	1·80
1558	5k. Sweden, Denmark and Norway, 1662 (A. Bureus and J. Blaeu) (40×43 mm)	2·30	1·80
1559	5k. Star globe, 1759 (Anders Akerman)	2·30	1·80
1560	5k. Relief map of Areskutan, 1938	2·30	1·80
1561	5k. Stockholm old town, 1989 (40×43 mm)	2·30	1·80
1562	5k. Bed-rock map of Areskutan, 1984	2·30	1·80

445 Queen Silvia

1991

1564	-	2k.80 blue	1·30	45
1565	-	2k.90 green	1·50	45
1566	-	3k.20 violet	1·40	45
1568	**445**	5k. purple	2·30	65
1569	**445**	6k. red	2·75	65
1570	**445**	6k.50 violet	3·00	90

DESIGN: 2k.80 to 3k.20, King Carl XVI Gustav.

446 Drottningholm Palace (after Erik Dahlbergh)

1991. Royal Residence at Drottningholm Palace.

| 1576 | **446** | 25k. brown, black & grn | 11·50 | 2·20 |

447 Seglora Church

1991. Rebate stamps. Centenary of Skansen Park, Stockholm. Multicoloured.

1577	2k.40 Type **447**	1·50	45
1578	2k.40 Celebration of Swedish Flag and National Days at Skansen	1·50	45
1579	2k.40 Wedding at Skansen	1·50	45
1580	2k.40 Animals, Skansen Zoo	1·50	45

448 Park Entrance

1991. Centenary of Public Amusement Parks. Each blue.

| 1581 | 2k.50 Type **448** | 1·40 | 45 |
| 1582 | 2k.50 Dancers and violinist | 1·40 | 45 |

449 Polar Bears

1991. Nordic Countries' Postal Co-operation. Tourism. Animals in Kolmarden Zoo.

| 1583 | **449** | 2k.50 black, brown & bl | 1·70 | 65 |
| 1584 | - | 4k. red and purple | 2·30 | 1·10 |

DESIGN: 4k. Dolphins and trainer.

450 "Hermes" Rocket

1991. Europa. Europe in Space. Multicoloured.

1585	4k. Type **450**	2·50	1·50
1586	4k. "Freja" Northern Lights research satellite	2·50	1·50
1587	4k. "Tele-X" television satellite	2·50	1·50

451 Magda Julin (figure skating, Antwerp, 1920)

1991. Olympic Games Gold Medallists (1st issue). Multicoloured.

1588	2k.50 Type **451**	1·20	70
1589	2k.50 Toini Gustafsson (cross-country skiing, Grenoble, 1968)	1·20	70
1590	2k.50 Agneta Andersson and Anna Olsson (canoeing, Los Angeles, 1984)	1·20	70
1591	2k.50 Ulrika Knape (high diving, Munich, 1972)	1·20	70

See also Nos. 1619/22 and 1635/8.

452 Spetal Mine, Norberg (after Carl David af Uhr)

1991. Bergslagen Iron Industry. Multicoloured.

1592	2k.50 Type **452**	1·20	90
1593	2k.50 Walloon smithy, Forsmark Mill (after J. Wilhem Wallender)	1·20	90
1594	2k.50 Forge (27×24 mm)	1·20	90
1595	2k.50 Foundry (after Johann Ahlback) (27×24 mm)	1·20	90
1596	2k.50 Dannemora Mine (after Elias Martin) (27×37 mm)	1·20	90
1597	2k.50 Pershyttan Mill (27×37 mm)	1·20	90

453 Stromsholm Castle

1991

| 1598 | **453** | 10k. green and black | 4·25 | 65 |

454 Lena Philipsson

1991. Rock and Pop Music. Multicoloured.

1599	2k.50 Type **454**	1·50	90
1600	2k.50 Roxette (duo)	1·50	90
1601	2k.50 Jerry Williams	1·50	90

455 Close-up of Gustav III

1991. 70th Birthday of Czeslaw Slania (engraver). Designs showing "Coronation of King Gustav III" by Carl Gustav Pilo.

1602	**455**	10k. blue	5·25	5·00
1603	-	10k. violet	5·25	5·00
1604	-	10k. black	5·25	5·00

DESIGNS—As T **455**: No. 1603, Close-up of lowering of crown onto King's head. 76×44 mm: 1604, Complete picture.

438 Moa Martinson

1990. Birth Centenary of Moa Martinson (novelist).

| 1532 | **438** | 2k.50 black and red | 1·30 | 45 |
| 1533 | - | 2k.50 black and violet | 1·30 | 45 |

DESIGN: No. 1533, Fredrika and Sofi bathing (from "Women and Apple Trees").

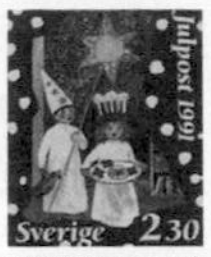

456 "Mans and Mari from Spring to Winter" (Kaj Beckman)

1991. Christmas. Illustrations from children's books. Multicoloured.

1605	2k.30 Type **456**	1·10	55
1606	2k.30 Family dancing round Christmas tree ("Peter and Lottas's Christmas", Elsa Beskow)	1·10	55
1607	2k.30 Dressed cat by Christmas tree ("Pettersson gets a Christmas Visit", Sven Nordqvist)	1·10	55
1608	2k.30 Girl by bed ("Little Anna's Christmas Present", Lasse Sandberg)	1·10	55

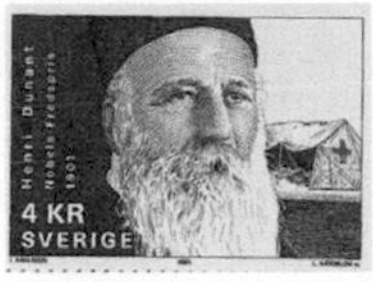

457 Henri Dunant (founder of Red Cross), 1901

1991. Nobel Prize Winners for Peace.

1609	**457**	4k. red	1·90	1·30
1610	-	4k. green	1·90	1·30
1611	-	4k. blue	1·90	1·30
1612	-	4k. lilac	1·90	1·30

DESIGNS: No. 1610, Albert Schweitzer (medical missionary), 1953; 1611, Alva Myrdal (disarmament negotiator), 1982; 1612, Andrei Sakharov (human rights activist), 1975.

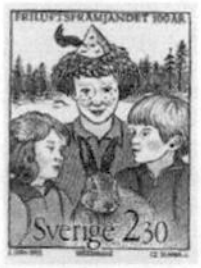

458 Mulle, the Forest Elf, with Children

1992. Centenary of Outdoor Life Association.

1613	**458**	2k.30 brown, red & grn	1·20	35

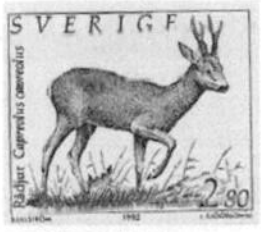

459 Roe Buck

1992. Wildlife.

1614	**459**	2k.80 brown, agate & grn	1·50	35
1615	-	2k.80 agate, brn & grn	1·50	35
1617	-	6k. brown and agate	3·00	1·10
1618	-	7k. brown and green	3·50	1·00

DESIGNS—As T **459**: No. 1615, Roe deer ("Capreolus capreolus") with fawn. 20×28 mm: No. 1617, Eurasian red squirrel ("Sciurus vulgaris"); 1618, Elk ("Alces alces").

1992. Olympic Games Gold medallists (2nd issue). As T **451**. Multicoloured.

1619	2k.80 Gunde Svan (cross-country skiing, Sarajevo, 1984, and Calgary, 1988)	1·30	70
1620	2k.80 Thomas Wassberg (cross-country skiing, Lake Placid, 1980, and Sarajevo, 1984)	1·30	70
1621	2k.80 Tomas Gustafson (speed skating, Sarajevo, 1984, and Calgary, 1988)	1·30	70
1622	2k.80 Ingemar Stenmark (slalom, Lake Placid, 1980)	1·30	70

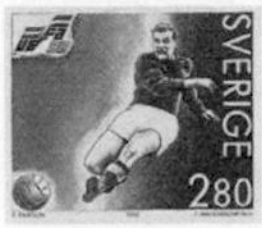

460 Gunnar Nordahl (Sweden)

1992. European Football Championship, Sweden. Each blue and green.

1623	2k.80 Type **460**	1·70	45
1624	2k.80 Lothar Matthaus (Germany) and Tomas Brolin (Sweden)	1·70	45

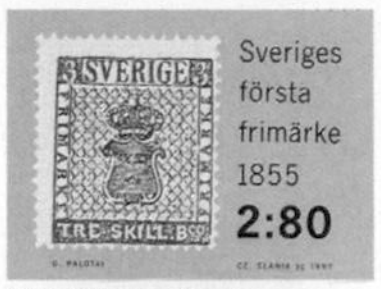

461 1855 3s. Green

1992. Stamp Year.

1625	**461**	2k.80 green, yellow & blk	2·75	2·75
1626	**461**	4k.50 green, yellow & blk	3·25	3·00
1627	-	5k.50 yellow, grey & blk	2·50	2·30

DESIGN: 5k.50, 1857 3s. yellow error.

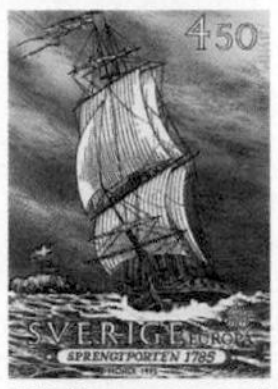

462 "Sprengtporten" (frigate), 1785

1992. Europa. 500th Anniv of Discovery of America by Columbus. Multicoloured.

1628	4k.50 Type **462**	3·00	1·80
1629	4k.50 "Superb" (brig), 1855	3·00	1·80
1630	4k.50 "Big T" (yacht) (competitor in Discovery Race)	3·00	1·80

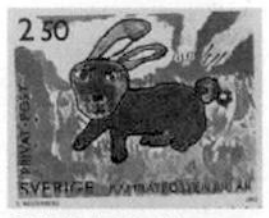

463 Rabbit (Emma Westerberg)

1992. Rebate stamps. Centenary of "Kamratposten" (children's magazine) showing children's drawings. Multicoloured.

1631	2k.50 Type **463**	1·50	45
1632	2k.50 Horses (Helena Johansson)	1·50	45
1633	2k.50 Kitten (Sabina Ostermark)	1·50	45
1634	2k.50 Elephant (Hanna Bengtsson)	1·50	45

1992. Olympic Games Gold Medallists (3rd series). As T **451**. Multicoloured.

1635	5k.50 Gunnar Larsson (swimming, Munich, 1972)	2·30	1·70
1636	5k.50 Bernt Johansson (cycling, Montreal, 1976)	2·30	1·70
1637	5k.50 Anders Garderud (steeplechase, Montreal, 1976)	2·30	1·70
1638	5k.50 Gert Fredriksson (canoeing, London, 1948)	2·30	1·70

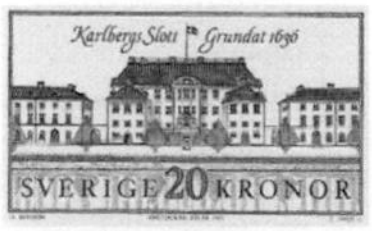

464 Karlberg Castle

1992

1639	**464**	20k. black, green and blue	8·00	1·30

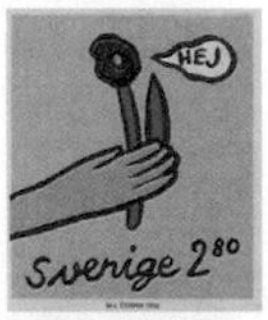

465 Hand holding Flower

1992. Greetings Stamps. Multicoloured.

1640	2k.80 Type **465**	1·20	55
1641	2k.80 Wedge of cheese ("Lyckans ost")	1·20	55
1642	2k.80 New-born baby ("Lev val!")	1·20	55
1643	2k.80 Writing with feather ("Gratulerar")	1·20	55

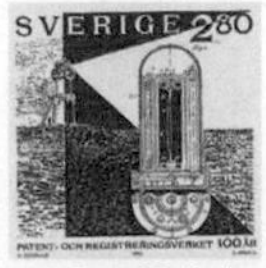

466 Gustaf Dalen's Sun Valve and First Automated Lighthouse, Gasfeten

1992. Centenary of Patent and Registration Office.

1644	**466**	2k.80 black and blue	1·20	45

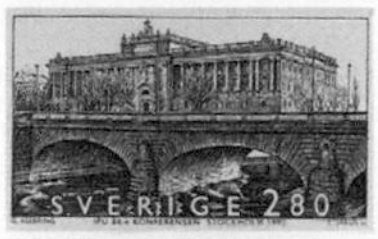

467 Riksdag (Parliament), Helgeandsholmen Island

1992. 88th Interparliamentary Union Conference, Stockholm.

1645	**467**	2k.80 violet on buff	1·20	45

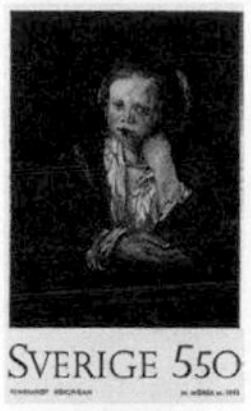

468 "Kitchen Maid" (Rembrandt)

1992. Bicentenary of National Museum of Fine Arts. Multicoloured.

1646	5k.50 Type **468**	2·75	2·00
1647	5k.50 "Triumph of Venus" (Francois Boucher) (40×44 mm)	2·75	2·00
1648	5k.50 "Portrait of a Girl" (Albrecht Durer)	2·75	2·00
1649	5k.50 Rorstrand vase decorated by Erik Wahlberg	2·75	2·00
1650	5k.50 "Seine Motif" (Carl Fredrik Hill) (40×44 mm)	2·75	2·00
1651	5k.50 "Sergel in his Studio" (Carl Larsson)	2·75	2·00

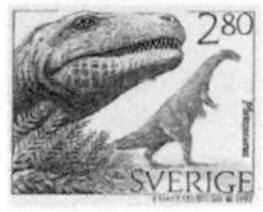

469 Plateosaurus

1992. Prehistoric Animals. Multicoloured.

1652	2k.80 Type **469**	1·80	1·40
1653	2k.80 Crocodile ("Thoracosaurus scanicus")	1·80	1·40
1654	2k.80 Woolly-haired rhino ("Coelodonta antiquitatis")	1·80	1·40
1655	2k.80 Mammoth ("Mammuthus primigenius")	1·80	1·40

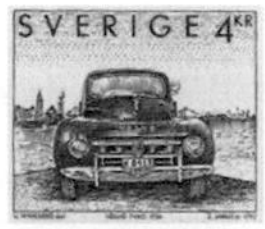

470 Volvo "PV831", 1950

1992. Swedish Cars.

1656	**470**	4k. blue	2·00	1·00
1657	-	4k. green and blue	2·00	1·00

DESIGN: No. 1657 Saab "92", 1950.

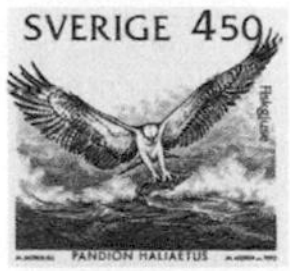

471 Osprey ("Pandion haliaetus")

1992. Birds of the Baltic.

1658	**471**	4k.50 black and blue	2·10	1·60
1659	-	4k.50 brown, black & bl	2·10	1·60
1660	-	4k.50 deep brown, brown and blue	2·10	1·60
1661	-	4k.50 black, brown & bl	2·10	1·60

DESIGNS: No. 1659, Black-tailed godwit ("Limosa limosa"); 1660, Goosander ("Mergus merganser"); 1661, Common shelducks ("Tadorna tadorna").

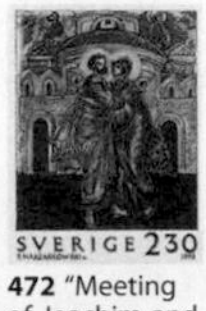

472 "Meeting of Joachim and Anna"

1992. Christmas. Icons. Multicoloured.

1662	2k.30 Type **472**	1·10	55
1663	2k.30 "Madonna and Child"	1·10	55
1664	2k.30 "Archangel Gabriel" (head)	1·10	55
1665	2k.30 "Saint Nicholas" (½-length portrait)	1·10	55

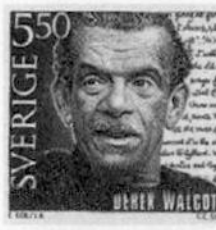

473 Walcott

1992. Award of Nobel Literature Prize to Derek Walcott.

1666	**473**	5k.50 purple, blue & brn	2·75	1·40
1667	-	5k.50 purple, brown & bl	2·75	1·40

DESIGN: No. 1667, Palm trees, ocean and text.

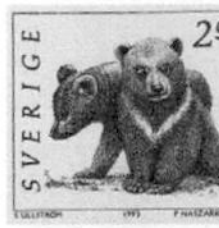

474 Brown Bear Cubs

1993. Wildlife.

1668	**474**	2k.90 brown and black	1·30	45
1669	-	2k.90 brown and black	1·30	45
1671	-	3k. multicoloured	1·40	70
1672	-	5k.80 black, grey & brn	3·25	70
1673	-	12k. brown, blue and red	4·50	1·80

DESIGNS—As T **474**: No. 1669, Brown bear. 27×21 mm: No. 1671, Polecat; 1672, Wolf. 21×27 mm: No. 1673, Lynx.

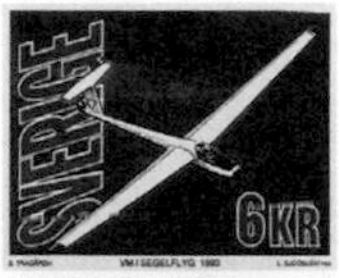

475 "Big Bird" Glider (World Gliding Championships, Borlange)

1993. Int Sports Championships in Sweden. Multicoloured.

1674	6k. Type **475**	3·00	2·20
1675	6k. Martin Kornbakk (World Wrestling Championships, Stockholm)	3·00	2·20
1676	6k. Jorgen Persson (World Table Tennis Championships, Gothenburg)	3·00	2·20
1677	6k. Lars Erik Andersson (European Bowling Championships, Malmo)	3·00	2·20
1678	6k. Per Carlen (World Handball Championships, Gothenburg)	3·00	2·20
1679	6k. Marie Helene Westin (World Cross-country Skiing Championships, Falun)	3·00	2·20

Nos. 1675/9 show Swedish competitors.

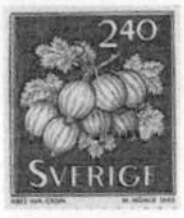

476 Gooseberries ("Ribes uva-crispa")

1993. Fruit.

1680	**476**	2k.40 green	1·20	35
1681	-	2k.40 green	1·20	45
1682	-	2k.40 red	1·20	45

DESIGNS: No. 1681, Pears ("Pryus communis"); 1682, Cherries ("Prunus avium").

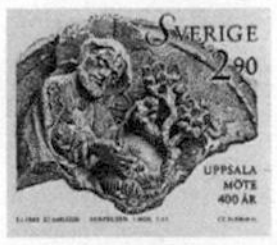

477 The Creation (relief, Uppsala Cathedral)

1993. 400th Anniv of Uppsala Convocation.

1683	**477**	2k.90 violet and buff	1·50	65
1684	-	2k.90 red and buff	1·50	65

DESIGN: No. 1684, Uppsala Cathedral before fire of 1702.

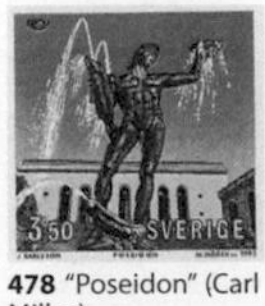

478 "Poseidon" (Carl Milles)

1993. Nordic Countries' Postal Co-operation. Tourism. Tourist Attractions in Gothenburg.

1685	**478**	3k.50 green, yellow & bl	1·80	1·10
1686	-	3k.50 indigo, yellow and blue	1·80	1·10

DESIGN: No. 1686, Liseberg Loop (fairground ride).

479 Ox-eye
Daisies

1993. Rebate stamps. Flowers. Multicoloured.

1687	2k.60 Type **479**	1·30	45
1688	2k.60 Poppies	1·30	45
1689	2k.60 Buttercups	1·30	45
1690	2k.60 Harebells	1·30	45

480 "Oguasark" (Ölle
Baertling)

1993. Europa. Contemporary Art. Multicoloured.

1691	5k. Type **480**	2·10	1·70
1692	5k. "Ade-Ledic-Nander II" (Oyvind Fahlstrom) (horiz)	2·10	1·70
1693	5k. "The Cubist Chair" (Otto Carlsund)	2·10	1·70

481 Swallowtail ("Papilio
machaon")

1993. Butterflies. Multicoloured.

1694	6k. Type **481**	3·00	1·80
1695	6k. Camberwell beauty ("Nymphalis antiopa")	3·00	1·80
1696	6k. Moorland clouded yellow ("Colias palaeno")	3·00	1·80
1697	6k. Scarce fritillary ("Euphydryas maturna")	3·00	1·80

482 Fireworks
("Hurray")

1993. Greetings Stamps. Multicoloured.

1698	2k.90 Type **482**	1·40	45
1699	2k.90 "Hor av Dig" ("Get in touch")	1·40	55
1700	2k.90 "Tycker om Dig" ("I like you")	1·40	45
1701	2k.90 "Lycka Till" ("Good luck")	1·40	55

483 Red-breasted Merganser
("Mergus serrator")

1993. Sea Birds. Multicoloured.

1702	5k. Type **483**	2·50	1·70
1703	5k. Velvet scoter ("Melanitta fusca")	2·50	1·70
1704	5k. Tufted duck ("Aythya fuligula")	2·50	1·70
1705	5k. Eider ("Somateria mollissima")	2·50	1·70

484 Surveyor, 1643
(cover of Johan
Mansson's nautical
book)

1993. 350th Anniv of Hydrographic Service.

1706	**484** 2k.90 brown, blue & blk	1·50	45
1707	- 2k.90 brown, blue & blk	1·50	45

DESIGN: No. 1707, Survey ship "Nils Stromcrona", 1993.

485 King Carl
Gustav

1993. 20th Anniv of Accession of King Carl XVI Gustav and Queen Silvia's 50th Birthday.

1708	8k. Type **485**	3·25	3·00
1709	10k. King Carl Gustav wearing medals	5·25	3·50
1710	10k. Queen Silvia	5·25	3·50
1711	12k. Family group and Stockholm and Drottningholm Palaces (75×44 mm)	6·25	4·50

486 Plaited
Heart

1993. Christmas.

1712	**486** 2k.40 green	1·20	55
1713	- 2k.40 red	1·20	55

DESIGN: No. 1713, Straw goat.

487 Stockholm City
Hall

1993. Award of Nobel Literature Prize to Toni Morrison.

1714	**487** 6k. red and blue	3·00	1·60
1715	- 6k. brown and red	3·00	1·60

DESIGN: No. 1715, Toni Morrison.

488 Victoria
Plums

1994. Fruit.

1716	**488** 2k.80 multicoloured	1·50	35
1717	- 2k.80 multicoloured	1·50	65
1718	- 2k.80 light green & green	1·50	65

DESIGNS: No. 1717, Opal plums; 1718, "James Grieve" apples.

489 North
Sweden Horse's
Head

1994. Domestic Animals (1st series).

1719	**489** 3k.20 brown, agate and red	1·60	55
1720	- 3k.20 brown, agate and red	1·60	55
1721	- 3k.20 black, brown & bl	1·60	55
1722	- 6k.40 black and green	3·00	1·00

DESIGNS—VERT: No. 1720, North Sweden horses in harness. HORIZ: 1721, Gotland sheep; 1722, Mountain cow. See also Nos. 1787/91 and 1802/3.

490 Mother Svea
and European
Union Emblem

1994. Single European Market.

1723	**490** 5k. blue	2·75	1·10

491 Siamese

1994. Cats. Multicoloured.

1724	**491** 4k.50 Type **491**	2·50	1·60
1725	4k.50 Persian	2·50	1·60
1726	4k.50 European	2·50	1·60
1727	4k.50 Abyssinian	2·50	1·60

492 Illustration
from "Le Roman de
la Rose"

1994. Franco–Swedish Cultural Relations. Multicoloured.

1728	5k. Type **492**	2·50	2·00
1729	5k. Swedish and French flags	2·50	2·00
1730	5k. Sketch by De la Vallee of Knight's House (40×43 mm)	2·50	2·00
1731	5k. "Household Chores" (Pehr Hillestrom)	2·50	2·00
1732	5k. "Banquet for Gustav III at the Trianon, 1784" (Niclas Lafrensen the younger) (40×43 mm)	2·50	2·00
1733	5k. "Carl XIV Johan" (Francois Gerard)	2·50	2·00

493 Martin Dahlin during
Match

1994. World Cup Football Championship, U.S.A.

1734	**493** 3k.20 blue and red	2·00	55

494 Wild Rose
("Rosa
dumalis")

1994. Roses. Multicoloured.

1735	3k.20 Type **494**	1·80	45
1736	3k.20 "Rosa alba maxima"	1·80	45
1737	3k.20 "Tuscany Superb"	1·80	45
1738	3k.20 "Peace"	1·80	45
1739	3k.20 "Four Seasons"	1·80	45

495 Lunar Module "Eagle"
and Astronauts

1994. 25th Anniv of First Manned Moon Landing.

1740	**495** 6k.50 orange, black & bl	3·25	1·80

496 Iris Vase
(Gunnar
Wennerberg), 1897

1994. 150th Annivs of Stockholm College of Arts, Crafts and Design and of Swedish Society of Crafts and Design. Multicoloured.

1741	6k.50 Type **496**	3·00	2·20
1742	6k.50 Wallpaper (Uno Ahren) and Chair (Carl Malmsten), 1917	3·00	2·20
1743	6k.50 Aralia cloth, 1920, and cabinet, 1940 (Josef Frank)	3·00	2·20
1744	6k.50 Crystal bowl engraved with fireworks design (Edward Hald), 1921	3·00	2·20
1745	6k.50 Silver water jug, 1941, and sketch of coffee pot, 1970s (Wiwen Nilsson)	3·00	2·20
1746	6k.50 Linen towel (Astrid Sampe), plate (Stig Lindberg) and cutlery (Sigurd Persson), 1955	3·00	2·20

497 Cat ("Love and
Kisses")

1994. Greetings Stamps. Multicoloured.

1747	3k.20 Type **497**	1·60	65
1748	3k.20 Snail ("You've got time")	1·60	65
1749	3k.20 Frog ("You're lovely just as you are")	1·70	70
1750	3k.20 Dog ("Hi there!")	1·70	70

498 Musicians
(sketch, Johan
Silvius) and
Opening Bars of
"Drottningholm
Music"

1994. 300th Birth Anniv of Johan Helmich Roman (composer) (1751) and Inauguration of Gothenburg Opera House (1752).

1751	**498** 3k.20 brown and blue	1·60	55
1752	- 3k.20 multicoloured	1·60	55

DESIGN: No. 1752, Opera House (designed Jan Izikowitz) and opening bars of opera "Aniara" by Karl Birger (inaugural programme).

499 Sepo Raty
(javelin)

1994. Sweden-Finland Athletics Meeting, Stockholm. Multicoloured.

1753	4k.50 Type **499**	2·30	1·50
1754	4k.50 Patrik Sjoberg (high jump)	2·30	1·50

500 Erland
Nordenskiold
(South America)

1994. Europa. Swedish Explorers. Multicoloured.

1755	5k.50 Type **500**	3·00	2·20
1756	5k.50 Eric von Rosen (Africa)	3·00	2·20
1757	5k.50 Sten Bergman (Asia and Australasia)	3·00	2·20

501 Caspian Tern
("Sterna caspia")

1994. Endangered Birds. Multicoloured.

1758	5k.50 Type **501**	2·75	2·20
1759	5k.50 White-tailed sea eagle ("Haliaeetus albicilla")	2·75	2·20
1760	5k.50 White-backed woodpecker ("Dendrocopos leucotos")	2·75	2·20
1761	5k.50 Lesser white-fronted goose ("Anser erythropus")	2·75	2·20

502 Bengtsson and Illustration from "The
Longships" (novel)

1994. Birth Centenary of Frans Bengtsson (writer).

1762	**502** 6k.40 violet, red and black	3·25	2·00

503 "Ja" ("Yes")

1994. European Union Membership Referendum (1st issue). Multicoloured.

1763	3k.20 Type **503**	1·70	55
1764	3k.20 "Nej" ("No")	1·70	55

See also Nos. 1785/6.

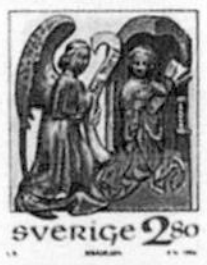

504 "The Annunciation"

1994. Christmas. Details from Askeby altarpiece. Multicoloured.

1765	2k.80 Type **504**	1·40	55
1766	2k.80 "Flight into Egypt"	1·40	55

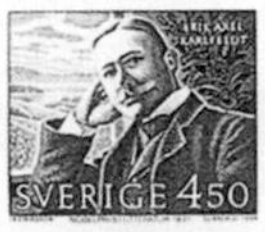

505 Erik Axel Karlfeldt (1931)

1994. Swedish Winners of the Nobel Literature Prize.

1767	**505**	4k.50 brown, dp bl & bl	2·10	1·20
1768	-	5k.50 deep brn, bl & brn	2·75	1·60
1769	-	6k.50 brn, dp grn & grn	3·25	2·00

DESIGNS: 5k.50, Eyvind Johnson (1974); 6k.50, Harry Martinsson (1974).

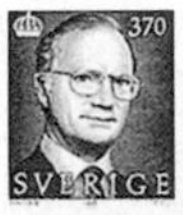

506 King Carl XVI Gustav

1995

1772	**506**	3k.70 red	1·70	55
1773	**506**	3k.85 black	1·70	70
1775	-	6k. green	2·50	1·20
1776	-	7k.50 purple	3·25	2·20
1777	-	8k. red	3·25	1·60

DESIGN: 6k., 7k.50, 8k. Queen Silvia.

1995. European Union Membership Referendum (2nd issue). Designs as Nos. 1763/4 but colours and values changed. Multicoloured.

1785	3k.70 Type **503**	1·70	70
1786	3k.70 "Nej" ("No")	1·70	70

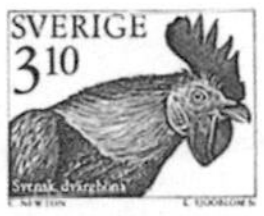

507 Swedish Dwarf Cock

1995. Domestic Animals (2nd series).

1787	**507**	3k.10 brown, chocolate and red	1·60	65
1788	-	3k.70 chestnut, brown and red	1·70	65
1789	-	3k.70 chestnut, brown and red	1·70	65

DESIGNS—VERT: No. 1788, Red poll cow; 1789, Goat.

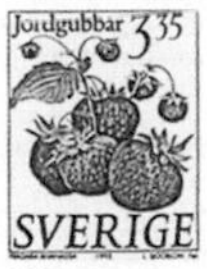

508 Strawberries

1995. Berries.

1790	**508**	3k.35 red, green and black on cream	1·50	55
1791	-	3k.35 black, green and purple on cream	1·50	55
1792	-	3k.35 red, green and black on cream	1·50	55

DESIGNS: No. 1791, Blackberries; 1792, Raspberries.

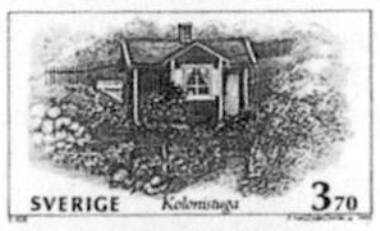

509 Cottage with Allotment, Sodermanland

1995. Traditional Buildings (1st series). Rural Houses. Multicoloured.

1793	3k.70 Type **509**	1·70	70
1794	3k.70 Soldier's smallholding, Skanegard	1·70	70
1795	3k.70 17th-century farmhouse, Scania	1·70	70
1796	3k.70 19th-century farmhouse, Jamtland	1·70	70
1797	3k.70 18th-century manor house, Dalarna	1·70	70

See also Nos. 1856/64, 1905/10 and 1961/5.

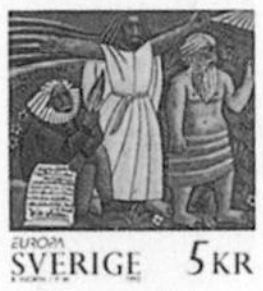

510 Jesus, Walt Whitman and Socrates

1995. Europa. Peace and Freedom. "Love, Peace and Labour" (wooden relief, Bror Hjorth). Multicoloured.

1798	5k. Type **510**	2·30	1·80
1799	5k. Lumumba, Albert Schweitzer and people of different races	2·30	1·80
1800	6k. Type **510**	2·75	2·20
1801	6k. As No. 1799	2·75	2·20

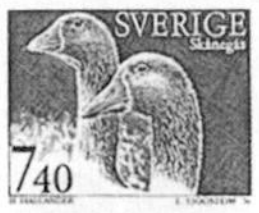

511 Scanian Geese

1995. Domestic Animals.

1802	**511**	7k.40 deep brown, brown and green	3·50	1·20
1803	-	7k.50 brown, green and blue	3·50	1·80

DESIGN: 7k.50, Swedish yellow duck.

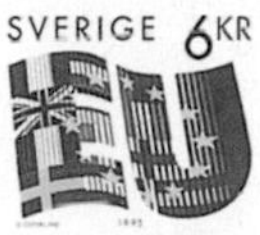

512 Members' Flags forming "EU"

1995. Admission of Sweden to European Union.

1804	**512**	6k. multicoloured	3·00	1·40

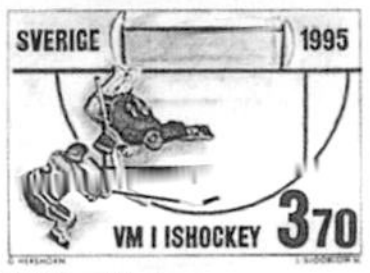

513 Ice Hockey

1995. World Ice Hockey Championship, Stockholm and Gavle (1805) and World Athletics Championships, Gothenburg (1806). Multicoloured.

1805	3k.70 Type **513**	3·25	90
1806	3k.70 Erica Johansson (1992 junior long jump champion) (27½×28 mm)	1·90	70

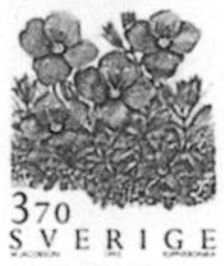

514 Rock Speedwell

1995. Mountain Flowers. Multicoloured.

1807	3k.70 Type **514**	1·80	65
1808	3k.70 Cloudberry (white flowers)	1·80	65
1809	3k.70 Mountain heath (pink flowers) and black bearberry	1·80	65
1810	3k.70 Alpine arnica (yellow flowers) and crowberry	1·80	65

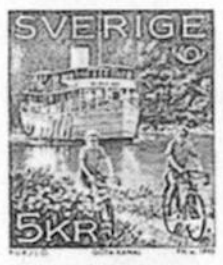

515 "Wilhelm Tham" (motor barge) on Gota Canal

1995. Nordic Countries' Postal Co-operation. Tourism.

1811	**515**	5k. green	2·30	1·50
1812	-	5k. violet	2·30	1·50

DESIGN: No. 1812, Moored yacht, Lake Vattern.

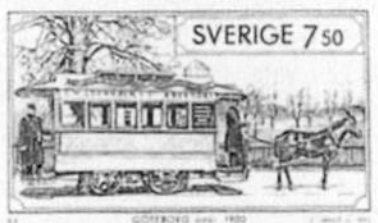

516 English Horse-drawn Tram, Gothenburg

1995. Trams.

1813	**516**	7k.50 red	3·25	2·50
1814	-	7k.50 purple	3·25	2·50
1815	-	7k.50 green	3·25	2·50
1816	-	7k.50 lilac	3·25	2·50
1817	-	7k.50 blue	3·25	2·50

DESIGNS: No. 1814, Electric tram, Norrkoping; 1815, Commuter tram, Helsingborg; 1816, Narrow gauge tram, Kiruna; 1817, Mustang tram, Stockholm.

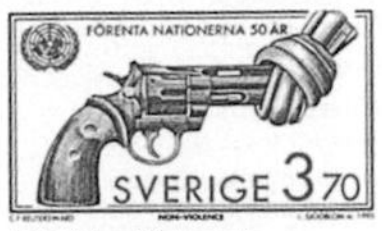

517 "Non-Violence" (sculpture, Carl Frederik Reutersward) (U.N. Building, New York)

1995. 50th Anniv of U.N.O.

1818	**517**	3k.70 deep blue and blue	1·80	70

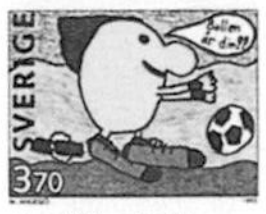

518 "The Ball is Yours!" (Mikael Angesjo)

1995. Greetings Stamps. Winning Entries in Children's Drawing Competition. Multicoloured.

1819	3k.70 Type **518**	1·80	65
1820	3k.70 Happy man saying "Hello" (Erica Sandstrom)	1·80	65
1821	3k.70 Teddy bear saying "I miss you" (Linda Nordenhem)	1·80	65
1822	3k.70 Shy mussel saying "Hello" (Christoffer Stenbom)	1·80	65

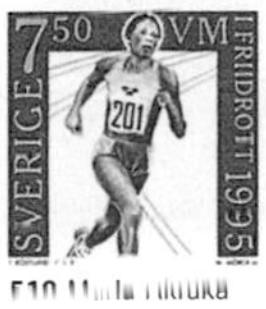

519

1995. World Athletics Championships, Gothenburg.

1823	**519**	7k.50 multicoloured	3·25	2·20

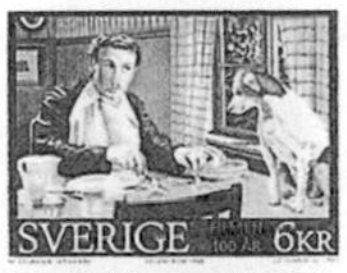

520 "Soldier Bom" (1948)

1995. Centenary of Motion Pictures. Scenes from Swedish Films. Multicoloured.

1824	6k. Type **520**	3·00	2·75
1825	6k. "Sir Arne's Treasure" (1919)	3·00	2·75
1826	6k. "Wild Strawberries" (1957)	3·00	2·75
1827	6k. "House of Angels" (1992)	3·00	2·75
1828	6k. "One Summer of Happiness" (1951)	3·00	2·75
1829	6k. "The Apple War" (1971)	3·00	2·75

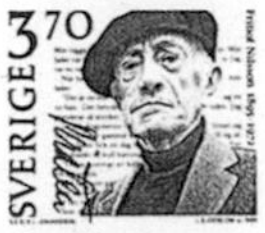

521 Nilsson

1995. Birth Centenary of Fritiof Nilsson (writer).

1830	**521**	3k.70 blue and red	1·80	90

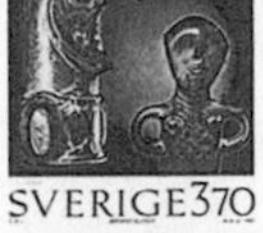

522 Bronze Figures (Bronze Age)

1995. Ancient Treasures from Museum of National Antiquities, Stockholm. Multicoloured.

1831	3k.70 Type **522**	1·80	1·10
1832	3k.70 Gold collar (400–550 A.D.)	1·80	1·10
1833	3k.70 Pendant (400–550 A.D.)	1·80	1·10
1834	3k.70 Bronze drum (Bronze Age)	1·80	1·10

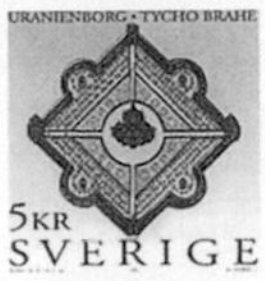

523 Uraniborg Observatory

1995. 450th Birth Anniv of Tycho Brahe (astronomer). Multicoloured.

1835	5k. Type **523**	2·50	1·20
1836	6k. Instrument for measuring positions in Space	2·75	1·80

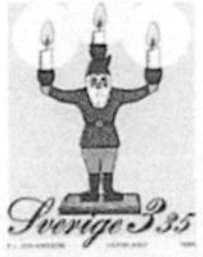

524 Santa Candlestick, Varmland

1995. Christmas. Candlesticks. Multicoloured.

1837	3k.35 Type **524**	1·70	80
1838	3k.35 Apple candlestick, Smaland	1·70	80
1839	3k.35 Wrought iron candlestick, Dalarna	1·70	80
1840	3k.35 Three-armed candlestick, Bergslagen	1·70	80

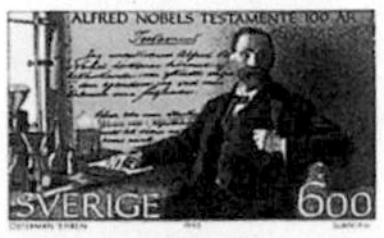

525 Nobel and Will

1995. Centenary of Nobel Prize Trust Fund. Multicoloured.

1841	6k. Type **525**	3·25	2·30
1842	6k. Nobel's home in Paris	3·25	2·30
1843	6k. Laboratory, Bjorkborn Manor, Karlskoga	3·25	2·30
1844	6k. Medal and award ceremony for Wilhelm Rontgen, 1901	3·25	2·30

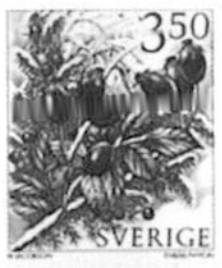

526 Rose Hips and Juniper

1996. Winter Berries. Multicoloured.

1845	3k.50 Type **526**	1·80	70
1846	3k.50 Cowberries and sloes	1·80	70
1847	3k.50 Holly	1·80	70
1848	7k.50 Rowan	3·50	2·30

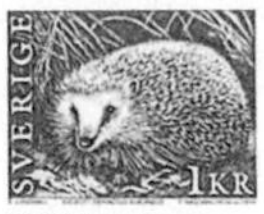

527 West European Hedgehog ("Erinaceus europaeus")

1996. Wildlife.

1849	**527**	1k. sepia, brown and green	55	35
1850	-	3k.20 multicoloured	1·50	1·10
1851	-	3k.85 multicoloured	1·60	65
1852	-	7k.70 brown, deep brown and chocolate	3·25	1·20
1854	-	3k.85 green, olive and black	1·80	65

DESIGNS—VERT: No. 1850, Eurasian beaver ("Castor fiber"). HORIZ: No. 1851, Stoat ("Mustela erminea"); 1852, Red fox ("Vulpes vulpes"); 1854, European otter ("Lutra lutra").

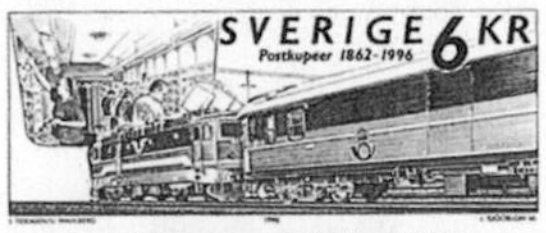

528 Postal Sorters and Modern Mail Carriage

1996. Discontinuation of Mail Sorting on Train Travelling Post Offices.

1855	**528**	6k. black, blue and red	3·00	1·70

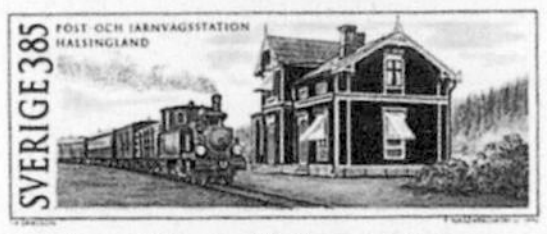

529 Post Office and Railway Station, Halsingland

1996. Traditional Buildings (2nd series). Business and Commercial Premises. Multicoloured.

1856	3k.85 Type **529**	1·80	1·00
1857	3k.85 Motala Assembly Hall, Ostergotland	1·80	1·00
1858	3k.85 Parish storehouse, Smaland (27×23 mm)	1·80	1·00
1859	3k.85 Octagonal log barn, Vasterbotten (27×23 mm)	1·80	1·00
1860	3k.85 Sheep shelter, Gotland (27×36 mm)	1·80	1·00
1861	3k.85 Old Town Hall, Lidkoping (27×36 mm)	1·80	1·00

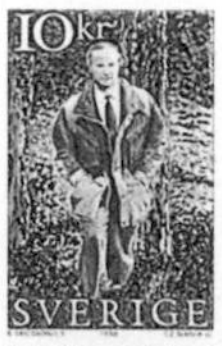

530 King Carl Gustav opening Tyresta National Park, 1993

1996. 50th Birthday of King Carl XVI Gustaf. Multicoloured.

1862	10k. Type **530**	4·50	4·50
1863	10k. In Bernadotte Gallery with painting of King Karl XIV Johan	4·50	4·50
1864	10k. With King Albert of Belgium, 1994	4·50	4·50
1865	20k. With royal family, 1995 (76×43 mm)	9·00	7·25

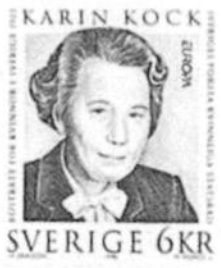

531 Karin Kock (politician)

1996. Europa. Famous Women.

1866	**531**	6k. brown and red	2·75	2·00
1867	-	6k. blue and red	2·75	2·00

DESIGN: No. 1867, Astrid Lindgren (children's writer).

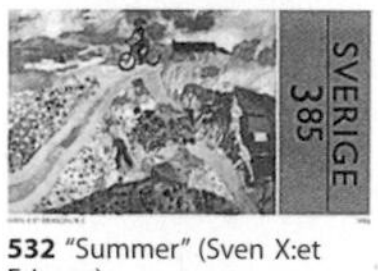

532 "Summer" (Sven X:et Erixson)

1996. Summer Paintings. Multicoloured.

1868	3k.85 Type **532**	1·80	65
1869	3k.85 "Summer Evening in Stora Nassa" (Roland Svensson)	1·80	65
1870	3k.85 "On The Island" (Eric Hallstrom)	1·80	65
1871	3k.85 "Rallarros" (Thage Nordholm)	1·80	65
1872	3k.85 "On the Bridge" (Ragnar Sandberg)	1·80	65

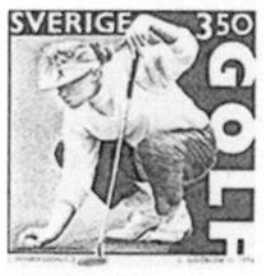

533 Annika Sorenstam

1996. Golf.

1873	**533**	3k.50 green on cream	2·30	1·00

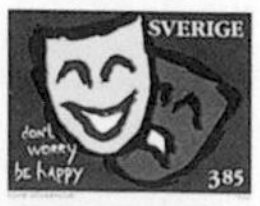

534 Theatre Masks

1996. Greetings Stamps.

1874	**534**	3k.85 multicoloured	1·90	70
1875	-	3k.85 blue, yellow and black	1·90	70
1876	-	3k.85 violet, yellow and black	1·90	70
1877	-	3k.85 red, black and pink	1·90	70

DESIGNS: No. 1875, Hearts forming four-leaved clover ("Be Happy!"); 1876, Heart within posthorn; 1877, Girl and hearts ("Do you remember me?").

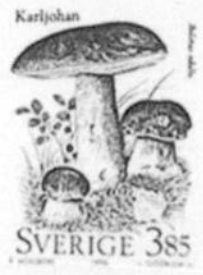

535 Cep ("Boletus edulis")

1996. Fungi. Multicoloured.

1878	3k.85 Type **535**	1·90	70
1879	5k. "Russula integra"	2·10	1·30
1880	5k. Chanterelle ("Cantherellus cibarius")	2·10	1·30
1881	5k. Death trumpets ("Craterellus cornucopioides")	2·10	1·30
1882	5k. Shaggy ink caps ("Coprinus comatus")	2·10	1·30

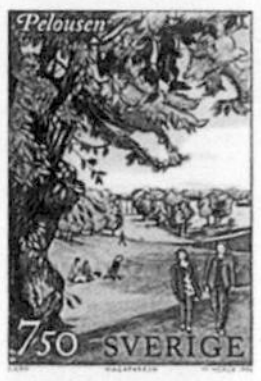

536 Grass Slopes, Haga Park

1996. The Ecopark, Stockholm. Multicoloured.

1883	7k.50 Type **536**	3·25	2·50
1884	7k.50 Copper tents, Haga Park	3·25	2·50
1885	7k.50 Rosendal Palace	3·25	2·50
1886	7k.50 Herons, Isbladskarret Swamp	3·25	2·50

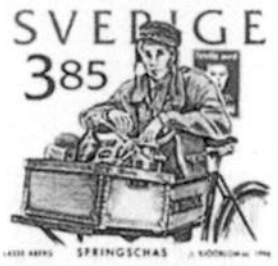

537 Errand Boy, 1930s

1996. Four Decades of Youth. Multicoloured.

1887	3k.85 Type **537**	2·00	1·50
1888	3k.85 Hippy, 1960s	2·00	1·50
1889	3k.85 Zoot-suiter, 1940s	2·00	1·50
1890	3k.85 Biker, 1950s	2·00	1·50

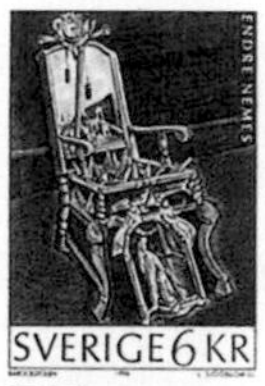

538 "Baroque Chair" (Endre Nemes)

1996. Art.

1891	**538**	6k. multicoloured	2·75	1·80

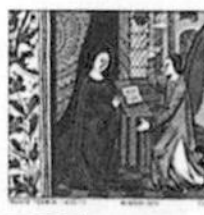

539 The Annunciation

1996. Christmas. Illustrations from 15th-century Book of Hours. Multicoloured.

1892	3k.50 Type **539**	1·70	90
1893	3k.50 Nativity	1·70	90
1894	3k.50 Adoration of the Wise Men	1·70	90

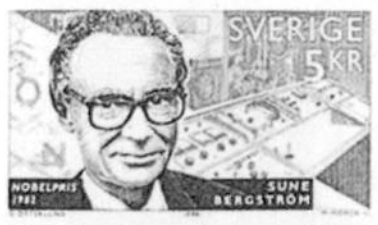

540 Sune Bergstrom (1982)

1996. Swedish Winners of the Nobel Physiology and Medicine Prize.

1895	**540**	5k. black, blue and green	2·75	1·60
1896	-	5k. black and green	2·75	1·60
1897	-	5k. black, blue and green	2·75	1·60
1898	-	5k. blue, green and black	2·75	1·60

DESIGNS: No. 1896, Bengt Samuelsson (1982); 1897, Hugo Theorell (1955); 1898, Ragnar Granit (1967).

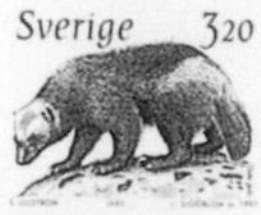

541 Wolverine ("Gulo gulo")

1997. Wildlife.

1899	**541**	3k.20 black, green and blue	1·70	1·20
1900	-	3k.50 black, green and red	1·90	1·10
1901	-	7k.70 black, red and green	3·50	2·30

DESIGNS—HORIZ: 3k.50, Snowy owl ("Nyctea scandiaca"). VERT: 7k.70, White stork ("Ciconia ciconia").

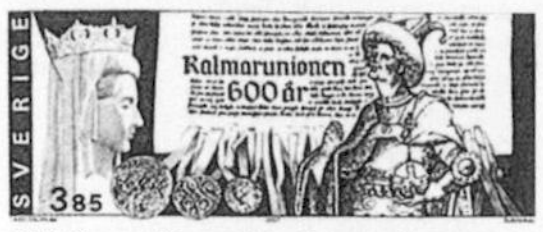

542 Queen Margareta, Coronation Document and Erik of Pommern

1997. 600th Anniv of Kalmar Union (of Sweden, Denmark and Norway).

1902	**542**	3k.85 blue	1·80	1·00

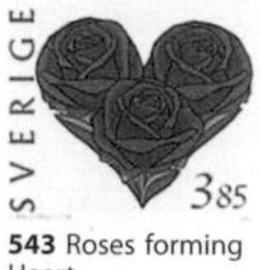

543 Roses forming Heart

1997. Greetings Stamps.

1903	**543**	3k.85 multicoloured (red roses)	1·90	80
1904	**543**	3k.85 multicoloured (pink roses)	1·90	80

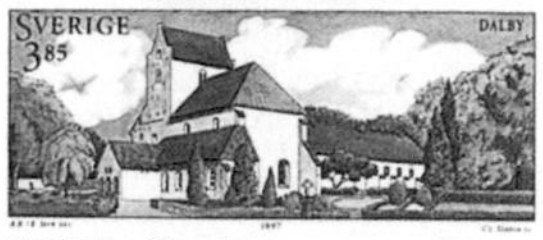

544 Dalby Church

1997. Traditional Buildings (3rd series). Churches. Multicoloured.

1905	3k.85 Type **544**	1·80	1·20
1906	3k.85 Vendel	1·80	1·20
1907	3k.85 Hagby (27×23 mm)	1·80	1·20
1908	3k.85 Overtornea (27×23 mm)	1·80	1·20
1909	3k.85 Varnhem (27×37 mm)	1·80	1·20
1910	3k.85 Ostra Amtervik (27×23 mm)	1·80	1·20

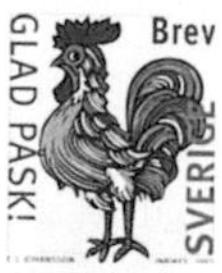

545 Cockerel

1997. Easter. Inscr "INRIKES BREV". Multicoloured.

1911	(5k.) Type **545**	2·50	90
1912	(5k.) Daffodils	2·50	90

Nos. 1911/12 were for use on domestic first class mail.

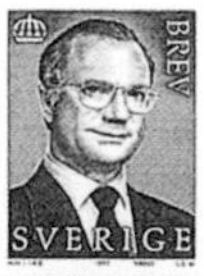

546 King Carl XVI Gustav

1997. Inscr "INRIKES BREV".

1913	**546**	(5k.) blue	2·50	80

No. 1913 was for use on domestic first class mail.

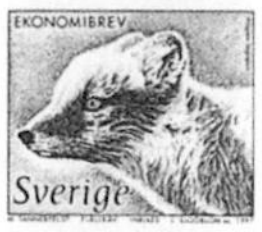

547 Arctic Fox ("Alopex lagopus")

1997. Wildlife (2nd series). (a) Inscr "EKONOMIBREV".

1914	**547**	(4k.50) black, brn & bl	2·00	80

(b) Inscr "BREV INRIKES" (1915/16) or "INRIKES BREV" (1917).

1915	(5k.) brown, black & grn	2·50	1·00
1916	(5k.) black and blue	2·50	1·00
1917	(5k.) black and red	2·50	1·00

DESIGNS: No. 1915, Przewalski's horses; 1916, Snow leopard; 1917, Snow leopard cubs.

No. 1914 was for use on domestic second class mail and Nos. 1915/17 on domestic first class mail.

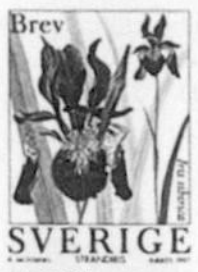

548 Siberian Iris ("Iris sibirica")

1997. Garden Flowers. Inscr "INRIKES BREV". Multicoloured.

1918	(5k.) Type **548**	2·30	1·20
1919	(5k.) Honeysuckle ("Lonicera periclymenum")	2·30	1·20
1920	(5k.) Columbine ("Aquilegia vulgaris")	2·30	1·20
1921	(5k.) Day lily ("Hemerocallis flava")	2·30	1·20
1922	(5k.) Pansy ("Viola wittrockiana")	2·30	1·20

Nos. 1918/22 were for use on domestic first class mail.

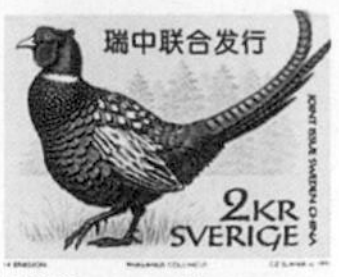

549 Common Pheasant ("Phasianus colchicus")

1997. Pheasants. Multicoloured.

1923	2k. Type **549**	95	65
1924	2k. Lady Amherst's pheasants ("Chrysolophus amherstiae")	95	65

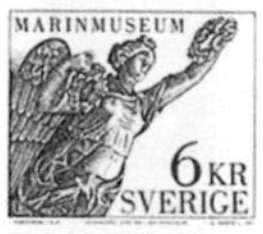

550 Figurehead from "Carl XIII" (ship of the line)

1997. Inauguration of Naval Museum, Karlskrona.

1925	**550**	6k. blue, brown and red	2·75	1·60

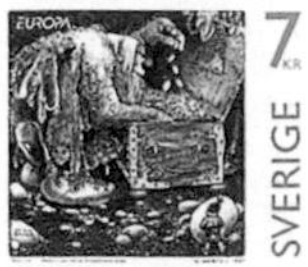

551 Troll with Treasure Chest ("The Troll and the Gnome Boy")

1997. Europa. Tales and Legends. Illustrations by John Bauer. Multicoloured.

1926	7k. Type **551**	3·25	2·20
1927	7k. Trolls gazing at fairy ("The Boy and the Trolls or the Adventure")	3·25	2·20
1928	7k. Boy before troll ("The Fearless Boy")	3·25	2·20

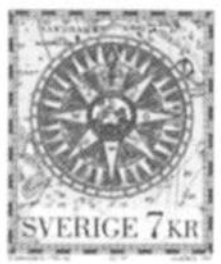

552 18th-century Compass Rose (Sven Billing)

1997. 18th International Cartographic Conference, Stockholm. Multicoloured.

1929	7k. Type **552**	3·25	1·50
1930	8k. Compass rose, 1568 (from atlas by Diego Homem)	3·75	1·80

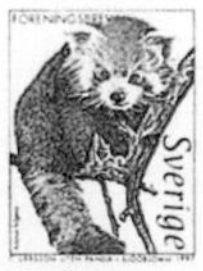

553 Lesser Panda

1997. Inscr "FORENINGSBREV".

1931	**553**	(3k.50) choc, brn & red	1·80	1·00

No. 1931 was for use on bulk rate mail from societies.

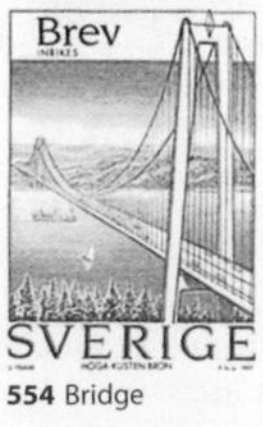

554 Bridge

1997. Inauguration of High Coast Suspension Bridge. Inscr "INRIKES Brev".

1932	**554**	(5k.) blue, green & dp bl	2·50	80

No. 1932 was for use on domestic first class mail.

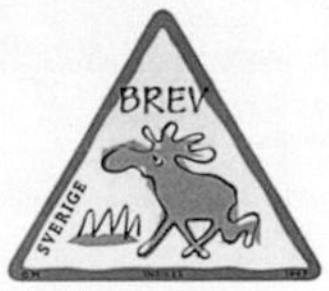

555 Elk and Mountains

1997. Greeting Stamps. Elk. Inscr "INRIKES BREV".

1933	**555**	(5k.) multicoloured	2·30	1·20
1934	-	(5k.) multicoloured	2·30	1·20
1935	-	(5k.) multicoloured	2·30	1·20
1936	-	(5k.) multicoloured	2·30	1·20
1937	-	(5k.) black, yellow and red	2·30	1·20
1938	-	(5k.) black and red	2·30	1·20

DESIGNS: No. 1934, Elk-shaped bar code; 1935, Striped elk; 1936, Running elk; 1937, Running elk (different); 1938, Elk and young.

Nos. 1933/8 were for use on domestic first class mail.

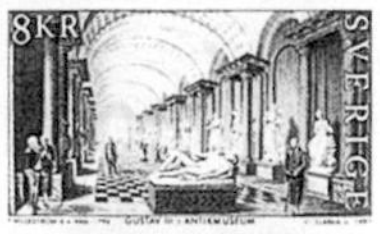

556 "Gallery of the Muses" (Peter Hillerstrom)

1997. Gustav III's Museum of Antiquities, Stockholm. Multicoloured.

1939	8k. Type **556**	3·50	2·50
1940	8k. "Endymion"	3·50	2·50

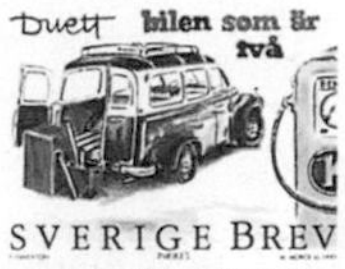

557 Volvo "Duett", 1958

1997. Cars. Inscr "INRIKES BREV". Multicoloured.

1941	(5k.) Type **557**	2·30	1·70
1942	(5k.) Chevrolet "Bel Air", 1955	2·30	1·70
1943	(5k.) Porsche "356", 1959	2·30	1·70
1944	(5k.) Citroen "B11", 1952	2·30	1·70
1945	(5k.) Saab "Monte Carlo" (Erik Carlsson's rally car)	2·30	1·70
1946	(5k.) Jaguar "E-type", 1961	2·30	1·70

Nos. 1941/6 were for use on domestic first class mail.

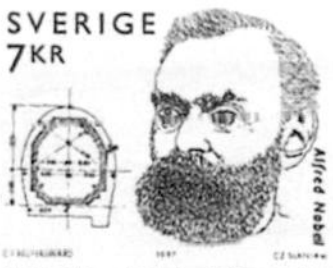

558 Alfred Nobel (founder of Prize Fund)

1997. The Nobel Prize.

1947	**558**	7k. black and pink	3·25	2·50
1948	-	7k. black and grey	3·25	2·50

DESIGN: No. 1948, Paul Karrer and molecular structure of Vitamin A (Chemistry Prize, 1937).

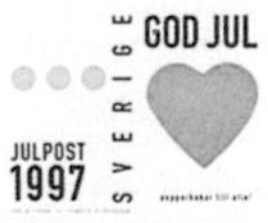

559 Heart

1997. Christmas Gingerbread Biscuits. Each brown, ochre and silver on yellow. Inscr "JULPOST".

1949	(3k.50) Type **559**	1·80	1·20
1950	(3k.50) Pigs	1·80	1·20
1951	(3k.50) Gingerbread men	1·80	1·20

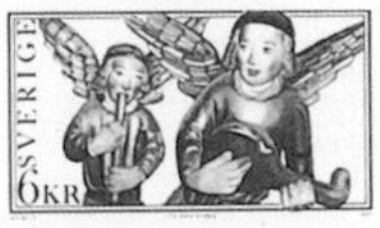

560 Angels with Pipe and Lute

1997. Christmas. Angels from altarpiece, Litslena Church. Multicoloured.

1952	6k. Type **560**	2·75	2·20
1953	6k. Angels with pipes and harp	2·75	2·20

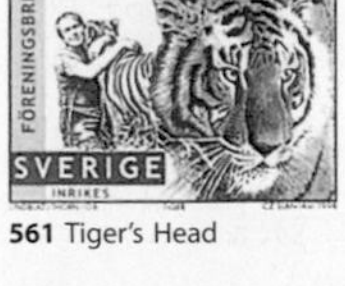

561 Tiger's Head

1998. Wildlife Photographs by Jan Lindblad. Inscr "FORENINGSBREV". Multicoloured.

1954	(3k.50) Type **561**	1·80	1·10
1955	(3k.50) Two tigers on rock	1·80	1·10

Nos. 1954/5 were for use on bulk rate mail from societies.

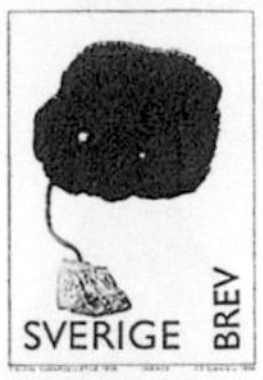

562 "Sponge Sculpture" (Yves Klein)

1998. Modern Art. Inscr "INRIKES BREV". Multicoloured.

1956	(5k.) Type **562**	2·30	1·30
1957	(5k.) "Skeppsholmen" (Goran Gidenstam)	2·30	1·30
1958	(5k.) "Monogram" (Robert Rauschenberg)	2·30	1·30

Nos. 1956/8 were for use on domestic first class mail.

563 Heart with Love Birds

1998. St. Valentine's Day. Inscr "INRIKES Brev".

1959	**563**	(5k.) red and green	2·30	1·00
1960	**563**	(5k.) mauve and blue	2·30	1·00

Nos. 1959/60 were for use on domestic first class mail.

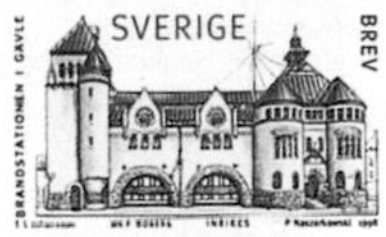

564 Fire Station, Gavle

1998. Traditional Buildings (4th series). Town Houses. Inscr "INRIKES BREV". Multicoloured.

1961	(5k.) Type **564**	2·30	1·00
1962	(5k.) Shoe shop, Askersund	2·30	1·00
1963	(5k.) Fish and delicatessen market hall, Gothenburg	2·30	1·00
1964	(5k.) Red Mill Cinema, Halmstad	2·30	1·00
1965	(5k.) Stads Hotel, Eksjo	2·30	1·00

Nos 1961/5 were for use on domestic first class mail.

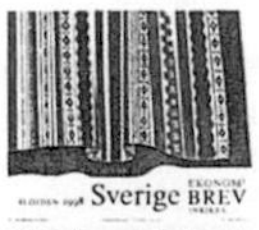

565 Apron, Dalarna

1998. Handicrafts. (a) Inscr "EKONOMI BREV INRIKES".

1966	**565**	(4k.50) scarlet, blk & red	2·10	1·00

(b) Inscr "INRIKES BREV".

1967	(5k.) black and brown	2·30	1·10

(c) With face value.

1968	8k. orange, violet and red	3·25	2·75
1969	8k. violet and red	3·25	2·75

DESIGNS: No. 1967, Iron candlestick, Skane; 1968, Lumberjack's woollen glove; 1969, Decorative wooden box.

No. 1966 was for use on domestic second class mail and No. 1967 on domestic first class mail.

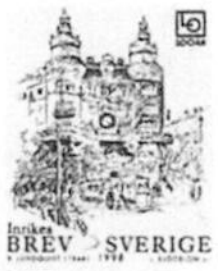

566 Confederation Building, Stockholm (after Birger Lundquist)

1998. Centenary of Swedish Confederation of Trade Unions. Inscr "Inrikes BREV".

1970	**566**	(5k.) black, stone & red	2·30	80

No. 1970 was for use on domestic first class mail.

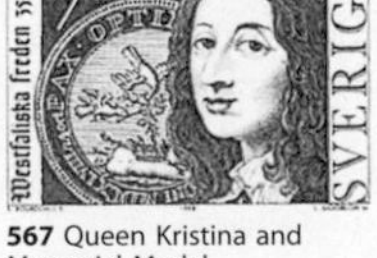

567 Queen Kristina and Memorial Medal

1998. 350th Anniv of Peace of Westphalia.

1971	**567**	7k. green and red	3·25	2·00

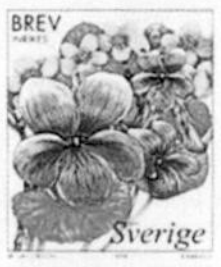

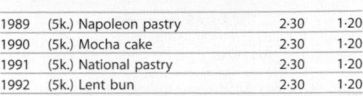

568 Marsh Violet

1998. Wetland Flowers. Inscr "BREV INRIKES". Multicoloured.

1972	(5k.) Type **568**	2·30	90
1973	(5k.) Great willow herb	2·30	90

Nos. 1972/3 were for use on domestic first class mail.

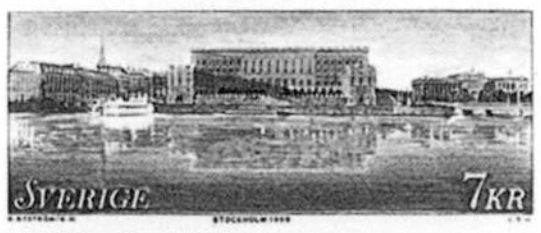

569 The Royal Palace

1998. Stockholm, Cultural Capital of Europe. Multicoloured. (a) Inscr "INRIKES BREV".

1974	(5k.) Type **569**	2·30	90
1975	(5k.) Archipelago ferries	2·30	1·40
1976	(5k.) Fisherman in front of Opera House (31×26 mm)	2·30	1·40
1977	(5k.) Yachts (31×26 mm)	2·30	1·40
1978	(5k.) Open-air swimming (31×39 mm)	2·30	1·40
1979	(5k.) City Hall (31×39 mm)	2·30	1·40

(b) With face value.

1980	7k. Type **569**	3·25	2·30
1981	7k. As No. 1975	3·25	2·30

Nos. 1974/9 were for use on domestic first class mail.

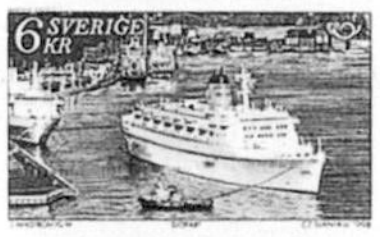

570 "Albatros" (cruise ship) in Stadsgard Harbour

1998. Nordic Countries, Postal Co-operation. Shipping.

1982	**570**	6k. multicoloured	3·25	1·50

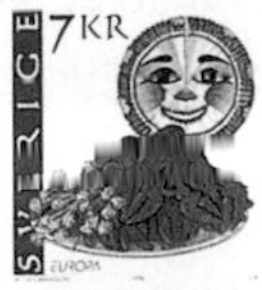

571 Paper Moon and Plate of Crayfish ("Crayfish Party")

1998. Europa. National Festivals. Multicoloured.

1983	7k. Type **571**	3·25	2·30
1984	7k. Children dancing around midsummer pole	3·25	2·30

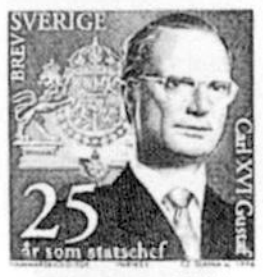

572 King Carl XVI Gustav and Coat of Arms

1998. 25th Anniv of Accession of King Carl XVI Gustav. Inscr "INRIKES BREV".

1985	**572**	(5k.) purple, green and red	2·30	1·00

No. 1985 was for use on domestic first class mail.

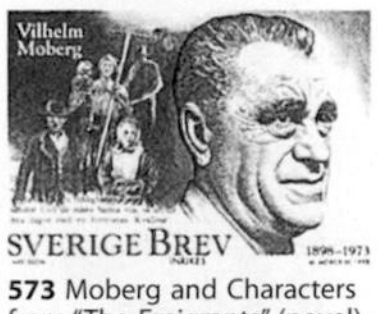

573 Moberg and Characters from "The Emigrants" (novel)

1998. Birth Centenary of Vilhelm Moberg (writer). Inscr "BREV INRIKES".

1986	**573**	(5k.) multicoloured	2·50	1·10

No. 1986 was for use on domestic first class mail.

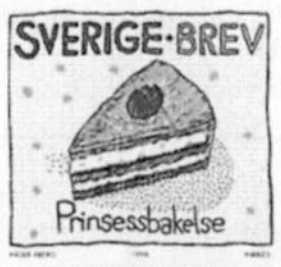

574 Princess Cake

1998. Greetings Stamps. Pastries. Inscr "BREV". Multicoloured.

1987	(5k.) Type **574**	2·30	1·20
1988	(5k.) Gustav Adolf pastry	2·30	1·20
1989	(5k.) Napoleon pastry	2·30	1·20
1990	(5k.) Mocha cake	2·30	1·20
1991	(5k.) National pastry	2·30	1·20
1992	(5k.) Lent bun	2·30	1·20

Nos. 1987/92 were for use on domestic first class mail.

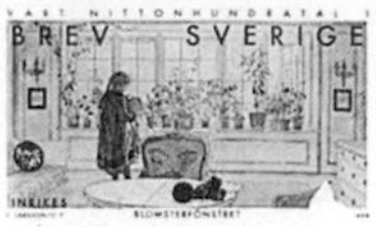

575 "Flowers in the window" (Carl Larsson)

1998. The Twentieth Century (1st series). 1900–1938. Inscr "INRIKES BREV". Multicoloured.

1993	(5k.) Type **575**	3·00	1·80
1994	(5k.) Stockholm Stadium and poster (Olympic Games, 1912)	3·00	1·80
1995	(5k.) Porjus hydro-electric power station and electric iron-ore. train on Lulea (Sweden)–Narvik (Norway) railway line	3·00	1·80
1996	(5k.) Zip, ball-bearing, vacuum cleaner and refrigerator (Swedish inventions)	3·00	1·80
1997	(5k.) Map of trans-ocean shipping routes and liner	3·00	1·80
1998	(5k.) Sven Jerring (first Swedish radio reporter)	3·00	1·80
1999	(5k.) Jazz musicians and Charleston dancers	3·00	1·80
2000	(5k.) Ellen Key (writer and suffragist) and Kerstin Hesselgren (first woman member of parliament)	3·00	1·80
2001	(5k.) Arne Borg (swimmer) and Gillis Grafstrom (figure skater) (Olympic and world champions)	3·00	1·80
2002	(5k.) Ernst Rolf (entertainer)	3·00	1·80

Nos. 1993/2002 were for use on domestic first class mail.

See also Nos. 2026/35 and 2083/92.

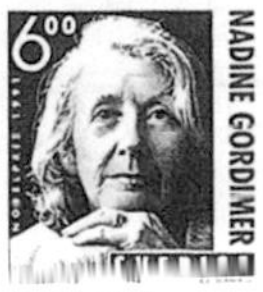

576 Nadine Gordimer (1991)

1998. The Nobel Literature Prize.

2003	**576**	6k. violet and blue	2·50	2·20
2004	-	6k. violet and red	2·50	2·20

DESIGN: No. 2004, Sigrid Undset (1928).

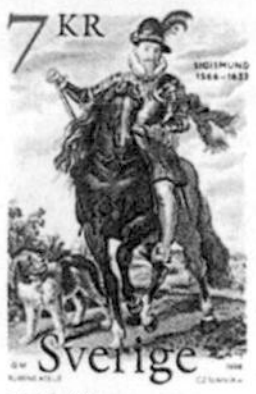

577 "King Sigismund of Sweden and Poland" (Studio of Rubens)

1998. 400th Anniv of Battle of Stangebro.

2005	**577**	7k. multicoloured	3·00	2·00

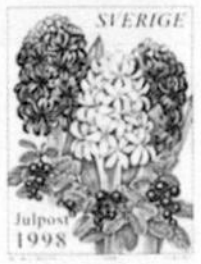

578 Hyacinths

1998. Christmas. Flowers. (a) No value expressed. Inscr "Julpost". Size 21×28 mm. Multicoloured.

2006	(4k.) Type **578**	1·80	1·00
2007	(4k.) Mistletoe	1·80	1·00
2008	(4k.) Amaryllis	1·80	1·00

(b) With face value. Size 23×27½ mm.

2009	6k. Lingonberry wreath	2·50	1·50
2010	6k. Azaleas	2·50	1·50

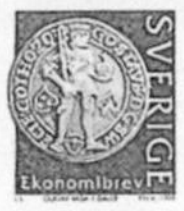

579 King Gustav Vasa 1 Daler, 1540

1999. Coins. (a) Inscr "Ekonomibrev".

2011	**579**	(4k.50) green	1·80	1·00

(b) Inscr "Brev inrikes".
2012 (5k.) blue 2·10 1·00
DESIGN: No. 2012, King Carl XIV John 1 riksdaler, 1831–43.
No. 2011 was for use on domestic second class mail and No. 2012 on domestic first class mail.

580 Harbour and Katarina Lift, Stockholm

1999. Centenary of Co-operative Union. Inscr "INRIKES BREV".
2013 **580** (5k.) multicoloured 2·10 1·60
No. 2013 was for use on domestic first class mail.

581 Easter Egg and Rabbit

1999. Easter. Inscr "INRIKES Brev". Multicoloured.
2014 (5k.) Type **581** 2·10 1·60
2015 (5k.) Easter eggs and chicks 2·10 1·60
Nos. 2014/15 were for use on domestic first class mail.

582 Rabbit cooking

1999. Rabbits. Drawings by Eva Eriksson from "Little Sister Rabbit" by Ulf Nilsson. Inscr "INRIKES BREV". Multicoloured.
2016 (5k.) Type **582** 2·10 1·60
2017 (5k.) Rabbit feeding baby rabbit 2·10 1·60
2018 (5k.) Rabbits dancing 2·10 1·60
2019 (5k.) Rabbits running through grass 2·10 1·60
Nos. 2016/19 were for use on domestic first class mail.

583 "East Indies" (anon)

1999. "Australia 99" International Stamp Exhibition, Melbourne. Paintings of Ships. Multicoloured.
2020 8k. Type **583** 3·25 2·50
2021 8k. "Mary Anne" (brigantine) (Folke Sjogren) 3·25 2·50
2022 8k. "Beatrice" (barque) (A. V. Gregory) 3·25 2·50
2023 8k. "Australic" (steamship) (T. G. Purvis) 3·25 2·50

584 Pontoon "Swan" at Dresund Bridge

1999. Construction of Oresund Bridge between Sweden and Denmark. (a) Inscr "INRIKES BREV". Multicoloured.
2024 (5k.) Type **584** 2·10 1·00

(b) With face value.
2025 6k. Bridge under construction (different) 2·50 2·20
No. 2024 was for use on domestic first class mail.

585 Eva Dahlbeck and Gunnar Bjornstrand in "Smiles of a Summer Night" (director Ingmar Bergman), 1955

1999. The Twentieth Century (2nd series). 1939–1969. Inscr "INRIKES BREV". Multicoloured.
2026 (5k.) Type **585** 2·00 1·40
2027 (5k.) Vallingby (first satellite town of Stockholm) 2·00 1·40

2028 (5k.) Ulla Billquist and scene from "My Soldier somewhere in Sweden" (song) (emergency military service, 1939–45) 2·00 1·40
2029 (5k.) Cobra telephone (L.M. Ericsson), three-point seat belt (Nils Bohlins), high voltage cables and Tetra Pak milk carton (Swedish inventions) 2·00 1·40
2030 (5k.) Douglas DC-4 airliner (first scheduled flight of state airline SAS) 2·00 1·40
2031 (5k.) Jester, Carl-Gustaf Lindstedt, host of "Hyland's Corner", and Prime Minister Tage Erlander (television) 2·00 1·40
2032 (5k.) Demonstrators, girl wearing optical-patterned dress and pop group Hep Stars (the 60s) 2·00 1·40
2033 (5k.) Volvo Amazon Car and family camping (leisure time) 2·00 1·40
2034 (5k.) Ingemar Johansson (world heavy-weight boxing champion), Mora-Nisse Karlsson (skier) and Gunder Hagg (athlete) 2·00 1·40
2035 (5k.) Alice Babs (jazz singer) and Jussi Bjorling (opera tenor) 2·00 1·40
Nos. 2026/35 were for use on domestic first class mail.

586 Postman's Bicycle

1999. Bicycles. (a) Inscr "FORENINGSBREV".
2036 **586** (3k.50) bl, ultram & yell 1·90 1·20

(b) Inscr "INRIKES BREV".
2037 (5k.) multicoloured 2·10 1·00

(c) With face value.
2038 6k. blue, purple and black 2·10 1·40
2039 8k. green, lt green & red 3·25 2·20
DESIGNS: No. 2037, Racing cyclist; 2038, City bike; 2039, Bike messenger.
No. 2036 was for use on bulk rate mail from societies; No. 2037 for use on domestic first class mail.

587 Pyramidal Orchid ("Salepsrot")

1999. Orchids. Inscr "INRIKES BREV". Multicoloured.
2040 (5k.) Type **587** 2·30 1·20
2041 (5k.) Lady's slipper ("Guckusko") 2·30 1·20
2042 (5k.) Marsh helleborine ("Karrknipprot") 2·30 1·20
2043 (5k.) Green-winged orchid ("Goknycklar") 2·30 1·20
Nos. 2040/3 were for use on domestic first class mail.

588 Plant Shoot

1999. 50th Anniv of Council of Europe.
2044 **588** 7k. multicoloured 3·25 2·20

589 Eurasian Pygmy Owl and Tyresta National Park

1999. Europa. Parks and Gardens. Multicoloured.
2045 7k. Type **589** 3·25 2·50
2046 7k. Pink helleborine and Gotska Sandon National Park 3·25 2·50

590 Peacock ("Inachis io")

1999. Butterflies. Multicoloured.
2047 6k. Type **590** 2·75 2·00
2048 6k. Blue argus ("Junonia orithya") 2·75 2·00
2049 6k. Common eggfly ("Hypolimnas bolina") 2·75 2·00
2050 6k. Red admiral ("Vanessa atalanta") 2·75 2·00

591 "Pisces"

1999. Signs of the Zodiac. Inscr "INRIKES Brev".
2051 **591** (5k.) blue, ultram and orge 2·30 1·40
2052 - (5k.) multicoloured 2·30 1·40
2053 - (5k.) blue, ultram and orge 2·30 1·40
2054 - (5k.) multicoloured 2·30 1·40
2055 - (5k.) blue, ultram and orge 2·30 1·40
2056 - (5k.) multicoloured 2·30 1·40
2057 - (5k.) multicoloured 2·30 1·40
2058 - (5k.) blue, ultram and orge 2·30 1·40
2059 - (5k.) orange, ultram and bl 2·30 1·40
2060 - (5k.) blue, ultram and orge 2·30 1·40
2061 - (5k.) orange, ultram and bl 2·30 1·40
2062 - (5k.) blue, ultram and orge 2·30 1·40
DESIGNS: No. 2052, "Aries"; 2053, "Taurus"; 2054, "Gemini"; 2055, "Cancer"; 2056, "Aquarius"; 2057, "Virgo"; 2058, "Libra"; 2059, "Scorpio"; 2060, "Sagittarius"; 2061, "Capricorn"; 2062, "Leo".
Nos. 2051/62 were for use on domestic first class mail.

592 Auguste Beernaert (Prime Minister of Belgium 1884–94), 1909

1999. Belgian Winners of Nobel Peace Prize.
2063 **592** 7k. blue and gold 3·00 2·30
2064 - 7k. red and gold 3·00 2·30
DESIGN: No. 2064, Henri la Fontaine (President of International Peace Bureau), 1913.

593 Thorleifs

1999. Swedish Dance Bands. Inscr "INRIKES BREV". Multicoloured.
2065 (5k.) Type **593** 2·30 1·40
2066 (5k.) Arvingara 2·30 1·40
2067 (5k.) Lotta Engbergs 2·30 1·40
2068 (5k.) Sten and Stanley 2·30 1·40
Nos. 2065/8 were for use on domestic first class mail.

594 "Nativity"

1999. Christmas. Stained-glass Windows (2069/71) and Wood Sculptures (2072/3). Multicoloured. (a) Inscr "JULPOST".
2069 (4k.) Type **594** 2·00 1·00
2070 (4k.) "Nativity" (different) 2·00 1·00
2071 (4k.) "Adoration of the Wise Men" 2·00 1·00

(b) With face value. Size 27½×30 mm.
2072 6k. Crowned Madonna with child 2·75 1·60
2073 6k. Madonna (in white cloak) and child 2·75 1·60
Nos. 2069/71 were for use on domestic first class mail.

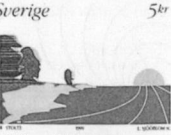
595 Sun rising over Heligholmen

1999. Dawning of New Millennium. Multicoloured.
2074 5k. Type **595** 3·00 2·00
2075 5k. Sun rising over coast at Gotland 3·00 2·00

596 Watch Mechanism

2000. Recovery of King Karl XII's Pocket Watch. (a) Inscr "EKONOMIBREV".
2076 **596** (4k.50) blue 1·90 90

(b) Inscr "INRIKES BREV".
2077 (5k.) brown 2·10 80
DESIGN: 5k. Watch face.
No. 2076 was for use on domestic second class mail and No. 2077 on domestic first class mail.

597 Heart

2000. Valentine's Day. Inscr "INRIKES BREV". Multicoloured.
2078 (5k.) Type **597** 2·10 1·20
2079 (5k.) Scribbled line in heart 2·10 1·20
Nos. 2078/9 were for use on domestic first class mail.

598 Dragon

2000. Chinese New Year. Year of the Dragon. Illustrations from "The Little Dragon with Red Eyes" by Astrid Lindgren. Inscr "INRIKES BREV". Multicoloured.
2080 (5k.) Type **598** 2·10 1·30
2081 (5k.) Dragon with basket 2·10 1·30
2082 (5k.) Dragon flying 2·10 1·30
Nos. 2080/2 were for use on domestic first class mail.

599 Modern Art, Stockholm Underground Railway

2000. The Twentieth Century (3rd series). 1970–1999. Inscr "INRIKES BREV". Multicoloured.
2083 (5k.) Type **599** 2·10 1·50
2084 (5k.) Swedish soldiers in United Nations peace- keeping force 2·10 1·50
2085 (5k.) Computer screen, mouse and voice-activated mobile phone (Swedish inventions) 2·10 1·50
2086 (5k.) Cullberg Ballet dancer and Hans Alfredson and Tage Danielsson (sketch writers) 2·10 1·50
2087 (5k.) Jonkoping Railway Station and high-speed train 2·10 1·50
2088 (5k.) Punk and Abba (pop group) 2·10 1·50
2089 (5k.) European flag and map of Europe (European Union membership, 1994) 2·10 1·50
2090 (5k.) Couple in orchard (film "The Apple War, 1971") 2·10 1·50
2091 (5k.) Pernilla Wiberg (slalom skier), Ingemar Stenmark (downhill skier) and Björn Borg (tennis player) 2·10 1·50
2092 (5k.) Child in womb (photograph, Lennart Nilsson) 2·10 1·50
Nos. 2083/92 were for use on domestic first class mail.

600 Parent and Child walking through Forest (public access)

2000. Swedish Forests. Multicoloured. (a) Inscr "Foreningsbrev".
2093 (3k.80) Type **600** 2·00 1·10

(b) Inscr "INRIKES BREV".

2094 (5k.) Felled trees and elk (forestry) 2·30 1·20
2095 (5k.) Western capercaillie in fir forest 2·30 1·20

(c) With face value.

2096 6k. Birch trees 2·30 1·80

No. 2093 was for use on bulk rate mail from societies. Nos. 2094/5 were for use on domestic first class mail.

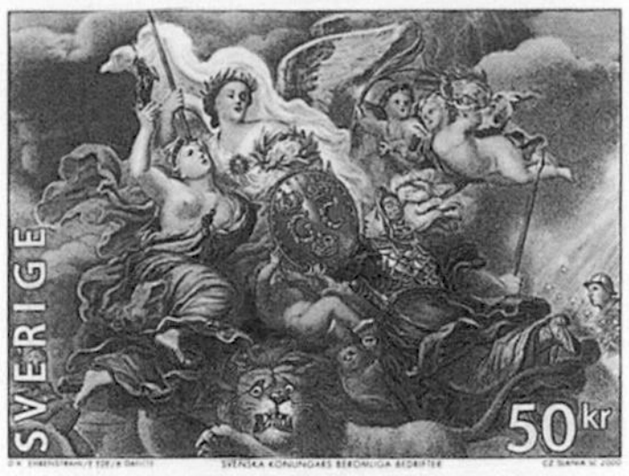

601 "Great deeds by Swedish Kings" (David Klocker Ehrenstrahl)

2000. 1000th Stamp Engraving by Czeslew Slanis. Sheet 94×126 mm.

MS2097 **601** 50k. multicoloured 20·00 19·00

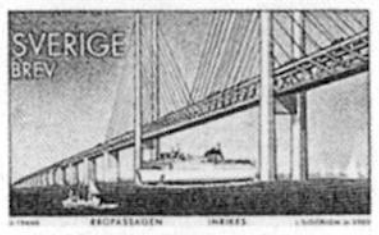

602 Oresund Bridge

2000. Inauguration of Oresund Link (Sweden–Denmark road and rail system). (a) Inscr "INRIKES BREV".

2098 **602** (5k.) black, bl & ultram 2·10 1·00

(b) Size 58×24 mm.

2099 6k. multicoloured 2·50 2·00
2100 6k. ultramarine and green 2·50 2·00

DESIGNS: No. 2099, Oresund Bridge, 2100, Map of Oresund Region.

No. 2098 was for use on domestic first class mail.

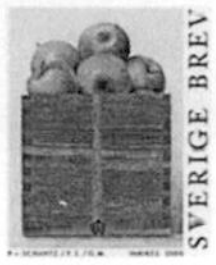

603 "A Peck of Apples"

2000. Modern Paintings by Philip von Schantz. Inscr "INRIKES BREV". Multicoloured.

2101 (5k.) Type **603** 2·10 1·20
2102 (5k.) "A Bowl of Blueberries" 2·10 1·20

Nos. 2101/2 were for use on domestic first class mail.

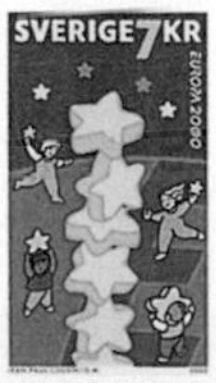

604 "Building Europe"

2000. Europa.

2103 **604** 7k. multicoloured 3·75 2·20

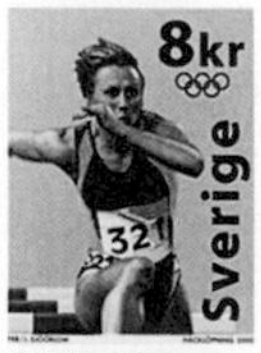

605 Hurdling

2000. Olympic Games, Sydney. Multicoloured.

2104 8k. Type **605** 3·25 2·75
2105 8k. Archery 3·25 2·75
2106 8k. Wind surfing 3·25 2·75
2107 8k. Beach volleyball 3·25 2·75

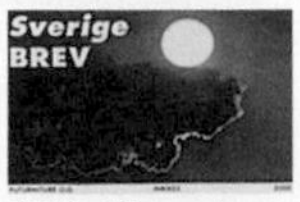

606 Red Sun and Clouds

2000. Weather. Inscr "INRIKES BREV". Multicoloured. Self-adhesive.

2108 (5k.) Type **606** 2·10 1·10
2109 (5k.) Lightning 2·10 1·10
2110 (5k.) Black clouds 2·10 1·10
2111 (5k.) Northern lights 2·10 1·10
2112 (5k.) Rainbow 2·10 1·10
2113 (5k.) Blue sky and white clouds 2·10 1·10

Nos. 2108/13 were for use on domestic first class mail.

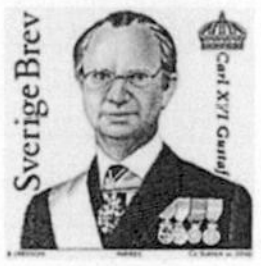

607 King Carl Gustaf XVI

2000. (a) Inscr "INRIKES Brev".

2114 **607** (5k.) blue 2·10 1·10
2115 **607** (5k.50) lake 2·30 1·80

(b) With face values.

2118 8k. red 3·25 2·30
2119 10k. mauve 4·25 3·50

DESIGN: 8k. Queen Silvia.

No. 2114/15 were for use on domestic first class mail.

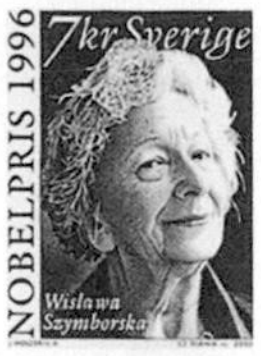

608 Wislawa Szymborska (poet), 1996

2000. Nobel Prize Winners for Literature.

2120 **608** 7k. purple and green 3·25 2·20
2121 - 7k. green and purple 3·25 2·20

DESIGN: No. 2121, Nelly Sachs (author), 1966.

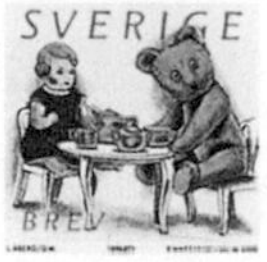

609 Teddy Bear and Doll

2000. Children's Toys. Booklet stamps. Inscr "BREV". Multicoloured.

2122 (5k.) Type **609** 2·30 2·20
2123 (5k.) Skipping rope, marbles and tin soldier 2·30 2·20
2124 (5k.) Toy horses pulling cart, doll and flag 2·30 2·20
2125 (5k.) Toy cars and policeman 2·30 2·20
2126 (5k.) Railway carriages and porter 2·30 2·20
2127 (5k.) Modern toys 2·30 2·20

Nos. 2122/27 were for use on domestic first class mail.

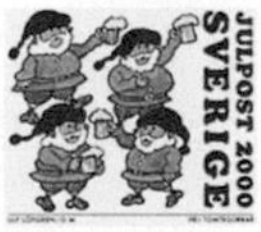

610 Elves drinking

2000. Christmas. Traditional Songs (2128/32) or Snowflakes (2133/4) (others). (a) No value expressed. Inscr "JULPOST".

2128 (4k.30) Type **610** 1·80 1·20
2129 (4k.30) Children dancing around tree (vert) 1·80 1·20
2130 (4k.30) Three gingerbread men (vert) 1·80 1·20
2131 (4k.30) Fox running (vert) 1·80 1·20
2132 (4k.30) Children dancing around candles (vert) 1·80 1·20

(b) With face value. Size 28×29 mm.

2133 6k. silver and blue (face value in blue) 2·50 1·80
2134 6k. silver and blue (face value in white) 2·50 1·80

DESIGNS: Nos. 2133/34 Snowflakes.

Nos. 2128/32 were for use on domestic first class mail.

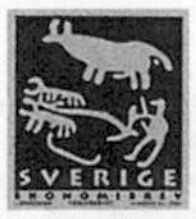

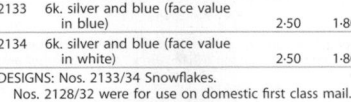

611 Farming

2001. UNESCO World Heritage Sites. Rock Carvings, Tanum. (a) Inscr "EKONOMIBREV".

2135 **611** (4k.50) blue on grey 2·00 1·30

(b) Inscr "INRIKES BREV".

2136 (5k.) red on grey 2·10 90

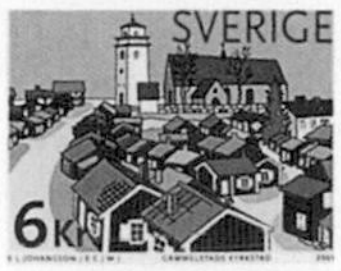

612 Gammelstad Church Village

(c) With face value 35×28 mm.

2137 6k. Type **612** 2·30 2·00
2138 6k. Karlskrona Naval Base 2·30 2·00
2139 6k. Interior of Drottningholm Palace Theatre 2·30 2·00
2140 6k. Ironworks, Engelsberg 2·30 2·00

DESIGN: No. 2136, Men in ships.

No. 2135 was for use on domestic second class mail and No. 2136 on domestic first class mail.

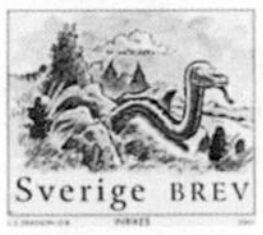

613 Rosa

2001. Chinese New Year. Year of the Snake. Depicting scenes from Nelson the Snake (book) by Ulf Stark. Multicoloured. Inscr "INRIKES BREV".

2141 (5k.) Type **613** 2·30 1·50
2142 (5k.) Nelson coiled on rock 2·30 1·50

Nos. 2141/2 were for use on domestic first class mail.

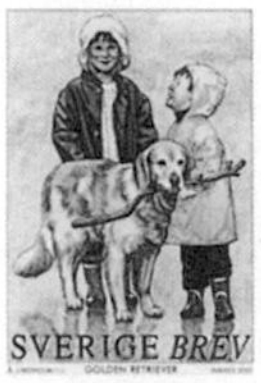

614 Children with Golden Retriever

2001. Working Dogs. Multicoloured. Inscr "INRIKES BREV".

2143 (5k.) Type **614** 2·10 1·70
2144 (5k.) German shepherds hunting in snow 2·10 1·70
2145 (5k.) Labrador guide dog with blind woman 2·10 1·70
2146 (5k.) Dachshunds and man 2·10 1·70

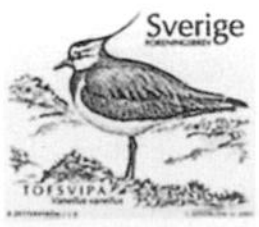

615 Northern Lapwing (*Vanellus vanellus*)

2001. Birds. (a) Inscr "FORENINGSBREV".

2147 **615** (3k.80) blue, green and brown 1·90 1·30

(b) Inscr "INRIKES Brev".

2148 (5k.) blue and black 2·10 1·50

(c) With face value.

2149 6k. green, black and orange 2·50 2·00
2150 7k. purple, brown and green 3·00 2·20

DESIGNS: No. 2148, Black-billed magpie (*Pica pica*); 2149, Herring gull (*Larus argentatus*); 2150, Long-tailed tit (*Aegithalos caudatus*).

No. 2147 was for use on bulk rate mail from societies and No. 2148 for use on domestic first class mail.

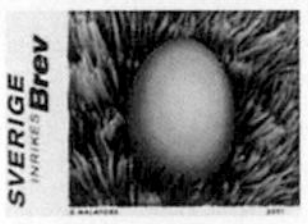

616 Yellow Egg

2001. Easter. Multicoloured. Self-adhesive. Inscr "INRIKES Brev".

2151 (5k.) Type **616** 2·10 1·50
2152 (5k.) Purple egg 2·10 1·50
2153 (5k.) Chick 2·10 1·50

Nos. 2151/3 were for use on domestic first class mail.

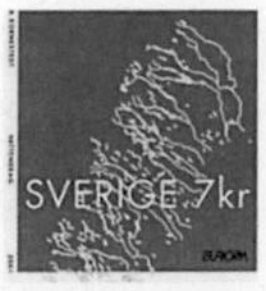

617 Waterways of Northern Sweden

2001. Europa. Water Resources.

2154 **617** 7k. blue, green and black 3·25 2·50
2155 - 7k. blue, green and black 3·25 2·50
2156 - 7k. multicoloured 3·25 2·50
2157 - 7k. multicoloured 3·25 2·50

DESIGNS: No. 2155, Waterways of Southern Sweden; 2156, Freighter entering lock, Trollhatte Canal; 2157 *Juno* (canal boat) leaving lock, Trollhatte Canal.

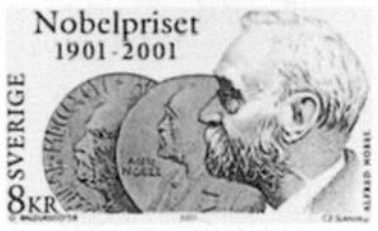

618 Obverse of Medals and Alfred Nobel (founder)

2001. Centenary of Nobel Prizes (1st issue). Each yellow and brown.

2158 8k. Type **618** 3·25 2·75
2159 8k. Reverse of medal for Medicine 3·25 2·75
2160 8k. Reverse of medal for Physics and Chemistry 3·25 2·75
2161 8k. Reverse of medal for Literature 3·25 2·75

See also Nos. 2172/3.

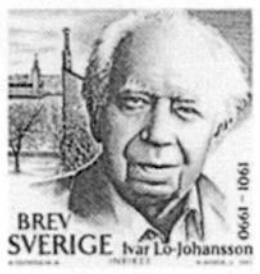

619 Lo-Johansson

2001. Birth Centenary of Ivar Lo-Johansson (writer). Each indigo, red and blue. Inscr "INRIKES BREV".

2162 (5k.) Type **619** 2·30 1·40
2163 (5k.) "The Last Vanload of Furniture of the Agricultural Labourers, 1945" (Svenolov Ehren) 2·30 1·40

Nos. 2162/3 were for use on domestic first class mail.

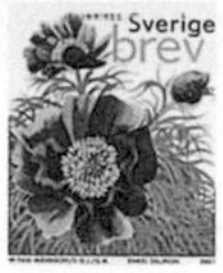

620 Fern Leaf Peony

2001. Peonies. Multicoloured. Inscr "INRIKES brev".

2164 (5k.) Type **620** 2·30 1·10
2165 (5k.) Garden peony "Monsieur Jules Elie" 2·30 1·10
2166 (5k.) Herbaceous peony 2·30 1·10
2167 (5k.) Common peony 2·30 1·10
2168 (5k.) Tree peony 2·30 1·10

Nos. 2164/8 were for use on domestic first class mail.

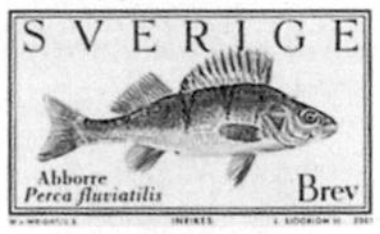

621 Eurasian Perch (*Perca fluviatilis*)

2001. Fish. Illustrations by Wilhelm von Wright from The Fishes of Scandinavia. Inscr "INRIKES Brev". Multicoloured. Self-adhesive.

2169 (5k.) Type **621** 2·30 1·40
2170 (5k.) Bream (*Abramis brama*) 2·30 1·40
2171 (5k.) Four-horned sculpin (*Triglopsis quadricornis*) 2·30 1·40

Nos. 2169/71 were for use on domestic first class mail.

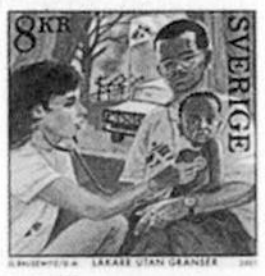

622 Doctors (Medicins sans Frontiers (1999))

2001. Centenary of Nobel Prize (2nd issue). Organizations. Peace Prize Winners. Multicoloured.

2172 8k. Type **622** 3·25 2·50
2173 8k. Relief workers distributing food (Red Cross (1901, 1917, 1944 and 1963)) 3·25 2·50

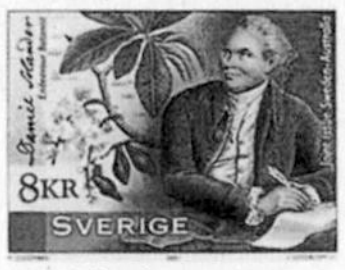

623 Solander

2001. 230th Anniv of Daniel Solander's (botanist) Voyage on H.M.S. Endeavour. Multicoloured.

2174 8k. Type **623** 3·25 2·75
2175 8k. Plant and H.M.S. *Endeavour* 3·25 2·75

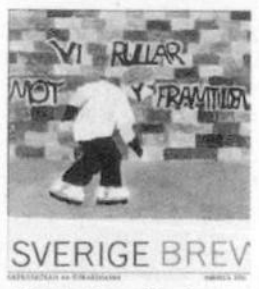

624 Inline Skater and Wall with Graffiti (Emelie Kilstrom)

2001. Design a Stamp Prize Winners. Inscr "BREV INRIKES". Multicoloured.

2176	(5k.) Type **624**	2·30	1·50
2177	(5k.) Letter dropping through letter-box (Thomas Frohling)	2·30	1·50

Nos. 2176/7 were for use on domestic first class mail.

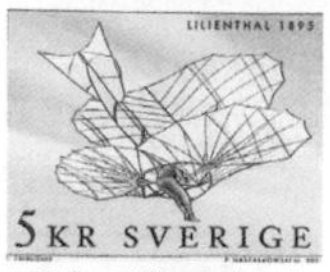

625 Otto Lilienthal and Biplane Glider, 1895

2001. Aviation. Multicoloured.

2178	5k. Type **625**	2·30	1·80
2179	5k. DFS Weihl glider and emblem of Royal Swedish Flying Club	2·30	1·80
2180	5k. SAAB J29, 1962	2·30	1·80
2181	5k. Friedrichshafen FF-49, 1920	2·30	1·80
2182	5k. Nyberg Flugan, 1999	2·30	1·80
2183	5k. Douglas DC-3, 1938	2·30	1·80

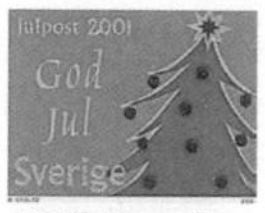

626 Christmas Tree

2001. Christmas. Decorations (2184/9) or Presents (2190/1). Multicoloured. (a) Inscr "julpost" (i) Ordinary gum.

2184	(4k.50) Type **626**	1·90	1·40

(ii) Size 26×20 mm. Self-adhesive.

2185	(4k.50) Star	1·90	1·40
2186	(4k.50) Home-made candy	1·90	1·40
2187	(4k.50) Angel	1·90	1·40
2188	(4k.50) Heart-shaped decoration	1·90	1·40
2189	(4k.50) Cone filled with sweets	1·90	1·40

(b) With face value. Size 26×29 mm. Ordinary gum.

2190	6k. Goat-shaped parcel	3·00	1·80
2191	6k. Christmas tree-shaped parcel	3·00	1·80

Nos. 2184/9 were for domestic first class mail.

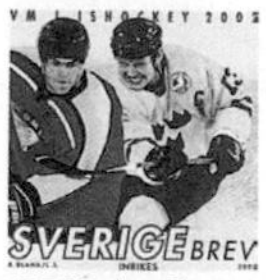

627 Hockey Players

2002. World Ice Hockey Championship, Sweden. Inscr "INRIKES BREV".

2192	**627**	(5k.) multicoloured	2·30	14·50

No. 2192 was for use on domestic first class mail.

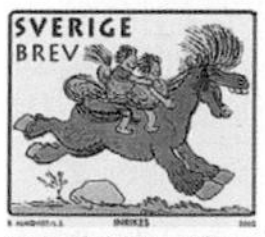

628 Children riding Horse

2002. Year of the Horse. Showing illustrations from Fairhair the Horse (cartoon character) by Bertil Almquist. Multicoloured. Inscr "INRIKES BREV".

2193	(5k.) Type **628**	2·30	1·40
2194	(5k.) Child leading Fairhair	2·30	1·40

Nos. 2193/4 were for use on domestic first class mail.

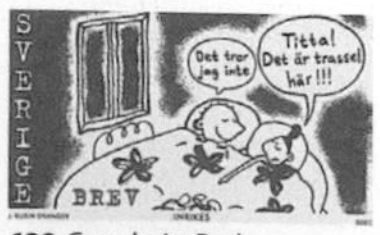

629 Couple in Bed

2002. Illustrations from Love and Miss Terrified by Joanna Dranger (book). Self-adhesive.

2195	**629**	(5k.) pink, mauve and orange	2·30	1·40
2196	**629**	(5k.) mauve, pink and orange	2·30	1·40
2197	**629**	(5k.) orange, mauve and pink	2·30	1·40

Nos. 2195/7 were for use on domestic first class mail.

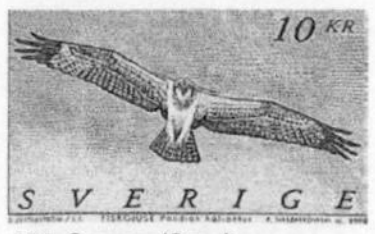

630 Osprey (*Pandion haliaetus*)

2002

2198	**630**	10k. brown and blue	5·25	1·80

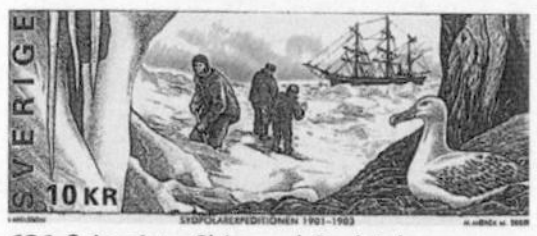

631 Scientists, Ship and Seabird

2002. Swedish Antarctic Expedition (1901–03). Multicoloured.

2199	10k. Type **631**	5·00	3·50
2200	10k. Icebergs, ship and Gentoo penguin	5·00	3·50

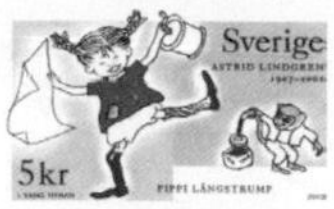

632 Pippi Longstocking (Ingrid Vang Nyman)

2002. Astrid Lindgren (children's writer) Commemoration. Depicting book illustrations by named artists.

2201	**632**	5k. multicoloured	2·75	1·80
2202	-	5k. multicoloured	2·75	1·80
2203	-	5k. multicoloured	2·75	1·80
2204	-	5k. brown and black	2·75	1·80
2205	-	5k. multicoloured	2·75	1·80
2206	-	5k. multicoloured	2·75	1·80
2207	-	5k. multicoloured	2·75	1·80

DESIGNS: No. 2202, Karlsson Pa Taket (Ilon Wikland); 2206, Lotta Pa Brakmakargatan (I. Wikland); 2207, Madicken (I. Wikland). 24×31 mm-No. 2203, Broderna Lejonhjarta (I. Wikland); 2205, Emil I Lonneberga (Bjorn Berg). 27×31 mm—No. 2204, Astrid Lindgren.

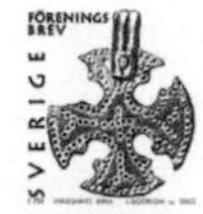

633 Cross (pendant, Birka)

2002. World Heritage Sites. (a) Birka and Hovgarden. (i) Inscr "FORENINGS BREV".

2208	**633**	(3k.80) lilac	2·10	1·30

(ii) Inscr "EKONOMI BREV".

2209	(4k.50) blue	2·30	1·40

(iii) Inscr "INRIKES BREV".

2210	(5k.) brown and mauve	2·75	1·50

DESIGNS: No. 2209, Runic stone, Hovgarden; 2210, Face-shaped pendant, Birka.

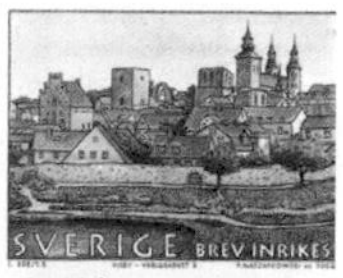

634 Visby

(b) Visby. Multicoloured. Inscr "INRIKES BREV".

2211	(5k.) Type **634**	2·50	1·50
2212	(5k.) Part of town wall	2·50	1·50
2213	(5k.) Burmeister building	2·50	1·50
2214	(5k.) Ruins of St. Catherine's Church	2·50	1·50

No. 2208 was for use on bulk rate mail from societies, No. 2209 was for domestic second class mail and Nos. 2210/14 were for domestic first class mail.

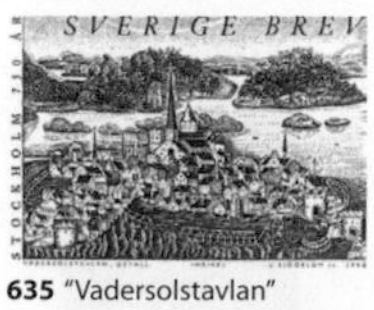

635 "Vadersolstavlan"

2002. 750th Anniv of Stockholm. (a) Inscr "INRIKES BREV".

2215	**635**	(5k.) green and mauve	2·75	1·50

(b) With face value. Size 30×31 mm.

2216	10k. mauve	4·50	3·00

DESIGN: 10k. Stadsholmen Island ("Vadersolstavlan" (detail)).

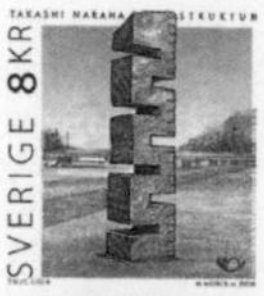

636 "Structure" (Takashi Naraha)

2002. Nordic Countries' Postal Co-operation. Modern Art. Sculptures. Multicoloured.

2217	8k. Type **636**	3·50	2·50
2218	8k. "Sprung From" (Pal Svensson)	3·50	2·50

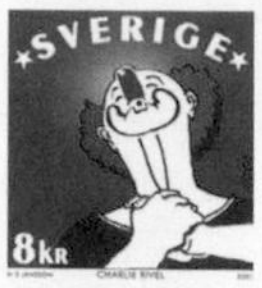

637 Charlie Rivel (clown)

2002. Europa. Circus. Multicoloured.

2219	8k. Type **637**	3·50	2·50
2220	8k. Clown with child (Clowns without Borders)	3·50	2·50
2221	8k. Man in balloon (Cirkus Cirkor)	3·50	2·50
2222	8k. Elephant and rider (Cirkus Scott)	3·50	2·50

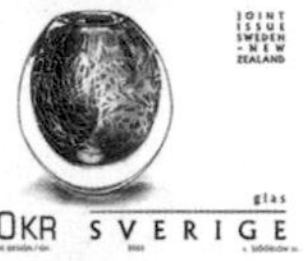

638 "Rain Forest" (glass vase) (Marie and Ola Hoglund)

2002. Artistic Crafts. Joint Issue with New Zealand. Multicoloured.

2223	10k. Type **638**	4·50	3·50
2224	10k. Flax basket (Willa Rogers)	4·50	3·50

Nos. 2223/4 are additionally inscr "JOINT ISSUE SWEDEN–NEW ZEALAND".

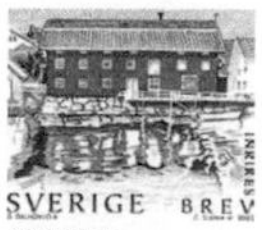

639 Haro Warehouse

2002. Bohuslan Province. Inscr "INRIKES BREV". (a) Ordinary gum.

2225	**639**	(5k.) multicoloured	2·50	1·50

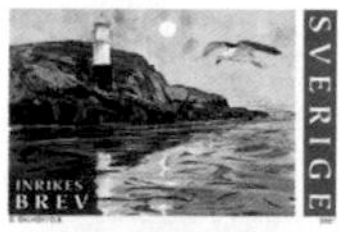

640 Lighthouse and Cliffs

(b) Multicoloured. Self-adhesive.

2226	(5k.) Type **640**	2·50	1·50
2227	(5k.) Lighthouse, rocks and birds	2·50	1·50
2228	(5k.) Yacht and waterfront houses	2·50	1·50
2229	(5k.) Dinghy with outboard engine	2·50	1·50

Nos. 2225/9 were for use on domestic first class mail.

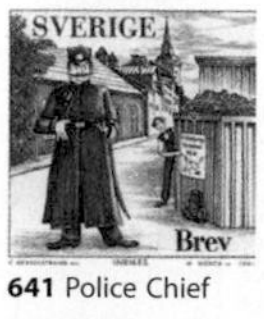

641 Police Chief

2002. Centenary of Gronkopings Veckoblad (satirical newspaper). Inscr "INRIKES Brev". Each blue, buff and red.

2230	(5k.) Type **641**	2·50	1·70
2231	(5k.) Postman	2·50	1·70

Nos. 2230/1 were for use on domestic first class mail.

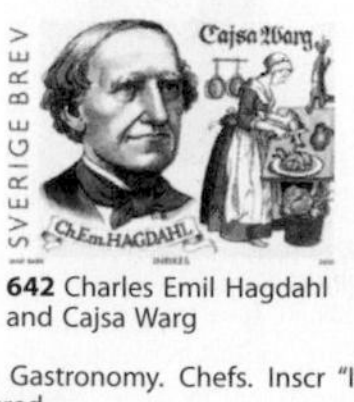

642 Charles Emil Hagdahl and Cajsa Warg

2002. Swedish Gastronomy. Chefs. Inscr "INRIKES BREV". Multicoloured.

2232	(5 k.) Type **642**	2·50	1·70
2233	(5k.) Marit "Hiram" Huldt	2·50	1·70
2234	(5k.) Tore Wretman	2·50	1·70
2235	(5k.) Leif Mannerstrom	2·50	1·70
2236	(5k.) Gert Klotzke	2·50	1·70
2237	(5k.) Christer Lingstrom	2·50	1·70

Nos. 2232/7 were for use on domestic first class mail.

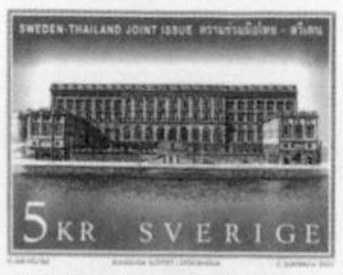

643 The Royal Palace, Stockholm

2002. Palaces. Joint Issue with Thailand. Multicoloured.

2238	5k. Type **643**	3·00	2·30
2239	5k. Dusit Maha Prasat Throne Hall	3·00	2·30

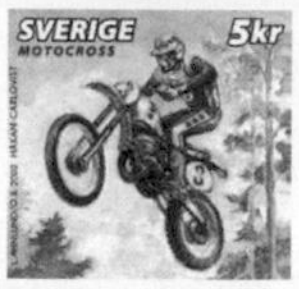

644 Hakan Carlqvist (motocross)

2002. Motorcycle Sports. Multicoloured.

2240	5k. Type **644**	2·50	2·30
2241	5k. Sten Lundin (motocross)	2·50	2·30
2242	5k. Anders Eriksson (enduro)	2·50	2·30
2243	5k. Ulf Karlsson (trial)	2·50	2·30
2244	5k. Ove Fundin (speedway)	2·50	2·30
2245	5k. Tony Rickardsson (speedway)	2·50	2·30
2246	5k. Peter Linden (road racing)	2·50	2·30
2247	5k. Varg-Olle Nygren (road racing)	2·50	2·30

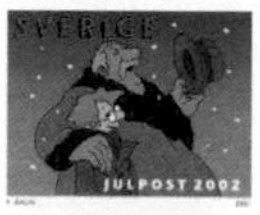

645 Karl-Bertil Jonsson and Father

2002. Christmas. Karl-Bertil Jonsson's Christmas (animated film by Per Ahlin). Scenes from the film. Inscr "julpost" Multicoloured. (a) Ordinary gum.

2248	(4k. 50) Type **645**	2·10	1·50

Nos. 2248/52 were for domestic first class mail.

(b) Self-adhesive gum.

2249	(4k.50) With sack of presents	2·10	1·50
2250	(4k.50) Asleep wearing cap with feather	2·10	1·50
2251	(4k.50) Shaking hands with man	2·10	1·50
2252	(4k.50) Surrounded by family	2·10	1·50

Nos. 2248/52 were for domestic first class mail.

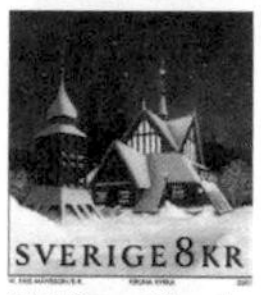

646 Kiruna Church

2002. Christmas. Churches. Multicoloured.

2253	8k. Type **646**	4·00	2·75
2254	8k. Habo	4·00	2·75
2255	8k. Sundborns	4·00	2·75
2256	8k. Tensta	4·00	2·75

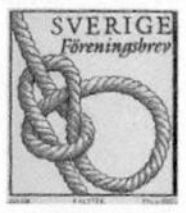

647 Bowline

2003. Knots. Coil stamps. (a) Inscr "Forenings brev".

2257	**647**	(4k.80) green	2·10	1·50

(b) Inscr "Ekonomibrev".

2258	-	(5k.) blue	2·30	1·70

(c) Inscr "Brev inrikes".

2259	-	(5k.50) redon	2·50	1·80

DESIGNS: (5k.) Sheet bend; (5k.50) Reef knot.

No. 2257 was for use on bulk rate mail from societies, No. 2258 was for domestic second-class mail and No. 2259 were for domestic first class mail.

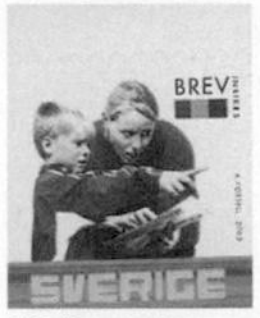

648 Boy and Teacher

2003. Centenary of Swedish Sports Federation. Multicoloured. Self-adhesive.

2260	(5k.50) Type **648**	2·50	1·80
2261	(5k.50) Wheelchair racing	2·50	1·80
2262	(5k.50) Snowboarding and deaf sign for sport	2·50	1·80
2263	(5k.50) Girl running	2·50	1·80

Nos. 2260/3 were for use on domestic first class mail.

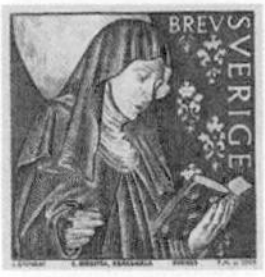

649 St. Birgitta (Bridget) (sculpture) (Johannes Stanrat)

2003. 700th Birth Anniv of St. Birgitta (1st issue). Inscr "INRIKES BREV".

2264	**649**	(5k.50) sepia and scarlet	2·50	1·80

Nos. 2264 was for use on domestic first class mail.

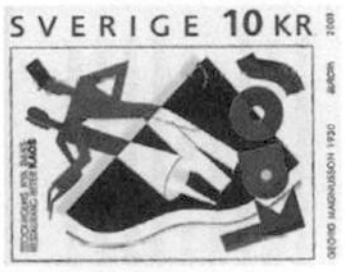

650 "Kaos" (Georg Magnusson)

2003. Europa. Poster Art. Multicoloured.

2265	10k. Type **650**	4·50	3·50
2266	10k. "Biologika Museum" (Carina Lank)	4·50	3·50
2267	10k. "Aerotransport" (Anders Beckman)	4·50	3·50
2268	10k. "Levande Lantbruk" (Owe Gustafson)	4·50	3·50

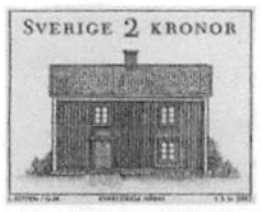

651 Cottage, Narke

2003. Provincial Houses (1st series). Designs from watercolour paintings by Laila Reppen.

2269	**651**	2k. lake, chestnut and green	95	70
2270	-	4k. green, lake and indigo	2·10	1·50
2271	-	5k. sepia, blue and emerald	2·50	1·80

DESIGNS: 4k. Double cottage, Bohuslan; 5k. Hall house, Medelpad.

See also Nos. 2338/40 and 2357/60.

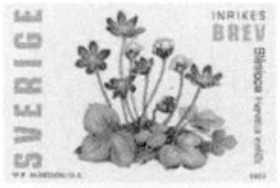

652 Hepatica (*Hepatica nobilis*)

2003. Flowers. Inscr "INRIKES BREV". Multicoloured. Self-adhesive.

2272	(5k.50) Type **652**	2·50	1·80
2273	(5k.50) Cowslip (*Primula veris*)	2·50	1·80
2274	(5k.50) Coltsfoot (*Tussilago farfara*)	2·50	1·80

Nos. 2272/4 were for use on domestic first class mail.

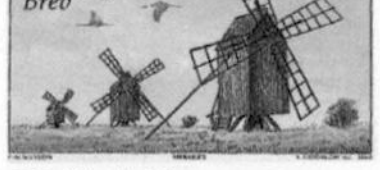

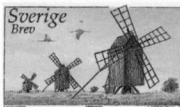

653 Windmills

2003. World Heritage Sites. Oland. Inscr "INRIKES BREV".

2275	(5k.50) Type **653**	2·50	1·80
2276	(5k.50) Stone circle, Stora Alvar	2·50	1·80
2277	(5k.50) Village	2·50	1·80
2278	(5k.50) Sheep grazing coastal wetlands	2·50	1·80

Nos. 2275/8 were for use on domestic first class mail.

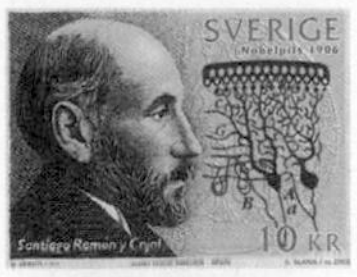

654 Santiago Ramon y Cajal (1906)

2003. Nobel Prize Winners for Medicine. Joint Issue with Spain. Multicoloured.

2279	10k. Type **654**	4·50	3·50
2280	10k. Severo Ochoa (1959)	4·50	3·50

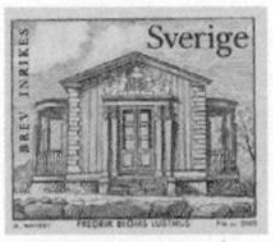

655 Frederik Blom's 19th-century Folly

2003. Garden Follies. Multicoloured. (a) Ordinary gum.

2281	(5k.50) Type **655**	2·50	1·80

(b) Self-adhesive gum.

2282	(5k.50) Emanuel Swedenborg's 18th-century folly	2·50	1·80
2283	(5k.50) Ebba Brahe's folly	2·50	1·80
2284	(5k.50) Raised folly	2·50	1·80
2285	(5k.50) Godegard manor folly, Ostergotland	2·50	1·80

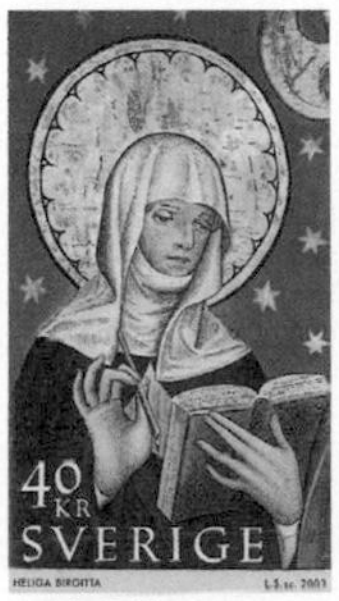

656 St. Bridget

2003. 700th Birth Anniv of St. Bridget. Sheet 94×128 mm.

MS2286 **656**	40k. multicoloured	19·00	17·00

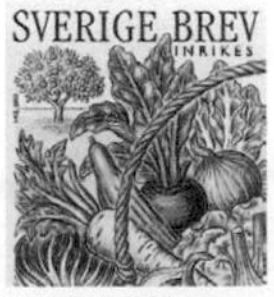

657 Red Cabbage, Parsnip, Cucumber, Beetroot and Onion

2003. Harvest. Multicoloured. Self-adhesive.

2287	(5k.50) Type **657**	2·50	1·80
2288	(5k.50) Melon, apple, raspberries and pumpkin	2·50	1·80
2289	(5k.50) Cabbage, potatoes, carrots and tomato	2·50	1·80
2290	(5k.50) Cherries, strawberries, plums and pear	2·50	1·80

Nos. 2287/90 form a composite design of a basket of fruit and vegetables.

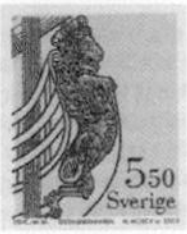

658 Lion (figurehead)

2003. 250th Anniv of Sinking of Gotheborg (East Indiaman). Reconstruction of Gotheborg. Multicoloured.

2291	5k.50 Type **658**	2·50	1·80
2292	5k.50 Interior of hull (44×26 mm)	2·50	1·80
2293	10k. Side elevation (43×53 mm)	4·50	3·50
2294	30k. "Under Sail" (Marc Grieves)	14·50	11·50

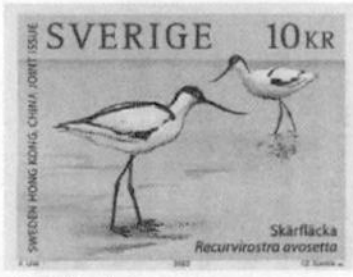

659 Pied Avocet (*Recurvirostra avosetta*)

2003. Water Birds. Multicoloured.

2295	10k. Type **659**	4·25	3·50
2296	10k. Slavonian grebe (*Podiceps auritus*)	4·25	3·50
2297	10k. Black-throated diver (*Gavia artica*)	4·25	3·50
2298	10k. Great crested grebe (*Podiceps cristatus*)	4·25	3·50

Stamps of the same design were issued by Hong Kong.

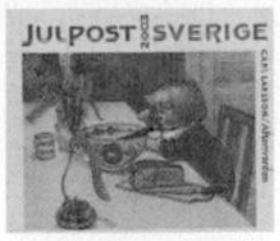

660 "Evening Meal"

2003. Christmas. Birth Centenary of Carl Larsson (artist). Paintings. Multicoloured. (a) Inscr "Julpost". (i) Coil stamp. Ordinary gum.

2299	(5k.) Type **660**	2·20	1·70

(ii) Size 23×27 mm. Self-adhesive.

2300	(5k.) "Esbjorn on Skis"	2·20	1·70
2301	(5k.) "Brita as Idun"	2·20	1·70
2302	(5k.) "Esbjorn"	2·20	1·70
2303	(5k.) "Front-yard and Wash-house" (detail)	2·20	1·70

(b) With face value. Size 27×30 mm. Ordinary gum.

2304	9k. "Martina with Breakfast Tray"	3·75	3·00
2305	9k. "Kersti's Sleigh Ride"	3·75	3·00

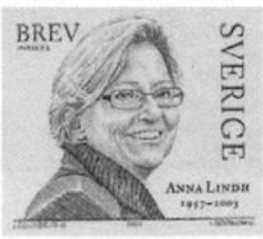

661 Anna Lindh

2003. Anna Lindh (foreign minister) Commemoration.

2306	**661**	(5k.50) purple	2·50	2·00
2307	**661**	10k. indigo	4·50	3·50

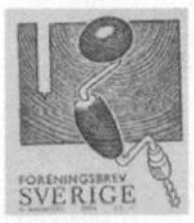

662 Brace and Bit

2004. Woodworking Tools. Coil stamps. (a) Inscr "Forenings brev".

2308	**662**	(4k.80) green	2·30	2·00

(b) Inscr "Ekonomibrev".

2309	(5k.) blue	2·30	2·00

(c) Inscr "Brev inrikes".

2310	(5k.50) red	2·75	2·20

DESIGNS: Saw (5k.); Plane (5k.50).

No. 2308 was for use on bulk rate mail from societies, No. 2309 was for domestic second-class mail and No. 2310 was for domestic first class mail.

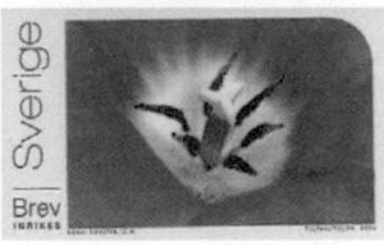

663 Tulip

2004. Flowers. Multicoloured.

2311	(5k.50) Type **663**	2·75	2·20
2312	(5k.50) Lily	2·75	2·20
2313	(5k.50) Hibiscus	2·75	2·20
2314	(5k.50) Amaryllis	2·75	2·20
2315	(5k.50) Zantedeschia	2·75	2·20

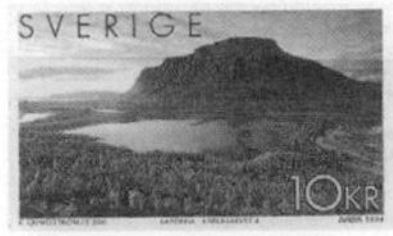

664 Lake and Mountain

2004. World Heritage Sites. Lapona. Multicoloured.

2316	10k. Type **664**	5·00	4·00
2317	10k. Tents	5·00	4·00

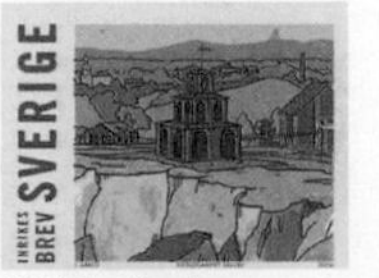

665 Mine Head

2004. World Heritage Sites. Falun. Multicoloured.

2318	(5k.50) Type **665**	2·75	2·20
2319	(5k.50) Water tower and buildings	2·75	2·20
2320	(5k.50) Doorway	2·75	2·20
2321	(5k.50) Miners	2·75	2·20

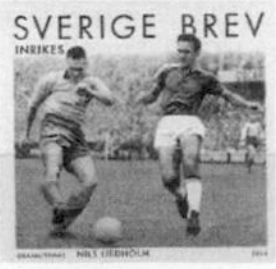

666 Two Footballers (Nils Liedholm)

2004. Centenary of Swedish Football Association. Multicoloured. Self-adhesive.

2322	(5k.50) Type **666**	2·75	2·20
2323	(5k.50) Women players (Hanna Ljungberg)	2·75	2·20
2324	(5k.50) Two players chasing ball (Fredrik Ljungberg)	2·75	2·20
2325	(5k.50) Player with raised arm (Henrik Larsson)	2·75	2·20
2326	(5k.50) Women players tackling (Victoria Svensson)	2·75	2·20
2327	(5k.50) Goalkeeper (Thomas Ravelli)	2·75	2·20

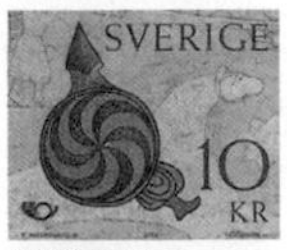

667 Returning Warrior

2004. Nordic Mythology. Sheet 104×70 mm containing T **667** and similar multicoloured design.

MS2328	10k. ×2, Type **667**; Welcoming Valkyrie	9·50	9·00

Stamps of a similar theme were issued by Aland Islands, Denmark, Faroe Islands, Finland, Greenland, Iceland and Norway.

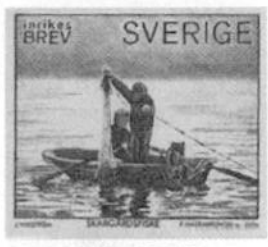

668 Night Fishing

2004. "Northern Light".

2329	**668**	(5k.50) blue	2·75	2·20
2330	-	(5k.50) brown	2·75	2·20

DESIGN: No. 2330 Lighthouse.

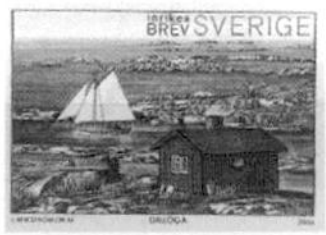

669 Yacht and Hut (Gilloga)

2004. Stockholm Archipelago. Multicoloured.

2331	(5k.50) Type **669**	2·75	2·20
2332	(5k.50) Rowing boat (Lang viksskar)	2·75	2·20
2333	(5k.50) Saltsjon (steam boat) (Stora Nassa)	2·75	2·20
2334	(5k.50) Yacht and lighthouse (Namdofjarden)	2·75	2·20

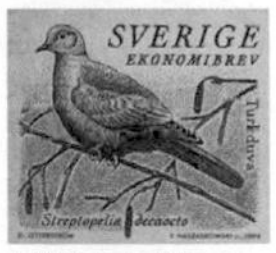

670 Collared Dove (*Streptopelia decaocto*)

2004. Centenary of Swedish Pigeon Society. (a) Inscr "EKONOMIBREV".

2335	**670**	(5k.) blue and agate	2·30	2·00

(b) Inscr "Brev inrikes".

2336	(5k.50) multicoloured	2·75	2·20

(c) With face value.

2337	10k. multicoloured	5·00	4·00

DESIGNS: (5k.50) Swedish tumbler; 10k Wood pigeon (*Columba palumbus*).

No. 2335 was for use on bulk rate mail from societies and No. 2336 was for domestic second-class mail.

2004. Provincial Houses (2nd series). As T **651** showing watercolour paintings by Laila Reppen.

2338	3k. yellow, red and brown	1·50	1·30
2339	6k. red, brown and green	3·00	2·50
2340	8k. deep green, brown and green	4·00	3·25

DESIGNS: 3k. Blacksmith's cottage, Uppland; 6k. Dalstand cottage; 8k. Gotland cottage.

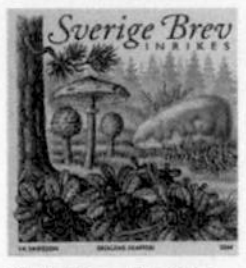

671 Tree, Berries, Fungi and Flowers

2004. Forest Food. Multicoloured. Self-adhesive.

2341	(5k.50) Type **671**	2·75	2·20
2342	(5k.50) Tree stump, butterfly and berries	2·75	2·20
2343	(5k.50) Basket of fungi	2·75	2·20
2344	(5k.50) Flowers, pond, berries and tree	2·75	2·20

Nos. 2341/2 and 2343/4, respectively, form composite designs.

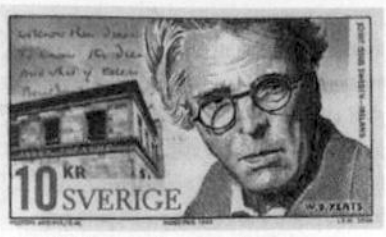

672 William Butler Yeats

2004. Irish Winners of Nobel Prize for Literature. Multicoloured.

2345	10k. Type **672**	5·00	4·00
2346	10k. George Bernard Shaw	5·00	4·00
2347	10k. Samuel Beckett	5·00	4·00
2348	10k. Seamus Heaney	5·00	4·00

Stamps of similar designs were issued by Ireland.

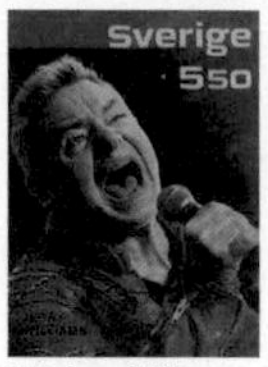

673 Jerry Williams

2004. Rock 54–04. 50th Anniv of "That's alright Mama" (record by Elvis Presley). Multicoloured.

2349	5k.50 Type **673**	2·75	2·20
2350	5k.50 Elvis Presley	2·75	2·20
2351	5k.50 Eve Dahlgren	2·75	2·20
2352	5k.50 Ulf Lundell	2·75	2·20
2353	5k.50 Tomas Leon	2·75	2·20
2354	5k.50 Pugh Rogefeldt	2·75	2·20
2355	5k.50 Maria Anderson (Sahara Hotnights)	2·75	2·20
2356	5k.50 Louise Hoffsten	2·75	2·20

2004. Provincial Houses (3rd series). Designs as T **651** showing watercolour paintings by Laila Reppen.

2357	50ore. blue and black (21×24 mm)	15	15
2358	1k. brown, green and black (31×24 mm)	60	50
2359	7k. black, brown and green	3·25	2·75
2360	9k. black, green and grey	4·00	3·25

DESIGNS: 50ore. Log cabin, Lapland; 1k. Miner's house, Västmanland; 7k. Scanian farm house; 9k. Blekinge cottage.

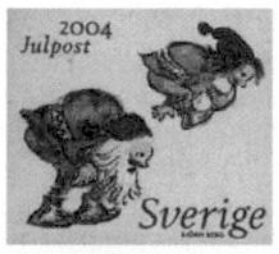

674 Gnomes playing Leap-frog

2004. Christmas. Designs showing gnomes. Multicoloured. Inscr "Julpost". (a) Ordinary gum.

2361	(5k.) Type **674**	2·10	1·80

(b) Self-adhesive gum.

2362	(5k.) Talking on cell phone	2·10	1·80
2363	(5k.) Carrying tree	2·10	1·80
2364	(5k.) Sledding	2·10	1·80
2365	(5k.) Collecting post	2·10	1·80

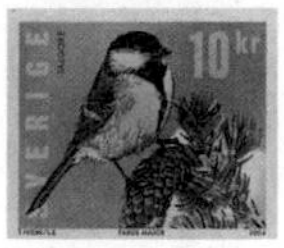

675 Great Tit (*Parus major*)

2004. Winter Birds. Multicoloured.

2366	10k. Type **675**	4·50	3·75
2367	10k. Yellowhammer (*Emberiza citronella*)	4·50	3·75
2368	10k. Pine grosbeak (*Pinicola enucleator*)	4·50	3·75
2369	10k. Bullfinch (*Pyrrhula pyrrhula*)	4·50	3·75

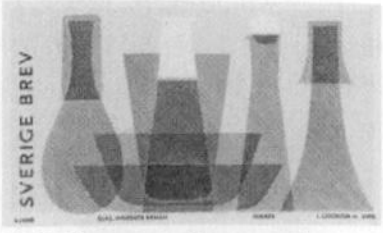

676 Glassware (Ingegerd Raman)

2005. Swedish Design. Self-adhesive. Inscr "INRIKES BREV".

2370	**676**	(5k.50) indigo and azure	2·50	2·10
2371	-	(5k.50) multicoloured	2·50	2·10
2372	-	(5k.50) azure, black and magenta	2·50	2·10
2373	-	(5k.50) azure, black and vermilion	2·50	2·10
2374	-	(5k.50) green and black	2·50	2·10
2375	-	(5k.50) multicoloured	2·50	2·10

DESIGNS: (5k.50)×6, Type **676**; Turn-o-matic ticket machine (Tom Ahlstrom and Hans Ehrich); Welding helmet (Carl-Goran Crafoord); Chair and shelves (John Kandell); Watch (Vivianna Torun Bulow-Hube); Streamliner toy car (Ulf Hanes).

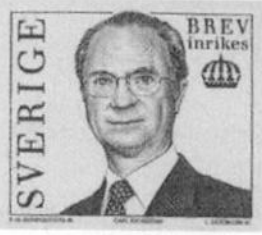

677 King Carl XVI Gustaf

2005. Coil stamps. (a) Inscr "Brev".

2376	**677**	(5k.50) violet and magenta	2·50	2·10

(b) With face value.

2377	10k. agate and brown	4·50	3·75

DESIGNS: Type **677**; 10k. Queen Silvia.

No. 2376 was for use on domestic mail and No. 2377 was for use on international mail.

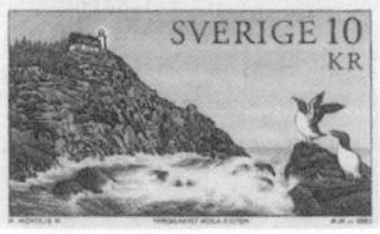

678 Hogbonden Lighthouse

2005. World Heritage Sites. High Coast. Multicoloured.

2378	10k. Type **678**	4·50	3·75
2379	10k. Eagles and cliffs, Storon Nature Reserve	4·50	3·75
2380	10k. Fishing village, Ulvon	4·50	3·75
2381	10k. Lakes, Haggvik	4·50	3·75

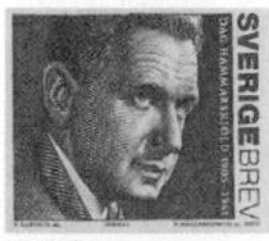

679 Dag Hammarskjold

2005. Birth Centenary of Dag Hammarskjold (Secretary-General of the United Nations, 1953–61). Inscr "INRIKES BREV".

2382	**679**	(5k.50) red-brown	2·50	2·10
2383	-	(5k.50) blue	2·50	2·10

DESIGNS: Type **679**; No. 2383 United Nations emblem.

No. 2382/3 were for use on domestic mail.

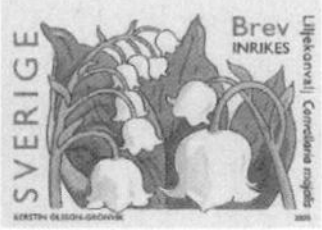

680 Lily of the Valley (*Convallaria majalis*)

2005. Spring Flowers. Self-adhesive. Inscr "INRIKES BREV". Multicoloured.

2384	(5k.50) Type **680**	2·50	2·10
2385	(5k.50) Yellow Star of Bethlehem (*Gagea lutea*)	2·50	2·10
2386	(5k.50) Pasque Flower (*Pulsatilla vulgaris*)	2·50	2·10
2387	(5k.50) Wood Anemone (*Anemone nemorosa*)	2·50	2·10

Nos. 2384/7 were for use on domestic first class mail.

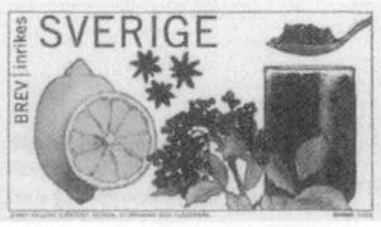

681 Lemon, Star Anise and Elderberry Marmalade

2005. Europa. Gastronomy. Multicoloured.

2388	10k. Type **681**	2·50	2·10
2389	10k. Katja apples, rosemary and Jerusalem artichoke	2·50	2·10
2390	10k. Chives, cheese and beets	2·50	2·10

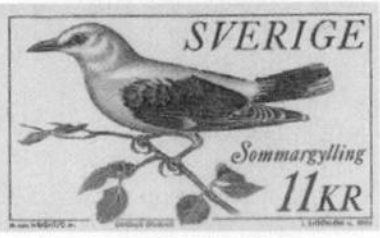

682 Golden Oriole (*Oriolus oriolus*) (Magnus Von Wright)

2005. Birds

2391	**682**	11k. multicoloured	5·00	4·25

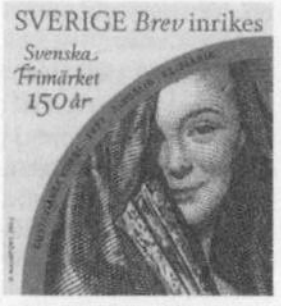

683 "Lady with a Veil" (A. Roslin) (As No. 709)

2005. 150th Anniv of First Swedish Stamp. Inscr "INRIKES BREV". Designs showing details of earlier stamps (Nos. 2392/5). Multicoloured.

2392	(5k.50) Type **683**	2·50	2·10
2393	(5k.50) Numeral (As No. 331)	2·50	2·10
2394	(5k.50) Post rider (As. No. 190)	2·50	2·10
2395	(5k.50) Angelica (As No. 1187)	2·50	2·10
2396	(5k.50) Pehr Ambjorn Sparre (creator of first stamps)	2·50	2·10
2397	(5k.50) Woman reading letter	2·50	2·10
2398	(5k.50) Airplane and train	2·50	2·10
2399	(5k.50) Modern postman	2·50	2·10

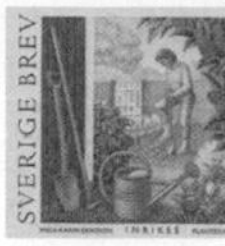

684 Woman digging

2005. Allotments. Inscr "INRIKES BREV". Multicoloured. (a) Ordinary gum.

2400	(4k.50) Type **684**	2·50	2·10

(b) Size 23×26 mm. Self-adhesive.

2401	(5k.50) Man weeding	2·50	2·10
2402	(5k.50) Woman sat at table	2·50	2·10
2403	(5k.50) Woman, basket of vegetables and onions	2·50	2·10
2404	(5k.50) Man watering	2·50	2·10

Nos. 2400/4 were for use on domestic first class mail.

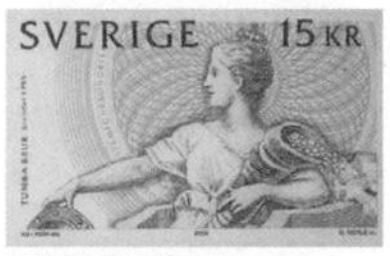

685 Mother Svea

2005. 250th Anniv of Tumba Bruk Bank.

2405	**685**	15k. black, silver and lavender	6·50	5·50

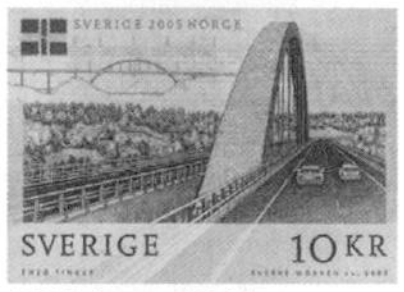

686 Svinesund Bridge

2005. Inauguration of Svinesund Bridge over Ides Fjord (joining Sweden and Norway). Sheet 162×94 mm containing T **686** and similar horiz design. Multicoloured.

MS2406	10k.×2 Type **686**; Bridge from side	8·75	8·50

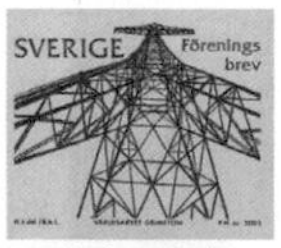

687 Varberg Radio Station, Grimeton

2005. World Heritage Sites. Coil stamps. (a) Inscr "Ekonomibrev".

2407	**687**	(4k.80) violet and green	2·00	1·70

(b) Inscr "Forenings brev".

2408	(5k.) multicoloured (40×23 mm)	2·10	1·80

DESIGNS: Type **687**; (5k.) Skogskyrkogarden cemetery.

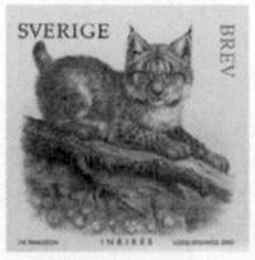

688 Lynx

2005. Animal Cubs. Self-adhesive. Inscr "INRIKES BREV". Multicoloured.

2409	(5k.50) Type **688**	2·50	2·10
2410	(5k.50) Bear	2·50	2·10
2411	(5k.50) Wolf	2·50	2·10
2412	(5k.50) Fox	2·50	2·10

Nos. 2409/12 were for use on domestic first class mail.

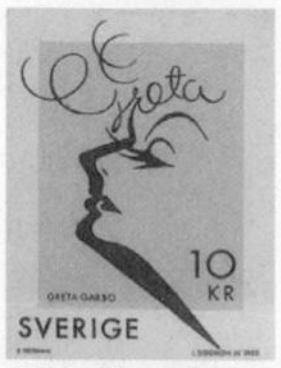

689 Profile and Signature

2005. Birth Centenary of Greta Garbo (actress).

2413	**689**	10k. azure and sepia	4·50	3·75
2414	-	10k. sepia	4·50	3·75

DESIGNS: Type **689**; 10k. Greta Garbo.

Stamps of similar designs were issued by USA.

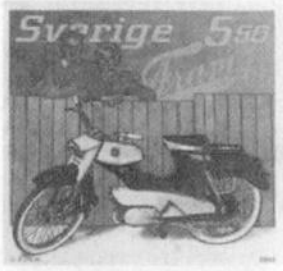

690 Fram-King Moped

2005. Mopeds. Multicoloured.

2415	5k.50 Type **690**	2·50	2·10
2416	5k.50 Husqvarna	2·50	2·10
2417	5k.50 Kuli rear-wheel and engine	2·50	2·10
2418	5k.50 Two mopeds and riders	2·50	2·10
2419	5k.50 Mechanic and moped	2·50	2·10
2420	5k.50 Three-wheel delivery moped	2·50	2·10
2421	5k.50 Frame-hung Zundapp engine	2·50	2·10
2422	5k.50 Modern Peugeot	2·50	2·10

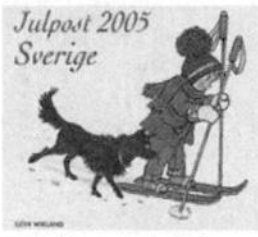

691 Kerstin's Skiing Tour

2005. Christmas. Illustrations by Ilon Wikland from Christmas in Noisy Village by Astrid Lindgren. Inscr "Julpost". Designs showing children. Multicoloured. (a) Ordinary gum.

2423	(5k.) Type **691**	2·10	1·80

(b) Self-adhesive.

2424	(5k.) Opening gate and feeding birds	2·10	1·80
2425	(5k.) Fetching tree on sled	2·10	1·80
2426	(5k.) Wrapping presents	2·10	1·80
2427	(5k.) Children and decorated tree	2·10	1·80

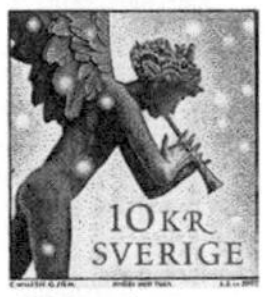

692 Angel

2005. Angel Sculptures by Carl Milles. Each deep blue, blue and red.

2428	10k. Type **692**	4·50	3·75
2429	10k. Playing horn facing left	4·50	3·75
2430	10k. Playing flute	4·50	3·75
2431	10k. Playing crooked horn	4·50	3·75

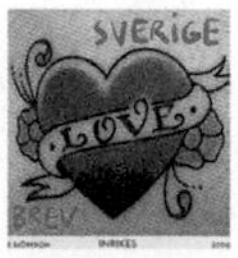

693 Tattooed Heart

2006. St. Valentine's Day. Multicoloured. Self-adhesive. Inscr "INRIKES BREV".

2432	(5k.50) Type **693**	2·50	2·10
2433	(5k.50) Painted heart	2·50	2·10
2434	(5k.50) Heart-shaped leaf	2·50	2·10
2435	(5k.50) Graffiti	2·50	2·10

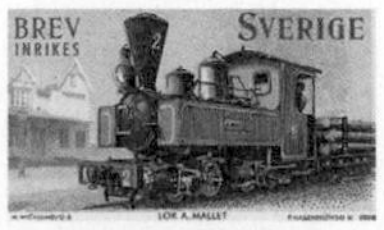

694 Steam Locomotive *A. Mallet*

2006. 150th Anniv of Swedish Railways. Inscr "INRIKES BREV". Multicoloured.

2436	(5k.50) Type **694**	2·50	2·10
2437	(5k.50) Rail bus	2·50	2·10
2438	(5k.50) D electric locomotive	2·50	2·10
2439	(5k.50) R steam locomotive	2·50	2·10

| 2440 | (5k.50) Electric locomotive 1281 | 2·50 | 2·10 |
| 2441 | 10k. Train on viaduct | 4·50 | 3·75 |

695 Coffee Cups

2006. Coffee Drinking. Multicoloured. Self-adhesive. Inscr "BREV".

2442	(5k.50) Type **695**	2·50	2·10
2443	(5k.50) Cafe latte and menu	2·50	2·10
2444	(5k.50) Coffee machine and cup	2·50	2·10
2445	(5k.50) Steam machine	2·50	2·10

696 Skogsraet

2006. Nordic Mythology. Sheet 105×70 mm containing T **696** and similar vert design. Multicoloured.

MS2446 10k.×2, Type **696**; Nacken ... 8·75 ... 8·50

Stamps of a similar theme were issued by Aland Islands, Denmark, Faröe Islands, Finland, Greenland, Iceland and Norway.

697 King Carl XVI Gustaf

2006. 60th Birthday of King Carl XVI Gustaf. Sheet 126×126 mm containing T **697** and similar vert design. slate black (Type **697**) or slate blue (As Type **697**).

MS2447 10k.r.×2, slate black; 10kr.
slate black ... 13·00 ... 12·00
DESIGNS: 10k. Type **697**×2 10k. As Type **697**

698 Stefan Holm

2006. Swedish Track and Field Athletes. Multicoloured. (i) Inscr "FORENINGS BREV".

| 2448 | (4k.80) Type **698** | 2·00 | 1·70 |

(ii) Inscr "BREV".

| 2449 | (5k.50) Carolina Kluft | 2·50 | 2·10 |
| 2450 | (5k.50) Kaja Bergqvist | 2·50 | 2·10 |

(iii) With face value.

| 2451 | 10k. Christian Olsson | 4·50 | 3·75 |

699 Mother and Children paddling

2006. Summer by the Lake. Inscr "INRIKES BREV". Multicoloured. (a) Ordinary gum.

| 2452 | (5k.50) Type **699** | 2·50 | 2·10 |

(b) Self-adhesive.

2453	(5k.50) Women picnicking	2·50	2·10
2454	(5k.50) Man and girl fishing	2·50	2·10
2455	(5k.50) Dog watching swimmers	2·50	2·10
2456	(5k.50) Frog and couple in boat	2·50	2·10

700 Faces (Linda Wong)

2006. Europa. Integration. Winning Designs in Children's Design a Stamp Competition. Multicoloured.

| 2457 | 10k. Type **700** | 4·50 | 3·75 |
| 2458 | 10k. Swedish flag as map (Alexandros Terzis) | 4·50 | 3·75 |

701 Kungsporten and Pojama Class Frigate

2006. Sveaborg Fortress, Suomenlinna—World Heritage Site. Multicoloured.

2459	10k. Type **701**	4·50	3·75
2460	10k. Tenaljen von Fersen and Turkoma class frigate	4·50	3·75
2461	10k. Bastion Hjärne and Udenma class frigate	4·50	3·75

Stamps of the same design were issued by Finland.

702 Musicians (Carl Michael Bellman)

2006. Composers. Coil Stamps. (i) Inscr "FORENINGSBREV".

(ii) Inscr "EKONOMIBREV".

| 2462 | **702** | (4k.80) red, chocolate and blue | 2·00 | 1·70 |
| 2463 | | (5k.) blue, chocolate and vermilion | 2·10 | 1·80 |

(iii) Inscr "BREV".

| 2464 | (5k.50) green, chocolate and vermilion | 2·50 | 2·10 |

DESIGNS: Type **702**; (5k.) Joseph Martin Kraus; (5k.50) Papageno (character from "The Magic Flute") (Wolfgang Amadeus Mozart).

703 Shipping and Trade

2006. 650th Anniv of Hanseatic League. Multicoloured.

2465	10k. Type **703**	4·50	3·75
2466	10k. Visby	4·50	3·75
2467	10k. Stockholm	4·50	3·75

Stamps of a similar design were issued by Germany.

704

705

706

707

708

709

710

711

2006. Children's Television Programmes. Multicoloured.

2468	**704**	5k.50 multicoloured	2·50	2·10
2469	**705**	5k.50 multicoloured	2·50	2·10
2470	**706**	5k.50 multicoloured	2·50	2·10
2471	**707**	5k.50 multicoloured	2·50	2·10
2472	**708**	5k.50 multicoloured	2·50	2·10
2473	**709**	5k.50 multicoloured	2·50	2·10
2474	**710**	5k.50 multicoloured	2·50	2·10
2475	**711**	5k.50 multicoloured	2·50	2·10

712 Santa and Candles

2006. Christmas. Inscr "Julpost 2006". Multicoloured. (a) Ordinary gum.

| 2476 | (5k.) Type **712** | 2·10 | 1·80 |

(b) Size 28×26 mm. Self-adhesive.

2477	(5k.) Star	2·10	1·80
2478	(5k.) Spiced orange and heart	2·10	1·80
2479	(5k.) Bullfinch on fat ball and poinsettia	2·10	1·80
2480	(5k.) Candle bridge	2·10	1·80

713 "Bordelle's Heracles in Snow" (Prince Eugen Napolean)

2006. Winter in Art. Multicoloured.

2481	10k. Type **713**	4·50	3·75
2482	10k. "LelleKalle" (Sven Ljungberg)	4·50	3·75
2483	10k. "Modification of Winter Landscape by W. O. Petersen" (Philip von Schantz)	4·50	3·75
2484	10k. "Rime Frost on Ice" (Gustaf Adolf Fjaestad)	4·50	3·75

714 Heart and Two Birds (Fagelhalsning)

2007. Spring. Inscribed "Inrikes Brev". Multicoloured. Self-adhesive.

2485	(5k.50) Type **714**	2·50	2·10
2486	(5k.50) Sun (Ljusare tider)	2·50	2·10
2487	(5k.50) Flowers, heart and dancer (Varyra)	2·50	2·10
2488	(5k.50) Bird in flight (Kvitter)	2·50	2·10

715 Linnaea borealis (J. W. Palmstruch)

2007. 300th Birth Anniv of Carl von Linné (Linnaeus) (scientist and plant and animal classification deviser) (1st issue). Multicoloured. (a) Inscribed "Inrikes Brev".

| 2489 | (5k.50) Type **715** | 2·50 | 2·10 |

(b) With face value.

| 2490 | 11k. Linnaeus (Gustaf Lundberg) (43×27 mm) | 5·00 | 4·25 |

See also No. **MS**2502.

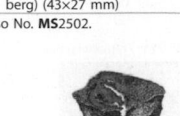

716 "Stenfragment I" (Svenerik Jakobsson)

2007. International Polar Year. Sheet 105×68 mm containing T **716** and similar multicoloured design.

MS2491 10k. Type **716**; 10k. "Arctic Ocean 2001 88° N 145° E" (Johan Petterson) (horiz) ... 8·75 ... 8·00

717 Anna Wallenberg Lifeboat and Modern Rescue Runner

2007. Centenary of Swedish Sea Rescue Society. Multicoloured. (i) Inscr "FORENINGSBREV".

| 2492 | (4k.80) Type **717** | 2·00 | 1·70 |

(ii) Inscr "EKONOMIBREV".

| 2493 | (5k.) Agusta-Bell AB-206 Jet Ranger (Air sea rescue) | 2·10 | 1·80 |

(iii) Inscr "BREV".

| 2494 | (5k.50) Victoria class rescue vessel | 2·50 | 2·10 |

718 Thorsman Plug (Oswald Thorsman) (1957)

2007. Swedish Innovation. Inscr "Ekonomibrev". Multicoloured. Self-adhesive.

2495	(5k.) Type **718**	2·10	1·80
2496	(5k.) "Aloyloben" (Elizabeth Gagnemyhr) (2002)	2·10	1·80
2497	(5k.) "Cool globe" (Birgitta Folker-Sundell) (1997)	2·10	1·80
2498	(5k.) Adjustable spanner (Johan Petter Johansson) (1892)	2·10	1·80

719 "JAMBOREE"

2007. Europa. Centenary of Scouting. Inscr "BREV".

| 2499 | (5k.50) Type **719** | 2·50 | 2·10 |
| 2500 | (5k.50) Scouts | 2·50 | 2·10 |

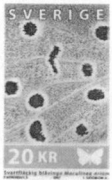

720 Wing (detail)

2007. Large Blue Butterfly (*Myrmica sabuleti*). Self-adhesive.

| 2501 | **720** | 20k. multicoloured | 8·75 | 7·25 |

721 *Musa×paradisiaca*

2007. 300th Birth Anniv of Carl von Linne (Linnaeus) (scientist and plant and animal classification deviser) (2nd issue). Drawings by Georg Dionys Ehret. Sheet 125×94 mm containing T **721** and similar vert design.

MS2502	11k.×2, Type **721**; *Podophyllum peltatum*	10·00	9·00

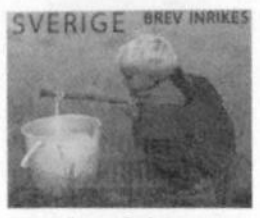

722 Boy fishing in Bucket

2007. Summer Stamps. Fishing. Inscribed 'IRIKES BREV'. Multicoloured. (a) Ordinary gum.

2503	(5k.50) Type **722**	2·50	2·10

(b) Size 38×27 mm. Self-adhesive.

2504	(5k.50) Boy fishing from jetty ('Bryggfiske')	2·50	2·10
2505	(5k.50) Girl kissing fish ('Fiskpuss')	2·50	2·10
2506	(5k.50) Girls each holding fish ('Dubbellycka')	2·50	2·10
2507	(5k.50) Two boys holding rod with fish ('Kompifiske')	2·50	2·10

2007. As T **677**.

2508	11k. ultramarine and green	5·00	4·25

DESIGN: Queen Silvia (as No. 2377).

No. 2508 was for use on international mail.

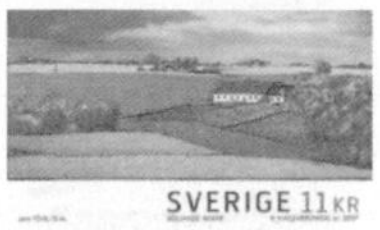

723 Farmhouse and Rape Fields, Skane

2007. Landscapes. Multicoloured.

2509	11k. Type **723**	5·00	4·25
2510	11k. Lake, Muddus National Park, Norrbotten	5·00	4·25
2511	11k. Elk in forest, Sveafallen Nature Reserve, Narke	5·00	4·25
2512	11k. Kallsjon lake, hayfield and huts, Jamtland	5·00	4·25

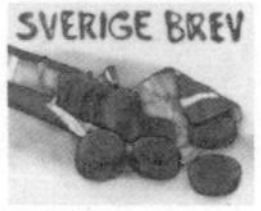

724 Chocolate Sweets

2007. Chocolate. Inscribed 'IRIKES BREV'. Multicoloured. (a) Ordinary gum.

2513	(5k.50) Type **724**	2·50	2·10

(b) Size 28×28 mm. Self-adhesive.

2514	(5k.50) Chocolate cake	2·50	2·10
2515	(5k.50) Chocolate covered strawberry	2·50	2·10
2516	(5k.50) Cocoa beans	2·50	2·10
2517	(5k.50) Cup of hot chocolate	2·50	2·10

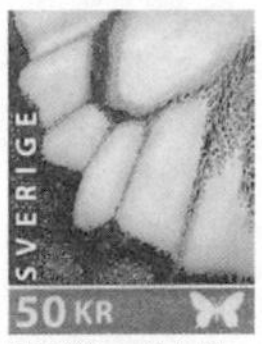

725 Wing (detail)

2007. Swallowtail Butterfly (*Papilio machaon*). Self-adhesive.

2518 **725**	50k. multicoloured	21·00	19·00

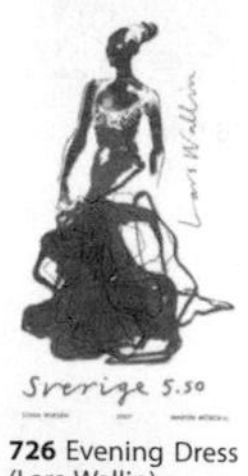

726 Evening Dress (Lars Wallin)

2007. Swedish Fashion Design. Multicoloured.

2519	5k.50 Type **726**	2·50	2·10
2520	5k.50 Wrap jacket (Ann-Sofie Back)	2·50	2·10
2521	5k.50 Halter-neck dress (Katja of Sweden)	2·50	2·10
2522	5k.50 Halter-neck dress (Behnaz Aram)	2·50	2·10
2523	5k.50 Ball gown (Gunilla Ponten)	2·50	2·10
2524	5k.50 Dress with tie-neck and bolero (Carin Rodebjer)	2·50	2·10
2525	5k.50 Coat (Rohdi Heintz)	2·50	2·10
2526	5k.50 Jacket (Nakkna)	2·50	2·10

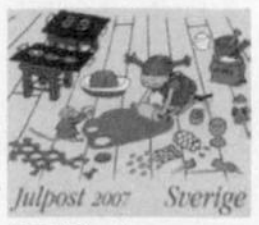

727 Pippi Longstocking making Cakes

2007. Christmas. Inscr 'Julpost 2007'. Multicoloured. (a) Ordinary gum.

2527	(5k) Type **727**	2·10	1·80

(b) Size 28×26 mm. Self-adhesive.

2528	(5k) The Big Red House	2·10	1·80
2529	(5k) Children playing snowballs	2·10	1·80
2530	(5k) Lotta and Christmas tree	2·10	1·80
2531	(5k) Children and sleigh	2·10	1·80

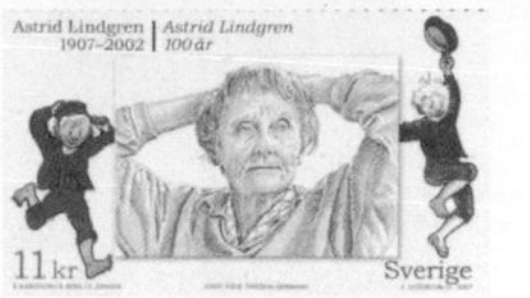

728 Astrid Lindgren and Emil from Lonneberga (character from book)

2007. Birth Centenary of Astrid Lindgren (children's author). Sheet 126×83 mm.

MS2532 **728**	11k. multicoloured	4·50	4·00

A stamp of the same design was issued by Germany.

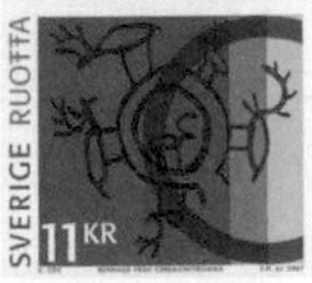

729 Stylized Reindeer and Sami Flag

2007. Sami Culture. Multicoloured.

2533	11k. Type **729**	4·25	3·50
2534	11k. Silver button (designed by Bertil Ahlin)	4·25	3·50
2535	11k. Glass plate (designed by Monica Edmondson)	4·25	3·50

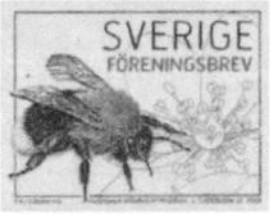

730 *Bombus hypnorum* (bumble bee)

2008. Insects. Multicoloured. (a) Size 30×24 mm. Inscr 'FORENINGSBREV'.

2536	(4k.80) Type **730**	2·00	1·70

(b) Size 30×26 mm. Inscr 'EKONOMIBREV'.

2537	(5k.) *Formica rufa* (ants)	2·10	1·80

(c) Size 30×31 mm. Inscr 'BREV INRIKES'.

2538	(5k.50) *Cocconella septempunctata* (ladybird)	2·50	2·10

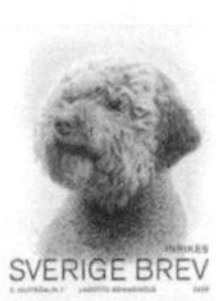

731 Lagatto Romagnola

2008. Dogs. Inscr 'INRIKES BREV'. Multicoloured. Self-adhesive.

2539	(5k.50) Type **731**	2·50	2·10
2540	(5k.50) Saluki	2·50	2·10
2541	(5k.50) Pug	2·50	2·10
2542	(5k.50) Great Dane	2·50	2·10

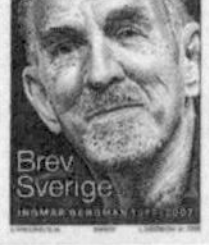

732 Ingmar Bergman

2008. 90th Birth Anniv of Ingmar Bergman (film and theatre director).

2543 **732**	(5k.50) slate	2·50	2·10
MS2544	125×83 mm. 11k. indigo (55×36 mm)	5·00	4·50

DESIGNS: 2543, Ingmar Bergman; **MS**2544, Scene from *Fanny and Alexander*.

No. 2543 was inscribed 'Brev'.

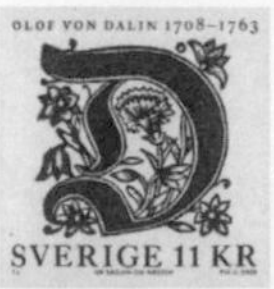

733 'D'

2008. 300th Birth Anniv of Olaf von Dalin (historian and writer). Each black and maroon.

2545	11k. Type **733**	5·00	4·25
2546	11k. Flautist and drover (Title page of *Then Swanska Argus*)	5·00	4·25

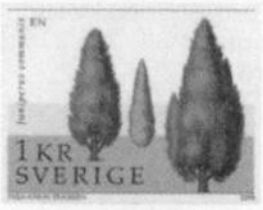

734 *Juniperus communis* (juniper)

2008. Trees. Multicoloured.

2547	1k. Type **734**	50	40
2548	1k. Juniper leaves and berries	50	40
2549	2k. *Betula pendula* (birch)	1·10	90
2550	2k. Birch leaves and catkins	1·10	90

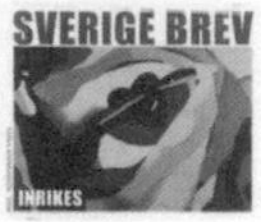

735 Eye

2008. 'Want to see You'. Inscr 'INRIKES BREV'. Multicoloured. Self-adhesive.

2551	(5k.50) Type **735**	2·75	2·40
2552	(5k.50) Eye behind glasses and heart on cheek	2·75	2·40
2553	(5k.50) Eye with heart shaped lashes	2·75	2·40
2554	(5k.50) Eye with heart shaped tears	2·75	2·40

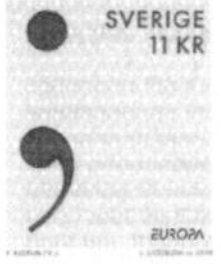

736 Semi-Colon

2008. Europa. The Letter. Each ochre, vermilion and black.

2555	11k. Type **736**	5·00	4·25
2556	11k. Comma	5·00	4·25

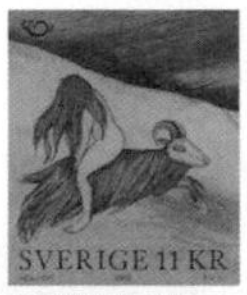

737 Witch riding backwards on Goat

2008. Norse Mythology. Mythical Places. Bakulla (Blue Mountain) (place of witches sabbath). Sheet 105×70 mm containig T **737** and similar vert design. Multicoloured.

MS2557	11k.×2, Type **737**; Bat	10·50	9·50

The stamps and margins of **MS**2557 form a composite design.

Stamps of a similar theme were issued by Aland Islands, Denmark, Faroe Islands, Greenland, Finland, Norway and Iceland.

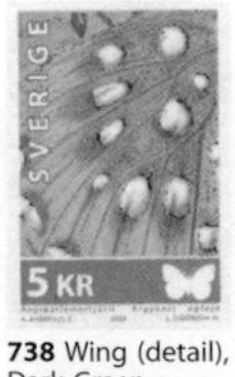

738 Wing (detail), Dark Green Fritillary (*Argynnis aglaja*)

2008. Butterflies. Multicoloured. Self-adhesive.

2558	5k. Type **738**	2·10	1·80
2559	10k. Apollo (*Parnassius apollo*)	4·25	3·50

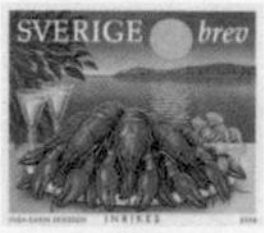

739 Crawfish

2008. Summer Stamps. Summer Tables. Inscribed 'IRIKES BREV'. Multicoloured. (a) Ordinary gum.

2560	(5k.50) Type **739**	2·30	1·90

(b) Size 37×26 mm. Self-adhesive.

2561	(5k.50) Strawberry gateau	2·30	1·90
2562	(5k.50) Fish on barbeque	2·30	1·90
2563	(5k.50) Coffee and pastries	2·30	1·90
2564	(5k.50) Ham, bread and melon	2·30	1·90

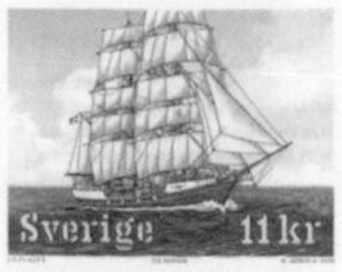

740 *Gunilla*

2008. Sailing Ships. Booklet stamps. Multicoloured.

2565	11k. Type **740**	4·50	3·75
2566	11k. *Tre Kronor af Stockholm*	4·50	3·75
2567	11k. *Gratitude*	4·50	3·75
2568	11k. *Gladan* and *Falken*	4·50	3·75

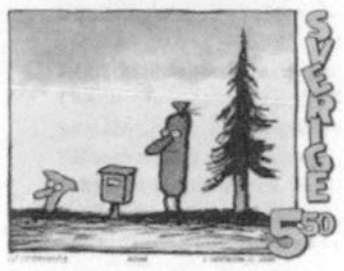

741 *Assar* (Ulf Lundkvist)

2008. Comic Strips. Scenes from comic strips. Multicoloured.

2569	5k.50 Type **741**	2·30	1·90
2570	5k.50 *Ensamma mamman* (Cecilia Torudd)	2·30	1·90
2571	5k.50 *Arne Anka* (Charlie Christensen)	2·30	1·90
2572	5k.50 *Rocky* (Martin Kellerman)	2·30	1·90
2573	5k.50 *nameless gloomy girl* (Nina Hemmingsson)	2·30	1·90
2574	5k.50 *Halge* (Lars Mortimer)	2·30	1·90
2575	5k.50 *Socker-Conny* (Joakim Pirinen)	2·30	1·90
2576	5k.50 *Swedish manga* (Asa Ekstrom)	2·30	1·90

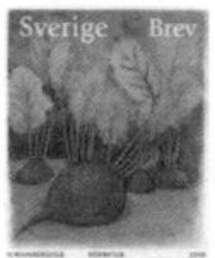

742 Beetroot

2008. Autumn Harvest. Organic Growing. Multicoloured. (a) Size 26×31 mm. Inscr 'Brev'. Self-adhesive.

2577	(5k.50) Type **742**	2·30	1·90
2578	(5k.50) Cabbage	2·30	1·90
2579	(5k.50) Pumpkin	2·30	1·90
2580	(5k.50) Potatoes	2·30	1·90

(b) Inscr 'Brev'. (i) Size 31×27 mm

2581	(5k.50) Apples	2·30	1·90

(ii) Size 31×24 mm.

2582	11k. Carrots	4·50	3·75

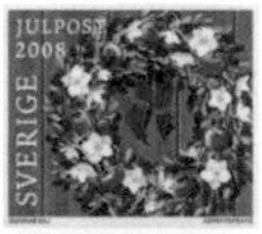

743 Wreath

2008. Christmas Wreaths. Inscr 'Julpost 2008'. Multicoloured. (a) Ordinary gum.

2583	(5k.) Type **743**	2·10	1·80

(b) Size 28×28 mm. Self-adhesive.

2584	(5k.) Heart shaped wreath	2·10	1·80
2585	(5k.) Mistletoe and wheat stems tied with bow	2·10	1·80
2586	(5k.) Red, white and green wreath	2·10	1·80
2587	(5k.) Star shaped wreath with lights	2·10	1·80

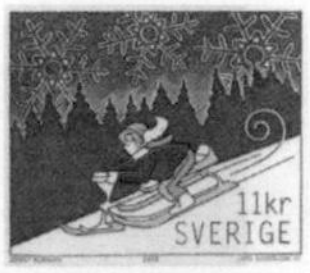

744 Tobogganing

2008. Winter Games. Multicoloured.

2588	11k. Type **744**	4·75	4·00
2589	11k. Snow ball pile and house	4·75	4·00
2590	11k. Making snow man	4·75	4·00

745 Dario Fo

2008. Dario Fo–1997 Nobel Prize for Literature Winner. Sheet 125×83 mm containing T **745** and similar vert design. Multicoloured.

MS2591 11k.×2 Type **745**; Nobel Prize diploma designed by Bo Larsson (34×50 mm) · · · · · · · · 9·50 · 9·00

746 Volkswagen Beetle

2009. Classic Cars. Multicoloured. (a) Inscr 'INRIKES BREV'.
2592 (6k.) Type **746** · · · · · · 2·50 · 2·10
2593 (6k.) Volvo PV 444 · · · · 2·50 · 2·10
2594 (6k.) Cadillac Coupe de Ville · 2·50 · 2·10
2595 (6k.) Citroen DS 19 · · · · 2·50 · 2·10
2596 (6k.) Ford Mustang convertible · 2·50 · 2·10

(b) Coil stamp.
2597 12k. Volvo Amazon · · · · 5·00 · 4·25

747 Mouth

2009. Greetings Stamps. Inscr 'BREV'. Multicoloured. (a) Ordinary gum.
2598 (6k.) Type **747** · · · · · · 2·50 · 2·10

(b) Size 32×26 mm. Self-adhesive.
2599 (6k.) Stylized swans · · · · 2·10
2600 (6k.) Stylized skaters · · · · 2·50 · 2·10
2601 (6k.) Heart-shaped clouds · · 2·50 · 2·10
2602 (6k.) Heart-shaped flowers · · 2·50 · 2·10

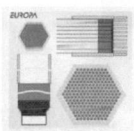

748 Polarimeter

2009. Europa. Astronomy. Multicoloured.
2603 12k. Type **748** · · · · · · 5·00 · 4·25
2604 12k. Crab Nebula and balloon carrying instruments · · · 5·00 · 4·25

749 Holding Envelope

2009. Bananas. Inscr 'BREV'. Designs showing banana-shaped clay figures. Multicoloured. Self-adhesive.
2605 (6k.) Type **749** · · · · · · 2·50 · 2·10
2606 (6k.) Mother and child · · · 2·50 · 2·10
2607 (6k.) Male figure carrying parcel · 2·50 · 2·10
2608 (6k.) Child offering flower to older male figure · · · · 2·50 · 2·10

750 'ONE KINGDOM BECAME TWO LANDS...'

2009. Bicentenary of Sweden–Finland Separation (Two Countries–One Future). Multicoloured.
2609 12k. Type **750** · · · · · · 5·00 · 4·25
2610 12k. Together we are a song... · 5·00 · 4·25

751 Up

2009. 500th Death Anniv of Albertus Pictor (artist). Sheet 105×75 mm containing T **751** and similar vert designs showing part of Wheel of Life (fresco), Harkeberga Church, Stockholm. Multicoloured.

MS2611 12k.×3, Type **751**; Top; Down · 15·00 · 14·50

752 Pandion haliaetus (osprey)

2009. Raptors. Multicoloured. (a) Size 25×33 mm. Inscr 'FORENINGSBREV'.
2612 (5k.) Type **752** · · · · · · 2·10 · 1·80

(b) Size 31×27 mm. Inscr 'EKONOMIBREV'.
2613 (5k.50) Accipiter nisus (Eurasian sparrowhawk) · · · · 2·30 · 1·90

(c) Size 30×32 mm. Inscr 'BREV'.
2614 (6k.) Haliaeetus albicilla (white-tailed eagle) · · · · 2·50 · 2·10
2615 (6k.) Asio flammeus (short-eared owl) · · · · · · · 2·50 · 2·10

753 Sand Star, Kosterhavet

2009. Nature. Inscr 'INRIKES BREV'. Multicoloured. (a) Ordinary gum.
2616 (6k.) Type **753** · · · · · · 2·30 · 1·90

(b) Size 38×26 mm. Self-adhesive.
2617 (6k.) Globe flower, Abisko National Park · · · · 2·30 · 1·90
2618 (6k.) Tree frog, Stenshuvud National Park · · · · 2·30 · 1·90
2619 (6k.) Dormouse, Garphyttan National Park · · · · 2·30 · 1·90
2620 (6k.) Cranberries, Store Mosse National Park · · · · 2·30 · 1·90

754 Braille writing

2009. Through the Eyes of Others. Birth Bicentenary of Louis Braille (inventor of Braille writing for the blind). Sheet 83×125 mm containing T **754** and similar horiz design. Inscr 'INRIKES BREV'. Multicoloured.

MS2621 (6k.)×2, Type **754**; As Type **754** (dull magenta background) · · 4·50 · 4·25

755 Kaknäs Tower, Stockholm

2009. Architecture.
2622 12k. slate grey · · · · · 4·25 · 3·75
2623 12k. agate · · · · · · 4·25 · 3·75
2624 12k. agate · · · · · · 4·25 · 3·75
2625 12k. slate grey · · · · · 4·25 · 3·75
DESIGNS: 2622, Type **755**; 2623, Lugnet ski jump, Falun; 2624, Balder roller coaster, Gothenburg; 2625, Turning Torso, Malmo.

2009. Coil Stamp. As T **677**.
2626 12k. slate green and agate · 4·25 · 3·75
DESIGN: Queen Silvia (as No. 2377).
No. 2626 was for use on international mail.

756 Christer Fuglesang

2009. Journey into Space. Christer Fuglesang—First Swedish Astronaut. Booklet Stamps. Multicoloured.
2627 6k. Type **756** · · · · · 2·30 · 1·90
2628 6k. Space walk · · · · 2·30 · 1·90
2629 6k. Space shuttle Discovery · 2·30 · 1·90
2630 6k. Christer Fuglesang with helmet on lap · · · · 2·30 · 1·90
2631 6k. Christer Fuglesang floating in space (38×38 mm) (rhomboid) · · · · 2·30 · 1·90

757 Ocimum basilicum (basil)

2009. Herbs and Spices. (a) Inscr 'INRIKES BREV'. Multicoloured. Self-adhesive.
2632 (6k.) Type **757** · · · · · 2·30 · 1·90
2633 (6k.) Capsicum (chilli) · · · 2·30 · 1·90
2634 (6k.) Rosmarinus officinalis (rosemary) · · · · 2·30 · 1·90
2635 (6k.) Allium sativum (garlic) · 2·30 · 1·90

(b) Ordinary gum.
2636 (6k.) bronze-green and light green (30×22 mm) · · 2·30 · 1·90
2637 12k. emerald and deep mauve (42×27 mm) · · · 4·25 · 3·75
DESIGNS: No. 2636, Anethum graveolens; No. 2637, Allium schoenoprasum.

758 Parcels

2009. Christmas (a) Inscr 'JUL POST'. Multicoloured. Self-adhesive.
2638 (5k.50) Type **758** · · · · 2·10 · 1·80
2639 (5k.50) Parcels including saw and ball · · · · · 2·10 · 1·80
2640 (5k.50) Parcels including teddy bear · · · · · 2·10 · 1·80
2641 (5k.50) Parcels including train engine · · · · · 2·10 · 1·80

(b) Ordinary gum.
2642 (5k.50) Wax seal (31×33 mm) · 2·10 · 1·80

759 Lagopus muta (ptarmigan)

2009. Snow-White Animals. Each indigo.
2643 12k. Type **759** · · · · · 4·25 · 3·75
2644 12k. Mustela erminea (ermine) · 4·25 · 3·75
2645 12k. Lepus timidus (alpine hare) · 4·25 · 3·75

760 Children of the Forest (written and illustrated by Elsa Beskow)

2010. Europa. Children's Books. Multicoloured.
2646 12k. Type **760** · · · · · 4·25 · 3·75
2647 12k. Maja's Alphabet (written and illustrated by Lena Anderson) · · · · 4·25 · 3·75

761 Cat

2010. Cats. Inscr 'BREV'. Designs showing cats. Multicoloured. Self-adhesive.
2648 (6k.) Type **761** · · · · · 2·30 · 1·90

2649 (6k.) Playing with ball · · · 2·30 · 1·90
2650 (6k.) Angry with arched back · 2·30 · 1·90
2651 (6k.) Stretching · · · · · 2·30 · 1·90

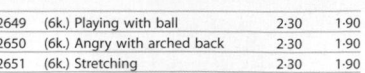

762 Vadstena Castle

2010. Castles and Palaces. Each grey-olive and black.
2652 12k. Type **762** · · · · · 4·25 · 3·75
2653 12k. Ulriksdal Palace · · · 4·25 · 3·75
2654 12k. TjolOholm Castles · · 4·25 · 3·75
2655 12k. LAckO Castle (30×38 mm) · 4·25 · 3·75
2656 12k. Sofiero Palace (30×38 mm) · 4·25 · 3·75

763 Rings

2010. Greeting Stamps. Multicoloured.

(a) Coil stamp
2657 (6k.) Type **763** · · · · · 2·30 · 1·90

(b) Size 38×26 mm. Booklet stamps. Self-adhesive. Die-cut wavy edge
2658 (6k.) Cake · · · · · · 2·30 · 1·90
2659 (6k.) Two birds holding heart · 2·30 · 1·90
2660 (6k.) Hands and 'TRUE LOVE' · 2·30 · 1·90
2661 (6k.) Champagne glasses · · 2·30 · 1·90

764 King Carl XVI Gustav

2010. King Carl XVI Gustav and Queen Silvia
2662 (6k.) blackish olive · · · 2·30 · 1·90
2663 12k. agate · · · · · · 4·25 · 3·75
Designs: Type **764**; 2663, Queen Silvia
No. 2662 is inscribed 'BRFV' and was originally on sale for 6k.

765 Mytilus edulis (blue mussel)

2010. Life at the Coast. Multicoloured.
MS2664 12k.×2, Type **765**; SD 141 Emelie · · · · · · 8·50 · 8·00
Stamps of a similar theme were issued by Denmark, Aland Islands, Faröe Islands, Finland, Iceland, Norway and Greenland.

766 Selenium Crystals

2010. Bicentenary of Karolinska Institute. Each deep mauve and new blue.
2665 (5k.50) Type **766** · · · · 2·10 · 1·80
2666 (5k.50) Silicon · · · · · 2·10 · 1·80

767 Crown Princess Victoria

2010. Wedding of Crown Princess Victoria and Daniel Westling. Each deep blue, grey-blue and silver.
MS2667 6k.×3, Type **767**; Royal monogram; Royal couple (84×126 mm) · 6·75 · 6·50

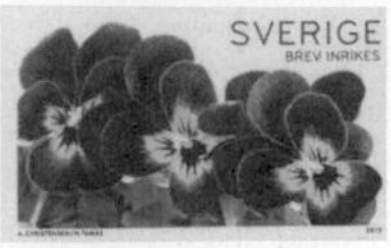

768 Pansies

2010. Greetings Stamps. Multicoloured.

(a) Coil stamp

2668	(6k.) Type **768**	2·30	1·90

(b) Size 29×29 mm. Booklet Stamps. Self-adhesive

2669	(6k.) Yellow pansy	2·30	1·90
2670	(6k.) Blue pansy	2·30	1·90
2671	(6k.) Red pansy	2·30	1·90
2672	(6k.) Multicoloured pansy	2·30	1·90

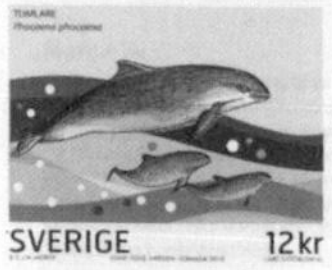

769 *Phocoena phocoena* (harbour porpoise)

2010. Marine Life. Booklet Stamps. Each black, dull ultramarine and turquoise-blue.

2673	12k. Type **769**	4·25	3·75
2674	12k. *Enhydra lutris* (sea otter)	4·25	3·75
2675	12k. *Balaenoptera musculus* (blue whale)	4·25	3·75
2676	12k. *Pusa hispida* (ringed seal)	4·25	3·75

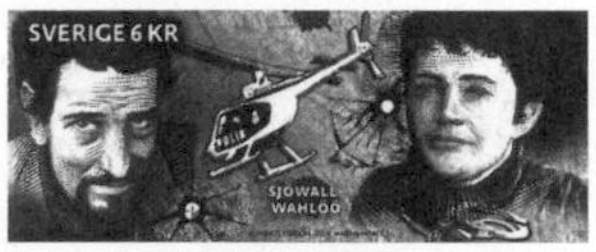

770 Maj Sjöwall and Per Wahlöö

2010. Crime Writers. Multicoloured.

2677	6k. Type **770**	2·50	2·10
2678	6k. Henning Mankell	2·50	2·10
2679	6k. Liza Marklund	2·50	2·10
2680	6k. Håkan Nesser (33×30 mm)	2·50	2·10
2681	6k. Steig Larsson (33×30 mm)	2·50	2·10

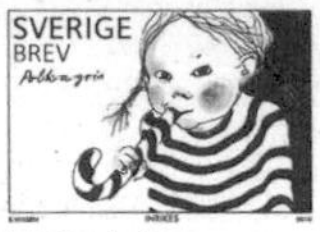

771 Candy Cane

2010. Local Foods

(a) Booklet stamps. Self-adhesive. Die-cut wavy edge

2682	(6k.) multicoloured	2·30	1·90
2683	(6k.) multicoloured	2·30	1·90
2684	(6k.) multicoloured	2·30	1·90
2685	(6k.) multicoloured	2·30	1·90

(b) Coil stamps.

2686	(6k.) yellow-brown and yellow-orange (31×27 mm)	2·30	1·90
2687	12k. deep brown and buff (44×27 mm)	4·25	3·75

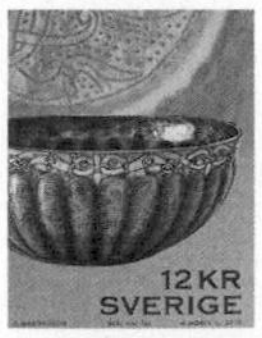

772 Bowl

2010. Art of Engraving. Multicoloured.

MS2688	12k.×3, Type **772**; Armour; Anneli Alhanko and Per-Arthur Segerström in *Romeo and Juliet* (As No. 850)	14·50	14·00

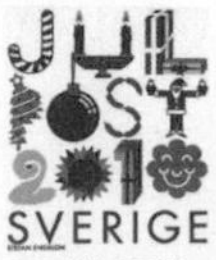

773 'JUL POST 2010'

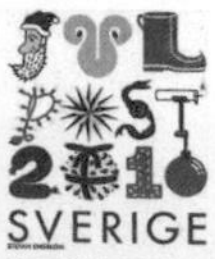

774 'JUL POST 2010'

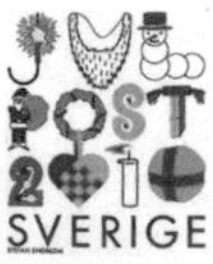

775 'JUL POST 2010'

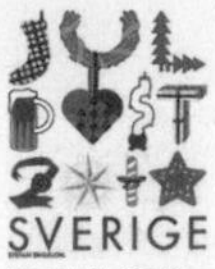

776 'JUL POST 2010'

2010. Christmas. Booklet Stamps

2689	**773**	(55c.) multicoloured	2·30	1·90
2690	**774**	(55c.) multicoloured	2·30	1·90
2691	**775**	(55c.) multicoloured	2·30	1·90
2692	**776**	(55c.) multicoloured	2·30	1·90

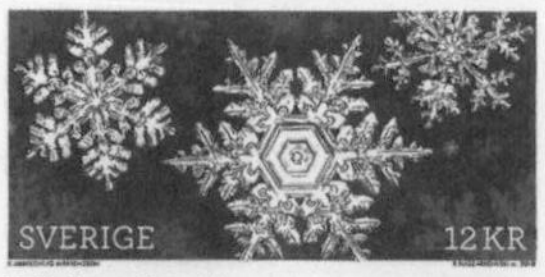

777 Snow Crystals

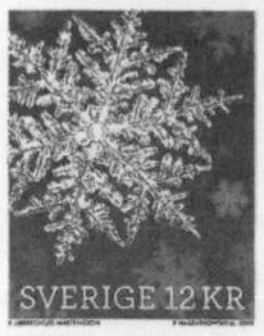

778 Snow Crystal

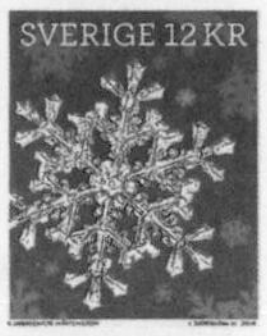

779 Snow Crystal

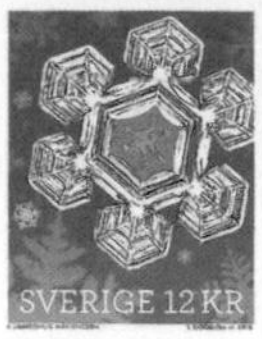

780 Snow Crystal

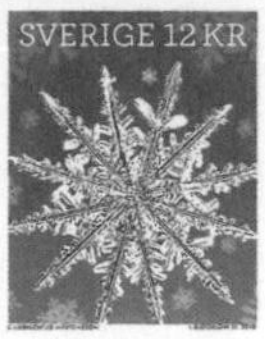

781 Snow Crystal

2010. Snow Crystals. Booklet Stamps

2693	**777**	12k. multicoloured	4·75	4·00
2694	**778**	12k. multicoloured	4·75	4·00
2695	**779**	12k. multicoloured	4·75	4·00
2696	**780**	12k. multicoloured	4·75	4·00
2697	**781**	12k. multicoloured	4·75	4·00

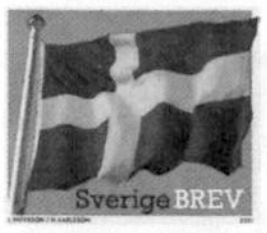

782 National Flag

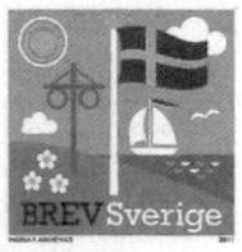

783 Flag at Lakeside

2011. Blue and Yellow (Swedish colours). Multicoloured.

(a) Coil Stamp. Ordinary gum

2698	(60c.) Type **782**	2·30	1·90

(b) Booklet stamps. Self-adhesive

2699	(60c.) Type **783**	2·30	1·90
2700	(60c.) Arms waving flags	2·30	1·90
2701	(60c.) Child exclaiming 'Heja' (Hurrah)	2·30	1·90
2702	(60c.) Flag from vehicle	2·30	1·90

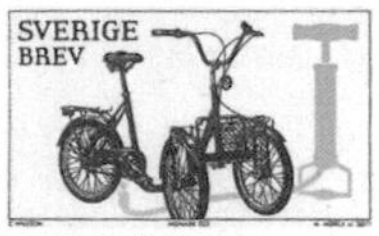

784 Monark 523 Three-wheeler

2011. Bicycles. Booklet Stamps. Each steel blue, bright mauve and grey.

2703	(60c.) Type **784**	2·30	1·90
2704	(60c.) Crescent's folding bicycle	2·30	1·90
2705	(60c.) Women's tourer	2·30	1·90
2706	(60c.) City bicycle	2·30	1·90
2707	(60c.) Child's tricycle	2·30	1·90

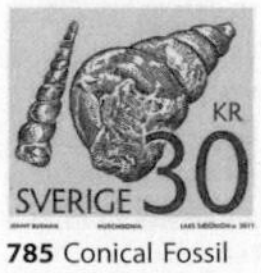

785 Conical Fossil

2011. Fossils. Multicoloured.

2708	30k. Type **785**	12·00	10·00
2709	40k. Ammonite (32×30 mm)	16·00	13·50

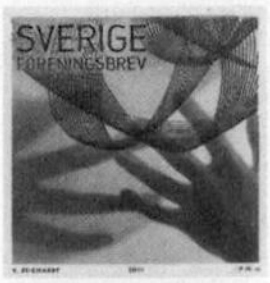

786 Hand and Web

2011. Networks. Multicoloured.

2710	FORENINGSBREV (5k.) Type **786**	2·10	1·80
2711	FORENINGSBREV (5k.) Hand, at left, and web (red)	2·10	1·80

Nos. 2710/1 are inscribed 'FORENINGSBREV' and were originally on sale for 5k.

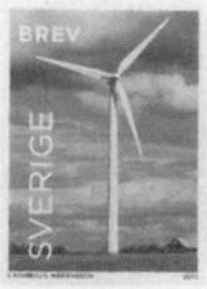

787 Wind Turbine

2011. Renewable Energy. Multicoloured.

(a) Coil Stamp

2712	BREV (6k.) Type **787**	2·30	1·90

(b) Booklet Stamps. Size 33×22 mm. Self-adhesive

2713	BREV (6k.) Cloud, sun and solar panels	2·30	1·90
2714	BREV (6k.) Grasses and wind turbine	2·30	1·90
2715	BREV (6k.) Bio-energy generator and trees	2·30	1·90
2716	BREV (6k.) Wave power collectors and sea bed	2·30	1·90

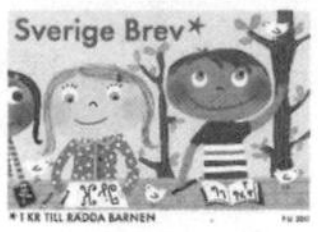

788 Girl and Boy with raised Arm

2011. Save the Children. Charity Stamps. Multicoloured.

2717	Brev (6k.+1k.) Type **788**	2·75	2·40
2718	Brev (6k.+1k.) Dark haired girl with slate, boy writing and girl reading	2·75	2·40

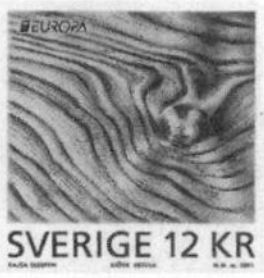

789 Section of Birch Tree (Betula)

2011. Europa. Forests. Multicoloured.

2719	12k. Type **789**	4·75	4·00
2720	12k. Section of spruce tree (*Pica abies*)	4·75	4·00

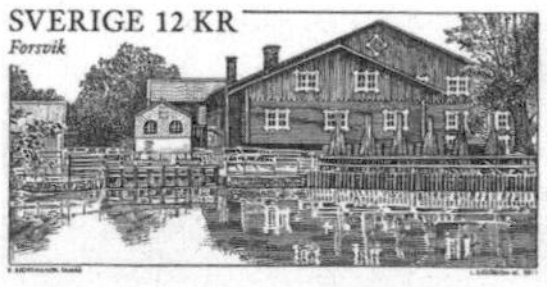

790 Forsvik

2011. Industrial Heritage. Mills

2721	12k. black and reddish brown	4·75	4·00
2722	12k. black and reddish brown (27×35 mm)	4·75	4·00
2723	12k. black and deep brown (27×35 mm)	4·75	4·00
2724	12k. black and reddish brown (27×35 mm)	4·75	4·00
2725	12k. black and reddish brown (27×35 mm)	4·75	4·00

Designs: 2721, Type **790**; 2722, Glass blower, Glasriket; 2723, Chimney and arched windows, Avesta; 2724, Chimney, building and bridge, Jonsered; 2725, Mackmyra Mill

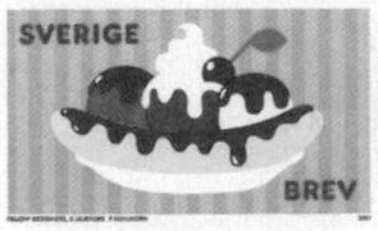

791 Banana Split

2011. Greetings Stamps. Ice Cream. Multicoloured.

(a) Coil Stamp

2726	Type **791**	2·30	1·90

(b) Booklet Stamps. Size 25×26 mm. Self-adhesive

2727	BREV (6k.) Pink lolly with ice cream filling	2·30	1·90
2728	BREV (6k.) Ice cream cone	2·30	1·90
2729	BREV (6k.) Tub with cherries	2·30	1·90
2730	BREV (6k.) Chocolate topped vanilla cone	2·30	1·90

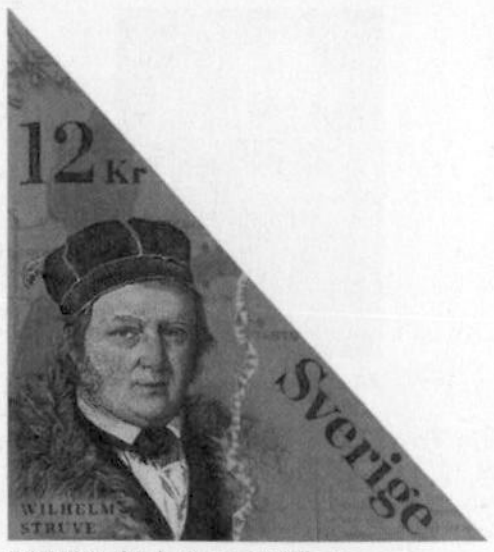

792 Friedrich Georg Wilhelm von Struve

2011. Struve Geodetic Arc. UNESCO World Heritage Site. Multicoloured.

MS2731	12k.×2, Type **792**; Theodolite	9·50	9·00

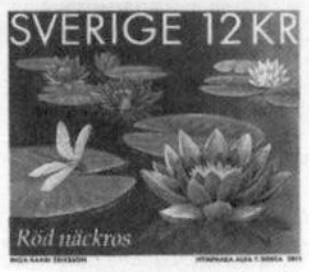

793 Red Waterlily

2011. Waterlilies. Booklet Stamps. Multicoloured.

2732	12k. Type **793**	4·25	3·75
2733	12k. Dragonfly and waterlilies	4·25	3·75
2734	12k. Single yellow flower	4·25	3·75
2735	12k. Single white flower	4·25	3·75

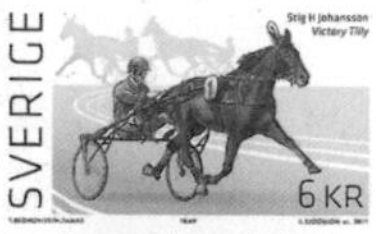

794 Victory Tilly and Stig H. Johansson (harness racing)

2011. Equestrian Sports. Booklet Stamps. Multicoloured.

2736	**777**	6k. Type **794**	2·75	2·20
2737	**778**	6k. Butterfly Flip and Malin Baryard-Johnsson (show jumping)	2·75	2·20
2738	**779**	6k. Norrskenets Grim and Ebba Stigenberg (pony racing)	2·75	2·20
2739	**780**	6k. Briar and Jan Brink (dressage)	2·75	2·20
2740	**781**	6k. Gaston KLG and Hannes Melin (eventing)	2·75	2·20

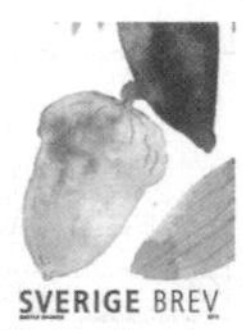

795 Seed Capsules

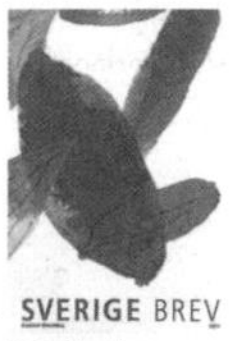

796 Seed Capsules

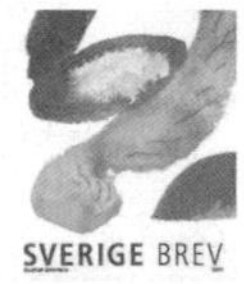

797 Seed Capsules

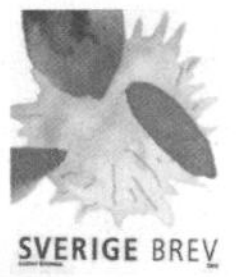

798 Seed Capsules

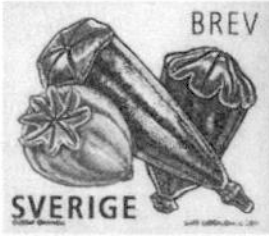

799 Poppy Seeds

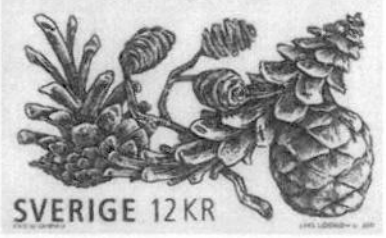

800 Cones

2011. Seed Capsules

(b) Booklet Stamps. Size 27×32 mm. Self-adhesive

2741	**795**	BREV (6k.) multicoloured	2·75	2·20
2742	**796**	BREV (6k.) multicoloured	2·75	2·20
2743	**797**	BREV (6k.) multicoloured	2·75	2·20
2744	**798**	BREV (6k.) multicoloured	2·75	2·20

(a) Coil Stamp

2745	**799**	BREV (6k.) multicoloured	2·75	2·20
2746	**800**	12k. multicoloured	5·25	4·50

2011. Christmas Flowers. Booklet Stamps. Multicoloured.

2747	JULPOST (5k.50) Type **801**	2·30	1·90
2748	JULPOST (5k.50) *Euphorbia pulcherrima*	2·30	1·90
2749	JULPOST (5k.50) *Hippeastrum x hortorum*	2·30	1·90
2750	JULPOST (5k.50) *Helleborus niger*	2·30	1·90

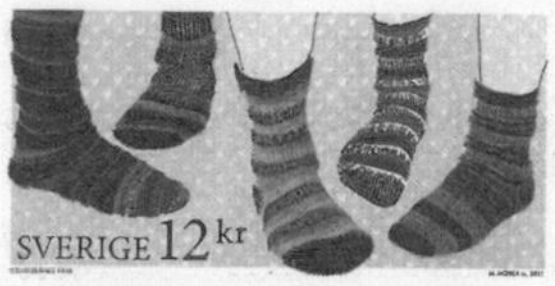

802 Socks

2011. Patterned Knitting. Booklet Stamps

2751	12k. Hat (32×27 mm)	4·75	4·00
2752	12k. Scarf (32×27 mm)	4·75	4·00
2753	12k. Green sweater (32×27 mm)	4·75	4·00
2754	12k. Mittens (32×27 mm)	4·75	4·00
2755	12k. Type **802**	4·75	4·00

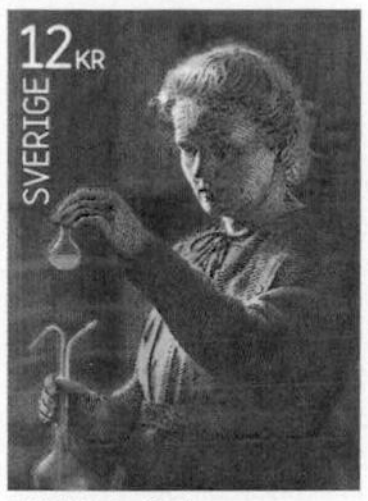

803 Marie Curie

2011. Centenary of Marie Skłodowska Curie's Nobel Prize for Chemistry

MS2756 12k.×2, Type **803**; Nobel medal (40×55 mm) 9·50 9·00

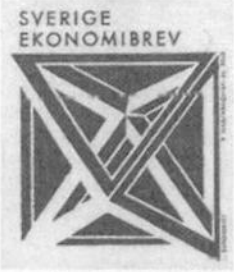

804 Octahedron

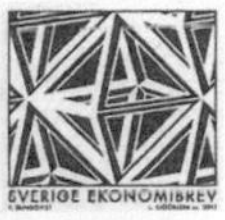

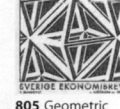

805 Geometric Figure

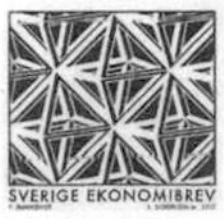

806 Geometric Figure

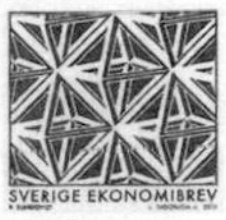

807 Geometric Figure

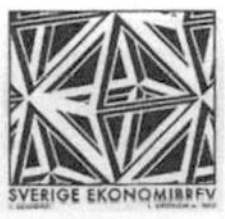

808 Geometric Figure

2012. Geometric Figures

(a) Coil Stamp

2757	**804**	(5K.50) emerald	2·30	1·90

(b) Booklet Stamps. Size 33×22 mm. Self-adhesive

2758	**805**	(5k.50) deep blue	2·30	1·90
2759	**806**	(5k.50) vermilion	2·30	1·90
2760	**807**	(5k.50) deep blue	2·30	1·90
2761	**808**	(5k.50) vermilion	2·30	1·90

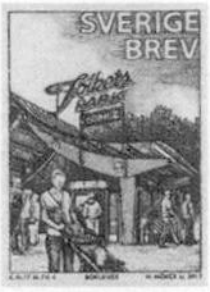

809 Families entering People's Park, Borlänge

2012. People's Parks

(a) Coil Stamp

2762	BREV (6k.) reddish violet	2·50	2·10

(b) Booklet Stamps. Size 37×27 mm. Self-adhesive

2763	BREV (6k.) dull ultramarine	2·50	2·10
2764	BREV (6k.) cerise	2·50	2·10
2765	BREV (6k.) dull ultramarine	2·50	2·10
2766	BREV (6k.) cerise	2·50	2·10

Designs: Type **809**; Families entering People's Park, Björneborg (Pori); Dancers, Arvika; Lill-Babs (Barbro Svensson); Chocolate wheel, Kolsnäs

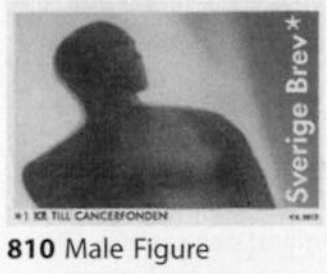

810 Male Figure

2012. Swedish Cancer Society. Charity Stamps. Booklet Stamps. Multicoloured.

2767	Brev (6k.+1k.) Type **810**	2·75	2·40
2768	Brev (6k.+1k.) Ripples	2·75	2·40

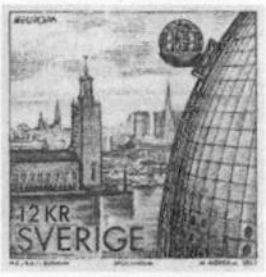

811 Globe and Cityscape, Stockholm

2012. Europa. Visit Sweden. Coil Stamps. Multicoloured.

2769	12k. Type **811**	4·75	4·00
2770	12k. Lake and houses, Dalarna	4·75	4·00

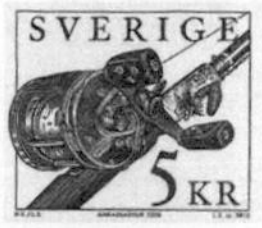

812 Ambassadeur 5000 Fishing Reel

2012. Fishing. 90th (2011) Anniv of ABU Garcia, Svängsta (fishing equipment developer and manufacturer). Coil Stamps

2771	5k. deep carmine-red and black	2·10	1·80
2772	10k. emerald and black (30×30 mm)	4·25	3·50
2773	20k. orange-brown, emerald and black (36×30 mm)	8·25	7·00

Designs: 5k. Type **812**; 10k. Salmon fly; 20k. Toby spoon spinner and Hi-Lo wobbler bait hooks

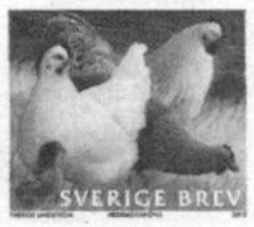

813 Hedemora Hens

2012. Swedish Poultry. Booklet Stamps. Multicoloured.

2774	BREV (6k.) Type **813**	2·50	2·10
2775	BREV (6k.) Old Swedish Dwarf cockerel and hens	2·50	2·10
2776	BREV (6k.) Swedish Spotted cockerel and hen	2·50	2·10
2777	BREV (6k.) Orust cockerel and hen	2·50	2·10

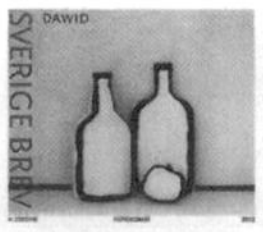

814 Still Life (Dawid (Björn Dawidsson))

2012. Fine Art Photography. Multicoloured.

(a) Coil Stamp

2778	BREV (6k.) Type **814**	2·30	1·90

(b) Booklet Stamps. Self-adhesive

2779	12k. Leaf in glass (Gunnar Smoliansky) (30×38 mm)	5·00	4·25
2780	12k. Woman in water wearing flowered hat (Denise Grünstein) (30×38 mm)	5·00	4·25
2781	12k. Woman clasping large balloon (Annika von Hausswolff) (30×38 mm)	5·00	4·25
2782	12k. Kissing (Christer Strömholm) (30×38 mm)	5·00	4·25
2783	12k. 'Dreamer in the Blue House', bachelor and Esperantist Johan Engman (Sune Jonsson) (63×32 mm)	5·00	4·25

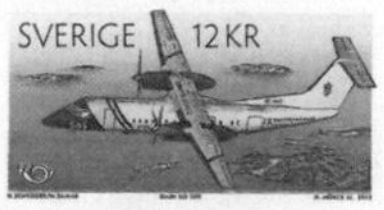

815 Bombardier Dash 8Q-300

2012. Life at the Coast. Multicoloured.

MS2784 12k.×2, Type **815**; Häradskär lighthouse and *Arkö* 833 (pilot boat) 10·00 9·50

Stamps of a similar theme were issued by Denmark, Aland Islands, Faröe Islands, Finland, Iceland, Norway and Greenland.

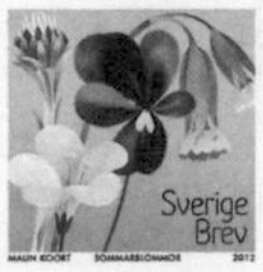

816 Meadow Flowers

2012. Meadow Flowers. Multicoloured.

(a) Coil Stamp

2785	BREV (6k.) Type **816**	2·50	2·10

(b) Size 29×29 mm. Booklet Stamps. Self-adhesive

2786	BREV (6k.) Cowslip	2·50	2·10
2787	BREV (6k.) Hairy Violet	2·50	2·10
2788	BREV (6k.) Catsfoot (*Antennaria dioica*)	2·50	2·10
2789	BREV (6k.) Meadow Saxifrage ('Mandelblommaa')	2·50	2·10

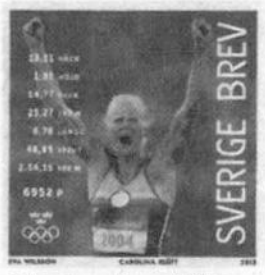

817 Carolina Klüft (heptathlon gold medalist, 2004 Olympic Games, Athens)

2012. Swedish Gold Medal Olympians. Coil Stamps. Multicoloured.

2790	BREV (6k.) Type **811**	2·50	2·10
2791	BREV (6k.) Ragnar Skanåker (pistol shooting gold medalist, 1972 Olympic Games, Munich)	2·50	2·10
2792	12k. Eric Lemming (javelin gold medallist, 1912 Olympic Games, Stockholm) (43×28 mm)	5·00	4·25

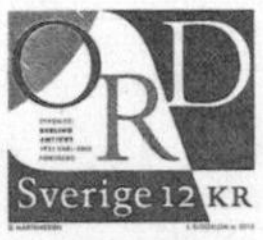

818 Berling Antiqua Font (Karl-Frik Forsberg)

2012. Swedish Designed Type Fonts

2793	12k. deep turquoise blue	5·00	4·25
2794	12k. deep turquoise blue	5·00	4·25
2795	12k. yellowish green	5·00	4·25
2796	12k. deep turquoise blue, yellowish green andreddish lilac	5·00	4·25
2797	12k. reddish lilac	5·00	4·25

Designs: 2793, Type **818**; 2794, Indigo Antiqua (Johan Ström); 2795, Sispos (Bo Berndal); 2796, Satura (Göran Söderström and Peter Bruhn); 2797, Tratic (Tom Hultgren)

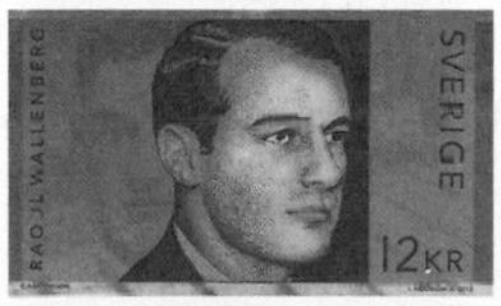

819 Raoul Wallenberg

2012. Birth Centenary of Raoul Wallenberg (saviour of thousands of Budapest Jews during WWII). Sheet 84×125 mm

MS2798 **819** 12k. multicoloured 5·00 4·75

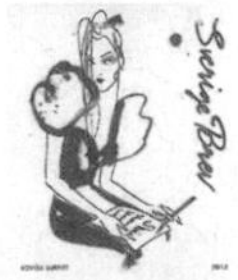

820 Girl writing

2012. Write! Booklet Stamps. Multicoloured.

2799	BREV (6k.) Type **820**	2·50	2·10
2800	BREV (6k.) Writing under lamp wearing green top	2·50	2·10
2801	BREV (6k.) Writing on laptop	2·50	2·10
2802	BREV (6k.) Red haired girl with head in hand wearing blue top	2·50	2·10

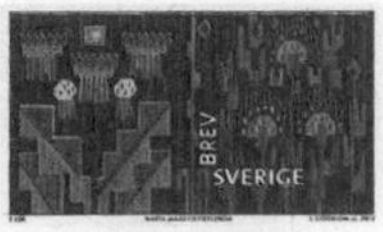

821 *June Flowers* (Märta Måås-Fjetterström)

2012. Textiles. Booklet Stamps. Multicoloured.

2803	BREV (6k.) Type **821**	2·50	2·10
2804	BREV (6k.) *Hommage à tuskaft* (Laris Stunke)	2·50	2·10
2805	BREV (6k.) *Ooomph* (Viola Gråsten)	2·50	2·10
2806	BREV (6k.) *Peace in the valley-at last* (Teresa Oscarsson)	2·50	2·10
2807	BREV (6k.) Lennart Rodhe	2·50	2·10

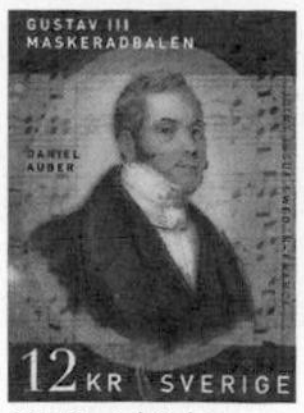

822 Daniel Auber

2012. Opera - *Gustav III*, or *The Masked Ball* (music by Daniel Auber, libretto by Eugène Scribe). Multicoloured.

MS2808 12k.×2, Type **822**; Olof Westring, principal dancer, in the role of Gustav III 10·00 9·50

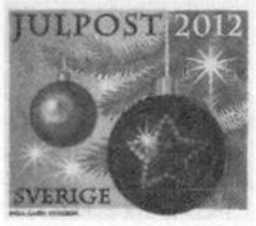

823 Baubles

2012. Christmas Tree Decorations. Booklet Stamps. Multicoloured.

2809	(5k.50) Type **823**	2·30	1·90
2810	(5k.50) Straw star	2·30	1·90
2811	(5k.50) Woven heart	2·30	1·90
2812	(5k.50) Candle and angel	2·30	1·90

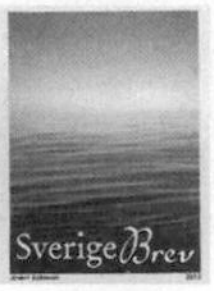

824 Horizon

2013. Heart in Nature. Multicoloured.

(a) Coil Stamp

2813	(6k.) Type **824**	2·00	

(b) Size 26×23 mm. Booklet Stamps. Self-adhesive

2814	(6k.) Heart-shaped pebbles	2·00	2·00
2815	(6k.) Heart-shaped leaves	2·00	2·00
2816	(6k.) Heart-shaped water drop-let in centre of leaf	2·00	2·00
2817	(6k.) Heart-shaped flower petals	2·00	2·00

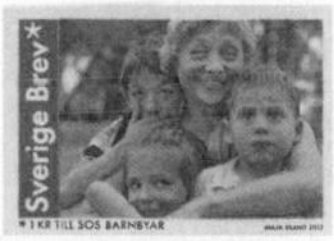

825 Children and Carer

2013. S.O.S. Children's Villages. Multicoloured.

2818	(6k.) (+1k.) Type **825**	3·00	3·00
2819	(6k.) (+1k.) Child and carer	3·00	3·00

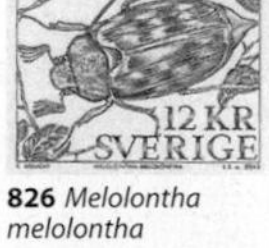

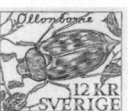

826 *Melolontha melolontha*

2013. Insects. Coil Stamps. Each steel-blue, carmine-red and deep dull green.

2820	12k. Type **826** (official insect of Halland)	4·25	4·25
2821	12k. *Aeshna osiliensis* (official insect of Närke)	4·25	4·25
2822	12k. *Lygaeus equestris* (official insect of Gotland)	4·25	4·25
2823	12k. *Bryodema tuberculata* (official insect of Öland)	4·25	4·25

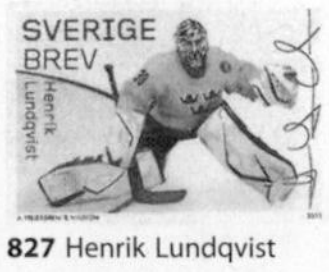

827 Henrik Lundqvist

2013. Ice Hockey World Championships. Hockey Heores. Booklet Stamps. Multicoloured.

2824	(6k.) Type **827**	2·00	2·00
2825	(6k.) Jörgen Jönsson	2·00	2·00
2826	(6k.) Börje Salming	2·00	2·00
2827	(6k.) Nicklas Lidström	2·00	2·00

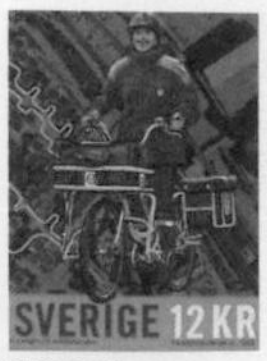

828 Postwoman riding Bicycle

2013. Europa. Postal Transport. Multicoloured.

MS2828	12k.×2, Type **828**; Postwoman and Clubcar electric vehicle (horiz)	10·00	9·50

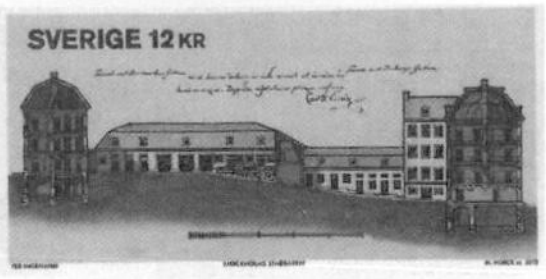

829 Spice Shopkeeper Ericsson's Building

2013. 300th Anniv of Stockholm City Planning Committee Archives. UNESCO Memory of the World Register. Booklet Stamps. Multicoloured.

2829	12k. Type **829** (63×32 mm)	4·25	4·25
2830	12k. Gröna Gården in Barnängen (30×38 mm)	4·25	4·25
2831	12k. Kulturhuset (30×38 mm)	4·25	4·25
2832	12k. House, Södra Ängby (30×38 mm)	4·25	4·25
2833	12k. Bredenberg's Department Store (30×38 mm)	4·25	4·25

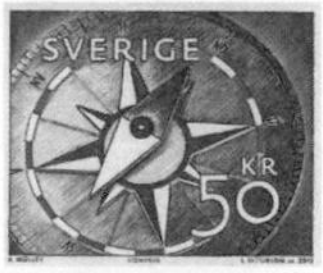

830 Compass

2013. Measure Time and Space. Coil Stamp

2834	**830**	50k. multicoloured	15·00	15·00

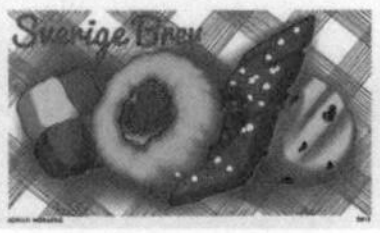

831 Cookies

2013. Cookies. Multicoloured.

(a) Coil Stamp

2835	(6k.) Type **831**	2·00	2·00

(b) Size 25×25 mm. Booklet Stamps. Self-adhesive

2836	(6k.) Jam-filled thumbprint cookies	2·00	2·00
2837	(6k.) Chocolate roll	2·00	2·00
2838	(6k.) Pretzel-shaped cookies	2·00	2·00
2839	(6k.) Battenberg	2·00	2·00

2013. Measure Time and Space (2nd issue). Coil Stamps. Multicoloured.

2840	30k. Barometer (26×31 mm)	12·00	12·00
2841	40k. Sundial (31×31 mm)	13·50	13·50

OFFICIAL STAMPS

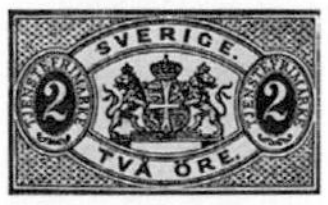

O6

1874

O27	**O6**	2ore orange	1·40	2·10
O28a	**O6**	3ore bistre	1·20	2·50
O29c	**O6**	4ore grey	2·75	90
O30a	**O6**	5ore green	6·00	1·50
O31a	**O6**	6ore lilac	£120	£190
O32	**O6**	6ore grey	£500	£225
O33b	**O6**	10ore red	2·40	40
O34a	**O6**	12ore blue	55·00	25·00
O35a	**O6**	20ore red	£200	2·75
O36	**O6**	20ore blue	5·50	50
O37a	**O6**	24ore yellow	60·00	28·00
O38ca	**O6**	30ore brown	£120	65
O39a	**O6**	50ore red	£170	28·00
O40	**O6**	50ore grey	18·00	1·90
O41d	**O6**	1k. blue and bistre	8·50	2·75

1889. Surch **TJENSTE FRIMARKE**, two crowns, and **TIO 10 ORE** on scroll.

O42	10ore on 12ore blue	13·00	19·00
O43	10ore on 24ore yellow	18·00	28·00

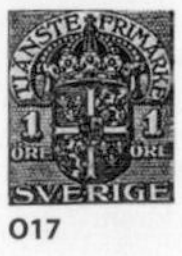

O17

1910

O87	**O17**	1ore black	45	60
O101	**O17**	2ore yellow	45	55
O102	**O17**	3ore brown	60	1·30
O103	**O17**	4ore lilac	45	55
O104	**O17**	5ore green	45	55
O105	**O17**	7ore green	60	1·70
O91	**O17**	8ore purple	80	1·30
O107	**O17**	10ore red	45	35
O108	**O17**	12ore red	45	55
O109	**O17**	15ore brown	60	55
O110	**O17**	20ore blue	60	55
O111	**O17**	25ore orange	1·20	55
O112	**O17**	30ore brown	80	55
O113	**O17**	35ore violet	1·20	1·30
O114	**O17**	50ore grey	4·75	2·75
O98	**O17**	1k. black on yellow	11·50	8·25
O99	**O17**	5k. purple on yellow	16·00	4·00

POSTAGE DUE STAMPS

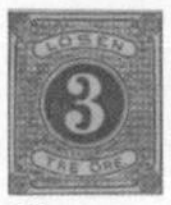

D6

1874

D27a	**D6**	1ore black	2·40	3·75
D28ab	**D6**	3ore red	4·75	7·00
D29ba	**D6**	5ore brown	3·50	4·50
D30a	**D6**	6ore yellow	9·50	10·00
D31	**D6**	12ore red	7·25	5·00
D32a	**D6**	20ore blue	4·75	4·50
D33	**D6**	24ore lilac	80·00	50·00
D34b	**D6**	24ore grey	24·00	28·00
D35b	**D6**	30ore green	6·00	4·50
D36a	**D6**	50ore brown	14·50	8·75
D37a	**D6**	1k. blue and bistre	95·00	38·00

Pt. 8

SWITZERLAND

A federal republic in central Europe between France, Germany and Italy.

100 rappen = 1 franken.
100 centimes = 1 franc.
100 centesimi = 1 franco.

These are expressions of the same currency in three languages.

For the issues under the Cantonal Administrations of Basel, Geneva and Zurich, see Stanley Gibbons' Part 8 (Italy and Switzerland) Catalogue.

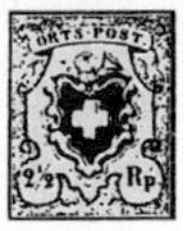

1

1850. Imperf. (a) Inscr "ORTS-POST".

1	**1**	2½r. black and red	£3500	£1900

(b) Inscr "POSTE LOCALE".

3	2½r. black and red	£3000	£1800

1850. As T **1** but inscr "RAYON I", "II" or "III". Imperf.

6	5r. red, black and blue (I)	£2500	£750
13	5r. red and blue (I)	£650	£170
10	10r. red, black and yellow (II)	£1100	£170
24	15rp. red (III)	£3000	£170
21	15 cts. red (III)	£20000	£1300

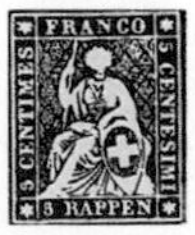

6

1854. Imperf.

46	**6**	2r. grey	£300	£650
47a	**6**	5r. brown	£275	25·00
48	**6**	10r. blue	£275	25·00
49a	**6**	15r. pink	£450	75·00
50	**6**	20r. orange	£550	85·00
51	**6**	40r. green	£500	£100
38a	**6**	1f. lilac	£1700	£1100

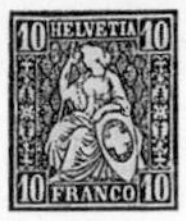

7

1862. Perf.

52	**7**	2c. grey	£190	5·00
61	**7**	2c. brown	3·00	2·10
61a	**7**	2c. bistre	3·00	2·10
53	**7**	3c. black	17·00	£170
54b	**7**	5c. brown	4·25	1·00
55	**7**	10c. blue	£850	1·00
62	**7**	10c. pink	10·00	1·30
63	**7**	15c. yellow	8·25	50·00
56a	**7**	20c. orange	3·00	4·25
64	**7**	25c. green	2·10	5·00
57	**7**	30c. red	£2000	50·00
65a	**7**	30c. blue	£650	17·00
58	**7**	40c. green	£1800	85·00
66	**7**	40c. grey	2·10	£180
67	**7**	50c. purple	60·00	65·00
59	**7**	60c. bronze	£1700	£225
60a	**7**	1f. gold	£1700	£600

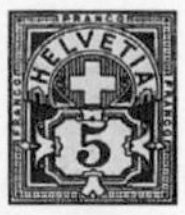

9

1882

126Bd	**9**	2c. brown	2·50	1·30
127Bc	**9**	3c. brown	3·25	17·00
128Bd	**9**	5c. purple	38·00	7·50
196a	**9**	5c. green	11·00	85
130Be	**9**	10c. red	14·00	6·75
131Be	**9**	12c. blue	12·50	1·30
132A	**9**	15c. yellow	£200	42·00
133Bc	**9**	15c. violet	£130	18·00

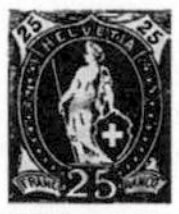

10

1882

214	**10**	20c. orange	4·25	6·75
146B	**10**	25c. green	20·00	2·50
207	**10**	25c. blue	10·00	3·00
209	**10**	40c. grey	50·00	25·00
202	**10**	30c. brown	12·50	3·25
150B	**10**	50c. blue	75·00	25·00
218	**10**	50c. green	8·75	33·00
152B	**10**	1f. purple	65·00	6·75
219	**10**	1f. red	50·00	17·00
154B	**10**	3f. brown	£250	42·00

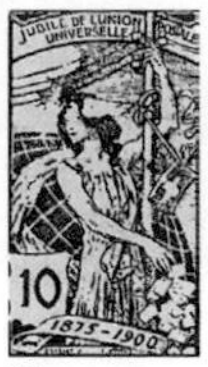

11

1900. 25th Anniv of U.P.U.

191	**11**	5c. green	4·25	3·25
189	**11**	10c. red	21·00	3·25
190	**11**	25c. blue	42·00	65·00

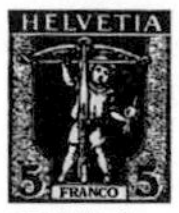

15 Tell's Son

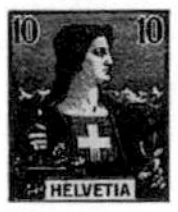

16

1907

225	**15**	2c. yellow	40	1·70
226	**15**	3c. brown	40	17·00
227	**15**	5c. green	5·00	85
228	**16**	10c. red	2·50	85
229	**16**	12c. brown	40	6·75
230	**16**	15c. mauve	5·00	21·00

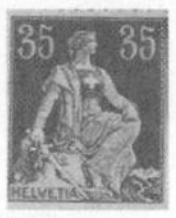

17

1908

232	**17**	20c. yellow and red	3·25	1·70
233	**17**	25c. blue and deep blue	3·00	1·30
234	**17**	30c. green and brown	2·30	85
235	**17**	35c. yellow and green	3·00	3·75
236	**17**	40c. yellow and purple	18·00	1·70
238	**17**	40c. blue	2·30	85
239a	**17**	40c. green	42·00	2·50
240a	**17**	50c. green and deep green	11·00	2·50
241	**17**	60c. brown	15·00	1·70
242	**17**	70c. yellow and brown	85·00	29·00
243	**17**	70c. buff and violet	22·00	5·75
244	**17**	80c. buff and grey	14·50	3·00
245	**17**	1f. green and purple	12·50	85
246	**17**	3f. yellow and bistre	£425	4·25

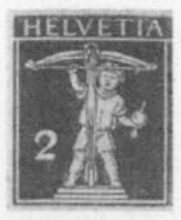

18 Cord in front of Shaft

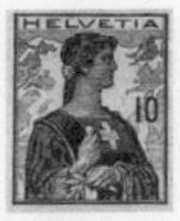

19

1908

247	**18**	2c. bistre	40	2·30
248	**18**	3c. violet	40	25·00
249	**18**	5c. green	12·50	40
250	**19**	10c. red	1·70	85
251	**19**	12c. brown	85	1·70
252	**19**	15c. mauve	42·00	1·70

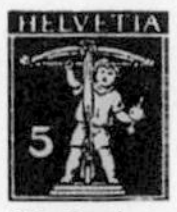

20a Cord behind Shaft

1910

260	**20a**	2c. brown	40	85
261	**20a**	2½c. purple	40	2·10
262	**20a**	2½c. bistre on buff	40	4·25
254	**20a**	3c. violet	40	85
255	**20a**	3c. brown	40	40
256a	**20a**	3c. blue on buff	7·50	38·00
263	**20a**	5c. green	1·20	40
264	**20a**	5c. orange on buff	15	15
265	**20a**	5c. grey on buff	15	15
266	**20a**	5c. purple on buff	15	15
267	**20a**	5c. green on buff	40	65
258	**20a**	7½c. grey	1·50	40
259	**20a**	7½c. green on buff	40	5·75

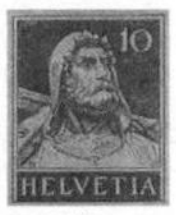

21 William Tell

1914

279	**21**	10c. red on buff	40	35
280	**21**	10c. green on buff	15	15
282	**21**	10c. violet on buff	1·00	40
283	**21**	12c. brown on buff	40	7·50
284	**21**	13c. green on buff	1·90	85
285	**21**	15c. purple on buff	3·00	85
286	**21**	15c. red on buff	3·75	7·50
287	**21**	20c. purple on buff	2·30	40
289	**21**	20c. red on buff	25	15
291	**21**	25c. red on buff	85	1·70
292	**21**	25c. brown on buff	4·25	2·50
293	**21**	30c. blue on buff	15·00	85

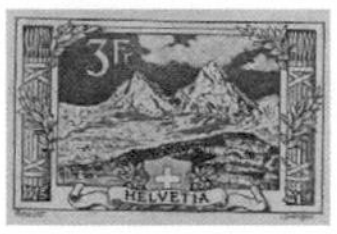

22 The Mythen

1914. Mountain Views.

294	**22**	3f. green	£1000	10·00
295	**22**	3f. red	£130	2·50
296	-	5f. blue	50·00	4·25
297	-	10f. mauve	£130	4·25
337	-	10f. green	£325	65·00

DESIGNS: 5f. The Rutli; 10f. The Jungfrau and girl holding shield.

1915. Surch.

298	**20a**	1c. on 2c. brown	15	2·10
307	**20a**	2½c. on 3c. brown	15	1·70
308	**20a**	3c. on 2½c. bistre on buff	15	5·00
309	**20a**	5c. on 2c. brown	15	7·50
310	**20a**	5c. on 7½c. grey	40	85
312	**20a**	5c. on 7½c. green on buff	40	17·00
313	**21**	10c. on 13c. green on buff	40	4·25
299	**19**	13c. on 12c. brown	15	18·00
300	**21**	13c. on 12c. brn on buff	15	1·30
314a	**21**	20c. on 15c. purple on buff	85	4·25
315	**17**	20c. on 25c. bl & dp bl	40	85
301	**17**	80c. on 70c. yell & brn	42·00	32·00

1919. Air. Optd with wings and propeller.

302	30c. green and brown	£170	£1900
303	50c. green and deep green	60·00	£180

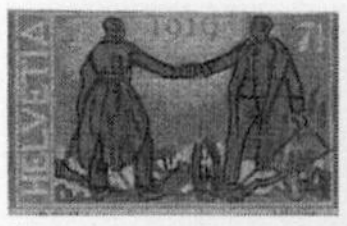

31

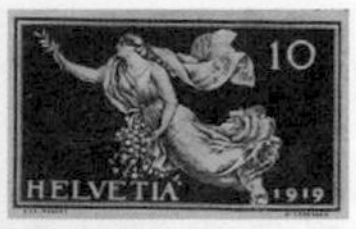

32

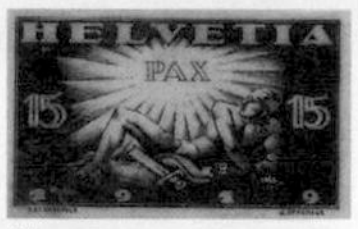

33

1919. Peace Celebrations.

304	**31**	7½c. green and black	1·20	3·25
305	**32**	10c. yellow and red	1·70	12·50
306	**33**	15c. yellow and violet	3·00	4·25

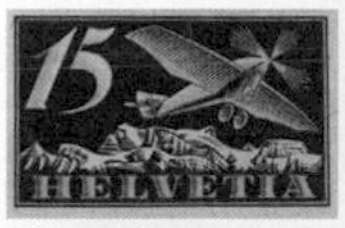

35 Monoplane

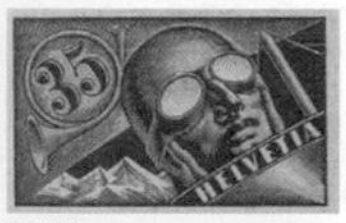

36 Pilot

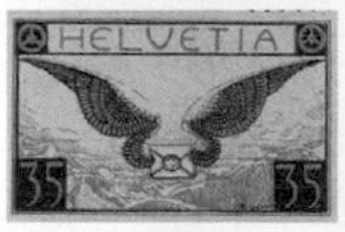

37

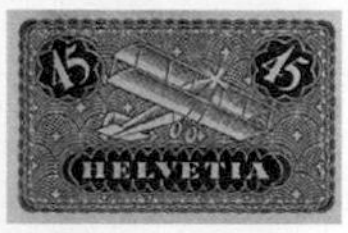

38 Biplane

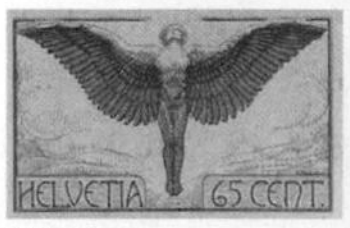

39 Icarus

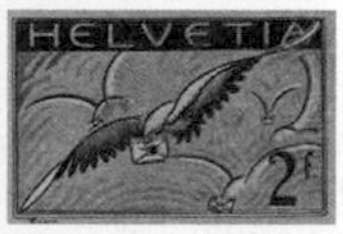

40

1923. Air.

316	**35**	15c. green and red	4·25	12·50
317a	**35**	20c. green and deep green	40	85
318	**35**	25c. grey and blue	11·50	33·00
319	**36**	35c. cinnamon and brown	17·00	75·00
320a	**37**	35c. brown and ochre	12·50	75·00
321	**36**	40c. lilac and violet	21·00	85·00
322a	**37**	40c. blue and green	65·00	£120
323	**38**	45c. red and blue	2·50	17·00
324a	**38**	50c. grey and red	1·70	3·25
325a	**39**	65c. blue and deep blue	4·25	12·50
326	**39**	75c. orange and purple	21·00	£110
327a	**39**	1f. lilac and purple	2·10	5·00
328a	**40**	2f. chestnut, sepia & brn	12·50	25·00

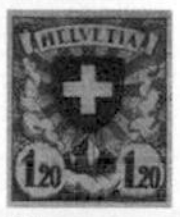

41

1924

329	**41**	90c. red, dp green & grn	23·00	4·25
330	**41**	1f.20 red, lake and pink	8·25	8·25
331a	**41**	1f.50 red, blue & turq	50·00	10·00
332a	**41**	2f. red, black and grey	46·00	14·00

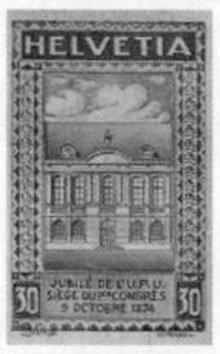

42 Seat of First U.P.U. Congress

1924. 50th Anniv of U.P.U.

333	-	20c. red	85	2·50
334	**42**	30c. blue	1·70	9·00

DESIGN: 20c. As T **42** but with different frame.

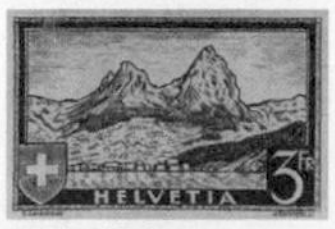

43 The Mythen

1931

335	**43**	3f. brown	70·00	8·25

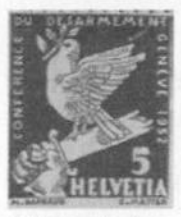

44 Symbol of Peace

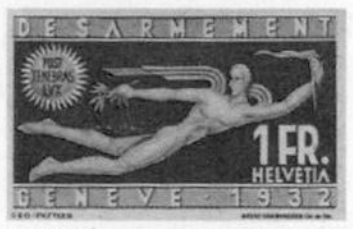

45 "After the Darkness, Light"

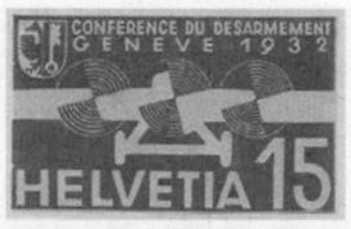

46 Peace and the Air Post

1932. International Disarmament Conference.

338	**44**	5c. green (postage)	40	85
339	**44**	10c. orange	40	40
340	**44**	20c. mauve	40	40
341	**44**	30c. blue	3·00	2·50
342	**44**	60c. brown	25·00	15·00
343	**45**	1f. grey and blue	25·00	16·00
344	**46**	15c. lt green & green (air)	85	3·75
345	**46**	20c. pink and red	1·70	5·00
346	**46**	90c. light blue and blue	9·25	65·00

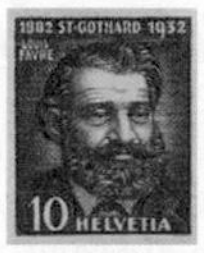

47 Louis Favre (engineer)

1932. 50th Anniv of St. Gotthard Railway.

347	**47**	10c. brown	15	15
348	-	20c. red	40	35
349	-	30c. blue	85	5·00

DESIGNS: 20c. Alfred Escher (President of Railway); 30c. Emil Welti (surveyor).

For redrawn designs, see Nos. 368 etc.

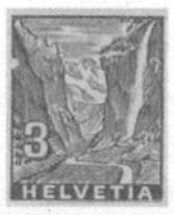

48 Staubbach Falls

1934. Landscapes.

350	**48**	3c. green	40	5·75
351	-	5c. green	25	25
352	-	10c. mauve	60	40
353	-	15c. orange	60	5·75
354	-	20c. red	1·00	85
355	-	25c. brown	10·00	12·50
356	-	30c. blue	38·00	3·25

DESIGNS: 5c. Mt. Pilatus; 10c. Chillon Castle and Dents du Midi; 15c. Grimsel Pass; 20c. St. Gotthard Railway, Biaschina Gorge; 25c. Viamala Gorge; 30c. Rhine Falls, Schaffhausen.

1934. National Philatelic Exhibition, Zurich ("NABA"). Sheet 62×72 mm.

MS357	Nos 351/4	£550	£1000

1935. Air. Surch.

358	**35**	10 on 15c. green and red	6·75	60·00
359	**46**	10 on 15c. light green and green	40	85
360	**46**	10 on 20c. pink and red	40	2·50
361	**46**	30 on 90c. light blue & blue	3·75	29·00
362	**46**	40 on 20c. pink and red	5·00	29·00
363	**46**	40 on 90c. light blue & blue	4·25	29·00
381	**39**	10 on 65c. blue & deep blue	40	85

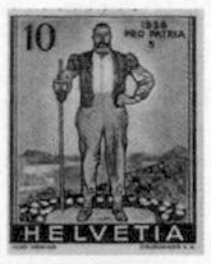

51 Freiburg Cowherd

1936. National Defence Fund.

364	**51**	10c.+5c. violet	85	1·70
365	**51**	20c.+10c. red	1·30	6·75
366	**51**	30c.+10c. blue	5·75	33·00
MS367		109×102 mm. Nos. 364/6	65·00	£325

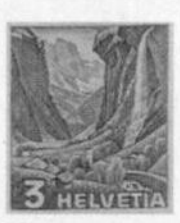

52 Staubbach Falls

1936. As T **48** but redrawn with figure of value lower down. Various landscapes.

368A	**52**	3c. green	15	15
369A	-	5c. green	15	15
489	-	5c. brown	40	25
370Ad	-	10c. purple	1·30	85
372A	-	10c. brown	25	25
490	-	10c. green	40	25
373A	-	15c. orange	60	1·70
374Ad	-	20c. red (Railway)	5·75	40
375A	-	20c. red (Lake)	25	25
491	-	20c. brown	40	25
376A	-	25c. brown	85	1·70
492	-	25c. red	3·00	4·50
377A	-	30c. blue	1·30	40
378A	-	35c. green	1·70	3·25
379A	-	40c. grey	7·50	40
494	-	40c. blue	50·00	2·50

DESIGNS: 5c. Mt. Pilatus; 10c. Chillon Castle and Dents du Midi; 15c. Grimsel Pass; 20c. (374d) St. Gotthard Railway, Biaschina Gorge; 20c. (Nos. 375, 491) Lake Lugano and Mt. San Salvatore; 25c. (No. 376) Viamala Gorge; 25c. (No. 492) National Park; 30c. Rhine Falls, Schaffhausen; 35c. Mt. Neufalkenstein and Klus; 40c. Mt. Santis and Lake Seealp.

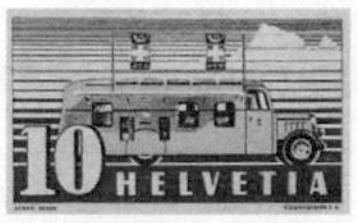

53 Mobile P.O.

1937. For Mobile P.O. Mail.

380	**53**	10c. yellow and black	40	80

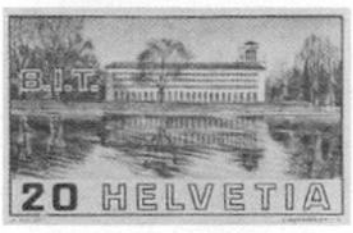

55 International Labour Bureau

1938

382	**55**	20c. red and buff	40	40
383	-	30c. blue and light blue	65	40
384	-	60c. brown and buff	2·75	4·25
385	-	1f. black and buff	10·50	28·00

DESIGNS: 30c. Palace of League of Nations; 60c. Inner courtyard of Palace of League of Nations; 1f. International Labour Bureau (different).

1938. Air. Special Flights. Surch **1938 "PRO AERO" 75 75** and bars.

386	**38**	75c. on 50c. green and red	†	9·25

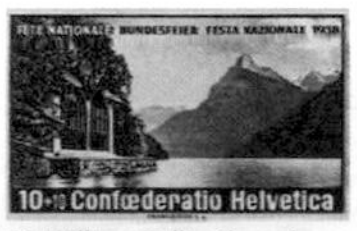

60 William Tell's Chapel

1938. National Fete. Fund for Swiss Subjects Abroad.

387	**60**	10c.+10c. violet & yellow	40	3·00

1938. National Philatelic Exhibition, Aarau and 25th Anniv of Swiss Air Mail Service. Sheet 74×87 mm.

MS387a	Nos. 375 and 381 (sold at 1f.50)	46·00	55·00

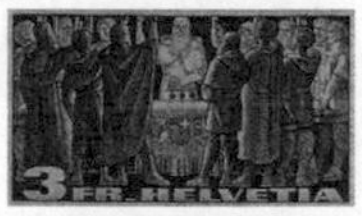

61 First Act of Federal Parliament

1938

388A	**61**	3f. brown on blue	17·00	15·00
388C	**61**	3f. brown on buff	4·25	1·70
389A	-	5f. blue on blue	11·50	10·00
389C	-	5f. blue on buff	6·75	1·70
390B	-	10f. green on blue	47·00	4·25
390C	-	10f. green on buff	13·50	5·75

DESIGNS: 5f. "The Assembly at Stans"; 10f. Polling booth.

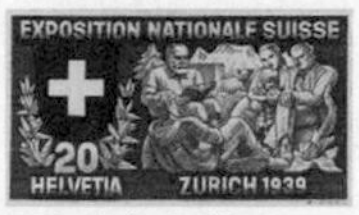

62 Symbolical of Swiss Culture

1939. National Exhibition, Zurich. Inscr in French (F), German (G) or Italian (I).

391F		10c. violet	40	40
391G		10c.	40	40
391I		10c.	40	40
392F	**62**	20c. carmine	40	40
392G	-	20c.	85	40
392I	-	20c.	8·25	40
393F	-	30c. blue and buff	3·25	5·00
393G	-	30c.	3·50	14·00
393I	-	30c.	2·50	16·00

DESIGNS: 10c. Group symbolic of Swiss Industry and Agriculture; 30c. Piz Rosegg and Tschirva Glacier.

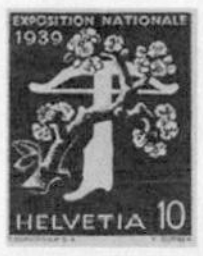

64 Crossbow and Floral Branch

1939. National Exhibition, Zurich. Inscr in French (F), German (G) or Italian (I).

394F		5c. emerald	60	4·25
394G		5c. emerald	60	3·25
394I		5c. emerald	85	6·75
395F	**64**	10c. brown	60	4·25
395G	**64**	10c. brown	60	3·00
395I	**64**	10c. brown	60	5·75
396F	**64**	20c. scarlet	1·30	5·75
396G	**64**	20c. scarlet	1·20	3·25
396I	**64**	20c. scarlet	1·20	8·25
397F	**64**	30c. blue	3·50	16·00
397G	**64**	30c. blue	3·25	13·50
397I	**64**	30c. blue	3·50	17·00

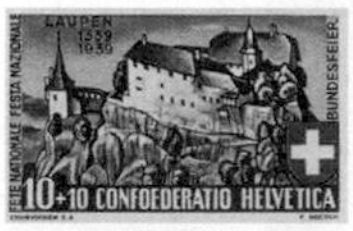

65 Laupen Castle

1939. National Fete. Fund for Destitute Mothers.

398	**65**	10c.+10c. brn, grey & red	40	2·10

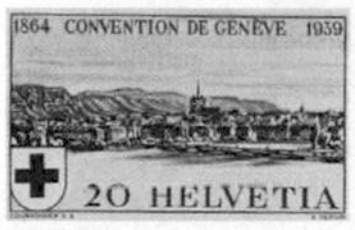

66 Geneva

1939. 75th Anniv of Geneva (Red Cross) Convention.

399	**66**	20c. red and buff	40	40
400	**66**	30c. blue, grey and red	40	4·50

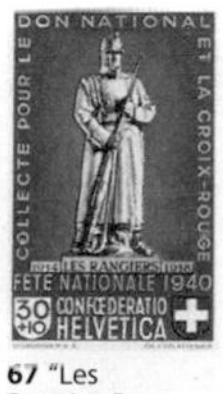

67 "Les Rangiers"

1940. National Fete and Red Cross Fund. Memorial designs inscr "FETE NATIONALE 1940" in German (5c., 20c.), Italian (10c.) and French (30c.).

401	-	5c.+5c. black and green	40	1·70
402	-	10c.+5c. black & orange	40	1·30
403	-	20c.+5c. black and red	3·25	2·10
404	**67**	30c.+10c. black and blue	2·10	12·50
MS404a		125×65 mm. Nos. 401/2, 403/4. Imperf (sold at 5f.)	£400	£900

DESIGNS—Battle Memorials: 5c. Sempach; 10c. Giornico; 20c. Calven.

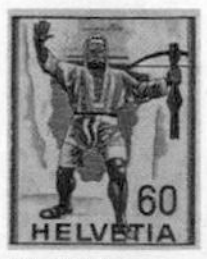

68 "William Tell" (Ferdinand Hodler)

1941. Historical Designs.

405	-	50c. blue on green	7·00	40
406	**68**	60c. brown on cinnamon	12·50	40
407	-	70c. purple on mauve	3·00	2·50
408	-	80c. black on grey	65	40
408a	-	80c. black on mauve	3·25	85
409	-	90c. red on pink	75	40
409a	-	90c. red on buff	4·25	4·25
410	-	1f. green on green	1·20	40
411	-	1f.20 purple on grey	1·20	40
411a	-	1f.20 purple on lilac	5·00	85
412	-	1f.50 blue on buff	2·10	40
413	-	2f. red on pink	2·50	40
413a	-	2f. red on cream	7·50	85

DESIGNS—(Works of art): 50c. "Oath of Union" (James Vibert); 70c. "Kneeling Warrior" (Ferdinand Hodler); 80c. "Dying Ensign" (Hodler); 90c. "Standard Bearer" (Niklaus Deutsch). Portraits: 1f. Col. Louis Pfyffer; 1f.20, George Jenatsch; 1f.50, Lt. Gen. Francois de Reynold; 2f. Col. Joachim Forrer.

www.robstine-stamps.com

GOOD NEWS!

For collectors of *fine used* stamps
A fantastic array of fine used material is now available through

www.robstine-stamps.com

My web site contains lists of several countries, including fine used stamps from early issues up to the present day. Most stamps are priced individually. Here is a list of the main countries I stock:

Australia	Germany 1872-1945	Malta
Austria	West and Unified Germany	Netherlands
Belgium	Berlin and the Zones	New Zealand
Canada	(East Germany) DDR	Norway
Czechoslovakia	Greenland	Portugal and Colonies
Denmark	Hungary	Spain
Faroes	Iceland	Sweden
Finland	Ireland	Switzerland
France	Italy and Colonies	USA
	Luxembourg	

Additionally I hold stocks of other areas, including British Commonwealth. I am regularly expanding my stock as suitable material becomes available.

www.robstine-stamps.com
also shows
✦ a photo Gallery of many better items in stock
✦ a monthly newsletter detailing new stock and other developments
✦ a potted history of Robstine Stamps
✦ an order form with terms and conditions
✦ a list of Fairs I attend. You will find me at Fairs on about 50 days during the year, including the twice yearly York fair

Contact me now for:
• **comprehensive stocks**
• **superb quality**
• **easy ordering**
• **quick response**

www.robstine-stamps.com

Stanley Gibbons

www.stanleygibbons.com

BY APPOINTMENT TO
HER MAJESTY THE QUEEN
PHILATELISTS
STANLEY GIBBONS LTD
LONDON

Stanley Gibbons - the home of stamp collecting since 1856 and today's market leader for all your philatelic needs.

For the best quality in stamps, catalogues, albums and all other accessories log on to our website today and explore our unrivalled range of products all available at the touch of a button.

visit **www.stanleygibbons.com**

Est 1856
STANLEY GIBBONS

Stanley Gibbons Limited
399 Strand, London, WC2R 0LX
+44 (0)20 7557 4444
www.stanleygibbons.com

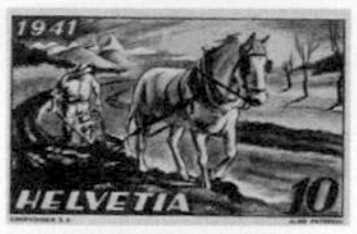

69 Ploughing

1941. Agricultural Development Plan.

414	69	10c. brown and buff	40	85

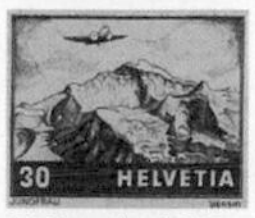

70 Douglas DC-2 The Jungfrau

1941. Air. Landscapes.

415	70	30c. blue on orange	85	40
415a	-	30c. grey on orange	12·50	21·00
416	-	40c. grey on orange	85	40
416a	-	40c. blue on orange	85·00	4·25
417	-	50c. green on orange	85	40
418	-	60c. brown on orange	1·20	40
419	-	70c. violet on orange	85	85
420	-	1f. green on buff	2·50	85
421	-	2f. red on buff	6·75	5·75
422	-	5f. blue on buff	28·00	25·00

DESIGNS: 40f. Valais; 50c. Lac Leman; 60c. Alpstein; 70c. Ticino; 1f. Lake Lucerne; 2f. Engadin; 5f. Churfirsten.

1941. Air. Special (Buochs–Payerne) Flights. No. 420 with "PRO AERO 28.V.1941" added.

423	1f. green on buff	8·25	31·00

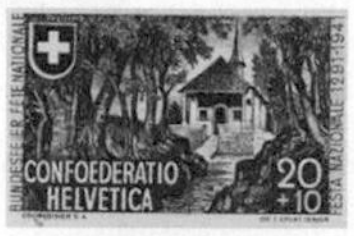

71 Chemin Creux near Kussnacht

1941. National Fete and 650th Anniv of Swiss Confederation.

424	-	10c.+10c. blue, red & yell	40	1·70
425	71	20c.+10c. scarlet, red and buff	40	3·00

DESIGN: 10c. Relief map of Lake Lucerne with Arms of Uri, Schwyz and Unterwalden.

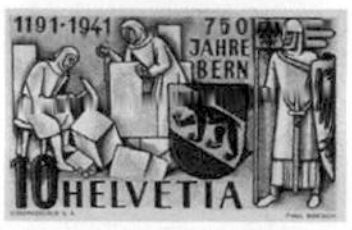

72 Arms of Berne, Masons laying Cornerstone and Knight

1941. 750th Anniv of Berne.

426	72	10c. multicoloured	40	1·70

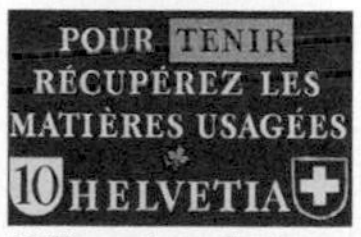

73 "To survive collect salvage"

1942. Salvage Campaign. Inscr in French (F.), German (G.) or Italian (I.). Value and coat of arms in red, tablets in blue. F.

427F	73	10c. brown	40	1·70

G.

427G	10c. brown	40	85

I.

427I	10c. brown	7·25	7·50

INSCRIPTIONS: (G) "Zum Durchhalten/Alstoffe sammeln"; (I) "PER RESISTERE/RACCOGLIETE/LA ROBA VECCHIA".

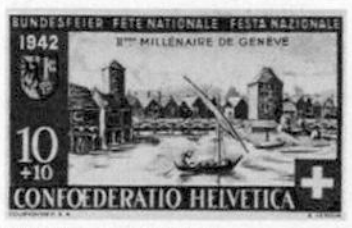

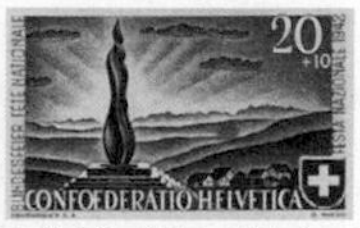

74 View of Old Geneva

75 Soldiers' Memorial at Forch, near Zurich

1942. National Fete, National Relief Fund and Bimillenary of Geneva.

428	74	10c.+10c. black, yellow and red	40	1·30
429	75	20c.+10c. red and yellow	40	3·75
MS429a 105×62 mm. Nos. 428/9. Imperf (sold at 2f.)			80·00	£375

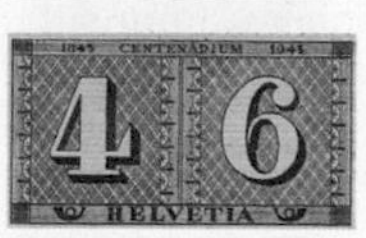

76

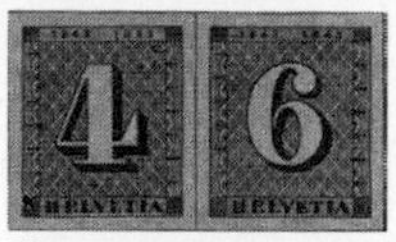

76a

1943. Cent of Swiss Cantonal Postage Stamps.

430	76	10c.(4+6) black	40	40
MS430a 160×140 mm. No. 430. Imperf (sold at 5f.)			75·00	90·00
MS430b 70×75 mm. T **76a** 4 and 6 (c.) black. Imperf (sold at 3f.)			70·00	90·00

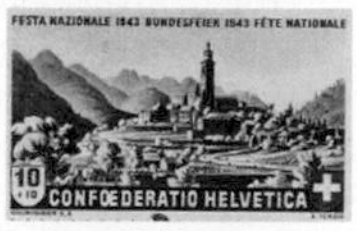

77 Intragna (Ticino)

1943. National Fete and Youth's Vocational Training Fund.

431	77	10c.+10c. black, buff and red	40	1·30
432	-	20c.+10c. red and buff	40	3·75

DESIGN: 20c. Federal Palace, Berne.

1943. Air. Special Flights. 30th Anniv of First Flight across Alps by Oscar Bider. As No. 432, optd **PRO AERO 13.VII.1943** and value.

433	1f. red and buff	65·00	65·00

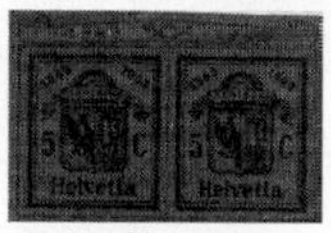

77a "Double Geneva"

1943. National Philatelic Exhibition Geneva ('GEPH') and Centenary of Geneva Cantonal Stamp. Sheet 72×73 mm. Imperf.

MS433a 5c. black and green (sold at 3f.)	3·00	17·00

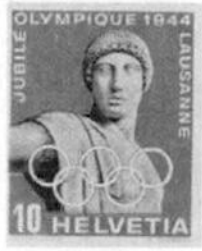

78 Apollo of Olympia

1944. Olympic Games Jubilee.

434	78	10c. black and orange	40	1·70
435	78	20c. black and red	40	1·70
436	78	30c. black and blue	85	13·50

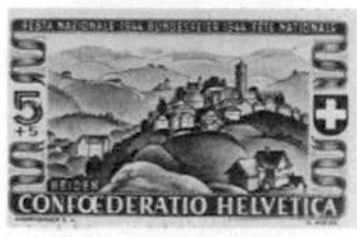

79 Heiden

1944. National Fete and Red Cross Fund.

437	79	5c.+5c. green, buff & red	40	3·75
438	-	10c.+10c. grey, buff and red	40	85
439	-	20c.+10c. red and buff	40	1·70
440	-	30c.+10c. blue, buff and red	3·00	29·00

DESIGNS: 10c. St. Jacques on the R. Birs; 20c. Castle Ruins, Mesocco; 30c. Basel.

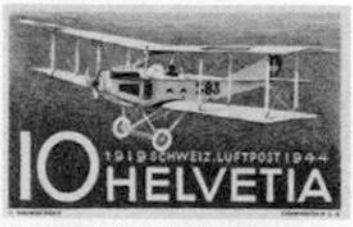

80 Haefeli DH-3 Biplane

1944. Air. 25th Anniv of National Air Post.

441	80	10c. brown and green	40	85
442	-	20c. red and stone	40	85
443	-	30c. ultramarine and blue	40	3·00
444	-	1f.50 agate, brown and red	8·25	29·00

AIRCRAFT: 20c. Fokker F.VIIb/3m CH-157; 30c. Lockheed 9B Orion; 1f.50, Douglas DC-3 HB-IRI.

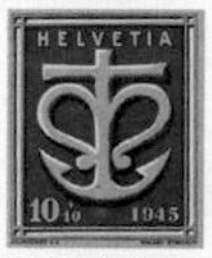

81 Symbolical of Faith, Hope and Charity

1945. War Relief Fund.

445	81	10c.+10c. green, black and grey	40	85
446	81	20c.+60c. red, black and grey	1·30	10·00

MS446a 70×110 mm. Imperf. 3f.+7f. blue	£170	£325

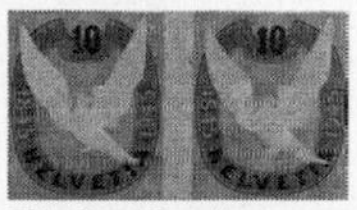

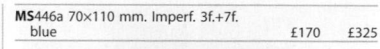

81b "Basel Dove"

1945. Centenary of Basel Cantonal Stamp Issue. Sheet 71×63 mm.

MS446b **81b** 10 (c.) green, red and black (sold at 3f.)	85·00	£150

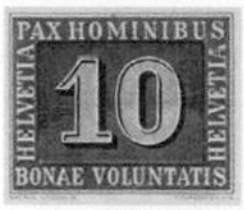

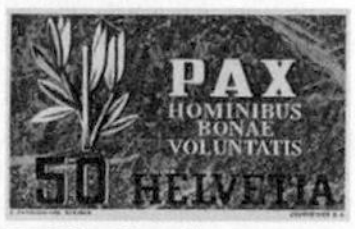

82 Trans "Peace to men of good will"

83 Olive Branch

1945. Peace. Inscr "PAX".

447	82	5c. green and grey	40	85
448	82	10c. brown and grey	40	35
449	82	20c. red and grey	40	25
450	82	30c. blue and grey	85	5·00
451	82	40c. orange and grey	1·70	18·00
452	83	50c. red and buff	3·25	38·00
453	-	60c. grey and light grey	2·50	25·00
454	-	80c. green and buff	5·00	£120
455	-	1f. blue and buff	8·25	£140
456	-	2f. brown and buff	25·00	£250
457	-	3f. green on buff	33·00	£130
458	-	5f. brown on buff	£120	£450
459	-	10f. violet on buff	95·00	£170

DESIGNS—As Type **83**: 60c. Keys; 80c. Horn of plenty; 1f. Dove; 2f. Spade and flowers in ploughed field. 38×21 mm: 3f. Crocuses; 5f. Clasped hands; 10f. Aged couple.

1945. Red Cross. As T **82**, but red cross and "5+10" in centre of stamp.

460	5c.+10c. green	40	1·30

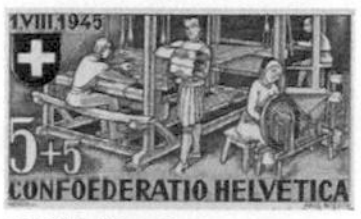

85 Silk Weaving

1945. National Fete.

461	85	5c.+5c. green and red	40	3·25
462	-	10c.+10c. brown, grey and red	40	1·30
463	-	20c.+10c. red and buff	85	1·30
464	-	30c.+10c. blue, grey and red	8·25	75·00

DESIGNS: 10, 20c. Jura and Emmental farmhouses; 30c. Timbered house.

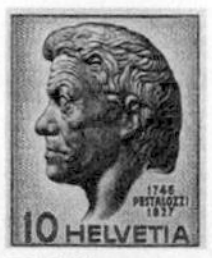

86 J. H. Pestalozzi

1946. Birth Bicentenary of J. H. Pestalozzi (educational reformer).

465	86	10c. purple	40	35

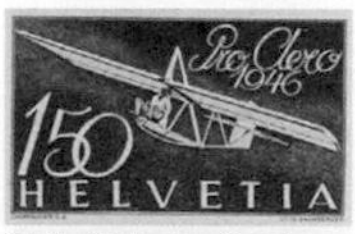

87 Zoglig Instructional Glider

1946. Air. Special (Lausanne, Lucerne, Locarno) Flights.

466	87	1f.50 red and grey	42·00	46·00

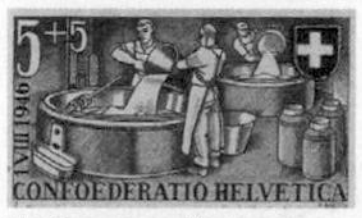

88 Cheese-making

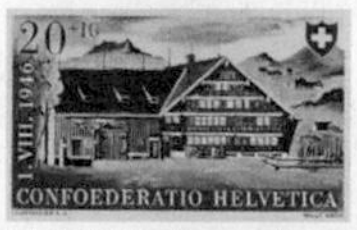

89 Chalet in Appenzell

1946. National Fete and Fund for Swiss Citizens Abroad.

467	88	5c.+5c. green and red	1·30	5·00
468	-	10c.+10c. brown, buff and red	85	1·30
469	89	20c.+10c. red and buff	1·40	1·30
470	-	30c.+10c. blue, grey and red	12·50	21·00

DESIGNS: 10c. Chalet in Vaud; 30c. Chalet in Engadine.

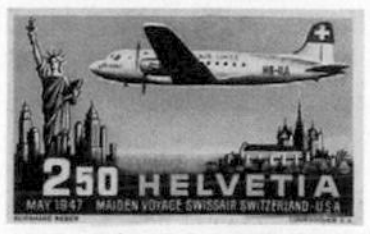

90 Douglas DC-4 Airliner, Statue of Liberty and St. Peter's Cathedral, Geneva

1947. Air. First Geneva–New York "Swissair" Flight.

472	90	2f.50 deep blue, blue & red	29·00	33·00

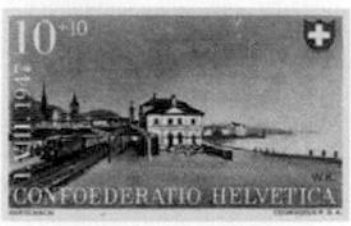

92 Rorschach Station

1947. National Fete. Professional Education of Invalids and Anti-cancer Funds. Inscr "I VIII 1947". Arms in red.

473	-	5c.+5c. green	85	4·25
474	92	10c.+10c. black and buff	1·70	1·30
475	-	20c.+10c. red and buff	1·70	1·70
476	-	30c.+10c. blue and grey	12·50	20·00

DESIGNS: 5c. Platelayers; 20c. Luen-Castiel station; 30c. Fluelen station.

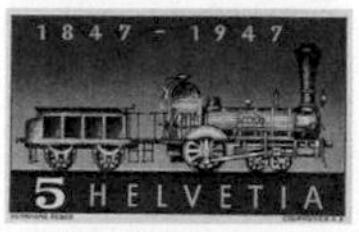

93 "Limmat" (first locomotive in Switzerland)

1947. Centenary of Swiss Federal Railways.

477	93	5c. green, yellow and black	1·70	85
478	-	10c. black and brown	1·70	85
479	-	20c. red, buff and lake	85	85
480	-	30c. blue, grey & light blue	4·25	4·25

DESIGNS: 10c. Class C5/62-10-0 steam locomotive, 1913; 20c. Type Ae8/14 electric locomotive crossing Melide Causeway; 30c. Lorraine Bridge, Berne.

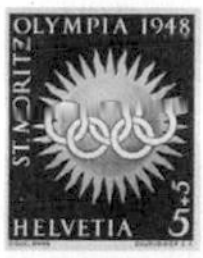

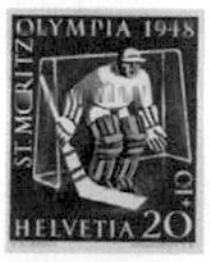

95 Sun of St. Moritz

96 Ice Hockey

1948. Fifth Winter Olympic Games.

481	95	5c.+5c. brown, yell & grn	85	2·50
482	-	10c.+10c. blue, light blue and brown	85	1·70
483	96	20c.+10c. yellow, black and purple	1·70	3·25
484	-	30c.+10c. black, light blue and blue	5·75	10·00

DESIGN: 10c. Snow crystals; 30c. Ski-runner.

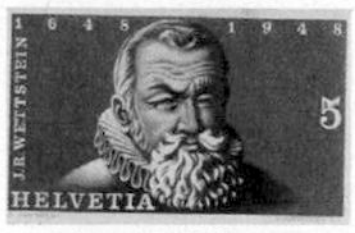

97 Johann Rudolf Wettstein

1948. Tercentenary of Treaty of Westphalia and Centenaries of the Neuchatel Revolution and Swiss Federation.

485	97	5c. green and deep green	40	85
486	-	10c. black and grey	40	35
487	-	20c. red and pink	85	40
488	-	30c. blue, grey and brown	1·70	2·50

DESIGNS: 10c. Neuchatel Castle; 20c. Symbol of Helvetia; 30c. Symbol of Federal State.

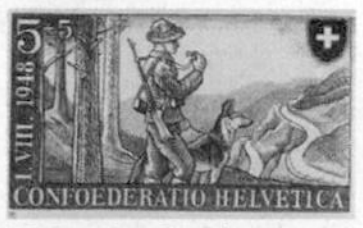

99 Frontier Guard

1948. National Fete and Anti-Tuberculosis Fund. Coat of arms in red.

495	99	5c.+5c. green	1·30	2·10
496	-	10c.+10c. slate and grey	85	1·30
497	-	20c.+10c. red and buff	1·30	1·70
498	-	30c.+10c. blue and grey	6·75	12·50

DESIGNS: 10c., 20c., 30c. Typical houses in Fribourg, Valais and Ticino respectively.

1948. National Philatelic Exhibition, Basel ("IMABA"). Sheet 110×61 mm. T **97**.

MS498a 10c. purple and gery; 20c. blue and grey (sold at 3f.)	£130	£100

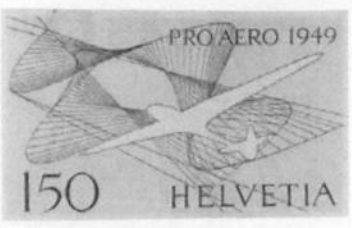

101 Glider

1949. Air. Special (La Chaux-de-Fonds–St. Gallen–Lugano) Flights.

499	**101**	1f.50 purple and yellow	65·00	65·00

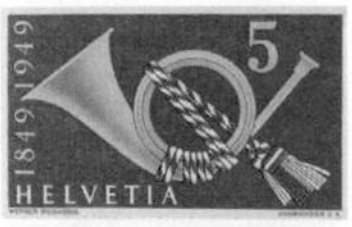

102 Posthorn

1949. Centenary of Federal Post.

500	**102**	5c. yellow, pink and grey	40	85
501	-	20c. yellow, violet and grey	40	40
502	-	30c. yellow, brown & grey	1·70	14·50

DESIGNS: 20c. Mail coach drawn by five horses; 30c. Postal motor coach and trailer.

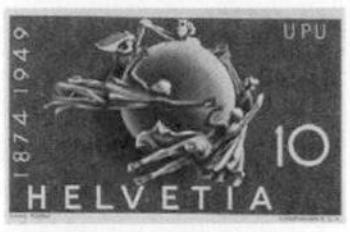

103 Main Motif of U.P.U. Monument, Berne

1949. 75th Anniv of U.P.U.

503	**103**	10c. green	40	85
504	-	25c. purple	85	10·00
505	-	40c. blue	1·70	11·50

DESIGNS: 25c. Globe and ribbon; 40c. Globe and pigeons.

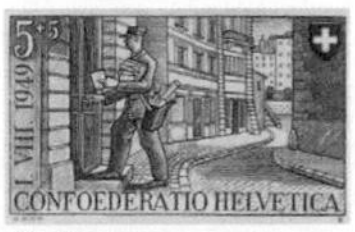

104 Postman

1949. National Fete and Youth Fund. T **104** and designs as T **89**, but dated "I. VIII. 1949". Arms in red.

506	**104**	5c.+5c. purple	1·30	2·50
507	-	10c.+10c. green & buff	85	1·30
508	-	20c.+10c. brown & buff	1·30	1·30
509	-	40c.+10c. blue & lt blue	9·25	23·00

DESIGNS—Typical houses in: 10c. Basel; 20c. Lucerne; 40c. Prattigau.

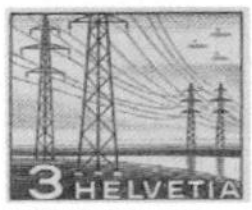

106 High-tension Pylons

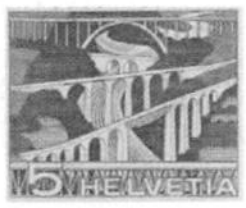

107 Railway Viaducts over River Sitter, near St. Gall

1949. Landscapes.

510	**106**	3c. black	4·25	4·25
511	**107**	5c. orange	50	25
512	-	10c. green	40	25
513	-	15c. turquoise	85	85
514a	-	20c. purple	60	25
515	-	25c. red	50	25
516	-	30c. green	85	25
517	-	35c. brown	1·70	1·70
518	-	40c. blue	4·25	40
519	-	50c. grey	4·25	40
520	-	60c. green	13·50	1·30
521	-	70c. violet	4·25	85

DESIGNS: 10c. Rack railway, Rochers de Naye; 15c. Rotary snowplough; 20c. Grimsel Reservoir; 25c. Lake Lugano and Melide railway causeway; 30c. Verbois hydro-electric power station; 35c. Alpine road (Val d'Anniviers); 40c. Rhine harbour, Basel; 50c. Suspension railway, Santis; 60c. Railway viaduct, Landwasser; 70c. Survey mark, Finsteraarhorn.

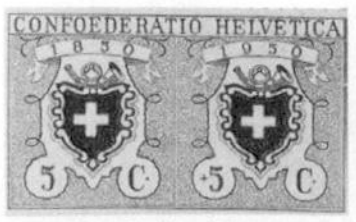

110 First Federal Postage Stamps

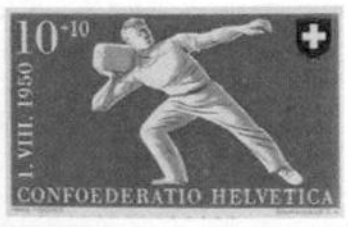

111 Putting the Weight

1950. National Fete, Red Cross Fund and Centenary of First Federal Postage Stamps. T **110** and designs, as T **111**, inscr "I. VIII. 1950". Coat of arms in red.

522	**110**	5c.+5c. black	85	1·30
523	**111**	10c.+10c. green & grey	2·10	1·30
524	-	20c.+10c. green & grey	3·00	1·70
525	-	30c.+10c. mauve & grey	8·25	38·00
526	-	40c.+10c. blue and grey	12·50	21·00

DESIGNS: 20c. Wrestling; 30c. Sprinting; 40c. Rifle-shooting.

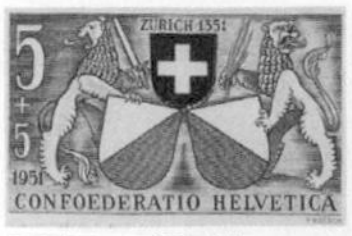

112 Arms of Zurich

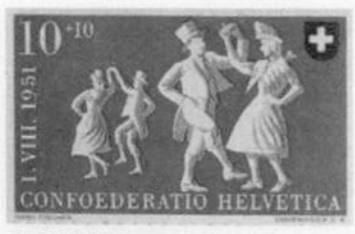

113 Valaisan Polka

1951. National Fete, Mothers' Fund and 600th Anniv of Zurich. Coat of arms in red.

527	**112**	5c.+5c. black	85	1·30
528	**113**	10c.+10c. green & grey	85	85
529	-	20c.+10c. green & grey	1·70	2·10
530	-	30c.+10c. mauve & grey	8·25	21·00
531	-	40c.+10c. blue and grey	12·50	25·00

DESIGNS—As Type **113**: 20c. Flag-swinging; 30c. "Hornussen" (game); 40c. Blowing alphorn.

1951. National Philatelic Exhibition, Lucerne ("LUNABA"). Sheet 74×54 mm. As No. 529. Imperf.

MS531a	40c. multicoloured (sold at 3f.)	£375	£275

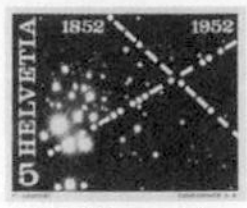

114 "Telegraph"

1952. Centenary of Swiss Telecommunications.

532	**114**	5c. orange and yellow	40	1·70
533	-	10c. green and pink	40	25
534	-	20c. mauve and lilac	1·70	25
535	-	40c. blue and light blue	4·25	11·00

DESIGNS: 10c. "Telephone"; 20c. "Radio"; 40c. "Television".

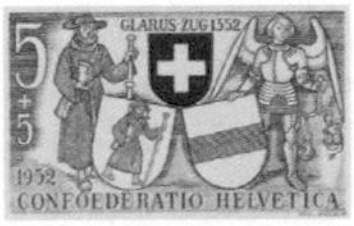

115 Arms of Glarus and Zug

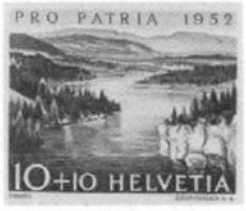

116 River Doubs

1952. Pro Patria. Cultural Funds and 600th Anniv of Glarus and Zug joining Confederation.

536	**115**	5c.+5c. red and black	85	1·70
537	**116**	10c.+10c. green and cream	85	85
538	-	20c.+10c. purple & pink	85	85
539	-	30c.+10c. brown & buff	5·75	17·00
540	-	40c.+10c. blue & lt blue	8·25	15·00

DESIGNS—As T **116**: 20c. St. Gotthard Lake; 30c. River Moesa; 40c. Marjelen Lake.

1953. Pro Patria. Emigrants' Fund and 600th Anniv of Berne joining Confederation.

541	5c.+5c. red and black	1·30	1·30
542	10c.+10c. green and cream	85	85
543	20c.+10c. purple and pink	1·30	1·30
544	30c.+10c. brown and buff	8·25	17·00
545	40c.+10c. blue & light blue	10·00	15·00

DESIGNS—As T **115**: 5c. Arms of Berne (inscr "BERN 1353"). As T **116** (inscr "PRO PATRIA 1953"): 10c. Rapids, R. Reuss; 20c. Lake Sihl; 30c. Aqueduct, Bisse; 40c. Lac Leman.

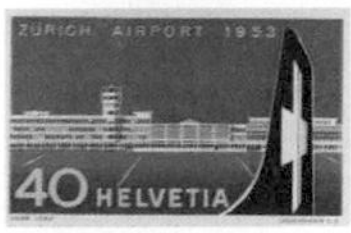

119 Zurich Airport

1953. Inauguration of Zurich Airport.

546	**119**	40c. blue, grey and red	7·50	17·00

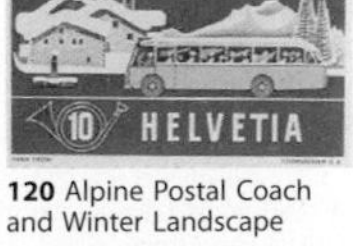

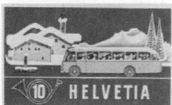

120 Alpine Postal Coach and Winter Landscape

1953. For Mobile P.O. Mail.

547	**120**	10c. yellow, green and emerald	85	40
548	-	20c. yellow, red and scarlet	85	40

DESIGN: 10c. Alpine postal coach and summer landscape.

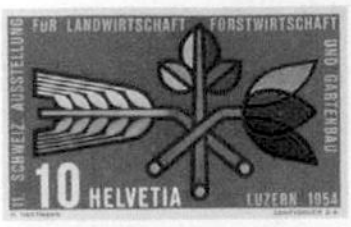

121 Ear of Wheat and Flower

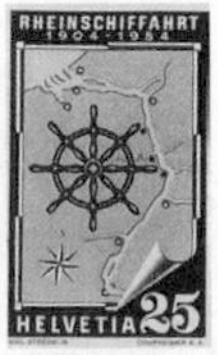

122 Rhine Map and Steering Wheel

1954. Publicity Issue.

549	**121**	10c. multicoloured	40	25
550	-	20c. multicoloured	2·50	40
551	**122**	25c. green, blue and red	1·70	4·25
552	-	40c. blue, yellow and black	5·50	5·75

DESIGNS—HORIZ: 10c. Type **121** (Agricultural Exhibition, Lucerne); 20c. Winged spoon (Cooking Exhibition, Berne); 40c. Football and world map (World Football Championship). VERT: 25c. Type **122** (50th anniv of navigation of River Rhine).

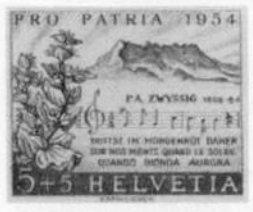

123 Opening Bars of "Swiss Hymn"

1954. Pro Patria. Youth Fund and Death Centenary of Father Zwyssig (composer of "Swiss Hymn").

553	**123**	5c.+5c. green	85	1·70
554	-	10c.+10c. green & turq	85	85
555	-	20c.+10c. purple and cream	1·70	85
556	-	30c.+10c. brown & buff	6·25	14·00
557	-	40c.+10c. deep blue and blue	7·00	17·00

DESIGNS: 10c. Lake Neuchatel; 20c. Maggia River; 30c. Taubenloch Gorge Waterfall; Schuss River; 40c. Lake Sils.

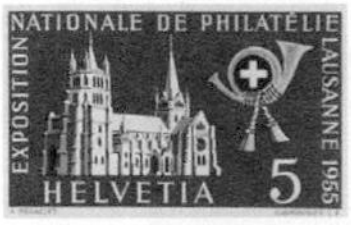

124 Lausanne Cathedral

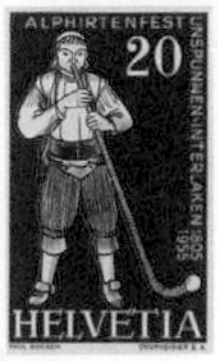

125 Alphorn Blower

1955. Publicity Issue. Inscr "1955".

558	**124**	5c. multicoloured	85	1·30
559	-	10c. multicoloured	85	85
560	**125**	20c. brown and red	2·10	85
561	-	40c. pink, black and blue	5·50	5·00

DESIGNS—HORIZ: 5c. Type **124** (National Philatelic Exhibition, Lausanne); 10c. Vaud girl's hat (Vevey Winegrowers' Festival); 40c. Car steering-wheel (25th International Motor Show, Geneva). VERT: 20c. Type **125** (Alpine Herdsman and Costume Festival, Interlaken).

1955. National Philatelic Exhibition, Lausanne. Sheet 103×52 mm. T **124**. Imperf.

MS561a	10c. and 20c. multicoloured (sold at 2f.)	£140	£130

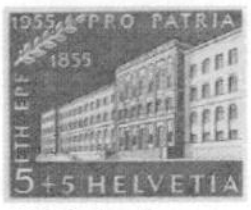

126 Federal Institute of Technology, Zurich

1955. Pro Patria. Mountain Population Fund and Centenary of Federal Institute of Technology.

562	**126**	5c.+5c. grey	85	1·30
563	-	10c.+10c. green and cream	85	85
564	-	20c.+10c. red and pink	1·70	1·30
565	-	30c.+10c. brown & buff	5·75	10·00
566	-	40c.+10c. blue and light blue	5·75	13·50

DESIGNS: 10c. Grandfey railway viaduct over River Saane, near Fribourg; 20c. Lake Aegeri; 30c. Lake Grappelensee; 40c. Lake Bienne.

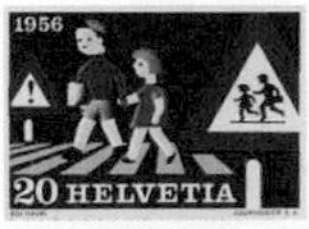

127 "Road Safety"

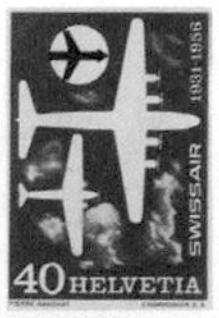

128 Fokker F.VIIb/3m and Douglas DC-6 Aircraft

1956. Publicity Issue. Inscr "1956".

567		5c. yellow, black and green	55	35
568		10c. black, green and red	85	40
569	**127**	20c. multicoloured	2·50	85
570	**128**	40c. blue and red	3·75	3·25

DESIGNS—HORIZ: 5c. First postal motor coach (50th anniv of postal motor coach service); 10c. Electric train emerging from Simplon Tunnel and Stockalper Palace (50th anniv of opening of Simplon Tunnel).

The 40c. commemorates the 25th anniv of Swissair.

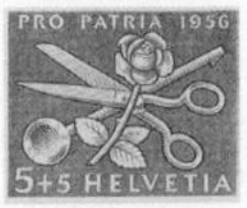

129 Rose, Scissors and Tape-measure

1956. Pro Patria. Swiss Women's Fund. T **129** and design as T **116** but inscr "PRO PATRIA 1956".

571	**129**	5c.+5c. green	85	2·10
572	-	10c.+10c. emerald and green	85	85
573	-	20c.+10c. purple & pink	1·70	1·30
574	-	30c.+10c. brown and light brown	4·25	10·00
575	-	40c.+10c. blue and light blue	5·00	13·50

DESIGNS: 10c. R. Rhone at St. Maurice; 20c. Katzensee; 30c. R. Rhine at Trin; 40c. Walensee.

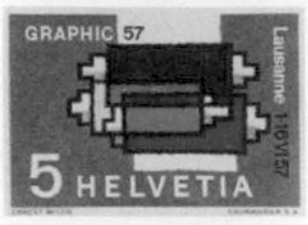

130 Printing Machine's Inking Rollers

1957. Publicity Issue. Inscr "1957".

576	**130**	5c. multicoloured	40	25
577	-	10c. brown, green & turq	4·25	40
578	-	20c. grey and red	40	85
579	-	40c. multicoloured	2·50	1·70

DESIGNS: 10c. Electric train crossing bridge over River Ticino (75th anniv of St. Gotthard Railway); 20c. Civil Defence shield and coat of arms ("Civil Defence"); 40c. Munatius Plancus, Basel and Rhine (2000th anniv of Basel).

The 5c. commemorates "Graphic 57" International Exhibition, Lausanne.

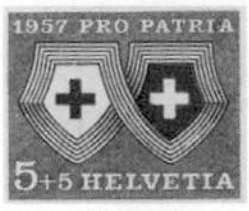

131 Shields of Switzerland and the Red Cross

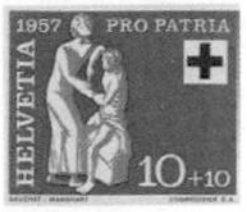

132 "Charity"

1957. Pro Patria. Swiss Red Cross and National Cancer League Funds. Cross in red.

580	**131**	5c.+5c. red and grey	40	1·30
581	**132**	10c.+10c. purple & grn	85	55
582	**132**	20c.+10c. grey and red	85	85
583	**132**	30c.+10c. blue & brown	4·50	7·50
584	**132**	40c.+10c. brown & blue	5·75	10·00

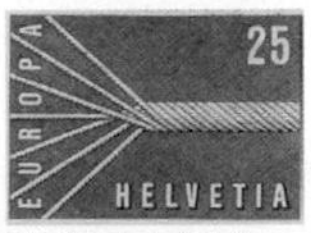

133 Symbol of Unity

1957. Europa.

585	**133**	25c. red	1·30	1·30
586	**133**	40c. blue	4·50	1·30

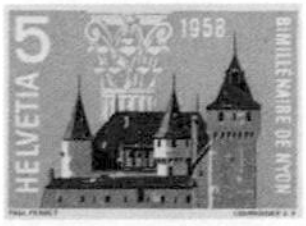

134 Nyon Castle (2000th anniv of Nyon)

1958. Publicity Issue. Inscr "1958".

587	**134**	5c. violet, buff and green	40	25
588	-	10c. myrtle, red and green	40	25
589	-	20c. red, lilac and vermilion	85	35
590	-	40c. multicoloured	1·70	2·10

DESIGNS: 10c. Woman's head with ribbons (Saffa Exhibition, Zurich); 20c. Crossbow (25th anniv as symbol of Swiss manufacture); 40c. Salvation Army bonnet (75th anniv of Salvation Army in Switzerland).

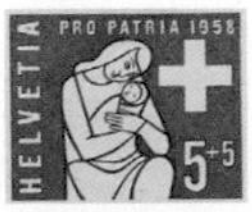

135 "Needy Mother"

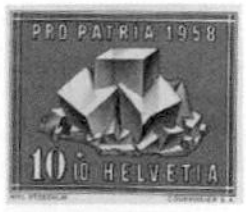

136 Fluorite

1958. Pro Patria. For Needy Mothers, T **135** and designs showing minerals, rocks and fossils as T **136**. Inscr "PRO PATRIA 1958".

591	5c.+5c. purple	50	40
592	10c.+10c. yellow, grn & blk	90	40
593	20c.+10c. bistre, red & blk	1·00	1·30
594	30c.+10c. purple, brn & blk	3·50	7·50
595	40c.+10c. blue, ultram & blk	3·50	8·25

DESIGNS: 20c. "Lytoceras fimbriatus" ammonite; 30c. Garnet; 40c. Rock crystal.

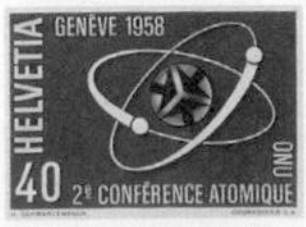

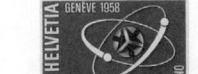

137 Atomic Symbol

1958. Second U.N. Atomic Conference, Geneva.

596	**137**	40c. red, blue and cream	85	85

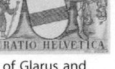

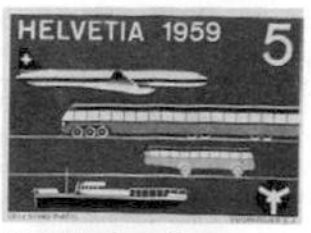

138 Modern Transport

1959. Publicity Issue. Inscr "1959".

597	5c. multicoloured	40	25
598	10c. yellow, grey and green	40	25
599	20c. multicoloured	85	40
600	50c. blue, violet and light blue	1·70	1·30

DESIGNS: 5c. Type **138** (opening of "The Swiss House of Transport and Communications"); 10c. Lictor's fasces of the Coat of Arms of St. Gall and posthorn (NABAG—National Philatelic Exhibition, St. Gall); 20c. Owl, hare and fish (Protection of Animals); 50c. J. Calvin, Th. de Beze and University building (4th centenary of University of Geneva).

1959. National Philatelic Exhibtion, St. Gallen ("NABAG"). Sheet 94×57 mm. As No. 598. Imperf.

MS600a 10c. and 20c. multicoloured (sold at 2f.) 21·00 21·00

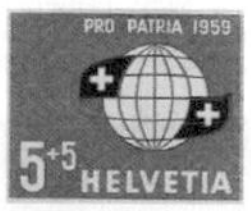

139 "Swiss Citizens Abroad"

1959. Pro Patria. For Swiss Citizens Abroad. T **139** and other designs showing minerals, rocks and fossils as T **136**, and inscr "PRO PATRIA 1959".

601	5c.+5c. red and grey	60	85
602	10c.+10c. multicoloured	65	85
603	20c.+10c. multicoloured	85	85
604	30c.+10c. violet, brn & blk	2·50	5·00
605	40c.+10c. blue, turquoise and black	3·00	5·00

DESIGNS: 10c. Agate; 20c. Tourmaline; 30c. Amethyst; 40c. Fossilized giant salamander.

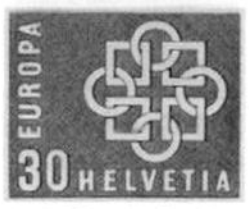

140 "Europa"

1959. Europa.

606	**140**	30c. red	1·70	85
607	**140**	50c. blue	2·50	1·70

1959. European P.T.T. Conference, Montreux. Optd **REUNION DES PTT D'EUROPE 1959.**

608	30c. red	21·00	11·50
609	50c. blue	21·00	11·50

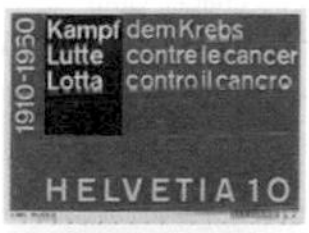

142 "Campaign against Cancer"

1960. Publicity Issue. Inscr "1460–1960" (20c.) or "1960" (50c., 75c.).

610	10c. red, light green and green	85	25
611	20c. multicoloured	85	25
612	50c. yellow, ultramarine & blue	85	1·70
613	75c. red, black and blue	5·75	5·75

DESIGNS: 10c. Type **142** (50th anniv of Swiss National League for Cancer Control); 20c. Charter and sceptre (500th anniv of Basel University); 50c. "Uprooted tree" (World Refugee Year); 75c. Douglas DC-8 jetliner ("Swissair enters the jet age").

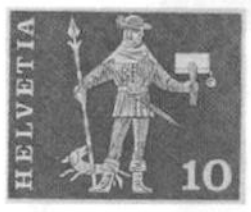

143 15th-century Schwyz Cantonal Messenger

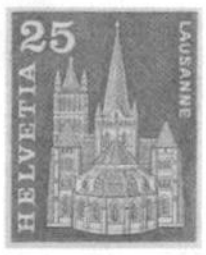

143a Lausanne Cathedral

1960. Postal History and "Architectural Monuments" (1st series).

614	-	5c. blue	25	15
615	**143**	10c. green	25	15
616	-	15c. red	25	15
617	-	20c. mauve	40	25
618	**143a**	25c. green	90	25
619p	-	30c. red	50	25
620	-	35c. red	1·30	1·30
621	-	40c. purple	1·10	25
622	-	50c. blue	1·40	35
623	-	60c. red	1·70	40
624	-	70c. orange	1·80	1·80
625	-	75c. blue	2·50	1·70
626	-	80c. purple	2·30	40
627	-	90c. green	1·80	40
628	-	1f. orange	1·80	25
629	-	1f.20 red	2·30	35
632	-	1f.30 brown on lilac	2·20	40
630	-	1f.50 green	2·75	85
633	-	1f.70 purple on lilac	2·75	40
631	-	2f. blue	4·25	1·70
634	-	2f.20 green on green	3·75	1·70
635	-	2f.80 orange on orange	4·75	1·70

DESIGNS—HORIZ: 5c. 17th-century Fribourg Cantonal messenger; 15c. 17th-century mule-driver; 20c. 19th-century mounted postman; 1f. Fribourg Town Hall; 1f.20, Basel Gate, Solothurn; 1f.50, Ital Reding's house, Schwyz; 1f.70, 2f., 2f.20, Abbey Church, Einsiedeln. VERT: 30c. Grossmunster, Zurich; 35c., 1f.30, Woodcutters Guildhall, Bienne; 40c. St. Peter's Cathedral, Geneva; 50c. Spalentor (gate), Basel; 60c. Clock Tower, Berne; 70c. Collegiate Church of St. Peter and St. Stephen, Bellinzona; 75c. Kapellbrucke (bridge) and Wasserturm, Lucerne; 80c. St. Gall Cathedral; 90c. Munot Fort, Schaffhausen; 2f.80, as 70c. but redrawn without bell-tower.

See also Nos. 698/713 and 1276.

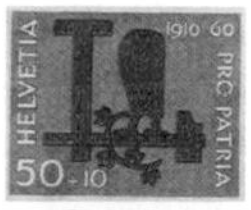

144 Symbols of Occupational Trades

1960. Pro Patria. For Swiss Youth. T **144** and other designs showing minerals, rocks and fossils as T **136** and inscr "PRO PATRIA 1960".

636		5c.+5c. multicoloured	85	1·30
637		10c.+10c. pink, green and black	85	85
638		20c.+10c. yellow, purple and black	85	85
639		30c.+10c. blue, brown and black	4·00	7·00
640	**144**	50c.+10c. gold & blue	4·25	6·75

DESIGNS: 5c. Smoky quartz; 10c. Orthoclase (feldspar); 20c. Devil's toenail (fossil shell); 30c. Azurite; 50c. Type **144** ("50 Years of National Day Collection").

1960. 50th Anniv of Pro Patria Charity Fund. Sheet 85×75 mm. As No. 640. Imperf.

MS641 50c.+10c. gold and blue (block of 4) (sold at 3f.) 55·00 30·00

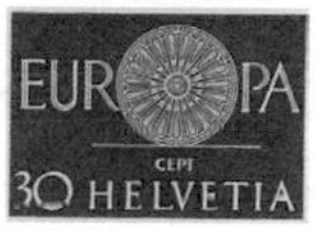

144a Conference Emblem

1960. Europa.

642	**144a**	30c. red	1·10	50
643	**144a**	50c. blue	1·60	1·50

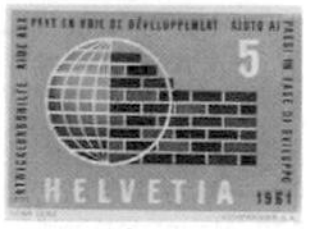

145 "Aid for Development"

1961. Publicity Issue.

644	**145**	5c. red, blue and grey	55	30
645	-	10c. yellow and blue	55	20
646	-	20c. multicoloured	3·25	1·00
647	-	50c. red, green and blue	2·20	2·00

DESIGNS: 5c. Type **145** ("Aid to countries in process of development"); 10c. Circular emblem ("Hyspa" Exhibition of 20th-century Hygiene, Gymnastics and Sport, Berne); 20c. Hockey stick (World and European Ice Hockey Championships, Geneva and Lausanne); 50c. Map of Switzerland with telephone centres as wiring diagram (inauguration of Swiss fully automatic telephone service).

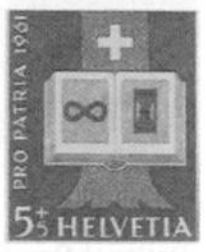

146 "Cultural Works of Eternity"

1961. Pro Patria. For Swiss Cultural Works, T **146** and other designs showing minerals, rocks and fossils as T **136** and inscr "PRO PATRIA 1961".

648	5c.+5c. blue	80	1·00
649	10c.+10c. purple, green and black	1·10	70
650	20c.+10c. red, blue and black	1·10	80
651	30c.+10c. blue, orange and black	2·75	5·00
652	50c.+10c. bistre, blue and black	3·25	7·00

DESIGNS: 10c. Fluorite; 20c. Glarone rabbitfish; 30c. Lazulite; 50c. Fossilized fern.

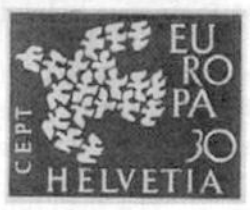

147 Doves

1961. Europa.

653	**147**	30c. red	1·10	50
654	**147**	50c. blue	1·60	1·50

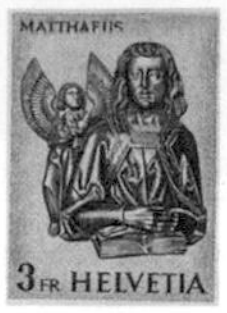

148 St. Matthew

1961. Wood Carvings from St. Oswald's Church, Zug.

655	**148**	3f. red	6·50	50
656	-	5f. blue	11·00	50
657	-	10f. brown	22·00	50
658	-	20f. red	43·00	7·00

DESIGNS: 5f. St. Mark; 10f. St. Luke; 20f. St. John.

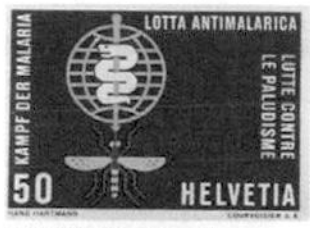

149 W.H.O. Emblem and Mosquito

1962. Publicity Issue.

659		5c. multicoloured	1·10	50
660		10c. bistre, purple and green	1·10	50
661		20c. multicoloured	4·25	1·00
662	**149**	50c. green, mauve and blue	2·20	2·00

DESIGNS: 5c. Electric train (introduction of Trans-Europe Express); 10c. Oarsman (World Rowing Championship, Lucerne); 20c. Jungfraujoch and Monch (50th anniv of Jungfraujoch rack railway station); 50c. Type **149** (malaria eradication).

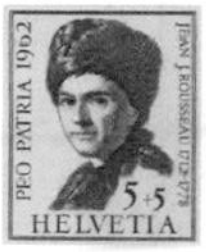

150 Rousseau

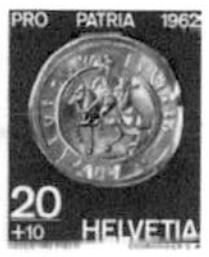

151 Schwyz Gold Ducat

1962. Pro Patria. For Swiss Old People's Homes and Cultural Works.

663	**150**	5c.+5c. blue	55	50
664	-	10c.+10c. blue, black and green	75	50
665	**151**	20c.+10c. yellow, black and red	1·10	1·00
666	-	30c.+10c. green, blue and red	1·60	3·00
667	-	50c.+10c. violet, black and blue	1·60	3·00

COINS—As Type **151**. 10c. Obwalden silver-half taler; 30c. Uri batzen; 50c. Nidwalden batzen.

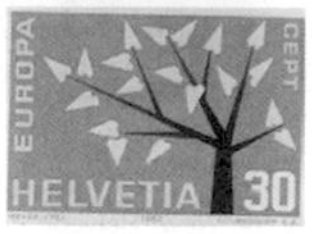

152 Europa "Tree"

1962. Europa.

668	**152**	30c. orange, yellow & brn	1·40	1·30
669	**152**	50c. blue, green and brown	2·20	1·50

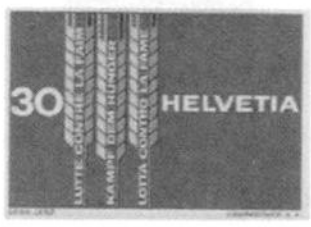

153 Campaign Emblem (Freedom from Hunger)

1963. Publicity Issue.

670	-	5c. brown, red and blue	55	40
671	-	10c. red, grey and green	1·10	30
672	-	20c. lake, red and grey	3·75	50
673	**153**	30c. yellow, brown & green	1·60	1·50
674	-	50c. red, silver and blue	2·40	2·20
675	-	50c. multicoloured	3·00	2·75

DESIGNS: No. 670, Boy scout (50th anniv of Swiss Boy Scout League); 671, Badge (Swiss Alpine Club cent); 672, Luegelkinn Viaduct (50th anniv of Lotschberg Railway); 674, Jubilee Emblem (Red Cross cent); 675, Hotel des Postes, Paris, 1863 (Paris Postal Conference).

1963. International Red Cross Centenary. Sheet 100×80 mm. As No. 674. Imperf.

MS675a 50c. multicoloured (block of 4) (sold at 3f.) 11·00 10·50

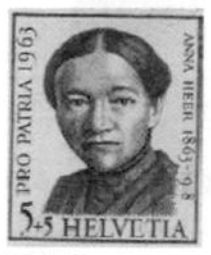

154 Dr. Anna Heer (nursing pioneer)

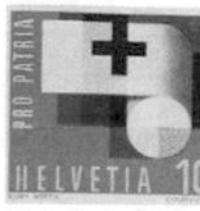

155 Roll of Bandage

1963. Pro Patria. For Swiss Medical and Refugee Aid. T **154** and other designs as T **155** showing Red Cross activities. Inscr "PRO PATRIA 1963".

676	5c.+5c. blue	55	50
677	10c.+10c. red, grey and green	80	50
678	20c.+10c. multicoloured	1·10	50
679	30c.+10c. multicoloured	1·70	3·00
680	50c.+10c. red, indigo & blue	2·30	3·00

DESIGNS: 20c. Gift parcel; 30c. Blood plasma; 50c. Red Cross brassard.

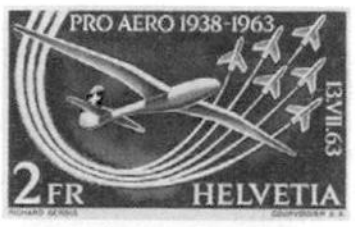

156 Glider and Jet Aircraft

1963. Air. 25th Anniv of Swiss "Pro Aero" Foundation. Berne–Locarno or Langenbruck–Berne (helicopter feeder) Special Flights.

681	**156**	2f. multicoloured	6·75	6·00

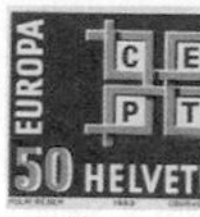

157 "Co-operation"

1963. Europa.

682	**157**	50c. brown and blue	1·10	1·00

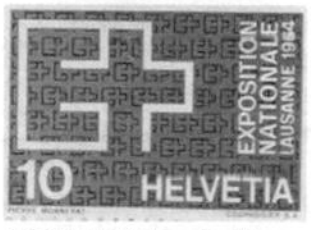

158 Exhibition Emblem

1963. Swiss National Exhibition, Lausanne.

683	**158**	10c. green and olive	55	20
684	**158**	20c. red and brown	55	20
685	-	50c. blue, grey and red	1·10	50
686	-	75c. violet, grey and red	1·70	1·50

DESIGNS: 50c. "Outlook" (emblem on globe and smaller globe); 75c. "Insight" (emblem on large globe).

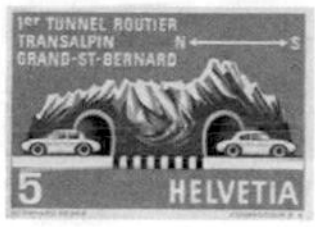

159 Great St. Bernard Tunnel

1964. Publicity Issue.

687	5c. blue, red and green	60	20
688	10c. green and blue	55	20
689	20c. multicoloured	85	30
690	50c. multicoloured	2·50	2·00

DESIGNS: 5c. Type **159** (Opening of Great St. Bernard Road Tunnel); 10c. Ancient "god of the waters" (Protection of water supplies); 20c. Swiss soldiers of 1864 and 1964 (Centenary of Swiss Association of Non-commissioned Officers); 50c. Standards of Geneva and Swiss Confederation (150th anniv of arrival of Swiss in Geneva).

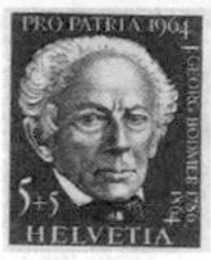

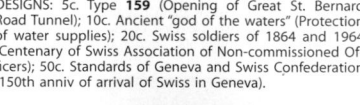

160 Johann Georg Bodmer (inventor)

1964. Pro Patria. For Swiss Mountain Aid and Cultural Funds. T **160** and vert designs of Swiss coins as T **151**. Inscr "PRO PATRIA 1964".

691	5c.+5c. blue	55	30
692	10c.+10c. drab, black & grn	55	30
693	20c.+10c. blue, black & mve	80	50
694	30c.+10c. blue, black & orge	1·10	1·00
695	50c.+10c. yellow, brn & bl	1·70	1·50

COINS: 10c. Zurich copper; 20c. Basel "doppeldicken"; 30c. Geneva silver thaler; 50c. Berne half gold florin.

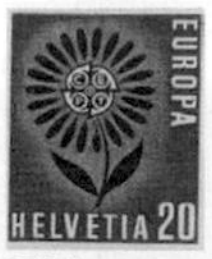

161 Europa "Flower"

305 Mouth of River Rhine and Caspian Tern

1992. Publicity Issue. Multicoloured.

1238	50c. Type **305** (centenary of Treaty for International Regulation of the Rhine)	1·20	55
1239	80c. Family (50th anniv of Pro Familia)	1·90	1·50
1240	90c. Chemical formula and model of difluorobutane molecule (centenary of International Chemical Nomenclature Conference, Geneva)	2·20	2·00

306 Map of Americas and "Santa Maria"

1992. Europa. 500th Anniv of Discovery of America by Columbus. Multicoloured.

1241	50c. Type **306**	2·40	55
1242	90c. Route map of first voyage and sketch for statue of Columbus (Vincenzo Vela)	3·00	2·30

307 Skier

1992. Sierre Int Comics Festival. Multicoloured.

1243	50c. Type **307**	1·50	55
1244	80c. Mouse-artist drawing strip	2·40	1·10
1245	90c. Love-struck man holding bunch of stamp-flowers behind back	2·75	2·30

308 1780s Earthenware Plate, Heimberg

1992. Pro Patria. Folk Art. Multicoloured.

1246	50c.+20c. Type **308**	1·80	1·10
1247	70c.+30c. Paper cut-out by Johann Jakob Hauswirth	3·00	2·30
1248	80c.+40c. Maplewood cream spoon, Gruyeres	3·75	3·50
1249	90c.+40c. Carnation from 1780 embroidered saddle cloth, Grisons	4·25	4·00

309 Flags and Alps

1992. Alpine Protection Convention.

1250	**309** 90c. multicoloured	2·75	2·00

310 Clowns on Trapeze

1992. The Circus. Multicoloured.

1251	50c. Type **310**	1·50	55
1252	70c. Sealion with Auguste the clown	2·20	1·10
1253	80c. Chalky the clown and elephant	2·75	1·70
1254	90c. Harlequin and horse	2·75	2·30

311 Sport Pictograms

1992. Pro Sport.

1255	**311** 50c.+20c. black & blue	1·70	1·10

312 Train and Map

1992. Centenary (1993) of Central Office for International Rail Carriage.

1256	**312** 90c. multicoloured	3·00	2·00

313 "A" (first class) Mail

1993

1257	– 60c. dp blue, yellow & bl	1·80	55
1258	**313** 80c. red, orange and scarlet	2·40	55

DESIGN: 60c. Lake Tanay.

314 Zurich and Geneva 1843 Stamps

1993. 150th Anniv of Swiss Postage Stamps. Multicoloured.

1259	60c. Type **314**	1·50	55
1260	80c. Postal cancellation (stamps for postage)	1·90	1·50
1261	100c. Magnifying glass (stamp collecting)	2·40	2·30

315 Paracelsus (after Augustin Hirschvogel) (500th birth anniv)

1993. Publicity Issue.

1262	**315** 60c. brown, grey and blue	1·80	55
1263	– 80c. multicoloured	2·40	1·70
1264	– 180c. multicoloured	5·50	4·50

DESIGNS—VERT: 80c. Discus thrower (from Greek vase) (inauguration of Olympic Museum, Lausanne). HORIZ: 180c. Worker's head (cent of International Metalworkers' Federation).

316 "Hohentwiel" (lake steamer) and Flags

1993. Lake Constance European Region.

1265	**316** 60c. multicoloured	1·80	1·00

317 Interior of Media House, Villeurbanne, France

1993. Europa. Contemporary Architecture.

1266	**317** 60c. ultramarine, blk & bl	1·80	55
1267	80c. red, black and grey	3·00	2·30

DESIGN: 80c. House, Breganzona, Ticino.

318 Appenzell Dairyman's Earring

1993. Pro Patria. Folk Art. Multicoloured.

1268	60c.+30c. Type **318**	2·40	1·70
1269	60c.+30c. Fluhli enamelled glass bottle, 1738	2·40	1·70
1270	80c.+40c. Driving cows to summer pasture (detail of mural, Sylvestre Pidoux)	3·75	3·50
1271	100c.+40c. Straw hat ornaments	4·25	4·00

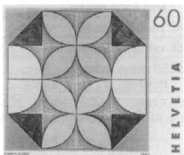

319 "Work No. 095" (Emma Kunz)

1993. Paintings by Swiss Women Artists. Multicoloured.

1272	60c. Type **319**	1·80	55
1273	80c. "Great Singer Lilas Goergens" (Aloise) (33×33 mm)	2·40	1·10
1274	100c. "Under the Rain Cloud" (Meret Oppenheim) (33×33 mm)	3·00	2·30
1275	120c. "Four Spaces with Horizontal Bands" (Sophi Taeuber-Arp) (33×33 mm)	3·75	2·75

320 Kapell Bridge and Water Tower, Lucerne

1993. Kapell Bridge Restoration Fund.

1276	**320** 80c.+20c. carmine and red	2·40	1·10

321 Hieroglyphic, Cuneiform and Roman Scripts

1994. "Books and the Press" Exhibition, Geneva. Multicoloured.

1277	60c. Type **321**	1·80	55
1278	80c. Gothic letterpress script	1·90	1·70
1279	100c. Modern electronic fonts	2·40	2·30

322 Athletes

1994. Publicity Issue. Multicoloured.

1280	60c. Type **322** (50th Anniv of National Sports School, Magglingen)	1·80	55
1281	80c. Jakob Bernoulli (mathematician) (after Nicolas Bernoulli) and formula and diagram of the law of large numbers (Int Mathematicians' Congress, Zurich)	1·90	1·60
1282	100c. Heads, Unisource emblem, globe and flags (collaboration of Swiss, Dutch and Swedish telecommunications companies)	2·40	2·30
1283	180c. Radar image, airliner and globe (50th anniv of I.C.A.O.)	4·75	4·00

323 Footballers

1994. World Cup Football Championship, U.S.A., and Cent (1995) of Swiss Football Association.

1284	**323** 80c. multicoloured	3·00	1·70

324 "Trieste" (bathyscaphe)

1994. Europa. Discoveries and Inventions. Vehicles used by Auguste Piccard in Stratospheric and Deep-sea Explorations. Multicoloured.

1285	60c. Type **324**	1·80	55
1286	100c. "F.N.R.S." (stratosphere balloon)	3·75	2·75

325 Neuchatel Weight-driven Clock (Jacques Matthey-Jonais)

1994. Pro Patria. Folk Art. Multicoloured.

1287	60c.+30c. Type **325**	2·40	1·70
1288	60c.+30c. Embroidered pomegranate on linen	2·40	1·70
1289	80c.+40c. Mould for Krafli pastry	3·75	3·50
1290	100c.+40c. Paper-bird cradle mobile	4·25	4·00

326 Symbolic Condom

1994. Anti-AIDS Campaign.

1291	**326** 60c. multicoloured	1·50	70

327 Simenon and his Home, Echandens Castle, Lausanne

1994. Fifth Death Anniv of Georges Simenon (novelist).

1292	**327** 100c. multicoloured	3·00	2·30

Schweizer Elektrizität Electricité Suisse Eletricità Svizzera 1895–1995 Helvetia 60

328 "Swiss Electricity"

1995. Publicity Issue.

1293	**328** 60c. multicoloured	1·80	55
1294	– 60c. blue and black	1·50	55
1295	– 80c. multicoloured	1·90	1·10
1296	– 180c. multicoloured	4·25	4·00

DESIGNS—HORIZ: No. 1293, Type **328** (centenary of Swiss Association of Electricity Producers and Distributors); 1295, "(sda ats)" (centenary of Swiss News Agency); 1296, "ONU UNO" (50th anniv of U.N.O.). VERT: No. 1294, Wrestlers (centenary of Swiss Wrestling Association and National Wrestling and Alpine Herdsmen's Festival, Chur).

329 European Beaver

1995. Endangered Animals. Multicoloured.

1297	60c. Type **329**	1·80	55
1298	80c. Map butterfly	2·40	1·80
1299	100c. Green tree frog	3·00	2·30
1300	120c. Little owl	3·75	2·75

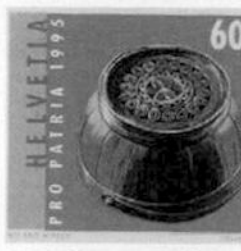

330 Cream Pail, 1776

1995. Pro Patria. Folk Art. Multicoloured.

1301	60c.+30c. Type **330**	2·40	1·70
1302	60c.+30c. Neuchatel straw hat	2·40	1·70
1303	80c.+40c. Detail of chest lock, 1580	3·75	3·50
1304	100c.+40c. Langnau ceramic sugar bowl	4·25	4·00

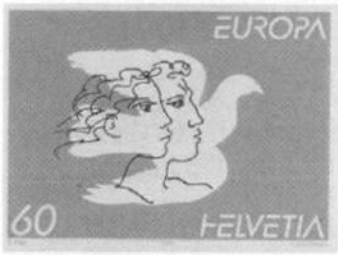

331 Couple and Dove

1995. Europa. Peace and Freedom.

1305	**331**	60c. blue and cobalt	3·75	55
1306	-	100c. brown and ochre	6·00	2·75

DESIGN: 100c. Europa with Zeus as bull.

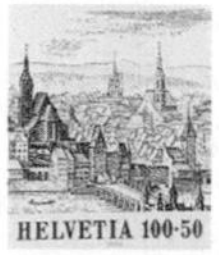

332 Basel (right-hand part)

1995. "Basler Taube 1995" Stamp Exhibition, Basel. Sheet 100×131 mm. containing T **332** and similar vert designs.

MS1307 60c.+30c. black, violet and blue; 80c+30c. multicoloured; 100c.+50c. black, violet and blue; 100c+50c. black, violet and blue 13·50 13·00

DESIGNS: 80c.+30c. Basel 2½ Dove stamp (150th Anniv of issue); 60c+30c., 100c.+50c. (2) Panorama of Basel by Matthaus Meriam (composite design).

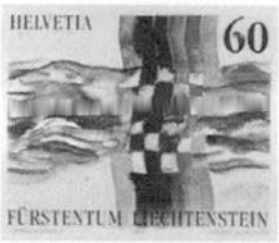

333 Coloured Ribbons woven through River

1995. Switzerland–Liechtenstein Co-operation.

1308	**333**	60c. multicoloured	1·50	55

No. 1308 was valid for use in both Switzerland and Liechtenstein (see No. 1106 of Liechtenstein).

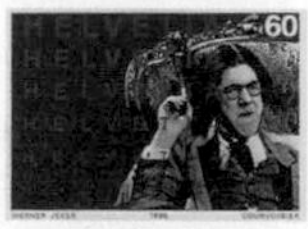

334 "The Vocation of Andre Carrel" (1925)

1995. Centenary of Motion Pictures. Multicoloured.

1309	60c. Type **334**	1·50	55
1310	80c. "Anna Goldin – The Last Witch"	1·90	1·70
1311	150c. "Pipilotti's Mistakes – Absolution"	3·75	3·50

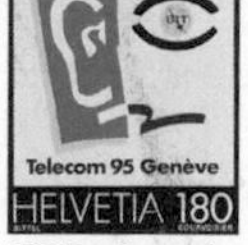

335 Ear, Eye and Mouth

1995. "Telecom 95" International Telecommunications Exhibition, Geneva.

1312	**335**	180c. multicoloured	4·25	4·00

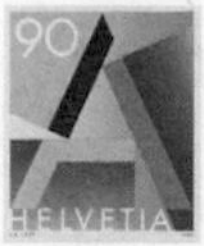

336 "A" (first class) Mail

1995

1313	**336**	90c. blue, red and yellow	2·20	55

See also No. 1480.

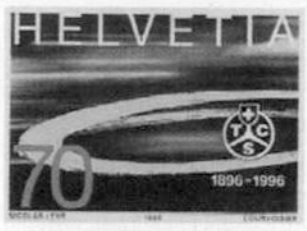

337 Emblem

1996. Publicity Issue. Multicoloured.

1314	70c. Type **337** (centenary of Touring Club of Switzerland)	1·70	80
1315	70c. Heart (50th anniv of charity organizations)	1·70	80
1316	90c. Brass band (30th Federal Music Festival, Interlaken)	2·20	2·00
1317	90c. Young girls (centenary of Pro Filia (girls' aid society))	2·20	2·00
1318	180c. Jean Piaget (child psychologist, birth centenary)	4·25	4·00

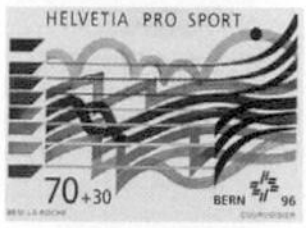

338 Coloured Ribbons and "Bern 96" Gymnastic Festival Emblem

1996. Pro Sport.

1319	**338**	70c.+30c. multicoloured	2·40	2·30

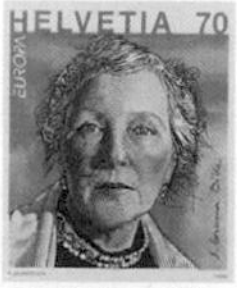

339 Corinna Bille (writer)

1996. Europa. Famous Women. Multicoloured.

1320	70c. Type **339**	1·70	55
1321	110c. Iris von Roten-Meyer (feminist writer)	2·75	2·75

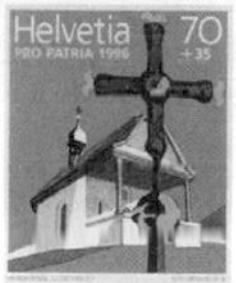

340 Magdalena Chapel, Wolfenschiessen, and Cross

1996. Pro Patria. Heritage. Multicoloured.

1322	70c.+35c. Type **340**	3·00	1·70
1323	70c.+35c. Underground sawmill and workshop, Col-des-Roches	3·00	1·70
1324	90c.+40c. Baroque baths, Pfafers	4·25	4·00
1325	110c.+50c. Roman road and milestone, Great St. Bernhard	4·75	4·50

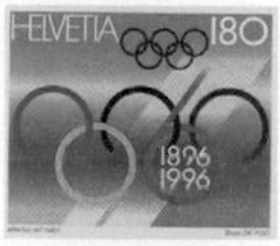

341 Olympic Rings

1996. Centenary of Modern Olympic Games.

1326	**341**	180c. multicoloured	5·50	4·00

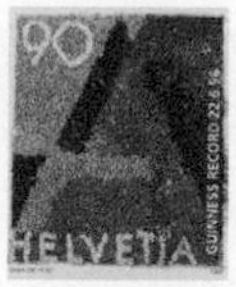

342 Representation of 1995 "A" Mail Stamp

1996. Guinness World Record for Largest "Living" Postage Stamp represented by Human Beings (arrangement of people to represent stamp design).

1327	**342**	90c. multicoloured	2·40	2·30

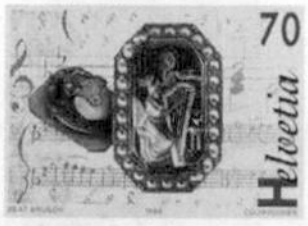

343 Musical Movement and Mechanical Ring (Isaac-Daniel Piguet)

1996. Bicentenary of Antoine Favre-Salomon's Invention of the Metal Teeth System for Music Boxes. Multicoloured.

1328	70c. Type **343**	1·80	80
1329	90c. "Basso-piccolo mandolin" cylinder music box (Eduard Jaccard)	2·40	2·30
1330	110c. Station automaton (Paillard & Co)	3·00	2·75
1331	180c. Kalllope disc music box	4·75	4·50

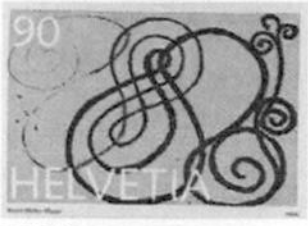

344 Pattern

1996. Greetings Stamps. Multicoloured. Self-adhesive.

1332	90c. Type **344**	3·00	2·75
1333	90c. Mottled pattern	3·00	2·75
1334	90c. Coil pattern	3·00	2·75
1335	90c. Flower and leaf pattern	3·00	2·75

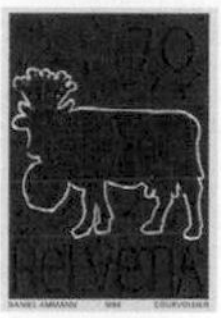

345 "The Golden Cow" (Daniel Ammann)

1996. Winning Entries in Stamp Design Competition.

1336	**345**	70c. gold and blue	1·70	80
1337	-	90c. multicoloured	2·20	2·00
1338	-	110c. multicoloured	2·75	2·50
1339	-	180c. brown, black and blue	4·25	4·00

DESIGNS: 90c. "Wake with a Smile" (Max Sprick); 110c. "Leaves" (Elena Emma-Pugliese); 180c. "Dove" (Rene Conscience).

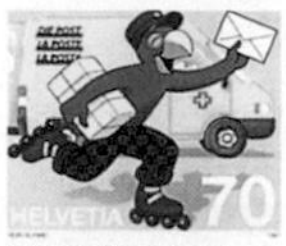

346 Globi delivering Mail

1997. Globi (cartoon character by Robert Lips).

1340	**346**	70c. multicoloured	1·70	30

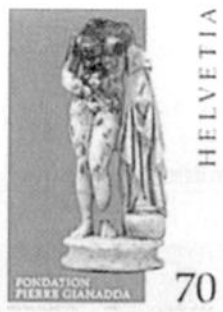

347 Venus of Octodurus

1997. Gallo-Roman Works of Art. Multicoloured.

1341	70c. Type **347** (from Forum Claudii Vallensium (now Martigny))	1·70	1·10
1342	90c. Bust of Bacchus (from Augusta Raurica (now Augst))	2·20	2·30
1343	110c. Ceramic fragment showing "Victory" (from Iulio Magus (now Schleitheim))	2·75	2·75
1344	180c. Mosaic showing female theatrical mask (from Vallon)	4·25	4·50

Each stamp is inscribed with the name of the Foundation bearing responsibility for the preservation of the respective archaeological sites.

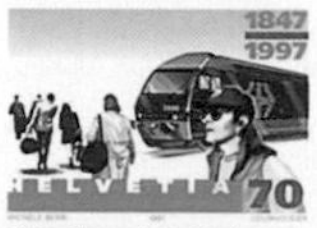

348 Class 460 Series 2000 Electric Locomotive

1997. 150th Anniv of Zurich–Barden Railway. Multicoloured.

1345	70c. Type **348**	2·20	1·10
1346	90c. Electric "Red Arrow" railcar set, 1935	2·75	2·30
1347	1f.40 Pullman coach, 1930s	4·25	3·50
1348	1f.70 "Limmat", 1847 (first locomotive in Switzerland)	4·75	4·50

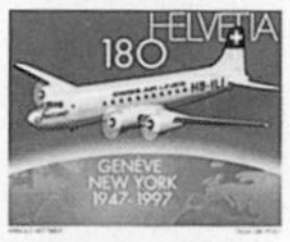

349 Douglas DC-4 "Grand Old Lady" over Globe

1997. 50th Anniv of Swissair's North Atlantic Service.

1349	**349**	180c. multicoloured	5·50	4·00

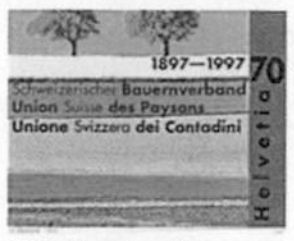

350 Farmland

1997. Publicity Issue. Multicoloured.

1350	70c. Type **350** (centenary of Swiss Farmers' Union)	1·70	70
1351	90c. Street plan (centenary of Swiss Municipalities' Union)	2·20	2·00

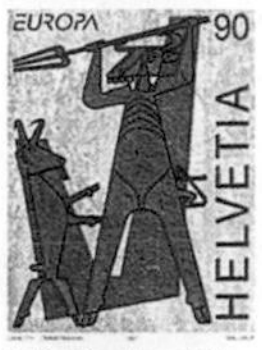

351 "Devil and the Goat" (painting by Heinrich Danioth on rock face of Schollenen Gorge)

1997. Europa. Tales and Legends. The Devil's Bridge.

1352	**351**	90c. brown and yellow	2·40	2·30

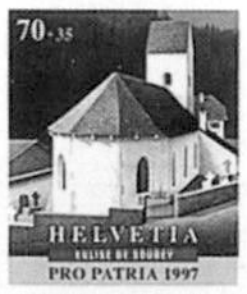

352 St. Valbert's Church, Soubey (Jura)

1997. Pro Patria. Heritage and Landscapes. Multicoloured.

1353	70c.+35c. Type **352**	3·00	1·70
1354	70c.+35c. Culture mill, Lutzelfluh (Berne)	3·00	1·70
1355	90c.+40c. Ittingen Charterhouse (Thurgau)	4·25	4·00
1356	110c.+50c. Casa Patriziale, Russo (Ticino)	4·75	4·50

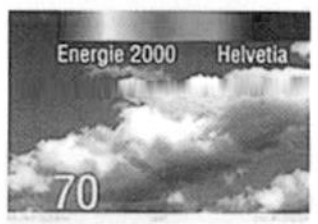

353 Clouds (Air)

1997. Energy 2000 (energy efficiency programme). The Elements. Multicoloured.

1357	70c. Type **353**	1·70	90
1358	90c. Burning wood (Fire)	2·20	2·30
1359	110c. Water droplets (Water)	2·75	2·75
1360	180c. Pile of soil (Earth)	4·25	4·50

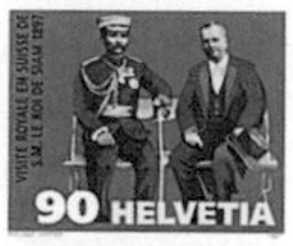

354 King Rama V and President Adolf Deucher

1997. Centenary of Visit of King Rama V of Siam.

1361	**354**	90c. multicoloured	2·20	2·00

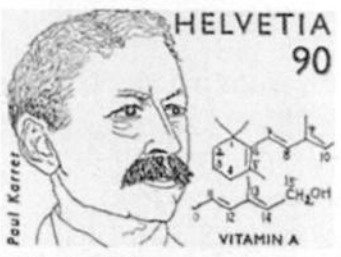

355 Paul Karrer and Molecular Structure of Vitamin A

1997. The Nobel Prize.

1362	**355**	90c. black and grey	2·75	2·00
1363	-	110c. black and purple	3·25	2·50

DESIGNS: 90c. Type **355** (Chemistry Prize, 1937); 110c. Alfred Nobel (founder of Prize Fund).

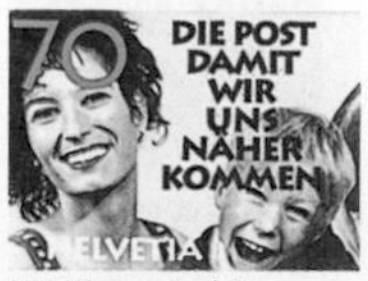

356 Woman and Boy (German)

1997. "The Post keeps Us in Touch".

1364	**356**	70c. black, red and blue	2·20	70
1365	-	70c. black, yellow and blue	2·20	70
1366	-	70c. black, yellow and green	2·20	70

1367	-	70c. black, green and red	2·20	70

DESIGNS: No. 1365, Boy wearing baseball cap with woman (French); 1366, Young couple (Italian); 1367, Girl and man (Romansch).

357 Postal Service Emblem

1998. Separation of Swiss Post and Swisscom (telecommunications).

1368	**357**	90c. black, yellow and red	2·20	2·00
1369	-	90c. deep blue, blue and red	2·20	2·00

DESIGN: No. 1369, Swisscom emblem.

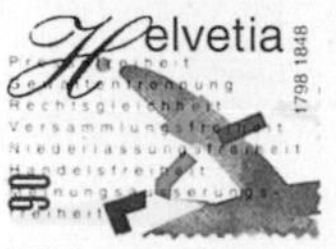

358 Arrows

1998. Bicentenary of Declaration of Helvetic Republic and 150th Anniv of Swiss Federal State. Multicoloured.

1370	90c. Type **358**	2·40	2·30
1371	90c. Face value at bottom right	2·40	2·30
1372	90c. Face value at top left	2·40	2·30
1373	90c. Face value at top right	2·40	2·30

359 Winter Olympics 2006

1998. Swiss Candidacy for Winter Olympic Games.

1374	**359**	90c. multicoloured	2·40	2·30

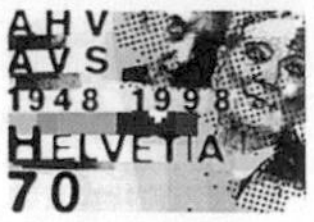

360 Elderly Couple

1998. Publicity Issues. Multicoloured.

1375	70c. Type **360** (Old Age and Survivor's Insurance)	1·70	90
1376	70c. National Museum, Prangins Castle (centenary of Swiss National Museum, Zurich, and inauguration of Prangins branch)	1·70	90
1377	90c. Fingerprints (centenary of St. Gallen University)	2·20	1·10

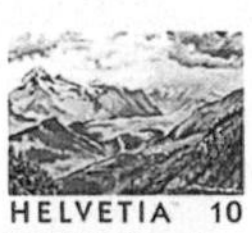

361 "On Top of the Simplon Pass"

1998. Paintings by Jean-Frederic Schnyder. Multicoloured.

1378	10c. Type **361**	35	25
1379	20c. "Snowdrift near Neuthal"	60	35
1380	50c. "Franches Montagnes"	1·50	55
1381	70c. "Two Horses"	1·70	60
1382	90c. "En Route"	2·20	70
1383	110c. "Winter Morning by the Alpnachersee"	2·75	1·00
1385	140c. "Zug"	3·50	1·10
1386	170c. "Olive Grove"	4·00	1·40
1387	180c. "Near Reutigen"	4·25	2·00

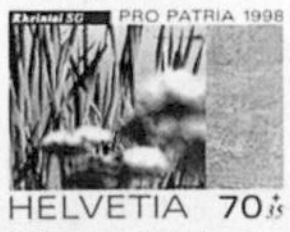

362 St. Gall, Rhine Valley

1998. Pro Patria. Heritage and Landscapes. Multicoloured.

1390	70c.+35c. Type **362**	3·00	2·30
1391	70c.+35c. Round church, Saas Balen	3·00	2·30
1392	90c.+40c. Forest, Bodmeren	3·75	3·50
1393	90c.+40c. The old Refuge (museum), St. Gotthard	4·25	3·50
1394	110c.+50c. Smithy, Corcelles	4·75	5·00

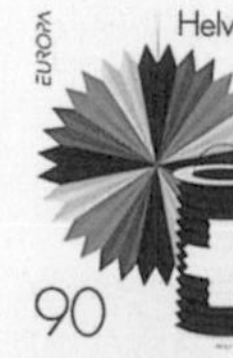

363 Lanterns

1998. Europa. National Festivals. National Day.

1395	**363**	90c. multicoloured	3·00	2·30

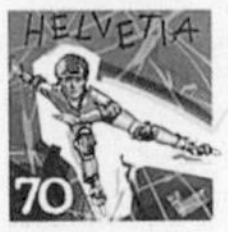

364 In-line Skating

1998. Sports. Multicoloured. Self-adhesive.

1396	70c. Type **364**	2·20	2·00
1397	70c. Snow-boarding	2·20	2·00
1398	70c. Mountain biking	2·20	2·00
1399	70c. Basketball	2·20	2·00
1400	70c. Beach volleyball	2·20	2·00

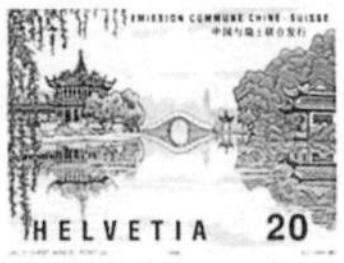

365 Bridge 24, Slender West Lake, Yangzhou, China

1998. Lakes. Multicoloured.

1401	20c. Type **365**	60	55
1402	70c. Chillon Castle, Lake Geneva	1·70	1·60
MS1403	96×70 mm. 90c. Chillion Castle and Bridge 24 (52×44 mm)	3·75	3·50

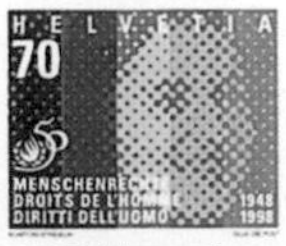

366 Emblem and Face

1998. 50th Anniv of Universal Declaration of Human Rights.

1404	**366**	70c. multicoloured	1·70	1·10

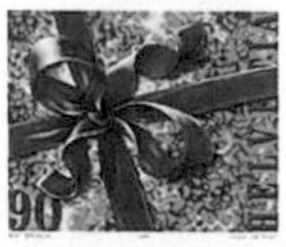

367 Christmas Wrapping

1998. Christmas.

1405	**367**	90c. multicoloured	2·20	2·30

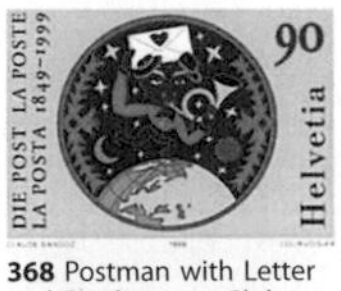

368 Postman with Letter and Posthorn on Globe

1999. 150th Anniv of Swiss Postal Service.

1406	**368**	90c. multicoloured	2·40	2·30

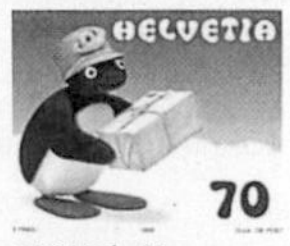

369 Little Pingu carrying Parcel

1999. Youth Stamps. Pingu (cartoon character). Multicoloured.

1407	70c. Type **369**	1·70	1·10
1408	90c. Papa Pingu driving snowmobile	2·20	2·30

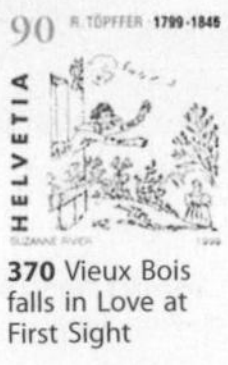

370 Vieux Bois falls in Love at First Sight

1999. Birth Bicentenary of Rodolphe Topffer (cartoonist). Scenes from "The Love of Monsieur Vieux Boris". Multicoloured. Self-adhesive.

1409	90c. Type **370**	2·75	2·50
1410	90c. Vieux Bois declares his love	2·75	2·50
1411	90c. Vieux Bois jumps in air with joy, knocking over furniture	2·75	2·50
1412	90c. Vieux Bois helping his love over wall	2·75	2·50
1413	90c. Wedding of Vieux Bois	2·75	2·50

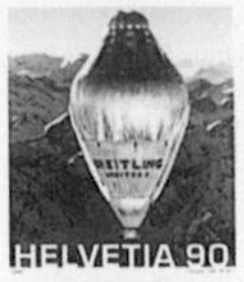

371 "Breitling Orbiter 3"

1999. First World Circumnavigation by Balloon, by Bertrand Piccard and Brian Jones.

1414	**371**	90c. multicoloured	3·00	2·00

372 Envelope Flap

1999. 125th Anniv of Universal Postal Union.

1415	**372**	20c. yellow and black	1·20	1·10
1416	-	70c. black, red and yellow	2·40	2·30

DESIGN—55×29 mm: 70c. U.P.U. emblem on card in envelope.

Nos. 1415/16 were printed, *se-tenant*, forming a composite design.

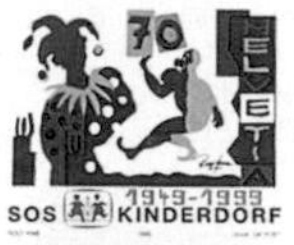

373 Jester and Clown

1999. Publicity Issue.

1417	**373**	70c. multicoloured	1·70	1·10
1418	-	90c. multicoloured	2·20	2·30
1419	-	90c. multicoloured	2·20	2·30
1420	-	1f.10 red and black	2·75	2·50

DESIGNS: No. 1417, Type **373** (50th anniv of SOS Children's Villages); 1418, Sketch of giant puppets (Winegrowers' Festival, Vevey); 1419, Flags of member countries and emblem (50th anniv of Council of Europe); 1420, Red Cross and emblem (50th anniv of Geneva Conventions).

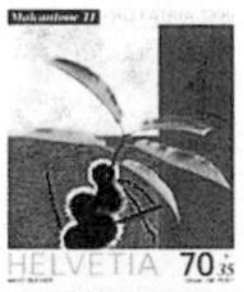

374 Chestnuts from Malcantone

1999. Pro Patria. Heritage and Landscapes. Multicoloured.

1421	70c.+35c. Type **374**	3·00	2·30
1422	70c.+35c. La Sarraz Castle	3·00	2·30
1423	90c.+40c. "Uri" (lake steamer)	4·25	4·00
1424	110c.+50c. St. Christopher carrying Baby Jesus (detail of fresco, St. Paul's Chapel, Rhazuns)	4·75	4·50

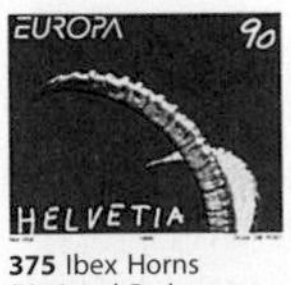

375 Ibex Horns (National Park, Engadine)

1999. Europa. Parks and Gardens.

1425	**375**	90c. black and blue	3·00	2·30

376 Roofs of Buildings

1999. "naba 2000" National Stamp Exhibition, St. Gallen (1st issue). Sheet 66×85 mm containing T **376** and similar vert designs. Multicoloured.

MS1426	20c.+10c. Type **376**; 70c.+30c. Spire of St. Laurenzen's Church; 90c.+30c. Oriel window	9·75	9·50

See also No. **MS**1442.

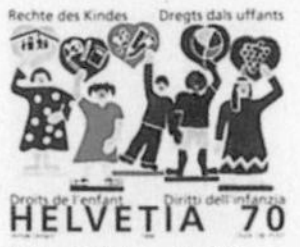

377 Children holding Pictures

1999. Publicity Issue. Multicoloured.

1427	70c. Type **377** (Children's Rights)	1·70	1·10
1428	90c. Carl Lutz (Swiss diplomat in Budapest during Second World War) (24th death anniv)	2·40	2·30
1429	1f.10 Chemical model of ozone and globe (birth bicentenary of Christian Schönbein (chemist))	2·75	2·50
1430	180c. "Midday in the Alps" (death centenary of Giovanni Segantini (painter))	4·50	4·25

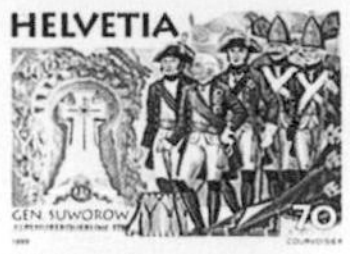

378 Schollenen Gorge Monument, Suvorov and Soldiers

1999. Bicentenary of General Aleksandr Suvorov's Crossing of the Alps. Multicoloured.

1431	70c. Type **378**	2·20	1·60
1432	110c. Suvorov vanguard (after engraving by L. Hess) passing Lake Klontal	3·25	2·50

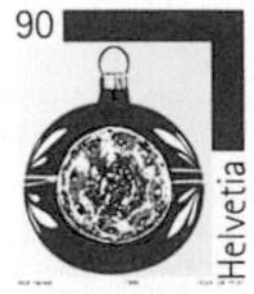

379 Christmas Bauble

1999. Christmas.

1433	**379**	90c. multicoloured	2·20	2·00

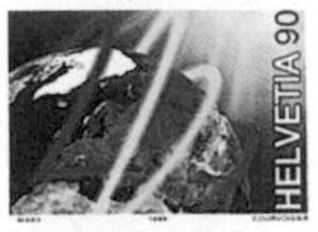

380 "2000" around Globe

1999. Year 2000.

1434	**380**	90c. multicoloured	2·20	2·00

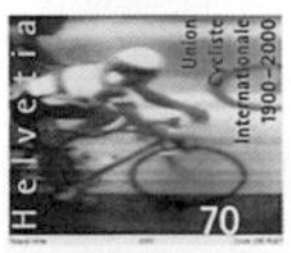

381 Cyclist

2000. Centenary of International Cycling Union.

1435	**381**	70c. multicoloured	2·20	1·10

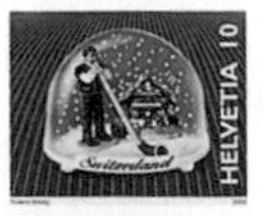

382 Alphorn Player

2000. Snow Storms. Multicoloured.

1436	10c. Type **382**	25	10
1437	20c. Fondue	50	35
1438	30c. Jugs and grapes on tray	85	70
1439	50c. Mountain goat	1·20	1·10
1440	60c. Clock	1·50	1·40
1441	70c. St. Bernards	1·70	1·00

See also No. 1479.

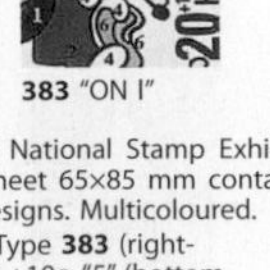

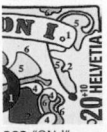

383 "ON I"

2000. "naba 2000" National Stamp Exhibition, St. Gallen (2nd issue). Sheet 65×85 mm containing T **383** and similar vert designs. Multicoloured.

MS1442	20c.+10c. Type **383** (right-hand corner); 20c.+10c. "5" (bottom left-hand corner); 70c.+35c. "RAY" (top left-hand corner), 90c.+45c. "Rp" (bottom right-hand corner.	11·00	10·50

The four stamps in **MS**1448 were issued together to form a composite design depiting a modern representation of a 1850 5r. Federal Administration stamp.

384 "frau" and Emblem

2000. Centenary of National Council of Women.
| 1443 | **384** | 70c. multicoloured | 1·70 | 1·10 |

385 "Building Europe"

2000. Europa.
| 1444 | **385** | 90c. multicoloured | 2·40 | 2·30 |

386 Town Square, Nafels

2000. Pro Patria. "Townscapes 2000" (rejuvenation projects). Multicoloured.
1445	70c.+35c. Type **386**	3·75	3·50
1446	70c.+35c. Main road, Tengia	3·75	3·50
1447	90c.+40c. Main road, Brugg	4·75	4·50
1448	90c.+40c. Marketplace, Carouge	4·75	4·50

387 Payerne Church and Violin

2000. Tourism. Multicoloured (except 1451, blue, turquoise and red).
1449	90c. Willisan farmhouse and horse	2·75	2·44
1450	100c. LD Suisse (lake steamer) and woman looking over Lake Geneva	3·00	2·75
1451	110c. Kleine Matterhorn glacier and skier	3·50	3·25
1452	120c. Type **387**	3·00	2·30
1453	130c. St. Saphorin Church and bottle of wine	3·25	2·30
1454	180c. National spring and bather, Vals	4·25	3·50
1455	200c. Landscape and walker	4·75	3·50
1456	220c. Bus and children	6·75	6·25
1457	300c. Stone bridge and mountain bike	7·25	4·50
1459	400c. Airplane fin and man with suitcase	12·00	11·50

388 Embroidery

2000. St. Gallen Embroidery. Self-adhesive.
| 1460 | **388** | 5f. cobalt and blue | 14·50 | 13·50 |
| MS1461 | 158×132 mm. No. 1460 ×4 | £375 | £450 |

389 Emblem

2000. Population Census.
| 1462 | **389** | 70c. multicoloured | 1·70 | 1·10 |

390 "Alien from Outer Space" (Yannick Kehrli)

2000. "Stampin' the Future". Winning Entries in Children's International Painting Competition. Multicoloured. Self-adhesive.
1463	70c. Type **390**	3·75	3·50
1464	70c. "Looks below the Sun" (Charlotte Battig)	3·75	3·50
1465	70c. "The Perfect World" (Sandra Dohler)	3·75	3·50
1466	70c. "My Town" (Stephanie Aerschmann)	3·75	3·50

391 Swimming

2000. Olympic Games, Sydney. Multicoloured. Self-adhesive.
1467	90c. Type **391**	3·75	3·50
1468	90c. Cycling	3·75	3·50
1469	90c. Running	3·75	3·50

392 Cathedral and Horsemen

2000. Stamp Day.
| 1470 | **392** | 70c. multicoloured | 2·20 | 1·60 |

393 Dresden-style Tree Decoration

2000. Christmas.
| 1471 | **393** | 90c. multicoloured | 3·50 | 2·00 |

394 Alice Rivaz

2001. Anniversaries.
1472	**394**	70c. multicoloured	1·70	1·10
1473	–	90c. multicoloured	2·75	2·30
1474	–	110c. red, grey and black	2·75	2·50
1475	–	130c. multicoloured	3·25	3·25

DESIGNS—As Type **394**:70c. Type **394** (writer, birth centenary); 110c. "CARITAS" and jigsaw pieces (centenary of Caritas (Christian charity organization)); 130c. Refugees (50th Anniv of United Nations High Commissioner for Refugees). Size 39×30 mm: 90c. Airplane (centenary of Aero-Club of Switzerland).

395 Flowers and Envelope

2001. Greetings Stamp.
| 1476 | **395** | 90c. multicoloured | 3·00 | 2·75 |

396 Woman's Head

2001. Anniversary and Event. Multicoloured.
| 1477 | 70c. Type **396** (re-opening of Vela Museum, Ligornetto) | 2·20 | 2·00 |
| 1478 | 90c. Chocolate segment (centenary of Chocosuisse) | 3·75 | 3·50 |

No. 1478 is impregnated with the scent of chocolate.

2001. Self-adhesive Stamps.
| 1479 | – | 70c. mult (as No. 1441) | 2·20 | 2·00 |
| 1480 | **336** | 90c. blue, orge & lemon | 2·75 | 2·50 |

397 Italian Theatre, La Chaux-de-Fonds

2001. Pro Patria. Cultural Heritage.
1481	70c.+35c. black, orange and red	3·25	3·00
1482	70c.+35c. black, brown and green	3·25	3·00
1483	90c.+40c. black, brown and lemon	4·00	3·75
1484	90c.+40c. multicoloured	4·00	3·75

DESIGNS: No. 1482, Hauterive Monastery; 1483, Leuk Castle; 1484, Rorschach Granary.

398 Water

2001. Europa. Water Resources.
| 1485 | **398** | 90c. multicoloured | 2·75 | 2·50 |

399 Blue Rainbow Fish

2001. Illustrations from *Rainbow Fish* (book by Martin Pfister). Multicoloured.
| 1486 | 70c. Type **399** | 2·00 | 1·90 |
| 1487 | 90c. Purple rainbow fish | 2·75 | 2·50 |

400 Straits Rhododendron (*Melastoma malabathricum*)

2001. Switzerland–Singapore Joint Issue. Flowers. Sheet 98×68 mm, containing T **400** and similar horiz designs. Multicoloured.
| MS1488 70c. Type **400**; 90c. *Saraca cauliflora*; 110c. Edelweiss (*Leontopodium alpinum*); 130c. Gentian (*Gentiana clusii*) | 13·50 | 13·00 |

401 "The Birth of Venus"

2001. Death Centenary of Arnold Bocklin (artist).
| 1489 | **401** | 180c. multicoloured | 5·00 | 4·75 |

402 Buildings (Beat Kehrli)

2001. Stamp Day. Winning entry in stamp design competition.
| 1490 | **402** | 70c. multicoloured | 2·20 | 2·10 |

403 Gablonz-style Christmas Tree Ornament

2001. Christmas.
| 1491 | **403** | 90c. multicoloured | 2·75 | 2·50 |

404 Ladder, Wall and Stars

2002. Escalade (festival) (celebrating 400th anniv of defeat of Savoyard attack on the city), Geneva.
| 1492 | **404** | 70c. multicoloured | 2·20 | 2·10 |

405 "E" and Towers, Biel

2002. "Expo '02" National Exhibition, Biel, Murten, Neuchatel and Yverdon-les-Bains (1st issue). Each featuring "Arteplage" (exhibition platform) of each host town. Multicoloured.
1493	70c. Type **405**	2·20	2·10
1494	70c. Reversed "P" and Monolith, Murten	2·20	2·10
1495	70c. "O", pebble-shaped construction over water, Neuchatel	2·20	2·10
1496	70c. "2" and artificial cloud, Yverdon-les-Bains	2·20	2·10

See also No. MS1509.

406 RABDe 500 InterCity Tilting Train (ICN)

2002. Centenary of Swiss Federal Railways (SBB) (national railway operator). Multicoloured.
1497	70c. Type **406**	2·20	2·10
1498	90c. InterCity 2000 double-deck train	3·00	3·00
1499	120c. Railcar, Lucerne–Lenzburg Seetal line	3·00	3·00
1500	130c. 119 Re 460 locomotive	4·50	4·25

407 Facade

2002. Centenary of Federal Parliament Building.
| 1501 | **407** | 90c. multicoloured | 3·00 | 2·75 |

408 Augusta A-109-K2 Helicopter and Hawker 800B Air Ambulance

2002. 50th Anniv of Swiss Air Rescue (Rega).
| 1502 | **408** | 180c. multicoloured | 5·00 | 4·75 |

409 Clown

2002. Europa. Circus. Multicoloured.
| 1503 | 70c. Type **409** | 2·40 | 2·20 |
| 1504 | 90c. Clown (different) | 2·75 | 2·50 |

410 Bruzella, Ticino Canton

2002. Pro Patria. Water Mills Preservation. Water mills. Multicoloured.
1505	70c.+35c. Type **410**	2·75	2·50
1506	70c.+35c. Oberdorf, Basel Canton	2·75	2·50
1507	90c.+40c. Lussery-Villars, de Vaud Canton	4·00	3·75
1508	90c.+40c. Buren a. d. Aare, Berne Canton	4·00	3·75

411 "X"

2002. "Expo '02", 6th National Exhibition, Biel, Murten, Neuchatel and Yverdon-les-Bains (2nd issue). Sheet 95×70 mm.
| MS1509 **411** 90c. multicoloured | 4·25 | 4·00 |

412 Two Teddies
(Switzerland, c.
1950)

2002. Centenary of the Teddy Bear. Multicoloured. Self-
adhesive.
1510	90c. White teddy with pink bow (France, 1925) (26×26 mm, round)	2·75	2·50
1511	90c. Type **412**	2·75	2·50
1512	90c. Teddy with grey-brown bow (Germany, 1904) (22×32 mm, oval)	2·75	2·50
1513	90c. "Philibert", Swiss Post Teddy (Switzerland, 2002) (26×22 mm, rectangle)	2·75	2·50
1514	90c. Teddy with grey paws (England, c. 1920) (26×26 mm, round)	2·75	2·50

413 Emblem

2002. Switzerland's Acccesssion to the United Nations.
| 1515 | **413** | 90c. multicoloured | 2·75 | 2·50 |

414 Emperor
Dragonfly (*Anax
imperator*)

2002. Insects. Multicoloured.
1516	10c. Type **414**	70	65
1517	20c. Dark green fritillary (*Mesoacidalia aglaja*)	1·00	95
1518	50c. Alpine longhorn beetle (*Rosalia alpina*)	1·40	1·30
1519	100c. Striped bug (*Graphosoma lineatum*)	3·00	3·00

415 Printing Press (copper
engraving, Abraham Bosse)

2002. Swiss Post Stamp Printers, Berne Commemoration.
| 1520 | **415** | 70c. multicoloured | 2·75 | 2·50 |

416 Ladybird on Leaf

2002. Greeting Stamp. Self-adhesive.
| 1521 | **416** | 90c. multicoloured | 3·00 | 3·00 |

417 Quartz

2002. Minerals. Multicoloured.
1522	200c. Type **417**	6·00	5·50
1523	300c. Rutilated quartz	9·25	8·75
1524	400c. Fluorite	12·00	11·00
1525	500c. Titanite	16·00	15·00
1525a	500c. Titanite	16·00	15·00

418 Kingfisher and
Jura Water
Engineering System
(Michele Berri)

2002. Stamp Day. Winning Entry in Stamp Design
Competition.
| 1535 | **418** | 70c. multicoloured | 2·20 | 2·10 |

419 Bohemian
Cardboard Tree
Decoration, c.
1900

2002. Christmas.
| 1536 | **419** | 90c. multicoloured | 2·50 | 2·40 |

420 Skier

2002. World Alpine Skiing Championship, St. Moritz.
| 1537 | **420** | 90c. multicoloured | 2·50 | 2·40 |

421 "70"

2003. Centenary of Swiss National Association of the
Blind and Library for the Blind and Visually Impaired.
| 1538 | **421** | 70c. orange | 2·20 | 2·10 |
No. 1538 was embossed with 70 in Braille.

422 Hypericum
(*Hypericum
perforatum*)

2003. Medicinal Plants. Multicoloured.
1539	70c. Type **422**	2·00	1·90
1540	90c. Periwinkle (*Vinca minor*)	2·75	2·50
1541	110c. Valerian (*Valeriana officinalis*)	3·25	3·00
1542	120c. *Arnica Montana*	3·50	3·25
1543	130c. Centaury (*Centaurium minus*)	3·75	3·50
1544	180c. Mallow (*Malva sylvestris*)	5·50	5·00
1545	220c. Chamomile (*Matricaria chamomilla*)	6·00	5·75

423 Waterfall

2003. International Year of Water.
| 1546 | **423** | 90c. multicoloured | 2·50 | 2·40 |

424 Contour Lines,
Compass and Runner

2003. World Orienteering Championships, Rapperswil-
Jona.
| 1547 | **424** | 90c. multicoloured | 2·50 | 2·40 |

425 Horse's Head

2003. Centenary of Marche-Concours (horse show and
market), Saignelegier.
| 1548 | **425** | 90c. multicoloured | 2·50 | 2·40 |

426 *Alinghi* (yacht)

2003. Switzerland, America's Cup Winners, 2003.
| 1549 | **426** | 90c. multicoloured | 4·25 | 4·00 |

427 Eagle

2003. Ticino 2003 International Stamp Exhibition,
Locarno. Sheet 96×70 mm containing T **427** and
similar vert design. Multicoloured.
| MS1550 | 20c. Type **427**; 70c. Gentians | 3·50 | 3·25 |

428 Laura

2003. 20th International Comics Festival, Sierre.
Characters created by Tom Tirabosco. Multicoloured.
1551	70c. Type **428**	2·20	2·10
1552	70c. Marco	2·20	2·10
1553	70c. Louis	2·20	2·10
1554	70c. Djema	2·20	2·10
MS1555	96×70 mm. 90c. Heidi	3·50	3·25

429 Innere Wynigen
Bridge, Burgdorf,
Berne Canton

2003. Historic Bridges and Footbridges. Multicoloured.
1556	70c.+35c. Type **429**	3·00	3·00
1557	70c.+35c. Salginatobel, Schiers, Grisons	3·00	3·00
1558	90c.+40c. Pont St-Jean, Saint Ursanne, Jura Canton	3·75	3·50
1559	90c.+40c. Reuss, Rottenschwil, Aargau Canton	3·75	3·50

430 "Don't
Forget
the Discount
Stamp" (Donald
Brun)

2003. Europa. Poster Art.
| 1560 | **430** | 90c. multicoloured | 2·50 | 2·40 |

431 Diddl and
Diddlina

2003. Diddl (cartoon character created by Thomas
Goletz). Multicoloured.
| 1561 | 70c. Type **431** | 2·00 | 1·90 |
| 1562 | 90c. Diddl chasing winged envelopes | 2·75 | 2·50 |

432 Jungfrau-
Aletsch-Bietschhorn
Region

2003. UNESCO World Heritage Sites. Multicoloured.
1563	90c. Type **432**	2·75	2·50
1564	90c. Three Castles, Bellinzona	2·75	2·50
1565	90c. Berne Old City	2·75	2·50
1566	90c. St. Gall Abbey Precinct	2·75	2·50
1567	90c. Mustair Convent	2·75	2·50

433 Onion market,
Berne

2003. Stamp Day. Winning Entry in Stamp Design
Competition.
| 1568 | **433** | 70c. multicoloured | 1·90 | 1·80 |

434 Wooden
Horseman
(Erzgebirge)

2003. Christmas. Regional Tree Decorations.
Multicoloured.
| 1569 | 70c. Type **434** | 2·00 | 1·90 |
| 1570 | 90c. Glass Father Christmas (Thuringa) | 2·75 | 2·50 |

435 Four-leafed Clover

2003. Greetings Stamp.
| 1571 | **435** | 1f.30 multicoloured | 3·75 | 3·50 |

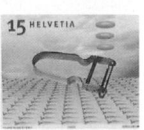

436 Rex Potato Peeler
(Alfred Neweczeral,
1947)

2003. Swiss Design Classics. Multicoloured.

(a) Booklet Stamps
1572	15c. Type **436**	70	65
1583	85c. Station clock (Hans Hilfiker, 1944)	2·75	2·50
1584	100c. Armchair (Heidi Weber (1959) after Le Corbusier (1928)	6·75	6·50
1585	100c. "Landi" (chair) (Hans Coray, 1939)	2·75	2·50
1586	220c. "Fixpencil" (Caran d'Ache 1929)	6·75	6·50

(b) Coil stamps
| 1590 | 50c. "Riri" (zip fastener) | 1·50 | 1·40 |
| 1591 | 220c. As No. 1586 | 2·00 | 1·50 |

437 Titeuf and Nadia

2004. Titeuf (cartoon created by Philippe Chappuis
(Zep)). Multicoloured.
1595	85c. Type **437** (Spring)	2·40	2·20
1596	85c. Sitting in refrigerator (Summer)	2·40	2·20
1597	85c. Kicking leaves (Autumn)	2·40	2·20
1598	85c. With snowman (Winter)	2·40	2·20

438 Centenary Emblem

2004. Centenary of FIFA (Federation Internationale de
Football Association).
| 1599 | **438** | 1f. multicoloured | 3·00 | 3·00 |

439 Family

2004. Cycling. Sheet 96×70 mm containing T **439** and
similar horiz design. Multicoloured.
| MS1600 | 1f. ×2, Type **439**; Two cyclists reading map | 6·00 | 5·75 |

440 Past and Present Players

2004. 50th Anniv of UEFA (Union of European Football Associations).
1601 **440** 1f.30 multicoloured 3·50 3·25

441 Rays

2004. 50th Anniv of CERN (European Organization for Nuclear Research).
1602 **441** 1f.80 gold, light blue and black 5·50 5·00

442 Doorbell and "Helvetia" (Emil Steinberger)

2004. Humour.
1603 **442** 85c. multicoloured 2·75 2·50

443 Bathing Pavilion, Gorgier

2004. Pro Patria. Small Buildings Preservation. Multicoloured.
1604 85c.+ 40c. Type **443** 3·50 3·25
1605 85c.+ 40c. Granary, Obermarsern 3·50 3·25
1606 1f.+50c. Seeburg landing stage, Lucerne 4·25 4·00
1607 1f.+50c. Ossuary, Gentilino 4·25 4·00

444 Diddl holding Pimboli

2004. Diddl (cartoon character created by Thomas Goletz) (2nd series). Multicoloured.
1608 85c. Type **444** 2·20 2·10
1609 1f. Diddl holding flower 3·00 2·75

445 Olympic Rings, Stadium and Runner

2004. Olympic Games, Athens.
1610 **445** 1f. multicoloured 2·75 2·50

446 Sun Lounger and Parasol

2004. Europa. Holidays.
1611 **446** 1f. multicoloured 2·75 2·50

447 Zeppelin NT Type Z No. 7

2004
1612 **447** 1f.80 multicoloured 5·00 4·75

448 Boy leapfrogging Pumpkin

2004. Suisse Balance (healthy eating campaign).
1613 **448** 85c. multicoloured 2·40 2·20

449 1854 10r. Stamp

2004. 150th Anniv of Strubeli (dishevelled) Stamps (first stamps showing seated Helvetia ("Mother of the Nation")). Sheet 96×70 mm containing T **449** and similar vert design. Multicoloured.
MS1614 85c. ×2, Type **449**; Coin showing Helvetia 5·00 4·75

450 Cat

2004. Swiss Animal Protection (SAP). Mult.
1615 85c. Type **450** 3·00 2·75
1616 1f. Hedgehog 3·00 3·00
1617 1f.30 Pig 3·75 3·50

451 Fossil and Mountains

2004. UNESCO World Heritage Site. Mount San Giorgio.
1618 **451** 1f. mauve and black 3·00 3·00

452 Making Cheese

2004. Traditional Food. Cheese. Multicoloured.
1619 1f. Type **452** 2·75 2·50
1620 1f.30 Cheeses and grapes 3·50 3·25

453 Wood Grain

2004. Sustainable Wood Production. Self-adhesive.
1621 **453** 5f. ochre 13·50 13·00
No. 1621 was made from wood veneer which has to be peeled from the backing paper.

454 Hydro Electric Power

2004. Stamp Day. Winning Entry in Stamp Design Competition.
1622 **454** 85c. multicoloured 2·20 2·10

455 Star

2004. Christmas. Tree Decorations. Sheet 160×56 mm containing T **455** and similar vert designs. Multicoloured.
MS1623 85c. Type **455**; 85c. Church; 1f. Angel; 1f. Horse and rider; 1f. Father Christmas 13·00 12·50
No. 1624 and T **456** have been left for stamp not yet received.

457 Children Kissing

2005. Greetings Stamps. Self-adhesive.
1625 **457** 100c. black and vermilion 3·00 2·75
1626 - 100c. multicoloured 3·00 2·75
1627 - 100c. multicoloured 3·00 2·75
1628 - 100c. black and scarlet-vermilion 3·00 2·75
DESIGNS: Type **457**; No. 1626, Couple riding bicycle; 1627, Couple embracing; 1628, Couple in dodgem car.
Nos. 1625/8 were issued with a label inscribed Priority attached at foot.

458 Double Helix, Faces and Building Facade

2005. 150th Anniv of Federal Technology Institute, Zurich.
1629 **458** 85c. multicoloured 2·40 2·20

459 Matterhorn superimposed on Inverted Map of Africa

2005
1630 **459** 85c. multicoloured 2·40 2·20

460 Cheeky Mouse typing Letter

2005. Cheeky Mouse (cartoon character created by Uli Stein). Multicoloured.
1631 85c. Type **460** 2·75 2·50
1632 100c. Playing golf 3·00 2·75

461 Traditional Costume and Unspunnen Stone

2005. Bicentenary of Folklore Festival, Unspunnen.
1633 **461** 100c. multicoloured 2·75 2·50

462 Coach-built Car

2005. Centenary of Motor Show, Geneva. Sheet 96×70 mm containing T **462** and similar horiz design. Multicoloured.
MS1634 100c. Type **462**; 130c. Futuristic car 6·75 6·50

463 Albert Einstein

2005. Centenary of Publication of "Special Theory of Relativity" by Albert Einstein.
1635 **463** 130c. multicoloured 3·50 3·25

464 Felix and Goats

2005. "Letters from Felix" (children's book written by Annette Langen and illustrated by Constanza Droop. Multicoloured.
1636 85c. Type **464** 2·20 2·10

465 Rotach Houses, Wasserwerkstrasse, Zurich

2005. Pro Patria. Multicoloured.
1638 85c.+40c. Type **465** 3·50 3·25
1639 85c.+40c. Monte Carasso Abbey, Bellinzona, Ticino 3·50 3·25
1640 100c.+50c. St. Katherinenthal Abbey, Diessenhofen 4·00 3·75
1641 100c.+50c. Palais Wilson, Geneva 4·00 3·75

466 Butterflies

2005. Greeting Stamp. Self-adhesive.
1642 **466** 100c. multicoloured 3·00 2·75

467 Player

2005. European Football Championship—2008, Switzerland and Austria (1st issue). Football for the Visually Impaired.
1643 **467** 100c. multicoloured 3·00 2·75
See also No. 1681, 1708, 1760 and 1761.

468 "Big-eared Clown" and "Monument in a Fertile Country"

2005. Inauguration of Zentrum Paul Klee Exhibition Centre, Berne.
1644 **468** 100c. multicoloured 3·00 2·75

469 Europe reflected in Dish Cover

2005. Europa. Gastronomy.
1645 **469** 100c. multicoloured 3·00 2·75

470 Subtractive Colours

2005. My Stamp. Colour. Multicoloured. Self-adhesive.
1646 50c. Type **470** 1·90 1·80
1647 100c. Additive colours 3·00 2·75

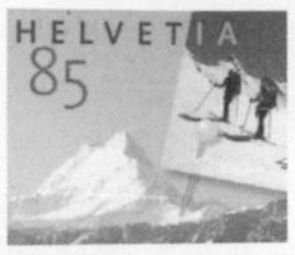

471 Skiers

2005. Centenary of NaturFreunde Schweiz (conservation organization). Sheet 110×90 mm containing T **471** and similar multicoloured designs.

MS1648 85c. Type **471**; 100c. Chalet (vert); 110c. Hikers; 130c. Rock climber (vert)	12·00	11·50

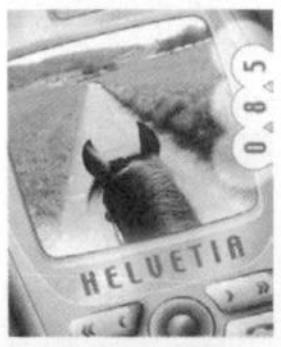

472 Horse's Head (Brigit Rohrbach)

2005. MMS (multimedia messaging). Multicoloured.

1649	85c. Type **472**	3·00	2·75
1650	100c. Hiker (Peter Schumacher)	3·50	3·25
1651	130c. Sign post (Remy Sager)	4·00	3·75
1652	180c. Footprint (Debora Ronchi)	4·25	4·00

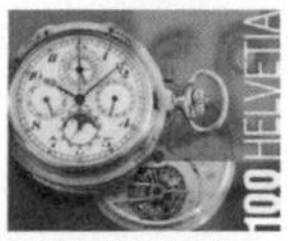

473 Pocket Watch

2005. Watches. Multicoloured.

1653	100c. Type **473**	3·00	3·00
1654	130c. Wristwatch	4·00	3·75

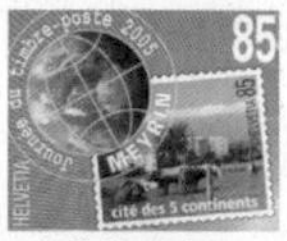

474 Globe and Landscape

2005. Stamp Day. Winning Entry in Stamp Design Competition.

1655	**474**	85c. multicoloured	2·50	2·40

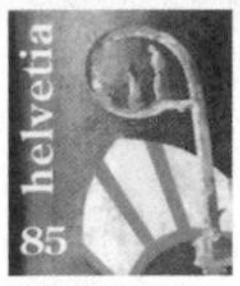

475 Mitre and Crosier

2005. Christmas. Multicoloured.

1656	85c. Type **475**	2·40	2·20
1657	100c. Gingerbread man	2·75	2·50

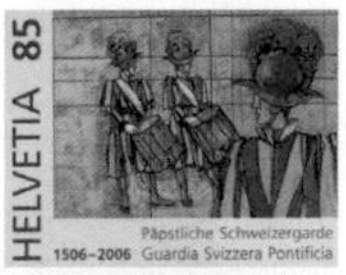

476 Swiss Papal Guard

2005. 500th Anniv of Swiss Papal Guard. Multicoloured.

1658	85c. Type **476**	2·40	2·20
1659	100c. Three guards facing left	4·00	3·75

Stamps of a similar design were issued by Vatican City.

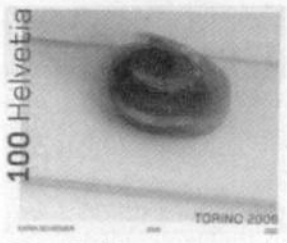

477 Curling

2005. Winter Olympic Games, Turin.

1660	**477**	100c. multicoloured	2·75	2·50

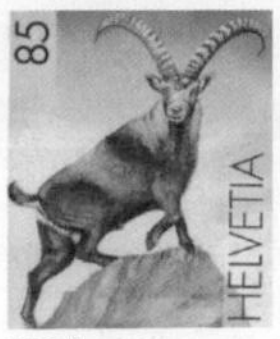

478 Ibex

2006. Centenary of Ibex Re-introduction Programme.

1661	**478**	85c. multicoloured	2·50	2·40

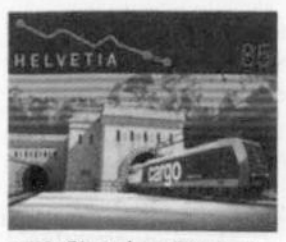

479 Simplon Tunnel between Rhone Valley and Val d'Ossola

2006. Railway Centenaries. Multicoloured.

1662	85c. Type **479**	2·40	2·20
1663	100c. Bern–Lotschberg–Simplon Railway (rapid train service)	2·75	2·50

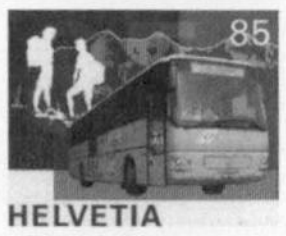

480 Post Bus

2006. Centenary of the Post Bus Service. Multicoloured. Self-adhesive.

1664	85c. Type **480**	2·00	1·90
1665	100c. Double bus	2·50	2·40
1666	130c. School minibus	3·00	2·75

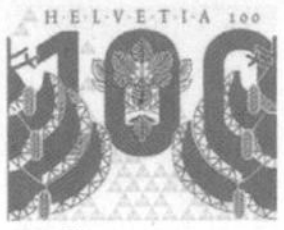

481 Fir

2006. Art Nouveau Exhibition, La Chaux-de-Fonds. Multicoloured.

1667	100c. Type **481**	2·75	2·50
1668	180c. Petals	5·00	4·75

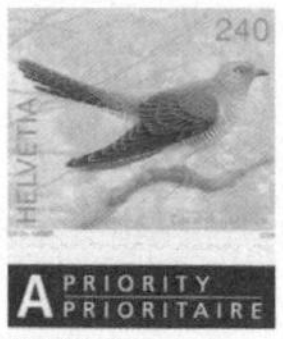

482 Cuckoo

2006. Birds. Multicoloured. Self-adhesive.

1669	85c. Chaffinch (*Fringilla coelebs*)	2·50	2·10
1670	100c. Great tit (*Parus major*)	2·50	2·40
1671	110c. Wall creeper (*Tichodroma muraria*)	3·00	3·00
1672	120c. Grey-headed wood pecker (*Picus canus*)	2·50	2·40
1673	130c. Rufus-tailed rockthrush (*Monticola saxatills*)	2·75	2·50
1676	140c. Rock partridge (*Alectoris milivus*) (1.4.09)	3·25	3·00
1676a	180c. Tengmalm's owl (*Aegolius funereus*) (different) (1.7.09)	3·25	3·00
1677	180c. Tengmalm's owl (*Aegolius funereus*)	4·25	4·00
1678	190c. Red kite (*Milivus milivus*) (1.4.09)	4·25	4·00
1679	220c. Great crested grebe (*Podiceps cristatus*)	5·00	4·75
1680	240c. Type **482**	6·75	6·50

No. 1673, 1674b, 1676 and 1679 have a label inscribed "Prioritaire" attached at foot.

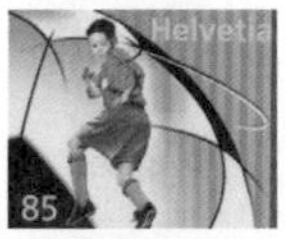

483 Player

2006. European Football Championship—2008, Switzerland and Austria (2nd issue). Youth Football.

1681	**483**	85c. multicoloured	2·50	2·40

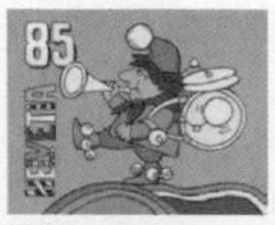

484 Kasperli

2006. Kasperli (children's character) written by Jorg Schneider and drawn by Heinz Steiger.

1682	**484**	85c. multicoloured	2·40	2·20

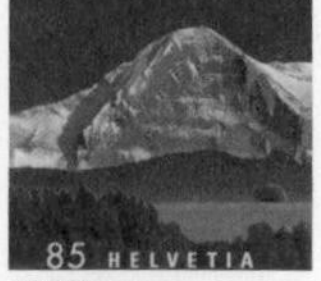

485 Eiger

2006. Mountains. Multicoloured.

1683	85c. Type **485**	2·20	2·10
1684	85c. Monch (30×35 mm)	2·20	2·10
1685	85c. Jungfrau (39×35 mm)	2·20	2·10

Nos. 1683/5 were issued together, *se-tenant*, forming a composite design of a panorama of the mountain range.

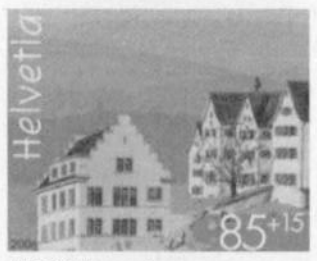

486 Monastery Buildings

2006. NABA National Stamp Exhibition, Baden (1st issue). Wettingen Monastery. Sheet 105×70 mm containing T **486** and similar horiz designs. Multicoloured.

MS1686 85c.+15c. Type **486**; 85c.+15c. Covered bridge; 100c.+50c. Building containing clock tower	9·25	8·75

The stamps and margins of **MS**1686 form a composite design of the monastery.

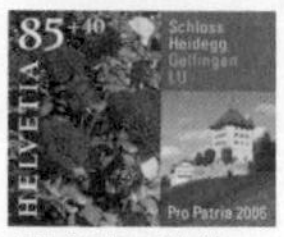

487 Schloss Heidegg, Gelfingen

2006. Pro Patria. Multicoloured.

1687	85c.+40c. Type **487**	3·50	3·25
1688	85c.+40c. Chateau de Prangins, Prangins	3·50	3·25
1689	100c.+50c. Villa Garbald, Castasegna	4·00	3·75
1690	100c.+50c. Schloss Birseck, Arlesheim	4·00	3·25

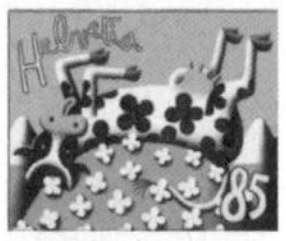

488 Cow

2006. Switzerland through the Eyes of Foreign Artists (1st issue). Patrice Killofer (France). Multicoloured.

1691	85c. Type **488**	2·20	2·10
1692	100c. Brown cow in water	2·50	2·40
1693	130c. Seated cow losing its spots	3·00	3·00
1694	180c. Snow covered white cow	4·25	4·00

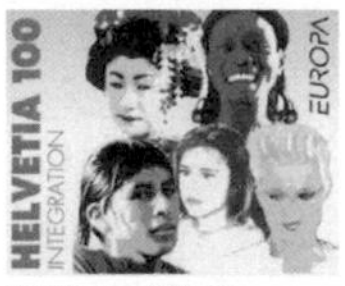

489 Faces of Many Nations

2006. Europa. Integration.

1695	**489**	100c. multicoloured	2·50	2·40

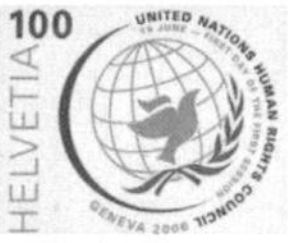

490 Emblem

2006. United Nations Human Rights Council, Geneva.

1696	**490**	100c. multicoloured	3·00	3·00

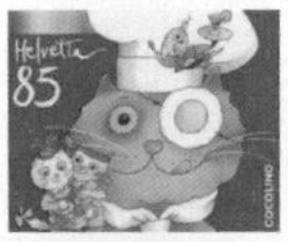

491 Cocolino

2006. Cocolino (cartoon character created by Oskar Weiss and Oskar Marti). Self-adhesive.

1697	**491**	85c. multicoloured	2·50	2·40

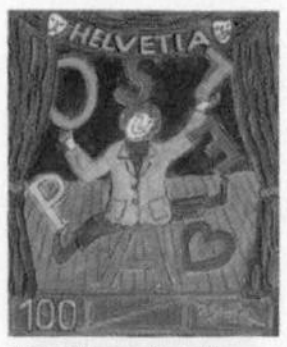

492 Clown juggling Letters

2006. Dimtri the Clown.

1698	**492**	100c. multicoloured	2·50	2·40

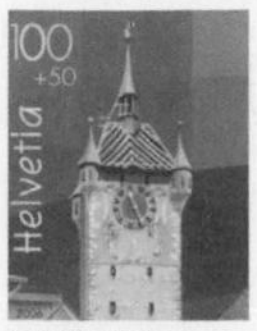

493 Clock Face

2006. Baden City Tower. Sheet 105×70 mm containing T **493** and similar vert design. Multicoloured.

MS1699 100c.+50c.×2, Type **493**; Base of tower and fountain	8·50	8·00

The stamps and margins of **MS**1699 form a composite design.

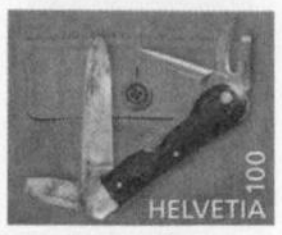

494 First Knife

2006. Victorinox Swiss Officer's Knife. Multicoloured.

1700	100c. Type **494**	2·50	2·40
1701	130c. Modern knife	3·50	3·25

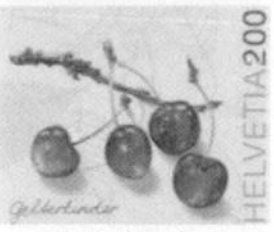

495 Gelterkinder Cherries

2006. ProSpecieRara (rare breeds association) (1st issue). Multicoloured. Self-adhesive.

1702	200c. Type **495**	5·00	4·75
1703	300c. Spatlauber apple	7·75	7·25

See also No. 1707 and 1782.

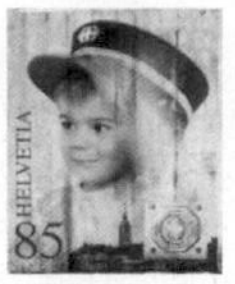

496 Boy wearing Conductor's Cap

2006. Stamp Day. Winning Entry in Stamp Design Competition. 150th Anniv of Olten, the Railway Town.

1704	**496**	85c. multicoloured	2·20	2·10

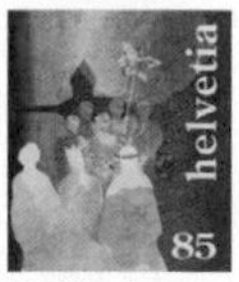

497 Star Singers

2006. Christmas Customs. Multicoloured.

1705	85c. Type **497**	2·20	2·10
1706	100c. Candles on Advent wreath	3·00	2·75

2006. ProSpecieRara (rare breeds association) (2nd issue). As T **495**. Multicoloured. Self-adhesive.

1707	400c. Hauszwetschge plums	10·00	9·50

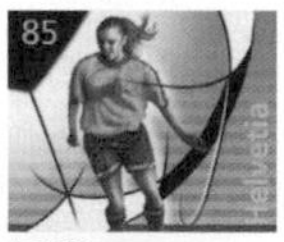

498 Player

2007. European Football Championship—2008, Switzerland and Austria (3rd issue). Women's Football.

1708	**498**	85c. multicoloured	2·40	2·20

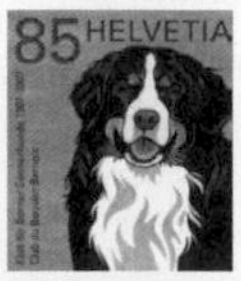

499 Bernese Mountain Dog

2007. Centenary of Swiss Club for Bernese Mountain Dogs. Self-adhesive.

1709	**499**	85c. multicoloured	2·40	2·20

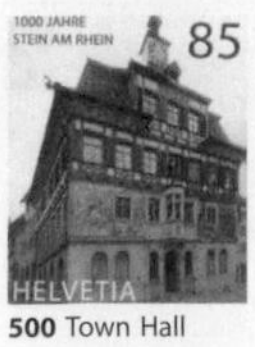

500 Town Hall

2007. Stein am Rhein Millenary. Multicoloured.

1710	85c. Type **500**	2·40	2·20
1711	85c. Painted houses (41×36 mm)	2·40	2·20
1712	85c. Municipal (market) fountain and Zur Meise (guildhall) (34×36 mm)	2·40	2·20

Nos. 1710/12 were issued together, *se-tenant*, forming a composite design.

501 Security Features

2007. Centenary of National Bank. Multicoloured. Self-adhesive.

| 1713 | 85c. Type **501** | 2·20 | 2·10 |
| 1714 | 100c. Banknote | 2·75 | 2·50 |

502 Cup, Jewel and Snake ('Legend of Charlemagne and the Snake')

2007. Legends and Stories. Multicoloured.

1715	85c. Type **502**	2·20	2·10
1716	100c. Girl and water lilies ('Fenetta, the Island Maiden')	2·50	2·40
1717	130c. Horse and rider ('The Judge of Bellinzona')	3·50	3·25
1718	180c. Woman flying over lake and mountains ('Margaretha')	5·00	4·75

503 Leonhard Euler

2007. 300th Birth Anniv of Leonhard Euler (mathematician and scientist).

| 1719 | **503** | 130c. multicoloured | 4·00 | 3·75 |

503a Roger Federer and Trophy

2007. Roger Federer—Tennis World Champion.

| 1720 | **503a** | 100c. multicoloured | 3·00 | 3·00 |

504 Coloured Balls

2007. Centenary of Swiss Association of Day Care Centres.

| 1721 | **504** | 85c. multicoloured | 2·20 | 2·10 |

505 Three Adults and Two Children

2007. Centenary of Museum of Communication, Berne. Multicoloured. Self-adhesive.

| 1722 | 85c. Type **505** | 2·20 | 2·10 |
| 1723 | 100c. Five adults | 3·75 | 3·50 |

506 Via Jacobi

2007. Pro Patria. Traditional Routes. Multicoloured.

1724	85c.+40c. Type **506**	3·50	3·25
1725	85c.+40c. Via Jura	3·50	3·25
1726	100c.+50c. Via Cook	4·25	4·00
1727	100c.+50c. Via Gottardo	4·25	4·00

508 Scouts

2007. Europa. Centenary of Scouting.

| 1728 | **508** | 100c. multicoloured | 2·40 | 2·20 |

509 *Skt. Adolf Thron-Fluhe-Blume* (Adolf Wolfli)

2007. Outsider Art. Multicoloured.

| 1729 | 100c. Type **509** | 2·50 | 2·40 |
| 1730 | 180c. Untitled (Carlo Zinelli) | 4·25 | 4·00 |

510 Schellen-Ursli on Bridge

2007. Schellen-Ursli (children's book character created by Selina Chonz and illustrated by Alois Carigiet). Self-adhesive.

| 1731 | **510** | 85c. multicoloured | 2·00 | 1·90 |

511 The Dancer

2007. Nina Corti (flamenco dancer).

| 1732 | **511** | 85c. multicoloured | 2·20 | 2·10 |

512 Family and Hearts

2007. Greetings Stamps. 'Congratulations'. Multicoloured. Self-adhesive.

1733	85c. Type **512**	2·20	2·10
1734	100c. Boy and stars	2·50	2·40
1735	130c. Woman and flowers	3·50	3·25

513 Monch (*Frankenstein* (Mary Shelley))

2007. Switzerland through the Eyes of Foreign Artists. Swiss Landscape and English Literature. Photographs by James Peel (British artist). Multicoloured.

1736	85c. Type **513**	2·20	2·10
1737	100c. Lauterbrunnen (*At Staubbach Falls* (William Wordsworth)) (vert)	2·50	2·40
1738	130c. Lac Leman (*The Prisoner of Chillon* (Lord Byron)) (vert)	3·50	3·25
1739	180c. Reichenbach Fall (*The Final Problem* (Sir Arthur Conan Doyle))	5·00	4·75

514 Skiers and Bee Tagg

2007. Internet Stamp. Self-adhesive.

| 1740 | **514** | 100c. multicoloured | 3·50 | 3·25 |

No. 1740 contains a Bee Tag (a two dimensional code which, when used with the appropriate software, connects a mobile telephone to the internet). The code gives entry to a competition to win Swiss Tourism prize.

515 Monastery

2007. Einsiedeln. Sheet 105×70 mm.

| MS1741 | **515** | 85c. multicoloured | 12·00 | 11·00 |

The stamps and margins of **MS**1741 form a composite design.

2007. Christmas. Multicoloured.

| 1743 | 100c. Decorated tree | 2·50 | 2·40 |
| 1744 | 130c. Presents | 3·00 | 3·00 |

No. 1742 and Type **516** have been left for 85c. stamp not yet received.

517 Heart-shaped Silhouette

2007. Silhouettes.

1745	**517**	85c. black and vermilion	2·20	2·10
1746	–	100c. black and emerald	2·50	2·40
1747	–	130c. black and blue	3·00	3·00
1748	–	180c. black and orange	4·25	4·00

DESIGNS: 85c. Type **517**; 100c. Tree shaped in circle; 130c. Tree with family cycling below; 180c. Symetrical tree of peacock feathers with dancers below.

518 Potato

2008. International Year of the Potato.

| 1749 | **518** | 85c. multicoloured | 2·30 | 2·20 |

519 Lars

2008. The Little Polar Bear Lars (created by Hans de Beer). Self-adhesive.

| 1750 | **519** | 85c. multicoloured | 2·30 | 2·20 |

520 Albrecht von Haller

2008. 300th Birth Anniv of Albrecht von Haller (physician, botanist and poet).

| 1751 | **520** | 85c. multicoloured | 2·30 | 2·20 |

521 Horses

2008. 50th Anniv of Horse Foundation (refuge), Jura. Multicoloured.

1752	85c. Type **521**	2·30	2·20
1753	85c. Track and four horses	2·30	2·20
1754	85c. Two horses and building	2·30	2·20

Nos. 1752/4 were issued together, se-tenant, forming a composite design.

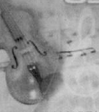

522 Violin

2008. Musical Instruments. Multicoloured.

1755	85c. Type **522**	2·40	2·20
1756	100c. Accordian	2·75	2·50
1757	130c. Electric guitar	3·50	3·25
1758	180c. Saxophone	4·50	4·25

523 Puck in Net

2008. Centenary of Swiss Ice Hockey Association.

| 1759 | **523** | 100c. multicoloured | 2·75 | 2·50 |

524 Player

2008. Euro 2008–European Football Championships, Austria and Switzerland (4th issue). Local Football.

| 1760 | **524** | 100c. multicoloured | 2·75 | 2·50 |

Nos. 1643, 1681, 1708 and 1760 together form a composite design of a football enclosing players.

525 Pitch

2008. Euro 2008–European Football Championships, Austria and Switzerland (5th issue). Self-adhesive.

| 1761 | **525** | 100c. emerald | 2·75 | 2·50 |

No. 1762 and Type **526** have been left for 'Euro 2008', issued on 8 May 2008, not yet received.

527 Birds in Flight forming Envelope

2008. Europa. The Letter.

| 1763 | **527** | 100c. multicoloured | 2·75 | 2·50 |

528 '100'

2008. Centenary of Swiss Life Saving Society.

| 1764 | **528** | 100c. multicoloured | 2·75 | 2·50 |

529 Mountain Biking

2008. Olympic Games, Beijing. Multicoloured.

| 1765 | 100c. Type **529** | 2·75 | 2·50 |

No. 1766 is vacant.

530 Via Sbrinz and Schitzturm Tower, Stansstad

2008. Pro Patria. Traditional Routes. Multicoloured.

1767	85c.+40c. Type **530**	3·50	3·25
1768	85c.+40c. East Gate, Avenches and Columns, Nyon	3·50	3·25
1769	100c.+50c. Via Valtellina, Cavaglia and Dürrboden restaurant	4·50	4·00
1770	100c.+50c. Via Stockalper, Engi and Old Hospice	4·50	4·00

531 Centre International de Conferences Geneve (conference venue)

2008. 24th UPU Congress, Geneva.
1771 **531** 130c. multicoloured 3·25 3·25

532 Wheat

2008. Cereals. Multicoloured. Self-adhesive.
1772 10c. Type **532** 45 40
1773 15c. Barley 55 50
1774 20c. Rye 65 60
1775 50c. Oats 1·50 1·40

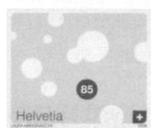

533 Cheese

2008. Switzerland through the Eyes of Foreign Artists. Multicoloured.
1776 85c. Type **533** 2·40 2·20
1777 100c. Chocolate 2·75 2·50
1778 130c. Clock 3·75 3·50
1779 180c. Tools (Swiss army pocket knives) 5·00 4·50

534 Old Bridge, Bad Sackingen—Stein/Aargau

2008. Bridges.
1780 **534** 100c. multicoloured 2·75 2·50
A stamp of a similar design was issued by Germany.

535 Stylized Figures

2008. Fredi Murer (film maker).
1781 **535** 100c. multicoloured 2·75 2·50

2008. ProSpecieRara (rare breeds association) (3rd issue). As T **495**. Multicoloured. Self-adhesive.
1782 500c. Catillac pear 14·50 13·00

536 Local Food

2008. Stamp Day, Bellinzona. Sheet 105×70 mm.
MS1783 **536** 85c. multicoloured 3·00 2·75

537 Bauble

2008. Christmas Baubles. Multicoloured.
1784 85c. Type **537** 3·00 2·75
1785 100c. Star shaped bauble 3·25 3·00
1786 130c. Bell shaped bauble 4·25 4·00

538 Rotes Quadrat (Max Bill)

2008. Art. Each black and scarlet.
1787 100c. Type **538** 3·25 3·00
1788 130c. Eier im Spiegel (eggs in a mirror) (Hans Finsler) (30×42 mm) 4·25 4·00

539 Brown Bear

2009. Centenary of Pro Natura (conservation organization).
1789 **539** 85c. multicoloured 3·00 2·75

540 Rigi (steam ship)

2009. 50th Anniv of Verkehrshaus Transport Museum. Multicoloured.
1790 85c. Type **540** 3·00 2·75
1791 100c. Dufaux race car 3·25 3·00
1792 130c. Lockheed Orion 9C Special aircraft 4·25 3·75

541 Boot

2009. International Ice Hockey Federation World Championships, Berne and Zurich–Kloten. Self-adhesive.
1793 **541** 100c. multicoloured 3·25 3·00

542 Vadret da Morteratsch

2009. Glacial Shrinkage.
1794 **542** 100c. multicoloured 3·25 3·00
The printing method allows No. 1794 to show the glacier as it is now, or as it was in 1850 when the stamp is tilted.

543 John Calvin

2009. 500th Birth Anniv of John Calvin (theologian).
1795 **543** 100c. multicoloured 3·25 3·00

544 The Human Mind

2009. Birth Centenary of Hans Erni (stamp designer). Multicoloured.
1796 100c. Type **544** 3·25 3·00
1797 130c. Human Hands 4·25 4·00

545 Hans Ulrich Grubenmann

2009. 300th Birth Anniv of Hans Ulrich Grubenmann (engineer).
1798 **545** 85c. multicoloured 3·00 2·75

546 Kittens

2009. European Wild Cat (Felis silvestris). Self-adhesive.
1799 **546** 85c. multicoloured 3·00 2·75

547 Birch

2009. Ancient Trees. Multicoloured. Self-adhesive.
1800 85c. Type **547** 3·25 3·00
1801 100c. Oak 3·75 3·50
1802 130c. Willow 4·75 4·50

548 Via Francigena and Great St. Bernhard Hospice

2009. Pro Patria. Traditional Routes. Multicoloured.
1803 85c.+40c. Type **548** 4·50 4·25
1804 85c.+40c. Via Salina, track and Berne Gate, Murten 4·50 4·25
1805 100c.+50c. Via Spluga, Viamala, Zillis-Reischen and Albertini House, SplÜgen 5·25 5·00
1806 100c.+50c. Via Rhenana, Basel Old Town and salt drilling towers, Rheinfelden 5·25 5·00
MS1807 105×70 mm. 100c.+50c. Illuminated roads (centenary of Pro Patria organization) 5·25 5·00

549 '@' and Type

2009. Graphics–From Guttenberg to the Internet.
1808 **549** 100c. multicoloured 3·75 3·50

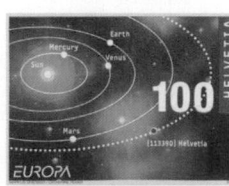

550 Planets and Helvetia Asteroid

2009. Europa. Astronomy.
1809 **550** 100c. multicoloured 3·75 3·50

551 Stiva da Morts (Place of Mourning, Vrin)

2009. Architecture. Multicoloured.
1810 100c. Type **551** 3·75 3·50
1811 180c. Pentorama Community Centre, Amriswil 6·50 6·25

552 Princess Lillifee

2009. Princess Lillifee (character created by Monika Finsterbusch). Self-adhesive.
1812 **552** 85c. multicoloured 3·25 3·00

553 Goats and Lead Cows

2009. Alpaufahrt (moving animals to and from alpine pastures), Appenzell. Multicoloured.
1813 85c. Type **553** 3·25 3·00
1814 85c. Cows and calves (32×37 mm) 3·25 3·00
1815 85c. Bull and horse drawn cart (34×37 mm) 3·25 3·00
Nos. 1813/15 were printed, se-tenant, forming a composite design of the procession.

554 'Den Zwang abwrft' (independence)

2009. Switzerland through the Eyes of Foreign Artists. Designs showing red flowers with a central white cross and parts of a poem by Friedrich Schiller describing Swiss virtues. Multicoloured. P 14×13.
1816 85c. Type **554** 3·25 3·00
1817 100c. Sich selbst genug 3·75 3·50
1818 130c. die Menschlichkeit noch ehrt 4·75 4·50
1819 180c. sich bescheidet 6·25 6·00

555 Design as 1903 Stamp (Type 18)

2009. Centenary of Swiss Stamp Dealers' Association.
1820 **555** 100c. light bright green and bright yellowish green 3·75 3·50

556 Refugees and Red Cross

2009. 60th Anniv of Geneva Conventions.
1821 **556** 100c. multicoloured 3·75 3·50

557 'Wedding'

2009. Greetings Stamps. Multicoloured. Self-adhesive.
1822 100c. Type **557** 3·75 3·50
1823 100c. Birth 3·75 3·50
1824 100c. Anniversary 3·75 3·50

558 Crane (emblem of Gruyères)

2009. Stamp Day, Gruyères. Sheet 70×105 mm.
MS1825 **558** 85c. multicoloured 3·50 3·25

559 Santa Hat

2009. Christmas. Multicoloured.
1826	85c. Type **559**	3·25	3·00
1827	100c. Tree	3·75	3·50
1828	130c. Parcel	4·75	4·50

560 Alpine Skier

2009. Paralympic Games, Vancouver.
1829	**560** 130c. multicoloured	4·75	4·50

561 Procession

2010. Centenary of Basel Carnival
1830	100c. Type **561**	3·75	3·50
1831	100c. Four figures and float (44×37 mm)	3·75	3·50
1832	100c. Band	3·75	3·50

No 1833 is vacant.

562 Emblem

2010. 550th Anniv of Basel University
1834	**562** 85c. deep turquoise-green, orange-red and black	3·25	3·00

563 Peacock Goats

2010. International Year of Biodiversity
1835	**563** 85c. multicoloured	3·25	3·00

564 Grandjean Monoplane and Ernest Failloubaz

2010. Centenary of Swiss Aviation. Multicoloured.
1836	85c. Type **564** (1st flight of Swiss aircraft by Swiss pilot)	3·25	3·00
1837	100c. Airbus A340 (modern civil aviation)	3·75	3·50
1838	130c. Geo Chavez flying Bleriot XI monoplane (first flight over Alps)	4·75	4·50
1839	180c. Acrobatic airplane, glider and air balloon (aviation sport)	6·50	6·25

565 Script

2010. Centenary of Swiss Cancer League
1840	**565** 100c. multicoloured	3·75	3·50

566 Dancers and Headdress (Federal Costume Festival, Schwyz)

2010. Traditional Swiss Customs. Multicoloured.
1841	100c. Type **566**	3·75	3·50
1842	100c. Alphorn and yodellers (centenary of Swiss Yodelling Association)	3·75	3·50
1843	100c. Drum (Federal Drumming and Piping Festival, Interlaken)	3·75	3·50
1844	100c. Marksman and target (Federal Marksmen's Festival, Aarau)	3·75	3·50

567 Neissen Funicular Railway

2010. Centenary of Bernina Railway
1845	85c. Type **567**	3·25	3·00
1846	100c. Bernina railway line	3·75	3·50

568 School Boy

2010. Death Centenary of Albert Anker (artist)
1847	**568** 85c. multicoloured	3·25	3·00

569 Johann Hebel and Basel

2010. 250th Birth Anniv of Johann Peter Hebel (theologian and writer)
1848	**569** 85c. multicoloured	3·25	3·00

570 Charles the Bold in Flight

2010. Pro Patria. Battle of Murten Panorama by Louis Braun. Multicoloured.
1849	85c.+40c. Type **570**	4·50	4·25
1850	85c.+40c. Archers and Duke of Somerset and mount dead by his tent	4·50	4·25
1851	100c.+50c. Burgundian cavalry under attack	5·25	5·00
1852	100c.+50c. Confederate troops with flags and halberds	5·25	5·00

571 Equilibres (Peter Fischli and David Weiss)

2010. Centenary of Kunsthaus (musuem of fine arts), Zurich
1853	**571** 100c. multicoloured	3·75	3·50

572 Figures

2010. Bicentenary of Public Welfare Society
1854	**572** 100c. new blue and pale grey	3·75	3·50

573 Heidi and Goats (*Heidi* by Johanna Spyri)

2010. Europa. Children's Books.
1855	**573** 100c. multticoloured	3·75	3·50

574 Big Top from Below

2010. World Circus 2010, Geneva
1856	**574** 140c. multicoloured	5·00	4·75

575 Jimmy Flitz

2010. Jimmy Flitz (cartoon character created by Roland Zoss). Booklet Stamp
1857	**575** 85c. multicoloured	3·25	3·00

helvetia | 85
576 Sphere

2010. Optical Art Designs by Youri Massen Juschin (artist). Multicoloured.
1858	85c. Type **576**	3·25	3·00
1859	100c. Blue, black and red squares	3·75	3·50
1860	140c. Circles within a lined square	5·00	4·75

577 Therapod

2010. Swiss Paleontology. Saurians. Multicoloured.
1861	85c. Type **577**	3·25	3·00
1862	100c. Ichthyosaur	3·75	3·50
1863	140c. Raeticodactylus filisurensis	5·00	4·75

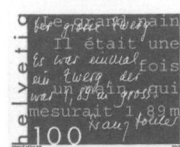
578 Words

2010. Franz Hohler (writer)
1864	**578** 100c. bright yellowish, green lemon and black	3·75	3·50

579 Jeanne Hersch

2010. Birth Centenary of Jeanne Hersch (philosopher)
1865	**579** 100c. multicoloured	3·75	3·50

580 Rolf Liebermann

2010. Swiss Composers Birth Centenaries. Multicoloured.
1866	100c. Type **580**	3·75	3·50
1867	140c. Heinrich Sutermeister	5·00	4·75

581 'TA' and 'EFT'

2010. 50th Anniv of European Free Trade Association
1868	**581** 140c. greenish yellow and black	5·00	4·75

582 Gustave Moynier and Henry Dunant

2010. Death Centenaries of Henry Dunant and Gustave Moynier (founders of precursor of Red Cross)
1869	**582** 190c. multicoloured	6·75	6·50

583 Zahringer Fountain and Zytglogge Medieval Clock Tower, Berne

2010. Stamp Day. Sheet 70×105 mm
MS1870 **583** 85c. multicoloured		3·75	3·50

584 Candle and Star

2010. Christmas. Multicoloured.
1871	85c. Type **584**	3·50	3·25
1872	100c. Snowflake	4·25	4·00
1873	140c. Angel and star	5·75	5·50

585 Lace-making Bobbins

2010. Traditional Swiss Handicrafts. Multicoloured.
1874	200c. Type **585**	7·75	7·50
1875	300c. Hands holding tools and carving of fox	11·50	11·50

586 Findus, Chicken, Mouse and Cheese

2011. Pettersson and Findus (Pettson och Findus) (created by Sven Nordqvist)
1876	**586** 85c. multicoloured	3·50	3·25

587 Bee and Flower

2011. Bees
1877	**587** 85c. multicoloured	3·50	3·25

588 Able-bodied and Disabled Children

2011. 50th Anniv of Cerebral Foundation
1878 **588** 85c. multicoloured   3·50   3·25

589 Gymnasts

2011. World Gymnaestrada, Lausanne
1879 **589** 85c. multicoloured   3·50   3·25

590 *Curcubita pepo* (courgette flower)

2011. Vegetable Flowers. Multicoloured.
1880   85c. Type **590**   3·50   3·25
1881   100c. *Pisum sativum* (snow pea)   4·00   3·75
1882   110c. *Allium ursinum* (wild
          garlic)   4·50   4·25
1883   260c. *Cynara scolymus*
          (artichoke)   10·50   10·00

591 Maison de Halles

2011. Neuchatel Millenary
1884 **591** 100c. multicoloured   4·00   3·75

592 Panda

2011. 50th Anniv of World Wide Fund for Nature (WWF)
1885 **592** 100c. multicoloured   4·00   3·75

593 Max Frisch

2011. Birth Centenary of Max Frisch (writer)
1886 **593** 100c. black   4·00   3·75

594 Vitamin C Molecule Construct

2011. International Year of Chemistry
1887 **594** 100c multicoloured   4·00   3·75

595 Mountains and Valley (Urnerboden)

2011. 50th Anniv of National Anthem. Multicoloured.
MS1888 25c.×4, Type **595**; Lake and mountains (Urnersee bei Flüelen); Tree on hillock (Urigen); Sunset over mountains (Schächentaler Windgällen)   4·25   4·00

596 Sunlight through Trees

2011. Europa. Forests
1889 **596** 100c. multicoloured   4·00   3·75

597 'ART IS RESISTANCE'

2011. Art. Venice Biennale
1890 **597** 100c. multicoloured   4·00   3·75

598 PS *Piemonte*

2011. Pro Patria. Steam Navigation in Switzerland. Multicoloured.
1891   85c.+40c. Type **598**   5·00   4·75
1892   85c.+40c. PS *Gallia*   5·00   4·75
1893   100c.+50c. PS *Blümlisalp*   6·00   5·75
1894   100c.+50c. PS *LA Suisse*   6·00   5·75

2011. Traditional Swiss Handicrafts. Coil Stamps. Multicoloured.
1895   400c. Potter 'throwing' pot
          on wheel   16·00   15·00
1896   500c. Blacksmith working
          at anvil   20·00   19·00

599 Muggestutz

2011. *Muggestutz* (written and drawn by Susanna Schmid-Germann). Booklet Stamp
1897 **599** 85c. multicoloured   4·25   4·00

600 Paul Burkhard

2011. Birth Centenary of Paul Burkhard (composer)
1898 **600** 100c. multicoloured   4·75   4·50

601 *Frucht 07*

2011. Art
1899 **601** 100c. multicoloured   4·75   4·50

602 Terraces and Erosion Prevention Walls

2011. World Heritage Site. Lavaux Vineyard Terraces. Multicoloured.
1900   100c. Type **602**   4·75   4·50
1901   100c. Terraces, Saint-Saphorin
          and Lake Geneva (41×36
          mm)   4·75   4·50
1902   100c. Lake Geneva, Le Gram-
          mont and gateway (37×36
          mm)   4·75   4·50

603 Baby's Dummy

2011. Greetings Stamps. Multicoloured.
1903   100c. Type **603**   4·75   4·50
1904   100c. Heart   4·75   4·50
1905   100c. Two glasses of cham-
          pagne   4·75   4·50
1906   100c. Two rings   4·75   4·50

604 *Dungarees* (Bajram Mahmuti)

2011. Art. Disabled Artists. Multicoloured.
1907   85c. Type **604**   4·25   4·00
1908   100c. *Emmental* (Claudia Aebi-
          Torre) (horiz)   4·75   4·50
1909   140c. *Mond* (Christian Oppliger)
          (horiz)   6·75   6·50
1910   190c. Untitled (Flavia Trachsel)   9·00   8·75

605 Chapel

2011. Christmas. Multicoloured.
1911   85c. Type **605**   3·75   3·50
1912   100c. Sleigh carrying presents
          and decorated tree   4·50   4·25
1913   140c. Chalet, wreath, presents
          and tree   6·00   5·75

606 Chateau de Villa, Sierre

2011. Stamp Day. Philasierre 2011 Stamp Exhibition. Sheet 70×105 mm
MS1914 **606** 85c. multicoloured   4·00   3·75

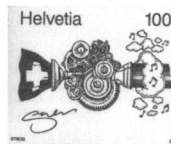
607 Flag in Music out

2011. Stress (Andres Andrekson) (rapper)
1915 **607** 100c. multicoloured   4·50   4·25

608 Locomotive

2012. Centenary of Jungfrau Railway
1916 **608** 100c. multicoloured   4·50   4·25

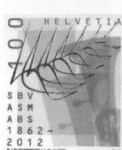
609 Emblem

2012. 150th Anniv of Swiss Brass Band Association
1917 **609** 100c. multicoloured   4·50   4·25

610 Beaver

2012. Fauna
1918 **610** 100c. multicoloured   4·50   4·25

611 Abstract from Civil Code

2012. Centenary of Swiss Civil Code
1919 **611** 100c. multicoloured   4·50   4·25

612 St. Gallus

2012. 1400th Birth Anniv of St. Gallus
1920 **612** 100c. Multicoloured   4·50   4·25

613 Little Tiger, Little Bear and Tigerduck

2012. 80th Birth Anniv of Janosch (Horst Eckert) (chidren's writer and illustrator). Booklet Stamp
1921 **613** 100c. multicoloured   4·50   4·25

614 Elm Village

2012. World Heritage Site. Martinsloch 'Window' (hole (21 metres high by 18 metres wide) in mountains of Tectonic Areana Sardona). Multicoloured.
1922   100c. Type **614**   4·50   4·25
1923   100c. Sunlight through
          'window' on 13/14 March
          or 30 September 1 October
          (41×36 mm)   4·50   4·25
1924   100c. Sunlight through
          'window' shining on church
          tower, Elm (37×36 mm)   4·50   4·25

615 *Lycopersicion lycopersicum* (tomato)

2012. Vegetable Flowers. Multicoloured.
1925   140c. Type **615**   6·00   5·75
1926   180c. *Phaseolus coccineus* (run-
          ner bean)   7·75   7·50
1927   190c. *Allium cepa* (onion)   8·25   8·00

616 Station Clock (Hans Hilfiker, 1944) and Station Clock Tidied Up

2012. Art. Tidying up Art - Ursus Wehrli
1928 **616** 100c. multicoloured   4·50   4·25

617 Blood Droplet as Balloon

2012. Blood Donation Campaign
1929 **617** 100c. multicoloured   4·50   4·25

618 Mother-in-Law's Visit

2012. Europa. Visit

1930	**618**	100c. multicoloured	4·50	4·25

619 Cabrio Cable Car

2012. Opening of Staserhorn Cabrio Cable Car

1931	**619**	100c. multicoloured	4·50	4·25

620 Survey

2012. Centenary of Cadastral (Official) Surveying

1932	**620**	100c. multicoloured	4·50	4·25

621 William Tell with Crossbow

2012. Anniversaries of the William Tell Plays at Altdorf and Interlaken. Multicoloured.

1933	100c. Type **621** (500th anniv)	4·50	4·25
1934	100c. Outdoor production of *William Tell* at Interlaken (centenary)	4·50	4·25

622 Löwenbrunnen Fountain, Utendorf

2012. Pro Patria. Small Buildings. Multicoloured.

1935	85c. +40c. Type **622**	5·00	4·75
1936	85c.. +40c. 'Fermes des Troncs' building, Mézières, Vaud	5·00	4·75
1937	100c. +50c. Villa Abendstern Summer House, Wädenswil	6·00	5·75
1938	100c. +50c. Crotti (cold store), Brusio, Poschiavo	6·00	5·75

628 Altstätten

2012. Stamp Day. Rhine Valley Stamp Exhibition. Sheet 105×70 mm

MS1952 **628**	85c. multicoloured	4·00	3·75

629 Tree-shaped Christmas Lights

2012. Christmas. Multicoloured.

1953	85c. Type **629**	3·75	3·50
1954	100c. Star-shaped Christmas lights (green)	4·50	4·25
1955	140c. Arched Christmas lights (blue)	6·25	6·00

630 Yakari and Butterfly

2012. Yakari (cartoon character created by Derib & Job (Claude de Ribaupierre and André Jobin))

1956	100c. Type **630**	4·50	4·25
1957	100c. Yakari riding Little Thunder	4·50	4·25

FRANK STAMPS

Issued to charity hospitals for free transmission of their mails.

F21

1911. With control figures at top.

F268	**F 21**	2c. red and green	15	15
F269	**F 21**	3c. red and green	3·50	85
F270	**F 21**	5c. red and green	1·60	15
F271	**F 21**	10c. red and green	2·10	15
F272	**F 21**	15c. red and green	29·00	5·75
F273	**F 21**	20c. red and green	5·25	85

F49 Deaconess

1935. With or without control figures.

F358A	**F49**	5c. green	4·25	2·10
F359A	-	10c. violet	4·25	2·10
F360A	-	20c. red	4·25	2·10

DESIGNS: 10c. Sister of the Ingenbohl Order; 20c. Henri Dunant (founder of Red Cross).

OFFICIAL STAMPS

1918. Optd **Industrielle Kriegs-wirtschaft**.

O308	**18b**	3c. brown	5·00	55·00
O300	**18b**	5c. green	15·00	65·00
O310	**18b**	7½c. grey	5·00	38·00
O303	**21**	10c. red on buff	[illegible]	[illegible]
O304	**21**	[illegible] purple on buff	18·00	90·00
O313	**17**	20c. yellow and red	12·50	85·00
O314	**17**	25c. blue and deep blue	12·50	85·00
O315	**17**	30c. green and brown	20·00	£150

1938. Optd with Geneva Cross.

O381A	**52**	3c. green	40	40
O382A	-	5c. green (No. 369)	40	40
O383A	-	10c. purple (No. 370)	1·30	65
O384A	-	15c. orange (No. 373)	40	2·50
O385A	-	20c. red (No. 375)	65	40
O386A	-	25c. brown (No. 376)	65	2·10
O387A	-	30c. blue (No. 377)	85	1·50
O388A	-	35c. green (No. 378)	85	1·90
O389A	-	40c. grey (No. 379)	85	1·50
O390	**17**	50c. green and deep green	3·25	2·10
O391	**17**	60c. brown	3·25	3·75
O392	**17**	70c. buff and violet	3·25	6·25
O393	**17**	80c. buff and grey	3·25	5·00
O395	**41**	90c. red, dp green & green	4·25	5·00
O394	**17**	1f. green and purple	4·25	5·00
O396	**41**	1f.20 red, lake and pink	4·25	6·75
O397	**41**	1f.50 red, blue & turquoise	7·50	9·25
O398	-	2f. red, black and grey	8·25	10·50

1942. Optd **Officiel**. (a) Landscape designs of 1936.

O427	**52**	3c. green	40	3·25
O428	-	5c. green	40	40
O430	-	10c. brown	40	65
O431	-	15c. orange	85	3·00
O432	-	20c. red (Lake)	85	65
O433	-	25c. brown	85	3·25
O434	-	30c. blue	1·30	1·30
O435	-	35c. green	1·70	4·25
O436	-	40c. grey	1·70	85

(b) Historical designs of 1941.

O437		50c. blue on green	5·75	6·75
O438	**68**	60c. brown on brown	6·75	6·75
O439	-	70c. purple on mauve	7·50	12·50
O440	-	80c. black on grey	2·10	2·50
O441	-	90c. red on pink	2·50	3·25
O442	-	1f. green on green	2·50	2·50
O443	-	1f.20 purple on grey	3·25	4·25
O444	-	1f.50 blue on buff	3·25	5·00
O445	-	2f. red on pink	4·25	5·75

1950. Landscape designs of 1949 optd **Officiel**.

O522	**107**	5c. orange	85	1·70
O523	-	10c. green	1·70	1·70
O524	-	15c. turquoise	14·00	25·00
O525	-	20c. purple	5·00	1·70
O526	-	25c. red	8·25	15·00
O527	-	30c. green	5·75	6·75
O528	-	35c. brown	8·25	17·00
O529	-	40c. blue	6·75	7·50
O530	-	50c. grey	10·00	11·50
O531	-	60c. green	12·50	12·50
O532	-	70c. violet	39·00	38·00

For Swiss stamps overprinted for the use of officials of the League of Nations, International Labour Office and other special U.N. Agencies having their headquarters at Geneva, see sub-section INTERNATIONAL ORGANIZATIONS SITUATED IN SWITZERLAND.

POSTAGE DUE STAMPS

D10

1878

D89	**D10**	1c. blue	2·50	2·10
D90	**D10**	2c. blue	2·50	2·10
D98B	**D10**	3c. blue	17·00	14·50
D92	**D10**	5c. blue	23·00	17·00
D99B	**D10**	5c. blue	21·00	9·25
D100B	**D10**	10c. blue	£225	9·25
D101A	**D10**	20c. blue	£275	6·75
D102A	**D10**	50c. blue	£550	29·00
D96	**D10**	100c. blue	£750	21·00
D97	**D10**	500c. blue	£650	33·00

Nos. D89 and D92a have raised backgrounds behind the figure of value.

1883. Numerals in red.

D268	1c. green	50	1·70
D181C	3c. green	7·50	15·00
D269B	5c. green	1·40	1·30
D270A	10c. green	4·50	2·50
D271B	20c. green	17·00	7·50
D204B	50c. green	18·00	5·75
D205B	100c. green	21·00	4·25
D187B	500c. green	£170	[illegible]

The above were issued in a wide range of shades from pale turquoise to olive between 1883 and 1910. A detailed list of these appears in the Stanley Gibbons Part 8 (Italy and Switzerland) Catalogue.

D21

1910

D274	**D21**	1c. green and red	15	15
D275	**D21**	3c. green and red	15	15
D276	**D21**	5c. green and red	15	15
D277	**D21**	10c. green and red	17·00	40
D278	**D21**	15c. green and red	1·00	1·70
D279	**D21**	20c. green and red	27·00	40
D280	**D21**	25c. green and red	1·70	85
D281	**D21**	30c. green and red	1·70	85
D282	**D21**	50c. green and red	2·10	1·70

1916. Surch.

D299	**D 21**	5 on 3c. red and green	15	15
D300	**D 21**	10 on 1c. red and green	40	12·50
D301	**D 21**	10 on 3c. red and green	35	2·10
D302	**D 21**	20 on 50c. red & green	1·20	2·10

D41

1924

D329	**D41**	5c. red and green	1·00	40
D330	**D41**	10c. red and green	4·25	75
D331	**D41**	15c. red and green	3·75	85
D332a	**D41**	20c. red and green	6·75	2·30
D333	**D41**	25c. red and green	4·25	85
D334	**D41**	30c. red and green	4·25	1·20
D335	**D41**	40c. red and green	5·75	1·00
D336	**D41**	50c. red and green	5·75	1·00

1937. Surch.

D380	**D41**	5 on 15c. red and green	1·30	5·50
D381	**D41**	10 on 30c. red & green	1·30	2·10
D382	**D41**	20 on 50c. red & green	2·10	6·75
D383	**D41**	40 on 50c. red & green	3·25	17·00

D54

1938

D384A	**D54**	5c. red	60	25
D385A	**D54**	10c. red	85	10
D386A	**D54**	15c. red	1·70	3·00
D387A	**D54**	20c. red	1·30	40
D388A	**D54**	25c. red	2·00	3·00
D389A	**D54**	30c. red	1·90	1·70
D390A	**D54**	40c. red	2·30	65
D391A	**D54**	50c. red	2·75	3·25

POSTCARD STAMPS

P1 Tourism Emblem

2002. Self-adhesive gum. No value expressed.

P1	**P1**	(1f.30) multicoloured	3·50	3·25
P2	**P1**	(1f.80) multicoloured	5·00	4·50

No. P1 was for use only on postcards sent to countries within Europe and No. P2 to overseas countries. They were not valid for use on other mail or in combination with other stamps.

"PRO JUVENTUTE" CHARITY STAMPS

PREMIUMS. All "Pro Juventute" stamps are sold at an additional premium which goes to Benevolent Societies. Until 1937 these premiums were not shown on the stamps, but were as follows:

2c. for all 3c. franking values; 5c. for all 5, 71/2, 10, 15 and 20c. values and 10c. for all 30 and 40c. values.

From 1937, when the premium first appeared on the designs, we show it in the catalogue listing.

C1 Helvetia and Matterhorn

1913. Children's Fund.

J1	**C1**	5c. green	4·50	13·00

C2 Appenzell

1915. Children's Fund.

J1a	**C2**	5c. green on buff	4·50	16·00
J2	-	10c. red on buff	£160	£130

DESIGN: 10c. Girl from Lucerne.

C4 Berne

1916. Children's Fund.

J3		3c. violet on buff	9·00	65·00
J4	**C 4**	5c. green on buff	20·00	16·00
J5	-	10c. red on buff	85·00	£110

DESIGNS: 3, 10c. Girls of Freiburg and Vaud.

C6 Valais

1917. Children's Fund.

J6	**C6**	3c. violet on buff	4·75	90·00
J7	-	5c. green on buff	12·50	8·00
J8	-	10c. red on buff	32·00	40·00

DESIGNS: 5c. Man of Unterwalden; 10c. Girl of Ticino.

9 Uri

1918. Children's Fund. Dated "1918".

J9	**C9**	10c. red, yellow and black on buff	13·50	40·00
J10	-	15c. multicoloured on buff	18·00	20·00

ARMS: 15c. Geneva.

1919. Children's Fund. As Type **C9** but dated "1919". Cream paper.

J11		7½c. red, grey and black	4·50	22·00
J12		10c. green, red and black	4·50	22·00
J13		15c. red, violet and black	9·00	11·00

ARMS: 7½c. Nidwalden; 10c. Vaud; 15c. Obwalden.

1920. Children's Fund. As Type **C9** but dated "1920". Cream paper.

J14		7½c. red, grey and black	5·50	24·00
J15		10c. blue, red and black	9·00	26·00
J16		15c. red, blue, violet and black	5·50	12·00

ARMS: 7½c. Schwyz; 10c. Zurich; 15c. Ticino.

1921. Children's Fund. As Type **C9** but dated "1921". Cream paper.

J17		10c. red, black and green	90	4·75
J18		20c. multicoloured	3·50	7·25
J19		40c. red and blue	14·50	90·00

ARMS: 10c. Valais; 20c. Berne; 40c. Switzerland.

1922. Children's Fund. As Type **C9** but dated "1922". Cream paper.

J20		5c. orange, blue and black	90	4·00
J21		10c. green and black	90	4·00
J22		20c. violet, blue and black	1·80	4·00
J23		40c. blue, red and black	16·00	£100

ARMS: 5c. Zug; 10c. Freiburg; 20c. Lucerne; 40c. Switzerland.

1923. Children's Fund. As Type **C9** but dated "1923". Cream paper.

J24		5c. orange and black	45	8·00
J25		10c. multicoloured	45	4·00
J26		20c. multicoloured	90	4·00
J27		40c. blue, red and black	12·50	80·00

ARMS: 5c. Basel; 10c. Glarus; 20c. Neuchatel; 40c. Switzerland.

1924. Children's Fund. As Type **C9** but dated "1924". Cream paper.

J28		5c. black and lilac	45	2·75
J29		10c. red, green and black	90	1·60
J30		20c. black, yellow and red	90	2·00
J31		30c. red, blue and black	2·75	24·00

ARMS: 5c. Appenzell; 10c. Solothurn; 20c. Schaffhausen; 30c. Switzerland.

1925. Children's Fund. As Type **C9** but dated "1925". Cream paper.

J32		5c. green, black and violet	45	2·40
J33		10c. black and green	45	1·60
J34		20c. multicoloured	65	1·60
J35		30c. red, blue and black	1·60	16·00

ARMS: 5c. St. Gall; 10c. Appenzell-Ausser-Rhoden; 20c. Graubunden; 30c. Switzerland.

1926. Children's Fund. As Type **C9** but dated "1926". Cream paper.

J36		5c. multicoloured	45	2·00
J37		10c. green, black and red	45	2·00
J38		20c. red, black and blue	65	2·40
J39		30c. blue, red and black	1·60	19·00

ARMS: 5c. Thurgau; 10c. Basel; 20c. Aargau; 30c. Switzerland and Lion of Lucerne.

C40 Forsaken Orphan

C42 J. H. Pestalozzi

C43 J. H. Pestalozzi

1927. Children's Fund. Dated "1927".

J40	**C40**	5c. purple & yell on grey	45	4·00
J41	-	10c. green & pink on green	45	80
J42	**C 42**	20c. red	65	80
J43	**C 43**	30c. blue and black	1·60	13·00

DESIGN—As Type C **40**: 40c. Orphan at Pestalozzi School.

C44 Lausanne

C47 J. H. Dunant

1928. Children's Fund. Dated "1928".

J44	**C44**	5c. red, purple and black on buff	45	3·25
J45	-	10c. red, green and black on buff	45	1·60
J46	-	20c. black, yellow and red on buff	45	1·60
J47	**C 47**	30c. blue and red	1·80	12·00

DESIGNS—As Type C **44**: 10c. Arms of Winterthur; 20c. Arms of St. Gall.

C48 Mt. San Salvatore, Lake Lugano

1929. Children's Fund. Dated "1929".

J48	**C 48**	5c. red and violet	45	2·00
J49	-	10c. blue and brown	45	2·00
J50	-	20c. blue and red	45	2·00
J51	-	30c. blue	2·00	20·00

DESIGNS: 10c. Mt. Titlis, Lake Engstlen; 20c. Mt. Lyskamm from Riffelberg; 30c. Nicholas de Flue.

C50 Freiburg

C51 A. Bitzius—"Jeremias Gotthelf"

1930. Children's Fund. Dated "1930".

J52	**C 50**	5c. blue, black and green on buff	45	2·00
J53	-	10c. multicoloured on buff	45	1·20
J54	-	20c. multicoloured on buff	45	1·20
J55	**C 51**	30c. blue	1·80	8·75

ARMS—As Type C **51**: 10c. Altdorf; 20c. Schaff-hausen.

C52 St. Moritz and Silvaplana Lakes

1931. Children's Fund. Dated "1931".

J56	**C 52**	5c. green	70	2·40
J57	-	10c. violet	45	1·20
J58	-	20c. red	1·10	2·00
J59	-	30c. blue	7·25	29·00

DESIGNS: 10c. The Wetterhorn; 20c. Lac Leman; 30c. Alexandre Vinet.

C54 Flag swinging

1932. Children's Fund. Dated "1932".

J60	**C 54**	5c. red and green	55	2·75
J61	-	10c. orange	70	3·25
J62	-	20c. red	90	2·75
J63	-	30c. blue	3·25	13·00

DESIGNS: 10c. Putting the weight; 20c. Wrestlers; 30c. Eugen Huber.

C56 Vaud

1933. Children's Fund. Dated "1933".

J64	**C 56**	5c. green and buff	55	2·40
J65	-	10c. violet and buff	55	2·40
J66	-	20c. scarlet and buff	70	3·25
J67	-	30c. blue	3·50	13·50

DESIGNS: 10c. Swiss girl from Berne; 20c. Swiss girl from Ticino; 30c. Father Gregoire Girard.

C59 A. von Haller

1934. Children's Fund. Dated "1934".

J68		5c. green and buff	45	2·40
J69		10c. violet and buff	65	1·60
J70		20c. red and buff	70	2·40
J71	**C 59**	30c. blue	3·50	13·00

SWISS GIRL DESIGNS—As Type C **56**: 5c. Appenzell; 10c. Valais; 20c. Graubunden.

C61 Stefano Franscini

1935. Children's Fund. Dated "1935".

J72	-	5c. green and buff	45	2·75
J73	-	10c. violet and buff	65	1·60
J74	-	20c. red and buff	70	4·75
J75	**C 61**	30c. blue	3·50	16·00

SWISS GIRL DESIGNS—As Type C **56**: 5c. Basel; 10c. Lucerne; 20c. Geneva.

C62 H. G. Nageli

1936. Children's Fund.

J76	**C62**	5c. green	45	1·30
J77	-	10c. purple and buff	90	1·30
J78	-	20c. red and buff	55	3·25
J79	-	30c. blue and buff	5·75	50·00

SWISS GIRL DESIGNS—As Type C **56**: 10c. Neuchatel; 20c. Schwyz; 30c. Zurich.

C64 Gen. Henri Dufour

C66 "Youth"

1937. Children's Fund.

J80	**C 64**	5c.+5c. green	45	85
J81	-	10c.+5c. purple	45	85
J82	**C 66**	20c.+5c. red, buff and silver	70	85
J83	-	30c.+10c. blue, buff and silver	2·00	9·25

DESIGNS: 10c. Nicholas de Flue; 30c. as Type C **66**, but girl's head facing other way.

1937. 25th Anniv of 'Pro Juventute' Stamp Issues. Sheet 105×55 mm. As Nos. J82/3. Imperf.

MSJ83a	20c.+5c. red and silver, 30c.+10c. ultramarine and silver	10·50	85·00

C67 Salomon Gessner

1938. Children's Fund. Dated "1938".

J84	**C 67**	5c.+5c. green	45	85
J85	-	10c.+5c. violet & buff	45	85
J86	-	20c.+5c. red and buff	65	85
J87	-	30c.+10c. blue & buff	2·50	10·00

SWISS GIRL DESIGNS—As Type C **56**: 10c. St. Gall; 20c. Uri; 30c. Aargau.

C69 Gen. Herzog

1939. Children's Fund.

J88	**C 69**	5c.+5c. green	45	85
J89	-	10c.+5c. violet & buff	45	85
J90	-	20c.+5c. red and buff	45	2·50
J91	-	30c.+10c. blue & buff	2·30	23·00

SWISS GIRL DESIGNS—As Type C **56**: 10c. Freibourg; 20c. Nidwalden; 30c. Basel.

C71 Gottfried Keller

1940. Children's Fund. Dated "1940".

J92	**C 71**	5c.+5c. green	45	85
J93	-	10c.+5c. brown & buff	45	85
J94	-	20c.+5c. red and buff	55	85
J95	-	30c.+10c. blue & buff	2·20	14·00

SWISS GIRL DESIGNS—As Type C **56**: 10c. Thurgau; 20c. Solothurn; 30c. Zug.

C73 Johann Kasper Lavater

1941. Children's Fund. Bicentenary of Birth of Lavater (philosopher) and of Death of Richard (clockmaker). Dated "1941".

J96	**C 73**	5c.+5c. green	45	50
J97	-	10c.+5c. brown & buff	45	60
J98	-	20c.+5c. red and buff	65	60
J99	-	30c.+10c. blue	1·40	11·00
MSJ99a		75×70 mm. Nos J97/8. Imperf	£140	£550

DESIGNS—As Type C **56**: 10c., 20c. Girls in national costumes of Schaffhausen and Obwalden. As Type C **73**: 30c. Daniel Jean Richard.

C74 Niklaus Riggenbach (rack railway pioneer)

1942. Children's Fund. Dated "1942".

J100	**C 74**	5c.+5c. green	45	85
J101	-	10c.+5c. brn & buff	45	85
J102	-	20c.+5c. red and buff	45	85
J103	-	30c.+10c. blue	2·30	7·50

DESIGNS: 10c. and 20c. Girls in national costumes of Appenzell Ausser-Rhoden and Glarus; 30c. Conrad Escher von der Linth (statesman).

C75 Emanuel von Fellenberg

C76 Silver Thistle

1943. Death Centenary of Philip Emanuel von Fellenberg (economist).

J104	**C 75**	5c.+5c. green	45	85
J105	**C 76**	10c.+5c. green, buff and grey	45	85
J106	-	20c.+5c. red, yellow and pink	45	85
J107	-	30c.+10c. blue, light blue and black	1·80	14·00

FLOWERS: As Type C **76**: 20c. "Ladies slipper"; 30c. Gentian.

C77 Numa Droz

1944. Birth Centenary of Droz (statesman).

J108	**C77**	5c.+5c. green	45	85
J109	-	10c.+5c. olive, yellow and green	45	85
J110	-	20c.+5c. red, yellow and grey	45	85
J111	-	30c.+10c. blue, grey and blue	1·80	15·00

DESIGNS: 10c. Edelweiss; 20c. Martagon lily; 30c. "Aquilegia alpina".

C78 Ludwig Forrer

1945. Children's Fund. Centenary of Births of Ludwig Forrer (statesman) and Susanna Orelli (social reformer). Dated "1945".

J112	**C 78**	5c.+5c. green	90	85
J113	-	10c.+10c. brown	90	85
J114	-	20c.+10c. red, pink and yellow	1·40	85
J115	-	30c.+10c. blue, mauve and grey	5·50	15·00

DESIGNS: 10c. Susanna Orelli; 20c. Alpine dog rose; 30c. Spring crocus.

C79 Rudolf Toepffer

1946. Death Centenary of Rudolf Toepffer (author and painter). Type **C79** and floral designs inscr "PRO JUVENTUTE 1946".

J116	**C79**	5c.+5c. green	90	85
J117	-	10c.+10c. green, grey and orange	90	85
J118	-	20c.+10c. red, grey and yellow	90	1·30
J119	-	30c.+10c. blue, grey and mauve	5·00	12·50

DESIGNS—As Type C **76**: 10c. Narcissus; 20c. Houseleek; 30c. Blue thistle.

C80 Jacob Burckhardt (historian)

1947. Children's Fund. Type **C80** and floral designs inscr "PRO JUVENTUTE 1947".

J120	**C80**	5c.+5c. green	90	85
J121	-	10c.+10c. black, yellow and grey	90	85
J122	-	20c.+10c. brown, orange and grey	90	85
J123	-	30c.+10c. blue, pink and grey	4·00	13·50

DESIGNS—As Type C **76**: 10c. Alpine primrose; 20c. Orange lily; 30c. Cyclamen.

C81 Gen. U. Wille

1948. Children's Fund. Type **C81** and floral designs as Type **C76**. Dated "1948".

J124	**C81**	5c.+5c. purple	90	85
J125	-	10c.+10c. green, yellow and grey	1·10	85
J126	-	20c.+10c. brown, red and buff	1·40	85
J127	-	40c.+10c. blue, yellow and grey	5·50	13·50

FLOWERS: 10c. Yellow foxglove; 20c. Rust-leaved Alpine rose; 40c. Lily of Paradise.

C82 Nicholas Wengi

1949. Children's Fund. Type **C82** and floral designs inscr "PRO JUVENTUTE 1949".

J128	**C82**	5c.+5c. red	90	85
J129	-	10c.+10c. green, grey and yellow	90	85
J130	-	20c.+10c. brown, blue and buff	90	85
J131	-	40c. blue, mauve and yellow	5·50	12·50

DESIGNS—As Type C **76**: 10c. "Pulsatilla alpina"; 20c. Alpine clematis; 40c. Superb pink.

C83 General Theophil Sprecher von Bernegg

C84 Red Admiral Butterfly

1950. Children's Fund. Inscr "PRO JUVENTUTE 1950".

J132	**C83**	5c.+5c. brown	90	40
J133	**C 84**	10c.+10c. mult	90	85
J134	-	20c.+10c. black, blue and orange	1·40	1·30
J135	-	30c.+10c. brown, grey and mauve	6·75	25·00
J136	-	40c.+10c. yellow, brown and blue	6·75	21·00

DESIGNS: 20c. Clifden's nonpareil (moth); 30c. Honey bee; 40c. Moorland clouded yellow (butterfly).

C85 Johanna Spyri (authoress)

1951. Children's Fund. Type **C85** and various insects as Type **C84**. Inscr "PRO JUVENTUTE 1951".

J137	**C85**	5c.+5c. purple	90	40
J138	-	10c.+10c. blue & grn	90	85
J139	-	20c.+10c. black, cream and mauve	1·40	85
J140	-	30c.+10c. black, orange and green	4·50	11·50
J141	-	40c.+10c. brown, red and blue	6·25	11·50

INSECTS: 10c. Banded agrion (dragonfly); 20c. Scarce swallowtail (butterfly); 30c. Orange-tip (butterfly); 40c. Viennese emperor moth.

C86 "Portrait of a Boy" (Anker)

1952. Children's Fund. Type **C86** and insects as Type **C84**. Inscr "PRO JUVENTUTE 1952".

J142	**C86**	5c.+5c. red	90	40
J143	-	10c.+10c. orange, black and green	90	85
J144	-	20c.+10c. cream, black and mauve	90	1·30
J145	-	30c.+10c. blue, black and brown	4·50	11·50
J146	-	40c.+10c. buff, brown and blue	4·50	11·50

INSECTS: 10c. Seven-spotted ladybird; 20c. Marbled white (butterfly); 30c. Chalk-hill blue (butterfly); 40c. Oak eggar moth.

1953. Children's Fund. Portraits as Type **C86** and insects as Type **C84**. Inscr "PRO JUVENTUTE 1953".

J147	5c.+5c. red	70	40
J148	10c.+10c. pink, brown and green	90	85
J149	20c.+10c. black, buff and mauve	1·10	1·30
J150	30c.+10c. black, red & grn	4·50	11·50
J151	40c.+10c. blue	6·25	11·50

DESIGNS: 5c. "Portrait of a girl" (Anker); 10c. Black arches moth; 20c. Camberwell beauty (butterfly); 30c. "Purpureus kaehleri" (longhorn beetle); 40c. F. Hodler (self-portrait).

1954. Children's Fund. Portrait as Type **C85** and insects as Type **C84**. Inscr "PRO JUVENTUTE 1954".

J152	5c.+5c. brown	90	40
J153	10c.+10c. multicoloured	90	85
J154	20c.+10c. multicoloured	1·80	85
J155	30c.+10c. multicoloured	5·50	11·50
J156	40c.+10c. multicoloured	5·50	11·50

DESIGNS: 5c. Jeremias Gotthelf (novelist) (after Albert Bitzius); 10c. Garden tiger moth; 20c. Buff-tailed bumble bee; 30c. "Ascalaphus libelluloides" (owl-fly); 40c. Swallowtail (butterfly).

1955. Children's Fund. Portrait as Type **C85** and insects as Type **C84**. Inscr "PRO JUVENTUTE 1955".

J157	5c.+5c. purple	90	40
J158	10c.+10c. multicoloured	90	85
J159	20c.+10c. multicoloured	1·40	85
J160	30c.+10c. multicoloured	5·50	8·25
J161	40c.+10c. black red & blue	6·25	9·25

DESIGNS: 5c. C. Pictet de Rochemont; 10c. Peacock (butterfly); 20c. Great horntail; 30c. Yellow tiger moth; 40c. Apollo (butterfly).

1956. Children's Fund. Portrait as Type **C85** and insects as Type **C84**. Inscr "PRO JUVENTUTE 1956".

J162	5c.+5c. purple	90	40
J163	10c.+10c. deep green, red and green	90	85
J164	20c.+10c. multicoloured	90	85
J165	30c.+10c. blue, indigo and yellow	3·50	7·50
J166	40c.+10c. yellow, brn & bl	4·00	8·00

DESIGNS: 5c. Carlo Maderno (architect); 10c. Common burnet (moth); 20c. Lesser purple emperor (butterfly); 30c. Blue ground beetle; 40c. Large white (butterfly).

1957. Children's Fund. Portrait as Type **C85** and insects as Type **C84**. Inscr "PRO JUVENTUTE 1957".

J167	5c.+5c. purple	90	40
J168	10c.+10c. multicoloured	90	85
J169	20c.+10c. yellow, brown and mauve	90	85
J170	30c.+10c. emerald, green and purple	3·50	6·75
J171	40c.+10c. multicoloured	2·75	5·50

DESIGNS: 5c. L. Euler (mathematician); 10c. Clouded yellow (butterfly); 20c. Magpie moth; 30c. Rose chafer (beetle); 40c. Rosy underwing (moth).

C92 Albrecht von Haller (naturalist)

C93 Pansy

1958. Children's Fund. Type **C92** and flowers as Type **C93**. Inscr "PRO JUVENTUTE 1958".

J172	**C92**	5c.+5c. purple	90	40
J173	**C 93**	10c.+10c. yellow, brown and green	90	85
J174	-	20c.+10c. mult	90	85
J175	-	30c.+10c. mult	2·30	4·25
J176	-	40c.+10c. mult	2·30	4·25

FLOWERS: 20c. Chinese aster; 30c. Morning Glory; 40c. Christmas rose.

1959. Children's Fund. Portrait as Type **C92** and flowers as Type **C93**. Inscr "PRO JUVENTUTE 1959".

J177	5c.+5c. purple	45	40
J178	10c.+10c. multicoloured	45	40
J179	20c.+10c. red, green and purple	45	40
J180	30c.+10c. multicoloured	2·75	4·25
J181	50c.+10c. multicoloured	2·75	3·75

DESIGNS: 5c. Karl Hilty (lawyer); 10c. Marsh marigold; 20c. Poppy; 30c. Nasturtium; 50c. Sweet pea.

1960. Children's Fund. Portrait as Type **C92** and flowers as Type **C93**. Inscr "PRO JUVENTUTE 1960".

J182	5c.+5c. blue	45	40
J183	10c.+10c. yellow, drab and green	45	40
J184	20c.+10c. green, brown and mauve	45	40
J185	30c.+10c. green, blue and brown	2·75	5·75
J186	50c.+10c. yellow, grn & bl	2·75	6·25

DESIGNS: 5c. Alexandre Calame (painter); 10c. Dandelion; 20c. Phlox; 30c. Larkspur; 50c. Thorn apple.

1961. Children's Fund. Portrait as Type **C92** and flowers as Type **C93**. Inscr "PRO JUVENTUTE 1961".

J187	5c.+5c. blue	45	40
J188	10c.+10c. multicoloured	45	40
J189	20c.+10c. multicoloured	45	40
J190	30c.+10c. multicoloured	1·90	3·25
J191	50c.+10c. multicoloured	2·30	3·75

DESIGNS: 5c. J. Furrer (first President of Swiss Confederation); 10c. Sunflower; 20c. Lily-of-the-Valley; 30c. Iris; 50c. Silverweed.

C97 "Child's World"

C98 Mother and Child

1962. Children's Fund. 50th Anniv of Pro Juventute Foundation. Inscr "1912–1962".

J192	-	5c.+5c. multicoloured	45	40
J193	**C 97**	10c.+10c. red & green	45	40
J194	**C 98**	20c.+10c. mult	45	85
J195	-	30c.+10c. red, mauve and yellow	1·40	1·70
J196	-	50c.+10c. yellow, brown and blue	1·90	1·70
MSJ196a		82×62 mm. 100c.+20c. multicoloured (×2) (sold at 3f.)	8·50	6·75

DESIGNS—As Type C **97**: 5c. Apple blossom; 30c. "Child's World" (child in meadow); 50c. Forsythia.

1963. Children's Fund. Portrait as Type **C86** and flowers as Type **C93**. Inscr "PRO JUVENTUTE 1963".

J197	5c.+5c. blue	45	40
J198a	10c.+10c. multicoloured	1·90	1·30
J199a	20c.+10c. red, green and carmine	1·90	1·30
J200	30c.+10c. multicoloured	2·30	2·50
J201	50c.+10c. purple, green and blue	2·30	2·50

DESIGNS: 5c. "Portrait of a Boy" (Anker); 10c. Oxeye daisy; 20c. Geranium; 30c. Cornflower; 50c. Carnation.

1964. Children's Fund. Portrait as Type **C86** and flowers as Type **C93**. Inscr "PRO JUVENTUTE 1964".

J202	5c.+5c. blue	45	40
J203	10c.+10c. orange, yellow and green	45	40
J204	20c.+10c. red, green and carmine	55	40
J205	30c.+10c. purple, green and brown	1·00	85
J206	50c.+10c. multicoloured	1·40	1·30

DESIGNS: 5c. "Portrait of a Girl" (Anker); 10c. Daffodil; 20c. Rose; 30c. Red clover; 50c. White water-lily.

C101 Western European Hedgehogs

1965. Children's Fund. Animals. Inscr "PRO JUVENTUTE 1965".

J207	**C101**	5c.+5c. ochre, brown and red	45	40
J208	-	10c.+10c. mult	45	40
J209	-	20c.+10c. blue, brown and chestnut	55	40
J210	-	30c.+10c. blue, black and yellow	95	85
J211	-	50c.+10c. black, brown and blue	1·10	85

ANIMALS: 10c. Alpine marmots; 20c. Red deer; 30c. Eurasian badgers; 50c. Arctic hares.

1966. Children's Fund. Animals. As Type **C101** but inscr "PRO JUVENTUTE 1966". Multicoloured.

J212	5c.+5c. Stoat	45	40
J213	10c.+10c. Eurasian red squirrel	45	40
J214	20c.+10c. Red fox	55	40
J215	30c.+10c. Brown hare	95	85
J216	50c.+10c. Chamois	1·10	85

C102 Roe Deer

1967. Children's Fund. Animals. Inscr "PRO JUVENTUTE 1967". Multicoloured.

J217	10c.+10c. Type **C102**	45	25
J218	20c.+10c. Pine marten	55	40
J219	30c.+10c. Ibex	95	40
J220	50c.+20c. European otter	1·30	85

1968. Children's Fund. Birds. As Type **C102** but inscr "1968". Multicoloured.

J221	10c.+10c. Western capercaillie	45	25
J222	20c.+10c. Northern bullfinch	55	40
J223	30c.+10c. Woodchat shrike	95	40
J224	50c.+20c. Firecrest	1·30	85

1969. Children's Fund. Birds. As Type **C102**. Inscr "1969". Multicoloured.

J225	10c.+10c. Eurasian goldfinch	45	25
J226	20c.+10c. Golden oriole	55	40
J227	30c.+10c. Wallcreeper	95	40
J228	50c.+20c. Jay	1·30	85

1970. Children's Fund. Birds. As Type **C102**. Inscr "1970". Multicoloured.

J229	10c.+10c. Blue tits	45	25
J230	20c.+10c. Hoopoe	55	40
J231	30c.+10c. Great spotted woodpecker	95	40
J232	50c.+20c. Great crested grebes	1·30	85

1971. Children's Fund. Birds. As Type **C102**. Inscr "1971". Multicoloured.

J233	10c.+10c. Common redstarts	45	15
J234	20c.+10c. Bluethroats	55	25
J235	30c.+10c. Peregrine falcon	95	40
J236	40c.+20c. Mallards	2·10	1·80

C104 "McGredy's Sunset" Rose

1972. Children's Fund. Roses. Multicoloured.

J237	10c.+10c. Type **C104**	45	15
J238	20c.+10c. "Miracle"	55	25
J239	30c.+10c. "Papa Meilland"	95	40
J240	40c.+20c. "Madame Dimitriu"	2·10	1·80

See also Nos. J258/61 and J279/82.

C105 Chestnut

1973. Children's Fund. "Fruits of the Forest". Multicoloured.

J241	15c.+5c. Type **C105**	45	25
J242	30c.+10c. Cherries	55	35
J243	40c.+20c. Blackberries	1·30	1·00
J244	60c.+20c. Bilberries	2·30	2·10

See also Nos. J245/8, J250/3 and J254/7.

1974. Children's Fund. "Fruits of the Forest". Poisonous Plants. As Type **C105**. Inscr "1974". Multicoloured.

J245	15c.+10c. Daphne	45	25
J246	30c.+20c. Belladonna	95	35
J247	50c.+20c. Laburnum	1·40	1·30
J248	60c.+25c. Mistletoe	1·90	1·50

1975. Children's Fund. As Type **C105**. Inscr "1975". Multicoloured.

J249	10c.+5c. "Post-Brent" (postman's hamper)	55	50
J250	15c.+10c. Hepatica	45	35
J251	30c.+20c. Rowan	95	40
J252	50c.+20c. Yellow deadnettle	1·30	1·20
J253	60c.+25c. Sycamore	1·90	1·50

1976. Children's Fund. "Fruits of the Forest". As Type **C105**. Inscr "1976". Multicoloured.

J254	20c.+10c. Barberry	55	25
J255	40c.+20c. Black elder	1·10	35
J256	40c.+20c. Lime	1·10	40
J257	80c.+40c. Lungwort	2·30	2·10

1977. Children's Fund. Roses. As Type **C104**. Inscr "1977". Multicoloured.

J258	20c.+10c. "Rosa foetida bicolor"	55	35
J259	40c.+20c. "Parfum de l'Hay"	1·10	40
J260	70c.+30c. "R. foetida persiana"	1·90	1·70
J261	80c.+40c. "R. centifolia muscosa"	2·30	2·10

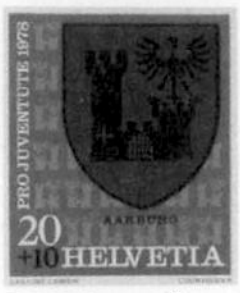

C106 Arms of Aarburg

1978. Children's Fund. Arms of the Communes (1st series). Multicoloured.

J262	20c.+10c. Type **C106**	55	35
J263	40c.+20c. Gruyeres	1·10	40
J264	70c.+30c. Castasegna	1·90	1·70
J265	80c.+40c. Wangen	2·75	2·10

See also Nos. J266/9, J270/3 and J274/7.

1979. Children's Fund. Arms of the Communes (2nd series). As Type **C106**. Multicoloured.

J266	20c.+10c. Cadro	55	35
J267	40c.+20c. Rute	1·10	40
J268	70c.+30c. Schwamendingen	1·90	1·70
J269	80c.+40c. Perroy	2·75	2·10

1980. Children's Fund. Arms of the Communes (3rd series). As Type **C106**. Multicoloured.

J270	20c.+10c. Cortaillod	55	35
J271	40c.+20c. Sierre	1·10	40
J272	70c.+30c. Scuol	1·90	1·70
J273	80c.+40c. Wolfenschiessen	2·75	2·10

1981. Children's Fund. Arms of the Communes (4th series). As Type **C106**. Multicoloured.

J274	20c.+10c. Uffikon	55	35
J275	40c.+20c. Torre	1·10	40
J276	70c.+30c. Benken	1·90	1·70
J277	80c.+40c. Preverenges	2·75	2·10

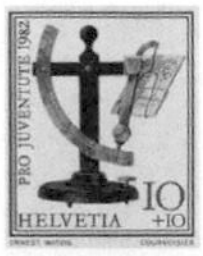

C107 Letter Balance

1982. Children's Fund. Type **C107** and roses as Type **C 104**. Multicoloured.

J278	10c.+10c. Type **C107**	95	25
J279	20c.+10c. "La Belle Portugaise"	55	25
J280	40c.+20c. "Hugh Dickson"	1·10	40
J281	70c.+30c. "Mermaid"	1·90	1·70
J282	80c.+40c. "Madame Caroline"	2·75	2·10

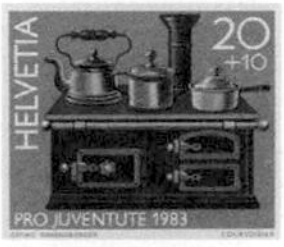

C108 Kitchen Stove, c. 1850

1983. Children's Fund. Toys. Multicoloured.

J283	20c.+10c. Type **C108**	1·10	45
J284	40c.+20c. Rocking horse, 1826	1·60	45
J285	70c.+30c. Doll, c. 1870	2·10	1·90
J286	80c.+40c. Steam locomotive, c. 1900	3·25	2·30

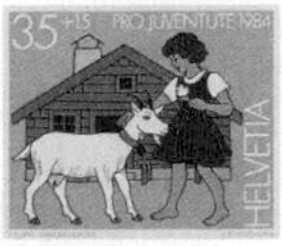

C109 Heidi and Goat (Johanna Spyri)

1984. Children's Fund. Characters from Children's Books. Multicoloured.

J287	35c.+15c. Type **C109**	1·10	1·00
J288	50c.+20c. Pinocchio and kite (Carlo Collodi)	1·50	50
J289	70c.+30c. Pippi Long-stocking (Astrid Lindgren)	2·75	2·50
J290	80c.+40c. Max and Moritz on roof (Wilhelm Busch)	3·25	3·00

1985. Children's Fund. Characters from Children's Books. As Type **C109**. Multicoloured.

J291	35c.+15c. Hansel, Gretel and Witch	1·10	1·00
J292	50c.+20c. Snow White and the Seven Dwarfs	1·60	50
J293	80c.+40c. Red Riding Hood and Wolf	3·25	2·50
J294	90c.+40c. Cinderella and Prince Charming	3·75	3·00

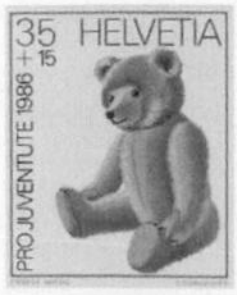

C110 Teddy Bear

1986. Children's Fund. Toys. Multicoloured.

J295	35c.+15c. Type **C110**	1·10	1·00
J296	50c.+20c. Spinning top	1·60	50
J297	80c.+40c. Steamroller	3·25	3·00
J298	90c.+40c. Doll	3·75	3·50

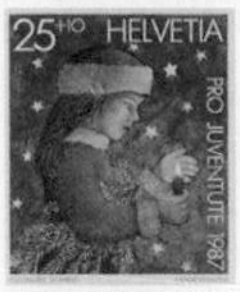

C111 Girl carrying Pine Branch and Candle

1987. Children's Fund. Child Development. Pre-school Age. Multicoloured.

J299	25c.+10c. Type **C111**	75	1·00
J300	35c.+15c. Mother breast-feeding baby	1·40	1·00
J301	50c.+20c. Toddler playing with bricks	1·60	50
J302	80c.+40c. Children playing in sand	2·75	2·50
J303	90c.+40c. Father with child on his shoulders	3·25	3·00

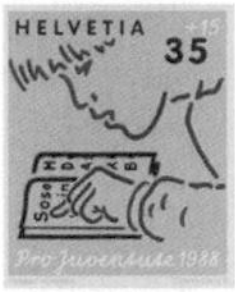

C112 Learning to Read

1988. Children's Fund. Child Development. School Age. Multicoloured.

J304	35c.+15c. Type **C112**	1·10	1·00
J305	50c.+20c. Playing triangle	1·60	50
J306	80c.+40c. Learning arithmetic	3·25	3·00
J307	90c.+40c. Drawing	3·75	3·50

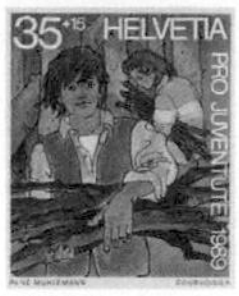

C113 Community Work

1989. Children's Fund. Child Development. Adolescence. Multicoloured.

J308	35c.+15c. Type **C113**	1·10	1·00
J309	50c.+20c. Young couple (friendship)	1·60	50
J310	80c.+40c. Boy at computer screen (vocational training)	3·25	3·00
J311	90c.+40c. Girl in laboratory (higher education and research)	3·75	3·50

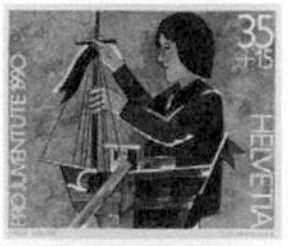

C114 Building Model Ship (hobbies)

1990. Child Development. Leisure Activities. Multicoloured.

J312	35c.+15c. Type **C114**	1·60	1·30
J313	50c.+20c. Youth group	1·60	70
J314	80c.+40c. Sport	3·25	3·00
J315	90c.+40c. Music	3·75	3·50

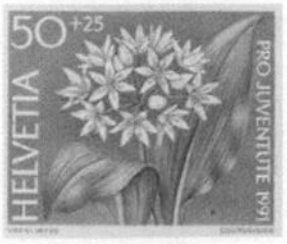

C115 Ramsons

1991. Woodland Flowers. Multicoloured.

J316	50c.+25c. Type **C115**	1·60	1·00
J317	70c.+30c. Wood cranesbill	2·10	2·00
J318	80c.+40c. Nettle-leaved bellflower	3·25	3·00
J319	90c.+40c. Few-leaved hawk-weed	3·25	3·00

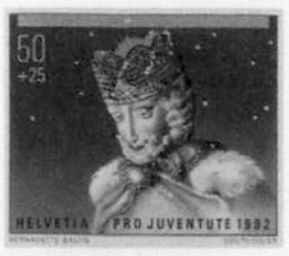

C116 Melchior (wood puppet)

1992. Christmas (J320) and Trees (others). Multicoloured.

J320	50c.+25c. Type **C116**	1·90	75
J321	50c.+25c. Beech	1·90	75
J322	70c.+30c. Norway maple	3·00	2·00
J323	80c.+40c. Pedunculate oak	3·25	2·50
J324	90c.+40c. Norway spruce	3·50	3·00

Nos. J321/4 show silhouette of tree and close-up of its leaves and fruit.

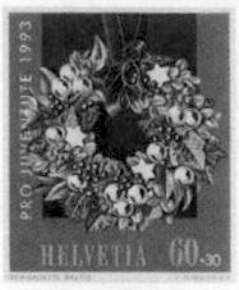

C117 Christmas Wreath

1993. Christmas (J325) and Woodland Plants (others). Multicoloured.

J325	60c.+30c. Type **C117**	2·30	1·40
J326	60c.+30c. Male fern	2·30	1·40
J327	80c.+40c. Guelder rose	3·25	2·75
J328	100c.+50c. "Mnium punctatum"	3·75	3·00

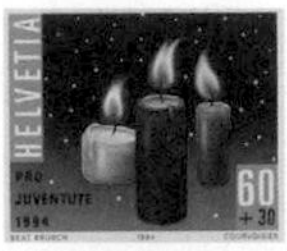

C118 Candles

1994. Christmas (J329) and Fungi (others). Multicoloured.

J329	60c.+30c. Type **C118**	2·30	1·40
J330	60c.+30c. Wood blewit	2·30	1·40
J331	80c.+40c. Red boletus	3·25	2·75
J332	100c.+50c. Shaggy pholiota	3·75	3·00

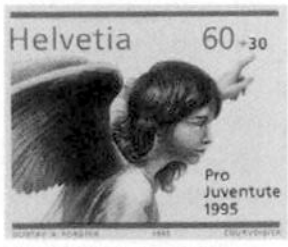

C119 Detail of "The Annunciation" (Bartolome Murillo)

1995. Christmas (J333) and Wildlife (others). Multicoloured.

J333	60c.+30c. Type **C119**	2·30	1·40
J334	60c.+30c. Brown trout	2·30	1·40
J335	80c.+40c. Grey wagtail	3·25	2·75
J336	100c.+50c. Spotted salamander	3·75	3·00

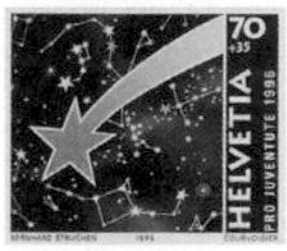

C120 Shooting Star and Constellations

1996. Christmas (J337) and Wildlife (others). Multicoloured.

J337	70c.+35c. Type **C120**	3·00	2·10
J338	70c.+35c. European graylings (fish)	3·00	2·10
J339	90c.+45c. Crayfish	3·75	3·25
J340	110c.+55c. European otter	4·25	4·00

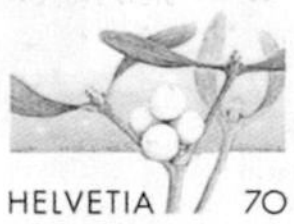

C121 Mistletoe

1997. Christmas (J341) and Wildlife (others). Multicoloured.

J341	70c.+35c. Type **C121**	3·00	2·10
J342	70c.+35c. Three-spined stickleback	3·00	2·10
J343	90c.+45c. Yellow-bellied toad	3·75	3·25
J344	110c.+55c. Ruff	4·25	4·00

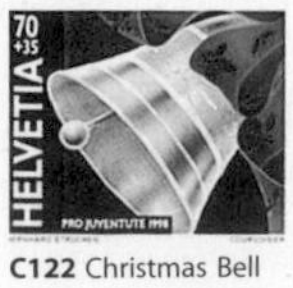

C122 Christmas Bell

1998. Christmas (J345) and Wildlife (others). Multicoloured.

J345	70c.+35c. Type **C122**	3·00	2·10
J346	70c.+35c. Ramshorn snail	3·00	2·10
J347	90c.+45c. Great crested grebe	3·75	3·25
J348	110c.+55c. Pike	4·25	4·00

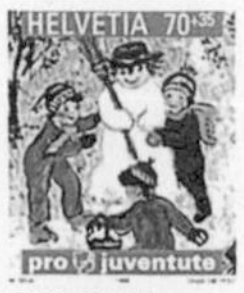

C123 Children and Snowman (Margaret Strub)

1999. Christmas (J349) and Illustrations from "Nicolo the Clown" (picture book by Verena Pavoni) (others). Multicoloured.

J349	70c.+35c. Type **C123**	3·00	2·10
J350	70c.+35c. Nicolo holding guitar	3·00	2·10
J351	90c.+45c. Nicolo with his father	3·75	3·25
J352	110c.+55c. Nicolo with donkey	4·25	4·00

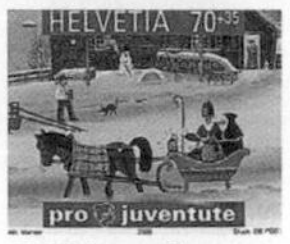

C124 Santa Claus

2000. Christmas. Illustrations from Little Albert (book) by Albert Manser. Multicoloured.

J353	70c.+35c. Type **C124**	3·25	3·00
J354	70c.+35c. Boys sitting on fence and girl	3·25	3·00
J355	90c.+45c. Little Albert with umbrella	4·25	4·00
J356	90c.+45c. Children sledging	4·25	4·00

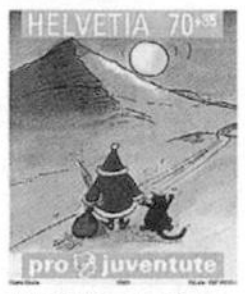

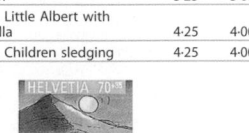

C125 Santa Claus and Cat

2001. Illustrations from Children's Books. Multicoloured.

J357	70c.+35c. Type **C125** (*What's Santa Claus Doing?* (text by Karin von Oldersausen, illustrations by Gabi Fluck))	3·25	3·00
J358	70c.+35c. Leopold the leopard in tree (*Leopold and the Sun* by Stephan Brülhart)	3·25	3·00
J359	90c.+45c. Bear on scooter (*Honey Bear by S. Brulhart*)	4·25	4·00
J360	90c.+45c. Tom the monkey in tree (*Leopold and the Sun*)	4·25	4·00

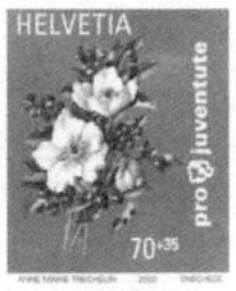

C126 "Christmas rose"

2002. Roses. Multicoloured.

J361	70c.+35c. Type **C126**	3·25	3·00
J362	70c.+35c. "Ingrid Bergman"	3·25	3·00
J363	90c.+45c. "Belle Vaudoise"	4·25	4·00
J364	90c.+45c. "Charmian"	4·25	4·00
J365	130c.+65c. "Fruhlingsgold"	6·50	6·00

No. J361 is impregnated with the fragrance of cinnamon and cloves and Nos. J362/5 with the perfume of roses.

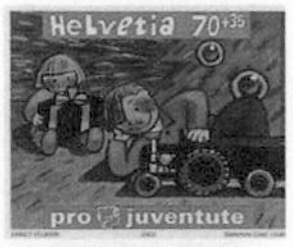

C127 Playing with Christmas Toys

2003. Children's Rights. The Right to Play. Multicoloured. Self-adhesive gum.

J366	70c.+35c. Type **C127**	3·25	3·00
J367	85c.+ 35c. Playing shop	3·75	3·50
J368	90c.+45c. Skateboarding	4·25	4·00
J369	100c.+45c. Playing music	4·50	4·25

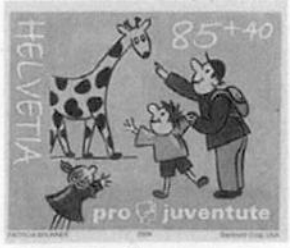

C128 Family and Giraffe

2004. Children's Rights. Right to Education. Multicoloured. Self-adhesive gum.

J370	85c.+40c. Type **C128**	4·00	3·75
J371	85c.+ 40c. Playing cards	4·00	3·75
J372	100c.+50c. Listening to older person read	4·75	4·50
J373	100c.+50c. Teacher and pupils	4·75	4·50

C129 Children enclosed in Lifebuoy

2005. Children's Rights. Right to Leisure and Play. Multicoloured. Self-adhesive.

J374	85c.+40c. Type **C1291**	4·00	3·75
J375	85c.+40c. Boy and girl catching cherries in mouth	4·00	3·75
J376	100c.+50c. Children and laptop computer	4·75	4·50
J377	100c.+50c. Boy wishing	4·75	4·50

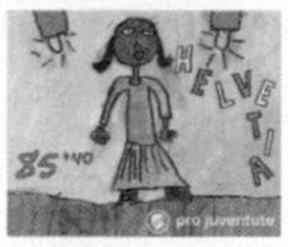

C130 Singer (Veronica Jesus Garcia Pinto)

2006. Winning Designs in Children's Painting Competition "My Dream Profession". Multicoloured. Self-adhesive.

J378	85c.+40c. Type **C130**	4·00	3·75
J379	85c.+40c. Workshop (garage owner) (Stephane Arada)	4·00	3·75
J380	100c.+50c. Dog with bandaged leg (vet) (Lea Mayer)	4·75	4·50
J381	100c.+50c. Angel	4·75	4·50

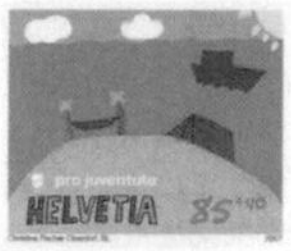

C131 *Camping* (Christine Fischer)

2007. Winning Designs in Children's Design a Stamp Competition. "Holiday Fun". Multicoloured.

J382	85c.+40c. Type **C131**	4·00	3·75
J383	85c.+40c. *Mountains* (Jonathon Balest)	4·00	3·75
J384	100c.+50c. *Sunshine* (Morena Rufatti)	4·75	4·50
J385	100c.+50c. Angels carrying heart	4·75	4·50

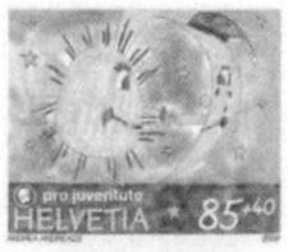

C132 *Friendship unites* (Andrea Andreazzi)

2008. Winning Designs in Children's Design a Stamp Competition. "Friendship". Multicoloured.

J386	85c.+40c. Type **C132**	4·00	3·75
J387	85c.+40c. *Friendship provides support* (Manon Peng)	4·00	3·75
J388	100c.+50c. *Friendship is a source of happiness* (Delia Candolo)	4·75	4·50
J389	100+50c. *Friendship is uplifting*	4·75	4·50

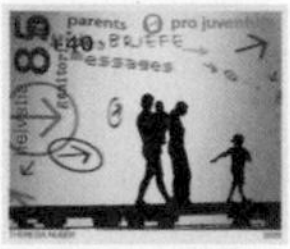

C133 Letters to Parents

2009. Pro Juventute Foundation. Multicoloured. Self-adhesive.

J390	85c.+40c. Type **C133**	4·00	3·75
J391	85c.+40c. Tree branches and children (holiday pass scheme)	4·00	3·75
J392	100c.+50c. Parents back to back (Tel. 147 advice line)	4·75	4·50
J393	100c.+50c. Children and stamps (stamp sales)	4·75	4·50

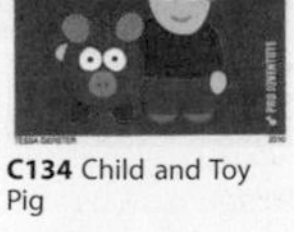

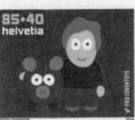

C134 Child and Toy Pig

2010. Children and Money. Multicoloured.

J394	85c. +40c. Type **C134**	4·00	3·75
J395	85c. +40c. Child thinking of teddy bear	4·00	3·75
J396	100c. +50c. Child with toy pig and teddy bear	4·75	4·50
J397	100c. +50c. Child with toy pig carrying present	4·75	4·50

INTERNATIONAL ORGANIZATIONS SITUATED IN SWITZERLAND

The stamps listed under this heading were issued by the Swiss Post Office primarily for the use of officials of the Organizations named, situated in Geneva.

These stamps could not be legitimately obtained unused before Feburary 1944.

A. LEAGUE OF NATIONS

1922. Optd **SOCIETE DES NATIONS**.

LN1	**18b**	2½c. bistre on buff		1·30
LN2	**18b**	3c. blue on buff		16·00
LN3	**18b**	5c. orange on buff		8·75
LN4	**18b**	5c. grey on buff		6·25
LN5	**18b**	5c. purple on buff		3·75
LN5a	**18b**	5c. green on buff		38·00
LN6	**18b**	7½c. green on buff		1·30
LN7	**21**	10c. green on buff		1·30
LN8	**21**	10c. violet on buff		2·50
LN9	**21**	15c. red on buff		2·50
LN10	**21**	20c. purple on buff		14·00
LN11	**21**	20c. red on buff		5·00
LN13	**21**	25c. red on buff		2·50
LN14	**21**	25c. brown on buff		31·00
LN15	**17**	30c. green and brown		23·00
LN16	**21**	30c. blue on buff		11·50
LN17	**17**	35c. yellow and green		15·00
LN18	**17**	40c. blue		2·50
LN19	**17**	40c. green and mauve		31·00
LN20a	**17**	50c. green & dp green	1·30	3·75
LN21	**17**	60c. brown	50·00	2·50
LN22a	**17**	70c. buff and violet	2·50	3·75
LN23a	**17**	80c. buff and grey	3·75	5·00
LN24a	**41**	90c. red, dp green & grn		7·50
LN25a	**17**	1f. green and purple		8·75
LN26b	**41**	1f.20 red, lake and pink	3·75	6·25
LN27a	**41**	1f.50 red, bl & turq	3·75	7·50
LN28a	**41**	2f. red, black and grey	4·50	8·25
LN29	**22**	3f. red		50·00
LN29a	**43**	3f. brown		£250
LN30	-	5f. blue (No. 296)		£110
LN32	-	10f. mauve (No. 297)		£225
LN33	-	10f. green (No. 337)		£300

1932. International Disarmament Conference. Optd **SOCIETE DES NATIONS**.

LN34	**44**	5c. green		28·00
LN35	**44**	10c. orange		2·50
LN36	**44**	20c. mauve		2·50
LN37	**44**	30c. blue		80·00
LN38	**44**	60c. brown		20·00
LN39	**45**	1f. grey and blue		19·00

1934. Landscape designs of 1934 optd **SOCIETE DES NATIONS**.

LN40	**48**	3c. green		80
LN41	-	5c. green		90
LN42	-	15c. orange		2·10
LN43	-	25c. brown		30·00
LN44	-	30c. blue		2·50

1937. Landscape designs of 1936 optd **SOCIETE DES NATIONS**.

LN45A	**52**	3c. green	25	90
LN46A	-	5c. green	25	90
LN47Ac	-	10c. purple		1·60
LN49	-	10c. brown	65	1·60
LN50A	-	15c. orange	50	90
LN51A	-	20c. red (railway)		3·25
LN51Ac	-	20c. red (lake)	90	2·50
LN52A	-	25c. brown	75	1·60
LN53A	-	30c. blue	75	1·50
LN54A	-	35c. green	75	1·50
LN55A	-	40c. grey	1·00	1·60

1938. Nos. 382/5 optd **SOCIETE DES NATIONS**.

LN56	**55**	20c. red and buff		2·50
LN57	-	30c. blue and light blue		5·00
LN58	-	60c. brown and buff		8·75
LN59	-	1f. black and buff		15·00

1938. Nos. 382/5 optd **SERVICE DE LA SOCIETE DES NATIONS** in circle.

LN60	**55**	20c. red and buff		3·25
LN61	-	30c. blue and light blue		6·25
LN62	-	60c. brown and buff		10·50
LN63	-	1f. black and buff		18·00

1939. Nos. 388c/90c optd **SOCIETE DES NATIONS**.

LN64	**61**	3f. brown on buff	4·50	15·00
LN65	-	5f. blue on buff	7·00	25·00
LN66	-	10f. green on buff	16·00	48·00

1944. Optd **COURRIER DE LA SOCIETE DES NATIONS**. (a) Landscape designs of 1936.

LN67	**52**	3c. green	40	65
LN68	-	5c. green	40	65
LN69	-	10c. brown	1·10	65
LN70	-	15c. orange	45	75
LN71	-	20c. red (lake)	55	1·30
LN72	-	25c. brown	65	1·60
LN73	-	30c. blue	75	1·60
LN74	-	35c. green	75	1·60
LN75	-	40c. grey	80	3·25

(b) Historical designs of 1941.

LN76		50c. blue on green	1·60	3·75
LN77	**68**	60c. brown on brown	1·90	5·00
LN78	-	70c. purple on mauve	1·90	5·00
LN79	-	80c. black on grey	1·60	3·75
LN80	-	90c. red on pink	1·60	3·75
LN81	-	1f. green on green	1·60	3·75
LN82	-	1f.20 purple on grey	2·50	5·75
LN83	-	1f.50 blue on buff	2·75	6·25
LN84	-	2f. red on pink	3·75	8·25

(c) Parliament designs of 1938.

LN85	**61**	3f. brown on buff	7·00	16·00
LN86	-	5f. blue on buff	11·50	25·00
LN87	-	10f. green on buff	19·00	50·00

B. INTERNATIONAL LABOUR OFFICE

Optd **S.d.N Bureau international du Travail** (Nos. LB1/47).

1923

LB1	**18b**	2½c. bistre on buff		75
LB2	**18b**	3c. blue on buff		2·50
LB3	**18b**	5c. orange on buff		90
LB4	**18b**	5c. purple on buff		75
LB5	**18b**	7½c. green on buff		75
LB6	**21**	10c. green on buff		90
LB8	**21**	15c. red on buff		2·50
LB9	**21**	20c. purple on buff		25·00
LB10	**21**	20c. red on buff		6·25
LB11	**21**	25c. red on buff		1·60
LB12	**21**	25c. brown on buff		4·50
LB13	**17**	30c. green and brown		£100
LB14	**21**	30c. blue on buff		3·75
LB15	**17**	35c. yellow and green		16·00
LB16	**17**	40c. blue		1·60
LB17	**17**	40c. green and mauve		33·00
LB18a	**17**	50c. green & deep green	2·50	3·25
LB19	**17**	60c. brown	2·50	2·50
LB20a	**17**	70c. buff and violet	2·30	3·75
LB21	**17**	80c. buff and grey	20·00	3·25
LB22	**41**	90c. red, dp grn & grn		6·25
LB23	**17**	1f. green and purple		4·00
LB24b	**38**	1f.20 red, lake and pink	20·00	5·75
LB25a	**38**	1f.50 red, bl & turq	3·75	4·50
LB26a	**38**	2f. red, black and grey	3·75	4·50
LB27	**22**	3f. red		31·00
LB27a	**43**	3f. brown		£250
LB28	-	5f. blue (No. 296)		50·00
LB30	-	10f. mauve (No. 297)		£225
LB31	-	10f. green (No. 337)		£200

1932. International Disarmament Conference.

LB32	**44**	5c. green		1·90
LB33	**44**	10c. orange		1·90
LB34	**44**	20c. mauve		1·90
LB35	**44**	30c. blue		12·50
LB36	**44**	60c. brown		12·50
LB37	**45**	1f. grey and blue		15·00

1937. Landscape design of 1934.

LB38	**48**	3c. green		8·25

1937. Landscape designs of 1936.

LB39A	**52**	3c. green	40	1·10
LB40A	-	5c. green	40	1·10
LB41B	-	10c. purple		3·25
LB41e	-	10c. brown	75	1·60
LB42A	-	15c. orange	50	1·90
LB43A	-	20c. red (railway)		3·75
LB43c	-	20c. red (lake)	90	1·60
LB44A	-	25c. brown	65	2·50
LB45A	-	30c. blue	65	2·00
LB46A	-	35c. green	75	2·75
LB47A	-	40c. grey	1·30	3·75

1938. Nos. 382/5 optd **S.d.N. Bureau international du Travail**.

LB48	**55**	20c. red and buff		2·50
LB49	-	30c. blue and light blue		5·00
LB50	-	60c. brown and buff		8·25
LB51	-	1f. black and buff		12·50

1938. Nos. 382/5 optd **SERVICE DU BUREAU INTERNATIONAL DU TRAVAIL** in circle.

LB52	**55**	20c. red and buff		5·75
LB53	-	30c. blue and light blue		5·00
LB54	-	60c. brown and buff		10·00
LB55	-	1f. black and buff		10·00

1939. Nos. 388c/90c optd **S.d.N. Bureau international du Travail**.

LB56	**61**	3f. brown on buff	6·25	12·50
LB57	-	5f. blue on buff	7·50	25·00
LB58	-	10f. green on buff	12·50	44·00

1944. Optd **COURRIER DU BUREAU INTERNATIONAL DU TRAVAIL**. (a) Landscape designs of 1936.

LB59	**52**	3c. green	40	65
LB60	-	5c. green	40	65
LB61	-	10c. brown	40	65
LB62	-	15c. orange	75	90
LB63	-	20c. red (lake)	65	90
LB64	-	25c. brown	75	1·00
LB65	-	30c. blue	90	2·00
LB66	-	35c. green	1·00	2·20
LB67	-	40c. grey	1·10	2·50

(b) Historical designs of 1941.

LB68		50c. blue on green	2·50	12·50
LB69	**68**	60c. brown on brown	2·50	12·50
LB70	-	70c. purple on mauve	3·00	12·50
LB71	-	80c. black on grey	75	2·00
LB72	-	90c. red on pink	75	2·00
LB73	-	1f. green on green	45	2·00
LB74	-	1f.20 purple on grey	1·10	2·50
LB75	-	1f.50 blue on buff	1·50	3·75
LB76	-	2f. red on pink	1·90	4·50

(c) Parliament designs of 1938.

LB77	**61**	3f. brown on buff	4·75	9·50
LB78	-	5f. blue on buff	7·00	16·00
LB79	-	10f. green on buff	15·00	38·00

1950. Landscape designs of 1949 optd **BUREAU INTERNATIONAL DU TRAVAIL**.

LB80	**107**	5c. orange	8·75	8·75
LB81	-	10c. green	8·75	8·75
LB82	-	15c. turquoise	12·50	15·00
LB83	-	20c. purple	12·50	15·00
LB84	-	25c. red	15·00	15·00
LB85	-	30c. green	15·00	15·00
LB86	-	35c. brown	15·00	15·00
LB87	-	40c. blue	15·00	15·00
LB88	-	50c. grey	23·00	15·00
LB89	-	60c. green	23·00	23·00
LB90	-	70c. violet	28·00	33·00

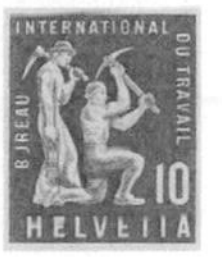

LB4 Miners (bas-relief)

1952. Inscr as in Type **LB4**.

LB91	**LB4**	5c. purple	40	25
LB92	**LB4**	10c. green	40	25
LB94	-	20c. red	40	40
LB95	-	30c. orange	65	65
LB96	**LB 4**	40c. blue	3·75	3·75
LB97	**LB 4**	50c. blue	90	90
LB98	-	60c. brown	75	75
LB99	-	2f. purple	2·30	2·30

DESIGN—HORIZ: 20, 30, 60c., 2f. Globe, flywheel and factory chimney.

1969. Pope Paul's Visit to Geneva. No. LB95 optd **Visite du Pape Paul VI Geneve 10 juin 1969**.

LB100	30c. orange	50	50

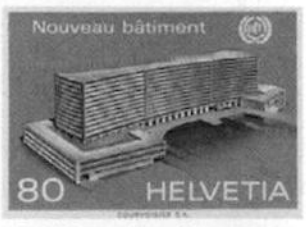

LB6 New Headquarters Building

1974. Inaug of New I.L.O. Headquarters, Geneva.

LB101	**LB6**	80c. multicoloured	1·00	1·00

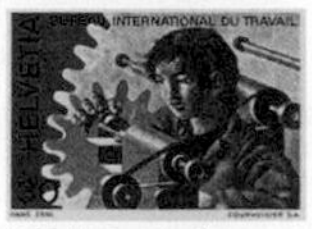

LB7 Man at Lathe

1975

LB102	**LB7**	30c. brown	40	40
LB103	-	60c. blue	65	65
LB104	-	90c. brown, red & grn	1·90	1·90
LB105	-	100c. green	1·00	1·00
LB106	-	120c. ochre and brown	1·60	1·60

DESIGNS: 60c. Woman at drilling machine; 90c. Welder and laboratory assistant; 100c. Surveyor with theodolite; 120c. Apprentice and instructor with slide rule.

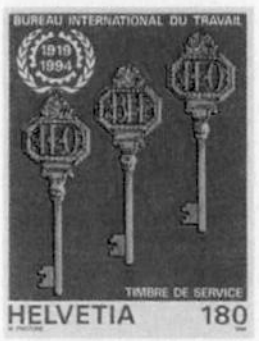

LB8 Keys

1994. 75th Anniv of I.L.O.

LB107	LB8	180c. multicoloured	3·75	3·75

C. INTERNATIONAL EDUCATION OFFICE

1944. Optd **COURRIER DU BUREAU INTERNATIONAL D'EDUCATION**. (a) Landscape designs of 1936.

LE1	52	3c. green	65	1·60
LE2	-	5c. green	75	2·50
LE3	-	10c. brown	75	2·50
LE4	-	15c. orange	75	2·50
LE5	-	20c. red (lake)	75	2·50
LE6	-	25c. brown	75	2·50
LE7	-	30c. blue	1·30	3·75
LE8	-	35c. green	1·30	3·75
LE9	-	40c. grey	1·50	3·75

(b) Historical designs of 1941.

LE10		50c. blue on green	7·50	25·00
LE11	68	60c. brown on brown	7·50	25·00
LE12	-	70c. purple on mauve	7·50	25·00
LE13	-	80c. black on grey	75	2·50
LE14	-	90c. red on pink	1·00	3·75
LE15	-	1f. green on green	1·30	3·75
LE16	-	1f.20 purple on grey	1·40	5·00
LE17	-	1f.50 blue on buff	1·80	5·75
LE18	-	2f. red on pink	2·10	6·25

(c) Parliament designs of 1938.

LE19	61	3f. brown on buff	9·50	25·00
LE20	-	5f. blue on buff	14·00	44·00
LE21	-	10f. green on buff	21·00	65·00

1946. Optd **BIE** vert.

LE22	86	10c. purple	90	90

Optd **BUREAU INTERNATIONAL D'EDUCATION** (Nos. LE23/39)

1948. Landscape designs of 1936.

LE23	5c. brown	5·00	5·00
LE24	10c. green	5·00	5·00
LE25	20c. brown	5·00	5·00
LE26	25c. red	5·00	5·00
LE27	30c. blue	5·75	5·75
LE28	40c. blue	5·75	5·75

1950. Landscape designs of 1949.

LE29	107	5c. orange	2·10	2·50
LE30	-	10c. green	2·10	3·25
LE31	-	15c. turquoise	2·10	3·25
LE32	-	20c. purple	5·25	12·50
LE33	-	25c. red	14·00	24·00
LE34	-	30c. green	14·00	24·00
LE35	-	35c. brown	10·00	16·00
LE36	-	40c. blue	10·00	16·00
LE37	-	50c. grey	12·50	18·00
LE38	-	60c. green	14·00	21·00
LE39	-	70c. violet	15·00	25·00

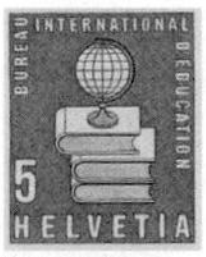

LE3 Globe on Books

1958. Inscr as in Type **LE3**.

LE40	LE3	5c. purple	15	15
LE41	LE3	10c. green	25	25
LE43	-	20c. red	50	50
LE44	-	30c. orange	65	65
LE45	LE 3	40c. blue	4·50	4·50
LE46	LE 3	50c. blue	75	75
LE47	-	60c. brown	90	90
LE48	-	2f. purple	2·50	2·50

DESIGN—VERT: 20, 30, 60c., 2f. Pestalozzi Monument, Yverdon.

D. WORLD HEALTH ORGANIZATION

1948. Optd **ORGANISATION MONDIALE DE LA SANTE**. (a) Landscape designs of 1936.

LH1	5c. brown (No. 489)	6·25	5·00
LH2	10c. green (No. 490)	6·25	6·25
LH3	20c. brown (No. 491)	6·25	6·25
LH4	25c. red (No. 492)	6·25	7·50
LH5	40c. blue (No. 494)	6·25	8·75

(b) Landscape designs of 1949.

LH6	107	5c. orange	1·90	1·60
LH7	-	10c. green	2·50	2·50
LH8	-	15c. turquoise	2·75	3·25
LH9	-	20c. purple	6·25	9·50
LH10	-	25c. red	6·25	9·50
LH11	-	30c. green	5·00	7·50
LH12	-	35c. brown	5·75	11·50
LH13	-	40c. blue	5·00	5·75
LH14	-	50c. grey	6·25	9·50
LH15	-	60c. green	7·00	15·00
LH16	-	70c. violet	8·25	15·00

(c) Historical designs of 1941 (Nos. 408/13).

LH17	80c. black on grey	6·25	5·75
LH18	90c. red on pink	12·50	15·00
LH19	1f. green on green	8·25	6·25
LH20	1f.20 purple on grey	16·00	21·00
LH21	1f.50 blue on buff	31·00	21·00
LH22	2f. red on pink	12·50	10·00

(d) Parliament designs of 1938.

LH23	61	3f. brown on buff	65·00	55·00
LH24	-	5f. blue on buff	25·00	18·00
LH25	-	10f. green on buff	£130	£100

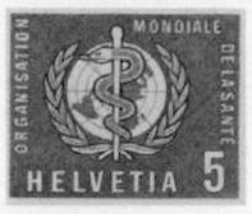

LH2 Staff of Aesculapius

1957

LH26	LH2	5c. purple	15	15
LH27	LH2	10c. green	25	25
LH29	LH2	20c. red	50	50
LH30	LH2	30c. orange	65	65
LH31	LH2	40c. blue	4·50	4·50
LH32	LH2	50c. blue	75	75
LH33	LH2	60c. brown	90	90
LH34	LH2	2f. purple	2·50	2·50

1962. Malaria Eradication. Optd **ERADICATION DU PALUDISME**.

LH35	50c. blue	1·10	1·10

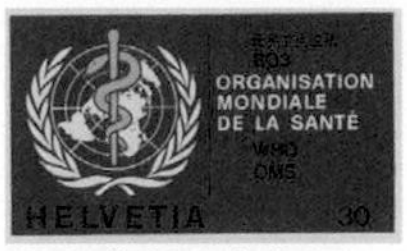

LH4 Staff of Aesculapius

1975

LH36	LH4	30c. green, purple and pink	50	50
LH37	LH4	60c. yellow, blue and light blue	90	90
LH38	LH4	90c. yellow, violet and light violet	1·30	1·30
LH39	LH4	100c. blue, brown and orange	1·50	1·50
LH40	LH4	140c. green, turquoise and red	1·90	1·90

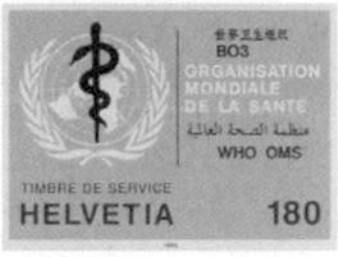

LH5 Staff of Aesculapius

1995

LH41	LH5	180c. yellow, brown and red	3·75	3·75

E. INTERNATIONAL REFUGEES ORGANIZATION

Optd **ORGANISATION INTERNATIONALE POUR LES REFUGIES.**

1950. (a) Landscape designs of 1949.

LR1	107	5c. orange	38·00	25·00
LR2	-	10c. green	38·00	25·00
LR3	-	20c. purple	38·00	25·00
LR4	-	25c. red	38·00	25·00
LR5	-	40c. blue	38·00	25·00

(b) Historical designs of 1941 (Nos. 408/13).

LR6	80c. black on grey	38·00	65·00
LR7	1f. green on green	38·00	19·00
LR8	2f. red on pink	38·00	19·00

F. WORLD METEOROLOGICAL ORGANIZATION

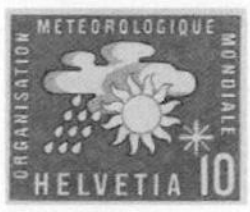

LM1 "The Elements"

1956. Inscr as in Type **LM1**.

LM1	LM1	5c. purple	15	15
LM2	LM1	10c. green	25	25
LM4	-	20c. red	50	50
LM5	-	30c. orange	65	65
LM6	LM 1	40c. blue	4·50	4·50
LM7	LM 1	50c. blue	75	75
LM8	-	60c. brown	90	90
LM9	-	2f. purple	3·75	3·75

DESIGN: 20, 30, 60c., 2f. Weathervane.

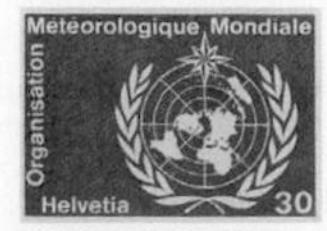

LM2 W.M.O. Emblem

1973. Cent of World Meteorological Organization.

LM10	LM2	30c. red	50	50
LM11	LM2	40c. blue	65	65
LM12	-	80c. violet and gold	1·10	1·10
LM13	LM2	1f. brown	1·50	1·50

DESIGN: 80c. Emblem and "OMI OMM 1873 1973".

G. UNIVERSAL POSTAL UNION

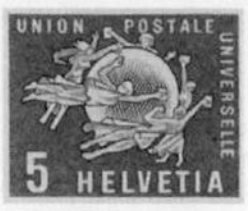

LP1 U.P.U. Monument, Berne

1957. Inscr as in Type **LP1**.

LP1	LP1	5c. purple	5·00	15
LP2	-	10c. green	25	25
LP4	-	20c. red	50	50
LP5	-	30c. orange	65	65
LP6	LP 1	40c. blue	4·50	4·50
LP7	LP 1	50c. blue	75	75
LP8	-	60c. brown	90	90
LP9	LP 1	2f. purple	2·50	2·50

DESIGN: 10, 20, 30, 60c. Pegasus (sculpture).

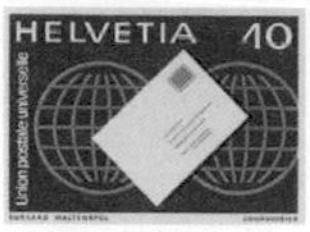

LP2 "Letter Post"

1976

LP10	LP2	40c. purple, blue and claret	65	65
LP11	-	80c. multicoloured	1·00	1·00
LP12	-	90c. multicoloured	1·30	1·30
LP13	-	100c. multicoloured	1·40	1·40
LP14	-	120c. multicoloured	2·00	2·00
LP15	-	140c. grey, blue and red	2·50	2·50

DESIGNS: 80c. "Parcel Post"; 90c. "Financial Services"; 100c. Technical co-operation; 120c. Carrier pigeon, international reply coupon and postal money order; 140c. Express Mail Service.

The 120 and 140c. are additionally inscribed "TIMBRE DE SERVICE".

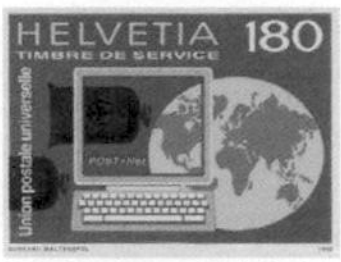

LP3 Computer, Mail Sacks and Globe

1995

LP16	LP 3	180c. multicoloured	3·25	3·25

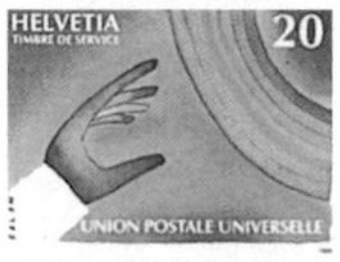

LP4 Hand reaching for Rainbow

1999. 125th Anniv of Universal Postal Union. Multicoloured.

LP17	20c. Type **LP4**	40	40
LP18	70c. Hand holding rainbow	1·20	1·20

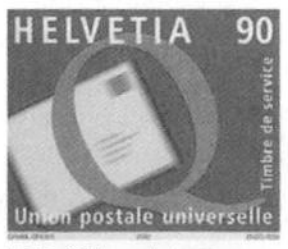

LP5 "Q" and Letter

2003

LP19	LP5	90c. multicoloured	3·00	3·00

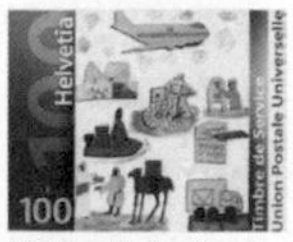

LP6 Symbols of Communication (Nasir Tahir)

2005

LP20	LP6	100c. multicoloured	2·40	2·40

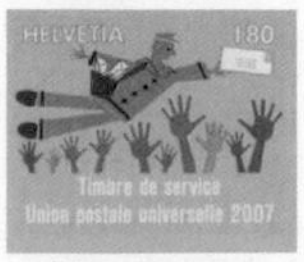

LP7 Flying Postman and Hands

2007

LP21	LP7	180c. multicoloured	4·75	4·75

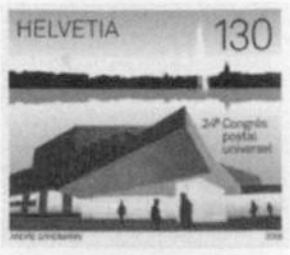

LP8 Centre International de Conferences Geneve (conference venue)

2008. 24th UPU Congress, Geneva.

LP22	LP8	130c. multicoloured	3·75	3·75

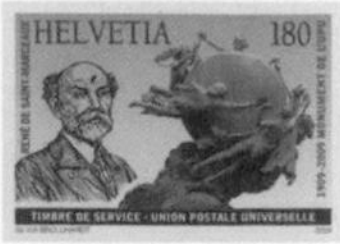

LP9 Rene de Saint-Marceaux (sculptor and creator of statue used as emblem of Universal Postal Union) and UPU Monument

2008. Centenary of UPU Monument. Rene de Saint-Marceaux (sculptor and creator of statue used as emblem of Universal Postal Union) Commemoration.

LP23	LP9	180c. multicoloured	4·75	4·75

H. UNITED NATIONS

1950. Optd **NATIONS UNIES OFFICE EUROPEEN**. (a) Landscape designs of 1949.

LU1	107	5c. orange	1·00	4·00
LU2	-	10c. green	1·30	4·00
LU3	-	15c. turquoise	2·00	5·25
LU4	-	20c. purple	2·50	7·25
LU5	-	25c. red	4·50	13·00
LU6	-	30c. green	4·50	13·00
LU7	-	35c. brown	4·50	13·00
LU8	-	40c. blue	6·50	14·50
LU9	-	50c. grey	7·75	20·00
LU10	-	60c. green	10·50	20·00
LU11	-	70c. violet	13·00	20·00

(b) Historical designs of 1941 (Nos. 408/13).

LU12	80c. black on grey	16·00	16·00
LU13	90c. red on pink	20·00	20·00
LU14	1f. green on green	20·00	20·00
LU15	1f.20 purple on grey	23·00	23·00
LU16	1f.50 blue on buff	23·00	23·00
LU17	2f. red on pink	23·00	23·00

(c) Parliament designs of 1938.

LU18	61	3f. brown on buff	£180	£200
LU19	-	5f. blue on buff	£180	£200
LU20	-	10f. green on buff	£225	£250

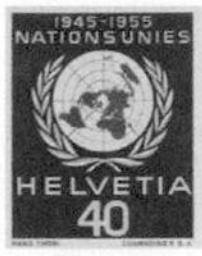

LU2

1955. Tenth Anniv of U.N.O.

LU21	LU2	40c. blue and yellow	5·25	6·50

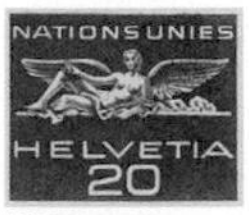

LU4

1955. Nos. LU22/3 and LU27/8 are as Type **LU2** but without dates.

LU22	-	5c. purple	25	25
LU23	-	10c. green	40	40
LU25	LU 4	20c. red	50	50
LU26	LU 4	30c. orange	65	65
LU27	-	40c. blue	8·50	8·50
LU28	-	50c. blue	80	80
LU29	LU 4	60c. brown	90	90
LU30	LU 4	2f. purple	3·50	3·50

1960. World Refugee Year. Nos. LU25 and LU28 optd **ANNEE MONDIALE DU REFUGIE 1959 1960.**

LU31	20c. red	50	50
LU32	50c. blue	80	80

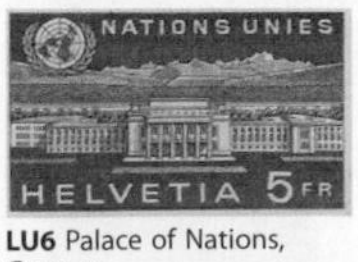

LU6 Palace of Nations, Geneva

1960. 15th Anniv of U.N.O.

LU33	LU6	5f. blue	7·75	7·75

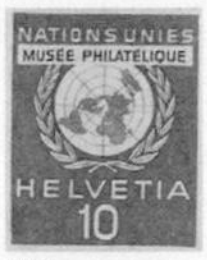

LU7

1962. Opening of U.N. Philatelic Museum, Geneva.

LU34	**LU7**	10c. green and red	25	25
LU35	-	30c. red and blue	50	50
LU36	**LU 7**	50c. blue and red	80	80
LU37	-	60c. brown and green	1·00	1·00

DESIGN—HORIZ: 30, 60c. As Type LU **4** but inscr "ONU MUSEE PHILATELIQUE".

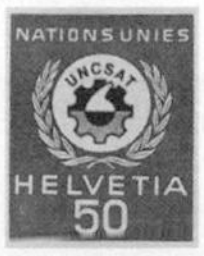

LU8 UNCSAT Emblem

1963. U.N. Scientific and Technological Conf, Geneva.

LU38	**LU8**	50c. red and blue	80	80
LU39	-	2f. green and purple	3·00	3·00

DESIGN—HORIZ: 2f. As Type LU **4**, but with emblem.

From 1969 stamps for the Geneva Headquarters were issued by the United Nations (q.v.)

I. INTERNATIONAL TELECOMMUNICATION UNION

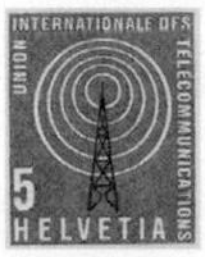

LT1 Transmitting Aerial

1958. Inscr as in Type **LT1**.

LT1	**LT1**	5c. purple	15	15
LT2	**LT1**	10c. green	25	25
LT4	-	20c. red	50	50
LT5	-	30c. orange	65	65
LT6	**LT1**	40c. blue	4·50	4·50
LT7	**LT1**	50c. blue	80	80
LT8	-	60c. brown	90	90
LT9	-	2f. purple	2·50	2·50

DESIGN: 20, 30, 60c., 2f. Receiving aerials

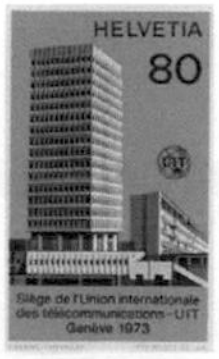

LT2 New H.Q. Building

1973. Inaug of New I.T.U. Headquarters, Geneva.

LT10	**LT2**	80c. black and blue	1·30	1·30

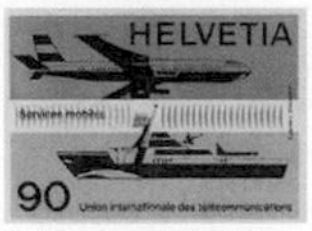

LT3 Boeing 747 Jetliner and Ocean Liner

1976. World Telecommunications Network.

LT11	-	40c. blue and red	65	65
LT12	**LT3**	90c. violet, blue & yellow	1·30	1·30
LT13	-	1f. red, green & yellow	1·60	1·60

DESIGNS: 40c. "Sound waves"; 1f. Face and microphone in television screen.

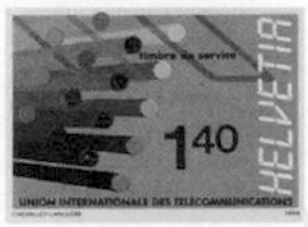

LT4 Optical Fibre Cables

1988

LT14	**LT4**	1f.40 multicoloured	2·20	2·20

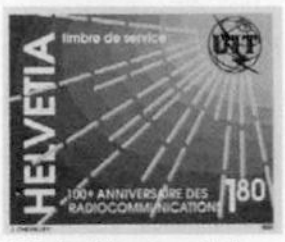

LT5 Emblem emitting Radio Signals

1994. 100 Years of Radio.

LT15	**LT5**	1f.80 multicoloured	3·00	3·00

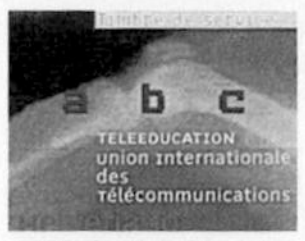

LT6 "a b c" and X-ray of Bone Joint ("Teleeducation")

1999. Multicoloured

LT16	10c. Type LT **6**		40	40
LT17	100c. Arrow and X-ray of bone joint ("Telemedicine")		1·70	1·70

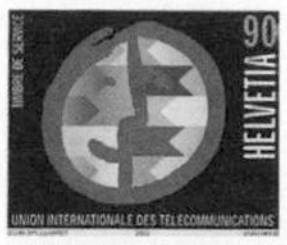

LT7 Stylized Face

2003

LT18	**LT7**	90c. multicoloured	2·50	2·50

J. WORLD INTELLECTUAL PROPERTY ORGANIZATION

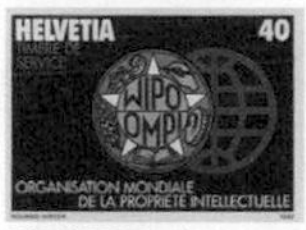

LV1 WIPO Seal

1989. Multicoloured.. Multicoloured..

LV1	40c. Type LV **1**		65	65
LV2	50c. Face and symbolic representation of intellect		90	90
LV3	80c. WIPO building, Geneva		1·00	1·00
LV4	100c. Hand pressing buttons, retort and cogwheel (industrial property)		1·60	1·60
LV5	120c. Head, ballet dancer, cello and book (copyright)		2·00	2·00

K. INTERNATIONAL OLYMPIC COMMITTEE

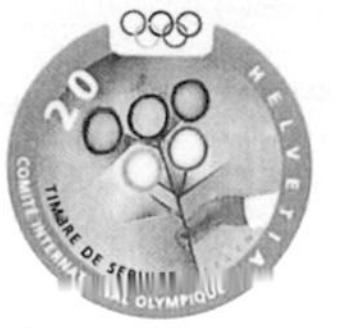

LW1 Olympic Rings

2000. Olympic Games, Sydney. Self-adhesive.

LW1	**LW1**	20c. multicoloured	1·60	1·60
LW2	**LW1**	70c. multicoloured	2·00	2·00

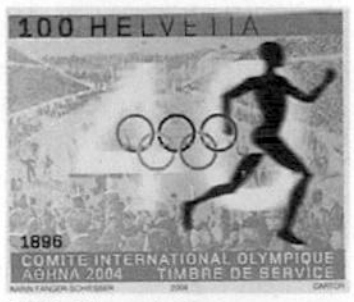

LW2 Olympic Rings, Stadium and Runner

2004. Olympic Games, Athens.

LW3	**LW2**	1f. multicoloured	2·50	2·50

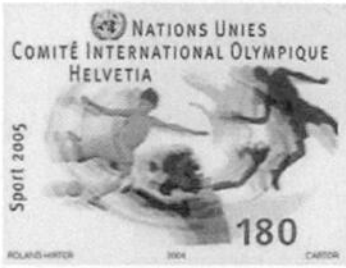

LW3 Sport

2004. International Year of Sport and Physical Education–2005.

LW4	**LW3**	180c. multicoloured	4·00	4·00

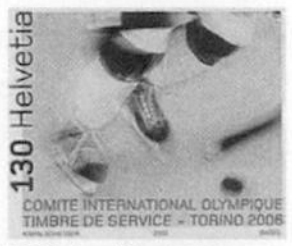

LW4 Ice Hockey

2005. Winter Olympic Games, Turin.

LW5	**LW4**	130c. multicoloured	3·25	3·25

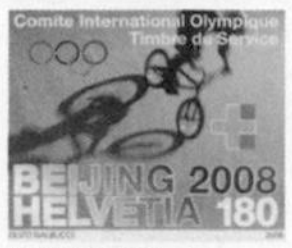

LW5 BMX Cyclist

2008. Olympic Games, Beijing.

LW6	**LW5**	180c. multicoloured	3·75	3·75

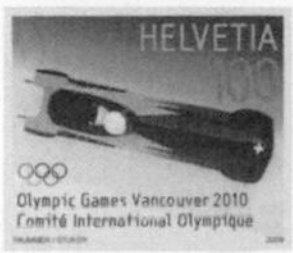

LW6 Bobsleigh

2009. Winter Olympic Games, Vancouver.

LW7	**LW6**	100c. multicoloured	1·80	1·80

Pt. 6, Pt. 19

SYRIA

A country at the E. end of the Mediterranean Sea, formerly Turkish territory. Occupied by the Allies in 1918 and administered under French Military Occupation. An Arab kingdom was set up in the Aleppo and Damascus area during 1919, but the Emir Faisal came into conflict with the French and was defeated in July 1920. In April 1920, the Mandate was offered to France, becoming effective in September 1923. Separate governments were established for the Territories of Damascus, Aleppo, the Alaouites (including Latakia), Great Lebanon and the Jebel Druze. Syria became a republic in 1934, and the Mandate ended with full Independence in 1942.

In 1958 the United Arab Republic was formed which comprised Egypt and Syria but separate stamps were issued for each territory as they employed different currencies. In 1961 Syria left the U.A.R. and the Syrian Arab Republic was established.

1919. 40 paras = 10 milliemes = 1 piastre.
1920. 100 centimes (or centiemes) = 1 piastre;
100 piastres = 1 Syrian Pound.

A. FRENCH MILITARY OCCUPATION

1919. Stamps of France surch **T. E. O.** and value in "MILLIEMES" or "PIASTRES".

1	**11**	1m. on 1c. grey	£200	£200
2	**11**	2m. on 2c. purple	£550	£550
3	**11**	3m. on 3c. orange	£250	£250
4	**15**	4m. on 15c. green	75·00	75·00
5	**18**	5m. on 5c. green	48·00	60·00
6	**18**	1p. on 10c. red	65·00	38·00
7	**18**	2p. on 25c. blue	34·00	30·00
8	**13**	5p. on 40c. red and blue	48·00	55·00
9	**13**	9p. on 50c. brown and lilac	90·00	95·00
10	**13**	10p. on 1f. red and yellow	£100	£130

1919. Nos. 9/13a and 19/23 of French Post Offices in the Turkish Empire ("Blanc", "Mouchon" and "Merson" key-types inscr "LEVANT") optd **T. E. O.** or surch in "MILLIEMES" also.

11	**A**	1m. on 1c. grey	3·75	4·00
12	**A**	2m. on 2c. purple	3·00	3·75
13	**A**	3m. on 3c. red	5·00	5·25
14	**B**	4m. on 15c. red	2·00	3·25
15	**A**	5m. on 5c. green	1·80	1·60
16	**B**	1p. on 25c. blue	1·30	1·50
17	**C**	2p. on 50c. brown and lilac	1·10	5·25
18	**C**	4p. on 1f. red and green	5·00	7·00
19	**C**	8p. on 2f. lilac and buff	16·00	17·00
20	**C**	20p. on 5f. blue and buff	£275	£275
MS16a		106×16 mm. Nos. 15/16. No gum	14·00	38·00

1920. Stamps of France surch **O. M. F. Syrie** and value in "MILLIEMES" or "PIASTRES".

25	**11**	1m. on 1c. grey	2·10	3·00
26	**11**	2m. on 2c. purple	5·75	7·00
27	**18**	3m. on 5c. green	3·75	5·75
28	**18**	5m. on 10c. red	2·10	5·00
29	**13**	20p. on 5f. blue and buff	80·00	£140

1920. Stamps of France surch **O. M. F. Syrie** and value. (a) Value in "CENTIMES" or "PIASTRES".

31	**11**	25c. on 1c. grey	4·00	3·25
32	**11**	50c. on 2c. purple	3·25	3·25
33	**11**	75c. on 3c. orange	3·50	5·75
35	**18**	1p. on 5c. green	3·50	40
36	**18**	2p. on 10c. red	3·00	3·00
37	**18**	2p. on 25c. blue	3·50	45
38	**18**	3p. on 25c. blue	3·75	3·50
39	**15**	5p. on 15c. green	4·50	4·75
40	**13**	10p. on 40c. red and blue	6·25	7·50
41	**13**	25p. on 50c. brown and lilac	7·50	8·50
42	**13**	50p. on 1f. red and yellow	35·00	50·00
44	**13**	100p. on 5f. blue and buff	70·00	80·00

(b) Value in "CENTIEMES".

45	**11**	25c. on 1c. grey	1·80	75
46	**11**	50c. on 2c. purple	1·60	25
47	**11**	75c. on 3c. orange	2·50	6·50

1920. Air. Nos. 35 and 39/40 optd **POSTE PAR AVION** in frame.

57	**18**	1p. on 5c. green	£200	75·00
58	**15**	5p. on 15c. green	£325	75·00
59	**13**	10p. on 40c. red and blue	£450	£130

1921. Issued at Damascus. Nos. K88/95 of Arab Kingdom surch **O. M. F. Syrie** and value in "CENTIEMES" or "PIASTRES".

60	**K3**	25c. on 1m. brown	7·00	5·25
61	**K3**	50c.on²⁄₁₀p green.	6·25	5·25
62	**K3**	1p.on³⁄₁₀p. yellow	5·25	4·00
63	**K 4**	1p. on 5m. red	16·00	11·50
64a	**K 4**	2p. on 5m. red	8·75	8·50
65	**K 3**	3p. on 1p. blue	11·50	4·75
66	**K 3**	5p. on 2p. green	12·00	23·00
67	**K 3**	10p. on 5p. purple	9·00	12·50
68	**K 3**	25p. on 10p. grey	15·00	28·00

1921. Stamps of France surch **O. M. F. Syrie** and value in "CENTIEMES" or "PIASTRES" (in two lines).

69	**18**	25c. on 5c. green	4·00	1·80
70	**18**	50c. on 10c. red	1·00	20
71	**15**	75c. on 15c. green	1·30	1·60
72	**18**	1p. on 20c. red	4·00	15
73	**13**	2p. on 40c. red and blue	2·50	15
74	**13**	3p. on 60c. violet and blue	3·75	25
75	**13**	5p. on 1f. red and yellow	7·25	7·00
76	**13**	10p. on 2f. orange and green	11·00	9·00
77	**13**	25p. on 5f. blue and buff	£140	£150

See also Nos. 81/5.

1921. Air. Nos. 72 and 75/6 optd **POSTE PAR AVION** in frame.

78	**18**	1p. on 20c. red	£140	60·00
79	**13**	5p. on 1f. red and yellow	£475	£200
80	**13**	10p. on 2f. orange and green	£450	£200

1921. Stamps of France surch **O.M.F. Syrie** and value in "PIASTRES" in one line.

81	**13**	2p. on 40c. red and blue	3·25	15
82	**13**	3p. on 60c. violet and blue	3·25	20
83	**13**	5p. on 1f. red and yellow	13·00	8·75
84	**13**	10p. on 2f. orange and green	20·00	21·00
85	**13**	25p. on 5f. blue and buff	17·00	18·00

1921. Air. Nos 72 and 75/6 optd **AVION**.

86	**18**	1p. on 20c. red	90·00	45·00
87	**13**	5p. on 1f. red and yellow	£160	75·00
88	**13**	10p. on 2f. orange and green	£200	80·00

1922. Air. Stamps of France surch **Poste par Avion O. M. F. Syrie** and value.

89	**13**	2p. on 40c. red and blue	25·00	65·00
90	**13**	3p. on 60c. violet and blue	21·00	65·00
91	**13**	5p. on 1f. red and yellow	30·00	65·00
92	**13**	10p. on 2f. orange and green	25·00	65·00

1922. Stamps of France surch **O. M. F. Syrie** and value in "CENTIEMES" or "PIASTRES".

93	**11**	10c. on 2c. purple	4·50	5·75
94	**18**	10c. on 5c. orange	3·50	6·00
95	**18**	25c. on 5c. orange	2·50	30
96	**18**	50c. on 10c. green	4·00	20
96b	**18**	1,25p. on 25c. blue	3·50	70
96c	**18**	1,50p. on 30c. orange	4·75	1·90
96d	**13**	2,50p. on 50c. brn & lilac	4·00	3·00
96e	**15**	2,50p. on 50c. blue	4·50	30

B. ARAB KINGDOM

Prior to the issues listed below, the Kingdom used stamps of Turkey variously overprinted. These are listed in Part 19 (Middle East) of the Stanley Gibbons Catalogue.

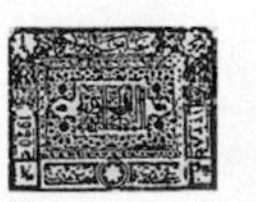

K3

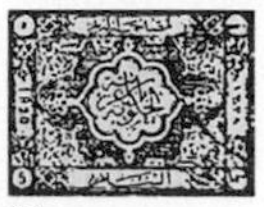

K4

1920. As Type **K3** and Type **K4**.

K88	**K3**	1m. brown (22×17 mm)	45	1·10
K89	**K3**	²⁄₁₀p. green (27×21 mm)	1·00	75
K90	**K3**	³⁄₁₀p. yellow (27×21 mm)	65	65
K91	**K4**	5m. red	65	40
K92	**K3**	1p. blue (27×21 mm)	65	65
K93	**K3**	2p. green (27×21 mm)	3·75	1·30
K94	**K3**	5p. purple (32×35 mm)	5·00	2·50
K95	**K3**	10p. grey (32×35 mm)	5·00	3·75

For 1p. black as Type **K3**, see Postage Due No. KD96.

1920. Independence Commemoration Optd with Arabic inscription.

K98	**K4**	5m. red	£700	£375

C. FRENCH MANDATED TERRITORY

Issues for Lebanon and Syria.
Nos. 97/174 are all stamps of France surch.

1923. (a) Surch **Syrie Grand Liban** in two lines and value.

97	**11**	10c. on 2c. purple	30	75
98	**18**	25c. on 5c. orange	2·00	3·50
99	**18**	50c. on 10c. green	1·60	1·30

100	15	75c. on 15c. green	3·25	6·00
101	18	1p. on 20c. brown	3·25	2·30
102	18	1,25p. on 25c. blue	3·00	2·50
103	18	1,50p. on 30c. orange	1·90	4·00
104	18	1,50p. on 30c. red	1·60	5·25
105	15	2,50p. on 50c. blue	1·60	75

(b) Surch **Syrie-Grand Liban** in one line and value.

106	13	2p. on 40c. red and blue	3·00	70
107	13	3p. on 60c. violet and blue	4·75	6·50
108	13	5p. on 1f. red and yellow	5·75	7·25
109	13	10p. on 2f. orange & green	18·00	28·00
110	13	25p. on 5f. blue and buff	65·00	75·00

(c) "Pasteur" issue surch Syrie Grand Liban in two lines and value.

111	30	50c. on 10c. green	3·00	5·75
112	30	1,50p. on 30c. red	2·40	5·25
113	30	2,50p. on 50c. blue	1·50	5·75

1923. Air. Surch **Post par Avion Syrie-Grand Liban** and value.

114	13	2p. on 40c. red and blue	60·00	60·00
115	13	3p. on 60c. violet and blue	40·00	60·00
116	13	5p. on 1f. red and yellow	65·00	45·00
117	13	10p. on 2f. orange and green	55·00	60·00

Issues for Syria only.

1924. Surch **SYRIE** and value in two lines. (a) Stamps of 1900–20.

118	11	10c. on 2c. purple	1·50	1·00
119	18	25c. on 5c. orange	1·90	80
120	18	50c. on 10c. green	1·90	1·00
121	15	75c. on 15c. green	3·75	3·00
122	18	1p. on 20c. brown	2·50	20
123	18	1.25p. on 25c. blue	3·50	4·50
124	18	1.50p. on 30c. orange	4·50	6·00
125	18	1.50p. on 30c. red	3·25	5·25
127	13	2p. on 40c. red and blue	1·50	40
126	15	2.50p. on 50c. blue	2·50	1·00
128	13	3p. on 60c. violet and blue	3·50	4·75
129	13	5p. on 1f. red and yellow	5·75	5·25
130	13	10p. on 2f. orange and green	7·50	9·75
131	13	25p. on 5f. blue and yellow	11·00	16·00

(b) "Pasteur issue".

132	30	50c. on 10c. green	2·00	3·50
133	30	1,50p. on 30c. red	3·00	6·50
134	30	2.50p. on 50c. blue	3·00	4·75

1924. Air. Surch **Poste par Avion Syrie** and value.

135	13	2p. on 40c. red and blue	5·00	10·50
136	13	3p. on 60c. violet and blue	4·50	10·00
137	13	5p. on 1f. red and yellow	3·75	10·50
138	13	10p. on 2f. orange & green	3·50	10·50

1924. Olympic Games issue (Nos. 401/4) surch **SYRIE** and value.

139	31	50c. on 10c. green and light green	18·00	34·00
140	-	1.25p. on 25c. carmine and red	12·00	48·00
141	-	1.50p. on 30c. red & black	12·50	70·00
142	-	2.50p. on 50c. ultramarine and blue	23·00	60·00

1924. Surch **Syrie** and value in French and Arabic. (a) Issues of 1900–20.

143	11	0,p.10 on 2c. red	80	2·00
144	18	0,p.25 on 5c. orange	1·00	3·75
145	18	0,p.50 on 10c. green	1·10	5·25
146	15	0,p.75 on 15c. green	2·50	6·00
147	18	1p. on 20c. brown	2·00	15
148	18	1,p.25 on 25c. blue	3·75	5·25
149	18	1p.50 on 30c. red (no comma)	3·25	3·50
150	18	1,p.50 on 30c. orange	8·25	9·00
151	18	2p. on 35c. violet	3·25	6·25
152	13	2p. on 40c. red and blue	3·75	90
153	13	2p. on 45c. green and blue	8·50	14·50
154	13	3p. on 60c. violet and blue	3·75	2·50
155	15	3p. on 60c. violet	3·75	7·25
156	15	4p. on 85c. red	2·10	4·50
157	13	5p. on 1f. red and yellow	3·00	5·00
158	13	10p. on 2f. orange & green	4·75	8·75
159	13	25p. on 5f. blue and buff	5·25	9·00

(b) "Pasteur" issue.

160	30	0,p.50 on 10c. green	90	30
161	30	0p.75 on 15c. green	4·00	6·50
162	30	1,p.50 on 30c. red	3·00	5·25
163	30	2p. on 45c. red	3·50	6·25
164	30	2p.50 on 50c. blue	2·10	1·60
165	30	4p. on 75c. blue	3·50	7·00

(c) Olympic Games Issue (Nos. 401/4).

166	31	0,p.50 on 10c. green and light green	12·50	60·00
167	-	1p.25 on 25c. carmine and red	12·50	36·00
168	-	1p.50 on 30c. red & black	12·50	34·00
169	-	2p.50 on 50c. ultramarine and blue	14·00	34·00

(d) Ronsard stamp.

170	35	4p. on 75c. blue on blue	70	6·50

1924. Air. Surch **Syrie Avion** and new value in French and Arabic.

171	13	2p. on 40c. red and blue	3·75	12·00
172	13	3p. on 60c. violet and blue	5·25	23·00
173	13	5p. on 1f. red and yellow	3·00	23·00
174	13	10p. on 2f. orange & green	3·50	17·00

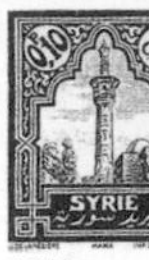

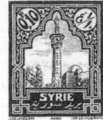

16 Hama

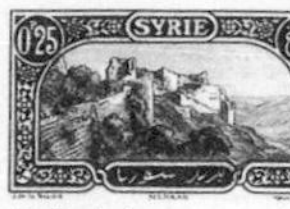

17 Merkab

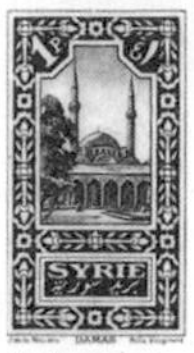

18 Damascus

1925. Views.

175	16	0p.10 violet	15	1·10
176	17	0p.25 black	1·90	1·60
177	-	0p.50 green	1·10	25
178	-	0p.75 red	1·60	2·10
179	18	1p. purple	70	15
180	-	1p.25 green	4·00	4·00
181	-	1p.50 pink	45	80
182	-	2p. brown	3·75	45
183	-	2p.50 blue	3·25	3·25
184	-	3p. brown	1·60	15
185	-	5p. violet	1·50	15
186	-	10p. purple	5·75	1·30
187	-	25p. blue	5·25	7·25

DESIGNS—As Type **17**: 0p.50, Alexandretta; 0p.75, Hama; 1p.25, Latakia; 1p.50, Damascus; 2, 25p. Palmyra (different views); 2p.50, Kalat Yamoun; 3p. Bridge of Daphne; 5, 10p. Aleppo (different views).

1925. Air. Nos. 182 and 184/6 optd **AVION** in French and Arabic.

188	2p. brown	3·25	7·75
189	3p. brown	2·10	7·75
190	5p. violet	1·50	3·75
191	10p. purple	2·00	4·75

1926. Air. Nos. 182 and 184/6 optd with Bleriot XI airplane.

192	2p. brown	3·75	5·75
193	3p. brown	1·40	3·50
194	5p. violet	3·00	4·50
195	10p. purple	3·25	7·50

1926. War Refugees Fund. Nos. 176 etc and 192/5 surch **Secours aux Refugies Afft** and value in French and Arabic.

196	17	0p.25 on 0p.25 black (postage)	2·50	7·25
197	-	0p.25 on 0p.50 green	3·25	8·25
198	-	0p.25 on 0p.75 red	1·00	6·50
199	18	0p.50 on 1p. purple	2·30	6·25
200	-	0p.50 on 1p.25 green	3·50	8·75
201	-	0p.50 on 1p.50 pink	1·60	7·75
202	-	0p.75 on 2p. brown	3·25	8·75
203	-	0p.75 on 2p.50 blue	3·25	8·25
208	-	1p. on 2p. brown (air)	2·50	9·50
204	-	1p. on 3p. brown	2·00	7·25
205	-	1p. on 5p. violet	1·90	4·00
209	-	2p. on 3p. brown	1·90	9·50
206	-	2p. on 10p. purple	2·00	7·75
210	-	3p. on 5p. violet	1·90	5·00
211	-	5p. on 10p. purple	1·90	8·25
207	-	5p. on 25p. blue	1·80	9·00

1926. No. 175 etc surch with new value in English and Arabic.

221	05 on 0p.10 violet	15	95
222	1p. on 3p. brown	3·00	1·10
223	2p. on 1p.25 green	4·50	55
212	3p.50 on 0p.75 red	1·40	4·50
224	4p. on 0p.25 black	3·50	1·30
215	4p.50 on 0p.75 red	55	15
216	6p. on 2p.50 blue	1·20	1·90
217	7p.50 on 2p.50 blue	1·30	30
218	12p. on 1p.25 green	3·00	5·00
219	15p. on 25p. blue	1·50	15
220	20p. on 1p.25 green	3·50	6·00

1929. Air. Nos. 177 etc, optd with Bleriot XI airplane or surch also in English and Arabic.

225	0p.50 green	75	1·60
226	1p. purple	2·40	3·00
227	2p. on 1p.25 green	4·75	5·00
228	15p. on 25p. blue	4·50	8·25
229	25p. blue	7·50	8·50

1929. Damascus Industrial Exhibition. Nos. 177 etc and various air stamps optd **EXPOSITION INDUSTRIELLE DAMAS 1929** in French and Arabic.

230	0p.50 green (postage)	3·25	4·00
237	0p.50 green (No. 225) (air)	4·00	8·25
231	1p. purple	3·00	3·50
238	1p. purple (No. 226)	3·50	8·50
232	1p.50 pink	3·00	3·50
239	2p. brown (No. 192)	4·00	4·75
233	3p. brown	3·00	4·50
240	3p. brown (No. 193)	3·25	4·50
234	5p. violet	3·50	3·50
241	5p. violet (No. 194)	3·00	8·50
235	10p. purple	4·50	4·50
242	10p. purple (No. 195)	3·25	6·00
236	25p. blue	3·75	4·50
243	25p. blue (No. 229)	3·25	6·00

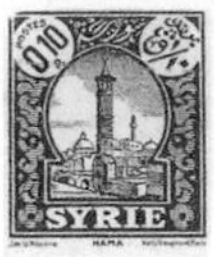

26 Hama

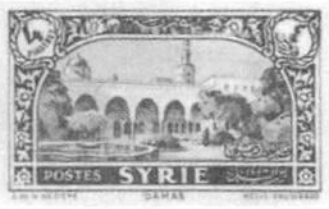

27 Damascus

1930. Views.

244	26	0p.10 mauve	75	50
244b	26	0p.10 purple	15	1·60
245	-	0p.20 blue	40	3·25
245a	-	0p.20 red	65	3·25
246	-	0p.25 green	3·25	2·30
246a	-	0p.25 violet	2·50	4·50
247	-	0p.50 violet	2·00	15
247a	-	0p.75 red	2·00	1·10
248	-	1p. green	3·50	15
248a	-	1p. brown	4·00	15
249	-	1p.50 brown	9·75	4·00
249a	-	1p.50 green	14·50	4·50
250	-	2p. violet	4·00	15
251	-	3p. green	4·00	4·50
252	27	4p. orange	2·10	15
253	-	4p.50 red	3·50	50
254	-	6p. black	3·00	95
255	-	7p.50 blue	3·75	25
256	-	10p. brown	4·50	55
257	-	15p. green	6·25	1·10
258	-	25p. purple	3·25	2·50
259	-	50p. brown	65·00	48·00
260	-	100p. red	70·00	70·00

DESIGNS—As Type **26**: 0p.20, Aleppo; 0p.25, Hama (different). As Type **27**: 0p.50, Alexandretta; 0p.75, 4p.50, Homs; 1p., 7p.50, Aleppo (different); 1p.50, 100p. Damascus (different); 2, 10p. Antioch; 3p. Bosra; 5p. Sednaya; 15p. Hama; 25p. St. Simeon; 50p. Palmyra.

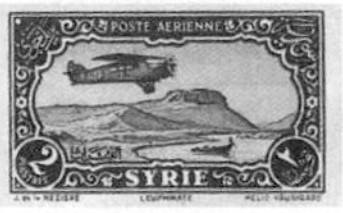

28 River Euphrates

1931. Air. Views with Potez 29-4 biplane.

261	-	0p.50 yellow (Homs)	1·60	1·60
261a	-	0p.50 brown (Homs)	3·75	3·75
262	-	1p. brown (Damascus)	3·50	2·40
263	28	2p. blue	4·00	3·75
264	-	3p. green (Palmyra)	2·50	1·60
265	-	5p. purple (Deir-el-Zor)	1·90	1·50
266	-	10p. blue (Damascus)	2·40	1·10
267	-	15p. red (Aleppo citadel)	3·00	2·50
268	-	25p. orange (Hama)	5·25	3·75
269	-	50p. black (Zebdani)	6·50	6·50
270	-	100p. mauve (Telebisse)	7·75	5·25

D. REPUBLIC UNDER FRENCH MANDATE

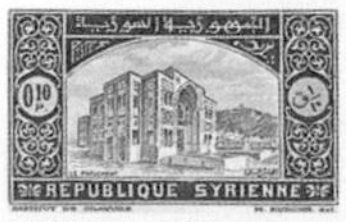

29 Parliament House, Damascus

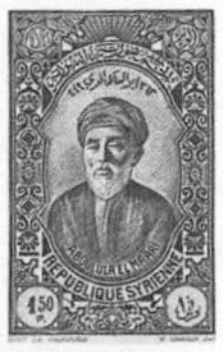

30 Aboulula el Maari

1934. Establishment of Republic.

271	29	0p.10 green (postage)	2·50	2·30
272	29	0p.20 black	1·50	2·00
273	29	0p.25 red	2·40	2·00
274	29	0p.50 blue	2·30	2·50
275	29	0p.75 purple	2·50	2·40
276	30	1p. red	3·75	5·00
277	30	1p.50 green	6·00	6·00
278	30	2p. brown	6·25	6·25
279	30	3p. blue	65·00	12·50
280	30	4p. violet	8·75	6·25
281	30	4p.50 red	11·50	9·00
282	30	5p. blue	7·00	9·00
283	30	6p. brown	7·25	8·25
284	30	7p.50 blue	11·50	12·50
285	-	10p. brown	14·50	15·00
286	-	15p. blue	16·00	12·50
287	-	25p. red	36·00	48·00
288	-	50p. brown	70·00	75·00
289	-	100p. red	35·00	65·00

DESIGNS—As Type **30**: Nos. 285/7, President Mohammed Ali Bey el-Abed; 288/9, Sultan Saladin.

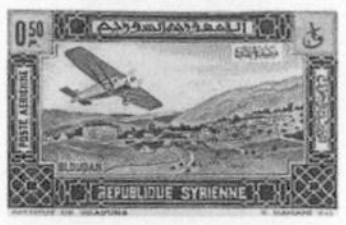

31 Farman F.190 Airplane over Bloudan

290	31	0p.50 brown (air)	3·75	4·50
291	31	1p. green	3·50	3·00
292	31	2p. blue	3·75	3·75
293	31	3p. red	4·00	7·50
294	31	5p. purple	7·50	7·75
295	31	10p. violet	55·00	55·00
296	31	15p. brown	50·00	40·00
297	31	25p. blue	65·00	60·00
298	31	50p. black	70·00	75·00
299	31	100p. brown	£100	£100

1936. Damascus Fair. Optd **1936 FOIRE DE DAMAS** in Arabic and French. (a) Postage stamps of 1930.

300	-	0p.50 violet	4·75	6·00
301	-	1p. brown	4·50	4·50
302	-	2p. violet	3·50	3·75
303	-	3p. green	3·25	3·50
304	27	4p. orange	4·50	7·25
305	-	4p.50 red	4·75	7·00
306	-	6p. green	3·50	5·25
307	-	7p. blue	3·75	5·00
308	-	10p. brown	5·75	5·75

(b) Air stamps of 1931.

309	-	0p.50 brown	4·75	9·75
310	-	1p. brown	3·50	3·50
311	28	2p. blue	4·00	6·50
312	-	3p. green	4·00	6·50
313	-	5p. purple	4·50	7·50

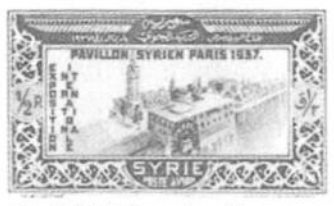

33 Exhibition Pavilion

1937. Air. Paris International Exhibition.

314	33	½p. green	2·10	2·50
315	33	1p. green	3·50	4·00
316	33	2p. brown	3·00	2·50
317	33	3p. red	2·40	3·50
318	33	5p. orange	4·50	3·75
319	33	10p. green	7·25	16·00
320	33	15p. blue	8·50	19·00
321	33	25p. violet	8·50	18·00

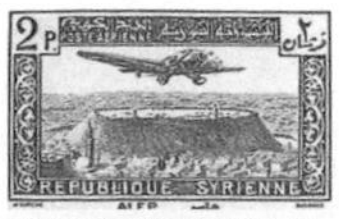

34 Savoia Marchetti S-73 over Aleppo

1937. Air.

322	34	½p. violet	15	55
323	-	1p. black	1·40	1·40
324	34	2p. green	2·10	1·90
325	-	3p. blue	1·90	2·10
326	34	5p. mauve	3·00	1·10
327	-	10p. brown	2·00	1·40
328	34	15p. brown	3·50	2·40
329	-	25p. blue	6·25	7·75

DESIGN: 1, 3, 10, 25p. Potez 62 airplane over Damascus.

1938. Stamps of 1930 surch in English and Arabic.

330	0p.25 on 0p.75 red	15	1·40
331	0p.50 on 1p.50 green	55	80
332	2p. on 7p.50 blue	1·10	70
333	2p.50 on 4p. orange	1·50	15
334	5p. on 7p.50 blue	1·80	40
335	10p. on 50p. brown	1·80	1·40
336	10p. on 100p. red	1·60	75

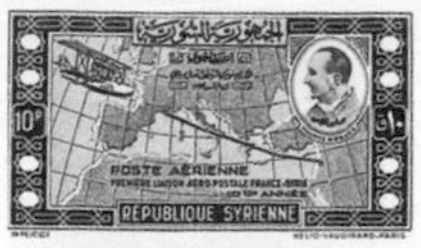

38 CAMS 53H Flying Boat, Maurice Nogues and Flight Route

1938. Air. Tenth Anniv of First Air Service Flight between France and Syria.

337	**38**	10p. green	3·25	9·75
MS337a 160×120 mm. No. 337 in block of four			65·00	95·00

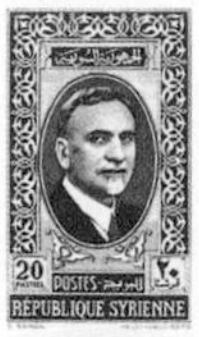

39 Pres. Atasi

1938. Unissued stamp surch **12.50** and in Arabic figures.

338	**39**	12p.50 on 10p. blue	3·00	20

1938

339	**39**	10p. blue	3·50	1·40
339a	**39**	20p. brown	3·75	80

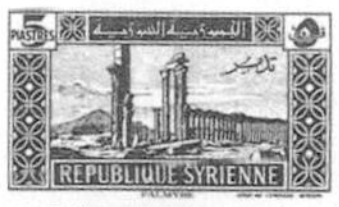

41 Palmyra

1940

340	**41**	5p. pink	4·50	95

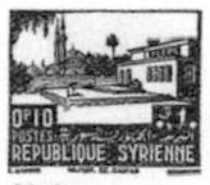

42 Damascus Museum

1940

341	**42**	0p.10 red (postage)	15	80
342	**42**	0p.20 blue	15	95
343	**42**	0p.25 brown	15	1·60
344	**42**	0p.50 blue	15	15
345	-	1p. blue	20	25
346	-	1p.50 brown	45	1·50
347	-	2p.50 green	15	45
348	-	5p. violet	65	15
349	-	7p.50 red	45	55
350	-	50p. purple	4·50	7·25

DESIGNS—As Type **45**: 1p., 1p.50, 2p.50, Hotel de Bloudan; 5p., 7p.50, 50p. Kasr-el-Heir Fortress.

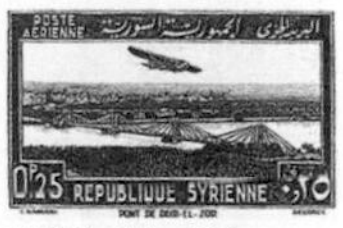

45 Deir-el-Zor Bridge

351	**45**	0p.25 black (air)	15	1·90
352	**45**	0p.50 blue	15	1·60
353	**45**	1p. blue	45	2·10
354	**45**	2p. brown	65	2·10
355	**45**	5p. green	1·20	2·30
356	**45**	10p. red	1·40	1·10
357	**45**	50p. violet	6·25	7·50

E. SYRIAN REPUBLIC

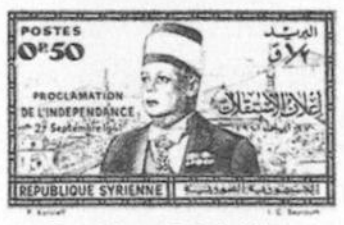

46 President Taj Addin el-Husni

1942. National Independence. Inscr "PROCLAMATION DE L'INDEPENDENCE 27 Septembre 1941".

358	**46**	0p.50 green (postage)	5·25	5·25
359	**46**	1p.50 brown	5·25	5·25
360	**46**	6p. red	5·25	5·25
361	**46**	15p. blue	5·25	5·25
362	-	10p. blue (air)	4·50	4·50
363	-	50p. purple	4·50	4·50
MS363a 205×138 mm. Nos. 358/63. Imperf			£700	

DESIGN: 10, 50p. As Type **46**, but President bareheaded and airplane inset.

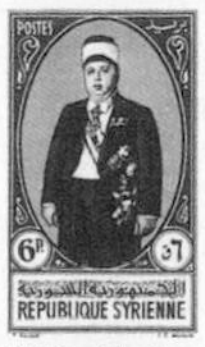

47 President Taj Addin el-Husni

1942. (a) Postage. Portrait in oval frame.

364	**47**	6p. purple and pink	3·25	3·25
365	**47**	15p. blue and light blue	3·25	3·25

(b) Air. Portrait in rectangular frame.

366	10p. green and emerald	5·25	5·25

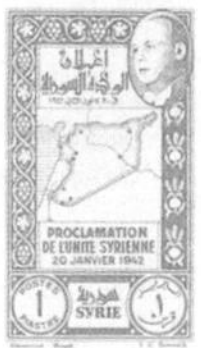

48 Syria and late President's portrait

1943. Union of Latakia and Jebel Druze with Syria. (a) President bare-headed.

367	**48**	1p. green (postage)	3·00	3·00
368	**48**	4p. brown	3·00	3·00
369	**48**	8p. violet	3·00	3·00
370	**48**	10p. orange	3·00	3·00
371	**48**	20p. blue	3·00	3·00

(b) President wearing turban.

372	2p. brown (air)	3·50	3·50
373	10p. purple	3·50	3·50
374	20p. blue	3·50	3·50
375	50p. pink	3·50	3·50

1943. Death of President Taj Addin el-Husni. Nos. 367/75 optd with narrow black border.

376	**48**	1p. green (postage)	3·00	3·00
377	**48**	4p. brown	3·00	3·00
378	**48**	8p. violet	3·00	3·00
379	**48**	10p. orange	3·00	3·00
380	**48**	20p. blue	3·00	3·00
381	-	2p. brown (air)	3·50	3·50
382	-	10p. purple	3·50	3·50
383	-	20p. blue	3·50	3·50
384	-	50p. pink	3·50	3·50

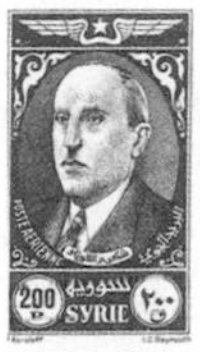

49 Pres. Shukri Bey al-Quwatli

1944. Air.

385	**49**	200p. purple	14·00	14·00
386	**49**	500p. blue	20·00	20·00

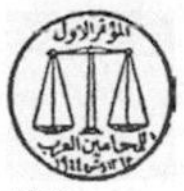

50 Trans. "First Congress of Arab Lawyers, Damascus"

1944. Air. First Arab Lawyers' Congress. Optd with T **50**.

387	-	10p. brown (No. 327)	4·25	4·25
388	-	15p. red (No. 267)	4·25	4·25
389	-	25p. orange (No. 268)	4·25	4·25
390	-	100p. mauve (No. 270)	10·50	10·50
391	**49**	200p. purple	18·00	18·00

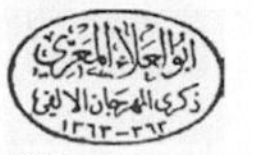

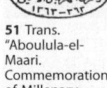

51 Trans. "Aboulula-el-Maari. Commemoration of Millenary, 363–1363"

1945. Millenary of Aboulula-el-Maari (Arab poet and philosopher). Optd with T **51**.

392	-	2p.50 green (No. 347) (postage)	3·75	3·75
393	-	7p.50 red (No. 349)	3·75	3·75
394	-	15p. red (No. 267) (air)	4·50	4·50
395	-	25p. orange (No. 268)	4·50	4·50
396	**49**	500p. blue	34·00	34·00

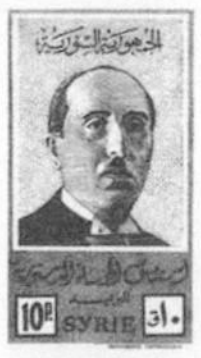

52 Pres. Shukri Bey al-Quwatli

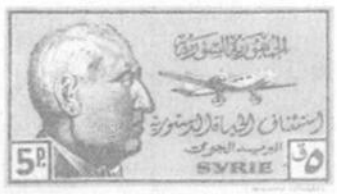

53 Pres. Shukri Bey al-Quwatli

1945. Resumption of Constitutional Govt.

397	**52**	4p. violet (postage)	55	55
398	**52**	6p. blue	65	65
399	**52**	10p. red	75	75
400	**52**	15p. brown	1·40	1·40
401	**52**	20p. green	1·50	1·50
402	**52**	40p. orange	1·90	1·90
403	**53**	5p. green (air)	55	55
404	**53**	10p. red	75	55
405	**53**	15p. orange	1·10	75
406	**53**	25p. blue	1·90	1·20
407	**53**	50p. violet	2·75	1·20
408	**53**	100p. brown	5·25	2·00
409	**53**	200p. red	13·00	6·50

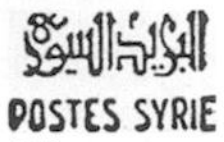
POSTES SYRIE

(54)

1945. Fiscal stamps inscr "TIMBRE FISCAL". (a) Optd with T **54** (No. 411 surch also).

410	25p. brown	7·00	7·00
411	50p. on 75p. brown	8·00	8·00
412	75p. brown	10·00	10·00
413	100p. green	15·00	15·00

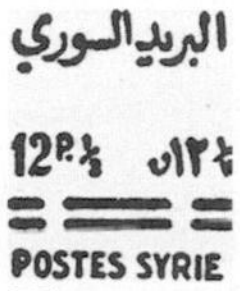
POSTES SYRIE

(55)

(b) Surch as T **55**.

414	12½p. on 15p. green	4·00	4·00
415	25p. on 25s. purple	4·00	4·00

(c) Optd or surch (416) with T **54** and with additional Arabic inscription at top.

416	50p. on 75p. brown	4·50	4·50
417	50p. mauve	4·00	4·00
418	100p. green	5·25	5·25

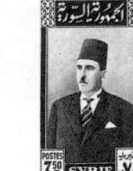

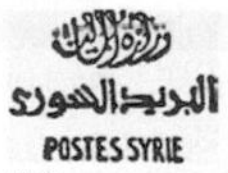
POSTES SYRIE

(56)

1946. Fiscal stamp optd with T **56**.

419	200p. blue	30·00	18·00

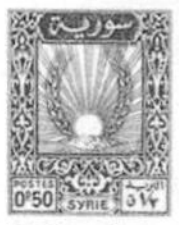

57 Ear of Wheat

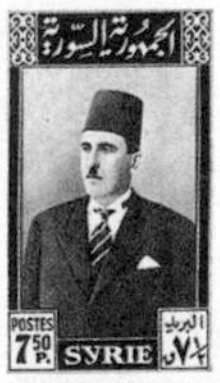

58 Pres. Shukri Bey al-Quwatli

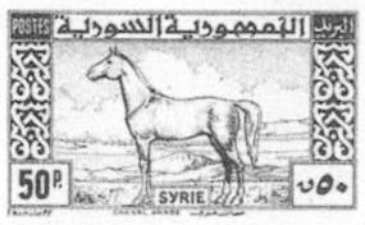

60 Arab Horse

1946

420	**57**	0p.50 orange (postage)	20	10
421	**57**	1p. violet	75	20
422	**57**	2p.50 grey	85	20
423	**57**	5p. green	1·20	30
424	**58**	7p.50 brown	30	10
425	**58**	10p. blue	30	20
426	**58**	12p.50 violet	1·40	20
427	-	15p. red	55	20
428	-	20p. violet	85	55
429	-	25p. blue	1·40	55
430	**60**	50p. brown	7·00	1·20
431	**60**	100p. green	15·00	2·75
432a	**60**	200p. purple	80·00	7·50

DESIGN—As Type **58**: 15, 20, 25p. Pres. Shukri Bey al-Quwatli bareheaded.

433	-	3p. red (air)	75	20
434	-	5p. green	75	20
435	-	6p. orange	75	20
436	-	10p. grey	55	20
437	-	15p. red	55	20
438	-	25p. blue	65	30
439	-	50p. violet	1·10	30
440	-	100p. blue	2·50	55
441	-	200p. brown	5·25	1·60
442	-	300p. brown	19·00	3·25
443	-	500p. green	21·00	4·75

DESIGNS—HORIZ: 3, 5, 6p. Flock of sheep; 10, 15, 25p. Kattineh Dam; 50, 100, 200p. Temple ruins, Kanaouat; 300, 500p. Sultan Ibrahim Mosque.

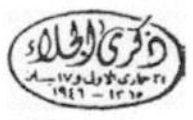

(65)

1946. Evacuation of Foreign Troops from Syria. Optd with T **65**.

444	**58**	10p. blue (postage)	75	75
445	**58**	12p.50 violet	1·10	1·10
446	**60**	50p. brown	3·25	3·25
447	-	25p. blue (No. 438) (air)	2·75	1·60

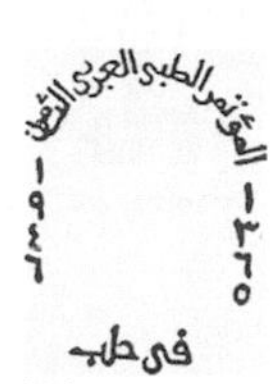

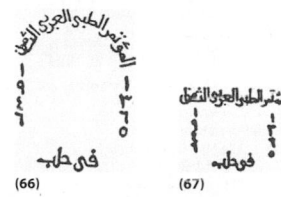

(66)

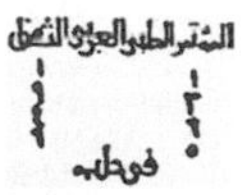

(67)

1946. Eighth Arab Medical Congress, Aleppo. (a) Postage. Optd with T **66**.

448	25p. blue (No. 429)	2·10	1·80

(b) Air. Optd with T **67**.

449	25p. blue (No. 438)	2·75	1·60
450	50p. violet (No. 439)	3·50	2·10
451	100p. blue (No. 440)	6·50	3·75

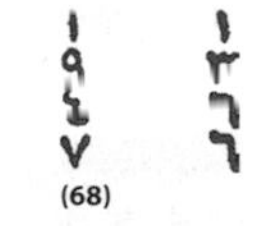

(68)

1947. First Anniv of Evacuation of Allied Forces. Nos. 444/7 optd as T **68** (= "1947 1366").

452	**58**	10p. blue (postage)	75	20
453	**58**	12p.50 violet	1·10	30
454	**60**	50p. brown	2·75	1·10
455	-	25p. blue (air)	2·75	1·60

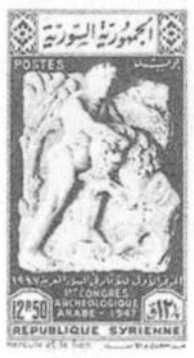

69 Hercules and Lion

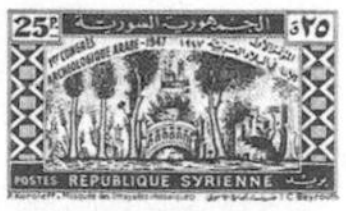

70 Mosaic of the Mosque of the Omayades

1947. First Arab Archaeological Congress, Damascus.

456	**69**	12p.50 green (postage)	1·10	85
457	**70**	25p. blue	2·10	1·40
458	-	12p.50 violet (air)	1·60	85
459	-	50p. brown	5·25	2·50
MS459a 138×188 mm. Nos. 456/9			65·00	65·00

DESIGNS—As T **70**: 12p.50, Window at Kasr El-Heir El-Gharbi; 50p. King Hazael's throne.

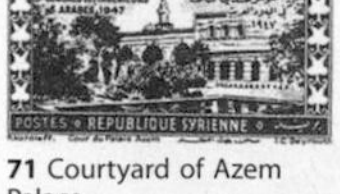

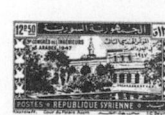

71 Courtyard of Azem Palace

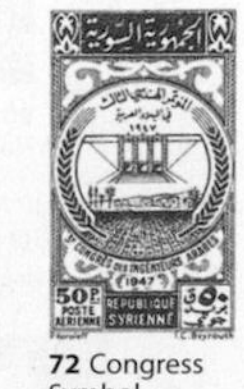

72 Congress Symbol

1947. Third Arab Engineers' Congress, Damascus. Inscr "3e CONGRES DES INGENIEURS ARABES 1947".

460	**71**	12p.50 purple (postage)	1·10	85
461	-	25p. blue	2·10	1·40
462	-	12p.50 green (air)	1·60	85
463	**72**	50p. violet	5·25	2·50
MS463a 138×188 mm. Nos. 460/3			65·00	65·00

DESIGNS—HORIZ: No. 461, Telephone Exchange Building; 462, Fortress at Kasr El-Heir El-Charqui.

73 Parliament Building

74 Pres. Shukri Bey al-Quwatli

1948. Re-election of Pres. Shukri Bey al-Quwatli.

464	**73**	12p.50 brown and grey (postage)	85	30
465	**74**	25p. mauve	1·30	85
466	**73**	12p.50 blue and violet (air)	85	45
467	**74**	50p. purple and green	3·50	1·60

MS467a 139×186 mm. Nos. 464/7. Imperf £275 £275

75 Syrian Arms

76 Soldier and Flag

1948. Compulsory Military Service.

468	**75**	12p.50 brown and grey (postage)	85	55
469	**76**	25p. multicoloured	1·30	85
470	**75**	12p.50 blue and light blue (air)	1·10	55
471	**76**	50p. green, red and black	4·50	1·30

MS471a 137×190 mm. Nos. 468/71. Imperf £225 £225

1948. Surch. (a) Postage.

472	-	0p.50 on 0p.75 red (No. 247a)	30	10
472ab	**60**	2p.50 on 200p. purple	55	30
472b	**60**	10p. on 100p. green	75	30
473	**60**	25p. on 200p. purple	5·25	65

(b) Air.

474	-	2p.50 on 3p. (No. 433)	10	10
475	-	2p.50 on 6p. (No. 435)	10	10
475a	-	2p.50 on 100p. (No. 440)	20	10
476	-	25p. on 200p. (No. 441)	1·10	45
477	-	50p. on 300p. (No. 442)	24·00	1·10
478	-	50p. on 500p. (No. 443)	24·00	1·10

78 Palmyra

79 President Husni el-Zaim and Lockheed Super Constellation over Damascus

1949. 75th Anniv of U.P.U.

479	-	12p.50 violet (postage)	2·75	2·75
480	**78**	25p. blue	4·75	4·75
481	-	12p.50 purple (air)	10·50	10·50
482	**79**	50p. black	28·00	19·00

DESIGNS—HORIZ: No. 479, Ain-el-Arous; 481, Globe and mountains.

80 President Husni el-Zaim

1949. Revolution of 30 March 1949.

483	**80**	25p. blue (postage)	1·30	85
484	**80**	50p. brown (air)	5·25	3·75

81 Pres. Husni el-Zaim and Map

1949. Presidential Election.

485	**81**	25p. brown & bl (postage)	5·25	3·25
486	**81**	50p. green and pink (air)	6·00	4·25

MS486a 125×188 mm. Nos. 485/6. Imperf £325 £325

82 Tel-Chehab

83 Damascus

1949

487	**82**	5p. grey	55	10
488	**82**	7p.50 brown	75	25
524	**82**	7p.50 green	55	20
489	**83**	12p.50 purple	95	25
490	**83**	25p. blue	1·80	60

84 Syrian Arms

85 G.P.O., Damascus

1950

491	**84**	0p.50 brown	20	10
492	**84**	2p.50 pink	20	20
493	-	10p. violet	55	35
494	-	12p.50 green	1·10	60
495	**85**	25p. blue	1·80	35
496	**85**	50p. black	6·00	1·20

DESIGN—HORIZ: 10, 12p.50, Abous–Damascus road.

86 Port of Latakia

1950. Air.

497	**86**	2p.50 violet	75	25
526	**86**	10p. blue	75	25
499	**86**	15p. brown	3·75	35
500	**86**	25p. blue	8·00	60

87 Parliament Building

88 Book and Torch

1951. New Constitution, 1950.

501	**87**	12p.50 black (postage)	55	35
502	**87**	25p. blue	85	70
503	**88**	12p.50 red (air)	55	35
504	**88**	50p. purple	1·80	1·70

89 Hama

1952

505	**89**	0p.50 brown (postage)	10	10
506	**89**	2p.50 blue	30	10
507	**89**	5p. green	30	10
508	**89**	10p. red	30	20
509	-	12p.50 black	95	25
510	-	15p. purple	6·00	35
511	-	25p. blue	2·75	60
512	-	100p. brown	10·50	3·00
513	-	2p.50 red (air)	25	10
514	-	5p. green	55	10
515	-	15p. violet	80	25
516	-	25p. blue	1·10	60
517	-	100p. purple	8·00	1·40

DESIGNS—Postage: 12p.50 to 100p. Palace of Justice, Damascus. Air: 2p.50 to 15p. Palmyra; 25, 100p. Citadel, Aleppo.

1952. Air. United Nations Social Welfare Seminar, Damascus. Optd **U. N. S. W. S. Damascus 8-20 Dec. 1952** and curved line of Arabic.

518	**86**	10p. blue	2·75	1·70
519	-	15p. violet (No. 515)	2·75	1·70
520	-	25p. blue (No. 516)	4·75	2·50
521	-	50p. violet (No. 439)	12·00	3·75

91 Qalaat el Hasn Fortress

1953

522	**91**	0p.50 red (postage)	20	10
523	-	2p.50 brown	30	10
525	**91**	12p.50 blue	2·50	25
527	-	50p. brown (air)	2·40	35

DESIGNS: 2p,50, Qalaat el Hasn fortress (different); 50p. G.P.O., Aleppo.

92 "Labour"

93 "Family"

94 "Communications"

1954

528	**92**	1p. green (postage)	20	10
529	**92**	2½p. red	20	10
530	**92**	5p. blue	30	10
531	**93**	7½p. red	45	10
532	**93**	10p. black	55	15
533	**93**	12½p. violet	55	20
534	-	20p. purple	1·10	25
535	-	25p. violet	2·10	80
536	-	50p. green	5·25	1·40
537	**94**	5p. violet (air)	20	15
538	**94**	10p. brown	30	15
539	**94**	15p. green	45	20
540	-	30p. brown	55	30
541	-	35p. blue	1·10	35
542	-	40p. orange	2·40	60
543	-	50p. purple	1·80	1·20
544	-	70p. violet	5·00	1·40

DESIGNS—As Type **93**. Postage: 20 to 50p. "Industry". Air: 30 to 70p. Syrian University.

95 Monument to Hejaz Railway

1954. Air. Damascus Fair. Inscr as in T **95**.

545	**95**	40p. mauve	1·40	80
546	-	50p. green	1·80	95

DESIGN—VERT: 50p. Mosque and Syrian flag.

1954. Cotton Festival, Aleppo. Optd **FESTIVAL du COTON. Alep. oct. 1954** and Arab inscription.

547	**93**	10p. black (postage)	85	35
548	-	25p. violet (No. 535)	1·10	60
549	-	50p. brown (No. 527) (air)	1·60	1·20
550	-	100p. purple (No. 517)	3·00	2·50

96a

1955. Arab Postal Union.

551	**96a**	12½p. green (postage)	75	35
552	**96a**	25p. violet	1·40	60
553	**96a**	5p. brown (air)	45	35

97

1955. Air. Middle East Rotary Congress.

554	**97**	35p. red	1·30	95
555	**97**	65p. green	2·75	1·70

98

1955. Air. 50th Anniv of Rotary International.

556	**98**	25p. violet	85	70
557	**98**	75p. blue	2·75	2·00

99 "Facing the Future"

1955. Air. Ninth Anniv of Evacuation of Foreign Troops from Syria.

558	**99**	40p. mauve	75	75
559	-	60p. blue	3·25	95

DESIGN: 60p. Tank and infantry attack.

See also Nos. 847/9.

100 Mother and Child

1955. Mothers' Day.

560	**100**	25p. red (postage)	75	60
561	**100**	35p. violet (air)	1·40	1·20
562	**100**	40p. black	2·10	1·70

101 Lockheed Super Constellation Airliner, Flag and Crowd

1955. Air. Emigrants' Congress.

563	**101**	5p. mauve	75	35
564	-	15p. blue	95	60

DESIGN: 15p. Lockheed Super Constellation over globe.

102 Syrian Pavilion

1955. Air. International Fair, Damascus.

565	**102**	25p.+5p. black	75	75
566	-	35p.+5p. blue	1·10	1·10
567	-	40p.+10p. purple	1·40	1·40
568	-	70p.+10p. green	2·10	2·10

DESIGNS: 35, 40p. "Industry and Agriculture"; 70p. Exhibition pavilions and flags.

103 Mother and Baby

1955. Air. International Children's Day.

569	**103**	25p. blue	95	60
570	**103**	50p. purple	1·80	80

104 U.N. Emblem and Torch

1955. Tenth Anniv of U.N.O.

571	**104**	7½p. red (postage)	75	60
572	**104**	12½p. green	1·40	85
573	-	15p. blue (air)	1·10	60
574	-	35p. brown	2·10	85

DESIGN: 15, 35p. Globe, dove and Scales of Justice.

105 Saracen Gate, Aleppo Citadel

1955. Installation of Aleppo Water Supply from River Euphrates.

575	**105**	7p.50 violet (postage)	45	10

576	105	12p.50 red	65	25
577	105	30p. blue (air)	2·75	1·70

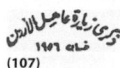

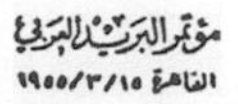

(106)

1955. Second Arab Postal Union Congress, Cairo. Nos. 551/3 optd with T **106**.

578	105	12½p. green (postage)	65	60
579		25p. violet	2·10	95
580		5p. brown (air)	85	25

(107)

1956. Visit of King Hussein of Jordan. Nos. 551/3 optd with T **107**.

581		12½p. green (postage)	75	70
582		25p. violet	1·30	1·30
583		5p. brown (air)	2·10	95

108
Monument

1956. Air. Tenth Anniv of Evacuation of Foreign Troops from Syria.

584	**108**	35p. sepia	85	70
585	-	65p. red	1·40	95
586	-	75p. grey	2·75	1·50

DESIGNS: 65p. Winged female figure; 75p. Pres. Shukri Bey al-Quwatli.

109 Pres.
Shukri Bey
al-Quwatli

1956. Air.

587	109	100p. black	1·80	1·50
588	109	200p. violet	3·75	2·00
589	109	300p. red	5·25	4·75
590	109	500p. green	10·50	8·75
MS590a 139×100 mm. Nos. 587/90.				
		Imperf. Without gum	90·00	90·00

110 Cotton

1956. Aleppo Cotton Festival.

591	110	2½p. green	75	35

1956. Air. Nos. 565/8 with premiums obliterated by bars.

592	102	25p. black	75	35
593	-	35p. blue	85	60
594	-	40p. purple	1·80	80
595	-	70p. green	2·10	1·70

111 Gate of
Kasr al-Heir,
Palmyra

1956. Air. Third International Fair, Damascus.

596	111	15p. brown	75	75
597	-	20p. blue	85	85
598	-	30p. green	1·20	1·20
599	-	35p. blue	1·30	1·30
600	-	50p. purple	1·60	1·60
MS600a 101×136 mm. Nos. 596/600.				
		Imperf. Without gum	75·00	75·00

DESIGNS: 20p. Cotton mill; 30p. Tractor; 35p. Phoenician galley and cogwheels; 50p. Textiles, carpets and pottery.

112 Clay Alphabetical
Tablet

1956. Air. International Campaign for Museums.

601	112	20p. black	1·30	80
602	-	30p. red	1·40	80
603	-	50p. brown	2·75	1·50
MS603a 139×100 mm. Nos. 601/3.				
		Imperf. Without gum	75	75

DESIGNS—VERT: 30p. Syrian legionary's helmet. HORIZ: 50p. Lintel of Belshamine Temple, Palmyra.

1956. 11th Anniv of U.N.O. Nos. 571/4 optd 11**eme ANNIVERSAIRE de L'ONU** in French and Arabic.

604	104	7½p. red (postage)	85	60
605	-	12½p. green	1·10	80
606	-	15p. blue (air)	1·80	95
607	-	35p. brown	3·50	2·30

114 Oaks and Mosque

1956. Air. Afforestation Day.

608	114	10p. brown	55	35
609	114	40p. green	1·30	80

115 Azem Palace,
Damascus

1957

610	115	12½p. purple	55	20
611	115	15p. black	75	25

116 "Resistance"

1957. Syrian Defence Force.

612	116	5p. mauve	45	20
613	116	20p. green	75	60

1957. Evacuation of Port Said. Optd **22.12.56 EVACUATION PORT SAID** in French and Arabic.

614	116	5p. mauve	45	20
615	116	20p. green	75	60

118 Mother
and Child

1957. Air. Mothers' Day.

616		40p. blue	1·20	1·20
617	118	60p. red	2·10	1·50

DESIGN: 40p. Mother fondling child.

119 "Sword of
Liberty"

1957. Air. 11th Anniv of Evacuation of Foreign Troops from Syria.

618	119	10p. brown	20	20
619	-	15p. green	55	35
620	-	25p. violet	75	45
621	-	35p. mauve	1·10	80
622	119	40p. black	1·70	1·40

DESIGNS: 15, 35p. Map and woman holding torch; 25p. Pres. Shukri Bey al-Quwatli.

120 Freighter
"Latakia" and Fair
Emblem

1957. Air. Fourth Damascus Fair.

623	120	25p. mauve	65	45
624	-	30p. brown	75	60
625	-	35p. blue	1·10	80
626	-	40p. green	1·50	95
627	120	70p. green	1·80	1·40

DESIGNS—VERT: 30, 40p. Girls harvesting and cotton picking. HORIZ: 35p. Interior of processing plant.

121 "Cotton"

1957. Aleppo Cotton Festival.

628	121	12½p. black & grn (postage)	75	35
629	121	17½p. black & orange (air)	85	60
630	121	40p. black and blue	1·80	80

122 Children at
Work and Play

1957. International Children's Day.

631	122	12½p. green (postage)	85	35
632	122	17½ blue (air)	1·80	80
633	122	20p. brown	1·80	80

123 Letter and Post-box

1957. International Correspondence Week.

634	123	5p. mauve (postage)	75	40
635	-	5p. green (air)	75	30

DESIGN: 5p. (air) Family writing letters.

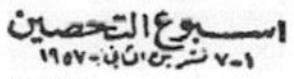

(124)

1957. National Defence Week. Optd with T **124**.

636	116	5p. mauve	20	20
637	116	20p. green	75	35

125 Scales of
Justice, Map and
Damascus
Silhouette

1957. Third Arab Lawyers Union Congress, Damascus.

638	125	12½p. green (postage)	55	35
639	125	17½p. red (air)	65	45
640	125	40p. black	1·30	80

126 Glider

1957. Air. Gliding Festival.

641	126	25p. brown	1·60	35

642	126	35p. green	2·10	60
643	126	40p. blue	3·25	1·20

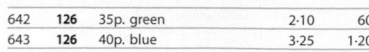

127 Torch and Map

1957. Afro-Asian Jurists' Congress, Damascus.

644	127	20p. brown (postage)	75	45
645	127	30p. green (air)	75	60
646	127	50p. violet	1·10	80

128 Khaled
Ibn el- Walid
Mosque, Homs

1957

647	128	2½p. brown	30	10

UNITED ARAB REPUBLIC

129 Telecommunications
Building

1958. Five Year Plan.

648	129	25p. blue (postage)	65	35
649	129	10p. green (air)	65	25
650	-	15p. brown	65	35

DESIGN—VERT: 15p. Telephone, radio tower and telegraph pole.

129a Union of
Egypt and Syria

1958. Birth of United Arab Republic.

651	129a	12½p. green and yellow (postage)	30	25
652	129a	17½p. brown & blue (air)	45	35

130 "Eternal Flame"

1958. 12th Anniv of Evacuation of Foreign Troops from Syria.

653	130	5p. violet & yellow (postage)	75	35
654	130	15p. red and green	1·10	80
655	-	35p. black and red (air)	1·80	80
656	-	45p. brown and blue	2·75	1·20

DESIGN: 35, 45p. Broken chain, dove and olive branch.

131 Scout fixing Tent-peg

1958. Air. Third Pan-Arab Scout Jamboree.

657	131	35p. brown	3·25	3·25
658	131	40p. blue	3·75	3·75

132 Mosque, Chimneys and Cogwheel

1958. Air. Fifth Int Fair, Damascus. Inscr "1.9.58".

659	-	25p. red	1·40	1·00
660	-	30p. green	2·10	1·50
661	**132**	45p. violet	2·40	2·00

MS661a 80×80 mm. 100p. black, red and green showing UAR flag and Fair Emblem. Imperf £160 £160

DESIGNS—HORIZ: 25p. View of Fair. VERT: 30p. Minaret, vase and emblem.

133 Bronze Rattle

1958. Ancient Syrian Art.

662	**133**	10p. green	20	15
663	-	15p. brown	30	15
664	-	20p. purple	45	20
665	-	30p. brown	55	25
666	-	40p. grey	65	35
667	-	60p. green	1·10	60
668	-	75p. blue	1·60	80
669	-	100p. purple	2·40	1·40
670	-	150p. purple	4·75	1·70

DESIGNS: 15p. Goddess of Spring; 20p. "Lamgi Mari" (statue); 30p. Mithras fighting bull; 40p. Aspasia; 60p. Minerva; 75p. Ancient gourd; 100p. Enamelled vase; 150p. Mosaic from Omayyad Mosque, Damascus.

1958. International Children's Day. Optd **R A U** and Arabic inscription.

670a	**122**	12½p. green (postage)	90·00	90·00
670b	**122**	17½p. blue (air)	70·00	70·00
670c	**122**	20p. brown	70·00	70·00

134 Cotton and Textiles

1958. Air. Aleppo Cotton Festival.

671	**134**	25p. yellow and brown	1·10	1·10
672	**134**	35p. red and brown	1·60	1·40

134a Hand holding Torch, and Iraqi Flag

1958. Republic of Iraq Commemoration.

673	**134a**	12½p. red	45	35

135 Light Airplane and Children with Model Airplane

1958. Air. Gliding Festival.

674	**135**	7½p. green	1·40	95
675	**135**	12½p. green	5·00	3·00

136 Damascus

1958. Fourth N.E. Regional Conference, Damascus.

676	**136**	12½p. green (postage)	65	35
677	**136**	17½p. violet (air)	65	60

137 U.N. Emblem and Charter

1958. Air. Tenth Anniv of Declaration of Human Rights.

678	**137**	25p. purple	55	45
679	**137**	35p. grey	75	60
680	**137**	40p. brown	1·10	80

137a U.A.R. Postal Emblem

1959. Post Day and Postal Employees' Social Fund.

681	**137a**	20p.+10p. red, black and green	1·10	1·10

137b

1959. First Anniv of United Arab Republic.

682	**137b**	12½p. red, black and green	50	35

138 Secondary School, Damascus

1959

683	**138**	12½p. green	35	25

138a "Telecommunications"

1959. Air. Arab Telecommunications Union Commemoration.

684	**138a**	40p. black and green	1·20	70

1959. Second Damascus Conference. No. 684 optd **2nd CONFERANCE DAMASCUS 1-3-1959** in English and Arabic.

685	**138a**	40p. black and green	1·30	80

139a U.A.R. and Yemeni Flags

1959. First Anniv of Proclamation of United Arab States (U.A.R. and Yemen).

686	**139a**	12½p. red and green	60	35

140 Mother with Children

1959. Arab Mothers' Day.

687	**140**	15p. red	50	35
688	**140**	25p. green	70	45

1959. Surch **U.A.R 2½p** and also in Arabic.

689	**92**	2½p. on 1p. green	25	25

142

1959. Air. 13th Anniv of Evacuation of Foreign Troops from Syria.

690	**142**	15p. green and yellow	35	25
691	**142**	35p. red and grey	85	45

DESIGN: 35p. Broken chain and flame.

143

1959. Patterns as T **143**.

692	**143**	2½p. violet	10	10
693	-	5p. brown	20	10
694	-	7½p. blue	25	10
695	-	10p. green	30	10

DESIGNS: 5 to 10p. Different styles of ornamental scrollwork.

144 "Emigration"

1959. Air. Emigrants' Congress.

696	**144**	80p. black, red and green	1·80	1·20

الجمهوريةالعربيةالمتحدة
U·A·R
(145)

1959. Optd as T **145**.

697	**115**	15p. black (postage)	70	35
698	-	50p. green (No. 536)	1·70	1·20
699	-	5p. green (No. 635) (air)	25	25
700	-	50p. purple (No. 543)	95	45
701	-	70p. violet (No. 544)	1·60	60

146 Oil Refinery

1959. Air. Inauguration of Oil Refinery.

702	**146**	50p. red, black and blue	2·75	1·00

147

1959. Sixth Damascus Fair.

703	**147**	35p. green, violet and grey	1·20	70

MS703a 80×80 mm. 30p. yellow and green showing Fair Emblem and Globe 3·00 3·00

148

1959. Air. Aleppo Cotton Festival.

704	**148**	45p. blue	95	60
705	**148**	50p. purple	95	80

149 Child and Factory

1959. Air. Children's Day.

706	**149**	25p. red, blue and lilac	70	35

150 Boys' College, Damascus

1959

707	**150**	25p. blue	95	35
708	-	35p. brown	1·30	60

DESIGN: 35p. Girls' College, Damascus.

150a "Shield against Aggression"

1959. Army Day.

709	**150a**	50p. brown	1·20	60

151 Ears of Corn, Cotton, Cogwheel and Factories

1959. Industrial and Agricultural Production Fair, Aleppo.

710	**151**	35p. brown, blue and grey	1·20	60

152 Mosque and Oaks

1959. Tree Day.

711	**152**	12½p. brown and green	50	25

153 A. R. Kawakbi

1960. 50th Death Anniv of A. R. Kawakbi (writer).

712	**153**	15p. green	50	35

153a

1960. Second Anniv of U.A.R.
713 153a 12½p. green and red 50 35

154 Diesel Train

1960. Latakia–Aleppo Railway Project.
714 154 12½p. brown, black & blue 3·50 1·30

154a Arab League Centre, Cairo

1960. Inaug of Arab League Centre, Cairo.
715 154a 12½p. black and green 50 35

1960. Mothers' Day. Optd **ARAB MOTHERS DAY 1960** in English and Arabic.
716 140 15p. red 50 35
717 140 25p. green 85 45

155a Mother, Child and Map of Palestine

1960. World Refugee Year,
718 155a 12½p. red 50 35
719 155a 50p. green 1·20 80

156 Government Building and Inscription

1960. 14th Anniv of Evacuation of Foreign Troops from Syria.
720 156 12½p. multicoloured 70 25

157 Hittin School

1960
721 157 17½p. lilac 85 35

1960. Industrial and Agricultural Production Fair, Aleppo. Optd **1960** and in Arabic.
722 151 35p. brown, blue and grey 70 60

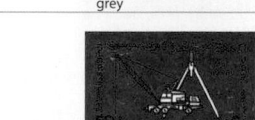

159 Mobile Crane and Compasses

1960. Air. Seventh International Damascus Fair.
723 159 50p. black, bistre and red 1·20 80
MS723a 70×160 mm. 100p. green, blue and brown (Fair emblem containing flags of all nations). Imperf 4·25 4·25

(160)

1960. Air. Aleppo Cotton Festival. Optd with T **160**.
724 148 45p. blue 95 60
725 148 50p. purple 1·20 80

161

1960. Children's Day.
726 161 35p. brown and green 1·20 70

162 Basketball

1960. Air. Olympic Games.
727 162 15p. brown, black and blue 70 25
728 - 20p. brown, black and blue 85 35
729 - 25p. multicoloured 85 35
730 - 40p. violet, pink and black 1·70 95
DESIGNS: 20p. Swimming; 25p. Fencing (Arab-style); 40p. Horse-jumping.

(163)

1960. Tree Day. Optd with T **163**.
731 152 12½p. brown and green 70 35

164 "UN" and Globe

1960. Air. 15th Anniv of U.N.O.
732 164 35p. red, green and blue 85 45
733 164 50p. blue, brown and red 1·20 70

165 Hanano

1961. Air. 25th Death Anniv (1960) of Ibrahim Hanano (patriot).
734 165 50p. green and brown 1·20 70

165a State Emblem

1961. Third Anniv of U.A.R.
735 165a 12½p. violet 50 35

166 St. Simeon's Monastery

1961
736 166 12½p. blue (postage) 35 25
746 - 200p. blue (air) 4·25 2·50
DESIGN—VERT: 200p. Entrance to St. Simeon's Monastery.

167 Raising the Flag

1961. Air. 15th Anniv of Evacuation of Foreign Troops from Syria.
737 167 40p. green 1·20 70

168 Eye and Hand "reading" Braille

1961. Air. U.N. Campaign for Welfare of Blind.
738 168 40p.+10p. black & grn 95 80

169 Palestinian and Map

1961. Air. Palestine Day.
739 169 50p. blue and black 1·20 70

170 Cogwheel and Corn

1961. Industrial and Agricultural Production Fair, Aleppo.
740 170 12½p. multicoloured 50 35

171 Abou Tammam (796–846)

1961. Air. Abou Tammam (writer) Commem.
741 171 50p. brown 95 45

172 Damascus University, Discus-thrower and Lyre

1961. Air. Fifth Universities Youth Festival.
742 172 15p. black and red 50 25
743 172 35p. violet and green 1·60 60
MS743a 100×63 mm. Nos. 742/3. Imperf 13·50 13·50

173 Open Window on World

1961. Air. Eighth International Damascus Fair.
744 173 17½p. violet and green 35 25
745 - 50p. violet and black 85 45
DESIGN: 50p. U.A.R. Pavilion.

SYRIAN ARAB REPUBLIC

175 Assembly Chamber

1961. Establishment of Syrian Arab Republic.
747 175 15p. red 50 50
748 175 35p. green 1·20 60
MS748a 80×80 mm. 50p. red, green, black and blue (Syrian flag). Imperf 6·00 6·00

176 The Noria, Hama

177 Arch of Triumph, Latakia

1961
749 176 2½p. red (postage) 20 20
750 176 5p. blue 25 20
751 - 7½p. green 40 20
752 - 10p. orange 60 20
753 177 12½p. brown 95 10
754 - 12½p. green 70 10
755 - 15p. blue 70 10
756 - 17½p. brown 1·00 15
757 - 22½p. turquoise 95 25
758 177 25p. brown 1·30 25
759 - 45p. yellow (air) 70 45
760 - 50p. red 95 60
761 - 85p. purple 1·70 70
762 - 100p. purple 2·20 80
763 - 200p. green 3·75 1·50
764 - 300p. blue 5·00 1·60
764a - 500p. purple 7·75 3·75
764b - 1000p. black 17·00 7·00
DESIGNS: 7½, 10p. Khaled ibn-el-Walid Mosque, Homs; 12½p. (No. 754), 15, 17½, 22½, 45, 50p. "The Beauty of Palmyra" (statue); 85, 100p. Archway and columns, Palmyra; 200 to 1000p. King Zahir Bibar's tomb.
See also Nos. 799/800.

178 Arab League Emblem and Headquarters, Cairo

1962. Air. Arab League Week.
765 178 17½p. turquoise and green 35 25
766 178 22½p. violet and blue 50 45
767 178 50p. brown and orange 1·30 80

179 Campaign Emblem

1962. Air. Malaria Eradication.
768 179 12½p. violet, brown & blue 50 35
769 179 50p. green, brown & yell 1·20 80

180 Prancing
Horse

1962. Air. 16th Anniv of Evacuation of Foreign Troops from Syria.

770	**180**	45p. orange and violet	70	35
771	–	55p. violet and blue	1·20	45

DESIGN: 55p. Military commander.

181 Qalb Lozah Church

1962

772	**181**	17½p. green	60	25
773	**181**	35p. green	95	35

182 Martyrs'
Memorial, Swaida

1962. Syrian Revolution Commemoration.

774	**182**	12½p. brown and drab	35	10
775	**182**	35p. green and turquoise	85	35

183 Jupiter
Temple Gate

1962

776	**183**	2½p. turquoise	25	10
777	**183**	5p. brown	35	10
778	**183**	7½p. brown	50	15
779	**183**	10p. purple	35	15

184 Globe,
Monument to
Hejaz Railway and
Handclasp

1962. Air. Ninth International Fair, Damascus.

780	**184**	17½p. brown and purple	35	25
781	**184**	22½p. mauve and red	50	35
782	–	40p. purple and brown	60	45
783	–	45p. blue and green	1·20	60

DESIGN: 40, 45p. Fair entrance.

185 Festival
Emblem

1962. Air. Aleppo Cotton Festival.

784	**185**	12½p. multicoloured	50	30
785	**185**	50p. multicoloured	95	70

See also Nos. 820/1.

186 Pres. Kudsi

1962. Presidential Elections.

786	**186**	12½p. brown and blue (postage)	50	10
787	**186**	50p. blue and buff (air)	95	60

187 Zenobia

1962. Air.

788	**187**	45p. violet	1·80	60
789	**187**	50p. red	1·80	60
790	**187**	85p. green	1·80	80
791	**187**	100p. purple	2·10	1·20

See also Nos. 801/4.

188 Saadallah
el-Jabiri

1962. Air. 15th Death Anniv of Saadallah el-Jabiri (revolutionary).

792	**188**	50p. blue	70	45

189 Moharde
Woman

1962. Air. Women in Regional Costumes. Multicoloured.

793	40p. Marje Sultan		70	60
794	45p. Kalamoun		85	65
795	50p. Type **189**		95	70
796	55p. Jabal al-Arab		1·20	80
797	60p. Afrine		1·30	85
798	65p. Hauran		1·80	1·20

1963. As previous designs but size 20×26 mm.

799	–	2½p. violet	25	10
800	–	5p. purple	30	10
801	**187**	7½p. grey	50	10
802	**187**	10p. brown	95	15
803	**187**	12½p. blue	1·40	20
804	**187**	15p. brown	2·40	25

DESIGN: Nos. 799/800, "The Beauty of Palmyra" (statue).

190 Ears of
Wheat, Hand and
Globe

1963. Freedom from Hunger.

805	**190**	12½p. black & bl (postage)	35	25
806	–	50p. black and red (air)	70	35

MS806a 90×65 mm. Nos. 805/6.   3·00   3·00

DESIGN: 50p. Bird feeding young in nest.

191 Faris el-Khouri   **192** S.A.R. Emblem
(politician)

1963. Air. 17th Anniv of Evacuation of Foreign Troops from Syria.

807	**191**	17½p. brown	50	25
808	**192**	22½p. green and black	70	35

193 Eagle

1963. Air. Baathist Revolution Commemoration.

809	**193**	12½p. green	25	25
810	**193**	50p. mauve	85	45

194 Ala el-Ma'ari
(bust)

1963. Air. 990th Birth Anniv of Ala el-Ma'ari (poet).

811	**194**	50p. violet	85	70

195 Copper Water
Jug

1963. Air. Tenth International Fair, Damascus.

812	**195**	37½p. multicoloured	85	45
813	**195**	50p. multicoloured	1·10	60

196 Central Bank

1963. Damascus Buildings.

814	–	17½p. violet	1·80	45
815	–	22½p. violet	50	35
816	**196**	25p. brown	35	25
817	–	35p. purple	60	35

BUILDINGS: 17½p. Hejaz Railway Station; 22½p. Mouassat Hospital; 35p. Post Office, Al-Jalaa.

197 "Red
Crescent" and
Centenary
Emblem

1963. Air. Red Cross Centenary. Crescent in red.

818	**197**	15p. black and blue	50	35
819	–	50p. black and green	95	60

DESIGN: 50p. "Red Crescent", globe and centenary emblem.

1963. Aleppo Cotton Festival. As T **185** but inscr "POSTAGE" and "1963" in place of "AIRMAIL" and "1962".

820	**185**	17½p. multicoloured	35	25
821	**185**	22½p. multicoloured	60	35

198 Child with
Ball

1963. Children's Day.

822	**198**	12½p. green and deep green	25	25
823	**198**	22½p. green and red	60	30

199 Firas
el-Hamadani

1963. Air. Death Millenary of Abou Firas el-Hamadani (poet).

824	**199**	50p. brown and bistre	85	70

200 Flame on
Head

1963. Air. 15th Anniv of Declaration of Human Rights. Flame in red.

825	**200**	17½p. black and grey	25	20
826	**200**	22½p. black and green	60	25
827	**200**	50p. black and violet	85	60

MS827a 110×70 mm. Nos. 825/7.
Imperf   2·40   2·40

201 Emblem and Flag

1964. Air. First Anniv of Baathist Revolution of 8 March 1963. Emblem and flag in red, black and green; inscr in black.

828	**201**	15p. green	25	15
829	**201**	17½p. pink	35	25
830	**201**	22½p. grey	60	35

202 Ugharit   **203** Chahba, Thalassa,
Princess   Mosaic

1964

831	**202**	2½p. grey (postage)	10	10
832	**202**	5p. brown	10	10
833	**202**	7½p. purple	10	10
834	**202**	10p. green	20	10
835	**202**	12½p. violet	25	15
836	**202**	17½p. blue	35	20
837	**202**	20p. red	70	25
838	**202**	25p. orange	1·20	30
839	**203**	27½p. red (air)	35	20
840	**203**	45p. brown	70	25
841	**203**	50p. green	95	30
842	**203**	55p. green	1·00	35
843	**203**	60p. blue	1·20	45

204 Kaaba, Mecca, and
Mosque, Damascus

1964. Air. First Arab Moslem Wakf Ministers' Conference.

844	**204**	12½p. black and blue	25	10
845	**204**	22½p. black and purple	35	25
846	**204**	50p. black and green	85	60

1964. Air. 18th Anniv of Evacuation of Foreign Troops from Syria. As T **99** but larger, 38½×26 mm. Inscr "1964".

847	**99**	20p. brown	25	25
848	**99**	25p. purple	35	35
849	**99**	60p. green	85	60

205 Abou al
Zahrawi

1964. Air. Fourth Arab Dental and Oral Surgery Congress, Damascus.

850	205	60p. brown	95	70

206 Bronze Chimes

1964. Air. 11th International Fair, Damascus.

851	206	20p. multicoloured	70	25
852	-	25p. multicoloured	85	35

DESIGN: 25p. Fair emblem.

207 Cotton Plant and Symbols 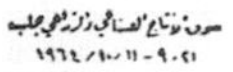   **(208)**

1964. Air. Aleppo Cotton Festival. No. 854 is optd with T **208**.

853	207	25p. multicoloured	60	35
854	207	25p. multicoloured	60	35

209 Aero Club Emblem

1964. Air. Tenth Anniv of Syrian Aero Club.

855	209	12½p. black and green	35	10
856	209	17½p. black and red	50	20
857	209	20p. black and blue	1·20	25

210 A.P.U. Emblem

1964. Air. Tenth Anniv of Arab Postal Union's Permanent Office, Cairo.

858	210	12½p. black and orange	25	10
859	210	20p. black and green	35	20
860	210	25p. black and mauve	50	25

211 Book within Hands

1964. Air. Burning of Algiers Library.

861	211	12½p. black and green	25	10
862	211	17½p. black and red	35	20
863	211	20p. black and blue	50	25

212 Tennis

1965. Air. Olympic Games, Tokyo. Multicoloured.

864	12½p. Type **212**		25	15
865	17½p. Wrestling		60	20
866	20p. Weightlifting		70	25
MS866a	90×57 mm. 100p. Wrestlers and drummer. Imperf		3·50	3·50

213 Flag, Map and Revolutionaries

1965. Second Anniv of Baathist Revolution of 8 March 1963.

867	213	12½p. multicoloured	25	15
868	213	17½p. multicoloured	35	20
869	213	20p. multicoloured	50	25

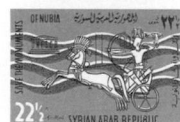

214 Rameses II in War Chariot, Abu Simbel

1965. Air. Nubian Monuments Preservation.

870	214	22½p. black, blue and green	50	25
871	-	50p. black, green and blue	95	45

DESIGN: 50p. Heads of Rameses II.

215 Weather Instruments and Map

1965. World Meteorological Day.

872	215	12½p. black and purple	25	15
873	215	27½p. black and blue	50	35

216 Al-Radi

1965. Air. 950th Death Anniv of Al-Sharif al-Radi (writer).

874	216	50p. black	95	60

217 Evacuation Symbol

1965. 19th Anniv of Evacuation of Foreign Troops from Syria.

875	217	12½p. green and blue	25	15
876	217	27½p. lilac and red	50	25

218 Hippocrates and Avicenna

1965. Air. "Medical Days of the Near and Middle East".

877	218	60p. black and green	1·20	80

219 Dagger on Deir Yassin, Palestine

1965. Air. Deir Yassin Massacre on 9 April 1948.

878	219	12½p. multicoloured	35	15
879	219	60p. multicoloured	85	45

220 I.T.U. Emblem and Symbols

1965. Air. Centenary of I.T.U.

880	220	12½p. multicoloured	35	20
881	220	27½p. multicoloured	70	25
882	220	60p. multicoloured	1·30	80

221 Arab Family, Flags and Map

1965. Palestine Week.

883	221	12½p.+5p. multicoloured	35	30
884	221	25p.+5p. multicoloured	40	35

222 Hands holding Hoe and Pick

1965. Peasants' Union.

885	222	2½p. green	10	10
886	222	12½p. violet	20	10
887	222	15p. purple	25	10

The above stamps are inscr "RERUBLIC" for "RFPUBLIC".

223 Welcoming Emigrant

1965. Air "Welcome Arab Emigrants".

888	223	25p. multicoloured	35	25
889	223	100p. multicoloured	1·60	95

224 Fair Entrance

1965. Air. 12th Int Fair, Damascus. Multicoloured.

890	12½p. Type **224**		10	10
891	27½p. Globe and compasses		50	25
892	60p. Syrian brassware		85	60

1965. Air. Aleppo Industrial and Agricultural Production Fair. Optd **INDUSTRIAL & AGRICULTURAL PRODUCTION FAIR-ALEPPO 1965** in English and Arabic.

893	226	25p. multicoloured	70	25

226 Cotton Boll and Shuttles

1965. Air. Aleppo Cotton Festival.

894	226	25p. multicoloured	70	25

227 I.C.Y. Emblem and View of Damascus

1965. Air. International Co-operation Year.

895	227	25p. multicoloured	70	25

228 Arabs, Torch and Map

1965. National Revolution Council.

896	228	12½p. multicoloured	25	20
897	228	25p. multicoloured	60	25

229 Industrial Workers

1966. Labour Unions.

898	229	12½p. blue	10	10
899	229	15p. red	25	15
900	229	20p. lilac	35	20
901	229	25p. brown	50	25

230 Radio Aerial, Globe and Flag

1966. Air. Arab Information Ministers' Conf, Damascus.

902	230	25p. multicoloured	35	25
903	230	60p. multicoloured	85	60

231 Dove-shaped Hand holding Flower

1966. Air. Third Anniv of Baathist Revolution of 8 March 1963. Multicoloured.

904	12½p. Type **231**		10	10
905	17½p. Revolutionaries (horiz)		25	15
906	50p. Type **231**		1·60	60

232 Colossi, Abu Simbel

1966. Air. Nubian Monuments Preservation Week.

907	232	25p. blue	50	25
908	232	60p. grey	95	35

233 Roman Lamp

1966

909	233	2½p. green	10	10
910	233	5p. purple	35	25
911	-	7½p. brown	25	15
912	-	10p. violet	25	15

DESIGN: 7½, 10p. 12th-century Islamic vessel.

234 U.N. Emblem and Headquarters

1966. Air. 20th Anniv of U.N.O.

913	**234**	25p. black and grey	25	25
914	**234**	50p. black and green	70	60
MS915	90×70 mm. **235** 100p. yellow, blue and black. Imperf		2·40	2·40

236 "Evacuation" (abstract)

1966. 20th Anniv of Evacuation of Foreign Troops from Syria.

916	**236**	12½p. multicoloured	25	10
917	**236**	27½p. multicoloured	50	35

237 Workers marching across Globe

1966. Air. Labour Day.

918	**237**	60p. multicoloured	85	60

238 W.H.O. Building

1966. Air. Inauguration of W.H.O. Headquarters, Geneva.

919	**238**	60p. black, blue and yellow	70	35

239 Traffic Signals and Map on Hand

1966. Air. Traffic Day.

920	**239**	25p. multicoloured	50	25

240 Astarte and Tyche (wrongly inscr "ASTRATE")

1966. Air.

921	**240**	50p. brown	70	35
922	**240**	60p. grey	1·20	60

241 Fair Emblem

1966. Air. 13th International Fair, Damascus.

923	**241**	12½p. multicoloured	25	10
924	**241**	60p. multicoloured	85	70

242 Shuttle (stylized)

1966. Air. Aleppo Cotton Festival.

925	**242**	50p. black, red and grey	85	60

243 Decade Emblem

1966. Air. International Hydrological Decade.

926	**243**	12½p. black, orange & green	25	10
927	**243**	60p. black, orange and blue	95	45

244 Emir Abd-el-Kader

1966. Air. Return of Emir Abd-el-Kader's Remains to Algiers.

928	**244**	12½p. black and green	50	15
929	**244**	50p. brown and green	70	45

245 U.N.R.W.A. Emblem

1966. Air. 21st Anniv of U.N. Day and Refugee Week.

930	**245**	12½p.+2½p. black and blue	25	25
931	**245**	50p.+5p. black and green	85	85

246 Handclasp and Map

1967. Air. Solidarity Congress, Damascus.

932	**246**	20p. multicoloured	35	20
933	**246**	25p. multicoloured	50	25

247 Doves and Oil Pipelines

1967. Air. Fourth Anniv of Baathist Revolution of 8 March 1963.

934	**247**	17½p. multicoloured	35	20
935	**247**	25p. multicoloured	50	25
936	**247**	27½p. multicoloured	70	35

248 Soldier and Citizens with Banner

1967. Air. 21st Anniv of Evacuation of Foreign Troops from Syria.

937	**248**	17½p. green	25	15
938	**248**	25p. purple	35	20
939	**248**	27½p. blue	50	25

249 Workers' Monument, Damascus

1967. Air. Labour Day.

940	**249**	12½p. turquoise	25	10
941	**249**	50p. mauve	85	60

250 Core Bust    **251** "African Woman" (vase)    **252** Head of a Young Man from Amrith

1967.

942	**250**	2½p. green (postage)	10	10
943	**250**	5p. red	10	10
944	**250**	10p. blue	20	10
945	**250**	12½p. brown	25	15
946	**251**	15p. purple	30	20
947	**251**	20p. blue	35	20
948	**251**	25p. green	40	25
949	**251**	27½p. blue	50	30
950	**252**	45p. red (air)	60	35
951	**252**	50p. mauve	85	40
952	**252**	60p. green	95	60
953	–	100p. green	1·20	70
954	–	500p. red	6·00	3·75

DESIGN—VERT: 100, 500p. Bust of Princess (2nd-century bronze).

253 Flags and Fair Entrance

1967. Air. 14th International Damascus Fair.

955	**253**	12½p. multicoloured	25	10
956	**253**	60p. multicoloured	85	60

254 Statue of Ur-Nina and Tourist Emblem

1967. Air. International Tourist Year.

957	**254**	12½p. purple, black & blue	25	15
958	**254**	25p. red, black and blue	30	20
959	**254**	27½p. blue, black & lt blue	50	25
MS960	105×80 mm. **254** 60p. blue, black and light blue. Imperf		2·20	2·20

255 Cotton Boll and Cogwheel

1967. Air. Aleppo Cotton Festival.

961	**255**	12½p. black, brown and yellow	25	15
962	**255**	60p. black, brown and yellow	85	60

1967. Air. Industrial and Agricultural Production Fair, Aleppo. Optd **INDUSTRIAL & AGRICULTURAL PRODUCTION FAIR ALEPPO 1967** in English and Arabic.

963	**255**	12½p. black, brown & yellow	25	15
964	**255**	60p. black, brown & yell	85	60

257 Ibn el-Naphis (scientist)

1967. Air. Sciences Week.

965	**257**	12½p. red and green	25	20
966	**257**	27½p. mauve and blue	70	25

258 Acclaiming Human Rights

1968. Air. Human Rights Year.

967	**258**	12½p. black, turquoise and blue	25	15
968	**258**	60p. black, red and pink	85	70
MS969	105×80 mm. 100p. multicoloured (Human Rights emblem and outlines of faces). Imperf		1·80	1·80

259 Learning to Read

1968. Air. Literacy Campaign.

970	**259**	12½p. multicoloured	10	10
971	–	17½p. multicoloured	25	15
972	**259**	25p. multicoloured	50	20
973	–	45p. multicoloured	70	45

DESIGN: 17½, 45p. Flaming torch and open book.

260 "The Arab Revolutionary" (Damascus statue)

1968. Fifth Anniv of Baathist Revolution of 8 March 1963.

974	**260**	12½p. brown, yellow & black	25	15
975	**260**	25p. mauve, pink and black	60	25
976	**260**	27½p. green, light green and black	65	35

261 Map of North Africa and Arabia

1968. 21st Anniv of Baath Arab Socialist Party.

977	**261**	12½p. multicoloured	25	15
978	**261**	60p. multicoloured	85	60

262 Euphrates Dam

1968. Air. Euphrates Dam Project.

979	262	12½p. multicoloured	25	15
980	262	17½p. multicoloured	35	20
981	262	25p. multicoloured	85	55

263 Hands holding Spanner, Rifle and Torch

1968. "Mobilisation Efforts".

982	263	12½p. multicoloured	10	10
983	263	17½p. multicoloured	25	20
984	263	25p. multicoloured	50	25

264 Railway Track and Sun

1968. 22nd Anniv of Evacuation of Foreign Troops from Syria.

985	264	12½p. multicoloured	95	25
986	264	27½p. multicoloured	2·40	35

265 Oil Pipeline Map

1968. Syrian Oil Exploration.

987	265	12½p. blue, green and light green	35	15
988	265	17½p. blue, brown and pink	85	25

266 Torch, Map and Laurel

1968. Palestine Day.

989	266	12½p. multicoloured	25	10
990	266	25p. multicoloured	35	20
991	266	27½p. multicoloured	50	25

267 Refugee Family

1968. Red Crescent Refugees Fund.

992	267	12½p.+2½p. black, purple and blue	60	60
993	267	27½p.+7½p. black, red and violet	60	60

268 Avenzoar (physician) and W.H.O. Emblem

1968. Air. 20th Anniv of W.H.O.

994	268	12½p. multicoloured	25	10
995	-	25p. multicoloured	35	25
996	-	60p. multicoloured	85	60

DESIGNS—As Type **268**, but with different portraits of Arab physicians: 25p. Razi; 60p. Jabir.

269 Ear of Corn, Cogwheel and Saracen Gate, Aleppo Citadel

1968. Industrial and Agricultural Production Fair, Aleppo.

997	269	12½p. multicoloured	25	15
998	269	27½p. multicoloured	35	25

270 Emblems of Fair, Agriculture and Industry

1968. 15th International Damascus Fair.

999	270	12½p. black, green & brown	10	10
1000	-	27½p. multicoloured	50	25
1001	270	60p. black, orange & blue	85	60

DESIGN—HORIZ: 27½p. Flag, hand with torch and emblems.

271 Gathering Cotton

1968. Aleppo Cotton Festival.

1002	271	12½p. multicoloured	25	20
1003	271	27½p. multicoloured	35	25

272 Monastery of St. Simeon the Stylite

1968. Air. Ancient Monuments (1st series).

1004	272	15p. multicoloured	10	10
1005	-	17½p. deep brown, brown and chocolate	25	15
1006	-	22½p. multicoloured	30	25
1007	-	45p. multicoloured	60	45
1008	-	50p. brown, sepia and blue	70	60

DESIGNS—VERT: 17½p. El Tekkieh Mosque, Damascus; 22½p. Temple columns, Palmyra. HORIZ: 45p. Chapel of St. Paul, Bab Kisan; 50p. Amphitheatre, Bosra.
See also Nos. 1026/30.

273 Oil Derrick

1968

1009	273	2½p. green and blue	10	10
1010	273	5p. blue and green	10	10
1011	273	7½p. blue and green	20	10
1012	273	10p. green and yellow	20	10
1013	273	12½p. red and yellow	25	15
1014	273	15p. brown and bistre	35	20
1015	273	27½p. brown and orange	50	25

274 Al-Jahez (scientist)

1968. Ninth Science Week.

1016	274	12½p. black and green	30	25
1017	274	27½p. black and grey	70	35

275 Throwing the Hammer

1968. Air. Olympic Games, Mexico.

1018	275	12½p. black, mauve and green	25	20
1019	-	25p. black, red and green	35	25
1020	-	27½p. black, grey and green	50	35
1021	-	60p. multicoloured	70	45

MS1022 105×80 mm. 50p. multicoloured. Imperf — 3·50 3·50

DESIGNS—VERT: 25p. Throwing the discus; 27½p. Running; 60p. Basketball. HORIZ (53×36 mm)—50p. Polo.

276 Aerial View of Airport

1969. Air. Construction of Damascus Int Airport.

1023	276	12½p. green, blue & yellow	25	15
1024	276	17½p. violet, red and green	60	25
1025	276	60p. black, mauve and yellow	1·60	45

277 Baal-Shamin Temple, Palmyra

1969. Air. Ancient Monuments (2nd series). Multicoloured.

1026	277	25p. Type **277**	35	25
1027		45p. Omayyad Mosque, Damascus	55	35
1028		50p. Amphitheatre, Palmyra	60	45
1029		60p. Khaled ibn el-Walid Mosque, Homs (vert)	70	50
1030		100p. St. Simeon's Column, Jebel Samaan	1·20	95

278 "Sun" and Clenched Fists in Broken Handcuffs

1969. Sixth Anniv of Baathist Revolution of 8 March 1963.

1031	278	12½p. multicoloured	25	15
1032	278	25p. multicoloured	50	20
1033	278	27½p. multicoloured	55	25

279 "Sun of Freedom"

1969. Fifth Youth Festival, Homs.

1034	279	12½p. red, yellow and blue	25	20
1035	279	25p. red, yellow and green	35	25

280 Symbols of Progress

1969. 23rd Anniv of Evacuation of Foreign Troops from Syria.

1036	280	12½p. multicoloured	25	20
1037	280	27½p. multicoloured	35	25

281 "Workers", Cogwheel and I.L.O. Emblem

1969. Air. 50th Anniv of I.L.O.

1038	281	12½p. multicoloured	25	20
1039	281	27½p. multicoloured	50	25

MS1040 76×54 mm. 60p. multicoloured — 2·40 2·40

DESIGN: Larger (54×37 mm)—60p. ILO emblem.

282 Russian Dancers

1969. Air. 16th Int Damascus Fair. Multicoloured.

1041		12½p. Type **282**	25	10
1042		27½p. Ballet dancers	60	25
1043		45p. Lebanese dancers	70	45
1044		55p. Egyptian dancers	85	50
1045		60p. Bulgarian dancers	1·20	70

283 "Fortune" (statue)

1969. Air. Ninth International Archaeological Congress, Damascus. Multicoloured.

1046	283	17½p. Type **283**	35	20
1047		45p. "Agriculture" (statue)	60	25
1048		60p. "Motherhood" (statue)	1·20	35

284 Children dancing

1969. Air. Children's Day.

1049	284	12½p. green, blue and turquoise	25	15
1050	284	25p. violet, blue and red	35	20
1051	284	27½p. grey, dp blue & blue	50	25

285 Mahatma Gandhi

1969. Birth Centenary of Mahatma Gandhi.

1052	285	12½p. brown and buff	25	20
1053	285	27½p. green and yellow	35	25

286 Cotton

1969. Aleppo Cotton Festival.

1054	286	12½p. multicoloured	10	10
1055	286	17½p. multicoloured	25	20
1056	286	25p. multicoloured	35	25

287 "Arab World" (6th Arab Science Congress)

1969. Tenth Science Week.

1057	**287**	12½p. blue and green	35	15
1058	-	25p. violet and pink	35	25
1059	-	27½p. brown and green	70	60

DESIGNS: 25p. Arab Academy (50th anniv); 27½p. Damascus University (50th anniv of Faculty of Medicine).

288 Cockerel

1969. Air. Damascus Agricultural Museum. Multicoloured.

1060	12½p. Type **288**	25	15
1061	17½p. Cow	35	20
1062	20p. Maize	50	25
1063	50p. Olives	70	35

289 Rising Sun, Hand and Book

1970. Seventh Anniv of Baathist Revolution of 8 March 1963.

1064	**289**	17½p. black, brown & blue	25	20
1065	**289**	25p. black, blue and red	35	25
1066	**289**	27½p. black, brown & green	70	35

290 Map of Arab World, League Emblem and Flag

1970. Silver Jubilee of Arab League.

1067	**290**	12½p. multicoloured	25	20
1068	**290**	25p. multicoloured	35	25
1069	**290**	27½p. multicoloured	70	35

291 Dish Aerial and Hand on Book

1970. Air. World Meteorological Day.

1070	**291**	25p. black, yellow & green	85	25
1071	**291**	60p. black, yellow & blue	1·30	80

292 Lenin

1970. Air. Birth Centenary of Lenin.

1072	**292**	15p. brown and red	25	15
1073	**292**	60p. green and red	95	70

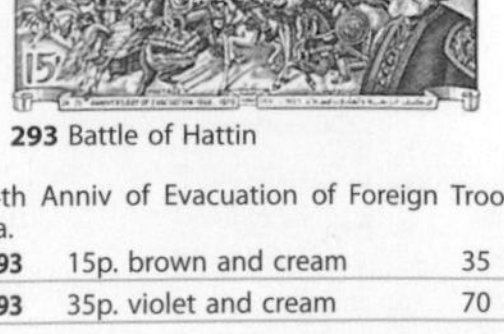

293 Battle of Hattin

1970. 24th Anniv of Evacuation of Foreign Troops from Syria.

1074	**293**	15p. brown and cream	35	25
1075	**293**	35p. violet and cream	70	35

294 Emblem of Workers' Syndicate

1970. Air. Labour Day.

1076	**294**	15p. brown and green	25	15
1077	**294**	60p. brown and orange	1·20	80

295 Young Syrians and Map

1970. Revolution's Youth Union, 1st Youth Week.

1078	**295**	15p. green and brown	10	10
1079	**295**	25p. brown and ochre	35	35

This issue is inscr "YOUTH'S FIRST WEAK" in error.

296 Refugee Family

1970. World Arab Refugee Week.

1080	**296**	15p. multicoloured	30	25
1081	**296**	25p. multicoloured	60	25
1082	**296**	35p. multicoloured	65	35

297 Dish Aerial and Open Book

1970. Air. World Telecommunications Day.

1083	**297**	15p. black and lilac	30	25
1084	**297**	60p. black and blue	1·20	80

298 New U.P.U. Headquarters Building

1970. Air. New U.P.U. Headquarters Building.

1085	**298**	15p. multicoloured	20	10
1086	**298**	60p. multicoloured	95	70

299 "Industry" and Graph

300 Khaled ibn el-Walid

1970

1087	**299**	2½p. red and brown (postage)	20	10
1088	**299**	5p. blue and orange	25	25
1089	**299**	7½p. grey and purple	20	10
1090	**299**	10p. brown and light brown	20	10
1091	**299**	12½p. red and blue	20	10
1092	**299**	15p. mauve and green	25	15
1093	**299**	20p. brown and blue	25	15
1094	**299**	22½p. green and brown	30	20
1095	**299**	25p. blue and grey	35	25
1096	**299**	27½p. brown and green	40	30
1097	**299**	35p. green and red	50	35
1098	**300**	45p. mauve (air)	60	25
1099	**300**	50p. green	70	35
1100	**300**	60p. brown	95	45
1101	**300**	100p. blue	1·30	60
1102	**300**	200p. green	2·40	1·30
1103	**300**	300p. violet	3·50	2·30
1104	**300**	500p. grey	6·00	4·75

301 Medieval Warriors

1970. Air. Folk Tales and Legends.

1105	**301**	5p. multicoloured	20	20
1106	-	10p. multicoloured	25	20
1107	-	15p. multicoloured	30	25
1108	-	20p. multicoloured	40	35
1109	-	60p. multicoloured	95	80

Nos. 1106/9 show horsemen similar to Type **301**.

302 Cotton

1970. Aleppo Agricultural and Industrial Fair. Multicoloured.

1110	5p. Type **302**	20	20
1111	10p. Tomatoes	25	20
1112	15p. Tobacco	30	20
1113	20p. Sugar beet	35	25
1114	35p. Wheat	70	60

303 Mosque in Flames

1970. Air. First Anniv of Burning of Al-Aqsa Mosque, Jerusalem.

1115	**303**	15p. multicoloured	30	25
1116	**303**	60p. multicoloured	95	45

304 Wood-carving

1970. Air. 17th Damascus Int Fair. Multicoloured.

1117	15p. Type **304**	25	20
1118	20p. Jewellery	30	25
1119	25p. Glass-making	35	30
1120	30p. Copper-engraving	70	35
1121	60p. Shell-work	1·60	60

305 Scout, Encampment and Badge

1970. Pan-Arab Scout Jamboree, Damascus.

1122	**305**	15p. green	50	25

306 Olive Tree and Emblem

1970. World Year of Olive-oil Production.

1123	**306**	15p. multicoloured	25	15
1124	**306**	25p. multicoloured	60	25

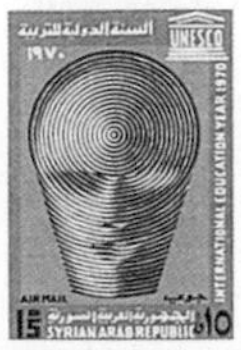

307 I.E.Y. Emblem

1970. Air. International Education Year.

1125	**307**	15p. brown, green & black	30	25
1126	**307**	60p. brown, blue & black	1·20	80

308 U.N. Emblems

1970. Air. 25th Anniv of U.N.O.

1127	**308**	15p. multicoloured	30	25
1128	**308**	60p. multicoloured	1·20	80

309 Protective Shield

1971. Eighth Anniv of Baathist Revolution of 8 March 1963.

1129	**309**	15p. blue, yellow & green	20	10
1130	**309**	22½p. green, yellow & brown	30	25
1131	**309**	27½p. brown, yellow & blue	50	35

310 Girl holding Garland

1971. Air. 25th Anniv of Evacuation of Foreign Troops from Syria.

1132	**310**	15p. multicoloured	25	15
1133	**310**	60p. multicoloured	85	45

311 Globe and World Races

1971. Air. Racial Equality Year.

1134	**311**	15p. multicoloured	20	10
1135	**311**	60p. multicoloured	85	60

312 Soldier, Worker and Labour Emblems

1971. Labour Day.

1136	**312**	15p. purple, blue & yell	25	20
1137	**312**	25p. deep blue, blue and yellow	50	25

313 Hailing Traffic

1971. World Traffic Day.

1138	**313**	15p. red, blue and black	25	10
1139	-	25p. multicoloured	35	25
1140	**313**	45p. red, yellow and black	70	45

DESIGN—VERT: 25p. Traffic signs and signal lights.

314 Cotton, Cogwheel and Factories

1971. Aleppo Agricultural and Industrial Fair.

1141	**314**	15p. black, blue and green	25	15
1142	**314**	30p. black, scarlet and red	55	45

315 A.P.U. Emblem

1971. 25th Anniv of Sofar Conference and Founding of Arab Postal Union.

1143	**315**	15p. multicoloured	30	25
1144	**315**	20p. multicoloured	60	30

316 Peppers and Fertilizer Plant

1971. 18th Damascus International Fair. Industries. Multicoloured.

1145	5p. Type **316**		10	10
1146	15p. TV set and telephone ("Electronics")		15	10
1147	35p. Oil lamp and dish ("Glassware")		70	45
1148	50p. Part of carpet ("Carpets")		1·20	70

317 Flag and Federation Map

1971. Arab Federation Referendum.

1149	**317**	15p. green, black and red	25	10

318 Pres. Hafez al-Assad and People's Council Chamber

1971. Air. People's Council and Presidential Election.

1150	**318**	15p. multicoloured	30	25
1151	**318**	65p. multicoloured	1·20	70

319 Pres. Nasser

1971. Air. First Death Anniv of Pres. Nasser of Egypt.

1152	**319**	15p. brown and green	25	10
1153	**319**	20p. brown and grey	60	25

320 "Telstar" and Dish Aerial

1971. 25th Anniv of UNESCO.

1154	**320**	15p. multicoloured	25	10
1155	**320**	50p. multicoloured	70	45

321 Flaming Torch

1971. "Movement of 16 November 1970".

1156	**321**	15p. multicoloured	10	10
1157	**321**	20p. multicoloured	35	30

322 Quill-pen and Open Book

1971. Eighth Writers' Congress.

1158	**322**	15p. brown, orange and green	25	10

323 Children with Ball

1971. 25th Anniv of UNICEF.

1159	**323**	15p. red, blue and deep blue	25	10
1160	**323**	25p. brown, green & blue	50	35

324 Book Year Emblem

1972. International Book Year.

1161	**324**	15p. violet, blue & brown	25	10
1162	**324**	20p. green, light green and brown	50	35

325 Emblems of Reconstruction

1972. Ninth Anniv of Baathist Revolution of 8 March 1963.

1163	**325**	15p. violet and green	10	10
1164	**325**	20p. red and bistre	35	25

326 Baath Party Emblem

1972. 25th Anniv of Baath Party.

1165	**326**	15p. multicoloured	10	10
1166	**326**	20p. multicoloured	35	25

327 Eagle, Factory Chimneys and Rifles

1972. First Anniv of Arab Republics Federation.

1167	**327**	15p. gold, black and red	35	10

328 Flowers and Broken Chain

1972. 26th Anniv of Evacuation of Foreign Troops from Syria.

1168	**328**	15p. grey and red	25	10
1169	**328**	50p. grey and green	70	45

329 Hand with Spanner

1972. Labour Day.

1170	**329**	15p. multicoloured	30	25
1171	**329**	50p. multicoloured	95	80

330 Telecommunications Emblem

1972. Air. World Telecommunications Day.

1172	**330**	15p. multicoloured	25	10
1173	**330**	50p. multicoloured	95	35

331 Environment Emblem

1972. United Nations Environmental Conservation Conference, Stockholm.

1174	**331**	15p. blue, azure and pink	25	10
1175	**331**	50p. purple, orange & yellow	95	45

332 Discus, Football and Swimming

333 Horsemen

1972. Olympic Games, Munich.

1176	**332**	15p. violet, black & bistre	35	25
1177	-	60p. orange, black & blue	1·20	70
MS1178		100×81 mm. **333** 75p. multi-coloured. Imperf	3·00	3·00

DESIGN: 60p. Running, gymnastics and fencing.

334 Dove and Factory

1972. Aleppo Agricultural and Industrial Fair.

1179	**334**	15p. multicoloured	25	10
1180	**334**	20p. multicoloured	35	25

335 President Hafez al-Assad

1972. Air.

1181	**335**	100p. green	1·80	80
1182	**335**	500p. brown	8·50	3·50

336 Women's Dance

1972. 19th Damascus International Fair. Multicoloured.

1183	**336**	15p. Type **336**	25	10
1184		20p. Tambourine dance	30	25
1185		50p. Men's drum dance	95	45

337 Airline Emblem

1972. Air. 25th Anniv of "Syrianair" Airline.

1186	**337**	15p. blue, light blue and black	35	15
1187	**337**	50p. blue, grey and black	1·10	35

338 Emblem of Revolution

1973. Tenth Anniv of Baathist Revolution of 8 March 1963.

1188	**338**	15p. green, red and black	10	10
1189	**338**	20p. orange, red & black	25	15
1190	**338**	25p. blue, red and black	35	25

339 Human Heart

1973. 25th Anniv of W.H.O.

1191	**339**	15p. blue, purple and grey	25	10
1192	**339**	20p. blue, purple & brn	70	35

340 Emblems of Agriculture and Industry

1973. 27th Anniv of Evacuation of Foreign Troops from Syria.

1193	**340**	15p. multicoloured	25	10
1194	**340**	20p. multicoloured	30	15

341 Globe and Workers

1973. Labour Day.

1195	**341**	15p. black, purple and stone	10	10
1196	**341**	50p. black, blue and buff	70	45

342 Family and Emblems

1973. Tenth Anniv of World Food Programme.

1197	**342**	15p. red and green	25	10
1198	**342**	50p. blue and lilac	85	45

343 Three Heads

1973

1199	**343**	2½p. green	10	10
1200	**343**	5p. orange	10	10
1201	-	7½p. brown	20	10
1202	-	10p. red	20	10
1203	**343**	15p. blue	25	15
1204	-	25p. blue	30	20
1205	-	35p. blue	35	25
1206	-	55p. green	50	30
1207	-	70p. purple	70	35

DESIGNS—HORIZ: 7½, 10, 55p. As Type **343** but with one head above the other two. VERT: 25, 35, 70p. Similar to Type **343**, but with heads in vertical arrangement.

344 Stock

1973. Int Flower Show, Damascus. Multicoloured.

1208	5p. Type **344**	25	20
1209	10p. Gardenia	30	20
1210	15p. Jasmine	35	20
1211	20p. Rose	40	20
1212	25p. Narcissus	50	25

345 Cogs and Flowers

1973. Aleppo Agricultural and Industrial Fair.

1213	**345**	15p. multicoloured	25	10

346 Euphrates Dam

1973. Euphrates Dam Project. Diversion of the River.

1214	**346**	15p. multicoloured	35	25
1215	**346**	50p. multicoloured	70	35

347 Deir Ezzor Costume

1973. 20th Damascus International Fair. Costumes. Multicoloured.

1216	5p. Type **347**	20	20
1217	10p. Hassake	20	20
1218	20p. As Sahel	30	25
1219	25p. Zakie	50	30
1220	50p. Sarakeb	70	35

348 Anniversary Emblem

1973. 25th Anniv of Declaration of Human Rights.

1221	**348**	15p. black, red and green	10	10
1222	**348**	50p. black, red and blue	60	35

349 Citadel of Ja'abar

1973. "Save the Euphrates Monuments" Campaign. Multicoloured.

1223	10p. Type **349**	20	10
1224	15p. Meskeneh Minaret (vert)	25	20
1225	25p. Psyche, Anab al-Safinah (vert)	35	25

350 W.M.O. Emblem

1973. Centenary of W.M.O.

1226	**350**	70p. multicoloured	70	35

351 Ancient City of Maalula

1973. Arab Emigrants' Congress, Buenos Aires.

1227	**351**	15p. black and blue	25	10
1228	-	50p. black and brown	70	35

DESIGN: 50p. Ruins of Afamia.

352 Soldier and Workers

1973. Third Anniv of Revolution of 16 November 1970.

1229	**352**	15p. blue and bistre	30	25
1230	**352**	25p. violet and red	50	30

353 Copernicus

1973. 14th Science Week.

1231	**353**	15p. black and gold	60	25
1232	-	25p. black and gold	1·10	35

DESIGN: 25p. Al-Biruni.

354 National Symbols

1973. 11th Anniv of Baathist Revolution of 8 March 1963.

1233	**354**	10p. blue and green	25	10
1234	**354**	25p. blue and green	30	25

355 U.P.U. Monument, Berne

1974. Centenary of U.P.U. Multicoloured.

1235	15p. Type **355**	25	20
1236	20p. Emblem on airmail letter (horiz)	30	25
1237	70p. Type **355**	95	80

356 Postal Institute

1974. Inauguration of Higher Arab Postal Institute, Damascus.

1238	**356**	15p. multicoloured	25	10

357 Sun and Monument

1974. 28th Anniv of Evacuation of Foreign Troops from Syria.

1239	**357**	15p. multicoloured	25	20
1240	**357**	20p. multicoloured	30	25

358 Machine Fitter

1974. Labour Day.

1241	**358**	15p. multicoloured	30	25
1242	**358**	50p. multicoloured	70	45

359 Abul Fida (historian)

1974. Famous Arabs.

1243	**359**	100p. green	1·20	70
1244	-	200p. brown	2·75	1·40

DESIGN: 200p. Al-Farabi (philosopher and encyclopedist).

360 Diamond and Part of Cogwheel

1974. 21st Damascus International Fair. Multicoloured.

1245	15p. Type **360**	25	20
1246	25p. "Sun" within cogwheel	30	25

361 Figs

1974. Aleppo Agricultural and Industrial Fair. Fruits. Multicoloured.

1247	5p. Type **361**	20	20
1248	15p. Grapes	25	20
1249	20p. Pomegranates	30	25
1250	25p. Cherries	35	30
1251	35p. Rose-hips	60	35

362 Flowers within Drop of Blood

1974. First Anniv of October Liberation War. Multicoloured.

1252	15p. Type **362**	50	25
1253	20p. Flower and stars	70	30

363 Knight and Rook

1974. 50th Anniv of International Chess Federation.

1254	**363**	15p. blue, lt blue & black	95	25
1255	-	50p. multicoloured	3·25	1·90

DESIGN: 50p. Knight on chessboard.

364 Symbolic Figure, Globe and Emblem

1974. World Population Year.

1256	**364**	50p. multicoloured	70	45

365 Ishtup-ilum

1974. Statuettes.

1257	**365**	20p. green	25	20
1258	-	55p. brown	60	25
1259	-	70p. blue	95	45

DESIGNS: 55p. Woman with vase; 70p. Ur-nina.

366 Oil Rig and Crowd

1975. 12th Anniv of Baathist Revolution of 8 March 1963.

1260	**366**	15p. multicoloured	25	10

367 Savings Emblem and Family ("Savings Certificates")

1975. Savings Campaign.

1261	**367**	15p. black, orange & green	25	10
1262	-	20p. brown, black & orange	35	15

DESIGN: 20p. Family with savings box and letter ("Postal Savings Bank").

368 Dove Emblem

1975. 29th Anniv of Evacuation of Foreign Troops from Syria.

1263	**368**	15p. multicoloured	25	20
1264	**368**	25p. multicoloured	25	20

369 Worker supporting Cog

1975. Labour Day.

1265	**369**	15p. multicoloured	25	20
1266	**369**	25p. multicoloured	25	20

370 Camomile

1975. Int Flower Show, Damascus. Multicoloured.

1267	5p. Type **370**	20	20
1268	10p. Chincherinchi	25	20
1269	15p. Carnations	30	20
1270	20p. Poppy	35	25
1271	25p. Honeysuckle	70	30

371 "Destruction and Reconstruction"

1975. Reoccupation of Qneitra.

| 1272 | 371 | 50p. multicoloured | 70 | 45 |

372 Apples

1975. Aleppo Agricultural and Industrial Fair. Fruits. Multicoloured.

1273		5p. Type 372	20	20
1274		10p. Quinces	25	20
1275		15p. Apricots	30	20
1276		20p. Mulberries	35	25
1277		25p. Loquats	60	30

373 Arabesque Pattern

1975. 22nd International Damascus Fair.

| 1278 | 373 | 15p. multicoloured | 30 | 25 |
| 1279 | 373 | 35p. multicoloured | 60 | 30 |

374 Pres. Hafez al-Assad

1975. Fifth Anniv of "Movement of 16 November 1970".

| 1280 | 374 | 15p. multicoloured | 30 | 25 |
| 1281 | 374 | 50p. multicoloured | 85 | 45 |

375 Symbolic Woman

1976. International Women's Year. Multicoloured.

1282		10p. Type 375	10	10
1283		15p. "Motherhood"	20	15
1284		25p. "Education"	30	25
1285		50p. "Science"	50	35

376 Bronze "Horse" Lamp

1976

1286	-	5p. green	10	10
1287	376	10p. green	20	10
1288	-	10p. blue	20	10
1289	-	15p. brown	20	10
1290	376	20p. red	25	15
1291	376	25p. blue	30	15
1292	-	30p. brown	35	20
1293	-	35p. green	40	20
1294	-	40p. orange	50	25
1295	-	50p. blue	70	35
1296	-	55p. mauve	60	25
1297	-	60p. violet	65	30
1298	-	70p. red	70	35
1299	-	75p. orange	85	45
1300	-	80p. green	95	50
1301	-	100p. mauve	1·20	60
1302	-	200p. blue	3·00	80
1303	-	300p. mauve	3·75	1·40
1304	-	500p. grey	6·75	4·50
1305	-	1000p. green	12·00	7·00

DESIGNS—VERT: 5p. Wall-painting showing figure of a man; 10p. (No. 1288) Flying goddess with wreath; 30, 35, 40p. Man's head inkstand; 50, 55, 60p. Statue of Nike; 70, 75, 80p. Statue of Hera; 100p. Imdugub-Mari (bird goddess); 200p. Arab astrolabe; 500p. Palmyrean coin of Valabathus; 1000p. Abraxas stone. HORIZ: 15p. Wall-painting showing figures; 300p. Herodian coin from Palmyra.

377 National Theatre, Damascus

1976. 13th Anniv of Baathist Revolution of 8 March 1963.

| 1306 | 377 | 25p. green, black & silver | 30 | 25 |
| 1307 | 377 | 35p. green, black & silver | 40 | 35 |

378 Nurse and Emblem

1976. Eighth Arab Red Crescent Societies' Conf, Damascus.

| 1308 | 378 | 25p. blue, black and red | 50 | 25 |
| 1309 | 378 | 100p. violet, black and red | 1·20 | 80 |

379 Syrian 5m. Stamp of 1920

1976. Arab Post Day.

| 1310 | 379 | 25p. multicoloured | 50 | 25 |
| 1311 | 379 | 35p. multicoloured | 60 | 45 |

380 Eagle and Stars

1976. 30th Anniv of Evacuation of Foreign Troops from Syria.

| 1312 | 380 | 25p. multicoloured | 50 | 25 |
| 1313 | 380 | 35p. multicoloured | 60 | 45 |

381 Hand gripping Spanner

1976. Labour Day.

| 1314 | 381 | 25p. blue and black | 50 | 25 |
| 1315 | | 60p. multicoloured | 70 | 45 |

DESIGN: 60p. Hand supporting globe.

382 Cotton Boll

1976. Aleppo Agricultural and Industrial Fair.

| 1316 | 382 | 25p. multicoloured | 50 | 25 |
| 1317 | 382 | 35p. multicoloured | 60 | 45 |

383 Tulips

1976. Int Flower Show, Damascus. Multicoloured.

1318		5p. Type 383	20	10
1319		15p. Yellow daisies	25	20
1320		20p. Turk's-cap lilies	35	25
1321		25p. Irises	60	30
1322		35p. Honeysuckle	70	35

384 Pottery

1976. Air. 23rd International Damascus Fair. Handicraft Industries. Multicoloured.

1323		10p. Type 384	25	20
1324		25p. Rug-making	40	35
1325		30p. Metalware	65	50
1326		35p. Wickerware	70	60
1327		100p. Wood-carving	1·20	1·00

385 People supporting Olive Branch

1976. Non-aligned Countries Summit Conference, Colombo. Multicoloured.

| 1328 | | 40p. Type 385 | 65 | 60 |
| 1329 | | 60p. Symbolic arrow penetrating "grey curtain" | 85 | 70 |

386 Football

1976. Fifth Pan-Arab Games. Multicoloured.

1330		5p. Type 386	25	20
1331		10p. Swimming	50	25
1332		25p. Running	55	30
1333		35p. Basketball	60	35
1334		50p. Throwing the javelin	70	60

MS1335 75×56 mm. 100p. Horse-jumping (56×36 mm). Imperf | 3·25 | 3·25 |

387 Construction Emblems

1976. Sixth Anniv of Movement of 16 November 1970.

| 1336 | 387 | 35p. multicoloured | 35 | 25 |

388 "The Fox and the Crow"

1976. Fairy Tales. Multicoloured.

1337		10p. Type 388	25	20
1338		15p. "The Hare and the Tortoise" (horiz)	30	25
1339		20p. "Little Red Riding Hood"	40	30
1340		25p. "The Wolf and the Goats" (horiz)	50	35
1341		35p. "The Wolf and the Lamb"	70	60

389 Muhammad Kurd-Ali (philosopher)

1976. Birth Centenary of Muhammad Kurd-Ali.

| 1342 | 389 | 25p. multicoloured | 35 | 25 |

390 Boeing 747SP

1977. Civil Aviation Day.

| 1343 | 390 | 35p. multicoloured | 1·40 | 45 |

391 Woman hoisting Flag

1977. 14th Anniv of Baathist Revolution of 8 March 1963.

| 1344 | 391 | 35p. multicoloured | 70 | 45 |

392 A.P.U. Emblem

1977. 25th Anniv of Arab Postal Union.

| 1345 | 392 | 35p. multicoloured | 60 | 25 |

393 Mounted Horseman

1977. 31st Anniv of Evacuation of Foreign Troops from Syria.

| 1346 | 393 | 100p. multicoloured | 1·40 | 80 |

394 Industrial Scene and Tools

1977. Labour Day.

| 1347 | 394 | 60p. multicoloured | 70 | 60 |

395 I.C.A.O. Emblem, Boeing 747SP and Globe

1977. 30th Anniv of I.C.A.O.

| 1348 | 395 | 100p. multicoloured | 1·90 | 1·40 |

396 Lemon

1977. International Agricultural Fair, Aleppo. Multicoloured.

1349		10p. Type 396	25	20
1350		20p. Lime	30	20
1351		25p. Grapefruit	50	25
1352		35p. Oranges	70	30
1353		60p. Tangerines	90	60

397 Mallows

1977. International Flower Show. Multicoloured.
1354		10p. Type **397**	25	15
1355		20p. Cockscomb	40	30
1356		25p. Convolvulus	50	35
1357		35p. Balsam	70	40
1358		60p. Lilac	85	70

398 Young Pioneers and Emblem

1977. Al Baath Pioneers Organization.
1359	**398**	35p. multicoloured	60	45

399 Arabesque Pattern and Coffee Pot

1977. 24th International Damascus Fair.
1360	**399**	25p. red, blue and black	30	25
1361	**399**	60p. brown, green & black	70	60

400 Globe and Measures

1977. World Standards Day.
1362	**400**	15p. multicoloured	25	10

401 Microscope, Book and Lyre

1977. 30th Anniv of UNESCO.
1363	**401**	25p. multicoloured	35	15

402 Shield, Surgeon and Crab

1977. Fighting Cancer Week.
1364	**402**	100p. multicoloured	1·20	45

403 Archbishop Capucci and Map of Palestine

1977. Third Anniv of Archbishop Capucci's Arrest.
1365	**403**	60p. multicoloured	70	25

404 Blind Man, Eye and Globe

1977. World Blind Week.
1366	**404**	55p. multicoloured	35	20
1367	**404**	70p. multicoloured	60	25

405 Dome of the Rock, Jerusalem

1977. Palestinian Welfare.
1368	**405**	5p. multicoloured	25	15
1369	**405**	10p. multicoloured	35	20

406 Pres. Hafez al-Assad and Government Palace, Damascus

1977. Seventh Anniv of Movement of 16 November 1970.
1370	**406**	50p. multicoloured	60	25

407 Eurasian Goldfinch

1978. Birds. Multicoloured.
1371		10p. Type **407**	2·10	1·20
1372		20p. Peregrine falcon	2·40	1·40
1373		25p. Feral rock dove	3·00	1·40
1374		35p. Hoopoe	6·00	1·70
1375		60p. Chukar partridge	7·25	3·25

408 Arrow and Blood Circulation

1978. World Health Day. "Fighting Blood Pressure".
1376	**408**	100p. multicoloured	95	45

409 Factory, Moon and Stars

1978. 32nd Anniv of Evacuation of Foreign Troops from Syria.
1377	**409**	35p. green, orange & black	35	20

410 Geometric Design

1978. 14th Arab Engineering Conf, Damascus.
1378	**410**	25p. green and black	35	10

411 Map of Arab Countries, Flag, Eye and Police

1978. Sixth Arab Conference of Police Commanders.
1379	**411**	35p. multicoloured	35	20

412 Brown Trout

1978. Fish. Multicoloured.
1380		10p. Type **412**	70	25
1381		20p. Seabream	90	30
1382		25p. Grouper	95	35
1383		35p. Striped red mullet	1·20	45
1384		60p. Wels	1·30	60

413 President Assad

1978. Air. Re-election of President Hafez al-Assad.
1385	**413**	25p. multicoloured	50	20
1386	**413**	35p. multicoloured	60	25
1387	**413**	60p. multicoloured	70	30

MS1388 79×105 mm. **413** 100p. multi-coloured. Imperf ... 1·60 ... 1·60

414 "Lobivia sp."

1978. International Flower Show, Damascus. Multicoloured.
1389		25p. Type **414**	35	15
1390		30p. "Mamillaria sp."	40	20
1391		35p. "Opuntia sp."	50	25
1392		50p. "Chamaecereus sp."	60	35
1393		60p. "Mamillaria sp." (different)	70	60

415 President Hafez al-Assad

1978. Eighth Anniv of Movement of 16 November 1970.
1394	**415**	60p. multicoloured	70	60

416 Euphrates Dam

1978. Inauguration of Euphrates Dam.
1395	**416**	60p. multicoloured	95	60

417 Fair Emblem

1979. 25th International Damascus Fair.
1396	**417**	25p. multicoloured	25	10
1397	**417**	35p. black, violet and silver	35	20

MS1398 105×80 mm. 100p. multicol-oured. Imperf ... 1·60 ... 1·60
DESIGN: **MS**1398, Arabesque pattern.

418 Averroes (philosopher)

1979. Averroes Commemoration.
1399	**418**	100p. multicoloured	1·90	1·20

419 Standing Figures within Globe

1979. International Year to Combat Racism.
1400	**419**	35p. multicoloured	35	20

420 Pyramid and Flower

1979. 16th Anniv of Baathist Revolution of 8 March 1963.
1401	**420**	100p. multicoloured	1·30	25

421 Hands supporting Globe

1979. 30th Anniv of Declaration of Human Rights.
1402	**421**	60p. multicoloured	70	60

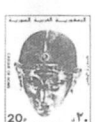
422 Helmet of Homs

1979. Exhibits from National Museum, Damascus.
1403	-	5p. red	20	10
1404	-	10p. green	35	10
1405	-	15p. mauve	35	20
1406	**422**	20p. green	25	10
1407	-	25p. red	25	10
1408	-	35p. brown	35	10
1409	-	75p. blue	70	35
1410	-	160p. green	1·40	60
1411	-	500p. brown	5·25	1·90

DESIGNS—VERT: 5, 160p. Umayyad window; 10p. Figurine; 15p. Rakka horseman (Abbcid ceramic); 25p. Head of Clipeata (Cleopatra); 35p. Seated statue of Ishtar (Astarte). HORIZ: 75p. Abdul Malik gold coin; 500p. Umar B. Abdul Aziz gold coin.

423 Geometric Design and Flame

1979. 33rd Anniv of Evacuation of Foreign Troops from Syria.
1416	**423**	35p. multicoloured	35	20

424 Ibn Assaker

1979. 900th Anniv of Ibn Assaker (historian and biographer).
| 1417 | **424** | 75p. brown, blue & green | 80 | 35 |

425 Tooth, Emblem and Mosque

1979. International Middle East Dental Congress.
| 1418 | **425** | 35p. multicoloured | 70 | 25 |

426 Welder working on Power Pylon

1979. Labour Day.
| 1419 | **426** | 50p. multicoloured | 60 | 45 |
| 1420 | **426** | 75p. multicoloured | 85 | 60 |

427 Girl holding Emblem with Flowers

1979. International Year of the Child. Multicoloured.
| 1421 | **427** | 10p. Type **427** | 25 | 10 |
| 1422 | | 15p. Boy and globe | 35 | 15 |

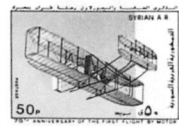

428 Wright Type A

1979. 75th Anniv of First Powered Flight. Multicoloured.
1423	**428**	50p. Type **428**	1·40	35
1424		75p. Bleriot's plane crossing English Channel	1·90	60
1425		100p. Lindbergh's "Spirit of St. Louis"	2·75	70

429 Power Station

1979
1426	**429**	5p. blue	20	10
1427	**429**	10p. mauve	20	10
1428	**429**	15p. green	25	10

430 Flags and Pavilion

1979. 26th International Damascus Fair. Multicoloured.
| 1429 | **430** | 60p. Type **430** | 50 | 20 |
| 1430 | | 75p. Lamp post and flags | 60 | 25 |

431 Running

1979. Eighth Mediterranean Games, Split. Multicoloured.
1431		25p. Type **431**	25	15
1432		35p. Swimmer on starting-block	35	20
1433		50p. Football	50	35

432 President Assad with Symbols of Agriculture and Industry

1979. Ninth Anniv of Movement of 16 November 1970.
| 1434 | **432** | 100p. multicoloured | 1·30 | 35 |

433 Swallowtail

1979. Butterflies. Multicoloured.
1435	**433**	20p. Type **433**	1·70	25
1436		25p. Peacock	2·10	30
1437		30p. White admiral	2·75	35
1438		35p. Blue morpho	3·25	40
1439		50p. Apollo	4·25	70

1979. International Flower Show, Damascus. Designs similar to T **414** showing various roses.
1440		5p. multicoloured	10	10
1441		10p. multicoloured	20	10
1442		15p. multicoloured	25	15
1443		50p. multicoloured	35	25
1444		75p. multicoloured	70	35
1445		100p. multicoloured	1·10	45

434 Astrolabe

1980. Second International Symposium on History of Arab Science.
1446	**434**	50p. violet	50	20
1447	**434**	100p. brown	85	45
1448	**434**	1000p. green	9·00	5·00

435 "8" over Buildings

1980. 17th Anniv of Baathist Revolution of 8 March 1963.
| 1449 | **435** | 40p. multicoloured | 35 | 20 |

436 Smoker

1980. World Health Day. Anti-smoking Campaign.
| 1450 | **436** | 60p. brown, green & black | 70 | 35 |
| 1451 | - | 100p. multicoloured | 1·20 | 45 |

DESIGN: 100p. Skull and cigarette.

437 Monument

1980. 34th Anniv of Evacuation of Foreign Troops from Syria.
| 1452 | **437** | 40p. multicoloured | 50 | 20 |
| 1453 | **437** | 60p. multicoloured | 60 | 35 |

438 Wrestling

1980. Olympic Games, Moscow. Multicoloured.
1454		15p. Type **438**	25	10
1455		25p. Fencing	30	15
1456		35p. Weightlifting	35	20
1457		50p. Judo	60	20
1458		75p. Boxing	85	25

MS1459 105×80 mm. 300p. Discus thrower, Games emblem and runner. Imperf | 22·00 | 22·00 |

439 "Savings"

1980. Savings Certificates.
| 1460 | **439** | 25p. violet, red and blue | 25 | 10 |

440 "Aladdin and the Magic Lamp"

1980. Popular Stories. Multicoloured.
1461		15p. "Sinbad the Sailor"	25	10
1462		20p. "Shahrazad and Shahrayar"	50	20
1463		35p. "Ali Baba and the Forty Thieves"	60	25
1464		50p. "Hassan the Clever"	70	60
1465		100p. Type **440**	95	80

441 Kaaba and Mosque, Mecca

1980. 1400th Anniv of Hegira.
| 1466 | **441** | 35p. multicoloured | 50 | 20 |

442 Daffodils

1980. International Flower Show, Damascus. Multicoloured.
1467		20p. Type **442**	50	35
1468		30p. Dahlias	60	45
1469		40p. Bergamot	70	60
1470		60p. Globe flowers	85	70
1471		100p. Cornflowers	1·10	95

443 "Industry"

1980. Tenth Anniv of Movement of 16 November 1970.
| 1472 | **443** | 100p. multicoloured | 1·20 | 60 |

444 Construction Worker

1980. Labour Day.
| 1473 | **444** | 35p. multicoloured | 35 | 20 |

445 Children encircling Globe

1980. International Children's Day.
| 1474 | **445** | 25p. green, black & yell | 35 | 10 |

446 Steam-powered Passenger Wagon, 1830

1980. Cars. Multicoloured.
1475		25p. Type **446**	60	45
1476		35p. Benz, 1899	65	50
1477		40p. Rolls-Royce, 1903	70	60
1478		50p. Mercedes, 1906	85	70
1479		60p. Austin, 1915	95	80

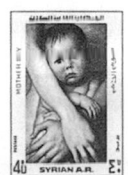

447 Mother's Arms around Child

1980. Mothers' Day. Multicoloured.
| 1480 | **447** | 40p. Type **447** | 50 | 20 |
| 1481 | | 100p. Faces of mother and child | 95 | 60 |

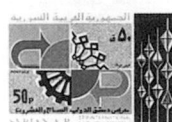

448 Fair Emblem

1980. 27th International Damascus Fair. Multicoloured.
| 1482 | **448** | 50p. Type **448** | 60 | 25 |
| 1483 | | 100p. As T **448** but with different motif on right | 1·20 | 60 |

449 Armed Forces

1980. Army Day.
| 1484 | **449** | 50p. multicoloured | 1·60 | 45 |

450 Arabesque Pattern

1981. 18th Anniv of Baathist Revolution of 8 March 1963.
| 1485 | **450** | 50p. multicoloured | 70 | 25 |

451 Geometric Design, Laurel and Hand holding Torch

1981. 35th Anniv of Evacuation of Foreign Troops from Syria.

1486	**451**	50p. multicoloured	70	25

452 Mosque and Script

1981. History of Arab-Islamic Civilization World Conference, Damascus.

1487	**452**	100p. green, deep green and black	1·30	70

453 Marching Workers and Emblem

1981. May Day.

1488	**453**	100p. multicoloured	1·20	60

454 Human Figure and House on Graph

1981. Housing and Population Census.

1489	**454**	50p. multicoloured	70	25

455 Family and Savings Emblem

1981. Savings Certificates.

1490	**455**	50p. black and brown	70	25

456 Dove and Map on Globe

1981. International Syrian and Palestinian Solidarity Conference, Damascus.

1491	**456**	160p. multicoloured	3·50	1·70

457 Avicenna

1981. Birth Millenary of Avicenna (philosopher and physician).

1492	**457**	100p. multicoloured	1·20	45

458 Glass Lamp

1981. Damascus Museum Exhibits.

1493	**458**	50p. red	85	35
1494	-	180p. multicoloured	2·40	1·20
1495	-	180p. multicoloured	2·40	1·20

DESIGNS: No. 1494, "Grand Mosque, Damascus" (painting); 1495, Hunting scene (tapestry).

459 Festival Emblem

1981. Youth Festival.

1496	**459**	60p. multicoloured	70	25

460 Decorative Pattern

1981. 28th International Damascus Fair.

1497	**460**	50p. mauve, blue & green	50	20
1498	-	160p. brown, yell & lilac	1·40	70

DESIGN: 160p. Globe encircled by wheat and cogwheel.

461 Palestinians and Dome of the Rock

1981. Palestinian Solidarity.

1499	**461**	100p. multicoloured	1·20	45

462 F.A.O. Emblem

1981. World Food Day.

1500	**462**	180p. blue, green and black	2·40	1·30

463 Tobacco Flowers

1981. International Flower Show, Damascus. Multicoloured.

1501		25p. Type **463**	70	60
1502		40p. Mimosa	1·10	70
1503		50p. Ixias	1·10	75
1504		60p. Passion flower	1·20	80
1505		100p. Dendrobium	1·40	1·20

464 Hands releasing Dove and Horseman

1981. 1300th Anniv of Bulgarian State.

1506	**464**	380p. multicoloured	3·50	1·40

465 Classroom

1981. International Children's Day.

1507	**465**	180p. black, red & green	2·40	1·30

466 Reading the Koran and Pres. Assad (image scaled to 45% of original size)

1981. Koran Reading Competition. Sheet 105×80 mm.

MS1508	500p. multicoloured	12·00	12·00

467 President Assad and Diesel Train

1981. 11th Anniv of Movement of 16 November 1970.

1509	**467**	60p. blue, black and brown	2·40	45

468 Symbols of Development

1982. 19th Anniv of Baathist Revolution of 8 March 1963.

1510	**468**	50p. grey, red and black	70	25

469 Robert Koch and Microscope

1982. Cent of Discovery of Tubercle Bacillus.

1511	**469**	180p. blue, brown and black	3·00	1·00

470 Pattern and Hand holding Rifle

1982. 36th Anniv of Evacuation of Foreign Troops from Syria.

1512	**470**	70p. red and blue	70	35

471 Disabled People and Emblem

1982. International Year of Disabled Persons (1981).

1513	**471**	90p. black, blue and yellow	1·20	45

472 A.P.U. Emblem

1982. 30th Anniv of Arab Postal Union.

1514	**472**	60p. red, green and yellow	95	35

473 Traffic Lights

1982. World Traffic Day.

1515	**473**	180p. black, red and blue	2·40	95

474 Geometric Pattern

1982. World Telecommunications Day.

1516	**474**	180p. light yellow, brown and yellow	1·90	95

475 Oil Rig, Factory Chimneys and Hand holding Torch

1982. Labour Day.

1517	**475**	180p. red, blue and light blue	1·90	95

476 Mother and Children

1982. Mothers' Day.

1518	**476**	40p. green	35	10
1519	**476**	75p. brown	70	35

477 Olives   **478** Pres. Assad

1982

1520	**477**	50p. green	50	20
1521	**477**	60p. grey	60	25
1522	-	100p. mauve	85	45
1523	**478**	150p. blue	1·20	70
1524	-	180p. red	1·80	80

DESIGN: 100, 180p. Harbour.

479 Footballer

1982. World Cup Football Championship, Spain. Multicoloured.

1525		40p. Type **479**	60	25
1526		60p. Two footballers	85	35
1527		100p. Two footballers (different)	1·60	1·20
MS1528	75×54 mm. 300p. World Cup emblem. Imperf		21·00	21·00

480 Policeman

1982. Police Day.
| 1529 | **480** | 50p. black, red and green | 70 | 25 |

481 Government Building

1982
1530	**481**	30p. brown	25	10
1531	–	70p. green	70	35
1532	–	200p. red	2·20	1·00

DESIGNS—HORIZ: 200p. Ruins. VERT: 70p. Arched wall.

482 Communications Emblem and Map

1982. Arab Telecommunication Day.
| 1533 | **482** | 50p. blue, ultramarine and red | 70 | 25 |

483 Scout pitching Tent

1982. 75th Anniv of Boy Scout Movement.
| 1534 | **483** | 160p. green | 2·20 | 95 |

484 Dish Aerial and World Map

1982. I.T.U. Delegates' Conference, Nairobi.
| 1535 | **484** | 180p. blue, ultramarine and red | 2·40 | 1·20 |

485 President Assad

1982. 12th Anniv of Movement of 16 November 1970.
| 1536 | **485** | 50p. blue and grey | 70 | 25 |

486 Water-wheel, Hama

1982
1537	**486**	5p. brown	10	10
1538	**486**	10p. violet	20	10
1539	**486**	20p. red	35	10
1540	**486**	50p. turquoise	70	25

487 Dragonfly

1982. Insects. Multicoloured.
1541	Type **487**	5p.	50	35
1542		10p. Stag beetle	60	45
1543		20p. Seven-spotted ladybird	85	70
1544		40p. Desert locust	1·60	1·40
1545		50p. Honey bee	1·70	1·50

488 Honeysuckle

1982. Int Flower Show, Damascus. Multicoloured.
| 1546 | | 50p. Type **488** | 70 | 35 |
| 1547 | | 60p. Geranium | 95 | 60 |

489 Satellites within Dove

1982. U.N. Conference on Exploration and Peaceful Uses of Outer Space, Vienna.
| 1548 | **489** | 50p. multicoloured | 70 | 25 |

490 Dove on Gun

1982. International Palestine Day.
| 1549 | **490** | 50p. multicoloured | 1·20 | 45 |

491 Damascus International Airport

1983. 20th Anniv of Baathist Revolution of 8 March 1963.
| 1550 | **491** | 60p. multicoloured | 1·90 | 80 |

492 Communications Emblems

1983. World Communications Year.
| 1551 | **492** | 180p. multicoloured | 2·40 | 1·00 |

493 Figurine

1983
| 1552 | **493** | 380p. brown and green | 6·00 | 2·30 |

494 Pharmacist

1983. Arab Pharmacists' Day.
| 1553 | **494** | 100p. multicoloured | 1·60 | 60 |

495 Liberation Monument, Qneitra

1983. Ninth Anniv of Liberation of Qneitra.
| 1554 | **495** | 50p. green | 1·40 | 60 |
| 1555 | | 100p. brown | 3·00 | 80 |

DESIGN: 100p. Ruined buildings.

496 Wave within Ship's Wheel

1983. 25th Anniv of I.M.O.
| 1556 | **496** | 180p. multicoloured | 2·75 | 95 |

497 Flame on Map

1983. Namibia Day.
| 1557 | **497** | 180p. blue, mauve and black | 2·10 | 95 |

498 I.S.O. Emblem and Factory

1983. World Standards Day.
| 1558 | **498** | 50p. multicoloured | 70 | 35 |
| 1559 | – | 100p. violet, green & black | 1·60 | 95 |

DESIGN: 100p. I.S.O. emblem and measuring equipment.

499 Gateway, Bosra

1983. Tenth Anniv of World Heritage Agreement.
| 1560 | **499** | 60p. brown | 85 | 35 |

500 Flowers

1983. Int Flower Show, Damascus. Multicoloured.
| 1561 | | 50p. Type **500** | 85 | 35 |
| 1562 | | 60p. Hibiscus | 95 | 70 |

501 Farmland

1983. World Food Day.
| 1563 | **501** | 180p. green, cream and deep green | 2·40 | 1·20 |

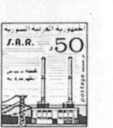

502 Factory

1983
| 1564 | **502** | 50p. green | 70 | 35 |

503 Statuette

1984. International Deir Ez-Zor History and Archaeology Symposium.
| 1565 | **503** | 225p. brown | 3·50 | 1·70 |

504 Aleppo

1984. International Symposium for the Conservation of Aleppo.
| 1566 | **504** | 245p. multicoloured | 3·50 | 1·70 |

505 Alassad Library

1984. 21st Anniv of Baathist Revolution of 8 March 1963.
| 1567 | **505** | 60p. multicoloured | 1·20 | 60 |

506 Bodies and mourning Woman with Child

1984. Sabra and Shatila (refugee camps in Lebanon) Massacres.
| 1568 | **506** | 225p. multicoloured | 3·25 | 1·50 |

507 Mother and Child

1984. Mothers' Day.
| 1569 | **507** | 245p. brown and green | 3·25 | 1·70 |

508 Dam, Emblem and Pioneers

1984. Ninth Regional Festival of Al Baath Pioneers. Multicoloured.
| 1570 | | 50p. Type **508** | 85 | 60 |
| 1571 | | 60p. Pioneers, ruins and emblems | 1·20 | 70 |

509 Swimming

1984. Olympic Games, Los Angeles. Multicoloured.
1572		30p. Type **509**	70	60
1573		50p. Wrestling	85	70
1574		60p. Running	95	80
1575		70p. Boxing	1·10	95
1576		90p. Football	1·40	1·30

MS1577 77×55 mm. 200p. Footballer within football. Imperf 13·50 13·50

510 Flowers

1984. Int Flower Show, Damascus. Multicoloured.
| 1578 | | 245p. Type **510** | 3·50 | 1·70 |
| 1579 | | 285p. Flowers (different) | 4·25 | 2·30 |

511 Pres. Assad and Text

1984. Fourth Revolutionary Youth Union Congress.
| 1580 | 511 | 50p. brown, deep brown and green | 70 | 35 |
| 1581 | - | 60p. multicoloured | 80 | 60 |

DESIGN—37×25 mm: 60p. Pres. Assad and saluting youth.

512 Emblem and Administration Building, Damascus

1984. Arab Postal Union Day.
| 1582 | 512 | 60p. multicoloured | 70 | 45 |

513 Globe, Dish Aerial and Telephone

1984. World Telecommunications Day.
| 1583 | 513 | 245p. multicoloured | 3·50 | 2·00 |

514 Arabesque Pattern

1984. 31st International Damascus Fair. Multicoloured.
| 1584 | | 45p. Type **514** | 70 | 25 |
| 1585 | | 100p. Ornate gold decoration | 2·10 | 80 |

515 Stylized Aircraft and Emblem

1984. 40th Anniv of I.C.A.O.
| 1586 | 515 | 45p. blue and deep blue | 85 | 35 |
| 1587 | - | 245p. blue, ultramarine and deep blue | 3·50 | 2·00 |

DESIGN: 245p. Emblem and stylized building.

516 Text, Flag and Pres. Assad

1984. 14th Anniv of Movement of 16 November 1970.
| 1588 | 516 | 65p. orange, black and brown | 95 | 1·20 |

517 Palmyra Roman Arch and Colonnades

1984. International Tourism Day.
| 1589 | 517 | 100p. brown, black and blue | 1·40 | 70 |

518 Wooded Landscape

1985. Woodland Conservation.
| 1590 | 518 | 45p. multicoloured | 95 | 35 |

519 University and Students

1985. 26th Anniv (1984) of Aleppo University.
| 1591 | 519 | 45p. black, blue and brown | 85 | 35 |

520 Oil Lamp

1985. 26th Anniv (1984) of Supreme Council of Science.
| 1592 | 520 | 65p. green, red and black | 1·20 | 60 |

521 Soldier holding Flag

1985. Army Day.
| 1593 | 521 | 65p. brown and bistre | 1·20 | 60 |

522 Pres. Assad

1985. Re-election of President Assad.
1594	522	200p. multicoloured	3·00	2·00
1595	522	300p. multicoloured	3·75	2·30
1596	522	500p. multicoloured	7·25	3·50
MS1597		140×85 mm. Nos. 1594/6. Imperf	18·00	18·00

523 Flag and Party Emblem

1985. Eighth Baath Arab Socialist Party Congress.
| 1598 | 523 | 50p. multicoloured | 85 | 35 |

524 Torch and "22"

1985. 22nd Anniv of Baathist Revolution of 8 March 1963.
| 1599 | 524 | 60p. multicoloured | 85 | 35 |

525 Tractor and Cow

1985. Aleppo Industrial and Agricultural Fair (1984). Multicoloured.
| 1600 | | 65p. Type **525** | 95 | 35 |
| 1601 | | 150p. Fort and carrots (vert) | 2·75 | 1·40 |

526 Liberation Movement, Qneitra

1985. Tenth Anniv (1984) of Liberation of Qneitra.
| 1602 | 526 | 70p. multicoloured | 2·10 | 60 |

527 Parliament Building

1985. Tenth Anniv of Arab Parliamentary Union.
| 1603 | 527 | 245p. multicoloured | 3·75 | 2·00 |

528 U.P.U. Emblem and Pigeon with Letter

1985. World Post Day.
| 1604 | 528 | 285p. multicoloured | 5·00 | 1·40 |

529 A.P.U. Emblem

1985. 12th Arab Postal Union Conference, Damascus.
| 1605 | 529 | 60p. multicoloured | 85 | 60 |

530 Medal

1985. Labour Day.
| 1606 | 530 | 60p. multicoloured | 85 | 60 |

531 Steam and Diesel Locomotives

1985. Second Scientific Symposium.
| 1607 | 531 | 60p. blue | 2·10 | 70 |

532 Emblem and Child with empty Bowl

1985. U.N. Child Survival Campaign.
| 1608 | 532 | 60p. black, green & pink | 85 | 60 |

533 Pres. Assad and Road

1985. 15th Anniv of Movement of 16 November 1970.
| 1609 | 533 | 60p. multicoloured | 85 | 60 |

534 Emblem and "40"

1985. 40th Anniv of U.N.O.
| 1610 | 534 | 245p. multicoloured | 3·25 | 2·00 |

535 Lily-flowered Tulip

1986. Int Flower Show, Damascus (1985). Multicoloured.
| 1611 | | 30p. Type **535** | 60 | 30 |
| 1612 | | 60p. Tulip | 1·20 | 95 |

536 Flask

1986. 32nd International Damascus Fair (1985).
| 1613 | 536 | 60p. multicoloured | 95 | 60 |

537 Abd-er-Rahman I

1986. 1200th Anniv of Abd-er-Rahman I ad Dakhel, Emir of Cordoba.
| 1614 | 537 | 60p. brown, cinnamon and light brown | 95 | 60 |

538 Pres. Hafez al-Assad

1988
1615	538	10p. red	10	10
1616	538	30p. blue	20	10
1616a	538	50p. lilac	50	20
1617	538	100p. blue	85	60
1618	538	150p. brown	1·20	45
1619	538	175p. violet	1·40	60
1620	538	200p. brown	1·70	1·00
1621	538	300p. mauve	2·40	1·50
1622	538	500p. orange	4·25	2·50
1623	538	550p. pink	4·75	2·30
1624	538	600p. green	6·00	2·50
1625	538	1000p. mauve	9·75	5·25
1626	538	2000p. green	21·00	10·50

For similar design but with full-face portrait, see Nos. 1774/80.

539 Tooth and Map

1986. 19th Arab Dentists' Union Congress, Damascus.
| 1627 | 539 | 110p. multicoloured | 2·40 | 1·40 |

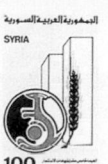

540 Tower Blocks, Ear of Wheat and Kangaroo

1986. 15th Anniv of Syrian Investment Certificates.
1628 **540** 100p. multicoloured 1·80 80

541 Traffic Policewoman, Globe and Traffic Lights

1986. World Traffic Day.
1629 **541** 330p. multicoloured 4·25 2·50

542 Policeman and Building in Laurel Wreath

1986. Police Day.
1630 **542** 110p. multicoloured 1·40 45

543 Industrial Symbols and Hand Holding Spanner

1986. Labour Day.
1631 **543** 330p. red, black and blue 3·75 3·00

544 Building

1986. 12th Anniv of Liberation of Qneitra.
1632 **544** 110p. multicoloured 1·30 45

545 Pictogram and Ball

1986. World Cup Football Championship, Mexico.
1633 **545** 330p. multicoloured 3·50 2·00
1634 **545** 370p. multicoloured 3·75 2·30
MS1635 105×80 mm. 500p. multicoloured (Ball and hemispheres). Imperf 7·25 7·25

546 Mother and Children

1986. Mothers' Day.
1636 **546** 100p. multicoloured 1·20 45

547 Pres. Assad and Diesel Train

1986. 23rd Anniv of Baathist Revolution of 8 March 1963.
1637 **547** 110p. multicoloured 2·40 1·20

548 A.P.U. Emblem, Post Office and Box

1986. Arab Post Day.
1638 **548** 110p. multicoloured 1·20 45

549 Fists, Map and Globe

1986. International Palestine Day.
1639 **549** 110p. multicoloured 1·20 45

550 Tulips

1986. Int Flower Show, Damascus. Multicoloured.
1640 10p. Type **550** 25 70
1641 50p. Mauve flowers 70 60
1642 100p. Yellow flowers 1·40 1·20
1643 110p. Pink flowers 1·60 1·30
1644 330p. Yellow flowers (different) 3·75 2·50

551 Pres. Assad and Tishreen Palace

1986. 16th Anniv of Movement of 16 November 1970.
1645 **551** 110p. multicoloured 1·20 45

552 Rocket and Flags

1986. First Anniv of Announcement of Syrian–Soviet Space Flight.
1646 **552** 330p. multicoloured 4·25 2·30

553 Jug and Star

1986. 33rd International Damascus Fair.
1647 **553** 110p. multicoloured 48·00 85
1648 – 330p. black, green and brown 1·80 1·20
DESIGN: 330p. Coffee pot.

554 Girls and National Flag

1987. International Children's Art Exhibition.
1649 **554** 330p. multicoloured 4·25 2·30

555 U.P.U. Emblem and Airmail Envelope

1987. World Post Day.
1650 **555** 330p. multicoloured 3·00 1·70

556 Children in Balloon over Town

1987. International Children's Day.
1651 **556** 330p. multicoloured 3·00 1·70

557 Citadel, Aleppo

1987. International Tourism Day.
1652 330p. Type **557** 3·25 1·70
1653 370p. Water-wheel, Hama 3·50 2·00

558 Industrial Symbols

1987. 24th Anniv of Baathist Revolution of 8 March 1963.
1654 **558** 100p. multicoloured 95 35

559 Doves flying from Globe

1987. International Peace Year.
1655 **559** 370p. multicoloured 3·25 2·00

560 Party Emblem

1987. 40th Anniv of Baath Arab Socialist Party.
1656 **560** 100p. multicoloured 95 35

561 Stars

1987. 41st Anniv of Evacuation of Foreign Troops from Syria.
1657 **561** 100p. multicoloured 95 35

562 Draughtsman

1987. Sixth Arab Ministers of Culture Conference.
1658 **562** 330p. blue, green & black 3·75 2·00

563 Map of Arab Postal Union Members

1987. Arab Post Day.
1659 **563** 110p. multicoloured 95 35

564 Couple within Cogwheel

1987. Labour Day.
1660 **564** 330p. multicoloured 3·25 2·00

565 Statue

1987. 13th Anniv of Liberation of Qneitra.
1661 **565** 100p. multicoloured 95 45

566 Pres. Assad with Children and Nurse

1987. Child Vaccination Campaign.
1662 **566** 100p. multicoloured 1·40 80
1663 **566** 330p. multicoloured 3·50 2·00

567 Dome of the Rock, Battle Scene and Saladin

1987. 800th Anniv of Battle of Hattin.
1664 **567** 110p. multicoloured 1·20 45

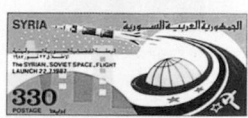

568 Rocket Launch and National Flags

1987. Syrian–Soviet Space Flight. Multicoloured.
1665 330p. Type **568** 3·25 2·00
1666 330p. Spacecraft docking with "Mir" space station (37×25 mm) 3·25 2·00
1667 330p. Space capsule re-entering Earth's atmosphere and group of cosmonauts (25×37 mm) 3·25 2·00
MS1668 150×110 mm. 300p. Rocket launch; 300p. Space capsule re-entering atmosphere; 300p. Spacecraft docked with space station; 300p. Stylized Syrian and Soviet cosmonauts. Imperf 18·00 18·00

569 Flags, Cosmonauts and Pres. Assad

1987. President's Space Conversation with Lt.-Col. Mohammed Faris (Syrian cosmonaut).
1669 **569** 500p. multicoloured   6·00   2·50

570 Stylized Flowers

1987. 34th International Damascus Fair.
1670 **570** 330p. multicoloured   3·00   2·00

571 Sports Pictograms

1987. Tenth Mediterranean Games, Latakia.
1671 **571** 100p. purple and black   85   60
1672 -   110p. multicoloured   1·20   70
1673 -   330p. multicoloured   3·00   1·70
1674 -   370p. multicoloured   3·50   2·30
MS1675 151×112 mm. 300p. ×4, multicoloured   16·00   16·00
DESIGNS: As Type **571**. HORIZ—110p. Swimming, bird and emblem. VERT—**MS**1671: Gymnastics, weightlifting, tennis and football. 52×23 mm—330p. Phoenician galley (Games emblem); 370p. Flags forming "SYRIA".

572 Soldier, Mikoyan Gurevich MiG-21D Fighter, Ship and Tank

1987. Army Day.
1676 **572** 100p. multicoloured   1·60   60

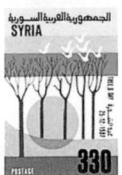

573 Trees, Sun and Birds

1987. Tree Day.
1677 **573** 330p. multicoloured   3·00   1·70

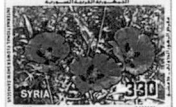

574 Poppies

1987. International Flower Show, Damascus.
1678   330p. Type **574**   3·50   1·40
1679   370p. Mauve flower   3·75   1·50

575 Pres. Assad acknowledging Applause

1987. 17th Anniv of Corrective Movement of 16 November 1970.
1680 **575** 150p. multicoloured   1·40   80

576 Barbed Wire around Map of Israel

1987. International Palestine Day.
1681 **576** 500p. multicoloured   5·00   2·50

577 U.P.U. and U.N. Emblems

1988. World Post Day.
1682 **577** 500p. multicoloured   5·50   3·00

578 Bosra Amphitheatre

1988. International Tourism Day. Multicoloured.
1683   500p. Type **578**   5·00   2·30
1684   500p. Palmyra ruins   5·00   2·30

579 Children as Cosmonauts

1988. International Children's Day.
1685 **579** 500p. multicoloured   5·00   2·30

580 Hand holding Torch

1988. 25th Anniv of Baathist Revolution of 8 March 1963.
1686 **580** 150p. multicoloured   1·30   80
MS1687 110×81 mm. 500p. No. 1686, map and flag. Imperf   6·00   6·00

581 Woman cradling Baby, Children and Adults

1988. Mothers' Day.
1688 **581** 500p. multicoloured   5·00   2·30

582 Arms, Cogwheel, Laurel Branch and Book

1988. 42nd Anniv of Evacuation of Foreign Troops from Syria.
1689 **582** 150p. multicoloured   1·30   70

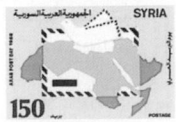

583 Dove, Airmail Envelope and Map

1988. Arab Post Day.
1690 **583** 150p. multicoloured   1·30   70

584 Spanner, Chimney, Cogwheel and Scroll

1988. Labour Day.
1691 **584** 550p. multicoloured   4·75   2·30

585 Modern Buildings

1988. Arab Engineers' Union.
1692 **585** 150p. multicoloured   1·30   70

586 Lily

1988. Int Flower Show, Damascus. Multicoloured.
1693   550p. Type **586**   5·00   2·30
1694   600p. Carnations   6·00   3·00

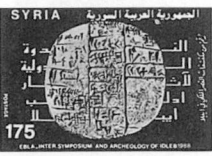

587 Clay Tablet

1988. Int Symposium on Archaeology of Ebla.
1695 **587** 175p. black and brown   1·80   80
1696 -   550p. brown, blue & black   5·00   2·30
1697 -   600p. multicoloured   5·50   2·50
DESIGNS: 550p. King making offering (carving from stone votive basin); 600p. Golden statue of goddess Ishtar.

588 Old City

1988. Preservation of Sana'a, Yemen.
1698 **588** 550p. multicoloured   5·50   2·30

589 Emblem

1988. Children's Day.
1699 **589** 600p. black, green and emerald   5·50   2·50

590 Sword, Shield and Emblems

1988. 35th International Damascus Fair.
1700 **590** 600p. multicoloured   5·50   2·50

591 Emblem and People

1988. 40th Anniv of W.H.O.
1701 **591** 600p. multicoloured   5·50   2·50

592 Emblems and Map

1988. 50th Anniv of Arab Scout Movement.
1702 **592** 150p. multicoloured   2·10   70

593 Cycling

1988. Olympic Games, Seoul. Multicoloured.
1703   550p. Type **593**   6·00   2·30
1704   600p. Football   6·25   2·50
MS1705 80×60 mm. 1200p. Emblem and Hodori (mascot). Imperf   19·00   19·00

594 Old Houses and Modern Flats

1988. Housing. Multicoloured.
1706   150p. Type **594** (Arab Housing Day)   1·70   95
1707   175p. House and makeshift shelter (International Year of Shelter for the Homeless (1987))   1·80   80
1708   550p. Types of housing (World Housing Day)   4·50   2·30
1709   600p. As No. 1707 but inscr for International Day for Housing the Homeless   4·75   2·50

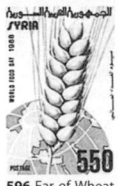

595 Euphrates Bridge, Deir el Zor

1988. International Tourism Day. Multicoloured.
1710   550p. Type **595**   4·75   2·30
1711   600p. Tetrapylon of Latakia   5·00   2·50
No. 1711 is erroneously inscribed "INTEPNATIONAL".

596 Ear of Wheat and Globe

1988. World Food Day.
1712 **596** 550p. multicoloured   5·00   2·10

597 Al-Assad University Hospital

1988. 18th Anniv of Corrective Movement of 16 November 1970.
1713 **597** 150p. multicoloured   1·40   70

598 Tree and Flowers

1988. Tree Day.
1714 **598** 600p. multicoloured 5·50 2·30

599 Dove with Envelope over Globe

1988. World Post Day.
1715 **599** 600p. multicoloured 5·00 2·30

600 Emblem and Doctor within Stethoscope

1989. Tenth Anniv of Arab Board for Medical Specializations.
1716 **600** 175p. multicoloured 1·60 70

601 Symbols of Agriculture and Industry

1989. 26th Anniv of Baathist Revolution of 8 March 1963.
1717 **601** 150p. multicoloured 60 35

602 Pres. Assad and Women

1989. Fifth General Congress of Union of Women.
1718 **602** 150p. multicoloured 60 35

603 Candle and Books

1989. Arab Teachers' Day.
1719 **603** 175p. multicoloured 70 45

604 Nehru

1989. Birth Centenary of Jarwaharlal Nehru (Indian statesman).
1720 **604** 550p. brown & lt brown 2·30 1·40

605 Mother and Children

1989. Mothers' Day.
1721 **605** 550p. multicoloured 2·30 1·40

606 Eurasian Goldfinch ("Goldfinch")

1989. Birds. Multicoloured.
1722 **606** 600p. Type 606 3·50 1·70
1723 600p. European bee eater ("Bee Eater") 3·50 1·70
1724 600p. Turtle dove 3·50 1·70

607 State Arms on Map

1989. 43rd Anniv of Evacuation of Foreign Troops from Syria.
1725 **607** 150p. multicoloured 60 35

608 Workers

1989. Labour Day.
1726 **608** 850p. green and black 3·50 2·20

609 Snapdragons

1989. Int Flower Show, Damascus. Multicoloured.
1727 **609** 150p. Type 609 60 35
1728 150p. "Canaria" 60 35
1729 450p. Cornflowers 1·80 1·20
1730 850p. "Clematis sackmani" 3·50 2·20
1731 900p. "Gesneriaceae" 3·75 2·30

610 Girl and Envelope

1989. Arab Post Day.
1732 **610** 175p. multicoloured 70 45

611 Emblem and Map

1989. 13th Arab Teachers' Union General Congress.
1733 **611** 175p. multicoloured 70 45

612 Painted Lady

1989. Butterflies. Multicoloured.
1734 **612** 550p. Type 612 2·75 1·50
1735 550p. Clouded yellow 2·75 1·50
1736 550p. Large (inscr "small") white 2·75 1·50

613 Symbols of International Co-operation

1989. World Telecommunications Day.
1737 **613** 550p. multicoloured 2·30 1·40

614 Emblem and Map

1989. 17th Arab Lawyers' Union Congress.
1738 **614** 175p. multicoloured 70 45

615 Monument and Al-Baath Pioneers

1989. 15th Anniv of Liberation of Qneitra.
1739 **615** 450p. multicoloured 1·80 1·20

616 Globe and Envelopes

1989. World Post Day,
1740 **616** 550p. multicoloured 2·30 1·40

617 Parliament Building

1989. Centenary of Interparliamentary Union.
1741 **617** 900p. multicoloured 3·50 2·30

618 Emblem and Monument

1989. 36th International Damascus Fair.
1742 **618** 450p. multicoloured 1·70 70

619 Jaabar Castle, Raqqa

1989. International Tourism Day. Multicoloured.
1743 **619** 550p. Type 619 2·30 1·40
1744 600p. Baal-Shamin Temple, Palmyra 2·40 1·50

620 Child's View of Intifada

1989. Palestinian "Intifada" Movement.
1745 **620** 550p. multicoloured 1·90 70

621 Common Carp

1989. Fish. Multicoloured.
1746 **621** 550p. Type 621 2·20 1·30
1747 600p. Brown trout 2·30 1·40

622 Omayyad Palace, Pres. Assad and Ebla Hotel

1989. 19th Anniv of Corrective Movement of 16 November 1970.
1748 **622** 150p. multicoloured 60 35

623 Children of Different Races taking Food from Large Bowl

1990. World Food Day (1989).
1749 **623** 850p. multicoloured 3·00 1·50

624 Dove, Globe and Children of Different Races

1990. International Children's Day.
1750 **624** 850p. multicoloured 3·00 1·50

625 Flag, Emblem and Ear of Wheat

1990. Fifth Revolutionary Youth Union Congress.
1751 **625** 150p. multicoloured 60 25

626 Tree-lined Road

1990. 27th Anniv of Baathist Revolution of 8 March 1963.
1752 **626** 600p. multicoloured 1·90 70

627 Flag and Arab Fighters

1990. 44th Anniv of Evacuation of Foreign Troops from Syria.
1753 **627** 175p. multicoloured 60 25

628 Woman carrying Child

1990. Mothers' Day.
| 1754 | **628** | 550p. multicoloured | 1·90 | 70 |

629 Globe and Couple

1990. Labour Day.
| 1755 | **629** | 550p. multicoloured | 1·80 | 95 |

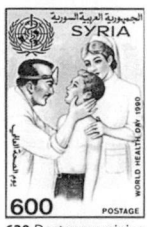

630 Doctor examining Boy

1990. World Health Day.
| 1756 | **630** | 600p. multicoloured | 1·90 | 1·00 |

631 Lilies

1990. Int Flower Show, Damascus. Multicoloured.
1757		600p. Type **631**	1·80	1·00
1758		600p. Cyclamen	1·80	1·00
1759		600p. Marigolds	1·80	1·00
1760		600p. "Viburnum opulus"	1·80	1·00
1761		600p. Swan river daisies	1·80	1·00

632 Goalkeeper saving Goal

1990. World Cup Football Championship, Italy. Multicoloured.
1762		550p. Type **632**	1·80	95
1763		550p. Players marking opponent	1·80	95
1764		600p. Map of Italy and ball (vert)	1·90	1·00
MS1765	74×55 mm. 1300p. Floodlit stadium and mascot. Imperf		13·50	13·50

633 Flag, Tree and City

1990. 16th Anniv of Liberation of Qneitra.
| 1766 | **633** | 550p. multicoloured | 1·80 | 95 |

634 Man and Book

1990. International Literacy Year.
| 1767 | **634** | 550p. multicoloured | 1·80 | 95 |

635 Weather Map

1990. World Meteorology Day.
| 1768 | **635** | 450p. multicoloured | 1·40 | 70 |

636 Emblem

1990. 37th International Damascus Fair.
| 1769 | **636** | 550p. multicoloured | 1·80 | 95 |

637 Old and Modern Methods of Ploughing

1990. United Nations Conference on Least Developed Countries.
| 1770 | **637** | 600p. multicoloured | 1·90 | 1·00 |

638 Boy watering Young Tree

1990. Tree Day.
| 1771 | **638** | 550p. multicoloured | 1·90 | 1·00 |

639 Children with Bread and Water in Wheat Field

1990. World Food Day.
| 1772 | **639** | 850p. multicoloured | 3·00 | 1·20 |

640 Al-Maqdisi and Map

1990. Death Millenary of Al-Maqdisi (geographer).
| 1773 | **640** | 550p. multicoloured | 1·90 | 1·00 |

1990. (a) As T **538** but with full-face portrait.
1774	50p. lilac	10	10
1775	70p. grey	20	10
1776	100p. blue	20	10
1777	150p. brown ("POSTAGE" in brown)	35	10
1777a	150p. brown ("POSTAGE" in white)	35	10
1778	300p. mauve	70	35
1779	350p. grey	95	45
1780	400p. red	1·00	50

641 Pres. Hafez al-Assad

(b) Type **641**.
1781	175p. multicoloured	50	20
1782	300p. multicoloured	85	25
1783	550p. multicoloured	1·40	35
1784	600p. multicoloured	1·90	70

(c) Horiz design with portrait as T **641** within decorative frame.
1786	1000p. multicoloured	3·00	95
1787	1500p. multicoloured	4·25	1·40
1788	2000p. multicoloured	6·00	1·90
1789	2500p. multicoloured	7·25	2·30

642 Pres. Assad with Scouts

1990. 20th Anniv of Corrective Movement of 16 November 1970. Sheet 120×95 mm. Imperf.
MS1795 550p. Type **642**; 550p. Pres. Assad and cheering crowd; 550p. Pres. Assad in uniform and Liberation Monument, Qneitra; 550p. Pres. Assad and Euphrates Dam   7·75   7·75

643 Control Tower, Douglas DC-9-80 Super Eighty Airliner and Emblem

1990. Arab Civil Aviation Day.
| 1796 | **643** | 175p. multicoloured | 70 | 35 |

644 Emblem, Open Book, Cogwheel and Ear of Wheat

1990. 40th Anniv of United Nations Development Programme.
| 1797 | **644** | 550p. multicoloured | 1·80 | 80 |

645 U.P.U. Emblem and Girl posting Letter

1990. World Post Day.
| 1798 | **645** | 550p. multicoloured | 1·80 | 80 |

646 Leapfrog

1990. World Children's Day.
| 1799 | **646** | 550p. multicoloured | 1·80 | 1·00 |

647 Emblem, Flames and Open Book

1990. Arab–Spanish Cultural Symposium.
| 1800 | **647** | 550p. multicoloured | 2·20 | 1·20 |

648 Paths to and away from AIDS

1990. World AIDS Day.
| 1801 | **648** | 550p. multicoloured | 2·20 | 1·20 |

649 Modern Roads and Buildings

1991. 28th Anniv of Baathist Revolution of 8 March 1963.
| 1802 | **649** | 150p. multicoloured | 1·20 | 25 |

650 Lesser Purple Emperor

1991. Butterflies. Multicoloured.
1803		550p. Type **650** (inscr "Change Ful Great Mars")	3·50	1·30
1804		550p. Small tortoiseshell	3·50	1·30
1805		550p. Swallowtail	3·50	1·30

651 Golden Orioles

1991. Birds. Multicoloured.
1806		600p. Type **651**	3·00	1·30
1807		600p. House sparrows	3·00	1·30
1808		600p. European roller	3·00	1·30

652 Three Generations

1991. Mothers' Day.
| 1809 | **652** | 550p. multicoloured | 2·20 | 95 |

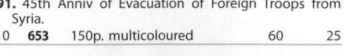

653 Statue

1991. 45th Anniv of Evacuation of Foreign Troops from Syria.
| 1810 | **653** | 150p. multicoloured | 60 | 25 |

654 Dividers and Spanner

1991. Labour Day.
1811 654 550p. multicoloured 2·20 95

655 Daffodils

1991. International Flower Show, Damascus. Multicoloured.
1812 550p. Type **655** 2·20 95
1813 600p. Bee balm 2·40 1·00

656 City and Ruins

1991. 17th Anniv of Liberation of Qneitra.
1814 656 550p. multicoloured 2·20 80

657 Running

1991. 11th Mediterranean Games, Athens. Multicoloured.
1815 550p. Type **657** 2·20 95
1816 550p. Football 2·20 95
1817 600p. Show jumping 2·40 1·20
MS1818 80×65 mm. 1300p. Dolphins playing water polo. Imperf 5·50 5·50

658 Hall

1991. 38th International Damascus Fair.
1819 658 550p. multicoloured 2·30 1·00

659 Courtyard, Azem Palace, Damascus

1991. International Tourism Day. Multicoloured.
1820 450p. Type **659** 1·80 80
1821 550p. Castle, Arwad Island 2·30 1·00

660 People encircling Block of Flats

1991. Housing Day.
1822 660 175p. multicoloured 70 35

661 Roller Skating

1991. International Children's Day.
1823 661 600p. multicoloured 2·40 1·00

662 Rhazes treating Patient

1991. Science Week.
1824 662 550p. multicoloured 2·30 1·00

663 Envelopes and Globe

1991. World Post Day.
1825 663 550p. multicoloured 2·30 1·00

664 Globe, Produce and Livestock

1991. World Food Day.
1826 664 550p. multicoloured 2·30 1·00

665 Tomb of Unknown Soldier, Damascus

1991
1827 665 600p. multicoloured 2·40 1·10
MS1828 65×80 mm. 1000p. Tomb, Imperf 4·25 4·25

666 Pres. Hafez-al-Assad

1991. 21st Anniv of Corrective Movement of 16 November 1970. Sheet 77×89 mm.
MS1829 666 2500p. multicoloured 10·00 10·00

667 Polluted and Clean Environments

1991. Environmental Protection.
1830 667 175p. multicoloured 85 45

668 Transmission Mast, Globe and Satellite

1991. International Telecommunications Fair.
1831 668 600p. multicoloured 2·40 1·10

669 Leaf and Port

1992. 29th Anniv of Baathist Revolution of 8 March 1963.
1832 669 600p. multicoloured 1·80 80

670 President Assad

1992. Re-election of President Hafez al-Assad. Multicoloured.
MS1833 Two sheets. (a) 65×95 mm. 5000p. Type **670**; (b) 100×85 mm. 5000p. Stamp portraits of Pres. Assad as in Type **670** but with state arms and inscriptions in right-hand margin 14·50 14·50

671 Chimneys, Gun-barrel, Ear of Wheat, Dove and Flag

1992. 45th Anniv of Baath Arab Socialist Party.
1834 671 850p. multicoloured 2·40 1·20

672 Crane and Mason building Wall

1992. Labour Day.
1835 672 900p. black, blue & mauve 2·75 1·30

673 Girls at Pedestrian Crossing

1992. Road Safety Campaign.
1836 673 850p. multicoloured 2·40 1·20

674 Girl listening to Mother's Stomach

1992. Mothers' Day.
1837 674 900p. multicoloured 2·75 1·30

675 Memorial

1992. 46th Anniv of Evacuation of Foreign Troops from Syria.
1838 675 900p. multicoloured 2·75 1·30

676 Flax

1992. International Flower Show, Damascus. Multicoloured.
1839 300p. Type **676** 85 35
1840 800p. "Yucca filamentosa" (vert) 2·30 1·00
1841 900p. "Zinnia elegans" (vert) 2·75 1·30

677 Football

1992. Olympic Games, Barcelona. Multicoloured.
1842 150p. Type **677** 35 25
1843 150p. Running 35 25
1844 450p. Swimming 1·20 60
1845 750p. Wrestling 2·10 95
MS1846 80×125 mm. 5000p. As Nos. 1842/5 but without face values. Imperf 7·25 7·25

678 Smoker standing in Ashtray

1992. Anti-smoking Campaign.
1847 678 750p. multicoloured 2·10 95

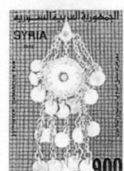

679 Pendant

1992. 39th International Damascus Fair.
1848 679 900p. multicoloured 2·40 1·20

680 Football

1992. Seventh Pan-Arab Games, Damascus. Multicoloured.
1849 750p. Type **680** 2·10 95
1850 850p. Gymnastics 2·40 1·20
1851 900p. Pole vaulting 2·75 1·30

681 Envelopes, Dove and Globe

1992. World Post Day.
1852 681 600p. multicoloured 1·80 80

682 Boy blowing
Dandelion Clock

1992. International Children's Day.
1853   **682**   850p. multicoloured   2·40   1·20

683 Sebtt
el-Mardini
(astronomer)

1992
1854   **683**   850p. multicoloured   3·00   1·30

684 Table Tennis

1992. Paralympic Games for Mentally Handicapped,
Madrid.
1855   **684**   850p. multicoloured   2·40   1·20

685 People's Square,
Damascus

1992. 22nd Anniv of Corrective Movement of 16
November 1970.
1856   **685**   450p. multicoloured   1·30   60

686 Tree

1992. Tree Day.
1857   **686**   600p. multicoloured   1·80   80

687 Statue of Pres. Assad,
Damascus

1993. 30th Anniv of Baathist Revolution of 8 March 1963.
1858   **687**   1100p. multicoloured   1·80   80

688 Common Blue

1993. Butterflies. Multicoloured.
1859   1000p. Type **688**   1·60   80
1860   1500p. Silver-washed fritillary   2·30   1·00
1861   2500p. Blue argus   4·00   1·90

689 Family

1993. Mothers' Day.
1862   **689**   1100p. multicoloured   1·80   80

690 Saladin Monument,
Damascus

1993. 47th Anniv of Evacuation of Foreign Troops from
Syria.
1863   **690**   1100p. multicoloured   1·80   80

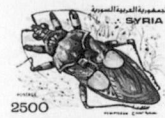

691 Bug

1993
1864   **691**   2500p. multicoloured   4·00   1·90

692 Tractor in Field of
Crops

1993. 25th Anniv of Arab Agrarian Union.
1865   **692**   1150p. multicoloured   1·80   80

693 Oil Workers

1993. Labour Day.
1866   **693**   1100p. multicoloured   1·80   80

694 Fye and Eye-chart

1993. Second Pan-Arab Ophthalmology International
Council Congress.
1867   **694**   1100p. multicoloured   1·80   80

695 Landscapes and Eye

1993. 25th Anniv of National Ophthalmological
Association.
1868   **695**   1150p. multicoloured   1·80   80

696 "Alcea setosa"

1993. 21st Int Flower Show, Damascus. Multicoloured.
1869   1000p. Type **696**   1·60   70
1870   1100p. Primulas   1·80   80
1871   1150p. Gesnerias   1·90   85

697 Prism Tomb

1993. International Tourism Day.
1872   **697**   1000p. multicoloured   1·80   80

698 Hand posting Letter
and Globe

1993. World Post Day.
1873   **698**   1000p. multicoloured   1·80   80

699 Boys playing Football

1993. International Children's Day.
1874   **699**   1150p. multicoloured   1·80   80

700 Ibn al-Bittar
(chemist)

1993. Science Week.
1875   **700**   1150p. multicoloured   1·80   80

701 Pres. Assad

1993. 23rd Anniv of Corrective Movement of 16
November 1970. Sheet 76×88 mm. Imperf.
MS1876 **701** 2500p. multicoloured   3·50   3·50

702 White Horse

1993. Arab Horses. Multicoloured.
1877   1000p. Type **702**   1·60   70
1878   1000p. Horse with white feet   1·60   70
1879   1500p. Black horse   2·10   95
1880   1500p. White horse with brown
           mane   2·10   95

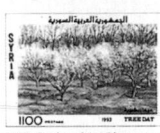

703 Orchard in Blossom

1993. Tree Day.
1881   **703**   1100p. multicoloured   1·80   80

704 Flags outside Venue

1993. 40th International Damascus Fair.
1882   **704**   1100p. multicoloured   1·80   80

705 Basel
al-Assad

1994. Basel al-Assad (President's son) Commem.
1883   **705**   2500p. multicoloured   3·50   1·70

706 Oranges

1994. 31st Anniv of Baathist Revolution of 8 March 1963.
Multicoloured.
1884   1500p. Type **706**   2·10   95
1885   1500p. Mandarins   2·10   95
1886   1500p. Lemons   2·10   95

707 Flags, Flame, Laurel
and Dates

1994. 48th Anniv of Evacuation of Foreign Troops from
Syria.
1887   **707**   1800p. multicoloured   2·40   1·20

708 Mechanical Digger
loading Truck

1994. Labour Day.
1888   **708**   1700p. multicoloured   2·40   1·20

709 Mother and Child at
Different Ages

1994. Mothers' Day.
1889   **709**   1800p. multicoloured   2·40   1·20

710 Emblem, "50" and "75"

1994. 75th Anniv of I.L.O. and 50th Anniv of Philadelphia
Declaration (social charter).
1890   **710**   1700p. multicoloured   2·10   95

711 Match Scene

1994. World Cup Football Championship, U.S.A.
Multicoloured.
1891   1700p. Type **711**   2·10   95
1892   1700p. Match scene (different)   2·10   95
MS1893 80×80 mm. 4000p. Match
scene (different). Imperf   5·00   5·00

712 Olympic Flag, Greek
Temple and "100"

1994. Cent of International Olympic Committee.
1894   **712**   1700p. multicoloured   1·80   95

713 Flags,
Lanterns and
Fountain

1994. 41st International Damascus Fair.
1895   **713**   1800p. multicoloured   2·10   1·00

714 Camomile

1994. Int Flower Show, Damascus. Multicoloured.
1896		1800p. Type **714**	2·10	1·00
1897		1800p. Gloxinia	2·10	1·00
1898		1800p. Mimosa	2·10	1·00

715 Apollo

1994. Butterflies. Multicoloured.
1899		1700p. Type **715**	2·10	1·00
1900		1700p. Purple emperor (value at right)	2·10	1·00
1901		1700p. Birdwing (value at left)	2·10	1·00

716 Symbols and Map

1994. Fourth Population Census.
| 1902 | **716** | 1000p. multicoloured | 1·10 | 50 |

717 Al-Kinsi (philosopher)

1994. ...
| 1903 | 717 | £S10 multicoloured | 1·30 | 65 |

718 Pres. Assad

1994. 24th Anniv of Corrective Movement of 16 November 1970. Sheet 76×88 mm. Imperf.
MS1904 £S25 multicoloured   3·25   3·25

719 Airport

1994. 50th Anniv of I.C.A.O.
| 1905 | **719** | £S17 multicoloured | 1·90 | 1·00 |

720 Al-Marjeh Square

1994
| 1906 | **720** | £S50 mauve | 5·75 | 2·75 |

721 Child with Tennis Racquet

1994. International Children's Day.
| 1907 | **721** | £S10 multicoloured | 1·30 | 65 |

722 Girl watching Birds with Envelopes

1994. World Post Day.
| 1908 | **722** | £S10 multicoloured | 1·30 | 65 |

723 Palmyra Roman Arch

1994. International Tourism Day.
| 1909 | **723** | £S17 multicoloured | 1·90 | 1·00 |

724 Modern Building

1995. 32nd Anniv of Baathist Revolution of 8 March 1963.
| 1910 | **724** | £S18 multicoloured | 1·60 | 1·10 |

725 League Emblem and Map

1995. 50th Anniv of Arab League.
| 1911 | **725** | £S17 multicoloured | 1·60 | 1·00 |

726 Water Pump

1995. World Water Day.
| 1912 | **726** | £S17 multicoloured | 1·60 | 1·00 |

727 Woman sheltering Figures

1995. Mothers' Day.
| 1913 | **727** | £S17 multicoloured | 1·60 | 1·00 |

728 Hand holding Tree

1995. Tree Day.
| 1914 | **728** | 1800p. multicoloured | 1·60 | 1·10 |

729 Family

1995. International Year of the Family (1994).
| 1915 | **729** | 1700p. multicoloured | 1·60 | 1·00 |

730 Statue and Flag

1995. 49th Anniv of Evacuation of Foreign Troops from Syria.
| 1916 | **730** | £S17 multicoloured | 1·60 | 1·00 |

731 ... on Flowers

1995. First Anniv of Arab Apiculturalists Union.
| 1917 | **731** | £S17 multicoloured | 2·30 | 1·10 |

732 Pres. Assad

1995
1920	**732**	£S10 purple	1·30	65
1921	**732**	£S17 lilac	1·60	1·00
1922	**732**	£S18 green	1·80	1·10
1923	**732**	£S100 blue	15	15
1924	**732**	£S500 yellow	40	25

733 Welder

1995. Labour Day.
| 1925 | **733** | £S10 multicoloured | 1·30 | 65 |

734 Anniversary Emblem

1995. 50th Anniv of F.A.O.
| 1926 | **734** | £S15 multicoloured | 1·40 | 90 |

735 Desert Festival

1995. Tourism Day.
| 1927 | **735** | £S18 multicoloured | 1·60 | 1·10 |

736 Astilbe

1995. 23rd Int Flower Show, Damascus. Multicoloured.
1928		£S10 Type **736**	1·00	90
1929		£S10 Evening primrose	1·00	90
1930		£S10 Campanula (blue carpet)	1·00	90

737 Anniversary Emblem on U.N. Headquarters

1995. 50th Anniv of U.N.O.
| 1931 | **737** | £S18 multicoloured | 1·60 | 1·10 |

738 Woman holding Globe

1995. Fourth World Conference on Women, Peking.
| 1932 | **738** | £S18 multicoloured | 1·60 | 1·10 |

739 ...

1995. 42nd International Damascus Fair.
| 1933 | **739** | £S15 multicoloured | 1·40 | 90 |

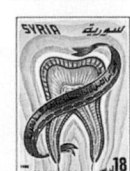
740 Tooth and Ribbon

1995. Second Congress of Arab Dentists' Association.
| 1934 | **740** | £S18 multicoloured | 1·60 | 1·10 |

741 Writing Letters and Air Mail Colours around Globe

1995. World Post Day.
| 1935 | **741** | £S15 multicoloured | 1·40 | 90 |

742 Children playing on Beach

1995. World Children's Day.
| 1936 | **742** | £S18 multicoloured | 1·60 | 1·10 |

743 Soldiers

1995. 50th Anniv of Syrian Army.
| 1937 | **743** | £S18 multicoloured | 1·60 | 1·10 |

744 Ahmed ben Maged

1995. 500th Death Anniv of Ahmed ben Maged (cartographer).
1938   **744**   £S18 multicoloured   1·60   1·10

745 Pres. Assad

1995. 25th Anniv of Corrective Movement of 16 November 1970.
1939   **745**   £S10 multicoloured   90   65
MS1940 111×75 mm. £S50 Pres. Assad and 1975, 1980, 1985 and 1990 stamps. Imperf   4·75   4·75

746 Great Tit and Chicks

1995. Birds. Multicoloured.
1941   £S18 Type **746**   1·90   1·40
1942   £S18 European robin in snow   1·90   1·40
1943   £S18 Bluethroat on post   1·90   1·40

747 Pasteur and Laboratory

1995. Death Centenary of Louis Pasteur (chemist).
1944   **747**   £S18 multicoloured   1·60   1·10

748 Olive Tree

1996. Tree Day.
1945   **748**   £S17 multicoloured   1·60   1·00

749 Pumping Station, Kudairan

1996. 33rd Anniv of Baathist Revolution of 8 March 1963.
1946   **749**   £S25 multicoloured   2·50   1·60

750 Woman and Horsemen

1996. 50th Anniv of Evacuation of Foreign Troops from Syria.
1947   **750**   £S10 multicoloured   90   65
1948   **750**   £S25 multicoloured   2·50   1·60
MS1949 80×60 mm. **750** £S25 multicoloured. Imperf   2·50   2·50

751 Woman and Baby

1996. Mothers' Day.
1950   **751**   £S10 multicoloured   90   65

752 Textile Factory Workers

1996. Labour Day.
1951   **752**   £S15 multicoloured   1·40   90

753 Memorial

1996. 22nd Anniv of Liberation of Qneitra.
1952   **753**   £S10 multicoloured   90   65

754 Map, Palestinian Flag and Arabic Script

1996. 50th Anniv of "Al-Baath" (newspaper).
1953   **754**   £S18 multicoloured   1·60   1·10

755 "Mammilaria erythosperma"

1996. 24th International Flower Show, Damascus. Cacti. Multicoloured.
1954   £S18 Type **755**   1·60   1·10
1955   £S18 "Notocactus graessnerii"   1·60   1·10

756 Wrestling

1996. Olympic Games, Atlanta, U.S.A. Multicoloured.
1956   £S17 Type **756**   1·60   1·00
1957   £S17 Swimming   1·60   1·00
1958   £S17 Running   1·60   1·00
MS1959 80×59 mm. £S25 Football. Imperf   2·50   2·50

757 Guglielmo Marconi and Transmitter

1996. Cent (1995) of First Radio Transmissions.
1960   **757**   £S17 multicoloured   1·60   1·00

758 Family protected from burning "AIDS"

1996. World AIDS Day.
1961   **758**   £S17 multicoloured   1·60   1·00

759 Fair Emblem, Pattern and Globe

1996. 43rd International Damascus Fair.
1962   **759**   £S17 multicoloured   1·60   1·00

760 Computer, Emblem and Globe

1996. Fifth Anniv of National Information Centre.
1963   **760**   £S18 multicoloured   1·60   1·10

761 Girls playing

1996. World Children's Day.
1964   **761**   £S10 multicoloured   90   65

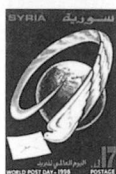

762 Globe and Dove with Letter

1996. World Post Day.
1965   **762**   £S17 multicoloured   1·60   1·00

763 Sons of Musa ibn Shaker

1996. Science Week.
1966   **763**   £S10 multicoloured   90   65

764 Pres. Assad

1996. 26th Anniv of Corrective Movement of 16 November 1970.
1967   **764**   £S10 multicoloured   90   65
MS1968 65×90 mm. **764** £S50 multicoloured. Imperf   4·75   4·75

765 Child sitting on Globe

1996. 50th Anniv of U.N.I.C.E.F.
1969   **765**   £S17 multicoloured   1·90   1·10

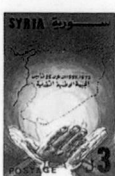

766 Hands and Map

767 Grain Silos and Wheat

1997. 25th Anniv of National Progressive Front.
1970   **766**   £S3 multicoloured   30   15

1997. 34th Anniv of Baathist Revolution of 8 March 1963.
1971   **767**   £S15 multicoloured   1·70   1·10

768 Party Emblem

1997. 50th Anniv of Baath Arab Socialist Party.
1972   **768**   £S25 multicoloured   3·50   2·10
MS1973 91×66 mm. No. 1972. Imperf   3·75   3·75

769 Apple Trees

1997. Tree Day.
1974   **769**   £S10 multicoloured   1·00   70

770 Mother and Daughter feeding Doves

1997. Mothers' Day.
1975   **770**   £S15 multicoloured   1·70   1·10

771 "Beautiful Woman from Palmyra" (relief)

1997. World Tourism Day (1996).
1976   **771**   £S17 multicoloured   1·90   1·10

772 Grey Mullet

1997. Fish. Multicoloured.
1977   £S17 Type **772**   2·10   1·30
1978   £S17 Mediterranean horse mackerel (country inscr at top)   2·10   1·30

773 Horsemen

1997. 51st Anniv of Evacuation of Foreign Troops from Syria.
1979   **773**   £S15 multicoloured   1·70   1·10

774 Building
Pipeline

1997. Labour Day.
1980 **774** £S15 multicoloured 1·70 1·10

775 Library and Books

1997. World Book Day.
1981 **775** £S10 multicoloured 1·00 70

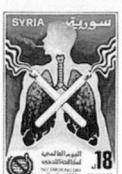

776 Smoker's
Diseased Lungs
and Cigarettes

1997. World "No Smoking" Day.
1982 **776** £S18 multicoloured 1·90 1·30

777 "Echinocereus
purporeus"

1997. International Flower Show, Damascus.
Multicoloured.
1983 £S18 Type **777** 1·90 1·30
1984 £S18 Irises 1·90 1·30

778 Emblem

1997. Fourth Arab Union of Dentists' Associations
Congress.
1985 **778** £S10 multicoloured 1·00 70

779 Flags and
Monument

1997. 44th International Damascus Fair.
1986 **779** £S17 multicoloured 1·90 1·10

780 Child reaching for
Landmine

1997. International Children's Day.
1987 **780** £S17 multicoloured 1·90 1·10

781 Post Rider and Dove

1997. World Post Day.
1988 **781** £S17 multicoloured 1·90 1·10

782 Tourists on Flying
Carpet

1997. International Tourism Day.
1989 **782** £S17 multicoloured 1·90 1·10

783 Jabir ibn
Haijan (alchemist)

1997. Science Week.
1990 **783** £S17 multicoloured 1·90 1·10

784 Pres. Assad

1997. 27th Anniv of Corrective Movement of 16
November 1991. Multicoloured.
1991 £S10 Type **784** 1·00 70
MS1992 109×85 mm. £S50 Portrait as
in T **784** with inscriptions arranged
beside it. Imperf 5·50 5·50

785 Emblem, Minarets and
Banner

1997. 30th Anniv of Organization of the Islamic
Conference.
1993 **785** £S10 multicoloured 1·00 70

786 Sewage Works

1998. 35th Anniv of Baathist Revolution of 8 March 1963.
1994 **786** £S17 multicoloured 1·90 1·10

787 Mother with Children

1998. Mothers' Day.
1995 **787** £S10 multicoloured 1·00 70

788 Warrior with
Raised Sword

1998. 52nd Anniv of Evacuation of Foreign Troops from
Syria.
1996 **788** £S10 multicoloured 1·00 70

789 Computer
and Industrial
Sites

1998. Labour Day.
1997 **789** £S18 multicoloured 2·00 1·30

790 Players
challenging for
Ball

1998. World Cup Football Championship, France.
1998 **790** £S10 multicoloured 1·00 70
MS1999 80×75 mm. £S25 Match scene.
Imperf 2·75 2·75

791 "Bougainvillea
glabra"

1998. International Flower Show, Damascus.
Multicoloured.
2000 £S17 Type **791** 1·90 1·10
2001 £S17 "Hibiscus rosa-sinensis" 2·00 1·30

792 Bust of
Princess of Raniar

1998. International Tourism Day.
2002 **792** £S17 multicoloured 2·00 1·30

793 Mother Teresa

1998. Death Commemoration of Mother Teresa (founder
of Missionaries of Charity).
2003 **793** £S18 multicoloured 2·20 1·40

794 Post Office

1998. Arab Post Day.
2004 **794** £S10 multicoloured 1·10 80

795 Cigarette
piercing Heart

1998. World "No Smoking" Day.
2005 **795** £S15 multicoloured 1·70 1·10

796 Doves and World Map

1998. World Post Day.
2006 **796** £S18 multicoloured 2·20 1·40

797 Child on
Globe and Dove

1998. International Children's Day.
2007 **797** £S18 multicoloured 2·20 1·40

798 Fish Fountain and Fair
Venue

1998. 45th International Damascus Fair.
2008 **798** £S18 multicoloured 2·20 1·40

799 Pres. Assad and Combat Scenes (image scaled to
44% of original size)

1998. 25th Anniv of October Offensive against Israel.
Sheet 110×75 mm.
MS2009 £S25 multicoloured 3·25 3·25

800 Ibn ad-Duranim
(mathematician)

1998. Science Week.
2010 **800** £S10 multicoloured 1·10 80

801 Pres. Assad

1998. 28th Anniv of Corrective Movement of 16
November 1970. Multicoloured.
2011 10p. Type **801** 1·10 80
MS2012 110×75 mm. £S25 Portrait as
in T **801** and state flag. Imperf 3·25 3·25

802 Dome of the Rock and Old City

1998. Jerusalem.
2013 **802** £S10 multicoloured 1·10 80

803 Dromedaries

1998
2014 **803** £S17 multicoloured 2·30 1·40

804 Pres. Assad

1999. Re-election of President Hafez al-Assad to Fifth Term.

2015	**804**	£S10 multicoloured	1·10	80
2016	**804**	£S17 multicoloured	1·90	1·30
2017	**804**	£S18 multicoloured	2·00	1·40

MS2018 149×119 mm. £S50 multi-coloured (Portrait as in T **804** and stamps of 1971, 1978, 1985 and 1992). Imperf ... 6·00 ... 6·00

805 New Communications Office Building

1990. 36th Baathist Revolution of 8 March 1963. Multicoloured.

2019		£S25 Type **805**	3·00	2·00

MS2020 75×110 mm. £S25 Commu-nications Office and statue of Pres. Assad. Imperf ... 3·25 ... 3·25

806 Fig Tree

1999. Tree Day.

2021	**806**	£S17 multicoloured	2·00	1·40

807 Mother breast-feeding Baby

1999. Mothers' Day.

2022	**807**	£S17 multicoloured	2·00	1·40

808 Woman in Baath Party Colours and Man with Rifle

1999. 53rd Anniv of Evacuation of Foreign Troops from Syria.

2023	**808**	£S18 multicoloured	2·20	1·50

809 16 November Workers' Further Education Institute

1999. Labour Day.

2024	**809**	£S10 multicoloured	1·20	85

810 Crowd with "Human Rights" Banner

1999. 50th Anniv (1998) of Universal Declaration of Human Rights.

2025	**810**	£S18 multicoloured	2·20	1·50

811 Jasmin

1999. International Flower Show, Damascus. Multicoloured.

2026		£S10 Type **811**	1·20	85
2027		£S10 Acanthus	1·20	85

812 Show Jumping and Crowd with Lighted Crowns

1999. Tenth Friendship Festival, Al Basel.

2028	**812**	£S10 multicoloured	1·20	85

813 Globes and Emblem

1999. 46th International Damascus Fair.

2029	**813**	£S15 multicoloured	1·90	1·20

814 Patient receiving Treatment and Emblem

1999. Seventh Arab Union of Dentists' Associations Congress.

2030	**814**	£S17 multicoloured	2·00	1·40

815 Postman and Map of Arab States

1999. Arab Post Day.

2031	**815**	£S10 multicoloured	1·20	85

816 Abu Hanifah al Deilouri (botanist)

1999. Science Week.

2032	**816**	£S17 multicoloured	2·00	1·40

817 Postal Transport, Emblem and Headquarters, Berne

1999. 125th Anniv of Universal Postal Union.

2033	**817**	£S17 multicoloured	2·00	1·40

818 Ummayed Mosque and Our Lady of Saydnaya Convent, Damascus

1999. 2000 Years of Religious Co-existence.

2034	**818**	£S17 multicoloured	2·00	1·40

819 October 1973 Liberation War Monument and Pres. Assad (statues)

1999. 29th Anniv of Corrective Movement of 16 November 1970. Multicoloured.

2035		£S17 Type **819**	2·00	2·00
2036		£S17 Close-up detail of statue (vert)	2·00	2·00

MS2037 110×76 mm. £S25 October 1973 Liberation War Monument and Fountains before statue. Imperf ... 3·00 ... 3·00

820 Children holding Hands around Globe

1999. International Children's Day.

2038	**820**	£S18 multicoloured	2·20	1·40

821 Factories, Corn and Family

2000. 37th Anniv of Baathist Revolution of 8 March 1963.

2039	**821**	£S18 multicoloured	2·00	2·00

822 Mother holding Child

2000. Mothers' Day.

2040	**822**	£S17 multicoloured	1·90	1·90

823 Battle Scene (image scaled to 50% of original size)

2000. 54th Anniv of Evacuation of Foreign Troops from Syria. Sheet 95×80 mm.

MS2041	£S25 multicoloured	2·75	2·75

824 Rose and Cog

2000. Labour Day.

2042	**824**	£S10 multicoloured	1·10	1·10

825 Foxy Charaxes

2000. Butterflies. Multicoloured.

2043		£S17 Type **825**	1·90	1·90
2044		£S18 Apaturairis	2·00	2·00

826 Tree and Fruit

2000. Tree Day.

2045	**826**	£S18 multicoloured	2·00	2·00

827 President Basher Al-Assad

2000. Election of President Basher Al-Assad.

2046	**827**	£S3 multicoloured	25	25
2047	**827**	£S10 multicoloured	1·20	1·20
2048	**827**	£S17 multicoloured	2·00	2·00
2049	**827**	£S18 multicoloured	2·10	2·10

MS2050 109×75 mm. £S50 President Al-Assad. Imperf ... 6·00 ... 6·00

828 Child with Balloons

2000

2051	**828**	£S10 multicoloured	1·20	1·20

829 Flags, Exhibition Building and Crowd

2000. 47th International Damascus Fair.

2052	**829**	£S15 multicoloured	1·70	1·70

830 U.P.U. Emblem, Envelope and Globe

2000. World Post Day.

2053	**830**	£S18 multicoloured	2·10	2·10

831 Map and Emblem

2000. Arab Post Day.
| 2054 | **831** | £S18 multicoloured | 2·10 | 2·10 |

832 Weight
Lifting

2000. Olympic Games, Sydney. Multicoloured.
2055		£S17 Type **832**	2·10	2·10
2056		£S18 Shot-put	2·30	2·30
MS2057	81×75 mm. £S25 Javelin		3·00	3·00

833 Nasir Al-din Altusi
(scientist)

2000. Science Week.
| 2058 | **833** | £S15 multicoloured | 2·40 | 2·40 |

834 Emblem and
Globe

2000. 50th Anniv of World Meteorological Organization.
| 2059 | **834** | £S10 multicoloured | 1·20 | 1·20 |

835 Cherubs in Rowing Boat and City (mosaic) (image
scaled to 43% of original size)

2000. World Tourism Day. Sheet 111×85 mm. Imperf.
| **MS**2060 | **835** | £S50 multicoloured | 6·00 | 6·00 |

836 Dam and Emblem

2001. 50th Anniv of Engineer Syndicate. Multicoloured.
| 2061 | | £S17 Type **836** | 2·00 | 2·00 |
| **MS**2062 | 85×95 mm. £S25 As No. 2061
but with design enlarged. Imperf | | 3·00 | 3·00 |

2001. Al-Marjeh Square. As T **720**.
2063	**720**	100p. light blue-green	40	40
2064	**720**	£S10 brown red	1·20	1·20
2065	**720**	£S50 deep blue	5·25	5·25

837 Computers

2001. 38th Anniv of Baathist Revolution of 8 March 1963.
| 2066 | **837** | £S25 multicoloured | 3·00 | 3·00 |

838 President Hafis al-Assad and
Agricultural Painting

2001. Ninth Agricultural Congress.
| 2067 | **838** | £S25 multicoloured | 3·00 | 3·00 |

839 Statue of
Mother and Baby

2001. Mother's Day.
| 2068 | **839** | £S10 multicoloured | 1·20 | 1·20 |

840 Horse's Head

2001. 55th Anniv of Evacuation of Foreign Troops from
Syria.
| 2069 | **840** | £S25 multicoloured | 3·00 | 3·00 |

841 Hand, Quill
and Emblem

2001. Book and Copyright Day.
| 2070 | **841** | £S10 multicoloured | 1·20 | 1·20 |

842 Statue of
Man holding
Spade and Globe

2001. Labour Day.
| 2071 | **842** | £S18 multicoloured | 2·10 | 2·10 |

843 Weigela

2001. International Flower Show, Damascus.
Multicoloured.
| 2072 | | £S10 Type **843** | 1·20 | 1·20 |
| 2073 | | £S10 Mertensia | 1·20 | 1·20 |

844 Ruined Building

2001. 27th Anniv of Liberation of Queneitra.
| 2074 | **844** | £S17 multicoloured | 1·70 | 1·70 |

845 President Bashar
Al-Assad

2001. First Anniv of Election of President Bashar Al-Assad.
| 2075 | **845** | £S17 multicoloured | 95 | 95 |

846 People climbing
Globe and UNHCR Emblem

2001. 50th Anniv of United Nations High Commissioner
for Refugees.
| 2076 | **846** | £S17 multicoloured | 1·70 | 1·70 |

847 Postman and Van

2001. Arab Post Day.
| 2077 | **847** | £S18 multicoloured | 1·70 | 1·70 |

848 Aerial View of
Damascus
surrounded by
Flags

2001. 48th International Damascus Fair.
| 2078 | **848** | £S10 multicoloured | 1·20 | 1·20 |

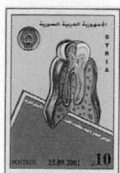

849 Skull, Cigarettes and
Ash Tray

2001. World "No Smoking" Day.
| 2079 | **849** | £S18 multicoloured | 2·10 | 2·10 |

850 Cross Section
of Tooth

2001. Tenth Arab Union of Dentists' Association Congress.
| 2080 | **850** | £S10 multicoloured | 1·20 | 1·20 |

851 Bust of Princess of
Banias

2001. World Tourism Day.
| 2081 | **851** | £S17 multicoloured | 1·70 | 1·70 |

852 Globe, Envelope and
UPU Emblem

2001. World Post Day.
| 2082 | **852** | £S10 multicoloured | 1·20 | 1·20 |

853 Boy

2001. International Children's Day.
| 2083 | **853** | £S18 multicoloured | 2·10 | 2·10 |

854 Inscribed
Scroll

2001. Arab Document Day. Multicoloured.
| 2084 | | £S10 Type **854** | 1·20 | 1·20 |
| **MS**2085 | 84×110 mm. £S25 As No. 2084
but with design enlarged. Imperf | | 3·00 | 3·00 |

855 The Citadel, Aleppo

2001. The Aga Khan Award for Architecture Presentation
Ceremony, Aleppo. Multicoloured.
2086		£S10 Type **855**	1·20	1·20
2087		£S17 The Citadel from below	2·00	2·00
2088		£S18 As No. 2087	2·10	2·10

856 Planning Commission
Building, Damascus

2001. 31st Anniv of Corrective Movement of 16
November 1970.
| 2089 | **856** | £S5 multicoloured | 55 | 55 |
| 2090 | **856** | £S15 multicoloured | 1·60 | 1·60 |

857 Youth
Stoning Tank

2001. Al Aqsa Intifada.
| 2091 | **857** | £S17 multicoloured | 1·70 | 1·70 |

858 Flowering
Tree

2001. Tree Day.
| 2092 | **858** | £S5 multicoloured | 55 | 55 |

859 Gazelle

2002
2093 859 £S15 multicoloured   1·60   1·60

860 Cement Factory

2002. 39th Anniv of Baathist Revolution of 8 March 1963.
2094 860 £S15 multicoloured   1·50   1·50

861 Mother holding Child

2002. Mothers' Day.
2095 861 £S25 multicoloured   2·40   2·40

862 Party Headquarters

2002. 55th Anniv of Al-Baath Party.
2096 862 £S15 multicoloured   1·50   1·50

863 Map and Emblem

2002. 56th Anniv of Evacuation of Foreign Troops from Syria.
2097 863 £S15 multicoloured   1·50   1·50

864 UNESCO Emblem

2002. Labour Day.
2098 864 £S10 multicoloured   1·10   1·10

865 Players

2002. World Cup Football Championships, Japan and South Korea. Multicoloured.
2099   £S5 Type **865**   55   55
2100   £S10 Player chasing ball   1·10   1·10
MS2101 79×65 mm £S25 Player jumping for ball. Imperf   2·00   2·00

866 Wallflower

2002. International Flower Show, Damascus. Multicoloured.
2102   £S15 Type **866**   1·50   1·50
2103   £S17 Narcissus   1·60   1·60

867 Envelopes circling Map of Arab States

2002. Arab Post Day.
2104 867 £S5 multicoloured   55   55
2105 867 £S10 multicoloured   1·10   1·10

868 Abdul-Rahman Al-Kawakibi

2002. Death Centenary of Abdul-Rahman Al-Kawakibi (wrlter).
2106 868 £S10 multicoloured   1·10   1·10

869 Emblem

2002. 49th International Damascus Fair. Multicoloured.
2107   £S5 Type **869**   55   55
2108   £S10 Mosaic   1·10   1·10

870 Map, Bridge and Train

2002. Centenary of First Syrian Railway.
2109 870 £S10 multicoloured   1·60   1·60

871 Sea Goddess, Shahba (mosaic)

2002. World Tourism Day.
2110 871 £S10 multicoloured   1·10   1·10

872 Protesters and Tank

2002. Second Anniv of Al Aqsa Intifada. Multicoloured.
2111   £S10 Type **872**   1·10   1·10
MS2112 64×80 mm. £S25 As No. 2111 but with design enlarged. Imperf   2·00   2·00

873 Dove holding Letter

2002. World Post Day. Multicoloured.
2113   £S10 Type **873**   1·10   1·10
2114   £S10 Envelope and UPU emblem (horiz)   1·10   1·10

874 Children

2002. International Children's Day.
2115 874 £S10 multicoloured   1·10   1·10

875 Techrin Thermal Power Plant

2002. 32nd Anniv of Corrective Movement of 16 November 1970.
2116 875 £S10 multicoloured   1·10   1·10

876 Sand Grouse

2002. Birds. Multicoloured.
2117   £S3 Type **876**   35   35
2118   £S5 Francolin   55   55
2119   £S10 Mallard   1·00   1·00
2120   £S15 Goose   1·50   1·50

877 Pine Tree

2002. Tree Day.
2121 877 £S10 multicoloured   1·10   1·10

2003. Al-Marjeh Square. As T **720**.
2122 720 300p. brown   40   40

878 Anniversary Emblem

2003. 40th Anniv of Baathist Revolution of 8 March 1963.
2123 878 £S15 multicoloured   1·20   1·20

879 Stylized Classroom

2003. Teachers' Day.
2124 879 £S17 multicoloured   1·30   1·30

880 Mother holding Sleeping Child

2003. Mothers' Day.
2125 880 £S32 multicoloured   2·75   2·75

881 Soldier

2003. 57th Anniv of Evacuation of Foreign Troops from Syria.
2126 881 £S15 multicoloured   1·20   1·20

882 Man and Machine

2003. Labour Day.
2127 882 £S10 multicoloured   2·00   2·00

883 Flower Border (inscr "Damask rose-violet")

2003. International Flower Show, Damascus. Multicoloured.
2128   £S10 Type **883**   80   80
2129   £S10 Red flowers (inscr "Anemone")   80   80
2130   £S10 White flowers (inscr "Daisy")   80   80
2131   £S10 Flower border (inscr "Damask rose-gillyflower")   80   80
2132   £S10 Sunflowers   80   80

884 Flags and Anniversary Emblem

2003. 50th International Damascus Fair. Multicoloured.
2133   £S32 Type **884**   2·40   2·40
MS2134 90×65 mm. £S50 Jewelled spheres. Imperf   4·00   4·00

885 Al Hamidieh Souk

2003. World Tourism Day.
2135 885 £S32 multicoloured   2·40   2·40

886 Flags and Globe

2003. World Post Day.
2136 886 £S10 multicoloured   80   80

887 Children Playing

2003. International Children's Day.
2137 **887** £S15 multicoloured 1·20 1·20

888 Building Facade and Pope John
Paul II

2003. 25th Anniv of the Pontificate of Pope John Paul II.
2138 **888** £S32 multicoloured 2·50 2·50

889 Flower, Map
and "33"

2003. 33rd Anniv of Corrective Movement of 16
November 1970.
2139 **889** £S15 multicoloured 1·20 1·20

890 President
Bashar
Al-Assad

2003
2140 **890** £S15 green 1·20 1·20
2141 **890** £S25 blue 2·00 2·00
2142 **890** £S50 magenta 4·25 4·25

891 Binaries,
Globe, Figures and
Computers

2003. World Information Technology Summit, Geneva.
2143 **891** £S15 multicoloured 1·20 1·20

892 Woodcock

2003. Birds. Multicoloured.
2144 £S5 Type **892** 40 40
2145 £S10 Lapwing 80 80
2146 £S15 European roller 1·20 1·20
2147 £S17 Teal 1·30 1·30
2148 £S18 Bustard 1·50 1·50

893 Pomegranate

2003. Tree Day.
2149 **893** £S25 multicoloured 2·10 2·10

894 Euphrates River Dam

2004. 41st Anniv of Baathist Revolution of 8 March 1963.
2150 **894** £S10 multicoloured 85 85

895 Teacher and
Pupil

2004. Teachers' Day.
2151 **895** £S5 multicoloured 45 45

896 Mother holding Baby

2004. Mothers' Day.
2152 **896** £S15 multicoloured 1·30 1·30

897 Map and "58"

2004. 58th Anniv of Evacuation of Foreign Troops from
Syria.
2153 **897** £S10 multicoloured 85 85

898 Factory and Cogs

2004. Labour Day.
2154 **898** £S10 multicoloured 85 85

899 Emblem and Players

2004. Centenary of FIFA (Federation Internationale de
Football Association) (1st issue). Multicoloured.
2155 £S10 Type **899** 45 45
2156 £S10 Two players and emblem 85 85
MS2157 81×66 mm. £S10 Emblem,
players and ball. Imperf 2·30 2·30
See also Nos. 2167/8.

900 Inscr "Gladiola
lavender"

2004. International Flower Show, Damascus.
Multicoloured.
2158 £S5 Type **900** 45 45
2159 £S5 Inscr "The Jasmine" 45 45
2160 £S5 Inscr "Iris" 45 45
2161 £S5 Inscr "Orange Nesrien" 45 45
2162 £S5 Tulips 45 45

901 Emblem

2004. International Red Cross Committee Campaign to
protect Children in War.
2163 **901** £S32 rosine and black 2·75 2·75

902 Runners

2004. Olympic Games, Athens. Multicoloured.
2164 £S5 Type **902** 45 45
2165 £S10 Boxers (horiz) 85 85
2166 £S25 Swimmer (horiz) 2·10 2·10

2004. Centenary of FIFA (Federation Internationale
de Football Association) (2nd issue). As T **899**.
Multicoloured.
2167 £S15 Emblem (vert) 1·30 1·30
2168 £S32 Emblem and "100" 2·75 2·75

903 Anniversary
Emblem

2004. 51st International Damascus Fair.
2169 **903** £S25 multicoloured 2·10 2·10

904 Family on Map

2004. Census.
2170 **904** £S10 multicoloured 85 85

905 Locomotive

2004. World Tourism Day. Multicoloured.
2171 £S5 Type **905** 45 45
2172 £S10 Building facade 85 85
2173 £S10 Locomotive with short
funnel 85 85

906 Envelopes

2004. World Post Day.
2174 **906** £S17 multicoloured 1·90 1·90

907 Babies

2004. International Children's Day.
2175 **907** £S18 multicoloured 1·60 1·60

908 Building and "34"

2004. 34th Anniv of Corrective Movement of 16
November1970.
2176 **908** £S25 multicoloured 2·75 2·75

909 Shami Goat

2004. Domestic Animals. Multicoloured.
2177 £S5 Type **909** 45 45
2178 £S15 Awassi sheep 1·40 1·40
2179 £S17 Buffalo 1·60 1·60
2180 £S18 Shami cow 1·70 1·70

910 Walnut

2004. Tree Day.
2181 **910** £S10 multicoloured 95 95

911 Northern Bald Ibis

2004
2182 **911** £S10 multicoloured 95 95

912 Port

2005. 42nd Anniv of Baathist Revolution of 8 March
1963.
2183 **912** £S17 multicoloured 1·60 1·60

913 Teacher and Pupil

2005. Teachers' Day.
2184 **913** £S25 multicoloured 2·30 2·30

914 Mother bathing
Child

2005. Mothers' Day.
2185 **914** £S18 multicoloured 1·70 1·70

915 Emblem

2005. 60th Anniv of Arab League.
2186 **915** £S10 multicoloured 80 80

916 Figures holding Flag

2005. 59th Anniv of Evacuation of Foreign Troops from Syria.
2187 **916** £S17 multicoloured 1·60 1·60

917 New Road

2005. Labour Day.
2188 **917** £S15 multicoloured 1·30 1·30

918 Hyacinth (inscr "Jacinthe")

2005. International Flower Show, Damascus. Multicoloured.
2189 £S5 Type **918** 65 65
2190 £S10 *Sternbergia clusiana* 95 95
2191 £S15 *Primula obconica* 1·40 1·40
2192 £S17 *Primula malacoides* 1·90 1·90
2193 £S18 Inscr "Canaria" 2·00 2·00

919 Inscr "Papilio Ulysses"

2005. Butterflies. Multicoloured.
2194 £S10 Type **919** 1·10 1·10
2195 £S10 Monarch 1·10 1·10
2196 £S10 *Baeotus baeotus* 1·10 1·10
2197 £S10 Inscr "Lace wing" 1·10 1·10
2198 £S10 Inscr "Tiger swallowtail" 1·10 1·10

920 Emblem

2005. 52nd International Damascus Fair.
2199 **920** £S15 multicoloured 1·90 1·90

921 Arwad Island

2005. World Tourism Day.
2200 **921** £S17 multicoloured 2·00 2·00

922 Rumi

923 Envelopes and Globe

2005. Mawlana Jalal Eddin Al-Rumi (Jalal al-Din Muhammad Rumi) (writer) Commemoration.
2201 **922** £S25 multicoloured 2·75 2·75

2005. World Post Day.
2202 **923** £S18 multicoloured 2·00 2·00

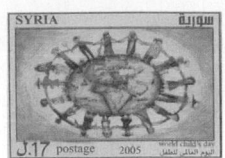

924 Children encircling Globe

2005. International Day of the Child.
2203 **924** £S17 multicoloured 1·70 1·70

925 Emblem and Stone Tablet

2005. World Information Society Summit, Tunis.
2204 **925** £S17 multicoloured 1·60 1·60

926 Teshreen Dam

2005. 35th Anniv of Corrective Movement of 16 November 1970.
2205 **926** £S25 multicoloured 2·30 2·30

927 Nizar Kabbani

2005. Writers Commemoration.
2206 £S10 Type **927** 1·10 1·10
2207 £S17 Sadalah Wannous 1·60 1·60
2208 £S18 Omar Abu Reisheh 1·70 1·70

928 Palm

2005. Tree Day.
2209 **928** £S17 multicoloured 1·60 1·60

929 Flags and Dove

2006. 43rd Anniv of Baathist Revolution of 8 March 1963.
2210 **929** £S18 multicoloured 1·70 1·70

930 Mosque, Aleppo

2006. Aleppo—Capital of Islamic Culture. Multicoloured.
2112 £S18 Type **927** 80 80
2211 £S17 Aleppo castle (horiz) 1·60 1·60
MS2213 80×60 mm. £S25 Script and buildings. Imperf 3·25 3·25

931 Mother and Child

2006. Mothers' Day.
2217 **931** £S17 multicoloured 1·60 1·60

932 Sultan Pasha al Atrach

2006. National Day. Personalities. Multicoloured.
2218 £S10 Type **932** 1·10 1·10
2219 £S10 Yousef al Azmeh 1·10 1·10
2220 £S10 Sheikh Saleh al Ali 1·10 1·10
2221 £S10 Ibrahim Hanano 1·10 1·10
2222 £S10 Ahmad Moraiwed 1·10 1·10

933 Figures and Emblem

2006. Labour Day.
2223 **933** £S17 multicoloured 1·60 1·60

934 *Hyoscyamus aureus*

2006. International Flower Show, Damascus. Multicoloured.
2224 £S5 Type **918** 45 45
2225 £S10 *Cistus salviaefolius* 95 95

935 Two Players

2006. World Cup Football Championship, Germany. Multicoloured.
2226 £S17 Type **935** 1·60 1·60
2227 £S18 Two players (different) 1·70 1·70
MS2228 60×82 mm. £S50 Players and trophy. Imperf 6·25 6·25

936 Great Walls and Ruins, Palmyra

2006. 50th Anniv of China—Syria Diplomatic Relations.
2229 **936** $10 multicoloured 1·10 1·10

937 Living and Dead Tree

2006. International Year of Deserts and Desertification.
2230 **937** $10 multicoloured 1·10 1·10

938 "53"

2006. 53rd International Fair, Damascus.
2231 **938** $10 multicoloured 1·10 1·10

939 Storyteller

2006. World Tourism Day. Multicoloured.
2232 £S10 Type **939** 1·10 1·10
2233 £S10 Baptism basin (28×58 mm) 1·10 1·10

940 Symbols of Postal Delivery

2006. World Post Day.
2234 **940** £S17 multicoloured 1·60 1·60

941 Building

2006. 36th Anniv of Corrective Movement of 16 November (1970).
2235 **941** £S15 multicoloured 1·40 1·40

942 Fateh Almudarres

2006. Artists. Multicoloured.
2236 £S10 Type **942** 1·10 1·10
2237 £S10 Adham Ismail 1·10 1·10
2238 £S10 Saheed Makhlouf 1·10 1·10
2239 £S10 Burhan Karkutli 1·10 1·10
2240 £S10 Michael Kirsheh 1·10 1·10

943 *Pistacia atlantica*

2006
2241 **943** £S15 multicoloured 1·40 1·40

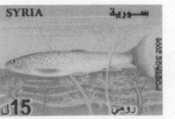

944 *Shabut* (barb)

2006. Fish. Multicoloured.
2242 £S15 Type **944** 1·40 1·40
2243 £S15 Catfish 1·40 1·40
2244 £S15 Mullet 1·40 1·40

945 Emblems

2007. 44th Anniv of Baathist Revolution of 8 March 1963.
2245 **945** £S17 multicoloured   1·60   1·60

946 Mother and Child
(statue)

2007. Mother's Day.
2246 **946** £S15 multicoloured   1·40   1·40

947 Torch and Map

2007. 60th Anniv of Baath Party.
2247 **947** £S25 multicoloured   2·30   2·30

948 Man holding
Banner

2007. National Day.
2248 **948** £S15 multicoloured   1·40   1·40

949 Workers holding
Emblem

2007. Labour Day.
2249 **949** £S10 multicoloured   1·10   1·10

950 Freesia

2007. International Flower Show, Damascus.
Multicoloured.
2250 £S15 Type **950**   1·40   1·40
2251 £S15 Ipomea purpurea   1·40   1·40
2252 £S15 Plumbago capensis   1·40   1·40

951 President Assad

2007. Second Term of President Bashar al-Assad.
Multicoloured.
2253 £S10 Type **951**   1·10   1·10
2254 £S15 President Assad (different)   1·40   1·40
MS2255 84×70 mm. £S25 President
  and assembly. Imperf   2·50   2·50

951a Emblems

2007. 54th International Fair, Damascus.
2255a **951a** £S15 multicoloured   1·40   1·40

952 St Paul's Church, Bab
Kissan, Damascus

2007. World Tourism Day.
2256 **952** £S10 multicoloured   1·10   1·10

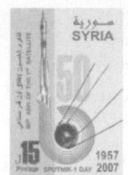

953 '50',
Spacecraft and
Sputnik I

2007. 50th Anniv of Space Exploration. Multicoloured.
2257 £S15 Type **953**   1·40   1·40
2258 £S25 50   2·30   2·30

954 Globe enclosed in
Envelope

2007. World Post Day.
2259 **954** £S25 multicoloured   2·30   2·30

955 Industrial Structure

2007. 37th Anniv of Corrective Movement of 16
November 1970.
2260 **955** £S15 multicoloured   1·40   1·40

956 Juniperus excelsa (inscr
'Juniperu excelsa')

2007. Tree Day.
2261 **956** £S18 multicoloured   1·70   1·70

957 Hussny
Sabah

2007. Personalities. Multicoloured.
2262 £S10 Type **957**   1·10   1·10
2263 £S10 Wajieh al Barudy   1·10   1·10
2264 £S10 Nadim Shoman   1·10   1·10
2265 £S10 Tawfik Izzeddin   1·10   1·10
2266 £S10 Abdussalam Al Ojaily   1·10   1·10

958 White Stork

2007. Birds. Multicoloured.
2267 £S10 Type **958**   1·10   1·10
2268 £S10 Woodpecker (inscr 'Syrian
  woodpecker')   1·10   1·10
2269 £S10 Shoveler   1·10   1·10
2270 £S10 Bee eater   1·10   1·10
2271 £S10 Turtle dove   1·10   1·10

959 Symbols of Industry
and Culture

2008. 45th Anniv of Baathist Revolution of 8 March 1963.
2272 **959** £S15 multicoloured   1·40   1·40

960 Mother and
Child

2008. Mothers' Day.
2273 **960** £S10 multicoloured   1·10   1·10

961 Emblem and Flags
of Members

2008. Arab Summit, Damascus. Multicoloured.
2274 £S10 Type **961**   1·10   1·10
MS2275 70×85 mm. £S25 Emblem and
  rider. Imperf   2·50   2·50

962 Al-Shamieh School

2008. Damascus, Arab Capital of Culture 2008.
Multicoloured.
2276 £S10 Type **962**   1·10   1·10
2277 £S15 Al-Thaheria Library   1·40   1·40
MS2278 70×85 mm. £S25 Damascus
  University. Imperf   2·50   2·50

963 Horse and Flag

2008. 62nd National Day.
2279 **963** £S10 multicoloured   1·10   1·10

964 Figures,
Emblem and Cog
Outline

2008. Labour Day.
2280 **964** £S20 multicoloured   2·00   2·00

965 Anniversary
Emblem

2008. 50th Anniv of Aleppo University.
2281 **965** £S15 multicoloured   1·40   1·40

966 Roses

2008. International Flower Show, Damascus.
Multicoloured.
2282 £S10 Type **966**   1·10   1·10
2283 £S10 Cacti   1·10   1·10
2284 £S10 Dahlias   1·10   1·10
2285 £S10 Primula (inscr 'wallflower')   1·10   1·10
2286 £S10 Marguerites   1·10   1·10

967 Camels

2008. Arab Post Day. Sheet 170×60 mm containing T **967**
and similar horiz design. Multicoloured.
MS2287 £S15 Type **967**; £S20 Pigeon   3·50   3·50

968 Weightlifting

2008. Olympic Games, Beijing. Multicoloured.
2288 £S5 Type **968**   45   45
2289 £S10 Long jump (vert)   1·10   1·10
MS2290 85×62 mm. £S25 Swimming.
  Imperf   2·50   2·50

969 Emblem

2008. 55th International Fair, Damascus.
2291 **969** £S25 multicoloured   2·30   2·30

969a Steam Locomotive

2008. Centenary of Hijaz Railway. Multicoloured.
2291a **969a** £S25 Type **969a**   2·30   2·30
MS2291b 70×85 mm. £S50 Route and
  locomotive emerging from tunnel.
  Imperf   5·00   5·00

970 Vase

2008. World Tourism Day. Multicoloured.
2292   £S10 Type **970**   1·10   1·10
2293   £S15 Dish (37×37 mm)   1·40   1·40

971 Dove, Envelope and Globe

2008. World Post Day.
2294   **971**   £S18 multicoloured   1·70   1·70

972 Sham (1st Syrian produced car)

2007. 38th Anniv of Corrective Movement of 16 November 1970.
2295   **972**   £S10 multicoloured   1·10   1·10

973 Hawthorn (inscr 'Howthorn')

2008. Tree Day.
2296   **973**   £S17 multicoloured   1·60   1·60

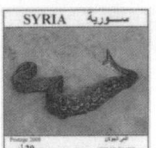

974 Inscr 'Golan Snake'

2008. Snakes. Multicoloured.
2297   £S20 Type **974**   1·90   1·90
2298   £S20 *Eryx jaculus*   1·90   1·90
2299   £S20 *Colubridae*   1·90   1·90
Nos. 2300/1 and Type **975** are vacant.

975a Louis Braille and Hands 'Reading'

2009. Birth Bicentenary of Louis Braille (inventor of Braille writing for the blind).
2301a   **975a**   £S17 multicoloured   1·80   1·80

2009. President Assad.
2301b   **890**   £S10 reddish lilac   1·20   1·20

976 Mustapha Akkad

2009. Personalities. Multicoloured.
2302   £S20 Type **976** (Syrian American film producer and director)   2·40   2·40
2303   £S20 Nihad Kalaai (actor)   2·40   2·40
2304   £S20 Maha al-Saleh (actress)   2·40   2·40
2305   £S20 Abd al-Latiff Fathy (actor)   2·40   2·40
2306   £S20 Inscr 'Fahd Kaaekati'   2·40   2·40

977 Emblem

2009. 46th Anniv of Baathist Revolution.
2307   **977**   £S10 multicoloured   1·20   1·20

978 Mother and Child

2009. Mothers' Day.
2308   **978**   £S18 multicoloured   1·90   1·90

979 Soldier, Woman, Dove and Flag

2009. 63rd National Day.
2309   **979**   £S17 multicoloured   1·80   1·80

980 Symbols of Labour

2009. Labour Day.
2310   **980**   £S15 multicoloured   1·40   1·40

981 Wallflowers

2009. International Flower Show, Damascus. Multicoloured.
2311   £S20 Type **981**   2·40   2·40
2312   £S20 Inscr 'Maemoza'   2·40   2·40
2313   £S20 Iris   2·40   2·40
2314   £S20 Inscr 'Lily'   2·40   2·40
2315   £S20 Inscr 'Adalia'   2·40   2·40

982 Emblem

2009. 56th Damascus Fair.
2316   **982**   £S15 multicoloured   1·40   1·40

983 Emblem

2009. al-Quds–2009 Capital of Arab Culture.
2317   **983**   £S10 multicoloured   1·20   1·20

984 Bab Al-Hawa

2009. Tourism. Multicoloured.
2318   £S25 Type **984**   2·75   2·75
2319   £S25 Mabrak al Naqa Mosque   2·75   2·75
2320   £S25 Amphitheatre, Bosra   2·75   2·75

985 Dove, Flower and Envelope

2009. World Post Day
2321   **985**   £S50 multicoloured   5·50   5·50

986 New Prime Ministry Headquarters

2009. 39th Anniv of Correctionist Movement of 16 November 1970.
2322   **986**   £S10 multicoloured   1·20   20

987 Trees in Blossom

2009. Tree Day
2323   **987**   £S15 multicoloured   1·40   1·40

988 Thrasher

2009. Birds. Multicoloured.
2324   £S20 Type **988**   2·40   2·40
2325   £S20 Redstart   2·40   2·40
2326   £S20 Blue headed yellow wagtail   2·40   2·40
2327   £S20 Honeyeater   2·40   2·40
2328   £S20 Syrian serin   2·40   2·40

989 Emblem

2010. 47th Anniv of Baathist Revolution
2329   **989**   £S25 multicoloured   2·75   2·75

990 Hand holding Rose

2010. Mothers' Day
2330   **990**   £S10 multicoloured   1·20   1·20

991 Flag, '64' and Outline of Prancing Horse

2010. 64th National Day
2331   **991**   £S50 multicoloured   5·50   5·50

992 Metal Workers

2010. Labour Day.
2332   **992**   £S25 multicoloured   2·75   2·75

993 Inscr 'Calendula'

2010. International Flower Show, Damascus. Multicoloured.
2333   £S25 Type **993**   2·75   2·75
2334   £S25 Inscr 'Cyeclamen'   2·75   2·75
2335   £S25 Rose   2·75   2·75
2336   £S25 Inscr 'Fuschia'   2·75   2·75
2337   £S25 Inscr "Roza bracteata"   2·75   2·75

994 Four Players

2010. World Cup Football Championships, South Africa. Multicoloured.
2338   £S25 Type **994**   2·75   2·75
2339   £S25 No. 3, No. 10 and No. 11 players tackling for ball   2·75   2·75
MS2340 85×63 mm. £S50 Championship emblem and trophy. Imperf   5·50   5·50

995 '2010' containing Symbols of Biodiversity

2010. International Year of Biodiversity
2341   **995**   £S50 multicoloured   5·50   5·50

996 Anniversary Emblem

2010. 50th Anniv of Aleppo Industrial and Agricultural Production Fair
2342   **996**   £S15 multicoloured   1·40   1·40

997 Rio de Janeiro, Brazil and Maalula, Syria

2010. Syria–Brazil Diplomatic Relationships
2343 **997** £S50 muticoloured 5·50 5·50

998 '57'

2010. 57th Damascus Fair
2344 **998** £S50 multicoloured 5·50 5·50

999 Clasped Hands

2010. Syria–Chile Diplomatic Relationships
2345 **999** £S25 multicoloured 2·75 2·75

1000 Square

2010. World Tourism Day. Multicoloured.
2346 £S25 Type **1000** 2·75 2·75
2347 £S25 Dancers 2·75 2·75

1001 Envelopes

2010. World Post Day
2348 **1001** £S25 multicoloured 2·75 2·75

1002 President Assad

2010. 40th Anniv of Correctionist Movement of 16 November 1970
2349 **1002** £S25 multicoloured 2·75 2·75
Nos. 2350 and Type **1003** are vacant

1004 Squirrel

2010. Fauna. Multicoloured.
2351 £S30 Type **1004** 3·25 3·25
2352 £S30 multicoloured 3·25 3·25
2353 £S40 Egyptian mongoose (inscr 'Ichnewmon') 3·50 3·50

1005 Almond Tree

2010. Tree Day
2354 **1005** £S50 multicoloured 5·50 5·50

1006 Fathullah Al-Sakal

2010. Lawyers. Multicoloured.
2355 £S25 Type **1006** 2·75 2·75
2356 £S25 Faris Al-Khouri 2·75 2·75
2357 £S25 Saeed Al-Gazi 2·75 2·75
2358 £S25 Abd-El-Salam Al-Tirmanini 2·75 2·75
2359 £S25 Mohammad Al-Fadel 2·75 2·75
2360 £S25 Ahmad Fouad Al-Koudmani 2·75 2·75

1007 Symbols of Progress

2011. 48th Anniv of Baathist Revolution
2361 **1007** £S25 multicoloured 2·75 2·75

1008 Child's Hand holding Mother's Hand

2011. Mothers' Day
2362 **1008** £S25 multicoloured 2·75 2·75

1009 Arm holding Flag

2011. 65th National Day
2363 **1009** £S25 multicoloured 2·75 2·75

1010 Baker

2011. Labour Day
2364 **1010** £S50 multicoloured 5·50 5·50

1011 Male and Female Outlines and AIDS Ribbon

2011. 30th Anniv of AIDS Prevention Campaign
2365 **1011** £S25 multicoloured 2·75 2·75

1012 *Nerium oleander*

2011. International Flower Show, Damascus. Multicoloured.
2366 £S50 Type **1012** 5·50 5·50
2367 £S50 Lily-of-the-Valley 5·50 5·50
2368 £S50 Lotus flower 5·50 5·50
2369 £S50 Bird of Paradise 5·50 5·50
2370 £S50 Dahlia 5·50 5·50

1013 Emblem

2011. 58th Damascus Fair
2371 **1013** £S15 multicoloured 1·40 1·40

1015 Sultan Ibrahim Mosque, Jableh

2011. World Tourism Day
2373 **1015** £S20 multicoloured 2·40 2·40

1016 Globe encircled by Envelopes

2011. World Post Day
2374 **1016** £S20 multicoloured 2·40 2·40

1017 Ariba – Latakia Highway (inscr 'Lattakia')

2011. 41st Anniv of Correctionist Movement of 16 November 1970
2375 **1017** £S15 multicoloured 1·40 1·40

1018 Olive Tree

2011. Tree Day
2376 **1018** £S15 multicoloured 1·40 1·40

1019 *Physeter macrocephalus* (Sperm Whale)

2011. Agreement on Conservation of Cetaceans of Mediterranean Sea
2377 £S25 Type **1019** 2·75 2·75
2378 £S25 *Globicephalus melas* (Long-finned Pilot Whale) 2·75 2·75
2379 £S25 *Stenella coeruleoalba* (Striped Dolphin) 2·75 2·75
2380 £S25 *Grampus griscus* (Risso's Dolphin) 2·75 2·75
2381 £S25 *Tursiops truncatus* (Bottlenose Dolphin) 2·75 2·75
2382 £S25 Killer Whale 2·75 2·75

1020 Nazek Al-Abed

2011. Pioneering Arab Women. Multicoloured.
2383 £S20 Type **1020** (campaigner for women's rights, volunteered for Syrian Army, and fought in Battle of Maysaloun, 1920) (inscr 'Abid') 2·40 2·40
2384 £S20 Inscr 'Fateema Solyman al-Ahmed' 2·40 2·40

2385 £S20 Adleh Bayhum Aljazairi (established 'Awakening of Shami Women's Society, 1927, founded the College of 'Dawhet Aaladab' and founded the nucleus for Syrian Women's Union, 1933) (inscr 'Adila Byham al-Jazairy') 2·40 2·40
2386 £S20 Thuraya al-Hafiz (feminist pioneer) (inscr 'Thorya') 2·40 2·40
2387 £S20 Mary Ajamy (writer, poet, and journalist) (inscr 'Marry Ajami') 2·40 2·40
2388 £S20 Inscr 'Souad Abdullah' 2·40 2·40

1021 '8'

2012. 49th Anniv of Baathist Revolution
2389 **1021** £S20 multicoloured 2·40 2·40

1022 Mother and Child

2012. Mothers' Day
2390 **1022** £S30 multicoloured 3·25 3·25

1023 Flowers and

2011. 66th National Day
2391 **1023** £S50 multicoloured 5·50 5·50

1024 Symbols of Work

2012. Labour Day.
2392 **1024** £S50 multicoloured 5·50 5·50

OBLIGATORY TAX STAMPS

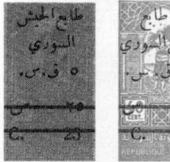

T57 **T58** **T59**

T60 **T61**

1945. Syrian Army Fund. Revenue Stamps surch or optd.
T419	**T57**	5p. on 25p. on 40p. pink	£190	32·00
T420	-	5p. on 25p. on 40p. pink	£190	65·00
T421	**T 58**	5p. on 25p. on 40p. pink	£190	43·00
T422	**T 59**	5p. blue	£325	32·00
T423	**T 60**	5p. blue	£180	27·00
T424	-	5p. blue	£200	21·00
T425	**T 61**	5p. blue	£200	35·00
T426	-	5p. blue	£225	38·00

No. T420 is as Type **57** but with additional overprint as top line of Type **61**.
No. T424 has top line of overprint as Type **59** and other lines as Type **60**.
No. T426 has top line overprinted as Type **61** and other lines as Type **60**.

POSTAGE DUE STAMPS.
A. FRENCH MILITARY OCCUPATION

1920. "Mouchon" and "Merson" key-types of French Post Offices in the Turkish Empire (inscr "LEVANT") surch **O. M. F. Syrie Ch. taxe** and value.

D48	**B**	1p. on 10c. red	£200	£200
D49	**B**	2p. on 20c. brown	£200	£200
D50	**B**	3p. on 30c. lilac	£200	£200
D51	**C**	4p. on 40c. red and blue	£200	£200

1920. Postage Due stamps of France surch **O. M. F. Syrie** and value.

D60	**D11**	50c. on 10c. brown	80	1·50
D52	**D11**	1p. on 10c. brown	4·00	8·25
D61	**D11**	1p. on 20c. green	1·50	1·50
D53	**D11**	2p. on 20c. green	3·00	8·50
D62	**D11**	2p. on 30c. red	5·75	9·50
D54	**D11**	3p. on 30c. red	2·50	8·25
D63	**D11**	3p. on 50c. purple	6·00	10·50
D55	**D11**	4p. on 50c. purple	6·50	19·00
D64	**D11**	5p. on 1f. purple on yellow	16·00	23·00

1921. Issued at Damascus. No. KD96 of Arab Kingdom surch **O. M. F. Syrie Chiffre Taxe** and value.

D69	**K 3**	50c. on 1p. black	6·00	12·50
D70	**K 3**	1p. on 1p. black	3·50	9·00

1921. Issued at Damascus. No. 64a/5 of Syria optd **TAXE**.

D89	**K 4**	2p. on 5m. red	14·50	18·00
D90	**K 3**	3p. on 1p. blue	36·00	36·00

B. ARAB KINGDOM

1920. As No. K92 but colour changed.

KD96	**K3**	1p. black	1·60	1·50

C. FRENCH MANDATED TERRITORY

1923. Postage Due stamps of France surch **Syrie Grand Liban** and value.

D118	**D11**	50c. on 10c. brown	5·00	7·25
D119	**D11**	1p. on 20c. green	5·00	8·50
D120	**D11**	2p. on 30c. red	3·50	7·50
D121	**D11**	3p. on 50c. purple	3·25	7·75
D122	**D11**	5p. on 1f. purple on yellow		

1924. Postage Due stamps of France surch **SYRIE** and value.

D139	**D11**	50c. on 10c. brown	90	6·50
D140	**D11**	1p. on 20c. green	2·50	6·50
D141	**D11**	2p. on 30c. red	3·00	7·50
D142	**D11**	3p. on 50c. purple	1·80	7·50
D143	**D11**	5p. on 1f. purple on yellow	2·40	7·75

1924. Postage Due stamps of France surch **Syrie** and value and also in Arabic.

D175	**D11**	0p.50 on 10c. brown	80	4·75
D176	**D11**	1p. on 20c. olive	2·00	6·50
D177	**D11**	2p. on 30c. red	2·50	6·25
D178	**D11**	3p. on 50c. purple	3·75	7·25
D179	**D11**	5p. on 1f. red on yellow	4·75	9·00

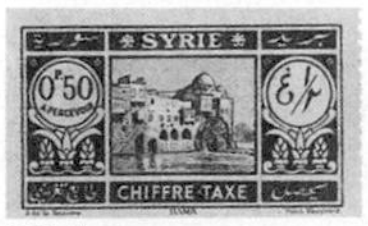

D20 Hama

1925

D192	**D20**	0p.50 brown on yellow	65	2·40
D193	-	1p. purple on pink	15	55
D194	-	2p. black on blue	1·20	3·25
D195	-	3p. black on red	1·50	1·90
D196	-	5p. black on green	1·50	3·50
D197	-	8p. black on blue	10·50	12·00
D198	-	15p. black on pink	16·00	21·00

DESIGNS—VERT: 1p. Antioch. HORIZ: 2p. Tarsus; 3p. Banias; 5p. Castle; 8p. Ornamental design; 15p. Lion.

E. SYRIAN REPUBLIC

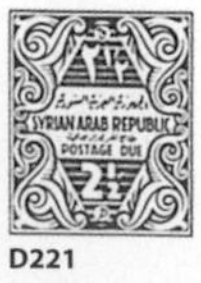

D221

1965

D883	**D221**	2½p. blue	35	20
D884	**D221**	5p. brown	60	25
D885	**D221**	10p. green	65	30
D886	**D221**	17½p. red	1·20	1·40
D887	**D221**	25p. blue	1·80	1·70

Pt. 6

TAHITI

The largest of the Society Islands in the S. Pacific Ocean. Later renamed Oceanic Settlements.

100 centimes = 1 franc.

1882. Stamps of French Colonies. "Peace and Commerce" type, surch **25c**.

1	**H**	25c. on 35c. black on orange	£275	£225
3a	**H**	25c. on 40c. red on yellow	£3250	£3750

1884. Stamps of French Colonies, "Commerce" (perf) and "Peace and Commerce" (imperf) types, surch **TAHITI** and value.

4	**J**	5c. on 20c. red on green	£200	£170
5	**J**	10c. on 20c. red on green	£225	£200
2	**H**	25c. on 35c. black on orange	£4500	£4500
6	**H**	25c. on 1f. green	£550	£450

1893. Stamps of French Colonies, "Commerce" type, optd **TAHITI**.

7	**J**	1c. black on blue	£600	£500
8	**J**	2c. brown on buff	£3000	£2500
9	**J**	4c. brown on grey	£1000	£850
10	**J**	5c. green on green	26·00	48·00
11	**J**	10c. black on lilac	44·00	60·00
12	**J**	15c. blue	47·00	55·00
13	**J**	20c. red on green	75·00	75·00
14	**J**	25c. brown	£8000	£7500
15	**J**	25c. black on pink	55·00	60·00
16	**J**	35c. black on orange	£2250	£2000
17	**J**	75c. red on pink	80·00	80·00
18	**J**	1f. green	£100	95·00

1893. Stamps of French Colonies, "Commerce" type, optd **1893 TAHITI**.

32	**J**	1c. black on blue	£950	£550
33	**J**	2c. brown on buff	£3500	£3250
34	**J**	4c. brown on grey	£1100	£1000
35	**J**	5c. green on green	£800	£700
36	**J**	10c. black on lilac	£250	£250
37	**J**	15c. blue	60·00	36·00
38	**J**	20c. red on green	65·00	65·00
39	**J**	25c. brown	£48000	£48000
40	**J**	25c. black on pink	65·00	65·00
41	**J**	35c. black on orange	£2250	£2000
42	**J**	75c. red on pink	60·00	60·00
43	**J**	1f. green	60·00	60·00

1903. Stamps of Oceanic Settlements, "Tablet" key-type, surch **TAHITI 10 centimes**.

57	**D**	10c. on 15c. blue and red	6·25	10·50
58	**D**	10c. on 25c. black and red on pink	5·25	7·25
59	**D**	10c. on 40c. red and blue on yellow	8·50	9·00

1915. Stamps of Oceanic Settlements, "Tablet" key-type, optd **TAHITI** and red cross.

60	15c. blue and red	£160	£160
61	15c. grey and red	45·00	55·00

POSTAGE DUE STAMPS

1893. Postage Due stamps of French Colonies optd **TAHITI**.

D19	**U**	1c. black	£275	£275
D20	**U**	2c. black	£275	£275
D21	**U**	3c. black	£275	£275
D22	**U**	4c. black	£325	£325
D23	**U**	5c. black	£325	£325
D24	**U**	10c. black	£325	£325
D25	**U**	15c. black	£325	£325
D26	**U**	20c. black	£325	£325
D27	**U**	30c. black	£325	£325
D28	**U**	40c. black	£325	£325
D29	**U**	60c. black	£350	£350
D30	**U**	1f. brown	£850	£850
D31	**U**	2f. brown	£850	£850

1893. Postage Due stamps of French Colonies optd **1893 TAHITI**.

D44	**U**	1c. black	£2250	£2250
D45	**U**	2c. black	£425	£425
D46	**U**	3c. black	£425	£425
D47	**U**	4c. black	£425	£425
D48	**U**	5c. black	£425	£425
D49	**U**	10c. black	£425	£425
D50	**U**	15c. black	£425	£425
D51	**U**	20c. black	£300	£300
D52	**U**	30c. black	£425	£425
D53	**U**	40c. black	£425	£425
D54	**U**	60c. black	£425	£425
D55	**U**	1f. brown	£425	£425
D56	**U**	2f. brown	£425	£425

For later issues see **OCEANIC SETTLEMENTS**.

Pt. 10

TAJIKISTAN

Formerly a constituent republic of the Soviet Union, Tajikistan became independent in 1991.

1992. 100 kopeks = 1 (Russian) rouble.
1995. 100 tanga = 1 (Tajik) rouble.
2001. 100 dirams (d) = 1 somoni (s).

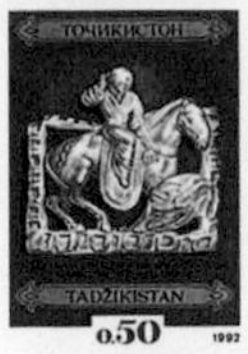

1 Hunter (gold relief)

1992

1	**1**	50k. multicoloured	80	75

Formerly a constituent republic of the Soviet Union, Tajikistan became independent in 1991.

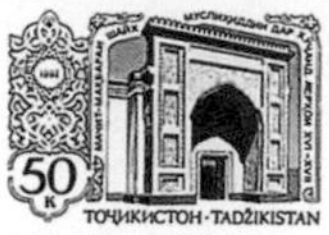

2 Sheikh Muslihiddin Mosque, Khudzand

1992

2	**2**	50k. multicoloured	80	75

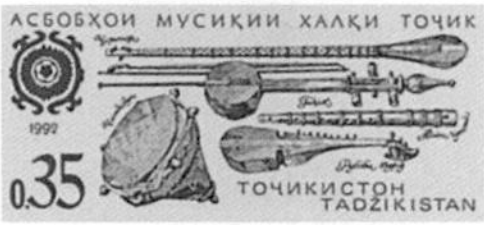

3 Traditional Musical Instruments

1992

3	**3**	35k. multicoloured	70	65

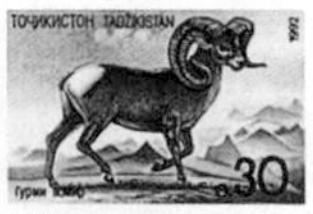

4 Argali

1992

4	**4**	30k. multicoloured	75	70

Точикистон
5.00
1992

(5)

1992. No. 2 surch as T **5**.

5	**2**	5r. on 50k. multicoloured	1·40	1·30
6	**2**	25r. on 50k. multicoloured	2·75	2·50

1992. No. 3 surch.

7	**3**	15r. on 35k. multicoloured	2·00	1·90
8	**3**	50r. on 35k. multicoloured	2·00	1·90

3.00

1992
Тадж.
(7)

1993. No. 6072 of Russia surch as T **7**.

9	**2410**	3r. on 1k. brown	95	90
10	**2410**	100r. on 1k. brown	3·75	3·50

Точикистон
10.00
(8)

1993. No. 6073 of Russia surch as T **8**.

11	10r. on 2k. brown	70	65
12	15r. on 2k. brown	3·50	3·25

60. 00

(9)

1993. No. 1 surch with T **9**.

15	**1**	60r. on 50k. multicoloured	2·75	2·50

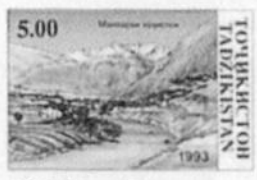

10 Mountain Landscape

1993. Multicoloured.. Multicoloured..

16	1r. Statue of Abuabdullokhi Rudaki, Dushanbe (vert)	30	20
17	5r. Type **10**	45	40
18	15r. Mausoleum of Sadriddin Aini (poet), Dushanbe (vert)	75	70
19	20r. State flag and map	1·10	1·00
20	25r. Hissar Fort	1·20	1·10
21	50r. Aini Opera and Ballet House, Dushanbe	1·70	1·50
22	100r. State flag and map (different)	3·75	3·50

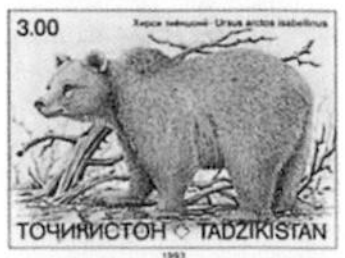

11 Brown Bear

1993. Mammals. Multicoloured.

23	3r. Type **11**	45	30
24	10r. Red deer	75	30
25	15r. Markhor	90	40
26	25r. Porcupine	1·50	1·10
27	100r. Snow leopard	4·50	2·75

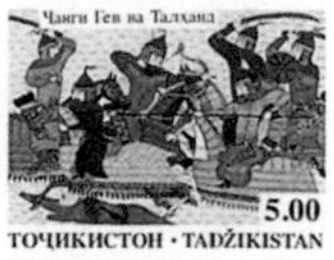

12 Geb and Talkhand in Battle

1993. Millenary of "Book of Kings" by Abu-l Kasim Mansur, Firdausi (Persian poet). Multicoloured.

28	5r. Type **12**	1·10	1·00
29	20r. Rustam and Sukhrov in combat	3·00	2·75
30	30r. Eagle Simurgh brings Zola to his father Som (vert)	4·50	4·25
MS31	100×81 mm. 50r. Portrait of Firdausi (29×44 mm)	7·50	7·00

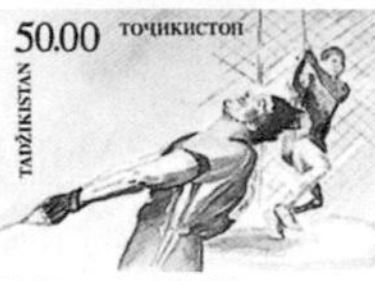

13 Throwing the Hammer

1993. Andrei Abduvaliev's Victory at Olympic Games, Barcelona. Sheet 70×70 mm.

MS32 **13** 50r. multicoloured	9·00	8·50

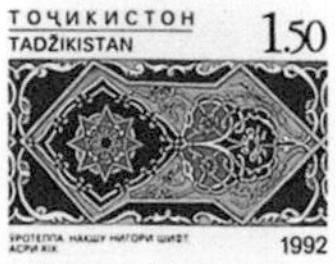

14 Ceiling Decoration

1993

33	**14**	1r.50 multicoloured	75	40

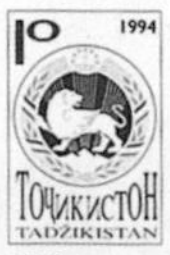

15 Arms

1994

34	**15**	10r. multicoloured	30	30
35	**15**	15r. multicoloured	40	35
36	**15**	35r. multicoloured	45	40
37	**15**	50r. multicoloured	60	55
38	**15**	100r. multicoloured	75	70

39	15	160r. multicoloured	1·10	1·00
40	15	500r. mult (23×37 mm)	1·50	1·40
41	15	1000r. mult (23×37 mm)	3·00	2·75

16 Hamadony (after Vafo Nazarovym)

1994. 680th Birth Anniv of Ali Hamadony (Persian mystic).

| 42 | 16 | 1000r. multicoloured (inscr in Roman alphabet) | 3·25 | 3·00 |
| 43 | 16 | 1000r. multicoloured (inscr in Cyrillic) | 3·25 | 3·00 |

(17)

1994. Andrei Abduvaliev's Victory at World Athletics Championships, Stuttgart. No. MS32 optd with T **17**.

| MS44 | 13 | 50r. multicoloured | 9·00 | 8·50 |

18 Post Office

1994. Historic Monuments. Multicoloured.

45		10r. Statue of Firdausi (vert)	30	30
46		35r. Type **18**	45	40
47		100r. Theatre	90	85
48		160r. Ulum Academy	1·40	1·30
49		160r. "Safar" building	1·40	1·30

19 Tyrannosaurus

1994. Prehistoric Animals. Multicoloured.

50		500r. Type **19**	1·10	75
51		500r. Stegosaurus	1·10	75
52		500r. Anatosaurus	1·10	75
53		500r. Parasaurolophus	1·10	75
54		500r. Triceratops	1·10	75
55		500r. Diatryma	1·10	75
56		500r. Tyrannosaurus (different)	1·10	75
57		500r. Spinosaurus	1·10	75

1995. No. 33 surch **1995** and value.

58	14	100r. on 1r.50 mult	30	25
59	14	600r. on 1r.50 mult	90	75
60	14	1000r. on 1r.50 mult	1·50	1·30
61	14	5000r. on 1r.50 mult	7·50	6·25

21 Gecko ("Alsophylax loricatus")

1995. Lizards. Multicoloured.

62		500r. Type **21**	1·20	1·00
63		500r. Sunwatcher ("Phrynocephalus helioscopus")	1·20	1·00
64		500r. Toad-headed agama ("Phrynocephalus mystaceus")	1·20	1·00
65		500r. Toad agama ("Phrynocephalus sogdianus")	1·20	1·00
66		500r. Plate-tailed gecko ("Teratoscincus scineus")	1·20	1·00
67		500r. Transcaspian desert monitor ("Varanus griseus")	1·20	1·00
MS68		80×55 mm. 5000r. Schneider's gold Skink ("Eumeces schneiden")	7·50	6·25

22 National Flag

1995. Membership of International Organizations. Multicoloured.

| 69 | | 1000r. Type **22** (Organization for Security and Co-operation in Europe) | 1·40 | 1·10 |

| 70 | | 1000r. National flag and New York Headquarters (United Nations) (horiz) | 1·40 | 1·10 |
| 71 | | 1000r. Emblem and national flag (Universal Postal Union) | 1·40 | 1·10 |

23 War Memorial, Dushanbe

1995. 50th Anniv of End of Second World War. Sheet 111×76 mm.

| MS72 | 23 | 5000r. multicoloured (gold inscr and rosette in margin) | 6·00 | 5·00 |

1995. "Beijing '95" International Stamp Exhibition, China (73) and "Singapore '95" International Stamp Exhibition (74). Nos. 64 and 67 optd with relevant exhibition emblem.

| 73 | | 500r. multicoloured | 4·50 | 3·75 |
| 74 | | 500r. multicoloured | 4·50 | 3·75 |

25 State Arms

1995

75	25	1r. multicoloured	25	15
76	25	2r. multicoloured	25	15
77	25	5r. multicoloured	25	15
78	25	12r. multicoloured	30	20
79	25	40r. multicoloured	60	50

26 Bar-headed Goose ("Anser indicus")

1996. Birds. Multicoloured.

80		200r. Type **26**	2·10	1·80
81		200r. Indian black-headed gull ("Larus brunnicephalus")	2·10	1·80
82		200r. Houbara bustard ("Otis undulata")	2·10	1·80
83		200r. Daurian partridge ("Perdix dauricae")	2·10	1·80
84		200r. Tibetan sandgrouse ("Syrrhaptes tibetana")	2·10	1·80
85		200r. Tibetan snowcock ("Tetraogallus tibetanus")	2·10	1·80
MS86		76×51 mm. 600r. Ring-necked pheasant ("Phasianus colchicus")	6·75	5·75

27 New York Headquarters

1996. 50th Anniv of UNO. Multicoloured.

| 87 | | 100r. Type **27** | 1·50 | 1·30 |
| MS88 | | 101×71 mm. 500r. Close-up view of New York headquarters | 6·75 | 6·00 |

28 Striped Hyena ("Hyaena hyaena")

1996. "Save the Aral Sea". Sheet 128×108 mm containing T **28** and similar horiz designs. Multicoloured.

| MS89 | | 100r. Caracal ("Felis caracal"); 100r. Aral trout ("Salmo trutta aralensis"); 100r. Type **28**; 100r. Kaufmann's shovelnose ("Pseudoscaphirhynchus kaufmanni"); 10r. Pike asp ("Aspiolucius esocinus") | 7·50 | 7·00 |

29 Pallas's Cat

1996. Wild Cats. Multicoloured. (a) With World Wildlife Fund emblem. Pallas's Cat.

90		100r. Type **29**	2·40	2·30
91		100r. Close-up	2·40	2·30
92		150r. Head	3·50	3·25
93		150r. Sitting	3·50	3·25

(b) Without W.W.F. emblem.

94		200r. Jungle cat ("Felis chaus")	4·00	3·75
95		200r. Lynx ("Felis lynx")	4·00	3·75
MS96		111×83 mm. 500r. Pallas's cat	8·00	7·50

30 Diving

1996. Olympic Games, Atlanta, U.S.A. Multicoloured.

97		200r. Type **30**	2·50	2·30
98		200r. Football	2·50	2·30
99		200r. Throwing the hammer	2·50	2·30
100		200r. Judo	2·50	2·30
101		200r. Baron Pierre de Coubertin (founder of modern Games)	2·50	2·30

31 Kamol Khujandi

1996. Kamol Khujandi (writer) Commemoration.

| 102 | 31 | 500r. multicoloured (inscr in Roman letters) | 6·75 | 6·00 |
| 103 | 31 | 500r. multicoloured (inscr in Cyrillic letters) | 6·75 | 6·00 |

32 Emblem

1996. Fifth Anniv of Central Asian Postal Union.

| 104 | 32 | 100r. Multicoloured | 6·00 | 5·25 |

33 Mt. Krozhenevskoi

1997. Mountains over 7000 m. Multicoloured.

105		100r. Type **33**	1·70	1·50
106		100r. Mt. Lenin	1·70	1·50
107		100r. Mt. Communism	1·70	1·50
MS108		100×69 mm. 500r. Mountain climber	9·25	8·25

1997. Nos. 58/61 surch A **1997**.

109		A (12r.) on 100r. on 1r.50 multicoloured	1·70	1·50
110		A (12r.) on 600r. on 1r.50 multicoloured	1·70	1·50
111		A (12r.) on 1000r. on 1r.50 multicoloured	1·70	1·50
112		A (12r.) on 5000r. on 1r.50 multicoloured	1·70	1·50

35 Copper Vessel

1998. Crafts. Multicoloured.

113		30r. Type **35**	85	75
114		100r. Cradles	2·50	2·30
MS115		64×64 mm. 300r. Painted dish. Imperf	5·00	4·50

36 Woman from Khujand

1998. Traditional Costumes. Multicoloured.

116		100r. Type **36**	1·70	1·50
117		100r. Woman from Darvoz carrying pot	1·70	1·50
118		150r. Man from Khujand (blue coat)	2·00	1·80
119		150r. Man from Darvoz (striped coat)	2·00	1·80

37 "Tulipa greigii"

1998. Flowers. Multicoloured.

120		12r. Type **37**	35	30
121		30r. "Crocus korolkowi"	70	60
122		70r. "Iris darwasica"	1·50	1·40
123		150r. "Petilium eduardll"	3·50	3·00
MS124		68×53 mm. 300r. "Juno nicolai"	6·00	5·25

38 "Catocala timur"

1998. Butterflies and Moths. Multicoloured.

125		12r. Type **38**	35	30
126		30r. "Celerio chamyla apocyni"	70	60
127		70r. "Colias sieversi"	1·50	1·40
128		100r. Southern swallowtail	3·50	3·00
MS129		68×53 mm. 300r. "Anthocharis tomyris"	6·00	5·25

39 Ruby

1998. Minerals. Multicoloured.

130		1r. Type **39**	35	30
131		1r. Sapphire	35	30
132		12r. Tourmaline	50	45
133		12r. Lapis lazuli	50	45
134		150r. Spinel	2·50	2·30
135		150r. Amethyst	2·50	2·30
MS136		126×85 mm. 350r. Agate	7·75	6·75

40 Ghafurov

1998. Death Commemoration of Bobojon Ghafurov (politician).

| 137 | 40 | 12r. multicoloured | 35 | 30 |
| 138 | 40 | 150r. multicoloured | 3·00 | 2·75 |

41 Centenary Poster

1999. Birth Bicentenary of Aleksandr Sergeevich Pushkin (poet). Multicoloured.

| 139 | | 100r. Type **41** | 85 | 75 |
| 140 | | 270r. Portrait of Pushkin | 2·00 | 1·80 |

42 Diamond Design

43 Key Design

44 Pyramid Design

1999. Carpet Designs. Value expressed by Cyrillic letter.

141	**42**	(A) multicoloured	35	30
142	**43**	(B) multicoloured	90	75
143	**44**	(B) multicoloured	2·30	2·00

45 Lion shaped figurine

1999. 1100th Anniv of Samanids State. Multicoloured.

144	30r. Type **45**	90	75
145	50r. Anniversary emblem	1·30	1·10
146	100r. Animal-shaped vessel	1·80	1·50
147	270r. Clay ornaments	4·50	3·75
MS148 124×105 mm. 500r. Ismoil Somoni (founder)		9·00	7·50

46 Ismoil Somoni

1999. Leaders. Sheet 114×77 mm containing T **46** and similar vert designs. Multicoloured.

MS149 100r. Type **46**; 500r. Pres. E. Rahmonov	12·50	10·50

47 Pleurotus eryngii

1999. Fungi. Multicoloured.

150	100r. Type **47**	70	60
151	270r. Naked mushroom	2·00	1·70
MS152 160×90 mm. As Nos. 150/1, each ×2		4·50	3·75
MS153 97×77 mm. 500r. Morchella steppicola		5·50	4·50

48 "125" and Parchment

2000. 125th Anniv of Universal Postal Union.

154	**48**	270t. multicoloured	1·80	1·50

49 Ophiocephalus argus (inscr "Arqus")

2000. Fish. Multicoloured.

155	40t. Type **49**	55	45
156	100t. Barbus brachycephalus	90	75
157	230t. Schizopygopsis stoliczkai	1·80	1·50
158	270t. Pseudoscaphirhynchus fedtschenkoi	2·20	1·80
MS159 150×104 mm. Nos. 155/8		6·25	5·25
MS160 100×68 mm. 500t. Pseudoscaphirhynchus Kaufmanni		4·50	3·75

50 Pandion haliaetus

2001. Birds. Multicoloured.

161	10d. Type **50**	55	45
162	27d. Aquila chrysaetus (vert)	1·40	1·20
163	50d. Gyps himalayensis	2·50	2·10
164	70d. Circaetus (inscr "ferox") (vert)	3·50	3·00
MS165 78×116 mm. 1s. Falco peregrinus (43×57 mm)		6·00	5·00

51 Mikhail Botvinnik

2001. Chess Champions. Multicoloured.

166	15d. Type **51**	70	60
167	41d. Robert Fischer (incr "Fisher")	2·00	1·70
MS168 136×136 mm. 10d. Wilhelm Steinitz; 25d. King and consorts playing chess; 50d. Jose Raul Capablanca; 70d. Emanuel Lasker; 90d. Arab chess players; 1s. Alexander Alekhine		17·00	14·50

2001. No. 20 surch.

169	A (6d.) on 25d. multicoloured	70	60
170	B (15d.) on 25d. multicoloured	2·00	1·70
171	B (41d.) on 25d. multicoloured	5·50	4·50

55 Satellite Dish

2001. Sputnik (satellite). Sheet 106×71 mm.

MS172 **55** 1s.50 multicoloured	6·25	5·25

57 TY-154M

2001. Transport. Multicoloured.

180	1s. Type **57**	4·50	3·75
MS181 140×85 mm. 41d. Road transport; 90d. Diesel locomotive; 1s. As No. 180		10·00	8·25

58 Emblem and Members' Flags

2001. Tenth Anniv of Union of Independent States.

182	**58**	50d. multicoloured	3·25	2·75

No. 182 also exists imperforate.

59 Anniversary Emblem

2001. Tenth Anniv of Regional Concord of Communications. Sheet 107×73 mm.

MS183 **59** 1s. multicoloured	6·25	5·25

60 Goddess Anahita

2002. 2700th Anniv of Avesta (holy book of Zoroastrianism). Multicoloured.

184	2d. Type **60**	55	45
185	3d. Priest	70	60
MS186 131×74 mm. Size 28×45 mm. 70d. Goddess Haoma; 90d. Farroh; 1s. God Surush; 2s. Goddess Din		17·00	14·00

61 Mother and Child

2002. 50th Anniv of United Nations High Commissioner for Refugees. Sheet 130×81 mm containing T **61** and similar vert designs. Multicoloured.

MS187 50d.×3, Type **61**; Refugees; Soldier, child and rainbow	8·00	6·75

62 Goldfinch

2002. Fauna and Flora. Sheet 77×172 mm containing T **62** and similar vert designs. Multicoloured.

MS188 6d. Type **62**; 15d. Hawfinch; 41d. Toadstool; 50d. Mouse; 95d. Moth with closed wings; 1s.50 Moth with open wings; 1s.50 Cat; 1s.50 Tulips	13·50	11·50

No. **MS**188 also exists imperforate.

63 Two Cats

2002. Reed Cat (Felis chaus). Multicoloured.

189	1s. Type **63**	2·20	1·80
190	1s.50 Adult cat	3·25	2·75
191	2s. Adult resting	4·50	3·75
192	2s. Kittens	4·50	3·75

64 Pan troglodytes

2002. 40th Anniv of Dushanbe Zoo. Multicoloured.

193	2d. Type **64**	25	25
194	3d. Cervus nippon hortulorum	35	30
195	10d. Panthera tigris altaica	45	40
196	41d. Diceros bicornis michaeli	1·60	1·40
197	50d. Giraffa camelopardalis (inscr "camelopardales") reticulata	2·00	1·70
198	1s. Panthera leo	4·00	3·25

65 Three Dancers

2002. Navruz Festival (spring). Sheet 108×72 mm containing T **65** and similar vert designs. Multicoloured.

MS199 50d. Type **65**; 1s. Navruz emblem; 1s. Two dancers	6·25	5·25

66 19th-century Mosque Entrance

2002. 2500th Anniv of Istaravshan. Multicoloured.

200	50d. Type **66**	1·40	1·20
201	50d. Entrance (Sari Mazor complex)	1·40	1·20
202	50d. Arched doorway (Sari Mazor complex)	1·40	1·20
203	50d. 16th-century Mosque entrance	1·40	1·20

2002. 2002. Chess Super Championship, Moscow. Stamps of No. **MS**168 optd 2002.

MS204 136×136 mm. 10d. Wilhelm Steinitz; 25d. King and consorts playing chess; 50d. Jose Raul Capablanca; 70d. Emanuel Lasker; 90d. Arab chess players; 1s. Alexander Alekhine	17·00	14·50

68 Flat Racing

2002. New Year. Year of the Horse. Multicoloured.

205	2d. Type **68**	20	15
206	3d. Two sulkies and drivers	20	15
207	50d. Dressage riders	1·40	1·20
208	50d. Fox hunting	1·40	1·20
209	95d. Carriage racing	2·75	2·30
210	95d. Polo	2·75	2·30
211	1s. Racing over jumps	3·00	2·40
212	1s. Show jumping	3·00	2·40
MS213 111×100 mm. 1s.50 Performing horses (vert)		6·25	5·25

69 Archery

2002. Traditional Sports. Multicoloured.

214	1d. Type **69**	25	20
215	20d. Horse racing	50	40
216	53d. Polo	1·30	1·00
217	65d. Feats of strength (stone carrying)	1·60	1·30
218	1s. Buzjashi	2·50	2·10
219	1s.24 Wrestling	3·00	2·50

70 Donkey Cart

2002. Oriental Bazaar. Multicoloured.

220	65d. Type **70**	1·60	1·30
221	65d. Trader carrying goods whilst riding donkey	1·60	1·30
222	65d. Melon trader	1·60	1·30
223	65d. Kebab seller	1·60	1·30

71 Monument

2003

224	**71**	1d. emerald	30	25
225	**71**	2d. purple	40	35

226	**71**	3d. green	50	40
227	**71**	4d. violet	55	45
228	**71**	12d. brown	80	65
229	**71**	20d. blue	1·60	1·30

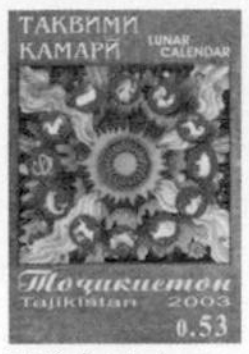
72 Solar System and Lunar Cycle

2003. New Year. Year of the Sheep. Multicoloured.

230	53d. Type **72**	1·60	1·30
231	65d. Sheep's head and lunar cycle	2·40	2·00
232	1s. Ram's head	3·25	2·50
MS233	107×71 mm. 1s.50 Sheep	4·50	4·25

2003. International Forum on Fresh Water (1st issue). No. **MS**159 surch.

MS234 150×104 mm. 8d. on 40d. multicoloured; 20d. on 100d. multicoloured; 53d. on 230d. multicoloured; 66d. on 270d. multicoloured 8·25 7·75

See also Nos. 237/8.

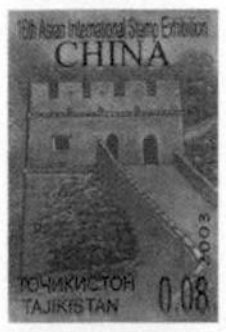
74 Great Wall, China

2003. Mianyang 2003 (China) and Bangkok 2003 (Thailand) International Stamp Exhibitions. Sheet 124×93 mm containing T **74** and similar vert designs. Multicoloured.

MS235 8d. Type **74**; 20d. *Panthera tigris*; 53d. *Inachis io*; 66d. Bangkok 2003 emblem and building; 1s. *Rupicapra rupicapra*; 1s50 *Ailuropoda melanoleuca*; 1s.50 *Leontopithecus rosalia*; 2s. *Elephas maximus* 15·00 13·00

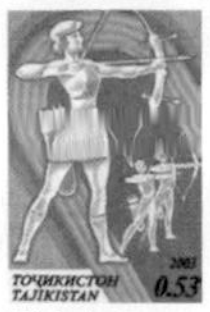
75 Archery

2003. Summer Olympic Games, Athens 2004 and Beijing 2008. Sheet 97×91 mm containing T **75** and similar vert designs. Multicoloured.

MS236 53d. Type **75**; 1s. Running; 1s.23. Football; 2s. Gymnastics 10·00 9·00

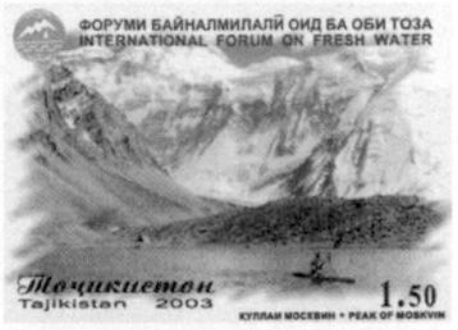
76 Moskvin Peak

2003. International Forum on Fresh Water (2nd issue). Multicoloured.

237	1s.50 Type **76**	3·00	2·75
238	1s.50 Iskanderkul lake	3·00	2·75

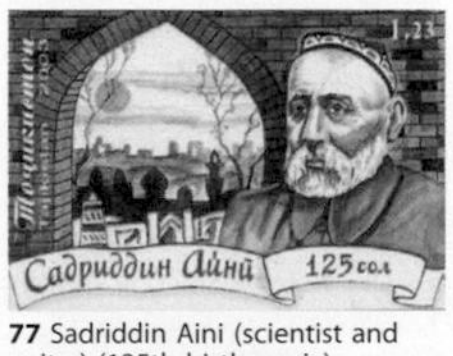
77 Sadriddin Aini (scientist and writer) (125th birth anniv)

2003. Anniversaries. Multicoloured.

239	1s.23 Type **77**	2·75	2·40
240	1s.23 Nosir Khusrav (writer and philosopher) (1000th (2004) birth anniv)	2·75	2·40

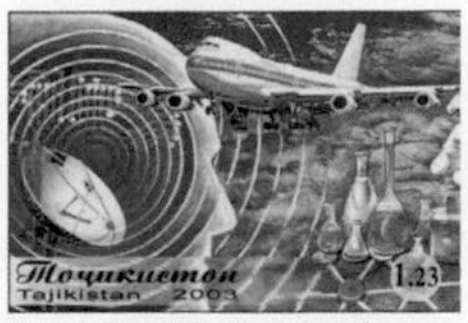
78 Satellite Dish, Aircraft and Chemicals

2003. Tenth Anniv of International Association of Academies of Sciences (IAAS). Multicoloured.

241	1s.23 Type **78**	2·75	2·40
242	1s.23 Spaceman, hand, emblem and VDU	2·75	2·40

Nos. 241/2 were issued together, se-tenant, forming a composite design.

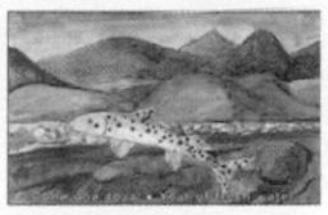
79 Trout (*Julja Shamsutdinova*)

2003. International Year of Fresh Water. Children's Paintings. Multicoloured.

243	66d. Type **79**	1·30	1·10
244	66d. Glacial river (Farrukh Djumaev)	1·30	1·10
245	66d. Mountain river (Ersin Bairak)	1·30	1·10
246	66d. River with waterfall (Ira Shkolenko)	1·30	1·10

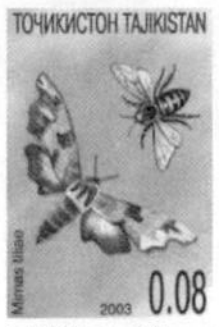
80 Mimas tiliae

2003. Fauna. Sheet 123×93 mm containing T **80** and similar vert designs. Multicoloured.

MS247 8d. Type **80**; 20d. *Mustela erminea*; 53d. *Testudo horsfieldii*; 64d. *Mantis religiosa*; 1s.23 *Lanius collurio*; 1s.27 *Canis aureus*; 1s.76 *Capra falconeri*; 2s.29 *Alcedo atthis* 14·00 12·00

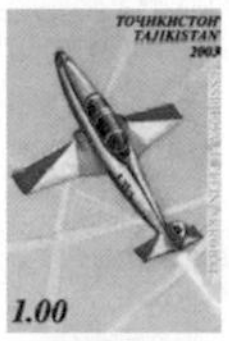
81 L-29A Delfin Akrobat (USSR)

2003. Aircraft. Sheet [illegible] mm containing T **81** and similar vert designs. Multicoloured.

MS248 1s.×8, Type **81**; Jak-55 (USA); Cessna-172 (USA); Siai Marchetti F-260 (Italy); Europa XS (UK); BO-209 Monsun (Germany); CAP-10 (France); Soko 2 (Bosnia and Herzgovina) 14·00 12·00

The stamps and margins of **MS**248 form a composite design of an airfield.

2004. No. **MS**152 surch.

MS249 20d.×2, on 100d.×2, multicoloured; 66d.×2 on 270d.×2 multicoloured 6·50 5·50

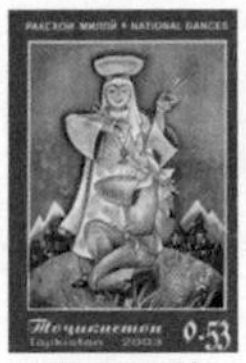
83 Woman with Castanets, Man playing Pipe

2004. Traditional Dances. Multicoloured.

250	53d. Type **83**	1·30	1·10
251	53d. Woman with tambourine, man with dutar	1·30	1·10
252	53d. Two men dancing	1·30	1·10
253	53d. Man playing drum, woman with arms raised	1·30	1·10

2004. No. 21 and No. 48 surch.

254	A (6d.) surch on 50d. multicoloured	1·00	85
255	B (15d.) surch on 160d. multicoloured	1·80	1·60

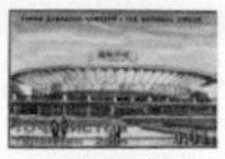
86 National Circus, Dushanbe

2004. Buildings. Multicoloured.

256	1d. Type **86**	20	20
257	2d. Firdavsi National Library	20	20
258	3d. National Bank	20	20
259	8d. Ministry of Finance	35	30
260	20d. Ministry of Communication	85	70
261	50d. Government Building	2·20	1·90

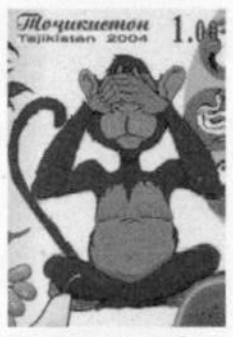
87 See no Evil

2004. New Year. Year of the Monkey. Sheet 103×65 mm containing T **87** and similar vert designs. Multicoloured.

MS262 1s. Type **87**; 1s.20 Hear no Evil and lunar cycle; 1s.50 Speak no Evil 6·75 5·75

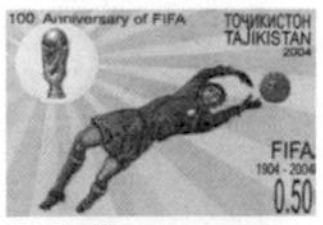
88 Goalkeeper

2004. Centenary of Federation Internationale de Football Association (FIFA). Multicoloured.

263	50d. Type **88**	1·00	85
264	70d. FIFA Secretariat Building, Zurich	1·50	1·30
265	1s. Stephane Chapuisat (Switzerland) (vert)	2·00	1·70
266	2s. Pele (Brazil) (vert)	4·00	3·25

Nos. 263/6 were also available imperforate.

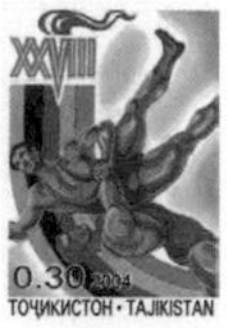
89 Wrestling

2004. Olympic Games, Athens. Sheet 126×110 mm containing T **89** and similar vert designs. Multicoloured.

MS267 30d. Type **89**; 45d. Running; 55d. Basketball; 60d. Shooting; 75d. Show jumping; 80d. Archery; 1s.50 Football; 2s.50 Gymnastics 12·00 10·00

No. **MS**267 also exists imperforate.

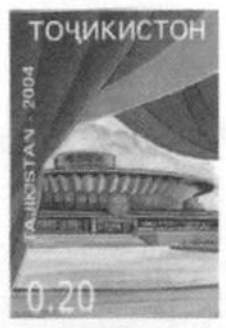
90 Curtains and National Circus, Dushanbe

2004. 80th Anniv of Dushanbe Circus. Sheet 96×92 mm containing T **90** and similar vert designs. Multicoloured.

MS271 20d. Type **90**; 50d. Tightrope walkers; 1s. Elephant and trainer; 1s.10 Conjurer, cat and lamp; 1s.50 Clown riding donkey; 1s.70 Equestrian acrobat 10·00 8·75

No. **MS**271 also exists imperforate.

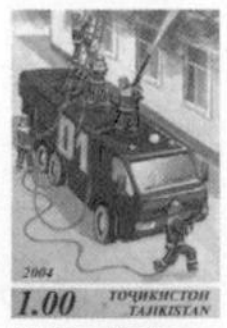
91 Fire Engine

2004. Transport. Multicoloured.

MS272 1s.×6 Type **91**; Air ambulance; Policemen and vehicles; Rail deliveries; Roadside rescue; Bus 9·25 7·50

Nos. 273/6 are vacant.

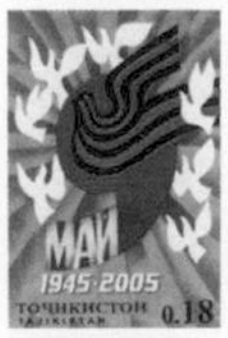
92 Doves

2005. 60th Anniv of End of World War II. Sheet 103×59 mm containing T **92** and similar vert design. Multicoloured.

MS277a 18t. Type **92**; 75t. As Type **92** 5·50 4·75

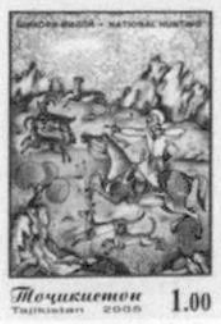
93 Huntsman

2005. Hunting (1st issue). Sheet 170×75 mm containing T **93** and similar vert designs. Multicoloured.

MS277b 1s. Type **93**; 1s.70 As Type **93** but with design reversed; 2s.30 As Type **93** 10·50 9·00

See also **MS**302.

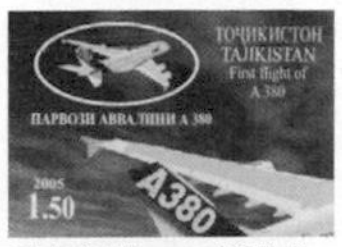
94 Left Wing and Tail Fin

2005. Maiden Flight of A380 Airbus. Designs showing part of the airplane. Multicoloured.

278	1s.50 Type **94**	2·75	2·30
278b	1s.50 Nose	2·75	2·30
279	1s.80 Tail section	3·25	2·75
280	1s.80 Right wing	3·25	2·75

Nos. 278/80 were issued together, *se-tenant*, forming a composite design.

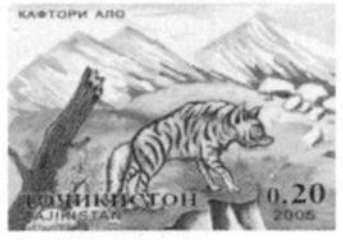
95 Hyena

2005. Fauna. Sheet 170×75 mm containing T **95** and similar horiz designs. Multicoloured.

MS281 20t. Type **95**; 20t. Lynx; 75t. Raccoon; 75t. Fox; 80t. Snow leopard; 1s. Bear; 1s.50 Leopard; 1s.80 Tiger 12·50 11·50

The stamps of **MS**281 form a composite design.

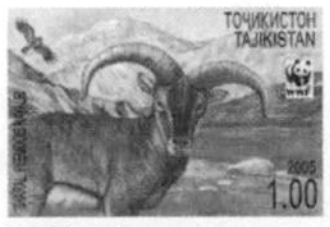
96 Bharal

2005. Himalayan Blue Sheep (Bharal) (*Pseudois nayaur*). Multicoloured.

282	1s. Type **96**	1·70	1·40
283	1s.45 Male and female	2·40	2·00
284	1s.70 Two females	2·75	2·40
285	2s.25 Two females in snow	3·75	3·25

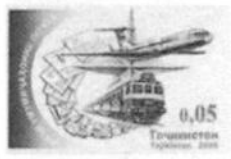
97 Airplane, Locomotive and Envelopes

2005. Transport.

286	**97**	5t. ultramarine and grey	30	25
287	**97**	7t. brown and bistre	40	35
288	**97**	11t. emerald and blue	55	50
289	**97**	20t. violet and lilac	70	60
290	**97**	55t. blue and slate	1·40	1·20
291	**97**	75t. orange and brown	1·80	1·60

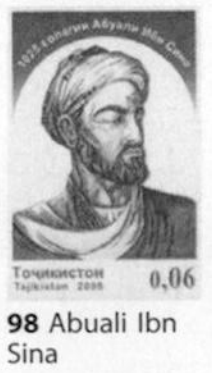
98 Abuali Ibn Sina

2005. Abuali Ibn Sina (Avicenna) (physician and polymath) Commemoration.

292	**98**	6t. green and slate	30	25
293	**98**	8t. brown and sepia	40	35
294	**98**	10t. violet and grey	55	50
295	**98**	12t. ultramarine and slate	70	60
296	**98**	50t. blue, slate and deep blue	1·40	1·20
297	**98**	1s. vermilion and yellow	1·80	1·60

99 Panchakent

2005. Mountains. Multicoloured.

298	1s. Type **99**		1·80	1·60
299	1s.50 Muminobod		2·50	2·20
300	2s. Pamir		3·50	3·00
301	2s.50 Isfara		4·25	3·50

2005. Hunting (2nd issue). Sheet 170×75 mm containing vert designs as T **93**. Multicoloured. Perf or imperf.

MS302 2s.50×2, Huntsman with falcon; Mounted huntsman wrestling with wildcat   9·75   8·75

100 Old Man and Bear

2006. Folk Tales. Multicoloured.

303	55t. Type **100**	1·10	95
304	75t. Traders and donkey	1·40	1·20
305	2s. Spearing dragon	3·50	3·00
306	3s. Man, tortoise, cockerel and fox	5·25	4·50

101 Man's Costume

2006. Traditional Costumes. Multicoloured.

307	75t. Type **101**	1·40	1·20
308	75t. Man wearing belted patterned coat and boots	1·40	1·20
309	1s. Woman wearing patterned coat, baggy trousers and large headscarf	1·80	1·60
310	1s. Woman wearing wide sleeved long dress and headdress	1·80	1·60

102 *Aquila chrysaetos* (golden eagle)

2006. Fauna. Sheet 120×90 mm containing T **102** and similar vert designs. Multicoloured.

MS311 8d. Type **102**; 20d. *Panthera tigris* (inscr 'longipilis') (tiger); 55d. *Hystrix hirsutirostris* (Indian crested porcupine); 70t. *Ailuropoda melanoleuca* (giant panda); 75d. *Meles meles* (badger); 1s.60 *Ursus arctos* (brown bear); 1s.92 *Mustela erminea* (stoat); 2s. *Bubo coromandus* (dusky eagle-owl)   14·00   12·00

103 Players

2006. World Cup Football Championship, Germany. Multicoloured.

312	1s.50 Type **103**	2·75	2·40
313	1s.50 Save in goalmouth	2·75	2·40
314	1s.50 Four players tackling	2·75	2·40
315	2s. Reverse kick towards goal	3·50	3·00

No. **MS**316 and Type **104** have been left for '15th Anniv of Republic', issued 30 August 2006, not yet received.

105 Anniversary Medal and Flag

2006. 2700th Anniv of Kulob. Sheet 111×50 mm containing T **105** and similar horiz design. Multicoloured.

MS317 2s.×2, Type **105**; Mir Said Ali Khamadoni's mausoleum   8·50   7·75

The stamps of No. **MS**317 share a composite background design.

106 Flags of Member States

2006. 15th Anniv of Commonwealth of Independent States. Sheet 111×50 mm containing T **106** and similar horiz design. Multicoloured.

MS318 1s.50×2, Type **106**; Symbols of communication   7·75   7·25

No. **MS**318 also contains a central stamp size label showing RCC emblem.

The stamps, label and margins of No. **MS**318 form a composite background design.

107 Cotton

2006. Cotton.

319	**107**	5t. multicoloured	30	25
320	**107**	6t. multicoloured	35	30
321	**107**	7t. multicoloured	40	35
322	**107**	8t. multicoloured	50	40
323	**107**	20t. multicoloured	1·00	85
324	**107**	75t. multicoloured	2·40	2·00

108 West Siberian Laika

2006. Dogs. Multicoloured.

325	20t. Type **108**	70	60
326	55t. Perdiguero de burgos (Spanish pointer)	1·10	95
327	75t. Afghan hound	1·40	1·20
328	1s. Sredneasiatskaia ovtcharka (inscr 'sredneasiatkaia') (Central Asia shepherd dog)	1·80	1·60
329	2s. Saluki hound	3·25	3·00
330	3s. Tosa	5·00	4·25

Nos. 325/30 also exist imperforate.

109 Cap

2006. Traditional Caps. Designs showing caps. Multicoloured.

331	1s.50 Type **109**	2·75	2·30
332	1s.50 With pointed crown	2·75	2·30
333	1s.50 With flat crown	2·75	2·30
334	1s.50 With raised crown and all-over design	2·75	2·30

Nos. 331/4 were issued together, *se-tenant* forming a composite background design.

(110)

2007. No. 49 surch as T **110**. Multicoloured.

335	75t. on 160r. Zafar Restaurant	2·40	2·00

No. 336 and Type **111** are left for Snakes, issued on 30 April 2007, not yet received.

112 Rumi

2007. 800th Birth Anniv of Jalal ad-Din Muhammad Balkhi (Mowlana) (Rumi).

337	**112**	5t. deep rose-red	30	25
338	**112**	10t. bright blue	40	35
339	**112**	20t. green	55	50
340	**112**	A indigo	70	60
341	**112**	☒ maroon	2·50	2·20
342	**112**	B deep magenta	4·25	3·50

No. 343 is vacant.

113 Earrings (Buhara and Kulyab

2007. Jewellery. Multicoloured.

344	50t. Type **113**	85	70
345	2s. Necklace (Buhara nad Kulyab)	3·25	3·00
346	2s.50 Tiered necklace with central pendant (mountain region)	4·25	3·50
347	3s. Earring (Buhara)	5·00	4·25

Nos. 348/54 and Type **114** are vacant.

115 *Aquila chrysaetos*

2007. Birds. Sheet 100×93 mm. Multicoloured.

MS355 1s. Type **115**; 1s.10 *Phasianinae*; 1s.20 *Aix galericulata*; 1s.30 *Otididae*; 1s.40 *Falco cherrug*; 1s.60 *Haliaeetus albicilla*   11·00   10·00

116 Football

2008. Olympic Games, Beijing. Multicoloured.

356	1s.50 Type **116**	2·10	1·80
357	2s. Boxing	2·75	2·40
358	2s. Throwing the hammer	2·75	2·40
359	2s. Judo	2·75	2·40

MS360 100×130mm. Nos. 336/9, each×2   21·00   19·00

117 Cooking Pot (Deg), 19th century, copper

2008. Cooking Pots. Multicoloured.

361	20t. Type **117**	55	50
362	25t. As Type **117**	70	60
363	50t. Cooking pot (Oftoba), 19th century, copper	1·10	95
364	1s. As No. 343	2·00	1·70
365	1s.35 Bucket (Satil), 19th century, copper	2·50	2·20
366	2s. As No. 363	3·75	3·25
367	2s.15 As No. 365	4·00	3·25
368	3s. As No. 363	5·25	4·50

118 Snow Slips, Pamir

2008. International Conference on Water Related Disaster Reduction. Sheet 105×72mm containing T **118** and similar vert design. Multicoloured.

MS369 2s.50×2 Type **118**; Tornado   7·75   7·75

119 Head of Buddha (statue)

2008. Ajinateppa Temple, 7th-8th Centuries AD. Sheet 116×82 mm containing T **119** and similarr square designs. Multicoloured.

MS370 2s.50 Type **119**; 3s.50 Supine torso of Buddha   9·75   9 00

~~**100**~~

120

2008. Opening of Russian Centre in Tajikistan. Nos. 139.140 surcharged and overprinted. Multicoloured.

371	1s. on 100r. Centenary poster	2·75	2·50
372	1s. on 270r. Portrait of Pushkin	2·75	2·50

121 Rudaki

2008. 1150th Birth Anniv of Abu Abdollah Jafar ibn Mohammad Rudaki (Rudaki). Sheet 102×58mm containing T **121** and similar vert design. Multicoloured.

MS373 2s.50×2 Type **121**; medallion showing Rudaki   9·00   8·50

122 Plantain and Grasshopper

2008. Flora and Fauna. Multicoloured.

374	1s.50 Type **122**	2·50	2·30
375	1s.50 Coltsfoot and ladybird	2·50	2·30
376	2s. Dandelion and beetle	3·25	3·00
377	2s. Marigold and bee	3·25	3·00

123 Viper

2008. Snakes. Sheet 98×59mm containing T **123** and similar horiz design. Multicoloured.

MS378 2s.50×2 Type **123**; Snake   9·75   9·00

124 Grapes

2008. Grapes. Multicoloured

379	1s.50 Type **124**	2·40	2·20
380	1s.50 Small narrow bluish grapes	2·40	2·20
381	2s. Pinkish grapes with pale leaf	3·25	3·00
382	2s. Long narrow cream grapes	3·25	3·00

No. 383 is vacant.

125 Gijack, Badahshon

2008. Musical Instruments. Multicoloured.
384	3s. Type 125	6·00	5·50
385	3s. Dotar Inscr "Dotaar"), Khorasan	6·00	5·50

No. 386 and Type **126** are vacant.

127 *Flowering Indian Lilac-Luchob* (Zuhur Habibuloev)

2009. Paintings. Sheet 109×104mm containing T **127** and similar vert design. Multicoloured.
MS387	4s.×2 Type 127; *My Mother - My Wings* (Sabzali Sharif)	13·00	12·00

128 Red Deer

2009. *Cervus elaphus bactrianus* (red deer). Multicoloured.
388	1s.50 Type 128	2·10	2·00
389	2s. Stag	2·75	2·50
390	2s.50 Stage and hinds	3·50	3·25
391	3s. Hind and fawn	4·25	4·00
MS392	92×155mm. Nos. 368/71 each×4	55·00	50·00

129 Panthera tigris tigris (tiger)

2009. Fauna. Multicoloured.
393	1s. Type 129	1·70	1·60
394	1s. Equus Przewalskii (Przewalski's horsel)	1·70	1·60
395	1s.50 Camelus bactrianus (Bactarian camel)	2·40	2·20
396	1s.50 Caracal caracal (caracal)	2·40	2·20
397	2s. Ailuropoda malanoleuca (giant panda)	3·25	3·00
398	2s. Macaca fuscata (Japanese macaque)	3·25	3·00
399	2s.30 Elephas maximus (elephant)	3·75	3·50
400	2s.30 Ovis vignei (urial)	3·75	3·50
MS401	155×93mm. Nos. 393/400	21·00	20·00

130 Mosque

2009. Al-Imam al-Azam Numan Thabit bin Zuta bin Mah (Abu Hanifa) (founder of Sunni Hanafi school of Islamic jurisprudence).
402	**130** 4s. multicoloured	6·25	5·75

131 Cat on Ball

2009. Circus Animals. Multicoloured.
MS403	3s.50×2, Type 131; Dog balancing ball on nose	12·50	11·50

132 Climbers on Abu ali ibn Sino (Pik Lenina)

2009. Glaciers of Tajikistan. Multicoloured.
MS404	4s.×2, Type 132; Ismoili Somoni (Garmo Peak)	13·00	12·00

0,15

133

2009. No. 143 surch as T **133**. Multicoloured.
405	15t. on (B) Type 44	55	50

134 Green Melon

2009. Melons. Multicoloured.
406	1s.50 Type 134	2·40	2·20
407	1s.50 Melon with mottled skin	2·40	2·20
408	2s. Long yellow melon	3·25	3·00
409	2s. Round, ridged yellowish melon	3·25	3·00

135 Peony and Butterfly

2010. Peonies. Multicoloured.
410	2s. Type 135	3·25	3·00
411	3s.20 Double peony and blue butterfly	5·25	4·75
MS412	91×63 mm. 3s.20 As No. 411	5·50	5·00

136 Year of the Tiger (image scaled to 27% of original size)

2010. Year of the Tiger. Fauna. No. **MS**281 overprinted as T **136**. Multicoloured.
MS413	20t. As Type 95; 20t. Lynx; 75t. Raccoon; 75t. Fox; 80t. Snow leopard; 1s. Bear; 1s.50 Leopard; 1s.80 Tiger	17·00	16·00

137 Soldier and Aircraft

2010. 65th Anniv of End of World War II. Multicoloured.
MS414	1s.35×3 Type 137×3; 2s.15×2 Parade in Red Square×2	14·00	13·00

138 Rogun Dam

2010. Hydroelectric Power Station at Rogun Dam. Multicoloured.
415	10d. Type 138	30	30
416	15d. Pylons and power lines	40	40
417	20d. Interior of power station	50	45
418	10s. Rail car and engineer	18·00	17·00

No. 419 and Type **139** are left for Khaje Abdullah Ansari, issued on 25 July 2010, not yet received.

140 Canis lupus (Wolf)

2010. Fauna. Bangkok 2010 and Portugal 2010 Philatelic Exhibitions. Multicoloured.
MS420	2.50s. Type 140; 3s. Lynx lynx (lynx); 3s.50 Elephas maximus (elephant); 4s.50 Panthera tigris (tiger)	26·00	24·00

141 Sasani Coin with Sacred Fire Image

2010. Coins. Multicoloured.
MS421	4s. Type 141; 5s. Shahanshoh Vasudeva gold coin	16·00	15·00

142 Musicians

2010. Traditional Men's Dance. Multicoloured.
MS422	4s.×2, Type 142; Men dancing	14·50	13·50

The stamps and margins of **MS**422 form a composite design.

143 Rabbit

2011. Chinese New Year. Year of the Rabbit. Multicoloured.
MS423	2s.×2, Type 143; Rabbit and cat	7·25	7·00

(144)

2011. Nos. 26 and 46 surch as T **144**
424	10d. on 25r. multicoloured	65	60
425	15d. on 35r. multicoloured	95	90

145 Steam Locomotive 1-5-0 L, 1947

2011. Steam Locomotives. Multicoloured.
426	1s.50 Type 145	2·75	2·50
427	1s.50 Steam locomotive 1-4-0 SCH, 1912	2·75	2·50
428	1s.50 Steam locomotive 1-3-1 Su, 1925	2·75	2·50
429	1s.50 Steam locomotive 2-3-1 Lp, 1925	2·75	2·50

146 Apricot Blossom

2011. Paintings. Apricot Blossom. Multicoloured.
430	3s.50 Type 146	6·50	6·00
431	4s. Birds and blossom	7·25	6·75

147 Norak Hydro Power Plant

2011. 20th Anniv of Independence
MS432	2s.50 Type147; 2s.50 Sangtuda hydro power plant; 2s.50 Rogun hydro power plant; 3s. President Emomali Rahmon (40×84 mm)	19·00	18·00

148 Anniversary Emblem

2011. 20th Anniv of Community of Independent States (CIS). Sheet 111×58 mm
MS433	148 3s.50 multicoloured	11·00	10·50

149 Satellite Receiver

2011. 20th Anniv of Regional Communication Community (RCC). Sheet 107×76 mm
MS434	149 2s.50 multicoloured	9·50	9·00

150 Man's Head

2011. Soguian Terracotta Figures of Fifth to Eighth Century. Multicoloured.
435	10d. Type 150	40	40
436	15d. Inscribed 'Head of Rurel'	50	45
437	20d. Head and shoulders inscribed 'Figure in high relief'	65	60
438	25d. Male head with elaborate headdress	70	70

151 Dragon

2012. Chinese New Year. Year of the Dragon. Multicoloured.
439	2s. Type 151	4·00	3·75
440	2s.50 Dolphin (inscr 'Fish')	4·75	4·50

152 Men and Woman, Darvoz District

2012. Traditional Costumes. Multicoloured.
441	1s.35 Type 152	2·75	2·50
442	2s.15 Woman and children, Kulob district	4·25	4·00

153 Judo

2012. Olympic Games, London. Multicoloured.
MS443	3s.×4, Type 153; Taekwondo; Hammer throwing; Boxing	16·00	15·00

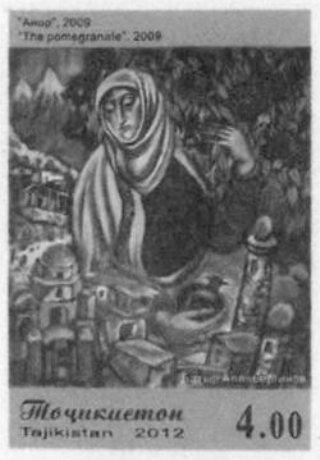

154 *The Pomegranate* (Batyr Allabergenov)

2012. Paintings. Multicoloured.

MS444 4s.×2, Type **154**; *Wake up* (Rakhim Safarov)		16·00	15·00

ТОЧИКИСТОН ИШТИРОКЧИИ ОЛИМПИАДАИ ЛОНДОН 2012

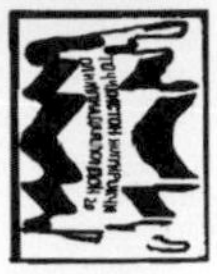

(155)

2012. MS236, Summer Olympic Games, Athens 2004 and Beijing 2008, overprinted in blue. Multicoloured.

MS445 53d. Type **75**; 1s. Running; 1s.23. Football; 2s. Gymnastics		29·00	27·00

2012. MS236, Summer Olympic Games, Athens 2004 and Beijing 2008, overprinted in violet or black. Multicoloured.

MS446 53d. Type **75**; 1s. Running; 1s.23. Football; 2s. Gymnastics		24·00	23·00

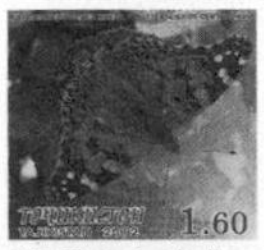

156 Tortoiseshell Butterfly on Rose

2012. Insects and Flowers. Multicoloured.

447	1s.60 Type **156**	3·25	3·00
448	1s.60 Grasshopper on deep pink rose	3·25	3·00
449	2s.50 Red Admiral butterfly on mimosa	5·00	4·75
450	2s.50 Swallowtail butterfly on mimosa	5·00	4·75
451	3s. Morpho butterfly on yellow rose with orange edges	6·00	5·50
452	3s. Monarch butterfly on yellow rose with orange edges	6·00	5·50
453	3s. Swallowtail butterfly on pink rose	6·00	5·50
454	3s. Ladybird on pink rose	6·00	5·50

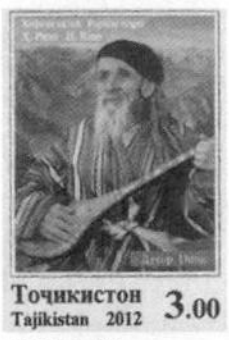

157 H. Rizo playing Dutor

2012. Musicians and Instruments. Multicoloured.

455	3s. Type **157**	6·00	5·50
456	3s. Gurminj Zavqibekov playing sitar	6·00	5·50

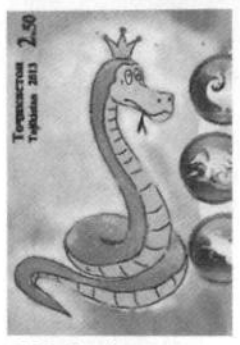

158 Snake

2012. Chinese New Year. Year of the Snake. Multicoloured.

MS547 2s.50×3, Type **158**; Snake and signs of the Zodiac; Snake facing left		15·00	14·25

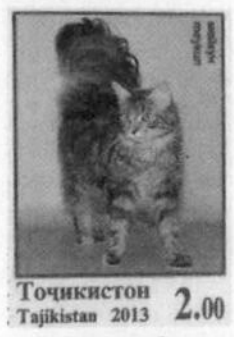

159 Maine Coon (inscr 'Meykun')

2013. Cat Breeds. Multicoloured.

458	2s. Type **156**	4·00	3·50
459	2s. British Blue	4·00	3·50
460	2s. LaPerm	4·00	3·50

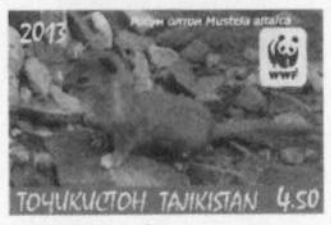

160 Weasel

2013. Endangered Species. Altai Weasel (*Mustela altaica*). Multicoloured.

461	4s.50 Type **160**	9·00	8·25
462	4s.50 Head of weasel	9·00	8·25
463	5s. Carrying pup	10·00	9·50
464	5s. Two weasels	10·00	9·50

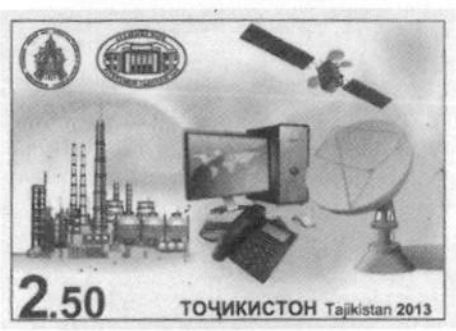

161 Satellite, reciever, computer and chemical plant

2013. 20th Anniv of Academy of Science. Multicoloured.

465	1s.60 Books, Microscope and Flasks	3·25	3·00
466	2s.50 Type **161**	5·00	4·75

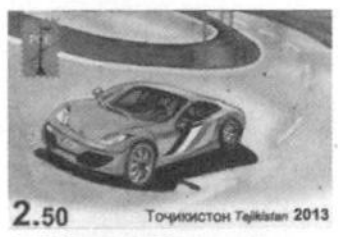

162 Sports Car

2013. Regional Communication Community (RCC). History of Communication. Multicoloured.

467	2s.50 Type **162**	5·00	4·75
468	2s.50 Aircraft and red car	5·00	4·75
469	2s.50 Aircraft and goods train	5·00	4·75
470	2s.50 Aircraft and passenger train	5·00	4·75

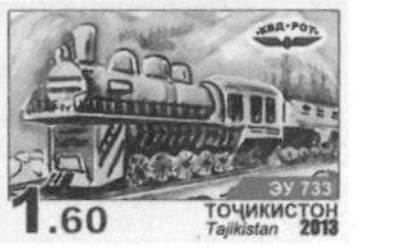

163 Locomotive EU733

2013. Trains. Multicoloured.

471	1s.60 Type **163**	3·25	3·00
472	1s.60 Locomotive TE 33A with electricity pylons in background	3·25	3·00
473	1s.60 Locomotive TE 33A emerging from tunnel	3·25	3·00
474	1s.60 Locomotive TE 33A crossing bridge over river	3·25	3·00

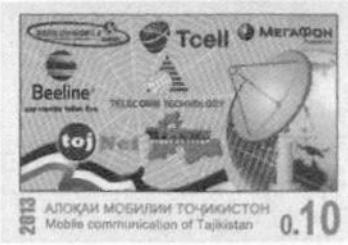

164 Transmitter and Mobile Technology Companies Emblems

2013. Mobile Communication in Tajikistan. Multicoloured.

475	10t. Type **164**	20	25
476	15t. As Type **164**	25	30
477	1s.60 Transmitter, emblems and Government Palace	3·25	3·00

50 с. парвози В. Терешкова ба каихон
2013
50 лет полету В.Терешковой в космос

(165) (image scaled to 58% of original size)

2013. 50th Anniv of First Woman's Space Flight. **MS**183, Tenth Anniv of RCC and **MS**172, *Sputnik* (satellite) over printed in red

MS478 1s. Type **59**		2·00	1·75
MS479 1s.50 Type **55**		3·00	2·50

Pt. 1

TANGANYIKA

Formerly the German colony of German East Africa. After the 1914–18 War it was under British mandate until 1946 and then administered by Britain under United Nations trusteeship until 1961 when it became independent within the British Commonwealth. It had a common postal service with Kenya and Uganda from 1935 to 1961 (for these issues see under Kenya, Uganda and Tanganyika). Renamed Tanzania in 1965.

1915. 16 annas = 1 rupee.
1917. 100 cents = 1 rupee.
1922. 100 cents = 1 shilling.

1915. Stamps of the Indian Expeditionary Forces optd **G. R. POST MAFIA**.

M33	**55**	3p. grey	40·00	£100
M34	**56**	½a. green	60·00	£100
M35	**57**	1a. red	65·00	90·00
M36	**59**	2a. lilac	£110	£190
M37	**61**	2½a. blue	£120	£200
M38	**62**	3a. orange	£130	£200
M39	**63**	4a. olive	£190	£275
M40	**65**	8a. mauve	£350	£450
M41	**66**	12a. red	£450	£600
M42	**67**	1r. brown and green	£475	£700

1916. Stamps of Nyasaland (King George V) optd **N.F.**

N1	½d. green	1·50	8·00
N2	1d. red	1·50	3·25
N3	3d. purple on yellow	25·00	17·00
N4	4d. black and red on yellow	50·00	40·00
N5	1s. black on green	70·00	70·00

1917. Stamps of Kenya and Uganda (King George V, 1912) optd **G.E.A.**

45	1c. black	15	80
47	3c. green	20	15
48	6c. red	20	10
49	10c. orange	50	60
50	12c. grey	50	3·00
51	15c. blue	1·50	4·75
52	25c. black and red on yellow	80	5·50
53	50c. black and lilac	2·00	4·75
54	75c. black on green	1·00	4·75
55	1r. black on green	5·50	7·00
56	2r. red and black on blue	13·00	60·00
57	3r. violet and green	16·00	80·00
58	4r. red and green on yellow	25·00	£120
59	5r. blue and purple	48·00	£140
60	10r. red and green on green	£150	£425
61	20r. black and purple on red	£375	£650
62	50r. red and green	£700	£1100

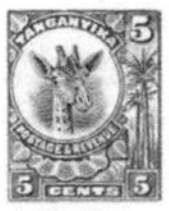

4 Giraffe

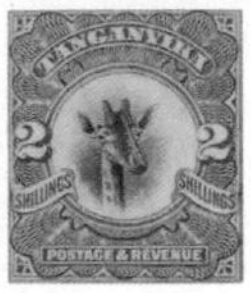

5

1922

83a	**5**	1s. green	6·00	11·00
86a	**5**	5s. black and red	38·00	95·00
87a	**5**	10s. black and blue	£100	£180
88a	**5**	£1 black and orange	£350	£550
74	**4**	5c. black and purple	2·25	20
89	**4**	5c. black and green	11·00	1·50
75	**4**	10c. black and green	3·50	85
90	**4**	10c. black and yellow	11·00	1·50
76	**4**	15c. black and red	4·00	10
77	**4**	20c. black and orange	5·00	10
78	**4**	25c. black	8·00	6·50
91	**4**	25c. black and blue	4·50	17·00
79	**4**	30c. black and blue	5·50	5·00
92	**4**	30c. black and purple	8·00	26·00
80	**4**	40c. black and brown	5·50	4·50
81	**4**	50c. black and grey	6·50	1·50
82	**4**	75c. black and yellow	5·50	22·00
84	**5**	2s. black and purple	9·00	26·00
85	**5**	3s. black	50·00	48·00

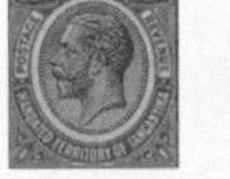

6

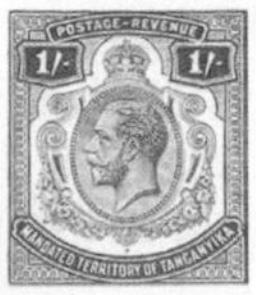

7

1927

93	**6**	5c. black and green	1·75	10
94	**6**	10c. black and yellow	2·00	10
95	**6**	15c. black and red	1·75	10
96	**6**	20c. black and orange	2·75	10
97	**6**	25c. black and blue	3·75	2·00
98	**6**	30c. black and purple	2·75	2·75
98a	**6**	30c. black and blue	25·00	30
99	**6**	40c. black and brown	2·00	8·50
100	**6**	50c. black and grey	2·50	1·00
101	**6**	75c. black and olive	2·00	24·00
102	**7**	1s. black and green	4·25	2·75
103	**7**	2s. black and purple	30·00	7·00
104	**7**	3s. black	48·00	95·00
105	**7**	5s. black and red	38·00	26·00
106	**7**	10s. black and blue	95·00	£150
107	**7**	£1 black and orange	£250	£400

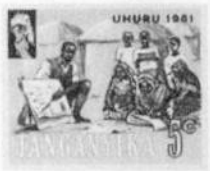

8 Teacher and Pupils

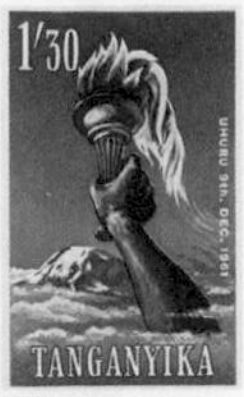

15 Freedom Torch over Mt. Kilimanjaro

1961. Independence. Inscr "UHURU 1961".

108	**8**	5c. sepia and green	10	10
109	-	10c. turquoise	10	10
110	-	15c. sepia and blue	10	10
111	-	20c. brown	10	10
112	-	30c. black, green and yellow	10	10
113	-	50c. black and yellow	10	10
114	-	1s. brown, blue and yellow	15	10
115	**15**	1s.30 multicoloured	4·25	10
116	-	2s. multicoloured	1·00	10
117	-	5s. turquoise and red	1·00	50
118	-	10s. black, purple and blue	15·00	4·75
119	**15**	20s. multicoloured	4·00	9·00

DESIGNS—VERT (as Type **8**): 10c. District nurse and child; 15c. Coffee picking; 20c. Harvesting maize; 50c. Serengeti lions. HORIZ (as Type **8**): 30c. Tanganyikan flag. (As Type **15**): 1s. "Maternity" (mother with nurse holding baby); 2s. Dar-es-Salaam waterfront; 5s. Land tillage; 10s. Diamond mine.

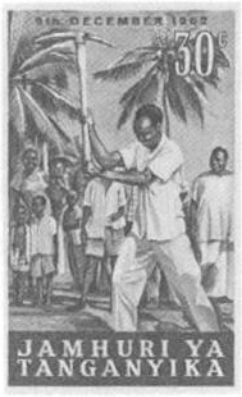

19 Pres. Nyerere inaugurating Self-help Project

1962. Inauguration of Republic.

120	**19**	30c. green	10	10
121	-	50c. multicoloured	10	10
122	-	1s.30 multicoloured	10	10
123	-	2s.50 black, red and blue	30	50

DESIGNS: 50c. Hoisting flag on Mt. Kilimanjaro; 1s.30, Presidential emblem; 2s.50, Independence monument.

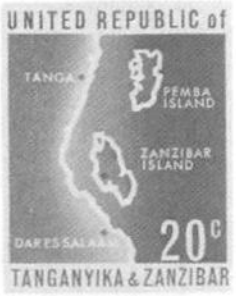

23 Map of Republic

1964. United Republic of Tanganyika and Zanzibar Commemoration.

124	**23**	20c. green and blue	30	10
125	-	30c. blue and sepia	10	10
126	-	1s.30 purple and blue	10	10
127	**23**	2s.50 purple and blue	2·00	1·75

DESIGN: 30c., 1s.30, Torch and spear emblem.

Despite the inscription on the stamps they had no validity in Zanzibar.

OFFICIAL STAMPS

1961. Independence stamps of 1961 optd **OFFICIAL**.

O1	5c. brown and green	10	10
O2	10c. turquoise	10	10
O3	15c. brown and blue	10	10
O4	20c. brown	10	10
O5	30c. black, green and yellow	10	10
O6	50c. black and yellow	10	10
O7	1s. brown, blue and yellow	10	10
O8	5s. turquoise and red	75	85

For later issues see **TANZANIA**.

Pt. 1

TANZANIA

A republic within the British Commonwealth formerly known as Tanganyika and incorporating Zanzibar.

100 cents = 1 shilling.

NOTE—Stamps inscribed "UGANDA KENYA TANGANYIKA & ZANZIBAR" (or "TANZANIA UGANDA KENYA") will be found listed under Kenya, Uganda and Tanganyika (Tanzania).

For use in Tanzania. Issues to No. 176 were also valid for use in Kenya and Uganda.

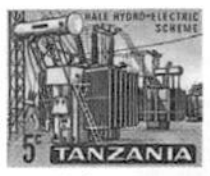

25 Hale Hydro-electric Scheme

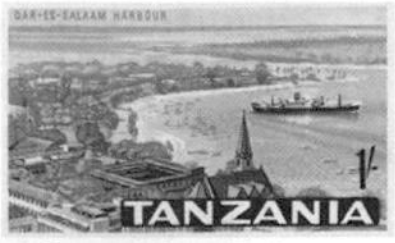

33 Dar-es-Salaam Harbour

1965

128	**25**	5c. blue and orange	10	10
129	-	10c. multicoloured	10	10
130	-	15c. multicoloured	10	10
131	-	20c. sepia, green and blue	10	10
132	-	30c. black and brown	10	10
133	-	40c. multicoloured	1·00	20
134	-	50c. multicoloured	1·00	10
135	-	65c. green, brown and blue	2·75	2·50
136	**33**	1s. multicoloured	1·50	10
137	-	1s.30 multicoloured	6·50	1·50
138	-	2s.50 blue and brown	6·50	1·25
139	-	5s. brown, green and blue	80	20
140	-	10s. yellow, green and blue	1·00	3·75
141	-	20s. multicoloured	7·00	18·00

DESIGNS—HORIZ (as Type **25**): 10c. Tanzania flag; 20c. Road-building; 50c. Common zebras, Manyara National Park; 65c. Mt. Kilimanjaro. (As Type **33**): 1s.30, Skull of "Zinjanthropus" and excavations, Olduvai Gorge; 2s.50, Fishing; 5s. Sisal industry; 10s. State House, Dar-es-Salaam. VERT (as Type **25**): 15c. National servicemen; 30c. Drum, spear, shield and stool; 40c. Giraffes, Mikumi National Park. (As Type **33**): 20s. Arms of Tanzania.

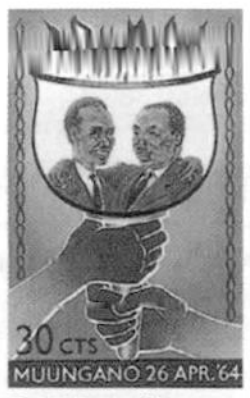

Z 39 Pres. Nyerere and First Vice-Pres. Karume within Bowl of Flame

1966. Second Anniv of United Republic. Multicoloured.

Z142	30c. Type Z **39**	20	45
Z143	50c. Hands supporting Bowl of Flame	20	45
Z144	1s.30 As 50c.	30	45
Z145	2s.50 Type Z **39**	40	1·25

Nos. Z142/5 were on sale in Zanzibar only.

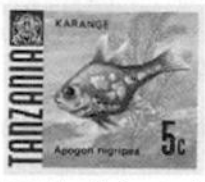

39 Black-footed Cardinalfish

1967. Fish. Multicoloured.

142	**39**	5c. mauve, green and black	10	2·75
143	-	10c. brown and bistre	10	10
144	-	15c. grey, blue and black	10	2·00
145	-	20c. brown and green	10	10
146	-	30c. green and black	20	10
147	-	40c. yellow, brown & green	1·00	10
148	-	50c. multicoloured	20	10
149	-	65c. yellow, green & black	2·00	4·50
150	-	70c. multicoloured	1·00	3·50
151	-	1s. brown, blue and purple	30	10
152	-	1s.30 multicoloured	4·00	10
153a	-	1s.50 multicoloured	2·25	10
154	-	2s.50 multicoloured	2·25	3·25
155a	-	5s. yellow, black and green	3·25	10
156a	-	10s. multicoloured	1·00	10
157a	-	20s. multicoloured	5·50	15

DESIGNS—As Type **39**: 10c. Sobrinus mud- skipper; 15c. White-spotted puffer; 20c. Thorny seahorse; 30c. Dusky batfish; 40c. Black-spotted sweetlips; 50c. Blue birdwrasse; 65c. Bennett's butterflyfish; 70c. Black-tipped grouper. 42×25 mm: 1s. Lionfish; 1s.30, Powder-blue surgeonfish; 1s.50, Yellow-finned fusilier; 2s.50, Emperor snapper; 5s. Moorish idol; 10s. Painted triggerfish; 20s. Horned squirrelfish.

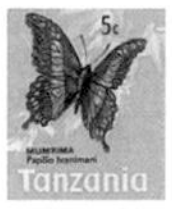

53 "Papilio hornimani"

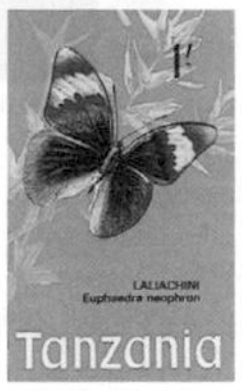

54 "Euphaedra neophron"

1973. Butterflies

(a) As T **53**

158	**53**	5c. green, blue and black	60	30
159	-	10c. multicoloured	60	15
160	-	15c. lavender and black	60	30
161	-	20c. brown, yellow & black	70	15
162	-	30c. yellow, orange & black	70	10
163	-	40c. multicoloured	70	15
164	-	50c. multicoloured	1·00	15
165	-	60c. brown, yellow and lake	1·50	60
166	-	70c. green, orange and black	1·50	20

(b) As T **54**

167	**54**	1s. multicoloured	1·50	15
168	-	1s.50 multicoloured	2·00	45
169	-	2s.50 multicoloured	2·25	80
170	-	5s. multicoloured	2·00	95
171	-	10s. multicoloured	2·25	6·00
172	-	20s. multicoloured	2·75	13·00

BUTTERFLIES: 10c. "Colotis ione"; 15c. "Amauris hyalites" (s sp. "makuyuenis"); 20c. "Libythea labdrea (s sp. "laius"); 30c. "Danaus chrysippus"; 40c. "Asterope rosa"; 50c. "Axiocerses styx"; 60c. "Terias hecabe"; 70c. "Acraea insignis"; 1s. "Euphaedra neophron"; 1s.50, "Precis octavia"; 2s.50, "Charaxes eupale"; 5s. "Charaxes pollux"; 10s. "Salamis parhassus"; 20s. "Papilio ophidicephalus".

1975. Nos. 165, 168/9 and 172 surch.

173	80c. on 60c. "Terias hecabe"	[illegible]	[illegible]
[illegible]	[illegible] on 1s.50 "Precis octavia"	4·00	7·00
175	3a. on 2s.50 "Charaxes eupale"	13·00	32·00
176	40s. on 20s. "Papilio ophidicephalus"	4·75	15·00

1976. Telecommunications Development. As Nos. 56/9 of Kenya.

177	50c. Microwave tower	10	10
178	1s. Cordless switchboard	15	10
179	2s. Telephones	25	30
180	3s. Message switching centre	30	40
MS181	120×120 mm. Nos. 177/80	1·10	1·50

1976. Olympic Games, Montreal. As Nos. 61/4 of Kenya.

182	50c. Akii Bua, Ugandan hurdler	10	10
183	1s. Filbert Bayi, Tanzanian runner	15	10
184	2s. Steve Muchoki, Kenyan boxer	25	40
185	3s. Olympic flame and East African flags	30	40
MS186	129×154 mm. Nos. 182/5	2·00	1·75

1976. Railway Transport. As Nos. 66/9 of Kenya.

187	50c. Diesel-hydraulic train, Tanzania–Zambia Railway	20	10
188	1s. Nile Bridge, Uganda	25	10
189	2s. Nakuru Station, Kenya	35	30
190	3s. Uganda Railway Class A locomotive, 1896	40	45
MS191	154×103 mm. Nos. 187/90	2·50	3·50

1977. Game Fish of East Africa. As Nos. 71/4 of Kenya.

192	50c. Nile perch	15	10
193	1s. Nile mouthbrooder	15	10
194	3s. Sailfish	50	40
195	5s. Black marlin	60	60
MS196	153×129 mm. Nos. 192/5	2·75	2·50

1977. Second World Black and African Festival of Arts and Culture. As Nos. 76/9 of Kenya.

197	50c. Maasai manyatta (village), Kenya	15	10
198	1s. "Heartbeat of Africa" (Ugandan dancers)	15	10
199	2s. Makonde sculpture	30	40
200	3s. "Early Man and Technology" (skinning hippopotamus)	75	1·60
MS201	132×190 mm. Nos. 197/200	1·40	2·00

1977. 25th Anniv of Safari Rally. As Nos. 81/4 of Kenya. Multicoloured.

202	50c. Rally-car and villagers	10	10
203	1s. Starting line	15	10
204	2s. Car fording river	30	40
205	5s. Car and elephants	1·00	1·10
MS206	126×93 mm. Nos. 202/5	1·40	2·00

1977. Centenary of Ugandan Church. As Nos. 86/9 of Kenya. Multicoloured.

207	50c. Canon Kivebulaya	10	10
208	1s. Modern Namirembe Cathedral	15	10
209	2s. The first Cathedral	30	40
210	5s. Early congregation Kigezi	60	1·75
MS211	126×89 mm. Nos. 207/10	1·00	2·00

1977. Endangered Species. As Nos. 96/100 of Kenya. Multicoloured.

212	50c. Pancake tortoise	40	10
213	1s. Nile crocodile	45	10
214	2s. Hunter's hartebeest	1·25	55
215	3s. Red colobus monkey	1·25	75
216	5s. Dugong	1·50	1·00
MS217	127×101 mm. Nos. 213/16	3·50	5·00

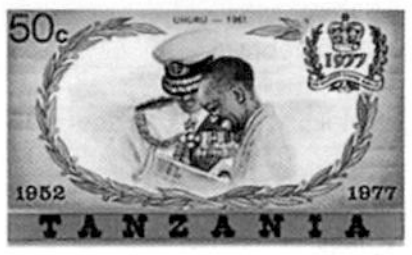

56 Prince Philip and President Nyerere

1977. Silver Jubilee. Multicoloured.

218	50c. Type **56**	10	10
219	5s. Pres. Nyerere with Queen and Prince Philip	15	25
220	10s. Jubilee emblem and Commonwealth flags	25	40
221	20s. The Crowning	40	60
MS222	128×102 mm. Nos. 218/21	75	1·50

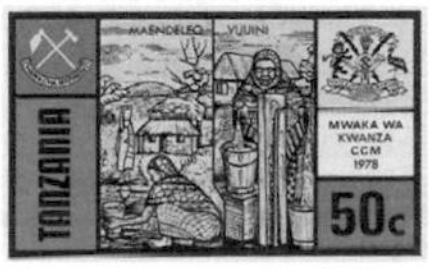

57 Improvements in Rural Living Standards

1978. First Anniv of Chama Cha Mapinduzi (New Revolutionary Party).

223	**57**	50c. multicoloured	10	10
224	-	1s. multicoloured	10	10
225	-	3s. multicoloured	25	60
226	-	5s. black, green and yellow	35	1·00
MS227		142×106 mm. Nos. 223/6	1·00	1·40

DESIGNS: 1s. Flag-raising ceremony, Zanzibar; 3s. Handing over of TANU headquarters, Dodoma; 5s. Chairman Julius Nyerere.

1978. World Cup Football Championship. As Nos. 122/5 of Kenya. Multicoloured.

228	50c. Joe Kadenge and forwards	10	10
229	1s. Mohamed Chuma and cup presentation	10	10
230	2s. Omari Kidevu and goal mouth scene	30	70
231	3s. Polly Ouma and forwards	40	1·00
MS232	136×81 mm. Nos. 228/31	2·00	1·75

1979. 25th Anniv of Coronation. Nos. 218/21 optd **25th ANNIVERSARY CORONATION 2nd JUNE 1953.**

233A	50c. Type **56**	10	10
234A	5s. Pres. Nyerere with Queen and Prince Philip	20	30
235A	10s. Jubilee emblem and Commonwealth flags	25	50
236A	20s. The Crowning	40	90
MS237A	128×102 mm. Nos. 233A/6A	75	1·50

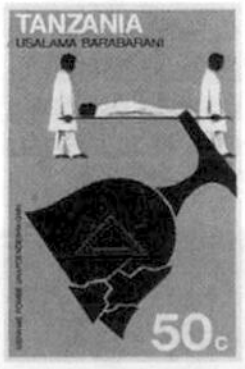

60 "Do not Drink and Drive"

1978. Road Safety.

238	**60**	50c. multicoloured	15	10
239	-	1s. multicoloured	20	10
240	-	3s. orange, black and brown	45	70
241	-	5s. multicoloured	75	1·40
MS242		92×129 mm. Nos. 238/41	1·40	2·00

DESIGNS: 1s. "Show courtesy to young, old and crippled"; 3s. "Observe the Highway Code"; 5s. "Do not drive a faulty vehicle.

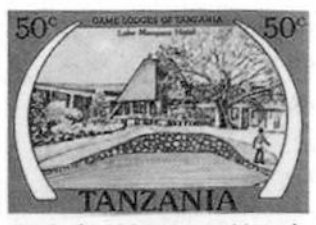

61 Lake Manyara Hotel

1978. Game Lodges. Multicoloured.

243	50c. Type **61**	10	10
244	1s. Lobo Wildlife Lodge	10	10
245	3s. Ngorongoro Crater Lodge	20	35
246	5s. Ngorongoro Wildlife Lodge	30	55
247	10s. Mafia Island Lodge	40	1·10
248	20s. Mikumi Wildlife Lodge	75	2·75
MS249	118×112 mm. Nos. 243/8	5·00	7·50

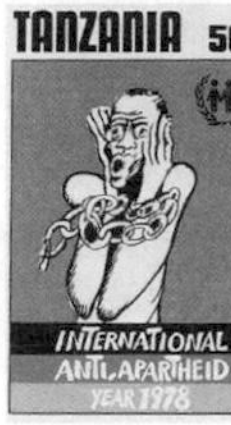

62 "Racial Suppression"

1978. International Anti-Apartheid Year.

250	**62**	50c. multicoloured	10	10
251	-	1s. black, green and yellow	10	10
252	-	2s.50 multicoloured	30	1·00
253	-	5s. multicoloured	60	1·75
MS254		127×132 mm. Nos. 250/3	1·25	2·75

DESIGNS: 1s. "Racial division"; 2s.50, "Racial harmony"; 5s. "Fall of suppression and rise of freedom".

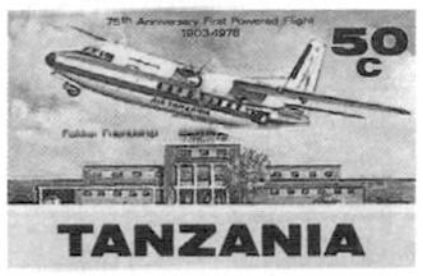

63 Fokker F.27 Friendship

1978. 75th Anniv of Powered Flight. Multicoloured.

255	50c. Type **63**	20	10
[illegible]	[illegible] on Zanzibar Island, 1930's	25	10
257	2s. Concorde	1·00	75
258	5s. Wright brothers' Flyer I, 1903	1·25	1·25
MS259	133×97 mm. Nos. 255/8	2·75	3·50

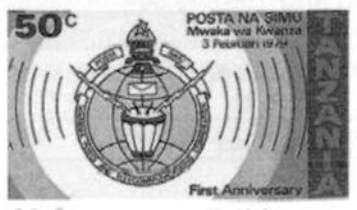

64 Corporation Emblem

1979. First Anniv of Tanzania Posts and Telecommunications Corporation. Multicoloured.

260	50c. Type **64**	10	10
261	5s. Headquarters buildings	50	70
MS262	82×97 mm. Nos. 260/1	1·00	1·50

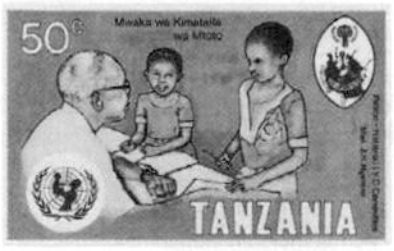

65 Pres. Nyerere (patron of National I.Y.C. Committee) with Children

1979. Int Year of the Child. Multicoloured.

263	50c. Type **65**	10	10
264	1s. Day care centre	15	10
265	2s. "Immunisation" (child being vaccinated)	25	45
266	5s. National I.Y.C. Committee emblem	40	1·00
MS267	127×91 mm. Nos. 263/6	1·25	1·50

1979. Nos. 159 and 166 surch.

268	10c. + 30c. multicoloured	2·25	2·25
269	50c. on 70c. green, orange and black	3·25	2·25

No. 268 was used as a 40c. value.

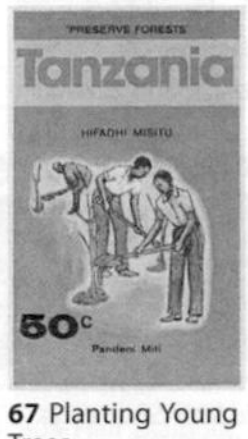

67 Planting Young Trees

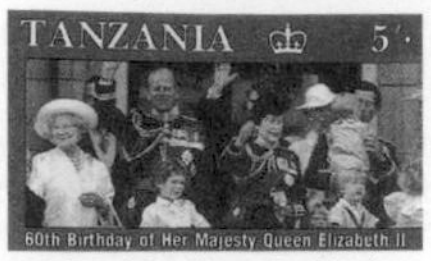

120 Royal Family on Buckingham Palace Balcony after Trooping the Colour

1987. 60th Birthday (1986) of Queen Elizabeth II. Multicoloured.

517	5s. Type **120**	15	20
518	10s. Queen and Prince Philip at Royal Ascot	20	25
519	40s. Queen Elizabeth II	50	1·50
520	60s. Queen Elizabeth with crowd	60	2·00
MS521	125×90 mm. Nos. 517/20	1·25	3·50

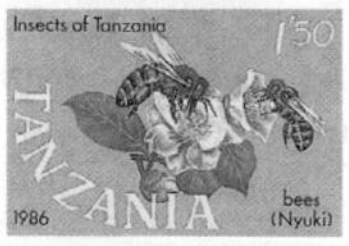

121 "Apis mellifera" (bee)

1987. Insects. Multicoloured.

522	1s.50 Type **121**	60	15
523	2s. "Prostephanus truncatus" (grain borer)	80	25
524	10s. "Glossina palpalis" (tsetse fly)	1·75	2·00
525	20s. "Polistes sp." (wasp)	2·50	4·25
MS526	110×101 mm. 30s. "Anopheles" sp (mosquito)	4·50	7·00

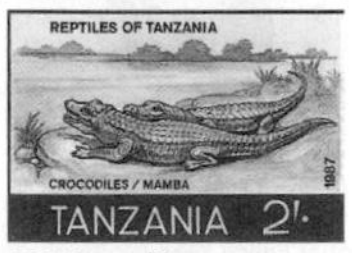

122 Crocodile

1987. Reptiles. Multicoloured.

527	2s. Type **122**	1·00	25
528	3s. Black-striped grass-snake	1·00	30
529	10s. Adder	2·25	2·00
530	20s. Green mamba	3·00	4·00
MS531	101×101 mm. 30s. Tortoise	1·50	1·25

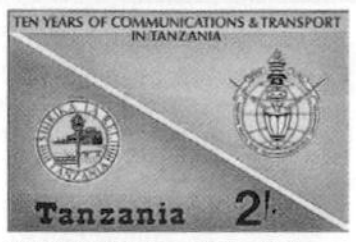

123 Emblems of Posts/ Telecommunications and Railways

1987. Tenth Anniv of Tanzania Communications and Transport Corporations. Multicoloured.

532	2s. Type **123**	50	30
533	8s. Emblems of Air Tanzania and Harbours Authority	1·25	1·25
MS534	100×66 mm. 20s. Methods of transport and communication	3·75	1·75

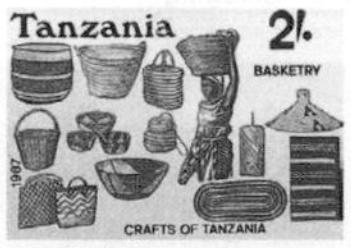

124 Basketry

1987. Traditional Handicrafts. Multicoloured.

535	2s. Type **124**	20	10
536	3s. Decorated gourds	20	15
537	10s. Stools	50	60
538	20s. Makonde carvings	75	85
MS539	89×89 mm. 40s. Makonde carver at work	1·00	1·25

1987. Tenth Anniv of Tanzania–Zambia Railway (1986). Nos. 445/9 optd **10th Anniversary of TANZANIA ZAMBIA RAILWAY AUTHORITY 1976-1986.**

540	**103**	1s.50 multicoloured	1·10	45
541	-	2s. multicoloured	1·10	45
542	-	5s. multicoloured	1·75	1·50
543	-	10s. multicoloured	2·50	2·50
544	-	30s. black, brown and red	4·00	7·50

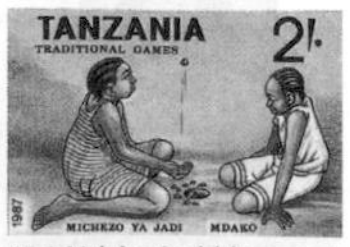

126 Mdako (pebble game)

1988. Traditional Pastimes. Multicoloured.

545	2s. Type **126**	15	10
546	3s. Wrestling	15	10
547	8s. Bull fighting, Zanzibar	35	30
548	20s. Bao (board game)	70	1·10
MS549	100×90 mm. 30s. Archery	1·25	1·40

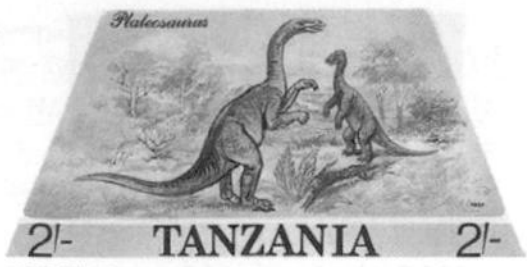

127 Plateosaurus

1988. Prehistoric and Modern Animals. Multicoloured.

550	2s. Type **127**	50	65
551	3s. Pteranodon	50	65
552	5s. Apatosaurus ("Brontosaurus")	60	65
553	7s. Lion	60	75
554	8s. Tiger	75	80
555	12s. Orang-utan	75	1·50
556	20s. Elephant	1·10	2·00
557	100s. Stegosaurus	1·75	3·00

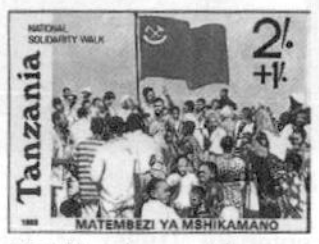

128 Marchers with Party Flag

1988. National Solidarity Walk. Multicoloured.

558	2s.+1s. +1s. Type **128**	25	25
559	3s.+1s. +1s. Pres. Mwinyi leading Walk	25	25
MS560	121×121 mm. 50s.+1s. Pres. Ali Hassan Mwinyi (35×25 mm)	75	85

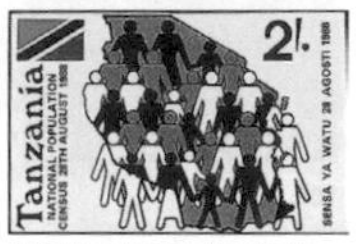

129 Population Symbols on Map

1988. Third National Population Census. Multicoloured.

561	2s. Type **129**	10	10
562	3s. Census official at work	10	10
563	10s. Community health care	15	15
564	20s. Population growth 1967–88	30	30
MS565	96×91 mm. 40s. Development of modern Tanzania	1·25	1·00

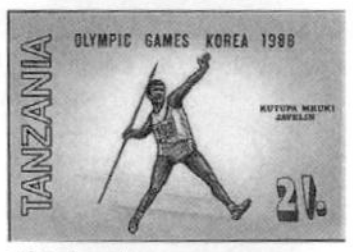

130 Javelin

1988. Olympic Games, Seoul (1st issue). Multicoloured.

566	2s. Type **130**	90	15
567	3s. Hurdling	90	15
568	7s. Long distance running	1·50	40
569	12s. Relay racing	1·75	70
MS570	100×70 mm. 40s. Badminton	4·00	1·50

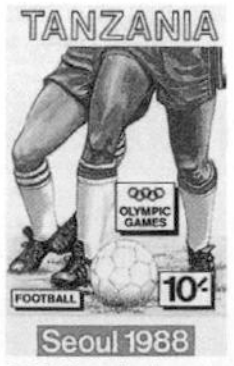

131 Football

1988. Olympic Games, Seoul (2nd issue). Multicoloured.

571	10s. Type **131**	30	10
572	20s. Cycling	1·50	25
573	50s. Fencing	70	50
574	70s. Volleyball	80	65
MS575	77×92 mm. 100s. Gymnastics	1·50	2·00

1988. Winter Olympic Games, Calgary. As T **131**. Multicoloured.

576	5s. Cross-country skiing	60	20
577	25s. Figure skating	1·25	30
578	50s. Downhill skiing	2·00	80
579	75s. Bobsleighing	2·25	2·50
MS580	77×92 mm. 100s. Ice hockey sticks wrapped in Olympic and Canadian colours	2·75	1·25

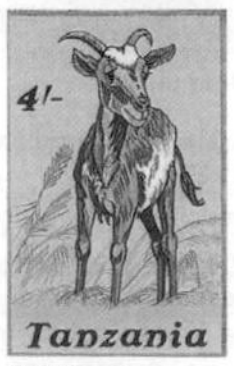

132 Goat

1988. Domestic Animals. Multicoloured.

581	4s. Type **132**	30	30
582	5s. Rabbit (horiz)	30	30
583	8s. Cows (horiz)	40	40
584	10s. Kitten (horiz)	1·00	70
585	12s. Pony	2·00	1·00
586	20s. Puppy	2·50	1·75
MS587	102×73 mm. 100s. Chicken (horiz)	2·50	1·75

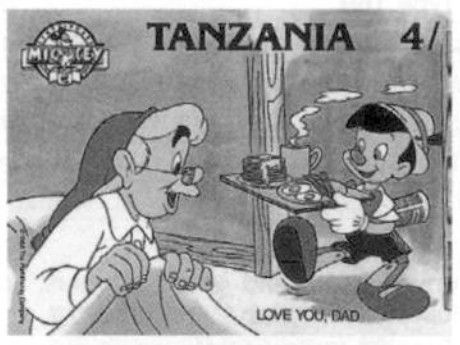

133 "Love You, Dad" (Pinocchio)

1988. Greetings Stamps. Walt Disney cartoon characters. Multicoloured.

588	4s. Type **133**	25	20
589	5s. "Happy Birthday" (Brer Rabbit and Chip n' Dale)	25	20
590	10s. "Trick or Treat" (Daisy and Donald Duck)	40	20
591	12s. "Be Kind to Animals" (Ferdie and Mordie with Pluto)	45	20
592	15s. "Love" (Daisy and Donald Duck)	55	35
593	20s. "Let's Celebrate" (Mickey Mouse and Goofy)	70	50
594	30s. "Keep in Touch" (Daisy and Donald Duck)	1·10	1·00
595	50s. "Love you, Mom" (Minnie Mouse with Ferdie and Mordie)	2·00	2·00
MS596	Two sheets, each 127×101 mm. (a) 150s. "Let's work together" (Goofy dressed as a fireman). (b) 150s. "Have a super Sunday" (Goofy dressed as American footballer) Set of 2 sheets	4·75	4·50

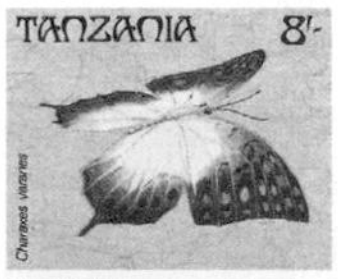

134 "Charaxes varanes"

1988. Butterflies. Multicoloured.

597	8s. Type **134**	60	10
598	30s. "Neptis melicerta"	1·10	30
599	40s. "Mylothris chloris"	1·25	40
600	50s. "Charaxes bohemani"	1·40	50
601	60s. "Myrina silenus"	1·50	1·00
602	75s. "Papilio phorcas"	2·00	1·50
603	90s. "Cyrestis camillus"	2·50	1·75
604	100s. "Salamis temora"	2·50	1·75
MS605	Two sheets, each 80×50 mm. (a) 200s. "Asterope rosa". (b) 250s. "Kallima rumia" Set of 2 sheets	8·00	6·00

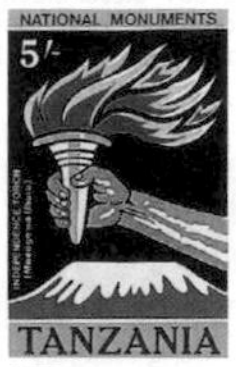

135 Independence Torch and Mt. Kilimanjaro

1988. National Monuments. Multicoloured.

606	5s. Type **135**	10	10
607	12s. Arusha Declaration Monument	20	15
608	30s. Askari Monument	35	40
609	60s. Independence Monument	55	80
MS610	100×89 mm. 100s. Askari Monument statue	1·25	1·40

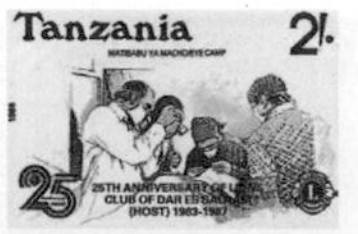

136 Eye Clinic

1988. 25th Anniv of Dar-es-Salaam Lions Club. Multicoloured.

611	2s. Type **136**	20	20
612	3s. Family at shallow water well	20	20
613	7s. Rhinoceros and outline map of Tanzania	3·75	30
614	12s. Club presenting school desks	30	45
MS615	100×65 mm. 40s. Lions International logo	1·00	1·00

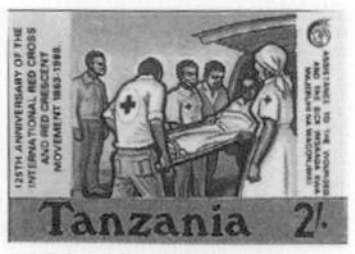

137 Loading Patient into Ambulance

1988. 125th Anniv of International Red Cross and Red Crescent. Multicoloured.

616	2s. Type **137**	50	20
617	3s. Mother and baby health clinic	50	20
618	7s. Red Cross flag	1·00	30
619	12s. Henri Dunant (founder)	1·00	45
MS620	90×90 mm. 40s. Members of Red Cross International Committee, 1863	1·00	1·00

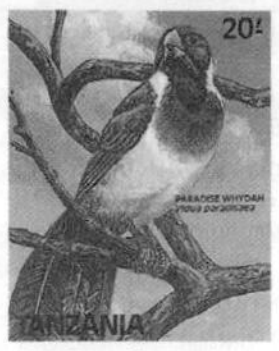

138 Paradise Whydah

1989. Birds. Multicoloured.

621	20s. Type **138**	1·00	85
622	20s. Black-collared barbet	1·00	85
623	20s. Bateleur	1·00	85
624	20s. Lilac-breasted roller and African open-bill storks in flight	1·00	85
625	20s. Red-tufted malachite sunbird and African open-bill stork in flight	1·00	85
626	20s. Dark chanting goshawk	1·00	85
627	20s. White-fronted bee eater, carmine bee eater and little bee eaters	1·00	85
628	20s. Narina's trogon and marabou stork in flight	1·00	85
629	20s. Grey parrot	1·00	85
630	20s. Hoopoe	1·00	85
631	20s. Masked lovebird ("Yellow-collared lovebird")	1·00	85
632	20s. Yellow-billed hornbill	1·00	85
633	20s. Hammerkop	1·00	85
634	20s. Violet-crested turaco and flamingos in flight	1·00	85
635	20s. Malachite kingfisher	1·00	85
636	20s. Greater flamingos	1·00	85
637	20s. Yellow-billed storks	1·00	85
638	20s. Whale-headed stork ("Shoebill stork")	1·00	85
639	20s. Saddle-bill stork and blacksmith plover	1·00	85
640	20s. South African crowned crane	1·00	85
MS641	Two sheets, each 105×75 mm. (a) 350s. Helmeted guineafowl (28×42 mm). (b) 350s. Ostrich (28×42 mm) Set of 2 sheets	13·00	7·00

Nos. 622/40 were printed together, *se-tenant*, forming a composite design of birds at a waterhole.

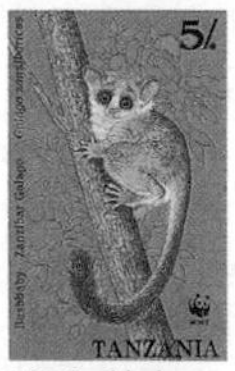

139 Bushbaby

1989. Fauna and Flora. Multicoloured.

642	5s. Type **139**	15	25
643	10s. Bushbaby holding insect (horiz)	20	25
644	20s. Bushbaby on forked branch	30	30
645	30s. Black cobra on umbrella acacia	60	60
646	45s. Bushbaby at night (horiz)	60	60
647	70s. Red-billed tropic bird and tree ferns	5·00	4·00
648	100s. African tree frog on cocoa tree	5·00	4·25
649	150s. Black-necked heron and Egyptian papyrus	8·00	8·50
MS650	Two sheets. (a) 115×85 mm. 350s. African palm civet (horiz). (b) 65×65 mm. 350s. Pink-backed pelican and baobab Tree (horiz) Set of 2 sheets	13·00	7·00

Nos. 646, 648/9 and **MS**650 are without the World Wildlife Fund logo.

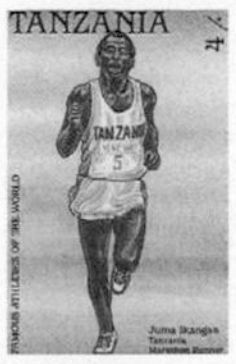

140 Juma Ikangaa (marathon runner)

1989. International Sporting Personalities. Multicoloured.

651	4s. Type **140**	15	15
652	8s.50 Steffi Graf (tennis player)	1·00	30
653	12s. Yannick Noah (tennis player)	80	40
654	40s. Pele (footballer)	90	65
655	100s. Erhard Keller (speed skater)	1·00	80
656	125s. Sadanoyama (sumo wrestler)	1·25	1·00
657	200s. Taino (sumo wrestler)	1·75	1·75
658	250s. T. Nakajima (golfer)	5·50	2·75
MS659	Two sheets. (a) 100×71 mm. 350s. Joe Louis (boxer). (b) 100×76 mm. 350s. I. Aoki (golfer) Set of 2 sheets	14·00	10·00

The captions on Nos. 658 and **MS**659b are transposed.

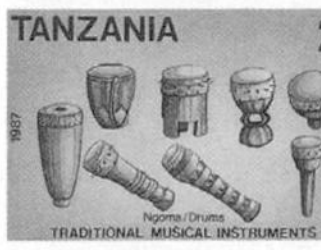

141 Drums

1989. Musical Instruments. Multicoloured.

660	2s. Type **141**	1·00	25
661	3s. Xylophones	1·00	25
662	10s. Thumbpiano	1·50	1·25
663	20s. Fiddles	1·50	3·75
MS664	91×80 mm. 40s. Violins with calebash resonators	1·00	1·00

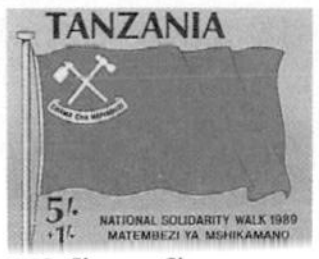

142 Chama Cha Mapinduzi Party Flag

1989. National Solidarity Walk. Multicoloured.

665	5s. +1s. Type **142**	25	25
666	10s. +1s. Marchers with party flag and President Mwinyi	25	25
MS667	122×122 mm. 50s.+1s. President Mwinyi (vert)	60	60

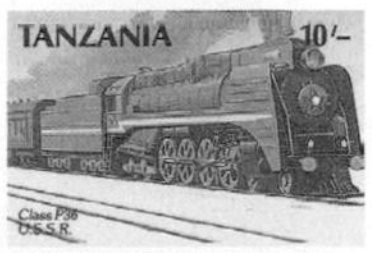

143 Class P36 Locomotive, Russia, 1953

1989. Steam Locomotives. Multicoloured.

668	10s. Type **143**	85	35
669	25s. Class 12 streamlined locomotive, Belgium, 1939	95	45
670	60s. Class C62 locomotive, Japan, 1948	1·50	1·00
671	75s. Pennsylvania Railroad Class T1 streamlined locomotive, U.S.A., 1942	1·60	1·25
672	80s. Class WP locomotive, India, 1946	1·75	1·25
673	90s. East African Railways Class 59 Garratt locomotive No. 5919	1·75	1·50
674	150s. Class "People" locomotive No. 1206, China	2·25	2·75
675	200s. Southern Pacific "Daylight" express, U.S.A	2·25	2·75
MS676	Two sheets, each 114×85 mm. (a) 350s. Stephenson's "Planet", Great Britain, 1830 (vert). (b) 350s. L.M.S. "Coronation Scot", Great Britain, 1937 (vert) Set of 2 sheets	7·00	8·50

1989. "World Stamp Expo '89" International Stamp Exhibition, Washington. Landmarks of Washington. sheet 78×62 mm, containing design as T **201b** of St. Vincent, but vert.

MS677	500s. Union Station	4·00	5·50

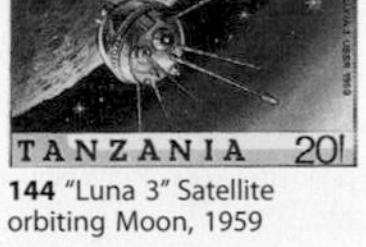

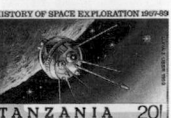

144 "Luna 3" Satellite orbiting Moon, 1959

1989. History of Space Exploration and 20th Anniv of First Manned Landing on Moon. Multicoloured.

678	20s. Type **144**	80	40
679	30s. "Gemini 6" and "7", 1965	90	45
680	40s. Astronaut Edward White in space, 1965	1·00	55
681	60s. Astronaut Aldrin on Moon, 1969	1·60	1·00
682	70s. Aldrin performing experiment, 1969	1·60	1·00
683	100s. "Apollo 15" astronaut and lunar rover, 1971	2·00	1·40
684	150s. "Apollo 18" and "Soyuz 19" docking in space, 1975	2·75	2·75
685	200s. Spacelab, 1983	2·75	2·75
MS686	Two sheets, each 110×90 mm. (a) 250s. Lunar module "Eagle" and "Apollo 11" emblem. (b) 250s. Projected U.S. space station Set of 2 sheets	7·50	8·00

1989. Olympic Medal Winners, Calgary and Seoul. Various stamps optd

(a) Nos. 571/4

687	10s. Type **131** (optd **Gold-USSR Silver-Brazil Bronze-W. Germany**)	90	40
688	20s. Cycling (optd **Men's Match Sprint, Lutz Hesslich, DDR**)	3·50	1·00
689	50s. Fencing (optd **Epee, Schmitt, W. Germany**)	2·25	1·60
690	70s. Volleyball (optd **Men's Team, USA**)	3·00	2·75
MS691	77×92 mm. 100s. Gymnastics (optd **Women's Team, Gold — USSR**)	3·75	4·25

(b) Nos. 576/9.

692	5s. Cross-country skiing (optd **Biathlon, Peter-Roetsch, DDR**)	75	40
693	25s. Figure skating (optd **Pairs, Gordeeva & Grinkov, USSR**)	1·75	75
694	50s. Downhill skiing (optd **Zurbriggen, Switzerland**)	2·50	1·75
695	75s. Bobsleighing (optd **Gold-USSR Silver-DDR Bronze-DDR**)	3·00	2·50
MS696	77×92 mm. 100s. Ice hockey sticks wrapped in Olympic and Canadian colours (optd **Ice Hockey: Gold — USSR**)	9·00	9·00

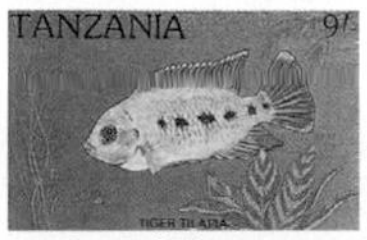

146 Spotted Tilapia

1989. Reef and Freshwater Fish of Tanzania. Multicoloured.

697	9s. Type **146**	75	40
698	13s. Painted triggerfish	75	40
699	20s. Powder-blue surgeonfish	1·00	50
700	40s. Red-tailed butterflyfish	1·60	75
701	70s. Red-tailed notho	2·00	1·25
702	100s. Ansorge's neolebias	2·50	1·75
703	150s. Blue panchax	2·75	3·00
704	200s. Regal angelfish	2·75	3·00
MS705	Two sheets, each 112×83 mm. (a) 350s. Jewel cichlid (50×38 mm). (b) 350s. Dusky batfish (38×50 mm) Set of 2 sheets	12·00	12·00

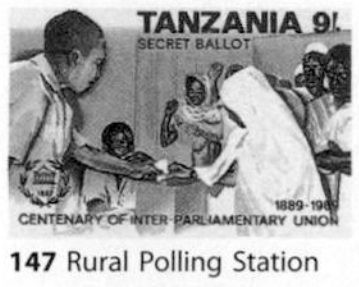

147 Rural Polling Station

1989. Centenary of Inter-Parliamentary Union.

706	**147**	9s. multicoloured	10	10
707	-	13s. multicoloured	10	10
708	-	80s. multicoloured	40	65
709	-	100s. black, ultram & bl	50	85
MS710		90×90 mm. 40s. multicoloured	70	1·25

DESIGNS: 13s. Parliament Building, Dar-es-Salaam; 40s. Sir William Randal Cremer and Frederic Passy (founders); 80s. Tanzania Parliament in session; 100s. Logo.

148 Logo

1990. Tenth Anniv of Pan-African Postal Union.

711	**148**	9s. yellow, green and black	30	20
712	-	13s. multicoloured	50	20
713	-	70s. multicoloured	2·00	1·40
714	-	100s. multicoloured	3·25	2·75
MS715		90×90 mm. 40s. multicoloured	1·75	2·75

DESIGNS: 13s. Collecting mail from post office box; 40s. Logos of Tanzania Posts and Telecommunications Corporation, P.A.P.U. and U.P.U.; 70s. Taking mail to post office; 100s. Mail transport.

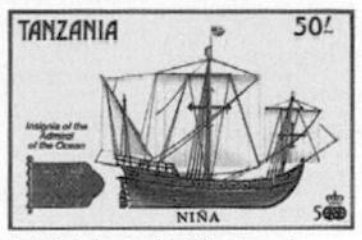

149 Admiral's Flag and "Nina"

1990. 500th Anniv (1992) of Discovery of America by Columbus (50, 60, 75, 200s.) and Modern Scientific Discoveries (others). Multicoloured.

716	9s. Bell XS-1 aircraft (first supersonic flight, 1947)	75	50
717	13s. "Trieste" (bathyscaphe) (first dive to depth of 35,000 ft, 1960)	75	50
718	50s. Type **149**	1·50	90
719	60s. Fleet flag and "Pinta"	1·50	1·10
720	75s. Standard of Castile and Leon and "Santa Maria"	1·50	1·25
721	150s. Transistor technology	1·25	2·00
722	200s. Arms of Columbus and map of First Voyage	2·75	3·00
723	250s. DNA molecule	2·75	3·00
MS724	Two sheets, each 106×78 mm. (a) 350s. Caravels in the Caribbean. (b) 350s. "Voyager II" and Neptune Set of 2 sheets	7·00	8·50

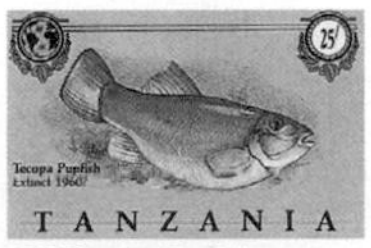

150 Tecopa Pupfish

1990. Extinct Species. Multicoloured.

725	25s. Type **150**	1·25	60
726	40s. Thylacine	1·75	1·00
727	50s. Quagga	2·00	1·10
728	60s. Passenger pigeon	3·00	1·75
729	75s. Rodriguez saddleback tortoise	2·25	1·75
730	100s. Toolache wallaby	2·50	2·00
731	150s. Texas red wolf	2·50	2·50
732	200s. Utah lake sculpin	2·50	2·50
MS733	Two sheets. (a) 102×74 mm. 350s. South Island Whekau. (b) 71×99 mm. 350s. Hawaii O-o (vert) Set of 2 sheets	15·00	12·00

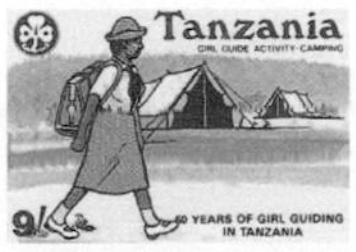

151 Camping

1990. 60th Anniv of Girl Guides Movement in Tanzania. Multicoloured.

734	9s. Type **151**	15	20
735	13s. Guides planting sapling	15	20
736	50s. Guide teaching woman to write	40	65
737	100s. Guide helping at child-care clinic	65	1·10
MS738	89×89 mm. 40s. Guide teaching child to read (vert)	1·00	1·25

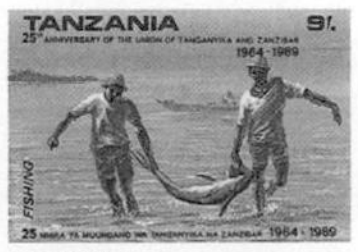

152 Fishing

1990. 25th Anniv of Union of Tanganyika and Zanzibar. Multicoloured.

739	9s. Type **152**	55	30
740	13s. Vineyard	55	30
741	50s. Cloves	1·75	1·50
742	100s. Presidents Nyerere and Karume exchanging Union instruments (vert)	2·75	4·50
MS743	90×90 mm. 40s. Arms (vert)	2·25	3·25

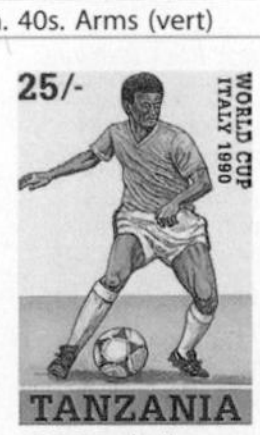

153 Footballer

1990. World Cup Football Championship, Italy (1st issue). Multicoloured.

744	25s. Type **153**	1·50	30
745	60s. Player passing ball	2·00	90
746	75s. Player turning	2·25	1·25
747	200s. Player kicking ball	4·50	5·50
MS748	Two sheets, each 105×76 mm. (a) 350s. Two players fighting for possession. (b) 350s. Player kicking ball Set of 2 sheets	12·00	10·00

See also Nos. 789/92 and 794/7.

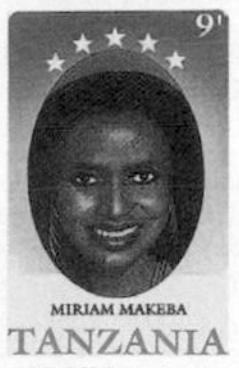

154 Miriam Makeba

1990. Famous Black Entertainers. Multicoloured.

749	9s. Type **154**	15	10
750	13s. Manu Dibango	15	10
751	25s. Fela	20	15
752	70s. Smokey Robinson	1·00	40
753	100s. Gladys Knight	1·10	55
754	150s. Eddie Murphy	2·25	2·25
755	200s. Sammy Davis Jnr.	2·50	2·75
756	250s. Stevie Wonder	2·50	3·00
MS757	Two sheets, each 69×88 mm. (a) 350s. Bill Cosby (30×39 mm). (b) 350s. Michael Jackson (30×39 mm) Set of 2 sheets	4·25	5·00

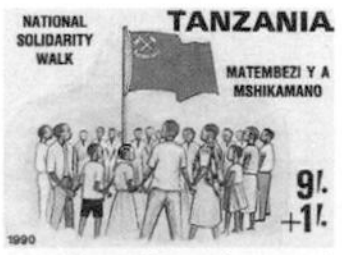

155 Ring of People round Party Flag

1990. Solidarity Walk, 1990. Multicoloured.

758	9s.+1s. +1s. Type **155**	1·00	1·25
759	13s.+1s. +1s. President Mwinyi	1·00	1·25
MS760	90×90 mm. 50s.+1s. Handclasp on map (vert)	1·75	2·25

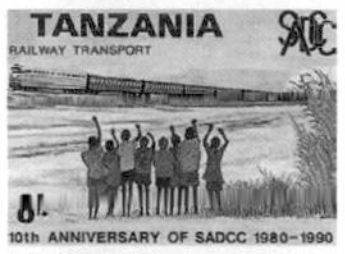

156 Diesel Train

1990. Tenth Anniv of Southern African Development Co-ordination Conference. Multicoloured.

761	8s. Type **156**	1·75	50
762	11s.50 Paper-making plant	30	20
763	25s. Tractor factory and ploughing	35	20
764	100s. Map and national flags	6·00	5·00
MS765	89×89 mm. 50s. Map of Southern Africa	3·25	3·75

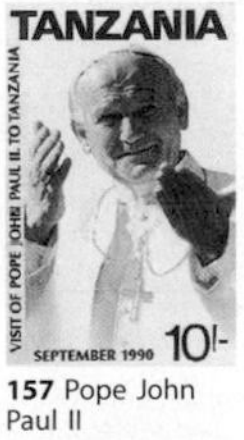

157 Pope John Paul II

1990. Papal Visit to Tanzania. Multicoloured.

766	10s. Type **157**	20	15
767	15s. Pope in ceremonial robes	25	15
768	20s. Pope giving blessing	30	15
769	100s. Papal coat of arms	80	1·10
MS770	172×143 mm. 50s. Pope John Paul II (horiz); 50s. St. Joseph's Cathedral, Dar-es-Salaam (horiz); 50s. Christ the King Cathedral, Moshi (horiz); 50s. Saint Theresa's Cathedral, Tabora (horiz); 50s. Cathedral of the Epiphany, Bugando Mwanza (horiz); 50s. St. Mathias Mulumba Kalemba Cathedral, Songea (horiz)	4·25	4·50

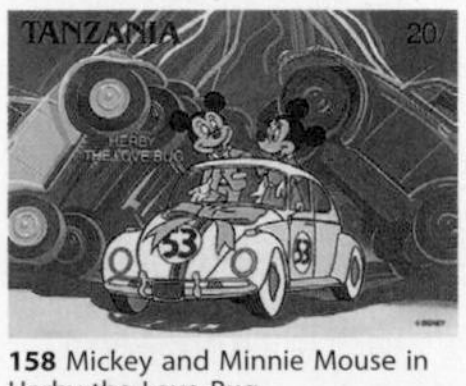

158 Mickey and Minnie Mouse in Herby the Love Bug

1990. Motor Cars from Disney Films. Multicoloured.

771	20s. Type **158**	30	30
772	30s. The Absent-minded Professor's car	35	35
773	45s. Chitty-Chitty Bang-Bang	45	45

774	60s. Mr. Toad's car	65	65
775	75s. Scrooge's limousine	75	75
776	100s. The Shaggy Dog's car	1·00	1·00
777	150s. Donald Duck's nephews cleaning car	1·60	1·60
778	200s. Fire engine from "Dumbo"	1·75	1·75
MS779	Two sheets, each 127×112 mm. (a) 350s. The Mickeymobile. (b) 350s. Cruella De Vil and dog wagon from "101 Dalmations" Set of 2 sheets	8·50	8·50

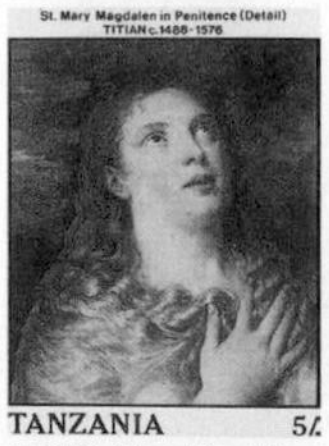

159 "St. Mary Magdalen in Penitence" (detail)

1990. Paintings by Titian. Multicoloured.

780	5s. Type **159**	10	10
781	10s. "Averoldi Polyptych" (detail)	10	10
782	15s. "Saint Margaret" (detail)	15	15
783	50s. "Venus and Adonis" (detail)	40	40
784	75s. "Venus and the Lutenist" (detail)	55	55
785	100s. "Tarquin and Lucretia" (detail)	70	70
786	125s. "Saint Jerome" (detail)	90	90
787	150s. "Madonna and Child in Glory with Saints" (detail)	1·00	1·00
MS788	Three sheets. (a) 95×110 mm. 300s. "Adoration of the Holy Trinity" (detail). (b) 95×110 mm. 300s. "St. Catherine of Alexandria at Prayer" (detail). (c) 110×95 mm. 300s. "The Supper at Emmaus" (detail) Set of 3 sheets	9·00	10·00

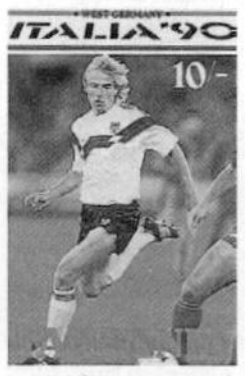

160 Klinsmann of West Germany

1990. World Cup Football Championship, Italy (2nd issue). Multicoloured.

789	10s. Type **160**	50	30
790	60s. Serena of Italy	90	60
791	100s. Nicol of Scotland	1·75	1·75
792	300s. Susic of Yugoslavia	3·25	4·00
MS793	Two sheets, each 85×95 mm. (a) 400s. Montero of Costa Rica. (b) 400s. Seifo of Belgium Set of 2 sheets	11·00	11·00

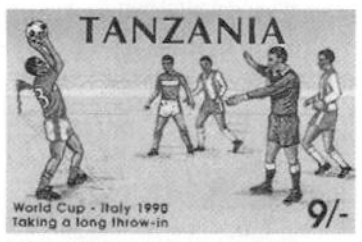

161 Throw-in

1990. World Cup Football Championship, Italy (3rd issue). Multicoloured.

794	9s. Type **161**	60	20
795	13s. Penalty kick	60	20
796	25s. Dribbling	85	25
797	100s. Corner kick	3·50	4·00
MS798	82×82 mm. 50s. World Cup and world map	3·50	3·75

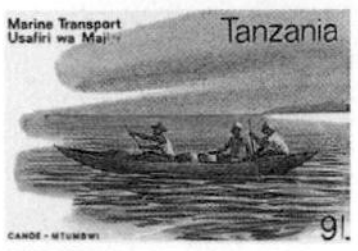

162 Canoe

1990. Marine Transport. Multicoloured.

799	9s. Type **162**	20	20
800	13s. Sailing canoe	25	20
801	25s. Dhow	90	25
802	100s. Freighter	3·75	4·25
MS803	90×90 mm. 40s. Mashua dhow	3·25	3·75

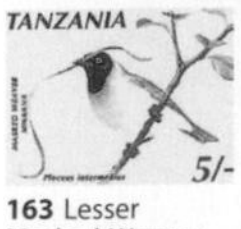

163 Lesser Masked Weaver

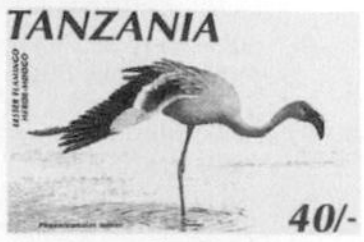

164 Lesser Flamingo

1990. Birds. Designs as T **163** (5s. to 30s.) or T **164** (40s. to 500s.). Multicoloured.

804	5s. Type **163**	20	60
805	9s. African emerald cuckoo	30	10
806	13s. Little bee eater	60	10
807	15s. Red bishop	40	10
808	20s. Bateleur	50	10
809	25s. Scarlet-chested sunbird	50	10
809a	30s. African wood pigeon	50	15
810	40s. Type **164**	50	15
811	70s. Helmeted guineafowl	60	30
812	100s. Eastern white pelican	75	30
813	170s. Saddle-bill stork	1·00	85
814	200s. South African crowned crane	1·00	90
814a	300s. Pied crow	1·00	1·50
814b	400s. White-headed vulture	1·00	1·75
815	500s. Ostrich	1·10	1·75
MS816	100×102 mm. 40s. Superb starling; 60s. Lilac-breasted roller	5·50	6·50

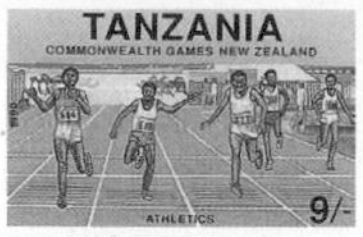

165 Athletics

1990. 14th Commonwealth Games, Auckland, New Zealand. Multicoloured.

817	9s. Type **165**	55	20
818	13s. Netball (vert)	80	20
819	25s. Pole vaulting	1·25	25
820	100s. Long jumping (vert)	2·50	3·50
MS821	100×100 mm. 40s. Boxing (vert)	1·75	2·50

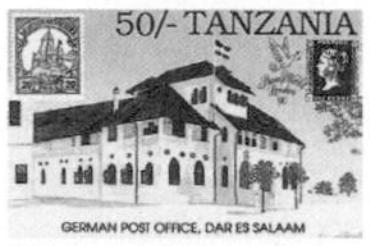

166 Former German Post Office, Dar-es-Salaam

1991. 150th Anniv of the Penny Black and "Stamp World London 90" International Stamp Exhibition. Multicoloured.

822	50s. Type **166**	90	90
823	50s. "Reichstag" (German mail steamer), 1890	90	90
824	75s. Dhows, Zanzibar	1·25	1·25
825	75s. Cobham's Short S.5 Singapore I flying boat, Mwanza, Lake Victoria, 1928	1·25	1·25
826	100s. Air Tanzania Fokker F.27 Friendship over Livingstone's house, Zanzibar	1·75	1·75
827	100s. Mail train at Moshi station	1·75	1·75
828	100s. English mail coach, 1840	1·75	1·75
829	150s. Stephenson's "Rocket" and mail coach, 1838	2·50	2·50
830	200s. Imperial Airways Handley Page H.P.42 at Croydon	2·50	2·50
MS831	Two sheets, each 85×65 mm. (a) 350s. Sir Rowland Hill and Penny Black. (b) 350s. Thurn and Taxis letter of 1860 Set of 2 sheets	10·00	12·00

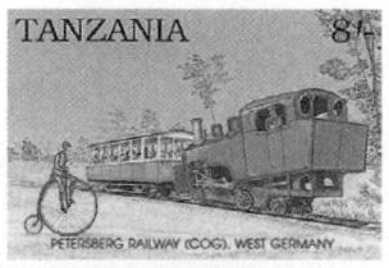

167 Petersberg Railway, Konigswinter, Germany

1991. Cog Railways. Multicoloured.

832	8s. Type **167**	50	30
833	25s. "Waumbek" (locomotive), Mt. Washington Railway, U.S.A	70	60
834	50s. Sarajevo–Dubrovnik line, Yugoslavia	85	75
835	100s. Budapest Rack Railway, Hungary	1·25	1·00
836	150s. Steam locomotive No. 97218, Vordenberg–Eisenerz line, Austria	1·75	1·75
837	200s. Last train on Rimutaka Incline, New Zealand, 1955	1·90	1·90
838	250s. "John Stevens" rack and pinion drive locomotive, U.S.A., 1825	1·90	2·00
839	300s. Mt. Pilatus Rack Railway steam railcar, Switzerland	2·00	2·00
MS840	Two sheets, each 117×87 mm. (a) 400s. Sylvester Marsh and Presidential excursion train, Mt. Washington Cog Railway, U.S.A., 1869 (51×38 mm). (b) 400s. Steam locomotive, Schneeberg Railway, Austria (51×38 mm) Set of 2 sheets	9·50	10·00

1991. International Literacy Year (1st issue). As T **226a** of St. Vincent, showing Walt Disney cartoon characters illustrating the Alphabet. Multicoloured.

841-67	1,2,3,5,10,15,18,20,25,30,35,40,45,50,55,60,75,80,90,100,120,125,140,150,160,175,200s. Set of 27	14·00	16·00
MS868	Two sheets, each 128×112 mm. (a) 600s. Tiger Lily and Lost Boys. (b) 600s. Mickey Mouse driving miniature railway locomotive (vert) Set of 2 sheets	11·00	12·00

See also Nos. 905/8.

1991. Olympic Games, Barcelona (1st issue). As T **239a** of Sierra Leone. Multicoloured.

869	5s. Archery	50	30
870	10s. Women's gymnastics	50	30
871	25s. Boxing	60	30
872	50s. Canoeing	85	55
873	100s. Volleyball	1·50	1·25
874	150s. Men's gymnastics	1·75	1·75
875	200s. 4×100 metres relay	2·25	2·25
876	300s. Judo	2·50	2·50
MS877	Two sheets, each 102×71 mm. (a) 400s. Cycling. (b) 400s. 400 metres men's hurdles Set of 2 sheets	11·00	11·00

See also Nos. 1309/12 and 1404/11.

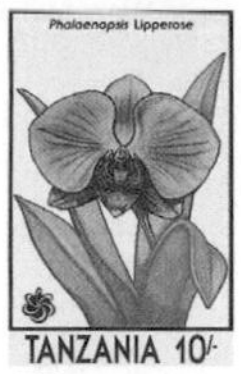

167a "Phalaenopsis Lipperose"

1991. "EXPO 90" International Garden and Greenery Exhibition, Osaka. Orchids. Multicoloured.

878	10s. Type **167a**	25	15
879	25s. "Lycoste Aquila"	35	20
880	30s. "Vuylstekeara Cambria Plush"	40	20
881	50s. "Vuylstekeara Monica Burnham"	55	35
882	90s. "Odontocidium Crowborough Plush"	1·00	1·00
883	100s. "Oncidioda Crowborough Chelsea"	1·00	1·00
884	250s. "Sophrolaeliocattleya Phena Saturn"	1·75	2·00
885	300s. "Laeliocattleya Lykas"	1·90	2·50
MS886	Two sheets, each 100×69 mm. (a) 400s. "Cymbidium Baldoyle Melbury". (b) 400s. "Cymbidium Tapestry Long Beach" Set of 2 sheets	5·50	6·50

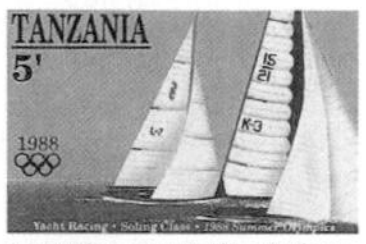

168 Olympic "Sailing" Class Yacht Racing

1991. Record-breaking Sports Events. Multicoloured.

887	5s. Type **168**	50	30
888	20s. Olympic downhill skiing	90	35
889	30s. "Tour de France" cycle race	2·50	70
890	40s. Le Mans 24-hour endurance motor race	1·75	75
891	75s. Olympic two man bob-sleighing	2·00	1·10
892	100s. Belgian Grand Prix motor cycle race	3·00	1·75
893	250s. Indianapolis 500 motor race	3·00	3·50
894	300s. Gold Cup power boat championship	3·00	3·75
MS895	Two sheets, each 85×64 mm. (a) 400s. Colorado 500 motor cycle race (vert). (b) 400s. Schneider Trophy air race (vert) Set of 2 sheets	9·50	11·00

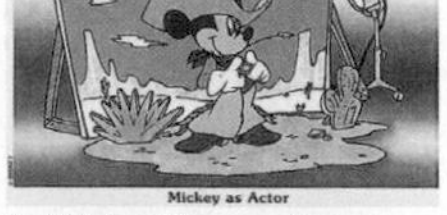

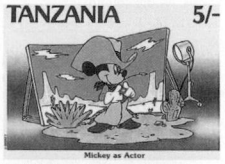

169 Mickey Mouse as Cowboy

1991. Mickey Mouse in Hollywood. Walt Disney cartoon characters as actors. Multicoloured.

896	5s. Type **169**	30	30
897	10s. Mickey as boxer	30	30
898	15s. Mickey as astronaut	30	30
899	20s. Mickey and Minnie as lovers	30	30
900	100s. Mickey as pirate rescuing Minnie	1·50	1·25
901	200s. Mickey and Donald Duck as policemen arresting Big Pete	2·75	2·50
902	350s. Mickey and Donald with Goofy in historical drama	3·00	2·75
903	450s. Mickey, Donald and Goofy as sailors	3·00	2·75
MS904	Two sheets, each 127×96 mm. (a) 600s. Mickey, Minnie and Donald in the mummy's tomb. (b) 600s. Mickey as Canadian Mountie rescuing Minnie from Big Pete Set of 2 sheets	12·00	12·00

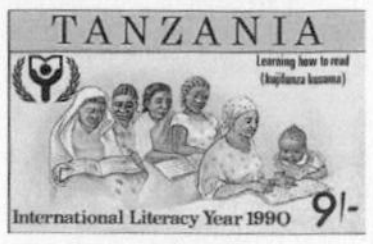

170 Women learning to Read

1991. International Literacy Year (2nd issue). Multicoloured.

905	9s. Type **170**	25	20
906	13s. Teacher with blackboard	30	20
907	25s. Literacy aids	40	25
908	100s. Reading newspaper	2·50	3·00
MS909	104×73 mm. 50s. Adult education class	2·00	2·50

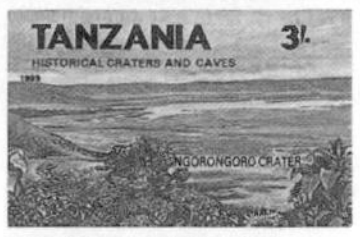

171 Ngorongoro Crater

1991. Historical Craters and Caves. Multicoloured.

910	3s. Type **171**	2·75	1·25
911	5s. Prehistoric rock painting, Kondoa Caves	3·25	1·25
912	9s. Inner crater, Mt. Kilimanjaro	3·75	1·50
913	12s. Olduvai Gorge	4·75	2·25
MS914	91×92 mm. 10s. Discarded bottles, Amboni Caves; 10s. Rock paintings, Amboni Caves; 10s. Entrance to Amboni Caves; 10s. Rock formation, Amboni Caves	20·00	11·00

1991. 350th Death Anniv of Rubens. Cartoons for Decius Mus Tapestries. As T **243** of Sierra Leone. Multicoloured.

915	85s. "Proclamation of the Vision"	1·75	2·00
916	85s. "Divining of the Entrails"	1·75	2·00
917	85s. "Dispatch of the Lictors"	1·75	2·00
918	85s. "Dedication to Death"	1·75	2·00
919	85s. "Victory and Death of Decius Mus"	1·75	2·00
920	85s. "Funeral Rites"	1·75	2·00
MS921	70×100 mm. 500s. "Trophy of War" (detail) (vert)	11·00	13·00

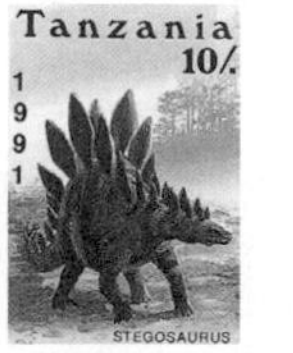

172 Stegosaurus

1991. Prehistoric Creatures. Multicoloured.

922	10s. Type **172**	25	25
923	15s. Triceratops	25	25
924	25s. Edmontosaurus	40	40
925	30s. Plateosaurus	40	40
926	35s. Diplodocus	45	45
927	100s. Iguanodon	1·40	1·50
928	200s. Silviasaurus	2·00	2·50
MS929	90×90 mm. 150s. Rhamphorhynchus	2·50	3·00

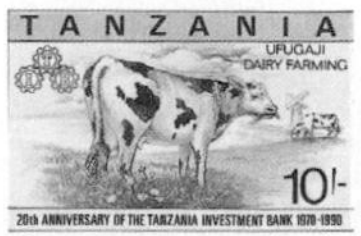

173 Dairy Farming

1991. 20th Anniv of Tanzania Investment Bank. Multicoloured.

930	10s. Type **173**	25	20
931	13s. Industrial development	30	20
932	25s. Engineering	35	20
933	100s. Tea picking	2·00	2·50
MS934	93×91 mm. Nos. 930/3	3·00	3·50

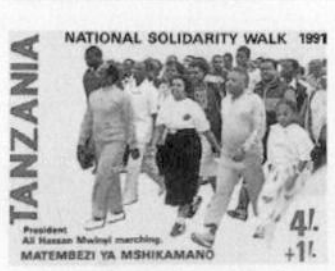

174 Pres. Mwinyi leading Walk

1991. National Solidarity Walk. Multicoloured.

935	4s.+1s. +1s. Type **174**	75	75

936	30s.+1s. +1s. Pres. Mwinyi planting sapling	1·50	1·50
MS937 91×91 mm. 50s.+1s. Pres. Mwinyi sorting cloves		2·50	3·00

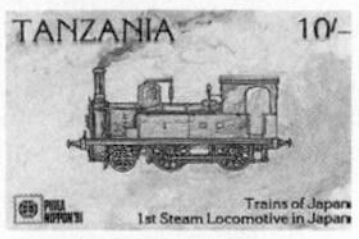

174a Class 150 Steam Locomotive, 1872 (first locomotive in Japan)

1991. "Phila Nippon '91" International Stamp Exhibition, Tokyo. Japanese Railway Loco-motives. Multicoloured.

938	10s. Type **174a**	1·25	65
939	25s. Class 4500 steam locomotive, 1902	1·60	90
940	35s. Class C 62 steam locomotive, 1948	1·75	1·00
941	50s. Mikado steam locomotive	1·90	1·25
942	75s. Class 6250 steam locomotive, 1915	2·50	1·50
943	100s. Class C 11 steam locomotive, 1932	2·75	1·75
944	200s. Class E 10 steam locomotive, 1948	3·25	3·25
945	300s. Class 8550 steam locomotive, 1899	3·75	4·00
MS946 Four sheets, each 102×71 mm. (a) 400s. Series 400 electric train. (b) 400s. Class EH10 electric locomotive, 1954. (c) 400s. Class DD51 diesel-hydraulic locomotive, 1962. (d) 400s. Class EF58 electric locomotive Set of 4 sheets		14·00	15·00

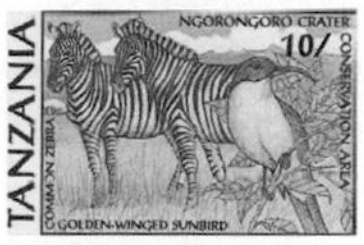

175 Zebra and Golden-winged Sunbird, Ngorongoro Crater

1991. National Game Parks. Multicoloured.

947	10s. Type **175**	1·50	70
948	25s. Greater kudu and elephant, Ruaha Park	2·00	1·00
949	30s. Sable antelope and red and yellow barbet, Mikumi [illegible]	[illegible]	[illegible]
950	50s. Leopard and wildebeest, Serengeti Park	1·50	1·25
951	90s. Giraffe and white starred robin, Ngurdoto Park	3·00	2·25
952	100s. Eland and Abbot's duiker, Kilimanjaro Park	2·00	1·75
953	250s. Lion and impala, Lake Manyara Park	3·00	3·75
954	300s. Black rhinoceros and ostrich, Tarangire Park	5·00	5·00
MS955 Two sheets, each 99×68 mm. (a) 400s. Blue-breasted kingfisher and defassa waterbuck, Selous Game Reserve. (b) 400s. Paradise whydah and oryx, Mkomazi Game Reserve Set of 2 sheets		17·00	14·00

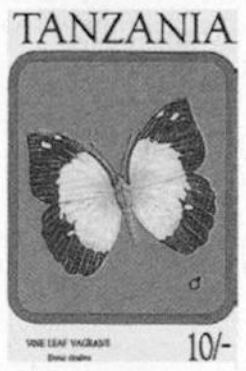

176 "Eronia cleodora"

1991. Butterflies. Multicoloured.

956	10s. Type **176**	55	45
957	15s. "Precis westermanni"	70	60
958	35s. "Antanartia delius"	1·00	90
959	75s. "Bematistes aganice"	1·75	1·60
960	100s. "Kallima jacksoni"	1·90	1·75
961	150s. "Apaturopsis cleocharis"	2·75	2·75
962	200s. "Colotis aurigineus"	3·00	3·00
963	300s. "Iolaus crawshayi"	3·25	3·50
MS964 Four sheets, each 117×76 mm. (a) 400s. "Charaxes zoolina". (b) 400s. "Papilio phorcas". (c) 400s. "Charaxes ethalion". (d) 400s. "Papilio nobilis" Set of 4 sheets		14·00	15·00

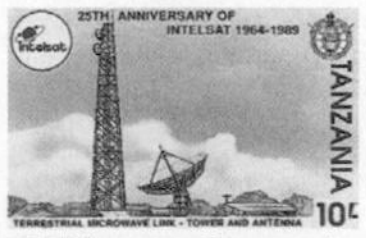

177 Microwave Tower and Dish Aerial

1991. 25th Anniv of Intelsat Satellite System. Multicoloured.

965	10s. Type **177**	50	20
966	25s. Satellite picture of Earth	65	30
967	100s. Mwenge "B" Earth station	2·25	1·50
968	500s. Mwenge "A" Earth station	7·75	10·00
MS969 90×86 mm. 50s. Satellite links on world map		3·75	3·75

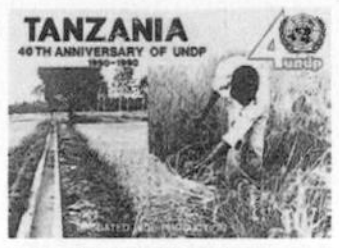

178 Rice Cultivation

1991. 40th Anniv of United Nations Development Programme. Multicoloured (except No. **MS**974).

970	10s. Type **178**	15	10
971	15s. Vocational and Civil Service training	20	10
972	100s. Terrace farming	1·50	1·60
973	500s. Renovated Arab door (vert)	5·50	8·00
MS974 90×90 mm. 40s. UNDP anniversary emblem (blue and black)		1·40	1·75

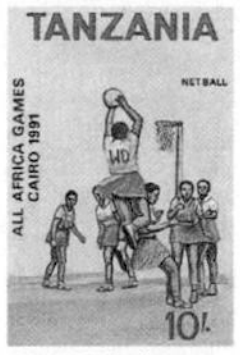

179 Netball

1991. All-Africa Games, Cairo. Multicoloured.

975	10s. Type **179**	50	30
976	15s. Football (horiz)	50	30
977	100s. Tennis	2·50	1·50
978	200s. Athletics	2·75	2·75
979	500s. Baseball (horiz)	6·00	8·50
MS980 80×60 mm. 500s. Basketball		12·00	10·00

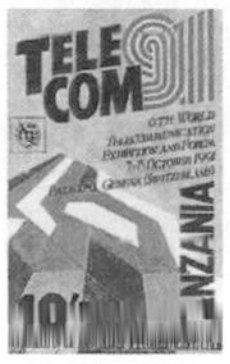

180 "TELECOM 91" Logo

1991. "TELECOM 91" International Telecom-munication Exhibition, Geneva (10, 15s.) and World Telecommunications Day (others). Multicoloured.

981	10s. Type **180**	20	10
982	15s. "TELECOM '91" logo and address on envelope (horiz)	20	10
983	35s. Symbolic telecommunication signals	40	30
984	100s. Symbolic telecommunication signals (horiz)	1·10	1·50

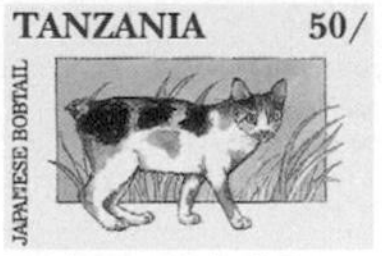

181 Japanese Bobtail Cat

1991. Cats. Multicoloured.

985	50s. Type **181**	90	80
986	50s. Cornish rex	90	80
987	50s. Malayan	90	80
988	50s. Tonkinese	90	80
989	50s. Abyssinian	90	80
990	50s. Russian blue	90	80
991	50s. Cymric	90	80
992	50s. Somali	90	80
993	50s. Siamese	90	80
994	50s. Himalayan	90	80
995	50s. Singapura	90	80
996	50s. Manx	90	80
997	50s. Oriental shorthair	90	80
998	50s. Maine coon	90	80
999	50s. Persian	90	80
1000	50s. Birman	90	80

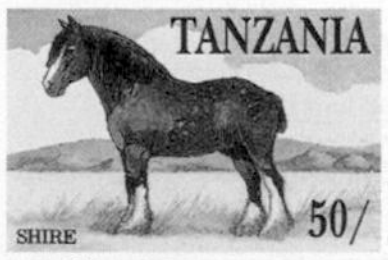

182 Shire Horse

1991. Horses and Ponies. Multicoloured.

1001	50s. Type **182**	90	80
1002	50s. Thoroughbred	90	80
1003	50s. Kladruber	90	80
1004	50s. Appaloosa	90	80
1005	50s. Hanoverian	90	80
1006	50s. Arab	90	80
1007	50s. Breton	90	80
1008	50s. Exmoor	90	80
1009	50s. Connemara	90	80
1010	50s. Lipizzaner	90	80
1011	50s. Shetland	90	80
1012	50s. Percheron	90	80
1013	50s. Pinto	90	80
1014	50s. Orlov	90	80
1015	50s. Palomino	90	80
1016	50s. Welsh cob	90	80

Nos. 1001/16 were printed together, *se-tenant*, as a sheetlet of 16 with the backgrounds of each horizontal strip of 4 forming a composite design.

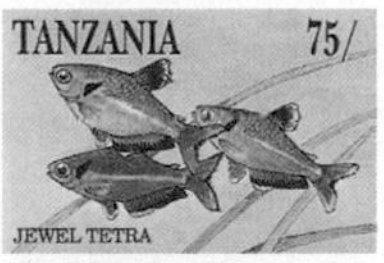

183 Yellow Tetra

1991. Aquarium Fish. Multicoloured.

1017	75s. Type **183**	75	75
1018	75s. Five-banded barb	75	75
1019	75s. Simpson platy	75	75
1020	75s. Guppy	75	75
1021	75s. Zebra danio	75	75
1022	75s. Neon tetra	75	75
1023	75s. Siamese fighting fish	75	75
1024	75s. Tiger barb	75	75
1025	75s. Two-striped lyretail	75	75
1026	75s. Fan-tailed goldfish	75	75
1027	75s. Pearl gourami	75	75
1028	75s. Freshwater angelfish	75	75
1029	75s. Clown loach	75	75
1030	75s. Red swordtail	75	75
1031	75s. Blue discus	75	75
1032	75s. Rosy barb	75	75

Nos. 1017/32 were printed together, *se-tenant*, with the backgrounds of each stamp forming a composite design.

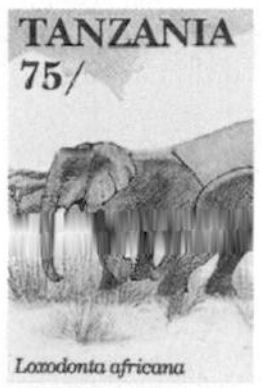

184 African Elephant

1991. African Elephants. Multicoloured.

1033	75s. Type **184**	1·25	1·10
1034	75s. Two elephants fighting	1·25	1·10
1035	75s. Elephant facing left and tree	1·25	1·10
1036	75s. Elephant facing forward and tree	1·25	1·10
1037	75s. Cow elephant and calf facing right standing in water	1·25	1·10
1038	75s. Cow watching over calf in water	1·25	1·10
1039	75s. Two adults and calf in water	1·25	1·10
1040	75s. Cow and calf facing left standing in water	1·25	1·10
1041	75s. Elephant facing right	1·25	1·10
1042	75s. Elephants feeding	1·25	1·10
1043	75s. Elephant feeding	1·25	1·10
1044	75s. Elephant and zebra	1·25	1·10
1045	75s. Cow and calf drinking	1·25	1·10
1046	75s. Calf suckling	1·25	1·10
1047	75s. Bull elephant	1·25	1·10
1048	75s. Cow with small calf	1·25	1·10

Nos. 1033/48 were printed together, *se-tenant*, as a sheetlet of 16 with each horizontal strip of 4 forming a composite design.

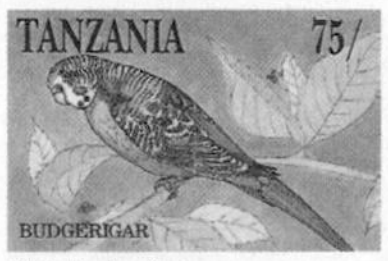

185 Budgerigar

1991. Pet Birds. Multicoloured.

1049	75s. Type **185**	90	80
1050	75s. Orange-breasted bunting ("Rainbow Bunting")	90	80
1051	75s. Golden-fronted leafbird	90	80
1052	75s. Black-headed caique	90	80
1053	75s. Java sparrow	90	80
1054	75s. Diamond firetail finch	90	80
1055	75s. Peach-faced lovebird	90	80
1056	75s. Golden conure	90	80
1057	75s. Military macaw	90	80
1058	75s. Yellow-faced parrotlet	90	80
1059	75s. Sulphur-crested cockatoo	90	80
1060	75s. White-fronted amazon ("Spectacled Amazon Parrot")	90	80
1061	75s. Paradise tanager	90	80
1062	75s. Gouldian finch	90	80
1063	75s. Masked lovebird	90	80
1064	75s. Southern grackle ("Hill Mynah")	90	80

Nos. 1049/64 were printed together, *se-tenant*, forming a composite design.

1991. Death Centenary (1990) of Vincent van Gogh (artist). As T **215a** of St. Vincent. Multicoloured.

1065	10s. "Peasant Woman Sewing"	70	30
1066	15s. "Head of Peasant Woman with Greenish Lace Cap"	75	35
1067	35s. "Flowering Orchard"	1·25	60
1068	75s. "Portrait of a Girl"	2·00	1·00
1069	100s. "Portrait of a Woman with Red Ribbon"	2·25	1·25
1070	150s. "Vase with Flowers"	3·00	3·00
1071	200s. "Houses in Antwerp"	3·25	3·50
1072	400s. "Seated Peasant Woman with White Cap"	6·00	7·50
MS1073 Two sheets, each 127×112 mm. (a) 400s. "Bulb Fields" (horiz). (b) 400s. "The Parsonage Garden at Nuenen in the Snow" (horiz). Imperf Set of 2 sheets		15·00	16·00

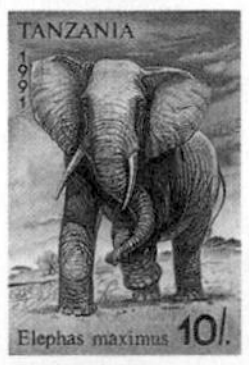

186 Indian Elephant

1991. Elephants. Multicoloured.

1074	10s. Type **186**	1·00	50
1075	15s. Indian elephant uprooting tree	1·25	65
1076	25s. Indian elephant with calf	1·60	80
1077	30s. African elephant	1·60	80
1078	35s. Head of African elephant (horiz)	1·60	85
1079	100s. African elephant and calf bathing (horiz)	3·50	2·50
[illegible]	[illegible] (horiz)	5·00	5·50
MS1081 90×90 mm. 400s. Mammoth (horiz)		4·00	4·50

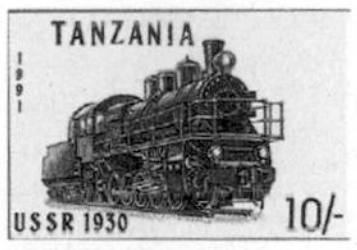

187 Class Em Steam Locomotive, Russia, 1930

1991. Locomotives of the World. Multicoloured.

1082	10s. Type **187**	20	25
1083	15s. "Hikari" express train, Japan, 1964	30	35
1084	25s. Russian steam locomotive, 1834 (vert)	35	45
1085	35s. TGV express train, France, 1979	45	55
1086	60s. Diesel railcar No. R16-01, France, 1972	70	80
1087	100s. High Speed Train 125, Great Britain, 1972	1·10	1·40
1088	300s. Russian steam locomotive, 1833 (vert)	2·50	3·00
MS1089 91×91 mm. French electric locomotive, 1952 (vert)		1·60	2·00

No. 1088 is inscribed "1837" in error.

1991. Christmas. Walt Disney Christmas Cards. As T **228** of St. Vincent. Multicoloured.

1090	10s. Disney characters in "JOY", 1968 (horiz)	40	20
1091	25s. Mickey, Donald, Pluto and Goofy hanging up stockings, 1981 (horiz)	65	40
1092	35s. Characters from Disney film "Robin Hood", 1973 (horiz)	80	45
1093	75s. Mickey looking at Christmas tree, 1967 (horiz)	1·40	90
1094	100s. Goofy, Mickey, Donald, Chip 'n' Dale on film set, 1969	1·75	1·25
1095	150s. Mickey on giant bubble, 1976	2·25	2·00
1096	200s. Clarabelle Cow with electric cow bell, 1935	2·50	2·50
1097	300s. Mickey's nephews with book, 1935	3·50	3·50
MS1098 Two sheets, each 127×102 mm. (a) 500s. Mickey handing out presents, 1935. (b) 500s. Disney cartoon characters, 1968 Set of 2 sheets		15·00	15·00

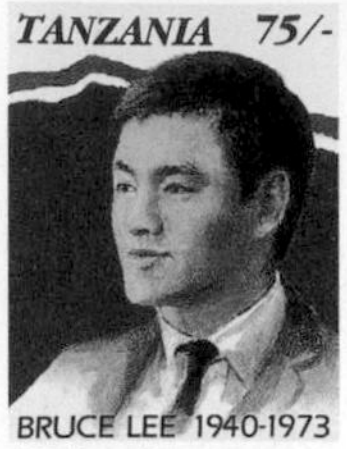

188 Bruce Lee

1992. Entertainers.

1099-134	75s.×36 multicoloured	25·00	27·00
MS1135	Four sheets, each 78×108 mm. 500s.×4 multicoloured (Bruce Lee, Marilyn Monroe, Elvis Presley, Kouyate & Kouyate, each 28×42 mm) Set of 4 sheets	23·00	26·00

Nos. 1099/1134 were issued as four sheetlets each of nine different designs, as Type **188**, depicting Bruce Lee, Marilyn Monroe, Elvis Presley and black entertainers (Scott Joplin, Sammy Davis Jnr, Joan Armatrading, Louis Armstrong, Miriam Makeba, Lionel Ritchie, Whitney Houston, Bob Marley, Tina Turner).

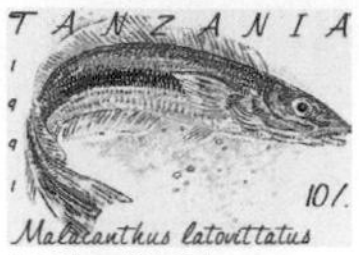

189 Sand Tilefish

1992. Fish. Multicoloured.

1136	10s. Type **189**	35	40
1137	15s. Five-banded cichlid	40	45
1138	25s. Pearly lamprologus	50	60
1139	35s. Jewel cichlid	60	70
1140	60s. Two-striped lyretail	80	1·00
1141	100s. Reef stonefish	1·25	1·50
1142	300s. Ahl's lyretail	2·50	4·00
MS1143	90×90 mm. 100s. Oarfish	1·60	2·00

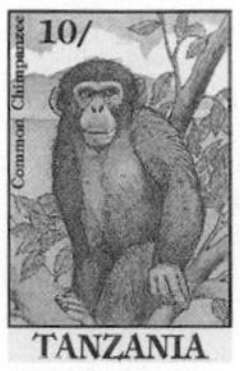

190 Chimpanzee in Tree

1992. Common Chimpanzee. Multicoloured.

1144	10s. Type **190**	75	50
1145	15s. Feeding	80	55
1146	35s. Two chimpanzees	1·40	85
1147	75s. Adult male with arms folded	2·00	1·25
1148	100s. Breaking branch	2·25	1·50
1149	150s. Young chimpanzee in tree	3·00	3·00
1150	200s. Female holding young	3·50	3·75
1151	300s. Chimpanzee sitting in tree	4·75	5·00
MS1152	Two sheets, each 99×68 mm. (a) 400s. Eating termites. (b) 400s. Swinging through trees Set of 2 sheets	7·00	7·00

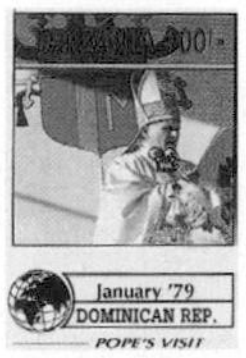

191 Pope John Paul II in Dominican Republic, 1979

1992. Papal Visits.

1153-272	100s.×120 multicoloured Set of 120	£110	75·00

DESIGNS: Nos. 1153/1272 Various scenes on Papal visits as Type **191**.

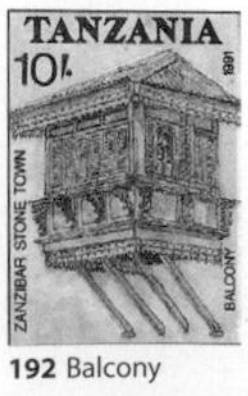

192 Balcony

1992. Zanzibar Stone Town. Multicoloured.

1273	10s. Type **192**	65	25
1274	20s. Bahlnara Mosque	90	35
1275	30s. High Court Building	1·25	40
1276	200s. National Museum (horiz)	7·00	8·50
MS1277	91×91 mm. 150s. Old Fort (horiz); 300s. Maruhubi ruins (horiz)	7·00	6·00

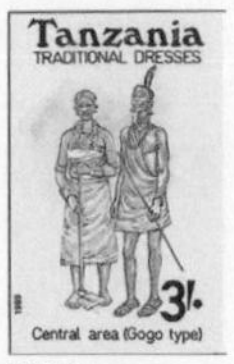

193 Gogo Costume

1992. Traditional Costumes. Multicoloured.

1278	3s. Type **193**	1·25	1·00
1279	5s. Swahili	1·25	1·00
1280	9s. Hehe and Makonde	1·75	1·10
1281	12s. Maasai	2·00	1·50
MS1282	91×91 mm. 40s. Mwarusha	4·50	4·75

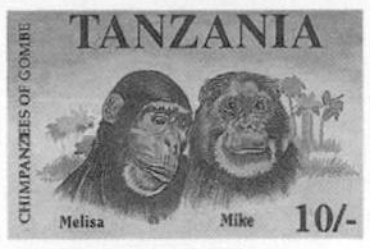

194 Melisa and Mike (chimpanzees)

1992. Chimpanzees of the Gombe. Multicoloured

(a) Horiz design as T **194**

1283	10s. Type **194**	1·00	55
1284	15s. Leakey and David Greybeard	1·25	65
1285	30s. Fifi termiting	1·60	1·10
1286	35s. Galahad	1·60	1·25
MS1287	90×90 mm. 100s. Fifi, Flo and Faben	2·50	2·75

(b) Vert design showing individual chimpanzees.

1288	10s. Leakey	1·00	1·00
1289	15s. Fifi	1·00	1·00
1290	20s. Faben	1·00	1·00
1291	30s. David Greybeard	1·00	1·00
1292	35s. Mike	1·00	1·00
1293	65s. Galahad	1·00	1·00
1294	100s. Melisa	1·25	1·25
1295	200s. Flo	1·75	1·75

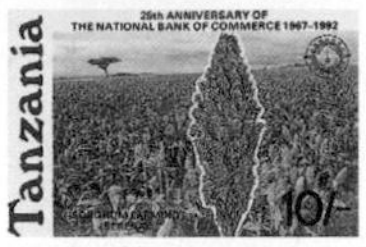

195 Sorghum Farming, Serena

1992. 25th Anniv of National Bank of Commerce. Multicoloured.

1296	10s. Type **195**	75	15
1297	15s. Samora Avenue branch and computer operator (vert)	85	25
1298	35s. Training centre	1·25	90
1299	40s. Women dyeing textiles	1·25	1·50
MS1300	111×117 mm. 30s. Bank head office	1·25	1·75

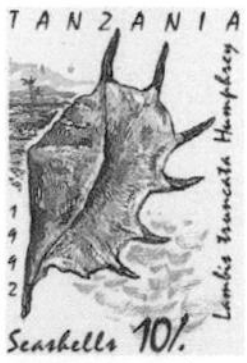

196 Giant Spider Conch

1992. Shells. Multicoloured.

1301	10s. Type **196**	25	30
1302	15s. Bull-mouth helmet	30	35
1303	25s. Rugose mitre	40	50
1304	30s. Lettered cone	40	50
1305	35s. True heart cockle	40	50
1306	50s. Ramose murex	50	70
1307	250s. Indian volute	1·50	3·25
MS1308	91×91 mm. 300s. Giant clam	2·75	4·00

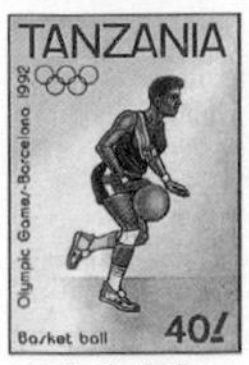

197 Basketball

1992. Olympic Games, Barcelona (2nd issue). Multicoloured.

1309	40s. Type **197**	45	30
1310	100s. Billiards	75	60
1311	200s. Table tennis	1·25	1·40
1312	400s. Darts	2·75	4·00
MS1313	90×85 mm. 500s. Weightlifting	3·00	4·25

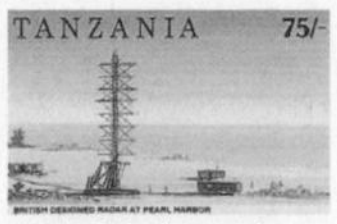

198 British-designed Radar, Pearl Harbor

1992. 50th Anniv of Japanese Attack on Pearl Harbor. Multicoloured.

1314	75s. Type **198**	2·25	1·40
1315	75s. Winston Churchill	2·25	1·40
1316	75s. Sinking of H.M.S. "Repulse" (battle cruiser)	2·25	1·40
1317	75s. Sinking of H.M.S. "Prince of Wales" (battleship)	2·25	1·40
1318	75s. Surrender of Singapore	2·25	1·40
1319	75s. Sinking of H.M.S. "Hermes" (aircraft carrier)	2·25	1·40
1320	75s. Japanese attack on Malayan airfield	2·25	1·40
1321	75s. Japanese gun crew, Hong Kong	2·25	1·40
1322	75s. Japanese landing craft	2·25	1·40
1323	75s. "Haguro" (Japanese cruiser)	2·25	1·40

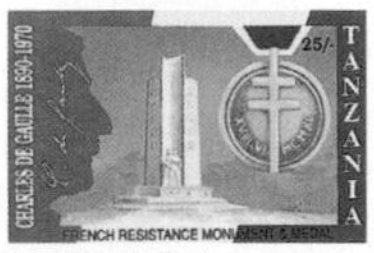

199 French Resistance Monument and Medal

1992. Birth Centenary (1990) of Charles de Gaulle (French statesman). Multicoloured.

1324	25s. Type **199**	50	40
1325	30s. Free French tank on Omaha beach, D-Day	50	40
1326	150s. Concorde at Charles de Gaulle Airport	10·00	7·50
MS1327	115×92 mm. 500s. Free French local Cross of Lorraine opt on Petain 1f.50 and De Gaulle label postmarked 25 August 1944 (39×51 mm)	10·00	12·00

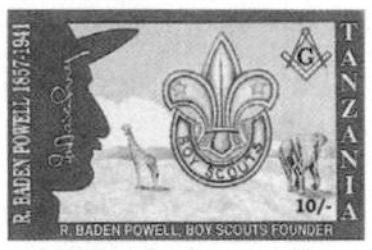

200 Scout Bridge, Giraffe and Elephant

1992. 50th Death Anniv (1991) of Lord Baden-Powell (founder of Boy Scout movement). Multicoloured.

1328	10s. Type **200**	80	50
1329	15s. Scouts in boat	80	50
1330	400s. John Glenn's space capsule	6·00	8·50
MS1331	90×117 mm. 500s. Tanzanian scout (39×51 mm)	4·25	6·50

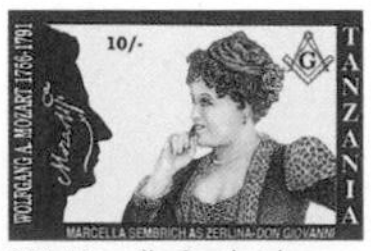

201 Marcella Sembrich as Zerlina in "Don Giovanni"

1992. Death Bicentenary of Mozart.

1332	**201**	10s. black and mauve	1·75	40
1333	-	50s. multicoloured	3·50	1·10
1334	-	300s. black and mauve	11·00	10·00
MS1335		115×87 mm. 500s. brown, stone and black	12·00	12·00

DESIGNS—HORIZ: 50s. Planet Jupiter (Symphony No. 41); 300s. Luciano Pavarotti as Idamente in "Idomeneo". VERT (35×47 mm): Wolfgang Amadeus Mozart.

1992. "Granada '92" International Stamp Exhibition, Spain. Paintings. As T **250b** of Sierra Leone.

1336	25s. red and black	60	40
1337	35s. multicoloured	70	50
1338	50s. multicoloured	85	60
1339	75s. multicoloured	1·25	1·00
1340	100s. black, brown and pink	1·75	1·25
1341	150s. red and black	2·25	2·25
1342	200s. red and black	2·50	2·50
1343	300s. multicoloured	3·00	3·50
MS1344	Two sheets, each 121×95 mm. (a) 400s. multicoloured. (b) 400s. multicoloured. Imperf Set of 2 sheets	9·50	11·00

DESIGNS—HORIZ (49½×36 mm): 25s. "A Picador, mounted on a Chulo's Shoulders, spears a Bull" (Goya); 150s. "Another Madness (of Martincho) in the Plaza de Zaragoza" (Goya); 200s. "Recklessness of Martincho in the Plaza de Zaragoza" (Goya). (111×86 mm): 400s. (**MS**1344a) "Two Men at Table" (Velasquez); 400s. (**MS**1344b) "Seascape" (Mariana Salvador Maella). VERT: 35s. "Philip IV at Fraga" (Velazquez); 50s. "Head of a Stag" (Velazquez); 75s. "The Cardinal-Infante Ferdinand as a Hunter" (Velazquez); 100s. "The Dream of Reason brings forth Monsters" (Goya); 300s. "Pablo de Valladolid" (Velazquez).

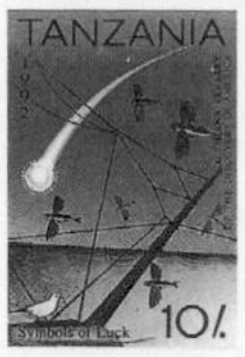

202 Lucky Omens

1992. 500th Anniv of Discovery of America by Columbus. Multicoloured.

1345	10s. Type **202**	20	20
1346	15s. Map and compass	25	25
1347	25s. Look-out in crow's nest	35	35
1348	30s. Amerindians sighting ships (horiz)	40	40
1349	35s. "Pinta" and "Nina" (horiz)	55	45
1350	75s. "Santa Maria" (horiz)	90	80
1351	250s. Wreck of "Santa Maria"	1·75	2·50
MS1352	93×93 mm. 200s. Columbus	1·75	2·50

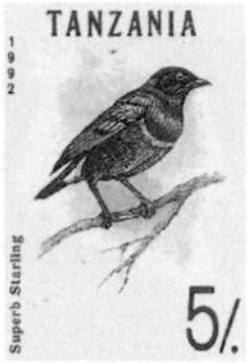

203 Superb Starling

1992. Birds. Multicoloured.

1353	5s. Type **203**	60	50
1354	10s. Golden Bishop ("Canary")	70	50
1355	15s. Four-coloured bush shrike	80	55
1356	25s. Grey-headed kingfisher	90	55
1357	30s. River kingfisher (Common Kingfisher")	90	55
1358	35s. Yellow-billed oxpecker	90	55
1359	150s. Black-throated honey-guide	2·50	3·00
MS1360	93×92 mm. 300s. European cuckoo (horiz)	2·75	3·50

1992. 15th Death Anniv of Elvis Presley. Nos. 1117/25 optd **15th Anniversary**.

1361	75s. Looking pensive	95	85
1362	75s. Wearing black and yellow striped shirt	95	85
1363	75s. Singing into microphone	95	85
1364	75s. Wearing wide-brimmed hat	95	85
1365	75s. With microphone in right hand	95	85
1366	75s. In Army uniform	95	85
1367	75s. Wearing pink shirt	95	85
1368	75s. In yellow shirt	95	85
1369	75s. In jacket and bow tie	95	85

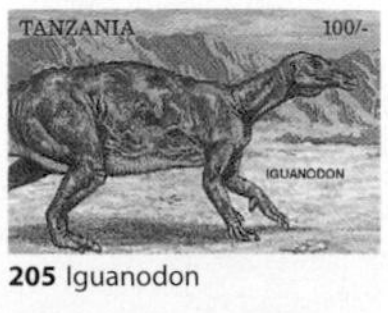

205 Iguanodon

1992. African Dinosaurs. Multicoloured.

1370	100s. Type **205**	1·10	90
1371	100s. Saltasaurus	1·10	90
1372	100s. Cetiosaurus	1·10	90
1373	100s. Camarasaurus	1·10	90
1374	100s. Spinosaurus	1·10	90
1375	100s. Stegosaurus	1·10	90
1376	100s. Allosaurus	1·10	90
1377	100s. Ceratosaurus	1·10	90
1378	100s. Lesothosaurus	1·10	90
1379	100s. Anchisaurus	1·10	90
1380	100s. Ornithomimus	1·10	90
1381	100s. Baronyx	1·10	90
1382	100s. Pachycephalosaurus	1·10	90
1383	100s. Heterodontosaurus	1·10	90
1384	100s. Dryosaurus	1·10	90
1385	100s. Coelophysis	1·10	90

Nos. 1370/85 were printed together, *se-tenant*, forming a composite design.

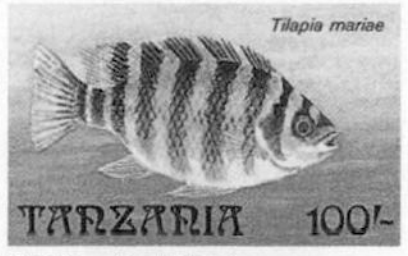

206 Spotted Tilapia

1992. Fish. Multicoloured.

1386	100s. Type **206**	1·00	1·00
1387	100s. Butterfly barb	1·00	1·00
1388	100s. Blunthead Molino cichlid	1·00	1·00
1389	100s. Angel squeaker	1·00	1·00
1390	100s. Dickfield's Julie	1·00	1·00
1391	100s. Nile mouthbrooder	1·00	1·00
1392	100s. Blue-finned notho	1·00	1·00
1393	100s. Crabro mbuna	1·00	1·00
1394	100s. Pearl-scaled lamprologus	1·00	1·00
1395	100s. Zebra mbuna	1·00	1·00
1396	100s. Marlier's Julie	1·00	1·00
1397	100s. Brichard's chalinochromis	1·00	1·00
MS1398	Three sheets, each 71×55 mm. (a) 500s. Palmqvist's notho. (b) 500s. Electric blue haplochromis. (c) 500s. Short lamprologus Set of 3 sheets	11·00	12·00

Nos. 1386/97 were printed together, *se-tenant*, forming a composite design.

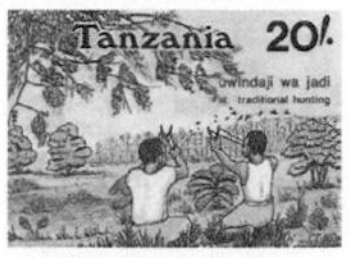

207 Hunting Birds with Catapults

1992. Traditional Hunting. Multicoloured.

1399	20s. Type **207**	1·75	50
1400	70s. Hunting antelope with bow and arrow	1·75	80
1401	100s. Hunting antelopes with dogs	3·00	1·50
1402	150s. Hunting lion with spears and shields	3·25	4·25
MS1403	100×100 mm. 40s. Traditional hunting weapons	3·75	4·50

1992. Olympic Games, Albertville and Barcelona (3rd issue). As T **251a** of Sierra Leone. Multicoloured.

1404	20s. Men's 4000 m pursuit cycling	2·00	85
1405	40s. Men's double sculls rowing (horiz)	70	20
1406	50s. Water polo (horiz)	80	20
1407	70s. Women's single luge (horiz)	90	30
1408	100s. Marathon (horiz)	95	50
1409	150s. Women's asymmetrical bars gymnastics (horiz)	2·00	2·25
1410	200s. Ice hockey	4·50	3·00
1411	400s. Men's rings gymnastics	4·50	6·00
MS1412	Two sheets, each 100×71 mm. (a) 500s. Tennis. (b) 500s. Football Set of 2 sheets	13·00	13·00

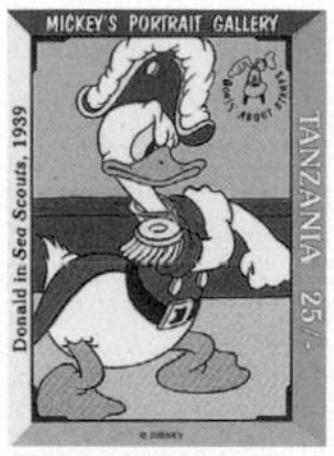

207a Donald Duck in "Sea Scout", 1939

1992. Mickey's Portrait Gallery. Walt Disney cartoon characters. Multicoloured.

1413	25s. Type **207a**	40	30
1414	25s. Minnie Mouse in "Hawaiian Holiday", 1937	40	30
1415	25s. Pluto in "Society Dog Show", 1939	40	30
1416	35s. Donald in "Fire Chief", 1940	55	40
1417	50s. Donald in "Truant Officer Donald", 1941	65	50
1418	75s. Goofy in "Clock Cleaners", 1937	85	60
1419	100s. Goofy in "Goofy and Wilbur", 1939	1·00	85
1420	100s. Mickey Mouse in "Magician Mickey", 1937	1·00	85
1421	200s. Minnie in "The Nifty Nineties", 1941	1·75	1·25
1422	300s. Mickey and Pluto in "Society Dog Show", 1939	2·00	1·75
1423	400s. Pluto and pups in "Pluto's Quin-Puplets", 1937	2·25	2·00
1424	500s. Daisy and Donald in "Mr. Duck Steps Out", 1940	2·25	2·00
MS1425	Three sheets. (a) 127×102 mm. 600s. Goofy in "Forever Goofy". (b) 127×102 mm. 600s. Daisy in "Don Donald", 1937. (c) 112×104 mm. 600s. Mickey and Minnie in "Brave Little Tailor", 1938 (horiz) Set of 3 sheets	9·50	11·00

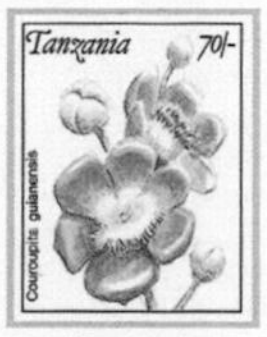

208 "Couroupita guinensis"

1993. Botanical Gardens of the World. Rio de Janeiro. African Plants. Vert designs as T **208**.

1426-1445	70s.×20 multicoloured Set of 20	16·00	18·00
MS1446	110×74 mm. 500s. Avenue of royal palms	4·75	5·50

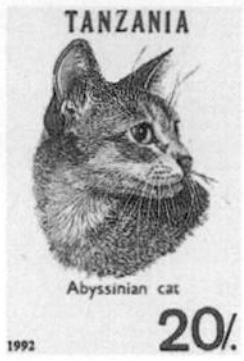

209 Abyssinian Cat

1992. Cats. Multicoloured.

1447	20s. Type **209**	55	45
1448	30s. Havana cat	55	45
1449	50s. Persian black cat	65	55
1450	70s. Persian blue cat	75	65
1451	100s. European silver tabby cat	1·00	85
1452	150s. Persian silver tabby cat	1·25	1·25
1453	200s. Maine coon cat	1·50	1·50
MS1454	90×90 mm. 300s. European cat	2·75	3·00

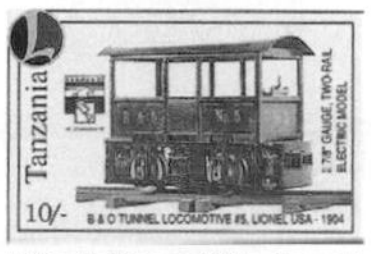

209a Baltimore Ohio Tunnel Locomotive No. 5, 1904

1992. "Genova '92" International Stamp Exhibition. Toy Trains manufactured by Lionel. Multicoloured.

1455	10s. Type **209a**	70	35
1456	20s. "Liberty Bell" locomotive No. 385E, 1930	80	45
1457	30s. Armoured rail car No. 203, 1917	85	40
1458	50s. Open trolley No. 202, 1910–14	1·25	60
1459	70s. "Macy Special" electric locomotive No. 405	1·50	85
1460	100s. "Milwaukee Road" bi-polar electric locomotive, 1929	1·60	95
1461	200s. New York Central Type S locomotive, 1912	2·00	2·25
1462	300s. Locomotive No. 7, 1914	2·25	3·25
MS1463	Two sheets. (a) 91×75 mm. 500s. Display model locomotive in clear plastic, 1947. (b) 71×89 mm. 500s. Mickey and Minnie Mouse on clockwork handcar, 1936 Set of 2 sheets	6·50	7·50

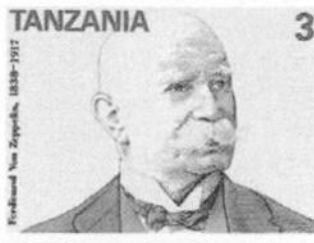

210 Count Ferdinand von Zeppelin

1992. Anniversaries and Events. Multicoloured.

1464	30s. Type **210**	60	30
1465	70s. "Santa Maria"	1·50	1·00
1466	70s. "Apollo–Soyuz" link-up, 1975	1·00	1·00
1467	150s. African elephant	3·00	1·50
1468	150s. Child being offered apple	1·00	1·50
1469	200s. Zebra	1·50	1·50
1470	200s. Trying on glasses	1·10	1·50
1471	300s. Airship "Graf Zeppelin", 1929	1·75	2·00
1472	300s. Christopher Columbus	2·00	2·00
1473	400s. Space shuttle	2·75	2·75
1474	400s. Wolfgang Amadeus Mozart (vert)	4·25	3·50
MS1475	Five sheets. (a) 110×82 mm. 500s. LZ-5 Zeppelin airship. (b) 114×81 mm. 500s. Head of Columbus. (c) 110×82 mm. 500s. "Voyager 2" space probe. (d) 114×81 mm. 500s. African elephant (different). (e) 110×68 mm. 500s. Queen of the Night from "The Magic Flute" (vert) Set of 5 sheets	17·00	19·00

ANNIVERSARIES AND EVENTS: Nos. 1464, 1471, **MS**1475a, 75th death anniv of Count Ferdinand von Zeppelin; 1465, 1472, **MS**1475b, 500th anniv of discovery of America by Columbus; 1466, 1473, **MS**1475c, International Space Year; 1467, 1469, **MS**1475d, Earth Summit '92, Rio; 1468, International Conference on Nutrition, Rome; 1470, 75th anniv of International Association of Lions Clubs; 1474, **MS**1475e, Death bicentenary of Mozart.

1992. Bicentenary of the Louvre, Paris. Paintings by Jean Chardin. As T **254a** of St Vincent. Multicoloured.

1476	100s. "Young Draughtsman sharpening Pencil"	85	85
1477	100s. "The Buffet"	85	85
1478	100s. "Return from the Market"	85	85
1479	100s. "The Hard-working Mother"	85	85
1480	100s. "Grace"	85	85
1481	100s. "The Copper Water Urn"	85	85
1482	100s. "The House of Cards"	85	85
1483	100s. "Boy with a Top"	85	85
MS1484	100×70 mm. 500s. "The Ray" (85×52 mm)	3·50	4·00

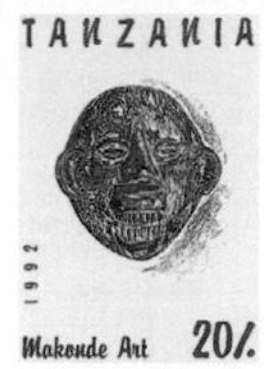

211 Carved Head

1992. Makonde Art.

1485	**211**	20s. multicoloured	15	15
1486	-	30s. multicoloured	15	15
1487	-	50s. multicoloured	20	20
1488	-	70s. multicoloured	30	30
1489	-	100s. multicoloured	40	40
1490	-	150s. multicoloured	70	70
1491	-	200s. multicoloured	80	80
MS1492		91×91 mm. 350s. multicoloured	1·75	2·25

DESIGNS: 30s. to 200s. Various carvings.

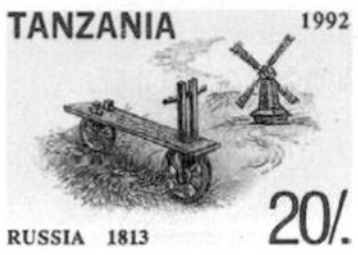

212 Russian Cycle, 1813

1992. Bicycles of the World. Multicoloured.

1493	20s. Type **212**	20	20
1494	30s. German, 1840	20	20
1495	50s. German, 1818	30	30
1496	70s. German, 1850	30	40
1497	100s. Italian, 1988	35	50
1498	150s. Swedish, 1982	50	80
1499	300s. Italian, 1989	70	1·25
MS1500	90×90 mm. 350s. British penny-farthing, 1887	1·00	2·50

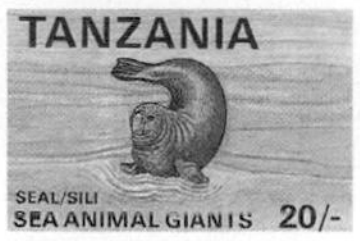

213 Seal

1993. Large Sea Creatures. Multicoloured.

1501	20s. Type **213**	75	50
1502	30s. Whale	2·25	80
1503	70s. Shark	1·25	1·00
1504	100s. Walrus	1·50	1·50
MS1505	99×91 mm. 500s. Sea turtle	6·50	6·50

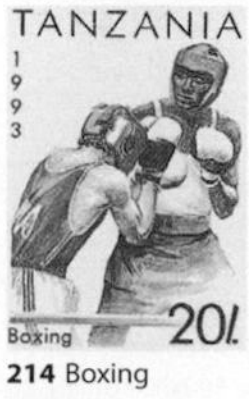

214 Boxing

1993. Sports. Multicoloured.

1506	20s. Type **214**	15	15
1507	50s. Hockey	1·00	30
1508	70s. Show jumping	40	40
1509	100s. Marathon running	45	45
1510	150s. Football	60	70
1511	200s. Diving	70	90
1512	400s. Basketball	2·00	2·50
MS1513	91×91 mm. 300s. High jumping (horiz)	1·75	2·25

1993. 40th Anniv of Coronation. As T **256a** of St. Vincent.

1514	100s. multicoloured	80	65
1515	150s. multicoloured	1·10	85
1516	200s. lilac and black	1·40	1·10
1517	300s. multicoloured	1·60	1·25
MS1518	102×70 mm. 500s. multicoloured	3·75	3·75

DESIGNS: 100s. Queen Elizabeth II at Coronation (photograph by Cecil Beaton); 150s. Gold salt-cellar; 200s. Prince Philip at Coronation; 300s. Queen Elizabeth II and Prince Andrew. (28½×42½ mm): 500s. "Princess Elizabeth opening the New Broadgate, Coventry" (detail) (Dame Laura Knight).

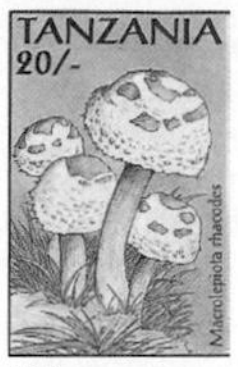

215 "Macrolepiota rhacodes"

1993. Fungi. Multicoloured.

1519	20s. Type **215**	60	35
1520	40s. "Mycena pura"	80	50
1521	50s. "Chlorophyllum molybdites"	80	50
1522	70s. "Agaricus campestris"	90	60
1523	100s. "Volvariella volvacea"	1·00	70
1524	150s. "Leucoagaricus naucinus"	1·40	1·25
1525	200s. "Oudemansiella radicata"	1·60	1·50
1526	300s. "Clitocybe nebularis"	1·75	2·00
MS1527	Two sheets, each 100×70 mm. (a) 500s. "Omphalotus olearius". (b) 500s. "Lepista nuda" Set of 2 sheets	6·50	7·50

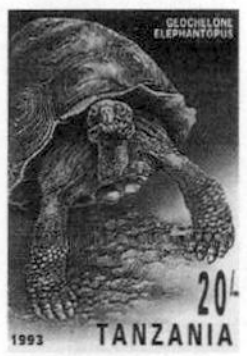

216 "Geochelone elephantopus" (tortoise)

1993. Reptiles. Multicoloured.

1528	20s. Type **216**	20	20
1529	50s. "Iguana iguana"	30	30
1530	70s. "Varanus salvator" (lizard) (horiz)	40	40
1531	100s. "Naja oxiana" (cobra)	45	45
1532	150s. "Chamaeleo jacksoni" (horiz)	70	70
1533	200s. "Eunectes murinus" (snake) (horiz)	80	80
1534	250s. "Alligator mississippensis" (horiz)	90	90
MS1535	90×90 mm. 500s. "Vipera berus" (snake)	2·50	3·50

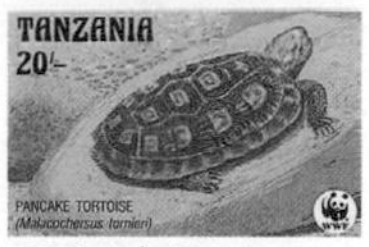

217 Pancake Tortoise on Rock

1993. Endangered Species. Pancake Tortoise. Multicoloured.

1536	20s. Type **217**	45	35
1537	30s. Drinking	50	40
1538	50s. Under rock	70	80
1539	70s. Tortoise hatching	90	1·00

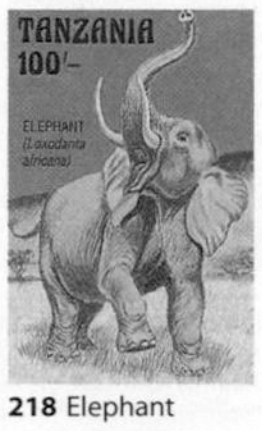

218 Elephant

1993. Wildlife.

1540-87	100s.×48 multicoloured	30·00	28·00
MS1588	Two sheets, each 100×71 mm. (a) 500s. Lion cub (horiz). (b) 500s. Elephant calf (horiz) Set of 2 sheets	7·50	8·50

Nos. 1540/87 were issued together, *se-tenant*, as four sheetlets each of twelve different vertical designs. The species depicted are, in addition to Type **218**, Gazelle, Hartebeest, Duiker, Genet, Civet, Eastern white pelican, Waterbuck, Blacksmith plover, Lesser pied kingfisher, Black-winged stilt, Bush pig, Brown-hooded kingfisher, Sable antelope, Impala, Buffalo, Leopard, Aardvark, Hippopotamus, Spotted hyena, South African crowned crane, Crocodile, Greater flamingo, Baboon, Potto, Lesser flamingo, Grey-headed kingfisher, Red colobus monkey, Dik-dik, Aardwolf (incorrectly inscribed "ARDWOLF"), Black-backed jackal, Tree pangolin, Serval, Yellow-billed hornbill, Pygmy mongoose, Bat-eared fox, Bushbaby, Egyptian vulture, Ostrich, Greater kudu, Diana monkey, Giraffe, Cheetah, Wildebeest, Chimpanzee, Warthog, Zebra and Rhinoceros.

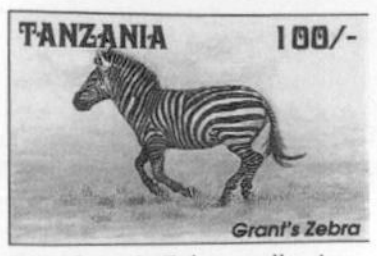

219 Grant's Zebra galloping

1992. Wild Animals. Multicoloured.

1589	100s. Type **219**	1·00	1·00
1590	100s. Grant's zebra standing	1·00	1·00
1591	100s. Grant's gazelle doe	1·00	1·00
1592	100s. Grant's gazelle buck	1·00	1·00
1593	100s. Thomson's gazelle	1·00	1·00
1594	100s. White-bearded gnu with calf	1·00	1·00
1595	100s. Female cheetah with cubs	1·00	1·00
1596	100s. Young cheetah drinking	1·00	1·00
1597	100s. Lioness carrying cub in mouth	1·00	1·00
1598	100s. Pair of hunting dogs	1·00	1·00
1599	100s. Three hunting dogs	1·00	1·00
1600	100s. Four hunting dogs	1·00	1·00
MS1601	Two sheets, each 106×76 mm. (a) 500s. African elephant. (b) 500s. Rhinoceros Set of 2 sheets	12·00	10·00

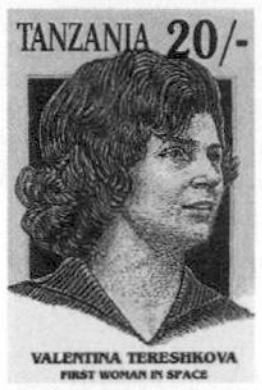

220 Valentina Tereshkova (first woman in space)

1993. Famous 20th-century Women. Multicoloured.

1602	20s. Type **220**	75	65
1603	40s. Marie Curie (physicist)	2·75	1·50
1604	50s. Indira Gandhi (Prime Minister of India)	4·00	1·50
1605	70s. Wilma Rudolph (Olympic athlete)	1·00	1·50
1606	100s. Margaret Mead (anthropologist)	1·00	1·50
1607	150s. Golda Meir (Prime Minister of Israel)	4·00	2·00
1608	200s. Dr. Elizabeth Blackwell (first female medical doctor)	1·75	2·00
1609	400s. Margaret Thatcher (Prime Minister of Great Britain)	3·75	3·25
MS1610	116×80 mm. 500s. Mother Teresa (humanitarian)	4·00	4·00

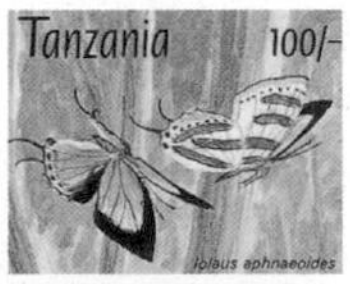

221 "Iolaus aphnaeoides"

1993. Butterflies.

1611-54	100s.×44 multicoloured	40·00	30·00
MS1655	Four sheets, each 69×58 mm. (a) 500s. "Cymothoe sangaris". (b) 500s. "Precis octavia". (c) 500s. "Charaxes violetta". (d) 500s. "Papilio nobilis" Set of 4 sheets	17·00	17·00

Nos. 1611/54 were printed *se-tenant* in two sheetlets of 12 (Nos. 1611/34) and one of 20 (Nos. 1635/54). The species depicted, in addition to Type **221**, are "Charaxes eupale", "Danaus formosa", "Antanartia hippomene", "Mylothris sagala", "Charaxes anticlea", "Salamis temora", "Nepheronia argia", "Acraea pseudolycia", "Hypolimnas antevorta", "Colotis hildebrandti", "Acraea bonasia", "Eurema desjardinsi", "Myrina silenus", "Iolaus ismenias", "Charaxes candiope", "Precis artaxia", "Danaus chrysippus", "Axiocerses bambana", "Precis orithya", "Pinacopteryx eriphia", "Iolaus coeculus", "Precis hierta", "Colotis regina", "Euphaedra neophron", "Mylothris poppea", "Aphaneus flavescens", "Eronia leda", "Charaxes zoolina", "Papilio bromius", "Cyrestis camillus", "Hypolycaena buxtoni", "Charaxes achaemenes", "Asterope rosa", "Graphium antheus", "Charaxes acuminatus", "Kallima rumia", "Leptosia alcesta", "Pseudacraea boisduvali", "Iolaus sidus", "Salamis parhassus", "Charaxes protoclea azota", "Charaxes bohemani" and "Papilio ophidicephalus".

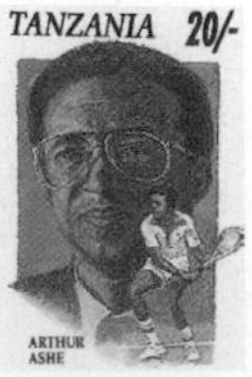

222 Arthur Ashe (tennis)

1993. Black Sporting Personalities. Multicoloured.

1656	20s. Type **222**	50	40
1657	40s. Michael Jordan (basketball)	60	60
1658	50s. Daley Thompson (decathlon)	60	40
1659	70s. Jackie Robinson (baseball)	60	40
1660	100s. Kareem Abdul-Jabbar (basketball)	75	60
1661	150s. Florence Joyner (athletics)	75	80
1662	200s. Jesse Owens (athletics)	75	1·00
1663	400s. Jack Johnson (boxing)	1·25	1·75
MS1664	72×101 mm. 500s. Muhammed Ali (boxing) (horiz)	2·50	3·25

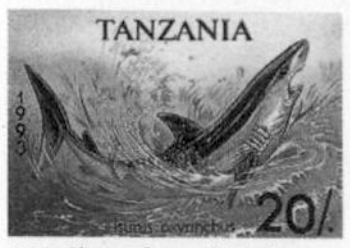

223 Short-finned Mako

1993. Sharks. Multicoloured.

1665	20s. Type **223**	15	15
1666	30s. Lantern shark	20	20
1667	50s. Tiger shark	20	25
1668	70s. African angelshark	30	35
1669	100s. Shark	35	45
1670	150s. White-tipped reef shark	50	65
1671	200s. Scalloped hammerhead	55	75
MS1672	91×91 mm. 350s. Six-gilled shark (vert)	1·75	2·00

No. is inscribed "Pristiophorus cirratus".

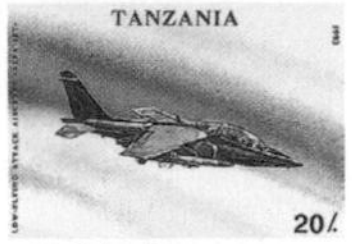

224 Alpha Jet

1993. Military Aircraft. Multicoloured.

1673	20s. Type **224**	20	20
1674	30s. Northrop F-5E	20	25
1675	50s. Dassault Mirage 3NG	25	30
1676	70s. MB 339C	35	45
1677	100s. MiG-31	35	50
1678	150s. C-101 Aviojet	40	70
1679	200s. General Dynamics F-16 Fighting Falcon	45	80
MS1680	91×91 mm. 500s. EAP fighter (vert)	1·40	2·00

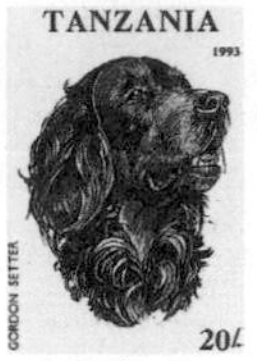

225 Gordon Setter

1993. Dogs. Multicoloured.

1681	20s. Type **225**	20	20
1682	30s. Zwergschnauzer	25	25
1683	50s. Labrador retriever	30	30
1684	70s. Wire fox terrier	35	45
1685	100s. English springer spaniel	40	50
1686	150s. Newfoundlander	60	70
1687	200s. Moscow toy terrier	70	80
MS1688	91×91 mm. 350s. Dobermann Pinscher	1·75	2·00

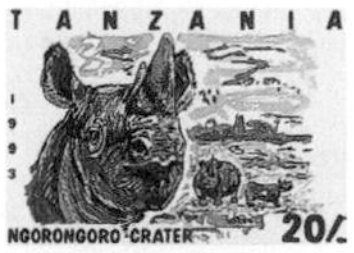

226 Rhinoceros, Ngorongoro Crater

1993. National Parks. Multicoloured.

1689	20s. Type **226**	20	20
1690	50s. Buffalo, Ngurdoto Crater	20	20
1691	70s. Leopard, Kilimanjaro	25	30
1692	100s. Baboon, Gombe	25	35
1693	150s. Lion, Selous	35	45
1694	200s. Giraffe, Mikumi	65	65
1695	250s. Zebra, Serengeti	65	70
MS1696	91×91 mm. 500s. Elephant, Lake Manyara (vert)	1·75	2·00

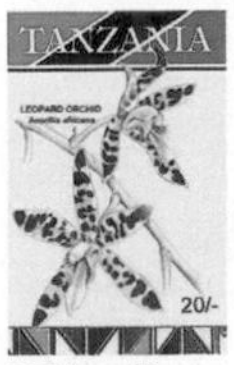

227 "Ansellia africana"

1993. Flowers. Multicoloured.

1697	20s. Type **227**	40	20
1698	30s. "Saintpaulia ionantha"	45	25
1699	40s. "Stapelia semota lutea"	50	30
1700	50s. "Impatiens walleriana"	50	30
1701	60s. "Senecio petraeus"	55	35
1702	70s. "Kalanchoe velutina"	65	40
1703	100s. "Kaempferia brachystemon"	85	60
1704	150s. "Nymphaea colorata"	1·25	1·25
1705	200s. "Thunbergia battiscombei"	1·40	1·40
1706	250s. "Crossandra nilotica"	1·40	1·50
1707	300s. "Spathodea campanulata"	1·60	1·75
1708	350s. "Ruttya fruticosa"	1·60	1·75
MS1709	Two sheets, each 100×70 mm. (a) 500s. "Streptocarpus saxorum". (b) 500s. "Glorioso verschurii" Set of 2 sheets	5·25	7·00

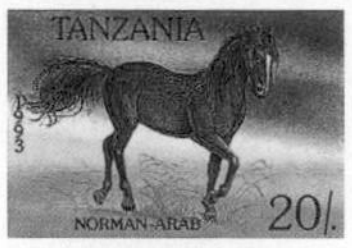

228 Norman-Arab

1993. Horses. Multicoloured.

1710	20s. Type **228**	40	30
1711	40s. Nonius	50	40
1712	50s. Boulonnais	50	40
1713	70s. Arab	60	60
1714	100s. Anglo-Arab	70	70
1715	150s. Tarpon	90	1·00
1716	200s. Thoroughbred	1·10	1·40
MS1717	91×91 mm. 400s. Anglo-Norman (vert)	1·75	2·00

No. 1716 is inscribed "THOROUGBLED" in error.

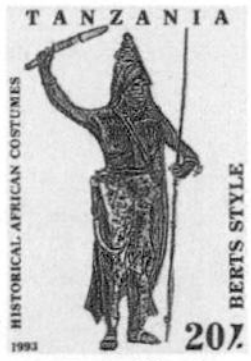

229 Berts Warrior

1993. Traditional African Costumes. Multicoloured.

1718	20s. Type **229**	10	10
1719	40s. Galla	15	15
1720	50s. Guinean	15	15
1721	70s. Goloff	20	25
1722	100s. Peul	30	30
1723	150s. Abyssinian	45	45
1724	200s. Pahuin	55	55
MS1725	91×91 mm. 350s. Zulu	1·10	1·25

1994. Hummel Figurines. As T **251b** of St. Vincent. Multicoloured.

1726	20s. Boy playing accordion	30	25
1727	40s. Girl with guitar and boy with lute	35	30
1728	50s. Boy playing euphonium	35	30
1729	70s. Boy playing mouth organ	40	35
1730	100s. Boy with trumpet on fence	50	45
1731	150s. Boy playing recorder	80	80
1732	200s. Boy with trumpet and bird on feet	90	90
1733	300s. Girl playing banjo	1·25	1·40
1734	350s. Boy carrying double bass on back	1·40	1·60
1735	400s. Girls with banjo and song sheet	1·40	1·60
MS1736	Two sheets, each 70×101 mm. (a) 500s. Carol singers. (b) 500s. Angels with trumpets in bell tower Set of 2 sheets	8·00	8·50

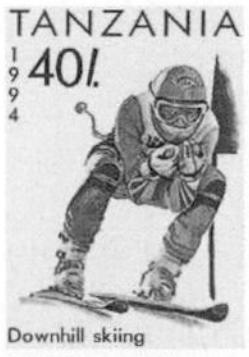

230 Downhill Skiing

1994. Winter Olympic Games, Lillehammer, Norway. Multicoloured.

1737	40s. Type **230**	20	20
1738	50s. Ice hockey	20	20
1739	70s. Speed skating	30	30
1740	100s. Bobsleighing	35	35
1741	120s. Figure skating	40	40
1742	170s. Free style skiing	55	55
1743	250s. Biathlon	75	75
MS1744	93×91 mm. 500s. Cross-country skiing	1·50	2·00

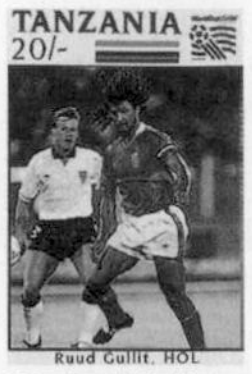

231 Ruud Gullit (Netherlands)

1994. World Cup Football Championship, U.S.A. (1st issue). Multicoloured.

1745	20s. Type **231**	50	30
1746	30s. Kevin Sheedy (Ireland)	50	30
1747	50s. Giuseppe Giannini (Italy)	60	40
1748	70s. Julio Cesar (Brazil)	65	45
1749	250s. John Barnes (England) and Grun (Belgium)	1·50	1·50
1750	300s. Chendo (Spain)	1·50	1·50
1751	350s. Frank Rijkaard (Netherlands)	1·60	2·00
1752	400s. Lothar Matthaeus (Germany)	1·60	2·00
MS1753	Two sheets. (a) 76×106 mm. 500s. Nicola Berti (Italy). (b) 106×76 mm. 500s. Des Walker (England) Set of 2 sheets	7·50	7·50

See also Nos. 1838/45 and 1892/8.

1994. "Hong Kong '94" International Stamp Exhibition. As T **271a** of St. Vincent. Multicoloured.

1754	350s. Blue-barred orange parrotfish and red cap white pearl-scale goldfish at right	1·40	1·40
1755	350s. Regal angelfish and red cap white pearl-scale goldfish at left	1·40	1·40

Nos. 1754/5 were printed together, *se-tenant*, forming a composite design.

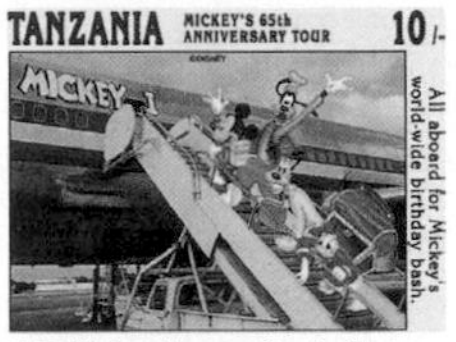

232 Mickey Mouse, Goofy, Pluto and Donald Duck boarding Airliner

1994. 65th Anniv of Mickey Mouse. Walt Disney Cartoon Characters on World Tour. Multicoloured.

1756	10s. Type **232**	55	25
1757	20s. Daisy Duck and Minnie Mouse dancing, Tonga	65	30
1758	30s. Mickey and Goofy playing bowls, Australia	70	35
1759	40s. Mickey, Donald and Goofy building igloo, Arctic Circle	75	40
1760	50s. Pluto, Goofy, Mickey and Donald on guard at Buckingham Palace, London	75	40
1761	60s. Pluto at Esna Bazaar, Egypt	80	55
1762	70s. Donald being chased by Zsambox herders, Hungary (vert)	80	55
1763	100s. Donald and Daisy on Grand Canal, Venice (vert)	1·25	70
1764	150s. Goofy dancing, Bali (vert)	1·75	1·50
1765	200s. Donald with monks, Thailand (vert)	2·00	1·75
1766	300s. Goofy water skiing at Taj Mahal, India (vert)	2·25	2·50
1767	400s. Mickey, Minnie, Goofy and Donald being carried by Sherpas, Nepal	2·50	2·75
MS1768	Three sheets. (a) 127×102 mm. 500s. Mickey at Livingstone's memorial, Ujiji (vert). (b) 127×102 mm. 500s. Mickey at Kigoma railway station, Tanzania (vert). (c) 102×127 mm. 500s. Mickey climbing Mt. Kilimanjaro (vert) Set of 3 sheets	11·00	12·00

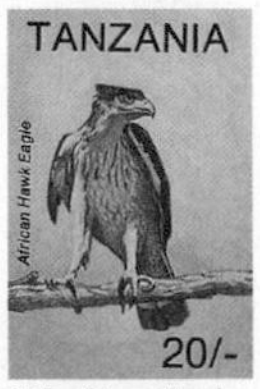

233 African Hawk Eagle

1994. Birds. Multicoloured.

1769	20s. Type **233**	1·25	95
1770	30s. Whale-headed stork ("Shoe-bill Stork")	1·25	95
1771	50s. Brown snake eagle ("Harrier Eagle")	1·50	1·10
1772	70s. Black-casqued hornbill ("Casqued Horn-Bill")	1·75	1·25
1773	100s. Crowned cranes	1·75	1·25
1774	150s. Greater flamingos	2·00	1·25
1775	200s. Pair of eastern white pelicans ("Pelicans") (horiz)	1·75	1·10

1776	250s. African jacana and African black crake (horiz)	1·75	1·10
1777	300s. Pair of ostriches (horiz)	1·75	1·25
1778	350s. Pair of helmeted guineafowl (horiz)	1·75	1·25
1779	400s. Malachite kingfisher (horiz)	1·75	1·25
1780	500s. Pair of saddle-bill storks ("Saddle-billed Stork") (horiz)	1·75	1·40

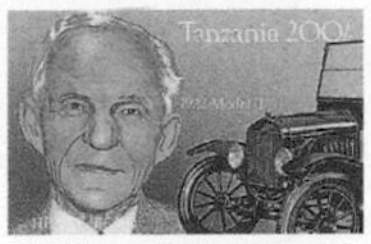

234 Henry Ford and Model "T"

1994. Centenaries of Henry Ford's First Petrol Engine (Nos. 1781 and 1783) and Karl Benz's First Four-wheeled Car (others). Multicoloured.

1781	200s. Type **234**	1·75	1·60
1782	200s. Benz, 1893, and "500 SEL", 1993	1·75	1·60
1783	400s. Ford, 1893, Mustang Cobra and emblem	2·75	2·50
1784	400s. Karl Benz and emblem	2·75	2·50
MS1785	Two sheets, each 106×71 mm. (a) 500s. Henry Ford outside first factory. (b) 500s. Benz emblem and bonnet of 1937 "540k" Set of 2 sheets	7·50	8·50

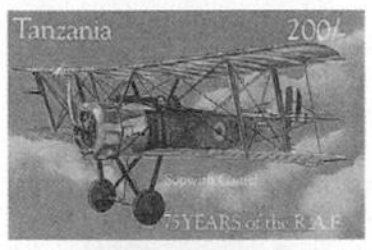

235 Sopwith Pup Biplane

1994. Aviation Anniversaries. Multicoloured.

1786	200s. Type **235**	2·50	1·75
1787	200s. Inflating hot-air balloons	2·50	1·75
1788	400s. Hawker Siddeley Harrier and design drawing	3·50	3·00
1789	400s. Jean-Pierre Blanchard and his balloon	3·50	3·00
MS1790	Two sheets, each 105×71 mm. (a) 500s. Supermarine Spitfire. (b) 500s. Hot-air balloons in flight (vert) Set of 2 sheets	10·00	9·00

ANNIVERSARIES: Nos. 1786, 1788, 75th anniv of Royal Air Force; Nos. 1787, 1789, Bicentenary of first balloon flight in the U.S.A.

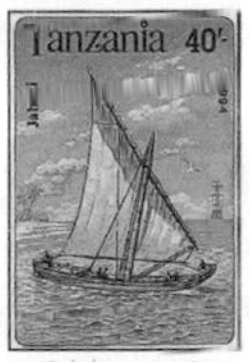

236 Jahazi (sailing canoe)

1994. Sailing Ships. Multicoloured.

1791	40s. Type **236**	15	15
1792	50s. Caravel	15	15
1793	70s. Pirate carrack	25	25
1794	100s. Baltic galeass	25	30
1795	170s. Frigate (inscr "Battle-ship")	35	55
1796	200s. British ship of the line (inscr "Frigate")	40	65
1797	250s. Brig	40	75
MS1798	91×91 mm. 500s. Clipper	1·25	2·00

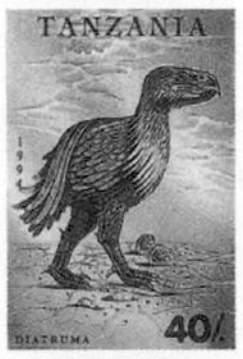

237 Diatryma

1994. Prehistoric Animals. Multicoloured.

1799	40s. Type **237**	60	30
1800	50s. Tyrannosaurus rex	60	30
1801	100s. Uintaterius	80	50
1802	120s. Stiracosaurus	90	80
1803	170s. Diplodocus	1·25	1·50
1804	250s. Archaeopteryx	1·40	1·60
1805	300s. Sordes	1·60	1·90
MS1806	91×91 mm. 500s. Dimetrodon	1·90	2·25

No. 1799 is inscribed "DIATRUMA" in error.

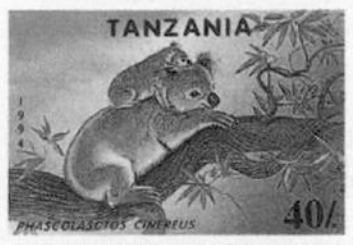

238 Koala Bear with Cub

1994. Endangered Species. Multicoloured.

1807	40s. Type **238**	25	25
1808	70s. Giant panda with cub	35	40
1809	100s. Golden eagles	45	55
1810	120s. African elephant with calf	60	70
1811	250s. Carribean monk seals	75	90
1812	400s. Dolphins	80	1·00
1813	500s. Whales	1·25	1·50
MS1814	90×90 mm. 500s. Tiger (vert)	2·75	2·75

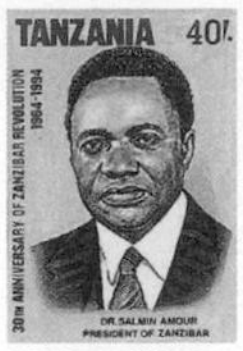

239 Pres. Salmin Amour of Zanzibar

1994. 30th Anniv of Zanzibar Revolution. Multicoloured.

1815	40s. Type **239**	40	10
1816	70s. Amani Karume (first President of Zanzibar)	60	20
1817	120s. Harvesting cloves (horiz)	1·00	1·00
1818	250s. Carved door	1·75	2·50
MS1819	91×91 mm. 500s. Hands clasped over map	2·00	2·50

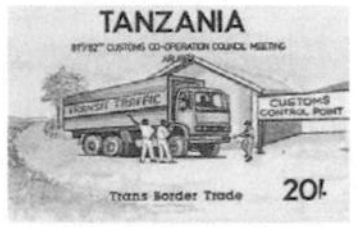

240 Lorry at Customs Post

1994. 81st/82nd Customs Co-Operation Council Meeting, Arusha. Multicoloured.

1820	20s. Type **240**	1·00	30
1821	50s. Container ship	1·50	40
1822	100s. Passengers and airliner	2·25	1·25
1823	150s. Customs and U.P.U. logos	2·25	2·50
MS1824	99×99 mm. 500s. Customs arms (30×40 mm)	3·75	3·50

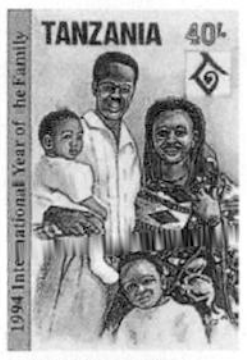

241 Tanzanian Family

1994. Int Year of the Family. Multicoloured.

1825	40s. Type **241**	35	15
1826	120s. Father playing with children	60	50
1827	170s. Family clinic (horiz)	75	1·00
1828	250s. Woman harvesting tobacco	90	1·50
MS1829	91×91 mm. 300s. Emblem	1·60	2·00

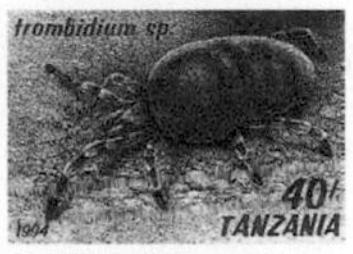

242 "Trombidium sp."

1994. Arachnids. Multicoloured.

1830	40s. Type **242**	20	20
1831	50s. "Eurypelma sp."	20	20
1832	100s. "Salticus sp."	30	30
1833	120s. "Micrommata rosea" (vert)	35	35
1834	170s. "Araneus sp." (vert)	50	50
1835	250s. "Micrathena sp." (vert)	70	70
1836	300s. "Araneus diadematus" (vert)	80	80
MS1837	92×92 mm. 500s. Claw of "Hadogenes" sp (vert)	1·75	2·00

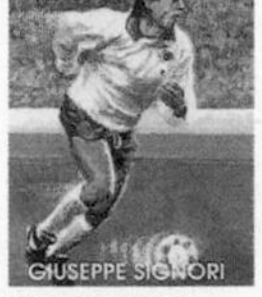

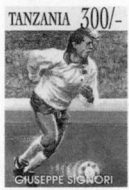

243 Giuseppe Signori (Italy)

1994. World Cup Football Championship, U.S.A. (2nd issue). Multicoloured.

1838	300s. Type **243**	1·00	1·00
1839	300s. Ruud Gullit (Netherlands)	1·00	1·00
1840	300s. Roberto Mancini (Italy)	1·00	1·00
1841	300s. Marco van Basten (Netherlands)	1·00	1·00
1842	300s. Dennis Bergkamp (Netherlands)	1·00	1·00
1843	300s. Oscar Ruggeri (Argentina)	1·00	1·00
1844	300s. Frank Rijkaard (Netherlands)	1·00	1·00
1845	300s. Peter Schmeichel (Denmark)	1·00	1·00
MS1846	100×70 mm. 1000s. World Cup trophy	4·00	4·50

See also Nos. 1892/8.

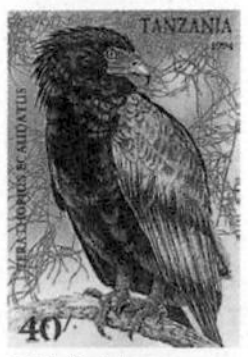

244 Bateleur

1994. Birds of Prey. Multicoloured.

1847	40s. Type **244**	65	40
1848	50s. Ornate hawk eagle	65	40
1849	100s. Osprey	85	60
1850	120s. Andean condor	85	65
1851	170s. African fish eagle (horiz)	1·00	90
1852	250s. King vulture	1·10	1·25
1853	400s. Peregrine falcon (horiz)	1·50	1·75
MS1854	90×90 mm. 500s. African white-backed vulture	2·25	2·50

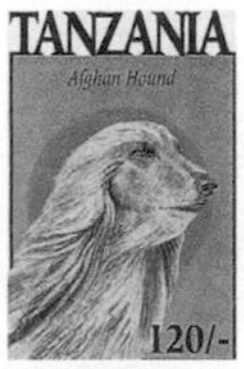

245 Afghan Hound

1994. Dogs of the World. Multicoloured.

1855/63	120s.×9 (Type **245**; Basenji; Siberian husky; Irish setter; Norwegian elkhound; Bracco Italiano; Australian cattle dog; German short-haired pointer; Rhodesian ridgeback)	5·00	5·50
1864/72	120s.×9 (Alsatian; Japanese chin; Shetland sheepdog; Italian spinone; Great dane; English setter; Welsh corgi; St. Bernard; Irish wolfhound)	5·00	5·50
1873/81	120s.×9 (Doberman pinscher; Chihuahua; Bloodhound; Keeshond; Tibetan spaniel; Japanese akita; Tervueren; Chow; Pharaoh hound)	5·00	5·50
1882/90	120s.×9 (Alaskan malamute; Scottish cairn terrier; American foxhound; British bulldog; Boston terrier; Borzoi; Shar pei; Saluki; Bernese mountain dog)	5·00	5·50
MS1891	Two sheets, each 76×106 mm. (a) 1000s. As No. 1856. (b) 1000s. As No. 1868 Set of 2 sheets	11·00	11·00

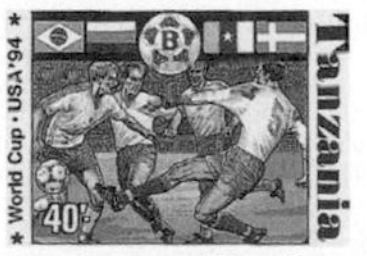

246 Players and Flags from Group B

1994. World Cup Football Championship, U.S.A. (3rd issue). Multicoloured.

1892	40s. Type **246**	45	45
1893	50s. Players and flags from Group C	50	50
1894	70s. Players and flags from Group D	60	60
1895	100s. Players and flags from Group E	65	65
1896	170s. Players and flags from Group A	90	90
1897	200s. Players and World Cup	1·10	1·10
1898	250s. Players and flags from Group F	1·40	1·40
MS1899	92×92 mm. 500s. Player heading ball	3·25	4·00

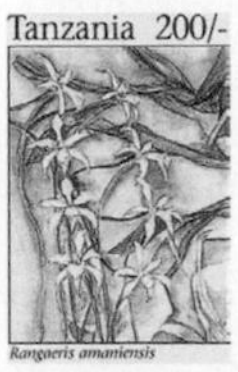

247 "Rangaeris amaniensis"

1994. Orchids. Multicoloured.

1900	200s. Type **247**	1·25	90
1901	200s. "Eulophia macowanii"	1·25	90
1902	200s. "Cytorchis arcuata"	1·25	90
1903	200s. "Centrostigma occultans"	1·25	90
1904	200s. "Cirrhopetalum umbellatum"	1·25	90
1905	200s. "Ansellia gigantea"	1·25	90
1906	200s. "Angraecum ramosum"	1·25	90
1907	200s. "Disa englerana"	1·25	90
1908	200s. "Nervilia stolziana"	1·25	90
1909	200s. "Satyrium orbiculare"	1·25	90
1910	200s. "Schizochilus sulphureus"	1·25	90
1911	200s. "Disa stolzii"	1·25	90
1912	200s. "Platycornye mediocris"	1·25	90
1913	200s. "Satyrium breve"	1·25	90
1914	200s. "Eulophia nuttii"	1·25	90
1915	200s. "Disa ornithantha"	1·25	90
MS1916	Two sheets, each 106×76 mm. (a) 1000s. "Phaius tankervilliae" (horiz). (b) 1000s. "Eulophia thomsonii" (horiz) Set of 2 sheets	8·00	8·50

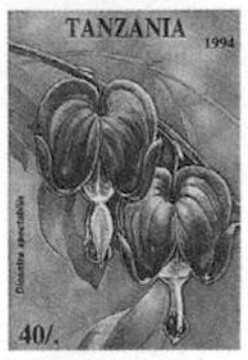

248 "Dicentra spectabilis"

1994. Flowers. Multicoloured.

1917	40s. Type **248**	25	30
1918	100s. "Thunbergia alata"	35	45
1919	120s. "Cyrtanthus minimiflorus"	35	50
1920	170s. "Nepenthes hybrida"	40	70
1921	250s. "Allamanda cathartica"	45	80
1922	300s. "Encyclia pentotis"	45	85
1923	400s. "Protea lacticolor"	50	90
MS1924	91×92 mm. 500s. Tradescantia	1·25	1·75

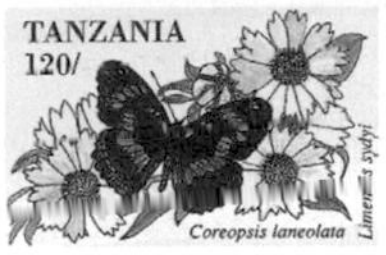

249 "Limenitis sydyi"

1994. Butterflies. Multicoloured.

1925	120s. Type **249**	70	70
1926	120s. "Agraulis vanillae"	70	70
1927	120s. "Danaus chrysippus"	70	70
1928	120s. "Eurytides marcellus"	70	70
1929	120s. "Artopoetes pryeri"	70	70
1930	120s. "Heliconius charitonius"	70	70
1931	120s. "Limenitis weidemeyerii"	70	70
1932	120s. "Phoebis sennae"	70	70
1933	120s. "Timelaea albescens"	70	70
1934	120s. "Papilio glaucus"	70	70
1935	120s. "Danaus plexippus"	70	70
1936	120s. "Papilio troilus"	70	70
1937	120s. "Hypolimnas antevorta"	70	70
1938	120s. "Cirrochroa imperatrix"	70	70
1939	120s. "Vanessa atalanta"	70	70
1940	120s. "Limenitis archippus"	70	70
1941	120s. "Hypolimnas pandarus"	70	70
1942	120s. "Anthocharis belia"	70	70
MS1943	Two sheets, each 101×70 mm. (a) 1000s. "Papilio polyxenes". (b) 1000s. "Vanessa cardui" Set of 2 sheets	8·50	9·00

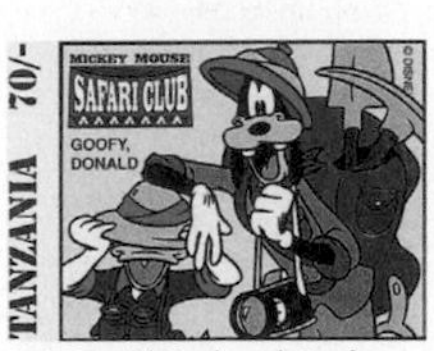

250 Donald Duck and Goofy with Safari Equipment

1994. Mickey Mouse Safari Club. Walt Disney Cartoon Characters on Safari. Multicoloured.

1944	70s. Type **250**	55	55
1945	70s. Donald and Mickey Mouse with leopard cubs	55	55
1946	100s. Donald photographing antelope	65	65
1947	100s. Donald between elephant's legs	65	65
1948	120s. Mickey with monkeys	70	70
1949	120s. Donald with hippopotamuses	70	70
1950	150s. Goofy carrying equipment	80	80
1951	150s. Mickey, Donald and Goofy sheltering under elephant's ears	80	80
1952	200s. Goofy with zebras	90	90

1953	200s. Donald, Goofy and Mickey with lion	90	90
1954	250s. Donald filming monkeys	1·00	1·00
1955	250s. Giraffe licking Mickey	1·00	1·00
MS1956	Three sheets, each 101×121 mm. (a) 1000s. Goofy in tree with camera (vert). (b) 1000s. Donald and Goofy with camera (vert). (c) 1000s. Donald and Mickey with camera (vert) Set of 3 sheets	11·00	12·00

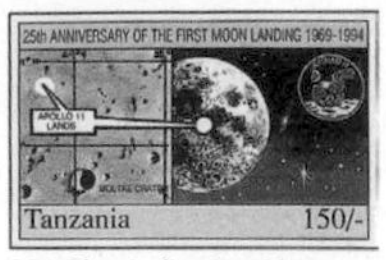

251 Plan indicating Moon Landing Point

1994. 25th Anniv of First Moon Landing. Multicoloured.

1957	150s. Type **251**	80	80
1958	150s. Photograph showing Sea of Tranquility	80	80
1959	150s. Lunar surface	80	80
1960	150s. Lift-off	80	80
1961	150s. Jettisoning first stage rocket	80	80
1962	150s. Jettisoning second stage rocket	80	80
1963	150s. Lunar module "Eagle" leaving command module	80	80
1964	150s. "Eagle" descending towards lunar surface	80	80
1965	150s. Armstrong and Aldrin (astronauts) inside "Eagle"	80	80
1966	150s. "Apollo 11" crew in space suits	80	80
1967	150s. "Eagle" on lunar surface	80	80
1968	150s. Armstrong descending to lunar surface	80	80
1969	150s. Astronaut, "Eagle" and experiment	80	80
1970	150s. Astronaut setting-up equipment	80	80
1971	150s. Reflection in astronaut's visor	80	80
1972	150s. Astronaut and U.S.A. flag	80	80
1973	150s. Astronaut carrying equipment	80	80
1974	150s. "Eagle" blasting off from Moon	80	80
1975	150s. Command module	80	80
1976	150s. "Eagle" leaving Moon	80	80
1977	150s. Capsule leaving Moon orbit	80	80
1978	150s. Capsule heading for Earth	80	80
1979	150s. Capsule re-entering Earth's atmosphere	80	80
1980	150s. Capsule in sea	80	80
1981	150s. Recovery crew opening hatch	80	80
1982	150s. Transferring astronauts by helicopter	80	80
1983	150s. Armstrong, Collins and Aldrin (astronauts) after recovery	80	80

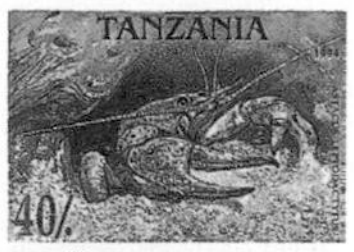

252 "Astacus leptodactytus"

1994. Crabs. Multicoloured.

1984	40s. Type **252**	20	30
1985	100s. "Eriocheir sinensis" (vert)	35	50
1986	120s. "Caneer opillo" (vert)	35	55
1987	170s. "Cardisoma quanhumi"	50	70
1988	250s. "Birgus latro" (vert)	65	85
1989	300s. "Menippe mercenaria"	65	90
1990	400s. "Dromia vulgaris" (vert)	75	95
MS1991	92×92 mm. 500s. Coral and crab's claw	1·60	2·00

1994. Centenary of International Olympic Committee. Gold Medal Winners. As T **285a** of St. Vincent. Multicoloured.

1992	350s. Kristin Otto (Germany) (50 metres freestyle swimming), 1988	1·00	1·00
1993	500s. Carl Lewis (U.S.A.) (various track and field events), 1984 and 1988	1·40	1·40
MS1994	74×104 mm. 1000s. Oksana Baiul (Ukraine) (figure skating), 1994	3·50	3·50

1994. 50th Anniv of D-Day (1st issue). As T **284b** of St. Vincent. Multicoloured.

1995	350s. Troops leaving landing craft	1·50	1·50
1996	600s. Amphibious tank and troops, Omaha Beach	2·00	2·00
MS1997	104×74 mm. 1000s. Loading landing craft in England	3·50	4·00

See also Nos. 1998/2016.

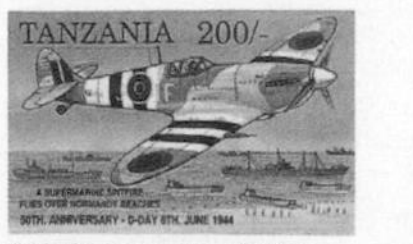

253 Supermarine Spitfire over Beaches

1994. 50th Anniv of D-Day (2nd issue). Multicoloured.

1998	200s. Type **253**	85	85
1999	200s. D.U.K.W.s landing on Gold Beach	85	85
2000	200s. Canadian troops landing on Juno Beach	85	85
2001	200s. Canadian cyclists disembarking, Juno Beach	85	85
2002	200s. Amphibious Sherman tank on beach	85	85
2003	200s. German gun emplacement	85	85
2004	200s. General Montgomery and British troops on beach	85	85
2005	200s. British engineers with AVRE Churchill tank, Gold Beach	85	85
2006	200s. U.S.S. "Thompson" (destroyer) being refuelled	85	85
2007	200s. H.M.S. "Warspite" (battleship)	85	85
2008	200s. Royal Marines on Juno Beach	85	85
2009	200s. Sherman Mark 1 flail tank leaving landing craft	85	85
2010	200s. General Eisenhower and U.S. troops on Omaha Beach	85	85
2011	200s. North American P-51 Mustang escorting ships	85	85
2012	200s. U.S. coastguard cutter alongside landing craft	85	85
2013	200s. U.S. troops in landing craft	85	85
2014	200s. U.S. troops landing on Omaha Beach	85	85
2015	200s. U.S. troops on Omaha Beach	85	85
MS2016	Two sheets, each 99×70 mm. (a) 1000s. U.S. marines amongst beach obstacles. (b) 1000s. U.S. troops landing on Utah Beach Set of 2 sheets	8·00	8·50

No. 2004 is inscribed "COMMANDER-IN-CHIEF" and No. 2010 "OPERATION OVERLOAD", both in error.

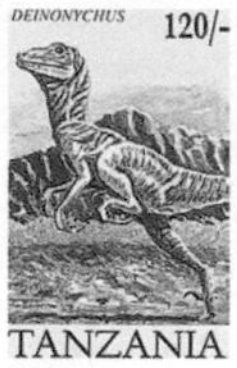

254 "Deinonychus"

1994. Prehistoric Animals.

2017/48	120s.×32 multicoloured	22·00	23·00
MS2049	80×110 mm. 1000s. multicoloured	4·50	5·00

DESIGNS—VERT: No. 2018, Styracosaurus; 2019, Anatosaurus; 2020, Plateosaurus; 2021, Iguanodon; 2022, Oviraptor; 2023, Dimorphodons; 2024, Ornithomimus; 2025, Lambeosaurus; 2026, Megalosaurus; 2027, Cetiosaurus; 2028, Hypsilophodon; 2029, Rhamphorynchus; 2030, Scelidosaurus; 2031, Antrodemus; 2032, Dimetrodon; **MS**2049, Brachiosaurus. HORIZ: No. 2033, Brontosaurus; 2034, Albertosaurus; 2035, Parasaurolophus; 2036, Pteranodons; 2037, Stegosaurus; 2038, Tyrannosaurus rex; 2039, Triceratops; 2040, Ornitholestes; 2041, Camarasaurus; 2042, Ankylosaurus; 2043, Trachodon; 2044, Allosaurus; 2045, Corythosaurus; 2046, Struthiomimus; 2047, Camptosaurus; 2048, Heterodontosaurus.

Nos. 2017/32 and 2033/48 respectively were printed together, se-tenant, Nos. 2033/48 forming a composite design.

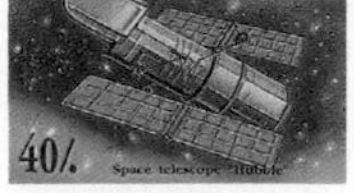

255 "Hubble" Space Telescope

1994. Space Research. Multicoloured.

2050	40s. Type **255**	20	30
2051	100s. "Mariner"	35	50
2052	120s. "Voyager 2"	40	55
2053	170s. "Work Package-03"	50	70
2054	250s. Orbiting solar observer	70	85
2055	300s. "Magellan"	70	90
2056	400s. "Galilei"	80	95
MS2057	91×91 mm. 500s. "Fobos"	1·90	2·25

It is understood that the following issues were freely available for postal purposes from Tanzanian post offices. Further issues, for which evidence of normal postal use cannot be found, could be obtained from the Philatelic Bureau in Dar-es-Salaam. Such issues will be found in the Appendix.

1995. No. 906 surch **70/-**.

2058	70s. on 13s. on 13s. Teacher with blackboard	3·00	1·00

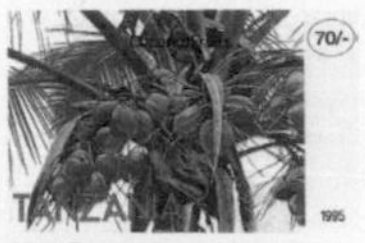

257 Coconuts

1995. Fruit. Multicoloured.

2059	70s. Type **257**	75	25
2060	100s. Pineapple	95	50
2061	150s. Pawpaw	1·40	1·50
2062	200s. Tomatoes	1·75	2·00
MS2063	91×91 mm. 500s. Type **257**	3·25	3·50

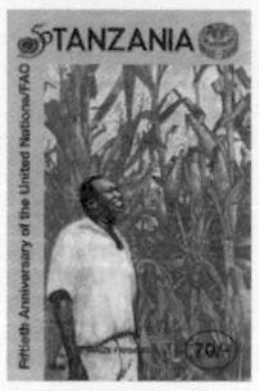

258 Farmer and Maize Crop

1995. 50th Anniv of United Nations and Food and Agriculture Organization. Multicoloured designs (except No. **MS**2068).

2064	70s. Type **258**	50	25
2065	100s. Ploughing with ox team (horiz)	65	40
2066	150s. Women in spinning mill (horiz)	90	1·25
2067	200s. Child drawing	1·25	1·60
MS2068	101×97 mm. 500s. U.N. 50th anniv logo (horiz) (black and blue)	3·00	3·75

1995. No. 810 surch **100/-**.

2069	100s. on 40s. on 40s. Lesser flamingo	3·00	1·00

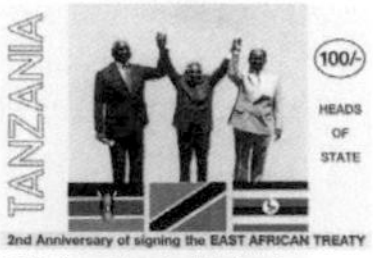

260 Presidents Mwinyi (Tanzania), Moi (Kenya) and Museveni (Uganda)

1995. Second Anniversary of East African Treaty. Multicoloured.

2070	100s. Type **260**	60	25
2071	150s. Map of East Africa and national flags (vert)	2·75	1·50
2072	180s. Cotton boll (vert)	1·50	1·75
2073	200s. Fishermen on Lake Victoria	1·75	2·00
MS2074	100×102 mm. 500s. Type **260**	3·50	4·00

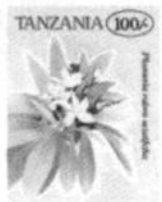

261 *Plumeria rubra acutifolia*

1996. Flowers. Multicoloured

(a) Without imprint date

2075	100s. Type **261**	35	15
2076	140s. *Lilaceae* (different)	50	25
2077	180s. *Alamanda*	60	25
2078	200s. *Lilaceae*	70	30
2079	210s. *Zinnia*	70	40
2080	260s. *Malvaviscus penduliflorus*	85	45
2081	300s. *Cannai*	1·00	50
2082	380s. *Nerium oleander carneum*	1·25	1·00
2083	400s. *Hibiscus rosa sinensis*	1·75	1·75
2084	600s. *Catharanthus roseus*	1·75	1·75
2085	700s. *Bougainvillea formosa*	2·00	2·25
2086	750s. *Acalypha*	2·00	2·25
MS2087	88×112 mm. 125s. ×4 in designs of 210, 300, 380 and 700s. (each 31×36 mm)	4·00	4·50

(b) With 1997 imprint date.

2088	150s. As 140s.	75	25
2088a	350s. As 210s.	1·25	90
2088b	400s. As 400s.	1·25	1·10
2088e	500s. As 600s.	1·10	1·25

Nos. 2081 and **MS**2087 are inscribed "Carna", both in error.

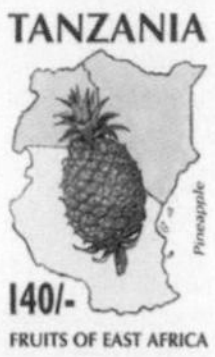

262 Pineapple

1996. East African Fruit. Multicoloured.

2089	140s. Type **262**	80	40
2090	180s. Orange and limes	1·00	90
2091	200s. Pear and apples	1·40	1·50
2092	300s. Bananas	2·00	2·25
MS2093	92×92 mm. 300s. No. 2092	2·75	3·00

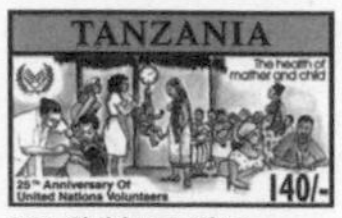

263 Children's Clinic

1996. 25th Anniv of U.N. Volunteers. Multicoloured.

2094	140s. Type **263**	1·25	40
2095	200s. Food distribution	1·50	1·00
2096	260s. Clean water supply	1·75	2·00
2097	300s. Public education	2·00	2·50
MS2098	95×95 mm. 500s. Refugee camp	4·75	5·00

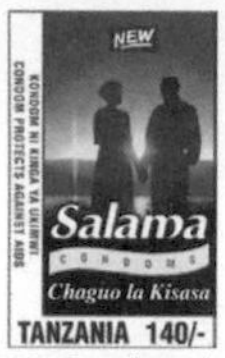

264 Couple and Setting Sun

1996. World Aids Day. Multicoloured.

2099	140s. Type **264**	1·50	45
2100	310s. People from various occupations (horiz)	2·25	2·25
2101	370s. Discussion group (horiz)	2·50	2·50
2102	410s. Orphans with foster mother (horiz)	2·75	2·75
MS2103	95×95 mm. 500s. Type **264**	5·00	5·00

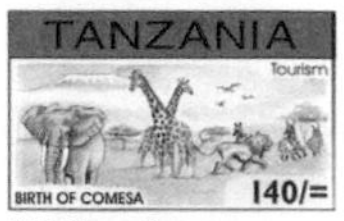

265 Game Reserve

1996. Second Anniv of Common Market for Eastern and Southern Africa (COMESA). Multicoloured.

2104	140s. Type **265**	2·00	60
2105	180s. Fishermen in canoe	1·50	1·00
2106	200s. Container ship at Dar-es-Salaam docks	2·25	1·75
2107	300s. Goods train on Tazara railway	4·00	3·50
MS2108	90×90 mm. 500s. Cotton bolls	4·25	5·00

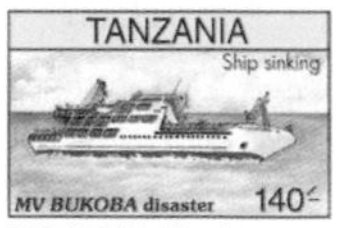

266 *Bukoba* (ferry) sinking

1997. First Anniv of Sinking of Bukoba (ferry). Multicoloured.

2109	140s. Type **266**	75	40
2110	350s. Recovering bodies from wreck	1·60	1·75
2111	370s. Identifying victims	1·75	2·00
2112	410s. Religious service for victims	1·90	2·25
MS2113	90×90 mm. 500s. *Bukoba* (ferry)	3·00	3·50

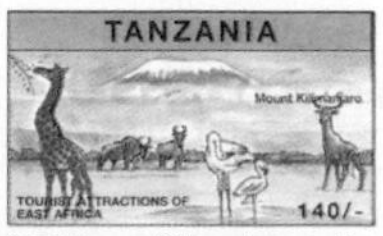

267 Mount Kilimanjaro and Animals

1997. Tourist Attractions. Multicoloured.

2114	140s. Type **267**	1·50	40
2115	310s. Members of the Masai tribe	1·75	2·00
2116	370s. Old Stone Town, Zanzibar	1·90	2·25
2117	410s. Buffalo on Ruaha Plains	2·25	2·50
MS2118	87×87 mm. 500s. Mount Kilimanjaro and elephant	3·00	3·50

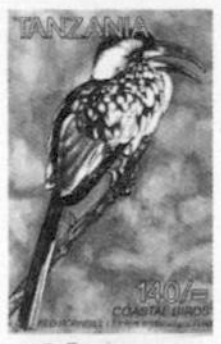

268 Red Hornbill

1997. Coastal Birds. Multicoloured.

2119	140s. Type **268**	1·25	50
2120	350s. Sacred ibis (horiz)	2·25	2·00
2121	370s. Gulls (horiz)	2·50	2·25
2122	410s. Ring-necked dove (horiz)	2·75	2·50
MS2123	90×90 mm. 500s. Red hornbill, sacred ibis, gulls and ring-necked dove	2·50	3·00

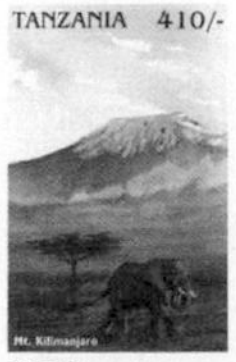

269 Mount Kilimanjaro and Elephant

1997

2124	**269** 410s. multicoloured	2·00	1·90

1998. Nos. 805/6 and 808 surch **150/-**.

2125	150s. on 9s. African emerald cuckoo	1·50	45
2126	150s. on 13s. Little bee eater	1·50	1·25
2127	150s. on 20s. Bateleur	2·50	2·50

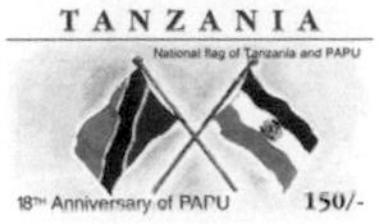

271 Tanzania and P.A.P.U. Flags

1998. 18th Anniv of Pan African Postal Union. Multicoloured.

2128	150s. Type **271**	3·50	3·00
2129	250s. P.A.P.U. logo	2·50	1·50
2130	400s. Postman making E.M.S. delivery	[illegible]	[illegible]
2131	500s. Two giraffes	2·50	1·50

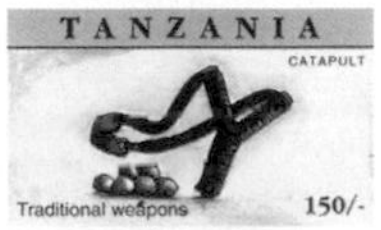

272 Catapult

1998. Traditional Weapons. Multicoloured.

2132	150s. Type **272**	1·00	45
2133	250s. Cutlass and club	1·40	1·10
2134	400s. Rifle and ammunition	1·90	2·00
2135	500s. Bow and arrows	2·25	2·50

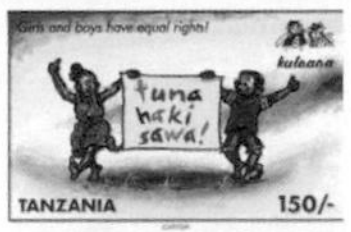

273 Children carrying Banner

1998. Children's Rights in Tanzania (1st series). Multicoloured.

2136	150s. Type **273**	80	40
2137	250s. Teacher with children	1·10	90
2138	400s. Adult with stick and child (vert)	1·75	1·90
2139	500s. Child hugging adult (vert)	2·00	2·25
MS2140	90×90 mm. 500s. As 250s.	2·00	2·25

See also Nos. 2428/**MS**2432.

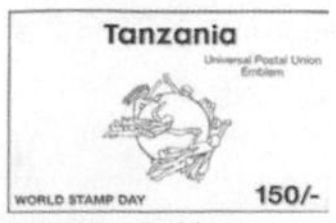

274 U.P.U. Emblem

1998. World Stamp Day. Multicoloured.

2141	150s. Type **274**	80	40
2142	250s. Cancelling mail	1·10	90
2143	400s. Dove carrying air mail letter	1·75	1·90
2144	500s. Woman posting letter	2·00	2·25
MS2145	90×90 mm. 500s. Woman posting letter, dove and U.P.U. emblem	2·00	2·25

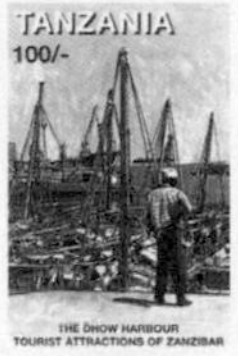

275 The Dhow Harbour

1998. Tourist Attractions of Zanzibar. Multicoloured.

2146	100s. Type **275**	55	20
2147	150s. Girl on giant tortoise in countryside	80	40
2148	250s. Children with giant tortoise (horiz)	1·10	90
2149	300s. Stone Town street	1·40	1·40
2150	400s. The Old Fort (horiz)	1·75	1·90
2151	500s. Red colobus monkeys (horiz)	2·00	2·25
MS2152	70×100 mm. 600s. Girl on giant tortoise in Stone Town street	2·25	2·50

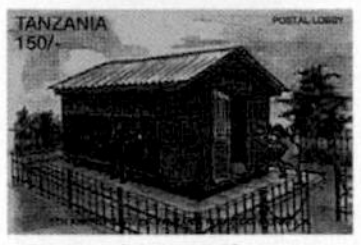

276 Local Post Office

1999. Fifth Anniv of Tanzania Posts Corporation. Multicoloured.

2153	150s. Type **276**	80	40
2154	250s. Post collection van	1·25	90
2155	350s. Counter services	1·60	1·75
2156	400s. Retail facilities	1·75	1·90
MS2157	76×117 mm. 500s. Headquarters (vert)	2·00	2·25

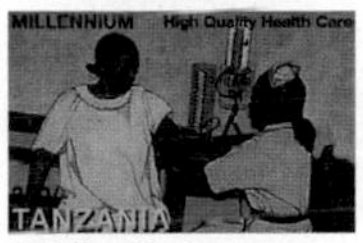

277 Blood Pressure Monitoring

1999. Millennium. Improvement in Living Standards. Multicoloured.

2158	350s. Type **277**	1·75	1·00
2159	400s. Children playing	1·75	1·10
2160	700s. Maize farming	3·25	3·75
2161	750s. Collecting clean water	3·25	3·75
MS2162	70×101 mm. 1500s. Ostriches (Tourism) (vert)	7·00	7·50

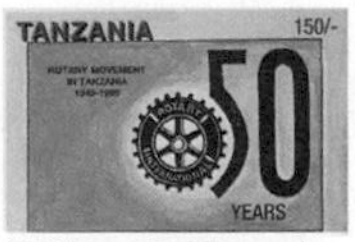

278 Rotary Emblem and "50"

1999. 50th Anniv of Rotary Club of Dar-es-Salaam. Multicoloured.

2163	150s. Type **278**	70	40
2164	250s. Giving child polio plus vaccine (vert)	90	75
2165	350s. Paul Harris (Rotary founder) (vert)	1·25	1·75
2166	400s. Women collecting clean drinking water from tap (vert)	1·50	2·25
MS2167	70×100 mm. 500s. Rotary emblem and "50" (vert)	2·00	2·75

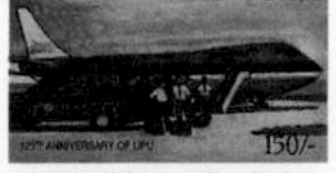

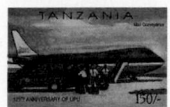

279 Mail being loaded onto Aeroplane

1999. 125th Anniv of Universal Postal Union. Multicoloured.

2168	150s. Type **279**	90	40
2169	300s. Children writing letters	1·25	1·00
2170	350s. UPU members committee meeting	1·40	1·60
2171	400s. Express Mail Service co-ordination	1·60	2·25
MS2172	90×90 mm. 500s. UPU logo	2·00	2·75

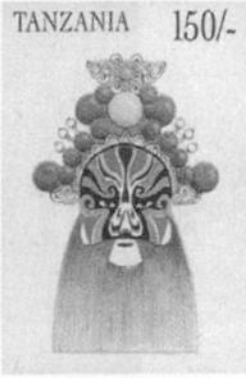

279a Mask

1999. Masks. Multicoloured.

2172a	150s. Type **279a**	70	35
2172b	250s. Mask with blue, red and white face	1·00	75
2172c	300s. Mask with red, black, brown and orange face	1·25	1·25
2172d	350s. Mask with black and white face and rouged cheeks	1·40	1·75
MS2172e	70×100 mm. 1500s. Firebird (two dancers)	4·75	5·50

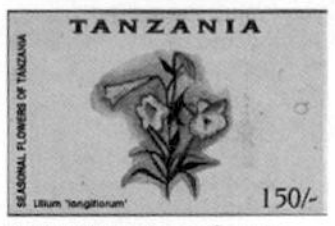

280 *Lilium longiflorum* (cool season)

1999. Seasonal Flowers. Multicoloured.

2173	150s. Type **280**	1·00	50
2174	250s. *Strelitzia reginae* (summer)	1·50	1·10
2175	400s. *Zantedeschia* (cool season)	2·00	2·00
2176	500s. Iris apollo (dry season)	2·25	2·50
MS2177	97×90 mm. 600s. As No. 2175	3·00	3·25

No. 2176 is inscribed "Ilis" in error.

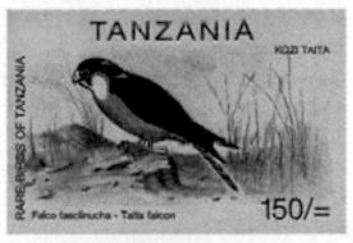

281 Taita Falcon

1999. Birds. Multicoloured.

2178	150s. Type **281**	1·50	55
2179	300s. Banded green sunbird	2·25	1·75
2180	400s. Spotted ground thrush	[illegible]	[illegible]
2181	500s. Fischer's turaco	3·00	3·00
MS2182	90×90 mm. 600s. Blue swallow	3·50	3·50

Nos. 2182and **MS**2183 are inscribed "Taulaco Fisheri" or "atrokaerulea", both in error.

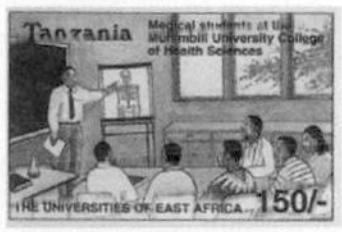

282 Medical Students, Muhimbili University, Tanzania

2000. Universities of East Africa. Multicoloured.

2183	150s. Type **282**	1·00	40
2184	200s. Students outside Zanzibar University	1·25	55
2185	600s. Makerere University, Uganda (vert)	2·50	2·75
2186	800s. Egerton university, Kenya	3·00	3·50
MS2187	87×87 mm. 500s. Inter University Council for East Africa emblem (84×82 mm)	2·75	3·25

2000. No. 813 surch **200/-**.

2188	200s. on 170s. Saddle-billed stork	1·75	65

2000. No. 815 surch **800/-**.

2189	800s. on 500s. Ostrich	4·00	3·50

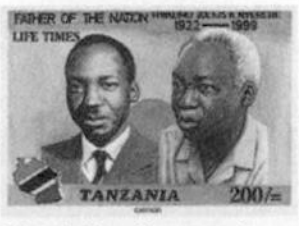

285 Julius Nyerere in Youth and Old Age

2000. Julius Nyerere (first president of Tanzania, 1962–85) Commemoration. Multicoloured.

2190	200s. Type **285**	90	45
2191	500s. With Edward Sakoine, Prime Minister	2·00	2·25
2192	600s. Nyerere (in close-up) (vert)	2·25	2·50
2193	800s. Wearing Mgolore, local cloth (vert)	2·50	2·75
MS2194	90×90 mm. 1000s. Nyerere's Mausoleum	3·25	4·50

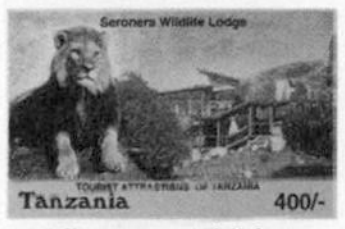

286 Seronera Wildlife Lodge, Serengeti and Lion

2000. Tourist Attractions of Tanzania. Multicoloured.

2195	400s. Type **286**	1·75	1·50
2196	400s. Lake Manyara National Park and elephant	1·75	1·50
2197	400s. Ngorongoro Crater, Wildlife Lodge and rhinoceros	1·75	1·50
2198	400s. Lobo Wildlife Lodge and giraffes	1·75	1·50
2199	400s. Kibo, the central cone of Kilimanjaro, and elephants	1·75	1·50
2200	400s. Fish off Mafia Island	1·75	1·50
2201	400s. Selous Game Reserve and wild dogs	1·75	1·50
2202	400s. Mikumi National Park and elephant	1·75	1·50
2203	500s. Seronera Wildlife Lodge, Serengeti and lion	1·75	1·60
2204	500s. Lake Manyara National Park and elephant	1·75	1·60
2205	500s. Ngorongoro Crater, Wildlife Lodge and rhinoceros	1·75	1·60
2206	500s. Lobo Wildlife Lodge and giraffes	1·75	1·60
2207	500s. Kibo, the central cone of Kilimanjaro, and elephants	1·75	1·60
2208	500s. Fish off Mafia Island	1·75	1·60
2209	500s. Selous Game Reserve and wild dogs	1·75	1·60
2210	500s. Mikumi National Park and elephant	1·75	1·60
2211	600s. Seronera Wildlife Lodge, Serengeti and lion	2·00	1·75
2212	600s. Lake Manyara National Park and elephant	2·00	1·75
2213	600s. Ngorongoro Crater, Wildlife Lodge and rhinoceros	2·00	1·75
2214	600s. Lobo Wildlife Lodge and giraffes	2·00	1·75
2215	600s. Kibo, the central cone of Kilimanjaro, and elephants	2·00	1·75
2216	600s. Fish off Mafia Island	2·00	1·75
2217	600s. Selous Game Reserve and wild dogs	2·00	1·75
2218	600s. Mikumi National Park and elephant	2·00	1·75
2219	800s. Seronera Wildlife Lodge, Serengeti and lion	2·25	2·00
2220	800s. Lake Manyara National Park and elephant	2·25	2·00
2221	800s. Ngorongoro Crater, Wildlife Lodge and rhinoceros	2·25	2·00
2222	800s. Lobo Wildlife Lodge and giraffes	2·25	2·00
2223	800s. Kibo, the central cone of Kilimanjaro, and elephants	2·25	2·00
2224	800s. Fish off Mafia Island	2·25	2·00
2225	800s. Selous Game Reserve and wild dogs	2·25	2·00
2226	800s. Mikumi National Park and elephant	2·25	2·00
MS2227	90×90 mm. 1000s. Lion, giraffes, elephant, rhinoceros and Kilimanjaro (vert)	3·75	3·50

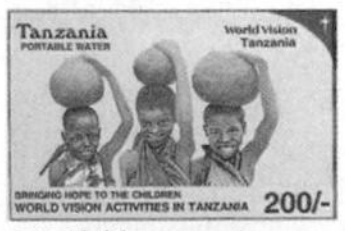

287 Children carrying Water Pots on their Heads

2000. Work of World Vision (aid organization) in Tanzania (1st series). Multicoloured.

2228	200s. Type **287**	80	40
2229	600s. Family making bread	2·00	1·75
2230	800s. Nurse weighing baby at clinic	2·25	2·50
2231	1000s. Children reading	2·50	2·75
MS2232	90×90 mm. 500s. Boy and girl	2·00	2·50

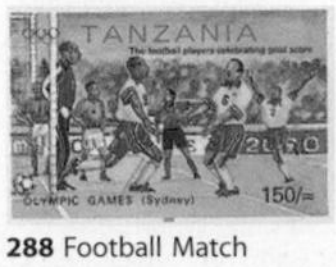

288 Football Match

2000. Olympic Games, Sydney. Multicoloured.

2233	150s. Type **288**	80	40
2234	350s. Basketball game (vert)	2·00	1·50
2235	400s. Athletics race (vert)	2·00	1·75
2236	800s. Boxing match	3·25	3·50
MS2237	90×90 mm. 500s. Presentation of medals (vert)	2·00	2·50

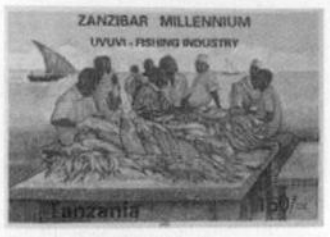

289 Gutting Fish

2000. Zanzibar Millennium. Multicoloured.

2238	150s. Type **289**	1·00	40
2239	200s. Tortoises, baskets of bread and logo	1·40	60
2240	400s. Boy and "Kukuza Hadhi ya Elimu na Uchumi Zanzibar" inscription (vert)	2·25	1·75
2241	800s. Girl studying and university graduates (vert)	3·75	5·00
MS2242	90×90 mm. 500s. Map and trophy (vert)	3·25	3·50

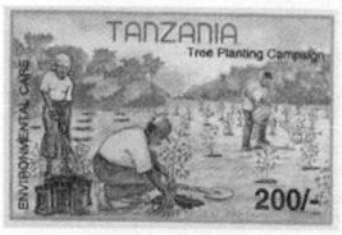

290 Planting Trees

2000. Environmental Protection. Multicoloured.

2243	200s. Type **290**	80	40
2244	400s. Forest stream	1·75	1·25
2245	600s. Maintenance of sewage works	2·00	2·50
2246	800s. River and forest	2·50	3·25
MS2247	90×90 mm. 1000s. Mt. Kilimanjaro	2·75	3·50

2000. No. 808 and 813 surch **230/-**.

2248	230s. on 170s. Bateleur	2·50	1·00
2248a	230s. on 170s. Saddle-billed stork	1·50	65

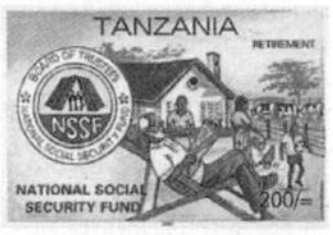

292 Old Man in Deckchair (Retirement)

2000. National Social Security Fund. Multicoloured.

2249	200s. Type **292**	80	40
2250	350s. Factory worker with eye injury (Employment injury)	1·50	1·00
2251	600s. Man holding prosthetic leg (Invalidity)	2·25	2·75
2252	800s. Mother and baby with nurse (Health insurance)	2·75	3·50
MS2253	90×90 mm. 500s. Pregnant woman (Maternity)	2·00	2·50

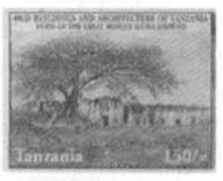

293 Ruins of the Great Mosque, Kilwa Kisiwani

2000. Old Buildings and Architecture of Tanzania. Multicoloured.

2254	150s. Type **293**	60	30
2255	200s. German Boma (fort), Mikindani, Mtwara	75	35
2256	250s. German Boma, Bagamoyo	80	40
2257	300s. Butiama Museum, Mara	90	50
2258	350s. Chief Government Chemist's Offices	95	55
2259	400s. The Old Post Office, Dar es Salaam	1·10	70
2260	500s. Dr. Livingstone's Tembe Lodge, Kwihara, Tabora	1·25	1·00
2261	600s. Original Governor's Palace and State House, Dar es Salaam (vert)	1·50	1·40
2262	700s. Traditional Houses of the Ngoni-Nyamwezi	1·60	1·60
2263	800s. Palace of Beit Elajaib, Stonetown, Zanzibar	1·75	2·00
2264	900s. Tongoni ruins, Tanga	2·00	2·50
2265	1000s. Karimjee Hall, Dar es Salaam	2·25	2·50
MS2266	100×100 mm. 1500s. The Old Boma, Mikindani, Southern Tanzania	3·75	5·00

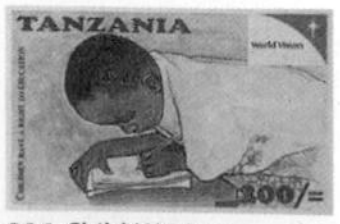

294 Child Writing

2001. Work of World Vision (aid organization) in Tanzania (2nd series). Multicoloured.

2267	200s. Type **294**	1·00	40
2268	600s. Children laughing	2·25	2·00
2269	800s. Child carrying bananas (vert)	2·50	3·00
2270	1000s. Child wearing grey t-shirt (vert)	2·75	3·50
MS2270a	90×90 mm. 500s. Children lying on grass	2·25	2·75

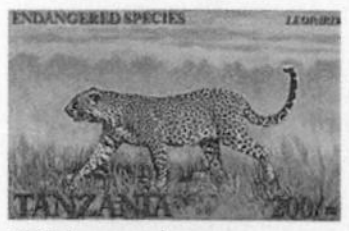

295 Leopard

2001. Endangered Species. Multicoloured.

2271	200s. Type **295**	1·00	50
2272	400s. Rhinoceros	2·75	1·75
2273	600s. Crocodile	2·75	2·75
2274	800s. Wild dogs	3·00	3·75
MS2275	90×90 mm. 600s. Cheetah	3·50	3·75

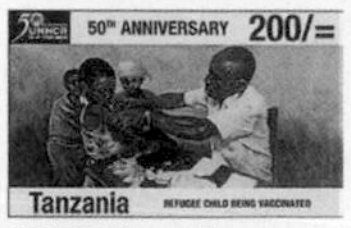

296 Child receiving Vaccination

2001. 50th Anniv of United Nations High Commission for Refugees. Multicoloured.

2276	200s. Type **296**	1·00	40
2277	400s. Refugees in boat on Lake Tanganyika	1·75	1·00
2278	600s. Female refugee (vert)	2·25	2·50
2279	800s. Refugees with possessions on bike	2·50	3·00
MS2280	90×90 mm. 600s. As No. 2278	2·25	3·00

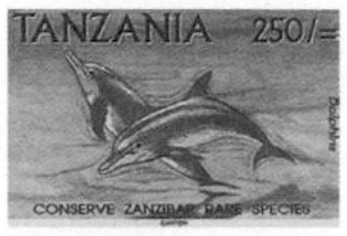

297 Dolphins

2001. Rare Species of Zanzibar. Multicoloured.

2281	250s. Type **297**	1·25	50
2282	300s. Coral plants	1·40	80
2283	450s. Coral reefs	1·90	1·90
2284	800s. Red colobus monkey (vert)	3·25	3·50
MS2285	90×90 mm. 700s. Colobus monkeys	3·50	3·75

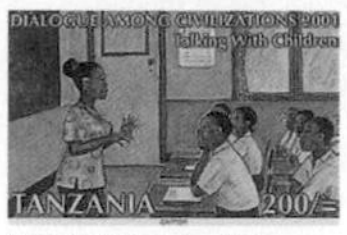

298 Children in Class

2001. United Nations Dialogue among Civilisations. Multicoloured.

2286	200s. Type **298**	80	40
2287	400s. People in different dress	1·25	90
2288	600s. Discussion group	2·00	2·50
2289	800s. Couple writing letters	2·25	2·75
MS2290	90×90 mm. 700s. Letter and handshake spanning globe (vert)	2·50	3·25

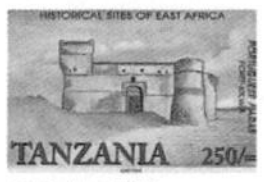

299 Fort Kilwa, Tanzania

2001. Historic Sites of East Africa. Multicoloured.

2291	250s. Type **299**	1·00	45
2292	300s. Ruins of Maruhubi Palace, Zanzibar	1·25	65
2293	400s. Old Provincial Office, Nairobi, Kenya (1913)	1·60	1·25
2294	800s. Mparu Tombs, Hoima, Uganda	3·00	3·75
MS2295	90×90 mm. 700s. Map of East Africa with sailing ship	4·25	4·50

2001. No. 808 surch.

2295a	230s. on 20s. Bateleur	8·00	6·00

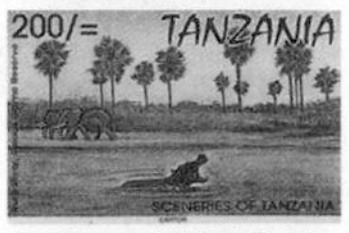

300 Hippo in River Rufiji, Selous Game Reserve

2001. Scenery of Tanzania. Multicoloured.

2296	200s. Type **300**	1·25	50
2297	400s. Mangapwani Beach, Zanzibar	1·50	1·00
2298	600s. Zebra and Mountains, Mikumi National Park	2·50	2·75
2299	800s. Balancing stones, Lake Victoria Mwanza (vert)	3·00	3·50
MS2300	90×90 mm. 700s. Giraffes, Ruaha National Park (vert)	5·00	5·00

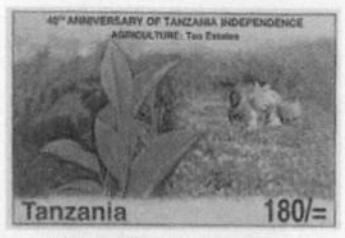

301 Tea Plantation

2001. 40th Anniv of Independence. Multicoloured.

2301	180s. Type **301**	80	30
2302	230s. Tanzania, Uganda and Kenya flags with triple handshake (vert)	2·25	1·00
2303	350s. University graduates (vert)	1·50	1·00
2304	450s. Lion, leopard, buffalo, rhinoceros, elephant and Mt. Kilimanjaro	3·75	2·25
2305	650s. Operating theatre	3·00	3·50
2306	950s. Minerals	5·50	6·50
MS2307	92×92 mm. 1000s. As 450s.	7·50	7·50

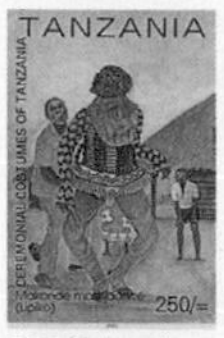

302 Makonde Masked Dancer

2002. Ceremonial Costumes. Multicoloured.

2308	250s. Type **302**	1·50	50
2309	350s. Mwaka Koga Festival dancers (Zanzibar)	1·75	1·00
2310	400s. Lizombe dancer	1·75	1·75
2311	450s. Zaramo bridal celebration	2·00	2·25
MS2312	90×90 mm. 500s. As No. 2299	2·50	3·00

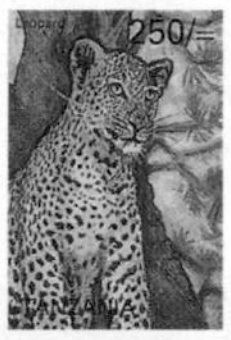

303 Leopard

2002. Animals of the National Parks. Sheet 105×150 mm containing T **303** and similar vert designs. Multicoloured.

MS2313	250s. Type **303**; 250s. Elephant; 250s. Rhinoceros; 250s. Lion; 250s. Buffalo	8·00	8·50

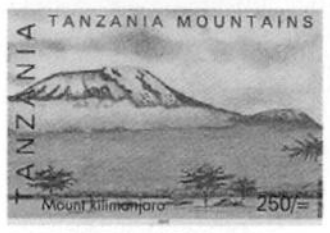

304 Mount Kilimanjaro

2002. International Year of Mountains. Multicoloured.

2314	250s. Type **304**	1·25	50
2315	350s. Usambara Mountains	1·50	1·00
2316	400s. Uluguru Mountains	1·75	1·50
2317	450s. Mwanihara Peak (Udzungwa Mountains)	1·90	2·25
MS2318	90×90 mm. 500s. As Type **303**	2·25	2·75

2002. No. 2077 surch **250/=**.

2319	250s. on 180s. Alamanda	1·25	65

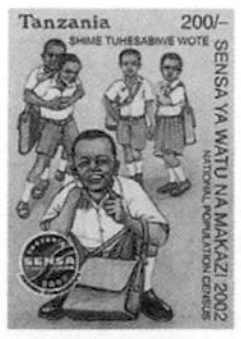

306 School Children

2002. National Population Census. Multicoloured.

2320	200s. Type **306**	90	40
2321	250s. Group of people (horiz)	95	45
2322	350s. Family (horiz)	1·10	70
2323	600s. Boy with emblem and statistics (horiz)	1·90	3·00

2002. No. 810 surch **250/=**.

2325	250s. on 40s. Lesser flamingo	1·25	65

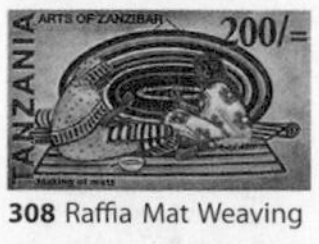

308 Raffia Mat Weaving

2002. Zanzibar Arts and Crafts. Multicoloured.

2326	200s. Type **308**	80	65
2327	250s. Sewing caps	90	65
2328	350s. Making chair	1·25	1·10
2329	600s. Henna tattoos	1·40	1·75
MS2330	90×90 mm. 800s. Carved wooden door	3·00	4·00

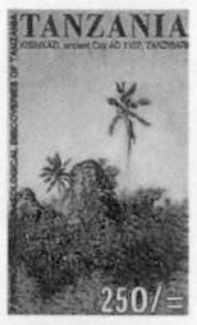

309 Ancient City of Kisimkazi, Zanzibar

2002. Paintings and Archaeology. Multicoloured.

2331	250s. Type **309**	1·25	50
2332	400s. Remains of Kaole Town, Bagamoyo (horiz)	1·75	1·25
2333	450s. Kondoa Irangi rock paintings	2·00	2·00
2334	600s. Great Mosque, Kilwa Kisiwani (horiz)	3·25	4·00
MS2335	90×90 mm. 1000s. As No. 2332	3·50	4·00

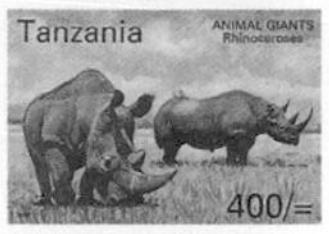

310 Rhinoceros

2003. The Big Five. Multicoloured.

2336	400s. Type **310**	2·00	1·25
2337	500s. Elephant	2·25	1·75
2338	600s. Lion	2·25	2·00
2339	800s. Leopard (vert)	2·75	3·25
2340	1000s. Buffalo	3·25	4·00
MS2341	85×115 mm. 1500m. The Big Five. Imperf	7·00	8·00

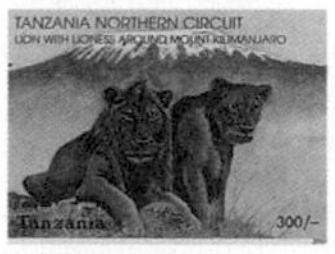

311 Lions

2003. Tourism. "The Northern Circuit". Multicoloured.

2342	300s. Type **311**	1·50	70
2343	350s. Mt. Kilimanjaro	1·50	80
2344	400s. Zebras	2·00	1·25
2345	500s. Elephants	2·50	1·75
2346	600s. Leopards	2·50	2·75
2347	800s. Rhinoceros	4·50	5·50
MS2348	97×75 mm. 1000s. Buffalo	4·00	5·00

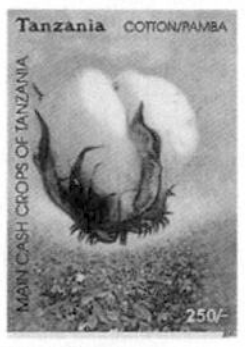

312 Cotton

2003. Cash Crops. Multicoloured.

2349	250s. Type **312**	80	40
2350	300s. Cashew nuts	90	50
2351	600s. Sisal	1·75	2·00
2352	800s. Cloves	2·50	3·75
MS2353	99×81 mm. 1000s. Tea (horiz)	4·00	4·50

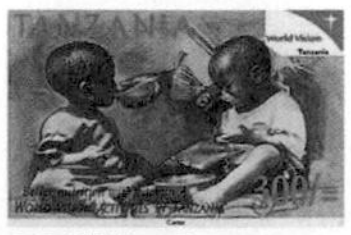

313 Children Eating

2003. Work of World Vision (aid organization) in Tanzania (3rd series). Multicoloured.

2354	300s. Type **313**	90	50
2355	600s. Children at school	1·75	2·00
2356	800s. Pumping water into bucket (vert)	2·25	2·75
2357	1000s. Distributing mosquito nets	2·50	3·25
MS2358	90×90 mm. 500s. Three children in ceremonial robes with microphone	2·00	2·50

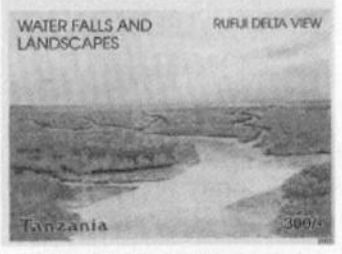

314 Rufiji Delta View

2003. Waterfalls and Landscapes. Multicoloured.

2359	300s. Type **314**	1·25	50

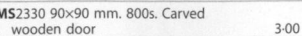

2360	400s. Shore line of Zanzibar coast	1·50	1·00
2361	500s. Riftvalley View (Lake Manyara)	1·75	1·75
2362	800s. Kalambo Falls (vert)	2·50	3·25
MS2363 105×87 mm. 1000s. Mangroves of coast		3·00	3·50

315 Nyamwezi Dance, Tabora

2003. Traditional Dances of East Africa. Multicoloured.

2364	300s. Type **315**	90	45
2365	500s. Luo dance, Kisumu	1·40	1·00
2366	600s. Pemba dance, Zanzibar	1·50	1·75
2367	800s. Baganda dance, Kampala	2·25	3·25
MS2368 99×81 mm. 1000s. Masai dance, Arusha		2·50	3·25

316 The Old Fort

2003. Sceneries of Zanzibar. Multicoloured.

2369	300s. Type **316**	1·00	50
2370	500s. Carved wooden door, Beit al Ajaib (vert)	1·40	1·25
2371	600s. Palm trees, Michamvi beach (vert)	1·50	1·75
2372	800s. Dhow, Beit al Ajaib	2·25	3·25
MS2373 95×149 mm. Nos. 2369 and 2371/2		4·50	5·50

317 Common Dolphin

2003. Marine Mammals. Multicoloured.

2374	300s. Type **317**	1·25	50
2375	350s. Sperm whale	2·00	1·25
2376	400s. Southern right whale	2·25	1·75
2377	600s. Dugong dugon	2·75	3·50
MS2378 105×71 mm. 300s. Bottlenose dolphin		2·25	2·50

318 Prayer on Hija (Tawaf)

2003. Religious Festivals. Multicoloured.

2379	300s. Type **318**	1·00	50
2380	500s. Choir at Christmas time	1·40	1·00
2381	600s. Birthday memorial of Prophet Muhammad (Maulid)	1·50	1·75
2382	800s. Christmas Day prayers	2·00	3·00
MS2383 90×90 mm. 1000s. Crucifixion		2·50	3·25

319 People working at Computer Terminals

2004. Tenth Anniv of Posts Corporation. Multicoloured.

2384	350s. Type **319**	1·00	45
2385	400s. Overnight mail van	2·00	1·50
2386	600s. Employees participating in meeting	2·00	2·25
2387	800s. EMS postal services mapped on globe	3·00	3·75
MS2388 130×98 mm. Nos. 2384/7		7·25	8·00
MS2389 90×90 mm. 1000s. Post Cargo lorry		4·50	4·75

320 Exchanging Money

2004. Western Union Money Transfer. Multicoloured.

2390	300s. Type **320**	1·00	40
2391	400s. Busalanga primary school	1·50	85
2392	500s. Mother and child with money (vert)	1·75	1·60
2393	600s. Globe inside emblem	2·00	2·25

MS2394 89×75 mm. 800s. As Type **320** but without Swahili inscription and Western Union emblem		2·50	3·00

Nos. 2390/MS2394 show "2003" inscription date.

321 Guides demonstrating Environmentally Friendly Cooker

2004. 75th Anniv of Girl Guides. Multicoloured.

2395	300s. Type **321**	1·00	45
2396	400s. Camp training	1·25	1·00
2397	600s. Bravery training	1·90	2·25
2398	800s. Guides assisting at Mother and Child clinic	2·50	3·50
MS2399 105×85 mm. 1000s. As No. 2397		2·75	3·50

Nos. 2395/MS2399 show "2003" inscription date.

322 Overland Vehicle

2004. 40th Anniv of Tanganyika Christian Refugee Service. Multicoloured.

2400	350s. Type **322**	90	45
2401	600s. Drawing fresh water	1·75	1·50
2402	800s. Children in school	2·25	2·50
2403	1000s. Planting saplings	2·50	3·00
MS2404 85×74 mm. 1200s. Combination of designs of Nos. 2400/3 (45×35 mm)		3·00	3·50

323 Cheering for Peddle Winners

2004. Dhow Events in Zanzibar. Multicoloured.

2405	350s. Type **323**	1·00	50
2406	400s. Punting race	1·10	75
2407	600s. Dhow race	1·75	2·00
2408	800s. Sail boat race	2·25	2·75
MS2409 91×90 mm. 1000s. Dhow (vert)		3·00	3·50
MS2409a 130×101 mm. Nos. 2405/8		6·00	6·00

324 Williamson Diamond Mine, Mwadui

2004. Mining. Multicoloured.

2410	350s. Type **324**	1·75	65
2411	500s. Semi processed jewels	2·25	1·50
2412	600s. Drillers	2·50	2·50
2413	800s. Small scale gold miners	4·00	4·25
MS2414 130×100 mm. Nos. 2416/19		9·50	9·50
MS2415 90×90 mm. 600s. Unprocessed gemstones		3·25	3·25

325 Removing Water Hyacinth, Mwanza City

2004. 24th Anniv of the Southern African Development Community. Multicoloured.

2416	350s. Type **325**	1·00	50
2417	500s. Irrigation of maize, Mbayali District, Mbeya	1·40	1·25
2418	600s. Paddy fields at Igomelo irrigation scheme	1·75	2·00
2419	800s. Installing pipes in new borehole, Mbeya Rural (vert)	2·25	3·00
MS2420 130×100 mm. Nos. 2410/13		5·75	6·25
MS2421 90×90 mm. 1000s. Men working in maize fields		3·00	3·50

326 Mwalimu Julius Kambarage Nyerere (facilitator in Burundi Peace negotiations)

2004. Law and Peace. Multicoloured.

2422	350s. Type **326**	1·00	45
2423	500s. Burundi returnees at Frontier Reception facility	1·40	1·25
2424	600s. Nelson Mandela and Pres. Benjamin W Mkapa	1·75	2·00
2425	800s. Presidents Yoweri Museveni of Uganda, Benjamin W Mkapa, and Domitien Ndayizeye of Burundi	2·25	3·00
MS2426 130×100 mm. Nos. 2422/5		5·75	6·25
MS2427 90×90 mm. 600s. Arusha International Conference Centre		1·90	2·25

2004. Nos. 2075, 2255 and 2079 surch.

2427a	350s. on 100s. Type **261**	2·50	1·25
2427b	350s. on 200s. German boma (fort), Mikindani, Mtwara	2·50	1·25
2427c	350s. on 210s. Zinnia	2·50	1·25

327 Family sitting outside House

2004. Children's Rights (2nd series). Multicoloured.

2428	350s. Type **327**	1·00	1·00
2429	350s. Teachers and student around table	1·00	1·00
2430	400s. Classroom scene	1·10	1·00
2431	500s. Students and child outside house	1·25	1·40
MS2432 90×90 mm. 1000s. As No. 2431		3·00	3·50

328 Mwalimu Julius Kambarage Nyerere

2005. Centenary of Rotary International. Multicoloured.

2433	350s. Type **328**	1·00	45
2434	500s. Emblems (vert)	1·25	80
2435	600s. Immunising child	1·75	2·00
2436	600s. Environmental project	1·75	2·00
2437	600s. Self reliance to the handicapped	1·75	2·00
2438	600s. Basic agriculture project (vert)	1·75	2·00
2439	600s. Jaipur Foot project	1·75	2·00
2440	600s. Malaria project	1·75	2·00
2441	600s. Eradication of River Blindness project	1·75	2·00
2442	800s. Map of East Africa (vert)	3·00	3·25
MS2443 44×59 mm. 1000s. Rotary emblem (vert)		3·25	3·75

329 Lionesses

2005. Safari Circuits. Multicoloured.

2444	350s. Type **329**	1·50	55
2445	500s. Cheetahs (horiz)	1·75	1·00
2446	600s. Red colobus monkey	2·00	2·00
2447	600s. Elephants (horiz)	2·25	2·25
2448	600s. Rhinoceroses (horiz)	2·25	2·25
2449	600s. Giraffes (horiz)	2·25	2·25
2450	600s. Crocodile (horiz)	2·25	2·25
2451	600s. Chimpanzees (horiz)	2·25	2·25
2452	600s. Buffaloes (horiz)	2·25	2·25
2453	800s. Zebras (horiz)	2·75	3·00
MS2454 90×90 mm. 1000s. Leopard (horiz); 1000s. Wild hunting dogs (horiz)		7·00	8·00

330 Baron Godefroy de Blonay

2005. Olympic Games, Athens (2004). Multicoloured.

2455	350s. Type **330**	1·00	80
2456	350s. Wrestling (horiz)	1·00	80
2457	500s. Medal, 1928	1·40	1·25
2458	1000s. Javelin throw (Grecian sculpture)	2·75	4·00

331 Map of Allied Invasion

2005. 60th Anniv of D-Day. Multicoloured.

MS2459 149×138 mm. 600s.×6, Type **331**; General Dwight D. Eisenhower; US troops landing at Omaha Beach; British Mosquitos; Fleet Admiral Ernest J. King; General George C. Marshall		11·00	11·00
MS2460 98×69 mm. 2500s. Battle at Green Beach, Normandy		8·00	8·50

332 West Side Lumber Company 3 Truck Shay

2005. Bicentenary of Steam Locomotives. Multicoloured.

MS2461 151×104 mm. 1000s.×4, Type **331**; LK & P Saddle tanker; Double headed C&T; Baldwin 4-6-0		10·00	11·00
MS2462 100×69 mm. 2500s. Union Pacific locomotive on Heber Valley railroad		7·50	8·00

333 Franco Baresi (Italy)

2005. Centenary of FIFA (Fédération Internationale de Football Association). Multicoloured.

MS2463 193×96 mm. 1000s.×4, Type **333**; Daniel Passarella (Argentina); Miroslav Klose (Germany); Michel Platini (France)		9·00	9·50
MS2464 107×86 mm. 2500s. Gianfranco Zola (Italy)		6·50	7·00

334 Pope John Paul II as Child and Mother, Emilia Kaczorowska

2005. Pope John Paul II Commemoration. Sheet, 94×117 mm, containing T **334** and similar horiz designs. Multicoloured.

MS2465 1000s.×4, Type **334**; Visit to Poland; With Pres. George W. Bush; Visit to Armenia		11·00	11·00

335 "Mathias Sandorf"

2005. Death Centenary of Jules Verne (writer).

MS2466 Five sheets, each 98×148 mm. (a) 800s.×4, multicoloured; multicoloured; multicoloured. (b) 800s.×4, multicoloured; multicoloured; multicoloured. (c) 800s.×4, multicoloured; blue, lilac and lemon; green, lilac and lemon. (d) 800s.×4, blue and lemon; lilac and lemon; and lemon; multicoloured. (e) 800s.×4, multicoloured; multicoloured; multicoloured; multicoloured

	27·00	32·00

MS2467 Five sheets. (a) 68×98 mm. 2000l. multicoloured. (b) 68×98 mm. 2000l. multicoloured. (c) 68×98 mm. 2000l. blue; lemon and violet. (d) 70×101 mm. 2000l. multicoloured. (e) 70×102 mm. 2000s. multicoloured

	20·00	23·00

DESIGNS: No. **MS**2467a, Type **334**; "The Steam House, The Demon of Cawnpore"; "Hector Servadac, The Career of a Comet"; "An Antarctic Mystery". No. **MS**2467b, "The Archipelago on Fire"; "The Vanished Diamond"; "Mistress Branican"; "The Castle of the Carpathians". No. **MS**2467c, "Around the World in Eighty Days"; "Dr. Ox's Experiment"; "The Purchase of the North Pole"; "Adrift in the Pacific". No. **MS**2467d, "Invasion of the Sea"; "The Floating Island"; "A Floating City"; "Dick Sands, Boy Captain". **MS**2467e, "Voyages Extraordinaires"; "Twenty Thousand Leagues under the Sea"; "A Floating City"; "Three Englishmen and Three Russians in South Africa". No. **MS**2468a "The Mysterious Island". No. **MS**24681b "Around the World in Eighty Days". No. **MS**2481c "The Invasion of the Sea". No. **MS**2468d "Five Weeks in a Balloon". **MS**2468e, "The Adventures of a Chinaman".

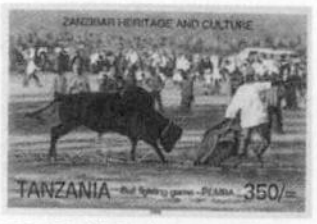

336 Bull Fighting

2005. Zanzibar Heritage and Culture. Multicoloured.

2468	350s. Type **336**	1·00	50
2469	400s. A narrow street, Stone Town (vert)	1·25	75
2470	600s. Buibui (outdoor traditional dress) (vert)	1·75	2·00
2471	600s. House of Wonders, Beit-al-Ajaib	1·75	2·00
2472	600s. Local Taarabu musicians	1·75	2·00
2473	600s. Fishing	1·75	2·00
2474	600s. Coconut tree	1·75	2·00
2475	600s. Khanga (indoor traditional dress)	1·75	2·00
2476	600s. Old museum building	1·75	2·00
2477	800s. Clove harvesting, Pemba Island	2·25	2·50
MS2478	90×90 mm. 500s. Modern power boat, Pemba Island	1·75	2·00

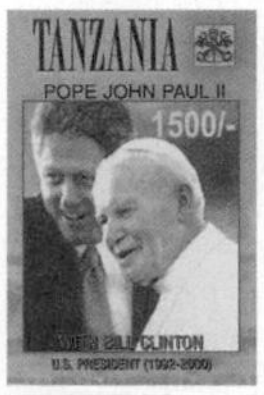

337 Pope John Paul II with Pres. Bill Clinton

2005. Pope John Paul II Commemoration.

2479	**337**	1500s. multicoloured	5·00	5·00

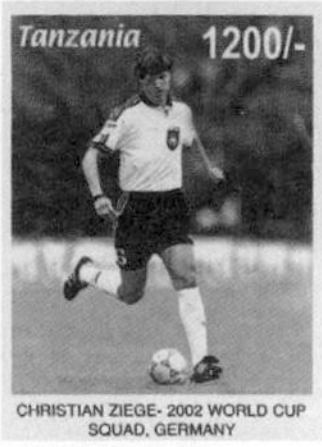

338 Christian Ziege

2005. 75th Anniv of First World Cup Football Championship, Uruguay. German Players. Multicoloured.

2480	1200s. Type **338**	2·75	3·25
2481	1200s. Marko Rehmer	2·75	3·25
2482	1200s. Jens Nowotny	2·75	3·25
MS2483	123×106 mm. 2500s. Rudi Voller	6·50	7·50

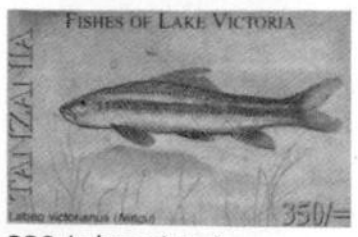

339 *Labeo victorianus*

2005. Fish of Lake Victoria. Multicoloured.

2484	350s. Type **339**	1·25	55
2485	350s. *Haplochromis sharpsnout*	1·25	1·25
2486	350s. *Haplochromis chilotes*	1·25	1·25
2487	350s. *Mormyrus kannume*	1·25	1·25
2488	350s. *Clarias gariepinus*	1·25	1·25
2489	350s. *Synodontis afrofischeri*	1·25	1·25
2490	350s. *Protopterus aethiopicius*	1·25	1·25
2491	400s. *Lates niloticus*	1·50	1·00
2492	600s. *Pundamilia nyererei*	2·25	2·00
2493	800s. *Brycinus sadleri*	3·00	3·25
MS2494	90×90 mm. 500s. *Oreochromis niloticus*	1·75	2·00

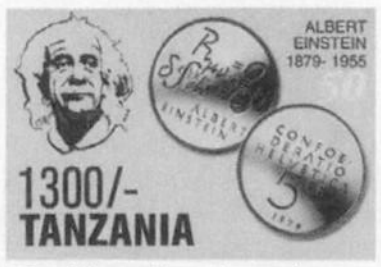

340 Albert Einstein and Commemorative Coins

2005. 50th Death Anniv of Albert Einstein (physicist). Multicoloured.

2495	1300s. Type **340**	4·00	4·00
2496	1300s. On the cover of *Time* magazine	4·00	4·00
2497	1300s. On early Israel stamp	4·00	4·00
MS2498	90×55 mm. 2500s. With hands clasped and inscription	8·00	8·50

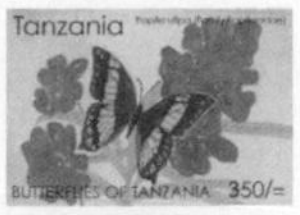

341 *Papilio ufipa*

2005. Butterflies of Tanzania. Multicoloured.

2499	350s. Type **341**	1·75	55
2500	500s. *Mylothris sagala mahale*	2·00	1·10
2501	600s. Type **341**	2·50	2·50
2502	600s. *Amauris tartarea tukuyuensis*	2·50	2·50
2503	600s. *Euphaedra neophron kiellandi*	2·50	2·50
2504	600s. *Charaxes lucyae gabriellae*	2·50	2·50
2505	600s. *Abisara zanzibarica*	2·50	2·50
2506	600s. *Acrae utengulensis*	2·50	2·50
2507	800s. As No. 2504	3·00	3·25
MS2508	90×90 mm. 500s. *Charaxes usambarae maridadi*	2·50	2·75

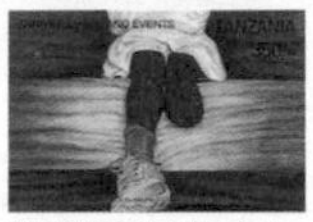

342 "Diabetes leads to Amputation" (World Diabetes Day)

2005. Anniversaries and Events. Multicoloured.

2509	350s. Type **342**	1·25	50
2510	500s. Voters queuing at polling station (General Election)	1·25	1·00
2511	600s. Pope John Paul II on arrival in Tanzania, 1990	2·75	2·25
2512	600s. Presidents J. K. Nyerere (Tanganyika) and Abeid Aman Kurume (Zanzibar) signing Act of Union, 1964	2·75	2·75
2513	600s. Woman casting vote (General Election)	2·75	2·75
2514	600s. Pope John Paul II greeted by former Pres. and Mrs. Nyerere, 1990	2·75	2·75
2515	600s. Pope John Paul II and Laurean Cardinal Rugambwa, 1990	2·75	2·75
2516	600s. Majimaji Museum, Songea (Cent of Majimaji rebellion)	2·75	2·75
2517	600s. Pres. B. W. Mkapa burning arms after ceasefire, 2001	2·75	2·75
2518	800s. Pope John Paul II, Pres. Mwinyi and Laurean Cardinal Rugambwa, 1990	3·50	3·50
MS2519	90×90 mm. 500s. Majimaji Monument (Cent of Majimaji rebellion) (vert)	1·75	2·00

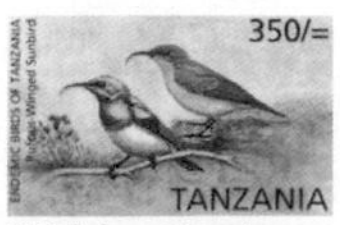

343 Rufous-winged Sunbird

2006. Endemic Birds of Tanzania. Multicoloured.

2520	350s. Type **343**	1·25	50
2521	500s. Pemba white-eye	1·75	1·00
2522	600s. Kilombero weaver	2·00	1·50
2523	600s. Pemba scops owl	2·25	2·25
2524	600s. Spike-heeled lark	2·25	2·25
2525	600s. Pemba green pigeon	2·25	2·25
2526	600s. Uluguru bush-shrike	2·25	2·25
2527	600s. Yellow collared love bird	2·25	2·25
2528	600s. Usambara nightjar	2·25	2·25
2529	800s. Usambara eagle owl	3·00	3·00
MS MS2530	121×82 mm. 500s. Moreau's sunbird (39×51 mm)	1·90	2·00

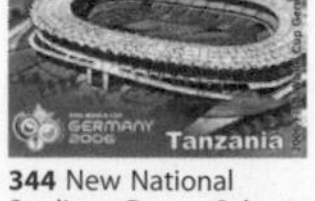

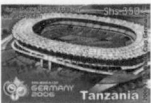

344 New National Stadium, Dar es Salaam

2006. World Cup Football Championship, Germany. Multicoloured.

2531	350s. Type **344**	80	65
2532	500s. Map of Africa with national flags and World Cup emblem (vert)	1·25	90
2533	600s. Pres. Kikwete unveiling World Cup trophy in Dar es Salaam	1·25	1·40
2534	800s. Official mascot (vert)	1·75	2·00
MS2535	93×72 mm. Nos. 2531/4	4·75	5·50
MS2536	85×58 mm. 600s. World Cup trophy	1·60	1·75

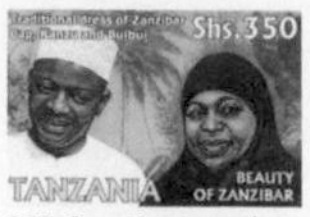

345 Cap, Kanzu and Buibui (traditional dress)

2006. Beauty of Zanzibar. Multicoloured.

2537	350s. Type **345**	80	65
2538	500s. Zanzibar Museum	1·25	90
2539	600s. Maruhubi Palace ruins	1·25	1·10
2540	600s. Green turtle, Mnemba Island	1·25	1·50
2541	600s. Red colobus monkey	6·75	8·00
2542	600s. Giant tortoise, Changgu Island	1·25	1·50
2543	600s. Zanzibar sunset	1·25	1·50
2544	600s. Dhow sailing near Matemwe	1·25	1·50
2545	600s. Coconut crab, Chumbe Island	1·25	1·50
2546	800s. Climbing a coconut tree	1·75	2·25
MS MS2547	61×103 mm. 500s. Clove foliage with flowerbuds enlarged (vert); 500s. Light Signal Tower (vert)	2·50	3·00

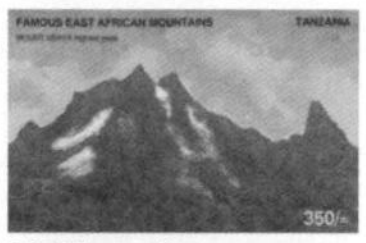

346 Mount Kenya

2006. Famous East African Mountains. Multicoloured.

2548	350s. Type **346**	80	65
2549	400s. Udzungwa Mountains	90	80
2550	600s. Sanje Falls, Udzungwa Mountains (vert)	1·50	1·75
2551	800s. Ruwenzori Range, Uganda	2·00	2·50
MS2552	Two sheets, each 130×100 mm. (a) 1000s. Kibo Summit and Mawenzi, Mount Kilimanjaro; 1000s. Giraffe and Mount Kilimanjaro. (b) 1000s. Herdsman with cattle and Ol Doinyo Lengai; 1000s. Summit and crater, Ol Doinyo Lengai (vert)	11·00	12·00

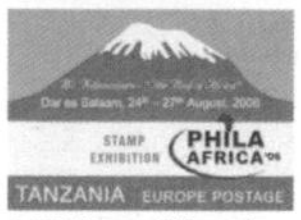

347 Mount Kilimanjaro

2006. Phila Africa 06 Stamp Exhibition, Dar-es-Salaam.

2553	**347**	(EUROPE POSTAGE) multicoloured	1·75	1·75
MS2554		100×100 mm. **347** 600s. multicoloured (49×34 mm)	1·75	2·00

2006. 30th Anniv of TAZARA Railways. As T **243** of Zambia. Multicoloured.

2555	350s. Map, signatories, Victoria Falls and Mount Kilimanjaro	1·50	1·50
2556	350s. Kenneth Kaunda (Zambian President) and Julius Nyerere (Tanzanian Prime Minister) at inauguration, 1975	1·50	1·50
2557	600s. TAZARA Headquarters, Dar-es-Salaam, Tanzania	2·00	2·00
2558	600s. New Kapiri Mposhi railway station	2·00	2·00
2559	800s. Train on viaduct	2·25	2·25
2560	800s. Train on river bridge	2·25	2·25

Stamps in similar designs were issued by Zambia.

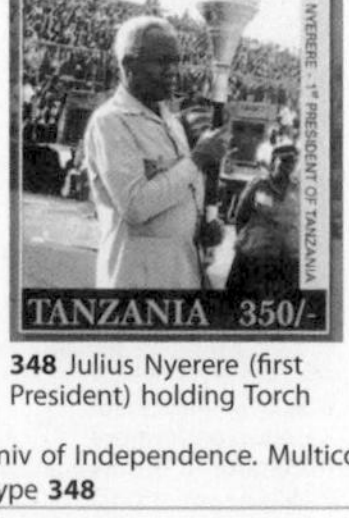

348 Julius Nyerere (first President) holding Torch

2006. 45th Anniv of Independence. Multicoloured.

2561	350s. Type **348**	80	65
2562	400s. University of Dar-es-Salaam (horiz)	90	75
2563	600s. Abeid A. Karume (first Vice President) (green border)	1·40	1·10
2564	600s. Rashidi Mfaume Kawawa (second Prime Minister)	1·40	1·60
2565	600s. Julius Nyerere	1·40	1·60
2566	600s. As No. 2563 but white border	1·40	1·60
2567	600s. Ali Hassan Mwinyi (second President)	1·40	1·60
2568	600s. Benjamin W. Mkapa (third President)	1·40	1·60
2569	600s. Jakaya Mrisho Kikwete (President)	1·40	1·60
2570	800s. Julius Nyerere wearing white hat	1·75	2·00
MS2571	90×110 mm. 400s. National Uhuru Monument, Arusha	1·40	1·60

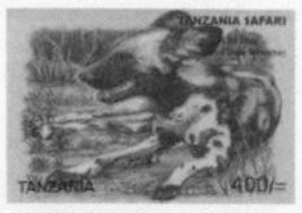

349 Wild Dog (Selous Game Reserve)

2007. Tanzania Safari. Multicoloured.

2572	400s. Type **349**	1·25	75
2573	600s. Warthog with young	1·75	1·50
2574	700s. Two zebras	2·25	2·00
2575	700s. Elephant	2·50	2·50
2576	700s. Cheetah (wrongly inscr 'Leopard Panthera pardus')	2·50	2·50
2577	700s. Leopard hiding in foliage (69×49 mm)	2·50	2·50
2578	700s. Two buffaloes	2·50	2·50
2579	700s. Lion and lioness	2·50	2·50
2580	800s. Two monkeys with young	2·50	2·50
MS2581	90×90 mm. 1000s. Two lionesses (49×34 mm)	3·00	3·50

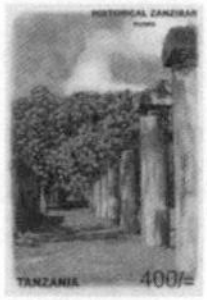

350 Ruins

2007. Historical Zanzibar. Multicoloured.

2582	400s. Type **350**	1·00	75
2583	600s. Coral reef fish (horiz)	1·40	1·10
2584	700s. Bet el Ajaib and cloves	1·50	1·50
2585	700s. Beach (horiz)	1·50	1·75
2586	700s. Kizimbani Persian Bath (horiz)	1·50	1·75
2587	700s. Maruhubi ruins (horiz)	1·50	1·75
2588	700s. Livingstone House (horiz)	1·50	1·75
2589	700s. The Old Dispensary (horiz)	1·50	1·75
2590	700s. Cave (horiz)	1·50	1·75
2591	800s. Coral formation (horiz)	1·60	1·75
MS2592	90×90 mm. 700s. Colobus monkey	1·75	2·00

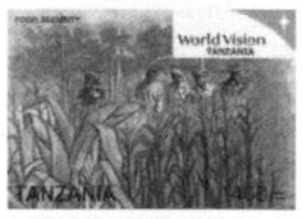

351 Crops ('Food Security')

2007. Work of World Vision (aid organization) in Tanzania (3rd series). Multicoloured.

2593	400s. Type **351**	1·00	75
2594	600s. Woman milking goat ('Income Generation and Nutrition')	1·40	1·25
2595	700s. Schoolgirls ('Advocating for Child and Rights')	1·50	1·50
2596	800s. Immunization	1·60	1·75
2597	1000s. Children in class ('Education for Development')	2·25	2·75
MS2598	90×90 mm. 400s. Type **351**	1·25	1·50
MS2599	100×130 mm. 700s.×3 No. 2595; As Nos. 2596/7	3·75	3·00

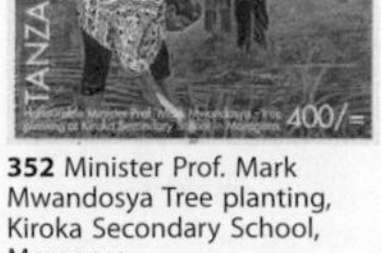

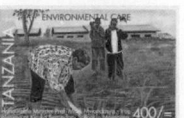

352 Minister Prof. Mark Mwandosya Tree planting, Kiroka Secondary School, Morogoro

2007. Environmental Care. Multicoloured.

2600	400s. Type **352**	1·25	75
2601	400s. Illegal mining causing land degradation and water pollution, Amani Nature Reserve, Tanga	1·50	1·50

2602	400s. Planting tree seedlings in degraded area, Morogoro	1·50	1·50
2603	400s. Planted trees growing in degraded area	1·50	1·50
2604	400s. Traditional soil and moisture conservation method	1·50	1·50
2605	400s. Tree seedlings	1·50	1·50
2606	400s. Soil erosion caused by agriculture on steep mountains	1·50	1·50
2607	500s. Indigenous fallow lands maintaining soil fertility, Shinyanga	1·25	1·25
2608	700s. Kihansi Waterfalls (habitat of endemic toad *Nectophrynoides aspergini*s)	2·25	2·50
2609	800s. Natural regeneration of forest area	2·50	2·75
MS2610	90×90 mm. 500s. Nguru Mountains catchment area for clean water	1·75	2·00

353 'Let us talk with our children about AIDS'

2007. AIDS Prevention Campaign. Multicoloured.

2611	400s. Type **353**	1·50	75
2612	700s. 'Be faithful in your marriage'	2·25	1·75
2613	800s. 'Fight against AIDS is our duty'	2·50	2·25
2614	1000s. 'Examine your health to be free'	3·00	3·50
MS2615	90×90 mm. 400s. 'world aids campaign' and emblem	2·00	2·00
MS2616	100×130 mm. 400s.×4 'Let us get education about AIDS'; 'Prevent yourself from new infection'; 'Let us sing to stop AIDS'; 'Let us not segregate the people with AIDS'	6·00	6·00

354 Children at Zanzibar Madrasa Resource Centre

2007. Golden Jubilee of the Aga Khan. Multicoloured.

2617	400s. Type **354**	1·25	75
2618	600s. Facade of Aga Khan Hospital, Dar es Salaam (gold border)	1·60	1·25
2619	600s. Facade of Stone Town Cultural Centre, Zanzibar	1·60	1·75
2620	600s. Balcony and window, Stone Town Cultural Centre, Zanzibar	1·60	1·75
2621	600s. Doctors with patient, Aga Khan Hospital, Dar es Salaam	1·60	1·75
2622	600s. As No. 2609 (white border)	1·60	1·75
2623	700s. Serena Safari Lodge, Lake Manyara	1·75	1·90
2624	800s. Serena Inn, Zanzibar	1·90	2·00
MS2625	90×90 mm. 1000s. Woman at Zanzibar Madrasa Resource Centre (vert)	2·50	3·00

355 Hehe Tribesman, Iringa

2007. Ceremonial Costumes. Multicoloured.

2626	400s. Type **355**	1·25	75
2627	600s. Haya girls wearing bark cloth	1·60	1·25
2628	700s. Msewe dancers, Pemba (horiz)	1·75	1·75
2629	700s. Maasai girls	1·75	1·75
2630	700s. Maasai dancing	1·75	1·75
2631	700s. Singida Nyaturu girl	1·75	1·75
2632	700s. Sambaa tribesman	1·75	1·75
2633	700s. Wabena woman grinding maize	1·75	1·75
2634	700s. Wairaq man and woman wearing leather	1·75	1·75
2635	800s. Wabena tribal ceremony	1·90	1·90
MS2636	90×90 mm. 400s. Wanyaturu girls	1·40	1·50

356 People of Tanzania

2007. Anti-Corruption Campaign. Multicoloured.

2637	400s. Type **356**	1·25	75
2638	400s. PCB emblem (yellow background)	1·75	2·00
2639	500s. Policeman and prisoner	2·00	1·50
2640	600s. Bus driver and policeman	4·00	4·25
2641	700s. Businessman on puppet strings (vert)	2·00	2·25
2642	800s. Official refusing bribe	2·25	2·50
MS2643	As No. 2638 (bistre background)	1·25	1·40

357 Wildebeest and Zebras grazing

2008. Animals. Multicoloured.

2644	400s. Type **357**	1·50	75
2645	600s. Lion and lioness (vert)	2·00	1·75
2646	700s. Lioness descending from tree, Manyara (vert)	2·00	2·00
2647	800s. Giraffes (vert)	3·00	3·50
MS2648	110×150 mm. 600s.×6 Leopard descending from tree (vert); Young chimpanzee (vert); Lioness resting on tree (vert); Adult male chimpanzee (vert); Cheetah with antelope kill; Baboons	11·00	13·00
MS2649	70×140 mm. 600s.×2 Leopard with cub; Impala	3·75	4·25

358 Basketball

2008. Olympic Games, Beijing. Multicoloured.

2650	700s. Type **358**	2·75	2·75
2651	700s. Marathon	2·75	2·75
2652	700s. Swimming	2·75	2·75
2653	700s. Javelin throw	2·75	2·75

359 Nutmeg

2008. Spices of Zanzibar. Multicoloured.

2654	400s. Type **359**	1·25	75
2655	600s. Picking cloves	1·75	1·25
2656	700s. Drying cloves (vert)	1·90	1·75
2657	1000s. Cardamom seeds	2·75	4·00
MS2658	116×115 mm. 600s.×6 Growing cardamom; Vanilla; Ginger; Mdalasini; Black pepper; Paprika	10·00	12·00
MS2659	101×101 mm. 600s. Binzari	1·90	2·25

360 Turtle

2008. Marine Parks of Tanzania. Multicoloured.

2660	400s. Type **360**	1·25	75
2661	600s. Dugongs	1·75	1·25
2662	700s. Octopus	1·90	1·75
2663	1000s. Whale shark	2·75	4·00
MS2664	150×140 mm. 600s.×6 Lizard fish; Moray eel; Turtle (facing right); Clear lion fish; Anemone fish; Coelacanth (all 42×32 mm)	12·00	14·00
MS2665	120×80 mm. 600s. Pair of seahorses (35×50 mm)	1·90	2·25

361 Kitulo National Park

2008. Botanical Gardens of Tanzania. Multicoloured.

2666	400s. Type **361**	1·25	75

2667	600s. Butterfly and chameleon in Amani Forest	2·00	1·50
2668	700s. Monkey and waterfall in Udzungwa Mountains Forest	2·00	2·00
2669	1000s. Forest in Saadani National Park	2·75	4·00
MS2670	127×77 mm. 600s.×6 Wild flowers ('Kitulo, the Garden of God'); Garden House, Vuga-Lushoto; Wild flowers and ferns, Udzungwa Mountains; Shoebill, Lake Rushwa Kagera; Riverside trees, Rufiji river, Selous Game Reserve; Rhinoceros, Ngorongoro crater	14·00	15·00
MS2671	100×150 mm. 600s. Denham's bustard and wild flowers ('Kitulo Botanical Wonderland') (50×35 mm)	2·75	3·00

362 Automated Post Office Counter

2009. 15th Anniv of Tanzania Posta Corporation. Multicoloured.

2672	400s. Type **362**	1·00	1·00
2673	600s. Posta Headquarters Building (vert)	1·50	1·50

363 Pres. George W. Bush

2009. Signing of Millennium Challenge Compact Aid Package by US President George Bush and Pres. Kikwete of Tanzania. Sheet 127×89 mm containing T **363** and similar vert design. Multicoloured.

MS2674	1500s.×2 Type **363**; Pres. Jakaya Kikwete	7·00	8·00

364 Mkuranga Moth

2009. Butterflies (and Moth) of Tanzania. Multicoloured.

2675	400s. Type **364**	1·50	1·00
2676	600s. Udzungwa Butterfly	1·75	1·25
2677	700s. *Acraea petraea* (butterfly red-brown)	1·90	1·90
2678	800s. *Acraea petraea* (butterfly pale brown)	2·25	2·50
MS2679	140×173 mm. 600s.×4 *Cymothoe alcimeda*; *Junonuia octavia sesamus*; *Junonia oenone oenone*; *Hypolimnas misippus*	6·50	7·00
MS2680	90×60 mm. 600s. *Vanessa cardui* and sunflowers	2·00	2·25
MS2681	120×90 mm. 600s. *Axiocerses tjoane* (vert)	2·00	2·25

The inscription 'Udzungwa Butterfly' on No. 2676 is printed upside down.

365 Red Colobus Monkey

2009. Zanzibar Attractions. Multicoloured.

2682	400s. Type **365**	1·25	60
2683	600s. House of Wonders (horiz)	1·50	1·00
2684	700s. Carved door	1·60	1·60
2685	1000s. Coffee seller	2·25	2·75
MS2686	150×115 mm. 600s.×6 Ngalawa (outrigger canoe); Zanzibar Seafront (horiz); Giant tortoise (horiz); Face of Red Colobus Monkey; Chake Chake's Courthouse (horiz); Zumari player (horiz)	9·00	9·00
MS2687	90×90 mm. 600s. Zanzibar Seafront with a Dhow (horiz)	1·40	1·40

366 Chimpanzees

2009. Wild Animals of Tanzania. Multicoloured.

2688	400s. Type **366**	1·00	50
2689	500s. Lion and lioness (horiz)	1·25	75
2690	600s. Grant's Red Colobus Monkeys (horiz)	1·25	85
2691	700s. Elephants	1·75	1·25
2692	800s. Migrating gnus (horiz)	1·75	1·25
2693	1000s. Water buck	2·25	1·75
2694	1800s. Elephant looking for tree foliage	5·00	4·50
2695	2000s. Migrating zebras (horiz)	5·50	5·50
2696	2500s. Hunting dogs (horiz)	6·00	7·00
2697	3000s. Buffalo (horiz)	7·00	8·00
2698	5000s. Zebras, gnu and gazelles grazing (horiz)	11·00	12·00
MS2699	150×115 mm. 600s.×6 Kirk's Red Colobus Monkey; Lioness guarding her cubs; The Udzungwa Monkey; Female Kongoni with her young; Female hippopotamus with baby; Leopard with her cub (all horiz)	9·00	9·00
MS2700	90×90 mm. 600s. Male Giraffe (horiz)	1·75	1·90

367 Mdako Game

2009. Youth and Sports. Multicoloured.

2701	400s. Type **367**	1·00	50
2702	600s. Girls playing tennis	1·25	75
2703	700s. Dancing	1·40	1·25
2704	1000s. Boy on swing	2·25	2·50
MS2705	145×90 mm. 600s.×6 Bao game; Boys playing basketball; Girls playing netball; Athletics (relay race); Girls skipping	9·00	9·00
MS2706	130×90 mm. 600s. Football game	1·40	1·40

OFFICIAL STAMPS

1965. Nos. 128 etc. optd **OFFICIAL**.

O9	**25**	5c. blue and orange	10	2·00
O10	–	10c. multicoloured	10	1·50
O11	–	15c. multicoloured	10	1·50
O12	–	20c. sepia, green and blue	10	2·00
O13	–	30c. black and brown	10	1·50
O14	–	50c. multicoloured	15	1·50
O15	**33**	1s. multicoloured	30	1·25
O16	–	5s. brown, green and blue	1·75	9·00

1967. Nos. 142, etc, optd **OFFICIAL**.

O20		5c. mauve, green and black	10	4·25
O21		10c. brown and bistre	10	1·00
O22		15c. grey, blue and black	10	6·00
O23		20c. brown and green	10	1·00
O24		30c. green and black	10	30
O36		40c. yellow, brown and green	45·00	4·00
O25		50c. multicoloured	15	1·60
O26		1s. brown, blue and purple	30	3·00
O27		5s. yellow, black and green	2·50	17·00

1973. Nos. 158 etc, optd **OFFICIAL**.

O40	**53**	5c. green, blue and black	50	3·25
O41	–	10c. multicoloured	75	40
O42	–	20c. brown, yellow & black	1·00	40
O43	–	40c. multicoloured	1·50	40
O44	–	50c. multicoloured	1·50	40
O45	–	70c. green, orange & black	1·50	1·00
O46	**54**	1s. multicoloured	1·50	40
O47	–	1s.50 multicoloured	2·75	3·25
O48	–	2s.50 multicoloured	3·25	8·50
O49	–	5s. multicoloured	3·50	14·00

1980. Nos. 307/13 and 315/17 optd **OFFICIAL**.

O54		10c. Type **75**	20	1·50
O55		20c. Large-spotted genet	25	1·00
O56		40c. Banded mongoose	30	1·00
O57		50c. Ratel	30	40
O58		75c. Large-toothed rock hyrax	40	60
O59		80c. Leopard	55	1·50
O60		1s. Impala	55	40
O66		1s.50 Giraffe	7·50	5·50
O61		2s. Common zebra	85	2·75

O62	3s. African buffalo	1·00	3·00
O63	5s. Lion	1·50	4·00

1990. Nos. 804/12 optd **OFFICIAL**.

O70	5s. Type **163**	65	2·75
O71	9s. African emerald cuckoo	80	1·75
O72	13s. Little bee eater	1·00	1·75
O73	15s. Red bishop	1·00	2·00
O74	20s. Bateleur	1·00	2·00
O75	25s. Scarlet-chested sunbird	1·00	2·00
O76	30s. African wood pigeon	1·50	2·50
O77	40s. Type **164**	1·25	2·00
O78	70s. Helmeted guineafowl	2·25	3·00
O79	100s. Eastern white pelican	2·75	4·00

1997. Nos. 2075/6, 2078 and 2081 optd **OFFICIAL**.

O80	100s. *Plumeria rubra acutifolia*	80	1·00
O81	140s. *Liliaceae*	1·00	1·40
O82	200s. *Liliaceae* (different)	1·50	1·75
O85	200s. *Nerium oleander carneum*	2·00	2·25
O83	260s. *Maluaviscus pendulilors*	1·50	1·75
O84	300s. *Canna*	1·75	2·25

No. O83 is inscribed "Carna" in error.

POSTAGE DUE STAMPS

The Postage Due stamps of Kenya, Uganda and Tanganyika were used in Tanganyika until 2 January 1967.

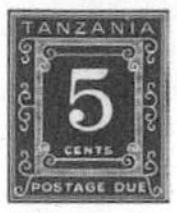
D1

1978

D19	**D1**	5c. red	15	2·75
D20	**D1**	10c. green	20	2·75
D21	**D1**	20c. blue	30	3·00
D22	**D1**	30c. brown	45	3·75
D23	**D1**	40c. purple	50	5·50
D24	**D1**	1s. orange	70	6·00

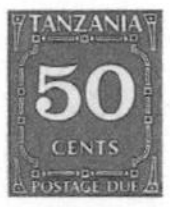
D2

1990

D30	**D2**	50c. green	10	75
D31	**D2**	80c. blue	10	50
D32	**D2**	1s. brown	15	75
D33	**D2**	2s. green	20	80
D34	**D2**	3s. purple	20	90
D35	**D2**	5s. brown	30	1·00
D36	**D2**	10s. brown	50	1·25
D37	**D2**	20s. brown	75	1·50
D38	**D2**	40s. blue	25	40
D39	**D2**	60s. green	30	60
D40	**D2**	80s. yellow	30	80
D41	**D2**	100s. blue	35	95

APPENDIX

The following stamps have either been issued in excess of postal needs, or have not been made available to the public in reasonable quantities at face value.

1985

Life and Times of Queen Elizabeth the Queen Mother. As Nos. 425/8 but embossed on gold foil. 20s.×2, 100s.×2.
Tanzanian Railway Locomotives (1st series). As Nos. 430/3 but embossed on gold foil. 5, 10, 20, 30s.

1986

Caribbean Royal Visit. Optd on previous issues. (a) On Nos. 425/8. 20s.×2, 100s.×2. (b) On Nos. 430/3. 5, 10, 20, 30s.
"Ameripex" International Stamp Exhibition, Chicago. Optd on Nos. 425/8. 20s.×2, 100s.×2.

1988

Cent of Statue of Liberty (1986). 1, 2, 3, 4, 5, 6, 7, 8, 10, 12, 15, 18, 20, 25, 30, 35, 40, 45, 50, 60s.
Royal Ruby Wedding. Optd on No. 378. 10s.
125th Anniv of Red Cross. Optd on Nos. 486/7. 5, 40s.
63rd Anniv of Rotary International in Africa. Optd on Nos. 422/3. 10s., 17s.50.

1995

The Beatles. 100s.×18.
Hoofed Animals. 70, 100, 150, 180, 200, 260, 380s.
Fauna of Coral Reefs. 70, 100, 150, 180, 200, 260, 380s.
"Singapore '95" International Stamp Exhibition. Trains of the World. 200s.×18.
Centof Sierra Club. 150s.×18.
Bats. 70, 100, 150, 180, 200, 260, 380s.
History of Rock and Roll. 250s.×9.
90th Anniv of Rotary International. 600s.
Winter Olympic Games, Lillehammer, Norway. 300, 400s.
Picasso Paintings. 30, 200, 300s.
450th Death Anniv of Copernicus (astronomer) (1993). 100, 300s.
"Polska '93" International Stamp Exhibition, Poznan. 200, 300s.
95th Birthday of Queen Elizabeth the Queen Mother. 250s.×4.
Olympic Games, Atlanta, 1996. Olympic History. 200s.×18.
50th Anniv of End of Second World War in the Pacific. 250s.×6.
50th Anniv of End of Second World War. 250s.×8.
Cacti. 70, 100, 150, 180, 200, 260, 380s.
African Reptiles. 200s.×12.
Predatory Animals. 70, 100, 150, 200, 250, 280, 300s.
50th Anniv of United Nations. 250s.×3.
50th Anniv of U.N. Food and Agriculture Organization. 250s.×3.
Cent of Cinema. Biblical Epics. 250s.×9.
20th Anniv of World Tourism Organization. 100, 300, 400s.
Gerry Garcia (rock musician) Commemoration. 200s.
Frogs. 100, 140, 180, 200, 210, 260, 300s.
Fauna of Kilimanjaro. 100s.×16, 250s.×4.
Butterflies. 200s.×19, 250, 370, 410s.

1996

Moths and Butterflies. 70, 100, 150, 200, 250, 260, 300s.
Chinese New Year ("Year of the Rat"). 200s.×4.
Horses. 250s.×9.
Cats. 100, 150, 200, 250s. × 9, 300s.×4.
Dogs. 70s, 250s.×10, 300s.×4, 600s.
Crocodiles. 100, 150, 200, 250, 260, 300, 380s.
125th Anniv of the Metropolitan Museum, New York. Paintings. 200s.×18.
Elvis Presley Commemoration. 200s.×9.
Snakes. 100, 140, 180, 200, 260, 300, 400s.
"China 96", International Stamp Exhibition. Deng Xiaoping. 250s.×6.
70th Birthday of Queen Elizabeth II. 300s.×3.
Famous People. 70, 100, 150, 200, 250s.×6.
Olympic Games, Atlanta. 100, 150, 200, 300s.
Birds. 300s.×16.
Cent of Radio. Famous People. 70, 100, 150, 200s.
Flowers. 300s.×16.
Fish. 100, 150, 200s.×9, 250, 500s.
Mercedes and Ferrari Cars. 250s.×12.
50th Anniv of UNESCO. 200, 250, 600s.
50th Anniv of UNICEF. 200, 250, 500s.
90th Anniv of Rotary. Nos. 985/1000 and 1589/600 optd **90th ANNIVERSARY OF ROTARY 1905–1995** and emblem. 50s.×16, 100s.×12.
International Scout Camp, Thailand and 34th World Scout Conf, Norway. Nos. 1001/16 and 1564/75 optd either **34th WORLD SCOUT CONFERENCE NORWAY JULY 8–12 1996** or **INTERNATIONAL SCOUT CAMP THAILAND MARCH 25–31 1996**, both with Scout emblem. 50s.×16, 100s.×12
Fungi. 300s.×16.

1997

"Hong Kong 97" International Stamp Exhibition. Portraits of Sun Yat-sen. 300s.×6.
Horses. 250s.×12.
Chernobyl's Children. 700s.×2.
Birds. 140s.×6, 150, 200, 370s.×6, 410, 500s.
Flowers. 200s.×6, 300s.×6.
175th Anniv of Brothers Grimm's Third Collection of Fairy Tales *Rumpelstiltskin*. 400s.×3.
Birth Bicent of Hiroshige (Japanese painter). 250s.× 6.
Golden Wedding of Queen Elizabeth and Prince Philip. 370s.×6.
Return of Hong Kong to China. 1000s.×5.
Winter Olympic Games, Nagano (1998). 100, 200, 250s.×4, 500, 600s.
World Cup Football Championship, France (1998). 100, 150, 200, 250s.×17, 500, 600s.
African Safari. 250s.×9.
Northern Wilderness (Arctic). 250s.×9.
Endangered Species. 250s.×24.
Seven Wonders of the Ancient World. 370s.×6.
Seven Wonders of the Modern World. 140s.×6.
Aviation. 100, 150s.×18, 200, 250s.×8, 300, 400, 500s.

1998

Diana, Princess of Wales Commemoration. 150, 250s.
Marine Life. 200s.×12, 250s.×18.
Chinese New Year ("Year of the Tiger"). 370s.×4.
Classic Cars. 370s.×12.
Aircraft. 300s.×18.
Exotic Flowers. 250s.×26.
Endangered Species. 200s.×12, 370s.×12.
Eagles. 370s.×6.
Fauna and Flora. 250, 370s. ×12, 410, 500, 600s.
International Year of the Ocean (1st issue). 150, 200s.×12, 250, 300s.×9, 400, 500s.
International Year of the Ocean (2nd issue). 1998 Marine Life overprinted with emblem. 200s. × 12, 250s.×18.
Fungi and Insects. 140, 150, 200, 250s.×19, 370, 410, 500, 600s.
Rudolph the Red-nosed Reindeer (cartoon film). 200s.×12.
25th Death Anniv of Pablo Picasso (painter). 400s.×2, 500s.
50th Death Anniv of Mahatma Gandhi. 370s.
1st Death Anniv of Diana, Princess of Wales. 600s.
19th World Scout Jamboree, Chile. 600s.×3.
80th Anniv of Royal Air Force 500s.×4.
John Denver Commemoration. 370s.×4.

1999

Chinese New Year ("Year of the Rabbit"). 4×250s.
Marine Life. 200, 250s.×19, 310, 410s.
Balloons. 370s.×6.
Tourism booklet. 150s. ×24.
Space. 70, 100, 150, 200, 250, 370s.
Early Flight. 20, 100, 140 s.×2, 150, 200, 250, 370s.×7.
Aircraft. 370s.×6.
Ships of the 19th Century. 370s.×12.
Endangered Species. 100s.×20.
Animals. 100, 140, 150, 200, 250, 370s.
Birds of the World. 370s.×12.
Birds. 370s.×12.
Flora and Fauna. 100, 140, 150, 200, 250, 370 s. × 13.
Orchids. 200, 250, 370s.×13.
Dogs of the World. 200s.×9.
Cats of the World. 100, 140, 150, 200, 250, 370s.×13.
Cats. 200, 250s.×9, 370, 410s.
Cats of the East. 500s.×4.
Prehistoric Animals. 400s.×6.
50th Anniv of Rotary in Tanzania. 150, 250, 350, 400s.
Queen Mother's Century. 600s.×4.
APS Stamp Show, Cleveland. Birds of Japan. 250s.×18.
Fashion Designers. 300s.×8.
Ballet. 300, 350, 400, 500s.
Hokusai (Japanese artist). 400s.×6.
Art of India. 500s.×8.
Military Exploits. 150, 250 s.×3, 300s.×3, 350s.×3, 400s.×3, 500s.×3.
Aircraft. 200, 250s.×9, 300, 400s.
Helicopters. 370s.×6.
UFOs. 370s.×12.
Locomotives. 400s.×6.
History of Trains. 400s.×12.
Sailing Vessels of the World. 400s.×12.
Fighting Machines of Second World War. 400s.×12.
Cars. 400s.×12.
"China '99". Paintings of Xu Beihong. 15 s.×10.
"China '99". Macau Returns to China. 300s.×4.
Underwater Creatures. 150, 250, 300s.×19, 350, 400, 500s.
Flowers. 150, 250, 350s.×18, 400, 500s.
Flowers of Africa. 150, 250, 300, 350, 400 s×13.
Flora and Fauna. 150s.×2, 250s.×2, 300s.×2, 350s.×2, 400s.×26, 500s.×2.
Fungi. 150, 250, 300, 350, 400s.×13, 500s.
Predators of the Deep. 200, 250, 370s.×7, 410s.
Prehistoric Animals. 200, 250, 370 s.×13, 410s.
Sea Birds. 150, 250s.×16, 300, 350, 400, 500s.
Marine Life. 250s.×12, 350, 400, 500s.
African Wildlife 300s.×8.
Central American Rainforest. 350s.×9.
Butterflies. 400s.×6.
Cats and Dogs. 400s.×12.

2000

Orchids. 200, 250, 370s.×13
Flowers. 150, 250, 300×19, 350, 400, 500s.
Flora and Fauna. 100, 140, 250, 370s.×13

2002

Queen Elizabeth the Queen Mother "In Memoriam". 95th Birthday of Queen Elizabeth the Queen Mother (1995 Appendix). Sheet margin inscribed "IN MEMORIAM 1900–2002". 250s.×4

2004

Mushrooms. 550s.×6
Animals. 550s.×6
Birds. 550s.×6
Butterflies. 550s.×6
Orchids. 550s.×6

2005

Rotary International. 1200s.×3

2006

80th Birthday of Queen Elizabeth II. 1200s.×4
250th Birth Anniv of Wolfgang Amadeus Mozart. 1200s.×4
50th Anniv of *Jailhouse Rock* (film) (Elvis Presley). 1200s.×4
Space: International Space Station. 800s.×6
Space: Mars Reconnaissance Orbiter. 1150s.×4
400th Birth Anniv of Rembrandt van Rijn. 1000s.×4
Endangered Species. Topi antelope (Damaliscus lunatus jimela). 600s.×4
Species of Zanzibar. 1000s.×8

2007

80th Birthday of Pope Benedict XVI. 600s.
Diamond Wedding of Queen Elizabeth II and Duke of Edinburgh. 750s.×2
10th Death Anniv of Diana, Princess of Wales. 750s.×6
50th Death Anniv of Qi Baishi (artist). 1000s.×4
Centenary of First Helicopter Flight. 1200s.×4

2008

Visit of Pope Benedict XVI to United States. 1000s.
Elivs Presley in the Movies. 1200s.×4

2009

Inauguration of US President Barack Obama. 1500s×4
50 Years of Space Exploration and Satellites. 750×6, 1200s.×17, 1500s.
China 2009 International Stamp Exhibiton, Luoyang. Peony. 570s.
Michael Jackson Commemoration. 1500s.×8

2010

Centenary of Chinese Aviation. 950s.×4

Pt. 1

TASMANIA

An island south of Australia, one of the States of the Australian Commonwealth, whose stamps it now uses.

12 pence = 1 schilling; 20 shillings = 1 pound.

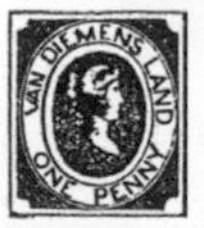
1

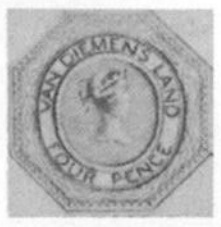
2

1853. Imperf.

3	**1**	1d. blue	£9500	£1300
11	**2**	4d. orange	£4750	£375

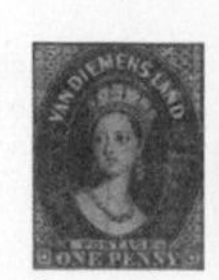
3

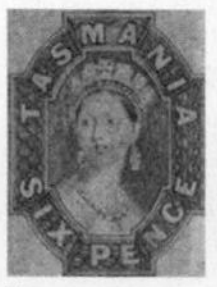
7

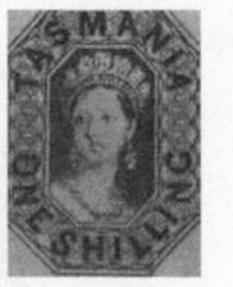
8

1855. Imperf.

28	**3**	1d. red	£325	32·00
34	**3**	2d. green	£325	85·00
36	**3**	4d. blue	£350	26·00
46	**7**	6d. purple	£600	80·00
41	**8**	1s. orange	£750	75·00

1864. Perf.

82	**3**	1d. red	90·00	24·00
71	**3**	2d. green	£550	95·00
72	**3**	4d. blue	£275	21·00
143	**7**	6d. purple	48·00	13·00
141	**8**	1s. orange	£250	65·00

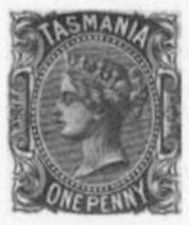
11

1870

159	**11**	½d. orange	3·00	3·25
156	**11**	1d. red	9·00	75
157	**11**	2d. green	10·00	75
165	**11**	3d. brown	8·00	8·00
130	**11**	4d. blue	£1100	£475
226	**11**	4d. yellow	14·00	7·00
158	**11**	8d. purple	14·00	9·00
256	**11**	9d. blue	7·50	5·50
131	**11**	10d. black	24·00	45·00
149*b*	**11**	5s. mauve	£275	70·00

1889. Surch **Halfpenny**.

167	½d. on 1d. red	10·00	20·00

1889. Surch **d. 2½**

169	2½d. on 9d. blue	5·00	3·50

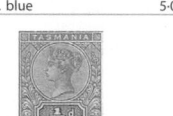

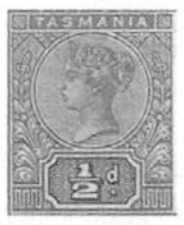
20

1892. Various frames.

216	**20**	½d. orange and mauve	2·50	1·25
217	**20**	2½d. purple	2·75	1·75
218	**20**	5d. blue and brown	7·00	3·75
219	**20**	6d. violet and black	14·00	4·75
220	**20**	10d. lake and green	10·00	14·00
221	**20**	1s. red and green	12·00	3·00
222	**20**	2s.6d. brown and blue	30·00	30·00
223	**20**	5s. purple and red	85·00	26·00
224	**20**	10s. mauve and brown	£180	£120
225	**20**	£1 green and yellow	£500	£450

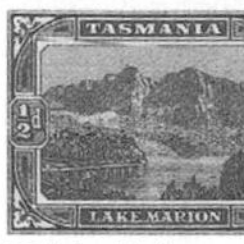
22 Lake Marion

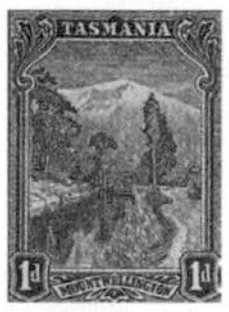
23 Mount Wellington

1899

249	**22**	½d. green	2·25	75
250	**23**	1d. red	5·50	30
251b	-	2d. violet	5·50	30
232	-	2½d. blue	22·00	3·75
246	-	3d. brown	10·00	4·50
247	-	4d. orange	20·00	4·50
235	-	5d. blue	35·00	11·00
236	-	6d. lake	32·00	30·00

DESIGNS—HORIZ: 2d. Hobart; 3d. Spring River, Port Davey; 5d. Mt. Gould, Lake St. Clair; 6d. Dilston Falls. VERT: 2½d. Tasman's Arch; 4d. Russell Falls.

1904. No. 218 surch **1½d.**

244	**20**	1½d. on 5d. blue and brown	1·50	1·75

1912. No. 251b surch **ONE PENNY**.

260	1d. on 2d. violet	1·00	1·00

Scan the QR code below
to get your FREE APPS
from Stanley Gibbons

Pt. 6; Pt. 17

TCHONGKING (CHUNGKING)

An Indo-Chinese Post Office was opened at Chungking in February 1902 and operated until it closed in December 1922.

1903. 100 centimes = 1 franc.
1919. 100 cents = 1 piastre.

Stamps of Indo-China surch.

1903. "Tablet" key-type surch with value in Chinese and TCHONGKING.

1	**D**	1c. black and red on blue	6·50	13·00
2	**D**	2c. brown and blue on buff	6·00	6·25
3	**D**	4c. brown and blue on grey	6·50	6·25
4	**D**	5c. green and red	5·50	8·75
5	**D**	10c. red and blue	5·50	8·75
6	**D**	15c. grey and red	5·00	9·00
7	**D**	20c. red and blue on green	7·25	12·50
8	**D**	25c. blue and red	70·00	85·00
9	**D**	25c. black and red on pink	8·50	23·00
10	**D**	30c. brown and blue on drab	22·00	30·00
11	**D**	40c. red and blue on yellow	85·00	90·00
12	**D**	50c. red and blue on pink	£250	£225
13	**D**	50c. brown and red on blue	£140	£150
14	**D**	75c. brown and red on orange	85·00	90·00
15	**D**	1f. green and red	90·00	£120
16	**D**	5f. mauve and blue on lilac	£140	£150

1906. Surch with value in Chinese and Tch'ong K'ing.

17	**8**	1c. green	3·00	9·50
18	**8**	2c. purple on yellow	2·75	6·50
19	**8**	4c. mauve on blue	3·00	3·75
20	**8**	5c. green	3·00	3·25
21	**8**	10c. pink	3·00	4·00
22	**8**	15c. brown on blue	18·00	21·00
23	**8**	20c. red on green	4·75	9·00
24	**8**	25c. blue	4·75	8·00
25	**8**	30c. brown on cream	6·25	11·00
26	**8**	35c. black on yellow	5·50	6·50
27	**8**	40c. black on grey	9·50	11·50
28	**8**	50c. brown on cream	10·00	24·00
29	**D**	75c. brown and red on orange	80·00	80·00
30	**8**	1f. green	[illegible]	[illegible]
31	**8**	2f. brown on yellow	42·00	70·00
32	**D**	5f. mauve and blue on lilac	£140	£150
33	**8**	10f. red on green	£160	£160

1908. Native types surch with value in Chinese and TCHONGKING.

34	**10**	1c. black and brown	1·40	1·00
35	**10**	2c. black and brown	1·40	1·00
36	**10**	4c. black and blue	1·70	1·80
37	**10**	5c. black and green	3·25	2·75
38	**10**	10c. black and red	3·00	3·00
39	**10**	15c. black and violet	3·50	8·00
40	**11**	20c. black and violet	6·25	11·50
41	**11**	25c. black and blue	5·50	11·00
42	**11**	30c. black and brown	5·50	12·50
43	**11**	35c. black and green	9·25	21·00
44	**11**	40c. black and brown	13·00	29·00
45	**11**	50c. black and red	12·50	24·00
46	**12**	75c. black and orange	12·50	28·00
47	-	1f. black and red	14·50	44·00
48	-	2f. black and green	£120	£150
49	-	5f. black and blue	55·00	75·00
50	-	10f. black and violet	£275	£300

1919. As last, but surch in addition in figures and words.

51	**10**	⅖c. on 1c. black and brown	1·20	1·40
52	**10**	⅘c. on 2c. black and brown	1·40	9·00
53	**10**	1⅗c. on 4c. black and blue	1·40	6·50
54	**10**	2c. on 5c. black and green	3·25	7·00
55	**10**	4c. on 10c. black and red	2·40	2·30
56	**10**	6c. on 15c. black and violet	5·00	4·50
57	**11**	8c. on 20c. black and violet	4·75	3·50
58	**11**	10c. on 25c. black and blue	6·50	5·25
59	**11**	12c. on 30c. black & brown	5·00	1·70
60	**11**	14c. on 35c. black and green	6·00	7·25
61	**11**	16c. on 40c. black and brown	6·25	7·50
62	**11**	20c. on 50c. black and red	34·00	28·00
63	**12**	30c. on 75c. black & orange	7·00	11·00
64	-	40c. on 1f. black and red	7·75	6·00
65	-	80c. on 2f. black and green	12·00	14·00
66	-	2p. on 5f. black and blue	17·00	24·00
67	-	4p. on 10f. black and violet	18·00	31·00

Pt. 9

TETE

Formerly using the stamps of Mozambique, this district of Mozambique was permitted to issue its own stamps from 1913 until 1920 when Mozambique stamps were again used.

100 centavos = 1 escudo.

1913. Surch **REPUBLICA TETE** and new value on "Vasco da Gama" issues of (a) Portuguese Colonies.

1	¼c. on 2½r. green	3·00	2·20
2	½c. on 5r. red	3·00	2·20
3	1c. on 10r. purple	3·00	2·20
4	2½c. on 25r. green	3·00	2·20
5	5c. on 50r. blue	3·00	2·20
6	7½c. on 75r. brown	4·25	2·50
7	10c. on 100r. brown	3·00	2·50
8	15c. on 150r. brown	3·00	2·50

(b) Macao.

9	¼c. on ½a. green	3·00	2·20
10	½c. on 1a. red	3·00	2·20
11	1c. on 2a. purple	3·00	2·20
12	2½c. on 4a. green	3·00	2·20
13	5c. on 8a. blue	3·00	2·20
14	7½c. on 12a. brown	4·25	2·50
15	10c. on 16a. brown	3·00	2·20
16	15c. on 24a. brown	3·00	2·20

(c) Timor.

17	¼c. on ½c. green	3·00	2·20
18	½c. on 1a. red	3·00	2·20
19	1c. on 2a. purple	3·00	2·20
20	2½c. on 4a. green	3·00	2·20
21	5c. on 8a. blue	3·00	2·20
22	7½c. on 12a. brown	4·25	2·50
23	10c. on 16a. brown	3·00	2·20
24	15c. on 24a. brown	3·00	2·20

1914. "Ceres" key-type inscr "TETE".

25	**U**	¼c. [illegible]	1·80	1·20
26	**U**	½c. black	1·80	1·20
27	**U**	1c. green	1·80	1·20
28	**U**	1½c. brown	1·80	1·20
29	**U**	2c. red	1·80	1·20
30	**U**	2½c. violet	1·80	1·20
31	**U**	5c. blue	1·80	1·20
32	**U**	7½c. brown	2·75	2·50
33	**U**	8c. grey	2·75	2·50
34	**U**	10c. red	3·50	2·50
35	**U**	15c. purple	4·25	4·00
36	**U**	20c. green	4·25	4·00
37	**U**	30c. brown on green	4·25	4·00
38	**U**	40c. brown on pink	5·00	4·25
39	**U**	50c. orange on orange	5·50	4·50
40	**U**	1e. green on blue	6·50	5·50

Pt. 21

THAILAND

An independent kingdom in S.E. Asia, previously known as Siam.

1883. 32 solot = 16 atts = 8 peinung (sio) = 4 songpy (sik) = 2 fuang = 1 salung; 4 salungs = 1 tical.
1909. 100 satangs = 1 tical.
1912. 100 satangs = 1 baht.

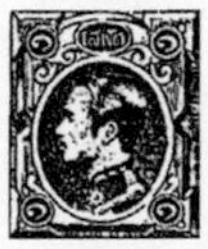

1 King Chulalongkorn

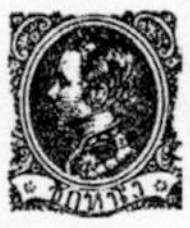

2

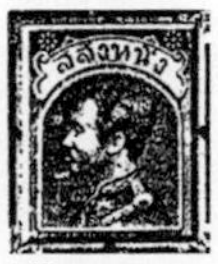

3 King Chulalongkorn

1883

1	**1**	1solot (⅛a.) blue	22·00	20·00
2	**1**	1att red	24·00	22·00
3	**1**	1sio (2a.) red	36·00	33·00
4	**2**	1sik (4a.) yellow	22·00	20·00
5	**3**	1salung (16a.) orange	65·00	60·00

1885. Surch. (a) **1 TICAL.**

6	**1**	1t. on 1solot blue	£4750	£4250

(b) **1 Tical.**

7	1t. on 1solot blue	£600	£550

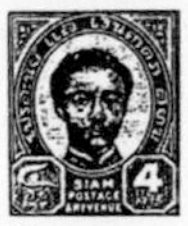

9

1887

11	**9**	1a. green	9·00	2·75
12	**9**	2a. green and red	9·75	2·75
13	**9**	3a. green and blue	17·00	6·00
14	**9**	4a. green and brown	18·00	6·50
15	**9**	8a. green and yellow	18·00	6·00
16	**9**	12a. purple and red	27·00	3·75
17	**9**	24a. purple and blue	30·00	5·00
18	**9**	64a. purple and brown	£120	33·00

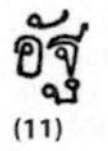

(11)

1889. Surch with T **11**.

19	**1**	1a. on 1sio red	34·00	30·00

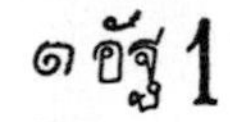

(12)

1889. (a) Surch as T **12**.

20	**9**	1a. on 2a. green and red	14·50	11·00
24	**9**	1a. on 3a. green and blue	19·00	13·00
26	**9**	2a. on 3a. green and blue	£130	85·00

(b) No. 24 further surch as T **12**.

28	2a. on 1a. on 3a. green & blue	£2500	£2250

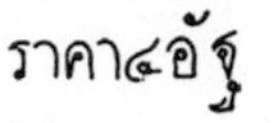

(23)

1892. Surch with T **23**.

32	4a. on 24a. purple and blue	60·00	43·00

1892. No. 32 further surch **4 atts** in English (with or without full point).

33	4a. on 24a. purple and blue	18·00	14·00

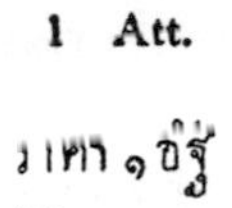

(42)

1892. Surch as T **42**.

54	1Att. on 12a. purple and red	£475	£450
63	1Att. on 12a. purple and red	24·00	6·50
37	1Att. on 64a. purple and brown	3·75	3·25
46	1Att. on 64a. purple & brown	2·75	2·20
44	2a. on 64a. purple and brown	2·40	2·20
58	3a. on 12a. purple and red	14·50	4·50
60	4a. on 12a. purple and red	18·00	5·00
50	10a. on 24a. purple and blue	9·75	1·60

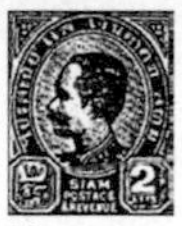

49

1899

67	**49**	1a. green	2·20	65
68	**49**	2a. green	2·40	65
69	**49**	2a. red and blue	11·00	1·80
70	**49**	3a. red and blue	9·00	1·60
71	**49**	3a. green	24·00	11·00
72	**49**	4a. red	9·75	2·20
73	**49**	4a. brown and pink	16·00	2·20
74	**49**	6a. red	65·00	16·00
75	**49**	8a. green and orange	27·00	2·75
76	**49**	10a. blue	11·00	2·20
77	**49**	12a. purple and red	48·00	2·20
78	**49**	14a. blue	24·00	16·00
79	**49**	24a. purple and blue	£325	27·00
80	**49**	28a. brown and blue	30·00	27·00
81	**49**	64a. purple and brown	80·00	11·00

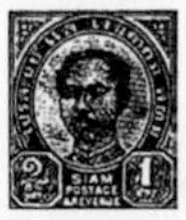

50

1899

82	**50**	1a. green	£300	£110
83	**50**	2a. green and red	£550	£160
84	**50**	3a. red and blue	£900	£225
85	**50**	4a. black and green	£3000	£750
86	**50**	10a. pink and green	£3250	£900

1905. Surch in English and Siamese.

90	**49**	1a. on 14a. blue	12·00	11·00
91	**49**	2a. on 28a. brown and blue	14·50	13·00

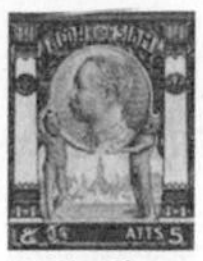

53 Wat Cheng "Temple of Light"

1905

92	**53**	1a. green and yellow	3·50	1·40
93	**53**	2a. grey and violet	3·50	1·40
94	**53**	2a. green	14·00	6·50
95	**53**	3a. green	4·75	2·30
96	**53**	3a. grey and violet	18·00	10·00
97	**53**	4a. red and brown	8·75	2·20
98	**53**	4a. red	14·00	3·00
99	**53**	5a. red	9·25	4·00
100	**53**	8a. bistre and black	13·00	2·10
101	**53**	9a. blue	33·00	10·50
102	**53**	12a. blue	18·00	4·75
103	**53**	18a. brown	90·00	33·00
104	**53**	24a. brown	35·00	8·75
105	**53**	1t. bistre and blue	47·00	7·50

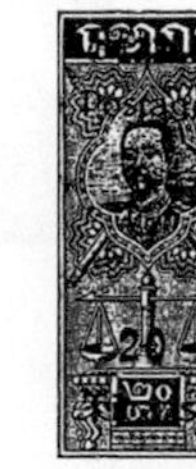

54

1907. Fiscal stamps optd **Siam. Postage** and new value.

106	**54**	10t. green	£900	£120
107	**54**	20t. green	£7000	£550
108	**54**	40t. green	£5500	£700

1907. Surch **1 att.** and thin line.

109	**9**	1a. on 24a. purple and blue	6·75	2·20

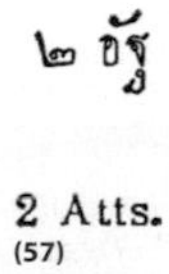

(57)

1908. Surch in English and Siamese as T **57**.

110		2a. on 24a. purple and blue	6·50	2·10
111	**53**	4a. on 5a. red	16·00	5·75
112	**49**	9a. on 10a. blue	20·00	5·75

1908. 40th Anniv of Reign of King Chulalongkorn. Optd **Jubilee 1868-1908** in English and Siamese.

113	**53**	1a. green and yellow	4·75	2·30
114	**53**	3a. green	7·00	3·75
115	**53**	4a. on 5a. (No. 111)	8·25	4·75
116	**53**	8a. bistre and black	23·00	23·00
117	**53**	18a. brown	47·00	35·00

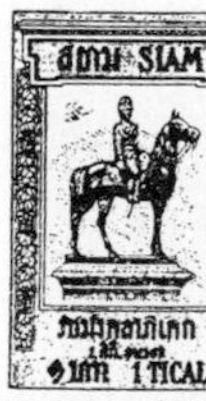

61 Statue of King Chulalongkorn, Bangkok

1908

118	**61**	1t. violet and green	75·00	11·50
119	**61**	2t. orange and purple	£110	29·00
120	**61**	3t. blue and green	£150	23·00
121	**61**	5t. green and lilac	£225	41·00
122	**61**	10t. red and green	£1300	£130
123	**61**	20t. brown and grey	£700	£140
124	**61**	40t. brown and blue	£750	£400

1909. Surch in satangs in English and Siamese.

125	**53**	2s. on 1a. green & yellow	3·50	1·80
127a	**53**	2s. on 2a. green	4·00	2·00
164	**53**	2s. on 2a. grey and violet	10·50	7·50
129	**53**	3s. on 3a. green	14·00	8·75
130	**53**	3s. on 3a. grey and violet	7·00	1·40
131	**53**	6s. on 4a. red and brown	42·00	37·00

132a	53	6s. on 4a. red	11·50	3·00
134	53	6s. on 5a. red	15·00	9·25
138	49	6s. on 6a. red	3·50	3·00
135	53	12s. on 8a. bistre & black	9·25	2·10
136	53	14s. on 9a. blue	13·00	2·30
137	53	14s. on 12a. blue	33·00	29·00
139	9	14s. on 12a. purple & red	£160	£150
140	49	14s. on 14a. blue	29·00	25·00

64 King Chulalongkorn

1910

141	64	2s. green and orange	3·50	2·30
142	64	3s. green	3·50	2·30
143	64	6s. red	7·00	3·00
144	64	12s. brown and black	18·00	3·50
145	64	14s. blue	29·00	4·00
146	64	28s. brown	47·00	10·50

65 King Vajiravudh    **66**

1912

166	65	2s. brown	3·25	1·80
167	65	3s. green	3·50	3·25
168	65	5s. red	5·75	1·80
149	65	6s. red	5·75	2·30
169	65	10s. brown and black	5·25	1·80
150	65	12s. brown and black	8·25	3·00
151	65	14s. blue	10·50	3·50
170	65	15s. blue	7·00	2·10
152	65	28s. brown	26·00	18·00
153	66	1b. brown and blue	44·00	3·00
154	66	2b. brown and red	55·00	5·75
155	66	3b. black and green	60·00	9·25
156	66	5b. black and violet	80·00	18·00
157	66	10b. purple and green	£450	£110
158	66	20b. brown and blue	£700	£130

1914. Surch in Satang in English and Siamese.

159		2s. on 14s. blue	4·00	1·10
165	64	2s. on 14s. blue	7·00	3·00
160		5s. on 6s. red	8·25	80
161		10s. on 12s. brown & black	8·25	95
162		15s. on 28s. brown	13·00	2·30

1918. Red Cross Fund. Optd with small cross in circle.

177	65	2s.(+3s.) brown	3·25	3·25
178	65	3s.(+2s.) green	3·50	3·50
179	65	5s.(+5s.) red	7·00	6·75
180	65	10s.(+5s.) brown and black	11·50	8·25
181	65	15s.(+5s.) blue	13·00	8·75
182	66	1b.(+25s.) brown & blue	65·00	47·00
183	66	2b.(+30s.) brown and red	70·00	55·00
184	66	3b.(+35s.) black and green	95·00	80·00
185	66	5b.(+40s.) black and violet	£375	£225
186	66	10b.(+1b.) purple & green	£600	£375
187	66	20b.(+1b.) brown & grn	£2250	£2000

1918. Optd **VICTORY** in English and Siamese.

188	65	2s. brown	5·00	4·75
189	65	3s. green	5·25	5·00
190	65	5s. red	7·00	6·75
191	65	10s. brown and black	10·00	9·25
192	65	15s. blue	10·50	10·00
193	66	1b. brown and blue	47·00	35·00
194	66	2b. brown and red	95·00	70·00
195	66	3b. black and green	£275	£180
196	66	5b. black and violet	£550	£475

1919. Surch in English and Siamese with figures only.

197	65	5s. on 6s. red	4·25	2·75
198	65	10s. on 12s. brown & black	8·25	2·20

(72a)    (72b)

1920. Scouts' Fund. Various stamps handstamped. (a) With Type **72a.**

199		2s.(+3s.) brown	65·00	65·00
200		3s.(+2s.) green	65·00	65·00
201		5s. on 6s. (+5s.) red (No. 160)	70·00	70·00
202		10s. on 12s. (+5s.) brown and black (No. 161)	70·00	70·00
203		15s.(+5s.) blue	£200	£180
204	53	1t.(+25s.) bistre and blue	£550	£550

(b) With Type **72b.**

205	65	2s.(+3s.) brown	47·00	47·00
206	65	3s.(+2s.) green	47·00	47·00
207	73	5s.(+5s.) red on pink	£120	£120
208	65	10s. on 12s. (+5s.) brown and black (No. 161)	95·00	95·00
209	65	15s.(+5s.) blue	95·00	95·00
210	53	1t.(+25s.) bistre and blue	£400	£400

These stamps were sold in aid of the "Wild Tiger" Scouts organization at the premium stated.

73

1920

211	73	2s. brown on yellow	4·75	1·10
212	73	3s. green on green	5·25	1·40
213	73	3s. brown	5·00	1·10
214	73	5s. red on pink	7·00	1·10
215	73	5s. green	28·00	6·50
216	73	5s. violet on mauve	10·50	1·40
217	73	10s. brown and black	10·00	1·10
218	73	15s. blue on blue	11·50	1·20
219	73	15s. red	47·00	8·25
220	73	25s. brown	23·00	4·00
221	73	25s. blue	41·00	2·50
222	73	50s. black and brown	47·00	2·30

บำรุงเสือป่า
[Scout's Fund logo]
SCOUT'S FUND
(73a)

1920. Scouts' Fund. Optd with T **73a.**

223		2s.(+3s.) brown on yellow	16·00	16·00
224		3s.(+2s.) green on green	16·00	16·00
225		5s.(+5s.) red on pink	16·00	16·00
226		10s.(+5s.) brown and black	16·00	16·00
227		15s.(+5s.) blue on blue	33·00	33·00
228		25s.(+25s.) brown	£110	£110
229		50s.(+30s.) black & brn	£300	£300

74 "Garuda" Bird

1925. Air.

230	74	2s. brown on yellow	9·25	70
231	74	3s. brown	9·25	70
239	74	5s. green	3·50	60
240	74	10s. orange and black	9·25	60
234	74	15s. red	11·50	1·40
242	74	25s. blue	5·75	1·80
243	74	50s. black and brown	5·75	2·30
237	74	1b. brown and blue	60·00	13·00

75 Coronation Stone

1926

244	75	1t. green and lilac	23·00	5·25
245	75	2t. red and carmine	55·00	8·75
246	75	3t. blue and green	£100	35·00
247	75	5t. green and violet	£140	65·00
248	75	10t. brown and red	£475	47·00
249	75	20t. brown and blue	£550	£160

1928. Surch in English and Siamese.

250	75	5s. on 15s. red	10·50	5·25
251	65	10s. on 28s. brown	18·00	3·00

76 King Prajadhipok   **77**

1928

252	76	2s. brown	80	35
253	76	3s. green	95	45
254	76	5s. violet	80	35
255	76	10s. red	95	45
256	76	15s. blue	1·10	60
257	76	25s. orange and black	5·75	1·50
258	76	50s. black and orange	3·00	2·00
259	76	80s. black and blue	5·75	3·25
260	77	1b. black and blue	8·25	3·50
261	77	2b. brown and red	11·50	7·50
262	77	3b. black and green	18·00	8·75
263	77	5b. brown and violet	26·00	10·00
264	77	10b. purple and green	65·00	15·00
265	77	20b. brown and green	£120	23·00
266	77	40b. brown and green	£225	£120

1930. Surch in English and Siamese.

267	64	10s. on 12s. brown & black	13·00	4·00
268	64	25s. on 28s. brown	41·00	3·25

79 Kings Prajadhipok and Chao Phya Chakri
81 Chao Phya Chakri (Rama I) 
80 Kings Prajadhipok and Chao Phya Chakri

1932. 150th Anniv of Chakri Dynasty and of Bangkok as Capital and Opening of Memorial Bridge over Menam.

269	79	2s. red	3·00	60
270	79	3s. green	4·75	1·30
271	79	5s. violet	3·00	60
272	80	10s. black and red	3·00	60
273	80	15s. black and blue	14·00	2·20
274	80	25s. black and mauve	19·00	3·00
275	80	50s. black and purple	75·00	6·50
276	81	1b. blue	£110	18·00

(82)

1939. Red Cross Fund. 75th Anniv of Membership of the International Red Cross. Surch as T **82.**

277	66	5+5s. on 1b. (153)	21·00	21·00
278	66	10+5s. on 2b. (154)	42·00	42·00
279	66	15+5s. on 3b. (155)*	42·00	42·00

83 National Assembly Hall

1939. Seventh Anniv of Constitution and National Day (1st issue).

280	83	2s. brown	7·00	3·00
281	83	3s. green	14·00	5·75
282	83	5s. purple	9·25	1·20
283	83	10s. red	21·00	1·40
284	83	15s. blue	49·00	3·00

84 Chakri Palace and "Garuda" Bird

1940. National Day (2nd issue).

285	84	2s. brown	6·50	1·20
286	84	3s. green	11·50	3·50
287	84	5s. purple	8·25	60
288	84	10s. red	21·00	60
289	84	15s. blue	41·00	1·80

85 King Ananda Mahidol   **86** Ploughing Rice Field   **87** Ban Pa'in Palace, Ayuthia

1941

290	85	2s. brown	3·00	70
291	85	3s. green	4·00	1·30
292	85	5s. violet	2·30	70
293	85	10s. red	2·30	70
294	86	15s. grey and blue	4·00	1·40
295	86	25s. orange and grey	5·25	1·60
296	86	50s. grey and orange	4·75	1·80
297	87	1b. grey and blue	22·00	5·25
298	87	2b. grey and red	14·00	3·00
299	87	3b. grey and green	55·00	7·00
300	87	5b. red and black	90·00	27·00
301	87	10b. yellow and green	£140	80·00

88 Monument of Democracy, Bangkok

1942. Air. With or without gum.

302	88	2s. brown	4·75	3·50
303	88	3s. green	35·00	34·00
304	88	5s. purple	4·75	1·80
305	88	10s. red	21·00	1·80
306	88	15s. blue	7·50	3·00

89 King Ananda Mahidol

1943

307	89	1b. blue	33·00	4·00

90 Indo-China War Monument, Bangkok

1943

310	90	3s. green	5·75	3·50

91 Bangkaen Monument and Ears of Rice

1943. Tenth Anniv of Failure of 1933 Revolt.

311	91	2s. orange	3·50	4·75
312	91	10s. red	4·75	1·20

92 King Bhumibol

1947

313	92	5s. violet	3·00	45
314	92	10s. red	3·25	45
315	92	20s. brown	3·50	45
316	92	50s. green	6·50	60
317	92	1b. blue and violet	23·00	70
318	92	2b. green and blue	80·00	2·30
319	92	3b. black and red	£110	4·50
320	92	5b. red and green	£120	8·75
321	92	10b. violet and brown	£350	3·25
322	92	20b. purple and black	£475	11·00

The baht values are larger, size 21½×27 mm.

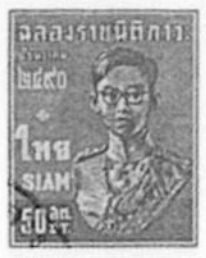

93

1947. Coming of Age of King Bhumibol. With gum (10, 50s.) or without gum (others).

323	**93**	5s. orange	5·25	4·50
324	**93**	10s. brown	£120	£100
325	**93**	10s. green	5·25	4·50
326	**93**	20s. blue	11·50	3·50
327	**93**	50s. green	21·00	7·00

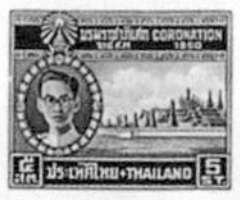

94 King and Palace

1950. King's Coronation.

328	**94**	5s. purple	3·00	45
329	**94**	10s. red	3·50	60
330	**94**	15s. violet	20·00	7·50
331	**94**	20s. brown	3·50	60
332	**94**	80s. green	37·00	8·25
333	**94**	1b. blue	8·75	1·20
334	**94**	2b. yellow	41·00	2·50
335	**94**	3b. grey	£120	14·00

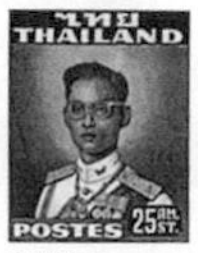

95 King Bhumibol

1951

336	**95**	5s. purple	3·50	25
337	**95**	10s. green	3·00	25
338	**95**	15s. brown	3·50	55
339	**95**	20s. brown	4·75	60
340	**95**	25s. red	1·80	25
341	**95**	50s. green	4·75	60
342	**95**	1b. blue	9·25	60
343	**95**	1b.15 blue	3·00	45
344	**95**	1b.25 red	15·00	70
345	**95**	2b. green	22·00	80
346	**95**	3b. grey	30·00	[illegible]
347	**95**	5b. red and blue	95·00	2·30
348	**95**	10b. violet and brown	£400	7·00
349	**95**	20b. green and black	£475	25·00

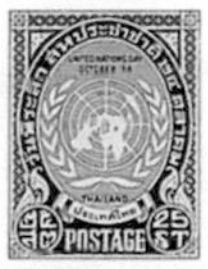

96 U.N. Emblem

1951. United Nations Day.

350	**96**	25s. blue	7·50	7·00

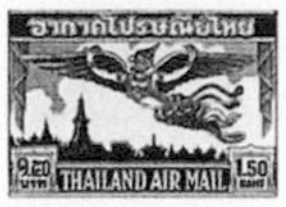

97 "Garuda" Bird

1952. Air.

351	**97**	1b.50 purple	8·00	1·80
352	**97**	2b. blue	23·00	3·50
353	**97**	3b. grey	29·00	2·30

1952. United Nations Day. Optd **1952**.

354	**96**	25s. blue	5·25	4·00

1952. 20th Anniv of Constitution. Surch with Vase emblem and **+ 20** in English and Siamese.

355	**76**	80s.+20s. black and blue	29·00	22·00

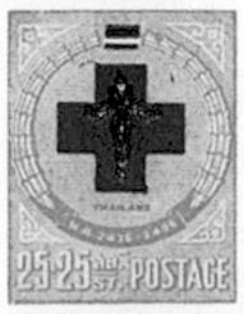

99 Dancer over Cross

1953. 60th Anniv of Thai Red Cross Society. Cross in red, figures in blue and red.

356	**99**	25s.+25s. cream & green	9·25	7·50
357	**99**	50s.+50s. cream and pink	29·00	27·00
358	**99**	1b.+1b. cream and blue	35·00	33·00

1953. United Nations Day. Optd **1953**.

359	**96**	25s. blue	4·25	3·00

1954. United Nations Day. Optd **1954** vert.

360		25s. blue	8·75	5·75

1955. Optd **THAILAND** in English and Siamese.

361	**76**	5s. violet	18·00	29·00
362	**76**	10s. red	18·00	29·00

1955. Surch.

363	**92**	5s. on 20s. brown	5·25	95
364	**92**	10s. on 20s. brown	8·25	1·20

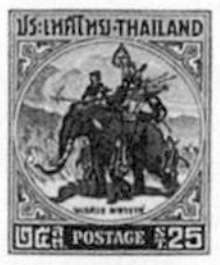

103 Processional Elephant

1955. 400th Birth Anniv of King Naresuan.

365	**103**	25s. red	4·25	70
366	**103**	80s. purple	37·00	6·50
367	**103**	1b.25 green	£110	4·75
368	**103**	2b. blue	23·00	2·30
369	**103**	3b. brown	90·00	3·50

1955. Red Cross Fair. Optd **24 98**.

370	**99**	25s.+25s. multicoloured	35·00	23·00
371	**99**	50s.+50s. multicoloured	£225	£160
372	**99**	1b.+1b. red, cream and blue	£325	£225

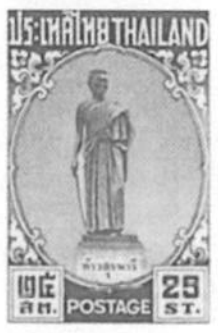

105 Tao Suranari

1955. Tao Suranari Commemoration.

373	**105**	10s. lilac	7·00	70
374	**105**	25s. green	4·75	45
375	**105**	1b. brown	60·00	4·75

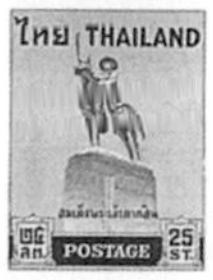

106 Equestrian Statue

1955. King Taksin Commemoration.

376	**106**	5s. blue	2·75	45
377	**106**	25s. green	16·00	60
378	**106**	1b.25 red	65·00	4·75

1955. U.N. Day. Optd **1955** vert.

379	**96**	25s. blue	8·75	5·75

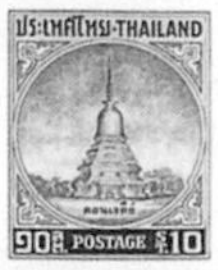

107 Don Chedi Pagoda

1956

380	**107**	10s. green	7·00	4·75
381	**107**	50s. brown	41·00	2·50
382	**107**	75s. violet	14·00	1·90
383	**107**	1b.50 brown	37·00	2·30

1956. United Nations Day. Optd **1956** vert.

384	**96**	25s. blue	8·75	6·50

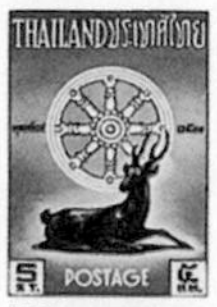

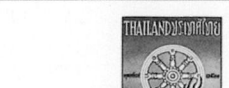

108 Dharmachakra and Sambar

1957. 2500th Anniv of Buddhist Era.

385	**108**	5s. brown	2·20	95
386	**108**	10s. purple	2·20	95
387	**108**	15s. green	5·00	2·50
388	-	20s. orange	5·25	3·00
389	-	25s. brown	1·60	75
390	-	50s. mauve	3·75	1·10
391	-	1b. brown	4·25	1·30
392	-	1b.25 blue	55·00	5·75
393	-	2b. purple	13·00	1·90

DESIGNS: 20s. to 50s. Hand of Peace and Dharmachakra; 1b. to 2b. Nakon Phatom pagoda.

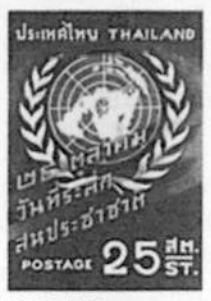

110 U.N. Emblem and Laurel Sprays

1957. United Nations Day.

394	**110**	25s. green	2·30	1·20
395	**110**	25s. brown (1958)	2·30	1·20
400	**110**	25s. blue (1959)	3·50	1·20

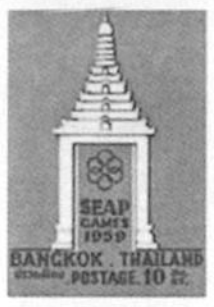

111 Gateway to Grand Palace

1959. First South-East Asia Peninsula Games.

396	**111**	10s. orange	1·60	25
397	-	25s. red	2·00	35
398	-	1b.25 green	8·25	2·20
399	-	2b. blue	7·00	1·30

DESIGNS: 25s. Royal parasols; 1b.25, Bowman; 2b. Wat Arun (temple) and prow of royal barge.

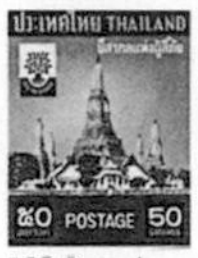

112 Pagoda

1960. World Refugee Year.

401	**112**	50s. brown	2·30	60
402	**112**	2b. green	3·50	1·80

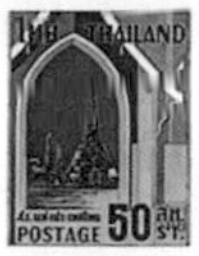

113 Wat Arun Temple

1960. Leprosy Relief Campaign.

403	**113**	50s. red	1·20	30
404	**113**	2b. blue	7·00	1·20

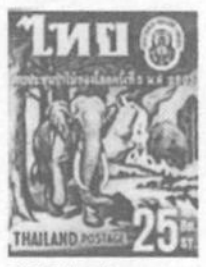

114 Indian Elephant

1960. Fifth World Forestry Congress, Seattle.

405	**114**	25s. green	2·30	60

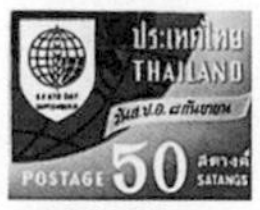

115 S.E.A.T.O. Emblem

1960. S.E.A.T.O. Day.

406	**115**	50s. brown	2·30	60

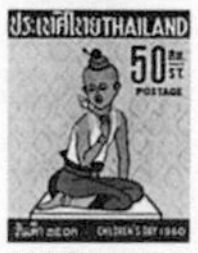

116 Siamese Child

1960. Children's Day.

407	**116**	50s. mauve	2·75	35
408	**116**	1b. brown	6·50	95

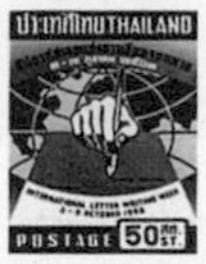

117 Letter-writing

1960. International Correspondence Week.

409	**117**	50s. mauve	2·30	80
410	**117**	2b. blue	7·00	2·30

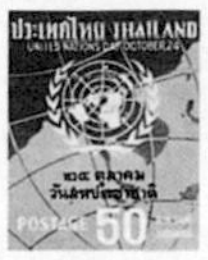

118 U.N. Emblem and Globe

1960. United Nations Day.

411	**118**	50s. violet	2·30	60
446	**118**	50s. red (1961)	2·30	1·10
467	**118**	50s. red (1962)	1·20	95

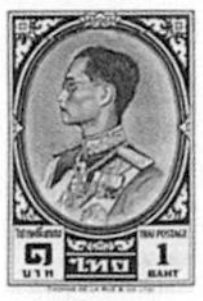

119 King Bhumibol

1961

422	**119**	5s. purple	95	45
423	**119**	10s. green	95	45
424	**119**	15s. brown	1·20	60
425	**119**	20s. brown	1·20	60
426	**119**	25s. red	1·20	60
427	**119**	50s. green	1·20	60
428	**119**	80s. orange	7·50	3·00
429	**119**	1b. brown and blue	7·00	1·20
430	**119**	1b.25 green and red	13·00	3·00
431	**119**	1b.50 green and violet	3·50	1·20
432	**119**	2b. violet and red	3·75	3·00
433	**119**	3b. blue and brown	20·00	1·20
434	**119**	4b. black and bistre	22·00	4·75
435	**119**	5b. green and blue	29·00	2·30
436	**119**	10b. black and red	£130	3·50
437	**119**	20b. blue and green	£150	7·00
438	**119**	25b. blue and green	70·00	5·75
439	**119**	40b. black and yellow	£160	10·50

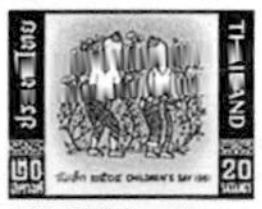

120 Children in Garden

1961. Children's Day.

440	**120**	20s. blue	2·50	1·10
441	**120**	2b. violet	7·50	2·30

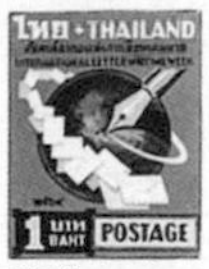

121 Pen, Letters and Globe

1961. International Correspondence Week.

442	-	25s. myrtle	1·10	30
443	-	50s. purple	45	25
444	**121**	1b. red	2·75	70
445	**121**	2b. blue	3·75	1·10

DESIGN: 25s., 50s. Pen, and world map on envelope.

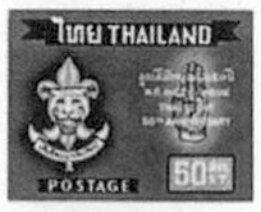

122 Thai Scout Badge and Saluting Hand

1961. 50th Anniv of Thai Scout Movement.

447	**122**	50s. red	1·10	45
448	-	1b. green	2·50	70
449	-	2b. blue	4·00	1·80

DESIGNS—VERT: 1b. Scout camp and scout saluting flag; 2b. King Vajiravudh in uniform, and scout, cub and guide marching.

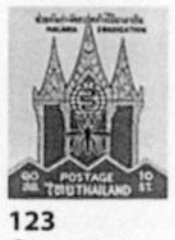

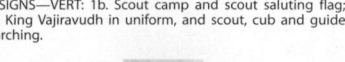

123 Campaign Emblem and Temple

1962. Malaria Eradication.

450	**123**	5s. brown	45	25
451	**123**	10s. brown	45	25

452	123	20s. blue	1·60	25
453	123	50s. red	45	25
454	-	1b. green	2·20	30
455	-	1b.50 purple	5·25	95
456	-	2b. blue	2·75	45
457	-	3b. violet	8·25	3·50

DESIGN: 1b. to 3b. Hanuman fighting mosquitoes.

124 Bangkok

1962. "Century 21" Exhibition, Seattle.

458	124	50s. purple	2·20	45
459	124	2b. blue	10·00	1·10

125 Thai Child with Doll

1962. Children's Day.

460	125	25s. green	2·00	25
461	125	50s. brown	2·10	30
462	125	2b. mauve	10·00	1·20

126 Correspondence Symbols

1962. International Correspondence Week.

463	126	25s. violet	1·10	35
464	126	50s. red	80	30
465	-	1b. bistre	5·25	45
466	-	2b. green	10·50	1·10

DESIGN: 1, 2b. Quill pen.

127 Exhibition Emblem

1962. Students' Exhibition, Bangkok.

468	127	50s. bistre	2·75	35

128 Harvesting

1963. Freedom from Hunger.

469	128	20s. green	2·75	95
470	128	50s. brown	2·00	35

129 "Temple Guardian"

1963. First Anniv of Asian–Oceanic Postal Union.

471	129	50s. green and brown	3·00	35

130 Centenary Emblem

1963. Red Cross Centenary.

472	130	50s.+10s. red and grey	1·20	60
473	-	50s.+10s. red and grey	1·20	60

DESIGN: No. 473, As Type **130**, but with positions of emblem and inscriptions reversed.

131 G.P.O. Bangkok and (inset) old P.O.

1963. 80th Anniv of Post and Telegraph Department.

474	131	50s. green, orange and violet	3·50	1·20
475	131	3b. brown, green and red	8·75	2·30

132 King Bhumibol

1963

476	132	5s. mauve	95	45
477	132	10s. green	95	45
478	132	15s. brown	95	45
479	132	20s. brown	1·20	60
480	132	25s. red	1·20	60
481	132	50s. green	2·30	70
482	132	75s. lilac	2·20	60
483	132	80s. orange	7·50	1·90
484	132	1b. brown and blue	5·75	60
485	132	1b.25 bistre and brown	23·00	7·00
486	132	1b.50 green and violet	7·00	1·20
487	132	2b. violet and red	7·00	60
488	132	3b. blue and brown	7·00	1·20
489	132	4b. black and bistre	10·50	3·50
490	132	5b. green and blue	8·25	1·20
491	132	10b. black and red	41·00	3·00
492	132	20b. blue and green	£250	9·25
493	132	25b. blue and green	18·00	2·30
494	132	40b. black and yellow	£325	14·00

133 Children with Dolls

1963. Children's Day.

505	133	50s. red	3·00	25
506	133	2b. blue	13·00	1·20

134 "Garuda" Bird with Scroll in Beak

1963. International Correspondence Week.

507	134	50s. purple and turquoise	4·00	70
508	134	1b. purple and green	6·50	1·20
509	-	2b. blue and brown	47·00	2·30
510	-	3b. green and brown	26·00	5·25

DESIGN: 2b., 3b. Thai women writing letters.

135 U.N. Emblem

1963. United Nations Day.

511	135	50s. blue	2·30	60

136 King Bhumibol

1963. King Bhumibol's 36th Birthday.

512	136	1b.50 indigo, yellow & bl	8·25	2·30
513	136	5b. blue, yellow & mauve	35·00	7·00

137 Mother and Child

1964. 17th Anniv of U.N.I.C.E.F.

514	137	50s. blue	1·50	60
515	137	2b. green	7·00	1·20

138 "Hand" of Flags, Pigeon and Globe

1964. International Correspondence Week.

516	138	50s. mauve and green	3·50	60
517	-	1b. brown and green	8·75	2·30
518	-	2b. violet and yellow	21·00	3·00
519	-	3b. brown and blue	14·00	4·75

DESIGNS: 1b. Thai girls and map; 2b. Map, pen and pencil; 3b. Hand with quill pen, and globe.

139 Globe and U.N. Emblem

1964. United Nations Day.

520	139	50s. grey	2·30	60

140 King Bhumibol and Queen Sirikit

1965. 15th Royal Wedding Anniv.

521	140	2b. multicoloured	23·00	1·20
522	140	5b. multicoloured	37·00	5·75

141 I.T.U. Emblem and Symbols

1965. I.T.U. Centenary.

523	141	1b. green	10·50	2·30

142 Goddess, Letters and Globes

1965. International Correspondence Week. Multicoloured.

524	50s. Type **142**		2·50	95
525	1b. Type **142**		7·50	1·20
526	2b. Handclasp, letters and world map		21·00	1·80
527	3b. As 2b.		26·00	5·75

143 Grand Palace, Bangkok

1965. International Co-operation Year and 20th Anniv of United Nations.

528	143	50s. lt blue, yellow & blue	3·00	60

145 U.P.U. Monument, Berne, and Map of Thailand

1965. 80th Anniv of Thailand's Admission to Universal Postal Union.

529	145	20s. blue and mauve	1·50	60
530	145	50s. black and blue	3·00	95
531	145	1b. brown and blue	10·50	1·20
532	145	3b. green and brown	21·00	3·75

146 Child and Lotus

1965. Children's Day.

533	146	50s. brown and black	2·30	60
534	-	1b. green and black	5·75	2·30

DESIGN: 1b. Child mounting stairs.

147 Cycling

1966. Publicity for Fifth Asian Games, Bangkok.

535	20s. red (Type **147**)		1·50	60
536	25s. violet (Tennis)		2·10	70
537	50s. red (Running)		1·50	60
538	1b. blue (Weightlifting)		6·50	2·30
539	1b.25 black (Boxing)		9·25	5·75
540	2b. blue (Swimming)		14·00	2·10
541	3b. brown (Basketball)		28·00	7·00
542	5b. purple (Football)		80·00	19·00

See also Nos. 553/6.

148 Emblem and Fair Buildings

1966. First International Trade Fair, Bangkok.

543	148	50s. purple	2·50	1·20
544	148	1b. brown	7·00	2·30

149 "Reading and Writing"

1966. International Correspondence Week.

545	-	50s. red	2·30	70
546	-	1b. brown	4·75	1·20
547	149	2b. violet	18·00	1·80
548	149	3b. green	10·50	3·50

DESIGN: 50s., 1b. "Map" envelope representing the five continents and pen.

150 U.N. Emblem

1966. United Nations Day.

549	150	50s. blue	2·30	60

151 Pra Buddha Bata (monastery)

1966. 20th Anniv of U.N.E.S.C.O.

550	151	50s. green and black	1·90	35

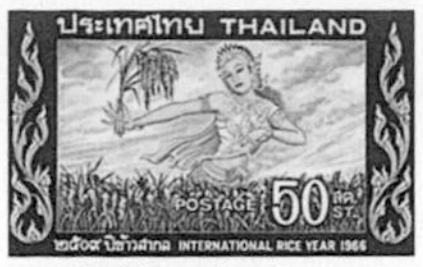

152 "Goddess of Rice"

1966. International Rice Year.

551	**152**	50s. blue and green	5·75	1·20
552	**152**	3b. red and purple	23·00	7·00

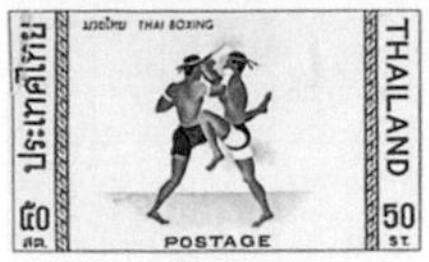

153 Thai Boxing

1966. Fifth Asian Games, Bangkok. Each black, red and brown.

553	50s. Type **153**	3·00	1·20
554	1b. Takraw (ball game)	9·25	2·50
555	2b. "Kite fighting"	41·00	5·75
556	3b. "Cudgel play"	35·00	15·00

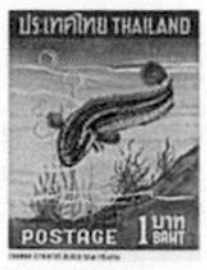

154 Chevron Snakehead

1967. Fish. Multicoloured.

557	1b. Type **154**	10·50	1·90
558	2b. Short mackerel	41·00	3·50
559	3b. Siamese barb	23·00	8·25
560	5b. Siamese fighting fish	29·00	9·25

The 2 and 3b. are size 45×26 mm.

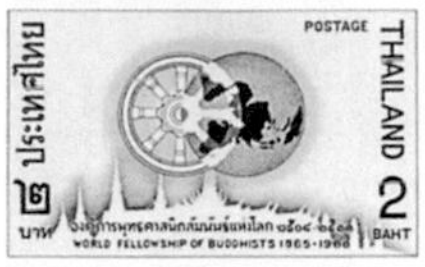

155 Djarmachakra and Globe

1967. Establishment of Buddhist World Fellowship Headquarters in Thailand.

561	**155**	2b. black and yellow	9·25	1·80

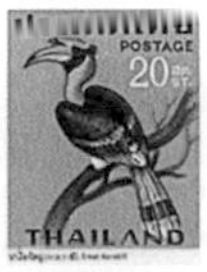

156 Great Indian Hornbill

1967. Birds. Multicoloured.

562	20s. Type **156**	2·30	1·20
563	25s. Southern grackle ("Talking Myna")	3·50	2·30
564	50s. White-rumped shama	5·75	1·80
565	1b. Siamese fireback pheasant ("Diard's Fireback Pheasant")	8·00	3·00
566	1b.50 Spotted-necked dove	8·25	3·50
567	2b. Sarus crane	41·00	5·75
568	3b. White-throated kingfisher ("White-breasted Kingfisher")	28·00	10·50
569	5b. Asian open-bill stork ("Open-billed Storks")	43·00	11·50

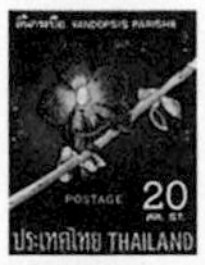

157 "Vandopsis parishii"

1967. Thai Orchids. Multicoloured.

570	20s. Type **157**	2·10	95
571	50s. "Ascocentrum curvifolium"	3·00	70
572	80s. "Rhynchostylis retusa"	5·25	2·30
573	1b. "Rhynchostylis gigantea"	7·25	2·50
574	1b.50 "Dendrobium alconeri"	7·50	2·75
575	2b. "Paphiopedilum callosum"	35·00	4·75
576	3b. "Dendrobium formosum"	26·00	9·25
577	5b. "Dendrobium primulinum"	41·00	9·25

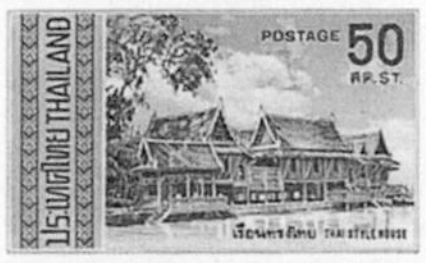

158 Thai House

1967. Thai Architecture.

578	**158**	50s. violet and blue	3·00	1·20
579	-	1b.50 chestnut and brown	8·25	4·50
580	-	2b. blue and turquoise	35·00	4·75
581	-	3b. brown and yellow	23·00	10·50

BUILDINGS: 1b.50, Pagodas; 2b. Temple bell-tower; 3b. Temple.

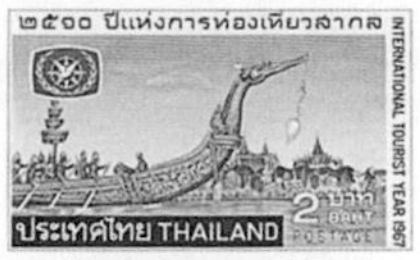

159 "Sri Suphanahong" (royal barge) and Palace

1967. International Tourist Year.

582	**159**	2b. brown and blue	14·00	3·00

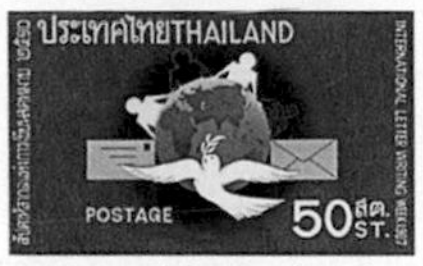

160 Dove, Globe, People and Letters

1967. International Correspondence Week.

583	**160**	50s. multicoloured	1·20	60
584	**160**	1b. multicoloured	4·75	95
585	-	2b. black and green	10·50	1·20
586	-	3b. black and brown	19·00	4·00

DESIGNS: 2, 3b. Handclasp, globe and doves.

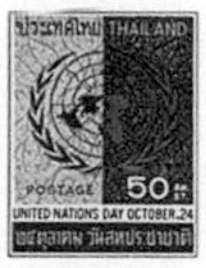

161 U.N. Emblem

1967. United Nations Day.

587	**161**	50s. multicoloured	2·10	35

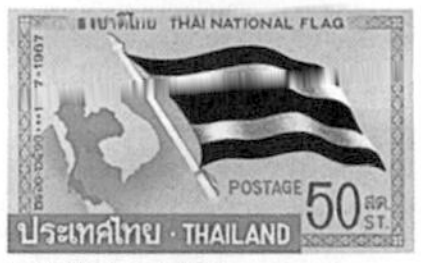

162 National Flag

1967. 50th Anniv of Thai National Flag.

588	**162**	50s. red, blue & turquoise	2·30	1·20
589	**162**	2b. red, blue and green	10·50	2·30

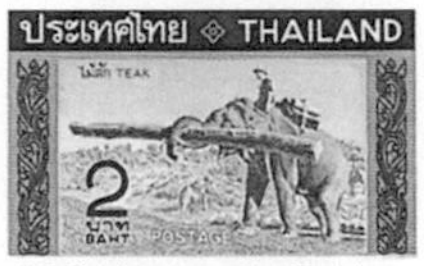

163 Elephant carrying Teak Log

1968. Export Promotion.

590	**163**	2b. brown and red	10·50	1·20

See also Nos. 630, 655 and 673.

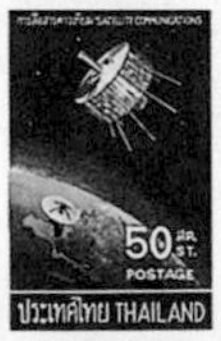

164 Satellite and Thai Tracking Station

1968. "Satellite Communications".

591	**164**	50s. multicoloured	1·10	25
592	**164**	3b. multicoloured	5·25	1·60

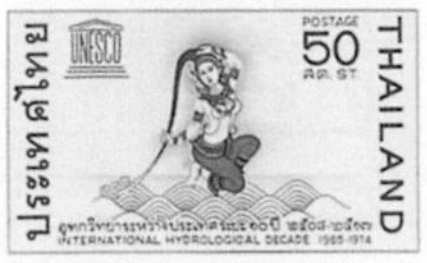

165 "Goddess of the Earth"

1968. International Hydrological Decade.

593	**165**	50s. multicoloured	3·50	60

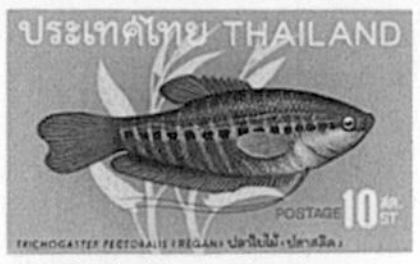

166 Snakeskin Gourami

1968. Thai Fish. Multicoloured.

594	10s. Type **166**	1·50	45
595	20s. Red-tailed black shark	2·30	60
596	25s. Thai mahseer	2·50	95
597	50s. Giant pangasius	6·50	1·20
598	80s. Bumblebee catfish	8·75	4·75
599	1b.25 Rambaia goby	9·25	7·00
600	1b.50 Giant carp	35·00	5·75
601	4b. Clown knifefish	70·00	21·00

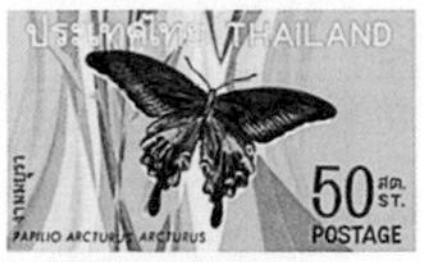

167 Blue Peacock

1968. Thai Butterflies. Multicoloured.

602	50s. Type **167**	2·50	1·20
603	1b. Golden birdwing	10·50	3·25
604	3b. Great mormon	30·00	9·25
605	4b. "Papilio palinurus"	42·00	18·00

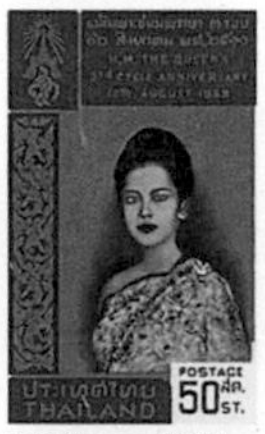

168 Queen Sirikit

1968. Queen Sirikit's "Third Cycle" Anniversary. Designs showing Queen Sirikit in different Thai costumes.

606	**168**	50s. multicoloured	1·20	70
607	-	2b. multicoloured	6·50	2·30
608	-	3b. multicoloured	15·00	4·75
609	-	5b. multicoloured	23·00	8·25

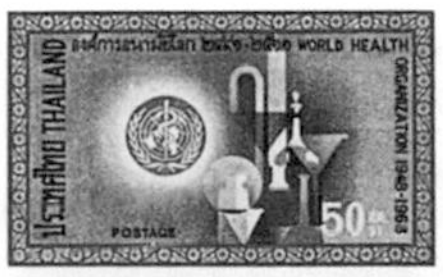

169 W.H.O. Emblem and Medical Equipment

1968. 20th Anniv of W.H.O.

610	**169**	50s. black and green	2·30	35

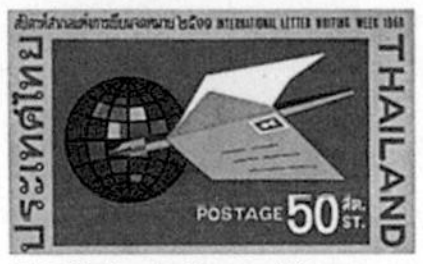

170 Globe, Letter and Pen

1968. International Correspondence Week. Multicoloured.

611	50s. Type **170**	60	45
612	1b. Globe on pen nib	2·10	80
613	2b. Type **170**	4·00	1·20
614	3b. Globe on pen nib	14·00	3·00

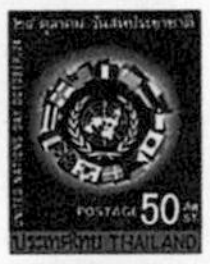

171 U.N. Emblem and Flags

1968. United Nations Day.

615	**171**	50s. multicoloured	1·80	35

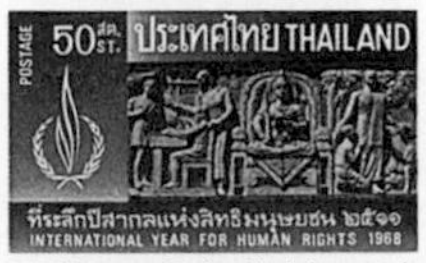

172 Human Rights Emblem and Sculpture

1968. 20th Anniv of Human Rights Year.

616	**172**	50s. violet, red and green	2·30	60

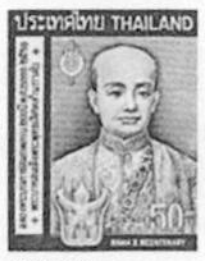

173 King Rama II

1968. Birth Bicentenary of King Rama II.

617	**173**	50s. yellow and brown	2·30	60

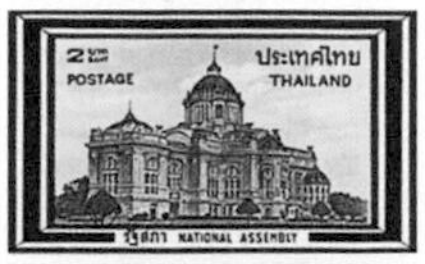

174 National Assembly Building

1969. First Election Day under New Constitution.

618	**174**	50s. multicoloured	1·30	35
619	**174**	2b. multicoloured	7·50	1·80

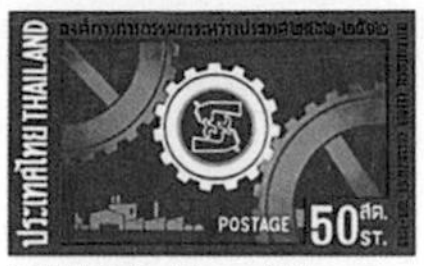

175 I.L.O. Emblem within Cogwheels

1969. 50th Anniv of I.L.O.

620	**175**	50s. blue, black and violet	1·30	35

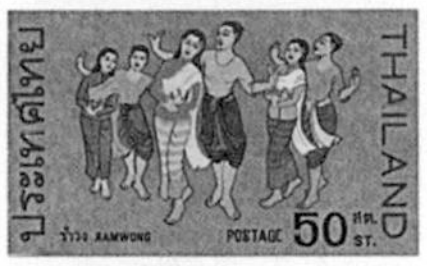

176 Ramwong Dance

1969. Thai Classical Dances. Multicoloured.

621	50s. Type **176**	95	45
622	1b. Candle dance	2·30	95
623	2b. Krathop Mai dance	5·25	1·20
624	3b. Nohra dance	[illegible]	[illegible]

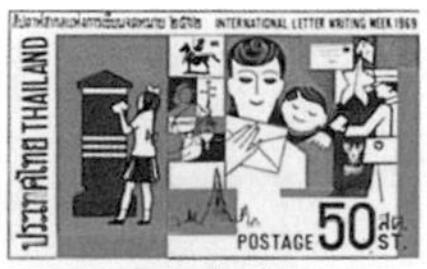

177 "Letters by Post"

1969. International Correspondence Week. Multicoloured.

625	50s. Type **177**	95	60
626	1b. Type **177**	2·00	70
627	2b. Writing and posting a letter	3·50	95
628	3b. As 2b.	4·75	2·10

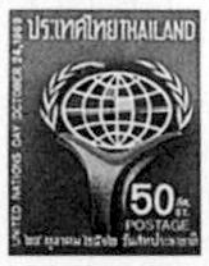

178 Globe in Hand

1969. United Nations Day.

629	**178**	50s. multicoloured	2·10	60

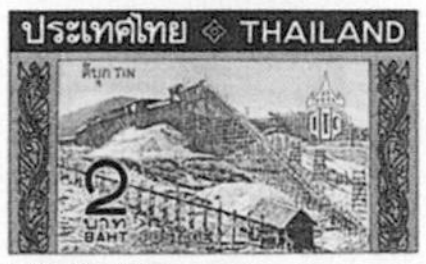

179 Tin Mine

1969. Export Promotion and Second Technical Conf of the International Tin Council, Bangkok.

630	**179**	2b. blue, brown and light blue	7·50	95

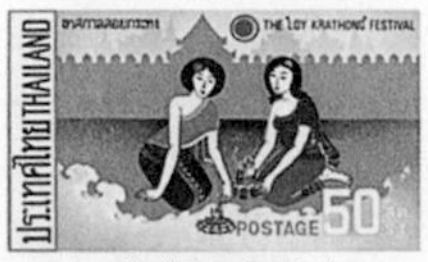

180 Loy Krathong Festival

1969. Thai Ceremonies and Festivals. Multicoloured.

631	50s. Type **180**	1·50	35
632	1b. Marriage ceremony	2·50	95
633	2b. Khwan ceremony	4·00	1·20
634	5b. Songkran festival	7·00	2·50

181 Breguet 14 Mail Plane

1969. 50th Anniv of Thai Airmail Services.
635   **181**   1b. brown, green and
blue   2·50   70

182 "Phra Rama"

1969. Nang Yai Shadow Theatre. Multicoloured.
636   50s. Type **182**   95   45
637   2b. "Ramasura"   5·00   60
638   3b. "Mekhala"   4·75   1·80
639   5b. "Ungkhut"   8·75   2·00

183 "Improvement of Productivity"

1969. Productivity Year.
640   **183**   50s. multicoloured   95   35

184 Thai Temples within I.C.W. Emblem

1970. 19th Triennial Conference of International Council of Women, Bangkok.
641   **184**   50s. black and blue   1·90   45

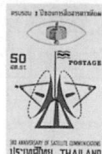

185 Dish Aerials

1970. Third Anniv of Thai Satellite Communications.
642   **185**   50s. multicoloured   95   35

186 Households and Data

1970. Seventh Population Census.
643   **186**   1b. multicoloured   1·40   60

187 New Headquarters Building

1970. Inauguration of New U.P.U. Headquarters Building, Berne.
644   **187**   50s. black, green and
blue   1·40   60

188 Khun Ram Kamhang as Teacher

1970. International Education Year.
645   **188**   50s. multicoloured   2·00   70

189 Swimming Stadium

1970. Sixth Asian Games, Bangkok.
646   **189**   50s. lilac, red and yellow   1·30   45
647   —   1b.50 green, red and
blue   3·00   95
648   —   3b. black, red and
bronze   3·75   1·60
649   —   5b. blue, red and green   5·75   1·80
STADIUMS: 1b.50, Velodrome; 3b. Subhajala-saya Stadium; 5b. Kittikachorn Indoor Stadium.
See also No. 660.

190 Boy and Girl writing Letter

1970. International Correspondence Week Multicoloured.
650   50s. Type **190**   95   45
651   1b. Woman writing letter   2·20   70
652   2b. Women reading letters   5·25   95
653   3b. Man reading letter   5·25   2·50
See also Nos. 683/6.

191 U.N. Emblem and Royal Palace, Bangkok

1970. 25th Anniv of United Nations.
654   **191**   50s. multicoloured   2·10   60

1970. Export Promotion. As T 163.
655   2b. brown, red and green   4·75   1·20
DESIGN: 2b. Rubber plantation.

193 The Heroes of Bangrachan

1970. Heroes and Heroines of Thai History.
656   **193**   50s. violet and red   95   70
657   —   1b. purple and violet   2·10   95
658   —   2b. brown and mauve   5·25   1·20
659   —   3b. green and blue   7·50   2·30
DESIGNS: 1b. Heroines Thao Thepkrasatri and Thao Srisunthorn on ramparts; 2b. Queen Suriyothai riding elephant; 3b. Phraya Phichaidaphak and battle scene.

194 King Bhumibol lighting Flame

1970. Inaug of 6th Asian Games, Bangkok.
660   **194**   1b. multicoloured   3·00   95

195 Woman playing So Sam Sai

1970. Classical Thai Musical Instruments. Multicoloured.
661   50s. Type **195**   95   60
662   1b. Khlui phiang-o (flute)   3·00   95
663   3b. Krachappi (guitar)   4·25   1·40
664   5b. Thon rammana (drums)   7·75   1·60

196 Chocolate-point Siamese

1971. Siamese Cats. Multicoloured.
665   50s. Type **196**   1·20   70
666   1b. Blue-point cat   5·75   1·40
667   2b. Seal-point cat   9·25   1·60
668   3b. Pure white cat and kittens   11·50   4·00

197 Pagoda, Nakhon Si Thammarat

1971. Buddhist Holy Places in Thailand. Pagodas.
669   **197**   50s. black, brown and
mauve   1·10   45
670   —   1b. brown, violet and
green   2·10   60
671   —   3b. sepia, brown &
orange   4·50   95
672   —   4b. brown, sepia and
blue   8·00   4·00
DESIGNS: 1b. Nakhon Phanom; 3b. Nakhon Pathom; 4b. Chiang Mai.

1971. Export Promotion. As T 163.
673   2b. multicoloured   3·00   95
DESIGN: 2b. Corncob and field.

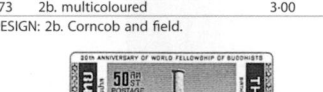

199 Buddha's Birthplace, Lumbini, Nepal

1971. 20th Anniv of World Fellowship of Buddhists.
674   **199**   50s. black and blue   1·50   45
675   —   1b. black and green   2·00   80
676   —   2b. black and brown   5·00   1·10
677   —   3b. black and red   4·00   2·20
DESIGNS: 1b. "Place of Enlightenment", Buddha Gaya, Bihar; 2b. "Place of First Sermon", Sarnath, Banaras; 3b. "Place of Final Passing Away", Kusinara.

200 King Bhumibol and Thai People

1971. 25th Anniv of Coronation.
678   **200**   50s. multicoloured   2·00   45

201 Floating Market, Wat Sai

1971. Visit ASEAN Year.
679   **201**   4b. multicoloured   4·00   95
ASEAN = Association of South East Asian Nations.

202 King and Queen in Scout Uniform

1971. 60th Anniv of Thai Boy Scout Movement.
680   **202**   50c. black, red and
yellow   2·00   60

1971. "THAILANDPEX '71" National Stamp Exhibition, Bangkok. Optd **4-8 AUGUST 1971 THAILANDPEX'71** in English and Thai and map within "perforations", covering four stamps.
681   **119**   80s. orange   11·50   12·50
682   **132**   80s. orange   11·50   12·50
Prices are for blocks of four stamps showing the entire overprint.

1971. International Correspondence Week. As T **190**. Multicoloured.
683   50s. Two girls writing a letter   70   25
684   1b. Two girls reading letters   1·80   45
685   2b. Women with letter on
veranda   2·50   60
686   3b. Man handing letter to
woman   5·00   2·00

205 Marble Temple, Bangkok

1971. United Nations Day.
687   **205**   50s. multicoloured   2·20   70

206 Raising Ducks

1971. Rural Life. Multicoloured.
688   50s. Type **206**   95   25
689   1b. Growing tobacco seedlings   1·50   45
690   2b. Cooping fish   2·00   60
691   3b. Cleaning rice-seed   4·75   2·30

207 Mother and Child

1971. 25th Anniv of U.N.I.C.E.F.
692   **207**   50s. multicoloured   95   25

208 Costumes from Chiang Saen Period (17th-century)

1972. Historical Costumes. Multicoloured.
693   50s. Type **208**   1·20   60
694   1b. Sukhothai period (13th–
14th centuries)   1·90   1·10
695   1b.50 Ayudhya period (14th–
17th centuries)   4·75   1·20
696   2b. Bangkok period (18th–19th
centuries)   8·75   2·50

209 Globe and A.O.P.U. Emblem

1972. Tenth Anniv of Asian–Oceanic Postal Union.
697   **209**   75s. blue   1·60   35

210 King Bhumibol

1972
698   **210**   10s. green   70   25
699   **210**   20s. blue   1·10   35
700   **210**   25s. red   1·20   40
701   **210**   50s. green   2·20   45
702   **210**   75s. lilac   2·30   45
703   **210**   1b.25 pink and green   4·25   60
704   **210**   2b. violet and red   4·50   65
705   **210**   2b.75 turquoise and
purple   4·00   95
706   **210**   3b. blue and brown   8·25   1·10
707   **210**   4b. red and blue   5·00   1·20
708   **210**   5b. brown and violet   5·25   1·30
709   **210**   6b. violet and green   11·00   1·40
710   **210**   10b. black and red   8·75   95

711	210	20b. green and orange	2·10	20
898d	210	40b. violet and brown	18·00	2·75
712a	210	50b. green and purple	65·00	5·25
713	210	100b. blue and orange	£100	8·25

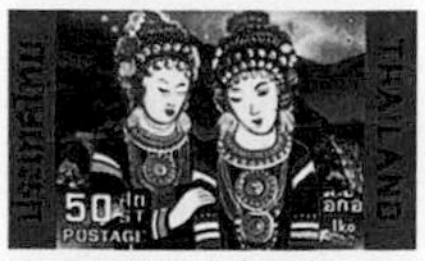

211 Two Women, Iko Tribe

1972. Hill Tribes of Thailand. Multicoloured.

714	50s. Type **211**	45	20
715	2b. Musician and children, Musoe tribe	2·30	60
716	4b. Woman embroidering, Yao tribe	11·50	5·25
717	5b. Woman with chickens, Maeo tribe	16·00	1·50

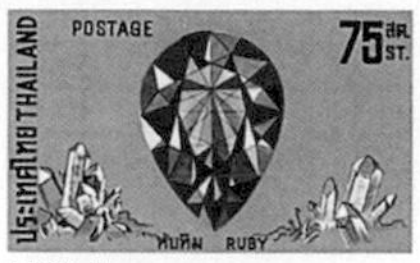

212 Ruby

1972. Precious Stones.

718	212	75s. multicoloured	2·50	35
719	-	2b. multicoloured	13·00	1·50
720	-	4b. black and green	16·00	5·75
721	-	6b. brown, black and red	18·00	5·25

DESIGNS: 2b. Yellow sapphire; 4b. Zircon; 6b. Star sapphire.

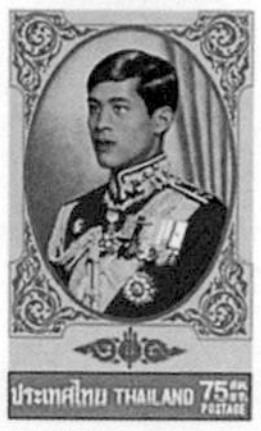

213 Prince Vajiralongkorn

1972. Prince Vajiralongkorn's 20th Birthday.

722	213	75s. multicoloured	3·00	60

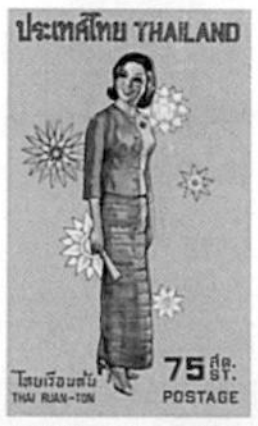

214 Thai Ruan-ton Costume

1972. Thai Women's National Costumes. Multicoloured.

723	75s. Type **214**	1·50	25
724	2b. Thai Chitrlada	3·00	1·10
725	4b. Thai Chakri	8·25	4·75
726	5b. Thai Borompimarn	8·75	3·75
MS727	120×160 mm. Nos. 723/6 (sold at 20b.)	70·00	60·00

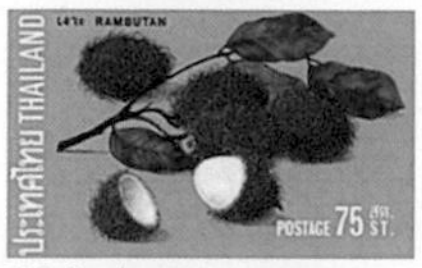

215 Rambutan

1972. Thai Fruit. Multicoloured.

728	75s. Type **215**	1·50	35
729	1b. Mangosteen	3·50	95
730	3b. Durian	7·50	2·10
731	5b. Mango	18·00	3·75

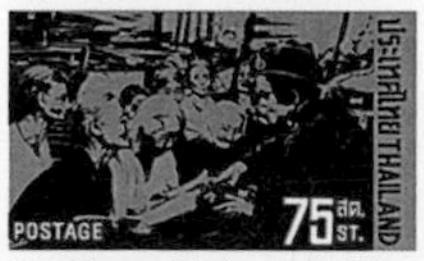

216 Princess-Mother with Old People

1972. Princess-Mother Sisangwan's 72nd Birthday.

732	216	75s. green and orange	7·50	1·50

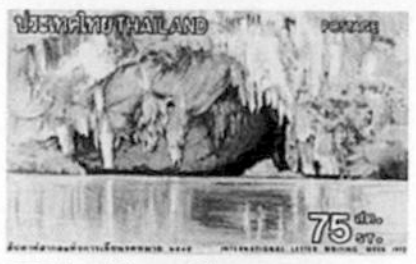

217 Lod Cave, Phangnga

1972. International Correspondence Week. Multicoloured.

733	75s. Type **217**	1·20	60
734	1b.25 Kang Kracharn Reservoir, Phetchaburi	2·50	1·40
735	2b.75 Erawan Waterfall, Kanchanaburi	8·25	95
736	3b. Nok-kaw Mountain, Loei	7·00	2·30

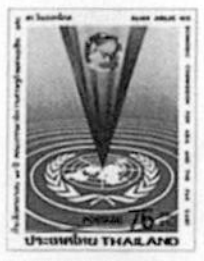

218 Globe on U.N. Emblem

1972. 25th Anniv of E.C.A.F.E.

737	218	75s. multicoloured	1·20	95

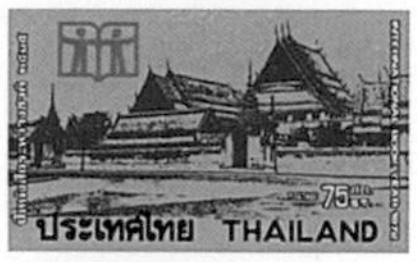

219 Watphrajetubon Vimolmanklaram Rajvaramahaviharn (ancient university)

1972. International Book Year.

738	219	75s. multicoloured	95	35

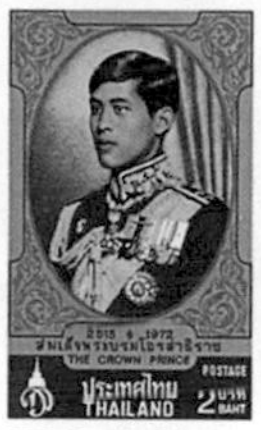

220 Crown Prince Vajiralongkorn

1972. Investiture of Crown Prince.

739	220	2b. multicoloured	2·75	60

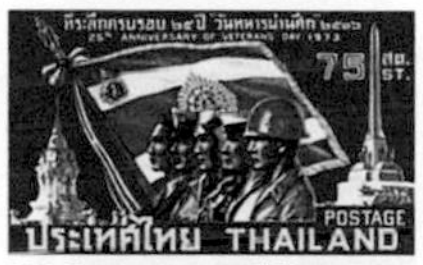

221 Servicemen and Flag

1973. 25th Anniv of Veterans' Day.

740	221	75s. multicoloured	1·80	35

1973. Red Cross Fair (1972). Nos. 472/3 surch **75+25 2515 1972.**

741	130	75s.+25s. on 50s.+10s.	1·40	1·40
742	-	75s.+25s. on 50s.+10s.	1·40	1·40

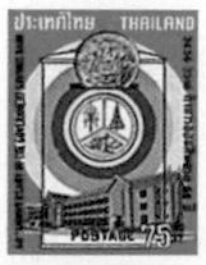

223 Emblem, Bank and Coin-box

1973. 60th Anniv of Government Savings Bank.

743	223	75s. multicoloured	1·30	35

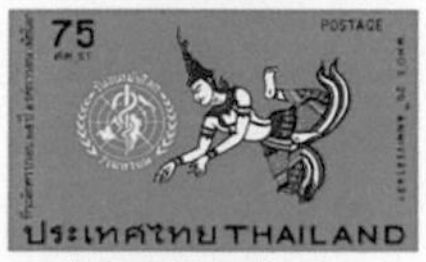

224 "Celestial Being" and Emblem

1973. 25th Anniv of W.H.O.

744	224	75s. multicoloured	1·20	35

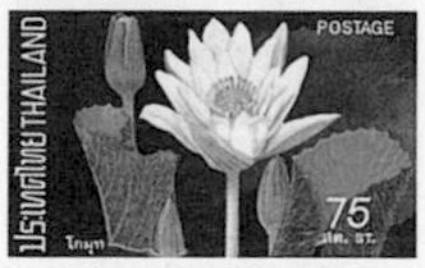

225 "Nymphaea pubescens"

1973. Lotus Flowers. Multicoloured.

745	75s. Type **225**	95	25
746	1b.50 "Nymphaea pubescens" (different)	1·50	70
747	2b. "Nelumbo nucifera"	5·25	80
748	4b. "Nelumbo nucifera" (different)	14·00	5·25

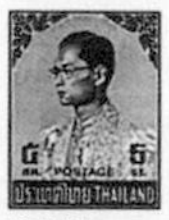

227 King Bhumibol

1973

749	227	5s. purple	2·30	70
1031	227	20s. blue	45	10
1031a	227	25s. red	55	20
1032	227	50s. green	4·75	35
1032a	227	75s. violet	1·50	35
753	227	5b. brown and violet	19·00	2·20
754	227	6b. violet and green	11·00	2·30
755	227	10b. brown and red	21·00	3·00
755a	227	20b. green and orange	£250	11·50

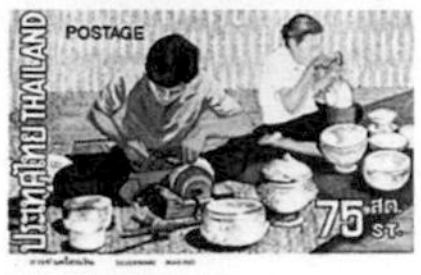

228 Silverware

1973. Thai Handicrafts. Multicoloured.

756	75s. Type **228**	95	25
757	2b.75 Lacquerware	3·50	60
758	4b. Pottery	8·25	4·00
759	5b. Paper umbrellas	7·50	1·50

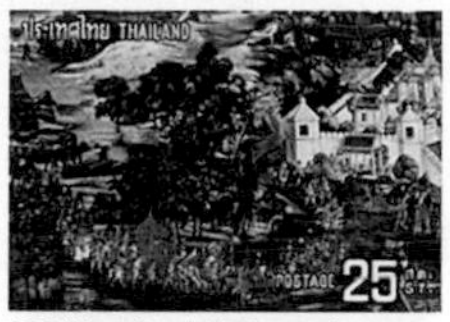

229 King Janaka's Procession

1973. "Ramayana" Mural, Temple of Emerald Buddha, Bangkok. Multicoloured.

760	25s. Type **229**	1·40	45
761	75s. Contest for Sita's hand	1·50	60
762	1b.50 Monkey prince toppling portico	5·00	2·00
763	2b. Monkey king breaking umbrella	8·25	2·50
764	2b.75 Maleenarj as Court chief	4·00	95
765	3b. Sprinkling holy water	14·00	3·00
766	5b. Tapansura fighting Rama	15·00	10·00
767	6b. Bharata on march	8·75	3·75

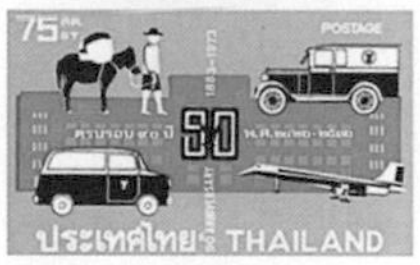

230 "Postal Services"

1973. 90th Anniv of Thai Post and Telegraph Department. Multicoloured.

768	75s. Type **230**	1·10	60
769	2b. "Telecommunication Services"	3·00	1·40

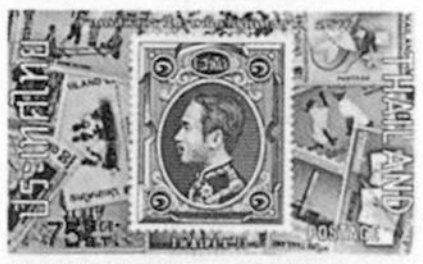

231 1 Solot Stamp of 1883

1973. "THAIPEX 73" National Stamp Exn.

770	231	75s. blue and red	95	25
771	-	1b.25 red and blue	2·30	80
772	-	1b.50 purple and green	8·25	2·30
773	-	2b. green and orange	5·75	95
MS774		191×97 mm. Nos. 770/3. Imperf (sold at 8b.)	30·00	28·00

DESIGNS: 1b.25, 6s. stamp of 1912; 1b.50, 5s. stamp of 1928; 2b. 3s. stamp of 1941.

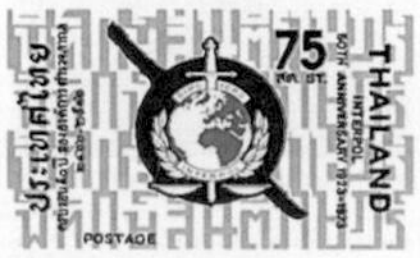

232 Interpol Emblem

1973. 50th Anniv of International Criminal Police Organization (Interpol).

775	232	75s. multicoloured	1·50	35

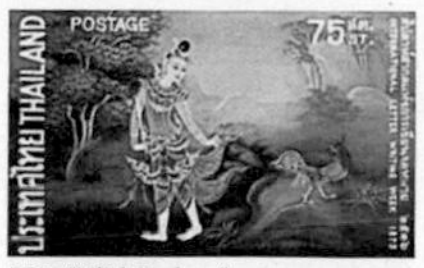

233 "Lilid Pralaw"

1973. Int Correspondence Week. Characters from Thai Literature. Multicoloured.

776	75s. Type **233**	60	25
777	1b.50 "Khun Chang Khun Phan"	2·30	70
778	2b. "Sang Thong"	5·25	2·10
779	5b. "Pha Apai Manee"	14·00	2·30
MS780	166×104 mm. Nos. 776/9 (sold at 15b.)	55·00	47·00

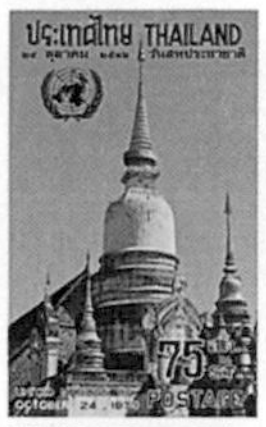

234 Wat Suan Dok Temple, Chiangmai

1973. United Nations Day.

781	234	75s. multicoloured	1·80	45

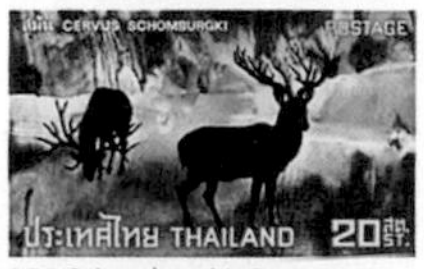

235 Schomburgk's Deer

1973. Protected Wild Animals. Multicoloured.

782	20s. Type **235**	95	35
783	25s. Kouprey	1·20	45
784	75r. Common gorals	2·10	60
785	1b.25 Water buffaloes	2·30	1·40
786	1b.50 Javan rhinoceros	11·50	4·00
787	2b. Thamin	15·00	4·75
788	2b.75 Sumatran rhinoceros	8·75	1·50
789	4b. Mainland serows	16·00	11·50

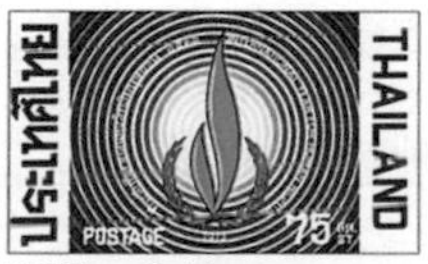

236 Flame Emblem

1973. 25th Anniv of Declaration of Human Rights.

790	236	75s. multicoloured	2·10	70

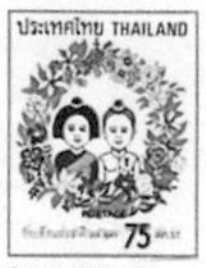

238 Children within Flowers

1973. Children's Day.

791	238	75s. multicoloured	2·20	45

1974. Red Cross Fair. Nos. 472/3 surch **75+25 1973** in English and Thai.

792	130	75s.+25s. on 50s.+10s.	2·00	2·00
793	-	75s.+25s. on 50s.+10s.	2·00	2·00

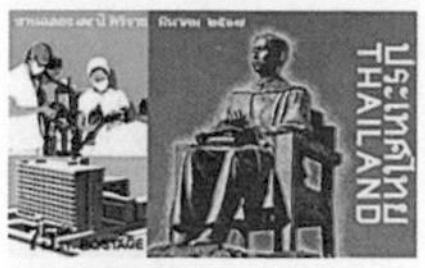

240 Statue of Krom Luang Songkia Nakarin

1974. 84th Anniv of Siriraj Hospital.

794	240	75s. multicoloured	1·90	60

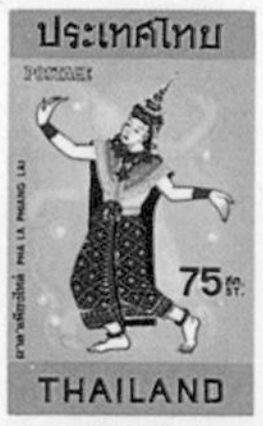

241 "Pha la Phiang Lai"

1974. Thai Classical Dance. Multicoloured.

795	75s. Type **241**	1·80	60
796	2b.75 "Phra Lak Phlaeng Rit"	4·50	95
797	4b. "Chin Sao Sai"	9·75	5·75
798	5b. "Charot Phra Sumen"	10·00	4·75

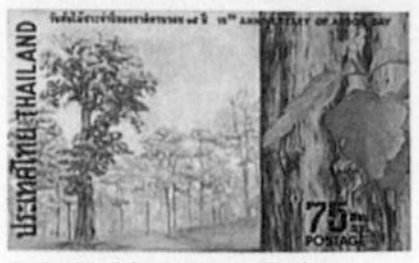

242 World's Largest Teak, Amphur Nam-Pad

1974. 15th Anniv of Arbor Day.

799	**242**	75s. multicoloured	1·50	60

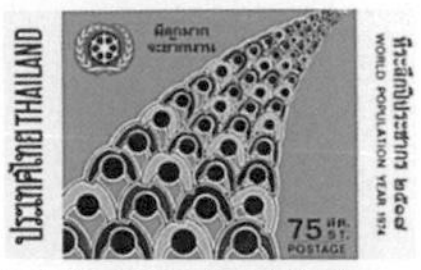

243 "Increasing Population"

1974. World Population Year.

800	**243**	75s. multicoloured	1·50	60

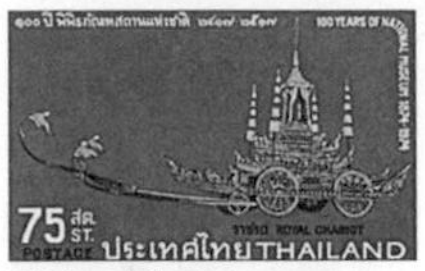

244 Royal Chariot

1974. Centenary of National Museum. Multicoloured.

801	75s. Type **244**	1·30	60
802	2b. Ban Chiang painted pottery vase	3·50	1·30
803	2b.75 Avalokitesavara Bodhisattva statue	4·50	1·10
804	3b. King Mongkut Rama IV	6·00	3·25

Nos. 802/4 have the face values incorrectly shown as "BATH".

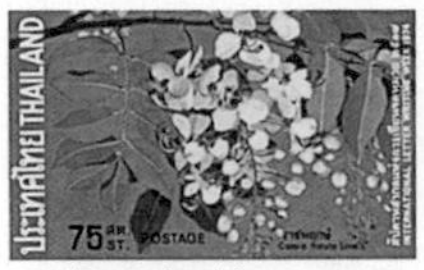

245 "Cassia fistula"

1974. International Correspondence Week. Tropical Plants. Multicoloured.

805	75s. Type **245**	95	25
806	2b.75 "Butea superba"	4·00	95
807	3b. "Jasminum sambac"	8·25	1·60
808	4b. "Lagerstroemia speciosa"	7·00	3·00
MS809	169×100 mm. Nos. 805/8 (sold at 15b.)	65·00	60·00

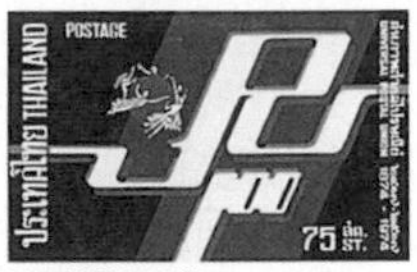

246 "UPU 100"

1974. Centenary of U.P.U.

810	**246**	75s. multicoloured	1·60	70

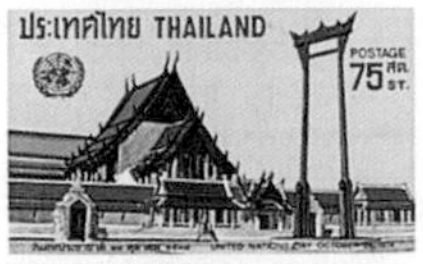

247 Wat Suthat Thepvararam

1974. United Nations Day.

811	**247**	75s. multicoloured	2·20	70

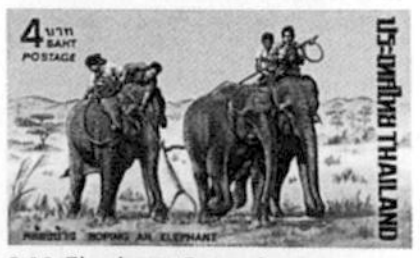

248 Elephant Round-up

1974. Tourism.

812	**248**	4b. multicoloured	7·00	3·00

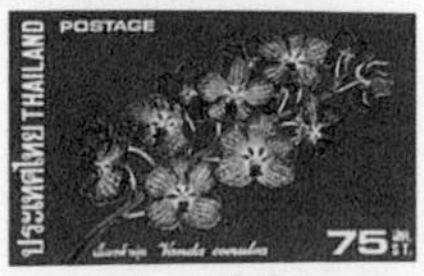

249 "Vanda coerulea"

1974. Thai Orchids (1st series). Multicoloured.

813	75s. Type **249**	1·40	45
814	2b.75 "Dendrobium aggregatum"	3·50	1·10
815	3b. "Dendrobium scabrilingue"	6·25	3·00
816	4b. "Aerides falcata" var "houlletiana"	6·50	3·50
MS817	138×105 mm. Nos. 813/16 (sold at 15b.)	70·00	65·00

See also Nos. 847/**MS**851.

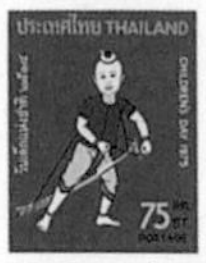

250 Boy riding Toy Horse

1974. Children's Day.

818	**250**	75c. multicoloured	2·30	80

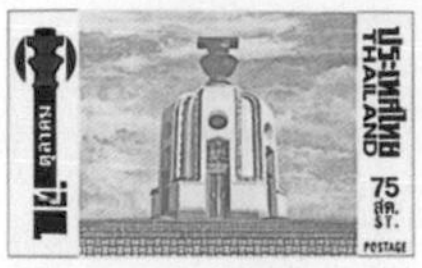

252 Democracy Monument

1975. Democratic Institutions Campaign. Multicoloured.

819	75s. Type **252**	1·40	45
820	2b. "Rights and Liberties"	3·75	95
821	2b.75 "Freedom to choose work"	6·50	1·20
822	5b. Top of monument and text	7·00	2·75

1975. Red Cross Fair 1974. Nos. 472/3 surch **1974 75+25** in English and Thai.

823	**130**	75s.+25s. on 50s.+10s. red and grey	2·00	2·00
824	-	75s.+25s. on 50s.+10s. red and grey	2·00	2·00

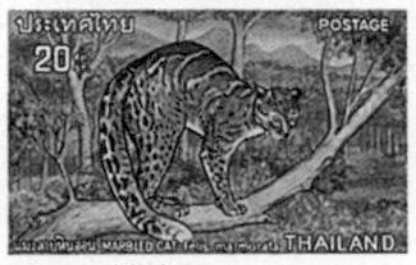

254 Marbled Cat

1975. Protected Wild Animals (1st series). Multicoloured.

825	20s. Type **254**	1·50	95
826	75s. Gaur	3·50	1·20
827	2b.75 Indian elephant	11·50	2·00
828	3b. Clouded leopard	8·75	5·00

See Nos. 913/16.

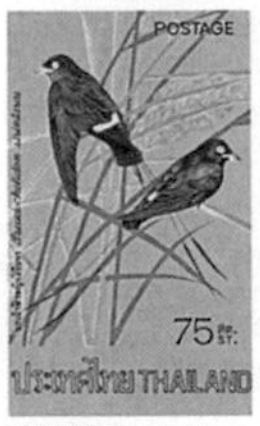

255 White-eyed River Martin

1975. Thailand Birds. Multicoloured.

829	75s. Type **255**	2·30	1·40
830	2b. Asiatic paradise fly catcher	5·50	2·30
831	2b.75 Long-tailed broadbill	7·00	2·75
832	5b. Sultan tit	11·50	4·25

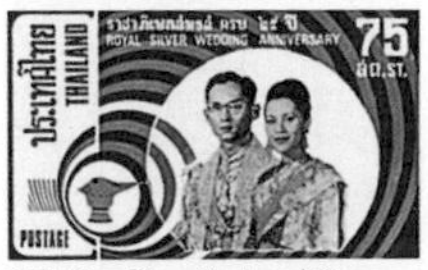

256 King Bhumibol and Queen Sirikit

1975. Silver Wedding of King Bhumibol and Queen Sirikit. Multicoloured.

833	75s. Type **256**	3·50	95
834	3b. As Type **256**, but different background	6·50	2·20

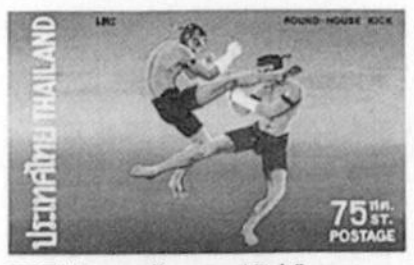

257 "Roundhouse Kick"

1975. Thai Boxing. Multicoloured.

835	75s. Type **257**	2·30	95
836	2b.75 "Reverse elbow"	5·75	1·80
837	3b. "Flying knee"	7·00	3·50
838	5b. "Ritual homage"	21·00	5·75

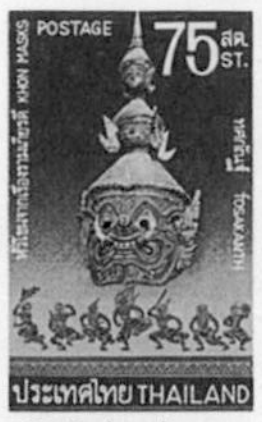

258 Toskanth

1975. Thai Culture. Masks. Multicoloured.

839	75s. Type **258**	2·50	45
840	2b. Kumbhakarn	7·00	95
841	3b. Rama	8·25	2·75
842	4b. Hanuman	20·00	8·75

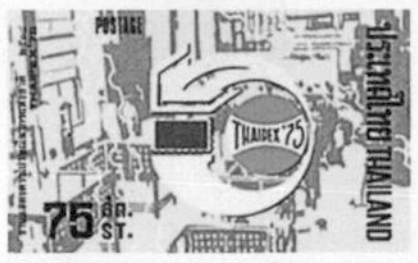

259 "Thaipex 75" Emblem

1975. "Thaipex 75" National Stamp Exhibition, Bangkok. Multicoloured.

843	75s. Type **259**	95	45
844	2b.75 Stamp designer	2·50	95
845	4b. Stamp printing works	4·00	2·50
846	5b. "Stamp collecting"	5·00	95

1975. Thai Orchids (2nd series). As T **249**. Multicoloured.

847	75s. "Dendrobium cruentum"	1·30	80
848	2b. "Dendrobium parishii"	3·50	2·10
849	2b.75 "Vanda teres"	6·00	2·30
850	5b. "Vanda denisoniana"	10·00	3·25
MS851	138×105 mm. Nos. 847/50	75·00	70·00

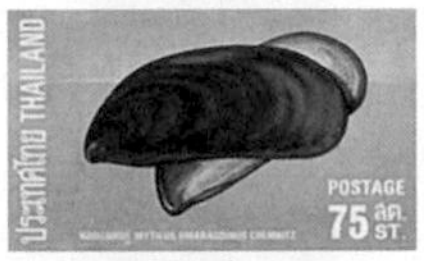

260 Green Mussel

1975. Sea Shells. Multicoloured.

852	75s. Type **260**	3·00	1·30
853	1b. Great green turban	2·50	25
854	2b.75 "Oliva mustelina"	8·25	60
855	5b. Money cowrie	16·00	5·25

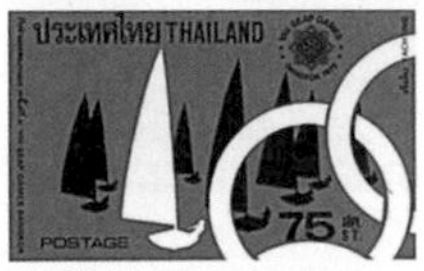

261 Yachting

1975. Eighth South-East Asian Peninsula Games, Bangkok (1st issue).

856	**261**	75s. black and blue	1·50	45
857	-	1b.25 black and mauve	2·00	1·40
858	-	1b.50 black and red	3·50	2·50
859	-	2b. black and green	5·25	2·75
MS860		118×133 mm. Nos. 856/9	60·00	55·00

DESIGNS: 1b.25, Badminton; 1b.50, Volleyball; 2b. Rifle and pistol shooting.

See also Nos. 878/**MS**882.

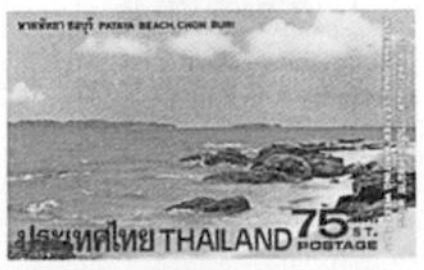

262 Pataya Beach

1975. International Correspondence Week. Multicoloured.

861	75s. Type **262**	1·80	95
862	2b. Samila Beach	3·50	2·20
863	3b. Prachuap Bay	8·75	1·30
864	5b. Laem Singha Bay	10·50	2·30

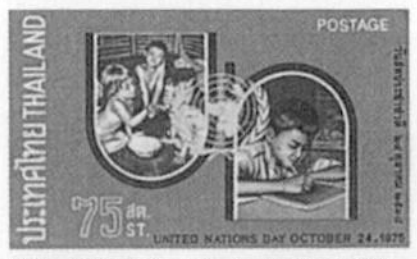

263 Children within Letters "U N"

1975. United Nations Day.

865	**263**	75s. multicoloured	2·10	70

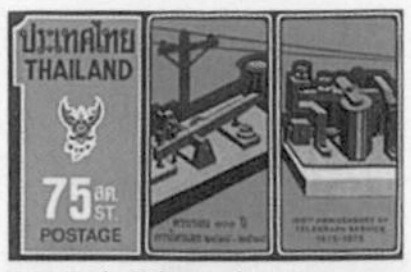

264 Early Telegraphs

1975. Centenary of Telegraph Service. Multicoloured.

866	75s. Type **264**	2·20	1·10
867	2b.75 Teleprinter and dish aerial	3·50	1·20

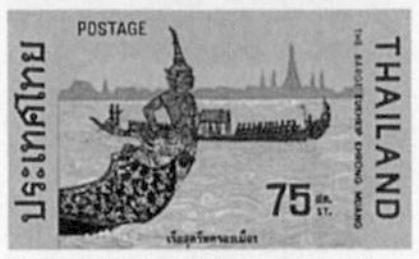

265 "Sukhrip Khrong Muang"

1975. Thai Ceremonial Barges. Multicoloured.

868	75s. Type **265**	3·50	70
869	1b. Royal barge "Anekchat Phuchong"	5·75	2·75
870	2b. Royal barge "Anantanakarat"	8·75	3·00
871	2b.75 "Krabi Ran Ron Rap	10·00	3·25
872	3b. "Asura Wayuphak"	11·50	3·50
873	4b. "Asura Paksi"	13·00	8·75
874	5b. Royal barge "Sri Suphanahong"	22·00	9·25
875	6b. "Phali Rang Thawip"	18·00	8·75

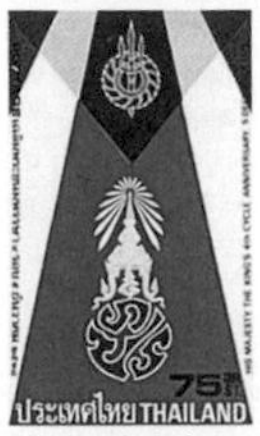

266 King's Cipher and Thai Crown

1975. King Bhumibol's 48th Birthday. Multicoloured.

876	75s. Type **266**	4·00	1·30
877	5b. King Bhumibol in uniform	7·50	2·20

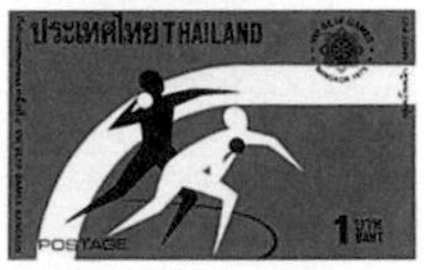

267 Putting the Shot

1975. Eighth South-East Asian Peninsula Games, Bangkok (2nd issue).

878	**267**	1b. black and orange	1·20	35
879	-	2b. black and green	4·00	2·30
880	-	3b. black and yellow	4·75	2·50
881	-	4b. black and violet	5·25	3·50
MS882		118×130 mm. Nos. 878/81	47·00	44·00

DESIGNS: 2b. Table tennis; 3b. Cycling; 4b. Relay-running.

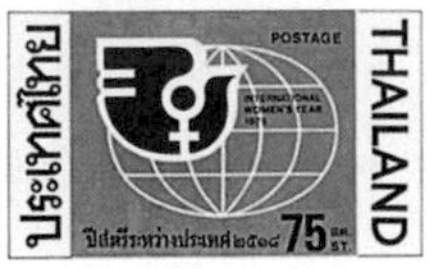

268 I.W.Y. Emblem on Globe

1975. International Women's Year.

883	**268**	75s. blue, orange and black	1·60	45

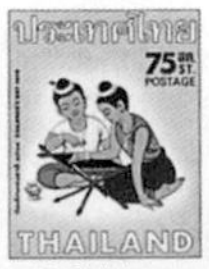

269 Children writing

1976. Children's Day.

884	**269**	75s. multicoloured	2·50	80

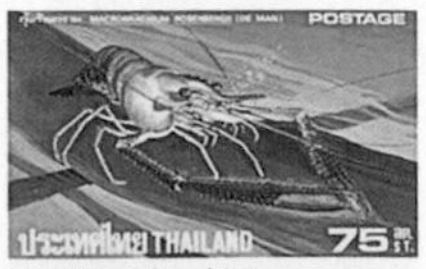

270 "Macrobrachium rosenbergii"

1976. Thai Lobsters and Shrimps. Multicoloured.

885	75s. Type **270**	3·75	45
886	2b. "Penaeus merguiensis"	5·50	3·00
887	2b.75 "Panulirus ornatus"	5·75	1·20
888	5b. "Penaeus monodon"	14·00	6·50

1976. Red Cross Fair 1975. Nos. 472/3 surch **75+25 2518 1975.**

889	**130**	75s.+25s. on 50s.+10s. red and grey	2·00	2·00
890	-	75s.+25s. on 50s.+10s. red and grey	2·00	2·00

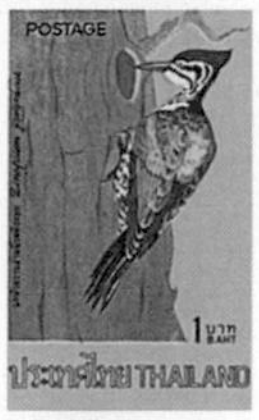

271 Common Gold-backed Woodpecker

1976. Thailand Birds. Multicoloured.

891	1b. Type **271**	95	70
892	1b.50 Greater green-billed malcoha	1·20	95
893	3b. Long-billed scimitar babbler	5·75	1·80
894	4b. Green magpie	4·25	1·40

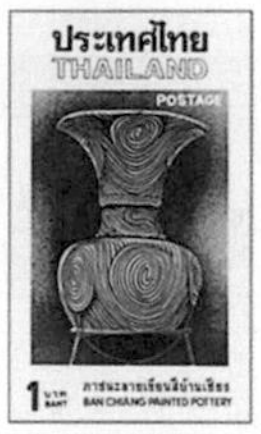

272 Ben Chiang Pot

1976. Ben Chiang Pottery.

895	**272**	1b. multicoloured	2·00	25
896	-	2b. milticoloured	7·50	1·20
897	-	3b. multicoloured	5·25	95
898	-	4b. multicoloured	7·00	5·25

DESIGNS: 2b. to 4b. Various items of pottery.

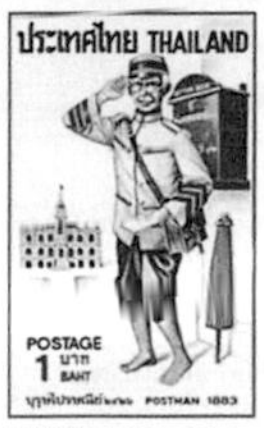

273 Postman of 1883

1976. Postmen's Uniforms. Multicoloured.

899	1b. Type **273**	1·40	45
900	3b. Postman of 1935	3·75	2·30
901	4b. Postman of 1950	5·25	3·50
902	5b. Postman of 1974	8·75	2·30

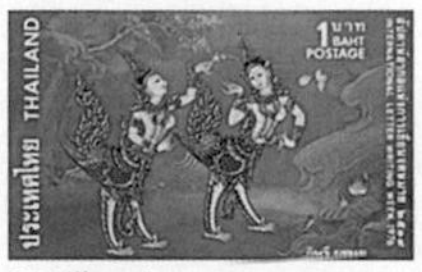

274 Kinnari

1976. Int Correspondence Week. Deities. Multicoloured.

903	1b. Type **274**	8·75	2·50
904	2b. Suphan-Mat-Cha	2·30	45
905	4b. Garuda	3·50	60
906	5b. Naga	5·00	1·20

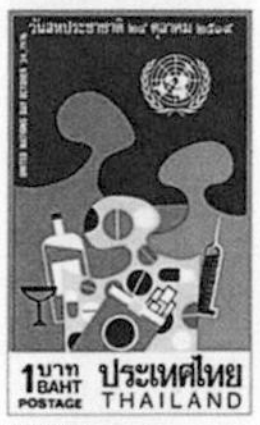

275 "Drug Addictions"

1976. United Nations Day.

907	**275**	1b. multicoloured	1·80	60

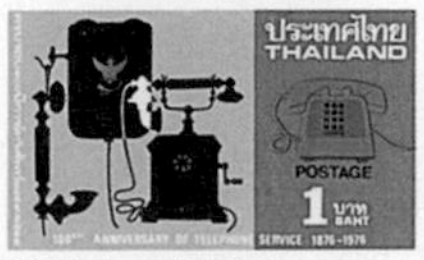

276 Early and Modern Telephones

1976. Telephone Centenary.

908	**276**	1b. multicoloured	1·80	60

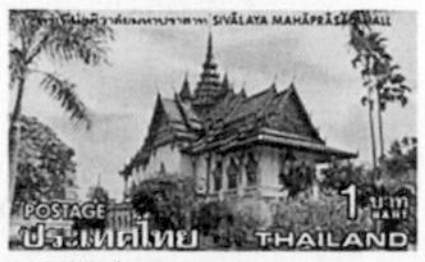

277 Sivalaya

1976. Thai Royal Halls. Multicoloured.

909	1b. Type **277**	1·40	25
910	2b. Cakri	10·00	95
911	4b. Mahisra	5·75	3·50
912	5b. Dusit	7·00	2·30

1976. Protected Wild Animals (2nd series). As T **254**. Multicoloured.

913	1b. Bangteng	8·25	3·50
914	2b. Malayan tapir	9·25	4·00
915	4b. Sambar	4·00	1·40
916	5b. Hog-deer	4·75	1·50

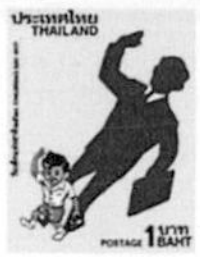

278 "From Child to Adult"

1977. Children's Day.

917	**278**	1b. multicoloured	2·10	45

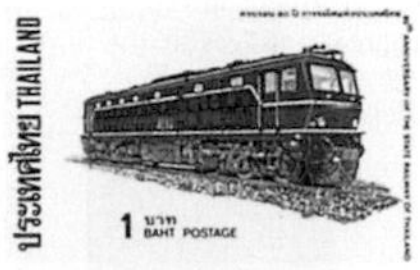

279 Alsthom Diesel-electric Locomotive No. 4101

1977. 80th Anniv of Thai State Railway. Multicoloured.

918	1b. Type **279**	2·10	1·40
919	2b. Davenport diesel locomotive No. 577	8·75	3·75
920	4b. Pacific steam locomotive No. 825, Japan	19·00	11·50
921	5b. George Egestoff's steam locomotive	29·00	8·75

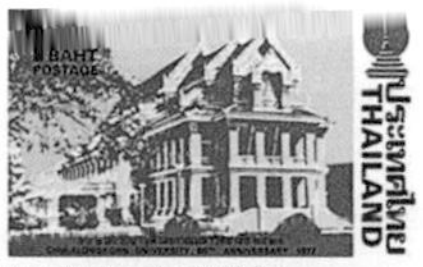

280 University Building

1977. 60th Anniv of Chulalongkorn University.

922	**280**	1b. multicoloured	2·20	60

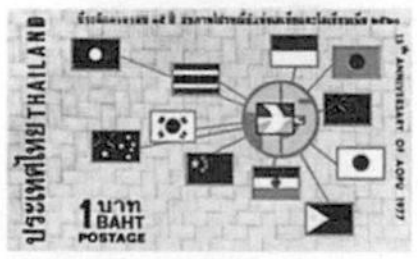

281 Flags of A.O.P.U. Countries

1977. 15th Anniv of Asian–Oceanic Postal Union.

923	**281**	1b. multicoloured	2·20	60

282 Crippled Ex-Serviceman

1977. Sai-Jai-Thai Foundation Day.

924	**282**	5b. multicoloured	2·75	70

1977. Red Cross Fair. Nos. 472/3 surch **75+25 2520-1977.**

925	**130**	75s.+25s. on 50s.+10s. red and grey	2·00	2·00
926	-	75s.+25s. on 50s.+10s. red and grey	2·00	2·00

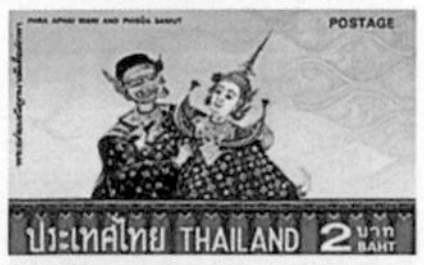

284 Phra Aphai Mani and Phisua Samut

1977. Puppet Shows. Multicoloured.

927	2b. Type **284**	1·20	25
928	3b. Rusi and Sutsakhon	3·00	60
929	4b. Nang Vali and Usren	2·30	45
930	5b. Phra Aphai Mani and Nang Laweng's portrait	3·50	95

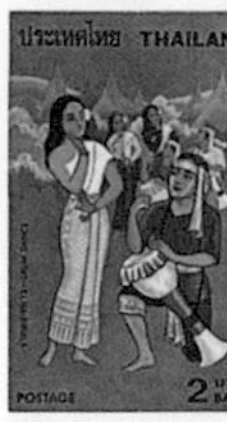

285 Drum Dance

1977. Thai Folk Dances. Multicoloured.

931	2b. Type **285**	45	25
932	3b. Dance of Dip-nets	2·30	70
933	4b. Harvesting dance	2·00	45
934	5b. Kan dance	2·30	70

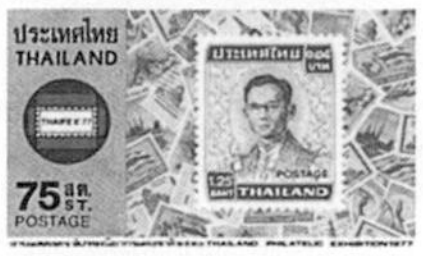

286 1b. Stamp of 1972

1977. "THAIPEX 77" National Stamp Exhibition.

935	**286**	75s. multicoloured	2·10	60

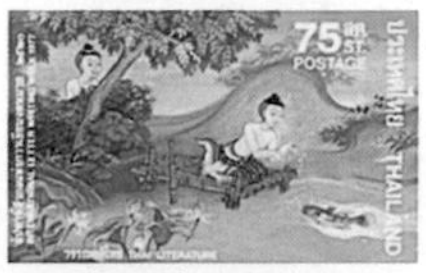

287 "Pla Bu Thong"

1977. International Correspondence Week. Scenes from Thai Literature. Multicoloured.

936	75s. Type **287**	3·00	45
937	2b. "Krai Thong"	3·50	1·20
938	5b. "Nang Kaew Na Ma"	4·25	70
939	6b. "Pra Rot Mali"	5·75	1·40

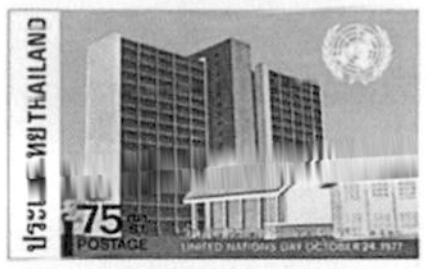

288 U.N. Building, Bangkok

1977. United Nations Day.

940	**288**	75s. multicoloured	2·75	45

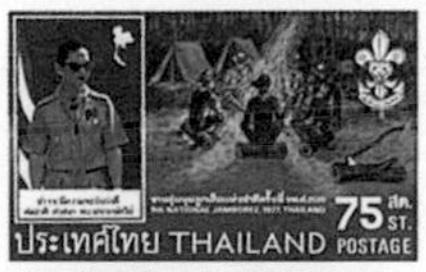

289 King Bhumibol in Scout Uniform, and Camp Fire

1977. Ninth National Scout Jamboree.

941	**289**	75s. multicoloured	3·75	45

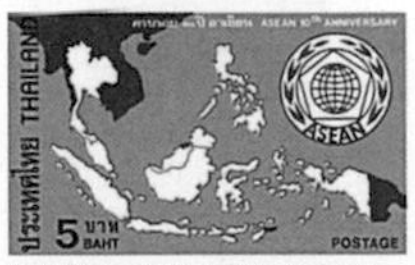

290 Map of A.S.E.A.N. Countries

1977. Tenth Anniv of Association of South East Asian Nations.

942	**290**	5b. multicoloured	3·25	70

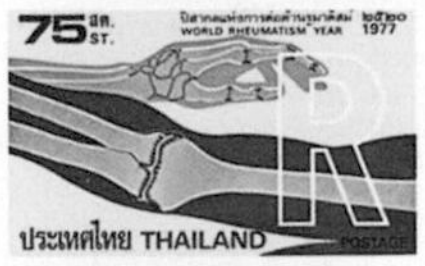

291 Elbow and Wrist Joints

1977. World Rheumatism Year.

943	**291**	75s. multicoloured	1·90	45

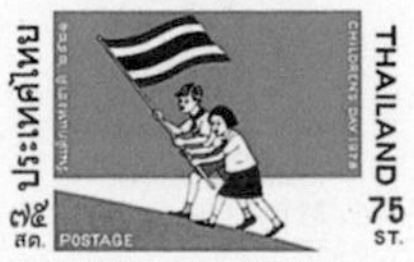

292 Children with Thai Flag

1978. Children's Day.

944	**292**	75s. multicoloured	2·50	70

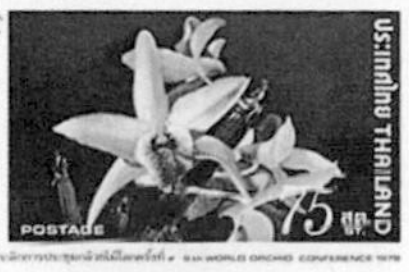

293 "Dendrobium heterocarpum"

1978. Ninth World Orchid Conference. Multicoloured.

945	75s. Type **293**	2·30	80
946	1b. "Dendrobium pulchellum"	3·75	1·50
947	1b.50 "Doritis pulcherrima var buyssoniana"	4·75	3·00
948	2b. "Dendrobium hercoglossum"	95	25
949	2b.75 "Aerides odorata"	8·25	60
950	3b. "Trichoglottis fasciata"	95	25
951	5b. "Dendrobium wardianum"	1·50	35
952	6b. "Dendrobium senile"	2·10	1·50

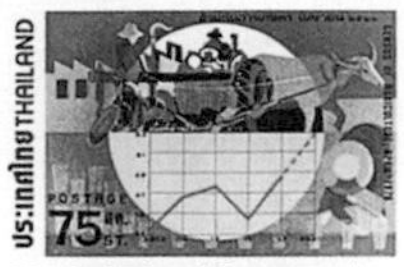

294 Agricultural Scenes and Rice Production Graph

1978. Agricultural Census.

953	**294**	75s. multicoloured	95	25

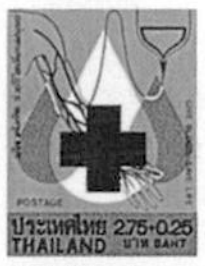

295 Blood Donation and Red Cross

1978. Red Cross.

954	**295**	2b.75+25s. multicoloured	3·50	3·00

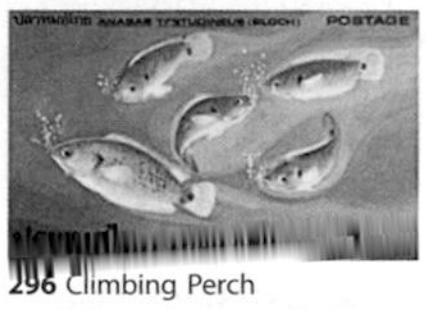

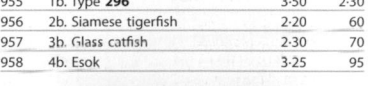

296 Climbing Perch

1978. Fish. Multicoloured.

955	1b. Type **296**	3·50	2·30
956	2b. Siamese tigerfish	2·20	60
957	3b. Glass catfish	2·30	70
958	4b. Esok	3·25	95

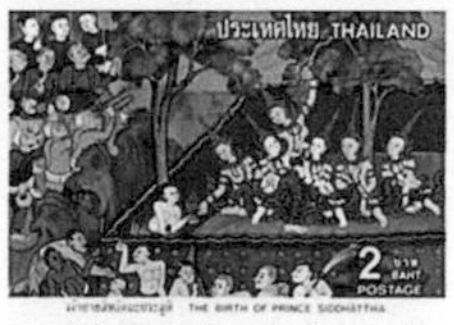

297 "Birth of Prince Siddhartha"

1978. "Buddha's Story" Mural, Puthi Savan Hall, National Museum. Multicoloured.

959	2b. Type **297**	3·50	1·10
960	3b. "Prince Siddhartha cuts his hair"	7·00	1·60
961	5b. "Buddha descends from Tavatimsa Heaven"	14·00	5·50
962	6b. "Buddha enters Nirvana"	8·25	3·50

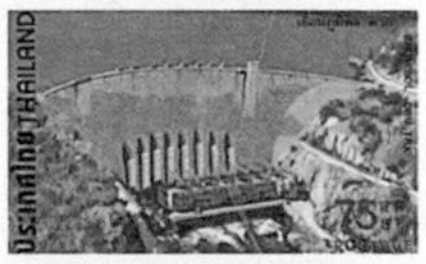

298 Bhumibol Dam

1978. Dams. Multicoloured.

963	75s. Type **298**	1·40	25
964	2b. Sirikit Dam	1·80	35
965	2b.75 Vajiralongkorn Dam	3·75	45
966	6b. Ubolratana Dam	5·75	3·00

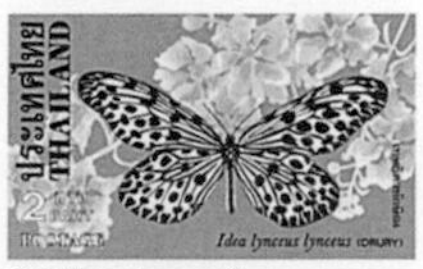

299 "Idea lynceus"

1978. Butterflies.

967	**299**	2b. black, violet and red	3·00	1·10
968	-	3b. multicoloured	4·75	1·20
969	-	5b. multicoloured	5·25	2·50
970	-	6b. multicoloured	7·00	4·00

DESIGNS: 3b. Eastern courtier; 5b. "Charaxes durnfordi"; 6b. "Cethosia penthesilea".

300 Phra Chedi Chai Mongkhon, Ayutthaya

1978. International Correspondence Week. Multicoloured.
971		75s. Type **300**	2·00	45
972		2b. Phra That Hariphunchai, Lamphun	3·00	60
973		2b.75 Phra Borom That Chaiya, Surat Thani	4·75	95
974		5b. Phra That Choeng Chum, Sakon Nakhon	5·00	2·00

301 Mother and Children

1978. United Nations Day.
975	**301**	75s. multicoloured	1·50	35

302 Basketball, Hockey and Boxing

1978. Eighth Asian Games, Bangkok. Multicoloured.
976		25s. Silhouettes of boxers, footballer and pole-vaulter	1·20	20
977		2b. Silhouettes of javelin-thrower, weightlifter and runner	1·60	80
978		3b. Football, shuttlecock, yacht and table-tennis bat and ball	3·00	1·20
979		5b. Type **302**	7·00	3·50

303 World Map and Different Races holding Hands

1978. International Anti-Apartheid Year.
980	**303**	75s. multicoloured	1·40	35

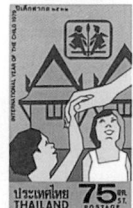

304 Children and S.O.S. Village, Tambol Bangpu

1979. International Year of the Child. Multicoloured.
981		75s. Children painting Thai flag (horiz)	95	25
982		75s. Type **304**	2·00	70

305 "Matuta lunaris"

1979. Crabs. Multicoloured.
983		2b. Type **305**	2·30	95
984		2b.75 "Matuta planipes"	7·00	1·20
985		3b. "Portunus pelagicus"	5·00	95
986		5b. "Scylla serrata"	7·00	4·00

306 Eye and Blind People

1979. Red Cross.
987	**306**	75s.+25s. multicoloured	1·30	70

307 Sugar Apples

1979. Fruit. Multicoloured.
988		1b. Type **307**	2·30	45
989		2b. Pineapple	2·50	1·40
990		5b. Bananas	4·75	1·50
991		6b. Longans	3·75	3·00

308 Planting Sapling

1979. 20th Arbor Day.
992	**308**	75s. multicoloured	1·20	35

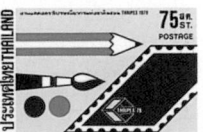

309 Pencil, Brush and Colours

1979. "Thaipex '79" National Stamp Exhibition, Bangkok. Multicoloured.
993		75s. Type **309**	95	20
994		2b. Envelopes	1·50	35
995		2b.75 Stamp stockbook	1·90	45
996		5b. Tweezers, stamps and magnifying glass	5·25	2·10

310 Baisi Pak Cham

1979. International Correspondence Week. Traditional Flower Arrangements. Multicoloured.
997		75s. Kruai upatcha (used at Buddhist ordination ceremony)	95	20
998		2b. Type **310** (used at Bramini-cal ceremonies)	1·50	35
999		2b.75 Krathong dokmai (for paying respects to elders or superiors)	2·10	45
1000		5b. Phum dokmai (altar decoration)	4·25	2·00

311 U.N.O. Emblem, Farmer, Cattle and Wheat

1979. United Nations Day.
1001	**311**	75s. multicoloured	1·30	35

312 "Makutrajakumarn" (frigate)

1979. Ships of the Royal Thai Navy. Multicoloured.
1002		2b. Type **312**	2·75	60
1003		3b. "Tapi" (frigate)	3·00	1·30
1004		5b. "Prabparapak" (missile craft)	7·00	3·00
1005		6b. T 91 (patrol boat)	11·00	4·00

313 Order of the Rajamitrabhorn

1979. Royal Orders and Decorations. Multicoloured.
1006		1b. Type **313**	2·00	60
1007		1b. Rajamitrabhorn ribbon	2·00	60
1008		2b. Order of the Royal House of Chakri	2·20	35
1009		2b. Royal House of Chakri ribbon	2·20	35
1010		5b. Order of the Nine Gems	3·00	1·20
1011		5b. Nine Gems ribbon	3·00	1·20
1012		6b. Knight Grand Cross of the Order of Chula Chom Klao	4·00	2·00
1013		6b. Chula Chom Klao ribbon	4·00	2·00

314 Transplanting Rice

1980. Children's Day. Multicoloured.
1014		75s. Type **314**	1·30	30
1015		75s. Harvesting rice	1·30	30

315 Family House and Map of Thailand

1980. Population and Housing Census.
1016	**315**	75s. multicoloured	1·10	25

316 Golden-fronted Leafbird

1980. Ninth Conference of Int Commission for Bird Preservation (Asian Section), Chiang Mai. Multicoloured.
1017		75s. Type **316**	1·10	25
1018		2b. Chinese yellow tit	1·50	45
1019		3b. Chestnut-tailed minla	3·75	60
1020		5b. Scarlet minivet	6·50	1·90

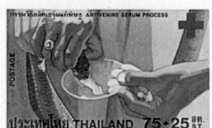

317 Extracting Snake Venom

1980. Red Cross.
1021	**317**	75s.+25s. multicoloured	1·60	1·40

318 Smokers and Diagram of Lungs

1980. World Health Day. Anti-smoking Campaign.
1022	**318**	75s. multicoloured	1·10	35

319 Garuda and Rotary Emblem

1980. 75th Anniv of Rotary International.
1023	**319**	5b. multicoloured	2·75	70

320 Sai Yok Falls, Kanchanaburi

1980. Waterfalls. Multicoloured.
1024		1b. Type **320**	95	20
1025		2b. Punyaban Falls, Ranong	1·20	35
1026		5b. Heo Suwat Falls, Nakhon Ratchasima	3·50	1·50
1027		6b. Siriphum Falls, Chiang Mai	3·00	2·10

321 Family and Reverse of F.A.O. Medal

1980. Queen Sirikit's "Fourth Cycle" Anniv (48th Birthday). Multicoloured.
1028		75s. Queen Sirikit (vert)	1·10	25
1029		5b. Type **321**	2·10	70
1030		5b. Thai family and obverse of F.A.O. medal	2·10	70

322 Khao Phanomrung Temple, Buri Ram

1980. Int Correspondence Week. Temples. Multicoloured.
1033		75s. Type **322**	95	35
1034		2b. Prang Ku Temple, Chai-yaphum	1·20	45
1035		2b.75 Phimai Temple, Nakhon Ratchasima	1·80	70
1036		5b. Srikhoraphum Temple, Surin	2·50	1·50

323 Princess Mother

1980. The Princess Mother's 80th Birthday.
1037	**323**	75s. multicoloured	4·00	80

324 Golden Mount Temple, Bangkok

1980. United Nations Day.
1038	324	75s. multicoloured	95	45

325 King Bhumibol

1980
1039	325	25s. red	2·50	35
1179	325	50s. green	2·30	40
1040	325	75s. violet	1·10	25
1041	325	1b. blue	1·10	45
1040a	325	1b.25 green	1·10	25
1180a	325	1b.50 orange	5·75	3·00
1041a	325	2b. purple and red	20·00	60
1235b	325	2b. brown	7·00	1·30
1042a	325	3b. blue and brown	1·10	35
1042b	325	4b. brown and blue	1·80	35
1043a	325	5b. brown and lilac	2·10	45
1044a	325	6b. lilac and green	2·10	35
1044b	325	6b.50 olive and green	2·20	1·10
1044c	325	7b. dp brown & brown	2·75	60
1044d	325	7b.50 blue and red	2·20	95
1044e	325	8b. green and brown	2·50	80
1045	325	8b.50 brown and green	2·75	95
1045a	325	9b. brown and blue	3·50	1·10
1046	325	9b.50 green and olive	3·50	1·20
1047	325	10b. green and red	3·50	1·30
1048	325	20b. green and orange	7·50	1·40
1049	325	50b. green and lilac	15·00	2·50
1050	325	100b. blue and orange	23·00	4·50

326 "King Rama VII signing Constitutional Document"

1980. Monument to King Prajadhipok (Rama VII).
1051	326	75s. multicoloured	95	45

327 Bowl

1980. Bencharong Ware. Multicoloured.
1052	2b.	Type 327	1·60	40
1053		2b.75 Covered bowls	1·80	45
1054		3b. Jar	2·00	70
1055		5b. Stem-plates	2·30	1·20

328 King Vajiravudh

1981. Birth Centenary of King Vajiravudh.
1056	328	75s. multicoloured	2·00	25

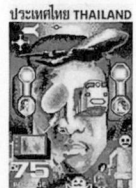

329 "Youth in Electronics Age" (Veth Maichun)

1981. Children's Day.
1057	329	75s. multicoloured	1·60	35

330 Mosque, Pattani Province

1981. 1400th Anniv of Hegira.
1058	330	5b. multicoloured	4·75	1·10

331 Palm Leaf Fish Mobile

1981. Int Handicraft Exhibition. Multicoloured.
1059		75s. Type 331	70	25
1060		75s. Carved teakwood elephant	70	25
1061		2b.75 Basketwork	1·80	70
1062		2b.75 Thai folk dolls	1·80	70

332 Scout aiding Cripple

1981. Int Year of Disabled Persons. Multicoloured.
1063		75s. Type 332	70	20
1064		5b. Disabled person cutting gem-stones	2·10	60

333 Red Cross Volunteer aiding Refugee

1981. Red Cross.
1065	333	75s.+25s. green and red	2·20	2·10

334 Ongkhot

1981. Khon (Thai classical dance) Masks. Multicoloured.
1066		75s. Type 334	60	10
1067		2b. Maiyarah	1·50	25
1068		3b. Sukrip	2·30	60
1069		5b. Indrajit	3·00	2·00

336 8a. Stamp, 1899

1981. "Thaipex '81" National Stamp Exn. Multicoloured.
1070		75s. Type 336	70	25
1071		75s. 28s. stamp, 1910	70	25
1072		2b.75 50s. stamp, 1919	1·80	70
1073		2b.75 3s. stamp, 1932	1·80	70

337 Luang Praditphairo

1981. Birth Centenary of Luang Praditphairo (musician).
1074	337	1b.25 multicoloured	1·30	35

338 Mai Hok-Hian

1981. International Correspondence Week. Dwarf Trees. Multicoloured.
1075		75s. Type 338	95	35
1076		2b. Mai Kam-Mao-Lo	1·50	60
1077		2b.75 Mai Khen	2·10	45
1078		5b. Mai Khabuan	3·75	1·50

339 Food Produce

1981. World Food Day.
1079	339	75s. multicoloured	95	25

340 Samran Mukhamat Pavilion, Bangkok

1981. United Nations Day.
1080	340	1b.25 multicoloured	1·30	35

341 Express_ _ _ _ _) at Muangtoey)

1981. Inaug of First Thai Expressway. Multicoloured.
1081		1b. Type 341	95	25
1082		5b. Expressway interchange	3·00	70

342 King Cobra

1981. Snakes. Multicoloured.
1083		75s. Type 342	95	20
1084		2b. Banded krait	2·00	95
1085		2b.75 Thai cobra	2·30	35
1086		5b. Malayan pit viper	3·00	1·50

343 Girl carrying Child

1982. Children's Day.
1087	343	1b.25 multicoloured	1·10	35

344 Scouts reaching for Peace

1982. 75th Anniv of Boy Scout Movement.
1088	344	1b.25 multicoloured	1·10	35

345 King Buddha Yod-Fa (Rama I)

1982. Bicentenary of Chakri Dynasty and of Bangkok. Multicoloured.
1089		1b. Type 345	1·60	45
1090		1b.25 Aerial view of Bangkok	1·80	60
1091		2b. King Buddha Lert La Naphalai (Rama II)	2·10	70
1092		3b. King Nang Klao (Rama III)	3·50	95
1093		4b. King Mongkut (Rama IV)	2·50	1·20
1094		5b. King Chulalongkorn (Rama V)	3·75	1·30
1095		6b. King Vajiravudh (Rama VI)	4·00	1·40
1096		7b. King Prajadhipok (Rama VII)	7·00	5·75
1097		8b. King Ananda Mahidol (Rama VIII)	3·50	1·80
1098		9b. King Bhumipol Adulyadej (Rama IX)	4·75	2·50

MS1099 Two sheets. (a) 205×145 mm. Nos. 1089/98; (b) 195×180 mm. Nos. 1089/98 (sold at 130b. pair) £150 £140

346 Dr. Robert Koch and Cross of Lorraine

1982. Cent of Discovery of Tubercle Bacillus.
1100	346	1b.25 multicoloured	1·40	35

347 "Quisqualis indica"

1982. Flowers. Multicoloured.
1101		1b.25 Type 347	45	25
1102		1b.50 "Murraya paniculata"	95	45
1103		6b.50 "Mesua ferrea"	2·50	1·40
1104		7b. "Desmos chinensis"	2·30	1·10

348 Wat Bowon Sathan Sutthawat

1982. "Bangkok 1983" International Stamp Exhibition (1st issue). Multicoloured.
1105		1b.25 Type 348	60	25
1106		4b.25 Wat Phra Chetuphon Wimon Mangkhalaram	1·50	60
1107		6b.50 Wat Mahathat Yuwarat Rangsarit	2·75	1·40
1108		7b. Wat Phra Sri Rattana Satsadaram	3·50	95

MS1109 160×140 mm. Nos. 1105/8 £130 £120
See also Nos. 1133/1135 and 1142/**MS**1146.

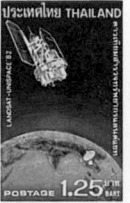

349 "Landsat" Satellite

1982. Second U.N. Conference on the Exploration and Peaceful Uses of Outer Space, Vienna.
1110	349	1b.25 multicoloured	1·40	45

350 Prince
Purachatra

1982. Birth Centenary of Prince Purachatra.

1111	**350**	1b.25 multicoloured	1·90	60

351 Covered Jar

1982. International Correspondence Week. Sangalok Pottery. Multicoloured.

1112		1b.25 Type **351**	45	25
1113		3b. Small jar	2·30	45
1114		4b.25 Celadon plate	1·90	1·10
1115		7b. Plate with fish design	2·50	1·90

352 Loha Prasat,
Bangkok

1982. United Nations Day.

1116	**352**	1b.25 multicoloured	1·30	35

353 Chap and Ching

1982. Thai Musical Instruments. Multicoloured.

1117		50s. Type **353**	25	10
1118		1b. Pi nok and pi nai (pipes)	1·10	35
1119		1b.25 Klong that and taphon (drums)	45	25
1120		1b.50 Khong mong (gong) and krap (wooden sticks)	60	45
1121		6b. Khong wong yai (glock-enspiel)	7·00	2·30
1122		7b. Khong wong lek (glock-enspiel)	3·00	95
1123		8b. Ranat ek (xylophone)	2·75	1·40
1124		9b. Ranat thum (xylophone)	3·00	1·60

354 Pileated
Gibbon

1982. National Wild Animal Preservation Day. Monkeys. Multicoloured.

1125		1b.25 Type **354**	1·20	25
1126		3b. Pigtail macaque	3·00	60
1127		5b. Slow loris	2·30	80
1128		7b. Silvered leaf monkey	2·50	1·20

355 Emblem and
Flags of Member
Countries

1982. 15th Anniv of Association of South-East Asian Nations.

1129	**355**	6b.50 multicoloured	2·50	95

356 Child
sweeping

1983. Children's Day.

1130	**356**	1b.25 multicoloured	1·10	35

357 Postcodes

1983. First Anniv of Postcodes. Multicoloured.

1131		1b.25 Type **357**	1·30	35
1132		1b.25 Postcoded envelope	1·30	35

358 Old General Post Office

1983. "Bangkok 1983" International Stamp Exhibition (2nd issue).

1133	**358**	7b. multicoloured	2·00	70
1134	**358**	10b. multicoloured	3·25	95
MS1135	142×100 mm. Nos. 1133/4. (sold at 30b.)		47·00	46·00

359 Junks

1983. 25th Anniv of International Maritime Organization.

1136	**359**	1b.25 multicoloured	1·10	35

360 Civil Servant's
Shoulder Strap

1983. Civil Servants' Day.

1137	**360**	1b.25 multicoloured	1·10	35

361 Giving and receiving Aid
and Red Cross

1983. Red Cross.

1138	**361**	1b.25+25s. multicoloured	1·80	1·50

362 Prince
Sithiporn Kridakara

1983. Birth Centenary of Prince Sithiporn Kridakara (agriculturalist).

1139	**362**	1b.25 multicoloured	1·10	35

363 Satellite, Map and Dish Aeria

1983. Domestic Satellite Communications System.

1140	**363**	2b. multicoloured	1·40	40

364 Prince
Bhanurangsi

1983. Prince Bhanurangsi (founder of Thai postal service) Commemoration.

1141	**364**	1b.25 multicoloured	1·20	25

365 Post Box Clearance

1983. "Bangkok 1983" International Stamp Exhibition (3rd issue). Multicoloured.

1142		1b.25 Type **365**	25	10
1143		7b.50 Post office counter	1·40	70
1144		8b.50 Mail transportation	2·00	80
1145		9b.50 Mail delivery	2·50	95
MS1146	162×140 mm. Nos. 1142/5 (sold at 50b.)		41·00	40·00

366 Cable Map of
A.S.E.A.N. Countries
and "Long Lines"
(cable ship)

1983. Inauguration of Malaysia–Singapore–Thailand Submarine Cable. Multicoloured.

1147		1b.25 Type **366**	35	25
1148		7b. Map of new cable	2·30	70

367 Flower Coral

1983. Int Correspondence Week. Corals. Multicoloured.

1149		2b. Type **367**	95	45
1150		3b. Lesser valley coral	2·00	60
1151		4b. Mushroom coral	1·50	80
1152		7b. Common lettuce coral	3·00	1·30

368 Satellite and Submarine
Cable Communications
Equipment

1983. World Communications Year. Multicoloured.

1153		2b. Type **368**	95	35
1154		3b. Telephone and telegraph service equipment	1·30	45

369 Fishing for Tuna

1983. United Nations Day.

1155	**369**	1b.25 multicoloured	95	35

370 Buddha
(sculpture)

1983. 700th Anniv of Thai Alphabet.

1156	**370**	3b. multicoloured	80	25
1157	-	7b. black and brown	2·00	70
1158	-	8b. multicoloured	2·30	80
1159	-	9b. multicoloured	2·50	95

DESIGNS—HORIZ: 3b. Sangkhalok pottery; 7b. Thai characters. VERT: 9b. Mahathat Temple.

371 Prince Mahidol
of Songkhla

1983. 60th Anniv of Co-operation between Siriraj Hospital and Rockefeller Foundation.

1160	**371**	9b.50 multicoloured	3·00	1·20

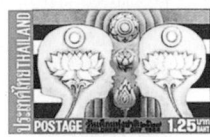

372 Lotus Blossoms within
Heads

1984. Children's Day.

1161	**372**	1b.25 multicoloured	1·20	40

373 Running

1984. 17th National Games, Phitsanulok Province. Multicoloured.

1162		1b.25 Type **373**	75	35
1163		3b. Football	95	40

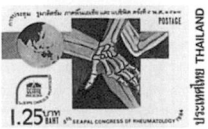

374 Skeletal Joints, Globe and
Emblem

1984. Fifth South East Asia and Pacific Area League against Rheumatism Congress.

1164	**374**	1b.25 multicoloured	1·10	40

375 Statue of King
Naresuan and
Modern Armed
Forces

1984. Armed Forces Day.

1165	**375**	1b.25 multicoloured	1·30	45

376 Royal Institute
Emblem in Door
Arch

1984. 50th Anniv of Royal Institute.
1166	**376**	1b.25 multicoloured	1·10	25

1984. Red Cross. No. 954 surch **3.25 + 0.25** in English
and Thai.
1167	**295**	3b.25+25s. on 2b.75+25s.		
		mult	3·50	6·00

378 King and Queen examining
Land Development Project

1984. Royal Initiated Projects. Multicoloured.
1168		1b.25 Type **378**	1·10	25
1169		1b.25 Improving barren area	1·10	25
1170		1b.25 Dam, terrace farming and		
		rain-making aircraft	1·10	25
1171		1b.25 Crops, fish and farm		
		animals	1·10	25
1172		1b.25 King and Queen of		
		Thailand	1·10	25

379 Dome Building and
University Emblem

1984. 50th Anniv of Thammasat University.
1173	**379**	1b.25 multicoloured	1·10	25

381 A.B.U. Emblem and Map

1984. 20th Anniv of Asia-Pacific Broadcasting Union.
1174	**381**	4b. multicoloured	1·80	80

382 Chiang Saen
Style Buddha

1984. Thai Sculptures of Buddhas. Multicoloured.
1175		1b.25 Type **382**	35	15
1176		7b. Sukhothai style	2·30	1·20
1177		8b.50 Thong style	2·50	1·50
1178		9b.50 Ayutthaya style	3·50	1·70

384 "Alocasia indica
var. metallica"

1984. International Correspondence Week. Medicinal
Plants. Multicoloured.
1181		1b.50 Type **384**	60	25
1182		2b. "Aloe barbadensis"	70	35
1183		4b. "Gynura pseudo-china"	1·40	65
1184		10b. "Rhoeo spathacea"	4·75	3·00

385 Princess
Mother

1984. 84th Birthday of Princess Mother.
1185	**385**	1b.50 multicoloured	1·10	40

386 Threshing Rice

1984. United Nations Day.
1186	**386**	1b.50 multicoloured	1·10	40

387 Bhutan Glory

1984. Butterflies. Multicoloured.
1187		2b. Type **387**	80	25
1188		3b. "Stichophthalma louisa"	1·20	40
1189		5b. Clipper	2·00	80
1190		7b. "Stichophthalma godfreyi"	3·00	1·20

388 "Crossing the
Road by Flyover"
(U-Tai Raksorn)

1985. Children's Day. Multicoloured.
1191		1b.50 Type **388**	60	25
1192		1b.50 "Crossing the Road by		
		Flyover" (Sravudh Charoen-		
		nawee) (horiz)	60	25

389 Bangkok Mail Centre

1985. Inauguration of Bangkok Mail-sorting Centre.
1193	**389**	1b.50 multicoloured	1·10	40

390 Monument to
Tao-Thep-Krasattri
and Tao-Sri-
Sundhorn

1985. Heroines of Phuket. Bicentennial Ceremony.
1194	**390**	2b. multicoloured	1·20	40

1985. Red Cross. No. 987 surch **2 + .25 BAHT.**
1195	**306**	2b.+25s. on 75s.+25s.		
		multicoloured	2·75	2·75

392 Bank Headquarters,
Bangkok, and King Vajiravudh
(Rama VI)

1985. 72nd Anniv of Government Savings Bank.
1196	**392**	1b.50 multicoloured	95	40

393 Satellite over Thai Buildings

1985. 20th Anniv of International Tele-communications
Satellite Organization.
1197	**393**	2b. multicoloured	1·10	55

394 Douglas DC-6 and DC-8
and Loi-Krathong Festival

1985. 25th Anniv of Thai Airways. Multicoloured.
1198		2b. Type **394**	60	25
1199		7b.50 Douglas DC-10-30 and		
		Thai classical dancing	2·30	1·30
1200		8b.50 Airbus Industrie A-300		
		and Thai buildings	3·00	1·50
1201		9b.50 Boeing 747-200 and		
		world landmarks	3·50	1·60

395 U.P.U. Emblem

1985. Centenary of Membership of U.P.U. and I.T.U.
Multicoloured.
1202		2b. Type **395**	80	25
1203		10b. I.T.U. Emblem	2·30	1·30

396 Pigeon

1985. National Communications Day.
1204	**396**	2b. blue, red & ultram	1·10	40

397 Aisvarya
Pavilion

1985. "Thaipex '85" Stamp Exhibition. Multicoloured.
1205		2b. Type **397**	60	25
1206		3b. Varopas Piman Pavilion		
		(horiz)	1·20	40
1207		7b. Vehas Camrun Pavilion		
		(horiz)	2·50	1·10
1208		10b. Vitoon Tassana Tower	3·75	1·60
MS1209		155×179 mm. Nos. 1205/8	95·00	95·00

398 King Mongkut, Solar Eclipse
and Telescope

1985. National Science Day.
1210	**398**	2b. multicoloured	1·80	40

399 Department Seals, 1885
and 1985

1985. Centenary of Royal Thai Survey Department.
1211	**399**	2b. multicoloured	1·10	25

400 Boxing

1985. 13th South-East Asia Games, Bangkok (1st issue).
Multicoloured.
1212		2b. Type **400**	1·30	40
1213		2b. Putting the shot	1·30	40
1214		2b. Badminton	1·30	40
1215		2b. Throwing the javelin	1·30	40
1216		2b. Weightlifting	1·30	40
MS1217		186×127 Nos. 1212/16 (sold		
		at 20)	55·00	55·00

See also Nos. 1229/**MS**1233.

401 Golden
Trumpet

1985. International Correspondence Week. Climbing
Plants Multicoloured.
1218		2b. Type **401**	60	25
1219		3b. "Jasminum auriculatum"	1·20	40
1220		7b. Passion flower	2·30	1·10
1221		10b. Coral-vine	3·00	1·50

402 Mothers and
Children at Clinic

1985. United Nations Day.
1222	**402**	2b. multicoloured	1·10	40

403 Prince Dhani
Nivat

1985. Birth Centenary of Prince Dhani Nivat, Kromamun
Bidyalabh Bridhyakorn.
1223	**403**	2b. multicoloured	2·10	40

404 Prince of
Jainad

1985. Birth Centenary of Rangsit, Prince of Jainad
(Minister of Health).
1224	**404**	1b.50 multicoloured	1·30	25

405 Emblem and Buildings

1985. Fifth Asian–Pacific Postal Union Congress.

| 1225 | **405** | 2b. multicoloured | 60 | 25 |
| 1226 | - | 10b. multicoloured | 3·00 | 1·50 |

DESIGN: 10b. As Type **405** but different buildings.

406 Emblem

1985. International Youth Year.

| 1227 | **406** | 2b. multicoloured | 1·50 | 55 |

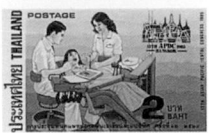

407 Dentist and Nurse tending Patient

1985. 12th Asian–Pacific Dental Congress.

| 1228 | **407** | 2b. multicoloured | 1·30 | 40 |

408 Volleyball

1985. 12th South-East Asia Games, Bangkok (2nd issue). Multicoloured.

1229	1b. Type **408**	25	15
1230	2b. Sepak-takraw (kick-ball)	70	40
1231	3b. Gymnastics	1·20	55
1232	4b. Bowls	1·40	65
MS1233 186×129 mm. Nos. 1229/32 plus label (sold at 20b.)		47·00	47·00

409 Chevalier de Chaumont presenting Message from Louis XIV to King Narai the Great, 1685

1985. 300th Anniv of Franco–Thai Relations. Multicoloured.

| 1234 | 2b. Type **409** | 80 | 25 |
| 1235 | 8b.50 Siamese emissaries carrying reply from King Narai to Louis XIV (horiz) | 2·30 | 1·20 |

410 Emblem

1986. Third Anniv of International and Inauguration of Domestic Express Mail Services.

| 1236 | **410** | 2b. multicoloured | 1·30 | 40 |

411 Green Turtle

1986. Turtles. Multicoloured.

1237	1b.50 Type **411**	1·20	55
1238	3b. Hawksbill turtle	2·30	65
1239	5b. Leatherback turtle	3·00	1·20
1240	10b. Olive turtle	2·75	1·70

412 "Family picking Lotus" (Areeya Makarabhundhu)

1986. Children's Day.

| 1241 | **412** | 2b. multicoloured | 1·10 | 25 |

1986. Red Cross. No. 1021 surch. **1986 2 + .25 BAHT** in English and Thai.

| 1242 | **317** | 2b.+25s. on 75s.+25s. multicoloured | 3·25 | 3·25 |

414 Statue of Sunthon Phu (Sukij Laidej), Amphoe Klaeng

1986. Birth Bicentenary of Sunthon Phu (poet).

| 1243 | **414** | 2b. multicoloured | 1·10 | 40 |

415 Watermelon

1986. Fruit. Multicoloured.

1244	2b. Type **415**	2·10	55
1245	2b. Malay apple ("Eugenia malaccensis")	2·10	55
1246	6b. Pomelo ("Citrus maxima")	2·30	80
1247	6b. Papaya ("Carica papaya")	2·30	80

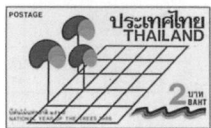

416 Trees on Grid and Water Line

1986. National Tree Year.

| 1248 | **416** | 2b. multicoloured | 1·10 | 40 |

417 Pigeon flying from Man's Head to Transmission Masts

1986. National Communications Day.

| 1249 | **417** | 2b. multicoloured | 1·10 | 25 |

418 Chalom

1986. International Correspondence Week. Bamboo Baskets. Multicoloured.

1250	2b. Type **418**	70	25
1251	2b. Krabung	70	25
1252	6b. Kratib	1·30	65
1253	6b. Kaleb	1·30	65

1986. No. 1031 surch **1 BAHT**.

| 1254 | **227** | 1b. on 20s. blue | 1·10 | 25 |

420 Emblem and War Scenes

1986. International Peace Year.

| 1255 | **420** | 2b. light blue, blue & red | 1·10 | 40 |

421 Industrial and Agricultural Scenes within Emblem

1986. Productivity Year.

| 1256 | **421** | 2b. multicoloured | 1·10 | 40 |

422 Scouts saluting and Scout helping Blind Man across Road

1986. 75th Anniv of Thai Scouting. Multicoloured.

1257	2b.+50s. Type **422**	70	40
1258	2b.+50s. Scouting activities	70	40
1259	2b.+50s. King and Queen making presentations to scouts	70	40
1260	2b.+50s. 15th Asia–Pacific Scout Conference, Thailand	70	40

423 Vanda "Varavuth"

1986. Sixth ASEAN Orchid Congress, Thailand. Multicoloured.

1261	2b. Type **423**	1·10	40
1262	3b. Ascocenda "Emma"	1·20	80
1263	4b. Dendrobium "Sri-Siam" (horiz)	2·10	1·90
1264	5b. Dendrobium "Ekapol Panda" (horiz)	2·30	1·60
MS1265 116×99 mm. Nos. 1261/4		£160	£160

424 Chinese Mushroom

1986. Edible Fungi. Multicoloured.

1266	2b. Type **424**	1·20	40
1267	2b. Oyster fungus ("Pleurotus ostreatus")	1·20	40
1268	6b. Ear mushroom ("Auricularia polytricha")	3·00	95
1269	6b. Abalone mushroom ("Pleurotus cystidiosus")	3·00	95

425 Black Sharkminnow

1986. 60th Anniv of Fisheries Department. Multicoloured.

1270	2b. Type **425**	80	40
1271	2b. Blanc's knifefish ("Notopterus blanci")	80	40
1272	7b. Asian bonytongue ("Scleropages formosus")	2·00	1·10
1273	7b. Giant catfish ("Pangasianodon gigas")	2·00	1·10

426 Children in Playground

1987. Children's Day. Multicoloured.

| 1274 | 2b. Type **426** | 1·10 | 40 |
| 1275 | 2b. Children in and around swimming pool | 1·10 | 40 |

Nos. 1274/5 were printed together, *se-tenant*, forming a composite design showing "Our School" by Lawan Maneenetr.

427 Northrop F-5 Tiger II and General Dynamics F-16 Fighting Falcon Fighters and Pilot

1987. 72nd Anniv of Royal Thai Air Force.

| 1276 | **427** | 2b. multicoloured | 1·80 | 40 |

428 King Rama III and Temples

1987. Birth Bicentenary of King Rama III.

| 1277 | **428** | 2b. multicoloured | 1·60 | 65 |

429 Communications and Transport Systems

1987. 75th Anniv of Ministry of Communications.

| 1278 | **429** | 2b. multicoloured | 1·10 | 40 |

1987. Red Cross. No. 1065 surch **2 + 0.50 BAHT**.

| 1279 | **333** | 2b.+50s. on 75s.+25s. green and red | 3·25 | 2·75 |

431 Tree-lined Street

1987. National Tree Year.

| 1280 | **431** | 2b. multicoloured | 1·10 | 40 |

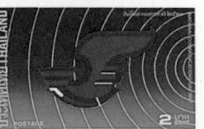

432 Gold Peacock

1987. "Thaipex'87" National Stamp Exhibition. Handicrafts. Multicoloured.

1281	2b. Type **432**	65	25
1282	2b. Gold hand-mirrors	65	25
1283	6b. Gold lustre water urn and finger bowls with trays (horiz)	1·30	65
1284	6b. Gold swan vase (horiz)	1·30	65
MS1285 160×175 mm. Nos. 1281/4 (sold at 40b.)		90·00	90·00

433 Flying Bird and Animal Horn (Somsak Junthavorn)

1987. National Communications Day.

| 1286 | **433** | 2b. multicoloured | 1·30 | 40 |

434 King Rama IX at Presentation Ceremony, King Rama V and Emblem

1987. Centenary of Chulachomklao Royal Military Academy, Khao Cha-Ngok.

| 1287 | **434** | 2b. multicoloured | 2·75 | 55 |

435 Spiral Ropes leading to Member Countries' Flags

1987. 20th Anniv of Association of South-East Asian Nations.

1288	**435**	2b. multicoloured	65	25
1289	**435**	3b. multicoloured	90	35
1290	**435**	4b. multicoloured	1·10	65
1291	**435**	5b. multicoloured	1·50	80

436 People and Open Book

1987. International Literacy Day.

| 1292 | **436** | 2b. multicoloured | 1·10 | 25 |

437 Flower-offering Ceremony, Saraburi

1987. Visit Thailand Year.. Multicoloured.

1293	2b. Type **437**		50	15
1294	3b. Duan Sib Festival (honouring ancestors), Nakhon Si Thammarat		65	25
1295	5b. Bang Fai (rain) Festival, Yasothon		1·10	55
1296	7b. Loi Krathong, Sukhothai		1·60	80

438 Ministry Building

1987. 72nd Anniv of Auditor General's Office.

| 1297 | **438** | 2b. multicoloured | 1·10 | 40 |

439 Temple of Dawn, "Sri Suphanahong" (royal barge) and Mt Fuji within "100"

1987. Centenary of Japan–Thailand Friendship Treaty.

| 1298 | **439** | 2b. multicoloured | 1·40 | 55 |

440 Tasselled Garland

1987. International Correspondence Week. Ceremonial Floral Garlands. Multicoloured.

1299	2b. Floral tassle		40	20
1300	3b. Type **440**		65	35
1301	5b. Wrist garland		1·30	55
1302	7b. Double-ended garland		1·50	80

1987. No. 1180a surch **2 BAHT**.

| 1303 | **325** | 2b. on 1b.50 orange | 1·40 | 25 |

442 Thai Pavilion

1987. Inauguration of Social Education and Cultural Centre.

| 1304 | **442** | 2b. multicoloured | 1·50 | 40 |

443 King Bhumibol Adulyadej as a Boy

1987. King Bhumibol Adulyadej's 60th Birthday. Multicoloured (except 1320).

1305	2b. Type **443**		1·10	55
1306	2b. Wedding photograph of King Bhumibol Adulyadej and Queen Sirikit, 1950		1·10	55
1307	2b. King on throne during Accession ceremony at Paisan Hall, 1950		1·10	55
1308	2b. King as monk on alms round		1·10	55
1309	2b. Elderly woman greeting King		1·10	55
1310	2b. King demonstrating to hill tribes how to take medicine		1·10	55
1311	2b. King and Queen presenting gift bag to wounded serviceman		1·10	55
1312	2b. King examining new system for small farms		1·10	55
1314	2b. Princess mother Somdej Phra Sri Nakarindra Boromrajjonnani		1·90	55
1315	2b. Crown Prince Maha Vajiralongkorn		1·90	55
1316	2b. Princess Maha Chakri Sirindhorn		1·90	55
1317	2b. Princess Chulabhorn		1·90	55
1318	2b. King Bhumibol Adulyadej and Queen Sirikit		1·90	55
1319	2b. King and family (48×33 mm)		1·90	55
1320	100b. gold and blue (King Bhumibol Adulyadej) (48×33 mm)		£100	£100

MS1313 190×144 mm. Nos. 1305/12 (sold at 40b.) | 55·00 | 55·00

444 "Teacher's Day" (Nutchaliya Suddhiprasit)

1988. Children's Day.

| 1321 | **444** | 2b. multicoloured | 1·10 | 25 |

445 Prince Kromamun Bridhyalongkorn (founder)

1988. 72nd Anniv of Thai Co-operatives.

| 1322 | **445** | 2b. multicoloured | 1·10 | 25 |

446 Society Building

1988. 84th Anniv of Siam Society (for promotion of arts and sciences).

| 1323 | **446** | 2b. multicoloured | 1·10 | 25 |

447 Phra Phai Luang Monastery

1988. Sukhothai Historical Park. Multicoloured.

1324	2b. Type **447**		65	20
1325	3b. Traphang Thonglang Monastery		75	35
1326	4b. Maha That Monastery		1·10	65
1327	6b. Thewalai Maha Kaset		1·90	80

1988. No. 1040a surch **1 BAHT**.

| 1557 | **325** | 1b. on 1b.25 green | 1·70 | 45 |

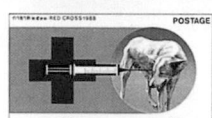

449 Syringe between Red Cross and Dog

1988. Red Cross Anti-rabies Campaign.

| 1329 | **449** | 2b. multicoloured | 1·10 | 40 |

450 King Rama V (founder)

1988. Centenary of Siriraj Hospital.

| 1330 | **450** | 5b. multicoloured | 4·25 | 1·20 |

451 Crested Fireback Pheasant

1988. Pheasants. Multicoloured.

1331	2b. Type **451**		50	20
1332	3b. Kalij pheasant		1·00	35
1333	6b. Silver pheasant		1·50	1·10
1334	7b. Mrs. Hume's pheasant		2·00	1·20

452 Hand holding Coloured Ribbons

1988. Centenary of International Women's Council.

| 1335 | **452** | 2b. multicoloured | 1·10 | 25 |

453 King Rama IX in King's Own Bodyguard Uniform

1988

1631	**453**	25s. brown	75	15
1336	**453**	50s. green	75	25
1337	**453**	1b. blue	90	20
1753	**453**	2b. red	1·10	30
1339	**453**	3b. blue and brown	1·30	40
1340	**453**	4b. red and blue	1·40	45

1341	**453**	5b. brown and lilac	1·50	55
1342	**453**	6b. purple and green	1·60	60
1343	**453**	7b. deep brown & brown	1·10	25
1344	**453**	8b. green and brown	1·80	40
1345	**453**	9b. brown and blue	2·75	65
1346	**453**	10b. green and red	2·50	25
1347	**453**	20b. green and orange	3·75	1·20
1348	**453**	25b. blue and green	6·25	1·60
1349	**453**	50b. green and lilac	11·50	2·00
1354	**453**	100b. blue and orange	19·00	4·00

454 King Rama IX in Full Robes

1988. 42nd Anniv of Accession to Throne of King Rama IX. Multicoloured. (a) T **454**.

| 1356 | 2b. Type **454** | | 4·00 | 65 |

(b) Royal Regalia. Size 33×48 mm (1357) or 48×33 mm (others).

1357	2b. Great Crown of Victory		1·00	40
1358	2b. Sword of Victory and scabbard (horiz)		1·00	40
1359	2b. Sceptre (horiz)		1·00	40
1360	2b. Royal Fan and Fly Whisk (horiz)		1·00	40
1361	2b. Slippers (horiz)		1·00	40

(c) Thrones.

1362	2b. Atthathit Uthumphon Ratchaat throne (octagonal base)		1·30	45
1363	2b. Phatthrabit throne (rectangular base)		1·30	45
1364	2b. Phuttan Kanchanasinghat throne (gold throne on angular steps)		1·30	45
1365	2b. Butsabokmala Mahachakkraphatphiman throne (ship shape)		1·30	45
1366	2b. Throne inlaid with mother-of-pearl (blue throne on angular steps)		1·30	45
1367	2b. Peony design niello throne (circular steps)		1·30	45

MS1368 130×172 mm. Nos. 1362/7 (sold at 25b.) | 95·00 | 95·00

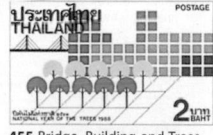

455 Bridge, Building and Trees

1988. National Tree Year.

| 1369 | **455** | 2b. multicoloured | 1·00 | 25 |

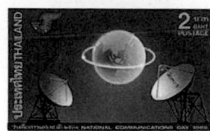

456 Globe and Dish Aerials

1988. National Communications Day.

| 1370 | **456** | 2b. multicoloured | 1·40 | 35 |

458 Grasshopper

1988. International Correspondence Week. Woven Coconut-leaf Folk Toys. Multicoloured.

1371	2b. Type **458**		50	20
1372	2b. Carp		50	20
1373	6b. Bird		1·40	65
1374	6b. Takro		1·40	65

459 Flats and Construction Workers

1988. Housing Development.

| 1375 | **459** | 2b. multicoloured | 1·00 | 25 |

460 King Rama V
in Full Uniform

1988. 120th Anniv of King's Own Bodyguard.
1376 **460** 2b. multicoloured   6·25   1·30

461 Road Signs

1988. Road Safety Campaign.
1377 **461** 2b. multicoloured   1·00   25

462 "Crotalaria
sessiliflora"

1988. New Year. Multicoloured.
1378   1b. Type **462**   1·00   55
1379   1b. "Uvaria grandiflora"   1·00   55
1380   1b. "Reinwardtia trigyna"   1·00   55
1381   1b. "Impatiens griffithii"   1·00   55

463 Buddha's Birthplace

1988. Buddhamonthon Celebrations. Multicoloured.
1382   2b. Type **463**   50   25
1383   3b. Buddha's place of enlight-
       enment   75   40
1384   4b. Site of Buddha's first
       sermon   90   55
1385   5b. Buddha's Place of Nirvana   1·00   65
1386   6b. Statue of Buddha (vert)   1·50   80
MS1386a 82×110 mm. No. 1386 (sold
       at 15b.)   44·00   44·00

464 Knight Grand
Commander of
Honourable Order
of Rama

1988. Insignia of Orders. Multicoloured.
1387   2b. Type **464**   50   25
1388   2b. Close-up of badge   50   25
1389   3b. Knight Grand Cordon (Spe-
       cial Class) of Most Exalted
       Order of the White Elephant   1·00   40
1390   3b. Close-up of badge   1·00   40
1391   5b. Knight Grand Cordon of
       Most Noble Order of Crown
       of Thailand   1·50   65
1392   5b. Close-up of badge   1·50   65
1393   7b. Close-up of Rarana Varab-
       horn Order of Merit   1·90   95
1394   7b. Badge on chain of office   1·90   95
   Stamps of the same value were issued together, se-
tenant, each pair forming a composite design.

465 "Floating Market" (Thongbai
Siyam)

1989. National Children's Day. Plasticine Paintings by
Blind People. Multicoloured.
1395   2b. Type **465**   65   25
1396   2b. "Flying Birds" (Kwanchai
       Kerd-Daeng)   65   25
1397   2b. "Little Mermaid" (Chalerm-
       pol Jiengmai)   65   25
1398   2b. "Golden Fish" (Natetip
       Korsantirak)   65   25

466 Emblem and Symbols of
Communication

1989. 12th Anniv of Thai Communications Authority.
1399 **466** 2b. multicoloured   1·10   40

467 Statue of Kings Rama V and
VI and Auditorium

1989. 72nd Anniv of Chulalongkorn University.
1400 **467** 2b. multicoloured   1·30   40

468 Red Cross
Worker

1989. 96th Anniv of Thai Red Cross (1401) and 125th
Anniv of Int Red Cross (1402). Multicoloured.
1401   2b. Type **468**   1·10   25
1402   10b. Red Cross and pillar   1·90   1·10

469 Phra Kaeo
Monastery

1989. Phra Nakhon Khiri Historical Park. Multicoloured.
1403   2b. Type **469**   90   40
1404   3b. Chatchawan Wiangchai
       Observatory   1·30   80
1405   5b. Phra That Chom Phet stupa   2·10   1·60
1406   6b. Wetchayan Wichian Phrasat
       Throne Hall   2·50   1·90

470 Lottery Office Building and
Profit Recipients

1989. 50th Anniv of Government Lottery Office.
1407 **470** 2b. multicoloured   1·00   25

471 Campaign
Emblem and
Figures

1989. International Anti-drugs Day.
1408 **471** 2b. multicoloured   1·00   25

472 Gold
Nielloware Figures

1989. National Arts and Crafts Year. Multicoloured.
1409   2b. Type **472**   50   25
1410   2b. Ceramics   50   25
1411   6b. Ornament inlaid with
       gemstones (horiz)   1·40   65
1412   6b. Triangular cushion (horiz)   1·40   65

473 Thailand Cone

1989. Shells. Multicoloured.
1413   2b. Type **473**   50   25
1414   3b. Thorny oyster   1·10   40
1415   6b. Great spotted cowrie   1·60   1·10
1416   10b. Chambered nautilus   4·75   2·75

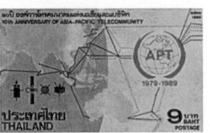

474 Satellites, Submarine Cable
Network and Emblem

1989. Tenth Anniv of Asia–Pacific Telecommunity.
1417 **474** 9b. multicoloured   2·00   1·20

475 Phya Anuman
Rajadhon

1989. Birth Centenary (1988) of Phya Anuman Rajadhon
(writer).
1418 **475** 2b. multicoloured   1·00   25

476 Emblem and School

1989. Centenary of Post and Telecommunications School.
1419 **476** 2b. multicoloured   1·10   25

477
Communications
Symbols

1989. National Communications Day.
1420 **477** 2b. multicoloured   1·00   25

478 Post Box

1989. "Thaipex '89" National Stamp Exhibition. Post
Boxes. Multicoloured.
1421   2b. Type **478**   65   25

1422   3b. Provincial box   75   40
1423   4b. City box   1·00   55
1424   5b. Imported English box   1·30   65
1425   6b. West German box sent as
       gift on introduction of Thai
       Postal Service   1·50   80
MS1425a 6b. 127×130 mm. Nos.
1421/5 (sold at 30b.)   50·00   50·00

479 Dragonfly

1989. Int Correspondence Week. Multicoloured.
1426   2b. Type **479**   1·00   25
1427   5b. Dragonfly (different)   1·40   65
1428   6b. Dragonfly (different)   1·50   80
1429   10b. Damselfly   2·40   1·30
MS1430 143×107 mm. Nos. 1426/9
(sold at 40b.)   44·00   44·00

480 Means of Transport and
Communications

1989. Asia–Pacific Transport and Communications
Decade.
1431 **480** 2b. multicoloured   90   25

481 Figure and
"Thoughts"

1989. Centenary of Mental Health Care.
1432 **481** 2b. multicoloured   90   25

482
"Hypericum
uralum"

1989. New Year. Flowers. Multicoloured.
1433   1b. Type **482**   65   55
1434   1b. "Uraria rufescens"   65   55
1435   1b. "Manglietia garrettii"   65   55
1436   1b. "Aeschynanthus macra-
       nthus"   65   55
MS1437 85×100 mm. Nos. 1433/6
(sold at 14b.)   10·00   10·00

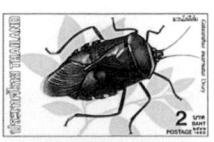

483 "Catacanthus incarnatus"
(shieldbug)

1989. Beetles. Multicoloured.
1438   2b. Type **483**   50   25
1439   3b. "Aristobia approximator"   75   40
1440   6b. "Chrysochroa chinensis"   1·50   65
1441   10b. "Enoplotrupes sharpi"   2·30   1·10

484 Medallists on
Rostrum

1989. Sports Welfare Fund. Multicoloured.
1442   2b.+1b. Type **484**   70   60
1443   2b.+1b. Nurse attending fallen
       cyclist   70   60
1444   2b.+1b. Boxing   70   60
1445   2b.+1b. Football   70   60

485 Official, Family and Graph

1990. Population and Housing Census.
1446   **485**   2b. multicoloured   1·10   25

486 Skipping (Phethai Setharangsi)

1990. National Children's Day. Multicoloured.
1447   2b. Type **486**   1·00   25
1448   2b. Various sports activities (Chalermpol Wongpim) (vert)   1·00   25

487 Skull splitting Heart

1990. Red Cross. Anti-AIDS Campaign.
1449   **487**   2b. blue, red and black   1·00   25

488 Tiap

1990. Heritage Conservation Day. Mother-of-Pearl Inlaid Containers. Multicoloured.
1450   2b. Type **488**   50   15
1451   2b. Phan waenfa   50   15
1452   8b. Lung (horiz)   1·40   80
1453   8b. Chiat (horiz)   1·40   80

489 Dental Students and Old Chair

1990. 50th Anniv of Chulalongkorn University Dentistry Faculty.
1454   **489**   2b. multicoloured   1·00   30

490 Tin

1990. Minerals. Multicoloured.
1460   2b. Type **490**   45   30
1461   3b. Zinc   75   35
1462   5b. Lead   1·20   55
1463   6b. Fluorite   2·10   1·00
MS1464 Two sheets, each 155×110 mm, each containing Nos. 1460/3 (a) Perf; (b) Imperf (pair sold at 60b.)   21·00   21·00

491 Pigeon

1990. National Communications Day.
1465   **491**   2b. blue, violet and purple   1·10   30

492 Pigeons and Envelopes

1990. 20th Anniv of Asian–Pacific Postal Training Centre, Bangkok.
1466   **492**   2b. green, blue and black   75   45
1467   **492**   8b. blue, green and black   2·30   1·10

493 Jaipur Foot Project

1990. 60th Anniv of Rotary International in Thailand. Multicoloured.
1468   2b. Type **493**   75   30
1469   3b. Child anti-polio vaccination campaign   1·20   35
1470   6b. Literacy campaign   1·50   70
1471   8b. King Chulalongkorn and his engraved cypher (Thai Museum, Nordkapp, Norway)   1·80   85

494 Account and Staff at Computer Terminals

1990. Centenary of Comptroller-General's Department.
1472   **494**   2b. multicoloured   1·70   45

495 Flowers in Dish (Cho Muang)

1990. Int Correspondence Week. Multicoloured.
1473   2b. Type **495**   60   20
1474   3b. Flowers on tray (Cha Mongkut)   75   30
1475   5b. Sweetmeats on tray with leaf design (Sane Chan)   1·40   35
1476   6b. Fruit in bowl (Luk Chup)   1·70   45
MS1477 Two sheets, each 152×127 mm, each containing Nos. 1473/6. (a) Perf; (b) Imperf (pair sold at 60b.)   23·00   23·00

496 Princess Mother with Flower

1990. 90th Birthday of Princess Mother.
1478   **496**   2b. multicoloured   6·75   1·00

497 "Cyrtandromoea grandiflora"

1990. New Year. Flowers. Multicoloured.
1479   1b. Type **497**   75   45
1480   1b. "Rhododendron arboreum sp. delavayi"   75   45
1481   1b. "Merremia vitifolia"   75   45
1482   1b. "Afgekia mahidolae"   75   45
MS1483 Two sheets, each 85×100 mm, each containing Nos. 1479/82. (a) Perf; (b) Imperf (pair sold at 20b.)   15·00   15·00

498 Wiman Mek Royal Hall

1990. Dusit Palace. Multicoloured.
1484   2b. Type **498**   75   30
1485   3b. Ratcharit Rungrot Royal House   90   35
1486   4b. Aphisek Dusit Royal Hall   1·10   45
1487   5b. Amphon Sathan Palace   1·20   50
1488   6b. Udon Phak Royal Hall   1·70   1·00
1489   8b. Anantasamakhom Throne Hall   2·75   1·40

499 Phrachetuphon Wimolmangkalaram Temple and Supreme Patriarch

1990. Birth Bicentenary of Supreme Patriarch Somdet Phra Maha Samanachao Kromphra Paramanuchitchinorot (formerly Prince Wasukri).
1490   **499**   2b. multicoloured   1·40   30

500 Judo

1990. Sports Welfare Fund. Multicoloured.
1491   2b.+1b. Type **500**   90   55
1492   2b.+1b. Archery   90   55
1493   2b.+1b. High jumping   90   55
1494   2b.+1b. Windsurfing   90   55

501 Aspects of Petroleum Industry

1990. 12th Anniv of Thai Petroleum Authority.
1495   **501**   2b. multicoloured   90   30

502 Mae Klong Railway Locomotive No. 6

1990. Steam Locomotives. Multicoloured.
1496   2b. Type **502**   1·50   30
1497   3b. "Sung Noen" locomotive No. 32   2·00   45
1498   5b. Class C 56 locomotive No. 715, Japan   2·50   2·30
1499   6b. Mikado locomotive No. 953, Japan   3·00   2·50
MS1500 Two sheets, each 152×123 mm, each containing Nos. 1496/9. (a) Perf; (b) Imperf (pair sold at 50b.)   26·00   24·00

503 Luk Khang (tops)

1991. Children's Day. Games. Multicoloured.
1501   2b. Type **503**   75   30
1502   3b. Pid Ta Ti Mo (blindfolded child smashing vase)   1·10   45
1503   5b. Doen Kala (walking on stones)   1·40   55
1504   6b. Phong Phang (blind man's buff)   2·00   70

504 Map, Surveyor and Cartographer

1991. Land Deeds Project.
1505   **504**   2b. multicoloured   90   30

505 Princess (patron) wearing Red Cross Uniform

1991. Red Cross. Princess Maha Chaki Sirindhorn's "Third Cycle" (36th) Birthday.
1506   **505**   2b. multicoloured   4·25   70
MS1507 Two sheets, each 80×105 mm, each containing No. 1506. (a) Perf; (b) Imperf (pair sold at 16b.)   23·00   21·00

506 "Indra's Heavenly Abode"

1991. Heritage Conservation Day. Floral Hanging Decorations. Multicoloured.
1508   2b. Type **506**   60   30
1509   3b. "Celestial Couch"   90   35
1510   4b. "Crystal Ladder"   1·20   45
1511   5b. "Crocodile"   1·50   55
MS1512 Two sheets, each 116×154 mm, each containing Nos. 1508/11. (a) Perf; (b) Imperf (pair sold at 60b.)   23·00   21·00

507 Goddess riding Goat

1991. Songkran (New Year) Day. Year of the Goat.
1513   **507**   2b. multicoloured   5·25   1·40
MS1514 Two sheets, each 80×100 mm, each containing No. 1513. (a) Perf; (b) Imperf (pair sold at 16b.)   55·00   50·00

508 Prince Narisranuvattivongs

1991. 44th Death Anniv of Prince Narisranuvattivongs.
1515   **508**   2b. brown, deep brown and yellow   75   30

509 Pink Lotus (Sutthiporn Wiset)

1991. Runners-up in International Correspondence Week Competition. Multicoloured.
1516   2b. Type **509**   60   20
1517   3b. Pink lotuses (Mathayom Suksa group, Khonkaen-vityayon School)   90   35
1518   5b. White lotus (Rattanaporn Sukhasem) (horiz)   1·40   55
1519   6b. Red lotuses (Phanupongs Sayasombat and Kanokwan Cholaphum) (horiz)   1·70   70

510 World Map, Communication Systems and Healthy Tree

1991. National Communications Day. "Communications and Preservation of the Environment".
1520   **510**   2b. multicoloured   1·20   35

511 Yok

1991. "Thaipex '91" National Stamp Exhibition. Textile Patterns. Multicoloured.

1521	2b. Type **511**	45	30
1522	4b. Mudmee	90	45
1523	6b. Khit	1·40	55
1524	8b. Chok	1·70	85
MS1525	110×145 mm. Nos. 1521/4 (sold at 30b.)	10·50	10·00

512 Workers and Productivity Arrow

1991. International Productivity Congress.

1526	**512**	2b. multicoloured	90	30

513 "Co-operation of Women around the World"

1991. 26th Int Council of Women Triennial.

1527	**513**	2b. multicoloured	90	30

514 Black

1991. International Correspondence Week. Japanese Bantams. Multicoloured.

1528	2b. Type **514**	75	20
1529	3b. Black-tailed buff	1·40	30
1530	6b. Buff	2·10	45
1531	8b. White	3·00	1·30
MS1532	Two sheets, each 145×110 mm, each containing Nos. 1528/31. (a) Perf; (b) Imperf (pair sold at 70b.)	23·00	21·00

515 Silver Coin of King Rama IV and Wat Phra Sri Rattana Satsadaram

1991. World Bank and International Monetary Fund Annual Meetings. Multicoloured.

1533	2b. Type **515**	45	30
1534	4b. Pod Duang money, Wat Mahathat Sukhothai and Wat Aroonrachawararam	60	45
1535	8b. Chieng and Hoi money and Wat Phrathat Doi Suthep	1·40	85
1536	10b. Funan, Dvaravati and Srivijaya money, Phra Pathom Chedi and Phra Borommathat Chaiya	1·80	1·10
MS1537	Two sheets, each 145×110 mm, each containing Nos. 1533/6. (a) Perf; (b) Imperf (pair sold at 70b.)	18·00	17·00

516 1908 1t. Stamp

1991. "Bangkok 1993" International Stamp Exhibition (1st series). Stamps from the 1908 King Chulalongkorn Issue. Multicoloured.

1538	2b. Type **516**	30	15
1539	3b. 2t. stamp	45	30
1540	4b. 3t. stamp	60	45
1541	5b. 5t. stamp	90	50
1542	6b. 10t. stamp	1·10	55
1543	7b. 20t. stamp	1·20	70
1544	8b. 40t. stamp	1·50	85
MS1545	Two sheets, each 80×129 mm, each containing No. 1544. (a) Perf; (b) Imperf (pair sold at 30b.)	15·00	14·00

See also Nos. 1618/**MS**1623, 1666/**MS**1670, 1700/**MS**1704 and **MS**1705.

517 Adult and Calves

1991. The Indian Elephant. Multicoloured.

1546	2b. Type **517**	75	30
1547	4b. Elephants pulling log	1·50	45
1548	6b. Adult male resting	1·80	70
1549	8b. Adults bathing	3·25	1·40
MS1550	Two sheets, each 96×78 mm, each containing No. 1549. (a) Perf; (b) Imperf (pair sold at 44b.)	23·00	21·00

518 "Dillenia obovata"

1991. New Year. Flowers. Multicoloured.

1551	1b. Type **518**	60	45
1552	1b. "Melastoma sanguineum"	60	45
1553	1b. "Commelina diffusa"	60	45
1554	1b. "Plumbago indica"	60	45
MS1555	Two sheets, each 85×100 mm, each containing Nos. 1551/4. (a) Perf; (b) Imperf (sold at 20b.)	15·00	14·00

520 Jogging

1991. Sports Welfare Fund. Multicoloured.

1558	2b.+1b. Type **520**	75	55
1559	2b.+1b. Cycling	75	55
1560	2b.+1b. Skipping	75	55
1561	2b.+1b. Swimming	75	55

521 Large Indian Civet

1991. Mammals. Multicoloured.

1562	2b. Type **521**	90	30
1563	3b. Banded linsang	1·20	35
1564	6b. Asiatic golden cat	1·70	55
1565	8b. Black giant squirrel	2·50	85
MS1566	Two sheets, each 146×110 mm, each containing Nos. 1562/5. (a) Perf; (b) Imperf (pair sold at 60b.)	24·00	23·00

522 Prince Mahidol

1992. Birth Centenary (1991) of Prince Mahidol of Songkla (pioneer of modern medicine in Thailand).

1567	**522**	2b. brown, gold & yellow	1·80	45

523 Archaeologists and Dinosaur Skeletons

1992. Centenary of Department of Mineral Resources. Multicoloured.

1568	2b. Type **523**	2·30	30
1569	2b. Mining excavation	2·30	30
1570	2b. Extracting natural gas and oil	2·30	30
1571	2b. Digging artesian wells	2·30	30

524 Drawing by Nachadong Bunprasoet

1992. Children's Day. "World under the Sea". Children's Drawings. Multicoloured.

1572	2b. Type **524**	60	30
1573	3b. Fishes and seaweed (Varaporn Phadkhan)	75	45
1574	5b. Mermaid (Phannipha Ngoenkon) (vert)	1·50	55

525 Battle Scene (mural, Chan Chittrakon)

1992. 400th Anniv of Duel between King Naresuan the Great of Thailand and Phra Maha Upparacha of Burma.

1575	**525**	2b. multicoloured	1·40	30

526 "Paphiopedilum bellatulum"

1992. Fourth Asia–Pacific Orchid Conf. Multicoloured.

1576	2b. Type **526**	45	15
1577	2b. "Paphiopedilum exul"	45	15
1578	3b. "Paphiopedilum godefroyae"	60	30
1579	3b. "Paphiopedilum concolor"	60	30
1580	6b. "Paphiopedilum niveum"	1·20	55
1581	6b. "Paphiopedilum villosum"	1·20	55
1582	10b. "Paphiopedilum parishii"	2·00	1·10
1583	10b. "Paphiopedilum sukhahulii"	2·00	1·10
MS1584	Four sheets, each 110×145 mm. (a) Nos. 1576, 1579/80 and 1582. Perf; (b) As a. but imperf; (c) Nos. 1577/8, 1581 and 1583. Perf; (d) As c. but imperf (4 sheets sold at 120b.)	30·00	28·00

527 Sugar Cane

1992. 21st International Sugar Cane Technologists Society Congress.

1585	**527**	2b. multicoloured	1·10	30

528 Prince Rabi Badhanasakdi (founder of School of Law)

1992. Centenary of Ministry of Justice. Legal Reformers. Multicoloured.

1586	3b. Type **528**	1·40	30
1587	5b. King Rama V (reformer of Courts system)	2·10	55

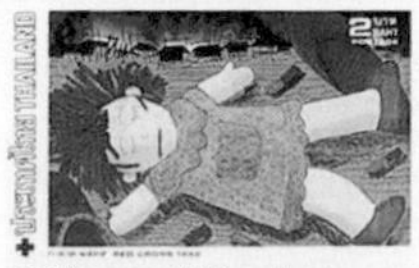

529 "Innocent" (Kamolporn Tapsuang)

1992. Red Cross.

1588	**529**	2b. multicoloured	90	15

530 Container Ships and Lorry

1992. 80th Anniv of Ministry of Transport and Communications. Multicoloured.

1589	2b. Type **530**	45	15
1590	3b. Diesel train and bus	60	30
1591	5b. Boeing 747-200 airliner and control tower	90	55
1592	6b. Lorry, satellites and aerials	1·10	70

531 Prince Damrong Rajanubharb (first Minister)

1992. Cent of Ministry of the Interior. Multicoloured.

1593	2b. Type **531**	60	30
1594	2b. Polling station	60	30
1595	2b. Emergency services and army	60	30
1596	2b. Child fetching water	60	30

532 Royal Ceremony of First Ploughing

1992. Centenary of Ministry of Agriculture and Co-operatives.

1597	**532**	2b. multicoloured	75	30
1598	**532**	3b. multicoloured	1·10	35
1599	**532**	4b. multicoloured	1·40	50
1600	**532**	5b. multicoloured	1·70	65

533 Ministry

1992. Centenary of Ministry of Education.

1601	**533**	2b. multicoloured	75	20

534 Western Region

1992. Thai Heritage Conservation Day. Traditional Carts. Multicoloured.

1602	2b. Type **534**	45	30
1603	3b. Northern region	60	45
1604	5b. North-eastern region	90	55
1605	10b. Eastern region	1·80	1·10
MS1606	Two sheets, each 145×110 mm, each containing Nos. 1602/5. (a) Perf; (b) Imperf (spair sold at 60b.)	13·50	13·00

535 Demon riding Monkey

1992. Songkran (New Year) Day. Year of the Monkey.

1607	**535**	2b. multicoloured	2·30	45

MS1608 Two sheets, each 80×100 mm,
each containing No. 1607. (a) Perf;
(b) Imperf (pair sold at 16b.)   13·50   13·00

536 American Brahman and
Livestock

1992. 50th Anniv of Department of Livestock
Development.
1609   **536**   2b. multicoloured   1·10   20

537 Birth of Buddha
(mural, Wat Angkaeo,
Bangkok)

1992. Wisakhabucha Day. Multicoloured.
1610   2b. Type **537**   60   30
1611   3b. "Enlightenment of Buddha"
(illustration by Phraya Thewa-
phinimmit from biography)   1·20   55
1612   5b. Death of Buddha (mural,
Wat Kanmatuyaram,
Bangkok)   1·70   1·10

538 Weather
Balloon, Dish Aerial,
Satellite and Map

1992. 50th Anniv of Meteorological Department.
1613   **538**   2b. multicoloured   1·10   20

539 Bua Tong Field,
Mae Hong Son
Province

1992. Association of South-East Asian Nations Tourism
Year. Multicoloured.
1614   2b. Type **539**   60   15
1615   3b. Klong Larn Waterfall, Kamphaeng Phet Province   75   30
1616   4b. Coral, Chumphon Province   90   45
1617   5b. Khao Ta-Poo, Phangnga
Province   1·10   55

540 1887 64a.
stamp

1992. "Bangkok 1993" International Stamp Exhibition
(2nd series). Multicoloured.
1618   2b. Type **540**   30   15
1619   3b. 1916 20b. stamp   45   30
1620   5b. 1928 40b. stamp   90   55
1621   7b. 1943 1b. stamp   1·20   70
1622   8b. 1947 20b. stamp   1·40   85
MS1623 Two sheets, each 123×185
mm, each containing Nos. 1618/22.
(a) Perf; (b) Imperf (pair sold at 70b.)   18·00   17·00

541 Prince   **543** Culture and
Chudadhuj   Sports
Dharadilok

1992. Birth Centenary of Prince Chudadhuj Dharadilok of
Bejraburna.
1624   **541**   2b. multicoloured   1·10   20

542 "Communications"

1992. National Communications Day.
1625   **542**   2b. multicoloured   90   15

543 Culture and
Sports

1992. 25th Anniv of Association of South-East Asian
Nations. Multicoloured.
1626   2b. Type **543**   45   15
1627   3b. Tourist sites   60   30
1628   5b. Transport and communications   90   55
1629   7b. Agriculture   1·40   85

544 Sirikit Medical Centre

1992. Inauguration of Sirikit Medical Centre.
1630   **544**   2b. multicoloured   75   15

545 Wedding Ceremony

546 Queen Sirikit and Cipher

1992. 60th Birthday of Queen Sirikit. (a) As T **545**.
Multicoloured.
1635   2b. Type **545**   1·20   45
1636   2b. Royal couple seated at
Coronation ceremony   1·20   45
1637   2b. Anointment as Queen   1·20   45
1638   2b. Seated on chair   1·20   45
1639   2b. Visiting hospital patient   1·20   45
1640   2b. Talking to subjects   1·20   45
MS1641 Two sheets, each 126×163
mm, each containing Nos. 1635/40.
(a) Perf; (b) Imperf (pair sold at 60b.)   21·00   20·00

(b) Royal Regalia. Enamelled gold objects. As T 546.
Multicoloured.
1642   2b. Bowls on footed tray (betel
and areca nut set)   75   30
1643   2b. Kettle   75   30
1644   2b. Water holder within bowl   75   30
1645   2b. Box on footed tray (betel
and areca nut set)   75   30
1646   2b. Vase   75   30

(c) Type **546**.
1647   100b. blue and gold   30·00   28·00

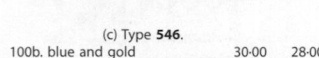

547 Prince Wan
Waithayakon

1992. Birth Centenary (1991) of Prince Wan Waithayakon,
Krommun Naradhip Bongsprabandh (diplomat).
1648   **547**   2b. multicoloured   1·10   15

548 Bhirasri

1992. Birth Centenary of Silpa Bhirasri (sculptor).
1649   **548**   2b. multicoloured   1·10   15

549 "Catalaphyllia jardinei"

1992. Int Correspondence Week. Corals. Multicoloured.
1650   2b. Type **549**   90   30
1651   3b. "Porites lutea"   1·40   45
1652   6b. "Tubastraea coccinea"   1·80   55
1653   8b. "Favia pallida"   2·75   85
MS1654 145×110 mm. Nos. 1650/3
(sold at 30b.)   7·50   7·00

550
"Rhododendron
simsii"

1992. New Year. Flowers. Multicoloured.
1655   1b. Type **550**   60   30
1656   1b. "Cynoglossum lanceolatum"   60   30
1657   1b. "Tithonia diversifolia"   60   30
1658   1b. "Agapetes parishii"   60   30
MS1659 Two sheets, each 100×85 mm,
each containing Nos. 1655/8. (a)
Perf; (b) Imperf (pair sold at 20b.)   9·00   8·50

551 Figures of Man
and Woman

1992. First Asian–Pacific Allergy and Immunology
Congress, Bangkok.
1660   **551**   2b. multicoloured   75   15

552 Anantasamakhom Throne
Hall, National Assembly Building
and King Prajadhipok's
Monument

1992. 60th Anniv of National Assembly.
1661   **552**   2b. multicoloured   1·10   20

553 Bank's Emblem and Bang
Khun Phrom Palace (old
headquarters)

1992. 50th Anniv of Bank of Thailand.
1662   **553**   2b. multicoloured   1·10   20

554 "River and Life" (Prathinthip
Mensin)

1993. Children's Day. Drawings. Multicoloured.
1663   2b. Type **554**   60   30
1664   2b. "Lovely Wild Animals and
Beautiful Forest" (Pratsani
Thammaprasert)   60   30
1665   2b. "Communications in the
Next Decade" (Natchaliya
Sutiprasit)   60   30

555 Kendi, Water Dropper and
Bottle

1993. "Bangkok 1993" International Stamp Exn (3rd
series). Traditional Pottery. Multicoloured.
1666   3b. Type **555**   60   30
1667   6b. Vase and bottles   1·10   55
1668   7b. Bowls   1·40   70
1669   8b. Jars   1·50   85
MS1670 145×110 mm. Nos. 1666/9
(sold at 35b.)   9·00   8·50

556
Anniversary
Emblem

1993. Centenary of Thai Teacher Training Institute.
1671   **556**   2b. multicoloured   75   30

557 Agricultural Produce

1993. 50th Anniv of Kasetsart University.
1672   **557**   2b. multicoloured   1·10   30

558 Buddha preaching
(mural, Wat
Kanmatuyaram,
Bangkok)

1993. Maghapuja Day.
1673   **558**   2b. multicoloured   3·00   70

559 Queen Sri
Bajarindra (first
royal patron)

1993. Centenary of Thai Red Cross.
1674   **559**   2b. multicoloured   1·40   45

560 Clock, Emblem and
Attorney General

1993. Centenary of Attorney General's Office.
| 1675 | **560** | 2b. multicoloured | 1·10 | 30 |

561 Wat Chedi Chet Thaeo

1993. Thai Heritage Conservation Day. Si Satchanalai Historical Park, Sukhothai Province. Multicoloured.
1676	3b. Type **561**	60	30
1677	4b. Wat Chang Lom	75	45
1678	6b. Wat Phra Si Rattanama-hathat	1·20	70
1679	7b. Wat Suan Kaeo Utthayan Noi	1·40	85
MS1680 145×110 mm. Nos. 1676/9 (sold at 25b.)	7·50	7·00

562 Demon riding Cock

1993. Songkran (New Year) Day. Year of the Cock.
| 1681 | **562** | 2b. multicoloured | 60 | 15 |
| **MS**1682 Two sheets, each 80×100 mm, each containing No. 1681. (a) Perf; (b) Imperf (pair sold at 16b.) | 7·50 | 7·00 |

563 "Marasmius sp."

1993. Fungi. Multicoloured.
1683	2b. Type **563**	30	15
1684	4b. "Coprinus sp."	75	45
1685	6b. "Mycena sp."	1·20	70
1686	8b. "Cyathus sp."	1·70	1·00
MS1687 145×110 mm. Nos. 1683/6 (sold at 30b.)	6·75	6·50

564 "Communications in the Next Decade"

1993. National Communications Day.
| 1688 | **564** | 2b. multicoloured | 75 | 30 |

565 Emblem, Morse Key and Satellite

1993. 110th Anniv of Post and Telegraph Department.
| 1689 | **565** | 2b. multicoloured | 1·80 | 45 |

566 Monument, Park and Reservoir

1993. Unveiling of Queen Suriyothai's Monument.
| 1690 | **566** | 2b. multicoloured | 1·10 | 30 |

567 Fawn Ridgeback

1993. International Correspondence Week. The Thai Ridgeback. Multicoloured.
1691	2b. Type **567**	75	30
1692	3b. Black	90	35
1693	5b. Tan	1·40	55
1694	10b. Grey	3·50	1·10
MS1695 145×110 mm. Nos. 1691/4 (sold at 30b.)	9·00	8·50

568 Tangerine

1993. Fruit. Multicoloured.
1696	2b. Type **568**	45	30
1697	3b. Bananas	75	35
1698	6b. Star gooseberry	1·20	70
1699	8b. Marian plum	1·50	1·00

569 Bencharong Cosmetic Jar

1993. "Bangkok 1993" International Stamp Exhibition (4th issue). Multicoloured.
1700	3b. Type **569**	60	30
1701	5b. Bencharong round cosmetic jar	90	55
1702	6b. Lai Nam Thong tall cosmetic jar	1·10	70
1703	7b. Lai Nam Thong cosmetic jar	1·40	85
MS1704 110×145 mm. Nos. 1700/3 (sold at 30b.)	6·00	5·75

1993. Bangkok 1993 International Stamp Exhibition (5th issue). Sheet 81×100 mm containing No. 1350.
| **MS**1705 25b. blue and olive | 13·50 | 13·00 |

570 Emblem and Oil Rigs

1993. Fifth Association of South East Asian Nations Council on Petroleum Conference and Exhibition.
| 1706 | **570** | 2b. multicoloured | 1·10 | 30 |

571 King Prajadhipok

1993. Birth Centenary of King Prajadhipok (Rama VII).
| 1707 | **571** | 2b. brown and gold | 1·70 | 45 |

572 "Ipomea cairica"

1993. New Year. Flowers. Multicoloured.
1708	1b. Type **572**	45	20
1709	1b. "Decaschistia parviflora"	45	20
1710	1b. "Hibiscus tiliaceus"	45	20
1711	1b. "Passiflora foetida"	45	20
MS1712 100×85 mm. Nos. 1708/11 (sold at 10b.)	3·75	3·50

1993. No. 1031a surch **1 BAHT**.
| 1713 | **227** | 1b. on 25s. red | 1·20 | 30 |

574 "Thaicom-1" Satellite, "Ariane 4" Rocket and Map of Thailand

1993. Launch of "Thaicom-1" (1st Thai communications satellite).
| 1714 | **574** | 2b. multicoloured | 75 | 30 |

575 "Play Land" (Piyathida Chapirom)

1994. Children's Day.
| 1715 | **575** | 2b. multicoloured | 90 | 30 |

576 Hospital Administrative Building

1994. Red Cross. 80th Anniv of Chulalongkorn Hospital.
| 1716 | **576** | 2b. multicoloured | 75 | 30 |

577 Emblem and Book

1994. 60th Anniv of Royal Institute.
| 1717 | **577** | 2b. multicoloured | 75 | 30 |

578 Wat Ratchaburana

1994. Thai Heritage Conservation Day. Phra Nakhon Si Ayutthaya Historical Park. Multicoloured.
1718	2b. Type **578**	55	30
1719	3b. Wat Maha That	70	45
1720	6b. Wat Maheyong	1·40	85
1721	9b. Wat Phra Si Sanphet	2·00	1·30
MS1722 145×110 mm. Nos. 1718/21 (sold at 25b.)	6·00	5·75

579 Friendship Bridge

1994. Inauguration of Friendship Bridge (between Thailand and Laos).
| 1723 | **579** | 9b. multicoloured | 3·00 | 70 |

580 Demon riding Dog

1994. Songkran (New Year) Day. Year of the Dog.
| 1724 | **580** | 2b. multicoloured | 60 | 30 |
| **MS**1725 Two sheets, each 80×100 mm, each containing No. 1724. (a) Perf; (b) Imperf (pair sold at 16b.) | 7·50 | 7·00 |

นิทรรศการตราไปรษณียากรไทย – จีน
泰國郵票展覽・北京
(581)

1994. Stamp Exhibition, Peking. As No. **MS**1725 but without sheet value and optd in bottom margin with T **581**.
| **MS**1726 Two sheets, each 80×100 mm. **580** 2b. multicoloured. (a) Perf; (b) Imperf | 13·50 | 13·00 |

582 Football

1994. Centenary of Int Olympic Committee. Multicoloured.
1727	2b. Type **582**	45	30
1728	3b. Running	60	45
1729	5b. Swimming	1·10	70
1730	6b. Weightlifting	1·40	85
1731	9b. Boxing	2·00	1·30

583 Dome Building

1994. 60th Anniv of Thammasat University.
| 1732 | **583** | 2b. multicoloured | 1·80 | 70 |

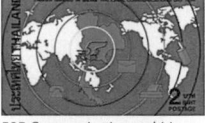
584 "Buddha giving First Sermon" (mural from Wat Thong Thammachat)

1994. Asalhapuja Day.
| 1733 | **584** | 2b. multicoloured | 75 | 30 |

585 Communications orbiting Thailand

1994. National Communications Day.
| 1734 | **585** | 2b. multicoloured | 75 | 30 |

586 "Phricotelphusa limula"

1994. Crabs. Multicoloured.
1735	3b. Type **586**	90	45
1736	5b. "Thaipotamon chulabhorn"	1·20	70
1737	6b. "Phricotelphusa sirindhorn"	1·40	85
1738	10b. "Thaiphusa sirikit"	2·75	1·40
MS1739 145×110 mm. Nos. 1735/8 (sold at 30b.)	7·50	7·00

587 Gold Niello Betel Nut Set

1994. International Correspondence Week. Betel Nut Sets.. Multicoloured.
1740	2b. Type **587**	45	30
1741	6b. Gold-plated silver niello set	1·40	85
1742	8b. Silver niello set	1·80	1·10
1743	9b. Gold niello set	2·00	1·30
MS1744 145×110 mm. Nos. 1740/3 (sold at 30b.)	6·75	6·50

588 Emblem and Workers

1994. 75th Anniv of I.L.O.
| 1745 | **588** | 2b. multicoloured | 45 | 30 |

589 "Eriocaulon odoratum"

1994. New Year. Flowers. Multicoloured.
| 1746 | 1b. Type **589** | 45 | 20 |
| 1747 | 1b. "Utricularia bifida" | 45 | 20 |

1748	1b. "Utricularia delphinioides"		45	20
1749	1b. "Utricularia minutissima"		45	20

MS1750 85×100 mm. Nos. 1746/9
(sold at 10b.) 3·75 3·50

590 Making Garland

1994. 60th Anniv of Suan Dusit Teachers' College.
| 1751 | **590** | 2b. multicoloured | 1·10 | 30 |

591 Chakri Mahaprasart Throne
Hall and Kings Chulalongkorn
and Bhumibol

1994. 120th Anniv of Council of State.
| 1754 | **591** | 2b. stone, blue and green | 2·40 | 45 |

592 Emblem and Airplane

1994. 50th Anniv of I.C.A.O.
| 1755 | **592** | 2b. multicoloured | 60 | 30 |

593 Dvaravati Grinding Stone
(7–11th century)

1994. 80th Anniv of Pharmacy in Thailand.. Multicoloured.
1756	2b. Type **593**		45	30
1757	6b. Lophuri grinding stone (11–13th century)		1·40	85
1758	9b. Bangkok period grinding stone (18–20th century)		2·00	1·30

594 Water Polo

1994. 18th South-East Asian Games, Chiang Mai. Multicoloured.
1759	2b.+1b. Type **594**		60	45
1760	2b.+1b. Tennis		60	45
1761	2b.+1b. Hurdling		60	45
1762	2b.+1b. Gymnastics		60	45

MS1763 145×110 mm. Nos. 1759/62
(sold at 15b.) 3·75 3·50

595 First Bar Building and
Kings Vajiravudh and Bhumibol

1995. 80th Anniv of the Bar.
| 1764 | **595** | 2b. multicoloured | 1·10 | 30 |

596 "Kites decorate
the Summer Sky"
(Kontorn Taechoran)

1995. Children's Day. Multicoloured.
1765	2b. Type **596**		90	30
1766	2b. "Trees and Streams" (Yuvadee Samutpong) (horiz)		90	30
1767	2b. "Youths and Religion" (Yutdanai Polyium) (horiz)		90	30

597 Front Page of
First Edition and
Pen Nib in Camera
Shutter

1995. 150th Anniv of "Bangkok Recorder" (newspaper).
| 1768 | **597** | 2b. multicoloured | 60 | 30 |

598 Breguet Biplane and
General Dynamics Fighting
Falcon Jet Fighter

1995. 80th Anniv of Royal Thai Airforce.
| 1769 | **598** | 2b. multicoloured | 75 | 35 |

599 "Wetchapha"

1995. Red Cross. 40th Anniv of "Wetchapha" (hospital ship).
| 1770 | **599** | 2b. multicoloured | 75 | 35 |

600 Naga Bridge

1995. Thai Heritage Conservation Day Phimai Historical Park. Multicoloured.
1771	3b. Type **600**		60	45
1772	5b. Brahmin Hall		1·10	55
1773	6b. Gateway in Inner wall		1·40	85
1774	9b. Main pagoda		2·00	1·30

MS1775 145×110 mm. Nos. 1771/4
(sold at 30b.) 6·75 6·50

601 Administration Hall

1995. 108th Anniv of Ministry of Defence.
| 1776 | **601** | 2b. multicoloured | 1·20 | 30 |

602 Woman
riding Boar

1995. Songkran (New Year) Day.
| 1777 | **602** | 2b. multicoloured | 45 | 30 |

MS1778 Two sheets, each 80×100 mm,
each containing No. 1777. (a) Perf;
(b) Imperf (sold at 16b.) 6·00 5·75

603 King Rama V and Saranrom
Palace

1995. 120th Anniv of Ministry of Foreign Affairs.
| 1779 | **603** | 2b. multicoloured | 1·40 | 45 |

604 Emerald Buddha

1995. Visakhapuja Day. Statues of Buddha. Multicoloured.
1780	2b. Type **604**		45	30
1781	6b. Phra Phuttha Chinnarat		1·40	85
1782	8b. Phra Phuttha Sihing		1·80	1·10
1783	9b. Phra Sukhothai Traimit		2·00	1·30

MS1784 127×151 mm. Nos. 1780/3
(sold at 35b.) 7·50 7·00

605 Emblem
forming Flower and
Globe

1995. Association of South East Asian Nations Environment Year.
| 1785 | **605** | 2b. multicoloured | 45 | 30 |

606 Emblem

1995. Thailand Information Technology Year.
| 1786 | **606** | 2b. multicoloured | 45 | 30 |

607 Asian Elephants and Young

1995. 20th Anniv of Thailand–China Diplomatic Relations. Multicoloured.
| 1787 | 2b. Type **607** | | 75 | 45 |
| 1788 | 2b. Asian elephants at river (face value at left) | | 75 | 45 |

MS1789 145×110 mm. Nos. 1787/8
(sold at 8b.) 5·25 5·00

Nos. 1787/8 were issued together, *se-tenant*, forming a composite design.

608 Optical Fibre Cables

1995. National Communications Day.
| 1790 | **608** | 2b. multicoloured | 45 | 30 |

609 Khoa Manee

1995. "Thaipex'95" National Stamp Exhibition. Cats. Multicoloured.
1791	3b. Type **609**		90	45
1792	6b. Korat		1·40	85
1793	7b. Sealpoint Siamese		1·80	1·00
1794	9b. Burmese		2·75	1·30

MS1795 110×145 mm. Nos. 1791/4
(sold at 35b.) 9·00 8·50

610 Headquarters

1995. 80th Anniv of Revenue Department.
| 1796 | **610** | 2b. multicoloured | 45 | 30 |

611 Money and Industry

1995. 120th Anniv of National Auditing.
| 1797 | **611** | 2b. multicoloured | 45 | 30 |

612 Khong

1995. International Correspondence Week. Wicker Aquatic Animal Baskets.. Multicoloured.
1798	2b. Type **612**		45	30
1799	2b. Krachangklom (round basket)		45	30
1800	9b. Sum (open-ended basket)		2·00	1·30
1801	9b. Ichu (jar)		2·00	1·30

MS1802 110×145 mm. Nos. 1798/1801
(sold at 35b.) 7·50 7·00

613 Foodstuffs and Anniversary
Emblem

1995. 50th Anniv of F.A.O.
| 1803 | **613** | 2b. multicoloured | 45 | 30 |

614 Telescope and Eclipse

1995. Total Solar Eclipse.
| 1804 | **614** | 2b. multicoloured | 75 | 30 |

615 U.N. Building, Thailand

1995. 50th Anniv of U.N.O.
| 1805 | **615** | 2b. multicoloured | 45 | 30 |

616 Tower

1995. "WORLDTECH'95" International Agricultural and Industrial Exhibition, Suranaree. Multicoloured.
1806	2b. Type **616**		45	30
1807	5b. Agriculture		1·10	70
1808	6b. Modern technology (horiz)		1·40	85
1809	9b. Reservoirs and coastline (horiz)		2·00	1·30

617 "Adenium
obesum"

1996. New Year. Flowers. Multicoloured.

1810	2b. Type **617**	45	30
1811	2b. "Bauhinia acuminata"	45	30
1812	2b. "Cananga odorata"	45	30
1813	2b. "Thunbergia erecta"	45	30
MS1814 100×85 mm. Nos. 1810/13 (sold at 15b.)		4·50	4·25

618 Vaccinating Cattle

1995. 60th Anniv of Veterinary Science in Thailand

1815	**618**	2b. multicoloured	90	45

619 Fencing

1995. 18th South-East Asian Games, Chiang Mai. Multicoloured.

1816	2b.+1b. Type **619**	60	45
1817	2b. Snooker	60	45
1818	2b. Diving	60	45
1819	2b.+1b. Pole vaulting	60	45
MS1820 145×110 mm. Nos. 1816/19 (sold at 15b.)		3·25	3·00

Nos. 1815/18 were issued together, *se-tenant*, forming a composite design.

620 Queen Somdej
Phra Sri Patcharin
(founder)

1996. Centenary of Siriraj School of Nursing and Midwifery.

1821	**620**	2b. multicoloured	90	30

621 Breguet Biplane and
Emblem

1996. National Aviation Day.

1822	**621**	2b. multicoloured	90	30

622 "Visakhapuja Day" (Malinee
Sanaewong)

1996. Children's Day. Children's Drawings. Multicoloured.

1823	2b. Type **622**	90	30
1824	2b. "Maghapuja Day" (Thirapon Deephlub) (tree in centre) (vert)	90	30
1825	2b. "Asalhapuja Day" (Voraphat Pankian) (tree at left) (vert)	90	30

623 Handshake
and Map of Asia
and Europe

1996. Asia–Europe Summit Meeting, Thailand.

1826	**623**	2b. multicoloured	60	30

624 Temiyajataka

1996. Maghapuja Day. Multicoloured.

1827	2b. Type **624**	45	30
1828	6b. Mahajanakajataka	1·40	85
1829	8b. Suvannasamjataka	1·80	1·10
1830	9b. Nemijataka	2·00	1·30
MS1831 152×127 mm. Nos. 1827/30 (sold at 36b.)		10·50	10·00

625 Princess Mother and
Golden Crematorium

1996. Princess Mother's Cremation.

1832	**625**	2b. multicoloured	2·00	35

626 Wat Phra Kaeo

1996. Thai Heritage Conservation Day. Kamphaeng Phet Historical Park. Multicoloured.

1833	2b. Type **626**	45	30
1834	3b. Wat Phra Non	75	45
1835	6b. Wat Chang Rop	1·40	85
1836	9b. Wat Pgra Si Iriyabot	2·00	1·30
MS1837 145×110 mm. Nos. 1833/6 (sold at 28b.)		6·25	6·00

627 Buddhist Pagoda, Wat
Chiang Man

1996. 700th Anniv of Chiang Mai. Multicoloured.

1838	2b. Type **627**	45	30
1839	6b. Angel sculpture, Wat Chet Yot's Pagoda	1·40	85
1840	8b. Insignia of Wat Phan Tao monastery	1·80	1·10
1841	9b. Sattaphanta	2·00	1·30
MS1842 145×110 mm. Nos. 1838/41 (sold at 37b.)		7·50	7·00

628 Rufous-necked
Hornbills

1996. Second International Asian Hornbill Workshop. Multicoloured.

1843	3b. Type **628**	60	45
1844	3b. Long-crested hornbill ("White-crowned Hornbill")	60	45
1845	9b. Blyth's hornbill ("Plain-pouched Hornbill")	2·00	1·30
1846	9b. Rhinoceros hornbill	2·00	1·30
MS1847 110×145 mm. Nos. 1843/6 (sold at 35b.)		9·00	8·50

629 Angel
riding Rat

1996. Songkran (New Year) Day.

1848	**629**	2b. multicoloured	45	30
MS1849 Two sheets, each 80×100 mm, containing No. 1848. (a) Perf; (b) Imperf (sold at 16b.)			9·00	8·50
MS1850 Two sheets, each 135×160 mm, Nos. 1513, 1607, 1681, 1724, 1777 and 1848. (a) Perf; (b) Imperf (sold at 40b.)			13·50	13·00

630 Royal Ablutions
Ceremony

631 King Bhumibol

1996. 50th Anniv of King Bhumibol's Accession to Throne as Rama IX (1st issue). Multicoloured. (a) Coronation Ceremony.

1851	3b. Type **630**	75	45
1852	3b. Pouring of the Libation	75	45
1853	3b. Grand Audience	75	45
1854	3b. Royal Progress by land	75	45
1855	3b. Making speech from balcony	75	45
MS1856 Five sheets, each 120×110 mm. (a) 3b. Type **630**; (b) 3b. No. 1852; (c) 3b. No. 1853; (d) 3b. No. 1854; (e) 3b. No. 1855 (five sheets sold for 40b.)		15·00	14·00

(b) Royal Regalia. As T **630**.

1857	3b. Betal and areca-nut set	75	45
1858	3b. Water urn	75	45
1859	3b. Gold-enamelled cuspidor and golden spittoon (horiz)	75	45
MS1860 110×145 mm. Nos. 1857/9 (sold at 17b.)		5·25	5·00

(c) National Development. As T **630** but horiz.

1861	3b. Cultivation of vetiver grass (prevention of soil erosion)	60	45
1862	3b. Chai Pattana aerator (improvement of water quality)	60	45
1863	3b. Airplane (rain-making project)	60	45
1864	3b. Dam (water resources development)	60	45
1865	3b. Sapling (Golden Jubilee Reforestation Campaign)	60	45
MS1866 185×122 mm. Nos. 1861/5 plus label (sold at 25b.)		6·75	6·50

(d) Type **631**.

1867	100b. multicoloured	23·00	14·00

See also No. 1885/**MS**1886.

632 Baron Pierre
de Coubertin
(founder) and
Grave

1996. Centenary of Modern Olympic Games. Multicoloured.

1868	2b. Type **632**	45	30
1869	3b. Lighting Olympic flame at Olympia, Greece	60	45
1870	5b. First modern Games and Olympic flag	1·10	70
1871	9b. Athlete and medal from 1896 Games	2·00	1·30

633 King Bhumibol
using Short-wave
Radio

1996. National Communications Day.

1872	**633**	2b. multicoloured	90	30

634 Tropical Rain Forest

1996. Centenary of Royal Forest Department. Multicoloured.

1873	3b. Type **634**	60	45
1874	6b. Evergreen mountain forest	1·40	85
1875	7b. Swamp forest	1·50	1·00
1876	9b. Mangrove forest	2·00	1·30
MS1877 144×108 mm. Nos. 1873/6 (sold at 35b.)		8·25	7·75

635 "Ramayana"

1996. International Correspondence Week. Thai Novels. Multicoloured.

1878	3b. Type **635**	60	45
1879	3b. Inao and Budsaba in cave ("Inao")	60	45
1880	9b. Lunhap being shown round forest ("Ngao Pa")	2·00	1·30
1881	9b. The cursing of Nang Mathanal ("Mathanapatha")	2·00	1·30
MS1882 145×110 mm. Nos. 1878/81 (sold at 36b.)		8·25	7·75

636 Youth
Activities

1996. Asia Regional Conference of Rotary International, Thailand.

1883	**636**	2b. multicoloured	75	30

637 Huoy Kha Khang National
Park

1996. 50th Anniv of U.N.E.S.C.O.

1884	**637**	2b. multicoloured	45	30

638 "Narai Song Suban H.M. King Rama IX" (new royal barge) (image scaled to 41% of original size)

1996. 50th Anniv of King Bhumibol's Accession to Throne as Rama IX (2nd issue). Multicoloured.

1885	**638**	9b. multicoloured	2·75	2·00
MS1886 170×110 mm. No. 1885 (sold at 16b.)			5·75	5·50

639 "Limnocharis
flava"

1996. New Year. Flowers. Multicoloured.

1887	2b. Type **639**	45	30
1888	2b. "Crinum thaianum" (vert)	45	30

1889 2b. "Monochoria hastata" (vert) 45 30
1890 2b. "Nymphoides indicum" 45 30
MS1891 85×100 mm. Nos. 1887/90 (sold at 15b.) 4·50 4·25

640 Indian Whistling Duck ("Dendrocygna javanica")

1996. Water Birds. Multicoloured.

1892	3b. Type **640**	75	45
1893	3b. Comb duck ("Sarkidiornis melanotos") (horiz)	75	45
1894	7b. Cotton teal ("Nettapus coromandelianus") (horiz)	1·50	1·00
1895	7b. White-winged wood duck ("Cairina scutulata")	1·50	1·00
MS1896	153×120 mm. Nos. 1892/5 (sold at 33b.)	9·00	8·50

641 King Rama IX in Admiral's Uniform

1996

2005	**641**	50s. green	60	15
2077	**641**	1b. blue	60	30
1897	**641**	2b. red	90	30
2078	**641**	4b. red and blue	1·80	45
1899	**641**	5b. red and lilac	3·25	70
2079	**641**	5b. brown and violet	2·30	55
1900	**641**	6b. lilac and green	2·75	55
1901	**641**	7b. green and pink	2·40	2·10
1902	**641**	9b. orange and blue	3·75	70
1903	**641**	10b. black and orange	3·75	1·40
1903a	**641**	12b. blue and green	2·10	1·30
1903b	**641**	[illegible] green and brown	3·50	70
1904	**641**	20b. red and violet	6·25	2·75
1905	**641**	25b. olive and green	12·00	5·00
1905a	**641**	30b. brown and pink	4·75	3·00
1906	**641**	50b. green and violet	12·00	3·50
1907	**641**	100b. blue and yellow	23·00	7·00
1908	**641**	200b. purple and mauve	38·00	14·00
1909	**641**	500b. mauve and orange (26×31 mm)	60·00	28·00

642 Children at Zoo (Ruangchai Khot-Tha)

1996. 50th Anniv of U.N.I.C.E.F.
1910 **642** 2b. multicoloured 45 30

643 Medal, Flag and Boxers

1996. First Thai Olympic Gold Medal (won by Somluck Khamsingh for boxing at Atlanta, U.S.A.).
1911 **643** 6b. multicoloured 1·40 85

644 School, King Rama V and Crown Prince Vajiravudh (Rama VI)

1997. Centenary of Mahavajiravudh School, Songkhla.
1912 **644** 62b. multicoloured 45 30

645 "Good Things in my Province" (Natamol Thongsai)

1997. Children's Day. Children's Drawings. Multicoloured.

1913	2b. Type **645** (dried fish, Samut Prakan)	60	30
1914	2b. "Tourist Sites in my Province", Chanthaburi (Somkiat Thongchomphu)	60	30

646 Old and New Buildings

1997. 20th Anniv of Communications Authority.
1915 **646** 2b. multicoloured 60 30

647 Statue

1997. Unveiling of Statue of Prince Bhanurangsi (founder of postal service) outside Communications Authority, Laksi (Bangkok).
1916 **647** 2b. multicoloured 60 30

648 Building

1997. Laksi Mail Centre. Multicoloured.

1917	2b. Type **648**	75	30
1918	2b. Letter sorting equipment	75	30

Nos. 1917/18 were issued together, se-tenant, forming a composite design.

649 Windsor Palace (University building)

1997. 80th Anniv of Chulalongkorn University. Multicoloured.

1919	2b. Type **649**	75	30
1920	2b. Faculty of Arts building	75	30

650 Early Steam Locomotive

1997. Cent of Thai State Railway. Multicoloured.

1921	3b. Type **650**	60	45
1922	4b. Garratt steam locomotive	90	55
1923	6b. Sulzer diesel-mechanic locomotive	1·40	85
1924	7b. Hitachi diesel-electric locomotive	1·70	1·00
MS1925	Two sheets. (a) 110×145 mm. No. 1921; (b) 145×110 mm. Nos. 1921/4 (pair sold at 50b.)	11·50	10·50

651 Rajakarun Museum

1997. Red Cross.
1926 **651** 3b. multicoloured 60 45

652 First Headquarters

1997. 84th Anniv of Government Savings Bank.
1927 **652** 2b. multicoloured 45 30

653 Outer Staircase

1997. Thai Heritage Conservation Day. Phanomrung Historical Park. Multicoloured.

1928	3b. Type **653**	60	45
1929	3b. Pavilion	60	45
1930	7b. Pathway and stairs to Sanctuary	1·50	1·00
1931	7b. Naga balustrade and Eastern Gallery central gate	1·50	1·00
MS1932	110×145 mm. Nos. 1928/31 (sold at 30b.)	6·75	6·50

654 Man riding Bull

1997. Songkran (New Year) Day. Year of the Bull.
1933 **654** 2b. multicoloured 75 30
MS1934 Two sheets, each 80×100 mm, each containing No. 1933. (a) Perf; (b) Imperf (sold at 16b.) 7·50 7·00

655 Pheasant-tailed Jacana

1997. Water Birds. Multicoloured.

1935	3b. Type **655**	90	85
1936	3b. Bronze-winged jacana	90	85
1937	7b. Painted stork	2·30	2·10
1938	7b. Black-winged stilt	2·30	2·10
MS1939	145×110 mm. Nos. 1935/8 (sold at 30b.)	9·75	9·25

656 Suthee Aerial and King Bhumibol using Radio

1997. Telecommunications. Multicoloured.

1940	2b. Type **656**	60	50
1941	3b. King using hand-held radio and various radios	90	75
1942	6b. King using computer	2·00	1·60
1943	9b. King, schoolchildren and "Thaicom" satellite (expanding secondary education to rural areas using satellite technology)	2·75	2·40
MS1944	145×110 mm. Nos. 1940/3 (sold at 30b.)	9·75	8·75

657 First Thai Cinema Advertisement, Equipment and Prince Sanbassatra

1997. Cent of Cinema in Thailand. Multicoloured.

1945	3b. King Prajadhipok filming and King Chulalongkorn's state visit to Europe, 1897 (first film documenting Thai history)	90	75
1946	3b. Type **657**	90	75
1947	7b. Poster for "Double Luck" (first movie with Thai producer) and band outside cinema	2·30	1·90
1948	7b. Open-air cinema and poster for "Going Astray" (first Thai sound film)	2·30	1·90

658 King Ananda Mahidol (Rama VIII) (founder), Building and Operation

1997. 50th Anniv of Faculty of Medicine, Chulalongkorn University.
1949 **658** 2b. multicoloured 75 30

659 Peterhof Palace and King Chulalongkorn

1997. Centenary of Thailand–Russia Diplomatic Relations and State Visit of King Chulalongkorn (Rama V) to Russia.
1950 **659** 2b. multicoloured 60 45

660 Mahosathajataka

1997. Asalhapuja Day. Designs illustrating ten Jataka stories. Multicoloured.

1951	3b. Type **660**	90	70
1952	4b. Bhuridattajataka	1·20	1·00
1953	6b. Candakumarajataka	2·00	1·70
1954	7b. Naradajataka	2·00	1·70
MS1955	Five sheets. (a) 152×127 mm. Nos. 1951/4; (b) 100×80 mm. No. 1951; (c) 100×80 mm. No. 1952; (d) 100×80 mm. No. 1953; (e) 100×80 mm. No. 1954 (set of 5 sold at 66b.)	23·00	21·00

661 Northern Region

1997. "Thaipex 97" Stamp Exhibition. Traditional Houses. Multicoloured.

1956	2b. Type **661**	45	30
1957	5b. Central region	1·20	1·00
1958	6b. North-eastern region	1·40	1·10
1959	9b. Southern region	2·10	1·80
MS1960	125×165 mm. Nos. 1956/9 (sold at 32b.)	6·00	5·75

662 Cape Blue Water-lily ("Nymphaea capensis")

1997. Greetings booklet stamps. No value indicated. Multicoloured.

1961	(2b.) Type **662**	1·50	70
1962	(2b.) Indian lotus ("Nymphaea stellata")	1·50	70

663 Means of Communications

1997. National Communications Day.
1963 **663** 2b. multicoloured 45 30

664 Luang Chiang Dao Mountain, Chiang Mai

1997. 30th Anniv of Association of South-East Asian Nations. Tourist Sights. Multicoloured.

1964	2b. Type **664**	45	30
1965	2b. Thi Lo Su Falls, Tak	45	30
1966	9b. Thalu Island, Chumphon	2·10	1·80
1967	9b. Phromthep Cape, Phuket	2·10	1·80

665 "Phuwiangosaurus sirindhornae"

1997. Dinosaurs. Multicoloured.

1968	2b. Type **665**	30	15
1969	3b. "Siamotyrannus isanensis"	60	30
1970	6b. "Siamosaurus suteethorni"	90	55
1971	9b. "Psittacosaurus sattayaraki"	1·80	1·00
MS1972 145×110 mm. Nos. 1968/71 (sold at 30b.)		5·25	5·00

666 King Chulalongkorn

1997. Centenary of Visit to Switzerland of King Chulalongkorn (Rama V).

1973	**666**	2b. multicoloured	75	30

667 Rickshaw and Bicycle Hybrid

1997. International Correspondence Week. Tricycles. Multicoloured.

1974	3b. Type **667**	45	30
1975	3b. Bicycle with attached side-seat and wheel	45	30
1976	9b. Motor tricycle No. 345	1·50	70
1977	9b. Tuk-tuk (open-sided three-wheel motor)	1·50	70
MS1978 144×110 mm. Nos. 1974/7 (sold at 30b.)		5·25	5·00

668 Purple Pacific Drupe

1997. World Post Day. Shells. Multicoloured.

1979	2b. Type **668**	45	30
1980	2b. "Nerita chamaelon"	45	30
1981	9b. "Littoraria melanostoma"	1·50	70
1982	9b. "Cryptospira elegans"	1·50	70
MS1983 144×110 mm. Nos. 1979/82 (sold at 30b.)		4·50	4·25

669 Chalerm Prakiat (energy efficient building), Khlong Har

1997. Energy Conservation.

1984	**669**	2b. multicoloured	45	30

670 "Suphannahong" (Royal Barge, 1911) (image scaled to 41% of original size)

1997

1985	**670**	9b. multicoloured	1·50	70
MS1986 157×95 mm. No. 1985 (sold at 20b.)			3·75	3·50

671 "Cassia alata"

1997. New Year. Flowers. Multicoloured.

1987	2b. Type **671**	45	30
1988	2b. "Strophanthus caudatus"	45	30
1989	2b. "Clinacanthus nutans"	45	30
1990	2b. "Acanthus ilicifolius"	45	30
MS1991 85×100 mm. Nos. 1987/90 (sold at 15b.)		3·00	2·75

672 Playing Saxophone and Score of his "Falling Rain"

1997. 70th Birthday of King Bhumibol. Multicoloured.

1992	2b. Type **672**	45	30
1993	2b. At easel and one of his paintings	45	30
1994	2b. Model airplane, "OK" class dinghy and bust and Bhumibol building boat	45	30
1995	2b. Sailing "OK" class dinghy and wearing team blazer with gold medal from South-East Asian Games	45	30
1996	6b. With camera and his photograph of Royal Water Development Project	90	55
1997	7b. Writing and his books "Nai In", "Tito" and "The Story of Mahajanaka"	1·20	70
1998	9b. Using computer, map from "The Story of Mahajanaka" and his New Year card	1·50	85

673 "Sport-minded in Maimed Bodies" (Sumonmarl Chaneiam)

1998. Children's Day. Children's Drawings. Multicoloured.

1999	2b. Type **673**	45	30
2000	2b. "Kite-flying Contest" (Pavinee Rodsawat)	45	30
2001	2b. "Gymnastics" (Kejsarin Nilwong)	45	30
2002	2b. "Windsurf Racing" (Voraphat Phankhian)	45	30

674 Dental Tools and Emblem on Tooth

1998. 20th Asia Pacific Dental Congress, Bangkok.

2003	**674**	2b. multicoloured	45	30

675 Victory Monument and Military and Civilian Representatives

1998. 50th Anniv of Veterans' Day.

2004	**675**	2b. multicoloured	75	30

676 Queen Sirikit (Red Cross president)

1998. Red Cross.

2015	**676**	2b. multicoloured	60	30

677 Shooting

1998. 13th Asian Games, Bangkok. Multicoloured.

2016	2b.+1b. Type **677**	45	30
2017	3b.+1b. Gymnastics	60	45
2018	4b.+1b. Swimming	75	55
2019	7b.+1b. Windsurfing	1·20	85

678 Main Tower

1998. Thai Heritage Conservation Day. Phanomrung Historical Park. Multicoloured.

2020	3b. Type **678**	45	30
2021	4b. Minor Tower	60	45
2022	6b. Scripture repository	90	70
2023	7b. Lintel depicting Vishnu sleeping in ocean (eastern doorway, Main Tower)	1·10	85
MS2024 110×145 mm. Nos. 2020/3		4·50	4·25

679 Woman riding Tiger

1998. Songkran (New Year) Day. Year of the Tiger.

2025	**679**	2b. multicoloured	60	30
MS2026 Two sheets, each 80×100 mm, each containing No. 2025. (a) Perf; (b) Imperf (pair sold at 16b.)			6·00	5·75

680 Fishing Cat

1998. Wild Cats. Multicoloured.

2027	2b. Type **680**	75	30
2028	4b. Tiger	1·10	45
2029	6b. Leopard	1·20	70
2030	8b. Jungle cat	1·50	85
MS2031 144×110 mm. Nos. 2027/30		6·00	5·75

681 Airliner and Radar Grid

1998. 50th Anniv of Aerothai (air-traffic control).

2032	**681**	2b. multicoloured	75	30

682 "Vidhurajataka" (Kritsana Moka-siri)

1998. Visakhapuja Day. Prize-winning Drawings of Ten Jataka Stories. Multicoloured.

2033	3b. Type **682**	60	30
2034	4b. "Vessantarajataka: Dana Kanda" (Chuttumrong Chalow-thorn-phises)	90	45
2035	6b. "Vessantarajataka: Kumara Kanda" (Surasin Chinna-wong)	1·20	70
2036	7b. "Vessantarajataka: Sakka-pabba Kanda" (Chuttumrong Chalow-thorn-phises)	1·50	85
MS2037 162×120 mm. Nos. 2033/6 (sold at 30b.)		4·50	4·25

683 Kiartiwongse and "Phra Ruang" (destroyer)

1998. 75th Death Anniv of Admiral Prince Abhakara Kiartiwongse, Prince of Jumborn.

2038	**683**	2b. multicoloured	75	30

684 Modern Technology (Porntiva Prasert)

1998. "Education Develops People and thus Nation". Under-9 Years Prize-winning Drawings.

2039	**684**	2b. multicoloured	75	30

685 Commemorative Coin and Map and Flags of Europe

1998. Centenary (1997) of First State Visit to Europe of King Chulalongkorn (Rama V).

2040	**685**	6b. multicoloured	1·20	70
2041	**685**	20b. multicoloured	3·00	2·10

686 Irrawaddy Dolphin

1998. International Year of the Ocean. Marine Mammals. Multicoloured.

2042	2b. Type **686**	55	20
2043	3b. Bottle-nosed dolphin	60	30
2044	6b. Sperm whale	90	70
2045	9b. Dugong	1·50	85
MS2046 164×110 mm. Nos. 2042/5 (sold at 30b.)		6·00	5·75

687 Dams

1998. 60th Anniv of Irrigation Engineering.

2047	**687**	2b. multicoloured	45	30

688 Model of Asynchronous Transfer Mode

1998. National Communications Day.

2048	**688**	2b. multicoloured	45	30

689 Faculty Building and Emblems

1998. 50th Anniv of Faculty of Political Science, Chulalongkorn University.

2049	**689**	2b. multicoloured	45	30

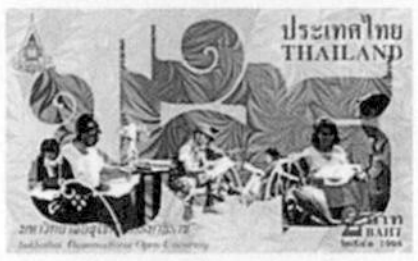

690 Correspondence Students

1998. 20th Anniv of Sukhothai Thammathirat Open University.
2050 **690** 2b. multicoloured 45 30

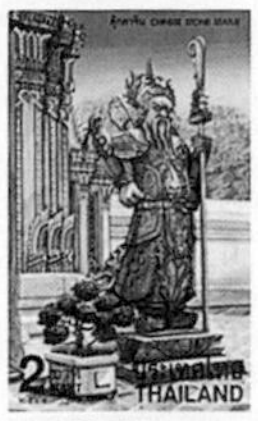

691 Warrior

1998. Chinese Stone Statues. Multicoloured.
2051 2b. Type **691** 45 30
2052 2b. Warrior holding barbed spear 45 30
2053 10b. Warrior holding mace 1·50 1·00
2054 10b. Warrior holding spear with jagged blade 1·50 1·00
MS2055 110×145 mm. Nos. 2051/4 (sold at 35b.) 5·25 5·00

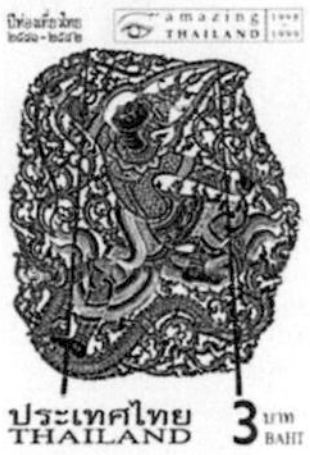

692 Archer

1998. "Amazing Thailand" Year. Perforated Hides. Multicoloured.
2056 3b. Type **692** 45 30
2057 3b. Warriors on elephants 45 30
2058 7b. [illegible] opponent 1·20 85
2059 7b. Deity hovering in sky 1·20 85

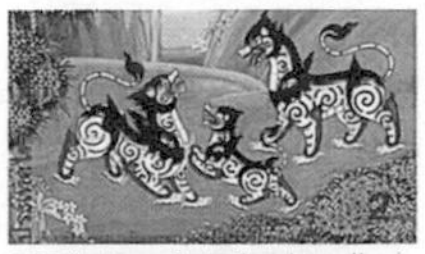
693 Kraisara Rajasiha (king lion)

1998. International Correspondence Week. Himavanta Mythical Animals of the Singha (lion) Family. Multicoloured.
2060 2b. Type **693** 45 30
2061 2b. Gajasiha (tusked lions) 45 30
2062 12b. Kesara Singha (hoofed lions) 1·70 1·10
2063 12b. Singhas 1·70 1·10
MS2064 140×99 mm. Nos. 2060/3 (sold at 40b.) 6·00 5·75

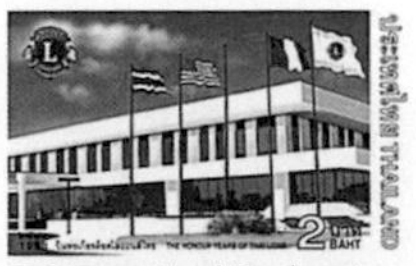
694 International Headquarters, Illinois

1998. Thai Presidency of International Association of Lions Clubs.
2065 **694** 2b. multicoloured 45 30

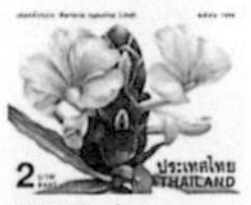

695 "Barleria lupulina"

1998. New Year. Flowers. Multcoloured.
2066 2b. Type **695** 45 30
2067 2b. Glory lily ("Gloriosa superba") 45 30
2068 2b. "Asclepias curassavica" 45 30
2069 2b. "Sesamum indicum" 45 30
MS2070 99×85 mm. Nos. 2066/9 (sold at 15b.) 3·75 3·50

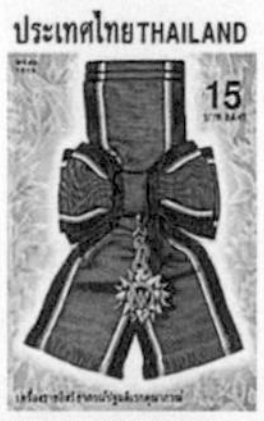

696 Knight Grand Cross (First Class)

1998. Most Admirable Order of the Direkgunabhorn. Multicoloured.
2071 15b. Type **696** 2·10 85
2072 15b. Close-up of badge 2·10 85

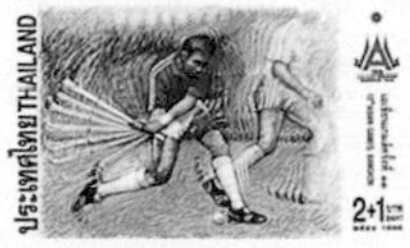

697 Hockey

1998. 13th Asian Games, Bangkok. Multicoloured.
2073 2b.+1b. Type **697** 60 30
2074 3b.+1b. Wrestling 75 45
2075 4b.+1b. Rowing 90 55
2076 7b.+1b. Show jumping 1·50 85

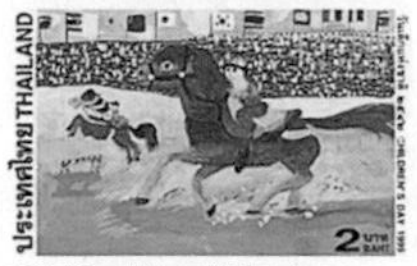

698 "Gymkhana" (Khontorn Taechoran)

1999. Children's Day. Children's Paintings. Multicoloured.
2081 2b. Type **698** 45 30
2082 2b. "Swimming" (Sunhapong Phitukburapa) 45 30
2083 2b. "Volleyball" (Vipharat Sae Lim) 45 30
2084 2b. "Sepak Takraw" (three-aside net game) (Phanot Ratanawongkae) 45 30

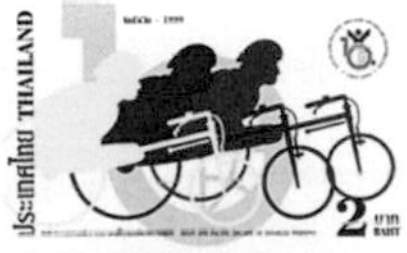

699 Wheel-chair Athletes

1999. Asian and Pacific Decade of Disabled Persons.
2085 **699** 2b. multicoloured 75 45

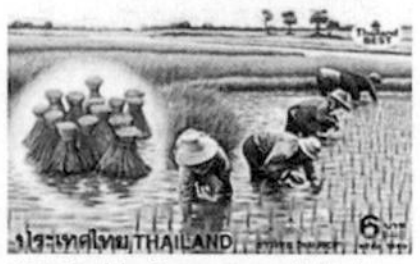

700 Paddy Sprouts and Workers planting Rice

1999. Rice Cultivation. Multicoloured.
2086 6b. Type **700** 1·10 70
2087 6b. Workers harvesting rice and ear of paddy 1·10 70
2088 12b. Paddy-threshing machine 1·80 1·40
2089 12b. Golden paddy field and bowl of cooked rice 1·80 1·40
MS2090 144×110 mm. Nos. 2086/90 (sold at 45b.) 6·00 5·75

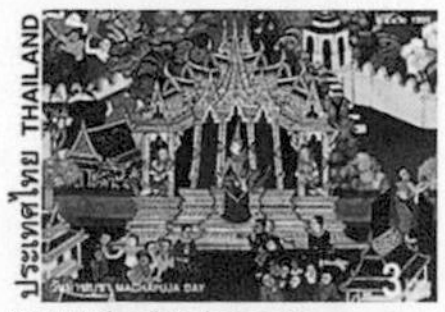

701 Birth of Mahajanaka

1999. Maghapuja Day. Showing murals from Wat Tha Sutthawat illustrating the story of Mahajanaka.. Multicoloured.
2091 3b. Type **701** 45 30
2092 6b. Mani Mekkhala carrying Mahajanaka to Mithila City 1·10 70
2093 9b. Two mango trees 1·40 1·00
2094 15b. Mahajanaka founding educational institute 2·30 1·70
MS2095 151×127 mm. Nos. 2091/4 (sold at 45b.) 6·75 6·50

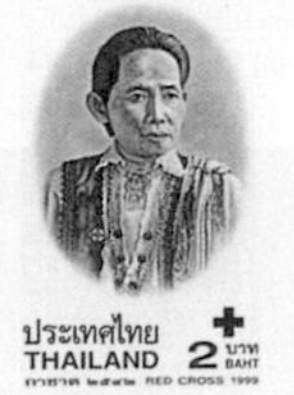

702 Queen Somdetch the Queen Grandmother

1999. Red Cross.
2096 **702** 2b. multicoloured 60 30

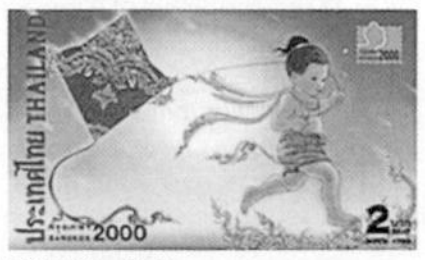

703 Kite Flying

1999. "BANGKOK 2000" World Youth Stamp Exhibition and 13th Asian International Stamp Exhibition, Bangkok. Children's Games (1st issue). Multicoloured.
2097 2b. Type **703** 60 30
2098 2b. Hoop rolling 60 30
2099 15b. Catching the last one in the line (children passing under arched arms) 2·10 1·70
2100 15b. Snatching a baby from Mother Snake 2·10 1·70
MS2101 145×110 mm. Nos. 2097/2100 (sold at 45b.) 6·75 6·50
See also Nos. 2119/**MS**2123 and 2195/**MS**2199.

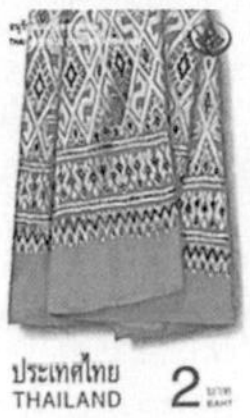

704 "Hooks and Squids" Motif

1999. Thai Heritage Conservation Day. Silk Mudmee Textiles. Multicoloured.
2102 2b. Type **704** 45 30
2103 4b. "Royal Umbrella" motif 75 45
2104 12b. "Naga upholding the Baisi" motif 1·80 1·40
2105 15b. "Naga upholding a flower pot" motif 2·40 1·80
MS2106 110×144 mm. Nos. 2102/5 (sold at 45b.) 6·75 6·50

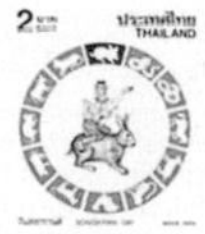

705 Woman riding Rabbit

1999. Songkran (New Year) Day. Year of the Rabbit.
2107 **705** 2b. multicoloured 45 30
MS2108 Two sheets, each 80×100 mm, each containing No. 2107. (a) Perf; (b) Imperf (sold at 16b.) 4·50 4·25

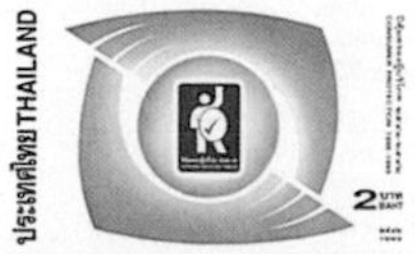

706 Hands encircling Emblem

1999. Consumer Protection Years, 1998–1999.
2109 **706** 2b. multicoloured 60 30

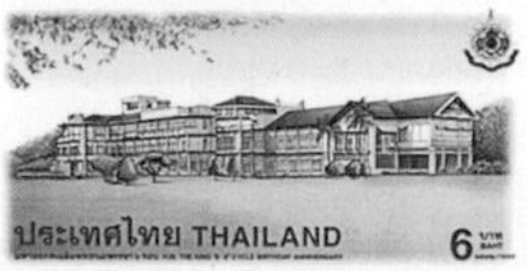

707 Chitralada Villa, Dusit Palace, Bangkok

1999. Sixth Cycle (72nd Birthday) of King Bhumibol. Royal Palaces (1st issue). Multicoloured.
2110 6b. Type **707** 1·20 70
2111 6b. Phu Phing Ratchaniwet Palace, Chieng Mai Province (red and green roofs) 1·20 70
2112 6b. Phu Phan Ratchaniwet Palace, Sakon Nakhon province (with large green lawn) 1·20 70
2113 6b. Thaksin Ratchaniwet Palace, Narathiwat Province (two-storey building with drive and ornamental trees) 1·20 70
MS2114 185×125 mm. Nos. 2110/13 (sold at 40b.) 6·75 6·50
See also Nos. 2130/**MS**2139, 2146/**MS**2155 and 2161/**MS**2164.

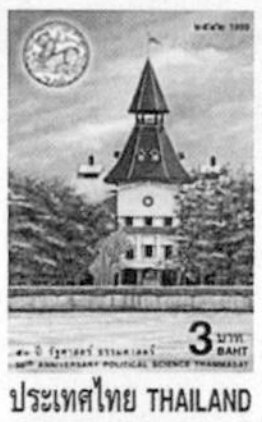

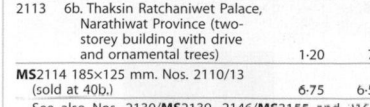

708 Administrative Building and Faculty Emblem

1999. 50th Anniv of Political Science Faculty, Thammasat University.
2115 **708** 3b. multicoloured 60 30

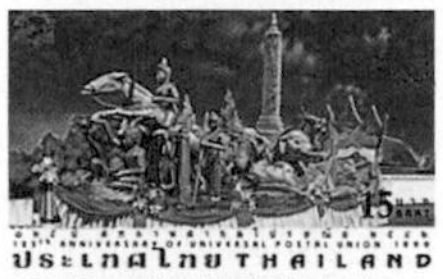

709 Float, Candle Festival, Ubon Ratchathani

1999. 125th Anniv of Universal Postal Union. Multicoloured.
2116 2b. Floating vessel, Light Festival 60 30
2117 15b. Type **709** 2·00 1·60

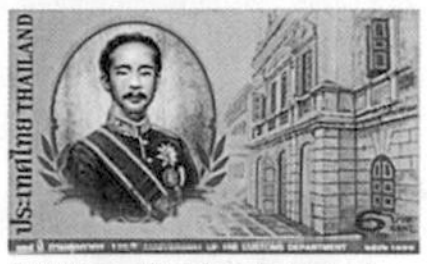

710 King Chulalongkorn and Customs Building

1999. 125th Anniv of the Customs Department
2118 **710** 6b. multicoloured 1·10 70

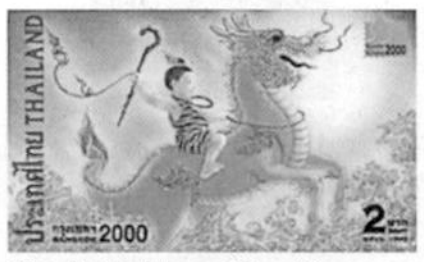

711 Sut Sakhon riding Dragon

1999. "BANGKOK 2000" World Youth Stamp Exhibition and 13th Asian International Stamp Exhibition, Bangkok (2nd issue). Folk Tales. Multicoloured.
2119 2b. Type **711** (Tale of Phra Aphai Mani) 60 30
2120 2b. Rishi transforming tiger cub and cow calf into children (Tale of Honwichai-Khawi) 60 30
2121 15b. Phra Sang climbing out of conch shell (Tale of Sang Thong) 2·00 1·60
2122 15b. Khun Chang, Khun Phaen and Nang Phim playing (Tale of Khun Chang and Khun Phaen) 2·00 1·60
MS2123 144×110 mm. Nos. 2119/22 (sold at 45b.) 7·50 7·00

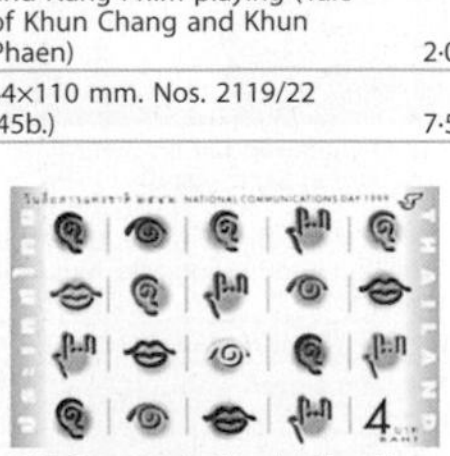

712 Communication by Eye, Ear, Mouth and Hand

1999. National Communications Day.
2124 **712** 4b. multicoloured 60 45

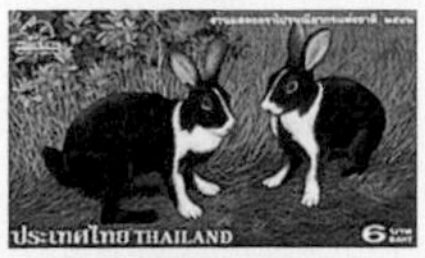

713 Rabbits

1999. "THAIPEX'99" 13th Thailand Stamp Exhibition, Bangkok. Domestic Rabbits. Multicoloured.
2125 6b. Type **713** 1·10 70
2126 6b. One golden and one brown rabbit 1·10 70
2127 12b. One grey and one grey and white rabbit 1·80 1·30
2128 12b. Two white rabbits 1·80 1·30

MS2129	144×110 mm. Nos. 2125/8 (sold at 50b.)	7·00	6·50

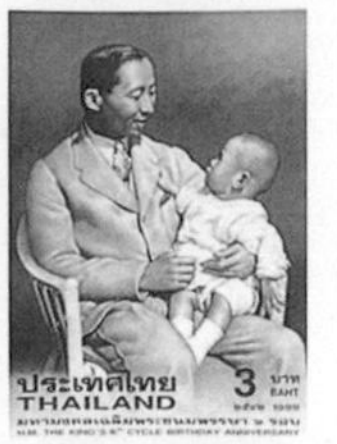
714 Prince Mahidol with Bhumibol as Baby

1999. Sixth Cycle (72nd Birthday) of King Bhumibol (2nd issue). Portraits of the King. Multicoloured.

2130	3b. Type **714**	60	30
2131	3b. Princess Mother and her children	60	30
2132	3b. With his brother King Ananda Mahidol	60	30
2133	6b. Bhumibol and King Ananda Mahidol in military uniform	1·10	55
2134	6b. On wedding day	1·10	55
2135	6b. Coronation ceremony	1·10	55
2136	12b. As a monk	2·30	1·30
2137	12b. King and Queen with their children	2·30	1·30
2138	12b. In royal robes	2·30	1·30
MS2139	134×214 mm. Nos. 2130/8 (sold at 90b.)	18·00	17·00

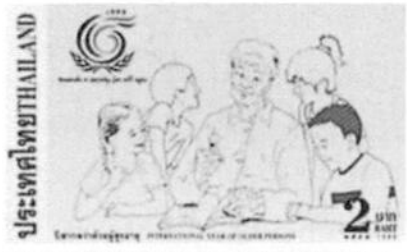
715 Older Person with Children

1999. International Year of the Elderly.

2140	**715**	2b. multicoloured	60	30

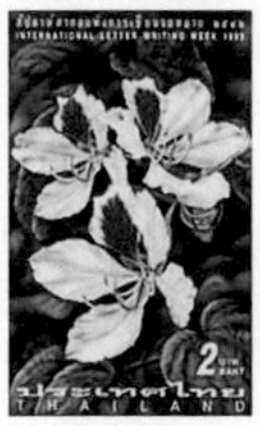
716 Orchid Tree

1999. International Correspondence Week. Flowers. Multicoloured.

2141	2b. Type **716**	60	30
2142	2b. "Bombax ceiba" (red flower)	60	30
2143	12b. "Radermachera ignea" (tubular yellow flowers)	1·80	1·30
2144	12b. "Bretschneidera sinensis" (pink bell flowers)	1·80	1·30
MS2145	110×145 mm. Nos. 2141/4 (sold at 35b.)	6·00	5·75

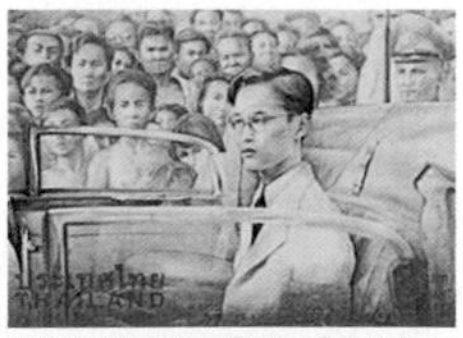
717 In Open-top Car on Returning to School in Switzerland

1999. Sixth Cycle (72nd Birthday) of King Bhumibol (3rd issue). The King and his Subjects. Multicoloured.

2146	3b. Type **717**	45	30
2147	3b. With Buddhist monks	45	30
2148	3b. King and Queen with students	45	30
2149	6b. With soldiers	90	55
2150	6b. With children prostrate at his feet	90	55
2151	6b. With boy on crutches	90	55
2152	12b. Visiting a hilltribe home	2·00	1·30
2153	12b. Drawing plan on ground	2·00	1·30
2154	12b. Talking to crowds	2·00	1·30
MS2155	215×135 mm. Nos. 2146/54 (sold at 90b.)	9·00	8·50

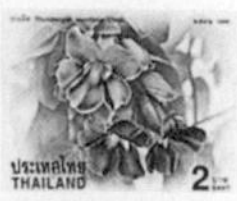
718 "Thunbergia laurifolia"

1999. New Year. Flowers. Multicoloured.

2156	2b. Type **718**	45	30
2157	2b. "Gmelina arborea"	45	30
2158	2b. "Prunus cerasoides"	45	30
2159	2b. "Fagraea fragans"	45	30
MS2160	99×85 mm. Nos. 2156/9 (sold at 15b.)	3·75	3·50

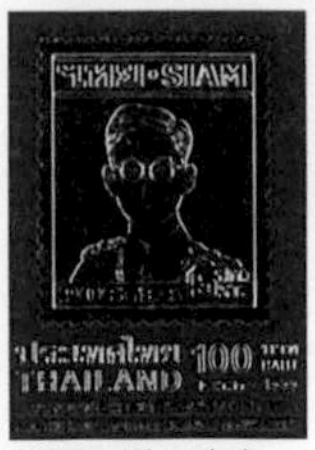
719 King Bhumibol

1999. Sixth Cycle (72nd Birthday) of King Bhumibol (4th issue).

2161	**719**	100b. gold and blue	12·00	11·50
2162	**719**	100b. silver and blue	12·00	11·50
2163	**719**	100b. bronze and blue	12·00	11·50
MS2164		175×140 mm. Nos. 2161/3 (sold at 350b.)	38·00	35·00

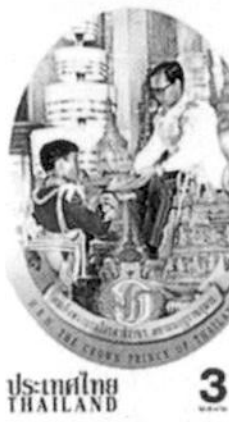
720 King Bhumibol and Prince Vajiralongkorn

1999. Investiture of Crown Prince Maha Vajiralongkorn.

2165	**720**	3b. multicoloured	1·40	45

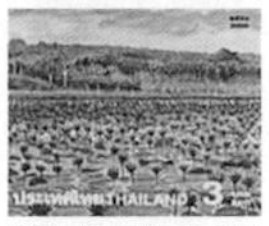
721 Lilies, Thale Noi

2000. Lake of Lilies, Phatthalung Province. Multicoloured.

2166	3b. Type **721**	75	45
2167	3b. Forest and lilies	75	45
2168	3b. Forest, buildings and lilies	75	45
2169	3b. Birds flying over lilies	75	45
2170	3b.15 lily flowers	75	45
2171	3b. Seven lily flowers	75	45
2172	3b. Six lily flowers	75	45
2173	3b. Eight lily flowers and three buds	75	45
2174	3b. Four lily flowers and two buds	75	45
2175	3b. Two lily flowers and eight lily pads	75	45
2176	3b. Two lily flowers	75	45
2177	3b. Three lily flowers	75	45

Nos. 2166/77 were issued together, *se-tenant*, forming a composite design of the lake.

The stamps are identified by the number of complete flowers shown.

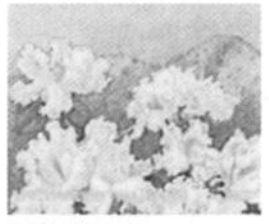
722 Flowers

2000. Kulap Khao Meadow, Chiang Mai Province. Multicoloured.

2178	3b. Type **722**	75	45
2179	3b. Flowers and two peaks	75	45
2180	3b. Flowers, four buds and mountains	75	45
2181	3b. Flowers, three buds and mountains	75	45
2182	3b. Three open flowers	75	45
2183	3b. Open flowers and seven buds	75	45
2184	3b. Open flowers and six buds	75	45
2185	3b. Open flowers and one bud	75	45
2186	3b. One open flower and five buds	75	45
2187	3b. Open flowers and four buds	75	45
2188	3b. Four open flowers	75	45
2189	3b. Four partially open flowers	75	45

Nos. 2178/89 were issued together, *se-tenant*, forming a composite design of the Kulap Khao meadow.

The stamps are identified by the number of complete flowers and buds shown.

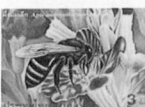

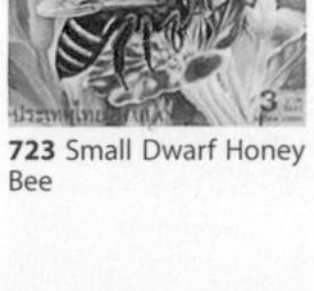
723 Small Dwarf Honey Bee

2000. Bees. Multicoloured.

2190	3b. Type **723**	75	45
2191	3b. Dwarf bee (*Apis florea*)	75	45
2192	3b. Asian honey bee (*Apis cerana*)	75	45
2193	3b. Giant bee (*Apis dorsata*)	75	45
MS2194	Four sheets, each 83×54 mm. (a) As Type **723**; (b) As No. 2191; (c) As No. 2192; (d) As No. 2193	6·00	5·75

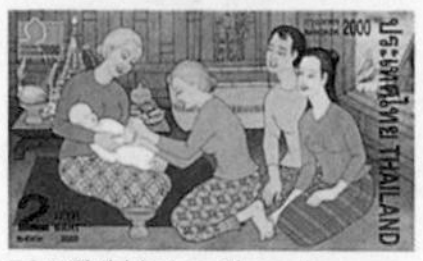
724 Child being Blessed

2000. "BANGKOK 2000" International Youth Stamp Exhibition and 13th Asian International Stamp Exhibition, Bangkok (3rd issue). Ceremonies. Multicoloured.

2195	2b. Type **724**	45	30
2196	2b. Woman cutting child's hair (Tonsure ceremony)	45	30
2197	15b. Pupils paying respects to teacher	2·30	1·80
2198	15b. Boy being carried aloft during ordination of novice	2·30	1·80
MS2199	110×144 mm. Nos. 2195/8 (sold at 45b.)	7·50	7·00

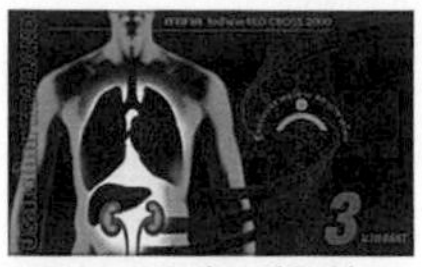
725 Human Body and Emblem

2000. Thai Red Cross Organ Donation Campaign.

2200	**725**	3b. multicoloured	60	45

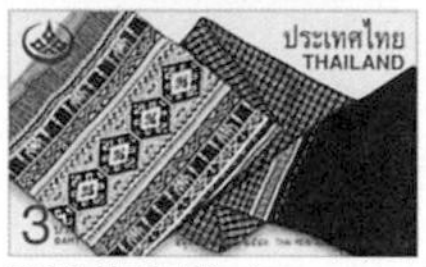
726 Sukhothai Province

2000. Thai Heritage Conservation. Chok Cloth Designs. Multicoloured.

2201	3b. Type **726**	75	45
2202	6b. Chiang Mai Province	1·20	85
2203	8b. Uthai Thani Province	2·00	1·30
2204	12b. Ratchaburi Province	2·30	1·70
MS2205	110×145 mm. Nos. 2201/4 (sold at 40b.)	7·50	7·00

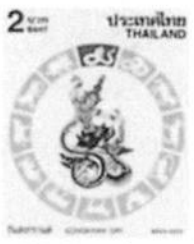
727 Angel riding Snake

2000. Songkran (New Year) Day. Year of the Snake.

2206	**727**	2b. multicoloured	45	30
MS2207		Two sheets, each 80×100 mm, each containing No. 2206. (a) Perf; (b) Imperf (pair sold at 16b.)	4·50	4·25

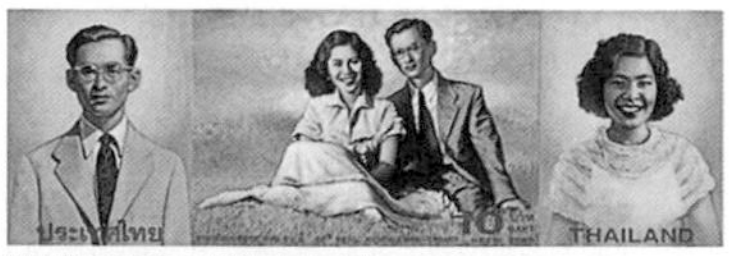
728 Engagement Photograph

2000. Golden Wedding Anniv of King Bhumibol and Queen Sirikit. Multicoloured.

2208	10b. Type **728**	1·80	1·30
2209	10b. Signing marriage register, 1950	1·80	1·30
2210	10b. Sitting on thrones during Coronation ceremony	1·80	1·30
2211	10b. With family	1·80	1·30
2212	10b. King Bhumibol and Queen Sirikit, 2000	1·80	1·30

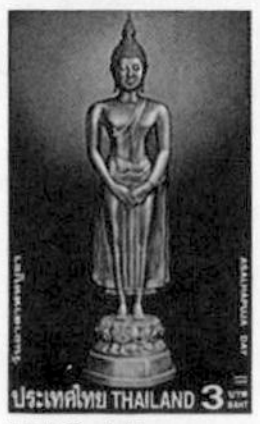
729 Buddha

2000. Asalhapuja Day.

2213	**729**	3b. multicoloured	90	45

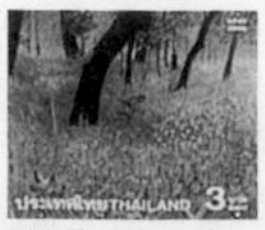
730 Flowers and Trees, Krachieo

2000. Krachieo Meadow, Pa Hin Ngam, Chaiyaphum Province. Multicoloured.

2214	3b. Type **730**	75	45
2215	3b. Flowers and sparse trees in distance	75	45
2216	3b. Flowers, two close trees and dense trees in distance	75	45
2217	3b. Flowers, four close trees and dense trees in distance	75	45
2218	3b. Six complete flowers	75	45
2219	3b. Eleven complete flowers	75	45
2220	3b. Seven complete flowers and half a flower at right-hand side	75	45
2221	3b. Six complete flowers and two incomplete flowers at bottom	75	45
2222	3b. Two flowers	75	45
2223	3b. Three flowers close together	75	45
2224	3b. One open and two partially open flowers	75	45
2225	3b. Two complete and three incomplete flowers	75	45

Nos. 2214/25 were issued together, *se-tenant*, forming a composite design of the meadow.

The stamps are identified by the number of trees or flowers shown.

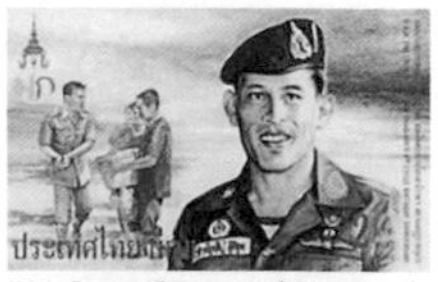
731 Crown Prince and Rice Seeds Sowing Ceremony

2000. Fourth Cycle (48th Birthday) of Crown Prince Maha Vajiralongkorn.

2226	**731**	2b. multicoloured	60	30
MS2227		125×90 mm. No. 2226 (sold at 8b.)	2·30	2·10

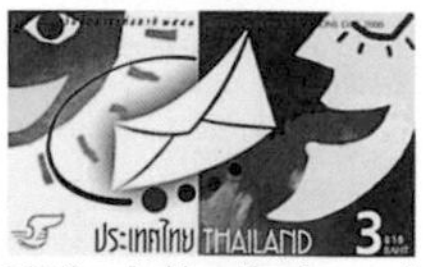
732 Sun, Emblem, Envelope and Moon

2000. National Communications Day.

2228	**732**	3b. multicoloured	60	30

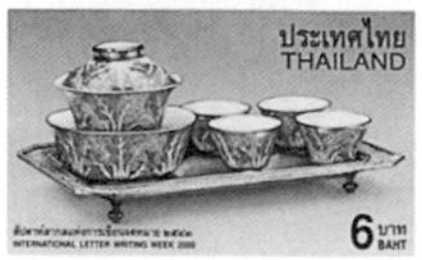
733 Cabbage Design Tea Set

2000. International Correspondence Week. Rattanakosin Period Tea Sets. Multicoloured.

2229	6b. Type **733**	90	70
2230	6b. Duck and animals in lotus pond design	90	70
2231	12b. Lotus bud design	1·80	1·40
2232	12b. Butterflies and bees design	1·80	1·40
MS2233	144×110 mm. Nos. 2229/32 (sold at 45b.)	6·75	6·50

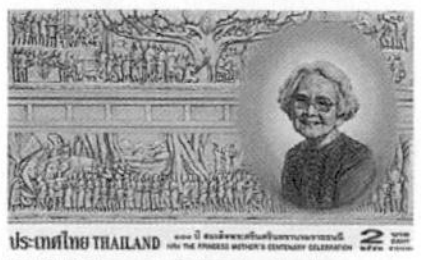
734 Princess Srinagarindra

2000. Birth Centenary of Princess Srinagarindra the Princess Mother.

2234	**734**	2b. multicoloured	60	30
MS2235		125×90 mm. **734** 2b. multicoloured	2·30	2·10

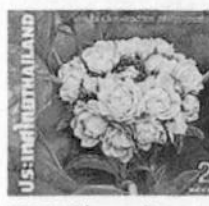
735 Glory Bower (*Clerodendrum philippinum*)

2000. New Year. Flowers. Multicoloured.

2236	2b. Type **735**	45	30
2237	2b. *Capparis micracantha*	45	30
2238	2b. Leopard lily (*Belamcanda chinensis*)	45	30

2239 2b. *Memecylon caeruleum* 45 30

MS2240 85×100 mm. Nos. 2236/9 (sold at 15b.) 3·00 2·75

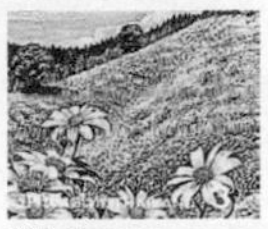

736 Flowers

2000. Bua Tong Meadow, Mae Hong Son Province. Multicoloured.

2241 3b. Type **736** 75 45
2242 3b. Meadow and trees (top left) 75 45
2243 3b. Meadow 75 45
2244 3b. Meadow and trees (top right) 75 45
2245 3b. Four flowers 75 45
2246 3b. Eleven flowers 75 45
2247 3b. Fifteen flowers 75 45
2248 3b. Twelve flowers 75 45
2249 3b. Three large flowers, two smaller flowers and one dead flower 75 45
2250 3b. Three large flowers 75 45
2251 3b. One large flower 75 45
2252 3b. Five flowers and one dead flower 75 45

Nos. 2241/52 were issued together, *se-tenant*, forming a composite design.

The stamps are identified by the number of complete flowers shown.

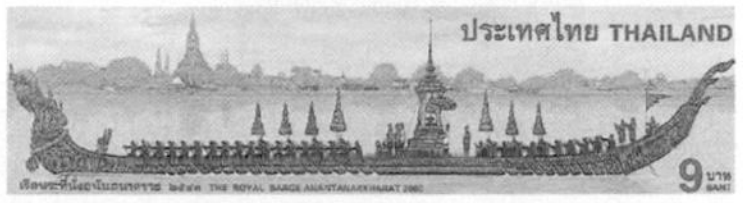

737 Anantanakkharat (Royal Barge, 1914) (image scaled to 41% of original size)

2000

2253 **737** 9b. multicoloured 1·40 1·00

MS2254 157×95 mm. No. 2253 (sold at 15b.) 3·00 2·75

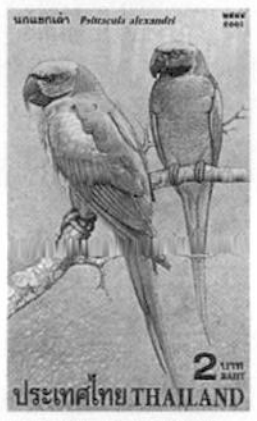

738 Moustached Parakeet (*Psittacula alexandri*)

2001. Parrots. Multicoloured.

2255 2b. Type **738** 60 30
2256 5b. Alexandrine parakeet (*Psittacula eupatria*) 90 55
2257 8b. *Psittacula cyanurus* 1·40 85
2258 10b. Blossom-headed parakeet (*Psittacula roseata*) 1·80 1·10

MS2259 110×144 mm. Nos. 2255/8 (sold at 35b.) 6·00 5·75

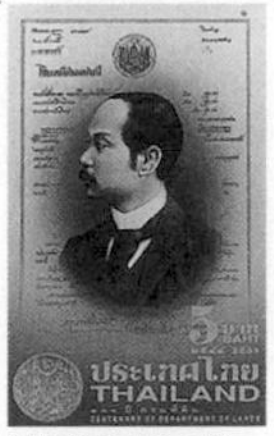

739 King Rama V and First Title Deed

2001. Centenary of Department of Lands.

2260 **739** 5b. multicoloured 90 55

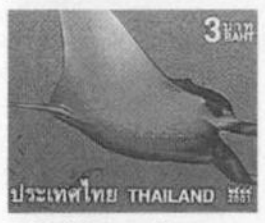

740 Manta Ray

2001. Marine Life. Multicoloured.

2261 3b. Type **740** 75 45
2262 3b. Fishes and jellyfish 75 45
2263 3b. Turtle 75 45
2264 3b. Coral and lionfish 75 45
2265 3b. Black and white fish and coral 75 45
2266 3b. Head of eel and yellow coral 75 45
2267 6b. Fishes and coral(28×47 mm) 1·10 70
2268 6b. Pufferfish and other fishes (28×47 mm) 1·10 70
2269 6b. Yellow and blue fish and coral (45×23 mm) 1·10 70

Nos. 2261/9 were issued together, *se-tenant*, forming a composite design.

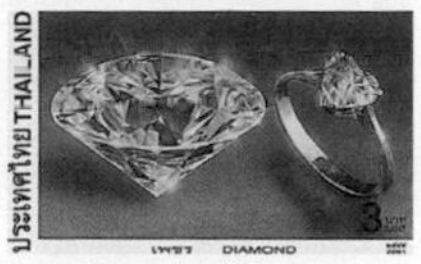

741 Diamond and Ring

2001. Precious Stones. Multicoloured.

2270 3b. Type **741** 60 30
2271 4b. Green sapphire and necklace 75 45
2272 6b. Pearl and necklace 1·10 70
2273 12b. Blue sapphire and necklace 1·80 1·30

MS2274 110×144 mm. Nos. 2270/3 (sold at 35b.) 6·00 5·75

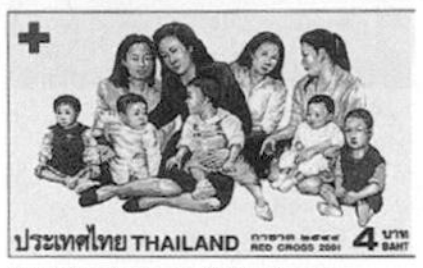

742 Women and Orphans

2001. Red Cross. 20th Anniv of Thai Red Cross Children's Homes.

2275 **742** 4b. multicoloured 75 45

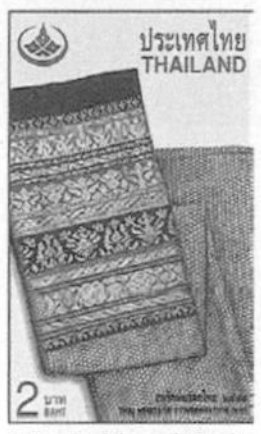

743 Gold and Red Brocade

2001. Thai Heritage Conservation Day. Showing different brocade designs. Multicoloured.

2276 2b. Type **743** 45 30
2277 3b. Green and gold design 75 45
2278 10b. Orange and gold design 1·50 1·10
2279 10b. Pink and gold design 1·50 1·10

MS2280 110×145 mm. Nos. 2276/9 (sold at 35b.) 6·00 5·75

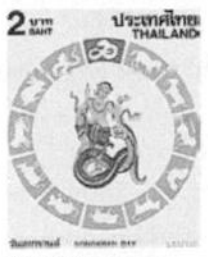

744 Woman riding Snake

2001. Songkran (New Year) Day. Year of the Snake.

2281 **744** 2b. multicoloured 45 30

MS2282 Two sheets, each 80×100 mm, each containing No. 2281. (a) Perf; (b) Imperf (pair sold at 16b.) 4·50 4·25

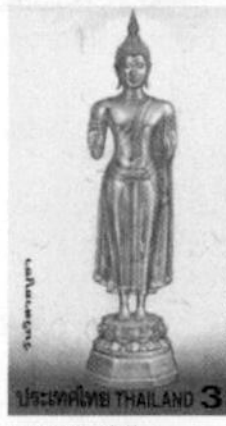

745 Buddha

2001. Visakhapuja Day.

2283 **745** 3b. multicoloured 90 45

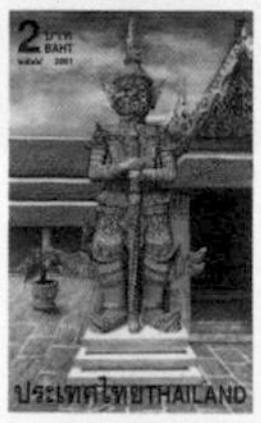

746 Maiyarap, Emerald Buddha Temple

2001. Demon Statues. Multicoloured.

2284 2b. Type **746** 45 30
2285 5b. Wirunchambang, Emerald Buddha Temple 75 55
2286 10b. Thotsakan, Temple of Dawn 1·50 1·10
2287 12b. Sahatsadecha, Temple of Dawn 2·00 1·40

MS2288 145×110 mm. Nos. 2284/7 (sold at 33b.) 6·00 5·75

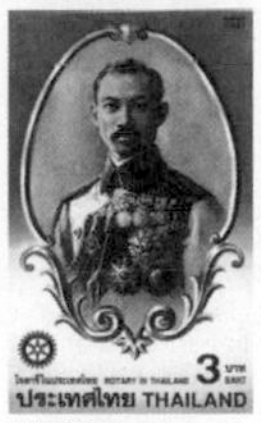

747 Prince Purachatra Jayakara (first governor)

2001. 66th Anniv of Rotary International in Thailand.

2289 **747** 3b. multicoloured 90 45

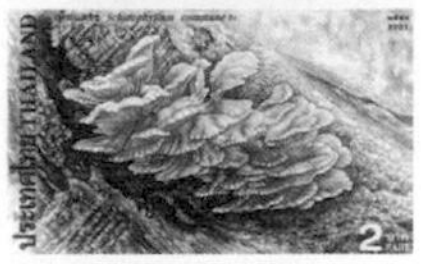

748 Split Gill (*Schizophyllum commune*)

2001. Fungi. Multicoloured.

2290 2b. Type **748** 60 30
2291 3b. *Lentinus giganteus* 75 45
2292 5b. *Pleurotus citrinopileatus* 90 55
2293 10b. *Pleurotus flabellatus* 1·70 1·10

MS2294 110×145 mm. Nos. 2290/3 (sold at 26b.) 6·00 5·75

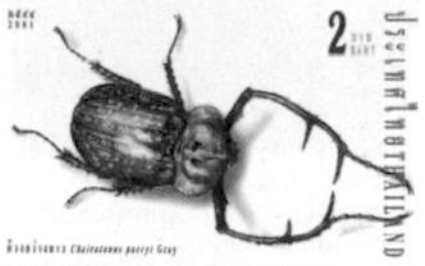

749 *Cheirotonus parryi*

2001. Insects. Multicoloured.

2295 2b. Type **749** 60 30
2296 5b. *Mouhotia batsei* 90 55
2297 6b. *Cladognathus giraffa* 1·10 70
2298 12b. Violin beetle (*Mormolyce phyllodes*) 1·80 1·30

MS2299 145×110 mm. Nos. 2295/8 (sold at 34b.) 7·50 7·00

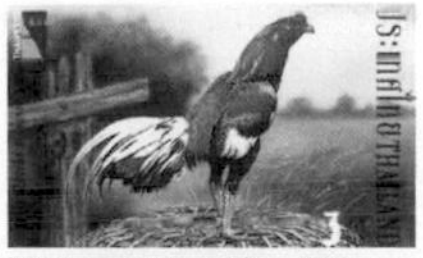

750 Lueng Hang Khoa (Aim-orn Saichumdee)

2001. THAIPEX '01, Thailand Philatelic Exhibition 2001. Domestic Fowl. Winning entries in the 1999 International Letter Writing Week painting competition. Multicoloured.

2300 3b. Type **750** 60 30
2301 4b. Lueng Hang Khoa (Rong Saichumdee) 75 45
2302 6b. Samae Dam (Rong Saichumdee) 1·10 70
2303 12b. Pradue Hang Dam (Chanthorn Niyomthum) 2·00 1·40

MS2304 145×110 mm. Nos. 2300/3. Perf or imperf (sold at 33b.) 6·00 5·75

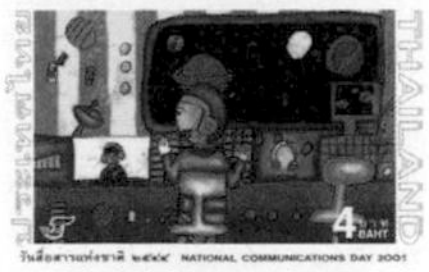

751 "Thai Children in the I.T. Era" (Sriarpha Kamlanglua)

2001. National Communications Day, 2000. Winning Entry in Children's International Letter Writing Week Painting Competition.

2305 **751** 4b. multicoloured 75 55

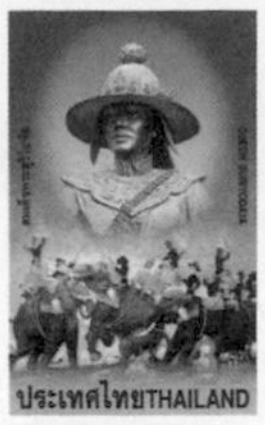

752 Queen Suriyodaya

2001. Queen Suriyodaya Commemoration.

2306 **752** 3b. multicoloured 90 55

MS2307 90×125 mm. No. 2306 (sold at 10b.) 3·75 3·50

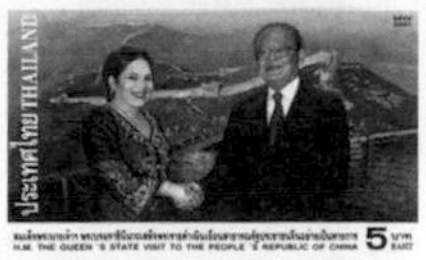

753 Queen meeting Pres. Jiang Ze Ming and Great Wall of China

2001. Visit by Queen Sirikit to People's Republic of China.

2308 **753** 5b. multicoloured 1·20 55

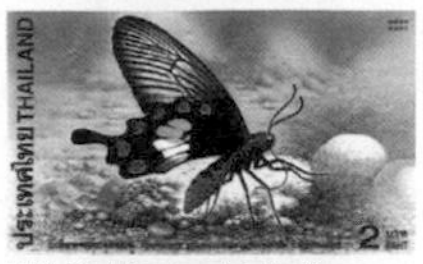

754 *Pachliopta aristolochiae goniopeltis*

2001. Butterflies. Multicoloured.

2309 2b. Type **754** 45 30
2310 4b. *Rhinopalpa polynice* 90 55
2311 10b. *Poritia erycinoides* 1·80 1·30
2312 12b. *Spindasis iohita* 2·30 1·40

MS2313 145×110 mm. Nos. 2309/2312 (sold at 40b.) 7·50 7·00

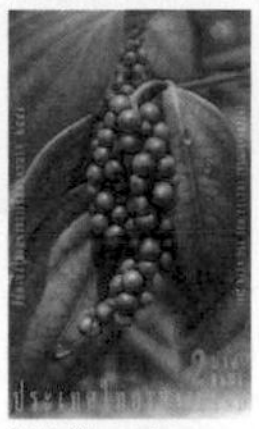

755 *Piper nigrum*

2001. International Correspondence Week. Plants. Multicoloured.

2314 2b. Type **755** 45 30
2315 3b. *Solanum trilobatum* 75 45
2316 5b. *Boesenbergia rotunda* 90 55
2317 10b. *Ocimum tenuiflorum* 1·70 1·10

MS2318 110×44 mm. Nos. 2314/17 (sold at 25b.) 5·25 5·00

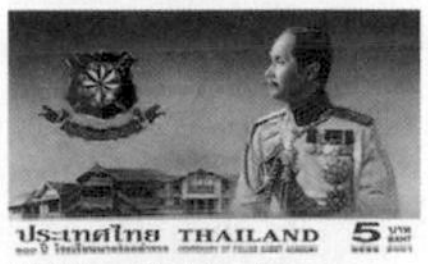

756 King Chulalongkorn, Academy Buildings and Logo

2001. Centenary of Police Cadet Academy.

2319 **756** 5b. multicoloured 1·10 70

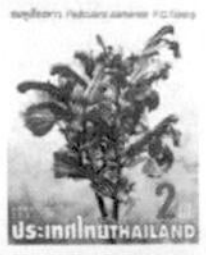

757 *Pedicularis siamensis*

2001. New Year. Flowers. Multicoloured.

2320 2b. Type **757** 45 30
2321 2b. *Schoutenia glomerata* 45 30
2322 2b. *Gentiana crassa* 45 30
2323 2b. *Colquhounia coccinea* 45 30

MS2324 85×100 mm. Nos. 2320/23 (sold at 11b.) 3·50 3·25

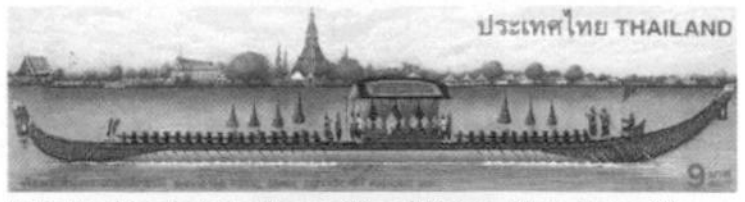

758 Anekkachat Puchong (Royal Barge, King Rama V) (image scaled to 41% of original size)

2001

2325 **758** 9b. multicoloured 1·80 1·30

MS2326 157×95 mm. No. 2325 (sold at 17b.) 5·25 4·75

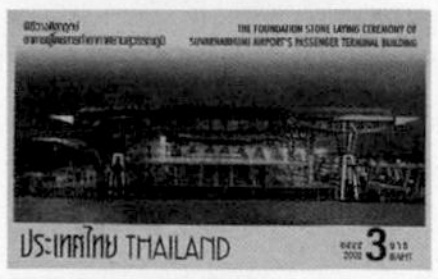

759 Terminal Building

2002. Foundation Stone Laying Ceremony, Suvarnabhumi Airport Passenger Terminal.

2327 **759** 3b. multicoloured 70 50

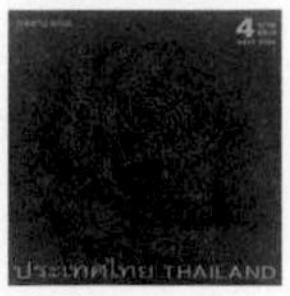

760 Rose

2002

2328 **760** 4b. multicoloured 6·25 2·20

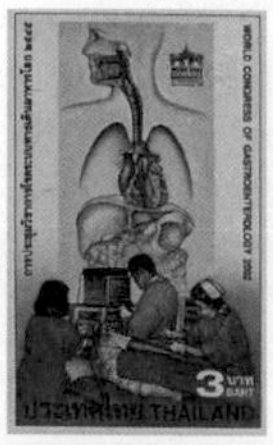

761 Operating Theatre

2002. World Gastroenterology Congress.

2329 **761** 3b. multicoloured 70 50

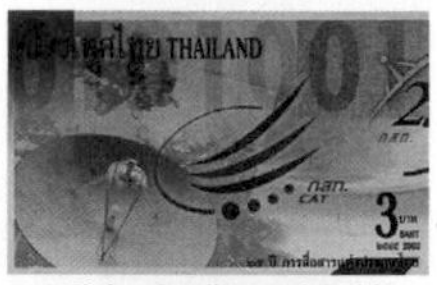

762 Globe, Satellite and Emblem

2002. 25th Anniv of Communications Authority. Multicoloured.

2330 3r. Type **762** 70 50

2331 3r. Envelope and post box 70 50

MS2332 110×86 mm. Nos. 2330/1 2·75 2·40

Nos. 2330/1 were issued together, *se-tenant*, forming a composite design.

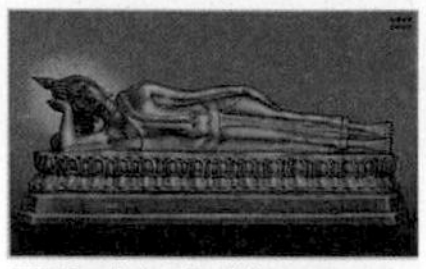

763 Reclining Buddha

2002. Maghapuja Day.

2333 **763** 3b. multicoloured 2·75 1·60

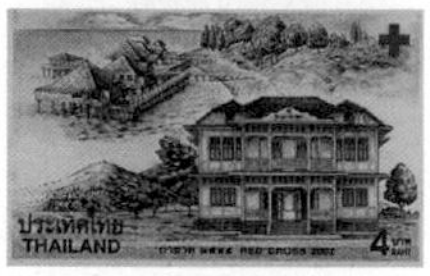

764 Queen Sawang Wadhana Memorial Hospital

2002. Red Cross.

2334 **764** 4b. multicoloured 90 65

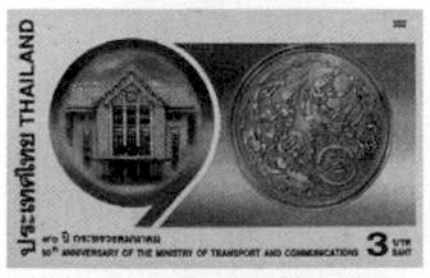

765 Headquarters and Emblem

2002. 90th Anniv of Ministry of Transport and Communications.

2335 **765** 3b. multicoloured 80 50

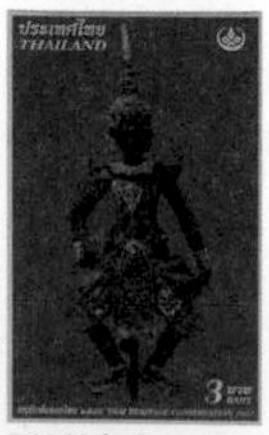

766 Male Puppet

2002. Heritage Conservation Day. Puppets. Multicoloured.

2336 3b. Type **766** 70 50

2337 3b. Female puppet 70 50

2338 4b. Demon 90 65

2339 15b. Monkey 2·50 2·10

MS2340 111×145 mm. Nos. 2336/9 (sold at 30b.) 7·00 6·25

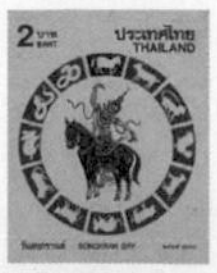

767 Female Angel riding Horse

2002. Songkran (New Year) Day. Year of the Horse. Multicoloured.

2341 2b. Type **767** 55 30

MS2342 Two sheets. (a) 80×100 mm. No. 2341 Perf or imperf (sold at 8b.) (b) 137×161 mm. 2b. No. 1933; 2b. No. 2025; 2b. No. 2107; 2b. No. 2206; 2b. No. 2281; 2b. No. 2341. Perf or imperf (sold at 14b.) 7·00 6·25

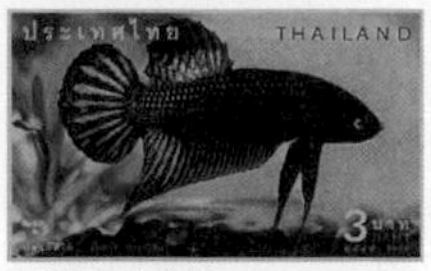

768 *Betta imbellis*

2002. Fighting Fish. Multicoloured.

2343 3b. Type **768** 90 50

2344 3b. *Betta splendens* (blue) 90 50

2345 4b. *Betta splendens* (red) 1·10 65

2346 15b. *Betta splendens* (bi-colour) 2·75 2·10

MS2347 144×110 mm. Nos. 2343/6 (sold at 30b.) 7·00 6·25

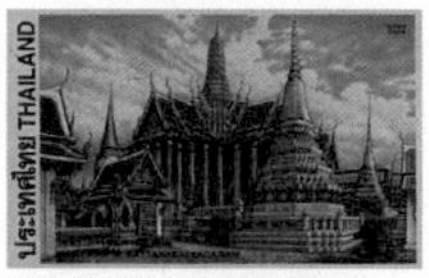

769 Wat Phra Si Rattanasatsadaram (Temple of the Emerald Buddha)

2002. Tourism. Multicoloured.

2348 3b. Type **769** 90 50

2349 3b. Wat Phra Chetuphon Wimon Mangkhalaram (Wat Pho) 90 50

2350 4b. Wat Arun Ratchawararam (The Temple of Dawn) 1·10 65

2351 12b. Wat Bechamabophit Dusit Wanaram (The Marble Temple) 2·10 1·60

MS2352 144×110 mm. Nos. 2348/51 (sold at 27b.) 5·25 4·75

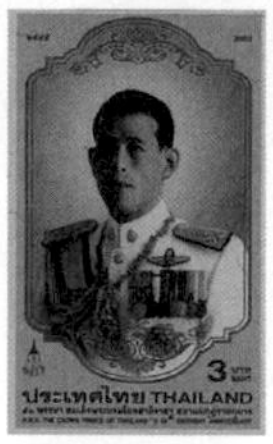

770 Crown Prince Maha Vajiralongkorn

2002. 50th Birthday of Crown Prince Maha Vajiralongkorn.

2353 **770** 3b. multicoloured 90 50

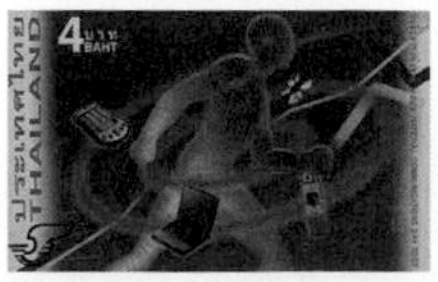

771 Figure and Communication Symbols

2002. National Communications Day.

2354 **771** 4b. multicoloured 1·10 65

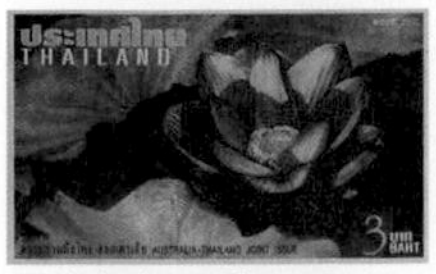

772 *Nelumba nucifera*

2002. Water Lilies. Multicoloured.

2355 3b. Type **772** 90 50

2356 3b. *Nymphaea immutablis* 90 50

MS2357 110×65 mm. Nos. 2355/6 (sold at 9b.) 2·75 2·40

Stamps of the same design were issued by Australia.

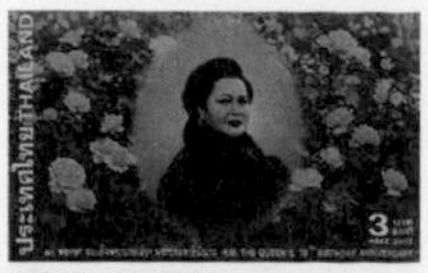

773 Queen Sirikit

2002. 70th Birthday of Queen Sirikit. Multicoloured.

2358 3b. Type **773** 70 50

2359 3b. "Queen Sirikit" rose 70 50

2360 4b. "Queen Sirikit" orchid 90 65

2361 15b. Dona "Queen Sirikit" (shrub) 2·50 1·90

MS2362 144×109 mm. Nos. 2358/61 (sold at 31b.) 6·00 5·50

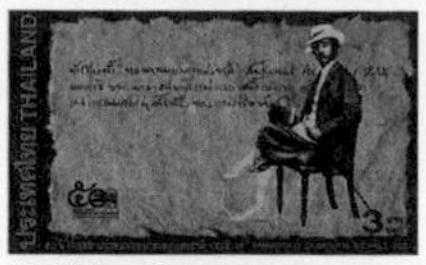

774 Prince Damrong Rajanubhab and Script

2002. 50th Anniv of National Archives.

2363 **774** 3b. multicoloured 70 50

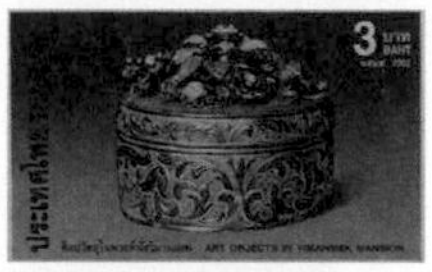

775 Betel Nut Box

2002. Royal Artefacts from Vimanmek Mansion. Multicoloured.

2364 3b. Type **775** 90 50

2365 3b. Pedestal tray 90 50

2366 4b. Betel nut bowl 1·10 50

2367 12b. Oblong betel nut box 2·10 1·60

MS2368 110×145 mm. Nos. 2364/7 (sold at 26b.) 5·25 4·75

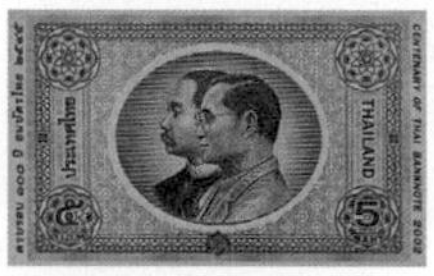

776 Portrait of Kings Rama V and Rama IX on Ancient Banknote

2002. Centenary of First Thai Banknote.

2369 **776** 5b. multicoloured 1·20 80

MS2370 162×120 mm. No. 2369 (sold at 11b.) 5·25 4·75

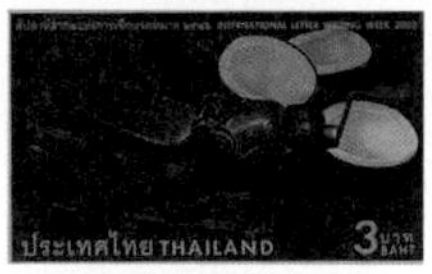

777 Animal-shaped Coconut Grater

2002. International Letter Writing Week. Thai Kitchenware. Multicoloured.

2371 3b. Type **777** 70 40

2372 3b. Bamboo strainer 70 40

2373 4b. Coconut shell ladles 1·10 50

2374 15b. Earthenware cooking stove 3·00 1·90

MS2375 144×110 mm. Nos. 2371/4 (sold at 31b.) 7·00 6·25

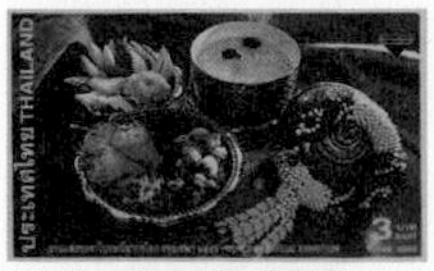

778 Khaochae (rice dish) (Central Region)

2002. Bangkok 2003 International Stamp Exhibition. Thai Food. Showing regional foods. Multicoloured.

2376 3b. Type **778** 70 40

2377 3b. Sato Phat Kung (prawn dish) and Kaenglueang (soup) (southern region) 70 40

2378 4b. Somtam (salad), Kaiyang (chicken dish) and Khaoniao Nueng (rice) (north-eastern region) 1·10 50

2379 15b. Khaepmu (pork), Namphrik Ong (chilli) and Sai-ua (sausage) (northern region) 3·00 1·90

MS2380 110×144 mm. Nos. 2376/9 (sold at 30b.) 7·00 6·25

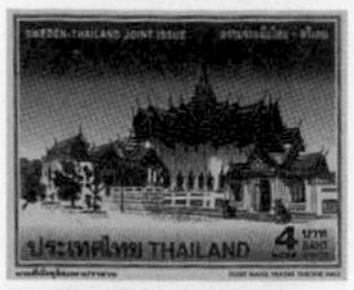

779 Dusit Maha Prasat Throne Hall

2002. Palaces. Joint Issue with Sweden. Multicoloured.

2381 4b. Type **779** 90 65

2382 4b. The Royal Palace, Stockholm 90 65

Stamps of the same design were issued by Sweden.

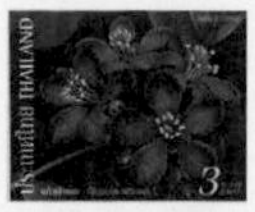

780 *Guaiacum officinale*

2002. New year. Flowers. Multicoloured.

2383 3b. Type **780** 70 40

2384 3b. *Nyctanthes arbor-tristis* 70 40

2385 3b. *Barleria cristata* 70 40

2386 3b. *Thevetia peruviana* 70 40

MS2387 99×85 mm Nos. 2383/6 (sold at 16b.) 4·50 4·00

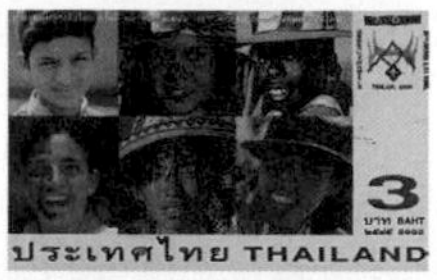

781 Young People

2002. 20th (2003) World Scout Jamboree. Multicoloured.

2388 3b. Type **781** 90 40

2389 12b. Beach (Jamboree camp site), Sattahip district 2·10 1·60

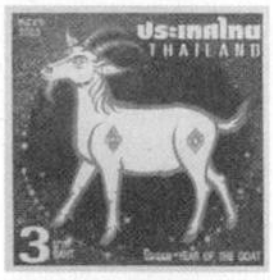

782 Goat

2003. Chinese New Year. "Year of the Goat".

2390 **782** 3b. multicoloured 90 30

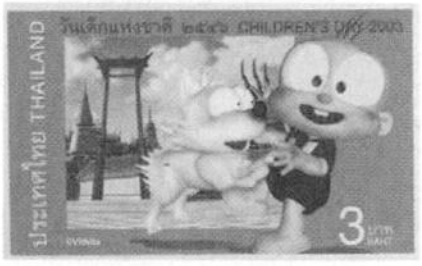

783 Pangpond and Dog

2003. National Children's Day. Cartoon characters. Multicoloured.

2391 3b. Type **783** 70 40

2392 3b. Pangpond and Hanuman 70 40

2393 3b. Pangpond and Namo 70 40

2394 3b. Pangpond and teacher 70 40

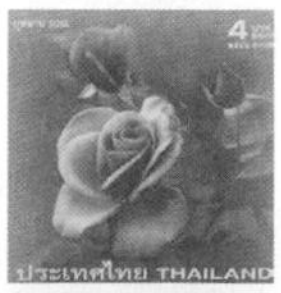

784 "Blue Nile" Rose

2003

2395 **784** 4b. multicoloured 1·80 80

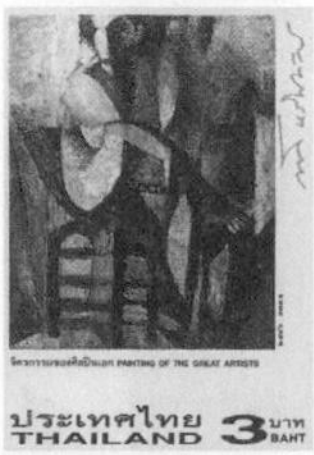

785 "Blue Green" (Fau Haribhitak)

2003. Art. Paintings. Multicoloured.

2396 3b. Type **785** 55 40

2397 3b. "Chira Chongkon" (Chamras Kietkong) 55 40

2398 3b. "Moonlight" (Prasong Padmanuja) 55 40

2399 15b. "Lotus Flowers" (Thawee Nandakwang) 2·75 1·90

786 Doi Inthanon, Chiang Mai

2003. Bangkok 2003 (2nd issue). Landscapes. Multicoloured.
2400	3b. Type **786**	55	40
2401	3b. Bridge over River Kwai, Kanchanaburi	55	40
2402	3b. Phu Kradung, Loei	55	40
2403	15b. Maya bay, Krabi	2·75	1·90
MS2404 110×145 mm. Nos. 2400/3 (sold at 29b.)		7·00	6·25

2003. As T 641.
| 2405 | **641** | 1b. blue | 70 | 30 |

787 Red Cross Worker carrying Flag

2003. Red Cross.
| 2430 | **787** | 3b. multicoloured | 70 | 50 |

788 Princess Maha Chakri Sirindhorn

2003. Princess Maha Chakri Sirindhorn's 48th Birthday.
| 2431 | **788** | 3b. multicoloured | 70 | 50 |

789 Erawan Suey Nga

2003. Cultural Heritage. Kick Boxing. Designs showing boxing moves. Multicoloured.
2432	3b. Type **789**	70	50
2433	3b. Hak kor aiyara (knee raised)	70	50
2434	3b. Hak nguang aiyara (right leg raised)	70	50
2435	15b. Jarakae fad hang (kick to head)	2·75	1·90
MS2436 127×152 mm. Nos. 2432/6 (sold at 29b.)		7·00	6·25

790 Princess Galyani Vadhana

2003. Princess Galyani Vadhana's 80th Birthday.
| 2437 | **790** | 3b. multicoloured | 1·60 | 80 |

791 Kings Rama V and VI

792 King Rama VII (Prajadhipok)

2003. Centenary of Inspector General Department.
| 2438 | **791** | 3b. multicoloured | 90 | 50 |

2003. King Prajadhipok Day.
| 2439 | **792** | 3b. multicoloured | 90 | 50 |

793 White-eared Jungle Fowl

2003. Bantam Fowl. Multicoloured.
2440	3b. Type **793**	70	40
2441	3b. Sugarcane husk coloured	70	40
2442	3b. Black-tailed white	70	40
2443	15b. Dark grey	2·75	1·90
MS2444 125×90 mm. Nos. 2440/3 (sold at 29b.)		7·00	6·25

794 Buddha holding Bowl

2003. Asalhapuja Day.
| 2445 | **794** | 3b. multicoloured | 2·50 | 65 |

795 Circuit Boards, Envelope with Wings and Statue

2003. National Communications Day.
| 2446 | **795** | 3b. multicoloured | 55 | 40 |

796 Thai Post Company Emblem

2003. Inauguration of Thailand Post Company and CAT Telecom Public Company. Multicoloured
2447	3b. Type **796**	55	40
2448	3b. Communications Authority emblem (24×28 mm)	55	40
2449	3b. CAT Telecom emblem	55	40

797 King Rama V (Chulalongkorn)

2003. 150th Birth Anniv of King Chulalongkorn.
| 2450 | **797** | 100b. multicoloured | 13·00 | 9·50 |
| **MS**2451 114×161 mm. No. 2450×4 Perf or imperf | | 55·00 | 48·00 |

798 House and Family

2003. 50th Anniv of Government Housing Bank.
| 2452 | **798** | 3b. multicoloured | 55 | 30 |

799 Cassis fistula (Ratchaphruek)

2003. National Emblems. Multicoloured.
2453	3b. Type **799**	90	40
2454	3b. Maple leaves, Canada	90	40
MS2455 110×85 mm. Nos. 2453/4 (sold at 9b.)		4·50	4·00

Stamps of the same design were issued by Canada.

800 Basket Maker, Phra Nakhon Si Ayutthaya

2003. Bangkok 2003 International Stamp Exhibition (3rd issue). Traditional Crafts. Multicoloured.
2456	3b. Type **800**	55	40
2457	3b. Potter, Nakhon Ratchasima	55	40
2458	3b. Leather worker, Nakhon Si Thammarat	55	40
2459	15b. Wood carver, Chiang Mai	2·75	1·90
MS2460 110×146 mm. Nos. 2456/9. Perf and imperf (sold at 29b.)		6·25	5·50

801 Lychee

2003. International Letter Writing Week. Fruits. Multicoloured.
2461	3b. Type **801**	70	40
2462	3b. Roseapple	70	40
2463	3b. Coconut	70	40
2464	15b. Jackfruit	2·75	1·90
MS2465 110×144 mm. Nos. 2461/4 (sold at 29b.)		7·00	6·25

802 Crowd surrounding Democracy Monument

2003. 30th Anniv of Democracy Day (student uprising).
| 2466 | **802** | 3b. multicoloured | 55 | 40 |

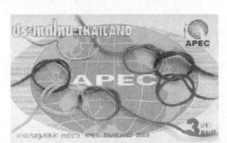

803 Globe and Linked String Loops

2003. Asian Pacific Economic Cooperation Meeting, Thailand.
| 2467 | **803** | 3b. multicoloured | 55 | 40 |

804 Bougainvillea spectabilis

2003. New Year. Flowers. Multicoloured.
2468	3b. Type **804**	55	40
2469	3b. Eucrosia bicolour	55	40
2470	3b. Cana xgeneralis	55	40
2471	3b. Zinnia violacea	55	40
MS2472 100×85 mm. Nos. 2468/71 (sold at 16b.)		3·50	3·25

805 Flag

2003. National Symbols. Multicoloured.
2473	3b. Type **805**	70	40
2474	3b. Cassis fistula (Ratchaphruek)	70	40
2475	3b. Pavilion	70	40
2476	3b. Elephant	70	40

806 Thai Elephant

2003. Tenth Anniv of Thailand—South Africa Diplomatic Relations. Multicoloured.
2477	3b. Type **806**	90	40
2478	3b. African elephant	90	40
MS2479 92×54 mm. No. 2477		4·50	4·00

807 Monkey

2004. New Year. Year of the Monkey.
| 2480 | **807** | 3b. multicoloured | 70 | 30 |

808 Phra Aphai Mani (animated cartoon)

2004. National Children's Day.
| 2481 | **808** | 3b. multicoloured | 90 | 50 |

809 Dancers ("A scene in Thai history")

2004. Art. Paintings by Hem Vejakorn. Multicoloured.
2482	3b. Type **809**	70	40
2483	3b. "Maha Bharatayudh"	70	40
2484	3b. "Khun Chang-Khun Phaen"	70	40
2485	3b. "Phra Lor"	70	40
MS2486 111×145 mm. Nos. 2482/5. (sold at 16b.)		5·25	4·75

810 "Sandra" Rose

2004
| 2487 | **810** | 4b. multicoloured | 1·10 | 50 |

811 Cuora amboinensis

2004. Turtles.
2488	3b. Type **811**	75	35
2489	3b. Platysternon megacephalum	75	35
2490	3b. Indotestudo elongate	75	35
2491	3b. Heosemys spinosa	75	35
MS2492 178×125 mm. Nos. 2488/91. (sold at 16b.)		5·50	5·25

812 Society Emblem and Khamthieng Memorial House

2004. Centenary of Siam Society (cultural organization).
| 2493 | 812 | 3b. multicoloured | 55 | 35 |

813 Horse and Vet (producing antibodics for immunization)

2004. Red Cross.
| 2494 | 813 | 3b. multicoloured | 55 | 35 |

814 Pink and Grey Brocade

2004. Thai Heritage Conservation Day. Showing different brocade designs. Multicoloured.
2495		3b. Type 814	75	35
2496		3b. Blue and white design	75	35
2497		3b. Green and gold design	75	35
2498		3b. Red and gold design	75	35
MS2499 110×145 mm. Nos. 2276/9. (sold at 16b.)			5·50	5·25

815 Sakate Temple, Bangkok

2004. Bangkok and Rome. Multicoloured.
2500		3b. Type 815	2·20	1·20
2501		3b. Colosseum, Rome	2·20	1·20
MS2502 142×71 mm 3b.×2, Nos. 2500/1			40·00	39·00

Stamps of a similar design were issued by Italy.

816 Drummer ("Ram-ma-na") (Chit Rienpracha)

2004. Sculpture. Multicoloured.
2503		3b. Type 816	75	35
2504		3b. Dancer ("Lakhon Ram") (Sitthidet Saenghiran)	75	35
2505		3b. Calf ("Luk Wua") (Paitun Muangsomboon) (horiz)	75	35
2506		3b. Flautist ("Khlui Thip") (Khien Yimsiri)	75	35

817 Non Ngai Buddha, Suphan Buri

2004. Tourism (1st issue). Multicoloured.
| 2507- 2526 | | 3b.×20 Type 817; Khao Laem Dam, Kanchanburi; Mural, Temple of the Emerald Buddha, Bangkok; Ko Li-Pe Satun; Buddha, Wat Phra Thong; Khao Luang National Park; Miracle Beach, Ko Dam Khwan, Krabi; Hornbill; Long Ru waterfall, Ubon Ratchathani; Prasat Hin Phanom Rung, Buri Ram; Maple leaves, Phu Kradueng National Park; Phukhao Ya, Ranong; Ko Kradat, Trat; Op Luang National Park; Dusky leaf monkey; Lalu, Sra Kaeo; Pu Kai, Mu Ko Similan, Phang-Nga; Tha-Le Noi Waterfowl Park, Phatthalung; Phu Pha Thoep, Mukdahan National Park; Phi Maen Cave, Mae Hong Son | 13·50 | 13·50 |

See also Nos. 2538/57, 2569/88 and 2601/16.

818 Phra Nangpava

2004. Statues of Buddha. Phra Khrueang Benchaphkhi. Multicoloured.
2527		9b. Type 818	4·00	3·00
2528		9b. Phra Kampaeng Soumkhor	4·00	3·00
2529		9b. Phra Somdej Wat Rakang-khositaram	4·00	3·00
2530		9b. Phra Rod	4·00	3·00
2531		9b. Phra Phongsuphan	4·00	3·00
MS2532 142×187 mm. Nos. 2527/31. (sold at 53b.)			37·00	35·00

819 Seated Buddha

2004. Visakhapuja Day.
| 2533 | 819 | 3b. multicoloured | 75 | 35 |

820 Phra Buddha Yod Fa Bridge

2004. Bridges. Multicoloured.
2534		5b. Type 820	90	55
2535		5b. Rama VI	90	55
2536		5b. Rama VIII	90	55
2537		5b. Rama IX	90	55

2004. Tourism (2nd issue). As T 817. Multicoloured.
| 2538- 2557 | | 3b.×20 Wat Pho Prathap Chang; Phra Prathan Chaturathit; Thalenai Angthong archipelago; Wat Na Phra Men; Sanam Chan Palace, Piyamitr tunnel; Ban Khamchanot; Pasak Cholasit dam; Khlong Lan waterfall; Mo-I Daeng cliff, Khao Phra Whan National Park; Changkra wild orchid park; Canoes, Ti Lo Re; Khao Ta Mong Lai; Suriya Patithin (solar calendar); Prasat Phu Phek; Traditional boat racing; Mae Wong National Park; Elephants; Khao National Park; Monks on horseback, Chiang Rai; Cyclists, Thung Salaeng LUang | 13·50 | 13·50 |

821 Jasmine

2004
| 2558 | 821 | 5b. multicoloured | 90 | 55 |

No. 2558 was impregnated with scent of Jasmine which was released when rubbed.

822 Circuit Board and ASEAN Emblem

2004. National Communications Day. ASEAN Telecommunications and Information Technology Ministers' Meeting, Bangkok.
| 2559 | 822 | 3b. multicoloured | 55 | 35 |

823 Princess Maha Chakri Sirindhorn

2004. Princess Maha Chakri Sirindhorn Information Technology Project.
| 2560 | 823 | 3b. multicoloured | 55 | 35 |

824 Locomotive

2004. First Underground Rapid Transit System (Chaloem Ratchamongkhon Line).
| 2561 | 824 | 3b. multicoloured | 55 | 35 |

825 Queen Sirikit

2004. Sixth Cycle (72nd birthday) of Queen Sirikit.
| 2562 | 825 | 100b. multicoloured | 12·00 | 7·00 |

826 Sampan

2004. Boats. Multicoloured.
2563		3b. Type 826	75	35
2564		3b. Krachaeng	75	35
2565		3b. Junk	75	35
2566		15b. Packet	1·80	1·20
MS2567 141×100 mm. Nos. 2563/6. (Sold at 29b)			5·50	5·25

The stamps and margins of **MS**2567 form a composite design.

2004. Tourism (3rd issue). As T 817. Multicoloured.
| 2568- 2587 | | 3b.×20 Phra Nang Din, Phayao; Phra That Kong Khao Noi, Yasothon; Phra Atchana, Wat Sri Chum; Wat Bang Kung, Samut Songkhram; Ku Kut, Wat Phrathat Chamthewi, Lamphun; Dolphin watching, Chachoengsao; Tak Bak Dok Mai tradition, Sarabui; Hat Chao Lao, Chanthaburi; Phu Kum Khao dinosaur fossils; Reversed stupa, Wat Phra That Lampang Luang; Khu Khut Waterfowl Park, Songkhla; Plant market Khlong 15, Nakhon Nayok; Huppatad, Uthai Thani; Thai Muang beach, Nakhon Phanom; Wild guar, Khao Yai National Park, Nakhon Ratchasima; Canoeing, Le Khao Kop cave, Trang; Flowers, Phu Soi Dao, Uttaradit; Kolae boat, Ban Paseyawo, Pattani; Mist, Thap Boek, Phu Hin Rongkla National Park, Phetchabun; Bats, Khao Chong Phran, Ratchaburi | 13·50 | 13·50 |

827 Chula Kite

2004. International Letter Writing Week. Kites. Multicoloured.
2588		3b. Type 827	75	35
2589		3b. Pakpao	75	35
2590		3b. Snake	75	35
2591		15b. Buffalo	1·80	1·20
MS2592 110×144 mm. Nos. 2588/91. (sold at 29b.)			5·50	5·25

828 King Rama IV

2004. Birth Bicentenary of King Rama IV.
| 2593 | 828 | 4b. multicoloured | 75 | 35 |

829 Globe, Keypad and Map

2004. E-Customs.
| 2594 | 829 | 3b. multicoloured | 55 | 35 |

830 Burmannia coelestis (inscr "coelestris")

2004. New Year. Flowers. Multicoloured.
2595		3b. Type 830	1·10	35
2596		3b. Wrightia sirikitiae	1·10	35
2597		3b. Utricularia bifida	1·10	35
2598		3b. Eria amica	1·10	35
MS2599 100×85 mm. Nos. 2595/8. (Sold at 16b.)			9·25	8·75

2004. Tourism (4th issue). As T 817. Multicoloured.
| 2600- 2615 | | 3b.×16 Phra That Cho Hae, Phrae; Wat Karuna, Chai Nat; Wat Nang Sao, Samut Sakhon; Phra Mutao Pagoda, Nonthaburi; Phu Kao Phraphan Kham National Park, Pang Bua Lam Phu; Airavata (Three headed elephant), Erawan Museum, Samut Prakan; Wat Chedi Hoi, Pathum Thani; White Krajiaw, Chaiyaphum; Chet Si Waterfall, Nong Khai; Summer Palace, Ko Si Chang, Chon Buri; Traditional Drum-making Village (Ban Bang Phae), Ang Thong; Ko Thalu, Rayong; Kosamphi Forest Park, Maha Sarakham; Cannonball Tree, Wat Phra Non Chaksi, Sing Buri; Kung Kula Rong Hai, Roi Et; Phu Sra Dok Bua, Amnat Charoen | 12·50 | 12·50 |

831 Couple

2004. Bangkok—Fashion City. Multicoloured.
2616		3b. Type 831	75	35
2617		3b. Sleeveless dress	75	35
2618		3b. Woman with head on hand	75	35
2619		3b. Woman facing right	1·80	1·20

MS2620 132×191 mm. Nos. 2617/19.
(Sold at 30b) 5·50 5·25
The stamps and margins of **MS**2620 form a composite design.

832 Queen Rambhai Barni

2004. Birth Centenary of Queen Rambhai Barni.
2621 **832** 3b. multicoloured 55 35

833 Rooster

2005. New Year. Year of the Rooster (1st issue).
2622 **833** 3b. multicoloured 55 35
See also Nos. 2684/7.

834 Characters from "Kaew Jom Kaen" (children's cartoon)

2005. National Children's Day.
2623 **834** 3b. multicoloured 55 35

835 Tango

2005. 50th Anniv of Thailand—Argentine Diplomatic Relations. Design showing dance. Multicoloured.
2624 3b. Type **835** 75 45
2625 3b. Tom Tom 75 45

836 Rose

2005
2626 **836** 10b. multicoloured 2·00 1·40
No. 2626 was impregnated with the scent of roses.

837 Emblem

2005. Centenary of Rotary International.
2627 **837** 3b. multicoloured 75 45

838 Buddha with clasped Hands

2005. Maghapuja Day.
2628 **838** 3b. multicoloured 75 45

839 Emblem and Gold Cloth

2005. Red Cross.
2629 **839** 3b. multicoloured 75 45

840 Princess Maha Chakri Sirindhorn

2005. 50th Birthday of Princess Maha Chakri Sirindhorn.
2630 **840** 3b. multicoloured 75 45

841 Hanging Decoration

2005. Cultural Heritage. Designs showing hanging decorations. Multicoloured.
2631 3b. Type **841** 55 45
2632 3b. Two-tiered 55 45
2633 3b. Circular with flame shapes 55 45
2634 3b. Chandelier shaped 2·40 90
MS2635 152×127 mm. Nos. 2631/4.
(Sold at 30b) 5·50 5·25

842 M. L. Buoha Nimmanhemin (Dokmaisod)

2005. Writers Birth Centenaries. Multicoloured.
2636 3b. Type **842** 55 45
2637 3b. Kularb Saipradit (Sri Burapha) 55 45
2638 3b. Kan Pungbun Na Ayudhya (Maimuangderm) 55 45
2639 3b. Arkatdumkeung Rabib-hadana 2·20 1·80
MS2640 144×110 mm. Nos. 2636/9.
(Sold at 17b.) 8·25 7·00

843 Coccinella transversalis

2005. Beetles. Multicoloured.
2641 5b. Type **843** 90 70
2642 5b. Chrysochroa buqueti rugicol-lis (48×29 mm) 90 70
2643 5b. Sagra femorata 90 70
2644 5b. Chrysochroa maruyama (inscr "maruyamai") (48×29 mm) 90 70

844 Phra Ruang Lang Rang Puen

2005. Benja—Pakee Amulets. Multicoloured.
2645 9b. Type **844** 1·70 1·40
2646 9b. Phra Hu Yan 1·70 1·40
2647 9b. Phra Chinnarat Bal Sema 1·70 1·40
2648 9b. Phra Mahesuan 1·70 1·40
2649 9b. Phra Tha Kradan 1·70 1·40
MS2650 142×186 mm. Nos. 2645/9.
(Sold at 55b.) 17·00 16·00
No. **MS**2650 was re-issued for Taipeh 2005 International Stamp Exhibition, the sheet face value overprinted with the exhibition emblem.

845 Panda

2005. 30th Anniv of Thailand—China Diplomatic Relations. Multicoloured.
2651 3b. Type **845** 75 55
2652 3b. Panda eating bamboo shoots 75 55
MS2653 100×145 mm. Nos. 2651/2.
(Sold at 15b.) 9·25 8·75
Nos. 2651/2 were issued in horizontal se-tenant pairs within the sheet, the pairs enclosed in rectangles (100×50 mm), each pair forming, with the background, a composite design.

846 Rama and Srida

2005. THAIPEX '05, Thailand Philatelic Exhibition 2005. Traditional Drama. Multicoloured.
2654 3b. Type **846** 55 35
2655 3b. Thotsakan 55 35
2656 3b. Hanuman 55 35
2657 15b. Rama and Thotsakan 2·75 2·10
MS2658 174×117 mm. Nos. 2654/7.
(Sold at 30b). Perf and imperf 7·25 7·00

847 Globe and Symbols of Communication

2005. National Communications Day.
2659 **847** 3b. multicoloured 75 35

848 Prasat Phanom Rung Gable

2005. Roof Gables. Multicoloured.
2660 5b. Type **848** 90 70
2661 5b. Wat Phra Phai Luang 90 70
2662 5b. Uposatha Hall, Wat Khao Bandai It 90 70
2663 5b. Scripture Library, Wat Phra Sing Woramahawihan 90 70

849 Rhynchostylis gigantea

2005. Orchids. Multicoloured.
2664 3b. Type **849** 75 55
2665 3b. Rhynchostylis gigantean (red) 75 55
2666 3b. Dendrobium gratiossimum 75 55
2667 15b. Dendrobium thyrsiflorum 2·75 2·30
MS2668 145×110 mm. Nos. 2664/7.
(Sold at 30b.) 5·75 5·50

850 Dove

2005. International Day of Peace.
2669 **850** 3b. multicoloured 75 55

851 Water Buffalo

2005. International Letter Writing Week. Water Buffalo. Multicoloured.
2670 3b. Type **851** 75 55
2671 3b. Standing 75 55
2672 3b. Lying 75 55
2673 15b. Ploughing 2·75 2·30
MS2674 110×145 mm. Nos. 2670/3.
(Sold at 30b.) 5·75 5·50

852 Library Building

2005. Centenary of National Library.
2675 **852** 3b. multicoloured 55 35

853 King Rama V and Slaves

2005. Centenary of the Abolition of Slavery in Thailand.
2676 **853** 3b. multicoloured 55 35

854 Beaumontia murtonii

2005. New Year. Flowers. Multicoloured.
2677 3b. Type **854** 55 35
2678 3b. Cochlospermum religiosum 55 35
2679 3b. Hibiscus mutabilis 55 35
2680 3b. Hibiscus rosa-sinensis 55 35
MS2681 100×85 mm. Nos. 2677/80.
(Sold at 17b.) 3·75 3·50

855 Princess Bejaratana

2005. 80th Birthday of Princess Bejaratana Ratsuda.
2682 **855** 3b. multicoloured 75 55

856 "Rooster at Dawn" (Prayat Pongdam)

2005. Year of the Rooster (2nd issue). Multicoloured
2683	3b. Type **856**	75	55
2684	3b. "Golden Rooster" (Pichai Nirand)	75	55
2685	3b. "Legendary Rooster" (girl dancing) (Chakrabhand Posayakrit)	75	55
2686	3b. "Divine Rooster" (Chalermchai Kositpipat) (horiz)	75	55

857 King Bhumibol Adulyadej and Workers

2005. Royal Development Project. Multicoloured.
2687	3b. Type **857**	75	55
2688	3b. Seated farmers and King Bhumibol Adulyadej	75	55

858 Somdet Phra Phutthachan

2005. Buddhist Monks. Multicoloured.
2689	5b. Type **858**	90	70
2690	5b. Phra Ratchamuni Samiram Khunupamachan	90	70
2691	5b. Phra Achan Man Bhuridatto	90	70
2692	5b. Khruba Si Wichai	90	70
MS2693 127×150 mm. Nos. 2689/92 (Sold at 305b.)		6·50	6·25

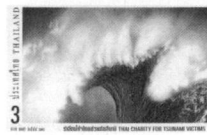

859 Wave

2005. Tsunami Victims' Charity. Multicoloured.
2694	3b. Type **859**	1·80	90
2695	3b. Children	1·80	90

860 Dog

2006. New Year. Year of the Dog. Granite paper.
2696	**860**	3b. multicoloured	75	55

861 Prince Chaturantarasmi

2006. 150th Birth Anniv of Prince Chaturantarasmi.
2697	**861**	3b. multicoloured	75	55

862 Working in Fields (Phanupong Tiaprasong)

2006. International Children's Day. Winning Designs in Children's Painting Competition. Multicoloured.
2698	3b. Type **862**	75	55
2699	3b. River commerce (Naraphon Daorueang)	75	55
2700	3b. River pleasure (Ruethairatana Suwanchang)	75	55
2701	3b. Family (Suchada Phakamsi)	75	55

863 Rose

2006
2702	**863**	3b. multicoloured	1·70	90

No. 2702 was impregnated with scent of roses.

864 Chaiwatthanaram Temple, Ayutthaya and Persepolis, Southern Iran

2006. 50th Anniv of Thailand—Iran Diplomatic Relations.
2703	**864**	3b. multicoloured	75	55

865 Queen Sirikit Centre for Breast Cancer

2006. Red Cross. Granite paper.
2704	**865**	3b. multicoloured	75	55

866 Monument

2006. Heritage Conservation Day. Multicoloured.
2705	3b. Type **866**	75	55
2706	3b. Ruins (horiz)	75	55
2707	3b. Balanced rock (horiz)	75	55
2708	15b. Nang Usa earth pillar	3·00	2·75
MS2709 150×85 mm. Nos. 2705/8 (Sold at 36b.)		7·25	7·00

867 Throne Hall

2006. Thon Buri Palace. Multicoloured.
2710	3b. Type **867**	75	55
2711	3b. King Taksin's shrine	75	55
2712	3b. Chinese style residences	75	55
2713	3b. King Pinklao's residence	75	55
MS2714 170×112 mm. Nos. 2710/13 (Sold at 17b.)		4·50	4·25

868 King Bhumibol Adulyadej

2006. 60th Anniv of Accession of King Bhumibol Adulyadej. Designs showing King Bhumibol Adulyadej. Multicoloured.
2715	3b. Type **868**	1·80	70
2716	3b. Orange background, suit and tie	1·80	70
2717	3b. Green background, collarless shirt, checked suit	1·80	70
2718	3b. Blue background, dark suit and tie	1·80	70
2719	3b. Bronze background, collarless shirt, blue suit	1·80	70
2720	3b. Purple background, collarless shirt, dark suit	1·80	70
MS2721 139×173 mm. Nos. 2715/20 (Sold at 30b.)		28·00	26·00

See also Nos. 2728 and 2752/MS2758.

869 Seated Buddha protected by Seven-headed Naga

2006. Visakhapuja Day.
2722	**869**	3b. multicoloured	75	55

870 Buddhadasa

2006. Birth Centenary of Buddhadasa (Nguam Panich). Multicoloured.
2723	3b. Type **870**	75	55
2724	3b. Facing left	75	55
2725	3b. Preaching	75	55
2726	3b. Sanctuary	75	55
MS2727 105×139 mm. Nos. 2723/6 (Sold at 17b.)		4·50	4·50

871 King Bhumibol Adulyadej

2006. 60th Anniv of Accession of King Bhumibol Adulyadej (2nd issue).
2728	**871**	100b. multicoloured	14·50	14·00

872 Amphiprion clarkii

2006. Fish. Multicoloured.
2729	3b. Type **872**	75	55
2730	3b. *Amphiprion perideraion*	75	55
2731	3b. *Amphiprion polymnus*	75	55
2732	3b. *Amphiprion ocellaris*	75	55
MS2733 177×91 mm. Nos. 2729/32 (Sold at 20b.)		4·50	4·50

The stamps and margins of **MS**2733 form a composite design of the sea bed.

873 Symbols of Communication

2006. National Communication Day.
2734	**873**	3b. multicoloured	75	55

874 *Mitrephora sirikitae*

2006
2735	**874**	5b. multicoloured	90	70

875 Khun Tongdaeng

2006. Khun Tongdaeng—King Bhumibol Adulyadej's Dog. Designs showing Khun Tongdaeng. Multicoloured.
2736	3b. Type **875**	75	55
2737	3b. Sitting	75	55
2738	3b. Standing	75	55
2739	3b. With puppies	75	55
MS2740 100×110 mm. Nos. 2736/9 (Sold at 17b.)		4·00	3·75

876 *Nepenthes mirabilis*

2006. International Letter Writing Week. Carnivorous Plants. Multicoloured.
2741	3b. Type **876**	75	55
2742	3b. *Rafflesia kerrii*	75	55
2743	3b. *Sapria poilanei*	75	55
2744	15b. *Drosera burmannii*	1·80	1·40
MS2745 110×145 mm. Nos. 2741/4 (Sold at 29b.)		5·50	5·25

877 *Impatiens phuluangensis*

2006. New Year. Flowers. Multicoloured.
2746	3b. Type **877**	75	55
2747	3b. *Murdannia gigantean*	75	55
2748	3b. *Hypoxis aurea*	75	55
2749	3b. *Caulokaemferia alba*	75	55
MS2750 99×85 mm. Nos. 2746/9 (Sold at 16b.)		4·25	4·00

878 King Rama V wearing Naval Uniform

2006. Centenary of Naval College.
2751	**878**	3b. multicoloured	75	55

879 King Bhumibol Adulyadej

2006. 60th Anniv of Accession of King Bhumibol Adulyadej (3rd issue). Designs showing King Bhumibol Adulyadej. Multicoloured.
2752	5b. Type **879**	1·10	70
2753	5b. On bridge carrying papers	1·10	70
2754	5b. Carrying camera	1·10	70
2755	5b. Taking notes	1·10	70

2756	5b.	Riding wearing uniform	1·10	70
2757	5b.	Facing left holding papers	1·10	70

MS2758 139×173 mm. Nos. 2752/7
(Sold at 44b.)   9·25   8·75

880 Friendship Bridge

2006. Inauguration of Second Thai–Lao Friendship Bridge between Mukdahan and Savannaket. Multicoloured.

2759	**880**	3b. Type **880**	75	55
2760		3b. Bridge at night	75	55

Nos. 2759/60 were issued together, se-tenant, forming a composite design.

881 Suvarnabhumi Airport

2006

2761	**881**	3b. multicoloured	75	55

882 Pig

2007. New Year. Year of the Pig.

2762	**882**	3b. multicoloured	75	55

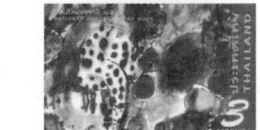

883 Animals (Supisara Kitpipit)

2007. Children's Drawings. Multicoloured.

2763	**883**	3b. Type **883**	75	55
2764		3b. Horse back riding (Parima Suriyasat)	75	55
2765		3b. Cats (Krongkwan Kitpipit)	75	55
2766		3b. Rainbow and animals (Sujeepat Sukchaiprakarn)	75	55

884 King Chulalongkorn and King Bhumibol Adulyadej

2007. Centenary of Siam Commercial Bank Company.

2767	**884**	3b. multicoloured	75	55

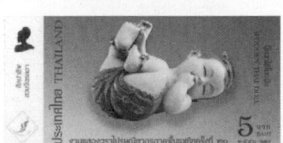

885 Child Doll: actual size 62×30 mm

2007. Wood Carving (1st issue). Designs showing child dolls. Multicoloured.

2768	5b.	Type **885**	90	70
2769	5b.	Sleeping with head on table	90	70
2770	5b.	With head and legs raised	90	70
2771	5b.	Sleeping with head on cushion	90	70

MS2772 141×110 mm. Nos. 2768/71.
(sold at 33b.)   6·50   6·25

See also Nos. 2774/**MS**2778.

886 Rose

2007

2773	**886**	5b. multicoloured	90	70

No. 2773 was impregnated with the scent of roses.

887 Flowers

2007. Wood Carving (2nd issue). Designs showing fruit and flowers. Multicoloured.

2774	5b.	Type **887**	90	70
2775	5b.	Decorated yellow fruit, white and yellow flowers	90	70
2776	5b.	Lotus flower	90	70
2777	5b.	Orange and white flowers	90	70

MS2778 141×110 mm. Nos. 2774/7.
(sold at 26b.)   5·75   5·50

888 Mahidol Wongsanusorn Building and Laboratory Technician

2007. Red Cross. Tuberculosis-free Zone.

2779	**888**	3b. multicoloured	75	55

888a Young Postman

2007. Young Postman.

2779a	3b.	**888a** multicoloured	90	55

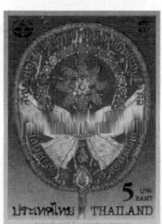

889 Fan

2007. Heritage Conservation Day. Ceremonial Fans. Multicoloured.

2780	5b.	Type **889**	90	70
2781	5b.	Blue fan	90	70
2782	5b.	Reddish-brown fan	90	70
2783	5b.	Scarlet and gold fan	90	70

MS2784 141×174 mm. Nos. 2780/3.
(sold at 27b.)   6·50   6·25

No. **MS**2784 was cut around in the shape of a fan.

890 King Bhumibol Adulyadej

2007. 80th Birth Anniv of King Bhumibol Adulyadej (1st issue).

2785	**890**	9b. multicoloured	2·40	2·30

See also No. **MS**2845.

891 Princess Galayani Vadhana

2007. 84th Birth Anniv of Princess Galayani Vadhana.

2786	**891**	3b. multicoloured	1·10	90

892 Scenes from Buddha's Life

2007. Visakhapuja Day.

2787	**892**	3b. multicoloured	75	55

893 Man Daeng Waterfall, Phu Hin Rong Kla National Park

2007. Waterfalls. Multicoloured.

2788		3b. Type **893**	75	55
2789		3b. Huai Mae Khamin, Khuean Srinagarindra National Park	75	55
2790		3b. Kaeng Sopha, Thung Salaeng Luang National Park	75	55
2791		3b. Mae Ya, Doi Inthanon National Park	75	55

MS2792 144×110 mm. Nos. 2788/91.
(sold at 16b.)   4·75   4·50

893a Mu Ko Similan National Park

2007. Amazing Thailand. Seaside. Multicoloured.

2792a	15b.	Type **1011**	1·60	1·60
2792b	15b.	Cliffs, Ko Kai	1·60	1·60
2792c	15b.	Sunset over sea, Ko Chang	1·60	1·60
2792d	15b.	Cliffs and rock formation in bay, Khao Tapu	1·60	1·60
2792e	15b.	Horse riders on beach, Hat Cha-Am	1·60	1·60
2792f	15b.	Cliffs and lagoon, Ao Maya	1·60	1·60
2792g	15b.	Waterside houses and boats, Ko Panyi	1·60	1·60
2792h	15b.	Boats on beach at evening, Hat Chao-Mai	1·60	1·60
2792i	15b.	White sand archipelago, Thale Waek	1·60	1·60
2792j	15b.	View over bay, Hat Pattaya	1·60	1·60

894 White Mask

2007. Phi Takhon Procession (Caravan of Devils), Loei Province. Multicoloured.

2793		3b. Type **894**	75	55
2794		3b. Black mask	75	55
2795		3b. Red mask	75	55
2796		3b. White mask (different)	75	55

MS2797 107×88 mm. 10b. Three masked dancers. (60×48 mm.)   3·50   3·25

The stamps and margins of **MS**2797 form a composite design.

895 Wat Rajaoraram

2007. Temples. Multicoloured.

2798	5b.	Type **895**	90	70
2799	5b.	Wat Rajapradit Sathitmahasimaram	90	70
2800	5b.	Wat Rajabopit Sathitmahasimaram	90	70
2801	5b.	Wat Suthatthepwararam	90	70

MS2802 144×110 mm. Nos. 2798/2801.
(sold at 27b.)   5·75   5·50

896 Rock Formations

2007. Pa Hin Ngam National Park. Multicoloured.

2803	5b.	Type **896**	90	70
2804	5b.	Horizontal rock formation	90	70
2805	5b.	Trophy shaped rock formation	90	70
2806	5b.	Pillared horizontal rock formation	90	70

MS2807 210×110 mm. Nos. 2803/6.
(sold at 27b.)   8·00   7·50

897 Pheasant

2007. Bangkok 2007 International Stamp Exhibition. Beetle Wings Collage. Multicoloured.

2808	5b.	Type **897**	1·10	70
2809	5b.	Duck	1·10	70
2810	5b.	Cockerel	1·10	70
2811	5b.	Heron	1·10	70

MS2812 110×145 mm. Nos. 2808/11
(sold at 33b.)   6·50   6·25

898 Transmitter and Communicator

2007. National Communications Day. Or Sor Radio Station.

2813	**898**	3b. multicoloured	75	55

899 Hand holding Medal

2007. 24th Universiade (International University Sports), Bangkok.

2814	**899**	3b. multicoloured	75	55

900 Secretariat Building, Bandar Seri Begawan, Brunei Darussalam

2007. Architecture. 40th Anniv of ASEAN (Association of South-east Asian Nations). Multicoloured.

2815		3b. Type **900**	75	55
2816		3b. National Museum, Cambodia	75	55
2817		3b. Fatahillah Museum, Jakarta	75	55
2818		3b. Traditional house, Laos	75	55
2819		3b. Railway Headquarters Building, Malaysia	75	55
2820		3b. Yangon Post Office, Union of Myanmar	75	55
2821		3b. Malacanang Palace, Manila	75	55
2822		3b. National Museum, Singapore	75	55
2823		3b. Vimanmek Mansion, Bangkok, Thailand	75	55
2824		3b. Presidential Palace, Hanoi, Vietnam	75	55

Stamps of a similar design were issued by all member countries.

901 Statue

2007. 120th Anniv of Thailand–Japan Diplomatic Relations. Multicoloured.

2825		3b. Type **901**	75	55
2826		3b. Pagoda	75	55
2827		3b. Elephant (mother of pearl inlay)	75	55

2828	3b. Dragon (woven)	75	55
2829	3b. Orchids	75	55
2830	3b. Cherry blossom	75	55
2831	3b. Thai dancer	75	55
2832	3b. Japanese dancer	75	55

902 Betel Nut Scissors

2007. Traditional Utensils. Multicoloured.

2833	3b. Type **902**	75	55
2834	3b. Cylinder and piston igniter	75	55
2835	3b. Betel nut masher	75	55
2836	3b. Oil lamp	75	55
MS2837	144×109 mm. Nos. 2833/6	5·25	5·00

903 Chaiyaphum

2007. Local Identity. Two sheets, each 254×126 mm containing T **903** and similar square designs showing provincial seals. Multicoloured.

MS2838 (a) 3b.×10, Type **903**; Chumphon; Chiang Rai; Chiang Mai; Trang; Trat; Tak; Nakhon Nayok; Nakhon Pathom; Nakhon Phanom. (b) 3b.×10, Bangkok; Krabi; Kanchanaburi; Kalasin; Kamphaeng Phet; Khon Kaen; Chanthaburi; Chachoengsao; Chonburi; Chai Nat. (sold at 18 baht.) 9·25 8·75

904 Phra Chula Chomklao Chaoyuhua (Chulalongkorn the Great (Rama V)) and King Bhumibol Adulyadej

2007. 120th Anniv of Ministry of Defence.

2839	**904** 3b. multicoloured	75	55

905 Pink Blooms

2007. Plumeria (frangipani). Multicoloured.

2840	3b. Type **905**	75	55
2841	3b. Magenta blooms	75	55
2842	3b. Yellow-tinged blooms	75	55
2843	3b. White blooms (inscr *Plumeria obtusa*)	75	55
MS2844	100×85 mm. Nos. 2840/3. (sold at 18 baht.)	4·75	4·50

906 King Bhumibol Adulyadej as Small Child

2007. 80th Birth Anniv of King Bhumibol Adulyadej (2nd issue). Sheet 150×180 mm containing T **906** and similar square designs. Multicoloured.

MS2845 5b.×8, Type **906**; As older child in wooden cart: As young man studying; As young man facing left; Wearing uniform; Wearing formal uniform; Wearing grey suit and red patterned tie; Wearing state robes; 80b. Wearing monk's robes during mourning for Queen Savang Vadhana (his grandmother) 28·00 26·00

The 5 baht stamps of **MS2845** are laid around the central holographic 80 baht stamp.

907 King anointing Elephant

2007. 80th Birth Anniv of King Bhumibol Adulyadej (3rd issue). Phr Sawer Adulyadej Phahon (royal white elephant). Multicoloured.

2846	5b. Type **907**	90	70
2847	5b. Riding elephant	90	70
2848	5b. King holding elephant's trunk (horiz)	90	70
2849	5b. Standing in compound (horiz)	90	70
MS2850	120×183 mm. 5b. As Type **907**	4·50	4·50

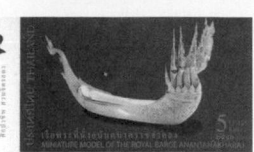

908 Model of Royal Barge *Anantanakharaj*

2007. Arts and Crafts from Queen Sirikit's Collection. Fifth Arts of the Kingdom Exhibition. Multicoloured.

2851	5b. Type **908**	90	80
2852	5b. Model of Royal Barge *Suphannahongse*	90	80
2853	5b. Sappagab Pharagajatarn	90	80
2854	5b. Sappagab Khram	90	80
2855	5b. Lustral water jars in gold niello	90	80
2856	5b. Gold niello miniature vanity set	90	80
2857	5b. Van Lipao basket	90	80
2858	5b. Gold niello evening bag	90	80
2859	20b. Miniature of Busabok Pavillion (41×69 mm)	3·75	3·50
MS2860	140×195 mm. No. 2859 (sold at 40b.)	10·00	9·75

909 Rat

2008. New Year. Year of the Rat. Multicoloured.

2861	3b. Type **909**	75	55
MS2862	120×45 mm. Nos. 2390 (goat), 2480 (monkey), 2622 (rooster), 2696 (dog), 2762 (pig) and 2861	5·75	5·50

910 Kok–Kek (stilt walking) (Kentis Kumsrijan)

2008. Children's Day. Cultural Heritage. Winning entries in Design a Stamp Competition. Multicoloured.

2863	3b. Type **910**	75	55
2864	3b. Kite flying (Natapol Saelim)	75	55
2865	3b. Hun Krabok (puppets) (Sirada Chokeyangkul)	75	55
2866	3b. Thien Phansa (candle sculpture) (Salinthip Narongpun)	75	55
2867	3b. Kwan Khao (rice plant (Mae Phosop) rites) (Amornthep Jitnak)	75	55

911 Yellow Dragon Costume

2008. Chinese New Year. Multicoloured.

2868	5b. Type **911**	90	70
2869	5b. Dragon costume with white fur eyelashes	90	70
2870	5b. Masks (26×21 mm)	90	70
2871	5b. Pageant float (26×21 mm)	90	70

MS2872	165×100 mm. 5b.×2, Nos. 2868/9	4·25	4·00

Nos. 2868/9 were issued together, *se-tenant*, forming a composite design.

912 Rose

2008. Rose.

2873	**912** 5b. multicoloured	90	70

Nos. 2873 was impregnated with the scent of roses.

2008. Young Postman. As Type **888a**

2874	3b. Post boy in boat holding envelope	90	55

913 Stylised Figures holding Heart

2008. Greeting Stamp. Love

2875	**913** 3b. grey and scarlet-vermilion	65	55

914 Chatukham

2008. Jatukham Rammathep (Chatukham Rammathep) Buddhist Amulets. Sheet 240×125 mm containing T **914** and similar vert designs. Multicoloured.

MS2876 9b.×12, Type **914**; Amulet ; Rammathep; As Type **914**; Amulet (grey ground); Rammathep (different); Amulet (olive-yellow ground); Amulet (dull violet-blue ground); Amulet (orange-brown ground); Amulet (light brown-olive ground); Amulet (light turquoise-green); Amulet (light rose red) 17·00 17·00

915 Portal Guardians

2008. Heritage Conservation Day. Portal Guardians. Multicoloured.

2877	3b. Type **915**	65	55
2878	3b. Painted guardians	65	55
2879	3b. Statues	65	55
2880	3b. Guardians with decorated background	65	55
MS2881	152×126 mm. Nos. 2877/80	5·25	5·00

2008. Local Identity. Sheet 254×126 mm containing square designs as T **903** showing provincial seals. Multicoloured.

MS2882 3b.×10, Nakhon Ratchasima; Nakhon Si Thammarat; Nakhon Sawan; Nonthaburii; Narathiwat; Nan ; Buri Ram; Pathum Thani; Prachuap Khiri; Prachin Buri 9·25 8·75

916 Wat Rajannada (Iron Castle)

2008. 50th Anniv of Thailand—Turkey Diplomatic Relations. Multicoloured.

2883	3b. Type **916**	55	35
2884	3b. Blue Mosque	55	35

916a Sunflowers

2008. Greetings Stamp. Sunflower

2884a	**916a** 3b. multicoloured	75	35

917 Scenes from Buddha's Life

2008. Visakhapuja Day.

2885	**917** 3b. multicoloured	75	55

918 Globe on Fire

2008. World Environment Day. Multicoloured.

2886	3b. Type **918**	55	35
2887	3b. People caring for globe as tree	55	35
2888	3b. Leaf on fire	55	35
2889	3b. Faces	55	35

919 *Brassocattleya*

2008. Orchids. Multicoloured.

2890	3b. Type **919**	55	35
2891	3b. *Aerides falcata*	55	35
2892	3b. *Arachnis hookeriana* x *Vanda*	55	35
2893	3b. *Phalaenopsis*	55	35
2894	3b. *Dendrobium sutiknoi*	55	35
2895	3b. *Paphiopedilum callosum*	55	35
2896	3b. *Grammatophyllum speciosum*	55	35
2897	3b. Inscr ('*Vascostylis* Prapawan')	55	35
2898	3b. *Vanda* Robert's Delight	55	35

920 Phra Buddha Saiyat (The Reclining Buddha Image), Wat Phra Chetuphon Wimon Mangkhalaram

2008. Amazing Thailand. Bangkok. Multicoloured.

2899	3b. Type **920**	55	35
2900	3b. The Giant Swing, Wat Suthat Thepwararam	55	35
2901	3b. Namphrik (chili dip)	55	35
2902	3b. Ring Road Bridges at night	55	35
2903	3b. Chao Phraya River, Wat Arun Ratchawararam	55	35
2904	3b. Phra Mondop, Wat Phra Si Rattanasatsadaram	55	35
2905	3b. Ramakian mural painting, enclosure gallery, Wat Phra Si Rattanasatsadaram	55	35
2906	3b. Trade and business centre	55	35
2907	3b. Ratchadamnoen Avenue at night	55	35
2908	3b. Chatuchak weekend market	55	35

Nos. 2909/18 and Type **921** are left for Mountains, issued on 11 July 2008, not yet received.

922 Young Postman

2008

| 2919 | **922** | 3b. multicoloured | 55 | 45 |

923 1883 1 solot
Stamp (As Type **1**)

2008. 125th Anniversary of Thai Postal Service (1st series). Sheet 125×168 mm containing T **923** and similar vert designs. Multicoloured.

MS2920 5b. Type **923**; 5b. 1883 1 solot Stamp (As Type **1**) (different); 5b. 1883 1 sik stamp (As Type **2**); 10b. 1883 1 salung stamp (As Type **3**); 25b. 1883 1 solot stamp (As Type **1**) (hologram). 7·25 7·00

924 Telegraph

2008. National Communications Day.

| 2921 | **924** | 3b. multicoloured | 55 | 45 |

925 Flowers

2008. Princess Maha Chakri Sirindhorn's Painting.

| 2922 | **925** | 5b. multicoloured | 90 | 75 |

926 Early and Modern Mail Vans

2008. 125th Anniv of Thai Postal Service (2nd series). Multicoloured.

2923	**926**	3b. Type **926**	55	45
2924		3b. Early and modern Post Offices	55	45
2925		3b. Early and modern postmen	55	45
2926		3b. Early and modern Post Office counters	55	45
2927		3b. 1883 1 solot Stamp (As Type **1**) and modern stamps	55	45

927 Thai Peacock

2008. Peacocks. Multicoloured.

| 2928 | 10b. Type **927** | 1·70 | 1·40 |
| 2929 | 10b. Perching | 1·70 | 1·40 |

MS2930 181×122 mm. Nos. 2928/9. Sold at 30b. 6·50 6·25

The stamps and margins of No. **MS**2930 form a composite design.

928 Grand Palace (Thailand)

2008. 50th Anniv of Thailand–Korea Diplomatic Relations. Multicoloured.

| 2931 | 3b. Type **928** | 55 | 45 |
| 2932 | 3b. Changdeokgung Palace (Korea) | 55 | 45 |

929 Shiva

2008. International Letter Writing Week. Thai Shadow Play Puppets. Multicoloured.

2933	3b. Type **929**	55	45
2934	3b. Preluder	55	45
2935	3b. Rishi	55	45
2936	3b. Theng the jester	55	45

MS2937 145×110 mm. Nos. 2933/6. Sold at 18b. 4·00 3·75

2008. Local Identity. Sheet 254×126 mm containing square designs as T **903** showing provincial seals. Multicoloured.

MS2938 3b.×10, Pattani; Pha Nakhon Si Ayutthaya; Phang-nga; Phatthalung; Phayao; Phichit; Pitsanulok; Phetch- aburi; Petchabun; Phrae 7·25 7·00

930 1908 2t. Stamp (As No. 119)

2008. Centenary of Equestrian Statue of King Chulalongkorn.

[line partly illegible]

931 Princess Galyani Vadhana as a Child

2008. Princess Galyani Vadhana's Cremation Ceremony. Sheet 170×127 mm containing T **931** and similar vert designs. Multicoloured.

MS2940 5b.×4, Type **931**; As a young woman; Wearing uniform; Wearing red dress 5·25 4·75

932 Suwanna Water Lily

2008. New Year. Flowers. Water Lilies. Multicoloured.

2941	3b. Type **932**	55	45
2942	3b. Tan-khwan	55	45
2943	3b. Tanpong	55	45
2944	3b. Mangala-ubol	55	45

MS2945 100×85 mm. Nos. 2941/4. Sold at 18b. 3·75 3·50

The stamps and margins of **MS**2945 form a composite design.

933 King Bhumibol Adulyadej

2008. 81st Birth Anniv of King Bhumibol Adulyadej.

| 2946 | **933** | 3b. multicoloured | 1·50 | 60 |

934 Chuang Bunnag

2008. Birth Bicentenary of Somdet Chao Phraya Borom Maha Sisuriyawong (Chuang Bunnag) (regent during the early years of the reign of King Chulalongkorn).

| 2947 | **934** | 3b. multicoloured | 55 | 45 |

935 Ox

2009. Chinese New Year. Year of the Ox.

| 2948 | **935** | 3b. multicoloured | 55 | 45 |

936 Phra Abhai Manee

2009. Children's Day. Scenes from *Phra Abhai Manee* by Phra Sunthorn. Multicoloured.

2949	3b. Type **936**	1·10	45
2950	3b. Phra Abhai Manee playing flute	1·10	45
2951	3b. Mermaid	1·10	45
2952	3b. Giantess	1·10	45
2953	3b. Falling	1·10	45
2954	3b. Phra Chao Ta (Old Hermit)	1·10	45
2955	3b. ... Hermit) (halted Manduk)	1·10	45
2956	3b. Nang Laveng	1·10	45

MS2956a 143×127 mm. 3b.×4, Nos. 2949/52 14·50 12·50

937 Prince Bhanurangsis as Child

2009. Prince Somdet Phra Raja Pitula Boromphongsabhimuk Chaofa, Bhanurangsiswangwong Krom Phraya Bhanuphandhuwongworadej (Prince Bhanurangsi) (Commander-in-Chief of Royal Siamese Army and founder of Thai postal service) Commemoration. Multicoloured.

2957	3b. Type **937**	55	45
2958	3b. As young man	55	45
2959	3b. Wearing uniform	55	45
2960	3b. Wearing uniform with white jacket	55	45

MS2961 180×130 mm. Nos. 2957/60. Sold at 20b. 3·75 3·50

938 Rose

2009

| 2962 | **938** | 5b. multicoloured | 1·10 | 60 |

Nos. 2962 was impregnated with the scent of roses.

939 Buildings

2009. 120th Anniv of Postal School.

| 2963 | **939** | 3b. multicoloured | 75 | 45 |

939a Harvesting Palm

2009. Amazing Thailand. Traditional Life. Multicoloured.

2963a	3b. Type **939a**	75	60
2963b	3b. Preparing and eating food outside	7·75	30
2963c	3b. Carving Erawan (many-headed elephant) statues	75	60
2963d	3b. Monk in boat receiving gifts of food	75	60
2963e	3b. Sky lanterns	75	60
2963f	3b. Craftworker	75	60
2963g	3b. Flower seller	75	60
2963h	3b. Men making fishing baskets	75	60
2963i	3b. Selling fruit from boats	75	60
2963j	3b. Elephants and riders with logs	75	60

940 Queen Sirikit Centre for Treatment of Cancer and Queen Sirikit

2009. Red Cross.

| 2964 | **940** | 3b. multicoloured | 75 | 45 |

941 Krom Luang Wongsa Dhiraj Snid

2009. Birth Bicentenary (2008) of Krom Luang Wongsa Dhiraj Snid (scholar, medical practitioner and poet).

| 2965 | **941** | 3b. multicoloured | 75 | 45 |

941a

941b

2009. Telecommunications. Nos. 1942 and 1943 surch as T **941a** (2965a) or **941b** (2965b)

| 2965a | 10b. on 6b. multicoloured (1942) | 10 | 10 |
| 2965b | 50b. on 9b. multicoloured (1943) | 10 | 10 |

942 Ta Muean Sanctuary

2009. Heritage Conservation Day. Stone Sanctuaries. Multicoloured.

2966	3b. Type **942**	75	45
2967	3b. Ta Muean Thom	75	45
2968	3b. Ta Muean Tot	75	45
2969	3b. Sadok kok Thom	75	45

MS2970 125×175 mm. Nos. 2966/9. Sold at 20b. 4·00 3·75

943 Gold Brocade Hat

2009. Royal Headgear. Multicoloured.

| 2971 | 5b. Type **943** | 90 | 60 |

2972	5b. Felt hat with feather	90	60
2973	5b. Battle helmet	90	60
2974	5b. Diamond covered hat	90	60

MS2975 101×129 mm. Nos. 2971/4.
Sold at 25b.   4·50   4·25

Nos. 2976/89 and Types **944/6** are vacant.

944 Dhammekka Stupa and Buddha teaching Disciples

2009. Visakhapuja Day
2976   **944**   3b. multicoloured   75   45

945 Ganesa (Ganesha)

2009. Hindu Gods. Multicoloured.

2977	5b. Type **945**	90	60
2978	5b. Brahma	90	60
2979	5b. Narayana	90	60
2980	5b. Siva	90	60

MS2981 150×105 mm. Nos. 2977/80
(Sold at 25b.)   4·00   3·75

946 *Cattleya* Queen Sirikit

2009. Orchids. Multicoloured.

2982	3b. Type **946**	55	45
2983	3b. *Paphiopedilum* Princess Sangwan	55	45
2984	3b. *Sirindhornia pulchella*	55	45
2985	3b. *Phalaenopsis* Princess Chulabhorn	55	45
2986	3b. *Dendrobium* Pink Nagarindra	55	45
2987	3b. *Ascocendo Sukontharat*	55	45
2988	3b. *Dendrobium* Soamsawal	55	45

MS2989 116×140 mm. Nos. 2982/8.
(Sold at 30b.)   13·00   12·50

947 Ten Krathop Sark, Thailand Folk Dance

2009. 60th Anniv of Thailand–Philippines Diplomatic Relations. Multicoloured.

2990	3b. Type **947**	55	45
2991	3b. Tinikling, Philippine Folk Dance	55	45

948 University Building and Pridi Banomyong (founder) (statue)

2009. 75th Anniv of Thammasat University.
2992   **948**   3b. multicoloured   75   45

949 Gods and Demons

2009. Traditional Festivals. Ubon Ratchaburi Candle Procession Festival. Multicoloured.

2993	3b. Type **949**	90	75
2994	3b. Hand	90	75
2995	3b. Riders on mythical beasts	90	75
2996	3b. Buddha and acolytes	90	75

MS2997 145×110 mm. Nos. 2993/6.
Sold at 20b.   5·25   5·00

950 Early Vehicles and Aircraft

2009. National Communications Day.
2998   **950**   3b. multicoloured   75   45

951 Puppetry

2009. THAIPEX '09, Thailand Philatelic Exhibition 2009. Multicoloured. Self-adhesive.

2999	25b. Type **951**	4·50	3·75
3000	25b. Puppets, puppeteers and stylized temple	4·50	3·75

2009. Local Identity. Sheet 254×126 mm containing square designs as T **903** showing provincial seals. Multicoloured.

MS3001 3b.×10, Phuket; Maha Sarakham; Mukdahan; Mae Hong Son; Yasothon; Yala; Roi Et; Ranong; Rayong; Ratchaburi   5·50   5·25

952 Guan Yin, Goddess of Mercy

2009. Stamp Day.
3002   9b. Type **952**   1·70   1·40

MS3003 85×120 mm. As Type **952**.
Sold at 15b.   2·75   2·50

953 Symbols of Communication

2009. Fifth Anniv of National Telecommunications Commission.
3004   **953**   3b. multicoloured   75   45

954 Four-wheeled Dog Cart

2009. Royal Carriages. Multicoloured.

3005	3b. Type **954**	55	45
3006	3b. C-Spring phaeton	55	45
3007	3b. State coach	55	45
3008	3b. Postillion landau	55	45

MS3009 101×111 mm. Nos. 3005/8.
Sold at 20b.   3·75   3·50

955 Kettle with Lid (Bai Thet)

2009. International Letter Writing Week. Golden Nielloware. Multicoloured.

3010	3b. Type **955**	55	45
3011	3b. Decanter with lid (Bai Thet)	55	45
3012	3b. Water bowl and ladle (Bai Thet)	55	45
3013	3b. Bowl and lid with lotus petal motif (Thepanom)	55	45

MS3014 110×145 mm. Nos. 3010/13.
Sold at 20b.   3·75   3·50

956 *Drosera peltata*

2009. New Year, 2010. Flowers. Multicoloured.

3015	3b. Type **956**	55	45
3016	3b. *Sonerila griffithii*	55	45
3017	3b. *Cyanotis arachnoidea*	55	45
3018	3b. *Caulokaempferia saxicola*	55	45

MS3019 99×85 mm Nos. 3015/18 (sold at 15b.)   2·75   2·50

957 Princess Bejaratana Ratsuda

2009. 84th Birth Anniv of Princess Bejaratana Ratsuda
3020   **957**   3b. multicoloured   75   60

958 Assisting Fallen Comrade (statue)

2009. 110th Anniv of Army Medical Department (RTA). Multicoloured.

3021	3b. Type **958**	55	45
3022	3b. Medical corps soldier carrying kit (cartoon) and medical helicopter	55	45
3023	3b. Assisting fallen comrade (cartoon) and operating theatre	55	45
3024	3b. Royal Thai Army Medical Department building	55	45

MS3024a 126×89 mm. Nos. 3021/4 (sold at 100b.)   28·00   4·50

959 THEOS and Earth from Space

2009. Thailand Earth Observation Systems Satellite (THEOS)
3025   **959**   3b. multicoloured   75   45

960 King Bhumibol Adulyadej and WIPO Award

2009. 82nd Birth Anniv of King Bhumibol Adulyadej
3026   **960**   9b. multicoloured   1·70   1·40

961 Miss Geneveve Caufield (founder of first school for the blind) and Students

2009. Thai Blind Education
3026a   **961**   3b. multicoloured   75   60

962 Tiger

2010. New Year. Year of the Tiger
3027   **962**   3b. multicoloured   75   60

963 Figures and Houses

2010. Population and Housing Census 2010
3028   **963**   3b. multicoloured   75   60

964 Phra Sang as Child and Birds

2010. National Children's Day 2010. *Sang Thong* (dramatic verse). Multicoloured.

3029	3b. Type **964**	75	60
3030	3b. Chao Ngo (Phra Sang diguised as ugly ogre) and Nang Rotchana	75	60
3031	3b. Phra Sang removing ogrecostume to reveal his true body	75	60
3032	3b. Phra Sang playing polo	75	60

965 Euah Suntornsanan

2010. Birth Centenary of Euah Suntornsanan (founder of Suntaraporn Orchestra, composer and musician)
3033   **965**   3b. multicoloured   75   60

966 Heart

2010. Greetings Stamps. Multicoloured.

(a) Ordinary gum

3034	3b. Type **966**	75	60
3035	3b. Balloons	75	60
3036	3b. Cake with three candles	75	60
3037	3b. Moon and stars as smiley face	75	60
3038	3b. Flowers	75	60
3039	3b. Child praying	75	60

(b) Self-adhesive

3040	3b. As Type **966**	75	60
3041	3b. Balloons	75	60
3042	3b. Cake with three candles	75	60
3043	3b. Moon and stars as smiley face	75	60
3044	3b. Flowers	75	60
3045	3b. Child praying	75	60

MS3045a 175×75 mm. Nos. 3040/5 (sold at 25b. in a plastic folder)   5·50   5·25

967 Red Rose

2010. Rose

3046	**967**	5b. multicoloured	90	75
MS3046a 120×160 mm. 5b. As Type				
967 (sold at 14b.)			5·50	5·25

968 Fu

2010. Chinese Gods. Fu (happiness) Lu (property) Shou (good health and long life). Multicoloured.

3047	5b. Type **968**	90	75
3048	5b. Lu	90	75
3049	5b. Shou	90	75
MS3049a 110×144 mm. Nos. 3047/9			
(sold at 24b.)		5·00	4·75

969 Paradise

2010. Bangkok 2010 International Stamp Exhibition. Fantasy World. Multicoloured.

3050	5b. Type **969**	90	75
3051	5b. Chinese Zodiac as tree of life enclosing people and surrounded by water	90	75
3052	5b. Garuda fighting a naga	90	75
3053	5b. Brahma riding Erawan (many-headed elephant)	90	75
MS3054 110×145 mm. Nos. 3050/3			
(sold at 28b.)		5·50	5·25

970 Chulalongkorn Hospital

2010. Red Cross

3055	**970**	3b. multicoloured	75	60

2010. Young Postman. As Type **888a**

3056	3b. Postboy carrying parcel	75	60

971 Jalimagalasana Residence

2010. Heritage Conservation Day. Royal Palaces. Multicoloured.

3057	3b. Type **971**	75	60
3058	3b. Phiman Chakri Hall, Phyat-hai Palace	75	60
3059	3b. Phra Ram Ratchaniwet Palace	75	60
3060	3b. Main Building, Srapathum Palace	75	60

972 King Rama I

2010. Death Bicentenary of King Rama I (Buddhayodfah Chulalok)

3061	**972**	3b. multicoloured	75	60

973 King Bhumibol Adulyadej and Queen Sirikit during Wedding Ceremony

2010. 60th Wedding Anniv of King Bhumibol Adulyadej and Queen Sirikit. Multicoloured.

3062	15b. Type **973**	3·50	3·00
3063	15b. King Bhumibol Adulyadej and Queen Sirikit in later life	3·50	3·00
MS3064 150×130 mm. Nos. 3062/3			
(Sold for 60b.)		13·00	12·50

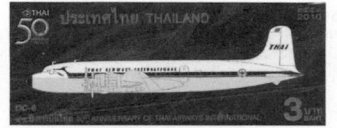

974 Douglas DC-6 Airliner

2010. 50th Anniv of Thai Airways International. Multicoloured.

3065	3b. Type **974**	90	75
3066	3b. McDonnell Douglas DC-10	90	75
3067	3b. Boeing 747-400	90	75
3068	3b. Airbus A340-600	90	75
MS3069 110×145 mm. Nos. 3065/8			
(sold for 22b.)		1·40	1·40

No. 3070 is vacant.

975 King Bhumibol Adulyadej

2010. 60th Anniv of Coronation

3071	**975**	9b. multicoloured	1·70	1·40

976 Pari Nirvana Shrine and Buddha Reclining entering Pari Nirvana

2010. Visakhapuja Day. Multicoloured.

3072	3b. Type **976**	75	60
MS3073 129×182 mm. 3b.×4, As Type			
892; As Type **917**; As Type **944**; As			
Type **976**;		6·50	6·25

977 Dragon Boat

2010. 50th Anniv of Tourism Authority of Thailand. Multicoloured.

3074	3b. Type **977**	75	60
3075	3b. Prang of Wat Arun at night, Bangkok	75	60
3076	3b. Canoeing	75	60
3077	3b. Elephants and riders crossing river	75	60

978 Ballot Box

2010. Office of Election Commission of Thailand

3078	**978**	3b. multicoloured	75	60

979

2010. 70th Anniversary of General Post Office Building. Multicoloured.

3079	3b. Type **979**	90	75
3080	3b. Stucco Post Office seal and statue of King Rama I	90	75
3081	5b. Building façade (58×24 mm)	90	75

980 King Nang Klao

2010. King Nang Klao Chao Youhua (Rama III), Father of Thai Trade

3082	**980**	3b. multicoloured	75	60

2010. Local Identity. Multicoloured.

MS3083 3b.×10, Lop Buri; Lampang;			
Lamphun; Loei; Si Sa Ket; Sakon			
Nakhon; Songkhla; Satun; Samut			
Prakan; Samut Songkhram		8·25	8·00

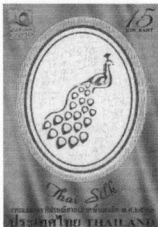

981 Peacock

2010. Bangkok 2010 International Stamp Exhibition (2nd issue). Thai Silk. Multicoloured, main colour given.

3084	**981**	15b. multicoloured	2·75	2·30
3085	**981**	15b. multicoloured (green)	2·75	2·30
3086	**981**	25b. multicoloured (gold and yellow)	4·50	3·75
3087	**981**	25b. multicoloured (silver)	4·50	3·75
MS3088 105×127 mm. As Type **981**			10·00	9·75

982 Prince Prisdang and UPU Emblem

2010. National Communications Day, 2010

3089	**982**	3b. multicoloured	75	60

983 *Rhynchostylis gigantean*

2010. Orchids. *Rhynchostylis gigantea.* Multicoloured.

3090	3b. Type **983**	75	60
3091	3b. Orange	75	60
3092	3b. White	75	60
3093	3b. Burgundy	75	60
MS3094 110×150 mm. Nos. 3090/3			
(sold for 20b.)		6·50	6·25

984 Thai Literature Conversation Contest

2010. Thai Literature Heritage. Winning Design in Painting Competition

3095	**984**	3b. multicoloured	75	60

985 National Flag

2010. National Identity. Multicoloured.

3096	3b. Type **985**	75	60
3097	3b. Cassia flowers	75	60

986 Queen Sri Savarindira at Royal Wedding Ceremony, Srapathum Palace, pouring water from conch shell on King Bhumibol Adulyadej's hands

2010. 150th Birth Anniv of Her Majesty Queen Sri Savarindira, Queen Grandmother. Multicoloured.

MS3102 125×156 mm. 3b.×4, Queen			
Sri Savarindira (vert); Prince Mahidol			
of Songkhla, Prince Father, and Prin-			
cess Sri Nagarindra, Princess Mother			
(vert); Type **986**; King Bhumibol			
Adulyadej and Queen Sirikit signing			
marriage certificate at Phra Tamnak			
Yai, Srapathum Palace		5·25	5·00

987 Obverse of First Hand-hammered Coin and Sitthikarn Mint (first Mint in Thailand)

2010. 150th Anniv of Royal Thai Mint. Multicoloured.

3103	5b. Type **987**	1·70	1·40
3104	5b. Reverse of first coin and Royal Thai Mint (present mint)	1·70	1·40
MS3105 145×115 mm. Nos. 3103/4			
(sold for 20b.)		6·50	6·25

988 Children

2010. 25th Anniv of National Youth Day. Participation, Development and Peace

3106	**988**	3b. multicoloured	75	60

989 Graphic

2010. Graphic Stamps

3107	**989**	3b. multicoloured	75	60
3108	**989**	3b. multicoloured (blue)	75	60
3109	**989**	3b. multicoloured (green)	75	60

990 Wind-up Animals

2010. International Letter Writing Week. Zinc Toys. Multicoloured.

3110	3b. Type **990**	75	60
3111	3b. Chinese rattle drums	75	60
3112	3b. Pistol	75	60
3113	3b. Boats	75	60
3114	3b. Boy riding tricycle	75	60
3115	3b. Spinning tops	75	60
MS3116 100×105 mm. Nos. 3110/12 (sold for 20b.)		4·50	4·25
MS3117 100×105 mm. Nos. 3113/15 (sold for 20b.)		4·50	4·25

991 Graph and Chest

2010. 120th Anniv of Comptroller-General's Department

3118	**991**	3b. multicoloured	75	60

992 Guan Yi

2010. Guan Yin (Buddhist goddess)

3119	**992**	9b. multicoloured	2·20	1·90
MS3120 87×125 mm. As Type **992** (sold for 15b.)			7·25	7·00

993 King Rama IX

2010. King Rama IX

3121	**993**	1b. blue	45	40
3122	**993**	2b. brown-red	75	60
3123	**993**	3b. green	1·80	1·50
3124	**993**	5b. brown	90	75
3125	**993**	6b. dull violet	1·70	1·40
3126	**993**	7b. magenta	2·20	1·90
3127	**993**	9b. yellow	2·40	2·00
3128	**993**	10b. bright orange and black	2·75	2·30
3129	**993**	12b. indigo and turquoise-blue	3·00	2·50
3130	**993**	15b. brown-olive and olive-yellow	3·50	3·00
3131	**993**	50b. lilac and grey-green (10.11.10)	9·25	6·25
3132	**993**	100b. apple-green and grey-green (10.11.10)	18·00	12·50
3133	**993**	200b. rose-carmine and agate (10.11.10)	37·00	23·00
3134	**993**	500b. orange and agate (25×29 mm) (10.11.10)	75·00	46·00

994 King Chulalongkorn

2010. Death Centenary of King Chulalongkorn

3135	**994**	9b. multicoloured	1·70	1·40

995 Vajiravudh College

2010. Centenary of of Vajiravudh College

3136	**995**	3b. multicoloured	75	60

996 Fireworks

2010. New Year. Fireworks. Multicoloured.

3137	3b. Type **996**	75	60
3138	3b. Twin burst gold firework	75	60
3139	3b. Large burst orange and yellow centred firework	75	60
3140	3b. Four smaller multicoloured bursts	75	60
MS3141 142×115 mm. Nos. 3137/40. Sold at 20b.		5·50	5·25

998 Rabbit

2011. Chinese New Year. Year of the Rabbit

3142	**998**	3b. multicoloured	75	60

999 Khun Phaen

2011. National Children's Day 2011. *Khun Chang-Khun Phaen.* Multicoloured.

3143	3b. Type **999**	75	60
3144	3b. Khun Chang	75	60
3145	3b. Kumara Thong and Hong Prai	75	60
3146	3b. Nang Phimpilailai	75	60

1000 Tomato

2011. Vegetables. Multicoloured.

3147	3b. Type **1000**	75	60
3148	3b. Lime	75	60
3149	3b. Bottle gourd	75	60
3150	3b. Pumpkin	75	60

1001 Li Tieguai

2011. The Eight Immortals. Multicoloured.

3151	3b. Type **1001**	75	60
3152	3b. Han Zhongli,	75	60
3153	3b. Lu Dongbin	75	60

3154	3b. Zhang Guo Lao	75	60
3155	3b. Lan Caihe	75	60
3156	3b. He Xiangu	75	60
3157	3b. Han Xiang Zi	75	60
3158	3b. Cao Guojiu	75	60
MS3159 90×200 mm. Nos. 3151/8 (sold for 40b.)		6·50	6·25

1002 Charoen Krung Road

2012. 150th Anniv of Charoen Krung Road (first road built with Western technology)

3160	**1002**	3b. multicoloured	75	60

1003 Heart of Roses

2011. Valetine's Day. Symbols of Love. Multicoloured.

3161	5b. Type **1003**	1·40	1·20
3162	5b. Graphic heart of hearts	75	60

1004 King Rama IX (King Bhumibol Adulyadej)

2011. 83rd Birth Anniv of King Bhumibol Adulyadej

3162a	**1004**	9b. multicoloured	1·80	1·50

1005 Suankularb Building

2011. Centenary of Suankularb Long Building (longest school building in Thailand)

3163	**1005**	3b. multicoloured	75	60

1006 Department Building

2011. Centenary of Fine Arts Department

3164	**1006**	3b. multicoloured	75	60

1007 Princess Maha Chakri Sirindhorn (Vice-President of Thai Red Cross Society)

2011. Red Cross

3165	**1007**	3b. multicoloured	75	60

1008 Uma-mahesvara Lintel

2011. Heritage Conservation Day. Muang Tam Religious Sanctuary. Multicoloured.

3166	3b. Type **1008**	75	60
3167	3b. Five towers	75	60
3168	3b. Entrance	75	60
3169	3b. Pond	75	60
MS3170 200×117 mm. Nos. 3166/9 (sold at 20b.)		6·50	6·25

1009 M.R. Kukrit Pramoj (during his term as Prime Minister of Thailand)

2011. Birth Centenary of Momrajawongse (M.R.) Kukrit Pramoj (journalist, educationalist, supporter of Thai art and culture, founder of Social Action Party and 13th prime minister). Multicoloured.

3171	3b. Type **1009**	75	60
3172	3b. Shaking hands with Mao Zedong, Chairman of the People's Republic of China (horiz)	75	60
3173	3b. Relaxing with his favourite dogs (horiz)	75	60
3174	3b. As younger man wearing traditional Khon costume	75	60

1010 Lao Traditional Dress

2011. 60th Anniversary of Thailand Lao PDR Diplomatic Relations. Multicoloured.

3175	3b. Type **1010**	75	60
3176	3b. Woman wearing Thai traditional dress	75	60
3177	3b. Cassia (golden shower) flowers (Thailand)	75	60
3178	3b. Plumeria (frangipani) flowers (Laos)	75	60

No. 3179 is vacant.

2011. Young Postman. As Type **888a**

(a) Ordinary gum. Granite paper

3180	3b. Postboy, utensils and food	75	60

(b) Booklet stamp. Self-adhesive

3181	3b. As No. 3180	75	60

Nos. 3182/91 are vacant.

1012 Pridi Banomyong being Awarded the Medal of Freedom (Gold Palm) at Ceremony in USA

2011. 111th Birth Anniv of Pridi Banomyong (founder of University of Moral and Political Sciences (Thammasat University) and Prime Minister March-August 1946). Multicoloured.

3192	3b. Type **1012**	75	60
3193	3b. As Prime Minister of Thailand, with Thammasat University in the background	75	60

1013 Panyananda Bhikkhu

2011. Birth Centenary of Panyananda Bhikkhu (monk and abbot of Chonpratan Rungsarit Temple). Multicoloured.

3194	3b. Type **1013**	75	60
3195	3b. Holding walking stick with temple in background	75	60
3196	3b. With statue of himself	75	60
3197	3b. At microphone	75	60

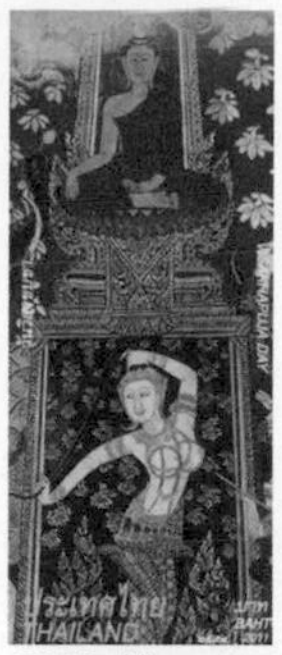

1014 Buddha and Mother Earth

2011. Visakhapuja Day

3198	**1014** 3b. multicoloured	75	60
MS3199	115×98 mm. As Type **1014**	3·75	3·50

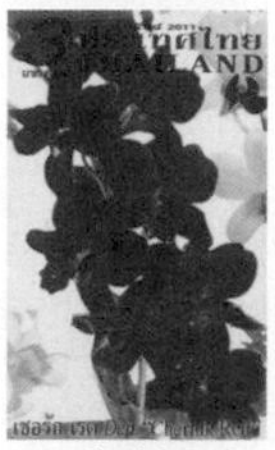

1015 Cherluk Red

2011. Orchids. *Dendrobium*. Multicoloured.

3200	3b. Type **1015**	75	60
3201	3b. Lai Sirin (pink)	75	60
3202	3b. Suree Peach (peach)	75	60
3203	3b. Cheetah (cream with burgandy lip)	75	60
MS3204	180×113 mm. Nos. 3200/3 (sold for 20b.)	4·50	4·25

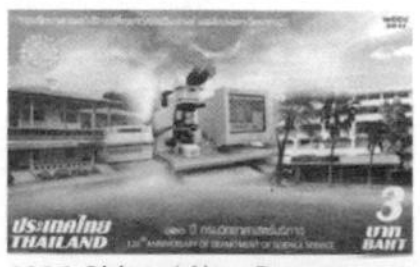

1016 Old and New Department of Science Service Building, Scientific Equipment and Department Emblem

2011. 120th Anniv of Department of Science Service

3205	**1016** 3b. multicoloured	75	60

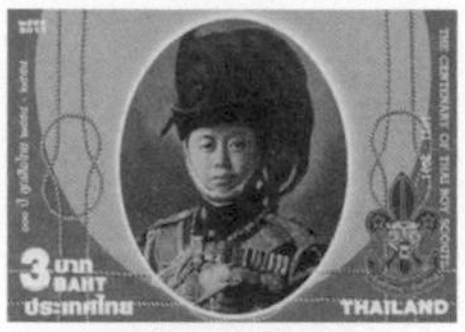

1017 King Rama VI (founder)

2011. Centenary of Thai Boy Scouts

3206	**1017** 3b. multicoloured	75	60

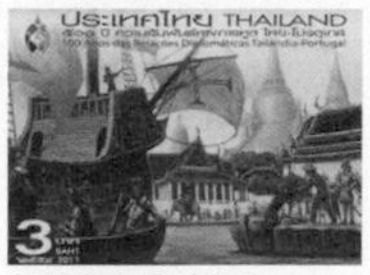

1018 Arrival of *Nau* (Portuguese ship) at Ayutthaya (left)

2011. 500th Anniv of Thailand - Portugal Diplomatic Relations. Multicoloured.

3207	3b. Type **1018**	75	60
3208	3b. Arrival of Nau (Portuguese ship) at Ayutthaya (right)	75	60
3209	3b. Portuguese ship and Thai landfall (left)	75	60
3210	3b. Portuguese ship and Thai landfall (right)	75	60

Nos. 3207/8 and 3209/10 were printed, *se-tenant*, in horizontal pairs forming composite designs.

2011. Local Identity. Multicoloured.

MS3211	3b.×10, Samut Sakhon; Sa Kaeo; Saraburi; Sing Buri; Sukhothai; Suphan Buri; Surat Thani; Surin; Nong Khai; Nong Bua Lam Phu	8·25	8·00

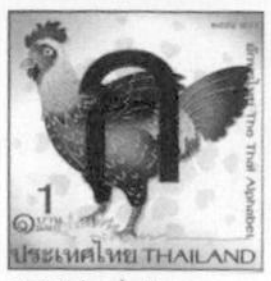

1019 ko kai (chicken)

2011. National Thai Language Day. The Thai Alphabet. Multicoloured.

3212	1b. Type **1019**	35	30
3213	1b. kho khai (egg)	35	30
3214	1b. kho khuat (bottle)	35	30
3215	1b. kho khwai (water buffalo)	35	30
3216	1b. kho khon (person)	35	30
3217	1b. kho ra-khang (bell)	35	30
3218	1b. ngo ngu (snake)	35	30
3219	1b. cho chan (plate)	35	30
3220	1b. cho ching (cymbals)	35	30
3221	1b. cho chang (elephant)	35	30
3222	1b. so so (chain)	35	30
3223	1b. cho choe (tree)	35	30
3224	1b. yo ying (woman)	35	30
3225	1b. yo ying (woman)	35	30
3226	1b. to pa-tak (javelin)	35	30
3227	1b. tho than (pedestal)	35	30
3228	1b. tho montho (Mandodari, character from Ramayana)	35	30
3229	1b. tho phu-thao (elder)	35	30
3230	1b. no nen (samanera, novice monk)	35	30
3231	1b. do dek (child)	35	30
3232	1b. to tao (turtle)	35	30
3233	1b. tho thung (sack)	35	30
3234	1b. tho thahan (soldier)	35	30
3235	1b. tho thong (flag)	35	30
3236	1b. no nu (mouse)	35	30
3237	1b. bo baimai (leaf)	35	30
3238	1b. po pla (fish)	35	30
3239	1b. pho phueng (bee)	35	30
3240	1b. fo fa (lid)	35	30
3241	1b. pho phan (tray)	35	30
3242	1b. fo fan (teeth)	35	30
3243	1b. pho sam-phao (sailboat)	35	30
3244	1b. mo ma (horse)	35	30
3245	1b. yo yak (yaksha)	35	30
3246	1b. ro ruea (boat)	35	30
3247	1b. lo ling (monkey)	35	30
3248	1b. wo waen (ring)	35	30
3249	1b. so sala (pavilion)	35	30
3250	1b. so rue-si (hermit)	35	30
3251	1b. so suea (tiger)	35	30
3252	1b. ho hip (chest)	35	30
3253	1b. lo chu-la (kite)	35	30
3254	1b. o ang (basin)	35	30
3255	1b. ho nok-huk (owl)	35	30

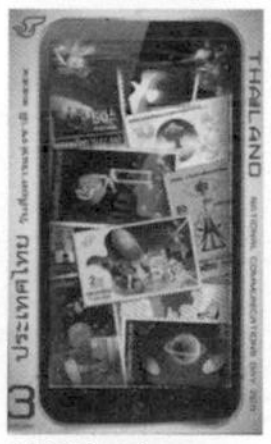

1020 Previous National Communications Day Stamps showing Symbols of Communications

2011. National Communications Day, 2011

3256	**1020** 3b. multicoloured	75	60

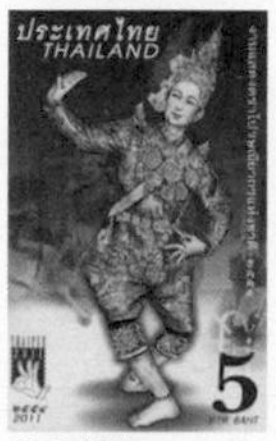

1021 Male Performer

2011. THAIPEX '11, Thailand Philatelic Exhibition 2011. Likay Folk Performers. Multicoloured.

3257	5b. Type **1021**	1·50	1·20
3258	5b. Male performer holding sword	1·50	1·20
3259	5b. Female performer wearing orange with arms crossed	1·50	1·20
3260	5b. Female performer wearing deep pink	1·50	1·20
MS3261	110×114 mm. Nos. 3257/60. Perf and imperf	7·25	7·00

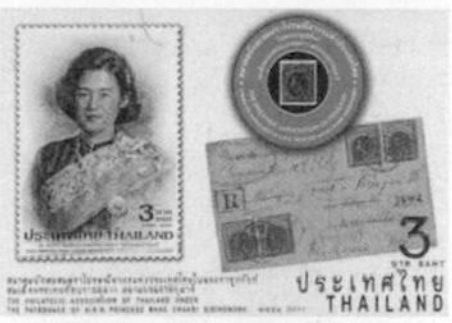

1022 2005 3b. Stamp (As Type **918**), Emblem and Early Envelope

2011. Philatelists Association of Thailand

3262	**1022** 3b. multicoloured	1·30	1·10

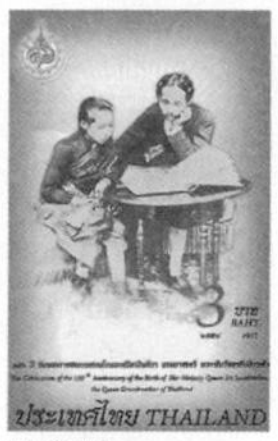

1023 King Chulalongkorn, King Rama V. and Her Majesty Queen Savang Vadhana

2011. 150th Birth Anniv of Her Majesty Queen Sri Savarindira, Queen Grandmother (2nd issue). Multicoloured.

MS3267	125×156 mm. 3b.×4, Type **1023**; Queen Savang Vadhana and Crown Prince Maha Vajirunhis; Queen Savang Vadhana, Prince Mahitala Dhibesra Adulyadej Vikrom, the Prince Father and Princess Valaya Alongkorn, Princess of Bejaburi; Queen Savang Vadhana, King Ananda Mahidol (King Rama VIII), King Bhumibol Adulyadej (King Rama IX), Princess Galyani Vadhana and Prince Rangsit Prayurasakdi, Prince of Jainad	3·00	2·50

Nos. 3263/6 are left for single stamps not yet received

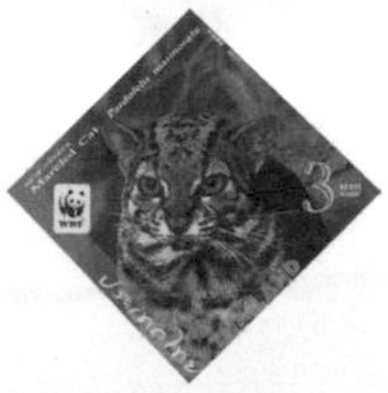

1024 *Pardofelis marmorata* (marbled cat)

2011. Endangered Species. Wild Cats. Multicoloured.

3268	5b. Type **1024**	90	75
3269	5b. *Pardofelis temminckii* (Asiatic golden cat)	90	75
3270	5b. *Prionailurus bengalsensis* (leopard cat)	90	75
3271	5b. *Prionailurus planiceps* (flat-headed cat)	90	75
MS3272	113×123 mm. Nos. 3268/711 (sold at 20b.)	5·50	4·75

OFFICIAL STAMPS

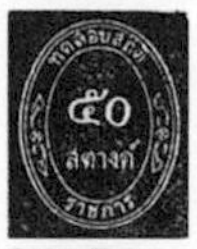

O133 (Trans "For Government Service Statistical Research")

1963

O495	**O133**	10s. red and pink	60	60
O496	**O133**	20s. red and green	70	70
O500	**O133**	20s. green	70	70
O497	**O133**	25s. red and blue	80	80
O501	**O133**	25s. blue	80	80
O502	**O133**	50s. red	1·60	1·60
O498	**O133**	1b. red and grey	1·90	1·90
O503	**O133**	1b. grey	1·90	1·90
O499	**O133**	2b. red and bronze	3·25	3·25
O504	**O133**	2b. bistre	3·75	3·75

The above were used compulsorily by Government Departments between 1 October 1963 and 31 January 1964, to determine the amount of mail sent out by the different departments for the purpose of charging them in the future. They were postmarked in the usual way.

Pt. 16

THESSALY

Special stamps issued during the Turkish occupation in the Graeco-Turkish War of 1898.

40 paras = 1 piastre.

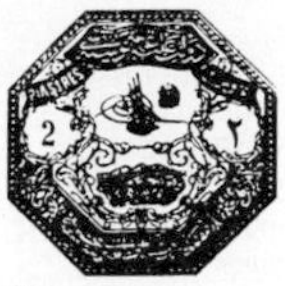

20

1898

M162	**20**	10pa. green	9·50	9·25
M163	**20**	20pa. red	9·50	9·25
M164	**20**	1pi. blue	9·50	9·25
M165	**20**	2pi. orange	9·50	9·25
M166	**20**	5pi. violet	9·50	9·25

Pt. 3

THRACE

A portion of Greece to the N. of the Aegean Sea for which stamps were issued by the Allies in 1919 and by the Greek Government in 1920. Now uses Greek stamps.

1919. 100 stotinki = 1 leva.
1920. 100 lepta = 1 drachma.

1920. Stamps of Bulgaria optd **THRACE INTERALLIEE** in two lines.

28	**49**	1s. black	35	30
29	**49**	2s. grey	35	30
30	**50**	5s. green	35	30
31	**50**	10s. red	35	30
32	**50**	15s. violet	35	30
33	-	25s. black and blue (No. 165)	35	30
34	-	1l. brown (No. 168)	5·50	5·25
35	-	2l. brown (No. 191)	8·75	8·50
36	-	3l. red (No. 192)	13·00	13·00

1920. Stamps of Bulgaria optd **THRACE INTERALLIEE** in one line.

40	**49**	1s. black	3·25	2·10
41	**49**	2s. grey	3·25	2·10
42	**50**	5s. green	1·10	55
43	**50**	10s. red	1·10	55
44	**50**	15s. violet	1·10	55
45	-	25s. black and blue (No. 165)	1·10	55

1920. Stamps of Bulgaria optd **THRACE Interalliee** in two lines vertically.

46	**50**	5s. green	35	30
47	**50**	10s. red	35	30
48	**50**	15s. violet	35	30
49	**50**	50s. brown	1·70	1·60

1920. Stamps of Bulgaria optd **THRACE OCCIDENTALE**.

50	5s. green	35	30
51	10s. red	35	30
52	15s. violet	35	30
53	25s. blue	35	30
54	30s. brown (imperf)	1·70	1·60
55	50s. brown	35	30

Διοίκησις
Δυτικῆς
Θράκης
(8)

1920. 1911 stamps of Greece optd with T **8**.

69	**29**	1l. green	35	85
70	**30**	2l. red	35	55
71	**29**	3l. red	35	55
72	**31**	5l. green	35	55
73	**29**	10l. red	55	1·10
74	**30**	15l. blue	35	55
75	**30**	25l. blue	55	1·10
76	**31**	30l. red	33·00	43·00
77	**30**	40l. blue	1·70	2·10
78	**31**	50l. purple	8·75	10·50
79	**32**	1d. blue	8·75	10·50
80	**32**	2d. red	33·00	37·00
65	**32**	3d. red	65·00	48·00
66	**32**	5d. blue	33·00	27·00
67	**32**	10d. blue	22·00	21·00
68	-	25d. blue (No. 212)	75·00	55·00

The opt on the 25d. is in capital letters.

1920. 1916 stamps of Greece, with opt Greece T 38, optd with T **8**.

81	**29**	1l. green (No. 269)	5·50	5·25
82	**30**	2l. red	35	55
83	**29**	10l. red	55	85
84	**30**	20l. purple	55	85
85	**31**	30l. red	55	85
86	**32**	2d. red	40·00	55·00
87	**32**	3d. red	55·00	32·00

88	32	5d. blue	46·00	65·00
89	32	10d. blue	33·00	60·00

Διοίκησις Θράκης (10)

Ὑπάτη Ἀρμοστεία Θράκης 5 Λεπτά 5 (11)

1920. Issue for E. Thrace. 1911 stamps of Greece optd with T **10**.

93	29	1l. green	35	1·10
94	30	2l. red	35	55
95	29	3l. red	35	55
96	31	5l. green	35	55
97	29	10l. red	55	85
98	30	20l. lilac	55	85
99	30	25l. blue	1·10	1·60
100	30	40l. blue	1·70	3·25
101	31	50l. purple	1·70	2·10
102	32	1d. blue	17·00	21·00
103	32	2d. red	33·00	37·00
92	-	25d. blue (No. 212)	65·00	95·00

1920. 1916 stamps of Greece with opt T **38** of Greece, optd with T **10**.

104	30	2l. red (No. 270)	35	55
105	31	5l. green	8·75	16·00
106	30	20l. purple	35	55
107	31	30l. red	35	55
108	32	3d. red	14·50	21·00
109	32	5d. blue	28·00	43·00
110	32	10d. blue	44·00	65·00

1920. Occupation of Adrianople. Stamps of Turkey surch as T **11**.

111	72	1l. on 5pa. orange	55	55
112	-	5l. on 3pi. blue (No. 965)	55	55
113	-	20l. on 1pi. grn (No. 964)	75	75
114	69	25l. on 5pi. on 2pa. blue	75	75
115	78	50l. on 5pi. black & grn	5·50	5·25
116	74	1d. on 20pa. red	2·75	2·10
117	30	2d. on 10pa. on 2pa. olive	2·75	2·75
118	85	3d. on 1pi. blue	13·00	13·00
119	31	5d. on 20pa. red	11·00	10·50

POSTAGE DUE STAMPS

1919. Postage Due stamps of Bulgaria optd **THRACE INTERALLIEE**. Perf.

D37	D37	5s. green	55	55
D38	D37	10s. violet	1·10	1·10
D39	D37	50s. blue	3·25	2·10

1920. Postage Due stamps of Bulgaria optd **THRACE OCCIDENTALE**. Imperf or perf (10s.).

D56	5s. green	35	30
D57	10s. violet	2·20	2·10
D58	20s. orange	55	55
D59	50s. blue	1·70	1·60

Pt. 7

THURN AND TAXIS

The Counts of Thurn and Taxis had a postal monopoly in parts of Germany and issued special stamps.

N. District. 30 silbergroschen = 1 thaler.
S. District. 60 kreuzer = 1 gulden.

NORTHERN DISTRICT

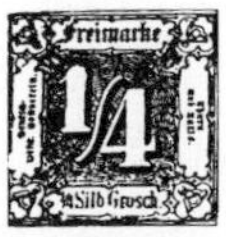

1

1852. Imperf.

1	1	¼sgr. black on brown	£225	41·00
2	1	⅓sgr. black on pink	£100	£180
4	1	½sgr. black on green	£600	35·00
5	1	1sgr. black on blue	£1100	£110
8	1	2sgr. black on pink	£700	23·00
11	1	3sgr. black on yellow	£850	60·00

1859. Imperf.

12	¼sgr. red	55·00	55·00
20	¼sgr. black	28·00	60·00
21	⅓sgr. green	39·00	£200
13	½sgr. green	£250	75·00
23	½sgr. orange	85·00	35·00
14	1sgr. blue	£250	35·00
25	1sgr. pink	55·00	18·00
15	2sgr. pink	£120	60·00
27	2sgr. blue	50·00	75·00
17	3sgr. red	£120	90·00
29	3sgr. brown	22·00	41·00
18	5sgr. mauve	2·20	£350
19	10sgr. orange	2·20	£700

1865. Rouletted.

31	¼sgr. black	11·00	£600
32	⅓sgr. green	17·00	£350
33	½sgr. yellow	33·00	55·00
34	1sgr. pink	36·00	23·00
35	2sgr. blue	2·20	80·00
36	3sgr. brown	4·00	35·00

SOUTHERN DISTRICT

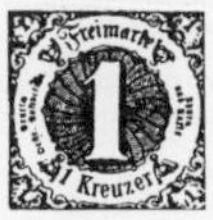

3

1852. Imperf.

51	3	1k. black on green	£200	11·50
53	3	3k. black on blue	£800	41·00
57	3	6k. black on pink	£1000	9·25
58	3	9k. black on yellow	£700	14·00

1859. Imperf.

60	1k. green	20·00	8·25
62	3k. blue	£475	18·00
68	3k. pink	11·00	21·00
63	6k. pink	£475	55·00
70	6k. blue	28·00	35·00
65	9k. yellow	£475	70·00
73	9k. brown	13·50	28·00
66	15k. purple	2·20	£140
67	30k. orange	2·20	£375

1865. Roul.

74	1k. green	19·00	18·00
81	3k. pink	2·20	23·00
76	6k. blue	2·20	29·00
77	9k. brown	4·50	41·00

Pt. 17

TIBET

Former independent state in the Himalayas, now part of China.

Chinese Empire.
12 pies = 1 anna;
16 annas = 1 Indian rupee.

Independent State.
6⅔ trangka = 1 sang.

A. CHINESE POST OFFICES

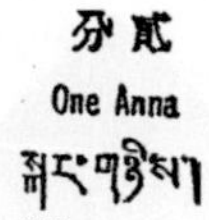

(C1)

1911. Stamps of China of 1898 surch as Type **C1**.

C1	32	3p. on 1c. brown	38·00	30·00
C2	32	½a. on 2c. green	45·00	35·00
C3	32	1a. on 4c. red	50·00	38·00
C4	32	2a. on 7c. red	55·00	40·00
C5	32	2½a. on 10c. blue	60·00	45·00
C6	33	3a. on 16c. green	£275	£160
C7	33	4a. on 20c. red	£180	£140
C8	33	6a. on 30c. red	£275	£180
C9	33	12a. on 50c. green	£900	£400
C10	34	1r. on $1 red and pink	£1800	£1200
C11	34	2r. on $2 red and yellow	£3250	£2750

These stamps were used in Post Offices set up by the Chinese army sent to Tibet in 1910. Following a revolt by the Tibetans these troops were withdrawn during 1912.

B. INDEPENDENT STATE

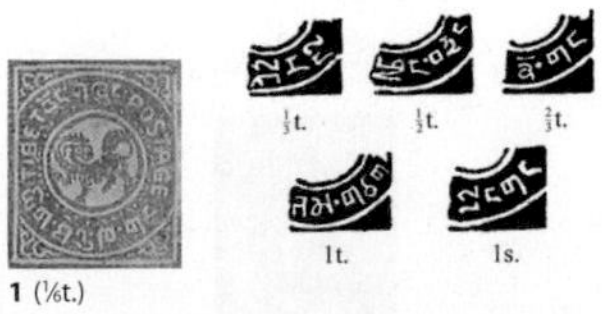

1 (⅙t.)

1912. Imperf.

1A	1	⅙t. green	27·00	20·00
2A	1	⅓t. blue	38·00	48·00
3Ab	1	½t. purple	£110	65·00
4A	1	⅔t. red	42·00	65·00
5A	1	1t. red	40·00	80·00
6A	1	1s. green	£120	£120

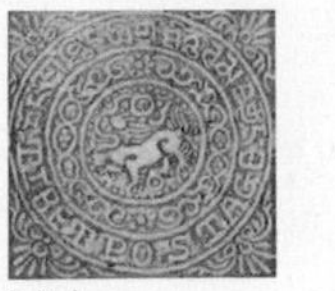

2 (4t.)

1914. Imperf.

7Ab	2	4t. blue	£1900	£1500
8Ab	2	8t. red	£170	£200

In the 8t. the rays from the circles in the corners of the stamp point outwards towards the corner.

3 (1t.) Tibetan Lion ½t. ⅔t.

1933. Perf or imperf.

9Ba	3	½t. yellow to orange	19·00	40·00
10B	3	⅔t. blue	18·00	35·00
11Ba	3	1t. red	20·00	16·00
11Bb	3	1t. orange	16·00	15·00
12Ba	3	2t. red	17·00	15·00
12Bc	3	2t. orange	16·00	16·00
13Bd	3	4t. green	14·00	12·00

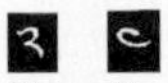

2t. 4t.

Pt. 20

TIERRA DEL FUEGO

An island at the extreme S. S. America. Stamp issued for use on correspondance to the mainland.

Currency is expressed in centigrammes of gold dust.

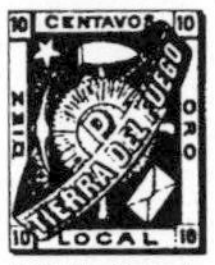

1 Gold-digger's Pick and Hammer

1891

1	1	10c. red	12·00

Pt. 1

TOBAGO

An island in the British West Indies, north-east of Trinidad. From 1896 to 1913 it used the stamps of Trinidad; from 1913 there were combined issues for Trinidad and Tobago.

12 pence = 1 shilling; 20 shillings = 1 pound.

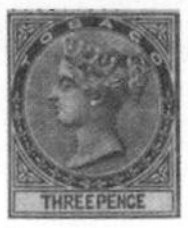

1

1879

1	1	1d. red	£140	£100
2		3d. blue	£140	85·00
3		6d. orange	65·00	80·00
4		1s. green	£400	80·00
5		5s. grey	£900	£800
6		£1 mauve	£4250	

In the above issue only stamps watermarked Crown CC were issued for postal use and our prices are for stamps bearing this watermark. Stamps with watermark Crown CA are fiscals and were never admitted to postal use.

1880. No. 3 divided vertically down the centre and surch with pen and ink.

7	1d. on half of 6d. orange	£5500	£800

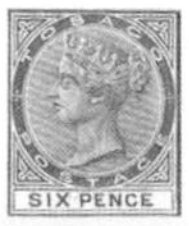

2

1880. "POSTAGE" added in design.

14	2	½d. brown	2·50	19·00
20	2	½d. green	4·50	1·75
21	2	1d. red	7·00	1·75
16*a*	2	2½d. blue	15·00	1·25
10	2	4d. green	£300	38·00
22	2	4d. grey	8·00	4·00
11	2	6d. buff	£400	£120
23	2	6d. brown	2·50	8·00
24	2	1s. yellow	4·00	26·00

1883. Surch in figures and words.

26	½d. on 2½d. blue	10·00	25·00
30	½d. on 4d. grey	29·00	85·00
27	½d. on 6d. buff	3·75	26·00
28	½d. on 6d. brown	£150	£200
29	1d. on 2½d. blue	£110	23·00
31	2½d. on 4d. grey	23·00	10·00
13	2½d. on 6d. buff	£100	£100

1896. Surch **½d POSTAGE**.

33	1	½d. on 4d. lilac and red	£100	55·00

Pt. 7; Pt. 1; Pt. 6; Pt. 14

TOGO

A territory in W. Africa, formerly a German Colony. Divided between France and Great Britain in 1919, the British portion being attached to the Gold Coast for administration and using the stamps of that country. In 1956 the French portion became an autonomous republic within the French Union. Full independence was achieved in April 1960.

100 pfennig = 1 mark.

GERMAN ISSUES

1897. Stamps of Germany optd **TOGO**.

G1	8	3pf. brown	7·25	9·25
G2	8	5pf. green	6·50	3·75
G3	9	10pf. red	7·75	4·25
G4	9	20pf. blue	7·75	18·00
G5	9	25pf. orange	49·00	75·00
G6	9	50pf. brown	49·00	75·00

1900. "Yacht" key-types inscr "TOGO".

G7	N	3pf. brown	1·30	1·60
G21	N	5pf. green	1·60	2·75
G9	N	10pf. red	29·00	2·20
G10	N	20pf. blue	1·30	2·00
G11	N	25pf. black & red on yell	1·30	13·00
G12	N	30pf. black & orge on buff	1·80	13·00
G13	N	40pf. black and red	1·30	13·00
G14	N	50pf. black & pur on buff	1·80	10·00
G15	N	80pf. black & red on pink	3·25	22·00
G16	O	1m. red	4·50	70·00
G17	O	2m. blue	7·25	£110
G18	O	3m. black	9·25	£200
G19	O	5m. red and black	£160	£650

ANGLO-FRENCH ISSUES

BRITISH ISSUES

1914. Nos. 7/21 (German Colonial Types) optd **TOGO** Anglo-French Occupation.

H1		3pf. brown	£130	£100
H2		5pf. green	£130	£100
H3		10pf. red	£130	£100
H17	N	20pf. blue	30·00	12·00
H18	N	25pf. black & red on yell	40·00	32·00
H19	N	30pf. blk & orge on buff	20·00	29·00
H7		40pf. black and red	£225	£250
H8		50pf. black & pur on buff	£12000	£10000
H9		80pf. black & red on rose	£275	£275
H10	O	1m. red	£5000	£2750
H11	O	2m. blue	£12000	£14000
H25	O	3m. black	†	£65000
H26	O	5m. lake and black	†	£65000

1914. Nos. 1/2 surch in words.

H27	N	½d on 3pf. brown	48·00	26·00
H28	N	1d. on 5pf. green	6·00	4·25

1915. Stamps of Gold Coast (King George V) optd **TOGO ANGLO-FRENCH OCCUPATION.**

H47	½d. green	30	2·75
H35	1d. red	30	60
H36	2d. grey	35	1·50
H50	2½d. blue	70	1·50
H51	3d. purple on yellow	6·00	1·25
H52	6d. purple	2·50	2·00
H41	1s. black on green	2·50	11·00
H54	2s. purple and blue on blue	4·50	8·50
H55	2s.6d. black and red on blue	4·50	7·00
H44	5s. green and red on yellow	9·50	15·00
H57	10s. green and red on green	27·00	65·00
H46	20s. purple and black on red	£150	£160

FRENCH ISSUES

1914. Stamps of German Colonies, "Yacht" key-type, optd **Togo Occupation franco-anglaise** or surch also.

1		05 on 3pf. brown	80·00	90·00
9		5pf. green	£1200	£550
10		10pf. red	£1400	£550
2		10 on 5pf. green	55·00	23·00
3		20pf. blue	80·00	65·00
4		25pf. black & red on yellow	£100	90·00
5		30pf. black & orge on orange	£130	£130
6		40pf. black and red	£550	£550
15		50pf. black & purple on buff	£27000	£17000
7		80pf. black and red on pink	£550	£550
16	O	1m. red		£60000
17	O	2m. blue	£34000	£28000
18	O	3m. black		£51000
19	O	5m. red and black	£51000	£60000

1916. Stamps of Dahomey optd **TOGO Occupation franco-anglaise**.

20	6	1c. black and violet	10	1·80
21	6	2c. pink and brown	10	1·60
22	6	4c. brown and black	30	2·00

23	6	5c. green and light green	80	2·50
24	6	10c. pink and orange	65	1·60
25	6	15c. purple and red	90	2·00
26	6	20c. brown and grey	1·00	3·00
27	6	25c. blue and ultramarine	1·50	2·75
28	6	30c. violet and brown	1·70	4·50
29	6	35c. black and brown	1·40	5·75
30	6	40c. orange and black	1·10	2·30
31	6	45c. blue and grey	90	3·50
32	6	50c. brown and chocolate	1·00	3·00
33	6	75c. violet and blue	6·50	13·00
34	6	1f. black and green	9·25	24·00
35	6	2f. brown and yellow	13·00	19·00
36	6	5f. blue and violet	14·00	40·00

FRENCH MANDATE

1921. Stamps of Dahomey optd **TOGO**.

37	1c. green and grey	20	5·25
38	2c. orange and blue	10	2·75
39	4c. orange and green	10	3·50
40	5c. black and red	35	1·60
41	10c. green and turquoise	45	1·60
42	15c. red and brown	75	2·00
43	20c. orange and green	2·00	2·30
44	25c. orange and grey	2·00	1·60
45	30c. red and carmine	1·50	5·00
46	35c. green and purple	2·75	8·50
47	40c. grey and green	2·75	10·00
48	45c. grey and purple	1·80	10·00
49	50c. blue	2·00	4·25
50	75c. blue and brown	1·70	6·00
51	1f. blue and grey	3·00	7·50
52	2f. red and green	8·00	17·00
53	5f. black and yellow	12·00	30·00

1922. Stamps of 1921 (No. 57 colour changed) surch.

54	25c. on 15c. red and brown	60	7·25
55	25c. on 2f. red and green	1·60	7·50
56	25c. on 5f. black and orange	1·50	7·00
57	60 on 75c. violet on pink	1·30	6·00
58	65 on 45c. grey and purple	2·75	9·50
59	85 on 75c. blue and brown	2·30	10·00

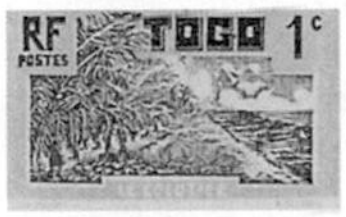

5 Coconut Palms

1924

60	5	1c. black and yellow	20	3·00
61	5	2c. black and red	20	2·30
62	5	4c. black and blue	65	4·00
63	5	5c. black and orange	20	50
64	5	10c. black and mauve	60	55
65	5	15c. black and green	65	45
66	-	20c. black and grey	85	30
67	-	25c. black and green on yellow	1·10	45
68	-	30c. black and green	1·10	1·00
69	-	30c. green and olive	1·10	70
70	-	35c. black and brown	2·30	5·75
71	-	35c. green and turquoise	90	6·50
72	-	40c. black and red	80	35
73	-	45c. black and red	55	90
74	-	50c. black and orange on blue	1·20	35
75	-	55c. red and blue	2·30	5·50
76	-	60c. black and purple on pink	2·30	5·50
77	-	60c. red	1·10	5·00
78	-	65c. brown and lilac	65	65
79	-	75c. black and blue	2·30	1·50
80	-	80c. lilac and blue	3·00	7·75
81	-	85c. brown and orange	2·00	4·50
82	-	90c. pink and red	2·75	3·75
83	-	1f. black and purple on blue	2·00	2·50
84	-	1f. blue	2·50	2·75
85	-	1f. green and lilac	3·50	2·75
86	-	1f. orange and red	1·90	2·75
87	-	1f.10 brown and mauve	7·00	5·00
88	-	1f.25 red and mauve	2·75	3·00
89	-	1f.50 blue	1·90	2·75
90	-	1f.75 pink and brown	21·00	5·50
91	-	1f.75 blue and ultramarine	2·20	6·50
92	-	2f. grey and black on blue	90	65
93	-	3f. red and green	2·00	1·70
94	-	5f. black and orange on blue	2·20	2·50
95	-	10f. pink and brown	3·00	3·25
96	-	20f. black and red on yellow	3·25	1·80

DESIGNS: 20c. to 90c. Cocoa trees; 1f. to 20f. Palm trees.

1926. No. 84 surch.

98	1f.25 on 1f. blue	1·50	2·00

1931. "Colonial Exhibition" key-types inscr "TOGO".

99	E	40c. green and black	6·00	8·50
100	F	50c. mauve and black	6·00	7·75
101	G	90c. red and black	5·50	20·00
102	H	1f.50 blue and black	7·75	20·00

1937. International Exhibition, Paris. As Nos. 168/73 of St.-Pierre et Miquelon.

103	20c. violet	1·70	9·00
104	30c. green	2·30	6·25
105	40c. red	1·00	4·75
106	50c. brown	1·00	8·50
107	90c. red	1·00	5·25
108	1f.50 blue	1·00	4·50
MS108a	120×100 mm. 3f. blue and agate. Imperf	7·25	28·00

1938. International Anti-cancer Fund. As T **38** of St. Pierre et Miquelon.

109	1f.75+50c. blue	14·00	55·00

1939. Centenary of Death of R. Caillie. As T **40** of Senegal.

110	90c. orange	55	90
111	2f. violet	55	4·00
112	2f.25 blue	55	6·25

1939. New York World's Fair. As T **41** of St. Pierre et Miquelon.

113	1f.25 red	1·50	7·25
114	2f.25 blue	90	7·50

1939. 150th Anniv of French Revolution. As T **42** of St. Pierre et Miquelon.

115	45c.+25c. green and black	8·50	21·00
116	70c.+30c. brown and black	8·50	21·00
117	90c.+35c. orange and black	8·50	21·00
118	1f.25+1f. red and black	8·50	21·00
119	2f.25+2f. blue and black	8·50	21·00

1940. Air. As T **48** of St. Pierre et Miquelon.

120	1f.90 blue	40	4·50
121	2f.90 red	45	6·50
122	4f.50 green	75	3·50
123	4f.90 olive	65	7·00
124	6f.90 orange	90	8·25

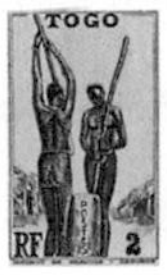

8 Pounding Meal

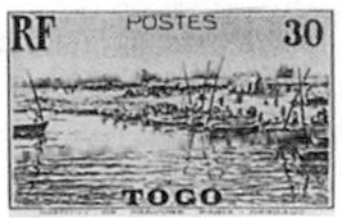

9 Riverside Village

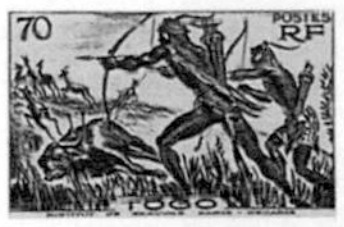

10 Hunting

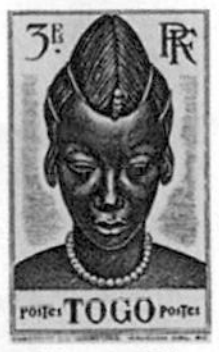

11 Young Girl

1940

125	8	2c. violet	30	5·75
126	8	3c. green	40	6·00
127	8	4c. black	75	6·00
128	8	5c. red	1·30	6·00
129	8	10c. blue	1·10	6·75
130	8	15c. brown	75	5·25
131	9	20c. plum	60	2·75
132	9	25c. blue	90	7·25
133	9	30c. black	60	4·00
134	9	40c. red	65	5·00
135	9	45c. green	80	7·00
136	9	50c. brown	60	7·50
137	9	60c. violet	80	5·25
138	10	70c. black	2·00	7·50
139	10	90c. violet	2·50	7·25
140	10	1f. green	2·75	6·50
141	10	1f.25 red	2·00	4·00
142	10	1f.40 brown	3·00	8·00
143	10	1f.60 orange	1·60	6·25
144	10	2f. blue	1·40	2·75
145	11	2f.25 blue	2·50	9·25
146	11	2f.50 red	1·30	4·00
147	11	3f. violet	1·40	2·75
148	11	5f. red	1·40	2·75
149	11	10f. violet	1·70	3·25
150	11	20f. black	2·30	3·50

1941. National Defence Fund. Surch **SECOURS NATIONAL** and value.

151	+1f. on 50c. (No. 136)	4·75	13·00
152	+2f. on 80c. (No. 80)	9·00	19·00
153	+2f. on 1f.50 (No. 89)	11·00	19·00
154	+3f. on 2f. (No. 144)	12·50	19·00

1942. Air. As T **40d** of Senegal.

154a	50f. violet and yellow	2·30	7·50

1944. Nos. 75 and 82 surch **1 fr. 50**.

155	1f.50 on 55c. red and blue	1·00	3·50
156	1f.50 on 90c. pink and red	65	2·00

1944. No. 139 surch in figures and ornament.

157	10	3f.50 on 90c. violet	2·00	4·75
158	10	4f. on 90c. violet	1·30	4·50
159	10	5f. on 90c. violet	2·75	7·25
160	10	5f.50 on 90c. violet	2·75	9·50
161	10	10f. on 90c. violet	3·75	7·75
162	10	20f. on 90c. violet	4·75	11·00

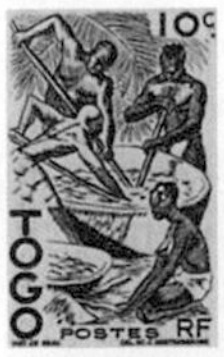

18 Oil Extraction Process

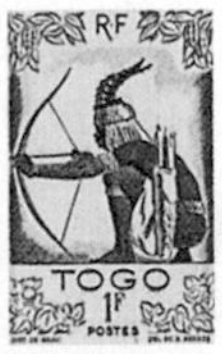

19 Archer

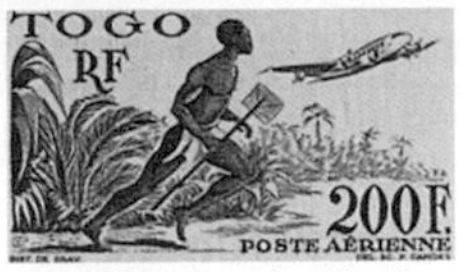

20 Postal Runner and Lockheed Constellation

1947

163	18	10c. red (postage)	20	6·00
164	18	30c. blue	20	6·00
165	18	50c. green	45	1·50
166	19	60c. pink	45	7·00
167	19	1f. brown	55	20
168	19	1f.20 green	90	6·25
169	-	1f.50 orange	1·60	5·25
170	-	2f. bistre	1·40	65
171	-	2f.50 black	2·00	9·25
172	-	3f. blue	1·30	55
173	-	3f.60 red	2·50	8·50
174	-	4f. blue	1·30	60
175	-	5f. brown	2·30	90
176	-	6f. blue	1·40	75
177	-	10f. red	2·00	75
178	-	15f. green	2·30	1·20
179	-	20f. green	2·00	1·70
180	-	25f. pink	1·80	1·40
181	-	40f. blue (air)	13·50	9·25
182	-	50f. mauve and violet	4·50	2·30
183	-	100f. brown and green	5·50	3·25
184	20	200f. pink	11·50	14·50

DESIGNS—As Type **10**: VERT: 1f.50 to 2f.50, Women hand-spinning cotton. HORIZ: 3f. to 4f. Drummer and village; 5f. to 10f. Red-fronted gazelles; 15f. to 25f. Trees and village. As Type **20**: 40f. African elephants and Sud Ouest SO.95 Corse II airplane; 50f. Airplane; 100f. Lockheed Constellation.

1949. Air. 75th Anniv of U.P.U. As T **58** of St. Pierre et Miquelon.

185	25f. multicoloured	3·75	20·00

1950. Colonial Welfare Fund. As T **59** of St. Pierre et Miquelon.

186	10f.+2f. blue and indigo	4·00	13·50

1952. Centenary of Military Medal. As T **60** of St. Pierre et Miquelon.

187	15f. brown, yellow and green	5·00	8·25

1954. Air. Tenth Anniv of Liberation. As T **66** of St. Pierre et Miquelon.

188	15f. violet and blue	7·75	5·50

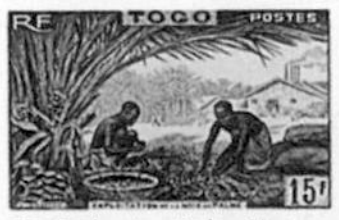

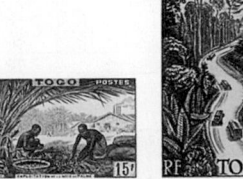

22 Gathering Palm Nuts

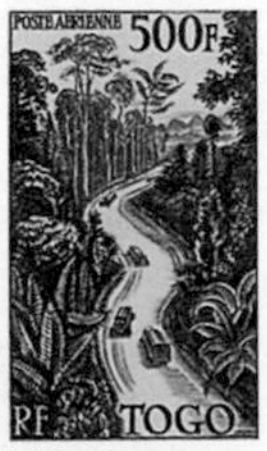

23 Roadway through Forest

1954

189	22	8f. purple, lake and violet (postage)	5·00	6·50
190	22	15f. brown, grey and blue	4·25	75
191	23	500f. blue and green (air)	60·00	80·00

AUTONOMOUS REPUBLIC

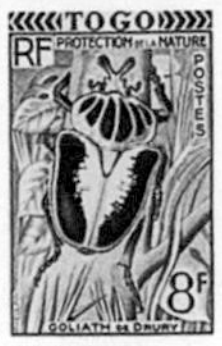

24 Goliath Beetle

1955. Nature Protection.

192	24	8f. black and green	3·00	9·50

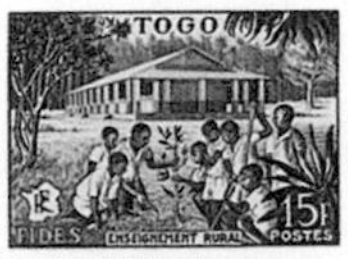

25 Rural School

1956. Economic and Social Fund Development Fund.

193	25	15f. brown and chestnut	2·00	90

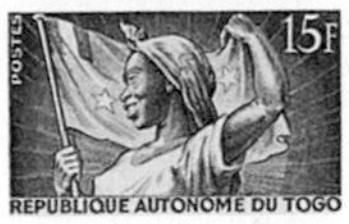

26 Togolese Woman and Flag

1957. New National Flag.

194	26	15f. brown, red & turquoise	1·60	80

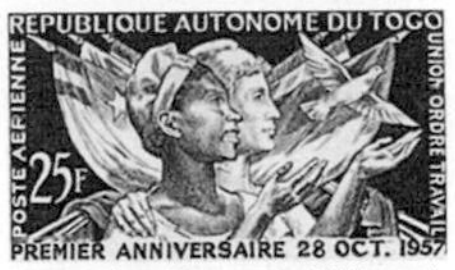

27 Togolese Woman and "Liberty" releasing Dove

1957. Air. First Anniv of Autonomous Republic.

195	27	25f. sepia, red and blue	75	2·75

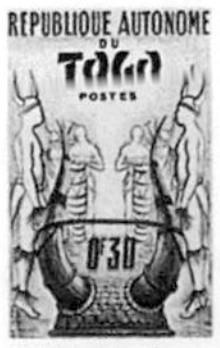

28 Konkomba Helmet

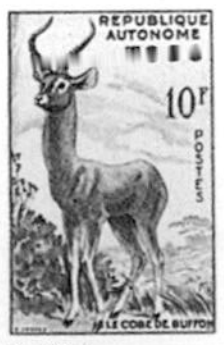

29 Kob

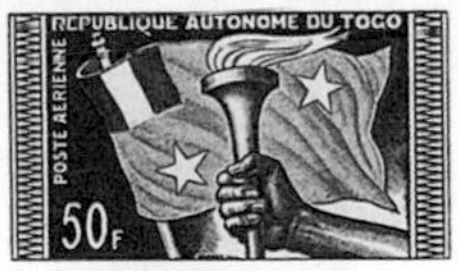

30 Torch and Flags

1957. Inscr "REPUBLIQUE AUTONOME DU TOGO".

196	28	30c. lilac and red (postage)	35	3·25
197	28	50c. indigo and blue	35	90
198	28	1f. lilac and purple	40	3·25
199	28	2f. brown and green	60	7·00
200	28	3f. black and green	65	3·75
201	29	4f. black and blue	90	4·50
202	29	5f. purple and grey	55	75
203	29	6f. grey and red	65	7·25
204	29	8f. violet and grey	1·00	5·25
205	29	10f. brown and green	2·30	1·60
206	-	15f. multicoloured	2·00	2·75
207	-	20f. multicoloured	2·50	55
208	-	25f. multicoloured	2·30	2·75
209	-	40f. multicoloured	2·75	3·50
210	30	50f. multicoloured (air)	2·75	4·00
211	30	100f. multicoloured	4·25	5·50
212	30	200f. multicoloured	3·50	3·00
213	-	500f. indigo, green and blue	20·00	55·00

DESIGNS—HORIZ: 15f. to 40f. Teak forest. 48×27 mm: 500f. Great egret.

See also Nos. 217/35.

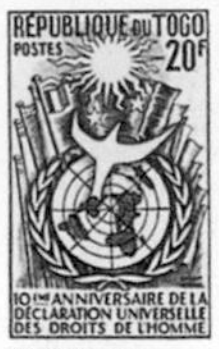

31 "Human Rights"

1958. Tenth Anniv of Human Rights Declaration.

214	**31**	20f. red and green	45	55

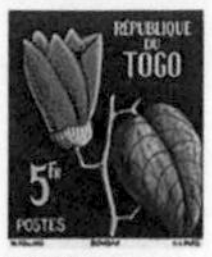

32 "Bombax"

1959. Tropical Flora.

215	**32**	5f. multicoloured	65	3·25
216	-	20f. yellow, green and black	90	1·80

DESIGN—HORIZ: 20f. "Tectona".

1959. As Nos. 196/213 but colours changed and inscr "REPUBLIQUE DU TOGO".

217	**28**	30c. blue & black (postage)	35	5·75
218	**28**	50c. green and green	35	6·75
219	**28**	1f. purple and green	45	1·80
220	**28**	2f. brown and green	45	35
221	**28**	3f. violet and purple	60	75
222	**29**	4f. violet and purple	1·80	1·40
223	**29**	5f. brown and green	1·90	1·80
224	**29**	6f. blue and ultramarine	2·00	1·30
225	**29**	8f. bistre and green	2·00	2·75
226	**29**	10f. brown and violet	1·70	1·80
227	-	15f. multicoloured	1·90	1·20
228	-	20f. multicoloured	1·10	20
229	-	25f. multicoloured	1·80	2·00
230	-	40f. multicoloured	1·50	90
231	-	25f. brown, grn & bl (air)	2·75	3·25
232	**30**	50f. multicoloured	75	90
233	**30**	100f. multicoloured	1·00	1·10
234	**30**	200f. multicoloured	2·00	4·75
235	-	500f. sepia, green & purple	11·00	2·50

DESIGN—VERT: 25f. (No. 231) Togo flag and shadow of airliner over Africa.

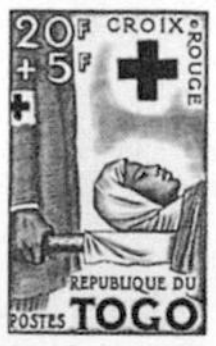

32a Patient on Stretcher

1959. Red Cross Commemoration.

236	**32a**	20f.+5f. red, orge & slate	2·50	6·50
237	-	30f.+5f. red, brown & bl	2·50	7·25
238	-	50f.+10f. red, brn & grn	2·50	7·25
MS238a		Three sheets each 78×106 mm. Nos. 236/8 in blocks of four. Perf or imperf	30·00	70·00

DESIGNS: 30f. Mother feeding child; 50f. Nurse superintending blood transfusion.

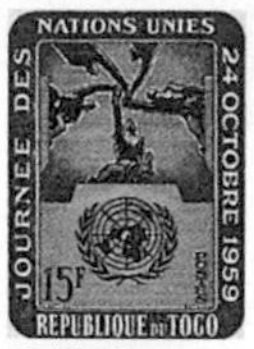

33 "The Five Continents"

1959. United Nations Day.

239	**33**	15f. blue and brown	1·80	5·75
240	**33**	20f. blue and violet	2·00	4·50
241	**33**	25f. blue and brown	1·90	6·50
242	**33**	40f. blue and green	2·00	3·75
243	**33**	60f. blue and red	2·30	6·50

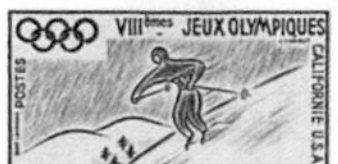

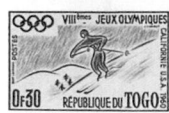

34 Skiing

1960. Olympic Games, California and Rome.

244	**34**	30c. turquoise, red & green	10	3·25
245	-	50c. purple, red and black	35	6·50
246	-	1f. green, red and black	65	6·50
247	-	10f. brown, blue and indigo	3·50	7·00
248	-	15f. purple and green	2·75	5·50
249	-	20f. chocolate, green & brown	2·75	5·50
250	-	25f. brown, red and orange	3·50	7·00

DESIGNS—HORIZ: 50c. Ice hockey; 1f. Tobogganing; 10f. Cycling; 25f. Running. VERT: 125f. Throwing the discus; 20f. Boxing.

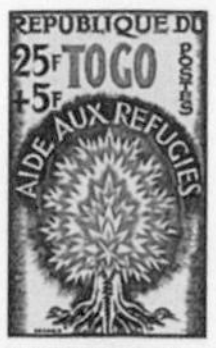

35 "Uprooted Tree"

1960. World Refugee Year.

251	**35**	25f.+5f. green, brown & bl	45	8·00
252	-	45f.+5f. olive, black & bl	55	8·25

DESIGN: 45f. As Type **35** but "TOGO" at foot.

INDEPENDENT REPUBLIC

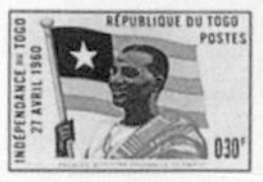

36 Prime Minister S. Olympio and Flag

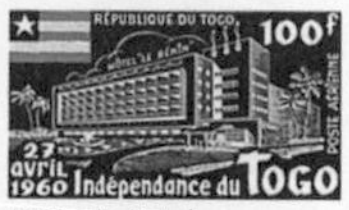

37 Benin Hotel

1960. Independence Commemoration. (a) Postage. Centres multicoloured; backgrounds cream; inscription and frame colours given.

253	**36**	30c. sepia	10	10
254	**36**	50c. brown	10	10
255	**36**	1f. purple	10	10
256	**36**	10f. blue	15	10
257	**36**	20f. red	40	15
258	**36**	25f. green	50	20

(b) Air.

259	**37**	100f. red, yellow and green	1·60	50
260	**37**	200f. multicoloured	2·75	90
261	-	500f. brown and green	9·50	3·25

DESIGN—As Type **37**: VERT: 500f. Palm-nut vulture and map of Togo.

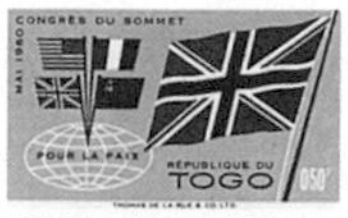

38 Union Jack and Flags

1960. Four-Power "Summit" Conference, Paris. Flags and inscr in red and blue.

262	**38**	50c. buff	10	10
263	-	1f. turquoise	10	10
264	-	20f. grey	35	20
265	-	25f. blue	40	20

DESIGNS—As Type **38** but flags of: 1f. Soviet Union; 20f. France; 25f. U.S.A. The Conference did not take place.

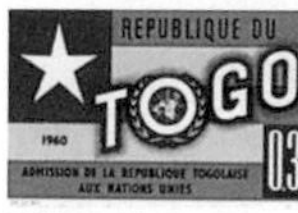

39 Togo Flag

1961. Admission of Togo into U.N.O. Flag in red, yellow and green.

266	**39**	30c. red	10	10
267	**39**	50c. brown	10	10
268	**39**	1f. blue	10	10
269	**39**	10f. purple	20	10
270	**39**	25f. black	40	15
271	**39**	30f. violet	45	20

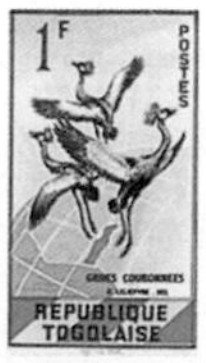

40 South African Crowned Cranes

1961

272	**40**	1f. multicoloured	50	10
273	**40**	10f. multicoloured	70	15
274	**40**	25f. multicoloured	1·10	40
275	**40**	30f. multicoloured	1·25	50

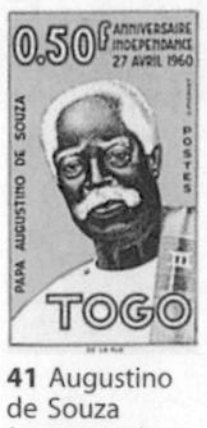

41 Augustino de Souza (statesman)

1961. First Anniv of Independence.

276	**41**	50c. black, red and yellow	10	10
277	**41**	1f. black, brown and green	10	10
278	**41**	10f. black, violet and blue	20	15
279	**41**	25f. black, green & salmon	40	10
280	**41**	30f. black, blue and mauve	50	20

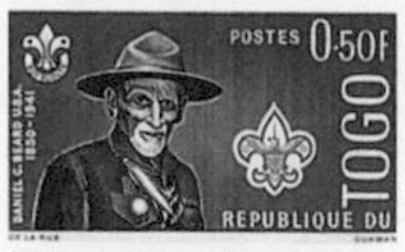

42 Daniel Beard (founder of American Boy Scout Movement) and Scout Badge

1961. Boy Scout Movement Commemoration.

281	**42**	50c. lake, green and red	10	10
282	-	1f. violet and red	10	10
283	-	10f. black and brown	20	10
284	-	25f. multicoloured	55	15
285	-	30f. red, brown and green	65	20
286	-	100f. mauve and blue	1·60	60
MS286a		121×147 mm. Nos. 281/6. Imperf	3·25	1·25

DESIGNS—HORIZ: 1f. Lord Baden-Powell; 10f. Daniel Mensah ("Rover" Scout Chief); 100f. Scout salute. VERT: 25f. Chief Daniel Wilson (Togolese Scout); 30f. Campfire on triangular emblem.

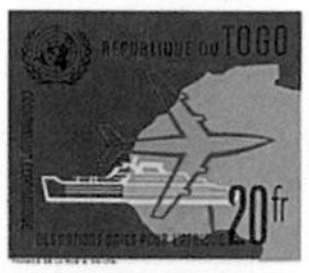

43 Jet Airliner and Motor Launch

1961. U.N. Economic Commission on Africa. Multicoloured.

287	20f. Type **43**	30	15
288	25f. Electric train and gantry	95	15
289	30f. Excavator and pylons	65	30
290	85f. Microscope and atomic symbol	1·25	50
MS290a	89×95 mm. Nos. 287/90. Imperf	3·25	1·10

The designs are superimposed on a map of Africa spread over the four stamps when the 30 and 85f. are mounted below the 20 and 25f.

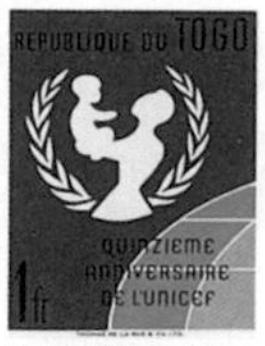

44 UNICEF Emblem

1961. 15th Anniv of UNICEF.

291	**44**	1f. blue, green and black	10	10
292	-	10f. multicoloured	15	10
293	-	20f. multicoloured	20	10
294	-	25f. multicoloured	45	20
295	-	30f. multicoloured	80	20
296	-	85f. multicoloured	1·25	60
MS296a		101×108 mm. Nos. 291/6. Imperf	3·00	1·25

DESIGNS: 10f. to 85f. Children dancing round the globe. The six stamps, arranged in the following order, form a composite picture: Upper row, 1, 25 and 20f. Lower row, 10, 85 and 30f.

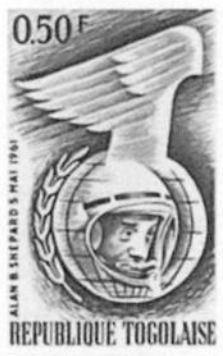

45 Alan Shepard

1962. Space Flights Commemoration.

297	**45**	50c. green	10	10
298	-	1f. mauve	15	10
299	**45**	25f. blue	35	20
300	-	30f. violet	50	30

DESIGN: 1, 30f. As Type **45** but portrait of Yuri Gagarin.

1962. Col. Glenn's Space Flight. Surch **100F COL. JOHN H. GLENN U S A VOL ORBITAL 20 FEVRIER 1962.**

301	**45**	100f. on 50c. green	2·00	2·00

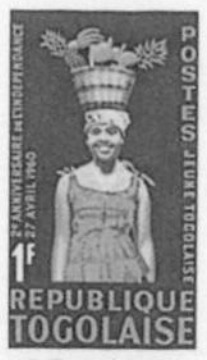

47 Togolese Girl

1962. Second Anniv of Independence.

303	-	50c. multicoloured	10	10
304	**47**	1f. green and pink	10	10
305	-	5f. multicoloured	20	15
306	**47**	20f. violet and yellow	30	15
307	-	25f. multicoloured	35	15
308	**47**	30f. red and yellow	35	15
MS308a		122×140 mm. Nos. 305, 306 and 308. Imperf	85	45

DESIGN: 50c., 5, 25f. Independence Monument.

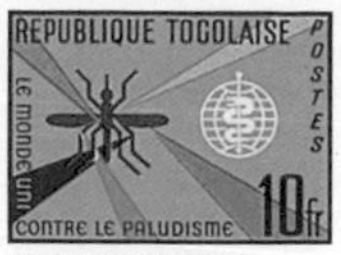

48 Arrows piercing Mosquito

1962. Malaria Eradication.

309	**48**	10f. multicoloured	30	10
310	**48**	25f. multicoloured	45	20
311	**48**	30f. multicoloured	50	35
312	**48**	85f. multicoloured	1·00	55

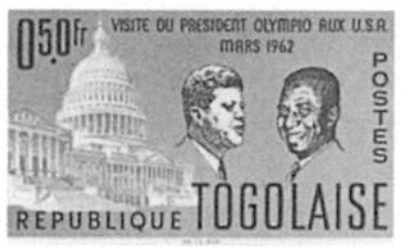

49 Presidents Kennedy and Olympio, and Capitol, Washington

1962. Visit of President Olympio to U.S.A.

313	**49**	50c. slate and ochre	10	10
314	**49**	1f. slate and blue	10	10
315	**49**	2f. slate and red	10	10
316	**49**	5f. slate and mauve	10	10
317	**49**	25f. slate and lilac	40	15
318	**49**	100f. slate and green	1·60	70
MS318a		105×75 mm. No. 318. Imperf	1·60	70

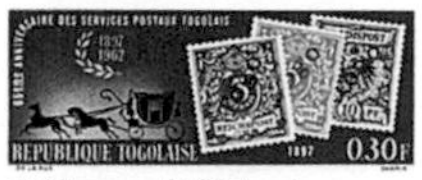

50 Stamps of 1897 and Mail-coach

1963. 65th Anniv of Togolese Postal Services.

319	**50**	30c. multicoloured (postage)	10	10
320	-	50c. multicoloured	10	10
321	-	1f. multicoloured	35	10
322	-	10f. multicoloured	45	15
323	-	25f. multicoloured	60	20
324	-	30f. multicoloured	85	40
325	-	100f. multicoloured (air)	2·40	1·00
MS325a		140×95 mm. Nos. 322/5. Imperf	1·90	75

DESIGNS (Togo stamps of): 50c. 1900 and German imperial yacht "Hohenzollern"; 1f. 1915 and steam mail train; 10f. 1924 and motor-cycle mail carrier; 25f. 1940 and mail-van; 30f. 1947 and Douglas DC-3 airplane; 100f. 1960 and Boeing 707 airplane.

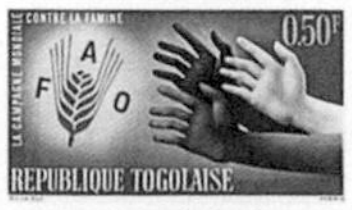

51 Hands reaching for F.A.O. Emblem

1963. Freedom from Hunger.

326	**51**	50c. multicoloured	10	10
327	**51**	1f. multicoloured	10	10
328	**51**	25f. multicoloured	60	20
329	**51**	30f. multicoloured	85	30

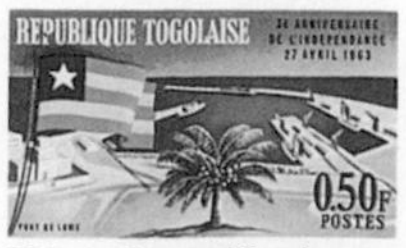

52 Lome Port and Togolese Flag

1963. Third Anniv of Independence. Flag in red, yellow and green.

330	**52**	50c. black and brown	10	10
331	**52**	1f. black and red	15	10
332	**52**	25f. black and blue	35	20
333	**52**	50f. black and ochre	70	35

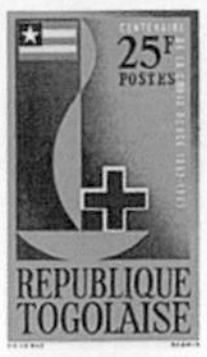

53 Centenary Emblem

1963. Red Cross Centenary. Flag in red, yellow and green; cross red.

334	**53**	25f. blue and black	85	30
335	**53**	30f. green and black	1·10	40

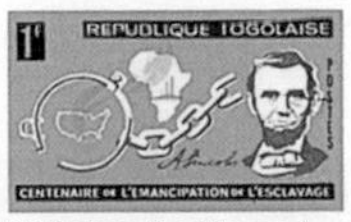

54 Broken Shackles and Abraham Lincoln

1963. Cent of American Slaves' Emancipation. Centre in grey and green.

336	**54**	50c. black & brn (postage)	10	10
337	**54**	1f. black and blue	10	10
338	**54**	25f. black and red	45	15
339	**54**	100f. black and orange (air)	1·40	60

MS339a 130×103 mm. Nos. 336/9. Imperf 1·60 95

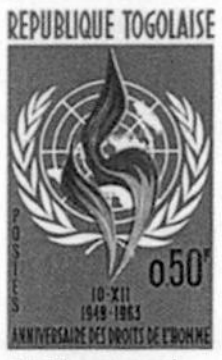

55 Flame and U.N. Emblem

1963. 15th Anniv of Declaration of Human Rights. Flame in red.

340	**55**	50c. blue and ultra [illegible]	10	10
341	**55**	1f. green and black	15	10
342	**55**	25f. lilac and blue	40	15
343	**55**	85f. gold and blue	1·10	60

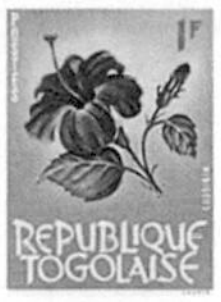

56 Hibiscus

1964. Multicoloured

344	50c. "Odontoglossum grande" (orchid) (postage)	10	10
345	1f. Type **56**	10	10
346	2f. "Papilio dardanus" (butterfly)	35	10
347	3f. "Morpho aega" (butterfly)	55	10
348	4f. "Pandinus imperator" (scorpion)	40	10
349	5f. Tortoise	20	15
350	6f. Strelitzia (flower)	55	15
351	8f. Python	45	15
352	10f. "Bunaea alcinde" (butterfly)	85	15
353	15f. Chameleon	1·25	15
354	20f. Common octopus	1·50	20
355	25f. John Dory (fish)	1·60	20
356	30f. French angelfish	2·00	35
357	40f. Pygmy hippopotamus	2·00	35
358	45f. African palm civet	3·25	60
359	60f. Bohar reedbuck	4·50	90
360	85f. Olive baboon	5·50	1·00
361	50f. Black-bellied seedcracker (air)	3·50	50
362	100f. Black and white mannikin	8·25	90
363	200f. Red-faced lovebird	12·00	1·90
364	250f. Grey parrot	28·00	4·25
365	500f. Yellow-breasted barbet	38·00	1·10

1964. President Kennedy Memorial Issue. Optd **En Memoire de JOHN F. KENNEDY 1917-1963**. Centre in grey and green.

366	**54**	50c. black & brn (postage)	15	10
367	**54**	1f. black and blue	15	10
368	**54**	25f. black and red	50	20
369	**54**	100f. black and orange (air)	1·60	80

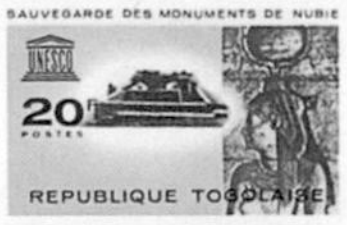

58 Temple and Isis

1964. Nubian Monuments Preservation.

370	**58**	20f. multicoloured	30	10
371	-	25f. mauve and black	35	20
372	-	30f. olive, black and yellow	50	30

MS372a 113×79 mm. Nos. 370/2. Imperf 1·10 60

DESIGNS: 25f. Head of Rameses II, Abu Simbel; 30f. Temple of Philae.

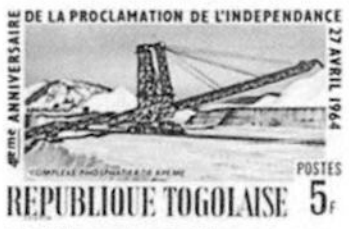

59 Phosphate Mine, Kpeme

1964. Fourth Anniv of Independence.

373	**59**	5f. ochre, bistre and brown	35	10
374	-	25f. lake, brown and violet	35	15
375	-	60f. yellow, olive and green	1·25	50
376	-	85f. blue, slate and violet	1·50	50

DESIGNS: 25f. Mine installations; 60f. Diesel phosphate train; 85f. Loading phosphate onto "Panama Maru" bulk carrier.

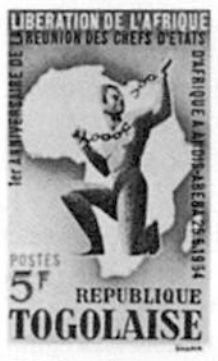

60 Togolese breaking Chain

1964. First Anniv of African Heads of State Conference, Addis Ababa.

377	**60**	5f. sepia & orange [illegible]	[illegible]	10
378	**60**	25f. sepia and green	35	15
379	**60**	85f. sepia and red	95	45
380	**60**	100f. sepia & turquoise (air)	1·25	65

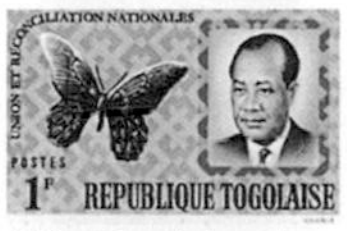

61 Pres. Grunitzky and "Papilio memnon"

1964. "National Union and Reconciliation".

381	**61**	1f. violet and mauve	20	10
382	-	5f. sepia and ochre	10	10
383	-	25f. violet and blue	45	15
384	**61**	45f. purple and red	1·75	50
385	-	85f. bronze and green	1·90	60

DESIGNS—President and: 5f. Dove; 25, 85f. Flowers.

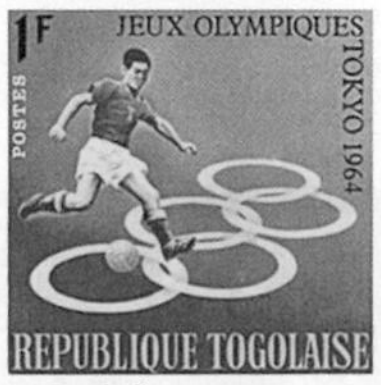

62 Football

1964. Olympic Games, Tokyo.

386	**62**	1f. green (postage)	10	10
387	-	5f. blue (Running)	25	15
388	-	25f. red (Throwing the discus)	75	15
389	**62**	45f. turquoise	1·00	40
390	-	100f. brown (Tennis) (air)	1·75	55

MS390a 105×112 mm. Nos. 388/390. Imperf 3·50 1·10

1964. French, African and Malagasy Co-operation. As T **60a** of Senegal.

391	25f. brown, bistre and purple	40	20

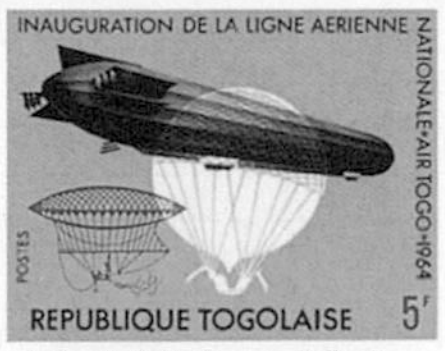

63 Charles's Hydrogen Balloon, Giffard's Steam-powered Dirigible Airship and Airship LZ-5

1964. Inaug of "Air Togo" (National Airline).

392	**63**	5f. multicoloured (postage)	10	10
393	**63**	10f. blue, lake and green	30	10
394	-	25f. ultramarine, orge & blue	50	15
395	-	45f. mauve, green and bl	1·10	35
396	-	100f. multicoloured (air)	1·90	80

MS396a 137×120 mm. Nos. 393/6. Imperf 3·75 1·25

DESIGNS: 25, 45f. Farman H.F. III biplane, Lilienthal biplane glider and Boeing 707; 100f. Boeing 707 and Togolese flag.

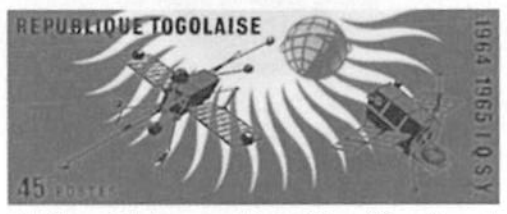

64 Sun, Globe and Satellites "Ogo" and "Mariner"

1964. International Quiet Sun Years. Sun yellow.

397	**64**	10f. blue and red	15	10
398	-	15f. blue, brown and mauve	20	10
399	-	20f. green and violet	30	10
400	-	25f. purple, green and blue	35	15
401	**64**	45f. blue and green	70	35
402	-	50f. green and red	80	40

MS402a 203×122 mm. Nos. 399/402. Imperf 2·10 1·00

SATELLITES: 15, 25f. "Tiros", "Telstar" and orbiting solar observatory; 20, 50f. "Nimbus", "Syncom" and "Relay".

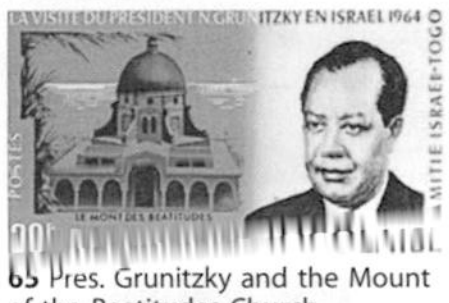

65 Pres. Grunitzky and the Mount of the Beatitudes Church

1965. Israel–Togo Friendship. Inscr "AMITIE ISRAEL–TOGO 1964".

403		5f. purple	10	10
404	**65**	20f. blue and purple	20	10
405	-	25f. turquoise and red	35	15
406	-	45f. olive, bistre and purple	70	35
407	-	85f. turquoise and purple	1·10	50

MS407a 138×102 mm. No. 407 in block of four. Imperf 3·75 3·75

DESIGNS—VERT: 5f. Togolese stamps being printed on Israel press. HORIZ: 25, 85f. Arms of Israel and Togo; 45f. As Type **65** but showing old synagogue, Capernaum.

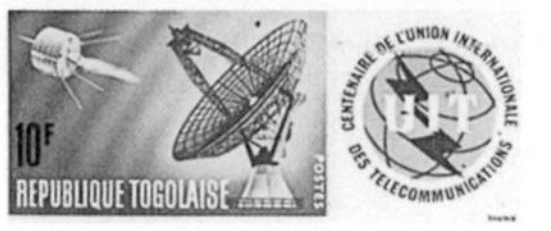

66 "Syncom 3", Dish Aerial and I.T.U. Emblem

1965. I.T.U. Centenary.

408	**66**	10f. turquoise and green	15	10
409	**66**	20f. olive and black	35	15
410	**66**	25f. blue and ultramarine	40	15
411	**66**	45f. rose and red	70	35
412	**66**	50f. green and black	90	45

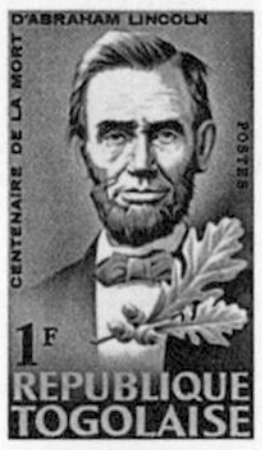

67 Abraham Lincoln

1965. Death Centenary of Lincoln.

413	**67**	1f. purple (postage)	10	10
414	**67**	5f. greeen	10	10
415	**67**	20f. brown	35	10
416	**67**	25f. blue	45	20
417	**67**	100f. olive (air)	1·60	70

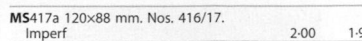

MS417a 120×88 mm. Nos. 416/17. Imperf 2·00 1·90

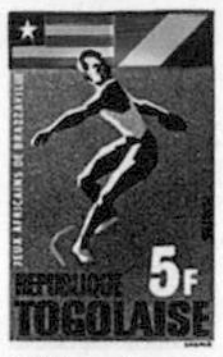

68 Throwing the Discus

1965. First African Games, Brazzaville. Flags in red, yellow and green.

418	**68**	5f. purple (postage)	10	10
419	-	10f. blue	15	10
420	-	15f. brown	35	10
421	-	25f. purple	90	20
422	-	100f. green (air)	1·50	65

SPORTS: 10f. Throwing the javelin; 15f. Hand-ball; 25f. Running; 100f. Football.

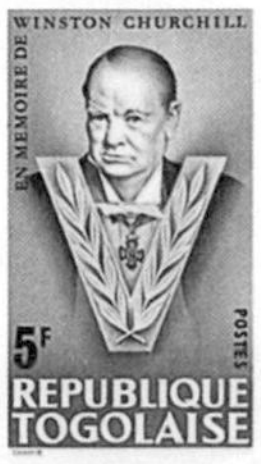

69 Sir Winston Churchill

1965. Churchill Commemoration.

423	**69**	5f. green (postage)	10	10
424	-	10f. violet and blue	15	10
425	**69**	20f. brown	40	15
426	-	45f. blue	65	35
427	**69**	85f. red (air)	1·50	65

MS427a 135×89 mm. Nos. 426/7. Imperf 2·10 1·00

DESIGNS—HORIZ: 10, 45f. Stalin, Roosevelt and Churchill at Teheran Conference, 1943

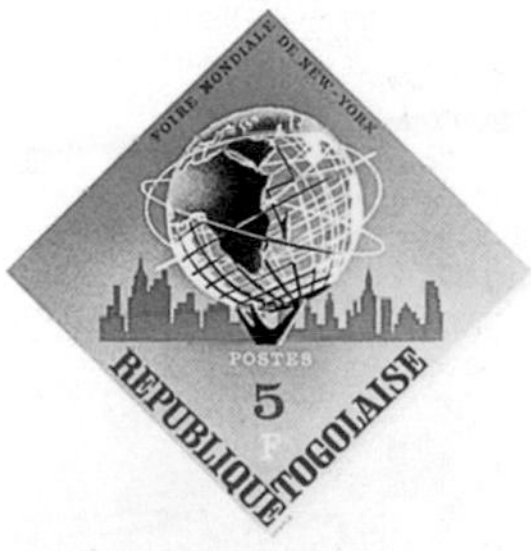

70 Unisphere

1965. New York World's Fair.

428	**70**	5f. plum and blue	15	10
429	-	10f. sepia and green	20	10
430	**70**	25f. myrtle and brown	35	20
431	-	50f. myrtle and violet	65	40
432	**70**	85f. brown and red	1·10	50

MS432a 140×96 mm. Nos. 431/2. Imperf 1·75 90

DESIGNS: 10f. Native dancers and drummer; 50f. Michelangelo's "Pieta".

71 "Laying Bricks of Peace"

1965. International Co-operation Year.

433	**71**	5f. multicoloured	10	10
434	**71**	15f. multicoloured	15	15
435	-	25f. multicoloured	30	15
436	-	40f. multicoloured	60	30
437	-	85f. multicoloured	1·00	50

DESIGNS: 25, 40f. Hands suppporting globe; 85f. I.C.Y. emblem.

72 Leonov with Camera

1965. Astronauts in Space.

| 438 | 72 | 25f. mauve and blue | 50 | 20 |
| 439 | - | 50f. brown and green | 90 | 40 |

DESIGN: 50f. White with rocket-gun.

73 "ONU" and Doves

1966. 20th Anniv of U.N.O.

440	73	5f. brown, yellow and blue (postage)	10	10
441	-	10f. blue, turquoise and orange	20	10
442	-	20f. orange, green and light green	35	15
443	-	25f. blue, turquoise & yell	45	20
444	-	100f. ochre, blue and light blue (air)	1·60	55
MS444a 90×129 mm. Nos. 443/4. Imperf			2·00	75

DESIGNS: 10f. U.N. Headquarters and emblem; 20f. "ONU" and orchids; 25f. U.N. Headquarters and Adlai Stevenson; 100f. "ONU", fruit and ears of wheat.

74 Pope Paul, Boeing 707 and U.N. Emblem

1966. Pope Paul's Visit to U.N. Organization. Multicoloured.

445	74	5f. Type **74** (postage)	10	10
446	-	15f. Pope before microphones at U.N. (vert)	20	10
447	-	20f. Pope and U.N. Head-quarters	35	15
448	-	30f. As 15f.	45	20
449	-	45f. Pope before microphones at U.N., and map (air)	80	30
450	-	90f. Type **74**	1·60	80
MS450a 100×117 mm. Nos. 449/50. Imperf			2·40	1·10

75 W.H.O. Building and Roses

1966. Inaug of W.H.O. Headquarters, Geneva. Multicoloured designs showing W.H.O. Building and flower as given.

451	75	5f. Type **75** (postage)	20	10
452	-	10f. Alstroemerias	35	10
453	-	15f. Asters	45	20
454	-	20f. Freesias	55	35
455	-	30f. Geraniums	65	35
456	-	45f. Asters (air)	95	35
457	-	50f. Type **75**	1·50	55
MS458 150×100 mm. Nos. 456/7. Imperf			2·40	90

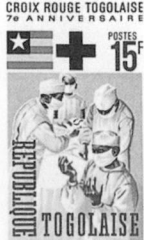

76 Surgical Operation

1966. Seventh Anniv of Togolese Red Cross. Multicoloured.

459	76	5f. Type **76** (postage)	10	10
460	-	10f. Blood transfusion	15	10
461	-	15f. Type **76**	30	15
462	-	30f. Blood transfusion	40	15
463	-	45f. African man and woman	70	45
464	-	100f. J. H. Dunant (air)	1·75	90

1966. Space Achievements. Nos. 438/9 optd as below or surch also.

465		50f. (**ENVOLEE SURVEYOR 1**)	85	40
466		50f. (**ENVOLEE GEMINI 9**)	85	40
467		100f. on 25f. (**ENVOLEE LUNA 9**)	1·60	70
468		100f. on 25f. (**ENVOLEE VENUS 3**)	1·60	70

78 Wood-carving

1966. Togolese Arts and Crafts.

469	78	5f. brn, yell & bl (postage)	10	10
470	-	10f. brown, salmon & green	15	10
471	-	15f. brown, yellow and red	30	15
472	-	30f. brown, bistre and violet	55	20
473	-	60f. brown, salmon and blue (air)	1·40	60
474	78	90f. brown, yellow and red	1·40	60

DESIGNS: 10, 60f. Basket-making; 15f. Weaving; 30f. Pottery.

79 Togolese Man

1966. Air. Inauguration of Douglas DC-8F Air Services. As T **76a** of Senegal.

| 475 | | 30f. black, green and yellow | 65 | 25 |

1966. Togolese Costumes and Dances. Multicoloured.

476	79	5f. Type **79** (postage)	10	10
477	-	10f. Togolese woman	10	10
478	-	20f. Female dancer	40	10
479	-	25f. Male dancer	50	15
480	-	30f. Dancer in horned helmet	65	20
481	-	45f. Drummer	1·00	50
482	-	50f. Female dancer (air)	85	45
483	-	60f. Dancer in horned helmet	1·40	60

80 Footballers and Jules Rimet Cup

1966. World Cup Football Championship, England. Showing football scenes and Jules Rimet Cup.

484	80	5f. multicoloured (postage)	20	10
485	-	10f. multicoloured	30	10
486	-	20f. multicoloured	50	10
487	-	25f. multicoloured	50	15
488	-	30f. multicoloured	65	20
489	-	45f. multicoloured	1·00	40
490	-	50f. multicoloured (air)	1·00	30
491	-	60f. multicoloured	1·50	40
MS492 159×111 mm. Nos. 489/91. Imperf			3·50	1·10

81 African Mouthbrooder

1967. Fish. Multicoloured designs showing fish with fishing craft in the background.

493	81	5f. Type **81** (postage)	30	10
494	-	10f. Golden trevally	50	15
495	-	15f. Six banded distichodus	60	25
496	-	25f. Jewel cichlid	85	30
497	-	30f. Type **81**	1·25	55
498	-	45f. As 10f. (air)	2·00	70
499	-	90f. As 15f.	2·75	1·00

82 African Boy and Greyhound

1967. 20th Anniv (1966) of UNICEF.

500	82	5f. multicoloured (postage)	20	10
501	-	10f. brown, green & lt grn	40	15
502	82	15f. black, brown & mauve	60	20
503	-	20f. black, ultramarine & blue	75	30
504	82	30f. black, blue and olive	1·10	35
505	-	45f. bronze, brown and yellow (air)	1·25	40
506	82	90c. black, bronze and blue	1·75	55
MS507 125×85 mm. Nos. 505/6. Imperf			3·00	95

DESIGNS: 10f. Boy and Irish setter; 20f. Girl and doberman; 45f. Girl and miniature poodle.

83 Launching "Diamant" Rocket

1967. French Space Achievements. Multicoloured.

508	83	5f. Type **83** (postage)	10	10
509	-	10f. Satellite "A-1" (horiz)	20	10
510	-	15f. Satellite "FR-1"	30	10
511	-	20f. Satellite "D-1" (horiz)	40	15
512	-	25f. As 10f.	50	30
513	-	40f. As 20f.	70	35
514	-	50f. Type **83** (air)	95	40
515	-	90f. As 15f.	1·50	55
MS516 91×120 mm. Nos. 514/15. Imperf			2·40	95

84 Bach and Organ

1967. 20th Anniv (1966) of UNESCO.

517	84	5f. multicoloured (postage)	10	10
518	-	10f. multicoloured	20	10
519	-	15f. multicoloured	45	20
520	-	20f. multicoloured	55	20
521	-	30f. multicoloured	90	45
522	84	45f. multicoloured (air)	1·10	40
523	-	90f. multicoloured	1·60	55
MS524 91×120 mm. Nos. 522/3. Imperf			2·75	95

DESIGNS: 10, 90f. Beethoven, violin and clarinets,, 15, 30f. Duke Ellington, saxophone, trumpet and drums; 20f. Debussy, grand piano and harp.

85 British Pavilion and Lilies

1967. World Fair, Montreal. Multicoloured.

525	85	5f. Type **85** (postage)	15	10
526	-	10f. French Pavilion and roses	30	10
527	-	30f. "Africa Place" and strelitzia	75	15
528	-	45f. As 10f. (air)	1·00	35
529	-	60f. Type **85**	1·10	45
530	-	90f. As 30f.	1·75	60
531	-	105f. U.S. Pavilion and daisies	2·25	65
MS532 160×110 mm. Nos. 528/30. Imperf			4·50	95

86 "Peace"

1967. Air. Disarmament. Designs showing sections of the "Peace" mural by J. Zanetti at the U.N. Headquarters Building Conference Room.

533	86	5f. multicoloured	15	10
534	A	15f. multicoloured	20	10
535	B	30f. multicoloured	40	10
536	86	45f. multicoloured	70	35
537	A	60f. multicoloured	1·25	45
538	B	90f. multicoloured	1·60	55
MS539 160×110 mm. Nos. 536/8. Imperf			3·50	1·25

87 Lions Emblem with Supporters

1967. 50th Anniv of Lions International. Multicoloured.

540	87	10f. Type **87**	20	10
541	-	20f. Flowers and Lions emblem	35	15
542	-	30f. Type **87**	45	20
543	-	45f. As 20f.	1·25	45

88 Bohar Reedbuck

1967. Wildlife.

544	88	5f. brown & pur (postage)	10	10
545	-	10f. blue, red and yellow	25	10
546	-	15f. black, lilac and green	45	15
547	-	20f. blue, sepia and yellow	55	25
548	-	25f. brown, yellow and olive	85	35
549	-	30f. blue, violet and yellow	1·75	50
550	-	45f. brown and blue (air)	90	35
551	-	60f. black, brown and green	1·25	50

DESIGNS: 10, 20, 30f. Montagu's harriers (birds of prey); 15f. Common zebra; 25f. Leopard; 45f. Lion; 60f. African elephants.

1967. Air. Fifth Anniv of U.A.M.P.T. As T **86a** of Senegal.

| 552 | | 100f. brown, blue and green | 1·60 | 1·10 |

89 Stamp Auction and Togo Stamps—1m. (German) of 1900 and 100f. Conference of 1964

1967. 70th Anniv of First Togolese Stamps. Multicoloured.

553	5f. Type **89** (postage)	15	10
554	10f. Exhibition and 1d. (British) of 1915 and 50f. I.T.U. of 1965	15	10
555	15f. Stamp shop and 50c. (French) of 1924	40	10
556	20f. Stamp-packet vending machine and 5f. U.N. of 1965	40	10
557	30f. As 15f.	60	30
558	45f. As 10f.	85	40
559	90f. Type **89** (air)	1·50	60
560	105f. Father and son with album and 1f. Kennedy of 1964	1·75	80
MS561	120×89 mm. Nos. 557/9. Imperf	3·00	1·25

89a Currency Tokens

1967. Fifth Anniv of West African Monetary Union.

562	**89a**	30f. blue and green	55	30

90 Long Jumping

1967. Olympic Games, Mexico and Grenoble (1968). Multicoloured.

563	5f. Type **90** (postage)	10	10
564	15f. Ski-jumping	20	10
565	30f. Relay runners	55	20
566	45f. Bob-sleighing	90	35
567	60f. As 30f. (air)	1·10	40
568	90f. Type **90**	1·00	55
MS569	90×120 mm. Nos. 566/8. Imperf	3·00	1·25

1967. National Day (29 Sept). Nos. 525/31 optd **JOURNEE NATIONALE DU TOGO 29 SEPTEMBRE 1967.**

570	5f. multicoloured (postage)	35	20
571	10f. multicoloured	35	20
572	30f. multicoloured	1·00	40
573	45f. multicoloured (air)	40	20
574	60f. multicoloured	80	35
575	90f. multicoloured	1·25	45
576	105f. multicoloured	2·25	65

92 "The Gleaners" (Millet) and Benin Phosphate Mine

1968. Paintings and Local Industries.

577	**92**	10f. multicoloured	20	10
578	-	20f. multicoloured	30	10
579	**92**	30f. multicoloured	60	15
580	-	45f. multicoloured	70	20
581	**92**	60f. multicoloured	1·25	45
582	-	90f. multicoloured	1·40	70

DESIGN: 20, 45, 90f. "The Weaver at the Loom" (Van Gogh) and textile plant, Dadia.

93 Brewing Beer

1968. Benin Brewery. Multicoloured.

583	20f. Type **93**	35	10
584	30f. "Drinking at a Bar" (detail from painting by Manet) (vert)	1·00	30
585	45f. Bottling-washing machine and bottle of Benin beer	70	40

94 Decade Emblem and Sunflowers

1968. International Hydrological Decade.

586	**94**	30f. multicoloured (postage)	60	30
587	**94**	60f. multicoloured (air)	85	40

95 Viking Longship and Portuguese Galleon

1968. Inaug of Lome Port. Multicoloured.

588	5f. Type **95** (postage)	15	10
589	10f. Paddle-steamer "Clermont" and Liner "Athlone Castle"	20	10
590	20f. Quayside, Lome Port	65	20
591	30f. Type **95**	90	35
592	45f. As 10f. (air)	1·10	40
593	90f. Nuclear-powered freighter "Savannah"	2·00	60
MS594	76×100 mm. Nos. 592/3. Imperf	3·10	1·00

96 Dr. Adenauer and Europa "Key"

1968. Adenauer (German statesman) Commem.

595	**96**	90f. multicoloured	1·60	80

97 "Dr. Turp's Anatomy Lesson" (Rembrandt)

1968. 20th Anniv of World Health Organization. Paintings. Multicoloured.

596	15f. "Expulsion from the Garden of Eden" (Michelangelo) (postage)	30	10
597	20f. Type **97**	40	15
598	30f. "Johann Deyman's Anatomy Lesson" (Rembrandt)	55	20
599	45f. "Christ healing the sick" (Raphael)	85	35
600	60f. As 30f. (air)	85	40
601	90f. As 45f.	1·10	55
MS602	76×100 mm. Nos. 600/1. Imperf	1·90	95

98 Wrestling

1968. Olympic Games, Mexico. Multicoloured.

603	15f. Type **98** (postage)	20	15
604	20f. Boxing	45	15
605	30f. Judo	65	20
606	45f. Running	80	35
607	60f. Type **98** (air)	90	40
608	90f. As 45f.	1·25	55
MS609	100×75 mm. Nos. 607/8. Imperf	2·10	95

99 "Try Your Luck"

1968. Second Anniv of National Lottery. Multicoloured.

610	30f. Type **99**	55	25
611	45f. Lottery ticket, horse-shoe and cloverleaf	80	30

100 Scout and Tent

1968. Air. "Philexafrique" Stamp Exhibition, Abidjan (Ivory Coast, 1969) (1st issue). As T **98a** of Senegal. Multicoloured.

612	100f. "The Letter" (J. A. Franquelin)	2·75	1·90

1968. Togolese Scouts. Multicoloured.

613	5f. Type **100** (postage)	10	10
614	10f. Scoutmaster with cubs	30	10
615	20f. Giving first aid	40	15
616	30f. Scout game	50	20
617	45f. As 10f.	65	35
618	60f. As 20f. (air)	90	45
619	90f. As 30f.	1·25	65
MS620	75×100 mm. Nos. 618/19. Imperf	2·10	1·10

The 10, 20, 45 and 60f. are horiz.

101 "The Adoration of the Shepherds" (Giorgione)

1968. Christmas. Paintings. Multicoloured.

621	15f. Type **101** (postage)	35	10
622	20f. "The Adoration of the Kings" (Brueghel)	45	10
623	30f. "The Adoration" (Botticelli)	55	15
624	45f. "The Adoration" (Durer)	90	35
625	60f. As 20f. (air)	1·00	40
626	90f. As 45f.	1·50	55
MS627	75×100 mm. Nos. 625/6. Imperf	2·50	95

102 Martin Luther King

1969. Human Rights Year.

628	**102**	15f. green & brown (postage)	20	10
629	-	20f. violet and turquoise	35	15
630	**102**	30f. blue and red	55	20
631	-	45f. red and olive	1·10	45
632	-	60f. blue and purple (air)	90	45
633	**102**	90f. brown and green	1·25	55
MS634		100×75 mm. Nos. 632/3. Imperf	2·10	95

PORTRAITS: 20f. Prof. Rene Cassin (Nobel Peace Prize-winner); 45f. Pope John XXIII; 60f. Robert E. Kennedy.

1969. Air. "Philexafrique" Stamp Exn, Abidjan, Ivory Coast (2nd issue). As T **101a** of Senegal.

635	50f. red, brown and green	80	80

DESIGN: 50f. Aledjo Rock and stamp of 1900.

103 Football

1969. Inaug of Sports Stadium, Lome.

636	**103**	10f. brown, red and green (postage)	10	10
637	-	15f. brown, blue and orange	30	10
638	-	20f. brown, green and yellow	40	15
639	-	30f. brown, blue and green	50	20
640	-	45f. brown, violet and orange	65	30
641	-	60f. brown, red and blue (air)	90	35
642	-	90f. brown, mauve and blue	1·25	55
MS643		76×100 mm. Nos. 641/2. Imperf	2·10	90

DESIGNS: 15f. Handball; 20f. Volleyball; 30f. Basketball; 45f. Tennis; 60f. Boxing; 90f. Cycling.

104 Module landing on Moon

1969. First Man on the Moon. Multicoloured.

644	1f. Type **104** (postage)	10	10
645	20f. Astronaut and module on Moon	20	10
646	30f. As Type **104**	40	15
647	45f. As 20f.	65	35
648	60f. Astronaut exploring lunar surface (air)	85	40
649	100f. Astronaut gathering Moon rock	1·40	70
MS650	100×140 mm. Nos. 646/9 with purple background. Imperf	3·25	1·60
MS650a	As above but with orange background. Imperf	3·25	1·60

105 "The Last Supper" (Tintoretto)

1969. Religious Paintings. Multicoloured.

651	5f. Type **105** (postage)	15	10
652	10f. "Christ's Vision at Emmaus" (Velazquez)	30	10
653	20f. "Pentecost" (El Greco)	50	20
654	30f. "The Annunciation" (Botticelli)	70	20
655	45f. As 10f.	1·10	45
656	90f. As 20f. (air)	1·90	65
MS657	95×92 mm. Nos. 655/6. Imperf	3·00	1·10

1969. Eisenhower Commem. Nos. 628/33 optd with Eisenhower's silhouette and **EN MEMOIRE DWIGHT D. EISENHOWER 1890-1968.**

658	**102**	15f. green & brown (postage)	25	15
659	-	20f. violet and turquoise	45	15
660	**102**	30f. blue and red	55	20
661	-	45f. red and olive	95	30
662	-	60f. blue and purple (air)	90	45
663	**102**	90f. brown and green	1·25	65
MS664		100×75 mm. Nos. 662/3. Imperf	2·10	1·10

107 Bank in Hand and Emblem

1969. Fifth Anniv of African Development Bank. Multicoloured.

665	30f. Type **107** (postage)	85	20
666	45f. Diesel locomotive in hand, and emblem	2·75	75
667	100f. Farmer and cattle in hand, and emblem (air)	1·25	55

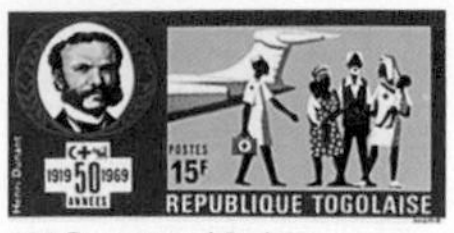

108 Dunant and Red Cross Workers

1969. 50th Anniv of League of Red Cross Societies. Multicoloured.

668	15f. Type **108** (postage)	35	10
669	20f. Pasteur and help for flood victims	40	10
670	30f. Fleming and flood control	75	20
671	45f. Rontgen and Red Cross post	95	30
672	60f. As 45f. (air)	90	45
673	90f. Type **108**	1·25	65
MS674	76×98 mm. Nos. 672/3. Imperf	2·10	1·10

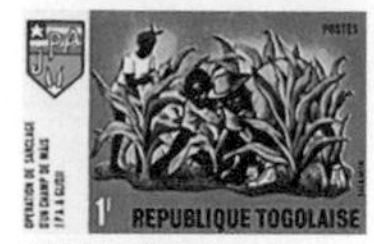

109 Weeding Corn

1969. Young Pioneers Agricultural Organization. Multicoloured.

675	1f. Type **109** (postage)	10	10
676	2f. Glidji Agricultural Centre	10	10
677	3f. Founding meeting	10	10
678	4f. Glidji class	15	10
679	5f. Student "pyramid"	15	10
680	7f. Students threshing	15	10
681	8f. Gardening instruction	15	10
682	10f. Co-op village	15	10
683	15f. Students gardening	30	15
684	20f. Cattle-breeding	35	15
685	25f. Poultry-farming	45	15
686	30f. Independence parade	45	20
687	40f. Boys on high-wire	65	35
688	45f. Tractor and trailer	80	35
689	50f. Co-op village	85	35
690	60f. Tractor-driving tuition	90	45
691	90f. Harvesting manioc (air)	1·10	45
692	100f. Gardening instruction	1·40	55
693	200f. Thinning-out corn	2·25	1·10
694	250f. Drummers marching	4·25	1·50
695	500f. Young pioneers marching	9·50	3·00

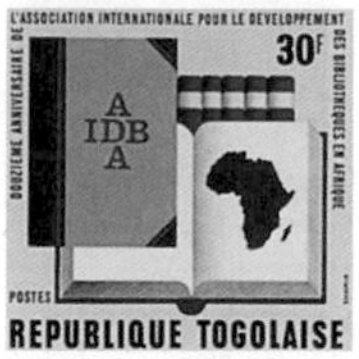

111 Books and Map

1969. 12th Anniv of International African Library Development Association.

700	**111**	30f. multicoloured	45	30

1969. Christmas. No. 644/5 and 647/9 optd **JOYEUX NOEL**.

701	1f. Type **104** (postage)	35	20
702	20f. Astronaut and module on Moon	1·10	45
703	45f. As 20f.	1·50	1·00
704	60f. Astronaut exploring lunar surface (air)	1·90	65
705	100f. Astronaut gathering Moon rock	3·00	1·00
MS706	95×92 mm. As Nos. 646/9. Imperf	3·25	1·60

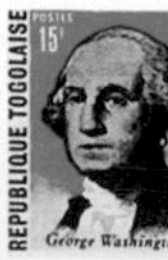

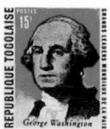

113 George Washington

1969. "Leaders of World Peace". Multicoloured.

707	15f. Type **113** (postage)	30	10
708	20f. Albert Luthule	35	10
709	30f. Mahatma Gandhi	55	15
710	45f. Simon Boliver	90	20
711	60f. Friedrich Ebert (air)	90	35
712	90f. As 30f.	1·25	50

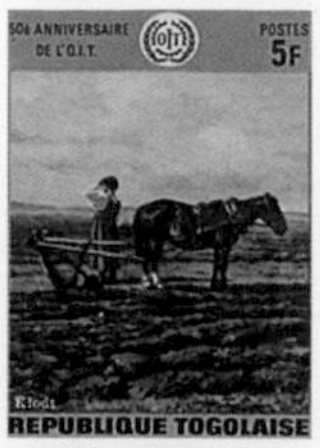

114 "Ploughing" (Klodt)

1970. 50th Anniv of I.L.O. Paintings. Multicoloured.

713	5f. Type **114** (postage)	10	10
714	10f. "Gardening" (Pissarro)	20	10
715	20f. "Harvesting Fruit" (Rivera)	35	10
716	30f. "Seeds of Spring" (Van Gogh)	80	35
717	45f. "Workers of the Fields" (Rivera)	80	35
718	60f. As 30f. (air)	1·00	35
719	90f. As 45f.	1·50	50
MS720	139×101 mm. Nos. 718/19. Imperf	2·50	85

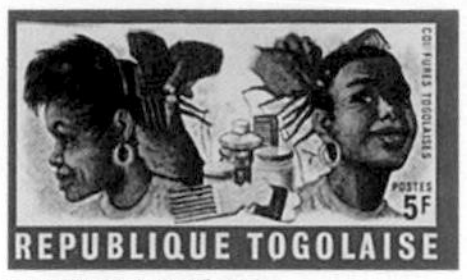

115 Model Coiffures

1970. Togolese Hair-styles. Multicoloured.

721	5f. Type **115** (postage)	15	10
722	10f. As T **115**, but different styles	35	10
723	20f. Fefe style	50	15
724	30f. Danmlongbedji style	1·25	20
725	45f. Blom style (air)	90	30
726	90f. Aklui and Danmlongbedji styles	1·60	65

Nos. 723/5 are vert.

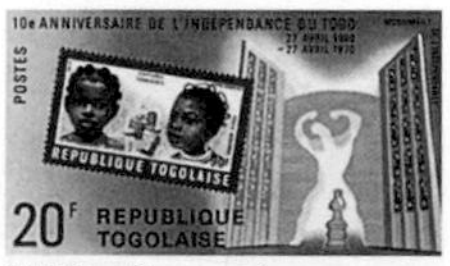

116 Togo Stamp and Independence Monument, Lome

1970. Tenth Anniv of Independence. Multicoloured.

727	20f. Type **116** (postage)	45	15
728	30f. Pres. Eyademe and Palace	65	20
729	50f. Map, dove and monument (vert)	1·10	35
730	60f. Togo stamp and monument (air)	80	40

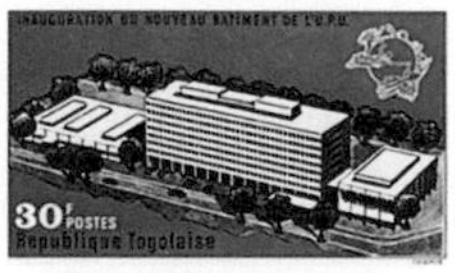

117 New U.P.U. Headquarters Building

1970. New U.P.U. Headquarters Building.

731	**117**	30f. violet and orange (postage)	1·00	35
732	**117**	50f. red and blue (air)	80	35

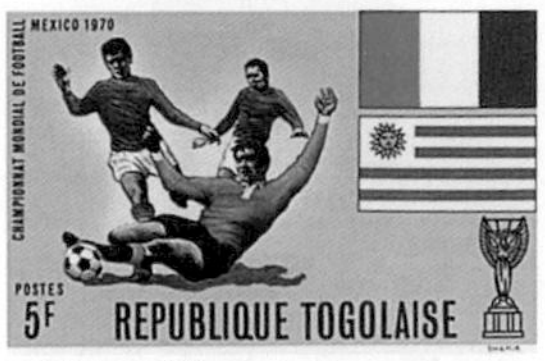

118 Italy and Uruguay

1970. World Cup Football Championships, Mexico. Multicoloured.

733	5f. Type **118** (postage)	10	10
734	10f. England and Brazil	20	10
735	15f. Russia and Mexico	35	10
736	20f. Germany and Morocco	45	10
737	30f. Rumania and Czechoslovakia	85	20
738	50f. Sweden and Israel (air)	55	30
739	60f. Bulgaria and Peru	65	35
740	90f. Belgium and El Salvador	1·25	50
MS741	140×105 mm. Nos. 737/40. Imperf	3·25	1·40

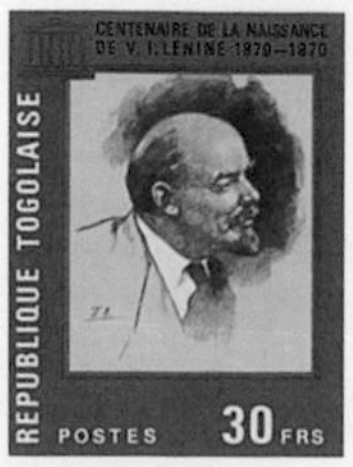

119 Lenin

1970. Birth Centenary of Lenin. Multicoloured.

742	30f. Type **119** (postage)	1·00	45
743	50f. "Peasant messengers with Lenin" (Serov) (air)	1·10	35

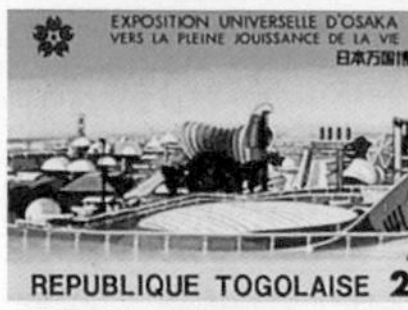

120 British Pavilion

1970. "Expo 70", Osaka, Japan. Multicoloured.

744	2f. Pennants, Sanyo Pavilion (57×36 mm)	15	10
745	20f. Type **120**	20	10
746	30f. French Pavilion	45	15
747	50f. Soviet Pavilion	85	30
748	60f. Japanese Pavilion	1·10	45
MS749	145×101 mm. 150f. Mitsubishi Pavilion (air)	2·50	1·00

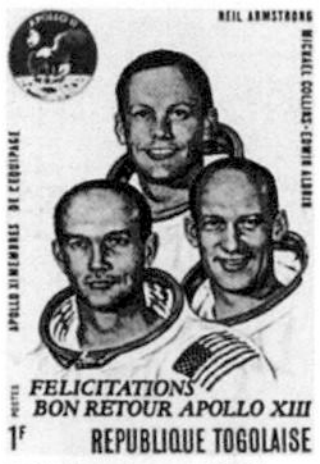

121 Armstrong, Collins and Aldrin

1970. "Apollo" Moon Flights. Multicoloured.

750	1f. Type **121** (postage)	10	10
751	2f. U.S. flag and moon-rock	10	10
752	20f. Astronaut and module on Moon	35	10
753	30f. Conrad, Gordon and Bean	65	20
754	50f. As 2f.	1·00	35
755	200f. Lovell, Haise and Swigert ("Apollo 13") (air)	2·50	1·40
MS756	129×100 mm. Nos. 750, 753 and 755. Imperf	3·25	1·75

1970. Safe Return of "Apollo 13". As Nos. 750/5, but additionally inscr "FELICITATIONS BON RETOUR APOLLO XIII".

757	**121**	1f. multicoloured (postage)	10	10
758	-	2f. multicoloured	10	10
759	-	20f. multicoloured	35	10
760	-	30f. multicoloured	65	20
761	-	50f. multicoloured	1·00	35
762	-	200f. multicoloured (air)	2·50	1·60
MS763		129×100 mm. Nos. 757, 760 and 762. Imperf	3·25	1·90

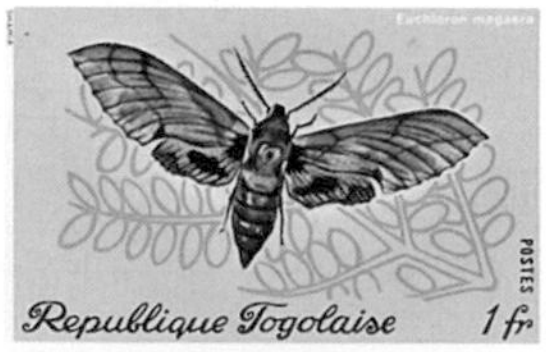

123 "Euchloron megaera"

1970. Butterflies and Moths. Multicoloured.

764	1f. Type **123** (postage)	15	10
765	2f. "Cymothoe sangaris"	30	10
766	30f. "Danaus chrysippus"	1·50	35
767	50f. "Morpho sp."	2·75	65
768	60f. Type **123** (air)	3·00	70
769	90f. "Pseudacraea boisiduvali"	4·25	95

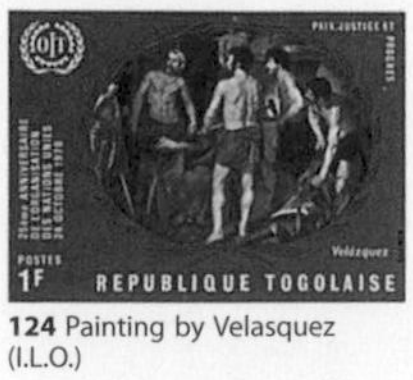

124 Painting by Velasquez (I.L.O.)

1970. 25th Anniv of U.N.O. Multicoloured.

770	1f. Type **124** (postage)	10	10
771	15f. Painting by Delacroix (F.A.O.)	10	10
772	20f. Painting by Holbein (UNESCO)	20	15
773	30f. Painting of U.N. H.Q., New York	60	15
774	50f. Painting by Renoir (UNICEF)	90	35
775	60f. Painting by Van Gogh (U.P.U.) (air)	1·00	35
776	90f. Painting by Carpaccio (W.H.O./O.M.S.)	1·50	50
MS777	139×100 mm. Nos. 773/6. Imperf	4·00	1·40

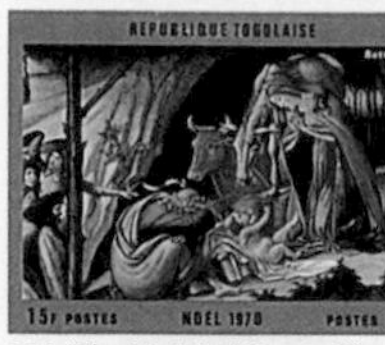

125 "The Nativity" (Botticelli)

1970. Christmas. "Nativity" Paintings by Old Masters. Multicoloured.

778	15f. Type **125** (postage)	15	10
779	20f. Veronese	15	10
780	30f. El Greco	55	15
781	50f. Fra Angelico	1·00	30
782	60f. Botticelli (different) (air)	1·25	30
783	90f. Tiepolo	1·75	45
MS784	186×115 mm. Nos. 782/3	3·00	85

1971. De Gaulle Commemoration (1st issue). Nos. 708/9 and 711/12 optd **EN MEMOIRE Charles De Gaulle 1890-1970** or surch in addition.

785	30f. multicoloured (postage)	1·10	35
786	30f. on 90f. multicoloured	1·10	35
787	150f. on 20f. multicoloured	6·75	1·75
788	200f. on 60f. mult (air)	5·25	2·50

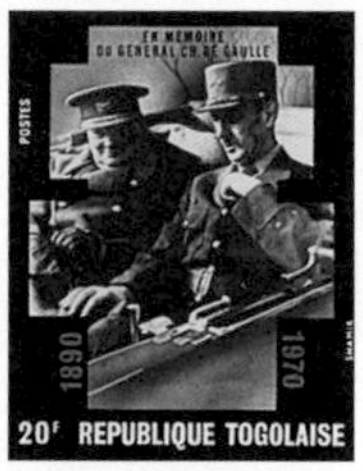

127 De Gaulle and Churchill

1971. De Gaulle Commemoration (2nd issue).

789	**127**	20f. blue & black (postage)	55	15
790	-	30f. red and black	65	20
791	-	40f. green and black	1·00	40
792	-	50f. brown and black	1·25	50
793	-	60f. violet and black (air)	2·25	55
794	-	90f. blue and black	3·25	80
MS795		105×145 mm. Nos. 791/4. Imperf	7·75	2·10

DESIGNS: 30f. De Gaulle with Eisenhower; 40f. With Pres. Kennedy; 50f. With Adenauer; 60f. With Pope Paul VI; 90f. General De Gaulle.

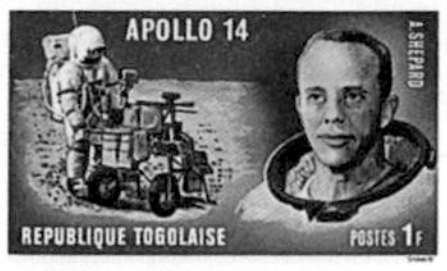

128 Shepard and Moon Exploration

1971. Moon Mission of "Apollo 14". Multicoloured.

796	1f. Type **128** (postage)	10	10
797	10f. Mitchell and rock-gathering	15	10
798	30f. Roosa and module approaching Moon	50	15
799	40f. Launch from Moon	90	30
800	50f. "Apollo 14" emblem (air)	60	20
801	100f. As 40f.	1·25	40
802	200f. As 50f.	2·10	80
MS803	139×100 mm. Nos. 799/802. Imperf	4·75	1·75

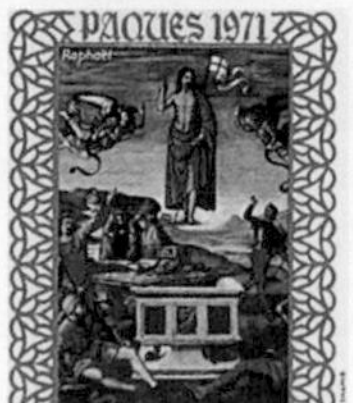

129 "The Resurrection" (after Raphael)

1971. Easter. Paintings of "The Resurrection" by various artists. Multicoloured.

804	1f. Type **129** (postage)	15	10
805	30f. Master of Trebon	55	15
806	40f. Type **129**	95	30
807	50f. M. Grunewald (air)	80	30
808	60f. As 30f.	1·00	40
809	90f. El Greco	1·50	55
MS810	199×154 mm. Nos. 806/9	4·25	1·50

130 Cocoa Tree and Pods

1971. International Cocoa Day. Multicoloured.

811	30f. Type **130** (postage)	55	15
812	40f. Sorting beans	85	20
813	50f. Drying beans	1·10	35
814	60f. Agricultural Ministry, Lome	60	30
815	90f. Type **130**	1·10	50
816	100f. As 40f.	1·25	60

131 Sud Aviation Caravelle over Control Tower

1971. Tenth Anniv of A.S.E.C.N.A. (Aerial Navigation Security Agency).

817	**131**	30f. multicoloured (postage)	90	35
818	**131**	100f. multicoloured (air)	1·50	65

132 Napoleon

1971. 150th Death Anniv of Napoleon. Embossed on gold foil.

819	**132**	1000f. gold	22·00	
MS820	100×119 mm. As T **132**. 1000f. gold. Embossed on card. Imperf		22·00	

133 Great Market, Lome

1971. Tourism. Multicoloured.

821	20f. Type **133** (postage)	35	10
822	30f. Wooden sculpture and protea	55	15
823	40f. Aledjo Gorge and olive baboon	80	20
824	50f. Vale Castle and red-fronted gazelle (air)	65	20
825	60f. Lake Togo and alligator	90	30
826	100f. Furnace, Tokpli, and hip-popotamus	1·25	40

134 Gbatchoume Image

1971. Togolese Religions. Multicoloured.

827	20f. Type **134** (postage)	35	15
828	30f. High priest, Temple of Atta Sakuma	50	20
829	40f. "Holy Stone" ceremony	85	30
830	50f. Moslem worshippers, Lome Mosque (air)	55	20
831	60f. Protestants	70	30

832	90f. Catholic ceremony, Djogbe-gan Monastery	95	40
MS833	128×102 mm. Nos. 829/32.	3·00	1·25

1971. Memorial Issue for "Soyuz 11" Astronauts. Nos. 799/MS803 optd **EN MEMOIRE DOBROVOLSKY - VOLKOV - PATSAYEV SOYUZ 11** or surch also.

834	40f. multicoloured (postage)	1·00	35
835	90f. on 50f. multicoloured (air)	90	35
836	100f. multicoloured	1·10	40
837	200f. multicoloured	2·00	65
MS838	139×100 mm. Nos. 834/7. Imperf	5·00	1·75

136 Speed-skating

1971. Winter Games, Sapporo, Japan (1972). Multicoloured.

839	1f. Type **136** (postage)	10	10
840	10f. Slalom skiing	10	10
841	20f. Figure-skating	35	10
842	30f. Bob-sleighing	55	20
843	50f. Ice-hockey	1·10	35
844	200f. Ski-jumping (air)	2·25	95
MS845	127×99 mm. Nos. 841/4. Imperf	5·25	1·60

1971. Air. Tenth Anniv of African and Malagasy Posts and Telecommunications Union. As T **141** of Senegal. Multicoloured.

846	100f. U.A.M.P.T. H.Q. and Adjogobo dancers	1·10	55

137 Togolese Child and Mask

1971. Air. "Children of the World". Embossed on gold foil.

847	**137**	1500f. gold	15·00	

138 Wooden Crocodile

1971. 25th Anniv of UNICEF. Multicoloured.

848	20f. Type **138** (postage)	20	10
849	30f. Toy "Bambi" and butterfly	45	15
850	50f. Toy monkey	80	30
851	50f. Wooden elephant on wheels	1·00	30
852	60f. Toy turtle (air)	55	20
853	90f. Toy parrot	85	35
MS854	115×97 mm. Nos. 850/3. Imperf	3·25	1·10

139 "Virgin and Child" (Botticelli)

1971. Christmas. "Virgin and Child" Paintings by Old Masters. Multicoloured.

855	10f. Type **139** (postage)	10	10
856	30f. (Maitre de la Vie de Marie)	65	20
857	40f. (Durer)	1·10	35
858	50f. (Veronese)	1·40	45
859	60f. (Giorgione) (air)	1·00	35
860	100f. (Raphael)	1·75	55
MS861	130×175 mm. Nos. 857/60. Imperf	5·25	1·75

140 St. Mark's Basilica, Venice

1972. UNESCO "Save Venice" Campaign. Multicoloured.

862	30f. Type **140** (postage)	90	30
863	40f. Rialto Bridge	1·25	40
864	100f. Doge's Palace (air)	1·40	65
MS865	100×131 mm. Nos. 862/4. Imperf	3·50	1·40

141 "The Crucifixion" (unknown artist)

1972. Easter. Religious Paintings. Multicoloured.

866	25f. Type **141** (postage)	45	15
867	30f. "The Deposition" (Botticelli)	70	15
868	40f. Type **141**	90	30
869	50f. "The Resurrection" (Thomas de Coloswar) (air)	85	20
870	100f. "The Ascension" (Mantegna)	1·60	40
MS871	120×148 mm. Nos. 867/70. Imperf	4·00	90

142 Heart Emblem and Blacksmith

1972. World Heart Month. Multicoloured.

872	30f. Type **142** (postage)	45	15
873	40f. Typist	55	20
874	60f. Javelin-thrower	85	35
875	100f. Type **142** (air)	1·25	45
MS876	77×91 mm. Nos. 874/5. Imperf	2·60	1·00

143 Hotel de la Paix, Lome

1972. O.C.A.M. Summit Conference, Lome. Embossed on gold foil.

877	**143**	1000f. gold, red and green	10·00	

1972. Pres. Nixon's Visit to China. Nos. 823/4 optd **VISITE DU PRESIDENT NIXON EN CHINE FEVRIER 1972** and additionally surch (No. 879).

878	300f. on 40f. mult (postage)	4·00	1·90
879	50f. multicoloured (air)	1·00	35

145 Woman preparing Cassava

1972. Cassava Industries. Multicoloured.

880	25f. Collecting cassava (horiz) (postage)	45	15
881	40f. Type **145**	65	20
882	60f. Cassava truck and factory (horiz) (air)	90	20
883	80f. Mother with Benin tapi-oca cake	1·25	45

146 Video-telephone

1972. World Telecommunications Day. Multicoloured.

884	40f. Type **146** (postage)	1·00	35

885	100f. "Intelsat 4" and map of Africa (air)	1·50	45

1972. Air. Pres. Nixon's Visit to Russia. No. 743 surch **VISITE DU PRESIDENT NIXON EN RUSSIE MAI 1972** and value.

886	300f. on 50f. multicoloured	5·00	2·75

148 Basketball

1972. Olympic Games, Munich. Multicoloured.

887	30f. Type **148** (postage)	50	15
888	40f. Running	65	20
889	50f. Throwing the discus	90	30
890	90f. Gymnastics (air)	65	35
891	200f. Type **148**	1·75	80
MS892	136×98 mm. Nos. 889/90. Imperf	1·50	65

149 Pin-tailed Whydah

1973. Exotic Birds. Multicoloured.

893	25f. Type **149** (postage)	75	25
894	30f. Broad-tailed paradise whydah	1·00	35
895	40f. Yellow-mantled whydah	1·10	55
896	60f. Long-tailed whydah	2·75	90
897	90f. Rose-ringed parakeet (air)	3·75	1·25
MS898	109×134 mm. Nos. 894/7. Imperf	7·75	3·00

150 Paul Harris (founder)

1972. Rotary International. Multicoloured.

899	40f. Type **150** (postage)	40	20
900	50f. Rotary and Togo flags	50	30
901	60f. Rotary emblem, map and laurel (air)	65	20
902	90f. As 50f.	90	35
903	100f. Type **150**	1·25	45
MS904	122×106 mm. Nos. 899/900. Imperf	3·75	1·50

151 "Mona Lisa" (L. da Vinci)

1972. Famous Paintings. Multicoloured.

905	25f. Type **151** (postage)	1·10	30
906	40f. "Virgin and Child" (Bellini)	1·25	30
907	60f. "Mystical Marriage of St. Catherine" (Master P.N.'s assistant) (air)	1·00	30
908	80f. "Self-portrait" (L. da Vinci)	1·25	35
909	100f. "St. Marie and Angels" (Botticelli)	1·60	50
MS910	112×140 mm. Nos. 906/9. Imperf	5·00	1·40

1972. Tenth Anniv of West African Monetary Union. As T **156** of Senegal.

| 911 | 40f. brown, grey and red | 55 | 40 |

152 Party H.Q. of R.P.T. and Presidents Pompidou and Eyadama

1972. Visit of President Pompidou to Togo. Multicoloured.

| 912 | 40f. Type **152** (postage) | 1·10 | 45 |
| 913 | 100f. Party H.Q. rear view and portraits as T **152** (air) | 1·75 | 55 |

153 Goethe

1972. Air. 140th Death Anniv of Goethe (poet).

| 914 | **153** | 100f. multicoloured | 1·50 | 65 |

154 "The Annunciation" (unknown artist)

1972. Christmas. Religious Paintings. Multicoloured.

915	25f. Type **154** (postage)	35	20
916	30f. "The Nativity" (Master Theodor of Prague)	55	20
917	40f. Type **154**	80	20
918	60f. As 30f. (air)	80	20
919	80f. "The Adoration of the Magi" (unknown artist)	1·00	30
920	100f. "The Flight into Egypt" (Giotto)	1·25	45
MS921 124×140 mm. Nos. 917/20. Imperf		3·75	1·10

155 R. Follerau and Allegory

1973. "World Day of the Leper". (a) Postage. 20th Anniv of Follereau Foundation.

| 922 | **155** | 40f. violet and green | 1·60 | 55 |

(b) Air. Cent of Hansen's Bacillus Discovery.

| 923 | | 100f. blue and red | 2·50 | 85 |

DESIGN: 100f. Dr. Hansen, microscope and bacillus slide.

156 W.H.O. Emblem

1973. 25th Anniv of W.H.O.

| 924 | **156** | 30f. multicoloured | 45 | 15 |
| 925 | **156** | 40f. multicoloured | 55 | 20 |

157 "The Crucifixion"

1973. Easter. Multicoloured.

926	25f. Type **157** (postage)	35	15
927	30f. "The Deposition"	55	20
928	40f. "The Resurrection"	80	20
929	90f. "Christ in Majesty" (air)	1·25	45
MS930 90×100 mm. Nos. 928/9. Imperf		2·00	65

158 Astronauts Cernan, Evans and Schmitt

1973. "Apollo 17" Moon Flight. Multicoloured.

931	30f. Type **158** (postage)	80	15
932	40f. Moon rover	1·00	30
933	100f. Discovery of "orange" rock (air)	1·10	40
934	200f. Pres. Kennedy and lift-off	2·25	85
MS935 108×100 mm. Nos. 933/4. Imperf		3·25	1·25

159 Erecting Tent

1973. International Scout Congress. Nairobi/Addis Ababa. Multicoloured.

936	10f. Type **159** (postage)	20	10
937	20f. Cooking meal (horiz)	45	10
938	30f. Rope-climbing	75	15
939	40f. Type **159**	1·00	20
940	100f. Canoeing (horiz) (air)	1·50	40
941	200f. As 20f.	2·75	85
MS942 108×98 mm. Nos. 940/1. Imperf		4·25	1·25

160 Heliocentric System

1973. 500th Birth Anniv of Copernicus. Multicoloured.

943	10f. Type **160** (postage)	15	10
944	20f. Copernicus	30	10
945	30f. "Astronomy" and "Astro-nautics"	65	15
946	40f. Astrolabe	85	20
947	90f. Type **160** (air)	1·25	35
948	100f. As 20f.	1·40	45
MS949 122×108 mm. Nos. 947/8. Imperf		2·60	80

161 Ambulance Team

1973. Togolese Red Cross. Multicoloured.

| 950 | 40f. Type **161** (postage) | 90 | 35 |
| 951 | 100f. Dove of peace, sun and map (air) | 1·90 | 65 |

1973. "Drought Relief". African Solidarity. No. 766 surch **SECHERESSE SOLIDARITE AFRICAINE 100F.**

| 952 | 100f. on 30f. multicoloured | 1·25 | 85 |

163 Classroom

1973. Literacy Campaign. Multicoloured.

953	30f. Type **163** (postage)	35	15
954	40f. African reading book (vert)	85	30
955	90f. Classroom (different) (air)	85	45

1973. African and Malagasy Posts and Telecommunications Union. As T **170** of Senegal.

| 956 | 100f. red, yellow and purple | 1·10 | 65 |

164 Interpol Emblem and H.Q. Paris

1973. 50th Anniv of Interpol.

| 957 | **164** | 30f. green, brown & yellow | 45 | 15 |
| 958 | **164** | 40f. blue, mauve and green | 65 | 20 |

165 W.M.O. Emblem in Weather-vane

1973. Centenary of W.M.O.

| 959 | **165** | 40f. grn, brn & yell (post) | 90 | 35 |
| 960 | **165** | 200f. brown, vio & bl (air) | 1·90 | 85 |

166 Togo Stamp and Steam and Diesel Locomotives

1973. 75th Anniv of Togolese Postal Services. Multicoloured.

961	25f. Type **166** (postage)	65	20
962	30f. Togo stamp and mail coaches	60	20
963	90f. Togo stamps and mail boats	1·75	45
964	100f. Togo stamps and mail-planes (air)	2·40	80
MS965 126×92 mm. Nos. 963/4. Imperf		4·00	1·25

167 Kennedy and A. Schaerf

1973. Tenth Death Anniv of Pres. Kennedy.

966	**167**	20f. violet and black on blue (postage)	35	10
967	-	30f. brown and black on brown	50	20
968	-	40f. green & black on green	85	30
969	-	90f. purple and black on mauve (air)	1·60	45
970	-	100f. blue & black on blue	1·60	45
971	-	200f. brown & blk on brown	2·75	80
MS972 114×72 mm. Nos. 970/1. Imperf			4·25	1·25

DESIGNS: 30f. Kennedy and Harold Macmillan; 40f. Kennedy and Konrad Adenauer; 90f. Kennedy and Charles de Gaulle; 100f. Kennedy and Nikita Kruschev; 200f. Kennedy and "Apollo" spacecraft.

168 Flame Emblem and "People"

1973. Air. 25th Anniv of Declaration of Human Rights.

| 973 | **168** | 250f. multicoloured | 2·75 | 1·40 |

169 "Virgin and Child" (anon)

1973. Christmas. Multicoloured.

974	25f. Type **169** (postage)	50	15
975	30f. "Adoration of the Magi" (Vivarini)	60	20
976	90f. "Virgin and Child" (S. di Pietro) (air)	1·00	35
977	100f. "Adoration of the Magi" (anon)	1·40	40
MS978 121×86 mm. Nos. 976/7. Imperf		2·75	75

1974. Lome District Rotary International Convention. Nos. 899, 901 and 903 optd **PREMIERE CONVENTION 210eme DISTRICT FEVRIER 1974 LOME.**

979	**150**	40f. mult (postage)	55	35
980	-	60f. multicoloured (air)	45	20
981	**150**	100f. multicoloured	90	35

171 Footballers

1974. World Cup Football Championship, West Germany.

982	**171**	20f. mult (postage)	35	15
983	-	30f. multicoloured	45	15
984	-	40f. multicoloured	55	20
985	-	90f. multicoloured (air)	90	35
986	-	100f. multicoloured	1·00	40
987	-	200f. multicoloured	2·00	70
MS988 69×110 mm. Nos. 986/7. Imperf		3·00	1·10

DESIGNS: Nos. 983/7, similar designs to Type **171**, showing footballers in action.

1974. Tenth Anniv of World Food Programme. Nos. 880/1 optd **10e ANNIVERSAIRE DU P. A. M.** or surch also.

| 989 | **145** | 40f. multicoloured | 55 | 35 |
| 990 | | 100f. on 25f. | 1·25 | 80 |

173 "Girl Before Mirror" (Picasso)

1974. Picasso Commemoration. Multicoloured.

991	20f. Type **173** (postage)	55	20
992	30f. "The Turkish Shawl"	80	35
993	40f. "Mandoline and Guitar"	1·10	35
994	90f. "The Muse" (air)	1·00	35
995	100f. "Les Demoiselles d'Avignon"	1·25	40
996	200f. "Sitting Nude"	2·50	85
MS997 155×104 mm. Nos. 994/6. Imperf		4·75	1·60

174 Kpeme Village

1974. Coastal Scenes. Multicoloured.

998	30f. Type **174** (postage)	45	20
999	40f. Tropicana tourist village	65	40
1000	90f. Fisherman on Lake Togo (air)	1·00	35
1001	100f. Mouth of Aneche River	1·25	40
MS1002 73×78 mm. Nos. 1000/1. Imperf		2·25	75

175 Togolese Postman

1974. Centenary of U.P.U. Multicoloured.

1003	30f. Type **175** (postage)	40	20
1004	40f. Postman with cleft carrying-stick	50	30
1005	50f. Type **175** (air)	60	30
1006	100f. As 40f.	1·25	45
MS1006a	Sheet 112×77 mm. Nos. 1005/6	1·75	75

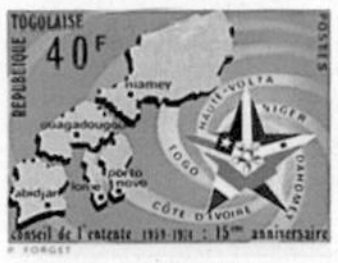

176 Map of Member Countries

1974. 15th Anniv of Council of Accord.

1007	**176** 40f. multicoloured	50	30

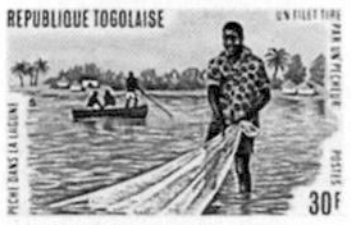

177 Hauling in Net

1974. Lagoon Fishing. Multicoloured.

1008	30f. Type **177** (postage)	45	20
1009	40f. Throwing net	65	30
1010	90f. Fishes in net (air)	1·00	30
1011	100f. Fishing with lines	1·25	35
1012	200f. Fishing with basket (vert)	2·75	70
MS1013	103×117 mm. Nos. 1010/12. Imperf	5·00	1·40

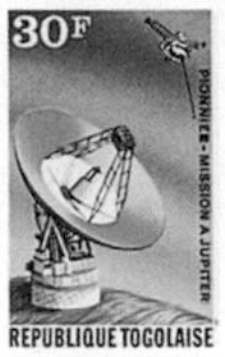

178 Earth Station and Probe

1974. U.S. "Jupiter" Space Mission. Multicoloured.

1014	30f. Type **178** (postage)	35	15
1015	40f. Probe transmitting to Earth (horiz)	45	20
1016	100f. Blast-off (air)	95	40
1017	200f. Jupiter probe (horiz)	1·75	70
MS1018	84×95 mm. Nos. 1016/17. Perf or imperf	2·75	1·10

1974. "Internaba 1974" Stamp Exhibition, Basel. Nos. 884/5 optd **INTERNABA 1974 CENTENARIUM U P U** and emblem.

1019	**146** 40f. mult (postage)	3·50	1·00
1020	- 100f. multicoloured (air)	4·25	1·40

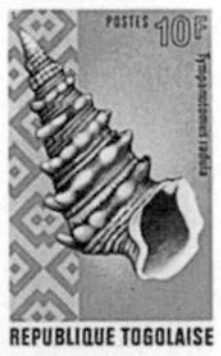

180 "Tympanotomus radula"

1974. Sea Shells. Multicoloured.

1021	10f. Type **180** (postage)	25	20
1022	20f. Giant tun	35	20
1023	30f. Trader cone	55	20
1024	40f. Great ribbed cockle	85	20
1025	90f. Ponsonbyi's volute (air)	1·40	40
1026	100f. Iredale's bonnet	1·90	40
MS1027	115×75 mm. Nos. 1025/6. Imperf	3·25	80

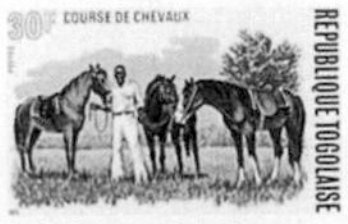

181 Groom with Horses

1974. Horse-racing. Multicoloured.

1028	30f. Type **181** (postage)	45	20
1029	40f. Exercising horses	65	30
1030	90f. Steeple-chaser taking fence (air)	1·00	35
1031	100f. Horses racing	1·50	45
MS1032	100×78 mm. Nos. 1030/1. Imperf	2·50	80

1974. Air. West Germany's Victory in World Cup Football Championship. Nos. 890/**MS**892 optd **COUPE DU MONDE DE FOOTBALL MUNICH 1974 VAINQUERS REPUBLIQUE FEDERALE ALLEMAGNE**.

1033	- 90f. multicoloured	90	35
1034	**148** 200f. multicoloured	1·75	80
MS1035	136×98 mm. 50, 90f. multicoloured. Imperf	1·25	55

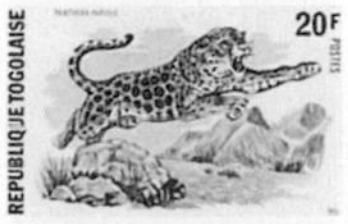

183 Leopard

1974. Wild Animals. Multicoloured.

1036	20f. Type **183** (postage)	50	15
1037	30f. Giraffes	75	20
1038	40f. Two African elephants	1·00	35
1039	90f. Lion and lioness (air)	1·50	45
1040	100f. Black rhinoceros and calf	2·00	45
MS1041	107×86 mm. Nos. 1038/40. Imperf	4·50	1·25

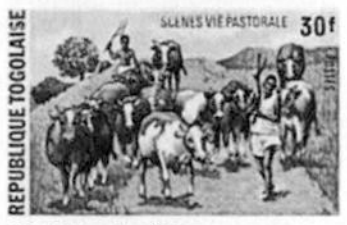

184 Herd of Cows

1974. Pastoral Economy. Multicoloured.

1042	30f. Type **184** (postage)	45	20
1043	40f. Milking	65	30
1044	90f. Cattle at water-hole (air)	85	45
1045	100f. Village cattle-pen	1·10	55
MS1046	85×78 mm. Nos. 1044/5. Imperf	1·90	1·00

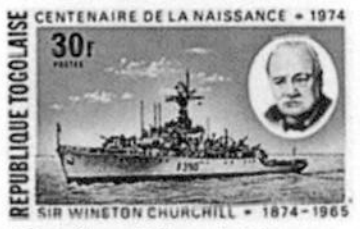

185 Churchill and Frigate H.M.S. "Loch Fada"

1974. Birth Centenary of Sir Winston Churchill. Multicoloured.

1047	30f. Type **185** (postage)	50	15
1048	40f. Churchill and Supermarine Spitfires	60	20
1049	100f. Type **185** (air)	1·40	35
1050	200f. As 40f.	2·25	80
MS1051	111×88 mm. Nos. 1049/50	2·60	1·10

1975. Opening of Hotel de la Paix, Lome. Optd **Inauguration de la l'hotel Paix 9-1-75.**

1051a	**143** 1000f. gold, red and green	9·50	

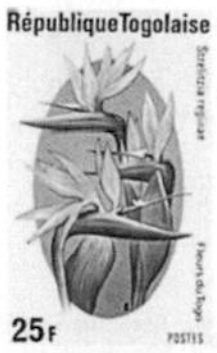

186 "Strelitzia reginae"

1975. Flowers of Togo. Multicoloured.

1052	25f. Type **186** (postage)	35	15
1053	30f. "Strophanthus sarmentosus"	45	15
1054	40f. "Chlamydocarya macrocarpa" (horiz)	55	20
1055	60f. "Clerodendrum scandens" (horiz)	90	35
1056	100f. "Clerodendrum thosonae" (horiz) (air)	1·40	45
1057	200f. "Gloriosa superba" (horiz)	2·50	65
MS1058	95×77 mm. Nos. 1056/7	3·75	1·10

1975. 70th Anniv of Rotary International. Optd **70e ANNIVERSAIRE 23 FEVRIER 1975.**

1059	**150** 40f. mult (postage)	30	25
1060	- 90f. multicoloured (No. 902) (air)	85	35
1061	**150** 100f. multicoloured	1·00	40

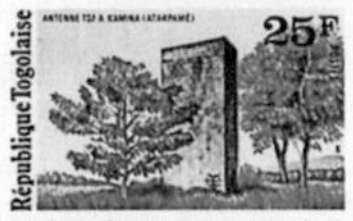

188 Radio Station, Kamina

1975. Tourism. Multicoloured.

1062	25f. Type **188**	20	10
1063	30f. Benedictine Monastery, Zogbegan	35	20
1064	40f. Causeway, Atchinedji	45	30
1065	60f. Ayome Waterfalls	80	40

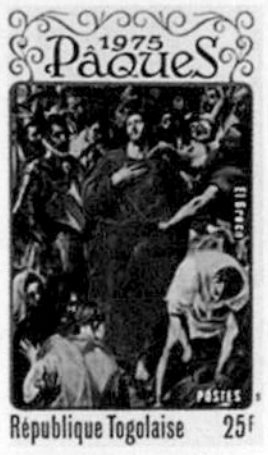

189 "Jesus Mocked" (El Greco)

1975. Easter. Multicoloured.

1066	25f. Type **189** (postage)	20	10
1067	30f. "The Crucifixion" (Master Janoslen)	35	10
1068	40f. "The Descent from the Cross" (Bellini)	55	20
1069	90f. "Pieta" (anon)	95	40
1070	100f. "Christ rising from the Grave" (Master MS) (air)	1·10	35
1071	200f. "The Holy Trinity" (detail) (Durer)	1·90	80
MS1072	106×88 mm. Nos. 1070/1. Imperf	3·00	1·10

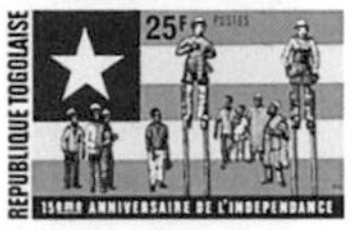

190 Stilt-walking

1975. 15th Anniv of Independence. Multicoloured.

1073	25f. Type **190** (postage)	30	10
1074	30f. Dancers	35	15
1075	50f. Independence parade (vert) (air)	40	15
1076	60f. Dancer	60	35
MS1077	115×108 mm. Nos. 1075/6. Imperf	1·00	50

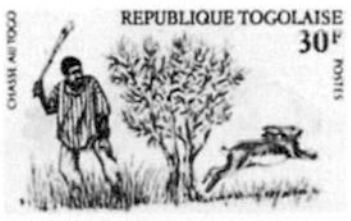

191 Hunting Bush Hare with Club

1975. Hunting. Multicoloured.

1078	30f. Type **191** (postage)	45	20
1079	40f. Hunting Eurasian beavers with bow	55	35
1080	90f. Hunting red deer with snare (air)	1·25	45
1081	100f. Hunting wild boar with gun	1·40	55

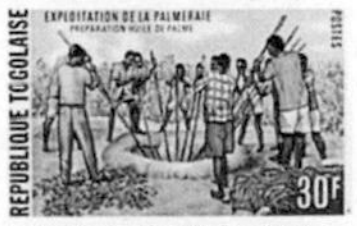

192 Pounding Palm Nuts

1975. Palm-oil Production. Multicoloured.

1082	30f. Type **192** (postage)	35	15
1083	40f. Extracting palm-oil (vert)	40	20
1084	85f. Selling palm-oil (vert) (air)	80	45
1085	100f. Oil-processing plant, Aloknegbe	90	55

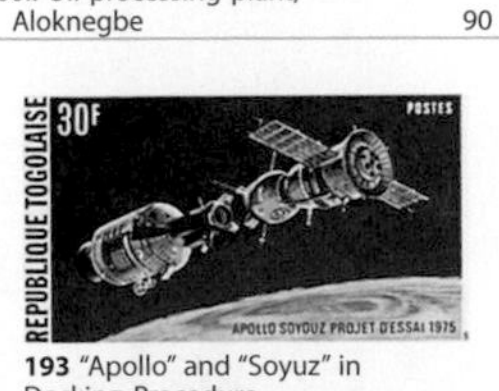

193 "Apollo" and "Soyuz" in Docking Procedure

1975. "Apollo–Soyuz" Space Link. Multicoloured.

1087	30f. Type **193** (postage)	45	15
1088	50f. "Soyuz" spacecraft (vert) (air)	40	15
1089	60f. Slaton, Brand and Stafford ("Apollo" astronauts)	55	20
1090	90f. Leonov and Kubasov ("Soyuz" cosmonauts)	70	30
1091	100f. U.S. and Soviet flags and "Apollo" and "Soyuz" linked	1·10	50
1092	200f. Emblem and globe	2·25	65
MS1093	150×105 mm. Nos. 1089/92	4·50	1·60

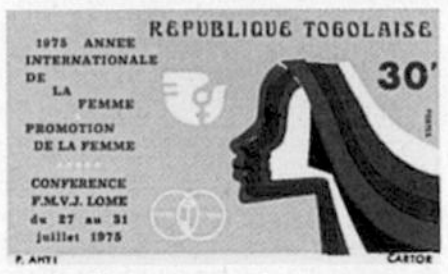

194 "African Women"

1975. International Women's Year.

1094	**194** 30f. multicoloured	40	15
1095	**194** 40f. multicoloured	45	20

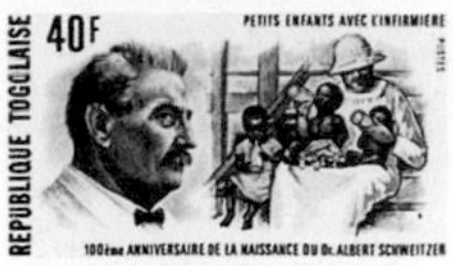

195 Dr. Schweitzer, and Children drinking Milk

1975. Birth Centenary of Dr. Albert Schweitzer. Multicoloured.

1096	40f. Type **195** (postage)	55	30
1097	80f. Schweitzer playing organ (vert) (air)	90	30
1098	90f. Schweitzer feeding Eastern white pelican (vert)	1·40	40
1099	100f. Schweitzer and Lambarene Hospital	1·25	35

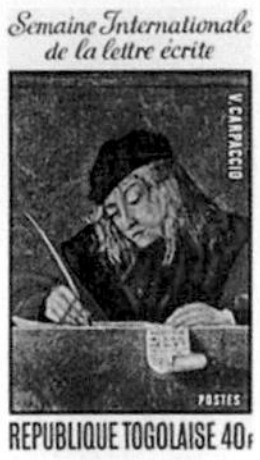

196 "Merchant writing Letter" (V. Carpaccio)

1975. International Letter-writing Week. Multicoloured.

1101	40f. Type **196** (postage)	55	30
1102	80f. "Erasmus writing Letter" (Holbein) (air)	90	35

1975. 30th Anniv of United Nations. Nos. 851/3 optd **30eme Anniversaire des Nations-Unies.**

1103	50f. multicoloured (postage)	55	30
1104	60f. multicoloured (air)	50	20
1105	90f. multicoloured	60	30
MS1106	115×97 mm. 40, 50, 60, 90f. Imperf	2·25	95

1975. Air. World Scout Jamboree, Norway. Nos. 940/1 optd **14eme JAMBOREE MONDIAL DES ECLAIREURS**.

1107	100f. multicoloured	95	45
1108	200f. multicoloured	1·75	80
MS1109	108×98 mm. Imperf	2·60	1·25

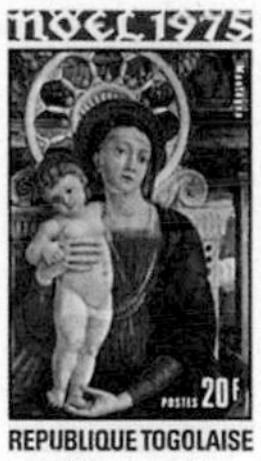

199 "Virgin and Child" (Mantegna)

1975. Christmas. "Virgin and Child" paintings by artists named. Multicoloured.

1110	20f. Type **199** (postage)	30	20
1111	30f. El Greco	40	20
1112	40f. Barend van Orley	45	20
1113	90f. Federigo Barocci (air)	80	30
1114	100f. Bellini	90	35
1115	200f. Correggio	1·60	55
MS1116	127×95 mm. Nos. 1114/15	2·50	90

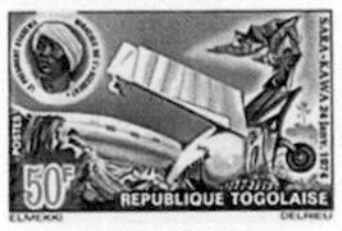

200 Crashed Airplane

1975. Pres. Eyadema's Escape in Air Crash at Sarakawa.

1117	**200** 50f. multicoloured	7·25	5·00
1118	**200** 60f. multicoloured	7·25	5·00

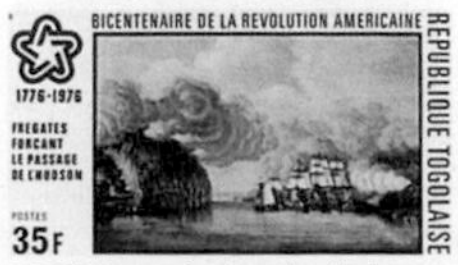

201 "Frigates forcing the Hudson Passage"

1976. Bicentenary of American Revolution. Multicoloured.

1119	35f. Type **201** (postage)	40	20
1120	50f. "George Washington" (G. Stuart) (vert)	55	30

1121	60f. "Surrender of Burgoyne" (Trumbull) (air)	65	20
1122	70f. "Surrender at Trenton" (Trumbull) (vert)	85	30
1123	100f. "Signing of Declaration of Independence" (Trumbull)	90	35
1124	200f. "Washington crossing the Delaware" (E. Leutze)	1·75	60
MS1125	138×95 mm. Nos. 1123/4	2·60	95

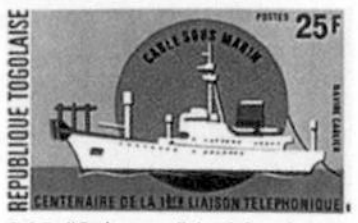

202 "Salerum" (cable ship)

1976. Telephone Centenary. Multicoloured.

1126	25f. Type **202** (postage)	30	15
1127	30f. Automatic telephone and tape-recording equipment	40	30
1128	70f. Edison and communications equipment (air)	55	30
1129	105f. Alexander Graham Bell, early and modern telephones	85	40
MS1130	130×100 mm. Nos. 1128/9	1·40	70

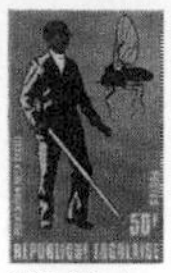

203 Blind Man and Mosquito

1976. World Health Day. Multicoloured.

1131	50f. Type **203** (postage)	65	30
1132	60f. Eye examination (air)	55	20

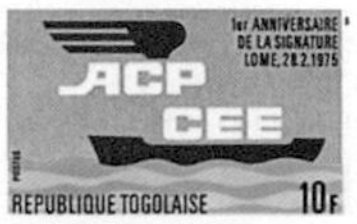

204 A.C.P. and C.E.E. Emblems

1976. First Anniv of A.C.P./C.E.E. Treaty (between Togo and European Common Market). Multicoloured.

1133	10f. Type **204** (postage)	15	10
1134	50f. Map of Africa, Europe and Asia	40	30
1135	60f. Type **204** (air)	45	20
1136	70f. As 50f.	55	30

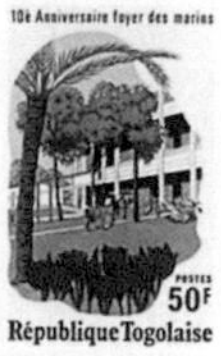

205 Exhibition Hall

1976. Anniversaries. Multicoloured.

1136a	5f. Type **205** (postage)	10	10
1136b	10f. Electricity pylon and flags	15	10
1137	50f. Type **205**	50	30
1138	60f. As 10f. (air)	50	30

The 5f. and 50f. commemorate the 10th anniv of the Marine Exhibition and the 10f. and 60f. the 1st anniv of the Ghana–Togo–Dahomey Electricity Link.

1976. Air. "Interphil '76" International Stamp Exhibition, Philadelphia. Nos. 1121/4 optd **INTERPHIL MAI 29 - JUIN 6.**

1139	60f. multicoloured	40	15
1140	70f. multicoloured	60	20
1141	100f. multicoloured	90	30
1142	200f. multicoloured	1·40	55
MS1143	138×95 mm	3·25	1·25

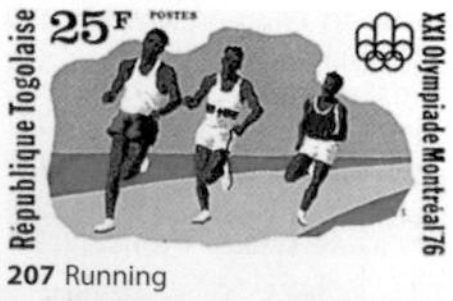

207 Running

1976. Olympic Games, Montreal. Multicoloured.

1144	25f. Type **207** (postage)	20	10
1145	30f. Canoeing	35	15
1146	50f. High-jumping	45	20
1147	70f. Sailing (air)	55	20
1148	105f. Motorcycling	85	35
1149	200f. Fencing	1·60	55
MS1150	133×116 mm. Nos. 1148/9	2·25	90

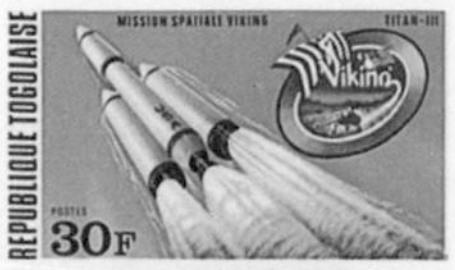

208 "Titan 3" and "Viking" Emblem

1976. "Viking" Space Mission. Multicoloured.

1151	30f. Type **208** (postage)	15	10
1152	50f. "Viking" en route between Earth and Mars	40	20
1153	60f. "Viking landing on Mars" (air)	55	20
1154	70f. Nodus Gordii, Mars	65	20
1155	100f. "Viking" over Mare Tyrrhenum	85	40
1156	200f. "Viking" landing on Mars (different)	1·50	55
MS1157	120×108 mm. Nos. 1155/6	2·25	95

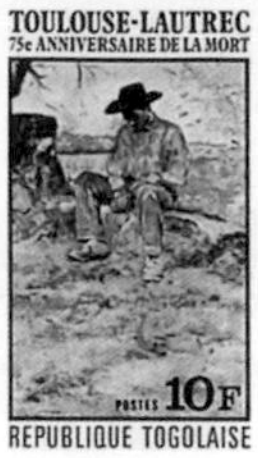

209 "Young Routy"

1976. 75th Death Anniv of Toulouse-Lautrec (painter). Multicoloured.

1158	10f. Type **209** (postage)	15	10
1159	20f. "Helene Vary"	50	15
1160	35f. "Louis Pascal"	75	15
1161	60f. "Carmen" (air)	1·00	20
1162	70f. "Maurice at the Somme"	1·00	30
1163	200f. "Messalina"	2·50	60
MS1164	122×82 mm. Nos. 1162/3	3·25	90

1976. International Children's Day. Nos. 950/1 optd **Journee Internationale de l'Enfance.**

1165	**161**	40f. mult (postage)	45	15
1166	-	100f. multicoloured (air)	80	45

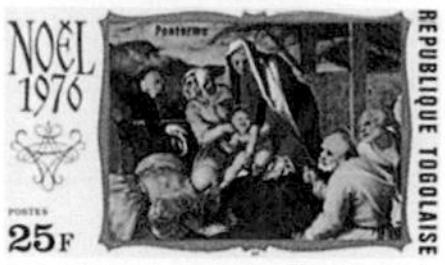

211 "Adoration of the Shepherds" (Pontormo)

1976. Christmas. Nativity scenes by artists named. Multicoloured.

1167	25f. Type **211** (postage)	35	15
1168	30f. Crivelli	45	15
1169	50f. Pontormo	80	20
1170	70f. Lotto (air)	65	20
1171	105f. Pontormo (different)	1·90	35
1172	200f. Lotto (different)	1·60	55
MS1173	151×108 mm. Nos. 1171/2	3·25	90

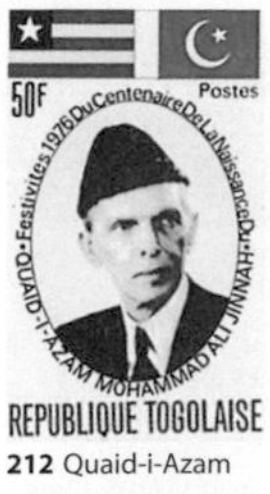

212 Quaid-i-Azam

1976. Birth Centenary of Mohammad Ali Jinnah, "Quaid-i-Azam".

1174	**212**	50f. multicoloured	55	30

1977. Gold Medal Winners, Montreal Olympic Games. Nos. 1146/7, 1149 and **MS**1150 optd **CHAMPIONS OLYMPIQUES** with events and countries.

1175	50f. multicoloured (postage)	60	20
1176	70f. multicoloured (air)	75	35
1177	200f. multicoloured	1·75	80
MS1178	133×116 mm	2·25	2·25

OPTD: 50f. **SAUT EN HAUTEUR POLOGNE**; 70f. **YACHTING - FLYING DUTCHMAN REPUBLIQUE FEDERALE ALLEMAGNE**; 200f. **ESCRIME-FLEURET PAR EQUIPES REPUBLIQUE FEDERALE ALLEMAGNE.**

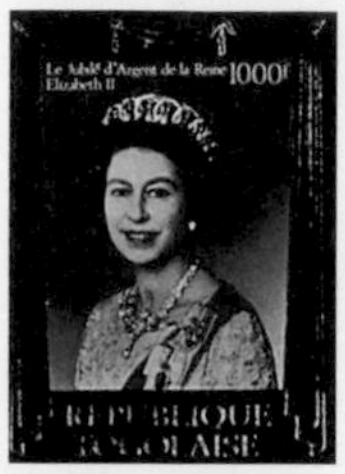

214 Queen Elizabeth II

1977. Silver Jubilee of Queen Elizabeth II. Multicoloured.

1179	1000f. Type **214**	7·75	
MS1180	108×130 mm. 1000f. Queen Elizabeth II in Coronation regalia	7·75	

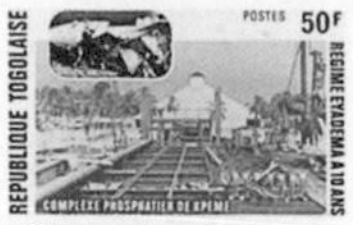

215 Phosphate Complex, Kpeme

1977. Tenth Anniv of Eyadema Regime. Multicoloured.

1181	50f. Type **215** (postage)	1·25	35
1182	60f. Parliament Building, Lome (air)	55	30
1183	100f. Crowd greeting Pres. Eyadema	80	40
MS1184	130×100 mm. Nos. 1182/3	1·40	1·40

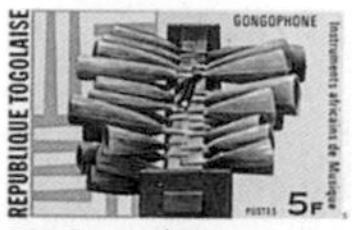

216 Gongophone

1977. Musical Instruments. Multicoloured.

1185	5f. Type **216** (postage)	15	10
1186	10f. Tamtam (vert)	20	10
1187	25f. Dondon	65	15
1188	60f. Atopani (air)	75	20
1189	80f. One-string fiddle (vert)	1·25	30
1190	105f. African flutes (vert)	1·75	35
MS1191	120×85 mm. Nos. 1189/90	3·00	3·00

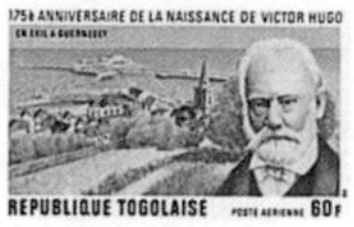

217 Victor Hugo and Guernsey Scene

1977. 175th Birth Anniv of Victor Hugo (writer). Multicoloured.

1192	50f. Victor Hugo as a young man, and residence (postage)	55	15
1193	60f. Type **217** (air)	60	30
MS1194	130×100 mm. Nos. 1192/3	1·10	1·10

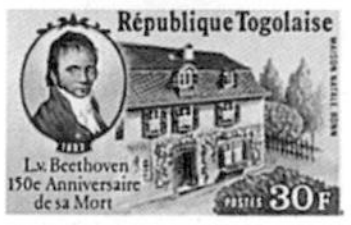

218 Beethoven and Birthplace, Bonn

1977. 150th Death Anniv of Ludwig van Beethoven. Multicoloured.

1195	30f. Type **218** (postage)	70	15
1196	50f. Beethoven's bust and Heiligenstadt residence	75	20
1197	100f. Young Beethoven and grand piano (air)	1·25	35
1198	200f. Beethoven on death-bed and Trinity Church, Vienna	2·25	65
MS1199	150×131 mm. Nos. 1197/8	3·50	3·50

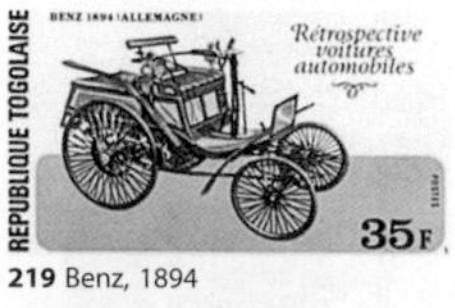

219 Benz, 1894

1977. Early Motor Cars. Multicoloured.

1200	35f. Type **219** (postage)	65	20
1201	50f. De Dion Bouton, 1903	1·00	30
1202	60f. Cannstatt-Daimler, 1899 (air)	80	20
1203	70f. Sunbeam, 1904	90	20
1204	100f. Renault, 1908	1·10	35
1205	200f. Rolls-Royce, 1909	1·90	65
MS1206	144×96 mm. Nos. 1204/5	3·00	3·00

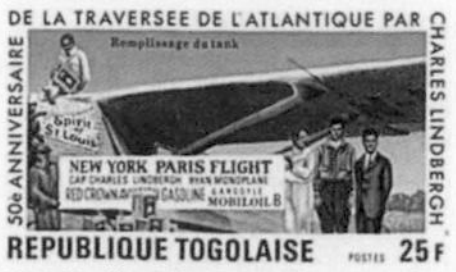

220 Lindbergh, Ground Crew and "Spirit of St. Louis"

1977. 50th Anniv of Lindbergh's Transatlantic Flight. Multicoloured.

1207	25f. Type **220** (postage)	35	15
1208	50f. Lindbergh before take-off	65	20
1209	60f. Lindbergh with son (air)	50	15
1210	85f. Lindbergh's home, Kent (England)	80	20
1211	90f. "Spirit of St. Louis" over Atlantic	80	30
1212	100f. Concorde over New York City	1·25	50
MS1213	120×95 mm. Nos. 1211/12	2·00	2·00

1977. Tenth Anniv of International French Language Council. Nos. 1192/3 optd **10eme ANNIVERSAIRE DU CONSEIL INTERNATIONAL DE LA LANGUE FRANCAISE.**

1214	**217**	50f. mult (postage)	60	40
1215	**217**	60f. multicoloured (air)	55	35

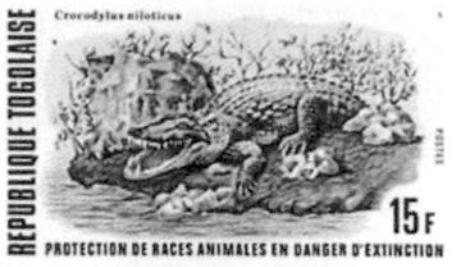

222 Nile Crocodile

1977. Endangered Wildlife. Multicoloured.

1216	5f. African crocodile (postage)	15	15
1217	15f. Type **222**	50	20
1218	60f. Western black-and-white colobus (air)	90	15
1219	90f. Chimpanzee (vert)	1·00	20
1220	100f. Leopard	1·25	30
1221	200f. African manatee	2·25	55
MS1222	153×120 mm. Nos. 1220/1	3·25	3·25

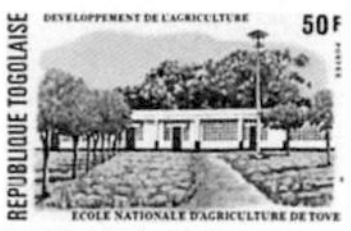

223 Agricultural School, Tove

1977. Agricultural Development. Multicoloured.

1223	50f. Type **223** (postage)	50	20
1224	60f. Corn silo (air)	55	15
1225	100f. Hoeing and planting	70	30
1226	200f. Tractor	1·50	55
MS1227	116×95 mm. Nos. 1225/6	2·00	2·00

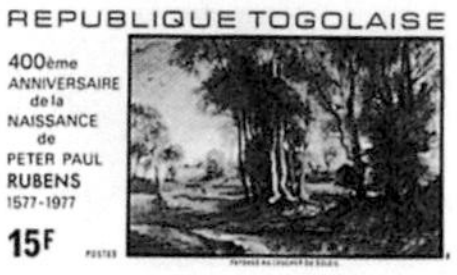

224 "Landscape at Sunset" (Rubens)

1977. 400th Birth Anniv of Rubens. Multicoloured.

1228	15f. Type **224** (postage)	35	10
1229	35f. "Exchange of the Princesses at Hendaye"	80	15
1230	60f. "Four Negro Heads" (air)	85	15
1231	100f. "Anne of Austria"	1·10	40
MS1232	151×97 mm. Nos. 1230/1	1·90	1·90

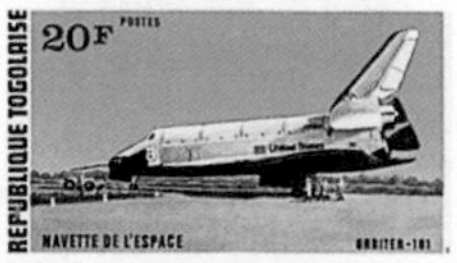

225 Shuttle after Landing

1977. Space Shuttle. Multicoloured.

1233	20f. Type **225** (postage)	20	10
1234	30f. Launching	35	15
1235	50f. Ejecting propellant tanks	55	15
1236	90f. Retrieving a satellite (air)	70	20
1237	100f. Ejecting repaired satellite	85	30
1238	200f. Shuttle landing	1·50	60
MS1239	111×140 mm. Nos. 1237/8	2·25	2·25

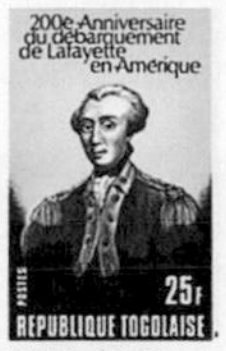

226 Lafayette at 19 (after Le Mire)

1977. Bicent of Lafayette's Arrival in America.

1240	**226**	25f. brown, yellow and purple (postage)	30	10
1241	-	50f. red, violet and pink	55	15
1242	-	60f. turquoise, green and deep green (air)	50	15
1243	-	105f. blue, light blue and purple	90	35
MS1244		129×100 mm. Nos. 1242/3	1·25	1·25

DESIGNS—HORIZ: 50f. Lafayette at Montpelier; 60f. Lafayette's arrival in New York; 105f. Lafayette with Washington at Valley Forge.

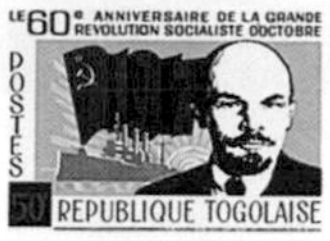

227 Lenin and Cruiser "Aurora"

1977. 60th Anniv of Russian Revolution.

1245	**227**	50f. multicoloured	80	30

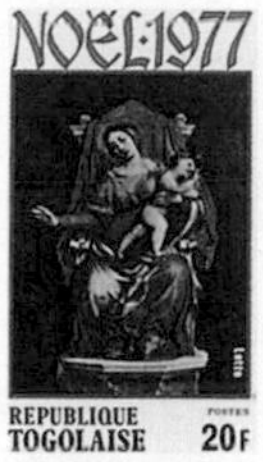

228 "Madonna and Child" (Lotto)

1977. Christmas. "Madonna and Child" by artists named. Multicoloured.

1246	20f. Type **228** (postage)	20	15
1247	30f. Crivelli	35	15
1248	50f. C. Tura	55	15
1249	90f. Crivelli (different) (air)	65	30
1250	100f. Bellini	90	35
1251	200f. Crivelli (different)	1·50	55
MS1252	132×102 mm. Nos. 1250/1	2·40	2·40

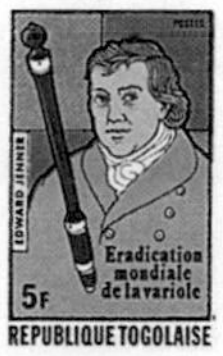

229 Edward Jenner

1978. World Eradication of Smallpox.

1253	**229**	5f. ochre, black and lilac (postage)	10	10
1254	-	20f. multicoloured	20	10
1255	**229**	50f. ochre, black and green (air)	35	15
1256	-	60f. multicoloured	40	15
MS1257		130×100 mm. Nos. 1255/6. Imperf	75	30

DESIGN—HORIZ: 20, 60f. Patients queuing for vaccination.

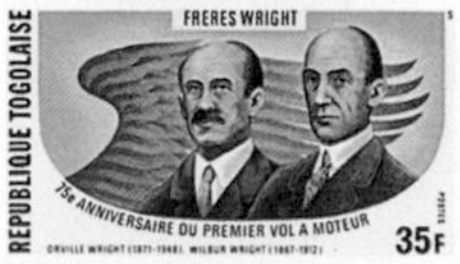

230 Wright Brothers

1978. 75th Anniv of First Flight by Wright Brothers. Multicoloured.

1258	35f. Type **230** (postage)	45	20
1259	50f. Wilbur Wright flying Glider No. III	85	35
1260	60f. Orville Wright Flight of 7 min 31 sec (air)	1·00	40
1261	70f. Wreckage of Wright Type A	1·10	40
1262	200f. Wright Brothers' cycle workshop, Dearborn, Michigan	1·40	55
1263	300f. Wright Flyer I (1st motorized flight)	2·00	85
MS1264	136×118 mm. Nos. 1262/3	3·25	1·40

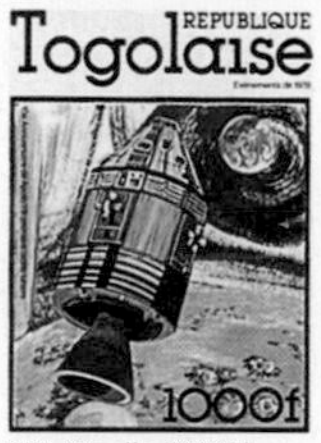

231 "Apollo 8" (10th anniv of first mission)

1978. Anniversaries and Events. Multicoloured.

1265	1000f. Type **231**	8·25
1266	1000f. High-jumping (Olympic Games, 1980)	8·25
1267	1000f. Westminster Abbey (25th anniv of Queen Elizabeth II's Coronation)	8·25
1268	1000f. "Duke of Wellington" (150th death anniv of Goya)	8·25
1269	1000f. Footballers and Cup (World Cup Football Championship)	8·25
MS1270	Five sheets each 101×95 mm. (a) 1000f. Launch of "Apollo 8"; (b) 1000f. Hurdling; (c) 1000f. Coronation coach; (d) 1000f. "Dona Isabel Cobos de Porcel" (Goya); (e) 1000f. Footballers with ball	40·00

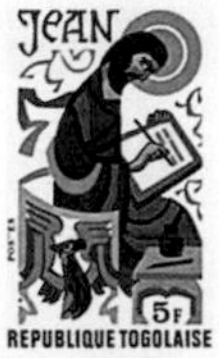

232 St. John

1978. The Evangelists. Multicoloured.

1271	5f. Type **232**	10	10
1272	10f. St. Luke	10	10
1273	25f. St. Mark	20	10
1274	30f. St. Mathew	30	10
MS1275	114×106 mm. Nos. 1271/4. Imperf	70	40

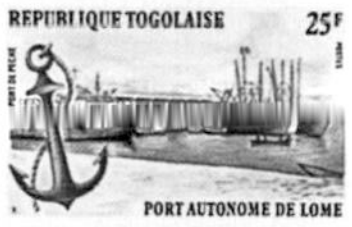

233 Fishing Harbour

1978. Autonomous Port of Lome. Multicoloured.

1276	25f. Type **233** (postage)	45	15
1277	60f. Industrial port (air)	80	25
1278	100f. Merchant port	1·25	40
1279	200f. General view	1·25	55
MS1280	130×101 mm. Nos. 1278/9	2·50	95

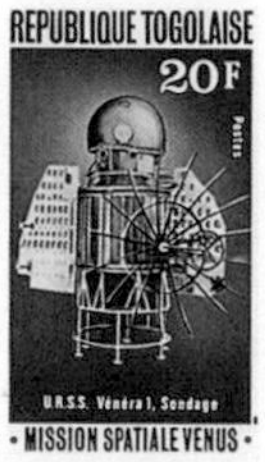

234 "Venera 1" Probe

1978. Space Mission—Venus. Multicoloured.

1281	20f. Type **234** (postage)	15	10
1282	30f. "Pioneer" (horiz)	20	15
1283	50f. Soviet fuel base and antenna	40	15
1284	90f. "Venera" blast jets (horiz) (air)	40	20
1285	100f. "Venera" antennae	55	30
1286	200f. "Pioneer" in orbit	1·00	55
MS1287	140×115 mm. Nos. 1285/6	1·50	85

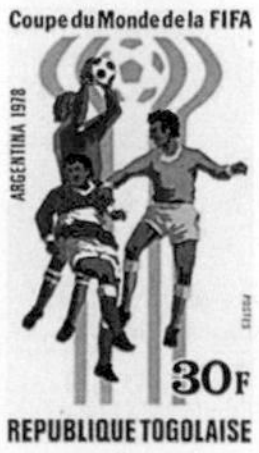

235 Goalkeeper catching Ball

1978. World Cup Football Championship, Argentina. Multicoloured.

1288	30f. Type **235** (postage)	30	10
1289	50f. Two players with ball	40	15
1290	60f. Heading the ball (air)	60	15
1291	80f. High kick	70	20
1292	200f. Chest stop	1·50	55
1293	300f. Player with ball	2·25	85
MS1294	133×96 mm. Nos. 1292/3	2·50	10

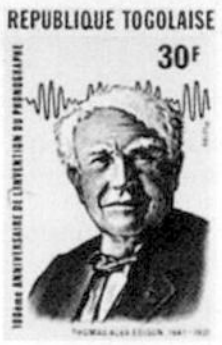

236 Thomas Edison (inventor)

1978. Centenary of Invention of the Phonograph. Multicoloured.

1295	30f. Type **236** (postage)	20	10
1296	50f. Couple dancing to H.M.V. "Victor", phonograph, 1905	45	15
1297	60f. Edison's original phonograph (horiz) (air)	40	15
1298	80f. Berliner's first phono-graph, 1888	50	20
1299	200f. Berliner's improved phonograph, 1894 (horiz)	1·25	55
1300	300f. "His Master's Voice" phonograph, c. 1900 (horiz)	2·00	85
MS1301	115×89 mm. Nos. 1299/1300	3·25	1·40

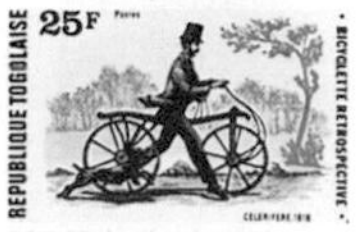

237 "Celerifere" 1818

1978. Early Bicycles. Multicoloured.

1302	25f. Type **237** (postage)	35	15
1303	50f. First bicycle side-car (vert)	65	20
1304	60f. Bantam bicycle (vert) (air)	55	15
1305	85f. Military folding bicycle	65	20
1306	90f. "La Draisienne" (vert)	90	35
1307	100f. Penny-farthing (vert)	95	40
MS1308	124×115 mm. Nos. 1306/7	1·90	75

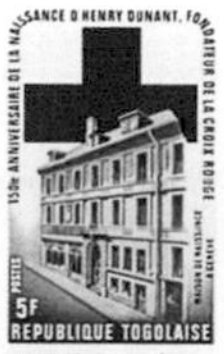

238 Dunant's Birthplace, Geneva

1978. 150th Birth Anniv of Henri Dunant (founder of Red Cross).

1309	**238**	5f. blue and red (postage)	10	10
1310	-	10f. brown and red	15	10
1311	-	25f. green and red	30	10
1312	-	60f. purple and red (air)	55	20
MS1313		146×99 mm. Nos. 1311/12	85	30

DESIGNS: 10f. Dunant at 35; 25f. Tending battle casualties, 1864; 60f. Red Cross pavilions, Paris Exhibition, 1867.

1978. Air. "Philexafrique" Stamp Exhibition, Libreville (Gabon), and Int Stamp Fair, Essen, West Germany. As T **237a** of Senegal. Multicoloured

1314	100f. Jay and Thurn and Taxis ¼sgr. stamp of 1854	2·75	2·25
1315	100f. Warthog and Togo 50f. stamp, 1964	2·75	2·25

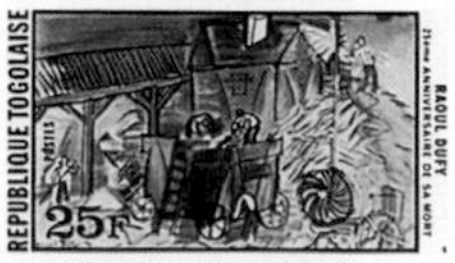

239 "Threshing" (Raoul Dufy)

1978. Artists' Anniversaries. Multicoloured.

1316	25f. Type **239** (25th death anniv) (postage)	50	15
1317	50f. "Horsemen on the Seashore" (Gauguin, 75th death anniv)	1·00	15
1318	60f. "Langlois Bridge" (Van Gogh, 125th birth anniv) (air)	60	15
1319	70f. "Sabbath of the Witches" (Goya, 150th death anniv)	75	20
1320	90f. "Christ Among the Doctors" (Durer, 450th death anniv)	85	20
1321	200f. "View of Arco" (Durer)	1·75	55
MS1322	101×131 mm. Nos. 1320/1	2·50	75

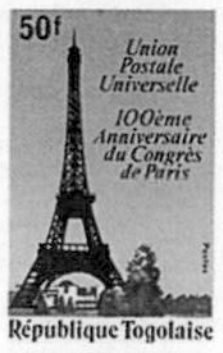

240 Eiffel Tower

1978. Centenary of Paris U.P.U. Congress. Multicoloured.

1323	50f. Type **240** (postage)	80	20
1324	60f. Full-rigged ship "Slieve Roe" (air)	85	25
1325	105f. Congress medallion	70	30
1326	200f. Steam locomotive, 1870	1·60	55
MS1327	115×88 mm. Nos. 1325/6	2·25	85

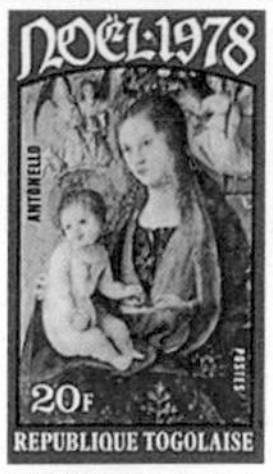

241 "Madonna and Child" (Antonello)

1978. Christmas. Paintings of the Virgin and Child by artists shown below. Multicoloured.

1328	20f. Type **241** (postage)	20	15
1329	30f. Crivelli	35	15
1330	50f. Tura	55	15
1331	90f. Crivelli (different) (air)	65	30
1332	100f. Tura (different)	90	30
1333	200f. Crivelli (different)	1·50	55
MS1334	122×90 mm. Nos. 1332/3	2·40	85

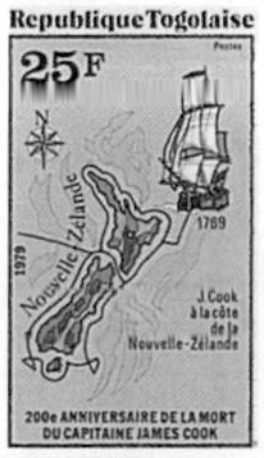

242 H.M.S. "Endeavour" and Route round New Zealand

1979. Death Bicentenary of Captain James Cook. Multicoloured.

1335	25f. Type **242** (postage)	80	25
1336	50f. Careening H.M.S. "Endeavour" (horiz)	1·00	35
1337	60f. "Freelove" at Whitby (horiz) (air)	1·25	35
1338	70f. Antarctic voyage of H.M.S. "Resolution" (horiz)	1·75	60
1339	90f. Capt. Cook	2·00	75
1340	200f. Sail plan of H.M.S. "Endeavour"	2·75	1·75
MS1341	142×98 mm. Nos. 1339/1400	4·75	2·50

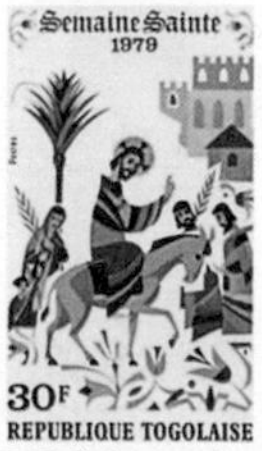

243 Christ entering Jerusalem

1979. Easter. Multicoloured.

1342	30f. Type **243** (postage)	20	10
1343	40f. The Last Supper (horiz)	30	15
1344	50f. Descent from the Cross (horiz)	40	15
1345	60f. Resurrection (air)	45	15
1346	100f. Ascension	65	30
1347	200f. Jesus appearing to Mary Magdalene	1·25	55
MS1348	94×109 mm. Nos. 1346/7	1·75	85

244 Statuette of Drummer

1979. Air. "Philexafrique 2" Stamp Exhibition, Libreville. Multicoloured.
1349	60f. Type **244**	1·10	55
1350	100f. Hands with letter	1·60	1·10

245 Einstein Observatory, Potsdam

1979. Birth Centenary of Albert Einstein (physicist).
1351	**245**	35f. red, yellow and black (postage)	20	10
1352	-	50f. green, mauve & black	35	10
1353	-	60f. multicoloured (air)	40	10
1354	-	85f. lilac, brown and black	60	15
1355	-	100f. multicoloured	65	20
1356	-	200f. green, brown & black	1·40	40
MS1357	127×90 mm. Nos. 1355/6		2·00	60

DESIGNS—HORIZ: 50f. Einstein and J. R. Mac-donald in Berlin, 1931; 60f. Sight and actuality diagram. VERT: 85f. Einstein playing violin; 100f. Atomic symbol and relativity formula; 200f. Albert Einstein.

246 Children with Flag

1979. International Year of the Child. Multicoloured.
1358	5f. Type **246**	10	10
1359	10f. Mother with children	10	10
1360	15f. Children's Village symbol on map of Africa (horiz)	15	10
1361	20f. Woman taking children to Children's Village (horiz)	15	10
1362	25f. Children sitting round Fan palm	30	10
1363	30f. Map of Togo showing Children's Villages	35	10
MS1364	111×89 mm. Nos. 1362/3	65	20

247 Planting Sapling

1979. Tree Day.
1365	**247**	50f. green and violet (postage)	50	15
1366	-	60f. brown & green (air)	55	20

DESIGN: 60f. Watering sapling.

248 Sir Rowland Hill

1979. Death Centenary of Sir Rowland Hill. Multicoloured.
1367	**248**	20f. Type **248** (postage)	15	10
1368		30f. French mail sorting office in the reign of Louis XV (horiz)	20	10
1369		40f. Parisian postbox, 1850	40	15
1370		90f. Bellman collecting letters, 1820 (air)	60	20
1371		100f. "Centre-cycles" used for mail delivery, 1880 (horiz)	65	20
1372		200f. French Post Office railway carriage, 1848 (horiz)	1·25	40
MS1373	138×105 mm. Nos. 1371/2		1·75	60

249 Stephenson's "Rocket", 1829

1979. Railway Locomotives. Multicoloured.
1374	35f. Type **249** (postage)	35	10
1375	50f. William Norris's "Austria", 1843 (horiz)	45	15
1376	60f. William Hudson's "General", 1855 (horiz) (air)	55	15
1377	85f. Stephenson locomotive, 1843 (horiz)	75	35
1378	100f. John Jarvis's "De Witt Clinton", 1831 (horiz)	85	35
1379	200f. David Joy's "Jenny Lind", 1847 (horiz)	1·75	55
MS1380	118×94 mm. Nos. 1378/9	2·50	90

250 Skiing

1979. Olympic Games, Lake Placid and Moscow. Multicoloured.
1381	20f. Type **250** (postage)	15	10
1382	30f. Olympic dinghies	20	15
1383	50f. Throwing the discus	40	10
1384	90f. Ski-jumping (air)	65	20
1385	100f. Canoeing	70	20
1386	200f. Gymnastics (rings exercise)	1·40	40
MS1387	96×90 mm. 100f. Bobsleighing (horiz); 200f. Gymnastics (horse exercise) (horiz)	3·00	85

See also Nos. 1418/MS1422 and 1423/MS1429.

251 Native praying

1979. Togo Religions.
1388	**251**	30f. brown, green and yellow (postage)	20	10
1389	-	50f. blue, brown and red	35	10
1390	-	60f. purple, blue and buff (air)	45	15
1391	-	70f. lilac, orange & green	50	20
MS1392	116×88 mm. Nos. 1390/1		95	35

DESIGNS—HORIZ: 50f. Catholic priests; 60f. Muslims at prayer; 70f. Protestant preachers.

252 Astronaut on Moon

1979. Tenth Anniv of First Moon Landing. Multicoloured.
1393	35f. Type **252** (postage)	30	10
1394	50f. Capsule orbiting Moon	40	10
1395	60f. Armstrong descending to Moon	45	10
1396	70f. Astronaut and flag (air)	50	15
1397	200f. Astronaut performing experiment	1·25	35
1398	300f. Module leaving Moon	2·00	50
MS1399	141×104 mm. Nos. 1397/8	3·00	85

253 Dish Aerial

1979. Third World Telecommunications Exposition, Geneva.
1400	-	50f. light brown, brown and green (postage)	35	10
1401	**253**	60f. green, blue and deep blue (air)	50	20

DESIGN—HORIZ: 50f. Television screen.

254 Pres. Eyadema

1979. Air. Tenth Anniv of R.P.T. Multicoloured.
1402	1000f. Pres. Eyadema and Party badge	6·75	
1403	1000f. Type **254**	6·75	

255 Holy Family

1979. Christmas. Multicoloured.
1404	20f. Type **255** (postage)	15	10
1405	30f. Madonna and Child and angels playing musical instruments	20	10
1406	50f. Adoration of the shepherds	40	10
1407	90f. Adoration of the Magi	55	20
1408	100f. Mother presenting Child	70	20
1409	200f. The Flight into Egypt	1·50	40
MS1410	133×104 mm. Nos. 1408/9	2·10	60

256 Rotary Emblem

1980. 75th Anniv of Rotary International. Multicoloured.
1411	25f. Type **256** (postage)	15	10
1412	30f. Anniversary emblem	30	10
1413	40f. Paul Harris (founder)	35	10
1414	90f. Figure exercising and sun (health) (air)	65	20
1415	100f. Fish and grain (food)	70	20
1416	200f. Family group (humanity)	1·40	40
MS1417	132×132 mm. Nos. 1415/16	2·00	60

257 Shooting (Biathlon)

1980. Winter Olympic Games, Lake Placid. Multicoloured.
1418	50f. Type **257** (postage)	50	10
1419	60f. Downhill skiing	40	10
1420	100f. Speed skating (air)	70	20
1421	200f. Cross-country skiing	1·40	40

MS1422	103×83 mm. 100f. Ski-jumping (horiz); 200f. Ice hockey (horiz)	70	20

258 Swimming

1980. Olympic Games, Moscow. Multicoloured.
1423	20f. Type **258** (postage)	15	10
1424	30f. Gymnastics	20	10
1425	50f. Running	40	10
1426	100f. Fencing (air)	65	20
1427	200f. Pole vaulting	1·25	45
1428	300f. Hurdles	2·00	55
MS1429	110×81 mm. Nos. 1427/8	3·25	95

259 Truck going to Market

1980. Market Scenes. Multicoloured.
1430	1f. Grinding savo (postage)	10	10
1431	2f. Women preparing meat	10	10
1432	3f. Type **259**	10	10
1433	4f. Unloading produce	10	10
1434	5f. Sugar-cane seller	10	10
1435	6f. Barber doing child's hair	10	10
1436	7f. Vegetable seller	10	10
1437	7f. Mangoes (vert)	10	10
1438	9f. Grain seller	10	10
1439	10f. Fish seller	10	10
1440	15f. Clay pot seller	10	10
1441	20f. Straw baskets	15	10
1442	25f. Lemon and onion seller (vert)	15	10
1443	30f. Straw baskets (different)	20	10
1444	40f. Shore market	30	15
1445	45f. Selling cooked food	35	15
1446	50f. Women carrying produce (vert)	35	15
1447	60f. Selling oil	45	15
1448	90f. Linen seller (air)	55	15
1449	100f. Bananas	65	20
1450	200f. Pottery	1·25	45
1451	250f. Setting-up stalls	1·60	55
1452	500f. Vegetable seller (different)	3·00	1·10
1453	1000f. Drink seller	6·00	2·25

See also Nos. D1454/7.

260 Concorde and Map of Africa

1980. 20th Anniv of African Air Safety Organization.
1458	**260**	50f. mult (postage)	55	20
1459	**260**	60f. multicoloured (air)	55	25

261 "Christ with Angels" (Mantegna)

1980. Easter. Multicoloured.
1460	30f. Type **261** (postage)	30	15
1461	40f. "Christ with Disciples" (Crivelli)	40	15
1462	50f. "Christ borne by His Followers" (Pontormo)	45	15
1463	60f. "The Deposition" (Lotto) (air)	50	10
1464	100f. "The Crucifixion" (El Greco)	70	20
1465	200f. "Christ with Angels" (Crivelli)	1·40	45
MS1466	127×109 mm. Nos. 1464/5	2·00	65

1980. "London 1980" International Stamp Exhibition. Nos. 1267 and MS1270c optd **Londres 1980**.
1467	1000f. Westminster Abbey	7·25	
MS1468	101×95 mm. 1000f. Coronation coach	7·25	

263 Radio Waves

1980. World Telecommuncations Day.

1469	-	50f. violet and green (postage)	45	10
1470	263	60f. pink, brown and blue (air)	50	15

DESIGN—HORIZ: 50f. Satellite.

264 Red Cross and Globe

1980. Togo Red Cross. Multicoloured.

1471		50f. Type 264 (postage)	55	10
1472		60f. Nurses and patient (air)	45	15

265 Jules Verne

1980. 75th Death Anniv of Jules Verne (writer). Multicoloured.

1473		30f. Type 265 (postage)	30	10
1474		50f. "20,000 Leagues under the Sea"	55	10
1475		60f. "From the Earth to the Moon" (air)	40	15
1476		80f. "Around the World in Eighty Days"	55	20
1477		100f. "From the Earth to the Moon" (different)	3·50	1·25
1478		200f. "20,000 Leagues under the Sea" (different)	1·75	60
MS1479		125×98 mm. Nos. 1477/8	5·00	1·90

266 "Baroness James de Rothschild"

1980. Birth Bicentenary of Jean Ingres (painter). Multicoloured.

1480		25f. Type 266 (postage)	35	10
1481		30f. "Napoleon I on the Imperial Throne"	55	10
1482		40f. "Don Pedro of Toledo putting down the Sword of Henry IV"	50	10
1483		90f. "Jupiter and Thetis" (air)	65	20
1484		100f. "The Countess of Hassonville"	85	20
1485		200f. "Tu Marcellus Eris"	1·50	35
MS1486		126×94 mm. Nos. 1484/5	2·25	75

267 Minnie holding Mirror for Leopard

1980. Walt Disney Characters and Wildlife.

1487		1f. Type 267	10	10
1488		2f. Goofy cleaning hippo's teeth	10	10
1489		3f. Donald clinging to crocodile	10	10
1490		4f. Donald hanging over cliff edge from rhino's horn	10	10
1491		5f. Goofy riding a water buffalo	10	10
1492		10f. Monkey photographing Mickey	10	10
1493		100f. Doctor Mickey examining giraffe	1·00	20
1494		300f. Elephant showering Goofy	2·00	40
MS1495		127×102 mm. 300f. Lion carrying off Goofy	2·00	40

1980. 50th Anniv of Pluto. As T 267. Multicoloured.

1496		200f. Pluto in party mood	1·60	40
MS1497		127×102 mm. 300f. Pluto in scene from film "Lend a Paw"	2·00	40

268 Wreath

1980. Famous Men of the Decade.

1498	268	25f. orange and green (postage)	15	10
1499	-	40f. deep green and green	65	20
1500	-	90f. dp blue & blue (air)	60	20
1501	-	100f. lilac and pink	1·10	20
1502	-	200f. brown and ochre	2·00	50
MS1503		115×117 mm. Nos. 1501/2	3·00	70

DESIGNS: 40f. Mao Tse-tung; 90f. Salvador Allende; 100f. Pope Paul VI; 200f. Jomo Kenyatta.

269 Tourist Hotel Emblem

1980. World Tourism Conference, Manila. Multicoloured.

1504		50f. Type 269	35	10
1505		150f. Conference emblem	1·00	35

270 Human Rights Emblem and Map of Australia

1980. 30th Anniv of Human Rights Convention.

1506	270	30f. violet, purple and black (postage)	30	10
1507	-	50f. green, light green and black	40	10
1508	-	60f. deep blue, blue and black (air)	40	15
1509	-	150f. brown, orange & black	1·00	35
MS1510		100×113 mm. Nos. 1508/9	1·40	50

DESIGNS: 50f. Map of Eurasia; 60f. Map of the Americas; 250f. Map of Africa.

271 Emblem

1980. Air. General Conclave of French-speaking Countries of the American Order of Rosicrucians, Lome.

1511	271	60f. multicoloured	50	15

272 Church at Melk, Austria

1980. Christmas. Multicoloured.

1512		20f. Type 272 (postage)	15	10
1513		30f. Tarragona Cathedral, Spain	20	10
1514		50f. Church of St. John the Baptist, Florence	35	10
1515		100f. Cologne Cathedral (air)	1·75	65
1516		150f. Notre-Dame, Paris	1·00	30
1517		200f. Canterbury Cathedral	1·40	35
MS1518		135×102 mm. Nos. 1516/17	2·25	60

272a U.A.P.T. Emblem

1980. Fifth Anniv of African Posts and Telecommunications Union.

1519	272a	100f. multicoloured	65	40

273 "February 2nd" Hotel

1981. Inauguration of "February 2nd" Hotel.

1520	273	50f. mult (postage)	45	15
1521	273	60f. multicoloured (air)	45	15

274 "Rembrandt's Father"

1981. Easter. Rembrandt Paintings. Multicoloured.

1522	274	30f. Type 274 (postage)	30	10
1523		40f. "Self-portrait"	35	10
1524		50f. "Rembrandt's Father as an Old Man"	40	10
1525		60f. "Rider on Horseback"	50	15
1526		100f. "Rembrandt's Mother" (air)	70	20
1527		200f. "Man in a Ruff"	1·50	45
MS1528		141×102 mm. Nos. 1526/7	2·10	65

275 Grey-necked Bald Crow

1981. Birds. Multicoloured.

1529		30f. Type 275 (postage)	40	10
1530		40f. Splendid sunbird	50	10
1531		60f. Violet starling	65	15
1532		90f. Red-collard whydah	1·10	20
1533		50f. Violet-backed sunbird (air)	65	15
1534		100f. Red bishop	1·40	25
MS1535		139×101 mm. Nos. 1532 and 1534	2·50	45

276 Dish Aerial

1981. Sixth African Postal Union Council Meeting. Multicoloured.

1536		70f. Type 276	50	15
1537		90f. Telecommunications control room	60	20
1538		105f. Map of Togo and Africa (vert)	70	30

277 Blind Man with Guide Dog

1981. International Year of Disabled People. Multicoloured.

1539		70f. Type 277 (postage)	85	30
1540		90f. One-legged carpenter (air)	60	15
1541		200f. Wheelchair basket-ball	1·60	55
MS1542		125×90 mm. 300f. Weaving from wheelchair	2·25	70

278 "Woman with Hat"

1981. Birth Centenary of Pablo Picasso. Multicoloured.

1543		25f. Type 278 (postage)	35	10
1544		50f. "She-goat"	45	10
1545		60f. "Violin"	55	15
1546		90f. "Violin and Bottle on Table" (air)	80	20
1547		100f. "Baboon with Young"	90	30
1548		200f. "Mandolin and Clarinet"	1·90	55
MS1549		139×101 mm. Nos. 1547/8	2·75	85

279 Aachen Cathedral, West Germany

1981. World Heritage Convention. Multicoloured.

1550		30f. Type 279 (postage)	20	10
1551		40f. Yellowstone National Park, U.S.A.	30	10
1552		50f. Nahanni National Park, Canada	35	10
1553		60f. Cruciform rock churches, Lalibela, Ethiopia	40	15
1554		100f. Old city centre, Cracow, Poland (air)	65	20
1555		200f. Goree Island, Senegal	1·25	35
MS1556		139×101 mm. Nos. 1554/5	1·75	55

280 "Vostok I" (20th anniv of first Manned Space Flight)

1981. Space Anniversaries. Multicoloured.

1557		25f. Type 280 (postage)	15	10
1558		50f. "Freedom 7", first American in space (20th anniv)	35	10
1559		60f. "Lunar Orbiter I" (15th anniv)	40	15
1560		90f. "Soyuz 10" (10th anniv) (air)	60	15
1561		100f. Astronauts on Moon ("Apollo XIV", 10th anniv)	65	20
MS1562		109×85 mm. 300f. "Voyager 1" (4th anniv) (vert)	1·75	65

281 "Adoration of the Magi"

1981. Christmas. Paintings by Rubens. Multicoloured.

1563	20f. Type **281** (postage)		15	10
1564	30f. "Adoration of the Shepherds"		20	10
1565	50f. "Coronation of St. Catherine"		40	10
1566	100f. "Adoration of the Magi" (different) (air)		60	20
1567	200f. "Madonna and Child"		1·40	45
1568	300f. "The Madonna giving the Robe to St. Idefonse"		2·25	65
MS1569	120×92 mm. Nos. 1567/8		3·50	1·10

282 Association Emblem and Togo Flag

1981. West African Rice Development Association.

1570	**282**	70f. mult (postage)	60	20
1571	**282**	105f. multicoloured (air)	65	30

283 Peace Dove and National Flag

1982. 15th Anniv of National Liberation. Multicoloured.

1572	70f. Type **283** (postage)		55	20
1573	90f. Pres. Eyadema and citizens (vert)		60	20
1574	105f. Pres. Eyadema and citizens holding hands (vert) (air)		65	35
1575	130f. Hotel complex		90	45

284 Scouts

1982. 75th Anniv of Boy Scout Movement. Multicoloured.

1576	70f. Type **284** (postage)		50	15
1577	90f. Signalling (air)		65	20
1578	120f. Constructing a tower		85	30
1579	130f. Scouts with canoe		90	50
1580	135f. Scouts and tent		95	35
MS1581	108×83 mm. 500f. Lord Baden-Powell		3·00	1·10

285 Moses and the Burning Bush

1982. Easter. The Ten Commandments. Multicoloured.

1582	10f. Type **285** (postage)		10	10
1583	25f. Jephtha's daughter		15	10
1584	30f. St. Vincent Ferrer preaching in Verona		20	10
1585	45f. The denouncing of Noah		30	10
1586	50f. Cain and Abel		35	10
1587	70f. Potiphar's wife		50	20
1588	90f. Isaac blessing Jacob		60	35
1589	105f. Susannah and the elders (air)		65	30
1590	120f. Bathsheba		85	35
MS1591	114×89 mm. 500f. Naboth's vineyard		3·00	1·10

286 Togo and Italy Olympic Stamps

1982. Air. "Romolymphil" Stamp Exhibition.

1592	**286**	105f. multicoloured	70	30

287 First Stamps of France and Togo

1982. Air. "Philexfrance '82" International Stamp Exhibition.

1593	**287**	90f. multicoloured	65	40

288 Goalkeeper

1982. World Cup Football Championship, Spain. Multicoloured.

1594	25f. Type **288** (postage)		15	10
1595	45f. Tackle		35	10
1596	105f. Heading ball (air)		65	20
1597	200f. Fighting for possession		1·25	45
1598	300f. Dribble		2·00	55
MS1599	121×89 mm. 500f. Footballer		3·00	1·10

289 "Papilio dardanus"

1982. Butterflies. Multicoloured.

1600	15f. Type **289** (postage)		20	10
1601	20f. "Belenois calypso"		35	10
1602	25f. "Palla decius"		50	10
1603	90f. "Euxanthe eurinome" (air)		1·60	90
1604	105f. "Mylothris rhodope"		1·75	1·00
MS1605	134×102 mm. 500f. "Papilio zalmoxis"		7·75	4·50

290 Infant Jesus

1982. Christmas. Details of Raphael's "Madonna del Baldacchino". Multicoloured.

1606	45f. Type **290** (postage)		40	10
1607	70f. Madonna		55	15
1608	105f. Angel		70	20
1609	130f. Angel (different)		1·00	30
1610	150f. Putti		1·10	35
MS1611	121×159 mm. 500f. Madonna and Child (vert)		3·50	1·00

291 Building, Sokode

1983. Visit of President Mitterrand of France. Multicoloured.

1612	35f. Type **291** (postage)		20	10
1613	45f. Children of different races and world map		35	15
1614	70f. French and Togolese soldiers (vert)		55	20
1615	90f. President Mitterrand (air) (vert)		70	30
1616	105f. Presidents Mitterrand and Eyadema shaking hands (vert)		80	35
1617	130f. Presidents Mitterrand and Eyadema and crowds		1·00	40

1983. World Cup Football Championship Results. Nos. 1594/8 optd **VAINQUEUR COUPE DU MONDE FOOTBALL 82 "ITALIE".**

1618	25f. Type **288** (postage)		15	10
1619	45f. Tackle		35	15
1620	105f. Heading ball (air)		65	35
1621	200f. Fighting for possession		1·25	55
1622	300f. Dribble		2·00	80
MS1623	121×89 mm. 500f. Footballer		3·00	1·25

293 Map of Africa showing W.A.M.U. Members

1983. 20th Anniv of West African Monetary Union. Multicoloured.

1624	70f. Type **293** (postage)		50	15
1625	90f. West African coin		60	20

294 Drummer

1983. World Communications Year. Multicoloured.

1626	70f. Type **294** (postage)		55	15
1627	90f. Modern post office and telecommunications system (air)		65	20

295 Boxing

1983. Air. Pre-Olympic Year. Multicoloured.

1628	70f. Type **295** (postage)		50	15
1629	90f. Hurdles		60	20
1630	105f. Pole vault		65	20
1631	130f. Sprinting		1·00	30
MS1632	110×81 mm. 500f. Running		3·00	1·10

296 Kondona Dance

1983. Traditional Dances. Multicoloured.

1633	70f. Type **296** (postage)		60	20
1634	90f. Kondona dance (different) (air)		80	20
1635	105f. Toubole dance		90	20
1636	130f. Adjogbo dance		1·10	20

297 Painting by Bellini

1983. Easter. Multicoloured.

1637	35f. Type **297** (postage)		30	10
1638	70f. Raphael (vert)		50	15
1639	90f. Carracci (air)		65	20
MS1640	100×77 mm. 500f. Reni (vert)		3·00	90

298 Catholic Church, Kante

1983. Christmas. Multicoloured.

1641	70f. Type **298** (postage)		50	15
1642	90f. Altar, Dapaong Cathedral (air)		60	20
1643	105f. Protestant church, Dapaong		70	20
MS1644	110×85 mm. 500f. Ecumenical church, Pya		3·00	90

299 Wrecked Airplane

1984. Tenth Anniv of Sarakawa Assassination Attempt. Multicoloured.

1645	70f. Type **299** (postage)		50	25
1646	90f. Wrecked airplane (different)		60	30
1647	120f. Memorial Hall (air)		85	40
1648	270f. Statue of President Eyadema (vert)		1·90	70

300 Picking Coffee Beans

1984. World Food Programme Day. Multicoloured.

1649	35f. Type **300**		20	10
1650	70f. Harvesting cocoa pods		50	15
1651	90f. Planting rice		65	20
MS1652	104×80 mm. 300f. Food storage containers (horiz)		1·90	65

301 Flags, Agriculture and Symbols of Unity Growth

1984. 25th Anniv of Council of Unity.

1653	**301**	70f. multicoloured	50	15
1654	**301**	90f. multicoloured	60	20

1984. Air. 19th Universal Postal Union Congress, Hamburg. Nos 1451/2 optd **19E CONGRES UPU HAMBOURG 1984.**

1655	250f. multicoloured		1·60	85
1656	500f. multicoloured		3·25	1·60

303 Tim Thorpe (gold, pentathlon and decathlon, 1912)

1984. Air. Olympic Games Medal Winners (1st series). Multicoloured.

1657	500f. Type **303**		4·50	85
1658	500f. Mathias Behr (silver, fencing, 1984)		4·50	85
1659	500f. Fredy Schmidtke (gold, cycling, 1984)		4·50	85
1660	500f. Dietmar Mogenburg (gold, high jumping, 1984)		4·50	85
1661	500f. Sabine Everts (bronze, heptathlon, 1984)		4·50	85

1662	500f. Jesse Owens (gold, 200 m, 1936)	4·50	85
1663	500f. Bob Beamon (gold, long jumping, 1968)	4·50	85
1664	500f. Muhammad Ali (gold, boxing, 1960)	22·00	85

See also Nos. 1825/32.

304 Thief on right-hand Cross

1984. Easter. Details from stained glass window in Norwich Cathedral. Multicoloured.

1665	70f. Roman guard (postage)	50	15
1666	90f. Mary Magdalene (air)	55	15
1667	120f. The Apostles comforting Mary	80	20
1668	270f. Type **304**	1·60	45
1669	300f. Thief on left-hand Cross	2·00	55
MS1670	63×114 mm. 500f. Christ on cross	3·00	90

305 Baguida (site of Protectorate Treaty signature, 1884)

1984. Centenary of Proclamation of German Protectorate. Multicoloured.

1671	35f. Type **305**	20	20
1672	35f. Degbenou School, 1893 (horiz)	20	20
1673	35f. Aneho Post Office extension, 1893 (horiz)	20	20
1674	35f. Kara suspension bridge, 1911 (horiz)	20	20
1675	35f. Adjido state school (horiz)	20	20
1676	35f. Administration post, Sansane Mango, 1908 (horiz)	20	20
1677	35f. Sokode cotton market, 1910 (horiz)	20	20
1678	45f. Main street, Lome, 1895, and 5m. "Yacht" stamp (horiz)	35	35
1679	45f. Governor's Palace, Lome, 1905 (horiz)	35	35
1680	45f. Drilling police squad, 1905 (horiz)	35	35
1681	45f. Guillaume fountain, Atakpame, 1906	35	35
1682	45f. Constructing Lome–Atakpame railway (horiz)	85	85
1683	45f. Rue de Commerce, Lome, and 10pf. "Yacht" stamp (horiz)	85	85
1684	70f. 20pf. and 2m. "Yacht" stamps, 1900 (horiz)	50	45
1685	70f. Lome wharf, 1903 (horiz)	1·10	1·10
1686	90f. Farming, Sansane Mango, 1908 (horiz)	60	55
1687	90f. Chancellor Otto von Bismarck	60	55
1688	90f. Emperor Wilhelm II	60	55
1689	90f. Commissoner J. von Puttkamer, 1891–3	60	55
1690	90f. Consul-General G. Nachtigal, 1884	60	55
1691	90f. Governor A. Koehler, 1895–1902	60	55
1692	90f. Governor W. Horn, 1902–5	60	55
1693	90f. Governor J. G. von Zech, 1905–10	60	55
1694	90f. Governor E. Bruckner, 1911–12	60	55
1695	90f. Governor A. F. von Mecklenberg, 1912–14	60	55
1696	90f. Governor H. G. von Doering, 1914	60	55
1697	120f. Signing of Protectorate Treaty, 1885 (horiz)	90	85
1698	120f. Postmen, 1885	90	85
1699	150f. Children dancing around maps and flags	1·10	95
1700	270f. German gunboat "Mowe", 1884 (horiz)	2·00	1·75
1701	270f. German sail corvette "Sophie", 1884	2·00	1·75
1702	270f. Steam train, Anecho railway, 1905 (horiz)	3·50	2·75
1703	270f. Mallet steam locomotive, Kpalime Railway, 1905 (dated "1907") (horiz)	3·50	2·75
1704	270f. Flags and Presidents of Togo and Germany (horiz)	2·25	1·90

306 High Jumping

1984. Air. Olympic Games, Los Angeles. Multicoloured.

1705	70f. Type **306**	45	25
1706	90f. Cycling	55	20
1707	120f. Football	80	30
1708	250f. Boxing (horiz)	1·60	50
1709	400f. Running (horiz)	2·75	80
MS1710	145×104 mm. 1000f. Football	6·00	1·75

307 Donald with Presents and Chip

1984. 50th Anniv of Donald Duck (cartoon character). Multicoloured.

1711	1f. Type **307** (postage)	10	10
1712	2f. Donald and Chip'n'Dale	10	10
1713	3f. Huey, Chip and Dale blowing up balloons	10	10
1714	5f. Donald and Chip holding birthday cake	10	10
1715	10f. Daisy kissing Donald	30	10
1716	15f. Goofy giving Donald his present	40	10
1717	105f. Huey, Dewey and Louie decorating cake (air)	85	15
1718	500f. Huey, Dewey, Louie and Donald with birthday cake	4·50	95
1719	1000f. Huey, Duey and Louie startling Donald	7·50	1·60
MS1720	126×102 mm. 1000f. Donald with present	7·50	1·60
MS1721	127×101 mm. 1000f. Donald Duck	7·50	1·60

308 West African Manatee

1984. Endangered Wildlife. Multicoloured.

1722	45f. Type **308** (postage)	1·50	20
1723	70f. Manatee (close up)	1·25	20
1724	90f. Manatees in water (air)	1·75	35
1725	105f. Manatee with cub	1·75	35
MS1726	Two sheets each 65×95 mm. (a) 1000f. Olive colobus "Colobus verus" (vert). (b) 1000f. Lesser bushbaby ("Galago senegalensis")	17·00	4·00

309 Flame and Eleanor Roosevelt

1984. Birth Cent of Eleanor Roosevelt. Multicoloured.

1727	70f. Type **309** (postage)	55	15
1728	90f. Eleanor Roosevelt and Statue of Liberty (air)	65	15

310 Lockheed Constellation, 1944

1984. 40th Anniv of International Civil Aviation Organization. Multicoloured.

1729	70f. Type **310** (postage)	55	30
1730	105f. Boeing 707, 1954 (air)	60	40
1731	200f. Douglas DC-8-61, 1966	1·25	80
1732	500f. Concorde, 1966	3·25	1·75

MS1733	111×81 mm. 1000f. "Icarus" (Hans Herni)	6·25	3·25

311 Bristol "400", 1947

1984. Classic Cars. Multicoloured.

1734	1f. Type **311** (postage)	10	10
1735	2f. Frazer Nash "Standard", 1925	10	10
1736	3f. Healey "Silverstone", 1950	10	10
1737	4f. Kissell "Gold Bug Speedstar", 1925	10	10
1738	50f. La Salle 5 litre, 1927	80	15
1739	90f. Minerva 30 h.p., 1921 (air)	70	15
1740	500f. Morgan "Plus 4", 1950	4·25	95
1741	1000f. Napier "40/50 T75 Six", 1921	7·75	2·25
MS1742	Two sheets each (a) 78×114 mm. 1000f. Peugeot Bebe, 1903. (b) 82×116 mm. 1000f. Nash Ambassador Six trunkback sedan, 1941	15·50	4·50

312 Pakistan (bronze, hockey, 1976)

1984. Air. Olympic Games Medal Winners (2nd series). Eight sheets, each 108×79 mm containing T **312** or similar vert designs. Multicoloured.

MS1743	(a) 500f. Type **312**. (b) 500f. Yukio Endo (gold, gymnastics, 1964). (c) 500f. Jurgen Hingsen (silver, decathlon, 1984). (d) 500f. Michael Gross (2 golds, 2 silver, swimming, 1984). (e) 500f. Bill Steinkraus (gold, equestrian events, 1968). (f) 500f. Pasquale Passarelli (gold, wrestling, 1984). (g) 500f. New Zealand (gold, hockey, 1976). (h) 500f. Karl-Heinz Rauschmayer (gold, equestrian events, 1984)	24·00	9·00

313 "Connestabile Madonna"

1984. Christmas. Paintings by Raphael. Multicoloured.

1744	70f. Type **313** (postage)	55	15
1745	290f. "The Cowper Madonna" (air)	1·90	65
1746	300f. "The Alba Madonna"	2·00	65
1747	500f. "Madonna of the Curtain"	3·25	1·10
MS1748	93×136 mm. 1000f. "Madonna with Saints John and Nicholas"	6·00	2·10

314 Rack Railway Steam Train, Madeira

1984. Railway Locomotives. Multicoloured.

1749	1f. Type **314** (postage)	10	10
1750	2f. British-built steam locomotive, Egypt	10	10
1751	3f. Garratt steam locomotive, Algeria	10	10
1752	4f. Diesel train, Congo-Ocean Railway	10	10
1753	50f. Italian-built steam locomotive, Libya	40	10
1754	90f. Northern Railway steam locomotive No. 49 (air)	70	15
1755	105f. Mallet steam locomotive, Togo	80	15
1756	500f. Steam locomotive, Rhodesia	3·75	70
1757	1000f. Beyer-Garratt steam locomotive, East African Railway	7·50	1·40

MS1758	Two sheets each 104×75 mm. (a) 1000f. First horse-drawn train to Dakar, Senegal railway. (b) 1000f. American-made locomotive, Ghana railway	11·00	4·00

315 Map of Americas and Flags

1984. Third E.E.C.–African States Convention, Lome. Multicoloured.

1759	100f. Type **315**	80	20
1760	130f. Map of Europe and Africa and flags	1·10	30
1761	270f. Map of Asia and Australasia and flags	2·00	60
MS1762	141×99 mm. 500f. Pres. Gnassinbe Ayadema	3·75	1·10

Nos. 1759/61 were printed in se-tenant strips of three, forming a composite design showing map of the world.

316 St. Paul

1984. The Twelve Apostles. Multicoloured.

1763	1f. Type **316** (postage)	10	10
1764	2f. St. Thomas	10	10
1765	3f. St. Matthew	10	10
1766	4f. St. James, the Less	10	10
1767	5f. St. Simon, the Zealot	10	10
1768	70f. St. Thaddeus	85	15
1769	90f. St. Bartholomew (air)	55	15
1770	105f. St. Philip	65	15
1771	200f. St. John	1·25	35
1772	270f. St. James, son of Zebedee	1·60	45
1773	400f. St. Andrew	2·50	80
1774	500f. St. Peter	3·25	90
MS1775	Two sheets each 116×78 mm. (a) 1000f. "The Last Supper" (detail) (Andrea del Castagno) (41×27 mm). (b) 1000f. "Coronation of the Virgin" (detail) (Raphael) (41×27 mm)	11·00	4·00

317 Allez France

1985. Racehorses. Multicoloured.

1776	1f. Type **317** (postage)	10	10
1777	2f. Arkle (vert)	10	10
1778	3f. Tingle Creek (vert)	10	10
1779	4f. Interco	10	10
1780	50f. Dawn Run	95	15
1781	90f. Seattle Slew (vert) (air)	85	20
1782	500f. Nijinsky	4·75	90
1783	1000f. Politician	7·75	2·25
MS1784	Two sheets each 100×70 mm. (a) 1000f. "Shergar"; (b) 1000f. "Red Rum"	11·00	4·00

318 Map, Globe and Doves

1985. Air. Peace and Human Rights. Multicoloured.

1785	230f. Type **318**	1·50	55
1786	270f. Palm tree by shore and emblem	1·75	55
1787	500f. Mining and emblem	3·25	1·10
1788	1000f. Human Rights monument	6·75	2·50

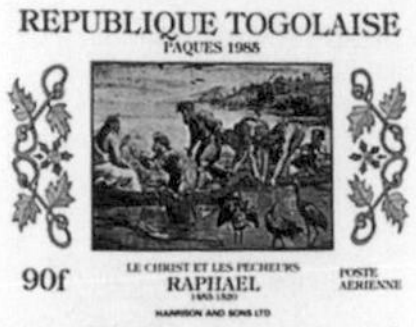
REPUBLIQUE TOGOLAISE
PAQUES 1985
90f
RAPHAEL
POSTE AERIENNE
319 "Christ and the Fisherman"

1985. Easter. Paintings by Raphael. Multicoloured.
1789 70f. "Christ and the Apostles" (postage) 55 15
1790 90f. Type **319** 60 20
1791 135f. "Christ making Benediction" (vert) (air) 1·00 20
1792 150f. "The Entombment" (vert) 1·10 30
1793 250f. "The Resurrection" (vert) 1·75 50
MS1794 75×105 mm. 1000f. "The Resurrection" (different) 7·00 2·00

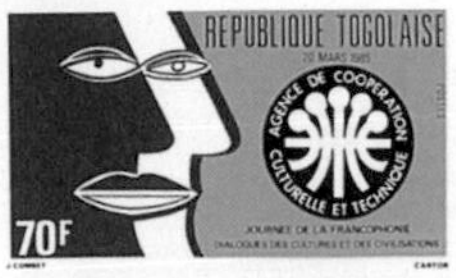
REPUBLIQUE TOGOLAISE
70F
320 Profiles and Emblem

1985. 15th Anniv of Cultural and Technical Co-operation Agency.
1795 **320** 70f. multicoloured 50 20
1796 **320** 90f. multicoloured 60 30

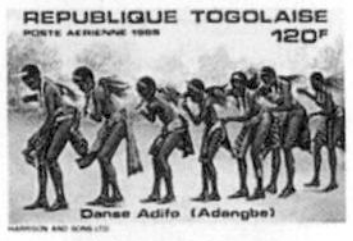
REPUBLIQUE TOGOLAISE
120F
321 Adifo Dance

1985. Air. Traditional Dances. Multicoloured.
1797 120f. Type **321** 80 30
1798 125f. Whip dance 90 35
1799 290f. Idjombi dance 1·90 65
1800 500f. Moba dance 3·25 95

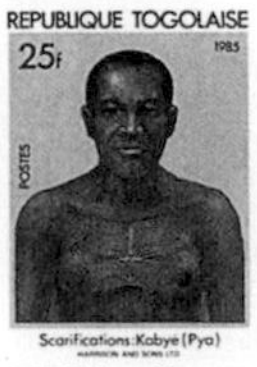
REPUBLIQUE TOGOLAISE
25F
1985
Scarifications: Kabye (Pya)
322 Kabye Man

1985. Tribal Markings. Multicoloured.
1801 25f. Type **322** (postage) 15 10
1802 70f. Mollah woman 50 20
1803 90f. Moba man (air) 60 20
1804 105f. Kabye woman 80 20
1805 270f. Peda woman 1·90 65

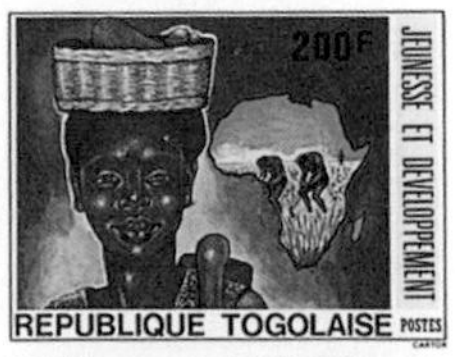
200F
JEUNESSE ET DEVELOPPEMENT
REPUBLIQUE TOGOLAISE
323 Woman carrying Basket on Head and Workers on Map

1985. "Philexafrique" Stamp Exhibition, Lome. "Youth and Development". Multicoloured.
1806 200f. Type **323** 1·60 90
1807 200f. Man ploughing field with oxen 1·60 90

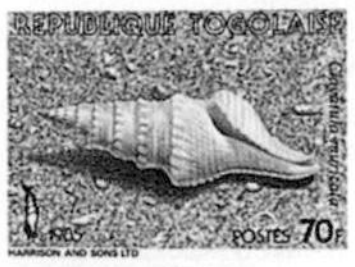
REPUBLIQUE TOGOLAISE
POSTES 70F
324 Muricate Turrid

1985. Sea Shells. Multicoloured.
1808 70f. Type **324** (postage) 95 20
1809 90f. Desjardin's marginalla (air) 1·00 25
1810 120f. Nifat turrid 1·25 25
1811 135f. Rat cowrie 1·50 25
1812 270f. Garter cone 3·00 60
MS1813 100×80 mm. 1000f. Traditional shell ("Conus genanus") headdress 7·00 2·00

1985. "Expo '85" World's Fair, Tsukuba, Japan. Nos. 1738 and 1741 optd **EXPOSITION MONDIALE 1985 TSUKUBA, JAPON.**
1814 50f. La Salle 5 litre, 1927 (postage) 85 20
1815 1000f. Napier "40/50 T75 Six", 1921 (air) 9·50 2·75

MS1816 Two sheets (a) 78×114 mm. 1000f. Peugeot "Bebe", 1903. (b) 82×116 mm. 1000f. Nash "Ambassador Six", 1941 15·00 10·00

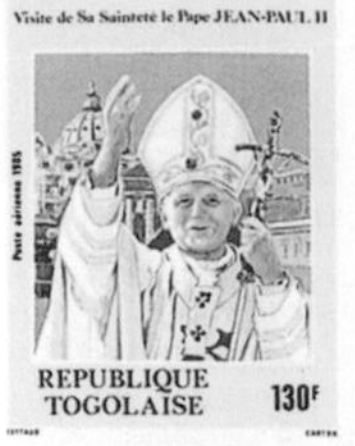
Visite de Sa Sainteté le Pape JEAN-PAUL II
REPUBLIQUE TOGOLAISE
130F
326 Pope giving Blessing

1985. Air. Visit of Pope John Paul II. Multicoloured.
1817 90f. Pope and children 85 20
1818 130f. Type **326** 1·10 35
1819 500f. Pres. Eyadema greeting Pope 4·25 2·25

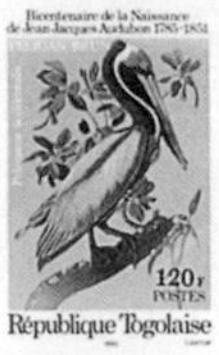
120F
POSTES
République Togolaise
327 Brown Pelican

1985. Birth Bicentenary of John J. Audubon (ornithologist). Multicoloured.
1820 120f. Type **327** (postage) 1·40 30
1821 270f. Golden eagle 3·50 70
1822 90f. Bonaparte's gulls (air) 1·10 20
1823 135f. Great-tailed grackle 1·75 30
1824 500f. Red-headed woodpecker 7·75 1·50
MS1825 80×104 mm. 1000f. Yellow warbler 15·00 10·00

1985. Air. Olympic Games Medal Winners (2nd series). Nos. 1657/64 optd.
1826 500f. **"ITALIE MEDAILLE D'OR"** 4·00 85
1827 500f. **"PHILIPPE BOISSE FRANCE MEDAILLE D'OR"** 4·00 85
1828 500f. **"ROLF GOLZ R.F.A. MEDAILLE D'ARGENT"** 4·00 85
1829 500f. **"PATRIK SJOBERG SUEDE MEDAILLE D'ARGENT"** 4·00 85
1830 500f. **"GLYNIS NUNN AUSTRALIE MEDAILLE D'OR"** 4·00 85
1831 500f. **"KIRK BAPTISTE ETATS UNIS MEDAILLE D'ARGENT"** 4·00 85
1832 500f. **"CARL LEWIS ETATS UNIS MEDAILLE D'OR"** 4·00 85
1833 500f. **"KEVIN BARRY NLE ZELANDE MEDAILLE D'ARGENT"** 4·00 85
MS1834 Eight sheets each 108×79 mm. (a) 500f. **R.F.A./MEDAILLE D'ARGENT**; (b) 500f. **KOJI GUSHIKEN/JAPON/MEDAILLE D'OR**; (c) 500f. **DALEY THOMPSON/GRANDE BRETAGNE/MEDAILLE D'OR**; (d) 500f. **FREDERIC DELCOURT/FRANCE/MEDAILLE D'ARGENT**; (e) 500f. **KAREN STIVES/ETATS UNIS/MEDAILLE D'ARGENT**; (f) 500f. **TAKASHI IRIE/JAPON/MEDAILLE D'ARGENT**; (g) 500f. **CANADA/MEDAILLE D'OR**; (h) 500f. **ROLF MILSER/R.F.A./MEDAILLE D'OR** 30·00 6·75

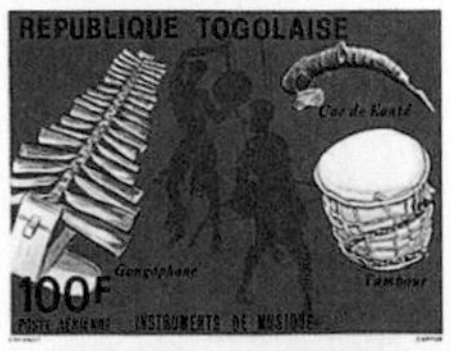
REPUBLIQUE TOGOLAISE
100F
POSTE AERIENNE INSTRUMENTS DE MUSIQUE
330 Gongophone, Kante Horn and Drum

1985. Air. "Philexafrique" Stamp Exhibition, Lome (2nd issue). Musical Instruments. Multicoloured.
1835 100f. Type **330** 1·40 65
1836 100f. Twin drums, Bassar horn and castanets 1·40 65

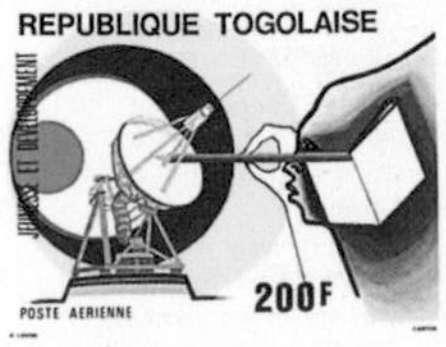
REPUBLIQUE TOGOLAISE
JEUNESSE ET DEVELOPPEMENT
POSTE AERIENNE
200F
331 Open Book, Profile, Hand holding Pencil and Dish Aerial

1985. Air. "Philexafrique" Stamp Exhibition, Lome (3rd issue). "Youth and Development". Multicoloured.
1837 200f. Type **331** 1·90 1·10
1838 200f. Profiles, factory, cogwheel and maize 1·90 1·10

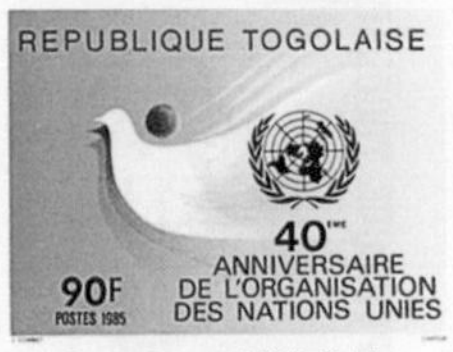
REPUBLIQUE TOGOLAISE
90F
POSTES 1985
40ème ANNIVERSAIRE DE L'ORGANISATION DES NATIONS UNIES
332 Dove, Sun and U.N. Emblem

1985. 40th Anniv of U.N.O. Multicoloured.
1839 90f. Type **332** (postage) 60 20
1840 115f. Hands reaching up to Emblem 90 20
1841 150f. Building new bridge on river Kara (air) 1·10 35
1842 250f. Preparing experimental field of millet at Atalote, Keran 1·60 50
1843 500f. Pres. Eyadema, U.N. Secretary-General, U.N. and national flags 3·25 85

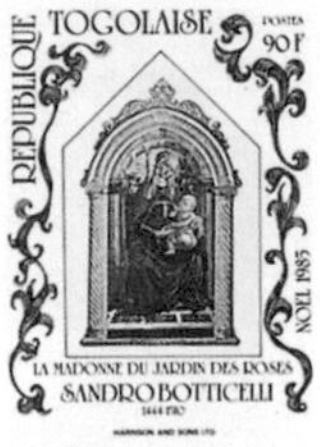
REPUBLIQUE TOGOLAISE
POSTES 90F
NOEL 1985
LA MADONE DU JARDIN DES ROSES
SANDRO BOTTICELLI
333 "Madonna of the Rose Garden" (Sandro Botticelli)

1985. Christmas. Multicoloured.
1844 90f. Type **333** (postage) 65 20
1845 115f. "Madonna and Child" (11th-century Byzantine painting) (air) 90 20
1846 150f. "Rest during the flight into Egypt" (Gerard David) 1·00 30
1847 160f. "African Madonna" (16th-century statue) 1·10 30
1848 250f. "African Madonna" (statue, 1900) 2·00 45
MS1849 105×75 mm. 500f. "Mystic Madonna" (Sandro Botticelli) (34×48 mm) 3·75 90

1985. Various stamps optd. (a) Nos. 1739/40 optd **10e ANNIVERSAIRE DE APOLLO-SOYUZ**.
1850 90f. Minerva 30 h.p., 1921 85 30
1851 500f. Morgan "Plus 4", 1950 4·75 1·40

(b) Nos. 1752, 1755 and 1757 optd **80e ANNIVERSAIRE du ROTARY INTERNATIONAL**.
1853 4f. Diesel train, Congo-Ocean Railway (postage) 55 35
1854 105f. Mallet steam locomotive, Togo (air) 1·10 1·00
1855 1000f. Beyer-Garratt steam locomotive, East African Railway 11·00 5·75
MS1856 Two sheets each 104×75 mm. (a) 1000f. First horse-drawn train to Dakar, Senegal railway; (b) 1000f. American-made locomotive, Ghana railway 17·00 10·50

(c) 150th Anniv of German Railways. Nos. 1753/4 and 1756 optd **150e ANNIVERSAIRE DE CHEMIN FER "LUDWIG"**.
1857 50f. Italian-built steam locomotive, Libya (postage) 1·00 35
1858 90f. Northern Railway steam locomotive No. 49 (air) 1·00 50
1859 500f. Steam locomotive, Rhodesia 6·25 2·75
MS1860 Two sheets each 104×75 mm. (a) 1000f. First horse-drawn train to Dakar, Senegal railway; (b) 1000f. American-made locomotive, Ghana railway 17·00 9·50

(d) Nos. 1773/4 optd **"75e ANNIVERSAIRE DE LA MORT DE HENRI DUNANT FONDATEUR DE LA CROIX ROUGE"**.
1861 400f. St. Andrew 3·25 1·10
1862 500f. St. Peter 4·00 1·40
MS1863 116×79 mm. 1000f. "Coronation of the Virgin" 7·75 5·25

(e) Nos. 1780 and 1783 optd **"75e ANNIVERSAIRE DU SCOUTISME FEMININ"**.
1864 50f. Dawn Run 85 20
1865 1000f. Politician 8·25 2·25
MS1866 Two sheets each 100×70 mm. (a) 1000f. "Shergar"; (b) 1000f. "Red Rum" 16·00 4·50

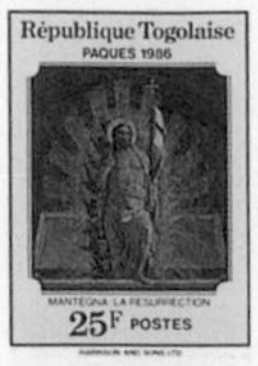
République Togolaise
PAQUES 1986
25F POSTES
335 "The Resurrection" (Andrea Mantegna)

1986. Easter. Multicoloured.
1867 25f. Type **335** (postage) 20 10
1868 70f. "Calvary" (Paul Veronese) 55 15
1869 90f. "The Last Supper" (Jacopo Robusti Tintoretto) (horiz) (air) 65 30
1870 200f. "Christ in the Tomb" (Berruguette) (horiz) 1·50 55
MS1871 80×100 mm. 1000f. Type **335** 7·50 2·75

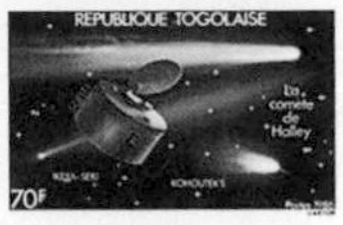
REPUBLIQUE TOGOLAISE
70F
336 "Suisie" Space Probe and Kohoutek's Comet

1986. Appearance of Halley's Comet (1st issue). Multicoloured.
1872 70f. Type **336** (postage) 55 15
1873 90f. "Vega I" space probe and people pointing at comet (air) 55 20
1874 150f. Comet and observation equipment 90 30
1875 200f. "Giotto" space probe and comet over town 1·25 40
MS1876 86×73 mm. 1000f. Comet, Edmond Halley and Sir Issac Newton 4·75 2·00
See also Nos. 1917/**MS**1921.

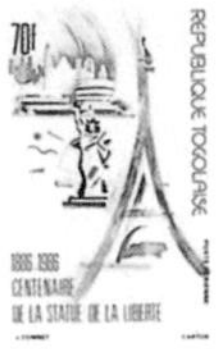
70F
REPUBLIQUE TOGOLAISE
337 New York, Statue and Eiffel Tower

1986. Air. Centenary of Statue of Liberty. Multicoloured.
1877 70f. Type **337** 50 15
1878 90f. Statue, Arc de Triomphe and Brooklyn Bridge 1·25 45
1879 500f. Statue, Pantheon and Empire State Building 3·25 1·10

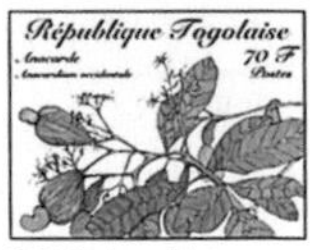
République Togolaise
70 F
338 Cashew Nut

1986. Fruit. Multicoloured.
1880 70f. Type **338** (postage) 55 15
1881 90f. Pineapple 80 20
1882 120f. Avocado (air) 90 20
1883 135f. Papaw 1·10 20
1884 290f. Mango (vert) 2·25 65

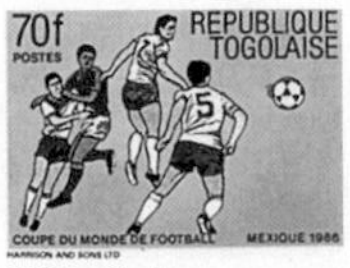
70f
REPUBLIQUE TOGOLAISE
POSTES
MEXIQUE 1986
339 Footballers

1986. World Cup Football Championship, Mexico.
1885 **339** 70f. mult (postage) 55 15
1886 - 90f. multicoloured (air) 55 30
1887 - 130f. multicoloured 85 35
1888 - 300f. multicoloured 1·90 70
MS1889 101×81 mm. 1000f. multicoloured 11·00 4·00
DESIGNS: 90f. to 1000f. Various footballing scenes.

1986. Air. "Ameripex '86" International Stamp Exhibition, Chicago. Nos. 1718/19 optd **AMERIPEX 86**.
1890 500f. Huey, Dewey, Louie and Donald with birthday cake 4·50 1·10
1891 1000f. Huey, Dewey and Louie startling Donald 8·25 2·25
MS1892 Two sheets each 126×102 mm. (a) 1000f. Donald with present; (b) 1000f. Donald Duck 8·25 2·25

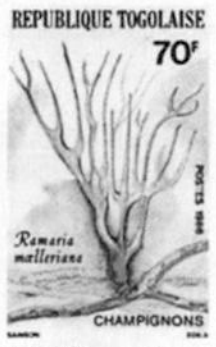

341 "Ramaria moelleriana"

1986. Fungi. Multicoloured.

1893	70f. Type **341**	1·25	50
1894	90f. "Hygrocybe firma"	1·50	70
1895	150f. "Kalchbrennera corallocephala"	2·50	1·25
1896	200f. "Cookeina tricholoma"	3·50	1·75

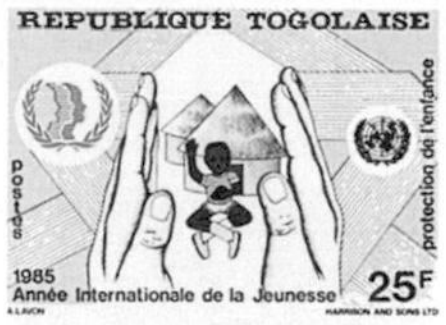

342 Hand framing Huts and Child

1986. International Youth Year (1985). Multicoloured.

1897	25f. Type **342**	30	15
1898	90f. Children feeding birds	1·10	40

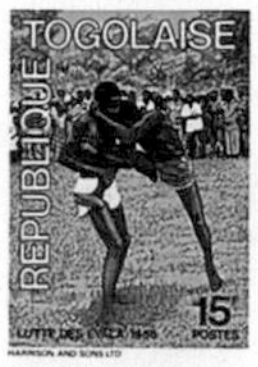

343 Wrestlers

1986. Evala Wrestling Contest.

1899	**343** 15f. mult (postage)	15	10
1900	- 20f. multicoloured	30	10
1901	- 70f. multicoloured	65	15
1902	- 90f. multicoloured (air)	40	35

DESIGNS: 20 to 90f. Wrestling scenes.

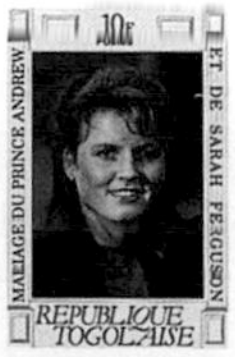

344 Miss Sarah Ferguson

1986. Wedding of Prince Andrew. Multicoloured.

1903	10f. Type **344** (postage)	55	10
1904	1000f. Prince Andrew (air)	6·75	2·25
MS1905	97×92 mm. 1000f. Prince Andrew and Miss Sarah Ferguson	6·75	2·25

1986. World Cup Winners. Nos. 1886/9 optd.

1906	70f. **DEMI-FINALE ARGENTINE 2 BELGIQUE 0** (postage)	55	35
1907	90f. **DEMI-FINALE ALLEMAGNE DE L'OUEST 2 FRANCE 0** (air)	55	20
1908	130f. **3 eme et 4 eme PLACE FRANCE 4 BELGIQUE 2**	85	35
1909	300f. **FINALE ARGENTINE 3 ALLEMAGNE DE L'OUEST 2**	1·90	80

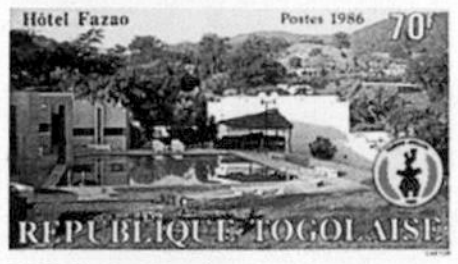

346 Fazao Hotel

1986. Hotels. Multicoloured.

1910	70f. Type **346** (postage)	55	15
1911	90f. Sarakawa Hotel (air)	65	30
1912	120f. The Lake Hotel	90	40

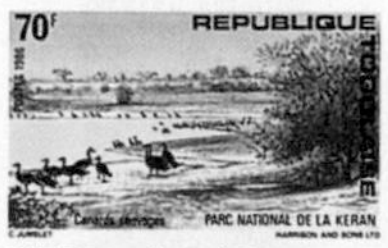

347 Spur-winged Geese

1986. Keran National Park. Multicoloured.

1913	70f. Type **347** (postage)	80	40
1914	90f. Antelope (air)	65	30
1915	100f. African elephant	80	35
1916	130f. Kob	1·00	45

1986. Appearance of Halley's Comet (2nd issue). Nos. 1872/5 optd as T **198a** of Sierra Leone.

1917	**336** 70f. mult (postage)	1·25	35
1918	- 90f. multicoloured (air)	1·00	30
1919	- 150f. multicoloured	1·50	40
1920	- 200f. multicoloured	1·90	70
MS1921	85×73 mm. 1000f. multicoloured	9·50	3·50

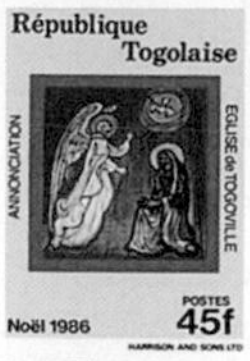

349 "The Annunciation"

1986. Christmas. Multicoloured.

1922	45f. Type **349** (postage)	45	15
1923	120f. "Nativity" (air)	90	35
1924	130f. "Adoration of the Magi"	1·10	45
1925	200f. "Flight into Egypt"	1·50	65
MS1926	80×100 mm. 1000f. Togoville church	7·50	3·25

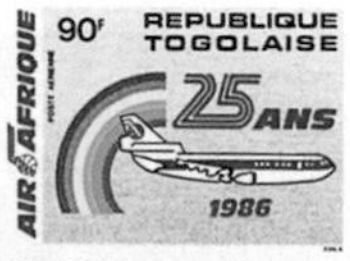

350 Rainbow and Douglas DC-10

1986. Air. 25th Anniv of Air Afrique.

1927	**350** 90f. multicoloured	75	45

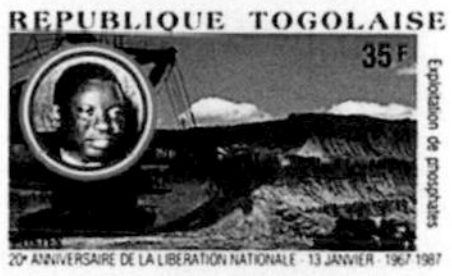

351 Pres. Eyadema and Phosphate Mine

1987. 20th Anniv of National Liberation. Multicoloured.

1928	35f. Type **351** (postage)	20	10
1929	50f. Anie sugar refinery	35	15
1930	70f. Nangbeto Dam	50	20
1931	90f. February 2 Hotel and Posts and Telecommunications building, Lome	60	20
1932	100f. Post and Telecommunications building, Kara (air)	55	15
1933	120f. Peace monument	80	30
1934	130f. Baby being vaccinated	90	35
MS1935	109×75 mm. 500f. Buildings and silos (48×36 mm)	2·75	1·10

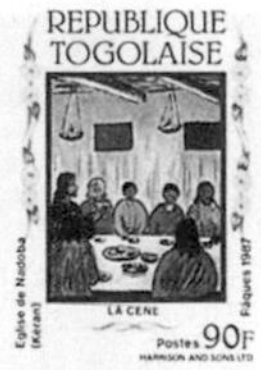

352 "The Last Supper"

1987. Easter. Paintings from Nadoba Church, Keran. Multicoloured.

1936	90f. Type **352** (postage)	65	30
1937	130f. "Christ on the Cross" (air)	90	30
1938	300f. "The Resurrection"	2·00	65
MS1939	100×80 mm. 500f. Fresco (detail) (40×29 mm)	3·00	1·50

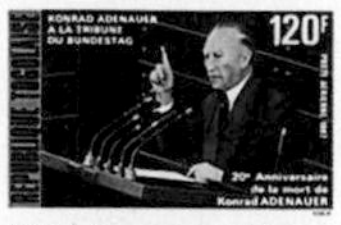

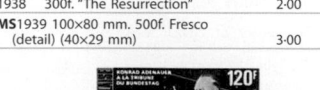

353 Adenauer speaking in the Bundestag

1987. Air. 20th Death Anniv of Konrad Adenauer (German Chancellor). Multicoloured.

1940	120f. Type **353**	85	30
1941	500f. Adenauer with John F. Kennedy	3·25	1·10
MS1942	118×88 mm. 500f. Adenauer (22×36 mm)	3·25	1·10

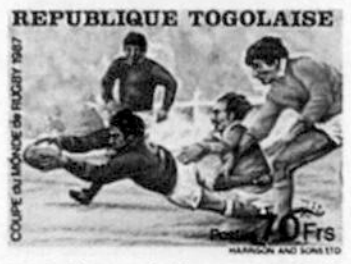

354 Player falling with Ball

1987. World Rugby Football Cup. Multicoloured.

1943	70f. Type **354** (postage)	80	30
1944	130f. Player running with ball (air)	1·25	35
1945	300f. Scrum	2·75	1·25
MS1946	80×100 mm. 1000f. Players around goal (26×37 mm)	9·00	4·00

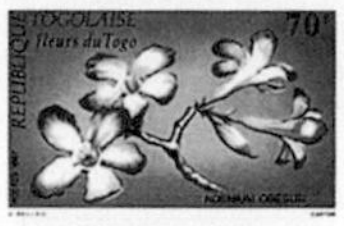

355 "Adenium obesum"

1987. Flowers. Multicoloured.

1947	70f. Type **355** (postage)	70	20
1948	90f. "Amorphophallus abyssinicus" (vert) (air)	85	30
1949	100f. "Ipomoea mauritiana"	1·00	30
1950	120f. "Salacia togoica" (vert)	1·25	35

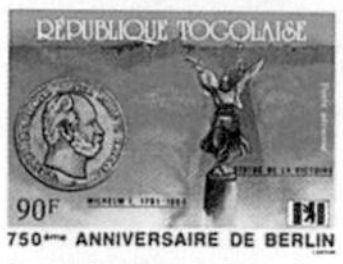

356 Wilhelm I Coin and Victory Statue

1987. Air. 750th Anniv of Berlin. Multicoloured.

1951	90f. Type **356**	65	30
1952	150f. Friedrich III coin and Brandenburg Gate	1·00	35
1953	300f. Wilhelm II coin and Place de la Republique	2·00	65
MS1954	129×89 mm. 750f. Otto von Bismarck and Charlottenburg Palace	4·75	1·75

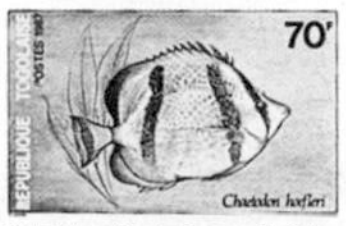

357 Hoefler's Butterflyfish

1987. Fish. Multicoloured.

1955	70f. Type **357**	1·00	35
1956	90f. Nile pufferfish	1·25	40
1957	120f. Guree spadefish	1·50	60
1958	130f. Dwarf labeo	1·75	60

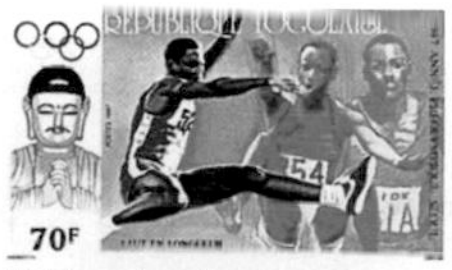

358 Long Jumping

1987. Olympic Games, Seoul (1988). Multicoloured.

1959	70f. Type **358** (postage)	60	20
1960	90f. Relay race (air)	60	20
1961	200f. Cycling	1·25	45
1962	250f. Javelin throwing	1·60	55
MS1963	111×84 mm. 1000f. Tennis (51×30 mm)	7·75	2·75

1987. Endangered Wildlife. As Nos. 1722/5 but values changed and size 37×24 mm.

1964	60f. Type **308** (postage)	1·00	20
1965	75f. Manatee (close up)	1·10	35
1966	80f. Manatees in water	1·50	35
1967	100f. Manatee with cub (air)	1·75	40

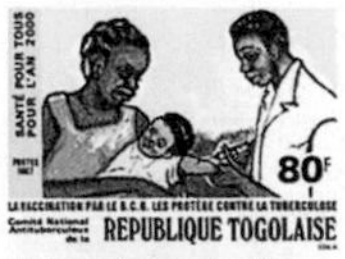

359 Doctor vaccinating Child

1987. "Health for All by Year 2000". Anti-tuberculosis Campaign. Multicoloured.

1968	80f. Type **359** (postage)	55	30
1969	90f. Family under umbrella (vert) (air)	60	30
1970	115f. Faculty of Medicine building, Lome University	80	35

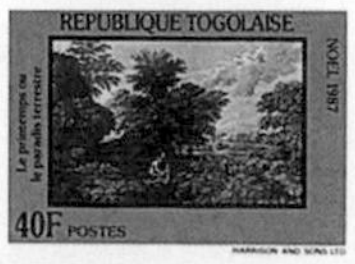

360 "Spring or the Earthly Paradise"

1987. Christmas. Multicoloured.

1971	40f. Type **360** (postage)	35	10
1972	45f. "The Creation of Adam" (Michelangelo)	35	10
1973	105f. "Presentation in the Temple" (vert) (air)	65	20
1974	270f. "The Original Sin" (vert)	1·75	65
MS1975	100×80 mm. 500f. "Nativity" (39×29 mm)	3·00	1·00

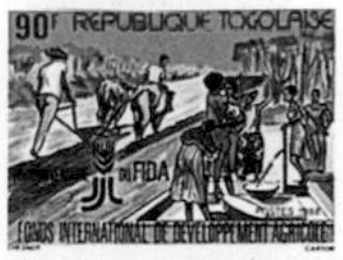

361 Men ploughing and Women collecting Water

1988. Tenth Anniv of Agricultural Development Fund.

1976	**361** 90f. multicoloured	65	20

1988. Stamp Exhibitions. Various miniature sheets optd and logo.

MS1977	Four sheets (a) 500f. **OLYMPHILEX '88**; (**MS**1743h); (b) 1000f. **Independence 40, Israel** (**MS**1742a); (c) 1000f. **Praga '88** (**MS**1758a); (d) 1000f. **Finlandia 88, Helsinki** (**MS**1758b)	18·00	10·50

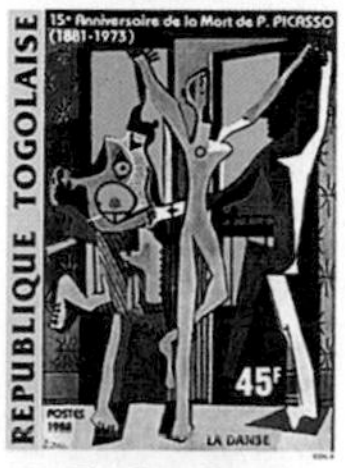

363 "The Dance"

1988. 15th Death Anniv of Pablo Picasso (painter). Multicoloured.

1978	45f. Type **363** (postage)	45	10
1979	160f. "Portrait of a Young Girl"	1·50	35
1980	300f. "Gueridon" (air)	2·75	85
MS1981	132×101 mm. 300f. "Mandolin and Guitar" (detail) (39×51 mm)	2·75	85

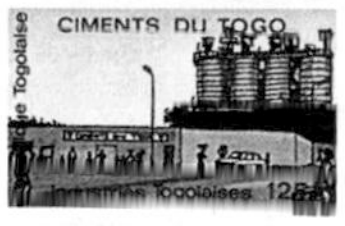

364 Cement

1988. Industries. Multicoloured.

1982	125f. Type **364**	85	30
1983	165f. Brewery	1·10	40
1984	195f. Phosphates	1·25	45
1985	200f. Plastics	1·25	45
1986	300f. Milling (vert)	2·10	65

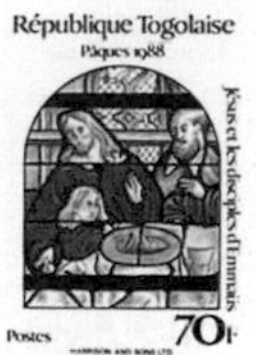

365 "Jesus and the Disciples at Emmaus"

1988. Easter. Stained Glass Windows. Multicoloured.

1987	70f. Type **365** (postage)	60	15
1988	90f. "Mary at the Foot of the Cross"	80	20
1989	120f. "Crucifixion" (air)	85	30
1990	200f. "St. Thomas and Resurrected Jesus"	1·40	45
MS1991	80×100 mm. 500f. "Agony of Jesus on Mount of Olives"	3·50	1·10

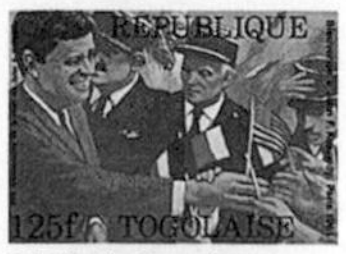

366 Paris Crowd welcoming Kennedy, 1961

1988. 25th Death Anniv of John F. Kennedy (U.S. President). Multicoloured.

1992	125f. Type **366**	1·00	20
1993	155f. Kennedy at Paris Town Hall (vert)	1·10	20
1994	165f. Kennedy and De Gaulle at Elysee Palace (vert)	1·25	40
1995	180f. John and Jacqueline Kennedy at Orly Airport	1·40	75
MS1996	100×72 mm. 750f. De Gaulle and Kennedy (vert)	5·50	2·75

367 Watchi Chief

1988. Traditional Tribal Costumes. Multicoloured.
1997	80f. Type **367**	55	20
1998	125f. Watchi woman	85	20
1999	165f. Kotokoli man	1·10	35
2000	175f. Ewe man	1·10	35
MS2001	104×78 mm. 500f. Moba man	3·00	95

368 Basketball

1988. Olympic Games, Seoul. Multicoloured.
2002	70f. Type **368** (postage)	50	15
2003	90f. Tennis	60	20
2004	120f. Archery (air)	85	30
2005	200f. Throwing the discus	1·40	45
MS2006	80×100 mm. 500f. Marathon	3·50	1·10

369 People with Candles

1988. 40th Anniv of W.H.O. Multicoloured.
2007	80f. Type **369**	55	15
2008	125f. Maps, emblem and "40"	85	20

370 Plaited Style

1988. Hairstyles. Multicoloured.
2009	80f. Type **370**	55	20
2010	125f. Knotted style	85	20
2011	170f. Plaited style with bow	1·00	40
2012	180f. Style with plaits all over head (vert)	1·25	40
MS2013	100×140 mm. 500f. Long and short styles	3·50	1·25

371 Collecting Water (B. Gossner)

1988. "Philtogo" National Stamp Exhibition. Designs depicting winning entries of a schools drawing competition. Multicoloured.
2014	10f. Type **371**	10	10
2015	35f. Villagers working on farm (K. Ekoue-Kouvahey)	20	10
2016	70f. Family (A. Abbey)	65	15
2017	90f. Village women preparing food (T. D. Lawson)	85	30
2018	120f. Fishermen and boats on shore (A. Tazzar)	1·10	30

372 "Adoration of the Magi" (Pieter Brueghel the Elder)

1988. Christmas. Multicoloured.
2019	80f. Type **372** (postage)	55	20

2020	150f. "The Virgin, The Infant Jesus, Saints Jerome and Dominic" (Fra. Filippo Lippi) (air)	1·00	20
2021	175f. "The Madonna, The Infant Jesus, St. Joseph and the Infant St. John the Baptist" (Federico Barocci)	1·25	35
2022	195f. "The Virgin and Child" (Gentile Bellini)	1·40	45
MS2023	100×80 mm. 750f. "Holy Family and a Shepherd" (Titian)	3·75	1·40

373 Wreckage of Airplane

1989. 15th Anniv of Sarakawa Assassination Attempt. Multicoloured.
2024	10f. Type **373**	10	10
2025	80f. Tail section (vert)	55	25
2026	125f. Soldiers and wreckage	85	50

374 Anniversary Emblem

1989. 20th Anniv of Benin Electricity Community.
2027	**374** 80f. multicoloured	60	20
2028	**374** 125f. multicoloured	95	20

375 Boxing

1989. Prince Emanuel of Liechtenstein Foundation. Multicoloured.
2029	80f. Type **375**	55	20
2030	125f. Long jumping	55	30
2031	165f. Running	1·10	40

376 Table Tennis

1989. Olympic Games, Barcelona (1992). Multicoloured.
2032	80f. Type **376** (postage)	65	20
2033	125f. Running (horiz)	90	20
2034	165f. Putting the shot	1·00	35
2035	175f. Basketball	1·25	35
2036	380f. High jumping (horiz) (air)	2·50	55
2037	425f. Boxing (horiz)	3·00	55
MS2038	90×69 mm. 650f. Show jumping (horiz)	4·00	1·25

377 Footballers and St. Janvier's Cathedral, Naples

1989. World Cup Football Championship, Italy. Multicoloured.
2039	80f. Type **377** (postage)	55	20
2040	125f. Milan Cathedral	85	20
2041	165f. Bevilacqua Palace, Verona	1·10	35
2042	175f. Baptistry, Florence	1·10	35
2043	380f. Madama Palace, Turin (air)	2·75	55
2044	425f. St. Laurent's Cathedral, Genoa	2·75	55
MS2045	68×90 mm. 650f. Colosseum, Rome	5·50	1·25

378 Bundestag

1989. 40th Anniv of Federal Republic of Germany. Multicoloured.
2046	90f. Type **378**	65	20
2047	125f. Konrad Adenauer (Chancellor, 1949–63) and Theodor Heuss (President, 1949–59) (vert)	95	30
2048	180f. West German flag and emblem	1·25	40

379 Tractor, Map and Woman at Water-pump

1989. 30th Anniv of Council of Unity.
2049	**379** 75f. multicoloured	55	20

380 Boys learning First Aid

1989. 125th Anniv of International Red Cross. Multicoloured.
2050	90f. Type **380**	50	20
2051	125f. Founding meeting	85	35

381 Storming the Bastille

1989. Bicentenary of French Revolution (1st issue). Multicoloured.
2052	90f. Type **381**	65	20
2053	125f. Oath of the Tennis Court (horiz)	1·00	35
2054	180f. Abolition of Privileges (horiz)	1·40	45
MS2055	82×67 mm. 1000f. Declaration of the Rights of Man	8·75	3·50

See also Nos. 2056/MS2060.

382 Jacques Necker (statesman) and The Three Orders

1989. Bicentenary of French Revolution (2nd issue). Multicoloured.
2056	90f. Type **382** (postage)	65	20
2057	190f. Guy le Chapelier and abolition of seigneurial rights	1·50	45
2058	425f. Talleyrand-Perigord (statesman) and La Fayette's oath (air)	2·75	55
2059	480f. Paul Barras (revolutionary) and overthrow of Robespierre	3·25	55
MS2060	131×95 mm. 750f. Georges Danton and return of royal family from Varennes (horiz)	5·00	1·10

383 People with Banners and Pres. Eyadema

1989. 20th Anniv of Kpalime Appeal. Multicoloured.
2061	90f. Type **383**	60	20

2062	125f. Pres. Eyadema addressing gathering	90	35

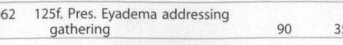

384 "Apollo II" Launch

1989. 20th Anniv of First Manned Landing on Moon. Multicoloured.
2063	40f. Type **384**	30	10
2064	90f. Space capsule in orbit	55	20
2065	150f. Landing capsule	1·10	35
2066	250f. Splashdown	1·60	45
MS2067	105×75 mm. 500f. Astronaut on Moon	3·25	90

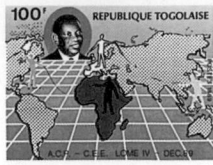

385 Figures on Map (dated "DEC.89")

1989. Fourth Lome Convention (on relations between European Community and African, Caribbean and Pacific countries). Multicoloured.
2068	100f. Type **385**	80	30
2069	100f. As T **385** but dated "15 DEC.89"	80	30

386 Emblem

1990. Tenth Anniv of Pan-African Postal Union.
2070	**386** 125f. gold, blue & brown	90	30

387 Party Headquarters, Kara

1990. 20th Anniv (1989) of Rally of Togolese People Party. Multicoloured.
2071	45f. Type **387**	35	15
2072	90f. Pres. Eyadema and anniversary emblem	60	20

388 "Myrina silenus" and Scout

1990. Scouts, Butterflies and Fungi. Multicoloured.
2073	80f. Type **388** (postage)	65	15
2074	90f. "Phlebobus silvaticus" (fungus)	65	15
2075	125f. "Volvariella esculenta" (fungus)	90	20
2076	165f. "Hypolycaena antifaunus" (butterfly)	1·10	35
2077	380f. "Termitomyces striatus" (fungus) (air)	3·00	55
2078	425f. "Axiocerces harpax" (butterfly)	3·00	55
MS2079	95×86 mm. 750f. "Cupidopsis jobates" (butterfly)	6·00	95

389 "Danaus chrysippus"

1990. Butterflies. Multicoloured.
2080	5f. Type **389**	50	10
2081	10f. "Morpho aega"	50	10

2082		15f. "Papilio demodocus"	50	10
2083		90f. "Papilio dardanus"	1·50	35
MS2084		132×106 mm. 500f. "Iterus zalmoxis" (33×26 mm) (air)	7·25	1·75

390 Emblem

1990. Ninth Convention of Lions Club Internationals District 403, Lome.

2085	**390**	90f. multicoloured	60	35
2086	**390**	125f. multicoloured	85	55
2087	**390**	165f. multicoloured	1·10	80

391 Nile Monitor

1990. Reptiles. Multicoloured.

2088		1f. Type **391**	50	10
2089		25f. Puff adder	75	10
2090		60f. Black-lipped cobra	1·00	15
2091		90f. African rock python	1·25	20

392 Pile of Cowrie Shells

1990. Money Cowrie Shells. Multicoloured.

2092		90f. Type **392**	1·00	20
2093		125f. Cowrie and bead ornament	1·50	25
2094		180f. Headdress with cowries and animal horns	2·00	55

393 Maps, Cogwheel and Arrows

1990. United States–Togo Friendship. Multicoloured.

2095		125f. Type **393**	90	35
2096		180f. Presidents Bush and Eyadema shaking hands (horiz)	1·25	35
MS2097		Two sheets. (a) 89×110 mm. 125f. Type **393** (64×78 mm); (b) 110×89 mm. 180f. As No. 2093 (80×67 mm)	2·10	70

394 Cinkasse Post Office

1990. Stamp Day.

2098	**394**	90f. multicoloured	60	35

395 Addressing Crowd, Brazzaville, 1944

1990. 20th Death Anniv of Charles de Gaulle (statesman).

2099	**395**	125f. multicoloured	85	45

396 Thatched Houses

1990. Traditional Housing. Multicoloured.

2100		90f. Type **396**	60	35
2101		125f. Village	85	45
2102		190f. Tamberma house	1·25	65

397 Airport, Airliners and Airline Emblems

1990. New Lome Airport.

2103	**397**	90f. multicoloured	1·00	35

398 Woman carrying Basket on Head (Sikou Dapau)

1990

2104	**398**	90f. multicoloured	60	35

399 Chimpanzee, Missahöuë Kloto

1991. Forests. Multicoloured.

2105		90f. Type **399**	60	35
2106		170f. Jardine's parrot, Aledjo Forest	1·25	75
2107		185f. Grey parrot, Chateau Vial Kloto Forest	1·40	75

400 Dancers

1992. Spirit Dances.

2108	**400**	90f. multicoloured	75	35
2109	-	125f. multicoloured	1·00	55
2110	-	190f. multicoloured	1·50	80

DESIGNS: 125, 190f. Various dances.

401 Royal Python hatching

1992. The Royal Python. Multicoloured.

2111		90f. Type **401**	75	35
2112		125f. Hatchlings emerging from shells	1·00	35
2113		190f. Hatchlings and empty shells	1·50	65
2114		300f. Close-up of hatchling and empty shell	2·25	90

402 Emblem

1994. 120th Anniv of U.P.U.

2115	**402**	180f. multicoloured	45	20

403 Postal Sorter

1994. World Post Day.

2117	**403**	90f. multicoloured	20	10
2118	**403**	120f. multicoloured	30	10

404 Footballers

1994. World Cup Football Championship, U.S.A.

2119	**404**	5f. multicoloured	10	10
2120	-	10f. multicoloured	10	10
2121	-	25f. multicoloured	10	10
2122	-	60f. multicoloured	15	10
2123	-	90f. multicoloured	20	10
2124	-	100f. multicoloured	25	10
2125	-	200f. multicoloured	50	20
2126	-	1000f. multicoloured	2·40	95
MS2127		Two sheets each 100×70 mm. (a) 1500f. multicoloured; (b) 3000f. multicoloured (horiz)	10·00	4·25

DESIGNS: 100f. to 3000f. Various footballing scenes.

405 Northern Pike

1995. Fish. Multicoloured.

2128		10f. Type **405**	10	10
2129		90f. Derbio	35	20
2130		180f. Common carp	75	40

406 "The Resurrection" (detail) (Andrea Mantegna)

1995. Easter. Multicoloured.

2131		90f. Type **406**	20	10
2132		180f. "Calvary" (Paolo Veronese)	45	20
2133		190f. "The Last Supper" (Jacopo Tintoretto) (horiz)	45	20

407 Hill

1995. Birth Bicentenary of Sir Rowland Hill (instigator of postage stamp).

2134	**407**	125f. multicoloured	30	10

408 Secretary Bird

1995. Birds. Multicoloured.

2135		5f. Type **408**	10	10
2136		10f. African paradise flycatcher ("Paradise Flycatcher")	10	10
2137		25f. African spoonbill (horiz)	10	10
2138		60f. Red-cheeked cordon-bleu ("Cordon Bleu") (horiz)	15	10
2139		90f. Orange-breasted sunbird	20	10

2140		100f. Yellow-billed hornbill	25	10
2141		180f. Barn owl (horiz)	45	20
2142		200f. Hoopoe feeding chick (horiz)	50	20
2143		300f. Red-crowned bishop ("Fire-crowned Bishop")	75	30
2144		1000f. Red-throated bee eater	2·40	95
MS2145		100×70 mm. 1500f. Ruppell's griffon (vulture) (horiz)	3·50	1·50

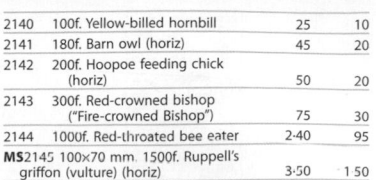

409 Madagascan Belvache

1995. Plants. Multicoloured.

2146		15f. Type **409**	10	10
2147		90f. Marigolds	20	10
2148		125f. Agave (horiz)	30	10

410 Anniversary Emblem

1995. 50th Anniv of U.N.O. (1st issue).

2149	**410**	180f. multicoloured	45	20

See also Nos. 2150/2.

411 Globe and Doves

1995. 50th Anniversaries. Multicoloured. (a) U.N.O. (2nd issue).

2150		25f. Type **411**	10	10
2151		90f. Doves and Headquarters building, New York	20	10
2152		400f. Globe and doves (different)	95	40
MS2153		72×102 mm. 1000f. Globe and dove	1·90	90

Nos. 2150/2 were issued together, se-tenant, forming a composite design.

(b) Food and Agriculture Organization.

2154		45f. Cattle	10	10
2155		125f. Cow	30	10
2156		125f. Mother and child collecting water (horiz)	30	10
2157		200f. Herdsmen	50	20
MS2158		Two sheets. (a) 90×60 mm. 300f. As No. 2156; (b) 72×102 mm. 1000f. Woman milking cow (horiz)	3·50	1·25

Nos. 2154/5 and 2157 were issued together, se-tenant, forming a composite design.

412 Montecassino, Italy

1995. 50th Anniv of End of Second World War (1st issue). Victory in Europe. Multicoloured.

2159		45f. Type **412**	10	10
2160		90f. Warsaw in ruins	20	10
2161		125f. Russian tanks in Berlin	30	10
2162		200f. German fighter planes	50	20
2163		200f. American cruiser in north Atlantic	50	20
2164		200f. Capture of Ludendorf Bridge	50	20
2165		200f. Russian "Katyusha" rockets	50	20
2166		500f. United Nations flag	2·50	90
MS2167		105×75 mm. 1500f. "U-236" (German submarine) surrenders to Royal Navy	7·50	2·75

See also Nos. 2191/**MS**2197.

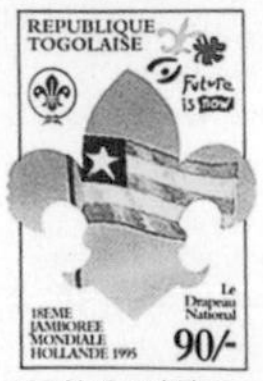

413 National Flag and Scout Badge

1995. 18th World Scout Jamboree, Dronten, Netherlands. Multicoloured.

2168	90f. Type **413**	20	10
2169	190f. Saluting scout and camp	45	20
2170	300f. Lord Baden-Powell (founder of Boy Scout Movement)	75	30
MS2171	70×100 mm. 1500f. Saluting scout and camp (different)	3·75	1·50

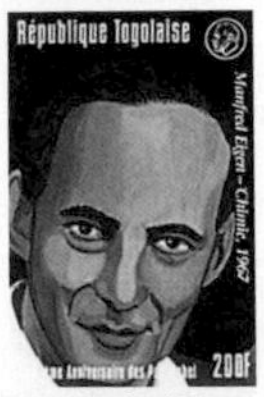

414 Manfred Eigen (Chemistry, 1967)

1995. Centenary of Nobel Prize Trust Fund. Multicoloured.

2172	200f. Type **414**	50	20
2173	200f. Donald J. Cram (Chemistry, 1987)	50	20
2174	200f. Paul J. Flory (Chemistry, 1974)	50	20
2175	200f. Johann Deisenhofer (Chemistry, 1988)	50	20
2176	200f. Percy Williams Bridgman (Physics, 1946)	50	20
2177	200f. Otto Stern (Physics, 1943)	50	20
2178	200f. Arne Tiselius (Chemistry, 1948)	50	20
2179	200f. J. Georg Bednorz (Physics, 1987)	50	20
2180	200f. Albert Claude (Medicine, 1974)	50	20
2181	200f. Elihu Root (Peace, 1912)	50	20
2182	200f. Alfred Fried (Peace, 1911)	50	20
2183	200f. Henri Moissan (Chemistry, 1906)	50	20
2184	200f. Charles Barkla (Physics, 1917)	50	20
2185	200f. Rudolf Eucken (Literature, 1908)	50	20
2186	200f. Carl von Ossietzky (Peace, 1935)	50	20
2187	200f. Sir Edward Appleton (Physics, 1947)	50	20
2188	200f. Camillo Golgi (Medicine, 1906)	50	20
2189	200f. Wilhelm Rontgen (Physics, 1901)	50	20
MS2190	Two sheets each 106×76 mm. (a) 1500f. Thomas Woodrow Wilson (Peace, 1919); (b) 1500f. Albert Einstein (Physics, 1921)	7·50	3·00

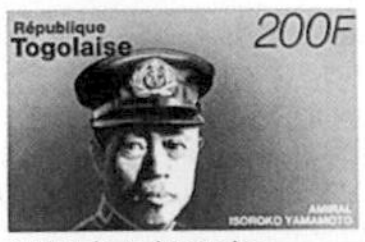

415 Admiral Isoroko Yamamoto

1995. 50th Anniv of End of Second World War (2nd issue). Victory in the Pacific. Japanese commanders. Multicoloured.

2191	200f. Type **415**	50	20
2192	200f. General Hideki Tojo (Minister of War, 1940–41 and Premier, 1941–44)	50	20
2193	200f. Vice-admiral Shigeru Fukudome	50	20
2194	200f. Admiral Shigetaro Shimada	50	20
2195	200f. Rear-admiral Chuichi Nagumo	50	20
2196	200f. General Shizu Ichi Tanaka	50	20
MS2197	107×76 mm. 1500f. Emperor Hirohito signing surrender	3·75	1·50

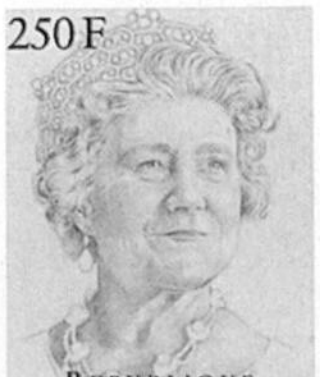

416 Drawing

1995. 95th Birthday of Queen Elizabeth the Queen Mother. Multicoloured.

2198	250f. Type **416**	60	25
2199	250f. Carrying umbrella	60	25
2200	250f. Seated at writing table (face value white)	60	25
2201	250f. As young woman	60	25
2202	250f. As No. 2200 but face value black	60	25
2203	250f. Cutting cake	60	25
2204	250f. Waving from car	60	25
MS2205	Two sheets each 101×127 mm. (a) 1000f. Wearing Garter robes; (b) 1000f. With King George VI	5·50	2·10

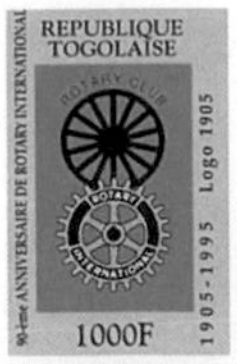

417 Original and Current Emblems

1995. 90th Anniv of Rotary International. Multicolured.

2206	1000f. Type **417**	2·40	90
MS2207	106×76 mm. 1000f. National flag and current emblem	2·40	90

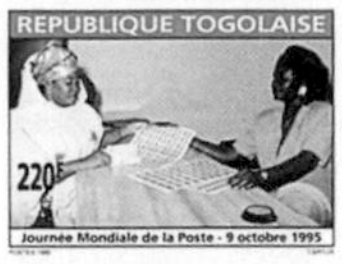

418 Woman buying Stamps

1995. World Post Day. Multicoloured.

2208	220f. Type **418**	55	20
2209	315f. Clerk arranging stamps on page	75	30
2210	335f. Sorting office	80	30

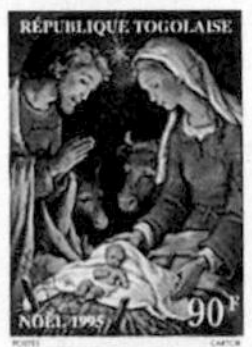

419 Nativity

1995. Christmas. Paintings. Multicoloured.

2211	90f. Type **419**	20	10
2212	325f. Adoration of the Wise Men	80	30
2213	340f. Adoration of the shepherds (horiz)	80	30
MS2214	98×71 mm. 500f. Close-up of painting on No. 2213	1·40	60

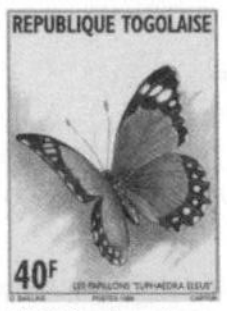

420 *Euphaedra eleus*

1996. Butterflies. Multicoloured.

2215	40f. Type **420**	10	10
2216	90f. *Papilio dardanus*	20	10
2217	220f. *Iolaus timon* (horiz)	55	20
2218	315f. *Charaxes cynthia* (horiz)	80	30

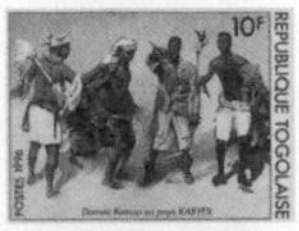

421 Kamou, Kabyes

1996. Traditional Dances. Multicoloured.

2219	10f. Type **421**	10	10
2220	90f. Kondona, Kabyes	20	10
2221	220f. Fire dance, Bassar	50	20
2222	315f. Hunters dance, Kloto	80	30
2223	335f. Women's voodoo dance	85	35

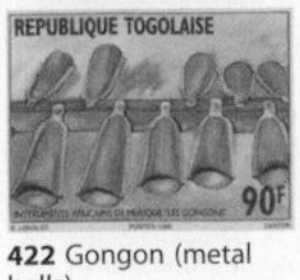

422 Gongon (metal bells)

1996. Traditional Musical Instruments. Multicoloured.

2224	90f. Type **422**	20	10
2225	220f. Balafon	55	20
2226	325f. Kora (inscr 'Cora')	80	30
2227	500f. Drums (inscr 'Tam-tams atopani')	1·10	40

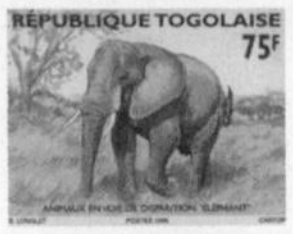

423 Elephant

1997. Endangered Species. Multicoloured.

2228	75f. Type **423**	20	10
2229	90f. Crocodile	20	10
2230	315f. Duiker (inscr 'Biche')	80	30

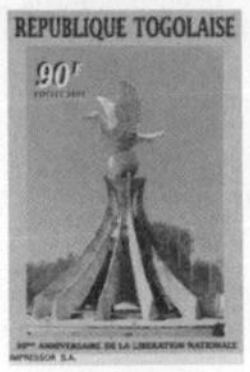

425 Monument

1997. 30th Anniv of National Liberation

2234	**425**	90f. multicoloured	20	10
2235		200f. multicoloured	55	20

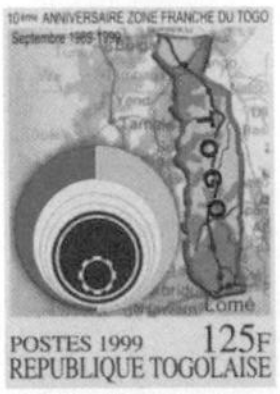

426 Emblem and Map of Togo

1999. Tenth Anniv of Free Trade Area in Togo. Multicoloured.

2236	125f. Type **426**	25	10
2237	240f. Emblem and sky	60	25
2238	340f. Emblem as iris in eye	85	35

Nos. 2239/56 are vacant.

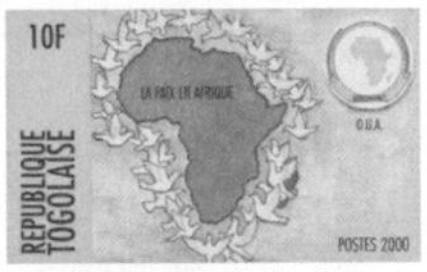

427 Map surrounded by Doves

2000. Organization for African Unity

2257	**427**	10f. multicoloured	10	10
2258		25f. multicoloured	10	10
2259		100f. multicoloured	20	10
2260		125f. multicoloured	25	15
2261		250f. multicoloured	55	20
2262		375f. multicoloured	90	40
2263		400f. multicoloured	90	45
2264		425f. multicoloured	95	45

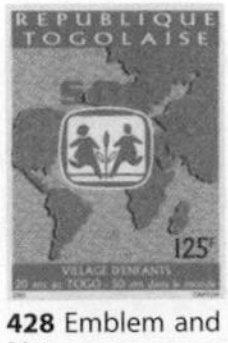

428 Emblem and Map

2001. 50th Anniv of International SOS Children's Villages

2265	**428**	125f. multicoloured	25	10

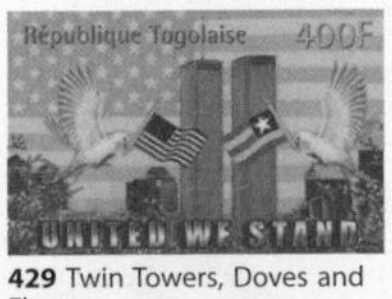

429 Twin Towers, Doves and Flags

2002. United We Stand

2266	**429**	400f. multicoloured	95	45

Nos. 2267/70 are left for Bella Bellow, issued in 2002, not yet received.

Nos. 2271/4 and Type **430** are left for 30th Anniv Togo-China Co-operation, issued on 1 March 2004, not yet received.

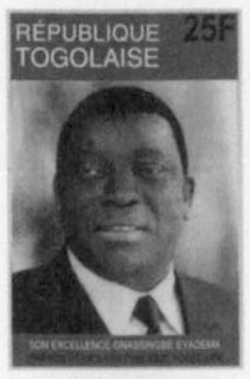

431 Gnassingbe Eyadema

2004. President Gnassingbe Eyadema

2275	**431**	25f. multicoloured	10	10
2276		50f. multicloured	10	10
2277		150f. multicoloured	25	10
2278		400f. multicoloured	95	45
2279		550f. multicoloured	1·00	45
2280		650f. multicoloured	1·10	50
2281		1000f. multicoloured	1·30	55
2282		2000f. multicoloured	1·60	70
2283		3000f. multicoloured	1·90	90

POSTAGE DUE STAMPS

1921. Postage Due stamps of Dahomy, "figure" key-type, optd **TOGO.**

D54	**M**	5c. green	45	6·75
D55	**M**	10c. red	35	6·50
D56	**M**	15c. grey	55	8·25
D57	**M**	20c. brown	2·00	9·00
D58	**M**	30c. blue	2·30	12·50
D59	**M**	50c. black	1·80	9·50
D60	**M**	60c. orange	2·50	10·50
D61	**M**	1f. violet	5·25	20·00

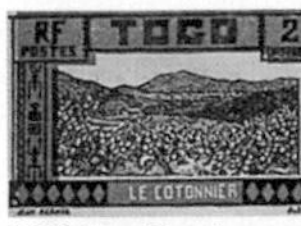

D8 Cotton Growing

1925. Centres and inscr in black.

D97	**D8**	2c. blue	10	6·75
D98	**D8**	4c. red	10	6·75
D99	**D8**	5c. greeen	35	7·00
D100	**D8**	10c. red	30	7·50
D101	**D8**	15c. yellow	55	7·50
D102	**D8**	20c. mauve	1·70	7·25
D103	**D8**	25c. grey	2·00	8·00
D104	**D8**	30c. yellow on blue	1·10	6·75
D105	**D8**	50c. brown	2·50	3·75
D106	**D8**	60c. green	1·70	7·25
D107	**D8**	1f. violet	1·70	6·50

1927. Surch.

D108	2f. on 1f. mauve and red	1·80	8·75
D109	3f. on 1f. blue and brown	2·30	13·50

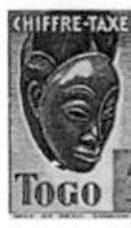

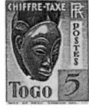

D12 Native Mask

1940

D151	**D12**	5c. black	1·40	7·75
D152	**D12**	10c. green	45	7·50
D153	**D12**	15c. red	30	7·75
D154	**D12**	20c. blue	30	7·75
D155	**D12**	30c. brown	45	7·75
D156	**D12**	50c. olive	90	11·00
D157	**D12**	60c. violet	45	7·75
D158	**D12**	1f. blue	1·50	9·00
D159	**D12**	2f. red	1·30	8·25
D160	**D12**	3f. violet	2·00	9·25

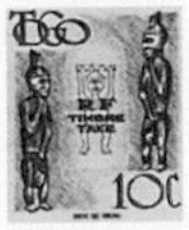

D21

1947

D185	**D21**	10c. blue	10	3·75
D186	**D21**	30c. red	10	6·00
D187	**D21**	50c. green	10	7·25
D188	**D21**	1f. brown	1·30	6·75
D189	**D21**	2f. red	1·10	5·75
D190	**D21**	3f. black	1·80	6·75
D191	**D21**	4f. blue	1·70	8·00
D192	**D21**	5f. brown	1·80	8·25
D193	**D21**	10f. orange	2·00	9·00
D194	**D21**	20f. blue	2·30	9·25

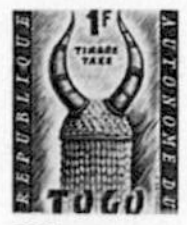

D31
Kon-komba
Helmet

1957

D214	**D31**	1f. violet	70	5·25
D215	**D31**	2f. orange	75	6·75
D216	**D31**	3f. grey	75	7·25
D217	**D31**	4f. red	65	7·25
D218	**D31**	5f. blue	65	7·25
D219	**D31**	10f. green	75·00	7·75
D220	**D31**	20f. purple	1·40	8·25

1959. As Nos. D214/20 but colours changed and inscr "REPUBLIQUE DU TOGO".

D244	1f. brown	45	1·10
D245	2f. turquoise	70	1·50
D246	3f. orange	70	5·25
D247	4f. blue	35	2·75
D248	5f. purple	35	6·50
D249	10f. violet	45	4·75
D250	20f. black	55	5·75

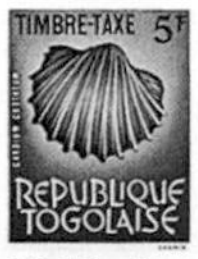

D57 "Cardium costatum"

1964. Sea Shells. Multicoloured.

D366	1f. Butterfly cone	20	20
D367	2f. Ermine marginella	20	20
D368	3f. Rat cowrie	20	20
D369	4f. Bubonian conch	30	30
D370	5f. Type D **57**	75	75
D371	10f. "Cancellaria cancellata"	1·00	1·00
D372	15f. African Neptue volute	2·00	2·00
D373	20f. "Tympanotomus radula"	2·50	2·50

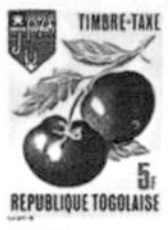

D110
Tomatoes

1969. Young Pioneers Agricultural Organization. Multicoloured.

D696	5f. Type D **110**	10	10
D697	10f. Corn on the cob	30	30
D698	19f. Red pepper	40	40
D699	20f. Peanuts	55	55

1980. As T **259**. Multicoloured.

D1454	5f. Women examining produce (vert)	10	10
D1455	10f. Market stall	10	10
D1456	25f. Poultry seller	15	10
D1457	50f. Carvings and ornaments	35	15

OFFICIAL STAMPS

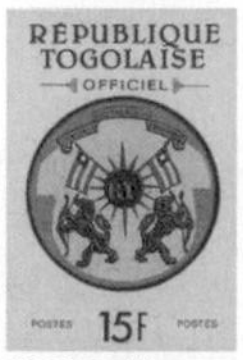

O400 Emblem

1991. Officials

O2108	**O400**	15f. multicoloured	10	10
O2109		50f. multicoloured	10	10
O2110		90f. multicoloured	15	15
O2111		100f. multicoloured	20	20
O2112		125f. multicoloured	25	25
O2113		180f. multicoloured	40	40
O2114		300f. multicoloured	80	80
O2115		500f. multicoloured	1·00	1·00

APPENDIX

The following stamps have either been issued in excess of postal needs or have not been available to the public in reasonable quantities at face value. Such stamps may later be given full listing if there is evidence of regular postal use.

All embossed on gold foil.

1989

Prince Emanuel of Liechtenstein Foundation. Air 1500f.×2.
Bicentenary of French Revolution (2nd issue). Air 1500f.
Scouts, Butterflies and Fungi. Air 1500f.

1994

Prehistoric Animals. 125f.; 180f.; 425f.; 480f.; 500f.; 1500f.
25th Anniv of Moon Landing. 600f.×3, Strip of 3; 600f.×3, Strip of 3

1995

World Cup Football Championship, France. 100f.; 150f.; 200f.; 300f.; 400f.; 500f.
Olympic Games, Atlanta. 100f.; 150f.; 200f., 300f.; 400f.; 500f. Insects. 100f.; 150f.; 200f.; 300f.; 400f.; 500f.
Fruit. 100f.; 150f.; 200f.; 300f.; 400f.; 500f.
Birds. 150f.; 200f.; 300f.; 400f.; 500f.; 1000f.
Tortoises. 150f.; 200f.; 300f.; 400f.; 500f.; 1000f.
Trains. 150f.; 200f.; 300f.; 400f.; 500f.; 1000f.
Deer. 180f.; 220f.; 325f.; 370f., Block of 4

1997

Return of Hong Kong to China. 220f.; 315f.; 325f.; 340f.; 370f.
Cats. 150f.; 200f.; 300f.; 400f.; 500f.; 1000f.
Military Uniforms. 150f.; 200f.; 300f.; 400f.; 500f.; 1000f.
Chinese New Year. Year of the Ox. 180f.×3, Strip of 3

1998

World Cup Football Championship, France. 370f.×6

1999

Birds. 100f.; 150f.; 200f.; 300f.; 400f.; 500f.
Cats. 100f.; 150f.; 200f.; 300f.; 400f.; 500f.
Ships. 100f.; 150f.; 200f.; 300f.; 400f.; 500f.
Fish. 100f.; 150f.; 200f.; 300f.; 400f.; 500f.
Fungi. 100f.; 150f.; 200f.; 300f.; 400f.; 500f.
Dogs. 100f.; 150f.; 200f.; 300f.; 400f.; 500f.
Flora. 100f.×3; 150f.×3; 200f.×2; 330f.×2; 500f.; 1000f.
Minerals. 100f.; 150f.; 200f.; 300f.; 400f.; 500f.
Butterflies. 100f.; 150f.; 200f.; 300f.; 400f.; 500f.
Cars. 100f.; 150f.; 200f.; 300f.; 400f.; 500f.

2000

Fauna. 100f.; 150f.; 200f.; 300f.; 400f.; 500f.

2001

Dogs. 100f.; 150f.; 200f.; 300f.; 400f.; 500f.
Fauna. 150f.; 200f.; 250f.; 300f.; 350f.; 400f.
Dogs and Cats. 275f.; 300f.; 325f.; 350f.; 375f.; 400f.
Birds. 200f.; 300f.; 500f.; 550f.; 600f.; 650f.

2004

Olympic Games, Athens. 150f.; 300f.; 450f.; 500f.

2006

Pope John Paul II. 550f.
Space Exploration. 150f.; 300f.; 450f.; 500f.
Birth Centenary of Senghor. 150f.; 550f.; 650f.; 1000f.; 2000f.; 3000f.; 5000f.; 10000f.

2010

Lions. 550f.×4
Predators. 550f.×4; 550f.×4
Monkeys. 550f.×4
Antilopes. 550f.×4
Elephants. 550f.×4
Hippopotami. 550f.×4
Owls. 550f.×4
Birds. 550f.×4
Raptors. 550f.×4
Birds. *Merops*. 550f.×4
Reptiles. 550f.×4
Turtles. 550f.×4
Marine Fauna. 550f.×4
Butterflies. 550f.×4
Fruit. 550f.×4
Flora. 550f.×4
Baobab Trees. 550f.×4
Pangolins. 550f.×4
Pope Benedict's Travels in Africa. 750f.×4
Birth Centenary of Jacques Cousteau. 750f.×4;
Charles Darwin. 750f.×4
Diana, Princess of Wales. 750f.×4
Death Centenary of Henry Dunant. 750f.×4
Natural Disasters, 2010. 750f.×4
75th Birth Anniv of Elvis Presley. 750f.×4
Togo's National Team The Hawks. 750f.×4
400th Anniv of discoveries of Galleleo. 750f.×4
Mahatma Ghandi. 750f.×4
George Stephenson. 750f.×4
Lech Kaczynski. 750f.×4
Marilyn Monroe. 750f.×4
Birth Bicentenary of Robert Schumann. 750f.×4
Centenary of American Scouts. 750f.×4
Expo 2010. 750f.×4
Vasily Smyslov. 750f.×4
Chinese New Year. Year of the Tiger. 750f.×4
350th Death Anniv of Diego Velasquez. 750f.×4
Centenary of First Commercial Dirigible. 750f.×4

Pt. 1

TOKELAU

Three islands situated north of Samoa. Formerly known as the Union Islands, they were administered as part of the Gilbert and Ellice Islands until transferred to New Zealand in 1925. Administered by Western Samoa (using stamps of Samoa) until they became a dependency of New Zealand in 1949. Adopted name of Tokelau in 1946.

1948. 12 pence = 1 shilling; 20 shillings = 1 pound.
1967. 100 cents or sene = 1 New Zealand dollar.

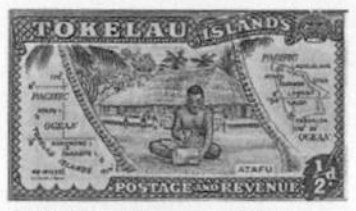

1 Atafu Village and Map

1948

1	**1**	½d. brown and purple	15	75
2	-	1d. red and green	15	50
3	-	2d. green and blue	15	50

DESIGNS: 1d. Nukunonu hut and map; 2d. Fakaofo village and map.

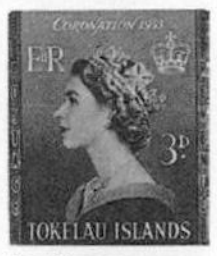

1a Queen Elizabeth II

1953. Coronation.

4	**1a**	3d. brown	1·50	1·50

1956. Surch **ONE SHILLING**.

5	**1**	1s. on ½d. brown and purple	75	1·25

1966. Arms types of New Zealand without value, surch **TOKELAU ISLANDS** and value in sterling.

6	**F6**	6d. blue	25	80
7	**F6**	8d. green	25	80
8	**F6**	2s. pink	30	80

1967. Decimal currency

(a) Nos. 1/3 surch

9	-	1c. on 1d. (No. 2)	20	1·00
10	-	2c. on 2d. (No. 3)	30	1·50
11	1	10c. on ½d. (No. 1)	70	2·00

(b) Arms types of New Zealand without value, surch **TOKELAU ISLANDS** and value in decimal currency

12	**F6**	3c. lilac	30	20
13	**F6**	5c. blue	30	20
14	**F6**	7c. green	30	20
15	**F6**	20c. pink	30	30

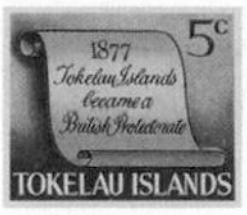

8 British Protectorate (1877)

1969. History of Tokelau Islands.

16	**8**	5c. blue, yellow and black	15	10
17	-	10c. red, yellow and black	15	10
18	-	15c. green, yellow and black	20	15
19	-	20c. brown, yellow and black	25	15

DESIGNS: 10c. Annexed to Gilbert and Ellice Islands (1916); 15c. New Zealand Administration (1925); 20c. New Zealand Territory (1948).

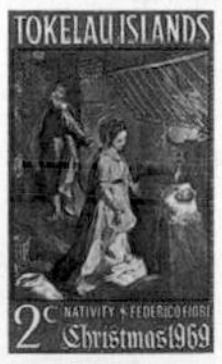

8a "The Nativity" (Federico Fiori (Barocci))

1969. Christmas.

20	**8a**	2c. multicoloured	10	15

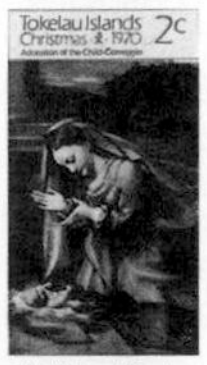

8b "The Virgin adoring the Child" (Correggio)

1970. Christmas.

21	**8b**	2c. multicoloured	10	20

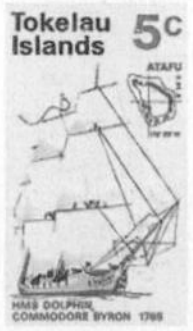

12 H.M.S. "Dolphin", 1765

1970. Discovery of Tokelau Islands. Multicoloured.

22	5c. Type **12**	65	35
23	10c. H.M.S. "Pandora", 1791	65	35
24	25c. "General Jackson" (American whaling ship), 1835 (horiz)	90	70

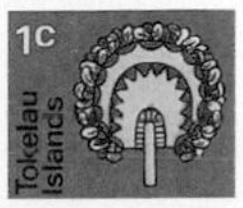

13 Fan

1971. Handicrafts. Multicoloured.

25	1c. Type **13**	15	20
26	2c. Hand-bag	20	30
27	3c. Basket	20	40
28	5c. Hand-bag	20	40
29	10c. Shopping-bag	20	45
30	15c. Hand-bag	25	1·00
31	20c. Canoe	25	1·10
32	25c. Fishing hooks	25	1·10

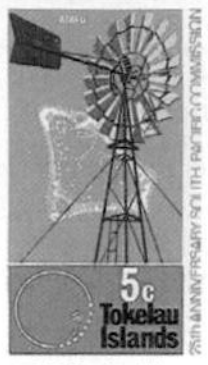

14 Windmill Pump

1972. 25th Anniv of South Pacific Commission. Multicoloured.

33	5c. Type **14**	30	60
34	10c. Community well	40	70
35	15c. Pest eradication	60	1·10
36	20c. Flags of member nations	85	1·10

On No. 35 "PACIFIC" is spelt "PACFIC".

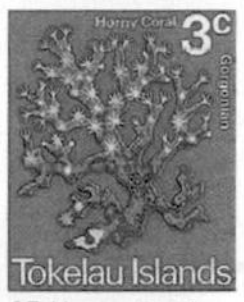

15 Horny Coral

1973. Coral. Multicoloured.

37	3c. Type **15**	50	70
38	5c. Soft coral	50	80
39	15c. Mushroom coral	75	1·00
40	25c. Staghorn coral	80	1·25

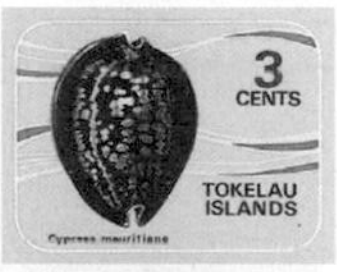

16 Hump-back Cowrie

1975. "Shells of the Coral Reef". Multicoloured.

41	3c. Type **16**	50	1·25
42	5c. Tiger cowrie	50	1·25
43	15c. Mole cowrie	65	1·50
44	25c. Eyed cowrie	70	1·75

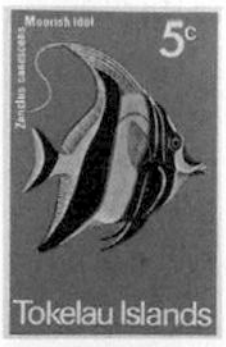

17 Moorish Idol

1975. Fish. Multicoloured.

45	5c. Type **17**	20	50
46	10c. Long-nosed butterflyfish	20	60
47	15c. Lined butterflyfish	30	80
48	25c. Lionfish ("Red-Fire Fish")	30	90

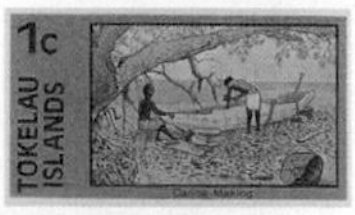

18 Canoe Building

1976. Multicoloured.

49a	1c. Type **18**	10	15
50	2c. Reef fishing	30	2·25
51a	3c. Weaving preparation	10	15
52a	5c. Uma (kitchen)	10	15
53a	9c. Carving (vert)	15	15
54a	20c. Husking coconuts (vert)	15	20
55a	50c. Wash day (vert)	20	20
56a	$1 Meal time (vert)	30	30

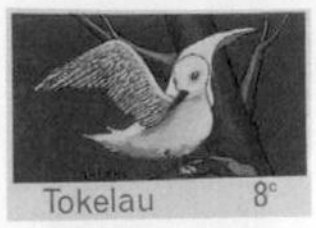

19 White Tern

1977. Birds of Tokelau. Multicoloured.

57	8c. Type **19**	30	40
58	10c. Ruddy turnstone	35	45
59	15c. White-capped noddy	45	70
60	30c. Common noddy	50	90

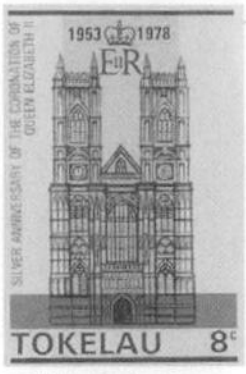

20 Westminster Abbey

1978. 25th Anniv of Coronation. Multicoloured.

61	8c. Type **20**	20	25
62	10c. King Edward's Chair	20	25
63	15c. Coronation regalia	30	40
64	30c. Queen Elizabeth II	50	65

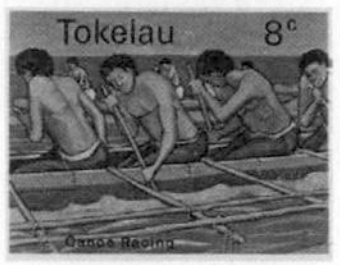

21 Canoe Race

1978. Canoe Racing.

65	**21**	8c. multicoloured	20	30
66	-	12c. multicoloured	20	35
67	-	15c. multicoloured	20	40
68	-	30c. multicoloured	30	70

DESIGNS: 12c. to 30c. Different scenes of canoe racing.

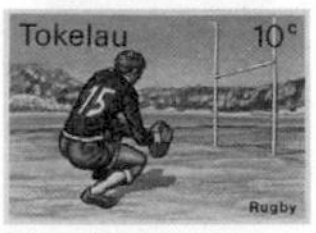

22 Rugby

1979. Local Sports. Multicoloured.

69	10c. Type **22**	20	30
70	15c. Cricket	75	60
71	20c. Rugby (different)	30	45
72	30c. Cricket (different)	75	80

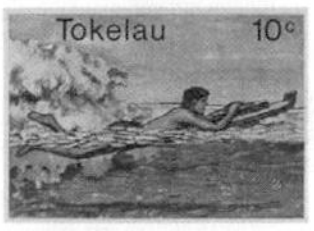

23 Surfing

1980. Water Sports. Multicoloured.

73	10c. Type **23**	10	15
74	20c. Surfing (different)	15	20
75	30c. Swimming	20	25
76	50c. Swimming (different)	25	35

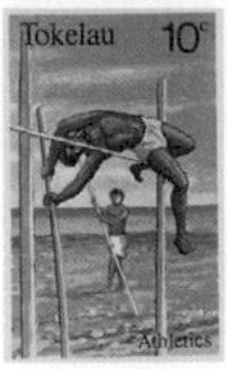

24 Pole Vaulting

1981. Sports. Multicoloured.

77	10c. Type **24**	10	10
78	20c. Volleyball	20	20
79	30c. Athletics (different)	25	30
80	50c. Volleyball (different)	30	35

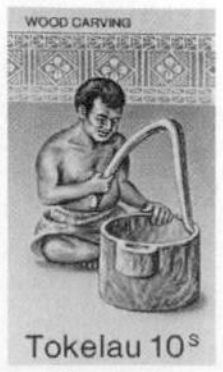

25 Wood Carving

1982. Handicrafts. Multicoloured.

81	10s. Type **25**	10	20
82	22s. Bow drilling sea shell	10	35
83	34s. Bowl finishing	15	45
84	60s. Basket weaving	25	80

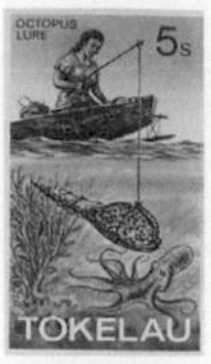

26 Octopus Lure

1982. Fishing Methods. Multicoloured.

85	5s. Type **26**	10	10
86	18s. Multiple-hook fishing	20	20
87	23s. Ruvettus fishing	25	25
88	34s. Netting flying fish	25	30
89	63s. Noose fishing	30	40
90	75s. Bonito fishing	40	45

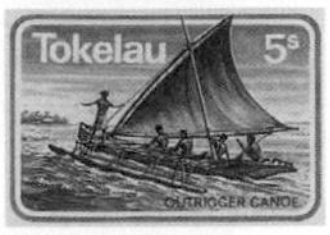

27 Outrigger Canoe

1983. Transport. Multicoloured.

91	5s. Type **27**	10	10
92	18s. Wooden whaleboat	10	15
93	23s. Aluminium whaleboat	10	20
94	34s. "Alia" (fishing catamaran)	15	25
95	63s. "Frysna" (freighter)	25	40
96	75s. Grumman MacKinnon Goose flying boat	30	50

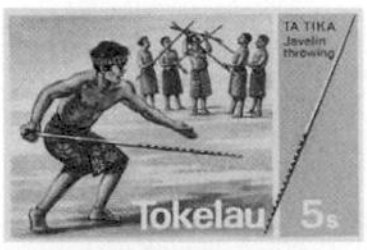

28 Javelin Throwing

1983. Traditional Pastimes. Multicoloured.

97	5s. Type **28**	10	10
98	18s. String game	10	15
99	23s. Fire making	10	20
100	34s. Shell throwing	15	25
101	63s. Hand-ball game	20	40
102	75s. Mass wrestling	25	50

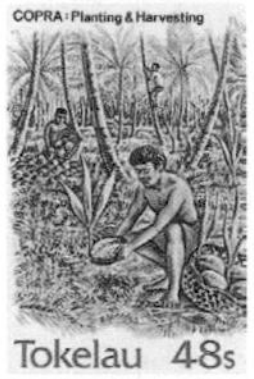

29 Planting and Harvesting

1984. Copra Industry. Multicoloured.

103	48s. Type **29**	30	40
104	48s. Husking and splitting	30	40
105	48s. Drying	30	40
106	48s. Bagging	30	40
107	48s. Shipping	30	40

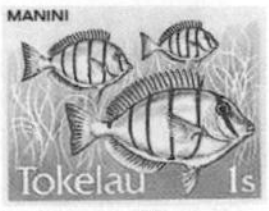

30 Convict Tang ("Manini")

1984. Fish. Multicoloured.

108	1s. Type **30**	10	10
109	2s. Flyingfish ("Hahave")	10	10
110	5s. Surge wrasse ("Uloulo")	15	10
111	9s. Unicornfish ("Ume ihu")	15	10
112	23s. Wrasse ("Lafilafi")	25	20
113	34s. Red snapper ("Fagamea")	30	25
114	50s. Yellow-finned tuna ("Kakahi")	40	40
115	75s. Oilfish ("Palu po")	55	55
116	$1 Grey shark ("Mokoha")	55	60
117	$2 Black marlin ("Hakula")	85	1·10

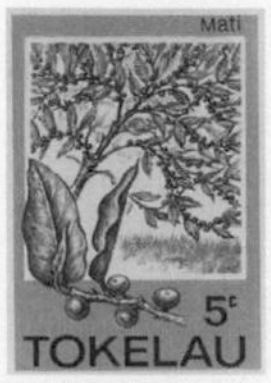

31 "Ficus tinctoria" ("Mati")

1985. Native Trees. Multicoloured.

118	5c. Type **31**	10	10
119	18c. "Morinda citrifolia" ("Nonu")	10	15
120	32c. Breadfruit tree ("Ulu")	15	25
121	48c. "Pandanus tectorius" ("Fala")	25	40
122	60c. "Cordia subcordata" ("Kanava")	30	45
123	75s. Coconut palm ("Niu")	35	55

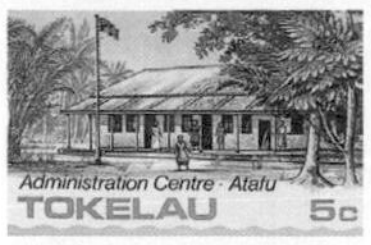

32 Administration Centre, Atafu

1985. Tokelau Architecture (1st series). Public Buildings. Multicoloured.

124	5c. Type **32**	10	10
125	18c. Administration Centre, Nukunonu	15	15
126	32c. Administration Centre, Fakaofo	15	25
127	48c. Congregational Church, Atafu	20	40
128	60c. Catholic Church, Nukunonu	25	45
129	75c. Congregational Church, Fakaofo	25	55

See also Nos. 130/5.

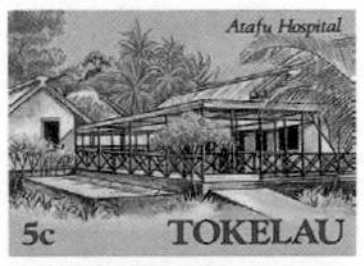

33 Atafu Hospital

1986. Tokelau Architecture (2nd series). Hospitals and Schools. Multicoloured.

130	5c. Type **33**	10	15
131	18c. St. Joseph's Hospital, Nukunonu	15	15
132	32c. Fenuafala Hospital, Fakaofo	15	30
133	48c. Matauala School, Atafu	20	45
134	60c. Matiti School, Nukunonu	25	60
135	75c. Fenuafala School, Fakaofo	25	90

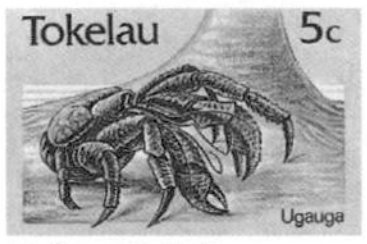

34 Coconut Crab

1986. Agricultural Livestock. Multicoloured.

136	5c. Type **34**	10	15
137	18c. Pigs	10	15
138	32c. Chickens	20	30
139	48c. Reef hawksbill turtle	25	45
140	60c. Goats	30	55
141	75c. Ducks	35	70

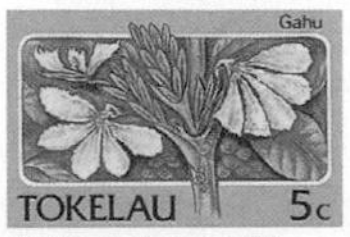

35 "Scaevola taccada" ("Gahu")

1987. Tokelau Flora. Multicoloured.

142	5c. Type **35**	35	50
143	18c. "Hernandia nymphaeifolia" ("Puka")	50	80
144	32c. "Pandanus tectorius" ("Higano")	65	1·10
145	48c. "Gardenia taitensis" (Tialetiale")	80	1·40
146	60c. "Pemphis acidula" ("Gagie")	1·00	1·75
147	75c. "Guettarda speciosa" ("Puapua")	1·10	1·90

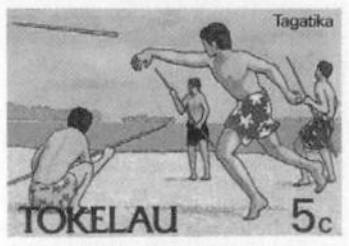

36 Javelin Throwing

1987. Tokelau Olympic Sports. Multicoloured.

148	5c. Type **36**	25	30
149	18c. Shot-putting	40	50
150	32c. Long jumping	50	90
151	48c. Hurdling	60	1·10
152	60c. Sprinting	65	1·75
153	75c. Wrestling	80	1·90

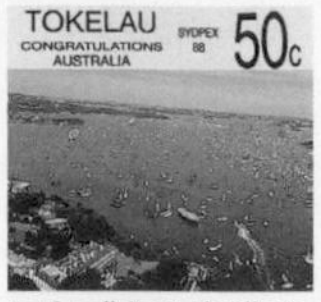

37 Small Boat Flotilla in Sydney Harbour

1988. Bicentenary of Australian Settlement and "Sydpex '88" National Stamp Exhibition, Sydney. Multicoloured.

154	50c. Type **37**	2·00	2·25
155	50c. Sailing ships and liners	2·00	2·25
156	50c. Sydney skyline and Opera House	2·00	2·25
157	50c. Sydney Harbour Bridge	2·00	2·25
158	50c. Sydney waterfront	2·00	2·25

Nos. 154/8 were printed together, se-tenant, forming a composite aerial view of the re-enactment of First Fleet's arrival.

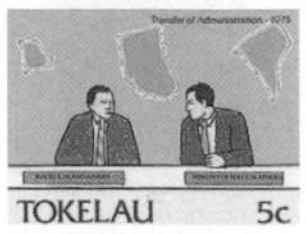

38 Island Maps and Ministerial Representatives

1988. Political Development. Multicoloured.

159	5c. Type **38** (administration transferred to N.Z. Foreign Affairs Ministry, 1975)	40	60
160	18c. General Fono (island assembly) meeting, 1977	45	55
161	32c. Arms of New Zealand (first visit by New Zealand Prime Minister, 1985)	70	80
162	48c. U.N. logo (first visit by U.N. representative, 1976)	80	1·00
163	60c. Canoe and U.N. logo (first Tokelau delegation to U.N., 1987)	1·00	1·40
164	75c. Secretary and N.Z. flag (first islander appointed as Official Secretary, 1987)	2·25	2·00

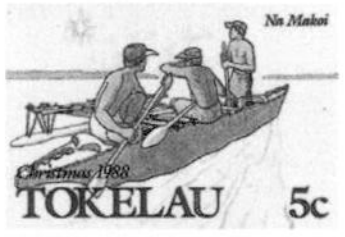

39 Three Wise Men in Canoe and Star

1988. Christmas. Designs showing Christmas in Tokelau. Multicoloured.

165	5c. Type **39**	25	35
166	20c. Tokelau Nativity	30	40
167	40c. Flight to Egypt by canoe	55	70
168	60c. Children's presents	60	1·00
169	70c. Christ Child in Tokelauan basket	70	1·10
170	$1 Christmas parade	85	1·40

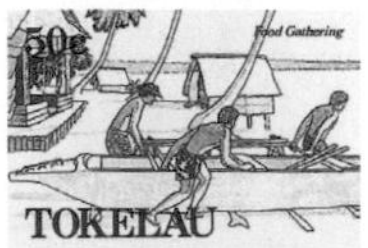

40 Launching Outrigger Canoe

1989. Food Gathering. Multicoloured.

171	50c. Type **40**	1·75	2·00
172	50c. Paddling canoe away from shore	1·75	2·00
173	50c. Fishing punt and sailing canoe	1·75	2·00
174	50c. Canoe on beach	1·75	2·00
175	50c. Loading coconuts into canoe	1·75	2·00
176	50c. Tokelauans with produce	1·75	2·00

Nos. 171/3 and 174/6 were each printed together, *se-tenant*, forming composite designs.

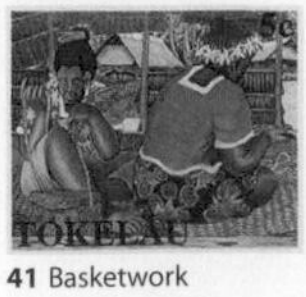

41 Basketwork

1990. Women's Handicrafts. Multicoloured.

177	5c. Type **41**	75	65

178	20c. Preparing cloth	1·25	1·10
179	40c. Tokelau fabrics	1·75	1·50
180	60c. Mat weaving	2·25	2·25
181	80c. Weaving palm fronds	3·00	3·25
182	$1 Basket making	3·25	3·50

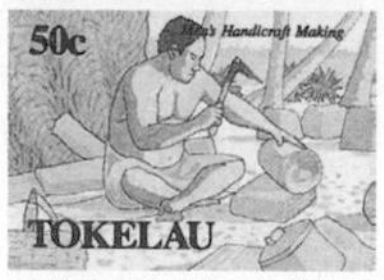

42 Man with Adze and Wood Blocks

1990. Men's Handicrafts. Multicoloured.

183	50c. Type **42**	2·00	2·25
184	50c. Making fishing boxes	2·00	2·25
185	50c. Fixing handles to fishing boxes	2·00	2·25
186	50c. Two men decorating fishing boxes	2·00	2·25
187	50c. Canoe building (two men)	2·00	2·25
188	50c. Canoe building (three men)	2·00	2·25

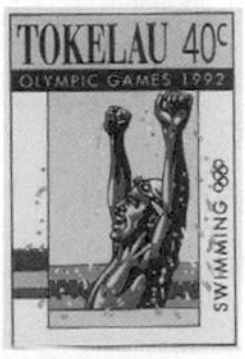

43 Swimming

1992. Olympic Games, Barcelona. Multicoloured.

189	40c. Type **43**	60	60
190	60c. Long jumping	80	90
191	$1 Volleyball	1·60	1·75
192	$1.80 Running	2·25	3·25

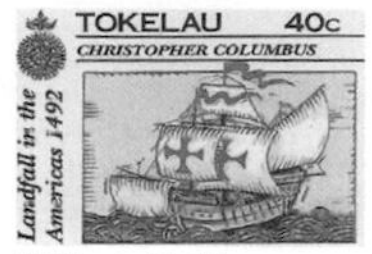

44 "Santa Maria"

1992. 500th Anniv of Discovery of America by Columbus. Multicoloured.

193	40c. Type **44**	1·00	1·00
194	60c. Christopher Columbus	1·25	1·40
195	$1.20 Fleet of Columbus	2·75	3·00
196	$1.80 Columbus landing in the New World	3·75	4·00

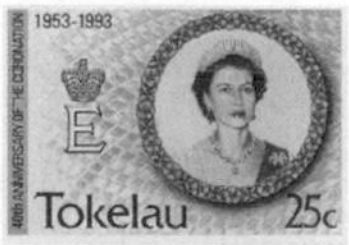

45 Queen Elizabeth II in 1953

1993. 40th Anniv of Coronation. Multicoloured.

197	25c. Type **45**	80	80
198	40c. Prince Philip	1·00	1·00
199	$1 Queen Elizabeth II in 1993	1·60	1·75
200	$2 Queen Elizabeth II and Prince Philip	2·50	3·25

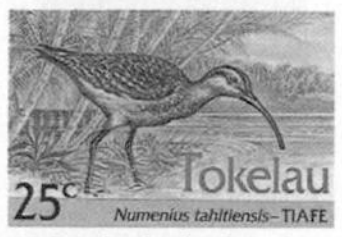

46 Bristle-thighed Curlew

1993. Birds of Tokelau. Multicoloured.

201	25c. Type **46**	75	75
202	40c. Red-tailed tropic bird	1·10	1·10
203	$1 Reef heron	1·75	1·75
204	$2 Pacific golden plover	2·50	3·25

1994. "Hong Kong '94" International Stamp Exhibition. Multicoloured.

MS205	125×100 mm. As Nos. 201/4 (sold at $5)	5·00	6·00

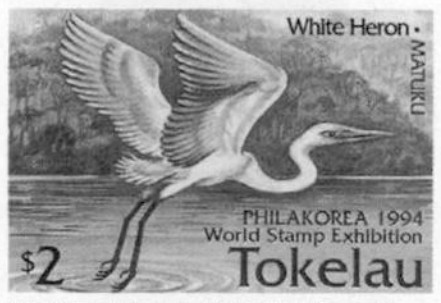

47 Great Egret ("White Heron")

1994. "Philakorea '94" International Stamp Exhibition, Seoul.

206	**47** $2 multicoloured	2·50	3·25
MS207	110×76 mm. No. 206	4·50	4·50

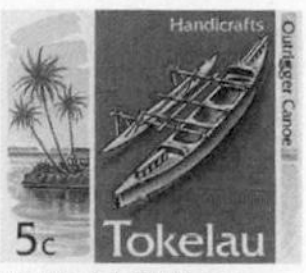

48 Model Outrigger Canoe

1994. Handicrafts. Multicoloured.

208	5c. Type **48**	10	10
209	25c. Plaited fan	20	25
210	40c. Plaited baskets	30	35
211	50c. Fishing box	35	40
212	80c. Water bottle	60	65
213	$1 Fishing hook	75	80
214	$2 Coconut gourds	1·50	1·60
215	$5 Shell necklace	3·75	4·00

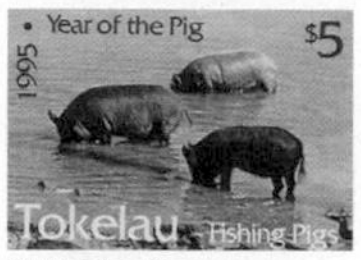

49 Fishing Pigs

1995. Chinese New Year ("Year of the Pig"). Sheet 100×75 mm.

MS218	**49** $5 multicoloured	7·00	7·50

1995. "PostX '95" National Stamp Exhibition, Auckland. No. **MS**218 optd with "PostX '95" emblem on sheet margin in red.

MS219	**49** $5 multicoloured	12·00	13·00

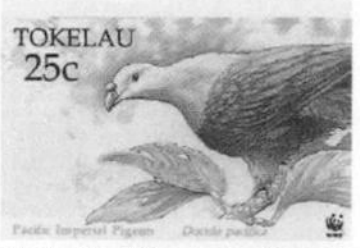

50 Pacific Pigeon on Branch

1995. Endangered Species. Pacific Pigeon. Multicoloured.

220	25c. Type **50**	60	65
221	40c. On branch (different)	85	90
222	$1 On branch with berries	1·40	1·75
223	$2 Chick in nest	2·40	3·25

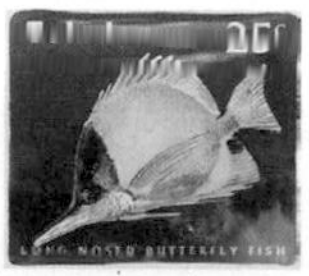

51 Long Nosed Butterflyfish

1995. Reef Fish. Multicoloured.

224	25c. Type **51**	45	55
225	40c. Emperor angelfish	70	75
226	$1 Moorish idol	1·40	1·60
227	$2 Lined butterflyfish	2·40	3·00
MS228	130×90 mm. Lionfish (39×34 mm)	2·75	4·00

1995. "Singapore '95" International Stamp Exhibition. No. **MS**218 optd with exhibition emblem on sheet margin.

MS229	**49** $5 multicoloured	5·50	7·00

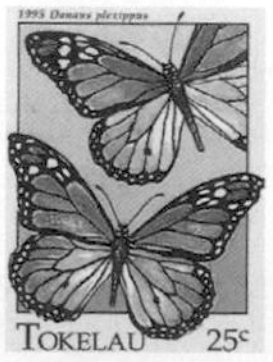

52 "Danaus plexippus"

1995. Butterflies and Moths. Multicoloured.

230	25c. Type **52**	65	65
231	40c. "Precis villida samoensis"	90	90
232	$1 "Hypolimnas bolina"	2·00	2·25
233	$2 "Euploea lewenii"	3·00	3·50

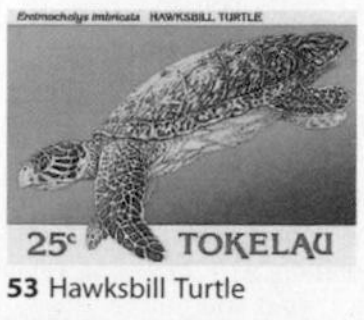

53 Hawksbill Turtle

1995. Year of the Sea Turtle. Multicoloured.

234	25c. Type **53**	65	65
235	40c. Leatherback turtle	90	90
236	$1 Green turtle	2·00	2·25
237	$2 Loggerhead turtle	3·00	3·50
MS238	130×90 mm. $3 As $2 (50×40 mm)	4·00	5·50

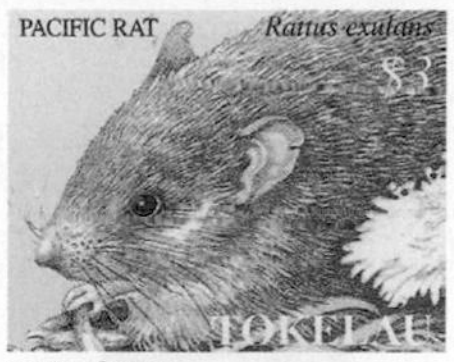

54 Pacific Rat

1996. Chinese New Year ("Year of the Rat"). Sheet 128×97 mm.

MS239	**54** $3 multicoloured	4·50	6·00

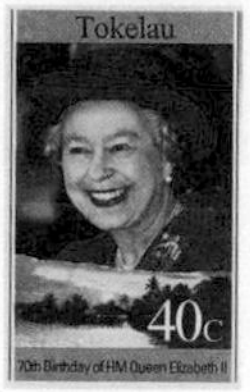

55 Queen Elizabeth II and Nukunonu

1996. 70th Birthday of Queen Elizabeth II. Each incorporating a different photograph of the Queen. Multicoloured.

240	40c. Type **55**	50	50
241	$1 Atafu at night	1·40	1·50
242	$1.25 Atafu	1·60	1·75
243	$2 Atafu village	2·00	2·50
MS244	64×66 mm. $3 Queen Elizabeth II	3·25	4·00

1996. "CHINA '96" Ninth Asian International Stamp Exhibition, Peking. No. **MS**239 optd with exhibition emblem on sheet margin in red.

MS245	128×97 mm. $3 Type **54**	4·00	5·50

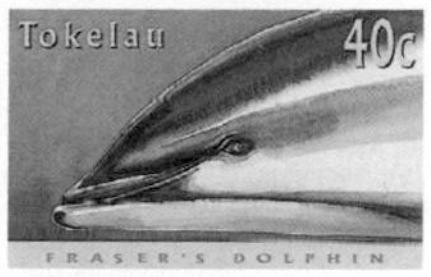

56 Fraser's Dolphin

1996. Dolphins. Multicoloured.

246	40c. Type **56**	1·00	1·00
247	$1 Common dolphin	2·50	2·50
248	$1.25 Striped dolphin	2·50	2·50
249	$2 Spotted dolphin	3·50	3·50

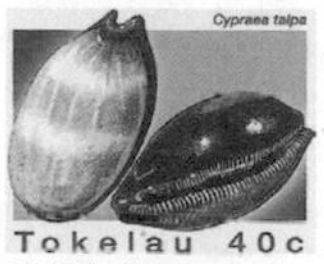

57 Mole Cowrie

1996. Sea Shells. Multicoloured.

250	40c. Type **57**	60	60
251	$1 Humpback cowrie	1·50	1·50
252	$1.25 Eyed cowrie	1·60	1·75
253	$2 Tiger cowrie	2·25	2·75
MS254	123×83 mm. $3 Humpback cowrie (different) (50×40 mm)	3·50	4·50

1996. "TAIPEI '96" Tenth Asian International Stamp Exhibition, Taiwan. No. **MS**239 optd with exhibition emblem on sheet margin.

MS255	128×97 mm. $3 Type **54**	3·25	4·00

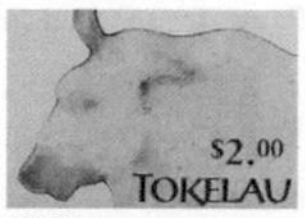

58 Ox

1997. Chinese New Year ("Year of the Ox"). Sheet 120×78 mm.

MS256	**58** $2 multicoloured	2·50	3·25

1997. "HONG KONG '97" International Stamp Exhibition. No. **MS**256 optd with **HONG KONG '97 STAMP EXHIBITION** in gold on sheet margin.

MS257	120×78 mm. **58** $2 multicoloured	3·00	3·50

1997. "Pacific '97" International Stamp Exhibition, San Francisco. No. **MS**256 optd with exhibition emblem on sheet margin.

MS258	120×78 mm. **58** $2 multicoloured	2·25	3·25

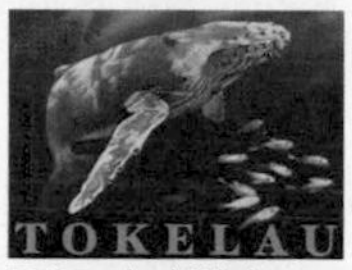

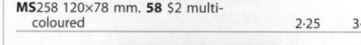

59 Humpback Whale

1997. Humpback Whales. Multicoloured.

259	40c. Type **59**	50	55
260	$1 Family of humpback whales	75	85
261	$1.25 Humpback whale feeding	1·00	1·50
262	$2 Humpback whale and calf	1·75	2·50
MS263	135×87 mm. Head of humpbacked whale	2·50	3·25

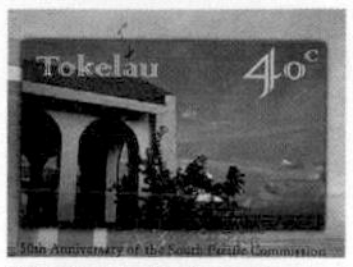

60 Church by Lagoon

1997. 50th Anniv of South Pacific Commission. Multicoloured.

264	40c. Type **60**	45	45
265	$1 Boy looking across lagoon	90	90
266	$1.25 Bungalow on small island	1·25	1·50
267	$2 Tokelau from the air	1·90	2·50

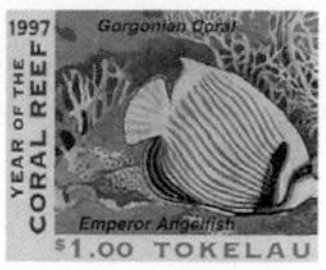

61 Gorgonian Coral and Emperor Angelfish

1997. Pacific Year of the Coral Reef. Multicoloured.

268	$1 Type **61**	1·00	1·25
269	$1 Soft coral	1·00	1·25
270	$1 Mushroom coral	1·00	1·25
271	$1 Staghorn coral	1·00	1·25
272	$1 Staghorn coral and moorish idols	1·00	1·25

Nos. 268/72 were printed together, se-tenant, with the backgrounds forming a composite design.

1997. "Aupex '97" National Stamp Exhibition, Auckland. No. **MS**263 optd **AUPEX '97, 13–16 NOVEMBER NZ NATIONAL STAMP EXHIBITION** on sheet margin in black.

MS273	135×87 mm. $3 Head of humpback whale	2·75	3·50

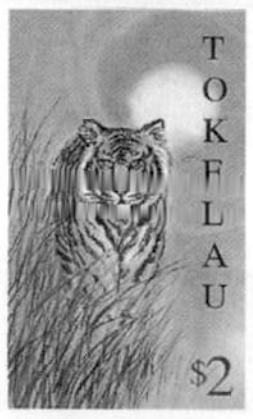

62 Tiger

1998. Chinese New Year ("Year of the Tiger"). Sheet 130×95 mm.

MS274	**62** $2 multicoloured	1·75	2·50

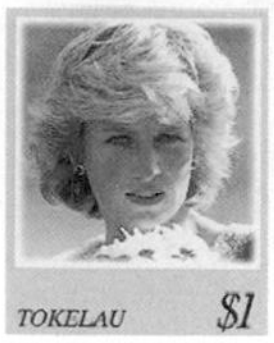

62a Carrying Yellow Bouquet

1998. Diana, Princess of Wales Commemoration. Multicoloured.

275	**62a** $1 Carrying yellow bouquet	1·00	1·25
MS276	145×70 mm. $1 Wearing red polka-dot dress; $1 Wearing matching pink hat and jacket; $1 No. 275; $1 In pink and yellow jacket with flowers (sold at $4+50c. charity premium)	2·50	4·00

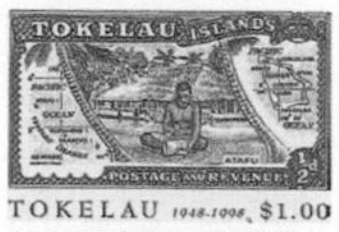

63 1948 ½d. Atafu Village Stamp

1998. 50th Anniv of Tokelau Postage Stamps. Sheet 105×80 mm, containing T **63** and similar horiz desings. Multicoloured.

MS277	$1 Type **63**; $1 1948 1d. Nukunono hut stamp; $1 1948 2d. Fakaofo village stamp	3·75	4·50

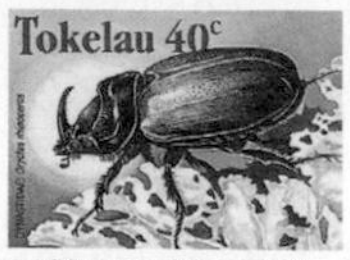

64 "Oryctes rhinoceros"

1998. Beetles. Multicoloured.

278	40c. Type **64**	85	85
279	$1 "Tribolium castaneum"	1·60	1·60
280	$1.25 "Coccinella repanda"	1·75	1·75
281	$2 "Amarygmus hydrophiloides"	2·75	3·25
MS282	125×86 mm. $3 Coccinella repanda (different)	2·50	3·25

65 "Ipomoea pes-caprae"

1998. Tropical Flowers. Multicoloured.

283	40c. Type **65**	40	50
284	$1 "Ipomoea littoralis"	85	95
285	$1.25 "Scaevola taccada"	1·00	1·40
286	$2 "Thespesia populnea"	1·60	2·25

66 Rabbit

1999. Chinese New Year ("Year of the Rabbit"). Sheet 105×70 mm.

MS287	**66** $3 multicoloured	2·25	3·00

67 H.M.S. *Pandora* (frigate)

1999. "Australia '99" International Stamp Exhibition, Melbourne. Sheet 119×80 mm.

MS288	**67** $3 multicoloured	2·75	3·25

1999. "iBRA '99" International Stamp Exhibition, Nuremberg. No. **MS**287 optd with the iBRA logo on the sheet margin.

MS289	105×70 mm. **66** $3 multicoloured	3·50	4·25

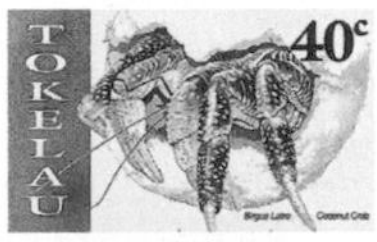

68 Coconut Crab

1999. Pacific Crabs. Multicoloured.

290	40c. Type **68**	40	40
291	$1 Ghost crab	85	95
292	$1.25 Land hermit crab	1·00	1·40
293	$2 Purple hermit crab	1·60	2·25
MS294	127×89 mm. $3 Ghost crab (different)	4·00	4·75

69 Lift-off

1999. 30th Anniv of First Manned Landing on Moon. Multicoloured.

295	25c. Type **69**	40	40
296	50c. Rocket stage separation	60	60
297	75c. Aldrin deploying experiment	70	70
298	$1 Planting the flag	85	85
299	$1.25 Separation of command module	1·00	1·25
300	$2 Recovery of astronauts	1·50	2·00
MS301	90×65 mm. $3 Lunar module, Earth and Jupiter	3·00	3·50

70 Black-naped Tern Chick and Egg

1999. Black-naped Tern. Multicoloured.

302	40c. Type **70**	45	45
303	$1 Black-naped tern perched on pebbles	90	90
304	$1.25 Two black-naped terns	1·10	1·10
305	$2 Two black-naped terns in flight	1·75	2·00

71 Dragon

2000. Chinese New Year ("Year of the Dragon"). Sheet 105×70 mm.

MS306	**71** $3 multicoloured	2·25	3·00

2000. "Bangkok 2000" World Youth Stamp Exhibition. No. **MS**306 optd on the margin with **WORLD YOUTH STAMP EXHIBITION BANGKOK 2000** in English and Thai.

MS307	105×70 mm. $3 Type **71**	2·25	3·00

72 Nukunonu

2000. "The Stamp Show 2000" International Stamp Exhibition, London. Sheet 105×85 mm.

MS308	**72** $6 multicoloured	3·75	5·00

2000. "EXPO 2000" World Stamp Exhibition, Anaheim, U.S.A. No. **MS**301 optd **WORLD STAMP EXPO 2000 7–16 JULY ANAHEIM – U.S.A.** on sheet margin.

MS309	90×65 mm. $3 Lunar module, Earth and Jupiter	2·75	3·50

73 Queen Elizabeth the Queen Mother

2000. Queen Elizabeth the Queen Mother's 100th Birthday. Multicoloured.

310	40c. Type **73**	55	35
311	$1.20 Queen Mother waving	1·00	1·00
312	$1.80 Wearing diamond ear-rings and pearl necklace	1·60	1·75
313	$3 Wearing blue hat and tartan scarf	2·25	2·75

74 *Gehyra oceanica*

2001. Lizards. Multicoloured.

314	40c. Type **74**	80	60
315	$1 *Lepidodactylus lugubris*	1·60	1·40
316	$1.25 *Gehyra mutilata*	1·75	1·75
317	$2 *Emoia cyanura*	2·75	2·75

75 Snake

2001. Chinese New Year ("Year of the Snake"). Sheet 105×73 mm.

MS318	**75** $3 multicoloured	3·50	4·00

2001. "Hong Kong 2001" Stamp Exhibition. No. **MS**318 optd **HONG KONG 2001** in English and Chinese on the sheet margin.

MS319	105×73 mm. $3 Type **75**	3·50	4·00

76 Yellow and Orange Seahorses

2001. Seahorses. Multicoloured.

320	40c. Type **76**	40	40
321	$1 Baby seahorses	70	80
322	$1.25 Pink seahorse	90	1·10
323	$2 Yellow seahorse	1·40	2·00
MS324	104×73 mm. $3 No. 320	2·25	3·00

77 Atafu Island

2001. Island Views. Multicoloured.

325	40c. Type **77**	70	60
326	$1 Fakaofo	1·25	1·25
327	$2 Sunrise over Nukunonu village	1·90	2·00
328	$2.50 Nukunonu beach	2·00	2·25

78 Princess Elizabeth and Lieutenant Philip Mountbatten, 1947

2002. Golden Jubilee.

329	**78**	40c. brown, red and gold	65	60
330	-	$1 multicoloured	1·10	1·10
331	-	$1.25 black, red and gold	1·40	1·50
332	-	$2 multicoloured	1·90	2·00
MS333		162×95 mm. Nos. 329/2 and $3 multicoloured	7·00	7·00

DESIGNS—HORIZ: $1 Queen Elizabeth in mauve hat; $1.25, Princess Elizabeth holding Prince Charles, 1948; $2 Queen Elizabeth in Poland, 1996. VERT:—(38×51 mm): $3 Queen Elizabeth after Annigoni.

79 Horse

2002. Chinese New Year ("Year of the Horse"). Sheet 105×70 mm.

MS334	**79** $4 multicoloured	4·00	5·00

2002. "Stampex 2002" Stamp Exhibition, Hong Kong. No. **MS**334 optd **STAMPEX 2002 HONG KONG 22–24 FEBRUARY 2002** in gold on the sheet margin.

MS335	105×70 mm. $4 Type **79**	4·00	5·00

80 Pelagic Thresher Sharks

2002. Endangered Species. Pelagic Thresher Shark.

336	**80**	40c. multicoloured	50	40
337	-	$1 multicoloured	90	90
338	-	$2 multicoloured	1·75	2·00
339	-	$2.50 multicoloured	1·90	2·50

DESIGNS: $1 to $2.50, Show sharks.

2002. Queen Elizabeth the Queen Mother Commemoration. As T **215** of St. Helena.

340	40c. black, gold and purple	50	40
341	$2 multicoloured	2·00	2·25
MS342	145×70 mm. $2.50 black and gold; $4 multicoloured	7·00	9·00

DESIGNS: 40c. Queen Elizabeth wearing wide-brimmed hat; $2 Queen Mother wearing mauve hat and coat; $2.50, Wearing feathered hat and pearls; $4 Queen Mother smiling. Designs in No. **MS**342 omit the "1900–2002" inscription and the coloured frame.

81 H.M.N.Z.S. *Kaniere* (frigate), 1958–59

2002. Royal New Zealand Navy Ships which have visited Tokelau. Multicoloured.

343	40c. Type **81**	1·00	80
344	$1 H.M.N.Z.S. *Endeavour* (supply ship), 1990	1·75	1·75
345	$2 H.M.N.Z.S. *Wellington* (frigate), 1987, 1988, 1990	3·25	3·50
346	$2.50 H.M.N.Z.S. *Monowai* (survey ship), 1979, 1985, 1994	4·00	4·25

82 Ram

2003. Chinese New Year ("Year of the Sheep"). Sheet 105×70 mm.

MS347	**82** $4 multicoloured	4·25	4·75

2003. 50th Anniv of Coronation. As T **219** of St. Helena. Multicoloured.

348	$2.50 Queen Elizabeth II with her Maids of Honour	3·00	3·25
349	$4 Queen and Duke of Edinburgh	4·00	4·75
MS350	95×115 mm. $2.50, As No. 348; $4 As No. 349	6·50	8·00

83 Prince William at Polo Match and at Sighthill Community Education Centre, 2001

2003. 21st Birthday of Prince William of Wales. Multicoloured.

351	$1.50 Type **83**	2·25	2·50
352	$3 At Tidworth Polo Club, 2002 and at Highgrove, 2000	3·25	3·50

2003. "Bangkok 2003" World Philatelic Exhibition. **MS**347 optd **BANGKOK 2003** in English and Thai in gold on the sheet margin.

MS353	105×70 mm. $4 Type **82**	3·25	4·00

84 Shoreline with Palm Trees

2003. "Welpex 2003" National Stamp Exhibition, Wellington, New Zealand. Sheet 119×80 mm.

MS354	**84** $4 multicoloured	3·75	4·50

85 Chinese Character and Monkeys

2004. Chinese New Year ("Year of the Monkey"). Sheet 105×71 mm.

MS355	**85** $4 red, black and gold	3·00	3·50

2004. Hong Kong Stamp Exhibition. No. **MS**355 optd **2004 Hong Kong Stamp Expo** in gold on the sheet margin.

MS356	**85** $4 red, black and gold	3·00	3·50

86 Dawn at Atafu

2004. Scenes. Multicoloured.

357	40c. Type **86**	1·00	80
358	$1 Fishermen returning to Nukunonu	1·75	1·75
359	$2 Early evening at Fakaofo	3·00	3·50
360	$2.50 Beach scene, Atafu	3·75	4·00

2004. Commemoration of Visit by Prime Minister of New Zealand. No. **MS**354 optd **NEW ZEALAND PRIME MINISTER'S VISIT AUGUST 2004** in silver with additional rectangular opt on sheet margin.

MS361	**84** $4 multicoloured	4·75	6·00

88 Lesser Frigate Bird

2004. Lesser Frigate Bird. Multicoloured.

362	40c. Type **88**	1·00	80
363	$1 Birds in flight	1·75	1·75
364	$2 Two birds in nest	3·25	3·50
365	$2.50 Juvenile bird	4·00	4·25

89 Rooster

2005. Chinese New Year ("Year of the Rooster"). Sheet 115×75 mm.

MS366	**89** $4 red, black and gold	7·00	7·50

2005. Pacific Explorer World Stamp Exhibition. No. **MS**366 optd with Pacific Explorer logo in gold on the margin.

MS367	**89** $4 vermilion, black and gold	6·00	7·00

2005. Pope John Paul II Commemoration. As T **231** of St Helena.

368	$1 multicoloured	2·00	2·00

90 HMNZS *Te Kaha* and Launch

2005. HMNZS Te Kaha (frigate). Multicoloured.

369	40c. Type **90**	1·25	1·00
370	$1 HMNZS *Te Kaha* offshore	2·00	1·75
371	$2 HMNZS *Te Kaha* at sunset	3·50	3·50
372	$2.50 Close up of HMNZS *Te Kaha*	4·25	4·50

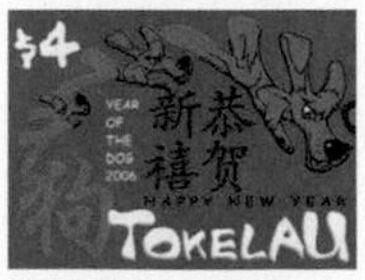

91 Leaping Dogs and Chinese Characters

2006. Chinese New Year ("Year of the Dog"). Sheet 115×75 mm.

MS373	**91** $4 vermilion, black and gold	6·00	7·00

92 Queen Elizabeth II

2006. 80th Birthday of Queen Elizabeth II. Multicoloured.

374	40c. Type **92**	1·00	85
375	$1 On wedding day	1·75	1·50
376	$2 Wearing tiara	3·25	3·25
377	$2.50 In close-up, wearing hat	3·50	3·75
MS378	144×75 mm. $2 As No. 375; $2.50 As No. 376	7·50	7·50

2006. Washington 2006 International Stamp Exhibition. Sheet 144×85 mm containing Nos. 325/8.

MS379	144×85 mm. 40c. Type **77**; $1 Fakaofo; $2 Sunrise over Nukunonu Village; $2.50 Nukunonu beach	10·00	12·00

2006. Kiwipex National Stamp Exhibition, Christchurch, New Zealand. No. **MS**378 optd **National Stamp Exhibition, Christchurch, New Zealand** in blue foil on the margin.

MS380	144×75 mm. $2 As No. 375 (optd **KIWIPEX**); $2.50 As No. 376 (optd **2006**)	6·00	7·00

93 Fishing Pig

2007. Chinese New Year ('Year of the Pig'). Sheet 105×70 mm.

MS381	**93** $4 multicoloured	6·00	7·00

94 Pacific Golden Plover

2007. Endangered Species. Pacific Golden Plover (*Pluvialis fulva*). Multicoloured.

382	40c. Type **94**	1·25	1·25
383	$1 Head of plover in breeding plumage	2·25	2·25
384	$2 On ground with wing outstretched (winter plumage)	4·00	4·00
385	$2.50 Pair in winter plumage	4·50	4·50

95 Bicolour Angelfish (*Centropyge bicolor*)

2007. Marine Life. Multicoloured.

386	10c. Type **95**	55	55
387	20c. Staghorn coral (*Acropora robusta*)	75	75
388	40c. Black-tipped reef shark (*Carcharhinus melanopterus*)	1·10	1·10
389	50c. Seastar (*Linckia multiflora*)	1·25	1·25
390	$1 Porcupine fish (*Diodon hystrix*)	1·75	1·75
391	$1.50 Thorny seahorse (*Hippocampus histrix*)	2·25	2·25
392	$2 Spotted eagle ray (*Aetobatis narinari*)	2·75	2·75
393	$2.50 Small giant clam (*Tridacna maxima*)	3·00	3·00
394	$5 Green turtle (*Chelonia mydas*)	5·50	5·50
395	$10 Slate pencil urchin (*Heterocentrotus mammillatus*)	11·00	11·00

96 Rat

2008. Chinese New Year ('Year of the Rat'). Sheet 105×70 mm.

MS396	**96** $4 multicoloured	6·00	7·00

97 Sir Edmund Hillary

2008. Sir Edmund Hillary Commemoration. Multicoloured.

397	50c. Type **97**	90	90
398	$1 Hillary on Mt. Everest (wearing checked shirt)	1·50	1·50
399	$2 Hillary on Mt. Everest (wearing jacket)	2·50	2·50
400	$2.50 As older man	2·75	2·75
MS401	110×68 mm. $5 Hillary and Tenzing Norgay on summit of Mt. Everest (horiz)	5·50	6·00

98 Houses on Seashore

2008. Scenes of Tokelau. Multicoloured.

402	50c. Type **98**	1·50	1·25
403	$1 Small boats off beach with palm trees	2·25	2·00
404	$2 Causeway lined with palm trees	3·75	3·75
405	$2.50 Houses at seashore	4·00	4·25
MS406	130×85 mm. $5 Landscape of tropical forest, beach and rocky islets	5·50	6·00

No. **MS**406 also commemorates Tarapex 2008 National Stamp Exhibition, New Plymouth, New Zealand.

99 Ox

2009. Chinese New Year. Year of the Ox. Sheet 106x70 mm

MS407	**99** $4 multicoloured	7·50	7·50

100 Chile 1875 One Peso Coin

2009. Coins of the Pacific. Multicoloured.

408	50c. Type **100**	1·00	1·00
409	$1 Great Britain 1911 one sovereign	1·75	1·75
410	$2 New Zealand 1950 half crown	3·25	3·25
411	$2.50 1997 Tokelau ten dollar	3·75	3·75
MS412	140×86 mm. Nos. 408/11	9·50	10·00

101 Tiger

2010. Chinese New Year. Year of the Tiger. Sheet 105x70 mm

MS413	**101** $4 multicoloured	11·50	11·50

2010. London 2010 International Stamp Exhibition. No. **MS**412 inscr 'London 2010 Stamp Exhibition' in gold on lower left sheet margin

MS414	140×86 mm. Nos. 408/11	8·75	8·75

102 Tokelauan Bible and Atafu Church

2010. Tokelauan Bible Translation. Multicoloured.

415	50c. Type **102**	1·00	1·00
416	$1 Tokelauan Bible and Fakaofo Church	2·00	2·00
417	$2 Tokelauan Bible and Nukunonu Church	3·00	3·00
418	$2.50 Tokelauan Bibles	3·50	3·50

103 Rabbits feeding on Carrots

2011. Chinese New Year. Year of the Rabbit. Sheet 105×71 mm

MS419	**103** $5 multicoloured	8·25	8·25

104 Yellow-bellied Sea Snake

2011. Endangered Species. Yellow-bellied Sea Snake (*Pelamis platura*). Multicoloured.

420	50c. Type **104**	1·00	1·00
421	$1 Sea snake on sandy beach	2·00	2·00
422	$2 Sea snake in sea	3·00	3·00
423	$2.50 Three sea snakes in sea	3·50	3·50

105 Prince William and Miss Catherine Middleton

2011. Royal Wedding. Sheet 118×90 mm.

MS424	**105** $6 multicoloured	10·00	10·00

106 Christmas Tree

2011. Christmas. Multicoloured.

425	40c. Type **106**	80	80
426	45c. Tree bauble	90	90
427	$1.40 Stocking	2·40	2·40
428	$2 Angel tree decoration	3·00	3·00

107 Gathering Coconuts

2012. Scenic. Multicoloured.

429	10c. Type **107**	20	20
430	20c. Atoll with palm trees and sandy beach	40	40
431	25c. Small offshore atoll with palm trees and hut	50	50
432	40c. Divers in lagoon	80	80
433	45c. Sailing canoe off coast	90	90
434	50c. Beached canoes and church	1·00	1·00
435	$1 Sandy beach backed by palm trees	2·00	2·00
436	$1.40 Angler and offshore atoll	2·40	2·40
437	$2 Palm forest and sandy beach	3·00	3·00

108 Queen Elizabeth II in Wellington, New Zealand, 1963

2012. Diamond Jubilee. Multicoloured.

438	$2 Type **108**	3·00	3·00
439	$3 Official New Zealand Portrait of Queen Elizabeth II, 2012	4·00	4·00
MS440	110×60 mm. Nos. 438/9	7·00	7·00

109 Yellowfin Tuna

2012. Fish of Tokelau. Multicoloured.

441	40c. Type **109**	80	80
442	45c. Ruby Snapper	90	90
443	$1.40 Wahoo	2·40	2·40
444	$2 Common Dolphinfish	3·00	3·00
MS445	110×90 mm. Nos. 441/4	7·00	7·00

110 Santa's Sleigh over Atafu

2012. Christmas. Multicoloured.

446	45c. Type **110**	90	90
447	$2 Reindeer flying over Nukunonu	3·00	3·00
448	$3 Reindeer flying over Fakaofo	4·00	4·00
MS449	105×62 mm. Nos. 446/8	7·50	7·50

111 Queen Elizabeth II and Duke of Edinburgh waving from Buckingham Palace Balcony after Coronation, 2 June 1953

2013. 60th Anniv of the Coronation. Multicoloured.

450	$2 Type **111**	3·00	3·00
451	$3 Coronation portrait of Royal family in Throne Room of Buckingham Palace, 1953	4·00	4·00
MS452	110×60 mm. Nos. 450/1	6·50	6·50

112 Blue Moon Butterfly (*Hypolimnas bolina pallescens*) (female)

2013. Tokelau Butterflies. Multicoloured.

453	45c. Type **112**	90	90
454	$1 Blue Moon Butterfly (*Hypolimnas bolina pallescens*) (male)	2·00	2·00
455	$1.40 Common Crow (*Euploea lewinii bourkei*)	2·40	2·40
456	$3 Meadow Argus (*Junonia villida*)	4·00	4·00
MS457	100×85 mm. Nos. 453/6	8·50	8·50

113 Mary and Joseph on Road to Bethlehem

2013. Christmas. Multicoloured.

458	45c. Type **113**	90	90
459	$1.40 Nativity	2·40	2·40
460	$2 Shepherds	3·00	3·00
461	$3 Wise men	4·00	4·00
MS462	135×63 mm. Nos. 458/61	9·00	9·00

Pt. 20

TOLIMA

One of the states of the Granadine Confederation. A department of Colombia from 1886, now uses Colombian stamps.

100 centavos = 1 peso.

1

1870. On white or coloured paper. Imperf.

6	1	5c. black	85·00	37·00
13	1	10c. black	85·00	37·00

2

3

1871. Various frames. Imperf.

14	2	5c. brown	2·75	2·75
15	3	10c. blue	8·25	8·00
16	3	50c. green	11·00	10·50
17	3	1p. red	17·00	16·00

6

7

8

9

1879. Imperf.

18a	6	5c. brown	55	55
19	7	10c. blue	65	65
20a	8	50c. green	65	65
21a	9	1p. red	2·20	2·10

10

1883. Imperf.

22	6	5c. orange	55	55
23	7	10c. red	1·20	1·20
24	10	20c. violet	2·00	1·90

11

1884. Imperf.

25	11	1c. grey	20	20
26	11	2c. red	20	20
27	11	2½c. orange	20	20
28	11	5c. brown	20	20
29a	11	10c. blue	35	30
30	11	20c. yellow	45	45
31	11	25c. black	45	45
32	11	50c. green	45	45
33	11	1p. red	55	55
34	11	2p. violet	75	75
35	11	5p. orange	55	55
36	11	10p. red	1·50	1·50

12

1886. Condor's wings touch Arms. Perf.

37	12	5c. brown	1·80	1·70
38	12	10c. blue	5·00	4·75
39	12	50c. green	4·00	3·75
40	12	1p. red	4·00	3·75

16

1886. Condor's wings do not touch Arms. Perf or imperf.

45	16	1c. grey	8·25	8·00
46	16	2c. red	8·75	8·50
47	16	2½c. pink	24·00	23·00
48	16	5c. brown	11·00	10·50
49	16	10c. blue	11·00	10·50
50	16	20c. yellow	8·75	8·50
51	16	25c. black	8·25	8·00
52	16	50c. green	5·00	4·75
53	16	1p. red	6·50	6·50
54	16	2p. violet	10·00	9·50
55	16	5p. orange	17·00	16·00
56	16	10p. red	10·00	9·50

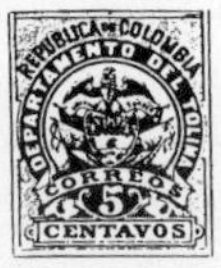

20

1888. Perf.

65	20	50c. blue	1·10	1·10
67	20	1c. blue on red	35	30
68	20	2c. green on green	35	30
69	20	5c. red	20	20
70	20	10c. green	65	65
71	20	20c. blue on yellow	35	30
72	20	1p. brown	2·75	2·75

21

1903. Imperf or perf.

85	21	4c. black on green	35	30
78	21	10c. green	20	20
87	21	20c. orange	65	65
88	21	50c. black on red	35	30
81	21	1p. brown	20	20
82	21	2p. grey	35	30
91	21	5p. red	20	20
92	21	10p. black on blue	35	30
92a	21	10p. black on green	35	30

Pt. 1

TONGA

(Or Friendly Is.). A group of islands in the S. Pacific Ocean. An independent Polynesian kingdom formerly under British protection. Tonga became a member of the Commonwealth in June 1970.

1886. 12 pence = 1 shilling; 20 shillings = 1 pound.
1967. 100 seniti = 1 pa'anga.

1 King George I

1886

1b	1	1d. red	10·00	3·25
2b	1	2d. violet	45·00	2·75
3ab	1	6d. blue	35·00	2·25
9	1	6d. orange	16·00	35·00
4ba	1	1s. green	55·00	3·25

(Or Friendly Is.). A group of islands in the S. Pacific Ocean. An independent Polynesian kingdom formerly under British protection, Tonga became a member of the Commonwealth in June 1970.

1891. Surch with value in words.

5	4d. on 1d. red	3·00	13·00
6	8d. on 2d. violet	45·00	£100

1891. Optd with stars in upper right and lower left corners.

7	1d. red	50·00	70·00
8	2d. violet	80·00	38·00

5 Arms of Tonga

6 King George I

1892

10a	5	1d. red	16·00	32·00
11	6	2d. olive	38·00	16·00
12	5	4d. brown	50·00	75·00
13	6	8d. mauve	65·00	£170
14	6	1s. brown	85·00	£130

1893. Surch in figures.

15	5	½d. on 1d. blue	23·00	27·00
16	6	2½d. on 2d. green	25·00	12·00
18	6	7½d. on 6d. red	30·00	80·00

1893. Surch **FIVE PENCE**.

17	5	5d. on 4d. orange	4·25	7·50

1894. Surch vert **SURCHARGE.** and value in words.

21		½d. on 4d. brown	2·00	7·00
22	6	½d. on 1s. brown	2·50	11·00
25	6	1d. on 2d. blue	50·00	38·00

1894. Surch vert **SURCHARGE.** and value in figures.

26b	6	1½d. on 2d. blue	50·00	50·00
27	6	2½d. on 2d. blue	40·00	50·00
23		2½d. on 8d. mauve	12·00	8·00
24b	1	2½d. on 1s. green	15·00	48·00
28b	6	7½d. on 2d. blue	65·00	50·00

13 King George II

1895. Surch **SURCHARGE** and new value.

29	13	½d. on 2½d. red	50·00	32·00
30	13	1d. on 2½d. red	£100	50·00
31	13	7½d. on 2½d. red	60·00	75·00

1895

32	1d. green	30·00	29·00
33	2½d. red	29·00	9·00
34b	5d. blue	23·00	60·00
35	7½d. yellow	42·00	50·00

1896. Nos. 26a and 28a surch with typewritten **Half-Penny**- and Tongan inscription.

36Aa	6	½d. on 1½d. on 2d. blue	£425	£425
37A	6	½d. on 7½d. on 2d. blue	85·00	£120

15 Arms

16 Ovava Tree, Kana-Kubolu

21 View of Haapai

1897

38a	15	½d. blue	70	3·00
55	15	½d. green	1·00	1·25
39	16	1d. black and red	80	80
40a	-	2d. sepia and bistre	20·00	3·50
43	-	2½d. black and blue	11·00	1·40
78	-	3d. black and green	65	6·00
45	-	4d. green and purple	4·50	4·00
46	-	5d. black and orange	32·00	12·00
79	-	6d. red	3·50	2·50
48	-	7½d. black and green	20·00	21·00
49	-	10d. black and lake	48·00	45·00
50	-	1s. black and brown	14·00	10·00
51a	21	2s. black and blue	32·00	32·00
81	-	2s.6d. purple	38·00	40·00
82	-	5s. black and red	16·00	60·00

DESIGNS—VERT (as Type **26**): 2, 2½, 5, 7½, 10d., 1s. King George II. (As Type **16**): 6d. Coral. (As Type **21**): 2s.6d. Red shining parrot. HORIZ (as Type **16**): 3d. Prehistoric trilith at Haamonga; 4d. Breadfruit. (As Type **21**): 5s. Vavau Harbour.

1899. Royal Wedding. Optd **T - L 1 June, 1899.**

54	16	1d. black and red	40·00	65·00

26 Queen Salote

1920

56	26	1½d. black	50	3·00
57	26	2d. purple and violet	15·00	13·00
76	26	2d. black and purple	7·00	2·75
58	26	2½d. black and blue	9·00	45·00
59	26	2½d. blue	8·00	1·00
60	26	5d. black and orange	3·25	7·00
61	26	7½d. black and green	1·75	1·75
62	26	10d. black and lake	2·50	4·75
63	26	1s. black and brown	1·25	2·50

1923. Nos. 46 and 48/82 surch **TWO PENCE PENI-E-UA.**

64	2d. on 5d. black and orange	1·00	85
65	2d. on 7½d. black and green	32·00	42·00
66	2d. on 10d. black and lake	22·00	65·00
67	2d. on 1s. black and brown	75·00	22·00
68a	2d. on 2s. black and blue	12·00	11·00
69	2d. on 2s.6d. purple	32·00	6·50
70a	2d. on 5s. black and red	3·25	2·50

29 Queen Salote

1938. 20th Anniv of Queen Salote's Accession. Dated "1918–1938" at foot.

71	29	1d. black and red	1·25	8·50
72	29	2d. black and purple	16·00	8·50
73	29	2½d. black and blue	16·00	10·00

1944. Silver Jubilee of Queen Salote's Accession. Tablet at foot dated "1918–1943".

83	1d. black and red	15	1·25
84	2d. black and violet	15	1·25
85	3d. black and green	15	1·25
86	6d. black and orange	1·00	2·00
87	1s. black and brown	75	2·00

1949. 75th Anniv of U.P.U. As T **33d/g** of St. Helena.

88	2½d. blue	20	1·00
89	3d. olive	2·00	3·75
90	6d. red	20	75
91	1s. brown	25	75

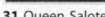

31 Queen Salote

32 Queen Salote

1950. 50th Birthday of Queen Salote.

92	**31**	1d. red	1·40	4·25
93	**32**	5d. green	1·40	3·75
94	-	1s. violet	1·40	4·00

DESIGN—VERT: 1s. Half-length portrait of Queen.

34 Map

35 Palace, Nuku'alofa

1951. 50th Anniv of Treaty of Friendship with Great Britain.

95	**34**	½d. green	30	4·25
96	**35**	1d. black and red	25	4·75
97	-	2½d. green and brown	30	4·00
98	-	3d. yellow and blue	2·50	3·00
99	-	5d. red and green	5·00	2·00
100	-	1s. orange and violet	4·50	2·00

DESIGNS—HORIZ: 2½d. Beach scene; 5d. Flag and island; 1s. Arms of Tonga and Great Britain. VERT: 3d. H.M.N.Z.S. "Bellona".

40 Royal Palace, Nuku'alofa

1953

101	**40**	1d. black and brown	10	10
102	-	1½d. blue and green	20	10
103	-	2d. turquoise and black	1·25	20
104	-	3d. blue and green	2·50	20
105	-	3½d. yellow and red	1·75	70
106	-	4d. yellow and red	2·50	10
107	-	5d. blue and brown	1·00	10
108	-	6d. black and blue	1·50	30
109	-	8d. green and violet	1·50	1·75
110	-	1s. blue and black	2·00	10
111	-	2s. green and brown	10·00	60
112	-	5s. yellow and lilac	25·00	9·50
113	-	10s. yellow and black	13·00	9·50
114	-	£1 yellow, red and blue	13·00	6·50

DESIGNS—HORIZ: 1½d. Shore fishing with throw-net; 2d. "Hifofua" and "Aoniu" (ketches); 3½d. Map of Tongatapu; 4d. Vava'u Harbour; 5d. Post Office, Nuku'alofa; 6d. Aerodrome, Fua'amotu; 8d. "Matua" (inter-island freighter) at Nuku'alofa Wharf; 2s. Lifuka, Ha'apai; 5s. Mutiny on the "Bounty". VERT: 3d. Swallows' Cave, Vava'u; 1s. Map of Tonga Islands; 10s. Queen Salote; £1 Arms of Tonga.

54 Stamp of 1886

1961. 75th Anniv of Tongan Postal Service.

115	**54**	1d. red and orange	10	10
116	-	2d. blue	1·25	45
117	-	4d. turquoise	20	45
118	-	5d. violet	1·25	45
119	-	1s. brown	1·25	45

DESIGNS: 2d. Whaling ship and whaleboat; 4d. Queen Salote and Post Office, Nuku'alofa; 5d. "Aoniu II" (inter-island freighter); 1s. Douglas DC-4 mail plane over Tongatapu.

1962. Centenary of Emancipation. Stamps of 1953 and No. 117 optd **1862 TAU'ATAINA EMANCIPATION 1962** or surch also.

120	1d. black and brown	10	2·00
121	4d. turquoise (No. 117)	10	90
122	5d. blue and brown	15	90
123	6d. black and blue	20	1·25
124	8d. green and violet	40	2·75
125	1s. blue and black	20	1·00
126	2s. on 3d. blue and green	40	7·00
127	5s. yellow and lilac	6·50	7·00

60 "Protein Foods"

1963. Freedom from Hunger.

128	**60**	11d. blue	50	15

61 Coat of Arms

1963. First Polynesian Gold Coinage Commem. Circular designs backed with paper, inscr overall "TONGA THE FRIENDLY ISLANDS". Imperf. (a) Postage ¼ koula coin. Diameter 158in.

129	**61**	1d. red on gold	10	10
130	**A**	2d. blue on gold	10	10
131	**61**	6d. green on gold	20	15
132	**A**	9d. purple on gold	20	15
133	**61**	1s.6d. violet on gold	30	30
134	**A**	2s. green on gold	40	40

(b) Air (i) ½ koula coin. Diameter 218in.

135	**B**	10d. red on gold	20	20
136	**61**	2s.4d. green on gold	30	30
137	**B**	1s.1d. blue on gold	30	30

(ii) 1 koula coin. Diameter 318in.

138		2s.1d. purple on gold	45	50
139	**61**	2s.4d. green on gold	50	60
140	**B**	2s.9d. violet on gold	50	60

DESIGNS: A, Queen Salote (head); B. Queen Salote (full length).

64 Red Cross Emblem

1963. Centenary of Red Cross.

141	**64**	2d. red and black	30	10
142	**64**	11d. red and blue	1·00	1·50

65 Queen Salote

66 Map of Tongatapu

1964. Pan-Pacific South-East Asia Women's Assn Meeting, Nuku'alofa. T **65/66** backed with paper inscr overall "TONGA THE FRIENDLY ISLANDS". Imperf.

143	**65**	3d. pink (postage)	25	40
144	**65**	9d. blue	35	40
145	**65**	2s. green	55	65
146	**65**	3s. lilac	90	1·50
147	**66**	10d. turquoise (air)	35	30
148	**66**	1s.2d. black	45	45
149	**66**	3s.6d. red	75	1·50
150	**66**	6s.6d. violet	1·10	2·75

1965. "Gold Coin" stamps of 1963 surch and with star over old value.

151	**61**	1s.3d. on 1s.6d. (postage)	25	25
152	**A**	1s.9d. on 9d.	25	25
153	**61**	2s.6d. on 6d.	30	50
154	**61**	5s. on 1d.	17·00	26·00
155	**A**	5s. on 2d.	2·75	3·75
156	**A**	5s. on 2s.	70	1·00
157	**B**	2s.3d. on 10d. (air)	25	40
158	**61**	2s.9d. on 11d.	30	55
159	**B**	4s.6d. on 2s.1d.	13·00	17·00
160	**61**	4s.6d. on 2s.4d.	13·00	17·00
161	**B**	4s.6d. on 2s.9d.	7·50	14·00

1966. Centenary of Tupou College and Secondary Education. Nos. 115/16 and 118/19 optd or surch **1866-1966 TUPOU COLLEGE & SECONDARY EDUCATION**.

162	**54**	1d. red and orange (postage)	10	10
163	**54**	3d. on 1d. red and orange	10	10
164	-	6d. on 2d. blue	15	10
165	-	1s.2d. on 2d. blue	25	10
166	-	2s. on 2d. blue	30	10
167	-	3s. on 2d. blue	30	15

As above opt but with additional **AIRMAIL** and **CENTENARY**.

168		5d. violet (air)	15	10
169	**54**	10d. on 1d. red and brown	15	10
170	-	1s. brown	30	10
171	-	2s.9d. on 2d. blue	35	15
172	-	3s.6d. on 5d. violet	35	15
173	-	4s.6d. on 1s. brown	45	15

1966. Queen Salote Commemoration. Nos. 143/4 and 147/8 optd. **IN MEMORIAM QUEEN SALOTE 1900+1965** (postage) or **1900 1965+ and laurel spray** (air) or surch also. Inscr and new figures of value in first colour and obliterating shapes in second colour given.

174	**65**	3d. (silver & blue) (postage)	30	20
175	**65**	5d. on 9d. (silver and black)	35	20
176	**65**	9d. (silver and black)	55	20
177	**65**	1s.7d. on 3d. (silver and blue)	1·25	1·00
178	**65**	3s.6d. on 9d. (silver & blk)	1·75	1·25
179	**65**	6s.6d. on 3d. (silver and blue)	2·25	3·00
180	**66**	10d. (silver and black) (air)	60	20
181	**66**	1s.2d. (black and gold)	70	35
182	**66**	4s. on 10d. (silver and black)	2·00	1·25
183	**66**	5s.6d. on 1s.2d. (black and gold)	2·25	2·50
184	**66**	10s.6d. on 1s.2d. (gold and black)	2·75	[illegible]

1967. Various stamps surch **SENITI** or **Seniti** and value. (a) Postage.

228	1s. on 1d. (No. 101)	10	10
229	2s. on 4d. (No. 106)	10	20
230	3s. on 3d. (No. 104)	10	20
187	3s. on 5d. (No. 107)	10	20
231	4s. on 5d. (No. 107)	10	20
232	5s. on 2d. (No. 108)	10	20
189	5s. on 3½d. (No. 105)	10	20
233	6s. on 6d. (No. 108)	10	20
190	6s. on 8d. (No. 109)	30	20
234	7s. on 1½d. (No. 102)	10	15
192	8s. on 6d. (No. 108)	30	20
235	8s. on 8d. (No. 109)	10	25
193	9s. on 3d. (No. 104)	15	20
236	9s. on 3½d. (No. 105)	20	30
239	2p. on 2s. (No. 111)	1·50	2·75
194	10s. on 1s. (No. 110)	15	20
195	11s. on 3d. on 1d. (No. 163)	30	30
238	20s. on 5s. (No. 112)	1·75	70
196	21s. on 3s. on 2d. (No. 167)	25	35
197	23s. on 1d. (No. 101)	25	35
198	30s. on 2s. (No. 111)*	2·75	3·50
199	30s. on 2s. (No. 111)*	2·75	3·75
200	50s. on 6d. (No. 108)	1·25	2·00
201	60s. on 2d. (No. 103)	1·50	2·25

*No. 198 has the surcharged value expressed horizontally; No. 199 has the figures "30" above and below "SENITI".

(b) Air. Surch with **AIRMAIL** added.

240	11s. on 10s. (No. 113)	25	30
241	21s. on 10s. (No. 113)	40	50
242	23s. on 10s. (No. 113)	40	50

74 Coat of Arms (reverse)

1967. Coronation of King Taufa'ahau IV. Circular designs backed with paper inscr overall "TONGA, THE FRIENDLY ISLANDS" etc. Imperf.

202	**74**	1s. orange & bl (b) (post)	10	30
203	**A**	2s. blue and mauve (c)	10	30
204	**74**	4s. green and purple (d)	15	25
205	**A**	15s. turquoise & vio (e)	55	25
206	**74**	28s. black and purple (a)	1·25	60
207	**A**	50s. red and blue (c)	2·00	2·00
208	**74**	1p. blue and red (f)	2·75	3·25
209	**A**	7s. red and black (b) (air)	25	10
210	**74**	9s. purple and green (c)	35	10
211	**A**	11s. blue and orange (d)	40	15
212	**74**	21s. black and green (e)	75	30
213	**A**	23s. purple and green (a)	85	45
214	**74**	29s. blue and green (c)	1·10	60
215	**A**	2p. purple and orange (f)	3·75	4·50

The commemorative coins depicted in reverse (Type **74**) are inscribed in various denominations as follows: 1s. "20 SENTIT"; 4s. "PA'ANGA"; 9s. "50 SENITI"; 21s. "TWO PA'ANGA"; 28s. "QUARTER HAU"; 29s. "HALF HAU"; 1p. "HAU".

Sizes: (a) Diameter 1½in.; (b) Diameter 1⁷⁄₁₀in.; (c) Diameter 2in.; (d) Diameter 2³⁄₁₀in.; (e) Diameter 2⁷⁄₁₀in.; (f) Diameter 2⁹⁄₁₀in.

1967. Arrival of U.S. Peace Corps in Tonga. As Nos. 101/13 but imperf in different colours and surch **The Friendly Islands welcome the United States Peace Corps** and new value (or S only).

216	1s. on 1d. black and yellow (postage)	10	20
217	2s. on 2d. blue and red	10	20
218	3s. on 3d. brown and yellow	10	20
219	4s. on 4d. violet and yellow	10	20
220	5s. on 5d. green and yellow	10	10
221	10s. on 1s. red and yellow	10	10
222	20s. on 2s. red and blue	30	15
223	50s. on 5s. sepia and yellow	2·75	1·50
224	1p. on 10s. yellow	70	1·75
225	11s. on 3½d. blue (air)	15	10
226	21s. on 1½d. green	30	20
227	23s. on 3½d. blue	30	20

1968. 50th Birthday of King Taufa'ahua IV. Nos. 202/15 optd **H.M'S BIRTHDAY 4 JULY 1968**.

243	**74**	1s. orange and blue (postage)	10	60
244	**A**	2s. blue and mauve	20	60
245	**74**	4s. green and purple	40	60
246	**A**	15s. turquoise and violet	1·75	35
247	**74**	28s. black and purple	2·50	45
248	**A**	50s. red and blue	3·25	2·00
249	**74**	1p. blue and red	6·50	7·50
250	**A**	7s. red and black (air)	80	20
251	**74**	9s. purple and green	85	20
252	**A**	11s. blue and orange	1·00	25
253	**74**	21s. black and green	2·25	30
254	**A**	23s. purple and green	2·25	30
255	**74**	29s. blue and green	2·50	40
256	**A**	2p. purple and orange	10·00	13·00

1968. South Pacific Games Field and Track Trials, Port Moresby, New Guinea. As Nos. 101/13 surch **Friendly Islands Field & Track Trials South Pacific Games Port Moresby 1969** and value.

257	5s. on 5d. green & yell (post)	10	15
258	10s. on 1s. red and yellow	10	15
259	15s. on 2s. red and blue	15	20
260	25s. on 2d. blue and red	25	25
261	50s. on 1d. black and yellow	35	55
262	75s. on 10s. orange and yellow	60	1·25
263	6s. on 6d. black & yellow (air)	10	15
264	7s. on 4d. violet and yellow	10	15
265	8s. on 8d. black and yellow	10	15
266	9s. on 1½d. green	10	15
267	11s. on 3d. brown and yellow	15	15
268	21s. on 3½d. blue	20	20
269	38s. on 5s. sepia and yellow	2·25	1·00
270	1p. on 10s. yellow	70	1·50

1969. Emergency Provisionals. Various stamps (Nos. 273/6 are imperf and in different colours) surch. (a) Postage.

271	1s. on 1s.2d. blue (No. 165)	2·75	4·50
272	1s. on 2s. on 3d. blue (No. 166)	2·75	4·50
273	1s. on 6d. blk & yell (No. 108)	70	1·75
274	2s. on 3½d. blue (No. 105)	75	1·75
275	3s. on 1½d. green (No. 102)	75	1·75
276	4s. on 8d. blk & yell (No. 109)	1·00	1·75

(b) Air. Nos. 171/3 surch.

277	1s. on 2s.9d. on 2d. blue	3·00	4·50
278	1s. on 3s.6d. on 5d. violet	3·00	4·50
279	1s. on 4s.6d. on 1s. brown	3·00	4·50

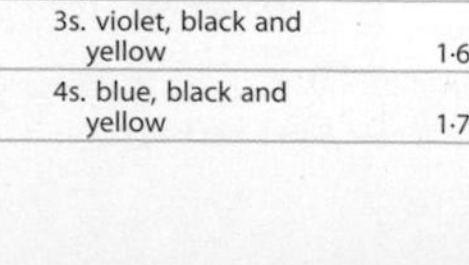

83 Banana

1969. Coil stamps. Self-adhesive.

280	**83**	1s. red, black and yellow	1·40	2·50
281	**83**	2s. green, black and yellow	1·50	2·50
282	**83**	3s. violet, black and yellow	1·60	2·50
283	**83**	4s. blue, black and yellow	1·75	2·50

| 284 | 83 | 5s. green, black and yellow | 1·90 | 2·50 |

See also Nos. 325/9, 413/17, 657/89, O45/9, O82/6 and O169/83.

84 Putting the Shot

1969. Third South Pacific Games, Port Moresby. Imperf. Self-adhesive.

285	84	1s. black, red & buff (postage)	10	15
286	84	3s. green, red and buff	10	15
287	84	6s. blue, red and buff	10	15
288	84	10s. violet, red and buff	15	15
289	84	30s. blue, red and buff	30	30
290	-	9s. black, vio & orge (air)	15	15
291	-	11s. black, blue and orange	15	15
292	-	20s. black, green and orange	25	25
293	-	60s. black, red and orange	75	1·25
294	-	1p. black, green and orange	1·10	2·00

DESIGN: Nos. 290/4, Boxing.

86 Oil Derrick and Map

1969. First Oil Search in Tonga. Imperf. Self-adhesive.

295	86	3s. multicoloured (postage)	55	15
296	86	7s. multicoloured	75	20
297	86	20s. multicoloured	1·25	50
298	86	25s. multicoloured	1·25	50
299	86	35s. multicoloured	1·50	80
300	-	9s. multicoloured (air)	75	25
301	-	10s. multicoloured	75	25
302	-	24s. multicoloured	1·25	50
303	-	29s. multicoloured	1·40	70
304	-	38s. multicoloured	1·50	80

DESIGN: Nos. 300/4, Oil derrick and island of Tongatapu.

87 Members of the British and Tongan Royal Families

1970. Royal Visit. Imperf. Self-adhesive.

305	87	3s. multicoloured (postage)	60	30
306	87	5s. multicoloured	70	30
307	87	10s. multicoloured	1·00	40
308	87	25s. multicoloured	2·50	75
309	87	50s. multicoloured	4·25	3·75
310	-	7s. multicoloured (air)	90	25
311	-	9s. multicoloured	1·00	30
312	-	24s. multicoloured	2·50	75
313	-	29s. multicoloured	2·75	80
314	-	38s. multicoloured	3·75	1·50

DESIGN: Nos. 310/14, Queen Elizabeth II and King Taufa'aha Tupou IV.

89 Book, Tongan Rulers and Flag

1970. Entry into British Commonwealth. Imperf. Self-adhesive.

315	89	3s. multicoloured (postage)	55	25
316	89	7s. multicoloured	80	30
317	89	15s. multicoloured	1·25	40
318	89	25s. multicoloured	1·50	50
319	89	50s. multicoloured	2·50	2·00
320	-	9s. blue, gold and red (air)	20	20
321	-	10s. purple, gold and blue	20	20
322	-	24s. yellow, gold and green	50	30
323	-	29s. blue, gold and red	55	30
324	-	38s. yellow, gold and green	70	55

DESIGN—"Star" shaped (size 44×51 mm): Nos. 320/4, Star and King Taufa'ahua Tupou IV.

90 Coconut

1970. Coil stamps. Imperf. Self-adhesive. (a) As T **83** but colours changed.

325	83	1s. yellow, purple and black	1·00	1·50
326	83	2s. yellow, blue and black	1·00	1·50
327	83	3s. yellow, brown and black	1·00	1·50
328	83	4s. yellow, green and black	1·00	1·50
329	83	5s. yellow, red and black	1·00	1·50

(b) Multicoloured; colour of face values given.

330	90	6s. red	1·00	1·50
331	90	7s. purple	1·10	1·50
332	90	8s. violet	1·25	1·50
333	90	9s. green	1·40	1·50
334	90	10s. orange	1·40	1·50

91 "Red Cross"

1970. Centenary of British Red Cross. Imperf. Self-adhesive.

335	91	3s. red, black and green (postage)	40	30
336	91	7s. red, black and blue	55	20
337	91	15s. red, black and purple	1·25	60
338	91	25s. red, black and blue	1·60	90
339	91	75s. red, black and brown	7·50	9·50
340	-	9s. red and turquoise (air)	60	20
341	-	10s. red and purple	60	20
342	-	18s. red and green	1·25	60
343	-	38s. red and blue	3·25	2·25
344	-	1p. red and silver	8·50	13·00

DESIGN—As Type **91**: Nos. 340/4, As Nos. 335/9 but with inscription rearranged and coat of arms omitted.

1971. 5th Death Anniv of Queen Salote. Nos. 174/80, 182/4 with part of old surch obliterated and further surch **1965 1970** and value. On air values the surch includes two laurel leaves.

345	65	2s. on 5d. on 9d. (postage)	35	35
346	65	3s. on 9d.	35	35
347	65	5s. on 3d.	55	35
348	65	15s. on 3s.6d. on 9d.	1·50	45
349	65	25s. on 6s.6d. on 3d.	2·50	90
350	65	50s. on 1s.7d. on 3d.	3·50	2·50
351	66	9s. on 10d. (air)	90	35
352	66	24s. on 4s. on 10d	2·50	75
353	66	29s. on 5s.6d. on 1s.2d.	2·75	1·25
354	66	38s. on 10s.6d. on 1s.2d.	3·25	1·75

1971. "Philatokyo '71" Stamp Exhibition, Japan. As Nos. 101 etc but imperf with colours changed and surch **PHILATOKYO '71**, emblem and value or **HONOURING JAPANESE POSTAL CENTENARY 1871-1971** (Nos. 357, 362, 364). Nos. 360/4 also surch **AIRMAIL**.

355		3s. on 8d. blk & yell (postage)	10	10
356		7s. on 4d. violet and yellow	15	10
357		15s. on 1s. red and yellow	30	20
358		25s. on 1d. black and yellow	40	30
359		75s. on 2s. red and blue	1·75	1·75
360		9s. on 1½d. green (air)	15	10
361		10s. on 4d. violet and yellow	15	10
362		18s. on 1s. red and yellow	35	25
363		38s. on 1d. black and yellow	70	50
364		1p. on 2s. red and blue	1·75	2·00

96 Wristwatch

1971. Air. Imperf. Self-adhesive.

365	96	14s. multicoloured	2·25	2·50
365a	96	17s. multicoloured	2·50	2·75
366	96	21s. multicoloured	2·50	2·75
366a	96	38s. multicoloured	3·50	3·75

See also Nos. O65/6a.

97 Pole-vaulter

1971. Fourth South Pacific Games, Tahiti. Imperf. Self-adhesive.

367	97	3s. multicoloured (postage)	10	10
368	97	7s. multicoloured	10	10
369	97	15s. multicoloured	20	20
370	97	25s. multicoloured	30	35
371	97	50s. multicoloured	60	90
372	-	9s. multicoloured (air)	10	10
373	-	10s. multicoloured	10	10
374	-	24s. multicoloured	30	35
375	-	29s. multicoloured	40	50
376	-	38s. multicoloured	55	70

DESIGN—HORIZ: Nos. 372/6, High-jumper.

98 Medal of Merit (reverse)

1971. Investiture of Royal Tongan Medal of Merit. Multicoloured, colour of medal given. Imperf. Self-adhesive.

377	98	3s. gold (postage)	10	20
378	98	24s. silver	25	25
379	-	38s. brown	60	50
380	-	10s. gold (air)	20	20
381	-	75s. silver	1·10	1·40
382	98	1p. brown	1·40	1·75

DESIGN—As Type **98**: Nos. 379/81, Obverse of the Medal of Merit.

99 Child

1971. 25th Anniv of UNICEF. Imperf. Self-adhesive.

383	99	2s. multicoloured (postage)	10	10
384	99	4s. multicoloured	10	10
385	99	8s. multicoloured	10	10
386	99	16s. multicoloured	25	25
387	99	30s. multicoloured	45	45
388	-	10s. multicoloured (air)	15	15
389	-	15s. multicoloured	25	25
390	-	25s. multicoloured	40	40
391	-	50s. multicoloured	85	1·00
392	-	1p. multicoloured	1·75	2·00

DESIGN—VERT (21×42 mm): Nos. 388/92, Woman.

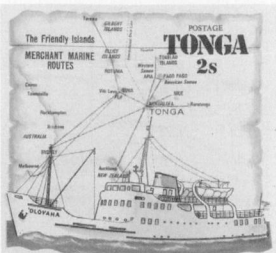

100 Map of South Pacific, and "Olovaha"

1972. Merchant Marine Routes. Imperf. Self-adhesive.

393	100	2s. multicoloured (postage)	30	40
394	100	10s. multicoloured	60	30
395	100	17s. multicoloured	90	30
396	100	21s. multicoloured	1·00	40
397	100	60s. multicoloured	4·25	3·50
398	-	9s. multicoloured (air)	60	30
399	-	12s. multicoloured	75	30
400	-	14s. multicoloured	85	30
401	-	75s. multicoloured	4·50	4·00
402	-	90s. multicoloured	4·75	5·50

DESIGN: Nos. 398/402, Map of South Pacific, and "Niuvakai".

101 Hau Coronation Coin

1972. Fifth Anniv of Coronation. Imperf. Self-adhesive.

403	101	5s. multicoloured (postage)	10	15
404	101	7s. multicoloured	10	15
405	101	10s. multicoloured	15	15
406	101	17s. multicoloured	30	20
407	101	60s. multicoloured	1·00	1·25
408	-	9s. multicoloured (air)	15	15
409	-	12s. multicoloured	20	15
410	-	14s. multicoloured	25	20
411	-	21s. multicoloured	35	20
412	-	75s. multicoloured	1·25	1·40

DESIGNS—(47×41 mm): Nos. 408/12, As T **101** but with coins above inscription instead of beneath it.

1972. Imperf. Self-adhesive. (a) As T **83** but inscription altered omitting "Best in the Pacific", and colours changed.

413	83	1s. yellow, red and black	60	60
414	83	2s. yellow, blue and black	65	60
415	83	3s. yellow, green and black	70	60
416	83	4s. yellow, blue and black	70	60
417	83	5s. yellow, brown and black	70	60

(b) As T **90** but colours changed. Multicoloured. Colour of face value given.

418	90	6s. orange	80	60
419	90	7s. blue	85	60
420	90	8s. purple	85	60
421	90	9s. orange	85	60
422	90	10s. blue	90	40

102 Water Melon

(c) Type **102**. Multicoloured. Colour of face value given.

423	102	15s. blue	1·75	65
424	102	20s. orange	2·00	85
425	102	25s. brown	2·25	95
426	102	40s. orange	3·50	2·00
427	102	50s. lemon	3·50	2·25

1972. Inauguration of Internal Airmail. No. 398 surch **7s NOVEMBER 1972 INAUGURAL Internal Airmail Nuku'alofa – Vava'u.**

| 428 | | 7s. on 9s. multicoloured | 1·00 | 2·50 |

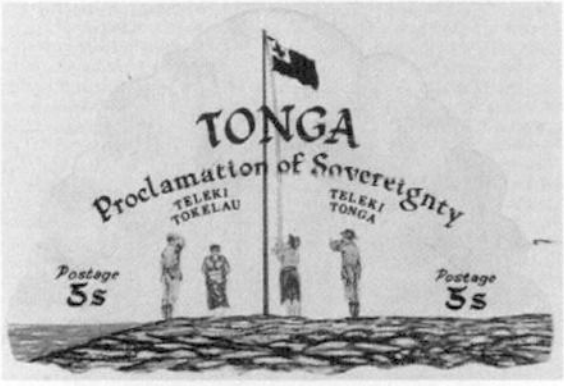

104 Hoisting Tongan Flag

1972. Proclamation of Sovereignty over Minerva Reefs. Imperf. Self-adhesive.

429	**104**	5s. multicoloured (postage)	10	15
430	**104**	7s. multicoloured	10	15
431	**104**	10s. multicoloured	15	15
432	**104**	15s. multicoloured	25	20
433	**104**	40s. multicoloured	80	65
434	-	9s. multicoloured (air)	15	15
435	-	12s. multicoloured	20	15
436	-	14s. multicoloured	25	15
437	-	38s. multicoloured	75	55
438	-	1p. multicoloured	2·00	2·75

DESIGN—SPHERICAL (52 mm diameter): Nos. 434/8, Proclamation in Govt Gazette.

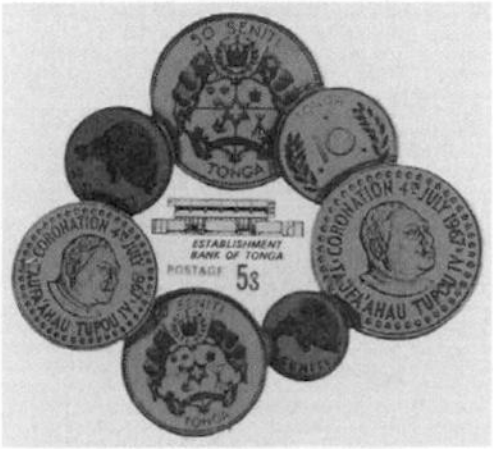

105 Coins around Bank

1973. Foundation of Bank of Tonga. Imperf. Self-adhesive.

439	**105**	5s. multicoloured (postage)	15	15
440	**105**	7s. multicoloured	15	15
441	**105**	10s. multicoloured	20	15
442	**105**	20s. multicoloured	50	30
443	**105**	30s. multicoloured	75	40
444	-	9s. multicoloured (air)	25	15
445	-	12s. multicoloured	25	15
446	-	17s. multicoloured	[illegible]	[illegible]
447	-	50s. multicoloured	1·50	1·50
448	-	90s. multicoloured	2·75	3·25

DESIGN—HORIZ (64×52 mm): Nos. 444/8, Bank and banknotes.

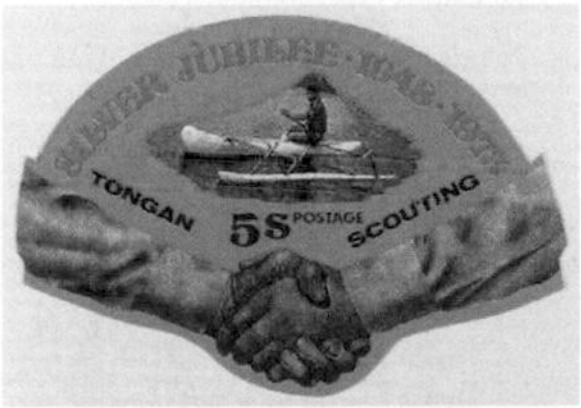

106 Handshake and Scout in Outrigger Canoe

1973. Silver Jubilee of Scouting in Tonga. Imperf. Self-adhesive.

449	**106**	5s. multicoloured (postage)	20	10
450	**106**	7s. multicoloured	30	15
451	**106**	15s. multicoloured	95	40
452	**106**	21s. multicoloured	1·25	50
453	**106**	50s. multicoloured	4·50	2·25
454	-	9s. multicoloured (air)	50	20
455	-	12s. multicoloured	60	30
456	-	14s. multicoloured	85	50
457	-	17s. multicoloured	95	60
458	-	1p. multicoloured	10·00	6·50

DESIGN—SQUARE (53×53 mm): Nos. 454/8, Scout badge.

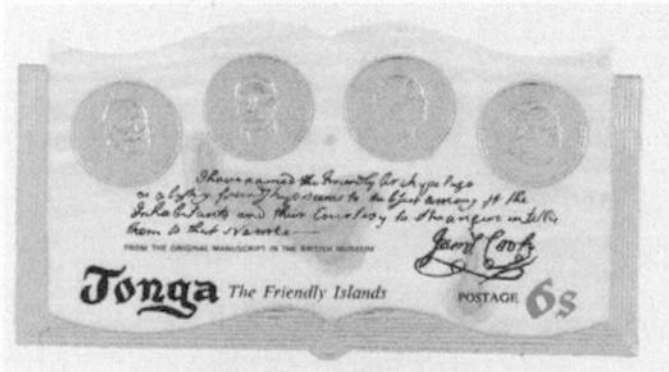

107 Excerpt from Cook's Log-book

1973. Bicentenary of Capt. Cook's Visit to Tonga. Imperf. Self-adhesive.

459	**107**	6s. multicoloured (postage)	40	30
460	**107**	8s. multicoloured	40	35
461	**107**	11s. multicoloured	60	40
462	**107**	35s. multicoloured	4·00	2·25
463	**107**	40s. multicoloured	4·00	2·50
464	-	9s. multicoloured (air)	70	30
465	-	14s. multicoloured	1·25	50
466	-	29s. multicoloured	4·00	2·00
467	-	38s. multicoloured	4·50	2·50
468	-	75s. multicoloured	8·50	4·50

DESIGN—VERT: Nos. 464/8, H.M.S. "Resolution".

1973. Commonwealth Games, Christchurch. Various stamps surch Commonwealth Games **CHRISTCHURCH 1974** and No. 474 optd **AIRMAIL** in addition.

469	**97**	5s. on 50s. multicoloured (No. 371) (postage)	15	10
470	-	12s. on 38s. mult (No. 379)	30	15
471	-	14s. on 75s. mult (No. 381)	30	15
472	**98**	20s. on 1p. mult (No. 382)	50	30
473	**98**	50s. on 24s. mult (No. 378)	1·00	1·00
474	**97**	7s. on 25s. mult (No. 370) (air)	15	10
475	-	9s. on 38s. mult (No. 376)	20	10
476	-	24s. mult (No. 374)	60	30
477	-	29s. on 9s. mult (No. 374)	70	40
478	-	40s. on 14s. mult (No. 456)	85	90

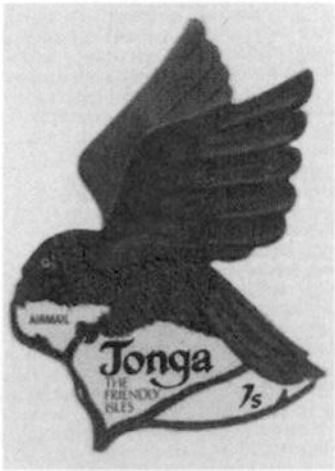

109 Red Shining Parrot

1974. Air. Imperf. Self-adhesive.

479	**109**	7s. multicoloured	95	65
480	**109**	9s. multicoloured	1·10	75
481	**109**	12s. multicoloured	1·25	75
482	**109**	14s. multicoloured	1·40	75
483	**109**	17s. multicoloured	1·50	1·00
484	**109**	29s. multicoloured	2·50	1·40
485	**109**	38s. multicoloured	3·00	1·50
486	**109**	50s. multicoloured	3·50	5·00
487	**109**	75s. multicoloured	[illegible]	[illegible]

For 25s. value in smaller design, 27×36 mm, see No. 1284.

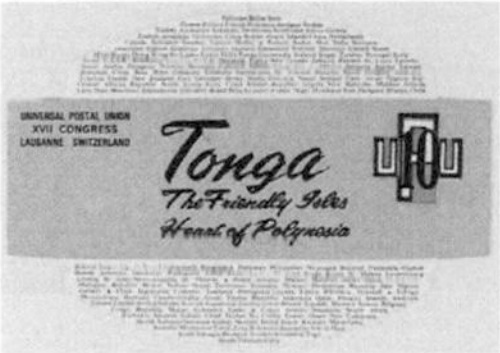

110 "Stamped Letter"

1974. Centenary of U.P.U. Imperf. Self-adhesive.

488	**110**	5s. multicoloured (postage)	10	30
489	**110**	10s. multicoloured	15	30
490	**110**	15s. multicoloured	25	40
491	**110**	20s. multicoloured	30	40
492	**110**	50s. multicoloured	1·00	1·60
493	-	14s. multicoloured (air)	25	30
494	-	21s. multicoloured	35	40
495	-	60s. multicoloured	1·10	1·75
496	-	75s. multicoloured	1·25	2·25
497	-	1p. multicoloured	1·50	2·50

DESIGN—HORIZ: Nos. 493/7, Carrier pigeon scattering letters over Tonga.

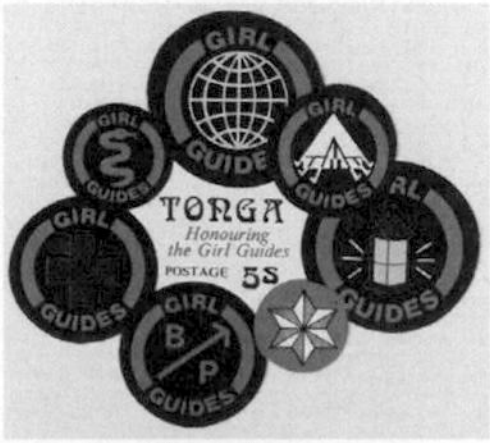

111 Girl Guides Badges

1974. Tongan Girl Guides. Imperf. Self-adhesive.

498	**111**	5s. multicoloured (postage)	40	30
499	**111**	10s. multicoloured	60	30
500	**111**	20s. multicoloured	1·50	65
501	**111**	40s. multicoloured	3·25	1·75
502	**111**	60s. multicoloured	4·00	2·75
503	-	14s. multicoloured (air)	1·00	45
504	-	16s. multicoloured	1·00	45
505	-	29s. multicoloured	2·00	1·00
506	-	31s. multicoloured	2·25	1·25
507	-	75s. multicoloured	5·50	3·50

DESIGN—VERT: Nos. 503/7, Girl Guide leaders.

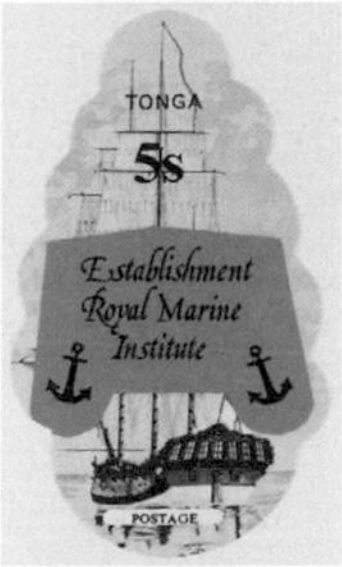

112 H.M.S. "Resolution"

1974. Establishment of Royal Marine Institute. Imperf. Self-adhesive.

508	**112**	5s. multicoloured (postage)	1·25	50
509	**112**	10s. multicoloured	1·40	50
510	**112**	25s. multicoloured	2·75	80
511	**112**	50s. multicoloured	4·00	3·00
512	**112**	75s. multicoloured	5·50	4·50
513	-	9s. multicoloured (air)	1·25	30
514	-	14s. multicoloured	1·75	55
515	-	17s. multicoloured	2·00	60
516	-	60s. multicoloured	4·25	3·75
517	-	90s. multicoloured	6·00	5·50

DESIGN—HORIZ (53×47 mm): Nos. 513/17, "James Cook" (LPG carrier).

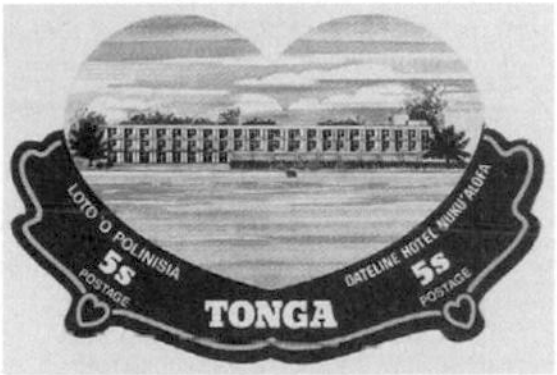

113 Dateline Hotel, Nuku'alofa

1975. South Pacific Forum and Tourism. Imperf. Self-adhesive.

518	**113**	5s. multicoloured (postage)	10	10
519	**113**	10s. multicoloured	10	10
520	**113**	[illegible] multicoloured	20	20
521	**113**	30s. multicoloured	45	45
522	**113**	1p. multicoloured	1·60	2·00
523	**113**	9s. multicoloured (air)	10	10
524	-	12s. multicoloured	15	15
525	-	14s. multicoloured	20	20
526	-	17s. multicoloured	20	20
527	-	38s. multicoloured	55	65

DESIGNS—(46×60 mm): 9, 12, 14s. Beach; 17, 38s. Surf and sea.

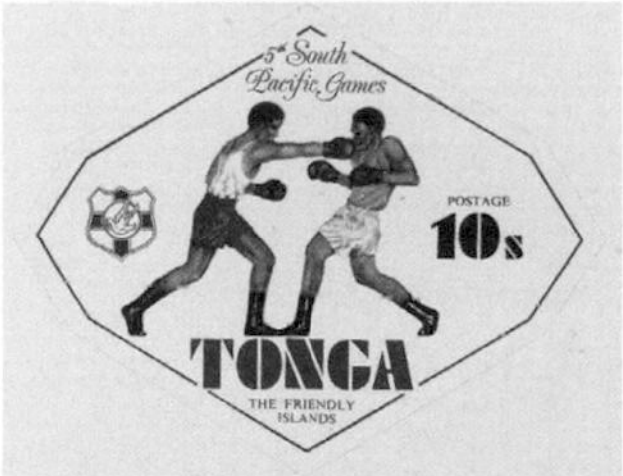

114 Boxing

1975. Fifth South Pacific Games, Guam. Imperf. Self-adhesive.

528	**114**	5s. multicoloured (postage)	20	30
529	**114**	10s. multicoloured	25	30
530	**114**	20s. multicoloured	40	45
531	**114**	25s. multicoloured	40	55
532	**114**	65s. multicoloured	1·00	2·00
533	-	9s. multicoloured (air)	25	25
534	-	12s. multicoloured	30	25
535	-	14s. multicoloured	30	25
536	-	17s. multicoloured	35	30
537	-	90s. multicoloured	1·40	2·25

DESIGN—(37×43 mm): Nos. 533/7, Throwing the discus.

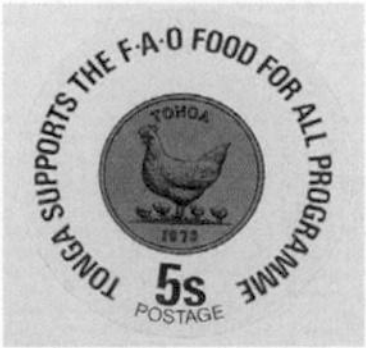

115 Commemorative Coin

1975. F.A.O. Commemoration. Imperf. Self-adhesive.

538	**115**	5s. multicoloured (postage)	15	10
539	-	20s. multicoloured	35	15
540	-	50s. blue, black and silver	75	35
541	-	1p. blue, black and silver	1·50	1·25
542	-	2p. black and silver	2·50	2·25
543	-	12s. multicoloured (air)	30	15
544	-	14s. multicoloured	30	15
545	-	25s. red, black and silver	45	20
546	-	50s. purple, black & silver	70	50
547	-	1p. black and silver	1·50	1·25

DESIGNS: Nos. 539/47 are as T **52** but showing different coins. Nos. 542 and 544 are horiz, size 75×42 mm.

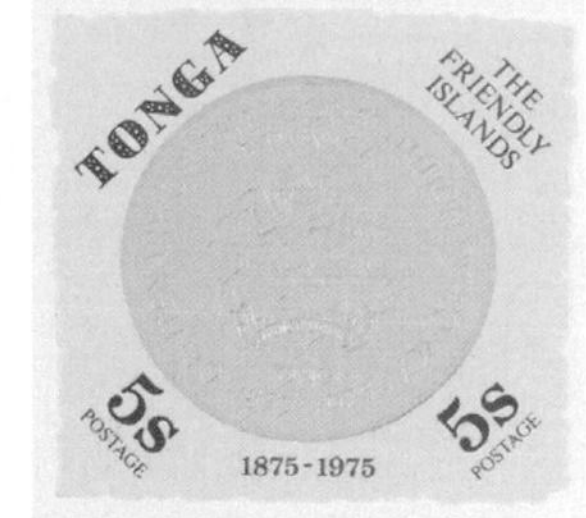

116 Commemorative Coin

1975. Centenary of Tongan Constitution. Mult. Imperf. Self-adhesive.

548	5s. Type **116** (postage)	40	35
549	10s. King George I	50	35
550	20s. King Taufa'ahau IV	85	50
551	50s. King George II	2·00	2·00
552	75s. Tongan arms	3·00	3·50
553	9s. King Taufa'ahau IV (air)	50	35
554	12s. Queen Salote	55	35
555	14s. Tongan arms	55	35
556	38s. King Taufa'ahau IV	1·50	70
557	1p. Four monarchs	3·50	4·50

SIZES: 60×40 mm, Nos. 549 and 551; 76×76 mm, Nos. 552 and 557; 57×56 mm, others.

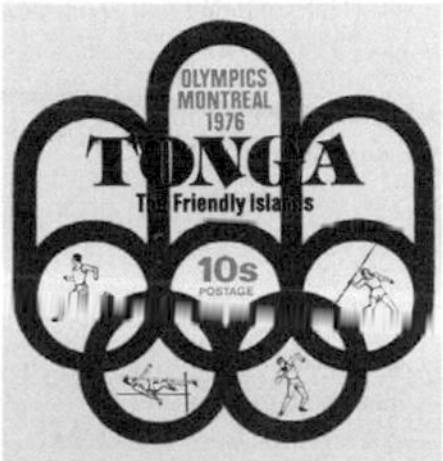

117 Montreal Logo

1976. First Participation in Olympic Games. Imperf. Self-adhesive. (a) Type **117**.

558	5s. red, black & blue (postage)	95	60
559	10s. red, black and green	1·10	60
560	25s. red, black and brown	2·25	90
561	35s. red, black and mauve	2·75	1·00
562	70s. red, black and green	5·50	4·50

(b) Montreal logo optd on Nos. 500/1, 504 and 507.

563	**111**	12s. on 20s. mult (air)	1·75	70
564	-	14s. on 16s. multicoloured	1·75	70
565	-	16s. multicoloured	1·75	70
566	**111**	38s. on 40s. multicoloured	3·50	75
567	-	75s. multicoloured	6·50	5·00

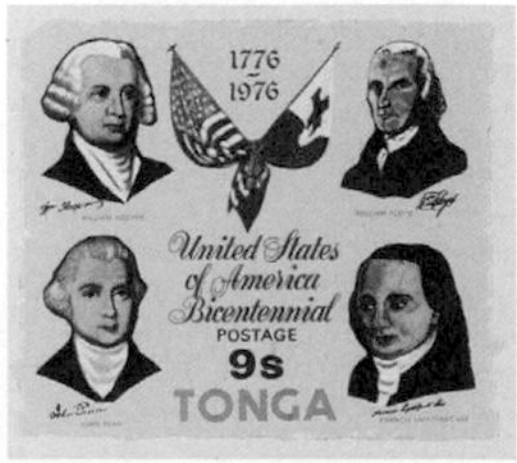

118 Signatories of Declaration of Independence

1976. Bicentenary of American Revolution. Imperf. Self-adhesive.

568	**118**	9s. multicoloured (postage)	30	15
569	-	10s. multicoloured	30	15
570	-	15s. multicoloured	45	45
571	-	25s. multicoloured	60	70
572	-	75s. multicoloured	1·50	2·50
573	-	12s. multicoloured (air)	40	15
574	-	14s. multicoloured	40	20
575	-	17s. multicoloured	50	35
576	-	38s. multicoloured	70	75
577	-	1p. multicoloured	1·75	3·50

DESIGNS: Nos. 569/77 show the signatories to the Declaration of Independence.

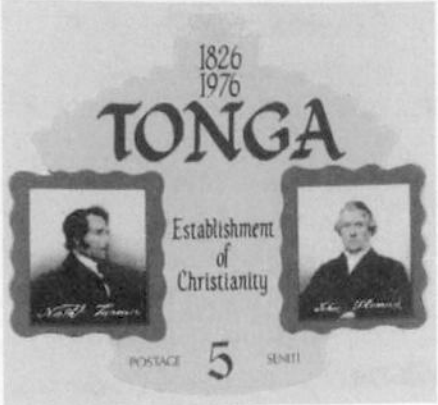

119 Nathaniel Turner and John Thomas (Methodist missionaries)

1976. 150th Anniv of Christianity in Tonga. Imperf. Self-adhesive.

578	**119**	5s. multicoloured (postage)	35	25
579	**119**	10s. multicoloured	50	25
580	**119**	20s. multicoloured	70	40
581	**119**	25s. multicoloured	75	45
582	**119**	85s. multicoloured	2·75	4·00
583	-	9s. multicoloured (air)	65	40
584	-	12s. multicoloured	70	45
585	-	14s. multicoloured	80	55
586	-	17s. multicoloured	1·00	60
587	-	38s. multicoloured	2·25	1·10

DESIGN: Nos. 583/7 show missionary ship "Triton".

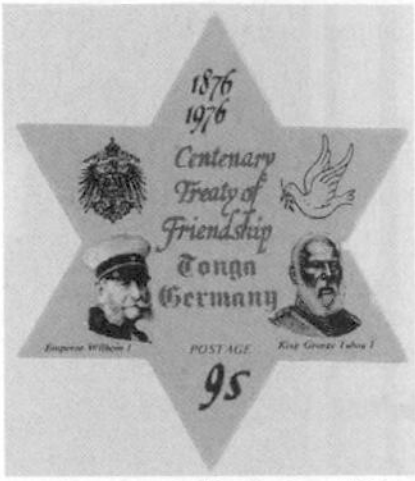

120 Emperor Wilhelm I and King George Tupou I

1976. Centenary of Treaty of Friendship with Germany. Imperf. Self-adhesive.

588	**120**	9s. multicoloured (postage)	20	20
589	**120**	15s. multicoloured	30	30
590	**120**	22s. multicoloured	40	45
591	**120**	50s. multicoloured	90	1·25
592	**120**	73s. multicoloured	1·40	1·90
593	-	11s. multicoloured (air)	25	25
594	-	17s. multicoloured	40	45
595	-	18s. multicoloured	40	45
596	-	31s. multicoloured	60	80
597	-	39s. multicoloured	70	90

DESIGNS—CIRCULAR (52 mm diameter): Nos. 593/7, Treaty signing.

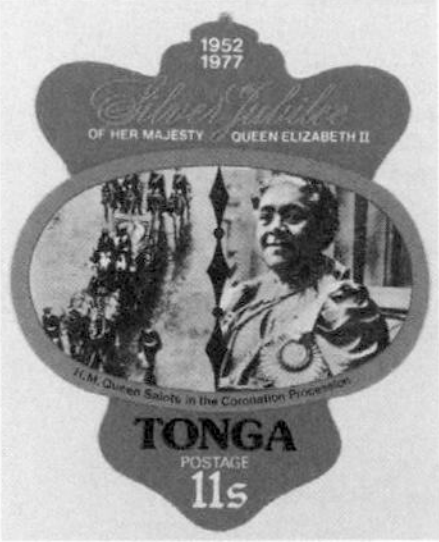

121 Queen Salote and Coronation Procession

1977. Silver Jubilee. Imperf. Self-adhesive.

598	**121**	11s. mult (postage)	40	40
599	**121**	20s. multicoloured	30	40
600	**121**	30s. multicoloured	30	40
601	**121**	50s. multicoloured	50	75
602	**121**	75s. multicoloured	65	1·00
603	-	15s. multicoloured (air)	30	35
604	-	17s. multicoloured	30	35
605	-	22s. multicoloured	3·00	1·50
606	-	31s. multicoloured	30	45
607	-	39s. multicoloured	30	45

DESIGN—SQUARE (59×59 mm): Nos. 603/7, Queen Elizabeth and King Taufa'ahau.

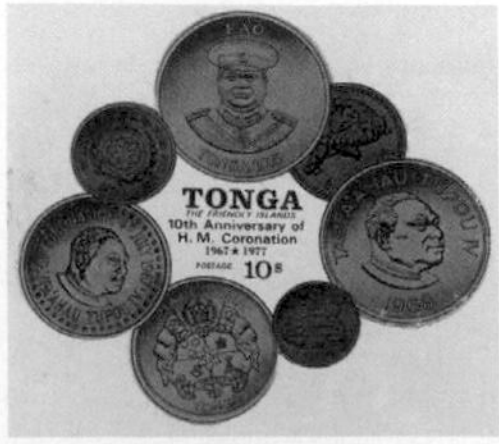

122 Tongan Coins

1977. Tenth Anniv of King's Coronation. Imperf. Self-adhesive.

608	**122**	10s. mult (postage)	20	20
609	**122**	15s. multicoloured	25	25
610	**122**	25s. multicoloured	35	45
611	**122**	50s. multicoloured	75	90
612	**122**	75s. multicoloured	1·00	1·50
613	-	11s. multicoloured (air)	25	20
614	-	17s. multicoloured	30	30
615	-	18s. multicoloured	30	30
616	-	39s. multicoloured	45	60
617	-	1p. multicoloured	1·50	2·25

DESIGN—OVAL (64×46 mm): Nos. 613/17, 1967 Coronation coin.

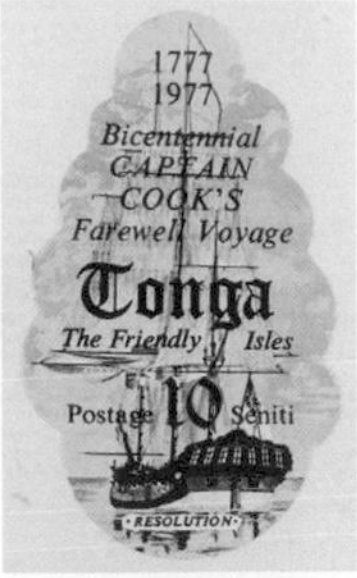

123 *H.M.S. Resolution*

1977. Bicentenary of Capt. Cook's Last Voyage. Imperf. Self-adhesive.

618	**123**	10s. mult (postage)	1·75	75
619	**123**	17s. multicoloured	2·25	1·10
620	**123**	25s. multicoloured	3·75	2·00
621	**123**	30s. multicoloured	3·75	2·75
622	**123**	40s. multicoloured	4·50	4·50
623	-	15s. multicoloured (air)	1·75	1·25
624	-	22s. multicoloured	2·75	2·25
625	-	31s. multicoloured	3·25	2·75
626	-	50s. multicoloured	4·50	4·75
627	-	1p. multicoloured	8·00	9·00

DESIGN—52×46 mm: Nos. 623/7, Medal and extract from Cook's journal.

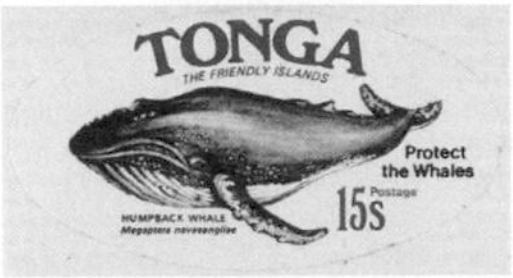

124 Humpback Whale

1977. Whale Conservation. Imperf. Self-adhesive.

628	**124**	15s. black, grey and blue (postage)	3·50	90
629	**124**	22s. black, grey and green	4·00	1·50
630	**124**	31s. black, grey and orange	4·50	2·00
631	**124**	38s. black, grey and lilac	4·75	2·50
632	**124**	64s. black, grey and brown	7·50	7·00
633	-	11s. multicoloured (air)	3·50	85
634	-	17s. multicoloured	4·00	90
635	-	18s. multicoloured	4·00	1·25
636	-	39s. multicoloured	5·50	2·25
637	-	50s. multicoloured	6·50	4·50

DESIGN—HEXAGONAL (66×51 mm): Nos. 633/7, Sei and fin whales.

For 60s. value as Type **124**, see No. 1282.

1978. Various stamps surch.

638	**115**	15s. on 5s. mult (postage)	1·50	1·75
639	**119**	15s. on 5s. multicoloured	1·50	1·75
640	**117**	15s. on 10s. red, blk & grn	1·50	1·75
641	**119**	15s. on 10s. multicoloured	1·50	1·75
642	**121**	15s. on 11s. multicoloured	1·50	2·75
643	**114**	15s. on 20s. multicoloured	1·50	1·75
644	-	15s. on 38s. multicoloured (No. O133)	1·50	1·75
645	-	17s. on 9s. multicoloured (No. 533) (air)	1·75	2·00
646	-	17s. on 9s. mult (No. 583)	1·75	2·00
647	-	17s. on 12s. mult (No. 534)	1·75	2·00
648	-	17s. on 12s. mult (No. 573)	1·75	2·00
649	-	17s. on 18s. mult (No. 595)	1·75	2·00
650	-	17s. on 38s. mult (No. 527)	1·75	2·00
651	-	17s. on 38s. mult (No. 556)	1·75	2·00
652	-	1p. on 35s. mult (No. O151)	20·00	27·00
653	-	1p. on 38s. mult (No. 576)	8·50	9·00
654	-	1p. on 75s. mult (No. 572)	8·50	9·00

The surcharges on Nos. 638/9 are formed by adding a "1" to the existing face value.

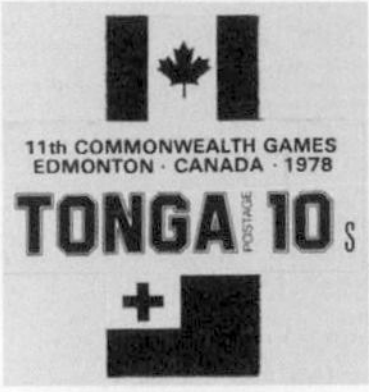

126 Flags of Canada and Tonga

1978. 11th Commonwealth Games, Edmonton. Imperf. Self-adhesive.

655	**126**	10s. blue, red and black (postage)	30	20
656	**126**	15s. multicoloured	40	30
657	**126**	20s. green, black and red	55	40
658	**126**	25s. red, blue and black	60	45
659	**126**	45s. black and red	1·40	1·25
660	-	17s. black and red (air)	45	30
661	-	35s. black, red and blue	75	65
662	-	38s. black, red and green	90	85
663	-	40s. black, red and green	95	90
664	-	65s. black, red and brown	1·75	2·00

DESIGN—LEAF-SHAPED (39×40 mm): Nos. 660/4, Maple leaf.

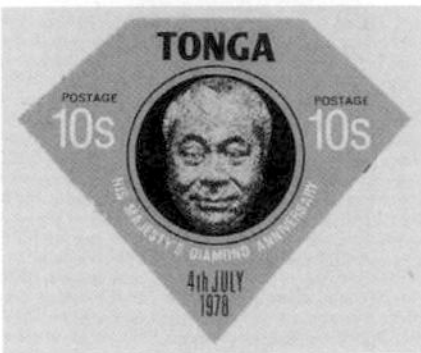

127 King Taufa'ahau Tupou IV

1978. 60th Birthday of King Taufa'ahau Tupou IV. Imperf. Self-adhesive.

665	**127**	2s. black, deep blue and blue (postage)	15	30
666	**127**	5s. black, blue and pink	15	30
667	**127**	10s. black, blue & mauve	25	25
668	**127**	25s. black, blue and grey	55	40
669	**127**	75s. black, blue and yellow	1·40	1·50
670	-	11s. black, bl & yell (air)	25	20
671	-	15s. black, blue and brown	35	25
672	-	17s. black, blue and lilac	40	25
673	-	39s. black, blue and green	80	55
674	-	1p. black, blue and pink	2·00	2·25

DESIGN—STAR SHAPED (44×51 mm): Nos. 670/4, Portrait of King.

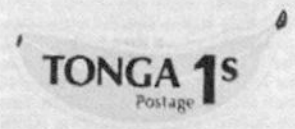

128 Banana

1978. Coil stamps. Imperf. Self-adhesive.

675	**128**	1s. black and yellow	40	60
676	-	2s. blue and yellow	40	60
677	-	3s. brown and yellow	50	60
678	-	4s. blue and yellow	50	60
679	-	5s. red and yellow	50	60
680	-	6s. purple, green & brown	60	60
681	-	7s. blue, green and brown	60	60
682	-	8s. red, green and brown	60	60
683	-	9s. mauve, green & brown	60	60
684	-	10s. green and brown	60	60
684a	-	13s. mauve, green & brown	10·00	5·00
685	-	15s. green and brown	1·50	1·25
686	-	20s. brown and green	1·75	1·40
687	-	30s. mauve, brown & green	2·00	2·00
688	-	50s. black, brown & grn	2·50	2·75
689	-	1p. purple, brown & grn	3·00	4·00
689a	-	2p. multicoloured	14·00	15·00
689b	-	3p. multicoloured	15·00	16·00

DESIGNS—As Type **128**: 2s. to 5s. Bananas, the number shown coinciding with the face value. 18×26 mm: 6s. to 10s. Coconuts. 17×30 mm: 13s. to 1p. Pineapple. 55×29 mm: 2, 3p. Mixed fruit.

For 10s. value as Type **128** but in smaller size (21×9 mm), see No. 1281.

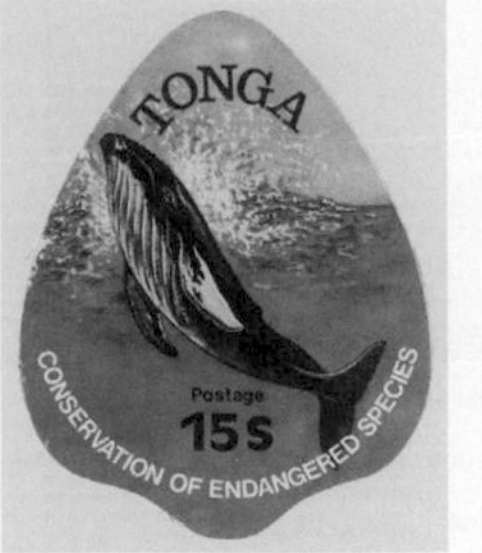

129 Humpback Whale

1978. Endangered Wildlife. Multicoloured. Self-adhesive.

690		15s. Type **129** (postage)	4·00	2·00
691		18s. Insular flying fox	3·00	2·00
692		25s. Turtle	3·00	2·00
693		28s. Red shining parrot	7·00	2·75
694		60s. Type **129**	9·00	8·00
695		17s. Type **129** (air)	4·00	2·00
696		22s. As 18s.	3·00	2·00
697		31s. As 25s.	3·00	2·00
698		39s. As 28s.	7·00	3·00
699		45s. As Type **129**	8·00	4·50

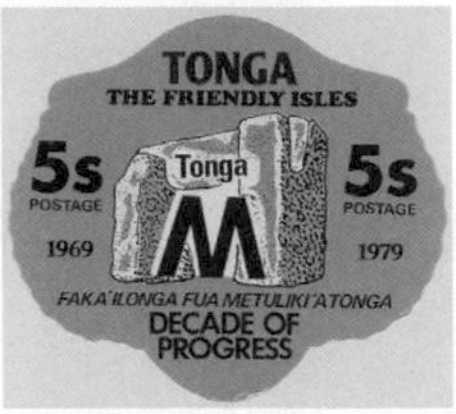

130 Metrication Symbol

1979. Decade of Progress. Self-adhesive.

700	**130**	5s. multicoloured (postage)	20	50
701	-	11s. multicoloured	1·40	50
702	-	18s. multicoloured	60	45
703	-	22s. multicoloured	60	45
704	-	50s. multicoloured	3·00	1·75
705	-	15s. multicoloured (air)	1·75	45
706	-	17s. multicoloured	1·75	45
707	-	31s. gold and blue	1·75	85
708	-	39s. multicoloured	1·25	90
709	-	1p. multicoloured	4·50	4·50

DESIGNS—VERT (58×55 mm): 11, 17s. Map of South Pacific Islands; 22s. New churches; 50, 15s. Air routes; 39s. Government offices; 1p. Communications. TEAR DROP (35×52 mm): 18s. Building wall of progress with the assistance of United States Peace Corps. As Type **130**: 31s. Rotary International emblem.

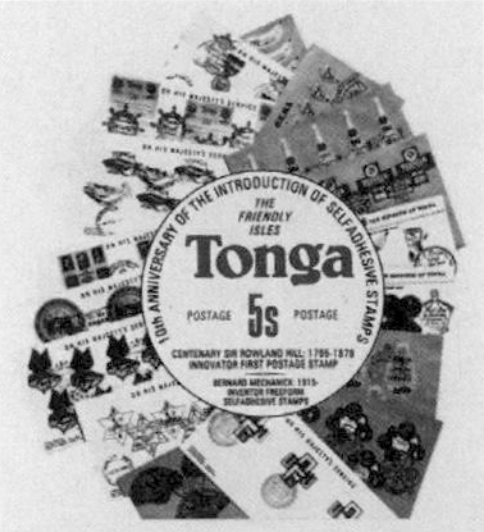

131 Various Envelopes bearing Self-adhesive Stamps

1979. Death Centenary of Sir Rowland Hill and 10th Anniv of Tongan Self-adhesive Stamps. Self-adhesive.

710	**131**	5s. multicoloured (postage)	20	10
711	**131**	10s. multicoloured	30	15
712	**131**	25s. multicoloured	50	35
713	**131**	50s. multicoloured	85	60
714	**131**	1p. multicoloured	1·50	1·25
715	-	15s. multicoloured (air)	40	20
716	-	17s. multicoloured	45	25
717	-	18s. multicoloured	45	25
718	-	31s. multicoloured	60	40
719	-	39s. multicoloured	70	45

DESIGN—MULTI-ANGULAR (53×53 mm): 15s. to 39s. Self-adhesive stamps.

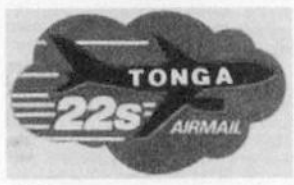

132

1979. Air. Coil stamps. Self-adhesive.

720	**132**	5s. black and blue	50	1·00
721	**132**	11s. black and blue	65	1·00
722	**132**	14s. black and violet	70	1·00
723	**132**	15s. black and mauve	70	1·00
724	**132**	17s. black and mauve	70	80
725	**132**	18s. black and red	70	70

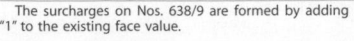

726	132	22s. black and red	80	70
726a	132	29s. black and red	15·00	5·50
727	132	31s. black and yellow	1·00	1·50
727a	132	32s. black and brown	15·00	6·00
728	132	39s. black and green	1·25	1·00
728a	132	47s. black and brown	15·00	7·50
729	132	75s. black and green	1·75	4·00
730	132	1p. black and green	2·25	5·00

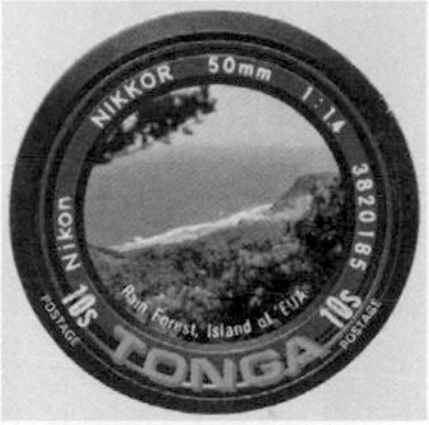

133 Rain Forest, Island of 'Eua

1979. Views as seen through the Lens of a Camera. Self-adhesive.

731	133	10s. mult (postage)	30	40
732	133	18s. multicoloured	30	40
733	133	31s. multicoloured	50	40
734	133	50s. multicoloured	70	1·50
735	133	60s. multicoloured	70	2·50
736	-	5s. multicoloured (air)	20	50
737	-	15s. multicoloured	30	30
738	-	17s. multicoloured	30	30
739	-	39s. multicoloured	60	60
740	-	75s. multicoloured	80	2·50

DESIGN: 5s. to 75s. Isle of Kao.

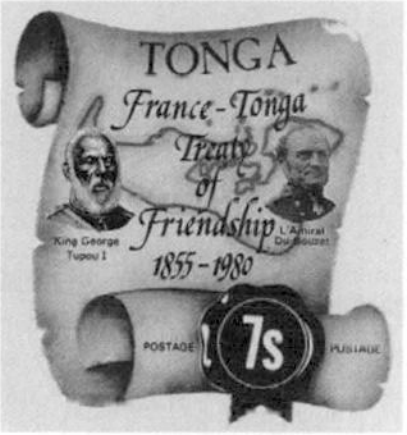

134 King Tupou I, Admiral Du Bouzet and Map of Tonga

1979. 125th Anniv of France–Tonga Treaty of Friendship. Self-adhesive.

741	134	7s. multicoloured (postage)	25	15
742	134	10s. multicoloured	30	20
743	134	14s. multicoloured	45	30
744	134	50s. multicoloured	1·25	1·25
745	134	75s. multicoloured	1·75	2·00
746	-	15s. multicoloured (air)	55	30
747	-	17s. multicoloured	60	35
748	-	22s. multicoloured	75	55
749	-	31s. multicoloured	1·10	90
750	-	39s. multicoloured	1·25	1·00

DESIGN: 15s. to 39s. King Tupou II, Napoleon III and "L'Aventure" (French warship).

1980. Olympic Games, Moscow. Nos. 710/19 surch or optd only (Nos. 753 and 755) **1980 OLYMPIC GAMES**, Olympic mascot and symbol.

751	131	13s. on 5s. multicoloured (postage)	35	35
752	-	20s. on 10s. multicoloured	55	55
753	-	25s. multicoloured	70	70
754	-	33s. on 50s. multicoloured	85	85
755	-	1p. multicoloured	3·25	3·50
756	-	9s. on 15s. multicoloured (air)	30	30
757	-	16s. on 17s. multicoloured	50	50
758	-	29s. on 18s. multicoloured	80	80
759	-	32s. on 31s. multicoloured	90	90
760	-	47s. on 39s. multicoloured	1·50	1·75

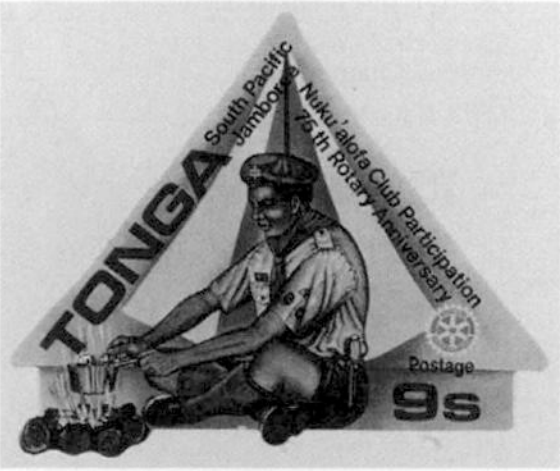

136 Scout at Campfire

1980. South Pacific Scout Jamboree, Tonga, and 75th Anniv of Rotary International. Self-adhesive.

761	136	9s. multicoloured (postage)	30	30
762	136	13s. multicoloured	40	30
763	136	15s. multicoloured	40	30
764	136	30s. multicoloured	75	60
765	-	29s. multicoloured (air)	75	45
766	-	32s. multicoloured	80	45
767	-	47s. multicoloured	1·10	70
768	-	1p. multicoloured	2·00	3·75

DESIGN: 29s. to 1p. Scout activities and Rotary emblem.

1980. Various stamps surch.

769	117	9s. on 35s. red, black and mauve (postage)	60	50
770	119	13s. on 20s. mult	60	90
771	119	13s. on 25s. mult	60	90
772	-	19s. on 25s. mult (No. 571)	85	1·50
773	114	1p. on 65s. mult	3·25	4·75
773a	-	5p. on 25s. mult (No. O214)	16·00	19·00
773b	-	5p. on 2p. mult (No. O215)	16·00	19·00
774	-	29s. on 14s. mult (No. 585) (air)	1·00	1·50
775	-	29s. on 39s. mult (No. 597)	1·00	1·50
776	-	32s. on 12s. mult (No. 554)	1·25	1·75
777	-	32s. on 14s. mult (No. 574)	1·25	1·75
778	-	47s. on 12s. mult (No. 524)	1·75	2·25
779	-	47s. on 12s. mult (No. 584)	1·75	2·25

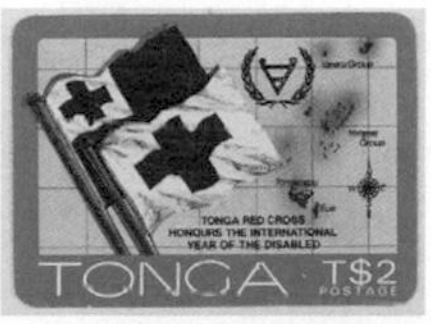

138 Red Cross and Tongan Flags, with Map of Tonga

1981. International Year of Disabled Persons. Self-adhesive.

780	138	2p. multicoloured (postage)	2·00	1·25
781	138	3p. multicoloured	2·25	1·50
782	-	29s. multicoloured (air)	50	20
783	-	32s. multicoloured	60	25
784	-	47s. multicoloured	70	30

DESIGN: Nos. 782/4, Red Cross flag and map depicting Tongatapu and Eua.

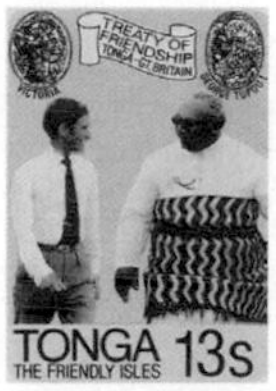

139 Prince Charles and King Taufa'ahau Tupou IV

1981. Royal Wedding and Centenary of Treaty of Friendship between Tonga and Great Britain. Multicoloured. Self-adhesive.

785		13s. Type **139**	50	50
786		47s. Prince Charles and Lady Diana Spencer	80	40
787		1p.50 Prince Charles and Lady Diana (different)	1·40	2·00
788		3p. Prince and Princess of Wales after wedding ceremony	1·60	3·00

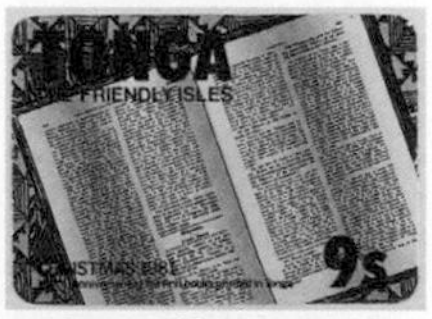

140 Report of Printing in "Missionary Notices"

1981. Christmas. 150th Anniv of First Books Printed in Tonga. Multicoloured. Self-adhesive.

789		9s. Type **140**	25	25
790		13s. "Missionary Notice" report (different)	30	40
791		32s. Type in chase	85	1·00
792		47s. Bible class	1·40	1·50

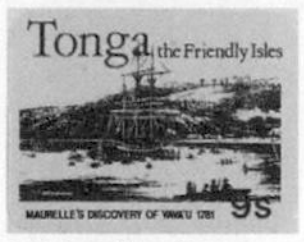

141 Landing Scene

1981. Bicentenary of Maurelle's Discovery of Vava'u. Multicoloured. Self-adhesive.

793		9s. Type **141**	55	40
794		13s. Map of Vava'u	70	50
795		47s. "La Princesa"	2·25	1·50
796		1p. "La Princesa" (different)	3·75	6·50
MS797		100×78 mm. As No. 796. Imperf	7·00	13·00

The stamp from No. **MS**797 is as No. 796 but without inscription at foot of design.

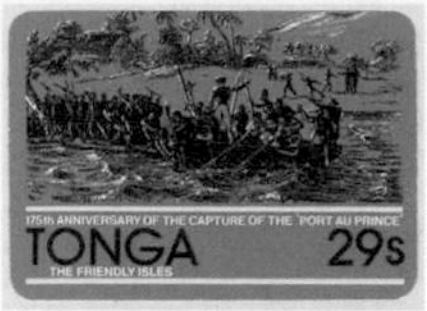

142 Battle Scene

1981. 175th Anniv of Capture of "Port au Prince" (ship). Each black and blue. Self-adhesive.

798		29s. Type **142**	1·00	50
799		32s. Battle scene (different)	1·00	55
800		47s. Map of the Ha'apai Group	1·40	1·40
801		47s. Native canoes preparing to attack	1·40	1·40
802		1p. "Port au Prince"	2·25	2·25

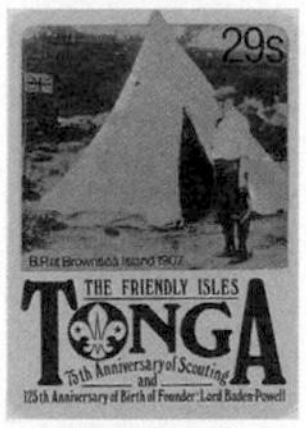

143 Baden-Powell at Brownsea Island, 1907

1982. 75th Anniv of Boy Scout Movement and 125th Birth Anniv of Lord Baden-Powell (founder). Multicoloured. Self-adhesive.

803		29s. Type **143**	75	30
804		32s. Baden-Powell on his charger "Black Prince"	80	35
805		47s. Baden-Powell at Imperial Jamboree, 1924	1·00	45
806		1p.50 Cover of first "Scouting for Boys" journal	2·25	2·25
807		2p.50 Newsboy, 1900, and Mafeking Siege 3d. stamp	3·50	5·50

1982. Cyclone Relief. No. 788 optd **CYCLONE RELIEF T$1+50s POSTAGE & RELIEF.**

808		1p.+50s. on 3p. Prince and Princess of Wales after wedding ceremony	80	2·00

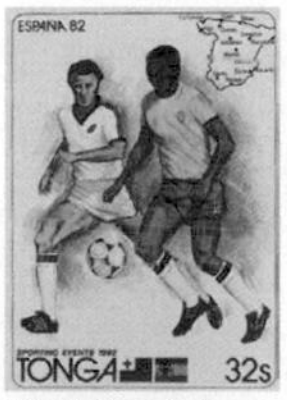

145 Ball Control

1982. World Cup Football Championship, Spain. Multicoloured. Self-adhesive.

809		32s. Type **145**	65	45
810		47s. Goalkeeping	75	60
811		75s. Heading	1·10	95
812		1p.50 Shooting	2·00	1·75

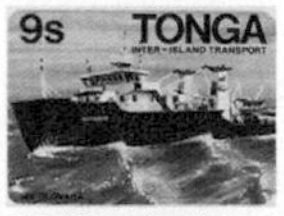

146 "Olovaha II" (inter-island freighter)

1982. Inter-Island Transport. Multicoloured. Self-adhesive.

813		9s. Type **146**	55	15
814		13s. Type **146**	60	25
815		47s. SPIA De Havilland Twin Otter 300	1·50	1·00
816		1p. As 47s.	2·40	3·00

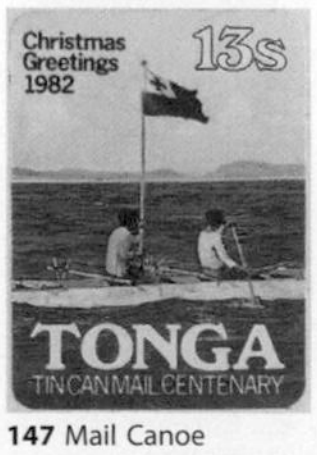

147 Mail Canoe

1982. Centenary of Tin Can Mail. Self-adhesive.

817	147	13s. multicoloured	15	25
818	-	32s. multicoloured	25	30
819	-	47s. multicoloured	35	35
820	-	2p. black and green	1·40	2·00
MS821		135×90 mm. Nos. 817/19. Imperf	1·25	2·50
MS822		135×89 mm. As No. 820 but with gold inscriptions. Imperf	3·00	5·00

DESIGNS: 32s. Mail canoe and ship; 47s. Collecting Tin Can mail; 2p. Map of Niuafo'ou.

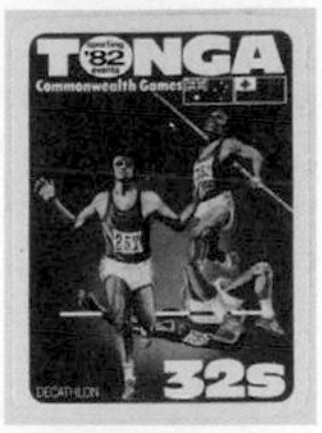

148 Decathlon

1982. Commonwealth Games, Brisbane. Multicoloured. Self-adhesive.

823		32s. Type **148**	50	50
824		$1.50 Tongan Police band at opening ceremony (horiz)	4·50	6·50

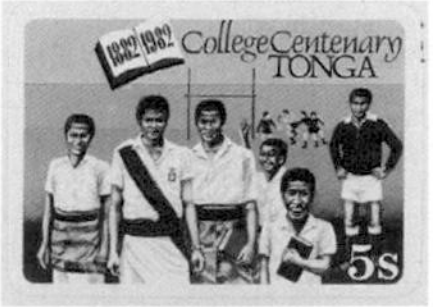

149 Pupils

1982. Cent of Tonga College. Multicoloured. Self-adhesive.

825		5s. Type **149** (Tongan inscription)	60	1·25
826		5s. Type **149** (English inscription)	60	1·25
827		29s. School crest and monument (Tongan inscr) (29×22 mm)	2·50	3·00
828		29s. As No. 827 but inscr in English	2·50	3·00
829		29s. King George Tupou I (founder) and school (Tongan inscr) (29×22 mm)	2·50	3·00
830		29s. As No. 829 but inscr in English	2·50	3·00

1982. Christmas. Nos. 817/9 optd Christmas Greetings 1982.

831		13s. Type **147**	25	50
832		32s. Mail boat and ship	60	75
833		47s. Collecting Tin Can mail	70	85

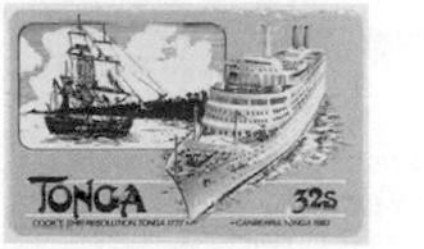

151 H.M.S. "Resolution" and S.S. "Canberra"

1983. Sea and Air Transport. Multicoloured. Self-adhesive.

834		29s. Type **151**	3·00	1·75
835		32s. Type **151**	3·00	1·75
836		47s. Montgolfier's balloon and Concorde	4·25	3·00
837		1p.50 As No. 836	6·50	10·00
MS838		120×165 mm. 2p.50 "Canberra" (liner) and Concorde	4·00	7·00

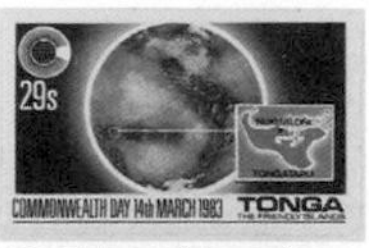

152 Globe and Inset of Tonga

1983. Commonwealth Day. Multicoloured. Self-adhesive.

839		29s. Type **152**	35	45
840		32s. Tongan dancers	4·75	4·25
841		47s. Trawler	50	80
842		1p.50 King Taufa'ahau Tupou IV and flag	1·75	5·00

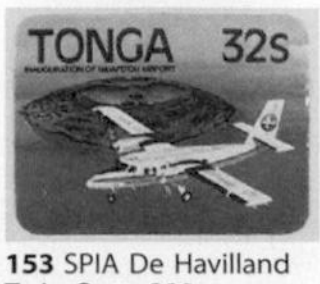

153 SPIA De Havilland Twin Otter 300

1983. Inauguration of Niuafo'ou Airport. Multicoloured. Self-adhesive.

843		32s. Type **153**	1·00	30
844		47s. Type **153**	1·10	35
845		1p. SPIA Boeing 707	1·75	1·25
846		1p.50 As No. 845	2·75	1·75

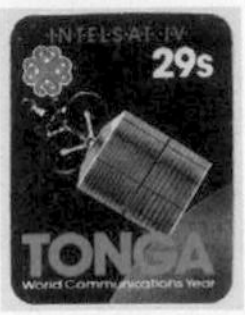

154 "Intelsat IV" Satellite

1983. World Communications Year. Multicoloured. Self-adhesive.

847	29s. Type **154**	40	20
848	32s. "Intelsat IVA" satellite	50	25
849	75s. "Intelsat V" satellite	1·00	70
850	2p. Moon post cover (45×32 mm)	1·50	2·00

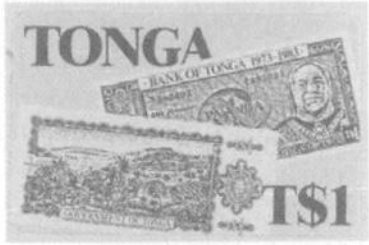

155 Obverse and Reverse of Pa'anga Banknote

1983. Tenth Anniv of Bank of Tonga. Self-adhesive.

851	**155**	1p. multicoloured	1·75	2·00
852	**155**	2p. multicoloured	2·25	3·25

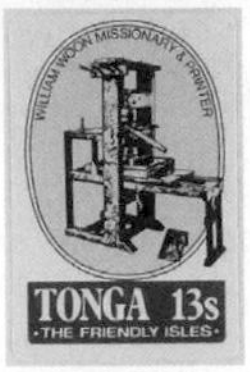

156 Early Printing Press

1983. Printing in Tonga. Multicoloured. Self-adhesive.

853	13s. Type **156**	20	15
854	32s. Arrival of W. Woon	40	30
855	1p. Early Tongan print	95	95
856	2p. "The Tonga Chronicle"	1·50	2·00

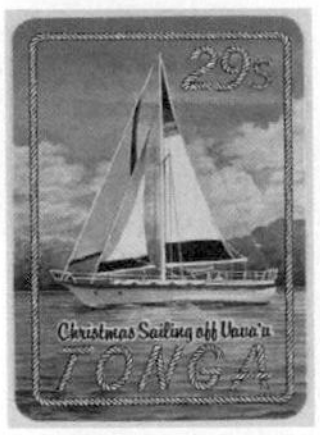

157 Yacht off Coast

1983. Christmas. Yachting off Vava'u. Mult. Self-adhesive.

857	29s. Type **157**	70	35
858	32s. View of yacht from cave	70	35
859	1p.50 Anchored yacht	2·00	2·25
860	2p.50 Yacht off coast (different)	2·75	3·50

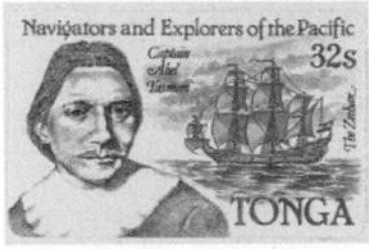

158 Abel Tasman and "Zeehan"

1984. Navigators and Explorers of the Pacific (1st series). Self-adhesive.

861	**158**	32s. green and black	1·75	1·50
862	-	47s. violet and black	2·25	2·00
863	-	90s. brown and black	4·50	3·75
864	-	1p.50 blue and black	6·00	5·00

DESIGNS: 47s. Capt. Samuel Wallis and H.M.S. "Dolphin"; 90s. Capt. William Bligh and H.M.S. "Bounty"; 1p.50, Capt. James Cook and H.M.S. "Resolution".

See also Nos. 896/9.

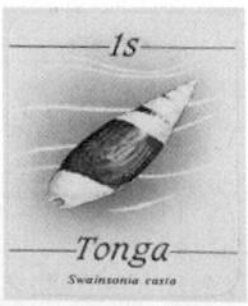

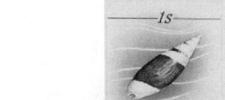

159 Chaste Mitre

1984. Marine Life. Multicoloured. Self-adhesive.

865	1s. Type **159**	40	1·75
866	2s. "Porites sp"	1·00	1·75
867	3s. Red squirrelfish	1·50	2·00
868	5s. Green map cowrie	50	1·75
869	6s. "Dardanus megistos" (crab)	1·50	2·00
870	9s. Variegated shark	1·50	1·00
871	10s. Bubble cone	1·00	1·75
872	13s. Lionfish	2·00	1·00
873	15s. Textile or cloth of gold cone	1·00	2·00
874	20s. White-tailed damselfish	2·50	2·50
875	29s. Princely cone	1·75	1·00
876	32s. Powder-blue surgeonfish	3·25	1·00
877	47s. Giant spider conch	3·00	1·60
878	1p. "Millepora dichotama"	11·00	9·50
879	2p. "Birgus latro" (crab)	16·00	16·00
880	3p. Rose-branch murex	9·00	16·00
881	5p. Yellow-finned tuna	11·00	19·00

Nos. 865/77 are 25×28 mm in size and Nos. 878/81 38×23 mm.

For these designs with normal gum but redrawn see Nos. 999/1017a and 1087/95. For similar designs but with face value at foot see Nos. 1218/34 and 1346/7.

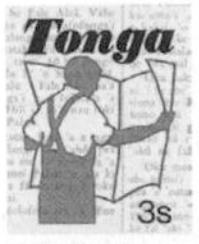

160 Printer checking Newspaper

1984. 20th Anniv of "Tonga Chronicle" (newspaper). Self-adhesive.

882	**160**	3s. brown and blue	15	20
883	**160**	32s. brown and red	45	65

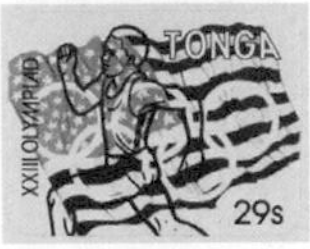

161 U.S.A. Flag and Running

1984. Olympic Games, Los Angeles. Each in black, red and blue. Self-adhesive.

884	29s. Type **161**	25	25
885	47s. Javelin-throwing	30	30
886	1p.50 Shot-putting	1·00	1·00
887	3p. Olympic torch	1·90	1·90

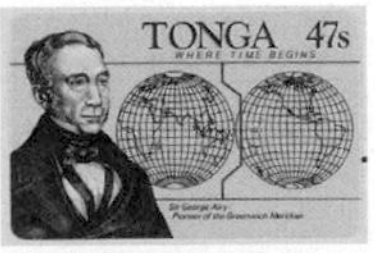

162 Sir George Airy and Dateline on World Map

1984. Centenary of International Dateline. Multicoloured. Self-adhesive.

888	47s. Type **162**	1·50	1·00
889	2p. Sir Sandford Fleming and Map of Pacific time zones	4·50	4·50

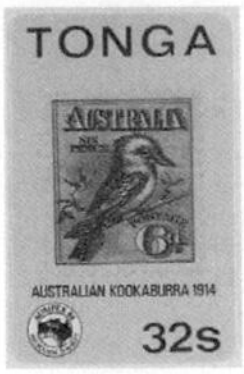

163 Australia 1914 Laughing Kookaburra 6d. Stamp

1984. "Ausipex" International Stamp Exhibition, Melbourne. Multicoloured. Self-adhesive.

890	32s. Type **163**	1·50	75
891	1p.50 Tonga 1897 Red shining parrot 2s.6d.	3·25	3·00
MS892	90×100 mm. As Nos. 890/1, but without exhibition logo and with "TONGA" and face values in gold.	4·00	4·00

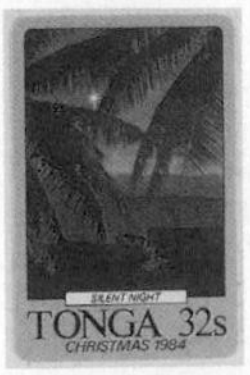

164 Beach at Sunset ("Silent Night")

1984. Christmas. Carols. Multicoloured. Self-adhesive.

893	32s. Type **164**	60	45
894	47s. Hut and palm trees ("Away in a Manger")	85	65
895	1p. Sailing boats ("I Saw Three Ships")	1·75	4·50

1985. Navigators and Explorers of the Pacific (2nd series). As T **158**. Self-adhesive.

896	32s. black and blue	3·00	1·25
897	47s. black and green	3·25	1·50
898	90s. black and red	7·00	4·00
899	1p.50 black and brown	7·50	6·50

DESIGNS: 32s. Willem Schouten and "Eendracht"; 47s. Jacob Le Maire and "Hoorn"; 90s. Fletcher Christian and "Bounty"; 1p.50, Francisco Maurelle and "La Princessa".

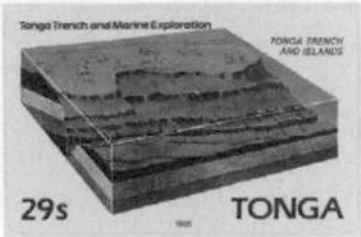

165 Section of Tonga Trench

1985. Geological Survey of the Tonga Trench. Multicoloured. Self-adhesive.

900	29s. Type **165**	1·25	1·00
901	32s. Diagram of marine seismic survey	1·25	1·00
902	47s. Diagram of aerial oil survey (vert)	1·60	1·50
903	1p.50 Diagram of sea bed survey (vert)	4·75	6·00
MS904	100×100 mm. 1p.50 Bearded angler (fish)	7·50	5·00

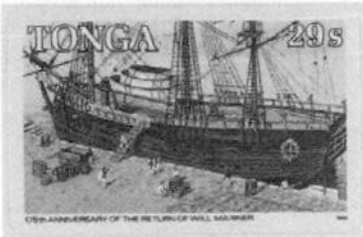

166 "Port au Prince" at Gravesend, 1805

1985. 175th Anniv of Will Mariner's Departure for England. Multicoloured. Self-adhesive.

905B	29s. Type **166**	60	50
906B	32s. Capture of "Port au Prince", Tonga, 1806	60	50
907B	47s. Will Mariner on Tongan canoe, 1807	80	70
908B	1p.50 Mariner boarding brig "Favourite", 1810	2·25	2·75
909B	2p.50 "Cuffnells" in English Channel, 1811	3·50	4·50

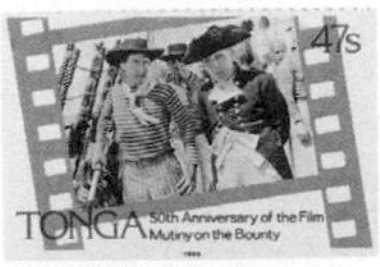

167 Quintal (Byron Russell) and Captain Bligh (Charles Laughton)

1985. 50th Anniv of Film "Mutiny on the Bounty". Multicoloured. Self-adhesive.

910	47s. Type **167**	8·50	8·50
911	47s. Captain Bligh and prisoners	8·50	8·50
912	47s. Fletcher Christian (Clark Gable)	8·50	8·50
913	47s. Mutineers threatening Bligh	8·50	8·50
914	47s. Bligh and Roger Byam (Franchot Tone) in boat	8·50	8·50

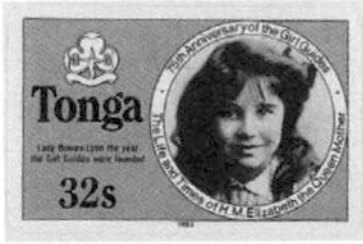

168 Lady Elizabeth Bowes-Lyon, 1910

1985. Life and Times of Queen Elizabeth the Queen Mother and 75th Anniv of Girl Guide Movement. Self-adhesive.

915A	**168**	32s. black, pink and brown	2·00	1·25
916A	-	47s. black, lilac and brown	2·25	1·50
917A	-	1p.50 black, yellow and brown	6·00	6·50
918A	-	2p.50 multicoloured	8·50	11·00

DESIGNS: 47s. Duchess of York at Hadfield Girl Guides' Rally, 1931; 1p.50, Duchess of York in Girl Guide uniform; 2p.50, Queen Mother in 1985 (from photo by Norman Parkinson).

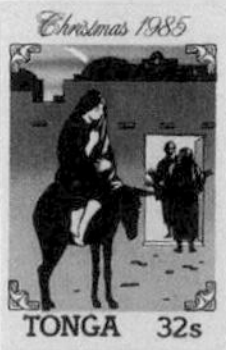

169 Mary and Joseph arriving at Inn

1985. Christmas. Multicoloured. Self-adhesive.

919	32s. Type **169**	55	30
920	42s. The Shepherds	60	40
921	1p.50 The Three Wise Men	2·25	3·00
922	2p.50 The Holy Family	3·25	4·00

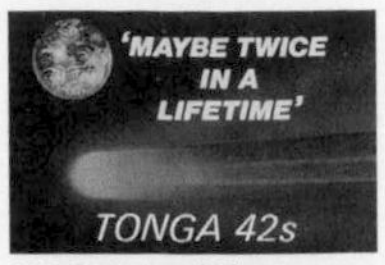

170 Comet and Slogan "Maybe Twice in a Lifetime"

1986. Appearance of Halley's Comet. Multicoloured.

923	42s. Type **170**	3·25	3·25
924	42s. Edmond Halley	3·25	3·25
925	42s. Solar System	3·25	3·25
926	42s. Telescope	3·25	3·25
927	42s. "Giotto" spacecraft	3·25	3·25
928	57s. Type **170**	3·25	3·25
929	57s. As No. 924	3·25	3·25
930	57s. As No. 925	3·25	3·25
931	57s. As No. 926	3·25	3·25
932	57s. As No. 927	3·25	3·25

Nos. 923/7 and 928/32 were each printed together, *se-tenant*, forming composite designs.

1986. Nos. 866/7, 869/70, 872, 874, 879 and 881 surch.

933	4s. on 2s. "Porites sp"	1·00	2·50
934	4s. on 13s. Lionfish	1·00	2·50
935	42s. on 3s. Red squirrelfish	2·50	1·75
936	42s. on 9s. Variegated shark	2·50	1·75
937	57s. on 6s. "Dardanus megistos"	3·00	2·25
938	57s. on 20s. White-tailed damselfish	3·00	2·25
939	2p.50 on 2p. "Birgus latro"	9·50	12·00
940	2p.50 on 5p. Yellow-finned tuna	9·50	12·00

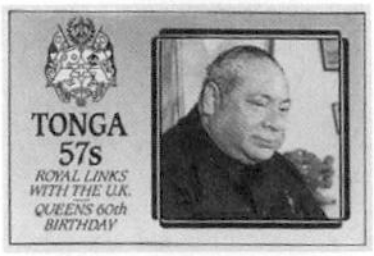

172 King Taufa'ahau Tupou IV of Tonga

1986. Royal Links with Great Britain and 60th Birthday of Queen Elizabeth II.

941	**172**	57s. multicoloured	75	1·00
942	-	57s. multicoloured	75	1·00
943	-	2p.50 brown, black and blue	3·25	4·00

DESIGNS—HORIZ (as Type **172**): No. 942, Queen Elizabeth II. SQUARE (40×40 mm): No. 943, Queen Elizabeth II and King Taufa'ahau Tupou IV, Tonga, 1970.

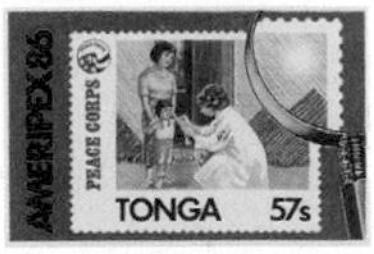

173 Peace Corps Nurse giving Injection

1986. "Ameripex '86" International Stamp Exhibition, Chicago. 25th Anniv of United States Peace Corps. Multicoloured.

944	57s. Type **173**	1·25	1·00
945	1p.50 Peace Corps teacher and pupil	2·25	3·25
MS946	90×90 mm. Nos. 944/5, magnifying glass and tweezers	3·00	4·50

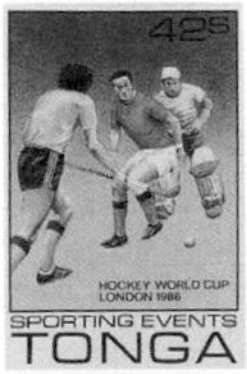

174 Hockey

1986. Sporting Events. Multicoloured.

947	42s. Type **174** (World Hockey Cup for Men, London)	1·75	1·00
948	57s. Handball (13th Commonwealth Games, Edinburgh)	1·50	1·00
949	1p. Boxing (13th Commonwealth Games, Edinburgh)	2·00	2·75
950	2p.50 Football (World Cup Football Championship, Mexico)	4·75	6·00

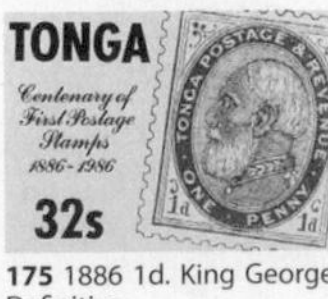

175 1886 1d. King George I Definitive

1986. Centenary of First Tonga Stamps. Multicoloured.

951	32s. Type **175**	1·75	1·10
952	42s. 1897 7½d. King George II inverted centre error	2·00	1·25
953	57s. 1950 Queen Salote's 50th Birthday 1d.	2·50	1·40

954	2p.50 1986 Royal Links with Great Britain 2p.50	4·25	7·00
MS955	132×104 mm. 50s.×8 Vert designs forming a montage of Tonga stamps	13·00	12·00

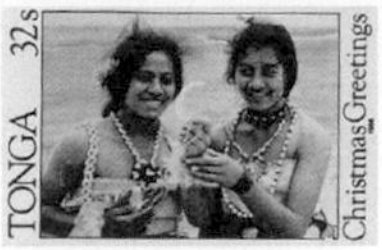

176 Girls wearing Shell Jewellery

1986. Christmas. Multicoloured.

956	32s. Type **176**	2·75	70
957	42s. Boy with wood carvings (vert)	3·00	75
958	57s. Children performing traditional dance (vert)	3·25	1·10
959	2p. Children in dugout canoe	7·50	11·00

1986. Scout Jamboree, Tongatapu. Nos. 957/8 optd **BOY SCOUT JAMBOREE 5TH-10TH DEC'86**.

960	42s. Boy with wood carvings (vert)	2·75	2·75
961	57s. Children performing traditional dance (vert)	3·25	3·25

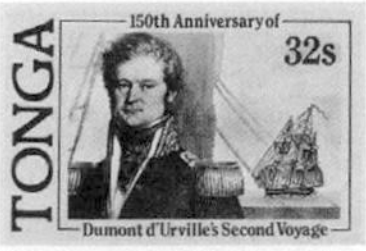

178 Dumont D'Urville and "L'Astrolabe"

1987. 150th Anniv of Dumont D'Urville's Second Voyage. Multicoloured.

962	32s. Type **178**	4·00	1·75
963	42s. Tongan girls (from "Voyage au Pole et dans l'Oceanie")	4·00	1·75
964	1p. Contemporary chart	9·00	6·50
965	2p.50 Wreck of "L'Astrolabe"	14·00	14·00

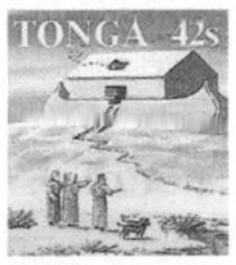

179 Noah's Ark

1987. World Wildlife Fund. Sheet 115×110 mm containing T **179** and similar vert designs. Multicoloured. P13½.

MS966	42s. Type **179**; 42s. American Bald Eagles; 42s. Giraffes and birds; 42s. Gulls; 42s. Ostriches and elephants; 42s. Elephant; 42s. Lions, zebras, antelopes and giraffes; 42s. Chimpanzees; 42s. Frogs and antelopes; 42s. Lizard and tigers; 42s. Snake and tiger; 42s. "Papilio machaon" (butterfly)	42·00	42·00

The stamps within No. **MS**966 show a composite design of animals entering Noah's Ark.

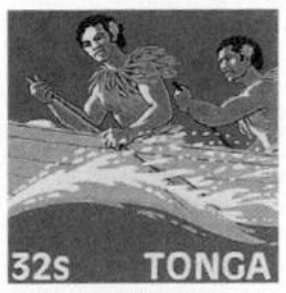

180 Two Paddlers in Canoe

1987. "Siv'a'alo" (Tonga-Fiji-Samoa) Canoe Race. Multicoloured.

967	32s. Type **180**	55	40
968	42s. Five paddlers	65	50
969	57s. Paddlers and canoe bow	80	65
970	1p.50 Two paddlers (different)	2·10	2·75
MS971	153×159 mm. Nos. 967/70	3·50	4·25

The stamps within **MS**971 show a composite design of two canoes racing.

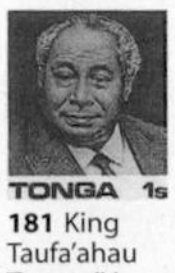

181 King Taufa'ahau Tupou IV

1987. 20th Anniv of Coronation of King Taufa'ahau Tupou IV. Self-adhesive.

972	**181**	1s. black and green	20	60
972d	**181**	2s. black and orange	2·50	3·25
973	**181**	5s. black and mauve	20	60
974	**181**	10s. black and lilac	25	60
975	**181**	15s. black and red	35	70
976	**181**	32s. black and blue	45	80

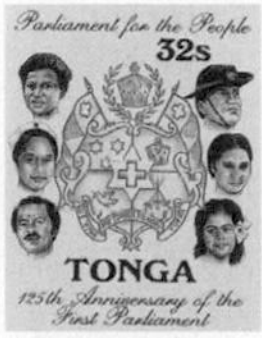

182 Arms and Tongan Citizens

1987. 125th Anniv of First Parliament.

977	**182**	32s. multicoloured	40	30
978	**182**	42s. multicoloured	50	40
979	**182**	75s. multicoloured	90	1·00
980	**182**	2p. multicoloured	2·25	3·25

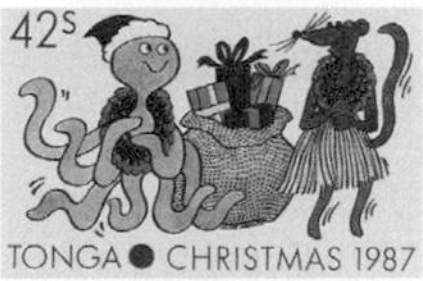

183 Father Christmas Octopus and Rat with Sack of Presents

1987. Christmas. Cartoons. Multicoloured.

981	42s. Type **183**	1·00	50
982	57s. Delivering presents by outrigger canoe	1·25	65
983	1p. Delivering presents by motorized tricycle	2·25	2·50
984	3p. Drinking cocktails	5·50	7·50

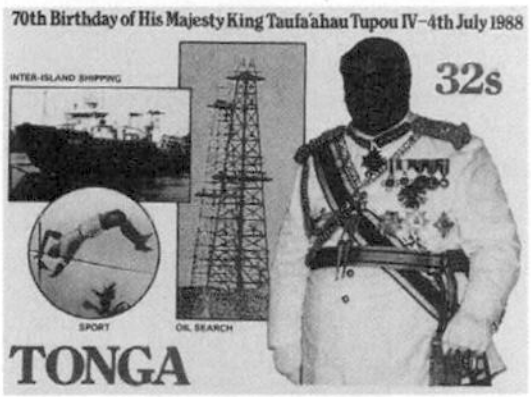

184 King Taufa'ahau Tupou IV, "Olovaha II" (inter-island freighter), Oil Rig and Pole Vaulting

1988. 70th Birthday of King Taufa'ahau Tupou IV. Designs each show portrait. Multicoloured.

985	32s. Type **184**	2·00	80
986	42s. Banknote, coins, Ha'amonga Trilithon and woodcarver	1·50	80
987	57s. Rowing, communications satellite and Red Cross worker	1·75	90
988	2p.50 Scout emblem, 1982 47s. Scout stamp and Friendly Islands Airways De Havilland Twin Otter 200/300 aircraft	7·50	8·50

See also Nos. 1082/5.

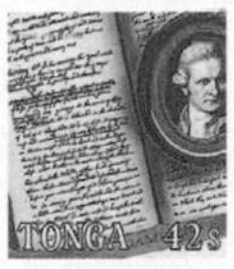

185 Capt. Cook and Journal

1988. Bicentenary of Australian Settlement. Sheet 115×110 mm containing T **185** and similar vert designs. Multicoloured.

MS989	42s. Type **185**; 42s. Ships in Sydney Harbour and Governor Philip; 42s. Australia 1952 2s.6d. aborigine definitive and early settlement; 42s. Burke and Wills (explorers); 42s. Emu, opals and gold prospector's licence; 42s. ANZAC cap badge and soldier; 42s. Cover from first overland mail by Trans Continental; 42s. Ross Smith, England–Australia flown cover and G.B. 1969 1s.9d. commemorative stamp; 42s. Don Bradman and Harold Larwood (cricketers); 42s. World War II campaign medals; 42s. Australia 1978 18c. Flying Doctor Service stamp and sheep station; 42s. Sydney Opera House	40·00	40·00

No. **MS**989 exists overprinted on the reverse as described below Nos. 985/8.

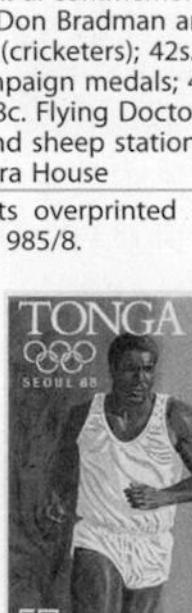

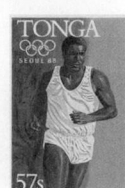

186 Athletics

1988. Olympic Games, Seoul. Multicoloured.

990	57s. Type **186**	70	65
991	75s. Sailing	1·10	95
992	2p. Cycling	8·00	3·75
993	3p. Tennis	6·50	5·00

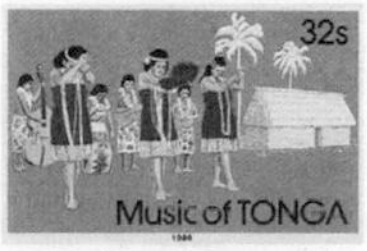

187 Traditional Tongan Fale

1988. Music in Tonga. Multicoloured.

994	32s. Type **187**	30	35
995	42s. Church choir	40	45
996	57s. Tonga Police Band outside Royal Palace	1·00	80
997	2p.50 "The Jets" pop group	2·40	3·25

188 Olympic Flame

1988. "Sport Aid '88". Sheet 105×75 mm, containing T **188** and design as No. 997. Multicoloured.

MS998	57s. Type **188**; 57s. As No. 997	1·40	2·25

1988. Redrawn designs (each showing wider gap between upper and lower lines) as Nos. 865/6, 868/9, 871/6 and 879/81 and new values, all normal gum. Multicoloured.

999	1s. Type **159**	30	1·50
1000	2s. "Porites sp"	40	2·00
1001	4s. Lionfish	2·75	2·75
1002	5s. Green map cowrie	50	1·75
1003	6s. "Dardanus megistos" (crab)	1·00	2·50
1004	7s. Wandering albatross	5·00	3·00
1005	10s. Bubble cone	60	1·00
1006	15s. Textile or cloth of gold cone	60	1·25
1007	20s. White-tailed damselfish	1·00	2·00
1008	32s. Powder-blue surgeonfish	1·00	70
1009	35s. Seahorse	4·50	3·25
1010	42s. Lesser frigate bird	4·75	70
1011	50s. Princely cone	5·00	2·25
1012	57s. Brown booby	5·50	1·00
1013	1p. "Chelonia mydas" (turtle)	7·00	4·75
1014	1p.50 Humpback whale	12·00	7·50
1015	2p. "Birgus latro" (crab)	8·00	8·50
1016	3p. Rose-branch murex	2·75	8·50
1017	5p. Yellow-finned tuna	13·00	17·00
1017a	10p. Variegated shark	22·00	26·00

Nos. 1013/17 are 41×22 mm and No. 1017a 26×41.

For smaller designs, 19×22 mm, see Nos. 1087/95.

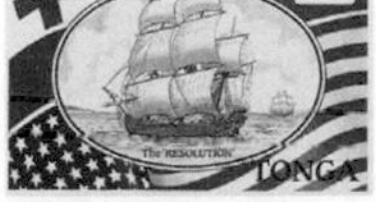

189 Capt. Cook's H.M.S. "Resolution"

1988. Centenary of Tonga–U.S.A. Treaty of Friendship. Multicoloured.

1018	42s. Type **189**	80	70
1019	57s. "Santa Maria"	1·00	80
1020	2p. Capt. Cook and Christopher Columbus	3·25	4·75
MS1021	140×115 mm. Nos. 1018/20	4·75	6·50

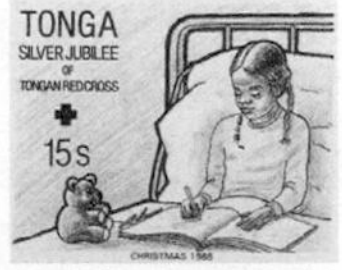

190 Girl in Hospital Bed

1988. Christmas. 125th Anniv of International Red Cross and 25th Anniv of Tongan Red Cross. Multicoloured.

1022	15s. Type **190** (A)	15	20
1023	15s. Type **190** (B)	15	20
1024	32s. Red Cross nurse reading to young boy (A)	30	35
1025	32s. Red Cross nurse reading to young boy (B)	30	35
1026	42s. Red Cross nurse taking pulse (A)	40	45
1027	42s. Red Cross nurse taking pulse (B)	40	45
1028	57s. Red Cross nurse with sleeping child (A)	55	65
1029	57s. Red Cross nurse with sleeping child (B)	55	65
1030	1p.50 Boy in wheelchair (A)	1·40	2·00
1031	1p.50 Boy in wheelchair (B)	1·40	2·00

Nos. 1022/3, 1024/5, 1026/7, 1028/9 and 1030/1 were printed together, *se-tenant*, in horizontal pairs throughout the sheets with the first stamp in each pair inscribed "INTERNATIONAL RED CROSS 125TH ANNIVERSARY" (A) and the second "SILVER JUBILEE OF TONGAN RED CROSS" (B).

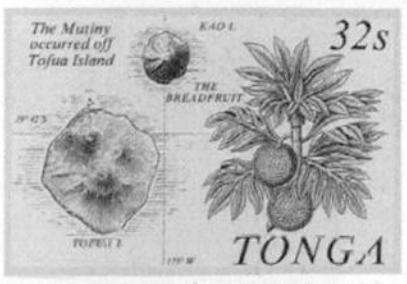

191 Map of Tofua Island and Breadfruit

1989. Bicentenary of Mutiny on the "Bounty". Multicoloured.

1032	32s. Type **191**	2·75	1·75
1033	42s. H.M.S. "Bounty" and chronometer	4·50	2·00
1034	57s. Captain Bligh and "Bounty's" launch cast adrift	6·00	3·00
MS1035	106×80 mm. 2p. Fletcher Christian on H.M.S. "Bounty" (vert); 3p. Bligh cast adrift.	10·00	11·00

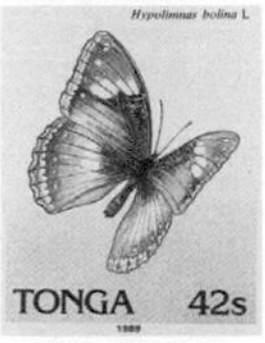

192 "Hypolimnas bolina"

1989. Butterflies. Multicoloured.

1036	42s. Type **192**	1·00	80
1037	57s. "Jamides bochus"	1·25	90
1038	1p.20 "Melanitis leda"	2·25	2·75
1039	2p.50 "Danaus plexippus"	3·75	5·50

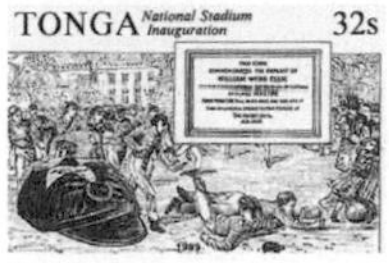

193 Football at Rugby School, 1870

1989. Inauguration of National Sports Stadium and South Pacific Mini Games, Tonga. Designs showing development of rugby, tennis and cricket. Multicoloured.

1040	32s. Type **193**	1·25	1·25
1041	32s. D. Gallaher (All Blacks' captain, 1905) and Springboks rugby match, 1906	1·25	1·25
1042	32s. King George V with Cambridge team, 1922, and W. Wakefield (England captain, 1926)	1·25	1·25
1043	32s. E. Crawford (Ireland captain, 1926) and players on cigarette cards	1·25	1·25
1044	32s. S. Mafi (Tonga captain, 1970s) and modern rugby match	1·25	1·25
1045	42s. Royal tennis, 1659	1·75	1·75
1046	42s. Major Wingfield and lawn tennis, 1873	1·75	1·75
1047	42s. Oxford and Cambridge tennis teams, 1884	1·75	1·75
1048	42s. Bunny Ryan, 1910, and players on cigarette cards	1·75	1·75
1049	42s. Boris Becker and modern tennis match	1·75	1·75
1050	57s. Cricket match, 1743, and F. Pilch memorial	3·75	3·00
1051	57s. W. G. Grace (19th-century cricketer)	3·75	3·00
1052	57s. "Boys Own Paper" cricket article, 1909	3·75	3·00
1053	57s. Australian cricket team, 1909, and players on cigarette cards	3·75	3·00
1054	57s. The Ashes urn, and modern cricket match	3·75	3·00

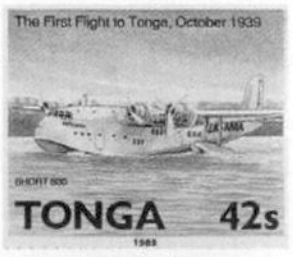

194 Short S.30 Modified "G" Class Flying Boat "Aotearoa", 1939 (50th anniv of first flight)

1989. Aviation in Tonga. Multicoloured.

1055	42s. Type **194**	2·75	1·10
1056	57s. Chance Vought F4U Corsair, 1943	3·25	1·50
1057	90s. Boeing 737 at Fua'amotu Airport	5·50	4·50
1058	3p. Montgolfier balloon, Wright Flyer I biplane, Concorde and space shuttle (97×26 mm)	14·00	14·00

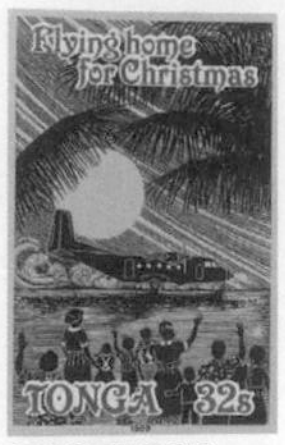

195 CASA C-212 Aviocar landing

1989. Christmas. "Flying Home".

1059	**195**	32s. green, brown & orange	2·00	80
1060	-	42s. green, brown & lt green	2·25	80
1061	-	57s. green, brown and red	2·50	90
1062	-	3p. green, brown & mve	8·00	10·00

DESIGNS: 42s. Villagers waving to CASA C-212 Aviocar aircraft; 57s. Outrigger canoe and CASA C-212 Aviocar aircraft; 3p. CASA C-212 Aviocar over headland.

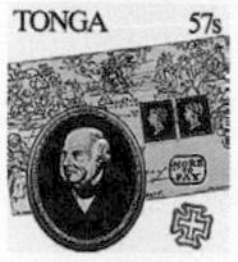

196 Rowland Hill, Mulready Cover and Penny Blacks

1989. 20th Universal Postal Union Congress, Washington. Sheet 115×110 mm containing T **196** and similar vert designs. Multicoloured.

MS1063 57s. Type **196**; 57s. Early train and steam ship; 57s. Stage coach, Pony Express poster and rider; 57s. French hot-air balloon and flown cover; 57s. Samuel Morse and telegraph key; 57s. Early British mail van and pillar box; 57s. Unloading de Havilland DH.4.M mail biplane; 57s. "Queen Mary" (liner) and Airship LZ-127 "Graf Zeppelin" flown cover; 57s. Westland Dragonfly helicopter and mail van; 57s. Computer and fax machine; 57s. "Apollo 11" emblem and space cover; 57s. U.P.U. Monument and space shuttle	45·00	45·00

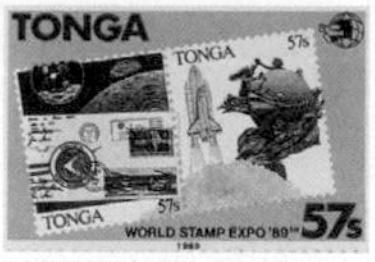

197 1989 U.P.U. Congress Stamps

1989. "World Stamp Expo '89" International Stamp Exhibition, Washington.

1064	**197**	57s. multicoloured	3·25	1·75

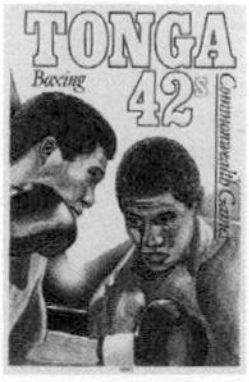

198 Boxing

1990. 14th Commonwealth Games, Auckland. Multicoloured.

1065	42s. Type **198**	90	70
1066	57s. Archery	1·50	1·10
1067	1p. Bowls	2·00	2·50
1068	2p. Swimming	3·50	5·00

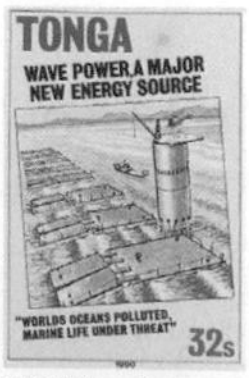

199 Wave Power Installation

1990. Alternative Sources of Electricity. Multicoloured.

1069	32s. Type **199**	1·00	65
1070	57s. Wind farm	1·50	1·10
1071	1p.20 Experimental solar cell vehicle	3·00	5·50
MS1072	110×90 mm. 2p.50 Planet Earth	7·00	8·50

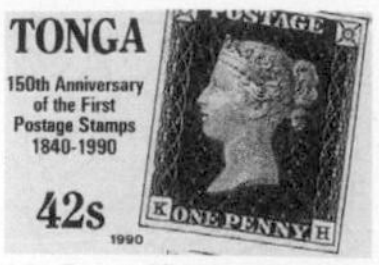

200 Penny Black

1990. 150th Anniv of the Penny Black.

1073	**200**	42s. multicoloured	1·50	1·50
1074	-	42s. multicoloured	1·50	1·50
1075	-	57s. red and black	1·75	1·25
1076	-	1p.50 multicoloured	3·75	4·25
1077	-	2p.50 multicoloured	5·50	6·00

DESIGNS: 42s. (1074) Great Britain 1840 Twopence Blue; 57s. Tonga 1886 1d.; 1p.50, 1980 South Pacific Scout Jamboree and Rotary 75th anniv 2p. official stamp; 2p.50, 1990 Alternative Sources of Electricity 57s.

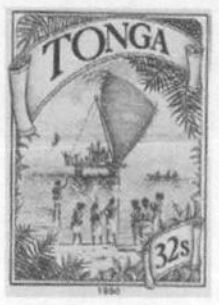

201 Departure of Canoe

1990. Polynesian Voyages of Discovery.

1078	**201**	32s. green	75	65
1079	-	42s. blue	1·00	80
1080	-	1p.20 brown	2·75	3·00
1081	-	3p. violet	5·50	8·00

DESIGNS: 42s. Navigating by night; 1p.20, Canoe and sea birds; 3p. Landfall.

1990. Silver Jubilee of King Taufa'ahau Tupou IV. As Nos. 985/8 but inscr "Silver Jubilee of His Majesty King Taufa'ahau Tupou IV. 1965–1990" and with "TONGA" and values in silver.

1082	32s. Type **184**	2·00	85
1083	42s. Banknote, coins Ha'amonga Trilithon and woodcarver	1·60	85
1084	57s. Rowing, communications satellite and Red Cross worker	1·75	95
1085	2p.50 Scout emblem, 1982 47s. Scout stamp and Friendly Island Airways de Havilland Twin Otter aircraft	8·50	9·00

1990. As Nos. 1000, 1002, 1003 (value changed), 1005 and 1008 redrawn smaller, 19×22 mm. Multicoloured.

1087	2s. "Porites sp."	40	75
1089	5s. Green map cowrie	40	75
1092	10s. Bubble cone	40	75
1093	15s. "Dardanus megistos" (crab)	5·50	2·25
1095	32s. Powder-blue surgeonfish	65	75

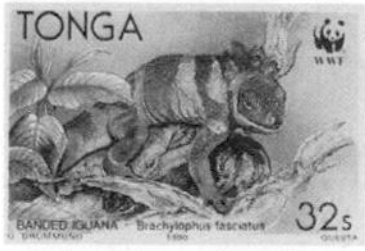

202 Iguana searching for Food

1990. Endangered Species. Banded Iguana. Multicoloured.

1105	32s. Type **202**	1·50	75
1106	42s. Head of male	1·75	85
1107	57s. Pair of iguanas during courtship	2·25	1·25
1108	1p.20 Iguana basking	5·00	6·50

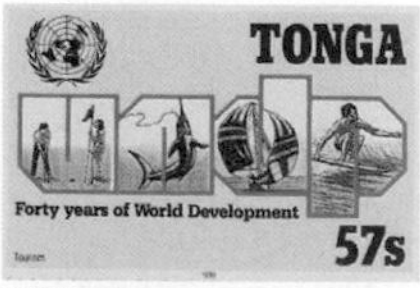

203 Tourism

1990. 40th Anniv of United Nations Development Programme. Multicoloured.

1109	57s. Type **203**	1·50	1·75
1110	57s. Agriculture and Fisheries	1·50	1·75
1111	3p. Education	7·00	9·50
1112	3p. Healthcare	7·00	9·50

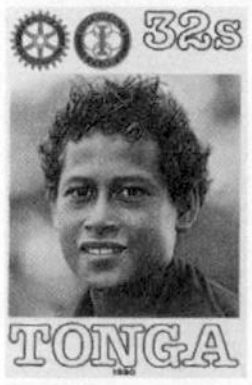

204 Boy

1990. Christmas. Rotary International Interact Project. Multicoloured.

1113	32s. Type **204**	80	40
1114	42s. Young boys	90	55
1115	2p. Girls in western clothes	3·50	4·25
1116	3p. Girls in traditional costumes	4·50	5·50

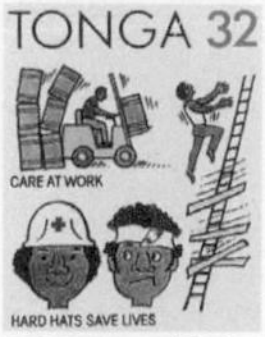

205 Safety at Work

1991. Accident Prevention. Multicoloured.

1117	32s. Type **205** (English inscription)	80	80
1118	32s. Safety at home (English inscription)	80	80
1119	32s. As No. 1118 (Tongan inscription)	80	80
1120	32s. As Type **205** (incorrectly inscr "Ngauo tokanga")	80	80
1120a	32s. As Type **205** (inscr corrected to "Ngaue tokanga")	22·00	22·00
1121	42s. Safety in cars (English inscription)	1·40	1·40
1122	42s. Safety on bikes (English inscription)	1·40	1·40
1123	42s. As No. 1122 (Tongan inscription)	1·40	1·40
1124	42s. As No. 1121 (Tongan inscription)	1·40	1·40
1125	57s. Safety at sea (English inscription)	1·50	1·50
1126	57s. Safety on the beach (English inscription)	1·50	1·50
1127	57s. As No. 1126 (Tongan inscription)	1·50	1·50
1128	57s. As No. 1125 (Tongan inscription)	1·50	1·50

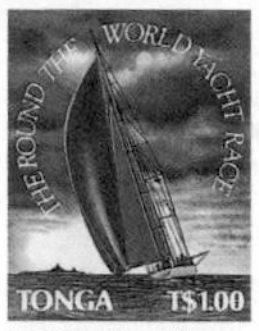

206 Yacht at Dawn

1991. Around the World Yacht Race. Sheet 120×103 mm containing T **206** and similar vert designs. Multicoloured.

MS1129 1p. Type **206**; 1p. Yacht in the morning; 1p. Yacht at midday; 1p. Yacht in the evening; 1p. Yacht at night	6·00	8·00

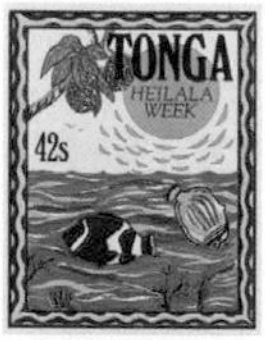

207 Fishes in the Sea

1991. Heilala Week. Multicoloured.

1130	42s. Type **207**	70	55
1131	57s. Island and yacht	90	65
1132	2p. Pile of fruit	2·75	3·50
1133	3p. Turtle on beach	3·50	4·25

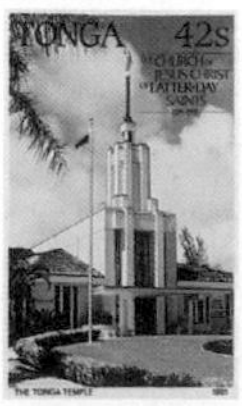

208 Tonga Temple

1991. Centenary of Church of Latter Day Saints in Tonga. Multicoloured.

1134	42s. Type **208**	1·10	1·10
1135	57s. Temple at night	1·40	1·40

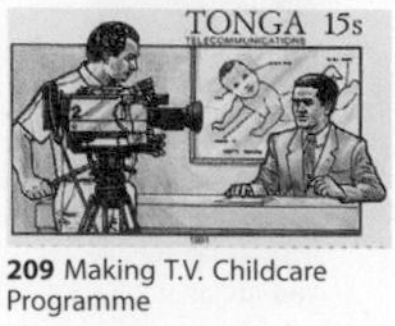

209 Making T.V. Childcare Programme

1991. Telecommunications in Tonga. Multicoloured.

1136	15s. Type **209**	35	45
1137	15s. T.V. satellite	35	45
1138	15s. Mothers watching programme	35	45
1139	32s. Man on telephone and woman with computer	65	75
1140	32s. Telecommunications satellite	65	75
1141	32s. Overseas customer on telephone	65	75
1142	42s. Sinking coaster	1·10	1·25
1143	42s. Coastguard controller	1·10	1·25
1144	42s. Maritime rescue	1·10	1·25
1145	57s. Weather satellite above Southern Hemisphere	1·25	1·40
1146	57s. Meteorologists collecting data	1·25	1·40
1147	57s. T.V. weather map and storm	1·25	1·40

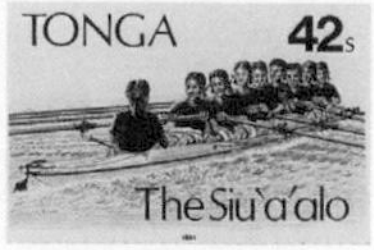

210 Women's Rowing Eight

1991. "Siu'a'alo" Rowing Festival. Multicoloured.

1148	42s. Type **210**	85	45
1149	57s. Longboat	1·00	55
1150	1p. Outrigger canoe	2·00	2·00
1151	2p. Stern of fautasi (large canoe)	3·25	4·25
1152	2p. Bow of fautasi	3·25	4·25

Nos. 1151/2 were printed together, *se-tenant*, forming a composite design.

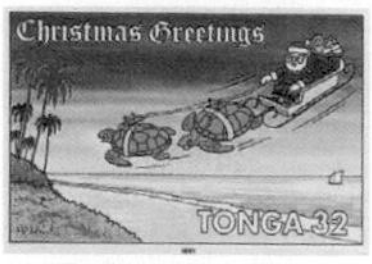

211 Turtles pulling Santa's Sledge

1991. Christmas. Multicoloured.

1153	32s. Type **211**	85	35
1154	42s. Santa Claus on roof of fala (Tongan house)	95	45
1155	57s. Family opening presents	1·10	60
1156	3p.50 Family waving goodbye to Santa	6·50	8·50

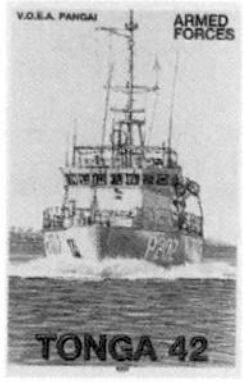

212 "Pangai" (patrol boat)

1991. Royal Tongan Defence Force. Multicoloured.

1157	42s. Type **212**	1·50	1·50
1158	42s. Marine in battle dress	1·50	1·50
1159	57s. Tonga Royal Guards	1·75	1·75
1160	57s. Raising the ensign on "Neiafu" (patrol boat)	1·75	1·75
1161	2p. "Savea" (patrol boat) (horiz)	3·50	4·25
1162	2p. King Taufa'ahau Tupou IV inspecting parade (horiz)	3·50	4·25

1992. No. 1007 surch **1s**.

1163	1s. on 20s. White-tailed damselfish	1·00	1·50

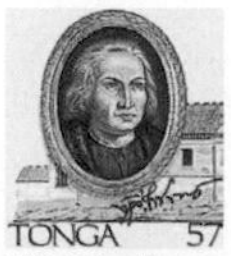

214 Columbus and Signature

1992. 500th Anniv of Discovery of America by Columbus. Sheet 119×109 mm containing T **214** and similar vert designs. Multicoloured.

MS1164 57s. Type **214**; 57s. Monastery of Santa Maria de la Chevas; 57s. Obverse and reverse of coin of Ferdinand and Isabella; 57s. Spain commemorative stamps of 1930; 57s. Compass and astrolabe; 57s. Model of "Santa Maria"; 57s. Sketch map and signature; 57s. 15th-century woodcut of Columbus arriving in New World; 57s. Lucayan artefacts and parrot; 57s. Pineapple, bird pendant and Indian nose ring; 57s. Columbus reporting to Spanish Court; 57s. Medal showing Columbus and signature	32·00	35·00

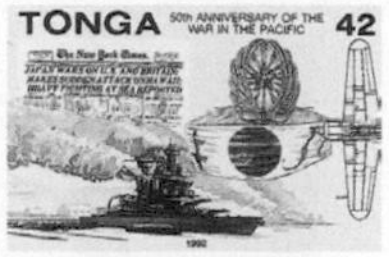

215 U.S.S. "Arizona" under attack, Pearl Harbor, 1941

1992. 50th Anniv of Outbreak of Pacific War. Multicoloured.

1165	42s. Type **215**	3·00	2·50
1166	42s. Japanese invasion of the Philippines	3·00	2·50
1167	42s. U.S. landings in the Gilbert Islands	3·00	2·50
1168	42s. Landing on Iwo Jima	3·00	2·50
1169	42s. Admiral Nimitz and Battle of Midway map	3·00	2·50
1170	42s. General MacArthur and liberation of Philippines map	3·00	2·50
1171	42s. Lt-Gen. Holland Smith and map of landings on Saipan and Tinian	3·00	2·50
1172	42s. Major-Gen. Curtis Lemay and bombing of Japan map	3·00	2·50
1173	42s. Japanese Mitsubishi A6M Zero-Sen	3·00	2·50
1174	42s. Douglas SBD Dauntless	3·00	2·50
1175	42s. Grumman FM-2 Wildcat	3·00	2·50
1176	42s. Supermarine Seafire Mk III	3·00	2·50

Nos. 1165/76 were printed togther, *se-tenant*, forming a composite design.

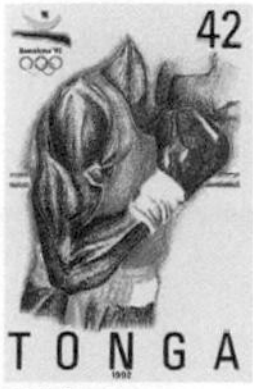

216 Boxing

1992. Olympic Games, Barcelona. Multicoloured.

1177	42s. Type **216**	75	50
1178	57s. Diving	95	55
1179	1p.50 Tennis	4·00	4·25
1180	3p. Cycling	6·00	6·50

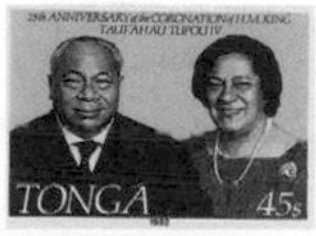

217 King Taufa'ahau Taupou IV and Queen Halaevalu

1992. 25th Anniv of the Coronation of King Tupou IV.

1181	217	45s. multicoloured	85	45
1182	-	80s. multicoloured	1·50	1·75
1183	-	80s. black and brown	1·50	1·75
1184	-	80s. multicoloured	1·50	1·75
1185	-	2p. multicoloured	3·50	4·00

DESIGNS—48×35 mm: No. 1182, King Tupou IV and Crown; 1183, Extract from Investiture ceremony; 1184, King Tupou IV and 1967 Coronation 2p. commemorative; 1185, As Type **217** but larger.

Nos. 1181/5 show the King's first name incorrectly spelt as "Tauf'ahau".

1992. No. 1095 surch **45s 45s.**

1186	45s. on 32s. Powder-blue surgeonfish	5·50	1·75

1992. Nos. 1121/4 surch **60.**

1187	60s. on 42s. Safety in cars (English inscr)	3·75	3·75
1188	60s. on 42s. Safety on bikes (English inscr)	3·75	3·75
1189	60s. on 42s. As No. 1187 (Tongan inscr)	3·75	3·75
1190	60s. on 42s. As No. 1188 (Tongan inscr)	3·75	3·75

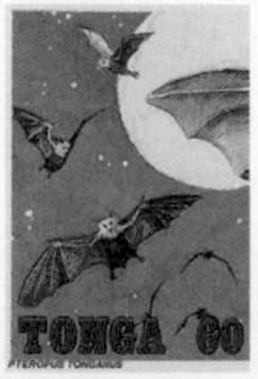

220 Bats flying Home

1992. Sacred Bats of Kolovai. Multicoloured.

1191	60s. Type **220**	1·60	1·75
1192	60s. Tongan fruit bat	1·60	1·75
1193	60s. Bats alighting on branches	1·60	1·75
1194	60s. Bats hanging from tree	1·60	1·75
1195	60s. Tongan fruit bat in tree	1·60	1·75

MS1196	96×112 mm. 45s. Kula leaving Tonga; 45s. Kula watching Chief's daughter dancing; 2p. Kula between fires and Hina; 2p. Kula leaving Samoa with bats (each 38×30 mm)	8·50	9·50

Nos. 1191/5 were printed together, *se-tenant*, forming a composite design.

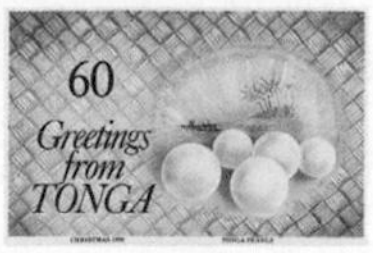

221 Tongan Pearls

1992. Christmas. Multicoloured.

1197	60s. Type **221**	70	65
1198	80s. Reef fish	90	80
1199	2p. Pacific orchids	4·25	5·00
1200	3p. Red shining parrots from Eua	5·50	7·00

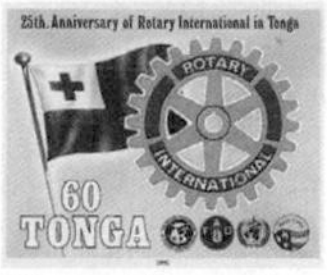

222 Tonga Flag and Rotary Emblem (25th anniv of Rotary International in Tonga)

1992. Anniversaries and Events.

1201	222	60s. multicoloured	1·00	65
1202	-	80s. multicoloured	1·25	90
1203	-	1p.50 violet, lilac & black	2·75	3·75
1204	-	3p.50 multicoloured	5·50	7·00

DESIGNS: 80s. Pres. Kennedy and Peace Corps emblem (25th anniv of Peace Corps in Tonga); 1p.50, F.A.O. and W.H.O. emblems (International Conference); 3p.50, Globe and Rotary Foundation emblem (75th anniv of Rotary Foundation).

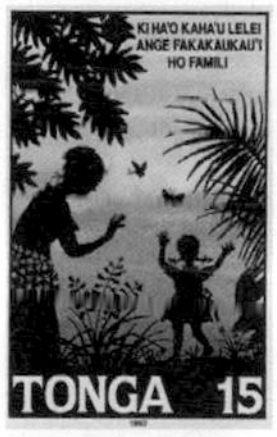

223 Mother and Child

1993. Family Planning.

1205	223	15s. black, blue and mauve (English inscr)	65	80
1206	-	15s. black, blue and mauve (Tongan inscr)	65	80
1207	-	45s. black, yellow and green (English inscr)	2·00	2·00
1208	-	45s. black, yellow and green (Tongan inscr)	2·00	2·00
1209	-	60s. black, red and yellow (English inscr)	2·25	2·50
1210	-	60s. black, red and yellow (Tongan inscr)	2·25	2·50
1211	-	2p. black, yellow & orange (English inscr)	8·00	8·50
1212	-	2p. black, yellow & orange (Tongan inscr)	8·00	8·50

DESIGNS: 45s. Child on bike; 60s. Girl with cats; 2p. Old man and boy playing chess.

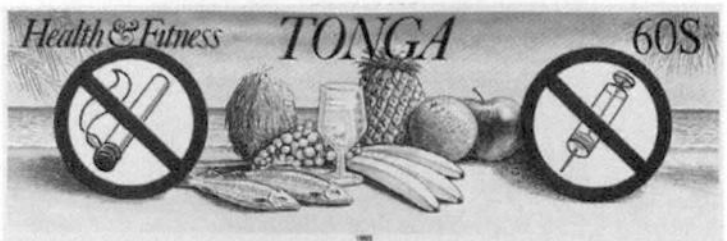

224 Anti-smoking and Anti-drugs Symbols with Healthy Food (image scaled to 58% of original size)

1993. Health and Fitness Campaign. Multicoloured.

1213	60s. Type **224**	1·25	90
1214	80s. Anti-smoking symbol and weight training	1·60	1·10
1215	1p.50 Anti-drugs symbol and water sports	2·75	3·50
1216	2p.50 Healthy food with cyclist and jogger	5·00	6·50

1993. Nos. 1001 and 1087 surch.

1217	10s. on 2s. "Porites sp."	60·00	15·00
1217a	20s. on 4s. Lionfish	£400	

For 1 to 10p. with species inscription at top left, see Nos. 1345/9.

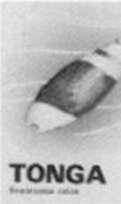

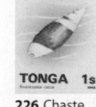

226 Chaste Mitre

1993. As Nos. 867, 872, 875, 877, 999, 1002, 1005, 1007, 1013/16 and 1017a, some with new face values, redrawn as in T **226** with species inscr at foot. Multicoloured.

1218	1s. Type **226**	25	1·00
1219	3s. Red squirrelfish	50	1·75
1220	5s. Green map cowrie	50	1·25
1221a	10s. Bubble cone	80	1·00
1223a	20s. White-tailed damselfish	1·00	1·00
1225a	45s. Giant spider conch (as No. 877)	1·25	70
1227a	60s. Princely cone (as No. 875)	1·50	1·25
1229a	80s. Lionfish (as No. 872)	1·50	1·25
1230	1p. "Chelonia mydas" (turtle)	1·25	1·50
1231	2p. "Birgus latro" (crab)	2·00	3·25
1232	3p. Rose-branch murex	2·75	5·50
1233	5p. Humpback whale (as No. 1014)	7·50	9·00
1234	10p. Variegated shark	28·00	32·00

Nos. 1218/29 are 19×22 mm, Nos. 1230/3 are 40×28 mm and No. 1234, 28×40 mm.

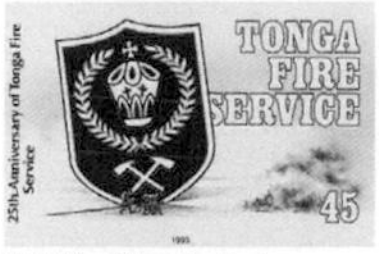

227 Fire Brigade Badge

1993. 25th Annivs of Police Training College and Fire Service. Multicoloured.

1235	45s. Type **227**	1·50	1·75
1236	45s. Police badge and van	1·50	1·75
1237	60s. Police band	1·75	2·00
1238	60s. Fire engine at fire	1·75	2·00
1239	2p. Fire engine at station	4·00	5·00
1240	2p. Policeman and dog handler	4·00	5·00

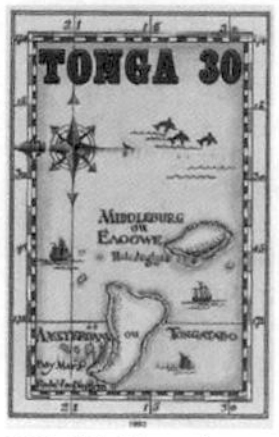

228 Old Map of Islands

1993. 300th Anniv of Abel Tasman's Discovery of Eua. Multicoloured.

1241	30s. Type **228**	85	55
1242	60s. "Heemskirk" and "Zeehaan" at sea	1·25	85
1243	80s. Tongan canoes welcoming ships	1·60	1·25
1244	3p.50 Tasman landing on Eua	6·00	8·00

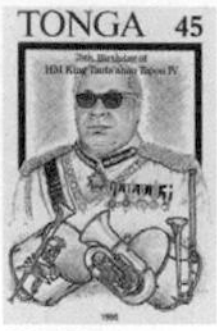

229 King Taufa'ahau Tupou IV and Musical Instruments

1993. 75th Birthday of King Taufa'ahau Tupou IV. Multicoloured.

1245	45s. Type **229**	60	45
1246	80s. King Tupou IV and sporting events	1·00	1·40
1247	80s. King Tupou IV and ancient landmarks	1·00	1·40
1248	80s. King Tupou IV and Royal Palace	1·00	1·40
1249	2p. As Type **229** but larger	2·50	3·25

Nos. 1246/9 are larger, 38½×51 mm.

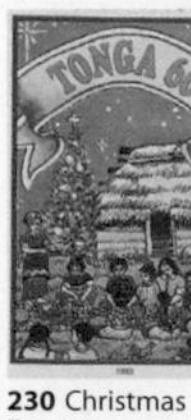

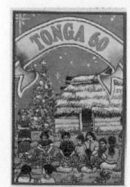

230 Christmas Feast

1993. Christmas. Multicoloured.

1250	60s. Type **230**	1·00	60
1251	80s. Firing home-made cannon	1·25	80
1252	1p.50 Band playing carols	2·50	3·25
1253	3p. Going to church	5·00	6·00

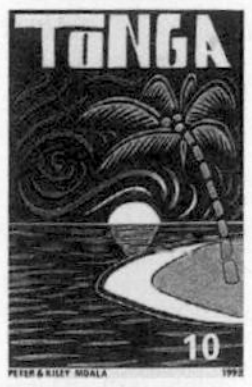

231 "Land of Sun, Sea and Sand" (Kiley and Peter Moala)

1993. Winners of Children's Painting Competition.

1254	231	10s. multicoloured	30	50
1255	-	10s. multicoloured	30	50
1256	-	10s. multicoloured	30	50
1257	-	10s. multicoloured	30	50
1258	-	10s. black and grey	30	50
1259	-	10s. black and grey	30	50
1260	231	80s. multicoloured	1·40	1·60
1261	-	80s. multicoloured	1·40	1·60
1262	-	80s. multicoloured	1·40	1·60
1263	-	80s. multicoloured	1·40	1·60
1264	-	80s. multicoloured	1·40	1·60
1265	-	80s. multicoloured	1·40	1·60

DESIGNS: Nos. 1255 and 1261, "Maui, Fisher God of Tonga" (Kiley and Peter Moala); 1256 and 1262, "Traditional Island Transport" (Kiley and Peter Moala); 1257 and 1263, "Young Girl making Kava" (Pulotu Pole'o); 1258 and 1264, "Maui and his Hook" (Salome Tapou); 1259 and 1265, "Communications in the South Pacific" (Fe'ofa'aki Taufa).

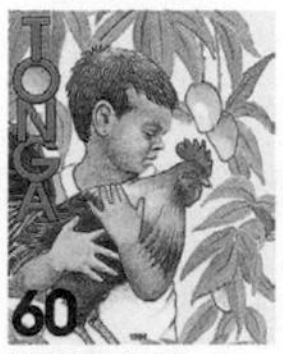

232 Boy holding Cockerel

1994. Animal Welfare. Sheet 122×100 mm, containing T **232** and similar vert designs. Multicoloured.

MS1266	60s. Type **232**; 60s. Girl with butterfly; 60s. Dog and puppies; 60s. Boy with puppy; 80s. Boy holding puppy; 80s. Girl holding cat	6·50	9·00

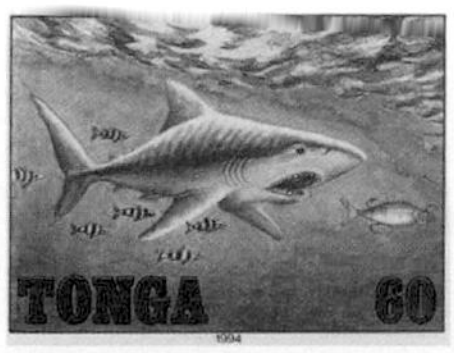

233 Tiger Shark

1994. Game Fishing. Multicoloured.

1267	60s. Type **233**	1·10	85
1268	80s. Dolphin (fish)	1·50	1·10
1269	1p.50 Yellow-finned tuna	2·75	3·50
1270	2p.50 Blue marlin	3·50	4·50

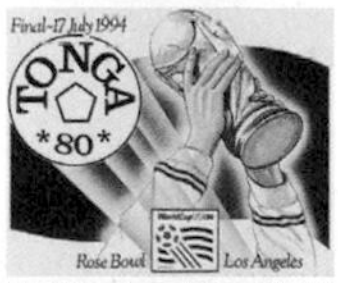

234 Hands holding World Cup

1994. World Cup Football Championship, U.S.A. Multicoloured.

1271	80s. Type **234**	1·50	1·50
1272	80s. Player's legs	1·50	1·50
1273	2p. German player (black shorts)	3·25	4·00
1274	2p. American player	3·25	4·00

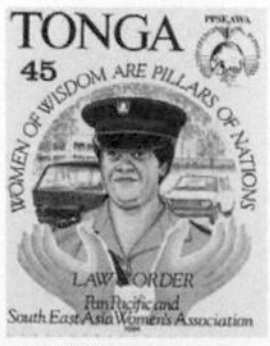

235 Policewoman

1994. Pan Pacific and South East Asia Women's Association Conference, Tonga. Multicoloured.

1275	45s. Type **235**	1·50	1·50
1276	45s. Woman barrister	1·50	1·50
1277	2p.50 Nurse	4·25	5·00
1278	2p.50 Woman doctor	4·25	5·00

1994. Christmas. No. **MS**1266 optd **MERRY CHRISTMAS** or equivalent in Tongan.

MS1279	60s. Type **232**; 60s. Girl with butterfly; 60s. Dog and puppies; 60s. Boy with puppy; 80s. Boy holding puppy; 80s. Girl holding cat	4·50	6·00

T **236** appears on five of the stamps from the miniature sheet.

The 60s. in the centre of the bottom row (dog and puppies) is overprinted "KILISIMASI FIEFIA".

1994. Visit South Pacific Year '95 (1st issue). No. 1204 surch **VISIT SOUTH PACIFIC YEAR '95 60** and emblem.

1280	60s. on 3p.50 multicoloured	1·50	1·50

See also Nos. 1297/1308.

1994. 25th Anniv of Tongan Self-adhesive Stamps. (a) Various previous self-adhesive designs, some in smaller size, with new values.

1281	**128**	10s. black and yellow (21×9 mm) (postage)	25	40
1282	**124**	60s. black, grey and brown	1·50	2·00
1283	-	60s. multicoloured (as Nos. O214/15)	1·50	2·00
1284	**109**	25s. multicoloured (27×36 mm) (air)	1·50	2·00

(b) As Nos. 915/18, but new face value and inscr "**SELF-ADHESIVE ANNIVERSARY 1969–1994**".

1285	**168**	45s. black, pink and brown	75	85
1286	-	45s. black, lilac and brown (as No. 916)	75	85
1287	-	45s. black, yellow and brown (as No. 917)	1·25	1·50
1288	-	45s. mult (as No. 918)	3·00	4·00

(c) Hologram design, 39×29 mm, showing "Tongastar 1" satellite.

1289	2p. multicoloured	6·50	7·50

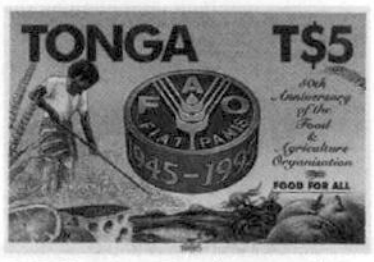

238 Farmer, Produce and Emblem

1995. 50th Anniv of F.A.O.

1290	**238**	5p. multicoloured	11·00	11·00

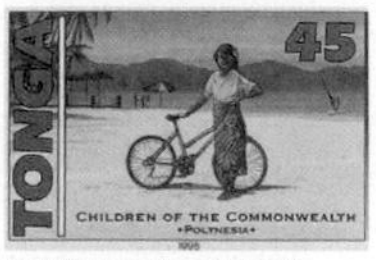

239 Polynesian Girl with Bicycle on Beach

1995. 25th Anniv of Tonga's Entry into Commonwealth. Children with Bicycles. Multicoloured.

1291	45s. Type **239**	75	55
1292	60s. Children and skyscrapers, Hong Kong	90	60
1293	80s. Boy in African village	1·25	80
1294	2p. Indian boy and palace	2·75	3·75
1295	2p.50 English children and village church	3·25	4·00

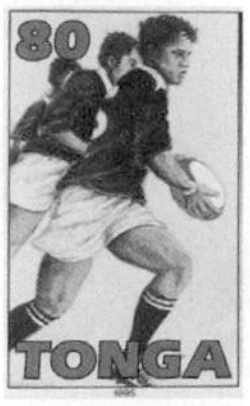

240 Three Players running with Ball

1995. World Cup Rugby Championship, South Africa. Two sheets, each 84×117 mm, containing T **240** and similar vert designs.

MS1296	(a) 80s.×2 Type **240**; 80s.×2 Two players running with ball. (b) 2p.×2 Player making pass; 2p.×2 Player receiving pass. Set of 2 sheets	15·00	16·00

The miniature sheets contain two of each design.

1995. Visit South Pacific Year '95 (2nd issue). (a) Nos. 1149/52, but inscr "VISIT SOUTH PACIFIC YEAR '95", optd or surch **WHERE TIME BEGINS** and emblem.

1297	60s. on 57s. Longboat	75	60
1298	80s. on 2p. Stern of fautasi (large canoe)	1·00	1·50
1299	80s. on 2p. Bow of fautasi	1·00	1·50
1300	1p. Outrigger canoe	1·40	1·75

(b) Nos. 1197/1200 inscr either (A) **"WHERE TIME BEGINS"** or (B) **"THE 21st CENTURY STARTS HERE"** and surch **WHERE TIME BEGINS 60** and emblem.

1301	60s. on 60s. Type **221** (A)	75	1·00
1302	60s. on 60s. Type **221** (B)	75	1·00
1303	60s. on 80s. Reef fish (A)	75	1·00
1304	60s. on 80s. Reef fish (B)	75	1·00
1305	60s. on 2p. Pacific orchids (A)	75	1·00
1306	60s. on 2p. Pacific orchids (B)	75	1·00
1307	60s. on 3p. Red shining parrots from Eua (A)	75	1·00
1308	60s. on 3p. Red shining parrots from Eua (B)	75	1·00

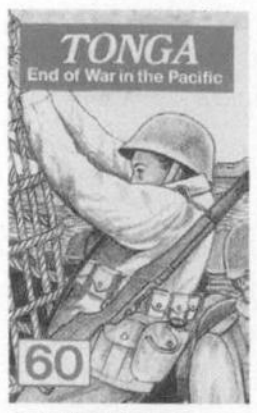

242 Soldier on Scrambling Net

1995. 50th Anniv of End of Second World War in the Pacific.

1309	**242**	60s. yellow, black & blue	1·40	1·75
1310	-	60s. yellow, black & blue	1·40	1·75
1311	-	60s. yellow, black & blue	1·40	1·75
1312	-	60s. multicoloured	1·40	1·75
1313	-	60s. multicoloured	1·40	1·75
1314	**242**	80s. yellow, black and red	1·40	1·75
1315	-	80s. yellow, black and red	1·40	1·75
1316	-	80s. yellow, black and red	1·40	1·75
1317	-	80s. multicoloured	1·40	1·75
1318	-	80s. multicoloured	1·40	1·75

DESIGNS: Nos. 1310 and 1315, U.S.S. "Nevada" (battleship) with troops in foreground; 1311 and 1316, U.S.S. "West Virginia" (battleship) and rear of landing craft; 1312 and 1317, U.S.S. "Idaho" (battleship) and front of landing craft; 1313 and 1318, Map of South-east Asia and Pacific.

Nos. 1309/18 were printed together, se-tenant, in sheetlets of 10 with the horizontal strips of 5 forming the same composite design.

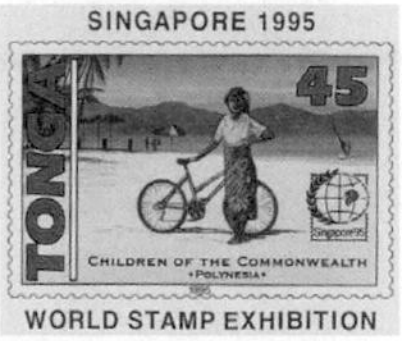

243 1995 Commonwealth 45s. Stamp and Exhibition Emblem

1995. "Singapore '95" International Stamp Exhibition. Multicoloured.

1319	45s. Type **243**	1·00	1·25
1320	60s. 1995 Commonwealth 60s. stamp and emblem	1·00	1·25

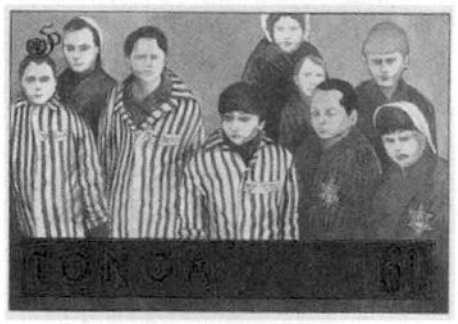

245 Holocaust Victims

1995. 50th Anniv of United Nations and End of Second World War.

1323	**245**	60s. multicoloured	1·00	1·25
1324	-	60s. black and blue	1·00	1·25
1325	-	60s. multicoloured	1·00	1·25
1326	-	80s. multicoloured	1·00	1·25
1327	-	80s. blue and black	1·00	1·25
1328	-	80s. multicoloured	1·00	1·25

DESIGNS—As T **245**: No. 1325, Children of Holocaust survivors with balloons; 1326, Atomic explosion, Hiroshima; 1328, U.S. Space Shuttle. 23×35 mm: Nos. 1324 and 1327, U.N. anniversary emblem.

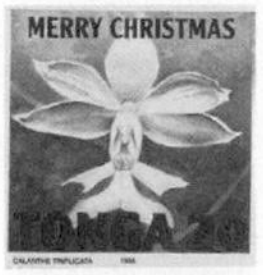

246 "Calanthe triplicata"

1995. Greetings Stamps. Orchids. Inscribed either "MERRY CHRISTMAS" (A) or "A HAPPY 1996" (B). Multicoloured.

1329	20s. Type **246** (A)	90	50
1330	45s. "Spathoglottis plicata" (A)	1·40	75
1331	45s. As No. 1330 (B)	1·40	75
1332	60s. "Dendrobium platygastrium" (A)	1·60	90
1333	60s. As No. 1332 (B)	1·60	90
1334	80s. "Goodyera rubicunda" (B)	1·75	1·25
1335	2p. "Dendrobium toki" (B)	3·75	4·50
1336	2p.50 "Phaius tankervillae" (A)	4·50	5·50

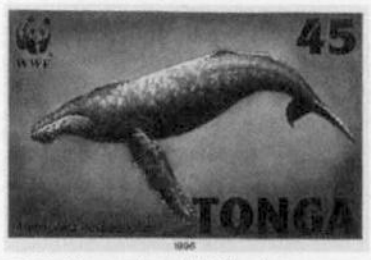

247 Humpback Whale

1996. Endangered Species. Humpback Whale. Multicoloured.

1337	45s. Type **247**	1·40	75
1338	60s. Whale and calf	1·75	90
1339	1p.50 Whale's tail and white-throated storm petrels	3·25	4·00
1340	2p.50 Whale breaking surface	4·75	6·50

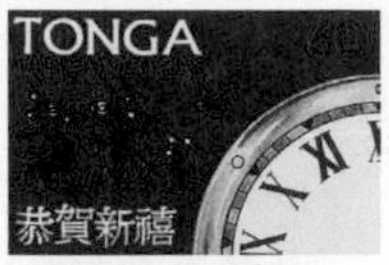

248 Rats and Top Left Quarter of Clock Face

1996. Chinese New Year ("Year of the Rat"). Sheets, 127×85 mm, containing T **248** and similar horiz designs showing rats and quarter segments of clock face. Multicoloured.

MS1341	10s. Type **248**; 10s. Top right quarter; 10s. Bottom left quarter; 10s. Bottom right quarter	75	1·00
MS1342	20s. Type **248**; 20s. Top right quarter; 20s. Bottom left quarter; 20s. Bottom right quarter	1·50	1·75
MS1343	45s. Type **248**; 45s. Top right quarter; 45s. Bottom left quarter; 45s. Bottom right quarter	2·00	3·00
MS1344	60s. Type **248**; 60s. Top right quarter; 60s. Bottom left quarter; 60s. Bottom right quarter	2·50	4·00

1996. Multicoloured designs as Nos. 1230/4, but redrawn with species inscriptions at top left.

1345	1p. "Chelonia mydas" (turtle)	5·00	2·75
1346	2p. "Birgus latro" (crab)	7·00	4·75
1347	3p. Rose branch murex	8·00	6·50
1348	5p. Humpback whale	18·00	17·00
1349	10p. Variegated shark (vert)	24·00	28·00

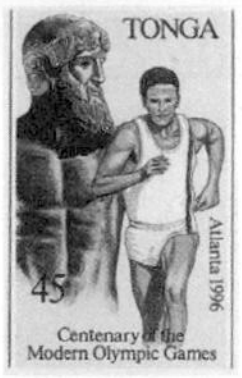

249 Running

1996. Centennial Olympic Games, Atlanta. Ancient Greek and Modern Athletes. Multicoloured.

1350	45s. Type **249**	90	65
1351	80s. Throwing the discus	1·50	1·25
1352	2p. Throwing the javelin	4·00	4·50
1353	3p. Equestrian dressage	5·50	6·50

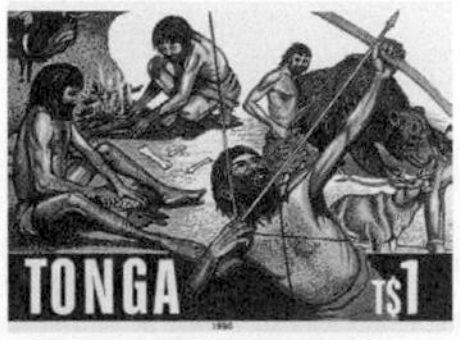

250 Aspects of Prehistoric Life

1996. 13th Congress of International Union of Prehistoric and Protohistoric Sciences, Forli, Italy. Multicoloured.

1354	1p. Type **250**	1·75	2·25
1355	1p. Aspects of Egyptian, Greek and Roman civilisations	1·75	2·25

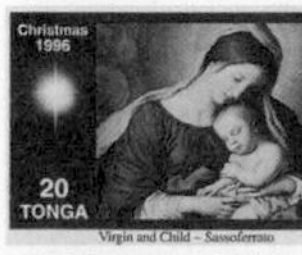

251 "Virgin and Child" (Sassoferrato)

1996. Christmas. Religious Paintings. Multicoloured.

1356	20s. Type **251**	45	45
1357	60s. "Adoration of the Shepherds" (Murillo)	1·10	75
1358	80s. "Virgin and Child" (Delaroche)	1·40	1·10
1359	3p. "Adoration of the Shepherds" (Champaigne)	4·50	6·00

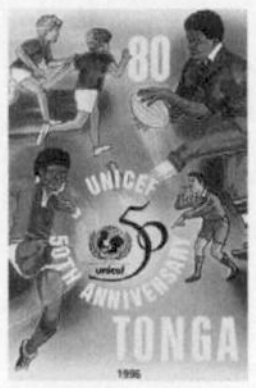

252 Athletics and Rugby

1996. 50th Anniv of UNICEF Children's Sports. Multicoloured.

1360	80s. Type **252**	1·60	2·00
1361	80s. Tennis	1·60	2·00
1362	80s. Cycling	1·60	2·00

Nos. 1360/2 were printed together, se-tenant, forming a composite design.

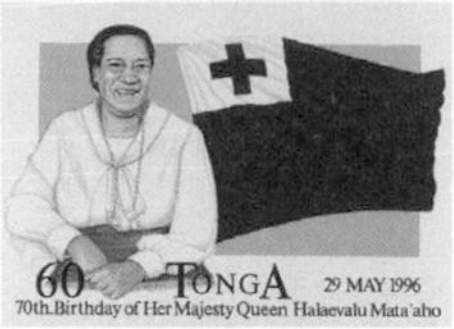

253 Queen Halaevalu Mata'aho and Flag

1996. 70th Birthday of Queen Halaevalu Mata'aho. Multicoloured.

1363	60s. Type **253**	1·00	65
1364	2p. Queen and obverse (portrait) of commemorative coin	3·25	4·00
1365	2p. Queen and reverse (arms) of commemorative coin	3·25	4·00

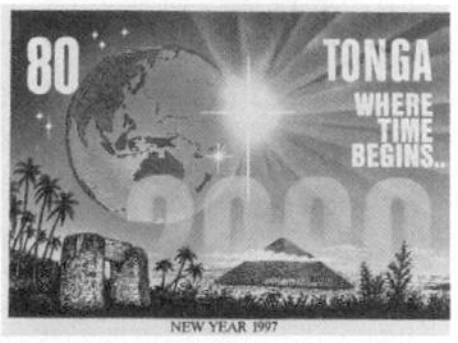

254 Globe, the Haamonga and Kao Island

1996. "Towards the Millennium". Multicoloured.

1366	80s. Type **254**	1·50	1·75
1367	80s. Mount Talau, Royal Palace and satellite	1·50	1·75
1368	2p. Type **254**	3·25	3·75
1369	2p. As No. 1367	3·25	3·75

1997. Chinese New Year ("Year of the Ox"). Sheet 126×85 mm, containing horiz designs as T **248**, showing ox and quarter segments of clock face. Multicoloured.

MS1370	60s. Top left quarter; 60s. Top right quarter; 80s. Bottom left quarter; 2p. Bottom right quarter	4·50	6·50

1997. Nos. 1235/40 surch.

1371	10s. on 45s. Type **227**	2·75	2·50
1372	10s. on 45s. Police badge and van	2·75	2·50
1373	10s. on 60s. Police band	2·75	2·50
1374	10s. on 60s. Fire engine at fire	2·75	2·50
1375	20s. on 2p. Fire engine at station	3·25	3·00
1376	20s. on 2p. Policeman and dog handler	3·25	3·00

1997. 75th Anniv of Tongan Rugby Union No. **MS**1296 surch (A) **FAKAMANATU TA'U 75 'OE 'AKAPULU 'IUNIONI 'I TONGA** or (B) **"75th ANNIVERSARY TONGA RUGBY FOOTBALL UNION".**

MS1377	Two sheets, each 84×117 mm. (a) 10s. on 80s. Type **240** (A); 10s. on 80s. Type **240** (B) 10s. on 80s. Two players running with ball (A); 10s. on 80s. Two players running with ball (B). (b) 1p. on 2p. Player making pass (A); 1p. on 2p. Player making pass (B); 1p. on 2p. Player receiving pass (A); 1p. on 2p. Player receiving pass (B) Set of 2 sheets	12·00	13·00

1997. Tongan Medal Winner at Atlanta Olympic Games. Nos. 1350/3 surch **A SILVER FOR TONGA.**

1378	10s. on 45s. Type **249**	70	90
1379	10s. on 80s. Throwing the discus	70	90
1380	10s. on 2p. Throwing the javelin	70	90
1381	3p. Equestrian dressage	9·00	10·00

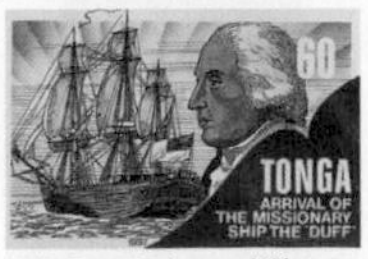

258 Captain James Wilson and "Duff" (full-rigged missionary ship)

1997. Birth Bicentenary of King George I and Bicentenary of Christianity in Tonga (1st issue). Multicoloured.

1382	10s. Type **258**	3·00	3·00

1383	10s. King George Tupou I	85	85
1384	10s. Missionaries landing at Tongatapu	3·00	3·00
1385	10s. Missionaries and Tongans	3·00	3·00
1386	60s. Type **258**	2·50	2·50
1387	60s. As No. 1384	2·50	2·50
1388	60s. As No. 1385	2·50	2·50
1389	80s. Type **258**	2·50	2·50
1390	80s. As No. 1384	2·50	2·50
1391	80s. As No. 1385	2·50	2·50

For 10s. (value as Nos. 1382/5, but smaller, 28×18 mm), see Nos. 1405/8.

259 Pacific Swallow

1997. "Pacific '97" International Stamp Exhibition, San Francisco. Sheet 84×110 mm.

| MS1392 **259** 2p. multicoloured | 3·00 | 4·00 |

260 Children and School Building

1997. 50th Anniv of Tonga High School. Multicoloured.

1393	20s. Type **260**	55	55
1394	60s. Athletic team	1·10	75
1395	80s. School band	1·60	1·00
1396	3p.50 Athletics meeting	4·25	6·50

Queen of Tonga during Coronation

1997. King and Queen of Tonga's Golden Wedding and 30th Anniv of the Coronation. Multicoloured. (a) Size 23×34 mm.

1397	10s. Type **261**	1·25	1·25
1398	10s. Moment of Crowning and procession	1·25	1·25
1399	10s. King and Queen of Tonga	1·25	1·25
1400	45s. Royal Crown	1·50	1·50

(b) Size 50×37 mm.

1401	60s. As T **261**	1·75	1·75
1402	60s. As No. 1398	1·75	1·75
1403	60s. As No. 1399	1·75	1·75
1404	2p. As No. 1400	3·75	4·25

1997. Birth Bicentenary of King George I and Bicentenary of Christianity in Tonga (2nd issue). As Nos. 1382/5, but smaller, 28×18 mm.

1405	10s. Type **258**	1·00	1·00
1406	10s. As No. 1384	1·00	1·00
1407	10s. As No. 1385	1·00	1·00
1408	10s. As No. 1383	60	60

262 "Lenzites elegans"

1997. Fungi. Multicoloured. (a) Size 18×28 mm.

1409	10s. Type **262**	2·00	2·00
1410	10s. "Marasmiellus semiustus"	2·00	2·00
1411	10s. "Aseroe rubra"	2·00	2·00
1412	10s. "Podoscypha involuta"	2·00	2·00
1413	10s. "Microporus xanthopus"	2·00	2·00
1414	10s. "Lentinus tuber-regium"	2·00	2·00

(b) Size 28×42 mm.

1415	20s. Type **262**	2·00	2·00
1416	20s. As No. 1410	2·00	2·00
1417	60s. As No. 1411	2·25	2·25
1418	60s. As No. 1412	2·25	2·25
1419	2p. As No. 1413	3·50	3·50
1420	2p. As No. 1414	3·50	3·50

Nos. 1409/14 were printed together, *se-tenant*, with the backgrounds forming a composite design.

1998. Diana, Princess of Wales Commemoration. Sheet, 145×170 mm, containing vert designs as T **194** of St. Helena. Multicoloured.

| MS1421 | 10s. Princess Diana, 1992; 80s. Wearing white jacket, 1992; 1p. Wearing black jacket, 1991; 2p.50, Wearing white top, 1993 (sold at 4p.40+50s. charity premium) | 2·00 | 3·50 |

263 King Taufa'ahua Tupou IV

1998. 80th Birthday of King Taufa'ahua Tupou IV.

| 1422 | **263** | 2p.70 multicoloured | 5·50 | 5·50 |
| MS1423 | 80×90 mm. 2p.70, No. 1422 2p.70, No. 276 of Niuafo'ou | | 7·50 | 8·00 |

1998. Chinese New Year ("Year of the Tiger"). Sheet, 126×85 mm, containing horiz designs as T **248**, each showing a tiger and quarter segment of clock face. Multicoloured.

| MS1424 | 55s. Top left quarter; 80s. Top right quarter; 1p. Bottom left quarter; 1p. Bottom right quarter | | 4·75 | 5·00 |

264 White Tern ("Fairy Tern")

1998. Birds. Multicoloured.

1425	5s. Type **264**	40	60
1426	10s. Tongan whistler	55	55
1427	15s. Barn owl	1·00	50
1428	20s. Purple swamphen	60	30
1429	30s. Red-footed booby	1·00	60
1430	40s. Buff-banded rail ("Banded Rail") (horiz)	1·25	60
1431	50s. Pacific marsh harrier ("Swamp Harrier") (horiz)	1·40	75
1432	55s. Blue-crowned lorikeet	1·40	75
1433	60s. Great frigate bird	1·50	1·00
1434	70s. Friendly quail dover ("Friendly Ground Dove") (horiz)	1·50	1·10
1435	80s. Red-tailed tropic bird	1·75	1·10
1436	1p. Red shining parrot	2·00	1·75
1437	2p. Pacific pigeon	3·50	3·50
1438	3p. Pacific golden plover (horiz)	4·50	5·00
1439	5p. Polynesian scrub hen ("Tongan Megapode") (horiz)	6·00	7·00

265 "Chaetodon pelewensis"

1998. International Year of the Ocean. Multicoloured.

1440	10s. Type **265**	55	75
1441	55s. "Chaetodon lunula"	1·10	1·40
1442	1p. "Chaetodon ephippium"	1·40	2·00

266 Angel (inscr in Tongan)

1998. Christmas. Multicoloured.

1443	10s. Type **266**	60	40
1444	80s. Angel (inscr in English)	2·25	1·00
1445	1p. Boy with candle (inscr in Tongan)	2·50	1·75
1446	1p.60 Girl holding candle (inscr in English)	3·50	4·50

267 Rabbit and Segment of Flower

1999. Chinese New Year ("Year of the Rabbit"). Sheet 126×85 mm, containing horiz designs as T **267**, showing rabbits and segments of flower. Multicoloured.

| MS1447 | 10s. Three rabbits; 55s. Rabbit eating leaf; 80s. Type **267**; 1p. Rabbit running | | 2·00 | 2·50 |

268 "Heemskerk" (Tasman), 1643

1999. Early Explorers. Multicoloured.

1448	55s. Type **268**	1·75	75
1449	80s. "L'Astrolabe" (La Perouse), 1788	2·25	1·00
1450	1p. H.M.S. "Bounty" (Bligh), 1789	3·25	2·50
1451	2p.50 H.M.S. "Resolution" (Cook), 1777	4·50	5·00
MS1452	118×60 mm. No. 1451	5·00	5·50

269 Neiafu

1999. Scenic Views of Vava'u. Multicoloured.

1453	10s. Type **269**	55	40
1454	55s. Yachts at Port of Refuge	1·00	50
1455	80s. Port of Refuge from the air	1·75	80
1456	1p. Sunset at Neiafu	2·00	1·75
1457	2p.50 Mounu Island	3·50	5·00

270 "Fagraea berteroana"

1999. Fragrant Flowers. Multicoloured.

1458	10s. Type **270**	30	25
1459	80s. "Garcinia pseudoguttfera"	90	65
1460	1p. "Phaleria disperma" (vert)	1·25	1·40
1461	2p.50 "Gardenia taitensis" (vert)	2·75	3·75

271 Crowd and Trilith at Haamonga

1999. New Millennium (1st issue). Multicoloured.

1462	55s. Type **271**	80	1·10
1463	80s. Crowd and doves	1·10	1·40
1464	1p. Tongans watching sunrise	1·25	1·60
1465	2p.50 King Tauf'ahau Tupou IV, dove and Millennium emblem	1·90	2·25

Nos. 1462/5 were printed together, *se-tenant*, with the backgrounds forming a composite design.

272 Dove and Heilala (flowers)

2000. New Millennium (2nd issue). Circular designs incorporating a clock face and inscribed "FIRST TO SEE THE MILLENNIUM". Multicoloured.

1466	10s. Type **272**	35	35
1467	1p. Haamonga Arch	1·40	1·40
1468	2p.50 Kalia (traditional canoe)	3·00	3·25
1469	2p.70 Royal Crown	3·00	3·25
MS1470	130×90 mm. Nos. 1468/9	6·50	7·00

273 Dragon

2000. Chinese New Year ("Year of the Dragon"). Sheet, 126×85 mm, containing T **273** and similar horiz designs. Multicoloured.

| MS1471 | 10s. Type **273**; 55s. Dragon blowing on sphere; 80s. Dragon on hills; 1p. Sea dragon | | 2·50 | 3·00 |

274 Queen Elizabeth the Queen Mother

2000. "The Stamp Show 2000" International Stamp Exhibition, London. Queen Elizabeth the Queen Mother's 100th Birthday. Sheet, 106×71 mm, containing T **274** and similar vert design. Multicoloured.

| MS1472 | 1p. Type **274**; 2p.50, Queen Salote Tupou III of Tonga | | 3·50 | 4·00 |

275 Launch of Proton RU500

2000. "EXPO 2000" World Stamp Exhibition, Anaheim, U.S.A. Geostationary Orbital Slot Space Programme. Multicoloured.

1473	10s. Type **275**	35	35
1474	1p. LM3 rocket for "Apstar 1" satellite (horiz)	1·25	1·75
1475	2p.50 "Apstar 1" satellite in orbit (horiz)	2·50	3·25
1476	2p.70 "Gorizont" satellite over Tonga (horiz)	2·50	3·25
MS1477	134×80 mm. (trapezium). Nos. 1475/6		5·50	6·50

276 Siulolo Liku (hurdling)

2000. Olympic Games, Sydney. Multicoloured.

1478	80s. Type **276**	1·10	1·25
1479	80s. Paea Wolfgramm (boxing)	1·10	1·25
1480	80s. Olympic Torch passing through Tonga (60×45 mm)	1·10	1·25
1481	80s. Mele Hifo Uhi (discus)	1·10	1·25
1482	80s. Viliami Toutai (weightlifting)	1·10	1·25

Nos. 1478/82 were printed together, *se-tenant*, with a composite series of Australian landmarks running along the bottom of each strip.

277 "Education"

2000. 30th Anniv of Tonga's Membership of the Commonwealth. Multicoloured.

1483	10s. Type **277**	25	25
1484	55s. "The Arts"	60	45
1485	80s. "Health"	85	65
1486	2p.70 "Agriculture"	2·50	3·50

278 Snake

2001. Chinese New Year ("Year of the Snake") and "Hong Kong 2001" Stamp Exhibition. Sheet 125×87 mm, containing T **278** and similar horiz designs showing different snakes.

MS1487 10s. multicoloured; 55s. multicoloured; 80s. multicoloured; 1p. multicoloured .... 3·25   3·50

279 Ma'ulu'ulu Dance

2001. Traditional Tongan Dances. Multicoloured.
1488	10s. Type **279**	30	20
1489	55s. Me'etupaki dance	70	45
1490	80s. Tau'olunga dance	85	65
1491	2p.70 Faha'iula dance	2·50	3·50

280 Fiddler Crab

2001. International Mangrove Environment Day. Multicoloured.
1492	10s. Type **280**	25	25
1493	55s. Spotbill duck ("Black Ducks") and grey mullet (vert)	65	45
1494	80s. Red mangrove and emperor fish (vert)	85	65
1495	1p. Mangrove flowers and reef heron	1·00	1·10
1496	2p.70 Mangrove crab	2·50	3·50
MS1497	165×75 mm. Nos. 1492/6	4·50	5·50

281 Fisherman catching Sailfish

2001. Game Fishing in Tonga. Multicoloured.
1498	45s. Type **281**	1·50	1·25
1499	80s. Blue marlin and fishing launch	1·75	1·75
1500	2p.40 Wahoo	3·00	3·25
1501	2p.60 Dorado	3·25	3·50

282 Banana

2001. Fruit. Multicoloured. Self-adhesive.
1502	10s. Type **282**	50	70
1503	45s. Coconut	90	1·00
1504	60s. Pineapple	1·00	1·10
1505	80s. Watermelon	1·10	1·25
1506	2p.40 Passion fruit	2·00	2·25

Nos. 1502/6 were printed together, *se-tenant*, with the surplus self-adhesive paper around each stamp showing a composite design of foliage.

283 *Haliotis ovina* Shell

2001. Shells. Multicoloured.
1507	10s. Type **283**	25	30
1508	80s. *Turbo petholatus*	85	85
1509	1p. *Trochus niloticus*	1·00	1·25
1510	2p.70 *Turbo marmoratus*	2·50	3·75

2002. Golden Jubilee. Sheet, 162×95 mm, containing designs as T **211** of St. Helena.

MS1511 15s. brownish black, rosine and gold; 90s. multicoloured; 1p.20, grey-black, rosine and gold; 1p.40, multicoloured; 2p.25, multicoloured .... 7·00   8·00

DESIGNS—HORIZ: (as Type **211** of St. Helena)—15s. Princess Elizabeth as a young girl; 90s. Queen Elizabeth in yellow outfit; 1p.20, Queen Elizabeth with Prince Charles and Princess Anne; 1p.40, Queen Elizabeth in evening dress. VERT: (38×51 mm)—2p.25, Queen Elizabeth after Annigoni.

284 Horses galloping

2002. Chinese New Year ("Year of the Horse"). Sheet 126×89 mm, containing T **284** and similar vert designs. Multicoloured.

MS1512 65s. Type **284**; 90s. Palomino and grey horses; 1p. Chestnut horse rearing; 2p.50 Pie-bald and bay horses .... 5·50   6·00

285 Surfer and Whale

2002. U.N. Year of Eco Tourism. Multicoloured.
1513	5s. Type **285**	45	45
1514	15s. Tongan girl and rocky coastline	45	45
1515	70s. Tropical fish and tourist beach	1·25	1·00
1516	1p.40 Island dancer and Haamonga trilith	2·00	2·00
1517	2p.25 Tongan man and canoes at sunset	3·00	3·50

286 Oyster Farm

2002. Development of Tonga Pearl Industry. Multicoloured.
1518	90s. Type **286**	1·10	1·25
1519	1p. Oysters on underwater frame	1·10	1·25
1520	1p.20 Tongan girl and pearls	1·40	1·75
1521	2p.50 Pearls and island scene	2·75	3·75
MS1522	Circular (97 mm diameter). Nos. 1520/1.	5·75	7·25

287 Leaping for Ball

2002. 17th Commonwealth Games, Manchester. Rugby Sevens. Multicoloured.
1523	15s. Type **287**	65	35
1524	30s. Players in a ruck	90	40
1525	90s. Running with ball	1·75	1·00
1526	4p. Scoring a try	6·50	8·50

288 Woman slitting Pandanus Leaves

2002. Weaving. Multicoloured.
1527	30s. Type **288**	50	25
1528	90s. Leaves drying and boy with large baskets	1·00	70
1529	1p.40 Women weaving baskets	1·60	1·75
1530	2p.50 Girl weaving basket lid	2·75	4·00

/ **15** 10s XX
(289) (290) (291)

10s XX 15¢
(292) (293)

XX XX XX

05s 45s 05s
(294) (295) (296)

XX

5s 60s 10s XX
(297) (298) (299)

XX

10s

XX 10s
(300) (301)

XX

XX

10s

10s XX 10s
(302) (303) (304)

XX

10s 10s XX
(305) (306)

XX

5c
(307)

2002. Various stamps surch as T **289/90**. (a) On Nos. 1432 and 1436.
1531	5s. on 55s. Blue-crowned lorikeet	25·00	20·00
1532	15s. on 1p. Red shining parrot	25·00	20·00

(b) On Nos. 1139/47 as T **291** (Nos. 1533/8) or **292**.
1533	10s. on 32s. Man on telephone and woman with computer	22·00	15·00
1534	10s. on 32s. Telecommunications satellite	22·00	15·00
1535	10s. on 32s. Overseas customer on telephone	22·00	15·00
1536	10s. on 42s. Sinking coaster		
1537	10s. on 42s. Coastguard controller		
1538	10s. on 42s. Maritime rescue		
1539	10s. on 57s. Weather satellite above Southern Hemisphere	32·00	25·00
1540	10s. on 57s. Meteorologist collecting data	32·00	25·00
1541	10s. on 57s. TV weather map and storm	32·00	25·00

On Nos. 1539/41 the new value is placed at the top left of the illustration, below "TONGA". On Nos. 1533/8 the relative positions of the new value and the X's vary but both are always placed above the illustration, level with "TONGA".

No. 1534 has been reported with overprint double.

(c) On No. 1432 as T **293**.
1542	15s. on 55s. Blue-crowned lorikeet	40·00	50·00
1543	20s. on 55s. Blue-crowned lorikeet	£300	25·00
1544	45s. on 55s. Blue-crowned lorikeet	25·00	

(d) No. 1432 surch as T **294** (No. 1545) or **295**.
1545	5s. on 55s. Blue-crowned lorikeet	25·00	75·00
1546	45s. on 55s. Blue-crowned lorikeet	40·00	

(e) On No. 1432 as T **296**.
1547	5s. on 55s. Blue-crowned lorikeet	£150	
1548	10s. on 55s. Blue-crowned lorikeet	25·00	
1549	15s. on 55s. Blue-crowned lorikeet	20·00	40·00
1550	20s. on 55s. Blue-crowned lorikeet	13·00	20·00

Examples of No. 1549 are known with the X's misplaced to the right and the original value obliterated in manuscript.

(f) On No. 1432 as T **297**.
1551	5s. on 55s. Blue-crowned lorikeet	10·00	20·00
1552	10s. on 55s. Blue-crowned lorikeet	24·00	
1553	15s. on 55s. Blue-crowned lorikeet	10·00	20·00
1554	20s. on 55s. Blue-crowned lorikeet	25·00	30·00

(g) On No. 1434 as T **298**.
1555	60s. on 70s. Friendly ground dove (horiz)	17·00	

(h) On Nos. 1153/4 as T **299** (Nos. 1556/7) or **300**.
1556	10s. on 32s. Type **211**	25·00	£100
1557	10s. on 42s. Santa Claus on roof of fala (Tongan house)	75·00	£100
1558	10s. on 42s. Santa Claus on roof of fala		

(i) On Nos. 1177/8 as T **301**.
1559	10s. on 42s. Type **216**	£180	£180
1560	10s. on 57s. Diving	45·00	

(j) On Nos. 1125/8 as T **302** (Nos. 1561/2) or **303**.
1561	10s. on 57s. Safety at sea (English inscription)	55·00	
1562	10s. on 57s. Safety on the beach (English inscription)	55·00	
1563	10s. on 57s. Safety on the beach (Tongan inscription)	55·00	
1564	10s. on 57s. Safety at sea (Tongan inscription)	55·00	

The new value is lower in relation to the "X's" on No. 1562 and higher on No. 1564 when compared to Nos. 1561 and 1563.

(k) On No. 162 of Niuafo'ou surch as T **304**.
1565	10s. on 42s. Heina crying over the eel's grave	45·00	75·00

(l) On Nos. 157/8 of Niuafo'ou surch as T **305** (No. 1566) or **306**.
1566	10s. on 42s. Type **30** of Niuafo'ou	£180	
1567	10s. on 57s. Adult beetle	£180	

Nos. 1566/7 on stamps of Niuafo'ou were used throughout Tonga.

(m) No. 1432 surch as T **307**.
1568	5s. on 55s. Blue-crowned lorikeet	10·00	
1569	10s. on 55s. Red-crowned lorikeet	18·00	
1570	15s. on 55s. Red-crowned lorikeet	24·00	

Surcharged values. Note that, to aid identification, for Nos. 1531/70 the surcharged values are shown as they appear on the stamps.

308 Red Shining Parrots in Tree Trunk Nest

2002. Tenth Anniv of Eua National Park. Red Shining Parrots. Multicoloured.
1571	45s. Type **308**	75	45
1572	1p. Eating fruit	1·25	1·00
1573	1p.50 Two parrots on branch	1·75	2·00
1574	2p.50 Red shining parrot with wings spread	2·75	3·75

309 Ram

2003. Chinese New Year ("Year of the Sheep"). Sheet 125×85 mm, containing T **309** and similar horiz designs. Multicoloured.

MS1575 65p. Type **309**; 80p. Three ewes; 1p. Three black-faced ewes; 2p.50 Two ewes	6·50	7·00

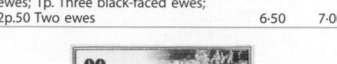

310 Queen Elizabeth II in Gold State Coach

2003. 50th Anniv of Coronation.

1576	**310**	90s. blue and gold	90	55
1577	-	1p.20 blue and gold	1·10	1·25
1578	-	1p.40 blue and gold	1·40	1·60
1579	-	2p.50 blue and gold	2·50	3·25

DESIGNS: 90s. Type **310**; 1p.20 Queen Salote; 1p.40 Queen Salote waving in carriage; 2p.50 Queen Elizabeth.

311 Fishing and Double-Hulled Canoes

2003. Abel Tasman Commemoration. In Search of the Great South Land.

1580	**311**	15s. drab, red and black	60	50
1581	-	75s. drab, red and black	1·25	80
1582	-	90s. stone, red and black	1·50	1·00
1583	-	2p.50 stone, red and black	6·75	7·00
MS1584		165×75 mm. Nos. 1540/3	9·00	9·00

DESIGNS: 15s. Type **311**; 75s. Men rowing ashore with barrels; 90s.Two double-hulled canoes; 2p.50 *Heemskerk* and *Zeehan*.

312 Euakafa Beach

2003. Scenic Beaches. Multicoloured.

1585	**312**	15s. Type **312**	50	35
1586		90s. Panqaimotu beach	1·25	70
1587		1p.40 Fafa beach	1·75	2·00
1588		2p.25 Nuku beach	3·00	3·50

313 Catholic Church, Neiafu, Vava'u

2003. Christmas. Churches. Multicoloured.

1589	**313**	15s. Type **313**	50	35
1590		90s. Wesleyan Church, Uiha, Ha'apai	1·25	70
1591		1p.40 Cathedral of the Immaculate Conception of Mary	1·75	2·25
1592		2p.25 Free Wesleyan Church, Nuku'alofa	3·00	4·00

314 Spider Monkey

2004. Chinese New Year ("Year of the Monkey"). Sheet 95×85 mm containing T **314** and similar horiz designs. Multicoloured.

MS1593 60s. Type **314**; 80s. Ring-tailed lemur; 1p. Cotton-top tamarin; 2p.50 White-cheeked gibbon	5·50	6·00

315 King George Tupou I (1875–93)

2004. Royal Succession. Multicoloured.

1594	65s. Type **315**	65	40
1595	90s. King George Tupou II (1893–1918)	85	60
1596	1p.40 Queen Salote Tupou III (1918–65)	1·25	1·50
1597	3p.05 King Taufa'ahau Tupou IV (1965–)	2·50	4·00
MS1598	160×65 mm. Nos. 1594/7	4·75	6·00

Stamps in the same designs were also issued by Niuafo'ou.

316 Mango Tree

2004. Trees. Multicoloured.

1599	45s. Type **316**	85	50
1600	60s. Pineapple tree	1·10	70
1601	80s. Coconut tree	1·40	90
1602	1p.80 Banana tree	3·00	4·25

317 Mary and Baby Jesus

2004. Christmas. Multicoloured.

1603	65s. Type **317**	1·25	60
1604	80s. Mary and Joseph on the way to Bethlehem	1·40	90
1605	1p.20 The Shepherds	2·25	2·00
1606	2p.50 The Three Wise Men	4·50	5·50

318 Rooster

2005. Chinese New Year ("Year of the Rooster"). Sheet 95×85 mm, containing T **318** and similar horiz designs. Multicoloured.

MS1607 65s. Type **318**; 80s. Rooster and palm trees; 1p. Rooster with wings spread; 2p.50 Three roosters	8·50	9·00

319 Humpback Whale

2005. Whales. Sheet, 160×85 mm, containing T **319** and similar horiz designs. Multicoloured.

MS1608 65s. Type **319**; 80s. Whale swimming; 1p. Two whales; 2p.50 Whale and diver	12·00	12·00

XX

XX

30s (**321**)	XX	30s (**322**)	30s (**323**)

XX

70s (**324**)	70s (**325**)	XX

XX

70s
(**326**)

2008. Various stamps surch by PO staff (Nos. 1609/12) or by the Government Printer, Nuku'alofa (others)

(a) Handstamped in two operations as T **320**

1609	30s. on 55s. Crowned Lorikeet (Niuafo'ou No. 271) (11.09)		

1610	30s. on 55s. Angel playing violin (Niuafo'ou No. 282)		
1611	30s. on 55s. *Jamides bochus* (butterfly) (Niuafo'ou No. 297) (7.08)		
1612	30s. on 55s. "The Arts" (No. 1484) (6.7.08)		

(b) Surch as T **321**

1613	30s. on 55s. Yachts at Port of Refuge (No. 1454) (10.11.08)	40·00	40·00

(c) Surch as T **322**

1614	30s. on 55s. Blue-crowned Lorikeet (No. 1432) (19.11.09)	25·00	25·00

(d) Surch as T **323**

1615	30s. on 55s. Black Ducks and Grey Mullet (No. 1493) (25.2.10)	25·00	25·00

(e) Surch as T **324**

1616	70s. on 55s. Blue-crowned Lory (Niuafo'ou No. 271)	50·00	50·00

(f) Surch as T **325**

1617	70s. on 55s. Barn Owls (Niuafo'ou No. 308) (10.5.10)	50·00	50·00

(g) Surch as T **326**

1618	70s. on 55s. Me'etupaki dance (No. 1489) (10.5.10)	32·00	32·00

327 King Siaosi Tupou V

2008. Coronation of King Siaosi Tupou V. Multicoloured.

1619	30s. Type **327**	43	43
1620	1p. King Siaosi Tupou V in evening dress	1·00	1·25
MS1621	120×91 mm. 5p. Coronation portrait (30×60 mm)	7·00	7·00

328 Christmas Decorations

2011. Christmas. Multicoloured.

1622	3p. Type **328**	3·00	3·50
1623	5p. Free Church of Tonga, Nuku'alofa	5·00	5·50

329 *Prosopeia tabuensis* (Red Shining Parrot)

2012. Birds (1st series). Multicoloured.

1624	60s. Type **329**	60	30
1625	2p.25 *Anas superciliosa* (Pacific Black Duck)	2·25	2·50
1626	2p.40 *Halcyon chloris* (White-collared Kingfisher)	2·40	2·75
1627	2p.50 *Egretta novaehollandiae* (White-faced Heron)	2·50	2·75
1628	2p.70 *Aplonis tabuensis* (Polynesian Starling)	2·75	3·00
1629	3p. *Megapodius pritchardii* (Polynesian Scrub Hen)	3·00	3·25
1630	3p.40 Honeyeater (wrongly inscr *Megapodius pritchardii*)	3·50	4·00
1631	4p. *Lalage maculosa* (Spotted Triller)	4·00	4·50
1632	5p. *Tyto alba* (Barn Owl)	5·00	5·50
1633	6p.60 Buff-banded Rail (wrongly inscr *Halcyon chloris*)	6·50	7·00
1634	7p.30 Purple Swamphen (wrongly inscr *Prosopeia tabuensis*)	7·50	8·00
1635	10p. Swamp Harrier	10·00	10·50
MS1636	152×137 mm. As Nos. 1624/35 but without white frames	50·00	55·00

Stamps from **MS1636** have no white frames.

330 Queen Elizabeth II

2012. Diamond Jubilee

1637	**330**	3p.40 multicoloured	3·50	4·00
MS1638		65×104 mm. $10 As No. 1637	10·00	10·00

331 Thorny Seahorse

2012. Endangered Species. Thorny Seahorse (*Hippocampus histrix*). Multicoloured.

1639	45s. Type **331**	45	30
1640	2p. Pair of Thorny Seahorses	2·00	2·50
1641	2p.40 Thorny Seahorse and sea fan	2·40	2·75
1642	3p.40 Infant Thorny Seahorse	3·50	4·00

332 Nuku'alofa Construction

2012. First Anniv of the Democracy. Multicoloured.

MS1643 45s. Type **332**; 85s. Vuna Wharf; 2p.70 Vaiola Hospital; 5p. New Construction; 8p. New Vuna Wharf; 10p. Nuku'alofa sidewalks	27·00	27·00

333 Titanic

2012. Centenary of the Sinking of the *Titanic*. Multicoloured.

MS1644	119× 88 mm. 45s. Type **333**; 3p.40 *Titanic* escorted by tug	3·75	3·75
MS1645	216×153 mm. 3p.40×4 As Type **333**; *Titanic* at quayside; *Titanic* escorted by tug, *Titanic* under way	13·50	13·50

334 Boy Scout Logo

2012. Anzac Day. Multicoloured.

1646	45s. Type **334**	45	30
1647	1p. Tonga Flag	1·00	90
1648	2p.40 Girl Guide logo (25th anniv of Tonga joining World Association of Scouts and Guides)	2·40	2·75
1649	3p.40 Rotary logo	3·50	4·00
MS1650	118×66 mm. 3p.40 Guides and leaders; 5p. Scouts and leaders (both after breakfast at Australian High Commissioner's Residence after ANZAC Day Dawn Service, 2011)	8·50	8·50

335 Boxing Match

2012. Olympic Games, London. Multicoloured.

1651	45s. Type **335**	45	30
1652	1p.40 Athlete on starting blocks	1·40	1·75
1653	3p.40 Swimmer	3·50	4·00
MS1654	112×133 mm. Nos. 1651/3, each ×2	10·50	10·50
MS1655	120×75 mm. Nos. 1651/3	5·25	5·25

336 Pencils

2012. Education

1656	**336**	3p. multicoloured	3·00	3·50

336a

2012. Personalized Stamp

1656a	**336a**	3p. black, grey and bright scarlet	3·00	3·50

337 Kings and Queen of Tonga and Royal Palace, Nuku'alofa (image scaled to 38% of original size)

2012. History of the Kings and Queen of Tonga: George Tupou I (1875-93), George Tupou II (1893-1918), Queen Salote Tupou III 1918-65), Taufa'ahau Tupou IV (1965-2006) and King George V (2006-12)

MS1657 **337** 20p. multicoloured 20·00 20·00

338 Australian Flag

2012. South Pacific Conference. Flags of Participating Nations (**MS**1658) and Key Dialogue Partners (**MS**1659). Multicoloured.

MS1658 2p.×16 Type **338**; Cook Islands; Fiji; Kiribati; Micronesia; Nauru; New Zealand; Niue; Palau; Papua New Guinea; Marshall Islands; Samoa; Solomon Islands; Tonga; Tuvalu; Vanuatu 32·00 32·00

MS1659 2p.×14 Canada; China (People's Republic); European Union; France; India; Indonesia; Italy; Japan; Republic of Korea; Malaysia; Philippines; Thailand; United Kingdom (wrongly inscr 'United Kindgom'); United States 28·00 28·00

In Loving Memory of Diana, Princess of Wales
31 August 1997
Her Legacy will live on forever
William snd Kate , Duke and Duchess of Cambridge
1st Anniversary of their Royal Wedding 2011

$5 X

339 (image scaled to 49% of original size)

2012. 15th Death Anniv of Princess Diana and First Wedding Anniv of the Duke and Duchess of Cambridge

MS1660 5p. on 10s. Princess Diana, 1992; 5p. on 80s. Wearing white jacket, 1992; 5p. on 1p. Wearing black jacket, 1991; 5p. on 2p.50, Wearing white top, 1993 20·00 20·00

No. **MS**1660 was optd across all four stamps with each stamp surch $5.

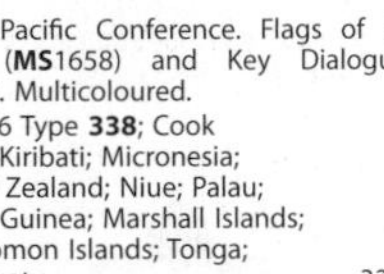

340 Angels dancing

2012. Christmas. *Mystical Nativity* (Sandro Botticelli, c. 1550). Multicoloured.

MS1661 1p.×11 Type **340**; Angels dancing (angel in black in centre holding olive branch); Angels dancing in circle (two angels in black); Three angels on roof of shelter; Virgin Mary praying, ox and ass; Angel (pointing towards Infant Jesus) and Three Kings; Infant Jesus (reaching towards Mary) and sleeping Joseph at left; Angel with two Shepherds; Angel (in green) embracing olive-crowned martyr; Angel (in white) embracing olive-crowned martyr; Angel (in red) embracing olive-crowned martyr 11·00 11·50

The stamps, margins and two stamp-size labels of **MS**1661 form a composite design showing the complete painting.

341 Prince Tupouto'a Vlukalala, Hon. Sinaitakala Tu'imatamoana Fakafanua and Family, 12 July 2012

2012. Royal Wedding

1662	3p. Type **341**	3·00	3·50

MS1663 120×95 mm. 3p.×5 Prince Tupouto'a Vlukalala and Hon. Sinaitakala Tu'imatamoana Fakafanua (in mauve dress) (36×36 mm); As Type **341** but without red border at top of stamp; Guests walking on ceremonial carpet (36×36 mm); Prince Tupouto'a Vlukalala and Hon. Sinaitakala Tu'imatamoana Fakafanua in traditional dress (36×36 mm); Wedding car (36×36 mm); 15·00 15·00

342 Snake

2013. Chinese New Year. Year of the Snake. Multicoloured.

MS1664 2p.45×4 Type **342**; As Type **342** but brown-purple snake on green background; Yellow snake on blue background; Purple and yellow snake on pink and yellow background 10·00 10·00

343 Head of Turtle

2013. Tonga Turtles from National Cultural Center, Nuku'alofa. Multicoloured.

1665	4p. Type **343**	4·00	4·50
1666	4p. Turtle in water, held by man	4·00	4·50
1667	4p. Man holding turtle, showing underside	4·00	4·50
1668	4p. Man in water, holding turtle	4·00	4·50
1669	5p. Turtle, side view	5·00	5·50
1670	5p. Underside of turtle	5·00	5·50
1671	5p. Turtle on rocks	5·00	5·50
1672	5p. Turtle, close-up of head and front flippers	5·00	5·50

MS1673 194×133 mm. As Nos. 1665/8 but with pale grey-brown and pale lavender-grey backgrounds 16·00 16·00

MS1674 198×127 mm. As Nos. 1669/72 but with pale grey-brown and pale lavender-grey backgrounds 20·00 20·00

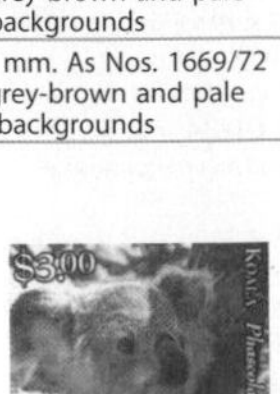

344 Koala (*Phascolarctos cinereus*)

2013. Australia 2013 World Stamp Expo, Melbourne. Multicoloured.

MS1675 $3×3 Type **344**; Royal Exhibition Building, Melbourne; Red Kangaroo (*Macropus rufus*) 9·00 9·00

345 Blow Holes in Reef, *Chaetodon flavirostris* and *Pseudanthias pleurotaenia*

2013. Blow Holes of Tonga (holes in coral reef), Houma. Each grey, black and turquoise-green.

MS1676 3p. Type **345**; 3p. Reef edge, *Pygoplites diacathus* and *Amblyglyphidodon melanopterus*; 4p. Reef edge, *Acanthurus guttatus* and *Myripristis hexagona*; 4p. Waves at reef edge, *Pseudanthias pleurotaenia* and *Zanclus comutus*; 5p. Blow holes, *Zanclus comutus* and *Pygoplites diacathus*; 5p. Blow holes, *Amblyglyphidodon melanopterus* and *Myripristis hexagona* 22·00 22·00

346 *Halcyon chloris* and *Adenanthera pavonina*

2013. Birds (2nd series). Multicoloured.

1677	10c. Type **346**	10	10
1678	20c. *Aplonis tabuensis* and *Myristica hypargyraea*	20	10
1679	30c. *Vini australis* and *Artocarpus altilis*	30	15
1680	40c. *Fregata minor* and *Hibiscus tilaceus*	40	30
1681	50c. *Sula sula* and *Terminalia catappa*	50	30
1682	80c. *Phaethon rubricauda* and *Cocos nucifera*	80	40
1683	90c. *Anous minatus* and *Elattostachys falcata*	90	50
1684	$1.10 *Lalage maculosa* and *Tarenna sambucina*	1·10	1·00
1685	$1.20 *Porzana tabuensis* and *Mimosa pigra*	1·25	1·25
1686	$2 *Foulehaio carunculatus* and *Solanum mauritianum*	2·00	2·50
1687	$12.50 *Prosopeia tabuensis* and *Adenanthera pavonina*	12·50	13·00
1688	$20 *Ptilinopus perousii* and *Psidium guajava*	18·00	18·00

MS1689 167×153 mm. As Nos. 1677/88 but without white frames 35·00 35·00

Stamps from **MS**1689 have no white frames.

EXPRESS STAMP

E1 Short-eared Owl in Flight

1990. Air.

E1	**E1**	10p. black, red and blue	9·50	10·00

E2 Short-eared Owl in Flight

2012. Short-eared Owl (*Asio flammeus*). Multicoloured.

E2	25p. Type E **2**	20·00	20·00
E3	25p. Short-eared owl on ground	20·00	20·00
E4	25p. Owl flying to right	20·00	20·00
E5	25p. Short-eared Owl	20·00	20·00
MSE6	161×135 mm. As Nos. E2/5	80·00	80·00

OFFICIAL STAMPS

1893. Optd **G.F.B.**

O1	**5**	1d. blue	24·00	50·00
O2	**6**	2d. blue	40·00	55·00
O3	**5**	4d. blue	50·00	£100
O4	**6**	8d. blue	95·00	£180
O5	**6**	1s. blue	£110	£200

1893. Nos. O1/5 variously surch.

O6	**5**	½d. on 1d. blue	26·00	50·00
O7	**6**	2½d. on 2d. blue	32·00	50·00
O8	**5**	5d. on 4d. blue	32·00	50·00
O9	**6**	7½d. on 8d. blue	32·00	80·00
O10	**6**	10d. on 1s. blue	40·00	85·00

1962. Air. Stamps of 1953 and 1961 optd as Nos. 120/7 but with **OFFICIAL AIRMAIL** in addition.

O11	2d. blue	23·00	7·50
O12	5d. violet	23·00	7·50
O13	1s. brown	18·00	4·50
O14	5s. yellow and lilac	£150	80·00
O15	10s. yellow and black	60·00	30·00
O16	£1 yellow, red and blue	85·00	50·00

1963. Air. First Polynesian Gold Coinage Commemoration. As No. 138 but additionally inscr "OFFICIAL". 1 koula coin. Diameter 338in. Imperf.

O17	**B**	15s. black on gold	12·00	13·00

1965. Air. Surch as Nos. 151/61.

O18	30s. on 15s. (No. O17)	3·75	5·00

1966. Air. Tupou College and Secondary Education Centenary. No. 117 surch **OFFICIAL AIRMAIL** and new value, with commemoration inscr as Nos. 168/73.

O19	10s. on 4d. green	50	35
O20	20s. on 4d. green	70	50

1967. Air. No. 112 surch **OFFICIAL AIRMAIL ONE PA'ANGA**.

O21	1p. on 5s. yellow and lilac	7·00	3·50

1967. Air. No. 114 surch **OFFICIAL AIRMAIL** and new value.

O22	40s. on £1 yellow, red & blue	60	75
O23	60s. on £1 yellow, red & blue	80	1·25
O24	1p. on £1 yellow, red and blue	1·10	2·25
O25	2p. on £1 yellow, red and blue	1·75	3·00

1967. Air. Arrival of U.S. Peace Corps in Tonga. As No. 114, but inperf and background colour changed, surch as Nos. 216/27 but with **Official Airmail** in addition.

O26	30s. on £1 multicoloured	50	30
O27	70s. on £1 multicoloured	70	1·50
O28	1p.50 on £1 multicoloured	1·00	2·50

1968. Air. 50th Birthday of King Taufa'ahua IV. No. 207 surch **HIS MAJESTY'S 50th BIRTHDAY OFFICIAL AIRMAIL** and new value.

O29	40s. on 50s. red and blue	3·25	80
O30	60s. on 50s. red and blue	3·75	1·75
O31	1p. on 50s. red and blue	5·00	4·75
O32	2p. on 50s. red and blue	9·00	11·00

1968. Air. South Pacific Games Field and Track Trials, Port Moresby, New Guinea. As No. 114 but imperf, background colour changed, surch **Friendly Islands Trials Field & Track South Pacific Games Port Moresby 1969 OFFICIAL AIRMAIL** and value.

O33	20s. on £1 multicoloured	20	25
O34	1p. on £1 multicoloured	70	1·50

1969. Air. Third South Pacific Games, Port Moresby. As Nos. 290/4 surch **OFFICIAL AIRMAIL**.

O35	70s. red, green and turquoise	75	1·60
O36	80s. red, orange and turquoise	85	1·60

1969. Air. Oil Search. As No. 114 but imperf, background colour changed and optd **1969 OIL SEARCH** and new value.

O37	90s. on £1 multicoloured	4·25	5·50
O38	1p.10 on £1 multicoloured	4·25	5·50

No. O37 is additionally optd **OFFICIAL AIRMAIL**.

1969. Air. Royal Visit. As No. 110, but imperf, colour changed, and surch **Royal Visit MARCH 1970 OFFICIAL AIRMAIL** and new value.

O39	75s. on 1s. red and yellow	8·50	6·00
O40	1p. on 1s. red and yellow	9·50	7·00
O41	1p.25 on 1s. red and yellow	10·00	8·50

1970. Air. Entry into British Commonwealth. As No. 112, but imperf and surch **Commonwealth Member JUNE 1970 OFFICIAL AIRMAIL** and value.

O42	50s. on 5s. yellow and brown	8·50	2·25
O43	90s. on 5s. yellow and brown	9·50	4·25
O44	1p.50 on 5s. yellow & brown	11·00	8·50

1970. Imperf. Self-adhesive. Colour of "TONGA" given for 6s. to 10s.

O45	**83**	1s. yellow, purple & black	90	1·60
O46	**83**	2s. yellow, blue and black	1·00	1·60
O47	**83**	3s. yellow, brown & black	1·00	1·60
O48	**83**	4s. yellow, green and black	1·00	1·60
O49	**83**	5s. yellow, red and black	1·00	1·60
O50	**90**	6s. blue	1·10	1·60
O51	**90**	7s. mauve	1·25	1·60
O52	**90**	8s. gold	1·25	1·60
O53	**90**	9s. red	1·40	1·60
O54	**90**	10s. silver	1·40	1·60

On the official issues Nos. O45 to O54, the value tablet is black (banana issue) or green (coconut issue). On the postage issues the colour is white.

See also Nos. O82/91.

1970. Air. Centenary of British Red Cross. As No. 102 and 112 but imperf in different colours and surch **Centenary British Red Cross 1870-1970 OFFICIAL AIRMAIL** and value.

O55	30s. on 1½d. green	2·00	2·25
O56	80s. on 5s. yellow and brown	13·00	8·50
O57	90s. on 5s. yellow and brown	13·00	8·50

1971. Air. Fifth Death Anniv of Queen Salote. As No. 113, but imperf and colour changed surch **OFFICIAL AIRMAIL 1965 IN MEMORIAM 1970** and value.

O58	20s. on 10s. orange	1·40	80
O59	30s. on 10s. orange	1·75	1·25
O60	50s. on 10s. orange	3·00	2·25
O61	2p. on 10s. orange	9·50	12·00

1971. Air. Philatokyo '71 Stamp Exhibition, Japan. Nos. O55/7 optd **PHILATOKYO '71** and emblem.

O62	30s. on 5d. green and yellow	90	65
O63	80s. on 5d. green and yellow	1·75	1·75
O64	90s. on 5d. green and yellow	2·00	2·00

1971. Air. As T **96** but inscr "OFFICIAL AIRMAIL".

O65	14s. multicoloured	2·25	2·50
O65a	17s. multicoloured	2·50	2·75
O66	21s. multicoloured	2·50	2·75
O66a	38s. multicoloured	3·50	3·75

O13

1971. Air. Fourth South Pacific Games, Tahiti. Imperf. Self-adhesive.

O67	**O13**	50s. multicoloured	60	90
O68	**O13**	90s. multicoloured	85	1·50
O69	**O13**	1p.50 multicoloured	1·25	1·75

1971. Air. Investiture of Royal Tongan Medal of Merit surch **INVESTITURE 1971 OFFICIAL AIRMAIL**.

O70	**89**	60s. on 3s. multicoloured	80	1·10
O71	**89**	80s. on 25s. multicoloured	1·10	1·40
O72	**89**	1p.10 on 7s. multicoloured	1·25	2·00

O15 "UNICEF" and Emblem

1971. Air. 25th Anniv of UNICEF. Imperf. Self-adhesive.

O73	**O15**	70s. multicoloured	1·00	1·75
O74	**O15**	80s. multicoloured	1·75	2·00
O75	**O15**	90s. multicoloured	1·90	2·25

1972. Air. Merchant Marine Routes. As T **100** but inscr "OFFICIAL AIRMAIL". Imperf. Self-adhesive.

O76	20s. multicoloured	1·25	80
O77	50s. multicoloured	2·75	2·50
O78	1p.20 multicoloured	5·50	7·00

DESIGN: Nos. O76/8, Map of South Pacific and "Aoniu".

1972. Air. Fifth Anniv of Coronation. Design similar to T **101**, but inscr "OFFICIAL AIRMAIL".

O79	50s. multicoloured	1·00	1·00
O80	70s. multicoloured	1·40	1·40
O81	1p.50 multicoloured	2·75	4·00

DESIGN—(47×57 mm): Nos. O79/81, As Type **101** but with different background.

1972. As Nos. 413/27 but inscr "OFFICIAL POST". (a) As Nos. 413/17.

O82	**83**	1s. yellow, red and black	30	50
O83	**83**	2s. yellow, green and black	35	50
O84	**83**	3s. yellow, green and black	40	50
O85	**83**	4s. yellow and black	40	50
O86	**83**	5s. yellow and black	40	50

(b) As Nos. O50/4 but colours changed. Multicoloured. Colour of "TONGA" given.

O87	**90**	6s. green	45	50
O88	**90**	7s. green	55	50
O89	**90**	8s. green	55	50
O90	**90**	9s. green	55	50
O91	**90**	10s. green	60	35

(c) As Nos. 423/7. Multicoloured. Colour of face value given.

O92	**102**	15s. blue	1·00	55
O93	**102**	20s. orange	1·25	75
O94	**102**	25s. brown	1·40	85
O95	**102**	40s. orange	2·50	1·75
O96	**102**	50s. blue	2·75	2·00

1972. Air. Proclamation of Sovereignty over Minerva Reefs. As T **104**, but inscr "OFFICIAL AIRMAIL".

O97	25s. multicoloured	40	35
O98	75s. multicoloured	1·25	1·50
O99	1p.50 multicoloured	2·50	3·00

1973. Air. Foundation of Bank of Tonga. No. 396 surch **TONGA 1973 ESTABLISHMENT BANK OF TONGA OFFICIAL AIRMAIL**, star and value.

O100	**100**	40s. on 21s. mult	1·50	1·25
O101	**100**	85s. on 21s. mult	3·00	3·25
O102	**100**	1p.25 on 21s. mult	3·75	7·00

1973. Silver Jubilee of Scouting in Tonga. Nos. O76, O74 and 319 surch or optd.

O103	-	30s. on 20s. mult	10·00	2·75
O104	**O15**	80s. multicoloured	25·00	10·00
O105	**89**	1p.40 on 50s. mult	35·00	25·00

OVERPRINT AND SURCHARGES: 30s. **SILVER JUBILEE TONGAN SCOUTING 1948-1973**, scout badge and value; 80c. **SILVER JUBILEE 1948-1973** and scout badge; 1p.40, **OFFICIAL AIRMAIL 1948-1973 SILVER JUBILEE TONGAN SCOUTING** and value.

1973. Air. Bicentenary of Capt. Cook's Visit. Design similar to T **107** but inscr "OFFICIAL AIRMAIL".

O106	25s. multicoloured	3·25	1·50
O107	80s. multicoloured	8·50	4·50
O108	1p.30 multicoloured	10·00	7·50

DESIGN—HORIZ (52×45 mm): Nos. O106/8, "James Cook" (bulk carrier).

1973. Air. Commonwealth Games, Christchurch. Nos. O67/9 optd **1974 Commonwealth Games Christchurch OFFICIAL AIRMAIL**.

O109	**O13**	50s. multicoloured	80	1·10
O110	**O13**	90s. multicoloured	1·40	1·75
O111	**O13**	1p.50 multicoloured	2·00	2·50

O19 Dove of Peace

1974. Air.

O112	**O19**	7s. green, violet and red	70	30
O113	**O19**	9s. green, violet & brn	75	35
O114	**O19**	12s. green, violet & brown	80	85
O115	**O19**	14s. green, violet & yellow	85	50
O116	**O19**	17s. multicoloured	95	70
O117	**O19**	29s. multicoloured	1·75	1·00
O118	**O19**	38s. multicoloured	2·25	1·25
O119	**O19**	50s. multicoloured	2·75	2·75
O120	**O19**	75s. multicoloured	4·00	4·50

1974. Air. Centenary of U.P.U. As Nos. 488/97 but inscr "OFFICIAL AIRMAIL".

O121	25s. orange, green and black	50	70
O122	35s. yellow, red and black	60	85
O123	70s. orange, blue and black	1·25	2·25

DESIGNS—HORIZ (43×40 mm): Nos. O121/3, Letters "UPU".

1974. Air. Tongan Girl Guides. As Nos. 498/507 inscr "OFFICIAL AIRMAIL".

O124	45s. multicoloured	4·00	2·00
O125	55s. multicoloured	4·25	2·25
O126	1p. multicoloured	7·50	5·50

DESIGNS—OVAL (36×52 mm): Nos. O124/6, Lady Baden-Powell.

1974. Air. Establishment of Royal Marine Institute. No. 446 surch **OFFICIAL AIRMAIL 80s** and RMI emblem and No. 451 surch **Establishment Royal Marine Institute Official Airmail TONGA TONGA**, RMI emblem and value.

O127	**106**	30s. on 15s. multicoloured	2·50	1·75
O128	-	35s. on 15s. multicoloured	2·75	2·00
O129	-	80s. on 17s. multicoloured	4·25	4·50

1975. Air. South Pacific Forum and Tourism. As T **113**. Imperf. Self-adhesive.

O130	50s. multicoloured	1·10	1·00
O131	75s. multicoloured	1·75	1·50
O132	1p.25 multicoloured	2·50	2·25

DESIGNS—(49×43 mm): 50s. Jungle arch; 75s., 1p.25, Sunset scene.

1975. Air. 5th South Pacific Games. As T **114**. Imperf. Self-adhesive.

O133	38s. multicoloured	65	50
O134	75s. multicoloured	1·10	1·75
O135	1p.20 multicoloured	1·75	3·50

DESIGN—OVAL (51×27 mm): Nos. O133/5, Runners on track.

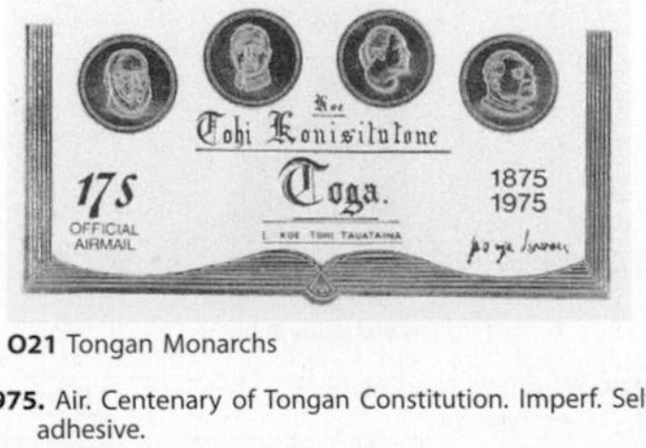

O21 Tongan Monarchs

1975. Air. Centenary of Tongan Constitution. Imperf. Self-adhesive.

O136	**O21**	17s. multicoloured	75	50
O137	**O21**	60s. multicoloured	1·90	2·25
O138	**O21**	90s. multicoloured	2·50	3·00

1976. Air. First Participation in Olympic Games. As Nos. 558/67 but inscr "OFFICIAL AIRMAIL".

O139	45s. multicoloured	4·50	1·75
O140	55s. multicoloured	4·50	1·90
O141	1p. multicoloured	8·50	9·50

DESIGN—OVAL (36×53 mm): Montreal logo.

1976. Air. Bicentenary of American Revolution. As Nos. 568/77 but inscr "OFFICIAL AIRMAIL".

O142	20s. multicoloured	75	50
O143	50s. multicoloured	1·00	1·50
O144	1p.15 multicoloured	2·00	3·50

1976. Air. 150th Anniv of Christianity in Tonga.

O145	65s. multicoloured	2·50	3·00
O146	85s. multicoloured	2·75	3·75
O147	1p.15 multicoloured	3·25	5·00

DESIGN—HEXAGONAL (65×52 mm): Lifuka Chapel.

1976. Air. Centenary of Treaty of Friendship with Germany.

O148	30s. multicoloured	60	70
O149	60s. multicoloured	1·40	1·75
O150	1p.25 multicoloured	2·75	3·50

DESIGN—RECTANGULAR (51×47 mm): Text.

1977. Air. Silver Jubilee.

O151	35s. multicoloured	70	40
O152	45s. multicoloured	30	30
O153	1p.10 multicoloured	45	50

DESIGN—57×66 mm: Flags of Tonga and the U.K.

1977. Air. Tenth Anniv of King's Coronation.

O154	20s. multicoloured	40	45
O155	40s. multicoloured	80	1·00
O156	80s. multicoloured	1·75	2·25

DESIGN—SQUARE (50×50 mm): 1967 Coronation coin.

1977. Air. Bicent of Capt. Cook's Last Voyage.

O157	20s. multicoloured	2·75	2·50
O158	55s. on 20s. multicoloured	6·00	6·50
O159	85s. on 20s. multicoloured	8·50	9·00

DESIGN—RECTANGULAR (52×46 mm): Text.

1977. Air. Whale Conservation.

O160	45s. multicoloured	5·50	3·00
O161	65s. multicoloured	7·50	5·50
O162	85s. multicoloured	9·00	6·50

DESIGN—HEXAGONAL (66×51 mm): Blue whale.

1978. Air. Commonwealth Games, Edmonton.

O163	30s. black, blue and red	60	60
O164	60s. black, red and blue	1·40	1·75
O165	1p. black, red and blue	1·75	2·00

DESIGN—TEAR-DROP (35×52 mm): Games emblem.

1978. Air. 60th Birthday of King Taufa'ahau Tupou IV.

O166	26s. black, red and yellow	50	30
O167	85s. black, brown and yellow	1·40	1·60
O168	90s. black, violet and yellow	1·50	1·60

DESIGN—MEDAL-SHAPED (21×45 mm): Portrait of King.

1978. Coil stamps. As Nos. 675/89 but inscr "OFFICIAL POST".

O169	1s. purple and yellow	20	50
O170	2s. brown and yellow	20	50
O171	3s. red and yellow	30	50
O172	4s. brown and yellow	30	50
O173	5s. green and yellow	30	50
O174	6s. brown and green	40	50
O175	7s. black, green and brown	40	50
O176	8s. red, green and brown	40	50
O177	9s. brown and green	40	50
O178	10s. green and brown	40	50
O179	15s. black, brown and green	1·00	1·00
O180	20s. red, brown and green	1·10	1·10
O181	30s. green and brown	1·25	1·50
O182	50s. blue, brown and green	1·50	2·00
O183	1p. violet, brown and green	2·25	3·00

1978. Air. Endangered Wildlife. Multicoloured.

O184	40s. Type **129**	6·50	4·00
O185	50s. Insular flying fox	5·50	4·00
O186	1p.10 Turtle	7·50	11·00

1979. Air. Decade of Progress. As Nos. 700/9, but inscr "OFFICIAL AIRMAIL".

O187	**G**	38s. multicoloured	1·50	65
O188	**E**	74s. multicoloured	1·60	1·75
O189	**A**	80s. multicoloured	3·00	2·50

1979. Air. Death Centenary of Sir Rowland Hill and Tenth Anniv of Tongan Self-adhesive Stamps.

O190	45s. multicoloured	75	60
O191	65s. multicoloured	1·10	85
O192	80s. multicoloured	1·25	1·10

DESIGN—HAND SHAPED (45×53 mm): 45s. to 80s. Removing self-adhesive stamp from backing paper.

O22 Blue-crowned Lory (with foliage)

1979. Air. Coil Stamps.

O193	**O22**	5s. multicoloured	60	70
O194	**O22**	11s. multicoloured	65	70
O195	**O22**	14s. multicoloured	65	70
O196	**O22**	15s. multicoloured	70	70
O197	**O22**	17s. multicoloured	70	70
O198	**O22**	18s. multicoloured	70	50
O199	**O22**	22s. multicoloured	80	50
O200	**O22**	31s. multicoloured	90	65
O201	**O22**	39s. multicoloured	1·25	80
O202	**O22**	75s. multicoloured	2·00	3·00
O203	**O22**	1p. multicoloured	2·50	4·00

1979. Air. Views as seen through the Lens of a Camera.

O204	35s. multicoloured	55	75
O205	45s. multicoloured	65	85
O206	1p. multicoloured	1·25	3·25

DESIGN: 35s. to 1p. Niuatoputapu and Tafahi.

1980. Air. 125th Anniv of France–Tonga Friendship Treaty.

O207	40s. multicoloured	75	1·00
O208	55s. multicoloured	1·00	1·25
O209	1p.25 multicoloured	2·00	2·75

DESIGN: 40s. to 1p.25, Establishment of the Principle of Religious Freedom in the Pacific Islands.

1980. Air. Olympic Games, Moscow. Nos. O190/2 surch mascot, **1980 OLYMPIC GAMES**, value and emblem.

O210	26s. on 45s. multicoloured	85	85
O211	40s. on 65s. multicoloured	1·40	1·40
O212	1p.10 on 1p. multicoloured	3·50	3·75

O23 Blue-crowned Lory (without foliage)

1980. No. O193 redrawn without foliage as Type **O23**.

O213	**O23**	5s. multicoloured	£110	80·00

1980. Air. South Pacific Scout Jamboree, Tonga and 75th Anniv of Rotary International.

O214	25s. multicoloured	75	65
O215	2p. multicoloured	3·50	6·50

DESIGN: 25s., 2p. Scout camp and Rotary emblem.

Nos. O214/15 show maps of Tonga on the reverse.

1980. Air. Nos. O145 surch **T$2**.

O216	2p. on 65s. multicoloured	4·50	6·50

1983. Nos. 834/6 optd **OFFICIAL**.

O217	29s. Type **151**	5·00	5·00
O218	32s. Type **151**	5·00	5·00
O219	47s. Montgolfier's balloon and Concorde	10·00	7·50

1984. Nos. 865/79 and 881 optd **OFFICIAL**.

O220	1s. Type **159**	50	1·60
O221	2s. "Porites sp"	50	1·60
O222	3s. Red squirrelfish	50	1·75
O223	5s. Green map cowrie	50	1·50
O224	6s. "Dardanus megistos"	50	1·75
O225	9s. Variegated shark	75	80
O226	10s. Bubble cone	80	1·25
O227	13s. Lionfish	1·25	80
O228	15s. Textile or cloth of gold cone	1·25	1·75
O229	20s. White-tailed damselfish	1·50	2·00
O230	29s. Princely cone	1·75	85
O231	32s. Powder-blue surgeonfish	1·75	85
O232	47s. Giant spider conch	2·00	90
O233	1p. "Millepora dichotama"	3·75	3·75
O234	2p. "Birgus latro"	7·00	7·50
O235	5p. Yellow-finned tuna	12·00	14·00

1986. Nos. 933/9 optd **OFFICIAL**.

O236	4s. on 2s. "Porites sp"	90	2·50
O237	4s. on 13s. Lionfish	90	2·50
O238	42s. on 3s. Red squirrelfish	2·75	2·50
O239	42s. on 9s. Variegated shark	2·75	2·50
O240	57s. on 6s. "Dardanus megistos"	3·00	2·75
O241	57s. on 20s. White-tailed damselfish	3·00	2·75
O242	2p.50 on 2p. "Birgus latro"	10·00	12·00

1994. Air. 25th Anniv of Tongan Self-adhesive Stamps. Design as No. O192, but inscr "25th ANNIVERSARY OF THE INTRODUCTION OF SELFADHESIVE STAMPS 1969–1994 BERNARD MECHANICK: 1915–80 INVENTOR FREEFORM SELFADHESIVE STAMPS" at centre foot.

O243	80s. multicoloured	7·00	7·00

O30 Bubble Cone

1995. Designs as Nos. 1221a, 1223a, 1225a, 1227a and 1229a, but inscr as Type **O30**.

O247	10s. Type O **30**	50	1·00
O249	20s. White-tailed dascyllus	75	1·00
O251	45s. Giant spider conch	1·00	60
O253	60s. Princely cone	1·25	75
O255	80s. Lionfish	1·50	1·00
O256	1p. "Chelonia mydas" (turtle)	2·00	1·75
O257	2p. "Birgus latro" (crab)	3·50	3·75
O258	3p. Rose branch murex	4·50	5·00
O259	5p. Humpback whale	8·50	9·50
O260	10p. Variegated shark (vert)	12·00	15·00

Pt. 10

TRANSCAUCASIAN FEDERATION

A Federation of Armenia, Azerbaijan and Georgia, which was absorbed into the U.S.S.R. in 1923.

100 kopeks = 1 rouble.

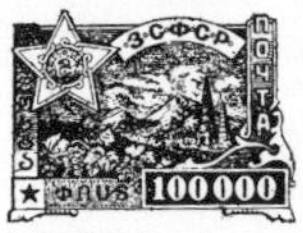

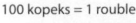

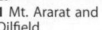

1 Mt. Ararat and Oilfield

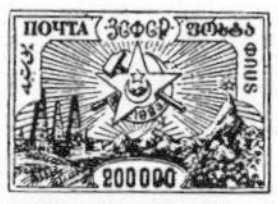

2 Mts. Ararat and Elbrus and Oil-derricks

1923

1	**1**	40,000r. purple	2·50	6·25
2	**1**	75,000r. green	2·50	6·25
3	**1**	100,000r. grey	2·50	6·25
4	**1**	150,000r. red	2·50	6·25
5	**2**	200,000r. green	2·50	6·25
6	**2**	300,000r. blue	2·50	6·25
7	**2**	350,000r. brown	2·30	6·25
8	**2**	500,000r. red	2·50	6·25

1923. Surch **700000 RYb**.

9	**1**	700,000r. on 40,000r. purple	8·25	8·25
10	**1**	700,000r. on 75,000r. green	8·25	8·25

1923. Values in gold kopeks.

11	**2**	1k. orange	3·00	5·75
12	**2**	2k. green	3·00	5·75
13	**2**	3k. red	4·50	5·75
14	**2**	4k. brown	2·50	5·75
15	**1**	5k. purple	2·50	5·75
16	**1**	9k. blue	2·50	5·75
17	**1**	18k. grey	2·50	5·75

Pt. 1

TRANSKEI

The Republic of Transkei was established on 26 October 1976, as the first of the independent "black homelands" constructed from the territory of the Republic of South Africa.

This independence did not receive international political recognition, but the stamps were accepted as valid on international mail.

Transkei was reincorporated with the Republic of South Africa on 27 April 1994.

100 cents = 1 rand.

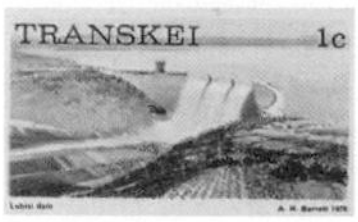

1 Lubisi Dam

1976. Transkei Scenes and Occupations. Multicoloured.

1	1c. Type **1**	10	10
2	2c. Soil cultivation	10	10
3	3c. Threshing sorghum	10	10
4a	4c. Transkei matron	15	10
5a	5c. Grinding maize	15	10
6	6c. Cutting "Phormium tenax"	15	10
7	7c. Herd-boy	40	10
8	8c. Felling timber	20	10
9	9c. Agricultural schooling	15	15
10a	10c. Tea picking	20	15
11a	15c. Carrying wood	30	15
12a	20c. Weaving industry	35	15
13	25c. Cattle	45	25
14a	30c. Sledge transportation	60	45
15	50c. Coat of arms and map	1·25	50
16	1r. Administration building, Umtata	50	1·25
17	2r. The Bunga (Parliamentary building), Umtata	75	2·25

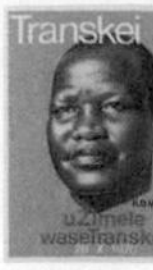

2 K. D. Matanzima

1976. Independence. Multicoloured.

18	4c. Type **2**	15	15
19	10c. Flag and mace	35	25
20	15c. K. D. Matanzima, Paramount Chief (different)	40	55
21	20c. Coat of arms	50	70

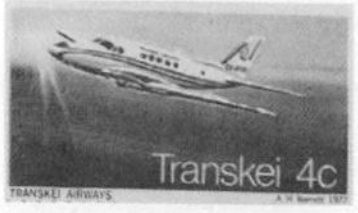

3 Beech 100 King Air of Transkei Airways

1977. Transkei Airways' Inaugural Flight. Multicoloured.

22	4c. Type **3**	25	15
23	15c. Beech King Air landing at Matanzima Airport	75	85

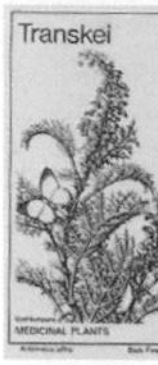

4 "Artemisia afra"

1977. Medicinal Plants (1st series). Multicoloured.

24	4c. Type **4**	15	10
25	10c. "Bulbine natalensis"	45	45
26	15c. "Melianthus major"	55	65
27	20c. "Cotyledon orbiculata"	65	90

See also Nos. 88/91.

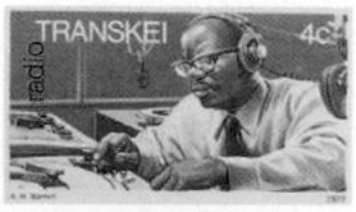

5 Disc Jockey

1977. First Anniv of Transkei Radio. Multicoloured.

28	4c. Type **5**	15	10
29	15c. Announcer	60	60

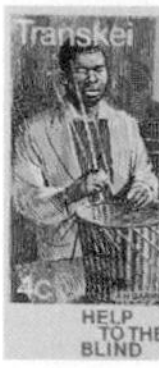

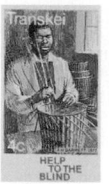

6 Blind Basket Weaver

1977. Help for the Blind.

30	**6**	4c. black, lilac and gold	15	10
31	-	15c. black, drab and gold	35	35
32	-	20c. black, brown and gold	75	80

DESIGNS: 15c. Hands reading braille; 20c. Blind woman spinning.

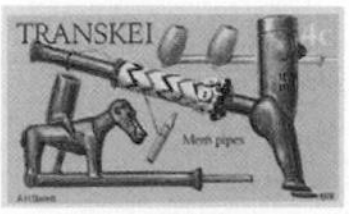

7 Men's Carved Pipes

1978. Carved Pipes. Multicoloured.

33	4c. Type **7**	10	10
34	10c. Two men's pipes	15	15
35	15c. Multi-bowled men's pipes	25	40
36	20c. Woman's and witch-doctor's pipes	30	50

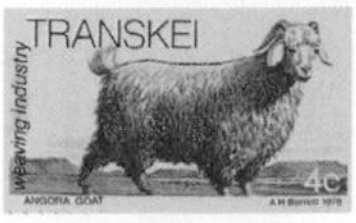

8 Angora Goat

1978. Weaving Industry. Multicoloured.

37	4c. Type **8**	10	10
38	10c. Spinning mohair	15	15
39	15c. Dyeing mohair	20	25
40	20c. Weaving a mohair rug	30	40

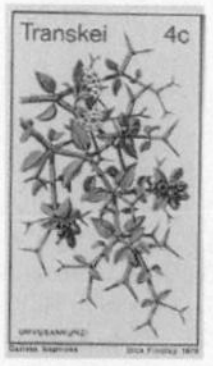

9 "Carissa bispinosa"

1978. Edible Wild Fruit. Multicoloured.

41	4c. Type **9**	10	10
42	10c. "Dovyalis caffra"	15	15
43	15c. "Harpephyllum caffrum"	25	40
44	20c. "Syzygium cordatum"	30	60

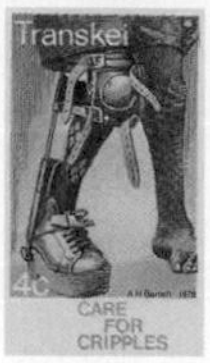

10 Calipers

1978. Care of Cripples.

45	**10**	4c. black, brown and gold	10	10
46	-	10c. black, grey and gold	25	25
47	-	15c. black, yellow and gold	40	50

DESIGNS: 10c. Child in wheelchair; 15c. Nurse examining child's leg.

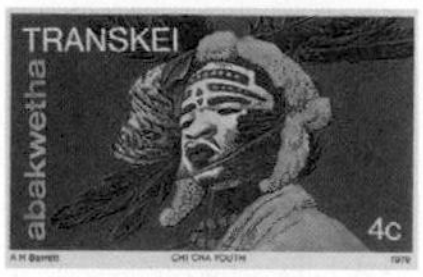

11 Chi Cha Youth

1979. Abakwetha (coming-of-age ceremony of Xhosa males). Multicoloured.

48	4c. Type **11**	10	10
49	10c. Youths in three-month seclusion	15	20
50	15c. Umtshilo dance	25	35
51	20c. Burning of seclusion hut at end of final ceremony	35	45

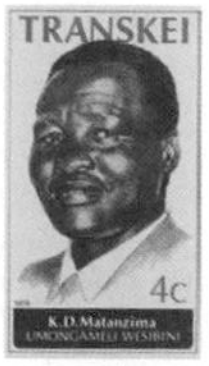

12 President K. D. Matanzima

1979. Inaug of Second State President.

52	**12**	4c. red and gold	15	10
53	**12**	15c. green and gold	50	45

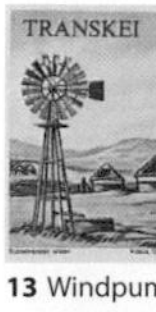

13 Windpump

1979. Water Resources. Multicoloured.

54	4c. Type **13**	15	10
55	10c. Woman ladling water into jar	20	25
56	15c. Indwe River Dam (horiz)	35	55
57	20c. Ncora Dam (horiz)	40	70

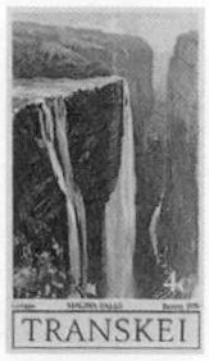

14 Magwa Falls

1979. Waterfalls. Multicoloured.

58	4c. Type **14**	15	10
59	10c. Bawa Falls	20	25
60	15c. Waterfall Bluff (horiz)	35	55
61	20c. Tsitsa Falls (horiz)	40	70

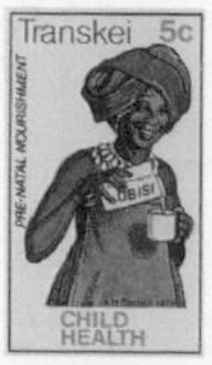

15 Expectant Mother pouring Milk

1979. Child Health. Multicoloured.

62	5c. Type **15**	15	10
63	15c. Mother breast-feeding baby	45	45
64	20c. Immunizing child	60	65

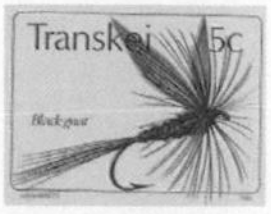

16 Black Gnat (dry fly)

1980. Fishing Flies (1st series). Multicoloured.

65	5c. Type **16**	25	35
66	5c. Zug Bug (nymph)	25	35
67	5c. March Brown (wet fly)	25	35
68	5c. Durham Ranger (salmon fly)	25	35
69	5c. Colonel Bates (streamer)	25	35

See also Nos. 83/7, 99/103, 116/20 and 133/7.

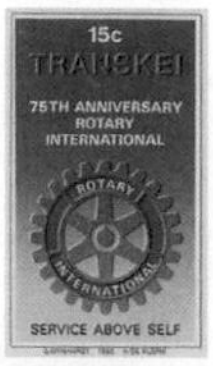

17 Rotary Emblem

1980. 75th Anniv of Rotary International.

70	**17**	15c. blue and gold	35	30

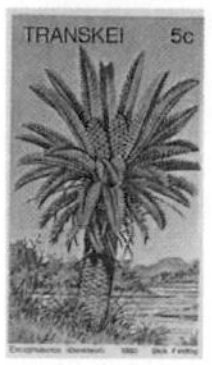

18 "Encephalartos altensteinii"

1980. Cycads. Multicoloured.

71	5c. Type **18**	15	10
72	10c. "Encephalartos princeps"	20	25
73	15c. "Encephalartos villosus"	25	40
74	20c. "Encephalartos friderici-guilielmi"	30	55

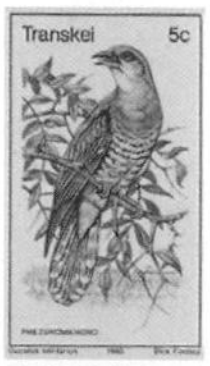

19 Red-chested Cuckoo

1980. Birds. Multicoloured.

75	5c. Type **19**	20	10
76	10c. Cape puff-back fly-catcher	35	25
77	15c. South African crowned crane	50	60
78	20c. Spectacled Weaver	55	70

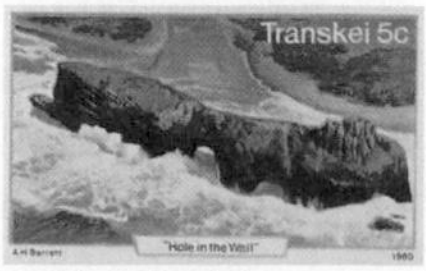

20 Hole in the Wall

1980. Tourism. Multicoloured.

79	5c. Type **20**	15	10
80	10c. Port St. Johns	20	25
81	15c. The Citadel (rock)	25	40
82	20c. The Archway (rock)	30	55

1981. Fishing Flies (2nd series). As T **16**. Multicoloured.

83	10c. Kent's Lightning (streamer)	25	25
84	10c. Wickham's Fancy (dry fly)	25	25
85	10c. Jock Scott (wet fly)	25	25

86	10c. Green Highlander (salmon fly)	25	25
87	10c. Tan Nymph	25	25

1981. Medicinal Plants (2nd series). As T **4**. Multicoloured.

88	5c. "Leonotis leonurus"	15	10
89	15c. "Euphorbia bupleurifolia"	20	30
90	20c. "Pelargonium reniforme"	20	35
91	25c. "Hibiscus trionum"	20	40

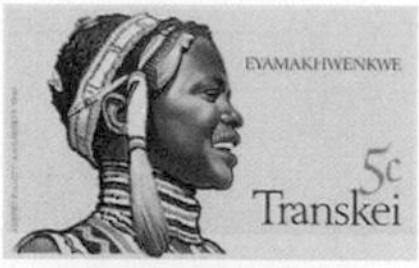

21 Eyamakhwenkwe

1981. Xhosa Women's Headdresses. Multicoloured.

92	5c. Type **21**	10	10
93	15c. Eyabafana	20	35
94	20c. Umfazana	25	45
95	25c. Ixhegokazi	30	55
MS96	126×91 mm. Nos. 92/5	1·00	1·25

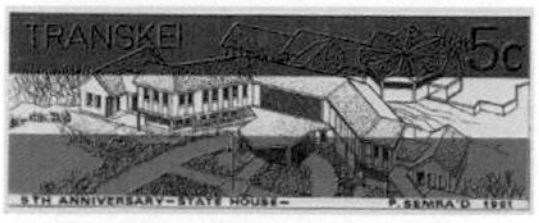

22 State House, Umtata

1981. Fifth Anniv of Independence.

97	22	5c. black, brown and green	15	10
98	-	15c. black, brown and green	45	30

DESIGN: 15c. University of Transkei.

1982. Fishing Flies (3rd series). As T **16**. Multicoloured.

99	10c. Blue Charm	25	30
100	10c. Royal Coachman	25	30
101	10c. Light Spruce	25	30
102	10c. Montana Nymph	25	30
103	10c. Butcher	25	30

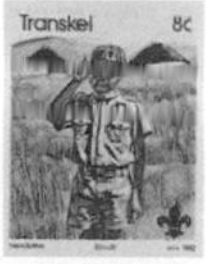

23 Cub Scout

1982. 75th Anniv of Boy Scout Movement. Multicoloured.

104	8c. Type **23**	15	10
105	10c. Scout planting tree	15	10
106	20c. Scout on raft	25	30
107	25c. Scout with dog	25	30

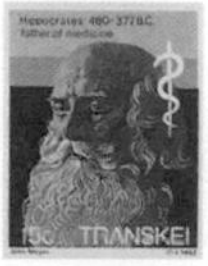

24 Hippocrates

1982. Celebrities of Medicine (1st series). Multicoloured.

108	15c. Type **24**	20	20
109	20c. Antonie van Leeuwenhoek	25	30
110	25c. William Harvey	30	40
111	30c. Joseph Lister	35	45

See also Nos. 125/8, 160/3, 176/9, 249/52, 273/6, 281/4 and 305/8.

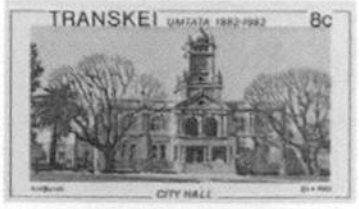

25 City Hall

1982. Centenary of Umtata. Multicoloured.

112	8c. Type **25**	10	10
113	15c. The Bunga	15	15
114	20c. Botha Sigcau Building	20	20
115	25c. Palace of Justice and K. D. Matanzima Building	25	30

1983. Fishing Flies (4th series). As T **16**. Multicoloured.

116	20c. Alexandra	25	30
117	20c. Kent's Marbled Sedge	25	30
118	20c. White Marabou	25	30
119	20c. Mayfly Nymph	25	30
120	20c. Silver Wilkinson	25	30

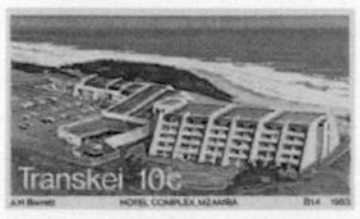

26 Hotel Complex, Mzamba

1983. Wildcoast Holiday Complex, Mzamba. Multicoloured.

121	10c. Type **26**	15	15
122	20c. Beach scene	25	25
123	25c. Casino	35	35
124	40c. Carousel	50	50

1983. Celebrities of Medicine (2nd series). As T **24**. Multicoloured.

125	10c. Edward Jenner	15	15
126	20c. Gregor Mendel	25	30
127	25c. Louis Pasteur	30	35
128	40c. Florence Nightingale	40	55

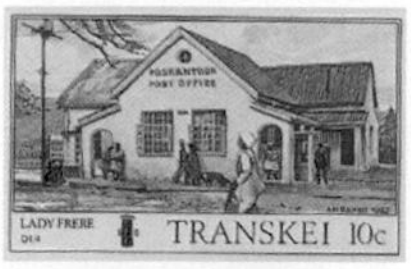

27 Lady Frere Post Office

1983. Transkei Post Offices (1st series). Multicoloured.

129	10c. Type **27**	15	15
130	20c. Idutywa	20	30
131	25c. Lusikisiki	20	35
132	40c. Cala	30	55

See also Nos. 156/9.

1984. Fishing Flies (5th series). As T **16**. Multicoloured.

133	20c. Silver Grey	35	45
134	20c. Ginger Quill	35	45
135	20c. Hardy's Favourite	35	45
136	20c. March Brown	35	45
137	20c. Kent's Spectrum Mohawk	35	45

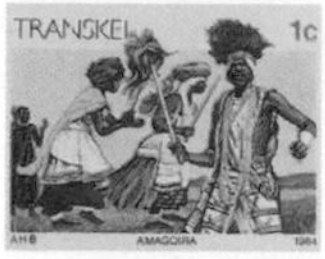

28 Amaqqira

1984. Xhosa Culture. Multicoloured.

138	1c. Type **28**	20	10
139	2c. Herdsman	20	10
140	3c. Mat making	20	10
141	4c. Xhosa dancers	20	10
142	5c. Shopping with donkeys	20	10
143	6c. Young musicians	30	15
144	7c. Fingo brides	30	20
145	8c. Tasting the beer	30	20
146	9c. Thinning the maize	30	30
147	10c. Dancing demonstration	30	15
148	11c. Water from the river	30	15
148a	12c. Preparing a meal	30	15
148b	14c. Weeding mealies	30	20
149	15c. National sport: stick fighting	20	20
149a	16c. Morning pasture	30	20
150	20c. Abakhwetha dance	30	25
150a	21c. Building of initiation hut	2·00	20
151	25c. Tribesman singing	30	25
152	30c. Jovial matrons	30	35
153	50c. Pipe making	35	60
154	1r. Intonjane	50	1·10
155	2r. Abakhwetha	70	2·00

1984. Transkei Post Offices (2nd series). As T **27**. Multicoloured.

156	11c. Umzimkulu	15	15
157	20c. Mount Fletcher	20	25
158	25c. Qumbu	20	25
159	50c. Umtata	30	50

1984. Celebrities of Medicine (3rd series). As T **24**. Multicoloured.

160	11c. Nicholas of Cusa	15	15
161	25c. William Morton	25	25
162	30c. Wilhelm Rontgen	30	40
163	45c. Karl Landsteiner	40	60

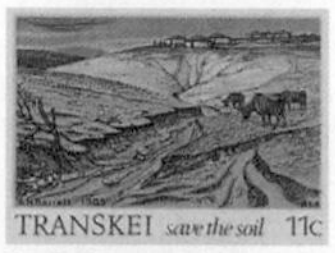

29 Soil Erosion by Overgrazing

1985. Soil Conservation. Multicoloured.

164	11c. Type **29**	15	15
165	25c. Removal of stock and construction of walls as sediment collectors	25	25
166	30c. Regeneration of vegetation	30	40
167	50c. Cattle grazing in lush landscape	40	60

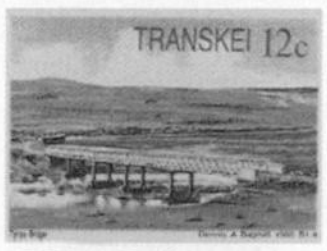

30 Tsitsa Bridge

1985. Bridges. Multicoloured.

168	12c. Type **30**	20	15
169	25c. White Kei Railway Bridge	25	25
170	30c. Mitchell Bridge	35	35
171	50c. Umzimvubu Bridge	55	60

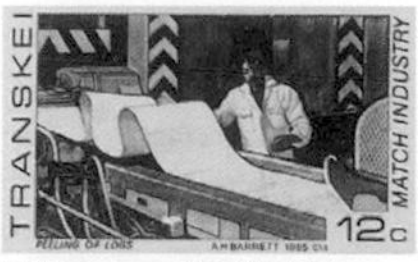

31 Veneer-peeling Machine

1985. Match Industry, Butterworth. Multicoloured.

172	12c. Type **31**	10	15
173	25c. Cutting wood to match-size	15	25
174	30c. Dipping splints in chemical to form match heads	20	35
175	50c. Boxing matches	35	65

1985. Celebrities of Medicine (4th series). As T **24**. Multicoloured.

176	12c. Andreas Vesalius	20	15
177	25c. Marcello Malpighi	30	40
178	30c. Francois Magendie	35	45
179	50c. William Stewart Halsted	50	70

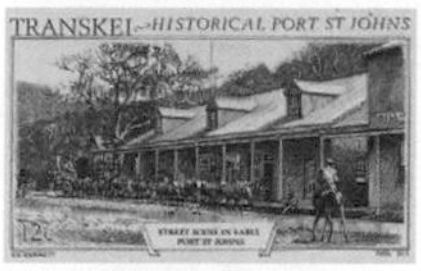

32 Early Street Scene

1986. Historic Port St. Johns. Multicoloured.

180	12c. Type **32**	20	15
181	20c. "Umzimvubu" (coaster) anchored at old jetty	45	45
182	25c. Wagons off-loading maize at jetty	50	50
183	30c. View of town at end of 19th century	50	55
MS184	130×94 mm. Nos. 180/3	1·50	1·50

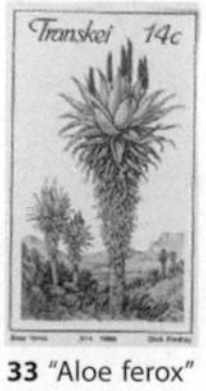

33 "Aloe ferox"

1986. Aloes. Multicoloured.

185	14c. Type **33**	20	15
186	20c. "Aloe arborescens"	30	30
187	25c. "Aloe maculata"	35	35
188	30c. "Aloe ecklonis"	45	45

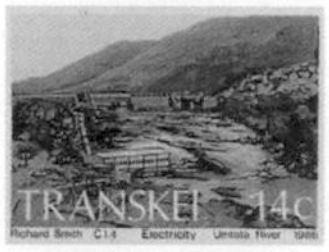

34 First Falls Station, Umtata River

1986. Hydro-electric Power Stations. Multicoloured.

189	14c. Type **34**	20	15
190	20c. Second Falls, Umtata River	25	25
191	25c. Ncora, Qumanco River	40	40
192	30c. Collywobbles, Mbashe River	50	50

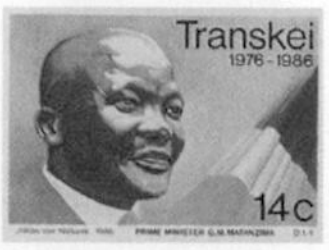

35 Prime Minister George Matanzima

1986. Tenth Anniv of Independence. Multicoloured.

193	14c. Type **35**	15	15
194	20c. Technical College, Umtata	25	30
195	25c. University of Transkei, Umtata	30	40
196	30c. Palace of Justice, Umtata	40	50

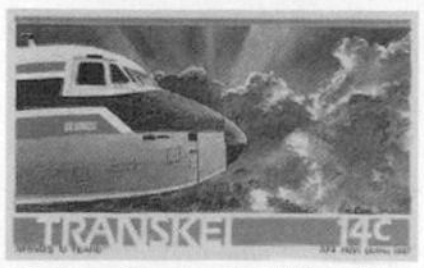

36 Piper Apache 235 "Ulundi" flying through Clouds

1987. Tenth Anniv of Transkei Airways Corporation. Multicoloured.

197	14c. Type **36**	20	15
198	20c. Tail fin of "Ulundi"	30	30
199	25c. Beech 100 King Air	40	40
200	30c. Control tower, K. D. Matanzima Airport	55	60

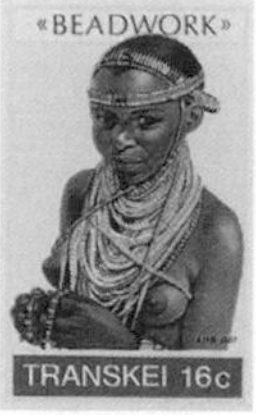

37 Pondo Girl

1987. Transkei Beadwork. Multicoloured.

201	16c. Type **37**	15	15
202	20c. Bomvana woman	25	30
203	25c. Xessibe woman	35	40
204	30c. Xhosa man	40	60

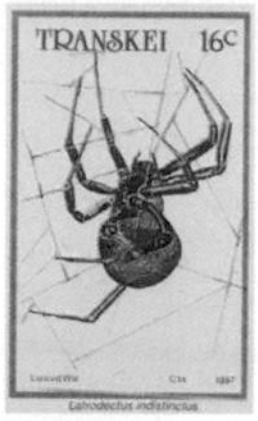

38 "Latrodectus indistinctus"

1987. Spiders. Multicoloured.

205	16c. Type **38**	15	15
206	20c. "Naephila pilipes"	25	30
207	25c. "Lycosidue sp"	30	40
208	30c. "Argiope nigrovittata"	40	55

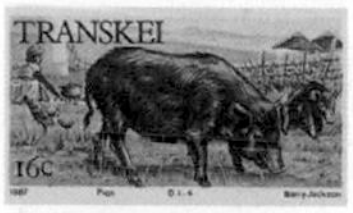

39 Common Black Pigs

1987. Domestic Animals. Multicoloured.

209	16c. Type **39**	15	15
210	30c. Goats	20	30
211	40c. Merino sheep	30	50
212	50c. Cattle	45	65

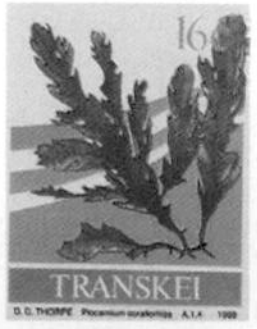

40 "Plocamium corallorhiza"

1988. Seaweed. Multicoloured.

213	16c. Type **40**	15	15
214	30c. "Gelidium amanzii"	25	30
215	40c. "Ecklonia biruncinata"	30	40
216	50c. "Halimeda cuneata"	40	55

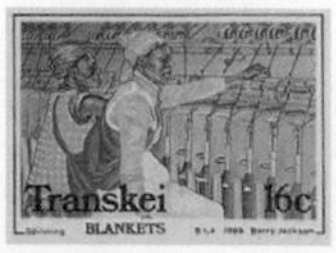

41 Spinning

1988. Blanket Factory, Butterworth. Multicoloured.

217	16c. Type **41**	10	10
218	30c. Warping	20	20
219	40c. Weaving	25	35
220	50c. Raising the nap	30	45

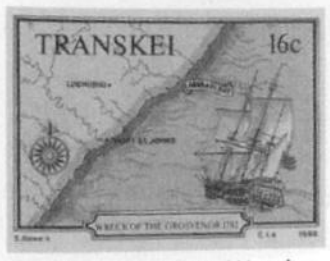

42 Map showing Wreck Site

1988. 206th Anniv of Shipwreck of "Grosvenor" (East Indiaman). Multicoloured.

221	16c. Type **42**	40	20
222	30c. "The Wreck of the 'Grosvenor'" (R. Smirke)	50	50
223	40c. Dirk hilt, dividers and coins from wreck	55	55
224	50c. "African Hospitality" (G. Morland)	60	70

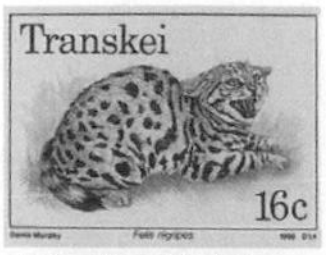

43 Small-spotted Cat

1988. Endangered Animals. Multicoloured.

225	16c. Type **43**	60	30
226	30c. Blue duiker	70	60
227	40c. Oribi	85	75
228	50c. Hunting dog	1·25	1·00

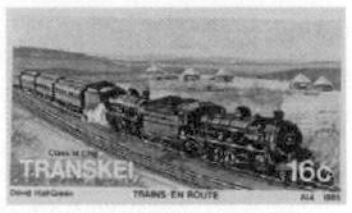

44 Class 14 CRB Steam Locomotives

1989. Trains. Multicoloured.

229	16c. Type **44**	20	20
230	30c. Class 14 CRB locomotive and passenger train at Toleni Halt	40	40
231	40c. Double-headed steam train on Great Kei River Bridge (vert)	60	70
232	50c. Double-headed steam train in Kei Valley (vert)	65	80

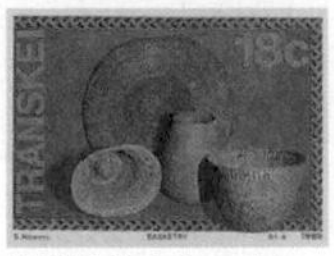

45 Mat, Baskets and Jar

1989. Basketry. Multicoloured.

233	18c. Type **45**	20	15
234	30c. Basket and jar	30	30
235	40c. Jars and bag	40	50
236	50c. Dish and jars	55	75

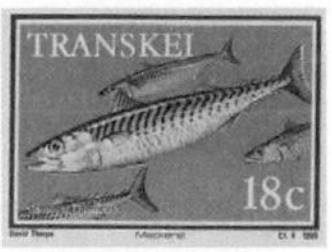

46 Chub Mackerel

1989. Seafood. Multicoloured.

237	18c. Type **46**	55	15
238	30c. Squid	70	50
239	40c. Perna or brown mussels	85	70
240	50c. Rock lobster	1·00	1·00

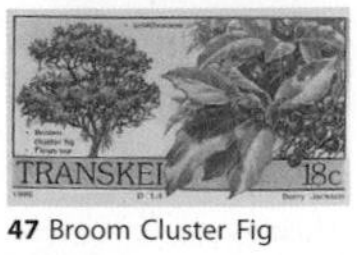

47 Broom Cluster Fig

1989. Trees. Multicoloured.

241	18c. Type **47**	50	20
242	30c. Natal fig	75	55
243	40c. Broad-leaved coral	85	85
244	50c. Cabbage tree	1·10	1·25

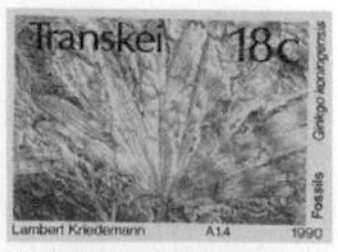

48 "Ginkgo koningensis"

1990. Plant Fossils. Multicoloured.

245	18c. Type **48**	80	25
246	30c. "Pseudoctenis spatulata"	1·10	80
247	40c. "Rissikia media"	1·25	1·10
248	50c. "Taeniopteris anavolans"	1·40	1·50

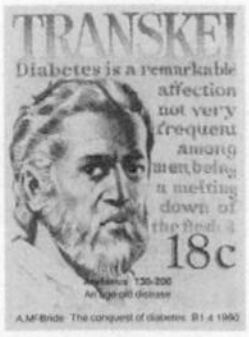

49 Aretaeus (discoverer of diabetes)

1990. Celebrities of Medicine (5th series). Diabetes Research. Multicoloured.

249	18c. Type **49**	70	20
250	30c. Claude Bernard (discovered sugar formation by liver)	1·10	70
251	40c. Oscar Minkowski (discovered pancreas removal caused diabetes)	1·25	90
252	50c. Frederick Banting (discoverer of insulin)	1·40	1·25

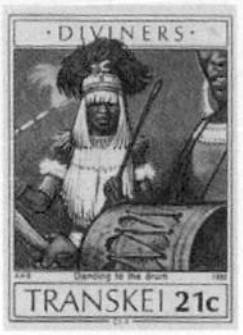

50 Diviner dancing to Drum

1990. Diviners. Multicoloured.

253	21c. Type **50**	50	20
254	35c. Lecturing Imichetywa (novitiates)	70	70
255	40c. Neophyte initiation	80	90
256	50c. Diviner's induction ceremony	95	1·40

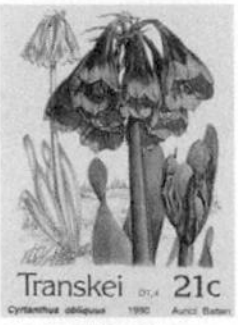

51 Soldier Lily

1990. Flowers. Multicoloured.

257	21c. Type **51**	65	20
258	35c. "Disa crassicornis"	90	65
259	40c. Christmas bells	1·00	90
260	50c. Port St. John's creeper	1·25	1·40

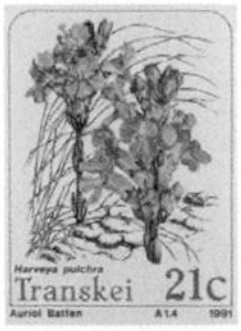

52 Pink Ink Plant

1991. Parasitic Plants. Multicoloured.

261	21c. Type **52**	60	20
262	35c. White harveya	90	70
263	40c. "Alectra sessiliflora"	1·00	1·10
264	50c. "Hydnora africana"	1·25	1·50

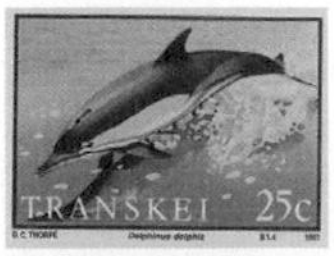

53 Common Dolphin

1991. Dolphins. Multicoloured.

265	25c. Type **53**	1·00	25
266	40c. Bottle-nosed dolphin	1·40	85
267	50c. Humpbacked dolphin	1·60	1·25
268	60c. Risso's dolphin	1·60	1·60

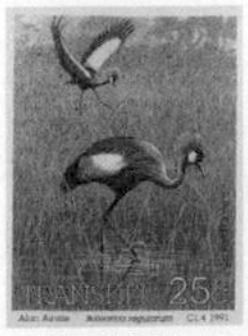

54 South African Crowned Cranes ("Crowned Cranes")

1991. Endangered Birds. Multicoloured.

269	25c. Type **54**	65	30
270	40c. Cape vulture	1·00	85
271	50c. Wattled crane	1·10	1·10
272	60c. Egyptian vulture	1·25	1·40

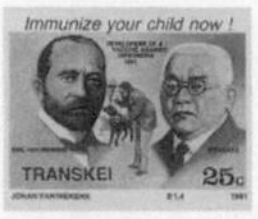

55 Emil von Behring and Shibasaburo Kitasao (diphtheria)

1991. Celebrities of Medicine (6th series). Vaccine Development. Multicoloured.

273	25c. Type **55**	1·00	25
274	40c. Camile Guerin and Albert Calmette (tuberculosis)	1·50	90
275	50c. Jonas Salk (poliomyelitis)	1·75	1·25
276	60c. John Enders (measles)	1·75	1·50

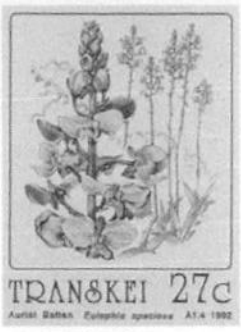

56 "Eulophia speciosa"

1992. Orchids. Multicoloured.

277	27c. Type **56**	25	20
278	45c. "Satyrium sphaerocarpum"	40	40
279	65c. "Disa scullyi"	60	70
280	85c. "Disa tysonii"	80	1·00

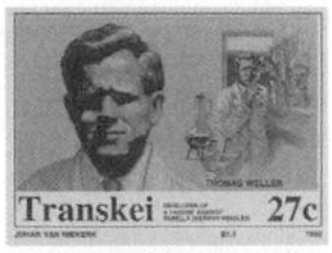

57 Thomas Weller (researcher into infectious viruses)

1992. Celebrities of Medicine (7th series). Multicoloured.

281	27c. Type **57**	75	25
282	45c. Ignaz Semmelweis	1·10	80
283	65c. Sir James Simpson	1·50	1·25
284	85c. Rene Laennec	1·75	1·60

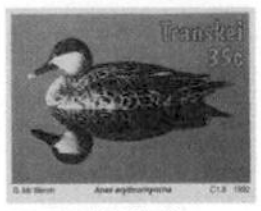

58 Red-billed Pintail

1992. Waterfowl. Multicoloured.

285	35c. Type **58**	60	60
286	35c. Hottentot teal	60	60
287	70c. Maccoa duck	90	90
288	70c. White-backed duck	90	90
289	90c. African black duck	1·10	1·10
290	90c. Egyptian goose	1·10	1·10
291	1r.05 Cape shoveler	1·40	1·40
292	1r.05 Cape teal	1·40	1·40

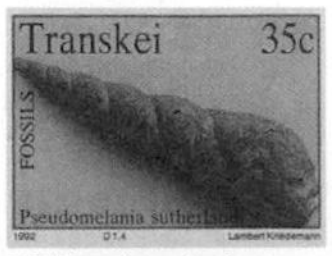

59 "Pseudomelania sutherlandi" (gastropod)

1992. Marine Fossils. Multicoloured.

293	35c. Type **59**	1·10	35
294	70c. "Gaudryceras denseplicatum" (ammonite)	1·50	1·10
295	90c. "Neithea quinquecostata" (bivalve)	1·60	1·50
296	1r.05 "Pugilina acuticarinatus" (gastropod)	1·75	1·60

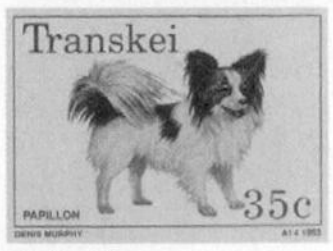

60 Papillon

1993. Dogs. Multicoloured.

297	35c. Type **60**	60	30
298	70c. Pekingese	90	90
299	90c. Chihuahua	1·10	1·25
300	1r.05 Dachshund	1·40	1·60

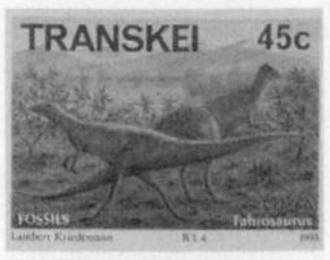

61 Fabrosaurus

1993. Prehistoric Animals. Multicoloured.

301	45c. Type **61**	1·10	40
302	65c. Diictodon	1·50	1·10
303	85c. Chasmatosaurus	1·75	1·60
304	1r.05 Rubidgea	1·75	1·75

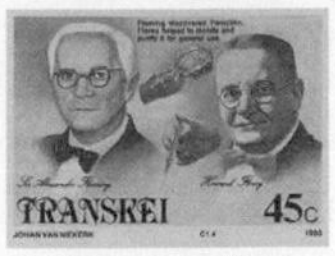

62 Sir Alexander Fleming and Howard Florey (discoverer and refiner of penicillin)

1993. Celebrities of Medicine (8th series). Multicoloured.

305	45c. Type **62**	70	40
306	65c. Alexis Carrel	1·10	1·10
307	85c. James Lind	1·25	1·50
308	1r.05 Santiago Ramon y Cajal	1·40	1·60

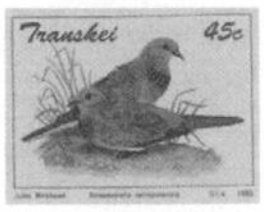

63 Laughing Doves

1993. Doves. Multicoloured.

309	45c. Type **63**	60	40
310	65c. Tambourine doves	90	90
311	85c. Emerald-spotted wood doves	1·25	1·25
312	1r.05 Namaqua doves	1·50	1·60
MS313	98×83 mm. Nos. 309/12	3·75	3·75

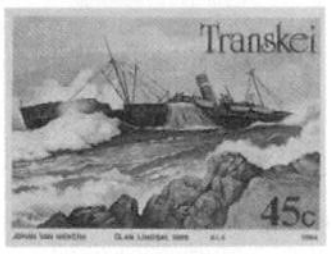

64 "Clan Lindsay" (steamer) on Rocks, Mazeppa Bay, 1898

1994. Shipwrecks. Multicoloured.

314	45c. Type **64**	1·25	60
315	65c. "Horizon" (freighter) on rocks near River Mngazi, 1967	1·60	1·25
316	85c. "Oceanos" (pleasure cruiser) sinking near Coffee Bay, 1991	1·90	1·60
317	1r.05 "Forresbank" (freighter) on fire near River Mtakatye, 1958	1·90	1·90

Pt. 1

TRANSVAAL

Formerly South African Republic under Boer rule, annexed by Gt. Britain in 1877, restored to the Boers in 1881 and again annexed in 1900 and since 1919 a province of the Union of S. Africa.

12 pence = 1 shilling; 20 shillings = 1 pound.

1

1870. Imperf or roul.

22	1	1d. black	30·00	40·00
61	1	1d. red	38·00	29·00
53	1	3d. lilac	80·00	55·00
54a	1	6d. blue	80·00	55·00
32	1	1s. green	£130	70·00

1874. Perf.

38	1d. red	£180	60·00
171	1d. grey	9·00	3·50
172	3d. black on red	38·00	8·50
173	3d. red	18·00	3·75
173c	3d. brown	38·00	7·50
41	6d. blue	£225	75·00
174	1s. green	90·00	8·50

1877. Optd **V. R. TRANSVAAL**. Imperf or roul.

101	1d. red	40·00	32·00
102	3d. lilac	£140	70·00
103	6d. blue	£160	42·00
113	6d. blue on red	£140	65·00
104	1s. green	£200	80·00

1877. Optd **V. R. Transvaal**. Imperf or roul.

116	1d. red on blue	80·00	40·00
117	1d. red on orange	38·00	28·00
118	3d. lilac on brown	85·00	38·00
119e	3d. lilac on green	£225	48·00
149	3d. lilac on blue	70·00	38·00
121	6d. blue on blue	£110	38·00
126	6d. blue on green	£130	38·00

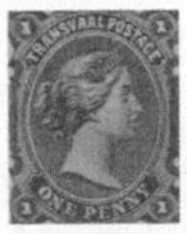

9

1878. Perf.

133	**9**	½d. red	30·00	95·00
134a	**9**	1d. brown	20·00	7·00
135	**9**	3d. red	29·00	9·50
136	**9**	4d. olive	40·00	11·00
137	**9**	6d. black	18·00	10·00
138	**9**	1s. green	£180	55·00
139	**9**	2s. blue	£300	£100

1879. Surch **1 Penny**.

145	1d. on 6d. black	65·00	27·00

1882. Surch **EEN PENNY**.

170	1d. on 4d. green	26·00	8·50

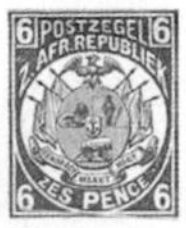

18

1885

175	**18**	½d. grey	2·50	10
176b	**18**	1d. red	2·00	10
177	**18**	2d. purple	3·50	4·75
178	**18**	2d. brown	3·50	10
179	**18**	2½d. mauve	4·50	55
180	**18**	3d. mauve	5·00	3·25
181	**18**	4d. olive	7·00	2·25
182	**18**	6d. blue	5·00	4·50
183	**18**	1s. green	4·75	2·50
184	**18**	2s.6d. yellow	17·00	4·25
185	**18**	5s. grey	10·00	7·50
186	**18**	10s. brown	45·00	17·00
187	**18**	£5 green	£3250	£190

1885. Surch **HALVE PENNY** vert, reading up or down.

188	**1**	½d. on 3d. red (No. 173)	9·50	14·00
192	**18**	½d. on 3d. mauve	9·50	9·50
189	**1**	½d. on 1s. green (No. 174)	38·00	65·00

1885. Surch with value in words and **Z. A. R.** both vert.

190	**9**	½d. on 6d. black	85·00	£120
191	**9**	2d. on 6d. black	14·00	19·00

1887. Surch **2d** and thick bar.

194	**18**	2d. on 3d. mauve	3·00	6·00

1893. Surch **Halve Penny** and bars.

196	½d. on 2d. pale brown	1·75	3·50

1893. Surch in figures and words between bars. (A) in one line, (B) in two.

197	1d. on 6d. blue (A)	2·75	2·50
198	2½d. on 1s. green (A)	3·25	8·00
199	2½d. on 1s. green (B)	11·00	8·50

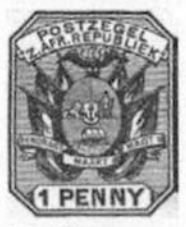

29 (Wagon with shafts)

1894

200	**29**	½d. grey	2·50	1·50
201	**29**	1d. red	4·00	20
202	**29**	2d. brown	4·00	30
203	**29**	6d. blue	4·50	1·00
204	**29**	1s. green	22·00	28·00

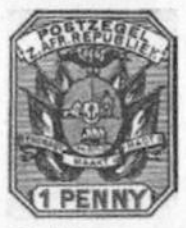

30 (Wagon with pole)

1895

205	**30**	½d. grey	2·25	10
206	**30**	1d. red	2·25	10
207	**30**	2d. brown	2·25	30
208	**30**	3d. mauve	3·75	1·25
209	**30**	4d. black	4·00	1·00
210	**30**	6d. blue	4·00	1·00
211	**30**	1s. green	5·00	1·50
212	**30**	5s. grey	22·00	40·00
212a	**30**	10s. brown	22·00	9·00

1895. Surch **Halve Penny** and bar.

213	½d. on 1s. green	2·25	40

1895. Surch **1d.** and thick bar.

214	**18**	1d. on 2½d. mauve	50	30

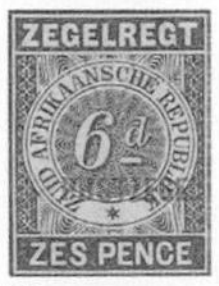

33

1895. Fiscal stamp optd **POSTZEGEL**.

215	**33**	6d. red	3·00	3·00

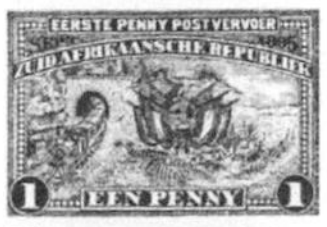

34

1895. Introduction of Penny Postage.

215c	**34**	1d. red	2·75	3·25

1896

216	**30**	½d. green	1·75	10
217	**30**	1d. red and green	1·75	10
218	**30**	2d. brown and green	2·00	20
219	**30**	2½d. blue and green	3·00	30
220	**30**	3d. purple and green	3·25	3·00
221	**30**	4d. olive and green	3·25	4·00
222	**30**	6d. lilac and green	3·00	2·75
223	**30**	1s. pale brown and green	2·50	1·50
224	**30**	2s.6d. violet and green	3·75	4·50

1900. Optd **V.R.I.**

226	½d. green	40	1·25
227	1d. red and green	75	1·25
228	2d. brown and green	4·25	3·50
229	2½d. blue and green	1·25	3·50
230	3d. purple and green	1·25	3·25
231	4d. olive and green	3·75	4·00
232	6d. lilac and green	4·00	2·75
233	1s. brown and green	4·00	4·50
234	2s.6d. violet and green	4·75	16·00
235	5s. grey	10·00	24·00
236	10s. brown	13·00	26·00
237 **18**	£5 green	£2000	£800

The majority of the £5 stamps, No. 237 on the market, are forgeries.

1901. Optd **E.R.I.**

238	**30**	½d. green	50	2·25
239	**30**	1d. red and green	50	10
240	**30**	3d. purple and green	2·25	4·75
241	**30**	4d. olive and green	2·75	9·00
242	**30**	2s.6d. violet and green	13·00	32·00

1901. Surch **E.R.I.** Half Penny.

243	½d. on 2d. brown and green	65	1·75

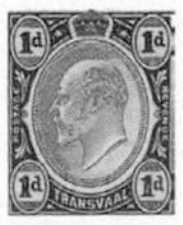

38

1902

244	**38**	½d. black and green	2·50	20
273	**38**	½d. green	3·50	10
245	**38**	1d. black and red	1·50	15
274	**38**	1d. red	1·25	10
246	**38**	2d. black and purple	7·00	1·00
275	**38**	2d. purple	3·50	60
247	**38**	2½d. black and blue	14·00	1·75
276	**38**	2½d. blue	24·00	12·00
264	**38**	3d. black and green	3·50	50
265	**38**	4d. black and brown	5·00	70
266a	**38**	6d. black and orange	5·50	50
251	**38**	1s. black and green	18·00	23·00
267	**38**	1s. grey and brown	13·00	50
252	**38**	2s. black and brown	70·00	80·00
257	**38**	2s. grey and yellow	19·00	22·00
253	**38**	2s.6d. mauve and black	17·00	18·00
270	**38**	5s. black & purple on yellow	29·00	1·75
271	**38**	10s. black & purple on red	90·00	4·25
272a	**38**	£1 green and violet	£300	22·00
259	**38**	£5 brown and violet	£2000	£900

Nos. 267, 268 and all values of 2s.6d. and above have the inscription "POSTAGE" on both sides. The rest are inscribed "POSTAGE" at left and "REVENUE" at right.

POSTAGE DUE STAMPS

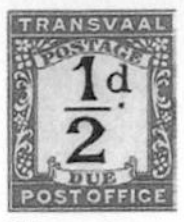

D1

1907

D1	**D1**	½d. black and green	3·50	1·25
D2	**D1**	1d. black and red	4·00	85
D3	**D1**	2d. brown	6·50	1·25
D4	**D1**	3d. black and blue	7·50	5·50
D5	**D1**	5d. black and violet	3·25	12·00
D6	**D1**	6d. black and brown	4·25	12·00
D7	**D1**	1s. red and black	17·00	10·00

Pt. 1

TRAVANCORE

A state in south-east India. In 1949 formed part of Travancore-Cochin.

16 cash = 1 chuckram; 28 chuckrams = 1 rupee.

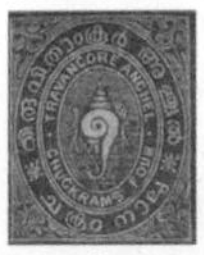

1 Conch or Chank Shell

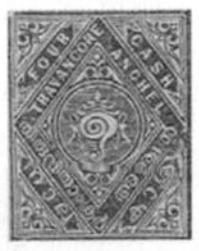

3

1888. Various frames.

9	**3**	4 cash pink	30	10
24	-	5 cash olive	80	30
34	-	5 cash brown	3·25	50
10	**1**	6 cash brown	30	10
27	-	10 cash pink	40	10
13	-	¾ch. black	2·25	25
39	-	¾ch. mauve	60	10
15	**1**	1¼ch. purple	55	55
42	**1**	1½ch. red	2·75	10
17	-	3ch. violet	2·75	20
19	-	7ch. purple	2·50	1·25
20	-	14ch. orange	2·75	3·00

1906. Surch in figures.

21a	¼ on ½ch. purple	1·00	20
22	⅜on ½ch. purple	1·00	35

1921. Surch in figures.

31	**3**	1c. on 4ca. pink	15	20
57	-	1c. on 5ca. brown	15	15
58	-	1c. on 5ca. purple	2·50	70
50	**1**	1c. on 1¼ch. purple	15	50
51	**1**	2c. on 1¼ch. purple	15	30
59	-	2c. on 10ca. pink	15	15
32	**1**	5c. on 1ch. blue	1·00	10

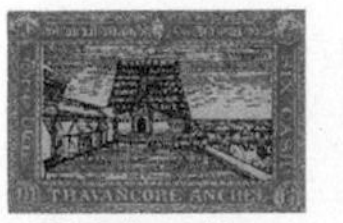

11 Sri Padmanabha Shrine

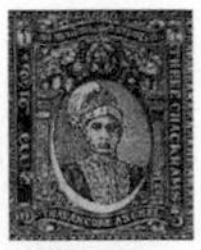

13 Maharaja Bala Rama Varma XI

1931. Coronation.

47	**11**	6 cash black and green	1·60	1·60
48	-	10 cash black and blue	1·25	70
49	**13**	3ch. black and purple	2·75	3·25

DESIGN—As Type **11**: 10 cash, State chariot.

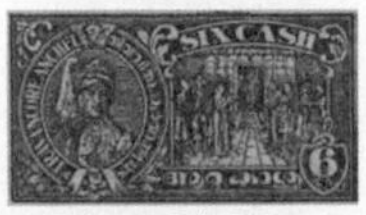

16 Maharaja Bala Rama Varma XI and Subramania Shrine

1937. Temple Entry Proclamation.

60	**16**	6 cash red	4·25	1·75
61	-	12 cash blue	6·00	1·25
62	-	1½ch. green	1·75	3·50
63	-	3ch. violet	6·50	3·00

DESIGNS: Portraits of the Maharaja and the temples of Sri Padmanabha (12 cash), Mahadeva (1½ch.) and Kanyakumari (3ch.).

1939. Maharaja's 27th Birthday

64	**20**	1ch. green	12·00	10
65	-	1½ch. red	7·00	7·00
66	**22**	2ch. orange	12·00	4·00
67	-	3ch. brown	11·00	10
68	-	4ch. red	14·00	40
69	-	7ch. blue	17·00	25·00
70	-	14ch. green	8·00	85·00

DESIGNS—As Type **22**: 1½, 3ch. Portraits of Maharaja. As Type **20**: 4ch. Sri Padmanabha Shrine; 7ch. Cape Comorin; 14ch. Pachipari Reservoir.

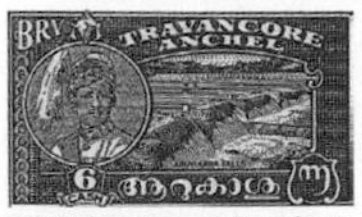

27 Maharaja and Aruvikara Falls

1941. 29th Birthday of Maharaja.

71a	**27**	6ca. violet	6·50	10
72	-	¾ch. brown	9·00	30

DESIGN: ¾ch. Maharaja and Marthanda Varma Bridge, Alwaye.

1943. Stamps of 1939 and 1941 surch in figures and capital letters.

73e		2ca. on 1½ch. red (No. 65)	40	50
74a		4ca. on ¾ch. brown (No. 72)	8·00	60
75	**19**	8ca. on 6ca. red (as No. 7)	5·00	30

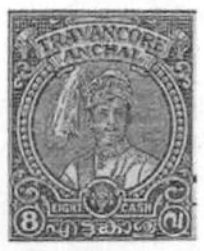

30 Maharaja Bala Rama Varma XI

1946. 34th Birthday of Maharaja.

76a	**30**	8ca. red	3·50	2·25

1946. No. O103 optd **SPECIAL**.

77	**27**	6 cash violet	8·50	5·00

OFFICIAL STAMPS

1911. Optd **On S S.**

O1	**3**	4 cash pink	20	10
O14	-	5 cash olive	2·25	10
O29	-	5 cash brown	25	75
O15	**1**	6 cash brown	30	10
O54	**1**	½ch. purple	20	10
O18	-	10 cash pink	2·00	10
O39	-	¾ch. black	35	15
O56	-	¾ch. mauve	60	15
O5	**1**	1ch. blue	2·00	10
O59	**1**	1½ch. red	40	10
O21	**1**	1¼ch. purple	50	10
O6	**1**	2ch. red	35	10
O8	-	3ch. violet	35	10
O10	**1**	4ch. green	55	10
O64	-	7ch. purple	1·50	30
O65	-	14ch. orange	2·25	40

1932. Official stamps surch in figures.

O74		6c. on 5ca. olive	1·75	2·00
O75		6c. on 5ca. brown	50	50
O83		12c. on 10ca. pink	20	15
O84	**1**	1ch.8c. on 1¼ch. red	35	25

1939. Optd **SERVICE**.

O85b		6 cash brown	70	30
O94	-	¾ch. mauve (No. 39)	24·00	20
O96	**20**	1ch. green	1·50	10
O95a	**1**	1½ch. red	6·50	1·00
O97b	-	1½ch. red (No. 65)	4·75	15
O98	**20**	2ch. orange	5·50	30
O99	-	3ch. brown (No. 67)	4·00	10
O100	-	4ch. red (No. 68)	5·50	1·00
O101	-	7ch. blue (No. 69)	10·00	35
O102	-	14ch. green (No. 70)	16·00	70

1942. Optd **SERVICE**.

O103	**27**	6 cash violet	60	50
O104	-	¾ch. brown (No. 72)	6·50	10

1942. Nos. 73a/5a optd **SERVICE**.

O106a	-	2ca. on 1½ch. red	50	15
O107a	-	4ca. on ¾ch.	3·00	20
O105a	**27**	8cash on 6ca. red	2·00	10

1947. Optd **SERVICE**.

O108	**30**	8 cash red	5·00	1·75

Pt. 1

TRAVANCORE-COCHIN

In 1949 the states of Cochin and Travancore in south-east India were united under the name of the United States of Travancore and Cochin. Now uses stamps of India.

12 pies = 1 anna; 16 annas = 1 rupee.

NO WATERMARK VARIETIES. These were formerly listed but we have now decided to omit them as they do not occur in full sheets. They are best collected in pairs, with and without watermarks.

COMPOUND PERFS. The notes above type **17** of Travancore also apply here.

VALIDITY OF STAMPS. From 6 June 1950 the stamps of Travancore-Cochin were valid on mail from both Indian and state post offices to destinations in India and abroad.

1949. Stamps of Travancore surch in PIES or ANNAS in English and native characters.

1e	**27**	2p. on 6ca. violet	1·00	20
2d	**30**	4p. on 8ca. red	1·50	30
3e	**20**	½a. on 1ch. green	1·00	40
4a	**22**	1a. on 2ch. orange	1·50	30
5d	**11**	2a. on 4ch. brown	5·00	55
6a	**25**	3a. on 7ch. blue (No. 69)	6·50	5·00
7b	**26**	6a. on 14ch. green (No. 70)	26·00	42·00

1949. No. 106 of Cochin optd **U.S.T.C.**

8	**21**	1a. orange	10·00	£110

1950. No. 106 of Cochin optd **T.-C.**

9	1a. orange	7·50	90·00

1950. No. 9 surch with new value.

10	6p. on 1a. orange	4·75	75·00
11	9p. on 1a. orange	4·50	75·00

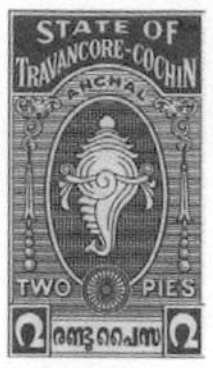

5 Conch or Chank Shell

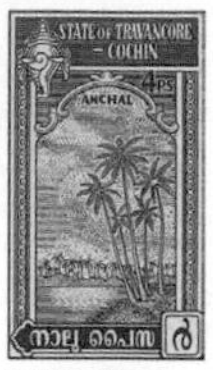

6 Palm Trees

1950

12	**5**	2p. red	3·00	4·75
13	**6**	4p. blue	5·00	18·00

OFFICIAL STAMPS

1949. Stamps of Travancore surch **SERVICE** and value in PIES or ANNAS in English and native characters.

O1f	**27**	2p. on 6ca. No. 71	1·75	75
O9a	**24**	2a. on 4ch. (No. 68)	1·75	1·10
O10f	**30**	4p. on 8ca. (No. 76a)	30	20
O11b	**20**	½a. on 1ch. (No. 64)	75	20
O14e	**25**	3a. on 7ch. (No. 69)	1·50	1·10
O12	**22**	1a. on 2ch. (No. 66)	40	30
O15	**26**	6a. on 14ch. (No. 70)	1·50	4·50

Pt. 1

TRENGGANU

A state of the Federation of Malaya, incorporated in Malaysia in 1963.

100 cents = 1 dollar (Straits or Malayan).

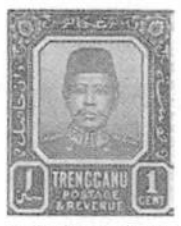

1 Sultan Zain ul ab din

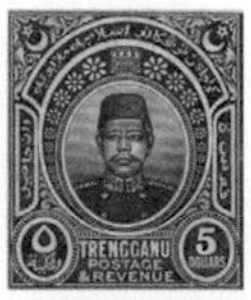

2 Sultan Zain ul ab din

1910

1	**1**	1c. green	1·75	1·00
2	**1**	2c. brown and purple	1·00	90
3	**1**	3c. red	2·25	2·25
4	**1**	4c. orange	3·50	6·00
5	**1**	4c. brown and green	2·00	4·00
5a	**1**	4c. red	1·25	2·00
6	**1**	5c. grey	1·25	6·00
7	**1**	5c. grey and brown	2·25	2·00
8	**1**	8c. blue	1·25	16·00
9a	**1**	10c. purple on yellow	3·25	14·00
10	**1**	10c. green and red on yellow	1·25	2·25
11	**1**	20c. mauve and purple	3·75	8·00
12	**1**	25c. green and purple	11·00	50·00
13	**1**	30c. purple and black	10·00	70·00
14	**1**	50c. black on green	4·50	14·00
15	**1**	$1 black and red on blue	17·00	25·00
16	**1**	$3 green and red on green	£225	£600
17	**2**	$5 green and purple	£250	£700
18	**2**	$25 red and green	£1600	£3500

1917. Surch **RED CROSS 2c.**

19	**1**	2c. on 3c. red	50	11·00
20	**1**	2c. on 4c. orange	1·50	20·00
21	**1**	2c. on 4c. brown and green	3·75	50·00
22	**1**	2c. on 8c. blue	1·25	38·00

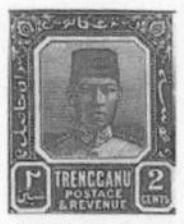

4 Sultan Suleiman

1921. As T **4**.

26	**4**	1c. black	1·75	1·50
27	**4**	2c. green	2·00	2·00
28	**4**	3c. green	2·00	1·00
29	**4**	3c. brown	40·00	14·00
30	**4**	4c. red	3·75	1·25
31	**4**	5c. grey and brown	2·00	5·00
32	**4**	5c. purple on yellow	1·75	1·25
33	**4**	6c. orange	6·50	70
34	**4**	8c. grey	50·00	8·00
35	**4**	10c. blue	3·25	1·00
36	**4**	12c. blue	4·25	1·75
37	**4**	20c. purple and orange	3·50	1·50
38	**4**	25c. green and purple	4·25	2·50
39	**4**	30c. purple and black	3·25	3·75
40	**4**	35c. red on yellow	4·75	3·25
41	**4**	50c. green and red	12·00	2·75
42	**4**	$1 purple and blue on blue	9·00	3·25
43	**4**	$3 green and red on green	60·00	£180

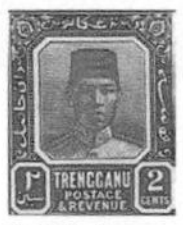

4 Sultan Suleiman

1921. Larger type, as T **2**, but portrait of Sultan Suleiman

25	$5 green and red on yellow	£160	£375
45	$25 purple and blue	£1200	£2750
46	$50 green and yellow	£3000	£4750
47	$100 green and red	£9000	£10000

1922. Optd **MALAYA-BORNEO EXHIBITION**.

48		2c. green	6·50	38·00
49		4c. red	6·50	50·00
50		5c. grey and brown	3·50	50·00
51	**1**	10c. green and red on yellow	5·50	45·00
52	**1**	20c. mauve and purple	8·50	48·00
53	**1**	25c. green and purple	5·00	48·00
54	**1**	30c. purple and black	5·50	48·00
55	**1**	50c. black on green	8·50	50·00
56	**1**	$1 black and red on blue	14·00	75·00
57	**1**	$3 green and red on green	£225	£475
58	**2**	$5 green and purple	£375	£700

1941. Surch.

59	**4**	2c. on 5c. purple on yellow	6·50	3·50
60	**4**	8c. on 10c. blue	7·00	7·50

1948. Silver Wedding. As T **33b/c** of St. Helena.

61	10c. violet	15	1·75
62	$5 red	26·00	42·00

1949. 75th Anniv of U.P.U. As T **33d/g** of St. Helena.

63	10c. purple	30	75
64	15c. blue	1·90	4·25
65	25c. orange	40	3·50
66	50c. black	1·00	3·50

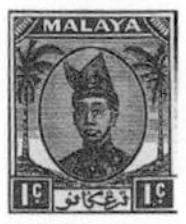

7 Sultan Ismail

1949

67	**7**	1c. black	1·00	75
68	**7**	2c. orange	1·00	75
69	**7**	3c. green	5·50	6·50
70	**7**	4c. brown	30	60
71	**7**	5c. purple	50	1·75
72	**7**	6c. grey	2·00	60
73	**7**	8c. red	1·00	3·75
74	**7**	8c. green	1·25	1·75
75	**7**	10c. purple	30	30
76	**7**	12c. red	1·25	3·00
77	**7**	15c. blue	9·00	30
78	**7**	20c. black and green	9·00	3·75
79	**7**	20c. blue	1·25	40
80	**7**	25c. purple and orange	2·50	2·00
81	**7**	30c. red and purple	1·25	2·25
82	**7**	35c. red and purple	1·50	2·25
83	**7**	40c. red and purple	12·00	26·00
84	**7**	50c. black and blue	2·25	2·25
85	**7**	$1 blue and green	7·00	15·00
86	**7**	$2 green and red	45·00	50·00
87	**7**	$3 green and brown	75·00	70·00

1953. Coronation. As T **33h** of St. Helena.

88	10c. black and purple	2·50	1·25

1957. As Nos. 92/102 of Kedah but inset portrait of Sultan Ismail.

89	1c. black	10	20
90	2c. red	1·50	30
91	4c. brown	15	10
92	5c. red	15	10
93	8c. green	4·00	60
94	10c. brown	2·75	10
94a	10c. purple	11·00	30
95	20c. blue	2·50	1·60
96a	50c. black and blue	55	2·00
97	$1 blue and purple	14·00	10·00
98	$2 green and red	17·00	9·00
99	$5 brown and green	32·00	22·00

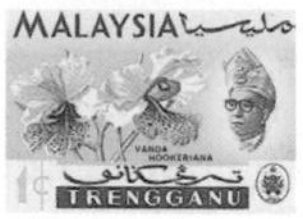

8 "Vanda hookeriana"

1965. As Nos. 115/21 of Kedah, but inset portrait of Sultan Ismail as in T **8**.

100	**8**	1c. multicoloured	10	2·00
101	-	2c. multicoloured	10	2·00
102	-	5c. multicoloured	15	1·00
103	-	6c. multicoloured	15	2·00
104	-	10c. multicoloured	20	25
105	-	15c. multicoloured	1·50	10
106	-	20c. multicoloured	1·50	1·50

The higher values used in Trengganu were Nos. 20/7 of Malaysia (National Issues).

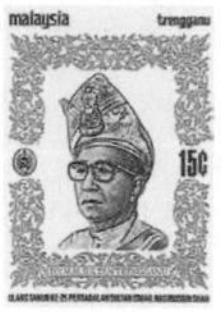

9 Sultan of Trengganu

1970. 25th Anniv of Installation of H.R.H. Tuanku Ismail Nasiruddin Shah as Sultan of Trengganu.

107	**9**	10c. multicoloured	1·00	3·00
108	**9**	15c. multicoloured	75	1·25
109	**9**	50c. multicoloured	1·25	3·00

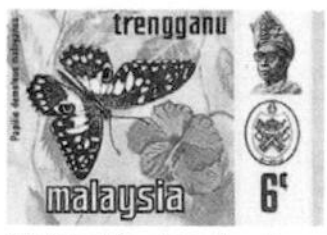

10 "Papilio demoleus"

1971. Butterflies. As Nos. 124/30 of Kedah but with portrait of Sultan Ismail Nasiruddin Shah as in T **10**.

110	-	1c. multicoloured	40	2·50
111	-	2c. multicoloured	80	2·50
112	-	5c. multicoloured	1·00	1·25
113	**10**	6c. multicoloured	1·75	2·75
114	-	10c. multicoloured	1·75	70
115	-	15c. multicoloured	1·75	20
116	-	20c. multicoloured	2·00	1·75

The high values in use with this issue were Nos. 64/71 of Malaysia (National Issues).

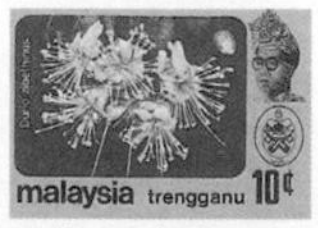

11 "Durio zibethinus"

1979. Flowers. As Nos. 135/41 of Kedah, but with portrait of Sultan Ismail Nasiruddin Shah as in T **11**.

118	1c. "Rafflesia hasseltii"	10	1·25
119	2c. "Pterocarpus indicus"	10	1·25
120	5c. "Lagerstroemia speciosa"	10	60
121	10c. Type **11**	15	10
122	15c. "Hibiscus rosa-sinensis"	15	10
123	20c. "Rhododendron scortechinii"	20	10
124	25c. "Etlingera elatior" (inscr "Phaeomeria speciosa")	40	50

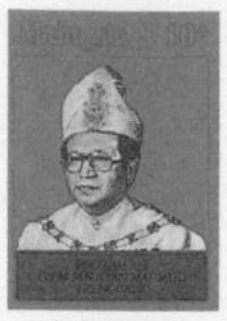

12 Sultan Mahmud

1981. Installation of Sultan Mahmud.

125	**12**	10c. black, blue and gold	35	1·50
126	**12**	15c. black, yellow and gold	45	50
127	**12**	50c. black, purple and gold	1·00	3·00

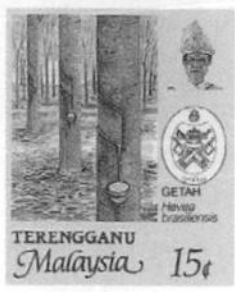

13 Rubber

1986. As Nos. 152/8 of Kedah but with portrait of Sultan Mahmud and inscr "TERENGGANU" as in T **13**.

135	1c. Coffee	10	30
136	2c. Coconuts	10	30
137	5c. Cocoa	15	30
138	10c. Black pepper	20	10
139	15c. Type **13**	30	10
140	20c. Oil palm	30	15
141	30c. Rice	40	15

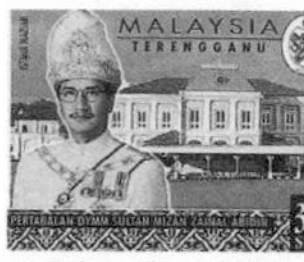

14 Sultan Mizan Zainal Abidin and Maziah Palace in 1999

1999. Installation of Sultan Mizan Zainal Abidin as Sultan of Trengganu. Multicoloured.

142	30c. Type **14**	50	25
143	50c. Maziah Palace, 1903	75	50
144	$1 Tengku Tengah Zahara Mosque at night	1·40	2·25

1999. As Nos. 137/8 and 140/1, but with portrait of Sultan Mizan.

147	5c. Cocoa	3·25	1·50
148	10c. Black pepper	3·25	1·50
150	20c. Oil palm	3·25	1·25
151	30c. Rice	80	85

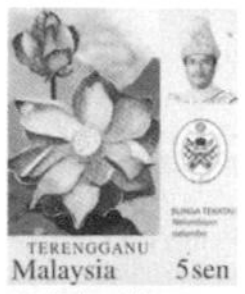

15 *Nelumbium nelumbo* (sacred lotus)

2007. Garden Flowers. As Nos. 210/15 of Johore, but with portrait of Sultan Mizan Zainal Abidin and Arms of Trengganu as in T **15**. Multicoloured.

152	5s. Type **15**	10	10
153	10s. *Hydrangea macrophylla*	15	10
154	20s. *Hippeastrum reticulatum*	25	15
155	30s. *Bougainvillea*	40	20
156	40s. *Ipomoea indica*	50	30
157	50s. *Hibiscus rosa-sinensis*	65	35
MS158	100×85 mm. Nos. 152/7	2·00	1·10

POSTAGE DUE STAMPS

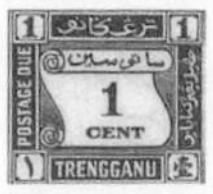

D1

1937

D1	**D1**	1c. red	8·50	55·00
D2	**D1**	4c. green	9·50	60·00
D3	**D1**	8c. yellow	55·00	£350
D4	**D1**	10c. brown	£120	£100

Pt. 8

TRIESTE

The Free Territory of Trieste situated on the Adriatic Coast between the frontiers of Italy and Yugoslavia. In 1954, when the Territory was divided between Italy and Yugoslavia, the overprinted issues were superseded by the ordinary issues of these countries in their respective zones.

For stamps of Italy surcharged **1.V.1945. TRIESTE TRST**, five-pointed star and value, see Venezia Giulia Nos. 20/32.

Allied Military Government.
100 centesimi = 1 lira.
1948. Yugoslav Military Government.
100 centesimi = 1 lira.
1949. 100 paras = 1 dinar.

ZONE A
ALLIED MILITARY GOVERNMENT

Stamps of Italy variously overprinted **A.M.G. F.T.T.** or **AMG-FTT** (Allied Military Government – Free Territory of Trieste) except where otherwise stated.

1947. Postage stamps of 1945, Nos. 647, etc.

1	25c. blue	30	2·50
2	50c. violet	30	2·50
3	1l. green	30	25
4	2l. brown	30	25
5	3l. red	30	25
6	4l. red	30	25
7	5l. blue	30	25
8	6l. violet	30	25
9	8l. green	5·00	6·25
10	10l. grey	65	30
11	10l. red	15·00	1·30
12	15l. blue	2·50	30
13	20l. violet	5·00	30
14	25l. green	10·00	10·00
15	30l. blue	£250	12·50
16	50l. purple	12·50	6·25
17	100l. red (No. 669)	70·00	44·00

1947. Air stamps of 1945, Nos. 670, etc.

18	1l. grey	40	25
19	2l. blue	40	25
20	5l. green	3·75	1·90
21	10l. red	3·75	1·90
22	25l. brown	12·50	6·25
23	50l. violet	55·00	12·50
24	100l. green	£110	10·00
25	300l. mauve	23·00	31·00
26	500l. blue	28·00	35·00
27	1000l. brown	£250	£250

1947. Air. 50th Anniv of Radio (Nos. 688/93).

59	6l. violet	2·50	2·20
60	10l. red	2·50	2·20
61	20l. orange	15·00	10·00
62	25l. blue	3·75	3·25
63	35l. blue	3·75	3·50
64	50l. purple	16·00	11·50

1948. Cent of 1848 Revolution (Nos. 706, etc).

65	3l. brown	30	25
66	4l. purple	30	25
67	5l. blue	30	25
68	6l. green	30	25
69	8l. brown	30	25
70	10l. red	50	30
71	12l. green	90	1·50
72	15l. black	24·00	12·50
73	20l. red	29·00	12·50
74	30l. blue	3·75	2·75
75	50l. violet	19·00	21·00
76	100l. blue	65·00	60·00

1948. Trieste Philatelic Congress stamps of 1945 optd **A.M.G. F.T.T. 1948 TRIESTE** and posthorn.

77	8l. green (postage)	25	25
78	10l. red	25	25
79	30l. blue	2·50	2·50
80	10l. red (air)	40	40
81	25l. brown	1·00	1·00
82	50l. violet	1·00	1·00

1948. Rebuilding of Bassano Bridge.

84	**209**	15l. green	2·75	2·30

1948. Donizetti.

85	**210**	15l. brown	15·00	3·25

1949. 25th Biennial Art Exhibition, Venice.

86	**212**	5l. red and flesh	1·60	2·00
87	-	15l. green and cream	12·50	14·00
88	-	20l. brown and buff	10·00	2·50
89	-	50l. blue and yellow	19·00	10·50

1949. 27th Milan Fair.

90	**211**	20l. brown	12·50	3·75

1949. 75th Anniv of U.P.U.

91	**213**	50l. blue	5·75	5·25

1949. Centenary of Roman Republic.

92	**214**	100l. brown	95·00	£110

1949. First Trieste Free Election.

93	**218**	20l. red	7·00	3·75

1949. European Recovery Plan.

94	**215**	5l. green	12·50	6·50
95	**215**	15l. violet	14·00	15·00
96	**215**	20l. brown	16·00	15·00

1949. Second World Health Congress, Rome.

97	**219**	20l. violet	16·00	7·50

1949. Giuseppe Mazzini.

98	**216**	20l. black	12·50	5·00

1949. Bicentenary of Vittorio Alfieri.

99	**217**	20l. brown	12·50	5·00

1949. 400th Anniv of Palladio's Basilica at Vicenza.

100	**220**	20l. violet	23·00	19·00

1949. 500th Birth Anniv of Lorenzo de Medici.

101	**221**	20l. blue	12·50	6·25

1949. 13th Bari Fair.

102	**222**	20l. red	12·50	5·75

1949. (a) Postage.

103	**195**	1l. green	30	30
104	-	2l. brown (No. 656)	30	30
105	-	3l. red (No. 657)	30	30
106	**193**	5l. blue	30	30
107	**195**	6l. violet	30	30
108	-	8l. green (No. 661)	35·00	14·00
109	**193**	10l. red	30	30
110	**195**	15l. blue	2·75	1·30
111	-	20l. purple (No. 665)	2·20	65
112	**196**	25l. green	44·00	5·00
113	**196**	50l. purple	65·00	5·00
114	**197**	100l. red	£150	23·00

(b) Air.

115	**198**	10l. red	40	25
116	-	25l. brown (No. 676)	40	25
117	**198**	50l. violet	40	25
118	-	100l. green (No. 911)	1·90	40
119	-	300l. mauve (No. 912)	23·00	14·00
120	-	500l. blue (No. 913)	25·00	16·00
121	-	1000l. purple (No. 914)	50·00	44·00

1949. 150th Anniv of Volta's Discovery of the Electric Cell.

135	[illegible]	20l. red	6·25	6·25
136	**224**	50l. blue	30·00	30·00

1949. Rebuilding of Holy Trinity Bridge, Florence.

137	**225**	20l. green	10·00	7·50

1949. Death Bimillenary of Catullus (poet).

138	**226**	20l. blue	7·50	5·75

1949. Birth Bicentenary of Domenico Cimarosa (composer).

153	**227**	20l. violet	8·75	5·00

1950. 28th Milan Fair.

154	**228**	20l. brown	8·75	5·00

1950. 32nd Int Automobile Exn, Turin.

155	**229**	20l. violet	4·50	3·75

1950. Fifth General UNESCO Conference.

156	-	20l. green	6·25	2·50
157	**230**	55l. blue	19·00	18·00

1950. Holy Year.

158	**231**	20l. violet	8·75	2·50
159	**231**	55l. blue	23·00	16·00

1950. Honouring Gaudenzio Ferrari (painter).

160	**232**	20l. green	6·25	4·50

1950. International Radio Conference.

161	**233**	20l. violet	10·00	8·75
162	**233**	55l. blue	30·00	29·00

1950. Death Bicentenary of Ludovico Murator (historian).

163	**234**	20l. brown	7·50	5·00

1950. 900th Death Anniv of D'Arezzo.

164	**235**	20l. green	8·25	5·00

1950. 14th Levant Fair, Bari.

165	**236**	20l. brown	5·00	5·00

1950. Second Trieste Fair. Optd **AMG FTT Fiera di Trieste 1950**.

166	**195**	15l. blue	7·50	3·25
167	-	20l. purple (No. 665)	7·50	3·25

1950. Wool Industry Pioneers.

168	**237**	20l. blue	5·00	4·75

1950. European Tobacco Conf (Nos. 755/7).

169	5l. green and mauve	2·50	1·90
170	20l. green and brown	5·00	4·50
171	55l. brown and blue	38·00	33·00

1950. Bicentenary of Fine Arts Academy.

172	**239**	20l. red and deep brown	5·75	5·00

1950. Birth Centenary of Augusto Righi.

173	**240**	20l. black and buff	7·50	5·75

1950. Provincial Occupations (Nos. 760/78).

176	50c. blue	40	25
177	1l. violet	40	25
178	2l. brown	1·30	25
179	5l. black	40	25
180	6l. brown	40	25
181	10l. green	1·90	25
182	12l. green	3·25	1·30
183	15l. blue	3·25	30
184	20l. violet	3·25	30
185	25l. brown	10·00	30
186	30l. purple	2·00	90
187	35l. red	3·50	2·00
188	40l. brown	3·50	75
189	50l. violet	40	25
190	55l. blue	40	30
191	60l. red	12·00	6·25
192	65l. green	40	30
193	100l. brown	8·75	65
194	200l. brown	7·00	6·25

1951. Centenary of First Tuscan Stamp.

195	**249**	20l. red and purple	6·25	5·00
196	**249**	55l. blue and ultramarine	70·00	65·00

1951. 33rd International Motor Show, Turin.

197	**243**	20l. green	3·75	3·50

1951. Consecration of Hall of Peace, Rome.

198	**244**	20l. violet	5·00	3·75

1951. 29th Milan Fair.

199	**245**	20l. brown	5·00	4·50
200	**246**	55l. blue	7·50	7·00

1951. Tenth International Textiles Exn, Turin.

201	**247**	20l. violet	5·00	3·75

1951. 500th Birth Anniv of Columbus.

202	**248**	20l. green	6·25	5·75

1951. International Gymnastic Festival, Florence.

203	**249**	5l. red and brown	11·00	44·00
204	**249**	10l. red and green	11·00	44·00
205	**249**	15l. red and blue	11·00	44·00

1951. Restoration of Montecassino Abbey.

206	**250**	20l. violet	1·90	1·30
207	-	55l. blue (No. 791)	5·00	3·25

1951. Third Trieste Fair. Optd **AMG-FTT FIERA di TRIESTE 1951** and shield.

208	6l. brown (No. 764)	1·50	1·10
209	20l. violet (No. 768)	1·60	1·30
210	55l. blue (No. 774)	2·20	2·00

1951. 500th Birth Anniv of Perugino.

211	**251**	20l. brown and sepia	3·25	3·25

1951. Triennial Art Exhibition, Milan.

212	**252**	20l. black and green	2·50	2·50
213	-	55l. pink and blue (No. 794)	5·00	5·00

1951. World Cycling Championship.

214	**253**	25l. black	11·50	5·00

1951. 15th Levant Fair, Bari.

215	**254**	25l. blue	3·25	2·50

1951. Birth Centenary of F. P. Michetti.

216	**255**	25l. brown	3·25	2·50

1951. Sardinian Stamp Centenary.

217	**256**	10l. black and brown	1·30	1·30
218	-	25l. green and red (No. 799)	1·30	1·30
219	-	60l. red and blue (No. 800)	3·25	3·25

1951. Third Industrial and Commercial Census.

220	**257**	10l. green	1·90	1·30

1951. Ninth National Census.

221	**258**	25l. black	1·90	1·30

1951. Forestry Festival.

222	**260**	10l. green and olive	2·20	1·60
223	**260**	25l. green (No. 807)	2·20	1·60

1951. Verdi.

224	-	10l. green and purple (No. 803)	1·90	1·40
225	**259**	25l. sepia and brown	1·90	1·40
226	-	60l. blue and green (No. 805)	3·25	2·50

1952. Bellini.

227	**261**	25l. black	1·90	1·30

1952. Caserta Palace.

228	**262**	25l. bistre and green	1·90	1·30

1952. First International Sports Stamps Exn, Rome.

229	**263**	25l. brown and black	2·50	1·30

1952. 30th Milan Fair.

230	**264**	60l. blue	4·50	5·00

1952. Leonardo da Vinci.

231	**265**	25l. orange	30	25
232	-	60l. blue (No. 813)	2·30	3·25
233	**265**	80l. red	3·75	3·25

1952. Overseas Fair, Naples.

234	**268**	25l. blue	1·90	1·30

1952. Modena and Parma Stamp Centenaries.

235	**267**	25l. black and brown	95	90
236	**267**	60l. indigo and blue	1·60	1·50

1952. Art Exhibition, Venice.

237	**269**	25l. black and cream	2·50	1·30

1952. 30th Padua Fair.

238	**270**	25l. red and blue	1·90	1·30

1952. Fourth Trieste Fair.

239	**271**	25l. green, red and brown	1·90	1·30

1952. 16th Levant Fair, Bari.

240	**272**	25l. green	1·90	1·30

1952. Savonarola.

241	**273**	25l. violet	1·90	1·30

1952. First Private Aeronautics Conf, Rome.

242	**274**	60l. blue and ultramarine	5·00	5·00

1952. Alpine Troops National Exhibition.

243	**275**	25l. black	2·50	1·30

1952. Armed Forces Day.

244	**276**	10l. green	1·00	1·00
245	**277**	25l. brown & light brown	1·30	1·30
246	-	60l. black and blue (No. 827)	3·75	3·75

1952. Mission to Ethiopia.

247	**278**	25l. deep brown and brown	2·50	1·30

1952. Birth Centenary of Gemito (sculptor).

248	**279**	25l. brown	1·90	1·30

1952. Birth Centenary of Mancini (painter).

249	**280**	25l. green	1·90	1·30

1952. Centenary of Martyrdom of Belfiore.

250	**281**	25l. blue and black	2·50	1·30

1953. Antonello Exhibition, Messina.

251	**282**	25l. red	2·50	1·30

1953. 20th "Mille Miglia" Car Race.

252	**283**	25l. violet	2·50	1·30

1953. Labour Orders of Merit.

253	**284**	25l. violet	2·50	1·30

1953. 300th Birth Anniv of Corelli.

254	**285**	25l. brown	2·50	1·30

1953. Coin type.

255	**286**	5l. grey	30	25
256	**286**	10l. red	30	25
257	**286**	12l. green	30	25
258	**286**	13l. purple	30	25
259	**286**	20l. brown	65	40
260	**286**	25l. violet	65	40
261	**286**	35l. red	5·00	3·25
262	**286**	60l. blue	5·00	3·25
263	**286**	80l. brown	7·50	6·25

1953. Seventh Death Centenary of St. Clare.

264	**287**	25l. red and brown	2·75	1·30

1953. Fifth Trieste Fair. Optd **V FIERA DI TRIESTE AMG FTT 1953.**

265	10l. green (No. 765)	1·30	50
266	25l. orange (No. 769)	1·30	50
267	60l. red (No. 775)	1·30	1·10

1953. Mountains Festival.

272	**288**	25l. green	2·75	1·30

1953. International Agricultural Exn, Rome.

273	**289**	25l. brown	75	55
274	**289**	60l. blue	1·30	1·00

1953. Fourth Anniv of Atlantic Pact.

275	**290**	25l. turquoise and orange	1·90	1·80
276	**290**	60l. blue and mauve	3·75	3·75

1953. Fifth Birth Centenary of Signorelli.

277	**291**	25l. green and brown	1·90	1·30

1953. Sixth Int Microbiological Congress, Rome.

278	**292**	25l. brown and black	1·90	1·30

1953. Tourist series (Nos. 855/60).

279	10l. brown and sepia	30	25
280	12l. black and blue	30	25
281	20l. brown and orange	30	25
282	25l. green and blue	1·00	1·00
283	35l. brown and buff	2·50	1·90
284	60l. blue and green	2·50	1·90

1954. 25th Anniv of Lateran Treaty.

285	**294**	25l. sepia and brown	90	50
286	**294**	60l. blue and light blue	1·10	1·00

1954. Introduction of Television in Italy.

287	**295**	25l. violet	75	65
288	**295**	60l. green	1·30	1·10

1954. Encouragement to Taxpayers.

289	**296**	25l. violet	2·50	1·50

1954. Milan–Turin Helicopter Mail Flight.

290	**297**	25l. green	1·40	1·30

1954. Tenth Anniv of Resistance Movement.

291	**298**	25l. black and brown	1·90	1·30

1954. Sixth Trieste Fair. Nos. 282 and 284 of Trieste additionally optd **FIERA DI TRIESTE 1954**.

292	-	25l. green and blue	1·90	1·80
293	**293**	60l. blue and green	2·50	2·50

1954. Birth Centenary of Catalani.

294	**299**	25l. green	1·90	1·30

1954. Seventh Birth Centenary of Marco Polo.

295	**300**	25l. brown	50	50
296	**300**	60l. green	1·50	1·00

1954. 60th Anniv of Italian Touring Club.

297	**301**	25l. green and red	1·90	1·60

1954. International Police Congress, Rome.

298	**302**	25l. red	75	55
299	**302**	60l. blue	1·30	1·00

CONCESSIONAL LETTER POST

1947. Optd **A.M.G. F.T.T.** in two lines.

CL44	-	1l. brn (No. CL649)	40	1·30
CL45	**CL201**	8l. red	12·00	2·50
CL46	**CL220**	15l. violet	65·00	11·50

1949. Optd **AMG-FTT**.

CL122	15l. violet	2·50	95
CL123	20l. violet	15·00	1·30

CONCESSIONAL PARCEL POST

1953

CP268	**CP288**	40l. orange	23·00	3·75
CP269	**CP288**	50l. blue	23·00	3·75
CP270	**CP288**	75l. brown	23·00	3·75
CP271	**CP288**	110l. pink	23·00	3·75

Unused prices are for the complete stamp, used prices for the left half of the stamp.

EXPRESS LETTER STAMPS

1947. Express Letter stamps optd **A.M.G. F.T.T.** in two lines.

E28	-	15l. red (No. E681)	30	40
E29	**200**	25l. orange	55·00	12·50
E30	**200**	30l. violet	75	90
E31	-	60l. red (No. E685)	48·00	19·00

1948. Centenary of 1848 Revolution. Express Letter stamp optd **A.M.G.-F.T.T.**

E83	**E209**	35l. violet	12·50	10·00

1950. Express Letter stamps optd **AMG-FTT** in one line.

E174		50l. purple	11·00	3·25
E175	-	60l. red (No. E685)	12·50	3·75

PARCEL POST STAMPS

Unused prices are for complete stamps, used prices for half-stamp.

1947. Parcel Post stamps optd **A.M.G. F.T.T.** in two lines on each half of stamp.

P32	**P201**	1l. brown	1·00	1·30
P33	**P201**	2l. blue	1·30	1·90
P34	**P201**	3l. orange	1·30	1·90
P35	**P201**	4l. grey	1·60	2·20
P36	**P201**	5l. purple	5·75	6·25
P37	**P201**	10l. violet	5·00	5·75
P38	**P201**	20l. purple	7·50	7·50
P39	**P201**	50l. red	12·50	14·00
P40	**P201**	100l. blue	15·00	19·00
P41	**P201**	200l. green	£550	£550
P42	**P201**	300l. purple	£325	£350
P43	**P201**	500l. brown	£190	£200

1949. Parcel Post stamps optd **AMG-FTT** in one line on each half of stamp.

P139		1l. brown	2·00	2·20
P140		2l. blue	75	1·00
P141		3l. orange	75	1·00
P142		4l. grey	75	1·00
P143		5l. purple	75	1·00
P144		10l. violet	2·50	2·75
P145		20l. purple	2·50	2·75
P146		30l. purple	1·00	1·30
P147		50l. red	2·50	2·75
P148		100l. blue	5·00	5·75
P149		200l. green	38·00	44·00
P150		300l. purple	£150	£190
P151		500l. brown	75·00	95·00
P152	**P928**	1000l. blue	£350	£400

POSTAGE DUE STAMPS

1947. Postage Due stamps optd **A.M.G. F.T.T.** in two lines.

D44	**D192**	1l. orange	1·00	1·00
D48	**D201**	1l. orange	50	90
D49	**D201**	2l. green	50	65
D50	**D201**	3l. red	1·30	1·50
D51	**D201**	4l. brown	10·00	12·50
D45	**D192**	5l. violet	5·00	1·30
D52	**D201**	5l. violet	£130	31·00
D53	**D201**	6l. blue	31·00	26·00
D54	**D201**	8l. mauve	75·00	80·00
D46	**D192**	10l. blue	15·00	2·50
D55	**D201**	10l. blue	£190	31·00
D56	**D201**	12l. brown	38·00	31·00
D47	**D192**	20l. red	31·00	3·25
D57	**D201**	20l. purple	38·00	10·00
D58	**D201**	50l. green	3·75	1·30

1949. Postage Due stamps optd **AMG-FTT** in one line.

D122	1l. orange	30	25
D123	2l. green	30	25
D124	3l. red	65	40
D125	5l. violet	1·30	65
D126	6l. blue	40	30
D127	8l. mauve	40	30
D128	10l. blue	65	30
D129	12l. brown	3·00	1·30
D130	20l. purple	5·00	65
D131	25l. red	7·50	3·25
D132	50l. green	7·50	1·30
D133	100l. orange	19·00	2·50
D134	500l. purple and blue	£100	65·00

ZONE B
YUGOSLAV MILITARY GOVERNMENT

Apart from the definitive issues illustrated below the following are stamps of Yugoslavia (sometimes in new colours), variously overprinted **STT VUJA** or **VUJA-STT** or (Nos. B65 onwards) **STT VUJNA** unless otherwise stated.

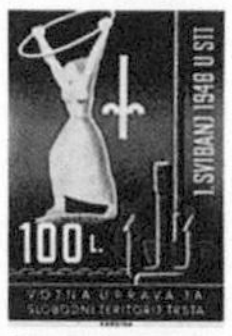

B1

1948. Labour Day.

B1	**B1**	100l. red and stone (A)	12·50	6·25
B2	**B1**	100l. red and stone (B)	12·50	6·25
B3	**B1**	100l. red and stone (C)	12·50	6·25

Inscr in Slovene (A) "I. MAJ 1948 V STO"; Italian (B) "I. MAGGIO 1948 NEL TLT"; or Croat (C) "I. SVIBANJ 1948 U STT".

1948. Red Cross. No. 545 optd and surch.

B3a	**131**	2l. on 50p. brown and red	50·00	50·00

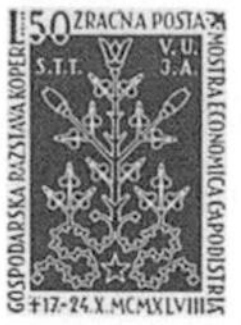

B2

1948. Air. Economic Exhibition, Capodistria.

B4	**B2**	25l. grey	1·90	1·80
B5	**B2**	50l. orange	1·90	1·80

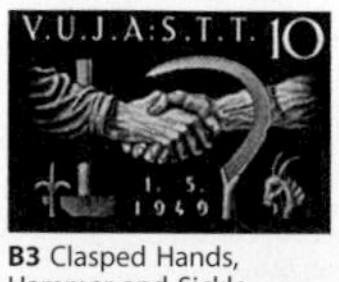

B3 Clasped Hands, Hammer and Sickle

1949. Labour Day.

B6	**B3**	10l. green	2·50	2·40

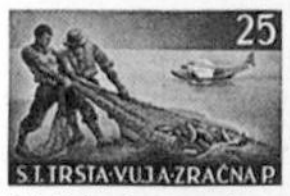

B4 Fishermen and Flying Boat

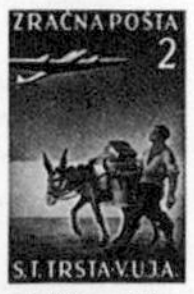

B5 Man with Donkey

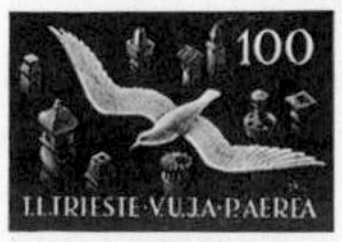

B6 Mediterranean Gull over Chimneys

1949. Air.

B7	**B4**	1l. turquoise	1·30	50
B8	**B5**	2l. brown	1·30	50
B9	**B4**	5l. blue	1·30	50
B10	**B5**	10l. violet	5·00	3·75
B11	**B4**	25l. brown	15·00	11·50
B12	**B5**	50l. green	15·00	11·50
B13	**B6**	100l. brown	23·00	16·00

1949. Partisans issue.

B14	**119**	50p. grey	75	50
B15	**119**	1d. green	75	50
B16	**120**	2d. red	90	50
B17	-	3d. red (No. 508)	1·30	50
B18	**120**	4d. blue	2·50	75
B19	-	5d. blue (No. 511)	2·50	75
B20	-	9d. mauve (No. 514)	12·50	2·50
B21	-	12d. blue (No. 515)	12·50	7·50
B22	**119**	16d. blue	19·00	10·00
B23	-	20d. red (No. 517)	38·00	12·50

1949. 75th Anniv of U.P.U.

B24		5d. blue (No. 612)	14·00	12·50
B25	**158**	12d. brown	14·00	12·50

1949. Air. Optd **DIN** or surch also.

B26	**B4**	1d. turquoise	70	65
B27	**B5**	2d. brown	70	65
B28	**B4**	5d. blue	70	65
B29	**B5**	10d. violet	70	65
B30	**B4**	15d. on 25l. brown	34·00	21·00
B31	**B5**	20d. on 50l. green	10·00	8·75
B32	**B6**	30d. on 100l. purple	14·00	10·00

1950. Centenary of Yugoslav Railways.

B33	**116**	2d. green	5·00	1·30
B34	-	3d. red (No. 632)	5·00	1·80
B35	-	5d. blue (No. 633)	6·25	4·50
B36	-	10d. orange (No. 633a)	25·00	12·50
MSB36Aa		10d. purple. Perf	£325	£250
MSB36Ba		10d. purple. Imperf	£325	£250

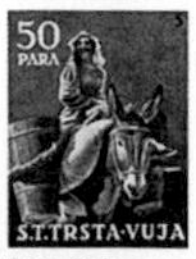

B10 Girl on Donkey

1950

B37	**B10**	50p. grey	1·30	65
B38	-	1d. red (Cockerel)	1·30	6·25
B38a	-	1d. brown (Cockerel)	2·50	65
B39	-	2d. blue (Geese)	1·30	65
B40	-	3d. brown (Bees)	1·30	65
B40a	-	3d. red (Bees)	5·00	65
B41	-	5d. green (Oxen)	8·75	65
B42	-	10d. brown (Turkey)	8·75	65
B43	-	15d. violet (Kids)	38·00	19·00
B44	-	20d. green (Silkworms)	19·00	10·00

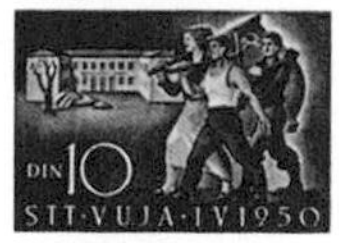

B11 Workers

1950. May Day.

B45	**B11**	3d. violet	1·30	90
B46	**B11**	10d. red	1·90	1·60

1950. Red Cross.

B47	**160**	50p. brown and red	2·50	1·90

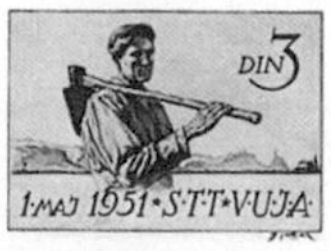

B12 Worker

1951. May Day.

B48	**B12**	3d. red	1·30	80
B49	**B12**	10d. green	2·50	1·30

1951. Red Cross.

B49a	**191**	0d.50 blue and red	38·00	31·00

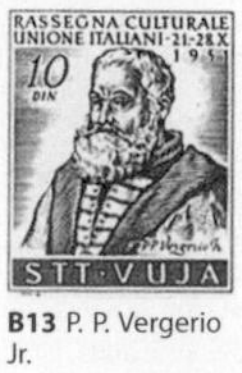

B13 P. P. Vergerio Jr.

1951. Festival of Italian Culture.

B50	**B13**	5d. blue	1·70	1·30
B51	**B13**	10d. purple	1·70	1·30
B52	**B13**	20d. brown	1·70	1·30

1951. Cultural Anniversaries.

B53	**189**	10d. orange	2·50	1·30
B54	-	12d. black (As No. 699)	12·50	12·50

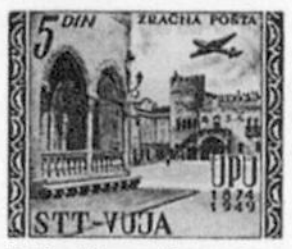

B14a Koper Square

1952. Air. 75th Anniv of U.P.U.

B54a	**B14a**	5d. brown	2·50	1·30
B54b	-	15d. blue	20·00	20·00
B54c	-	25d. green	12·50	12·50

DESIGNS—VERT: 15d. Lighthouse, Piran. HORIZ: 25d. Hotel, Portoroz.

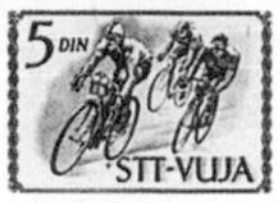

B15 Cyclists

1952. Physical Culture Propaganda.

B55	**B15**	5d. brown	65	50
B56	-	10d. green	65	50
B57	-	15d. red	65	50
B58	-	28d. blue	3·75	2·50
B59	-	50d. red	5·00	5·00
B60	-	100d. blue	23·00	15·00

DESIGNS: 10d. Footballers; 15d. Rowing four; 28d. Yachting; 50d. Netball players; 100d. Diver.

1952. Marshal Tito's 60th Birthday. As Nos. 727/9 of Yugoslavia additionally inscr "STT VUJA".

B61	**196**	15d. brown	5·00	3·75
B62	**197**	28d. red	7·50	5·00
B63	-	50d. green (No. 729)	12·50	10·00

1952. Children's Week.

B64	**198**	15d. pink	2·50	2·50

1952. 15th Olympic Games, Helsinki. As Nos. 731/6.

B65	**199**	5d. brown on flesh	3·75	1·30
B66	-	10d. green on cream	3·75	1·30
B67	-	15d. violet on mauve	3·75	1·30
B68	-	28d. brown on buff	5·00	3·75
B69	-	50d. brown on yellow	21·00	15·00
B70	-	100d. blue on pink	50·00	55·00

1952. Navy Day (Nos. 737/9).

B71		15d. purple	3·75	2·50
B72	**200**	28d. brown	6·25	3·75
B73	-	50d. black	8·75	6·25

1952. Red Cross.

B74	**201**	50p. red, grey and black	2·50	1·30

1952. Sixth Yugoslav Communist Party Congress.

B75	**202**	15d. brown	3·25	1·30
B76	**202**	15d. turquoise	3·25	1·30
B77	**202**	15d. brown	3·25	1·30
B78	**202**	15d. blue	3·25	1·30

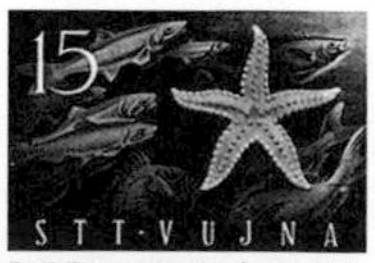

B17 European Anchovy and Starfish

1952. Philatelic Exhibition, Koper.

B78a	**B17**	15d. brown	6·25	6·25
MSB78b		48×70 mm. **B17** 50d. green. Imperf (sold at 85d.)	90·00	90·00

1953. Tenth Death Anniv of Tesla (inventor).

B79	**203**	15d. red	65	65
B80	**203**	30d. blue	2·50	2·50

1953. Pictorials of 1950.

B81	1d. grey (No. 705)	19·00	14·00
B86	2d. red (No. 718)	1·30	65
B82	3d. red (No. 655)	1·30	65
B87	5d. orange (No. 719)	1·30	65
B83	10d. green (No. 721)	1·30	65
B88	15d. red (No. 723)	2·50	1·10
B84	30d. blue (No. 712)	10·00	5·00
B85	50d. turquoise (No. 714)	15·00	10·00

1953. United Nations (Nos. 747/9).

B89	**204**	15d. green	30	25
B90	-	30d. blue	80	55
B91	-	50d. red	1·60	1·30

1953. Adriatic Car Rally. As Nos. 750/3.

B92	**205**	15d. brown and yellow	65	50
B93	-	30d. green and emerald	65	50
B94	-	50d. mauve and orange	65	50
B95	-	70d. deep blue and blue	4·50	3·25

1953. Marshal Tito.

B96	**206**	50d. green	6·25	6·25

1953. 38th Esperanto Congress, Zagreb.

B97	**207**	15d. grn & turq (postage)	12·50	12·50
B98	**207**	300d. green and violet (air)	£450	£450

1953. Tenth Anniv of Liberation of Istria and Slovene Coast.

B99	**209**	15d. blue	6·25	6·25

1953. Death Centenary of Radicevic (poet).

B100	**210**	15d. black	3·75	2·50

1953. Red Cross.

B101	**211**	2d. red and bistre	2·50	1·30

1953. Tenth Anniv of 1st Republican Legislative Assembly. As Nos. 762/4.

B102	**212**	15d. violet	1·80	1·00
B103	-	30d. red	2·00	1·30
B104	-	50d. green	2·75	1·90

1954. Air. As Nos. 675 etc.

B108	1d. lilac	1·30	65
B109	2d. green	1·30	65
B110	3d. purple	1·30	65
B111	5d. brown	1·30	65
B112	10d. turquoise	1·30	65
B113	20d. brown	1·30	65
B114	30d. blue	1·30	65
B115	50d. black	1·30	90
B116	100d. red	5·00	3·75
B117	200d. violet	7·50	6·25
B118	500d. orange	50·00	34·00

1954. Animals. As Nos. 765/76.

B119	2d. grey, buff and red	1·30	65
B120	5d. slate, buff and grey	1·30	65
B121	10d. brown and green	1·30	65
B122	15d. brown and blue	1·30	65
B123	17d. sepia and brown	1·30	65
B124	25d. yellow, blue and brown	1·30	65
B125	30d. brown and violet	1·30	65
B126	35d. black and purple	1·30	1·30
B127	50d. brown and green	2·50	1·90
B128	65d. black and brown	10·00	7·50
B129	70d. brown and blue	19·00	10·00
B130	100d. black and blue	50·00	40·00

1954. Serbian Insurrection. As Nos. 778/81.

B131	-	15d. multicoloured	1·30	90
B132	**214**	30d. multicoloured	1·30	90
B133	-	50d. multicoloured	1·40	1·20
B134	-	70d. multicoloured	2·50	1·90

POSTAGE DUE STAMPS

1948. Red Cross. No. D546 surch **VUJA STT** and new value.

BD4	**131**	2l. on 50p. green and red	£425	£400

1949. On 1946 issue.

BD26	**D126**	50p. orange	1·30	75
BD27	**D126**	1d. orange	1·30	75
BD74	**D126**	1d. brown	65	65
BD28	**D126**	2d. blue	1·30	75
BD75	**D126**	2d. green	65	65
BD29	**D126**	3d. green	2·50	75
BD30	**D126**	5d. violet	6·25	3·25
BD76	**D126**	5d. blue	65	65
BD77	**D126**	10d. red	65	65
BD78	**D126**	20d. violet	65	65
BD79	**D126**	30d. orange	65	65
BD80	**D126**	50d. blue	65	65
BD81	**D126**	100d. purple	28·00	21·00

Nos. BD26/30 optd **STT VUJA** and the rest **STT VUJNA**.

1950. Red Cross. No. D617 optd **VUJA STT**.

BD48	**160**	50p. purple and red	2·50	1·90

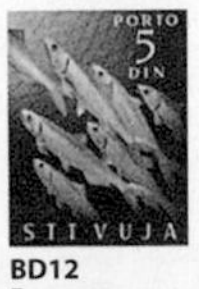

BD12 European Anchovy

1950. Fishe.

BD49	-	50p. brown	6·25	1·30
BD50	-	1d. green	8·75	3·75
BD51	**BD12**	2d. blue	8·75	3·75
BD52	**BD12**	3d. blue	11·50	5·00
BD53	**BD12**	5d. purple	38·00	14·00

DESIGN: 50p., 1d. Two meagres.

1951. Red Cross. No. D703 optd **STT VUJA**.

BD54	**191**	0d.50 green and red	£375	£350

1952. Red Cross. No. D741.

BD82	**D202**	50p. red and grey	2·50	1·30

1953. Red Cross. As No. D762.

BD102	**211**	2d. red and purple	2·50	1·30

Pt. 1

TRINIDAD

An island in the West Indies off the coast of Venezuela. Now uses stamps of Trinidad and Tobago.

12 pence = 1 shilling; 20 shillings = 1 pound.

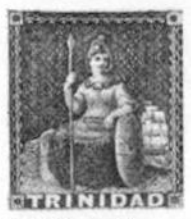

2 Britannia

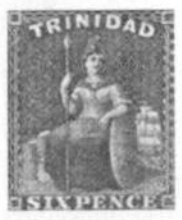

4 Britannia

1851. Imperf.

2	**2**	(1d.) purple	21·00	80·00
3	**2**	(1d.) blue	22·00	65·00
6	**2**	(1d.) grey	55·00	80·00
8	**2**	(1d.) red	£180	75·00
25	**4**	4d. lilac	£120	£325
28	**4**	6d. green	£12000	£425
29	**4**	1s. blue	£100	£350

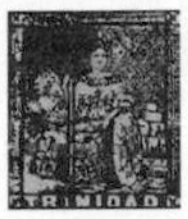

3

1853

18	**3**	(1d.) blue	£4000	£650
19	**3**	(1d.) grey	£4000	£400
20	**3**	(1d.) red	16·00	£600

1859

75	**2**	(1d.) red	50·00	2·75
70	**4**	4d. lilac	£130	20·00
76	**4**	4d. grey	£130	2·00
72*b*	**4**	6d. green	£110	6·00
63	**4**	1s. blue	£2250	£110
73*b*	**1**	1s. purple	£140	7·00
78	**4**	1s. yellow	£160	4·50

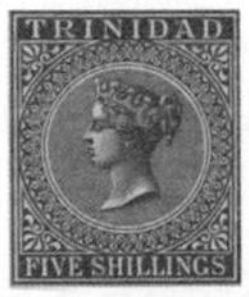

5

1869

113	**5**	5s. red	55·00	£110

1879. Surch in words.

98	**2**	½d. lilac	20·00	12·00
101	**2**	1d. red	75·00	2·50

1882. No. 95 surch **1d** with pen.

104	**4**	1d. on 6d. green	15·00	9·00

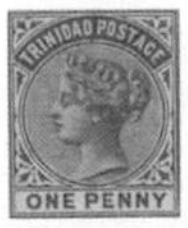

10

1883

106	**10**	½d. green	10·00	1·25
107	**10**	1d. red	22·00	50
108	**10**	2½d. blue	26·00	60
110	**10**	4d. grey	4·25	60
111	**10**	6d. black	7·50	6·50
112	**10**	1s. orange	13·00	6·00

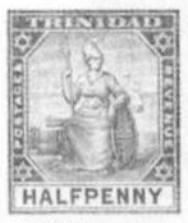

11 Britannia

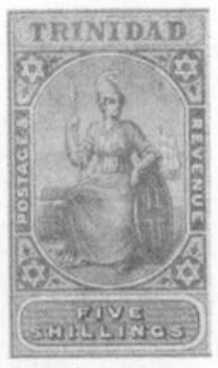

12 Britannia

1896

114	**11**	½d. purple and green	3·25	30
115	**11**	1d. purple and red	3·50	10
127	**11**	1d. black on red	1·00	2·00
135	**11**	1d. red	3·00	10
117	**11**	2½d. purple and blue	6·00	20
128	**11**	2½d. purple and blue on blue	4·50	10
137	**11**	2½d. blue	10·00	15
118	**11**	4d. purple and orange	8·00	25·00
129	**11**	4d. green and blue on buff	25·00	30
138	**11**	4d. grey and red on yellow	6·50	15·00
119	**11**	5d. purple and mauve	9·50	15·00
120	**11**	6d. purple and black	7·50	5·50
140	**11**	6d. purple and mauve	10·00	16·00
121	**11**	1s. green and brown	7·50	6·50
130	**11**	1s. black and blue on yellow	3·75	22·00
142	**11**	1s. purple & blue on yellow	16·00	26·00
143	**11**	1s. black on green	2·75	1·25
131	**12**	5s. purple and mauve	19·00	5·50
123	**12**	10s. green and blue	£325	£500
124	**12**	£1 green and red	£200	£325

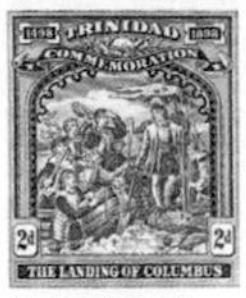

13 Landing of Columbus

1898. 400th Anniv of Discovery of Trinidad.

125	**13**	2d. brown and violet	2·75	1·25

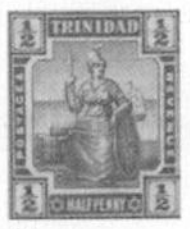

14

1909. Figures in corners.

146	**14**	½d. green	10·00	10
147	-	1d. red	11·00	10
148	-	2½d. blue	26·00	4·00

On the 1d. figures are in lower corners only.

POSTAGE DUE STAMPS

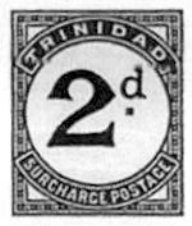

D1

1885

D1	**D1**	½d. black	19·00	50·00
D13	**D1**	4d. black	14·00	21·00
D14	**D1**	5d. black	20·00	22·00
D15	**D1**	6d. black	6·50	16·00
D16	**D1**	8d. black	18·00	20·00
D17	**D1**	1s. black	26·00	42·00
D18	**D1**	1d. black	4·00	4·00
D19	**D1**	2d. black	8·50	1·50
D20	**D1**	3d. black	9·00	6·00

OFFICIAL STAMPS

1894. Optd **O S.**

O1	**10**	½d. green	45·00	60·00
O2	**10**	1d. red	48·00	65·00
O3	**10**	2½d. blue	50·00	95·00
O4	**10**	4d. grey	55·00	£120
O5	**10**	6d. black	55·00	£130
O6	**10**	1s. orange	75·00	£180
O7	**5**	5s. red	£170	£800

1909. Optd **OFFICIAL**.

O8	**11**	½d. green	3·25	10·00
O9	**11**	1d. red	3·00	11·00

1910. Optd **OFFICIAL**.

O10	**14**	½d. green	11·00	15·00

Pt. 1

TRINIDAD AND TOBAGO

Combined issues for Trinidad and Tobago, administratively one colony. Part of the British Caribbean Federation from 1958 until 31 August 1962, when it became independent within the British Commonwealth.

1913. 12 pence = 1 shilling; 20 shillings = 1 pound.
1935. 100 cents = 1 West Indian dollar.

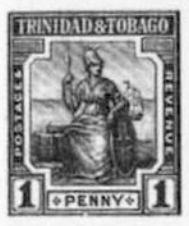

17

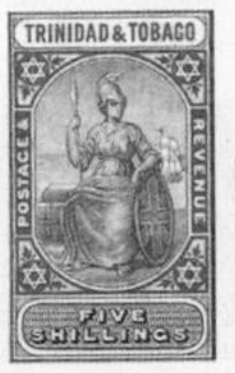

18

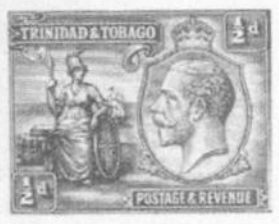

27

1913

149	**17**	½d. green	3·00	10
207	**17**	1d. red	60	30
208	**17**	1d. brown	60	1·50
209	**17**	2d. grey	1·00	1·25
151	**17**	2½d. blue	12·00	50
211	**17**	3d. blue	7·00	3·00
152a	**17**	4d. black and red on yellow		
153*a*	**17**	6d. purple and mauve	18·00	11·00
154*c*	**17**	1s. black on green	1·50	3·00
155d	**18**	5s. purple and mauve	£100	£130
156*a*	**18**	£1 green and red	£250	£300

1915. Optd cross over **21. 10. 15.**

174		1d. red	3·00	4·50

1916. Optd **19.10.16.** over cross.

175		1d. red	50	2·00

1917. Optd **WAR TAX** in one line (No. 176) or two lines (others).

177	½d. green	1·50	40
176	1d. red	4·00	3·25
180	1d. red	15	75

1918. Optd **War Tax** in two lines.

187	½d. green	10	3·00

1922

218	**27**	½d. green	50	10
219	**27**	1d. brown	50	10
220b	**27**	1½d. red	1·75	30
222	**27**	2d. grey	50	1·25
223	**27**	3d. blue	50	1·25
224	**27**	4d. black and red on yellow	3·25	3·25
225	**27**	6d. purple and mauve	2·25	26·00
226	**27**	6d. green and red on green	1·25	60
227	**27**	1s. black on green	5·50	1·75
228	**27**	5s. purple and mauve	27·00	38·00
229	**27**	£1 green and red	£150	£275

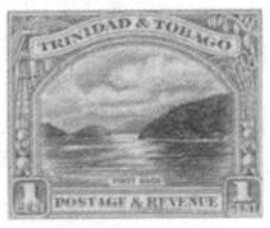

28 First Boca

1935

230a	**28**	1c. blue and green	30	10
231a	-	2c. blue and brown	1·75	10
232	-	3c. black and red	2·00	30
233	-	6c. brown and blue	4·25	2·50
234	-	8c. green and orange	3·75	3·50
235	-	12c. black and violet	4·25	1·75
236	-	24c. black and green	8·00	2·75
237	-	48c. green	9·50	15·00
238	-	72c. green and red	40·00	30·00

DESIGNS: 2c. Imperial College of Tropical Agriculture; 3c. Mt. Irvine Bay, Tobago; 6c. Discovery of Lake Asphalt; 8c. Queen's Park, Savannah; 12c. Town Hall, San Fernando; 24c. Govt. House; 48c. Memorial Park; 72c. Blue Basin.

1935. Silver Jubilee. As T **32a** of St. Helena.

239	2c. blue and black	30	75
240	3c. blue and red	30	2·50
241	6c. brown and blue	1·75	2·50
242	24c. grey and purple	12·00	24·00

1937. Coronation. As T **32b** of St. Helena.

243	1c. green	15	60
244	2c. brown	35	15
245	8c. orange	90	2·25

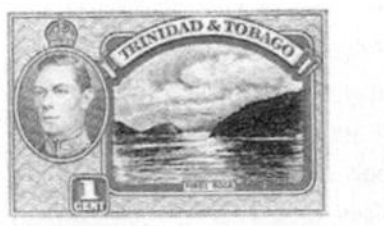

37 First Boca

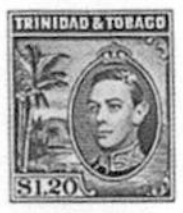

47 King George VI

1938. Designs as 1935 issue but with portrait of King George VI as in T **37** and without "POSTAGE & REVENUE", and T **47**.

(a) As T **37**

246	**37**	1c. blue and green	1·00	30
247	-	2c. blue and brown	1·25	20
248	-	3c. black and red	11·00	1·00
248a	-	3c. green and purple	30	20
249	-	4c. brown	30·00	2·75
249a	-	4c. red	50	1·00
249b	-	5c. mauve	50	15
250	-	6c. brown and blue	2·75	80
251	-	8c. green and orange	2·75	1·00
252a	-	12c. black and purple	4·50	10
253	-	24c. black and olive	7·00	10
254	-	60c. green and red	14·00	1·50

(b) As T **47**

255	**47**	$1.20 green	13·00	1·50
256	**47**	$4.80 red	40·00	55·00

NEW DESIGNS: 4c. Memorial Park; 5c. G.P.O. and Treasury; 60c. As No. 238.

1946. Victory. As T **33a** of St. Helena.

257	3c. brown	10	10
258	6c. blue	55	1·50

1948. Silver Wedding. As T **33b/c** of St. Helena.

259	3c. brown	10	10
260	$4.80 red	30·00	48·00

1949. 75th Anniv of U.P.U. As T **33d/g** of St. Helena.

261	5c. purple	35	1·00
262	6c. blue	2·00	2·25
263	12c. violet	55	1·50
264	24c. green	55	1·25

1951. B.W.I. University College. As T **10a/b** of St. Kitts-Nevis.

265	3c. green and brown	20	1·25
266	12c. black and violet	30	1·25

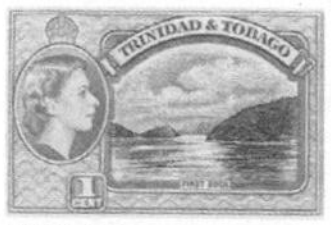

48 First Boca

1953. Designs as 1938 and 1940 issues but with portrait of Queen Elizabeth in place of King George VI as in T **48** (1c., 2c., 12c.) or facing left (others).

267	**48**	1c. blue and green	20	40
268	-	2c. blue and brown	20	40
269	-	3c. green and purple	20	10
270	-	4c. red	30	40
271	-	5c. mauve	40	30
272	-	6c. brown and blue	60	30
273	-	8c. olive and red	2·50	30
274	-	12c. black and purple	40	10
275	-	24c. black and olive	2·75	30
276	-	60c. green and red	27·00	1·75
277a	-	$1.20 green	1·50	30
278a	-	$4.80 red	11·00	18·00

1953. Coronation. As T **33h** of St. Helena.

279	3c. black and green	30	10

1956. No. 268 surch **ONE CENT**.

280	1c. on 2c. blue and brown	1·25	2·00

1958. Inaug of British Caribbean Federation. As T **27a** of St. Kitts-Nevis.

281	5c. green	50	10
282	6c. blue	55	1·50
283	12c. red	60	10

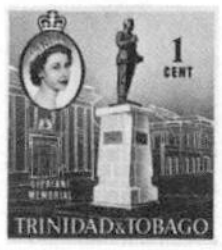

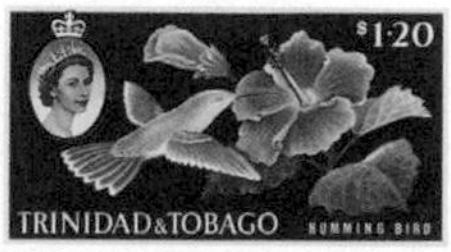

51 Cipriani Memorial

53 Copper-rumped Hummingbird ("Humming Bird")

1960

284	**51**	1c. stone and black	1·25	20
285	-	2c. blue	10	20
286	-	5c. blue	10	10
287	-	6c. brown	10	1·00
288	-	8c. green	10	1·50
289	-	10c. lilac	10	10
290	-	12c. red	10	1·25
291	-	15c. orange (A)	3·00	1·00
291a	-	15c. orange (B)	12·00	10
292	-	25c. red and blue	80	10
293	-	35c. green and black	3·75	10
294	-	50c. yellow, grey and blue	35	1·50
295	-	60c. red, green and blue	55	30
296	**53**	$1.20 multicoloured	15·00	4·00
297	-	$4.80 green and blue	22·00	21·00

DESIGNS—HORIZ (as Type **51**): 2c. Queen's Hall; 5c. Whitehall; 6c. Treasury Building; 8c. Governor-General's House; 10c. General Hospital, San Fernando; 12c. Oil refinery; 15c. (A) Crest, (B) Coat of arms; 25c. Scarlet ibis; 35c. Pitch Lake; 50c. Mohammed Jinnah Mosque. VERT (as Type **51**): 60c. Anthurium lilies. (As Type **53**): $4.80, Map of Trinidad and Tobago.

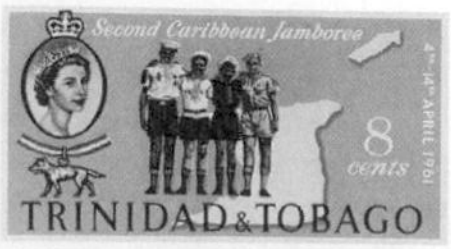

65 Scouts and Gold Wolf Badge

1961. Second Caribbean Scout Jamboree. Design multicoloured. Background colours given.

298	**65**	8c. green	15	10
299	**65**	25c. blue	15	10

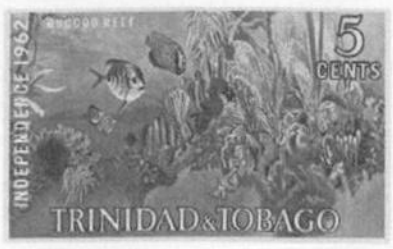

66 "Buccoo Reef" (painting by Carlisle Chang)

1962. Independence.

300	**66**	5c. turquoise	10	10
301	-	8c. grey	40	1·00
302	-	25c. violet	15	10
303	-	35c. multicoloured	2·25	15
304	-	60c. red, black and blue	2·75	3·75

DESIGNS: 8c. Piarco Air Terminal; 25c. Hilton Hotel, Port-of-Spain; 35c. Greater bird of paradise ("Bird of Paradise") and map; 60c. Scarlet ibis and map.

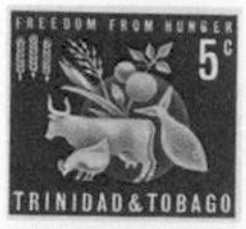

71 "Protein Foods"

1963. Freedom from Hunger.

305	**71**	5c. red	30	10
306	**71**	8c. bistre	40	85
307	**71**	25c. blue	65	20

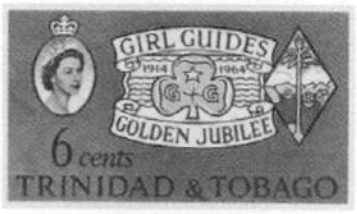

72 Jubilee Emblem

1964. Golden Jubilee of Trinidad and Tobago Girl Guides' Association.

308	**72**	6c. yellow, blue and red	10	70
309	**72**	25c. yellow, ultram & blue	15	20
310	**72**	35c. yellow, blue and green	20	20

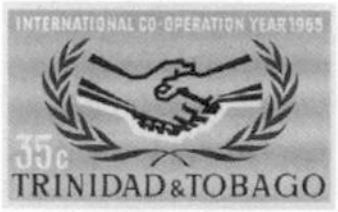

73 I.C.Y. Emblem

1965. International Co-operation Year.

311	**73**	35c. brown, green & yellow	65	20

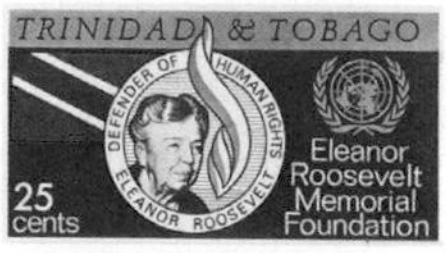

74 Eleanor Roosevelt, Flag and U.N. Emblem

1965. Eleanor Roosevelt Memorial Foundation.

312	**74**	25c. black, red and blue	15	10

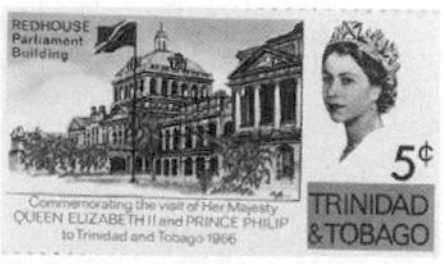

75 Parliament Building

1966. Royal Visit. Multicoloured.

313	5c. Type **75**	1·10	10
314	8c. Map, Royal Yacht "Britannia" and arms	1·90	1·00
315	25c. Map and flag	1·90	55
316	35c. Flag and panorama	1·90	70

1967. Fifth Year of Independence. Nos. 289, 291a and 295 optd **FIFTH YEAR OF INDEPENDENCE 31st AUGUST 1967.**

318	8c. green	10	10
319	10c. lilac	10	10
320	15c. orange	10	10
321	60c. blue, green and red	25	15

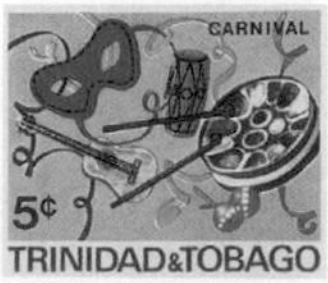

80 Musical Instruments

1968. Trinidad Carnival. Multicoloured.

322	5c. Type **80**	10	10
323	10c. Calypso King (vert)	10	10
324	15c. Steel band	10	10
325	25c. Carnival procession	15	10
326	35c. Carnival King (vert)	15	10
327	60c. Carnival Queen (vert)	20	1·00

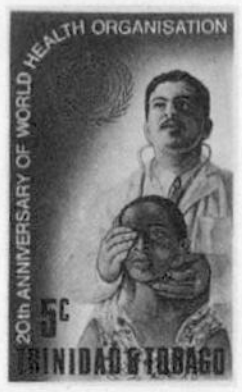

86 Doctor giving Eye-test

1968. 20th Anniv of World Health Organization.

328	**86**	5c. red, brown and gold	15	10
329	**86**	25c. orange, brown and gold	35	15
330	**86**	35c. blue, black and gold	40	25

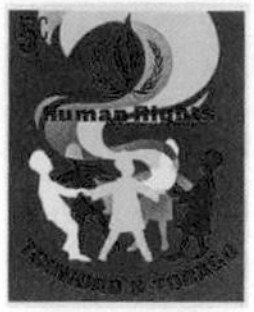

87 Peoples of the World and Emblem

1968. Human Rights Year.

331	**87**	5c. red, black and yellow	10	10
332	**87**	10c. blue, black and yellow	15	10
333	**87**	25c. green, black and yellow	30	15

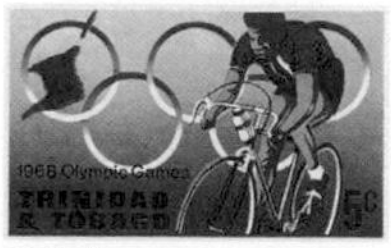

88 Cycling

1968. Olympic Games, Mexico. Multicoloured.

334	5c. Type **88**	70	10
335	15c. Weightlifting	20	10
336	25c. Relay-racing	20	10
337	35c. Sprinting	20	10
338	$1.20 Maps of Mexico and Trinidad	1·50	45

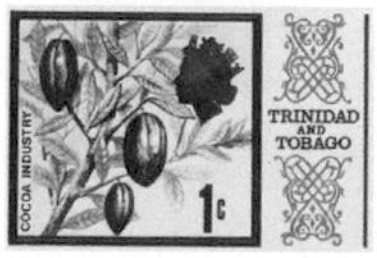

93 Cocoa Beans

1969. Multicoloured.

339c	1c. Type **93**	10	30
340	3c. Sugar refinery	10	10
341a	5c. Rufous-vented chachalaca ("Cocrico")	2·00	10
342	6c. Oil refinery	10	10
343	8c. Fertiliser plant	4·50	3·25
344a	10c. Green hermit	2·00	20
345	12c. Citrus fruit	15	3·50
346	15c. Arms of Trinidad and Tobago	10	10
347	20c. Flag and outline of Trinidad and Tobago	30	10
348	25c. As 20c.	30	1·00
349	30c. Chaconia plant	30	10
350	40c. Scarlet ibis	5·50	10
351	50c. Maracas Bay	30	4·25
352	$1 Poui tree	60	15
353	$2.50 Fishing	1·00	5·50
354	$5 Red house	1·00	5·50

Nos. 344/9 and 352 are vert.

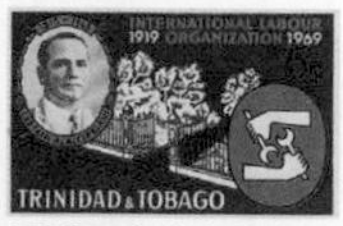

108 Captain A. A. Cipriani (labour leader) and Entrance to Woodford Square

1969. 50th Anniv of Int Labour Organization.

355	**108**	6c. black, gold and red	15	25
356	-	15c. black, gold and blue	15	25

DESIGN: 15c. Arms of Industrial Court and entrance to Woodford Square.

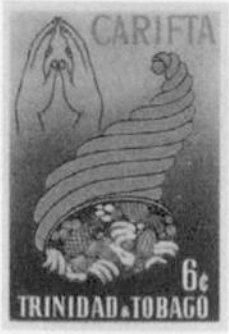

110 Cornucopia and Fruit

1969. First Anniv of C.A.R.I.F.T.A. Multicoloured.

357	6c. Type **110**	10	10
358	10c. Flags of Britain and member nations (horiz)	10	10
359	30c. Map showing C.A.R.I.F.T.A. countries	20	20
360	40c. Boeing 727-100 "Sunjet" in flight (horiz)	40	90

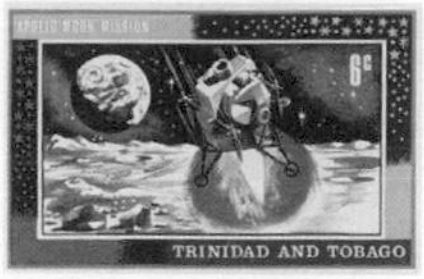

114 Space Module landing on Moon

1969. First Man on the Moon. Multicoloured.

361	6c. Type **114**	20	10
362	40c. Space module and astronauts on Moon (vert)	30	10
363	$1 Astronauts seen from inside space module	60	35

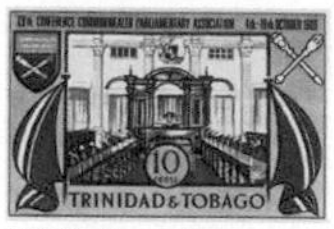

117 Parliamentary Chamber, Flags and Emblem

1969. 15th Commonwealth Parliamentary Association Conference, Port-of-Spain. Multicoloured.

364	10c. Type **117**	10	10
365	15c. J.F. Kennedy College	10	10
366	30c. Parliamentary maces	25	50
367	40c. Cannon and emblem	25	50

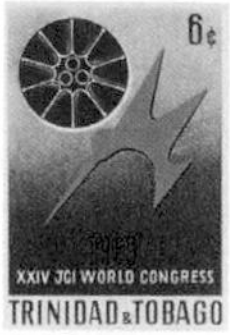

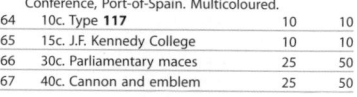

121 Congress Emblem

1969. International Congress of the Junior Chamber of Commerce.

368	**121**	6c. black, red and gold	10	10
369	-	30c. gold, lake and blue	25	40
370	-	40c. black, gold and blue	25	40

DESIGNS: (both incorporating the Congress emblem). HORIZ: 30c. Islands at daybreak. VERT: 40c. Palm trees and ruin.

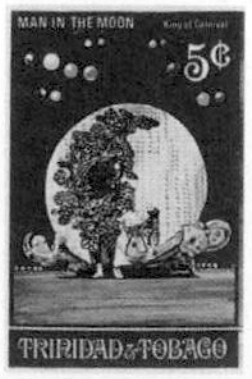

124 "Man in the Moon"

1970. Carnival Winners. Multicoloured.

371	5c. Type **124**	10	10
372	6c. "City beneath the Sea"	10	10
373	15c. "Antelope" God Bamibara	15	10
374	30c. "Chanticleer" Pheasant Queen of Malaya	25	10
375	40c. Steel Band of the Year	25	30

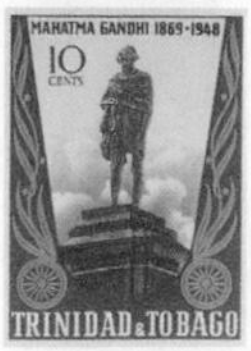

129 Statue of Gandhi

1970. Gandhi Centenary Year (1969). Multicoloured.

376	10c. Type **129**	40	10
377	30c. Head of Gandhi and flag of India (horiz)	85	20

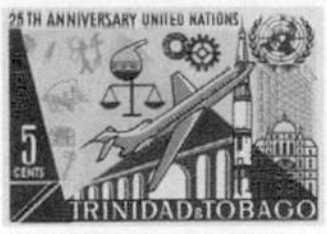

131 Symbols of Culture, Science, Arts and Technology

1970. 25th Anniv of U.N.

378	131	5c. multicoloured	10	10
379	-	10c. multicoloured	20	10
380	-	20c. multicoloured	20	45
381	-	30c. multicoloured	25	30

DESIGNS AND SIZES: 10c. Children of different races, map and flag (34×25 mm); 20c. Noah's Ark, rainbow and dove (34×23 mm); 30c. New U.P.U. H.Q. Building (46×27½ mm).

1970. Inauguration of National Commercial Bank. No. 341 optd **NATIONAL COMMERCIAL BANK ESTABLISHED 1.7.70.**

382	5c. multicoloured	30	10

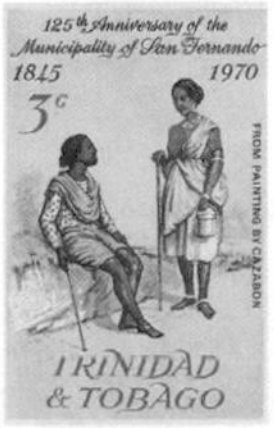

134 "East Indian Immigrants" (J. Cazabon)

1970. 125th Anniv of San Fernando. Paintings by Cazabon.

383	134	3c. multicoloured	10	90
384	-	5c. black, blue and ochre	10	10
385	-	40c. black, blue and ochre	95	20

DESIGNS—HORIZ: 5c. "San Fernando Town Hall"; 40c. "San Fernando Harbour, 1860".

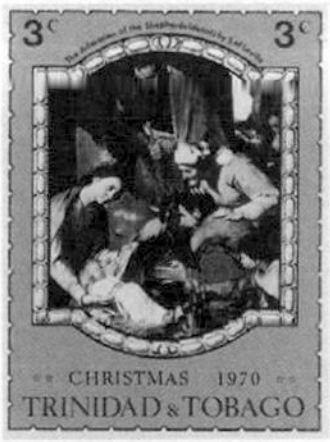

135 "The Adoration of the Shepherds" (detail, School of Seville)

1970. Christmas. Multicoloured.

386	3c. Type **135**	10	10
387	5c. "Madonna and Child with Saints" (detail, Titian)	10	10
388	30c. "The Adoration of the Shepherds" (detail, Le Nain)	15	20
389	40c. "The Virgin and Child, St. John and an Angel" (Morando)	15	10
390	$1 "The Adoration of the Kings" (detail, Veronese)	35	2·50
MS391	114×153 mm. Nos. 386/9	1·00	1·25

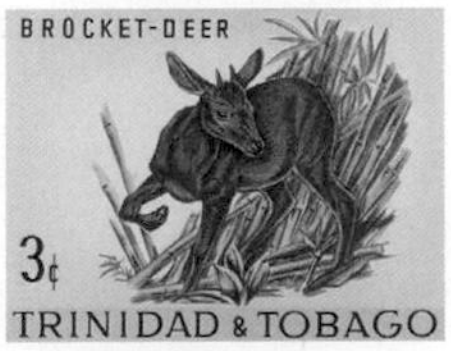

136 Red Brocket

1971. Trinidad Wildlife. Multicoloured.

392	3c. Type **136**	15	30
393	5c. Collared peccary	20	15
394	6c. Paca	20	50
395	30c. Brazilian agouti	60	3·50
396	40c. Ocelot	60	2·75

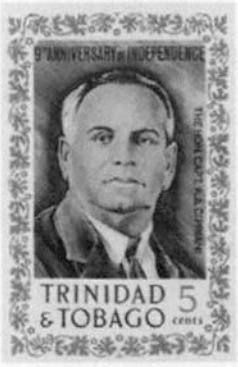

137 A. A. Cipriani

1971. Ninth Anniv of Independence. Multicoloured.

397	5c. Type **137**	10	10
398	30c. Chaconia medal	30	1·10

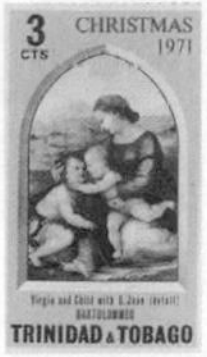

138 "Virgin and Child with St. John" (detail, Bartolommeo)

1971. Christmas.

399	138	3c. multicoloured	15	15
400	-	5c. multicoloured	20	10
401	-	10c. multicoloured	25	10
402	-	15c. multicoloured	30	20

DESIGNS: 5c. Local creche; 10c. "Virgin and Child with Saints Jerome and Dominic" (detail, Lippi); 15c. "Virgin and Child with St. Anne" (detail, Gerolamo dai Libri).

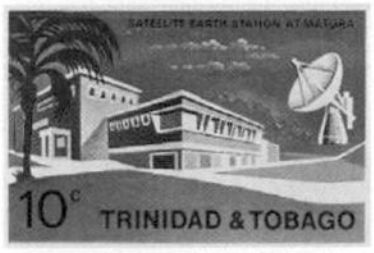

139 Satellite Earth Station, Matura

1971. Satellite Earth Station. Multicoloured.

403	10c. Type **139**	10	10
404	30c. Dish antennae	25	1·10
405	40c. Satellite and the Earth	35	1·10
MS406	140×76 mm. Nos. 403/5	65	2·10

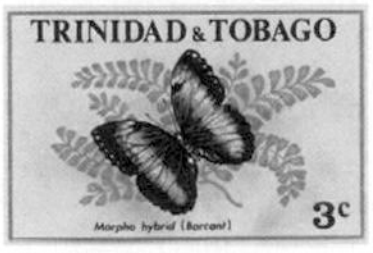

140 "Morpho peleides x achilleana"

1972. Butterflies. Multicoloured.

407	3c. Type **140**	75	1·00
408	5c. "Eryphanis polyxena"	80	10
409	6c. "Phoebis philea"	85	1·50
410	10c. "Prepona laertes"	1·00	15
411	20c. "Eurytides telesilaus"	1·75	2·25
412	30c. "Eurema proterpia"	2·00	2·75

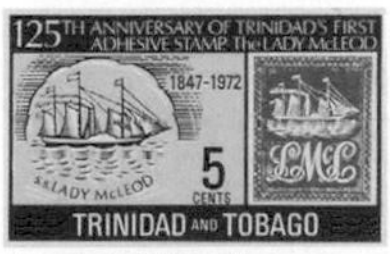

141 "Lady McLeod" (paddle-steamer) and McLeod Stamp

1972. 125th Anniv of First Trinidad Postage Stamp.

413	141	5c. multicoloured	20	10
414	-	10c. multicoloured	30	10
415	-	30c. blue, brown and black	60	45
MS416		83×140 mm. Nos. 413/15	1·00	1·25

DESIGNS: 10c. Lady McLeod stamp and map; 30c. Lady McLeod and inscription.

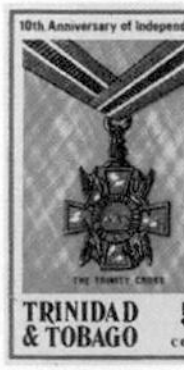

142 Trinity Cross

1972. Tenth Anniv of Independence. Multicoloured.

417	5c. Type **142**	10	10
418	10c. Chaconia Medal	10	10
419	20c. Humming-bird Medal	15	15
420	30c. Medal of Merit	15	20
MS421	93×121 mm. Nos. 417/20	60	1·00

See also Nos. 440/4.

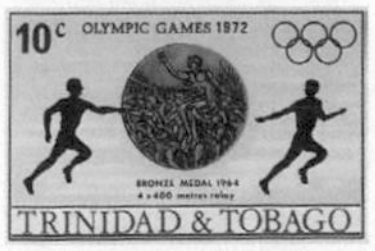

143 Bronze Medal, 1964 Relay

1972. Olympic Games, Munich. Multicoloured.

422	10c. Type **143**	15	10
423	20c. Bronze, 1964 200 m	25	25
424	30c. Silver, 1952 weightlifting	35	25
425	40c. Silver, 1964 400 m	35	25
426	50c. Silver, 1948 weightlifting	35	2·00
MS427	153×82 mm. Nos. 422/6	1·75	2·50

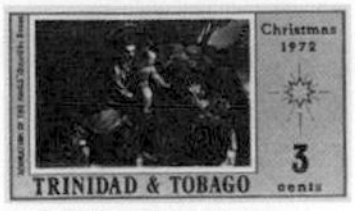

144 "Adoration of the Kings" (detail, Dosso)

1972. Christmas. Multicoloured.

431	3c. Type **144**	10	10
432	5c. "The Holy Family and a Shepherd" (Titian)	10	10
433	30c. As 5c.	70	55
MS434	73×99 mm. Nos. 431/3	1·00	2·00

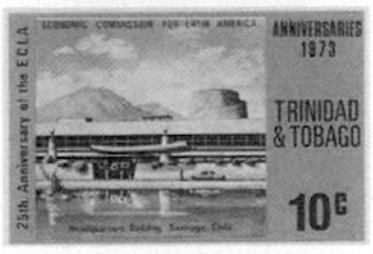

145 E.C.L.A. Building, Chile

1973. Anniversaries. Events described on stamps. Multicoloured.

435	10c. Type **145**	10	10
436	20c. Interpol emblem	45	30
437	30c. W.M.O. emblem	45	30
438	40c. University of the West Indies	45	1·00
MS439	155×92 mm. Nos. 435/8	1·25	1·40

1973. 11th Anniv of Independence. Medals as T **142**. Multicoloured.

440	10c. Trinity Cross	10	10
441	20c. Medal of Merit	20	40
442	30c. Chaconia Medal	20	50
443	40c. Hummingbird Medal	30	50
MS444	75×122 mm. Nos. 440/3	70	1·25

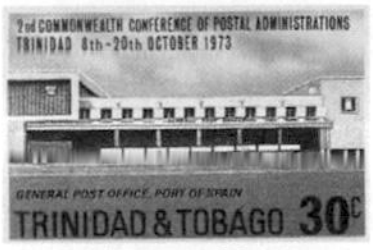

146 G.P.O., Port-of-Spain

1973. Second Commonwealth Conference of Postal Administrations, Trinidad. Multicoloured.

445	30c. Type **146**	20	75
446	40c. Conference Hall, Chaguaramas (wrongly inscr "Chagaramas")	30	75
MS447	115×115 mm. Nos. 445/6	60	1·50

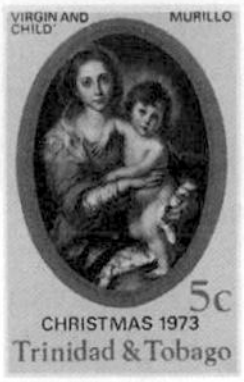

147 "Madonna with Child" (Murillo)

1973. Christmas.

448	147	5c. multicoloured	10	10
449	147	$1 multicoloured	60	1·25
MS450		94×88 mm. Nos. 448/9	85	1·75

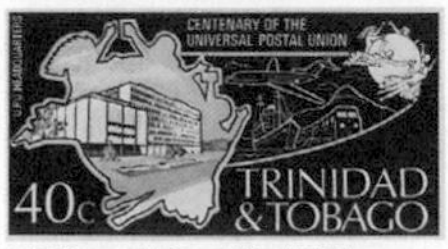

148 Berne H.Q. within U.P.U. Emblem

1974. Centenary of U.P.U. Multicoloured.

451	40c. Type **148**	30	15
452	50c. Map within emblem	30	85
MS453	117×104 mm. Nos. 451/2	10·00	20·00

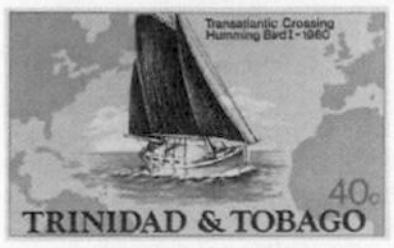

149 "Humming Bird I" (ketch) crossing Atlantic Ocean (1960)

1974. First Anniv of World Voyage by H. and K. La Borde. Multicoloured.

454	40c. Type **149**	50	15
455	50c. "Humming Bird II" (ketch) crossing globe	60	1·40
MS456	109×84 mm. Nos. 454/5	1·50	4·00

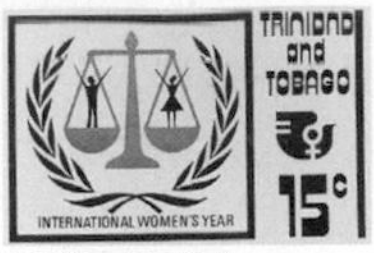

150 "Sex Equality"

1975. International Women's Year.

457	150	15c. multicoloured	15	30
458	150	30c. multicoloured	35	70

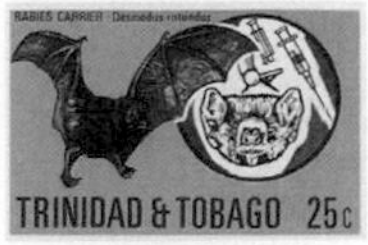

151 Common Vampire Bat, Microscope and Syringe

1975. Isolation of Rabies Virus. Multicoloured.

459	25c. Type **151**	45	1·25
460	30c. Dr. Pawan, instruments and book	55	55

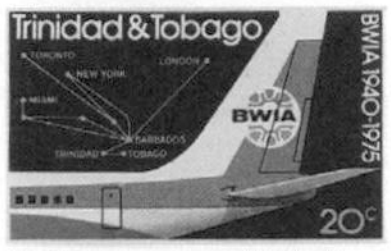

152 Route-map and Tail of Boeing 707

1975. 35th Anniv of British West Indian Airways. Multicoloured.

461	20c. Type **152**	40	80
462	30c. 707 on ground	60	90
463	40c. 707 in flight	70	1·10
MS464	119×110 mm. Nos. 461/3	1·50	2·50

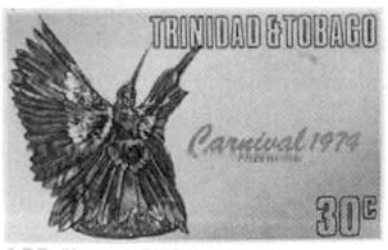

153 "From the Land of the Humming Bird"

1975. Carnival. 1974 Prize-winning Costumes. Multicoloured.

465	30c. Type **153**	10	10
466	$1 "The Little Carib"	40	50
MS467	83×108 mm. Nos. 465/6	1·10	1·10

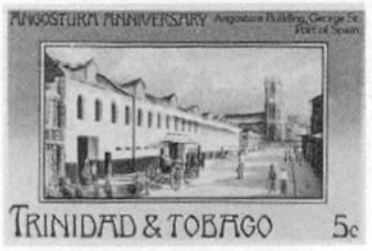

154 Angostura Building, Port-of-Spain

1976. 150th Anniv of Angostura Bitters. Multicoloured.

468	5c. Type **154**	10	40
469	35c. Medal, New Orleans, 1885/6	20	35
470	45c. Medal, Sydney, 1879	25	40
471	50c. Medal, Brussels, 1897	25	1·40
MS472	119×112 mm. Nos. 468/71	65	1·75

1976. West Indian Victory in World Cricket Cup. As T **126** of Barbados.

474	35c. Caribbean map	45	90
475	45c. Prudential Cup	55	90
MS476	80×80 mm. Nos. 474/5	1·75	4·00

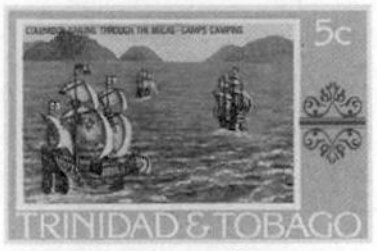

155 "Columbus sailing Through the Bocas" (Campins)

1976. Paintings, Hotels and Orchids. Multicoloured.

479	5c. Type **155**	2·50	30
480	6c. Robinson Crusoe Hotel, Tobago	20	2·75
482	10c. "San Fernando Hill" (J. Cazabon)	20	10
483	12c. "Paphinia cristata"	2·25	4·50
484	15c. Turtle Beach Hotel	50	3·25
485	20c. "East Indians in a Landscape" (J. Cazabon)	70	10
486	25c. Mt. Irvine Hotel	60	10
487	30c. "Caularthron bicornutum"	2·25	3·25

488		35c. "Los Gallos Point" (J. Cazabon)	1·75	10
489		40c. "Miltassia"	3·00	10
490		45c. "Corbeaux Town" (J. Cazabon)	1·00	10
491		50c. "Oncidium ampliatum"	2·25	20
492		70c. Beach facilities, Mt. Irvine Hotel	70	1·25
494		$2.50 "Oncidium papilio"	2·50	6·00
495		$5 Trinidad Holiday Inn	1·25	7·00
MS497		171×100 mm. Nos. 479, 482, 485, 488 and 490	2·00	1·50
MS498		171×88 mm. Nos. 480, 484, 486, 492 and 495	2·25	7·00
MS499		170×90 mm. Nos. 483, 487, 489, 491 and 494	4·50	5·00

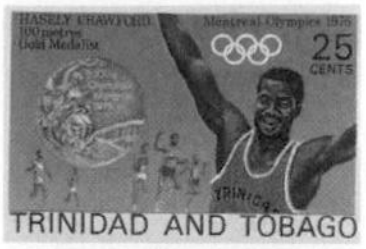

156 Hasely Crawford and Olympic Gold Medal

1977. Hasely Crawford Commemoration.

501	**156**	25c. multicoloured	30	50
MS502		93×70 mm. No. 501	60	1·25

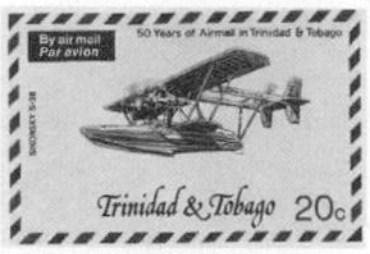

157 Lindbergh's Sikorsky S-38, 1929

1977. 50th Anniv of Airmail Service. Multicoloured.

503		20c. Type **157**	40	20
504		35c. Arrival of Charles and Anne Lindbergh	50	35
505		45c. Boeing 707, c. 1960	60	60
506		50c. Boeing 747-200, 1969	1·00	3·75
MS507		130×100 mm. Nos. 503/6	3·00	4·25

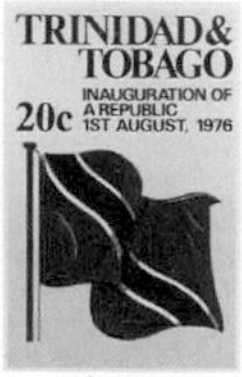

158 National Flag

1977. Inauguration of Republic. Multicoloured.

508		20c. Type **158**	40	15
509		35c. Coat of arms	60	65
510		45c. Government House	70	85
MS511		125×84 mm. Nos. 508/10	1·00	2·50

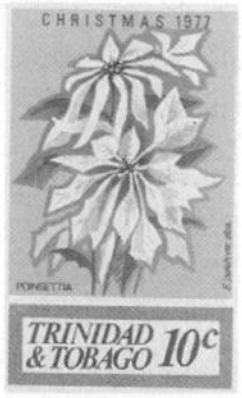

159 White Poinsettia

1977. Christmas. Multicoloured.

512		10c. Type **159**	20	10
513		35c. Type **159**	25	10
514		45c. Red poinsettia	30	30
515		50c. As 45c.	35	2·50
MS516		112×142 mm. Nos. 512/15	1·00	3·50

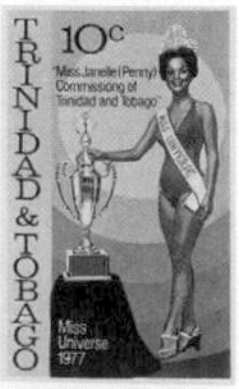

160 Miss Janelle (Penny) Commissioning with Trophy

1978. "Miss Universe 1977" Commemoration. Multicoloured.

517		10c. Type **160**	25	10
518		35c. Portrait	40	60
519		45c. In evening dress	45	75
MS520		186×120 mm. Nos. 517/19	1·00	2·00

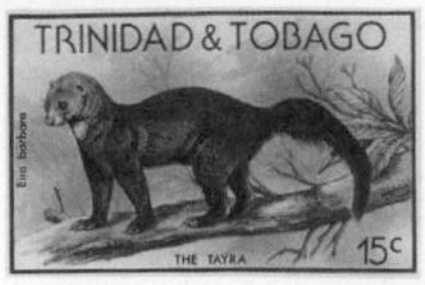

161 Tayra

1978. Wildlife. Multicoloured.

521		15c. Type **161**	20	20
522		25c. Ocelot	30	30
523		40c. Brazilian tree porcupine	50	30
524		70c. Tamandua	65	3·00
MS525		128×101 mm. Nos. 521/4	1·50	3·75

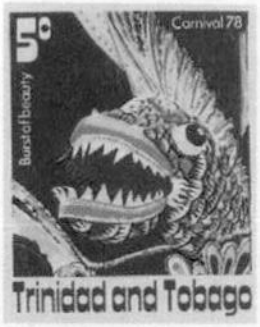

162 "Burst of Beauty"

1979. Carnival 1978.

526	**162**	5c. multicoloured	10	10
527	-	10c. multicoloured	10	10
528	-	35c. multicoloured	10	10
529	-	45c. multicoloured	10	10
530	-	50c. brown, red and lilac	10	15
531	-	$1 multicoloured	20	65

DESIGNS: 10c. Rain worshipper; 35c. "Zodiac"; 45c. Praying mantis; 50c. "Eye of the Hurricane"; $1 Steel orchestra.

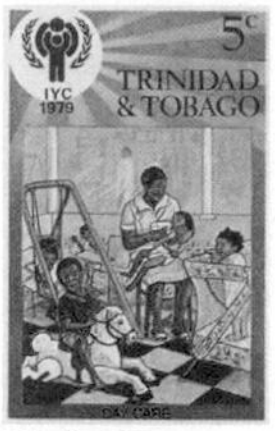

163 Day Care

1979. International Year of the Child. Multicoloured.

532		5c. Type **163**	10	10
533		10c. School feeding programme	10	10
534		35c. Dental care	30	15
535		45c. Nursery school	30	20
536		50c. Free bus transport	30	85
537		$1 Medical care	65	2·75
MS538		114×132 mm. Nos. 532/7	1·60	2·50

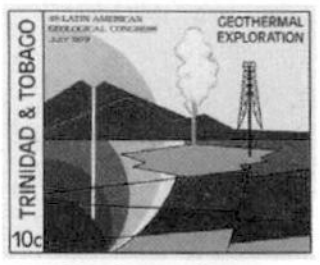

164 Geothermal Exploration

1979. Fourth Latin American Geological Congress. Multicoloured.

539		10c. Type **164**	20	10
540		35c. Hydrogeology	35	40
541		45c. Petroleum exploration	40	40
542		70c. Environmental preservation	55	1·60
MS543		185×89 mm. Nos. 539/42	1·50	2·25

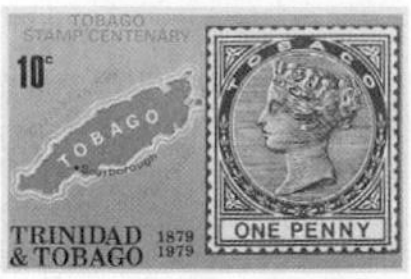

165 1879 1d. Stamp and Map of Tobago

1979. Tobago Stamp Centenary.

544	**165**	10c. multicoloured	10	10
545	-	15c. multicoloured	15	10
546	-	35c. multicoloured	20	20
547	-	45c. multicoloured	20	20
548	-	70c. multicoloured	25	1·50
549	-	$1 black, lilac and orange	25	1·75
MS550		165×155 mm. Nos. 544/9	1·25	4·00

DESIGNS: 15c. 1879 3d. and 1880 ½d. surcharged on half of 6d; 35c. 1879 6d. and 1886 ½d. surcharged on 6d; 45c. 1879 1s. and 1886 ½d. surcharged on 2½d; 70c. 1879 5s. and Great Britain 1856 1s. with "A14" (Scarborough, Tobago) postmark; $1 1879 £1 and General Post Office, Scarborough, Tobago.

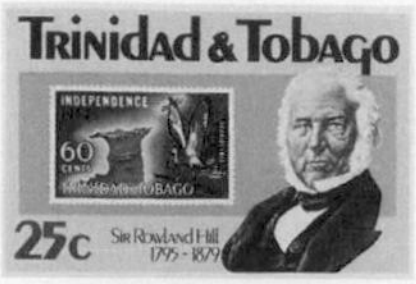

166 1962 60c. Independence Commemorative Stamp and Sir Rowland Hill

1979. Death Cent of Sir Rowland Hill. Multicoloured.

551		25c. Type **166**	30	15
552		45c. 1977 35c. Inauguration of Republic commemorative	35	20
553		$1 1879 Trinidad ½d. surcharge and Tobago, 1880 4d.	45	1·75
MS554		115×125 mm. No. 551/3	1·00	1·75

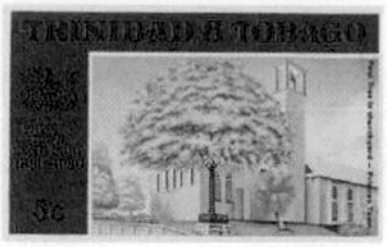

167 Poui Tree in Churchyard

1980. Centenary of Princes Town. Multicoloured.

555		5c. Type **167**	10	10
556		10c. Princes Town Court House	10	10
557		50c. Locomotive of the Royal Train, 1880	60	90
558		$1.50 H.M.S. "Bacchante" (screw corvette)	1·00	2·00
MS559		177×102 mm. Nos. 555/8	2·00	2·75

1980. Population Census. Nos. 479/80 and 482 optd **1844–1980 POPULATION CENSUS 12th MAY 1980**.

560		5c. Type **155**	20	20
561		6c. Robinson Crusoe Hotel, Tobago	20	80
562		10c. "San Fernando Hill" (J. Cazabon)	20	20

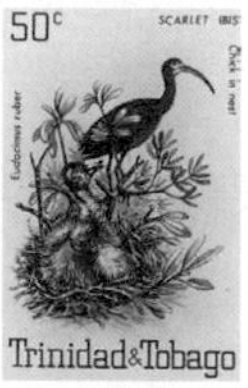

169 Scarlet Ibis (male)

1980. Scarlet Ibis. Multicoloured.

563		50c. Type **169**	50	1·40
564		50c. Male and female	50	1·40
565		50c. Hen and nest	50	1·40
566		50c. Nest and eggs	50	1·40
567		50c. Chick in nest	50	1·40

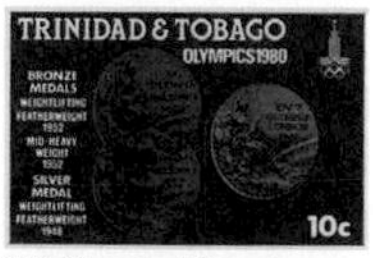

170 Silver and Bronze Medals for Weightlifting, 1948 and 1952

1980. Olympic Games, Moscow.

568	**170**	10c. multicoloured	10	10
569	-	15c. multicoloured	10	10
570	-	70c. multicoloured	45	1·25
MS571		110×149 mm. $2.50 black, silver and red	1·50	4·50

DESIGNS—HORIZ: 15c. Hasely Crawford (100 metres sprint winner, 1976) and gold medal; 70c. Silver medal for 400 metres and bronze medal for 4×400 metres relay, 1964. VERT: $2.50, Olympic Games emblems for Moscow, 1980, Olympia 776 B.C. and Athens, 1896.

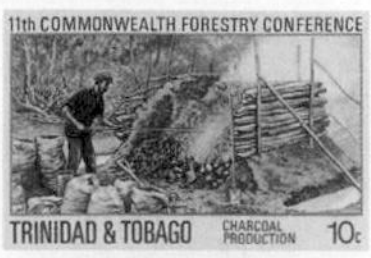

171 Charcoal Production

1980. 11th Commonwealth Forestry Conf. Multicoloured.

572		10c. Type **171**	10	10
573		55c. Logging	20	25
574		70c. Teak plantation	30	60
575		$2.50 Watershed management	60	2·25
MS576		135×87 mm. Nos. 572/5	1·75	2·75

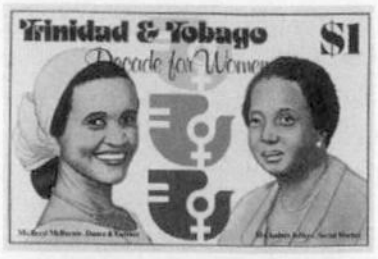

172 Beryl McBurnie (dance and culture) and Audrey Jeffers (social worker)

1980. Decade for Women (1st issue). Multicoloured.

577		$1 Type **172**	35	55
578		$1 Elizabeth Bourne (judiciary) and Isabella Teshier (government)	35	55
579		$1 Dr. Stella Abidh (public health) and Louise Horne (nutrition)	35	55

See also Nos. 680/2.

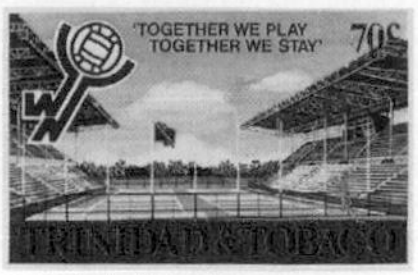

173 Netball Stadium

1980. World Netball Tournament.

580	**173**	70c. multicoloured	30	50

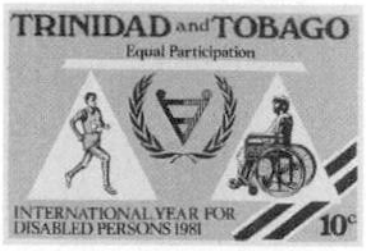

174 I.Y.D.P. Emblem, Athlete and Disabled Person

1981. International Year of Disabled Persons.

581	**174**	10c. green, black and red	15	10
582	-	70c. orange, black and red	30	70
583	-	$1.50 blue, black and red	40	1·40
584	-	$2 flesh, black and red	40	1·75

DESIGNS: 70c. I.Y.D.P. emblem and doctor with disabled person; $1.50, Emblem and blind man and woman; $2, Emblem and inscription.

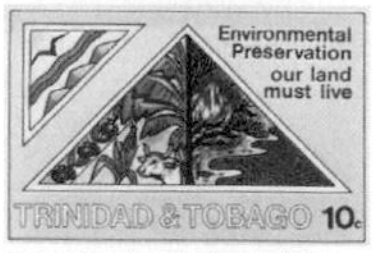

175 "Our Land Must Live"

1981. Environmental Preservation. Multicoloured.

585		10c. Type **175**	15	10
586		55c. "Our seas must live"	45	30
587		$3 "Our skies must live"	1·60	1·60
MS588		142×89 mm. Nos. 555/7	2·50	4·50

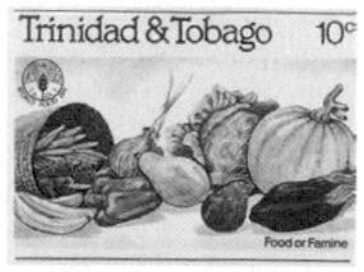

176 "Food For Famine"

1981. World Food Day. Multicoloured.

589		10c. Type **176**	10	10
590		15c. "Produce more" (threshing and milling rice)	10	10
591		45c. "Fish for food" (Bigeye)	30	20
592		55c. "Prevent hunger"	35	25
593		$1.50 "Fight malnutrition"	75	90
594		$2 "Fish for food" (Small-mouthed grunt)	90	1·25
MS595		164×98 mm. Nos. 589/94	2·25	5·00

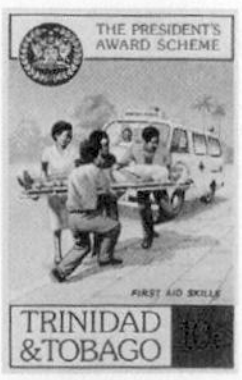

177 "First Aid Skills"

1981. President's Award Scheme. Multicoloured.

596		10c. Type **177**	20	10
597		70c. "Motor mechanics"	40	45
598		$1 "Expedition"	50	55
599		$2 Presenting an award	60	1·40

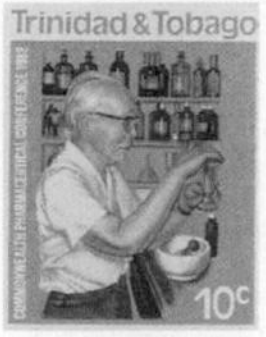

178 Pharmacist at Work

1982. Commonwealth Pharmaceutical Conference. Multicoloured.

600	10c. Type **178**	15	10
601	$1 Gerritoute (plant)	1·75	2·25
602	$2 Rachette (plant)	2·75	4·25

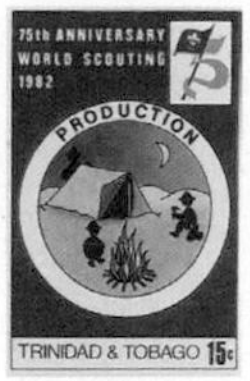

179 "Production"

1982. 75th Anniv of Boy Scout Movement. Multicoloured.

603	15c. Type **179**	60	10
604	55c. "Tolerance"	1·50	30
605	$5 "Discipline"	5·50	7·00

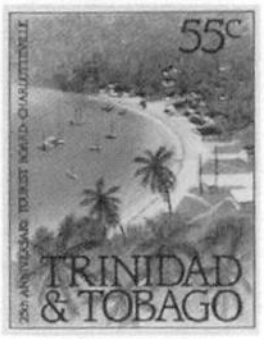

180 Charlotteville

1982. 25th Anniv of Tourist Board. Multicoloured.

606	55c. Type **180**	30	25
607	$1 Boating	40	55
608	$3 Fort George	1·25	2·50

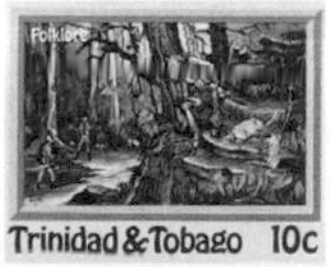

181 "Pa Pa Bois"

1982. Folklore. Local Spirits and Demons. Multicoloured.

609	10c. Type **181**	10	10
610	15c. "La Diablesse"	10	10
611	65c. "Lugarhoo", "Phantom" and "Soucouyant"	35	30
612	$5 "Bois de Soleil", "Davens" and "Mamma de l'Eau"	2·50	3·25
MS613	133×100 mm. Nos. 609/12	4·25	6·50

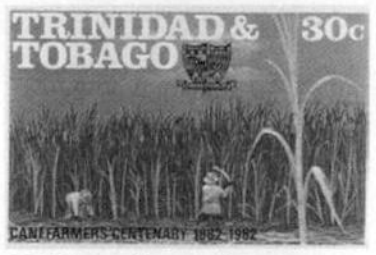

182 Cane Harvesting

1982. Cent of Canefarmers' Association. Multicoloured.

614	30c. Type **182**	30	15
615	70c. Farmers loading bullock cart	60	1·00
616	$1.50 Cane field in bloom	1·10	3·25
MS617	72×117 mm. Nos. 614/16	1·40	2·75

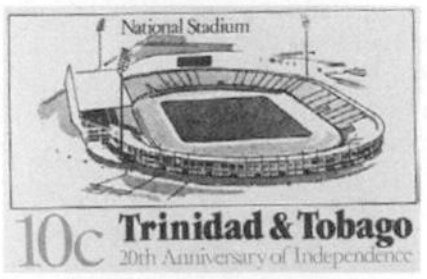

183 National Stadium

1982. 20th Anniv of Independence. Multicoloured.

618	10c. Type **183**	50	10
619	35c. Caroni water treatment plant	60	15
620	50c. Mount Hope Maternity Hospital	1·50	25
621	$2 National Insurance Board Mall, Tobago	1·75	2·00

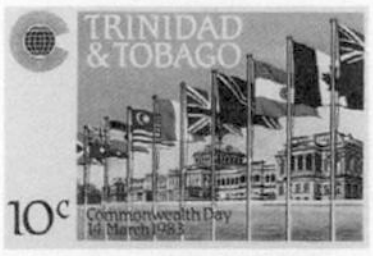

184 Commonwealth Flags

1983. Commonwealth Day. Multicoloured.

622	10c. Type **184**	10	10
623	55c. Satellite view of Trinidad and Tobago	25	20
624	$1 "Nodding donkey" oil pump (vert)	40	70
625	$2 Map of Trinidad and Tobago (vert)	85	1·50

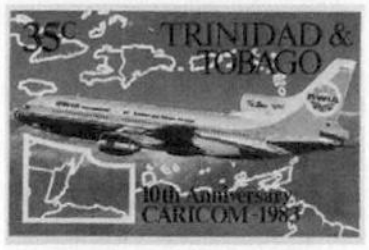

185 Lockheed Tristar 500 "Flamingo"

1983. Tenth Anniv of CARICOM.

626	**185** 35c. multicoloured	2·00	2·25

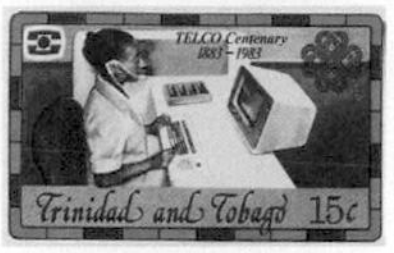

186 V.D.U. Operator

1983. World Communications Year. Multicoloured.

627	15c. Type **186**	20	10
628	55c. Scarborough Post Office, Tobago	30	20
629	$1 Textel building	60	70
630	$3 Morne Blue E.C.M.S. station	1·10	2·50

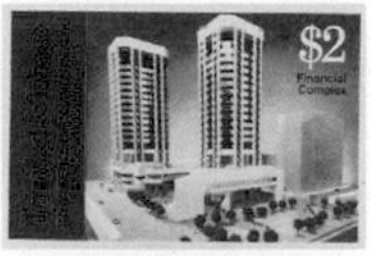

187 Financial Complex

1983. Conference of Commonwealth Finance Ministers.

631	**187** $2 multicoloured	60	1·25

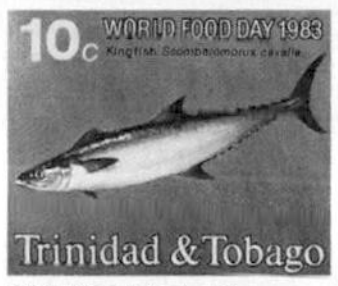

188 King Mackerel

1983. World Food Day. Multicoloured.

632	10c. Type **188**	20	10
633	55c. Four-winged flyingfish	1·00	40
634	70c. Queen or pink conch	1·25	1·40
635	$4 Red shrimp	4·50	7·50

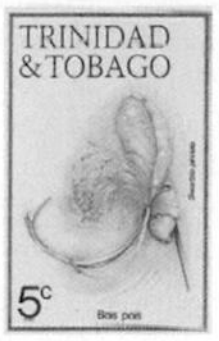

189 Bois Pois

1983. Flowers. Multicoloured.

636A	5c. Type **189**	1·00	2·00
687	10c. Maraval lily	30	30
638A	15c. Star grass	90	1·00
639A	20c. Bois caco	30	55
640A	25c. Strangling fig	1·10	2·50
641A	30c. "Cassia moschata"	50	40
642A	50c. Chalice flower	50	40
643A	65c. Black stick	55	1·00
644A	80c. "Columnea scandens"	65	2·00
695	95c. Cat's claw	65	70
696	$1 Bois l'agli	65	30
647A	$1.50 "Eustoma exaltatum"	1·25	2·50
648A	$2 Chaconia (39×29 mm)	1·50	3·00
649A	$2.50 "Chrysothemis pulchella" (39×29 mm)	1·25	4·00
700	$5 "Centratherum punctatum" (39×29 mm)	1·50	2·00
701	$10 Savanna flower (39×29 mm)	2·25	4·50

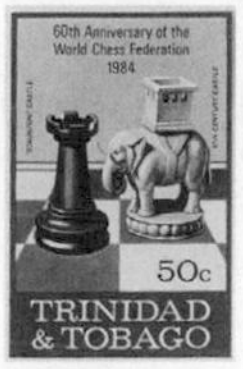

190 Rooks in Staunton and 17th-century Styles

1984. 60th Anniv of Int Chess Federation. Multicoloured.

652	50c. Type **190**	3·25	50
653	70c. Bishops in Staunton and 12th-century Lewis styles	3·50	2·00
654	$1.50 Queens in Staunton and 13th-century Swedish styles	4·50	6·00
655	$2 Kings in Staunton and 19th-century Chinese styles	6·00	7·50

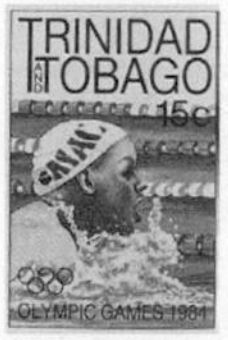

191 Swimming

1984. Olympic Games, Los Angeles. Multicoloured.

656	15c. Type **191**	10	10
657	55c. Track and field events	30	20
658	$1.50 Sailing	1·00	1·75
659	$4 Cycling	7·00	7·50
MS660	132×85 mm. Nos. 656/9	7·50	8·50

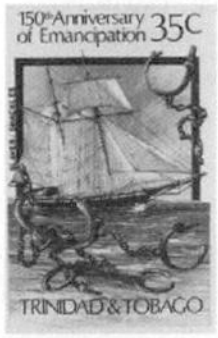

192 Slave Schooner and Shackles

1984. 150th Anniv of Abolition of Slavery. Multicoloured.

661	35c. Type **192**	1·50	40
662	55c. Slave and "Slave Triangle" map	2·50	60
663	$1 "Capitalism and Slavery" (book by Dr. Eric Williams)	2·50	2·50
664	$2 Toussaint l'Ouverture (Haitian revolutionary)	3·25	7·00
MS665	95×100 mm. Nos. 661/4	9·00	12·00

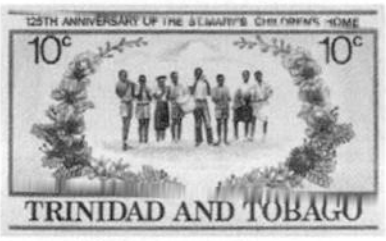

193 Children's Band

1984. 125th Anniv of St. Mary's Children's Home. Multicoloured.

666	10c. Type **193**	15	10
667	70c. St. Mary's Children's Home	50	50
668	$3 Group of children	2·25	4·00

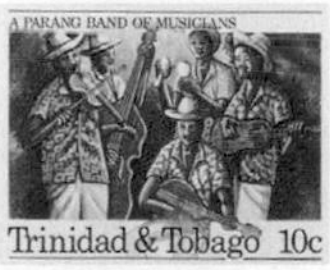

194 Parang Band

1984. Parang Festival. Multicoloured.

669	10c. Type **194**	25	10
670	30c. Music and poinsettia	60	15
671	$1 Bandola, bandolin and cuatro (musical instruments)	1·75	1·25
672	$3 Double bass, fiddle and guitar (musical instruments)	2·75	6·50

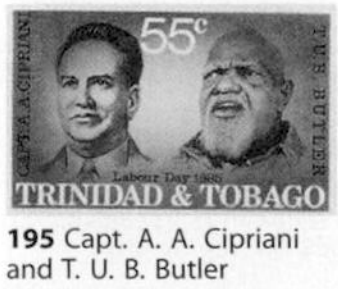

195 Capt. A. A. Cipriani and T. U. B. Butler

1985. Labour Day. Labour Leaders.

673	**195** 55c. black and red	1·60	1·60
674	- 55c. black and yellow	1·60	1·60
675	- 55c. black and green	1·60	1·60

DESIGNS: No. 674, C. P. Alexander and Q. O'Connor; 675, A. Cola Rienzi and C. T. W. E. Worrell.

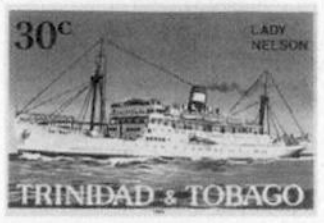

196 "Lady Nelson" (1928)

1985. Ships. Multicoloured.

676	30c. Type **196**	70	25
677	95c. "Lady Drake", (1928)	1·00	1·75
678	$1.50 "Federal Palm" (1961)	1·00	3·00
679	$2 "Federal Maple" (1961)	1·25	3·50

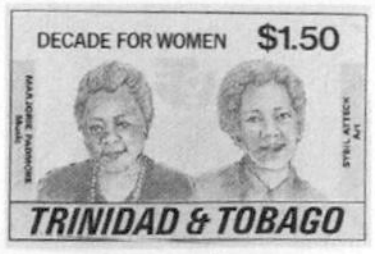

197 Marjorie Padmore (music) and Sybil Atteck (art)

1985. Decade for Women (2nd issue). Multicoloured.

680	$1.50 Type **197**	2·25	3·00
681	$1.50 May Cherrie (medical social worker) and Evelyn Tracey (social worker)	2·25	3·00
682	$1.50 Umilta McShine (education) and Jessica Smith-Phillips (public service)	2·25	3·00

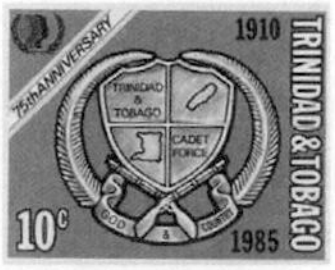

198 Badge of Trinidad and Tobago Cadet Force (75th Anniv)

1985. International Youth Year. Multicoloured.

683	10c. Type **198**	45	10
684	65c. Guide badges (75th anniv of Girl Guide movement)	2·00	2·75
685	95c. Young people of Trinidad	2·50	3·25

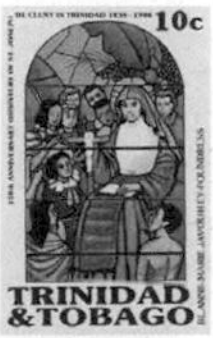

199 Anne-Marie Javouhey (foundress)

1986. 150th Anniv of Arrival of Sisters of St. Joseph de Cluny. Multicoloured.

702	10c. Type **199**	10	10
703	65c. St. Joseph's Convent, Port-of-Spain	45	1·40
704	95c. Children and statue of Anne-Marie Javouhey	65	1·75

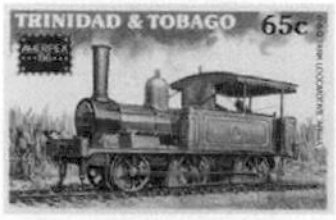

200 Tank Locomotive "Arima"

1986. "Ameripex 86" International Stamp Exhibition, Chicago. Trinidad Railway Loco-motives. Multicoloured.

705	65c. Type **200**	25	35
706	95c. Canadian-built steam locomotive No. 22	35	60
707	$1.10 Steam tender engine	40	1·40
708	$1.50 Saddle tank locomotive	60	2·00
MS709	105×80 mm. Nos. 705/8	1·40	3·75

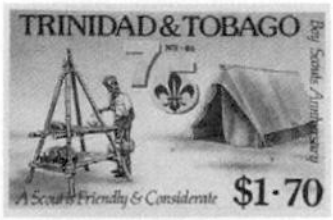

201 Scout Camp

1986. 75th Anniv of Trinidad and Tobago Boy Scouts. Multicoloured.

710	$1.70 Type **201**	1·00	2·00
711	$2 Scouts of 1911 and 1986	1·25	2·25

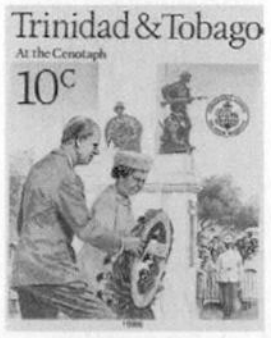

202 Queen and Duke of Edinburgh laying Wreath at War Memorial

1986. 60th Birthday of Queen Elizabeth II. Multicoloured.

712	10c. Type **202**	35	10
713	15c. Queen with Trinidadian dignitaries aboard "Britannia"	1·00	30
714	30c. With President Ellis Clarke	65	30
715	$5 Receiving bouquet	3·00	7·00

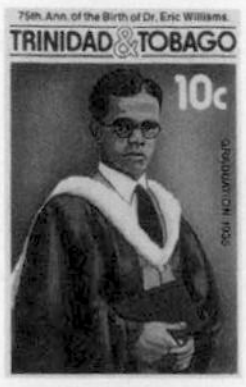

203 Eric Williams at Graduation, 1935

1986. 75th Birth Anniv of Dr. Eric Williams. Multicoloured.

716	10c. Type **203**	70	10
717	30c. Premier Eric Williams (wearing red tie)	1·10	30
718	30c. As No. 717 but wearing black and orange tie	1·10	30
719	95c. Arms of University of West Indies and Dr. Williams as Pro-Chancellor (horiz)	2·00	1·25
720	$5 Prime Minister Williams and Whitehall (horiz)	2·75	10·50
MS721	105×100 mm. Nos. 716/17 and 719/20	5·00	10·00

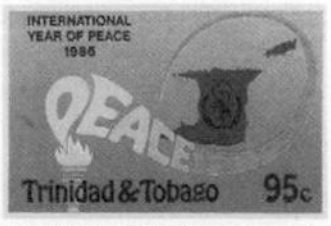

204 "PEACE" Slogan and Outline map of Trinidad and Tobago

1986. International Peace Year. Multicoloured.

722	95c. Type **204**	60	50
723	$3 Peace dove with olive branch	1·50	3·50

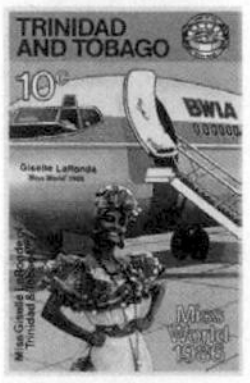

205 Miss Giselle La Ronde and BWIA Airliner

1987. Miss World 1986. Multicoloured.

724	10c. Type **205**	1·50	20
725	30c. In swimsuit on beach	2·25	30
726	95c. Miss Giselle La Ronde	3·75	2·50
727	$1.65 Wearing Miss World sash	4·75	7·50

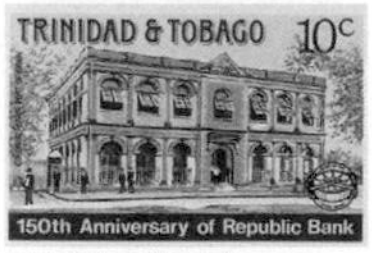

206 Colonial Bank, Port-of-Spain

1987. 150th Anniv of Republic Bank. Multicoloured.

728	10c. Type **206**	10	10
729	65c. Cocoa plantation	60	90
730	95c. Oil field	3·25	2·50
731	$1.10 Belmont Tramway Company tramcar	3·25	4·00

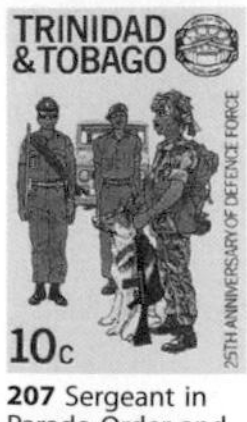

207 Sergeant in Parade Order and Soldiers in Work Dress and Battle Dress

1988. 25th Anniv of Defence Force. Multicoloured.

732	10c. Type **207**	1·50	20
733	30c. Women soldiers	2·75	30
734	$1.10 Defence Force officers	3·75	3·00
735	$1.50 Naval ratings and patrol boat	5·00	4·50

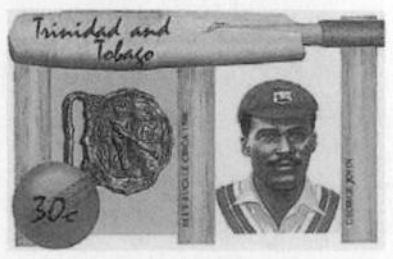

207a George John

1988. West Indian Cricket. Showing portrait, cricket equipment and early belt buckle. Multicoloured.

736	30c. Type **207a**	2·00	40
737	65c. Learie Constantine	3·00	1·00
738	95c. Sonny Ramadhin	3·25	1·75
739	$1.50 Gerry Gomez	3·75	4·00
740	$2.50 Jeffrey Stollmeyer	4·75	7·00

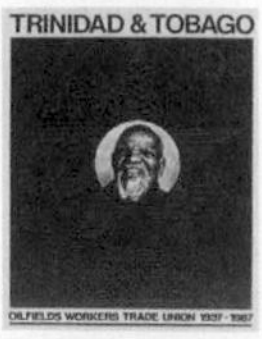

208 Uriah Butler (labour leader)

1988. 50th Anniv (1987) of Oilfield Workers Trade Union. Multicoloured.

741	10c. Type **208**	10	10
742	30c. Adrian Rienzi (O.W.T.U. president, 1937–42)	10	10
743	65c. John Rojas (O.W.T.U. president, 1943 62)	15	25
744	$5 George Weekes (O.W.T.U. president, 1962–87)	1·25	2·50

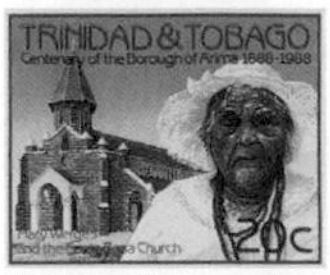

209 Mary Werges and Santa Rosa Church

1988. Centenary of Borough of Arima. Multicoloured.

745	20c. Type **209**	15	10
746	30c. Governor W. Robinson and Royal Charter	15	10
747	$1.10 Arrival of Governor Robinson at railway station	3·25	2·00
748	$1.50 Mayor J. F. Wallen and Centenary logo	1·00	2·50

1988. 300th Anniv of Lloyd's of London. As T **152a** of St. Helena. Multicoloured.

749	30c. Queen Mother at topping out of new building, 1984	1·50	20
750	$1.10 BWIA Lockheed Tristar 500 airliner "Flamingo" (horiz)	2·75	1·40
751	$1.55 Steel works, Trinidad (horiz)	1·75	2·00
752	$2 "Atlantic Empress" (tanker) on fire off Tobago, 1979	4·50	3·00

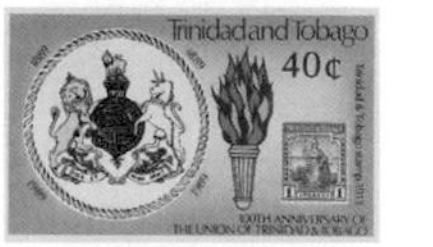

210 Colonial Arms of Trinidad & Tobago and 1913 1d. Stamp

1989. Centenary of Union of Trinidad and Tobago. Multicoloured.

753	40c. Type **210**	1·50	10
754	$1 Pre-1889 Tobago emblem and Tobago 1896 ½d. on 4d. stamp	3·00	1·00
755	$1.50 Pre-1889 Trinidad emblem and Trinidad 1883 4d. stamp	3·25	4·25
756	$2.25 Current Arms of Trinidad and Tobago and 1977 45c. Republic commemorative	3·75	6·50

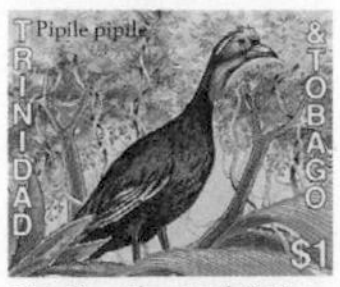

211 Blue-throated Piping Guan

1989. Rare Fauna of Trinidad and Tobago. Multicoloured.

757	$1 Type **211**	3·25	3·50
758	$1 "Phyllodytes auratus" (frog)	3·25	3·50
759	$1 "Cebus albifrons trinitatis" (monkey)	3·25	3·50
760	$1 Tamandua	3·25	3·50
761	$1 "Lutra longicaudis" (otter)	3·25	3·50

Nos. 757/61 were printed together, se-tenant, forming a composite background design.

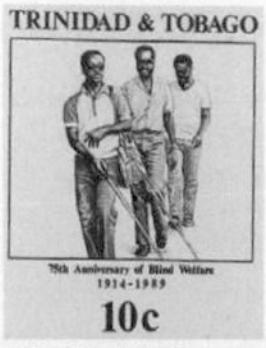

212 Blind Welfare

1989. Anniversaries. Multicoloured.

762	10c. Type **212** (75th anniv)	1·50	20
763	40c. Port-of-Spain City Hall (75th anniv)	40	20
764	$1 Guides and Brownies (75th anniv)	3·25	60
765	$2.25 Red Cross members (50th anniv)	4·25	3·00

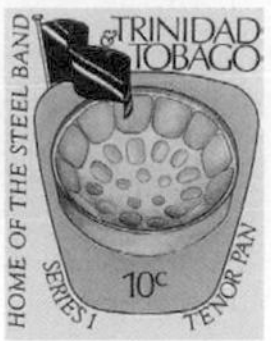

213 Tenor Pan

1990. Steel Pans (1st series). Multicoloured.

766	10c. Type **213**	15	10
767	40c. Guitar pans	30	15
768	$1 Cello pans	65	80
769	$2.25 Bass pans	1·25	3·50

See also Nos. 828/31.

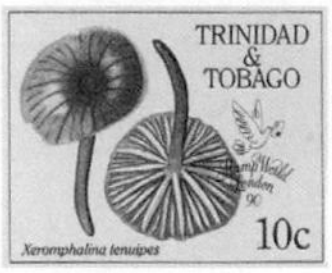

214 "Xeromphalina tenuipes"

1990. "Stamp World London 90" International Stamp Exhibition. Fungi. Multicoloured.

770	10c. Type **214**	35	20
771	40c. "Phallus indusiatus" ("Dictyophora indusiata")	65	25
772	$1 "Leucocoprinus birnbaumii"	1·25	1·00
773	$2.25 "Crinipellis perniciosa"	2·00	4·00

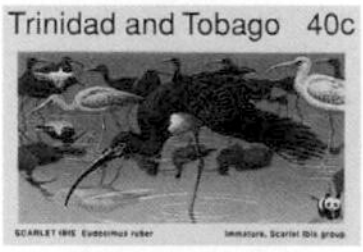

215 Scarlet Ibis in Immature Plumage

1990. Scarlet Ibis. Multicoloured.

774	40c. Type **215**	1·50	30
775	80c. Pair in pre-nuptial display	1·75	1·40
776	$1 Male in breeding plumage	1·75	1·40
777	$2.25 Adult on nest with chick	2·75	4·25

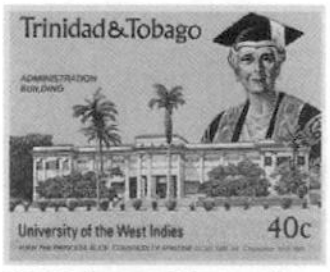

216 Princess Alice and Administration Building

1990. 40th Anniv of University of West Indies. Multicoloured.

778	40c. Type **216**	80	15
779	80c. Sir Hugh Wooding and Library	1·00	80
780	$1 Sir Allen Lewis and Faculty of Engineering	1·40	1·00
781	$2.25 Sir Shridath Ramphal and Faculty of Medical Sciences	3·75	6·50

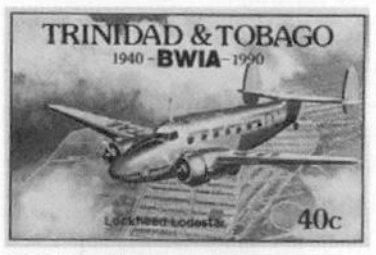

217 Lockheed Lodestar

1990. 50th Anniv of British West Indies Airways. Multicoloured.

782	40c. Type **217**	1·75	30
783	80c. Vickers Viking 1A	2·25	1·25
784	$1 Vickers Viscount 702	2·50	1·25
785	$2.25 Boeing 707	3·50	6·50
MS786	77×52 mm. $5 Lockheed L-1011 TriStar 500	4·75	7·00

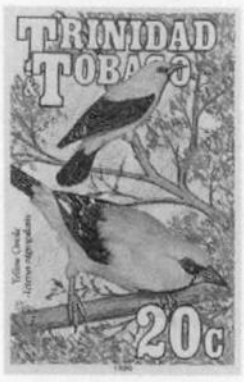

218 Yellow Oriole

1990. Birds. Multicoloured.

787	20c. Type **218**	1·00	50
837	25c. Green-rumped parrotlet	2·50	30
789	40c. Fork-tailed flycatcher	1·50	20
839	50c. Copper-rumped hummingbird	50	30
840	$1 Bananaquit	3·50	60
841	$2 Violaceous euphonia ("Semp")	4·00	1·50
793	$2.25 Channel-billed toucan	2·50	2·00
843	$2.50 Bay-headed tanager	3·00	2·50
844	$5 Green honeycreeper	2·75	2·75
845	$10 Cattle egret	3·50	5·00
846	$20 Golden-olive woodpecker	6·50	10·00
798	$50 Peregrine falcon	11·00	17·00

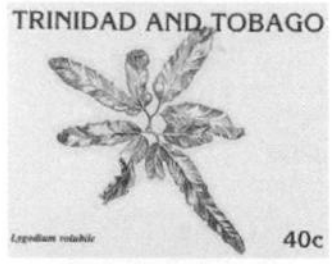

219 "Lygodium volubile"

1991. Ferns. Multicoloured.

799	40c. Type **219**	40	15
800	80c. "Blechnum occidentale"	75	70
801	$1 "Gleichenia bifida"	85	85
802	$2.25 "Polypodium lycopodioides"	2·00	3·50

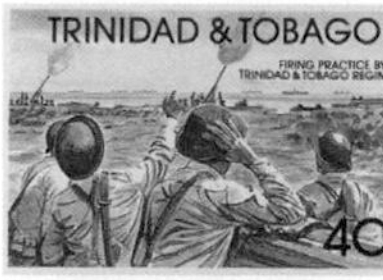

220 Trinidad and Tobago Regiment Anti-aircraft Battery

1991. 50th Anniv of Second World War. Multicoloured.

803	40c. Type **220**	1·75	30
804	80c. Fairey Barracuda Mk III attacking U-boat	2·75	1·25
805	$1 Avro Type 683 Lancaster	3·00	1·40
806	$2.25 H.M.S. "Wye" (frigate) escorting convoy	4·75	7·00
MS807	117×85 mm. $2.50, Presentation Supermarine Spitfire; $2.50, Presentation Vickers-Armstrong Wellington bomber	11·00	11·00

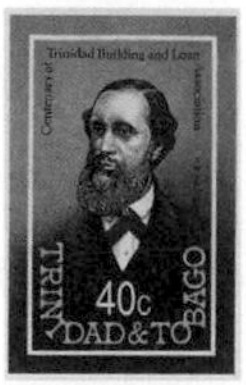

221 H. E. Rapsey (founder)

1992. Anniversaries. Multicoloured.

808	40c. Type **221** (centenary of Trinidad Building and Loan Association.)	30	15
809	80c. "Inca clathrata quesneli" (beetle) (Trinidad & Tobago Field Naturalists' Club)	1·00	1·40
810	$1 Holy Name Convent (centenary)	1·10	1·60

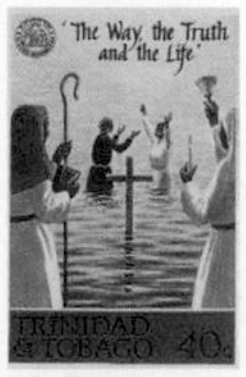

222 Baptism (Baptist)

1992. Religions of Trinidad and Tobago. Multicoloured.

811	40c. Type **222**	1·10	1·50
812	40c. Minaret with star and crescent (Islam)	1·10	1·50
813	40c. Logo (Hinduism)	1·10	1·50
814	40c. Cross (Christian)	1·10	1·50
815	40c. Logo (Baha'i)	1·10	1·50

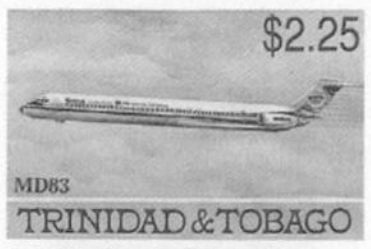

223 McDonnell Douglas MD-83

1992. Aircraft. Multicoloured.

816	$2.25 Type **223**	2·75	3·25
817	$2.25 Lockheed L-1011 TriStar aircraft	2·75	3·25

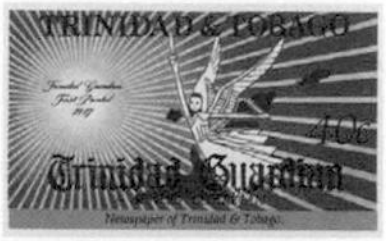

224 "Trinidad Guardian" Title (75th anniv of newspaper)

1992. Anniversaries. Multicoloured.

818	40c. Type **224**	10	10
819	40c. Nativity scene (Christmas) (vert)	10	10
820	$1 National Museum and Art Gallery (centenary)	35	50
821	$2.25 Cover to St. James Internment Camp, 1942 (50th anniv of Trinidad and Tobago Philatelic Society)	1·00	2·50

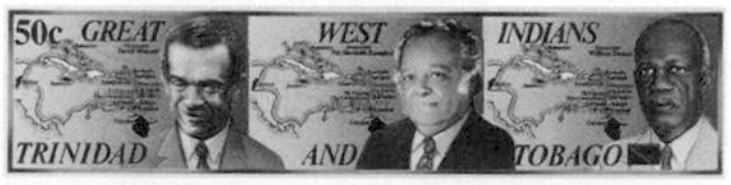

225 Derek Walcott, Sir Shridath Ramphal and William Demas with Caribbean Maps (image scaled to 48% of original size)

1994. 20th Anniv of CARICOM (Caribbean Economic Community). Recipients of Order of the Caribbean Community.

822	**225**	50c. multicoloured	40	20
823	**225**	$1.50 multicoloured	70	1·00
824	**225**	$2.75 multicoloured	1·10	2·00
825	**225**	$3 multicoloured	1·25	2·25
MS826		90×90 mm. $6 multicoloured (Insignia of the Order (34½×51½ mm))	2·25	3·50

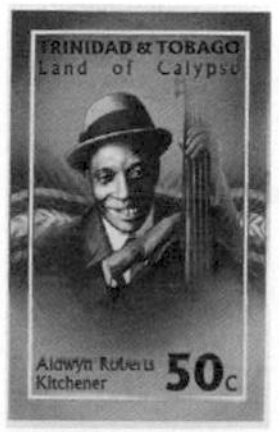

226 Aldwyn Roberts Kitchener (bass player)

1994. "Land of Calypso".

827	**226**	50c. multicoloured	2·00	1·00

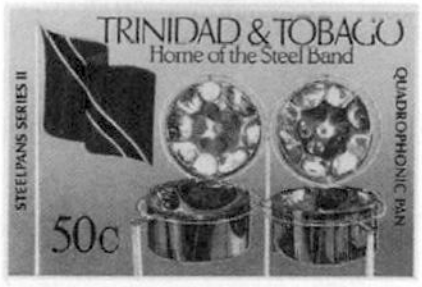

227 Quadrophonic Pans

1994. Steel Pans (2nd series). Multicoloured.

828	50c. Type **227**	40	20
829	$1 Tenor base pans	70	50
830	$2.25 Six pans	1·40	2·25
831	$2.50 Rocket pans	1·50	2·25

1994. "Hong Kong '94" International Stamp Exhibition. Nos. 837, 789, 841 and 796 optd **HONG KONG '94** and emblem.

832	25c. Green-rumped parrotlet	30	20
833	40c. Fork-tailed flycatcher	35	20
834	$2 Violaceous euphonia	95	1·25
835	$10 Cattle egret	3·25	6·00

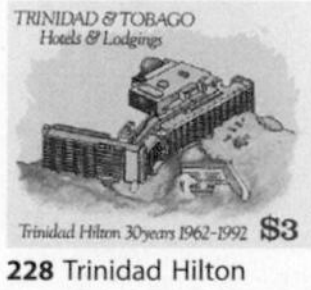

228 Trinidad Hilton

1994. Hotels and Lodgings. Multicoloured.

848	$3 Type **228**	90	1·40
849	$3 Sandy Point Village, Tobago	90	1·40
850	$3 Asa Wright Nature Centre and Lodge	90	1·40
851	$3 M.L.'s Bed and Breakfast	90	1·40

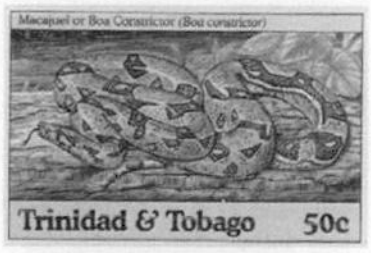

229 Boa Constrictor

1994. Snakes. Multicoloured.

852	50c. Type **229**	35	20
853	$1.25 Vine snake	75	70
854	$2.50 Bushmaster	1·40	1·75
855	$3 Large coral snake	1·60	2·00

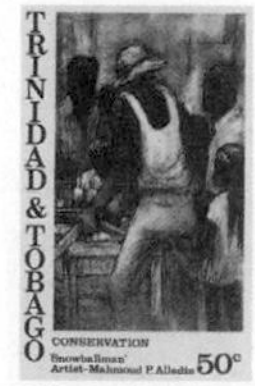

230 "Snowballman" (painting, Mahmoud Alladin)

1995. 50th Anniv of Trinidad Art Society. Multicoloured.

856	50c. Type **230**	40	70
857	50c. "Fishermen" (painting, Sybil Atteck)	40	70
858	50c. Copper sculpture (Ken Morris)	40	70

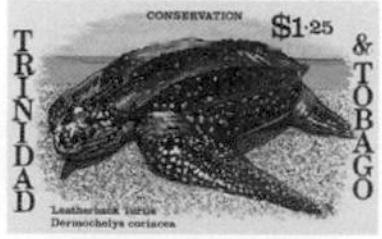

231 Loggerhead Turtle

1995. Conservation. Multicoloured.

859	$1.25 Type **231**	60	60
860	$2.50 Port-of-Spain Lighthouse (vert)	1·50	1·50
861	$3 "Knowsley" (location of Ministry of Foreign Affairs)	1·00	1·75

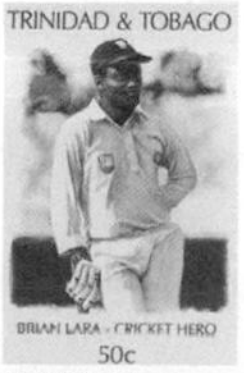

232 Brian Lara

1996. Brian Lara (cricketer) Commemoration.

862	**232**	50c. multicoloured	30	15
863	-	$1.25 multicoloured	60	50
864	-	$2.50 multicoloured	1·10	1·50
865	-	$3 multicoloured	1·25	1·75
MS866		62×75 mm. $3.75 multicoloured; $5.01 multicoloured	6·50	7·00

DESIGNS: $1.25 to $5.01, Cricket scenes.

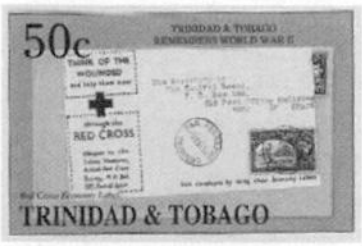

233 Red Cross Economy Label on Envelope

1996. 50th Anniv of End of Second World War (1995). Multicoloured.

867	50c. Type **233**	45	10
868	$1.25 U.S.S. "Missouri" (battleship), 1944	1·10	70
869	$2.50 U.S. servicemen playing baseball, 1942	1·40	1·90
870	$3 Fleet Air Arm Fulmar 1 (fighter)	1·60	2·25
MS871	116×85 mm. $3 Fleet Air Arm Grumman Mackinnon G-21C Goose flying boat; $3 U.S. Navy airship	3·50	4·50

1997. "HONG KONG '97" International Stamp Exhibition. Sheet 130×90 mm, containing design as No. 795. Multicoloured.

MS872	$5 Green honeycreeper	1·75	2·50

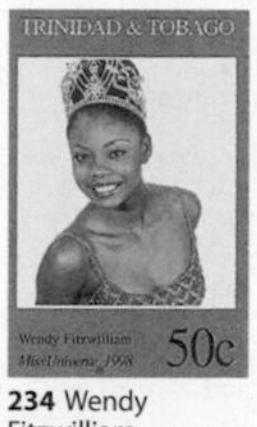

234 Wendy Fitzwilliam

1999. Wendy Fitzwilliam ("Miss Universe 1998"). Multicoloured.

873	50c. Type **234**	60	15
874	$1.25 Lying on beach	1·25	55
875	$2.50 In national costume	2·25	2·50
876	$3 In white evening gown	2·50	2·75
MS877	70×100 mm. $5 Wearing "Miss Universe" sash	6·00	6·00

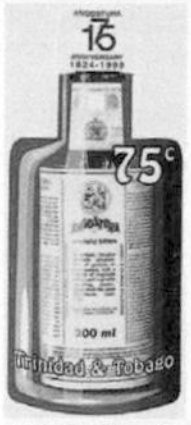

235 Bottle of Angostura Bitters

2000. 175th Anniv of Angostura Bitters. Mult. Self-adhesive.

878	75c. Type **235**	60	30
879	$3 Angostura Building inside bottle	2·25	2·25
880	$4.50 Cocktails and Angostura inside bottle (horiz)	3·25	4·00
MS881	120×80 mm. Nos. 878/80. Imperf	4·25	5·00

2000. Nos. 789 surch **75c**.

883	75c. on 40c. on 40c. Fork-tailed flycatcher	5·00	1·00

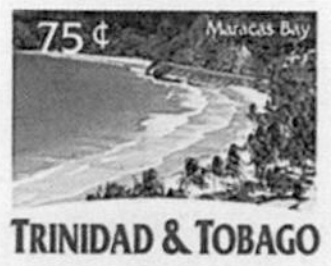

237 Maracas Bay

2000. Beaches of Trinidad and Tobago. Multicoloured.

884	75c. Type **237**	1·00	20
885	$1 Pirate's Bay	1·25	35
886	$3.75 Pigeon Point	2·75	3·50
887	$5 Toco, North Coast	3·50	4·25

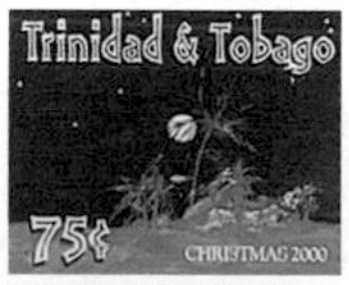

238 Moon over Caroni Landscape

2000. Christmas. Multicoloured.

888	75c. Type **238**	1·00	20
889	$3.75 Traditional food and drink	2·50	1·50
890	$4.50 Parang singers on beach	2·75	3·00
891	$5.25 Angels playing steel pans	3·25	3·75

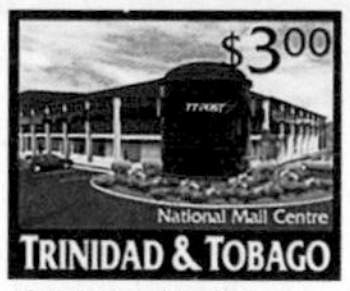

239 National Mail Centre

2000. New National Mail Centre. Multicoloured.

892	$3 Type **239**	2·00	1·00
893	$10 Side view of Centre	5·00	7·00

2001. No. 793 surch **75c**.

894	75c. on $2.25 Channel-billed toucan	11·00	3·75

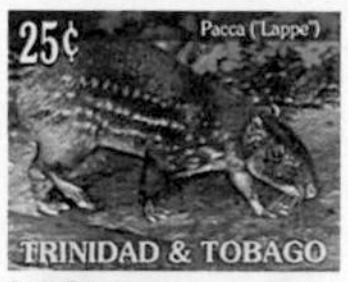

241 Pacca

2001. Endangered Wildlife. Multicoloured.

895	25c. Type **241**	70	20
896	50c. Prehensile-tailed porcupine	1·10	30
897	75c. Iguana	1·50	30
898	$1 Leatherback turtle	1·75	30
899	$2 Golden tegu	2·50	1·00
900	$3 Red howler monkey	3·00	1·25
901	$4 Weeping capuchin monkey (vert)	3·00	1·50
902	$5 River otter	3·25	1·75
903	$10 Ocelot	6·00	6·00
904	$20 Blue-throated piping guan ("Trinidad Piping Guan") (vert)	15·00	17·00

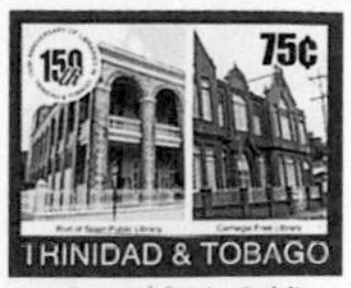

242 Port of Spain Public Library and Carnegie Library, San Fernando

2001. Anniversaries. Multicoloured.

905	75c. Type **242**	80	50
906	75c. National flag and Salvation Army emblem (vert)	2·25	80
907	$2 William Booth Memorial Hall (vert)	2·50	1·75
908	$3.25 New National Library	2·25	3·25
MS909	Two sheets each 125×85 mm. (a) Nos. 905 and 908. (b) Nos. 906/7	5·50	6·50

ANNIVERSARIES: Nos. 905 and 908, 150th anniv of public libraries; 906/7, centenary of Salvation Army in Trinidad and Tobago.

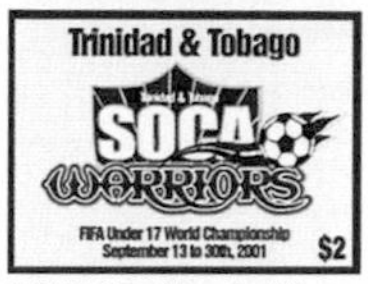

243 National Football Team Logo

2001. FIFA Under 17 World Football Championships. Multicoloured.

910	$2 Type **243**	1·00	90
911	$3.25 National flag and team slogan	1·75	1·75
912	$4.50 Stryka (team mascot) with national flag	2·50	2·75
913	$5.25 Four new football grounds	2·75	3·00
MS914	110×99 mm. Nos. 910/13	7·25	8·00

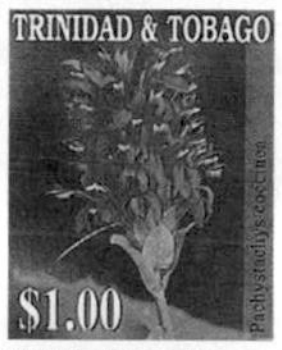

244 *Pachystachys coccinea*

2001. Flowers. Multicoloured designs.

915	$1 Type **244**	1·00	25
916	$2.50 *Heliconia psittacorum*	2·00	1·60
917	$3.25 *Brownea latifolia* (horiz)	2·25	2·25
918	$3.75 *Oncidium papilio*	3·25	3·50

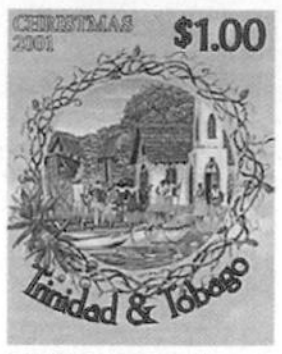

245 Congregation and Church inside Wreath

2001. Christmas. Multicoloured.

919	$1 Type **245**	80	25
920	$3.75 Musicians and dancers within Christmas tree	2·00	1·40
921	$4.50 Family and house inside wreath	2·25	2·50
922	$5.25 Church and choir within Christmas tree	2·50	3·25
MS923	118×157 mm. Nos. 919/22	7·00	8·00

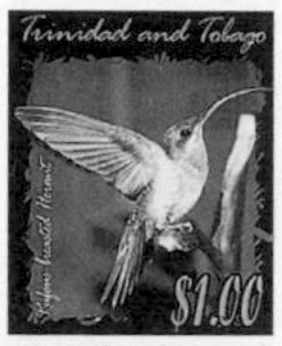

246 Rufous-breasted Hermit

2002. Hummingbirds. Multicoloured.

924	$1 Type **246**	1·25	35
925	$2.50 Black-throated mango	2·00	1·40
926	$3.25 Tufted coquette	2·75	3·00
927	$3.75 White-chested emerald	3·25	3·25

247 Cracker Butterfly

2002. Butterflies. Multicoloured.

928	$1 Type **247**	1·00	25
929	$3.75 Tiger butterfly	3·00	2·00
930	$4.50 Four continent butterfly	3·25	3·25
931	$5.25 89 butterfly	3·50	4·00

248 Fort Picton

2002. Forts. Multicoloured.

932	$1 Type **248**	70	25
933	$3.75 Fort George	2·00	1·40
934	$4.50 Fort King George	2·25	2·50
935	$5.25 Fort James	2·50	3·25
MS936	152×120 mm. Nos. 932/5	7·00	8·00

249 Dr. Eric Williams addressing Public Meeting, Woodford Square, Port of Spain

2002. 40th Anniv of Independence ($1) and Golden Jubilee (others). Showing the 1966 Royal Visit. Multicoloured.

937	$1 Type **249**	80	25
938	$3.75 Queen Elizabeth and Duke of Edinburgh with Dr. Williams and Governor-General	2·00	1·50
939	$4.50 Queen and Duke of Edinburgh with Mayor Taylor, Port of Spain	2·25	2·50
940	$5.25 Queen Elizabeth addressing Parliament	2·50	3·25
MS941	148×111 mm. $10 Queen Elizabeth in open car	7·00	8·50

250 Child playing on a Pan

2002. Christmas. Multicoloured.

942	$1 Type **250**	65	25
943	$2.50 Parranderos singers (horiz)	1·50	75
944	$3.75 Decorated hillside homes (horiz)	2·00	1·75
945	$5.25 Father Christmas in donkey cart	3·00	4·50

251 Centenary of P.A.H.O. Logo

2002. Centenary of Pan American Health Organisation. Multicoloured.

946	$1 Type **251**	90	30
947	$2.50 Port of Spain office	1·50	85
948	$3.25 Health images on pan	1·75	1·60
949	$4.50 Joseph Pawan (discoverer of vampire bat rabies)	2·25	2·75

252 Ian Bishop (bowler)

2003. Trinidad Cricketers. Multicoloured.

950	$1 Type **252**	85	35
951	$2.50 Deryck Murray (wicket-keeper)	1·75	1·10
952	$4.50 Augustine Logie (batsman)	2·50	2·75
953	$5.25 Ann John (female cricketer)	2·75	3·25

253 Mountain Immortelle

2003. "Treasures of the Rainforest". Multicoloured. Self-adhesive.

954	$1 Type **253**	90	1·10
955	$1 Blue-crowned motmot	90	1·10
956	$1 Red Howler monkey	90	1·10
957	$1 Butterfly orchid	90	1·10
958	$1 Channel-billed toucan	90	1·10
959	$1 Ocelot	90	1·10
960	$1 Bromeliads	90	1·10
961	$1 Lineated woodpecker	90	1·10
962	$1 Tamandua	90	1·10
963	$1 Emperor butterfly	90	1·10

254 Children dressed as Flowers

2003. Carnival. Multicoloured.

964	$1 Type **254**	70	25
965	$2.50 Group of minstrels	1·40	75
966	$3.75 Reveller in fly costume (vert)	1·75	1·50
967	$4.50 Buddha float (vert)	2·25	2·50
968	$5.25 Carnival dancers (vert)	2·50	3·00
MS969	90×90 mm. No. 968	2·75	3·25

255 President Robinson of Trinidad & Tobago with U.N. Secretary-General Kofi Annan

2003. Inauguration of International Criminal Court. Multicoloured.

970	$1 Type **255**	1·00	35
971	$2.50 Pres. Robinson with group of international lawyers	1·75	80
972	$3.75 Pres. Robinson with Ambassador Philippe Kirsch of Canada	2·00	2·25
973	$4.50 Pres. Robinson with Pres. Ciampi of Italy and Emma Bonino M.E.P.	2·25	3·50
MS974	90×90 mm. $6 President Arthur Robinson (vert)	3·50	4·00

256 Port of Spain Lighthouse

2003. Lighthouses. Multicoloured.

975	$1 Type **256**	1·75	45
976	$3.75 Chacachacare Lighthouse	2·50	1·50
977	$4.50 Port of Spain Lighthouse (different)	2·75	2·75
978	$5.25 Chacachacare Lighthouse (different)	3·50	4·00
MS979	119×151 mm. Nos. 975/8	9·50	9·50

257 Boulder Brain Coral

2003. Marine Life. Multicoloured.

980	$1 Type **257**	1·00	30
981	$2.50 Hawksbill turtle	1·75	1·00
982	$3.75 Green moray	2·00	1·75
983	$4.50 Creole wrasse	2·25	2·50
984	$5.25 Black-spotted sea goddess (sea slug)	2·50	3·50
MS985	100×100 mm. $10 Queen angelfish	8·00	8·50

258 "Dancing the cocoa"

2003. "Sweet Memories". Multicoloured.

986	$1 Type **258**	60	25
987	$2.50 Dirt oven	1·10	80
988	$3.75 Washing clothes in river	1·50	1·50
989	$4.50 Box-cart racing	1·60	2·00
990	$5.25 Pitching marbles	1·75	2·50
MS991	130×100 mm. Nos. 986/90	6·00	7·00

259 "View of Port of Spain from Laventille Hill"

2003. Christmas. Paintings by Cazaban. Multicoloured.

992	$1 Type **259**	75	25
993	$2.50 "View of Diego Martin from Fort George"	1·50	60
994	$3.75 "Corbeaux Town Trinidad"	2·10	1·10
995	$4.50 "Rain Clouds over Cedros"	2·25	2·25
996	$5.25 "Los Gallos, Icacos Bay"	2·50	3·50
MS997	150×112 mm. $5 "River at St. Ann's"; $6.50 "House in Trinidad"	6·50	7·50

260 Demonstration ("UNITE AGAINST AIDS")

2003. World AIDS Awareness Day. Multicoloured.

998	$1 Type **260**	80	30
999	$2.50 Despairing man ("STIGMA ISOLATES")	1·60	1·00
1000	$3.75 Nurse with girl ("CARE STOPS AIDS") (vert)	2·25	2·25
1001	$4.50 Man with family ("FAMILY PROTECTS") (vert)	2·75	3·50
MS1002	101×101 mm. $10 People of Trinidad	5·50	6·50

261 Aldric Farrel ("The Lord Pretender")

2004. Carnival. Vintage Calypso Singers. Multicoloured.

1003	$1 Type **261**	65	25
1004	$2.50 Roy Lewis ("The Mystic Prowler")	1·25	70
1005	$3.75 "Lord Kitchener", "The Mighty Sparrow" and "The Roaring Lion"	1·60	1·50
1006	$4.50 Rose McArthur Linda Sandy Lewis ("Calypso Rose")	1·75	2·25
1007	$5.25 "Nap Hepburne", "Lord Brynner" and "The Mighty Sparrow"	2·00	3·25

MS1008	150×110 mm. $10 "Calypso Rose"	5·00	6·00

262 Mango

2004. Fruit. Multicoloured.

1009	$1 Type **262**	65	25
1010	$2.50 Lime	1·25	80
1011	$3.75 Pineapple	1·60	1·50
1012	$4.50 Coconut (horiz)	1·75	2·25
1013	$5.25 Orange (horiz)	2·00	3·25
MS1014	100×100 mm. $10 Guava (horiz)	5·00	6·00

263 Sprinting

2004. Olympic Games, Athens, Greece. Multicoloured.

1015	$1 Type **263**	65	25
1016	$2.50 Boxing	1·25	90
1017	$3.75 Taekwondo	1·60	1·75
1018	$4.50 Swimming	1·75	3·00

264 Slave Ship

2004. Abolition of Slavery. Multicoloured.

1019	$1 Type **264**	75	25
1020	$2.50 Rada community, Belmont	1·40	80
1021	$3.75 Daaga, Prince of Popo	1·75	1·50
1022	$4.50 Slaves singing freedom songs (horiz)	2·00	2·50
1023	$5.25 Providence Estate aqueduct, Tobago (horiz)	2·25	3·25
MS1024	100×100 mm. $15 Sandy's escape (horiz)	7·00	8·00

265 "Lady with Ginger Lillies"

2004. Christmas. Paintings by Boscoe Holder. Multicoloured.

1025	$1 Type **265**	65	25
1026	$2.50 "View from Maracas Lookout"	1·25	50
1027	$3.75 "Lady in Peacock Chair"	1·60	1·25
1028	$4.50 "Caribbean Beauty in White" (horiz)	1·75	2·00
1029	$5.25 "Teteron Bay, Chaguaramas (horiz)	2·00	3·25
MS1030	100×100 mm. $10 Detail of "Creole Ladies in Straw Hats" (horiz)	4·00	4·50

266 "Dame Lorraine"

2005. Carnival. Paintings by Hayden Geeawan. Multicoloured.

1031	$1 Type **266**	55	25
1032	$2.50 "Jab Jab"	1·00	75
1033	$3.25 "Burrokeet" (horiz)	1·40	1·50
1034	$3.75 "Midnight Robber"	1·40	1·60
1035	$4.50 "Fancy Indian"	1·50	2·25
MS1036	121×101 mm. $15 "Fancy Sailor"	6·50	7·50

267 Brian Lara

2005. Brian Lara (Captain of West Indies Cricket Team)–Commemoration of Batting Record. Multicoloured.

1037	$1 Type **267**	1·00	40
1038	$2.50 Holding up bat	1·50	90
1039	$3.75 Running with bat	2·25	1·75
1040	$4.50 Running with helmet in hand	2·50	2·50
1041	$5.25 Swinging bat	2·75	3·25
MS1042 100×100 mm. $15 Walking under archway of bats		8·50	8·50

268 Foureye Butterfly Fish

2005. Coastal Dreamscape. Multicoloured. Self-adhesive.

1043	$1 Type **268**	1·00	1·10
1044	$1 Caribbean reef squid	1·00	1·10
1045	$1 Hawksbill turtle and diver	1·00	1·10
1046	$1 Southern sting ray	1·00	1·10
1047	$1 Queen angel fish	1·00	1·10
1048	$1 Giant anemone	1·00	1·10
1049	$1 Peppermint shrimp	1·00	1·10
1050	$1 Rough file clam	1·00	1·10
1051	$1 White speckled hermit crab	1·00	1·10
1052	$1 Christmas tree worm	1·00	1·10

269 Bele (Dance)

2005. Tobago Heritage Festival. Multicoloured.

1053	$1 Type **269**	55	25
1054	$2.50 Tobago Jig	1·10	70
1055	$3.75 Goat race (horiz)	1·50	1·25
1056	$4.50 Harvest Festival (horiz)	2·00	2·00
1057	$5.25 Drumming Festival (horiz)	2·25	2·50
MS1057a 100×100 mm. $15 Traditional Tobago wedding		6·00	6·50

270 Rachet

2005. Herbal Medicine. Multicoloured.

1058	25c. Type **270**	40	15
1059	50c. Chandelier	70	25
1060	75c. Worm grass	90	30
1061	$1 Black sage	1·00	30
1062	$3 Wonder of the world	1·75	1·25
1063	$3.25 Vervine	2·00	1·50
1064	$4 Aloe Vera	2·25	1·75
1065	$5 Senna	2·25	2·25
1066	$10 Bois bande	4·25	4·75
1067	$20 Herbal garden	8·00	11·00

271 Sir Solomon Hochoy and Dr Eric E. Williams (First Prime Minister, 1956–81)

2005. Birth Centenary of Sir Solomon Hochy (Governor and Governor General). Multicoloured.

1068	$1 Type **271**	60	25
1069	$2.50 With H.I.M Haile Selassie I	1·25	80
1070	$3.75 With Lady Thelma Hochoy	1·60	1·50
1071	$4.50 With Queen Elizabeth II	2·25	2·25
1072	$5.25 Inspecting Guard of Honour	2·50	3·25

MS1073 100×100 mm. $15 Sir Solomon Hochoy · 6·50 · 7·50

272 Women Police Officers

2005. 50th Anniv of Induction of Women Police. Sheet, 100×100 mm.
MS1074 **272** $15 black and bistre · 9·00 · 9·00

273 Anti-smoking Emblem

2005. "Children Against Cancer" Anti-smoking Campaign. Sheet 100×100 mm.
MS1075 **273** $15 multicoloured · 7·00 · 8·00

No. **MS**1075 was sold at $20 with a pink ribbon. The $5 premium goes to the Trinidad and Tobago Cancer Society.

274 Anansi, Snake and Rabbit planning to go to Cricket Match

2005. Christmas. Children's Stamps. "Anansi and the Cricket Match". Multicoloured.

1076	$1 Type **274**	55	25
1077	$2.50 Anansi, Snake and Rabbit on train hiding from ticket collector	1·00	80
1078	$3.75 Anansi, Snake and Rabbit with sun umbrella at match	1·40	1·40
1079	$4.50 Anansi telling snack vendor that Snake and Rabbit would pay	1·50	2·00
1080	$5.25 Snack vendor demanding payment from Snake and Rabbit and Anansi boarding train1	1·60	2·50
MS1081 100×100 mm. $15 Anansi full after eating all Rabbit's and Snake's breakfast		5·00	6·50

275 Pope John Paul II disembarking from Aircraft

2006. Pope John Paul II Commemoration. Multicoloured.

1082	$1 Type **275**	75	25
1083	$2.50 Kissing ground of Trinidad at Piarco Airport	1·25	80
1084	$3.75 Greeting monk	1·40	1·40
1085	$4.50 With Archbishop Pantin, hands raised in blessing	1·50	2·00
1086	$5.25 With Archbishop Pantin	1·75	2·50
MS1087 100×100 mm. $15 Riding in jeep with Archbishop Pantin		7·00	7·50

276 Jubilant Players

2006. World Cup Football Championship, Germany. Trinidad and Tobago's First World Cup Appearance. Multicoloured.

1088	$1 Type **276**	90	25
1089	$2.50 Two players	2·00	1·40
1090	$3.75 Three players	2·50	2·50
1091	$4.50 Player with flag	3·25	3·50

277 Palm Tree on Shoreline

2006. Inauguration of CSME Single Market and Economy. Multicoloured.

1092	$1 Type **277**	65	25
1093	$2.50 Lighthouse	1·75	1·10
1094	$3.75 Mobile phone	1·60	1·40
1095	$4.50 Sandy seashore (horiz)	1·75	2·25
1096	$5.25 Keyboard and globe (horiz)	1·90	2·75
MS1097 Diamond 142×140 mm. $15 Outline map of West Indies (horiz)		6·50	7·50

278 Aganesia pulchella (native orchid)

2006. 50th Anniv of Trinidad and Tobago Orchid Society. Sheet 100×100 mm.
MS1098 **278** $15 multicoloured · 6·50 · 7·50

279 "Guayaguayare Beach" (Ou Hing Wan)

2006. Bicentenary of the Arrival of Chinese Immigrants in Trinidad and Tobago. Multicoloured.

1099	$1 Type **279**	65	25
1100	$2.50 "Hosay" (Carlisle Chang)	1·25	80
1101	$3.75 "Saddle Road" (Amy Leong Pang) (vert)	1·60	1·40
1102	$4.50 "Mother and Child" (sculpture by Patrick Chu Foon) (vert)	1·75	2·25
1103	$5.25 "Still Life" (Sybil Atteck) (vert)	1·90	2·50
MS1104 100×100 mm. $15 "Inherent Nobility of Man" (Carlisle Chang) (vert)		5·50	6·50

280 Driving the Rim

2006. "Games We Used to Play". Multicoloured.

1105	$1 Type **280**	65	25
1106	$2.50 Spinning the top	1·25	80
1107	$3.75 Playing 3A	1·60	1·90
1108	$4.50 Farmer in the den	1·90	2·50
MS1109 100×100 mm. $15 Tyre swing		5·00	6·00

281 Batsman

2007. World Cup Cricket, West Indies. Multicoloured.

1110	$1 Type **281**	75	25
1111	$2 Bowler	1·25	60
1112	$3.75 Bowler (different)	1·40	1·00
1113	$3.75 Batsman (kneeling)	1·75	1·75
1114	$4.50 Wicket-keeper catching ball	2·00	2·50
MS1115 117×92 mm. $15 Cricket World Cup trophy (30×48 mm)		7·00	8·00

282 The Red House, c. 1907

2007. Centenary of the Re-opening of the Red House. Multicoloured.

1116	$1 Type **282**	50	30
1117	$2.50 The Parliament Chamber	1·10	80
1118	$3.75 The Cenotaph and Eternal Flame	1·75	1·40
1119	$5.25 The Red House Rotunda and Fountain	2·25	3·00
MS1120 100×100 mm. $15 Red House		5·50	6·50

283 Main Entrance of St. Mary's Children's Home, c. 1930

2007. 150th Anniv of St. Mary's Children's Home. Multicoloured.

1121	$1 Type **283**	50	30
1122	$2.50 The Fountain	1·10	80
1123	$3.75 St. Mary's Anglican Church	1·75	1·50
1124	$4.50 St. Mary's Children's Home Cubs Pack	2·00	2·50

284 Roomor

2007. Historical Buildings. Multicoloured.

1125	$1 Type **284**	60	30
1126	$2 Killarney	1·00	60
1127	$2.50 Queen's Royal College	1·25	75
1128	$3.25 Hayes Court	1·75	1·00
1129	$3.75 Knowsley	1·90	1·25
1130	$4.50 Mille Fleurs	2·00	1·40
1131	$10 Boissiere House ('The Ginger Bread House')	4·25	4·00
1132	$20 Archbishop's House	7·50	8·50
1133	$50 White Hall	17·00	19·00

285 Ozone Layer

2008. 20th Anniv (2007) of the Montreal Protocol. Sheet 70×160 mm.
MS1134 **285** $15 multicoloured · 5·50 · 6·50

286 Athletics

2008. Olympic Games, Beijing. Multicoloured.

1135	$3.50 Type **286**	1·90	1·90
1136	$3.50 Table tennis	1·90	1·90
1137	$3.50 Cycling	1·90	1·90
1138	$3.50 Swimming	1·90	1·90

287 Cubs

2008. Centenary (2007) of World Scouting. Multicoloured.

1139	$1 Type **287**	55	35
1140	$2.50 Scouts	1·10	1·00

1141	$3.75 Venture scouts	1·60	1·50
1142	$4.50 Scout leaders	2·00	2·50
MS1143	100×100 mm. $15 Lord Baden-Powell (vert)	5·50	6·00

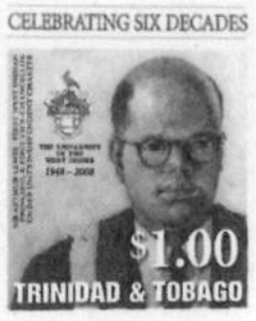

288 Sir Arthur Lewis (first West Indian principal)

2008. 60th Anniv of the University of the West Indies. Multicoloured.

1144	$1 Type **288**	50	40
1145	$2.50 Princess Alice (first Chancellor)	1·00	90
1146	$3.75 Sir Philip Sherlock (first Principal of St. Augustine Campus)	1·75	1·50
1147	$4.50 Administration Building, St. Augustine Campus (horiz)	2·25	2·25
1148	$5.25 The Samaan Tree, St. Augustine Campus (horiz)	2·50	2·50
MS1149	100×100 mm. $15 Administration Building, St. Augustine Campus at night	6·50	7·00

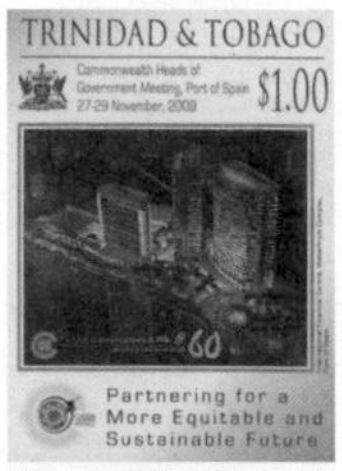

289 International Finacial Centre, Waterfront complex, Port of Spain

2009. Commonwealth Heads of Government Meeting, Port of Spain. Multicoloured

1150	$1 Type **289**	45	35
1151	$2.50 Steel pans	1·00	90
1152	$3.75 Pigeon Point, Tobafo	1·75	1·50
1153	$4.50 Queen Elizabeth II and Commonwealth Secretaries	2·25	2·25
1154	$5.25 Scarlet ibis (*Eudocimus ruber*)	2·50	2·50
MS1155	110×150 mm. $15 CHOGM 2009 emblem (33×45mm) P 14×13½	6·00	6·50

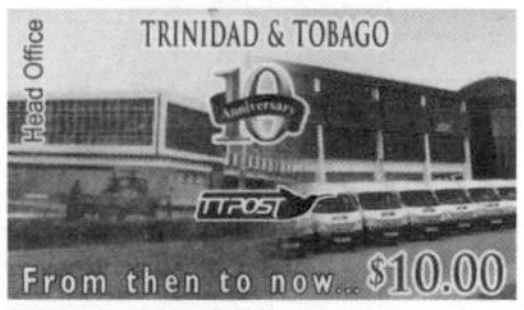

290 TTPost Head Office

2010. Tenth Anniv of Trinidad and Tobago Postal Corporation. Multicoloured.

MS1156	$10 Type **290**; $10 Post office counter	7·00	8·00

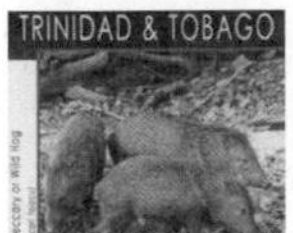

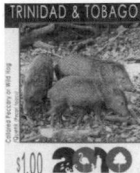

291 Collared Peccary or Wild Hog (*Pecari tajacu*)

2010. London 2010 Festival of Stamps. International Year of Biodiversity. Multicoloured.

MS1157	$1 Type **291**; $1 Beach with dead tree, No Man's Land, Bon Accord, Tobago; $2.50 Butterfly orchid (*Psychopsis papilio*); $2.50 Hot peppers (*Capsicum* sp.); $3.75 Paria Bay, north coast of Trinidad; $3.75 Ornate hawk eagle (*Spizaetus ornatus*); $4.50 Trinidad piping guan (*Aburria pipile*); $4.50 Royal poinciana or flamboyant tree (*Delonix regia*); $5.25 Trinidad Select hybrid cocoa pod (*Theobroma cacao* L.); $5.25 Water buffalo (*Bubalus bubalis*) at Aripo Livestock Station	14·00	15·00
MS1158	$1 Agouti (*Dasyprocta fuliginosa*); $1 Fishermen with catch at Grafton Beach, Tobago; $2.50 Caroni Swamp and Bird Sanctuary, west coast of Trinidad; $2.50 Red brocket deer (*Mazama americana*); $3.75 Turkey vulture (*Cathartes aura*); $3.75 White-chested emerald hummingbird (*Amazilia brevirostris*); $4.50 Leather back turtle (*Dermochelys coriacea*); $4.50 Nariva Swamp, east coast of Trinidad; $5.25 Soldado Rock, Gulf of Paria; $5.25 Orchid (*Selenipedium palmifolium*)	14·00	15·00

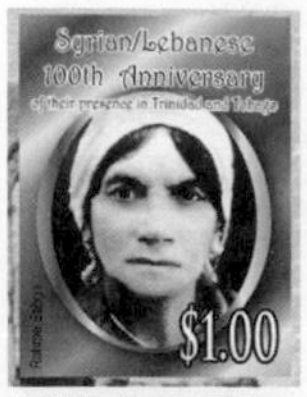

292 Mrs. Rahme Sabga (peddler, arrived 1908)

2010. Centenary of Syrians/Lebanese in Trinidad and Tobago. Multicoloured.

1159	$1 Type **292**	30	20
1160	$2.50 Kashish (peddler)	75	55
1161	$3.75 Grand Bazaar	1·25	1·25
1162	$4.50 Nicholas Tower	1·75	1·75
MS1163	100×100 mm. $15 Woman wearing traditional Arab headdress	6·00	6·50

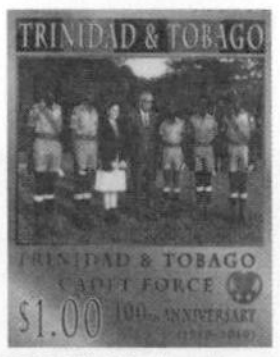

293 Trinidad and Tobago Cadets

2010. Centenary of Trinidad and Tobago Cadet Force. Multicoloured.

1164	$1 Type **293**	30	20
1165	$2.50 Young cadets (colour photo)	75	55
1166	$3.75 Cadets with shield	1·25	1·25
1167	$4.50 Cadets and leader	1·75	1·75
1168	$5.25 Seven adult cadets	2·00	2·00
MS1169	149×110 mm. $15 Governor Sir George Ruthven Le Hunte (founder) and Prof George Maxwell Richards (current President and Commander-in-Chief of Armed Forces)	6·00	6·50

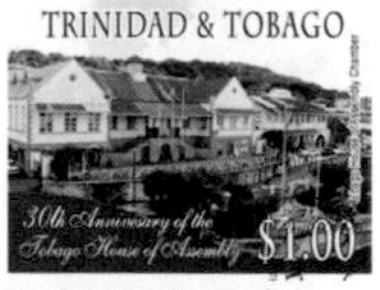

294 Tobago House of Assembly

2010. 30th Anniv of the Tobago House of Assembly. Multicoloured.

1170	$1 Type **294**	30	20
1171	$2.50 Englishman's Bay	75	55
1172	$3.75 St. Patrick's Anglican Church	1·25	1·25
1173	$4.50 Fort King George	1·75	1·75
1174	$5.25 Buccoo Goat Race	2·00	2·00
MS1175	100×100 mm. $15 Jetty at Pigeon Point Heritage Park	6·00	6·50

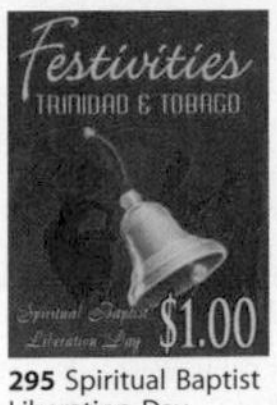

295 Spiritual Baptist Liberation Day

2010. Festivities. Multicoloured.

1176	$1 Type **295**	40	20
1177	$2.50 Eid-ul-Fitr	90	55
1178	$3.75 Christmas	1·25	1·25
1179	$4.50 Diwali	1·75	1·75
MS1180	100×100 mm. $15 Parang	6·00	6·50

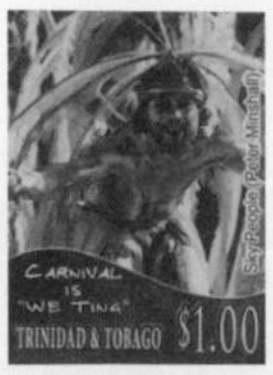

296 Man wearing Sky People Costume by Peter Minshall

2011. Carnival is 'We Ting'. Multicoloured.

1181	$1 Type **296**	30	20
1182	$2.50 Children portraying Pierrot Grenade	75	55
1183	$3.75 Junior Carnival Queen on Broadway	1·25	1·25
1184	$4.50 Children's carnival on Frederick Street	1·75	1·75
1185	$5.25 Man wearing Black Indian Chief costume by Larrie Approo	2·00	2·00
MS1186	100×100 mm. $15 Woman wearing Pan Woman costume by Wendy Kallicharan	6·00	6·50

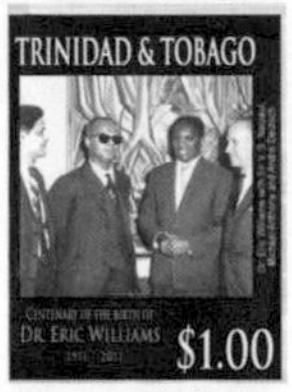

297 Dr. Eric Williams with Sir V. S. Naipaul, Michael Anthony and Andre Deutsch

2011. Birth Centenary of Dr. Eric Williams (1911-81, first Prime Minister 1962-81). Multicoloured.

1187	$1 Type **297**	30	20
1188	$1.50 Dr. Williams playing cricket with C. L. R. James and Learie Constantine	50	40
1189	$2.50 Dr. Williams with Kwame Nkrumah	75	55
1190	$3.75 Painting of Dr. Williams by Georgia M. Cordner	1·25	1·25
1191	$4.50 Dr. Williams with John Lennon and Ringo Starr	1·75	1·75
1192	$5.25 Dr. Williams and Jawaharlal Nehru	2·00	2·00
MS1193	100×150 mm. $15 Sir Winston Churchill and Dr. Eric Williams	6·00	6·50

$1.00

(298)

2012. No. 793 surch with T **298**

1194	$1 on $2.25 Channel-billed Toucan	30	20

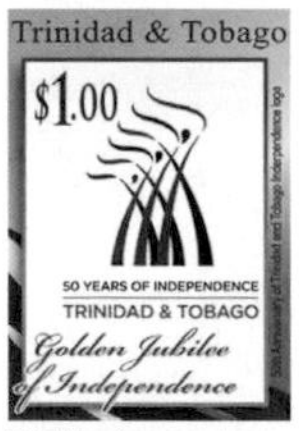

299 Anniversary Logo

2012. 50th Anniv of Independence. Multicoloured.

1195	$1 Type **299**	30	20
1196	$1 Trinidad and Tobago flag (horiz)	30	20
1197	$1 Sir Solomon Hochoy (first Governor-General) assisting Dr. Eric Williams (first Prime Minister) with signing of official documents (horiz)	30	20
1198	$1 First colonial seal and arms of Trinidad and Tobago (horiz)	30	20

$1.00
CARICOM
CARICOM 40TH ANNIVERSARY
(1973 - 2013)
HEADS OF GOVERNMENT CONFERENCE
PORT OF SPAIN, 4-6 JULY 2013

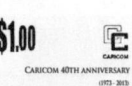

(300)

2013. 40th Anniv of CARICOM. Nos. 887, 1072, 1148 and 1154 surch as T **300**.

1199	$1 on $5 Toco, North Coast	30	20
1200	$1 on $5.25 Sir Solomon Hochoy inspecting Guard of Honour	30	20
1201	$1 on $5.25 The Samaan Tree, St. Augustine Campus	30	20
1202	$1 on $5.25 Scarlet Ibis	30	20

OFFICIAL STAMP

1913. Optd **OFFICIAL.**

O14	**17**	½d. green	4·75	8·50

POSTAGE DUE STAMPS

1947. As Type **D1** of Trinidad but value in cents.

D26a	2c. black	20	5·50
D27	4c. black	2·75	3·00
D28a	6c. black	30	7·50
D29a	8c. black	35	32·00
D30	10c. black	3·25	8·50
D31a	12c. black	40	25·00
D32	16c. black	2·00	55·00
D33	24c. black	13·00	14·00

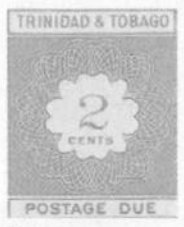

D2

1969. Size 19×24 mm.

D34	**D2**	2c. green	15	2·50
D35	**D2**	4c. red	25	8·00
D36	**D2**	6c. brown	50	4·50
D37	**D2**	8c. violet	65	4·75
D38	**D2**	10c. red	1·00	7·50
D39	**D2**	12c. yellow	80	5·00
D40	**D2**	16c. green	1·00	6·50
D41	**D2**	24c. grey	1·00	11·00
D42	**D2**	50c. blue	1·00	4·50
D43	**D2**	60c. green	1·00	4·00

1976. Smaller design, 17×21 mm.

D44	2c. green	20	2·00
D45	4c. red	25	1·25
D46	6c. brown	25	2·00
D47	8c. lilac	30	2·00
D48	10c. red	30	1·25
D49	12c. orange	50	1·50

Pt. 8

TRIPOLITANIA

One of the provinces into which the Italian colony of Libya was divided.

100 centesimi = 1 lira.

Stamps optd **Tripoli di Barberia**, formerly listed here, will be found under Italian P.O.s in the Levant Nos. 171/81.

Nos. 1/138, except where otherwise described, are Italian stamps, sometimes in new colours, overprinted **TRIPOLITANIA.**

1923. Propagation of the Faith.

1	**66**	20c. orange and green	8·75	40·00
2	**66**	30c. orange and red	8·75	40·00
3	**66**	50c. orange and violet	5·75	46·00
4	**66**	1l. orange and blue	5·75	65·00

1923. Fascist March on Rome.

5	**73**	10c. green	11·00	17·00
6	**73**	30c. violet	11·00	17·00
7	**73**	50c. red	11·00	17·00
8	**74**	1l. blue	11·00	46·00
9	**74**	2l. brown	11·00	60·00
10	**75**	5l. black and blue	11·00	90·00

1924. Manzoni.

11	**77**	10c. black and purple	8·75	40·00
12	-	15c. black and green	8·75	40·00
13	-	30c. black	8·75	40·00
14	-	50c. black and brown	8·75	40·00
15	-	1l. black and blue	70·00	£300
16	-	5l. black and purple	£900	£2750

1925. Holy Year.

17		20c.+10c. brown & green	4·50	29·00
18	**81**	30c.+15c. brown & choc	4·50	29·00
19	-	50c.+25c. brown & violet	4·50	29·00
20	-	60c.+30c. brown and red	4·50	35·00
21	-	1l.+50c. purple and blue	5·25	40·00
22	-	5l.+2l.50 purple and red	5·25	60·00

1925. Royal Jubilee.

23	**82**	60c. red	1·70	9·25
24	**82**	1l. blue	2·30	10·50
24c	**82**	1l.25 blue	4·50	31·00

1926. St. Francis of Assisi.

25	**83**	20c. green	3·50	17·00
26	-	40c. violet	3·50	17·00
27	-	60c. red	3·50	23·00
28	-	1l.25 blue	3·50	35·00
29	-	5l.+2l.50 green	8·00	70·00

1926. As Colonial Propaganda stamps of Somalia, T **21**, but inscr "TRIPOLITANIA".

30	5c.+5c. brown	1·20	8·00
31	10c.+5c. green	1·20	8·00
32	20c.+5c. green	1·20	8·00
33	40c.+5c. red	1·20	8·00

34		60c.+5c. orange	1·20	8·00
35		1l.+5c. blue	1·20	14·00

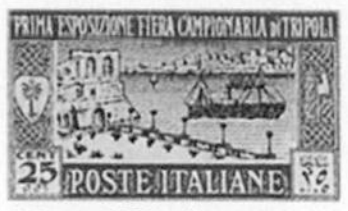

6 Port of Tripoli

1927. First Tripoli Trade Fair.

36	**6**	20c.+05c. black and purple	5·25	18·00
37	**6**	25c.+05c. black and green	5·25	18·00
38	-	40c.+10c. black and brown	5·25	18·00
39	-	60c.+10c. black and brown	5·25	18·00
40	-	75c.+20c. black and red	5·25	18·00
41	-	1l.25+20c. black and blue	31·00	60·00

DESIGNS: 40, 60c. Arch of Marcus Aurelius; 75c., 1l.25, View of Tripoli.

1927. First National Defence issue.

42	**89**	40+20c. black and brown	3·50	35·00
43	**89**	60+30c. brown and red	3·50	35·00
44	**89**	1l.25+60c. black and blue	3·50	60·00
45	**89**	5l.+2l.50 black and green	7·00	80·00

1927. Death Centenary of Volta.

46	**91**	20c. violet	8·75	35·00
47	**91**	50c. orange	12·50	23·00
48	**91**	1l.25 blue	20·00	60·00

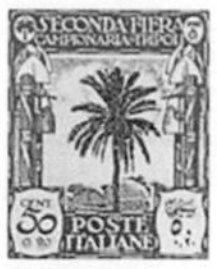

9 Palm Tree

1928. Second Tripoli Trade Fair.

49	-	30c.+20c. brown & purple	4·50	21·00
50	**9**	50c.+20c. brown and green	4·50	21·00
51	-	1l.25+20c. brown and red	4·50	21·00
52	-	1l.75+20c. brown and blue	4·50	21·00
53	-	2l.55+50c. sepia & brown	8·00	29·00
54	-	5l.+1l. brown and violet	12·50	40·00

DESIGNS. As T **9**: 30c. Tripoli; 1l.25, Camel riders. 38×22½ mm: 1l.75, Arab citadel; 2l.55, Tripoli; 5l. Desert outpost.

1928. 45th Anniv of Italian-African Society. As T **25** of Somalia.

55		20c.+5c. green	3·50	11·50
56		30c.+5c. red	3·50	11·50
57		50c.+10c. violet	3·50	17·00
58		1l.25+20c. blue	3·50	23·00

1929. Second National Defence issue.

59	**89**	30c.+10c. black and red	5·75	23·00
60	-	50c.+20c. grey	5·75	23·00
61	-	1l.25+50c. blue & brown	8·75	46·00
62	-	5l.+2l. black and olive	8·75	70·00

1929. Third Tripoli Trade Fair. Inscr "1929".

63		30c.+20c. black and purple	14·50	23·00
64		50c.+20c. black and green	14·50	23·00
65		1l.25+20c. black and red	14·50	23·00
66		1l.75+20c. black and blue	14·50	23·00
67		2l.55+50c. black and brown	14·50	23·00
68		5l.+1l. black and violet	£180	£350

DESIGNS—As T **9**: 30c., 1l.25, Different trees; 50c. Dorcas gazelle. 38×22½ mm: 1l.75, Goats; 2l.55, Camel caravan; 5l. Trees.

1929. Abbey of Montecassino.

69	**104**	20c. green	8·00	18·00
70	-	25c. red	8·00	18·00
71	-	50c.+10c. red	8·00	23·00
72	-	75c.+15c. brown	8·00	23·00
73	**104**	1l.25+25c. purple	16·00	40·00
74	-	5l.+1l. blue	16·00	46·00
75	-	10l.+2l. brown	16·00	70·00

1930. Fourth Tripoli Trade Fair. Inscr "1930".

76		30c. brown	3·50	14·00
77		50c. violet	3·50	14·00
78		1l.25 blue	3·50	14·00
79		1l.75+20c. red	4·50	25·00
80		2l.55+45c. green	20·00	40·00
81		5l.+1l. orange	20·00	50·00
82		10l.+2l. purple	20·00	65·00

DESIGNS—As T **9**: 30c. Gathering bananas; 50c. Tobacco plant; 1l.25, Venus of Cyrene. 38×22½ mm: 5l. Motor and camel transport; 10l. Rome pavilion, at exhibition entrance.

1930. Marriage of Prince Humbert and Princess Marie Jose.

83	**109**	20c. green	2·30	5·75
84	**109**	50c.+10c. red	1·70	9·25
85	**109**	1l.25+25c. red	1·70	21·00

1930. Ferrucci.

86	**114**	20c. violet (postage)	4·00	4·50
87	-	25c. green (No. 283)	4·00	4·50
88	-	50c. black (as No. 284)	4·00	11·50
89	-	1l.25 blue (No. 285)	4·00	17·00
90	-	5l.+2l. red (as No. 286)	12·50	32·00
91	**117**	50c. purple (air)	7·25	9·25
92	**117**	1l. blue	7·25	14·00
93	**117**	5l.+2l. red	27·00	60·00

1930. Third National Defence issue.

94	**89**	30c.+10c. green and deep green	29·00	35·00
95	-	50c.+10c. violet and green	29·00	50·00
96	-	1l.25+30c. brown and deep brown	29·00	70·00
97	-	5l.+1l.50 green and blue	90·00	£160

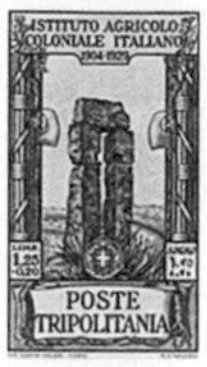

17 Roman Arch

1930. 25th Anniv (1929) of Italian Colonial Agricultural Institute.

98	**17**	50c.+20c. brown	4·00	21·00
99	**17**	1l.25+20c. blue	4·00	21·00
100	**17**	1l.75+20c. green	4·00	23·00
101	**17**	2l.55+50c. violet	8·75	40·00
102	**17**	5l.+1l. red	8·75	60·00

1930. Virgil.

103	-	15c. grey (postage)	1·20	7·00
104	-	20c. brown	1·20	3·50
105	-	25c. green	1·20	3·50
106	-	30c. brown	1·20	3·50
107	-	50c. purple	1·20	3·50
108	-	75c. red	1·20	4·50
109	-	1l.25 blue	1·20	9·25
110	-	5l.+1l.50 purple	8·75	46·00
111	-	10l.+2l.50 brown	8·75	80·00
112	**119**	50c. green (air)	4·50	11·50
113	**119**	1l. red	4·50	11·50
114	**119**	7l.70+1l.30 brown	10·50	50·00
115	**119**	9l.+2l. blue	10·50	50·00

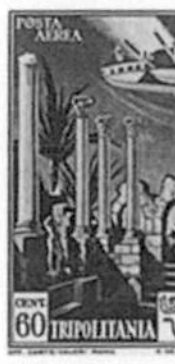

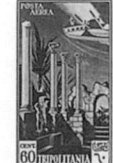

18 Columns of Leptis

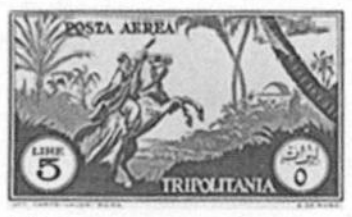

19

1931. Air.

116	**18**	50c. red	1·70	30
117	**18**	60c. red	4·50	10·50
117a	**18**	75c. blue	4·50	11·50
118	**18**	80c. purple	11·50	17·00
119	**19**	1l. blue	3·00	65
120	**19**	1l.20 brown	30·00	21·00
121	**19**	1l.50 red	14·50	21·00
122	**19**	5l. green	38·00	35·00

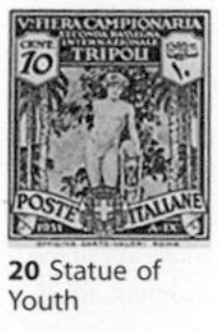

20 Statue of Youth

1931. Fifth Tripoli Trade Fair.

123	**20**	10c. black (postage)	5·75	11·50
124	-	25c. green	5·75	11·50
125	-	50c. violet	5·75	11·50
126	-	1l.25 blue	5·75	15·00
127	-	1l.75+25c. red	8·00	29·00
128	-	2l.75+45c. orange	8·00	35·00
129	-	5l.+1l. purple	20·00	46·00
130	-	10l.+2l. brown	60·00	80·00
131	-	50c. blue (air)	3·50	17·00

DESIGNS—As Type **20**: 25c. Arab musician; 50c. (postage) View of Zeughet; 1l.25, Snake charmer; 1l.75, House and windmill; 2l.75, Libyan "Zaptie"; 5l. Arab horseman. As Type E **21**: 10l. Exhibition Pavilion; 50c. (air) Airplane over desert.

1931. St. Antony of Padua.

132	**121**	20c. brown	3·00	16·00
133	-	25c. green	3·00	7·00
134	-	30c. black	3·00	7·00
135	-	50c. purple	3·00	7·00
136	-	75c. grey	3·00	18·00
137	-	1l.25 blue	3·00	37·00
138	-	5l.+2l.50 brown	8·75	80·00

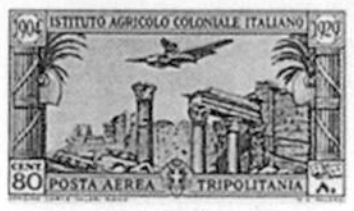

22 Savoia Marchetti S-55A Flying Boat over Ruins

1931. Air. 25th Anniv (1929) of Italian Colonial Agricultural Institute.

139	**22**	50c. blue	5·75	21·00
140	**22**	80c. violet	5·75	21·00
141	**22**	1l. black	5·75	30·00
142	**22**	2l. green	10·50	38·00
143	**22**	5l.+2l. red	12·50	75·00

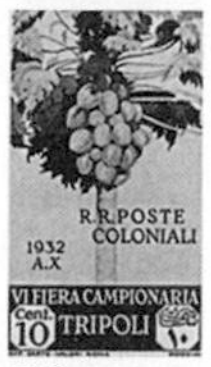

23 Paw-paw Tree

1932. Sixth Tripoli Trade Fair. Inscr "1932".

144	**23**	10c. brown (postage)	8·75	16·00
145	-	20c. brown	8·75	16·00
146	-	25c. green	8·75	16·00
147	-	30c. green	8·75	16·00
148	-	50c. violet	8·75	16·00
149	-	75c. red	11·50	17·00
150	-	1l.25 blue	11·50	23·00
151	-	1l.75+25c. brown	48·00	80·00
152	-	5l.+1l. blue	48·00	£150
153	-	10l.+2l. purple	£120	£300
154	-	50c. blue (air)	16·00	40·00
155	-	1l. brown	16·00	40·00
156	-	2l.+1l. black	40·00	£100
157	-	5l.+2l. red	£130	£225

DESIGNS—POSTAGE. VERT: 10c. to 50c. Various trees; 75c. Roman mausoleum at Ghirza; 10l. Dorcas gazelle. HORIZ: 1l.25, Mogadiscio aerodrome; 1l.75, Lioness; 5l. Arab and camel. AIR. HORIZ: 50c., 1l. Marina Fiat MF.5 flying boat over Bedouin camp; 2, 5l. Marina Fiat MF.5 flying boat over Tripoli.

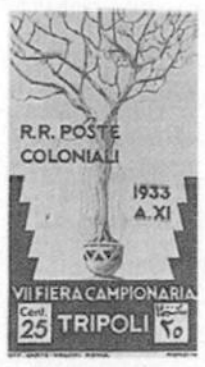

24 Incense Plant

1933. Seventh Tripoli Trade Fair. Inscr "1933".

158		10c. purple (postage)	50·00	35·00
159	**24**	25c. green	25·00	35·00
160	-	30c. brown	25·00	35·00
161	-	50c. violet	25·00	35·00
162	-	1l.25 blue	60·00	70·00
163	-	5l.+1l. brown	£100	£150
164	-	10l.+2l.50 red	£100	£225
165	-	50c. green (air)	11·50	25·00
166	-	75c. red	11·50	25·00
167	-	1l. blue	11·50	25·00
168	-	2l.+50c. violet	23·00	40·00
169	-	5l.+1l. brown	40·00	70·00
170	-	10l.+2l.50 black	40·00	£170

DESIGNS—POSTAGE. VERT: 10c. Ostrich; 50c. Arch of Marcus Aurelius; 1l.25, Golden eagle; 10l. Tripoli and Fascist emblem. HORIZ: 30c. Arab drummer; 5l. Leopard. AIR. HORIZ: 50c., 2l. Seaplane over Tripoli; 75c., 10l. Caproni Ca 101 airplane over Tagiura; 1, 5l. Seaplane leaving Tripoli.

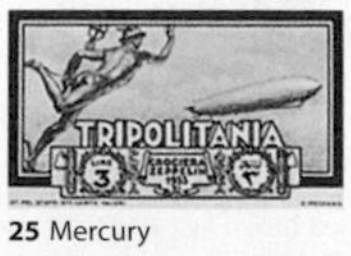

25 Mercury

1933. Airship "Graf Zeppelin".

171	**25**	3l. brown	12·50	£140
172	-	5l. violet	12·50	£140
173	-	10l. green	12·50	£250
174	**25**	12l. blue	12·50	£300
175	-	15l. red	12·50	£300
176	-	20l. black	12·50	£350

DESIGNS: 5, 15l. "Graf Zeppelin" and Arch of Marcus Aurelius; 10, 20l. "Graf Zeppelin" and allegory of "dawn".

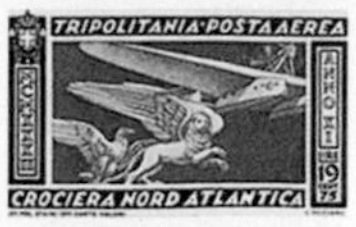

26 "Flight"

1933. Air. Balbo Transatlantic Mass Formation Flight.

177	**26**	19l.75 brown and black	26·00	£750
178	**26**	44l.75 green and blue	26·00	£750

1934. Air. Rome–Buenos Aires Flight. Optd with Savoia Marchetti S-71 airplane and **1934-XII PRIMO VOLO DIRETTO ROMA = BUENOS-AYRES TRIMOTORE LOMBARDI-MAZZOTTI** or surch also in Italian.

179	**19**	2l. on 5l. brown	4·50	75·00
180	**19**	3l. on 5l. green	4·50	75·00
181	**19**	5l. brown	4·50	85·00
182	**19**	10l. on 5l. red	4·50	85·00

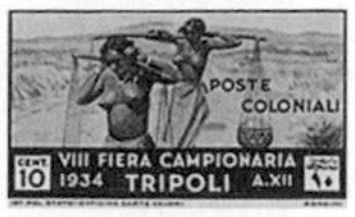

27 Water Carriers

1934. Eighth Tripoli Trade Fair.

183	**27**	10c. brown (postage)	8·00	17·00
184	-	20c. red	8·00	17·00
185	-	25c. green	8·00	17·00
186	-	30c. brown	8·00	17·00
187	-	50c. violet	8·00	17·00
188	-	75c. red	8·00	29·00
189	-	1l.25 blue	70·00	£120

DESIGNS—VERT: 20c. Arab; 25c. Minaret; 50c. Statue of Emperor Claudius. HORIZ: 30c., 1l.25, Moslem shrine; 75c. Ruins of Ghadames.

190		50c. blue (air)	14·50	29·00
191		75c. red	14·50	29·00
192		5l.+1l. green	£130	£200
193		10l.+2l. purple	£130	£200
194		25l.+3l. brown	£180	£250

DESIGNS—HORIZ: 50c., 5l. Marina Fiat MF.5 flying boat off Tripoli; 75c., 10l. Airplane over mosque. VERT: 25l. Caproni Ca 101 airplane and camel.

See also Nos. E195/6.

1934. Air. Oasis Flight. As Nos. 190/4 optd **CIRCUITO DELLE OASI TRIPOLI MAGGIO 1934 XII**.

197	50c. red	23·00	£140
198	75c. bistre	23·00	£140
199	5l.+1l. brown	23·00	£140
200	10l.+2l. blue	£425	£750
201	25l.+3l. violet	£425	£750

See also Nos. E202/3.

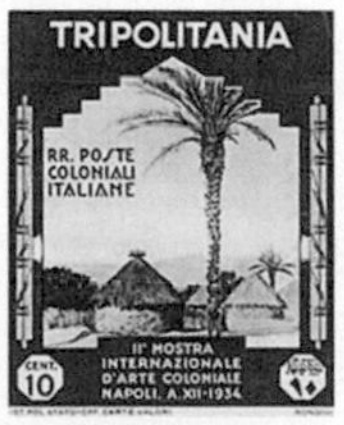

29 Village

1934. Second International Colonial Exn, Naples.

204	**29**	5c. brown and green (postage)	7·00	18·00
205	**29**	10c. black and brown	7·00	18·00
206	**29**	20c. blue and red	7·00	18·00
207	**29**	50c. brown and violet	7·00	18·00
208	**29**	60c. blue and brown	7·00	25·00
209	**29**	1l.25 green and blue	7·00	38·00
210	-	25c. orange and blue (air)	7·00	18·00
211	-	50c. blue and green	7·00	18·00
212	-	75c. orange and brown	7·00	18·00
213	-	80c. green and brown	7·00	18·00
214	-	1l. green and red	7·00	25·00
215	-	2l. brown and blue	7·00	38·00

DESIGNS: 25c. to 75c. Shadow of airplane over desert; 80c. to 2l. Arab camel corps and Caproni Ca 101 airplane.

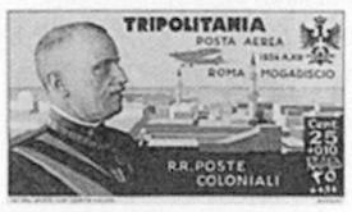

30

1934. Air. Rome–Mogadiscio Flight.

216	**30**	25c.+10c. green	8·75	17·00
217	**30**	50c.+10c. brown	8·75	17·00
218	**30**	75c.+15c. red	8·75	17·00
219	**30**	80c.+15c. black	8·75	17·00
220	**30**	1l.+20c. brown	8·75	17·00
221	**30**	2l.+20c. blue	8·75	17·00
222	**30**	3l.+25c. violet	35·00	90·00
223	**30**	5l.+25c. orange	35·00	90·00
224	**30**	10l.+30c. purple	35·00	90·00
225	**30**	25l.+2l. green	35·00	90·00

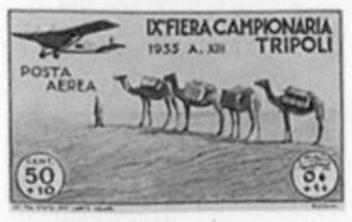

32 Camel Transport

1935. Ninth Tripoli Exhibition.

226	-	10c.+10c. brown (post)	1·70	5·75
227	-	20c.+10c. red	1·70	5·75
228	-	50c.+10c. violet	1·70	5·75
229	-	75c.+15c. red	1·70	5·75
230	-	1l.25+25c. blue	2·30	5·75
231	-	2l.+50c. green	2·30	11·50
232	-	25c.+10c. green (air)	1·40	5·75
233	**32**	50c.+10c. blue	1·40	5·75
234	-	1l.+25c. blue	1·40	5·75
235	-	2l.+30c. red	1·40	9·25
236	-	3l.+1l.50 brown	1·40	10·50
237	-	10l.+5l. purple	12·50	40·00

DESIGNS—POSTAGE. VERT: 10, 20c. Pomegranate tree; 50c., 2l. Arab flautist; 75c., 1l.25, Arab in burnous. AIR. VERT: 25c., 3l. Watch-tower. HORIZ: 1, 10l. Arab girl and Caproni Ca 101 airplane.

For issue inscr "XII FIERA CAMPIONARIA TRIPOLI" and dated "1938", see Libya Nos. 88/95.

CONCESSIONAL LETTER POST

1931. Optd **TRIPOLITANIA**.

CL123	**CL109**	10c. brown	20·00	23·00

EXPRESS LETTER STAMPS

Express stamps optd **TRIPOLI DI BARBERIA**, formerly listed here, will be found under Italian P.O.s in the Levant Nos. E6/7.

1927. First Tripoli Exhibition. Inscr "EXPRES".

E42	1l.25+30c. black and violet	17·00	46·00
E43	2l.50+1l. black and yellow	17·00	60·00

DESIGN—As T **6**: 1l.25, 2l.50, Camels and palm trees.

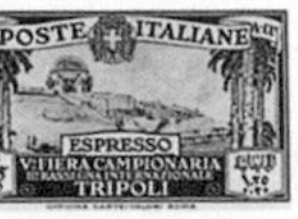

E21 War Memorial

1931. Fifth Tripoli Trade Fair.

E132	**E21**	1l.25+20c. red	14·50	29·00

1934. Air. Eighth Tripoli Trade Fair.

E195	2l.25 black	50·00	75·00
E196	4l.50+1l. blue	50·00	75·00

DESIGN—As T **27**: Nos. E195/6, Caproni Ca 101 airplane over Bedouins in desert.

1934. Air. Oasis Flight. As Nos. E195/6 optd **CIRCUITO DELLE OASI TRIPOLI MAGGIO 1934-XII**.

E202	2l.25 red	23·00	£140
E203	4l.50+1l. red	23·00	£140

OFFICIAL STAMPS

1934. No. 225 (colour changed) optd **SERVIZIO DI STATO** and Crown.

O226	**30**	25l.+2l. red	£4000	£6500

From 1943 to 1951 Tripolitania was under British administration; stamps issued during this period are listed under British Occupation of Italian Colonies. From 1952 it was part of independent Libya.

Pt. 1

TRISTAN DA CUNHA

An island in the south Atlantic Ocean west of S. Africa. Following a volcanic eruption the island was evacuated on 10 October 1961, but resettled in 1963.

1952. 12 pence = 1 shilling; 20 shilling = 1 pound.
1961. 100 cents = 1 rand.
1963. Reverted to sterling currency.

1952. Stamps of St. Helena optd **TRISTAN DA CUNHA**.

1	**33**	½d. violet	15	3·50
2	**33**	1d. black and green	1·00	1·50
3	**33**	1½d. black and red	1·00	1·50
4	**33**	2d. black and red	1·00	1·50
5	**33**	3d. grey	1·00	1·50
6	**33**	4d. blue	7·00	2·50
7	**33**	6d. blue	7·00	2·50
8	**33**	8d. green	7·00	8·50
9	**33**	1s. brown	5·50	2·00
10	**33**	2s.6d. purple	24·00	18·00
11	**33**	5s. brown	38·00	24·00
12	**33**	10s. purple	60·00	40·00

1953. Coronation. As T **33h** of St. Helena.

13	3d. black and green	1·25	2·00

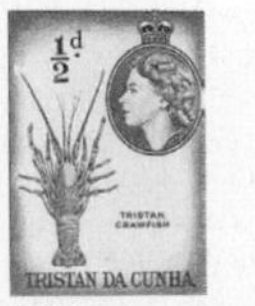

2 Tristan Crawfish

1954

14	**2**	½d. red and brown	10	10
15	-	1d. sepia and green	10	50
16	-	1½d. black and purple	1·75	1·75
17	-	2d. violet and orange	30	20
18	-	2½d. black and red	1·75	60
19	-	3d. blue and olive	2·50	1·75
20	-	4d. turquoise and blue	60	70
21	-	5d. green and black	60	70
22	-	6d. green and violet	60	75
23	-	9d. lilac and red	60	45
24	-	1s. green and sepia	60	45
25	-	2s.6d. sepia and blue	17·00	10·00
26	-	5s. black and orange	50·00	14·00
27	-	10s. orange and purple	24·00	14·00

DESIGNS—HORIZ: 1d. Carting flax; 2d. Big Beach factory; 2½d. Yellow-nosed albatross (sea birds); 4d. Tristan from S.W.; 5d. Girls on donkeys; 6d. Inaccessible Is. from Tristan; 9d. Nightingale Is; 1s. St. Mary's Church; 2s.6d. Southern elephant seal at Gough Is; 5s. Inaccessible Island rail (bird); 10s. Spinning wheel. VERT: 1½d. Rockhopper penguin; 3d. Island longboat.

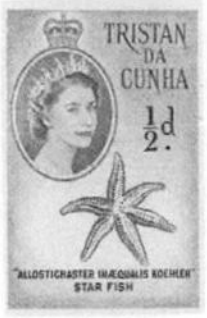

16 Starfish

1960. Marine Life. Value, fish and inscriptions in black.

28	**16**	½d. orange	15	40
29	-	1d. purple	15	20
30	-	1½d. turquoise	20	70
31	-	2d. green	30	1·00
32	-	2½d. sepia	55	60
33	-	3d. red	1·25	2·00
34	-	4d. olive	1·25	1·25
35	-	5d. yellow	1·50	1·00
36	-	6d. blue	1·75	1·00
37	-	9d. red	1·75	1·50
38	-	1s. brown	3·50	60
39	-	2s.6d. blue	11·00	11·00
40	-	5s. green	12·00	12·00
41	-	10s. violet	48·00	28·00

FISH: 1d. Concha wrasse; 1½d. Two-spined thornfish; 2d. Atlantic saury; 2½d. Bristle snipefish; 3d. Tristan crawfish; 4d. False jacopever; 5d. Five-fingered morwong; 6d. Long-finned scad; 9d. Christophersen's medusafish; 1s. Blue medusafish; 2s.6d. Snoek; 5s. Blue shark; 10s. Black right whale.

1961. As 1960 issue but values in new currency. Value, fish and inscriptions in black.

42	**16**	½c. orange	10	1·25
43	-	1c. purple (as 1d.)	15	1·25
44	-	1½c. turquoise (as 1½d.)	35	1·25
45	-	2c. sepia (as 2½d.)	65	1·25
46	-	2½c. red (as 3d.)	1·00	1·25
47	-	3c. olive (as 4d.)	1·00	1·25
48	-	4c. yellow (as 5d.)	1·25	1·25
49	-	5c. blue (as 6d.)	1·25	1·25
50	-	7½c. red (as 9d.)	1·25	1·25
51	-	10c. brown (as 1s.)	2·00	1·25
52	-	25c. blue (as 2s.6d.)	7·00	7·50
53	-	50c. green (as 5s.)	23·00	17·00
54	-	1r. violet (as 10s.)	50·00	32·00

1963. Tristan Resettlement. Nos. 176/88 of St. Helena optd **TRISTAN DA CUNHA RESETTLEMENT 1963**.

55	**50**	1d. multicoloured	15	1·00
56	-	1½d. multicoloured	1·50	70
57	-	2d. red and grey	25	1·00
58	-	3d. multicoloured	30	1·00
59	-	4½d. multicoloured	50	60
60	-	6d. red, sepia and olive	3·00	30
61	-	7d. brown, black and violet	50	30
62	-	10d. purple and blue	50	30
63	-	1s. yellow, green and brown	50	30
64	-	1s.6d. grey, black and blue	6·50	1·00
65	-	2s.6d. red, yellow & turquoise	1·00	45
66	-	5s. yellow, brown and green	6·00	1·00
67	-	10s. red, black and blue	6·00	1·00

1963. Freedom from Hunger. As T **63a** of St. Helena.

68	1s.6d. red	50	30

1964. Cent of Red Cross. As T **63b** of St. Helena.

69	3d. red and black	20	15
70	1s.6d. red and blue	30	20

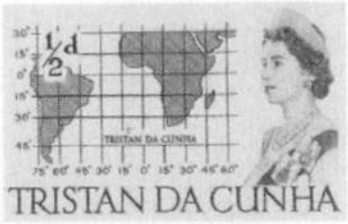

31 South Atlantic Map

1965

71	**31**	½d. black and blue	15	30
72	-	1d. black and green	1·00	15
73	-	1½d. black and blue	1·00	15
74	-	2d. black and purple	1·00	15
75	-	3d. black and turquoise	1·00	15
75a	-	4d. black and orange	4·00	4·00
76	-	4½d. black and brown	1·00	15
77	-	6d. black and green	1·25	15
78	-	7d. black and red	2·25	30
79	-	10d. black and brown	1·25	55
80	-	1s. black and red	1·25	30
81	-	1s.6d. black and olive	7·00	2·50
82	**31**	2s.6d. black and brown	3·50	3·75
83	-	5s. black and violet	9·50	3·50
84	-	10s. blue and red	1·75	1·25
84a	-	10s. black and blue	15·00	11·00
84b	-	£1 blue and brown	12·00	11·00

DESIGNS—HORIZ: 1d. Flagship of Tristao da Cunha, 1506; 1½d. "Heemstede" (Dutch East Indiaman), 1643; 2d. "Edward" (American whaling ship), 1864; 3d. "Shenandoah" (Confederate warship), 1862; 4d. H.M.S. "Challenger" (survey ship), 1873; 4½d. H.M.S. "Galatea" (screw frigate), 1867; 6d. H.M.S. "Cilicia" (transport), 1942; 7d. Royal Yacht "Britannia"; 10d. H.M.S. "Leopard" (frigate); 1s. "Tjisadane" (liner); 1s.6d. "Tristania" (crayfish trawler); 2s.6d. "Boissevain" (cargo liner); 5s. "Bornholm" (liner); 10s. (No. 84a), "R.S.A." (research vessel). VERT: 10s. (No. 84), £1 Queen Elizabeth II (portrait as in T **31** but larger).

1965. Cent of I.T.U. As T **64a** of St. Helena.

85	3d. red and grey	20	15
86	6d. violet and orange	30	15

1965. I.C.Y. As T **64b** of St. Helena.

87	1d. purple and turquoise	20	15
88	6d. green and lavender	50	25

1966. Churchill Commemoration. As T **64c** of St. Helena.

89	1d. blue	35	40
90	3d. green	1·00	50
91	6d. brown	1·25	65
92	1s.6d. violet	1·40	70

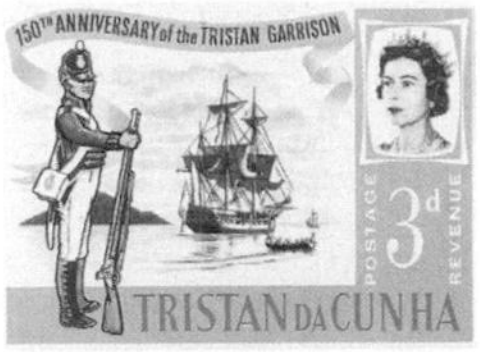

45 H.M.S. *Falmouth* (frigate) at Tristan and Soldier of 1816

1966. 150th Anniv of Tristan Garrison.

93	**45**	3d. multicoloured	15	10
94	**45**	6d. multicoloured	15	15
95	**45**	1s.6d. multicoloured	20	25
96	**45**	2s.6d. multicoloured	25	25

1966. World Cup Football Championship. As T **64d** of St. Helena.

97	3d. multicoloured	20	10
98	2s.6d. multicoloured	50	20

1966. Inauguration of W.H.O. Headquarters, Geneva. As T **64e** of St. Helena.

99	6d. black, green and blue	65	30
100	5s. black, purple and ochre	1·10	70

1966. 20th Anniv of UNESCO. As T **64f/h** of St. Helena.

101	10d. multicoloured	25	15
102	1s.6d. yellow, violet and olive	40	20
103	2s.6d. black, purple and orange	45	25

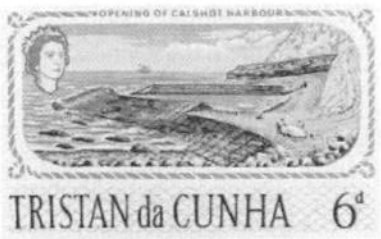

46 Calshot Harbour

1967. Opening of Calshot Harbour.

104	**46**	6d. multicoloured	10	10
105	**46**	10d. multicoloured	10	10
106	**46**	1s.6d. multicoloured	10	15
107	**46**	2s.6d. multicoloured	15	20

1967. No. 76 surch **4d** and bars.

108	4d. on 4½d. black and brown	10	10

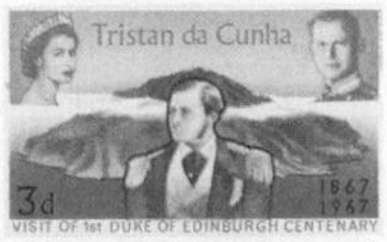

48 Prince Alfred, First Duke of Edinburgh

1967. Centenary of First Duke of Edinburgh's Visit to Tristan.

109	**48**	3d. multicoloured	10	10
110	**48**	6d. multicoloured	10	10
111	**48**	1s.6d. multicoloured	10	10
112	**48**	2s.6d. multicoloured	15	15

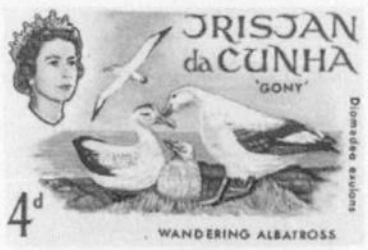

49 Wandering Albatross

1968. Birds. Multicoloured.

113	4d. Type **49**	30	30
114	1s. Wilkins's finch	35	30
115	1s.6d. Tristan thrush	40	55
116	2s.6d. Greater shearwater	60	65

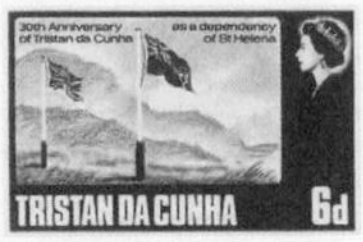

53 Union Jack and Dependency Flag

1968. 30th Anniv of Tristan da Cunha as a Dependency of St. Helena.

117	**53**	6d. multicoloured	20	30
118	-	9d. sepia and blue	20	35
119	**53**	1s.6d. multicoloured	30	40
120	-	2s.6d. red and blue	40	40

DESIGN: 9d. and 2s.6d. St. Helena and Tristan on chart.

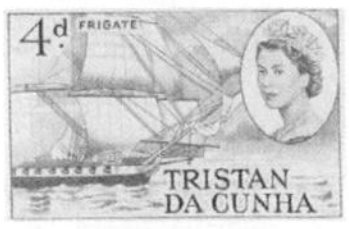

55 Frigate

1969. Clipper Ships.

121	**55**	4d. blue	60	40
122	-	1s. red	60	45
123	-	1s.6d. green	65	90
124	-	2s.6d. brown	70	95

DESIGNS: 1s. Full-rigged ship; 1s.6d. Barque; 2s.6d. Full-rigged clipper.

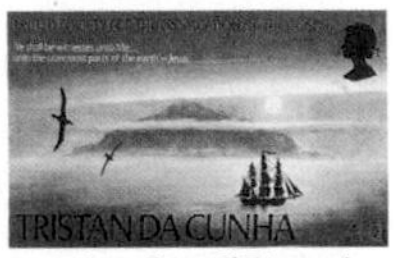

59 Sailing Ship off Tristan da Cunha

1969. United Society for the Propagation of the Gospel. Multicoloured.

125	4d. Type **59**	60	30
126	9d. Islanders going to first gospel service	15	30
127	1s.6d. Landing of the first minister	15	40
128	2s.6d. Procession outside St. Mary's Church	20	40

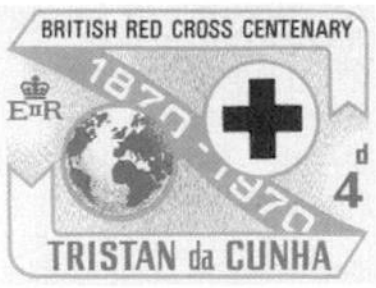

63 Globe and Red Cross Emblem

1970. Centenary of British Red Cross.

129	**63**	4d. deep green, red and green	10	25
130	**63**	9d. bistre, red and green	15	30
131	-	1s.9d. drab, red and blue	40	45
132	-	2s.6d. purple, red and blue	45	55

DESIGN—VERT: Nos. 131/2, "Union Jack" and Red Cross flag.

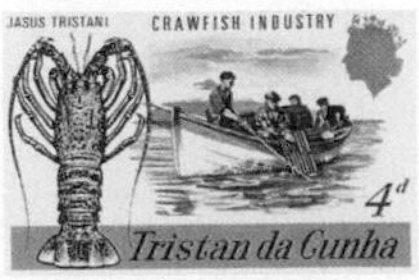

64 Crawfish and Longboat

1970. Crawfish Industry. Multicoloured.

133	4d. Type **64**	30	30
134	10d. Packing and storing crawfish	35	35
135	1s.6d. Type **64**	45	60
136	2s.6d. As 10d.	45	70

1971. Decimal Currency. Nos. 72, etc surch.

137	**31**	½p. on 1d. black and green	15	15
138	-	1p. on 2d. black and purple	15	15
139	-	1½p. on 4d. black and orange	30	15

140	-	2½p. on 6d. black and green	30	15
141	-	3p. on 7d. black and red	30	15
142	-	4p. on 10d. black and brown	30	20
143	-	5p. on 1s. black and red	30	20
144	-	7½p. on 1s.6d. black & olive	1·25	1·75
145	-	12½p. on 2s.6d. black & brown	1·25	2·25
146	-	15p. on 1½d. black and blue	1·25	2·50
147	-	25p. on 5s. black and violet	1·25	4·50
148	-	50p. on 10s. black and blue (No. 84a)	1·25	9·00

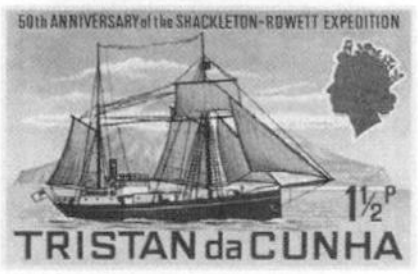

66 *Quest*

1971. 50th Anniv of Shackleton-Rowett Expedition.

149	**66**	1½p. multicoloured	70	30
150	-	4p. brown, green and light green	70	40
151	-	7½p. black, purple and green	70	40
152	-	12½p. multicoloured	75	45

DESIGNS—HORIZ: 4p. Presentation of Scout Troop flag; 7½p. Cachet on pair of 6d. G.B. stamps; 12½p. Shackleton, postmarks and longboat taking mail to the "Quest".

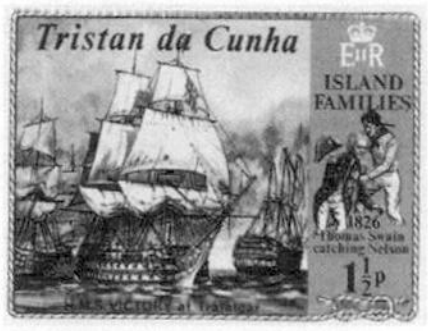

67 H.M.S. *Victory* at Trafalgar and Thomas Swain catching Nelson

1971. Island Families. Multicoloured.

153		1½p. Type **67**	20	40
154		2½p. "Emily of Stonington" (American schooner) (P. W. Green)	20	50
155		4p. "Italia" (barque) (Lavarello and Repetto)	25	60
156		7½p. H.M.S. "Falmouth" (frigate) (William Glass)	30	70
157		12½p. American whaling ship (Rogers and Hagan)	30	85

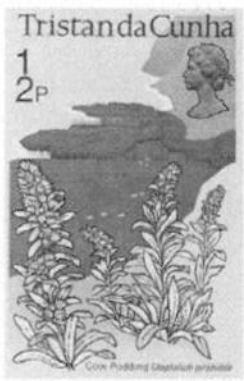

68 Cow Pudding

1972. Flowering Plants. Multicoloured.

158		½p. Type **68**	20	15
159		1p. Peak berry	40	15
160		1½p. Sand flower (horiz)	40	20
161		2½p. N.Z. flax (horiz)	40	20
162		3p. Island tree	40	20
163		4p. Bog fern	40	25
164		5p. Dog catcher	3·00	30
165		7½p. Celery	4·50	1·50
166		12½p. Pepper tree	1·25	60
167		25p. Foul berry (horiz)	1·25	1·50
168		50p. Tussock	7·00	2·50
169		£1 Tussac (horiz)	1·75	2·50

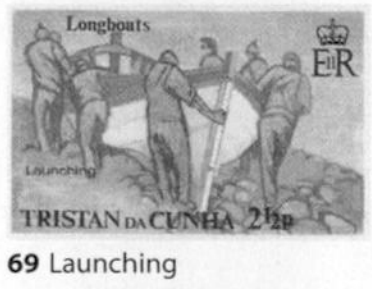

69 Launching

1972. Tristan Longboats. Multicoloured.

170		2½p. Type **69**	25	15
171		4p. Under oars	30	15
172		7½p. Coxswain Arthur Repetto (vert)	30	20
173		12½p. Under sail for Nightingale Island (vert)	35	25

1972. Royal Silver Wedding. As T **103** of St. Helena, but with Tristan thrushes and wandering albatrosses in background.

174		2½p. brown	25	30
175		7½p. blue	10	30

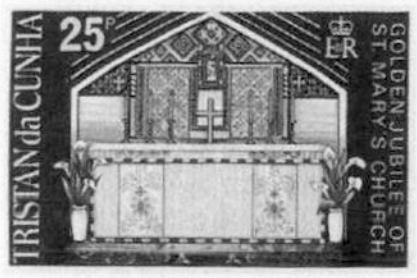

71 Church Altar

1973. Golden Jubilee of St. Mary's Church.

176	**71**	25p. multicoloured	40	40

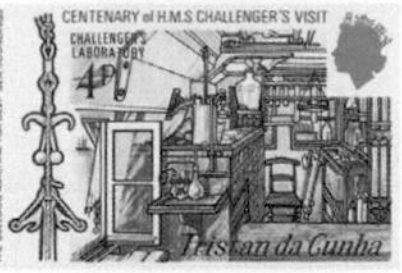

72 H.M.S. *Challenger's* Laboratory

1973. Cent of H.M.S. "Challenger's" Visit. Multicoloured.

177		4p. Type **72**	25	25
178		5p. H.M.S. "Challenger" off Tristan	25	25
179		7½p. "Challenger's" pinnace off Nightingale Is.	25	30
180		12½p. Survey route	35	40
MS181		145×96 mm. Nos. 177/80	1·10	2·75

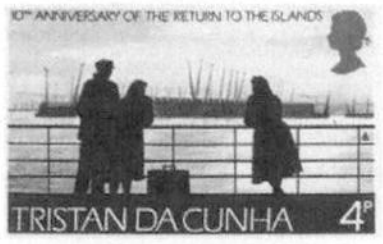

73 Approaching English Port

1973. Tenth Anniv of Return to Tristan da Cunha.

182	**73**	4p. brown, yellow and gold	20	25
183	-	5p. multicoloured	20	25
184	-	7½p. multicoloured	20	35
185	-	12½p. multicoloured	30	45

DESIGNS: 5p. Survey party; 7½p. Embarking on "Bornholm"; 12½p. Approaching Tristan.

1973. Royal Wedding. As T **103a** of St. Helena. Multicoloured, background colours given.

186		7½p. blue	15	10
187		12½p. green	15	10

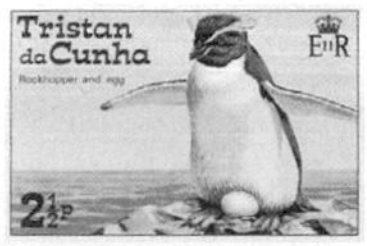

74 Rockhopper Penguin and Egg

1974. Rockhopper Penguins. Multicoloured.

188		2½p. Type **74**	1·00	75
189		5p. Rockhopper colony, Inaccessible Island	1·25	1·00
190		7½p. Penguin fishing	1·50	1·25
191		25p. Adult and fledgling	1·75	1·50

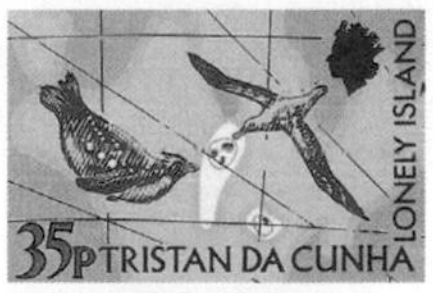

75 Map with Rockhopper Penguin and Wandering Albatross

1974. "The Lonely Island". Sheet 154×104 mm.

MS192	**75**	35p. multicoloured	3·50	4·00

76 Blenheim Palace

1974. Birth Centenary of Sir Winston Churchill.

193	**76**	7½p. yellow and black	10	10
194	-	25p. black, brown and grey	30	25
MS195		93×93 mm. Nos. 193/4	55	1·60

DESIGN: 25p. Churchill with Queen Elizabeth II.

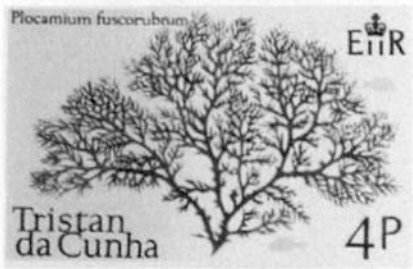

77 *Plocamium fuscorubrum*

1975. Sea Plants.

196	**77**	4p. red, lilac and black	15	10
197	-	5p. green, blue and turquoise	15	15
198	-	10p. orange, brown & purple	20	15
199	-	20p. multicoloured	30	25

DESIGNS: 5p. "Ulva lactua"; 10p. "Epymenia flabellata"; 20p. "Macrocystis pyrifera".

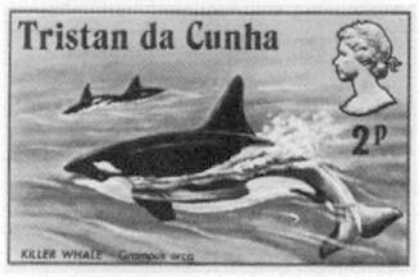

78 Killer Whale

1975. Whales. Multicoloured.

200		2p. Type **78**	65	35
201		3p. Rough-toothed dolphin	65	35
202		5p. Black right whale	75	40
203		20p. Fin whale	1·40	85

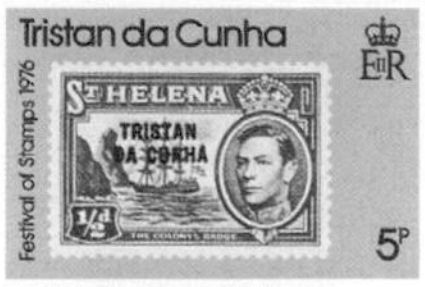

79 ½d. Stamp of 1952

1976. Festival of Stamps, London.

204	**79**	5p. black, violet and lilac	15	15
205	-	9p. black, green and blue	20	15
206	-	25p. multicoloured	30	40

DESIGNS—VERT: 9p. 1953 Coronation stamp. HORIZ: 25p. Mail carrier "Tristania II".

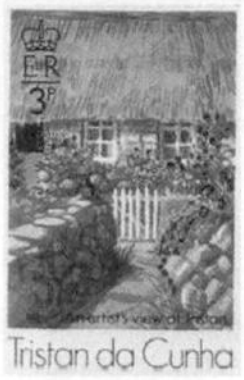

80 Island Cottage

1976. Paintings by Roland Svensson (1st series). Multicoloured.

207		3p. Type **80**	15	15
208		5p. The potato patches (horiz)	15	15
209		10p. Edinburgh from the sea (horiz)	20	20
210		20p. Huts, Nightingale Is.	30	35
MS211		125×112 mm. Nos. 207/10	1·50	2·00

See also Nos. 234/8 and 272/6.

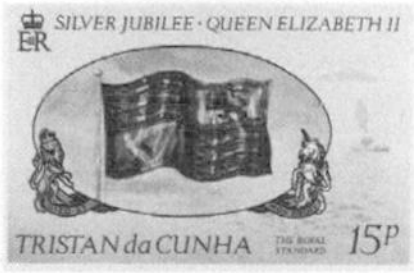

81 The Royal Standard

1977. Silver Jubilee. Multicoloured.

212		10p. Royal Yacht "Britannia"	15	20
213		15p. Type **81**	15	20
214		25p. Royal family	20	20

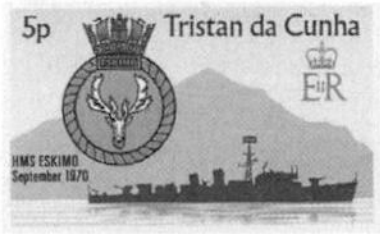

82 H.M.S. *Eskimo* (frigate)

1977. Ships' Crests (1st series). Multicoloured.

215		5p. Type **82**	15	15
216		10p. H.M.S. "Naiad" (frigate)	20	15
217		15p. H.M.S. "Jaguar" (frigate)	25	25
218		20p. H.M.S. "London" (destroyer)	30	30
MS219		142×140 mm. Nos. 215/18	1·00	1·50

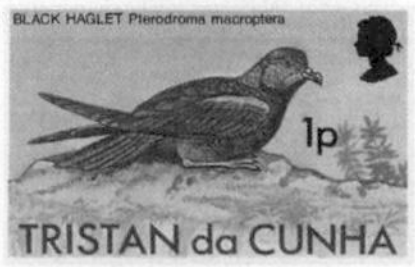

83 Great-winged Petrel

1977. Birds. Multicoloured.

220		1p. Type **83**	15	60
221		2p. White-faced storm petrel	20	90
222		3p. Hall's giant petrel	20	90
223		4p. Soft-plumaged petrel	60	1·00
224		5p. Wandering albatross	60	1·00
225		10p. Kerguelen petrel	60	1·00
226		15p. Antarctic tern	60	1·00
227		20p. Greater shearwater	1·00	1·00
228		25p. Broad-billed prion	1·00	1·00
229		50p. Antarctic skua	1·25	1·00
230		£1 Common diving petrel	1·50	1·00
231		£2 Yellow-nosed albatross	3·00	1·75

The 3p. to £2 designs are vert.

1978. Nos. 213/14 surch.

232		4p. on 15p. Type **81**	80	2·50
233		7½p. on 25p. Royal family	80	2·50

1978. Paintings by Roland Svensson (2nd series). As T **80**. Multicoloured.

234		5p. St. Mary's Church	15	15
235		10p. Longboats	15	15
236		15p. A Tristan home	20	25
237		20p. The harbour, 1970	20	25
MS238		115×128 mm. Nos. 234/7	1·50	2·00

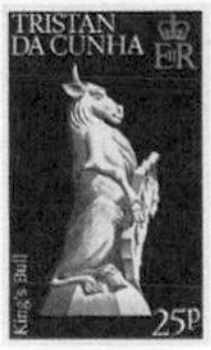

85 King's Bull

1978. 25th Anniv of Coronation.

239	**85**	25p. brown, violet and silver	25	30
240	-	25p. multicoloured	25	30
241	-	25p. brown, violet and silver	25	30

DESIGNS: No. 240, Queen Elizabeth II; 241, Tristan crawfish.

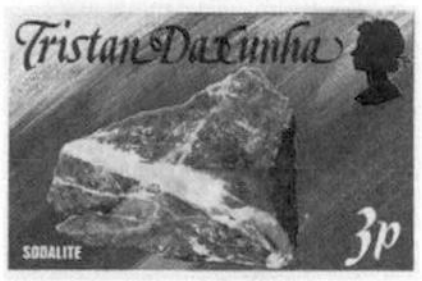

86 Sodalite

1978. Local Minerals. Multicoloured.

242		3p. Type **86**	25	25
243		5p. Aragonite	30	30
244		10p. Sulphur	45	45
245		20p. Lava containing pyroxene crystal	65	65

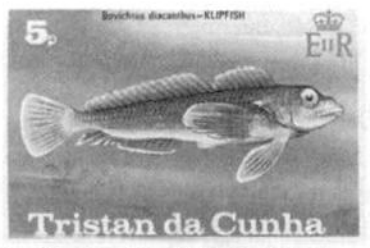

87 Two-spined Thornfish

1978. Fish.

246	**87**	5p. black, brown and green	10	10
247	-	10p. black, brown and green	15	15
248	-	15p. multicoloured	20	20
249	-	20p. multicoloured	30	25

DESIGNS: 10p. Five-fingered morwong; 15p. Concha wrasse; 20p. Tristan jacopever.

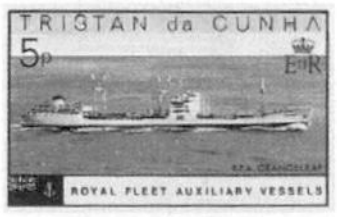

88 R.F.A. *Orangeleaf* (tanker)

1978. Royal Fleet Auxiliary Vessels. Multicoloured.

250		5p. Type **88**	15	10
251		10p. R.F.A. "Tarbatness" (store carrier)	15	10
252		20p. R.F.A. "Tidereach" (tanker)	20	25
253		25p. R.F.A. "Reliant" (store carrier)	25	30
MS254		136×140 mm. Nos. 250/3	65	2·75

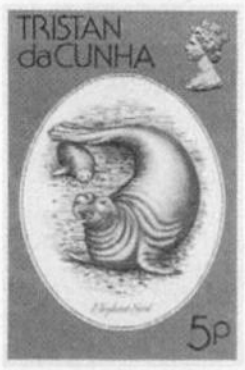

89 Southern Elephant Seal

1978. Wildlife Conservation. Multicoloured.

255		5p. Type **89**	10	10
256		10p. Afro-Australian fur seal	15	15
257		15p. Tristan thrush	25	20
258		20p. Nightingale finch ("Tristan Bunting")	35	25

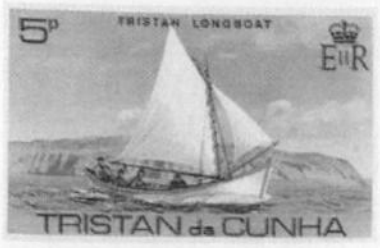

90 Tristan Longboat

1978. Visit of "Queen Elizabeth 2". Multicoloured.

259	5p. Type **90**	15	15
260	10p. "Queen Mary" (liner)	15	15
261	15p. "Queen Elizabeth" (liner)	20	25
262	20p. "Queen Elizabeth 2" (liner)	20	25
MS263	148×96 mm. 25p. Queen Elizabeth 2 (liner) (131×27 mm)	75	1·50

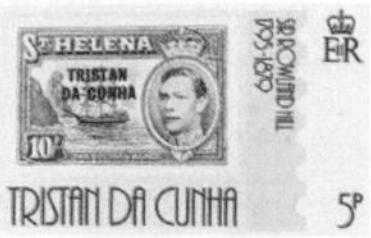

91 1952 "TRISTAN DA CUNHA" overprint on St. Helena 10s. Definitive

1979. Death Centenary of Sir Rowland Hill.

264	**91**	5p. black, lilac and yellow	10	15
265	-	10p. black, red and green	15	20
266	-	25p. multicoloured	30	30
MS267		83×103 mm. 50p. black and red	60	70

DESIGNS—HORIZ: 10p. 1954 5s. definitive. VERT: 25p. "TRISTAN DA CUNHA RESETTLEMENT 1963" overprint on St. Helena 3d. definitive; 50p. 1946 1d. 4 Potatoes local label.

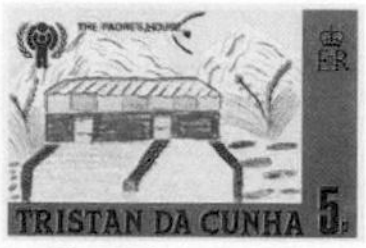

92 "The Padre's House"

1979. International Year of the Child. Children's Drawings. Multicoloured.

268	5p. Type **92**	10	10
269	10p. "Houses in the Village"	15	15
270	15p. "St. Mary's Church"	15	15
271	20p. "Rockhopper Penguins"	20	25

1980. Paintings by Roland Svensson (3rd series). As T **80**. Multicoloured.

272	5p. "Stoltenhoff Island" (horiz)	10	10
273	10p. "Nightingale from the East" (horiz)	15	20
274	15p. "The Administrator's Abode"	15	25
275	20p. "Ridge where the Goat jump off"	20	30
MS276	126×109 mm. Nos. 272/6	70	1·25

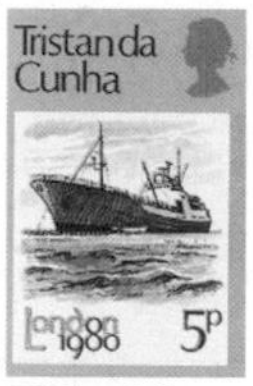

93 *Tristania II* (crayfish trawler)

1980. "London 1980" Int Stamp Exhibition. Multicoloured.

277	5p. Type **93**	10	10
278	10p. Mail being unloaded at Calshot Harbour	15	15
279	15p. Tractor transporting mail to Post Office	15	20
280	20p. Ringing the "dong" to summon people to Post Office	20	20
281	25p. Distributing mail	25	25

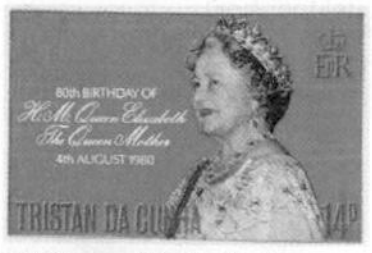
94 Queen Elizabeth the Queen Mother at Royal Opera House, 1976

1980. 80th Birthday of The Queen Mother.

282	**94**	14p. multicoloured	25	25

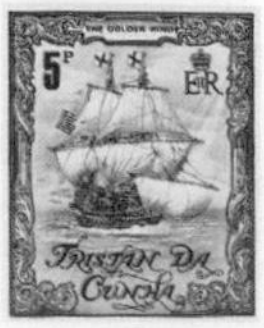
95 *Golden Hind*

1980. 400th Anniv of Sir Francis Drake's Circumnavigation of the World. Multicoloured.

283	5p. Type **95**	10	10
284	10p. Drake's route	15	15
285	20p. Sir Francis Drake	20	20
286	25p. Queen Elizabeth I	25	25

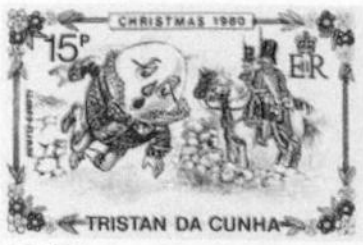

96 "Humpty Dumpty"

1980. Christmas. Scenes from Nursery Rhymes. Multicoloured.

287	15p. Type **96**	15	25
288	15p. "Mary had a little Lamb"	15	25
289	15p. "Little Jack Horner"	15	25
290	15p. "Hey Diddle Diddle"	15	25
291	15p. "London Bridge"	15	25
292	15p. "Old King Cole"	15	25
293	15p. "Sing a Song of Sixpence"	15	25
294	15p. "Tom, Tom the Piper's Son"	15	25
295	15p. "The Owl and the Pussy Cat"	15	25

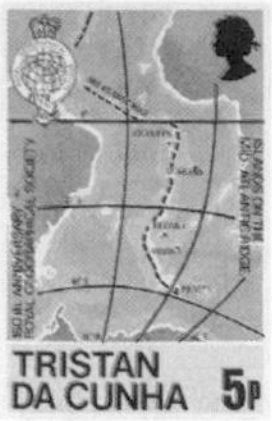

97 South Atlantic Ocean showing Islands on Mid-Atlantic Ridge

1980. 150th Anniv of Royal Geographical Society. Maps. Multicoloured.

296	5p. Type **97**	15	20
297	10p. Tristan da Cunha group (Beauforts Survey, 1806)	15	25
298	15p. Tristan Island (Crawford, 1937–38)	20	30
299	20p. Gough Island (1955–56)	25	40

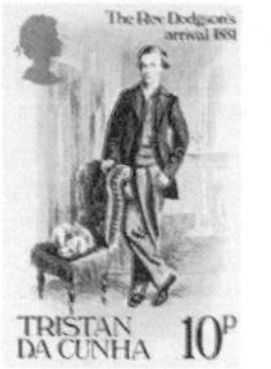

98 Revd. Dodgson as Young Man

1981. Centenary of Revd. Edwin Dodgson's Arrival on Tristan da Cunha. Multicoloured.

300	10p. Type **98**	10	15
301	20p. Dodgson and view of Tristan da Cunha (horiz)	20	30
302	30p. Dodgson with people of Tristan da Cunha	25	45
MS303	140×134 mm. Nos. 300/2	75	1·40

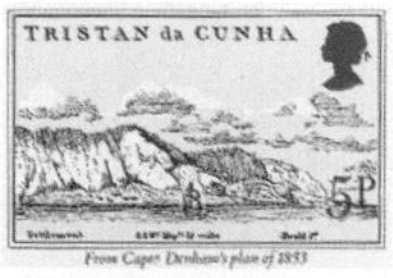

99 Detail from Captain Denham's Plan, 1853

1981. Early Maps. Multicoloured.

304	5p. Type **99**	15	10
305	14p. Detail from map by A. Dalrymple, 17 March 1781	20	20
306	21p. Detail from Captain Denham's plan, 1853 (different)	25	30
MS307	110×70 mm. 35p. Detail from map by J. van Keulen, circa 1700	50	60

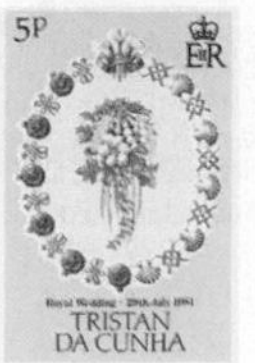

100 Wedding Bouquet from Tristan da Cunha

1981. Royal Wedding. Multicoloured.

308	5p. Type **100**	10	10
309	20p. Investiture of Prince of Wales	15	15
310	50p. Prince Charles and Lady Diana Spencer	45	45

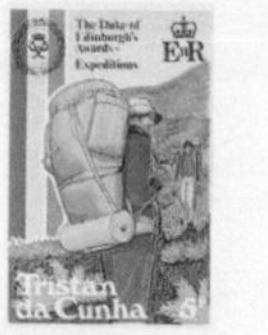
101 Explorer with Rucksack

1981. 25th Anniv of Duke of Edinburgh Award Scheme. Multicoloured.

311	5p. Type **101**	10	10
312	10p. Explorer at campsite	10	10
313	20p. Explorer map reading	20	20
314	25p. Duke of Edinburgh	25	25

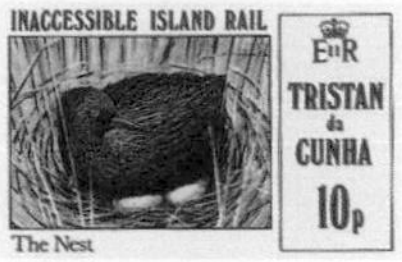

102 Inaccessible Island Rail on Nest

1981. Inaccessible Island Rail. Multicoloured.

315	10p. Type **102**	20	30
316	10p. Inaccessible Island rail eggs	20	30
317	10p. Rail chicks	20	30
318	10p. Adult rail	20	30

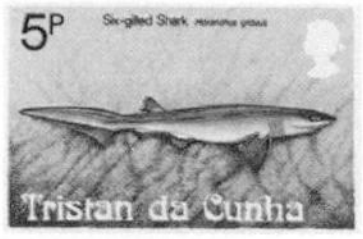

103 Six-gilled Shark

1982. Sharks. Multicoloured.

319	5p. Type **103**	25	10
320	14p. Porbeagle	25	20
321	21p. Blue shark	25	35
322	35p. Golden hammerhead	35	50

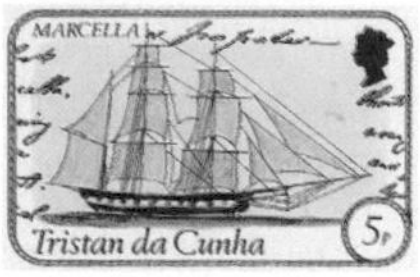

104 *Marcella* (barque)

1982. Sailing Ships (1st series). Multicoloured.

323	5p. Type **104**	20	20
324	15p. "Eliza Adams" (full-rigged ship)	20	20
325	30p. "Corinthian" (American whaling ship)	30	30
326	50p. "Samuel and Thomas" (American whaling ship)	40	40

See also Nos. 341/4.

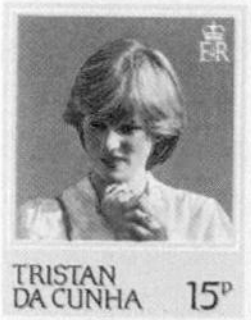

105 Lady Diana Spencer at Windsor, July 1981

1982. 21st Birthday of Princess of Wales. Multicoloured.

327	5p. Tristan da Cunha coat of arms	10	10
328	15p. Type **105**	25	20
329	30p. Prince and Princess of Wales in wedding portrait	30	40
330	50p. Formal portrait	60	60

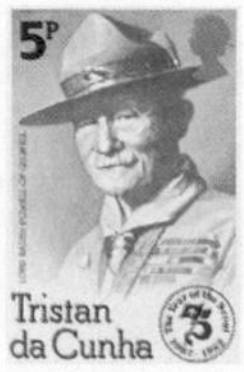

106 Lord Baden-Powell

1982. 75th Anniv of Boy Scout Movement. Multicoloured.

331	5p. Type **106**	15	15
332	20p. First Scout camp, Brownsea, 1907	20	35
333	50p. Local Scouts on parade (horiz)	45	75
MS334	88×104 mm. 50p. Moral of the Acorn and the Oak	75	1·40

1982. Commonwealth Games, Brisbane. Nos. 224 and 228 optd **1ST PARTICIPATION COMMONWEALTH GAMES 1982.**

335	5p. Wandering albatross	15	10
336	25p. Broad-billed prion	40	30

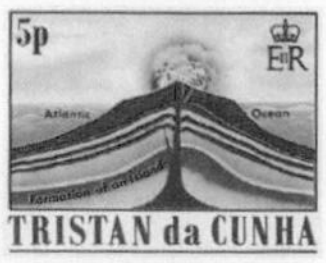

108 Formation of Island

1982. Volcanoes. Multicoloured.

337	5p. Type **108**	15	15
338	15p. Plan showing surface cinder cones and cross-section of volcano showing feeders	25	35
339	25p. Eruption	35	50
340	35p. 1961 Tristan eruption	40	70

1983. Sailing Ships (2nd series). As T **104**. Multicoloured.

341	5p. "Islander" (barque) (vert)	15	15
342	20p. "Roscoe" (full-rigged ship)	25	25
343	35p. "Columbia" (whaling ship)	35	40
344	50p. "Emeline" (schooner) (vert)	50	60

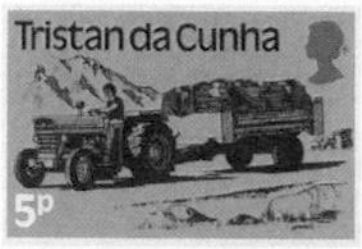

109 Tractor pulling Trailer

1983. Land Transport. Multicoloured.

345	5p. Type **109**	10	15
346	15p. Pack donkeys	15	25
347	30p. Bullock cart	20	40
348	50p. Landrover	30	60

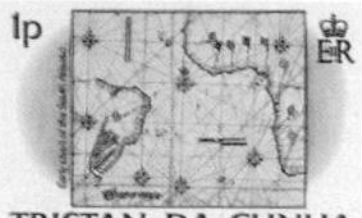

110 Early Chart of South Atlantic

1983. Island History. Multicoloured.

349	1p. Type **110**	30	50
350	3p. Tristao da Cunha's caravel	40	50
351	4p. Notice left by Dutch on first landing, 1643	40	50
352	5p. 17th-century views of the island	40	50
353	10p. British army landing party, 1815	45	50
354	15p. 19th-century view of the settlement	55	70
355	18p. Governor Glass's house	55	70
356	20p. The Revd. W. F. Taylor and Peter Green	65	75
357	25p. "John and Elizabeth" (American whaling ship)	85	75
358	50p. Letters Patent declaring Tristan da Cunha a dependency of St. Helena	1·10	1·50
359	£1 Commissioning of H.M.S. "Atlantic Isle", 1944	1·25	2·50
360	£2 Evacuation, 1961	2·00	4·00

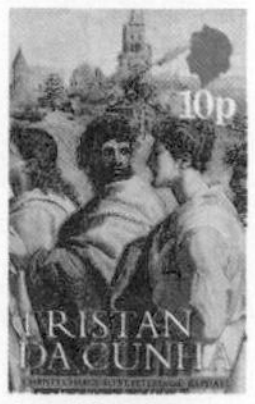

111 "Christ's Charge to St. Peter" (detail)

1983. 500th Birth Anniv of Raphael.

361	**111**	10p. multicoloured	15	20
362	-	25p. multicoloured	25	35
363	-	40p. multicoloured	45	60
MS364		115×90 mm. 50p. multicoloured (horiz)	70	80

DESIGNS: 25, 40p. Different details of "Christ's Charge to St. Peter" (Raphael).

On No. **MS**364 the Queen's head has been replaced by the Royal Cypher.

112 1952 6d. Stamp

1984. 150th Anniv of St. Helena as British Colony. Multicoloured.

365	10p. Type **112**	20	35
366	15p. 1952 1s. stamp	25	45
367	25p. 1952 2s.6d. stamp	30	70
368	60p. 1952 10s. stamp	60	1·25

113 Agrocybe praecox var. cutefracta

1984. Fungi. Multicoloured.

369	10p. Type **113**	30	70
370	20p. "Laccaria tetraspora"	40	90
371	30p. "Agrocybe cylindracea" (horiz)	45	1·00
372	50p. "Sacoscypha coccinea" (horiz)	55	1·25

114 Constellation of "Orion"

1984. The Night Sky. Multicoloured.

373	10p. Type **114**	35	80
374	20p. "Scorpius"	40	90
375	25p. "Canis Major"	45	95
376	50p. "Crux"	60	1·10

115 Sheep-shearing

1984. Tristan Woollens Industry. Multicoloured.

377	9p. Type **115**	15	45
378	17p. Carding wool	20	50
379	29p. Spinning	30	80
380	45p. Knitting	45	90
MS381	120×85 mm. As Nos. 377/80, but without white borders around the designs	1·00	3·00

116 "Christmas Dinner-table"

1984. Christmas. Children's Drawings. Multicoloured.

382	10p. Type **116**	20	35
383	20p. "Santa Claus in ox cart"	25	40
384	30p. "Santa Claus in longboat"	30	70
385	50p. "The Nativity"	50	80

117 "H.M.S. Julia (sloop) Ashore near Pigbite, 1817" (Midshipman C. W. Browne)

1985. Shipwrecks (1st series).

386	**117**	10p. blue and light blue	40	80

387	-	25p. brown and green	50	1·40
388	-	35p. brown and yellow	65	1·60
MS389	142×101 mm. 60p. multicoloured			75	2·25

DESIGNS—VERT: 25p. Bell from "Mabel Clark", St. Mary's Church. HORIZ: 35p. "Barque 'Glenhuntley' foundering, 1898" (John Hagan); 60p. Map of Tristan da Cunha showing site of shipwrecks.
See also Nos. 411/14 and 426/9.

118 The Queen Mother at Ascot with Princess Margaret

1985. Life and Times of Queen Elizabeth the Queen Mother. Multicoloured.

390	10p. The Queen Mother and Prince Charles, 1954	20	30
391	20p. Type **118**	30	60
392	30p. Queen Elizabeth the Queen Mother	40	85
393	50p. With Prince Henry at his christening	70	1·25
MS394	91×73 mm. 80p. The Queen Mother and the young Princess Anne at Trooping the Colour.	2·75	3·25

119 Jonathan Lambert and "Isles of Refreshment" Flag, 1811

1985. Flags. Multicoloured.

395	10p. Type **119**	40	90
396	15p. 21st Light Dragoons guidon and cannon from Fort Malcolm (1816–17) (vert)	50	1·00
397	25p. White Ensign and H.M.S. "Falmouth" (frigate) offshore, 1816 (vert)	60	1·40
398	60p. Union Jack and Tristan da Cunha (vert)	1·00	2·75

120 Lifeboat heading for Barque West Riding

1985. Cent of Loss of Island Lifeboat. Multicoloured.

399	10p. Type **120**	25	60
400	30p. Map of Tristan da Cunha	35	1·00
401	50p. Memorial plaque to lifeboat crew	50	1·50

121 Halley's Comet, 1066, from Bayeux Tapestry

1986. Appearance of Halley's Comet. Multicoloured.

402	10p. Type **121**	30	75
403	20p. Path of Comet	35	1·25
404	30p. Comet over Inaccessible Island	40	1·50
405	50p. H.M.S. "Paramour" (pink) and map of South Atlantic	75	2·00

1986. 60th Birthday of Queen Elizabeth II. As T **145a** of St. Helena. Multicoloured.

406	10p. With Prince Charles, 1950	15	35
407	15p. Queen at Trooping the Colour	20	45
408	25p. In robes of Order of the Bath, Westminster Abbey, 1972	25	70
409	45p. In Canada, 1977	40	1·25
410	65p. At Crown Agents Head Office, London, 1983	55	1·50

122 "Allanshaw wrecked on East Beach, 1893" (drawing by John Hagan)

1986. Shipwrecks (2nd series).

411	**122**	9p. blue, deep blue and black	65	1·00
412	-	20p. green, yellow and black	1·00	1·50
413	-	40p. blue, violet and black	1·25	2·00
MS414	142×80 mm. 65p. brown and black		2·25	4·00

DESIGNS—VERT: 20p. Church font from wreck of "Edward Vittery", 1881; 40p. Ship's figurehead. HORIZ: 65p. Gaetano Lavarello and Andrea Repetto, survivors from "Ilatia", 1892.

1986. Royal Wedding. As T **146a** of St. Helena. Multicoloured.

415	10p. Prince Andrew and Miss Sarah Ferguson	20	65
416	40p. Prince Andrew piloting helicopter, Digby, Canada, 1985	80	1·60

123 Wandering Albatross

1986. Flora and Fauna of Inaccessible Island. Multicoloured.

417	5p. Type **123**	30	80
418	10p. "Lagenophora nudicaulis" (daisy)	30	90
419	20p. "Cynthia virginiensis" (butterfly)	50	1·40
420	25p. Wilkins's finch ("Wilkins' Bunting")	55	1·40
421	50p. White-chinned petrel ("Ring-eye")	70	2·00

124 Dimorphinoctua cunhaensis (flightless moth)

1987. Island Flightless Insects and Birds. Multicoloured.

422	10p. Type **124**	25	70
423	25p. "Tristanomyia frustilifera" (fly) and Crater Lake	35	1·40
424	35p. Inaccessible Island rail ("Flightless Rail") and Inaccessible Island	65	2·25
425	50p. Gough Island coot ("Gough Island Moorhen") and Gough Island	80	2·50

125 Castaways from Blenden Hall attacking Sea Elephant, 1821

1987. Shipwrecks (3rd series).

426	**125**	11p. black and brown	65	1·25
427	-	17p. black and lilac	80	1·60
428	-	45p. black and green	1·00	2·00
MS429	131×70 mm. blue, green and light blue		3·00	3·00

DESIGNS—HORIZ: 17p. Barquentine "Henry A. Paull" stranded at Sandy Point, 1879; 70p. Map of Inaccessible Island showing sites of shipwrecks. VERT: 45p. Gustav Stoltenhoff, 1871, and Stoltenhoff Island.

126 Rockhopper Penguin swimming

1987. Rockhopper Penguins. Multicoloured.

430	10p. Type **126**	1·10	1·25
431	20p. Adult with egg	1·40	1·60
432	30p. Adult with juvenile	1·90	2·25
433	50p. Head of rockhopper penguin	2·50	2·75

127 Microscope and Published Report

1987. 50th Anniv of Norwegian Scientific Expedition. Multicoloured.

434	10p. Type **127**	90	1·25
435	20p. Scientists ringing yellow-nosed albatross ("Mollymawk")	1·90	2·25
436	30p. Expedition hut, Little Beach Point	2·25	2·75
437	50p. S.S. "Thorshammer" (whale factory ship)	3·25	3·75

1988. Royal Ruby Wedding. Nos. 406/10 optd **40TH WEDDING ANNIVERSARY**.

438	10p. Princess Elizabeth with Prince Charles, 1950	20	25
439	15p. Queen Elizabeth II at Trooping the Colour	25	35
440	25p. In robes of Order of the Bath, Westminster Abbey, 1972	35	55
441	45p. In Canada, 1977	60	95
442	65p. At Crown Agents Head Office, London, 1983	75	1·40

128 Nightingale Finch ("Tristan Bunting")

1988. Fauna of Nightingale Island. Multicoloured.

443	5p. Type **128**	40	65
444	10p. Tristan thrush (immature)	55	75
445	20p. Yellow-nosed albatross (chick)	70	1·10
446	25p. Greater shearwater ("Great Shearwater")	70	1·25
447	50p. Elephant seal	1·00	2·25

129 Painted Penguin Eggs

1988. Tristan da Cunha Handicrafts. Multicoloured.

448	10p. Type **129**	25	55
449	15p. Moccasins	35	70
450	35p. Knitwear	75	1·40
451	50p. Model longboat	1·10	1·75

130 Processing Blubber

1988. 19th-century Whaling. Multicoloured.

452	10p. Type **130**	1·00	75
453	20p. Harpoon guns	1·25	1·00
454	30p. Scrimshaw (carved whale bone)	1·50	1·25
455	50p. Whaling ships	3·00	2·00
MS456	76×56 mm. £1 Right whale	3·00	2·75

1988. 300th Anniv of Lloyd's of London. As T **152a** of St. Helena.

457	10p. multicoloured	40	40
458	25p. multicoloured	1·50	1·10
459	35p. black and green	2·00	1·50

460	50p. black and red	2·75	1·90

DESIGNS—VERT: 10p. New Lloyd's Building, 1988; 50p. "Kobenhavn" (cadet barque). HORIZ: 25p. "Tristania II" (crayfish trawler); 35p. "St. Helena" (mail ship).

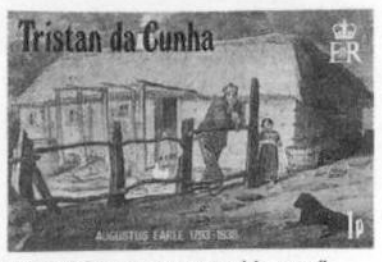

131 "Government House"

1988. Augustus Earle's Paintings, 1824. Multicoloured.

461	1p. Type **131**	30	75
462	3p. "Squall off Tristan"	45	75
463	4p. "Rafting Blubber"	50	75
464	5p. "View near Little Beach"	50	75
465	10p. "Man killing Albatross"	70	75
466	15p. "View on The Summit"	90	1·25
467	20p. "Nightingale Island"	1·00	1·40
468	25p. "Earle on Tristan"	1·00	1·60
469	35p. "Solitude–Watching the Horizon"	1·00	1·75
470	50p. "Northeaster"	1·00	2·00
471	£1 "Tristan Village"	1·25	1·75
472	£2 "Governor Glass at Dinner"	2·00	3·75

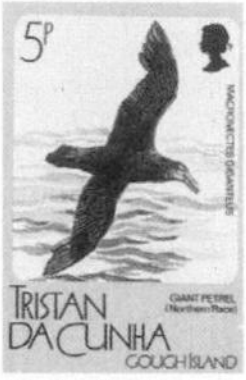

132 Hall's Giant Petrel

1989. Fauna of Gough Island. Multicoloured.

473	5p. Type **132**	1·00	1·50
474	10p. Gough Island coot ("Gough Island Moorhen")	1·10	1·50
475	20p. Gough Island finch ("Gough Bunting")	1·50	1·75
476	25p. Sooty albatross	1·60	1·75
477	50p. Amsterdam fur seal	2·00	3·00

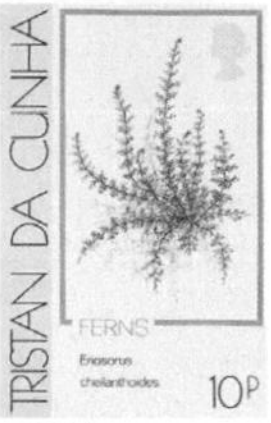

133 *Eriosorus cheilanthoides*

1989. Ferns. Multicoloured.

478	10p. Type **133**	65	65
479	25p. "Asplenium alvarezense"	1·10	1·10
480	35p. "Elaphoglossum hybridum"	1·40	1·40
481	50p. "Ophioglossum opacum"	1·60	1·60

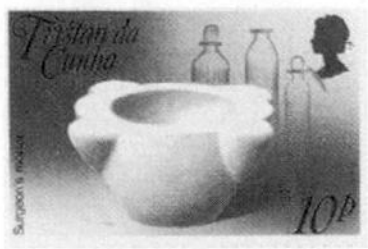

134 Surgeon's Mortar

1989. Nautical Museum Exhibits. Multicoloured.

482	10p. Type **134**	65	65
483	20p. Parts of darting-gun harpoon	1·10	1·10
484	30p. Ship's compass with binnacle-hood	1·40	1·40
485	60p. Rope-twisting device	1·75	1·75

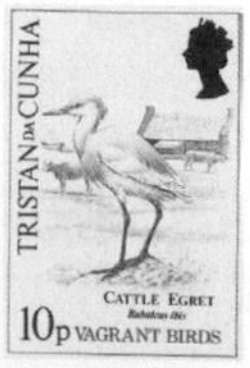

135 Cattle Egret

1989. Vagrant Birds. Multicoloured.

486	10p. Type **135**	1·50	1·50
487	25p. Spotted sandpiper	2·25	2·50
488	35p. American purple gallinule ("Purple Gallinule")	2·50	2·75
489	50p. Barn swallow	2·75	3·25

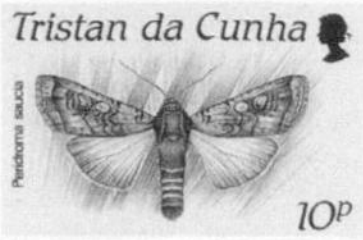

136 *Peridroma saucia*

1990. Moths. Multicoloured.

490	10p. Type **136**	90	1·00
491	15p. "Ascalapha odorata"	1·25	1·60
492	35p. "Agrius cingulata"	2·00	2·50
493	60p. "Eumorpha labruscae"	2·75	3·25

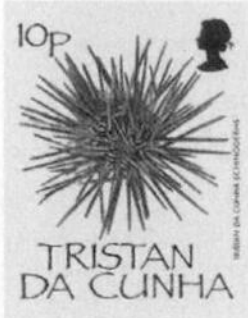

137 Sea Urchin

1990. Echinoderms.

494	**137** 10p. multicoloured	1·00	1·00
495	- 20p. multicoloured	1·50	2·00
496	- 30p. multicoloured	1·90	2·50
497	- 60p. multicoloured	2·50	3·25

DESIGNS: 20p. to 60p. Different starfish.

1990. 90th Birthday of Queen Elizabeth the Queen Mother. As T **161a** of St. Helena.

498	25p. multicoloured	1·00	1·25
499	£1 brown and blue	2·50	3·25

DESIGNS—21×36 mm: 25p. Queen Mother at the London Coliseum. 29×37 mm: £1 Queen Elizabeth broadcasting to women of the Empire, 1939.

1990. Maiden Voyage of "St. Helena II". As T **162** of St. Helena. Multicoloured.

500	10p. "Dunnottar Castle" (liner), 1942	1·50	1·25
501	15p. "St. Helena I" (mail ship) at Tristan	2·00	1·75
502	35p. Launch of "St. Helena II" (mail ship)	2·75	3·00
503	60p. Duke of York launching "St. Helena II"	3·75	4·00
MS504	100×100 mm. £1 "St. Helena II" and outline map of Tristan da Cunha	4·25	7·00

No. **MS**504 also contains two imperforate designs of similar stamps from Ascension and St. Helena without face values.

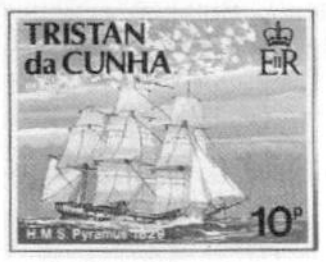

138 H.M.S. *Pyramus* (frigate), 1829

1990. Ships of the Royal Navy (1st series). Multicoloured.

505	10p. Type **138**	2·50	1·50
506	25p. H.M.S. "Penguin" (sloop), 1815	3·50	2·75
507	35p. H.M.S. "Thalia" (screw corvette), 1886	3·75	3·00
508	50p. H.M.S. "Sidon" (paddle frigate), 1858	4·75	3·75

See also Nos. 509/12 and 565/8.

1991. Ships of the Royal Navy (2nd series). As T **138**. Multicoloured.

509	10p. H.M.S. "Milford" (sloop), 1938	2·00	1·25
510	25p. H.M.S. "Dublin" (cruiser), 1923	3·00	2·50
511	35p. H.M.S. "Yarmouth" (cruiser), 1919	3·25	2·75
512	50p. H.M.S. "Carlisle" (cruiser), 1938	3·75	3·50

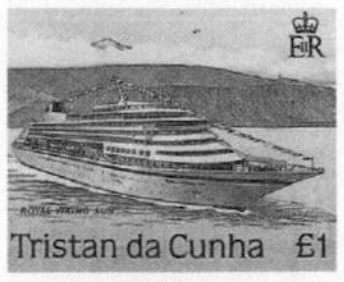

139 *Royal Viking sun* (cruise liner)

1991. Visit of "Royal Viking Sun". Sheet 62×47 mm.

MS513	**139** £1 multicoloured	6·00	8·00

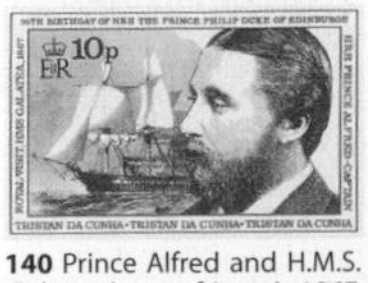

140 Prince Alfred and H.M.S. *Galatea* (screw frigate), 1867

1991. 70th Birthday of Prince Philip, Duke of Edinburgh.

514	**140** 10p. black, lt blue & blue	2·25	1·75
515	- 25p. black, lt green & green	3·25	2·50
516	- 30p. black, brown & yellow	3·50	3·25
517	- 50p. multicoloured	4·50	3·75

DESIGNS: 25p. Prince Philip meeting local inhabitants, 1957; 30p. Prince Philip and Royal Yacht "Britannia", 1957; 50p. Prince Philip and Edinburgh settlement.

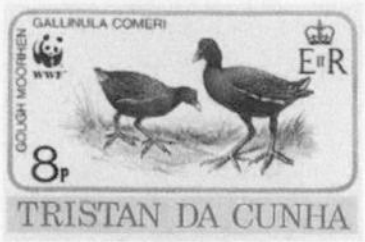

141 Pair of Gough Island coots ("Gough Island Moorhens")

1991. Endangered Species. Birds. Multicoloured.

518	8p. Type **141**	1·75	1·75
519	10p. Gough Island finch ("Gough Bunting")	1·75	1·75
520	12p. Gough Island coot ("Gough Island Moorhen") on nest	1·90	1·90
521	15p. Gough Island finch ("Gough Bunting") feeding chicks	1·90	1·90

1992. 500th Anniv of Discovery of America by Columbus and Re-enactment Voyages. As T **168** of St. Helena. Multicoloured.

522	10p. Map of re-enactment voyages and "Eye of the Wind" (cadet brig)	1·00	1·50
523	15p. Compass rose and "Soren Larsen" (cadet brigantine)	1·50	2·00
524	35p. Ships of Columbus	2·50	3·00
525	60p. Columbus and "Santa Maria"	2·75	3·25

1992. 40th Anniv of Queen Elizabeth II's Accession. As T **168a** of St. Helena. Multicoloured.

526	10p. Tristan from the sea	80	60
527	20p. Longboat under sail	1·25	90
528	25p. Aerial view of Edinburgh	1·25	1·00
529	35p. Three portraits of Queen Elizabeth	1·50	1·25
530	65p. Queen Elizabeth II	2·50	2·25

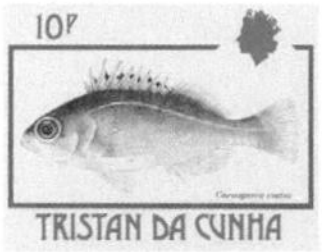

142 Coats' Perch

1992. Fish. Multicoloured.

531	10p. Type **142**	80	90
532	15p. Lined trumpeter	1·25	1·40
533	35p. Karrer's morid cod	2·25	2·75
534	60p. Long-finned scad	2·75	3·25

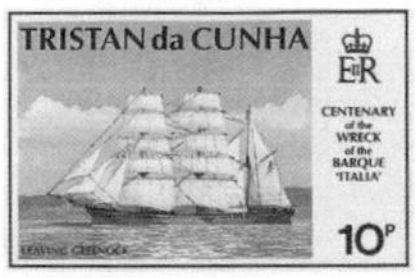

143 *Italia* leaving Greenock

1992. Cent of the Wreck of Barque "Italia". Multicoloured.

535	10p. Type **143**	1·25	1·50
536	45p. In mid-Atlantic	2·75	3·50
537	65p. Driving ashore on Stony Beach	3·25	4·00
MS538	101×75 mm. £1 "Italia" becalmed	8·50	11·00

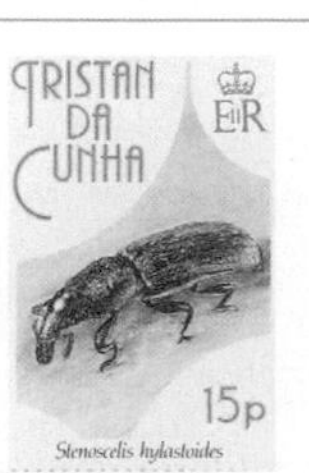

144 *Stenoscelis hylastoides*

1993. Insects. Multicoloured.

539	15p. Type **144**	1·50	1·50
540	45p. "Trogloscaptomyza brevilamellata"	2·75	3·00
541	60p. "Senilites tristanicola"	3·25	3·75

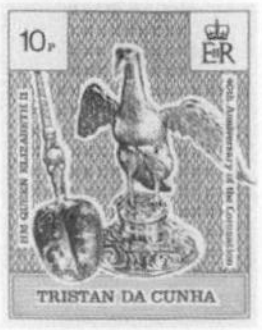

145 Ampulla and Anointing Spoon

1993. 40th Anniv of Coronation.

542	**145** 10p. green and black	90	1·00
543	- 15p. mauve and black	1·40	1·60
544	- 35p. violet and black	1·90	2·50
545	- 60p. blue and black	2·50	3·25

DESIGNS: 15p. Orb; 35p. Imperial State Crown; 60p. St. Edward's Crown.

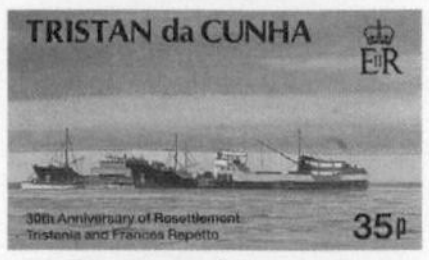

146 *Tristania* and *Frances Repetto* (crayfish trawlers)

1993. 30th Anniv of Resettlement of Tristan. Multicoloured.

546	35p. Type **146**	2·50	3·00
547	35p. "Boissevain" (cargo liner)	2·50	3·00
548	50p. "Bornholm" (liner) and longboat	3·25	3·75

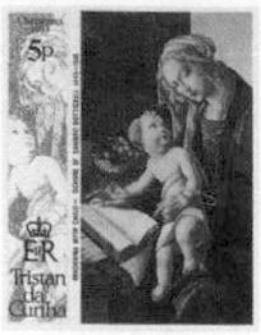

147 "Madonna with Child" (School of Botticelli)

1993. Christmas. Religious Paintings. Multicoloured.

549	5p. Type **147**	90	1·00
550	15p. "The Holy Family" (Daniel Gran)	2·00	2·00
551	35p. "The Holy Virgin and Child" (Rubens)	3·00	3·25
552	65p. "The Mystical Marriage of St. Catherine with the Holy Child" (Jan van Balen)	4·00	5·00

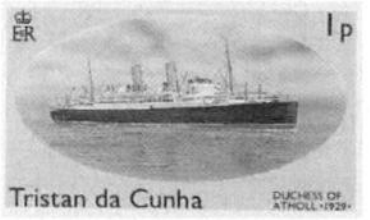

148 *Duchess of Atholl* (liner)

1994. Ships. Multicoloured.

553	1p. Type **148**	75	1·25
554	3p. "Empress of Australia" (liner)	1·00	1·25
555	5p. "Anatolia" (freighter)	1·00	1·25
556	8p. "Viceroy of India" (liner)	1·10	1·50
557	10p. "Rangitata" (transport)	1·10	1·50
558	15p. "Caronia" (liner)	1·40	1·50
559	20p. "Rotterdam" (liner)	1·50	1·50
560	25p. "Leonardo da Vinci" (liner)	1·50	1·50
561	35p. "Vistafjord" (liner)	1·75	1·75
562	£1 "World Discoverer" (liner)	4·00	4·50
563	£2 "Astor" (liner)	7·00	8·00
564	£5 "St. Helena II" (mail ship)	12·00	14·00

1994. Ships of the Royal Navy (3rd series). As T **138**. Multicoloured.

565	10p. H.M.S. "Nigeria" (cruiser), 1948	1·25	1·50
566	25p. H.M.S. "Phoebe" (cruiser), 1949	2·25	2·50
567	35p. H.M.S. "Liverpool" (cruiser), 1949	2·25	2·50
568	50p. H.M.S. "Magpie" (frigate), 1955	3·00	3·25

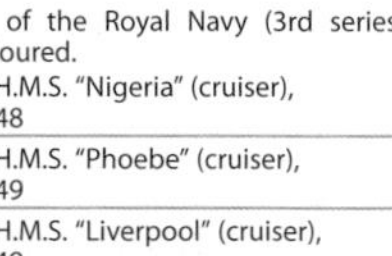

149 Blue Shark

1994. Sharks. Multicoloured.

569	10p. Type **149**	90	1·25
570	45p. Seven-gilled shark	2·50	3·25
571	65p. Short-finned mako	3·25	4·00

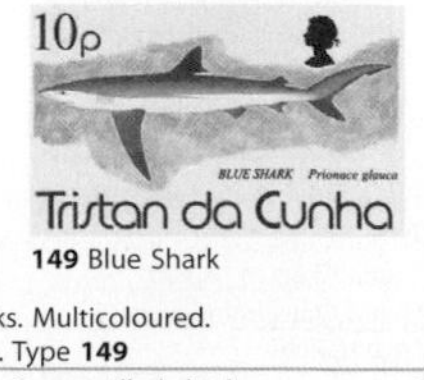

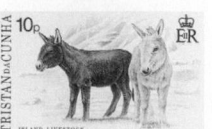

150 Pair of Donkeys

1994. Island Livestock (1st series). Multicoloured.

572	10p. Type **150**	1·10	1·25
573	20p. Cattle	1·40	1·50
574	35p. Ducks and geese	2·50	3·00
575	60p. Girl bottle-feeding lamb	3·25	4·00

See also Nos. 620/3.

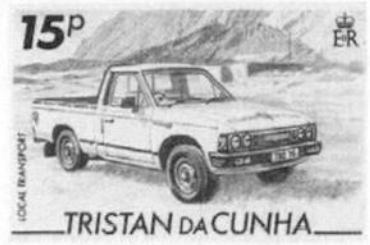

151 Pick-up Truck

1995. Local Transport. Multicoloured.

576	15p. Type **151**	1·10	1·25
577	20p. Sherpa van	1·50	1·50
578	45p. Scooter and Yamaha motorcycle	2·50	3·00
579	60p. Administrator's Land Rover	3·00	3·75

1995. 50th Anniv of End of Second World War. As T **182a** of St. Helena. Multicoloured.

580	15p. Sailors training on Lewis guns	1·75	1·50
581	20p. Tristan Defence Volunteers	1·75	1·60
582	45p. Wireless and meteorological station	2·75	2·75
583	60p. H.M.S. "Birmingham" (cruiser)	4·50	4·50
MS584	75×85 mm. £1 Reverse of 1939–45 War Medal (vert)	2·00	2·75

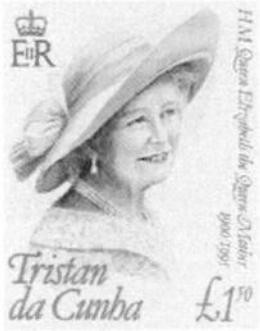

152 Queen Elizabeth the Queen Mother

1995. 95th Birthday of Queen Elizabeth the Queen Mother. Sheet 75×103 mm.

MS585	**152** £1.50 multicoloured	7·00	7·50

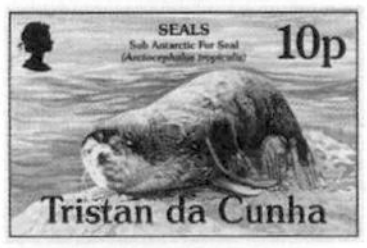

153 Sub-Antarctic Fur Seal on Rock

1995. Seals. Multicoloured.

586	10p. Type **153**	90	1·25
587	35p. Sub-Antarctic fur seals with pups	2·00	2·50
588	45p. Southern elephant seal asleep with pups	2·50	3·00
589	50p. Southern elephant seals in water	2·50	3·00

1996. 50th Anniv of United Nations. As T **201a** of St. Helena. Multicoloured.

590	20p. Bedford 4-ton lorry	1·75	1·75
591	30p. Saxon armoured personnel carrier	2·00	2·00
592	45p. Mi26 heavy lift helicopter	3·50	3·50
593	50p. R.F.A. "Sir Tristram" (landing ship)	3·50	3·50

1996. 70th Birthday of Queen Elizabeth II. As T **55** of Tokelau, each incorporating a different photograph of the Queen.

594	15p. Tristan from the sea	70	1·10
595	20p. Traditional cottage	80	1·40
596	45p. The Residency	1·75	2·75
597	60p. The Queen and Prince Philip	2·25	3·25

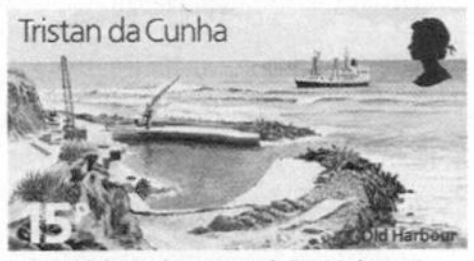

154 Old Harbour and *St. Helena I* (mail ship)

1996. Construction of New Harbour. Multicoloured.

598	15p. Type **154**	2·00	2·00
599	20p. Excavator and dump truck (44×27 mm)	2·00	2·00
600	45p. Construction of new mole (44×27 mm)	3·00	3·00
601	60p. New harbour and "St. Helena II" (mail ship)	4·00	4·50

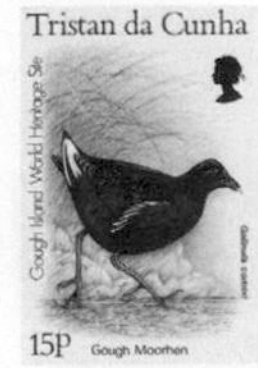

155 Gough Island coot ("Gough Island Moorhen")

1996. Declaration of Gough Island as World Heritage Site. Birds. Multicoloured.

602	15p. Type **155**	1·25	1·40
603	20p. Wandering albatross	1·40	1·50
604	45p. Sooty albatross	2·50	2·75
605	60p. Gough Island finch ("Gough Bunting")	3·35	3·50

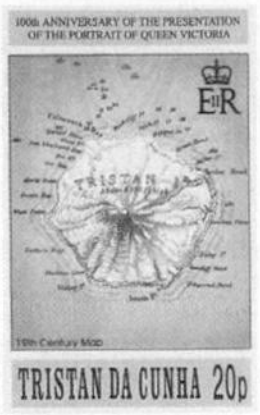

156 19th-century Map

1996. Centenary of the Presentation of the Queen Victoria Portrait to Tristan. Multicoloured.

606	20p. Type **156**	1·25	1·25
607	30p. H.M.S. "Magpie" (gunboat)	1·75	2·00
608	45p. Governor Peter Green	1·90	2·25
609	50p. "Queen Victoria" (H. von Angeli) (detail)	2·00	2·50

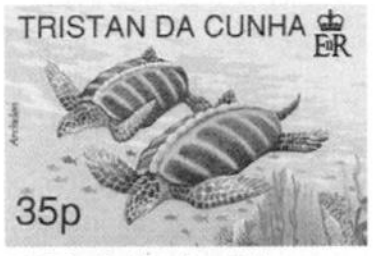

157 Archelon (turtle)

1997. Atlantic Marine Fauna (1st series). Cretaceous Period. Sheet 92×100 mm, containing T **157** and similar horiz designs. Multicoloured.

MS610	35p. Type **157**; 35p. Trinacromerum; 35p. Platecarpus; 35p. Clidastes	5·00	5·50

See also No. **MS**638.

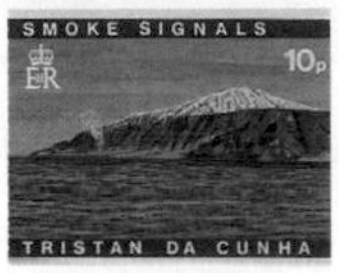

158 Smoke Signals

1997. Visual Communications. Multicoloured.

611	10p. Type **158**	40	75
612	10p. H.M.S. "Eurydice" (frigate)	40	75
613	15p. H.M.S. "Challenger" (survey ship)	60	1·00
614	15p. Flag hoists	60	1·00
615	20p. Semaphore	70	1·00
616	20p. H.M.S. "Carlisle" (cruiser)	70	1·00
617	35p. Aldis lamp	80	1·10
618	35p. H.M.S. "Cilicia" (transport)	80	1·10

Nos. 611/12, 613/14, 615/16 and 617/18 respectively were printed together, *se-tenant*, forming composite designs.

1997. Return of Hong Kong to China. Sheet 130×90 mm, containing designs as No. 605, but with "1997" imprint date.

MS619	60p. Gough Island finch ("Gough Bunting")	1·75	3·00

1997. Island Livestock (2nd series). As T **192** of St. Helena. Multicoloured.

620	20p. Chickens	1·00	1·10
621	30p. Bull	1·40	1·60
622	45p. Sheep	1·90	2·50
623	50p. Collie dogs	3·75	3·75

1997. Golden Wedding of Queen Elizabeth and Prince Philip. As T **192a** of St. Helena. Multicoloured.

624	15p. Queen Elizabeth	1·25	3·75
625	15p. Prince Philip playing polo	1·25	1·25
626	20p. Queen Elizabeth with horse	1·25	1·25
627	20p. Prince Philip	1·25	1·25
628	45p. Queen Elizabeth with Prince Philip in R.A.F. uniform	1·90	2·00
629	45p. Princess Anne on horseback	1·90	2·00
MS630	110×70 mm. £1.50, Queen Elizabeth and Prince Philip in landau (horiz)	10·00	11·00

Nos. 624/5, 626/7 and 628/9 respectively were printed together, *se-tenant*, with the backgrounds forming composite designs.

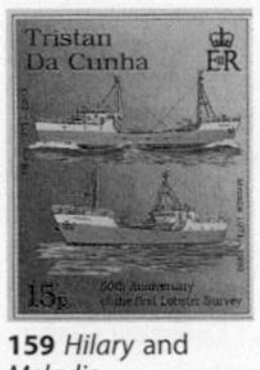

159 *Hilary* and *Melodie*

1998. 50th Anniv of First Lobster Survey. Lobster Trawlers. Multicoloured.

631	15p. Type **159**	60	80
632	20p. "Tristania II" and "Hekla"	70	90
633	30p. "Pequena" and "Frances Repetto"	90	1·25
634	45p. "Tristania" and "Gillian Gaggins"	1·50	1·75
635	50p. "Kelso" and "Edinburgh"	1·50	2·00
MS636	100×80 mm. £1.20, Revd. C. P. Lawrence and lobster	4·75	7·00

1998. Diana, Princess of Wales Commemoration. Sheet 145×70 mm, containing vert designs as T **149** of St. Helena. Multicoloured.

MS637	35p. Wearing pink jacket, 1993; 35p. Wearing white jacket, 1990; 35p. Laughing, in striped dress, 1991; 35p. Wearing blue and white dress, 1989 (sold at £1.40 + 20p. charity premium)	2·00	3·25

1998. Atlantic Marine Fauna (2nd series). Miocene Epoch. Sheet 92×100 mm, containing horiz designs as T **157**. Multicoloured.

MS638	45p. Carcharodon (shark); 45p. Orycterocetus (sperm whale); 45p. Eurhinodelphis (dolphin); 45p. Hexanchus (shark) and Myliobatis (ray)	14·00	15·00

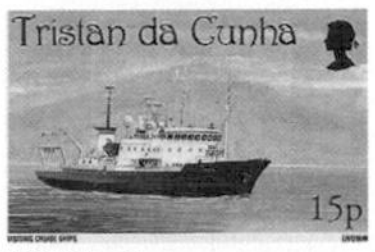

160 *Livonia*

1998. Cruise Ships. Multicoloured.

639	15p. Type **160**	2·00	2·25
640	20p. "Professor Molchanov"	2·25	2·50
641	45p. "Explorer"	2·75	3·25
642	60p. "Hanseatic"	3·00	3·50

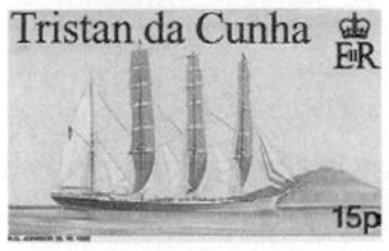

161 *H. G. Johnson* (barque)

1998. Maritime Heritage (1st series). Multicoloured.

643	15p. Type **161**	[illegible]	[illegible]
644	35p. "Theodore" (full-rigged ship)	2·75	3·00
645	45p. "Hesperides" (full-rigged ship)	3·25	3·50
646	50p. "Bessfield" (barque)	3·25	3·50

1999. Maritime Heritage (2nd series). As T **161**. Multicoloured.

647	20p. "Derwent" (full-rigged ship)	2·00	2·25
648	30p. "Strathgryfe" (full-rigged ship)	2·75	3·00
649	50p. "Celestial Empire" (full-rigged ship)	3·25	3·50
650	60p. "Lamorna" (full-rigged ship)	3·25	3·50

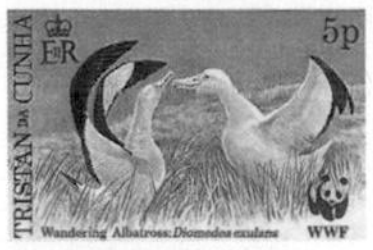

162 Wandering Albatross Courtship Dance

1999. Endangered Species. Wandering Albatross. Multicoloured.

651	5p. Type **162**	75	1·00
652	8p. Adult and chick	75	1·00
653	12p. Adult with spread wings	75	1·00
654	15p. Two adults in flight	75	1·00

1999. Royal Wedding. As T **197a** of St. Helena. Multicoloured.

655	45p. Photographs of Prince Edward and Miss Sophie Rhys-Jones	1·75	1·25
656	£1.20 Engagement photograph	3·75	4·50

1999. "Queen Elizabeth the Queen Mother's Century". As T **199** of St. Helena. Multicoloured (except £1.50).

657	20p. With King George VI and Princess Elizabeth, 1944	80	1·00
658	30p. King George and Queen Elizabeth at Balmoral, 1951	1·00	1·25
659	50p. Family group outside Clarence House, 1994	1·50	2·00
660	60p. Inspecting The Black Watch parade	2·00	2·25
MS661	145×70 mm. £1.50, Lady Elizabeth Bowes-Lyon, 1905, and Hurricane squadron, Battle of Britain, 1940 (black)	4·50	6·50

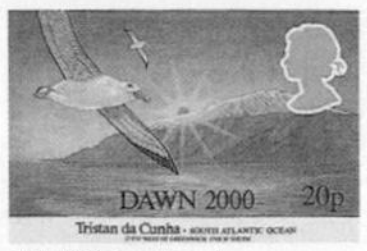

163 Winter Sunrise

2000. New Millennium. Multicoloured.

662	20p. Type **163**	2·75	2·00
663	30p. Spring sunrise	3·25	2·50
664	50p. Summer sunrise	4·00	3·50
665	60p. Autumn sunrise	4·50	4·00

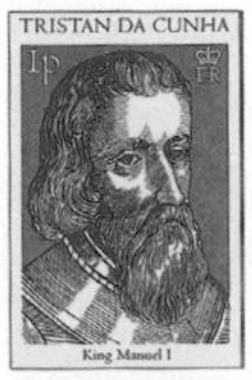

164 King Manuel I of Portugal

2000. Monarchs connected with Tristan da Cunha. Multicoloured (except 1p. and 5p.).

666	1p. Type **164** (black, stone and brown)	60	1·25
667	3p. Frederick Henry, Prince of Orange	80	1·25
668	5p. Empress Maria Theresa of Austria (green, stone and black)	1·00	1·25
669	8p. King George III	1·50	1·50
670	10p. King George IV	1·50	1·50
671	15p. King William IV	1·75	1·75
672	20p. Queen Victoria	1·75	1·75
673	25p. King Edward VII	1·75	1·75
674	35p. King George V	2·50	2·50
675	£1 King Edward VIII	5·50	6·00
676	£2 King George VI	9·00	9·50
677	£5 Queen Elizabeth II	15·00	17·00

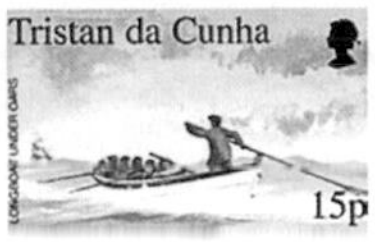

165 Longboat under Oars

2000. "The Stamp Show 2000" International Stamp Exhibition. Visit of Cutty Sark (clipper), 1876 Multicoloured.

678	15p. Type **165**	1·50	1·50
679	45p. Longboat under sail	2·50	3·75
680	50p. *Cutty Sark* at sea	5·50	5·50
681	60p. *Cutty Sark* on display at Greenwich	6·00	6·00
MS682	102×65 mm. £1.50, "Cutty Sark" off Tristan da Cunha	14·00	14·00

2000. 18th Birthday of Prince William. As T **48** of South Georgia and South Sandwich Islands. Multicoloured.

683	45p. Prince Charles with sons, 1985	2·00	2·25
684	45p. Prince William in 1995	2·00	2·25
685	45p. Prince William in 1999 (horiz)	2·00	2·25
686	45p. Prince William in overcoat and scarf (horiz)	2·00	2·25
MS687	175×95 mm. 45p. With Shetland pony, 1995 (horiz) and Nos. 683/6.	11·00	11·00

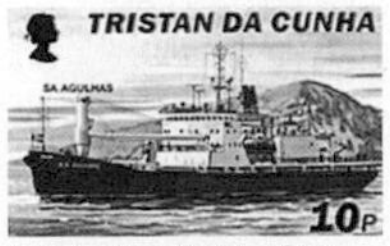

166 *Agulhas* (South African Antarctic research ship)

2000. Helicopters and Ships. Multicoloured.

688	10p. Type **166**	1·40	1·75
689	10p. S.A. 330J Puma helicopter, 1999	1·40	1·75
690	15p. H.M.S. *London* (destroyer)	1·50	1·75
691	15p. Westland Wessex HAS1 helicopter, 1964	1·50	1·75
692	20p. H.M.S. *Endurance II* (ice patrol ship)	1·50	1·75
693	20p. Westland Lynx HAS3 helicopter, 1996	1·50	1·75
694	50p. U.S.S. *Spiegel Grove* (landing ship)	1·75	2·00
695	50p. Sikorsky UH-19F helicopter, 1963	1·75	2·00

Nos. 688/9, 690/1, 692/3 and 694/5 were each printed together, *se-tenant*, with the backgrounds forming composite designs.

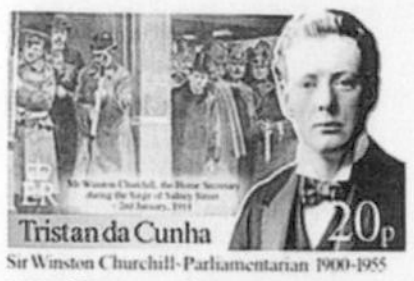

167 Winston Churchill as Home Secretary and Siege of Sidney Street, 1911

2000. Centenary of Sir Winston Churchill's Election to Parliament. Multicoloured.

696	20p. Type **167**	2·50	1·75
697	30p. As Chancellor of the Exchequer, 1925, and with Pres. Roosevelt at signing of Atlantic Treaty, 1941	2·75	2·50
698	50p. Showing Victory sign and making V.E. Day broadcast, 1945	3·50	3·25
699	60p. In retirement and greeting Queen Elizabeth II at 10 Downing Street, 1955	3·50	3·50

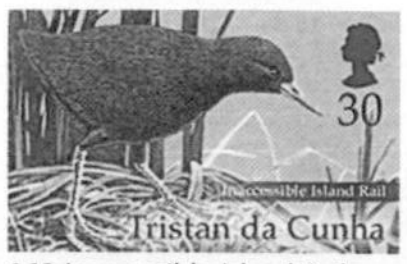

168 Inaccessible Island Rail

2001. "HONG KONG 2001" Stamp Exhibition. Sheet 150×90 mm, containing T **168** and similar horiz design showing island bird. Multicoloured.

MS700	30p. Type **168**; 45p. Black-faced spoonbill	7·50	8·50

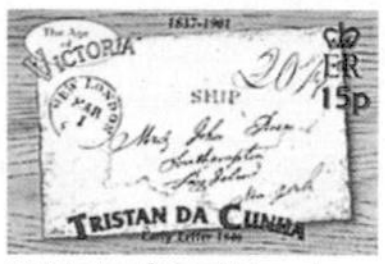

169 Letter from Tristan da Cunha, 1846

2001. Death Centenary of Queen Victoria. Multicoloured.

701	15p. Type **169**	95	95
702	20p. Prince Alfred, Duke of Edinburgh (vert)	1·10	1·10
703	30p. H.M.S. *Galatea* (screw frigate)	1·60	1·75
704	35p. Queen Victoria (vert)	1·60	1·75
705	50p. Charles Dickens (vert)	2·00	2·25
706	60p. Longboats re-supplying warship	2·00	2·25
MS707	104×80 mm. £1.50, Queen Victoria outside St. Paul's during Diamond Jubilee celebrations	4·50	6·50

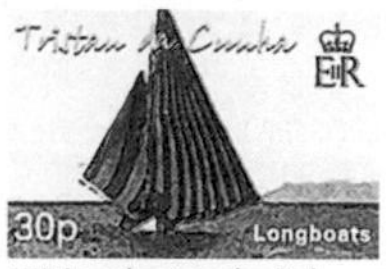

170 Longboat under Sail

2001. Tristan Longboats. Multicoloured.

708	30p. Type **170**	1·75	1·75
709	30p. Two longboats at sea (face value at bottom right)	1·75	1·75
710	30p. Two longboats at sea (face value at bottom left)	1·75	1·75
711	30p. Longboat with multicoloured mainsail near island	1·75	1·75
712	30p. Longboat with blue and white striped sail near island	1·75	1·75
713	30p. Longboat with white mainsail near island	1·75	1·75
714	30p. Longboat with blue mainsail near island	1·75	1·75
715	30p. Longboat in harbour	1·75	1·75

2001. Hurricane Relief. Nos. 688/95 optd **HURRICANE RELIEF 2001**. Multicoloured.

716	10p. Type **166**	2·00	2·25
717	10p. S.A. 330J Puma helicopter, 1999	2·00	2·25
718	15p. H.M.S. *London* (destroyer)	2·50	2·75
719	15p. Westland Wessex HAS1 helicopter, 1964	2·50	2·75
720	20p. H.M.S. *Endurance II* (ice patrol ship)	2·50	2·75
721	20p. Westland Lynx HAS3 helicopter, 1996	2·50	2·75
722	50p. U.S.S. *Spiegel Grove* (landing ship)	3·25	3·50
723	50p. Sikorsky UH-19F helicopter, 1963	3·25	3·50

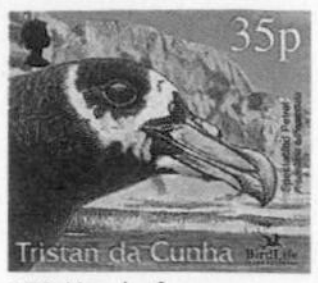

172 Head of White-chinned Petrel ("Spectacled Petrel")

2001. Birdlife World Bird Festival (1st series). White-chinned Petrel. Sheet 175×80 mm, containing T **172** and similar multicoloured designs.

MS724	35p. Type **172**; 35p. Petrel in front of cliffs (*vert*); 35p. Petrel, descending to sea (*vert*); 35p. Petrel flying; 35p. Petrel chick	15·00	16·00

See also Nos. 770/**MS**774.

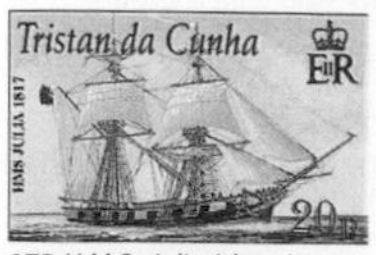

173 H.M.S. *Julia* (sloop), 1817

2001. Royal Navy Connections with Tristan da Cunha. Multicoloured.

725	20p. Type **173**	2·25	2·50
726	20p. H.M.S. *Penguin* (sloop), 1815	2·25	2·50
727	35p. H.M.S. *Beagle* (screw sloop), 1901	3·00	3·25
728	35p. H.M.S. *Puma* (frigate), 1962	3·00	3·25
729	60p. H.M.S. *Monmouth* (frigate), 1997	4·50	5·00
730	60p. H.M.S. *Somerset* (frigate), 1999	4·50	5·00

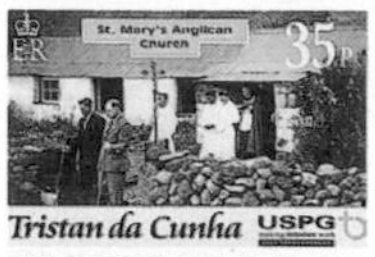

174 Procession at St. Mary's Anglican Church

2001. 150th Anniv of Arrival of First U.S.P.G. Missionary on Tristan da Cunha. Multicoloured (except No. 731).

731	35p. Type **174** (brown, black and yellow)	2·75	3·00
732	35p. St. Joseph's Catholic Church	2·75	3·00
733	60p. Altar, St. Mary's Church (vert)	5·00	5·50
734	60p. Stained glass, St. Joseph's Church (vert)	5·00	5·50

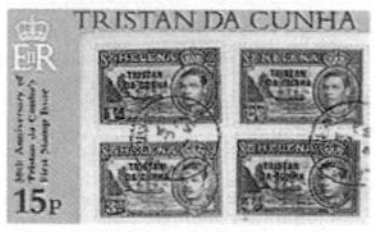

175 1952 Overprints on St. Helena 3d., 4d., 1s. and 2s.6d.

2002. 50th Anniv of First Stamp Issue. Multicoloured (except 60p.).

735	15p. Type **175**	2·50	1·75
736	20p. 1952 6d., 8d., 5s. and 10s. overprinted stamps	2·50	1·75
737	50p. 1952 ½d., 1d., 1½d. and 2d. overprinted stamps	5·50	6·00
738	60p. Buying stamps, 1952 (black, sepia and bistre)	6·00	6·50
MS739	146×90 mm. 45p. × 4 As Nos. 735/8, but each inscr "Tristan da Cunha" in mock manuscript	9·50	11·00

2002. Golden Jubilee. As T **211** of St. Helena.

740	15p. black, red and gold	1·25	1·00
741	30p. multicoloured	1·90	1·75
742	45p. multicoloured	2·50	2·75
743	50p. multicoloured	2·50	2·75
MS744	162×95 mm. Nos. 740/3 and 60p. multicoloured	8·50	9·00

DESIGNS—HORIZ: 15p. Princess Elizabeth, 1947; 30p. Queen Elizabeth in evening dress, Buckingham Palace, 1991; 45p. Queen Elizabeth in multicoloured turban; 50p. Queen Elizabeth at Newmarket, 1997. VERT: (38×51 mm)—50p. Queen Elizabeth after Annigoni.

DESIGNS as Nos. 740/3 in No. **MS**744 omit the gold frame around each stamp and the "Golden Jubilee 1952-2002" inscription.

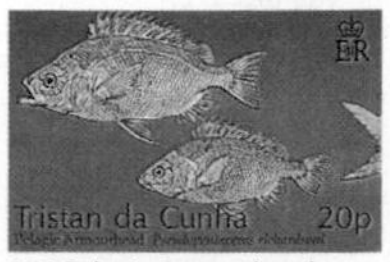

176 Pelagic Armourhead (fish)

2002. Extension of Fishing Industry to New Species. Multicoloured.

745	20p. Type **176**	1·50	1·25
746	35p. Yellowtail	2·25	2·25
747	50p. Splendid alfonsino	3·00	3·25
MS748	140×75 mm. 60p. *San Liberatore* (stern trawler) and Nos. 745/7	5·00	6·00

2002. Queen Elizabeth the Queen Mother Commemoration. As T **215** of St. Helena.

749	20p. black, gold and purple	1·50	70
750	£1.50 multicoloured	5·50	6·50
MS751	145×70 mm. 75p. black and gold; 75p. multicoloured	7·50	8·50

DESIGNS: 20p. Queen Elizabeth visiting a shipyard, 1942; 75p. black and gold (No. **MS**751) Duchess of York with Princess Margaret, 1930; 75p. multicoloured (No. **MS**751) Queen Mother at Cheltenham Races; £1.50, Queen Mother on her birthday, 1995.

Designs in No. **MS**751 omit the "1900–2002" inscription and the coloured frame.

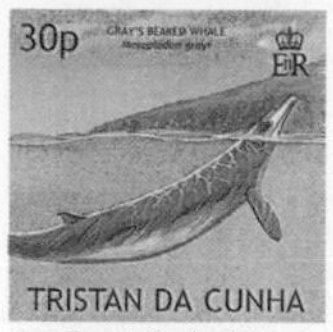

177 Gray's Beaked Whale

2002. Marine Mammals. Multicoloured.

752	30p. Type **177**	3·50	3·50
753	30p. Dusky dolphin	3·50	3·50
754	30p. False killer whale	3·50	3·50
755	30p. Long-finned pilot whale	3·50	3·50
756	30p. Sperm whale	3·50	3·50
757	30p. Shepherd's beaked whale	3·50	3·50
MS758	81×92 mm. £2 Humpback whale	16·00	17·00

Nos. 752/7 were printed together, *se-tenant*, forming a composite design.

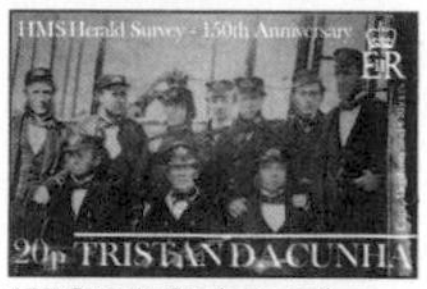

178 Captain Denham and Officers of H.M.S. *Herald* (survey ship)

2002. 150th Anniv of Survey by H.M.S. Herald. Multicoloured (except 20p.).

759	20p. Type **178** (ochre and agate)	1·50	1·10
760	35p. H.M.S. *Herald* in Bay of Biscay	2·00	2·00
761	50p. H.M.S. *Herald* off Tristan da Cunha, 1852	2·50	2·50
762	60p. H.M.S. *Herald* and H.M.S. *Torch* (paddle steamer) at sunset	2·75	3·25

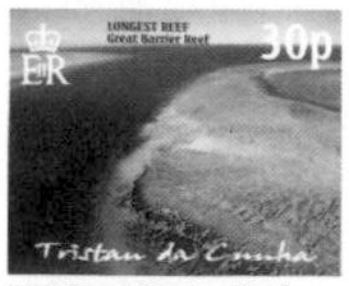

179 Great Barrier Reef, Australia (longest reef)

2003. World Geographical Records. Multicoloured.

763	30p. Type **179**	1·40	1·75
764	30p. Greenland (biggest island)	1·40	1·75
765	30p. Sahara (biggest desert)	1·40	1·75
766	30p. River Amazon (longest river)	1·40	1·75
767	30p. Mt Everest (highest mountain)	1·40	1·75
768	30p. Edinburgh, Tristan da Cunha (most remote inhabited island)	1·40	1·75
MS769	90×68 mm £2 Closer view of Edinburgh	8·50	10·00

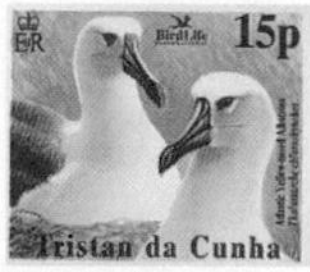

180 Atlantic Yellow-nosed Albatross (pair)

2003. BirdLife International (2nd series). Atlantic Yellow-nosed Albatross. Multicoloured.

770	15p. Type **180**	1·40	1·25
771	30p. Albatross on nest (vert)	2·25	2·25
772	45p. Albatross in flight (vert)	2·75	2·75
773	50p. Two albatrosses in flight	2·75	3·00
MS774	175×80 mm. Nos. 770/3 and £1 Pair in flight	8·50	9·50

2003. 50th Anniv of Coronation. As T **210** of St. Helena. Multicoloured.

775	20p. Queen Elizabeth II with Royal family	70	70
776	£1.50 Archbishop and bishops paying homage to Queen	4·25	4·50
MS777	95×115 mm. 75p. As 20p.; 75p. As £1.50	4·25	5·00

2003. As T **220** of St. Helena.

778	£2.80 black, mauve and cream	6·00	6·50

2003. 21st Birthday of Prince William of Wales. As T **55** of South Georgia and South Sandwich Islands. Multicoloured.

779	50p. Prince William at Sighthill Community Education Centre, 2001 and playing polo, 2002	2·00	2·00
780	50p. In Scotland, 2001 and on Raleigh International Expedition, 2000	2·00	2·00

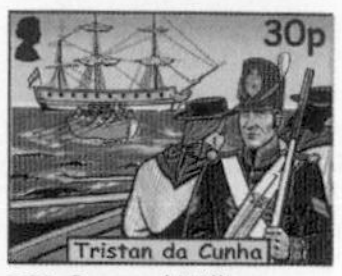

181 Corporal William Glass arriving on HMS *Falmouth* (1816)

2003. 150th Death Anniv of William Glass (founding settler of Tristan). Multicoloured.

781	30p. Type **181**	1·75	1·75
782	30p. Corporal Glass with other Royal Artillerymen	1·75	1·75
783	30p. William Glass and family remaining on Tristan (1817)	1·75	1·75
784	30p. William Glass and family	1·75	1·75
785	30p. Governor William Glass conducting marriage of eldest daughter Mary (1833)	1·75	1·75
786	30p. Governor William Glass as old man (1853)	1·75	1·75

Nos. 781/6 were printed together, *se-tenant*, with a small se-tenant label describing the stamp design at the foot of each stamp.

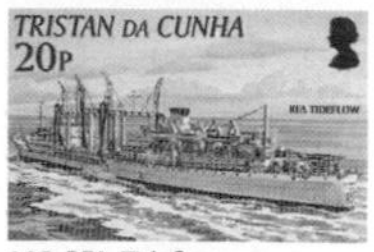

182 RFA *Tideflow*

2003. Royal Navy Connections with Tristan da Cunha (2nd series). Multicoloured.

787	20p. Type **182**	1·75	2·00
788	20p. RFA *Tidespring* (tanker)	1·75	2·00
789	35p. RFA *Gold Rover* (tanker)	2·50	2·75
790	35p. RFA *Diligence* (repair ship)	2·50	2·75
791	60p. RFA *Wave Chief*	4·00	4·50
792	60p. Royal Yacht *Britannia*	4·00	4·50

Nos. 791/2 have no white margins and form a composite background design.

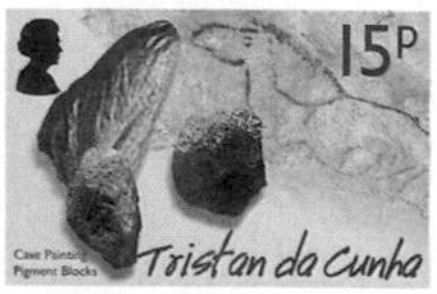

183 Pigment Blocks and Cave Painting

2004. History of Writing. Multicoloured.

793	15p. Type **183**	95	95
794	20p. Clay tablet	1·10	1·10
795	35p. Egyptian writing palette	1·90	2·00
796	45p. Goose quill pen	2·00	2·25
797	50p. Fountain pen	2·00	2·25
798	60p. Ballpoint pen	2·50	2·75
MS799	100×90 mm. £1.50 Word processing	6·50	7·50

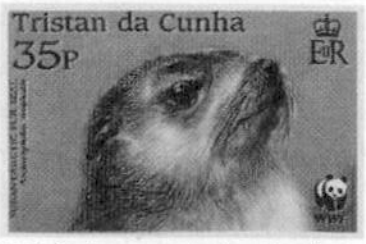

184 Subantarctic Fur Seal

2004. Endangered Species. Subantarctic Fur Seal. Multicoloured.

800	35p. Type **184**	1·40	1·60
801	35p. Seal swimming	1·40	1·60
802	35p. Two seals	1·40	1·60
803	35p. Seal on rocks	1·40	1·60

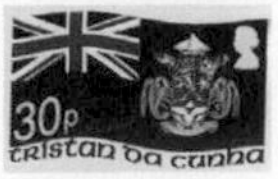

185 Flag

2004. New Island Flag. Self-adhesive.

804	**185** 30p. multicoloured	1·00	1·00

2004. Merchant Ships. As T **227** of St. Helena. Multicoloured.

805	20p. RMS *Dunnottar Castle*	1·75	1·90
806	20p. RMS *Caronia*	1·75	1·90
807	35p. MV *Edinburgh*	2·50	2·75
808	35p. SA *Agulhas*	2·50	2·75
809	60p. MV *Hanseatic*	4·00	4·50
810	60p. MV *Explorer*	4·00	4·50

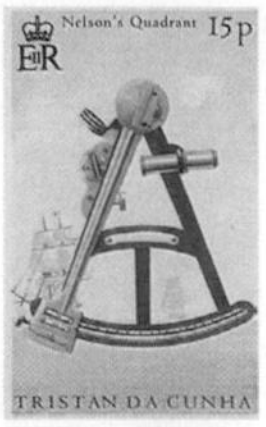

186 Nelson's Quadrant

2005. Bicentenary of the Battle of Trafalgar. Multicoloured.

811	15p. Type **186**	1·60	1·75
812	20p. HMS *Royal Sovereign* breaks the line (horiz)	2·25	2·50
813	25p. Thomas Swain helping wounded Lord Nelson (horiz)	2·25	2·50
814	35p. HMS *Victory* breaks the line (horiz)	3·25	3·50
815	50p. Lord Nelson	3·50	3·75
816	60p. HMS *Victory*	4·25	4·50
MS817	120×79 mm. 75p. Captain Sir Thomas Hardy; 75p. HMS *Victory* firing signal shot	11·00	12·00

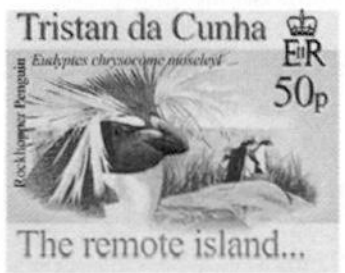

187 Rockhopper Penguins

2005. Islands (1st series). Tristan da Cunha. Multicoloured.

818	50p. Type **187**	2·00	2·25
819	50p. Southern elephant seals	2·00	2·25
820	50p. Tristan rock lobster	2·00	2·25
821	50p. Crowberry	2·00	2·25
822	50p. Island settlement and volcano	2·00	2·25

See also Nos. 823/7, 828/32, 850/4, 855/9, 866/70 and **MS**871 .

2005. Islands (2nd series). Gough Island. As T **187**. Multicoloured.

823	50p. Gough moorhen	2·00	2·25
824	50p. Subantarctic fur seal	2·00	2·25
825	50p. Bluefish	2·00	2·25
826	50p. Gough tree fern	2·00	2·25
827	50p. South African weather station	2·00	2·25

2005. Islands (3rd issue). Inaccessible Island. As T **187**. Multicoloured.

828	50p. Inaccessible Island rail	2·00	2·25
829	50p. Dusky dolphin	2·00	2·25
830	50p. Soldierfish	2·00	2·25
831	50p. Pepper tree	2·00	2·25
832	50p. Waterfall	2·00	2·25

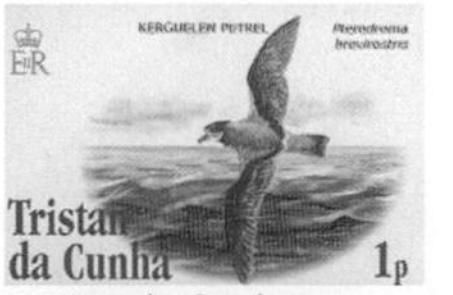

188 Kerguelen Petrel

2005. Birds. Multicoloured.

833	1p. Type **188**	45	60
834	3p. Sooty albatross	60	70
835	5p. Antarctic tern	75	80
836	8p. Nightingale finch ("Tristan Bunting")	1·00	1·25
837	10p. Pintado ("Cape") petrel	1·00	1·25
838	15p. Gough Island coot ("Tristan Moorhen")	1·50	1·25
839	20p. Giant petrel ("Fulmar")	1·75	1·25
840	25p. Brown skua	1·75	1·40
841	35p. Great-winged petrel	2·00	1·50
842	£1 Broad-billed prion	4·75	5·00
843	£2 Soft-plumaged petrel	8·50	9·50
844	£5 Rockhopper penguin	14·00	17·00

2005. Pope John Paul II Commemoration. As T **231** of St Helena.

845	50p multicoloured	2·75	3·00

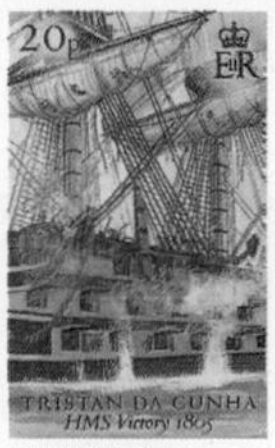

189 HMS *Victory*

2005. Bicentenary of the Battle of Trafalgar (2nd issue). Multicoloured.

846	20p. Type **189**	3·25	2·00
847	70p. Ships engaged in battle (horiz)	5·50	6·00
848	£1 Admiral Lord Nelson	7·00	7·50

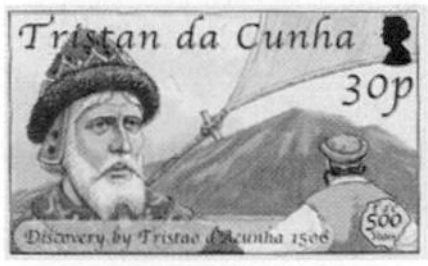

190 Portuguese Admiral Tristao d'Acunha and First Sighting of Tristan da Cunha

2006. 500th Anniv of Discovery of Tristan da Cunha (1st issue). Multicoloured.

MS849	Two sheets, each 160×100 mm. (a) 30p. Type **190**; 30p. French frigate *L'heure du Berger* (first survey), 1767; 30p. Jonathan Lambert and establishment of trading station, 1810; 50p. William Glass and elephant seal, 1816; 50p. Crew rowing away from wreck of *Emily*, 1836; 80p. *Duke of Gloucester*, 1824. (b) 30p. Thomas Swain as old man and with wounded Nelson at Battle of Trafalgar; 30p. HMS *Challenger*, 1873; 30p. Arrival of Reverend Dodgson, 1881; 50p. Crew of wrecked *Italia* coming ashore, 1892; 50p. HMS *Milford*, 1938; 80p. Outline map (Norwegian expedition, 1937/8)	20·00	22·00

See also No. **MS**865.

2006. Islands (4th issue). Nightingale Island. As T **187**. Multicoloured.

850	50p. Tristan thrush	2·00	2·25
851	50p. Southern right whales	2·00	2·25
852	50p. Fivefinger fish	2·00	2·25
853	50p. Tussock grass	2·00	2·25
854	50p. Nightingale Island	2·00	2·25

2006. Islands (5th issue). Middle Island. As T **187**. Multicoloured.

855	50p. Broad-billed prion	2·00	2·25
856	50p. False killer whale	2·00	2·25
857	50p. Wreckfish	2·00	2·25
858	50p. *Blechnum tabulare* (fern)	2·00	2·25
859	50p. Middle Island	2·00	2·25

2006. 80th Birthday of Queen Elizabeth II. As T **237** of St. Helena. Multicoloured.

860	60p. Princess Elizabeth as young girl	3·00	3·25
861	60p. Queen Elizabeth II wearing black hat, c. 1955	3·00	3·25
862	60p. Wearing red hat	3·00	3·25
863	60p. Recent photograph of Queen Elizabeth II	3·00	3·25
MS864	144×75 mm. 50p. As No. 861; 50p. As No. 862	5·50	6·00

Stamps from No. **MS**864 do not have white borders.

2006. 500th Anniv of Discovery of Tristan da Cunha (2nd issue). As T **190**. Multicoloured.

MS865	Two sheets, each 160×100 mm. (a) 30p. Tristan Defence Volunteers in training, World War II; 30p. HMS Atlantic Isle (radio and weather station), 1944; 30p. 1946 1d. "Potato Stamp"; 50p. First Tristan da Cunha stamp, 1952 (overprinted 3d. St. Helena stamp); 50p. Volcano eruption and evacuation, 1961; 80p. Gough Island Scientific Expedition, 1955. (b) 30p. Royal Society Expedition, 1962; 30p. Resettlement, 1963; 30p. Denstone Expedition to Inaccessible Island, 1982; 50p. RMS *St. Helena*, 1992; 50p. New Coat of Arms, 2002; 80p. Hurricane disaster, 2001	25·00	27·00

2006. Islands (6th issue). Stoltenhoff Island. As T **187**. Multicoloured.

866	50p. Brown skua	2·00	2·50
867	50p. Shepherd's beaked whales	2·00	2·50
868	50p. Snoek (fish)	2·00	2·50
869	50p. Sea bind weed	2·00	2·50
870	50p. Stoltenhoff Island	2·00	2·50

2007. Islands (7th series). Sheet 160×75 mm containing horiz designs as T **187**. Multicoloured.

MS871	50p.×6 Map and flag of Tristan da Cunha; Wandering albatross and Inaccessible Island; Tail of humpback whale and Nightingale Island; Traditional longboats and Middle Island; Mackerel and Stoltenhoff Island; Sub-Antarctic fur seal and Gough Island	19·00	21·00

The stamps within **MS**871 all show an outline map of the island depicted.

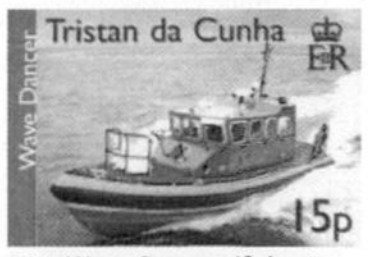

191 *Wave Dancer* (fisheries patrol boat)

2007. Local Vehicles. Multicoloured.

872	15p. Type **191**	1·00	1·00
873	20p. Ambulance	1·75	1·25
874	30p. Inshore rescue craft	2·00	1·50
875	45p. Police Land Rover	3·50	3·25
876	50p. Fire engine	3·50	3·25
877	85p. Administrator's Land Rover	4·50	5·00

2007. Diamond Wedding of Queen Elizabeth II and Duke of Edinburgh. As T **242** of St. Helena. Multicoloured.

878	50p. Princess Elizabeth and Duke of Edinburgh, c. 1947	2·25	2·50
879	50p. Princess Elizabeth looking out of carriage window on wedding day	2·25	2·50
880	50p. Princess Elizabeth on wedding day, waving from balcony	2·25	2·50
881	50p. Young Queen Elizabeth and Duke of Edinburgh in evening dress	2·25	2·50
MS882	125×85 mm. £2 Wedding photograph of Princess Elizabeth (42×56 mm)	8·00	8·50

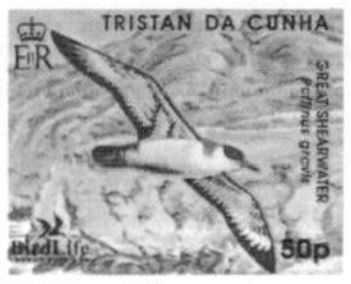

192 Great Shearwater

2007. Great Shearwater (*Puffinus gravis*). Sheet 170×85 mm containing T **192** and similar horiz designs. Multicoloured.

MS883	50p.×6 Type **192**; In flight, seen from above; On nest, head turned to left; In flight, wings raised; In close-up on nest, facing left; Chick	17·00	18·00

The stamps within **MS**883 form a composite design showing seabirds and headland.

2007. Centenary of Scouting. As T **244** of St. Helena. Multicoloured.

884	15p. Scout James Marr and his log of 1921–2 Antarctic expedition *Into the FrozenSouth*	1·50	1·00
885	20p. *Quest* frozen into Antarctic ice	1·75	1·25
886	£1.25 Scout Marr presenting Tristan Da Cunha Troop flag to Patrol Leader Donald Glass, May 1922	5·00	5·50
887	£1.40 Children of Tristan da Cunha outside schoolhouse, May 1922	5·00	5·50
MS888	90×65 mm. £1.50 Scout Marr and ship's cat 'Questie' (vert); £1.50 Lord Baden-Powell (150th birth anniv) (vert)	12·00	13·00

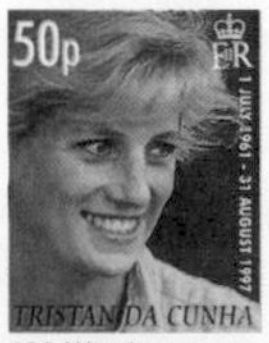

193 Wearing Turquoise Blouse

2007. Tenth Death Anniv of Diana, Princess of Wales. Multicoloured.

889	50p. Type **193**	1·90	1·90
890	50p. Wearing red dress (dark blue background)	1·90	1·90
891	50p. Wearing diamond and pearl earrings	1·90	1·90
892	50p. Wearing black	1·90	1·90
893	50p. Wearing dress with narrow straps and diamond necklace	1·90	1·90
894	50p. Wearing white dress, looking over shoulder	1·90	1·90

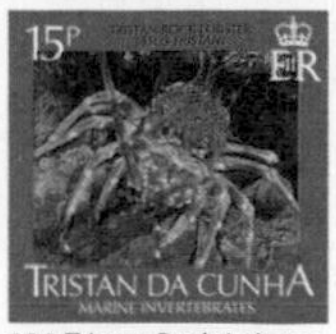

194 Tristan Rock Lobster (*Jasus tristani*)

2007. Marine Invertebrates. Multicoloured.

895	15p. Type **194**	80	80
896	20p. Trumpet anemone (*Parazoanthus hertwigi*)	90	90
897	35p. Starfish (*Henricia simplex*)	1·60	1·60
898	60p. Tristan urchin (*Arbacia crassispina*)	2·25	2·75
899	60p. Sponge	2·25	2·75
900	85p. Strawberry anemone (*Corynactis annulata*)	3·00	3·50

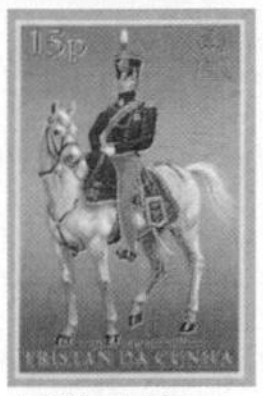

195 21st Light Dragoon Officer

2007. Military Uniforms. Multicoloured.

901	15p. Type **195**	2·00	2·00
902	15p. Corporal, Royal Artillery	2·00	2·00
903	20p. Privates, Royal Artillery	2·00	2·00
904	20p. Lieutenant, Royal Artillery	2·00	2·00
905	£1 Cape Regiment	6·50	7·00
906	£1 South Africa Army Engineering Corps	6·50	7·00

2008. 90th Anniv of the Royal Air Force. Horiz designs as T **247** of St. Helena. Multicoloured (except **MS**912).

907	30p. Hawker Hart	2·25	2·25
908	30p. Hawker Typhoon	2·25	2·25
909	30p. Royal Aircraft Factory S.E.5a	2·25	2·25
910	30p. Avro Vulcan	2·25	2·25
911	30p. SEPECAT Jaguar	2·25	2·25
MS912	110×70 mm. £1.50 Sir Hugh Trenchard ('father of the RAF') (brownish black and brownish grey) (vert)	7·50	8·00

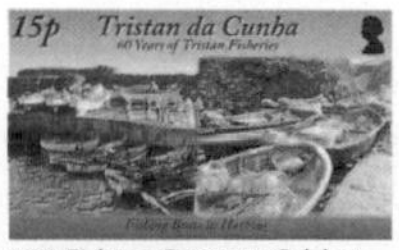

196 Fishing Boats in Calshot Harbour

2008. 60th Anniv of Tristan Fisheries. Multicoloured.

913	15p. Type **196**	1·25	1·25
914	20p. Fishing boats	1·40	1·40
915	30p. Offloading and loading fish	2·00	2·00
916	70p. Sorting crawfish tails	3·50	3·75
917	80p. Rock lobster tails wrapped and packed	3·50	3·75
918	£1.25 Shipping for export	6·00	6·50

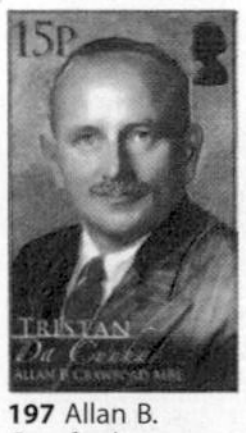

197 Allan B. Crawford

2008. Allan B. Crawford (founder of Tristan da Cunha Association and author) Commemoration. Multicoloured.

919	15p. Type **197**	80	80
920	20p. 1d. 'Potato stamp', 1946–7	1·00	1·00
921	50p. First map of Tristan da Cunha drawn by Allan Crawford, 1937–8	2·50	2·50
922	60p. Allan Crawford with Norwegian Scientific Expedition, 1937–8 and cover of *I Went to Tristan*, 1941 (horiz)	2·75	2·75
923	85p. Establishment of Meteorological Office at Marion Island, 1948 and cover of *Tristan da Cunha and the Roaring Forties*, 1982 (horiz)	3·25	3·50
924	£1.20 Allan Crawford on Royal Society Expedition, 1962 and cover of *Penguins, Potatoes and Postage Stamps*, 1999 (horiz)	4·75	5·50

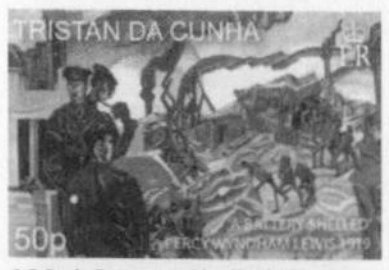

198 *A Battery Shelled* (Percy Wyndham Lewis) (1919)

2008. 90th Anniv of the End of World War I. Designs showing paintings. Multicoloured.

925	50p. Type **198**	2·50	2·50
926	50p. *The Angels of Mons* (R. Crowhurst) (1914) (vert)	2·50	2·50
927	50p. *Oppy Wood* (John Nash) (1917)	2·50	2·50
928	50p. *Lion leads in Jutland* (W. L. Wyllie) (1916)	2·50	2·50
929	50p. *End of Richthofen* (Charles H. Hubbell) (1918)	2·50	2·50
930	50p. *Somme Tank* (Louis Dauphin) (1916)	2·50	2·50
MS931	110×70 mm. £1 The UK Overseas Territories Wreath of Remembrance (vert)	4·00	4·50

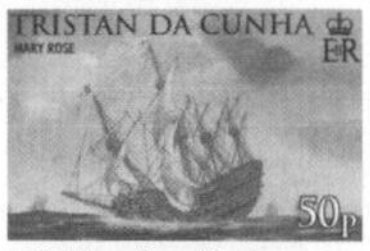

199 *Mary Rose* (Tudor carrack), 1509/10

2009. Seafaring and Exploration. Multicoloured.

932	50p. Type **199**	2·75	2·75
933	50p. *Cutty Sark* (clipper), 1869	2·75	2·75
934	50p. *Suomen Joutsen* (full-rigged ship), 1902	2·75	2·75
935	50p. *Endurance* (barquentine), 1912 (Shackleton)	2·75	2·75
936	50p. MS *Explorer*, 1969	2·75	2·75
937	50p. RFA *Lyme Bay* (Bay Class landing ship dock), 2005	2·75	2·75
MS938	110×70 mm. £1 Tristao da Cunha (discovered Tristan da Cunha, 1506) (vert)	4·75	5·50

2009. Centenary of Naval Aviation. As T **255** of St. Helena. Multicoloured.

939	25p. Felixstowe F.2A flying boat	2·00	2·00
940	35p. Short S.27	3·00	3·00
941	50p. Sikorsky Hoverfly helicopter	4·00	4·00
942	50p. Blackburn Dart	4·00	4·00
MS943	110×70 mm. £1.50 Lt. Cdr. C. R. Samson in Short S.27 taking off from HMS *Hibernia*, 1912	8·00	9·00

2009. International Year of Astronomy. 40th Anniv of First Moon Landing. As T **257** of St. Helena. Multicoloured.

944	25p. Goddard Rocket, 1936	1·40	1·40
945	35p. X-24B Spaceplane, 1972	1·90	1·90
946	60p. Apollo launch, 1969	3·25	3·25
947	90p. *Discovery* ferried by 747, 2005	4·50	5·00
948	£1 X-43C, experimental hypersonic aircraft	4·50	5·00
MS949	100×80 mm. £1.50 *The Fabulous Photo We Never Took* (astronauts Alan Bean and Pete Conrad in front of Surveyor III) (Alan Bean) (39×59 mm). Wmk upright	6·00	7·00

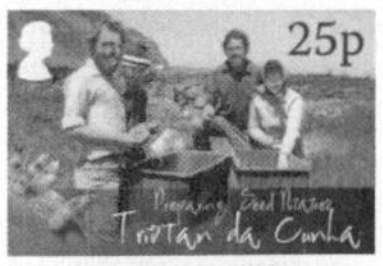

200 Preparing Seed Potatoes

2009. Potato Production. Multicoloured.

950	25p. Type **200**	1·50	1·75
951	25p. Women planting potatoes	1·50	1·75
952	35p. Digging out potatoes	2·00	2·25
953	35p. Tractor with trailer of harvested potatoes	2·00	2·25
954	£1.10 Potato flowers	4·00	4·50
955	£1.10 Potato patches	4·00	4·50

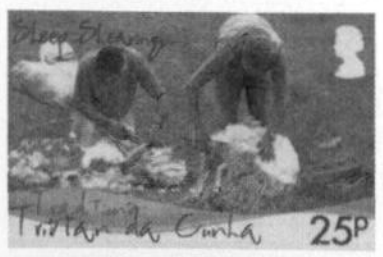

201 Sheep shearing

2009. Tristan da Cunha Traditions. Multicoloured.

956	25p. Type **201**	1·50	1·50
957	35p. Ratting Day	1·75	1·75
958	70p. Longboats to Nightingale Island	3·00	3·50
959	£1.60 Old Year's Night Okalolies (masked men)	5·50	6·50

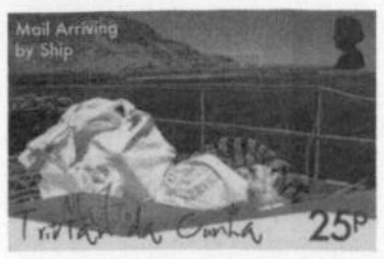

202 Mail Bags arriving on Ship's Deck

2009. Mail to Tristan da Cunha. Multicoloured.

960	25p. Type **202**	2·25	1·75
961	35p. Loading mail bags onto trailer at Calshot Harbour	3·00	2·25
962	£1 Hitting the gong to announce that post is ready for collection	7·00	7·50
963	£1.60 Giving out the mail, Prince Philip Hall	9·00	10·00

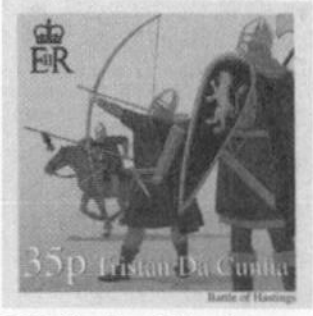

203 Battle of Hastings, 1066

2010. History of the British Isles (1st series). Multicoloured.

964	35p. Type **203**	1·50	1·50
965	35p. Peasants' Revolt, 1381	1·50	1·50
966	35p. King Henry VIII and Hampton Court Palace	1·50	1·50
967	35p. Thomas Cranmer ('English Reformation')	1·50	1·50
968	35p. Queen Elizabeth I and Columbus' ships ('Elizabethan Era')	1·50	1·50
969	35p. Oliver Cromwell and King Charles I ('English Civil War')	1·50	1·50
970	35p. Sir Isaac Newton ('Scientific Innovation')	1·50	1·50
971	35p. Bonnie Prince Charlie	1·50	1·50

2010. 70th Anniv of the Battle of Britain. As T **261** of St. Helena. Multicoloured.

972	25p. Pilots standing in front of plane	2·00	2·00
973	25p. Pilots running towards planes	2·00	2·00
974	50p. Group of pilots reading chart	3·50	3·50
975	50p. Pilots sat on grass in front of plane	3·50	3·50
976	70p. Pilots running to planes	4·50	4·50
977	70p. Group of pilots	4·50	4·50

No. **MS**978 is left for miniature sheet not yet received.

2010. Centenary of Accession of King George V. As T **262** of St. Helena. Multicoloured.

MS979	£1.50 Great Britain King George V 1912 ½d. green stamp	5·50	6·00

2010. History of the British Isles (2nd series). As T **203**. Multicoloured.

980	35p. Murder of Archbishop Thomas Becket by four knights in Canterbury Cathedral, 1170	1·90	1·90
981	35p. Bowmen and mounted knight (Battle of Agincourt, 1415)	1·90	1·90
982	35p. Vice Admiral Nelson and HMS *Victory* (Battle of Trafalgar, 1805)	1·90	1·90
983	35p. Isambard Kingdom Brunel and suspension bridge (Engineering & Transportation)	1·90	1·90
984	35p. Guglielmo Marconi and early wireless, 1901 (Wireless Age)	1·90	1·90
985	35p. Suffragettes (Votes for Women)	1·90	1·90
986	35p. Unemployed men (The Great Depression, 1930s)	1·90	1·90
987	35p. Joseph Stalin, Franklin D. Roosevelt, Winston Churchill and fighter planes (Second World War)	1·90	1·90

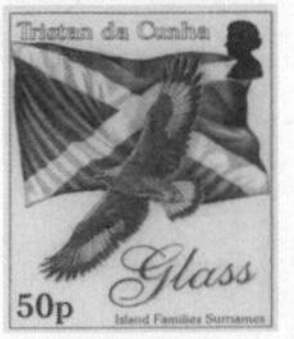

204 Golden Eagle and Scotland Flag (Glass)

2010. Island Families Surnames. Multicoloured.

988	50p. Type **204**	3·50	3·50
989	50p. American bald eagle and US flag (Hagan and Rogers)	3·50	3·50
990	50p. Oystercatcher and Dutch flag (Green)	3·50	3·50
991	50p. Hoopoe and Italian flag (Repetto and Lavarello)	3·50	3·50
992	50p. Avocet and England flag (Swain)	3·50	3·50

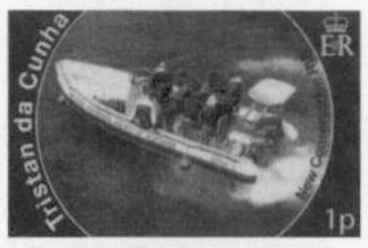

205 New Conservation RIB

2010. Conservation. Multicoloured.

993	1p. Type **205**	10	10
994	3p. Eradication of New Zealand flax on Nightingale Island	20	20
995	5p. Ringing Tristan albatross	35	35
996	8p. Hag's tooth (rock formation) on Gough Island (World Heritage site)	40	40
997	10p. Inaccessible rail	60	60
998	15p. Inaccessible Island (World Heritage site)	80	80
999	25p. Counting sub-Antarctic fur seals	1·00	1·00
1000	35p. Eradication of sagina plant on Gough Island	1·25	1·25
1001	70p. Eradication of loganberry plants at Sandy Point	2·40	2·40
1002	£1 Ringing Atlantic yellow-nosed albatross	5·50	5·50
1003	£2 Gough bunting	7·50	7·50
1004	£5 Counting northern rockhopper penguins	18·00	18·00

2010. Tristan Traditions (2nd series). As T **201**. Multicoloured.

1005	25p. Thatching	1·50	1·50
1006	35p. Bullock cart	2·25	2·25
1007	70p. Musicians (fiddle and accordion players)	3·25	3·50
1008	£1.60 Pillow dance	6·50	7·00

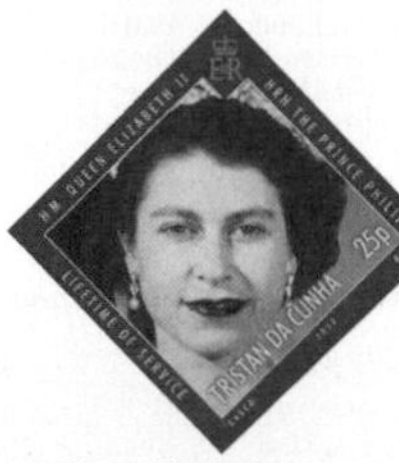

206 Queen Elizabeth II, c. 1952

2011. Queen Elizabeth II and Prince Philip. 'A Lifetime of Service'. Multicoloured.

1009	25p. Type **206**	1·10	1·10
1010	35p. Princess Elizabeth and Lieut. Philip Mountbatten laughing, Clydebank, 1947	1·50	1·50
1011	50p. Queen Eliizabeth II and Prince Philip, c. 2007	2·25	2·25
1012	50p. Queen Elizabeth II (wearing red coat and hat) and Prince Philip, 1990s	2·25	2·25
1013	70p. Queen Elizabeth II and Prince Philip, c. 1972	3·50	3·50
1014	70p. Lieut. Philip Mountbatten, c. 1947	3·50	3·50
MS1015	174×163 mm. Nos. 1009/14 and three stamp-size labels	12·00	13·00
MS1016	110×70 mm. £1.50 Queen Elizabeth II (wearing green checked dress) and Prince Philip, c. 2007	6·00	7·00

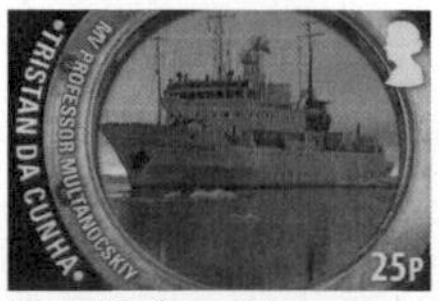

207 MV *Professor Multanocskiy*

2011. Atlantic Odyssey (voyages to Antarctica). Multicoloured.

1017	25p. Type **207**	1·25	1·25
1018	35p. MV *Aleksey Maryshev*	1·75	1·75
1019	70p. MV *Professor Molchanov*	3·25	3·25
1020	£1.10 MV *Plancius*	4·50	4·50
MS1021	100×80 mm. £1.50 As No. 1020	7·00	7·50

2011. Royal Wedding (1st issue). Multicoloured.

MS1022	£3 Prince William and Miss Catherine Middleton	11·00	12·00

2011. History of the British Isles (3rd series). Multicoloured.

1023	35p. King John signing Magna Carta, 1215		
1024	35p. Mounted knights carrying standards of Houses of Lancaster and York (Wars of the Roses, 145585)	1·10	1·10
1025	35p. Guy Fawkes (Gunpowder Plot), 1605	1·10	
1026	35p. Samuel Pepys writing in diary and London ablaze (Great Fire of London, 1666)	1·10	1·10
1027	35p. Duke of Wellington (Battle of Waterloo, 1815)	1·10	1·10
1028	35p. Factory and smoking chimneys (Industry & Commerce)	1·10	1·10
1029	35p. Queen Victoria, lion statue and Union Jack (Age of Empire)	1·10	1·10
1030	35p. Lord Kitchener and soldiers (First World War)	1·10	1·10

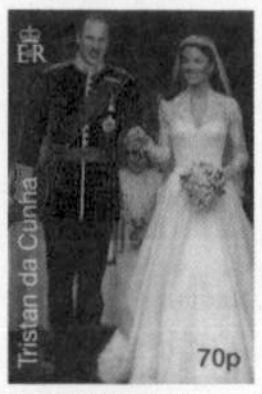

208 Duke and Duchess of Cambridge at Westminister Abbey after Wedding Ceremony

2011. Royal Wedding (2nd issue). Multicoloured.

1031	70p. Type **208**	2·25	2·25
1032	70p. Duke and Duchess of Cambridge waving from State Landau (horiz)	2·25	2·25
1033	70p. Duke and Duchess of Cambridge kissing on Buckingham Palace balcony	2·25	2·25
1034	70p. Leaving Buckingham Palace in car with 'JU5T WED' numberplate (horiz)	2·25	2·25

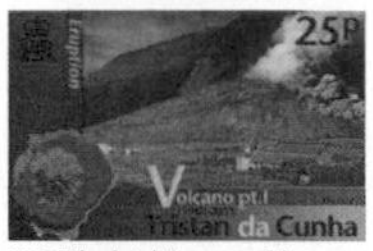

209 Tholoid (mass of lava rising above surface)

2011. Volcano (1st series). 50th Anniv of the Eruption and Evacuation of Tristan da Cunha. Multicoloured.

1035	25p. Type **209**	85	85
1036	35p. Volcanic eruption, October 1961	1·25	1·25
1037	95p. Islanders boarding *Tjisadane*, 1961	3·00	3·00
1038	£1.10 Arrival of Islanders at Cape Town	3·75	3·75
MS1039	94×64 mm. £2 MV *Tjisadane*	7·50	7·50

2012. Volcano (2nd series). 50th Anniv of the Royal Society Expedition. Multicoloured.

1040	25p. Rowing out to HMS *Protector* ('Returning with the Report')	85	85
1041	35p. Resettlement survey team	1·25	1·25
1042	95p. Whirlwind helicopter from HMS *Protector*	3·00	3·00
1043	£1.10 Royal Society members	3·75	3·75
MS1044	94×64 mm. £2 Landing party	7·50	7·50

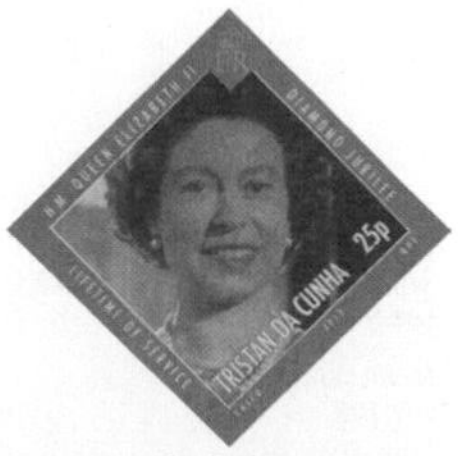

210 Queen Elizabeth II

2012. Diamond Jubilee. Multlcoloured.

1045	25p. Type **210**	85	85
1046	35p. Queen Elizabeth II wearing yellow, 1970s	1·75	1·75
1047	50p. Queen Elizabeth II, c. 1952	1·75	1·75
1048	50p. Queen Elizabeth II wearing blue, c. 2005	1·75	1·75
1049	70p. Queen Elizabeth II wearing tiara and drop earrings, c. 1955	2·50	2·50
1050	70p. Queen Elizabeth II wearing tiara and drop earrings, c. 2005	2·50	2·50
MS1051	174×164 mm. Nos. 1045/50 and three stamp-size labels	11·00	11·00
MS1052	110×70 mm. £1.50 Coronation photograph, 1953	4·50	4·50

211 Harland and Wolff Shipyard

2012. Centenary of the Sinking of the *Titanic*. Multicoloured.
MS1053 50p.×10 Type **211**; First class dining room; *Titanic*'s propellors; Sinking of the ship; Captain E. J. Smith and crew; Survivors in lifeboat; Setting sail; Newspaper reports; Passengers strolling on board; Discovery of the wreck ... 13·00 13·00

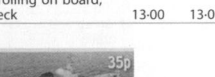

212 S.A. *Agulhas II*

2012. Maiden Voyage of S.A. *Agulhas II*. Multicoloured.
1054	35p. Type **212**	1·25	1·25
1055	35p. *S.A. Agulhas I*	1·25	1·25
1056	70p. *S.A. Agulhas I* off Tristan da Cunha	2·50	2·50
1057	£1.10 *S.A. Agulhas II* off Tristan da Cunha	3·75	3·75

213 HMS *Portland*, 2005

2012. Ships' Crests (2nd series). Multicoloured.
MS1058 35p. Type **213**; 35p. HMS *Edinburgh*, 2006; 70p. HMS *Clyde*, 2011; 70p. HMS *Montrose*, 2012 ... 7·50 7·50

214 James Marr and Tristan da Cunha

2012. Shackleton-Rowett Expedition, 1921-2. Multicoloured.
1059	70p. Type **214**	2·50	2·50
1060	70p. Frank Wild and Inaccessible Island	2·50	2·50
1061	70p. Frank Worsley and Nightingale Island	2·50	2·50
1062	70p. Hubert Wilkins and Gough Island	2·50	2·50

215 Tristan Albatross Chick

2013. Endangered Species. Tristan Albatross (*Diomedea dabbenena*). Multicoloured.
1063	35p. Type **215**	1·25	1·25
1064	45p. Adult and chick	1·50	1·50
1065	70p. Pair	2·50	2·50
1066	£1.10 Adult in flight	3·75	3·75
MS1067 94×64 mm. £3 Adult displaying ... 10·00 10·00

216 Recorders and 'When Fish Get the Flu'

2013. Tristan Song Project. Multicoloured.
1068	35p. Type **216**	1·25	1·25
1069	45p. Violin and 'Rockhopper Penguins'	1·50	1·50
1070	70p. Guitar and 'Volcano's Black'	2·50	2·50
1071	£1.10 Accordion and 'The Molly' (albatross)	3·75	3·75

217 Queen Victoria

2013. 60th Anniv of Coronation of Queen Elizabeth II. 'A Celebration of Coronation Commemoratives'. Multicoloured.
1072	35p. Type **217**	1·25	1·25
1073	45p. King Edward VII and Queen Alexandra and grandstand at Charing Cross Station for Coronation procession	1·50	1·50
1074	70p. King George V and Queen Mary	2·50	2·50
1075	£1.10 King George VI and Queen Elizabeth, crowned 12 May 1937	3·75	3·75
1076	£1.50 Queen Elizabeth II and Duke of Edinburgh	4·50	4·50
MS1077 110×70 mm. £2 Recent photograph of Queen Elizabeth II (32×48 mm) ... 7·50 7·50

2013. Volcano (3rd series). 50th Anniv of the Resettlement. Multicoloured.
1078	25p. Returned Islanders amongst their possessions	1·25	1·25
1079	35p. Islanders looking for their possessions amongst the unloaded stores	1·50	1·50
1080	95p. Islanders on shore, MV *Boissevain* and MV *Frances Repetto* offshore	3·25	3·25
1081	£1.10 Returning islanders transported by tractor and trailer	3·75	3·75
MS1082 94×64 mm. £2 Islanders hauling longboat up beach, MV *Boissevain* and MV *Tristania* offshore ... 8·00 8·00

218 St. Mary's Anglican Church, Tristan da Cunha

2013. Christmas. Churches. Multicoloured.
1083	35p. Type **218**	1·25	1·25
1084	35p. St. Joseph's Catholic Church, Tristan da Cunha	1·25	1·25
1085	£1.10 Canterbury Cathedral, England	3·00	3·00
1086	£1.10 St. Peter's Basilica, Vatican City	3·00	3·00

2013. Volcano (4th series). Ships of Volcano Period (1961-3). Multicoloured.
1087	25p. HMS *Puma*	1·25	1·25
1088	35p. HMS *Jaguar*	1·50	1·50
1089	95p. MV *Tristania*	3·25	3·25
1090	£1.10 HMMV *Stirling Castle*	3·75	3·75
MS1091 94×64 mm. £2 MV *Bornholm* ... 8·00 8·00

219 James Weddell and *Jane*

2014. Ships and Explorers. Multicoloured.
1092	35p. Type **219**	1·25	1·25
1093	45p. George Nares and *Challenger*	1·50	1·50
1094	70p. Carsten Borchgrevink and SS *Antarctic*	2·50	2·50
1095	£1.50 Dr. Alexander Macklin and *Quest*	4·50	4·50

POSTAGE DUE STAMPS

1957. As Type **D1** of St Lucia.
D1	1d. red	1·75	16·00
D2	2d. yellow	2·50	4·75
D3	3d. green	2·50	5·50
D4	4d. blue	4·50	7·00
D5	5d. lake	2·50	25·00

D2

1976
D11	**D2**	1p. purple	10	30
D12	**D2**	2p. green	10	30
D13	**D2**	4p. violet	15	35
D14	**D2**	5p. blue	15	40
D15	**D2**	10p. brown	15	45

D3 Outline Map of Tristan da Cunha

1986
D16	**D3**	1p. brown & light brown	10	80
D17	**D3**	2p. brown and orange	15	80
D18	**D3**	5p. brown and red	20	80
D19	**D3**	7p. black and violet	20	80
D20	**D3**	10p. black and blue	25	80
D21	**D3**	25p. black and green	65	1·40

LOOKING FOR THAT ELUSIVE STAMP?

Send a copy of your wants list or call:
Andrew Mansi on 020 7557 4455
email amansi@stanleygibbons.com
or Brian Lucas on 020 7557 4418
email blucas@stanleygibbons.com

Est 1856

STANLEY GIBBONS

Stanley Gibbons Limited
399 Strand
London, WC2R 0LX
+44 (0)20 7557 4444
www.stanleygibbons.com

Pt. 1

TRUCIAL STATES

Seven Arab shaikhdoms on the Persian Gulf abd Gulf of Oman, in treaty with Great Britain. The following stamps were issued at the British Postal Agency at Dubai until it closed on 14 June 1963.

Individual issues were later made by Abh Dhabi, Ajman, Dubai, Fujeira, Ras al Khaima, Sharjah and Umm al Qiwain.

100 naye paise = 1 rupee.

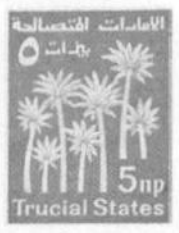

1 Palms

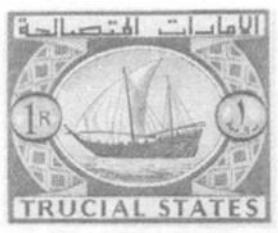

2 Dhow

1961

1	1	5n.p. green	1·75	1·25
2	1	15n.p. brown	60	75
3	1	20n.p. blue	1·75	1·50
4	1	30n.p. orange	60	20
5	1	40n.p. violet	60	40
6	1	50n.p. bistre	60	75
7	1	75n.p. grey	60	1·00
8	2	1r. green	9·50	4·25
9	2	2r. black	8·50	22·00
10	2	5r. red	12·00	28·00
11	2	10r. blue	15·00	28·00

Pt. 6, Pt. 14

TUNISIA

Formerly a French Protectorate in N. Africa, Tunisia became an independent kingdom in 1956 and a republic in 1957.

1888. 100 centimes = 1 franc.
1959. 1000 milliemes = 1 dinar.

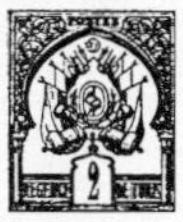
1

1888. Arms on plain background.

1	1	1c. black on blue	1·00	2·30
2	1	2c. brown on buff	45	90
3	1	5c. green on green	11·00	3·75
4	1	15c. blue on blue	30·00	3·25
5	1	25c. black on pink	85·00	18·00
6	1	40c. red on yellow	55·00	23·00
7	1	75c. pink on pink	65·00	70·00
8	1	5f. mauve on lilac	£375	£300

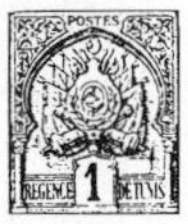
2

1888. Arms on shaded background.

9	2	1c. black on blue	55	10
10	2	2c. brown on buff	70	10
22	2	5c. green	2·75	30
12	2	10c. black on lilac	14·50	20
23	2	10c. red	4·00	30
14	2	15c. blue	85·00	55
24	2	15c. grey	4·75	35
15	2	20c. red on green	13·00	30
16	2	25c. black on pink	18·00	45
25	2	25c. blue	28·00	45
26	2	35c. brown	60·00	90
17	2	40c. red on yellow	11·00	35
18	2	75c. pink on pink	£140	55·00
19	2	75c. violet on yellow	13·00	2·00
20	2	1f. green	12·00	2·75
27	2	2f. lilac	£160	£130
21	2	5f. mauve on lilac	£160	80·00

1902. Surch **25** and bars.

28	25 on 15c. blue	1·60	2·30

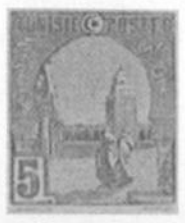
4 Mosque at Kairouan

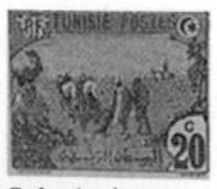
5 Agriculture

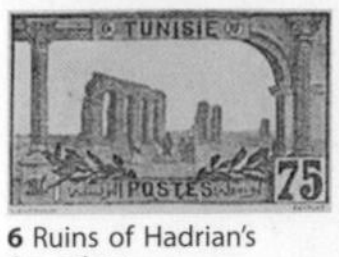

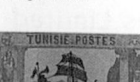

6 Ruins of Hadrian's Aqueduct

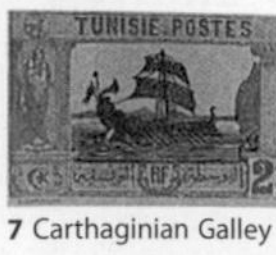
7 Carthaginian Galley

1906

30	4	1c. black on yellow	10	10
31	4	2c. brown	10	10
32	4	3c. red	30	2·30
33	4	5c. green on green	90	10
34	5	10c. red	1·40	10
35	5	15c. violet	1·70	10
36	5	20c. brown	60	30
37	5	25c. blue	3·00	20
38	6	35c. brown and green	14·00	1·00
39	6	40c. red and brown	4·50	85
40	6	75c. red and purple	90	35
41	7	1f. brown and red	1·50	80
42	7	2f. green and brown	6·00	2·75
43	7	5f. blue and violet	10·00	7·75

See also Nos. 72/8, 105 and 107/13.

1908. Surch.

44	2	10 on 15c. grey	75	30
45	2	35 on 1f. green	1·60	2·75
46	2	40 on 2f. lilac	3·25	4·75
47	2	75 on 5f. mauve on lilac	1·80	7·75

1911. Surch in figures and bar.

48	5	10 on 15c. violet	3·75	30
60	5	15c. on 10c. red	2·00	20
79	5	20c. on 15c. violet	2·50	20

1915. Red Cross Fund. Optd with red cross.

49	15c. violet	1·20	85

1916. Red Cross Fund. Optd with red cross and bars.

50	4	5c. green on green	1·60	2·75

1916. Prisoners-of-War Fund. Surch with red cross and **10c**.

51	5	10c. on 15c. brown on blue	1·00	4·75
52	5	10c. on 20c. brown on yellow	1·60	5·75
53	5	10c. on 25c. blue on green	2·50	8·75
54	6	10c. on 35c. violet and green	3·25	21·00
55	6	10c. on 40c. black and brown	2·50	8·50
56	6	10c. on 75c. green and red	5·25	30·00
57	7	10c. on 1f. green and red	5·75	14·00
58	7	10c. on 2f. blue and brown	75·00	£130
59	7	10c. on 5f. red and violet	90·00	£140

1918. Prisoners-of-War Fund. Surch **15c** and red cross.

61	5	15c. on 20c. black on green	2·00	6·00
62	5	15c. on 25c. blue	2·00	7·75
63	6	15c. on 35c. red and olive	3·00	11·50
64	6	15c. on 40c. blue and brown	2·50	14·50
65	6	15c. on 75c. black and red	9·25	26·00
66	7	15c. on 1f. violet and red	20·00	55·00
67	7	15c. on 2f. red and brown	85·00	£120
68	7	15c. on 5f. black and violet	£130	£130

1919. Air. Optd **Poste Aerienne** and wings or surch **30c** and bars also.

69	6	30c. on 35c. brown and green	1·70	3·50
70	6	30c. blue and olive	85	1·40

1920. New values and colours changed.

72	4	5c. orange	85	20
73	5	10c. green	50	35
74	5	25c. violet	65	10
75	6	30c. violet and purple	1·80	2·00
76	5	30c. red	1·90	3·25
77	5	50c. blue	1·10	80
78	6	60c. violet and green	1·10	85

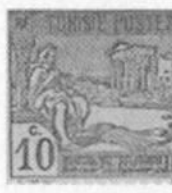
18 Ruin at Dougga

1922

80	18	10c. green	65	10
81	18	30c. red	1·30	3·25
82	18	50c. blue	60	45

See also Nos. 104 and 106.

1923. War Wounded Fund. Surch **AFFt**, medal and new value.

83	4	0c. on 1c. blue	35	6·50
84	4	0c. on 2c. brown	35	8·00
85	4	1c. on 3c. green	35	7·75
86	4	2c. on 5c. mauve	35	6·75
87	18	3c. on 10c. mauve on blue	65	6·50
88	5	5c. on 15c. green	1·20	7·75
89	5	5c. on 20c. blue on red	2·00	11·50
90	5	5c. on 25c. mauve on blue	2·30	10·50
91	18	5c. on 30c. orange	1·80	11·50
92	6	5c. on 35c. mauve and blue	3·50	10·50
93	6	5c. on 40c. brown and blue	2·50	8·25
94	18	10c. on 50c. black on blue	2·75	12·00
95	6	10c. on 60c. blue and brown	2·75	8·00
96	6	10c. on 75c. green & mauve	3·50	18·00
97	7	25c. on 1f. mauve and lake	4·25	18·00
98	7	25c. on 2f. red and blue	18·00	55·00
99	7	25c. on 5f. brown and green	32·00	£120

1923. Surch.

100	4	10 on 5c. green on green	70	45
101	5	20 on 15c. violet	2·00	1·80
102	5	30 on 20c. brown	60	20
103	5	50 on 25c. blue	1·00	10

1923. New values and colours.

104	18	10c. pink	45	20
105	5	15c. brown on orange	45	35
106	18	30c. mauve	40	55
107	5	40c. black on pink	85	1·30
108	5	40c. green	45	10
109	6	60c. carmine and red	1·20	3·50
110	6	75c. scarlet and red	1·30	1·60
111	7	1f. light blue and blue	50	30
112	7	2f. red and green on pink	1·20	2·30
113	7	5f. green and lilac	2·00	2·00

1925. Parcel Post stamps surch **PROTECTION DE L'ENFANCE POSTES** and value in figures.

114	P8	1c. on 5c. red and brown on rose	35	3·50
115	P8	2c. on 10c. blue and brown on yellow	60	2·75
116	P8	3c. on 20c. red and purple on mauve	75	8·00
117	P8	5c. on 25c. red and green on green	80	8·25
118	P8	5c. on 40c. green and red on yellow	90	7·25
119	P8	10c. on 50c. green and violet on mauve	1·40	11·50
120	P8	10c. on 75c. brown and green on green	1·40	9·25
121	P8	25c. on 1f. green and blue on blue	1·40	8·75
122	P8	25c. on 2f. purple and red on rose	2·75	21·00
123	P8	25c. on 5f. brown and red on green	18·00	80·00

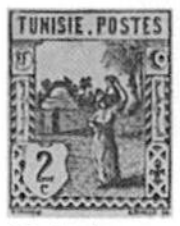

21 Arab Woman

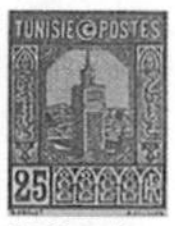

22 Grand Mosque, Tunis

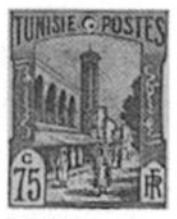

23 Mosque, Place Halfaouine, Tunis

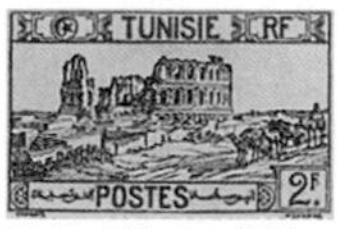

24 Amphitheatre, El Djem

1926

124	21	1c. red	10	45
125	21	2c. green	10	1·50
126	21	3c. blue	35	3·25
127	21	5c. green	40	20
128	21	10c. mauve	65	10
129	22	15c. lilac	60	10
130	22	20c. red	40	50
131	22	25c. green	65	35
131a	22	25c. mauve	1·10	10
132	22	30c. mauve	35	10
133	22	30c. green	1·00	35
134	22	40c. brown	40	10
134a	22	45c. green	3·75	7·50
135	23	50c. black	1·30	10
135a	23	50c. blue	3·75	10
135b	23	50c. green	90	75
135c	23	60c. red	45	1·10
135d	23	65c. blue	2·75	75
135e	23	70c. red	55	1·70
136	23	75c. red	1·80	1·40
136a	23	75c. mauve	1·20	10
137	23	80c. blue	1·00	4·00
137a	23	80c. brown	45	2·00
138	23	90c. red	40	10
138a	23	90c. blue	14·00	34·00
139	23	1f. purple	35	10
139a	23	1f. red	15	10
140	24	1f.05 pink and blue	1·00	2·30
141	24	1f.25 blue and light blue	1·10	3·25
141a	24	1f.25 red	3·50	7·00
141b	24	1f.30 violet and blue	1·10	2·75
141c	24	1f.40 purple	4·75	7·50
142	24	1f.50 blue and light blue	1·80	55
142a	24	1f.50 orange and red	1·00	2·00
143	24	2f. brown and red	1·00	10
143a	24	2f. red	60	30
143b	24	2f.25 blue	1·30	3·25
143c	24	2f.50 green	1·30	2·75
144	24	3f. orange and blue	1·50	10
144a	24	3f. violet	70	55
145	24	5f. green and red on green	1·50	80
145a	24	5f. brown	2·50	5·50
146	24	10f. grey and red on blue	4·50	4·50
146a	24	10f. pink	4·00	7·25
146b	24	20f. red and mauve on pink	2·30	1·40

For similar designs see Nos. 172/91, 220/31 and 257/286.

1927. Surch **1f 50**.

147	1f.50 on 1f.25 blue and ultramarine	80	1·80

1927. Air. Optd **Poste Aerienne** and airplane or surch in figures and bars also.

148	7	1f. light blue and blue	80	1·50
152	24	1f.30 mauve and orange	1·50	3·00
169	24	1f.50 on 1f.30 mve & orge	2·30	45
170	24	1f.50 on 1f.80 red and green	2·50	45
171	24	1f.50 on 2f.55 brn & mve	4·00	1·20
149	6	1f.75 on 75c. scarlet and red	1·10	1·80
150	7	1f.75 on 5f. green and lilac	2·75	10·00
153	24	1f.80 red and green	2·00	4·75
151	7	2f. red and green on pink	2·75	3·75
154	24	2f.55 brown and mauve	1·80	3·75

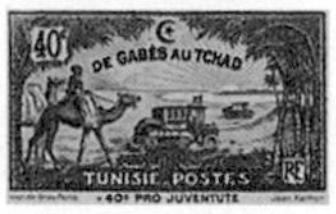

26 First Tunis–Chad Motor Service

1928. Child Welfare.

155	26	40c.+40c. brown	1·00	7·50
156	26	50c.+50c. purple	1·00	6·50
157	26	75c.+75c. blue	1·20	6·25
158	26	1f.+1f. red	1·30	8·50
159	26	1f.50+1f.50 blue	1·20	8·50
160	26	2f.+2f. green	1·40	8·25
161	26	5f.+5f. brown	1·40	5·50

1928. Surch.

162	4	3c. on 5c. orange	35	2·50
163	5	10c. on 15c. brown on orange	50	35
164	18	25c. on 30c. mauve	55	20
165	23	40c. on 80c. blue	75	2·50
166	22	50c. on 40c. brown	4·25	35
167	23	50c. on 75c. red	90	70

1929. Precancelled AFFRANCHts POSTES and surch **10**.

168	22	10 on 30c. mauve	1·10	7·75

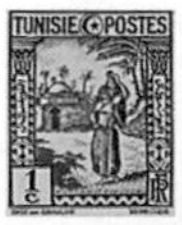

28

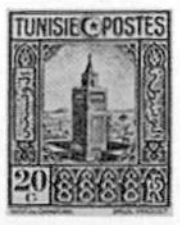

29

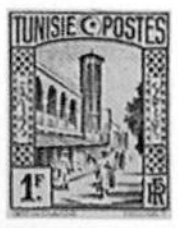

30

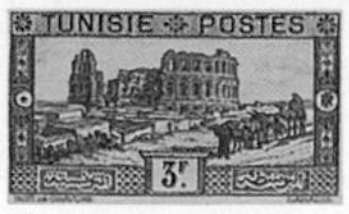

31

1931

172	28	1c. blue	10	4·25
173	28	2c. brown	10	3·00
174	28	3c. black	35	5·50
175	28	5c. green	10	75
176	28	10c. red	10	65
177	29	15c. purple	1·40	70
178	29	20c. brown	10	35
179	29	25c. red	1·00	20
180	29	30c. green	1·00	70
181	29	40c. orange	90	10
182	30	50c. blue	50	10
183	30	75c. yellow	1·00	35
184	30	90c. red	1·00	3·25
185	30	1f. olive	85	20

186	**31**	1f.50 blue	70	30
187	**31**	2f. brown	1·00	35
188	**31**	3f. green	11·00	20·00
189	**31**	5f. red	22·00	26·00
190	**31**	10f. black	30·00	70·00
191	**31**	20f. brown	55·00	80·00

1937. Surch.

191a	**23**	25c. on 65c. blue	50	60
192	**23**	0.65 on 50c. blue	1·40	20
193	**23**	65 on 50c. blue	3·25	50
193b	**23**	1FR on 90c. blue	2·30	60
193c	**24**	1F. on 1f.25 red	55	3·50
193d	**24**	1F. on 1f.40 purple	40	1·00
193e	**24**	1F. on 2f.25 blue	55	1·00
194	**24**	1f.75 on 1f.50 blue and light blue	5·25	1·80

1938. 50th Anniv of Tunisian Postal Service. Surch **1888 1938** and value.

196	**28**	1c.+1c. blue	2·30	9·50
197	**28**	2c.+2c. brown	1·80	8·00
198	**28**	3c.+3c. black	1·70	7·75
199	**28**	5c.+5c. green	2·50	8·00
200	**28**	10c.+10c. red	2·30	8·00
201	**29**	15c.+15c. purple	1·80	8·25
202	**29**	20c.+20c. brown	2·30	9·50
203	**29**	25c.+25c. red	2·00	8·00
204	**29**	30c.+30c. green	2·00	8·00
205	**29**	40c.+40c. orange	1·50	8·00
206	**30**	50c.+50c. blue	2·30	8·00
207	**30**	75c.+75c. yellow	2·30	8·00
208	**30**	90c.+90c. red	1·70	7·75
209	**30**	1f.+1f. olive	1·60	8·25
210	**31**	1f.50+1f. blue	2·75	6·50
211	**31**	2f.+1f.50 brown	3·00	9·75
212	**31**	3f.+2f. green	3·00	10·50
213	**31**	5f.+3f. red	11·00	44·00
214	**31**	10f.+5f. black	18·00	75·00
215	**31**	20f.+10f. brown	60·00	£100

1941. National Relief. Surch **SECOURS NATIONAL1941** and value.

216	**22**	1f. on 45c. green	1·70	8·25
217	**24**	1f.30 on 1f.25 red	1·80	10·50
218	**24**	1f.50 on 1f.40 purple	2·00	9·50
219	**24**	2f. on 2f.25 blue	1·00	12·00

1941. As stamps of 1926 but without monogram "RF".

220	**22**	30c. red	90	8·25
221	**23**	1f.20 grey	75	2·30
222	**23**	1f.50 brown	85	20
223	**24**	2f.40 pink and red	1·10	5·50
224	**24**	2f.50 light blue and blue	65	45
225	**24**	3f. violet	2·00	6·50
226	**24**	4f. blue and black	1·20	3·50
227	**24**	4f.50 brown and green	1·20	2·75
228	**24**	5f. black	70	1·10
229	**24**	10f. violet and purple	60	50
230	**24**	15f. red	8·50	15·00
231	**24**	20f. red and lilac	5·75	8·50

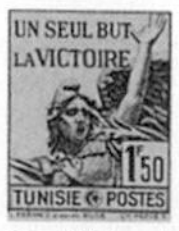

41a "Victory"

1943

232	**41a**	1f.50 red	45	40

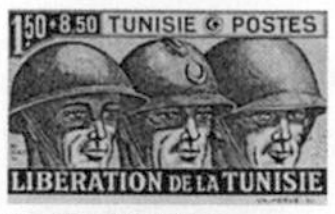

42 Allied Soldiers

1943. Charity. Tunisian Liberation.

233	**42**	1f.50+8f.50 red	35	3·50

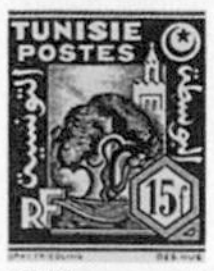

43 Mosque and Olive Trees

1944

234	**43**	30c. yellow	75	6·50
235	**43**	40c. brown	45	4·75
236	**43**	60c. orange	35	1·80
237	**43**	70c. red	45	5·50
238	**43**	80c. green	50	4·75
239	**43**	90c. violet	50	6·00
240	**43**	1f. red	45	65
241	**43**	1f.50 blue	35	35
242	**43**	2f.40 red	35	5·00
243	**43**	2f.50 brown	30	50
244	**43**	3f. violet	30	20
245	**43**	4f. blue	35	80
246	**43**	4f.50 green	45	35
247	**43**	5f. grey	20	70
248	**43**	6f. brown	35	45
249	**43**	10f. lake	45	1·60
250	**43**	15f. brown	55	1·70
251	**43**	20f. lilac	65	75

Nos. 234/41 are smaller, 15½×19 mm.

1944. Forces Welfare Fund. Surch **+ 48 frcs pour nos Combattants**.

252		2f.+48f. red (21¼×26½ mm)	1·20	8·00

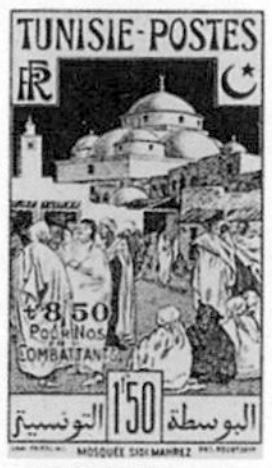

44 Sidi Mahrez Mosque

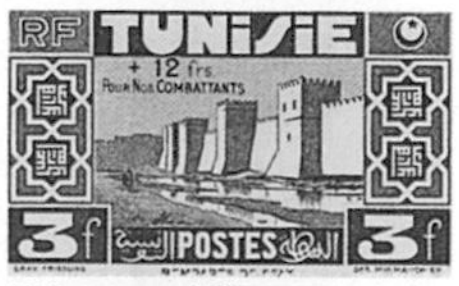

45 Ramparts of Sfax

1945. Forces Welfare Fund. Surch **POUR NOS COMBATTANTS** and value.

253	**44**	1f.50+8f.50 brown	75	7·25
254	**45**	3f.+12f. green	75	7·50
255	-	4f.+21f. brown	75	7·25
256	-	10f.+40f. red	75	8·25

DESIGNS—HORIZ: 4f. Camel patrol at Fort Saint; 10f. Mosque at Sidi-bou-Said.

1945. New values and colours.

257	**23**	10c. brown	35	2·50
258	**23**	30c. olive	35	1·70
259	**23**	40c. red	35	1·20
260	**23**	50c. turquoise	60	10
261	**23**	60c. blue	35	1·40
262	**23**	80c. green	1·30	4·00
263	**23**	1f.20 brown	1·60	3·50
264	**23**	1f.50 lilac	60	10
265	**23**	2f. green	35	10
267	**24**	2f.40 red	2·00	7·50
268	**23**	2f.50 brown	1·30	75
269	**24**	3f. brown	1·20	60
270	**23**	3f. red	60	10
271	**24**	4f. blue	2·75	2·30
272	**23**	4f. violet	1·60	35
273	**24**	4f. violet	1·80	1·60
273a	**23**	4f. orange	1·30	1·40
274	**23**	4f.50 blue	1·10	35
275	**24**	5f. green	1·00	60
275a	**23**	5f. blue	1·00	35
275b	**23**	5f. green	1·30	60
276	**24**	6f. blue	2·30	80
277	**24**	6f. red	1·80	1·40
278	**23**	6f. red	60	10
279	**24**	10f. orange	1·30	35
280	**24**	10f. blue	1·20	1·20
281	**24**	15f. mauve	90	85
281a	**23**	15f. red	1·50	10
282	**24**	20f. green	85	10
283	**24**	25f. violet	1·20	2·50
284	**24**	25f. orange	95	1·40
285	**24**	50f. red	1·50	85
286	**24**	100f. red	1·70	55

1945. Anti-tuberculosis Fund. Type of France optd **TUNISIE**.

287	**222**	2f.+1f. orange	20	4·00

1945. Postal Employees' War Victims' Fund. Type of France optd **TUNISIE**.

288	**223**	4f.+6f. brown	1·10	6·75

1945. Stamp Day. Type of France (Louis XI) optd **TUNISIE**.

289	**228**	2f.+3f. green	35	5·00

1945. War Veterans' Fund. Surch **ANCIENS COMBATTANTS R F** and value.

290	**21**	4f.+6f. on 10c. blue	80	6·50
291	**23**	10f.+30f. on 80c. green	1·00	6·75

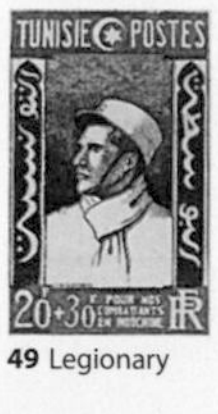

49 Legionary

1946. Welfare Fund for French Troops in Indo-China.

292	**49**	20f.+30f. black, red and green	1·20	6·75

1946. Red Cross Fund. Surch with cross **1946** and new values.

293	**23**	80c.+50c. green	65	7·00
294	**23**	1f.50+1f.50 lilac	65	7·00
295	**23**	2f.+2f. green	65	7·00
296	**24**	2f.40+2f. red	65	7·00
297	**24**	4f.+4f. blue	65	8·75

1946. Stamp Day. La Varane Type of France optd **TUNISIE**.

298	**241**	3f.+2f. blue	45	4·75

1947. Stamp Day. Louvois Type of France optd **TUNISIE**.

299	**253**	4f.50+5f.50 brown	1·30	7·50

1947. Naval Charities. Type of France surch **TUNISIE** and new value.

300	**234**	10+15 on 2f.+3f. blue	1·10	8·25

1947. Welfare Fund. Surch **SOLIDARITE 1947 +40 F**.

301	**24**	10f.+40f. black	55	7·50

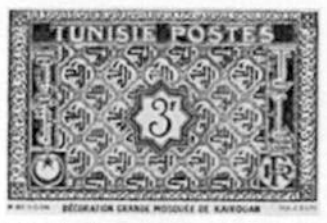

53 Arabesque Ornamentation from Great Mosque at Kairouan

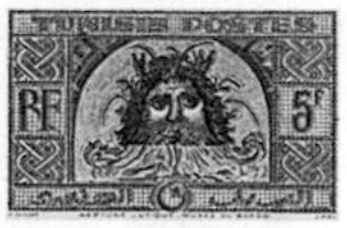

54 Neptune

1947

302	**53**	3f. green and turquoise	1·20	2·30
303	**53**	4f. red and purple	60	3·50
304	**54**	5f. black and green	1·20	2·75
305	**53**	6f. red and brown	50	85
306	**54**	10f. black and brown	85	65
306a	**53**	10f. violet	2·00	10
306b	**53**	12f. brown	2·50	2·75
306c	**53**	12f. orange and brown	1·20	1·50
306d	**53**	15f. red and brown	2·75	3·50
307	**54**	18f. blue and green	1·50	4·00
307a	**54**	25f. turquoise and blue	1·90	1·30
307b	**53**	30f. blue and deep blue	2·00	2·30

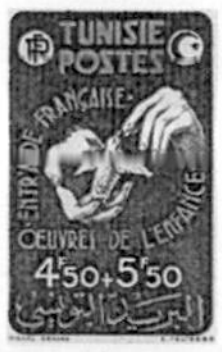

55 Feeding a Fledgling

1947. Infant Welfare Fund.

308	**55**	4f.50+5f.50 green	75	4·75
309	**55**	6f.+9f. blue	75	4·75
310	**55**	8f.+17f. red	75	4·75
311	**55**	10f.+40f. violet	75	4·75

1948. Stamp Day. Type of France (Arago) optd **TUNISIE**.

312	**253**	6f.+4f. red	1·00	8·50

1948. Anti-tuberculosis Fund. Surch **AIDEZ LES TUBERCULEUX +10f.**

313	**53**	4f.+10f. orange and green	70	7·25

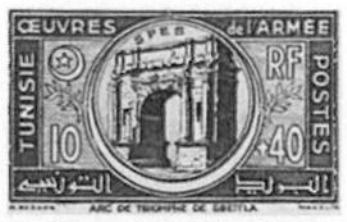

57 Triumphal Arch, Sbeitla

1948. Army Welfare Fund.

315	**57**	10f.+40f. green and bistre	1·10	9·00
316	**57**	18f.+42f. dp blue & blue	1·10	9·00

1949. Stamp Day. Type of France (Choiseul), optd **TUNISIE**.

317	**278**	15f.+5f. black	1·60	4·00

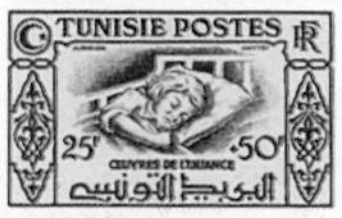

58 Child in Cot

1949. Child Welfare Fund.

318	**58**	25f.+50f. green	2·50	10·50

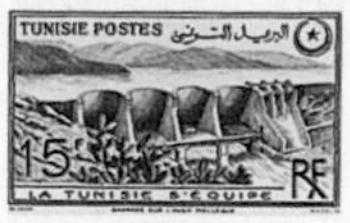

59 Oued Mellegue Barrage

1949. Tunisian Development.

319	**59**	15f. black	90	75

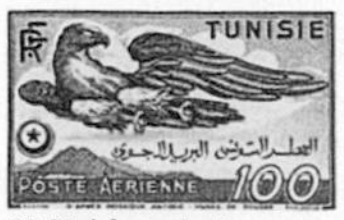

60 Bird from Antique Mosaic

1949. Air.

320	**60**	100f. brown and green	2·00	2·00
321	**60**	200f. black and blue (A)	3·00	2·50
322	**60**	200f. black and blue (B)	4·00	4·50

In A the Arabic inscription is in two lines and in B it is in one line.

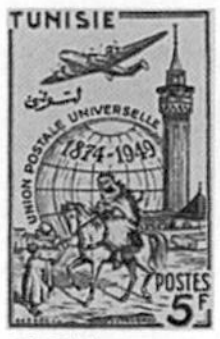

61 Globe, Mounted Postman and Sud Est Languedoc Airliner

1949. 75th Anniv of U.P.U.

323	**61**	5f. green on blue (postage)	1·00	8·00
324	**61**	15f. brown on blue	1·40	8·25
325	**61**	15f. blue on blue (air)	75	4·25

1949. Free French Association Fund. Surch Lorraine Cross and **FFL +15F.**

326	**54**	10f.+15f. red and blue	1·50	5·00

1950. Stamp Day. Type of France (Postman) optd **TUNISIE**.

327	**292**	12f.+3f. green	1·50	5·00

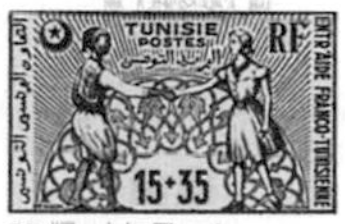

62 "Tunisia Thanks France"

1950. Franco-Tunisian Relief Fund.

328	**62**	15f.+35f. red	1·50	9·75
329	**62**	25f.+45f. blue	1·50	9·75

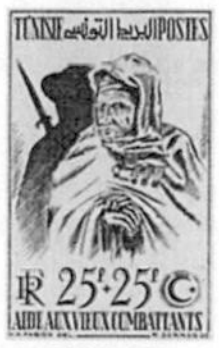

63 Old Soldier

1950. Veterans' Relief Fund.

330	**63**	25f.+25f. blue	1·90	9·75

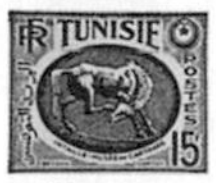

64 Horse (bas-relief)

1950. (a) Size 21½×17½ mm.

331	**64**	10c. blue	35	5·00
332	**64**	50c. brown	35	2·30
333	**64**	1f. violet	40	35
334	**64**	2f. grey	65	95
335	**64**	3f. brown	80	75
336	**64**	4f. orange	80	55
337	**64**	5f. green	70	35
338	**64**	8f. blue	1·20	1·70
340	**64**	12f. red	1·90	1·30
341	**64**	15f. red	40	10
342	**64**	15f. blue	1·90	10

(b) Size 22½×18¼ mm.

343		15f. red	2·75	4·00
344		15f. blue	2·75	3·75
345		30f. blue	3·00	75

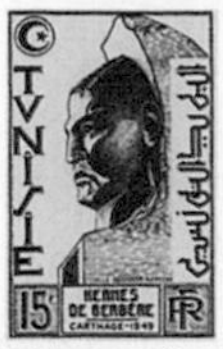

65 Hermes of Berbera

1950

346	**65**	15f. red	1·30	3·25
347	**65**	25f. blue	55	35
348	**65**	50f. green	1·40	45

1951. Stamp Day. Type of France (Sorting Van), but colour changed, optd **TUNISIE**.

349	**300**	12f.+3f. grey	1·50	6·50

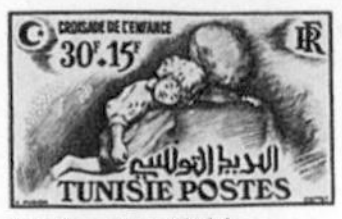

66 Sleeping Child

1951. Child Welfare Fund.

350	**66**	30f.+15f. blue	2·50	7·00

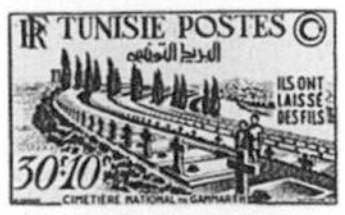

67 Gammarth National Cemetery

1951. War Orphans' Fund.

351	**67**	30f.+10f. blue	1·80	5·00

1952. Stamp Day. Type of France (Mail Coach), optd **TUNISIE**.

352	**319**	12f.+3f. violet	1·30	5·00

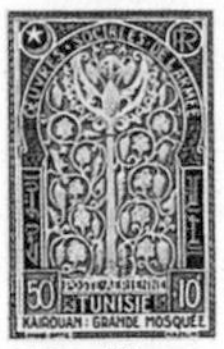

68 Panel from Great Mosque at Kairouan

1952. Army Welfare Fund. Inscr "OEUVRES SOCIALES DE L'ARMEE".

353	-	15f.+1f. indigo and blue (postage)	1·70	1·90
354	**68**	50f.+10f. green and black (air)	2·75	12·00

DESIGN: 15f. Ornamental stucco, Bardo Palace.

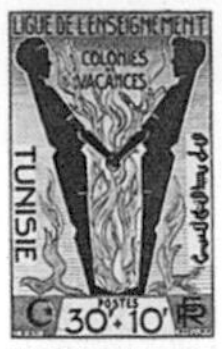

69 Schoolboys clasping Hands

1952. Holiday Camp Fund.

355	**69**	30f.+10f. green	2·50	7·50

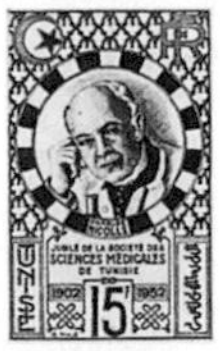

70 Charles Nicolle

1952. Golden Jubilee of Tunisian Medical Sciences Society.

356	**70**	15f. brown	1·40	1·40
357	**70**	30f. blue	1·90	2·00

1952. Centenary of Military Medal. Type of France surch **Tunisie +5F.**

358	**327**	15f.+5f. green	90	10·00

1953. Stamp Day. Type of France (Count D'Argenson), optd **TUNISIE**.

359	**334**	12f.+3f. red	2·75	7·00

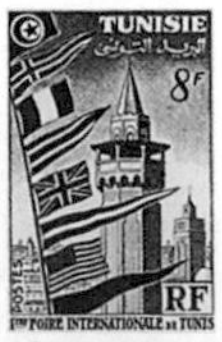

71 Tower and Flags

1953. First International Fair, Tunis.

360	**71**	8f. brown and deep brown	45	7·00
361	**71**	12f. green and emerald	50	7·00
362	**71**	15f. indigo and blue	55	1·80
363	**71**	18f. deep violet and violet	50	7·00
364	**71**	30f. red and carmine	55	8·00

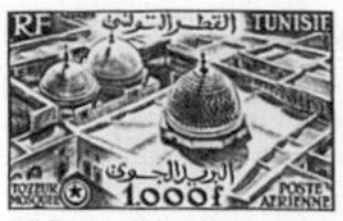

72 Tozeur Mosque

1953. Air.

365	-	100f. blue, turquoise & green	3·75	5·50
366	-	200f. sepia, purple & brown	5·00	8·50
367	-	500f. brown and blue	20·00	55·00
368	**72**	1000f. green	25·00	80·00

DESIGNS: 100, 200f. Monastir; 500f. View of Korbous.

For similar stamps but without "R F" see Nos. 423/6.

1954. Stamp Day. Type of France (Lavallette), optd **TUNISIE**.

369	**346**	12f.+3f. blue	1·50	8·00

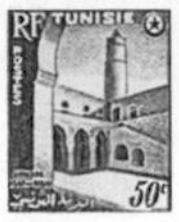

73 Courtyard, Sousse

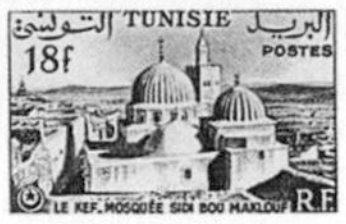

74 Sidi Bou Maklouf Mosque, Le Kef

1954

370	**73**	50c. green	35	5·75
371	**73**	1f. red	45	35
372	-	2f. purple	80	95
373	-	4f. turquoise	1·90	2·00
374	-	5f. violet	1·60	10
375	-	8f. brown	1·50	2·50
376	-	10f. green	2·50	2·50
377	-	12f. brown	2·30	1·60
378	-	15f. blue (18×22 mm)	2·50	2·75
386	-	15f. blue (17×21½ mm)	65	10
379	**74**	18f. brown	4·50	5·25
380	-	20f. blue	2·30	70
381	-	25f. blue	2·50	1·30
382	-	30f. purple	2·50	6·50
383	-	40f. green	2·50	2·75
384	-	50f. lilac	3·00	70
385	-	75f. red	6·25	8·75

DESIGNS—As Type **73**: 2, 4f. Takrouna ramparts; 5, 8f. Dwellings and Mosque, Tatahouine; 10, 12f. Cave dwellings, Matmata; 15f. Street, Sidi-bou-said. As Type **74**: 20, 25f. Genoese Fort, Tabarka; 30, 40f. Bab-el-Khadra Gate, Tunis; 50, 75f. Four-storey dwellings, Medenine.

For similar stamps but without "R F" see Nos. 406/22.

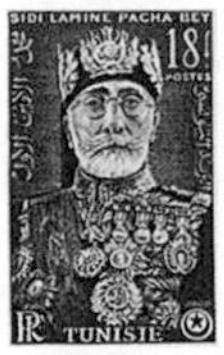

76 Bey of Tunisia

1954

387	**76**	8f. deep blue and blue	2·50	6·75
388	**76**	12f. indigo and blue	2·50	3·75
389	**76**	15f. red and carmine	2·50	6·50
390	**76**	18f. deep brown and brown	3·00	6·50
391	**76**	30f. deep green and green	3·50	9·25

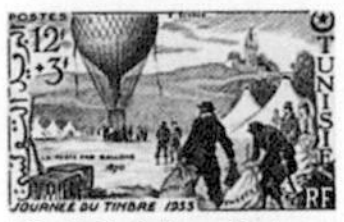

76a Paris Balloon Post, 1870

1955. Stamp Day.

392	**76a**	12f.+3f. brown	2·00	2·30

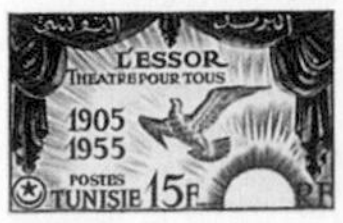

77

1955. 50th Anniv of "L'Essor" (Tunisian Amateur Dramatic Society).

393	**77**	15f. blue, red and orange	1·80	6·75

78 Tunisian Buildings and Rotary Emblem

1955. 50th Anniv of Rotary International.

394	**78**	12f. deep brown and brown	45	7·75
395	**78**	15f. brown and grey	45	7·75
396	**78**	18f. lilac and violet	45	7·75
397	**78**	25f. deep blue and blue	45	7·75
398	**78**	30f. indigo and blue	65	7·75

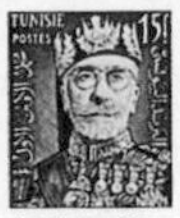

79 Bey of Tunisia

1955

399	**79**	15f. blue	1·30	35

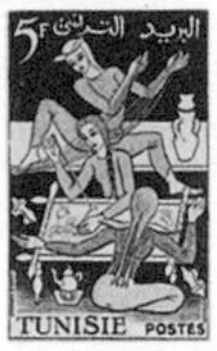

80 "Embroidery"

1955. Third International Fair, Tunis.

400	**80**	5f. lake	1·10	5·50
401	**80**	12f. blue	1·10	5·50
402	-	15f. green	1·40	5·75
403	-	18f. red	1·10	4·50
404	-	20f. violet	1·40	7·50
405	-	30f. purple	90	5·25

DESIGNS: 15, 18f. "Pottery"; 20, 30f. "Jasmin sellers".

1956. Nos. 365/6 and 368/86 re-engraved without "R F".

406	50c. green (postage)	10	3·50
407	1f. red	35	10
408	2f. purple	10	35
409	4f. blue	40	10
410	5f. violet	10	10
411	8f. brown	40	50
412	10f. green	35	10
413	12f. brown	35	15
414	15f. blue (18×22 mm)	3·00	3·50
415	15f. blue (17×21½ mm)	60	10
416	18f. brown	35	55
417	20f. blue	35	10
418	25f. blue	1·10	10
419	30f. purple	35	15
420	40f. green	35	10
421	50f. lilac	1·30	10
422	75f. red	85	55
423	100f. blue, turquoise and green (air)	2·75	45
424	200f. sepia, purple and brown	2·75	1·80
425	500f. brown and blue	7·25	14·00
426	1000f. green	8·25	36·00

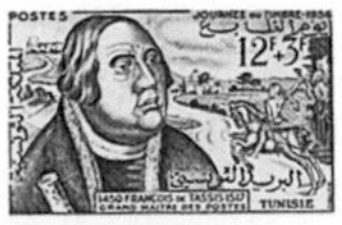

80a Francis of Taxis

1956. Stamp Day.

427	**80a**	12f.+3f. green	1·20	5·25

INDEPENDENT KINGDOM

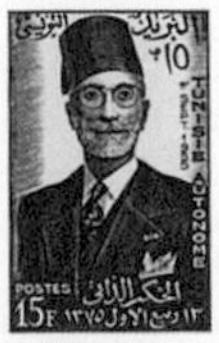

81 Bey of Tunisia

1956. Autonomous Government.

428	**81**	5f. blue	35	35
429	-	12f. purple	35	35
430	**81**	15f. red	35	35
431	-	18f. grey	45	35
432	**81**	20f. green	45	35
433	-	30f. brown	90	40

DESIGN: 12, 18, 30f. Tunisian girl releasing dove.

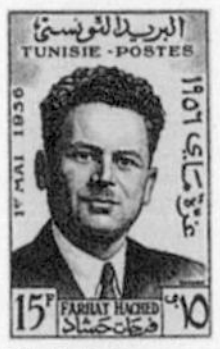

82 Farhat Hached

1956. Labour Day.

434	**82**	15f. lake	30	30
435	**82**	30f. blue	35	35

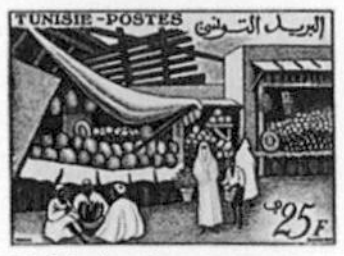

83 Market Scene

1956. Tunisian Products.

436	-	12f. violet, purple & mauve	60	20
437	-	15f. green, brown and blue	60	20
438	-	18f. blue	90	35
439	-	20f. brown	90	35
440	**83**	25f. brown	1·25	55
441	**83**	30f. blue	1·40	55

DESIGNS—VERT: 12f. Bunch of grapes; 15f. Sprig of olives; 18f. Harvesting; 20f. Man with basket containing wedding offering.

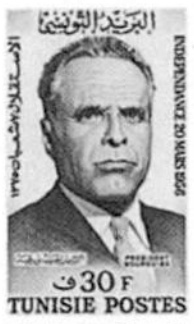

84 Pres. Habib Bourguiba

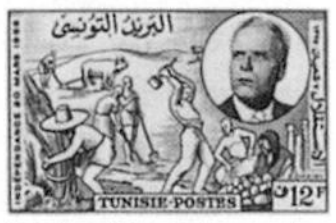

85 Pres. Bourguiba and Agricultural Workers

1957. First Anniv of Independence.

442	**84**	5f. blue	20	20
443	**85**	12f. pink	20	20
444	**84**	20f. blue	30	20
445	**85**	25f. green	35	20
446	**84**	30f. brown	40	30
447	**85**	50f. red	80	50

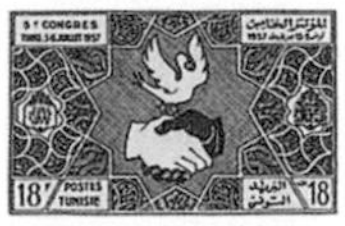

86 Dove and Handclasp

1957. Fifth International Confederation of Free Trade Unions Congress.

448	**86**	18f. purple	35	35
449	-	20f. red	40	40
450	**86**	25f. green	40	40
451	-	30f. blue	45	45

DESIGN—VERT: 20, 30f. Handclasp and Labour Exchange.

INDEPENDENT REPUBLIC

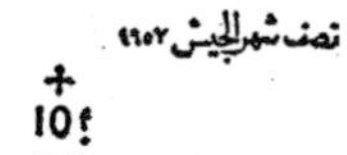

(87)

1957. Tunisian Army Fortnight. No. 417 optd with T **87**.

452		20f.+10f. blue	55	55

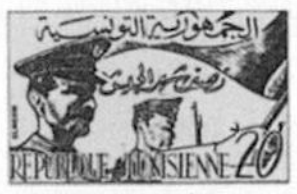

88 Tunisian Soldiers and Flag

1957. Proclamation of Republic.

453	**88**	20f. red	16·00	16·00
454	**88**	25f. violet	16·00	16·00
455	**88**	30f. brown	16·00	16·00

1957. Fifth International Fair, Tunis. As No. 404 but additionally inscr "5e FOIRE INTERNATIONALE" and Arabic inscriptions at sides, surch **+ 10F.**

456		20f.+10f. violet	45	45

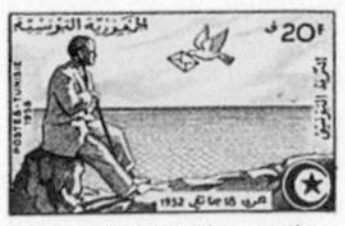

90 Pres Bourguiba on Ile de la Galite

1958. Sixth Anniv of Exile of Pres. Bourguiba.

457	**90**	20f. blue and brown	55	35
458	**90**	25f. blue and violet	55	35

91 Tunisian Emblems and Map

1958. Second Anniv of Independence.
459	**91**	20f. green and brown	35	15
460	-	25f. brown and blue	35	15
461	-	30f. brown, deep brown and red	45	20

DESIGNS: 25f. Mother and child; 30f. Clenched fist holding Tunisian flag.
For 20f. brown and blue see No. 464.

92 Andreas Vesalius (scientist) and A. ibn Khaldoun

1958. Brussels International Exhibition.
462	**92**	30f. green and bistre	45	20

93 Planting Olives

1958. Labour Day.
463	**93**	20f. multicoloured	45	45

1958. Third Anniv of Return of Pres. Bourguiba. As T **91** but with inscr altered.
464	**91**	20f. brown and blue	40	20

94

1958. First Anniv of Proclamation of Tunisian Republic.
465	**94**	5f. purple and bistre	45	20
466	**94**	10f. deep green & lt green	45	20
467	**94**	15f. brown and orange	45	20
468	**94**	20f. violet, olive and yellow	45	20
469	**94**	25f. purple	45	20

95 Pres. Bourguiba

1958. Pres. Bourguiba's 55th Birthday.
470	**95**	20f. purple and violet	35	20

96 Fishermen with Catch

1958. Sixth International Fair.
471	**96**	25f. purple, red and green	70	35

97 UNESCO Headquarters, Paris

1958. Inaug of UNESCO Building.
472	**97**	25f. myrtle	60	35

98 "Shedding the veil"

1959. Emancipation of Tunisian Women.
473	**98**	20m. turquoise	45	30

99 Hand holding plant

1959. 25th Anniv of Neo-Destour (Nationalist Party) and Victory Congress.
474	**99**	5m. red, brown and purple	30	10
475	-	10m. multicoloured	35	15
476	-	20m. blue	40	20
477	-	30m. blue, turquoise & brown	65	40

DESIGNS—VERT: 10m. Tunisians with flaming torch and flag on shield; 20m. Pres. Bourguiba in exile at Borj le Boeuf, 1954. HORIZ: 30m. Pres. Bourguiba and Borj le Boeuf, 1934.

100 "Tunisia"

1959. Third Anniv of Independence.
478	**100**	50m. multicoloured	65	35

101 Tunisian Horseman

1959. Designs as T **101**.
479		½m. brown, green and emerald	35	10
480		1m. bistre and blue	10	10
481		2m. brown, yellow and blue	15	10
482		3m. myrtle	10	10
483		4m. brown	30	15
484		5m. myrtle	20	10
485		6m. violet	20	15
486		8m. purple	65	30
487		10m. red, green and bistre	20	10
487a		12m. violet and bistre	65	20
488		15m. blue	60	10
489		16m. green	30	20
490		20m. turquoise	1·00	30
491		20m. purple, olive and myrtle	2·25	30
492		25m. blue, brown & turquoise	30	20
493		30m. brown, green & turq	45	10
494		40m. green	1·60	20
495		45m. green	70	30
496		50m. multicoloured	90	20
497		60m. brown and green	1·25	35
498		70m. multicoloured	1·40	50
499		75m. brown	1·25	55
500		90m. brown, green and blue	1·60	55
501		95m. multicoloured	1·90	1·00
502		100m. multicoloured	2·00	90
503		200m. red, bistre and blue	5·00	2·50
504		½d. brown	16·00	6·75
505		1d. ochre and green	25·00	13·50

DESIGNS—VERT: ½m. Ain Draham; 2m. Camel-driver; 3m. Saddler's shop; 5m. Type **101**; 6m. Weavers; 8m. Gafsa; 10m. Woman holding pomegranates; 12m. Turner; 20m. (No. 491), Gabes; 40m. Kairouan; 70m. Carpet weaver; 75m. Nabeul vase; 95m. Olive-gatherer; ½d. Sbeitla. HORIZ: 1m. Kairouan environs; 4m. Medenine; 15m. Monastir; 16m. Tunis; 20m. (No. 490), Room in Arab house, Sidi-Bou-Said; 25m. Sfax; 30m. Aqueduct, Medjerda Valley; 45m. Bizerta; 50m. Djerba; 60m. Le Jerid; 90m. Le Kef; 100m. Sidi-bou-Said highway; 200m. Old port of Sfax; 1d. Beja ploughman.

102 "Freedom"

1959. Africa Freedom Day.
506	**102**	40m. brown and blue	50	35

103 Postman

1959. Stamp Day.
507	**103**	20m.+5m. brown & orge	45	45

104 Clenched Hands

1959. U.N. Day.
508	**104**	80m. brown, blue & purple	65	45

105

1959. Red Crescent Day.
509	**105**	10m.+5m. multicoloured	35	35

106 Dancer and Coin

1959. First Anniv of Tunisian Central Bank.
510	**106**	50m. black and blue	50	50

107 "Uprooted Tree"

1960. World Refugee Year. Inscr "ANNEE MONDIALE DES REFUGIES 1959–1960".
511	**107**	20m. blue	40	20
512	-	40m. black and purple	50	35

DESIGN—HORIZ: 40m. Doves.

108 Camel Rider telephoning

1960. Stamp Day.
513	**108**	60m.+5m. orange, blue and olive	80	80

109 Pres. Bourguiba signing Promulgation

1960. Promulgation of Constitution.
514	**109**	20m. red, brown and green	40	35

110 Fair Emblems

1960. Fifth Sousse National Fair.
515	**110**	100m. black and green	65	45

111 President Bourguiba

1960
516	**111**	20m. black	20	10
517	**111**	30m. black, red and blue	35	10
518	**111**	40m. black, red and green	45	20

112 Jamboree Emblems

1960. Fourth Arab Scout Jamboree, Tunis.
519	**112**	10m. turquoise	35	35
520	-	25m. purple, red and green	40	35
521	-	30m. lake, violet and green	60	35
522	-	40m. black, blue and red	65	40
523	-	60m. violet, purple & sepia	1·25	55

DESIGNS: 25m. Saluting hand with scouts as fingers; 30m. Camp bugler; 40m. Scout peacock badge; 60m. Scout by camp fire.

113 Cyclist in Stadium

1960. Olympic Games.
524	**113**	5m. brown and olive	30	25
525	-	10m. purple, green & blue	35	30
526	-	15m. carmine and red	35	30
527	-	25m. slate and blue	45	40
528	-	50m. blue and green	85	65

DESIGNS: 10m. Flowers composed of Olympic rings; 15m. Girl with racquet; 25m. Runner; 50m. Handball player.

114

1960. Fifth World Forestry Congress, Seattle.
529	**114**	8m. lake, green and blue	35	15
530	-	15m. green	40	20

| 531 | - | 25m. red, green and violet | 65 | 30 |
| 532 | - | 50m. turquoise, brown & green | 1·10 | 50 |

DESIGNS: 15m. Removing bark from tree; 25m. Tree within leaf; 50m. Diamond pattern featuring palm.

115 U.N. Emblem and People's Arms

1960. U.N. Day.

| 533 | **115** | 40m. blue, red and black | 65 | 45 |

116 Dove of Peace

1961. Fifth Anniv of Independence.

534	**116**	20m. blue, bistre & purple	30	20
535	**116**	30m. brown, violet & blue	35	20
536	**116**	40m. ultramarine, blue & green	55	40
537	-	75m. blue, mauve and olive	80	45

DESIGN: 75m. Globe and Arms of Tunisia.

117 Tunisian Animals and Map of Africa

1961. Africa Day and Third Anniv of Accra Conference. Inscr "JOURNEE DE L'AFRIQUE 15.4.1961".

538	**117**	40m. green, brown and bistre	35	20
539	-	60m. black, brown & turquoise	40	30
540	-	100m. violet, emerald and grey	70	45
541	-	200m. brown and orange	1·40	1·00

DESIGNS (all showing outline of Africa): 50m. Profiles of Negress and Arab woman; 100m. Masks and "Africa Day" in Arabic; 200m. Clasped hands.

118 Stamps and Magnifier

1961. Stamp Day. Inscr "JOURNEE DU TIMBRE 1961". Multicoloured.

542		12m.+4m. Kerkennah dancer and costume of stamps (vert)	45	45
543		15m.+5m. Mobile postal delivery (vert)	60	60
544		20m.+6m. Type **118**	65	65
545		50m.+5m. Postman in shirt depicting stamps (vert)	80	80

119 "Celebration"

1961. National Day.

546	**119**	25m. brown, red and violet	45	15
547	-	50m. brown, choc & grn	45	20
548	-	95m. mauve, brown & blue	65	40

DESIGNS: 50m. Family celebrating in street; 95m. Girl astride crescent moon.

120 Dag Hammarskjoeld

1961. U.N. Day.

| 549 | **120** | 40m. blue | 60 | 35 |

121 Arms of Tunisia

1962. Tenth Anniv of Independence Campaign. Arms in red, yellow, blue and black.

550	**121**	1m. yellow and black	10	10
551	**121**	2m. pink and black	15	15
552	**121**	3m. blue and black	15	15
553	**121**	6m. grey and black	20	20

122 Mosquito in Web

1962. Malaria Eradication. Inscr "LE MONDE UNI CONTRE LE PALUDISME".

554	**122**	20m. brown	45	30
555	-	30m. brown, green & chocolate	45	30
556	-	40m. red, green and brown	80	35

DESIGNS—VERT: 30m. "Horseman" attacking mosquito; 40m. Hands destroying mosquito.

123 African

1962. Africa Day. Inscr "JOURNEE DE L'AFRIQUE 1962".

| 557 | **123** | 50m. brown and buff | 55 | 35 |
| 558 | - | 10m. multicoloured | 80 | 45 |

DESIGN: 100m. Symbolic figure clasping "Africa".

124 Dancer

1962. May Day. Inscr "FETE DU TRAVAIL 1962".

| 559 | **124** | 40m. multicoloured | 40 | 20 |
| 560 | - | 60m. brown | 45 | 30 |

DESIGN: 60m. Worker with pneumatic drill.

125 Rejoicing Tunisians

1962. National Day.

| 561 | **125** | 20m. black and salmon | 50 | 35 |

126 Gabes Costume

1962. Republic Festival. Regional Costumes. Multicoloured.

562	5m. Type **126**	55	20
563	10m. Mahdia	65	35
564	15m. Kairouan	90	45
565	20m. Hammamet	1·10	55
566	25m. Djerba	1·25	55
567	30m. As 10m.	1·25	65
568	40m. As 20m.	1·40	65
569	50m. Type **126**	1·40	85
570	55m. Ksar Hellal	2·50	1·00
571	60m. Tunis	3·00	1·40

127 U.N. Emblem and Tunisian Flag

1962. U.N. Day.

572	**127**	20m. red, black and grey	35	30
573	-	30m. multicoloured	40	30
574	-	40m. blue, black & brown	65	35

DESIGNS—HORIZ: 30m. "Plant" with three leaves and globe. VERT: 40m. Globe and dove.

128 A. Q. Chabbi (poet)

1962. Aboul Qasim Chabbi Commemoration.

| 575 | **128** | 15m. violet | 35 | 20 |

129 Pres. Bourguiba

1962

576	**129**	20m. blue	15	15
577	**129**	30m. red	15	10
578	**129**	40m. green	20	15

130 Hached Telephone Exchange

1962. Modernization of Telephone System.

579	**130**	5m. multicoloured	30	20
580	-	10m. multicoloured	35	20
581	-	15m. multicoloured	50	35
582	-	50m. flesh, brown & black	80	50
583	-	100m. blue, purple & black	2·00	90
584	-	200m. multicoloured	2·75	1·40

DESIGNS: 10m. Carthage Telephone Exchange; 15m. Aerial equipment; 50m. Telephone switchboard operators; 100m. Telephone equipment as human figure; 200m. Belvedere Telephone Exchange.

131 Runners

1963. 13th International Military Sports Council Cross-country Championships.

| 585 | **131** | 30m. brown, green & black | 60 | 45 |

132 Dove with Wheatear and Globe

1963. Freedom from Hunger.

| 586 | **132** | 20m. blue and brown | 30 | 20 |
| 587 | - | 40m. purple and brown | 40 | 20 |

DESIGN: 40m. Child taking nourishment.

133 Centenary Emblem

1963. Red Cross Centenary.

| 588 | **133** | 20m. red, grey and brown | 45 | 20 |

1963. U.N. Day. Nos. 542/5 optd **1963 O.N.U.** in English and Arabic.

589	12m.+4m. multicoloured	30	30
590	15m.+5m. multicoloured	35	35
591	20m.+6m. multicoloured	40	40
592	50m.+5m. multicoloured	65	65

135 "Miss World"

1963. 15th Anniv of Declaration of Human Rights.

| 593 | **135** | 30m. brown and green | 45 | 30 |

136 "Out of Reach"

1964. Nubian Monuments Preservation.

| 594 | **136** | 50m. ochre, brown & blue | 45 | 30 |

137 "Unsettled Forecast"

1964. World Meteorological Day.

| 595 | **137** | 40m. mauve, blue & brown | 45 | 20 |

138 Mohamed
Ali (trade union
leader)

1964. 70th Birth Anniv of Mohamed Ali.
596   **138**   50m. purple   45   35

139 Africa within
Flower

1964. First Anniv of Addis Ababa Conference of the
Organization of African Unity.
597   **139**   60m. multicoloured   50   30

140 Pres.
Bourguiba

1964. National Day.
598   **140**   20m. blue   15   10
599   **140**   30m. brown   20   10

141 "Bizerte"
("ship")

1964. Neo-Destour Congress, Bizerta.
600   **141**   50m. green and black   40   30

142 Fulvous
Babbler

1965. Air. Tunisian Birds. Multicoloured.
601   **142**   25m. Type **142**   1·50   50
602   55m. Great grey strike   2·25   75
603   55m. Cream-coloured courser   2·50   95
604   100m. Chaffinch   3·00   1·10
605   150m. Greater flamingoes   5·25   2·40
606   200m. Barbary partridge   8·00   2·75
607   300m. European roller   12·50   5·25
608   500m. Houbara bustard   18·00   6·25
SIZES—As Type **142**: 55m. (both). Others, 23×32½ mm.

143 Early Telegraphist
and Aerial Mast

1965. I.T.U. Centenary.
609   **143**   55m. blue and black   50   30

144 Carthaginian
Coin

1965. Festival of Popular Arts, Carthage.
610   **144**   5m. purple and green   15   10
611   **144**   10m. purple and yellow   30   20
612   **144**   75m. purple and blue   65   20

145 Girl reading
Book

1965. Opening of Students' Home, Tunis.
613   **145**   25m. blue, black and red   30   20
614   **145**   40m. black, blue and red   40   20
615   **145**   50m. red, black and blue   45   30
MS616 130×130 mm. Nos. 613/15.
Imperf or perf (sold at 200m.)   2·50   2·50

146 Joined
Hooks

1965. International Co-operation Year.
617   **146**   40m. blue, purple &
           black   45   25

147 Women
bathing

1966. Mineral Springs. Inscr "EAUX MINERALES".
618   **147**   10m. red, ochre and grey   30   20
619   20m. multicoloured   40   30
620   30m. red, blue and
           yellow   45   35
621   100m. olive, yellow
           & blue   1·10   55
DESIGNS: 20m. Man pouring water; 30m. Woman pouring water; 100m. Mountain and fronds of tree.

148 Pres. Bourguiba and   **149**
Hands   Independence

1966. Tenth Anniv of Independence.
622   **148**   5m. lilac and blue   15   10
623   **148**   10m. green and blue   20   15
624   **149**   25m. multicoloured   20   15
625   40m. multicoloured   55   20
626   60m. multicoloured   80   35
DESIGNS—As Type **149**: 40m. "Development".
VERT: 60m. "Promotion of Culture" ("man" draped in books, palette, musical instruments, etc).

150 Sectional
Map of Africa

1966. Second U.N. African Regional Cartographic
Conference, Tunisia.
627   **150**   15m. multicoloured   30   20
628   **150**   35m. multicoloured   35   20
629   **150**   40m. multicoloured   50   35
MS630 129×98 mm. Nos. 627/9. Imperf
or perf (sold at 150m.)   12·00   12·00

151 UNESCO Emblem of
the Muses

1966. 20th Anniv of UNESCO.
631   **151**   100m. brown and black   85   35

152 "Athletics"

1967. Publicity for Mediterranean Games (September, 1967).
632   **152**   20m. brown, blue
         and red   20   15
633   **152**   30m. black and blue   40   30

153 Gabes   **154** Emblems of
Costume and   Civilization
Fair Emblem

1967. "Expo 67" World Fair, Montreal. T **154** and earlier
designs redrawn as T **153**.
634   50m. mult (As No. 566)   35   15
635   **153**   75m. multicoloured   50   30
636   **154**   100m. green, black &
         turquoise   80   30
637   **154**   110m. red, sepia and
         blue   95   40
638   155m. mult (As No. 605)   1·60   60

155 Tunisian Pavilion, Pres.
Bourguiba and Map

1967. "National Day at World Fair, Montreal".
639   **155**   65m. purple and red   40   35
640   105m. brown, red and
         blue   50   35
641   120m. blue   60   40
642   200m. black, red &
         purple   1·25   50
DESIGNS: 105m. As Type **155**, but with profile bust of
Pres. Bourguiba. Tunisian pavilion (different view) with:
120m. Silhouette and 200m. Bust of Pres. Bourguiba.

156 "Tunisia" holding
Clover

1967. Tenth Anniv of Republic. Multicoloured.
643   **156**   25m. Type **156**   20   15
644   40m. Woman releasing doves
        (vert)   35   15

157 Tennis Club

1967. Mediterranean Games, Tunis.
645   **157**   5m. red and green   20   20
646   10m. multicoloured   20   15
647   15m. black   35   20
648   35m. turquoise, purple
        & black   45   20
649   75m. green, violet
        and red   80   40
DESIGNS—VERT: 10m. "Spring Triumphs" (squared panel).
HORIZ: 15m. Olympic swimming pool; 35m. Sports Palace; 75m. Olympic stadium.

158 Bas-relief from
Statue of Apollo

1967. Tunisian History. Punic period.
650   **158**   15m. red, black and
        green   30   20
651   20m. flesh, red and blue   35   20
652   25m. brown and olive   45   20

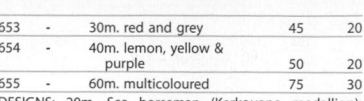

653   30m. red and grey   45   20
654   40m. lemon, yellow &
        purple   50   20
655   60m. multicoloured   75   30
DESIGNS: 20m. Sea horseman (Kerkouane medallion);
25m. Hannibal (bronze bust); 30m. "The Sacrifice" (votive
stele); 40m. Hamilcar (coin); 60m. Glass funeral pendant
mask.

159 "Human
Rights"

1968. Human Rights Year.
656   **159**   25m. red   40   35
657   **159**   60m. blue   45   20

160 "Electronic Man"

1968. Electronics in Postal Service.
658   **160**   25m. blue, brown &
        purple   35   30
659   **160**   40m. black, brown &
        green   35   30
660   **160**   60m. purple, slate and
        blue   45   35

161 "Doctor
and Patient"

1968. 20th Anniv of W.H.O.
661   **161**   25m. green and
        turquoise   40   35
662   **161**   60m. red and lake   45   35

162 Arabian
Jasmine

1968. Tunisian Flowers. Multicoloured.
663   5m. Flax   20   15
664   6m. Indian shot   20   15
665   10m. Pomegranate   30   15
666   12m. Type **162**   30   15
667   15m. Raponticum   35   15
668   20m. Geranium   40   20
669   25m. Madonna lily   40   30
670   40m. Almond   60   30
671   50m. Capers   80   45
672   60m. Ariana rose   1·25   70
673   100m. Jasmine   1·90   1·10

163 Globe on
"Sunflower"

1968. Red Crescent Day.
674   **163**   15m. red, green and
        blue   35   30
675   25m. red and purple   40   30
DESIGN: 25m. Red crescent on wings of dove.

164 Flautist

1968. Stamp Day.
676	**164**	20m. multicoloured	35	20
677	**164**	50m. multicoloured	40	35

165 Golden Jackal

1968. Fauna. Multicoloured.
678		5m. Type **165**	20	15
679		8m. North African crested porcupine	30	20
680		10m. Dromedary	40	20
681		15m. Dorcas gazelle	75	20
682		20m. Fennec fox	1·25	45
683		25m. Algerian hedgehog	1·50	55
684		40m. Horse	1·90	80
685		60m. Wild boar	2·50	1·25

166 Worker

1969. 50th Anniv of I.L.O. Multicoloured.
686		25m. Type **166**	35	30
687		60m. Youth and girl holding "May 1" banner	50	35

167 Musicians and Veiled Dancers

1969. Stamp Day.
688	**167**	100m. multicoloured	70	35

168 Tunisian Arms

1969
689	**168**	15m. multicoloured	20	20
690	**168**	25m. multicoloured	30	20
691	**168**	40m. multicoloured	35	20
692	**168**	60m. multicoloured	40	20

169 "Industrial Development"

1969. Fifth Anniv of African Development Bank.
693	**169**	60m. multicoloured	40	30

170 Lute

1970. Musical Instruments. Multicoloured.
694		25m. Type **170**	45	35
695		50m. Zither	55	35
696		70m. Rehab	80	35
697		90m. Naghrat (drums)	1·00	35

Nos. 695 and 697 are horiz, size 33×22 mm.

171 Nurse, Caduceus and Flags

1970. Sixth North-African Maghreb Medical Seminar, Tunis.
698	**171**	25m. multicoloured	35	20

172 New U.P.U. Headquarters Building

1970. New U.P.U. Headquarters Building, Berne.
699	**172**	25m. brown and red	40	20

173 Mounted Postman

1970. Stamp Day. Multicoloured.
700		25m. Type **173**	20	20
701		35m. "Postmen of yesterday and today" (23×38 mm)	35	20

174 U.N. Emblem, "N" and Dove forming "O.N.U."

1970. 25th Anniv of United Nations.
702	**174**	40m. multicoloured	40	20

175 "The Flower-seller"

1970. "Tunisian Life" (1st series). Multicoloured.
703		20m. Type **175**	20	15
704		25m. "The husband's third day of marriage"	30	20
705		35m. "The Perfumer"	45	35
706		40m. "The Fish-seller"	50	35
707		85m. "The Coffee-house keeper"	80	35
MS708		139×126 mm. Nos. 703/7. Imperf or perf	2·25	2·25

See also Nos. 715/**MS**719, 757/**MS**765 and 819/**MS**824.

176 Lenin

1970. Birth Centenary of Lenin.
709	**176**	60m. lake	1·25	35

177 Dish Aerial and Flags

1971. Maghreban Posts and Telecommunciations Co-ordination.
710	**177**	25m. multicoloured	40	35

178 U.N. Building and Symbol

1971. Racial Equality Year.
711	**178**	80m. multicoloured	45	30

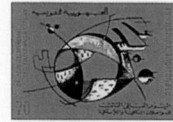

179 Globe and Satellites

1971. World Telecommunications Day.
712	**179**	70m. multicoloured	40	20

180 Moon, Earth and Satellites

1971. "Conquest of Space".
713	**180**	15m. black and blue	35	20
714	-	90m. black and red	60	30

DESIGN: 90m. Space allegory.

181 "The Pottery Dealer"

1971. "Tunisian Life" (2nd series). Multicoloured.
715		25m. Type **181**	35	20
716		30m. "The Esparto dealer"	35	20
717		40m. "The Poulterer"	45	20
718		50m. "The Dyer"	55	30
MS719		100×129 mm. Nos. 715/18. Imperf or perf (sold at 500m.)	2·50	2·50

182 Pres. Bourguiba

1971. Eighth P.S.D. Destourian Socialist Party Congress, Tunis. Multicoloured.
720		25m. Type **182**	20	20
721		30m. Bourguiba in bed, 1938 (horiz)	20	20
722		50m. Bourguiba acclaimed	35	30
723		80m. Bourguiba—"Builder of the Nation" (horiz)	45	30

SIZES: 30m., 80m. 13½×14; 50m. As Type **182**.

183 Shah Mohammed Riza Pahlavi and Achaemenidian Effigy

1971. 2500th Anniv of Persian Empire. Multicoloured.
724		25m. Type **183**	30	20
725		50m. "King Bahram-Gur hunting" (14th-century)	35	20
726		100m. "Coronation of Louhrasap" (Persian 11th-century miniature)	60	30
MS727		104×82 mm. Nos. 724/6. Imperf or perf (sold at 500m.)	2·50	2·50

184 Pimento

1971. "Flowers, Fruits and Folklore". Multicoloured.
728		1m. Type **184**	10	10
729		2m. Mint	20	15
730		5m. Pear	35	20
731		25m. Laurel rose	40	30
732		60m. Quince	80	20
733		100m. Grapefruit	1·50	35
MS734		130×160 mm. Nos. 728/33. Imperf or perf (sold at 500m.)	2·50	2·50

Each design includes a scene from Tunisian folklore.

185 "The Musicians of Kerkena"

1971. Stamp Day.
735	**185**	50m. multicoloured	40	20

186 Telephone

1971. Pan-African Telecommunications Network.
736	**186**	95m. multicoloured	50	45

187 UNICEF Emblem

1971. 25th Anniv of UNICEF.
737	**187**	110m. multicoloured	50	35

188 Rialto Bridge, Venice

1971. UNESCO "Save Venice" Campaign. Multicoloured.
738		25m. Gondolier (vert)	35	20
739		30m. De Medici and Palace (vert)	40	20
740		50m. Prow of gondola (vert)	45	35
741		80m. Type **188**	80	35

189 Olive-tree Emblem

1972. World Olive-oil Year.
742	**189**	60m. multicoloured	40	20

190 Tunisian reading Book

1972. International Book Year.
743	**190**	90m. multicoloured	50	40

191 Heart
Emblem

1972. World Health Day. Multicoloured.
744		25m. Type **191**	35	20
745		60m. Heart within "hour-glass"	55	35

192 "Old Age"

1972. Tunisian Red Crescent.
746	**192**	10m.+10m. violet & red	35	30
747	-	75m.+10m. brown & red	50	35

DESIGN: 75m. Mother and Child ("Child Care").

193 "Only One Earth"

1972. U.N. Environmental Conservation Conf, Stockholm.
748	**193**	60m. green and brown	50	20

194 Hurdling

1972. Olympic Games, Munich.
749	-	5m. multicoloured	10	10
750	**194**	15m. multicoloured	15	10
751	-	20m. black, green and gold	15	10
752	-	25m. multicoloured	15	15
753	-	60m. multicoloured	35	20
754	-	80m. multicoloured	45	30

MS755 130×95 mm. Nos. 749/54.
Imperf or perf (sold at 500m.)   2·50   2·50
DESIGNS—VERT: 5m. Handball; 20m. Athletes saluting. HORIZ: 25m. Football; 60m. Swimming; 80m. Running.

195 Chessboard

1972. 20th Chess Olympiad, Skopje, Yugoslavia.
756	**195**	60m. multicoloured	1·25	55

196 "The Fisherman"

1972. "Tunisian Life" (3rd series). Multicoloured.
757		5m. Type **196**	20	15
758		10m. "The Basket-maker"	20	15
759		25m. "The Musician"	30	15
760		50m. "The Berber Bride"	55	20
761		60m. "The Flower-seller"	80	20
762		80m. "The Mystic"	1·10	40

MS763 136×136 mm. Nos. 757/62. Perf
or imperf (sold at 500m.)   2·00   2·00

197 New P.T.T. H.Q., Tunis

1972. Stamp Day.
764	**197**	25m. multicoloured	30	20

198 Dome of the Rock, Jerusalem

1973. Dome of the Rock Commemoration.
765	**198**	25m. multicoloured	40	30

199 Globe and Beribboned Pen

1973. Ninth Writers' Congress and 11th Poetry Festival. Multicoloured.
766		25m. Type **199**	20	20
767		60m. Lyre emblem	35	20

200 Heads of Family

1973. Family Planning. Multicoloured.
768		20m. Type **200**	20	20
769		25m Family profiles and bird	35	30

201 Figures "10" and Bird feeding Young

1973. Tenth Anniv of World Food Programme. Multicoloured.
770		25m. Type **201**	60	20
771		60m. Symbolic "10"	60	20

202 Sculptured Roman Head

1973. UNESCO "Save Carthage" Campaign. Multicoloured.
772		5m. Type **202**	30	20
773		25m. Carthagian mosaics	45	35
774		30m. "Cycle of mosaics"	45	35
775		40m. "Goodwill" stele (vert)	60	35
776		60m. Preacher's hand (from Korba statue)	70	35
777		75m. "Malga" (17th-century potsherd) (vert)	85	40

MS778 144×100 mm. Nos. 772/7.
Imperf (sold at 500m.)   5·50   5·50

203 Red Crescent Nurse

1973. Tunisian Red Crescent.
779	**203**	25m.+10m. multicol-oured	45	35
780	-	60m.+10m. red and grey	65	35

DESIGN—HORIZ: 60m. Arms of blood donors.

204 "World Telecommunications"

1973. Fifth World Telecommunications Day. Multicoloured.
781		60m. Type **204**	35	20
782		75m. "The Universe"	40	20

205 Smiling Youth

1973. First Pan-African Festival of Youth. Multicoloured.
783		25m. Festival Map	35	30
784		40m. Type **205**	40	30

206 Scout Badge

1973. International Scouting.
785	**206**	25m. multicoloured	35	30

207 "Rover" in Car

1973. Second Pan-Arab Rover Rally.
786	**207**	60m. multicoloured	40	35

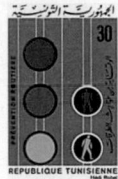

208 Traffic Lights

1973. Road Safety. Multicoloured.
787		25m. Motorway junction (horiz)	35	30
788		30m. Type **208**	40	30

209 Winged Camel

1973. Stamp Day. Multicoloured.
789		10m. Peacock ("collectors pride") (horiz)	35	20
790		65m. Type **209**	40	35

210 Copernicus

1973. 500th Birth Anniv of Copernicus.
791	**210**	60m. multicoloured	1·25	35

211 O.A.U. Emblems within Arms

1973. Tenth Anniv of Organization of African Unity.
792	**211**	25m. multicoloured	40	20

212 Interpol Emblem and Handclasp

1973. 50th Anniv of International Criminal Police Organization (Interpol).
793	**212**	65m. multicoloured	45	35

213 Flower Offering

1973. 25th Anniv of Declaration of Human Rights.
794	**213**	60m. multicoloured	55	35

214 W.M.O. H.Q., Geneva

1973. W.M.O. Centenary. Multicoloured.
795		25m. Type **214**	40	20
796		60m. Earth and emblems	45	30

215 President Bourguiba, 1934

1974. 40th Anniv of Neo-Destour Party.
797	**215**	15m. purple, red and black	20	20
798	-	25m. brown, orange & black	20	20
799	-	60m. blue, red and black	30	20
800	-	75m. brown, mauve & black	35	20
801	-	100m. green, orange & black	45	35

MS802 155×63 mm. Nos. 797/801.
Imperf or perf (sold at 500m.)   2·25   2·25
DESIGNS: Nos. 798/801, Various portraits of Pres. Bourguiba (founder), similar to Type **215**.

216 Scientist using Microscope

1974. Sixth African Micro-Palaeontological Conf, Tunis.
803	**216**	60m. multicoloured	1·40	60

217 "Blood Donation"

1974. Tunisian Red Crescent. Multicoloured.

804	25m.+10m. Type **217**	35	35
805	75m.+10m. "Blood Transfusion"	45	45

218 Telephonist holding Globe

1974. Inauguration of International Automatic Telephone Service. Multicoloured.

806	15m. Type **218**	20	20
807	60m. Telephone dial	45	35

219 Population Emblems

1974. World Population Year.

808	**219**	110m. multicoloured	55	35

220 Pres. Bourguiba and Emblem

1974. Destourian Socialist Party Congress.

809	**220**	25m. blue, turquoise & black	20	20
810	-	60m. red, yellow and black	30	25
811	-	200m. purple, green & black	90	50

MS812 135×66 mm. Nos. 809/11.
Imperf (sold at 500m.)   2·25   2·25

DESIGNS—HORIZ: 60m. Pres. Bourguiba and sunflower; 200m. Pres. Bourguiba and sunflower.

221 Aircraft crossing Globe

1974. 25th Anniv of Tunisian Aviation.

813	**221**	60m. multicoloured	45	35

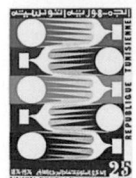

222 "Carrier-pigeons"

1974. Centenary of U.P.U. Multicoloured.

814	25m. Type **222**	35	25
815	60m. Handclasp	45	30

223 Bardo Palace as "Ballot Box"

1974. Legislative and Presidential Elections.

816	**223**	25m. blue, green and black	35	30
817	-	100m. black and orange	50	35

DESIGN: 100m. Pres. Bourguiba on poll card.

224 Postman with Parcels on Head

1974. Stamp Day.

818	**224**	75m. multicoloured	45	20

225 "The Water-carrier"

1975. "Scenes from Tunisian Life" (4th series). Multicoloured.

819	5m. Type **225**	15	15
820	15m. "The Scent Sprinkler"	20	20
821	25m. "The Washer-women"	20	20
822	60m. "The Potter"	35	20
823	110m. "The Fruit-seller"	85	50

MS824 124×118 mm. Nos. 819/23.
Imperf or perf (sold at 500m.)   2·40   2·40

226 Stylized Bird

1975. 13th Arab Engineers' Union Conference, Tunis. Multicoloured.

825	25m. Skyscraper and scaffolding (vert)	20	20
826	65m. Type **226**	75	30

227 Gold Coffee-pot and Tray

1975. Handicrafts. Multicoloured.

827	10m. Type **227**	20	20
828	15m. Horseman and saddlery (embroidery)	20	20
829	25m. Still life (painting)	30	20
830	30m. Bird-cage (fine-crafts) (vert)	35	20
831	40m. Silver head-dress (jewellery) (vert)	35	20
832	60m. Textile patterns	55	30

228 Man and Scales

1975. Tunisian Red Crescent Campaign against Malnutrition.

833	**228**	50m.+10m. mult	40	35

229 "Telecommunications"

1975. Seventh World Telecommunications Day.

834	**229**	50m. multicoloured	30	20

230 Allegory of Victory

1975. 20th Anniv of "Victory" (Return of Bourguiba). Multicoloured.

835	25m. Type **230**	20	20
836	65m. Return of President Bourguiba (horiz)	35	20

231 Tunisian Woman

1975. International Women's Year.

837	**231**	110m. multicoloured	55	30

232 Children on Road Crossing

1975. Road Safety Campaign.

838	**232**	25m. multicoloured	20	20

233 Djerba

1975. "Tunisia, Yesterday and Today" (1st series). Multicoloured.

839	10m. Type **233**	20	20
840	15m. Tunis	20	20
841	20m. Monastir	20	20
842	65m. Sousse	45	30
843	500m. Tozeur	3·75	35
844	1d. Kairouan	6·25	2·50

See also Nos. 864/7.

234 Figures representing Sport

1975. Seventh Mediterranean Games, Algiers. Multicoloured.

845	25m. Type **234**	20	20
846	50m. "Ship of sport" (horiz)	35	20

235 Bouquet of Flowers

1975. Stamp Day.

847	**235**	100m. multicoloured	45	20

236 College Building

1975. Centenary of Sadiki College.

848	**236**	25m. multicoloured	30	20

237 "Duck"

1976. Tunisian Mosaics. Multicoloured.

849	5m. Type **237**	30	20
850	10m. Fish	30	20
851	25m. Lioness (40×27 mm)	55	45
852	60m. Gorgon (40×27 mm)	60	45
853	75m. Circus spectators (27×40 mm)	65	45
854	100m. Virgil (27×40 mm)	1·25	45

MS855 95×123 mm. Nos. 849/54.
Imperf or perf (sold at 500m.)   1·90   1·90

238 Early and Modern Telephones

1976. Telephone Centenary.

856	**238**	150m. multicoloured	55	30

239 Figures "20" and Banners

1976. 20th Anniv of Independence. Multicoloured.

857	40m. Type **239**	20	20
858	100m. Figures "20" and flag emblem	40	20
859	150m. Floral allegory of "Tunisia"	60	30

MS860 120×82 mm. 50m. As No. 857; 200m. As No. 858; 250m. As No. 859.
Imperf or perf   3·75   3·75

240 Blind Man with Stick

1976. World Health Day.

861	**240**	100m. black and red	45	20

241 Blood Donation

1976. Tunisian Red Crescent.

862	**241**	40m.+10m. mult	40	30

242 "Urban Development"

1976. "Habitat" Human Settlements Conference, Vancouver.

863	**242**	40m. multicoloured	30	20

243 Henna Tradition

1976. "Tunisia, Yesterday and Today" (2nd series). Multicoloured.

864		40m. Type **243**	20	20
865		50m. Diving for sponges	55	20
866		65m. Weaving	35	20
867		110m. Pottery	50	35

244 "Spirit of 1776" (Willard)

1976. Bicentenary of American Revolution.

868	**244**	200m. multicoloured	1·40	65
MS869	130×100 mm. **244** 500m. multicoloured. Imperf or perf		3·00	3·00

245 Running

1976. Olympic Games, Montreal. Multicoloured.

870		50m. Type **245**	20	20
871		75m. Olympic flags and rings	35	20
872		120m. Olympic "dove"	55	30

246 Girl reading Book

1976. Literature for Children.

873	**246**	100m. multicoloured	45	20

247 Bird and Faces Emblem

1976. 15th Anniv of 1st Non-aligned Countries' Conference, Belgrade.

874	**247**	150m. multicoloured	60	20

248 Mausoleum, Tunis

1976. Cultural Heritage. Multicoloured.

875		85m. Type **248**	35	20
876		100m. Great Mosque, Kairouan	40	20
877		150m. Ribat Monastery, Monastir	60	20
878		200m. Barber's Mosque, Kairouan	90	35

249 Emblem and Globe

1976. 25th Anniv of U.N. Postal Administration.

879	**249**	150m. multicoloured	65	30

250 Red Crescent on Litter

1977. Tunisian Red Crescent.

880	**250**	50m.+10m. multicolored	40	35

251 Circuit Diagram

1977. World Telecommunications Day.

881	**251**	150m. multicoloured	65	40

252 "Dialogue"

1977. Tenth Anniv of International French Language Council.

882	**252**	100m. multicoloured	80	35

253 Footballers

1977. First World Junior Football Tournament.

883	**253**	150m. multicoloured	90	45

254 Gold Coin

1977. Cultural Patrimony. Multicoloured.

884		10m. Type **254**	10	10
885		15m. 13th-century stele	15	15
886		20m. 17th-century illuminated manuscript	20	15
887		30m. Glass painting	35	20
888		40m. Ceramic pot decor	40	20
889		50m. Gate, Sidi-Bou-Said	45	20

255 "The Young Republic"

1977. 20th Anniv of Republic. Multicoloured.

890		40m. Type **255**	35	20
891		100m. "The Confident Republic"	40	20
892		150m. "The Determined Republic"	65	30
MS893	117×113 mm. Nos. 890/2. Perf or imperf		1·40	1·40

256 A.P.U. Emblem within Postmark

1977. 25th Anniv of Arab Postal Union.

894	**256**	40m. multicoloured	20	20

257 Globe and Cogwheels

1977. World Rheumatism Year.

895	**257**	120m. brown, red & black	65	35

258 Harvester and Rural Cameos

1977. Rural Development.

896	**258**	40m. multicoloured	35	20

259 Factory Workers

1978. Employment Priority Plan. Multicoloured.

897		20m. Forms of transport and driver (horiz)	85	55
898		40m. Tractor driver and farm workers (horiz)	20	20
899		100m. Type **259**	45	30

260 Pres. Bourguiba and Flaming Torch within "9"

1978. 40th Anniv of 9 April Revolution.

900	**260**	40m. green, brown & olive	20	20
901	-	60m. red, brown and black	20	20

DESIGN. 60m. Pres. Bourguiba within figure "9".

261 Policeman in Safety Helmet

1978. Sixth African Regional Interpol Conference.

902	**261**	150m. multicoloured	80	35

262 "Blood Donors"

1978. Tunisian Red Crescent.

903	**262**	50m.+10m. mult	45	30

263 Goalkeeper catching World Cup Emblem

1978. World Cup Football Championship, Argentina. Multicoloured.

904		40m. Type **263**	30	20
905		150m. Footballer, map and flags	85	35

264 Hammer and Chisel chipping away Apartheid

1978. International Anti-Apartheid Year. Multicoloured.

906		50m. Type **264**	20	20
907		100m. Black and white doves	45	30

265 Flora, Fauna and Polluting Factory

1978. Protection of Nature and the Environment. Multicoloured.

908		10m. Type **265**	15	15
909		50m. "Pollution of the oceans"	40	20
910		120m. "Making the deserts green"	95	20

266 Crane removing Smallpox from Globe

1978. Global Eradication of Smallpox.

911	**266**	150m. multicoloured	65	35

267 Zlass Horseman

1978. Calligraphy, Art and Traditions. Multicoloured.

912		5m. Type **267**	10	10
913		60m. Djerba wedding	30	15
914		75m. Women potters from the Mogods	40	15
915		100m. Dove over cupolas of Marabout Sidi Mahrez	45	20
916		500m. Opening of the ploughing season, Jenduba	3 25	1·00
917		1d. Man on swing between palm trees (Spring Festival, Tozeur)	5·50	2·25

268 Lenin Banner

1978. 60th Anniv of Russian Revolution.

918	**268**	150m. multicoloured	1·10	45

269 Farhat Hached

1978. Farhat Hached (Trade Union leader). Commemoration.

919	**269**	50m. multicoloured	35	10

270 Family
Group

1978. Tenth Anniv of Tunisian Family Planning
Association.
920   **270**   50m. multicoloured   40   20

271 "The Sun"

1978. Solar Energy.
921   **271**   100m. multicoloured   60   20

272 Boeing 747 and Flags

1978. 20th Anniv of Tunisian Civil Aeronautics and
Meteorology.
922   **272**   50m. multicoloured   30   20

273 Hand
holding Bird

1979. Tunisian Red Crescent.
923   **273**   50m.+10m. mult   40   30

274 Pres.
Bourguiba

1979. 20th Anniv of Constitution.
924   **274**   50m. brown, yellow
               & black   20   20

275 Sun, Yacht and Golfer

1979. Inauguration of El Kantaoui Port.
925   **275**   150m. multicoloured   65   30

276 Korbous

1979. Tunisian Landscapes. Multicoloured.
926   50m. Type **276**   15   10
927   100m. Mides   35   15

277 Bow-net
Making

1979. Crafts. Multicoloured.
928   10m. Type **277**   15   10
929   50m. Bee-keeping   35   10

278 Pres.
Bourguiba and
"10"

1979. Tenth Congress of Socialist Destourian Party.
930   **278**   50m. multicoloured   30   10

279 Dish Aerial
and Satellite

1979. Third World Telecommunications Exhibition,
Geneva.
931   **279**   150m. multicoloured   65   35

280 World Map, Koran
and Symbols of Arab
Achievements

1979. The Arabs.
932   **280**   50m. multicoloured   20   15

281 Children
crossing Road

1979. International Year of the Child. Multicoloured.
933   50m. Type **281**   20   15
934   100m. Child, fruit and birds   50   20

282 Dove and
Olive Tree

1979. Second World Olive-oil Year.
935   **282**   150m. multicoloured   80   35

283 Symbolic
Figure

1979. 20th Anniv of Central Bank of Tunisia.
936   **283**   50m. multicolourd   20   20

284 Children and
Jujube Tree

1979. Animals and Plants. Multicoloured.
937   20m. Type **284**   20   10
938   30m. Common peafowl   40   25
939   70m. Goat   65   20
940   85m. Girl and date palm   70   20

285 Coded Letter

1980. Introduction of Postal Coding.
941   **285**   50m. multicoloured   30   20

286 Smoker

1980. World Health Day. Anti-smoking Campaign.
942   **286**   150m. multicoloured   65   30

287 Red Crescent
and Globe forming
an Eye

1980. Tunisian Red Crescent.
943   **287**   50m.+10m. mult   40   30

288 President
Bourguiba,
Flower and
Open Book

1980. 25th Anniv of Victory and Return of President
Bourguiba. Multicoloured.
944   50m. Type **288**   20   20
945   100m. Pres. Bourguiba, dove
             and mosque   85   35

289 Gymnast as Butterfly

1980. Turin Gymnastic Games.
946   **289**   100m. multicoloured   45   20

290 Tools

1980. Handicrafts. Multicoloured.
947   30m. Type **290**   30   20
948   75m. Woman embroidering   40   20

291 Ibn Khaldoun
(philosopher)

1980. Ibn Khaldoun Commemoration.
949   **291**   50m. multicoloured   20   20

292 Avicenna

1980. Birth Millenary of Avicenna (philosopher).
950   **292**   100m. sepia and brown   65   35

293 Al-Biruni and
Scientific Diagram

1980. The Arabs' Contribution to Science.
951   **293**   50m. multicoloured   35   20

294 Yachts at Sidi Bou Said

1980. Sidi Bou Said.
952   **294**   100m. multicoloured   65   35

295 "Tourists"

1980. World Tourism Conference, Manila.
953   **295**   150m. multicoloured   55   20

296 "Wedding at Djerba"

1980. Yahia (painter) Commemoration.
954   **296**   50m. multicoloured   40   30

297 Aircraft over
Tozeur

1980. Opening of Tozeur International Airport.
955   **297**   85m. multicoloured   35   20

298 "Eye"

1980. Seventh Afro-Asian Congress on Ophthalmology.
956   **298**   100m. multicoloured   55   35

299 Spider's Web

1980. 1400th Anniv of Hegira. Multicoloured.
957   50m. Type **299**   20   20
958   80m. Minarets   35   20

300 Face as
Camera

1980. Carthage Cinematographic Days.
959   **300**   100m. multicoloured   45   30

301 "Ophrys scolopax
scolopax"

1980. Flora and Fauna. Multicoloured.
960		20m. Type **301**	20	20
961		25m. "Cyclamen europaeum"	20	20
962		50m. Mouflon	20	20
963		100m. Golden eagle	90	40

302 Kairouan Mosque

1980. Conservation of Kairouan.
964	**302**	85m. multicoloured	35	20

303 H. von
Stephan

1981. 150th Birth Anniv of Heinrich von Stephan
(founder of U.P.U.).
965	**303**	150m. multicoloured	65	35

304 Hands
holding Bottle
containing Blood
Drop

1981. 20th Anniv of Tunisian Blood Donors Association.
966	**304**	75m. multicoloured	65	45

305 Flags and
Pres. Bourguiba

1981. 25th Anniv of Independence. Multicoloured.
967		50m. Type **305**	20	20
968		60m. Stork and ribbons form-
ing "25"	35	20
969		85m. Stylized birds	55	35
970		120m. Victory riding a winged
horse	55	35
MS971 96×130 mm. Nos. 976/70. Perf
or imperf			1·70	1·70

306 Flower and Pres.
Bourguiba

1981. Special Congress of Destourian Socialist Party.
Multicoloured.
972		50m. Type **306**	20	15
973		75m. Arrows forming flower	35	20

307 Mosque, Mahdia and
Galley

1981. Tourism. Multicoloured.
974		50m. Type **307**	20	20
975		85m. Djerid bride passing Great
Mosque of Tozeur (vert)	35	30
976		100m. Needle rocks, Tabarka	45	30

308 Stylized
Peacock hatching
Egg

1981. Red Crescent.
977	**308**	50m.+10m. mult	35	35

309 I.T.U. and
W.H.O. Emblems
and Ribbons
forming
Caduceus

1981. World Telecommunications Day.
978	**309**	150m. multicoloured	60	30

310 Flowers
and Youths

1981. Youth Festival.
979	**310**	100m. multicoloured	45	20

311 Kemal Ataturk

1981. Birth Centenary of Kemal Ataturk.
980	**311**	150m. multicoloured	65	35

312 Skifa Khala,
Mahdia

1981. Tunisian Monuments.
981	**312**	150m. multicoloured	65	35

313 Cheikh Mohamed Tahar
ben Achour and Minaret

1981. Cheikh Mohamed Tahar ben Achour (scholar and
teacher) Commemoration.
982	**313**	200m. multicoloured	1·00	45

314 Rejoicing
Woman

1981. 25th Anniv of Personal Status Code. Multicoloured.
983		50m. Type **314**	20	20
984		100m. Dove and head of
woman	40	30

315 Tree with
Broken Branch

1981. International Year of Disabled People.
985	**315**	250m. multicoloured	1·00	65

316 Stylized
Figure and
Ka'aba, Mecca

1981. Pilgrimage to Mecca.
986	**316**	50m. multicoloured	30	20

317 Food
Sources

1981. World Food Day.
987	**317**	200m. multicoloured	90	50

318 Dome of the Rock

1981. Palestinian Welfare.
988	**318**	50m.+5m. multicoloured	35	20
989	**318**	150m.+5m. multicol-
oured	60	35
990	**318**	200m.+5m. multicol-
oured	90	50

319 Mnaguech
(earring)

1981. Jewellery. Multicoloured.
991		150m. Type **319**	60	30
992		180m. Mahfdha (pendant)
(horiz)	70	35
993		200m. Essalta (hairnet)	90	40

320 Ship passing under
Bridge

1981. Bizerta Drawbridge.
994	**320**	230m. multicoloured	80	40

321 Chemist (detail
from 13th-century
manuscript)

1982. Arab Pharmacists' Union.
995	**321**	80m. multicoloured	55	35

322 Ring of People around
Red Crescent

1982. Red Crescent.
996	**322**	80m.+10m. multicol-
oured	40	30

323 "Ocean
Research"

1982. International Symposium "Ocean Venture", Tunis.
997	**323**	150m. multicoloured	80	45

324 "Productive
Family"

1982. The Productive Family.
998	**324**	80m. multicoloured	35	20

325 Pres.
Bourguiba and
Woman's Head

1982. 25th Anniv of Republic.
999	**325**	80m. blue and black	30	20
1000	-	100m. multicoloured	40	30
1001	-	200m. multicoloured	65	35
MS1002 138×90 mm. Nos. 999/1001.
(sold at 500m.)			2·40	2·40

DESIGNS: 100m. President and woman with "XXV" headband; 200m. President and woman with "25" in hair.

326 Scout within "50"

1982. 75th Anniv of Scout Movement and 50th Anniv of
Tunisian Scout Movement. Multicoloured.
1003		80m. Type **326**	35	20
1004		200m. Scout camp (vert)	65	20

327
"Pseudophillipsia
azzouzi"

1982. Fossils. Multicoloured.
1005		80m. Type **327**	45	35
1006		200m. "Mediterraneo-trigonia
cherahilensis"	1·40	65
1007		280m. "Numidiopleura enig-
matica" (fish) (horiz)	2·50	1·40
1008		300m. "Micreschara tunisiensis"	2·00	1·40
1009		500m. "Mantelliceras perv-
inquieri"	3·75	2·00
1010		1000m. "Elephas africanavus"
(horiz)	6·25	3·00

328 Tunisian
Woman

1982. 30th Anniv of Arab Postal Union.
1011   **328**   80m. multicoloured   40   20

329 I.T.U.
Emblem

1982. I.T.U. Delegates' Conference, Nairobi.
1012   **329**   200m. multicoloured   65   45

330 Tunisian
Buildings and
Congress Centre

1982. "Tunisia Land of Congresses".
1013   **330**   200m. multicoloured   65   30

331 "Feeding the
World"

1982. World Food Day.
1014   **331**   200m. multicoloured   65   30

332 Tahar
Haddad

1982. Tahar Haddad (social reformer) Commem.
1015   **332**   200m. brown   80   35

333 Microscope

1982. Cent of Discovery of Tubercle Bacillus.
1016   **333**   100m. multicoloured   55   30

334 Figure
dancing in Rain

1982. Stories and Songs from Tunisia. Multicoloured.
1017   20m. Type **334**   15   15
1018   30m. Woman with broom   15   15
1019   70m. Boy and fisherman   20   15
1020   80m. Chicken (horiz)   30   20
1021   100m. Woman admiring herself
       in mirror (horiz)   40   20
1022   120m. Two girls   45   30

335 Clasped Hands and
Palestine Flag

1982. Palestinian Solidarity Day.
1023   **335**   80m. multicoloured   30   20

336 Farhat Hached

1982. 30th Death Anniv of Farhat Hached.
1024   **336**   80m. red   35   20

337 Bourguiba
Sidi Saad Dam

1982. Inauguration of Bourguiba Sidi Saad Dam.
1025   **337**   80m. multicoloured   45   20

338
Environment
Emblem on
Blackboard

1982. Opening of Environment Training Work School.
1026   **338**   80m. multicoloured   35   15

339 Giving
Blood

1983. Red Crescent.
1027   **339**   80m.+10m. multicol-
                 oured   50   30

340 "Communications"

1983. World Communications Year.
1028   **340**   200m. multicoloured   55   30

341 Dove and
Map of Africa

1983. 20th Anniv of Organization of African Unity.
1029   **341**   230m. blue and deep
                 blue   65   40

342 Customs Officer, Globes
and Suitcases

1983. 20th Anniv of Customs Co-operation Council.
1030   **342**   100m. multicoloured   35   20

343 Aly Ben
Ayed

1983. Aly Ben Ayed (actor) Commemoration.
1031   **343**   80m. red, black and
                 deep red   30   30

344 Carved Face,
El Mekta

1983. Pre-historic Artefacts. Multicoloured.
1032   15m. Type **344**   20   20
1033   20m. Neolithic necklace, Kef el
       Agab (horiz)   30   20
1034   30m. Neolithic grindstone,
       Redeyef (horiz)   30   20
1035   40m. Animal petroglyph, Gafsa   35   20
1036   80m. Dolmen, Mactar (horiz)   40   30
1037   100m. Bi-face flint, El Mekta   55   30

345 Dove, Barbed Wire and
Dome of the Rock

1983. Palestinian Welfare.
1038   **345**   80m.+5m. multicoloured   40   40

346 Sporting Activities

1983. Sport for All.
1039   **346**   40m. multicoloured   15   10

347 Tunisian
with Flag and
"Destour" (French
freighter)

1983. 20th Anniv of Evacuation of Foreign Troops.
1040   **347**   80m. multicoloured   30   20

348 Fishing Boats and Fishes

1983. World Fishing Day.
1041   **348**   200m. multicoloured   1·00   25

349 "The Weaver" (Hedi Khayachi)

1983. Hedi Khayachi (painter) Commem.
1042   **349**   80m. multicoloured   45   35

350 Saluting the
Flag

1983. Salute to the Flag.
1043   **350**   100m. multicoloured   35   20

351 Air Hostess
and Airliner

1983. 25th Anniv of Tunisian Civil Aviation and
Meteorology.
1044   **351**   150m. multicoloured   55   20

352 Pres. Bourguiba
and Archway

1984. 50th Anniv of Neo-Destour Party. Multicoloured.
1045   40m. Type **352**   15   10
1046   70m. Bourguiba and torch   20   10
1047   80m. Bourguiba and flag   30   15
1048   150m. Bourguiba and wall   50   30
1049   200m. Bourguiba and dove
       (horiz)   60   35
1050   230m. Pres. Bourguiba (horiz)   70   45
MS1051 Three sheets, each 183×130
       mm. (a) Nos. 1045 and 1048; (b)
       Nos. 1046/7; (c) Nos. 1049/50. Perf
       or imperf   2·50   2·50

353 Map of Africa

1984. Fourth School of Molecular Biology.
1052   **353**   100m. multicoloured   55   30

354 First Aid

1984. Red Crescent.
1053   **354**   80m.+10m. multicol-
                 oured   40   30

355 Ibn el Jazzar

1984. Ibn el Jazzar (doctor) Commem.
1054   **355**   80m. multicoloured   40   30

356
"Co-operation"

1984. Economic Co-operation among Developing Countries.
| 1055 | 356 | 230m. multicoloured | 80 | 35 |

357 Witch, Maiden and Coquette

1984. Stories and Songs from Tunisia. Multicoloured.
1056		20m. Type **357**	10	10
1057		80m. Puppet, hands and mouse	30	20
1058		100m. Boy and horse (vert)	35	15

358 Family facing the Future

1984. 20th Anniv of Tunisian Education and Family Organization.
| 1059 | 358 | 80m. multicoloured | 30 | 20 |

359 Medina, Tunis

1984. National Heritage Protection.
| 1060 | 359 | 100m. multicoloured | 35 | 20 |

360 Aboul Qasim Chabbi

1984. 50th Death Anniv of Aboul Qasim Chabbi (poet).
| 1061 | 360 | 100m. sepia, light brown and brown | 35 | 20 |

361 Emblem, Stylized Bird and Airplane

1984. 40th Anniv of International Civil Aviation Organization.
| 1062 | 361 | 200m. multicoloured | 65 | 20 |

362 Band and Singers

1984. Sahara Festival.
| 1063 | 362 | 20m. multicoloured | 45 | 20 |

363 Telephonist, Satellite and Dish Aerial

1984. 20th Anniv of "Intelsat" Communication Satellite.
| 1064 | 363 | 100m. multicoloured | 35 | 15 |

364 "Mediterranean Countryside"

1984. Jilani Abdulwahelb (artist) Commem.
| 1065 | 364 | 100m. multicoloured | 55 | 35 |

365 Profile and Exterior of House

1985. "Expo 85" World's Fair, Tsukuba.
| 1066 | 365 | 200m. multicoloured | 65 | 35 |

366 Crescents and Stars within Circle

1985. Red Crescent.
| 1067 | 366 | 100m.+10m. mult | 35 | 30 |

367 Hands reaching from Sea and Flames

1985. Third Civil Protection Week.
| 1068 | 367 | 100m. multicoloured | 30 | 15 |

368 Pres. Bourguiba on Horseback

1985. 30th Anniv of Independence. Multicoloured.
1069		75m. Type **368**	20	10
1070		100m. Pres. Bourguiba in boat and crowd on quay (horiz)	30	10
1071		200m. Pres. Bourguiba in sombrero	55	20
1072		230m. Pres. Bourguiba waving to crowd from balcony (horiz)	60	20
MS1073	98×155 mm. Nos. 1069/72. Perf or imperf (sold at 700m.)		1·90	1·90

369 Pres. Bourguiba and Ancient Sculpture

1985. Tunisian Day at "Expo '85" World's Fair, Tsukuba.
| 1074 | 369 | 250m. multicoloured | 80 | 30 |

370 Images within Film

1985. International Amateur Film Festival, Kelibia.
| 1075 | 370 | 250m. multicoloured | 1·50 | 1·10 |

371 Dark Clouds, Sun and Flowers

1985. Stories and Songs from Tunisia. Multicoloured.
1076		25m. Type **371**	10	10
1077		50m. Man's profile and hand holding women	15	10
1078		100m. Man and cooking pot over fire	35	15

372 Heart as Dove and I.Y.Y. Emblem

1985. International Youth Year.
| 1079 | 372 | 250m. multicoloured | 80 | 30 |

373 "The Perfumiers' Hall"

1985. Painting by Hedi Larnaout.
| 1080 | 373 | 100m. multicoloured | 45 | 20 |

374 Matmata Wedding Dress

1985. Wedding Dresses (1st series). Multicoloured.
1081		20m. Type **374**	10	10
1082		50m. Moknine dress	15	10
1083		100m. Tunis dress	35	15

See also Nos. 1099/1101.

375 Stylized People and U.N. Emblem

1985. 40th Anniv of U.N.O.
| 1084 | 375 | 250m. multicoloured | 80 | 30 |

376 Harvest (Makthar stele)

1985. Food Self-sufficiency.
| 1085 | 376 | 100m. multicoloured | 35 | 20 |

377 Emblem illuminating Globe and Flags

1985. 40th Anniv of Arab League.
| 1086 | 377 | 100m. multicoloured | 30 | 15 |

378 Aziza Othmana

1985. Aziza Othmana (founder of hospitals) Commemoration.
| 1087 | 378 | 100m. brown, green and red | 45 | 20 |

379 Surveying Instruments and Books forming Face

1985. Centenary of Land Law.
| 1088 | 379 | 100m. multicoloured | 30 | 10 |

380 Dove and Pres. Bourguiba

1986. 30th Anniv of Independence.
1089	380	100m. multicoloured	30	10
1090	-	120m. black, blue and deep blue	35	15
1091	-	280m. blue, violet and black	80	35
1092	-	300m. multicoloured	85	40
MS1093	105×127 mm. Nos. 1089/92. Perf or imperf		2·40	2·40

DESIGNS—HORIZ: 120m. Rocket; 280m. Horse and rider. VERT: 300m. Balloons.

381 Hulusi Behcet (dermatologist)

1986. Third Mediterranean Rheumatology Days, Tunis, and Ninth International Society of Geographical Ophthalmology Congress, Monastir. Multicoloured.
| 1094 | | 300m. Type **381** | 1·25 | 35 |
| 1095 | | 380m. Behcet and sun and eye emblems | 1·60 | 45 |

382 Map and Red Crescent

1986. World Red Crescent and Red Cross Day.
| 1096 | 382 | 120m.+10m. multicoloured | 40 | 30 |

383 Pres. Bourguiba, Symbols and "12"

1986. 12th Destourian Socialist Party Congress, Tunis. Multicoloured.
| 1097 | | 120m. Type **383** | 30 | 10 |
| 1098 | | 300m. Flaming torch, Pres. Bourguiba and "12" | 85 | 30 |

442 Dougga

1990. Tourism.
| 1195 | **442** | 300m. multicoloured | 65 | 35 |

443 Adults learning to Read and Write

1990. International Literacy Year.
| 1196 | **443** | 120m. multicoloured | 30 | 15 |

444 Figures, Tree and Fishes in Water

1990. Water.
| 1197 | **444** | 150m. multicoloured | 45 | 30 |

445 Fireworks and Date

1990. Third Anniv of Declaration of 7 November 1987. Multicoloured.
| 1198 | | 150m. Type **445** | 35 | 15 |
| 1199 | | 150m. Clock tower | 35 | 15 |

446 Kheireddine et Tounsi

1990. Death Centenary of Kheireddine et Tounsi (political reformer).
| 1200 | **446** | 150m. green | 45 | 20 |

447 Red Deer

1990. Flora and Fauna. Multicoloured.
1201		150m. Type **447**	35	15
1202		200m. Thistle	45	15
1203		300m. Water buffalo	65	20
1204		600m. Orchid	1·40	55

448 Members' Flags forming Stars

1991. Second Anniv of Maghreb Union.
| 1205 | **448** | 180m. multicoloured | 45 | 20 |

449 Montazah Tabarka

1991. Tourism.
| 1206 | **449** | 450m. multicoloured | 1·00 | 45 |

450 Doves and Emblem

1991. Red Crescent. Help for War Victims.
| 1207 | **450** | 180m.+10m. multicoloured | 45 | 35 |

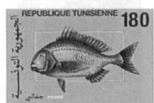

451 Common Seabream

1991. Fish. Multicoloured.
1208		180m. Type **451**	65	30
1209		350m. Striped red mullet	1·25	55
1210		450m. Atlantic mackerel	1·60	65
1211		550m. Common pandora	2·00	1·00

452 Vase of Flowers (Taieb Khlif)

1991. Children's Rights.
| 1212 | **452** | 450m. multicoloured | 1·25 | 35 |

453 "Plein-Sud" (anon.)

1991
| 1213 | **453** | 400m. multicoloured | 90 | 35 |

454 Bracelets and Ring

1991. Jewellery. Multicoloured.
1214		120m. Type **454**	30	15
1215		180m. Headdress and necklace (vert)	40	15
1216		220m. Headdress, earrings and collar (vert)	45	20
1217		730m. Key-ring (vert)	2·25	80

455 Date and Profile of Woman

1991. Fourth Anniv of Declaration of 7 November 1987.
| 1218 | **455** | 180m. multicoloured | 45 | 20 |

456 Sorting Office

1991. Tunis-Carthage Sorting Office.
| 1219 | **456** | 80m. blue, red and green | 20 | 10 |

457 Dove and Globe

1991. World Human Rights Day.
| 1220 | **457** | 450m. blue | 1·25 | 35 |

458 Bayram Ettounsi

1991. 31st Death Anniv of Bayram Ettounsi.
| 1221 | **458** | 200m. blue | 45 | 15 |

459 Emblem on Microchip

1992. "Expo '92" World's Fair, Seville.
| 1222 | **459** | 180m. multicoloured | 45 | 20 |

460 G.P.O.

1992. Centenary of General Post Office, Tunis.
| 1223 | **460** | 180m. brown | 45 | 20 |
| 1224 | - | 450m. brown | 1·25 | 35 |

DESIGN—VERT: 450m. Different view of G.P.O.

461 "When the Subconscious Awakes" (Moncef ben Amor)

1992
| 1225 | **461** | 500m. multicoloured | 1·40 | 45 |

462 Running

1992. Olympic Games, Barcelona. Multicoloured.
| 1226 | | 180m. Type **462** | 65 | 30 |
| 1227 | | 450m. Judo (vert) | 1·60 | 55 |

463 European Bee Eater

1992. Birds. Multicoloured.
1228		100m. Type **463**	55	20
1229		180m. Eurasian goldfinch	80	40
1230		200m. European serin	1·10	40
1231		500m. Western greenfinch	2·50	95

MS1232 77×108 mm. Nos. 1228/31. Perf or imperf (sold at 1000d.)
| | | | 2·40 | 2·40 |

464 President and Children

1992. United Nations Convention on Rights of the Child.
| 1233 | **464** | 180m. multicoloured | 45 | 30 |

465 Women and Open Book

1992. African Regional Human Rights Conference, Tunis.
| 1234 | **465** | 480m. multicoloured | 1·50 | 65 |

466 Ribbon forming "7"

1992. Fifth Anniv of Declaration of 7 November 1987. Multicoloured.
| 1235 | | 180m. Type **466** | 45 | 20 |
| 1236 | | 730m. President with people and doves | 2·10 | 90 |

467 "Acacia tortilis"

1992. National Tree Day.
| 1237 | **467** | 180m. multicoloured | 45 | 30 |

468 Stylized Figure and Emblems

1992. International Nutrition Conference, Rome.
| 1238 | **468** | 450m. multicoloured | 1·50 | 55 |

469 Chemesse

1992. Traditional Costumes. Multicoloured.
| 1239 | | 100m. Type **469** | 30 | 20 |
| 1240 | | 350m. Hanifites | 85 | 45 |

470 "Billy Goat between Two Bushes" (El Jem)

1992. Mosaics. Multicoloured.
1241	100m. Type **470**		30	15
1242	180m. "Wild Duck" (El Jem)		75	35
1243	350m. "Racehorse" (Sidi Abdallah)		1·25	45
1244	450m. "Gazelle in the Grass" (El Jem)		1·40	70

471 Wolf

1992. Flora and Fauna. Multicoloured.
1245	20m. Type **471**	10	10
1246	60m. "Hoya carnosa" (plant) (vert)	10	10

472 Line Graph on World Map

1993. United Nations World Conference on Human Rights, Vienna.
1247	**472**	450m. multicoloured	1·40	60

Open Brief-case

1993. Arab-African Fair, Tunis.
1248	**473**	450m. multicoloured	1·25	30

474 "Relaxing on the Patio" (Ali Guermassi)

1993
1249	**474**	450m. multicoloured	1·25	30

475 Conference Emblem

1993. Constitutional Democratic Assembly Party Conference.
1250	**475**	180m. red and black	50	15

476 Blood Transfusion

1993. Red Crescent. "Dignity for All".
1251	**476**	120m.+30m. multicoloured	60	35

477 Louis Pasteur and Charles Nicolle (former director)

1993. Centenary of Pasteur Institute, Tunis.
1252	**477**	450m. multicoloured	1·40	60

478 "7"

1993. Sixth Anniv of Declaration of 7 November 1987. Multicoloured.
1253	**478**	180m. Type **478**	50	15
1254	-	450m. "7"s and waves	1·25	50

479 Carpet

1993. Kairouan Carpets.
1255	**479**	100m. multicoloured	15	10
1256	-	120m. multicoloured	15	10
1257	-	180m. multicoloured	50	15
1258	-	350m. multicoloured	1·10	60

DESIGNS: 120m. to 350m. Different carpets.

480 Boy with Guitar (Donia Haik)

1993. School Cultural Activities. Children's drawings. Multicoloured.
1259	**480**	180m. Type **480**	50	15
1260	-	180m. Painting and reading (Anissa Chatbouri) (horiz)	50	15

481 Ballot Box, Hands and Map

1994. Presidential and Legislative Elections.
1261	**481**	180m. multicoloured	50	15

482 Players, Trophy and Mascot

1994. African Nations Cup Football Championship. Multicoloured.
1262	**482**	180m. Type **482**	50	15
1263	-	350m. Trophy, goalkeeper making save and mascot	1·00	25
1264	-	450m. Map of Africa, Olympic Rings, player, trophy and mascot	1·25	60

483 Workers, "75" and Emblem

1994. 75th Anniv of I.L.O.
1265	**483**	350m. multicoloured	1·10	25

484 Family within House

1994. International Year of the Family.
1266	**484**	180m. multicoloured	50	15

485 President Ben Ali

1994. Re-election of President Zine el Abidine Ben Ali.
1267	**485**	180m. multicoloured	50	15
1268	**485**	350m. multicoloured	1·00	75
MS1269	108×126 mm. Nos. 1267/8. Perf or imperf	1·50	1·50

486 Blackthorn

1994. Plants. Multicoloured.
1270	**486**	50m. Type **486**	10	10
1271	-	100m. "Xeranthemum inapertum"	15	10
1272	-	200m. "Orchis simia"	60	15
1273	-	1d. "Scilla peruviana"	2·75	1·50

487 Dove and Emblem

1994. 30th Organization of African Unity Summit Meeting, Tunis.
1274	**487**	480m. multicoloured	1·40	60

488 Torch with Map as Flame and Centenary Emblem

1994. Centenary of International Olympic Committee.
1275	**488**	450m. multicoloured	1·50	60

489 Pencil and Postal and Tourism Motifs

1994. "Philakorea 1994" International Stamp Exhibition, Seoul.
1276	**489**	450m. multicoloured	1·50	60

490 Clouded Yellow

1994. Butterflies. Multicoloured.
1277	**490**	100m. Type **490**	15	10
1278	-	180m. Red admiral	50	15
1279	-	300m. Scarce swallowtail (vert)	75	20
1280	-	350m. African monarch	1·00	50
1281	-	450m. Painted lady (vert)	1·25	60
1282	-	500m. Swallowtail (vert)	1·50	60

491 President Ben Ali and Anniversary Emblem

1994. Seventh Anniv of Declaration of 7 November 1987. Multicoloured.
1283	**491**	350m. Type **491**	1·00	25
1284	-	730m. "7", fireworks and state crest (vert)	1·90	50

492 Boxers and Globe

1994. 41st Military Boxing Championships, Tunis.
1285	**492**	450m. multicoloured	1·40	60

493 Tailfins

1994. 50th Anniv of I.C.A.O.
1286	**493**	450m. multicoloured	1·00	30

494 Greylag Geese

1994. Wildlife. Multicoloured.
1287	**494**	180m. Type **494**	25	15
1288	-	350m. Tufted duck and European pochard (horiz)	75	25
1289	-	500m. Water buffaloes	1·10	60
1290	-	1000m. European otters (horiz)	2·10	1·25

495 "Composition" (Ridha Bettaieb)

1994
1291	**495**	500m. multicoloured	1·10	35

496 "50", Map and Emblem

1995. 50th Anniv of League of Arab States.
1292	**496**	180m. multicoloured	25	15

497 Oil Lamp

1995. Glassware. Multicoloured.
| 1293 | 450m. Type 497 | 60 | 30 |
| 1294 | 730m. Oil lamp with handle | 95 | 50 |

498 Chebbi

1995. 60th Death Anniv (1994) of Aboulkacem Chebbi (poet).
| 1295 | 498 | 180m. multicoloured | 25 | 15 |

499 Earring

1995. Fourth World Conference on Women, Peking.
| 1296 | 499 | 180m. multicoloured | 25 | 15 |

500 Farming

1995. 50th Anniv of F.A.O.
| 1297 | 500 | 350m. multicoloured | 45 | 25 |

501 U.N. Workers and Anniversary Emblem over World Map

1995. 50th Anniv of U.N.O.
| 1298 | 501 | 350m. multicoloured | 45 | 25 |

502 Crops

1995. Anti-desertification Campaign.
| 1299 | 502 | 180m. multicoloured | 25 | 15 |

503 President Ben Ali visiting Village

1995. Eighth Anniv of Declaration of 7 November 1987. Multicoloured.
| 1300 | 180m. Type 503 | 25 | 15 |
| 1301 | 350m. President Ben Ali meeting children | 45 | 25 |

504 Hannibal (Carthaginian general)

1995
| 1302 | 504 | 180m. purple | 25 | 15 |
| MS1303 | 119×131 mm. No. 1032 Perf or imperf (sold at 1d.) | 2·40 | 2·40 |

505 Human Rights Award

1995. World Human Rights Day.
| 1304 | 505 | 350m. multicoloured | 45 | 25 |

506 Bird carrying Olive Branch and People crossing Road

1995. Safety of Pedestrians.
| 1305 | 506 | 350m. multicoloured | 45 | 25 |

507 "Ophrys lapethica"

1995. Flora and Fauna. Multicoloured.
1306	50m. Type 507	10	10
1307	180m. Dorcas gazelle	25	15
1308	300m. "Scupellaria cypria"	40	20
1309	350m. Houbara bustard	45	25

508 Modern and Traditional Work

1996. 50th Anniv of Tunisian General Workers' Union.
| 1310 | 508 | 440m. multicoloured | 55 | 30 |

509 Man's Jebba, Khamri

1996. National Traditional Costume Day. Multicoloured.
| 1311 | 170m. Type 509 | 20 | 10 |
| 1312 | 200m. Woman's embroidered kaftan, Hammamet | 25 | 15 |

510 "March 20 1996 1956"

1996. 40th Anniv of Independence. Multicoloured.
| 1313 | 200m. Type 510 | 25 | 15 |
| 1314 | 390m. "20", "40", dove and rainbow | 50 | 25 |

511 "Hannana" (Noureddine Khayachi)

1996
| 1315 | 511 | 810m. multicoloured | 1·00 | 50 |

512 Seven-spotted Ladybirds

1996. Insects. Multicoloured.
| 1316 | 200m. Type 512 | 25 | 15 |
| 1317 | 810m. Honey bee | 1·00 | 50 |

513 Mascot

1996. World Environment Day.
| 1318 | 513 | 390m. multicoloured | 50 | 25 |

514 Magnifying Glass on "Stamp"

1996. "Capex'96" International Stamp Exhibition, Toronto, Canada.
| 1319 | 514 | 200m. multicoloured | 25 | 15 |

515 Flags over Stadium

1996. Centenary of Olympic Games and Olympic Games, Atlanta. Multicoloured.
1320	20m. Type 515	10	10
1321	200m. Runner, fireworks and "100" (vert)	25	15
1322	390m. Mosaic of ancient Greek wrestlers	50	25

516 Woman's Hands holding Dove

1996. 40th Anniv of Code of Personal Status.
| 1323 | 516 | 200m. multicoloured | 25 | 15 |

517 Ramparts of Sousse

1996. Ancient Buildings. Multicoloured.
1324	20m. Type 517	10	10
1325	200m. Numide de Dougga mausoleum (vert)	25	15
1326	390m. Arch of Trajan, Makthar	50	25

518 Hammer breaking Chain on Anvil

1996. International Year against Poverty.
| 1327 | 518 | 390m. multicoloured | 50 | 25 |

519 Candles on "7" and Map

1996. Ninth Anniv of Declaration of 7 November 1987. Multicoloured.
| 1328 | 200m. Type 519 | 25 | 15 |
| 1329 | 390m. Girl with doves | 50 | 25 |

520 Camels outside Traditional Dwellings

1996. National Saharan Tourism Day. Multicoloured.
| 1330 | 200m. Type 520 | 25 | 15 |
| 1331 | 200m. Traditional pattern | 25 | 15 |

Nos. 1330/1 were issued together, se-tenant, forming a composite design.

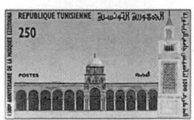

521 Facade

1996. 1300th Anniv of Ezzitouna Mosque.
| 1332 | 521 | 250m. multicoloured | 25 | 15 |

522 Campaign Symbols

1996. National Solidarity Day. Multicoloured.
| 1333 | 500m. Type 522 | 55 | 30 |
| 1334 | 500m. Jigsaw showing public services | 55 | 30 |

523 United Nations Emblem, Trophy and Open Book

1996. World Human Rights Day.
| 1335 | 523 | 500m. multicoloured | 55 | 30 |

524 Schoolchildren

1996. 50th Anniv of UNICEF.
| 1336 | 524 | 810m. multicoloured | 85 | 45 |

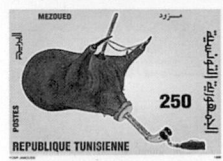

525 Mezoued (bagpipes)

1996. Musical Instruments. Multicoloured.

1337	250m. Type **525**	25	15
1338	300m. Gombri (stringed instrument)	30	15
1339	350m. Tabla (drum)	35	20
1340	500m. Tar tounsi (tambourine)	55	30

1997. As Nos. 1337/40 but smaller, 38×24 mm, and face values changed.

1341	20m. As No. 1339	10	10
1342	30m. Type **525**	10	10
1343	50m. As No. 1338	10	10
1344	100m. As No. 1340	10	10

526 Writing Implements and Open Book

1997. World Book and Authors' Rights Day.

1345	**526**	1d. multicoloured	1·00	50

527 Mediterranean Blue Mussels

1997. Molluscs. Multicoloured.

1346	50m. Type **527**	10	10
1347	70m. Clams	10	10
1348	350m. Common octopus	35	20
1349	500m. Common cuttlefish	55	30

528 San Francisco–Oakland Bay Bridge

1997. "Pacific 97" International Stamp Exhibition, San Francisco.

1350	**528**	250m. multicoloured	25	15

529 Tennis Player and Runner

1997. Mediterranean Games, Bari, Italy.

1351	**529**	350m. multicoloured	35	20

530 Emblems

1997. Tunis, Cultural Capital.

1352	**530**	250m. multicoloured	25	15

531 State Arms

1997. 40th Anniv of Republic. Multicoloured.

1353	130m. Type **531**	15	10
1354	500m. Airplane and flowers (horiz)	55	30

532 African Spiny-tailed Lizard

1997. Reptiles. Multicoloured.

1355	100m. Type **532**	10	10
1356	350m. Chameleon (vert)	40	20
1357	500m. Desert monitor	55	30

533 Ariana Rose

1997

1358	**533**	350m. multicoloured	40	20

534 Pres. Ben Ali with Elderly Woman

1997. World Day for Protection of the Elderly.

1359	**534**	250m. multicoloured	25	15

535 "Autumn" (Ammar Farhat)

1997. Art. Multicoloured.

1360	250m. Type **535**	25	15
1361	250m. "In Cafe Maure" (Farhat)	25	15
1362	250m. "Old Man" (Farhat)	25	15
1363	250m. "Fisher of Men" (sculpture, Hedi Selmi)	25	15
1364	500m. "Cafe des Nattes" (Sidi Bou Said) (horiz)	55	30
1365	500m. "Lesson" (Yahia Turki) (horiz)	55	30
1366	1000m. "Hand-spinner" (Farhat)	1·10	55

536 Pres. Ben Ali with Child, Flag and Doves forming "7"

1997. Tenth Anniv of Declaration of 7 November 1987.

1367	-	250m. violet and gold	25	15
1368	**536**	500m. multicoloured	50	25

DESIGN—VERT: 250m. "7", globe and laurel leaves.

537 Sandrose (mineral)

1997

1369	**537**	250m. multicoloured	25	15

538 Scales, Emblem and World Map

1997. International Day of Human Rights.

1370	**538**	500m. multicoloured	50	25

539 Arab

1997. Horses. Multicoloured.

1371	50m. Type **539**	10	10
1372	70m. Barbary	10	10
1373	250m. Arab-Barbary (vert)	25	15
1374	500m. Head of Arab (vert)	50	25

540 Memorial and Flowers

1998. 40th Anniv of Bombing of Sakiet Sidi Youssef.

1375	**540**	250m. multicoloured	25	15

541 Children and Flowers

1998. Fifth School Health Week.

1376	**541**	250m. multicoloured	25	15

542 Dove and Human Rights Emblem on Scales

1998. Centenary of Tunisian Bar.

1377	**542**	250m. multicoloured	25	15

543 Monument

1998. Martyrs' Day. Multicoloured.

1378	250m. Type **543**	25	15
1379	520m. Roses and "9"	55	30

544 Okba Ibn Nafaa Mosque, Kairouan

1998

1380	**544**	500m. multicoloured	50	25

545 National Team

1998. World Cup Football Championship, France. Multicoloured.

1381	250m. Type **545**	25	15
1382	500m. Player, ball and trophy (vert)	50	25

546 Crab

1998. Marine Life. Multicoloured.

1383	110m. Type **546**	10	10
1384	250m. King prawn	25	15
1385	1000m. Lobster	1·00	50

547 Dove, Flag and Torch Bearers

1998. Constitutional Democratic Assembly Party Congress. Multicoloured.

1386	250m. Type **547**	25	15
1387	250m. President Ben Ali, flag, torch bearers and banners (horiz)	25	15

548 Isaac ibn Soleimane, Ahmed ibn el Jazzar and Constantin the African (physicians)

1998. 36th International History of Medicine Congress.

1388	**548**	500m. multicoloured	50	25

549 "Weaver" (Ali Guermassi)

1998. Paintings. Multicoloured.

1389	250m. Type **549**	25	15
1390	250m. "Musician" (Noureddine Khayachi) (vert)	25	15
1391	500m. "Still Life" (Ali Khouja) (vert)	50	25

550 Bank and Anniversary Emblem

1998. 40th Anniv of Central Bank of Tunisia.

1392	**550**	250m. multicoloured	25	15

551 Symbols of Industry and Agriculture

1998. 11th Anniv of Declaration of 7 November 1987.

1393	**551**	250m. multicoloured	25	15

552 "Tunisia" in Arabic and Anniversary Emblem

1998. 50th Anniv of Universal Declaration of Human Rights.

1394	**552**	250m. multicoloured	25	15

553 Ibn Rushd

1998. 800th Death Anniv of Ibn Rushd (Averroes) (philosopher and physician).
| 1395 | **553** | 500m. multicoloured | 50 | 25 |

554 Saliha (singer)

1998. Musicians. Multicoloured.
1396		250m. Type **554**	25	15
1397		250m. Kaddour Srarfi (composer and violinist) (horiz)	25	15
1398		500m. Ali Riahi (singer and composer)	50	25

555 Mountain Gazelles

1998. Boukornine National Park. Multicoloured.
1399		70m. Type **555**	10	10
1400		110m. Brown hare	10	10
1401		250m. Bonelli's eagles	25	15
1402		500m. Persian cyclamen	50	25

556 Orange Tree

1999. Trees. Multicoloured.
1403		250m. Type **556**	25	15
1404		250m. Date palm (vert)	25	15
1405		500m. Olive tree	50	20

557 Thuburbo Majus

1999. Archaeological Sites. Multicoloured.
1406		50m. Type **557**	10	10
1407		250m. Baths at Bulla Regia (horiz)	25	15
1408		500m. Zaghouan aqueduct (horiz)	50	20

558 "L'Intemporel" (Moncef ben Amor)

1999. Paintings. Multicoloured.
1409		250m. Type **558**	25	15
1410		250m. "Betrothal" (Ali Guermassi)	25	15
1411		250m. "Pottery" (Ammar Farhat)	25	15
1412		250m. "Hat and Fan Seller" (Yahia Turki)	25	15

559 Arms, Columns and Legislative Chamber

1999. 40th Anniv of Constitution.
| 1413 | **559** | 250m. multicoloured | 25 | 15 |

560 Acacia

1999. Flowers. Multicoloured.
1414		70m. Type **560**	10	10
1415		250m. Bougainvillea ("Bougainvillea spectabilis")	25	15
1416		250m. Common poppy ("Papaver rhoeas")	25	15
1417		500m. Carnation	50	25
MS1418		81×109 mm. Nos. 1414/17. Imperf (sold at 1500m.)	1·50	1·50

561 Stamps, Globe as Eye and Emblem

1999. "Philexfrance 99" International Stamp Exhibition, Paris.
| 1419 | **561** | 500m. multicoloured | 50 | 25 |

562 Haddad and Women

1999. Birth Centenary of Tahar Haddad.
| 1420 | **562** | 500m. multicoloured | 50 | 25 |

563 Loggerhead Turtle

1999. Marine Life. Multicoloured.
| 1421 | | 250m. Type **563** | 25 | 15 |
| 1422 | | 500m. Grouper | 50 | 25 |

564 Body Parts as Jigsaw Puzzle of Dove

1999. National Organ Donation Awareness Day.
| 1423 | **564** | 250m. multicoloured | 25 | 15 |

565 U.P.U. Emblem

1999. 125th Anniv of Universal Postal Union.
| 1424 | **565** | 500m. multicoloured | 50 | 25 |

566 Ballot Box, Ear of Wheat and Sailing Boat

1999. Presidential and Legislative Elections.
| 1425 | **566** | 500m. multicoloured | 50 | 25 |

567 Tamarisk

1999. Flora and Fauna. Multicoloured.
| 1426 | | 250m. Type **567** | 25 | 15 |
| 1427 | | 500m. Dromedary | 50 | 25 |

568 Computer, Pencil and rising Sun

1999. 12th Anniv of Declaration of 7th November 1987.
| 1428 | **568** | 250m. multicoloured | 25 | 15 |

569 Emblem and Scales of Justice

1999. World Human Rights Day.
| 1429 | **569** | 250m. multicoloured | 25 | 15 |

570 Ahmed Ibn Abi Dhiaf

1999. Death Anniversaries. Multicoloured.
1430		250m. Type **570** (125th anniv)	25	15
1431		250m. Abdelaziz Thaalbi (55th anniv)	25	15
1432		500m. Khemaies Tarnane (35th anniv) (horiz)	50	25

571 "2000" and 20th-Century Symbols

1999. New Millennium.
| 1433 | **571** | 250m. multicoloured | 25 | 15 |

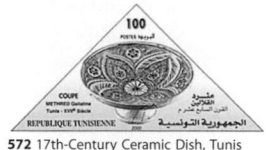

572 17th-Century Ceramic Dish, Tunis

2000. Archaeological Sites and Artefacts. Multicoloured.
1434		100m. Type **572**	10	10
1435		110m. 9th-century plate, Raqqada (triangular)	10	10
1436		250m. Water Temple, Zaghouan (35×35 mm)	20	10
1437		500m. "Ulysses and the Sirens" (mosaic), Dougga (35×35 mm)	45	25

573 Carthage (car ferry)

2000
| 1438 | **573** | 500m. multicoloured | 45 | 25 |

574 Archway and Palm Tree

2000. "EXPO 2000" World's Fair, Hanover, Germany.
| 1439 | **574** | 1000m. multicoloured | 95 | 50 |

575 Carob Tree

2000. Trees. Multicoloured.
1440		50m. Type **575**	10	10
1441		100m. Apricot	10	10
1442		250m. Avocado (vert)	25	10
1443		400m. Apple	35	15

576 Emblem

2000. Mediterranean Games, Tunis (1st series).
| 1444 | **576** | 500m. multicoloured | 45 | 20 |

See also Nos. 1473/4.

577 Emblem and Sydney Opera House

2000. Olympic Games, Sydney.
| 1445 | **577** | 500m. multicoloured | 45 | 20 |

578 Freesias

2000. Flowers. Multicoloured.
1446		110m. Type **578**	10	10
1447		200m. Chrysanthemums	20	10
1448		250m. Rose "Golden Times"	25	10
1449		250m. Vase of flowers (33×49 mm)	25	10
1450		500m. Rose "Calibra"	45	20

579 Dove, Sun and Symbols

2000. 13th Anniv of Declaration of 7 November 1987.
| 1451 | **579** | 250m. multicoloured | 25 | 10 |

580 "Still life" (Hedi Khayachi)

2000. Paintings. Multicoloured.
| 1452 | | 100m. Type **580** | 10 | 10 |

1453	250m. "Landscape" (Abdelaziz Berraies)	25	10
1454	250m. "The Sharpener" (Ali Guermassi)	25	10
1455	400m. "The Seller of Dates and Milk" (Yahia Turki) (vert)	35	15

581 Monument

2000. International Year of Human Rights.
| 1456 | **581** | 500m. multicoloured | 45 | 20 |

582 *Neverita josephinia*

2000. Shells. Multicoloured.
1457	50m. Type **582**	10	10
1458	250m. Trunculus murex (*Phyllonotus trunculus*)	25	10
1459	250m. *Columbella rustica*	25	10
1460	1d. *Arca noe*	95	45

583 Imam Sahnoun

2000. Personalities. Multicoloured.
1461	250m. Type **583**	25	10
1462	250m. Ibn Arafa	25	10
1463	250m. Ali Belhaouane	25	10
1464	1d. Mohamed Jamoussi (musician)	95	45

584 Map and Flags

2001. Tunisia's Presidency of NATO. Security Council.
| 1465 | **584** | 250m. multicoloured | 25 | 10 |

585 Globe, Clasped Hands and Dove

2001. World Solidarity Fund.
| 1466 | **585** | 500m. multicoloured | 50 | 25 |

586 Symbols of Communications

2001. Digital Culture Year.
| 1467 | **586** | 250m. multicoloured | 25 | 10 |

587 Flag, Father and Child

2001. Mohamed Dohra Commemoration.
| 1468 | **587** | 600m. multicoloured | 60 | 30 |

588 Tunis Town Hall

2001. Tourism. Multicoloured.
1469	250m. Type **588**	25	10
1470	250m. Gighis (Roman ruins), Djerba Island	25	10
1471	250m. 19th-century tile, Tunis (vert)	25	10
1472	500m. "The Needles", Tabarka (vert)	50	25

589 Emblem, Stadium and Running Track

2001. Mediterranean Games, Tunis (2nd series). Multicoloured.
| 1473 | 250m. Type **589** | 15 | 10 |
| 1474 | 500m. Runners and gold medal | 50 | 25 |

590 "Sidi Bou Said" (Pierre Boucherle)

2001. Paintings. Multicoloured.
1475	250m. Type **590**	25	10
1476	250m. "Still Life" (Pierre Boucherle)	25	10
1477	250m. "Dream" (Aly Ben Salem) (vert)	25	10
1478	500m. "Traditional Outdoor Marrlage" (Aly Ben Salem)	50	25

591 Stylized Faces and Arrows

2001. United Nations Year of Dialogue among Civilizations.
| 1479 | **591** | 500m. multicoloured | 50 | 25 |

592 Emblem and Symbols of Employment

2001. National Employment Fund.
| 1480 | **592** | 250m. multicoloured | 20 | 10 |

593 Anniversary Medal

2001. 14th Anniv of Declaration of 7th November.
| 1481 | **593** | 250m. multicoloured | 25 | 10 |

594 Marbled White Butterfly

2001. Butterflies and Moth. Multicoloured.
1482	250m. Type **594**	25	10
1483	250m. Butterfly (inscr "Ariane")	25	10
1484	250m. Butterfly (inscr "Pacha a deux queues")	25	10
1485	500m. Moth (inscr "Grand paan de nuit")	40	20
MS1486 137×126 mm. 250m. ×2, Nos. 1482/3; 500m. ×2, Nos. 1484/5. Imperf		1·30	1·30

595 Crossbill

2001. Birds. Multicoloured.
1487	250m. Type **595**	25	10
1488	500m. Great tit	40	20
1489	600m. Jay	50	25
1490	600m. Stork	50	25
MS1491 120×131 mm. 300m. No. 1487; 500m. No. 1488; 600m. ×2, No. 1489/90		1·20	1·20

596 Scales of Justice and Globe

2001. International Human Rights Day.
| 1492 | **596** | 250m. multicoloured |

597 Ibrahim Ibn Al Aghlab

2001. Personalities. Multicoloured.
1493	250m. Type **597**	25	10
1494	250m. Ibn Rachiq Al Kairaouani	25	10
1495	350m. Abdelaziz Laroui	30	15
1496	650m. Assad Ibn Al Fourat	55	25

598 Modern Script

2001. Calligraphy. Multicoloured.
| 1497 | 350m. Type **598** | 30 | 15 |
| 1498 | 350m. Ancient script (vert) | 30 | 15 |

599 Tower, El Kef Kasbah

2002. Archaeological Sites. Multicoloured.
1499	250m. Type **599**	25	10
1500	390m. Amphitheatre, Oudhna (horiz)	30	15
1501	600m. Hall, Baron d'Erlanger Palace	50	25
1502	600m. Figures, Virgil Mosaic	50	25

600 Rabbit (*Oryctolagus cuniculus*)

2002. Fauna of Zembra and Zembretta National Park. Multicoloured.
| 1503 | 250m. Type **600** | 20 | 10 |

601 Slender-horned Gazelle (*Gazella leptoceros*)

2002. Tourism. Multicoloured.
1508	250m. Type **601**	20	10
1509	390m. Sahara	30	15
1510	600m. Horseman	50	25
1511	600m. Tamghza	50	25
MS1512 141×140 mm. 400m. ×2, Nos. 1508/9; 600m. ×2, Nos. 1510/11. Imperf		1·75	1·75

1504	250m. Mouflon sheep (*Ovis musimon*)	20	10
1505	600m. Audouin's Gull (*Larus audouinii*)	50	25
1506	600m. Peregrine Falcon (*Falco peregrinus brookei*)	50	25
MS1507 127×131 mm. 400m. ×2, Nos. 1503/4; 600m. ×2, Nos. 1505/6		1·75	1·75

602 Player, Ball and Trophy

2002. World Cup Football Championships, Japan and South Korea. Multicoloured.
1513	390m. Type **602**	30	15
1514	600m. Trophy and ball	50	25
MS1515 116×116 mm. 500m. No. 1513; 1d. No. 1514		1·30	1·30

603 Sheikh Mohamed Senoussi

2002. Personalities. Multicoloured.
1516	100m. Type **603**	10	10
1517	250m. Mosbah Jarbou	20	10
1518	250m. Mohamed Daghbaji	20	10
1519	1d.100 Abou Al Hassen	95	45

604 Wheelchair Racer

2002. World Disabled Athletics Championship, Villeneuve d'Ascq. Multicoloured.
| 1520 | 100m. Type **604** | 10 | 10 |
| 1521 | 700m. Discus thrower (vert) | 60 | 30 |

605 Conference Emblem and Animals

2002. 27th World Veterinary Conference, Tunis.
| 1522 | **605** | 600m. multicoloured | 50 | 25 |

606 Club Emblem

2002. 20th Anniv of CIGV (international travellers club).
| 1523 | **606** | 600m. multicoloured | 50 | 25 |

607 Dove and Couple holding Torch

2002. 15th Anniv of Declaration of 7th November.
1524	**607**	390m. multicoloured	35	15

608 Farhat Hached

2002. 50th Death Anniv of Farhat Hached (founder of General Union of Tunisian Workers).
1525	**608**	390m. multicoloured	35	15

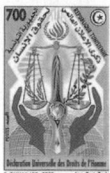

609 Scales and Globe

2002. International Human Rights Day.
1526	**609**	390m. multicoloured	35	15

610 "Wedding" (Habib Bouabana)

2002. Art. Multicoloured.
1527		250m. Type **610**	20	10
1528		250m. Folk Art (Ammar Farhat)	20	10
1529		250m. "Gazelles in Clearing" (Aly Ben Salem) (horiz)	20	10
1530		900m. "Still Life" (Pierre Boucherle)	80	40

611 Spinner

2003. Mosaics. Multicoloured.
1531		390m. Type **611**	35	20
1532		600m. Inscr "Africa"	55	30

612 Young Scouts

2003. 70th Anniv of Tunisian Scouting. Multicoloured.
1533		250m. Type **612**	20	10
1534		600m. Adult scouts (vert)	55	30

613 Open Book

2003. National Book Year.
1535	**613**	390m. multicoloured	35	20

614 "Washerwomen" (Yahia Turki)

2003. Yahia Turki (artist) Commemoration.
1536	**614**	1d. multicoloured	90	45

615 Horse and Buildings, Farhat Hached, Rades

2003. Parks. Multicoloured.
1537		200m. Type **615**	20	10
1538		250m. Animal park, Friguia	20	10
1539		390m. La Marsa park	35	20
1540		1d. Ennahli park	90	45

616 Air Balloons, Ruins and Coastal Development

2003. National Tourism Day.
1541	**616**	600m. multicoloured	55	30

617 Emblems

2003. Constitutional Rally.
1542	**617**	250m. multicoloured	20	10

618 Habib Bourguiba

2003. Birth Centenary of Habib Bourguiba (president, 1957—1987).
1543	**618**	390m. multicoloured	35	20

619 Oryx dammah

2003. Flora and Fauna. Multicoloured.
1544		50m. Type **619**	10	10
1545		50m. Nyanthes sambac	10	10
1546		100m. Ram	10	10
1547		100m. Myrtle communis	10	10
1548		100m. Rosa canina (36×36 mm)	10	10
1549		200m. Ostrich (Sruthio camelus)	20	10
1550		200m. No. 1548	20	10
1551		250m. No. 1545 (36×36 mm)	20	10
1552		250m. No. 1546 (36×36 mm)	20	10
1553		390m. No. 1549 (36×36 mm)	35	20
1554		600m. Type 619 (36×36 mm)	55	30
1555		1d. No. 1547 (36×36 mm)	90	45

620 Stylized Figures and Flag

2003. 16th Anniv of Declaration of 7th November.
1556	**620**	250m. multicoloured	20	10

621 "5+5" and Participants Flags

2003. First 5+5 Summit, Tunis.
1557	**621**	600m. multicoloured	55	30

622 Figures surrounding Globe

2003. 55th Anniv of Universal Declaration of Human Rights.
1558	**622**	350m. multicoloured	30	15

623 Machmoum El Fell

2003. Silverwork. Multicoloured.
1559		600m. Type **623**	55	30
1560		600m. Khelel brooch	55	30
MS1561	120×81 mm. Nos. 1559/60		1·00	1·00

624 Map of Africa, Stylized Players and Trophy

2004. African Nations Football Championship. Multicoloured.
1562		250m. Type **624**	20	10
1563		600m. Map as figure holding trophy	55	30

625 Flag and People holding Torch

2004. 70th Anniv of Ksar Helal Congress.
1564	**625**	250m. multicoloured	20	10

626 Conference Emblem

2004. League of Arab States Summit Conference, Tunis.
1565	**626**	600m. multicoloured	55	30

627 Brazier

2004. Copper Handicrafts. Multicoloured.
1566		50m. Type **627**	10	10
1567		100m. Water jug	10	10
1568		150m. Jug and bowl	10	10
1569		200m. Jug	20	10
1570		250m. Amphora	20	10
1571		250m. Bucket	20	10
1572		300m. No. 1571	25	15
1573		600m. Type 627	55	30
1574		700m. No. 1570	60	30
1575		1d. No. 1568	90	45

628 Husseinite Era Gold Coin (1767)

2004. Early Currency. Multicoloured.
1576		250m. Type **628**	20	10
1577		250m. Islamic era gold dinar (706)	20	10
1578		600m. Punic era gold coin (310 BC)	50	30
1579		600m. Punic era silver coin (300 BC)	55	30
1580		1d. Banknote (1847) (67×30 mm)	90	45

629 Anniversary Emblem

2004. 40th Anniv of African Development Bank.
1581	**629**	700m. multicoloured	60	30

630 Garden Rake, Teeth as Flowers and Watering Can (A. El Mediouni)

2004. Children's Drawings.
1582	**630**	250m. multicoloured	20	10

631 Ballot Envelopes and Ballot Box

2004. Presidential and Legislative Elections.
1583 **631** 250m. multicoloured 20 10

632 Clock Tower and Computer Operators

2004. 17th Anniv of Declaration of 7th November.
1584 **632** 250m. multicoloured 20 10

633 El Abidine Mosque, Carthage

2004
1585 **633** 250m. multicoloured 20 10

634 White-headed Duck (*Oxyura leucocephala*)

2004. Birds. Multicoloured.
1586 100m. Type **634** 10 10
1587 600m. Ferruginous duck (*Aythya nyroca*) 50 25
1588 600m. Moussier's redstart (*Phoenicurus moussieri*) 50 25
1589 1000m. Marbled teal (*Marmaronetta angustirostris*) 80 40

635 Emblem

2004. Universal Declaration of Human Rights.
1590 **635** 350m. multicoloured 30 15

636 Ibn Chabbat (scientist)

2004. Personalities. Multicoloured.
1591 250m. Type **636** 20 10
1592 500m. Ibn Charaf (writer) 40 20
1593 600m. Elyssa (Dido) (Queen of Carthage) 50 25
1594 600m. Mongi Ben Hmida (neurologist) 50 25
1595 600m. Hatem el Mekki (artist and stamp designer) 50 25

637 Stylized Player

2005. International Handball Championship, Tunisia.
1596 **637** 600m. multicoloured 60 30

638 Takhlila, Hammam Sousse

2005. Traditional Costumes. Multicoloured.
1597 250m. Type **638** 20 10
1598 390m. Tarf-Ras, Kerkennah 30 15
1599 390m. Jebba, Karmassoud 30 15
1600 600m. Women's costume, Matmata 50 25

639 Emblem and Map

2005. World Information Society Summit, Tunis (1st issue).
1601 **639** 600m. multicoloured 50 25
See also No. 1613.

640 Victory (bas-relief)

2005. Roman and Punic Period Sculpture. Multicoloured.
1602 250m. Type **640** 20 10
1603 250m. Aesculapius (god of medicine) (Roman statue) 20 10
1604 600m. Female terracotta mask 50 25
1605 1000m. Baal Hammon (god) (terracotta statue) 80 40

641 Globe with Hand Raised against Cigarettes

2005. International No Smoking Day.
1606 **641** 250m. multicoloured 20 10

642 Emblem

2005. Centenary of Rotary International.
1607 **642** 600m. multicoloured 50 25

643 Emblem and Runners

2005. International Year of Sport and Physical Education.
1608 **643** 600m. multicoloured 50 25

644 Emblem and Scout

2005. World Scouting Conference, Tunis.
1609 **644** 600m. multicoloured 50 25

645 Emblem and "E=mc²"

2005. International Year of Physics.
1610 **645** 2d. multicoloured 1·60 80

646 Tower Block, Olive Branch, Globe and Girl using Computer

2004. 18th Anniv of Declaration of 7th November.
1611 **646** 250m. multicoloured 20 10

647 Map and Arrows

2005. World Information Society Summit, Tunis (2nd issue).
1612 **647** 600m. multicoloured 50 25

648 Emblem

2005. Universal Declaration of Human Rights.
1613 **648** 350m. multicoloured 30 15

649 Foeniculum

2005. Medicinal Plants. Multicoloured.
1614 250m. Type **649** 20 10
1615 600m. *Lavandula angustifolia* 50 25
1616 600m. *Mentha aquatica* 50 25
1617 1d. *Origanum majorana* 80 40

650 Ibn Khaldun

2006. 600th Death Anniv of Abu Zayd Abdu l-Rahman ibn Muhammad ibn Khaldun al-Hadrami (Ibn Khaldun) (historian).
1618 **650** 390m. multicoloured 45 25

651 Emblems

2006. 50th Anniv of Independence. Multicoloured.
1619 250m. Type **651** 30 15
1620 250m. "50", flag and symbols of industry (horiz) 30 15
1621 250m. Doctor and child 30 15
1622 250m. Bridge 30 15
1623 390m. Flag as stylized woman holding torch 45 25
1624 390m. Woman's head and book 45 25
1625 390m. Flag as dove containing man, woman and computer 45 25
MS1626 99×151 mm. Nos. 1619/25 2·50 2·50

652 Ying Yang Symbol (3rd-century mosaic)

2006. Dialogue between Civilizations and Religions.
1627 **652** 1d.350 multicoloured 1·60 80

653 Earrings

2006. Jewellery. Multicoloured.
1628 250m. Type **653** 30 15
1629 250m. Earrings with red stones 30 15
1630 600m. Gold buckle 30 15
1631 600m. Pendant earrings with amethysts 30 15

654 Stylized Figures

2006. Disabled Employment Programme.
1632 **654** 2d.350 multicoloured 2·75 1·40

655 Town Centre

2006. National Cleanliness and Environmental Protection Programme.
1633 **655** 250m. multicoloured 30 15

656 Flags and Players Legs

2006. World Cup Football Championships, Germany. Multicoloured.
1634 250m. Type **656** 30 15
1635 600m. Player 70 35

657 Soldiers and Emblem

2006. 50th Anniv of Armed Forces.
1636 **657** 250m. multicoloured 30 15

658 Bridge

2006. 50th Anniv of Tunisia—Japan Diplomatic Relations.
1637 **658** 700m. multicoloured 75 40

659 Signs

2006. National Holiday Safety Campaign.
1638 **659** 250m. multicoloured 30 15

660 Working Women

2006. 50th Anniv of Code Personal of Status.
1639 **660** 2d.350 multicoloured 2·75 1·40

661 Globe, Scales and "19"

2006. 19th Anniv of Declaration of 7th November.
1640 **661** 250m. multicoloured 30 15

662 Emblems

2006. Declaration of Human Rights.
1641 **662** 700m. multicoloured 75 40

663 Jebba en Soie

2007. Traditional Textiles. Multicoloured.
1642 250m. Type **663** 30 15

1643 250m. Tenue de la Jelwa 30 15
1644 1d.100 Kilim 1·50 75
1645 1d.350 Woven wool cover 1·80 90

664 '51'

2007. 51st Anniv of Independence.
1646 **664** 250m. multicoloured 30 15

665 Digital Symbols

2007. Youth and Digital Culture.
1647 **665** 250m. multicoloured 30 15

666 Mascot

2007. National Energy Conservation Campaign.
1648 **666** 1d. multicoloured 1·30 65

667 Globe as Doves

2007. Dialogue between Civilizations and Religions.
1649 **667** 600m. multicoloured 80 40

668 Caracalla Baths, Dougga

2007. Archaeological Sites. Multicoloured.
1650 250m. Type **668** 30 15
1651 250m. Kerkouan (Punic town) 30 15
1652 600m. Great Baths, Makthar 80 40
1653 600m. Capitol, Sbeitla 80 40

669 Symbols of Investment

2007. Investment Forum, Carthage.
1654 **669** 600m. multicoloured 80 40

670 Tourist Resort

2007. Tourism. Multicoloured.
1655 250m. Type **670** 30 15
1656 250m. Sahara 30 15
1657 600m. Golf 40
1658 600m. Tabarka Jazz Festival 80 40

671 Arms and Script

2007. 50th Anniv of Republic. Multicoloured.
1659 250m. Type **671** 30 15
1660 250m. '50' and arms 30 15

672 '20' and City Skyline

2007. 20th Anniv of Declaration of 7th November.
1661 **672** 250m. multicoloured 30 15

673 Open Door, Flags, Handshake and '50'

2007. 50th Anniv of Tunisia–Germany Friendship.
1662 **673** 600m. multicoloured 80 40

674 Stylized Figures enclosing Emblem

2007. International Solidarity Day.
1663 **674** 1d.350 multicoloured 1·80 90

675 Doves and Emblem

2008. 50th Anniv of Bombing of Sakiet Sid Youcef, Tunisia.
1664 **675** 250m. multicoloured 30 15

A stamp of a similar design was issued by Algeria.

676 Emblems

2008. 40th Anniv of Court of Auditors.
1665 **676** 250m. multicoloured 35 20

677 Emblems

2008. 60th Anniv of Declaration of Human Rights.
1666 **677** 600m. multicoloured 85 45

678 Symbols of Meteorology

2008. World Meteorology Day.
1667 **678** 250m. multicoloured 35 20

679 Decorated Vase

2008. Cultural Heritage. Multicoloured.
1668 250m. Type **679** 35 20
1669 600m. Terracotta dish, Kairouan 85 45
1670 600m. Egg shaped goblet 85 45
1671 1d.100 Lamp with camel decoration 1·60 80

680 Emblem

2008. National Day of the Disabled.
1672 **680** 250m. multicoloured 35 20

681 Mugil cephalus

2008. Fish. Multicoloured.
1673 250m Type **681** 35 20
1674 250m. Thunnus thynnus 35 20
1675 600m. Dicentrarchus labrax 85 45
1676 600m. Sparus aurata 85 45

682 Emblem

2008. Democratic Constitutional Rally.
1677	**682**	250m. multicoloured	40	20

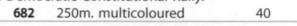

683 Pigeon

2008. Arab Post Day. Sheet 180×52 mm containing T **683** and similar horiz design. Multicoloured.
MS1678	600m.×2, Type **683**; Caravan of camels	1·80	1·80

The stamps and margins of **MS**1678 form a composite design.

684 Olympic Rings

2008. Olympic Games, Beijing. Multicoloured.
1679	250m. Type **684**	40	20
1680	600m. Olympic rings and symbols of disciplines	90	45

685 Stylized Young People

2008. Year of Dialogue with Youth.
1681	**685**	250m. multicoloured	40	20

686 '21', Emblem and Stylized Figures

2008. 21st Anniv of Declaration of 7th November.
1682	**686**	250m. multicoloured	40	20

687 '50', Students and Building

2008. 50th Anniv of University of Tunisia.
1683	**687**	250m. multicoloured	40	20

688 Ridha El Kalai (musician)

2008. Personalities. Multicoloured.
1684	250m. Type **688**	40	20
1685	250m. Anmar Farhat (artist)	40	20
1686	600m. Mahmoud Messadi (writer and politician) (vert)	95	45
1687	600m. Hedi Jouini (singer, oud player and composer) (vert)	90	45

689 '20'

2009. 20th Anniv of Arab Maghreb Union
1688	**689**	250m. multicoloured	45	25

690 Aboul Chebbi

2009. Birth Centenary of Aboul Qacem Chebbi (writer)
1689	**690**	250m. multicoloured	45	25

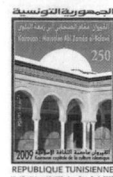

691 Abi Zamâa al Balawi's Mausoleum

2009. Kairouan–Capital of Islamic Culture. Multicoloured.
1690	250m. Type **691**	45	25
1691	250m. Okba Ibn Afaa Mosque	45	25
1692	1000m. Emblem	1·70	85
MS1693	126×83 mm. Nos. 1690/2	2·60	1·40

692 Rush Mat

2009. Plant Fibres Craftwork. Multicoloured.
1694	250m, Type **692**	45	25
1695	250m. Raffia covered bottle and woven bin	45	25
1696	600m. Decorated rush basket	95	45
1697	600m. Palm fibre fan	95	45

693 Emblem

2009. 18th Congress of International Military Law and Law of War Society
1698	**693**	700m. multicoloured	1·00	50

694 Anniversary Emblem

2009. 50th Anniv of Constitution
1699	**694**	250m. multicoloured	45	25

695 Eryobotrica japonica (medlar)

2009. Fruit. Multicoloured.
1700	250m. Type **695**	45	25
1701	600m. Cerasus (cherry)	95	45
1702	600m. Ficus carica (fig)	95	45
1703	600m. Prunus persica (peach)	95	45
MS1704	108×108 mm. Nos. 1700/3	2·75	1·40

696 Map and Stylized Athletes

2009. Mediterranean Games, Pescara
1705	**696**	600m. multicoloured	90	45

697 Emblems, Voting Papers and Ballot Box

2009. Presidential and Legislative Elections, 2009
1706	**697**	250m. multicoloured	45	25

698 '22', Emblem and Stylized Figures

2009. 22nd Anniv of Declaration of 7th November
1707	**698**	390m. multicoloured	60	40

699 Stylized Figures and Yacht

2009. 61st Anniv of Universal Declaration of Human Rights
1708	**699**	1d.350 multicoloured	1·60	80

700 Meat Tagine

2009. Local Foods. Multicoloured.
1709	250m. Type **700**	45	25
1710	700m. Mechoula salad	1·00	50
1711	1000m. Grilled fish	1·60	80
1712	1100m. Meat couscous	1·70	85
MS1713	107×107 mm. Nos. 1709/12	4·75	2·40

701 Skyline and Women's Profiles

2010. Arab Women's Day
1714	**701**	1d.350 multicoloured	25	15

702 Ying Yang Symbol (3rd-century mosaic)

2010. Year of Dialogue among Civilizations. The Ben Ali Chair for the Dialogue of Civilizations and Religions
1715	**702**	2d.350 multicoloured	40	25

703 Emblem

2010. International Year of Youth
1716	**703**	390m. multicoloured	60	35

704 Emblem

2010. Expo 2010, Shanghai
1717	**704**	390m. multicoloured	60	35

705 Punica granatum (Pomegranate)

2010. Organic Farming in Tunisia. Multicoloured.
1718	250m. Type **705**	40	25
1719	250m. Cynara scolymus (Artichoke)	40	25
1720	250m. Prunus dulcis (Almond)	40	25
1721	600m. Phoenix dactylifera (Dates)	90	45
1722	600m. Solanum lycopersicum (Tomato)	90	45
1723	600m. Olea europea (Olives and Olive oil)	90	45
1724	600m. Capiscum annum (Sweet Peppers)	90	45
1725	600m. Opuntia ficus-indica (Barbary Fig)	90	45
MS1726	181×121mm. 250m.×2, Nos. 1718/20; 600m. ×2, Nos. 1721/5	5·25	5·25

706 Symbols of Technology

2010. Tunisia - Technology in Presidential Programme
1727	**706**	390m. multicoloured	60	35

707 Emblem

2010. Year of Peace and Security in Africa
1728	**707**	250m. multicoloured	40	25

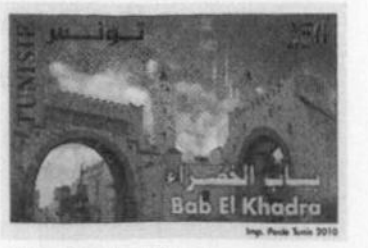

708 Bab El Khadra

2010. Monuments of the Medina of Tunis. Multicoloured.

1729	250m. Type **708**	40	25
1730	250m. Bab Jedid	40	25
1731	250m. Dar Hsine	40	25
1732	250m. Dar Ben Abdallah	40	25
1733	600m. Bab Bhar	90	45
1734	600m. Bab Saâdoun	90	45

No. 1735 and Type **709** are left for Singapore 2010, issued on 14 August 2010, not yet received.

Nos. 1736/40 and Type **710** are left for Personalities, issued on 10 October 2010, not yet received.

No. 1741 and Type **711** are left for Arab Women's Congress issued on 28 October 2010, not yet received.

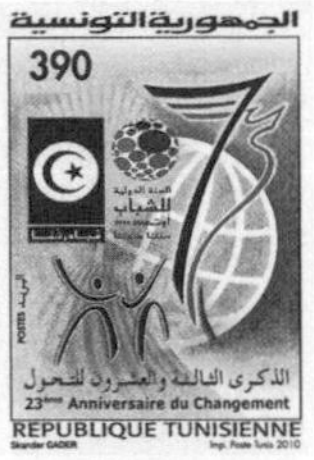

712 Emblem

2010. 22nd Anniv of Declaration of 7th November

1742	**712**	390m. multicoloured	60	35

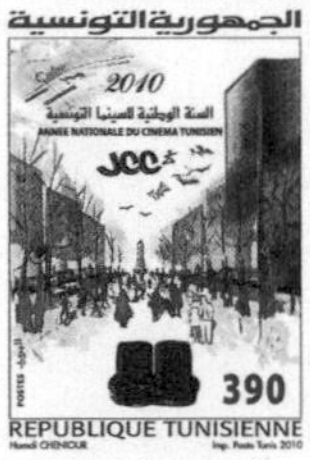

713 Street Scene and Cinema Seats

2010. National Year of Cinema

1743	**713**	390m. multicoloured	60	35

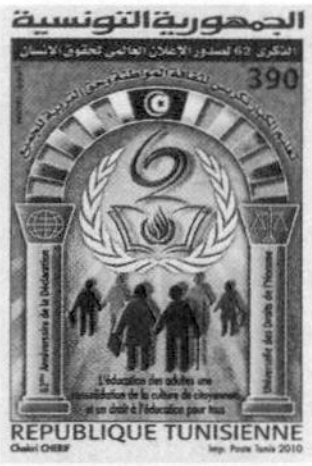

714 Emblem, People and Archway

2010. 62nd Anniv of Universal Declaration of Human Rights

1744	**714**	390m. multcoloured	60	35

PARCEL POST STAMPS

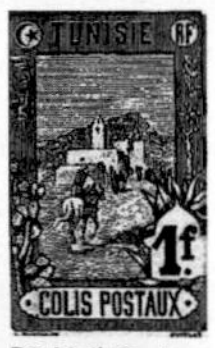

P8 Mail Carrier

1906

P44	**P8**	5c. purple and green	75	45
P45	**P8**	10c. pink and red	55	55
P46	**P8**	20c. red and brown	2·50	45
P47	**P8**	25c. brown and blue	4·25	45
P48	**P8**	40c. red and grey	4·75	1·00
P49	**P8**	50c. violet and brown	4·75	45
P50	**P8**	75c. blue and brown	8·75	45
P51	**P8**	1f. red and brown	3·75	35
P52	**P8**	2f. blue and red	9·25	45
P53	**P8**	5f. brown and violet	22·00	1·40

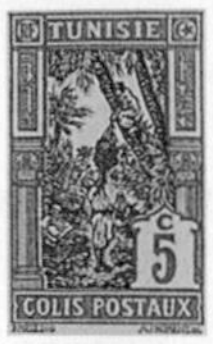

P25 Date Gathering

1926

P147	**P25**	5c. blue and brown	45	65
P148	**P25**	10c. mauve and red	45	1·00
P149	**P25**	20c. black and green	1·20	90
P150	**P25**	25c. black and brown	70	1·30
P151	**P25**	40c. green and red	1·00	85
P152	**P25**	50c. black and violet	1·10	75·00
P153	**P25**	60c. red and brown	1·43	2·00
P154	**P25**	75c. green and lilac	1·40	90
P155	**P25**	80c. brown and red	1·80	95
P156	**P25**	1f. pink and blue	1·80	45
P157	**P25**	2f. red and mauve	1·80	55
P158	**P25**	4f. black and red	2·75	75
P159	**P25**	5f. violet and brown	1·80	45
P160	**P25**	10f. grn & red on grn	2·75	1·00
P161	**P25**	20f. vio & grn on pink	12·00	2·75

POSTAGE DUE STAMPS

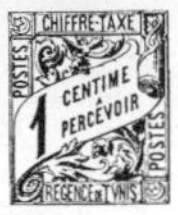

D3

1901

D28	**D3**	1c. black	30	30
D29	**D3**	2c. orange	35	55
D30	**D3**	5c. blue	45	55
D31	**D3**	10c. brown	1·10	35
D32	**D3**	20c. green	4·50	45
D33	**D3**	30c. red	4·00	65
D34	**D3**	50c. lake	1·30	85
D35	**D3**	1f. olive	1·10	65·00
D36	**D3**	2f. red on green	3·50	8·00
D37	**D3**	5f. black on yellow	40·00	60·00

1914. Surch **2 FRANCS**.

D49	2f. on 5f. black on yell	1·10	7·25

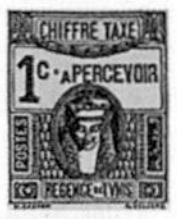

D20 Carthaginian Statue

1923

D100	**D20**	1c. black	10	4·50
D101	**D20**	2c. black on yellow	20	5·00
D102	**D20**	5c. purple	20	2·75
D103	**D20**	10c. blue	45	5·75
D104	**D20**	20c. orange on yellow	20	20
D105	**D20**	30c. brown	10	35
D106	**D20**	50c. red	55	1·00
D107	**D20**	60c. mauve	90·00	55·00
D108	**D20**	80c. brown	45	6·00
D109	**D20**	90c. red	55	1·10
D110	**D20**	1f. green	20	20
D111	**D20**	2f. green	70	3·25
D112	**D20**	3f. violet on pink	1·00	2·75
D113	**D20**	5f. violet	70	1·10

1945

D287	10c. green	10	7·25
D288	50c. violet	10	7·25
D289	2f. pink	50	1·00
D290	4f. blue	20	5·00
D291	10f. mauve	95	4·25
D292	20f. brown	1·30	1·40
D293	30f. blue	2·50	6·50

Nos. D293 is inscribed "TIMBRE TAXE".

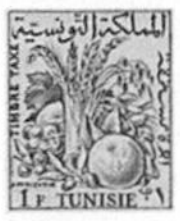

D86 Agricultural Produce

1957

D448	**D86**	1f. green	20	20
D449	**D86**	2f. brown	20	20
D450	**D86**	3f. green	40	40
D451	**D86**	4f. blue	45	45
D452	**D86**	5f. mauve	45	45
D453	**D86**	10f. red	45	45
D454	**D86**	20f. sepia	1·75	1·75
D455	**D86**	30f. blue	1·90	1·90

1960. Inscr "REPUBLIQUE TUNISIENNE" and new currency.

D534	1m. green	10	10
D535	2m. brown	10	10
D536	3m. green	15	15
D537	4m. blue	15	15
D538	5m. violet	20	20
D539	10m. red	40	40
D540	20m. brown	60	60
D541	30m. blue	70	70
D542	40m. brown	15	15
D543	100m. green	40	30

Pt. 16

TURKEY

Formerly an empire, this country is now a republic, the greater part of its territory lying in Asia Minor.

1863. 40 paras = 1 piastre or grush.
1942. 100 paras = 1 kurus.
1947. 100 kurus = 1 lira.
2005. 100 ykr. = 1 ytl.

For designs as Types **1**, **2**, **9**, **15**, **21**, **23**, **25**, **28** and **30** but in black or brown, see Postage Due stamps.

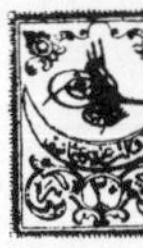

1

1863. Imperf.

1	**1**	20pa. black on yellow	80·00	32·00
2	**1**	1pi. black on purple	£120	36·00
3	**1**	2pi. black on blue	£130	55·00
4	**1**	5pi. black on red	£250	80·00

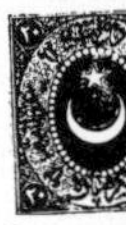

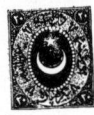

2

1865. Perf.

11	**2**	10pa. green	7·25	23·00
35a	**2**	10pa. brown	£130	7·75
64	**2**	10pa. mauve	1·40	60
12	**2**	20pa. yellow	3·75	3·75
65	**2**	20pa. green	1·40	60
94	**2**	20pa. grey	3·75	9·25
13	**2**	1pi. lilac	13·00	3·75
66	**2**	1pi. yellow	1·40	60
14	**2**	2pi. blue	4·75	60·00
95	**2**	2pi. red to brown	1·90	60
15	**2**	5pi. red	2·40	60·00
39c	**2**	5pi. grey	30·00	43·00
46	**2**	5pi. blue	1·40	12·00
16	**2**	25pi. orange	£300	£300
48	**2**	25pi. red	36·00	£150

1876. Surch with value in figures and Pres.

77	**2**	¼pre. on 10pa. mauve	2·40	3·00
78	**2**	½pre. on 20pa. green	6·00	3·00
79	**2**	1¼pre. on 50pa. red	1·40	3·00
80	**2**	2pre. on 2pi. brown	38·00	9·25
81	**2**	5pre. on 5pi. blue	3·00	£120

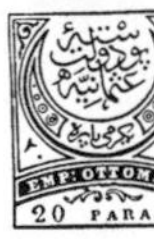

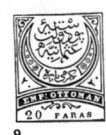

9

1876

89	**9**	5pa. black and yellow	2·40	9·25
96	**9**	5pa. lilac	£190	£180
109	**9**	5pa. black	1·20	3·00
113	**9**	5pa. green and yellow	2·40	6·00
82	**9**	10pa. black and mauve	1·90	9·25
90	**9**	10pa. black and green	1·90	4·50
97	**9**	10pa. green	1·20	1·50
83	**9**	20pa. purple and green	60·00	6·00
91	**9**	20pa. black and pink	31·00	1·60
103	**9**	20pa. pink	1·40	1·20
92	**9**	1pi. black and grey (A)	60·00	7·75
93	**9**	1pi. black and blue (B)	95·00	3·75
99	**9**	1pi. blue	1·20	1·50
85	**9**	2pi. black and flesh	1·20	6·00
110	**9**	2pi. orange and blue	1·20	2·40
114	**9**	2pi. mauve and grey	1·40	1·80
126a	**9**	2pi. yellow	75·00	5·00
86	**9**	5pi. pink and blue	3·00	18·00
111	**9**	5pi. green	3·00	31·00
115	**9**	5pi. brown	4·75	24·00
87	**9**	25pi. purple and mauve	14·50	£120
107	**9**	25pi. black	£300	£500
112	**9**	25pi. brown	29·00	£225
116	**9**	25pi. red and yellow	24·00	£225
84	**9**	50pa. blue and yellow	70	12·00

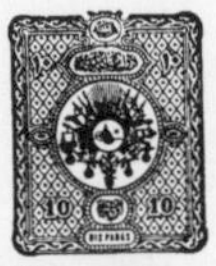

15

1892. Various frames.

141	**15**	10pa. green	1·40	60
142a	**15**	20pa. red	1·20	60
143	**15**	1pi. blue	95·00	60
144	**15**	2pi. brown	1·90	60
145	**15**	5pi. purple	2·40	18·00

1897. Surch **5 5 Cinq Paras**.

160	**15**	5pa. on 10pa. green	3·00	1·80

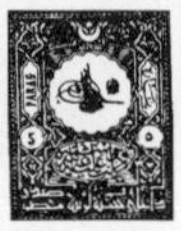

21

1901. For Internal Mail.

167	**21**	5pa. violet	70	60
168	**21**	10pa. green	70	60
169	**21**	20pa. red	70	60
170	**21**	1pi. blue	95	60
171	**21**	2pi. orange	1·90	60
203	**21**	5pi. mauve	7·25	3·00
173	**21**	25pi. brown	9·50	1·80
174	**21**	50pi. brown	31·00	48·00

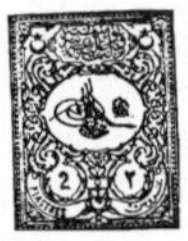

22

1901. For Foreign Mail.

175	**22**	5pa. brown	1·20	60
176	**22**	10pa. green	1·20	60
177	**22**	20pa. mauve	1·20	60
178	**22**	1pi. blue	1·20	60
179	**22**	2pi. blue	2·40	1·20
180	**22**	5pi. brown	9·50	5·00
181	**22**	25pi. green	95·00	37·00
182	**22**	50pi. yellow	£225	£110

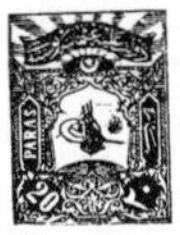

23

1905

212A	**23**	5pa. brown	95	60
213A	**23**	10pa. green	95	60
214A	**23**	20pa. pink	95	60
215A	**23**	1pi. blue	95	60
216B	**23**	2pi. blue	95	60
217B	**23**	2½pi. purple	95	60
218B	**23**	5pi. brown	1·10	95
219A	**23**	10pi. orange	3·50	1·20
220A	**23**	25pi. green	12·00	18·00
221A	**23**	50pi. purple	48·00	37·00

Type **24** is the Turkish letter "B" which stands for Behie = discount.

ب

(24)

1906. Optd with T **24**.

230B	**23**	10pa. green	1·50	1·40
231B	**23**	20pa. pink	1·50	1·40
232A	**23**	1pi. blue	3·00	1·20
233B	**23**	2pi. blue	13·00	5·75

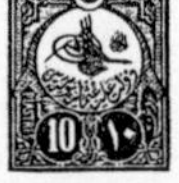

25

1908

234B	**25**	5pa. brown	40	50
235B	**25**	10pa. green	60	50
236B	**25**	20pa. red	30·00	50
237B	**25**	1pi. blue	3·75	50
238C	**25**	2pi. black	4·50	50
239B	**25**	2½pi. brown	3·00	50
240B	**25**	5pi. purple	55·00	50
241A	**25**	10pi. red	48·00	3·00
242A	**25**	25pi. green	9·50	6·00
243A	**25**	50pi. brown	36·00	55·00

1908. Optd as T **24** but smaller.

252B	**25**	10pa. green	3·75	4·75
253B	**25**	20pa. red	5·00	4·75
254B	**25**	1pi. blue	7·50	7·75
255A	**25**	2pi. black	24·00	15·00

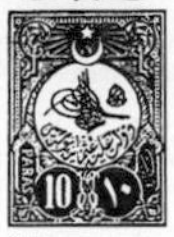

27

1908. Granting of Constitution.

256B	**27**	5pa. brown	55	50
257B	**27**	10pa. green	55	50
258B	**27**	20pa. red	1·50	95
259B	**27**	1pi. blue	1·50	1·20
260B	**27**	2pi. black	17·00	25·00

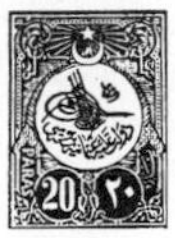

28

1909

271A	**28**	2pa. green	95	60
261B	**28**	5pa. brown	40	20
262B	**28**	10pa. green	40	20
263C	**28**	20pa. red	75	20
264B	**28**	1pi. blue	55	20
265B	**28**	2pi. black	1·10	30
266C	**28**	2½pi. brown	75·00	24·00
267B	**28**	5pi. purple	2·30	30
268B	**28**	10pi. red	12·00	60
269A	**28**	25pi. green	£350	90·00
270C	**28**	50pi. brown	£110	£120

1909. Optd as T **24** but smaller.

289B	**28**	10pa. green	2·30	1·40
290C	**28**	20pa. red	1·90	95
291A	**28**	1pi. blue	7·25	4·25
292A	**28**	2pi. black	60·00	31·00

1910. No. 261 surch **2** and Turkish inscr.

296A	**28**	2pa. on 5pa. brown	70	90

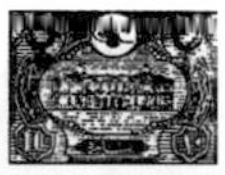

30 G.P.O., Constantinople

1913

333	**30**	2pa. green	95	60
334	**30**	5pa. bistre	95	60
335	**30**	10pa. green	95	60
336	**30**	20pa. pink	95	60
337	**30**	1pi. blue	95	60
338	**30**	2pi. grey	1·90	60
339	**30**	5pi. purple	3·25	60
340	**30**	10pi. red	7·25	1·20
341	**30**	25pi. green	22·00	28·00
342	**30**	50pi. brown	75·00	£150

1913. Optd as T **24** but smaller.

343	**30**	10pa. green	95	60
344	**30**	20pa. pink	95	60
345	**30**	1pi. blue	95	60
346	**30**	2pi. grey	17·00	9·25

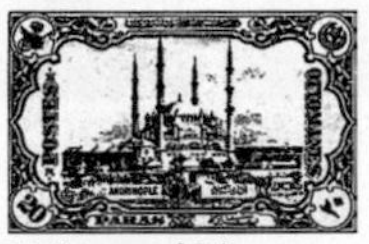

31 Mosque of Selim

1913. Recapture of Adrianople.

353	**31**	10pa. green	1·40	1·20
963	**31**	20pa. red	85	50
355	**31**	40pa. blue	5·75	3·75

For Type **31** surcharged, see Postage Due stamps.

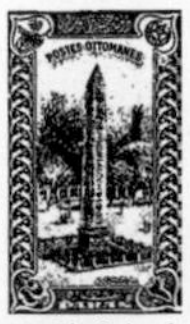

32 Obelisk of Theodosius

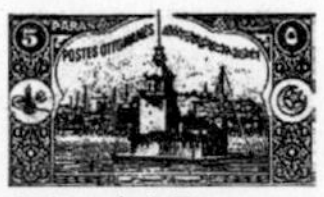

34 Leander's Tower

1914

499	**32**	2pa. purple	50	60
500	-	4pa. brown	50	60
501	**34**	5pa. purple	50	60
961	**34**	5pa. brown	85	50
502	-	6pa. blue	50	60
503	-	10pa. green	2·40	60
504	-	20pa. red	1·40	60
505	-	1pi. blue	50	60
964	-	1pi. green	3·50	50
506	-	1½pi. grey and red	95	60
507	-	1¾pi. brown and grey	95	60
508	-	2pi. black and green	1·90	60
509	-	2½pi. green and orange	1·40	60
965	-	3pi. blue	85	50
510	-	5pi. lilac	3·00	60
966	-	5pi. grey	48·00	50
511	-	10pi. brown	6·00	60
967	-	10pi. lilac	12·00	50
512	-	25pi. green	£120	6·00
968	-	25pi. purple	4·75	2·50
513	-	50pi. pink	4·75	3·00
969	-	50pi. brown	4·75	10·50
514	-	100pi. blue	70·00	24·00
515	-	200pi. black and green	£450	£275

DESIGNS—VERT: 4ps. Column of Constantine; 6pa. Seven Towers Castle, Yedikule. HORIZ: 10pa. Lighthouse Garden, Constantinople; 20pa. Castle of Europe; 1pi. Mosque of Sultan Ahmed; 11/2 piMonuments to Martyrs of Liberty; 1¾pi., 3pi. Fountains of Suleiman; 2pi. Cruiser 'Hamidiye'; 2½pi., 5pi. (966) Candilli, Bosphorus; 5pi. (510) Former Ministry of War; 10pi. Sweet Waters of Europe; 25pi. Suleiman Mosque; 50pi. Bosphorus at Rumeli Hisar; 100pi. Sultan Ahmed's Fountain; 200pi. Sultan Mohamed V

SIZES—As Type **32**: 4, 6pa; 31½×20 mm: 10pa. to 1pi; 26×21 mm: 1½pi. to 2½ pi; 38×24 mm: 5pi. to 50pi; 40×25½ mm: 100, 200pi.

1914. Stamps of 1914 optd with small star.

516		10pa. green	2·40	60
517		20pa. red	9·50	60
518		1pi. blue	1·90	60
519		1¾pi. brown and grey	1·20	1·80
520		2pi. black and green	43·00	3·00

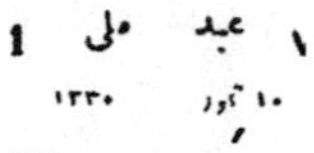

(49)

1914. Seventh Anniv of Constitution No. 506 surch with T **49**.

521	1pi. on 1½pi. grey and red	3·75	3·00

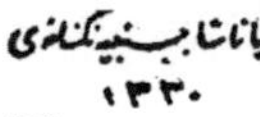

(50)

1914. Abrogation of the Capitulations. Nos. 501/11 optd with T **50**.

524	5pa. purple	1·90	60
526	10pa. green	3·75	60
527	20pa. red	3·75	60
528	1pi. blue	9·50	1·80
530	2pi. black and green	14·50	1·80
532	5pi. lilac	60·00	4·25
533	10pi. brown	£190	60·00

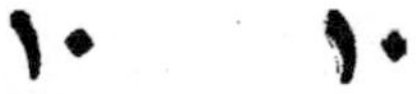

(51)

1915. Nos. 514/15 surch as T **51**.

534	10pi. on 100pi. blue	60·00	15·00
535	25pi. on 200pi. black & green	14·50	6·00

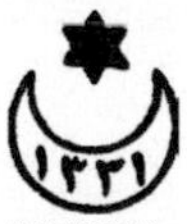

(53) ("1331" = 1915)

1915. Various issues optd with T **53**. I. On postage stamps. (a) 1892 and 1897 issues.

536	**15**	5pa. on 10pa. green	95	60
537	**15**	10pa. green	95	60
538	**15**	2pi. brown	1·40	60
539	**15**	5pi. purple	3·75	60

(b) 1901 issues. (i) For Internal mail.

540	**21**	5pa. violet	95	60
541	**21**	10pa. green	1·40	60
542	**21**	20pa. red	1·40	60
543	**21**	1pi. blue	1·40	60
544	**21**	2pi. orange	1·90	60
545	**21**	5pi. mauve	2·40	60
546	**21**	25pi. brown	12·00	2·40

(ii) For Foreign mail.

547	**22**	5pa. brown	95	60
548	**22**	1pi. blue	3·00	60
549	**22**	2pi. blue	2·40	60
550	**22**	5pi. brown	19·00	60
551	**22**	25pi. green	60·00	37·00

(c) 1905 and 1906 issues.

552	**23**	5pa. buff	95	60
553b	**23**	10pa. green	40	20
561	**23**	10pa. green (230)	1·90	60
554a	**23**	20pa. pink	65	40
555a	**23**	1pi. blue	75	30
556b	**23**	2pi. grey	1·30	50
562	**23**	2pi. grey (233)	4·75	60
557	**23**	2½pi. purple	1·40	60
558a	**23**	5pi. brown	45	30
559	**23**	10pi. orange	12·00	60
560	**23**	25pi. green	60·00	12·00

(d) 1908 issues.

563	**25**	5pa. brown	95·00	43·00
564	**25**	2pi. black	£300	60·00
569a	**25**	2pi. black (255)	9·00	3·00
565	**25**	2½pi. brown	3·00	60
566a	**25**	5pi. purple	75·00	35·00
567	**25**	10pi. red	14·50	6·00
568	**25**	25pi. green	29·00	6·00

(e) 1909 issues.

570	**28**	5pa. brown	25	20
572	**28**	20pa. red	1·90	60
579	**28**	20pa. red (290)	1·90	60
573	**28**	1pi. blue	1·90	60
581	**28**	1pi. blue (291)	1·90	60
574	**28**	2pi. black	1·90	60
582	**28**	2pi. black (292)	3·25	60
575	**28**	2½pi. brown	60·00	31·00
576	**28**	5pi. purple	40	20
577	**28**	10pi. red	9·50	60
578	**28**	25pi. green	£1900	£1400

(f) 1913 issues.

583	**30**	5pa. bistre	95	60
584	**30**	10pa. green	95	60
591	**30**	10pa. green (343)	95	60
585	**30**	20pa. pink	95	60
592	**30**	20pa. pink (344)	95	60
586	**30**	1pi. blue	95	60
593	**30**	1pi. blue (345)	1·90	60
587	**30**	2pi. grey	95	60
594	**30**	2pi. grey (346)	7·25	3·75
588	**30**	5pi. purple	3·00	60
589	**30**	10pi. red	9·50	60
590	**30**	25pi. green	29·00	24·00

II. On printed matter stamps (for use as postage stamps). (a) 1894 issue.

595	**15**	10pa. green	5·75	60
596	**15**	2pi. brown	1·40	60

(b) 1901 issues.

597	**21**	5pa. violet	95	1·20
600	**22**	10pa. green	95	60
598	**21**	20pa. red	1·90	1·20
599	**21**	5pi. mauve	19·00	6·00

(c) 1905 issues.

601b	**23**	5pa. buff	30	25
602	**23**	2pi. grey	17·00	6·00
603	**23**	5pi. brown	9·50	60

(d) 1908 issues.

604	**25**	2pi. black	£1300	£600
605a	**25**	5pi. purple	7·25	75

(e) 1909 issues.

606	**28**	5pa. brown	95	60
608	**28**	5pi. purple	95·00	43·00

(54)

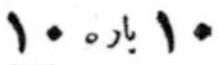

(56)

1915. Various issues optd with T **54** (star varies). I. On postage stamps. (a) 1892 issue, also surch with T **56**.

630	**15**	10pa. on 20pa. red	50	60

(b) 1901 issues.

631	**21**	1pi. blue	70	60
632a	**21**	5pi. mauve	8·00	1·30

(c) 1905 and 1906 issues, Nos. 633 and 636 also surch with T 56.

609a	**23**	10pa. green	35	35
611b	**23**	10pa. green (230)	30·00	25·00
633	**23**	10pa. on 20pa. pink	60	60
636a	**23**	10pa. on 20pa. pink (231)	45	45
634	**23**	1pi. blue	1·50	60
637	**23**	1pi. blue (232)	60	60
610	**23**	10pi. orange	12·00	60

(d) 1908 issues.

612	**25**	10pa. green	1·20	60
614a	**25**	10pa. green (252)	£225	£170
638	**25**	20pa. red		
640a	**25**	20pa. red (253)	70	60
641	**25**	1pi. blue (254)	70	60
613	**25**	5pi. purple	70·00	15·00
639	**25**	10pi. red	£475	£250

(e) 1909 issues.

616	**28**	10pa. green	60	60
620	**28**	10pa. green (289)	60	60
643	**28**	20pa. red	95	1·80
647	**28**	20pa. red (290)	70	60
645	**28**	1pi. blue	80	50
649	**28**	1pi. blue (291)	70	60
619	**28**	5pi. purple	8·50	1·80
646	**28**	10pi. red	50·00	50·00

(f) 1913 issues.

623	**30**	10pa. green	70	60
625	**30**	10pa. green (343)	70	60
650	**30**	20pa. pink	60	60
653	**30**	20pa. pink (344)	70	60
624	**30**	1pi. blue	70	60
652	**30**	10pi. red	15·00	7·50

(g) 1916 Postal Jubilee issue.

654	**60**	10pa. red	70	60
655	**60**	20pa. blue	70	60
656	**60**	1pi. black and violet	70	60
657	**60**	5pi. black and brown	95	60

II. On printed matter stamps (for use as postage stamps). (a) 1894 issue, also surch with T **56**.

658	**15**	10pa. on 20pa. red	50	60

(b) 1901 issue.

659	**22**	5pi. brown	11·00	3·00

(c) 1908 issue.

626	**25**	10pa. green	£350	£225
627	**25**	5pi. purple	70·00	15·00

(d) 1909 issue.

629	**28**	10pa. green	60	60

(57) ("1332" = 1916)

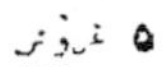

(58)

1916. Various issues optd with T **57**, some also surch in piastres as T **58**. I. On postage stamps. (a) 1892 and 1897 issues.

660	**15**	5pa. on 10pa. green (160)	60	60
661	**15**	10pa. green	95	60
662	**15**	20pa. red	60	60
663	**15**	1pi. blue	48·00	60·00
664	**15**	2pi. brown	4·75	1·20
665	**15**	5pi. purple	48·00	60·00

(b) 1901 issues. (i) Internal mail.

666	**21**	5pa. violet	70·00	60·00
667	**21**	10pa. green	1·40	1·80
668	**21**	20pa. red	60	60
669	**21**	1pi. blue	70	60
670	**21**	2pi. orange	1·40	60
671a	**21**	10pi. on 25pi. brown	5·75	1·40
672	**21**	10pi. on 50pi. brown	7·25	1·80
673a	**21**	25pi. brown	5·75	1·90
674	**21**	50pi. brown	9·50	2·50

(ii) Foreign mail.

675	**22**	5pa. brown	60	50
676	**22**	10pa. green	95	50
677	**22**	20pa. mauve	60	50
678	**22**	1pi. blue	95	50
679	**22**	2pi. blue	4·75	50
680	**22**	5pi. on 25pi. green	55·00	60·00
681	**22**	10pi. on 25pi. green	55·00	60·00
682	**22**	25pi. green	55·00	60·00

(c) 1905 and 1906 issues.

683	**23**	5pa. buff	60	50
692a	**23**	10pa. green (230)	90	60
684	**23**	20pa. pink	60	50
693	**23**	20pa. pink (231)	95	50
685a	**23**	1pi. blue	55	40
694a	**23**	1pi. blue (232)	75	60
686a	**23**	2pi. grey	1·90	60
687	**23**	2½pi. purple	7·25	1·60
688	**23**	10pi. on 25pi. green	7·25	2·50
689	**23**	10pi. on 50pi. purple	7·25	2·10
690	**23**	25pi. green	7·25	2·10
691	**23**	50pi. purple	4·75	1·60

(d) 1908 issues.

701	**25**	2pi. black (255)	60·00	65·00
695	**25**	2½pi. brown	60·00	65·00
696	**25**	10pi. on 25pi. green	19·00	13·00
697a	**25**	10pi. on 50pi. brown	55·00	60·00
699	**25**	25pi. green	7·25	2·50
698	**25**	25pi. on 50pi. brown	60·00	65·00
700	**25**	50pi. brown	60·00	65·00

(e) 1908 Constitution issue.

702	**27**	5pa. brown	60·00	65·00

(f) 1909 issues.

703	**28**	5pa. brown	50	50
704	**28**	10pa. green	48·00	50·00
705	**28**	20pa. red	48·00	50·00

707	**28**	1pi. blue	95	50
711	**28**	1pi. blue (291)	60·00	65·00
708	**28**	2pi. black	3·00	1·60
712	**28**	2pi. black (292)	48·00	50·00
709	**28**	2½pi. brown	48·00	50·00
710	**28**	5pi. purple	48·00	50·00

(g) 1913 issues.

713	**30**	5pa. bistre	60	50
714	**30**	20pa. pink	1·40	50
715	**30**	1pi. blue	1·40	50
720	**30**	1pi. blue (345)	95	1·00
716	**30**	2pi. grey	3·00	1·00
717	**30**	10pi. on 50pi. brown	12·00	10·50
718	**30**	25pi. green	7·25	5·25
719	**30**	50pi. brown	14·50	13·00

(h) 1913 Adrianople issue.

721	**31**	10pa. green	1·20	50
722	**31**	20pa. red	1·90	50
723	**31**	40pa. blue	5·75	2·50

(i) 1914 Constitution issue with further surch.

724		60pa. on 1pi.on 1½pi. grey and red	2·40	3·75

(j) 1916 Postal Jubilee issues.

725	**60**	5pi. black and brown	1·50	1·80

II. On printed matter stamps (for use as postage stamps).
(a) 1894 issues.

726	**15**	5pa. on 10pa. green	60	50
727	**15**	10pa. green	95	50
728	**15**	20pa. red	50	50
729	**15**	5pi. purple	48·00	50·00

(b) 1901 issues. (i) Internal mail.

730	**21**	5pa. violet	48·00	50·00
731	**21**	10pa. green	48·00	50·00
732	**21**	20pa. red	70	50
733	**21**	1pi. blue	70	50
734	**21**	2pi. orange	70	50

(ii) Foreign mail.

735	**22**	5pa. brown	60	50
736	**22**	10pa. green	60	50
737	**22**	20pa. mauve	60	50
738	**22**	1pi. blue	60	50

(c) 1905 issue.

739	**23**	5pa. buff	60	50
740	**23**	10pa. green	48·00	50·00
741	**23**	20pa. pink	48·00	50·00
742a	**23**	1pi. blue	1·40	50

(d) 1908 issue.

743a	**25**	5pa. brown	55·00	55·00

(e) 1909 issue.

744	**28**	5pa. brown	60·00	65·00

III. On 1913 Adrianople postage due issues (for use as postage stamps).

745	**31**	10 on 2pa. on 10pa. green	55·00	60·00
746	**31**	20 on 5pa. on 20pa. red	55·00	60·00
747	**31**	40 on 10pa. on 40pa. blue	55·00	60·00

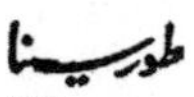

(59)

1916. Occupation of Sinai Peninsula. Optd with T **59**.

749	**21**	5pa. violet	95	50
750	**21**	10pa. green	95	50
751	**28**	20pa. red	1·90	50
752	**28**	1pi. blue	5·25	1·00
753	**30**	5pi. purple	12·00	3·25

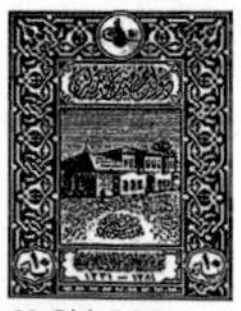

60 Old G.P.O., Constantinople

1916. Jubilee of Constantinople City Post.

754A	**60**	5pa. green	70	50
755A	**60**	10pa. red	70	50
756A	**60**	20pa. blue	70	50
757A	**60**	1pi. black and violet	1·40	50
758A	**60**	5pi. black and brown	19·00	50

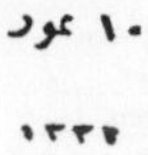

(61)

1916. National Fete. Optd with T **61**.

759	**15**	10pa. green	1·90	2·10
760b	**23**	20pa. red	1·40	1·10
761a	**23**	1pi. blue	9·50	5·25
762b	**23**	2pi. grey	10·00	70
763	**23**	2½pi. purple	19·00	1·60

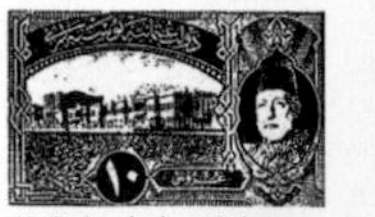

62 Dolmabahce Palace

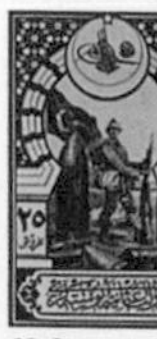

63 Sentry

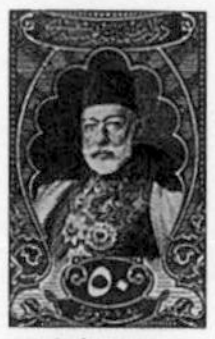

64 Sultan Mohamed V

1916

764	**62**	10pi. violet	8·50	5·25
765	**62**	10pi. green on grey	31·00	2·50
766	**62**	10pi. brown	13·00	2·50
767	**63**	25pi. red on buff	2·20	1·60
768	**64**	50pi. red	4·75	5·25
769	**64**	50pi. green on yellow	1·90	2·50
770	**64**	50pi. blue	2·40	10·50

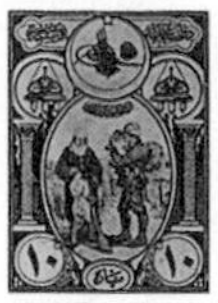

65 Off to the Front

1917. Charity.

771	**65**	10pa. purple	1·20	50

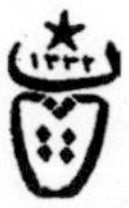

(66)

1917. Various issues optd with T **66** or surch in addition.
A. On postage stamp issue of 1865.

782	**2**	10pa. mauve	43·00	70·00
772a	**2**	20pa. yellow	43·00	70·00
783	**2**	20pa. green	43·00	70·00
785	**2**	20pa. grey	43·00	70·00
773b	**2**	1pi. lilac	40·00	40·00
784	**2**	1pi. yellow	43·00	70·00
774	**2**	2pi. blue	43·00	70·00
780	**2**	2pi. red to brown	43·00	70·00
775	**2**	5pi. red	43·00	70·00
778	**2**	5pi. blue	43·00	70·00
779	**2**	25pi. red	43·00	70·00

B. On surcharged postage stamp issue of 1876.

787	**2**	¼pre. on 10pa. mauve	43·00	70·00
788	**2**	½pre. on 20pa. green	43·00	70·00
789	**2**	1¼pre. on 50pa. red	43·00	70·00

C. On postage stamp issue of 1876.

790	**9**	5pa. black and yellow	43·00	70·00
791	**9**	5pa. black	70	80
792	**9**	10pa. black and green	43·00	70·00
793	**9**	10pa. green	43·00	70·00
794	**9**	50pa. black and yellow	43·00	70·00
795	**9**	2pi. black and flesh	43·00	70·00
796	**9**	2pi. ochre	43·00	70·00
797	**9**	2pi. orange and blue	1·70	1·80
798	**9**	5pi. brown	43·00	70·00
799	**9**	5pi. green	43·00	70·00
801	**9**	25pi. purple and mauve	43·00	70·00
802	**9**	25pi. brown	43·00	70·00

D. On postage stamp issue of 1892.

803	**15**	20pa. purple	1·20	1·30
804	**15**	2pi. brown	2·00	2·00

E. On postage stamp issue of 1901.

805	**21**	5pa. violet	38·00	50·00
806	**21**	10pa. green	3·75	4·25
807	**21**	20pa. red	70	80
808	**21**	1pi. blue	70	70
809	**21**	2pi. orange	2·20	2·40
810	**21**	5pi. mauve	38·00	50·00
811	**21**	10pi. on 50pi. brown	31·00	50·00
812	**21**	25pi. brown	4·75	5·25

F. On postage stamp issue of 1901.

813	**22**	5pa. brown	2·40	2·50
814	**22**	20pa. mauve	70	80
815	**22**	1pi. blue	1·90	2·10
816	**22**	2pi. blue	4·75	5·25
817	**22**	5pi. brown	31·00	50·00
818	**22**	10pi. on 50pi. yellow	43·00	70·00
819	**22**	25pi. green	31·00	50·00

G. On postage stamp issues of 1905 and 1906.

820	**23**	5pa. buff	55	40
821	**23**	10pa. green	31·00	50·00
830	**23**	10pa. green (No. 230)	55	60
822	**23**	20pa. pink	55	60
831	**23**	20pa. pink (No. 231)	60	60
823	**23**	1pi. blue	55	60
832	**23**	1pi. blue (No. 232)	95	1·00
824	**23**	2pi. grey	3·25	3·25
833	**23**	2pi. grey (No. 233)	31·00	50·00
825	**23**	2½pi. purple	4·75	5·25
826	**23**	5pi. brown	31·00	50·00
827	**23**	10pi. orange	31·00	50·00
828	**23**	10pi. on 50pi. purple	31·00	50·00
829	**23**	25pi. green	31·00	50·00

H. On postage stamp issues of 1908.

834a	**25**	5pa. brown	2·75	3·00
835	**25**	10pa. green	70	80
840	**25**	10pa. green (No. 252)	£140	£225
841	**25**	1pi. blue (No. 254)	38·00	50·00
836	**25**	2pi. black	31·00	50·00
842	**25**	2pi. black (No. 255)	43·00	70·00
837a	**25**	2½pi. brown	3·75	2·10
838	**25**	10pi. on 50pi. brown	31·00	50·00
839	**25**	25pi. green	31·00	50·00

I. On Constitution issue of 1908.

843	**27**	5pa. brown	1·10	1·10

J. On postage stamp issues of 1909.

844	**28**	5pa. brown	80	60
846	**28**	10pa. green	70	70
854	**28**	10pa. green (No. 289)	£140	£225
847	**28**	20pa. red	70	70
849	**28**	1pi. blue	55	55
856	**28**	1pi. blue (No. 291)	2·00	2·00
850	**28**	2pi. black	3·25	3·75
857	**28**	2pi. black (No. 292)	4·25	4·75
851	**28**	2½pi. brown	31·00	50·00
852a	**28**	5pi. purple	31·00	50·00
853	**28**	10pi. red	31·00	50·00

K. On postage stamp issues of 1913.

858	**30**	5pa. bistre	1·20	1·30
859	**30**	10pa. green	31·00	50·00
865	**30**	10pa. green (No. 343)	1·40	1·60
860	**30**	20pa. pink	1·40	1·60
861	**30**	1pi. blue	1·40	1·60
866	**30**	1pi. blue (No. 345)	3·00	3·25
862	**30**	2pi. grey	3·25	3·75
867	**30**	2pi. grey (No. 346)	31·00	50·00
863	**30**	5pi. purple	31·00	50·00
864	**30**	10pi. red	31·00	50·00

L. On Adrianople Commem stamps of 1913.

868	**31**	10pa. green	4·75	5·25
869	**31**	40pa. blue	6·75	7·25

M. On Constitution Commem of 1914 with additional surch in Turkish.

870		60pa. on 1pi. on 1½pi. grey and red (No. 521)	1·40	1·60

N. On postage stamp issues of 1916.

871	**63**	25pi. red on buff	4·75	5·25
872	**64**	50pi. red	17·00	18·00
873	**64**	50pi. green on yellow	31·00	50·00
874	**64**	50pi. blue	14·50	24·00

O. On stamps of Eastern Roumelia of 1881 (T **9** of Turkey, but inscr "ROUMELIE ORIENTALE" at left).

876		5pa. lilac	31·00	50·00
877		10pa. green	31·00	50·00
875		20pa. black and red	31·00	50·00
878		20pa. red	31·00	50·00

P. On printed matter stamps of 1893 optd with Type **N16**.

879	**15**	20pa. red (No. N 156a)	3·50	4·00
880	**15**	1pi. blue (No. N 157)	70	80

Q. On printed matter stamps of 1901 optd with Type **N23**.

881	**21**	5pa. violet (No. N183)	2·20	2·40
882	**21**	10pa. green (No. N184)	22·00	39·00
883	**21**	20pa. red (No. N185)	1·40	1·60
884	**21**	1pi. blue (No. N186)	3·00	3·25
885	**21**	2pi. orange (No. N187)	2·40	2·50
886	**21**	5pi. mauve (No. N188)	31·00	50·00

R. On printed matter stamps of 1901 optd with Type N 23.

887	**22**	5pa. brown (No. N189)	3·75	4·25
888	**22**	10pa. green (No. N190)	3·75	4·25
889	**22**	20pa. mauve (No. N191)	3·75	4·25
890	**22**	2pi. blue (No. N193)	43·00	70·00

S. On printed matter stamps of 1905 optd with Type **N23**.

891d	**23**	5pa. brown (No. N222)	70	80
892	**23**	10pa. green (No. N223)	1·40	1·60
893	**23**	20pa. pink (No. N224)	70	80
894	**23**	1pi. blue (No. N225)	50	40
895	**23**	2pi. grey (No. N226)	31·00	50·00
896	**23**	5pi. brown (No. N227)	31·00	50·00

T. On printed matter stamp of 1908 optd with Type **N27**.

897	**25**	5pa. brown (No. N244)	30·00	30·00

U. On postage due stamps of 1865.

898	**D 4**	20pa. brown	43·00	70·00
899	**D 4**	1pi. brown	43·00	70·00
900	**D 4**	2pi. brown	43·00	70·00
901	**D 4**	5pi. brown	43·00	70·00
902	**D 4**	25pi. brown	43·00	70·00

V. On postage due stamps of 1888.

904	**9**	1pi. black (D118)	43·00	70·00
905	**9**	2pi. black (D119)	43·00	70·00

W. On postage due stamps of 1892.

906	**15**	20pa. black (D146)	1·40	1·60
907	**15**	1pi. black (D148)	1·40	1·60
908	**15**	2pi. black (D149)	1·40	1·60

X. On Adrianople commemoration issue of 1913 (postage due stamps surch in Arabic further surch).

909	**31**	10 on 2pa. on 10pa. green (D356)	95	1·00
910	**31**	20 on 5pa. on 20pa. red (D357)	95	1·00
911	**31**	40 on 10pa. on 40pa. blue (D358)	1·40	1·60
912	**31**	40 on 20pa. on 40pa. blue (D359)	3·25	3·75

The overprints on printed matter and postage due stamps were used for ordinary postage.

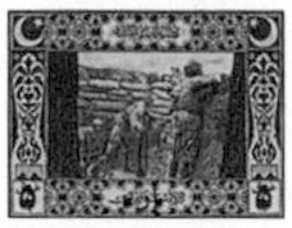

67 In the Trenches

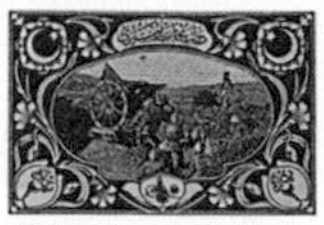

69 Howitzer at Sedd el Bahr

1917. Surch variously in Turkish.

913	**67**	5pa. on 1pi. red	70	50
914	**69**	5pi. on 2pa. blue	12·00	1·80
915	**65**	10pa. on 20pa. red	1·90	50

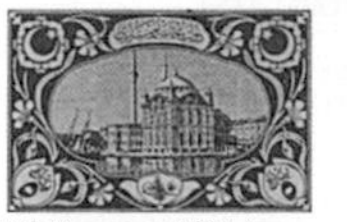

72 Mosque at Ortakoy

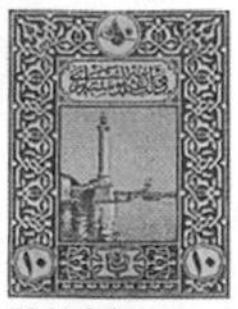

73 Lighthouse, Achir Kapu

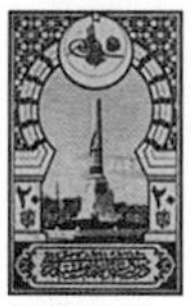

74 Martyrs' Column

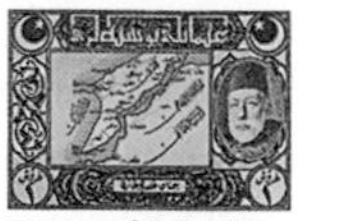

75 Map of Gallipoli

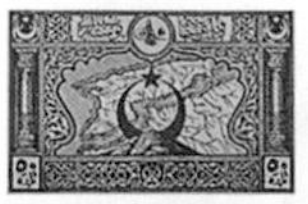

76 Map of Gallipoli

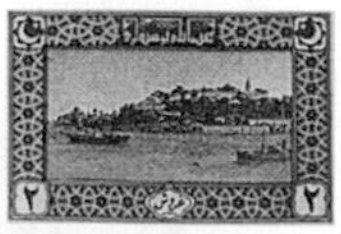

77 Seraglio Point

1917

916	**69**	2pa. violet	1·10	70
917	**72**	5pa. orange	1·10	30
918	**73**	10pa. green	1·10	30
919	**74**	20pa. red	85	50
920	**75**	1pi. blue	2·40	50
921	**76**	50pa. blue	1·20	50
921b	**77**	2pi. blue and brown	3·00	50
922	-	5pi. brown and blue	17·00	2·40

DESIGNS—As T **77**. 5pi. Pyramids.

1918. Surch **5 Piastres 5** and in Turkish.

923	**69**	5pi. on 2pa. blue	12·00	50

1918. No. 913 with additional surch.

924	**67**	2pa. on 5pa. on 1pi. red	1·40	1·60

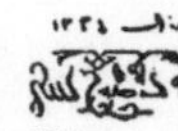

(81)

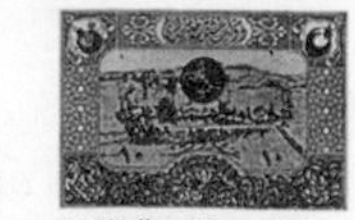

84 Wells at Beersheba

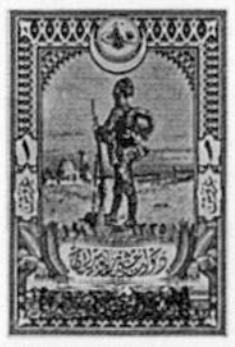

85 Sentry at Beersheba

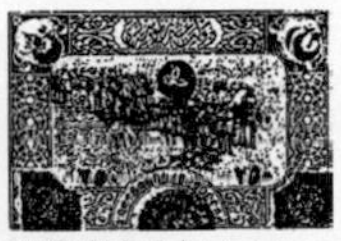

87 Turkish Column in Sinai

1918. Armistice. Optd as T **81**.

925	**84**	20pa. purple	70	1·60
926	**75**	1pi. blue	7·25	10·50
927	**85**	1pi. blue	£120	£160
937	**D51**	1pi. blue (No. D518)	£120	£160
928	**76**	50pa. blue	60	1·60
929	**77**	2pi. blue and brown	70	1·60
930	-	2½pi. green and orange (No. 509)	£120	£160
931	-	5pi. brown and blue (No. 922)	1·30	1·80
932	**62**	10pi. green on grey	6·00	10·50
933	**63**	25pi. red on buff	6·00	10·50
934	**87**	25pi. blue	£120	£160
935	-	50pi. pink (No. 513)	£120	£160
936	**64**	50pi. green on yellow	7·25	10·50

1918. Stamp of 1909 optd with Sultan's toughra and surch in Turkish.

938	**28**	5pa. on 2pa. green	70	80

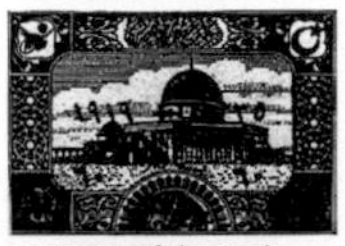

86 Dome of the Rock, Jerusalem

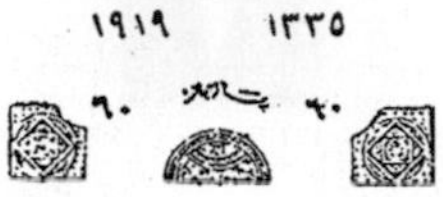

(88)

1919. Accession of Sultan Mohamed VI. Optd with date as in T **88** and ornaments or inscription.

939	**84**	20pa. purple	1·70	10·50
940	**85**	1pi. blue	2·40	18·00
941	**86**	60pa. on 10pa. green	1·10	7·75
942	**87**	25pi. blue	7·25	50·00

The illustrations Type **85** (optd with date and inscription at foot) and **86** (surch with T **88**) illustrate Nos. 940/1. Nos. 939 and 942 are overprinted with the date and the central motif only at bottom of Type **88**.

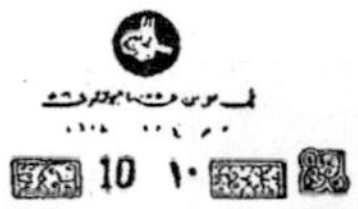

(89)

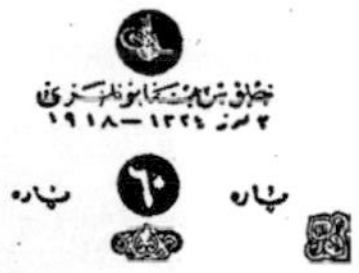

(90)

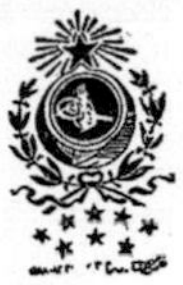

(91)

1919. First Anniv of Sultan's Accession. Optd or surch as T **89**, **90** or **91**.

943	**69**	2pa. violet	60	1·50
944	**72**	5pa. orange	35	35
945	**28**	5pa. on 2pa. green	50	50
947	**73**	10pa. green	75	1·00
946	**30**	10pa. on 2pa. green	50	50
960a	**D49**	10pa. on 5pa. brown	24·00	39·00
948	**74**	20pa. red	70	50
960b	**D50**	20pa. red	24·00	39·00
960c	**D51**	1pi. blue	24·00	39·00
949	**75**	1pi. blue	1·10	1·00
950	**76**	60pa. on 50pa. blue	85	1·00
951	**77**	60pa. on 2pi. blue and brown	50	50
960d	**D52**	2pi. blue	24·00	39·00
952	**77**	2pi. blue and brown	50	1·00
952a	-	2½pi. green and orange (No. 509)	24·00	39·00
953	-	5pi. brown and blue (No. 922)	40	65
954	**62**	10pi. brown	2·40	2·50
955	**84**	10pi. on 20pa. purple	50	1·00
956	**63**	25pi. red and buff	1·90	2·10
957	**85**	35pi. on 1pi. blue	1·40	2·50
958	**64**	50pi. green on yellow	3·00	5·25
958a	**64**	50pi. red	24·00	39·00
959	**86**	100pi. on 60pa. on 10pa. green	3·75	5·25
960	**87**	250pi. on 25pi. blue	3·75	5·25

Types **84** and **87** illustrate Nos. 955 and 960.

1921. Surch in figures and words and in Turkish characters.

970	**65**	30pa. on 10pa. purple	1·10	50
971	-	60pa. on 10pa. green (No. 503)	1·10	50
972	**67**	4½pi. on 1pi. red	2·40	50
973	-	7½ on 3pi. blue (No. 965)	12·00	1·00

Numerous fiscal and other stamps were surcharged or overprinted by the Turkish Nationalist Government at Angora during 1921, but as they are not often met with by general collectors we omit them. A full listing will be found in Part 16 (Central Asia) of the Stanley Gibbons catalogue.

Nos. A79/90 and A119/24 were the only definitive issue of the Angora Government at this period.

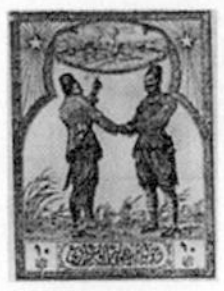

A24 National Pact

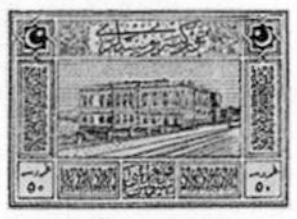

A25 Parliament House, Sivas

1921

A79	**A24**	10pa. purple	50	25
A80	-	20pa. green	50	25
A81	-	1pi. blue	50	25
A82	-	2pi. purple	3·00	50
A83	-	5pi. blue	3·00	50
A84	-	10pi. brown	9·50	80
A85	-	25pi. red	14·50	1·00
A86	**A25**	50pi. blue (A)	95	8·25
A87	**A25**	50pi. blue (B)	95	1·30
A88	-	100pi. violet	70·00	5·25
A89	-	200pi. violet	£190	65·00
A90	-	500pi. green	£110	29·00

DESIGNS—HORIZ: 20pa. Izmir Harbour; 1pi. Mosque, Adrianople; 10pi. Legendary grey wolf, Boz Kurt; 25pi. Castle Adana; 200pi. Map of Anatolia. VERT: 2pi. Mosque, Konya; 5pi. Soldier taking oath; 100pi. Mosque, Ourfa; 500pi. Declaration of faith from Koran.

Type (B) of the 50pi. as illustrated. In Type (A) the inscription at the top is similar to that of Type A **30** and the figures in the value tablets are above instead of below the Turkish inscription.

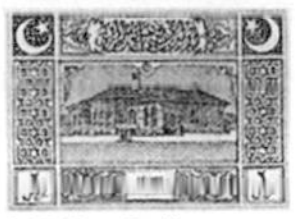

A30 First Parliament House, Angora

1922

A119	**A30**	5pa. mauve	50	2·50
A120	**A30**	10pa. green	95	2·50
A121	**A30**	20pa. red	1·40	2·10
A122	**A30**	1pi. orange	9·50	4·25
A123	**A30**	2pi. brown	19·00	4·50
A124	**A30**	3pi. red	2·40	50

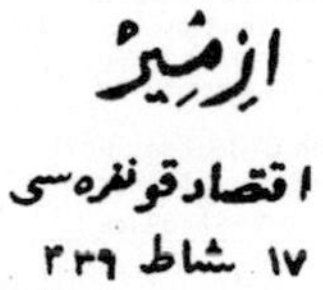

(94a)

1923. Izmir (Smyrna) Economic Congress. Nos. 918 and A80/4 optd with T **94a**.

973b	**73**	10pa. green	7·25	5·25
973c	-	20pa. green	7·25	6·50
973d	-	1pi. blue	9·50	10·50
973e	-	2pi. purple	9·50	21·00
973f	-	5pi. blue	14·50	16·00
973g	-	10pi. brown	24·00	37·00

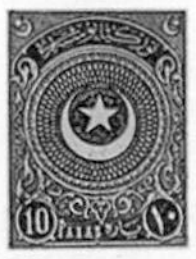

95

1923

974	**95**	10pa. grey	25	25
975	**95**	20pa. yellow	25	25
976	**95**	1pi. mauve	25	25
977	**95**	1½pi. green	25	80
978	**95**	2pi. green	70	25
979	**95**	3pi. brown	70	50
980	**95**	3¾pi. brown	2·40	2·50
1001	**95**	4½pi. red	1·20	50
1002	**95**	5pi. violet	3·00	25
1003	**95**	7½pi. blue	3·00	50
1004	**95**	10pi. grey	8·50	4·75
1012a	**95**	10pi. blue	£160	2·30
986	**95**	11¼pi. pink	2·40	2·10
1006	**95**	15pi. brown	8·50	5·25
988	**95**	18¾pi. green	3·25	3·25
989	**95**	22½pi. orange	5·75	2·10
990	**95**	25pi. brown	29·00	2·50
991	**95**	50pi. grey	70·00	4·25
992	**95**	100pi. purple	£140	9·25
993	**95**	500pi. green	£475	£160

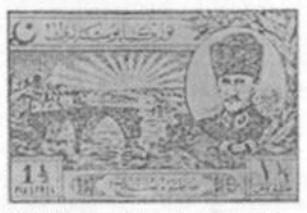

96 Kemal Ataturk and Sakarya Bridge

1924. Treaty of Lausanne.

1013	**96**	1½pi. green	1·40	1·60
1014	**96**	3pi. violet	1·40	2·10
1015	**96**	4½pi. pink	1·90	3·75
1016	**96**	5pi. brown	3·00	5·25
1017	**96**	7½pi. blue	2·40	3·75
1018	**96**	50pi. orange	9·50	34·00
1019	**96**	100pi. purple	55·00	47·00
1020	**96**	200pi. olive	70·00	70·00

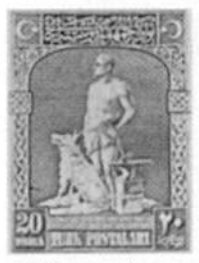

97 Legendary Blacksmith and Grey Wolf, Boz Kurt

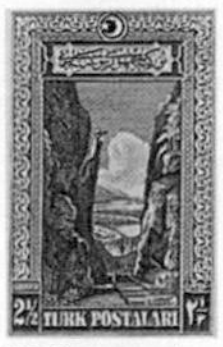

98 Gorge and River Sakarya

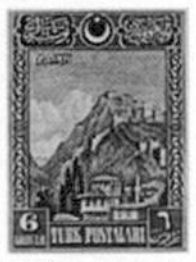

99 Fortress of Ankara

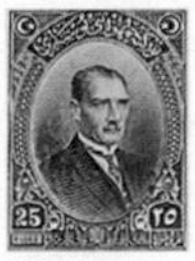

100 Kemal Ataturk

1926

1021	**97**	10pa. grey	50	10
1022	**97**	20pa. orange	50	15
1023	**97**	1gr. red	50	15
1024	**98**	2gr. green	1·40	25
1025	**98**	2½gr. black	1·90	25
1026	**98**	3gr. red	2·40	25
1027	**99**	5gr. violet	3·00	50
1028	**99**	6gr. red	95	25
1029	**99**	10gr. blue	7·25	50
1030	**99**	15gr. orange	9·50	50
1031	**100**	25gr. black and green	14·50	1·30
1032	**100**	50gr. black and red	19·00	1·60
1033	**100**	100gr. black and olive	34·00	2·10
1034	**100**	200gr. black and brown	85·00	5·75

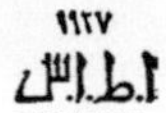

101 "1927 Izmir Exhibition"

1927. Izmir (Smyrna) Exhibition. Optd with T **101**.

1035	**97**	1gr. red	50	50
1036	**98**	2gr. green	50	1·00
1037	**98**	2½gr. black	1·40	2·10
1038	**98**	3gr. red	1·90	2·50
1039	**99**	5gr. violet	2·40	4·25
1040	**99**	6gr. red	1·40	1·60
1041	**99**	10gr. blue	3·25	3·75
1042	**99**	15gr. orange	4·75	5·25
1043	**100**	25gr. black and green	14·50	21·00
1044	**100**	50gr. black and red	26·00	39·00
1045	**100**	100gr. black and olive	60·00	80·00

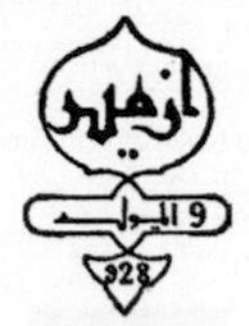

102 "Izmir, 9 Sept, 1928"

1928. Second Izmir Exhibition. T 97/9 optd with T **102** and T **100** optd **928** and 2 lines of Turkish.

1053	**97**	10pa. grey	50	40
1054	**97**	20pa. orange	50	40
1055	**97**	1gr. red	95	50
1056	**98**	2gr. green	1·40	1·60
1057	**98**	2½gr. black	1·40	1·60
1058	**98**	3gr. red	1·40	1·60
1059	**99**	5gr. violet	1·90	3·25
1060	**99**	6gr. red	50	50
1061	**99**	10gr. blue	3·25	3·25
1062	**99**	15gr. orange	4·75	2·10
1063	**100**	25gr. black and green	14·50	6·50
1064	**100**	50gr. black and red	17·00	21·00
1065	**100**	100gr. black and olive	38·00	50·00
1066	**100**	200gr. black and brown	60·00	65·00

1929. Surch with value in "Paradir" or "Kurustur".

1067	**97**	20par. on 1gr. red	50	25
1068	**99**	2½kur. on 5gr. violet	95	50
1069	**99**	6kur. on 10gr. blue	5·75	1·00

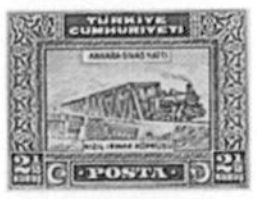

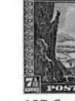

106 Bridge over Kizil-Irmak

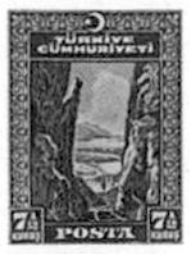

107 Gorge and River Sakarya

1929. T **106/7** and 1926 stamps but inscr "TURKIYE CUMHURIYETI".

1076	**97**	10pa. green	25	25
1077	**106**	20pa. violet	25	25
1078	**106**	1k. green	50	50
1079	**97**	1½k. green	50	40
1070	**106**	2k. black	4·75	1·00
1080	**106**	2k. violet	95	50
1081	**106**	2½k. green	1·90	50
1072	**106**	3k. purple	3·75	1·60
1082	**106**	3k. red	19·00	1·60
1083	**97**	4k. red	7·25	50
1084	**99**	5k. purple	11·00	50
1085	**97**	6k. blue	7·25	40
1086	**107**	7½k. red	25	25
1088	**99**	12½k. blue	70	25
1089	**99**	15k. orange	70	50
1090	**107**	17½k. black	70	50
1091	**99**	20k. brown	48·00	2·10
1092	**107**	25k. brown	95	1·00
1093	**99**	30k. brown	1·40	1·00
1094	**107**	40k. purple	1·40	1·00
1075	**100**	50k. black and red	60·00	9·25

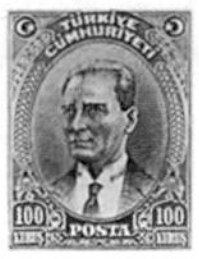

109

1930

1095	**109**	50k. black and red	3·00	1·30
1096	**109**	100k. black and olive	3·00	1·30
1097	**109**	200k. black and green	3·00	1·60
1098	**109**	500k. black and brown	17·00	24·00

1930. Opening of Ankara–Sivas Railway. Surch Sivas D. Y. 30ag. 930 and value.

1099	**97**	10pa. on 10pa. green	50	1·30
1100	**106**	10pa. on 20pa. violet	50	1·60
1101	**106**	20pa. on 1k. green	95	1·60
1102	**97**	1k. on 1½k. green	50	1·30
1103	**106**	1½k. on 2k. violet	50	1·30
1104	**106**	2k. on 2½k. green	95	1·60
1105	**106**	2½k. on 3k. red	2·40	2·10
1106	**97**	3k. on 4k. red	1·90	1·60
1107	**99**	4k. on 5k. purple	1·90	1·60
1108	**97**	5k. on 6k. blue	2·40	1·00
1109	**107**	6k. on 7½k. red	3·25	4·25
1110	**99**	7½k. on 12½k. blue	70	50
1111	**99**	12½k. on 15k. orange	1·20	1·00
1112	**107**	15k. on 17½k. black	4·75	4·25
1113	**99**	17½k. on 20k. brown	4·75	2·10
1114	**107**	20k. on 25k. brown	7·25	2·10
1115	**99**	25k. on 30k. brown	4·75	2·50
1116	**107**	30k. on 40k. purple	7·25	2·50
1117	**109**	40k. on 50k. black and red	14·50	7·75
1118	**109**	50k. on 100k. black and green	65·00	17·00
1119	**109**	100k. on 200k. black and green	80·00	29·00
1120	**109**	250k. on 500k. black and brown	70·00	37·00

1931. Surch **1 Kurus**.

1121	**97**	1k. on 1½k. green	95	50

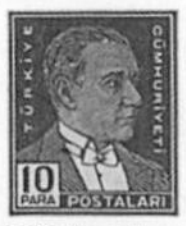

112 Kemal Ataturk

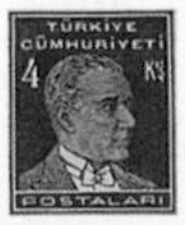

113

1931

1124	**113**	1k. green	10	10
1122	**112**	10pa. green	10	10
1444	**112**	10pa. brown	15	10

1444a	112	10pa. red	40	10
1123	112	20pa. orange	10	10
1445	112	20pa. green	25	10
1453b	112	20pa. yellow	15	10
1123a	112	30pa. violet	25	10
1453c	113	1k. orange	15	10
1124a	112	1½k. lilac	50	10
1125	113	2k. violet	50	10
1125a	113	2k. green	45	40
1447	113	2k. mauve	60	10
1447a	113	2k. yellow	1·10	10
1453d	113	2k. pink	15	10
1126	112	2½k. green	50	10
1126a	113	3k. brown	25	10
1448	113	3k. orange	1·00	10
1448a	113	3k. blue	70	10
1127	113	4k. black	2·40	10
1453f	113	4k. green	15	10
1128	113	5k. red	25	10
1128a	113	5k. black	1·70	40
1449a	113	5k. purple	5·00	10
1453g	113	5k. blue	75	10
1129	113	6k. blue	3·00	10
1129a	113	6k. red	25	40
1130	112	7½k. red	25	10
1130a	113	8k. blue	95	20
1453h	113	8k. violet	15	10
1131	112	10k. black	2·30	10
1131a	112	10k. blue	7·00	40
1450	112	10k. brown	3·00	10
1453i	112	10k. green	15	10
1132	112	12k. brown	35	15
1453j	112	12k. red	25	10
1133	112	12½k. blue	35	15
1134	112	15k. yellow	35	20
1451	112	15k. violet	5·25	10
1453k	112	15k. red	40	10
1135	112	20k. green	35	20
1452	112	20k. blue	26·00	15
1453la	112	20k. purple	11·50	10
1136	112	25k. blue	1·90	25
1137	112	30k. purple	4·25	30
1453	112	30k. pink	30·00	35
1453m	112	30k. green	1·50	10
1138	112	100k. brown	1·20	65
1139	112	200k. violet	3·50	2·10
1453a	112	200k. brown	7·50	1·60
1140	112	250k. brown	80·00	7·25

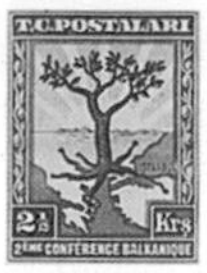

114 Tree with Roots in Six Balkan Capitals

1931. Second Balkan Conference.

1141	114	2½k. green	10	10
1142	114	4k. red	10	15
1143	114	6k. blue	10	15
1144	114	7½k. red	10	20
1145	114	12k. orange	50	25
1146	114	12½k. blue	50	25
1147	114	30k. violet	50	1·60
1148	114	50k. brown	95	80
1149	114	100k. purple	1·90	1·60

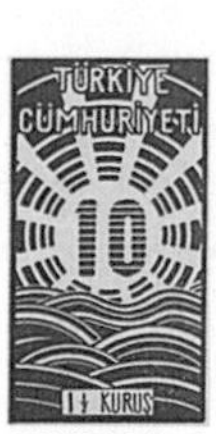

115 "Rebirth of Turkey"

1933. Tenth Anniv of Turkish Republic.

1150	115	1½k. green	50	1·00
1151	115	2k. bistre	50	1·30
1152	-	3k. red	70	1·00
1153	-	6k. blue	70	1·30
1154	115	12½k. blue	2·40	2·50
1155	115	25k. brown	3·50	5·25
1156	-	50k. brown	4·75	16·00

DESIGNS—HORIZ: 3, 6, 50k. Wheat, cogwheels, factory, "X" and Kemal Ataturk.

1934. Air. Optd **1934** and airplane or surch also.

1157	107	7½k. lake	30	20
1158	99	12½k. on 15k. orange	45	30
1159	107	20k. on 25k. brown	45	40
1160	107	25k. brown	70	50
1161	107	40k. purple	1·40	1·30

1934. Izmir International Fair. Optd **Izmir 9 Eylul 934 Sergisi** or surch also.

1162	97	10pa. green	50	1·00
1163	97	1k. on 1½k. green	95	80
1164	107	2k. on 25k. brown	1·40	1·30
1165	107	5k. on 7½k. red	4·75	5·25
1166	107	6k. on 17½k. black	2·40	2·10
1167	99	12½k. blue	7·25	5·25
1168	99	15k. on 20k. brown	48·00	47·00
1169	107	20k. on 25k. brown	34·00	39·00
1170	109	50k. on 100k. black and green	38·00	39·00

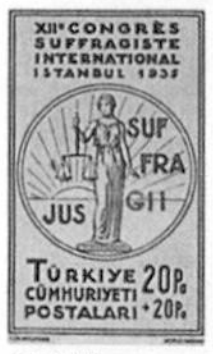

119 Alliance Badge

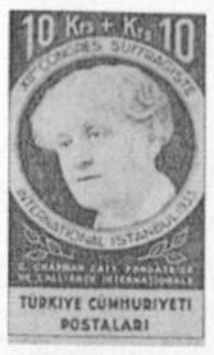

120 Mrs. C. Chapman Catt

1935. 12th Congress of the International Women's Alliance, Istanbul.

1171	119	20pa.+20pa. bistre	50	50
1172	-	1k.+1k. red	50	50
1173	-	2k.+2k. blue	95	80
1174	-	2½k.+2½k. green	95	80
1175	-	4k.+4k. blue	1·40	1·00
1176	-	5k.+5k. purple	2·40	2·10
1177	-	7½k.+7½k. red	2·40	2·10
1178	120	10k.+10k. orange	2·40	2·50
1179	-	12½k.+12½k. blue	2·40	2·50
1180	-	15k.+15k. violet	4·75	5·25
1181	-	20k.+20k. red	7·25	6·50
1182	-	25k.+25k. green	14·50	14·50
1183	-	30k.+30k. blue	85·00	£100
1184	-	50k.+50k. green	£170	£160
1185	-	100k.+100k. red	£120	£140

DESIGNS: 1k. Woman teacher; 2k. Woman farmer; 2½k. Typist; 4k. Woman pilot and policewoman; 5k. Women voters; 7½k. Yildiz Palace, Istanbul; 12½k. Jane Addams; 15k. Grazia Deledda; 20k. Selma Lagerlof; 25k. Bertha von Suttner; 30k. Sigrid Undset; 50k. Mme. Curie-Sklodowska; 100k. Kemal Ataturk.

1936. Remilitarization of Dardanelles. Surch **BOGAZLAR MUKAVELESININ IMZASI 20/7/1936** and value in figures.

1186	107	4k. on 17½k. black	95	50
1187	107	5k. on 25k. brown	1·40	50
1188	100	6k. on 50k. black and red	50	25
1189	109	10k. on 100k. black and olive	2·40	2·50
1190	109	20k. on 200k. black and green	3·50	5·25
1191	109	50k. on 500k. black and brown	3·50	5·25

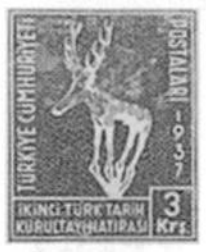

122 Stag

1937. Second Turkish Historical Congress.

1192	122	3k. violet	95	1·30
1193	-	6k. blue	1·40	2·10
1194	122	7½k. red	2·40	4·00
1195	-	12½k. blue	4·75	7·75

DESIGN: 6, 12½k. Bust of Ataturk.

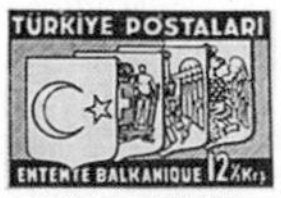

124 Arms of Turkey, Greece, Rumania and Yugoslavia

1937. Balkan Entente.

1196	124	8k. red	4·75	2·50
1197	124	12½k. blue	7·25	5·25

1938. Air. Surch **1937** with airplane above and value.

1198	107	4½k. on 7½k. lake	6·00	1·40
1199	99	9k. on 15k. orange	37·00	13·50
1200	107	35k. on 40k. purple	10·00	11·00

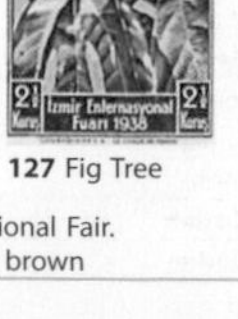

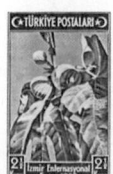

127 Fig Tree

1938. Izmir International Fair.

1201	-	10pa. brown	75	10
1202	-	30pa. violet	75	10
1203	127	2½k. green	1·90	40
1204	-	3k. orange	1·50	15
1205	-	5k. green	2·75	40
1206	-	6k. brown	13·50	3·25
1207	-	7½k. red	7·50	1·30
1208	-	8k. red	5·75	1·30
1209	-	12k. purple	7·50	1·60
1210	-	12½k. blue	15·00	7·75

DESIGNS—HORIZ: 10pa. An Izmir boulevard; 30pa. Izmir Fair; 6k. Woman gathering grapes. VERT: 3k. Clock Tower, Hukunet Square; 5k. Olive branch; 7½k. Woman gathering grapes; 8k. Izmir Harbour; 12k. Equestrian statue of Ataturk; 12½k. Ataturk.

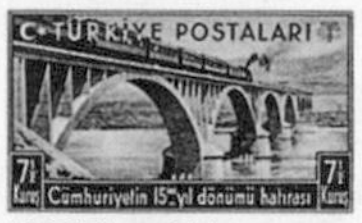

129 Railway Bridge

1938. 15th Anniv of Proclamation of Turkish Republic.

1211	-	2½k. green	1·10	4·00
1212	-	3k. red	90	40
1213	-	6k. bistre	1·30	60
1214	129	7½k. red	5·75	1·20
1215	-	8k. purple	6·50	3·25
1216	-	12½k. blue	3·75	2·50

DESIGNS—HORIZ: 2½k. Military display; 3k. Aerial view of Kayseri; 8k. Scout buglers. VERT: 6k. Ataturk driving a tractor; 12½k. Ataturk.

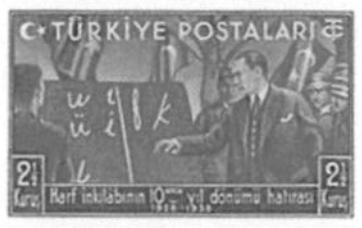

130 Kemal Ataturk teaching Alphabet

1938. Tenth Anniv of Introduction of Latin Alphabet into Turkey.

1217	130	2½k. green	1·10	60
1218	130	3k. orange	1·50	60
1219	130	6k. purple	1·90	80
1220	130	7½k. red	1·90	1·40
1221	130	8k. red	2·75	1·60
1222	130	12½k. blue	4·25	2·10

1938. Death of Kemal Ataturk. Mourning Issue. Optd **21-11-1938** and bar.

1223	113	3k. brown	45	15
1224	113	5k. red	45	15
1225	113	6k. blue	90	35
1226	112	7½k. red	90	60
1227	113	8k. blue	1·30	1·20
1228	112	12½k. blue	3·00	2·50

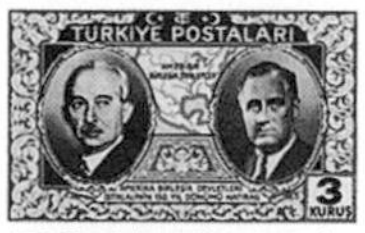

133 Presidents Inonu and Roosevelt and Map of North America

1939. 150th Anniv of U.S. Constitution.

1229	-	2½k. green, red and blue	45	25
1230	133	3k. brown and blue	45	40
1231	-	6k. violet, red and blue	90	60
1232	-	7½k. red and blue	90	65
1233	133	8k. purple and blue	1·30	80
1234	-	12½k. ultramarine & blue	3·00	2·30

DESIGNS—VERT: 2½, 6k. Turkish and U.S. flags. HORIZ: 7½, 12½k. Ataturk and George Washington.

1939. Cession of Hatay to Turkey. Surch **Hatayin Anavatana Kavusmasi 23/7/1939** and new values.

1235	107	3k. on 25k. brown	45	25
1236	109	6k. on 200k. black and green	45	40
1237	107	7½k. on 25k. brown	90	60
1238	109	12k. on 100k. (1096)	90	65
1239	109	12½k. on 200k. (1097)	1·30	80
1240	109	17½k. on 500k. (1098)	3·00	2·30

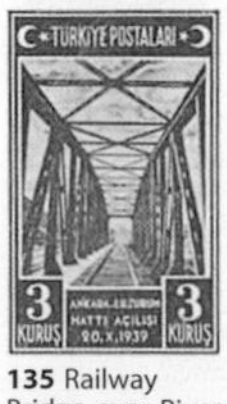

135 Railway Bridge over River Firat

1939. Opening of Ankara–Erzurum Railway.

1241	135	3k. red	3·75	3·00
1242	-	6k. brown	6·50	6·25
1243	-	7½k. red	6·50	6·25
1244	-	12½k. blue	6·50	9·75

DESIGNS—VERT: 6k. Steam locomotive. HORIZ: 7½k. Railway in Firat gorge; 12½k. Tunnel entrance at Atma-Bogazi.

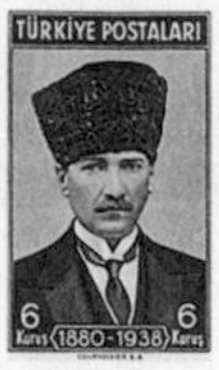

136 Kemal Ataturk

1939. First Death Anniv of Kemal Ataturk.

1245	-	2½k. green	75	40
1246	-	3k. blue	75	60
1247	-	5k. brown	90	60
1248	136	6k. brown	1·50	40
1249	-	7½k. red	2·40	1·20
1250	-	8k. olive	1·70	1·00
1251	-	12½k. blue	1·90	40
1252	-	17½k. red	3·50	1·60

MS1252a 90×119 mm. 100k. indigo — 70 — 60

DESIGN: 2½k. Ataturk's residence; 3k. to 17½k. Portraits of Kemal Ataturk as Type **136**.

1940. Balkan Entente. As T **103** of Yugoslavia, but with the torch and Arms of Turkey, Greece, Rumania and Yugoslavia rearranged.

1253	8k. blue	4·50	1·00
1254	10k. blue	6·75	1·00

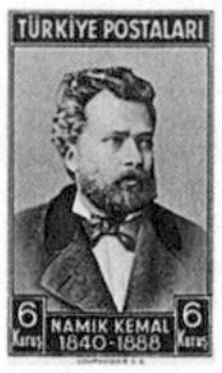

137 Namik Kemal

1940. Birth Centenary of Namik Kemal (poet).

1255	137	6k. brown	1·90	65
1256	137	8k. olive	2·75	1·50
1257	137	12k. red	3·00	1·20
1258	137	12½k. blue	7·50	3·00

1940. Izmir International Fair. Surch **IZMIR ENTERNASYONAL FUARI 1940** and value.

1259	109	6k. on 200k. black and green	55	60
1260	109	10k. on 200k. black and green	75	60
1261	109	12k. on 500k. black and brown	1·00	1·00

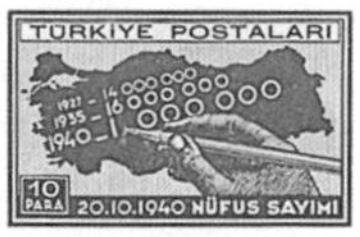

139 Map and Census Figures

1940. National Census.

1262	139	10pa. green	15	15
1263	139	3k. orange	45	35
1264	139	6k. red	90	60
1265	139	10k. blue	3·00	1·40

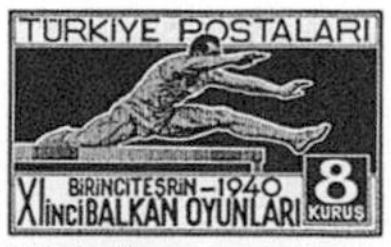

140 Hurdling

1940. 11th Balkan Games.

1266	-	3k. olive	1·90	2·10
1267	-	6k. red	6·75	6·50
1268	140	8k. brown	3·75	4·00
1269	-	10k. blue	6·75	6·50

DESIGNS—VERT: 3k. Running; 6k. Pole vaulting; 10k. Throwing the discus.

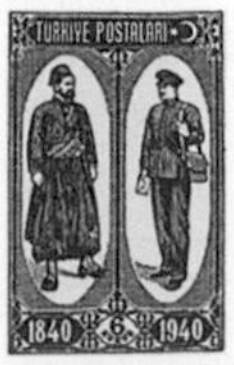

141 Postmen of 1840 and 1940

1940. Centenary of First Adhesive Postage Stamps.

1270	-	3k. green	45	25
1271	141	6k. red	60	35
1272	-	10k. blue	2·00	1·50

1273	-	12k. brown	1·50	1·20

DESIGNS—HORIZ: 3k. Mail carriers on horseback. VERT: 10k. Early paddle-steamer and modern mail launch; 12k. G.P.O., Istanbul.

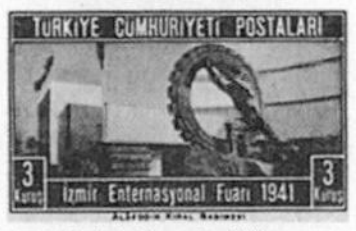
142 Exhibition Building

1941. Izmir International Fair.

1274	-	30pa. green	15	10
1275	142	3k. grey	15	10
1276	-	6k. red	45	25
1277	-	10k. blue	25	25
1278	-	12k. purple	45	15
1279	-	17½k. brown	85	60

DESIGNS—HORIZ: 30pa. Freighter "Etrusk" in Izmir harbour; 6, 17½k. Exhibition pavilions; 12k. Girl in field. VERT: 10k. Equestrian statue.

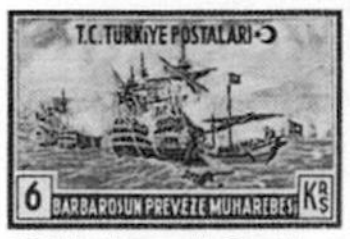
143 Barbarossa's Corsair Fleet

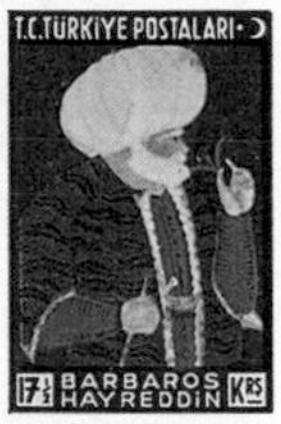
144 Barbarossa

1941. 400th Death Anniv of Barbarossa (Khair-ed-Din).

1280	-	20pa. violet	15	15
1281	143	3k. blue	40	15
1282	143	6k. red	90	40
1283	143	10k. blue	1·10	65
1284	143	12k. brown	1·30	65
1285	144	17½k. multicoloured	3·75	2·10

DESIGN—24×37 mm: 20pa. Barbarossa's tomb.

1941. Air. Surch with airplane and new value.

1286	107	4½k. on 25k. brown	1·90	1·60
1287	109	9k. on 200k. black & grn	9·00	9·00
1288	109	35k. on 500k. blk & brn	5·75	5·75

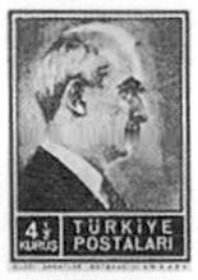
146 Pres. Inonu

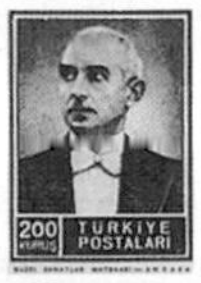
147

1942

1289	146	0.25k. bistre	10	10
1290	146	0.50k. green	10	10
1291	146	1k. grey	10	10
1292	146	1½k. mauve	10	10
1293	146	2k. green	10	10
1294	146	4k. brown	10	10
1295	146	4½k. black	15	10
1296	146	5k. blue	40	15
1297	146	6k. red	10	10
1298	146	6¾k. blue	1·10	10
1299	146	9k. violet	25	10
1300	146	10k. blue	25	10
1301	146	13½k. purple	15	10
1302	146	16k. green	25	10
1303	146	17½k. red	30	10
1304	146	20k. purple	85	25
1305	146	27½k. orange	60	15
1306	146	37k. brown	75	25
1307	146	50k. violet	2·75	35
1308	146	100k. brown	6·00	2·20
1309	147	200k. brown	13·50	1·60

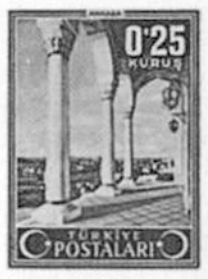
148 Ankara

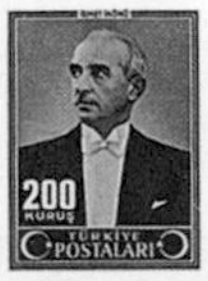
150 Pres. Inonu

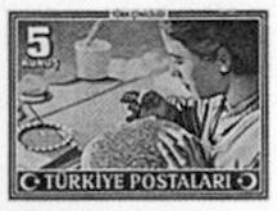
149 Tile-decorating

1943. Inscr "TURKIYE POSTALARI" between two crescents and stars.

1310	148	0.25k. yellow	10	10
1311	-	0.50k. green	40	10
1312	-	1k. olive	10	10
1313	-	1½k. violet	10	10
1314	-	2k. green	45	10
1315	-	4k. red	1·00	10
1316	-	4½k. black	90	10
1317	149	5k. blue	55	10
1318	-	6k. red	25	10
1319	-	6¾k. blue	25	10
1320	-	10k. blue	40	10
1321	-	13½k. mauve	40	10
1322	-	16k. green	2·30	10
1323	-	17½k. brown	90	10
1324	-	20k. brown	1·40	10
1325	-	27½k. orange	1·80	40
1326	-	37k. brown	1·10	10
1327	-	50k. purple	4·50	10
1328	-	100k. olive	12·00	1·20
1329	150	200k. brown	17·00	2·10
MS1329a 90×120 mm. **150** 200k. sepia			60·00	49·00

DESIGNS—VERT: 0.50k. Mohair goats; 2k. Oranges; 4k. Merino sheep; 4½k. Steam train entering tunnel; 6k. Statue of Kemal Ataturk, Ankara, 6¾, 10k. Full face portrait of Pres. Inonu; 17½k. Republic Monument, Istanbul; 20k. National Defence Monument, Ankara; 27½k. P.O., Istanbul; 37k. Monument at Afyon; 100k. Ataturk and Inonu. HORIZ: 1k. Antioch; 1½k. Ankara Reservoir; 13½k. National Assembly building; 16k. View of Arnavutkoy; 50k. People's House, Ankara.

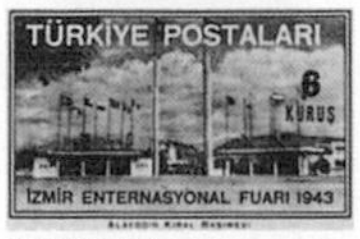
152 Fair Entrance

1943. Izmir International Fair.

1330	-	4½k. grey	45	40
1331	152	6k. red	40	25
1332	-	6¾k. blue	40	25
1333	152	10k. blue	40	25
1334	-	13½k. brown	1·30	80
1335	-	27½k. grey	90	1·00

DESIGNS—VERT: 4½, 13½k. Girl eating grapes. HORIZ: 6¾, 27½k. Fair Pavilion.

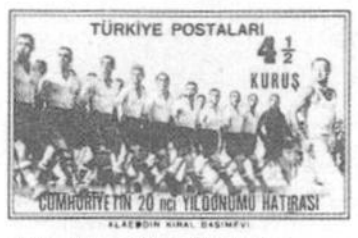
153 Marching Athletes

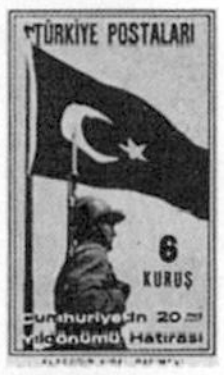
154 Soldier guarding Flag

1943. 20th Anniv of Republic.

1336	153	4½k. olive	1·40	1·40
1337	154	6k. red	70	25
1338	-	6¾k. blue	25	25
1339	-	10k. blue	75	15
1340	-	13½k. olive	45	25
1341	-	27½k. brown	90	1·00

DESIGNS—HORIZ: 6¾k. Railway bridge over River Firat; 10k. Hospital; 13½k. Ankara. VERT: 27½k. President Inonu.

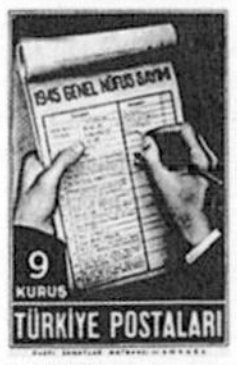
155 Filling Census Form

1945. National Census.

1342	155	4½k. olive	75	65
1343	155	9k. violet	75	65
1344	155	10k. blue	75	65
1345	155	18k. red	1·30	1·20
MS1345a 90×120 mm. **155** 1l. purple. Imperf			70·00	60·00

1945. Surch **4½ KURUS.**

1346		4½k. on 6¾k. blue (No. 1319)	40	15

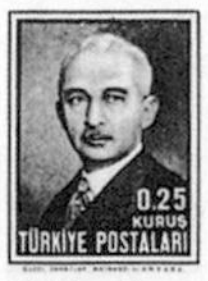
157 Pres. Inonu

1946

1347	157	0.25k. red	15	10
1348	157	1k. green	25	10
1349	157	1½k. purple	25	10
1350	157	9k. violet	55	10
1351	157	10k. blue	1·50	10
1352	157	50k. brown	5·00	40

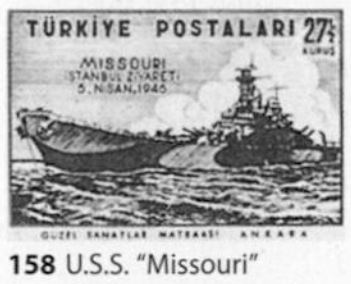
158 U.S.S. "Missouri"

1946. Visit of U.S. Battleship "Missouri" to Istanbul.

1353	158	9k. violet	25	10
1354	158	10k. blue	40	15
1355	158	27½k. grey	1·10	75

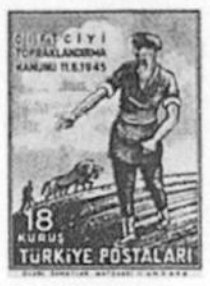
159 Sower

1946. Agrarian Reform.

1356	159	9k. violet	25	15
1357	159	10k. blue	25	15
1358	159	18k. olive	30	15
1359	159	27½k. orange	30	40

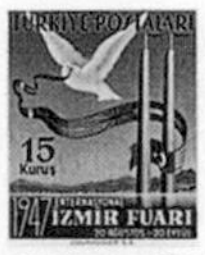
160 Dove of Peace

1947. Izmir International Fair.

1360	160	15k. purple and violet	15	15
1361	160	20k. blue and deep blue	15	15
1362	160	30k. brown and black	25	15
1363	160	1l. olive and green	1·40	1·20

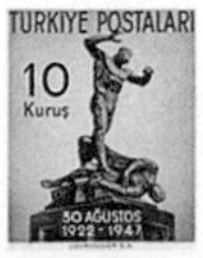
161 Monument at Afyon

1947. 25th Anniv of Battle of Dumlupinar.

1364	161	10k. brown & lt brown	25	15
1365	-	15k. violet and grey	25	15
1366	-	20k. blue and grey	30	15
1367	161	30k. green and grey	30	15
1368	-	60k. green and bistre	85	35
1369	-	1l. green and grey	1·50	1·20

DESIGN: 15, 60k. Ismet Inonu; 20k., 1l. Kemal Ataturk.

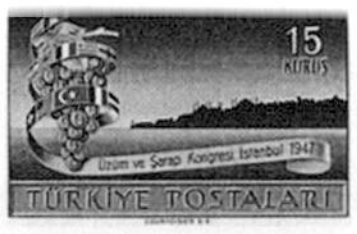
163 Istanbul, Grapes and Ribbon

1947. International Vintners' Congress.

1370	163	15k. purple	15	15
1371	163	20k. blue	25	25
1372	163	60k. brown	1·10	60

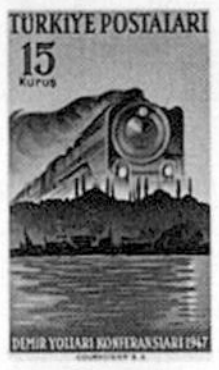
164 Steam Express Train

1947. International Railway Congress, Istanbul.

1373	164	15k. purple	55	25
1374	164	20k. blue	75	40
1375	164	60k. olive	2·30	1·80

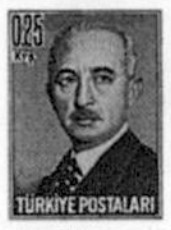
165 Pres. Inonu

1948

1376	165	0.25k. red	10	10
1377	165	1k. black	10	10
1378	165	2k. purple	10	10
1379	165	3k. orange	10	10
1380	165	4k. green	10	10
1381	165	5k. blue	10	10
1382	165	10k. brown	15	10
1383	165	12k. red	25	10
1384	165	15k. violet	15	10
1385	165	20k. blue	40	10
1386	165	30k. brown	90	15
1387	165	60k. black	1·40	25
1388	165	1l. olive	3·25	40
1389	165	2l. brown	27·00	4·50
1390	165	5l. purple	23·00	23·00

The lira values are larger.

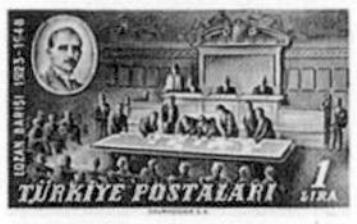
167 Signing the Treaty

1948. 25th Anniv of Treaty of Lausanne.

1391	167	15k. purple	25	15
1392	-	20k. blue	25	15
1393	-	40k. green	40	50
1394	167	1l. brown	1·40	1·00

DESIGN: 20, 40k. Lausanne Palace.

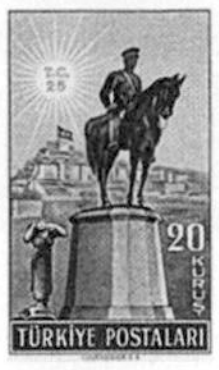
168 Statue of Kemal Ataturk

1948. 25th Anniv of Proclamation of Republic.

1395	168	15k. violet	25	15
1396	168	20k. blue	25	15
1397	168	40k. green	40	40
1398	168	1l. brown	1·80	1·80

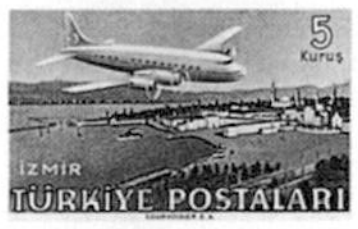
170 Douglas DC-6 over Izmir

1949. Air.

1399	170	5k. violet and lilac	25	10
1400	-	20k. brown and lilac	30	10
1401	-	30k. green and grey	55	10
1402	170	40k. blue and light blue	1·00	25
1403	-	50k. brown and mauve	1·00	25
1404	-	1l. green and blue	3·00	1·10

AIRCRAFT: 20, 50k. Vickers Viking 1B; 30k., 1l. Light monoplane.

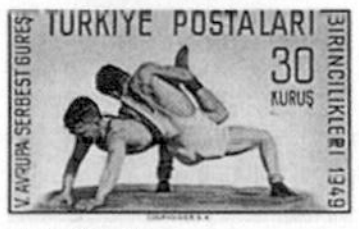
172 Wrestlers

1949. Fifth European Wrestling Championships. Designs depicting wrestling holds and inscr as in T **172**.

1405	-	15k. mauve (vert)	1·40	1·20
1406	-	20k. blue (vert)	2·75	1·80
1407	172	30k. brown	2·75	1·80
1408	-	60k. green (horiz)	4·50	4·50

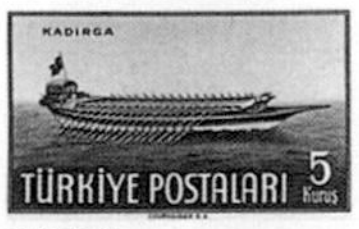
173 Galley

1949. Navy Day.

1409	173	5k. violet	25	10
1410	-	10k. brown	30	10
1411	-	15k. red	40	15
1412	-	20k. blue	45	35
1413	-	30k. slate	1·00	75
1414	-	40k. olive	1·30	1·20

DESIGNS—HORIZ: 15k. Cruiser "Hamidiye"; 20k. Submarine "Sakarya"; 30k. Battlecruiser "Yavuz". VERT: 10k. Ship of the line "Mahmudiye"; 40k. Statue of Barbarossa.

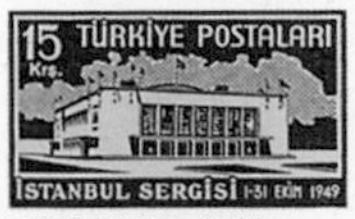
175 Exhibition Building

1949. Istanbul Fair.

1415	175	15k. brown	25	15
1416	175	20k. blue	30	35
1417	175	30k. olive	85	50

176 U.P.U. Monument,
Berne

1949. 75th Anniv of U.P.U.
1418	-	15k. violet	30	15
1419	-	20k. blue	40	35
1420	176	30k. red	60	40
1421	176	40k. green	1·40	90

DESIGN: 15, 20k. as Type **176** but vert.

177 Sud Est Languedoc
over Bogazia

1950. Air.
| 1422 | 177 | 2l.50 green and blue | 22·00 | 21·00 |

178 Youth,
Istanbul and
Ankara

1950. Second World Youth Union Meeting.
| 1423 | 178 | 15k. violet | 25 | 15 |
| 1424 | 178 | 20k. blue | 55 | 40 |

180 Voting

1950. General Election.
1425	180	15k. brown	25	25
1426	180	20k. blue	30	25
1427	-	30k. blue and green	45	50

DESIGNS—HORIZ: 30k. Kemal Ataturk and map of Turkey.

181 Hazel Nut

1950. Izmir Fair.
1428	181	8k. green and yellow	45	35
1429	-	12k. mauve	70	40
1430	-	15k. brown	90	60
1431	-	20k. blue and light blue	1·50	80
1432	-	30k. brown	2·10	1·60

DESIGN: 12k. Acorns; 15k. Cotton; 20k. Fair symbol; 30k. Tobacco.

182 Map and
Statistics

1950. National Census.
| 1433 | 182 | 15k. brown | 40 | 15 |
| 1434 | 182 | 20k. blue | 40 | 25 |

183 Hezarfen
Celebi's "Bird
Flight" and
Tower

1950. Air. International Civil Aviation Congress, Istanbul.
1435	183	20k. blue and green	40	25
1436	-	40k. blue and brown	70	75
1437	-	60k. blue and violet	1·20	1·30

DESIGNS—VERT: 40k. Biplane over Taurus Mountains.
HORIZ: 60k. Douglas DC-3 airplane over Istanbul.

184 Farabi (philosopher)

1950. 1000th Death Anniv of Farabi.
1438	184	15k. multicoloured	45	35
1439	184	20k. multicoloured	90	50
1440	184	60k. multicoloured	3·25	2·50
1441	184	1l. multicoloured	5·25	3·75

185 Mithat Pasha and Deposit
Bank

1950. Third Co-operative Congress, Istanbul.
| 1442 | 185 | 15k. violet | 90 | 60 |
| 1443 | - | 20k. blue | 90 | 60 |

DESIGN: 20k. Agricultural Bank.

1951. Air. Industrial Congress, Ankara. Nos. 1399, 1401
and 1403 optd **SANAYI KONGRESI 9-NISAN-1951.**
1454	170	5k. violet and lilac	90	1·00
1455	-	30k. green and grey	2·40	1·50
1456	-	50k. brown and mauve	2·75	2·50

187 "Iskendrun" (liner)

1951. 25th Anniv of Coastal Trading Rights.
1457	-	15k. blue	55	25
1458	187	20k. blue	55	25
1459	-	30k. grey	90	75
1460	-	1l. green	2·75	2·50

DESIGNS—HORIZ: 15k. Tug "Hora" and liner "Providence"; 30k. Diver and launch. VERT: 1l. Lighthouse.

188 Mosque of Sultan   **189** Count
Ahmed   Carton de Wiart

1951. 40th Interparliamentary Conference, Istanbul.
1461	188	15k. green	45	15
1462	-	20k. blue	45	15
1463	189	30k. brown	85	80
1464	-	60k. purple	1·70	1·30

DESIGNS—As Type **188**: 20k. Dolmabahce Palace; 60k. Rumeli Tower.

190 F.A.O. Emblem and
Silo

1952. U.N. Economic Conf, Ankara. Inscr "Ankara 1951".
1465	190	15k. green	75	40
1466	-	20k. violet	90	50
1467	-	30k. blue	1·90	1·20
1468	-	60k. red	2·75	2·50

MS1468a 132×110 mm. Nos. 1465/8.
| | | Imperf | 75·00 | 80·00 |

DESIGNS: 20k. Int Bank emblem and hydro-electric station; 30k. U.N. emblem and New York headquarters; 60k. Ankara University.

191 A. H. Tarhan

1952. Birth Centenary of Tarhan (writer).
1469	191	15k. purple	15	15
1470	191	20k. blue	15	15
1471	191	30k. brown	75	50
1472	191	60k. green	1·70	1·60

192 Bergama   **193** Kemal
Ataturk

1952. Views. Imperf or perf.
1473	192	1k. orange	10	10
1474	-	2k. green	10	10
1475	-	3k. brown	10	10
1476	-	4k. green	10	10
1477	-	5k. brown	10	10
1478	193	10k. brown	15	10
1479	193	12k. red	30	10
1480	193	15k. violet (medallion)	25	10
1481	193	20k. blue (medallion)	85	10
1482	-	30k. green	40	10
1483	-	40k. blue	75	10
1484	-	50k. green	75	10
1485	-	75k. black	1·10	40
1486	-	1l. violet	90	25
1487	-	2l. blue	1·80	40
1488	-	5l. brown	38·00	8·25

DESIGNS—VERT: 2k. Ruins at Milas; 3k. Karatay Gate, Konya; 4k. Trees on Kozak Plateau; 5k. Urgup; 30k. Emirsultan Mosque, Bursa; 40k. Yenicami (New Mosque), Istanbul. HORIZ: 50k. Waterfall, Tarsus; 75k. Rocks at Urgup; 1l. Dolmabahce Palace, Istanbul; 2l. Pavilion, Istanbul; 5l. Interior of Istanbul Museum.

1952. Surch **0.50 Kurus.**
| 1489 | 192 | 0.50k. on 1k. orange | 25 | 15 |

196 Congress Building

1952. Eighth Int Mechanics Congress, Istanbul.
1490	196	15k. violet	45	15
1491	196	20k. blue	60	35
1492	196	60k. brown	1·70	1·80

197 Turkish
Sentry

1952. Turkish Participation in Korean War.
1493	197	15k. slate	30	15
1494	-	20k. blue	40	15
1495	-	30k. brown	85	50
1496	-	60k. red and green	1·70	1·20

DESIGNS: 20k. Turkish soldier and flag; 30k. Soldier and Korean child reading comic paper; 60k. Soldiers planting Turkish flag.

198 Doves,
Hand and Red
Crescent

1952. 75th Anniv of Red Crescent Society.
| 1497 | 198 | 15k. red and green | 85 | 60 |
| 1498 | - | 20k. red and blue | 1·80 | 1·10 |

DESIGN: 20k. Red Crescent flag.

199 Bas-relief on
Monument

1952. 75th Anniv of Battle of Erzurum.
1499	199	15k. violet	30	15
1500	-	20k. blue	45	35
1501	-	40k. grey	1·10	1·20

DESIGNS—HORIZ: 20k. Azizye Monument, Erzurum; 40k. View of Erzurum.

200 Pigeon
carrying
Newspaper

1952
1502	200	0.50k. green	15	10
1503	200	0.50k. violet	15	10
1503a	200	0.50k. orange	15	10
1503b	200	0.50k. brown	15	10

201 Rumeli Fort   **202** Sultan
Mohammed II
(after Gentile
Bellini)

1953. 500th Anniv of Fall of Constantinople.
1504	201	5k. blue and ultramarine	55	15
1505	-	8k. grey	55	15
1506	-	10k. blue	75	15
1507	-	12k. purple	75	15
1508	-	15k. brown	75	15
1509	-	20k. red	1·20	15
1510	-	30k. green	2·30	15
1511	-	40k. violet	2·30	40
1512	-	60k. brown	2·30	60
1513	-	1l. green	3·75	1·60
1514	-	2l. multicoloured	9·00	5·25
1515	202	2½l. lt brn, yell & brn	13·50	7·50

MS1515a 100×125 mm. No. 1515.
| | | Imperf | 38·00 | 16·00 |

DESIGNS—As Type **201**: HORIZ: 8k. Turkish army at Edirne; 10k. Horsemen and fleet; 12k. Landing of Turkish Army; 15k. Topkapi ramparts; 40k. Sultan Mohammed II and Patriarch Yenadios; 60k.15th-century map of Constantinople; 1l. Mausoleum of Mohammed II. VERT: 20k. Turkish army entering Constantinople; 30k. Sultan Mohammed II Mosque. As Type **202**: 2l. Sultan Mohammed II (after miniature by Sinan).

203 Odeon Theatre,
Ephesus

1953. Views of Ephesus. Inscr "EFES". Multicoloured centres.
1516	203	12k. green	30	15
1517	-	15k. violet	30	15
1518	-	20k. slate	30	15
1519	-	40k. turquoise	45	25
1520	-	60k. blue	55	60
1521	-	1l. red	2·75	3·00

DESIGNS: 15k. St. John's Church and Acropolis; 20k. Statue of Blessed Virgin, Panaya Kapulu; 40k. Council Church ruins; 60k. Grotto of the Seven Sleepers; 1l. House of the Blessed Virgin, Panaya Kapulu.

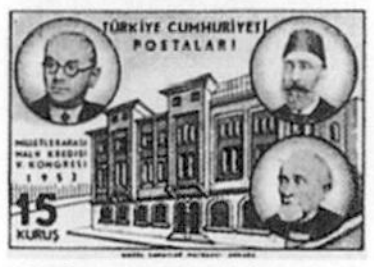

204 Pres. Bayar, Mithat Pasha, Dr. Delitsch and Ankara Bank

1953. Fifth International Public Credit Congress.

1522	**204**	15k. brown	40	25
1523	-	20k. turquoise	60	50

DESIGN: 20k. Pres. Bayar, Mithat Pasha and Ankara University.

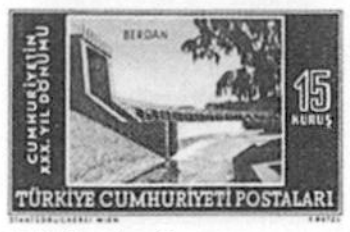

205 Berdan Barrage

1953. 30th Anniv of Republic.

1524	-	10k. bistre	25	15
1525	**205**	15k. slate	25	15
1526	-	20k. red	30	15
1527	-	30k. olive	1·20	1·00
1528	-	35k. blue	40	40
1529	-	55k. lilac	1·30	1·80

DESIGNS—HORIZ: 10k. Combine-harvester; 20k. Soldiers on parade; 30k. Diesel train; 35k. Yesilkoy airport. VERT: 55k. Kemal Ataturk.

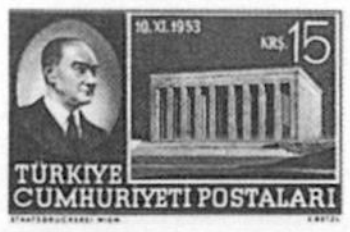

206 Kemal Ataturk and Mausoleum

1953. Transfer of Ashes of Kemal Ataturk to Mausoleum

1530	**206**	15k. black	45	40
[illegible]	[illegible]	[illegible]	[illegible]	[illegible]

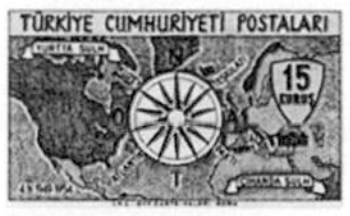

207 Map of World and Compass

1954. Fifth Anniv of N.A.T.O.

1532	**207**	15k. brown	2·00	2·10
1533	-	20k. blue	2·00	2·10
1534	-	40k. green	15·00	16·00

DESIGNS: 20k. Globe and stars; 40k. Allegory of growth of N.A.T.O.

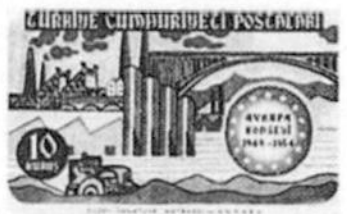

208 "Industry, Agriculture and Construction"

1954. Fifth Anniv of Council of Europe.

1535	**208**	10k. brown	3·75	4·00
1536	-	15k. green	2·30	2·50
1537	-	20k. blue	2·30	2·50
1538	**208**	30k. violet	15·00	16·00

DESIGN: 15, 20k. Flag and figure of "Peace and Justice".

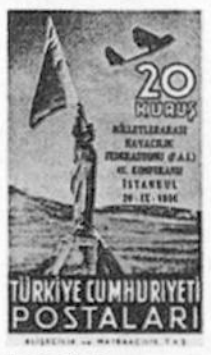

209 Flying Exercise

1954. 47th Conference of International Aeronautical Federation. Inscr "20.IX.1954".

1539	**209**	20k. black	25	15
1540	-	35k. lilac	45	35
1541	-	45k. blue	1·10	50

DESIGNS: 35k. Baron Delagrange and glider; 45k. Ataturk and formation of De Havilland Tiger Moth biplanes.

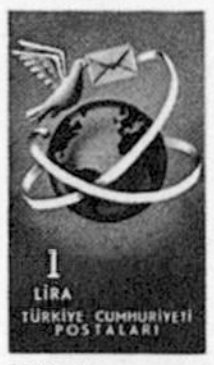

(209a)

1954. First Anniv of Reorganisation of Turkish Posts. Sheet 122×132 mm. T **209a** and similar vert designs.

MS1541a 20k. turquoise (telephone receivers); 30k. ultramarine (telegraph pole); 1l. purple (T **209a**)	15·00	16·00

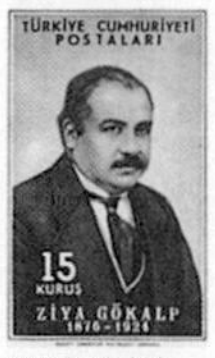

210 Z. Gokalp

1954. 30th Death Anniv of Gokalp (sociologist).

1542	**210**	15k. violet	15	15
1543	**210**	20k. green	30	25
1544	**210**	30k. red	70	40

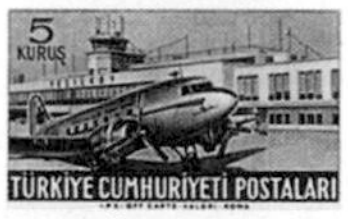

211 Yesilkoy Airport

1954. Air.

1545	**211**	5k. blue and brown	15	15
1546	-	20k. blue and brown	25	15
1547	-	35k. blue and green	45	15
1548	**211**	40k. blue and red	70	15
1549	-	45k. blue and violet	1·10	25
1550	-	55k. blue and black	1·90	50

DESIGNS: 20, 45k. Frontal view of Yesilkoy Airport; 35, 55k. Ankara Airport.

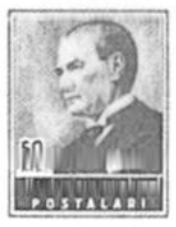

212 Kemal Ataturk

1955

1551	**212**	15k. red	15	10
1552	**212**	20k. blue	15	10
1553	**212**	40k. slate	40	10
1554	**212**	50k. green	40	10
1555	**212**	75k. brown	85	25

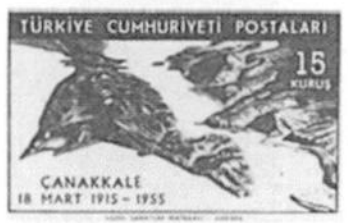

213 Relief Map of the Dardanelles

1955. 40th Anniv of Battle of Canakkale (Dardanelles).

1556	**213**	15k. green	15	10
1557	-	20k. brown	15	15
1558	-	30k. blue	45	35
1559	-	60k. drab	75	80

DESIGNS—VERT: 20k. Gunner Seyid loading gun; 60k. Ataturk in uniform. HORIZ: 30k. Minelayer "Nusret".

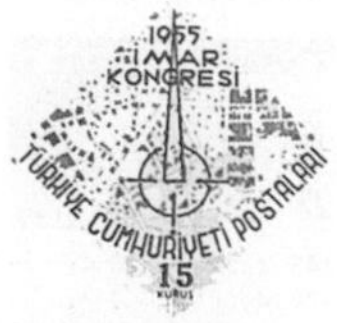

214 "Reconstruction"

1955. Town Planning Congress.

1560	**214**	15k. grey	15	15
1561	**214**	20k. blue	25	15
1562	**214**	50k. brown	45	35
1563	**214**	1l. violet	1·10	75

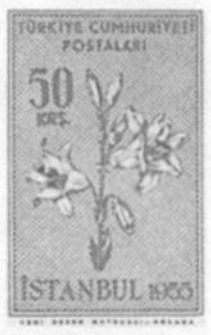

215 Lilies

1955. Spring Flower Festival. Inscr "ISTANBUL 1955".

1564	-	10k. red and green	55	15
1565	-	15k. yellow and green	40	15
1566	-	20k. red and green	40	15
1567	**215**	50k. green and yellow	2·75	35

FLOWERS: 10k. Carnations; 15k. Tulips; 20k. Roses.

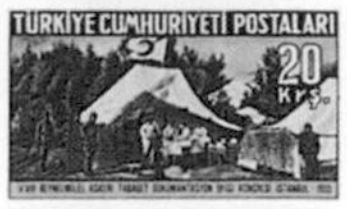

216 First-aid Centre

1955. 18th Congress of International Documentation Office of Military Medicine.

1568	**216**	20k. red and grey	40	25
1569	-	30k. green and light green	75	75

DESIGN: 30k. Gulhane Military Hospital, Ankara.

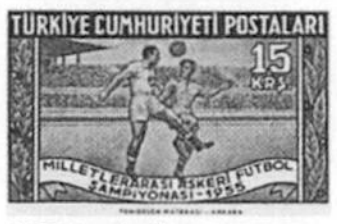

217 Footballers

1955. Int Military Football Championships.

1570	**217**	15k. blue	75	25
1571	-	20k. red	40	25
1572	-	1l. green	1·90	1·60

DESIGNS—VERT: 20k. Footballers' badge. HORIZ: 1l. Championship plaque.

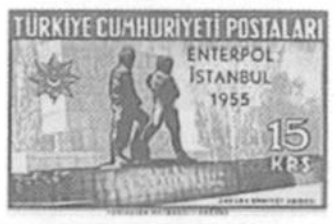

218 Police Monument, Ankara

1955. International Police Commission Meeting, Istanbul.

1573	**218**	15k. green and turquoise	15	10
1574	-	20k. violet and lilac	25	10
1575	-	30k. black and grey	55	15
1576	-	45k. brown & light brown	1·40	1·00

DESIGNS: 20k. Dolmabahce Palace, Istanbul; 30k. Police College, Ankara; 45k. Police Martyrs' Monument, Istanbul.

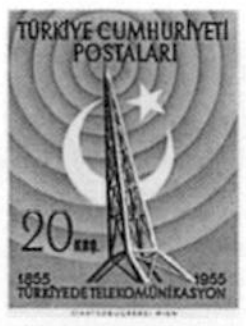

219 Radio Mast

1955. Cent of Telecommunications in Turkey.

1577	-	15k. olive	15	15
1578	**219**	20k. red	15	15
1579	-	45k. brown	55	35
1580	**219**	60k. blue	55	40

DESIGNS—HORIZ: 15, 45k. Telegraph table and pole.

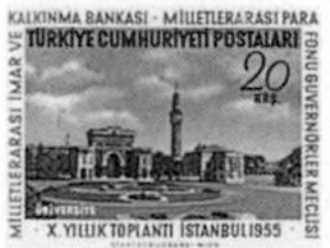

220 Istanbul University

1955. Tenth Meeting of Governors of Int Reconstruction and Development Bank and Int Monetary Fund.

1581	-	15k. orange	15	10
1582	**220**	20k. red	25	15
1583	-	60k. purple	45	50
1584	-	1l. blue	75	90

DESIGNS: 15k. Faculty of Letters, Istanbul; 60k. Hilton Hotel; 1l. Kiz Kulesi.

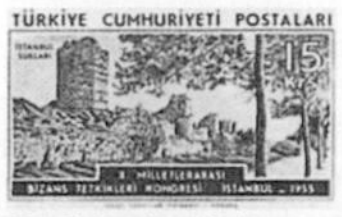

221 Ruins, Istanbul

1955. Tenth International Congress of Byzantine Research.

1585	**221**	15k. green and blue	25	15
1586	-	20k. red and orange	25	15
1587	-	30k. brown and pink	30	25
1588	-	75k. blue and lilac	90	80

DESIGNS—VERT: 20k. Obelisk and Sultan Ahmed Mosque; 75k. Map of Istanbul in 1422. HORIZ: 30k. Church of St. Sophia.

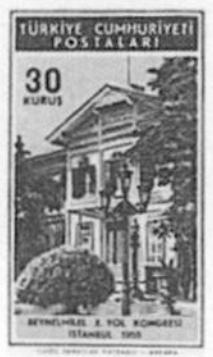

222

1955. Tenth International Road Planning Congress.

1589	-	20k. mauve	25	15
1590	**222**	30k. green	30	25
1591	-	55k. blue	1·00	1·00

DESIGNS: 20k. Congress emblem; 55k. Bridges.

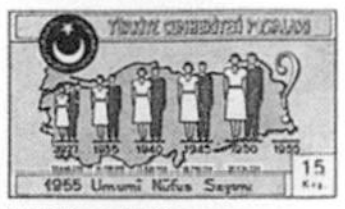

223 Population Pictograph

1955. National Census.

1592	**223**	15k. grey and red	30	15
1593	**223**	20k. lilac and red	25	15
1594	**223**	30k. blue and red	30	15
1595	**223**	60k. green and red	75	50

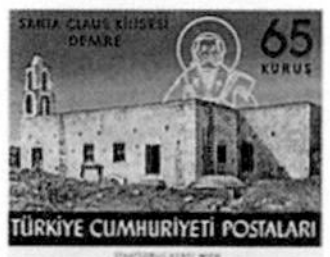

224 Santa Claus Church, Demre

1955. Tourism.

1596	-	18k. green and blue	25	15
1597	-	20k. brown and blue	25	20
1598	-	30k. brown and green	25	15
1599	-	45k. green and brown	1·70	1·00
1600	-	50k. brown and green	30	25
1601	**224**	65k. black and red	45	40

DESIGNS—VERT: 18k. Waterfall near Antalya; 45k. Theatre doorway ruins, Side; 50k. Countryside, Antalya. HORIZ: 20k. Alanya; 30k. Amphitheatre, Aspendos.

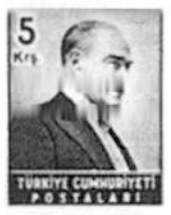

225 Kemal Ataturk

1955

1602	**225**	0.50k. pink	15	10
1603	**225**	1k. yellow	15	10
1604	**225**	2k. blue	15	10
1605	**225**	3k. red	15	10
1606	**225**	5k. brown	15	10
1606a	**225**	6k. green	15	10
1607	**225**	10k. green	15	10
1607a	**225**	18k. purple	15	10
1608	**225**	20k. blue	15	10
1609	**225**	25k. olive	25	10
1610	**225**	30k. violet	30	10
1611	**225**	40k. brown	40	10
1612	**225**	75k. slate	1·70	15

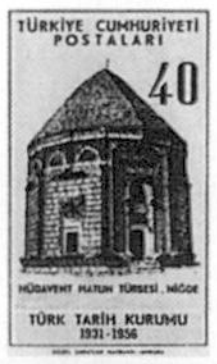

226 Mausoleum of Hudavent Hatum

1956. 25th Anniv of Turkish Historical Association.

1613	**226**	40k. deep blue and blue	25	15

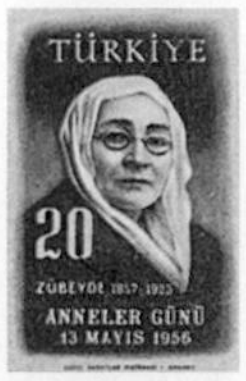

227 Zubeyde

1956. Mothers' Day.

1614	**227**	20k. brown & buff (perf)	25	15
1615	**227**	20k. olive and green (imperf)	90	65

228 Shah of Iran and Queen
Soraya

1956. Visit of Shah of Iran to Turkey.
| 1616 | **228** | 100k. green and light green (perf) | 1·25 | 15 |
| 1617 | **228** | 100k. red and green (imperf) | 12·50 | 8·25 |

229 Kemal
Ataturk

1956
1618	**229**	½k. green	15	10
1619	**229**	1k. orange	15	10
1620	**229**	3k. green	15	10
1621	**229**	5k. violet	15	10
1622	**229**	6k. mauve	15	10
1623	**229**	10k. purple	15	10
1624	**229**	12k. brown	15	10
1625	**229**	15k. blue	15	10
1626	**229**	18k. pink	15	10
1627	**229**	20k. brown	15	10
1628	**229**	25k. green	15	10
1629	**229**	30k. slate	15	10
1630	**229**	40k. olive	15	10
1631	**229**	50k. orange	40	10
1632	**229**	60k. blue	40	10
1633	**229**	70k. turquoise	1·00	
1634	**229**	75k. brown	50	10

See also Nos. 1659/78.

230 Erenkoy Sanatorium

1956. Turkish Post Office Health Service.
| 1635 | **230** | 50k. turquoise and pink | 80 | 30 |

231

1956. 25th Izmir International Fair.
| 1636 | **231** | 45k. green (postage) | 25 | 15 |
| 1637 | **231** | 25k. brown (air) | 15 | 15 |

Sheet 103×52 mm.
MS1637a 50k. red (cement works);
50k. ultramarine (harbour project)
(horiz). Imperf   4·00   3·75

232 Serpent
in Bottle

1956. International Anti-Alcoholism Congress.
| 1638 | **232** | 25k. multicoloured | 35 | 15 |

233 Medical
Clinic, Kayseri

1956. 750th Anniv of Medical Clinic, Kayseri.
| 1639 | **233** | 60k. violet and yellow | 35 | 15 |

234 Sariyar
Barrage

1956. Inauguration of Sariyar Dam.
| 1640 | **234** | 20k. red | 35 | 25 |
| 1641 | **234** | 20k. blue | 35 | 25 |

235 Wrestling

1956. Olympic Games. Inscr as in T **235**.
| 1642 | **235** | 40k. sepia on green | 50 | 40 |
| 1643 | - | 65k. red on grey | 75 | 40 |

DESIGN: 65k. Another wrestling match.

236 Mehmet
Akif Ersoy

1956. 20th Death Anniv of Ersoy (poet).
1644	**236**	20k. brown and green	15	10
1645	**236**	20k. red and grey	15	10
1646	**236**	20k. violet and pink	15	10

Each stamp is inscribed with a different line of verse
from the Turkish National Anthem composed by Ersoy.

237 Vase of Troy

1956. Troy Commemoration. Inscr "TRUVA (TROIA)".
1647	-	15k. green	1·20	1·10
1648	**237**	20k. purple	1·00	90
1649	-	30k. brown	2·00	1·80

DESIGNS—HORIZ: 15k. Troy Amphitheatre; 30k. Trojan
Horse.

238 Mobile X-ray Unit

1957. T.B. Relief Campaign.
| 1650 | **238** | 25k. red and drab | 25 | 15 |

239 Pres. Heuss

1957. Visit of President of West Germany.
| 1651 | **239** | 40k. brown and yellow (postage) | 25 | 10 |
| 1652 | **239** | 40k. purple and pink (air) | 25 | 10 |

240 View of Bergama

1957. Bergama Fair.
| 1653 | **240** | 20k. brown | 15 | 10 |
| 1654 | - | 40k. green | 25 | 10 |

DESIGN: 40k. Folk-dancing.

241

1957. Turkish-American Friendship.
| 1655 | **241** | 25k. violet | 40 | 10 |
| 1656 | **241** | 40k. blue | 40 | 10 |

242 Osman Hamdi Bey
(founder)

1957. 75th Anniv of Fine Arts Academy, Istanbul.
| 1657 | **242** | 20k. drab, buff and black | 25 | 15 |
| 1658 | - | 30k. grey, green & lt grn | 25 | 15 |

DESIGN—HORIZ: 30k. Hittite relic of Alacahoyuk; Inscr
"GUZEL SANATLAR AKADEMISI 75. YIL".

243 Kemal
Ataturk

1957
1659	**243**	½k. brown	10	10
1660	**243**	1k. blue	10	10
1661	**243**	2k. violet	10	10
1662	**243**	3k. orange	10	10
1663	**243**	5k. green	10	10
1664	**243**	6k. green	10	10
1665	**243**	10k. violet	10	10
1666	**243**	12k. green	10	10
1667	**243**	15k. green	10	10
1668	**243**	18k. mauve	10	10
1669	**243**	20k. sepia	10	10
1670	**243**	25k. brown	10	10
1671	**243**	30k. blue	10	10
1672	**243**	40k. slate	10	10
1673	**243**	50k. yellow	15	10
1674	**243**	60k. black	15	10
1675	**243**	70k. purple	25	15
1676	**243**	75k. olive	35	25
1677	-	100k. red	80	15
1678	-	250k. olive	2·10	55

Nos. 1677/8 are larger, 21×29 mm.

244
Mohammed
Zahir Shah

1957. Visit of Mohammed Zahir Shah of Afghanistan.
| 1679 | **244** | 45k. red and orange (postage) | 25 | 10 |
| 1680 | **244** | 25k. deep green and green (air) | 25 | 10 |

245 Amasya Medical
Centre

1957. 11th Congress of World Medical Association.
| 1681 | **245** | 25k. red and yellow | 10 | 10 |
| 1682 | - | 65k. blue and yellow | 50 | 10 |

DESIGN—HORIZ: 65k. Sultan Mohammed School, 1557.

246 Sultan Mohammed II
Mosque

1957. 400th Anniv of the Suleiman Mosque, Istanbul.
| 1683 | **246** | 20k. green | 15 | 10 |
| 1684 | - | 1l. brown | 65 | 25 |

DESIGN—VERT: 1l. Mimar Koca Sinan (architect).

| 1685 | | 50k. on 2l. blue (No. 1487) | 35 | 25 |

248 Forestry Map of
Turkey

1957. Centenary of Forestry Teaching.
| 1686 | **248** | 20k. green and brown | 10 | 10 |
| 1687 | | 25k. green and blue | 10 | 10 |

DESIGN—VERT: 25k. Planting fir-tree.

249 Fuzuli (poet)

1957. Fuzuli Year.
| 1688 | **249** | 50k. multicoloured | 60 | 25 |

250 Franklin

1957. 250th Birth Anniv of Benjamin Franklin.
| 1689 | **250** | 65k. purple | 35 | 15 |
| 1690 | **250** | 65k. blue | 35 | 15 |

251 Mevlana's   **251a**
Tomb, Konya

1957. 750th Birth Anniv of Mevlana (poet).
| 1691 | **251** | 50k. violet, blue and green | 25 | 15 |
| 1692 | - | 100k. deep blue and blue | 75 | 15 |

MS1692a 54×102 mm. **251a** 100k.
multicoloured. Imperf   1·80   1·70

DESIGN—HORIZ: 100k. Konya Museum.

252 Adana

1958. Turkish Towns. As T **252**. (a) 26×21 mm.
1693		5k. brown (Adana)	15	10
1694		5k. mauve (Adapazari)	15	10
1695		5k. red (Adiyaman)	15	10
1696		5k. brown (Afyon)	15	10
1697		5k. green (Amasya)	15	10
1698		5k. blue (Ankara)	15	10
1699		5k. green (Antakya)	15	10
1700		5k. green (Antalya)	15	10
1701		5k. lilac (Artvin)	15	10
1702		5k. orange (Aydin)	15	10
1703		5k. violet (Balikesir)	15	10
1704		5k. green (Bilecik)	15	10
1705		5k. purple (Bingol)	15	10
1706		5k. blue (Bitlis)	15	10
1707		5k. purple (Bolu)	15	10
1708		5k. brown (Burdur)	15	10
1709		5k. green (Bursa)	15	10
1710		5k. blue (Canakkale)	15	10
1711		5k. violet (Cankiri)	15	10
1712		5k. blue (Corum)	15	10
1713		5k. blue (Denizli)	15	10
1714		5k. orange (Diyrbakir)	15	10
1715		5k. violet (Edirne)	15	10
1716		5k. green (Elazig)	15	10
1717		5k. blue (Erzincan)	15	10
1718		5k. orange (Erzurum)	15	10
1719		5k. green (Eskisehur)	15	10
1720		5k. green (Gaziantep)	15	10
1721		5k. blue (Giresun)	15	10
1722		5k. blue (Gumusane)	15	10

1723	5k. purple (Hakkari)	15	10
1724	5k. mauve (Isparta)	15	10
1725	5k. blue (Istanbul)	15	10
1726	5k. blue (Izmir)	15	10
1727	5k. blue (Izmit)	15	10
1728	5k. violet (Karakose)	15	10
1729	5k. green (Kars)	15	10
1730	5k. mauve (Kastamonu)	15	10
1731	5k. green (Kayseri)	15	10
1732	5k. brown (Kirklareli)	15	10
1733	5k. orange (Kirsehir)	15	10
1734	5k. blue (Konya)	15	10
1735	5k. violet (Kutahya)	15	10
1736	5k. brown (Malatya)	15	10
1737	5k. green (Manisa)	15	10
1738	5k. purple (Maras)	15	10
1739	5k. red (Mardin)	15	10
1740	5k. green (Mersin)	15	10
1741	5k. green (Mugla)	15	10
1742	5k. green (Mus)	15	10
1743	5k. green (Nevsehir)	15	10
1744	5k. red (Nigde)	15	10
1745	5k. blue (Ordu)	15	10
1746	5k. violet (Rize)	15	10
1747	5k. purple (Samsun)	15	10
1748	5k. brown (Siirt)	15	10
1749	5k. blue (Sinop)	15	10
1750	5k. green (Sivas)	15	10
1751	5k. blue (Tekirdag)	15	10
1752	5k. red (Tokat)	15	10
1753	5k. blue (Trabzon)	15	10
1754	5k. orange (Tunceli)	15	10
1755	5k. brown (Urfa)	15	10
1756	5k. green (Usak)	15	10
1757	5k. red (Van)	15	10
1758	5k. mauve (Yozgat)	15	10
1759	5k. blue (Zonguldak)	15	10

(b) 32½×22 mm.

1760	20k. brown (Adana)	15	10
1761	20k. mauve (Adapazari)	15	10
1762	20k. red (Adiyaman)	15	10
1763	20k. brown (Afyon)	15	10
1764	20k. green (Amasya)	15	10
1765	20k. blue (Ankara)	15	10
1766	20k. blue (Antakya)	15	10
1767	20k. green (Antalya)	15	10
1768	20k. blue (Artvin)	15	10
1769	20k. orange (Aydin)	15	10
1770	20k. purple (Balikesir)	15	10
1771	20k. green (Bilecik)	15	10
1772	20k. grey (Bingol)	15	10
1773	20k. violet (Bitlis)	15	10
1774	20k. purple (Bolu)	15	10
1775	20k. brown (Burdur)	15	10
1776	20k. green (Bursa)	15	10
1777	20k. blue (Canakkale)	15	10
1778	20k. purple (Cankiri)	15	10
1779	20k. grey (Corum)	15	10
1780	20k. blue (Denizli)	15	10
1781	20k. red (Diyrbakir)	15	10
1782	20k. grey (Edirne)	15	10
1783	20k. green (Elazig)	15	10
1784	20k. blue (Erzincan)	15	10
1785	20k. orange (Erzurum)	15	10
1786	20k. green (Eskisehur)	15	10
1787	20k. green (Gaziantep)	15	10
1788	20k. blue (Giresun)	15	10
1789	20k. blue (Gumusane)	15	10
1790	20k. purple (Hakkari)	15	10
1791	20k. mauve (Isparta)	15	10
1792	20k. blue (Istanbul)	15	10
1793	20k. blue (Izmir)	15	10
1794	20k. green (Izmit)	15	10
1795	20k. violet (Karakose)	15	10
1796	20k. green (Kars)	15	10
1797	20k. mauve (Kastamonu)	15	10
1798	20k. green (Kayseri)	15	10
1799	20k. brown (Kirklareli)	15	10
1800	20k. brown (Kirsehir)	15	10
1801	20k. blue (Konya)	15	10
1802	20k. violet (Kutahya)	15	10
1803	20k. brown (Malatya)	15	15
1804	20k. green (Manisa)	15	10
1805	20k. purple (Maras)	15	10
1806	20k. red (Mardin)	15	10
1807	20k. green (Mersin)	15	10
1808	20k. green (Mugla)	15	10
1809	20k. green (Mus)	15	10
1810	20k. green (Nevsehir)	15	15
1811	20k. red (Nigde)	15	15
1812	20k. blue (Ordu)	15	15
1813	20k. violet (Rize)	15	15
1814	20k. purple (Samsun)	15	10
1815	20k. brown (Siirt)	15	10
1816	20k. blue (Sinop)	15	10
1817	20k. green (Sivas)	15	10
1818	20k. blue (Tekirdag)	15	10
1819	20k. red (Tokat)	15	10
1820	20k. blue (Trabzon)	15	10
1821	20k. red (Tunceli)	15	15
1822	20k. brown (Urfa)	15	15
1823	20k. grey (Usak)	15	15
1824	20k. red (Van)	15	15
1825	20k. red (Yozgat)	15	15
1826	20k. blue (Zonguldak)	15	15

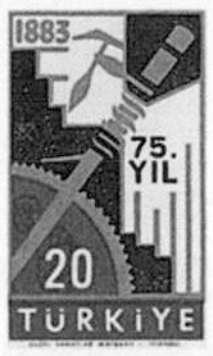

253

1958. 75th Anniv of the Institute of Economics and Commerce, Ankara.

1827	**253**	20k. orange, blue & bistre	15	10
1828	**253**	25k. blue, orange & bistre	15	10

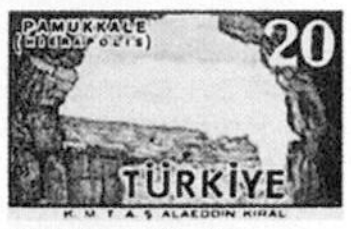

254 Hierapolis at Pamukkale

1958. Pamukkale Tourist Publicity. Inscr "PAMUKKALE".

1829	**254**	20k. brown	15	10
1830	-	25k. blue	25	10

DESIGN—HORIZ: 25k. Travertins (rocks) near Denizli.

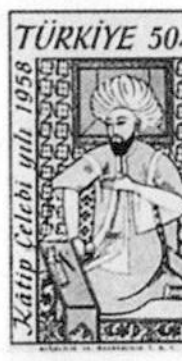

255 Katib Celebi

1958. 300th Death Anniv of Katib Celebi (author).

1831	**255**	50k.+10k. black	35	15

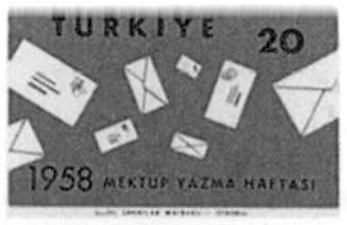

256 Letters

1958. International Correspondence Week.

1832	**256**	20k. orange and black	25	15

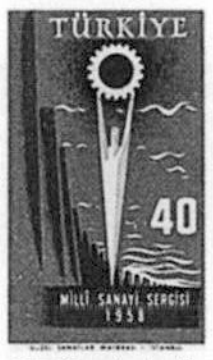

257 Symbol of Industry

1958. Industrial Fair, Istanbul.

1833	**257**	40k. black and blue	25	15

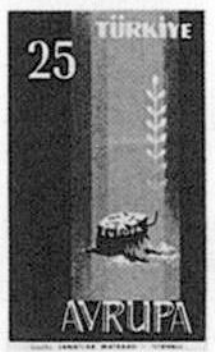

258 Symbol of "Europa"

1958. Europa.

1834	**258**	25k. lilac and violet	40	25
1835	**258**	40k. blue and ultramarine	80	55

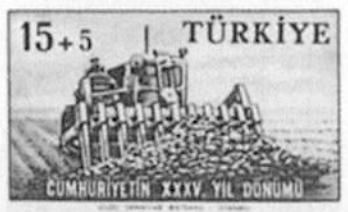

259 Bulldozer

1958. 35th Anniv of Republic.

1836	**259**	15k.+5k. orange	10	10
1837	-	20k.+5k. brown	15	15
1838	-	25k.+5k. green	25	25

DESIGNS—VERT: 20k. Portrait of Kemal Ataturk. HORIZ: 25k. Army tanks and Republic F-84G Thunderjets.

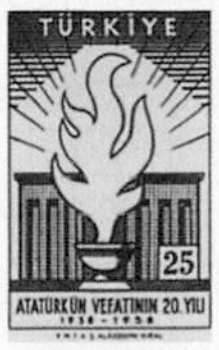

260 Flame of Remembrance

1958. 20th Death Anniv of Kemal Ataturk.

1839	**260**	25k. red	10	10
1840	-	75k. green	25	15

DESIGN: 75k. Sword, sprig and bust of Kemal Ataturk.

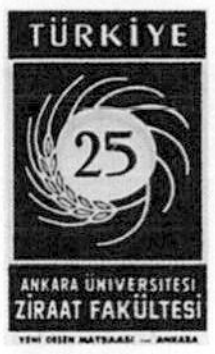

261

1959. 25th Anniv of Faculty of Agriculture, Ankara University.

1841	**261**	25k. yellow and violet	25	15

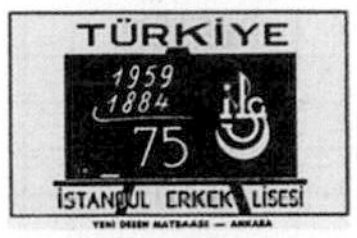

262 Blackboard

1959. 75th Anniv of Boys' High School, Istanbul.

1842	**262**	75k. black and yellow	35	15

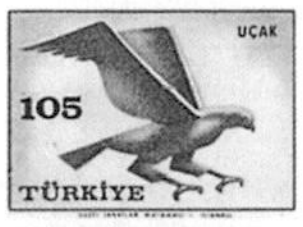

263 Eagle

1959. Air. Birds.

1843	-	40k. purple and mauve	15	10
1844	-	65k. myrtle and turquoise	35	25
1845	-	85k. blue and black	65	25
1846	**263**	105k. bistre and yellow	90	25
1847	-	125k. lilac and violet	1·20	40
1848	-	155k. green and yellow	1·40	55
1849	-	195k. blue and black	1·50	60
1850	-	245k. brown and orange	2·30	1·50

BIRDS (in flight)—HORIZ: 40k. Barn swallows; 65k. Cranes; 85k. Gulls. VERT: 125k. House martin; 155k. Demoiselle crane; 195k. Gulls; 245k. Turtle dove.

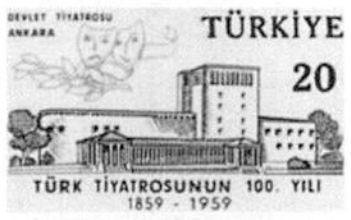

264 Theatre, Ankara

1959. Centenary of Turkish Theatre.

1851	**264**	20k. brown and green	15	10
1852	-	25k. green and orange	15	10

DESIGN: 25k. Portrait of Sinasi and masks.

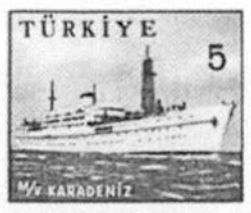

265 "Karadeniz" (liner)

1959

1853	-	1k. blue	10	10
1854	**265**	5k. blue	15	10
1855	-	10k. blue	10	10
1856	-	15k. brown	35	15
1857	-	20k. green	10	10
1858	-	25k. lilac	15	10
1859a	-	30k. purple	50	10
1860	-	40k. blue	60	10
1861	-	45k. violet	60	10
1862	-	55k. brown	80	10
1863	-	60k. green	1·20	10
1864	-	75k. olive	5·00	10
1865	-	90k. blue	5·00	15
1866	-	100k. grey	5·00	10
1867	-	120k. purple	5·00	15
1868	-	150k. orange	5·75	15
1869	-	200k. green	5·00	15
1870	-	250k. brown	2·50	25
1871	-	500k. blue	10·50	40

DESIGNS—HORIZ: 1k. Vickers Viscount 700 airliner; 10k. Grain silo; 15k. Steel works; 20k. Euphrates Bridge; 25k. Zonguldak Harbour; 30k. Oil refinery; 40k. Rumeli Hisari Fortress; 45k. Sugar factory; 55k. Coal mine; 150k. Combine-harvester. VERT: 60k. Telegraph pole; 75k. Railway; 90k. Crane loading "Kars" (container ship); 100k. Cement factory; 120k. Coast road; 200k. Electric transformer; 250, 500k. Portrait of Ataturk.

1959. Postage Due Stamps surch **20–20** for ordinary postage.

1872	**D121**	20k. on 20pa. brown	25	10
1873	**D121**	20k. on 2k. violet	25	10
1874	**D121**	20k. on 3k. violet	25	10
1875	**D121**	20k. on 5k. green	25	10
1876	**D121**	20k. on 12k. red	25	10

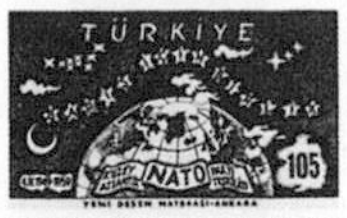

267 Northern Hemisphere and Stars

1959. Tenth Anniv of N.A.T.O.

1877	**267**	105k. red	40	25
1878	**267**	195k. green	80	60

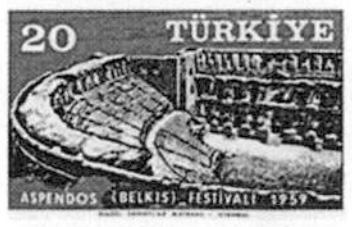

268 Amphitheatre, Aspendos

1959. Aspendos Festival.

1879	**268**	20k. violet and bistre	15	10
1880	**268**	20k. brown and green	15	10

1959. Tenth Anniv of Council of Europe. Surch **X. YIL** in circle of stars and **105 AVRUPA KONSEYI**.

1881	**259**	105k. on 15k.+5k. orange	60	45

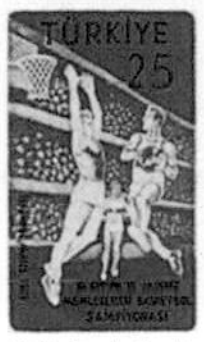

270 Basketball Players

1959. 11th European and Mediterranean Basketball Championships, Istanbul.

1882	**270**	25k. red and blue	25	15

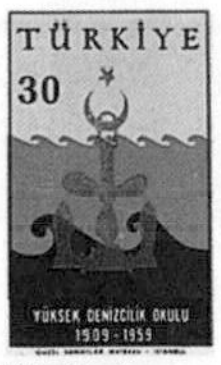

271 Marine Symbols

1959. 50th Anniv of Turkish Merchant Marine College.

1883	**271**	30k. multicoloured	15	10
1884	-	40k. multicoloured	25	15

DESIGN: 40k. As 30k. but seahorse in place of anchor symbol.

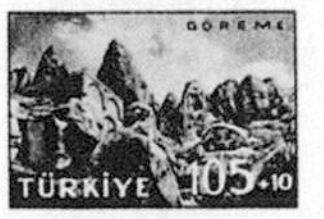

272 Goreme

1959. Tourist Publicity.

1885	**272**	105k.+10k. orange and violet	50	40

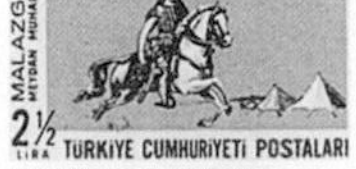

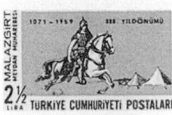

273 Mounted Warrior

1959. 888th Anniv of Battle of Malazgirt.

1886	**273**	2½l. purple and blue	1·10	1·00

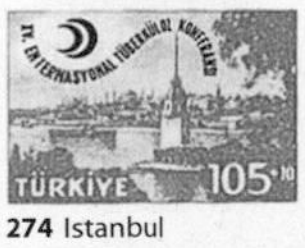

274 Istanbul

1959. 15th International T.B. Conf, Istanbul.

1887	**274**	105k.+10k. blue and red	50	60

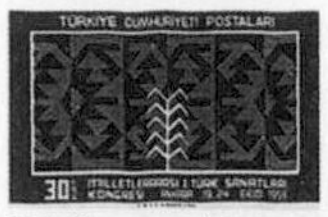

275 Ornamental Pattern

1959. First International Congress of Turkish Arts.

1888	**275**	30k. red and black	15	15
1889	-	40k. blue, black and ochre	25	15
1890	-	75k. blue, yellow and red	50	40

DESIGNS—HORIZ: 40k. Sultan Mohammed II Mosque in silhouette. VERT: 75k. Circular ornament.

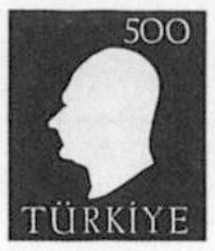

276 Kemal Ataturk

1959

1891	**276**	500k. blue	2·50	90
MS1891a 53×74 mm. **276** 500k. red. Imperf			2·50	2·30

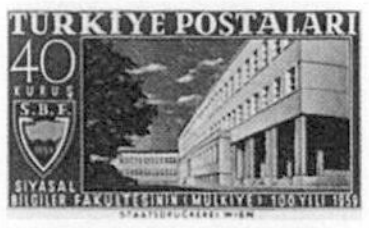

277 Faculty Building

1959. Centenary of Turkish Political Science Faculty.

1892	**277**	40k. brown and green	15	10
1893	**277**	40k. blue and brown	25	10
1894	-	1l. ochre and violet	75	45

DESIGN—VERT: 1l. "S.B.F." emblem of Faculty.

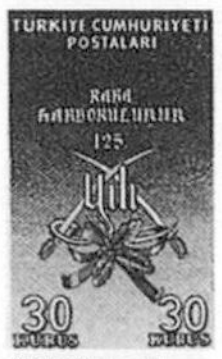

278 Crossed Sabres

1960. 125th Anniv of Territorial War College.

1895	**278**	30k. red and yellow	10	10
1896	-	40k. yellow, brown & red	15	10

DESIGN: 40k. Bayonet in bowl of fire.

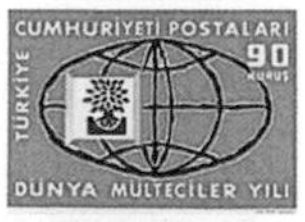

279 "Uprooted Tree" and Globe

1960. World Refugee Year.

1897	**279**	90k. black and turquoise	10	10
1898	-	105k. black and yellow	15	15

DESIGN: 105k. "Uprooted Tree" and houses representing refugee camp.

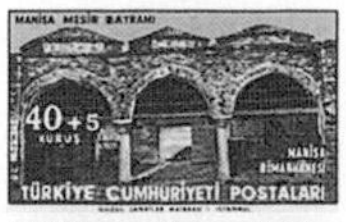

280 Mental Home, Manisa

1960. Manisa Fair. Inscr "MANISA MESIR BAYRAMI".

1899	**280**	40k.+5k. violet & mve	15	15
1900	**280**	40k.+5k. green & blue	15	15
1901	-	90k.+5k. purple & mve	60	30
1902	-	105k.+10k. mult	75	55

DESIGNS—VERT: 90k. Sultan Mosque, Manisa; 30½×42½ mm: 105k. Merkez Muslihittin Efendi (portrait).

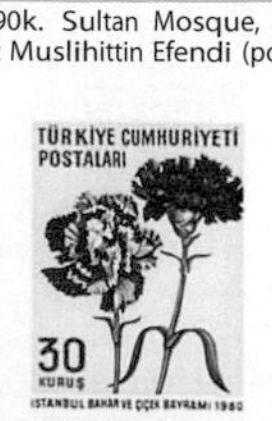

281 Carnations

1960. Spring Flowers Festival, Istanbul. Inscr "1960". Flowers in natural colours. Colours of inscriptions and backgrounds given.

1903	**281**	30k. red and yellow	40	15
1904	-	40k. green and grey	65	25
1905	-	75k. red and blue	1·00	40
1906	-	105k. green and pink	1·60	55

FLOWERS: 40k. Jasmine; 75k. Rose; 105k. Tulips.

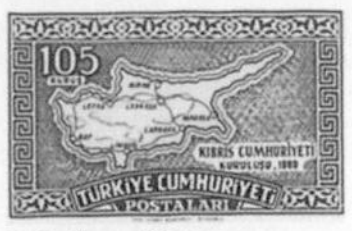

282 Map of Cyprus

1960. Proclamation of Cyprus Republic. Inscr "KIBRIS CUMHURIYETI".

1907	-	40k. mauve and blue	25	10
1908	**282**	105k. yellow, blue & grn	35	15

DESIGN: 40k. Town Centre, Nicosia.

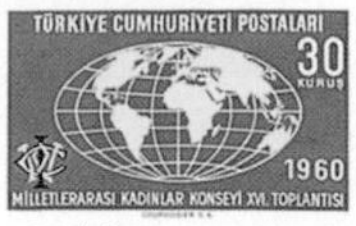

283 Globe

1960. 16th Women's Int Council Meeting.

1909	**283**	30k. yellow and lilac	25	10
1910	-	75k. drab and blue	35	15

DESIGN: 75k. Women, "W.I.C." emblem and nest.

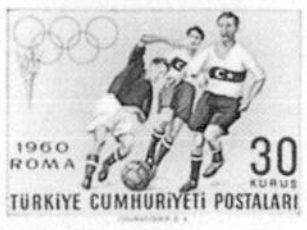

283a Football

1960. Olympic Games.

1911	30k. green (Type **283a**)	60	15
1912	30k. black (Basketball)	60	15
1913	30k. blue (Wrestling)	60	15
1914	30k. purple (Hurdling)	60	15
1915	30k. brown (Show jumping)	60	15
MS1915a 215×160 mm. Nos. 1911/15		18·00	

1960. Europa. As T **144a** of Switzerland but size 32½×22½ mm.

1916	75k. turquoise and green	80	75
1917	105k. light and deep blue	1·20	1·10

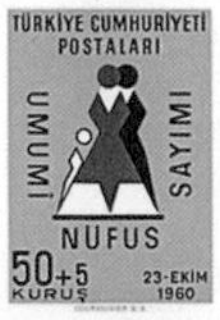

285 "Population"

1960. National Census.

1918	-	30k.+5k. red and blue	15	15
1919	**285**	50k.+5k. blue & turq	40	15

DESIGN—HORIZ: 30k. Graph showing outlines of human faces.

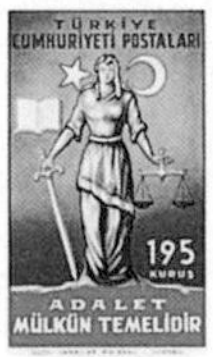

286 "Justice"

1960. Trial of Ex-Government Officials.

1920	-	40k. bistre and violet	15	15
1921	-	105k. red and green	25	15
1922	**286**	195k. red and green	60	25

DESIGNS—HORIZ: 40k. Badge of Turkish Army; 105k. Trial scene.

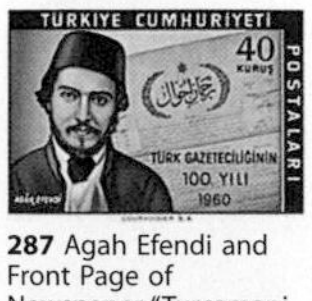

287 Agah Efendi and Front Page of Newspaper "Turcamani Ahval"

1960. Turkish Press Centenary.

1923	**287**	40k. purple and blue	25	15
1924	**287**	60k. purple and ochre	40	30

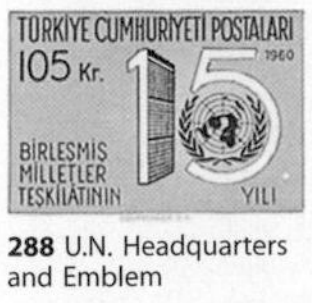

288 U.N. Headquarters and Emblem

1960. 15th Anniv of U.N.O.

1925	-	90k. ultramarine and blue	25	15
1926	**288**	105k. brown and green	35	25

DESIGN—VERT: 90k. U.N. emblem, "XV" and hand holding torch.

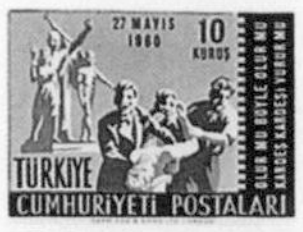

289 Revolutionaries

1960. Revolution of 27 May 1960.

1927	**289**	10k. grey and black	10	10
1928	-	30k. violet	15	10
1929	-	40k. red and black	15	15
1930	-	105k. multicoloured	40	25

DESIGNS—HORIZ: 30k. Kemal Ataturk and hand with torch; 105k. Soldiers and wounded youth. VERT: 40k. Prancing horse breaking chain.

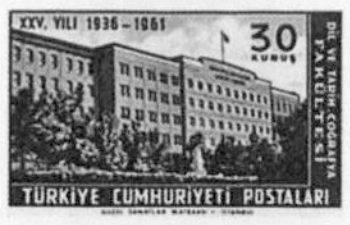

290 Faculty Building

1960. 25th Anniv of History and Geography Faculty.

1931	**290**	30k. black and green	15	10
1932	-	40k. black and buff	25	15
1933	-	60k. olive, buff and green	40	30

DESIGNS—HORIZ: 40k. Sun disc, cuneiform writing and map of Turkey. VERT: 60k. Ataturk's statue.

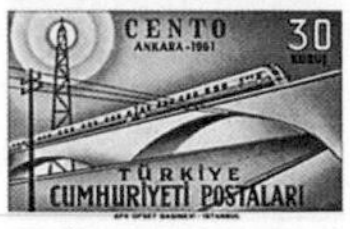

291 "Communications and Transport"

1961. Ninth Central Treaty Organization Ministers' Meeting, Ankara.

1934	**291**	30k. black and violet	15	10
1935	-	40k. black and green	25	15
1936	-	75k. black and blue	60	25

DESIGNS: 40k. Road and rail construction, telephone and telegraph; 75k. Parliament building, Ankara.

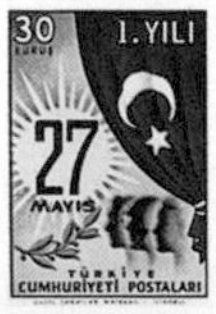

292

1961. First Anniv of 27 May Revolution.

1937	**292**	30k. multicoloured	15	10
1938	-	40k. green, cream & black	35	15
1939	-	60k. red, green and deep green	50	15

DESIGNS—HORIZ: 40k. Boz Kurt and warriors. VERT: 60k. "Progress".

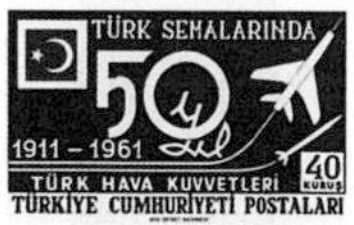

293 North American F100 Jet and Rocket

1961. 50th Anniv of Turkish Air Force.

1940	-	38k. orange, lake & black	15	15
1941	**293**	40k. violet and red	35	15
1942	-	75k. buff, grey and black	50	25

DESIGNS—HORIZ: 30k. Rockets. VERT: 75k. Ataturk, eagle and North American Super Sabre jets.

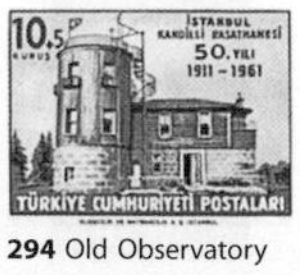

294 Old Observatory

1961. 50th Anniv of Kandilli Observatory, Istanbul.

1943	**294**	10k.+5k. turquoise and green	25	15
1944	-	30k.+5k. violet and black	25	15
1945	-	40k.+5k. brown and sepia	25	25
1946	-	75k.+5k. olive and green	65	25

DESIGNS—HORIZ: 30k. Observatory emblem; 75k. Observatory building. VERT: 40k. F. Gokmen.

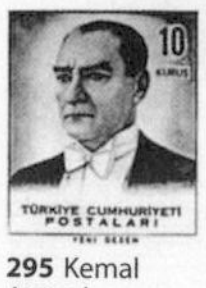

295 Kemal Ataturk

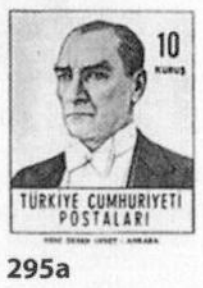

295a

1961

1947	**295a**	1k. brown	15	10
1948	**295a**	5k. blue	15	10
1949	**295**	10k. mauve	35	10
1950	**295a**	10k. sepia	35	10
1951	**295a**	30k. green	80	15
1952	**295a**	10l. violet (22×32 mm)	20·00	1·50

296 Doves

1961. Europa.

1960	**296**	30k. blue	40	55
1961	**296**	40k. grey	80	75
1962	**296**	75k. red	1·20	1·00

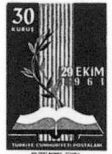

297 Tulip and Cogwheel

1961. Centenary of Professional and Technical Schools.

1963	**297**	30k. pink, silver and slate	15	15
1964	-	75k. red, black and blue	40	25

DESIGN—HORIZ: 75k. Inscr "100 Yili 1861–1961" and tulip and cogwheel emblem.

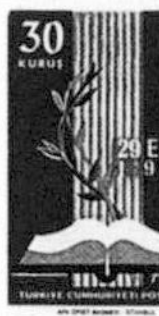

298 "The Constitution"

1961. Opening of Turkish Parliament.

1965	**298**	30k. black, bistre and red	15	15
1966	**298**	75k. black, green and blue	40	15

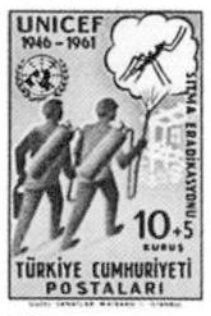

299 Insecticide-sprayers ("Malaria Eradication")

1961. 15th Anniv of UNICEF.

1967	**299**	10k.+5k. turquoise	15	15
1968	-	30k.+5k. violet	25	40
1969	-	75k.+5k. brown	60	55

DESIGNS—HORIZ: 30k. Mother and child ("Child Welfare"). VERT: 75k. Mother giving pasteurized milk to children ("Education on Nourishment").

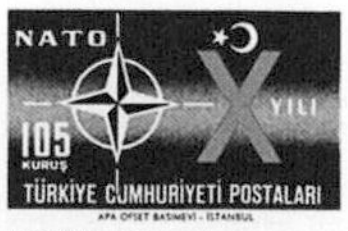

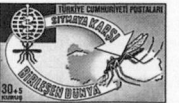

300 N.A.T.O. and Anniversary Emblem

1962. Tenth Anniv of Turkish Admission to N.A.T.O.

1970	-	75k. black, silver and blue	40	40
1971	**300**	105k. black, silver and red	40	40

DESIGN—VERT: 75k. Peace dove over N.A.T.O. and Anniv emblems.

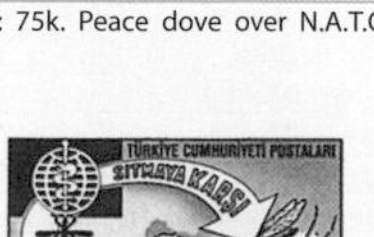

301 Mosquito on Map of Turkey

1962. Malaria Eradication.

1972	**301**	30k.+5k. brown	25	15
1973	**301**	75k.+5k. mauve & blk	25	25

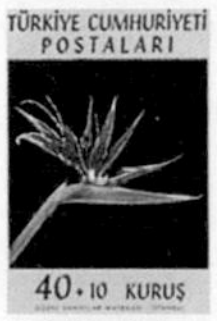

302 "Strelitzia reginae"

1962. Flowers. Multicoloured.

1974		30k.+10k. "Poinsettia pulcherrima"	25	15
1975		40k.+10k. Type **302**	60	30
1976		75k.+10k. "Nymphea alba"	80	45

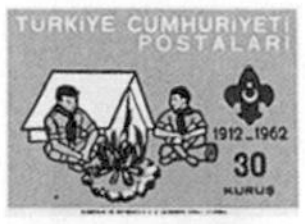

303 Scouts in Camp

1962. 50th Anniv of Turkish Scout Movement.

1977	**303**	30k. red, black and green	25	15
1978	-	60k. red, black and lilac	35	40
1979	-	105k. red, black & brown	80	60

DESIGNS: 60k. Two scouts with flag; 105k. Wolf Cub and Brownie.

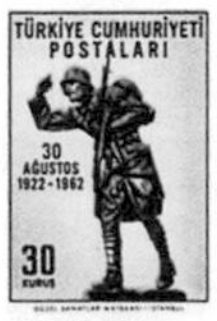

304 Soldier (Victory Monument, Ankara)

1962. 40th Anniv of Battle of Dumlupinar.

1980	**304**	30k. green	15	10
1981	-	40k. brown and black	40	10
1982	-	75k. grey	65	40

DESIGNS—HORIZ: 40k. Ox-cart carrying ammunition. (Victory Monument, Ankara). VERT: 75k. Kemal Ataturk.

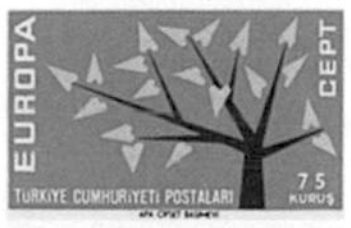

305 Europa "Tree"

1962. Europa.

1983	**305**	75k. sepia and green	40	25
1984	**305**	105k. sepia and red	80	55
1985	**305**	195k. sepia and blue	1·60	1·10

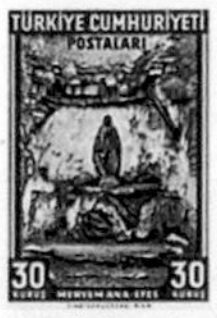

306 Shrine of the Virgin Mary

1962. Tourist Issue. Multicoloured.

1986		30k. Type **306**	15	15
1987		40k. Interior	25	25
1988		75k. Exterior	35	30
1989		105k. Statue of the Virgin	50	45

DESIGNS: The 40 and 75k. show horiz views of the Virgin Mary's house at Ephesus.

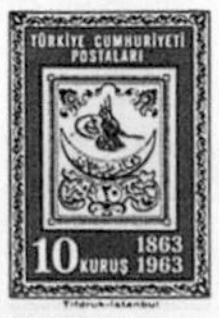

307 Turkish 20pa. Stamp of 1863

1963. Stamp Centenary.

1990	**307**	10k. black, yellow & brn	10	10
1991	-	30k. black, pink and violet	15	10
1992	-	40k. black, blue & turq	15	15
1993	-	75k. black, pink & brown	40	30

DESIGNS—Turkish stamps of 1863: 30k. (1pi.); 40k. (2pi.); 75k. (5pi.).

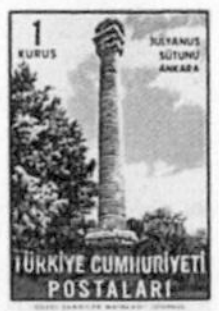

308 Julian's Column, Ankara

1963

1994	**308**	1k. green and olive	10	10
1995	**308**	1k. violet	15	10
1996	-	5k. sepia and brown	15	10
1997	-	10k. mauve and green	25	10
1998	-	30k. black and violet	65	10
1999	-	50k. green, brown & yell	1·60	15
2000	-	60k. grey	4·00	10
2001	-	100k. brown	2·50	10
2002	-	150k. green	12·50	40

DESIGNS—HORIZ: 5k. Ethnographic Museum; 10k. Citadel; 30k. Educational Establishment, Gazi; 50k. Ataturk's Mausoleum; 60k. Presidential Palace, Ankara; 100k. Ataturk's house; 150k. National Museum, Ankara.

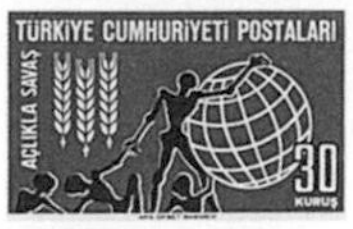

309 "Clinging to the World"

1963. Freedom from Hunger.

2010	**309**	30k. deep blue and blue	15	15
2011	-	40k. deep brown & brown	25	25
2012	-	75k. deep green and green	60	40

DESIGNS: 40k. Sowers; 75k. Emblem and Globe within hands.

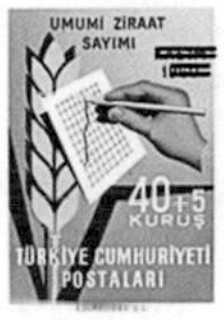

310 Wheat and Census Graph

1963. Agricultural Census. Unissued stamps with "KASIM 1960" obliterated with bars. Inscr "UMUMI ZIRAAT SAYIMI".

2013	**310**	40k.+5k. multicoloured	15	15
2014	-	60k.+5k. multicoloured	35	25

DESIGN—HORIZ: 60k. Wheat and chart.

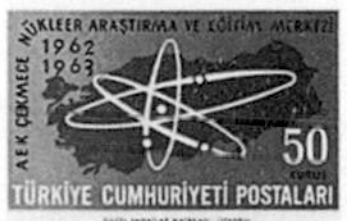

311 Atomic Symbol on Map

1963. First Anniv of Opening of Turkish Nuclear Research Centre.

2015	**311**	50k. brown & deep brown	15	15
2016	-	60k. multicoloured	35	25
2017	-	100k. blue & ultramarine	50	40

DESIGNS: 60k. Various symbols; 100k. Emblem of Turkish Atomic Energy Commission.

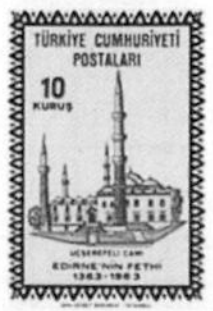

312 Ucserefili Mosque

1963. 600th Anniv of Conquest of Edirne.

2018	**312**	10k. green, ultramarine and blue	15	10
2019	-	30k. blue and red	25	15
2020	-	60k. multicoloured	40	15
2021	-	100k. multicoloured	1·00	40

DESIGNS—HORIZ: 30k. Meric Bridge; 60k. Kum Kasri (building). VERT: 100k. Sultan Amurat I.

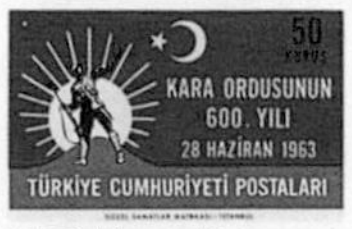

313 Soldier and Sun

1963. 600th Anniv of Turkish Army.

2022	**313**	50k. black, red and blue	15	10
2023	**313**	100k. black, red & bistre	40	40

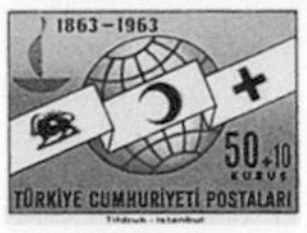

314 Globe and Emblems

1963. Red Cross Centenary. Multicoloured.

2024		50k.+10k. Type **314**	35	30
2025		60k.+10k. "Flowers" emblem (vert)	35	30
2026		100k.+10k. Three emblems on flags	60	55

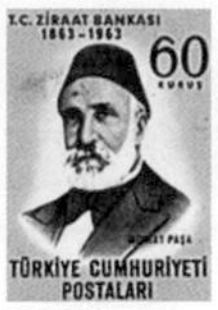

315 Mithat Pasha (founder)

1963. Centenary of Turkish Agricultural Bank.

2027	-	30k. brown, green and yellow	15	10
2028	-	50k. blue and lilac	25	15
2029	**315**	60k. green and black	40	25

DESIGNS—HORIZ: 30k. Ploughing and irrigation; 50k. Agricultural Bank, Ankara.

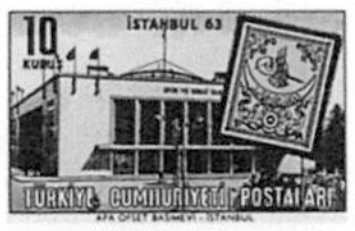

316 Exhibition Hall, Istanbul, and 5pi. stamp of 1863

1963. "Istanbul '63" International Stamp Exn.

2030	**316**	10k. salmon, black and yellow	15	10
2031	-	50k. green, red and black	25	15
2032	-	60k. sepia, black and blue	25	15
2033	-	100k. violet and purple	40	30
2034	-	130k. brown, orge & yell	60	45

DESIGNS: 50k. Sultan Ahmed's Mosque, Obelisk and 3pi. on 2pa. Nationalist Government (Angora) stamp of 1920; 60k. Istanbul skyline and 10pi. (Angora) stamp of 1922; 100k. Rumeli Fort and 6k. stamp of 1929/30; 130k. Ankara Fort and 12½k. air stamp of 1934.

1963. International Philatelic Exhibition, Istanbul ("F.I.P. GUNU"). Miniature sheets (88×116 mm) comprising reproductions of T **1**.

MS2034a	10k. yellow, brown and black (20pa.), 50k. lilac, pink and black (1pi.); 60k. green, blue and black (2pi.); 130k. brown, pink and black (5pi.)	1·60	1·90

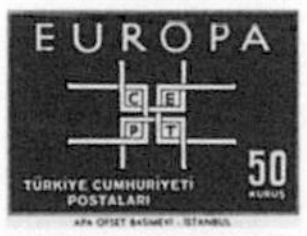

317 "Co-operation"

1963. Europa.

2035	**317**	50k. orange, black and red	40	40
2036	**317**	130k. blue, black & green	80	75

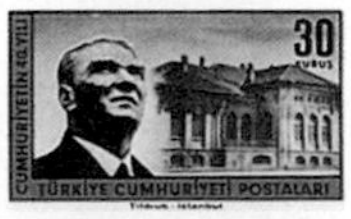

318 Ataturk and Old Parliament House

1963. 40th Anniv of Turkish Republic. Multicoloured.

2037		30k. Type **318**	15	15
2038		50k. Ataturk and flag	35	15
2039		60k. Ataturk and new Parliament House	50	25

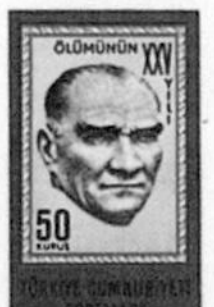

319 Kemal Ataturk

1963. 25th Death Anniv of Kemal Ataturk.

2040	**319**	50k. multicoloured	50	25
2041	**319**	60k. multicoloured	50	25

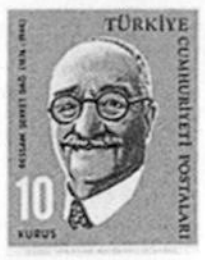

320 R.S. Dag (painter)

1964. Cultural Celebrities.

2042	-	1k. black and red	10	10
2043	-	5k. black and green	15	10
2044	**320**	10k. black and brown	25	10
2045	-	50k. black and blue	1·30	15
2046	-	60k. black and grey	1·80	15
2047	-	100k. ultramarine & blue	1·30	15
2048	-	130k. black and green	6·50	25

PORTRAITS: 1k. H. R. Gurpinar (romanticist, birth cent); 5k. J. H. Izmirli (savant, 20th death anniv); 10k. Type **320** (20th death anniv); 50k. R. Z. M. Ekrem (writer, 50th death anniv); 60k. A. M. Pasa (commander, 125th birth anniv); 100k. A. Rasim (writer, birth cent); 130k. S. Zeki (mathematician, birth cent).

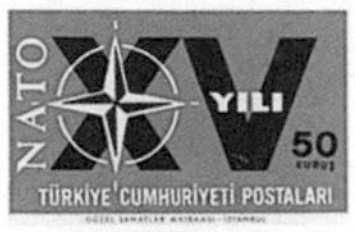

321 N.A.T.O. Emblem and "XV"

1964. 15th Anniv of N.A.T.O.

2049	**321**	50k. red, violet & turq	40	25
2050	-	130k. black and red	80	55

DESIGN: 130k. N.A.T.O. emblem and laurel sprig.

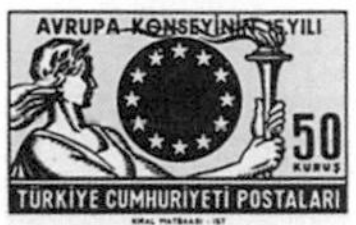

322 "Europa" holding Torch

1964. 15th Anniv of Council of Europe.

2051	**322**	50k. blue, brown & yell	25	15
2052	-	130k. orange, ultramarine and blue	60	45

DESIGN: 130k. Torch and circlet of stars.

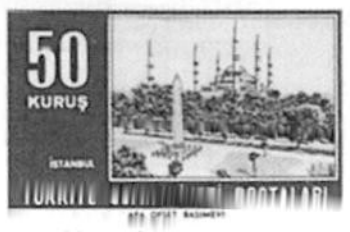

323 Haga Mosque, Istanbul

1964. Tourist Issue.

2053	**323**	50k. green and olive	25	15
2054	-	50k. red and purple	25	15
2055	-	50k. violet and blue	35	15
2056	-	60k. green, black & pur	40	15
2057	-	60k. brown and sepia	40	15

DESIGNS—HORIZ: No. 2054 Temple of Zeus, Silifke; 2055 Amasra. VERT: No. 2056 Mersin; 2057 Augustus' Temple, Ankara.

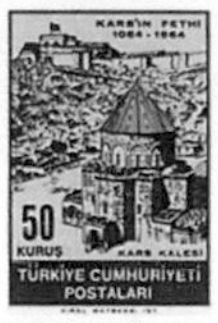

324 Kars Castle

1964. 900th Anniv of Conquest of Kars.

2058	**324**	50k. black and lilac	25	10
2059	-	130k. multicoloured	50	40

DESIGN: 130k. Alpaslan warrior.

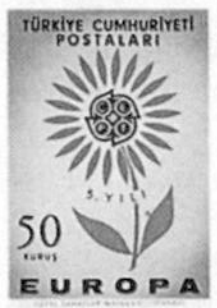

325 Europa "Flower"

1964. Europa.

2060	**325**	50k. blue, grey and orange	1·00	90
2061	**325**	130k. purple, green & bl	1·50	1·40

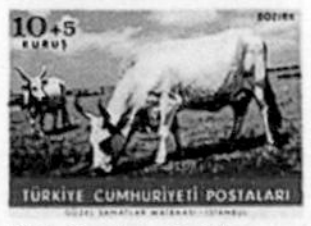

326 Grazing Cattle

1964. Animal Protection Fund. Multicoloured.

2062		10k.+5k. Type **326**	15	15

2063	30k.+5k. Horned sheep	35	15
2064	50k.+5k. Horses	50	25
2065	60k.+5k. Three horned sheep	80	40
2066	100k.+5k. Dairy cows	1·50	60

The 30k. and 60k. are vert.

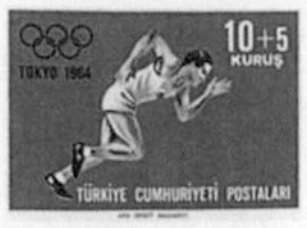

327 Running

1964. Olympic Games, Tokyo.

2067	**327**	10k.+5k. black, red and brown	15	15
2068	-	50k.+5k. black, red and olive	65	25
2069	-	60k.+5k. black, red and blue	1·00	40
2070	-	100k.+5k. black, red and violet	1·50	75

DESIGNS—VERT: 50k. Torch-bearer; 60k. Wrestling; 100k. Throwing the discus.

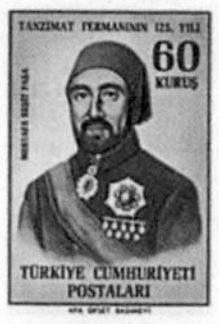

328 Mustafa Resit

1964. 125th Anniv of Reformation Decrees. Multicoloured.

2071	50k. Mustafa Resit and the pashas (horiz 48×32 mm)	65	25
2072	60k. Type **328**	65	30
2073	100k. As 50k.	1·20	60

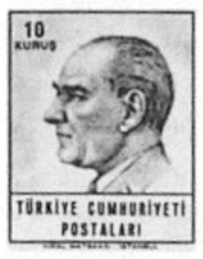

329 Kemal Ataturk

1964

2074	**329**	1k. green	25	10
2075	**329**	5k. blue	40	10
2076	**329**	10k. blue	1·00	10
2077	**329**	25k. green	1·80	25
2078	**329**	30k. purple	2·10	10
2079	**329**	50k. brown	3·00	10
2080	**329**	150k. orange	10·50	15

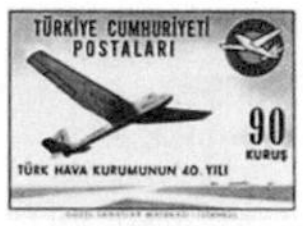

330 Glider

1965. 40th Anniv of Turkish Civil Aviation League. Multicoloured.

2081	60k. Parachutist (vert)	25	25
2082	90k. Type **330**	40	30
2083	130k. Ataturk and squadron of aircraft (vert)	80	45

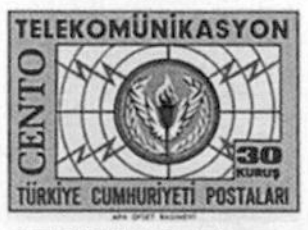

331 CENTO Emblem

1965. Completion of CENTO Telecommunications Projects. Multicoloured.

2084	30k. Type **331**	15	15
2085	50k. Aerial mast (vert)	35	15
2086	75k. Hand pressing button (inaugural ceremony)	50	25

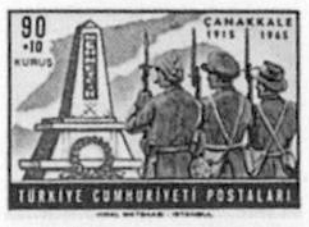

332 Monument and Soldiers

1965. 50th Anniv of Battle of the Dardanelles. Multicoloured.

2087	50k.+10k. Wreath and map	40	25
2088	90k.+10k. Type **332**	60	40
2089	130k.+10k. Dardanelles Monument and flag (vert)	1·10	75

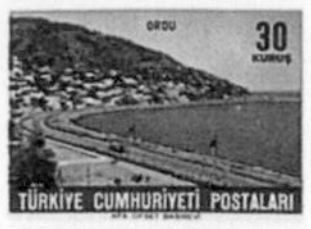

333 Beach at Ordu

1965. Tourism. Multicoloured.

2090	30k. Type **333**	25	15
2091	50k. Manavgat Falls	35	15
2092	60k. Istanbul	40	15
2093	100k. Urfa	65	30
2094	130k. Alanya	1·00	40

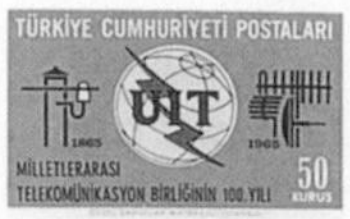

334 I.T.U. Emblem and Symbols

1965. I.T.U. Centenary.

2095	**334**	50k. multicoloured	25	15
2096	**334**	130k. multicoloured	60	45

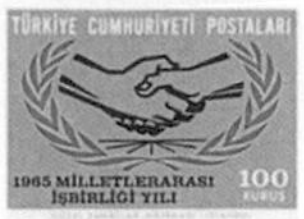

335 I.C.Y. Emblem

1965. International Co-operation Year.

2097	**335**	100k. red, green and salmon	50	40
2098	**335**	130k. violet, green and grey	60	45

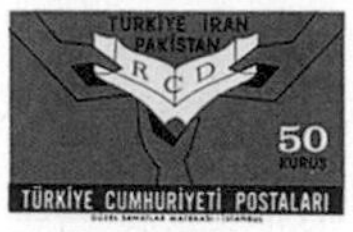

336 "Co-operation"

1965. First Anniv of Regional Development Co-operation Pact. Multicoloured.

2099	50k. Type **336**	35	25
2100	75k. Globe and flags of Turkey, Iran and Pakistan	50	30

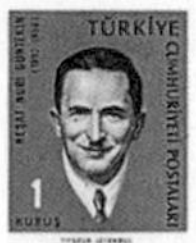

337 R. N. Guntekin

1965. Cultural Celebrities.

2101	**337**	1k. black and red	10	10
2102	-	5k. black and blue	10	10
2103	-	10k. black and ochre	40	10
2104	-	25k. black and brown	1·50	10
2105	-	30k. black and grey	1·50	10
2106	-	50k. black and yellow	2·10	10
2107	-	60k. black and purple	1·60	10
2108	-	150k. black and green	1·50	25
2109	-	220k. black and brown	1·60	45

PORTRAITS: 5k. Dr. B. O Akalin; 10k. T. Fikret; 25k. T. Cemil; 30k. Ahmet Vefik Pasa; 50k. O. Seyfettin; 60k. K. Mimaroglu; 150k. H. Z. Usakligil; 220k. Y. K. Beyatli.

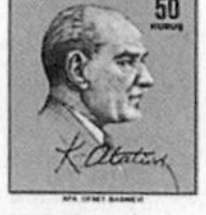

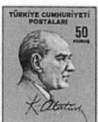

338 Kemal Ataturk and Signature

1965

2110	**338**	1k. black and mauve	35	10
2111	**338**	5k. black and green	35	10
2112	**338**	10k. black and blue	1·20	10
2113	**338**	50k. black and gold	1·80	10
2114	**338**	150k. black and silver	1·80	10

See also Nos. 2170/4.

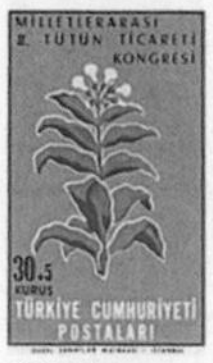

339 Tobacco Plant

1965. Second International Tobacco Congress. Multicoloured.

2115	30k.+5k. Type **339**	40	15
2116	50k.+5k. Leander's Tower and tobacco leaves (horiz)	60	25
2117	100k.+5k. Tobacco leaf	1·20	75

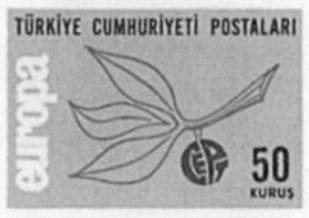

340 Europa "Sprig"

1965. Europa.

2118	**340**	50k. green, blue and grey	1·20	60
2119	**340**	130k. green, blk & ochre	2·50	90

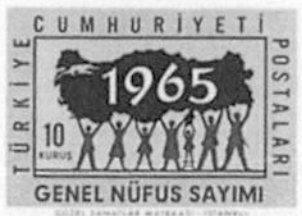

341 Civilians supporting Map

1965. National Census. Inscr "GENEL NUFUS SAYIMI".

2120	**341**	10k. multicoloured	15	15
2121	-	50k. light green, green and black	15	15
2122	-	100k. black, blue & orge	50	30

DESIGNS—HORIZ: 50k. Year "1965". VERT: 100k. Human eye and figure.

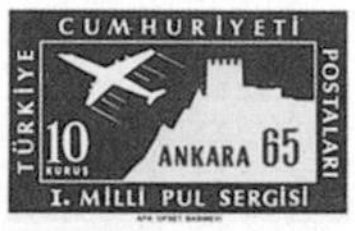

342 Ankara Castle and Airliner

1965. "Ankara '65" National Stamp Exn. Inscr "I. MILLI PUL SERGISI".

2123	**342**	10k. red, yellow and violet	10	10
2124	-	30k. multicoloured	15	10
2125	-	50k. blue, red and olive	25	10
2126	-	100k. multicoloured	80	40
MS2127		50×95 mm. 150k. multicoloured	3·00	3·50

DESIGNS—HORIZ: 30k. Archer; 50k. Horseman; 100k. Three thematic "stamps" and medal. VERT: 150k. Hands holding stamp album.

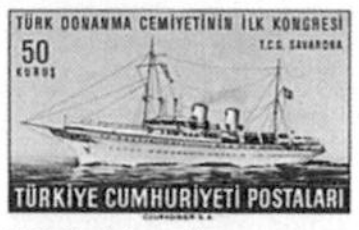

343 Training-ship "Savarona"

1965. Turkish Naval Society Congress.

2128	**343**	50k. brown and blue	35	25
2129	-	60k. indigo and blue	50	25
2130	-	100k. brown and blue	75	40
2131	-	130k. purple and blue	1·10	75
2132	-	220k. black and blue	2·30	1·10

DESIGNS: 60k. Submarine "Piri Reis"; 100k. Destroyer "Alpaslan"; 130k. Destroyer "Gelibolu"; 220k. Destroyer "Gemlik".

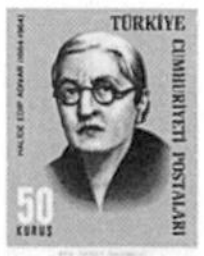

344 Halide E. Adivar

1966. Cultural Celebrities.

2133	-	25k. brown and grey	1·30	10
2134	-	30k. brown and mauve	1·20	10
2135	**344**	50k. black and blue	80	10
2136	-	60k. brown and green	80	15
2137	-	130k. black and blue	2·50	30

PORTRAITS: 25k. H. S. Arel; 30k. K. Akdik; 60k. Abdurrahman Seref; 130k. Naima.

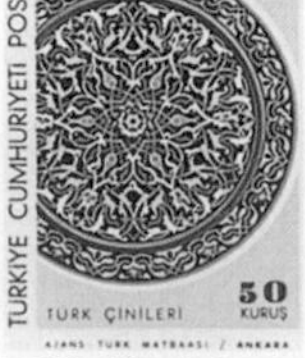

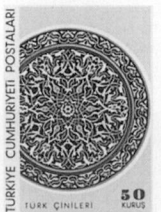

345 Roof Panel, Green Mausoleum, Burs

1966. Turkish Faience. Multicoloured.

2138	50k. Type **345**	50	25
2139	60k. "Spring Flowers", Sultan Mausoleum, Istanbul	3·00	1·80
2140	130k. 16th-cent tile, Iznik	1·10	60

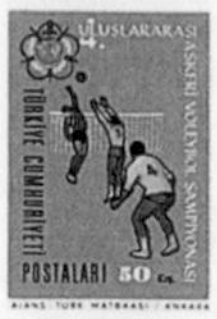

346 Volleyball

1966. Int Military Volleyball Championships.

2141	**346**	50k. multicoloured	40	15

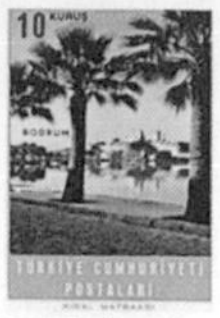

347 Bodrum

1966. Tourism. Multicoloured.

2142	10k. Type **347**	10	10
2143	30k. Kusadasi	1·10	55
2144	50k. Anadoluhisari (horiz)	25	10
2145	90k. Marmaris	35	15
2146	100k. Izmir (horiz)	35	15

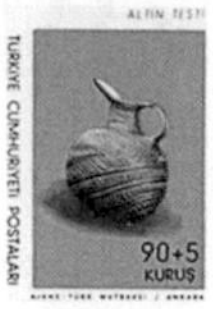

348 Golden Pitcher

1966. Ancient Works of Art. Multicoloured.

2147	30k.+5k. Ivory eagle and rabbit (horiz)	40	30
2148	50k.+5k. Deity in basalt	60	45
2149	60k.+5k. Bronze bull	80	55
2150	90k.+5k. Type **348**	1·10	85

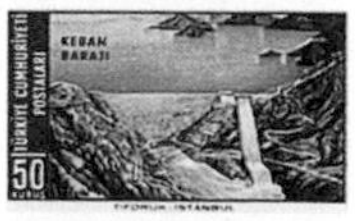

349 View of Dam

1966. Inaug of Keban Dam. Multicoloured.

2151	50k. Type **349**	25	10
2152	60k. Keban valley and bridge	60	45

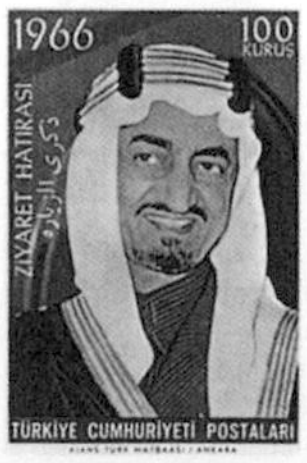

350 King Faisal

1966. Visit of King of Saudi Arabia.

2153	**350**	100k. deep red and red	80	40

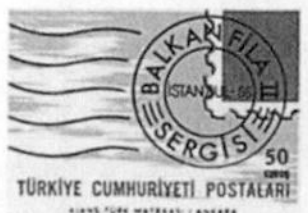

351 "Stamp" and "Postmark"

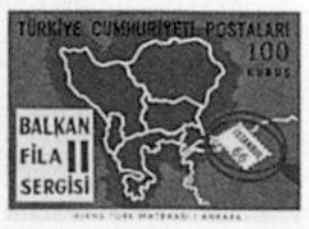

352

1966. "Balkanfila" Stamp Exhibition, Istanbul. Multicoloured.

2154	50k. Type **351**	25	15
2155	60k. Stamp "flower"	35	25
2156	75k. "Stamps" in form of display frames	40	40
MS2157	75×50 mm. **352** 100k. chestnut, blue and yellow. Imperf	2·50	2·30

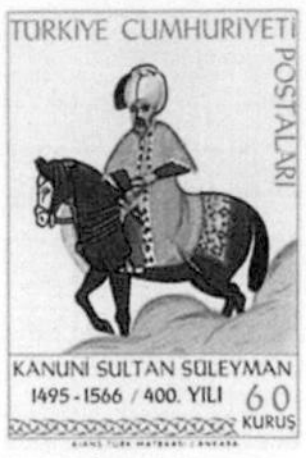

353 Sultan Suleiman on Horseback

1966. 400th Death Anniv of Sultan Suleiman. Multicoloured.

2158		60k. Type **353**	50	40
2159		90k. Mausoleum, Istanbul	1·20	85
2160		130k. Sultan Suleiman (profile)	2·50	1·40

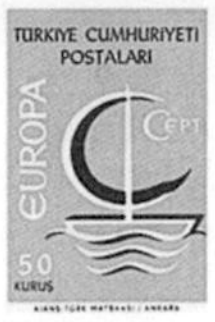

354 Europa "Ship"

1966. Europa.

2161	**354**	50k. ultramarine, bl & blk	1·20	75
2162	**354**	130k. purple, lilac & black	2·10	1·50

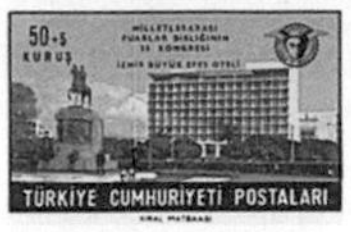

355 Grand Hotel Ephesus, Izmir

1966. 33rd International Fairs Union Congress, Izmir. Multicoloured.

2163		50k.+5k. Type **355**	35	25
2164		60k.+5k. Konak Square, Izmir (vert)	50	45
2165		130k.+5k. Izmir Fair	90	75

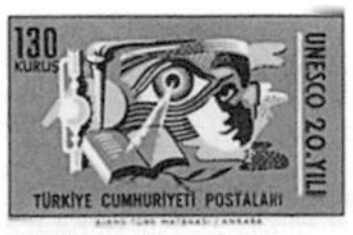

356 "Education, Science and Culture"

1966. 20th Anniv of UNESCO.

2166	**356**	130k. chestnut, yellow and brown	50	30

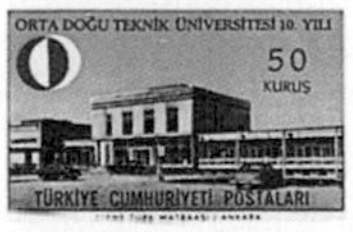

357 University of Technology

1966. Tenth Anniv of Middle East University of Technology. Multicoloured.

2167		50k. Type **357**	25	15
2168		100k. Atomic symbol	60	40
2169		130k. Symbols of the sciences	80	45

1966. As Nos. 2110/14.

2170	**338**	25k. black and green	35	10
2171	**338**	30k. black and pink	35	10
2172	**338**	50k. black and violet	1·20	10
2173	**338**	90k. black and brown	1·80	10
2174	**338**	100k. black and drab	1·80	10

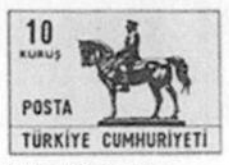

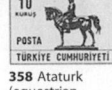

358 Ataturk (equestrian statue)

1966. Greetings Card Stamp.

2175	**358**	10k. black and yellow	25	15

See also Nos. 2218/9, 2257/8, 2303 and 2418.

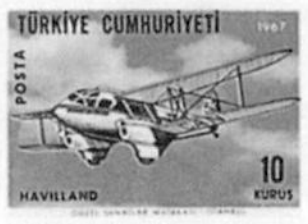

359 De Havilland Dragon Rapide

1967. Air. Aircraft.

2176	**359**	10k. black and pink	25	10
2177	-	60k. red, black and green	35	10
2178	-	130k. red, black and blue	1·10	25
2179	-	220k. red, sepia and ochre	1·60	40
2180	-	270k. red, blue and salmon	2·50	55

DESIGNS: 60k. Fokker F27 Friendship; 130k. Douglas DC-9-30; 220k. Douglas DC-3; 270k. Vickers Viscount 700.

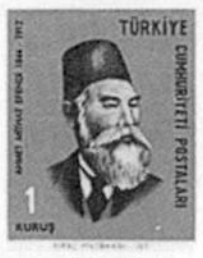

360 A. Mithat (author)

1967. Cultural Celebrities.

2181	**360**	1k. black and green	10	10
2182	-	5k. black and ochre	25	10
2183	-	50k. black and violet	1·60	10
2184	-	100k. black and yellow	5·00	25
2185	-	150k. black and yellow	3·25	40

PORTRAITS: 5k. T. Reis (naval commander); 50k. S. Mehmet (statesman); 100k. Nedim (philosopher); 150k. O. Hamdi (painter).

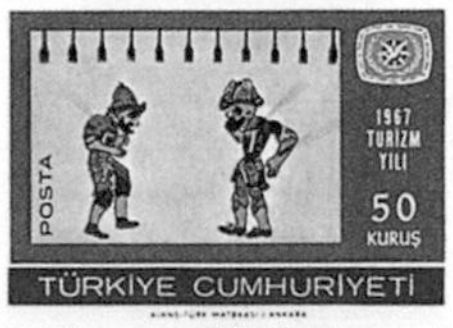

361 Karogoz and Hacivat (puppets)

1967. International Tourist Year. Multicoloured.

2186		50k. Type **361**	1·40	45
2187		60k. Sword and shield game	1·40	55
2188		90k. Military Band	1·60	75
2189		100k. Karagoz (puppet) (vert)	2·10	1·30

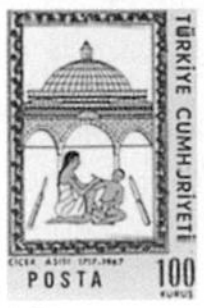

362 "Vaccination"

1967. 250th Anniv of 1st Smallpox Vaccination, Edirne.

2190	**362**	100k. multicoloured	60	40

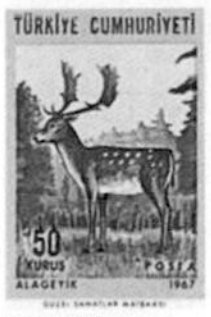

363 Fallow Deer

1967. Game Animals. Multicoloured.

2191		50k. Type **363**	40	15
2192		60k. Wild goat	50	30
2193		100k. Brown bear	80	60
2194		130k. Wild boar	1·20	75

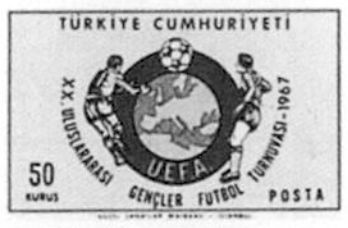

364 Emblem and Footballers

1967. 20th Int Junior Football Tournament. Multicoloured.

2195		50k. Type **364**	1·00	60
2196		130k. Footballers and emblem	1·50	90

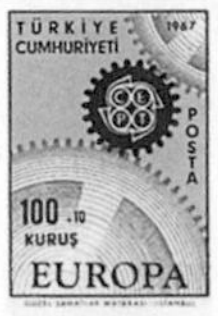

365 Cogwheels

1967. Europa.

2197	**365**	100k.+10k. mult	1·60	1·10
2198	**365**	130k.+10k. mult	1·60	1·10

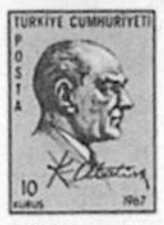

366 Kemal Ataturk

1967

2199	**366**	10k. black and green	3·25	10
2200	**366**	50k. black and pink	3·25	30

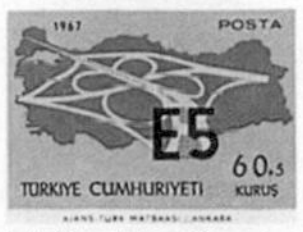

367 Road Junction on Map

1967. Opening of "E 5" Motorway. Multicoloured.

2201		60k.+5k. Type **367**	40	40
2202		130k.+5k. Motorway map and emblem (vert)	1·20	1·10

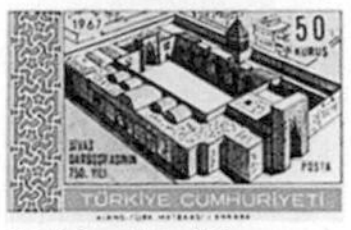

368 Sivas Hospital

1967. 750th Anniv of Sivas Hospital.

2203	**368**	50k. multicoloured	35	15

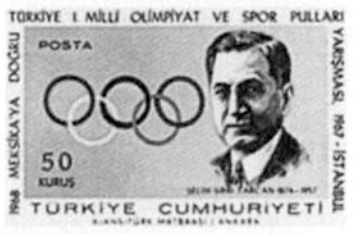

369 Selim Tarcan and Olympic Rings

1967. First Turkish Olympic Competitions, Istanbul. Multicoloured.

2204		50k. Type **369**	40	40
2205		60k. Pierre de Coubertin and Olympic Rings	40	40

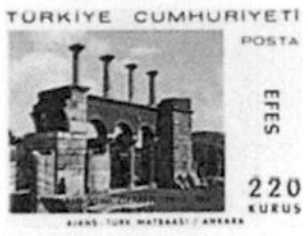

370 St. John's Church, Ephesus

1967. Pope Paul VI's Visit to Virgin Mary's House, Ephesus. Multicoloured.

2206		130k. Interior of Virgin Mary's House, Ephesus	40	40
2207		220k. Type **370**	1·00	90

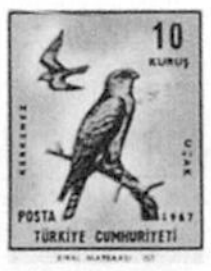

371 Common Kestrel

1967. Air. Birds.

2208	**371**	10k. brown and salmon	1·10	10
2209	-	60k. brown and yellow	65	10
2210	-	130k. purple and blue	1·80	15
2211	-	220k. sepia and green	2·75	30
2212	-	270k. brown and lilac	3·75	40

DESIGNS: 60k. Imperial eagle; 130k. Pallid harrier; 220k. Northern sparrow hawk; 270k. Common buzzard.

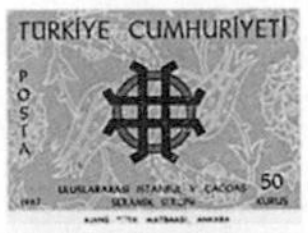

372 Exhibition Emblem

1967. International Ceramics Exn, Istanbul.

2213	**372**	50k. multicoloured	50	25

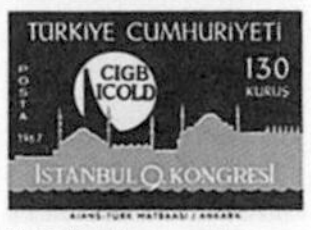

373 Emblem and Istanbul Skyline

1967. Congress of International Large Dams Commission, Istanbul.

2214	**373**	130k. blue and drab	75	40

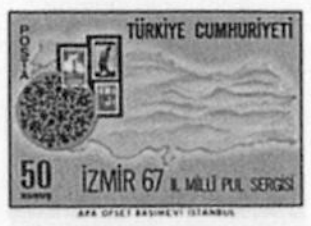

374 "Stamps" and Map

1967. "Izmir '67" Stamp Exhibition. Multicoloured.

2215		50k. Type **374**	35	15
2216		60k. "Stamps" and grapes	50	25
MS2217		100×52 mm. Nos. 2215/16	2·50	2·75

1967. Greetings Card Stamps. As T **358**.

2218		10k. black and green	25	10
2219		10k. black and red	25	10

DESIGNS: Equestrian statues of Ataturk at: No. 2218 Samsun; No. 2219 Izmir.

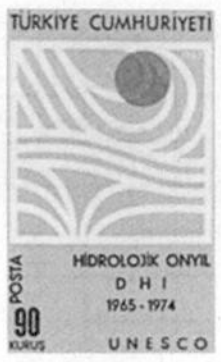

375 Decade Emblem

1967. International Hydrological Decade.

2220	**375**	90k. yellow, black & grn	60	45
2221	**375**	130k. yellow, black & lilac	75	55

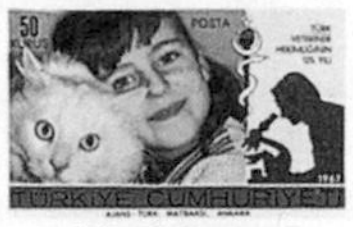

376 Girl with Angora Cat

1967. 125th Anniv of Turkish Veterinary Medical Service. Multicoloured.

2222		50k. Type **376**	50	30
2223		60k. Horse	50	30

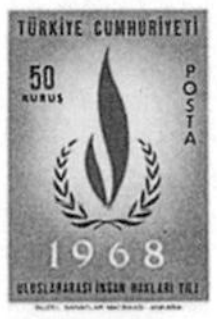

377 Human Rights Emblem

1968. Human Rights Year.

2224	**377**	50k. multicoloured	35	15
2225	**377**	130k. multicoloured	65	30

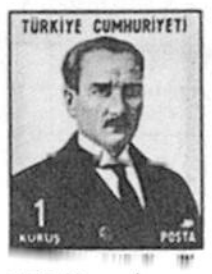

378 Kemal Ataturk

1968

2226	**378**	1k. blue and light blue	10	10
2227	**378**	5k. green and light green	40	10
2228	**378**	50k. brown and yellow	4·50	15
2229	**378**	200k. brown and pink	3·25	25

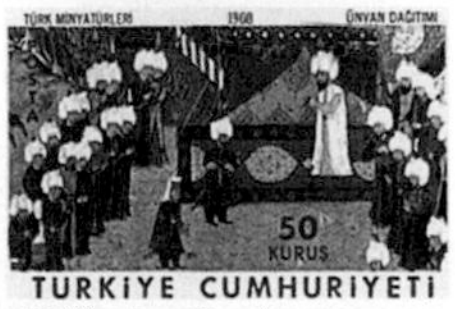

379 "The Investiture"

1968. Turkish Book Miniatures. Multicoloured.

2230		50k. Type **379**	1·00	30
2231		60k. "Suleiman the Magnificent receiving an ambassador" (vert)	1·10	30
2232		90k. "The Sultan's Archery Practice"	1·60	55
2233		100k. "The Musicians"	2·50	75

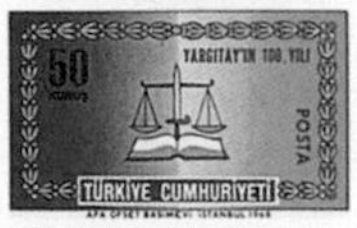

380 Scales of Justice

1968. Turkish Courts Centenary. Multicoloured. (a) Supreme Court.

2234		50k. Type **380**	40	15
2235		60k. Ahmet Cevdet Pasha (president) and scroll	40	15

(b) Court of Appeal.

2236		50k. Book	40	15
2237		60k. Mithat Pasha (first president) and scroll	40	15

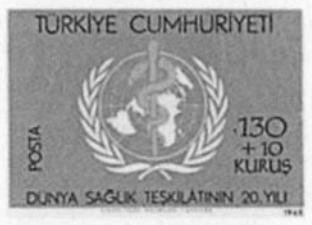

381 W.H.O. Emblem

1968. 20th Anniv of W.H.O.
| 2238 | **381** | 130k.+10k. yellow, black and blue | 80 | 45 |

382 Europa "Key"

1968. Europa.
| 2239 | **382** | 100k. yellow, red and blue | 2·10 | 1·10 |
| 2240 | **382** | 130k. yellow, red & green | 3·00 | 2·30 |

383 Etem Pasha and Dr. Marko

1968. Turkish Red Crescent Fund. Multicoloured.
2241	50k.+10k. Type **383**	40	30
2242	60k.+10k. Omer Pasha and Dr. Abdullah	65	45
2243	100k.+10k. Kemal Ataturk and Dr. Refik Saydam in front of Red Crescent Headquarters (vert)	1·00	60

384 "Kismet"

1968. Sadun Boro's World Voyage in Ketch "Kismet".
| 2244 | **384** | 50k. multicoloured | 80 | 25 |

385 "Protection against Usury" (after Koseoglu)

1968. Centenary of Pawnbroking Office, Istanbul.
| 2245 | **385** | 50k. multicoloured | 50 | 40 |

386 Battle of Sakarya and Obverse of Medal

1968. Independence Medal. Multicoloured.
| 2246 | 50k. Type **386** | 25 | 15 |
| 2247 | 130k. National Anthem and reverse of medal | 1·00 | 60 |

387 Old and New Emblems within "100"

1968. Centenary of Galatasaray High School. Multicoloured.
2248	50k. Type **387**	25	25
2249	60k. Gulbaba offering flowers to Bayazet II	40	30
2250	100k. Kemal Ataturk and School Building	1·00	60

388 President De Gaulle

1968. President De Gaulle's Visit to Turkey.
| 2251 | **388** | 130k. multicoloured | 1·20 | 85 |

389 Kemal Ataturk

1968. 30th Death Anniv of Kemal Ataturk.
2252	**389**	30k. black and yellow	25	10
2253	-	50k. black and green	25	15
2254	-	60k. black and turquoise	40	25
2255	-	100k. black, green and bistre	90	40
2256	-	250k. multicoloured	2·30	85

DESIGNS: 50k. Ataturk's Cenotaph; 60k. Ataturk at railway carriage window. (32½×43 mm): 100k. Ataturk's portrait and "address to youth"; 250k. Ataturk in military uniform.

1968. Greetings Card Stamps. As T **358** but dated "1968".
| 2257 | 10k. black and mauve | 15 | 10 |
| 2258 | 10k. black and blue | 15 | 10 |

DESIGNS: Equestrian statues of Ataturk at: No. 2257 Antakya; No. 2258 Zonguldak.

390 Ince Minara Mosque, Konya

1968. Historic Buildings.
2259	**390**	1k. sepia and brown	10	15
2260	-	10k. maroon and purple	25	10
2261	-	50k. green and grey	90	10
2262	-	100k. green & light green	3·00	15
2263	-	200k. blue and light blue	2·00	25

DESIGNS: 10k. Doner Kumbet (tomb), Kayseri; 50k. Karatay University, Konya; 100k. Ortakoy Mosque, Istanbul; 200k. Ulu Mosque, Divrigi.

391 Dove and N.A.T.O. Emblem

1969. 20th Anniv of N.A.T.O.
| 2264 | **391** | 50k.+10k. black, blue and green | 40 | 40 |
| 2265 | - | 130k.+10k. gold, blue and deep blue | 80 | 75 |

DESIGN: 130k. Stars around globe and N.A.T.O. emblem.

392 "Education"

1969. Turkish Economy.
2266	**392**	1k. black and red	10	10
2267	**392**	1k. black and green	10	10
2268	**392**	1k. black and violet	10	10
2269	**392**	1k. black and brown	10	10
2270	**392**	1k. black and grey	10	10
2271	-	50k. brown and ochre	80	10
2272	-	90k. black and olive	1·20	10
2273	-	100k. red and black	1·60	10
2274	-	180k. violet and orange	3·25	30

DESIGNS: 50k. Farm workers and tractor ("Agriculture"); 90k. Ladle, factory and cogwheel ("Industry"); 100k. Road sign and graph ("Highways"); 180k. Derricks ("Oil Industry").

393 I.L.O. Emblem

1969. 50th Anniv of I.L.O.
| 2275 | **393** | 130k. red and black | 60 | 40 |

394 "Hafsa Sultan" (unknown artist)

1969. Hafsa Sultan (medical pioneer) Commem.
| 2276 | **394** | 60k. multicoloured | 50 | 40 |

395 Colonnade

1969. Europa.
| 2277 | **395** | 100k. multicoloured | 1·20 | 1·10 |
| 2278 | **395** | 130k. multicoloured | 2·10 | 1·90 |

396 Kemal Ataturk in 1919

1969. 50th Anniv of Kemal Ataturk's Landing at Samsun. Multicoloured.
| 2279 | 50k. Type **396** | 35 | 15 |
| 2280 | 60k. Cargo liner "Bandirma" (horiz) | 50 | 25 |

397 Symbolic Map of Istanbul

1969. 22nd Int Chambers of Commerce Congress, Istanbul.
| 2281 | **397** | 130k. multicoloured | 60 | 25 |

398 "Suleiman the Great holding Audience" (16th-cent Turkish miniature)

1969. Fifth Anniv of Regional Co-operation for Development Pact Miniatures. Multicoloured.
2282	50k. Type **398**	25	15
2283	80k. "Kneeling Servant" (17th-cent Persian)	65	40
2284	130k. "Lady on Balcony" (18th-cent Mogul–Pakistan)	1·50	75

399 Kemal Ataturk in Civilian Dress

1969. 50th Anniv of Erzurum Congress.
| 2285 | **399** | 50k. black and violet | 40 | 25 |
| 2286 | - | 60k. black and green | 40 | 25 |

DESIGN—HORIZ: 60k. Ataturk's statue, Erzurum.

401 Red Cross Societies' Emblems

1969. 21st International Red Cross Conf, Istanbul.
| 2291 | **401** | 100k.+10k. red, blue and ultramarine | 40 | 40 |
| 2292 | - | 130k.+10k. mult | 60 | 45 |

DESIGN: 130k. Conference emblem and silhouette of Istanbul.

402 Congress Hall

1969. 50th Anniv of Sivas Congress.
| 2293 | **402** | 50k. purple, black and red | 40 | 25 |
| 2294 | - | 60k. olive, black & yellow | 40 | 25 |

DESIGN: 60k. Congress delegates.

403 Halay Scarf Dance

1969. Turkish Folk-dances. Multicoloured.
2295	30k. Bar dancers	35	15
2296	50k. Caydacira "candle" dance	50	25
2297	60k. Type **403**	75	25
2298	100k. Kilic-Kalkan sword dance	1·30	45
2299	130k. Zeybek dance (vert)	1·60	85

404 Bleriot XI "Prince Celaladdin"

1969. 55th Anniv of First Turkish Airmail Service.
| 2300 | **404** | 60k. deep blue and blue | 35 | 25 |
| 2301 | - | 75k. black and bistre | 35 | 25 |

DESIGN: 75k. 1914 First Flight cover.

405 "Kutadgu Bilig"

1969. 900th Anniv of "Kutadgu Bilig" (political manual) Compilation.
| 2302 | **405** | 130k. brown, gold and bistre | 60 | 40 |

1969. Greetings Card Stamp. As T **358**.
| 2303 | 10k. brown and green | 10 | 10 |

DESIGN: 10k. Equestrian statue of Ataturk at Bursa.

406 "Ataturk's Arrival" (S. Tuna)

1969. 50th Anniv of Kemal Ataturk's Arrival in Ankara. Multicoloured.
| 2304 | 50k. Type **406** | 65 | 30 |
| 2305 | 60k. Ataturk's motorcade | 1·00 | 45 |

407 "Erosion Control"

1970. Nature Conservation Year. Multicoloured.
2306	50k.+10k. Type **407**	40	40
2307	60k.+10k. "Protection of Flora"	40	40
2308	130k.+10k. "Protection of Wildlife"	1·60	1·10

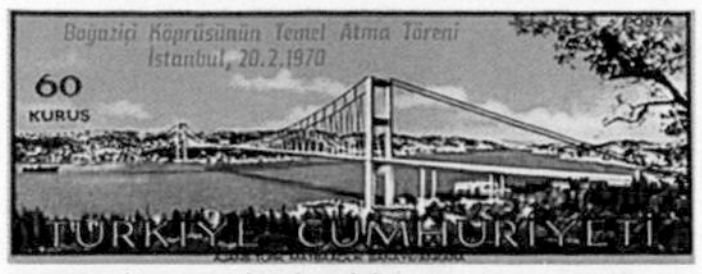

408 Bosphorus Bridge (model)

1970. Commencement of Work on Bosphorus Bridge. Multicoloured.

2309		60k. Type **408**	60	40
2310		130k. Symbolic bridge linking Europe and Asia	1·50	1·10

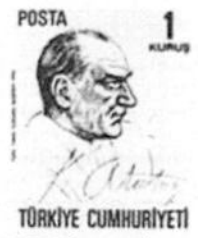

409 Ataturk and Signature

1970

2311	**409**	1k. brown and red	25	10
2312	**409**	50k. green and olive	60	10

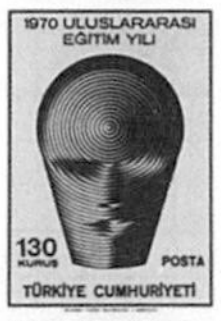

410 Education Year Emblem

1970. International Education Year.

2313	**410**	130k. blue, purple & mve	75	55

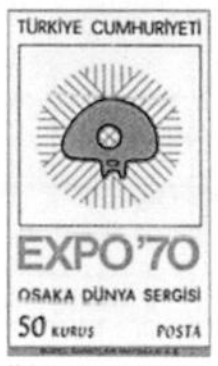

[illegible] Pavilion Emblem

1970. World Fair "Expo '70", Osaka, Japan. Multicoloured.

2314		50k. Type **411**	35	15
2315		100k. Turkish pavilion and Expo emblem	50	30

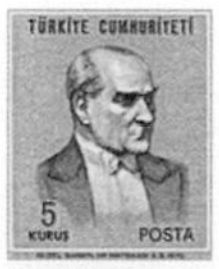

412 Kemal Ataturk

1970. Kemal Ataturk

2316	**412**	5k. black and silver	15	10
2317	**412**	30k. black and bistre	25	10
2318	**412**	50k. black and pink	75	10
2319	**412**	75k. black and lilac	1·50	10
2320	**412**	100k. black and blue	1·10	10

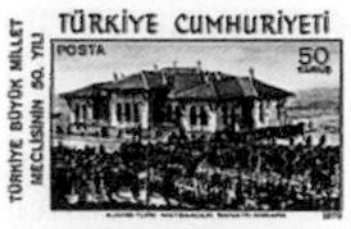

413 Opening Ceremony

1970. 50th Anniv of Turkish National Assembly. Multicoloured.

2321		50k. Type **413**	40	15
2322		60k. First Assembly in session	40	15

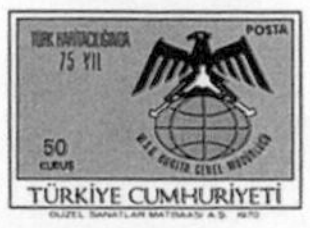

414 Emblem of Cartography Directorate

1970. "75 Years of Turkish Cartography". Multicoloured.

2323		50k. Type **414**	35	15
2324		60k. Dornier Do-28 airplane and contour map	40	25
2325		100k. Survey equipment	75	40
2326		130k. Lt.-Gen. Mehmet Sevki Pasha and relief map of Turkey	1·00	60

Nos. 2324 and 2326 are larger, size 48×33 mm.

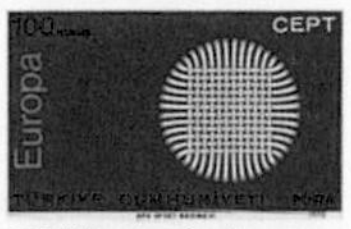

415 "Flaming Sun"

1970. Europa.

2327	**415**	100k. red, orange & black	2·10	1·10
2328	**415**	130k. green, orange & blk	2·10	1·10

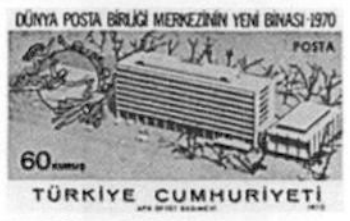

416 New U.P.U. Headquarters Building

1970. New U.P.U. Headquarters Building, Berne.

2329	**416**	60k. black, blue & lt blue	35	25
2330	**416**	130k. black, green and light green	65	40

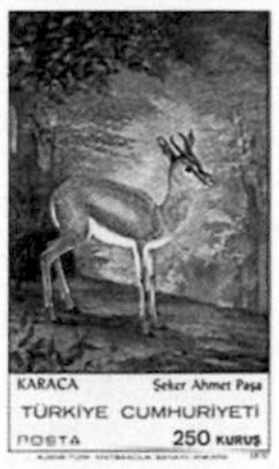

417 "Roe-deer" (Seker Ahmet Pasha)

1970. Turkish Paintings. Multicoloured.

2331		250k. Type **417**	1·20	90
2332		250k. "Lady with Mimosa" (Osman Hamdi)	1·20	90

See also Nos. 2349/50, 2364/5, 2396/7, 2416/17 and 2443/4.

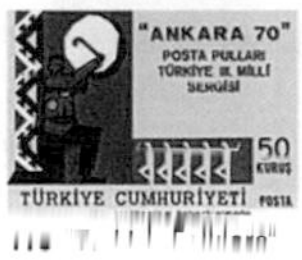

[illegible]

1970. "Ankara 70" National Stamp Exhibition. Multicoloured.

2333		10k. "Tree" of stamps and open album (vert)	15	10
2334		50k. Type **418**	35	15
2335		60k. Ataturk statue and "stamps"	40	15
MS2336		79×109 mm. 130k. Symbolic dove	2·50	2·75

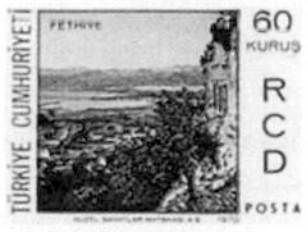

419 Fethiye (Turkey)

1970. Sixth Anniv of Regional Co-operation for Development. Multicoloured.

2337		60k. Type **419**	35	15
2338		80k. Seeyo-Se-Pol Bridge, Isfahan (Iran)	50	30
2339		130k. Saiful Malook Lake (Pakistan)	80	45

No. 2338 is larger 41×26 mm.

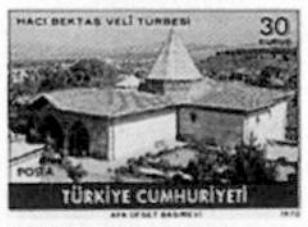

420 Tomb of Haci Bektas Veli

1970. 700th Death Anniv of Haci Bektas Veli (mystic). Multicoloured.

2340		30k. Type **420**	25	15
2341		100k. Sultan Balim's tomb (vert)	80	40
2342		180k. Haci Bektas Veli (vert)	1·40	60

No. 2342 is larger, size 32×49 mm.

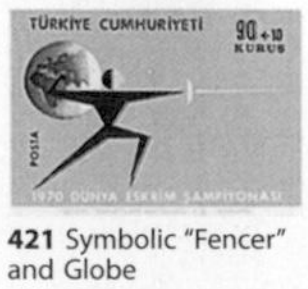

421 Symbolic "Fencer" and Globe

1970. World Fencing Championships.

2343	**421**	90k.+10k. black, blue and light blue	50	30
2344	-	130k.+10k. orange, green, black and blue	75	70

DESIGN: 130k. Modern fencer, folk-dancer and globe.

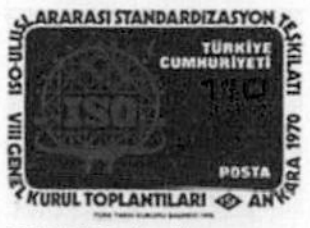

422 I.S.O. Emblem

1970. Eighth International Standardization Organization General Assembly, Ankara.

2345	**422**	110k. red, gold and black	35	15
2346	**422**	150k. blue, gold and black	60	30

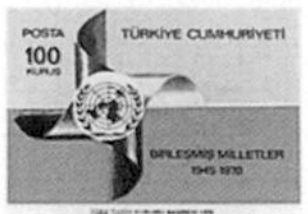

423 U.N. Emblem within Windmill

1970. 25th Anniv of United Nations. Multicoloured.

2347		100k. Type **423**	40	25
2348		220k. World's people supporting U.N. (vert)	80	55

1970. Turkish Paintings. As T **417**. Multicoloured.

2349		250k. "Fevzi Cakmak" (Avni Lifij) (vert)	1·20	90
2350		250k. "Fishing-boats" (Nazmi Ziya) (75×33 mm)	1·20	90

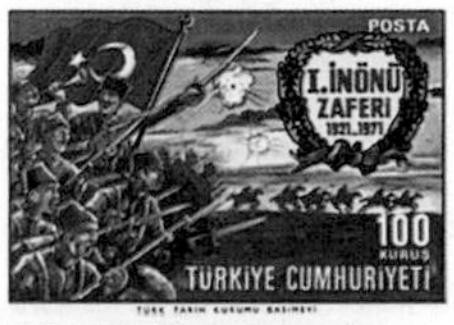

424 Turkish Troops Advancing

1971. 50th Anniv of First Battle of Inonu.

2351	**424**	100k. multicoloured	80	40

See also No. 2368.

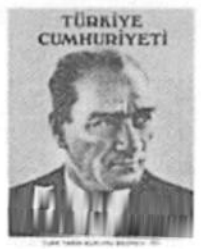

425 Kemal Ataturk

1971. Kemal Ataturk

2352	**425**	5k. blue and grey	15	10
2353	**425**	25k. red and grey	1·10	10
2354	-	25k. brown and pink	40	10
2355	**425**	100k. violet and grey	2·50	10
2356	-	100k. green and flesh	2·10	15
2357	-	250k. blue and drab	3·00	15
2358	**425**	400k. green and bistre	3·75	15

DESIGNS: Nos. 2354, 2356 and 2357, Portraits similar to Type **425** but larger, 21×26 mm, and with face value at bottom right.

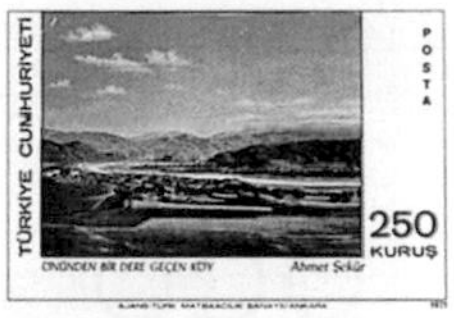

428 "Turkish Village" (A. Sekur)

1971. Turkish Paintings. Multicoloured.

2364		250k. Type **428**	1·20	1·10
2365		250k. "Yildiz Palace Garden" (A. R. Bicakcilar)	1·20	1·10

See also Nos. 2396/7, 2416/17 and 2443/4.

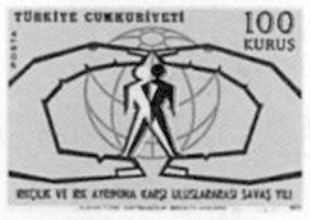

429 Hands enclosing "Four Races"

1971. Racial Equality Year.

2366	**429**	100k. multicoloured	35	15
2367	**429**	250k. multicoloured	1·00	60

1971. 50th Anniv of Second Battle of Inonu. Design similar to T **424**. Multicoloured.

2368		100k. Turkish machine-gunners	80	40

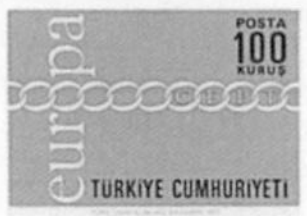

430 Europa Chain

1971. Europa.

2369	**430**	100k. violet, yellow & bl	1·60	75
2370	**430**	150k. green, red & orange	3·25	1·50

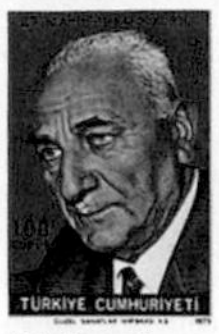

431 Pres. C. Gursel

1971. 11th Anniv of 27 May 1960 Revolution.

2371	**431**	100k. multicoloured	50	25

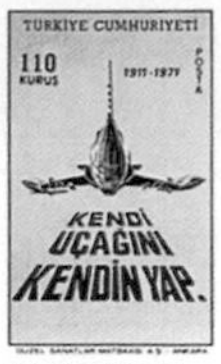

432 Lockhead Super Starfighter

1971. Air. "60 Years of Turkish Aviation". Multicoloured.

2372		110k. Type **432**	1·00	15
2373		200k. Victory Monument, Afyon and aircraft	2·10	25
2374		250k. Air Force emblem and jet fighters (horiz)	2·10	25
2375		325k. Lockheed Super Starfighters and pilot	3·00	30
2376		400k. Bleriot XI airplane of 1911 (horiz)	3·50	45
2377		475k. Hezarfen Celebi's "bird flight" from Galata Tower (horiz)	4·00	55

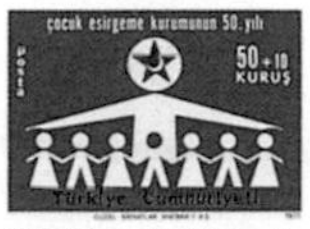

433 "Care of Children"

1971. 50th Anniv of Children's Protection Society.

[illegible]			15	15
2379	-	100k.+15k. mult	35	30
2380	-	110k.+15k. mult	50	30

DESIGNS—VERT: 100k. Child standing on protective hand. HORIZ: 110k. Mother and child.

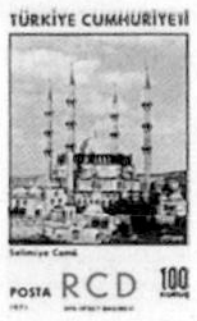

434 Selimiye Mosque, Edirne

1971. Seventh Anniv of Regional Co-operation for Development Pact Mosques. Multicoloured.

2381		100k. Type **434**	50	15
2382		150k. Chalharbagh Mosque School (Iran)	50	30
2383		200k. Badshahi Mosque (Pakistan) (horiz)	80	40

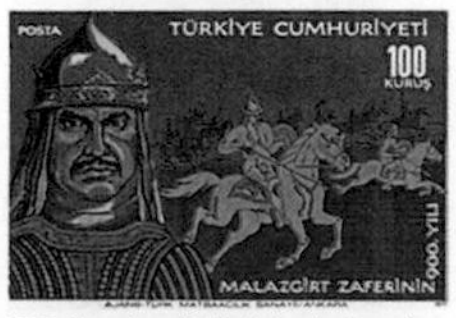

435 Alpaslan (Seljuk leader) and Cavalry

1971. 900th Anniv of Battle of Malazgirt.

2384	**435**	100k. multicoloured	50	25
2385	-	250k. red, yellow & black	1·20	55

DESIGN: 250k. Seljuk mounted archer.

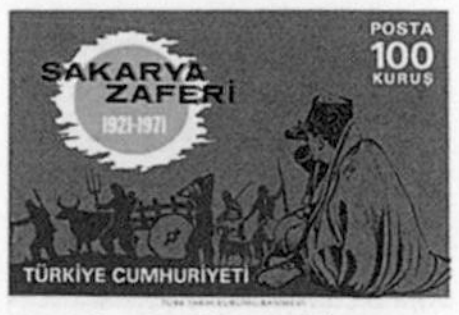

436 Officer and Troop Column

1971. 50th Anniv of Battle of Sakarya.

2386	**436**	100k. multicoloured	80	40

437 Diesel Train and Map
(Turkey–Iran Line)

1971. International Rail Links.

2387	-	100k. multicoloured	60	25
2388	-	110k. violet and blue	60	25
2389	**437**	250k. multicoloured	1·30	40

DESIGNS: 100k. Diesel train crossing bridge (Turkey–Bulgaria line); 110k. Train ferry "Orhan Atliman", Lake Van (Turkey–Iran line).

438 Football

1971. Mediterranean Games, Izmir.

2390	**438**	100k. black, violet & blue	40	15
2391	-	200k. multicoloured	80	40

MS2392 50×95 mm. 250k. multicoloured. Imperf | | 2·10 | 1·90

DESIGNS—VERT: 200k. "Athlete and stadium"; 250k. "Athlete putting the shot, and map".

439 Tomb of Cyrus the Great

1971. 2500th Anniv of Persian Empire.

2393	**439**	25k. multicoloured	25	15
2394	-	100k. multicoloured	50	25
2395	-	150k. brown and drab	1·30	40

DESIGNS—VERT: 100k. Persian mosaic of woman. HORIZ: 150k. Kemal Ataturk and Riza Shah Pahlavi.

1971. Turkish Paintings. As T **428**. Multicoloured.

2396		250k. "Sultan Mohammed I and Entourage"	1·00	75
2397		250k. "Cinili Kosk Palace"	1·00	75

441 UNICEF
Emblem

1971. 25th Anniv of UNICEF.

2404	**441**	100k.+10k. mult	40	25
2405	**441**	250k.+15k. mult	1·00	55

442 Yunus Emre

1971. 650th Death Anniv of Yunus Emre (folk-poet).

2406	**442**	100k. multicoloured	50	30

443 First Turkish Map of the World (1072) and Book Year Emblem

1972. International Book Year.

2407	**443**	100k. multicoloured	50	25

444 Doves and
N.A.T.O.
Emblem

1972. 20th Anniv of Turkey's Membership of N.A.T.O.

2408	**444**	100k. black, grey & green	1·30	75
2409	**444**	250k. black, grey and blue	2·00	1·10

445 Human
Heart

1972. World Health Day.

2410	**445**	250k.+25k. red, black and grey	80	60

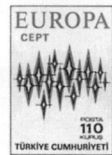

447 "Communications"

1972. Europa.

2414	**447**	110k. multicoloured	3·25	90
2415	**447**	250k. multicoloured	5·00	1·40

1972. Turkish Paintings. As T **428**. Multicoloured.

2416		250k. "Gebze" (Osman Hamdi)	1·20	75
2417		250k. "Forest" (S. A. Pasa)	1·20	75

1972. As T **358**.

2418		25k. black and brown	10	10

DESIGN: 25k. Equestrian statue of Ataturk at Ankara.

448 "Fisherman" (G. Dareli)

1972. Regional Co-operation for Development. Multicoloured.

2419		100k. Type **448**	1·00	30
2420		125k. "Will and Power" (Chughtai)	1·20	70
2421		150k. "Iranian Woman" (Behzad)	1·50	90

449 Olympic Rings

1972. Olympic Games, Munich.

2422	**449**	100k.+15k. mult	40	30
2423	-	110k.+25k. mult	40	30
2424	-	250k.+25k. mult	90	85

DESIGNS: 110k. "Athletes"; 250k. "Stadium".

450 Ataturk at Observation Post

1972. 50th Anniv of Turkish War of Liberation. Multicoloured. (a) The Great Offensive.

2425		100k. Type **450**	80	15
2426		110k. Artillery	80	15

(b) Commander-in-Chief's Offensive.

2427		100k. Hand-to-hand fighting	80	40

(c) Entry into Izmir.

2428		100k. Commanders in open car	80	40

451 "Diagnosis and
Cure"

1972. Fight against Cancer.

2429	**451**	100k. red, black and blue	40	15

452 Kemal
Ataturk

1972. Various sizes.

2430	**452**	5k. light blue on blue	10	10
2430a	**452**	25k. orange on orange	10	10
2431	**452**	100k. lake on blue	1·50	10
2431a	**452**	100k. light grey on grey	25	10
2431b	**452**	100k. olive on green	25	10
2432	**452**	110k. blue on blue	1·50	10
2432a	**452**	125k. green and grey	1·50	10
2433	**452**	150k. brown on buff	1·50	10
2433a	**452**	150k. green on green	35	10
2434	**452**	175k. purple on yellow	1·50	10
2434a	**452**	200k. red on buff	1·50	10
2434b	**452**	200k. brown on buff	60	10
2435	**452**	250k. lilac on pink	60	10
2435a	**452**	400k. turquoise on blue	65	40
2436	**452**	500k. violet on pink	3·75	25
2437	**452**	500k. blue on blue	1·20	30
2438	**452**	10l. mauve on pink	2·50	45

453 U.I.C.
Emblem

1972. 50th Anniv of International Railway Union.

2439	**453**	100k. brown, buff & grn	50	15

454 University Emblem

1973. Bicent of Technical University, Istanbul.

2440	**454**	100k.+25k. mult	50	40

455 Europa "Posthorn"

1973. Europa.

2441	**455**	110k. multicoloured	3·00	85
2442	**455**	250k. multicoloured	5·25	1·40

1973. Turkish Painters. As T **428**. Multicoloured.

2443		250k. "Old Almshouses, Istanbul" (Ahmet Ziya Akbulut) (horiz)	1·20	75
2444		250k. "Flowers in Vase" (Suleyman Seyyit) (vert)	1·20	75

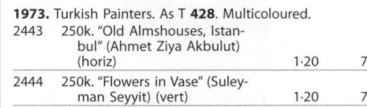

456 Helmet and
Sword

1973. Land Forces' Day.

2445	**456**	90k. green, brown & grey	25	25
2446	-	100k. green, brown and light green	35	25

DESIGN: 100k. As Type **456**, but wreath enclosing design.

457 Carved
Head, Tomb of
Antiochus I
(Turkey)

1973. Regional Co-operation for Development. Multicoloured.

2447		100k. Type **457**	35	15
2448		150k. Statue, Lut excavations (Iran)	60	30
2449		200k. Street in Moenjodaro (Pakistan)	75	45

458 Peace Dove and "50"

1973. 50th Anniv of Lausanne Peace Treaty.

2450	**458**	100k.+25k. mult	50	25

459 Minelayer "Nusret
II"

1973. Bicentenary of Turkish Navy. Multicoloured.

2451		5k. Type **459**	10	10
2452		25k. Destroyer "Istanbul"	15	10
2453		100k. Motor torpedo-boat "Simsek"	60	15
2454		250k. Cadet brig "Nurud-i-Futuh" (48×32 mm)	3·25	55

460 "Al-Biruni"
(from
16th-century
miniature)

1973. Millenary of Abu Reihan al-Biruni.

2455	**460**	250k. multicoloured	75	40

461 "Equal
Opportunity"

1973. Centenary of Darussafaka High School.

2456	**461**	100k. multicoloured	35	25

463 "Balkanfila"
Emblem

1973. "Balkanfila IV" Stamp Exhibition, Izmir (1st issue).

2458	**463**	100k. multicoloured	35	25

See also Nos. 2462/3.

464 Sivas Sheepdog

1973. Animals.

2459	**464**	25k. blue, yellow & black	25	15
2460	-	100k. yellow, black & bl	1·00	15

DESIGN: 100k. Angora cat.

465 Kemal Ataturk

1973. 35th Death Anniv of Kemal Ataturk.
| 2461 | 465 | 100k. brown and drab | 50 | 25 |

466 Bosphorus and "Stamps"

1973. "Balkanfila IV" Stamp Exhibition (2nd issue). Multicoloured.
| 2462 | | 110k. Type 466 | 25 | 15 |
| 2463 | | 250k. "Balkanfila" in decorative script | 60 | 45 |

467 "Flower" Emblem

1973. 50th Anniv of Republic.
2464	467	100k. red, violet and blue	25	15
2465	-	250k. multicoloured	75	40
2466	-	475k. yellow and blue	1·10	75
MS2467		79×110 mm. 500k. multicoloured	3·75	3·50

DESIGNS: As T **467**—250k. "Hands" supporting "50"; 475k. Cogwheel and ears of corn. 32×49 mm. 500k. Kemal Ataturk.

468 Bosphorus Bridge

1973. Opening of Bosphorus Bridge, Istanbul. Multicoloured.
| 2468 | | 100k. Type 468 | 40 | 25 |
| 2469 | | 150k. View of Bosphorus and bridge | 60 | 30 |

469 Bosphorus Bridge and UNICEF Emblem

1973. UNICEF Ceremony. Children of Europe and Asia linked by Bosphorus Bridge.
| 2470 | 469 | 200k. multicoloured | 60 | 45 |

470 Mevlana Celaleddin

1973. 700th Death Anniv of Mevlana Celaleddin (poet and mystic).
| 2471 | - | 100k. green, blue & black | 35 | 10 |
| 2472 | 470 | 250k. multicoloured | 60 | 45 |

DESIGN: 100k. Tomb and dancing dervishes.

471 Cotton

1973. Export Products.
| 2473 | 471 | 75k. grey, blue and black | 25 | 10 |

2474	-	90k. bistre, blue and black	25	15
2475	-	100k. black, blue & green	35	15
2476	-	250k. multicoloured	1·80	25
2477	-	325k. yellow, blue & blk	1·50	40
2478	-	475k. black, blue & brn	2·30	55

DESIGNS: 90k. Grapes; 100k. Figs; 250k. Citrus fruits; 325k. Tobacco; 475k. Hazelnuts.

472 Fokker Fellowship

1973. Air. Multicoloured.
| 2479 | | 110k. Type 472 | 50 | 15 |
| 2480 | | 250k. Douglas DC-10 | 1·00 | 40 |

473 President Inonu

1973. President Inonu's Death.
| 2481 | 473 | 100k. brown and buff | 40 | 15 |

474 "Statue of a King" (Hittite era)

1974. Europa. Sculptures. Multicoloured.
| 2482 | | 110k. Type 474 | 8·25 | 1·10 |
| 2483 | | 250k. "Statuette of a Child" (c. 2000 B.C.) | 8·25 | 1·90 |

475 Doctor and Patient

1974. 75th Anniv of Sisli Paediatrics Hospital.
| 2484 | 475 | 110k. black, grey and blue | 35 | 15 |

476 Silver and Gold Idol

1974. Archaeological Treasures. Multicoloured.
2485		125k. Type 476	25	15
2486		175k. Painted jar (horiz)	40	25
2487		200k. Bulls (statuettes) (horiz)	60	30
2488		250k. Jug	80	45

477 Population Year Emblem

1974. World Population Year.
| 2489 | 477 | 250k.+25k. mult | 75 | 55 |

479 Turkish Carpet

1974. Regional Co-operation for Development. Multicoloured.
2496		100k. Type 479	1·20	55
2497		150k. Iranian carpet	1·60	1·20
2498		200k. Pakistani carpet	3·00	55

480 Dove and Map of Cyprus

1974. Turkish Intervention in Cyprus.
| 2499 | 480 | 250k. multicoloured | 1·00 | 45 |

481 "Getting to Grips"

1974. World Free-style Wrestling Championships, Ankara. Multicoloured.
2500		90k. Type 481	15	15
2501		100k. "Throw" (vert)	35	25
2502		250k. "Lock"	75	55

482 Dove with Letter

1974. Centenary of Universal Postal Union.
2503	482	110k. gold, dp blue & bl	25	15
2504	-	200k. brown and green	50	30
2505	-	250k. multicoloured	60	55

DESIGNS: 200k. Dove; 250k. Arrows encircling globe.

483 Open Book (Law Reform)

1974. Works and Reforms of Ataturk (1st series).
2506	483	50k. black and blue	10	10
2507	-	150k. multicoloured	35	25
2508	-	400k. multicoloured	1·00	70

DESIGNS—VERT: 150k. "Tree" ("National Economy"); 400k. Students facing sun ("Reform of Education").
See also Nos. 2543/5, 2566/8, 2597/9, 2639/41 and 2670/2.

484 Marconi

1974. Birth Centenary of Marconi (radio pioneer).
| 2509 | 484 | 250k.+25k. black, brown and red | 75 | 55 |

485 Arrows (3rd Five Year Development Programme)

1974. "Turkish Development".
| 2510 | 485 | 25k. black and brown | 15 | 10 |
| 2511 | - | 100k. grey and brown | 50 | 10 |

DESIGNS—HORIZ: 100k. Map of Turkey within cogwheel (industrialization).

486 Volleyball

1974. Ball Games.
2512	486	125k. black and blue	35	10
2513	-	175k. black and orange	40	15
2514	-	250k. black and green	65	30

DESIGNS: 175k. Basketball; 250k. Football.

487 Dr. Albert Schweitzer

1975. Birth Centenary of Dr. Albert Schweitzer.
| 2515 | 487 | 250k.+50k. mult | 1·00 | 85 |

488 Automatic Telex Network

1975. Posts and Telecommunications.
2516	488	5k. black and yellow	15	10
2517	-	50k. green and orange	15	10
2518	-	100k. black and blue	15	15

DESIGNS: 50k. Postal cheques; 100k. Radio link.

489 "Going to the Classroom" (I. Sivga)

1975. Children's Drawings. Multicoloured.
2519	489	25k. Type 489	10	10
2520		50k. "View from a Village" (H. Dogru)	15	10
2521		100k. "Folklore" (B. Aktan)	40	25

490 Karacaoglan Monument (H. Tuzun)

1975. Karacaoglan (musician) Commem.
| 2522 | 490 | 110k. mauve, green & brn | 40 | 15 |

491 "Orange-gathering in Hatay" (C. Tollu)

1975. Europa. Paintings. Multicoloured.
| 2523 | | 110k. Type 491 | 3·75 | 75 |
| 2524 | | 250k. "The Yoruks" (T. Zaim) | 3·75 | 1·10 |

492 Turkish Porcelain Vase

1975. Regional Co-operation for Development. Traditional Crafts. Multicoloured.
2525		110k. Type 492	1·20	30
2526		200k. Ceramic plate (Iran) (horiz)	1·60	45
2527		250k. Camel-skin vase (Pakistan)	2·10	75

493 Namibia located on Map of Africa

1975. Namibia Day.

2528	**493**	250k.+50k. mult	75	60

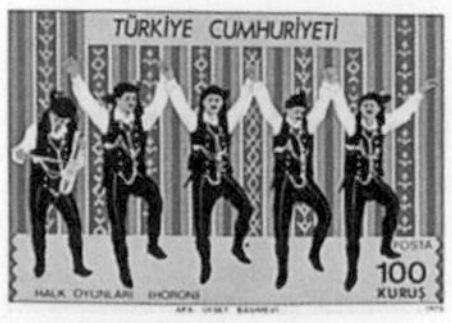

494 Horon Folk-dancers

1975. Turkish Folk Dances. Multicoloured.

2529	100k. Type **494**	40	15
2530	125k. Kasik	65	25
2531	175k. Bengi	1·00	30
2532	250k. Kasap	1·20	45
2533	325k. Kafkas (vert)	1·60	75

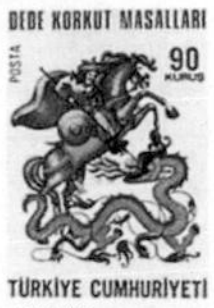

495 "Oguz Khan slaying Dragon"

1975. Tales of Dede Korkut. Multicoloured.

2534	90k. Type **495**	15	15
2535	175k. Tale of Duha Koca Oglu Deli Dumrul Hikayesi (horiz)	40	25
2536	200k. "Pillaging the Home of Salur Kazan"	50	30

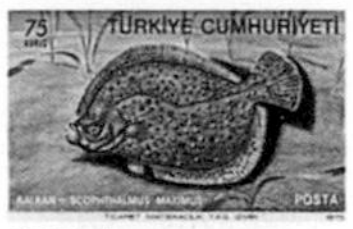

497 Turbot

1975. Fish. Multicoloured.

2538	75k. Type **497**	1·60	15
2539	90k. Common carp	2·10	15
2540	175k. Brown trout	2·50	25
2541	250k. Red mullet	3·25	60
2542	475k. Gilthead seabream	5·00	75

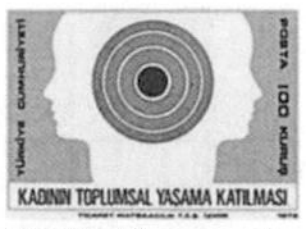

498 Two Women and Symbol (Women's Participation in Public Life)

1975. Works and Reforms of Ataturk (2nd series).

2543	**498**	100k. red, black and stone	15	10
2544	-	110k. multicoloured	25	15
2545	-	250k. multicoloured	60	25

DESIGNS—VERT: 110k. Symbol and inscription (Nationalization of Insurance Companies). HORIZ: 250k. Arrows (Orientation of the Fine Arts).

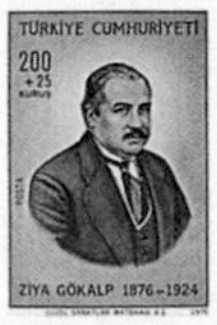

499 Z. Gokalp

1976. Birth Cent of Ziya Gokalp (philosopher).

2546	**499**	200k.+25k. mult	60	40

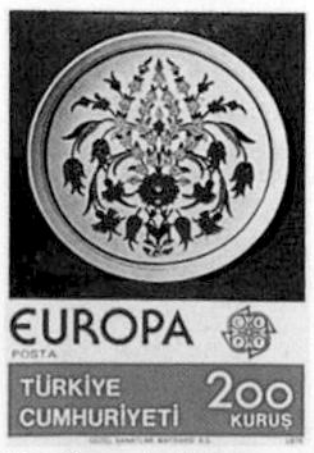

500 Ceramic Plate

1976. Europa. Multicoloured.

2547	200k. Type **500**	6·50	75
2548	400k. Dessert jug	8·25	1·90

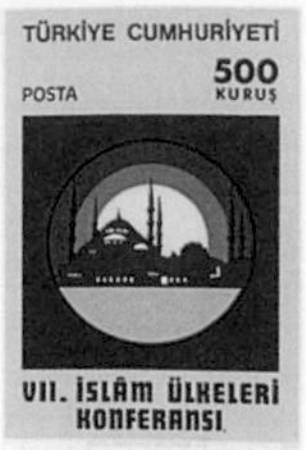

501 Silhouette of Istanbul

1976. Seventh Islamic Conference, Istanbul.

2549	**501**	500k. multicoloured	1·00	55

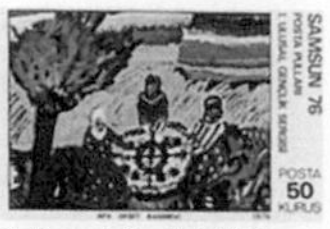

502 "Lunch in Field" (S. Yucel)

1976. "Samsun '76" Youth Stamp Exn. Multicoloured.

2550	50k. Type **502**	15	15
2551	200k. "Boats on the Bosphorus" (E. Kosemen) (vert)	25	25
2552	400k. "Winter View" (R. Cetinkaya)	60	40

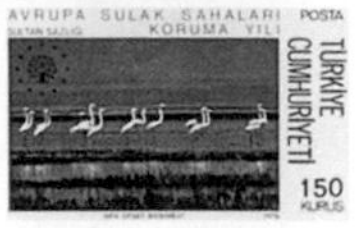

503 Sultan Marshes

1976. European Wetlands Conservation Year. Turkish Landscapes. Multicoloured.

2553	150k. Type **503**	1·60	1·40
2554	200k. Lake Manyas	1·20	55
2555	250k. Lake Borabey	1·60	75
2556	400k. Manavgat waterfalls	2·10	1·40

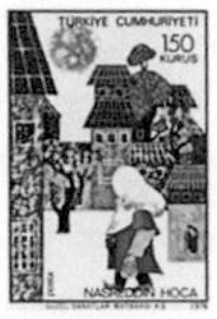

504 "Hodja with Liver"

1976. Nasreddin Hodja (humourist) Commem. "The Liver and the Kite". Multicoloured.

2557	150k. Type **504**	35	15
2558	250k. "Friend offers recipe"	65	30
2559	600k. "Kite takes liver, leaving recipe"	1·50	75

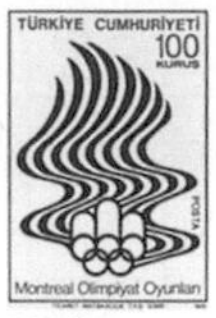

505 Games Emblem and Flame

1976. Olympic Games, Montreal.

2560	**505**	100k. red and blue	25	15
2561	-	400k. multicoloured	90	45
2562	-	600k. multicoloured	1·40	60

DESIGNS—HORIZ: 400k. "Athlete" as "76". VERT: 600k. Games emblem.

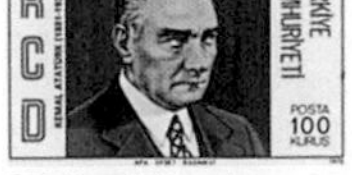

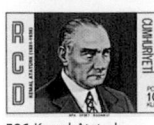

506 Kemal Ataturk (Turkey)

1976. Regional Co-operation for Development. Heads of State. Multicoloured.

2563	100k. Type **506**	15	10
2564	200k. Riza Shah Pahlavi (Iran)	50	25
2565	250k. Mohammed Ali Jinnah (Pakistan)	65	40

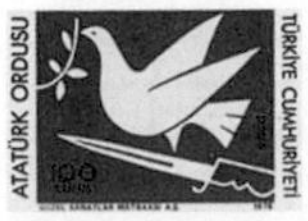

507 Peace Dove and Sword (Army Reform)

1976. Works and Reforms of Ataturk (3rd series).

2566	**507**	100k. black and red	15	10
2567	-	200k. multicoloured	40	15
2568	-	400k. multicoloured	65	40

DESIGNS: 200k. Words, books and listeners (Ataturk's speeches); 400k. Peace doves and globe ("Peace through-out the World").

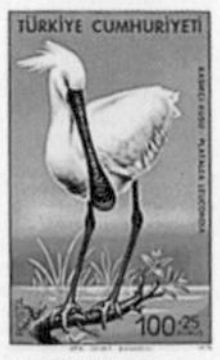

508 White Spoonbill

1976. Turkish Birds. Multicoloured.

2569	100k.+25k. Type **508**	40	25
2570	150k.+25k. European roller	65	55
2571	200k.+25k. Greater flamingo	1·10	60
2572	400k.+25k. Waldrapp (horiz)	3·00	1·70

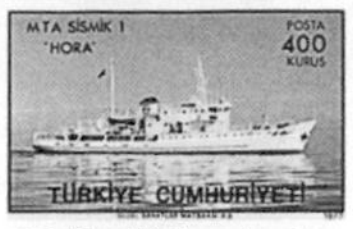

509 "Hora" (oil exploration ship)

1977

2573	**509**	400k. multicoloured	1·00	45

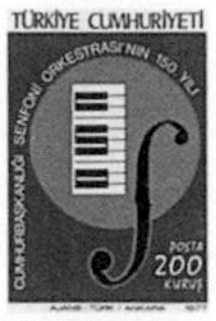

510 Musical Symbols

1977. 150th Anniv of Presidential Symphony Orchestra.

2574	**510**	200k. multicoloured	50	25

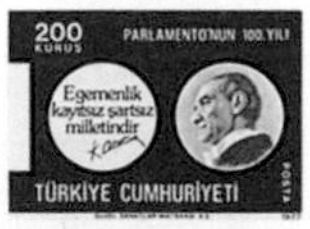

511 Kemal Ataturk in "100"

1977. Centenary of Parliament.

2575	**511**	200k. black and red	50	25
2576	-	400k. black and brown	1·00	45

DESIGN: 400k. Hand placing ballot-paper in box.

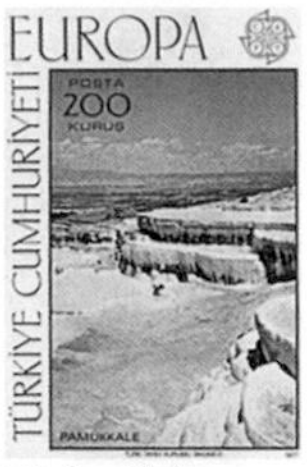

512 Pamukkale

1977. Europa. Landscapes. Multicoloured.

2577	200k. Type **512**	8·25	1·10
2578	400k. Zelve	8·25	1·90

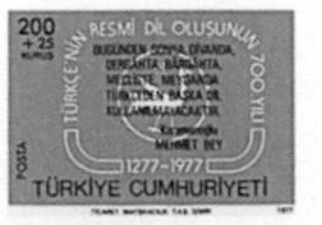

513 Edict of Karamanoglu Mehmet Bey and "Ongun" Bird

1977. 700th Anniv of Official Turkish Language.

2579	**513**	200k.+25k. black and green	50	40

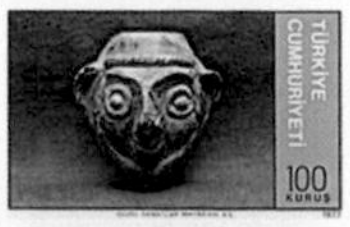

514 Head-shaped Vase, Turkey

1977. Regional Co-operation for Development. Pottery. Multicoloured.

2580	100k. Type **514**	60	15
2581	255k. Earthenware pot (Iran)	1·10	25
2582	675k. Model bullock cart (Pakistan)	2·10	75
MS2583	107×78 mm. Nos. 2580/2	8·25	7·50

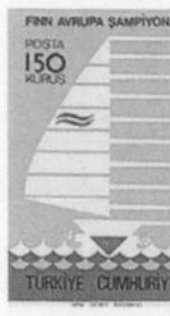

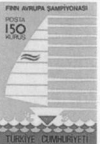

515 Stylized Sailing Yacht

1977. European Finn Class Sailing Championships.

2584	**515**	150k. black, blue and light blue	35	15
2585	-	200k. blue and deep blue	60	25
2586	-	250k. black and blue	75	40

DESIGNS—HORIZ: 200k. VERT: 250k. Both showing stylized sailing yachts.

1977. Surch **10 KURUS**.

2592	**409**	10k. on 1k. brn & red	10	10

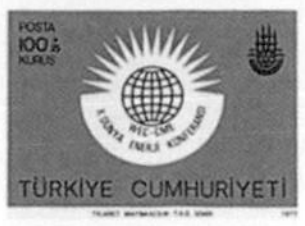

522 "Globe" and Emblem

1977. Tenth World Energy Conference.

2593	**522**	100k.+25k. black, brown and pink	35	10
2594	-	600k.+50k. red, black and blue	1·10	70

DESIGN: 600k. Similar design showing a "globe" and emblem.

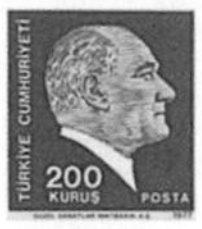

523 Kemal Ataturk

1977. Size 20½×22½ mm.

2595	**523**	200k. blue on light blue	40	10
2596	**523**	250k. turquoise on blue	60	10

See also Nos. 2619/25.

524 "Head and Book" (Rationalism)

1977. Works and Reform of Ataturk (4th series). Multicoloured.

2597	100k. Type **524**	15	10
2598	200k. Words by Ataturk (National Sovereignty)	25	15
2599	400k. Symbol (Leadership for Liberation of Nations)	65	25

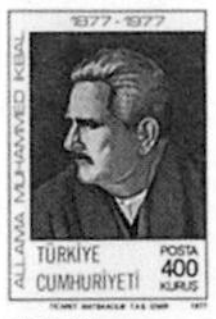

525 Allama Muhammad Iqbal

1977. Birth Centenary of Allama Muhammad Iqbal (Pakistani poet).

2600	**525**	400k. multicoloured	75	40

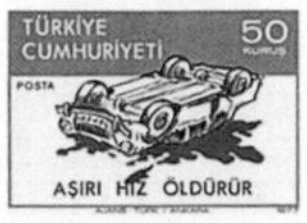

526 Overturned Car

1977. Road Safety.

2601	**526**	50k. black, blue and red	40	15
2602	-	150k. black, grey and red	15	15
2603	-	250k. black, brown & red	40	15
2604	-	500k. black, grey and red	60	15
2605	-	800k. deep green, green and red	1·10	15
2606	-	10l. green, red and black	1·20	25

DESIGNS—VERT: 150k. Arrow crossing white lines and pool of blood; 500k. "Children crossing" sign; 800k. "No overtaking" sign; 10l. Footprints in road and on pedestrian crossing. HORIZ: 250k. Tractor pulling trailer loaded with people.

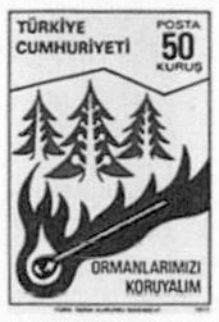

527 Lighted Match and Trees

1977. Forest Conservation.

2607	527	50k. black, red and green	25	10
2608	-	250k. black, green & grey	40	25

DESIGN: 250k. "Tree germination".
See also No. 2699.

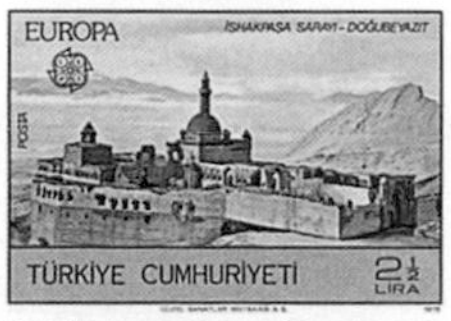

530 Ishakpasa Palace, Dogubeyazit

1978. Europa. Multicoloured.

2616	2½l. Type **530**	8·25	75
2617	5l. Anamur Castle	8·25	1·90

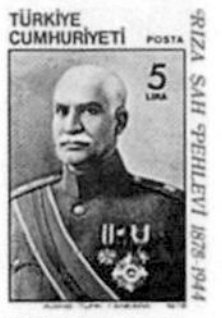

531 Riza Shah Pahlavi of Iran

1978. Birth Centenary of Riza Shah Pahlavi of Iran.

2618	531	5l. multicoloured	50	15

1978. As Type **523** but larger, 19×25 mm.

2619	10k. brown	10	10
2620	50k. grey	10	10
2621	1l. red	10	10
2622	2½l. lilac	15	10
2623	5l. blue	40	10
2624	25l. blue and light blue	1·80	40
2625	50l. orange and light orange	3·75	60

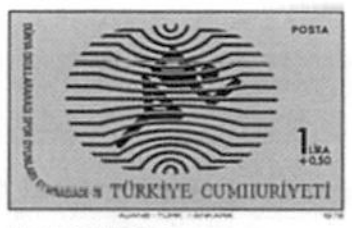

532 Athletics

1978. "Gymnasiade '78" World School Games.

2626	532	1l.+50k. deep green and green	15	10
2627	-	2½l.+50k. blue & orge	25	25
2628	-	5l.+50k. blue and pink	60	30
2629	-	8l.+50k. blue and green	1·10	75

DESIGNS: 2½l. Gymnastics; 5l. Table tennis; 8l. Swimming.

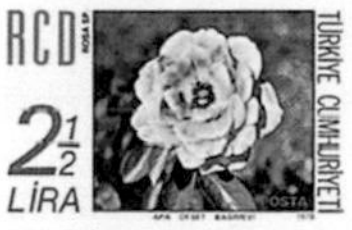

533 Salmon Rose

1978. Regional Co-operation for Development. Multicoloured.

2630	2½l. Type **533**	50	15
2631	3½l. Pink roses	75	30
2632	8l. Red roses	1·20	30

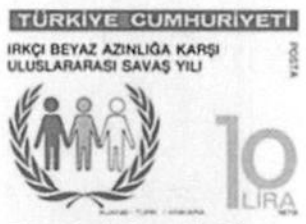

534 Anti-Apartheid Year Emblem

1978. International Anti-Apartheid Year.

2633	534	10l. multicoloured	80	40

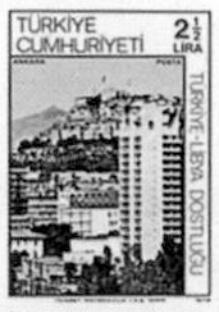

535 View of Ankara

1978. Turkish–Libyan Friendship. Multicoloured.

2634	2½l. Type **535**	40	15
2635	5l. View of Tripoli	60	25

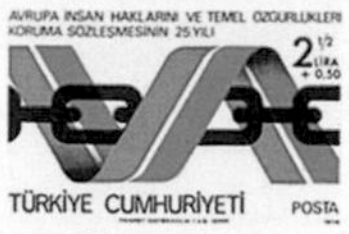

536 Ribbon and Chain

1978. 25th Anniv of European Convention on Human Rights.

2636	536	2½l.+50k. blue, green and black	40	40
2637	-	5l.+50k. red, blue and black	1·20	1·10

DESIGN: 5l. Ribbon and flower.

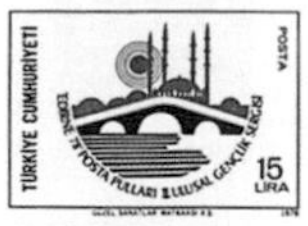

537 Mosque and Bridge

1978. "Edirne 78" Youth Philatelic Exhibition. Sheet 72×52 mm. Imperf.

MS2638 **537**	15l. blue, black and red	1·60	1·50

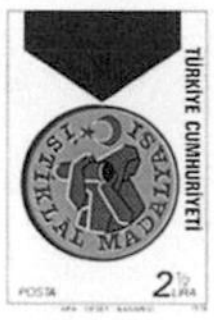

538 Independence Medal

1978. Works and Reforms of Ataturk (5th series).

2639	538	2½l. multicoloured	15	10
2640	-	3½l. red and black	35	10
2641	-	5l. multicoloured	50	25

DESIGNS—HORIZ: 3½l. Talking heads (Language reform). VERT: 5l. "ABC" in Arabic and Roman scripts (Adoption of Latin alphabet).

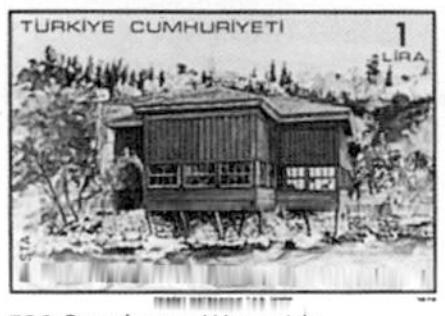

539 Bosphorus Waterside Residence of Koprulu Huseyin Pasa, Istanbul (1699)

1978. Traditional Turkish Houses. Multicoloured.

2642	1l. Type **539**	15	15
2643	2½l. Residence of Saatci Ali Efendi, Izmit, 1774	40	25
2644	3½l. House of Bey, Kula (vert)	65	45
2645	5l. House of Bahaeddin Aga, Milas (vert)	80	55
2646	8l. House of Safranbolu	2·10	1·40

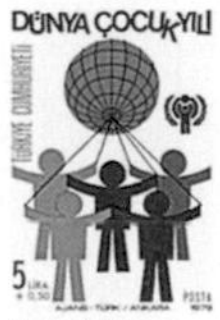

541 Children with Globe as Balloon

1979. International Year of the Child.

2649	-	2½l.+50k. black, gold and red	25	15
2650	541	5l.+50k. multicoloured	60	40
2651	-	8l.+50k. multicoloured	1·00	85

DESIGNS: 2½l. Children embracing beneath hearts; 8l. Adult and child balancing globe.

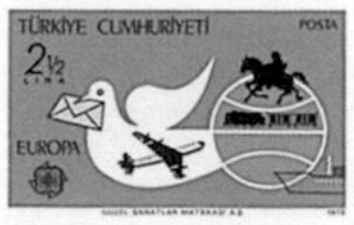

542 Mail Transport

1979. Europa.

2652	542	2½l. black, green and blue	5·00	60
2653	-	5l. orange and black	5·00	60
2654	-	7½l. black and blue	5·00	1·10

DESIGNS: 5l. Telex keyboard, morse key and telegraph poles; 7½l. Telephone dial and dish aerial.

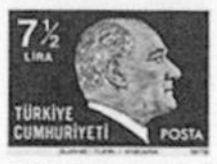

543 Kemal Ataturk

1979

2655	543	50k. green	15	10
2656	543	1l. green and light green	10	10
2657	543	2½l. lilac	10	10
2657a	543	2½l. blue	15	10
2658	543	5l. blue and light blue	25	10
2659	543	7½l. brown	60	15
2659a	543	7½l. red	60	10
2660	543	10l. mauve	1·20	40
2661	543	20l. grey	60	15
2661a	543	10l. mauve (22×22 mm)	40	10
2748	543	2½l. orange	10	10

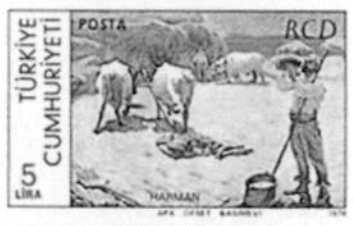

544 "Turkish Harvest" (Namik Ismail)

1979. Regional Co-operation for Development. Paintings. Multicoloured.

2662	5l. Type **544**	25	15
2663	7½l. "Iranian Goldsmith" (Kamal el Molk)	40	25
2664	10l. "Pakistan Village Scene" (Ustad Baksh)	80	40

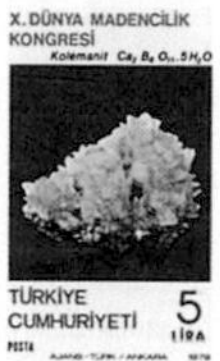

545 Colemanite

1979. Tenth World Mining Congress. Multicoloured.

2665	5l. Type **545**	35	15
2666	7½l. Chromite	50	25
2667	10l. Antimonite	75	45
2668	15l. Sulphur	1·10	70

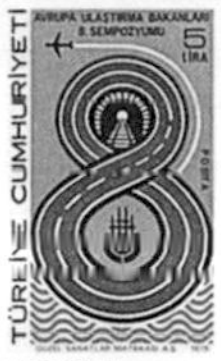

546 Highway forming Figure 8

1979. Eighth European Communications Ministers' Symposium.

2669	546	5l. multicoloured	40	40

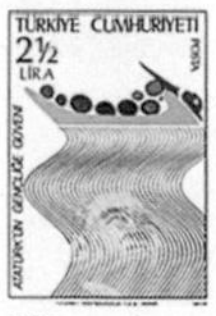

547 "Confidence in Youth"

1979. Works and Reforms of Ataturk (6th series).

2670	547	2½l. multicoloured	15	10
2671	-	3½l. multicoloured	25	10
2672	-	5l. black and orange	40	25

DESIGNS—HORIZ: 3½l. "Secularism". VERT: 5l. "National Oath".

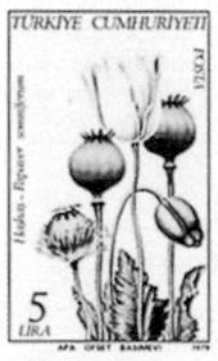

548 Poppy ("Papaver somniferum")

1979. Flowers (1st series). Multicoloured.

2673	5l. Type **548**	35	15
2674	7½l. Oleander ("Nerium oleander")	50	25
2675	10l. Late spider orchid ("Ophrys holosericea")	65	30
2676	15l. Mandrake ("Mandragora autumnalis")	1·00	45

See also Nos. 2705/8.

1979. "Ankara 79" Stamp Exhibition. Sheet 122×57 mm.

MS2677	No. 2658 ×8	12·00	10·00

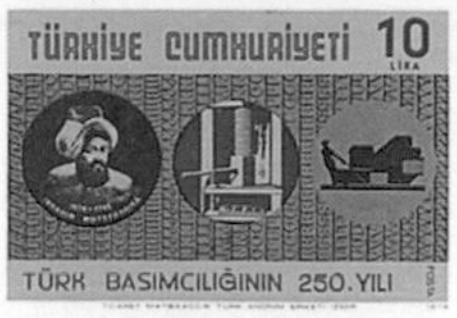

549 Ibrahim Muteferrika (first printer) and Presses

1979. 250th Anniv of Turkish Printing.

2678	549	10l. multicoloured	50	40

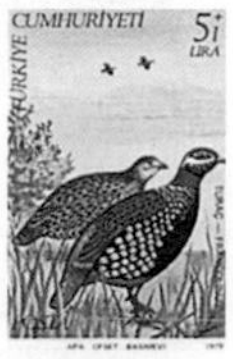

550 Black Partridge

1979. Wildlife Conservation. Multicoloured.

2679	5l.+1l. Type **550**	60	55
2680	5l.+1l. Great bustard	60	55
2681	5l.+1l. Demoiselle crane	60	55
2682	5l.+1l. Goitred gazelle	60	55
2683	5l.+1l. Mouflon	60	55

Nos. 2679/83 were issued together, se-tenant, forming a composite design.

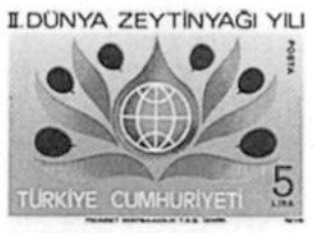

551 Olives, Leaves and Globe in Oil-drop

1979. Second World Olive-oil Year.

2684	551	5l. multicoloured	25	10
2685	-	10l. yellow and green	50	30

DESIGN. 10l. Globe in oil drop.

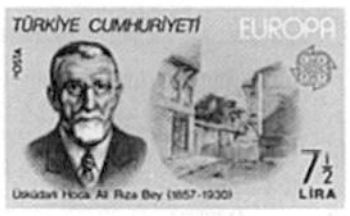

553 Uskudarli Hoca Ali Riza (artist)

1980. Europa. Multicoloured.

2692	7½l. Type **553**	2·50	40
2693	10l. Ali Sami Boyar (artist)	2·50	40
2694	20l. Dr. Hulusi Behcet (skin specialist)	2·50	75

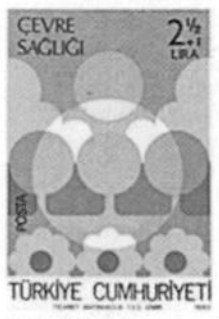

554 Flowers and Trees

1980. Environmental Protection. Multicoloured.

2695	2½l.+1l. Type **554**	10	10
2696	7½l.+1l. Sun and water	25	15
2697	15l.+1l. Factory polluting atmosphere	40	25
2698	20l.+1l. Flower surrounded by oil	50	40

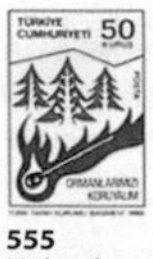

555 Lighted Match and Trees

1980. Forest Conservation.

2699	555	50k. green, red and brown	10	10

See also No. 2607.

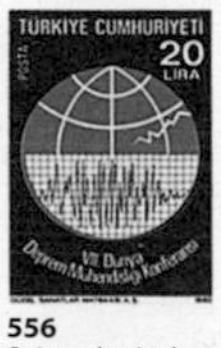

556 Seismological Graph

1980. Seventh World Conference on Earthquake Engineering.

2700	-	7½l. brown, blue & orange	25	15
2701	556	20l. black, orange & blue	60	25

DESIGN: 7½l. Pictorial representation of earthquake within globe.

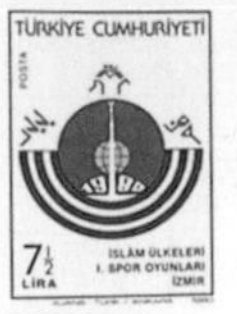

557 Games Emblem and Pictograms

1980. First Islamic Games, Izmir. Multicoloured.

2702	7½l. Type **557**	25	15
2703	20l. As No. 2702 but with different sports around emblem	60	25

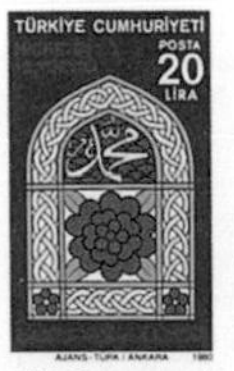

558 Ornamental Window

1980. 1400th Anniv of Hegira.

2704	558	20l. multicoloured	80	40

1980. Flowers (2nd series). As T **548**. Multicoloured.

2705	2½l. Manisa tulip ("Tulipa hayatii")	15	15
2706	7½l. Ephesian bellflower ("Campanula ephesia")	40	25
2707	15l. Crocus ("Crocus ancyrensis")	65	40
2708	20l. Anatolian orchid ("Orchis anatolica")	1·20	75

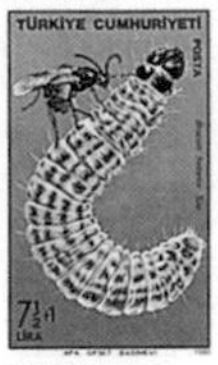

559 "Bracon hebetor" and Larva of Dark Arches Moth

1980. Useful Insects (1st series). Multicoloured.

2709	2½l.+1l. "Rodolia cardinalis" (ladybird) and cottony cushion scale	15	15
2710	7½l.+1l. Type **559**	40	25
2711	15l.+1l. Caterpillar-hunter and larva of gypsy moth	65	40
2712	20l.+1l. "Deraeocoris rutilus" (leaf bug)	1·20	75

See also Nos. 2763/6.

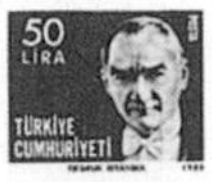

560 Kemal Ataturk

1980

2713	560	7½l. brown and pink	25	10
2714	560	10l. brown & lt brown	25	10
2715	560	20l. violet and mauve	50	10
2716	560	30l. grey and light grey	80	25
2717	560	50l. red and yellow	1·20	15
2718	560	75l. green and lt green	1·80	15
2719	560	100l. blue and light blue	3·25	30
2719a	560	15l. blue	60	10
2719b	560	20l. orange	35	10
2719c	560	65l. green	2·00	15
2719d	560	90l. mauve	2·50	30

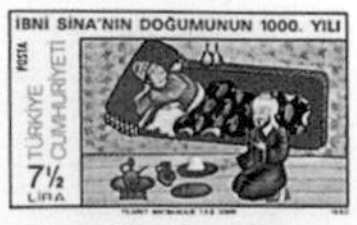

561 Ibn Sina Teaching

1980. Birth Millenary of Ibn Sina (Avicenna) (philosopher and physician). Multicoloured.

2720	7½l. Type **561**	25	15
2721	20l. Ibn Sina (vert)	1·00	25

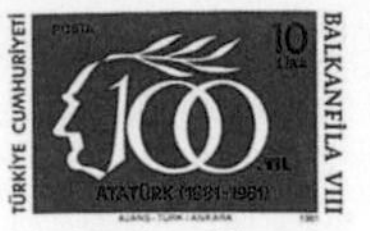

562 Ataturk and Figures "100"

1981. "Balkanfila VIII" Stamp Exhibition, Ankara.

2722	562	10l. red and black	60	25

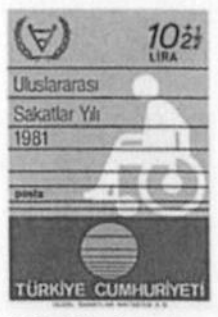

563 Disabled Person in Wheelchair

1981. International Year of Disabled Persons.

2723	563	10l.+2½l. multicoloured	25	15
2724	563	20l.+2½l. multicoloured	50	30

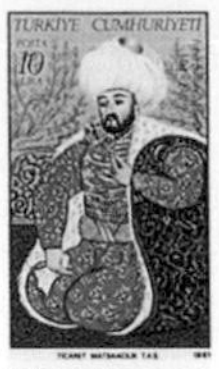

564 Sultan Mohammed the Conqueror

1981. 500th Death Anniv of Mohammed the Conqueror.

2725	564	10l. multicoloured	35	15
2726	564	20l. multicoloured	90	55

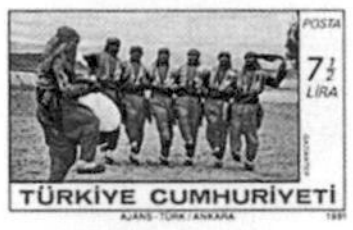

565 Gaziantep

1981. Folk Dances and Europa (35, 70l.). Multicoloured.

2727	½l. Type **565**	25	15
2728	10l. Balikesir	40	15
2729	15l. Kahramanmaras	75	30
2730	35l. Antalya	3·25	75
2731	70l. Burdur	5·00	75

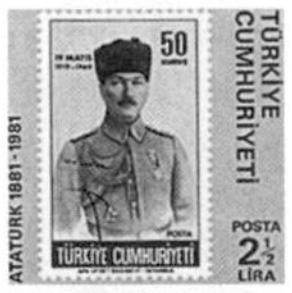

566 Ataturk in 1919 (S.G. 2279)

1981. Birth Centenary of Kemal Ataturk. Previous stamps showing Ataturk. Multicoloured.

2732	566	2½l. multicoloured	60	30
2733	-	7½l. black and brown	60	30
2734	-	10l. multicoloured	60	30
2735	-	20l. blue, red and black	60	30
2736	-	25l. black, red and orange	60	30
2737	-	35l. multicoloured	60	30
MS2738		120×120 mm. As No. 2732; 37½l. As No. 2733; 50l. As No. 2734; 100l. As No. 2735; 125l. As No. 2736; 175l. As No. 2737	16·00	15·00

DESIGNS: 7½l. Ataturk in civilian dress (S.G. No. 2285); 10l. Ataturk and old Parliament House (S.G. No. 2037); 20l. Ataturk teaching Latin alphabet (S.G. No. 1222); 25l. Remilitarization of Dardanelles surcharged stamp (S.G. No. 1188); 35l. Ataturk in evening dress (from miniature sheet).

1981. Various stamps surch **10 LIRA**.

2739		10l. on 60k. red, black and green (No. 2177)	80	15
2740	452	10l. on 110k. blue on blue	80	15
2741	452	10l. on 400k. turquoise on blue	80	15
2742	-	10l. on 800k. green, turq & red (No. 2605)	80	15

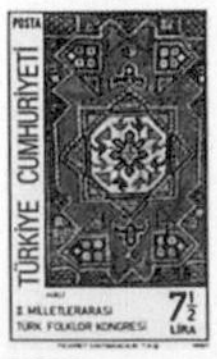

568 Carpet

1981. Second International Congress of Turkish Folklore. Multicoloured.

2743	7½l. Type **568**	15	15
2744	10l. Embroidery	25	15
2745	15l. Drum and "zurna"	40	25
2746	20l. Embroidered napkin	50	30
2747	30l. Rug	1·00	45

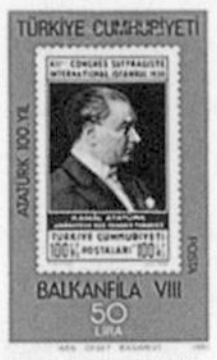

569 Ataturk (SG 1185)

1981. "Balkanfila VIII" Stamp Exhibition, Ankara (2nd issue). Sheet 104×82 mm containing T **569** and similar vert designs.

MS2749	50l. red, blue and black; 50l. indigo, red and black (Tree (SG No. 1146))	3·25	3·00

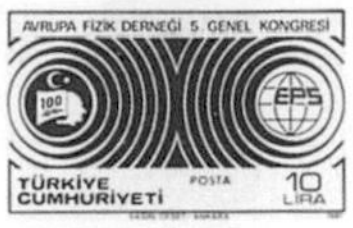

570 Ataturk Centenary and E.P.S. Emblem

1981. Fifth European Physical Society General Congress.

2750	570	10l. multicoloured	35	15
2751	570	30l. multicoloured	1·30	45

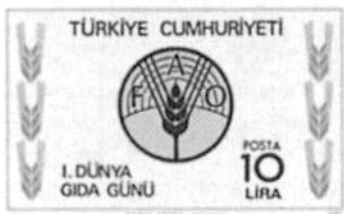

571 F.A.O. Emblem

1981. World Food Day.

2752	571	10l. multicoloured	40	15
2753	571	30l. multicoloured	80	30

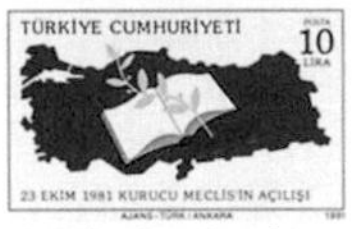

572 Olive Branch and Constitution on Map of Turkey

1981. Inauguration of Constituent Assembly.

2754	572	10l. multicoloured	35	15
2755	572	30l. multicoloured	1·30	60

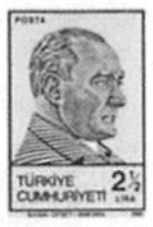

574 Kemal Ataturk

1981

2762	574	2½l. red on grey	10	10

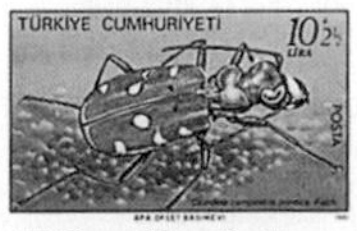

575 Green Tiger Beetle

1981. Useful Insects (2nd series). Multicoloured.

2763	10l.+2½l. Type **575**	40	40
2764	20l.+2½l. "Syrphus vitripennis" (hover fly)	1·10	75
2765	30l.+2½l. "Ascalaphus macaronius" (owl-fly)	1·20	1·00
2766	40l.+2½l. "Empusa fasciata"	1·40	1·10

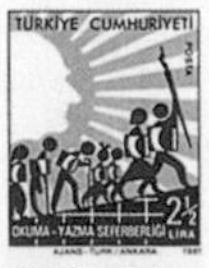

576 Students and Silhouette of Ataturk

1981. Literacy Campaign.

2767	576	2½l. orange and blue	10	10

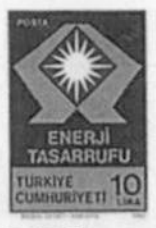

577 Sun

1982. Energy Conservation.

2768	577	10l. yellow, blue & green	40	10

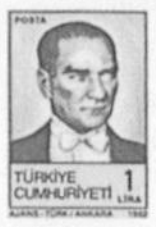

578 Kemal Ataturk

1982

2769	578	1l. green	15	10
2770	-	2½l. lilac	25	10
2771	-	5l. blue	35	10
2772	-	10l. red	40	10
2773	-	35l. brown	1·30	10

DESIGNS: 2½ to 35l. Different portraits of Ataturk.

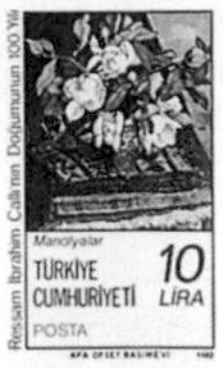

579 "Magnolias"

1982. Birth Centenary of Ibrahim Calli (painter). Multicoloured.

2774	10l. Type **579**	2·20	15
2775	20l. "Fishermen" (horiz)	75	25
2776	30l. "Sewing Woman"	1·20	40

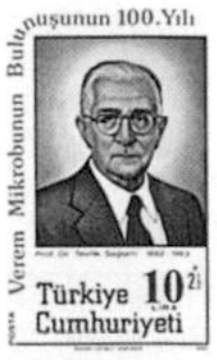

580 Dr. Tevfik Saglam

1982. Centenary of Discovery of Tubercle Bacillus. Multicoloured.

2777	10l.+2½l. Type **580**	35	25
2778	30l.+2½l. Dr. Robert Koch	65	45

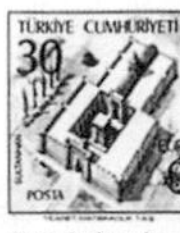

581 Sultanhan Caravanserai

1982. Europa. Sheet 78×80 mm containing T **581** and similar square design. Multicoloured.

MS2779	30l. ×2, Type **581**; 70l. ×2, Map of silk route	6·50	3·75

The two values form a composite design.

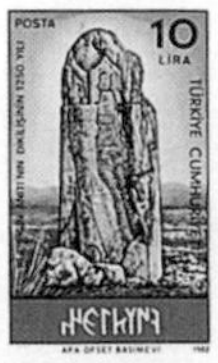

582 Kul Tigin Monument

1982. 1250th Anniv of Kul Tigin Monument. Multicoloured.

2780	10l. Type **582**	25	15
2781	30l. Head of Kul Tigin	60	30

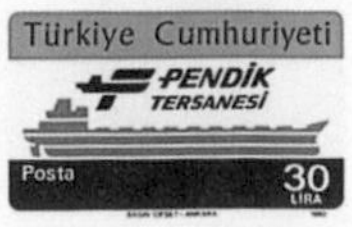

583 Tanker and Emblem

1982. Inauguration of Pendik Shipyard.

2782	583	30l. multicoloured	60	25

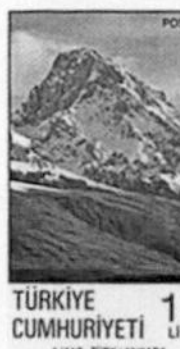

584 Demirkazik

1982. Anatolian Mountains. Multicoloured.

2783	7½l. Agri Dagi	40	15
2784	10l. Buzul Dagi (horiz)	60	25
2785	15l. Type **584**	80	40
2786	20l. Erciyes (horiz)	1·10	40
2787	30l. Kackar Dagi	1·20	60
2788	35l. Uludag (horiz)	2·10	90

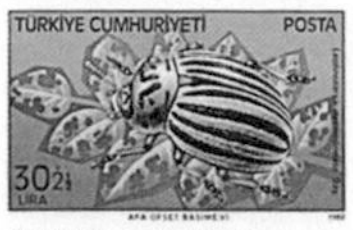

585 Colorado Potato Beetle

1982. Insect Pests (1st series). Multicoloured.

2789	10l.+2½l. "Eurydema spectabile" (shield-bug)	40	15
2790	15l.+2½l. Olive fruit-fly	60	25
2791	20l.+2½l. "Klapperichicen viridissima" (cicada)	80	40
2792	20l.+2½l. Type **585**	1·10	60
2793	35l.+2½l. "Rhynchites auratus" (weevil)	1·20	60

See also Nos. 2830/4.

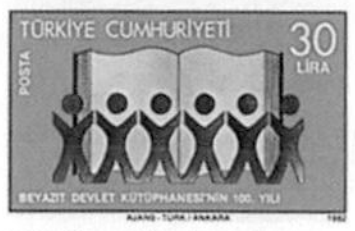

586 Open Book and Figures

1982. Centenary of Beyazit State Library.

2794	**586**	30l. multicoloured	65	25

1982. "Antalya 82" Youth Philatelic Exhibition. Sheet 75×61 mm.

MS2795	No. 2713 ×4	3·00	2·75

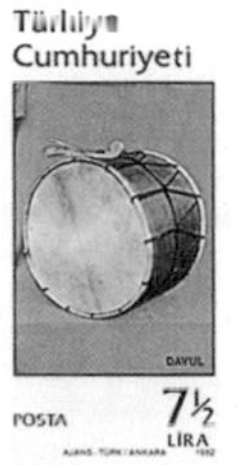

587 Drum

1982. Musical Instruments. Multicoloured.

2796	7½l. Type **587**	40	25
2797	10l. Lute ("Baglama")	60	25
2798	15l. Horn ("Zurna") (horiz)	65	25
2799	20l. Stringed instrument ("Kemence") (horiz)	80	40
2800	30l. Flute ("Mey")	1·60	45

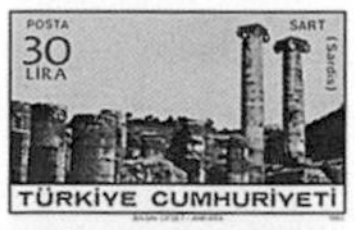

588 Temple of Artemis, Sart

1982. Ancient Cities.

2801	**588**	30l. multicoloured	65	25

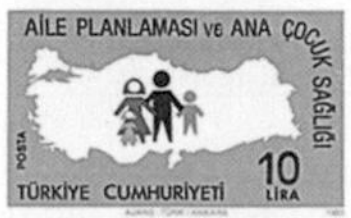

589 Family on Map

1983. Family Planning and Mother and Child Health. Multicoloured.

2802	10l. Type **589**	15	10
2803	35l. Mother and child	80	25

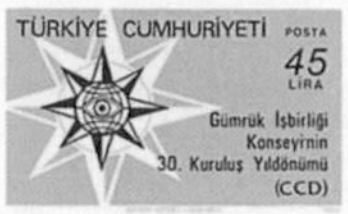

590 Council Emblem

1983. 30th Anniv of Customs Co-operation Council.

2804	**590**	45l. multicoloured	1·00	40

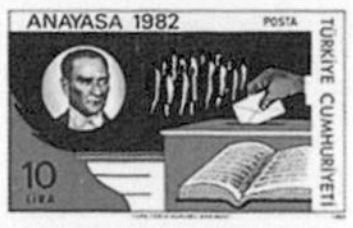

591 People, Ballot Box and Constitution

1983. 1982 Constitution. Multicoloured.

2805	10l. Type **591**	15	10
2806	30l. Constitution, scales and olive branch	65	30

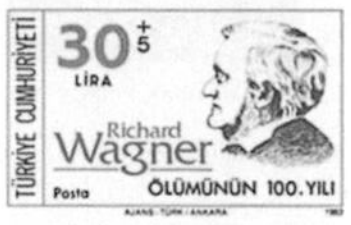

592 Richard Wagner

1983. Death Cent of Richard Wagner (composer).

2807	**592**	30l.+5l. multicoloured	80	40

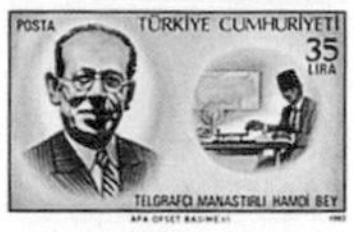

593 Hamdi Bey

1983. 38th Death Anniv of Hamdi Bey (telegraphist).

2808	**593**	35l. multicoloured	80	25

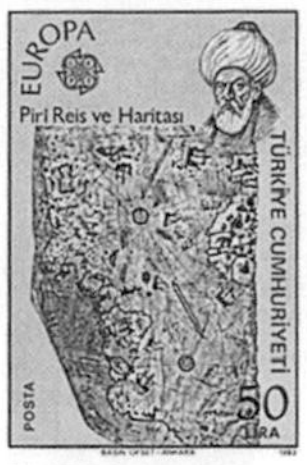

594 Piri Reis (geographer) and Map

1983. Europa. Multicoloured.

2809	50l. Type **594**	20·00	7·50
2810	100l. Ulugh Bey (Central Asian ruler) and observatory	20·00	7·50

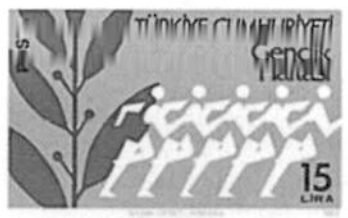

595 Olive Branch and Athletes

1983. Youth Week.

2811	**595**	15l. multicoloured	40	15

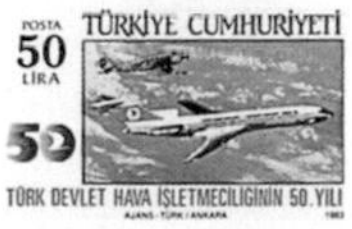

596 Junkers Ju 52/3m and Boeing 727

1983. 50th Anniv of Turkish State Airline. Multicoloured.

2812	50l. Type **596**	1·10	40
2813	70l. Airport at night	1·40	75

No. 2812 is wrongly inscribed "F-13".

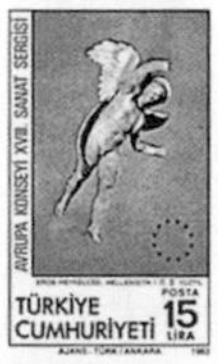

597 Hellenic Statue of Eros

1983. 18th Council of Europe Art Exhibition, Istanbul. Multicoloured.

2814	15l. Type **597**	60	15
2815	35l. Hittite carving of two-headed duck (horiz)	1·00	40
2816	50l. Ottoman zinc flask and jug	1·40	45
2817	70l. Busts of Marcus Aurelius and his wife Faustina (horiz)	2·00	60

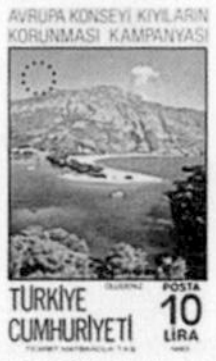

598 Oludeniz

1983. Coastal Protection. Multicoloured.

2818	10l. Type **598**	40	15
2819	25l. Olimpos	80	25
2820	35l. Kekova	1·20	40

1983. Nos. 2655 and 2699 surch **5 LIRA**.

2821	**543**	5l. on 50k. green	10	10
2822	**555**	5l. on 50k. green, red and brown	15	10

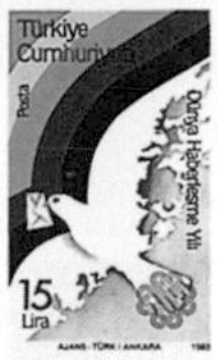

600 Dove carrying Letter

1983. World Communications Year. Multicoloured.

2823	15l. Type **600**	40	15
2824	50l. Telephone pole and telephone wires (horiz)	75	30
2825	70l. Telephone dial and letter within ornamental design	1·30	45

See also **MS**2835.

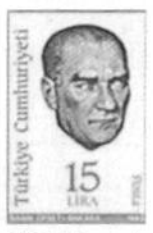

601 Kemal Ataturk

1983

2826	**601**	15l. blue and light blue	60	10
2827	**601**	50l. blue and green	1·10	15
2828	**601**	100l. blue and orange	3·25	25

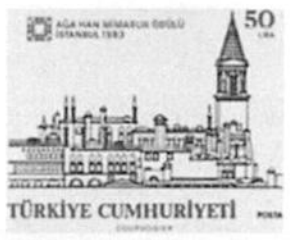

602 Topkapi Serail, Istanbul

1983. Aga Khan Award for Architecture.

2829	**602**	50l. yellow, black & green	1·00	40

1983. Insect Pests (2nd series). As T **585**. Multicoloured.

2830	15l.+5l. Sun pest	40	25
2831	25l.+5l. "Phyllobius nigrofasciatus" (weevil)	60	40
2832	35l.+5l. "Cercopsis intermedia" (froghopper)	75	55
2833	50l.+10l. Striped bug	90	75
2834	75l.+10l. "Capnodis miliaris"	1·50	1·10

1983. "Izmir 83" National Stamp Exhibition. Sheet 76×78 mm.

MS2835	No. 2826 ×5 plus label	2·10	1·90

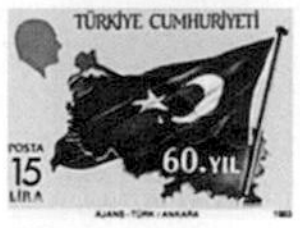

603 Map and Flag of Turkey

1983. 60th Anniv of Republic.

2836	**603**	15l. multicoloured	25	10
2837	**603**	50l. multicoloured	90	25

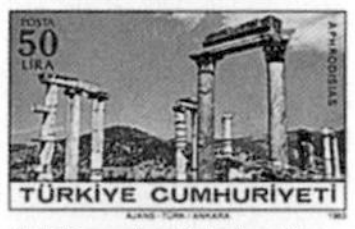

605 Temple of Aphrodite, Aphrodisias

1983. Ancient Cities.

2838	**605**	50l. multicoloured	1·00	30

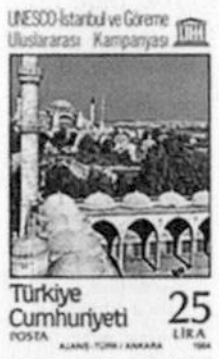

607 St. Sophia's from Sultan Ahmed Mosque, Istanbul

1984. UNESCO International Campaign for Istanbul and Goreme. Multicoloured.

2850	25l. Type **607**	50	25
2851	35l. Rock dwellings and chapels, Goreme	60	30
2852	50l. Suleymaniye district, Istanbul	1·00	40

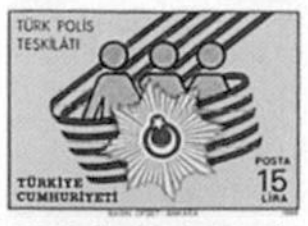

608 Police Badge and Ribbon protecting Citizens

1984. Turkish Police Organization.

2853	**608**	15l. multicoloured	35	10

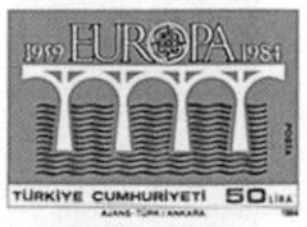

609 Bridge

1984. Europa. 25th Anniv of C.E.P.T.

2854	**609**	50l. multicoloured	21·00	1·10
2855	**609**	100l. multicoloured	21·00	1·50

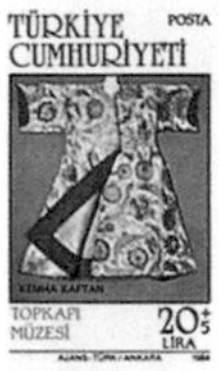

610 Kaftan (16th-century)

1984. Topkapi Museum (1st series). Multicoloured.

2856	20l.+5l. Type **610**	75	25
2857	70l.+15l. Ceremonial ewer	1·80	70
2858	90l.+20l. Gold inlaid and jewelled swords	3·00	1·00
2859	100l.+25l. Kaaba lock	3·00	1·10

See also Nos. 2892/5, 2925/8 and 2967/70.

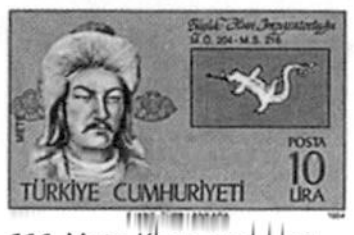

611 Mete Khan and Flag of Great Hun Empire

1984. Turkic States (1st series). Multicoloured.

2860	10l. Type **611**	50	15
2861	20l. Panu and flag of Western Hun Empire	1·00	25
2862	50l. Attila and flag of European Hun Empire	1·80	30
2863	70l. Aksunvar and flag of Ak Hun Empire	3·00	45

See also Nos. 2896/9, 2930/3 and 2971/4.

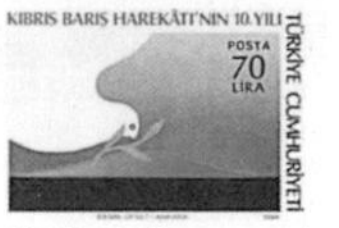

612 Peace Dove

1984. Tenth Anniv of Turkish Forces in Cyprus.

2864	**612**	70l. multicoloured	1·50	40

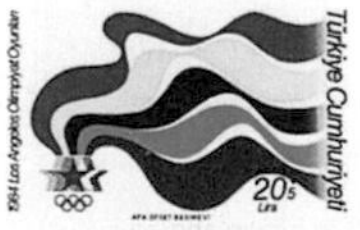

613 Olympic Colours

1984. Olympic Games, Los Angeles. Multicoloured.

2865	20l.+5l. Type **613**	40	25
2866	70l.+15l. Medallion of wrestler (vert)	1·40	1·10
2867	100l.+20l. Stylized athlete	4·00	3·00

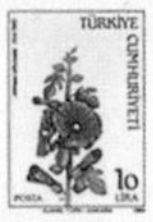

614 Marsh Mallow

1984. Wild Flowers. Multicoloured.

2868	5l. "Narcissus tazetta"	15	15
2868a	10l. Type **614**	15	15
2869	20l. Common poppy	40	15
2870	70l. "Cyclamen pseudoibericum"	1·10	15
2870a	100l. False chamomile	1·20	30
2871	200l. Snowdrops	2·50	25
2872	300l. "Tulipa sintenesii"	4·00	25

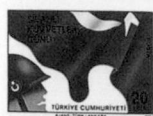

615 Soldier and Flag

1984. Armed Forces Day.

2873	**615**	20l. multicoloured	40	15
2874	-	50l. multicoloured	75	25
2875	-	70l. red, blue and black	1·30	30
2876	-	90l. multicoloured	1·60	45

DESIGNS: 50l. Olive branch as sword hilt; 70l. Emblem, soldier and flag; 90l. Soldier, olive branch and map.

616
Liquidamber

1984. Forest Resources. Multicoloured.

2877	**616**	10l. Type **616**	25	15
2878	-	20l. Oriental spruce	65	15
2879	-	70l. Oriental beech	1·20	40
2880	-	90l. Cedar of Lebanon	2·00	55

617 Pres.
Inonu

1984. Birth Cent of Ismet Inonu (Prime Minister 1923–37 and 1962–65; President 1938–50).

| 2881 | **617** | 20l. multicoloured | 1·00 | 15 |

618 Detail of
13th-century
Seljukian Carpet

1984. First Int Congress on Turkish Carpets.

| 2882 | **618** | 70l. multicoloured | 1·00 | 45 |

619 Great Mosque and
University, Harran

1984. Ancient Cities.

| 2883 | **619** | 70l. multicoloured | 1·60 | 60 |

620 Women and Ballot
Box

1984. 50th Anniv of Turkish Women's Suffrage.

| 2884 | **620** | 20l. multicoloured | 40 | 15 |

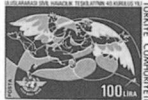

621 "Icarus" (Hans
Herni)

1984. 40th Anniv of I.C.A.O.

| 2885 | **621** | 100l. multicoloured | 1·60 | 60 |

622 1951
Interpliamentary
Conference 15k. Stamp

1985. "Istanbul '87" International Stamp Exhibition. Sheet 116×82 mm containing T **622** and similar design.

| MS2886 | 70l. ×4, multicoloured | 3·75 | 3·50 |

623 Glider and Parachutist

1985. 60th Anniv of Turkish Aviation League. Multicoloured.

| 2887 | | 10l. Type **623** | 40 | 15 |
| 2888 | | 20l. Cameron Viva 77 hot-air balloon (vert) | 60 | 25 |

624 Globe and
Satellite

1985. 20th Anniv of International Telecommunications Satellite Organization.

| 2889 | **624** | 100l. multicoloured | 1·60 | 75 |

625 Score and Ulvi Cemal
Erkin (composer)

1985. Europa. Music Year. Multicoloured.

| 2890 | | 100l. Type **625** | 29·00 | 2·30 |
| 2891 | | 200l. Score and Mithat Fenmen (composer and pianist) | 29·00 | 2·30 |

1985. Topkapi Museum (2nd series). As T **610**. Multicoloured.

2892		10l.+5l. Plate decorated with peacock	60	15
2893		20l.+10l. Jug and cup	80	40
2894		100l.+15l. Porcelain ewer and bowl	2·10	1·10
2895		120l.+20l. Chinese porcelain plate	3·00	1·40

1985. Turkic States (2nd series). As T **611**. Multicoloured.

2896		10l. Bilge Kagan and flag of Gokturk Empire	60	15
2897		20l. Bayan Kagan and flag of Avar Empire	1·10	25
2898		70l. Hazar Kagan and flag of Hazar Empire	2·50	60
2899		100l. Kutlug Kul Bilge Kagan and flag of Uygur Empire	3·25	90

626 Louis
Pasteur working
in Laboratory

1985. Centenary of Discovery of Anti-rabies Vaccine.

| 2900 | **626** | 100l.+15l. mult | 1·60 | 90 |

627 I.Y.Y. Emblem within
Globe and Profiles

1985. International Youth Year. Multicoloured.

| 2901 | | 100l. Type **627** | 1·20 | 60 |
| 2902 | | 120l. Globe and I.Y.Y. Emblem | 1·60 | 75 |

628 Postman
and Couple
Dancing

1985. Introduction of Post Codes.

2903	**628**	10l. black, yellow & brn	40	15
2904	**628**	20l. black, yellow and red	40	15
2905	**628**	20l. black, yellow & green	40	15
2906	**628**	20l. black, yellow and blue	40	15
2907	**628**	70l. blue, yellow & purple	1·00	40
2908	**628**	100l. black, yellow and grey	2·30	40

629 Aynalikavak Palace

1985. National Palaces Symposium. Multicoloured.

| 2909 | | 20l. Type **629** | 40 | 15 |
| 2910 | | 100l. Beylerbeyi Palace | 1·60 | 60 |

630 U.N. Emblem,
Headquarters and Flags in
"40"

1985. 40th Anniv of U.N.O.

| 2911 | **630** | 100l. multicoloured | 1·20 | 60 |

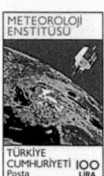

631 Alanya

1985. Ancient Cities.

| 2912 | **631** | 100l. multicoloured | 1·60 | 60 |

632 Satellite
and Infra-red
Picture of
Earth's Surface

1985. 60th Anniv of Meteorological Institute.

| 2913 | **632** | 100l. multicoloured | 1·60 | 60 |

633 Emblem

1985. Centenary of Isik Lyceum, Istanbul.

| 2914 | **633** | 20l. gold, blue and red | 40 | 15 |

634 Kemal
Ataturk

1985

2915	**634**	10l. blue and cobalt	15	10
2916	**634**	20l. brown and lilac	25	15
2917	**634**	100l. purple and lilac	1·60	40

635 Girl and Flower

1986. International 23rd April Children's Festival, Ankara. Multicoloured.

2918		20l. Type **635**	25	15
2919		100l. Family	1·20	40
2920		120l. Balloon seller	1·50	45

636 Boy drawing in Smoke
from Chimney

1986. Europa. Multicoloured.

| 2921 | | 100l. Type **636** | 16·00 | 75 |
| 2922 | | 200l. Plaster on dead half of leaf (vert) | 16·00 | 1·90 |

637 Trophy

1986. Ataturk International Peace Prize. Multicoloured.

| 2923 | | 20l. Type **637** | 40 | 15 |
| 2924 | | 100l. Front view of trophy | 1·20 | 40 |

1986. Topkapi Museum (3rd series). As T **610**. Multicoloured.

2925		20l.+5l. Censer	80	25
2926		100l.+10l. Jade and jewelled tankard	1·60	60
2927		120l.+15l. Dagger and sheath	2·10	75
2928		200l.+30l. Willow buckler	3·75	1·10

638 "Abdulhamit"

1986. Centenary of Turkish Submarine Fleet.

| 2929 | **638** | 20l. multicoloured | 80 | 40 |

1986. Turkic States (3rd series). As T **611**. Multicoloured.

2930		10l. Bilge Kul Kadir Khan and flag of Kara Khanids Empire	50	15
2931		20l. Alp Tekin and flag of Ghaznavids Empire	65	25
2932		100l. Seljuk and flag of Great Seljuk Empire	2·10	40
2933		120l. Muhammed Harezmsah and flag of Harezmsah State	3·25	55

639 Wrestlers
oiling
Themselves

1986. Kirkpinar Wrestling. Multicoloured.

2934		10l. Type **639**	40	10
2935		20l. Opening ceremony	65	15
2936		100l. Wrestlers	1·60	40

640 Chateau de la Muette,
Paris (headquarters)

1986. 25th Anniv of Organization for Economic Co-operation and Development.

| 2937 | **640** | 100l. multicoloured | 1·00 | 30 |

641 Benz "Einspur" Tricar,
1886

1986. Centenary of Motor Car. Multicoloured.

2938		10l. Type **641**	50	15
2939		20l. Rolls-Royce "Silver Ghost", 1906	60	15
2940		100l. Mercedes touring car, 1928	1·60	45
2941		200l. Impression of speed-ing car	3·50	90

642 "Arrangement with Tulips" (Feyhaman Duran)

1986. Artists' Birth Centenaries. Multicoloured.
2942	100l.	Type **642**	1·20	40
2943	120l.	"Landscape with Fountain" (Huseyin Avni Lifij) (horiz)	1·60	55

643 Celal Bayar

1986. Celal Bayar (Prime Minister 1937–39; President 1950–60) Commemoration.
2944	**643**	20l. brown, gold and mauve	25	25
2945	-	100l. green, gold and mauve	1·40	45

DESIGN: 100l. Profile of Celal Bayar.

645 Kubad-Abad

1986. Ancient Cities.
2950	**645**	100l. multicoloured	1·20	40

646 N.A.T.O. Emblem and Dove with Olive Branch

1986. 32nd N.A.T.O. Assembly, Istanbul.
2951	**646**	100l.+20l. mult	2·10	40

647 Ersoy and National Flag

1986. 50th Death Anniv of Mehmet Akif Ersoy (composer of national anthem).
2952	**647**	20l. multicoloured	40	15

648 Driver wearing Seat Belt

1987. Road Safety.
2953	**648**	10l. violet, red and blue	25	25
2954	-	20l. red, blue and brown	35	15
2955	-	150l. brown, red & green	1·10	40

DESIGNS: 20l. Smashed drinking glass and road; 150l. Broken speed limit sign and road.

649 Spurge Hawk Moth

1987. Moths and Butterflies. Multicoloured.
2956	10l.	Type **649**	40	15
2957	20l.	Red admiral	1·20	25
2958	100l.	Jersey tiger moth	4·00	1·20
2959	120l.	Clouded yellow	5·00	1·40

650 Modern Housing and Emblem

1987. International Year of Shelter for the Homeless.
2960	**650**	200l. multicoloured	1·40	60

651 Casting

1987. 50th Anniv of Turkish Iron and Steel Works. Multicoloured.
2961	50l.	Type **651**	40	15
2962	200l.	Karabuk Works	1·20	60

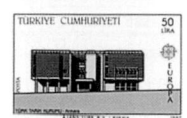

652 Map of Turkey and Grand National Assembly Building, Ankara

1987. "Sovereignty belongs to the People".
2963	**652**	50l. multicoloured	50	15

653 Turkish History Institution, Ankara (Turgut Cansever and Ertur Yener)

1987. Europa. Architecture. Multicoloured.
2964	50l.	Type **653**	16·00	75
2965	200l.	Social Insurance Institution, Zeyrek (Şedad Hakki Eldem)	16·00	2·30

654 Olympic Rings as Flames

1987. 92nd Session of International Olympic Committee, Istanbul.
2966	**654**	200l. multicoloured	1·60	75

1987. Topkapi Museum (4th series). As T **610**. Multicoloured.
2967	20l.+5l.	Crystals and jewelled ewer	40	15
2968	50l.+10l.	Emerald, gold and diamond ceiling pendant (horiz)	60	25
2969	200l.+15l.	Sherbet jug	1·50	90
2970	250l.+30l.	Crystal, gold and jewelled writing drawer (horiz)	2·50	1·00

1987. Turkic States (4th series). As T **611**. Multicoloured.
2971	10l.	Batu Khan and flag of Golden Horde State	60	25
2972	20l.	Timur (Tamerlane) and flag of Great Timur Empire	65	30
2973	50l.	Babur Shah and flag of Mughal Empire	1·20	30
2974	200l.	Osman Bey and flag of Ottoman Empire	3·75	1·10

655 Men

1987. Paintings from Mehmet Siyah Kalem's "Album of the Conqueror". Multicoloured.
2975	10l.	Type **655**	15	40

1987.
2976	20l.	Donkey rider and attendants (horiz)	25	40
2977	50l.	Man whipping fallen horse (horiz)	60	40
2978	200l.	Demon	2·30	1·10

656 Cancer Cells and Pipette holding Drug

1987. 15th International Chemotherapy Congress, Istanbul.
2979	**656**	200l.+25l. mult	1·20	75

657 Ihlamur Pavilion

1987. Royal Pavilions (1st series). Multicoloured.
2980	50l.	Type **657**	40	15
2981	200l.	Kucuksu Pavilion	1·00	45

See also Nos. 3019/20.

658 Suleiman receiving Barbarossa (miniature)

1987. Suleiman the Magnificent. Multicoloured.
2982	30l.	Suleiman	35	40
2983	50l.	Suleiman's tougra (horiz)	40	40
2984	200l.	Type **658**	1·60	75
2985	270l.	Sculpture of Suleiman from U.S. House of Representatives and inscribed scroll	2·75	75

659 Cemal Gursel 1960–66

1987. Turkish Presidents. Sheet 111×143 mm containing T **659** and similar vert designs, each sepia, vermilion and gold.
MS2986 50l. Type **659**; 50l. Cevdet Sunay, 1966–73; 50l. Fahri S. Koruturk, 1973–80; 50l. Kenan Evren (current President); 50l. Ismet Inonu, 1938–50; 50l. Celal Bayar, 1950–60; 100l. Kemal Ataturk, 1923–38 (29×39 mm)   6·25   5·75

660 Sinan and Selimiye Mosque, Edrine

1988. 400th Death Anniv of Mimar Sinan (architect). Multicoloured.
2987	50l.	Type **660**	15	15
2988	200l.	Suleiman Mosque	75	70

661 Means of Transport

1988. Europa. Transport and Communications. Multicoloured.
2989	200l.	Type **661**	6·25	2·30

1988.
2990	600l.	Electric impulses forming globe between telephone and computer terminal (horiz)	6·25	2·30

662 Syringes between Healthy and Sick Children

1988. Health. Multicoloured.
2991	50l.	Type **662**	25	15
2992	200l.	Capsules forming cross on bottle (vert)	60	25
2993	300l.	Heart in cogwheel and heart-shaped worker	90	40
2994	600l.	Organs for transplant on open hands (vert)	1·60	75

663 American Standard Steam Locomotive, 1850s

1988. Locomotives. Each agate, light brown and brown.
2995	50l.	Type **663**	1·60	30
2996	100l.	Saronno side-tank locomotive No. 3328, 1897	2·50	45
2997	200l.	Henschel Krupp steam locomotive No. 46020, 1933	3·25	75
2998	300l.	Type E 43001 electric locomotive, 1987	4·00	90
2999	600l.	MTE-Tulomsas diesel locomotive, 1984	6·50	2·10

664 Articulated Lorry

1988. 21st International Road Transport Union World Congress, Istanbul
3000	**664**	200l.+25l. mult	60	55

665 Scales and Map

1988. 120th Anniv of Court of Cassation (appeal court).
3001	**665**	50l. multicoloured	40	40

666 Fatih Sultan Mohamed Bridge, Bosphorus

1988. Completion of Bridges. Multicoloured.
3002	200l.	Type **666**	1·60	1·50
3003	300l.	Seto Great road and rail Bridge, Japan	2·10	1·50

667 Telephone Dial and Wires over Villages

1988. Completion of Telephone Network to Every Village.
3004	**667**	100l. multicoloured	40	25

669 Running

1988. Olympic Games, Seoul. Multicoloured.
3005	100l.	Type **669**	40	15
3006	200l.	Archery	60	40
3007	400l.	Weightlifting	1·10	75
3008	600l.	Football (vert)	1·60	1·40

670
Weightlifting

1988. Naim Suleymanoglu, Olympic and World Heavyweight Record Holder for Weightlifting.
| 3009 | **670** | 1000l. multicoloured | 6·25 | 2·30 |

671 Lush Scene in Hands surrounded by Barren Earth

1988. European Campaign for Rural Areas. Multicoloured.
| 3010 | | 100l.+25l. Type **671** | 65 | 60 |
| 3011 | | 400l.+50l. Rural scene in eye | 1·40 | 1·30 |

672 General Dynamics F-16 Fighters and Cogwheel

1988. Turkish Aerospace Industries. Multicoloured.
| 3012 | | 50l. Type **672** | 15 | 15 |
| 3013 | | 200l. Birds forming jet fighter (horiz) | 80 | 25 |

673 "Gonepteryx cleopatra"

1988. Butterflies. Multicoloured.
3014		100l. Type **673** (wrongly inscr "G. rhamni")	1·60	70
3015		200l. Hermit	3·00	1·40
3016		400l. Eastern festoon	5·25	2·75
3017		600l. Camberwell beauty	8·25	4·25
MS3018	122×79 mm. Nos. 3014/17		21·00	15·00

1988. Royal Pavilions (2nd series). As T **657**. Multicoloured.
| 3019 | | 100l. Kasr-i Humayun Imperial Lodge, Maslak | 40 | 15 |
| 3020 | | 400l. Sale Pavilion, Yildiz | 1·20 | 60 |

674 Ataturk

1988. 50th Death Anniv of Kemal Ataturk (President, 1923–38). Sheet 105×70 mm.
| MS3021 | 400l. chestnut and violet | | 1·60 | 1·50 |

675 Large-leaved Lime

1988. Medicinal Plants. Multicoloured.
3022		150l. Type **675**	40	25
3023		300l. Common mallow	80	45
3024		600l. Henbane	1·20	90
3025		900l. Deadly nightshade	2·50	1·40

676 Seated Goddess with Child (clay statuette)

1989. Archaeology (1st series). Multicoloured.
| 3026 | | 150l. Type **676** | 80 | 15 |
| 3027 | | 300l. Lead figurine of god and goddess | 1·20 | 45 |

| 3028 | | 600l. Clay human-shaped vase | 1·60 | 90 |
| 3029 | | 1000l. Hittite ivory figurine of mountain god | 3·75 | 1·50 |
See also Nos. 3062/5, 3104/7 and 3134/7.

1989. Nos. 2826, 2915 and 2916 surch.
3030	**601**	50l. on 15l. blue and light blue	40	15
3031	**634**	75l. on 10l. blue and cobalt	40	15
3032	**634**	150l. on 20l. brown and lilac	80	25

678 Dove and Emblem

1989. 40th Anniv of N.A.T.O.
| 3033 | **678** | 600l. ultram, blue & red | 1·20 | 75 |

679 Silkworm Moth Larva on Leaf

1989. Silk Industry. Multicoloured.
| 3034 | | 150l.+50l. Type **679** | 40 | 40 |
| 3035 | | 600l.+100l. Silkworm moth cocoon and lengths of cloth | 1·20 | 75 |

680 Leap-frog

1989. Europa. Children's Games. Multicoloured.
| 3036 | | 600l. Type **680** | 23·00 | 1·50 |
| 3037 | | 1000l. Children going under arch formed by other children ("Open the Door, Head Bezirgan") | 23·00 | 2·30 |

681 Arrow and Anniversary Emblem

1989. 40th Anniv of Council of Europe.
| 3038 | **681** | 600l.+100l. mult | 1·20 | 90 |

683 Paddle-steamer "Sahilbent"

1989. Steamers. Multicoloured.
3045		150l. Type **683**	1·60	45
3046		300l. "Ragbet" (paddle-steamer)	3·00	75
3047		600l. "Tari" (freighter)	6·25	1·50
3048		1000l. "Guzelhisar" (ferry)	9·75	2·50

684 Birds

1989. Bicentenary of French Revolution.
| 3049 | **684** | 600l. multicoloured | 1·60 | 75 |

685 Kemal Ataturk

1989
| 3050 | **685** | 2000l. blue and grey | 2·10 | 1·70 |
| 3051 | **685** | 5000l. brown and grey | 5·00 | 4·25 |
See also Nos. 3093/4, 3144 and 3199/3200.

1989. No. 2916 surch **LIRA 500**.
| 3052 | **634** | 500l. on 20l. brown and lilac | 60 | 45 |

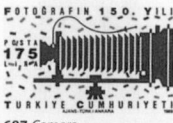

687 Camera

1989. 150th Anniv of Photography. Multicoloured.
| 3053 | | 175l. Type **687** | 25 | 25 |
| 3054 | | 700l. Coloured lens shutter | 1·00 | 90 |

688 "Manzara" (Hikmet Onat)

1989. State Exhibition of Paintings and Sculpture. Multicoloured.
3055		200l. Type **688**	25	15
3056		700l. "Sari Saz" (Bedri Rahmi Eyuboglu)	1·10	70
3057		1000l. "Kadin" (sculpture, Zuhtu Muridoglu)	1·60	1·10

689 Nehru

1989. Birth Centenary of Jawaharlal Nehru (Indian statesman).
| 3058 | **689** | 700l. multicoloured | 80 | 75 |

690 Loggerhead Turtle

1989. Sea Turtles. Multicoloured.
3059		700l. Type **690**	3·25	1·90
3060		1000l. Common green turtle	5·00	2·30
MS3061	82×78 mm. Nos. 3059/60		9·75	9·00

1990. Archaeology (2nd series). As T **676**. Multicoloured.
3062		100l. Ivory statuette of goddess (vert)	35	30
3063		200l. Clay ram's head and antelope's head twin ceremonial vessel	50	45
3064		500l. Gold goddess pendant (vert)	65	60
3065		700l. Ivory statuette of lion	1·40	1·30

691 Turkish Memorial

1990. 75th Anniv of Gallipoli Campaign.
| 3066 | **691** | 1000l. multicoloured | 1·00 | 90 |

692 Turkish Garden (left half)

1990. International Garden and Greenery Exposition, Osaka. Multicoloured.
| 3067 | | 1000l. Type **692** | 1·00 | 90 |
| 3068 | | 1000l. Right half of garden | 1·00 | 90 |
Nos. 3067/8 were issued together, *se-tenant*, forming a composite design.

1990. Various stamps surch.
3069	–	50l. on 5l. mult (No. 2868)	1·20	25
3070	**648**	100l. on 10l. red, violet & bl	1·60	25
3071	**648**	150l. on 10l. red, violet & bl	80	15
3072	–	200l. on 70l. mult (No. 2870)	2·10	30
3073	–	300l. on 20l. red, blue and brown (No. 2954)	1·60	15

| 3074 | – | 300l. on 70l. mult (No. 2870) | 1·60 | 15 |
| 3075 | – | 1500l. on 20l. mult (No. 2869) | 9·75 | 1·10 |

694 "70" and Ataturk

1990. 70th Anniv of Establishment of Nationalist Provisional Government.
| 3076 | **694** | 300l. multicoloured | 50 | 45 |

695 Antalya

1990. European Tourism Year. Multicoloured.
| 3077 | | 300l.+50l. Type **695** | 40 | 40 |
| 3078 | | 1000l.+100l. Istanbul | 1·00 | 90 |

696 Ankara Post Office

1990. Europa. Post Office Buildings. Multicoloured.
| 3079 | | 700l. Type **696** | 8·25 | 1·50 |
| 3080 | | 1000l. Istanbul Post Office (horiz) | 8·25 | 1·50 |

697 Map and Dove as Open Book

1990. European Supreme Courts' Conference, Ankara.
| 3081 | **697** | 1000l. blue, dp blue & red | 1·60 | 1·50 |

698 Fire Salamander

1990. World Environment Day. Multicoloured.
3082		300l. Type **698**	60	30
3083		500l. Banded newt	80	45
3084		1000l. Fire-bellied toads	1·20	90
3085		1500l. Common tree frog (vert)	2·30	1·80

699 "Ertugrul" (frigate) and Turkish and Japanese Women

1990. Centenary of First Turkish Envoy to Japan.
| 3086 | **699** | 1000l. multicoloured | 1·60 | 90 |

701 Smoker's Body shattering

1990. Anti-addiction Campaign. Multicoloured.
| 3087 | | 300l. on 50l. Type **701** | 40 | 40 |
| 3088 | | 1000l. on 100l. Addict injecting drug into skeletal arm (horiz) | 1·20 | 1·10 |

702 "Self-portrait"

1990. Death Centenary of Vincent van Gogh (painter). Multicoloured.

3089	300l. Type **702**	1·60	75
3090	700l. "Boats in Saintes Maries" (horiz)	2·50	1·50
3091	1000l. "Sunflowers"	2·50	1·50
3092	1500l. "Road with Cypress"	4·00	2·30

1990. As T **685** but inscription redrawn and dated "1990".

3093	**685**	500l. green and grey	80	30
3094	**685**	1000l. mauve and grey	1·20	45

703 Emblem, Pen, Open Book and Globe

1990. International Literacy Year.

3095	**703**	300l. multicoloured	40	40

704 "Portrait" (Nurullah Berk)

1990. State Exhibition of Painting and Sculpture. Multicoloured.

3096	300l. Type **704**	40	25
3097	700l. "Derya Kuzulari" (Cevat Dereli)	65	55
3098	1000l. "Artist's Mother" (bust) (Nijad Sirel)	1·40	90

705 Tatar Courier and Modern Postal Transport

1990. 150th Anniv of Ministry of Posts and Telecommunications. Multicoloured.

3099	200l. Type **705**	35	25
3100	250l. Computer terminal and Morse key	50	30
3101	400l. Manual and digital telephone exchanges	65	40
3102	1500l. Telegraph wires, dish aerial and satellite	1·80	1·40
MS3103	108×78 mm. Nos. 3099/3102	3·75	3·50

1991. Archaeology (3rd series). As T **676**. Multicoloured.

3104	300l. Clay figurine of woman (vert)	50	15
3105	500l. Bronze sistrum (vert)	60	30
3106	1000l. Clay kettle on stand (vert)	1·00	55
3107	1500l. Clay ceremonial vessel (vert)	2·10	90

707 Lake Abant

1991. Lakes. Multicoloured.

3110	250l. Type **707**	25	15
3111	500l. Lake Egirdir	60	40
3112	1500l. Lake Van	1·60	1·40

708 Satellite and Map of Europe

1991. Europa. Europe in Space. Multicoloured.

3113	1000l. Type **708**	16·00	1·10
3114	1500l. Satellite and map of Europe (different)	16·00	1·90

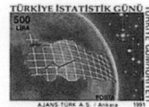

709 Graph on Globe

1991. National Statistics Day.

3115	**709**	500l. multicoloured	40	30

710 Cable Ship, Map, Cable and Telephone Handset

1991. Eastern Mediterranean Fibre Optic Cable System (EMOS-1).

3116	**710**	500l. multicoloured	40	25

711 Emblem

1991. European Transport Ministers' Conference, Antalya.

3117	**711**	500l. multicoloured	40	40

712 Emre

1991. "Yunus Emre (13th-century poet) Year of Love". Multicoloured.

3118	500l.+100l. Type **712**	50	45
3119	1500l.+100l. Globe, and Emre as tree	1·30	1·10

713 Harpsichord, Score and Mozart

1991. Death Bicentenary of Wolfgang Amadeus Mozart (composer).

3120	**713**	1500l.+100l. mult	1·40	1·30

714 "Abdulcanbaz" (Turhan Selcuk)

1991. Caricature. Multicoloured.

3121	500l. "Amcabey" (Cemal Nadir Guler) (horiz)	40	25
3122	1000l. Type **714**	1·00	55

715 13th-century Seljukian Wall Plaque

1991. Turkish Ceramics. Multicoloured.

3123	500l. Type **715**	40	30
3124	1500l. Late 16th-century Ottoman wall plaque	1·00	75

716 Emblem

1991. Turkish Grand National Assembly's Protection of Human Rights International Symposium, Ankara.

3125	**716**	500l. multicoloured	40	25

717 Dam, Water and Sun

1991. South-eastern Anatolia Project (hydro-electric power and irrigation development).

3126	**717**	500l. multicoloured	40	25

718 Keloglan and Genie with Tray of Food

1991. "Keloglan" (fairy tale). Multicoloured.

3127	500l. Type **718**	35	25
3128	1000l. Keloglan and dinner guests	65	55
3129	1500l. Keloglan ploughing	1·50	1·10

719 Sand Boa

1991. World Environment Day. Snakes. Multicoloured.

3130	250l. Type **719**	1·60	45
3131	500l. Four-lined snake	2·50	90
3132	1000l. Ottoman viper	5·00	1·70
3133	1500l. Caucasus viper	7·50	2·75

1992. Archaeology (4th series). As T **676**. Multicoloured.

3134	300l. Clay statuette of Mother Goddess (vert)	25	15
3135	500l. Bronze statuette (vert)	40	25
3136	1000l. Hittite clay vase (vert)	60	40
3137	1500l. Urartian lion (vert)	1·20	90

721 Emblem and People

1992. 30th Anniv of Supreme Court.

3140	**721**	500l.+100l. mult	40	40

722 Balloons

1992. Europa. 500th Anniv of Discovery of America by Columbus.

3141	—	1500l. blue and red	8·25	1·50
3142	**722**	2000l. multicoloured	8·25	1·90

DESIGN—HORIZ: 1500l. Stylized caravel.

723 Immigrant Ship

1992. 500th Anniv of Jewish Immigration.

3143	**723**	1500l. multicoloured	80	75

724 Kemal Ataturk

1992

3144	—	250l. orange, ochre and gold	80	75
3145	**724**	10000l. blue, grey & gold	4·00	3·75

DESIGN: 250l. Portrait of Ataturk as in Type **685**.

725 Court Emblem

1992. 130th Anniv of Court of Accounts.

3146	**725**	500l. multicoloured	40	40

726 Congress Emblem

1992. Third Turkish Economy Congress, Izmir.

3147	**726**	1500l. multicoloured	80	55

727 Northern Lapwing

1992. World Environment Day. Birds. Multicoloured.

3148	500l. Type **727**	40	40
3149	1000l. Golden oriole	60	55
3150	1500l. Common shelduck	80	75
3151	2000l. White-throated kingfisher (vert)	1·50	1·40

728 Ears of Grain, Cogwheel and Hands

1992. Black Sea Economic Co-operation Conference, Istanbul.

3152	**728**	1500l. multicoloured	50	45

729 Doves forming Olympic Flame

1992. Olympic Games, Barcelona. Multicoloured.

3153	500l. Type **729**	40	40
3154	1000l. Boxing	60	55
3155	1500l. Weightlifting	80	75
3156	2000l. Wrestling	1·50	1·40

730 Soldiers and Old Woman

1992. Legend of Anatolia. Multicoloured.

3157	500l. Type **730**	25	15
3158	1000l. Old woman filling trough with buttermilk	40	25
3159	1500l. Soldiers drinking from trough	75	55

731 Bride and Mother-in-law Dolls from Merkez Kapikaya

1992. Traditional Crafts. Multicoloured.

3160	500l. Knitted flowers from Icel-Namrun (horiz)	25	15
3161	1000l. Type **731**	50	40
3162	3000l. Woven saddlebag from Hakkari (horiz)	1·10	75

732 Cherries

1992. Fruit (1st series). Multicoloured.

3163	500l. Type **732**	40	30
3164	1000l. Apricots	65	45
3165	3000l. Grapes	1·20	90
3166	5000l. Apples	1·80	1·40

See also Nos. 3176/9.

734 Mountaineering

1992. 26th Anniv of Turkish Mountaineering Federation (3169) and 80th Anniv of Turkish Scout Movement (3170). Multicoloured.

3169	1000l.+200l. Type **734**	60	55
3170	3000l.+200l. Scouts watering sapling (horiz)	1·50	1·40

735 Sait Faik Abasiyanik

1992. Anniversaries. No value expressed.

3171	**735** (T) blue, indigo and red	1·20	15
3172	- (T) blue, orange and violet	1·20	15
3173	- (M) blue, green & orange	1·20	15
3174	- (M) blue, red and indigo	1·20	15
3175	- (M) blue, red and green	1·20	15

DESIGNS: No. 3171, Type **935** (writer, 86th birth anniv); 3172, Fikret Mualla Saygi (painter, 25th death anniv); 3173, Muhsin Ertugrul (actor and producer, birth centenary); 3174, Cevat Sakir Kabaagaeli (writer, 19th death anniv); 3175, Asik Veysel Satiroglu (poet, 98th birth anniv).

Nos. 3171/2 were intended for greeting cards and Nos. 3173/5 for inland letters.

1993. Fruit (2nd series). As T **732**. Multicoloured.

3176	500l. Bananas	40	30
3177	1000l. Oranges	60	45
3178	3000l. Pears	1·10	75
3179	5000l. Pomegranates	1·60	1·40

736 Sculpture (Hadi Bara)

1993. Europa. Contemporary Art. Multicoloured.

3180	1000l. Type **736**	1·20	60
3181	3000l. Carved figure (Zuhtu Muridoglu)	1·20	60

737 Terraces

1993. Campaign for the Preservation of Pamukkale. Multicoloured.

3182	1000l.+200l. Type **737**	60	25
3183	3000l.+500l. Close-up of terrace	1·10	70

738 Buildings and Emblem

1993. Economic Co-operation Organization Conference, Istanbul.

3184	**738** 2500l. ultramarine, blue and gold	65	60

739 Rize

1993. Traditional Houses (1st series). Multicoloured.

3185	1000l. Type **739**	25	15
3186	2500l. Rize (different) (horiz)	50	40
3187	3000l. Trabzon	80	60
3188	5000l. Black Sea houses (horiz)	1·30	75

See also Nos. 3222/5, 3256/9, 3283/6 and 3318/21.

740 Mausoleum

1993. 900th Birth Anniv of Hoca Ahmet Yesevi (philosopher).

3189	**740** 3000l. gold, blue & lt blue	60	55

741 Haci Arif Bey

1993. Death Anniversaries. No value expressed. Each brown and red.

3190	(T) Type **741** (composer, 109th)	1·20	15
3191	(T) Neyzen Tevfik Kolayli (singer, 40th)	1·20	15
3192	(M) Orhan Veli Kanik (poet, 43rd)	1·20	15
3193	(M) Cahit Sitki Taranci (poet, 27th)	1·20	15
3194	(M) Munir Nurettin Seluk (composer, 12th)	1·20	15

Nos. 3190/1 were intended for greetings cards and Nos. 3192/4 for inland letters.

742 Emblem

1993. Istanbul's Bid to host Summer Olympic Games in Year 2000.

3195	**742** 2500l. multicoloured	60	45

1993. As T **685** but inscription redrawn and dated "1993".

3199	**685** 5000l. violet and gold	3·00	75
3200	**685** 20000l. mauve and gold	5·25	2·75

744 Amphora on Sea-bed

1993. Mediterranean Treaty. Multicoloured.

3201	1000l. Type **744**	40	25
3202	3000l. Dolphin	80	70

745 Emblem

1993. U.N. Natural Disaster Relief Day.

3203	**745** 3000l.+500l. mult	80	55

746 Prayer Mat

1993. Handicrafts. Multicoloured.

3204	1000l. Type **746**	40	25
3205	2500l. Silver earrings	60	40
3206	5000l. Crocheted purse	1·10	90

747 Laurel Wreath, Torch and Silhouette of Kemal Ataturk

1993. 70th Anniv of Republic.

3207	**747** 1000l. multicoloured	25	25

748 Man in Gas Mask and Fire

1993. Civil Defence.

3208	**748** 1000l. multicoloured	25	25

749 Satellite, Globe and Map

1994. "Turksat" Communications Satellite. Multicoloured.

3209	1500l. Type **749**	35	30
3210	5000l. Satellite and map showing satellite's "foot- print"	50	45

750 Ears of Corn

1994. 40th Anniv of Water Supply Company.

3211	**750** 1500l. multicoloured	40	25

751 Ezogelin Corbasi

1994. Traditional Dishes. Multicoloured.

3212	1000l. Type **751**	40	30
3213	1500l. Karisik dolma	40	30
3214	3500l. Shish kebabs	65	45
3215	5000l. Baklava	80	60

752 Marie Curie

1994. Europa. Discoveries. Multicoloured.

3216	1500l. Type **752** (discoverer of radium)	80	75
3217	5000l. Albert Einstein and equation (formulator of Theory of Relativity) (horiz)	80	75

754 Faselis, Antalya

1994. Environment Day. Multicoloured.

3220	6000l. Type **754**	1·00	75
3221	8500l. Gocek, Mugla (vert)	1·50	90

755 Bursa

1994. Traditional Houses (2nd series). Multicoloured.

3222	2500l. Type **755**	65	40
3223	3500l. Uskudar	65	45
3224	6000l. Anadolu Hisari	80	70
3225	8500l. Edirne	1·20	75

756 Trekking in Mountains

1994. Tourism. Multicoloured.

3226	5000l. Type **756**	80	55
3227	10000l. White-water rafting (horiz)	1·20	1·00

757 Centenary Emblem over City

1994. Centenary of International Olympic Committee.

3228	**757** 12500l.+500l. mult	1·40	1·10

758 "2001"

1994. Seven Year Plan.

3229	**758** 2500l. multicoloured	40	25

759 Kusak Design

1994. Embroidery. Multicoloured.

3230	7500l. Type **759**	1·80	1·70
3231	12500l. Paalik design (horiz)	1·20	75

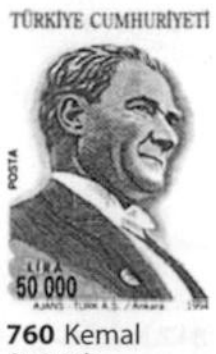
760 Kemal Ataturk

1994

3232	**760**	50000l. violet, mve & red	3·75	2·30

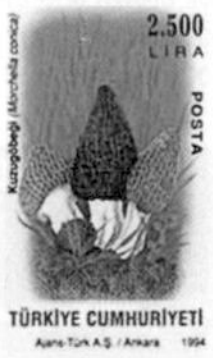
761 Common Morel

1994. Fungi. Multicoloured.

3233	2500l. Type **761**	60	45
3234	5000l. "Agaricus bernardii"	80	60
3235	7500l. Saffron milk cap	1·50	1·20
3236	12500l. Parasol mushroom	2·10	1·50

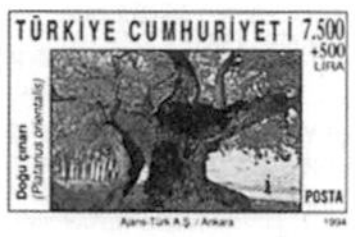
762 "Platanus orientalis"

1994. Trees. Multicoloured.

3237	7500l.+500l. Type **762**	1·00	75
3238	12500l.+1000l. "Cupressus sempervirens" (vert)	2·00	1·50

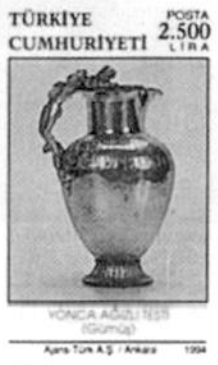
763 Silver Jug

1994. Traditional Crafts. Multicoloured.

3239	2500l. Type **763**	65	40
3240	5000l. Silver censer	80	45
3241	7500l. Necklace (horiz)	1·00	60
3242	12500l. Gold brooch (half horse and half fish) (horiz)	1·60	1·20

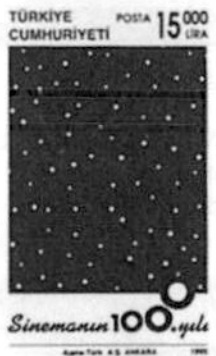
765 Starry Sky

1995. Centenary of Motion Pictures.

3245	**765**	15000l. blue and red	1·20	1·10

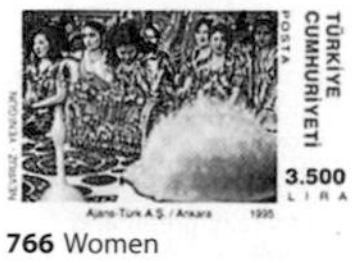
766 Women

1995. Nevruz Festival.

3246	**766**	3500l. multicoloured	40	40

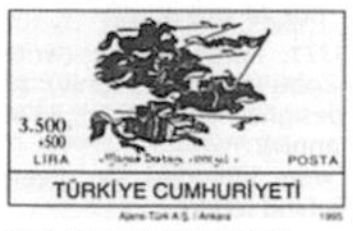
767 "Ballad of Manas" (Kirghiz epic, millenary)

1995. Anniversaries.

3247	**767**	3500l.+500l. brown, yellow and red	25	25
3248	-	3500l.+500l. mult	35	30

DESIGN—VERT: No. 3248, Abay Kunanbay and books (Kazakh philosopher and politician, 150th birth anniv).

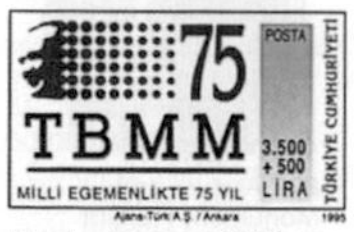
768 Anniversary Emblem

1995. 75th Anniv of National Assembly.

3249	**768**	3500l.+500l. black, red and blue	25	25

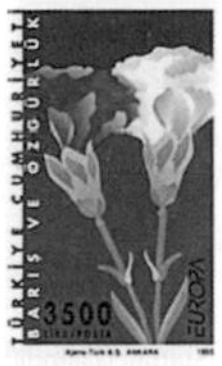
769 Carnations

1995. Europa. Peace and Freedom. Multicoloured.

3250	3500l. Type **769**	80	75
3251	15000l. Leaves	1·20	1·10

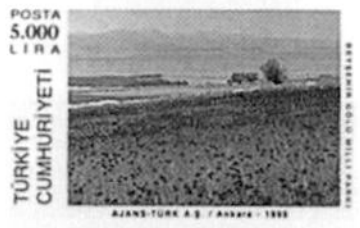
771 Beysehir Coast

1995. World Environment Day. National Parks. Multicoloured.

3253	5000l. Type **771**	40	40
3254	15000l. Yedigoller	1·00	90
3255	25000l. Ilgaz mountains	2·00	1·80

1995. Traditional Houses (3rd series). As T **755**. Multicoloured.

3256	5000l. Izmir (vert)	35	30
3257	10000l. Kula (vert)	65	60
3258	15000l. Mugla	1·00	90
3259	20000l. Birgi	1·30	1·20

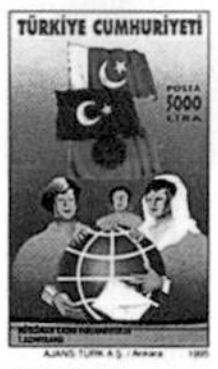
772 Delegates, Flags and Globe

1995. First Muslim Parliamentary Members Congress, Islamabad.

3260	**772**	5000l. multicoloured	40	40

773 Painting of Townscape (left detail)

1995. "Istanbul 96" International Stamp Exhibition. Multicoloured.

3261	7000l. Type **773**	60	55
3262	7000l. Aerial photo of bay (left detail)	60	55
3263	25000l. Painting of townscape (right detail)	1·50	1·40
3264	25000l. Aerial photo of bay (right detail)	1·50	1·40

Nos. 3261/4 were issued together, *se-tenant*, forming two composite designs.

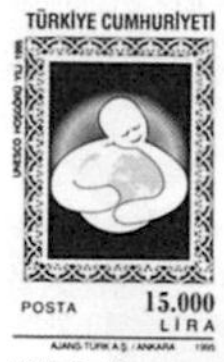
774 Spirit embracing Earth

1995. 50th Anniversaries. Multicoloured.

3265	15000l. Type **774** (UNESCO)	60	55
3266	30000l. Anniversary emblem (U.N.O.)	1·10	1·00

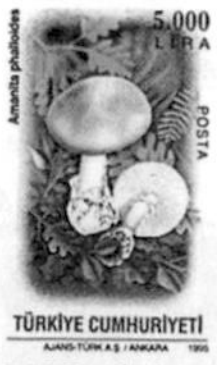
776 Death Cap

1995. Fungi. Multicoloured.

3268	5000l. Type **776**	65	60
3269	10000l. "Lepiota helveola"	80	75
3270	20000l. Beefsteak morel	1·40	1·30
3271	30000l. "Amanita gemmata"	2·10	1·90

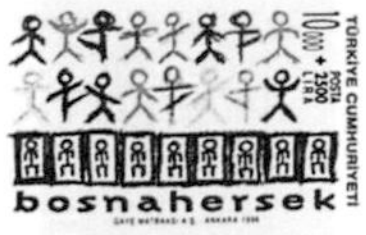
777 Living in Harmony

1996. Aid for Bosnia and Herzegovina.

3272	**777**	10000l.+2500l. mult	40	40

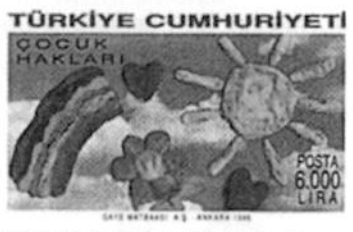
778 Rainbow, Flower, Sun and Hearts

1996. Children's Rights. Multicoloured.

3273	6000l. Type **778**	25	25
3274	10000l. Child drawing "A"	60	55

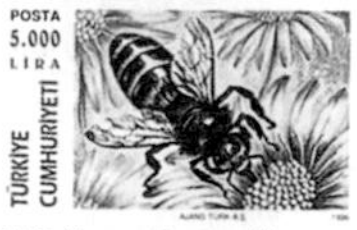
779 Honey Bee on Flower

1996. "Istanbul '96" International Stamp Exhibition (2nd issue). Sheet 118×78 mm containing T **779** and similar horiz designs. Multicoloured.

MS3275	5000l. Type **779**; 10000l. Anatolian karabash (dog); 15000l. Black cockerel; 30000l. Trout	4·00	3·75

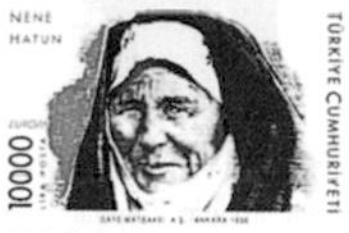
780 Nene Hatun (revolutionary)

1996. Europa. Famous Women. Multicoloured.

3276	10000l. Type **780**	1·20	1·10
3277	40000l. Halide Edip Adivar (writer and politician)	2·10	1·90

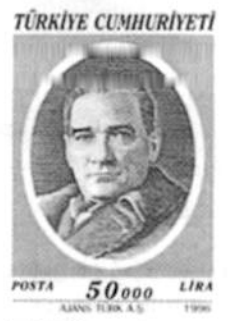
781 Kemal Ataturk

1996

3278	**781**	50000l. brown and pink	1·20	1·10
3279	-	100000l. blue and orange	2·50	2·30

DESIGN: 100000l. Ataturk (different).

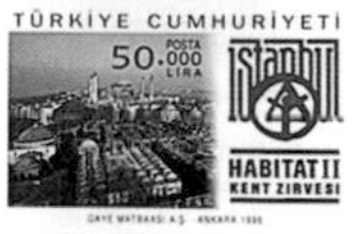
782 Istanbul

1996. "HABITAT II" Second United Nations Conference on Human Settlements, Istanbul.

3280	**782**	50000l. multicoloured	1·20	1·10

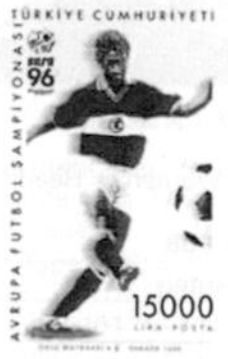
783 Player with Ball

1996. European Football Championship, England. Multicoloured.

3281	15000l. Type **783**	80	75
3282	50000l. Football composed of participating countries' flags (horiz)	1·60	1·50

1996. Traditional Houses (4th series). As T **755**. Multicoloured.

3283	10000l. Kayseri	25	25
3284	15000l. Konya	40	40
3285	25000l. Ankara (vert)	60	55
3286	50000l. Konya (vert)	1·60	1·50

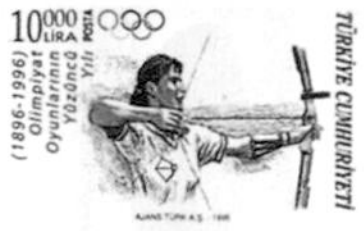
784 Archery

1996. Centenary of Modern Olympic Games and "Istanbul '96" International Stamp Exhibition (3rd issue). Sheet 118×78 mm containing T **784** and similar horiz designs. Multicoloured.

MS3287	10000l. Type **784**; 15000l. Wrestling; 25000l. Weightlifting; 50000l. Hurdling	5·00	4·50

1996. Various stamps surch. (a) Postcard Rate. Surch T and emblem.

3292	-	T (10000l.) on 250l. orange, brown and gold (No. 3144)	65	40
3293	**685**	T (10000l.) on 2000l. blue and grey	65	40

(b) Domestic Letter Rate. Nos. 3099 and 3101/2 surch **M.**

3294	**705**	M (15000l.) on 200l. multicoloured	1·20	90
3295	-	M (15000l.) on 400l. multicoloured	1·20	90
3296	-	M (15000l.) on 1500l. multicoloured	1·20	90

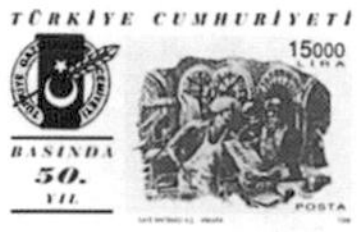
788 Printing Works and Association Emblem

1996. 50th Anniv of Journalists' Association.

3297	**788**	15000l. multicoloured	40	40

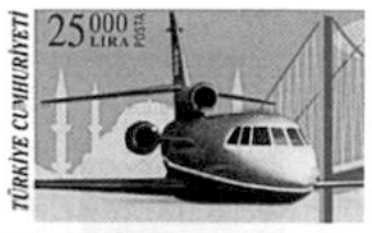
789 Airplane

1996. "Istanbul '96" Stamp Exhibition. Sheet 118×78 mm containing T **789** and similar horiz designs. Multicoloured.

MS3298	Type **789**: 50000l. Helicopter and liner superstructure; 75000l. Railway locomotive; 100000l. Coach and liner hull	9·75	9·00

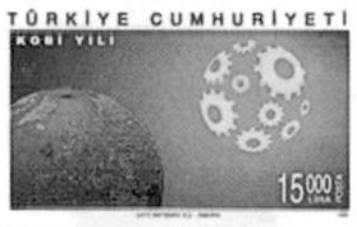
790 Cogwheels on Sphere and Globe

1996. Year of Small and Medium Businesses.

3299	**790**	15000l. multicoloured	40	40

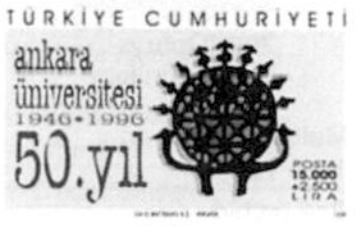
791 Emblem

1996. 50th Anniv of Ankara University.

3300	**791**	15000l.+2500l. mult	40	40

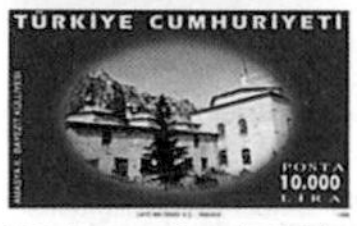
792 Amasya Bayezit Public Library

1996. Historical Buildings. Multicoloured.

3301	10000l. Type **792** (500th anniv)	15	15
3302	15000l. Divrigi Mosque and Hospital	40	40

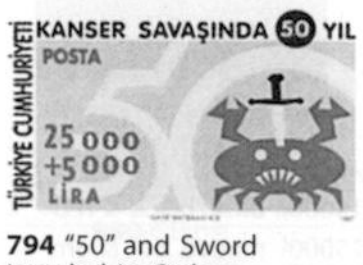
794 "50" and Sword impaled in Crab

1997. 50th Anniv of National Cancer Research and Prevention Association.

3304	**794**	25000l.+5000l. mult	40	40

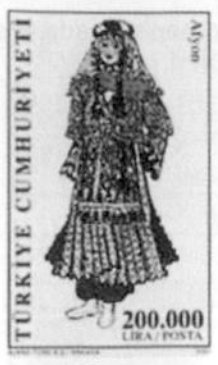

851 Afyon

2001. Women's Regional Costumes (1st series). Multicoloured.

3451	200000l. Type **851**	65	60
3452	200000l. Balikesir	65	60
3453	325000l. Kars	1·00	90
3454	325000l. Tokat	1·00	90

See also Nos. 3494/7.

2001. Traditional Women's Headdresses (5th series). As T **808**. Multicoloured.

3455	200000l. Mersin-Silifke	50	45
3456	250000l. Sivas	65	60
3457	425000l. Aydin	1·10	1·00
3458	450000l. Hakkari	1·20	1·10

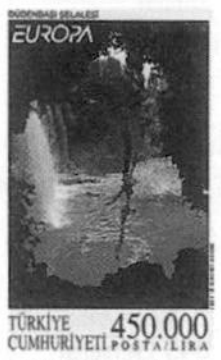

852 Dudenbasi Waterfalls

2001. Europa. Water Resources. Multicoloured.

3459	450000l. Type **852**	1·10	1·00
3460	500000l. Yerkopru Falls	1·10	1·00

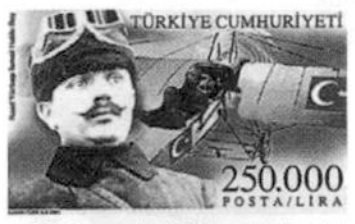

853 Captain Mehmet Fethi Bey (pilot) and Muaret-I-Milliye

2001. 87th Anniv of First Istanbul–Cairo Flights by Turkish Crews. Multicoloured.

3461	250000l. Type **853**	40	40
3462	300000l. First Lieutenant Sadik Bey (navigator) and Muaret-I-Miliye	50	45
3463	450000l. First Lieutenant Nuri Bey (pilot) and Prince Celaleddin	75	70
3464	500000l. Captain Ismail Hakki Bey (navigator) and Prince Celaleddin	80	75

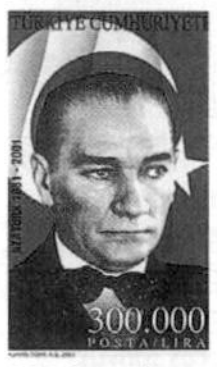

854 Ataturk and Turkish Flag

2001. 120th Birth Anniv of Kemal Ataturk (President, 1923–38). Multicoloured.

3465	200000l. Type **854**	65	60
3466	450000l. Ataturk and building (horiz)	1·00	90

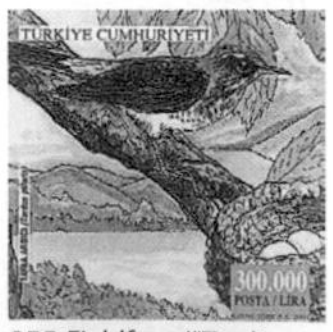

855 Fieldfare ("Turdis pilaris")

2001. World Environment Day. Birds. Two sheets, 109×73 mm containing square designs as T **855**. Multicoloured.

MS3467	Two sheets (a) 300000l. Type **855**; 300000l. Goldfinch ("Carduelis carduelis"). (b) 450000l. European bee eater ("Merops apiaster"); 450000l. Hoopoe ("Upupa epops")	3·75	3·50

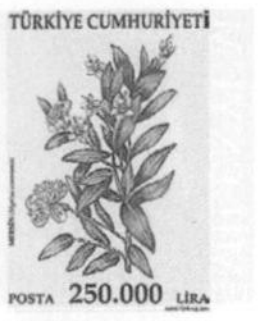

856 Myrtle (*Myrtus communis*)

2001. Plants. Multicoloured.

3468	250000l. Type **856**	40	40
3469	300000l. Yarrow (*Achillea millefolium*)	50	45
3470	450000l. St. John's Wort (*Hypericum perforatum*)	80	75
3471	500000l. Moyes rose (*Rosa moyesii*)	80	75
3472	1750000l. Whitethorn (*Crataegus oxyacantha*)	3·00	2·75

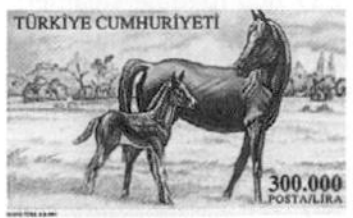

857 Mare and Foal

2001. Horses. Multicoloured.

3473	300000l. Type **857**	50	45
3474	450000l. Horses galloping	80	75
3475	450000l. Heads of three horses	80	75
3476	500000l. Horse (vert)	80	75

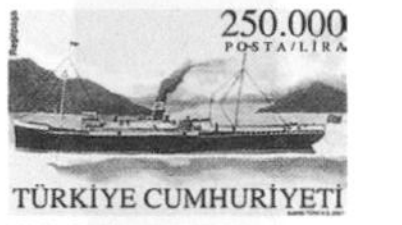

858 *Resitpasa*

2001. Merchant Ships. Multicoloured.

3477	250000l. Type **858**	50	45
3478	300000l. *Gulnihal*	60	55
3479	300000l. *Mithatpasa*	60	55
3480	500000l. *Aydin*	80	75

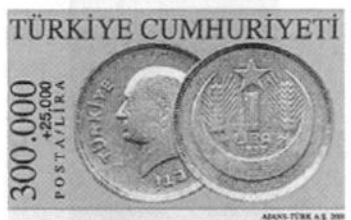

859 Obverse and Reverse of 1 Lira Coin, 1937

2001. Coins. Multicoloured.

3481	300000l.+25000l. Type **859**	75	70
3482	300000l.+25000l. Obverse and reverse of 100 Kurus coin, 1934	75	70
3483	450000l.+25000l. Obverse and reverse of Sultan Mehmet II gold coin, 1451	80	75
3484	500000l.+25000l. Obverse and reverse of Sultan Meliksah gold coin, 467	1·00	90

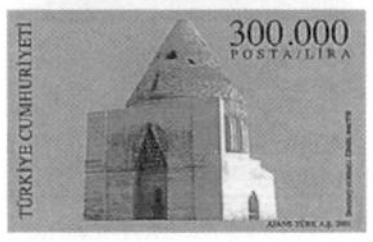

860 Sultan Tekes's Tomb, Turkmenistan

2001. Buildings.

3485	860	300000l. green and black	75	70
3486	-	300000l. red, yellow and black	75	70
3487	-	450000l. red, lilac and black	80	75
3488	-	500000l. blue and black	1·00	90

DESIGNS: No. 3486, Sirvansahlar Palace; 3487, Timur's Tomb, Samarkand; 3488, Yildirim Beyazit's Tomb.

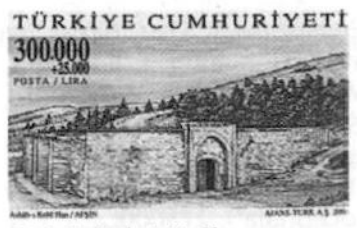

861 Ashab-I Keff (13th-century)

2001. Caravanserais (inns) along the Silk Road. Multicoloured.

3489	300000l. + 25000l. Type **861**	80	75
3490	500000l. + 25000l. Horozlu (13th-century)	1·20	1·10

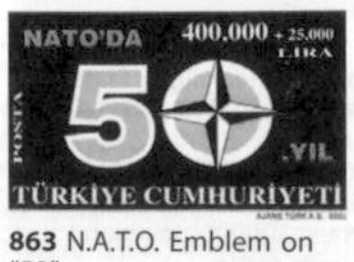

863 N.A.T.O. Emblem on "50"

2002. 50th Anniv of Turkey's Membership of North Atlantic Treaty Organization.

3492	**863**	400000l. + 25000l. multicoloured	80	75

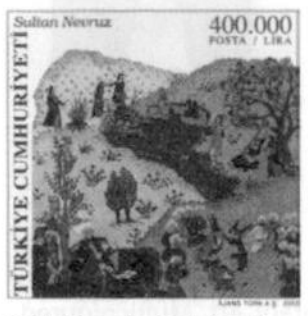

864 People Celebrating in Garden

2002. Sultan Nevruz Festival.

3493	**864**	400000l. multicoloured	80	75

2002. Women's Regional Costumes (2nd series). As T **851**. Multicoloured.

3494	350000l. Kastamonu	65	60
3495	400000l. Canakkale	80	75
3496	500000l. Amasya-Ilisu	80	75
3497	600000l. Elazig	1·00	90

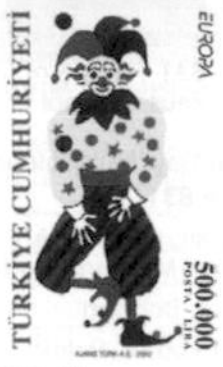

865 Clown

2002. Europa. Circus.

3498	**865**	500000l. multicoloured	1·20	1·10

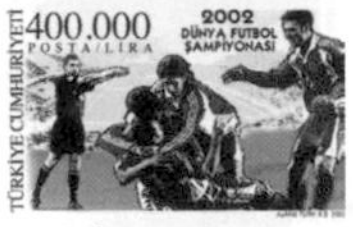

866 Referee and Footballers

2002. World Cup Football Championship, Japan and South Korea (1st issue). Multicoloured.

3499	400000l. Type **866**	80	75
3500	600000l. World cup, football and player	1·20	1·10

See also Nos. 3508/9.

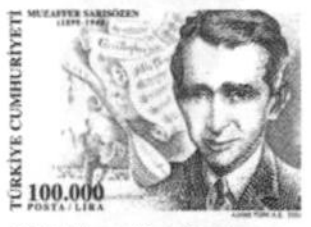

867 Muzaffer Sarisozen (musician)

2002. Personalities.

3501	**867**	100000l. red, brown and black	15	15
3502	-	400000l. blue, indigo and black	60	55
3503	-	500000l. brown, deep brown and black	75	70
3504	-	600000l. lilac, purple and black	80	75
3505	-	2500000l. green, olive and black	3·50	3·25

DESIGNS: 400000l. Arif Nihat Asya (teacher, writer and politician); 500000l. Vedat Tek (architect); 600000l. Hilmi Ziya Ulken (philosopher); 2500000l. Ibrahim Calli (artist).

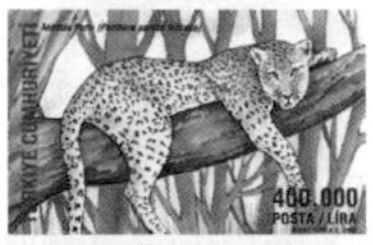

868 Anatolian Leopard (*Panthera pardus tulliana*)

2002. World Environment Day. Sheet 109×80 mm, containing T **868** and similar horiz designs. Multicoloured.

MS3506	400000l. Type **868**; 400000l. Eurasian lynx (*Lynx lynx*); 400000l. Tiger (*Panthera tigris*); 400000l. Caracal (*Felis caracal*)	3·00	2·75

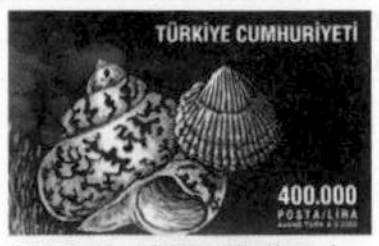

869 Painted Top Shell and Edible Cockle

2002. Shells. Sheet 103×78 mm, containing T **869** and similar horiz designs. Multicoloured.

MS3507	400000l. Type **869**; 500000l. *Netted nassa*; 600000l. Common northern whelk; 750000l. Common periwinkle	4·00	3·75

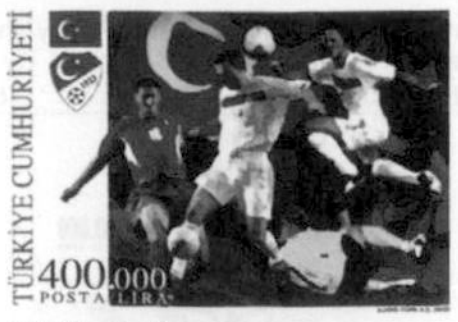

870 Footballers

2002. World Cup Football Championship, Japan and South Korea (2nd issue). Multicoloured.

3508	400000l. Type **870**	80	75
3509	700000l. Turkish team (third place play-off winners)	1·60	1·50

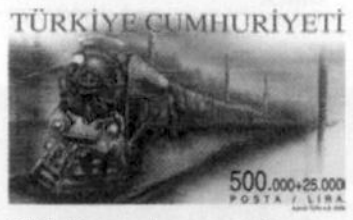

871 Steam Locomotive

2002. Railways. Multicoloured.

3510	500000l.+25000l. Type **871**	1·00	90
3511	700000l.+25000l. Modern locomotive	1·50	1·40

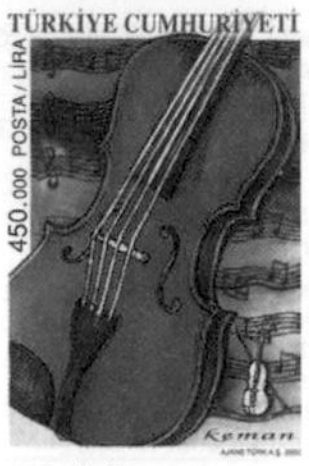

872 Violin

2002. Musical Instruments. Multicoloured.

3512	450000l. Type **872**	80	75
3513	700000l. Double bass	1·20	1·10

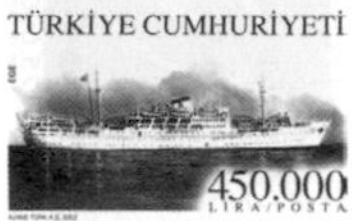

873 *Ege*

2002. Merchant Ships. Multicoloured.

3514	450000l. Type **873**	65	60
3515	500000l. *Ayvalik*	65	60
3516	700000l. *Marakaz*	80	75
3517	700000l. *Karadeniz*	80	75

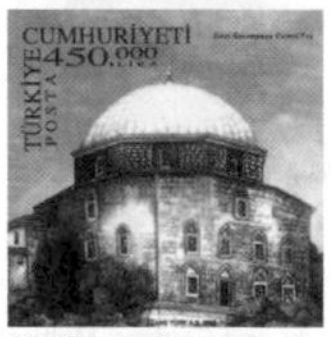

874 Pasha Gazi Kasim Mosque, Pecs

2002. Cultural Heritage. Sheet 105×65 mm, containing T **874** and similar square designs. Multicoloured.

MS3518	450l. Type **874**; 700l. Rakoczi Mansion, Tekirdag	1·60	1·50

Stamps of a similar design were issued by Hungary.

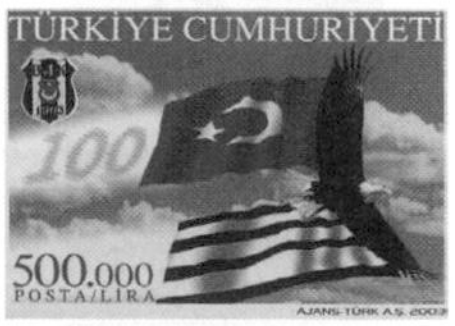

876 Eagle and Flags

2003. Centenary of Besiktas Gymnastic Club. Multicoloured.

3524	500000l. Type **876**	50	45
3525	700000l. Eagle, stars, badge and stadium	65	60
3526	750000l. Badge and footballers	75	70
3527	1000000l. Emblem	1·00	90

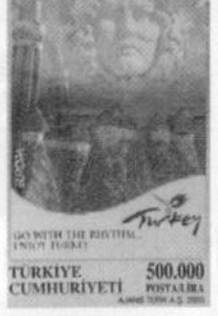

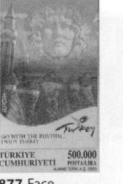

877 Face, Minarets and Mountains

2003. Europa. Poster Art. Multicoloured.

3528	500000l. Type **877**	65	60

3529 700000l. Trees and children
(theatre poster) 1·00 90

878 Siege of
Constantinople

2003. 550th Anniv of Conquest of Istanbul
(Constantinople). Multicoloured.
3530 500000l. Type **878** 50 45
3531 500000l. Sultan Mehmet II 50 45
3532 700000l. Sultan's robe 65 60
3533 1500000l. Sultan Mehmet II
(different) 1·40 1·30

879 Gazelle (*Gazella
subgutturosa*)

2003. World Environment Day. Sheet 111×78 mm
containing T **879** and similar horiz designs.
Multicoloured.
MS3534 500000l. ×4, Type **879**; Red
deer (*Cervus elephus*); Roe deer
(*Capreolus capreolus*); Fallow deer
(*Cervus dama*) 2·00 1·80

880 Western Zodiac

2003
3535 **880** 500000l. multicoloured 50 45

2003. Women's Regional Costumes (3rd series). As T **851**.
Multicoloured.
3536 500000l. Gaziantep 50 45
3537 500000l. Sivas 50 45
3538 700000l. Erzincan 65 60
3539 700000l. Ankara-Beyazari 65 60

881 Quince
Flowers

2003. Flowering Trees. Multicoloured.
3540 500000l. Type **881** 50 45
3541 700000l. Wild cherry 75 70
3542 750000l. Plum 75 70
3543 1000000l. Pomegranate 1·00 90
3544 3000000l. Orange 3·00 2·75

883 Tram

2003. Rail Transport. Multicoloured.
3549 600000l.+50000l. Type **883** 75 70
3550 800000l.+50000l. Subway train 90 85

884 Horn

2003. Brass Instruments. Multicoloured.
3551 600000l. Type **884** 65 60
3552 800000l. Trumpet 80 75

886 Kemal Ataturk (first
president) and National
Flag

2003. 80th Anniv of Republic. Multicoloured.
3554 600000l. Type **886** 65 60
3555 600000l. Kemal Ataturk and
cavalry 65 60

887 *Karadeniz*

2003. Ships. Frigates. Multicoloured.
3556 600000l. Type **887** 65 60
3557 600000l. *Gediz* 65 60
3558 700000l. *Salihreis* 75 70
3559 700000l. *Kocatepe* 75 70

888 Mithat Pasha, Bank Facade
and Farmers

2003. 140th Anniv of Ziraat Bank.
3560 **888** 600000l. multicoloured 65 60

889 Villa,
Trabzon

2003. Cultural Heritage. Multicoloured.
3561 600000l. Type **889** 65 60
3562 700000l. Museum, Adapazari 75 70
3563 800000l. House, Saloniki 80 75
3564 1000000l. Museum, Ankara 1·10 1·00

890 Ibrahim
Erzurumlu

2003. 300th Birth Anniv of Ibrahim Hakki Erzurumlu
(writer and mystic).
3565 **890** 600000l.+50000l. multicoloured 65 60

891 "PttBank"

2004. PTT (post office) Bank.
3566 **891** 600000l. multicoloured 60 55

892 Kerempe
Lighthouse,
Kastamonu

2004. Lighthouses. Multicoloured.
3567 600000l.+50000l. Type **892** 65 60
3568 700000l.+50000l. Gelidonya,
Antalya 75 70

2004. Women's Regional Costumes (4th series). As T **851**.
Multicoloured.
3569 60000l. Edirne 60 55
3570 60000l. Tunceli 65 60

3571 700000l. Burdur 65 60
3572 800000l. Trabzon 75 70

893 Skiing and
Windsurfing

2004. Europa. Holidays. Multicoloured.
3573 700000l. Type **893** 65 60
3574 800000l. Yachts and ruins 75 70

894 Common Kestrel (*Falco
tinnunculus*)

2004. World Environment Day. Sheet 108×78 mm
containing T **894** and similar horiz designs.
Multicoloured.
MS3575 700000l.×4, Type **894**; Common buzzard (*Buteo buteo*); Golden
eagle (*Aquila chrysaetos*); Red kite
(*Milvus migrans*) 2·75 2·40
The stamps and margins of No. **MS**3575 form a composite design.

895 Mamahatun

2004. Caravanserais (inns) along the Silk Road.
Multicoloured.
3576 600000l. Type **895** 60 55
3577 700000l. Cardakhan 65 60

896 Child,
Policeman and
Dog

2004. 165th Anniv of Gendarmerie.
3578 **896** 600000l. multicoloured 60 55

897 Goldcrest (*Regulus
regulus*)

2004. Birds. Multicoloured.
3579 100000l. Type **897** 10 10
3580 250000l. *Sylvia rueppelli* 25 25
3581 600000l. *Hippolais polyglotta* 60 55
3582 700000l. House sparrow (*Passer
domesticus*) 65 60
3583 800000l. *Emberiza bruniceps* 75 70
3584 1000000l. Chaffinch (*Fringella
coelebs*) 90 85
3585 1500000l. Common redstart
(*Phoenicurus phoenicurus*) 1·40 1·30
3586 3500000l. Robin (*Erithacus
rubecula*) 3·25 3·00

898 Wrestling

2004. Olympic Games, Athens. Multicoloured.
3587 600000l. Type **898** 60 55
3588 700000l. Running (vert) 65 60
3589 700000l. Weightlifting 65 60
3590 800000l. Wrestling (different) 90 85

2004. Ships. Fleet Vessels. As T **887**. Multicoloured.
3591 600000l. TCG 18 Mart (S-356) 60 55
3592 700000l. TCG Preveze (S-363) 65 60
3593 700000l. TCG Anafartalar (S-356) 65 60
3594 800000l. TCG Atilay (S-347) 75 70

899 Piri Reis

2004. 450th Death Anniv of Piri Reis (admiral).
3595 **899** 600000l. multicoloured 60 55

900 Guide

2004. Guide and Scouting Movement. Multicoloured.
3596 600000l.+50000l. Type **900** 60 55
3597 700000l.+50000l. Boy scout 75 70

902 Kapuzbasi Waterfall

2004. Waterfalls. Multicoloured.
3603 600000l. Type **902** 60 55
3604 700000l. Sudusen (vert) 65 60

903 Villa, Bursa

2004. Cultural Heritage. Multicoloured.
3605 600000l. Type **903** 65 60
3606 700000l. House, Havza 75 60
3607 700000l. Museum, Erzurum 75 70
3608 800000l. Ministry building,
Ankara 80 75

904 Two Aircraft

2004. Turkish Stars (air display team). Sheet 108×78
mm containing T **904** and similar horiz designs.
Multicoloured.
MS3609 600000l. Type **904**; 700000l.
Five aircraft with coloured exhausts;
800000l Aircraft in vertical flight;
900000l. Aircraft in level flight 2·75 2·50

905 Adana

2005. Provinces. Multicoloured.
3610 1ykr. Type **905** 10 10
3611 5ykr. Adiyaman 10 10
3612 10ykr. Aeyon 10 10
3613 25ykr. Agri 25 25
3614 50ykr. Amaysa 40 40
3615 60ykr. Ankara 50 45
3616 60ykr. Bitlis 50 45
3617 70ykr. Antalya 60 55
3618 70ykr. Bolu 60 55
3619 80ykr. Artvin 65 60
3620 80ykr. Burdur 65 60
3621 90ykr. Aydin 75 70
3622 1ytl. Balikesir 80 75
3623 1.5ytl. Bilecik 1·20 1·10
3624 3.5ytl. Bursa 3·00 2·75
3625 3.5ytl. Bingol 3·00 2·75

906 Emblems

2005. Centenary of Rotary International.
| 3627 | **906** | 80ykr.+10ykr. Multicoloured | 75 | 70 |

2005. Lighthouses. As T **892**. Multicoloured.
| 3628 | 60ykr. Batiburnu, Canakkale | 50 | 45 |
| 3629 | 70ykr. Zonguldak | 60 | 55 |

907 Catamaran

2005. International Maritime Festival, Marmaris. Multicoloured.
| 3630 | 70ykr. Type **907** | 60 | 55 |
| 3631 | 80ykr. Yacht at sunset | 65 | 60 |

908 Child and Woman Police Officer

2005. 160th Anniv of the Turkish Police Organization.
| 3632 | **908** | 70ykr. Multicoloured | 60 | 55 |

909 Flag as Flame

2005. 85th Anniv of National Sovereignty. Multicoloured.
| 3633 | 60ykr. Type **909** | 50 | 45 |
| 3634 | 70ykr. Fireworks | 60 | 55 |

910 Vegetables as Landscape

2005. Europa. Gastronomy.
| 3635 | **910** | 70ykr. Multicoloured | 60 | 55 |

911 Yavuz Sultan Selim

2005. Sultans' Kaftans. Multicoloured.
3636	70ykr. Type **911**	60	55
3637	70ykr. Muram III	60	55
3638	70ykr. Ahmed I	60	55
3639	70ykr. Ahmed I (different)	60	55

912 *Pagellus bogaraveo*

2005. World Environment Day. Fish. Sheet 113×78 mm containing T **912** and similar horiz designs. Multicoloured.
| MS3640 | 60ykr. Type **912**; 70ykr. *Epinephelus guaza*; 70ykr. *Merlangus euxinus* (inscr "Merlanyus"); 80ykr. *Maena smaris* | 2·75 | 2·50 |

913 Carpet, Hereke, Turkey

2005. Carpets and Tapestries. Multicoloured.
| 3641 | 60ykr. Type **913** | 50 | 45 |
| 3642 | 70ykr. "L'humanitie assaillie par les sept Peches capiteux" (Seven Deadly Sins) (16th-century tapestry, Brussels) | 60 | 55 |

Stamps of a similar design were issued by Belgium.

914 Istanbul

2005. World Architecture Congress, Istanbul.
| 3643 | **914** | 70ykr. Multicoloured | 60 | 55 |

916 Achelous

2005. Zeugma (archaeological site). Multicoloured.
3650	60ykr. Type **916**	50	45
3651	70ykr. Achilles	60	55
3652	70ykr. Oceanus and Thetys	60	55
3653	80ykr. Maenad	65	60

917 Musical Clock (Britain, 1770)

2005. Clocks. Multicoloured.
| 3654 | 60ykr. Type **917** | 50 | 45 |
| 3655 | 70ykr. Perpetual clock (France, 1867) | 60 | 55 |

918 Race Car

2005. Turkish Formula I Grand Prix, Istanbul.
| 3656 | **918** | 70ykr. multicoloured | 60 | 55 |

919 Albert Einstein and Atomic Model

2005. International Year of Physics.
| 3657 | **919** | 70ykr.+10ykr. multicoloured | 75 | 70 |

920 Sakip Sabanci

2005. Business Personalities. Multicoloured.
| 3658 | 60ykr. Type **920** | 50 | 45 |
| 3659 | 70ykr. Vehbi Koc | 60 | 55 |

2005. Provinces. As T **905**. Multicoloured.
3660	50ykr. Canakkale	40	40
3661	60ykr. Corum	50	45
3662	60ykr. Cankiri	50	45
3663	60ykr. Edirne	50	45
3664	60ykr. Diyarbakir	50	45
3665	60ykr. Denizli	50	45
3666	60ykr. Elazig	50	45
3667	70ykr. Erzincan	60	50
3668	70ykr. Erzurum	60	55
3669	70ykr. Eskisehir	60	55
3670	70ykr. Gaziantep	60	55
3671	70ykr. Giresun	60	55
3672	70ykr. Gumushane	60	55
3673	1ytl. Hakkari	80	75
3674	1ytl.50 Hatay	1·20	1·10
3675	2ytl.50 Isparta	1·40	1·30

921 Rumi and Dervish Dancers

2005. 800th Birth Anniv (2007) of Mevlana Celaleddin (Rumi) (poet and philosopher).
| 3676 | **921** | 70ykr. multicoloured | 60 | 55 |

922 Fans and Club Arms

2005. Centenary of Galatasary Sports Club. Multicoloured.
3677	60ykr. Type **922**	50	45
3678	70ykr. Arms, stadium and trophy	60	55
MS3679	108×78 mm. 60ykr. Ali Sami Yen (founder); 70ykr. Entrance; 80ykr. Celebrating fans; 1ytl. Celebrating fans (different)	2·75	2·50

923 Turkish Flag and European Union Stars

2005. Negotiations for Membership of European Union.
| 3680 | **923** | 70ykr. multicoloured | 60 | 55 |

924 Leek (*Allium porrum*)

2005. Medicinal Plants. Multicoloured.
3681	60ykr. Type **924**	50	45
3682	70ykr. Garlic (*Allium sativum*)	60	55
3683	80ykr. Onion (*Allium cepa*)	65	60

925 As No. 2415

2005. 50th Anniv of Europa Stamps. Multicoloured.
3684	60ykr. Type **925**	75	70
3685	70ykr. As Type **325**	90	80
3686	80ykr. As Type **365**	1·00	90
3687	1ykl. As No. 2162	1·20	1·10
MS3688	Two sheets, each 111×79 mm. All horiz. (a) 10ykr. As No. 1962; 25ykr. As No. 2278; 60ykr. As Type **305**; 70ykr. As Type **382**. (b) 10ykr. As Type **284**; 25ykr. As No. 2442; 60ykr. As Type **317**; 70ykr. As Type **430**	4·50	4·50

926 Speed Skater

2006. Winter Olympic Games, Turin. Multicoloured.
| 3689 | 60ykr. Type **926** | 75 | 70 |
| 3690 | 70ykr. Skier | 90 | 80 |

927 Forest and Lake

2006. World Forest Day.
| 3691 | **927** | 60ykr.+10ykr. multicoloured | 90 | 90 |

928 Boy wearing Protective Glasses

2006. Solar Eclipse.
| 3692 | **928** | 70ykr. multicoloured | 90 | 80 |

929 Hands holding Pencil

2006. Support for Education.
| 3693 | **929** | 60ykr. multicoloured | 75 | 70 |

931 Karaoglan

2006. Cartoons. Karaoglan created by Suat Yalaz. Multicoloured.
3699	60ykr. Type **931**	75	70
3700	70ykr. On horseback holding whip	90	80
3701	70ykr. With sword and shield	90	80
3702	80ykr. On horseback holding sword	1·00	90

931a Izzet Baysal

2006. Izzet Baysal Commemoration.
| 3702a | **931a** | 60ykr. multicoloured | 1·00 | 1·00 |

932 Soldiers

2006. 125th Birth Anniv of Mustafa Kemal Ataturk. Multicoloured.
3703	60ykr. Type **932**	75	70
3704	60ykr. Bandirma and Ataturk in uniform	75	70
3705	60ykr. Train and Ataturk in formal dress	75	70
3706	60ykr. With leaders	75	70
3707	60ykr. Wearing lounge suit	75	70
3708	60ykr. Wearing overcoat and on horseback	75	70
3709	60ykr. Facing right and with crowd	75	70
3710	60ykr. Holding papers and with military leaders	75	70
3711	60ykr. With child	75	70
3712	60ykr. Crowd and Ataturk facing left	75	70

933 Linked Hands

2006. Europa. Integration.
| 3713 | **933** | 70ykr. multicoloured | 90 | 80 |

934 Cracked Earth

2006. International Year of Deserts and Desertification. Sheet 79×112 mm containing T **934** and similar vert designs. Multicoloured.

MS3714 25ykr. Type **934**; 50ykr. Conifer and rocky ground; 70ykr. Remains of forest; 70ykr. New forest growth   2·60   2·60

935 Player and Ball

2006. World Cup Football Championship, Germany. Multicoloured.

| 3715 | 70ykr. Type **935** | 90 | 80 |
| 3716 | 70ykr. Player and ball (vert) | 90 | 80 |

936 Deperdussin Monoplane

2006. Early Aircraft of the Turkish Airforce 1912–14. Multicoloured.

3717	60ykr. Type **936**	75	70
3718	70ykr. R E P parasol monoplane	90	80
3719	70ykr. Bleriot monoplane	90	80

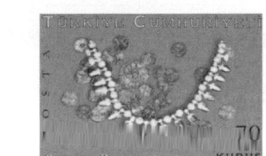

937 Necklace

2006. Karun's Treasure. Multicoloured.

3720	70ykr. Type **937**	90	80
3721	70ykr. Winged necklace and bracelet	90	80
3722	80ykr. Two lion-headed cuffs	1·00	90

938 Bride and Groom

2006. Turkish Cinema. Showing scenes from films. Multicoloured.

| 3723 | 60ykr. Type **938** | 75 | 70 |
| 3724 | 70ykr. Woman and two men | 90 | 80 |

2006. Provinces. As T **905**. Multicoloured.

3725	10ykr. Kahramanmaras	15	15
3726	10ykr. Manisa	15	15
3727	50ykr. Koscali	45	45
3728	50ykr. Kirsgehir	45	45
3729	60ykr. Izmir	50	50
3730	60ykr. Konya	50	50
3731	60ykr. Mugla	50	50
3732	60ykr. Mardin	50	50
3733	70ykr. Istanbul	65	65
3734	70ykr. Mersin	65	65
3735	1ytl. Kutahya	90	90
3736	1ytl. Kirklareli	90	90
3737	1ytl.60 Kastamonu	1·50	1·50
3738	2ytl. Kayseri	1·70	1·70
3739	4ytl. Malatya	3·75	3·75
3740	4ytl. Kars	3·75	3·75

939 Steam Locomotive

2006. 150th Anniv of Railways. Multicoloured.

| 3741 | 60ykr. Type **939** | 75 | 70 |
| 3742 | 70ykr. Modern locomotive | 90 | 80 |

940 Mehmet Ersoy and Script

2006. 70th Death Anniv of Mehmet Akif Ersoy (poet). Multicoloured.

| 3743 | 60ykr.+10ykr. Type **940** | 90 | 90 |
| 3744 | 70ykr.+10ykr. Script and Mehmet Ersoy | 1·00 | 1·00 |

940a Building Facade

2006. 75th Anniv of National Central Bank (TNB).

| 3745 | **940a** 60ykr. multicoloured | 1·00 | 1·00 |

941 Globe and Shaft of Energy

2006. ITU Conference, Tunis. Multicoloured.

| 3746 | 60ykr. Type **941** | 75 | 70 |
| 3747 | 70ykr. Rays emanating from map | 90 | 80 |

942 Statue

2006. 50th Anniv of Middle East Technical University.

| 3748 | **942** 60ykr. multicoloured | 75 | 70 |

942a Emblems

2006. 50th Anniv of National Atomic Energy Authority.

| 3749 | **942a** 60ykr. multicoloured | 1·00 | 1·00 |

943 Vents

2006. Geothermal Energy. Multicoloured.

| 3750 | 60ykr. Type **943** | 75 | 75 |
| 3751 | 70ykr. Power station | 85 | 85 |

2007. Early Aircraft of the Turkish Airforce 1912–14. As T **936**. Multicoloured.

3757	60ykr. Breguet XIV B-2	80	80
3758	70ykr. Albatros C-XV	85	85
3759	70ykr. Fiat R2	85	85

945 Carved Relief

2007. Anatolian Civilizations. Hittites. Multicoloured.

3760	60ykr. Type **945**	75	75
3761	60ykr. Sulumeli'nin	75	75
3762	60ykr. Charioteer	75	75
3763	60ykr. Coin	75	75

946 Flags and Map

2007. Post Office Directorate Meeting.

| 3764 | **946** 60ykr. multicoloured | 75 | 75 |

947 Battle Scene

2007. 650th Anniversary of Tekirdag.

| 3765 | **947** 60ykr. multicoloured | 75 | 75 |

948 Committee

2007. Centenary of Fenerbachce Sports Club. Multicoloured.

| 3766 | 60ykr. Type **948** | 75 | 75 |
| 3767 | 60ykr. Document | 75 | 75 |

MS3768 192×78 mm. Size 41×25 mm. Women's football team; Runner; Yachtsman; Boxer; Rower; Basketball and table tennis. Imperf   6·00   6·00

MS3769 112×85 mm. 60ykr. Lighthouse, Fenerbache Burnu; 70ykr. Meeting of three; 80ykr. Pitch; 90ykr. Stadium   3·75   3·75

949 Mevlana

2007. 800th Birth anniv of Mawlana Jalal-ad-Din Muhammad Rumi (Mevlana or Rumi) (philosopher and writer). Sheet 130×70 mm containing T **949** and similar vert designs. Multicoloured.

MS3770 25ykr. Type **949**; 50ykr Script; 60ykr. Mevlevi (Sufi order founded by the followers of Rumi) Dervishes dancing; 70ykr. Konya (domicile for last fifty years of life)   2·75   2·75

950 Campfire

2007. Europa. Centenary of Scouting. Multicoloured.

| 3771 | 60ykr. Type **950** | 80 | 80 |
| 3772 | 70ykr. Scouts saluting | 85 | 85 |

951 Soldier and Flag

2007. 25th Anniv of Armed Forces.

| 3773 | **951** 60ykr. multicoloured | 75 | 75 |

952 Goats

2007. Domestic Animals. Sheet 112×77 mm containing T **952** and similar horiz designs. Multicoloured.

MS3774 25ykr. Type **952**; 50ykr. Cattle; 60ykr. Sheep; 70ykr. Chickens   3·00   3·00

The stamps and margins of MS3774 form a composite design of a farmyard.

953 Noah's Pudding

2007. Traditonal Cuisine. Multicoloured.

3775	1ytl. Type **953**	1·30	1·30
3776	1ytl. Bulghur	1·30	1·30
3777	2ytl. Baked ravioli	2·75	2·75

954 Emblem

2007. 15th Anniversary Summit of Black Sea Econonmic Cooperation Organization.

| 3778 | **954** 60ykr. multicoloured | 1·00 | 1·00 |

2007. Provinces. As T **905**. Multicoloured.

3779	10ykr. Siirt	15	15
3780	50ykr. Ordu	55	55
3781	60ykr. Rize	75	75
3782	1ytl. Nigde	1·20	1·20
3783	1ytl. Samsun	1·20	1·20
3784	2ytl. Nevsehir	2·20	2·20
3785	4ytl. Mus	4·50	4·50
3786	4ytl. Saksrya	4·50	4·50

955 Committee

2007. 75th Anniv of Language Society.

| 3787 | **955** 70ykr. multicoloured | 1·00 | 1·00 |

956 Flag, Coastguard Vessel and Ataturk

2007. 25th Anniv of Coastguard Control.

| 3788 | **956** 60ykr.+10ykr. multicoloured | 1·00 | 1·00 |

957 White Rose

2007. Roses. Multicoloured.

3789	60ykr. Type **957**	2·10	2·10
3790	60ykr. Red rose	2·10	2·10
3791	60ykr. Yellow rose	2·10	2·10

958 Tuzsuz Deli Bekir and Efe

2007. Cultural Heritage. Shadow Play Characters. Multicoloured.

3792	60ykr. Type **958**	85	85
3793	70ykr. Hacivat and Karagoz	95	95
3794	80ykr. Tiryaki and Celebi	1·20	1·20

959 Blue Mosque

2007. Balkanfila 2007 Stamp Exhibition, Istanbul. Two sheets, each 116×87 mm, containing T **959** and similar horiz designs. Multicoloured.
MS3795 (a) 60ykr. Type **959**; 70ykr. Hagia Sophia; 80ykr. City wall; 1ykl. Bridge over Bosphorus. (b) 60ykr. Dove and flags; 70ykr. Stylized bridge; 80ykr. Flags; 1ykl. Map and flags. Imperf .... 4·50 ... 4·50

The stamps of **MS**3795a/b, each form a composite design.
Nos. 3796/802 are vacant.

960 Mimar Sinan and Buyukcekmece Bridge

2007. 420th (2008) Death Anniv of Mimar Sinan (architect and early earthquake engineer). Multicoloured.

3803	60ykr. Type **960**	90	90
3804	70ykr. Selimiye Mosque	95	95
3805	70ykr. Haseki Hurrem Sultan Hamam (Bath of Roxelana), Ayasofya	95	95
3806	80ykr. Suleymaniye Mosque	1·20	1·20

961 Head

2007. World Philosophy Day.
3807	**961** 60ykr. multicoloured	1·00	1·00

962 Keloglan

2007. Cartoons. Keloglan. Multicoloured.

3808	60ykr. Type **962**	90	90
3809	70ykr. Riding donkey	95	95
3810	70ykr. Saying farewell to mother	95	95
3811	80ykr. Releasing birds	1·20	1·20

2007. Provinces. As T **905**. Multicoloured.

3812	5ykr. Tunceli	20	20
3813	10ykr. Tokat	30	30
3814	65ykr. Trab-zon	1·10	1·10
3815	65ykr. Sanliurfa	1·10	1·10
3816	80ykr. Sivas	1·20	1·20
3817	85ykr. Usak	1·40	1·40
3818	1ytl. Tekirdag	1·70	1·70
3819	4ytl.50 Sinop	5·00	5·00

964 White Flowers

2007. Traditional Arts. Paper Marbling. Multicoloured.
3821	60ykr.+10ykr. Type **964**	1·10	1·10
3822	70ykr.+10ykr. Tulips	1·20	1·20

965 Emblem

2008. 40th Anniv of TRT Television Channel. Multicoloured.
3823	40ykr. Type **965**	65	65
3824	80ykr. Building	1·30	1·30

966 Seated at Table

2008. 800th Birth Anniv of Nasreddin Hoca'nin (Mulla Nasrudin). Multicoloured.
3825	25ykr. Type **966**	30	30
3826	65ykr. Riding donkey backwards	80	80
3827	80ykr. Holding two pots	1·30	1·30
3828	85ykr. At river's edge	1·40	1·40

967 Couple and Flowers

2008. Valentine's Day. Multicoloured.
3829	65ykr. Type **967**	80	80
3830	80ykr. Envelope and flowers	1·30	1·30

Nos. 3831/6 and Type **968** are vacant.

969 Hospital

2008. 700th Anniv of Darussifa (Bimarhane) Mental Hospital (built by Ildus Hatun, wife of Sultan Olcaytu), Amasya. Sheet 130×63 mm containing T **969** and similar vert designs. Multicoloured.
MS3837 50ykr. Type **969**; 65ykr. Playing music; 80ykr. Lecture; 85ykr. Healing ... 3·75 ... 3·75

Nos. 3831/6 and Type **968** have been left for 'Attaturk', issued on 29 February 2008, not yet received.

970 Pendant, Pin and Necklace

2008. Anatolian Civilizations. Urartians. Multicoloured.
3838	65ykr. Type **970**	75	75
3839	65ykr. Statue	75	75
3840	80ykr. Harput Castle, Elazig	1·40	1·40
3841	80ykr. Pot on stand	1·40	1·40

971 Kasgarli Mahmut on Horseback

2008. Birth Millenary (2005) of Mahmud ibn Muhammad al-Kashgari (Kasgarli Mahmut) (linguist and lexicographer of Turkic dialects). Multicoloured.
3842	65ykr.+10ykr. Type **971**	1·10	1·10
3843	80ykr.+10ykr. Reading	1·30	1·30

972 B24 D (Consolidated B-24D LIBERATOR)

2008. Aircraft. Multicoloured.
3844	65ykr. Type **972**	75	75
3845	80ykr. Curtiss Hawk	1·20	1·20
3846	85ykr. PZL XXIV	1·30	1·30

973 Hands forming Heart

2008. Europa. The Letter. Multicoloured.
3847	65ykr. Type **973**	80	80
3848	80ykr. Ink bottle, pen and letter	1·30	1·30

974 Temple

2008. 50th Anniv of Turkey–Thailand Diplomatic Relations. Multicoloured.
3849	65ykr. Type **974**	80	80
3850	80ykr. Mosque	1·30	1·30

975 Olympic Rings, Dove and Emblem

2008. Centenary of National Olympic Committee. Multicoloured.
3851	65ykr. Type **975**	80	80
3852	80ykr. Athletes in parade	1·30	1·30
3853	85ykr. Stadium	1·40	1·40
3854	1ytl. Athlete	1·70	1·70

2008. Provinces. As T **905**. Multicoloured.
3855	5ykr. Zonguldak	10	10
3856	50ykr. Yozgat	55	55
3857	65ykr. Kirikale	80	80
3858	65ykr. Aksaray	80	80
3859	80ykr. Karaman	1·30	1·30
3860	85ykr. Van	1·40	1·40
3861	1ytl. Bayburt	1·70	1·70
3862	4ytl.50 Batman	6·50	6·50

976 Child and Polar Bears

2008. World Environment Day. Global Warming Awareness Campaign. Sheet 130×65 mm containing T **976** and similar vert designs. Multicoloured.
MS3863 25ykr. Type **976**; 65ykr. Melting ice; 80ykr. Glacial valley; 85ykr. Flower, face and parched, cracked earth ... 3·75 ... 3·75

977 Selahattin Ulkumen

2008. Humanitarians (who assisted Jews to escape the holocaust). Multicoloured.
3864	65ykr. Type **977**	80	80
3865	80ykr. Necdet Kent	1·20	1·20

978 Archery

2008. Olympic Games, Beijing. Multicoloured.
3866	25ykr. Type **978**	20	20
3867	65ykr. Taekwondo (vert)	80	80
3868	80ykr. Wrestling	80	80
3869	80ykr. Weightlifting	80	80

2008. Provinces. As T **905**. Multicoloured.
3870	50ykr. Kilis	40	40
3871	65ykr. Bartin (vert)	80	80
3872	1ytl. Ardahan	1·50	1·50
3873	1ytl. Igdir	1·50	1·50
3874	1ytl.50 Yalova	1·70	1·70
3875	2ytl. Karabuk	2·75	2·75
3876	2ytl. Osmaniye	2·75	2·75
3877	4ytl.50 Duzce	5·75	5·75
3878	4ytl.50 Sirnak	5·75	5·75

979 Bowl

2008. Turkish Arts and Crafts. Glassware. Multicoloured. P 13½.
3879	65ykr. Type **979**	80	80
3880	80ykr. Decorated vase	1·20	1·20

980 Barbarossa Hayreddin Pasha (fleet commander)

2008. 470th Anniv of Perveza Naval Victory. Naval Forces Day. Multicoloured.
3881	65ykr. Type **980**	80	80
3882	80ykr. Battle scene and Attaturk	1·20	1·20

981 Haydarpasa Railway Station and Locomotive

2008. Istanbul Railway Stations. Multicoloured.
3883	65ykr.+10ykr. Type **981**	90	90
3884	80ykr.+10ykr. Sirkeci	1·30	1·30

982 Istiqlal Mosque, Jakarta, Indonesia

2008. Turkey and Indonesia. Sheet 225×210 mm containing T **982** and similar horiz designs. Multicoloured.

MS3885 65ykr. Type **982**; 65ykr. Barelang bridge, Indonesia; 65ykr. Drummers, Saman dance, Indonesia; 65ykr. *Mucuna benettii*; 65ykr. Flat-headed cat; 80ykr. Sultan Ahmed Mosque, Istanbul, Turkey ; 80ykr. Bosphorus Bridge, Turkey; 80ykr. Whirling Dervishes; 80ykr. Tulips; 80ykr. Turkish Van cat 10·00 10·00

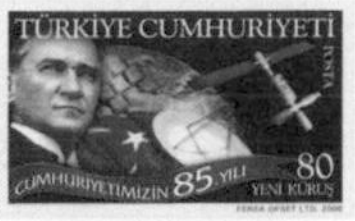

983 Attatürk and Symbols of Space

2008. 85th Anniv of Turkish Republic. Multicoloured.

3886 80ykr. Type **983** 1·20 1·20
3887 80ykr. Attaturk and symbols of transport 1·20 1·20

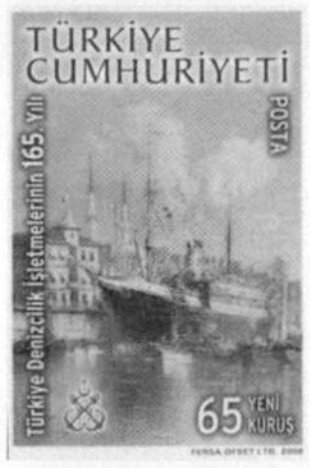

984 Ship in Port

2008. 165th Anniv of Turkish Maritime Organization. Multicoloured.

3888 65ykr. Type **984** 80 80
3889 80ykr. Ship at sea (horiz) 1·20 1·20
3890 80ykr. Organization emblem 1·20 1·20

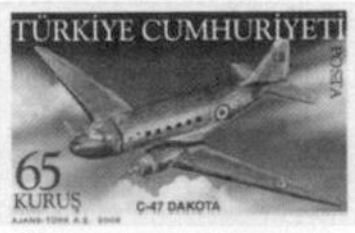

986 Douglas C-47 Skytrain (inscr 'C-47 Dakota')

2009. Aircraft. Multicoloured.

[illegible] 80 80
3896 80ykr. North American F-100 Super Sabre (inscr 'F-100 D Super Sabre') 1·20 1·20
3897 1ytl. North American F-86 Sabre 1·70 1·70

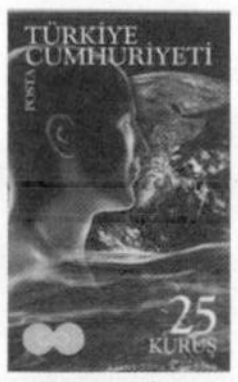

987 Face of Water and Globe

2009. Fifth World Water Forum, Istanbul. Sheet 131×65 mm containing T **987** and similar vert designs. Multicoloured.

MS3898 25ykr. Type **987**; 65ykr. Water droplet containing emblem; 80ykr. Waterfall; 80ykr. Pouring water 3·50 3·50

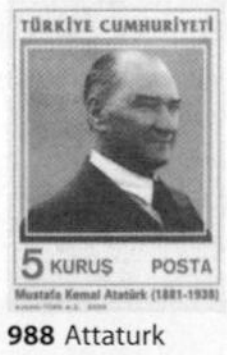

988 Attaturk

2009. Mustafa Kemal Attaturk Commemoration. Multicoloured.

3899 5ykr. Type **988** 20 20
3900 10ykr. Looking left 35 35
3901 25ykr. Walking with small girl 55 55
3902 50ykr. Seated at desk 60 60
3903 65ykr. Facing right 70 70
3903a 75ykr. Facing left 80 80
3904 80ykr. Wearing bowler hat facing left 80 80
3905 85ykr. Wearing evening dress facing left 1·20 1·20
3905a 90ykr. Wearing bowler hat facing right 1·20 1·20
3906 1ytl. Wearing evening dress with medal and carrying hat 1·50 1·50
3907 2ytl. Wearing evening dress, head and shoulders 2·75 2·75
3908 4ytl.50 Wearing cap facing left 5·50 5·50
3908a 5ytl. Wearing high collar facing right 5·50 5·50

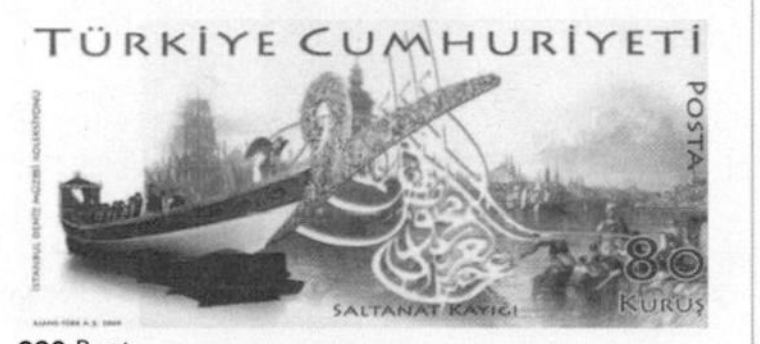

990 Boat

2009. Ottoman Royal Boats of Sultan Kayigi. Multicoloured.

3918 80ykr. Type **990** 1·20 1·20
3919 80ykr. With pointed prow 1·20 1·20

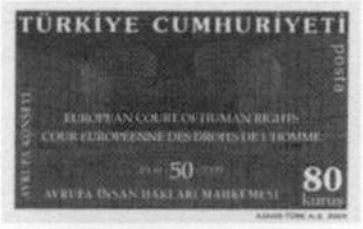

991 Court of Human Rights

2009. 50th Anniv of European Court of Human Rights (3911) or 60th Anniv of Council of Europe (3912). Multicoloured.

3920 80ykr. Type **991** 1·20 1·20
3921 80ykr. 60 1·20 1·20

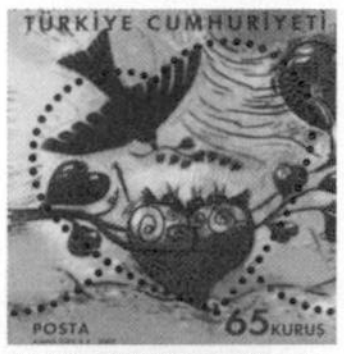

992 Blackbirds nesting in Heart

2009. Mothers' Day. Multicoloured.

3922 65ykr. Type **992** 80 80
3923 80ykr. Baby enclosed in hands 1·20 1·20
3924 1ytl. Mother and child 1·40 1·40
3925 1ytl. Child's hand enclosed in adult hand 1·40 1·40

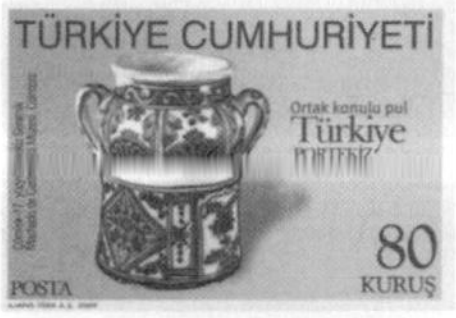

993 Portuguese Ceramic Jar

2009. Ceramics of Turkey and Portugal. Multicoloured.

3926 80ykr. Type **993** 1·20 1·20
3927 85ykr. Turkish Iznik Mosque lamp 1·30 1·30

Stamps of a similar design were issued by Portugal.

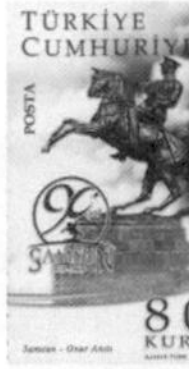

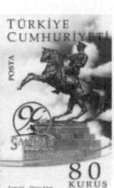

994 Congress Building and Ethnographic Museum, Samsun

2009. 90th Anniv of the Arrival of Attaturk in Samsun and Congresses of Erzurum and Sivas. Sheet 130×66 mm containing T **994** and similar vert designs. Multicoloured.

MS3928 25ykr. Type **994**; 65ykr. Congress Building and Attaturk Museum, Erzurum; 65ykr. Sarayduzu Barracks Building ; 80ykr. Attaturk Memorial Statue, Samsun 2·75 2·75

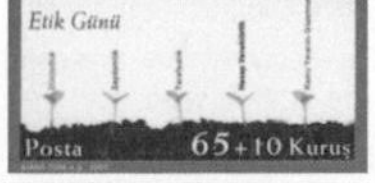

995 Ethics as Flowers

2009. Day of Ethics.

3929 **995** 65ykr.+10ykr. multicoloured 90 90

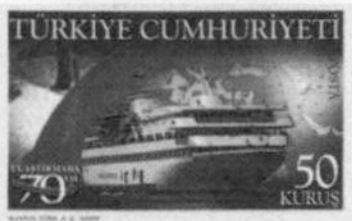

996 Liner

2009. 70th Anniv of Ministry of Transport and Communication. Multicoloured.

3930 50ykr. Type **996** 45 45
3931 65ykr. Suspension bridge and coach 80 80
3932 80ykr. Satellite, receiver, envelope, PC and video phone 80 80
3933 1ytl. Delivering parcel, envelope, aircraft and globe 1·50 1·50
3934 1ytl. High speed locomotive 1·50 1·50

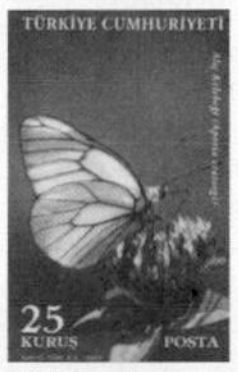

997 *Aporia crataegi*

2009. World Environment Day. Butterflies. Sheet 130×67 mm containing T **997** and similar vert designs. Multicoloured.

MS3935 25ykr. Type **997**; 65ykr. *Lasiommate megera*; 80ykr. *Plebeius agestis*; 80ykr. *Gonepteryx rhamni* 2·25 2·25

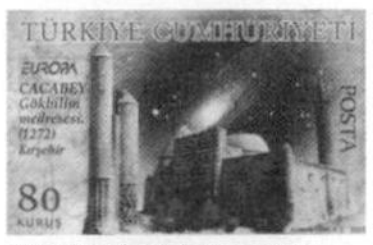

998 Cacabey Astronomy Medresse, Kirsehir (built 1272– 1273 and used as observatory)

2009. Europa. Astronomy. Multicoloured.

3936 80ykr. Type **998** 1·30 1·30
3937 1ytl. Globe and Ali Kuscu (1403–1474) (astronomer) 1·50 1·50

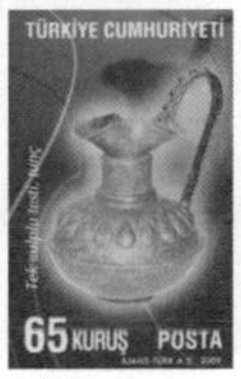

999 Bronze Jug

2009. Anatolian Civilizations. Phrygia. Multicoloured.

3938 65ykr. Type **999** 80 80
3939 80ykr. Ceremonial terracotta drinking vessel with birds at top 1·30 1·30
3940 1ytl. Goose-shaped terracotta drinking vessel 1·50 1·50
3941 1ytl. Four handled bronze bowl 1·50 1·50

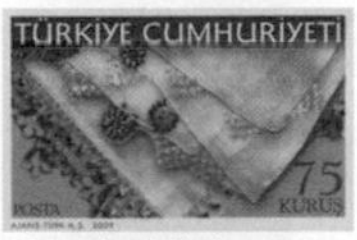

1000 Edged Cloths

2009. Turkish Arts and Crafts. Needlework. Multicoloured.

3942 75ykr. Type **1000** 85 85
3943 90ykr. Embroidered cloths 90 90

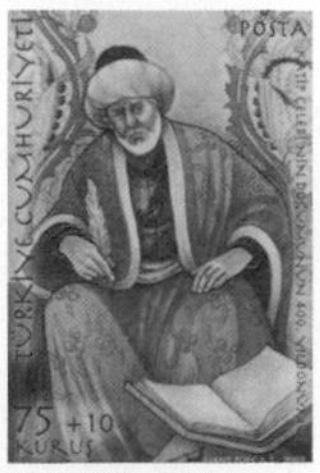

1001 Katip Celebi

2009. 400th Birth Anniv of Katip Celebi (Mustafa bin Abdallah, Haji Khalifa or Kalfa) (scholar, historian, geographer and writer). Multicoloured.

3944 75ykr.+10ykr. Type **1001** 90 90
3945 90ykr.+10ykr. Katip Celebi and ships 1·10 1·10

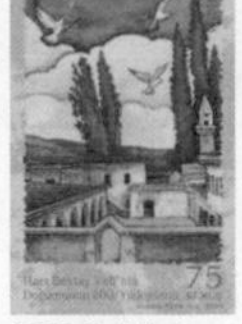

1002 Buildings and Doves

2009. 800th Birth Anniv of Haci Bektas Veli (mystic, humanist and philosopher). Sheet 130×71 mm containing T **1002** and similar vert designs. Multicoloured.

MS3946 75ykr. Type **1002**; 75ykr. Haci Bektas Veli with doves; 90ykr. Haci Bektas Veli with deer and lion; 90ykr. Dancers 4·50 4·50

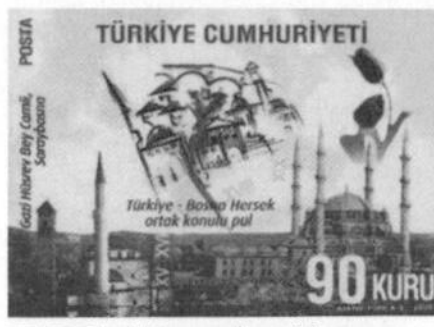

1003 Gazi Husrev-beg Mosque, Sarajevo and Selimiye Mosque, Edirne

2009. BH Post Sarajevo and Turkish Post Co-operation.

3947 **1003** 90ykr. multicoloured 1·40 1·40

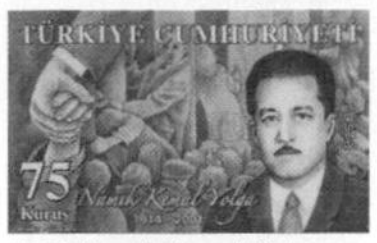

1004 Namik Kemal Yolga

2009. Humanitarians (who assisted Jews to escape the holocaust) (2nd series).

3948 **1004** 75ykr. multicoloured 1·20 1·20

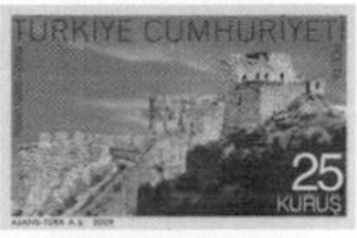

1005 Kozan Castle, Adana

2009. Castles. Multicoloured.

3949 25ykr. Type **1005** 15 15
3950 75ykr. Afyon 75 75
3951 90ykr. Amasya 1·20 1·20
3952 1ytl. Ankara 1·30 1·30

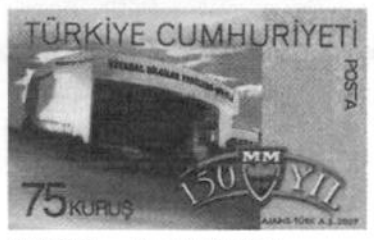

1006 Faculty Building

2009. 150th Anniv of Faculty of Political Science. Multicoloured.

3953 75ykr. Type **1006** 75 75
3954 90ykr. Anniversary emblem 1·30 1·30

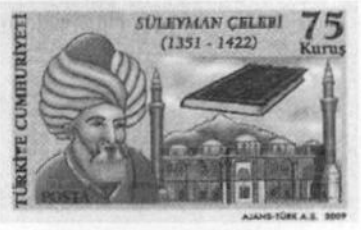

1007 Süleyman Çelebi

20019. Personalities. Multicoloured.

3955 75ykr. Type **1007** (co-ruler of empire during Ottoman Interregnum) 75 75
3956 90ykr. Chinghiz Aitmatov (inscr 'Lengiz Aytmatov') (writer) 1·30 1·30

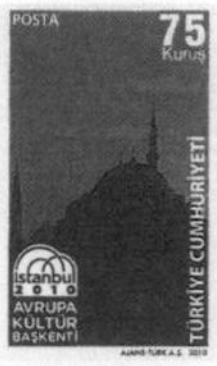

1008 Skyline at Night

2010. Istanbul 2010 European Capital of Culture

3957 75ykr. Type **1008** 75 75
3958 75ykr. Face and snakes (bas-relief) 75 75
3959 75ykr. Dome, interior 75 75
3960 75ykr. Mosque, aerial view 75 75
3961 75ykr. Kiz Kulesi 75 75
3962 75ykr. Bread rings 75 75
3963 75ykr. Tram 75 75
3964 75ykr. Haydarpasa Station Building 75 75
3965 90ykr. City skyline against pink sky (horiz) 1·30 1·30
3966 90ykr. Virgin Mary (mural) (detail) (horiz) 1·30 1·30
3967 90ykr. Fishermen in half-light (horiz) 1·30 1·30
3968 90ykr. Waterside at dusk (horiz) 1·30 1·30
3969 90ykr. Ship on Bosphorus at dusk (horiz) 1·30 1·30

3970	90ykr. Seabirds flying over Bosphorus (horiz)	1·30	1·30
3971	90ykr. Aerial view of city (horiz)	1·30	1·30
3972	90ykr. Skyline with mosques at night (horiz)	1·30	1·30

1009 Ski Jump

2010. Winter Olympic Games, Vancouver. Multicoloured.

3973	25ykr. Type **1009**	50	50
3974	75ykr. Snow boarding	75	75
3975	90ykr. Cross country skiing	1·30	1·30
3976	90ykr. Speed skating	1·30	1·30

1010 McDonnell Douglas F-4 Phantom

2010. Aircraft. Multicoloured.

3977	75ykr. Type **1010**	75	75
3978	90ykr. General Dynamics F-16 Fighting Falcon	1·30	1·30
3979	1ytl. CASA/IPTN CN-235	1·50	1·50

1011 Gold Conjoined Figures

2010. Anatolian Civilizations. Early Bronze Age

3980	75ykr. Type **1011**	75	75
3981	90ykr. Bronze Hittite sun disk	1·30	1·30
3982	1ytl. Gold necklace	1·50	1·50
3983	1ytl. Bronze woman breastfeeding child	1·50	1·50

1012 Anniversary Emblem

2010. 90th Anniv of Anadolu Agency

3984	**1012** 75ykr. multicoloured	75	75

1013 Anniversary Emblem

2010. 90th Anniv of of TBMM (Turkish National Grand Assembly)

3985	75ykr. Type **1013**	75	75
3986	90ykr. Early building, modern building and Atatürk (78×36 mm)	1·30	1·30

1014 Sile Lighthouse

2010. 150th Anniv of Sile Lighthouse

3987	**1014** 75k. multicoloured	75	75

1015 Dove

2010. Labour and Solidarity Day. Multicoloured.

3988	90ykr. Type **1015**	1·30	1·30
3989	90ykr. Hands holding globe	1·30	1·30
3990	110ykr. Dove carrying banner	1·60	1·60
3991	110ykr. Workman	1·60	1·60

1016 Yunus Emre and Tomb

2010

3992	75ykr. Type **1016**	75	75
3993	90ykr. Yunus Emre, parched ground and poem	1·30	1·30

1017 Flags of Turkey and Europe Combined

2010. Europe Day

3994	**1017** 75ykr. multicoloured	75	75

1018 *Balik Çobani* (Fish Herder)

2010. Europa 2010. Children's Books. Multicoloured.

3995	80ykr. Type **1018**	1·20	1·20
3996	110ykr. *Dede Kokut*	1·60	1·60

1019 Satellite

2010. RASAT Satellite Research and Development Project

3997	**1019** 75ykr. multicoloured	75	75

1020 *Crocus stevenii*

2010. World Environment Day. Multicoloured.

MS3998 110ykr.×4, Type **1020**; *Crocus mathewii; Astragalus lineatus; Erica bocquetii* 5·00 5·00

1021 Sultan's Barge with Canopy

2010. The Sultan's Boats. Multicoloured.

3999	80ykr. Type **1021**	1·20	1·20
4000	110ykr. White barge with gold decoration and bird-shaped figurehead	1·60	1·60

1022 Atatürk

2010. Mustafa Kemal Atatürk Commemoration. Multicoloured.

4001	25ykr. Type **1022**	50	50
4002	80ykr. Wearing cap and overcoat, facing right	1·20	1·20
4003	110ykr. Smiling, facing left	1·60	1·60
4004	155ykr. With moustache and wearing glasses, facing front	1·70	1·70

1023 Steam Locomotive

2010. Steam Locomotives. Multicoloured.

4005	80ykr. +10ykr. Type **1023**	1·30	1·30
4006	110ykr. +10ykr. Steam locomotive 242	1·65	1·65

1025 Two Players

2010. FIBA World Basketball Championship for Men, 2010. Multicoloured.

4012	80ykr. Type **1025**	1·20	1·20
4013	80ykr. Two players at net	1·20	1·20
4014	110ykr. As Type **1025**	1·60	1·60
4015	110ykr. As No. 4013	1·60	1·60

1026 Ritsurin Gardens

2010. Japan Year in Turkey, 2010. Multicoloured.

MS4016 80ykr.×5, Type **1026**; Traditional Japanese dance (woman); Traditional Japanese folk dance troup; Tokyo skyline and Mount Fuji; Noh theatre actor. 100ykr.×5, Kabuto Samurai war mask; Mount Fuji: Kokeshi dolls; *Ertugrul* frigate; Sushi 4·00 4·00

1027 Collegiate Church of Santa María la Mayor, Toro, Zamora

2010. The Alliance of Civilizations, Turkey and Spain. Multicoloured.

MS4017 80ykr. Type **1027**; 110ykr. Ortakoy Mosque, Istanbul 3·50 3·50

1028 Rug from Uşak

2010. Traditional Turkish Arts - Rugs. Multicoloured.

4018	80ykr. +10ykr. Type **1028**	1·20	1·20
4019	110ykr. +10ykr. Kayseri	1·60	1·60

1030 Emblem on Map of Turkey

2010. Economic Cooperation Organisation (ECO) Summit. Multicoloured.

MS4025 90ykr. Type **1030**;100ykr. As Type **1030**; 130ykr. As Type **1030**; 150ykr. As Type **1030** 5·25 5·25

1032 Lily

2011. Lilies. Multicoloured.

4030	25ykr. Type **1032**	50	50
4031	1ylr. Two pale mauve blooms	1·50	1·50
4032	3ytl.65 One green tinged bloom	3·50	3·50
4033	6ytl. One red, orange and pink bloom	5·00	5·00

1033 Government Institution, Moscow

2011. 90th Anniv of Moscow Agreement. Multicoloured.

MS4034 90ykr.×2, Type **1033**; Negotiators around conference table 2·65 2·65

1035 Evliya Celebi

2011. 400th Birth Anniv of Evliya Celebi (traveller and adventurer). Multicoloured.

4039	90ykr. Type **1035**	1·30	1·30
4040	1ylr.30 On horseback	1·65	1·65

1036 *Diplodus vulgaris*

2011. Fish. Multicoloured.

4041	1ytl.30 Type **1036**	1·65	1·65
4042	1ytl.30 *Trigla lucerna*	1·65	1·65
4043	1ytl.30 *Xiphias gladius*	1·65	1·65

1037 Anniversary Emblem

2011. 50th Anniv of OECD

4044	**1037** 1ytl. multicoloured	1·50	1·50

1038 Woodpecker and Forest

2011. Europa 2011. Forests. Multicoloured.

4045	90ykr. Type **1038**	1·30	1·30
4046	1ytl.30 Deer and forest	1·65	1·65

1039 Emblem

2011. Week of the Disabled. Multicoloured.

4047	90ykr. Type **1039**	1·30	1·30
4048	1ytl.30 Emblem (different)	1·65	1·65

1040 Atatürk

2011. 130th Birth Anniv of Atatürk. Sheet 94×64 mm
MS4049 1040 90ykr. multicoloured

1041 Military Aircraft

2011. Centenary of Turkish Air Force. Multicoloured.
MS4050 1ytl.30×4, Type **1041**; Aircraft
over river; Aircraft at sunrise; Aircraft
taking off (all horiz) 5·50 5·50
MS4051 1ytl.30×4, Aircraft over three
figures looking up; Aircraft, flag
and eagle (statue, Air Force war
academy, Istanbul); Aircraft in flight
above clouds; Aircraft above buildings (all vert) 25·00 25·00

1042 *Anas acuta*
(Northern Pintail)

2011. World Environment Day. Multicoloured.
MS4052 25ykr. Type **1042**; 90ykr.
Streptopelia turtur (European Turtle
Dove); 1ytl.30 *Phasianus colchicus*
(Common Pheasant); 1ytl.30 *Alec-
toris chukar* (Chukar Partridge) 4·75 4·75

2011. 60th Anniv of Korean War
4053 **1043** 1ytl. multicoloured 1·50 1·50

1044 Adult Hand clasping Child's
Hand

2011. 90th Anniv of Social Services and Child Protection
Agency
4054 **1044** 90ykr. multicoloured 1·30 1·30

1045 Wrestlers

2011. 650th Year of Kirkpinar Oil Wrestling. Multicoloured.
MS4055 90ykr. Type **1045**; 90ykr.
Falling wrestlers; 1ytl.30 Standing
wrestlers with heads lowered; 1ytl.30
Wrestlers and referee 5·00 5·00

1046 Van Castle

2011. City of Van, History and Natural Assets.
Multicoloured.
MS4056 25ykr. Type **1046**; 90ykr.
Husrev Pasha Mosque; 1ytl.30 Catak
Bridge and Pearl Mullet; 1ytl.30
Akdamar Island Church and Van Cat 4·75 4·75

1047 Emblem (partial) and
Mascot

2011. Trabzon 2011, European Youth Olympic Festival.
Multicoloured.

4057	25ykr. Type **1047**		50	50
4058	90ykr. Emblem (full) and mascot		1·30	1·30
4059	1ytl.30 Mascot and partial emblem on banner		1·65	1·65
4060	1ytl.30 Mascot (vert)		1·65	1·65

1048 Building and Emblem

2011. Centenary of Yildiz Technical University.
Multicoloured.

4061	90ykr. Type **1048**		1·30	1·30
4062	1ytl.30 Anniversary emblem enclosed in star and building		1·65	1·65

1049 *Pyracantha
coccinea*

2011. Fruiting Trees and Shrubs. Multicoloured.

4063	10ykr. Type **1049**		30	30
4064	1ytl. *Prunus persica* (peach)		1·50	1·50
4065	1ytl.30 *Prunus avium* (wild cherry)		1·65	1·65
4066	3ytl.65 *Rubus fruticosus* (blackberry)		3·50	3·50

1050 Ancient City of Hasankeyf

2011. Cultural Heritage
4067 **1050** 1ytl.30 +10ykr. multicoloured 1·85 1·85

1051 Soldiers on
Parade

2011. Otuzdokuzlular (military unit). Multicoloured.

4068	50ykr. Type **1051**		60	60
4069	90ykr. Parading soldiers fac-ing left		1·30	1·30
4070	1ytl.30 Soldiers on transport ship (horiz)		1·65	1·65

1052 White Barge with Gold Decoration

2011. The Sultan's Boats. Multicoloured.

4071	90ykr. Type **1052**		1·30	1·30
4072	1ytl.30 White barge with gold decoration, rear canopy and gold-coloured on prow		1·65	1·65

1054 Anniversary
Emblem

2011. 50th Anniv of State Personnel Presidency
4077 **1054** 100ykr. +10ykr. multicoloured 1·60 1·60

1055 Farmer's
wife seated
below Drying
Chillies

2011. People and Agriculture. Multicoloured.

4078	10ykr. Type **1055**		30	30
4079	1ytl. Women working in field of cloches		1·50	1·50
4080	1ytl.30 Boy and Water Buffaloes in river (horiz)		1·65	1·65
4081	3ytl.65 Man and poly-houses in evening (horiz)		3·50	3·50

1056 Emblem and
Runners

2012. Istanbul 2012 European Capital of Sports.
Multicoloured.

4082	50ykr. Type **1056**		60	60
4083	1ytl. Tennis player		1·50	1·50
4084	1ytl. Yachts		1·50	1·50
4085	2ytl. Cyclists		2·00	2·00

1057 Globe

2012. Provision of Equality of Opportunities between
Men and Women in Turkey. Multicoloured.

4086	10ykr. Type **1057**		30	30
4087	1ytl. Outline of woman's face and flower		1·50	1·50
4088	2ytl. Globe (As Type **1057** but pink background)		2·00	2·00

1058 Hurdler

2012. World Indoor Athletics Championships, 2012,
Athletics Gymnasium, Ataköy. Multicoloured.
MS4089 50ykr. Type **1058**; 1ytl. Female
long jumper; 1ytl. Male high jumper;
2ytl. Male hurdler 4·00 4·00

1059 Association Building

2012. Centenary of Turkish Hearth Association
4090 **1059** 1ytl. multicoloured 1·50 1·50

1060 Early School Building

2012. 140th Anniv of Pertevniyal High School
4091 **1060** 1ytl. multicoloured 1·50 1·50

1061 Hands encircling Emblem

2012. The Morality and Law of Brotherhood.
Multicoloured.
MS4092 1ytl. Type **1061**; 1ytl. Red rose 2·25 2·25

1062 Anniversary Emblem

2012. 50th Anniv of Constitutional Court. Multicoloured.

4093	1ytl. Type **1062**		1·50	1·50
4094	2ytl. Court Building		2·00	2·00

1063 Yat Limani,
Anatalya

2012. Tourism. Multicoloured.

4095	2ytl. Type **1063**		2·00	2·00
4096	2ytl. Aspendos, Anatalya		2·00	2·00
4097	2ytl. Ortaköy, Istanbul		2·00	2·00
4098	2ytl. Kiz Kulesi, Istanbul		2·00	2·00
4099	2ytl. Göreme, Nevşehir		2·00	2·00
4100	2ytl. Zelve, Nevşehir		2·00	2·00
4101	2ytl. Saat Kulesi (clock tower), Izmir		2·00	2·00
4102	2ytl. Efes, Izmir		2·00	2·00

1065 Hang Glider, Skier
and Symbols of Turkey

2012. Europa. Visit Turkey. Multicoloured.

4108	2ytl. Type **1063**		2·00	2·00
4109	2ytl. Fresco (partial), dervish, Mosque and heads		2·00	2·00

1066 TOBB Building

2012. 60th Anniv of Union of Chambers and Commodity
Exchanges of Turkey (TOBB). Multicoloured.
4110 **1066** 1ytl. multicoloured 1·50 1·50

1067 '150' and Court Building

2012. 150th Anniv of Court of Accounts. Multicoloured.

4111	1ytl. Type **1067**		1·50	1·50
4112	2ytl. Emblem and '150'		2·00	2·00

OBLIGATORY TAX STAMPS

T101 Nurse
bandaging Patient

1926. Red Crescent.

T1035	-	1g. red, yellow & blk	50	20
T1036	**T101**	2½g. multicoloured	50	20
T1037	-	5g. multicoloured	50	2·50
T1038	-	10g. multicoloured	1·40	5·75

DESIGNS—VERT: 1g. Red crescent and decorative archway; 5g. Refugees. HORIZ: 10g. Stretcher bearers.

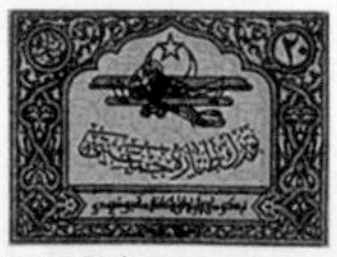

T102 Biplane

1926. Aviation Fund.

T1039	**T102**	20pa. brown & green	95	1·00
T1040	**T102**	1g. green and stone	95	1·00
T1041	**T102**	5g. violet and green	1·90	2·10
T1042	**T102**	5g. red and green	70·00	9·25

The 5g. stamps are 40×29 mm.

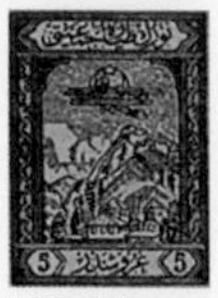

T103 Biplane over Ankara

1927. Aviation Fund.

T1043	**T102**	20pa. red and green	25	50
T1044	**T102**	1g. green and ochre	25	50
T1045	**T103**	2g. brown and green	25	1·00
T1046	**T103**	2½g. red and green	2·40	1·80
T1047	**T103**	5g. blue and buff	50	50
T1048	**T103**	10g. blue and pink	2·40	2·10
T1049	**T103**	15g. green and yellow	2·40	1·60
T1050	**T103**	20g. brown and ochre	4·75	2·50
T1051	**T103**	50g. blue & light blue	4·75	10·50
T1052	**T103**	100g. red and blue	£110	70·00

The 20pa. and 1g. are 25×15 mm.

(T104)

1927. Red Crescent No. T1035 and charity labels surch with Type **T104** or similar types.

T1053	20pa. on 1g. red, yell & blk	3·25	2·10
T1054	20pa. on 1g. brown	1·90	6·50
T1055	20pa. on 2½g. lilac	1·90	2·50

DESIGNS: 26×21 mm. No. T1054 Hospital ship. No. T1055 Nurse tending patient.

No. T1053 has an extra line of Turkish characters in the surcharge.

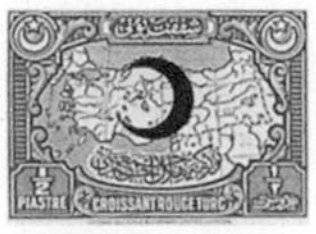

T105 Red Crescent on Map of Turkey

1928. Red Crescent. Various frames. Crescent in red.

T1067	**T105**	½pi. brown	25	50
T1068	**T105**	1pi. purple	25	15
T1069	**T105**	2½pi. orange	25	25
T1070	**T105**	5pi. brown	50	50
T1071	**T105**	10pi. green	50	80
T1072	**T105**	20pi. blue	70	1·00
T1073	**T105**	50pi. purple	2·40	1·60

See also Nos. T1171/4 and T1198/1212.

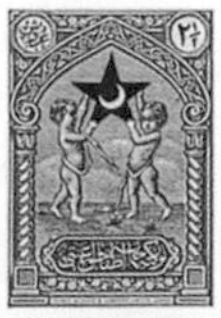

T106 Cherubs holding Star

1928. Child Welfare.

T1074	**T106**	1g. olive and red	15	15
T1075	**T106**	2½g. brown and red	20	25
T1076	**T106**	5g. green and red	50	3·25
T1077	**T106**	25g. black and red	1·70	10·50

See also Nos. T1160/1 and T1165/6.

1930. Aviation Fund. Nos. T1039, T1043, T1045 and T1049 surch.

T1099	**T102**	Bir (1)k. on 20pa. brown and green	£225	75·00
T1100	**T102**	Bir (1)k. on 20pa. red and green	50	1·00
T1101	**T103**	Yuz (100)pa. on 2g. brown and green	50	1·00
T1102	**T102**	5k. on 20pa. red and green	50	1·00
T1103	**T102**	Bes (5)k. on 20pa. red and green	4·75	2·50
T1104	**T103**	On (10)k. on 2g. brown and green	95	1·00
T1105	**T103**	Elli (50)k. on 2g. brown and green	19·00	21·00
T1106	**T103**	Bir (1)l. on 2g. brown and green	55·00	60·00
T1107	**T103**	Bes (5)l. on 15g. green and yellow	£2500	£1400

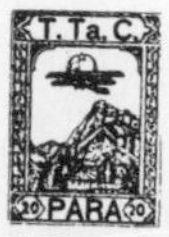

T114 Biplane over Ankara

1931. Aviation Fund.

T1141	**T114**	20pa. black	1·40	5·25

See also Nos. T1154/6.

1932. Child Welfare. No. T1074 surch.

T1150	**T106**	20pa. on 1g. olive and red	70	2·50
T1153	**T106**	3k. on 1g. olive and red	1·70	2·50

1932. Aviation Fund. As Type **T114** but larger, 22×30 mm, and with sky shaded.

T1154	1k. purple	95	1·60
T1155	5k. red	1·40	3·75
T1156	10k. green	2·40	7·75

1932. Red Crescent. Nos. T1067, T1069 and T1071 surch.

T1157	**T105**	1k. on 2½pi. orange	25	50
T1158	**T105**	5k. on ½pi. brown	50	2·50
T1159	**T105**	5k. on 10pi. green	50	5·25

1933. Child Welfare. As Type **T106** but inscr "IZMIR HIMAYEI ETFAL CEMIYETI".

T1160	1k. violet and red	1·40	2·50
T1161	5k. brown and red	3·25	8·50

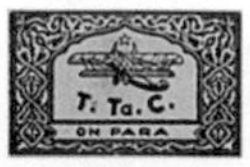

T118 Biplane

1933. Aviation Fund.

T1162	**T118**	On (10)pa. green	95	1·80
T1163	**T118**	Bir (1)k. red	2·40	4·00
T1164	**T118**	Bes (5)k. lilac	7·25	9·25

1934. Child Welfare. As Type **T106** but inscr "Turkiye Himayeietfal Cemiyeti".

T1165	20pa. purple and red	1·40	2·50
T1166	15k. green and red	3·25	7·75

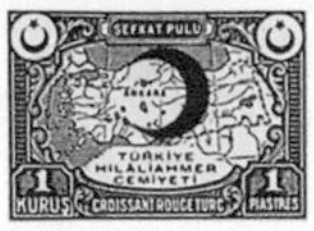

T119 Red Crescent and Map of Turkey

1934. Inscr "TURKIYE HILALIAHMER CEMIYETI" (different frame on 5k.).

T1171	**T119**	½k. blue and red	10	50
T1172	**T119**	1k. brown and red	15	15
T1173	**T119**	2½k. brown and red	25	50
T1174	**T119**	5k. green and red	2·40	2·50

See also Nos. T1198/1212.

1936. Child Welfare. Nos. T1074/5 and T1165 optd **P.Y.S.** or surch also.

T1186	**T106**	20pa. purple and red	1·90	3·25
T1187	**T106**	1g. olive and red	50	1·00
T1188	**T106**	3k. on 2½g. brn & red	95	3·25

1937. Red Crescent. As Types **T105** and **T119** but inscr "TURKIYE KIZILAY CEMIYETI". Various frames.

T1204	½k. blue and red	6·75	50
T1199	1k. mauve and red	25	25
T1200	2½k. orange and red	50	80
T1201	5k. green and red	50	1·30
T1209	5k. brown and red	3·50	50
T1202	10k. green and red	95	4·00
T1203	20k. black and red	1·70	7·75
T1211	50k. purple and red	26·00	2·40
T1212	1l. blue and red	85·00	7·50

1938. Child Welfare. No. T1075 surch. (a) Value in figures and words above **P. Y. S.**

T1213	**T106**	20pa. on 2½g. brown and red	2·30	1·20
T1214	**T106**	1k. on 2½g. brown and red	2·30	1·20

(b) **P. Y. S.** above value in figures and words.

T1215	**T106**	20pa. on 2½g. brown and red	2·30	1·50
T1216	**T106**	1k. on 2½g. brown and red	2·30	1·50

(c) **1 kurus**.

T1217	**T106**	1k. on 2½g. brown and red	3·00	1·60

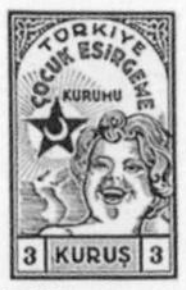

T138 Laughing Child

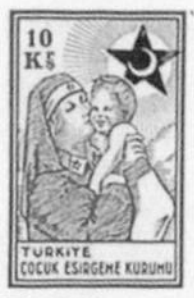

T139 Nurse and Baby

1940. Child Welfare. Star in red.

T1259	**T138**	20pa. green	40	15
T1260	**T138**	1k. lilac	40	15
T1261	**T139**	1k. blue	40	15
T1262	**T139**	2½k. mauve	40	15
T1263	**T138**	3k. black	90	40
T1264	**T139**	5k. lilac	90	40
T1265	**T139**	10k. green	3·75	60
T1266	**T138**	15k. blue	1·90	80
T1267	**T139**	25k. olive	4·25	3·00
T1268	**T139**	50k. olive	9·75	9·75

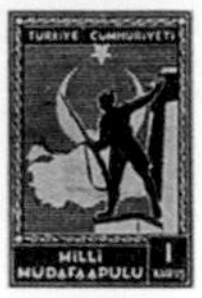

T145 Soldier and Map of Turkey

1941. National Defence.

T1289	**T145**	1k. violet	3·00	15
T1290	**T145**	2k. blue	4·50	25
T1291	**T145**	3k. brown	7·50	80
T1292	**T145**	4k. mauve	15·00	80
T1293	**T145**	5k. pink	15·00	1·60
T1294	**T145**	10k. blue	38·00	2·50

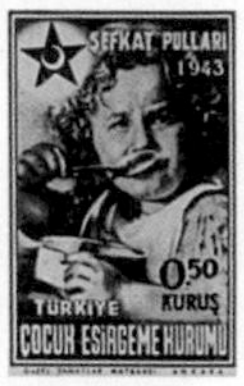

T151 Child eating

1943. Child Welfare. Inscr "SEFKAT PULLARI 1943".

T1330	**T151**	0.50k. violet and red	40	25
T1331	**T151**	0.50k. green and red	40	25
T1332	-	1k. blue and red	40	40
T1333	-	3k. red and orange	55	60
T1334	-	15k. black, buff and red	75	60
T1335	-	100k. blue and red	1·40	1·20
MST1336		140×118 mm. Nos. T1330/5	11·50	12·50

DESIGNS—VERT: 1k. Nurse with baby; 15k. Baby and emblem; 100k. President Inonu and child. HORIZ: 3k. Nurse and child.

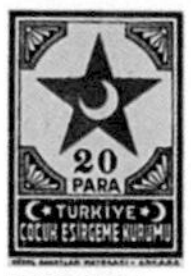

T152 Child Welfare Emblem

1943. Child Welfare. Star in red.

T1337	**T152**	20pa. blue	15	10
T1338	-	1k. green	15	10
T1339	-	3k. brown	25	15
T1340	-	5k. orange	2·30	2·10
T1341	-	5k. brown	1·50	80
T1342	-	10k. red	1·70	50
T1343	-	15k. lilac	2·75	50
T1344	-	25k. violet	3·50	80
T1345	-	50k. blue	4·50	1·20
T1346	-	100k. green	6·00	2·10

DESIGNS—VERT: 1k. Hospital; 3k. Nurse and children; 5k. Baby in cot; 10k. Nurse bathing baby; 15k. Nurse helping child to drink; 50k. Child. HORIZ: 25k. Baby with bottle; 100k. Hospital.

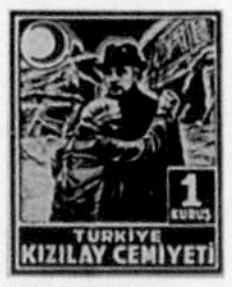

T155 Pres. Inonu and Victim

1944. Red Crescent. Inscr "TURKIYE KIZILAY CEMIYETI".

T1347	-	20pa. brown, flesh, red and blue	1·50	10
T1348	**T155**	1k. olive, yellow, green and red	1·50	10
T1349	-	2½k. blue and red	1·50	10
T1350	-	5k. blue and red	3·75	60
T1351	-	10k. blue, green and red	3·00	60
T1352	-	50k. green, black and red	7·50	1·00
T1353	-	1l. yellow, black and red	23·00	3·75

DESIGNS—VERT: 20pa. Nurse tending dreaming patient; 5k. Soldier and nurse; 10k. Feeding victims; 50k. Wounded soldiers on raft; 1l. Nurse within red crescent. HORIZ: 2½k. Stretcher bearers and hospital ship.

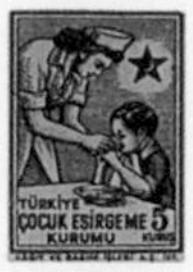

T156 Nurse helping Child to Drink

1945. Child Welfare. Star in red.

T1354	-	1k. lilac	15	10
T1355	-	2½k. blue	75	25
T1356	**T156**	5k. green	40	25
T1357	-	10k. brown	75	40
T1358	-	250k. black	23·00	6·25
T1359	-	500k. violet	60·00	23·00

DESIGNS—VERT (21×20 mm): 1k. Nurse carrying baby; 2½k. Nurse holding child; 10k. Child sucking thumb. HORIZ (28×22 mm): 250, 500k. Emblem.

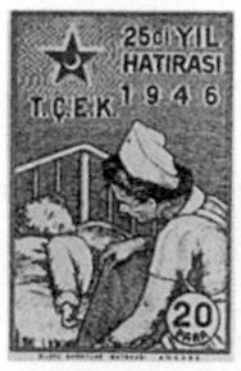

T159 Nurse tucking Baby in Cot

1946. 25th Anniv of Child Welfare Organization.

T1360	**T159**	20pa. brown and red	15	15
T1361	-	1k. blue and red	15	15
T1362	-	2½k. red	15	60
T1363	-	5k. brown and red	55	60
T1364	-	15k. purple and red	55	1·40
T1365	-	25k. green and red	2·30	2·50
T1366	-	50k. green and red	2·75	3·00
T1367	-	150k. brown and red	8·25	9·00
MST1368		80×105 mm. 250k. blue, pink and red	38·00	41·00

DESIGNS: 1k. Mother and baby; 2½k. Nurse holding child above head; 5k. Doctor examining baby; 15k. Nurse feeding baby; 25k. Nurse bathing baby; 50k. Nurse weighing baby; 150k. Nurse, and child in cot; 250k. Pres Inonu and child.

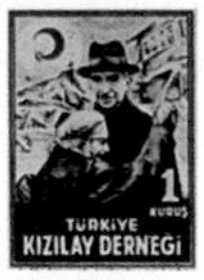

T160 Pres. Inonu and Victim

1946. Red Crescent. As Nos. T1347/8, T1350 and T1353 and new design inscr "TURKIYE KIZILAY DERNEGI".

T1369	-	20pa. yellow, grey, blue and red	25	15
T1532	-	20pa. brown, yellow, violet and red	15	10
T1370	**T155**	1k. multicoloured	3·75	1·20
T1371	**T160**	1k. brown, blue and red	75	25
T1533	-	1k. green, blk & red	25	10
T1372	-	5k. blue and red	45	25
T1373	-	20k. red, blue & pur	1·50	80
T1374	-	1l. black, yell & red	7·50	2·50
T1375	-	250k. black, green and red	11·50	5·00
T1376	-	5l. black, pink and red	19·00	6·50
T1377	-	10l. blue and red	38·00	25·00

DESIGNS—VERT: 20pa. As No. T1347; 1k. (T1533), As No. T1352; 5k. As No. T1350; 1l. As No. T1353; 5l. Nurse tending patient; 10l. Soldier, red crescent and figure symbolizing Victory. HORIZ: 20k. Ankara Hospital; 250k. Nurse helping injured soldier.

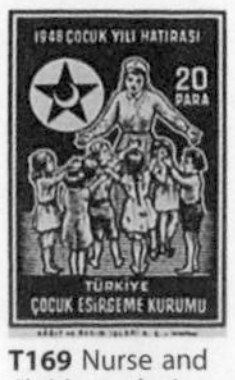

T169 Nurse and Children playing

1948. Child Welfare. Star in red.

T1399	**T169**	20pa. blue	15	15
T1400	-	20pa. mauve	15	15

T1401	-	1k. green	45	50
T1402	-	3k. purple	1·30	1·40
T1403	-	15k. grey	4·50	5·00
T1404	-	30k. orange	6·75	7·50
T1405	-	150k. green	9·00	9·75
T1406	-	300k. red	13·00	14·00

DESIGNS—VERT: 20pa. (No. 1400) Nurse and children walking; 1k. Nurse feeding two children; 3k. Nurse with three children; 15k. Parents and two children; 150k. Nurse holding baby; 300k. Heads of nurse and child. HORIZ: 30k. Father handing baby to nurse.

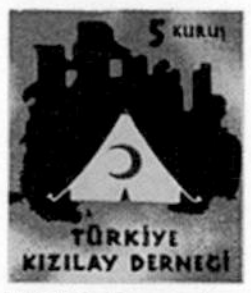

T177 Ruins and Tent

1949. Red Crescent.

T1422	**T177**	5k. black, red & pur	75	30
T1423	**T177**	10k. purple, red and flesh	75	30

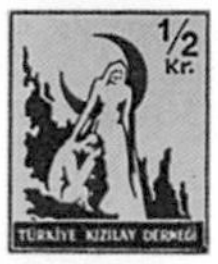

T179 "Grief"

1950. Red Crescent. Crescent in red.

T1425	**T179**	½k. blue	90	25
T1426	**T179**	1k. blue	55	10
T1427	**T179**	2k. mauve	55	10
T1428	**T179**	2½k. orange	55	10
T1429	**T179**	3k. green	55	10
T1430	**T179**	4k. drab	75	15
T1431	**T179**	5k. blue	75	15
T1432	**T179**	10k. pink	3·00	60
T1433	**T179**	25k. brown	5·75	1·00
T1434	-	50k. blue	5·75	1·00
T1435	-	100k. green	11·50	2·30

DESIGN: 50, 100k. Plant with broken stem.

1952. (a) Red Crescent. Nos. T1427 and T1429/30 surch.

T1489	**T179**	20pa. on 2k. mauve and red	45	25
T1490	**T179**	20pa. on 3k. green and red	25	15
T1491	**T179**	20pa. on 4k. drab and red	25	25

(b) Child Welfare. Nos. T1355, T1362 and T1339 surch.

T1492	1k. on 2½k. blue and red	25	15
T1493	1k. on 2½k. red	70	50
T1494	1k. on 3k. brown and red	25	15

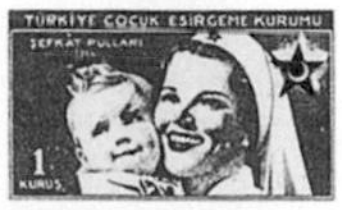

T208 Nurse and Baby

1954. Child Welfare. Inscr "SEFKAT PULLARI 1954".

T1534	-	20pa. yellow & orange	15	10
T1535	-	20pa. green and red	25	15
T1536	**T208**	1k. blue and red	40	15

DESIGN: Nos. 1534/5, Nurse with two children.
See also Nos. T1569 and T1573/4.

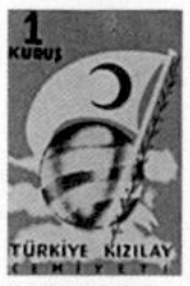

T211 Globe and Flag

1954. Red Crescent.

T1545	**T211**	1k. multicoloured	25	10
T1546	-	5k. red, grey and green	30	10
T1547	-	10k. grey, green and red	40	10

DESIGNS: 5k. Nurse with wings on cloud; 10k. Arm and hand.
See also Nos. T1652, T1656/8, T1838 and T1840/3.

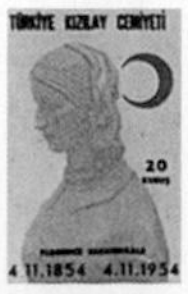

T212 Florence Nightingale

1954. Red Crescent. Centenary of Florence Nightingale's Arrival at Scutari.

T1551	**T212**	20k. green, brown and red	75	60
T1552	-	30k. brown, black and red	75	65
T1553	-	50k. stone, black and red	75	80

DESIGNS: 30k. Florence Nightingale (three-quarter face); 50k. Selimiye Barracks.

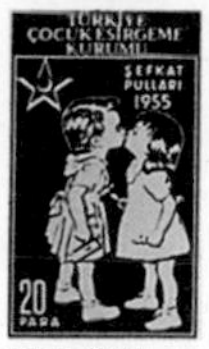

T215 Children Kissing

1955. Child Welfare. Inscr "SEFKAT PULLARI 1955". Star in red.

T1564	**T215**	20pa. blue	15	10
T1565	**T215**	20pa. brown	15	10
T1566	**T215**	1k. purple	15	10
T1567	**T215**	3k. bistre	15	10
T1568	**T215**	5k. orange	15	10
T1569	**T208**	10k. green	75	15
T1570	-	15k. blue	55	15
T1571	-	25k. lake	1·10	40
T1572	-	50k. green	1·90	80
T1573	**T208**	2½l. brown	£375	£110
T1574	**T208**	10l. violet	£550	£275

DESIGN: 15 to 50k. Nurse carrying baby.

1955. Red Crescent. Nos. T1373 and T1435 surch.

T1575	20pa. on 20k. red, blue and purple	55	40
T1576	20pa. on 100k. green and red	40	15

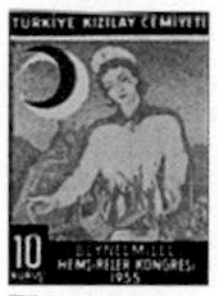

T219 Nurse

1955. Red Crescent. Congress of International Council of Nurses.

T1578	**T219**	10k. brown, red and black	1·10	65
T1579	-	15k. green, red and black	1·10	65
T1580	-	100k. blue and red	2·30	2·10

DESIGNS—HORIZ: 15k. Nurses marching. VERT: [illegible] blem, Red Cross and Red Crescent flags and nurses.

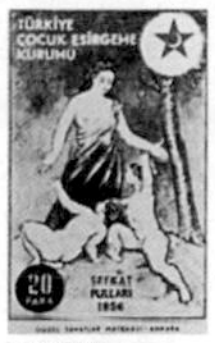

T227 Woman and Children

1956. Child Welfare. Star in red.

T1614	**T227**	20pa. salmon	55	15
T1615	**T227**	20pa. olive	55	15
T1616	**T227**	1k. blue	55	15
T1617	**T227**	1k. violet	55	15
T1618	**T227**	3k. brown	75	80
T1619	-	10k. red	7·50	4·00
T1620	-	25k. green	11·50	7·50
T1621	-	50k. blue	15·00	7·50
T1622	-	2½l. lilac	26·00	16·00
T1623	-	5l. brown	38·00	35·00
T1624	-	10l. green	55·00	45·00

DESIGNS: 10k. to 50k. Flag and building; 2½l. to 10l. Mother and baby.

1956. Red Crescent. No. T1545 surch.

T1625	**T211**	20pa. on 1k. mult	15	15
T1626	**T211**	2.5k. on 1k. mult	25	25

1956. Child Welfare. Nos. 1399/1406 optd **IV. DUNYA Cocuk Gunu 1 Ekim 1956**. Nos. 1644/6 surch, also.

T1639	**T169**	20pa. red and blue	15·00	13·50
T1640	-	20pa. mauve and red	15·00	13·50
T1641	-	1k. green and red	15·00	13·50
T1642	-	3k. purple and red	15·00	13·50
T1643	-	15k. grey and red	15·00	13·50
T1644	-	25k. on 30k. orange and red	15·00	13·50
T1645	-	100k. on 150k. green and red	15·00	13·50
T1646	-	250k. on 300k. deep red and red	15·00	13·50

1957. Red Crescent. As No. T1373 but inscr "TURKIYE KIZILAY CEMIYETI", new design and as Nos. T1545/6. Crescent in red.

T1651	-	½k. drab and brown	60	15
T1652	**T211**	1k. black, bis & green	60	15
T1653	-	2½k. green & dp green	60	15
T1655	-	20k. red, brown and blue	1·00	40
T1656	**T211**	25k. grey, black and green	2·50	90
T1657	**T211**	50k. blue and green	3·00	1·50
T1658	**T211**	100k. violet, black and green	6·25	2·40

DESIGNS—VERT: ½, 2½k. Flower being watered. HORIZ: 20k. Ankara hospital.

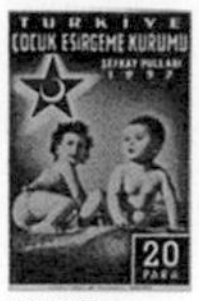

T239 Two Babies

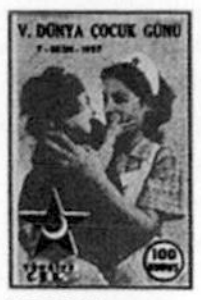

T246 Nurse and Child

1957. Child Welfare.

T1659	**T239**	20pa. green and red	10	10
T1660	**T239**	20pa. pink and red	10	10
T1661	**T239**	1k. blue and red	15	10
T1662	**T239**	3k. orange and red	50	30
T1683	**T246**	100k. brown and red	1·40	1·30
T1684	**T246**	150k. green and red	1·50	1·20
T1685	**T246**	250k. violet and red	1·60	1·30

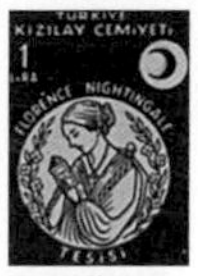

T254 Florence Nightingale

1958. Florence Nightingale Foundation. Crescent in red.

T1829	**T254**	1l. green	60	40
T1830	**T254**	1½l. grey	1·00	75
T1831	**T254**	2½l. blue	1·40	1·10

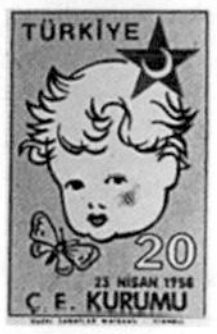

T255 Child's Head and Butterfly

1958. Child Welfare. [illegible] Multicoloured.

T1832	20k. Type T **255**	20	10
T1833	25k. Brimstone	20	10
T1834	50k. Little tiger blue (horiz)	25	20
T1835	75k. Green-veined white (horiz)	70	55
T1836	150k. Peacock	1·60	1·10

1958. Red Crescent. As Nos. T1651/3, T1546 and T1656/8 but colours changed. Crescent in red.

T1837	-	½k. lilac	20	15
T1838	**T 211**	1k. black, brown and green	20	15
T1839	-	2½k. grey and red	30	15
T1840	-	5k. red, brown and green	40	15
T1841	**T 211**	25k. black, green and brown	60	25
T1842	**T 211**	50k. purple, black and green	1·90	30
T1843	**T 211**	100k. drab, black and green	3·00	80

OFFICIAL STAMPS

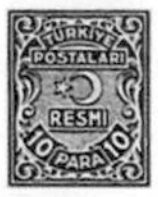

O160

1947

O1360	**O160**	10pa. brown	15	10
O1361	**O160**	1k. green	25	10
O1362	**O160**	2k. purple	45	10
O1363	**O160**	3k. orange	60	10
O1364	**O160**	5k. turquoise	15·00	10
O1365	**O160**	10k. brown	11·50	10
O1366	**O160**	15k. violet	3·50	10
O1367	**O160**	20k. blue	4·25	10
O1368	**O160**	30k. olive	4·25	10
O1369	**O160**	50k. blue	4·25	10
O1370	**O160**	1l. green	5·25	15
O1371	**O160**	2l. red	7·50	50

1951. Postage stamps optd **RESMI** between bars with star and crescent above.

O1458	**165**	0.25k. red	15	10
O1454	**165**	5k. blue	15	10
O1461	**165**	10k. brown	55	10
O1462	**165**	15k. violet	90	10
O1456	**165**	20k. blue	75	10
O1469	**165**	30k. brown	30	10
O1470	**165**	60k. black	1·20	25

1955. Postage stamps optd **RESMI** between wavy bars with star and crescent above or surch also.

O1568	**165**	0.25k. red	10	10
O1587	**165**	½k. on 1k. black	15	10
O1569	**165**	1k. black	10	10
O1570	**165**	2k. purple	10	10
O1593	**165**	2k. on 4k. green	10	10
O1571	**165**	3k. orange	10	10
O1594	**165**	3k. on 4k. green	10	10
O1572	**165**	4k. green	10	10
O1581	**165**	5k. blue	10	10
O1573	**165**	5k. on 15k. violet	10	10
O1595	**165**	10k. on 12k. red	30	15
O1574	**165**	10k. on 15k. violet	10	10
O1575	**165**	15k. violet	25	15
O1576	**165**	20k. blue	70	25
O1585	**165**	30k. brown	70	25
O1577	**165**	40k. on 1l. olive	70	40
O1590	**165**	75k. on 1l. olive	1·20	25
O1578	**165**	75k. on 2l. brown	1·50	1·00
O1579	**165**	75k. on 5l. purple	15·00	16·00

Nos. O1577-9 and O1590 are larger.

O241

1957

O1655	**O241**	5k. blue	10	10
O1843	**O241**	5k. red	10	10
O1656	**O241**	10k. brown	10	10
O1844	**O241**	10k. olive	10	10
O1657	**O241**	15k. violet	10	10
O1845	**O241**	15k. red	10	10
O1658	**O241**	20k. red	10	10
O1846	**O241**	20k. violet	10	10
O1659	**O241**	30k. olive	25	10
O1660	**O241**	40k. purple	25	10
O1847	**O241**	40k. blue	15	10
O1661	**O241**	50k. grey	40	10
O1662	**O241**	60k. green	50	10
O1848	**O241**	60k. orange	50	10
O1663	**O241**	75k. orange	65	10
O1849	**O241**	75k. grey	50	10
O1664	**O241**	100k. green	80	10
O1850	**O241**	100k. violet	1·00	25
O1665	**O241**	200k. lake	1·80	40
O1851	**O241**	200k. brown	2·10	40

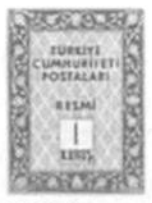

O284

1960

O1916	**O284**	1k. orange	10	10
O1917	**O284**	5k. red	10	10
O1918	**O284**	10k. green	40	10
O1919	**O284**	30k. brown	25	10
O1920	**O284**	60k. green	60	10
O1921	**O284**	1l. purple	1·10	10
O1922	**O284**	1½l. blue	2·50	10
O1923	**O284**	2½l. violet	3·25	25
O1924	**O284**	5l. blue	6·50	45

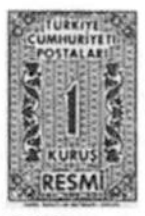

O303

1962

O1977	**O303**	1k. brown	10	10
O1978	**O303**	5k. green	10	10
O1979	**O303**	10k. brown	10	10
O1980	**O303**	15k. blue	15	10
O1981	**O303**	25k. red	15	10
O1982	**O303**	30k. blue	35	10

1963. Surch.

O2003	**O303**	50k. on 30k. blue	60	15
O2004	**O284**	100k. on 60k. green	60	15

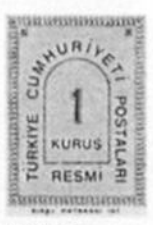

O320

1963

O2042	**O320**	1k. green	10	10
O2043	**O320**	5k. brown	10	10
O2044	**O320**	10k. green	10	10
O2045	**O320**	50k. red	25	10
O2046	**O320**	100k. blue	80	10

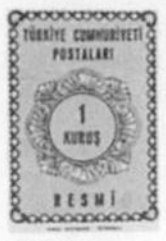

O329

1964

O2074	**O329**	1k. grey	10	10
O2075	**O329**	5k. blue	15	10
O2076	**O329**	10k. yellow	15	10
O2077	**O329**	30k. red	1·00	10
O2078	**O329**	50k. green	1·80	10
O2079	**O329**	60k. brown	1·80	10
O2080	**O329**	80k. turquoise	3·00	10
O2081	**O329**	130k. blue	6·25	25
O2082	**O329**	200k. purple	10·50	45

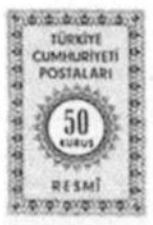

O344

1965

O2133	**O344**	1k. green	10	10
O2134	**O344**	10k. blue	10	10
O2135	**O344**	50k. orange	35	10

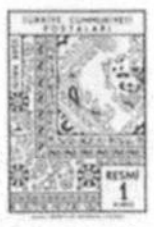

O358 Usak Carpet

1966. Turkish Carpets.

O2175	**O358**	1k. orange	10	10
O2176	-	50k. green	25	10
O2177	-	100k. red	50	10
O2178	-	150k. blue	75	15
O2179	-	200k. bistre	1·20	25
O2180	-	500k. lilac	2·75	90

DESIGNS (Carpets of): 50k. Bergama; 100k. Ladik; 150k. Selcuk; 200k. Nomad; 500k. Anatolia.

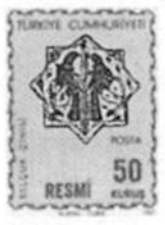

O372 Doves Emblem

1967

O2213	**O372**	1k. blue & light blue	10	10
O2214	**O372**	50k. blue and orange	25	10
O2215	**O372**	100k. blue & mauve	50	10

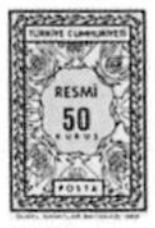

O383

1968

O2241	**O383**	50k. brown and green	25	10
O2242	**O383**	150k. black & orange	80	15
O2243	**O383**	500k. brown and blue	2·75	25

O400

1969

O2287	**O400**	1k. red and green	10	10
O2288	**O400**	10k. blue and green	10	10
O2289	**O400**	50k. brown and green	25	10
O2290	**O400**	100k. mauve & green	60	10

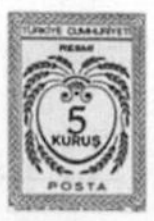

O427

1971

O2359	**O427**	5k. blue and brown	10	10
O2360	**O427**	10k. red and blue	15	10
O2361	**O427**	30k. violet & orange	50	10
O2362	**O427**	50k. brown and blue	50	15
O2363	**O427**	75k. green and buff	80	30

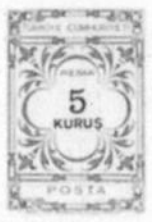

O440

1971. Face-value and border colour given first.

O2398	**O440**	5k. blue and grey	10	10
O2399	**O440**	25k. green and brown	10	10
O2400	**O440**	100k. brown & green	50	10
O2401	**O440**	200k. brown & ochre	1·10	10
O2402	**O440**	250k. purple & violet	1·50	15
O2403	**O440**	500k. blue & light blue	3·00	45

O446

1972

O2411	**O446**	5k. blue and brown	15	10
O2412	**O446**	100k. green & brown	40	10
O2413	**O446**	200k. red and brown	1·10	15

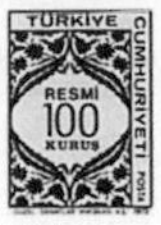

O462

1973

O2457	**O462**	100k. blue and cream	25	15

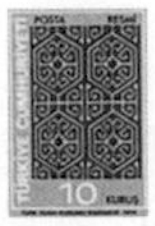

O478 Trellis Motif

1974

O2490	**O478**	10k. brown on pink	10	10
O2491	**O478**	25k. purple on blue	10	10
O2492	**O478**	50k. red on mauve	10	10
O2493	**O478**	150k. brown on grn	35	10
O2494	**O478**	250k. red on pink	65	15
O2495	**O478**	500k. brown on yell	1·20	25

O496

1975

O2537	**O496**	100k. red and blue	25	15

1977. Surch.

O2587	**O320**	5k. on 1k. green	10	10
O2588	**O329**	5k. on 1k. grey	10	10
O2589	**O344**	5k. on 1k. green	10	10
O2590	**O358**	5k. on 1k. orange	10	10
O2591	**O372**	5k. on 1k. blue and light blue	10	10

O528

1977

O2609	**O528**	250k. green and blue	25	15

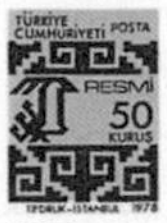

O529

1978

O2610	**O529**	50k. pink and red	10	10
O2611	**O529**	2½l. buff and brown	35	10
O2612	**O529**	4½l. lilac and green	60	10
O2613	**O529**	5l. blue and violet	60	10
O2614	**O529**	10l. light green and green	1·10	15
O2615	**O529**	25l. yellow and red	3·00	45

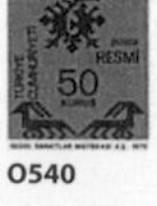

O540

1979

O2647	**O540**	50k. deep orange and orange	10	10
O2648	**O540**	2½l. blue & light blue	10	10

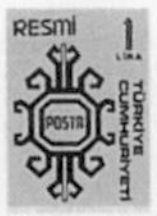

O552

1979

O2686	**O552**	50k. violet and pink	10	10
O2687	**O552**	1l. red and green	10	10
O2688	**O552**	2½l. mauve and light mauve	10	10
O2689	**O552**	5l. purple and blue	25	15
O2690	**O552**	7½l. blue and lilac	40	25
O2691	**O552**	10l. blue and buff	75	45
O2692	**O552**	35l. purple and silver	80	75
O2693	**O552**	50l. blue and pink	1·20	1·10

O573

1981

O2756	**O573**	5l. red and yellow	2·50	75
O2757	**O573**	10l. red and pink	3·25	1·50
O2758	**O573**	35l. mauve and grey	5·75	3·00
O2759	**O573**	50l. blue and pink	5·75	3·00
O2760	**O573**	75l. emerald & green	8·25	6·00
O2761	**O573**	100l. blue & lt blue	8·25	6·00

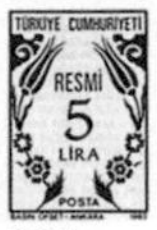

O606

1983

O2839	**O606**	5l. blue and yellow	1·60	15
O2840	**O606**	15l. blue and yellow	2·50	25
O2841	**O606**	20l. blue and grey	40	15
O2842	**O606**	50l. blue & light blue	3·25	75
O2843	**O606**	65l. blue and mauve	4·00	1·00
O2844	**O606**	70l. blue and pink	1·20	60
O2845	**O606**	90l. blue and brown	5·00	1·30
O2846	**O606**	90l. blue & light blue	1·60	75
O2847	**O606**	100l. blue and green	1·60	1·10
O2848	**O606**	125l. blue and green	5·00	2·30
O2849	**O606**	230l. blue and orange	3·75	2·30

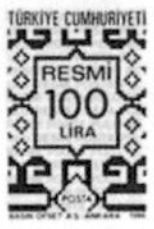

O644

1986

O2946	**O644**	5l. blue and yellow	40	25
O2947	**O644**	10l. blue and pink	40	25
O2948	**O644**	20l. blue and grey	80	25
O2949	**O644**	50l. blue & light blue	40	25
O2950	**O644**	100l. blue and green	1·60	55
O2951	**O644**	300l. blue and lilac	2·50	90

1989. Various stamps surch.

O3039	**O644**	500l. on 10l. blue and pink	2·10	1·90
O3040	**O606**	500l. on 15l. blue and yellow	80	75
O3041	**O644**	500l. on 20l. blue and grey	2·10	1·90
O3042	**O606**	1000l. on 70l. blue and pink	3·75	3·50
O3043	**O606**	1000l. on 90l. blue and brown	3·75	3·50
O3044	**O606**	1250l. on 230l. blue and orange	5·00	4·50

1991. Nos. O2843 and O2846 surch.

O3108	**O606**	100l. on 65l. blue and mauve	65	60
O3109	**O606**	250l. on 90l. blue and light blue	65	60

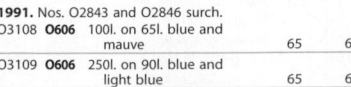

O720

1992

O3138	**O720**	3000l. deep brown and brown	2·30	2·10
O3139	**O720**	5000l. green & lt grn	4·00	3·50

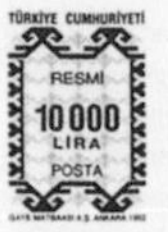

O733

1992

O3167	**O733**	1000l. blue and green	80	75
O3168	**O733**	10000l. green & blue	4·00	3·75

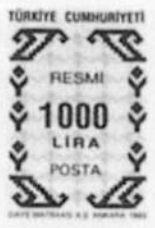

O743

1993

O3196	**O743**	1000l. green & brown	80	75
O3197	**O743**	1500l. green & brown	1·60	1·50
O3198	**O743**	5000l. brown & green	2·50	2·30

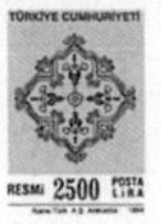

O753

1994

O3218	**O753**	2500l. dp mve & mve	80	75
O3219	**O753**	25000l. brn & stone	3·75	3·50

O764

1995

O3243	**O764**	3500l. violet and light violet	80	75
O3244	**O764**	17500l. green and light green	3·75	3·50

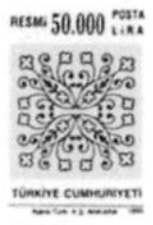

O770

1995

O3252	**O770**	50000l. green and olive	3·25	3·00

O775

1995

O3267	**O775**	5000l. red and orange	40	40

O785

1996

O3288	**O785**	15000l. red and blue	40	40
O3289	-	20000l. violet and green	80	75
O3290	-	50000l. green and violet	1·60	1·50
O3291	-	100000l. blue and red	3·25	3·00

DESIGNS: 20000l. Hearts forming pattern; 50000l. Leaves forming pattern; 100000l. Ornate scroll pattern.

O793

1997

O3303	**O793**	25000l. blue and mauve	60	55

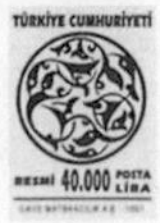

O803

1997

O3322	**O803**	40000l. violet and red	80	75
O3323	-	250000l. green and red	4·00	3·75

DESIGN: 250000l. Diamond-shaped pattern.

O815

1998

O3348	O815	40000l. light blue and blue	40	40
O3349	-	75000l. lilac and orange	80	75
O3350	-	100000l. purple	80	75
O3351	-	200000l. green and brown	1·60	1·50
O3352	-	500000l. green and brown	3·75	3·50

DESIGNS: 75000l. Pattern forming St. Andrew's cross with fleur-de-lis finials; 100000l. Diamond-shaped pattern; 200000l. Pattern with central circle; 500000l. Pattern forming five crosses.

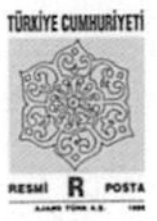

O827

1999

O3384	O827	R (75000l.) lilac and blue	1·20	1·10
O3385	-	RT (275000l.) grey and pink	3·75	3·50

DESIGN: No. O3385, Pattern of flowers.

No. O3384 was for use on Official letters and No. O3385 for use on Official registered letters.

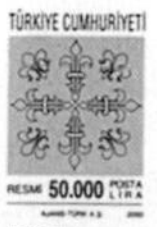

O838

2000

O3414	O838	50000l. pink and blue	40	40
O3415	-	75000l. grey and brown	40	40
O3416	-	500000l. blue and brown	1·60	1·50
O3417	-	1250000l. buff and blue	3·75	3·50

DESIGNS: 75000l. Squares and triangles; 500000l. Clover leaf pattern; 1250000l. Fleur de Lys pattern.

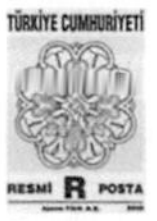

O849

2000

O3448	O 849	R yellow and blue	80	75
O3449	O 849	RT blue and ultramarine	1·60	1·50

No. O3448 was for use on Official letters and No. O3449 for use on Official registered letters.

O862

2001

O3491	O 862	R yellow and blue	60	55

No. O3491 was for use on Official letters.

O875

2002

O3519	O 875	50000l. blue and red	15	15
O3520	-	100000l. yellow and green	25	25
O3521	-	250000l. blue and red	40	40
O3522	-	500000l. orange and blue	80	75
O3523	-	1500000l. yellow, light green and green	1·60	1·50

DESIGNS: 100000l. Pattern of curved lines; 250000l. Pattern of leaves; 50000l. Pattern with diamond shape in centre; 1500000l. Oval shaped pattern.

O882

2003

O3545	O 882	500000l. red and blue	60	55
O3546	-	750000l. blue and buff	80	75
O3547	-	1000000l. green and blue	1·10	1·00
O3548	-	3000000l. buff and blue	3·00	2·75

DESIGNS: 750000l. Cross-shaped pattern; 1000000l. Diamond-shaped pattern; 3000000l. Pattern of four holly leaves.

O885

2003

O3553	O885	mauve and pink	65	60

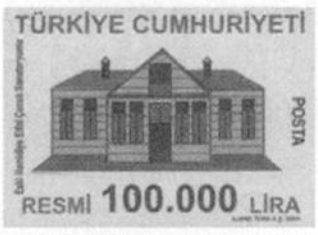

O901 Children's Hospital, Hamidiye Etfal

2004. Multicoloured.. Multicoloured..

O3598	100000l. Type O **901**	10	10
O3599	500000l. Combined Heat and Power Station, Silahtaraga	50	45
O3600	600000l. PTT building, Ankara (vert)	60	55
O3601	1000000l. Ministry of Finance building, Ankara	90	85
O3602	1500000l. Head Post Office. Istanbul (vert)	3·25	3·00

2005. As Type O 901. Multicoloured.

O3626	60ykr. Main post office, Ankara	50	45

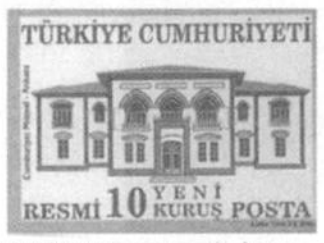

O915 Museum, Ankara

2005. Multicoloured.. Multicoloured..

O3644	10ykr. Type O **915**	10	10
O3645	25ykr. Culture and Tourism Ministry, Ankara	25	25
O3646	50ykr. Government building, Ankara	65	60
O3647	60ykr. [illegible] Culture museum, Ankara	75	70
O3648	1ytl. Ethnographic museum, Ankara	90	85
O3649	3ytl. 50 National library, Ankara	1·40	1·30

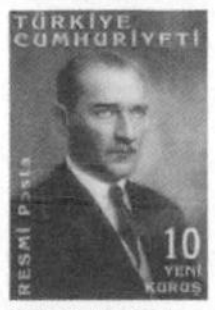

O930 Ataturk

2006. Mustafa Kemal Ataturk. Multicoloured.

O3694	10ykr. Type O **930**	10	10
O3695	50ykr. With hand out-stretched	65	60
O3696	60ykr. Wearing hat	75	70
O3697	1ykl. Wearing blue tie	1·60	1·50
O3698	3ykl.5 Wearing dress suit	4·00	3·25

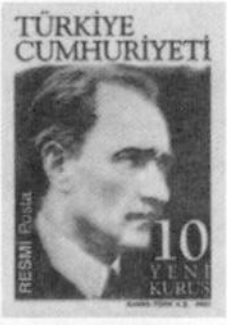

O944 Ataturk

2007. Mustafa Kemal Ataturk. Multicoloured.

O3752	10ykr. Type O **944**	20	20
O3753	50ykr. Seated	55	55
O3754	60ykr. With moustache	75	75
O3755	1ykl. Facing left	1·20	1·20
O3756	4ykl. Wearing high-collared shirt and tie	3·75	3·75

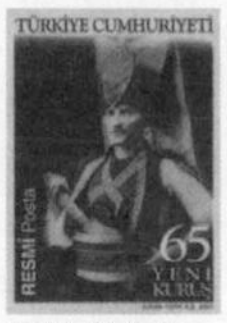

O963 Ataturk

2007. Mustafa Kemal Ataturk.

O3820	**O963**	65ykr. multicoloured	1·00	1·00

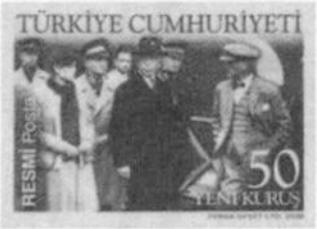

O 985 Attaturk with Leaders

2008. Mustafa Kemal Attatürk. Multicoloured.

O3891	50ykr. Type O **985**	65	65
O3892	65ykr. Attaturk (vert)	80	80
O3893	1ytl. With workers (vert)	1·30	1·30
O3894	5ytl. Wearing evening dress (vert)	4·25	4·25

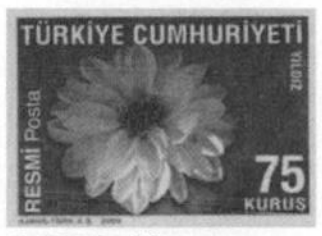

O 989 Dahlia

2009. Flowers. Multicoloured.

O3913a	75ykr. Type **989**	85	85
O3917	5ykl. Geranium	4·25	4·25

Numbers are left for stamps not received.

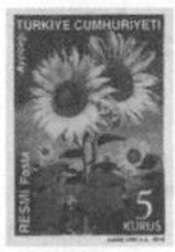

O1024 Sunflowers

2010. Official Stamps. Flowers. Multicoloured.

O4007	5ykr. Type O**1024**	20	20
O4008	10ykr. Poppies	30	30
O4009	25ykr. Passion flower	50	50
O4010	80ykr. Zinnia	1·20	1·20
O4011	1ytl. Rose	1·50	1·50

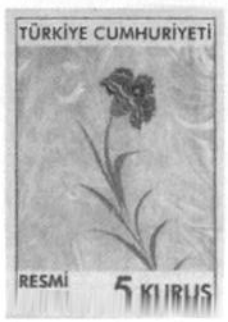

O1029 Dianthus

2010. Official Stamps. Flowers. Multicoloured.

O4020	5ykr. Type O**1029**	20	20
O4021	50ykr. Orange and yellow pansy-shaped flowers	60	60
O4022	80ykr. Dark pink salvia-shaped flowers, blue background	1·20	1·20
O4023	90ykr. Yellow composite flowers, blue background	1·30	1·30
O4024	1ytl. White tulip-shaped flowers, blue background	1·50	1·50

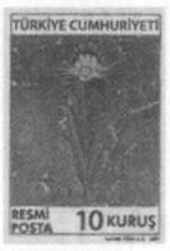

O1034 Flower

2011. Official Stamps. Multicoloured.

O4035	10ykr. Type O**1034**	30	30
O4036	1ytl. Orange and yellow composite flowers	1·50	1·50
O4037	2ytl.80 Stylized peacock feathers, blue background	3·00	3·00
O4038	6ytl. Stylized peacock feathers, multicoloured background	5·00	5·00

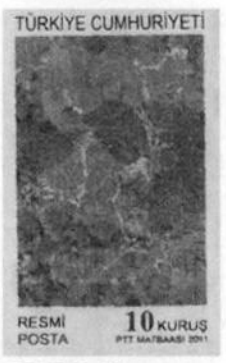

O1053 Abstract

2011. Official Stamps. Multicoloured.

O4073	10ykr. Type O**1053**	30	30
O4074	1ytl. Fluid heart-shapes around a circular centre, darker blue background	1·50	1·50
O4075	2ytl. Fluid shapes and two circular shapes, pale blue marbled background	2·00	2·00
O4076	7ytl. Multicoloured marbled design with central magenta splashes	5·50	5·50

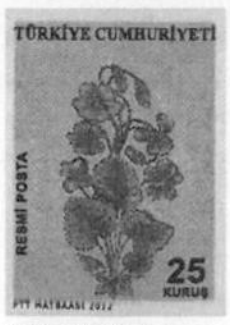

O1064 Violets

2012. Official Stamps. Flowers. Multicoloured.

O4103	25ykr. Type **O1064**	50	50
O4104	50ykr. Red and blue tied bouquet	60	60
O4105	1ytl. Multicoloured bouquet in blue patterned vase	1·50	1·50
O4106	3ytl.75 Two blue rose-shaped blooms tied with red ribbon	3·50	3·50
O4107	7ytl. Pink single roses tied bouquet	5·50	5·50

POSTAGE DUE STAMPS

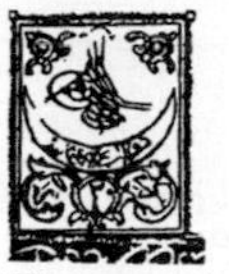

D2

1863. Imperf.

D7	D2	20pa. black on brown	£300	75·00
D8	D2	1pi. black on brown	£550	60·00
D9	D2	2pi. black on brown	£3500	£180
D10	D2	5pi. black on brown	£2500	£225

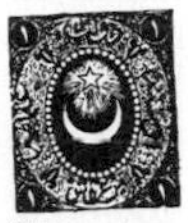

D4

1865

D18	D4	20pa. brown	2·40	6·00
D19	D4	1pi. brown	2·40	6·00
D74B	D4	2pi. brown	5·75	11·00
D70A	D4	5pi. brown	1·40	9·25
D76B	D4	25pi. brown	38·00	£150

1888. As T **9**.

D117	9	20pa. black	3·00	15·00
D118	9	1pi. black	3·00	15·00
D119	9	2pi. black	3·00	18·00

1892. As T **15**.

D146	15	20pa. black	6·75	15·00
D147	15	20pa. black on red	2·40	24·00
D148	15	1pi. black	22·00	15·00
D149	15	2pi. black	17·00	15·00

1901. As T **21**.

D195	21	10pa. black on red	3·75	7·25
D196	21	20pa. black on red	3·50	10·50
D197	21	1pi. black on red	3·00	12·00
D198	21	2pi. black on red	1·70	18·00

1905. As T **23**.

D228	23	1pi. black on red	3·00	12·00
D229	23	2pi. black on red	4·25	24·00

1908. As T **25**.

D250A	25	1pi. black on red	75·00	9·25
D251B	25	2pi. black on red	7·50	65·00

1909. As T **28**.

D288A	28	1pi. black on red	14·50	60·00
D287B	28	2pi. black on red	£120	£200

1913. As T **30**.

D347	30	2pa. black on red	95	1·40
D348	30	5pa. black on red	95	1·40
D349	30	10pa. black on red	95	1·40
D350	30	20pa. black on red	95	1·40
D351	30	1pi. black on red	4·25	12·00
D352	30	2pi. black on red	7·75	21·00

1913. Adrianople Issue surch.

D356	31	2pa. on 10pa. green	3·00	1·40
D357	31	5pa. on 20pa. red	3·00	1·40
D358	31	10pa. on 40pa. blue	9·50	4·75
D359	31	20pa. on 40pa. blue	31·00	21·00

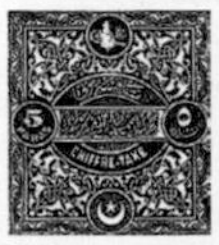

D49

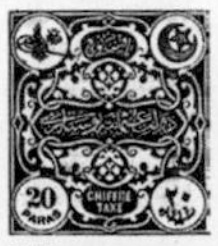

D50

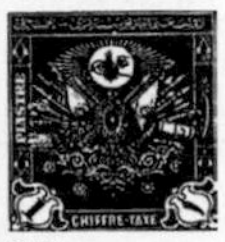

D51

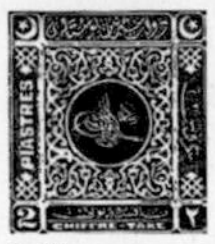

D52

1914

D516	**D49**	5pa. brown	1·20	12·00
D517	**D50**	20pa. red	1·20	12·00
D518	**D51**	1pi. blue	1·20	12·00
D519	**D52**	2pi. blue	1·20	12·00

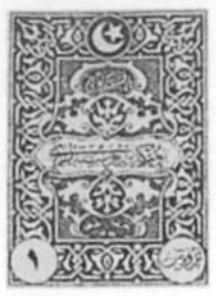

AD26

1921

AD91	**AD 26**	20pa. green	1·40	3·25
AD92	**AD 26**	1pi. green	3·00	3·50
AD93	**AD 26**	2pi. brown	3·75	11·00
AD94	**AD 26**	3pi. red	10·00	17·00
AD95	**AD 26**	5pi. blue	12·00	34·00

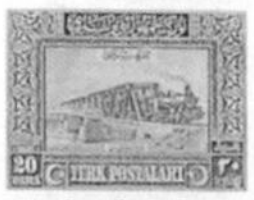

D101 Bridge over Kizil-Irmak

1926

D1035	**D101**	20pa. orange	95	2·50
D1036	**D101**	1gr. red	1·40	5·25
D1037	**D101**	2gr. green	1·40	5·25
D1038	**D101**	3gr. purple	2·40	13·00
D1039	**D101**	5gr. violet	4·75	21·00

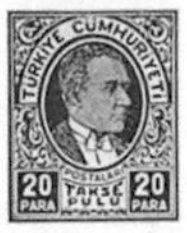

D121

1936

D1186	**D121**	20pa. brown	10	50
D1187	**D121**	2k. blue	10	1·00
D1188	**D121**	3k. violet	10	1·30
D1189	**D121**	5k. green	10	1·60
D1190	**D121**	12k. red	10	3·75

PRINTED MATTER STAMPS

1879. Optd **IMPRIMES** in scroll.

N88	**9**	10pa. black and mauve	£225	£275

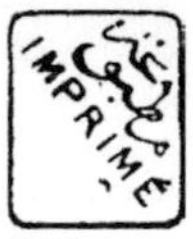

(N14)

1891. Stamps of 1876 optd with Type **N14**.

N132	**9**	10pa. green	38·00	15·00
N134	**9**	20pa. pink	70·00	18·00
N136	**9**	1pi. blue	£190	£180
N138	**9**	2pi. yellow	£475	£500
N139	**9**	5pi. brown	£950	£900

1892. Stamps of 1892 optd with Type **N14**.

N150	**15**	10pa. green	£275	12·00
N151	**15**	20pa. red	£800	£450
N152	**15**	1pi. blue	£130	£180
N153	**15**	2pi. brown	£140	£225
N154	**15**	5pi. purple	£1500	£1500

مطبوعه

(N16)

1894. Stamps of 1892 optd with Type **N16**.

N155	**15**	10pa. green	3·50	3·00
N156a	**15**	20pa. red	2·30	1·40
N157	**15**	1pi. blue	3·00	1·80
N158	**15**	2pi. brown	26·00	15·00
N159	**15**	5pi. purple	80·00	65·00
N161	**15**	5pa. on 10pa. grn (160)	3·75	2·40

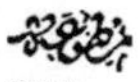

(N23)

1901. Stamps of 1901 optd with Type **N23**.

N183	**21**	5pa. violet	8·50	2·40
N184	**21**	10pa. green	31·00	3·00
N185	**21**	20pa. red	8·50	1·80
N186	**21**	1pi. blue	24·00	2·40
N187	**21**	2pi. orange	85·00	5·00
N188	**21**	5pi. mauve	£160	34·00

1901. Stamps of 1901 optd with Type **N23**.

N189	**22**	5pa. brown	95	1·20
N190	**22**	10pa. green	6·00	7·75
N191	**22**	20pa. mauve	31·00	9·25
N192	**22**	1pi. blue	60·00	28·00
N193	**22**	2pi. blue	£140	46·00
N194	**22**	5pi. brown	£325	£110

1905. Stamps of 1905 optd with Type **N23**.

N222B	**23**	5pa. brown	85	65
N223B	**23**	10pa. green	23·00	3·00
N224A	**23**	20pa. pink	2·40	1·50
N225B	**23**	1pi. blue	1·90	1·60
N226A	**23**	2pi. blue	65·00	31·00
N227A	**23**	5pi. brown	£120	24·00

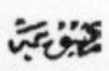

(N27)

1908. Stamps of 1908 optd with Type **N27**.

N244A	**25**	5pa. brown	9·50	60
N245B	**25**	10pa. green	13·00	50
N246B	**25**	20pa. red	13·00	50
N247A	**25**	1pi. blue	95·00	3·00
N248A	**25**	2pi. black	£140	9·25
N249B	**25**	5pi. purple	£170	29·00

1909. Stamps of 1909 optd with Type **N27**.

N276A	**28**	5pa. brown	2·40	60
N277C	**28**	10pa. green	3·75	60
N278C	**28**	20pa. red	30·00	3·25
N279A	**28**	1pi. blue	95·00	6·00
N280A	**28**	2pi. black	£250	37·00
N281A	**28**	5pi. purple	£475	80·00

1911. New value of 1909 issue.

N332	**28**	2pa. olive		

1920. No. 500 surch.

N961	5 on 4pa. brown	1·20	50

Pt. 10

TURKMENISTAN

Formerly a constituent republic of the Soviet Union, Turkmenistan became independent on 27 October 1991.

1992. 100 kopeks = 1 rouble.
1994. 100 tenge = 1 manat.

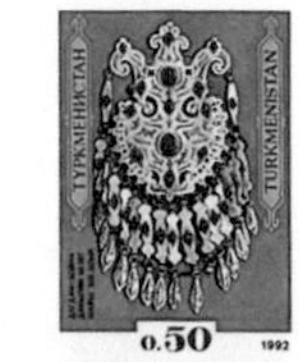

1 19th-century Gold and Jewelled Bib

1992. Treasure in National Museum.

1	**1**	50k. multicoloured	70	65

See also No. 4.

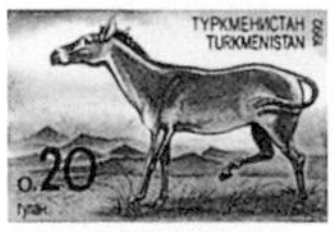

2 Asiatic Wild Ass

1992. Animals of Central Asia. Multicoloured.

2	20k. Type **2**	40	40
3	40k. Cobra (vert)	55	50

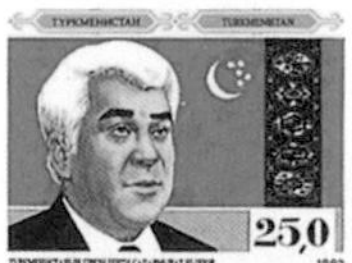

3 President Saparmyrat Niyazov and Reverse of National Flag

1992. History and Culture. Multicoloured.

4	10r. Type **1**	1·40	1·30
5	10r. Girl in traditional dress and Kopet-Daga Mountains	1·40	1·30
6	10r. Mollanepes Drama Theatre, Ashkhabad	1·40	1·30
7	10r. Akhaltekin horseman (vert)	1·40	1·30
8	15r. Arms (vert)	1·80	1·60
9	25r. Type **3**	2·50	2·30
MS10	111×79 mm. 10r. Map of Turkmenistan. Imperf	8·50	7·50

For similar design to Type **3** but with flag reversed, see No. 12.

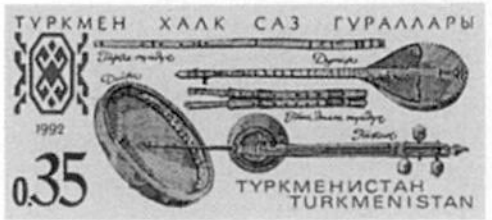

4 Traditional Musical Instruments

1992

11	**4**	35k. multicoloured	55	50

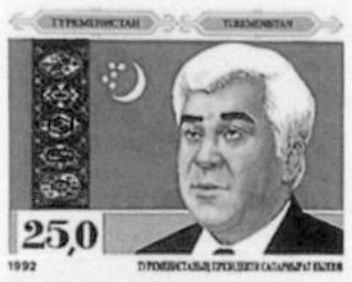

5 National Flag and President Saparmyrat Niyazov

1992. First Anniv of Independence.

12	**5**	25r. multicoloured	5·50	5·00

For similar design but with flag reversed, see No 9.

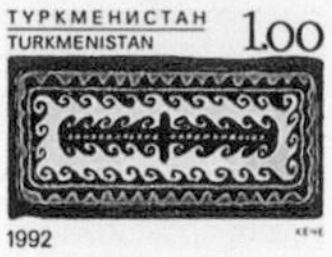

6 Carpet

1992

13	**6**	1r. multicoloured	55	50

1992. Nos. 7/8 optd with horse's head.

14	10r. multicoloured	1·10	1·00
15	15r. multicoloured	1·40	1·30

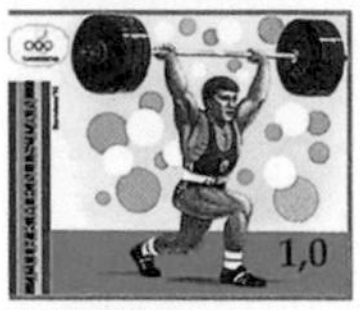

8 Weightlifting

1993. Olympic Games, Barcelona. Multicoloured.

16	1r. Type **8**	30	25
17	3r. Show jumping	55	50
18	5r. Wrestling	85	75
19	10r. Canoeing	2·10	1·90
20	15r. National Olympic emblem	3·50	3·25
MS21	108×82 mm. 15r. Flags and sports pictograms. Imperf	17·00	15·00

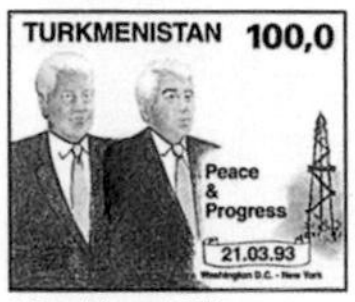

9 Presidents William Clinton and Niyazov

1993. Visit of President Saparmyrat Niyazov to United States of America. Type **9** with different dates. Multicoloured.

22	**9**	100r. Dated "21.03.93"	2·10	1·90
23	**9**	100r. Dated "22.03.93"	2·10	1·90
24	**9**	100r. Dated "23.03.93"	2·10	1·90
25	**9**	100r. Dated "24.03.93"	2·10	1·90
26	**9**	100r. Dated "25.03.93"	2·10	1·90

1993. Nos. 16/20 surch.

27	10r. on 3r. Show jumping	30	25
28	15r. on 5r. Wrestling	55	50
29	15r. on 10r. Canoeing	85	75
30	25r. on 1r. Type **8**	2·10	1·90
31	50r. on 15r. National Olympic emblem	3·50	3·25

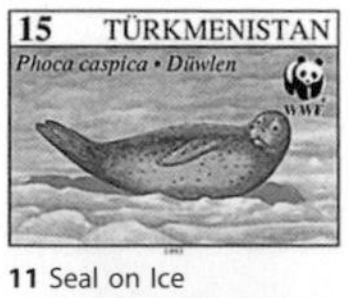

11 Seal on Ice

1993. The Caspian Seal (*Phoca caspica*). Multicoloured.

32	15r. Type **11**	40	40
33	25r. Seal on sandy beach	70	65
34	50r. Seal on pebble beach	1·00	90
35	100r. Adult with young	1·50	1·40
36	150r. Seal swimming	2·40	2·10
37	500r. Seal on sandy beach (different)	5·50	5·00

Nos. 33 and 37 were issued together, *se-tenant*, forming a composite design.

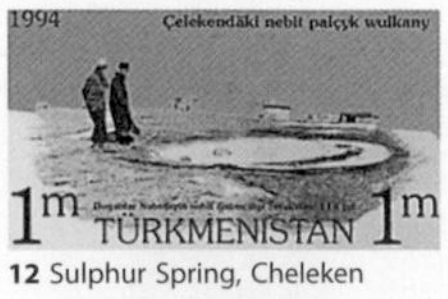

12 Sulphur Spring, Cheleken

1994. 115th Anniv of Nobel Partnership to Exploit Black Sea Oil. Multicoloured.

38	1m. Type **12**	85	75
39	1m.50 "Turkmen" (oil tanker)	1·40	1·30
40	2m. Drilling in Cheleken	1·80	1·60
41	3m. Nobel brothers and Petr Bilderling (partners) (vert)	3·00	2·75
MS42	93×68 mm. 5m. Statue and oil derricks	7·00	6·25

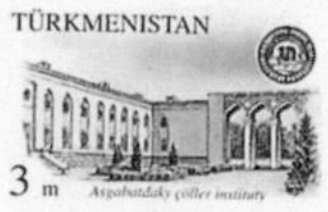

13 Repetek Institute

1994. Repetek Nature Reserve. Multicoloured.

43	3m. Type **13**	70	65
44	5m. Dromedaries in Repetek Desert	85	75
45	5m. Saw-scaled viper	85	75
46	10m. Transcaspian desert monitor	2·00	1·80
47	20m. Tortoise	4·25	3·75
MS48	86×69 mm. 10m. *Haloxylon amodendron*	3·50	3·25

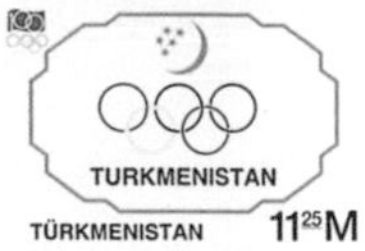

14 National Olympic Committee Emblem

1994. Centenary of International Olympic Committee.

49	**14**	11m.25 multicoloured	4·00	3·50
MS50		106×76 mm. **14** 20m. multicoloured	6·25	5·75

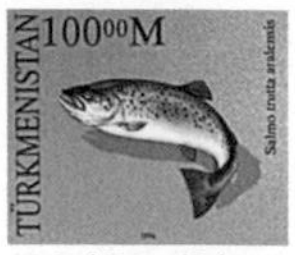

15 Aral Trout (*Salmo trutta aralensis*)

1996. "Save the Aral Sea". Sheet 128×108 mm containing T **15** and similar horiz designs. Multicoloured.

MS51	100m. Caracal (*Felis caracal*); 100m. Type **15**; 100m. Striped hyena; (*Hyaena hyaena*); 100m. Kaufmann's shovelnose (*Pseudoscaphirhynchus Kaufmanni*); 100m. Pike asp (*Aspiolucius esocinus*)	10·50	9·50

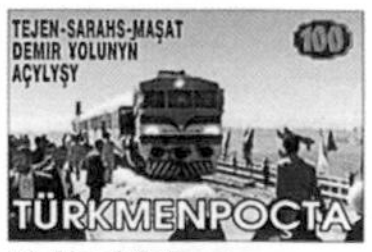

16 Diesel Train

1996. Fifth Anniv of Independence. Multicoloured.

52	100m. Type **16** (inauguration of Turkmenistan–Iran railway)	70	65
53	100m. Turkmenistan highlighted on globe (vert)	70	65
54	300m. Presidents Rafsanjani of Iran, Niyazov of Turkmenistan and Demirel of Turkey (opening of Turkmenistan–Iran–Turkey gas pipeline)	1·80	1·60
55	300m. Saparmyrat International Airport, Ashgabat (vert)	1·80	1·60
56	500m. Boutros Boutros-Ghali (United Nations Secretary General) and President Saparmyrat Niyazov (vert)	2·75	2·40
57	1000m. National flag and arms	5·00	4·50

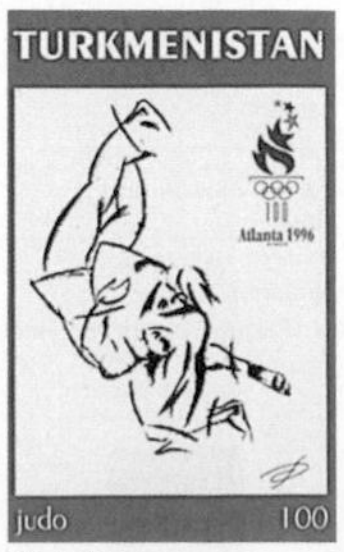

17 Judo

1997. Olympic Games, Atlanta, U.S.A. Multicoloured.

58	100m. Type **17**	70	65
59	300m. Athletics	2·75	2·50
60	300m. Greco-Roman wrestling	2·75	2·50
61	300m. Boxing	2·75	2·50
62	500m. Shooting	5·00	4·50
MS63	86×105 mm. 1000m. Olympic torch	9·75	8·75

18 Woman in Red Dress and Blue Shawl

1999. National Costumes. Multicoloured.

64	500m. Type **18**	70	65
65	1000m. Woman in red dress	1·40	1·30
66	1200m. Woman in pink dress	1·70	1·50
67	2500m. Woman in red dress and embroidered shawl	3·25	3·00
68	3000m. Woman in green dress	3·75	3·50

19 Common Kestrel

1999. Birds of Prey. Multicoloured.

69	1000m. Type **19**	1·50	1·40
70	1000m. Peregrine falcon "Falco peregrinus" facing left	1·50	1·40
71	1000m. Peregrine falcon facing right	1·50	1·40
72	2500m. Common kestrel on branch	3·75	3·25
73	3000m. Peregrine falcon on branch	4·25	3·75

Nos. 69/73 were issued together, *se-tenant*, with the backgrounds forming a composite design.

20 Afghanistan

2000. Fifth Anniv of Neutrality. Designs showing country flags. Multicoloured.

74-97	3000m. Type **20**; Armenia; Azerbaijan; Bangladesh; Belarus; Colombia; Czech Republic; Egypt; France; Georgia; India; Indonesia; Iran; Kenya; Kyrgyzstan; Malaysia; Mauritius; Pakistan; Moldova; Russian Federation; Senegal; Tajikistan; Turkey; Ukraine	75·00	70·00

21 "A"

2000. No value expressed. Self-adhesive. Imperf.

98	**21**	(A) brown and buff	1·80	1·60

22 Altyn Asyr Trade Centre

2001. National Symbols. No value expressed. Multicoloured. Self-adhesive. Imperf.

99	B (1000m.) Type **22**	85	75
100	U (3000m.) Flag and arms	2·00	1·80

23 Perenli

2001. Akhal-Teke Horses. Multicoloured.

101-106	3000m.×6, Type **23**; Garader; Pyyada; Tyllanur; Arkadas; Yanardag	19·00	18·00

MS107 112×80 mm. 5000m.×2, Bitarap; Yanardag (vert)	21·00	19·00

MS108 Two sheets, each 117×90 mm. (a) 5000m. Yanardag and mountains. (b) 500m. Yanardag and herd in cornfield. Imperf	21·00	19·00

24 500m. Coin showing President Saparmurat Niyazov (obverse) and Castle (reverse)

2001. Tenth Anniv of Independence. Seven sheets, each 210×157 mm containing T **24** and similar multicoloured designs. Imperf.

MS109 (a) Coins. 500m.×6, Type **24** and **5** other designs showing 500m. coins with Pres. Niyazov (obverse) and various castles (reverse). (b) Buildings. Size 32×11 mm. 1000m.×6, Soltan Sanjar; Nusay; Gyz Gala; Urgenc; Anew; Kone Urgenc. (c) Cultural Heritage. Size 29×43 mm. 1200m.×6, Horn; Cloth; Musical instruments; Rodogunda (statue); Vase; Chest ornament. (d) Hotels. Size 38×31 mm. 1250m.×6, Ahal; Gara Altyn; Demiryolcy; Altyn Suw; Kopetdag; Aziya. (e) Buildings. Size 29×43 mm. 1250m.×6, Skyscraper; Arch of Neutrality; Turkmengosstrakh; Office tower; Turkmenbashibank; Altyn Asyr trade centre. (f) Statues. Size 29×43 mm. 3000m.×6, Oguz Han; Seljuk Bay; Bayram Han; Soltan Sanjur; Gorkut Ata; Gorogly Beg. (g) Statues. Size 29×43 mm. 3000m.×6, Bayram Han; Sahyrlary Kemine; Sahylary Zelili; Sahyrlary Seydi; Sahyrlary Mollanepes; Sahyrlary Mataji | 75·00 | 70·00 |

25 Quaid E Azam Mohammad Ali Jinnah

2001. 125th Birth Anniv of Quaid E Azam Mohammad Ali Jinnah (founder of Pakistan). Turkmenistan-Pakistan Relations.

110	**25**	500m. multicoloured	1·10	1·00

26 Sylvia communis

2002. Birds. Four sheets containing T **26** and similar horiz designs. Multicoloured.

MS111 Two sheets, each 125×124 mm. (a) 3000m.×6, Type **26**; *Cuculus canorus; Sylvia curruca; Corvus pica; Corvus frugilegus; Corvus corax.* (b) 3000m.×6, *Motacilla flava; Lanius isabellinus; Oenanthe oenanthe; Corvus monedula; Corvus cornix; Upupa pyrrhocorax* | 25·00 | 23·00 |

MS112 Two sheets, each 101×72 mm. (a) 5000m. *Anas crecca.* (b) 5000m. *Riparia riparia* | 7·50 | 6·75 |

The stamps and margins of **MS**111/112a/b each form composite designs.

27 *Pandoriana pandora*

2002. Butterflies. Four sheets containing T **27** and similar horiz designs. Multicoloured.

MS113 Two sheets, each 118×125 mm (a) 3000m.×6, Type **27**; *Chazara briseis; Aphantopus hyperantus; Iolana iolas; Pararge schakra; Maniola jurtina.* (b) 3000m.×6, *Vanessa indica; Cynthia cardui; Pararge aegeria; Pieris rapae; Lysandra bellargus; Anthocharis cardamines* | 25·00 | 23·00 |

MS114 98×69 mm. (a) 5000m. *Quercusia quercus* (horiz) | 3·75 | 3·50 |

MS115 69×98 mm. (a) 5000m. *Hamearis lucina* (horiz) | 3·75 | 3·50 |

The stamps and margins of **MS**113/115 each form composite designs.

28 Mosque

2003. Self-adhesive.

116	**28**	B multicoloured	1·70	1·50

29 Dome and Tower

2003. Self-adhesive.

117	**29**	G multicoloured	2·10	1·90

30 Building Facade

2004. Self-adhesive.

118	**30**	B multicoloured	1·70	1·50

31 Dog

2004. Dogs.

119	**31**	A multicoloured	1·70	1·50

31a Spacecraft

2005. Book in Space. 'Ruhnama' (book by Pres. Saparmyrat Niyazov) jettisoned from Russian Shuttle. Multicoloured.

MS119a 5000m.×2, Type **31a**; 'Ruhnama'

32 Dun

2005. Akhal-Teke Horses. Four sheets containing T **32** and similar multicoloured designs.

MS120 227×154 mm. (a) 2500m.×2, Type **32**; Palamino. (b) (c) 2500m.×2, Foal suckling; Bright bay facing left | 8·50 | 7·50 |

MS120a 227×154 mm. 2500m.×2, Head of horse wearing decorative bridle (vert); Dark bay rearing (vert) | 8·50 | 7·50 |

MS120b 227×154 mm. 2500m.×2, Foal suckling; Bright bay facing left | 8·50 | 7·50 |

MS121 154×227 mm. 2500m.×2, Grey facing right; Bright bay facing right | 17·00 | 15·00 |

33 Kofi Annan, Secretary General of United Nations and Saparmurat Niyazov, President of Turkmenistan

---

2005. Fifth Anniv of Turkmenistan's Permanent Neutrality. Sheet 207×277 mm containing T **33** and similar horiz design. Multicoloured.

MS122 5000m.×2, Type **33**; Emblem and monument to president of Turkmenistan | 20·00 | 18·00 |

34 Building

2006. Architecture. Sheet 211×160 mm containing T **34** and similar multicoloured designs.

MS123 3000m.×8, Type **34**; Arts Palace, Independence Square; National Theatre; Geke-tep Mosque; Gypjak Moaque; Akhal-Teke Horse Monument; Ministry of Defence; Building. 5000m.×4, Arch of Neutrality (40×60 mm.); Oil and Gas Ministry (40×60 mm.); President Hotel (40×60 mm.); Independence Monument (40×60 mm.) | 31·00 | 28·00 |

2007. President Saparmurat Niyazov (Turkmenbashy) Commemoration. Multicoloured.

MS124 A×13, Size 33×47 mm, President Saparmurat Niyazov×4 Size 33×25 mm, President Saparmurat Niyazov×8 Size 51×24 mm President Saparmurat Niyazov

MS125 A×13, Size 33×47 mm, President Saparmurat Niyazov×4 Size 33×25 mm, Saparmurat Niyazov×8 Size 51×24 mm Saparmurat Niyazov

36 Leopard

2007. Leopard

126	**36**	A multicoloured		

2008. Fauna. Multicoloured.

128	A Leopard (As Type **36**)
129	D Ram
130	G Pelican
131	G Lynx
132	O Crane
133	S Stag
134	T Partridge

2008. Architecture. Ministry of Health Building, Ashqabat

135	**38**	S multicoloured

2009. Fauna. Multicoloured.

136	A Leopard (As Type **36**)
137	D Ram (As No. 129)
138	G Pelican (As No. 130)
139	G Lynx (As No. 131)
140	O Crane (As No. 132)
141	S Stag (As No. 133)
142	T Partridge (As No. 134)

39 Goitered Gazelle Buck

2009. Fauna. Ungulates. Multicoloured.

143	D Type **39**
144	G Moflon ram
145	K Goitered gazelle, does and buck

2010. 65th Anniv of Victory. Multicoloured.

MS146 Y.×4, Two soldiers marching holding wreath; Monument; Guard of honour beside monument; Veterans of WWII

41 Gas Plant

2010. Turkmenistan - China Gas Main. Multicoloured.

147	G Type **41**
148	G Flags of participating countries

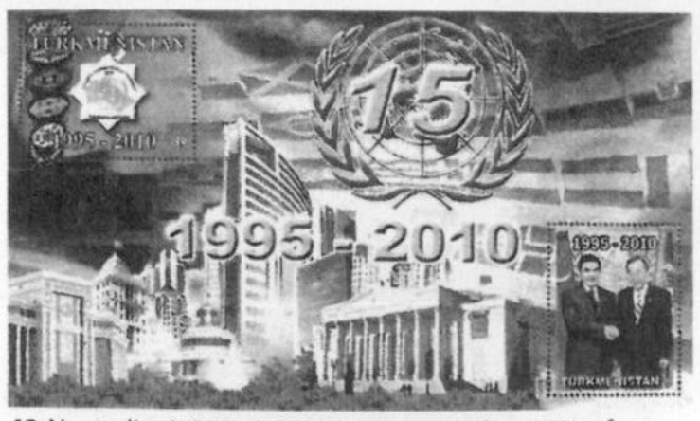

42 Neutrality '1995 - 2010' (image scaled to 57% of original size)

2010. 15th Anniv of Neutrality. Multicoloured.
MS149 B.×2, Symbols (horiz); President Berdymuhamedov with Li Zhaoxing (vert)

2013. Dogs. Alabai Turkmenian Sheep Dog. Multicoloured.
MS150 A.×6, Fawn dog, standing, facing right; Bright brown dog, standing, facing right; Young white dog with brown markings on head, seated; Head and shoulders of long haired bi-coloured dog; Fawn dog looking left over right shoulder; Mother dog facing left

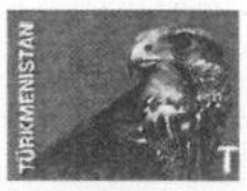

43 Falcon

2013. Falconry. Multicoloured.
MS151 T.×3, Sight hound, facing left; Type **43;** Sight hound, head and shoulders, facing right

Pt. 1

TURKS ISLANDS

A group of islands in the British West Indies, S.E. of the Bahamas, now grouped with the Caicos Islands and using the stamps of Turks and Caicos Islands. A dependency of Jamaica until August 1962, when it became a Crown Colony.

12 pence = 1 shilling.

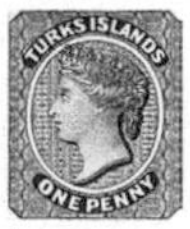

1

1867

55	**1**	1d. brown	£100	38·00
63	**1**	1d. red	7·00	4·50
2	**1**	6d. black	£120	£140
59	**1**	6d. brown	4·75	6·00
3	**1**	1s. blue	£100	60·00
6	**1**	1s. lilac	£5000	£2000
52	**1**	1s. green	£200	£150
60	**1**	1s. brown	6·50	4·75

1881. Surch with large figures.

17	½ on 1d. red	60·00	£150
8	½ on 6d. black	£100	£150
9	½ on 1s. blue	£140	£200
19	½ on 1s. lilac	£100	£225
34	2½ on 1d. red	£750	
28	2½ on 6d. black	£250	£450
36	2½ on 1s. lilac	£600	£900
38	2½ on 1s. blue	£1100	
47	4 on 1d. red	£750	£475
43	4 on 6d. black	£110	£160
45	4 on 1s. lilac	£475	£750

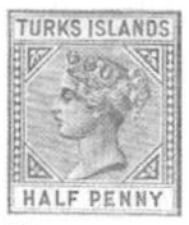

31

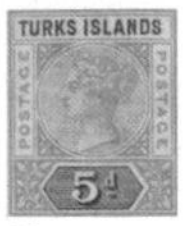

34

1881

70	**31**	½d. green	6·50	4·25
56	**31**	2½d. brown	45·00	17·00
65	**31**	2½d. blue	6·50	4·50
50	**31**	4d. blue	£170	60·00
57	**31**	4d. grey	40·00	4·25
71	**31**	4d. purple and blue	24·00	26·00
72	**34**	5d. olive and red	11·00	26·00

1889. Surch **One Penny**.

61	**31**	1d. on 2½d. brown	23·00	20·00

1893. Surch ½**d.** and bar.

68	½d. on 4d. grey	£180	£190

Pt. 1

TURKS AND CAICOS ISLANDS

(see TURKS ISLANDS)

1900. 12 pence = 1 shilling; 20 shillings = 1 pound.
1969. 100 cents = 1 dollar.

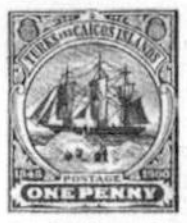

35 Badge of the Islands

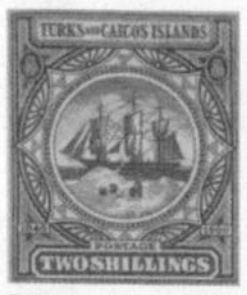

36

1900

110	**35**	½d. green	5·00	15
102	**35**	1d. red	3·50	75
103	**35**	2d. brown	1·00	1·25
104a	**35**	2½d. blue	1·75	1·00
112	**35**	3d. purple on yellow	2·25	6·00
105	**35**	4d. orange	3·75	7·00
106	**35**	6d. mauve	2·50	6·50
107	**35**	1s. brown	3·25	22·00
108	**36**	2s. purple	50·00	80·00
109	**36**	3s. red	80·00	£110

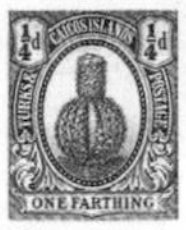

37 Turk's-head Cactus

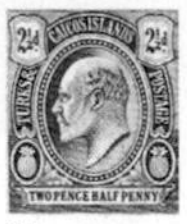

38

1909

115	**37**	¼d. mauve	1·75	1·00
116	**37**	¼d. red	60	40
162	**37**	¼d. black	80	1·00
117	**38**	½d. green	75	40
118	**38**	1d. red	1·25	40
119	**38**	2d. grey	5·50	1·40
120	**38**	2½d. blue	8·00	2·25
121	**38**	3d. purple on yellow	2·50	2·00
122	**38**	4d. red on yellow	3·25	6·00
123	**38**	6d. purple	7·00	3·00
124	**38**	1s. black on green	7·50	5·50
125	**38**	2s. red and green	45·00	65·00
126	**38**	3s. black on red	48·00	40·00

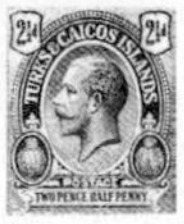

39

1913

129	**39**	½d. green	50	1·75
130a	**39**	1d. red	1·10	2·00
131	**39**	2d. grey	2·25	3·50
132	**39**	2½d. blue	2·25	3·00
133	**39**	3d. purple on yellow	2·25	11·00
134a	**39**	4d. red on yellow	1·75	7·50
135	**39**	5d. green	6·50	22·00
136	**39**	6d. purple	2·50	3·50
137	**39**	1s. orange	1·50	5·00
138	**39**	2s. red on green	21·00	45·00
139	**39**	3s. black on red	15·00	26·00

1917. Optd **WAR TAX** in one line.

143	1d. red	10	1·25
144	3d. purple on yellow	60	1·75

1918. Optd **WAR TAX** in two lines.

150	1d. red	10	2·00
148	3d. purple on yellow	20	5·50

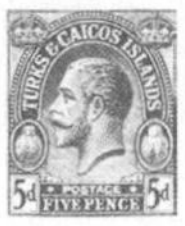

44

1922. Inscr "POSTAGE".

166	**44**	2d. grey	50	5·00
167	**44**	2½d. purple on yellow	50	1·75
168	**44**	3d. blue	50	5·00
169	**44**	4d. red on yellow	1·25	18·00
170	**44**	5d. green	85	22·00
171	**44**	6d. purple	70	13·00
172	**44**	1s. orange	80	23·00
173	**44**	2s. red on green	2·00	9·50
175	**44**	3s. black on red	5·00	38·00
163	**44**	½d. green	5·00	4·50
164	**44**	1d. brown	50	3·25
165	**44**	1½d. red	9·00	17·00

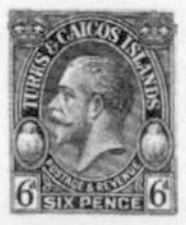

45

1928. Inscr "POSTAGE & REVENUE".

176	**45**	½d. green	75	50
177	**45**	1d. brown	75	70
178	**45**	1½d. red	75	4·50
179	**45**	2d. grey	75	50
180	**45**	2½d. purple on yellow	75	5·00
181	**45**	3d. blue	75	10·00
182	**45**	6d. purple	75	7·50
183	**45**	1s. orange	3·75	7·50
184	**45**	2s. red on green	7·00	38·00
185	**45**	5s. green on yellow	13·00	35·00
186	**45**	10s. purple on blue	60·00	£120

1935. Silver Jubilee. As T **32a** of St. Helena.

187	½d. black and green	30	1·00
188	3d. brown and blue	5·50	5·00
189	6d. blue and green	1·75	5·50
190	1s. grey and purple	1·75	4·00

1937. Coronation. As T **32b/c** of St. Helena.

191	½d. green	10	10
192	2d. grey	80	65
193	3d. blue	80	65

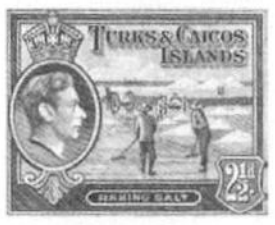

46 Raking Salt

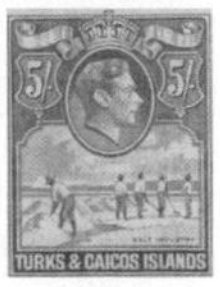

47 Salt Industry

1938

194	**46**	¼d. black	20	10
195a	**46**	½d. green	2·75	70
196	**46**	1d. brown	75	10
197	**46**	1½d. red	75	15
198	**46**	2d. grey	1·00	30
199a	**46**	2½d. orange	6·00	3·50
200	**46**	3d. blue	70	30
201	**46**	6d. mauve	22·00	3·50
201a	**46**	6d. sepia	50	20
202	**46**	1s. bistre	5·00	13·00
202a	**46**	1s. olive	50	20
203a	**47**	2s. red	22·00	22·00
204a	**47**	5s. green	55·00	29·00
205	**47**	10s. violet	30·00	7·50

1946. Victory. As T **33a** of St. Helena.

206	2d. grey	10	15
207	3d. blue	15	20

1948. Silver Wedding. As T **33b/c** of St. Helena.

208	1d. brown	15	10
209	10s. violet	14·00	20·00

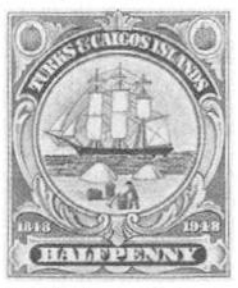

50 Badge of the Islands

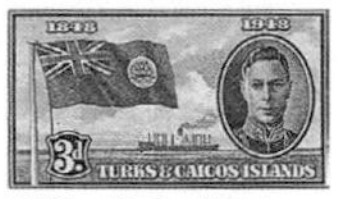

51 Blue Ensign bearing Dependency Badge

1948. Centenary of Dependency's Separation from the Bahamas.

210	**50**	½d. green	2·00	15
211	**50**	2d. red	2·00	15
212	**51**	3d. blue	1·75	15
213	-	6d. violet	1·75	30
214	-	2s. black and blue	1·25	2·25
215	-	5s. black and green	1·50	7·50
216	-	10s. black and brown	4·25	7·50

DESIGNS—HORIZ: 6d. Map of Turks and Caicos Is; 2, 5, 10s. Queen Victoria and King George VI.

1949. 75th Anniv of U.P.U. As T **33d/g** of St. Helena.

217	2½d. orange	20	2·25
218	3d. blue	2·25	1·00
219	6d. brown	30	1·00
220	1s. olive	20	35

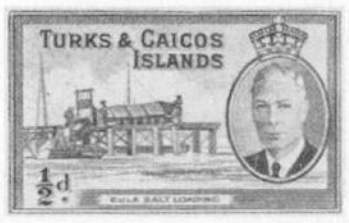

54 Bulk Salt Loading

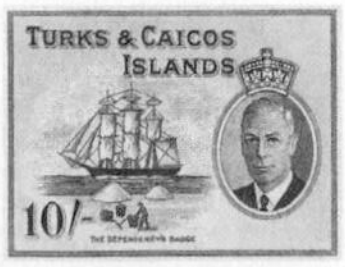

66 Dependency's Badge

1950

221	**54**	½d. green	85	40
222	-	1d. brown	80	75
223	-	1½d. red	1·25	55
224	-	2d. orange	1·00	40
225	-	2½d. olive	1·25	50
226	-	3d. blue	60	40
227	-	4d. black and pink	3·75	70
228	-	6d. black and blue	3·25	50
229	-	1s. black and turquoise	3·00	40
230	-	1s.6d. black and red	16·00	3·25
231	-	2s. green and blue	7·00	4·50
232	-	5s. blue and black	27·00	8·50
233	**66**	10s. black and violet	28·00	26·00

DESIGNS—As Type **65**: 1d. Salt Cay; 1½d. Caicos mail; 2d. Grand Turk; 2½d. Diving for sponges; 3d. South Creek; 4d. Map; 6d. Grand Turk Light; 1s. Government House; 1s.6d. Cockburn Harbour; 2s. Govt Offices; 5s. Loading salt.

1953. Coronation. As T **33h** of St. Helena.

234	2d. black and orange	60	1·25

1955. As 1950 but with portrait of Queen Elizabeth II.

235	5d. black and green	1·75	70
236	8d. black and brown	2·75	70

DESIGNS—HORIZ—As Type **65**: 5d. M.V. "Kirksons"; 8d. Greater flamingos in flight.

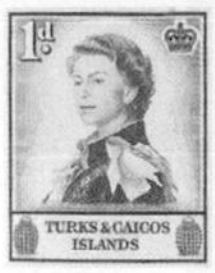

69 Queen Elizabeth II (after Annigoni)

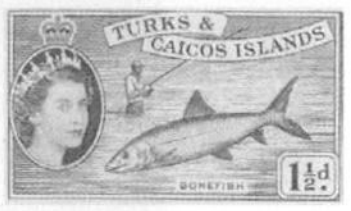

70 Bonefish

1957

237	**69**	1d. blue and red	40	20
238	**70**	1½d. grey and orange	30	30
239	-	2d. brown and olive	30	15
240	-	2½d. red and green	30	15
241	-	3d. turquoise and purple	30	15
242	-	4d. lake and black	1·25	15
243	-	5d. green and brown	1·25	40
244	-	6d. red and blue	2·00	55
245	-	8d. red and black	3·25	20
246	-	1s. blue and black	1·25	10
247	-	1s.6d. sepia and blue	19·00	1·50
248	-	2s. blue and brown	16·00	2·50
249	-	5s. black and red	8·50	2·00
250	-	10s. black and purple	25·00	8·00

DESIGNS—As Type **70**: 2d. Red grouper; 2½d. Spiny lobster; 3d. Albacore; 4d. Mutton snapper; 5d. Permit; 6d. Queen or pink conch; 8d. Greater flamingoes; 1s. Spanish mackeral; 1s.6d. Salt Cay; 2s. "Uakon" (Caicos sloop); 5s. Cable Office. As Type **84**: 10s. Dependency's badge.

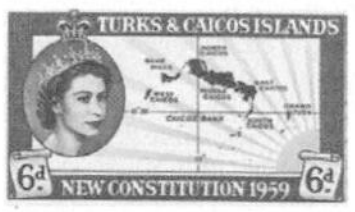

83 Map of the Turks and Caicos Is.

1959. New Constitution.

251	**83**	6d. olive and orange	80	70
252	**83**	8d. violet and orange	80	40

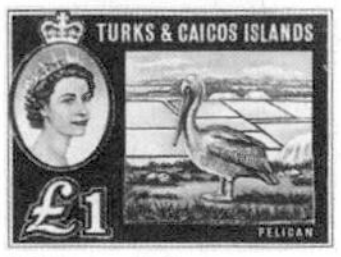

84 Brown Pelican

1960

253	**84**	£1 brown and red	45·00	16·00

1963. Freedom from Hunger. As T **63a** of St. Helena.

254	8d. red	30	15

1963. Cent of Red Cross. As T **63b** of St. Helena.

255	2d. red and black	15	50
256	8d. red and blue	30	50

1964. 400th Birth Anniv of Shakespeare. As T **45a** of St. Lucia.

257	8d. green	30	10

1965. Cent of I.T.U. As T **64a** of St. Helena.

258	1d. red and brown	10	10
259	2s. green and blue	20	20

1965. I.C.Y. As T **64b** of St. Helena.

260	1d. purple and turquoise	10	15
261	8d. green and blue	20	15

1966. Churchill Commemoration. As T **64c** of St. Helena.

262	1d. blue	10	10
263	2d. green	20	10
264	8d. brown	35	10
265	1s.6d. violet	50	1·10

1966. Royal Visit. As T **48a** of St. Kitts-Nevis.

266	8d. black and blue	40	10
267	1s.6d. black and mauve	60	20

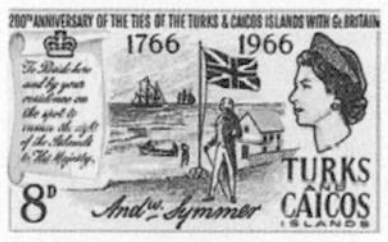

86 Andrew Symmer and Royal Warrant

1966. Bicent of "Ties with Britain".

268	-	1d. blue and orange	10	10
269	**86**	8d. red, blue and yellow	20	15
270	-	1s.6d. multicoloured	25	20

DESIGNS: 1d. Andrew Symmer going ashore; 1s.6d. Arms and Royal Cypher.

1966. 20th Anniv of UNESCO. As T **64f/h** of St. Helena.

271	1d. multicoloured	10	10
272	8d. yellow, violet and olive	40	10
273	1s.6d. black, purple and orange	65	40

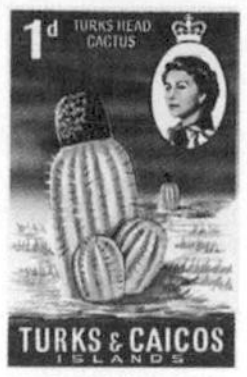

88 Turk's-head Cactus

1967

274	**88**	1d. yellow, red and violet	10	10
275	-	1½d. brown and yellow	1·50	10
276	-	2d. grey and yellow	20	10
277	-	3d. agate and green	20	10
278	-	4d. mauve, black & turq	2·75	10
279	-	6d. brown and blue	2·25	10
280	-	8d. yellow, turquoise & blue	55	10
281	-	1s. purple and turquoise	20	10
282	-	1s.6d. yellow, brown & blue	50	20
283	-	2s. multicoloured	1·25	2·00
284	-	3s. mauve and blue	2·50	40
285	-	5s. ochre, blue and light blue	2·00	2·75
286	-	10s. multicoloured	4·00	3·00
287		[illegible] silver and red	4·50	10·00

DESIGNS—HORIZ: 1½d. Boat-building; 4d. [illegible] try; 1s. Fishing; 2s. Crawfish industry; 3s. Maps of Turks and Caicos Islands and West Indies; 5s. Fishing industry; 10s. Arms of Turks and Caicos Islands. VERT: 2d. Donkey; 3d. Sisal industry; 6d. Salt industry; 8d. Skin-diving; 1s.6d. Water-skiing; £1 Queen Elizabeth II.

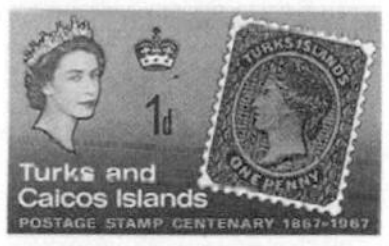

102 Turks Islands 1d. Stamp of 1867

1967. Stamp Centenary.

288	**102**	1d. black and mauve	15	10
289	-	6d. black and grey	25	15
290	-	1s. black and blue	25	15

DESIGNS: 6d. Queen Elizabeth "stamp" and Turks Islands 6d. stamp of 1867; 1s. Turks Islands 1s. of 1867.

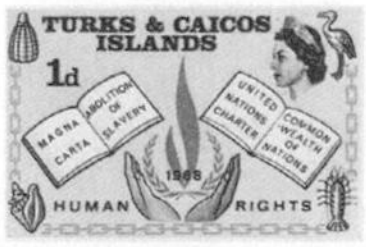

104 Human Rights Emblem and Charter

1968. Human Rights Year.

291	**104**	1d. multicoloured	10	10
292	**104**	8d. multicoloured	15	15
293	**104**	1s.6d. multicoloured	15	15

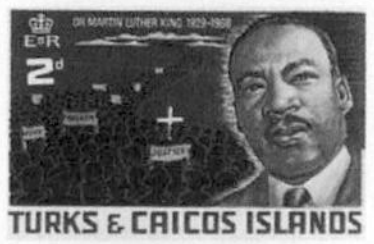

105 Dr. Martin Luther King and "Freedom March"

1968. Martin Luther King. Commem.

294	**105**	2d. brown and blue	10	10
295	**105**	8d. brown and lake	15	15
296	**105**	1s.6d. brown and violet	15	15

1969. Decimal Currency. Nos. 274/87 surch, and new value in old design (¼c.).

297	¼c. multicoloured (as No. 286)	10	10
298	1c. on 1d. yellow, red & violet	10	10
299	2c. on 2d. grey and yellow	10	10
300	3c. on 3d. agate and green	10	10
301	4c. on 4d. mauve, blk & turq	2·75	10
302	5c. on 6d. brown and blue	10	10
303	7c. on 8d. yellow, turq & bl	10	10
304	8c. on 1½d. brown and yellow	10	10
305	10c. on 1s. purple & turquoise	20	10
306	15c. on 1s.6d. yell, brn & bl	25	10
307	20c. on 2s. multicoloured	30	25
308	30c. on 3s. mauve and blue	55	35
309	50c. on 5s. ochre, blue & lt bl	1·25	45
310	$1 on 10s. multicoloured	2·50	1·25
311a	$2 on £1 blue, silver and red	2·25	6·50

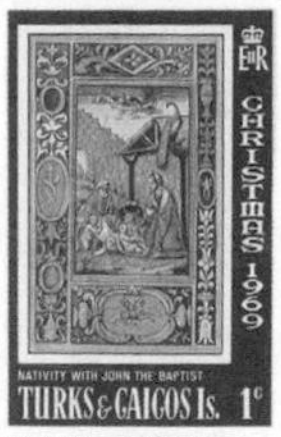

107 "The Nativity with John the Baptist"

1969. Christmas. Scenes from 16th-century "Book of Hours". Multicoloured.

312	1c. Type **107**	10	10
313	3c. "The Flight into Egypt"	10	10
314	15c. Type **107**	15	10
315	30c. As 3c.	25	20

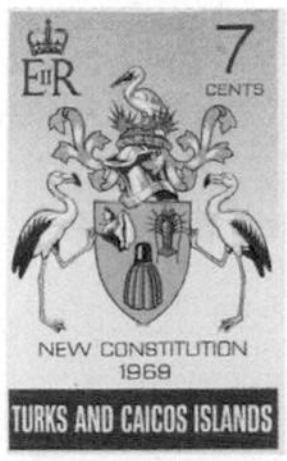

109 Coat of Arms

1970. New Constitution.

316	**109**	7c. multicoloured	20	25
317	[illegible]	[illegible] multicoloured	35	25

For similar $10 design but without comm[illegible] scription, see No. 946.

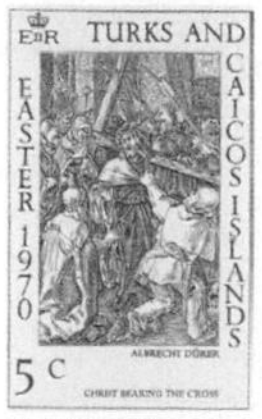

110 "Christ bearing the Cross"

1970. Easter. Details from the "Small Engraved Passion" by Durer.

318	**110**	5c. grey and blue	10	10
319	-	7c. grey and red	10	10
320	-	50c. grey and brown	60	1·00

DESIGNS: 7c. "Christ on the Cross" ; 50c. "The Lamentation of Christ".

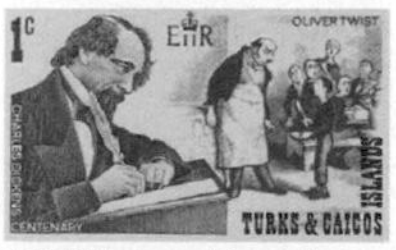

113 Dickens and Scene from "Oliver Twist"

1970. Death Cent of Charles Dickens.

321	**113**	1c. black & blue on yellow	10	50
322	-	3c. black and blue on flesh	20	40
323	-	15c. black & blue on flesh	60	20
324	-	30c. black & drab on blue	80	40

DESIGNS (showing Dickens and scene): 3c. "A Christmas Carol"; 15c. "Pickwick Papers"; 30c. "The Old Curiosity Shop".

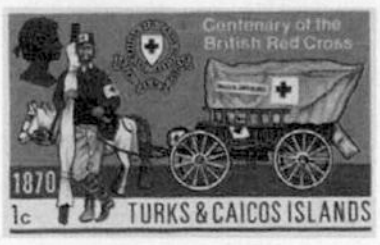

114 Ambulance, 1870

1970. Cent of British Red Cross. Multicoloured.

325	1c. Type **114**	10	20
326	5c. Ambulance, 1970	20	10
327	15c. Type **114**	40	15
328	30c. As 5c.	50	20

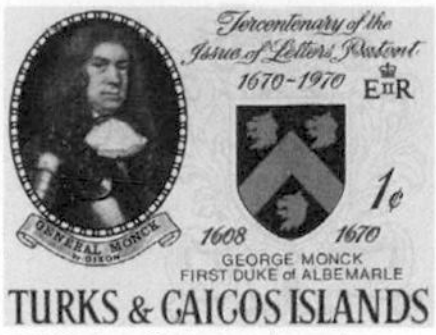

115 Duke of Albemarle and Coat-of-Arms

1970. Tercentenary of Issue of Letters Patent. Multicoloured.

329	1c. Type **115**	10	30
330	8c. Arms of Charles II and Elizabeth II	25	40
331	10c. Type **115**	25	15
332	35c. As 8c.	55	75

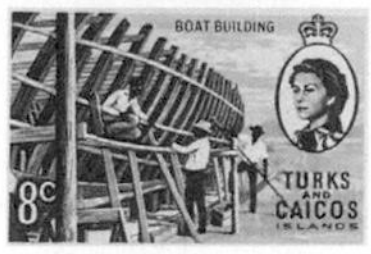

116 Boat-building

1971. Designs as Nos. 274/87 but values in decimal currency as T **116**.

333	**88**	1c. yellow, red and violet	10	10
334	-	2c. grey and yellow (as No. 276)	10	10
335	-	3c. agate and green (as No. 277)	15	10
336	-	4c. mauve, black and turquoise (as No. 278)	1·25	10
337	-	5c. brown and blue (as No. 279)	40	10
338	-	7c. yellow, turquoise and blue (as No. 280)	30	10
339	**116**	8c. brown and yellow	1·25	10
340	-	10c. purple and turquoise (as No. 281)	75	10
341	-	15c. yellow, brown and blue (as No. 282)	1·00	65
342	-	20c. mult (as No. 283)	1·50	2·50
343	-	30c. purple and blue (as [illegible] 284)	2·00	1·25
344	-	50c. ochre, blue and light blue (as No. 285)	3·00	2·00
345	-	$1 mult (as No. 286)	3·00	3·00
346	-	$2 blue, silver and red (as No. 287)	4·00	8·00

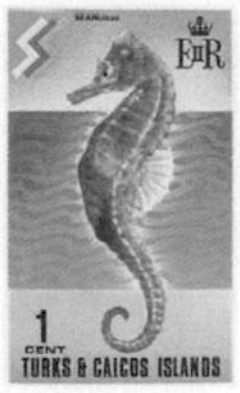

117 Lined Seahorse

1971. Tourist Development. Multicoloured.

347	1c. Type **117**	10	10
348	3c. Queen or pink conch shell	15	10
349	15c. Oystercatcher (horiz)	50	20
350	30c. Sailfish ("Blue marlin") (horiz)	35	25

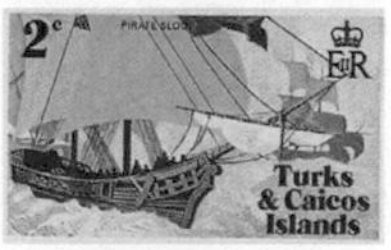

118 Pirate Sloop

1971. Pirates. Multicoloured.

351	2c. Type **118**	10	10
352	3c. Pirate treasure	10	10
353	15c. Marooned sailor	45	15
354	30c. Buccaneers	70	45

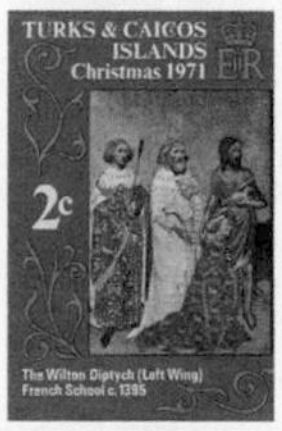

119 The Wilton Diptych (Left Wing)

1971. Christmas. Multicoloured.

355	2c. Type **119**	10	10
356	2c. The Wilton Diptych (Right Wing)	10	10
357	8c. Type **119**	10	10
358	8c. As No. 356	10	10
359	15c. Type **119**	20	10
360	15c. As No. 356	20	10

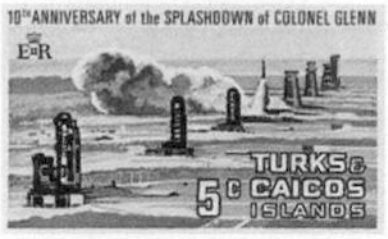

120 Cape Kennedy Launching Area

1972. Tenth Anniv of Colonel Glenn's Splashdown. Multicoloured.

361	5c. Type **120**	10	10
362	10c. "Friendship 7" space capsule	10	10
363	15c. Map of Islands and splashdown	15	10
364	20c. N.A.S.A. space medal (vert)	15	10

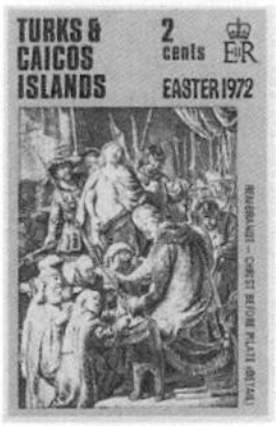

121 "Christ before Pilate" (Rembrandt)

1972. Easter.

365	**121**	2c. black and lilac	10	10
366	-	15c. black and pink	20	10
367	-	30c. black and yellow	30	15

DESIGNS—HORIZ: 15c. "The Three Crosses" (Rembrandt). VERT: 30c. "The Descent from the Cross" (Rembrandt).

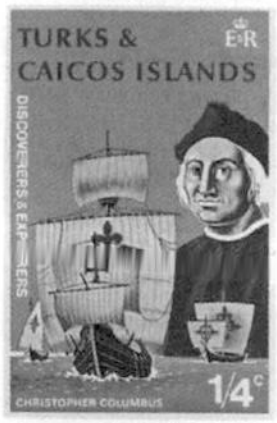

122 Christopher Columbus

1972. Discoverers and Explorers. Multicoloured.

368	¼c. Type **122**	20	75
369	8c. Sir Richard Grenville (horiz)	1·00	30
370	10c. Capt. John Smith	1·00	10
371	30c. Juan Ponce de Leon (horiz)	1·75	90

1972. Royal Silver Wedding. As T **103** of St. Helena, but with Turk's-head cactus and spiny lobster in background.

372	10c. blue	15	10
373	20c. green	15	10

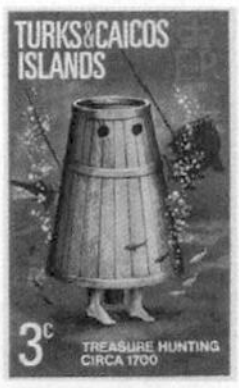

124 Treasure Hunting, c. 1700

1973. Treasure.

374	**124**	3c. multicoloured	10	10
375	-	5c. purple, silver and black	10	10
376	-	10c. purple, silver & black	20	10
377	-	30c. multicoloured	60	30
MS378		127×108 mm. Nos. 374/7	1·10	2·25

DESIGNS: 5c. Silver Bank medallion (obverse); 10c. Silver Bank medallion (reverse); 30c. Treasure hunting, 1973.

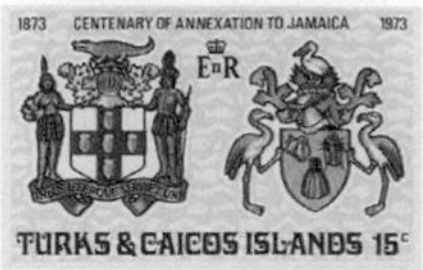

125 Arms of Jamaica and Turks and Caicos Islands

1973. Centenary of Annexation by Jamaica.

379	125	15c. multicoloured	25	10
380	125	35c. multicoloured	45	20

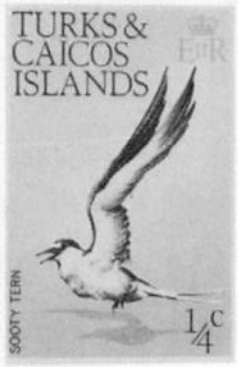

126 Sooty Tern

1973

381	¼c. Type **126**	10	40
382	1c. Magnificent frigate bird	30	60
383	2c. Common noddy	30	60
384	3c. Blue-grey gnatcatcher	85	50
385	4c. Little blue heron	35	1·50
386	5c. Catbird	30	30
387	7c. Black-whiskered vireo	4·50	30
388	8c. Osprey	5·00	3·25
389	10c. Greater flamingo	70	1·25
390	15c. Brown pelican	1·25	50
392	30c. Northern mockingbird	1·75	90
459	20c. Parula warbler	1·50	75
461	50c. Ruby-throated hummingbird	1·50	2·25
462	$1 Bananaquit	2·50	2·75
463	$2 Cedar waxwing	6·00	4·50
464	$5 Painted bunting	1·75	2·25

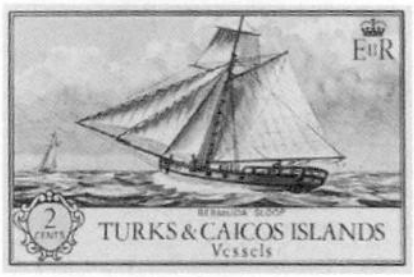

127 Bermuda Sloop

1973. Vessels. Multicoloured.

396	2c. Type **127**	15	1·00
397	5c. H.M.S. "Blanche" (screw sloop)	20	10
398	8c. "Grand Turk" (American privateer) and "Hinchinbrook II" (British packet), 1813	25	1·00
399	10c. H.M.S. "Endymion" (frigate), 1790	25	15
400	15c. "Medina" (paddle-steamer)	25	80
401	20c. H.M.S. "Daring" (brig), 1804	30	1·25
MS402	198×101 mm. Nos. 296/401	1·10	3·75

1973. Royal Wedding. As T **103a** of St. Helena.

403	12c. blue	10	10
404	18c. blue	10	10

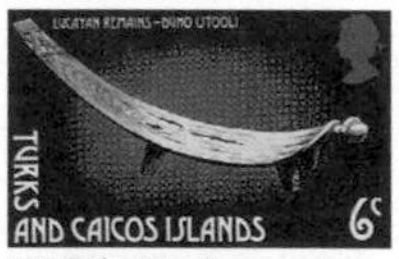

128 Duho (stool)

1974. Lucayan Remains. Multicoloured.

405	6c. Type **128**	10	10
406	10c. Broken wood bowl	15	10
407	12c. Greenstone axe	15	10
408	18c. Wood bowl	15	10
409	35c. Fragment of duho	20	20
MS410	240×90 mm. Nos. 405/9	1·10	1·75

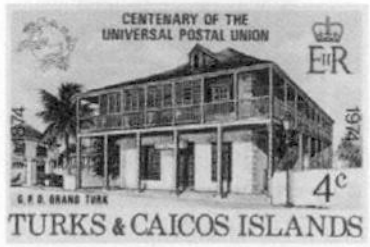

129 G.P.O., Grand Turk

1974. Centenary of U.P.U. Multicoloured.

426	4c. Type **129**	10	10
427	12c. Sloop and island map	20	10
428	18c. "U.P.U." and globe	20	10
429	55c. Posthorn and emblem	35	35

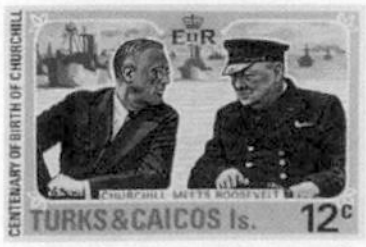

130 Churchill and Roosevelt

1974. Birth Cent of Sir Winston Churchill. Multicoloured.

430	12c. Type **130**	15	15
431	18c. Churchill and vapour-trails	15	15
MS432	85×85 mm. Nos. 430/1	40	45

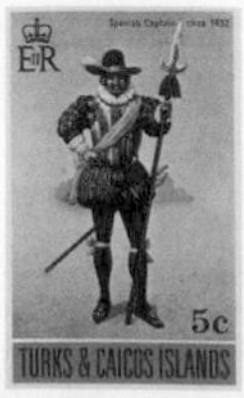

131 Spanish Captain circa 1492

1975. Military Uniforms. Multicoloured.

433	5c. Type **131**	10	10
434	20c. Officer, Royal Artillery, 1783	20	15
435	25c. Officer, 67th Foot, 1798	25	15
436	35c. Private, 1st West India Regiment, 1833	35	25
MS437	145×88 mm. Nos. 433/6	1·00	2·00

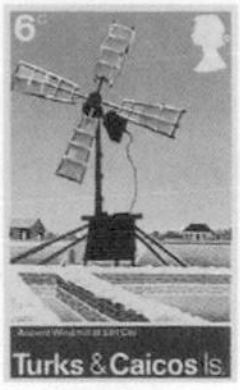

132 Ancient Windmill Salt Cay

1975. Salt-raking Industry. Multicoloured.

438	6c. Type **132**	15	10
439	10c. Salt pans drying in sun (horiz)	15	10
440	20c. Salt-raking (horiz)	25	25
441	25c. Unprocessed salt heaps	30	30

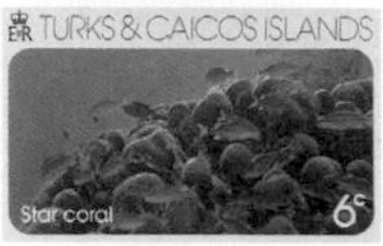

133 Star Coral

1975. Island Coral. Multicoloured.

442	6c. Type **133**	15	10
443	10c. Elkhorn coral	20	10
444	20c. Brain coral	35	15
445	25c. Staghorn coral	40	20

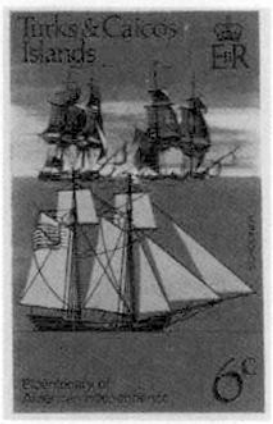

134 American Schooner

1976. Bicent of American Revolution. Multicoloured.

446	6c. Type **134**	25	15
447	20c. British ship of the line	30	20
448	25c. American privateer "Grand Turk"	30	25
449	55c. British ketch	40	65
MS450	95×151 mm. Nos. 446/9	1·00	4·00

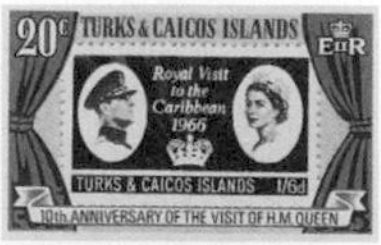

135 1s.6d. Royal Visit Stamp of 1966

1976. Tenth Anniv of Royal Visit. Multicoloured

466	20c. Type **135**	30	30
467	25c. 8d. Royal Visit stamp	40	30

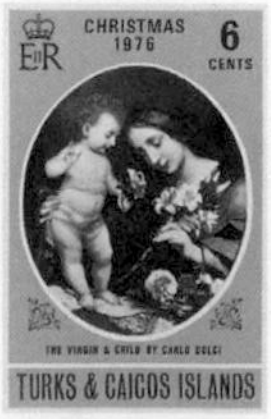

136 "The Virgin and Child with Flowers" (C. Dolci)

1976. Christmas. Multicoloured.

468	6c. Type **136**	10	10
469	10c. "Virgin and Child" with St. John and an Angel" (Studio of Botticelli)	10	10
470	20c. "Adoration of the Magi" (Master of Paraiso)	30	15
471	25c. "Adoration of the Magi" (French miniature)	30	20

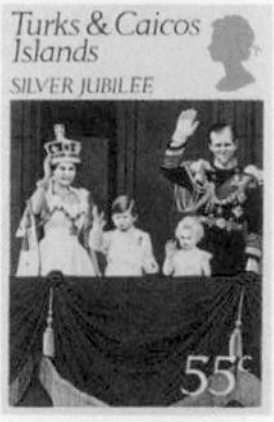

137 Balcony Scene, Buckingham Palace

1977. Silver Jubilee. Multicoloured.

472	6c. Queen presenting O.B.E. to E. T. Wood	10	10
473	25c. Queen with regalia	15	20
474	55c. Type **137**	30	45
MS475	120×97 mm. $5 Queen Elizabeth II	1·00	80

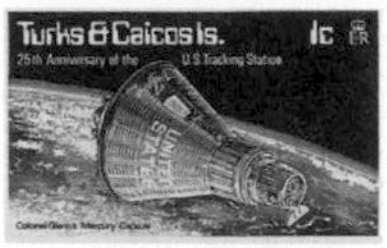

138 Col. Glenn's "Mercury" Capsule

1977. 25th Anniv of U.S. Tracking Station. Multicoloured.

476	1c. Type **138**	10	10
477	3c. Moon buggy "Rover" (vert)	10	10
478	6c. Tracking Station, Grand Turk	10	10
479	20c. Moon landing craft (vert)	15	15
480	25c. Col. Glenn's rocket launch (vert)	20	20
481	50c. "Telstar 1" satellite	30	40

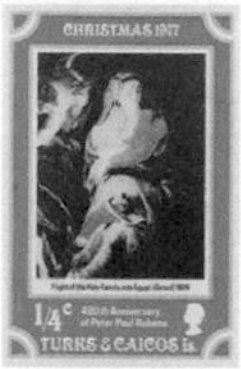

139 "Flight of the Holy Family" (Rubens)

1977. Christmas. 400th Birth Anniv of Rubens. Multicoloured.

482	¼c. Type **139**	10	10
483	½c. "Adoration of the Magi" (1634)	10	10
484	1c. "Adoration of the Magi" (1624)	10	10
485	6c. "Virgin within Garland"	10	10
486	20c. "Madonna and Child Adored by Angels"	15	10
487	$2 "Adoration of the Magi" (1618)	1·25	1·25
MS488	100×81 mm. $1 detail of 20c.	1·00	1·40

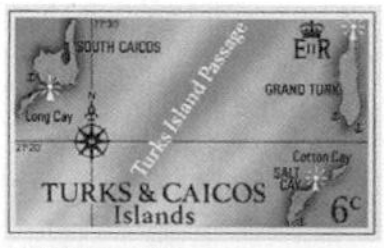

140 Map of Passage

1978. Turks Islands Passage. Multicoloured.

489A	6c. Type **140**	15	20
490A	20c. Caicos sloop passing Grand Turk Lighthouse	45	75
491A	25c. Motor cruiser	45	85
492A	55c. "Jamaica Planter" (freighter)	95	2·25
MS493A	136×88 mm. Nos. 489A/92A	1·10	2·75

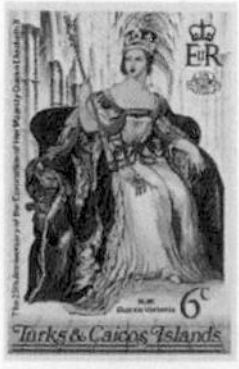

141 "Queen Victoria" (Sir George Hayter)

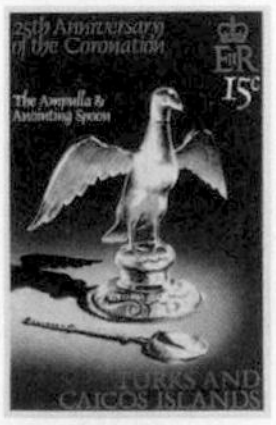

142 Ampulla and Anointing Spoon

1978. 25th Anniv of Coronation. Multicoloured. (a) Monarchs in Coronation robes.

494	6c. Type **141**	10	10
495	10c. "King Edward VII" (Sir Samuel Fildes)	10	10
496	25c. King George V	20	10
497	$2 King George VI	50	70
MS498	161×113 mm. $2.50 Queen Elizabeth II	75	75

(b) Coronation regalia. Self-adhesive.

499	15c. Type **142**	15	30
500	25c. St. Edward's Crown	15	30
501	$2 Queen Elizabeth II in Coronation robes	1·00	2·50

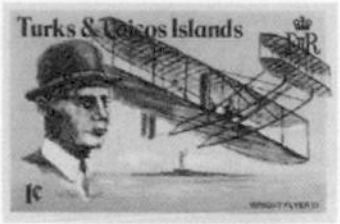

143 Wilbur Wright and Wright Type A

1978. 75th Anniv of Powered Flight. Multicoloured.

502	1c. Type **143**	10	10
503	6c. Wright brothers and Cessna 337 Super Skymaster	10	10
504	10c. Orville Wright and Lockheed L.188 Electra	10	10
505	15c. Wilbur Wright and Douglas C-47 Skytrain	15	15
506	35c. Wilbur Wright and Britten Norman Islander	35	35
507	$2 Wilbur Wright and Wright Type A	1·00	2·00
MS508	111×84 mm. $1 Orville Wright and Wright glider No. III	60	1·60

No. 502 is inscr "FLYER III" in error.

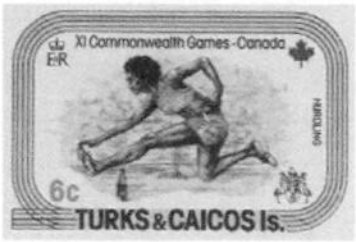

144 Hurdling

1978. 11th Commonwealth Games, Edmonton. Multicoloured.

509	6c. Type **144**	10	10
510	20c. Weightlifting	15	15
511	55c. Boxing	20	30
512	$2 Cycling	50	1·25
MS513	105×79 mm. $1 Sprinting	55	1·50

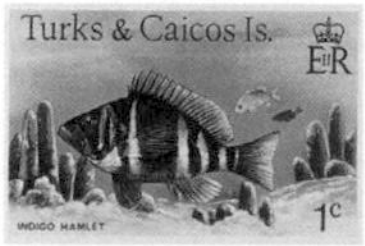

145 Indigo Hamlet

1978. Fish. Multicoloured.

514A	1c. Type **145**	15	50
515A	2c. Tobacco fish	75	50
516A	3c. Bar jack	50	30
517A	4c. Porkfish	75	50
518A	5c. Spanish grunt	50	40
519A	7c. Yellow-tailed snapper	1·00	1·25
520A	8c. Four-eyed butterflyfish	1·00	15
521A	10c. Yellow-finned grouper	50	15
522A	15c. Beau Gregory	1·50	30
523A	20c. Queen angelfish	50	30
524A	30c. Hogfish	1·75	40
525A	50c. Royal gramma ("Fairy basslet")	1·00	65
526A	$1 Fin-spot wrasse	1·50	1·60
527A	$2 Stoplight parrotfish	1·50	2·50
528A	$5 Queen triggerfish	1·50	6·50

Some values exist both with or without imprint date at foot.

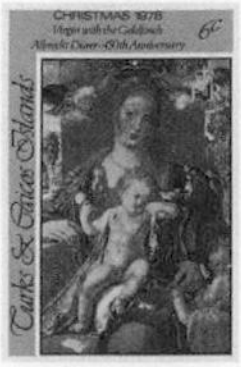

146 "Madonna of the Siskin"

1978. Christmas. Paintings by Durer. Multicoloured.

529	6c. Type **146**	15	10
530	20c. "The Virgin and Child with St. Anne"	20	15
531	35c. "Paumgartner Nativity" (horiz)	35	15
532	$2 "Praying Hands"	85	1·40
MS533	137×124 mm. $1 "Adoration of The Magi" (horiz)	2·25	3·25

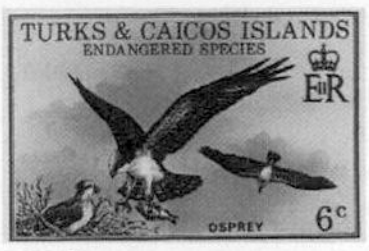

147 Osprey

1979. Endangered Wildlife. Multicoloured.

534	6c. Type **147**	75	20
535	20c. Green turtle	65	20
536	25c. Queen or pink conch	75	25
537	55c. Rough-toothed dolphin	90	50
538	$1 Humpback whale	2·00	2·50
MS539	117×85 mm. $2 Iguana	2·50	4·25

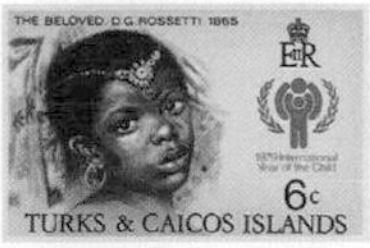

148 "The Beloved" (painting by D. G. Rossetti)

1979. International Year of the Child. Multicoloured.

540	6c. Type **148**	10	10
541	25c. "Tahitian Girl" (P. Gauguin)	15	10
542	55c. "Calmady Children" (Sir Thomas Lawrence)	25	20
543	$1 "Mother and Daughter" (detail, P. Gauguin)	45	45
MS544	112×85 mm. $2 "Marchesa Elena Grimalda" (A. van Dyck)	55	1·50

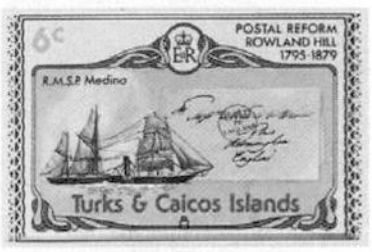

149 "Medina" (paddle-steamer) and Handstamped Cover

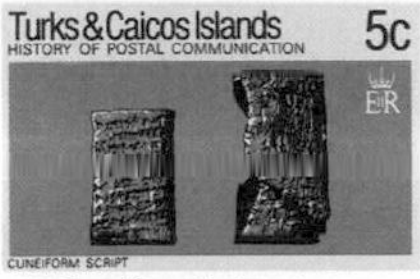

150 Cuneiform Script

1979. Death Centenary of Sir Rowland Hill. (a) As T **149**. Multicoloured.

545	6c. Type **149**	10	10
546	20c. Sir Rowland Hill and map of Caribbean	15	15
547	45c. "Orinoco I" (mail paddle-steamer) and cover bearing Penny Black stamp	20	20
548	75c. "Shannon" (screw steamer) and letter to Grand Turk	30	30
549	$1 "Trent I" (paddle-steamer) and map of Caribbean	35	35
550	$2 Turks Islands 1867 and Turks and Caicos Islands 1900 1d. stamps	3·50	4·00
MS551	170×113 mm. As No. 550	70	1·50

(b) As T **150**. Self-adhesive.

552	**150**	5c. black and green	10	10
553	-	5c. black and green	10	10
554	-	5c. black and green	10	10
555	-	15c. black and blue	20	20
556	-	15c. black and blue	20	20
557	-	15c. black and blue	20	20
558	-	25c. black and blue	30	30
559	-	25c. black and blue	60	45
560	-	25c. black and blue	30	30
561	-	40c. black and red	45	45
562	-	40c. black and red	45	45
563	-	40c. black and red	45	45
564	-	$1 black and yellow	70	1·25

DESIGNS—HORIZ: No. 533, Egyptian papyrus; No. 554, Chinese paper; No. 555, Greek runner; No. 556, Roman post horse; No. 557, Roman post ship; No. 558, Pigeon post; No. 559, Railway post; No. 560, Packet paddle-steamer; No. 561, Balloon post; No. 562, First airmail; No. 563, Supersonic airmail. VERT: No. 564, Original stamp press.

1979. "Brasiliana 79" International Stamp Exhibition, Rio de Janeiro. No. **MS**551 optd **BRASILIAN 79**.

MS565	170×113 mm. $2 Turks Islands 1867 and Turks and Caicos Islands 1900 1d. stamps	65	1·50

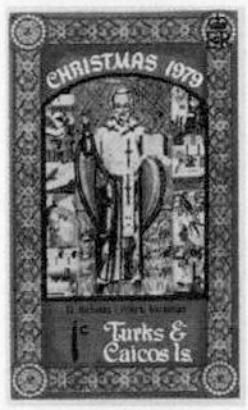

152 "St. Nicholas", Prikra, Ukraine

1979. Christmas. Religious Art. Multicoloured.

566	1c. Type **152**	10	10
567	3c. "Emperor Otto II with Symbols of Empire" (Master of the Registrum Gregorii)	10	10
568	6c. "Portrait of St. John" (Book of Lindisfarne)	10	10
569	15c. "Adoration of the Majestas Domini" (prayer book of Otto II)	10	10
570	20c. "Christ attended by Angels" (Book of Kells)	15	15
571	25c. "St. John the Evangelist" (Gospels of St. Medard of Soissons), Charlemagne	20	15
572	65c. "Christ Pantocrator", Trocany, Ukraine	30	35
573	$1 "Portrait of St. John" (Canterbury Codex Aureus)	45	60
MS574	106×133 mm. $2 "Portrait of St. Matthew" (Book of Lindisfarne)	70	1·50

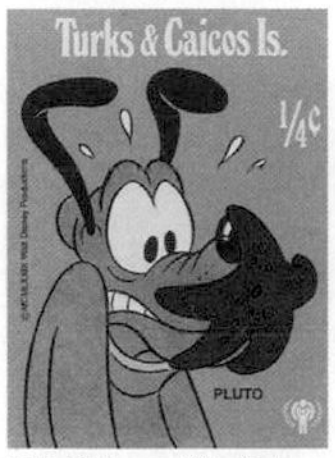

153 Pluto and Starfish

1979. International Year of the Child. Walt Disney cartoon characters. At the Seaside. Multicoloured.

575	¼c. Type **153**	10	10
576	½c. Minnie Mouse in summer outfit	10	10
577	1c. Mickey Mouse underwater	10	10
578	2c. Goofy and turtle	10	10
579	3c. Donald Duck and dolphin	10	10
580	4c. Mickey Mouse fishing	10	10
581	5c. Goofy surfing	10	10
582	25c. Pluto and crab	45	20
583	$1 Daisy water-skiing	75	2·25
MS584	126×96 mm. $1.50 Goofy after water-skiing accident	1·00	1·60

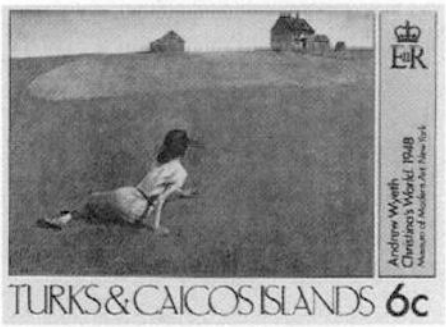

154 "Christina's World" (painting by Andrew Wyeth)

1979. Works of Art. Multicoloured.

585	6c. Type **154**	10	10
586	10c. Ivory leopards, Benin (19th-cent)	10	10
587	20c. "The Kiss" (painting by Gustav Klimt) (vert)	15	15
588	25c. "Portrait of a Lady" (painting by R. van der Weyden) (vert)	15	15
589	80c. Bull's head harp, Sumer, c. 2600 B.C. (vert)	20	30
590	$1 "The Wave" (painting by Hokusai)	25	50
MS591	110×140 mm. $2 "Holy Family" (painting by Rembrant) (vert)	70	1·25

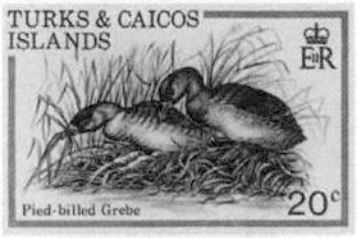

155 Pied-billed Grebe

1980. Birds. Multicoloured.

592	20c. Type **155**	70	55
593	25c. Ovenbirds at nest	75	55
594	35c. Hen harrier	1·00	60
595	55c. Yellow-bellied sapsucker	1·25	65
596	$1 Blue-winged teal	1·50	3·00
MS597	107×81 mm. $2 Glossy ibis	2·75	2·25

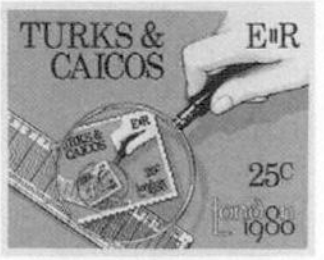

156 Stamp, Magnifying Glass and Perforation Gauge

1980. "London 1980" Int Stamp Exhibition. Multicoloured.

598	**156**	25c. black and yellow	15	15
599	-	40c. black and green	15	25
MS600		76×97 mm. $2 red, black and blue	70	1·10

DESIGN: 40c. Tweezers, stamp and perforation gauge; $2 Earls Court Exhibition Centre.

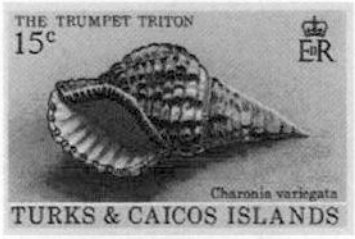

157 Atlantic Trumpet Triton

1980. Shells. Multicoloured.

601	14c. Type **157**	15	20
602	20c. Measled cowrie	15	25
603	30c. True tulip	20	35
604	45c. Lion's-paw scallop	25	45
605	55c. Sunrise tellin	30	55
606	70c. Crown cone	35	70

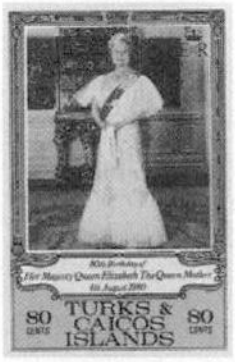

158 Queen Elizabeth the Queen Mother

1980. 80th Birthday of The Queen Mother.

607	**158**	80c. multicoloured	50	1·40
MS608		57×80 mm. **158** $1.50 multicoloured	80	2·00

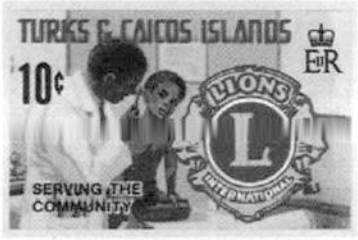

159 Doctor examining Child and Lions International Emblem

1980. "Serving the Community". Multicoloured.

609	10c. Type **159**	15	10
610	15c. Students receiving scholarships and Kiwanis International emblem	20	10
611	45c. Teacher with students and Soroptimist emblem	40	35
612	$1 Lobster trawler and Rotary International emblem	75	80
MS613	101×74 mm. $2 School receiving funds and Rotary International emblem	1·00	2·00

No. **MS**613 also commemorates the 75th anniv of Rotary International.

1980. Christmas. Scenes from Walt Disney's "Pinocchio". As T **153**. Multicoloured.

614	¼c. Scene from "Pinocchio"	10	10
615	½c. As puppet	10	10
616	1c. Pinocchio changed into a boy	10	10
617	2c. Captured by fox	10	10
618	3c. Pinocchio and puppeteer	10	10
619	4c. Pinocchio and bird's nest nose	10	10
620	5c. Pinocchio eating	10	10
621	75c. Pinocchio with ass ears	1·00	90
622	$1 Pinocchio underwater	1·25	1·00
MS623	127×102 mm. $2 Pinocchio dancing (vert)	2·50	2·50

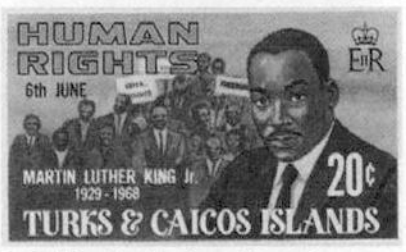

160 Martin Luther King Jr

1980. Human Rights. Personalities. Multicoloured.

624	20c. Type **160**	15	10
625	30c. John F. Kennedy	30	25
626	45c. Roberto Clemente (baseball player)	45	35
627	70c. Sir Frank Worrel (cricketer)	2·00	1·50
628	$1 Harriet Tubman	1·10	1·25
MS629	103×80 mm. $2 Marcus Garvey	1·10	1·25

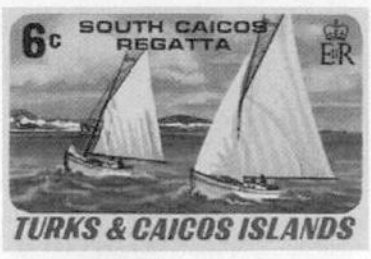

161 Yachts

1980. South Caicos Regatta. Multicoloured.

630	6c. Type **161**	10	10
631	15c. Trophy and yachts	15	15
632	35c. Spectators watching speedboat race	25	20
633	$1 Caicos sloops	60	65
MS634	113×85 mm. $2 Queen Elizabeth II and map of South Caicos (vert)	80	1·75

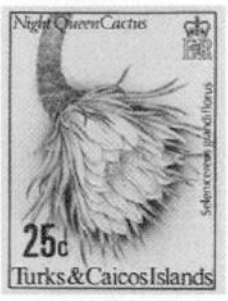

162 Night Queen Cactus

1981. Flowering Cacti. Multicoloured.

635	25c. Type **162**	20	25
636	35c. Ripsaw cactus	25	35
637	55c. Royal strawberry cactus	30	60
638	80c. Caicos cactus	40	1·00
MS639	72×68 mm. $2 Turks head cactus	1·00	2·00

1981. 50th Anniv of Walt Disney's Pluto (cartoon character). As T **153**. Multicoloured.

640	10c. Pluto listening to queen or pink conch shell	10	10
641	75c. Pluto on raft and porpoise	50	90
MS642	127×101 mm. $1.50 Pluto in scene from film "Simple Things"	1·00	2·25

1981. Easter. Walt Disney Cartoon Characters. As T **153**. Multicoloured.

643	10c. Donald Duck and Louie	20	20
644	25c. Goofy and Donald Duck	25	40
645	60c. Chip and Dale	30	1·00
646	80c. Scrooge McDuck and Huey	35	1·40
MS647	126×101 mm. $4 Chip (or Dale)	4·00	3·50

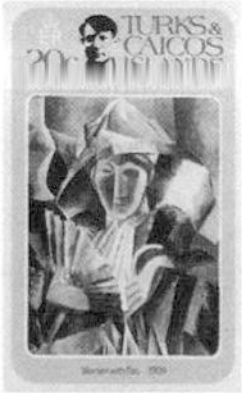

163 "Woman with Fan"

1981. Birth Centenary of Picasso. Multicoloured.

648	20c. Type **163**	15	15
649	45c. "Woman with Pears"	20	15
650	80c. "The Accordionist"	30	40
651	$1 "The Aficionado"	45	60
MS652	102×127 mm. $2 "Girl with a Mandolin"	1·00	1·00

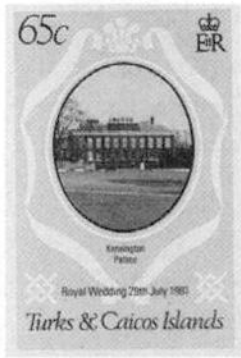

164 Kensington Palace

1981. Royal Wedding. Multicoloured.

653	35c. Prince Charles and Lady Diana Spencer	15	10
654	65c. Type **164**	20	20
655	90c. Prince Charles as Colonel of the Welsh Guards	25	30
MS656	90×82 mm. $2 Glass Coach	50	55

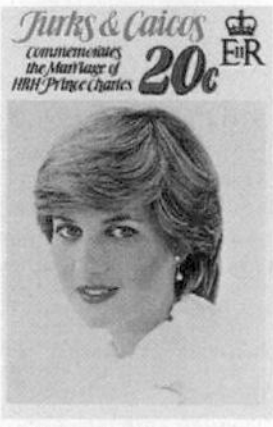

165 Lady Diana Spencer

1981. Royal Wedding. Multicoloured. Self-adhesive.

657	20c. Type **165**	25	30
658	$1 Prince Charles	35	70
659	$2 Prince Charles and Lady Diana Spencer	1·10	2·25

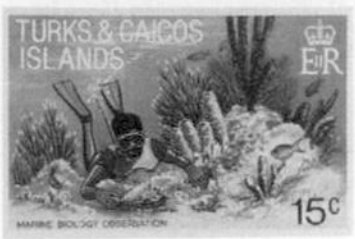

166 Marine Biology Observation

1981. Diving. Multicoloured.

660	15c. Type **166**	20	15
661	40c. Underwater photography	35	35
662	75c. Wreck diving	60	70
663	$1 Diving with dolphins	80	1·00
MS664	91×75 mm. $2 Diving flag	1·75	2·25

1981. Christmas. As T **153** showing scenes from Walt Disney's cartoon film "Uncle Remus".

665	¼c. multicoloured	10	10
666	½c. multicoloured	10	10
667	1c. multicoloured	10	10
668	2c. multicoloured	10	10
669	3c. multicoloured	10	10
670	4c. multicoloured	10	10
671	5c. multicoloured	10	10
672	75c. multicoloured	1·00	80
673	$1 multicoloured	1·25	1·00
MS674	128×103 mm. multicoloured	1·75	2·25

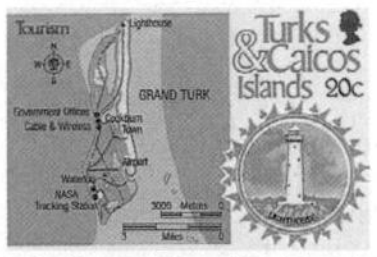

167 Map of Grand Turk, and Lighthouse

1981. Tourism. Multicoloured.

675	20c. Type **167**	60	50
676	20c. Map of Salt Cay, and "industrial archaeology"	60	50
677	20c. Map of South Caicos, and "island flying"	60	50
678	20c. Map of East Caicos, and "beach combing"	60	50
679	20c. Map of Central Grand Caicos, and cave exploring	60	50
680	20c. Map of North Caicos and camping and hiking	60	50
681	20c. Map of North Caicos, Parrot Cay, Dellis Cay, Fort George Cay, Pine Cay and Water Cay, and "environmental studies"	60	50
682	20c. Map of Providenciales, and scuba diving	60	50
683	20c. Map of West Caicos, and "cruising and bird sanctuary"	60	50
684	20c. Turks and Caicos Islands flag	60	50

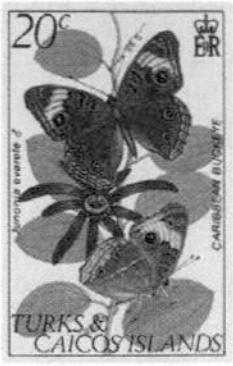

168 "Junonia evarete"

1982. Butterflies. Multicoloured.

685	20c. Type **168**	30	30
686	35c. "Strymon maesites"	45	55
687	65c. "Agraulis vanillae"	70	1·25
688	$1 "Eurema dina"	1·00	2·00
MS689	72×56 mm. $2 "Anaea intermedia"	2·50	3·75

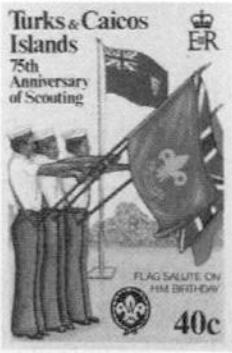

169 Flag Salute on Queen's Birthday

1982. 75th Anniv of Boy Scout Movement. Multicoloured.

690	40c. Type **169**	50	50
691	50c. Raft building	60	60
692	75c. Sea scout cricket match	1·10	1·60
693	$1 Nature study	1·50	1·75
MS694	100×70 mm. $2 Lord Baden-Powell and scout salute	1·50	3·00

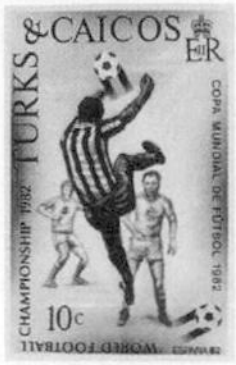

170 Footballer

1982. World Cup Football Championship, Spain.

695	**170**	10c. multicoloured	15	15
696	-	25c. multicoloured	20	20
697	-	45c. multicoloured	25	25
698	-	$1 multicoloured	80	80
MS699		117×83 mm. $2 multicoloured	1·25	2·00

DESIGNS: 25c. to $2, Various footballers.

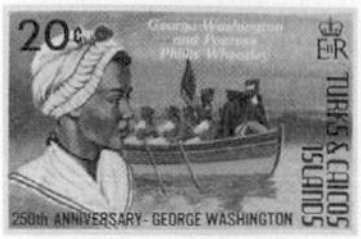

171 Washington crossing the Delaware and Phillis Wheatley (poetess)

1982. 250th Birth Anniv of George Washington and Birth Centenary of Franklin D. Roosevelt.

700	20c. Type **171**	20	30
701	35c. George Washington and Benjamin Banneker (surveyor)	30	45
702	65c. Franklin D. Roosevelt meeting George Washington Carver (agricultural researcher)	35	80
703	80c. Roosevelt as stamp collector	45	1·00
MS704	100×70 mm. $2 Roosevelt with stamp showing profile of Washington	1·00	2·50

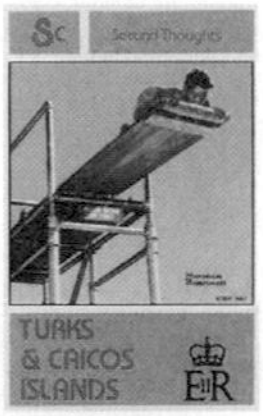

172 "Second Thoughts"

1982. Norman Rockwell (painter) Commemoration. Multicoloured.

705	8c. Type **172**	15	10
706	15c. "The Proper Gratuity"	20	20
707	20c. "Doctor's Office" (inscr "Before the Shot")	25	30
708	25c. "Bottom of the Sixth" (inscr "The Three Umpires")	25	30

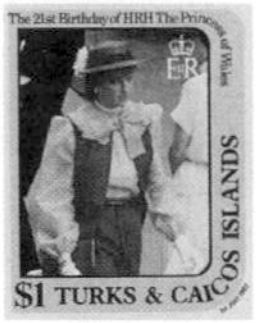

173 Princess of Wales

1982. 21st Birthday of Princess of Wales. Multicoloured.

709	55c. As 8c.	35	45
710	70c. As 35c.	60	55
711	$1 Type **173**	90	80
MS712	102×76 mm. $2 Princess Diana (different)	1·50	1·75
713	8c. Sandringham	15	35
714	35c. Prince and Princess of Wales	55	1·00
715	$1.10 Type **173**	80	2·00

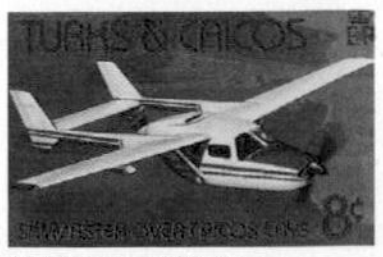

174 Cessna 337 Super Skymaster over Caicos Cays

1982. Aircraft. Multicoloured.

716	8c. Type **174**	15	15
717	15c. Lockheed JetStar II over Grand Turk	20	25
718	65c. Sikorsky S.58 helicopter over South Caicos	65	80
719	$1.10 Cessna 182 Skylan over Providenciales	1·10	1·25
MS720	99×69 mm. $2 Boeing 727-200 over Turks and Caicos Islands	2·00	2·50

1982. Christmas. Scenes from Walt Disney's Cartoon film "Mickey's Christmas Carol". As T **153**. Multicoloured.

721	1c. Donald Duck, Mickey Mouse and Scrooge	10	10
722	1c. Goofy (Marley's ghost) and Scrooge	10	10
723	2c. Jiminy Cricket and Scrooge	10	10
724	2c. Huey, Dewey and Louie	10	10
725	3c. Daisy Duck and youthful Scrooge	10	10
726	3c. Giant and Scrooge	10	10
727	4c. Two bad wolves, a wise pig and a reformed Scrooge	10	10
728	65c. Donald Duck and Scrooge	1·00	75
729	$1.10 Mortie and Scrooge	1·60	1·25
MS730	126×101 mm. $2 Mickey and Minnie Mouse with Mortie	2·75	2·50

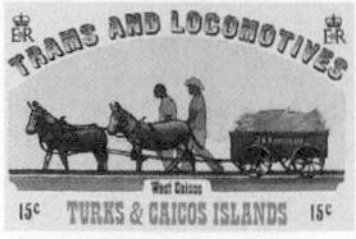

175 West Caicos Mule-drawn Wagon

1983. Trams and Locomotives. Multicoloured.

731	15c. Type **175**	20	25
732	55c. West Caicos steam locomotive	65	70
733	90c. East Caicos mule-drawn sisal train	90	1·00
734	$1.60 East Caicos steam locomotive	1·75	1·90
MS735	99×69 mm. $2.50 Steam sisal train	2·25	2·25

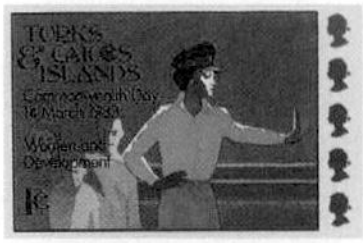

176 Policewoman on Traffic Duty

1983. Commonwealth Day. Multicoloured.

736	1c. Type **176**	85	50
737	8c. Stylized sun and weather vane	30	20
738	65c. Yacht	85	1·00
739	$1 Cricket	2·00	2·00

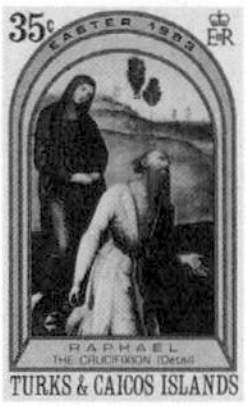

177 "St. John and the Virgin Mary" (detail)

1983. Easter. Designs showing details from the "Mond Crucifixion" by Raphael. Multicoloured.

740	35c. Type **177**	20	25
741	50c. "Two Women"	30	35
742	95c. "Angel with two jars"	40	60
743	$1.10 "Angel with one jar"	60	80
MS744	100×130 mm. $2.50 "Christ on the Cross"	2·00	2·00

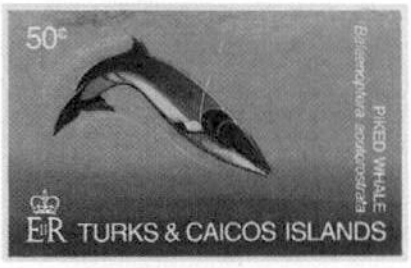

178 Minke Whale

1983. Whales. Multicoloured.

745	50c. Type **178**	2·00	2·00
746	65c. Black right whale	2·25	2·25
747	70c. Killer whale	2·50	2·50
748	95c. Sperm whale	2·75	2·75
749	$1.10 Cuvier's beaked whale	3·00	3·00
750	$2 Blue whale	5·00	5·00
751	$2.20 Humpback whale	5·50	5·50
752	$3 Long-finned pilot whale	6·25	6·25
MS753	112×82 mm. $3 Fin whale	7·00	5·00

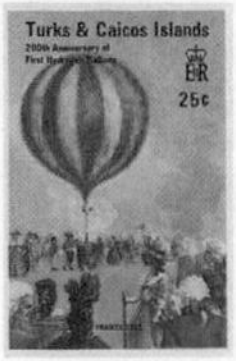

179 First Hydrogen Balloon "The Globe", 1783

1983. Bicentenary of Manned Flight. Multicoloured.

754	25c. Type **179**	20	25
755	35c. "Friendship 7"	25	35
756	70c. First hot air balloon "Le Martial", 1783	40	70
757	95c. Space shuttle "Columbia"	55	90
MS758	112×76 mm. $2 Montgolfier balloon and space shuttle	1·25	2·00

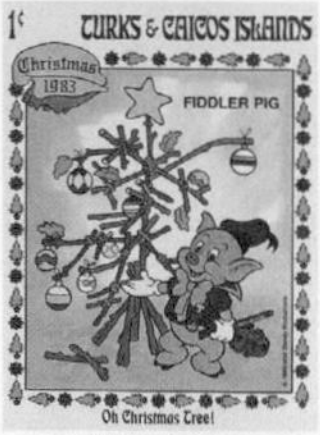

180 Fiddler Pig

1983. Christmas. Walt Disney Cartoon Characters. Multicoloured.

759	1c. Type **180**	10	10
760	1c. Fifer Pig	10	10
761	2c. Practical Pig	10	10
762	2c. Pluto	10	10
763	3c. Goofy	10	10
764	3c. Mickey Mouse	10	10
765	35c. Gyro Gearloose	70	35
766	50c. Ludwig von Drake	1·00	60
767	$1.10 Huey, Dewey and Louie	1·40	1·25
MS768	127×102 mm. $2.50 Mickey and Minnie Mouse with Huey, Dewey and Louie	3·25	4·00

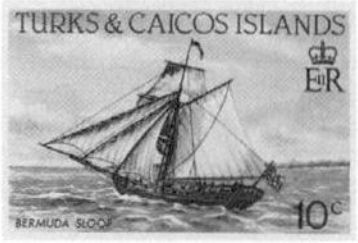

181 Bermudan Sloop

1983. Ships. Multicoloured.

769	4c. Arawak dug-out canoe	1·00	2·75
770	5c. "Santa Maria"	1·00	2·75
771	8c. British and Spanish ships in battle	2·25	2·75
772	10c. Type **181**	2·25	1·50
773a	20c. U.S. privateer "Grand Turk"	50	2·25
774a	25c. H.M.S. "Boreas" (frigate)	60	2·25
775	30c. H.M.S. "Endymion" (frigate) attacking French ship, 1790s	3·00	1·50
776a	35c. "Caesar" (barque)	60	2·75
777a	50c. "Grapeshot" (American schooner)	60	2·25
778a	65c. H.M.S. "Invincible" (battle cruiser)	2·50	3·50
779a	95c. H.M.S. "Magicienne" (cruiser)	2·50	3·50
780	$1.10 H.M.S. "Durban" (cruiser)	6·00	3·75
781a	$2 "Sentinel" (cable ship)	2·50	6·50
782	$3 H.M.S. "Minerva" (frigate)	7·50	7·50
783	$5 Caicos sloop	7·50	13·00

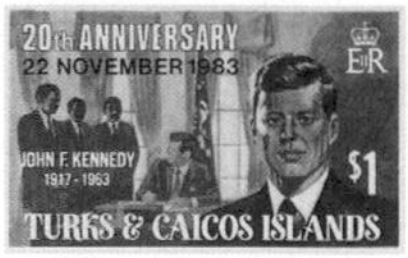

182 Pres. Kennedy and Signing of Civil Rights Legislation

1983. 20th Death Anniv of J. F. Kennedy (U.S. President).

784	**182**	20c. multicoloured	20	15
785	**182**	$1 multicoloured	50	1·25

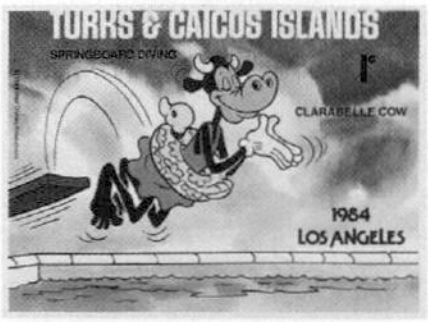

183 Clarabelle Cow Diving

1984. Olympic Games, Los Angeles. Multicoloured. A. Inscr "1984 LOS ANGELES".

786A	1c. Type **183**	10	10
787A	1c. Donald Duck in 500 m kayak race	10	10
788A	2c. Huey, Dewey and Louie in 1000m kayak race	10	10
789A	2c. Mickey Mouse in single kayak	10	10
790A	3c. Donald Duck highboard diving	10	10
791A	3c. Minnie Mouse in kayak slalom	10	10
792A	25c. Mickey Mouse freestyle swimming	70	45
793A	75c. Donald Duck playing water-polo	2·00	2·00

794A $1 Uncle Scrooge and Donald Duck yachting 2·00 2·00
MS795A 117×90 mm. $2 Pluto platform diving 4·00 4·50

B. Inscr "1984 OLYMPICS LOS ANGELES" and Olympic emblem.

786B 1c. Type 183 10 10
787B 1c. Donald Duck in 500 m kayak race 10 10
788B 2c. Huey, Dewey and Louie in 1000m kayak race 10 10
789B 2c. Mickey Mouse in single kayak 10 10
790B 3c. Donald Duck highboard diving 10 10
791B 3c. Minnie Mouse in kayak slalom 10 10
792B 25c. Mickey Mouse freestyle swimming 70 45
793B 75c. Donald Duck playing water-polo 2·00 2·00
794B $1 Uncle Scrooge and Donald Duck yachting 2·00 2·00
MS795B 117×90 mm. $2 Pluto platform diving 4·00 6·00

184 "Cadillac V-16", 1933

1984. Classic Cars and 125th Anniv of first Commercial Oil Well. Multicoloured.

796 4c. Type 184 30 10
797 8c. Rolls-Royce "Phanton III", 1937 40 15
798 10c. Saab "99", 1969 40 15
799 25c. Maserati "Bora", 1973 90 40
800 40c. Datsun "260Z", 1970 1·25 65
801 55c. Porsche "917", 1971 1·40 80
802 80c. Lincoln "Continental", 1939 1·50 90
803 $1 Triumph "TR3A", 1957 1·60 1·25
MS804 70×100 mm. $2 Daimler, 1886 2·00 2·50

185 "Rest during the Flight to Egypt, with St. Francis"

1984. Easter. 450th Death Anniv of Correggio (painter). Multicoloured.

805 15c. Type 185 20 15
806 40c. "St. Luke and St Ambrose" 45 40
807 60c. "Diana and her Chariot" 65 65
808 95c. "The Deposition of Christ" 80 80
MS809 100×79 mm. $2 "The Nativity with Saints Elizabeth and John the Younger" (horiz) 1·25 2·50

1984. Universal Postal Union Congress, Hamburg. Nos. 748/9 optd 19TH UPU CONGRESS, HAMBURG, WEST GERMANY.1874–1984 and emblem. Multicoloured.

810 95c. Sperm whale 2·50 3·00
811 $1.10 Goosebeak whale 2·50 3·00
MS812 112×82 mm. $3 Fin whale 4·25 4·25

 *(appears in column 2 at top — Orange Clownfish)*

187 "The Adventure of the Second Stain"

1984. 125th Birth Anniv of Sir Arthur Conan Doyle (author). Multicoloured.

813 25c. Type 187 2·75 1·50
814 45c. "The Adventure of the Final Problem" 3·50 2·25
815 70c. "The Adventure of the Empty House" 5·50 3·50
816 85c. "The Adventure of the Greek Interpreter" 6·50 4·00
MS817 100×70 mm. $2 Sir Arthur Conan Doyle 11·00 11·00

188 Orange Clownfish

1984. "Ausipex" International Stamp Exhibition, Melbourne. 175th Birth Anniv of Charles Darwin. Multicoloured.

818 5c. Type 188 60 50
819 35c. Monitor lizard 2·25 1·75
820 50c. Rainbow lory 3·50 3·25
821 $1.10 Koalas 3·75 4·25
MS822 100×70 mm. $2 Eastern grey kangaroo 2·50 4·50

189 Donald Duck cutting down Christmas Tree

1984. Christmas. Walt Disney Cartoon Characters. Designs showing scenes form "Toy Tinkers". Multicoloured.

823 20c. Type 189 85 45
824 35c. Donald Duck and Chip n' Dale playing with train set 1·10 75
825 50c. Donald Duck and Chip n' Dale playing with catapult 1·60 1·10
826 75c. Donald Duck, Chip n' Dale and Christmas tree 2·25 1·75
827 $1.10 Donald Duck, toy soldier and Chip 'n' Dale 2·50 2·50
MS828 126×102 mm. $2 Donald Duck as Father Christmas 3·25 4·00

190 Magnolia Warbler

1985. Birth Bicentenary of John J. Audubon (ornithologist). Multicoloured.

829 25c. Type 190 2·00 75
830 45c. Short-eared owl 3·00 1·50
831 70c. Mourning dove and eggs 3·50 2·75
832 85c. Caribbean martin 3·50 3·00
MS833 100×70 mm. $2 Oystercatcher and chicks 4·50 4·50

191 Leonardo da Vinci and Illustration of Glider Wing (15th century)

1985. 40th Anniv of International Civil Aviation Organization. Pioneers. Multicoloured.

834 8c. Type 191 65 40
835 25c. Sir Alliott Verdon Roe and Avro (Canada) CF-102 jetliner (1949) 1·75 55
836 65c. Robert H. Goddard and first liquid fuel rocket (1926) 2·50 1·75
837 $1 Igor Sikorsky and Vought-Sikorsky VS-300 helicopter prototype (1939) 6·00 4·25
MS838 100×70 mm. $2 Amelia Earhart's Lockheed 10E Electra (1937) 2·75 3·25

192 Benjamin Franklin and Marquis de Lafayette

1985. Centenary of Statue of Liberty's Arrival in New York. Multicoloured.

839 20c. Type 192 80 50
840 30c. Frederic Bartholdi (designer) and Gustave Eiffel (engineer) 1·10 80

841 65c. "Isere" (French screw warship) arriving in New York with statue, 1885 2·50 1·75
842 $1.10 United States fund raisers Louis Agassiz, Charles Sumner, H. W. Longfellow and Joseph Pulitzer 2·50 2·00
MS843 99×69 mm. $2 Dedication ceremony, 1886 3·00 3·50

193 Sir Edward Hawke and H.M.S. "Royal George" (ship of the line), 1782

1985. Salute to Royal Navy. Multicoloured.

844 20c. Type 193 2·50 2·25
845 30c. Lord Nelson and H.M.S. "Victory" (ship of the line), 1805 3·00 2·50
846 65c. Admiral Sir George Cockburn and H.M.S. "Albion" (ship of the line), 1802 4·00 3·50
847 95c. Admiral Sir David Beatty and H.M.S. "Indefatigable" (battle cruiser), 1916 5·00 5·50
MS848 99×69 mm. $2 18th-century sailor and cannon (vert) 3·25 4·00

194 Mark Twain riding on Halley's Comet

1985. International Youth Year. Birth Annivs of Mark Twain (150th) and Jakob Grimm (Bicentenary). Multicoloured.

849 25c. Type 194 1·25 65
850 35c. "Grand Turk" (Mississippi river steamer) 2·00 80
851 50c. Hansel and Gretel and gingerbread house (vert) 2·25 1·75
852 95c. Rumpelstiltskin (vert) 3·00 3·25
MS853 99×68 mm. $2 Mark Twain and the Brothers Grimm 3·50 5·00

195 The Queen Mother outside Clarence House

1985. Life and Times of Queen Elizabeth the Queen Mother. Multicoloured.

854 30c. Type 195 70 45
855 50c. Visiting Biggin Hill airfield (horiz) 2·25 1·00
856 $1.10 80th birthday portrait 2·25 2·50
MS857 56×85 mm. $2 With Prince Charles at Garter ceremony, Windsor Castle, 1968 2·00 3·00

196 King George II and Score of "Zadok the Priest" (1727)

1985. 300th Birth Anniv of George Frederick Handel (composer).

858 196 4c. multicoloured 65 50
859 - 10c. multicoloured 1·00 50
860 - 50c. multicoloured 2·50 2·50
861 - $1.10 multicoloured 3·00 5·50
MS862 101×76 mm. $2 black, purple-blue 5·00 7·50

DESIGNS: 10c. Queen Caroline and score of "Funeral Anthem" (1737); 50c. King George I and score of "Water Music" (1714); $1.10, Queen Anne and score of "Or la Tromba" from "Rinaldo" (1711); $2 George Frederick Handel.

1985. 300th Birth Anniv of Johann Sebastian Bach (composer). As T 189a of Sierra Leone. Multicoloured.

863 15c. Bassoon 1·00 40
864 40c. Natural horn 1·50 85
865 60c. Viola d'amore 2·00 1·25

866 95c. Clavichord 2·25 2·25
MS867 102×76 mm. $2 Johann Sebastian Bach 4·00 4·00

197 Harley-Davidson Dual Cylinder (1915) on Middle Caicos

1985. Centenary of the Motor Cycle. Multicoloured.

868 8c. Type 197 85 30
869 25c. Triumph "Thunderbird" (1950) on Grand Turk 1·75 70
870 55c. BMW "K100RS" (1985) on North Caicos 2·75 1·75
871 $1.20 Honda "1100 Shadow" (1985) on South Caicos 3·75 7·00
MS872 100×77 mm. $2 Daimler single track (1885) (vert) 4·50 4·50

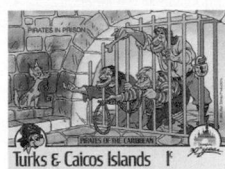

198 Pirates in Prison

1985. 30th Anniv of Disneyland, U.S.A. Designs showing scenes from "Pirates of the Caribbean" exhibition. Multicoloured.

873 1c. Type 198 10 10
874 1c. The fate of Captain William Kidd 10 10
875 2c. Bartholomew Roberts 10 10
876 2c. Two buccaneers 10 10
877 3c. Privateers looting 10 10
878 3c. Auction of captives 10 10
879 35c. Singing pirates 1·50 80
880 75c. Edward Teach—"Blackbeard" 3·00 3·25
881 $1.10 Sir Henry Morgan 3·50 4·00
MS882 123×86 mm. $2.50 Mary Read and Anne Bonney 5·00 4·50

199 Brownies from China, Turks and Caicos and Papua New Guinea

1985. 75th Anniv of Girl Guide Movement and 35th Anniv of Grand Turk Company. Multicoloured.

883 10c. Type 199 75 40
884 40c. Brownies from Surinam, Turks and Caicos and Korea 1·75 1·25
885 70c. Guides from Australia, Turks and Caicos and Canada 2·50 3·00
886 80c. Guides from West Germany, Turks and Caicos and Israel 2·75 3·00
MS887 107×76 mm. $2 75th anniv emblem 3·00 3·50

200 Iguana and Log

1986. Turks and Caicos Ground Iguana. Multicoloured.

888 8c. Type 200 2·25 1·25
889 10c. Iguana on beach 2·25 1·25
890 20c. Iguana at nest 3·50 2·50
891 35c. Iguana eating flowers 6·50 4·50
MS892 105×76 mm. $2 Map showing habitat 13·00 14·00

201 Duke and Duchess of York after Wedding

1986. Royal Wedding. Multicoloured.

893 35c. Type 201 1·50 55
894 65c. Miss Sarah Ferguson in wedding carriage 2·50 1·40

895	$1.10 Duke and Duchess of York on Palace balcony after wedding	3·00	2·75
MS896	85×85 mm. $2 Duke and Duchess leaving Westsminster Abbey	4·25	4·50

202 "Prophecy of Birth of Christ to King Achaz"

1987. Christmas. Illuminated illustrations by Giorgio Clovio from "Farnese Book of Hours". Multicoloured.

897	35c. Type **202**	1·25	85
898	50c. "The Annunciation"	1·75	1·75
899	65c. "The Circumcision"	2·25	2·25
900	95c. "Adoration of the Kings"	3·25	4·00
MS901	76×106 mm. $2 "The Nativity"	4·75	6·00

203 H.M.S. "Victoria" (ship of the line), 1859, and Victoria Cross

1987. 150th Anniv of Accession of Queen Victoria. Multicoloured.

902	8c. Type **203**	1·75	1·00
903	35c. "Victoria" (paddle-steamer) and gold sovereign	3·00	2·25
904	55c. Royal Yacht "Victoria and Albert I" and 1840 Penny Black stamp	3·25	2·75
905	95c. Royal Yacht "Victoria and Albert II" and Victoria Public Library	5·00	5·00
MS906	129×76 mm. $2 "Victoria" (barque)	6·00	7·00

1987. Bicentenary of U.S. Constitution. As T **210a** of Sierra Leone. Multicoloured.

907	10c. State Seal, New Jersey	25	35
908	35c. 18th-century family going to church ("Freedom of Worship") (vert)	75	75
909	65c. U.S. Supreme Court, Judicial Branch, Washington (vert)	1·40	1·75
910	80c. John Adams (statesman) (vert)	1·60	2·50
MS911	105×75 mm. $2 George Mason (Virginia delegate) (vert)	1·75	4·00

204 "Santa Maria"

1988. 500th Anniv (1992) of Discovery of America by Columbus (1st issue). Multicoloured.

912	4c. Type **204**	45	30
913	25c. Columbus meeting Tainos Indians	95	60
914	70c. "Santa Maria" anchored off Indian village	2·75	3·25
915	$1 Columbus in field of grain	2·75	3·25
MS916	105×76 mm. $2 "Santa Maria", "Pinta" and "Nina"	3·50	4·50

See also Nos. 947/51, 1028/36, 1072/80 and 1166/76.

205 Arawak Artifact and Scouts in Cave, Middle Caicos

1988. World Scout Jamboree, Australia. Multicoloured.

917	8c. Type **205**	20	15
918	35c. "Santa Maria" scouts and Hawks Nest Island (horiz)	55	55
919	65c. Scouts diving to wreck of galleon	95	1·25
920	95c. Visiting ruins of 19th-century sisal plantation (horiz)	1·40	1·75
MS921	118×82 mm. $2 Splashdown of John Glenn's "Mercury" capsule, 1962	3·75	5·00

No. **MS**921 is inscribed "Sight" in error.

1988. Royal Ruby Wedding. Nos. 772, 774 and 781 optd **40TH WEDDING ANNIVERSARY H.M. QUEEN ELIZABETH II H.R.H. THE DUKE OF EDINBURGH.**

922	10c. Type **181**	75	50
923	25c. H.M.S. "Boreas" (frigate)	1·25	55
924	$2 "Sentinel" (cable ship)	4·00	4·50

207 Football

1988. Olympic Games, Seoul. Multicoloured.

925	8c. Type **207**	45	15
926	30c. Yachting	80	50
927	70c. Cycling	6·00	2·00
928	$1 Athletics	1·75	2·25
MS929	102×71 mm. $2 Swimming	2·75	3·75

208 Game-fishing Launch and Swordfish

1988. Billfish Tournament. Multicoloured.

930	8c. Type **208**	55	30
931	10c. Competitors with swordfish catch	55	30
932	70c. Game-fishing launch	2·25	3·00
933	$1 Atlantic blue marlin	2·75	3·50
MS934	119×85 mm. $2 Stylized sailfish	4·00	6·00

1988. Christmas. 500th Birth Anniv of Titian (artist). As T **183a** of St. Vincent, inscr "CHRISTMAS 1988" and with royal cypher at top right. Multicoloured.

935	15c. "Madonna and Child with Saint Catherine"	40	30
936	25c. "Madonna with a Rabbit"	50	40
937	35c. "Virgin and Child with Saints"	60	50
938	40c. "The Gypsy Madonna"	70	60
939	50c. "The Holy Family and a Shepherd"	80	70
940	65c. "Madonna and Child"	95	85
941	$3 "Madonna and Child with Saints"	4·25	6·00
MS942	Two sheets, each 110×95 mm. (a) $2 "Adoration of the Magi" (detail). (b) $2 "The Annunciation" (detail) Set of 2 sheets	6·00	7·50

209 Princess Alexandra and Government House

1988. Visit of Princess Alexandra. Multicoloured.

943	70c. Type **209**	2·50	1·50
944	$1.40 Princess Alexandra and map of islands	7·50	4·50
MS945	92×72 mm. $2 Princess Alexandra (vert)	11·00	10·00

210 Coat of Arms

1988

946	**210**	$10 multicoloured	11·00	13·00

210a Cutting Tree Bark for Canoe

1989. 500th Anniv (1992) of Discovery of America by Columbus (2nd issue). Pre-Columbian Carib Society. Multicoloured.

947	10c. Type **210a**	15	15
948	50c. Body painting	80	80
949	65c. Religious ceremony	95	1·10
950	$1 Canoeing (vert)	1·50	1·75
MS951	87×70 mm. $2 Cave pictograph (horiz)	3·50	5·00

1989. "World Stamp Expo '89" International Stamp Exhibition, Washington (1st issue). Sheet 77×62 mm containing horiz design as T **201b** of St. Vincent. Multicoloured.

MS952	$1.50 Lincoln Memorial	2·50	3·50

210c Andrew Jackson and Railway Locomotive "DeWitt Clinton"

1989. "World Stamp Expo '89" International Stamp Exhibition, Washington. Bicentenary of the U.S. Presidency. Multicoloured.

953	50c. Type **210c**	1·25	1·25
954	50c. Martin van Buren, Moses Walker and early baseball game	1·25	1·25
955	50c. William H. Harrison and campaign parade	1·25	1·25
956	50c. John Tyler, Davy Crockett and the Alamo, Texas	1·25	1·25
957	50c. James K. Polk, California gold miner and first U.S. postage stamp	1·25	1·25
958	50c. Zachary Taylor and Battle of Buena Vista, 1846	1·25	1·25
959	50c. Rutherford B. Hayes and end of Confederate Reconstruction	1·25	1·25
960	50c. James A. Garfield and Battle of Shiloh	1·25	1·25
961	50c. Chester A. Arthur and opening of Brooklyn Bridge, 1883	1·25	1·25
962	50c. Grover Cleveland, Columbian Exposition, Chicago, 1893, and commemorative stamp	1·25	1·25
963	50c. Benjamin Harrison, Pan-American Union Building and map of Americas	1·25	1·25
964	50c. William McKinley and Rough Rider Monument	1·25	1·25
965	50c. Hebert Hoover, Sonya Heine (skater) and Ralph Metcalf (athlete)	1·25	1·25
966	50c. Franklin D. Roosevelt with dog and in wheelchair	1·25	1·25
967	50c. Statue of Washington by Frazer and New York World's Fair, 1939	1·25	1·25
968	50c. Harry S. Truman, Veterans Memorial Building, San Francisco, and U.N. emblem	1·25	1·25
969	50c. Dwight D. Eisenhower and U.S. troops landing in Normandy, 1944	1·25	1·25
970	50c. John F. Kennedy and "Apollo 11" astronauts on Moon, 1969	1·25	1·25

1989. Christmas. Paintings by Bellini. As T **204a** of St. Vincent. Multicoloured.

971	15c. "Madonna and Child"	80	50
972	25c. "The Madonna of the Shrubs"	90	50
973	35c. "The Virgin and Child"	1·00	60
974	40c. "The Virgin and Child with a Greek Inscription"	1·10	70
975	50c. "The Madonna of the Meadow"	1·25	80
976	65c. "The Madonna of the Pear"	2·25	2·25
977	70c. "The Virgin and Child" (different)	2·50	2·50
978	$1 "Madonna and Child" (different)	3·50	3·75
MS979	Two sheets, each 96×72 mm. (a) $2 "The Virgin and Child enthroned". (b) $2 "The Madonna with John the Baptist and another Saint" Set of 2 sheets	11·00	13·00

211 Lift-off "Apollo 11"

1990. 20th Anniv of First Manned Landing on Moon. Multicoloured.

980	50c. Type **211**	1·40	1·40
981	50c. Lunar module "Eagle" on Moon	1·40	1·40
982	50c. Aldrin gathering dust sample	1·40	1·40
983	50c. Neil Armstrong with camera	1·40	1·40
984	50c. "Eagle" re-united with command module "Columbia"	1·40	1·40

Nos. 980/4 were printed together, se-tenant, with Nos. 981/3 forming a composite design.

212 "Zephyranthes rosea"

1990. Island Flowers. Multicoloured.

985	8c. Type **212**	30	20
986	10c. "Sophora tomentosa"	30	20
987	15c. "Coccoloba uvifera"	40	25
988	20c. "Encyclia gracilis"	40	30
989	25c. "Tillandsia streptophylla"	50	35
990a	30c. "Maurandella antirrhiniflora"	70	60
991	35c. "Tillandsia balbisiana"	60	50
992a	50c. "Encyclia rufa"	1·00	1·00
993a	65c. "Aechmea lingulata"	1·25	1·25
994	80c. "Asclepias curassavica"	1·40	1·50
995	$1 "Caesalpinia bahamensis"	1·50	1·60
996	$1.10 "Capparis cynophallophora"	2·00	2·75
997	$1.25 "Stachytarpheta jamaicensis"	2·50	3·00
998	$2 "Cassia biflora"	3·00	4·00
999	$5 "Clusia rosea"	7·00	10·00
1000	$10 "Opuntia bahamana"	14·00	18·00

213 Queen Parrotfish

1990. Fish. Multicoloured.

1001	8c. Type **213**	25	20
1002	10c. Queen triggerfish	25	20
1003	25c. Sergeant major	60	45
1004	40c. Spotted goatfish	85	75
1005	50c. Neon goby	1·00	85
1006	75c. Nassau grouper	1·50	1·50
1007	80c. Yellow-headed jawfish	1·75	2·00
1008	$1 Blue tang	1·75	2·00
MS1009	Two sheets, each 115×80 mm. (a) $2 Butter hamlet. (b) $2 Queen angelfish Set of 2 sheets	13·00	14·00

214 Yellow-billed Cuckoo

1990. Birds (1st series). Multicoloured.

1010	10c. Type **214**	1·10	60
1011	15c. White-tailed tropic bird	1·50	60
1012	20c. Kirtland's warbler	2·25	85
1013	30c. Yellow-crowned night heron	2·25	85
1014	50c. Black-billed whistling duck ("West Indian tree duck")	2·50	1·10
1015	80c. Yellow-bellied sapsucker	3·25	2·50
1016	$1 American kestrel	3·25	2·50
1017	$1.40 Northern mockingbird	3·75	4·00
MS1018	Two sheets, each 104×78 mm. (a) $2 Yellow warbler. (b) $2 Osprey Set of 2 sheets	20·00	20·00

See also Nos. 1050/8.

215 "Anartia jatrophae"

1990. Butterflies (1st series). Multicoloured.

1019	15c. Type **215**	80	45
1020	25c. "Phoebis sennae" (horiz)	1·00	60
1021	35c. "Euptoieta hegesia" (horiz)	1·25	75

1022	40c. "Hylephila phylaeus" (horiz)	1·40	80
1023	50c. "Eurema chamberlaini" (horiz)	1·40	1·00
1024	60c. "Brephidium exilis"	1·60	1·40
1025	90c. "Papilio aristodemus" (horiz)	2·75	3·00
1026	$1 "Marpesia eleuchea"	2·75	3·00
MS1027	Two sheets, each 106×76 mm. (a) $2 "Hemiargus thomast" (horiz). (b) $2 "Danaus gilippus (horiz) Set of 2 sheets	11·00	12·00

See also Nos. 1081/9.

215a Rock Beauty

1990. 500th Anniv (1992) of Discovery of America by Columbus (3rd issue). New World Natural History–Fish. Multicoloured.

1028	10c. Type **215a**	60	30
1029	15c. Coney	70	40
1030	25c. Red hind	95	60
1031	50c. Banded butterflyfish	1·50	1·25
1032	60c. French angelfish	1·90	1·50
1033	75c. Black-barred soldierfish	2·00	1·90
1034	90c. Stoplight parrotfish	2·25	2·25
1035	$1 French grunt	2·25	2·40
MS1036	Two sheets, each 109×75 mm. (a) $2 Blue chrornis. (b) $2 Grey angelfish Set of 2 sheets	9·00	10·00

216 Penny "Rainbow Trial" in Blue

1990. 150th Anniv of the Penny Black.

1037	**216**	25c. blue	1·50	80
1038	-	75c. brown	3·00	2·50
1039	-	$1 blue	3·75	3·25
MS1040		144×111 mm. $2 black	5·00	6·00

DESIGNS: 75c. 1d. red-brown colour trial of December, 1840; $1 2d. blue of 1840; $2 Penny black.

217 Pillar Box No. 1, 1855

1990. "Stamp World London 90" Int Stamp Exhibition. British Pillar Boxes.

1041	**217**	35c. brown and grey	1·25	65
1042	-	50c. blue and grey	1·60	1·10
1043	-	$1.25 blue and grey	3·50	4·00
MS1044		143×111 mm. $2 red and black	6·00	6·50

DESIGNS: 50c. Penfold box, 1866; $1.25, Air mail box, 1935; $2 "k" type box, 1979.

218 Queen Elizabeth the Queen Mother

1990. 90th Birthday of Queen Elizabeth the Queen Mother.

1045	**218**	10c. multicoloured	35	15
1046	-	25c. multicoloured	75	50
1047	-	75c. multicoloured	1·40	1·60
1048	-	$1.25 multicoloured	2·00	2·50
MS1049		70×73 mm. $2 multicoloured	4·00	5·00

DESIGNS: 25, 75c., $2, Recent photographs of the Queen Mother.

219 Stripe-headed Tanager

1990. Birds (2nd series). Multicoloured.

1050	8c. Type **219**	90	55
1051	10c. Black-whiskered vireo (horiz)	90	55
1052	25c. Blue-grey gnatcatcher (horiz)	1·50	60
1053	40c. Lesser scaup (horiz)	2·00	1·00
1054	50c. Bahama pintail (horiz)	2·00	1·10
1055	75c. Black-necked stilt (horiz)	2·50	2·50
1056	80c. Oystercatcher	2·50	2·75
1057	$1 Louisiana heron (horiz)	3·00	3·25
MS1058	Two sheets, each 98×69 mm. (a) $2 American coot (horiz). (b) $2 Bahama woodstar (horiz) Set of 2 sheets	7·50	8·50

220 "Triumph of Christ over Sin and Death" (detail, Rubens)

1990. Christmas. 350th Death Anniv of Rubens. Multicoloured.

1059	10c. Type **220**	50	20
1060	35c. "St. Theresa Praying" (detail)	1·00	45
1061	45c. "St. Theresa Praying" (different detail)	1·10	60
1062	50c. "Triumph of Christ over Sin and Death" (different detail)	1·25	65
1063	65c. "St. Theresa Praying" (different detail)	1·75	1·10
1064	75c. "Triumph of Christ over Sin and Death" (different detail)	2·00	1·40
1065	$1.25 "St. Theresa Praying" (different detail)	2·50	3·75
MS1066	Two sheets, each 70×100 mm. (a) $2 "Triumph of Christ over Sin and Death" (different detail). (b) $2 "St. Theresa Praying" (different detail) Set of 2 sheets	11·00	12·00

221 Canoeing

1991. Olympic Games, Barcelona (1992). Multicoloured.

1067	10c. Type **221**	35	25
1068	25c. 100 metre sprint	70	50
1069	75c. Pole vaulting	1·60	1·60
1070	$1.25 Javelin	2·25	3·00
MS1071	109×70 mm. $2 Basketball	6·50	6·50

1991. 500th Anniv (1992) of Discovery of America by Columbus (4th issue). History of Exploration. As T **220a** of St. Vincent. Multicoloured.

1072	5c. Henry Hudson in Hudson's Bay, 1611	85	55
1073	10c. Roald Amundsen's airship N.1 "Norge", 1926	85	55
1074	15c. Amundsen's "Gjoa" in the Northwest Passage, 1906	1·40	70
1075	50c. Submarine U.S.S. "Nautilus" under North Pole, 1958	1·75	70
1076	75c. Robert Scott's "Terra Nova", 1911	3·00	1·25
1077	$1 Byrd and Bennett's Fokker F.VIIa/3m "Josephine Ford" aircraft over North Pole, 1926	3·25	2·00
1078	$1.25 Lincoln Ellsworth's Northrop Gamma "Polar Star" on trans-Antarctic flight, 1935	3·50	3·50
1079	$1.50 Capt. James Cook in the Antarctic, 1772–75	4·50	5·00
MS1080	Two sheets, each 116×76 mm. (a) "Santa Maria" (vert). (b) $2 Bow of "Nina" (vert) Set of 2 sheets	9·00	10·00

222 "Anartia jatrophae"

1991. Butterflies (2nd series). Multicoloured.

1081	5c. Type **222**	35	40
1082	25c. "Historis osius"	80	50
1083	35c. "Agraulis vanillae"	90	65
1084	45c. "Junonia evarete"	1·10	90
1085	55c. "Dryas julia"	1·25	1·25
1086	65c. "Siproeta stelenes"	1·60	1·60
1087	70c. "Appias drusilla"	1·75	1·75
1088	$1 "Ascia monuste"	1·90	2·00
MS1089	Two sheets, each 114×72 mm. (a) $2 "Phoebis philea". (b) "Pseudolycaena marsyas" Set of 2 sheets	10·00	11·00

223 Protohydrochoerus

1991. Extinct Species of Fauna. Multicoloured.

1090	5c. Type **223**	70	60
1091	10c. Phororhacos	70	60
1092	15c. Prothylacynus	85	60
1093	50c. Borhyaena	2·00	1·10
1094	75c. Smilodon	2·50	1·60
1095	$1 Thoatherium	2·75	2·00
1096	$1.25 Cuvieronius	3·00	3·25
1097	$1.50 Toxodon	3·00	3·50
MS1098	Two sheets, each 79×59 mm. (a) $2 Astrapotherium. (b) $2 Mesosaurus Set of 2 sheets	11·00	12·00

1991. 65th Birthday of Queen Elizabeth II. As T **220b** of St. Vincent. Multicoloured.

1099	25c. Queen and Prince Philip at St. Paul's Cathedral, 1988	65	45
1100	35c. Queen and Prince Philip	80	60
1101	65c. Queen and Prince Philip at Garter Ceremony, 1988	1·40	1·40
1102	80c. Queen at Windsor, May 1988	1·75	2·00
MS1103	68×90 mm. $2 Separate photographs of Queen and Prince Philip	4·00	5·00

224 "Pluteus chrysophlebius"

1991. Fungi. Multicoloured.

1104	10c. Type **224**	40	30
1105	15c. "Leucopaxillus gracillimus	55	30
1106	20c. "Marasmius haematocephalus"	65	40
1107	35c. "Collybia subpruinosa"	85	45
1108	50c. "Marasmius atrorubens" (vert)	1·25	75
1109	65c. "Leucocoprinus birnbaumii" (vert)	1·50	1·25
1110	$1.10 "Trogia cantharelloides" (vert)	2·00	2·50
1111	$1.25 "Boletellus cubensis" (vert)	2·00	2·75
MS1112	Two sheets, each 85×59 mm. (a) $2 "Pynrhoglossum pyrrhum" (vert). (b) $2 "Gerronema cirtinum" Set of 2 sheets	10·00	11·00

1991. Tenth Wedding Anniv of the Prince and Princess of Wales. As T **220b** of St. Vincent. Multicoloured.

1113	10c. Prince and Princess of Wales, 1987	80	25
1114	45c. Separate photographs of Prince, Princess and sons	2·50	90
1115	50c. Prince Henry in fire engine and Prince William applauding	3·50	1·50
1116	$1 Princess Diana in Derbyshire, 1990, and Prince Charles	3·25	3·00
MS1117	68×90 mm. $2 Prince, Princess and Family, Majorca, 1990	5·50	6·00

1991. Death Centenary (1990) of Vincent van Gogh (artist). As T **215a** of St. Vincent. Multicoloured.

1118	15c. "Weaver with Spinning Wheel"	1·00	60
1119	25c. "Head of a Young Peasant with Pipe" (vert)	1·25	60
1120	35c. "Old Cemetery Tower at Nuenen" (vert)	1·40	60
1121	45c. "Cottage at Nightfall"	1·50	70
1122	50c. "Still Life with Open Bible"	1·50	75
1123	65c. "Lane, Jardin du Luxembourg"	2·25	1·60
1124	80c. "Pont du Carrousel and Louvre, Paris"	2·75	3·25
1125	$1 "Vase with Poppies, Cornflowers, Peonies and Chrysanthemums" (vert)	3·00	3·25
MS1126	Two sheets, each 117×80 mm. (a) $2 "Ploughed Field" (horiz). (b) $2 "Entrance to the Public Park" (horiz). Imperf Set of 2 sheets	12·00	13·00

225 Series "8550" Steam Locomotive, 1899

1991. "Phila Nippon '91" International Stamp Exhibition, Tokyo. Japanese Steam Locomotives. Multicoloured.

1127	8c. Type **225**	70	60
1128	10c. Class C57, 1937	70	50
1129	45c. Series 4110, 1913	1·50	70
1130	50c. Class C55, 1935	1·50	70
1131	65c. Series 6250, 1915	2·00	1·40
1132	80c. Class E10, 1948	2·25	2·25
1133	$1 Series 4500, 1902	2·25	2·50
1134	$1.25 Class C11, 1932	2·50	3·50
MS1135	Two sheets, each 112×80 mm. (a) $2 Class C58, 1938. (b) $2 Class C62, 1948 Set of 2 sheets	9·00	9·00

1991. Christmas. Religious Paintings by Gerard David. As T **241a** of St. Vincent. Multicoloured.

1136	8c. "Adoration of the Shepherds" (detail)	55	20
1137	15c. "Virgin and Child Enthroned with Two Angels"	75	25
1138	35c. "The Annunciation" (outer wings)	1·25	50
1139	45c. "The Rest on the Flight to Egypt" (different)	1·40	75
1140	50c. "The Rest on the Flight to Egypt" (different)	1·40	90
1141	65c. "Virgin and Child with Angels"	2·00	1·25
1142	80c. "Adoration of the Shepherds"	2·50	2·75
1143	$1.25 "Perussis Altarpiece" (detail)	3·00	3·75
MS1144	Two sheets, each 102×127 mm. (a) $2 "The Nativity" (b) $2 "Adoration of the Kings" Set of 2 sheets	9·00	10·00

1992. 40th Anniv of Queen Elizabeth II's Accession. As T **229a** of St. Vincent. Multicoloured.

1145	10c. Garden overlooking sea	65	40
1146	20c. Jetty	1·00	55
1147	25c. Small bay	1·25	60
1148	35c. Island road	1·40	75
1149	50c. Grand Turk	1·75	1·10
1150	65c. Beach	2·00	1·60
1151	80c. Marina	2·25	2·25
1152	$1.10 Grand Turk (different)	2·50	2·75
MS1153	Two sheets, each 75×97 mm. (a) $2 Beach (different). (b) $2 Foreshore, Grand Turk Set of 2 sheets	11·00	12·00

1992. "Granada '92" Int Stamp Exn, Spain. Religious Paintings. As T **250b** of Sierra Leone. Multicoloured.

1154	8c. "St. Monica" (Luis Tristan)	70	20
1155	20c. "The Vision of Ezekiel: The Resurrection of the Flesh" (detail) (Francisco Collantes)	1·00	30
1156	45c. "The Vision of Ezekiel: The Resurrection of the Flesh" (different detail) (Collantes)	1·50	65
1157	50c. "The Martyrdom of St. Phillip" (Jose de Ribera)	1·50	65
1158	65c. "St. John the Evangelist" (Juan Ribalta)	2·00	1·25
1159	80c. "Archimedes" (De Ribera)	2·25	2·50
1160	$1 "St. John the Baptist in the Desert" (De Ribera)	2·50	2·75
1161	$1.25 "The Martyrdom of St. Phillip" (detail) (De Ribera)	2·75	3·25
MS1162	Two sheets, each 95×120 mm. (a) $2 "The Baptism of Christ" (Juan Fernández Navarrete). (b) $2 "Battle at EL Sotillo" (Francisco Zurbarán). Imperf Set of 2 sheets	11·00	12·00

226 Boy Scout on Duty at New York World's Fair, 1964

1992. 17th World Scout Jamboree, Korea. Multicoloured.

1163	$1 Type **226**	2·75	3·00
1164	$1 Lord Baden-Powell (vert)	2·75	3·00
MS1165	117×89 mm. $2 Silver Buffalo award	6·50	7·00

227 "Nina" and Commemorative Coin

1992. 500th Anniv of Discovery of America by Columbus (5th issue). Multicoloured.

1166	10c. Type **227**	85	55
1167	15c. Departure from Palos	1·00	55
1168	20c. Coat of arms of Columbus	1·00	65
1169	25c. Ships of Columbus	1·50	65
1170	30c. "Pinta"	1·50	65
1171	35c. Landfall in the New World	1·50	70
1172	50c. Christopher Columbus	1·75	1·00
1173	65c. "Santa Maria"	2·00	1·25
1174	80c. Erecting commemorative cross	2·00	2·25
1175	$1.10 Columbus meeting Amerindian	2·25	2·75
MS1176	Two sheets, each 70×100 mm. (a) $2 Coins showing ships of Columbus. (b) $2 Coins showing landing in the New World Set of 2 sheets	11·00	11·00

1992. Christmas. Religious Paintings. As T **241a** of St. Vincent. Multicoloured.

1177	8c. "Nativity" (detail) (Simon Bening)	70	15
1178	15c. "Circumcision" (detail) (Bening)	1·00	30
1179	35c. "Flight to Egypt" (detail) (Bening)	1·60	60
1180	50c. "Massacre of the Innocents" (detail) (Bening)	1·75	80
1181	65c. "The Annunciation" (Dieric Bouts)	2·00	1·25
1182	80c. "The Visitation" (Bouts)	2·50	2·75
1183	$1.10 "Adoration of the Angels" (Bouts)	2·75	3·00
1184	$1.25 "Adoration of the Wise Men" (Bouts)	2·75	3·25
MS1185	Two sheets, each 77×102 mm. (a) $2 "The Virgin seated with the Child" (detail) (Bouts). (b) $2 "The Virgin and Child" (detail) (Bouts) Set of 2 sheets	12·00	13·00

228 American Astronaut repairing Satellite

1993. Anniversaries and Events. Multicoloured.

1186	25c. Type **228**	2·00	60
1187	50c. Dead and flourishing trees	2·25	90
1188	65c. Food and World map	2·75	1·60
1189	80c. Polluted and clean seas	3·25	3·00
1190	$1 Lions Club emblem	3·25	3·00
1191	$1.25 Projected orbiting quarantine modules	3·75	4·00
MS1192	Two sheets, each 107×80 mm. (a) $2 Projected orbital Martian vehicle. (b) $2 Industrialised town and clean beach Set of 2 sheets	13·00	14·00

ANNIVERSARIES AND EVENTS: Nos. 1186, 1191, **MS**1192a, International Space Year; 1187, 1189, **MS**1192b, Earth Summit '92, Rio; 1188, International Conference on Nutrition, Rome; 1190, 75th anniv of International Association of Lions Clubs.

1993. Visit of the Duke of Edinburgh. Nos. 1100/1 optd **Royal Visit HRH Duke of Edinburgh 20th March 1993**.

1193	35c. Queen and Prince Philip	2·25	1·25
1194	65c. Queen and Prince Philip at Garter Ceremony, 1988	3·00	2·00
MS1195	68×90 mm. $2 Separate photographs of Queen and Prince Philip	6·50	6·50

1993. 40th Anniv of Coronation. As T **256a** of St. Vincent.

1196	15c. multicoloured	40	40
1197	50c. multicoloured	1·10	1·40
1198	$1 green and black	1·60	1·75
1199	$1.25 multicoloured	1·60	1·75
MS1200	70×100 mm. $2 multicoloured	5·50	6·00

DESIGNS: 15c. Communion Chalice and Plate; 50c. Queen Elizabeth II at Coronation (photograph by Cecil Beaton); $1 Queen Elizabeth during Coronation ceremony; $1.25, Queen Elizabeth and Prince Philip. (28½×42½ mm.)—$2 "Queen Elizabeth II" (detail).

230 Omphalosaurus

1993. Prehistoric Animals. Multicoloured.

1201	8c. Type **230**	30	30
1202	15c. Coelophysis	40	30
1203	20c. Triceratops	45	30
1204	35c. Dilophosaurus	65	50
1205	50c. Pterodactylus	80	65
1206	65c. Elasmosaurus	1·10	1·00
1207	80c. Stegosaurus	1·25	1·40
1208	$1.25 Euoplocephalus	1·60	2·25
MS1209	Two sheets, each 100×70 mm. (a) $2 As 20c. (b) $2 As 35c. Set of 2 sheets	11·00	12·00

1993. Christmas. Religious Paintings. As T **256b** of St. Vincent. Black, yellow and red (Nos. 1210/12, 1217) or multicoloured (others).

1210	8c. "Mary, Queen of the Angels" (detail) (Durer)	60	20
1211	20c. "Mary, Queen of the Angels" (different detail) (Durer)	90	30
1212	35c. "Mary, Queen of the Angels" (different detail) (Durer)	1·25	50
1213	50c. "Virgin and Child with St. John the Baptist" (Raphael)	1·60	70
1214	65c. "The Canagiani Holy Family" (detail) (Raphael)	2·00	1·25
1215	80c. "The Holy Family with the Lamb" (detail) (Raphael)	2·25	2·25
1216	$1 "Virgin and Child with St. John the Baptist" (different detail) (Raphael)	2·75	2·75
1217	$1.25 "Mary, Queen of the Angels" (different detail) (Durer)	3·00	3·50
MS1218	Two sheets, each 102×127 mm. (a) $2 "Mary, Queen of the Angels" (different detail) (Durer). (b) $2 "The Canagiani Holy Family" (different detail) (Raphael) (horiz) Set of 2 sheets	9·00	10·00

231 Blue-headed Wrasse

1993. Fish. Multicoloured.

1219	10c. Type **231**	40	30
1220	20c. Honeycomb cowfish	60	40
1221	25c. Glass-eyed snapper	60	40
1222	35c. Spotted drum	75	50
1223	50c. Jolt-headed porgy	1·00	70
1224	65c. Small-mouthed grunt	1·25	1·00
1225	80c. Candy basslet ("Peppermint bass")	1·40	1·75
1226	$1.10 Indigo hamlet	1·75	2·75
MS1227	Two sheets, each 106×75 mm. (a) $2 Bonnethead. (b) $2 Atlantic sharp-nosed shark Set of 2 sheets	7·50	8·50

The captions on No. **MS**1227 have been transposed in error.

232 Killdeer Plover ("Killdeer")

1993. Birds. Multicoloured.

1228	10c. Type **232**	1·00	75
1229	15c. Yellow-crowned night heron (vert)	1·40	75
1230	35c. Northern mockingbird	2·00	75
1231	50c. Eastern kingbird (vert)	2·25	1·00
1232	65c. Magnolia warbler	2·75	1·50
1233	80c. Cedar waxwing (vert)	3·00	3·00
1234	$1.10 Ruby-throated hummingbird	3·00	3·00
1235	$1.25 Painted bunting (vert)	3·25	3·50
MS1236	Two sheets, each 100×70 mm. (a) $2 Ruddy duck. (b) $2 American kestrel (vert) Set of 2 sheets	11·00	12·00

233 Sergio Goycoechea (Argentina)

1994. World Cup Football Championship, U.S.A. Multicoloured.

1237	8c. Type **233**	40	20
1238	10c. Bodo Illgner (Germany)	40	20
1239	50c. Nico Claesen (Belgium), Bossis and Amoros (France)	1·50	70
1240	65c. German players celebrating	1·75	1·10
1241	80c. Cameroun players celebrating	2·00	2·00
1242	$1 Cuciuffo (Argentina), Santin and Francescoli (Uruguay)	2·00	2·25
1243	$1.10 Hugo Sanchez (Mexico)	2·00	2·50
MS1244	Two sheets, each 100×70 mm. (a) $2 The Silverdome, Michigan. (b) $2 Michel Platini (France) (vert) Set of 2 sheets	6·50	7·50

No. 1237 is inscribed "Segio" and No. 1238 "Bado", both in error.

234 "Xerocomus guadelupae"

1994. Fungi. Multicoloured.

1245	5c. Type **234**	30	30
1246	10c. "Volvariella volvacea"	30	30
1247	35c. "Hygrocybe atrosquamosa" (horiz)	65	50
1248	50c. "Pleurotus ostreatus" (horiz)	90	65
1249	65c. "Marasmius pallescens" (horiz)	1·25	1·00
1250	80c. "Coprinus plicatilis"	1·40	1·50
1251	$1.10 "Bolbitius vitellinus" (horiz)	1·60	1·90
1252	$1.50 "Pyrrhoglossum lilaceipes"	2·00	2·50
MS1253	Two sheets, each 102×72 mm. (a) $2 "Russula cremeolilacina". (b) $2 "Lentinus edodes" (horiz) Set of 2 sheets	8·00	8·00

235 "The Annunciation"

1994. Christmas. Illustrations from 15th-century French Book of Hours. Multicoloured.

1254	25c. Type **235**	1·10	35
1255	50c. "The Visitation"	1·90	75
1256	65c. "Annunciation to the Shepherds"	2·25	1·25
1257	80c. "The Nativity"	2·50	2·50
1258	$1 "Flight into Egypt"	2·75	2·50
MS1259	63×86 mm. $2 "The Adoration of the Magi"	5·00	6·00

236 "Dryas julia"

1994. Butterflies. Multicoloured.

1260	15c. Type **236**	40	35
1261	20c. "Urbanus proteus"	45	40
1262	25c. "Colobura dirce"	50	40
1263	50c. "Papilio homerus"	90	65
1264	65c. "Chiodes catillus"	1·25	1·00
1265	80c. "Eurytides zonaria"	1·50	1·75
1266	$1 "Hypolymnas misippus"	1·60	1·75
1267	$1.25 "Phoebis avellaneda"	1·75	2·00
MS1268	Two sheets, each 100×70 mm. (a) $2 "Eurema adamst". (b) $2 "Morpho peleides" Set of 2 sheets	6·50	7·00

237 General Montgomery and British Troops landing on Juno Beach

1994. 50th Anniv of D-Day. Multicoloured.

1269	10c. Type **237**	30	30
1270	15c. Admiral Ramsay and British commandos at Sword Beach	45	35
1271	35c. Gun crew on H.M.S. "Belfast" (cruiser)	65	45
1272	50c. Montgomery and Eisenhower with Air Chief Marshal Tedder	90	65
1273	65c. General Eisenhower and men of U.S. 101st Airborne Division	1·25	1·00
1274	80c. Lt-Gen. Bradley and U.S. troops landing on Omaha Beach	1·40	1·50
1275	$1.10 Arrival of U.S. reinforcements	1·60	1·75
1276	$1.25 Eisenhower at briefing	1·75	1·90
MS1277	Two sheets, each 100×70 mm. (a) $2 Landing craft and barrage balloon. (b) $2 Eisenhower and Montgomery Set of 2 sheets	6·50	7·00

238 "Cattleya deckeri"

1995. Orchids. Multicoloured.

1278	8c. Type **238**	50	20
1279	20c. "Epidendrum carpophorum"	70	30
1280	25c. "Epidendrum ciliare"	70	35
1281	50c. "Encyclia phoenicea"	95	70
1282	65c. "Bletia patula"	1·25	1·10
1283	80c. "Brassia caudata"	1·40	1·50
1284	$1 "Brassavola nodosa"	1·60	1·60
1285	$1.25 "Bletia purpurea"	1·90	2·25
MS1286	Two sheets, each 100×70 mm. (a) $2 "Vanilla planifolia". (b) $2 "Ionopsis utricularioides" Set of 2 sheets	7·50	8·00

1995. 25th Anniv of First Manned Moon Landing. As T **284a** of St. Vincent. Multicoloured.

1287	10c. "Apollo 11"	30	30
1288	20c. Moon landing simulation	45	35
1289	25c. "Astronauts on the Moon" (detail) (Kovales)	50	35
1290	35c. First human foot on Moon	65	45
1291	50c. Astronaut Aldrin conducting solar wind experiment	90	65
1292	65c. Astronauts planting U.S.A. flag	1·25	1·00
1293	80c. Space module "Columbia" over lunar surface	1·40	1·50
1294	$1.10 "Apollo 11" after splashdown	1·60	1·90
MS1295	Two sheets, each 104×84 mm. (a) $2 Sample of Moon rock. (b) $2 "Apollo 11" lift-off, Cape Canaveral (vert) Set of 2 sheets	7·00	7·50

239 Elasmosaurus

1995. Jurassic Marine Reptiles. Multicoloured.

1296	35c. Type **239**	65	65
1297	35c. Plesiosaurus	65	65
1298	35c. Ichthyosaurus	65	65
1299	35c. Archelon	65	65
1300	35c. Askeptosaurus	65	65
1301	35c. Macroplata	65	65
1302	35c. Ceresiosaurus	65	65
1303	35c. Liopleurodon	65	65
1304	35c. Henodus	65	65
1305	35c. Muraenosaurus	65	65
1306	35c. Placodus	65	65
1307	35c. Kronosaurus	65	65

Nos. 1296/1307 were printed together, se-tenant, forming a composite design.

No. 1303 is inscribed "Lipoleurodon" in error.

240 Fencing

1995. Centenary of Int Olympic Committee. Multicoloured.

1308	8c. Type **240**	40	30
1309	10c. Speed skating	40	30
1310	15c. Diving	60	30
1311	20c. Cycling	2·75	85
1312	25c. Ice hockey	2·75	85
1313	35c. Figure skating	1·25	70
1314	50c. Football	1·50	90
1315	65c. Bobsleighing	1·50	1·25
1316	80c. Supergiant slalom	1·50	1·60
1317	$1.25 Show jumping	2·50	3·00
MS1318	Two sheets, each 89×110 mm. (a) $2 Downhill skiing. (b) $2 Gymnastics Set of 2 sheets	6·50	7·50

Both miniature sheets are incorrectly dated "1984–1994" on the margin.

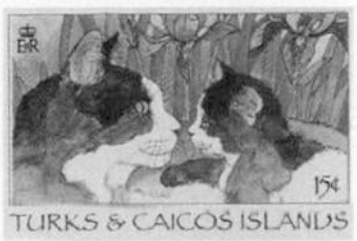

241 Cat and Kitten

1995. Cats. Multicoloured.

1319	15c. Type **241**	1·00	65
1320	20c. Tabby on branch	1·10	65
1321	35c. Cat and ladybird	1·60	65
1322	50c. Black and white cat	2·00	75
1323	65c. Red cat with flower in paw	2·25	1·25
1324	80c. White cat on pink pillow	2·50	1·75
1325	$1 Siamese with flower in paws	2·50	2·50
1326	$1.25 Cats preening	2·75	3·50
MS1327	Two sheets, each 106×76 mm. (a) $2 Kitten and ladybirds. (b) $2 Kittens asleep Set of 2 sheets	8·50	8·50

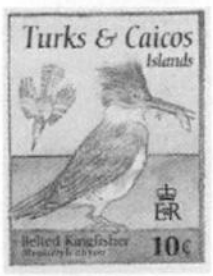

242 Belted Kingfisher

1995. Birds. Multicoloured.

1328	10c. Type **242**	80	75
1329	15c. Clapper rail	1·00	60
1330	20c. American redstart	1·25	60
1331	25c. Roseate tern	1·40	60
1332	35c. American purple gallinule ("Purple Gallinule")	1·40	60
1333	45c. Ruddy turnstone	1·50	70
1334	50c. Barn owl	2·25	1·25
1335	60c. Brown booby	1·75	90
1336	80c. Great blue heron	2·00	1·25
1337	$1 Antillean nighthawk	2·75	2·00
1338	$1.25 Thick-billed vireo	3·00	2·25
1339	$1.40 Greater flamingo ("American Flamingo")	4·00	3·50
1340	$2 Wilson's plover	4·25	4·50
1341	$5 Blue-winged teal	8·00	9·50
1342	$10 Pair of reddish egrets (50×28 mm)	14·00	16·00

[illegible] Birthday of Queen Elizabeth the Queen Mother. As T **299a** of St. Vincent.

1344	50c. brown, light brown and black	2·00	1·75
1345	50c. multicoloured	2·00	1·75
1346	50c. multicoloured	2·00	1·75
1347	50c. multicoloured	2·00	1·75
MS1348	102×127 mm. $2 multicoloured	6·50	6·50

DESIGNS: No. 1344, Queen Elizabeth the Queen Mother (pastel drawing); 1345, Wearing tiara; 1346, At desk (oil painting); 1347, Wearing blue dress; **MS**1348, wearing pale blue dress and hat.

1995. 50th Anniv of End of Second World War in Europe. As T **296a** of St. Vincent. Multicoloured.

1349	10c. Churchill, Roosevelt and Stalin at Yalta Conference	50	50
1350	15c. Liberated Allied prisoners of war	50	50
1351	20c. Meeting of American and Soviet soldiers at River Elbe	55	50
1352	25c. Pres. Roosevelt's funeral cortege	55	35
1353	60c. U.S. bugler sounding cease-fire	1·10	1·10
1354	80c. U.S. sailor kissing nurse, New York	1·50	1·75
1355	$1 Nuremburg Trials	1·75	2·00
MS1356	104×74 mm. $2 Fireworks over Allied capital	3·00	3·75

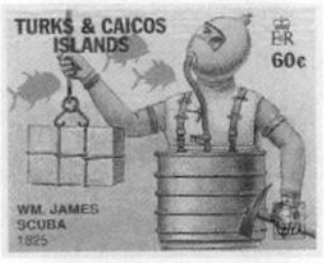

243 William James Scuba, 1825

1995. "Singapore '95" International Stamp Exhibition. Deep Sea Diving. Multicoloured.

1357	60c. Type **243**	1·50	1·50
1358	60c. Rouquayrol apparatus, 1864	1·50	1·50
1359	60c. Fluess oxygen-rebreathing apparatus, 1878	1·50	1·50
1360	60c. Armoured diving suit, 1900	1·50	1·50
1361	60c. Diving on the "Lusitania" in Peress armoured diving suit, 1935	1·50	1·50
1362	60c. Cousteau Gagnan aqualung, 1943	1·50	1·50
1363	60c. Underwater camera, 1955	1·50	1·50
1364	60c. Sylvia Earle's record dive, 1979	1·50	1·50
1365	60c. Spider propeller-driven rigid suit, 1984	1·50	1·50
MS1366	Two sheets, each 107×77 mm. (a) $2 Helmet diver, 1935. (b) $2 Jacques-Yves Cousteau (aqualung pioneer) Set of 2 sheets	6·00	6·50

1995. Christmas. Religious Paintings by Piero di Cosimo. As T **281a** of Sierra Leone. Multicoloured.

1367	20c. "Madonna and Child with St. Giovannino"	90	50
1368	25c. "Adoration of the Child"	90	50
1369	60c. "Madonna and Child with St. Giovannino, St. Margherita and Angel"	2·00	1·25
1370	$1 "Madonna and Child with Angel"	2·25	2·75
MS1371	76×106 mm. $2 "Madonna and Child with Angels and Saints" (detail)	6·50	7·00

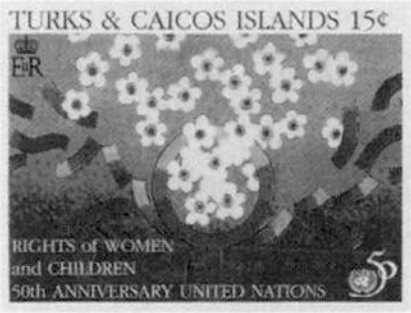

244 Daisies and Female Symbol ("Rights of Women and Children")

1996. 50th Anniv of the United Nations. Multicoloured.

1372	15c. Type **244**	30	25
1373	60c. Peace dove escaping from prison	80	80
1374	80c. Symbolic candles ("Human Rights")	1·10	1·50
1375	$1 People on open book	1·40	1·75
MS1376	107×78 mm. $2 National flags forming "50"	3·25	4·25

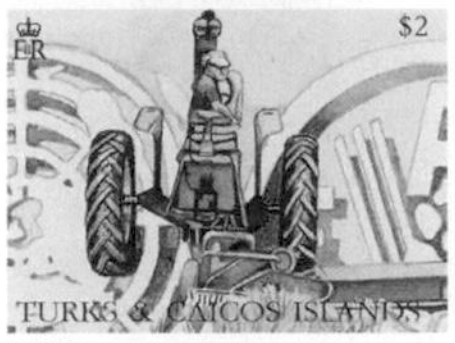

245 Farmer on Tractor

1996. 50th Anniv of Food and Agriculture Organization. Sheet 111×80 mm.

MS1377	**245** $2 multicoloured	[illegible]	[illegible]

1996. 70th Birthday of Queen Elizabeth II. As T **323a** of St. Vincent. Multicoloured.

1378	80c. As Type **323a** of St. Vincent	1·25	1·40
1379	80c. In blue coat and hat	1·25	1·40
1380	80c. At Trooping the Colour	1·25	1·40
MS1381	125×104 mm. $2 In yellow dress and hat	3·75	4·00

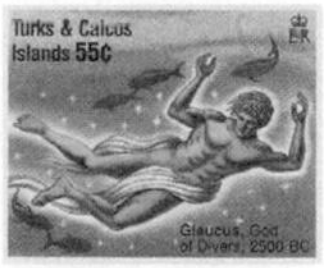

246 Glaucus, God of Divers, 2500 B.C.

1996. "China '96" Asian International Philatelic Exhibition, Beijing. Underwater Exploration (1st series). Multicoloured.

1382	55c. Type **246**	1·40	1·40
1383	55c. Alexander the Great, 332 B.C.	1·40	1·40
1384	55c. Salvage diver, 1430	1·40	1·40
1385	55c. Borelli's rebreathing device, 1680	1·40	1·40
1386	55c. Edmund Halley's diving bell, 1690	1·40	1·40
1387	55c. John Lethbridge's diving machine, 1715	1·40	1·40
1388	55c. Klingert's diving apparatus, 1789	1·40	1·40
1389	55c. Drieberg's triton, 1808	1·40	1·40
1390	55c. Seibe's diving helmet, 1819	1·40	1·40
MS1391	Two sheets, each 102×77 mm. (a) $2 12th-century Arab diver. (b) $2 Caribbean pearl diver, 1498 Set of 2 sheets	7·50	8·50

See also Nos. 1392/1401 and 1460/9.

1996. "Capex '96" World Stamp Exhibition, Toronto. Underwater Exploration (2nd series). As T **246**. Multicoloured.

1392	60c. Jim Jarrat exploring "Lusitania", 1935	1·00	1·00
1393	60c. Cousteau's first use of scuba gear for exploration, 1952	1·00	1·00
1394	60c. Discovery of oldest shipwreck, 1959	1·00	1·00
1395	60c. Raising of the "Vasa", 1961	1·00	1·00
1396	60c. Mel Fisher discovering "Atocha", 1971	1·00	1·00
1397	60c. Barry Clifford discovering "Whydah", 1984	1·00	1·00
1398	60c. Argo robot over the "Bismarck", 1989	1·00	1·00
1399	60c. Discovery of "Land Tortoise" in Lake George, New York, 1991	1·00	1·00
1400	60c. Nuclear submarine recovering artefacts from Roman shipwreck, 1994	1·00	1·00
MS1401	Two sheets, each 102×77 mm. (a) $2 Diver investigates the "Edmund Fitzgerald". (b) $2 Alvin exploring the "Titanic" Set of 2 sheets	5·50	7·00

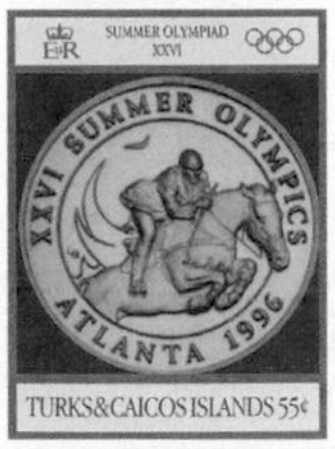

247 Show Jumping

1996. Olympic Games, Atlanta. Sports on Medals. Multicoloured.

1402	55c. Type **247**	90	1·00
1403	55c. Cycling	90	1·00
1404	55c. Fencing	90	1·00
1405	55c. Gymnastics	90	1·00
1406	55c. Pole vaulting	90	1·00
1407	55c. Sprinting	90	1·00
1408	55c. Swimming	90	1·00
1409	55c. Diving	90	1·00
1410	55c. Hurdling	90	1·00
1411	55c. Long-distance running	90	1·00

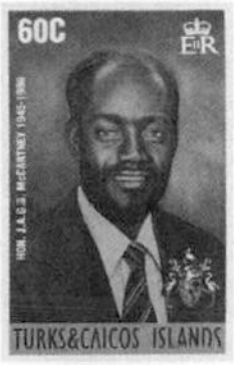

248 James McCartney (First Chief Minister)

[illegible]. 20th Anniv of [illegible]

1412	**248**	60c. multicoloured	70	75

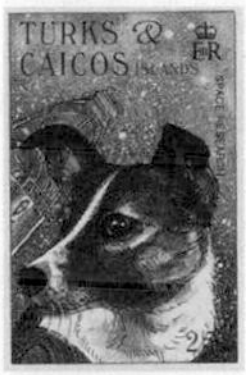

249 Space Dog

1996. Working Dogs. Multicoloured.

1413	25c. Type **249**	70	70
1414	25c. Greyhound	70	70
1415	25c. St. Bernard	70	70
1416	25c. Dog with medals	70	70
1417	25c. Retriever	70	70
1418	25c. Dog with bone	70	70
1419	25c. "Hearing ear" dog	70	70
1420	25c. Husky	70	70
1421	25c. Police alsatian	70	70
1422	25c. Guard dog	70	70
1423	25c. Boxer	70	70
1424	25c. Sniffer dog	70	70
MS1425	Two sheets, each 106×76 mm. (a) $2 Labrador guide dog. (b) $2 Border sheep dog Set of 2 sheets	8·50	8·50

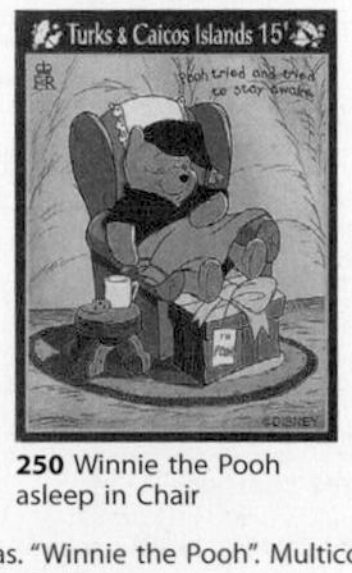

250 Winnie the Pooh asleep in Chair

1996. Christmas. "Winnie the Pooh". Multicoloured.

1426	15c. Type **250**	70	40
1427	20c. Piglet holding star decoration	70	40
1428	35c. Tigger carrying presents	90	55
1429	50c. Pooh, Tigger and Piglet singing carols	1·25	80
1430	60c. Winnie and Rabbit	1·40	1·10
1431	80c. Tigger and Roo	2·00	1·75
1432	$1 Santa Pooh filling stockings	2·25	2·25
1433	$1.25 Christopher Robin and Winnie the Pooh	2·50	3·00
MS1434	Two sheets. (a) 124×98 mm. $2 Piglet decorating biscuits. (b) 98×124 mm. $2.60, Piglet placing star on tree Set of 2 sheets	11·00	11·00

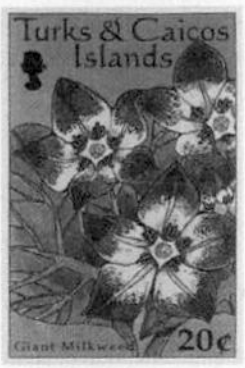

251 Giant Milkweed

1997. Flowers. Multicoloured.

1435	20c. Type **251**	55	65
1436	20c. Geiger tree	55	65
1437	20c. Passion flower	55	65
1438	20c. Hibiscus	55	65
1439	60c. Yellow elder	80	90
1440	60c. Prickly poppy	80	90
1441	60c. Frangipani	80	90
1442	60c. Seaside mahoe	80	90
MS1443	Two sheets, each 105×76 mm. (a) $2 Firecracker. (b) $2 Chain of love Set of 2 sheets	5·50	6·50

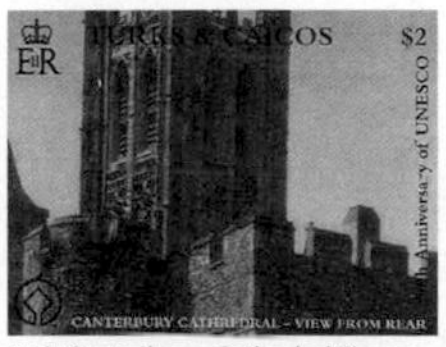

252 Canterbury Cathedral Tower

1997. 50th Anniv of UNESCO. Two sheets, each 127×102 mm, containing T **252** and similar horiz design. Multicoloured.

MS1444	(a) $2 Type **252**; (b) $2 High Altar, Canterbury Cathedral Set of 2 sheets	5·50	6·50

The miniature sheets of No. **MS**1444 are inscribed "CATHEDRAL" in error.

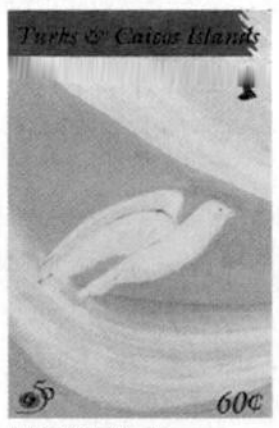

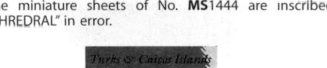

253 White Dove (face value at right)

1997. 50th Anniv of UNICEF. Multicoloured.

1445	60c. Type **253**	1·50	1·75
1446	60c. White dove (with face value at left)	1·50	1·75
1447	60c. Three children	1·50	1·75
1448	60c. Two children with pets	1·50	1·75

1997. Golden Wedding of Queen Elizabeth and Prince Philip. As T **347a** of St. Vincent. Multicoloured.

1449	60c. Queen Elizabeth II	1·50	1·50
1450	60c. Royal coat of arms	1·50	1·50
1451	60c. Queen Elizabeth and Prince Philip in carriage	1·50	1·50
1452	60c. Queen Elizabeth and Prince Philip on royal visit	1·50	1·50
1453	60c. Windsor Castle	1·50	1·50
1454	60c. Prince Philip	1·50	1·50
MS1455	100×70 mm. $2 Princess Elizabeth and Duke of Edinburgh on wedding day	5·50	6·00

1997. "Pacific '97" International Stamp Exhibition, San Francisco. Death Centenary of Heinrich von Stephan (founder of the U.P.U.). As T **347c** of St. Vincent.

1456	50c. mauve	1·25	1·40
1457	50c. brown	1·25	1·40
1458	50c. blue	1·25	1·40
MS1459	80×117 mm. $2 mauve and black	2·75	3·50

DESIGNS: No. 1456, British mail coach, 1700s; 1457, Von Stephan and Mercury; 1458, Space Shuttle; **MS**1459, Von Stephan and Ancient Greek messenger.

1997. "STAMPSHOW '97" 111th Annual A.P.S. Convention, Milwaukee. Underwater Exploration (3rd series). As T **246**. Multicoloured.

1460	20c. Edgerton underwater camera, 1954	60	70
1461	20c. Conshelf habitat, 1963	60	70
1462	20c. "Sealab II", 1965	60	70
1463	20c. Research habitat Tektite, 1970	60	70

1464	20c. Galapagos volcanic rift, 1974	60	70
1465	20c. Epaulard robot survey craft, 1979	60	70
1466	20c. Underwater sealife, 1995	60	70
1467	20c. One-man research vessel, 1996	60	70
1468	20c. Okhotsk Tower, Japan, 1996	60	70
MS1469	Two sheets, each 72×103 mm. (a) $2 Coelacanth. (b) John Williamson making underwater movie Set of 2 sheets	6·00	7·00

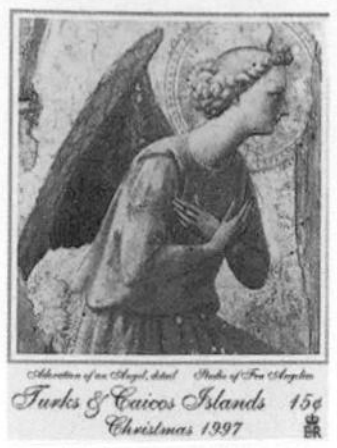

254 "Adoration of an Angel" (detail) (Studio of Fra Angelico)

1997. Christmas. Religious Paintings. Multicoloured.

1470	15c. Type **254**	35	25
1471	20c. "Scenes from the life of St. John the Baptist" (detail) (Master of Saint Severin)	40	30
1472	35c. "Archangel Gabriel" (Masolino de Panicale)	65	45
1473	50c. "Jeremiah with two Angels" (detail) (Gherardo Starnina)	85	65
1474	60c. "Jeremiah with Two Angels" (different detail) (Starnina)	95	75
1475	80c. "The Annunciation" (detail) (Giovanni di Palo di Grazia)	1·25	1·40
1476	$1 "The Annunciation" (detail) (Carlo di Braccesco)	1·40	1·50
1477	$1.25 "The Nativity" (detail) (Benvenuto di Giovanni Guasta)	1·75	2·50
MS1478	Two sheets. (a) 130×105 mm. $2 "The Journey of the Magi" (detail) (Benozzo Gozzoli). (b) 105×130 mm. $2 "The Wilton Diptych" (right panel) (anon) Set of 2 sheets	6·00	7·00

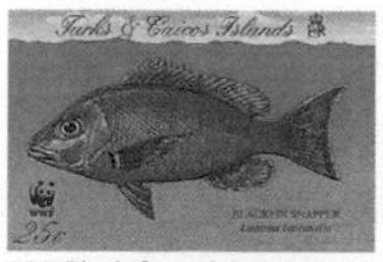

255 Black-finned Snapper

1998. Endangered Species. International Year of the Reef. Fish. Multicoloured.

1479	25c. Type **255**	55	65
1480	25c. Dog snapper	55	65
1481	25c. Cubera snapper	55	65
1482	25c. Mahogany snapper	55	65

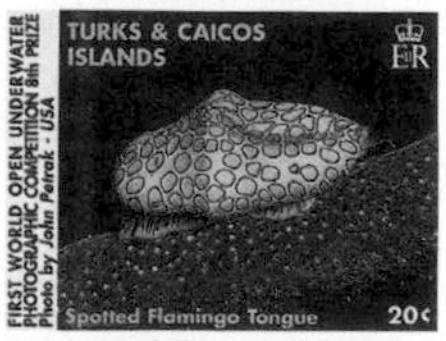

256 Spotted Flamingo Tongue (John Petrak)

1998. First World Open Underwater Photographic Competition Prizewinners (1997). Multicoloured.

1483	20c. Type **256**	40	35
1484	50c. Feather duster (Dave Bothwell)	80	75
1485	60c. Squirrel fish (Waldermar Seifert)	95	90
1486	80c. Queen angelfish (Ralph Oberlander)	1·25	1·40
1487	$1 Barracuda (Steve Rosenburg)	1·50	1·60
1488	$1.25 Royal gramma ("Fairy Basslet") (John Petrak)	1·90	2·25
MS1489	Two sheets, each 148×85 mm. (a) $2 Spotted Cleaning Shrimp (Micheal Boyer). (b) $2 Rough File Clam (Steve Rosenburg) Set of 2 sheets	6·00	7·00

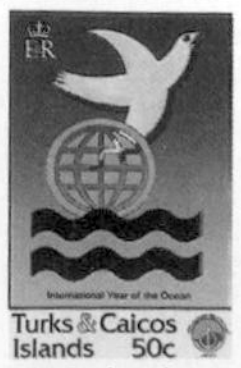

257 Bird and Logo

1998. International Year of the Ocean. Multicoloured.

1490	50c. Type **257**	1·25	1·40
1491	50c. Stylized crab	1·25	1·40
1492	50c. Fish	1·25	1·40
1493	50c. Logo in cloverleaf	1·25	1·40
MS1494	102×71 mm. $2 Queen and globe logo	3·50	4·00

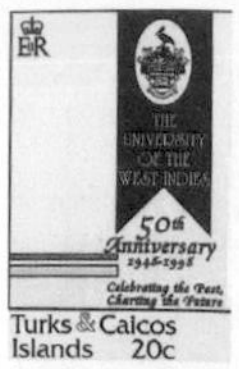

258 University Arms on Banner (50th anniv of University of West Indies)

1998. Anniversaries and Events. Multicoloured.

1495	20c. Type **258**	50	35
1496	60c. Global logo (UNESCO World Solar Energy Programme Summit)	1·25	1·25
1497	80c. Flame (50th anniv of Universal Declaration of Human Rights)	1·50	1·75
1498	$1 John Glenn (astronaut) (second space flight)	2·00	2·25
MS1499	100×72 mm. $2 Space shuttle (John Glen's second space flight)	3·00	3·50

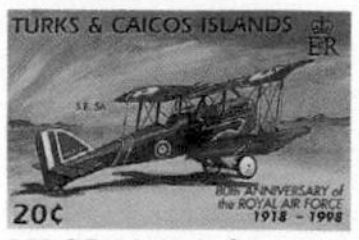

259 S.E. 5A Aircraft

1998. 80th Anniv of Royal Air Force. Multicoloured.

1500	20c. Type **259**	1·00	40
1501	50c. Sopwith Camel	1·50	85
1502	60c. Supermarine Spitfire	1·60	1·25
1503	80c. Avro Lancaster	2·00	2·00
1504	$1 Panavia Tornado	2·25	2·25
1505	$1.25 Hawker Hurricane	2·50	3·00
MS1506	Two sheets, each 100×80 mm. (a) $2 Hawker Siddley Harrier. (b) $2 Avro Vulcan Set of 2 sheets	9·00	9·00

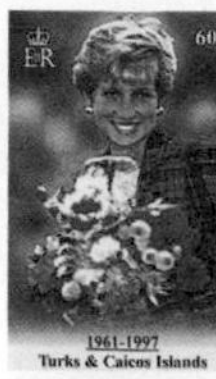

260 Diana, Princess of Wales

1998. First Death Anniv of Diana, Princess of Wales.

1507	**260**	60c. multicoloured	1·50	1·25

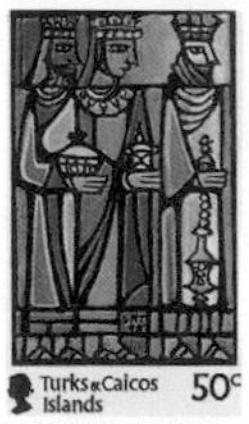

261 "Magi's Visit"

1998. Christmas. Paintings by Thomasita Fessler. Multicoloured.

1508	50c. Type **261**	1·10	1·25
1509	50c. "Flight into Egypt"	1·10	1·25
1510	50c. "Wedding Feast"	1·10	1·25
1511	50c. "Maria"	1·10	1·25
1512	50c. "Annunciation and Visitation" (57×46 mm)	1·10	1·25
1513	50c. "Nativity" (57×46 mm)	1·10	1·25
MS1514	105×103 mm. $2 "Queen of Mothers"	3·25	3·75

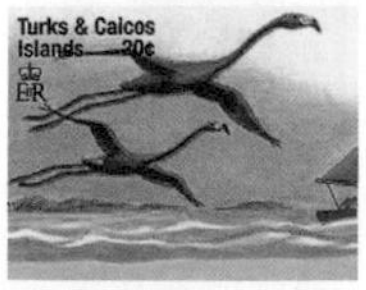

262 Flamingos

1999. Marine Life. Multicoloured.

1515	20c. Type **262**	70	70
1516	20c. Sailing dinghies	70	70
1517	20c. Seagulls and lighthouse	70	70
1518	20c. House on beach	70	70
1519	20c. Yellowtail snapper and pillar coral	70	70
1520	20c. Yellowtail snapper and elliptical star coral	70	70
1521	20c. Porkfish	70	70
1522	20c. Spotted eagle ray	70	70
1523	20c. Large ivory coral	70	70
1524	20c. Shy hamlet and mustard hill coral	70	70
1525	20c. Blue crust coral	70	70
1526	20c. Fused staghorn coral	70	70
1527	20c. Queen angelfish and massive starlet coral	70	70
1528	20c. Pinnate spiny sea fan	70	70
1529	20c. Knobby star coral	70	70
1530	20c. Lowridge cactus coral	70	70
1531	20c. Orange telesto coral	70	70
1532	20c. Spanish hogfish and knobby ten-ray star coral	70	70
1533	20c. Clown wrasse and boulder brain coral	70	70
1534	20c. Rainbow parrotfish and regal sea fan	70	70
1535	20c. Bluestriped grunt and great star coral	70	70
1536	20c. Blue tang and stinging coral	70	70
1537	20c. Lavender thin finger coral	70	70
1538	20c. Juvenile French grunt and brilliant sea fingers	70	70
MS1539	Two sheets, each 100×70 mm. (a) $2 Elkhorn coral. (b) Sea fan Set of 2 sheets	11·00	12·00

Nos. 1515/38 were printed together, *se-tenant*, with the backgrounds forming a composite design.

No. 1520 is inscribed "ELIPITICAL STAR CORAL" in error.

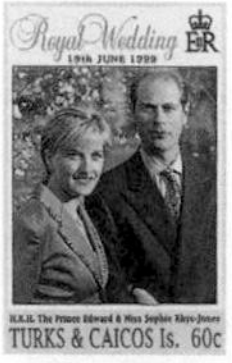

263 Prince Edward and Miss Sophie Rhys-Jones

1999. Royal Wedding. Multicoloured.

1540	60c. Type **263**	1·40	1·40
1541	60c. Prince Edward	1·40	1·40
1542	60c. Miss Sophie Rhys-Jones	1·40	1·40
1543	60c. Prince Edward and Miss Sophie Rhys-Jones (different)	1·40	1·40
MS1544	Two sheets, each 75×60 mm. (a) $2 Prince Edward and Miss Sophie Rhys Jones in front of bulid-ing. (b) $2 Prince Edward and Miss Sophie Rhys-Jones in front of tree Set of 2 sheets	7·00	8·00

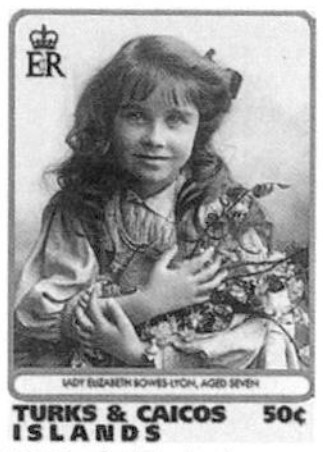

264 Lady Elizabeth Bowes-Lyon, 1907

1999. Queen Elizabeth the Queen Mother's 99th Birthday. Multicoloured.

1545	50c. Type **264**	1·25	1·25
1546	50c. Lady Elizabeth Bowes-Lyon, 1919	1·25	1·25
1547	50c. On wedding day, 1923	1·25	1·25
1548	50c. With Princesses Elizabeth and Margaret, 1936	1·25	1·25
1549	50c. King George VI and Queen Elizabeth during Second World War	1·25	1·25
1550	50c. Queen Elizabeth the Queen Mother, 1958	1·25	1·25
1551	50c. Wearing blue outfit, 1960	1·25	1·25
1552	50c. Wearing floral dress, 1970	1·25	1·25
1553	50c. With Princes Charles and William, 1983	1·25	1·25
1554	50c. Queen Mother, 1999	1·25	1·25

No. 1549 is inscribed "GEORGE IV" in error.

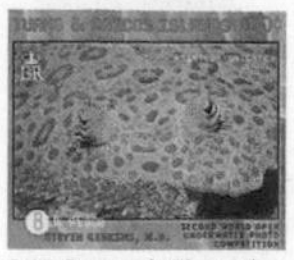

265 Peacock Flounder (M. Lynn)

1999. Winning Entries from Second World Open Underwater Photographic Competition. Multicoloured.

1555	10c. Type **265** (inscr "Painted Tunicates (S. Genkins)" in error)	40	40
1555b	10c. Painted Tunicates (S. Genkins)	40	40
1556	20c. Peacock flounder (S. Genkins) (inscr "Peacock Flounder (M. Lynn)" in error)	60	60
1556b	20c. Type **265**	60	60
1557	50c. Squat anemone shrimps (M. Boyer)	1·25	80
1558	60c. Juvenile drum (N. Army)	1·40	1·10
1559	80c. Batwing coral crab (R. Jarnutowski)	1·60	1·60
1560	$1 Moon jellyfish (R. Kaufman)	1·75	1·90
MS1561	Two sheets, each 85×68 mm. (a) $2 Christmas Tree Worms (B. Joubert) (48½×36 mm). (b) $2 Longhorn Nudibranch (Trina Lochlear) (48½×36 mm) Set of 2 sheets	10·00	11·00

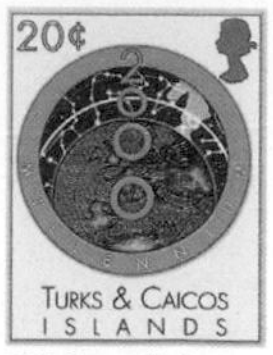

266 Constellations over Earth and "2000"

1999. New Millennium. Multicoloured.

1562	20c. Type **266**	80	40
1563	50c. Big Ben, London (30×47 mm)	1·50	1·25
1564	50c. Flamingo, Turks and Caicos Islands (30×47 mm)	1·50	1·25
1565	50c. Empire State Building, New York (30×47 mm)	1·50	1·25
1566	50c. Roman Coliseum, Rome (30×47 mm)	1·50	1·25
1567	50c. Dome of the Rock, Jerusalem (30×47 mm)	1·50	1·25
1568	50c. Eiffel Tower, Paris (30×47 mm)	1·50	1·25
1569	$1 As 20c.	2·00	2·25
MS1570	Two sheets, each 106×86 mm. (a) $2 Part of globe and Turks and Caicos Islands flag (30×47 mm). (b) $2 Part of globe and Turks and Caicos Islands coat of arms (30×47 mm). Set of 2 sheets	11·00	12·00

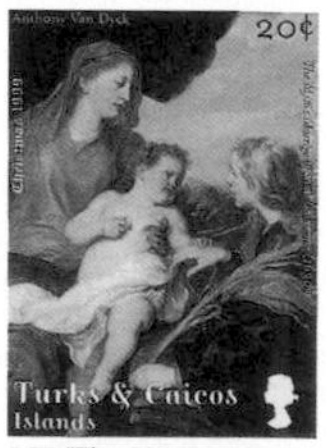

267 "The Mystic Marriage of Saint Catherine" (Anthony Van Dyck)

1999. Christmas. Multicoloured.

1571	20c. Type **267**	75	35
1572	50c. "Rest on the Flight into Egypt"	1·50	75
1573	$2 "Holy Family with Saints John and Elizabeth"	4·50	5·00
MS1574	102×122 mm. $2 "The Madonna of the Rosary"	6·00	6·50

No. 1571 is inscribed "Marrige" in error.

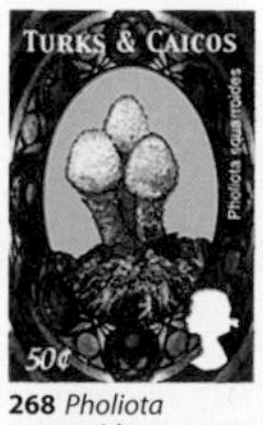

268 *Pholiota squarroides*

2000. Fungi. Multicoloured.

1575	50c. Type **268**	1·25	1·40
1576	50c. *Psilocybe squmosa*	1·25	1·40
1577	50c. *Spathularia velutipes*	1·25	1·40
1578	50c. *Russula*	1·25	1·40
1579	50c. *Clitocybe clavipes*	1·25	1·40
1580	50c. *Boletus frostii*	1·25	1·40
MS1581	Two sheets, each 108×71 mm. (a) $2 *Strobilurus conigenoides* (horiz). (b) $2 *Stereum ostrea* (horiz) Set of 2 sheets	8·00	8·50

Nos. 1575/80 were printed together, *se-tenant*, with the background forming a composite design.

2000. Olympic Games, Sydney. As T **396b** of St. Vincent. Multicoloured.

1582	50c. Johan Oxenstierna (Swedish swimmer), 1932	1·25	1·40
1583	50c. Javelin	1·25	1·40
1584	50c. Aztec Stadium, Mexico City, 1968, and Mexican flag	1·25	1·40
1585	50c. Ancient Greek long- distance running	1·25	1·40

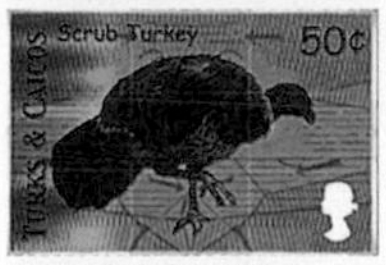

269 Bush Turkey ("Scrub Turkey")

2000. Caribbean Birds. Multicoloured.

1586	50c. Type **269**	1·60	1·60
1587	50c. Glaucous-winged gull ("Sickle Bill Gull")	1·60	1·60
1588	50c. Black-capped chickadee ("Chickadee")	1·60	1·60
1589	60c. Cattle egret ("Egret")	1·60	1·60
1590	60c. Royal tern ("Tern")	1·60	1·60
1591	60c. Osprey	1·60	1·60
1592	60c. Great blue heron	1·60	1·60
1593	60c. Brown pelican ("Pelican")	1·60	1·60
1594	60c. Bahama pintail	1·60	1·50
MS1595	Two sheets, each 95×82 mm. (a) $2 Greater flamingo ("Flamingo"). (b) $2 Hyacinth macaw ("Macaw") Set of 2 sheets	9·00	10·00

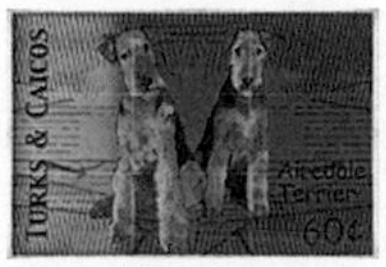

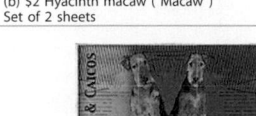

270 Airedale Terriers

2000. Cats and Dogs of the World. Multicoloured.

1596	60c. Type **270**	1·50	1·60
1597	60c. Beagle	1·50	1·60
1598	60c. Dalmatian	1·50	1·60
1599	60c. Chow chow	1·50	1·60
1600	60c. Chihuahua	1·50	1·60
1601	60c. Pug	1·50	1·60
1602	80c. Egyptian mau	1·60	1·75
1603	80c. Manx	1·60	1·75
1604	80c. Burmese	1·60	1·75
1605	80c. Korat	1·60	1·75
1606	80c. Maine coon	1·60	1·75
1607	80c. American shorthair	1·60	1·75
MS1608	Two sheets, each 95×82 mm. (a) $2 Collie. (b) Devon rex Set of 2 sheets	8·50	9·50

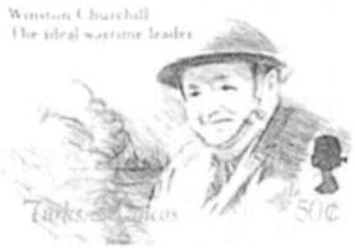
271 Sir Winston Churchill

2000. 60th Anniv of the Battle of Britain. Multicoloured (except No. MS1625a).

1609	50c. Type **271**	1·25	1·25
1610	50c. Barrage balloon	1·25	1·25
1611	50c. Heinkel He-III/Casa 2 IIIE (fighter)	1·25	1·25
1612	50c. Saying goodbye to young evacuee	1·25	1·25
1613	50c. Hawker Hurricane (fighter)	1·25	1·25
1614	50c. Dr. Jocelyn Peakins (clergyman) in Home Guard	1·10	1·25
1615	50c. R.A.F. squadron scramble	1·25	1·25
1616	50c. Members of Royal Observer Corps watching sky	1·25	1·25
1617	50c. James "Ginger" Lacey	1·25	1·25
1618	50c. Douglas Bader	1·25	1·25
1619	50c. Edgar "Cobber" Kain	1·25	1·25
1620	50c. Air Vice-Marshal Keith Park (commander, No. 11 Group)	1·25	1·25
1621	50c. James "Johnny" Johnson	1·25	1·25
1622	50c. Adolph "Sailor" Malan	1·25	1·25
1623	50c. Alan "Al" Deere	1·25	1·25
1624	50c. Air Vice-Marshal, Trafford Leigh-Mallory (commander, No. 12 Group)	1·25	1·25
MS1625	Two sheets. (a) 86×136 mm. $2 Child evacuees (pink, grey and black). (b) 118×85 mm. $2 Winston Churchill, Union Jack and pilots Set of 2 sheets	8·50	8·50

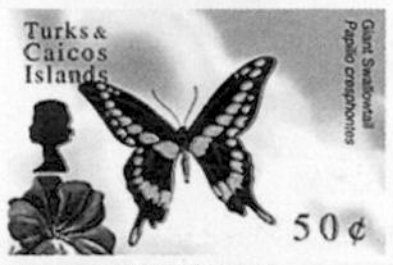

272 Giant Swallowtail

2000. Caribbean Butterflies. Multicoloured.

1626	50c. Type **272**	1·40	1·40
1627	50c. Common morpho	1·40	1·40
1628	50c. Tiger pierid	1·40	1·40
1629	50c. Banded king shoemaker	1·40	1·40
1630	50c. Figure-of-eight butterfly	1·40	1·40
1631	50c. Polydamas swallowtail	1·40	1·40
1632	50c. Clorinde	1·40	1·40
1633	50c. Blue night butterfly	1·40	1·40
1634	50c. Small lace-wing	1·40	1·40
1635	50c. Mosaic	1·40	1·40
1636	50c. Monarch	1·40	1·40
1637	50c. Grecian shoemaker	1·40	1·40
MS1638	Two sheets, each 68×98 mm. (a) $2 Orange-barred sulphur. (b) $2 White peacock Set of 2 sheets	8·50	8·75

Nos. 1626/31 and 1632/37 were each printed together, *se-tenant*, with the backgrounds forming composite designs.

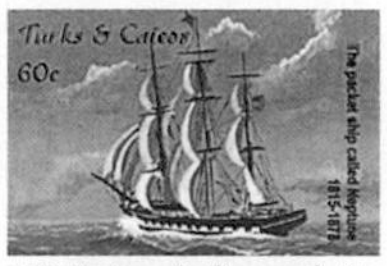

273 *Neptune* (sailing packet)

2001. Sailing Ships of the World. Multicoloured.

1639	60c. Type **273**	1·50	1·50
1640	60c. American clipper (vert)	1·50	1·50
1641	60c. U.S.C.G. *Eagle* (cadet barque)	1·50	1·50
1642	60c. *Gloria* (Colombian cadet ship)	1·50	1·50
1643	60c. Viking longship	1·50	1·50
1644	60c. *Henri Grace a Dieu* (English galleon)	1·50	1·50
1645	60c. *Golden Hind* (Drake)	1·50	1·50
1646	60c. H.M.S. *Endeavour* (Cook)	1·50	1·50
1647	60c. *Anglo-Norman* (British barque)	1·50	1·50
1648	60c. *Libertad* (Argentine full-rigged cadet ship)	1·50	1·50
1649	60c. Northern European cog	1·50	1·50
1650	60c. 16th-century carrack	1·50	1·50
1651	60c. *Mayflower* (Pilgrim Fathers)	1·50	1·50
1652	60c. *Queen Anne's Revenge* (Blackbeard)	1·50	1·50
1653	60c. *Holkar* (British barque)	1·50	1·50
1654	60c. *Amerigo Vespucci* (Italian cadet ship)	1·50	1·50
MS1655	Two sheets, each 48×67 mm. (a) $2 U.S.S. Constitution (frigate) (vert). (b) $2 Danmark (full-rigged Danish cadet ship) (vert) Set of 2 sheets	9·50	10·00

No 1642 is inscribed "Columbia" and 1648 "Liberated", both in error.

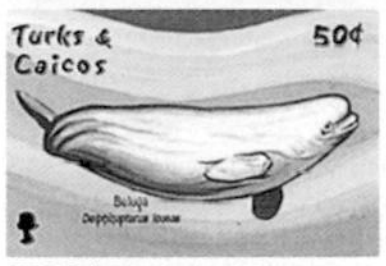

274 Beluga

2001. Whales and Dolphins. Multicoloured.

1656	50c. Type **274**	1·50	1·50
1657	50c. Dwarf sperm whale	1·50	1·50
1658	50c. Killer whale, swimming underwater	1·50	1·50
1659	50c. Shortfin pilot whale	1·50	1·50
1660	50c. Bowhead whale	1·50	1·50
1661	50c. Two killer whales	1·50	1·50
1662	50c. Pygmy sperm whale	1·50	1·50
1663	50c. Right whale	1·50	1·50
1664	50c. Sperm whale with calf	1·50	1·50
1665	50c. California grey whale	1·50	1·50
1666	50c. Narwhal	1·50	1·50
1667	50c. Killer whale leaping	1·50	1·50
1668	50c. Bryde's whale	1·50	1·50
1669	50c. Two belugas	1·50	1·50
1670	50c. Sperm whale	1·50	1·50
1671	50c. Three pilot whales	1·50	1·50
MS1672	Two sheets, each 92×69 mm. (a) $2 Humpback whale and calf. (b) $2 Cuviers beacked whale Set of 2 sheets	9·50	9·50

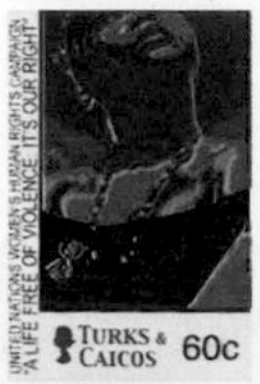

274a "Caribbean Woman II"

2001. United Nations Women's Human Rights Campaign. Multicoloured.

1673	60c. Type **274a**	1·40	1·40
1674	80c. Woman on beach	1·60	1·60

2001. Death Centenary of Queen Victoria. As T **425** of St. Vincent. Multicoloured.

1675	60c. Queen Victoria in old age, wearing white cap	1·40	1·40
1676	60c. As a girl in evening dress	1·40	1·40
1677	60c. Bare-headed	1·40	1·40
1678	60c. Wearing diadem	1·40	1·40
1679	60c. Holding fan	1·40	1·40
1680	60c. In Coronation robes (after Franz Winterhalter)	1·40	1·40
1681	60c. In carriage	1·40	1·40
1682	60c. As Empress of India	1·40	1·40
MS1683	Two sheets, each 82×113 mm. (a) $2 Queen Victoria carrying umbrella. (b) $2 Wearing white hat and veil Set of 2 sheets	7·50	8·00

2001. 75th Birthday of Queen Elizabeth II. As T **428** of St. Vincent. Multicoloured.

1684	60c. Queen Elizabeth wearing purple hat and coat	1·50	1·50
1685	60c. Wearing tiara and evening dress	1·50	1·50
1686	60c. In green hat and coat	1·50	1·50
1687	60c. Wearing diadem and ruby necklace	1·50	1·50
1688	60c. In red hat and coat	1·50	1·50
1689	60c. Wearing tiara and veil	1·50	1·50
MS1690	78×140 mm. $2 Queen Elizabeth robes of the Order of the Bath	4·25	4·50

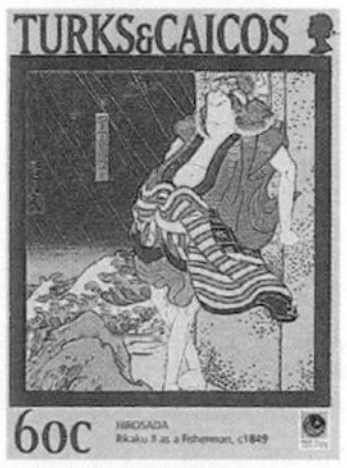

275 "Rikaku II as a Fisherman" (Hirosada)

2001. "Philanippon '01" International Stamp Exhibition, Tokyo. Japanese Art. Multicoloured.

1691	60c. Type **275**	1·10	1·25
1692	60c. "Autumn Moon in Mirror" (Suzuki Harunobu)	1·10	1·25
1693	60c. "Musical Party" (Hishikawa Morunobu)	1·10	1·25
1694	60c. "Kannon and Four Farmers" (H. Gatto)	1·10	1·25
1695	60c. "Rain in Fifth Month" (I. Kuninobu)	1·10	1·25
1696	60c. "The Lives of Women" (Utagawa Kuniyoshi)	1·10	1·25

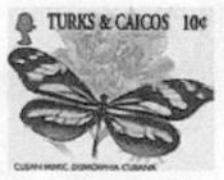

276 *Dismorphia cubana*

2001. Butterflies. Multicoloured.

1697	10c. Type **276**	25	20
1698	15c. *Parides gundalachianus* (vert)	35	20
1699	20c. *Graphium androcles*	40	30
1700	25c. Eastern black swallowtail	75	55
1701	35c. *Papilio velvois* (vert)	90	60
1702	45c. Schaus swallowtail (vert)	50	55
1703	50c. Pipevine swallowtail (vert)	60	65
1704	60c. *Euploea Mniszechii* (vert)	70	75
1705	80c. *Papilio caiguanabus* (vert)	90	95
1706	$1 *Graphium encelades* (vert)	1·20	1·30
1707	$1.25 *Calisto zangis*	1·40	1·50
1708	$1.40 Eastern tiger swallowtail	1·60	1·70
1709	$2 *Graphium milon* (vert)	2·30	2·40
1710	$5 Palamedes swallowtail	8·00	8·50
1711	$10 Zebra swallowtail	15·00	16·00

No. 1704 is inscribed "MNISZECKI", in error.

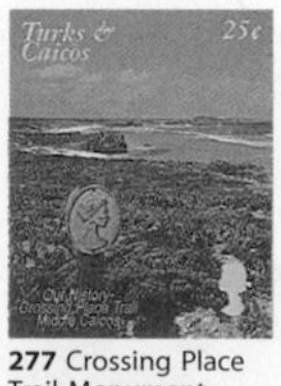

277 Crossing Place Trail Monument, Middle Caicos

2002. Golden Jubilee. Multicoloured (except Nos. 1718/19).

1712	25c. Type **277**	60	70
1713	25c. Wades Green Plantation, North Caicos	60	70
1714	25c. Underwater scenery, Grand Turk	60	70
1715	25c. St. Thomas Anglican Church, Grand Turk	60	70
1716	25c. Ripsaw Band, Grand Turk	60	70
1717	25c. Basket weaving	60	70
1718	60c. Princess Mary with cannon, Grand Turk, 1960 (black and gold)	1·25	1·40
1719	60c. Queen Elizabeth on South Caicos, 1966 (black, gold and blue)	1·25	1·40
1720	60c. Princess Alexandra on Providenciales, 1988	1·25	1·40
1721	60c. Duke of Edinburgh on Grand Turk, 1998	1·25	1·40
1722	60c. Prince Andrew and aquarium, Grand Turk, 2000	1·25	1·40
1723	80c. Salt gathering, Salt Cay	1·60	1·70
1724	80c. Space capsule, Grand Turk	1·60	1·70
1725	80c. Legislative Council Chamber, Grand Turk	1·60	1·70
1726	80c. Map of Turks and Caicos Islands	1·60	1·70
1727	80c. National Museum, Grand Turk	1·60	1·70

2002. 20th World Scout Jamboree, Thailand. As T **116** of St. Kitts. Multicoloured.

1728	80c. Scout wood-working	1·40	1·50
1729	80c. Rifle shooting	1·40	1·50
1730	80c. Swinging over river	1·40	1·50
1731	80c. Scouts in tent at night	1·40	1·50
MS1732	107×127 mm. $2 Disabled scouts playing football	3·25	3·50

2002. International Year of Mountains. As T **115** of St. Kitts, but vert. Multicoloured.

1733	80c. Devil's Peak, South Africa	1·40	1·50
1734	80c. Drakensburg Mountains, South Africa	1·40	1·50
1735	80c. Mont Blanc, France	1·40	1·50
1736	80c. Roan Mountain, Tennessee, U.S.A.	1·40	1·50
1737	80c. Mount Sefton, New Zealand	1·40	1·50
1738	80c. Mount Cook, New Zealand	1·40	1·50
MS1739	107×127 mm. $2 North-west Highlands, Scotland	3·25	3·50

2002. U.N. Year of Eco Tourism. As T **449** of St. Vincent. Multicoloured.

1740	60c. Humpback whale and lighthouse	1·60	1·60
1741	60c. Yacht	1·60	1·60
1742	60c. Two yachts racing	1·60	1·60
1743	60c. Queen angelfish	1·60	1·60
1744	60c. Manta and tropical fish	1·60	1·60
1745	60c. Turtle with boy wearing snorkle	1·60	1·60
MS1746	98×70 mm. $2 "Jojo" (Bottlenose Dolphin) (85×28 mm)	3·25	3·50

Nos. 1740/5 were printed together, *se-tenant*, forming a composite design.

2002. "United We Stand". Support for Victims of 11 September 2001 Terrorist Attacks. As T **114** of St. Kitts. Multicoloured.

1747	50c. U.S. and Turks and Caicos flags with Statue of Liberty's torch	1·00	1·10

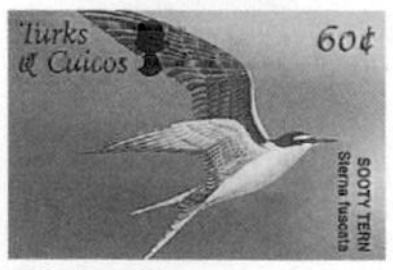

278 Sooty Tern

2002. Birds and Insects. Multicoloured.

1748	60c. Type **278**	1·40	1·40
1749	60c. Magnificent frigatebird	1·40	1·40
1750	60c. American white pelican	1·40	1·40
1751	60c. Northern shoveler	1·40	1·40
1752	60c. Northern oriole ("Baltimore Oriole")	1·40	1·40
1753	60c. Roseate spoonbill	1·40	1·40
1754	60c. Hawk moth	1·40	1·40
1755	60c. Burnet moth	1·40	1·40
1756	60c. Mammoth wasp	1·40	1·40
1757	60c. Branch-boring beetle	1·10	1·25
1758	60c. Flower mantid on leaf	1·40	1·40
1759	60c. Flower mantid on tree trunk	1·40	1·40
MS1760	Two sheets, each 95×93 mm. (a) $2 Greater flamingo (vert). (b) $2 Tiphiid wasp Set of 2 sheets	6·50	7·00

Nos. 1748/53 (birds) and 1754/9 (insects) were each printed together, *se-tenant*, with the backgrounds forming composite designs.

No. 1753 is inscribed "ROSTATE" in error.

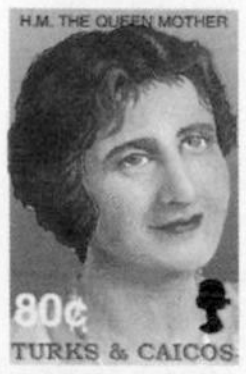

279 Duchess of York, 1923

2002. Queen Elizabeth the Queen Mother Commemoration. Multicoloured.

1761	80c. Type **279**	1·75	1·75
1762	80c. Queen Elizabeth the Queen Mother on Remembrance Day	1·75	1·75

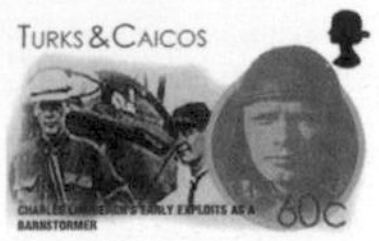

280 Charles Lindbergh as a Young Man

2002. 75th Anniv of First Solo Transatlantic Flight. Multicoloured.

1763	60c. Type **280**	1·50	1·50
1764	60c. Lindbergh with *Spirit of St. Louis*	1·50	1·50
1765	60c. *Spirit of St. Louis*	1·50	1·50
1766	60c. *Spirit of St. Louis* taking off from Roosevelt Field	1·50	1·50
1767	60c. *Spirit of St. Louis* above Atlantic	1·50	1·50
1768	60c. Lindbergh in Paris	1·50	1·50

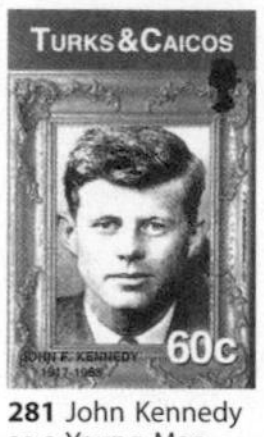

281 John Kennedy as a Young Man

2002. Pres John Kennedy Commemoration. Multicoloured, centre colours given.

1769	**281**	60c. brown	1·50	1·50
1770	-	60c. mauve	1·10	1·25
1771	-	60c. grey	1·50	1·50
1772	-	60c. blue	1·50	1·50
1773	-	60c. violet	1·50	1·50
1774	-	60c. bistre	1·50	1·50

DESIGNS: Nos. 1770/4, Showing different portraits.

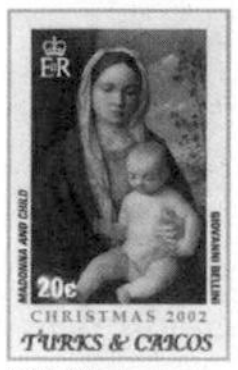

282 "Madonna and Child" (Giovanni Bellini)

2002. Christmas. Religious Paintings. Multicoloured.

1775	20c. Type **282**	50	25
1776	25c. "Adoration of the Magi" (Antonio Correggio) (horiz)	55	30
1777	60c. "Transfiguration of Christ" (Bellini)	1·40	80
1778	80c. "Polyptych of St. Vincent Ferrer," (Bellini)	1·60	1·25
1779	$1 "Miraculous Mass" (Simone Martini)	2·00	2·25
MS1780	90×125 $2 "Christ in Heaven with Four Saints" (Domenico Ghirlandaio) (horiz)	3·00	3·25

No. 1776 is inscribed "ADORATIO" in error.

2003. Japanese Art. As T **467** of St. Vincent. Multicoloured.

1781	25c. "Nagata no Taro Nagamune" (detail) (Utagawa Kuniyoshi)	50	30
1782	35c. "Ichikawa Danjuro VII" (Utagawa Kunisada)	70	40
1783	60c. "Nagata no Taro Nagamune" (different detail) (Utagawa Kuniyoshi)	1·25	1·00
1784	$1 "Nagata no Taro Nagamune" (different detail) (Utagawa Kuniyoshi)	1·90	2·25
MS1785	150×150 mm. 80c. Kabuki theatre actor (looking forwards); 80c. Actor with sword in mouth; 80c. Actor holding sword; 80c. Actor with red and yellow quilt	4·50	5·00
MS1786	85×115 mm. $2 "Two Women by a River" (Hashimoto Chikanobu)	3·25	3·50

Stamps from No. **MS**1785 all show details from "Scroll of Actors" by Toyohara Chikanobu et al.

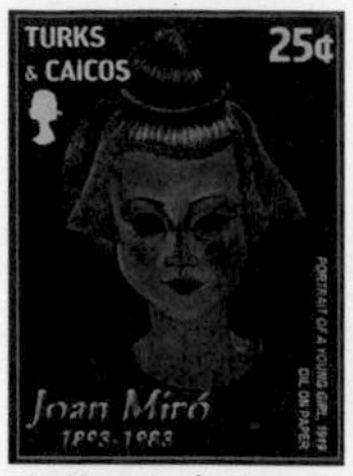

283 "Portrait of a Young Girl"

2003. 20th Death Anniv of Joan Miro (artist). Multicoloured.

1787	25c. Type **283**	50	30
1788	50c. "Table with Glove"	90	70
1789	60c. "Self-portrait, 1917"	1·00	90
1790	$1 "The Farmer's Wife"	1·60	2·00
MS1791	200×135 mm. 80c. "Portrait of Ramon Sunyer"; 80c. "Self Portrait, 1919"; 80c. "Portrait of a Spanish Dancer"; 80c. "Portrait of Joana Obrador"	4·50	5·00
MS1792	Two sheets. (a) 83×104 mm. $2 "Flowers and Butterfly". Imperf. (b) 104×83 mm. $2 "Still Life of the Coffee Grinder". Imperf Set of 2 sheets	6·00	7·00

2003. Rembrandt (artist) Commemoration. As T **466** of St. Vincent. Multicoloured.

1793	25c. "Portrait of a Young Man resting his Chin on his Hand"	50	30
1794	50c. "A Woman at an Open Door"	90	60
1795	$1 "The Return of the Prodigal Son"	1·75	2·25
1796	$1 "Portrait of an Elderly Man"	1·75	2·25
MS1797	185×182 mm. 60c. "Nicolaas van Bambeeck"; 60c. "Agatha Bas, Wife of Nicolaas van Bambeeck"; 60c. "Portrait of a Man holding his Hat"; 60c. "Saskia in a Red Hat" (all 35×47 mm)	3·25	3·50
MS1798	96×128 mm. $2 "Christ driving the Money-changers from the Temple"	3·25	3·50

2003. 30th Anniv of CARICOM. As T **122** of St. Kitts. Multicoloured.

1799	60c. Union Jack, flamingo and emblem	1·75	1·40

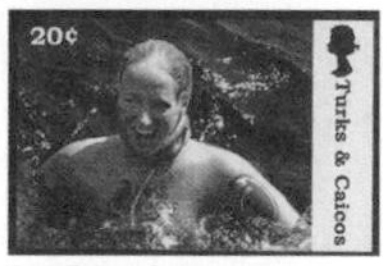

284 Tanya Streeter

2003. Tanya Streeter's Freediving World Record (2002). Multicoloured.

MS1800	98×179 mm. 20c. Type **284**; 20c. Tanya Streeter and practice dive; 20c. At seashore; 20c. With map of Turks and Caicos; 20c. Descending dive rope	1·60	1·75

2003. Centenary of Tour de France Cycle Race. As T **127** of St. Kitts. Multicoloured.

MS1801	160×100 mm. $1 Eddy Merckx (1974); $1 Bernard Thevenet (1975); $1 Lucien van Impe (1976); $1 Bernard Thevenet (1977)	6·50	7·00
MS1802	100×70 mm. $2 Bernard Hinault (1979)	3·25	3·50

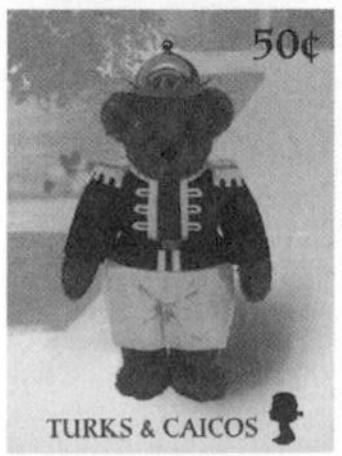

285 Teddy Bear in Military Uniform

2003. Centenary of the Teddy Bear. German Teddy Bears. Multicoloured.

MS1803	184×129 mm. 50c. Type **285**; 50c. Teddy bear wearing blue dress, apron and headscarf; 50c. Musician bear carrying violin; 50c. Marching teddy bear wearing sword	3·25	3·50
MS1804	70×96 mm. $2 Beer mug with teddy bear pattern	3·25	3·50

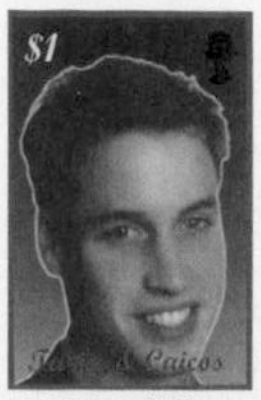

286 Prince William

2003. 21st Birthday of Prince William of Wales. Multicoloured.

MS1805	167×118 mm. $1 Type **286** (blue background); $1 Type **286** (pink background); $1 Prince William (head and shoulders)	5·00	5·50
MS1806	76×101 mm. $2 Prince William	3·25	3·50

2003. Centenary of Powered Flight. As T **126** of St. Kitts. Multicoloured.

MS1807	116×136 mm. 60c. Vought F4U Corsair; 60c. Messerschmitt Me 262; 60c. A6M; 60c. Hawker Hurricane	5·00	5·50
MS1808	101×76 mm. $2 Supermarine Spitfire Mk IX	3·50	3·75

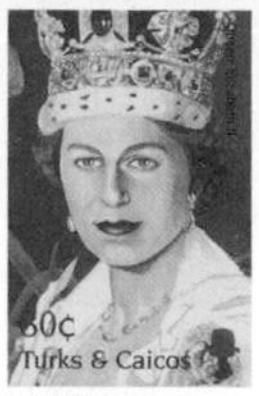

287 Queen Elizabeth II wearing Imperial State Crown

2003. 50th Anniv of Coronation. Multicoloured.

MS1809	147×91 mm. 80c. Type **287**; 80c. Wearing lilac dress; 80c. Wearing diadem	3·75	4·00
MS1810	Two sheets, each 76×101 mm. (a) $2 Queen in Garter robes. (b) $5 In profile	10·00	11·00

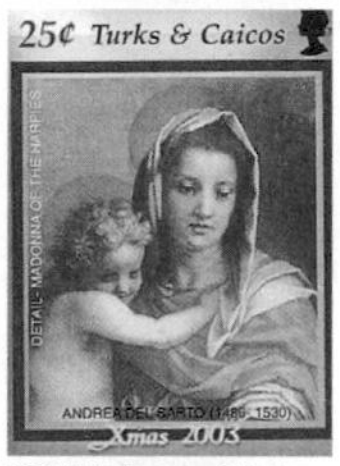

288 "Madonna of the Harpies" (detail, Andrea del Sarto)

2003. Christmas. Multicoloured.

1811	25c. Type **288**	50	30
1812	60c. "Madonna and Child with St. Giovannino" (detail, del Sarto)	1·00	75
1813	80c. "Madonna and Child with St. Giuseppe and St. Pietro Martre" (detail, del Sarto)	1·40	1·25
1814	$1 "Madonna and Child with the Angels" (detail, del Sarto)	1·60	2·00
MS1815	81×115 mm. $2 Montefeltro Altarpiece (Piero della Francesca)	3·25	3·50

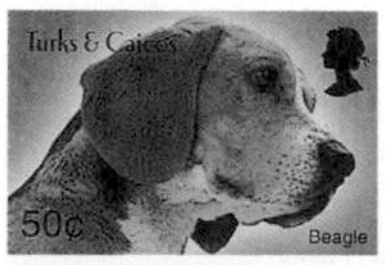

289 Beagle

2003. Dogs and Cats. Multicoloured.

1816	50c. Type **289**	1·10	1·10
1817	50c. Persian	1·10	1·10
1818	60c. Sabueso Espagnol (dog) (vert)	1·25	1·25
1819	60c. Cymric (cat)	1·25	1·25
1820	80c. Basset hound (vert)	1·60	1·60
1821	80c. Maine coon (cat) (vert)	1·60	1·60
1822	$1 Jack Russell terrier (vert)	1·75	1·90
1823	$1 Tiffany (cat)	1·75	1·90
MS1824	Two sheets. (a) 96×66 mm. $2 Dachshund. (b) 66×96 mm. $2 Kurile Island Bobtail (cat) (vert)	6·50	7·00

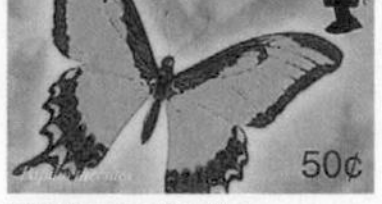

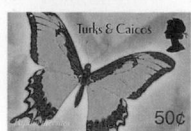

290 *Papilio thersites*

2003. Butterflies. Multicoloured.

1825	50c. Type **290**	1·10	75
1826	60c. *Papilio andraemon*	1·25	85
1827	80c. *Papilio pelaus*	1·60	1·40
1828	$1 *Consul hippona*	1·90	2·00
MS1829	96×66 mm. $2 *Papilio pelaus*	3·75	4·00

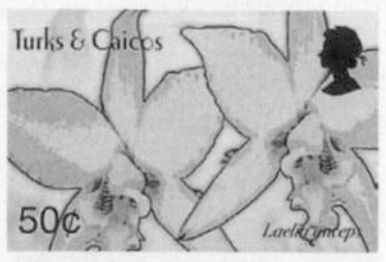

291 *Laelia anceps*

2003. Orchids. Multicoloured.

1830	50c. Type **291**	1·10	75
1831	60c. *Laelia briegeri*	1·25	85
1832	80c. *Laelia fidelensis*	1·60	1·40
1833	$1 *Laelia cinnabarina*	1·90	2·00
MS1834	96×66 mm. $2 *Laelia rubescens*	3·75	4·00

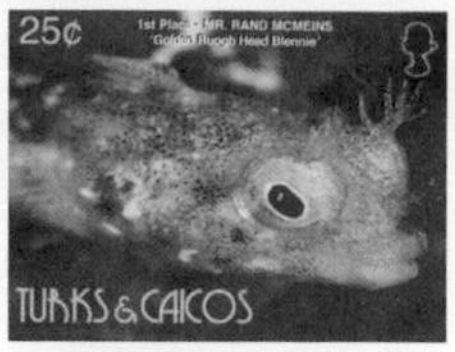

292 Golden Rough Head Blennie (Rand McMeins)

2006. First Annual (2005) Turks and Caicos Underwater Photography Competition Entries. Designs showing entries in photography competition. Multicoloured.

1835	25c. Type **292**	55	55
1836	50c. Octopus at night (Marc van Driessche)	1·10	1·00
1837	60c. Sea turtle (Mike Nebel)	1·20	1·20
1838	80c. Juvenile octopus (Amber Blecker)	1·60	1·60
1839	$1 School of horse eye jacks (Amber Blecker)	2·00	2·00
MS1840	261×102 mm. Nos. 1835/9	6·50	6·50
MS1841	120×120 mm. $2 Coral reef (Keith Caplan) (vert)	4·00	4·00

Stamps from **MS**1840 have narrow blue borders.

No. 1835 is wrongly inscribed "Ruogh". The 25c. stamp from **MS**1840 is correctly spelled "Rough".

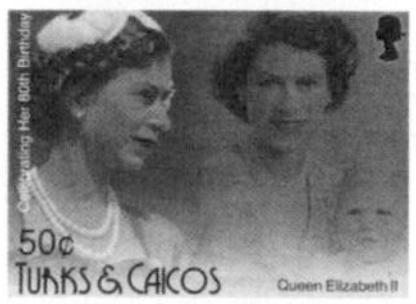

293 Young Queen Elizabeth II and Queen with Young Princess Anne

2006. 80th Birthday of Queen Elizabeth II. Multicoloured.

MS1842	152×164 mm. 50c. Type **293**; 60c. Queen in recent years wearing white and wearing tiara; 80c. Queen in recent years wearing tiara and young Queen Elizabeth wearing white jacket and hat; $1 Painting of Princess Elizabeth in white dress and young Queen Elizabeth	5·75	5·75
MS1843	120×120 mm. $6 Young Queen Elizabeth II wearing diadem (vert)	12·00	12·00

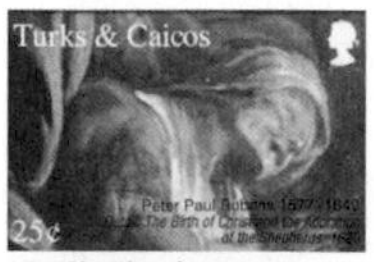

294 Shepherd

2006. Christmas. Paintings by Peter Paul Rubens. Multicoloured.

1844	25c. Type **294**	55	55
1845	60c. Baby Jesus	1·20	1·20
1846	80c. Two shepherds	1·60	1·60
1847	$1 Virgin Mary	2·00	2·00
MS1848	100×150 mm. As Nos. 1844/7	5·25	5·25
MS1849	70×100 mm. $6 *Our Lady, the Christ Child and Saints* (detail) (vert)	12·00	12·00

Nos. 1844/7 show details from *The Birth of Christ and the Adoration of the Shepherds*, and the margin of **MS**1849 shows the complete painting.

Nos. 1844/7 are inscribed with the title of the painting. Stamps from **MS**1849 omit this inscription.

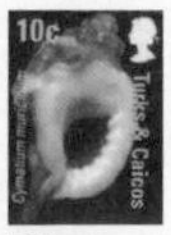

295 *Cymatium muricinum*

2007. Shells. Multicoloured.

1850	10c. Type **295**	20	20
1851	15c. *Tellina radiate*	30	30
1852	20c. *Tonna maculosa*	40	40

1853	25c. *Leucozonia nassa*	50	50
1854	35c. *Trachycardium magnum*	70	70
1855	45c. *Papyridea soleniformis*	95	95
1856	50c. *Epitonium lamellosum*	1·00	1·00
1857	60c. *Astraea brevispina*	1·20	1·20
1858	80c. *Bulla striata*	1·60	1·60
1859	$1 *Murex margaritensis*	2·00	2·00
1860	$1.25 *Chama macerophylla*	2·50	2·50
1861	$1.40 *Vasum capitellum*	2·75	2·75
1862	$2 *Coralliophila abbreviate*	4·00	4·00
1863	$5 *Trachycardium isocardia*	10·00	10·00
1864	$10 *Oliva reticularis*	20·00	20·00

2007. Christmas. As T **460** of Sierra Leone. Multicoloured.

1865	25c. *The Virgin and Child* (Carlo Maratta) (*vert*)	50	50
1866	60c. *The Adoration of the Magi* (detail) (Vincent Malo)	1·20	1·20
1867	80c. *The Annunciation* (detail) (Robert Campin)	1·60	1·60
1868	$1 *The Adoration of the Magi* (detail) Giovanni di Paolo)	2·00	2·00
MS1869	70×100 mm. $6 *The Adoration of the Magi* (Quentin Massys)	12·00	12·00

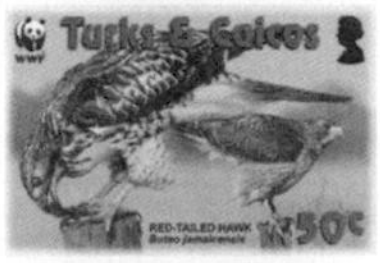

296 Red-tailed Hawks

2007. Endangered Species. Red-tailed Hawk (*Buteo jamaicensis*). Multicoloured.

1870	50c. Type **296**	1·00	1·00
1871	50c. Adult at nest feeding young	1·00	1·00
1872	50c. Perched at edge of cliff, wings outstretched	1·00	1·00
1873	50c. Close-up of head	1·00	1·00
MS1874	115×168 mm. Nos. 1870/3, each ×2	8·00	8·00

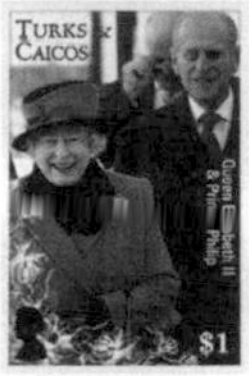

297 Queen Elizabeth II and Prince Philip

2007. Diamond Wedding of Queen Elizabeth II and Prince Philip. Multicoloured.

1875	$1 Type **297** (purple inscr)	2·00	2·00
1876	$1 Queen Elizabeth II (purple inscr)	2·00	2·00
1877	$1 As No. 1876 (turquoise inscr)	2·00	2·00
1878	$1 As Type **297** (turquoise inscr)	2·00	2·00
1879	$1 As Type **297** (black inscr)	2·00	2·00
1880	$1 As No. 1876 (black inscr)	2·00	2·00
MS1881	100×70 mm. $6 Queen Elizabeth II and Prince Philip on balcony (*horiz*)	12·00	12·00

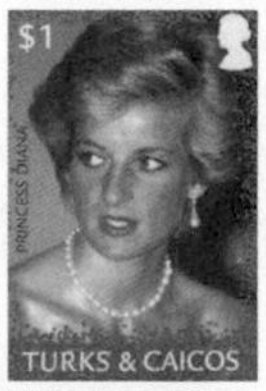

298 Princess Diana

2007. Tenth Death Anniv of Princess Diana. Multicoloured.

1882	$1 Type **298**	2·00	2·00
1883	$1 Seen in profile, wearing red dress	2·00	2·00
1884	$1 Seen in profile, wearing tiara	2·00	2·00
1885	$1 Wearing diamond and pearl drop earrings	2·00	2·00
MS1886	101×70 mm. $6 Wearing fawn hat and green jacket	12·00	12·00

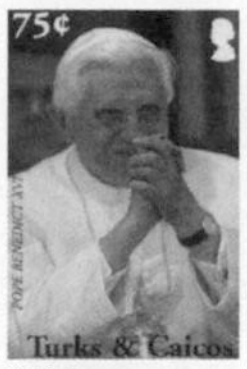

299 Pope Benedict XVI

2008. 80th Birthday of Pope Benedict XVI (2007).

1887	**299**	75c. multicoloured	1·40	1·40

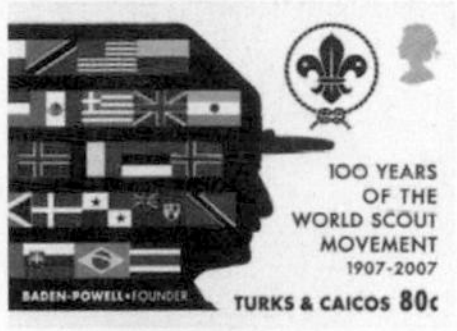

300 Silhouette of Lord Baden-Powell and National Flags

2008. Centenary of World Scouting and 21st World Scout Jamboree, England (2007). Multicoloured.

1888	80c. Type **300**	1·50	1·50
1889	80c. Badge silhouette and jamboree emblems (peace dove emblem at bottom right)	1·50	1·50
1890	80c. Badge silhouette and jamboree emblems (red and white chequered emblem at top right)	1·50	1·50
1891	80c. Lord Baden-Powell silhouette and flags (white cross on red flag of Switzerland at bottom left)	1·50	1·50
1892	80c. Lord Baden-Powell silhouette and flags (Philippines at top right, blue and red with sun in white triangle at left)	1·50	1·50
1893	80c. Badge silhouette and jamboree emblems (blue, white and red on green maple leaf badge at top right)	1·50	1·50
MS1894	110×80 mm. $6 Lord Baden-Powell (vert)	11·00	11·00

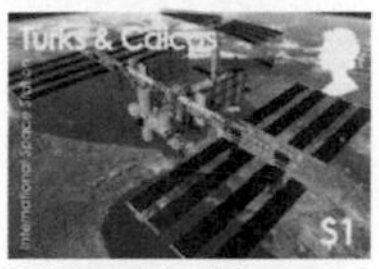

301 International Space Station

2008. 50 Years of Space Exploration and Satellites. International Space Station. Multicoloured.

1895	$1 Type **301**	1·90	1·90
1896	$1 Seen from above, over dry land	1·90	1·90
1897	$1 Seen from above, over land and ocean	1·90	1·90
1898	$1 Side view of International Space Station	1·90	1·90
MS1899	100×70 mm. $6 International Space Station	11·00	11·00

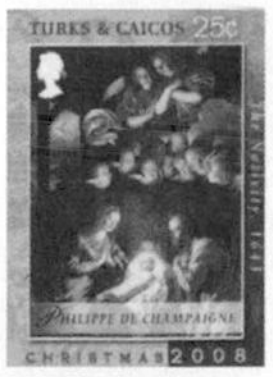

302 *The Nativity* (Phillippe de Champaigne), 1643

2008. Christmas. Designs showing paintings. Multicoloured.

1900	25c. Type **302**	45	45
1901	60c. *Mystic Nativity* (Sandro Botticelli), c. 1500	1·10	1·10
1902	80c. *The Virgin in a Rose Arbor* (Stefan Lochner), c. 1440	1·50	1·50
1903	$1 *The Adoration of the Shepherds* (Francisco Zurbáran), 1638–9	1·90	1·90
MS1904	70×100 mm. $6 *The Virgin with Angels* (William Bougereau)	11·00	11·00

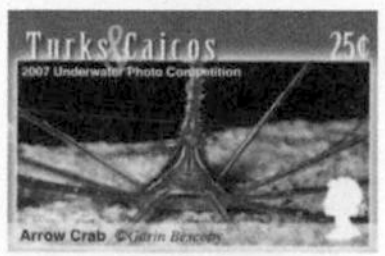

303 Arrow Crab (Garin Bescoby)

2008. Third Annual (2007) Turks and Caicos Underwater Photography Competition. Designs showing entries. Multicoloured.

1905	25c. Type **303**	45	45
1906	60c. Trumpet fish (Karin Nargis) (3rd)	1·10	1·10
1907	80c. Sting ray (Barbara Shively) (2nd)	1·50	1·50
1908	$1 Giant anemone (Roddy Mcleod) (1st)	1·90	1·90
MS1909	130×100 mm. Nos. 1905/8	4·75	4·75
MS1910	100×70 mm. $6 Red banded lobster (Jayne Baker)	11·00	11·00

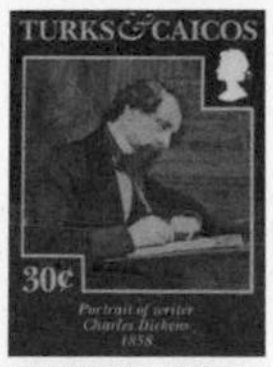

304 Charles Dickens, 1858

2012. Birth Bicentenary of Charles Dickens (writer). Multicoloured.

MS1911	200×100 mm. 30c.×6 Type **304**; Illustration from *A Tale of Two Cities*; Charles Dickens, c. 1860; Statue of Charles Dickens in Philadelphia; Illustration from *Oliver Twist*; Illustration from *A Christmas Carol*	3·00	3·00
MS1912	100×70 mm. $5 Portrait of Charles Dickens in his study (51×38 mm)	9·00	9·00

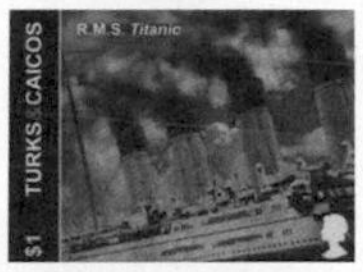

305 *Titanic*

2012. Centenary of Sinking of the *Titanic*. Multicoloured.

MS1913	100×140 mm. $1×8 Type **305**; Bow of *Titanic*; Smokestacks of *Titanic* and crest of wave; Crest of wave and top of iceberg; *Titanic* (midsection with cabins); Iceberg; Survivors in lifeboat; *Titanic* sinking and survivors in lifeboat	13·00	13·00
MS1914	101×70 mm. $5 *Titanic*	9·00	9·00
MS1915	101×70 mm. $5 *Titanic* sinking and survivors in lifeboat	9·00	9·00

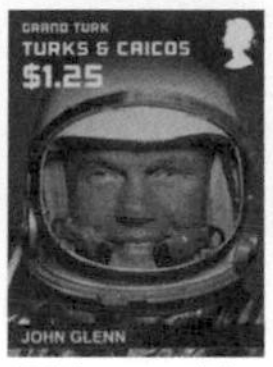

306 Astronaut John Glenn

2012. 50th Anniv of John Glenn's Orbit in *Friendship* 7. Multicoloured.

MS1916	150×110 mm. $1.25×4 Type **306**;On launch pad; Blast off ; Splashdown	9·00	9·00
MS1917	100×70 mm. $6 Astronaut John Glenn and US flags	11·00	11·00

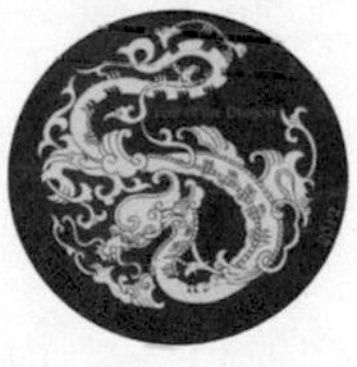

307 Dragon

2012. Chinese New Year. Year of the Dragon

MS1918	130×70 mm. **307** $3 multi-coloured	5·00	5·00

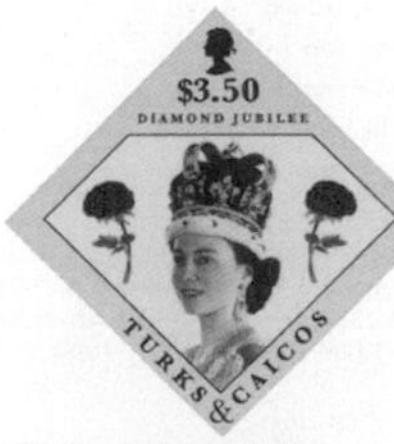

308 Queen Elizabeth II

2012. Diamond Jubilee. Multicoloured.

MS1919	125×130 mm. $3.50 Type **308**×4	20·00	20·00
MS1920	81×80 mm. $9 Queen Elizabeth II wearing tiara	14·00	14·00

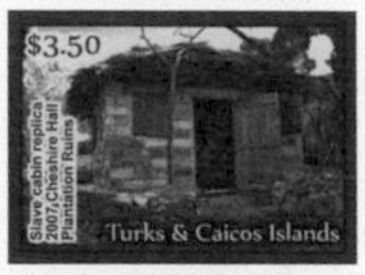

309 Slave Cabin Replica, 2007, Cheshire Hall Plantation Ruins

2013. 20th Anniv of Turks and Caicos National Trust. Sheet 65×65 mm

MS1921	**309**	$3.50 multicoloured	5·50	5·50

Pt. 8

TUSCANY

Formerly an independent duchy in C. Italy, now part of Italy.

1851. 60 quattrini = 20 soldi = 12 crazie = 1 Tuscan lira.
1859. 1 Tuscan lira = 1 Italian lira.

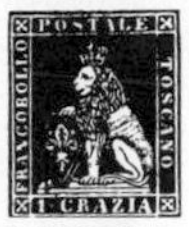

1 Arms of Tuscany

1851. Imperf.

1	1	1q. black on blue	£17000	£19000
2	1	1q. black on grey	£13000	£1800
24	1	1q. black	£1800	£1100
4	1	1s. orange on blue	£20000	£2250
5	1	1s. orange on grey	£17000	£2000
25	1	1s. buff	£54000	£6500
6	1	2s. red on blue	£54000	£8000
7	1	1c. red on blue	£9500	£325
9	1	1c. red on grey	£9000	£140
26	1	1c. red	£12000	£700
10	1	2c. blue on blue	£8500	£325
11	1	2c. blue on grey	£5000	£160
28	1	2c. blue	£4000	£160
13	1	4c. green on blue	£12000	£325
14	1	4c. green on grey	£9000	£170
30	1	4c. green	£9000	£190
16	1	6c. blue on blue	£12000	£400
17	1	6c. blue on grey	£9500	£300
31	1	6c. blue	£12000	£300
20	1	9c. purple on blue	£22000	£650
22	1	9c. purple on grey	£22000	£275
33	1	9c. brown	£51000	£6000
23	1	60c. red on blue	£97000	£27000

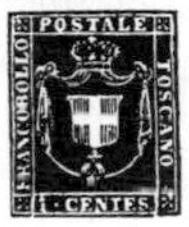

5 Arms of Tuscany

1860. Imperf.

36	5	1c. purple	£3500	£1000
40	5	5c. green	£13000	£275
43	5	10c. brown	£3750	65·00
45	5	20c. blue	£12000	£225
48	5	40c. red	£18000	£350
50	5	80c. red	£33000	£1600
51	5	3l. buff	£225000	£110000

NEWSPAPER STAMP TAX

N3

1854

N1	**N3**	2s. black	£130

Pt. 10

TUVA

A province lying between the Sajan and Tannu Ola range. Formerly known as North Mongolia and Tannu, Tuva was incorporated into the U.S.S.R. on 11 October 1944.

1926. 100 kopeks = 1 rouble.
1934. 100 kopeks = 1 tugrik.
1936. 100 kopeks = 1 aksha.

PRICES. The prices quoted in the used column are for stamps cancelled to order where these occur. Postally used copies are worth considerably more.

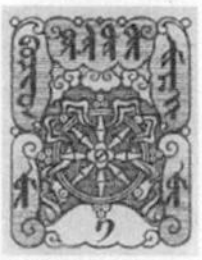

1 Wheel of Eternity

1926

1	1	1k. red	2·20	2·00
2	1	2k. blue	2·20	2·00
3	1	5k. orange	2·20	2·00
4	1	8k. green	2·50	2·20

5	1	10k. violet	2·50	2·20
6	1	30k. brown	3·00	2·20
7	1	50k. black	3·00	2·20
8	1	1r. turquoise	7·50	4·00
9	1	3r. red	10·50	7·50
10	1	5r. blue	17·00	10·50

The rouble values are larger, 22½×30 mm.

1927. Surch **TOUVA POSTAGE** and value.

11		8k. on 50k. black	28·00	14·00
12		14k. on 1r. turquoise	29·00	14·00
13		18k. on 3r. red	30·00	15·00
14		28k. on 5r. blue	32·00	16·00

4 Tuvan Woman

5 Map of Tuva

6 Mongolian Sheep and Tents

7 Fording a River

8 Reindeer

1927

15	4	1k. brown, red and black	1·00	60
16	-	2k. brown, green and violet	1·60	80
17	-	3k. green, yellow and black	2·30	90
18	-	4k. brown and blue	1·00	70
19	-	5k. blue, black and orange	1·20	90
20	5	8k. sepia, blue and red	1·20	90
21	-	10k. red, black and green	7·50	1·30
22	-	14k. orange and blue	14·00	5·50
23	6	18k. brown and blue	14·00	5·75
24	-	28k. sepia and green	10·50	2·75
25	7	40k. green and red	7·00	3·50
26	-	50k. brown, black and green	5·25	3·00
27	-	70k. bistre and red	8·75	4·75
28	8	1r. violet and brown	15·00	9·25

DESIGNS—As Type **4**: 2k. Red deer; 3k. Common goral; 4k. Mongolian tent; 5k. Tuvan man. As Type **5**: 10k. Archers; 14k. Camel caravan. As Type **6**: 28k. Landscape. As Type **7**: 50k. Girl carpet-weaver; 70k. Horseman.

1932. Stamps of 1927 surch **TbBA POSTA** and value (10k. optd only).

29	7	1k. on 40k. green and red	11·50	12·50
30	-	2k. on 50k. brown, black and green	12·50	12·50
31	-	3k. on 70k. bistre and red	12·50	12·50
32	5	5k. on 8k. sepia, blue and red	15·00	12·50
33	-	10k. red, black and green	17·00	14·00
34	-	15k. on 14k. orange and blue	20·00	20·00

1932. Stamps of 1927 surch.

35	5	10k. on 8k. brown	£250	£130
36	-	15k. on 14k. orange and blue	£425	£250
37	6	35k. on 18k. brown and blue	£180	£130
38	-	35k. on 28k. sepia and green	£180	£130

1933. Fiscal stamps (20×39 mm) surch **Posta** and value.
(a) Numerals 6¾ mm tall.

39		15k. on 6k. yellow	£400	£200
40		35k. on 15k. brown	£1100	£5500

(b) Numerals 5¼ mm tall.

41		15k. on 6k. yellow	£500	£275
42		35k. on 15k. brown	£2000	£1000

12 Mounted Hunter

13 Interior of Tent

14 Yak

1934. Perf or imperf.

43A	12	1k. orange	1·70	1·20
44A	-	2k. green	1·70	1·30
45A	13	3k. red	1·70	1·30
46A	-	4k. purple	4·25	2·50
47A	14	5k. blue	4·25	2·50
48A	-	10k. brown	4·25	2·50
49A	-	15k. lake	4·25	2·50
50A	-	20k. black	5·25	3·50

DESIGNS—As Type **12**: 2k. Hunter. As Type **13**: 4k. Tractor. As Type **14**: 10k. Camel caravan; 15k. Lassoing reindeer; 20k. Corsac fox-hunting.

The 2t. also comes larger, 61×31 mm.

15 Kalinin K-5 over Yaks

16 Western Capercaillie

1934. Air.

51	15	1k. red	1·70	1·30
52	-	5k. green	1·70	1·30
53	16	10k. brown	7·00	4·00
54	-	15k. red	3·50	1·30
55	-	25k. purple	3·50	1·30
56	15	50k. green	3·50	1·30
57	-	75k. red	3·50	1·30
58	15	1t. blue	4·50	1·30
59a	-	2t. blue (55×28 mm)	25·00	32·00

DESIGNS—As Type **15**: 5, 15k. Tupolev ANT-25 over camels. As Type **16**: 25k. Junkers F-13 with skis over argali; 75k. Junkers F-13 over ox-cart; 2t. Tupolev ANT-9 over roe deer.

1935. No. 49 surch.

60		20k. on 15k. lake	£225	£425

18 Map of Tuva

19 Rocky Outcrop

1935. Landscapes.

61	18	1k. orange	1·60	1·30
62	-	3k. green	1·60	1·30
63	-	5k. red	2·00	1·30
64	-	10k. violet	2·00	1·30
65	19	15k. green	2·20	1·60
66	-	25k. blue	2·50	1·60
67	-	50k. sepia	4·00	2·00

DESIGNS—As Type **18**: 3, 5, 10k. Views of River Yenisei. As Type **19**: 25k. Bei-kem rapids; 50k. Mounted hunter.

See also No. 115.

20 Eurasian Badger

21 Corsac Fox

22 Elk

1935. Animals.

68	20	1k. orange	2·00	1·50
69	-	3k. green	2·00	1·50
70	-	5k. mauve	2·00	1·50
71	21	10k. red	2·00	1·50
72	-	25k. red	3·25	1·70
73	-	50k. blue	3·25	1·70
74	22	1t. violet	3·25	1·70
75	-	2t. blue	4·50	1·70
76	-	3t. brown	5·25	2·00
77	-	5t. blue	6·25	2·20

DESIGNS—As Type **20**—VERT: 3k. Eurasian red squirrel. HORIZ: 5k. Sable. As Type **21**: 25k. European otter; 50k. Lynx. LARGER (61×31 mm): 2t. Yak; 3k. Bactrian camel. As Type **22**: 5t. Brown bear.

23 Arms of Republic

24 Wrestlers

25 Herdsman

26 Sports Meeting   **27** Partisans

28 Yak Transport

29 Horseman and Airship

30 Seaplane over Waves

1936. 15th Anniv of Independence. (a) Postage.

78A	23	1k. green	2·20	90
79A	-	2k. sepia	2·20	90
80B	-	3k. blue	3·00	1·00
81B	24	4k. red	3·50	1·00
82A	-	5k. purple	5·50	90
83A	24	6k. green	5·25	90
84A	-	8k. purple	5·25	90
85B	-	10k. red	5·75	90
86A	-	12k. agate	7·00	1·30
87B	-	15k. green	8·75	90
88A	-	20k. blue	8·75	1·40
89B	25	25k. red	8·75	90
90A	-	30k. purple	25·00	1·70
91B	25	35k. red	8·75	90
92B	-	40k. sepia	8·75	90
93B	-	50k. blue	8·75	90
94B	26	70k. plum	10·50	1·70
95B	-	80k. green	9·75	1·70
96B	27	1a. red	9·75	2·00
97B	27	2a. red	9·75	2·00
98B	-	3a. blue	10·50	2·30
99A	-	5a. agate	10·50	2·30

DESIGNS—As Type **23**: 2k. President Gyrmittazi; 3k. Camel and driver. As Type **24**: 5, 8k. Archers; 10, 15k. Fishermen; 12, 20k. Brown bear hunt. As Type **25**: 30k. Bactrian camel and steam goods train; 40, 50k. Horse-racing. As Type **26**: 8k., 5a. 1921 war scene; 3a. Confiscation of cattle.
See also Nos. 116 and 118/19.

(b) Air.

100	28	5k. blue and flesh	3·50	1·30
101	-	10k. purple and brown	5·25	1·40
102	28	15k. agate and grey	5·25	1·40
103	29	25k. purple and cream	7·00	1·70
104	-	50k. red and cream	7·00	2·00
105	29	75k. green and yellow	7·00	2·00
106	30	1a. green and turquoise	8·00	3·25
107	30	2a. red and cream	8·75	3·50
108	30	3a. sepia and flesh	9·25	3·50

DESIGNS—As Type **28**: 10k. Horse-drawn reaper. As Type **29**: 50k. Feast of the women.
See also No. 117.

1938. Various stamps surch with large numerals and old values obliterated.

109		5k. on 2a. red (No. 97)	£425
110		5k. on 2a. red and cream (No. 107)	£375
111		10k. on 1t. blue (No. 58)	£325
112		20k. on 5k. sepia (No. 67)	£325
113		30k. on 2a. red and cream (No. 107)	£325
114		30k. on 3a. sepia and flesh (No. 108)	£325

See also Nos. 120/1.

1938. Previous types with designs modified and colours changed.

115	5k. green (No. 70)	£170
116	10k. blue (No. 85)	£170
117	15k. brown (No. 102)	£170
118	20k. red (No. 88)	£400
119	30k. purple (as No. 95)	£170

In Nos. 116/19 the dates have been removed and in No. 117 "AIR MAIL" also.

1939. Nos. 58 and 67 surch with small thick numerals and old values obliterated.

120	1k. on 1t. blue	£300
121	20k. on 50k. sepia	£250

See also Nos. 122/3.

1940. Various stamps surch.

122	10k. on 1t. blue (No. 58)	£130
123	20k. on 50k. sepia (No. 67)	£130
124	20k. on 50k. blue (No. 73)	£400
125	20k. on 50k. blue (No. 93)	£400
126	20k. on 50k. red and cream (No. 104)	£100
127	20k. on 75k. green and yellow (No. 105)	£110
128	20k. on 80k. green (No. 95)	£600

1942. Nos. 98/9 surch.

129	25k. on 3a. blue	£1600
130	25k. on 5a. agate	

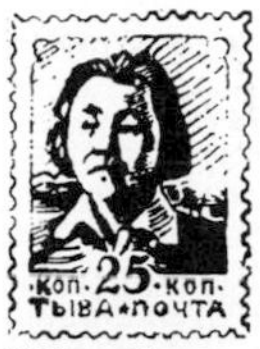

34 Tuvan Woman

1942. 21st Anniv of Independence. Imperf.

131	**34**	25k. blue	£1000	£200
132	-	25k. blue	£1000	£200
133	-	25k. blue	£1000	£200

DESIGNS: No. 132 Agricultural Exhibition building; No. 133 Government building.

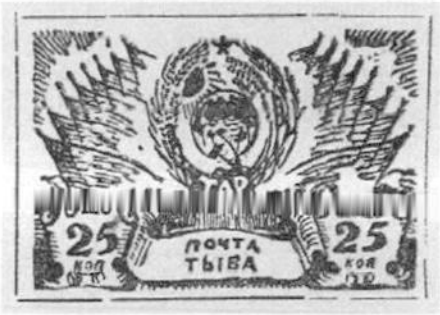

35 Coat of Arms

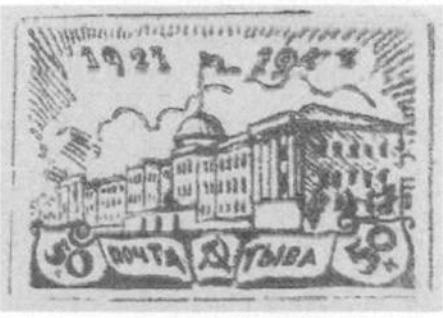

36 Government Building

1943. 22nd Anniv of Independence. With or without gum.

134	**35**	25k. blue	£120
135	**35**	25k. black	£130
136	**35**	25k. green	£150
137	**36**	50k. green	£150

Pt. 1

TUVALU

Formerly known as Ellice Islands and sharing a joint administration with the Gilbert group. On 1 January 1976 the two island groups separated and the Ellice Islands were renamed Tuvalu.

100 cents = $1 Australian.

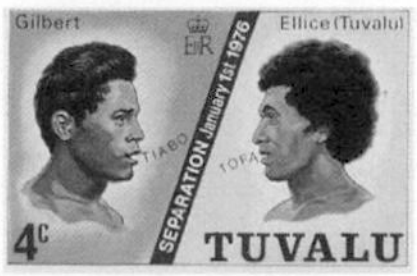

1 Tuvaluan and Gilbertese

1976. Separation. Multicoloured.

1	4c. Type **1**	35	80
2	10c. Map of the islands (vert)	50	1·00
3	35c. Gilbert and Ellice canoes	70	1·50

1976. Nos. 173/87 of Gilbert and Ellice Islands optd **TUVALU.**

14	1c. Cutting toddy	30	30
20	2c. Lagoon fishing	30	40
21	3c. Cleaning pandanus leaves	30	70
22	4c. Casting nets	30	45
5	5c. Gilbertese canoe	50	1·00
15	6c. De-husking coconuts	30	30
6	8c. Weaving pandanus fronds	45	60
7	10c. Weaving a basket	30	65
16	15c. Tiger shark	1·00	40
23	20c. Beating a rolled pandanus leaf	30	55
24	25c. Loading copra	30	55
25	35c. Fishing at night	70	60
17	50c. Local handicrafts	30	50
18	$1 Weaving coconut screen	35	60
19	$2 Coat of arms	50	60

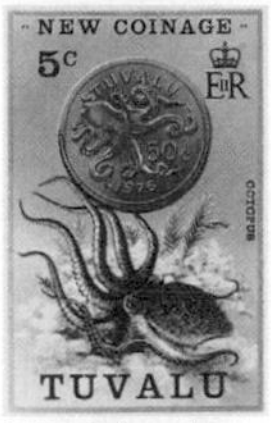

3 50c. Coin and Octopus

1976. New Coinage. Multicoloured.

26	5c. Type **3**	25	25
27	10c. Red-eyed crab	35	30
28	15c. Flying fish	45	40
29	35c. Green turtle	60	50

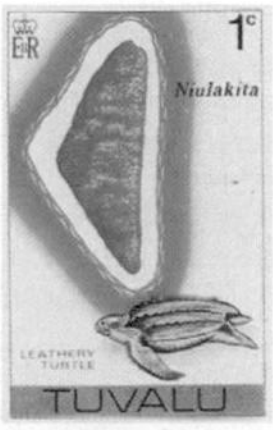

4 Niulakita and Seven-ridged Leathery Turtle

1976. Multicoloured

58	1c. Type **4**	50	15
59	2c. Nukulaelae and sleeping mat	20	25
[illegible]	[illegible]	30	15
61	5c. Nanumanga and grass skirt	25	15
62	6c. Nukufetau and coconut crab	20	35
63	8c. Funafuti and banana tree	20	25
64	10c. Map of Tuvalu	20	20
37	15c. Niutao and flying fish	75	20
38	20c. Vaitupu and maneapa (meeting hall)	35	40
66	25c. Nanumea and fish-hook	80	20
67	30c. Fatele (local dancing)	30	20
40	35c. Te Ano (game)	35	20
68	40c. Screw pine	30	15
41	50c. Canoe pole fishing	35	20
42	$1 Reef fishing by flare	35	20
43	$2 Living house	35	20
69	$5 M.V. "Nivanga"	1·00	2·25

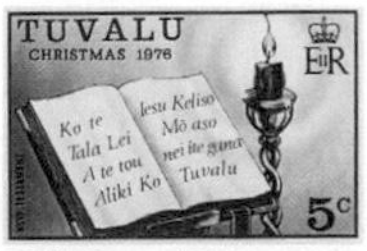

5 Title Page of New Testament

1976. Christmas. Multicoloured.

45	5c. Type **5**	20	25
46	20c. Lotolelei Church	20	25
47	25c. Kelupi Church	20	25
48	30c. Mataloa o Tuvala Church	25	25
49	35c. Palataise o Keliso Church	25	25

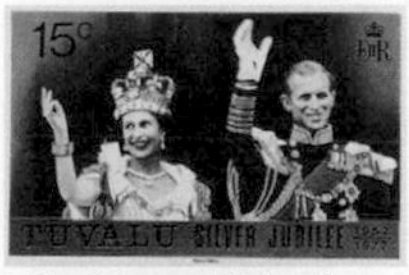

6 The Queen and Duke of Edinburgh after Coronation

1977. Silver Jubilee. Multicoloured.

50	15c. Type **6**	15	10
51	35c. Prince Philip carried ashore at Vaitupu	20	15
52	50c. The Queen and attendants	30	20
MS53	98×144 mm. Nos. 50/2	1·00	1·00

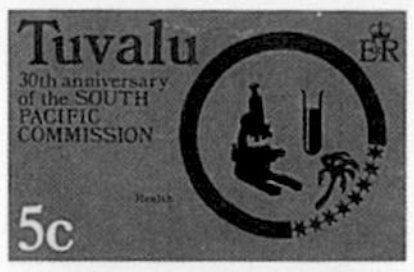

7 "Health"

1977. 30th Anniv of South Pacific Commission. Multicoloured.

54	5c. Type **7**	15	20
55	20c. "Education"	15	20
56	30c. "Fruit-growing"	15	20
57	35c. Map of S.P.C. area	35	25

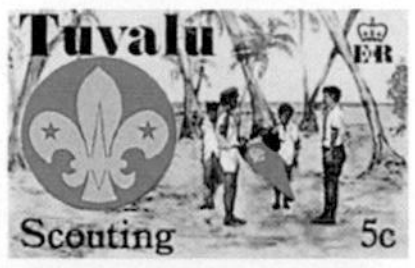

8 Scout Promise

1977. 50th Anniv of Scouting in the Central Pacific. Multicoloured.

73	5c. Type **8**	15	20
74	20c. Canoeing	15	20
75	30c. Scout shelter	20	25
76	35c. Lord Baden-Powell	20	25

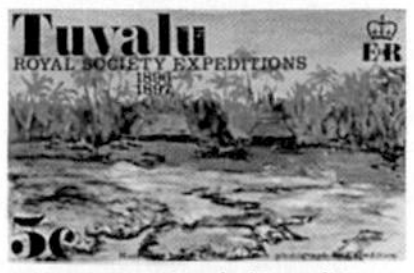

9 Hurricane Beach (Expedition photo)

1977. Royal Society Expeditions, 1896–97.

77	**9**	5c. multicoloured	15	15
78	-	20c. black and blue	15	20
79	-	30c. black and blue	20	20
80	-	35c. multicoloured	20	20

DESIGNS—VERT: 20c. Boring apparatus on H.M.S. "Porpoise"; 30c. Dredging chart. HORIZ: 35c. Charles Darwin and H.M.S. "Beagle".

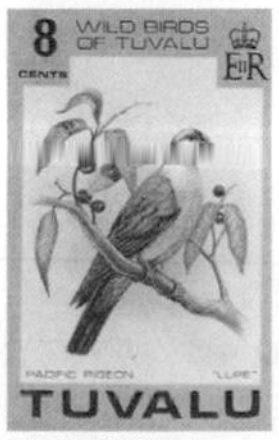

10 Pacific Pigeon

1978. Wild Birds. Multicoloured.

81	8c. Type **10**	25	25
82	20c. Reef heron	30	40
83	30c. White tern ("Fairy Tern")	35	50
84	40c. Lesser frigate bird	35	55

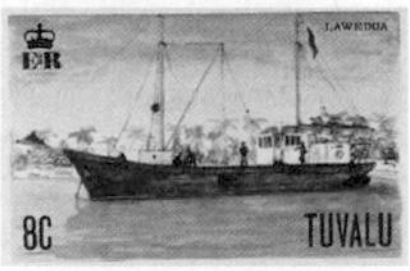

11 "Lawedua" (inter-island coaster)

1978. Ships. Multicoloured.

85	8c. Type **11**	15	15
86	20c. "Wallacia" (tug)	15	15
87	30c. "Cenpac Rounder" (freighter)	20	20
88	40c. "Pacific Explorer" (freighter)	20	20

1978. 25th Anniv of Coronation. As Nos. 422/5 of Montserrat. Multicoloured.

89	8c. Canterbury Cathedral	10	10
90	30c. Salisbury Cathedral	10	10
91	40c. Wells Cathedral	10	10
92	$1 Hereford Cathedral	30	30
MS93	137×108 mm. Nos. 89/92	45	70

1978. Independence. Nos. 63/4, 37/8, 67/40 and 68 optd **INDEPENDENCE 1ST OCTOBER 1978.**

94	8c. Funafuti and banana tree	10	10
95	10c. Map of Tuvalu	10	10
96	15c. Niutao and four-winged flyingfish	10	10
97	20c. Vaitupu and maneapa (house)	10	10
98	30c. Fatele (local dancing)	15	15
99	35c. Te Ano (game)	15	15
100	40c. Screw pine	15	15

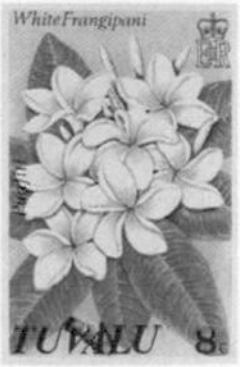

13 White Frangipani

1978. Wild Flowers. Multicoloured.

101	8c. Type **13**	10	10
102	20c. Susana	10	10
103	30c. Tiale	15	15
104	40c. Inato	20	25

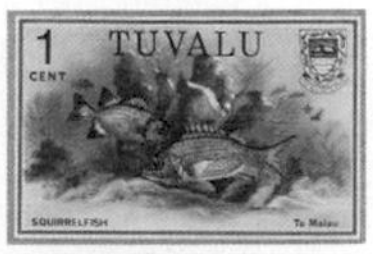

14 Squirrelfish

1979. Fish (1st series). Multicoloured.

105	1c. Type **14**	10	10
106	2c. Band-tailed goatfish	10	10
107	4c. Regal angelfish	10	10
108	5c. Melon butterflyfish	10	10
109	6c. Semi-circle angelfish	10	10
110	8c. Blue-striped snapper	10	10
111	10c. Clown anemonefish	15	10
112	15c. Chevron butterflyfish	20	10
113	20c. Yellow-edged lyretail ("Fairy cod")	25	15
114	25c. Clown triggerfish	25	20
115	30c. Long-nosed butterflyfish	25	10
116	35c. Yellow-finned tuna	30	15
117	40c. Spotted eagle ray	30	10
117b	45c. Black-tipped grouper	1·50	2·25
118	50c. Hammerhead	30	20
119	70c. Lionfish (vert)	30	30
120	$1 Painted triggerfish (vert)	30	30
121	$2 Copper-banded butterflyfish ("Beaked coralfish") (vert)	50	30
122	$5 Tiger shark (vert)	70	35

See also Nos. 770/81.

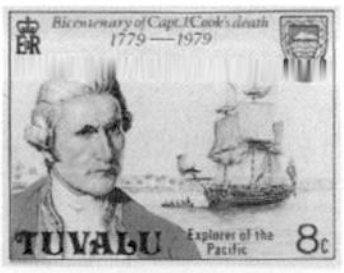

15 "Explorer of the Pacific"

1979. Death Bicent of Capt. James Cook. Multicoloured.

123	8c. Type **15**	15	20
124	30c. "A new island is discovered"	15	20
125	40c. "Transit of Venus, Tahiti, 3 June, 1769"	15	20
126	$1 Cook's death	15	30

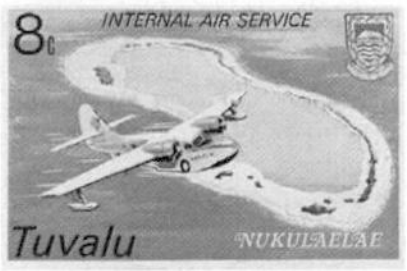

16 Grumman Mackinnon Goose Flying Boat and Nukulaelae Island

1979. Internal Air Service. Multicoloured.

127	8c. Type **16**	15	15
128	20c. Goose and Vaitupu	15	15
129	30c. Goose and Nui	20	20
130	40c. Goose and Funafuti	25	30

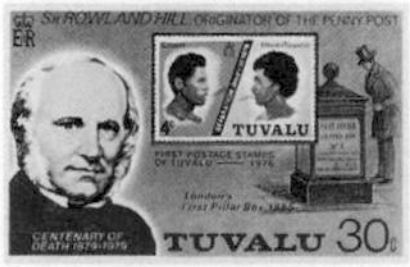

17 Sir Rowland Hill, 1976 4c. Separation Commemorative and London's First Pillar Box, 1855

1979. Death Cent of Sir Rowland Hill. Multicoloured.

131	30c. Type **17**	15	15
132	40c. Sir Rowland Hill, 1976 10c. Separation commemorative and Penny Black	15	15
133	$1 Sir Rowland Hill, 1976 35c. Separation commemorative and mail coach	25	30
MS134	148×140 mm. Nos. 131/3	70	1·25

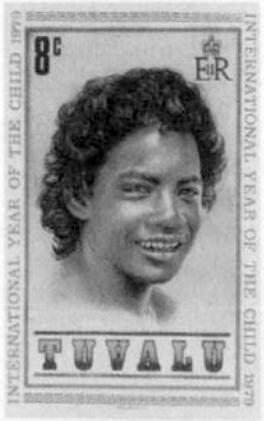

18 Child's Face

1979. International Year of the Child.

135	**18**	8c. multicoloured	10	10
136	-	20c. multicoloured	10	10
137	-	30c. multicoloured	10	15
138	-	40c. multicoloured	15	25

DESIGN: 20c. to 40c. Children's faces.

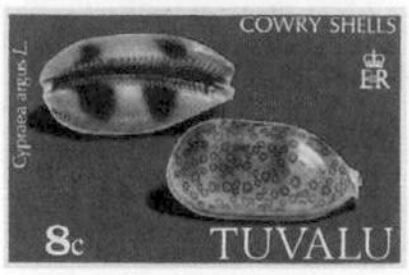

19 Eyed Cowrie

1980. Cowrie Shells. Multicoloured.

139	8c. Type **19**	10	10
140	20c. Jester cowrie	10	10
141	30c. Closely-related carnelian cowrie	15	15
142	40c. Golden cowrie	25	20

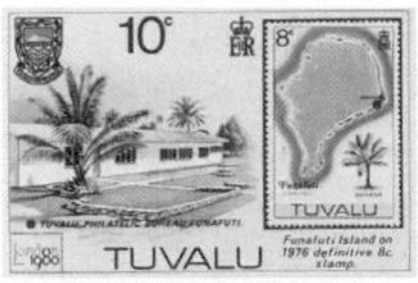

20 Philatelic Bureau, Funafuti, and 1976 8c. Definitive

1980. "London 1980" Int Stamp Exhibition. Multicoloured.

143	10c. Type **20**	10	10
144	20c. Nukulaelae postmark and 1976 2c. definitive	15	15
145	30c. Fleet Post Office, U.S. Navy, airmail cover, 1943	15	20
146	$1 Map and arms of Tuvalu	35	40
MS147	160×136 mm. Nos. 143/6	65	1·10

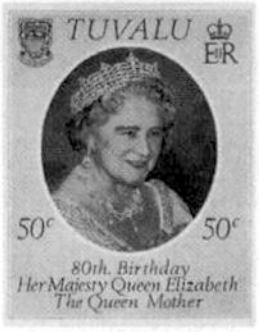

21 Queen Elizabeth the Queen Mother at Royal Variety Performance, 1978

1980. 80th Birthday of The Queen Mother.

148	**21**	15c. multicoloured	25	20

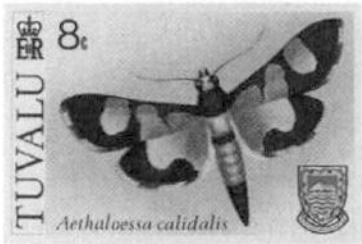

22 "Aethaloessa calidalis"

1980. Moths. Multicoloured.

149	8c. Type **22**	10	10
150	20c. "Parotis suralis"	15	10
151	30c. "Dudua aprobola"	20	15
152	40c. "Decadarchis simulans"	20	15

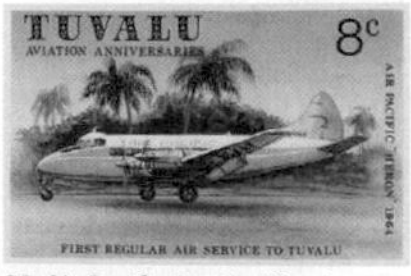

23 Air Pacific De Havilland Heron 2

1980. Aviation Commemorations. Multicoloured.

153	8c. Type **23**	10	10
154	20c. Hawker Siddeley H.S.748	15	10
155	30c. Short S.25 Sunderland flying boat	15	15
156	40c. Orville Wright and Wright Flyer III	20	15

COMMEMORATIONS: 8c. 1st regular air service to Tuvalu, 1964; 20c. Air service to Tuvalu; 30c. Wartime R.N.Z.A.F. flying boat service to Funafuti, 1945; 40c. Wright Brothers' 1st flight, 17 December, 1903.

1981. No. 118 surch **45 CENTS**.

157	45c. on 50c. Hammerhead	25	40

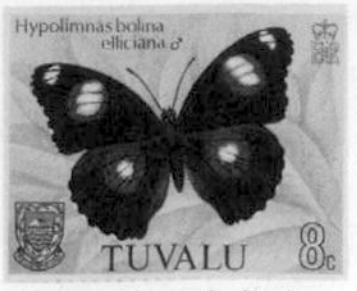

25 "Hypolimnas bolina" (male)

1981. Butterflies. Multicoloured.

158	8c. Type **25**	15	10
159	20c. "Hypolimnas bolina" (female)	20	15
160	30c. "Hypolimnas bolina" (female) (different)	20	20
161	40c. "Precis villida" (male)	25	20

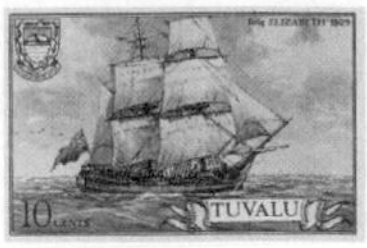

26 "Elizabeth" (brig), 1809

1981. Ships (1st series). Multicoloured.

162	10c. Type **26**	15	15
163	25c. "Rebecca" (brigantine), 1819	15	20
164	35c. "Independence II" (whaling ship), 1821	20	25
165	40c. H.M.S. "Basilisk" (paddle-sloop), 1872	25	30
166	45c. H.M.S. "Royalist" (screw-corvette), 1890	30	35
167	50c. "Olivebank" (barque), 1920	30	35

See also Nos. 235/40, 377/80, 442/5, 809/12 and 832/6.

1981. Royal Wedding. Royal Yachts. As T **14a/b** of St. Kitts. Multicoloured.

168	10c. "Carolina"	10	15
169	10c. Prince Charles and Lady Diana Spencer	35	50
170	45c. "Victoria and Albert III"	10	15
171	45c. As No. 169	40	65
172	$2 "Britannia"	25	50
173	$2 As No. 169	75	1·50
MS174	120×109 mm. $1.50, As No. 169	50	75

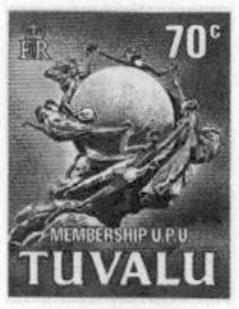

27 U.P.U. Emblem

1981. U.P.U. Membership.

177	**27**	70c. blue	20	30
178	**27**	$1 brown	30	45
MS179		86×71 mm. Nos. 177/8	70	2·25

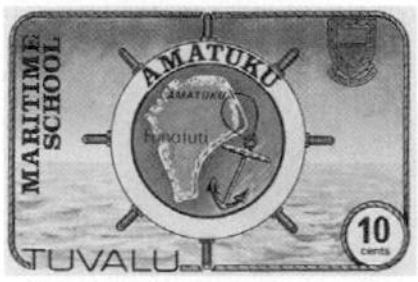

28 Map of Funafuti, and Anchor

1982. Amatuku Maritime School. Multicoloured.

180	10c. Type **28**	10	10
181	25c. Motor launch	20	20
182	35c. School buildings and jetty	25	30
183	45c. School flag and freighter	30	35

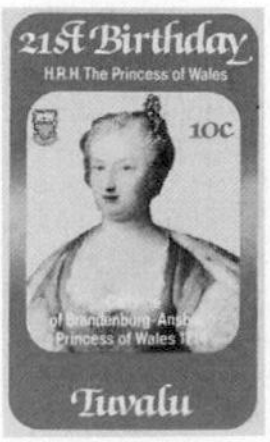

29 Caroline of Brandenburg-Ansbach, Princess of Wales, 1714

1982. 21st Birthday of Princess of Wales. Multicoloured.

184	10c. Type **29**	10	10
185	45c. Coat of arms of Caroline of Brandenburg-Ansbach	10	10
186	$1.50 Diana, Princess of Wales	50	30

1982. Tonga Cyclone Relief. Nos. 170/1 optd **TONGA CYCLONE RELIEF 1982 +20c.**

187	45c.+20c. "Victoria and Albert III"	10	30
188	45c.+20c. Prince Charles and Lady Diana Spencer	30	1·10

1982. Birth of Prince William of Wales. Nos. 184/6 optd **ROYAL BABY.**

189	10c. Type **29**	10	10
190	45c. Coat of arms of Caroline of Brandenburg-Ansbach	10	10
191	$1.50 Diana, Princess of Wales	30	30

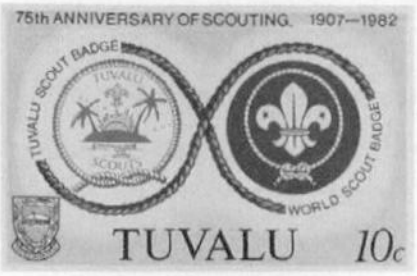

31 Tuvalu and World Scout Badge

1982. 75th Anniv of Boy Scout Movement. Multicoloured.

192	10c. Type **31**	15	15
193	25c. Campfire	25	40
194	35c. Parade	30	45
195	45c. Boy scout	40	55

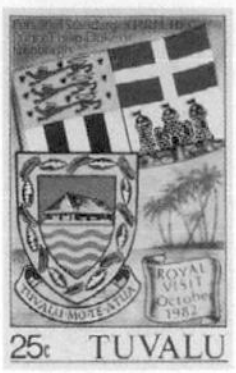

32 Tuvalu Crest and Duke of Edinburgh's Standard

1982. Royal Visit. Multicoloured.

196	25c. Type **32**	15	20
197	45c. Tuvalu flag and Queen's Royal Standard	25	30
198	50c. Portrait of Queen Elizabeth II	25	30
MS199	104×85 mm. Nos. 196/8	60	1·75

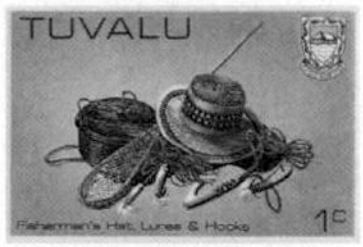

33 Fisherman's Hat and Equipment

1983. Handicrafts. Multicoloured.

200	1c. Type **33**	15	10
201	2c. Cowrie shell handbags	15	10
202	5c. Wedding and baby food baskets	15	10
203	10c. Model canoe	15	10
203a	15c. Ladies' sun hats	1·75	2·00
204	20c. Palm climbing rope and platform with toddy pot	15	20
205	25c. Pandanus baskets	15	20
205a	30c. Basket tray and coconut stand	1·50	1·40
206	35c. Pandanus pillows and shell necklaces	25	30
207	40c. Round baskets and fans	20	35
208	45c. Reef sandals and fish trap	20	40
209	50c. Rat trap (vert)	20	45
209a	60c. Fisherman's waterproof boxes (vert)	1·75	1·40
210	$1 Pump drill and adze (vert)	20	45
211	$2 Fisherman's hat and canoe bailers (vert)	30	55
212	$5 Fishing rod, lures and scoop nets (vert)	60	75

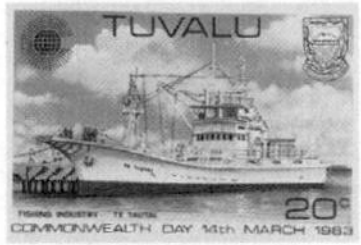

34 "Te Tautai" (trawler)

1983. Commonwealth Day. Multicoloured.

213	20c. Type **34**	15	15
214	35c. Traditional dancing, Motufoua School	15	25
215	45c. Satellite view of Pacific	20	30
216	50c. "Morning Star" (container ship)	25	40

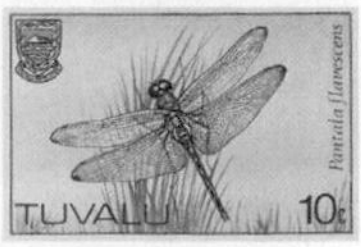

35 "Pantala flavescens"

1983. Dragonflies. Multicoloured.

217	10c. Type **35**	15	10
218	35c. "Anax guttatus"	20	35
219	40c. "Tholymis tillarga"	20	40
220	50c. "Diplacodes bipunctata"	25	50

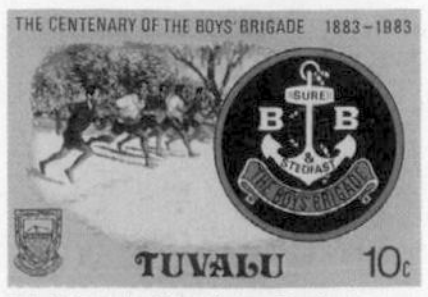

36 Brigade Members Racing

1983. Centenary of Boys' Brigade. Multicoloured.

221	10c. Type **36**	10	10
222	35c. B.B. members in outrigger canoe	20	30
223	$1 On parade	50	1·00

1983. No. 210 surch **60c.**

224	60c. on $1 Pump drill and adze	70	70

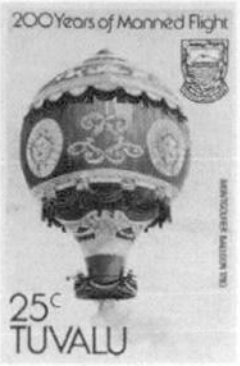

38 Montgolfier Balloon, 1783

1983. Bicentenary of Manned Flight. Multicoloured.

225	25c. Type **38**	20	20
226	35c. Grumman Mackinnon Turbo Goose (horiz)	20	25
227	45c. Beech 200 Super King Air (horiz)	25	30
228	50c. "Double Eagle II" balloon	25	35
MS229	114×145 mm. Nos. 225/8	70	1·00

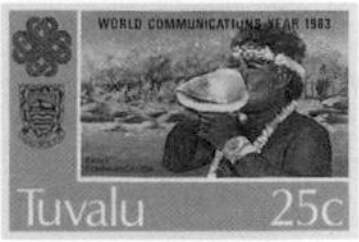

39 Early Communications

1983. World Communications Year. Multicoloured.

230	25c. Type **39**	15	15
231	35c. Radio operator	20	20
232	45c. Modern teleprinter	20	20
233	50c. Funafuti transmitting station	25	25

1984. No. 208 surch **30c.**

234	30c. on 45c. Reef sandals and fish trap	35	40

1984. Ships (2nd series). As T **26**. Multicoloured.

235	10c. "Titus" (freighter), 1897	25	15
236	20c. "Malaita" (freighter), 1905	25	15
237	25c. "Aymeric" (freighter), 1906	25	15
238	35c. "Anshun" (freighter), 1965	30	25
239	45c. "Beaverbank" (freighter), 1970	30	30
240	50c. "Benjamin Bowring" (freighter), 1981	30	30

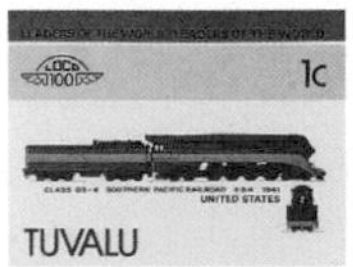

41 Southern Pacific Railroad Class GS-4

1984. Leaders of the World. Railway Locomotives (1st series). As T **41**. The first in each pair shows technical drawings and the second the locomotive at work.

241	1c. multicoloured	10	10
242	1c. multicoloured	10	10
243	15c. multicoloured	20	25
244	15c. multicoloured	20	25
245	40c. multicoloured	25	30
246	40c. multicoloured	25	30
247	60c. multicoloured	35	40
248	60c. multicoloured	35	40

DESIGNS: Nos. 241/2, Southern Pacific Railroad Class GS-4, U.S.A. (1941); 243/4, New South Wales Govt Class AD 60, Australia (1952); 245/6, New South Wales Govt Class C38, Australia (1943); 247/8, Class "Achilles" "Lord of the Isles", Great Britain (1892).

See also Nos. 253/68, 273/80, 313/20 and 348/55.

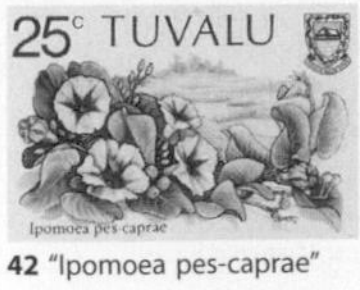

42 "Ipomoea pes-caprae"

1984. Beach Flowers. Multicoloured.

249	25c. Type **42**	25	25
250	45c. "Ipomoea macrantha"	40	40
251	50c. "Triumfetta procumbens"	45	45
252	60c. "Portulaca quadrifida"	50	50

1984. Leaders of the World. Railway Locomotives (2nd series). As T **41**. The first design in each pair shows technical drawings and the second the locomotive at work.

253	10c. multicoloured	10	10
254	10c. multicoloured	10	10
255	15c. multicoloured	10	15
256	15c. multicoloured	10	15
257	20c. multicoloured	10	15
258	20c. multicoloured	10	15
259	25c. multicoloured	10	15
260	25c. multicoloured	10	15
261	40c. multicoloured	10	20
262	40c. multicoloured	10	20
263	50c. multicoloured	10	20
264	50c. multicoloured	10	20
265	60c. multicoloured	10	20
266	60c. multicoloured	10	20
267	$1 multicoloured	15	25
268	$1 multicoloured	15	25

DESIGNS: Nos. 253/4, Illinois Central Railroad "Casey Jones" type locomotive No. 382, U.S.A. (1896); 255/6, Erie Railroad Triplex type, U.S.A. (1914); 257/8, Class 370 Advanced Passenger Train, Great Britain (1981); 259/60, LMS Class 4F, Great Britain (1924); 261/2, GWR Class "Tornado Rover", Great Britain (1888); 263/4, Class 73 electric locomotive "Broadlands", Great Britain (1967); 265/6, "Locomotion", Great Britain (1825); 267/8, Class C57, Japan (1937).

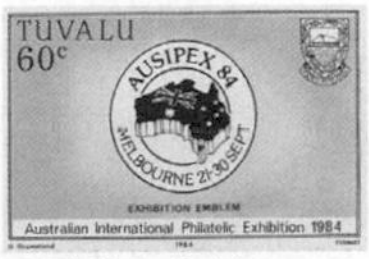

43 Exhibition Emblem

1984. "Ausipex" International Stamp Exhibition, Melbourne. Multicoloured.

269	60c. Type **43**	20	30
270	60c. Arms of Tuvalu	20	30
271	60c. Tuvalu flag	20	30
272	60c. Royal Exhibition Building, Melbourne	20	30

1984. Leaders of the World. Railway Locomotives (3rd series). As T **41**. The first in each pair shows technical drawings and the second the locomotive at work.

273	1c. multicoloured	10	10
274	1c. multicoloured	10	10
275	15c. multicoloured	15	20
276	15c. multicoloured	15	20
277	30c. multicoloured	20	25
278	30c. multicoloured	20	25
279	$1 multicoloured	40	65
280	$1 multicoloured	40	65

DESIGNS: Nos. 273/4, Class 9700, Japan (1897); 275/6, Paris-Lyon-Mediterranee Class 231C/K, France (1909); 277/8, Class 640, Italy (1907); 279/80, Paris-Orleans Class 4500, France (1906).

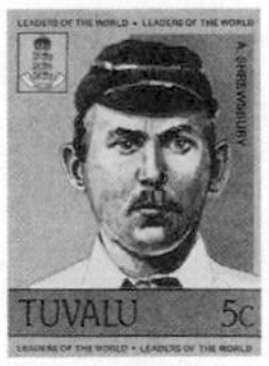

44 A. Shrewsbury

1984. Leaders of the World. Cricketers. As T **44**. The first in each pair shows the cricketer in action and the second a head portrait.

281	5c. multicoloured	15	40
282	5c. multicoloured	15	40
283	30c. multicoloured	25	45
284	30c. multicoloured	25	45
285	50c. multicoloured	25	45
286	50c. multicoloured	25	45
287	60c. multicoloured	30	45
288	60c. multicoloured	30	45

DESIGNS: 281/2, A. Shrewsbury; 283/4, H. Verity; 285/6, E. H. Hendren; 287/8, J. Briggs.

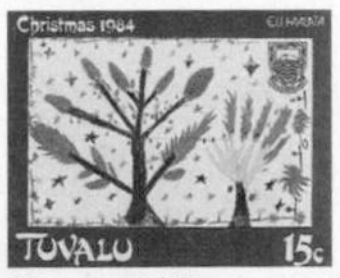

45 Trees and Stars

1984. Christmas. Children's Drawings. Multicoloured.

289	15c. Type **45**	10	10
290	40c. Fishing from outrigger canoes	20	20
291	50c. Three Wise Men bearing gifts	25	25
292	60c. The Holy Family	35	35

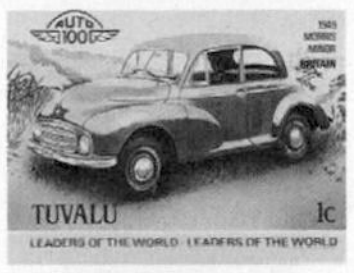

46 Morris Minor

1984. Leaders of the World. Automobiles (1st series). As T **46**. The first in each pair shows technical drawings and the second paintings.

293	1c. black, brown and yellow	10	10
294	1c. multicoloured	10	10
295	15c. black, pink and lilac	10	15
296	15c. multicoloured	10	15
297	50c. black, brown and mauve	20	20
298	50c. multicoloured	20	30
299	$1 black, green and blue	30	40
300	$1 multicoloured	30	40

DESIGNS: Nos. 293/4, "Morris Minor"; 295/6, Studebaker "Avanti"; 297/8, Chevrolet "Inter-national Six"; 299/300, Allard "J2".

See also Nos. 321/8, 356/71, 421/32 and 446/69.

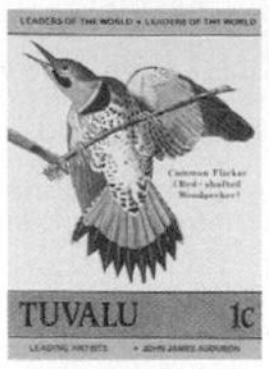

47 Common Flicker

1985. Leaders of the World. Birth Bicentenary of John J. Audubon (ornithologist). Multicoloured.

301	1c. Type **47**	10	10
302	1c. Say's phoebe	10	10
303	25c. Townsend's warbler	20	30
304	25c. Bohemian waxwing	20	30
305	50c. Prothonotary warbler	20	50
306	50c. Worm eating warbler	20	50
307	70c. Broad-winged hawk	30	65
308	70c. Hen harrier	30	65

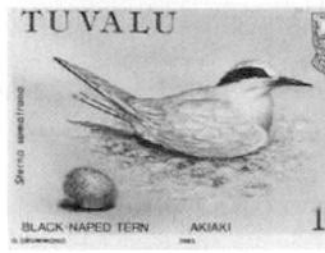

48 Black-naped Tern

1985. Birds and their Eggs. Multicoloured.

309	15c. Type **48**	40	20
310	40c. White-capped noddy	55	50
311	50c. White-tailed tropicbird	60	60
312	60c. Sooty tern	65	70

1985. Leaders of the World. Railway Locomotives (4th series). As T **41**. The first in each pair shows technical drawings and the second the locomotive at work.

313	5c. multicoloured	10	10
314	5c. multicoloured	10	10
315	10c. multicoloured	10	10
316	10c. multicoloured	10	10
317	30c. multicoloured	30	35
318	30c. multicoloured	30	35
319	$1 multicoloured	50	80
320	$1 multicoloured	50	80

DESIGNS: Nos. 313/14, GWR "Churchward 28XX", Great Britain (1905); 315/16, Class KF No. 605, China (1935); 317/18, Class 99.77 No. 99773, Germany (1952); 319/20, Pearson type, Great Britain (1853).

1985. Leaders of the World. Automobiles (2nd series). As T **46**. The first in each pair shows technical drawings and the second paintings.

321	1c. black, green and deep green	10	10
322	1c. multicoloured	10	10
323	20c. black, pink and red	15	20
324	20c. multicoloured	15	20
325	50c. black, blue and violet	20	30
326	50c. multicoloured	20	30
327	70c. black, pink and brown	20	35
328	70c. multicoloured	20	35

DESIGNS: No. 321/2, Rickenbacker (1923); 323/4, Detroit-Electric two door brougham (1914); 325/6, Packard "Clipper" (1941); 327/8, Audi "Quattro" (1982).

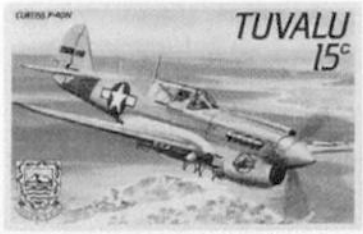

49 Curtiss P-40N Warhawk

1985. World War II Aircraft. Multicoloured.

329	15c. Type **49**	2·00	1·00
330	40c. Consolidated B-24 Liberator	2·50	1·75
331	50c. Lockhead PV-1 Ventura	2·50	2·00
332	60c. Douglas C-54	2·50	2·25
MS333	110×108 mm. Nos. 329/32	5·00	4·00

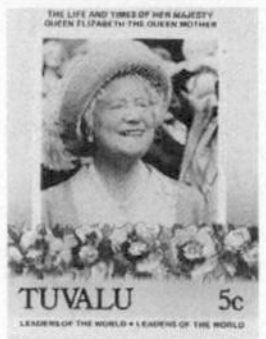

50 Queen Elizabeth the Queen Mother

1985. Leaders of the World. Life and Times of Queen Elizabeth the Queen Mother. Various portraits.

334	**50**	5c. multicoloured	10	20
335	-	5c. multicoloured	10	20
336	-	30c. multicoloured	10	20
337	-	30c. multicoloured	10	20
338	-	60c. multicoloured	15	25
339	-	60c. multicoloured	15	25
340	-	$1 multicoloured	15	40
341	-	$1 multicoloured	15	40
MS342		85×114 mm. $1.20 multicoloured; $1.20 multicoloured	60	1·50

Each value issued in pairs showing a floral pattern across the bottom of the portraits which stops short of the left-hand edge on the first stamp and of the right-hand edge on the second.

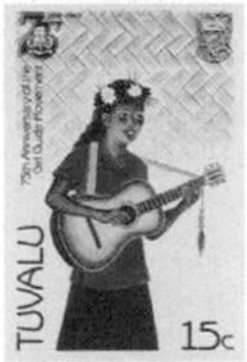

51 Guide playing Guitar

1985. 75th Anniv of Girl Guide Movement. Multicoloured.

343	15c. Type **51**	15	20
344	40c. Building camp-fire	40	45
345	50c. Patrol leader with Guide flag	50	55
346	60c. Guide saluting	60	65
MS347	141×77 mm. Nos. 343/6	1·50	2·00

1985. Leaders of the World. Railway Locomotives (5th series). As T **41**. The first in each pair shows technical drawings and the second the locomotive at work.

348	10c. multicoloured	10	15
349	10c. multicoloured	10	15
350	40c. multicoloured	20	30
351	40c. multicoloured	20	30
352	65c. multicoloured	25	40
353	65c. multicoloured	25	40
354	$1 multicoloured	30	55
355	$1 multicoloured	30	55

DESIGNS: Nos. 348/49, LNER "Green Arrow", Great Britain (1936); 350/1, Conrail Class SD-50 diesel locomotive No. 6729, U.S.A. (1982); 352/3, "Flying Hamburger", Germany (1932); 354/5, Class 1070, Japan (1925. Dated "1908" in error).

1985. Leaders of the World. Automobiles (3rd series). As T **46**. The first in each pair shows technical drawings and the second paintings.

356	5c. black, grey and mauve	10	15
357	5c. multicoloured	10	15
358	10c. black, pink and red	10	20
359	10c. multicoloured	10	20
360	15c. black, brown and red	10	20
361	15c. multicoloured	10	20
362	35c. black, red and blue	15	30
363	35c. multicoloured	15	30
364	40c. black, light green & green	15	30
365	40c. multicoloured	15	30
366	55c. black, stone and green	15	30
367	55c. multicoloured	15	30
368	$1 black, deep brown & brown	25	40
369	$1 multicoloured	25	40
370	$1.50 black, pink and red	30	45
371	$1.50 multicoloured	30	45

DESIGNS: Nos. 356/7, Cord "L-29" (1929); 358/9, Horch "670 V-12" (1932); 360/1, Lanchester (1901); 362/3, Citroen "2 CV" (1950); 364/5, MGA (1957); 366/7, Ferrari "250 GTO" (1962); 368/9, Ford "V-8" (1932); 370/1, Aston Martin "Lagonda" (1977).

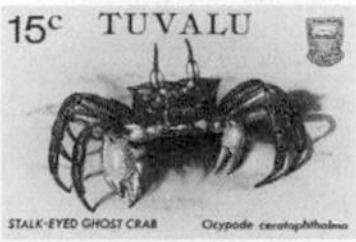

52 Stalk-eyed Ghost Crab

1986. Crabs. Multicoloured.

372	15c. Type **52**	70	90
373	40c. Red and white painted crab	80	1·25
374	50c. Red-spotted crab	80	1·75
375	60c. Red hermit crab	80	2·00

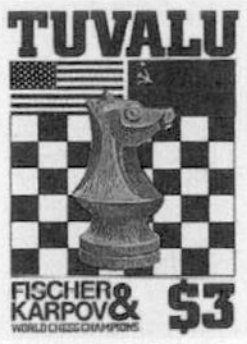

53 Chess Knight on Board and Flags of U.S. and U.S.S.R. (World Chess Championships)

1986. International Events. Sheet 148×127 mm, containing T **53** and similar vert design. Multicoloured.

MS376	$3 Type **53**; $3 Emblem (80th anniv of Rotary)	5·50	8·00

1986. Ships (3rd series). Missionary Vessels. As T **26**. Multicoloured.

377	15c. "Messenger of Peace" (schooner)	60	70
378	40c. "John Wesley" (brig)	70	1·00
379	50c. "Duff" (full-rigged ship)	70	1·25
380	60c. "Triton" (brigantine)	70	1·75

1986. 60th Birthday of Queen Elizabeth II. As T **167** of British Virgin Islands. Multicoloured.

381	10c. Queen wearing ceremonial cloak, New Zealand, 1977	15	15
382	90c. Before visit to France, 1957	30	35
383	$1.50 Queen in 1982	45	80
384	$3 In Canberra, 1982 (vert)	60	1·50
MS385	85×115 mm. $4 Queen carring bouquet	2·50	6·00

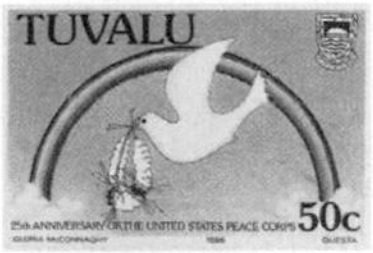

54 Peace Dove carrying Wreath and Rainbow

1986. 25th Anniv of United States Peace Corps.

386	**54**	50c. multicoloured	80	1·00

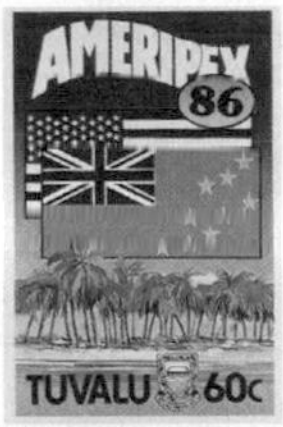

55 Island and Flags of Tuvalu and U.S.A

1986. "Ameripex" Int Stamp Exhibition, Chicago.

387	**55**	60c. multicoloured	85	1·00

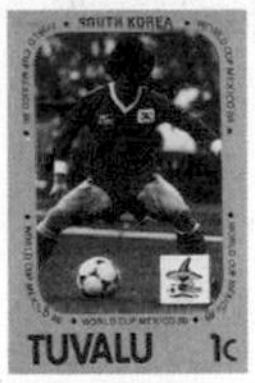

56 South Korean Player

1986. World Cup Football Championship, Mexico. Multicoloured.

388	1c. Type **56**	10	10
389	5c. French player	10	10
390	10c. West German captain with World Cup trophy, 1974	10	10
391	40c. Italian player	40	50
392	60c. World Cup final, 1974 (59×39 mm)	50	65
393	$1 Canadian team (59×39 mm)	70	90
394	$2 Northern Irish team (59×39 mm)	90	1·50
395	$3 English team (59×39 mm)	1·25	2·50
MS396	Two sheets, each 85×114 mm. (a) $1.50 As No. 393; (b) $2.50 As No. 394 Set of 2 sheets	3·25	6·00

1986. Royal Wedding (1st issue). As T **164a** of St. Lucia. Multicoloured.

397	60c. Prince Andrew and Miss Sarah Ferguson	25	45
398	60c. Prince Andrew with prize-winning bull	25	45
399	$1 Prince Andrew at horse trials (horiz)	30	70
400	$1 Miss Sarah Ferguson and Princess Diana (horiz)	30	70
MS401	85×115 mm. $6 Duke and Duchess of York after wedding (horiz)	1·75	5·00

See also Nos. 433/6.

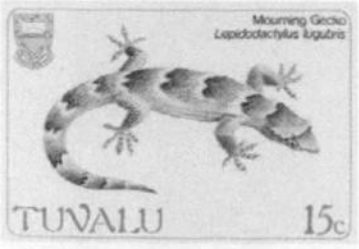

57 Mourning Gecko

1986. Lizards. Multicoloured.

402	15c. Type **57**	55	55
403	40c. Oceanic stump-toed gecko	1·00	1·00
404	50c. Azure-tailed skink	1·25	1·50
405	60c. Moth skink	1·50	2·00

1986. "Stampex '86" Stamp Exhibition, Adelaide. No. 386 optd **STAMPEX 86 ADELAIDE** and kangaroo.

406	**54**	50c. multicoloured	55	65

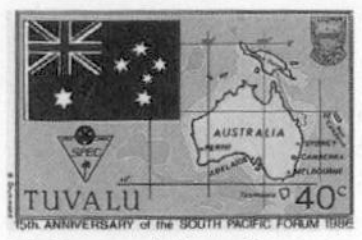

59 Map and Flag of Australia

1986. 15th Anniv of South Pacific Forum. Maps and national flags. Multicoloured.

407	40c. Type **59**	70	70
408	40c. Cook Islands	70	70
409	40c. Micronesia	70	70
410	40c. Fiji	70	70
411	40c. Kiribati	70	70
412	40c. Western Samoa	70	70
413	40c. Nauru	70	70
414	40c. Vanuatu	70	70
415	40c. New Zealand	70	70
416	40c. Tuvalu	70	70
417	40c. Tonga	70	70
418	40c. Solomon Islands	70	70
419	40c. Papua New Guinea	70	70
420	40c. Niue	70	70

1986. Automobiles (4th series). As T **46**. The first in each pair show technical drawings and the second paintings.

421	15c. multicoloured	15	15
422	15c. multicoloured	15	15
423	40c. multicoloured	20	25
424	40c. multicoloured	20	25
425	50c. multicoloured	20	30
426	50c. multicoloured	20	30
427	60c. multicoloured	20	35
428	60c. multicoloured	20	35
429	90c. multicoloured	25	35
430	90c. multicoloured	25	35
431	$1.50 multicoloured	30	45
432	$1.50 multicoloured	30	45

DESIGNS: Nos. 421/2, Copper "500" (1953); 423/4, Rover "2000" (1964); 425/6, Ruxton (1930); 427/8, Jowett "Jupiter" (1950); 429/30, Cobra "Daytona Coupe" (1964); 431/2, Packard Model F "Old Pacific" (1903).

1986. Royal Wedding (2nd issue). Nos. 397/400 optd **Congratulations to T.R.H. The Duke & Duchess of York**.

433	60c. Prince Andrew and Miss Sarah Ferguson	1·00	1·50
434	60c. Prince Andrew with prize-winning bull	1·00	1·50
435	$1 Prince Andrew at horse trials (horiz)	1·60	1·75
436	$1 Miss Sarah Ferguson and Princess Diana (horiz)	1·60	1·75

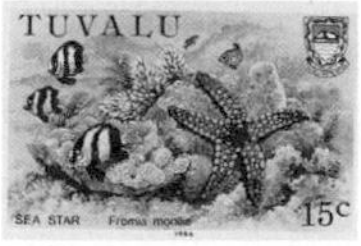

60 Sea Star

1986. Coral Reef Life (1st series). Multicoloured.

437	15c. Type **60**	85	85
438	40c. Pencil urchin	1·60	1·90
439	50c. Fragile coral	1·75	2·00
440	60c. Pink coral	2·00	2·25

See also Nos. 498/501, 558/62 and 822/6.

1986. Centenary of Statue of Liberty. Vert views of Statue as T **121a** of Montserrat in separate miniature sheets. Multicoloured.

MS441 Nine sheets, each 85×115 mm. $1.25; $1.50; $1.80; $2; $2.25; $2.50; $3; $3.25; $3.50 Set of 9 sheets 6·00 9·00

1987. Ships (4th series). Missionary Steamers. As T **26**. Multicoloured.

442	15c. "Southern Cross IV"	1·10	1·10
443	40c. "John Williams VI"	2·25	2·50
444	50c. "John Williams IV"	2·50	2·75
445	60c. M.S. "Southern Cross"	2·50	2·75

1987. Automobiles (5th series). As T **46**. The first in each pair shows technical drawings and the second paintings.

446	1c. multicoloured	10	10
447	1c. multicoloured	10	10
448	2c. multicoloured	10	10
449	2c. multicoloured	10	10
450	5c. multicoloured	10	10
451	5c. multicoloured	10	10
452	10c. multicoloured	15	20
453	10c. multicoloured	15	20
454	20c. multicoloured	20	25
455	20c. multicoloured	20	25
456	30c. multicoloured	25	30
457	30c. multicoloured	25	30
458	40c. multicoloured	30	35
459	40c. multicoloured	30	35
460	50c. multicoloured	30	40
461	50c. multicoloured	30	40
462	60c. multicoloured	30	40
463	60c. multicoloured	30	40
464	70c. multicoloured	30	45
465	70c. multicoloured	30	45
466	75c. multicoloured	30	45
467	75c. multicoloured	30	45
468	$1 multicoloured	40	70
469	$1 multicoloured	40	70
MS470	100×85 mm. Nos. 468/9	2·25	6·50

DESIGNS: Nos. 446/7, Talbot-Lago (1938); 448/9, Du Pont "Model G" (1930); 450/1, Riley "RM" (1950); 452/3, Chevrolet "Baby Grand" (1915); 454/5, Shelby "Mustang GT 500 KR" (1968); 456/7, Ferrari "212 Export Barchetta" (1952); 458/9, Peerless "Model 48-Six" (1912); 460/1, Sunbeam "Alpine" (1954); 462/3, Matra-Ford "MS 80" (1969); 464/5, Squire 1½ Litre (1934); 466/7, Talbot "105" (1931); 468/9, Plymouth "Model Q" (1928).

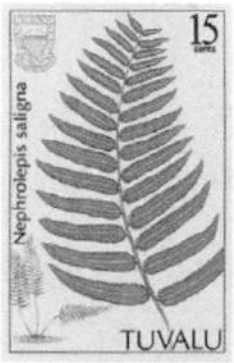

61 "Nephrolepis saligna"

1987. Ferns. Multicoloured.

471	15c. Type **61**	40	65
472	40c. "Asplenium nidus"	70	1·00
473	50c. "Microsorum scolopendria"	80	1·25
474	60c. "Pteris tripartita"	90	1·50
MS475	62×62 mm. $1.50 "Psilotum nuclum"	2·25	3·50

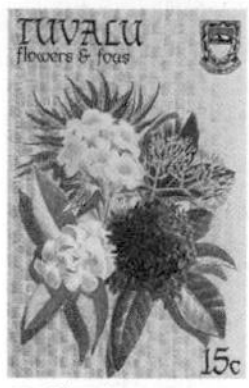

62 Floral Arrangement

1987. Flowers and "Fous". Designs showing either floral arrangements or "fous" (women's headdresses). Multicoloured.

476	15c. Type **62**	25	35
477	15c. "Fou"	25	35
478	40c. "Fou"	40	75
479	40c. Floral arrangement	40	75
480	50c. Floral arrangement	50	80
481	50c. "Fou"	50	80
482	60c. "Fou"	55	90
483	60c. Floral arrangement	55	90

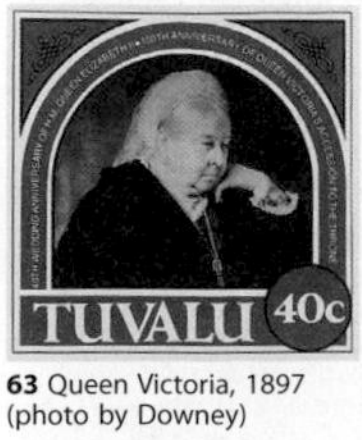

63 Queen Victoria, 1897 (photo by Downey)

1987. Royal Ruby Wedding and 150th Anniv of Queen Victoria's Accession.

484	**63**	40c. brown, black and green	45	55
485	-	60c. purple, black and green	60	75
486	-	80c. brown, black and blue	70	1·40
487	-	$1 brown, black and purple	90	1·60
488	-	$2 multicoloured	1·40	2·75
MS489		86×101 mm. $3 black	2·50	4·00

DESIGNS: 60c. Wedding of Princess Elizabeth and Duke of Edinburgh, 1947; 80c. Queen, Duke of Edinburgh and Prince Charles, 1950; $1 Queen with Princess Anne, 1950; $2 Queen Elizabeth II, 1970; $3 Queen and Prince Charles at Princess Anne's christening, 1950.

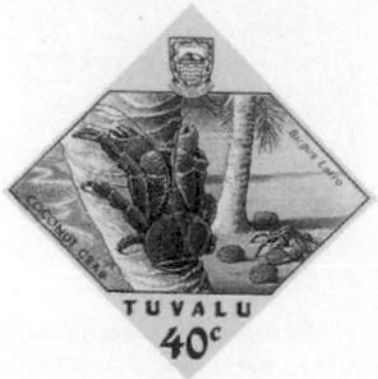

64 Coconut Crab

1987. Crustaceans. Multicoloured.

490	40c. Type **64**	1·00	1·25
491	50c. Painted crayfish	1·25	1·50
492	60c. Ocean crayfish	1·40	1·75

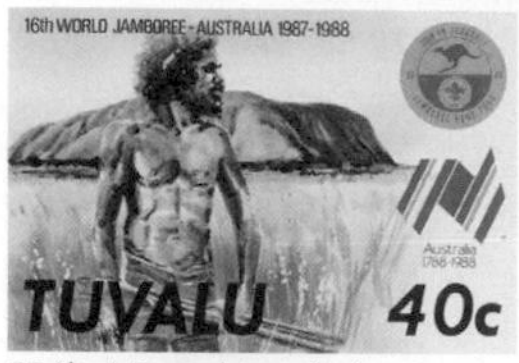

65 Aborigine and Ayers Rock

1987. World Scout Jamboree, Australia, and Bicent of Australian Settlement. Multicoloured.

493	40c. Type **65**	30	45
494	60c. Capt. Cook and H.M.S. "Endeavour"	70	90
495	$1 Scout saluting and Scout Park entrance	70	95
496	$1.50 Koala and kangaroo	80	1·25
MS497	115×85 mm. $2.50 Lord and Lady Baden Powell	2·00	3·25

1988. Coral Reef Life (2nd series). As T **60**. Multicoloured.

498	15c. Spanish dancer	65	85
499	40c. Hard corals	75	1·40
500	50c. Feather stars	75	1·60
501	60c. Staghorn corals	75	1·60

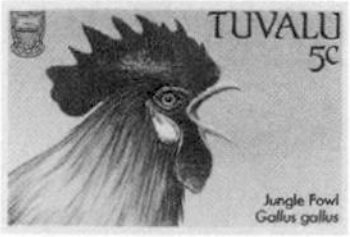

66 Red Junglefowl

1988. Birds. Multicoloured.

502	5c. Type **66**	10	15
503	10c. White tern	10	20
504	15c. Common noddy	15	20
505	20c. Phoenix petrel	20	40
506	25c. Pacific golden plover	20	45
507	30c. Crested tern	25	45
508	35c. Sooty tern	25	50
509	40c. Bristle-thighed curlew	25	40
510	45c. Bar-tailed godwit ("Eastern Bar-tailed Godwit")	25	45
511	50c. Eastern reef heron	25	50
512	55c. Great frigate bird ("Greater Frigate-bird")	30	70
513	60c. Red-footed booby	30	75
514	70c. Rufous-necked sandpiper ("Red-necked Stint")	30	1·00
515	$1 Long-tailed koel ("New Zealand Long-tailed Cuckoo")	30	1·50
516	$2 Red-tailed tropic bird	35	2·50
517	$5 Buff-banded rail ("Banded Rail")	65	4·00

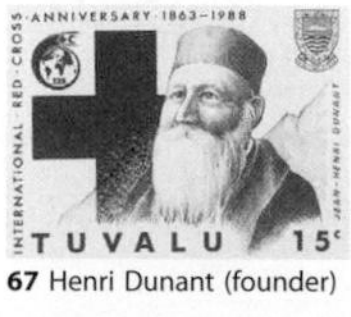

67 Henri Dunant (founder)

1988. 125th Anniv of International Red Cross.

518	**67**	15c. red and brown	10	20
519	-	40c. red and blue	20	40
520	-	50c. red and green	25	50
521	-	60c. red and purple	35	70
MS522		96×66 mm. $1.50 red and green	90	2·50

DESIGNS: 40c. Junior Red Cross members on parade; 50c. Red Cross worker with boy in wheelchair; 60c. First aid training; $1.50, Lecture.

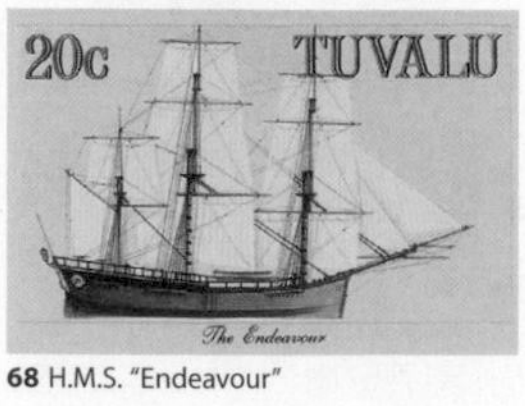

68 H.M.S. "Endeavour"

1988. Voyages of Captain Cook. Multicoloured.

523	20c. Type **68**	60	80
524	40c. Stern of H.M.S. "Endeavour"	70	1·10
525	50c. Cook preparing to land at Tahiti (vert)	80	1·25
526	60c. Maori chief (vert)	80	1·40
527	80c. H.M.S. "Resolution" and Hawaiian canoe	80	1·75
528	$1 "Captain Cook" (after Nathaniel Dance) (vert)	90	1·90
MS529	115×85 mm. $2.50 H.M.S. "Resolution" in Antarctic	7·50	8·00

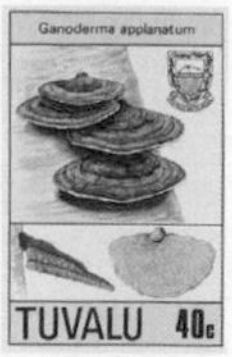

69 "Ganoderma applanatum"

1988. Fungi (1st series). Multicoloured.

530	40c. Type **69**	45	1·10
531	50c. "Pseudoepicoccum cocos" (brown leaf spot)	55	1·25
532	60c. "Rigidoporus lineatus" ("Rigidoporus zonalis")	60	1·50
533	90c. "Rigidoporus microporus"	65	1·75

See also Nos. 554/7.

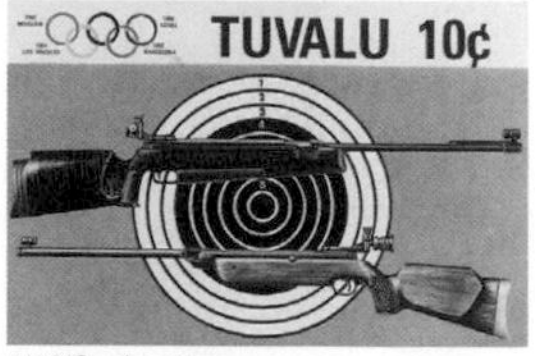

70 Rifle-shooting

1988. Olympic Games, Seoul. Multicoloured.

534	10c. Type **70**	35	65
535	20c. Judo	45	70
536	40c. Canoeing	60	90
537	60c. Swimming	70	1·25
538	80c. Sailing	80	1·75
539	$1 Gymnastics	1·10	1·75

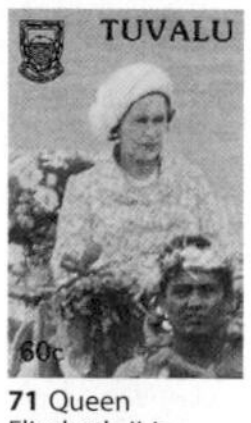

71 Queen Elizabeth II in Ceremonial Canoe

1988. Tenth Anniv of Independence.

540	**71**	60c. multicoloured	60	70
541	-	90c. multicoloured	90	1·10
542	-	$1 multicoloured (horiz)	1·00	1·40
543	-	$1.20 multicoloured	1·25	1·75
MS544		Designs as Nos. 540/3 in separate miniature sheets, each 85×85 mm. Set of 4 sheets	3·50	5·00

DESIGNS: 90c. to $1.20, Scenes from Royal Visit of 1982.

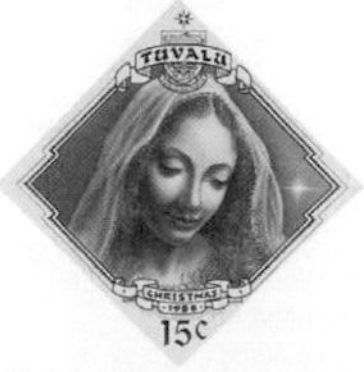

72 Virgin Mary

1988. Christmas. Multicoloured.

545	15c. Type **72**	45	55
546	40c. Christ Child	70	80
547	60c. Joseph	85	1·75
MS548	73×99 mm. $1.50 Angel	1·75	2·50

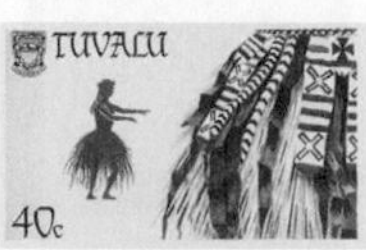

73 Dancing Skirt and Dancer

1989. Traditional Dancing Skirts. Designs showing skirts and dancer silhouettes.

549	**73**	40c. multicoloured	60	90
550	-	50c. multicoloured	70	1·00
551	-	60c. multicoloured	75	1·25
552	-	90c. multicoloured	1·10	1·75

MS553 110×75 mm. $1.50 multicoloured (dancer) (vert) 3·00 5·00

1989. Fungi (2nd series). As T **69**. Multicoloured.
554 40c. "Trametes marianna" ("Trametes muelleri") 1·50 1·75
555 50c. "Pestalotiopsis palmarum" (grey leaf spot) 1·75 1·90
556 60c. "Trametes cingulata" 1·75 2·00
557 90c. "Schizophyllum commune" 2·50 2·75

1989. Coral Reef Life (3rd series). As T **60**. Multicoloured.
558 40c. Pennant coralfish 1·50 1·75
559 50c. Orange-finned anemonefish 1·75 2·00
560 60c. Narrow-banded batfish 2·00 2·25
561 90c. Thread-finned butterflyfish 2·50 2·75
MS562 110×85 mm. Nos. 558/61 7·00 9·00

74 "Nivaga II"

1989. Delivery of "Nivaga II" (new inter-island ship). Sheet 116×85 mm.
MS563 **74** $1.50 multicoloured 4·50 6·00

75 Trumpet Triton Shell

1989. Christmas. Multicoloured.
564 40c. Type **75** 75 75
565 50c. Posy of flowers 85 85
566 60c. Germinating coconut 1·00 1·00
567 90c. Jewellery 1·75 2·50

76 "Cocus nucifera"

1990. Tropical Trees. Multicoloured.
568 15c. Type **76** 80 90
569 30c. "Rhizophora samoensis" 1·00 1·25
570 40c. "Messerschmidia argentea" 1·25 1·40
571 50c. "Pandanus tectorius" 1·40 1·75
572 60c. "Hernandia nymphaeifolia" 1·50 1·90
573 90c. "Pisonia grandis" 2·00 2·75

77 Penny Black with "Stamp World London 90" Emblem

1990. 150th Anniv of the Penny Black, and "Stamp World London 90" International Stamp Exhibition.
574 **77** 15c. multicoloured 1·50 1·50
575 **77** 40c. multicoloured 2·75 2·75
576 **77** 90c. multicoloured 4·50 5·00
MS577 115×85 mm. **77** $2 multicoloured 8·00 9·50

78 Japanese Camouflaged Freighter

1990. Second World War Ships (1st series). Multicoloured.
578 15c. Type **78** 1·50 1·50
579 30c. U.S.S. "Unimack" (seaplane tender) 2·25 2·25
580 40c. "Amagiri" (Japanese destroyer) 2·25 2·25
581 50c. U.S.S. "Platte" (attack transport) 2·50 2·50
582 60c. Japanese "Shumushu" Class escort 2·75 2·75

583 90c. U.S.S. "Independence" (aircraft carrier) 3·25 3·25
See also Nos. 613/16.

79 "Erythrina fusca"

1990. Flowers. Multicoloured.
584 15c. Type **79** 30 50
585 30c. "Capparis cordifolia" 50 70
586 40c. "Portulaca pilosa" 60 80
587 50c. "Cordia subcordata" 75 90
588 60c. "Scaevola taccada" 80 1·00
589 90c. "Suriana maritima" 1·25 2·00

80 Land Resources Survey

1990. 40th Anniv of United Nations Development Programme. Multicoloured.
590 40c. Type **80** 80 80
591 60c. Satellite earth station 1·50 1·50
592 $1.20 "Te Tautai" (trawler) 3·25 4·25

81 Mary and Joseph travelling to Bethlehem

1990. Christmas. Multicoloured.
593 15c. Type **81** 55 55
594 40c. The Nativity 1·00 1·00
595 60c. Shepherds with flock 1·50 1·50
596 90c. Wise Men bearing gifts 2·00 2·50

82 Ramose Murex

1991. Sea Shells. Multicoloured.
597 40c. Type **82** 1·50 1·50
598 50c. Marble cone 1·60 1·60
599 60c. Commercial trochus 1·75 1·75
600 $1.50 Green map cowrie 3·50 4·00

83 "Cylas formicarius" (beetle)

1991. Insects. Multicoloured.
601 40c. Type **83** 2·25 1·60
602 50c. "Heliothis armiger" (moth) 2·50 1·75
603 60c. "Spodoptera litura" (moth) 2·75 2·00
604 $1.50 "Agrius convolvuli" (moth) 7·00 8·50

84 Green Turtle

1991. Endangered Marine Life. Multicoloured.
605 40c. Type **84** 1·75 1·25
606 50c. Humpback whale 2·25 1·50
607 60c. Hawksbill turtle 2·25 1·60
608 $1.50 Sperm whale 5·00 6·50

85 Football

1991. Ninth South Pacific Games. Multicoloured.
609 40c. Type **85** 1·75 1·25
610 50c. Volleyball 2·25 1·75
611 60c. Lawn tennis 3·50 2·50
612 $1.50 Cricket 8·50 8·50

86 U.S.S. "Tennessee" (battleship)

1991. Second World War Ships (2nd series). Multicoloured.
613 40c. Type **86** 3·25 2·25
614 50c. "Haguro" (Japanese cruiser) 3·50 2·25
615 60c. H.M.N.Z.S. "Achilles" (cruiser) 3·75 2·50
616 $1.50 U.S.S. "North Carolina" (battleship) 8·00 11·00

87 Traditional Dancers

1991. Christmas. Multicoloured.
617 40c. Type **87** 1·75 1·25
618 50c. Solo dancer 2·00 1·50
619 60c. Dancers in green costumes 2·50 1·75
620 $1.50 Dancers in multicoloured costumes 5·00 7·00

88 Southern Fish Constellation

1992. Pacific Star Constellations. Multicoloured.
621 40c. Type **88** 2·50 2·00
622 50c. Scorpion 2·75 2·00
623 60c. Archer 3·25 2·25
624 $1.50 Southern Cross 7·00 8·50

89 King George VI and Cargo Liner

1992. Cent of British Occupation of Tuvalu. Multicoloured.
625 40c. Type **89** 2·50 2·00
626 50c. King George V and freighter with barges at wharf 2·75 2·00
627 60c. King Edward VII and freighter 3·00 2·25
628 $1.50 Queen Victoria and warship 5·50 6·50

90 Columbus with King Ferdinand and Queen Isabella of Spain

1992. 500th Anniv of Discovery of America by Columbus.
629 **90** 40c. blue and black 70 80
630 - 50c. purple and black 80 90
631 - 60c. green and black 90 1·10
632 - $1.50 purple and black 2·25 3·50
DESIGNS: 50c. Columbus and Polynesians; 60c. Columbus and South American Indians; $1.50, Columbus and North American Indians.

91 Blue-spotted Butterflyfish

1992. Fish. Multicoloured.
633 15c. Type **91** 65 65
634 20c. Bridled parrotfish 70 70
635 25c. Clown surgeonfish 70 70
636 30c. Moon wrasse 80 80
637 35c. Harlequin filefish 90 80
638 40c. Bird wrasse 1·00 50
639 45c. Black-finned pigfish 1·00 50
640 50c. Blue damselfish 1·00 60
641 60c. Hump-headed wrasse 1·25 70
642 70c. Ornate butterflyfish (vert) 1·25 1·25
643 90c. Saddle butterflyfish (vert) 1·50 1·50
644 $1 Vagabond butterflyfish (vert) 1·50 1·60
645 $2 Pennant coralfish (vert) 2·00 3·25
646 $3 Moorish idol (vert) 2·50 4·25

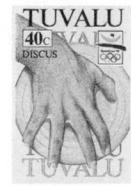
92 Discus Throwing

1992. Olympic Games, Barcelona. Multicoloured.
647 40c. Type **92** 1·25 1·00
648 50c. Javelin throwing 1·50 1·25
649 60c. Shotput 1·75 1·50
650 $1.50 Competitor's foot 3·25 4·50
MS651 100×71 mm. $2 Olympic stadium, Barcelona 4·25 5·00

93 Blue Coral

1992. Endangered Species. Blue Coral.
652 **93** 10c. multicoloured 1·00 1·00
653 - 25c. multicoloured 2·00 2·00
654 - 30c. multicoloured 2·00 2·00
655 - 35c. multicoloured 2·25 2·25
DESIGNS: 25c. to 35c. Different coral formations.

1992. "Kuala Lumpur '92" International Philatelic Exhibition. Nos. 636, 638 and 640/1 optd **KL92 KUALA LUMPUR '92** and emblem.
656 30c. Moon wrasse 1·60 1·60
657 40c. Bird wrasse 1·75 1·75
658 50c. Blue damselfish 2·00 2·00
659 60c. Hump-headed wrasse 2·00 2·00

95 Fishermen and Angel

1992. Christmas. Multicoloured.
660 40c. Type **95** 90 70
661 50c. Fishing canoes following star 1·00 80
662 60c. Nativity scene 1·25 1·00
663 $1.50 Christmas gifts 2·25 3·25

96 "Calophyllum inophyllum"

1993. Flowers. Multicoloured.
664 40c. Type **96** 1·25 1·10
665 50c. "Hibiscus tiliaceus" 1·50 1·10
666 60c. "Lantana camara" 1·60 1·10
667 $1.50 "Plumeria rubra" 2·75 3·25

97 Japanese Nakajima B5N "Kate" Bombers attacking Island

1993. 50th Anniv of War in the Pacific. Multicoloured.

668	40c. Type **97**		2·00	1·40
669	50c. Japanese anti-aircraft gun (vert)		2·25	1·40
670	60c. American troops storming beach		2·50	1·40
671	$1.50 Map of Funafuti Atoll (vert)		6·50	6·50

98 "Cepora perimale"

1993. "Indopex '93" International Stamp Exhibition", Surabaya, Indonesia. Sheet 81×111 mm.

MS672 **98** $1.50 multicoloured   3·50   3·75

99 Fluted Giant Clam

1993. Marine Life. Multicoloured.

673	40c. Type **99**	50	50
674	50c. Anemone crab	60	60
675	60c. Octopus	70	70
676	$1.50 Green turtle	1·50	1·75

100 Queen Elizabeth II and Prince Philip in Land Rover

1993. 40th Anniv of Coronation.

677	**100**	40c. multicoloured	50	50
678	–	50c. multicoloured	60	60
679	–	60c. multicoloured	70	70
680	–	$1.50 multicoloured	1·50	1·75

MS681 88×88 mm. $2 green, yellow and black   7·00   8·00

DESIGNS: 50c. Queen Elizabeth drinking kava; 60c. Queen Elizabeth with parasol; $1.50, Ceremonial welcome; $2 Crowning of Queen Elizabeth II, 1953.

1993. "Taipei '93" International Stamp Exhibition, Taiwan. Sheet, 85×85 mm, containing multicoloured design as T **98**.

MS682 $1.50, "Geoffroyi godart" (vert)   3·75   5·00

1993. "Bangkok 1993" International Stamp Exhibition, Thailand. Sheet, 86×86 mm, containing horiz design as T **98**.

MS683 $1.50 "Paradisea staudinger"   2·00   2·50

101 Hermit Crab and Shells on Beach

1993. Environmental Protection. Multicoloured.

684	40c. Type **101**	50	50
685	50c. Conch shell and starfish	60	60
686	60c. Crab, seaweed and shells	70	70
687	$1.50 Herring gull and human footprint on beach	1·75	1·75

MS688 126×80 mm. Nos. 684/7   5·50   6·00

102 Virgin and Child with Christmas Tree

1993. Christmas. Multicoloured.

689	40c. Type **102**	50	50
690	50c. Candle	60	60
691	60c. Angel	70	70
692	$1.50 Decorated palm tree	1·50	1·75

1994. "Hong Kong '94" International Stamp Exhibition. Sheet 85×85 mm containing multicoloured design as T **98**.

MS693 $2 "Danaus plexippus" (vert)   3·25   3·75

103 Beach

1994. Island Scenery. Multicoloured.

694	40c. Type **103**	60	50
695	50c. Lagoon	70	60
696	60c. Distant island	80	70
697	$1.50 Launch and outrigger canoes on beach	1·50	1·75

104 Irish Red Setter

1994. Chinese New Year ("Year of the Dog"). Multicoloured.

698	40c. Type **104**	1·25	90
699	50c. Golden retriever	1·40	1·00
700	60c. West Highland terrier	1·60	1·10
701	$1.50 German shepherd	3·00	3·25

105 World Cup, Australian Player and Sydney Opera House

1994. World Cup Football Championship, U.S.A. Multicoloured.

702	40c. Type **105**	50	50
703	50c. English player and Big Ben, London	60	60
704	60c. Argentinian player and House of Assembly, Buenos Aires	70	70
705	$1.50 German player and Brandenburg Gate, Berlin	1·50	1·75

MS706 105×99 mm. $2 American player and Statue of Liberty, New York   4·25   5·50

106 Giant Button Top

1994. Sea Snails. Multicoloured.

707	40c. Type **106**	50	50
708	50c. Tapestry turban	60	60
709	60c. "Planaxis savignyi"	70	70
710	$1.50 Green-lined paper bubble	1·50	1·75

107 Pekingese and Logo

1994. "Philakorea '94" International Stamp Exhibition, Seoul. Sheet 106×72 mm.

MS711 **107** $1.50 multicoloured   2·50   3·25

1994. "Singpex '94" Stamp Exhibition. Nos. 502/3 and 509/10 optd **SINGPEX '94 AUG 31-SEP 5 SINGAPORE** and emblem.

712	5c. Type **66**	25	40
713	10c. White tern	30	40
714	40c. Bristle-thighed curlew	60	70
715	45c. Bar-tailed godwit	60	70

109 "Saturn V" Launch

1994. 25th Anniv of First Manned Moon Landing. Multicoloured.

716	40c. Type **109**	60	60
717	50c. "Apollo 11" capsule	70	70
718	60c. Neil Armstrong and American flag	90	90
719	$1.50 Capsule re-entry	1·75	2·00

110 Boys swimming with Log

1994. Christmas. Local Customs. Multicoloured.

720	40c. Type **110**	50	50
721	50c. Fishermen landing catch	60	60
722	60c. Christmas dinner	70	70
723	$1.50 Traditional dancers	1·50	1·75

111 Pig asleep

1995. Chinese New Year ("Year of the Pig"). Multicoloured.

724	40c. Type **111**	50	50
725	50c. Two pigs and vegetation	60	60
726	60c. Three pigs	70	70
727	$1.50 Sow suckling piglets	1·50	1·75

112 Emblem and Man with Produce in Wheelbarrow

1995. 50th Anniv of F.A.O. Multicoloured.

728	40c. Type **112**	50	50
729	50c. Man holding basket of food	60	60
730	60c. Woman slicing produce	70	70
731	$1.50 Woman mixing food	1·50	1·75

113 Beach and Lagoon

1995. Visit South Pacific Year. Multicoloured.

732	40c. Type **113**	50	50
733	50c. Catamaran	60	60
734	60c. Traditional hut	70	70
735	$1.50 Village on beach	1·50	1·75

114 "Dendrobium comptonii"

1995. Pacific Coastal Orchids. Multicoloured.

736	40c. Type **114**	65	65
737	50c. "Dendrobium involutum"	75	75
738	60c. "Dendrobium rarum"	85	85
739	$1.50 "Grammatophyllum scriptum"	2·00	2·50

115 Japanese Soldier and Maps of Tuvalu and Japan

1995. 50th Anniv of End of Second World War. Multicoloured.

740	40c. Type **115**	1·25	90
741	50c. American soldier and beach landing	1·40	1·10
742	60c. American marine and tree	1·60	1·25
743	$1.50 American soldier and atomic explosion	4·00	4·50

116 Tuvalu Dancer

1995. "JAKARTA '95" Stamp Exhibition, Indonesia. Sheet 85×85 mm.

MS744 **116** $1 multicoloured   2·00   2·25

117 "Phalaenopsis amabillis"

1995. "Singapore '95" International Stamp Exhibition. Sheet 85×85 mm.

MS745 **117** $1 multicoloured   2·75   3·00

118 Tuvaluans in Outrigger Canoes

1995. 50th Anniv of United Nations. Sheet 83×70 mm, containing T **118** and similar vert design. Multicoloured.

MS746 $1 Type **118**; $1 U.N. headquarters, New York   2·50   3·00

119 "Silent Night" and Aerial View of Airfield

1995. Christmas. Christmas Carols. Multicoloured.

747	40c. Type **119**	50	50
748	50c. "O Come all ye Faithful" and choir boys	60	60
749	60c. "The First Nowell" and choir girls	70	70
750	$1.50 "Hark the Herald Angels sing" and angel	1·50	1·75

120 1976 Separation 4c. Stamp

1996. 20th Anniv of Separation from Gilbert Islands and of First Tuvalu Postage Stamps. Sheet 108×82 mm, containing T **120** and similar horiz designs showing values from 1976 Separation issue.

MS751 40c. Type **120**; 60c. 1976 10c. stamp; $1 1976 35c. stamp   4·25   4·50

121 Rat with Jar

1996. Chinese New Year ("Year of the Rat"). Sheet 130×87 mm containing T **121** and similar vert design. Multicoloured.

MS752	50c. Type **121**; 50c. Rat drinking from jar	1·40	1·75

1996. "HONGPEX '96" International Stamp Exhibition. Sheet as No. **MS**752, but additionally inscr with "HONGPEX '96" emblem on sheet margin.

MS753	50c. Type **121**; 50c. Rat drinking from jar	1·75	2·00

1996. "indonesia 96" International Youth Stamp Exhibition, Bandung. No. **MS**744 optd indonesia 96.

MS754	85×85 mm. **116** $1 multicoloured	2·00	2·50

1996. "CHINA '96" Ninth Asian International Stamp Exhibition, Peking. Sheet as No. **MS**752, but additionally inscr with "CHINA '96" emblem and puppet holding envelope on sheet margin.

MS755	50c. Type **121**; 50c. Rat drinking from jar	1·40	2·00

123 Volleyball

1996. Olympic Games, Atlanta. Multicoloured.

756	40c. Type **123**	50	50
757	50c. Swimming	60	60
758	60c. Weightlifting	70	70
759	$1.50 Boxing	1·50	1·75

1996. "TAIPEI '96" Tenth Asian International Stamp Exhibition, Taiwan. No. 639 surch **$1.00 TAIPEI '96 21-27 OCTOBER** and emblem.

760	$1 on 45c. Black-finned pigfish	1·75	2·00

125 Children being immunised

1996. 50th Anniv of UNICEF. Multicoloured.

761	40c. Type **125**	50	50
762	50c. Teacher and children	60	60
763	60c. Domestic water tanks and child	70	70
764	$1.50 Children in hydroponic greenhouse	1·50	1·75

126 Wise Men following Star

1996. Christmas. Multicoloured.

765	40c. Type **126**	50	50
766	50c. Shepherds and star	60	60
767	60c. Wise men presenting gifts	70	70
768	$1.50 The Nativity	1·50	1·75

127 Ox ploughing

1997. HONG KONG '97 International Stamp Exhibition. Chinese New Year ("Year of the Ox"). Sheet 97×83 mm. P 14.

MS769	$2 multicoloured	2·40	3·25

1997. Fish (2nd series). As T **14**. Multicoloured.

770	25c. Sehel's grey mullet	40	40
771	30c. Leatherback	45	45
772	40c. Hump-backed snapper ("Paddletail")	55	50
773	45c. Long-nosed emperor	60	50
774	50c. Blue-spined unicornfish	60	50
775	55c. Oblique-banded snapper	65	55
776	60c. Twin-spotted snapper ("Red bass")	70	60
777	70c. Rusty jobfish	80	75
778	90c. Leopard flounder	1·00	90
779	$1 Ruby snapper	1·25	1·25
780	$2 Yellow-striped snapper	1·90	2·25
781	$3 Black jack	2·75	3·25

128 White Pekin Ducks

1997. "Pacific '97" International Stamp Exhibition, San Francisco. Ducks. Multicoloured.

782	40c. Type **128**	50	50
783	50c. Muscovy ducks	60	60
784	60c. Pacific black ducks	70	70
785	$1.50 Mandarin ducks	1·50	1·75

129 Korat King Cat

1997. Cats. Multicoloured.

786	40c. Type **129**	50	50
787	50c. Long-haired ginger kitten	60	60
788	60c. Shaded cameo	70	70
789	$1.50 Maine coon	1·50	1·75

1997. Return of Hong Kong to China. Sheet, 130×90 mm, containing design as No. 780.

MS790	$2 Yellow-striped snapper	1·50	2·50

1997. Golden Wedding of Queen Elizabeth and Prince Philip. As T **87** of Kiribati. Multicoloured.

791	40c. Queen Elizabeth and Prince Philip in Land Rover	50	55
792	40c. Queen Elizabeth	50	55
793	50c. Queen Elizabeth accepting ceremonial gift	60	70
794	50c. Prince Philip	60	70
795	60c. Three portraits of Queen Elizabeth	70	80
796	60c. Queen Elizabeth and Prince Philip leaving Philatelic Bureau	70	80
MS797	110×70 mm. $2 Queen Elizabeth and Prince Philip in landau (horiz)	2·10	2·75

Nos. 791/2, 793/4 and 795/6 respectively were printed together, *se-tenant*, with the backgrounds forming composite designs.

130 Turtle Hunting

1997. Christmas. Multicoloured.

798	40c. Type **130**	40	40
799	50c. Pole fishing	50	50
800	60c. Canoe racing	60	60
801	$1.50 Traditional dancing	1·40	1·75

131 Tiger

1998. Chinese New Year ("Year of the Tiger"). Sheet 110×69 mm.

MS802	**131** $1.40 multicoloured	1·50	2·25

1998. Diana, Princess of Wales Commemoration. Sheet, 145×70 mm, containing vert designs as T **194** of St. Helena. Multicoloured.

MS803	80c. Wearing pearl drop earrings, 1990; 80c. Wearing black evening dress, 1995; 80c. Wearing tiara, 1992; 80c. Wearing beige coat (sold at $3.20 + 20c. charity premium)	1·75	2·50

1998. 80th Anniv of the Royal Air Force. As T **270** of Samoa. Multicoloured.

804	40c. Hawker Woodcock	60	50
805	50c. Vickers Victoria	65	60
806	60c. Bristol Brigand	75	70
807	$1.50 De Havilland D.H.C.1 Chipmunk	2·00	2·25
MS808	110×77 mm. $1 Sopwith Pup; $1 Armstrong Whitworth F.K.S; $1 North American Harvard; $1 Vultee Vengeance	3·75	5·00

132 "Los Reyes" and "Santiago" (Alvare Mendana)

1998. Ships (5th series). Multicoloured.

809	40c. Type **132**	50	50
810	50c. "Morning Star II" (missionary schooner)	60	60
811	60c. "The Light" (missionary brigantine)	70	70
812	$1.50 New Zealand missionary schooner	1·75	2·00

133 Bottlenose Dolphin

1998. Dolphins and Porpoises. Multicoloured.

813	40c. Type **133**	50	50
814	50c. Dall's porpoise	60	60
815	60c. Harbour porpoise	70	70
816	$1.50 Common dolphin	1·50	1·75

134 Bikenibeu Paeniu, Teacher and Class

1998. 20th Anniv of Independence. Prime Ministers of Tuvalu. Multicoloured.

817	40c. Type **134**	50	50
818	60c. Kamuta Latasi and diagram of communications network	60	60
819	90c. Sir Tomasi Puapua and emblem of Trust Fund	85	85
820	$1.50 Sir Toaripi Lauti and emblem of Maritime School	1·50	1·75
MS821	115×81 mm. Nos. 817/20	3·00	3·25

135 "Psammocra digitata" and Bleached "Platygyra daedalea"

1998. Coral Reef Life (4th series). Multicoloured.

822	20c. Type **135**	30	30
823	30c. Bleached "Acropora robusta"	40	40
824	50c. Bleached "Acropora hyacinthus"	60	60
825	$1 Bleached "Acropora danai" and "Montastrea curta"	1·10	1·25
MS826	74×54 mm. $1.50, Bleached "Seriatopora" and Bleached "Stylophora"	2·00	2·25

136 Mary and Joseph travelling to Bethlehem

1998. Christmas. Multicoloured.

827	40c. Type **136**	50	50
828	50c. Shepherds and angel	60	60
829	60c. The Nativity	70	70
830	$1.50 Visit of Wise Men	1·50	1·75

137 Rabbit playing Pipa and Chinese Lantern

1999. Chinese New Year ("Year of the Rabbit"). Sheet 115×75 mm.

MS831	**137** $2 multicoloured	2·25	2·75

138 "Heemskerk" (Tasman), 1642

1999. "Australia '99" World Stamp Exhibition, Melbourne. Ships (6th series). Multicoloured.

832	40c. Type **138**	60	50
833	50c. H.M.S. "Endeavour" (Cook), 1769	75	65
834	90c. "Sophia Jane" (paddle-steamer), 1831	1·00	90
835	$1.50 "Chusan I" (screw steamer), 1852	1·75	2·00
MS836	135×75 mm. $2 H.M.S. "Supply" (brig), 1788	2·25	2·75

1999. Kosovo Relief Campaign. Nos. 505, 508, 512 and 515 optd **Kosovo Relief Fund**.

837	20c. Phoenix petrel	35	40
838	35c. Sooty tern	50	55
839	55c. Great frigate bird	65	75
840	$1 Long-tailed koel	1·25	1·40

1999. 30th Anniv of the First Manned Landing on Moon. As T **94a** of St. Kitts. Multicoloured.

841	40c. Lift-off	50	50
842	60c. Lander approaches Moon	70	70
843	90c. Lander leaving Moon	1·10	90
844	$1.50 Crew recovery	1·75	2·00
MS845	90×80 mm. $2 Earth as seen from Moon (circular, 40 mm diameter)	2·50	3·00

1999. "Queen Elizabeth the Queen Mother's Century". As T **199** of St. Helena. Multicoloured.

846	40c. King George VI and Queen Elizabeth inspecting bomb damage, 1940	60	60
847	60c. Queen Elizabeth with her daughters, 1951	75	75
848	90c. With Princes William and Harry, 1995	90	90
849	$1.50 Inspecting the Queen's Dragoon Guards	1·50	2·00
MS850	145×70 mm. $2 Lady Elizabeth Bowes-Lyon aged 6, and Yuri Gagarin (first cosmonaut)	2·25	2·75

140 "Solandra maxima" (flower)

1999. Flowers. Multicoloured.

851	90c. Type **140**	1·10	1·25
852	90c. "Cistus" sp.	1·10	1·25
853	90c. "Pandorea jasminoides"	1·10	1·25
854	90c. "Grewia caffra"	1·10	1·25
855	90c. "Mandevilla x amabilis"	1·10	1·25
856	90c. "Punica granatum" (open flowers)	1·10	1·25
857	90c. "Cassylha filiformis"	1·10	1·25
858	90c. "Wollastonia biflora"	1·10	1·25
859	90c. "Portulacacae lueta" (without local inscr)	1·10	1·25
860	90c. "Portulacacae lueta" (also inscr "TAMOLOC")	1·10	1·25
861	90c. "Vigna marina"	1·10	1·25
862	90c. "Punica granatum" (closed flowers)	1·10	1·25
MS863	97×104 mm. $3 "Cassia surattensis" (vert)	2·75	3·50

No. **MS**863 is inscribed "SCRAMBLED EGGES" in error.
Nos. 851/6 and 857/62 were each printed together, *se-tenant*, with the backgrounds forming composite designs.

141 Lady of Peace

1999. New Millennium. Allegories of Peace. Multicoloured.

864	90c. Type **141**	1·25	1·25
865	90c. Olive branch	1·25	1·25
866	90c. Dove	1·25	1·25
867	90c. Lion	1·25	1·25
868	90c. Lamb	1·25	1·25
869	90c. Cherub with bouquet ("War crowning Peace")	1·25	1·25

870	90c. As Type **142**, but with white frame	1·25	1·25

MS871 94×75 mm. $2 Sunrise and "2000" (46×28 mm). 4·75 5·00

Nos. 864/9 were printed together, se-tenant, forming a composite design.

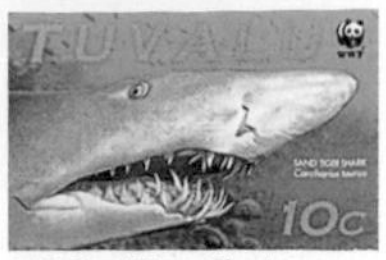

142 Sand Tiger Shark showing Teeth

2000. Endangered Species. Sand Tiger Shark. Multicoloured.

872	10c. Type **142**	30	25
873	30c. Sand tiger shark swimming	50	45
874	50c. Sand tiger shark over seaweed	75	75
875	60c. Group of sand tiger sharks	90	1·00

MS876 207×135 mm. As Nos. 872/5, but without WWF pander emblem 2·50 2·75

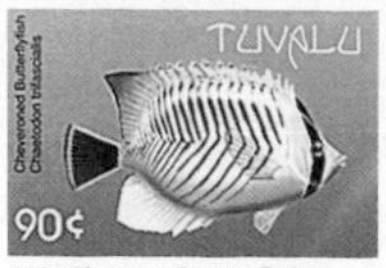

143 Chevron Butterflyfish

2000. Marine Life. Multicoloured.

877	90c. Type **143**	1·75	1·75
878	90c. Mandarin fish	1·75	1·75
879	90c. Bicoloured angelfish	1·75	1·75
880	90c. Copper-banded butterflyfish	1·75	1·75
881	90c. Clown anemonefish	1·75	1·75
882	90c. Lemon-peel angelfish	1·75	1·75
883	90c. Manta ray	1·75	1·75
884	90c. White shark	1·75	1·75
885	90c. Hammerhead shark	1·75	1·75
886	90c. Tiger shark	1·75	1·75
887	90c. Great barracuda	1·75	1·75
888	90c. Leatherback turtle	1·75	1·75
889	90c. Common tern	1·75	1·75
890	90c. Red-billed tropic bird ("White-tailed Tropicbird")	1·75	1·75
891	90c. Emperor snapper	1·75	1·75
892	90c. Clown triggerfish	1·75	1·75
893	90c. Pennant coralfish ("Longfin Bannerfish")	1·75	1·75
894	90c. Harlequin tuskfish	1·75	1·75
895	90c. Wilson's storm petrel	1·75	1·75
896	90c. Common dolphin	1·75	1·75
897	90c. Yellow seahorse ("Spotted Seahorse")	1·75	1·75
898	90c. Threeband demoiselle	1·75	1·75
899	90c. Coral hind	1·75	1·75
900	90c. Palette surgeonfish	1·75	1·75
901	90c. Great frigatebird	1·75	1·75
902	90c. Brown booby	1·75	1·75
903	90c. Dugong	1·75	1·75
904	90c. Red knot	1·75	1·75
905	90c. Common starfish	1·75	1·75
906	90c. Hawksbill turtle	1·75	1·75
907	90c. Whale shark	1·75	1·75
908	90c. Six-blotched hind ("Sixspot Grouper")	1·75	1·75
909	90c. Blue-streaked cleaner wrasse	1·75	1·75
910	90c. Lemon shark	1·75	1·75
911	90c. Spotted boxfish ("Spotted Trunkfish")	1·75	1·75
912	90c. Forceps butterflyfish ("Long-nosed Butterflyfish")	1·75	1·75

MS913 Three sheets, each 103×73 mm. (a) $3 Pygmy parrotfish. (b) $3 Picasso triggerfish. (c) $3 Sailfish Set of 3 sheets 20·00 22·00

Nos. 877/82, 883/8, 889/94, 895/900, 901/6 and 907/12 were each printed together, se-tenant, with the backgrounds forming composite designs.

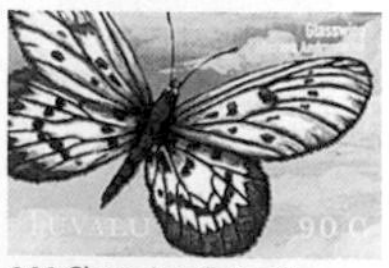

144 Glasswing Butterfly

2000. South Pacific Butterflies. Multicoloured.

914	90c. Type **144**	2·00	2·00
915	90c. Leftwing butterfly	2·00	2·00
916	90c. Moth butterfly	2·00	2·00
917	90c. Blue triangle	2·00	2·00
918	90c. Beak butterfly	2·00	2·00
919	90c. Plane butterfly	2·00	2·00
920	90c. Birdwing (vert)	2·00	2·00
921	90c. Tailed emperor (vert)	2·00	2·00
922	90c. Orchard shallowtail (vert)	2·00	2·00
923	90c. Union jack (vert)	2·00	2·00
924	90c. Long-tailed blue (vert)	2·00	2·00
925	90c. Common jezebel (vert)	2·00	2·00
926	90c. Caper white (vert)	2·00	2·00
927	90c. Common Indian crow (vert)	2·00	2·00
928	90c. Eastern flat (vert)	2·00	2·00
929	90c. Cairns birdwing (vert)	2·00	2·00
930	90c. Monarch (vert)	2·00	2·00
931	90c. Meadow argus (vert)	2·00	2·00

MS932 Two sheets, each 70×100 mm. (a) $3 Great egg-fly (vert). (b) $3 Palmfly Set of 2 sheets 16·00 18·00

Nos. 914/19, 920/5 and 926/31 were each printed together, se-tenant, with the backgrounds forming composite designs.

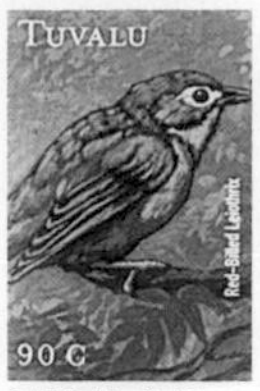

145 Pekin Robin ("Red-Billed Leiothrix")

2000. South Pacific Birds. Multicoloured.

933	90c. Type **145**	2·50	2·50
934	90c. Grey shrike-thrush	2·50	2·50
935	90c. Great frigatebird	2·50	2·50
936	90c. River kingfisher ("Common Kingfisher")	2·50	2·50
937	90c. Chestnut-breasted mannikin ("Chestnut-breasted Finch")	2·50	2·50
938	90c. White tern	2·50	2·50
939	90c. Rainbow lorikeet	2·50	2·50
940	90c. White-throated tree creeper	2·50	2·50
941	90c. White-tailed kingfisher	2·50	2·50
942	90c. Golden whistler	2·50	2·50
943	90c. Grey plover ("Black-bellied Plover")	2·50	2·50
944	90c. Australian stone-curlew ("Beach Thick-knee")	2·50	2·50
945	90c. White-collared kingfisher	2·50	2·50
946	90c. Peale's petrel ("Scaled Petrel")	2·50	2·50
947	90c. Blue wren ("Superb Blue Wren")	2·50	2·50
948	90c. Osprey	2·50	2·50
949	90c. Great cormorant	2·50	2·50
950	90c. Peregrine falcon	2·50	2·50

MS951 Two sheets. (a) 100×70 mm. $3 Broad-billed prion (horiz). (b) 70×100 mm $3 Morepork Set of 2 sheets 20·00 21·00

Nos. 933/8, 939/44 and 945/50 were each printed together, se-tenant, with the backgrounds forming composite designs.

No. 945 is inscribed "Kingisher" in error.

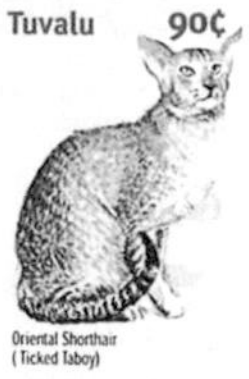

146 Oriental Shorthair

2000. Cats and Dogs. Multicoloured.

952	90c. Type **146**	1·50	1·50
953	90c. Balinese	1·50	1·50
954	90c. Somali	1·50	1·50
955	90c. Chinchilla Persian	1·50	1·50
956	90c. Tonkinese	1·50	1·50
957	90c. Japanese bobtail	1·50	1·50
958	90c. Oriental shorthair (head)	1·50	1·50
959	90c. Balinese (head)	1·50	1·50
960	90c. Somali (head)	1·50	1·50
961	90c. Chinchilla Persian (head)	1·50	1·50
962	90c. Tonkinese (head)	1·50	1·50
963	90c. Japanese bobtail (head)	1·50	1·50
964	90c. Fox terrier (horiz)	1·50	1·50
965	90c. Collie (horiz)	1·50	1·50
966	90c. Boston terrier (horiz)	1·50	1·50
967	90c. Welsh corgie (horiz)	1·50	1·50
968	90c. Pointer (horiz)	1·50	1·50
969	90c. Dalmatian (horiz)	1·50	1·50
970	90c. Dalmatian (head)	1·50	1·50
971	90c. Boston terrier (head)	1·50	1·50
972	90c. Fox terrier (head)	1·50	1·50
973	90c. Pointer (head)	1·50	1·50
974	90c. Welsh corgi (head)	1·50	1·50
975	90c. Collie (head)	1·50	1·50

MS976 Two sheets. (a) 96×70 mm. $3 Oriental shorthair. (b) 70×96 mm. $3 Scottish terrier (horiz) Set of 2 sheets 9·00 10·00

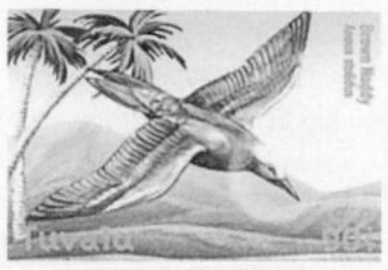

147 Common Noddy ("Brown Noddy")

2000. Fauna. Multicoloured.

977	90c. Type **147**	1·75	1·75
978	90c. Great frigatebird	1·75	1·75
979	90c. Emperor angelfish	1·75	1·75
980	90c. Common dolphin	1·75	1·75
981	90c. Hermit crab	1·75	1·75
982	90c. Threadfin butterflyfish	1·75	1·75
983	90c. Red-footed booby	1·75	1·75
984	90c. Red-tailed tropicbird	1·75	1·75
985	90c. Grey plover ("Black-bellied Plover")	1·75	1·75
986	90c. Common tern	1·75	1·75
987	90c. Ruddy turnstone	1·75	1·75
988	90c. Sanderling	1·75	1·75

MS989 70×93 mm. $3 Great frigatebird (vert) 5·50 6·00

Nos. 977/82 and 983/8 were each printed together, se-tenant, with the backgrounds forming composite designs.

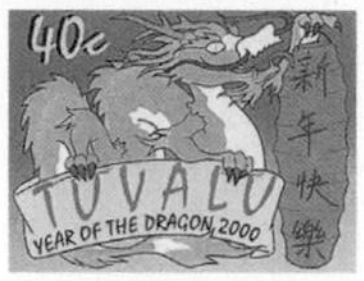

148 Green Dragon

2001. Chinese New Year ("Years of the Dragon and Snake"). Multicoloured.

990	40c. Type **148**	90	65
991	60c. Green snake with orange markings	1·25	85
992	90c. Orange snake with green markings	1·75	1·40
993	$1.05 Blue dragon	2·25	2·75

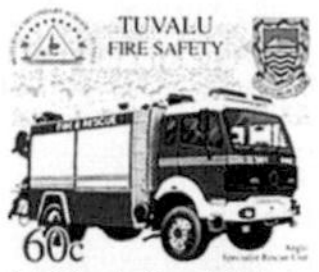

149 Anglo Specialist Rescue Unit

2001. Fire Service. Multicoloured.

994	60c. Type **149**	1·25	60
995	90c. Anglo 4800 water/foam tender	1·75	85
996	$1.50 Bronto 33-2T1 combined telescopic ladder/hydraulic platform	2·75	2·75
997	$2 Anglo 450 LRX water tenders	3·00	3·50

MS998 105×55 mm. $3 Wormald "Arrestor" ARFFV in gateway to Motufoua Secondary School 5·50 6·00

Nos. 994/7 also commemorate the first anniv of the fire tragedy at Motufoua Secondary School.

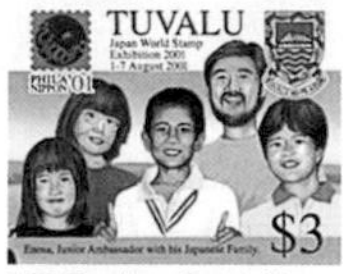

150 Tuvaluan Boy with Japanese Family

2001. "Philanippon '01" International Stamp Exhibition, Tokyo. 13th Asian-Pacific Children's Convention, Fukuoka. Sheet 94×80 mm.

MS999 **150** $3 multicoloured 3·50 3·75

2001. 101st Birthday of Queen Elizabeth the Queen Mother. Nos. 846/9 optd or surch **101 birthday**.

1000	60c. Queen Elizabeth with her daughters, 1951	75	60
1001	90c. With Princes William and Harry, 1995	1·10	85
1002	$1.50 Inspecting the Queen's Dragoon Guards	2·00	2·25
1003	$2 on 40c. King George VI and Queen Elizabeth inspecting bomb damage, 1940	2·75	3·00

MS1004 145×70 mm. $5 on $2 Lady Elizabeth Bowes-Lyon aged 6, and Yuri Gagarin (first cosmonaut) 7·00 8·00

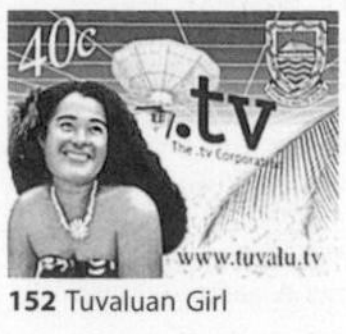

152 Tuvaluan Girl

2001. Inauguration of .tv Corporation (Internet Service Provider). Each featuring satellite dish and web address. Multicoloured.

1005	40c. Type **152**	70	60
1006	60c. Local dancers	85	70
1007	90c. Tuvaluan man blowing conch shell	1·25	1·00
1008	$1.50 Young child with flower garland around head	2·25	2·75

MS1009 85×50 mm. $2 Satellite dishes and web address 2·75 3·00

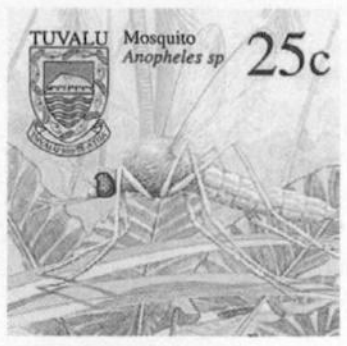

153 Mosquito

2001. Insects. Multicoloured.

1010	25c. Type **153**	90	80
1011	30c. Giant African snail	1·00	1·00
1012	40c. Cockroach	1·25	60
1013	45c. Stick insect	1·40	75
1014	50c. Green stink bug	1·40	75
1015	55c. Dragonfly	1·50	80
1016	60c. Caterpillar of monarch butterfly	1·60	70
1017	70c. Coconut beetle	1·75	1·50
1018	90c. Honey bee	1·90	90
1019	$1 Monarch butterfly	2·50	1·75
1020	$2 Common eggfly butterfly	4·50	5·50
1021	$3 Painted lady butterfly	6·50	7·50

2002. "United We Stand". Support for Victims of 11 September 2001 Terrorist Attacks. As T **445** of St. Vincent.

1022	$2 multicoloured (blue background)	2·25	2·50
1023	$2 multicoloured (yellow background)	2·25	2·50

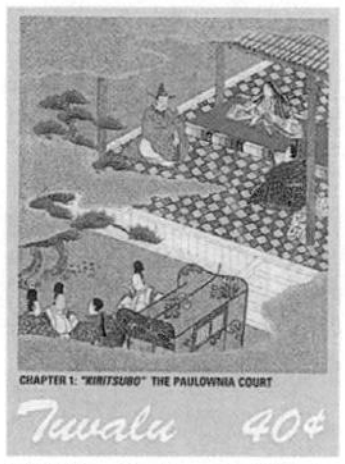

154 The Paulownia Court

2002. Japanese Art. "The Tale of Genji" (Murasaki Shikibu). Multicoloured.

1024	40c. Type **154**	60	65
1025	40c. The Broom Tree	60	65
1026	40c. The Shell of the Locust	60	65
1027	40c. Evening Faces	60	65
1028	40c. Lavender	60	65
1029	40c. The Safflower	60	65
1030	60c. The Festival of the Cherry Blossoms	75	80
1031	60c. Heartvine	75	80
1032	60c. The Sacred Tree	75	80
1033	60c. The Orange Blossoms	75	80
1034	60c. Suma	75	80
1035	60c. Akashi	75	80
1036	90c. The Wormwood Patch	95	1·00
1037	90c. The Gate House	95	1·00
1038	90c. A Picture Contest	95	1·00
1039	90c. The Wind in the Pines	95	1·00
1040	90c. A Rack of Cloud	95	1·00
1041	90c. The Morning Glory	95	1·00

MS1042 Three sheets, each 93×124 mm. (a) $4 An Autumn Excursion (chapter 7). (b) $4 Channel Buoys (chapter 14). (c) $4 The Maiden (chapter 21). Imperf Set of 3 sheets 12·00 14·00

Nos. 1024/9 (chapters 1/6), 1030/5 (chapters 8/13) and 1036/41 (chapters 15/20).

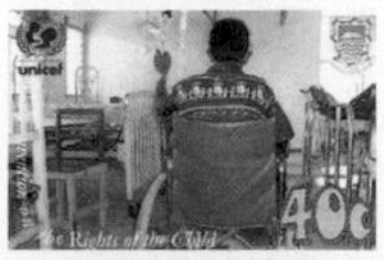

155 Young Hospital Patient in Wheelchair

2002. UNICEF. Rights of the Child. Multicoloured.

1043	40c. Type **155**	75	60
1044	60c. Children by roadside	1·00	70
1045	90c. Nauti Primary School, Funafuti	1·50	1·00
1046	$1.50 Mother and baby	2·50	3·25

MS1047 110×80 mm. $1 Taulosa Karl; $1 Simalua Jacinta Enele (Tuvalu representatives at UN special session on children) 4·50 5·00

2002. Golden Jubilee. As T **110** of St. Kitts. Multicoloured.

1048 $1.50 Princes William and Harry as young boys 2·75 2·75

1049 $1.50 Queen Elizabeth at garden party 2·75 2·75

1050 $1.50 Queen Elizabeth with Prince Philip wearing robes of Order of the Bath 2·75 2·75

1051 $1.50 Queen Elizabeth in red hat and coat 2·75 2·75

MS1052 76×108 mm. $4 Queen Elizabeth on horseback for Trooping the Colour 6·50 6·50

2002. World Cup Football Championship, Japan and Korea. As T **113** of St. Kitts. Multicoloured.

1053 90c. Tom Finney (England) 1·25 1·40

1054 90c. Publicity poster, Germany, 1974 1·25 1·40

1055 90c. Portuguese player 1·25 1·40

1056 90c. Uruguayan player 1·25 1·40

1057 90c. Suwon Stadium, Korea (56×42 mm) 1·25 1·40

MS1058 64×86 mm. $4 Johann Cruyff (Holland) 4·75 6·00

No. **MS**1058 is inscribed "JOHAN CRUFF" in error.

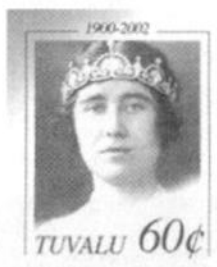

156 Duchess of York, 1923

2002. Queen Elizabeth the Queen Mother Commemoration. Each multicoloured ($1.50) or black and lilac (others).

1059 60c. Type **156** 75 75

1060 60c. Duchess of York, 1923 (different) (face value at left) 75 75

1061 90c. Queen Mother at Sandringham, 1992 (29×25 mm) 1·10 1·25

1062 90c. Queen Mother accepting posy from child, 1989 (29×25 mm) 1·10 1·25

1063 90c. Queen Mother with teddy bear, Queen Charlotte's Hospital, 1989 (29×25 mm) 1·10 1·25

[illegible] Didcot, 1989 (29×25 mm) 1·10 1·25

1065 $1.50 Queen Mother at Tower Hamlets Memorial Garden, 2001 (40×30 mm) 2·00 2·25

MS1066 Two sheets, each 65×101 mm. (a) $2 Lady Elizabeth Bowes-Lyon with her brother David; $2 Queen Mother in old age. (b) $2 Queen Elizabeth smelling rose, 1950s; $2 Queen Mother, 1971(each 26×40 mm). Set of 2 sheets 9·50 10·00

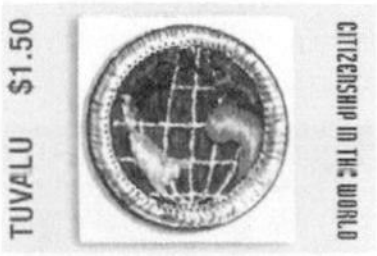

157 Citizen of the World Badge

2002. 20th World Scout Jamboree, Thailand. Multicoloured.

1067 $1.50 Type **157** 1·75 2·00

1068 $1.50 First Aid badge 1·75 2·00

1069 $1.50 Personal Fitness badge 1·75 2·00

1070 $1.50 Environmental Science badge 1·75 2·00

MS1071 66×85 mm. $5 Lord Baden-Powell (vert) 7·00 7·50

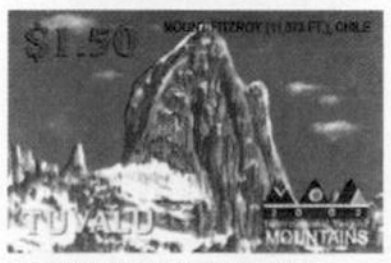

158 Mt Fitzroy, Argentina

2002. International Year of Mountains. Multicoloured.

1072 $1.50 Type **158** 1·75 2·00

1073 $1.50 Mt Foraker, U.S.A. 1·75 2·00

1074 $1.50 Mt Fujiyama, Japan 1·75 2·00

1075 $1.50 Mt Makalu, Nepal 1·75 2·00

MS1076 63×84 mm. $4 Mt Godwin-Austen (K2), Kashmir (vert) 7·00 7·50

No. 1072 is inscribed "CHILE" in error.

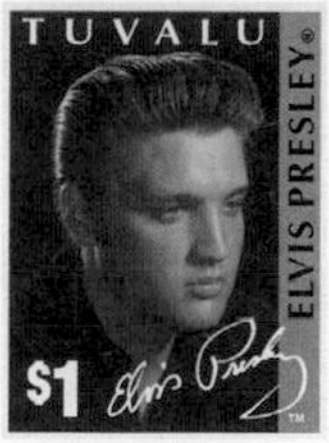

159 Elvis Presley

2002. 25th Death Anniv of Elvis Presley.

1077 **159** $1 multicoloured 1·40 1·40

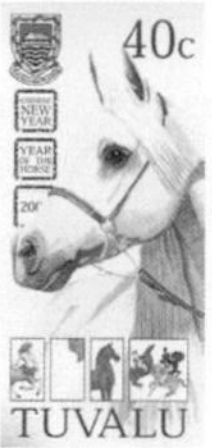

160 Palomino Horse

2003. End of Chinese "Year of the Horse". Multicoloured.

1078 40c. Type **160** 60 50

1079 60c. White Arab horse 75 60

1080 90c. Wild horse 1·10 90

1081 $2 Chestnut horse 2·75 3·50

MS1082 75×75 mm. $1.50 Seahorse; $1.50 Group of seahorses 4·25 4·75

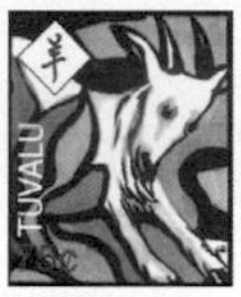

161 Ram in Bushes

2003. Chinese New Year ("Year of the Ram"). Multicoloured.

1083 75c. Type **161** 1·10 1·25

1084 75c. Side view of ram's head 1·10 1·25

[illegible]

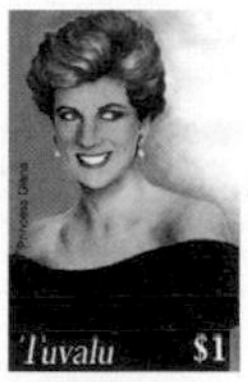

162 Diana, Princess of Wales

2003. Fifth Death Anniv of Diana, Princess of Wales. Multicoloured.

1086 $1 Type **162** 1·40 1·60

1087 $1 Princess Diana wearing emerald necklace 1·40 1·60

1088 $1 Wearing blue evening dress 1·40 1·60

1089 $1 Wearing turquoise scarf 1·40 1·60

1090 $1 Wearing pink blouse 1·40 1·60

1091 $1 Wearing lace dress 1·40 1·60

MS1092 90×105 mm. $4 Princess Diana and rose 5·00 6·00

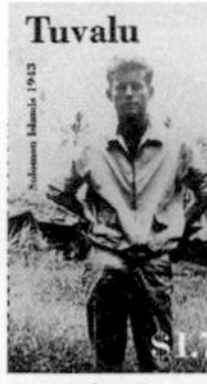

163 John F. Kennedy in Solomon Islands, 1943

2003. Life and Times of President John F. Kennedy. Two sheets containing T **163** and similar vert designs.

MS1093 127×142 mm. $1.75 Type **163** (green and black); $1.75 As Commander of USS *PT109* (motor torpedo boat) (deep brown, brown and black); $1.75 Receiving Medal for Gallantry, 1941 (deep blue, deep blue and black); $1.75 On crutches in Senate Campaign, 1952 (lilac and black) 9·00 10·00

MS1094 70×77 mm. $4 With father and brothers (lavender, violet and black) 4·50 5·00

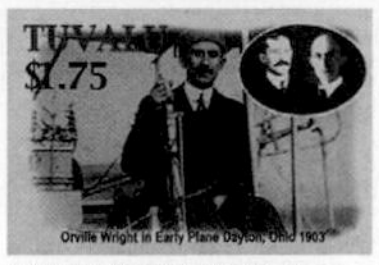

164 Orville Wright, Dayton, Ohio, 1903

2003. Centenary of Powered Flight. Sheets containing T **164** and similar horiz designs. Multicoloured.

MS1095 178×96 mm. $1.75 Type **164**; $1.75 Wilbur Wright with King Alphonso of Spain, Pau, France, 1909; $1.75 Wright Type A biplane, Le Mans, France, 1908; $1.75 Voisin "Boxkite", France, 1907 9·00 9·50

MS1096 178×96 mm. $1.75 Gabriel Voisin's motor boat powered glider, France, 1905; $1.75 Trajan Vuia in *Vuia No. 1*, France, 1906; $1.75 Santos-Dumont's biplane 14 bis, France, 1906; $1.75 Wright Type A biplane, Virginia, 1908 9·00 9·50

MS1097 Two sheets, each 95×65 mm. (a) $4 Wright Type A biplane, Virginia, 1908. (b) $4 Curtiss *June Bug*, 1908 Set of two sheets 9·00 9·50

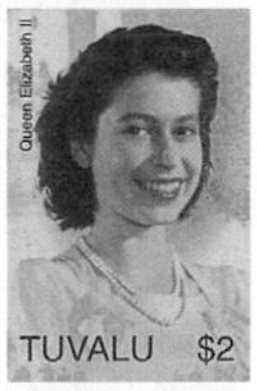

165 Princess Elizabeth

2003. 50th Anniv of Coronation. Multicoloured.

MS1098 155×93 mm. $2 Type **165**; $2 Queen wearing diadem; $2 Queen wearing yellow hat and coat 8·00 8·50

MS1099 76×106 mm. $4 Queen Elizabeth II 5·50 6·00

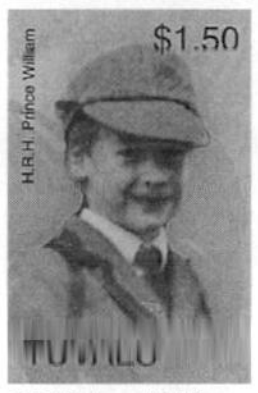

166 Prince William as Schoolboy

2003. 21st Birthday of Prince William of Wales. Multicoloured.

MS1100 156×86 mm. $1.50 Type **166**; $1.50 Wearing blue shirt; $1.50 Wearing polo helmet 6·50 7·00

MS1101 76×105 mm. $4 Prince William 6·00 6·50

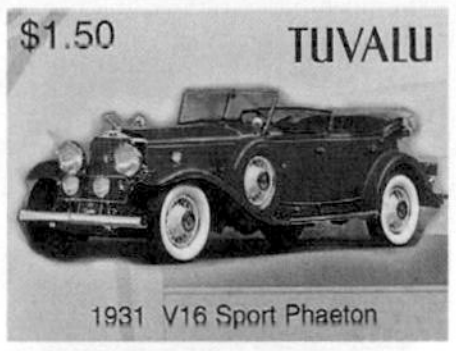

167 V16 Sport Phaeton (1931)

2003. Centenary of General Motors Cadillac. Multicoloured.

MS1102 126×176 mm. $1.50 Type **167**; $1.50 Eldorado Convertible (1959); $1.50 Seville Elegante (1979); $1.50 Seville Elegante (1983) 8·50 9·50

MS1103 89×125 mm. $4 Cadillac 5·50 6·00

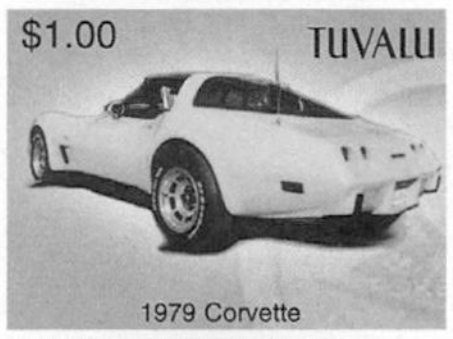

168 Yellow Corvette (1979)

2003. 50th Anniv of General Motors Chevrolet Corvette. Multicoloured.

MS1104 126×146 mm. $1 Type **168**; $1 Red Corvette (1979); $1 Silver Corvette (1979); $1 Corvette (1980) 8·00 8·50

MS1105 126×90 mm. $4 Corvette (1990) 8·00 8·50

2003. Centenary of Tour de France Cycle Race. As T **127** of St. Kitts. Multicoloured.

MS1106 158×98 mm. $1 Gastone Nencini (1960); $1 Jacques Anquetil (1961); $1 Jacques Anquetil (1962); $1 Jacques Anquetil (1963) 7·50 7·50

MS1107 98×68 mm. $4 Jan Janssen (1968) 7·50 7·50

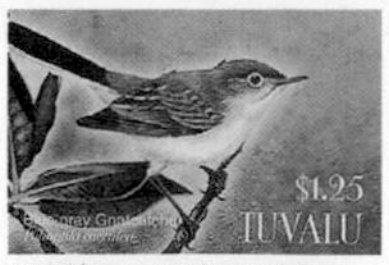

169 Blue grey Gnatcatcher

2003. Birds, Butterflies, Flowers and Orchids. Multicoloured.

MS1108 115×115 mm. $1.25 Type **169**; $1.25 White-eyed vireo; $1.25 Clapper rail; $1.25 Sandhill crane 9·50 9·50

MS1109 135×115 mm. $1.25 Malachite; $1.25 White hairstreak; $1.25 Giant swallowtail; $1.25 Bahamian swallowtail 9·50 9·50

MS1110 91×135 mm. $1.25 *Rhododendron yakushimanum*; $1.25 *Tulipa* "Golden Artist"; $1.25 *Lilium* "Golden Splendor"; $1.25 *Anthurium andraeanum* (all vert) 9·50 9·50

MS1111 107×116 mm. $1.25 *Dimerandra emarginata*; $1.25 *Oncidium lanceanum*; $1.25 *Isochilus linearis*; $1.25 *Oeceoclades maculate* (all vert) 9·50 9·50

MS1112 Four sheets. (a) 95×65 mm. $3 Grasshopper sparrow. (b) 65×95 mm. $3 Polydamas swallowtail. Imperf. (c) 65×95 mm. $3 *Rosa* "Candy Bianca". Imperf. (d) 95×65 mm. $3 *Oncidium ampliatum* Set of 4 sheets 22·00 24·00

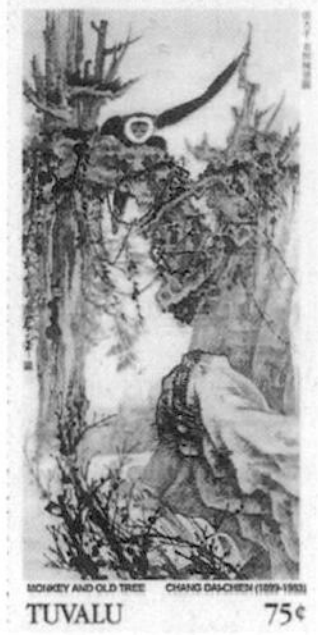

170 "Monkey and Old Tree"

2004. Chinese New Year ("Year of the Monkey"). Paintings by Chang Dai-Chien. Multicoloured.

MS1113 117×106 mm. 75c. ×4 Type **170** 4·00 4·25

[illegible] Monkeys" 3·25 3·50

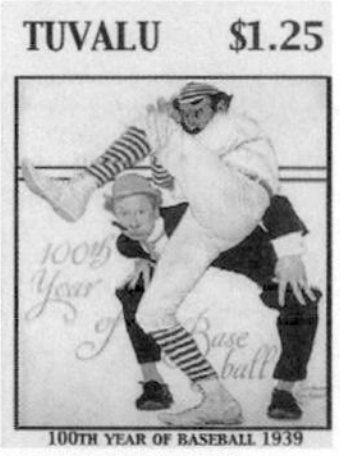

171 "100th Year of Baseball", 1939

2004. 25th Death Anniv of Norman Rockwell (artist) (2003). Designs showing covers for Saturday Evening Post. Multicoloured.

MS1115 146×178 mm. $1.25 Type **171**; $1.25 "The Locker Room (The Rookie)", 1957; $1.25 "The Dugout", 1948; $1.25 "Game Called because of Rain", 1949 3·50 7·00

MS1116 91×98 mm. $3 "New Kids in the Neighborhood", 1967 (detail) (horiz) 4·50 5·00

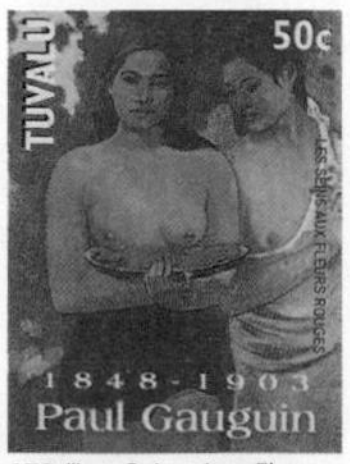

172 "Les Seins Aux Fleurs Rouges"

2004. Death Centenary of Paul Gauguin (artist). Multicoloured.

1117 50c. Type **172** 75 65

1118 60c. "Famille Tahitienne" 85 70

1119 $1 "Tahitiennes Sur La Plage" 1·60 1·40

1120 $2 "Jeune Fille a L'Eventail" 3·00 3·50

MS1121 129×154 mm. $1 "Nafea Faa Ipoipo"; $1 "Le Cheval Blanc"; $1 "Pape Moe"; $1 "Contes Barbares" 6·00 6·50

MS1122 93×73 mm. $4 "Femmes de Tahiti". Imperf 6·00 6·50

173 "Philadelphia and
Elizabeth Wharton"
(Anthony Van Dyck)

2004. 300th Anniv of St. Petersburg. "Treasures of the
Hermitage". Multicoloured.

1123	50c. Type **173**	75	60
1124	80c. "A Glass of Lemonade" (Gerard Terboch)	1·10	1·10
1125	$1 "A Mistress and Her Servant" (Pieter De Hooch)	1·60	1·60
1126	$1.20 "Portrait of a Man and His Three Sons" (Bartholomaeus Bruyn the Elder)	1·75	2·00
MS1127	80×68 mm. $4 "The Milkmaid's Family" (Louis Le Nain). Imperf	6·50	7·00

174 "Seated Woman,
1945"

2004. 30th Death Anniv (2003) of Pablo Picasso (artist).
Multicoloured.

| **MS**1128 | 131×166 mm. $1.50 Type **174**; $1.50 "Woman in Armchair, 1949"; $1.50 "Bust of Francoise, 1946"; $1.50 "Head of a Woman, 1046" | 11·00 | 12·00 |
| **MS**1129 | 97×70 mm. $4 "Françoise Gilot with Paloma and Claude, 1951". Imperf | 6·50 | 7·50 |

175 Girl Reading Speech

2004. AIDS Awareness. Multicoloured.

1130	60c. Type **175**	1·00	60
1131	90c. School girl and panellists at table	1·50	90
1132	$1.50 Kilogatasi drama group	2·50	2·75
1133	$2 Panellists at table	3·25	3·75
MS1134	110×80 mm. $3 Group discussion	6·00	7·00

176 Chen
Shui-bian (Pres. of
Republic of China)

2004. Inauguration of Chen Shui-bian, Pres. of the
Republic of China (Taiwan). Sheet 110×80
mm containing T **176** and similar vert design.
Multicoloured.

| **MS**1135 | $2 Type **176**; $2 Honourable Saufatu Sopoanga (Prime Minister of Tuvalu) | 5·00 | 6·00 |

176a Handshake and National Flags
of Tuvalu and Taiwan

2004. 25th Anniv of Diplomatic Relations between Tuvalu
and the Republic of China (Taiwan). Sheet 110×80
mm.

| **MS**1135a | $5 multicoloured | 6·00 | 7·00 |

177 Sebastiano Rossi (Italy)

2004. Centenary of FIFA (Federation Internationale de
Football Association). Multicoloured.

| **MS**1136 | 193×97 mm. $1×4, Type **177**; Clarence Seedorf (Holland); Zico (Brazil); Jack Charlton (England) | 6·50 | 7·00 |
| **MS**1137 | 108×87 mm. $3 Geoff Hurst | 5·50 | 6·00 |

178 Pope John Paul II

2005. 25th Anniv of the Pontificate of Pope John Paul II.
Multicoloured.

1138	$1.50 Type **178**	4·00	4·00
1139	$1.50 Speaking into microphone	4·00	4·00
1140	$1.50 With hand raised	4·00	4·00
1141	$1.50 At the Wailing Wall	4·00	4·00

179 Alfred Nobel

2005. International Year of Peace. Multicoloured.

1142	$1.50 Type **179**	2·50	3·00
1143	$1.50 Peace doves	2·50	3·00
1144	$1.50 Nelson Mandela	2·50	3·00

180 General
George C. Marshall

2005. 60th Anniv of D-Day Landings. Multicoloured.

1145	$1.50 Type **180**	3·50	3·50
1146	$1.50 Admiral Sir Ramsay Bertram Home	3·50	3·50
1147	$1.50 Chief of Staff Walter Bedell Smith	3·50	3·50
1148	$1.50 Field Marshall Alan Francis Brooke	3·50	3·50
MS1149	70×100 mm. $3 George Smith Patton Jr. (Commander of the 1st US Army Group)	6·00	7·00

181 Striped-faced unicornfish

2005. Marine Life. Multicoloured.

| **MS**1150 | 137×107 mm. $1×4, Type **181**; Great barracuda; Blue-ringed octopus; Giant clam | 7·50 | 8·00 |
| **MS**1151 | 98×68 mm. $3 Humpback whale | 7·00 | 7·50 |

182 Rat Terrier

2005. Dogs. Multicoloured.

1152	20c. Type **182**	75	55
1153	75c. Large Spanish hound	1·75	1·00
1154	$1 Lundehund	2·00	1·50
1155	$3 Beagle harrier	5·50	7·00
MS1156	98×68 mm. $3 Old Danish pointer	6·50	7·00

183 Common
Toadflax

2005. Medicinal Plants. Multicoloured.

| **MS**1157 | 137×127 mm. $1×4, Type **183**; Pomegranate; Black horehound; Agnus castus | 6·50 | 7·00 |
| **MS**1158 | 68×98 mm. $3 Black henbane | 5·50 | 6·00 |

184 Louse Fly

2005. Insects. Multicoloured.

| **MS**1159 | 136×106 mm. $1×4, Type **184**; Predacious diving beetle; Ladybird; Mosquito | 6·00 | 6·50 |
| **MS**1160 | 98×68 mm. $3 House fly (horiz) | 5·00 | 5·50 |

184a President Chen Shui-bian

2005. Visit of Chen Shui-bian (President of the Republic
of China (Taiwan)). Sheet 110×80 mm.

| **MS**1160a | **184a** $5 multicoloured | 6·00 | 7·00 |

2005. Centenary of Motufoua Secondary School. No.
MS1047 optd **Motufoua 100th Anniversary 1905
– 2005**.

| **MS**1160b | 110×80 mm. $1 Taulosa Karl; $1 Simalua Jacinta Enele (Tuvalu representatives at UN special session on children) | 3·00 | 3·50 |

No. **MS**1160b is overprinted **Motufoua 100th Anniversary 1905–2005** in an ellipse across the tops of the
two stamps and the sheet margin. The sheet is also overprinted **Celebrating 100th Anniversary of Motufoua
Secondary School** on the lower sheet margin.

185 Pope John
Paul II and Queen
Elizabeth II

2005. Pope John Paul II Commemoration.

| 1161 | **185** $4 multicoloured | 8·00 | 8·00 |

186 HMS Victory and
Redoubtable

2005. Bicentenary of the Battle of Trafalgar.
Multicoloured.

| **MS**1162 | 144×122 mm. $1.50×4, Type **186**; Admiral Lord Horatio Nelson; HMS Victory and British Fleet; Admiral Nelson fatally wounded below deck | 15·00 | 15·00 |
| **MS**1163 | 70×100 mm. $3 Admiral Lord Cuthbert Collingwood | 6·50 | 7·00 |

187 Thomas Berthold,
Germany

2005. 75th Anniv of First World Cup Football
Championship, Uruguay. Multicoloured.

1164	$2 Type **187**	3·00	3·25
1165	$2 Bobby Charlton, England	3·00	3·25
1166	$2 Klaus Augenthaler, Germany	3·00	3·25
MS1167	123×105 mm. $3 Thomas Strunz, Germany	5·00	5·50

188 Winston Churchill

2005. 60th Anniv of Victory in Europe. Multicoloured.

| **MS**1168 | 137×85 mm. $2×3, Type **188**; Charles de Gaulle; "Hitler Dead" headline | 12·00 | 12·00 |
| **MS**1169 | 100×70 mm. $3 General George S. Patton | 5·50 | 6·00 |

189 Harry Truman (US
President 1945–53)

2005. 60th Anniv of Victory in Japan. Multicoloured.

| **MS**1170 | 137×85 mm. $2 Type **189**; $2 "PEACE!" headline; $2 General Eisenhower | 10·00 | 11·00 |
| **MS**1171 | 100×70 mm. $3 Brigadier General Paul Tibbets Jnr and B-29 bomber Enola Gay | 6·50 | 7·00 |

190 Albert Einstein with
Hendrik Lorentz (physicist)

2005. 50th Death Anniv of Albert Einstein (physicist).
Multicoloured.

1172	$2 Type **190**	4·00	4·00
1173	$2 With Fritz Haber (physical chemist)	4·00	4·00
1174	$2 With David ben Gurion (former Israeli Prime Minister)	4·00	4·00
MS1175	70×100 mm. $3 With Thomas Mann (writer)	6·50	7·00

191 Young Child

2005. Centenary of Rotary International. Multicoloured.

1176	$2 Type **191**	3·50	4·00
1177	$2 Handful of medicines	3·50	4·00
1178	$2 Children	3·50	4·00
MS1179	100×70 mm. $3 Paul Harris (founder) and centenary emblem	6·00	7·00

192 Hans Christian
Andersen

2005. Birth Bicentenary of Hans Christian Andersen
(writer). Multicoloured.

1180	$2 Type **192**	3·00	3·50
1181	$2 Statue of Hans Christian Andersen seated, Rosenborg Garden, Copenhagen	3·00	3·50
1182	$2 Hans Christian Andersen (seen in profile)	3·00	3·50

MS1183 70×100 mm. $3 Statue of Hans Christian Andersen (standing), Odense — 4·75 5·50

193 Elvis Presley

2006. 70th Birthday (2005) of Elvis Presley. Multicoloured.
MS1184 129×104 mm. $3×4 Type **193**; Part of roof; Bushes to left and right of portrait; Part of window — 16·00 17·00
MS1185 135×111 mm. $3×4 Elvis Presley wearing Stetson — 16·00 17·00

The stamps and margins of No. MS1184 form a composite background design showing Gracelands.

The stamps within No. MS1184 each show the portrait photograph in Type **193** and different parts of the Gracelands building.

194 Wally Szczerbiak, Minnesota Timberwolves

2006. US National Basketball Association Players. Multicoloured.

1186	35c. Type **194**	50	55
1187	35c. Minnesota Timberwolves emblem	1·50	2·00
1188	35c. Stephen Jackson, Indiana Pacers	50	55
1189	35c. Indiana Pacers emblem	1·50	2·00
1190	35c. Udonis Haslem, Miami Heat	50	55
1191	35c. Miami Heat emblem	1·50	2·00
1192	35c. Paul Pierce, Boston Celtics	1·50	2·00
1193	35c. Ricky Davis, Boston Celtics	50	55
1194	35c. Rodney Buford, New Jersey Nets	50	55
1195	35c. New Jersey Nets emblem	1·50	2·00
1196	35c. Detroit Pistons emblem	1·50	2·00
1197	35c. Chauncey Billups, Detroit Pistons	50	55

195 Stylized Spanish Player and Strip

2006. World Cup Football Championship, Germany. T **195** and similar vert designs showing team strip, cartoon player and World Cup trophy. Multicoloured.
MS1198 127×102 mm. 90c. Type **195**; $1 South Korea; $1.50 France; $2 USA — 4·50 5·00

196 Princess Elizabeth holding Corgi

2006. 80th Birthday of Queen Elizabeth II. Multicoloured.

1199	$1.30 Type **196**	2·50	2·50
1200	$1.30 Queen in Coronation robes and crown	2·50	2·50
1201	$1.30 Wearing hat and coat, 1960s	2·50	2·50
1202	$1.30 Wearing tiara and sash	2·50	2·50
MS1203	120×120 mm. $3 Young Queen Elizabeth wearing diadem	6·00	6·50

197 Space Shuttle *Discovery* (top portion)

2006. Space Anniversaries. Multicoloured. (a) Return of Space Shuttle Discovery, 2005.
MS1204 150×100 mm. $1×6 Type **197**; *Discovery* in orbit; *Discovery* (rear portion with tail fins); Astronaut on robotic arm; Nose of *Discovery*; Robotic arm of *Discovery* — 10·00 10·00

(b) International Space Station.
MS1205 150×100 mm. $1.30×4 First parts of ISS launched, 1998 (rocket); International Space Station (large solar arrays); First parts of ISS launched, 1998 (shuttle); International Space Station (modules and small solar arrays) — 10·00 10·00

(c) Calipso–Cloudsat Satellites.
MS1206 100×71 mm. $3 Calipso Satellite — 6·00 6·00

198 John Kennedy in *PT109*, 1942

2006. 90th Birth Anniv of John F. Kennedy (US President 1960–3) (1st issue). Multicoloured.
MS1207 Two sheets, each 108×130 mm. (a) $1.30×4 Type **198**; Receiving medal for gallantry, 1944; John F. Kennedy (facing right); As Navy Ensign, 1941. (b) $1.30×4 Young John Kennedy (wearing bow tie); John Kennedy (wearing gold coloured jacket and tie); With Eleanor Roosevelt; John Kennedy and Capitol, Washington DC — 17·00 18·00

The two stamps at the foot of MS1207a/b each form composite designs showing badge of US Navy (a) or the ...

See also Nos. 1282/5.

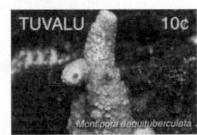

199 *Montipora aequituberculata*

2006. Corals. Multicoloured.

1208	10c. Type **199**	50	60
1209	25c. *Montipora capricornis*	85	80
1210	30c. *Montipora verrucosa*	90	80
1211	40c. *Acropora caroliniana*	1·25	60
1212	50c. *Acropora aculeus*	1·40	85
1213	60c. *Acropora anthocercis*	1·60	1·10
1214	65c. *Acropora granulosa*	1·75	1·40
1215	80c. *Acropora Rosaria*	2·50	1·75
1216	90c. *Acropora cerealis*	2·50	1·75
1217	$1 *Acropora yongei*	2·50	2·00
1218	$2 *Acropora echinata*	4·50	5·00
1219	$5 *Astreopora myriophthalma*	9·50	11·00

200 Mozart gazing out of Window

2006. 250th Birth Anniv of Wolfgang Amadeus Mozart (composer). Multicoloured.

1220	$1.30 Type **200**	3·75	3·75
1221	$1.30 Mozart family, 1780	3·75	3·75
1222	$1.30 Mozart as young boy playing piano, 1763	3·75	3·75
1223	$1.30 French Art Deco illustration of young Mozart playing piano	3·75	3·75

201 Four Pygmy Killer Whales

2006. Endangered Species. Pygmy Killer Whale (*Feresa attenuata*). Multicoloured.

1224	40c. Type **201**	1·50	1·50
1225	60c. Two pygmy killer whales	1·75	1·75
1226	90c. Group of pygmy killer whales	2·00	2·00
1227	$5 Pygmy killer whale near surface of water	7·50	7·50
MS1228	100×152 mm. Nos. 1224/7, each ×2	20·00	20·00

Nos. 1224/7 have cobalt borders and stamps from MS1228 have lavender margins.

2006. 400th Birth Anniv of Rembrandt Harmenszoon van Rijn (artist). As T **157** of St. Kitts showing paintings. Multicoloured.

1229	10c. *Woman in Bed* (detail)	15	15
1230	20c. *The Flight into Egypt* (detail)	30	30
1231	35c. *The Suicide of Lucretia* (detail)	50	50
1232	95c. *Esther Preparing to Intercede with Ahasuerus* (detail)	1·30	1·30
1233	$1 *Rembrandt's Mother* (detail)	1·50	1·50
1234	$2 *Child with Dead Peacocks* (detail)	3·00	3·00
MS1235	76×106 mm. $3 *The Abduction of Ganymede* (detail). Imperf	4·25	4·25

202 Reed Warbler

2006. Birds. Multicoloured.
MS1236 131×108 mm. $1×4 Type **202**; Indian pitta; Gurney's pitta; Northern shrike — 9·00 9·00
MS1237 70×100 mm. $3 Black-backed fairy wren — 7·00 7·00

203 *Graphium agamemnon* (tailed jay)

2006. Butterflies. Multicoloured.
MS1238 131×108 mm. $1×4 Type **203**; Ixias undatus; Hebomoia leucippe detanii, Trogonoptera brookiana (Rajah Brooke's birdwing) — 9·00 9·00
MS1239 70×100 mm. $3 Cynthia cardui (painted lady) — 7·00 7·00

The stamps and margins of No. MS1238 form a composite design of a flowering meadow.

204 On Wedding Day, 1947

2007. Diamond Wedding of Queen Elizabeth II and Duke of Edinburgh. Multicoloured.

1240	$1 Type **204**	2·00	2·00
1241	$1 Queen Elizabeth (wearing tiara) and Duke of Edinburgh (wearing military uniform), c. 1960	2·00	2·00

205 Diana, Princess of Wales

2007. Tenth Death Anniv of Diana, Princess of Wales. Multicoloured.

1242	$1 Type **205**	1·50	1·50
1243	$1 Looking upwards, wearing beige dress with white collar (head and shoulders)	1·50	1·50
1244	$1 Wearing pale pink dress and hat (head and shoulders)	1·50	1·50
1245	$1 As No. 1244 but seen three-quarter length	1·50	1·50
1246	$1 As No. 1243 but seen half-length	1·50	1·50

1247	$1 As Type **205** but seen three-quarter length	1·50	1·50
MS1248	100×70 mm. $3 Wearing beige dress with white collar, standing in front of Egyptian wall painting	4·25	4·25

206 BO-105 Tank-destroyer

2007. Centenary of First Helicopter Flight. Multicoloured.

1249	20c. Type **206**	1·25	1·00
1250	75c. NH 90 utility helicopter (horiz)	2·50	1·50
1251	$1 S-65/RH-53D hostage rescue helicopter (horiz)	2·75	1·50
1252	$1.30 BO-105 tank-destroyer (different) (horiz)	2·75	3·00
1253	$1.30 S-65/RH-53D hostage rescue helicopter (different) (horiz)	2·75	3·00
1254	$1.30 AH 64 Apache armoured gunship (horiz)	2·75	3·00
1255	$1.30 NH 90 utility helicopter (different) (horiz)	2·75	3·00
1256	$2 AH 64 Apache armoured gunship (different) (horiz)	3·50	3·75
MS1257	100×70 mm. $3 HUP Retriever utility helicopter (horiz)	8·50	8·50

207 '100', Scout Badge and Cyclist

2007. Centenary of World Scouting. Multicoloured.

1258	20c. Type **207**	1·00	75
1259	75c. Scout cooking over campfire	1·50	1·25
1260	$1 Scouts playing cricket	2·75	2·00
1261	$2 Archer	3·25	3·50
MS1262	100×70 mm. $3 Boy and scout flag (horiz)	5·50	6·00

Nos. 1258/61 all show Scout badge and scout activity contained in '100' as Type **207**.

208 Deforestation

2007. Global Warming (1st series). Multicoloured.

1263	$1 Type **208**	2·00	2·00
1264	$1 Melting ice-cap	2·00	2·00
1265	$1 Chimney emitting pollution ('Industrialization')	2·00	2·00
1266	$1 Globe ('Warmer Temperature')	2·00	2·00
1267	$1 Traffic	2·00	2·00
1268	$1 Storm ('Extreme Weather')	2·00	2·00
MS1269	100×70 mm. $3 Globe in flames	6·00	6·50

See also Nos. MS1291/MS1292 and 1293/MS1299.

209 Ships ('A Good Wind for Thousands of Miles')

2007. 50th Death Anniv of Qi Baishi (artist). Multicoloured.
MS1270 115×150 mm. $1×6 Type **209**; $1 Top of waterfall ('The Yuxia and Lianhua Mountains'); $1 Mountains and setting sun ('Autumn Landscape with Cormorants'); $1 Forested coastline ('A Good Wind for Thousands of Miles'); $1 Trees and foot of waterfall ('The Yuxia and Lianhua Mountains'); $1 Autumn trees and coastal rocks with cormorants ('Autumn Landscape with Cormorants') — 15·00 16·00

MS1271	Two sheets, each 70×100 mm. (a) $2.50×2 'Grasshopper on a Branch'; 'Fish and Catfish'. (b) $3 Ink Landscape	6·75	7·50

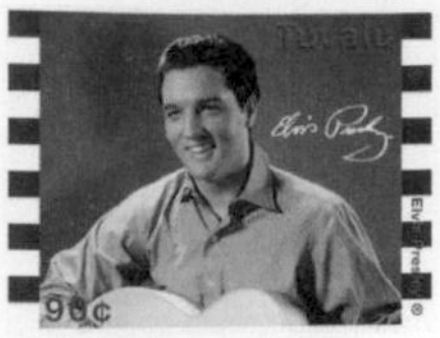

210 Elvis Presley

2007. 30th Death Anniv of Elvis Presley. Multicoloured.

1272	90c. Type **210**	1·40	1·40
1273	90c. Wearing white shirt	1·40	1·40
1274	90c. Wearing jacket and tie	1·40	1·40
1275	90c. Wearing floral shirt	1·40	1·40
1276	90c. Wearing pale blue shirt	1·40	1·40
1277	90c. Wearing army uniform	1·40	1·40

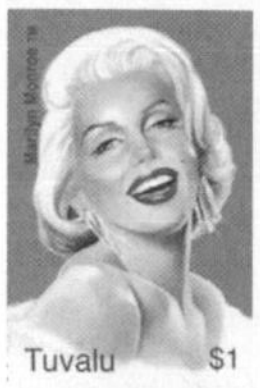

211 Marilyn Monroe

2007. 80th Birth Anniv of Marilyn Monroe. Multicoloured.

1278	$1 Type **211**	1·50	1·50
1279	$1 Wearing black dress with diamante straps	1·50	1·50
1280	$1 Wearing black halter neck dress	1·50	1·50
1281	$1 Wearing cream wrap	1·50	1·50

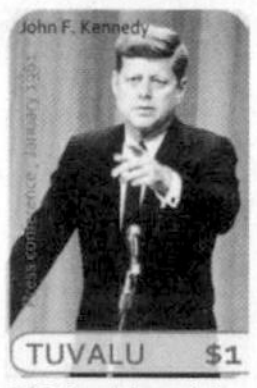

212 President John Kennedy

2007. 90th Birth Anniv (2006) of John F. Kennedy (US President 1960–3) (2nd issue). Designs showing him speaking at Press Conference, January 1961. Multicoloured.

1282	$1 Type **212**	1·75	1·75
1283	$1 Speaking, with right hand raised	1·75	1·75
1284	$1 Speaking	1·75	1·75
1285	$1 Smiling	1·75	1·75

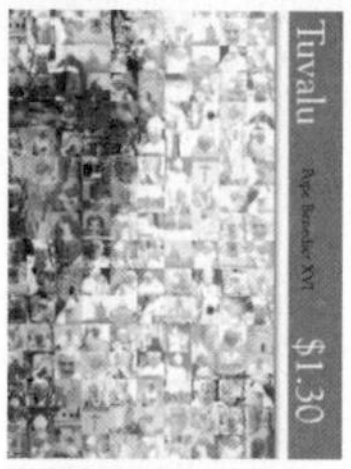

213 Miniature Photographs forming Part of Ear

2007. 80th Birthday of Pope Benedict XVI. Sheet 160×220 mm containing T **213** and similar vert designs. Multicoloured.

MS1286	$1.30×4 Type **213**; Robes (margin at right); Robes (margin at foot); Pope Benedict XVI	9·50	9·50

The bottom right stamp shows a photograph of Pope Benedict XVI. The remainder of the stamps and the margins of the sheet show a collage of miniature photographs forming a portrait of the Pope when viewed as a whole sheet.

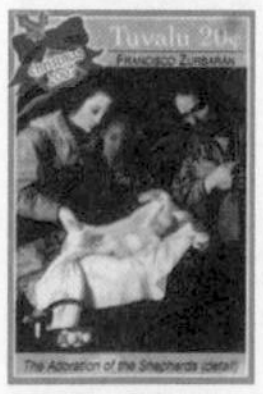

214 'The Adoration of the Shepherds' (detail) (Francisco Zurbaran)

2007. Christmas. Paintings. Multicoloured.

1287	20c. Type **214**	45	30
1288	75c. 'Madonna and Child with Angels' (Hans Memling)	1·40	1·10
1289	$1 'The Nativity' (detail) (Maestro Esiguo)	1·75	1·50
1290	$2 'The Nativity' (Philippe de Champaigne)	3·25	4·00

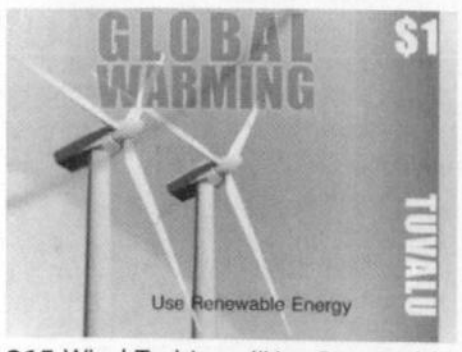

215 Wind Turbines ('Use Renewable Energy')

2007. Global Warming (2nd series). Multicoloured.

MS1291	177×132 mm. $1×6 Type **215**; Power station ('Atmospheric Carbon Dioxide'); Seedling ('Plant Trees'); Harvesting timber (deforestation); Emblem (recycling); Globe and rising thermometer (greenhouse gases)	11·00	11·00
MS1292	70×100 mm. $3 Seedling growing from cracked earth (vert)	5·50	6·00

No. **MS**1291 contains six stamps, 2×3, the three left-hand stamps forming a composite background design showing the Earth and its atmosphere.

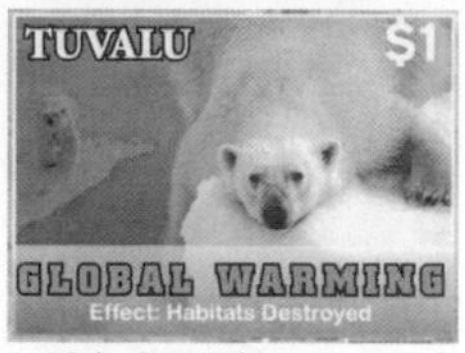

216 Polar Bear (Habitats Destroyed)

2008. Global Warming (3rd series). Multicoloured.

1293	$1 Type **216**	2·25	2·25
1294	$1 Solar panels (Renewable Energy)	2·25	2·25
1295	$1 Corals (Coral Reef Bleaching)	2·25	2·25
1296	$1 Emblem (Recycle)	2·25	2·25
1297	$1 Tornado and lightning (Erratic Weather Patterns)	2·25	2·25
1298	$1 Growing seedlings (Plant Trees)	2·25	2·25
MS1299	100×70 mm. $3 Wind turbines ('Use Renewable Green Energy')	6·00	6·50

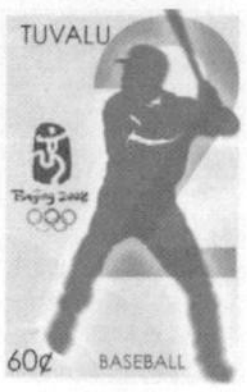

217 Baseball

2008. Olympic Games, Beijing. Multicoloured.

1300	60c. Type **217**	1·40	1·40
1301	60c. Fencing	1·40	1·40
1302	60c. Hockey	1·40	1·40
1303	60c. Gymnastics	1·40	1·40

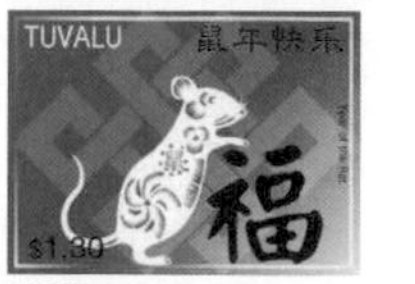

218 Rat

2008. Chinese New Year ('Year of the Rat'). Sheet 130×100 mm containing T **218** and similar horiz designs.

MS1304	$1.30×4 Type **218** and as Type **218** with yellow shading at bottom left, top right and top left	8·00	8·00

The stamps and margins of No. **MS**1304 form a composite design of a pattern with yellow shading in the centre.

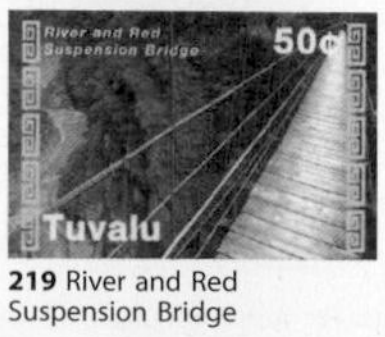

219 River and Red Suspension Bridge

2008. Taipei 2008 International Stamp Exhibition. Multicoloured.

1305	50c. Type **219**	70	70
1306	50c. Chinese New Year dragon	70	70
1307	50c. National Palace Museum	70	70
1308	50c. Taipei Main Station	70	70
1309	50c. Golden Waterfall at Jin Gua Shi	70	70
1310	50c. National Concert Hall, Taipei	70	70
MS1311	100×70 mm. $2 Buddhist Temple (vert)	2·75	3·00

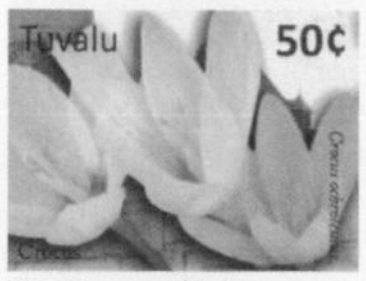

220 *Crocus ochroleucus*

2008. Israel 2008 World Stamp Championship, Tel-Aviv. Flowers of the Holy Land. Multicoloured.

MS1312	150×100 mm. 50c.×6 Type **220**; Aleppo adonis (*Adonis palaestina*); Wild chamomile (*Matricaria recutita*); Fig buttercup (*Ranunculus ficaria*); Dwarf chicory (*Cichorium pumilum*); Queen mallow (*Lavatera trimestris*)	5·00	5·50
MS1313	100×70 mm. $2 *Crocus vitellinus*	4·00	4·50

The stamps and margins of No. **MS**1312 form a composite design showing a Holy Land landscape.

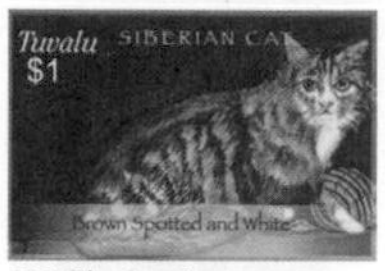

221 Siberian Cat

2008. Cats of the World. Multicoloured.

MS1314	130×100 mm. $1×6 Type **221**; California spangled; Siamese; Burmilla; European shorthair; Devon Rex	9·00	9·00
MS1315	100×70 mm. $3 Calico American wirehair	4·75	4·75

The stamps and margins of No. **MS**1314 form a composite design showing cats on and in front of a sofa.

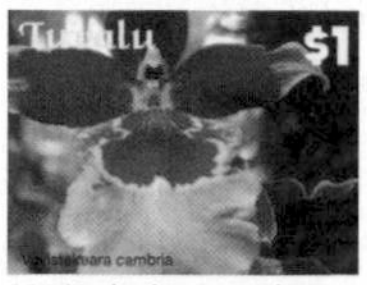

222 *Vuylstekeara cambria*

2008. Orchids of the South Pacific. Multicoloured.

1316	$1 Type **222**	2·00	2·00
1317	$1 *Dendrobium nobile* (pale pink)	2·00	2·00
1318	$1 *Phalaenopsis nivacolor*	2·00	2·00
1319	$1 *Cattleya trianae*	2·00	2·00
1320	$1 *Dendrobium nobile* (green and magenta)	2·00	2·00
1321	$1 *Cymbidium* Alexanderi	2·00	2·00

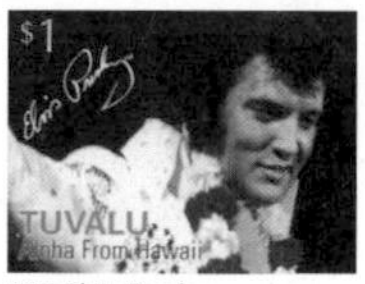

223 Elvis Presley

2008. 35th Anniv of Elvis Presley's 'Aloha from Hawaii' Concert. Multicoloured.

1322	$1 Type **223**	1·50	1·50
1323	$1 Singing, both hands raised, one clasping microphone	1·50	1·50
1324	$1 Singing, both hands clasped around microphone	1·50	1·50

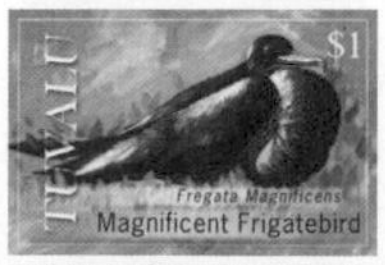

224 Magnificent Frigatebird (*Fregata magnificens*)

2008. Birds of Tuvalu. Multicoloured.

1325	$1 Type **224**	2·00	2·00
1326	$1 Townsend's warbler (*Dendroica townsendi*)	2·00	2·00
1327	$1 Sooty tern (*Onychoprion fuscatus nubilosus*)	2·00	2·00
1328	$1 Common noddy (*Anous stolidus*)	2·00	2·00
1329	$1 Masked booby (*Sula dactylatra*)	2·00	2·00
1330	$1 Red-tailed tropicbird (*Phaethon rubricauda*)	2·00	2·00

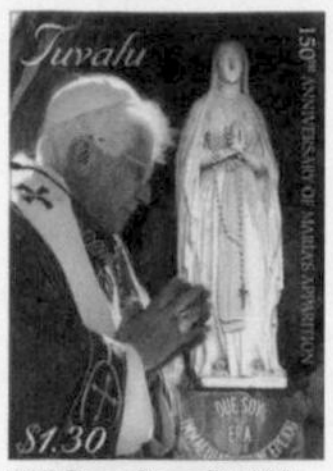

225 Pope Benedict XVI praying at Lourdes

2008. 150th Anniv of the Apparition of the Virgin Mary to St. Bernadette and Visit of Pope Benedict XVI to Lourdes.

1331	**225**	$1.30 multicoloured	2·75	2·75

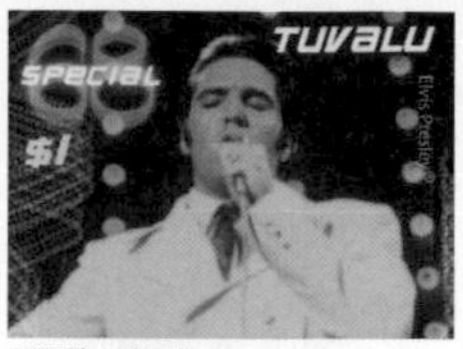

226 Elvis Presley

2008. 40th Anniv of '68 Special' (TV programme). Multicoloured.

1332	$1 Type **226**	1·50	1·50
1333	$1 Wearing leather jacket (front view)	1·50	1·50
1334	$1 Wearing white jacket (side view)	1·50	1·50
1335	$1 Wearing white jacket (side view, leaning forward)	1·50	1·50
1336	$1 Wearing leather jacket (side view)	1·50	1·50
1337	$1 Wearing white jacket (front view, right hand raised)	1·50	1·50

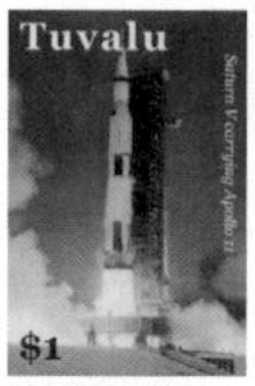

227 Saturn V Rocket carrying Apollo 11, 1969

2008. 50 Years of Space Exploration and Satellites. Multicoloured.

1338	$1 Type **227**	2·00	2·00
1339	$1 Buzz Aldrin's bootprint on Moon	2·00	2·00
1340	$1 Apollo 11 Command module	2·00	2·00
1341	$1 Neil Armstrong (commander)	2·00	2·00
1342	$1 Michael Collins (command module pilot)	2·00	2·00
1343	$1 Edwin E. Aldrin (lunar module pilot)	2·00	2·00
1344	$1.30 Cassini-Huygens spacecraft	3·00	3·00
1345	$1.30 Titan IV-B/Centaur launch vehicle, 1997	3·00	3·00
1346	$1.30 Cassini-Huygens spacecraft and Saturn's rings	3·00	3·00
1347	$1.30 Cassini spacecraft, Saturn and Huygens probe entering moon Titan's atmosphere, 2005	3·00	3·00
1348	$1.30 Inside Sputnik 1	3·00	3·00
1349	$1.30 Sputnik 1 and planet Earth	3·00	3·00
1350	$1.30 R-7 Semyorka Sputnik 1's rocket	3·00	3·00
1351	$1.30 Sputnik 1 above Earth	3·00	3·00
1352	$1.30 Galileo in laboratory	3·00	3·00
1353	$1.30 Galileo, Jupiter and moons Europa and Io	3·00	3·00
1354	$1.30 Galileo probe	3·00	3·00
1355	$1.30 Galileo, Jupiter and moons Io and Ganymede	3·00	3·00
1356	$1.30 Chandra X-ray Observatory, star and nebula	3·00	3·00
1357	$1.30 Chandra X-ray Observatory and stars	3·00	3·00
1358	$1.30 Chandra X-ray Observatory and galaxy (pink cloud)	3·00	3·00
1359	$1.30 Chandra X-ray Observatory (turquoise-green cloud)	3·00	3·00

228 Wiley Post wearing Pressure Suit

2008. 75th Anniv of Wiley Post's First Solo Round-the-World Flight. Multicoloured.

1360	$1.30 Type 228	2·25	2·25
1361	$1.30 Wiley Post and *Winnie Mae*	2·25	2·25
1362	$1.30 Lockheed Vega V *Winnie Mae*	2·25	2·25
1363	$1.30 Wiley Post atop plane	2·25	2·25
1364	$1.30 Wiley and Mae Post	2·25	2·25
1365	$1.30 Harold Gatty (navigator) and world map	2·25	2·25

229 Diana, Princess of Wales

2008. Tenth Death Anniv (2007) of Diana, Princess of Wales. Sheet 100×150 mm containing T **229** and similar horiz designs. Multicoloured.

MS1366 Type **229**; Wearing white dress with fan detail at shoulder, looking down; Wearing white jacket with stand up collar; Princess Diana (white scroll at right)   7·25   7·25

The stamps and margins of No. MS1366 form a composite design.

Tuvalu $1.30
230 Pres. Abraham Lincoln

2009. Inauguration of President Barack Obama. Sheet 190×130 mm containing T **230** and similar vert designs. Multicoloured.

MS1367 $1.30×6 Type **230**; Emancipation Proclamation signed by Pres. Lincoln, 1862; Dr. Martin Luther King; Dr. King at the March on Washington, 1963; Pres. Barack Obama; Pres. Obama giving Victory Speech   9·50   10·00

231 Holly with Berries

2009. Christmas. Multicoloured.

1368	60c. Type 231	75	55
1369	90c. Bauble	1·25	80
1370	$1 Wrapped present	1·50	1·50
1371	$2.50 Candy cane tree decoration	3·25	3·75

232 Ox

2009. Chinese New Year. Year of the Ox. Sheet 190×90 mm.

MS1372 60c. Type **232**; 90c., $1.20, $2.50, each As Type **232**   6·50   7·00

233 Elvis Presley and Symbolic Dove

2009. Elvis Presley Commemoration. Sheet 127×190 mm containing T **233** and similar vert designs. Multicoloured.

MS1373 Type **233**; Elvis Presley in gold medallion; With black dove; With red and gold flames; With spangled dove; With blue and gold peacock   8·00   8·00

234 Pope Benedict XVI

2009. Visit of Pope Benedict XVI to Israel. Sheet 100×150 mm. Multicoloured.

MS1374 60c. Type **234**; 90c. As Type **234** (window at right); $1.20 As Type **234** (exterior of dome at left); $2.50 As Type **234** (carved stonework in right background)   8·50   8·50

The stamps within MS1374 all show a portrait of Pope Benedict XVI as in Type **234** but have different background designs showing the interior of the dome and exterior of the Church of the Holy Sepulchre, Jerusalem.

235 Michael Jackson

2009. Michael Jackson Commemoration. Multicoloured.

MS1375 178×127 mm. $1.30×4 Type **235**; Wearing white, holding microphone; Wearing white shirt with black tie, smiling; Wearing black jacket, hat and tie (inscr 'MICHAEL JACKSON' at right)   6·50   6·50

MS1376 178×127 mm. $1.30×4 Wearing blue shirt, stage with lights in foreground; Wearing white, audience with raised hands in foreground; Wearing blue shirt, audience in foreground; Wearing white, audience and fireworks in foreground (all vert)   6·50   6·50

236 Moe and Larry shutting Curly's Head in Door

2009. The Three Stooges. Sheet 140×130 mm containing T **236** and similar vert designs. Multicoloured.

MS1377 Type **236**; Moe banging Larry and Curly's heads together; Larry with dog on lead and Moe and Curly pointing; Moe, Curly and Larry (green background)   6·50   6·50

237 Michelle Obama

2009. 'The First Family of the United States'. Sheet 135×80 mm containing T **237** and similar horiz designs. Multicoloured.

MS1378 Type **237**; Pres. Barack Obama; Pres. Obama and Bo the dog; Pres. Obama and family   6·50   6·50

238 Golden Olive Branch left on the Moon

2009. 40th Anniv of the First Moon Landing. Multicoloured.

MS1379 Type **237a**; Apollo 11 Command Module above Moon's surface; Saturn V rocket; Astronaut Neil Armstrong; Congressional Space Medal of Honor; Apollo 11 Lunar Module   10·00   10·00

MS1380 Photograph of Buzz Aldrin and Lunar Module on Moon taken by Neil Armstrong; Saturn V with Apollo 11; Apollo 11 Command Module orbiting Moon; Apollo 11 crewmen await pick-up from sea   8·50   8·50

239 Prince Harry with Girl at Harlem Children's Zone

2009. Visit of Prince Harry to New York. Sheet 140×100 mm containing T **238** and similar vert designs. Multicoloured.

MS1381 Type **238**; Wreath laid by Prince Harry at Ground Zero; Prince Harry competing in Polo Classic; On visit to Veterans Affairs Medical Center   8·50   8·50

239a Prime Minister Apisai Ielemia (Tuvalu) and Pres. Ma Ying-jeou (Taiwan)

2009. 30th Anniv of Diplomatic Relations between Tuvalu and Republic of China (Taiwan)

MS1381a **239a** $5 multicoloured   8·00   8·00

240 Pres. John F. Kennedy

2009. Tenth Death Anniv of John Kennedy Jnr. Sheet 130×100 mm containing T **240** and similar vert designs. Multicoloured.

MS1382 Type **240**; Pres. John Kennedy and Jacqueline Kennedy; Pres. Kennedy with John Jnr. as young child; Pres. Kennedy making speech   8·50   8·50

241 Toy Reindeer and Santa Outfit

2009. Christmas. Multicoloured.

1383	60c. Type 241	75	55
1384	90c. Gold leaves and bells	1·25	80
1385	$1 Snowman felt decoration	1·50	1·50
1386	$2 Christmas cake	2·75	3·25

242 *Hyposcada kezia*

2009. Butterflies. Multicoloured.

1387	60c. Type 242	1·10	60
1388	90c. *Heteronympha mirifica*	1·50	85
1389	$1 *Libythea geoffroy*	1·75	1·50
1390	$2.50 *Protographium leosthenes*	3·25	3·75

MS1391 152×98 mm. $1×6 *Horaga selina; Ornithoptera victoriae; Polyura eudamippus; Catopsilia scylla; Graphium mendana; Melanitis amabilis*   9·00   9·00

The stamps and margins of No. MS1391 form a composite design.

243 Pope Benedict XVI

2009. Fifth Anniv of Pontificate of Pope Benedict XVI. Multicoloured.

MS1392 Type **243**; Head and shoulders portrait, wearing white skullcap; Wearing white skullcap and red and gold robes; With staff and mitre   8·50   8·50

244 Princess Diana holding Baby

2009. Diana, Princess of Wales Commemoration. Multicoloured.

MS1393 $1.30×4 Type **244**; Wearing Halo Trust protective vest; Wearing landmine protection vest and visor; With boy   8·00   8·00

245 Elvis Presley

2010. 75th Birth Anniv of Elvis Presley. Multicoloured.

MS1394 $1.30×4 Type **245**; Head turned to left, Smiling, facing camera; Singing   8·00   8·00

246 Scout Salute

2010. Centenary of Boy Scouts of America. Multicoloured.

MS1395 $1.30 Type **246**×2; $1.30 Scout planting tree×2   8·00   8·00

MS1396 $1.30 Scout hiking×2; $1.30 Scout angling×2   8·00   8·00

246a Road, Village, Trees and Clouds (Elisapeta Nelu)

2010. 40th Anniv of Earth Day. Multicoloured.

MS1396a 50c. Beach, palm trees, sunrise over ocean and marine life (Taupule Junavaka); 60c. Buildings and trees by seashore and marine life; 90c. Type **246a**; $1.50 Village by seashore (Alapi Afesoi)   5·00   5·00

247 Winston Churchill

2010. 70th Anniv of the Battle of Britain. Multicoloured.

MS1397 $1.30×4 Type **247**; Churchill visiting ruins of Coventry Cathedral; Passers-by with pram and bicycle and ruins of building; Vehicles and pedestrians in bomb damaged street   10·00   10·00

MS1398 $1.30×4 Winston Churchill (in close up); Messerschmitt BF109E; Symbols of Luftwaffe and RAF; Supermarine Spitfire   10·00   10·00

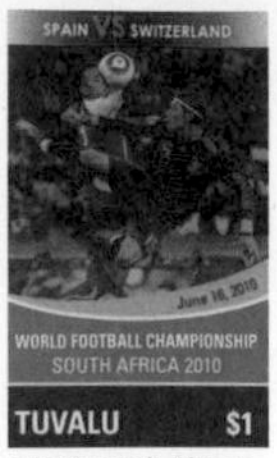

248 Spanish Player No. 15, Spain vs. Switzerland

2010. World Cup Football Championship, South Africa. Multicoloured.

MS1399 130×154 mm. $1×4 Spain vs. Switzerland: Type **248**; Players Spain No. 22 and Switzerland No. 17 tackling; Spanish player dribbling ball, Switzerland Nos. 8 and 6 in background; Spain No. 3 and Switzerland No. 16 competing for ball 5·50 6·00

MS1400 130×154 mm. $1×4 Spain vs. Honduras: Spanish players Nos. 8 and 7; Spain No. 10 and Honduras No. 22 competing for ball; Spain No. 8 and Honduras No. 8; Spain No. 11, Honduras No. 22 and Spain No. 16 5·50 6·00

MS1401 130×154 mm. $1×4 Spain vs. Chile: Spain Nos. 7 and 10; Spain No. 9 and Chile No. 3; Spain No. 5, Chile No. 10 and Spain No. 16 tackling for ball; Spain No. 11 (heading ball) and Chile No. 7 5·50 6·00

MS1402 130×154 mm. $1×4 Spain vs. Portugal: Spain No. 19 carrying victorious team mate; Spain No. 16 and Portugal No. 23 competing for ball; Spanish player kicking ball; Spanish player and Portugal No. 23 competing for ball 5·50 6·00

MS1403 130×154 mm. $1×4 Spain vs. Paraguay: Spain No. 10, Paraguay No. 16 and Spain No. 8 pursuing ball; Goalkeeper throwing ball; Spain No. 16 and Paraguay No. 3; Paraguay No. 21 and Spain No. 15 5·50 6·00

MS1404 130×154 mm. $1×4 Spain vs. Germany: No. 23 and Germany No. 15; Spain No. 8 and Germany No. 7 kicking ball; Germany No. 6 and Spain No. 6 pursuing ball; Spain No. 11 and Germany No. 15 5·50 6·00

MS1405 130×154 mm. $1×4 Spain vs. Netherlands: Netherlands No. 4 (heading ball) and Spain No. 15; Spain No. 15 (kneeling, with arms outstretched in victory); Spain No. 7 and Netherlands No. 4; Spain No. 10 and Netherlands player 5·50 6·00

MS1406 85×89 mm. $3 Victorious Spanish team 4·50 5·00

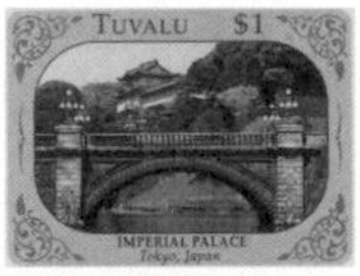

249 Spanish Player No. 15, Spain vs. Switzerland

2010. Palaces of the World. Multicoloured.

MS1407 139×100 mm. $1×6 Type **249**; Dolmabahçe Palace, Istanbul, Turkey; Winter Palace, St. Petersburg, Russia; Schönbrunn Palace, Vienna, Austria; Summer Palace, Beijing, China; Buckingham Palace, London, England 8·50 8·50

MS1408 100×70 mm. $3 Palace of Versailles, Versailles, France (vert) 4·50 4·50

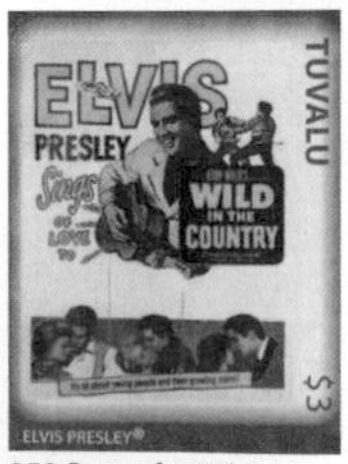

250 Poster for *Wild in the Country*

2010. Elvis Presley in Film *Wild in the Country*, 1961. Multicoloured.

MS1409 125×90 mm. $3 Type **250** 4·50 4·50

MS1410 90×125 mm. $3 As Glenn Tyler (in barn) 4·50 4·50

MS1411 90×125 mm. $3 Elvis Presley (brown background) 4·50 4·50

MS1412 125×90 mm. $3 Elvis Presley (yellow background) 4·50 4·50

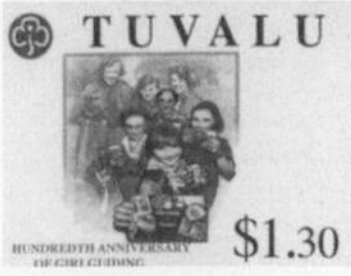

251 Modern and Early Guides

2010. Centenary of Girlguiding. Multicoloured.

MS1413 150×100 mm. $1.30×4 Type **251**; Modern guide and two early guides; Modern guide playing drum and early guides; Two modern guides and early guides 8·00 8·00

MS1414 70×100 mm. $3 Six guides and centenary emblem (vert) 4·50 4·50

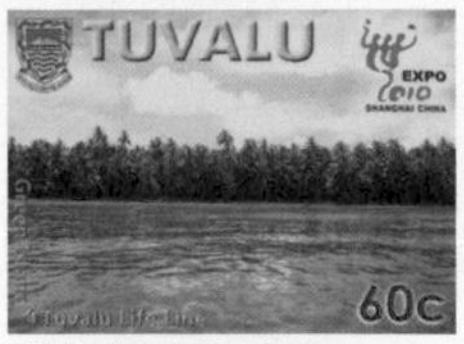

252 Atoll with Palm Trees

2010. Expo 2010, Shanghai, China. Year of the Tiger. 'Green Island is Tuvalu Life Line'. Multicoloured.

MS1415 60c. Type **252**; 90c. Sandy beach and lagoon; $1.50 Palm trees growing on beach; $2 Sandy beach and palm trees 8·00 8·00

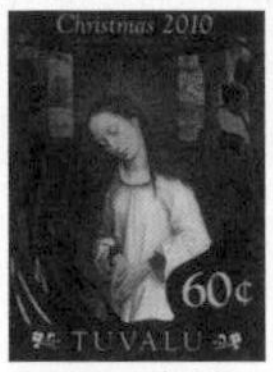

253 Pierre Bladelin Triptych (Rogier van der Weyden), 1445

2010. Christmas. Multicoloured.

1416	60c. Type **253**	75	55
1417	90c. *Annunciation* (Pietro Cavallini), c. 1291	1·25	80
1418	$1 Altarpiece of the Nativity (Jacques Daret), c. 1433	1·50	1·50
1419	$2 *Nativity* (Matthias Grunewald), c. 1515	2·75	3·25

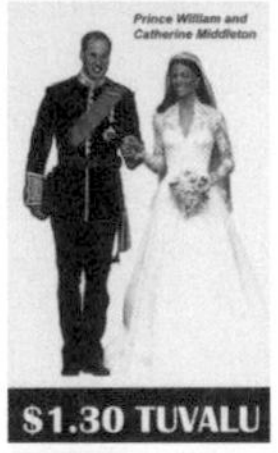

254 Duke and Duchess of Cambridge

2011. Royal Wedding. Multicoloured.

MS1420 100×150 mm. $1.30 Type **254**×2; $1.30 Duchess of Cambridge×2 8·00 8·00

MS1421 100×150 mm. $1.30 Prince William, Duke of Cambridge×2; $1.30 Duke (looking to right) and Duchess of Cambridge×2 8·00 8·00

MS1422 75×128 mm. $3 Duke and Duchess of Cambridge kissing (30×80 mm) 4·50 4·50

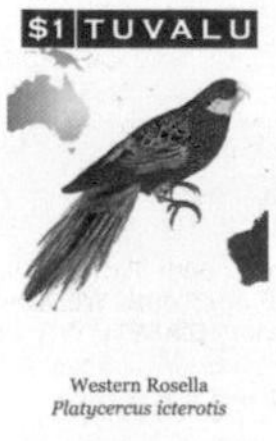

255 Western Rosella (*Platycercus icterotis*)

2011. Parrots of the South Pacific. Multicoloured.

MS1423 230×85 mm. $1×6 Type **255**; Australian Ringneck (*Barnardius zonarius*); Budgerigar (*Melopsittacus undulatus*); Northern Rosella (*Platycercus venustus*). Red-capped Parrot (*Purpureicephalus spurius*); Regent Parrot (*Polytelis anthopeplus*) 8·50 8·50

MS1424 110×60 mm. $3 Red-winged Parrot (*Aprosmictus erythropterus*) 4·50 4·50

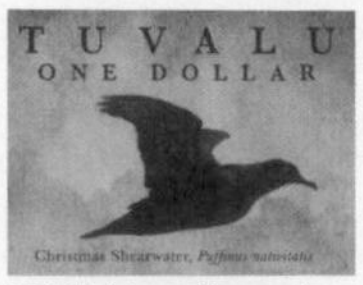

256 Christmas Shearwater (*Puffinus nativitatus*)

2012. Marine Life. Multicoloured.

MS1425 101×201 mm. $1×5 Type **256**; Flying Fish (*Parexocoetus brachypterus*); Albacore Tuna (*Thunnus alalunga*); Pantropical Spotted Dolphin (*Stenella attenuata*); Pygmy Killer Whale (*Feresa attenuata*) 8·00 8·00

MS1426 71×101 mm. $3 Parrotfish (*Scarus pectoralis*) (50×38 mm) 4·50 4·50

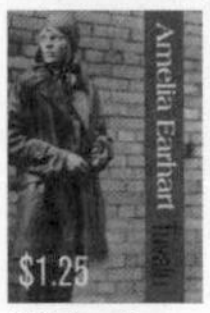

257 Amelia Earhart

2012. 75th Anniv of the Disappearance of Amelia Earhart (aviator). Multicoloured.

MS1427 200×81 mm. $1.25×4 Type **257**; Amelia Earhart smiling, aircraft in background; Amelia Earhart, aircraft propellor and airfield in background; Amelia Earhart smiling, aircraft propellor in background 8·00 8·00

MS1428 130×61 mm. $3.50 Amelia Earhart and aircraft 4·50 4·50

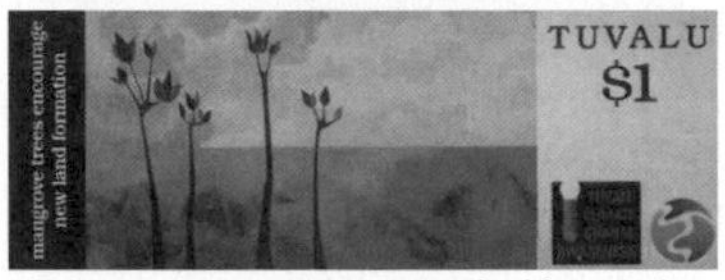

258 'mangrove trees encourage new land formation'

2012. Climate Change Awareness. Multicoloured.

1429	$1 Type **258**	1·50	1·50
1430	$1 'distillation plants turn seas into clean drinking water'	1·50	1·50
1431	$1 'crops that are genetically enhanced to grow near salt water'	1·50	1·50
1432	$1 'turning off lights to save energy'	1·50	1·50
1433	$1 'plant a tree to help reduce greenhouse gases'	1·50	1·50

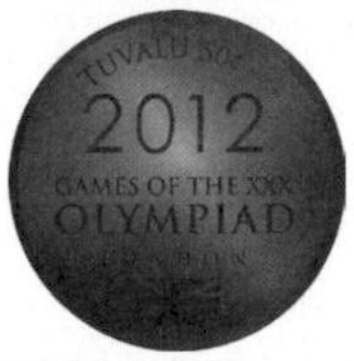

259 Bronze Medal

2012. Olympic Games, London. Multicoloured.

MS1434 149×100 mm. 50c.×3 Type **259**; Silver medal; Gold medal 2·10 2·10

MS1435 70×101 mm. $1.50 '2012', London skyline and Olympic rings (30×50 mm) 2·10 2·10

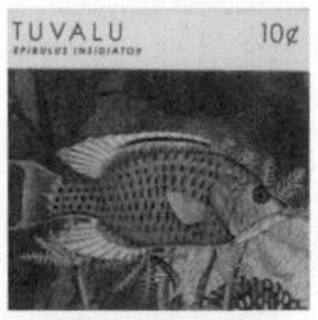

260 *Epibulus insidiator*

2012. Fish. Multicoloured.

1436	10c. Type **260**	15	10
1437	40c. *Zanclus cornutus*	50	30
1438	60c. *Anampses cuvier*	75	55
1439	90c. *Rhinecanthus verrucosus*	1·25	80
1440	$1 *Lactoria fornasini*	1·50	1·50
1441	$1.25 *Enchelycore pardalis*	1·75	1·75
1442	$1.50 *Diodon liturosus*	2·00	2·00
1443	$1.75 *Anampses elegans*	2·25	2·25
1444	$2 *Thalassoma trilobatum*	2·75	3·00
1445	$2.75 *Pomacanthus imperator*	3·50	4·00
1446	$3.25 *Pomacanthus semicirculatus*	4·50	4·50
1447	$5 *Cheilinus fasciatus*	7·25	7·25

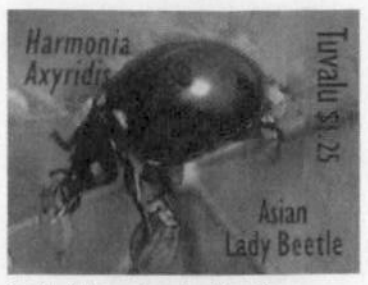

261 Asian Lady Beetle (*Harmonia axyridis*)

2012. Tuvaluan Beetles. Multicoloured.

MS1448 150×101 mm. $1.25×4 Type **261**; Blister Beetle (*Mylabris pustulate*); Water Beetle (*Acilius sulcatus*); Gemeiner Widderbock (*Clytus arietis*) 8·00 8·00

MS1449 100×70 mm. $3 Firefly (*Photinus pyralis*) 4·50 4·50

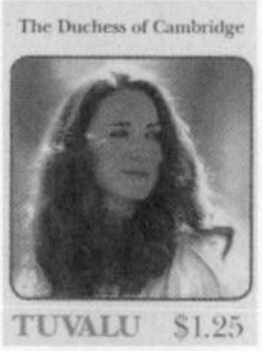

262 Catherine, Duchess of Cambridge

2012. The Duke and Duchess of Cambridge visit Tuvalu. Multicoloured.

MS1450 190×100 mm. $1.25×5 Type **262**; Crest of Tuvalu; Duke and Duchess of Cambridge; Queen Elizabeth II visits Tuvalu, 1982; Prince William, Duke of Cambridge 8·50 8·50

MS1451 100×100 mm. $3.50 Duke and Duchess of Cambridge (50×30 mm) 4·50 4·50

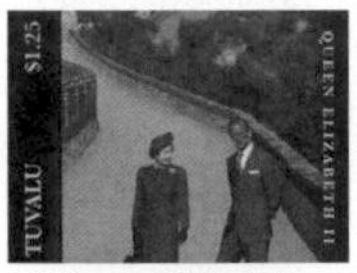

263 Queen Elizabeth II and Prince Philip visit the Great Wall of China, 1986

2012. Diamond Jubilee. Multicoloured.

MS1452 180×120 mm. $1.25×4 Type **263**; Queen Elizabeth II visit Yosemite National Park, USA, 1983; Queen Elizabeth II and Emperor Haile Selassie, Tissisal Falls, Ethiopia, 1965; Queen Elizabeth II and Prince Philip visit the Taj Mahal, India, 1961 8·00 8·00

MS1453 70×100 mm. $3.50 Queen Elizabeth II visits Tuvalu, 1982 (vert) 4·50 4·50

Nos. **MS**1454/5, Type **264** are left for UN World Humanitarian Day, not yet received

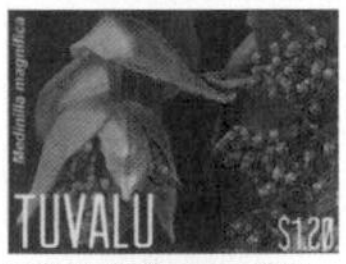

265 *Medinilla magnifica*

2013. Blossoming Plants of the Pacific. Multicoloured.

MS1456 134×106 mm. $1.20×4 Type **265**; *Alpinia purpurata*; *Nymphaea rubra*; *Crotalaria retusa* 7·50 7·50

MS1457 134×107 mm. $1.20×4 *Hibiscus rosa-sinensis*; *Gardenia taitensis*; *Hibiscus brackenridgei*; *Ranunculus lyallii* 7·50 7·50

MS1458 94×64 mm. $3.50 *Etlingera elatior* 4·50 4·50

MS1459 93×64 mm. $3.50 *Tecomanthe speciosa* (vert) 4·50 4·50

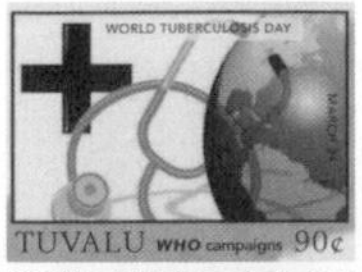

266 World Tuberculosis Day

2013. 65th Anniv of World Health Organization. Multicoloured.

MS1460 190×140 mm. 90c.×6 Type **266**; World Immunization Week; World Health Day; World Aids Day; World No Tobacco Day; World Blood Donor Day 8·00 8·00

MS1461 110×70 mm. $3.50 ECG and Globe 4·50 4·50

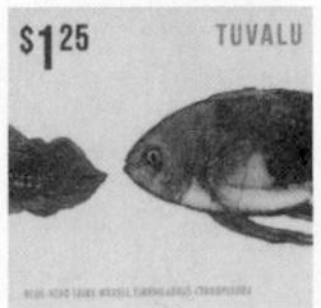

267 Blue-head Fairy Wrasse (*Cirrhirabrus cyanopleura*)

2013. Fish of the Pacific. Multicoloured.

MS1462 $1.25×4 Type **267**; Clownfish (*Amphirion ocellaris*); Clown Triggerfish (*Balistoides conspicillum*); Copperband Butterflyfish (*Chelmon rostratus*)   8·00   8·00

MS1463 $1.25×4 Scribbled Angelfish (*Chaetodontoplus duboulayi*); Flame Angelfish (*Centropyge loricula*); Harlequin Tuskfish (*Choerodon fasciatus*); Flameback Angelfish (*Centropyge aurantonotus*)   8·00   8·00

268 Duke and Duchess of Cambridge with Prince George

2013. Birth of Prince George of Cambridge. Multicoloured.

MS1464 150×100 mm. $1.20×4 Type **268**; Prince Charles (holding baby Prince William) and Princess Diana; Princess Diana and baby Prince William; Catherine, Duchess of Cambridge and Prince George   7·50   7·50

MS1465 70×100 mm. $3.50 Duke and Duchess of Cambridge with baby Prince George   4·50   4·50

269 Queen Elizabeth II waving from Car, c. 1952

2013. 60th Anniv of the Coronation. Multicoloured.

MS1466 150×120 mm. $1.20×4 Type **269**; Queen Elizabeth II wearing diadem, c. 1952; Queen Elizabeth II in recent years; Queen Elizabeth II with young Prince Charles in toy car, c. 1952   7·50   7·50

MS1467 70×100 mm. $3.50 Princess Elizabeth   4·50   4·50

OFFICIAL STAMPS

1981. Nos. 105/22 optd **OFFICIAL**.

O1	**14**	1c. multicoloured	10	10
O2	-	2c. multicoloured	10	10
O3	-	4c. multicoloured	10	10
O4	-	5c. multicoloured	10	10
O5	-	6c. multicoloured	10	10
O6	-	8c. multicoloured	10	10
O7	-	10c. multicoloured	15	15
O8	-	15c. multicoloured	15	15
O9	-	20c. multicoloured	20	20
O10a	-	25c. multicoloured	25·00	25
O11	-	30c. multicoloured	20	20
O12	-	35c. multicoloured	20	20
O13	-	40c. multicoloured	20	20
O14	-	45c. multicoloured	25	25
O15	-	50c. multicoloured	30	30
O16	-	70c. multicoloured	40	40
O17	-	$1 multicoloured	40	40
O18a	-	$2 multicoloured	75	75
O19	-	$5 multicoloured	1·00	75

1983. Nos. 202/3a, 205/12, 224 and 234 optd **OFFICIAL**.

O20	5c. Wedding and baby food baskets		10	40
O21	10c. Hand-carved model of canoe		10	40
O22	15c. Ladies' sun hats		15	70
O23	25c. Pandanus baskets		25	60
O24	30c. on 45c. Reef sandals and fish trap		50	70
O25	30c. Basket tray and coconut stand		30	70
O26	35c. Pandanus pillows and shell necklaces		40	75
O27	40c. Round baskets and fans		45	75
O28	45c. Reef sandals and fish trap		45	75
O29	50c. Rat trap		50	75
O30	60c. on $1 Pump drill and adze		75	75
O31	60c. Fisherman's waterproof boxes		60	1·00
O32	$1 Pump drill and adze		75	1·00
O33	$2 Fisherman's hat and canoe bailers		80	1·00
O34	$5 Fishing rod, lures and scoop nets		1·25	2·50

1989. Nos. 502/17 optd **OFFICIAL**.

O35	5c. Type **66**		30	55
O36	10c. White tern		30	55

O37	15c. Common noddy		45	55
O38	20c. Phoenix petrel		45	55
O39	25c. Pacific golden plover		50	75
O40	30c. Crested tern		50	75
O41	35c. Sooty tern		55	80
O42	40c. Bristle-thighed curlew		55	80
O43	45c. Bar-tailed godwit		65	85
O44	50c. Reef heron		70	90
O45	55c. Great frigate bird		70	90
O46	60c. Red-footed booby		70	90
O47	70c. Rufous-necked sandpiper		80	1·00
O48	$1 Long-tailed koel		1·10	1·10
O49	$2 Red-tailed tropic bird		2·00	1·90
O50	$5 Buff-banded rail		4·25	4·50

POSTAGE DUE STAMPS

D1 Tuvalu Crest

1981.

D1	**D1**	1c. black and purple	10	10
D2	**D1**	2c. black and blue	10	10
D3	**D1**	5c. black and brown	10	10
D13	**D1**	10c. black and green	10	10
D14	**D1**	20c. black and brown	15	20
D6	**D1**	30c. black and orange	15	30
D7	**D1**	40c. black and blue	15	40
D8	**D1**	50c. black and green	20	45
D9	**D1**	$1 black and mauve	30	80

Some values exist with or without the imprint date at foot.

APPENDIX

The following stamps for individual islands of Tuvalu have either been issued in excess of postal needs, or have not been made available to the public in reasonable quantities at face value.

FUNAFUTI

1984

Leaders of the World. Railway Locomotives (1st series). Two designs for each value, the first showing technical drawings and the second the locomotive at work. 15, 20, 30, 40, 50, 60c. each×2.

Leaders of the World. Automobiles (1st series). Two designs for each value, the first showing technical drawings and the second the car in action. 1, 10, 40c., $1 each×2.

Leaders of the World. Railway Locomotives (2nd series). Two designs for each value, the first showing technical drawings and the second the locomotive at work. 5, 15, 25, 35, 40, 55, 60c., $1 each×2.

1985

Leaders of the World. Automobiles (2nd series). Two designs for each value, the first showing technical drawings and the second the car in action. 1, 30, 55, 60c. each×2.

Leaders of the World. Railway Locomotives (3rd series). Two designs for each value, the first showing technical drawings and the second the locomotive at work. 5, 15, 35, 40, 50c., $1 each×2.

Leaders of the World. Life and Times of Queen Elizabeth the Queen Mother. Two designs for each value, showing different portraits. 5, 25, 80c., $1.05 each×2.

1986

60th Birthday of Queen Elizabeth II. 10, 50c., $1.50, $3.50.

Royal Wedding (1st issue). 60c., $1 each×2.

Royal Wedding (2nd issue). Previous Royal Wedding stamps optd **Congratulations T.R.H. The Duke & Duchess of York**. 60c., $1 each×2.

Railway Locomotives (4th series). Two designs for each value, the first showing technical drawings and the second the locomotive at work. 20, 40, 60c., $1.50 each×2.

1987

Automobiles (3rd series). Two designs for each value, the first showing technical drawings and the second the car in action. 10, 20, 40, 60, 75, 80c., $1.50 each×2.

Royal Ruby Wedding. 20, 50, 75c., $1.20, $1.75.

1988

Olympic Games, Seoul. 10, 20, 40, 50, 80, 90c.

NANUMAGA

1984

Leaders of the World. Automobiles (1st series). Two designs for each value, the first showing technical drawings and the second the car in action. 5, 10, 25, 30, 40c., $1 each×2.

Leaders of the World. British Monarchs. Two designs for each value, forming a composite picture. 10, 20, 30, 40, 50c., $1 each×2.

Leaders of the World. Automobiles (2nd series). Two designs for each value, the first showing technical drawings and the second the car in action. 5, 10, 50c., $1 each×2.

1985

Leaders of the World. Railway Locomotives. Two designs for each value, the first showing technical drawings and the second the locomotive at work. 10, 25, 50, 60c. each×2.

Leaders of the World. Flowers. 25, 30, 40, 50c. each×2.

Leaders of the World. Automobiles (3rd series). Two designs for each value, the first showing technical drawings and the second the car in action. 10, 25, 75c., $1 each×2.

Leaders of the World. Life and Times of Queen Elizabeth the Queen Mother. Two designs for each value, showing different portraits. 15, 55, 65, 90c. each×2.

1986

60th Birthday of Queen Elizabeth II. 5c., $1, $1.75, $2.50.

World Cup Football Championship, Mexico. 1, 2, 5, 5, 10, 20, 35, 50, 60, 75c., $1, $2, $4.

Royal Wedding (1st issue). 60c., $1 each×2.

Royal Wedding (2nd issue). Previous Royal Wedding stamps optd as for Funafuti. 60c., $1 each×2.

1987

Automobiles (4th series). Two designs for each value, the first showing technical drawings and the second the car in action. 5, 10, 15, 20, 25, 40, 60c., $1 each×2.

Royal Ruby Wedding. 15, 35, 60c., $1.50, $1.75.

NANUMEA

1984

Leaders of the World. Railway Locomotives (1st series). Two designs for each value, the first showing technical drawings and the second the locomotive at work. 15, 20, 30, 40, 50, 60c. each×2.

Leaders of the World. Famous Cricketers. Two designs for each value, the first showing a portrait and the second the cricketer in action. 1, 10, 40c., $1 each×2.

1985

Leaders of the World. Automobiles (1st series). Two designs for each value, the first showing technical drawings and the second the car in action. 5, 40, 50, 60c. each×2.

Leaders of the World. Railway Locomotives (2nd series). Two designs for each value, the first showing technical drawings and the second the locomotive at work. 1, 35, 50, 60c. each×2.

Leaders of the World. Automobiles (2nd series). Two designs for each value, the first showing technical drawings and the second the car in action. 15, 20, 50, 60c. each×2.

Leaders of the World. Cats. 5, 30, 50c., $1 each×2.

Leaders of the World. Life and Times of Queen Elizabeth the Queen Mother. Two designs for each value, showing different portraits. 5, 30, 75c., $1.05 each×2.

1986

60th Birthday of Queen Elizabeth II. 10, 80c., $1.75, $3.

World Cup Football Championship, Mexico. 1, 2, 5, 10, 25, 40, 50, 75, 90c., $1, $2.50, $4.

Royal Wedding (1st issue). 60c., $1 each×2.

Royal Wedding (2nd issue). Previous Royal Wedding stamps optd as for Funafuti. 60c., $1 each×2.

Automobiles (3rd series). Two designs for each value, the first showing technical drawings and the second the car in action. 10, 20, 35, 50, 75c., $2 each×2.

1987

Royal Ruby Wedding. 40, 60, 80c., $1, $2.

NIUTAO

1984

Leaders of the World. Automobiles (1st series). Two designs for each value, the first showing technical drawings and the second the car in action. 15, 30, 40, 50c. each×2.

Leaders of the World. Railway Locomotives (1st series). Two designs for each value, the first showing technical drawings and the second the locomotive at work. 5, 10, 20, 40, 50c., $1 each×2.

1985

Leaders of the World. Famous Cricketers. Two designs for each value, the first showing a portrait and the second the cricketer in action. 1, 15, 50c., $1 each×2.

Leaders of the World. Birth Bicent of John J. Audubon (ornithologist). Birds. 5, 15, 25c., $1 each×2.

Leaders of the World. Automobiles (2nd series). Two designs for each value, the first showing technical drawings and the second the car in action. 20, 25, 40, 60c. each×2.

Leaders of the World. Railway Locomotives (2nd series). Two designs for each value, the first showing technical drawings and the second the locomotive at work. 10, 30, 45, 60, 75c., $1.20 each×2.

Leaders of the World. Life and Times of Queen Elizabeth the Queen Mother. Two designs for each value, showing different portraits. 15, 35, 70, 95c. each×2.

1986

60th Birthday of Queen Elizabeth II. 5, 60c., $1.50, $3.50.

Royal Wedding (1st issue). 60c., $1 each×2.

Royal Wedding (2nd series). Previous Royal Wedding stamps optd as for Funafuti. 60c., $1 each×2.

1987

Royal Ruby Wedding. 60th Birthday of Queen Elizabeth II issue of 1986 optd **40th WEDDING ANNIVERSARY OF H.M. QUEEN ELIZABETH II**. 5, 60c., $1.50, $3.50.

NUI

1984

Leaders of the World. Railway Locomotives (1st series). Two designs for each value, the first showing technical drawings and the second the locomotive at work. 15, 25, 30, 50c. each×2.

Leaders of the World. British Monarchs. Two designs for each value, forming a composite picture. 1, 5, 15, 40, 50c., $1 each×2.

1985

Leaders of the World. Railway Locomotives (2nd series). Two designs for each value, the first showing techni-

---

cal drawings and the second the locomotive at work. 5, 15, 25c., $1 each×2.

Leaders of the World. Automobiles (1st series). Two designs for each value, the first showing technical drawings and the second the car in action. 25, 30, 40, 50c. each×2.

Leaders of the World. Famous Cricketers. Two designs for each value, the first showing a portrait and the second the cricketer in action. 25, 30, 40, 70c., each×2.

Leaders of the World. Life and Times of Queen Elizabeth the Queen Mother. Two designs for each value, showing different portraits. 5, 50, 75, 85c. each×2.

Leaders of the World. Automobiles (2nd series). Two designs for each value, the first showing technical drawings and the second the car in action. 5, 15, 40, 60, 90c., $1.10 each×2.

1986

60th Birthday of Queen Elizabeth II. 10, 80c., $1.75, $3.

Royal Wedding (1st issue). 60c., $1 each×2.

Royal Wedding (2nd issue). Previous Royal Wedding stamps optd as for Funafuti. 60c., $1 each×2.

1987

Railway Locomotives (3rd series). Two designs for each value, the first showing technical drawings and the second the locomotive at work. 10, 25, 35, 40, 60, 75c., $1, $1.25 each×2.

Royal Ruby Wedding. 20, 50, 75c., $1.20, $1.75.

1988

Railway Locomotives (4th series). Two designs for each value, the first showing technical drawings and the second the locomotive at work. 5, 10, 20, 25, 40, 50, 60, 75c. each×2.

NUKUFETAU

1984

Leaders of the World. Automobiles (1st series). Two designs for each value, the first showing technical drawings and the second the car in action. 10, 25, 30, 50, 60c. each×2.

Leaders of the World. British Monarchs. Two designs for each value, forming a composite picture. 1, 10, 30, 50, 60c., $1 each×2.

1985

Leaders of the World. Famous Cricketers. Two designs for each value, the first showing a portrait and the second the cricketer in action. 1, 10, 55c., $1 each×2.

Leaders of the World. Railway Locomotives (1st series). Two designs for each value, the first showing technical drawings and the second the locomotive at work. 1, 10, 60, 70c. each×2.

Leaders of the World. Automobiles (2nd series). Two designs for each value, the first showing technical drawings and the second the car in action. 5, 10, 15, 20, 50, 60, 70c., $1.50 each×2.

Leaders of the World. Life and Times of Queen Elizabeth the Queen Mother. Two designs for each value, showing different portraits. 5, 30, 75c., $1.05 each×2.

1986

Leaders of the World. Railway Locomotives (2nd series). Two designs for each value, the first showing technical drawings and the second the locomotive at work. 20, 40, 60c., $1.50 each×2.

60th Birthday of Queen Elizabeth II. 5, 40c., $2, $4.

Royal Wedding (1st issue). 60c., $1 each×2.

Royal Wedding (2nd issue). Previous Royal Wedding stamps optd as for Funafuti. 60c., $1 each×2.

1987

Railway Locomotives (3rd series). Two designs for each value, the first showing technical drawings and the second the locomotive at work. 5, 10, 15, 25, 30, 50, 60c., $1 each×2.

Royal Ruby Wedding. 60th Birthday of Queen Elizabeth II issue of 1986 optd as for Niutao. 5, 40c., $2, $4.

NUKULAELAE

1984

Leaders of the World. Railway Locomotives (1st series). Two designs for each value, the first showing technical drawings and the second the locomotive at work. 5, 15, 40c., $1 each×2.

Leaders of the World. Famous Cricketers. Two designs for each value, the first showing a portrait and the second the cricketer in action. 5, 15, 30c., $1 each×2.

Leaders of the World. Railway Locomotives (2nd series). Two designs for each value, the first showing technical drawings and the second the locomotive at work. 5, 20, 40c., $1 each×2.

1985

Leaders of the World. Automobiles (1st series). Two designs for each value, the first showing technical drawings and the second the car in action. 5, 35, 50, 70c. each×2.

Leaders of the World. Dogs. 5, 20, 50, 70c. each×2.

Leaders of the World. Railway Locomotives (3rd series). Two designs for each value, the first showing technical drawings and the second the locomotive at work. 10, 25, 50c. each×2.

Leaders of the World. Automobiles (2nd series). Two designs for each value, the first showing technical drawings and the second the car in action. 10, 25, 35, 50, 75c., $1 each×2.

Leaders of the World. Life and Times of Queen Elizabeth the Queen Mother. Two designs for each value, showing different portraits. 5, 25, 85c., $1 each×2.

1986

60th Birthday of Queen Elizabeth II. 10c., $1, $1.50, $3.

Railway Locomotives (4th series). Two designs for each value, the first showing technical drawings and the second the locomotive at work. 10, 15, 25, 40, 50, 80c., $1, $1.50 each×2.

Royal Wedding (1st issue). 60c., $1 each×2.

Royal Wedding (2nd issue). Previous Royal Wedding stamps optd as for Funafuti. 60c., $1 each×2.

1987

Royal Ruby Wedding. 15, 35, 60c., $1.50, $1.75.

VAITUPU

1984

Leaders of the World. Automobiles (1st series). Two designs for each value, the first showing technical drawings and the second the car in action. 15, 25, 30, 50c. each×2.
Leaders of the World. British Monarchs. Two designs for each value, forming a composite picture. 1, 5, 15, 40, 50c., $1 each×2.
Leaders of the World. Automobiles (2nd series). Two designs for each value, the first showing technical drawings and the second the car in action. 5, 15, 25, 30, 40, 50, 60c. $1 each×2.

1985

Leaders of the World. Railway Locomotives (1st series). Two designs for each value, the first showing technical drawings and the second the locomotive at work. 10, 25, 50, 60c. each×2.
Leaders of the World. Butterflies. 5, 15, 50, 75c. each×2.
Leaders of the World. Automobiles (3rd series). Two designs for each value, the first showing technical drawings and the second the car in action. 15, 30, 40, 60c. each×2.
Leaders of the World. Life and Times of Queen Elizabeth the Queen Mother. Two designs for each value, showing different portraits. 15, 40, 65, 90c. each×2.

1986

Leaders of the World. Railway Locomotives (2nd series). Two designs for each value, the first showing technical drawings and the second the locomotives at work. 5, 25, 80c., $1 each×2.
60th Birthday of Queen Elizabeth II. 5, 60c., $2, $3.50.
Royal Wedding (1st issue). 60c., $1 each×2.
Royal Wedding (2nd issue). Previous Royal Wedding stamps optd as for Funafuti. 60c., $1 each×2.

1987

Railway Locomotives (3rd series). Two designs for each value, the first showing technical drawings and the second the locomotive at work. 10, 15, 25, 35, 45, 65, 85c., $1 each×2.
Royal Ruby Wedding. 60th Birthday of Queen Elizabeth II issue of 1986 optd as for Niutao. 5, 60c., $2, $3.50.

2010

Abraham Lincoln Commemoration $1.30×4
50th Anniv of Election of Pres. John F. Kennedy $1.30×12
Birth Bicent of Frédéric Chopin $1.30×4
Fifth Anniv of Pontificate of Pope Benedict XVI $1.30×4
Fifth Death Anniv of Pope John Paul II $1.30×8
Princess Diana Commemoration $1.30×4
35th Anniv of 'Thrilla in Manila' (boxing match between Mohammad Ali and Joe Frazier) $1.30×8

2011

Whales of the World $1×6
Indipex 2011 International Stamp Exhibition, New Delhi. Personalities of India $1.30×4
Elvis Presley Commemoration $1.30×8
Abraham Lincoln and the American Civil War $1.30×4
125th Anniv of the Statue of Liberty $1.30×4
Beatification of Pope John Paul II $1×2
Personalisable Stamp 20c.
US Pres. Barack Obama meets Australian Prime Minister Julia Gillard $1.30×4
50th Anniv of the First Man in Space $1.30×8
Birth Cent of Ronald Reagan $1×4
150th Anniv of the American Civil War $1.30×12
Birth Cent (2010) of Mother Teresa $1.30×4
Philanippon '11 International Stamp Exhibition. Japanese Woodblock Paintings $1×6; $1.30×4
50th Birth Anniv of Princess Diana $1.30×4
Women's World Cup Football Final $1.30×4

2012

Cent of the Sinking of the *Titanic* $1.50×3
Dog Breeds of the World $1×5
Cat Breeds of the World 80c.×5
Paintings by Raphael $1×4

2013

Mushrooms $1.20×4
Election of Pope Francis I $1.20×4
Pacific Seashells $1×5
Dolphins $1.25×4
Temples of Thailand $1.20×8

Pt. 6

UBANGI-SHARI

Formerly part of the French Congo. Ubangi-Shari became a separate colony in 1904 (although stamps of the French Congo continued to be used until 1915). From 1915 to 1922 it shared a postal administration with Chad.

From 1936 to 1958 Ubangi-Shari was part of French Equatorial Africa. In December 1958 it became the autonomous state of the Central African Republic.

100 centimes = 1 franc.

A. UBANGI-SHARI-CHAD

1915. Stamps of Middle Congo optd **OUBANGUI-CHARI-TCHAD**.

1	1	1c. green and brown	35	5·00
2	1	2c. violet and brown	45	7·50
3	1	4c. blue and brown	55	6·50
4	1	5c. green and blue	55	5·25
19	1	5c. yellow and blue	3·25	8·50
5	1	10c. red and blue	1·00	5·50
20	1	10c. green and turquoise	3·25	8·50
5a	1	15c. purple and pink	2·75	10·00
6	1	20c. brown and blue	3·50	13·50
7	2	25c. blue and green	3·25	5·00
21	2	25c. green and black	3·00	7·00
8	2	30c. red and green	3·25	7·75
22	2	30c. red	2·30	8·25
9	2	35c. brown and blue	6·50	26·00
10	2	40c. green and brown	6·00	26·00
11	2	45c. violet and orange	6·75	32·00
12	2	50c. green and orange	4·50	32·00
23	2	50c. blue and green	3·50	8·75
13	2	75c. brown and blue	11·50	37·00
14	3	1f. green and violet	11·00	33·00
15	3	2f. violet and green	14·50	37·00
16	3	5f. blue and pink	55·00	95·00

1916. No. 5 surch **5c** and cross.

18	3	10c.+5c. red and blue	2·75	7·00

B. UBANGI-SHARI

1922. Stamps of Middle Congo, new colours, optd **OUBANGUI-CHARI**.

24	1	1c. violet and green	40	5·50
25	1	2c. green and pink	35	7·50
26	1	4c. brown and purple	2·00	8·00
27	1	5c. blue and pink	2·50	8·25
28	1	10c. green and turquoise	3·50	10·50
29	1	15c. pink and blue	2·25	11·50
30	1	20c. brown and pink	10·00	36·00
31	1	25c. violet and pink	5·50	21·00
32	1	30c. red	2·75	18·00
33	1	35c. violet and green	7·50	34·00
34	1	40c. blue and mauve	5·00	29·00
35	1	45c. brown and mauve	5·00	27·00
36	1	50c. blue and light blue	3·00	14·00
37	1	60 on 75c. violet on pink	5·00	20·00
38	1	75c. brown and pink	5·50	34·00
39	3	1f. green and blue	7·25	36·00
40	3	2f. green and pink	8·25	50·00
41	3	5f. green and brown	17·00	70·00

1924. Stamps of 1922 and similar stamps additionally optd **AFRIQUE EQUATORIALE FRANCAISE.**

42	1	1c. violet and green	20	5·75
43	1	2c. green and pink	20	7·75
44	1	4c. brown and chocolate	30	7·00
44c	1	4c. brown	2·50	10·50
45	1	5c. blue and pink	35	2·50
46	1	10c. green and turquoise	55	7·25
47	1	10c. red and blue	65	2·30
48	1	15c. pink and blue	1·10	9·00
49	1	20c. brown and pink	1·10	6·00
50	2	25c. violet and pink	1·80	1·40
51	2	30c. red	1·30	5·25
52	2	30c. brown and pink	55	1·00
53	2	30c. olive and green	2·75	7·75
54	2	35c. violet and green	90	5·75
55	2	40c. blue and mauve	1·90	2·30
56	2	45c. brown and mauve	2·30	7·25
57	2	50c. blue and light blue	1·70	4·00
58	2	50c. grey and blue	2·30	1·60
59	2	60 on 75c. violet on pink	1·70	4·00
60	2	65c. brown and blue	3·25	11·00
61	2	75c. brown and pink	2·75	8·75
62	2	75c. blue and light blue	2·00	5·00
63	2	75c. purple and brown	4·50	6·75
64	2	90c. pink and red	6·75	36·00
65a	3	1f. green and blue	1·00	1·30
66	3	1f.10 brown and blue	3·50	13·50
67	3	1f.25 mauve and green	11·50	12·00
68	3	1f.50 ultramarine and blue	6·50	42·00
69	3	1f.75 brown and orange	14·00	12·50
70	3	2f. green and pink	4·25	4·00
71	3	3f. mauve on pink	7·00	27·00
72	3	5f. green and brown	5·75	8·25

1925. As last but new colours and surch.

73	65 on 1f. violet and brown	1·20	5·75
74	85 on 1f. violet and brown	1·00	10·00
75	90 on 75c. pink and red	2·50	3·75
76	1f.25 on 1f. blue & ultram	1·00	1·20
77	1f.50 on 1f. ultramarine & bl	2·75	2·75
78	3f. on 5f. brown and red	4·25	13·50
79	10f. on 5f. red and mauve	14·00	30·00
80	20f. on 5f. mauve and grey	23·00	70·00

1931. "International Colonial Exhibition" key-types inscr "OUBANGUI-CHARI".

103	E	40c. green	5·50	14·00
104	F	50c. mauve	5·50	14·00
105	G	90c. red	5·50	14·00
106	H	1f.50 blue	7·50	14·00

POSTAGE DUE STAMPS

1928. Postage Due type of France optd **OUBANGUI-CHARI A. E. F.**

D81	D11	5c. blue	1·20	7·75
D82	D11	10c. brown	1·50	5·50
D83	D11	20c. olive	1·80	3·50
D84	D11	25c. red	1·80	7·75
D85	D11	30c. red	1·80	6·50
D86	D11	45c. green	1·80	5·00
D87	D11	50c. purple	2·30	11·00
D88	D11	60c. brown on cream	2·50	6·75
D89	D11	1f. red on cream	3·25	11·50
D90	D11	2f. red	4·00	19·00
D91	D11	3f. violet	4·00	19·00

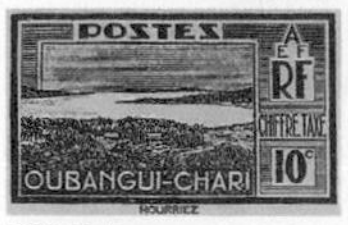

D12 Mobaye

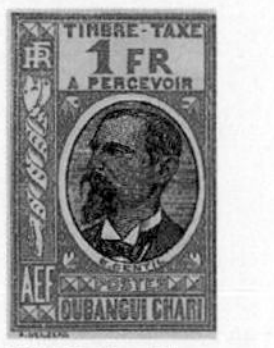

D13 E. Gentil

1930

D92	D12	5c. olive and blue	2·30	4·75
D93	D12	10c. brown and red	2·00	7·00
D94	D12	20c. brown and green	3·75	8·25
D95	D12	25c. brown and blue	6·50	7·25
D96	D12	30c. green and brown	5·75	12·50
D97	D12	45c. olive and green	7·00	14·50
D98	D12	50c. brown and mauve	11·00	27·00
D99	D12	60c. black and violet	16·00	29·00
D100	D13	1f. black and brown	8·50	16·00
D101	D13	2f. brown and mauve	8·50	24·00
D102	D13	3f. brown and red	8·75	36·00

Pt. 1

UGANDA

A Br. Protectorate in Central Africa until it attained independence within the British Commonwealth in 1962. From 1903 to 1962 used the stamps listed under "Kenya, Uganda and Tanganyika".

1895. 200 cowries = 1 rupee.
1896. 16 annas = 1 rupee.
1962. 100 cents = 1 shilling.

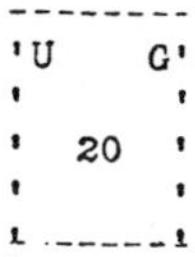

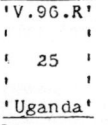

2

1895. Typewritten in black.

17	2	5 (c.) black	£3250	£1300
18	2	10 (c.) black	£3250	£1600
19	2	15 (c.) black	£2000	£1500
20	2	20 (c.) black	£3250	£1500
21	2	25 (c.) black	£1800	£1600
6	2	30 (c.) black	£2500	£2250
4	2	40 (c.) black	£6000	£2250
8	2	50 (c.) on 10 (c.) black	†	£70000
9	2	60 (c.) on 30 (c.) black	†	£70000

1895. Typewritten in violet.

35	5 (c.) violet	£700	£650
36	10 (c.) violet	£650	£650
37	15 (c.) violet	£1100	£600
38	20 (c.) violet	£475	£300
39	25 (c.) violet	£1800	£1600
40	30 (c.) violet	£2250	£1100
41	40 (c.) violet	£2250	£1500
42	50 (c.) violet	£2000	£1500
43	100 (c.) violet	£2500	£3000

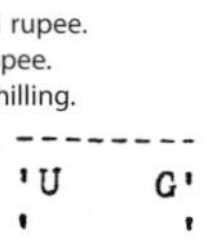

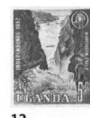

3

1896. Typewritten in violet.

44	3	5 (c.) violet	£750	£1000
45	3	10 (c.) violet	£850	£650
46	3	15 (c.) violet	£750	£750
47	3	20 (c.) violet	£400	£225
48	3	25 (c.) violet	£700	£900
49	3	30 (c.) violet	£750	£850
50	3	40 (c.) violet	£900	£900
51	3	50 (c.) violet	£750	£800
52	3	60 (c.) violet	£1600	£2000
53	3	100 (c.) violet	£1500	£2000

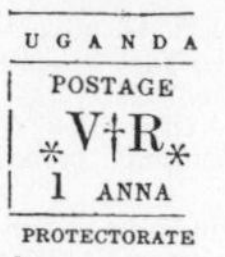

4

1896

(a) As Type **4**

55	4	1a. black	23·00	26·00
56	4	2a. black	29·00	35·00
57	4	3a. black	29·00	45·00
58	4	4a. black	32·00	38·00
59	4	8a. black	40·00	48·00
60	4	1r. black	85·00	£100
61	4	5r. black	£275	£350

(b) Optd with large **L**

70	1a. black	£190	£170
71	2a. black	£120	£120
72	3a. black	£375	£325
73	4a. black	£120	£160
74	8a. black	£200	£300
75	1r. black	£375	£450
76	5r. black	£22000	£22000

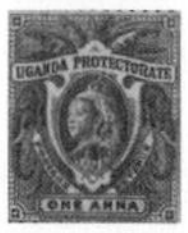

8

1898

(a) As Type **8**

84*a*	8	1a. red	2·25	1·75
86	8	2a. brown	9·00	11·00
87*a*	8	3a. grey	21·00	20·00
88	8	4a. green	13·00	10·00
89	8	8a. green	15·00	30·00

(b) Larger type with lions at either side of portrait.

90	1r. blue	55·00	55·00
91	5r. brown	£100	£120

1902. Stamps of British East Africa optd **UGANDA**.

92	11	½a. green	3·00	2·00
93	11	2½a. blue	4·50	3·00

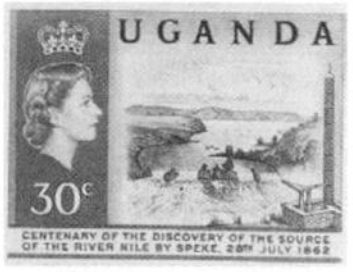

11 Ripon Falls and Speke Memorial

1962. Centenary of Speke's Discovery of Source of Nile.

95	11	30c. black and red	20	25
96	11	50c. black and violet	20	10
97	11	1s.30 black and green	1·00	25
98	11	2s.50 black and blue	2·25	2·25

12 Murchison Falls

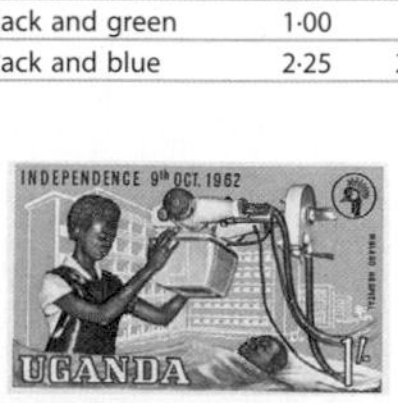

14 Mulago Hospital

1962. Independence.

99	12	5c. green	10	10
100	-	10c. brown	10	10
101	-	15c. black, red and green	10	10
102	-	20c. plum and buff	10	10
103	-	30c. blue	10	10
104	-	50c. black and turquoise	10	10
105	14	1s. sepia, red and turquoise	1·25	20
106	-	1s.30 orange and violet	25	10
107	-	2s. black, red and blue	50	70
108	-	5s. red and deep green	8·00	1·50
109	-	10s. slate and brown	4·25	4·00
110	-	20s. brown and blue	4·50	21·00

DESIGNS—As Type **12**: 10c. Tobacco growing; 15c. Coffee growing; 20c. Ankole cattle; 30c. Cotton; 50c. Mountains of the Moon. As Type **14**: 1s.30, Cathedrals and mosque; 2s. Makerere College; 5s. Copper mining; 10s. Cement industry; 20s. Parliament Buildings.

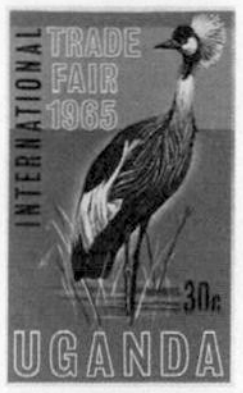

15 South African Crowned Crane

1965. International Trade Fair, Kampala.

111	15	30c. multicoloured	15	10
112	15	1s.30 multicoloured	25	10

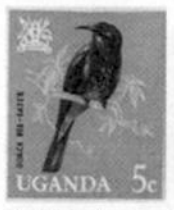

16 Black BeeEater

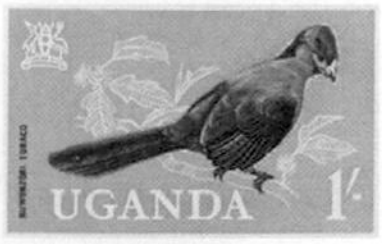

18 Ruwenzori Turaco

1965. Birds.

113	16	5c. multicoloured	10	10
114	-	10c. brown, black and blue	10	10
115	-	15c. yellow and brown	20	10
116	-	20c. multicoloured	20	10
117	-	30c. black and brown	1·50	10
118	-	40c. multicoloured	1·00	1·75
119	-	50c. blue and violet	25	10
120	-	65c. red, black and grey	2·50	2·75
121	18	1s. multicoloured	50	10
122	-	1s.30 brown, black & yell	5·50	30
123	-	2s.50 multicoloured	4·25	65
124	-	5s. multicoloured	7·00	4·00
125	-	10s. multicoloured	11·00	11·00
126	-	20s. multicoloured	21·00	38·00

DESIGNS—HORIZ (as Type **16**): 10c. African jacana; 30c. Sacred ibis; 65c. Red-crowned bishop. (As Type **18**): 2s.50, Great blue turaco; 10s. Black-collared lovebird. 20s. South African crowned crane ("Crowned Crane"). VERT (as Type **16**): 15c. Orange weaver; 20c. Narina's trogon ("Narina Trogon"); 40c. Blue-breasted kingfisher; 50c. Whale-headed stork. (As Type **18**): 1s.30, African fish eagle; 5s. Lilac-breasted roller.

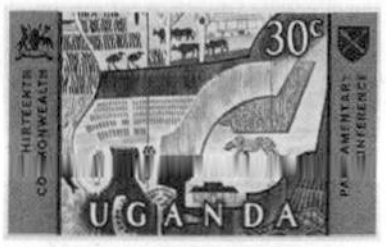

19 Carved Screen

1967. 13th Commonwealth Parliamentary Association Conference. Multicoloured.

127	30c. Type **19**	10	10
128	50c. Arms of Uganda	10	10
129	1s.30 Parliamentary Building	10	10
130	2s.50 Conference Chamber	15	1·75

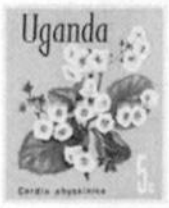

20 "Cordia abyssinica"

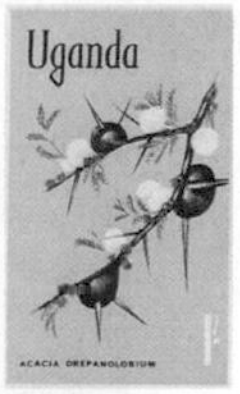

21 "Acacia drepanolobium"

1969. Flowers.

131a	20	5c. brown, green and yellow	40	10
132	-	10c. multicoloured	10	10
133	-	15c. multicoloured	40	10
134	-	20c. violet, olive and green	15	10
135	-	30c. multicoloured	20	10
136	-	40c. violet, green and grey	20	10
137	-	50c. multicoloured	20	10
138	-	60c. multicoloured	45	2·50
139	-	70c. multicoloured	25	30
140	21	1s. multicoloured	20	10
141	-	1s.50 multicoloured	25	10
142a	-	2s.50 multicoloured	1·25	10
143a	-	5s. multicoloured	1·75	10
144a	-	10s. multicoloured	3·75	10
145	-	20s. multicoloured	1·00	6·00

DESIGNS—As Type **20**: 10c. "Grewia similis"; 15c. "Cassia didymobotrya"; 20c. "Coleus barbatus"; 30c. "Ochna ovata"; 40c. "Ipomoea spathulata"; 50c. "Spathodea nilotica"; 60c. "Oncoba spinosa"; 70c. "Carissa edulis". As Type **21**: 1s.50, "Clerodendrum myricoides"; 2s.50, "Acanthus arboreus"; 5s. "Kigelia aethiopium"; 10s. "Erythrina abyssinica"; 20s. "Monodora myristica".

1975. Nos. 140, 142a and 145 surch.

146	2s. on 1s. on 1s.50 multicoloured	2·00	1·50
147	3s. on 2s.50 on 2s.50 multicoloured	18·00	42·00
148	40s. on 20s. on 20s. multicoloured	4·00	3·50

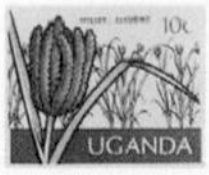

23 Millet

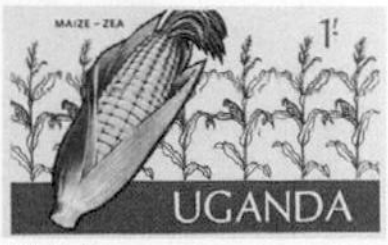

24 Maize

1975. Ugandan Crops.

149	23	10c. black, green and brown	10	10
150	-	20c. multicoloured	10	10
151	-	30c. multicoloured	10	10
152	-	40c. multicoloured	10	10
153	-	50c. multicoloured	10	10
154	-	70c. black, green & turq	10	15
155	-	80c. multicoloured	10	15
156	24	1s. multicoloured	10	10
157	-	2s. multicoloured	30	30
158	-	3s. multicoloured	50	45
159	-	5s. multicoloured	50	75
160	-	10s. multicoloured	50	1·25
161	-	20s. green, black and purple	70	2·50
162	-	40s. green, blue and orange	1·10	4·50

DESIGNS—As Type **23**: 20c. Sugar; 30c. Tobacco; 40c. Onions; 50c. Tomatoes; 70c. Tea; 80c. Bananas. As Type **24**: 2s. Pineapples; 3s. Coffee; 5s. Oranges; 10s. Groundnuts; 20s. Cotton; 40s. Runner beans.

Face value colours: 5s. green; 10s. brown; 20s. mauve; 40s. orange.

For these values with colours changed, see Nos. 220/3.

1976. Telecommunications Development. As Nos. 56/60 of Kenya.

163	50c. Microwave tower	10	10
164	1s. Cordless switchboard	10	10
165	2s. Telephone	20	25
166	3s. Message Switching Centre	30	45
MS167	120×120 mm. Nos. 163/6	90	1·25

1976. Olympic Games, Montreal. As Nos. 61/5 of Kenya.

168	50c. Akii Bua, hurdler	10	10
169	1s. Filbert Bayi, runner	10	10
170	2s. Steve Muchoki, boxer	30	30
171	3s. East African flags	40	45
MS172	129×154 mm. Nos. 168/71	4·00	5·00

1976. Railway Transport. As Nos. 66/70 of Kenya.

173	50c. Diesel-hydraulic train, Tanzania–Zambia railway	15	10
174	1s. Nile Bridge, Uganda	15	10
175	2s. Nakuru Station, Kenya	50	45
176	3s. Uganda Railway Class A locomotive, 1896	55	55
MS177	154×103 mm. Nos. 173/6	2·25	2·50

1977. Game Fish of East Africa. As Nos. 71/5 of Kenya. Multicoloured.

178	50c. Nile perch	15	10
179	1s. Nile mouthbrooder	20	10
180	3s. Sailfish	60	40
181	5s. Black marlin	80	60
MS182	153×129 mm. Nos. 178/81	3·25	2·00

1977. Second World Black and African Festival of Arts and Culture. As Nos. 76/80 of Kenya. Multicoloured.

183	50c. Maasai manyatta (village), Kenya	10	10
184	1s. "Heartbeat of Africa" (Ugandan dancers)	10	10
185	2s. Makonde sculpture, Tanzania	25	55
186	3s. "Early man and technology" (skinning hippopotamus)	35	85
MS187	132×109 mm. Nos. 183/6	1·25	2·25

1977. 25th Anniv of Safari Rally. As Nos. 81/5 of Kenya. Multicoloured.

188	50c. Rally-car and villagers	10	10
189	1s. Starting-line	10	10
190	2s. Car fording river	25	35
191	5s. Car and elephants	80	1·00
MS192	126×93 mm. Nos. 188/91	1·50	2·50

1977. Centenary of Ugandan Church. As Nos. 86/90 of Kenya. Multicoloured.

193	50c. Canon Kivebulaya	10	10
194	1s. Modern Namirembe Cathedral	10	10
195	2s. Old Namirembe Cathedral	20	40
196	5s. Early congregation, Kigezi	45	1·10
MS197	126×89 mm. Nos. 193/6	1·00	1·75

1977. Design as No. 155 surch **80c**.

198	80c. on 60c. on 60c. multicoloured	30	20

1977. Endangered Species. As Nos. 96/101 of Kenya. Multicoloured.

199	50c. Pancake tortoise	30	10
200	1s. Nile crocodile	45	10
201	2s. Hunter's hartebeest	80	40
202	3s. Red colobus monkey	1·00	75
203	5s. Dugong	1·00	1·00
MS204	127×101 mm. Nos. 200/3	3·75	3·00

1978. World Cup Football Championship, Argentina (1st issue). As Nos. 122/6 of Kenya. Multicoloured.

205	50c. Joe Kadenge and forwards	15	10
206	1s. Mohamed Chuma and cup presentation	15	10
207	2s. Omari Kidevu and goal-mouth scene	30	45
208	5s. Polly Ouma and forwards	50	1·25
MS209	136×81 mm. Nos. 205/8	1·50	2·50

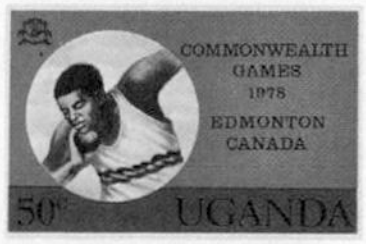

26 Shot Putting

1978. Commonwealth Games, Edmonton. Multicoloured.

210	50c. Type **26**	10	10
211	1s. Long jumping	15	10
212	2s. Running	20	40
213	5s. Boxing	40	1·10
MS214	114×85 mm. Nos. 210/13	1·25	3·00

1978. World Cup Football Championship, Argentina (2nd issue). As Nos. 205/8, but additionally inscr "WORLD CUP 1978".

215	50c. Polly Ouma and forwards	10	10
216	2s. Omari Kidevu and goal-mouth scene	20	50
217	5s. Joe Kadenge and forwards	40	85
218	10s. Mohamed Chuma and cup presentation	70	1·75
MS219	140×87 mm. Nos. 215/18	1·50	2·75

1978. As Nos. 159/62, but colours changed.

220	5s. mult (face value in blue)	50	70
221	10s. mult (face value in mauve)	50	85
222	20s. mult (face value in brown)	55	85
223	40s. mult (face value in red)	65	1·10

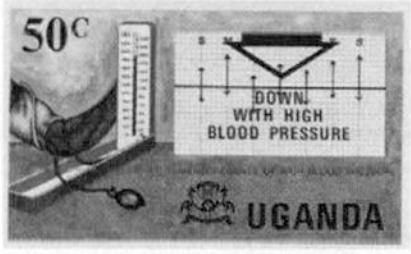

27 Measurements of High Blood Pressure

1978. "Down with High Blood Pressure". Multicoloured.

224	50c. Type **27**	15	10
225	1s. Hypertension and the heart	15	10
226	2s. Fundus of the eye in hypertension	40	45
227	5s. Kidney and high blood pressure	75	1·40
MS228	180×115 mm. Nos. 224/7	1·25	2·75

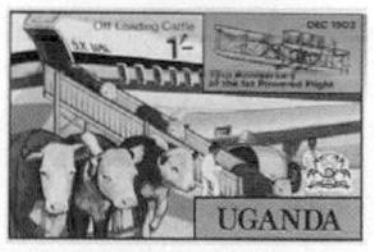

28 Off Loading Cattle

1978. 75th Anniv of Powered Flight. Multicoloured.

229	1s. Type **28**	15	10
230	1s.50 "Domestic services" (passengers boarding Britten Norman Islander)	25	15
231	2s.70 Export of Uganda coffee	25	35
232	10s. "Time machines in the air" (Wright Flyer III and Concorde)	75	1·50
MS233	166×110 mm. Nos. 299/32	1·50	2·75

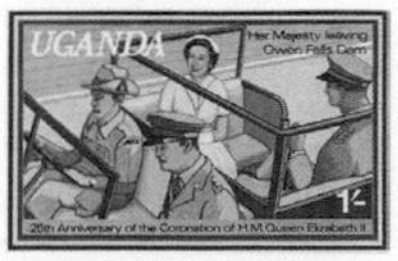

29 Queen Elizabeth II leaving Owen Falls Dam

1979. 25th Anniv of Coronation (1978). Multicoloured.

234	1s. Type **29**	15	10
235	1s.50 Regalia	15	10
236	2s.70 Coronation ceremony	30	20
237	10s. Royal family on balcony of Buckingham Palace	50	1·25
MS238	150×102 mm. Nos. 234/7	1·40	1·25

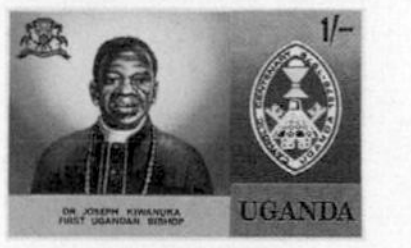

30 Dr. Joseph Kiwanuka (first Ugandan bishop)

1979. Centenary of Catholic Church in Uganda. Multicoloured.

239	1s. Type **30**	10	10
240	1s.50 Lubaga Cathedral	10	10
241	2s.70 Ugandan pilgrimage to Rome, Holy Year, 1975	15	25
242	10s. Friar Lourdel-Mapeera (early missionary)	50	80
MS243	128×91 mm. Nos. 239/42	1·00	2·00

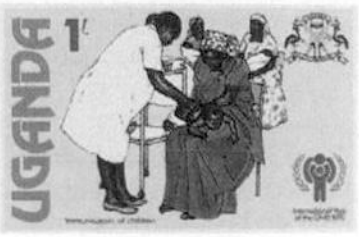

31 Immunization of Children

1979. International Year of the Child. Multicoloured.

244	1s. Type **31**	10	10
245	1s.50 Handicapped children at play	15	20
246	2s.70 Ugandan I.Y.C. emblem	15	35
247	10s. Children in class	40	1·10
MS248	136×113 mm. Nos. 244/7	1·10	2·00

1979. Liberation. Optd **UGANDA LIBERATED 1979**

249	23	10c. black, green and brown	10	10
250	-	20c. multicoloured	10	10
251	-	30c. multicoloured	10	10
252	-	40c. multicoloured	10	10
253	-	50c. multicoloured	10	10
254	-	70c. black, green & turq	10	10
255	-	80c. multicoloured	10	10
256	24	1s. multicoloured	15	15
257	-	2s. multicoloured	20	25
258	-	3s. multicoloured	35	40
259	-	5s. multicoloured	55	60
260	-	10s. multicoloured	80	1·25
261	-	20s. green, black and purple	1·00	2·40
262	-	40s. green, black and orange	1·50	4·75

(b) Nos. 210/13.

263	50c. Type **26**	10	10
264	1s. Long jumping	15	20
265	2s. Running	25	30
266	5s. Boxing	60	65

(c) Nos. 207, 215, 217/18.

[illegible]	[illegible]	[illegible]	[illegible]
268	2s. Omari Kidevu and goal-mouth scene	20	30
269	5s. Joe Kadenge and forwards	55	65
270	10s. Mohamed Chuma and cup presentation	1·00	1·40

(d) Nos. 220/3.

271	5s. multicoloured	55	60
272	10s. multicoloured	60	1·25
273	20s. multicoloured	60	2·40
274	40s. multicoloured	75	4·75

(e) Nos. 229/32.

275	1s. Type **28**	35	20
276	1s.50 "Domestic services"	45	25
277	2s.70 Export of Uganda coffee	55	55
278	10s. "Time machines in the air"	2·00	2·50

(f) Nos. 234/7.

279	1s. Type **29**	10	20
280	1s.50 Regalia	15	20
281	2s.70 Coronation ceremony	20	40
282	10s. Royal family on balcony of Buckingham Palace	85	1·75
MS283	150×102 mm. Nos. 234/6 and 15s. as No. 237	1·50	3·25

(g) Nos. 239/42.

284	1s. Type **30**	10	20
285	1s.50 Lubaga Cathedral	15	25
286	2s.70 Ugandan pilgrimage to Rome, Holy Year, 1975	30	50
287	10s. Friar Lourdel-Mapeera (early missionary)	90	1·75
MS288	128×91 mm. Nos. 239/42	1·75	2·75

(h) Nos. 244/8.

289	1s. Type **31**	20	20
290	1s.50 Handicapped children at play	25	25
291	2s.70 Ugandan I.Y.C. emblem	50	60
292	10s. Children in class	1·40	1·75
MS293	136×113 mm. Nos. 289/92	2·25	3·50

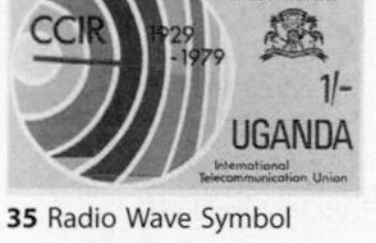

35 Radio Wave Symbol

1979. 50th Anniv of International Consultative Radio Committee and International Telecom-munications Union.

294	35	1s. multicoloured	10	10
295	35	1s.50 multicoloured	15	10
296	35	2s.70 multicoloured	15	35
297	35	10s. multicoloured	40	1·10

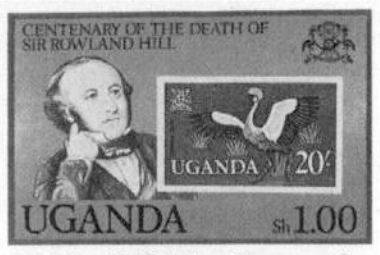

36 20s. Definitive Stamp of 1965 and Sir Rowland Hill

1979. Death Cent of Sir Rowland Hill. Multicoloured.

298	1s. Type **36**	10	10
299	1s.50 1967 13th Common-wealth Parliamentary Association Conference 50c. commemorative	15	10
300	2s.70 1962 Independence 20s. commemorative	15	30
301	10s. Uganda Protectorate 1898 1a.	40	1·25
MS302	154×98 mm. Nos. 298/301	65	1·50

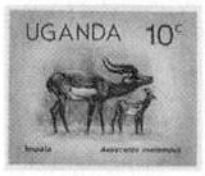

37 Impala

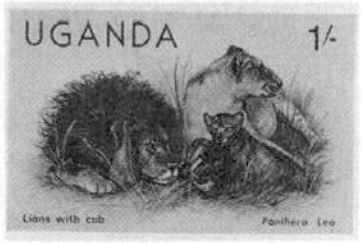

38 Lions with Cub

1979. Wildlife.
SIZES—As Type **37**: 10c. to 80c. As Type **38**: 1s. to 40s.
See also Nos. 433/9.

A. Without imprint date

303A	10c. Type **37**	10	20
304A	20c. Large-spotted genet	10	20
305A	30c. Thomson's gazelle	10	20
306A	50c. Lesser bushbaby	10	10
307A	80c. Hunting dog	10	10
308A	1s. Type **38**	10	10
309A	1s.50 Gorilla	40	10
311A	2s.70 Leopard with cub	40	20
312A	3s.50 Black rhinoceros	50	55
313A	5s. Waterbuck	25	55
314A	10s. African buffalo	30	1·00
315A	20s. Hippopotamus	65	2·00
316A	40s. African elephant	1·00	3·50

B. With imprint date

310B	2s. Common zebra	40	35

1980. "London 1980" International Stamp Exhibition. Nos. 298/301 optd **LONDON 1980**.

317	36	1s. multicoloured	15	10
318	-	1s.50 multicoloured	15	10
319	-	2s.70 multicoloured	25	25
320	-	10s. multicoloured	55	80
MS321		154×99 mm. Nos. 317/20	1·00	1·75

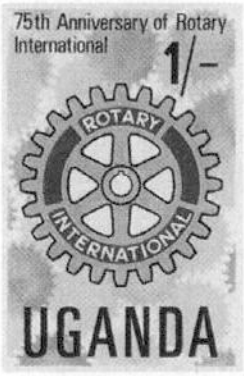

40 Rotary Emblem

1980. 75th Anniv of Rotary International. Multicoloured.

322	1s. Type **40**	10	10
323	20s. Paul P. Harris (founder) with wheel-barrow contain-ing "Rotary projects" (horiz)	1·25	2·00
MS324	100×76 mm. Nos. 322/3. Imperf	1·25	2·50

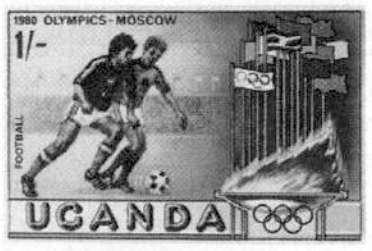

41 Football

1980. Olympic Games, Moscow. Multicoloured.

325	1s. Type **41**	10	10
326	2s. Relay	10	10
327	10s. Hurdles	35	75
328	20s. Boxing	55	2·00
MS329	118×90 mm. 2s.70, 3s., 5s., 25s. As Nos. 325/8	1·25	2·25

1981. Olympic Medal Winners. Nos. 325/8 optd.

330	41	1s. multicoloured	10	10
331	-	2s. multicoloured	20	25
332	-	10s. multicoloured	55	90
333	-	20s. multicoloured	85	2·25
MS334		118×90 mm. 2s.70, 3s. 5s., 25s. As Nos. 330/3	1·00	2·50

OVERPRINTS: 1s. **FOOTBALL GOLD MEDALISTS, C.S.S.R.**; 2s. **RELAY GOLD MEDALIST U.S.S.R.**; 10s. **HURDLES 110m. GOLD MEDALIST THOMAS MUNKELT, D.D.R.**; 20s. **BOXING WELTERWEIGHT SILVER MEDALIST JOHN MUGABI, UGANDA.**

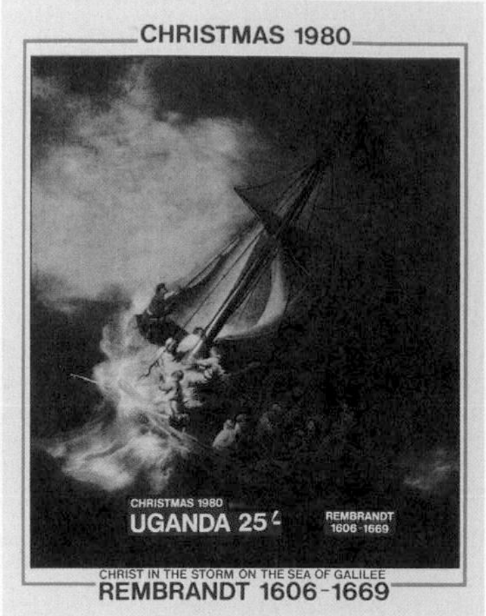

43 "Christ in the Storm on the Sea of Galilee" (painting, Rembrandt)

1980. Christmas. Sheet 79×101 mm. Imperf.

MS335	**43**	25s. multicoloured	4·25	4·75

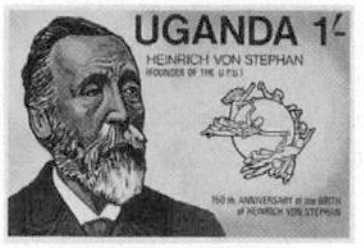

44 Heinrich von Stephan and U.P.U. Emblem

1981. 150th Birth Anniv of Heinrich von Stephan (founder of U.P.U.). Multicoloured.

336	1s. Type **44**	10	10
337	2s. U.P.U. Headquarters	15	15
338	2s.70 Air mail, 1935	40	20
339	10s. Mail transport by train, 1927	1·10	80
MS340	112×95 mm. Nos. 336/9	2·25	1·90

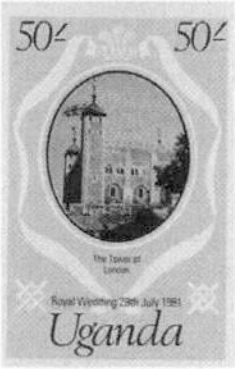

45 Tower of London

1981. Royal Wedding. Multicoloured

(a) Previously unissued stamps surch

341	10s. on 1s. on 1s. Prince Charles and Lady Diana Spencer	20	50
342	50s. on 5s. on 5s. Type **45**	30	70
343	200s. on 20s. on 20s. Prince Charles at Balmoral	60	2·00
MS344	95×80 mm. 250s. on 25s. Royal Mews	3·00	5·50

(b) Stamps reissued with new face values.

345	10s. As No. 341	10	15
346	50s. Type **45**	15	20
347	200s. As No. 343	30	40
MS348	95×80 mm. 250s. As No. **MS**344	50	65

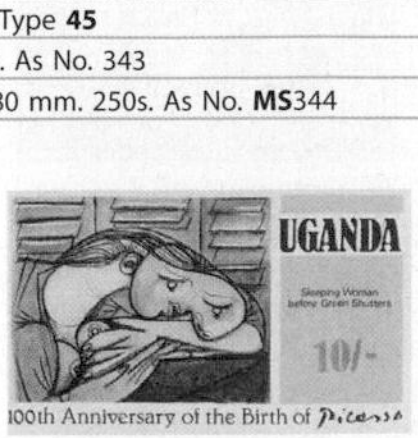

48 "Sleeping Woman before Green Shutters"

1981. Birth Centenary of Picasso. Multicoloured.

349	10s. Type **48**	10	10
350	20s. "Bullfight"	20	20
351	30s. "Detail of a Nude asleep in a Landscape"	25	30
352	200s. "Interior with a Girl Drawing"	1·10	3·25
MS353	120×146 mm. 250s. "Minotaure" (112×139 mm). Imperf	2·00	4·00

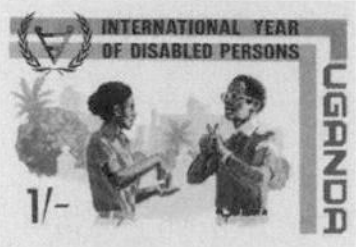

49 Deaf People using Sign Language

1981. Int Year of Disabled Persons. Multicoloured.

354	1s. Type **49**	10	10
355	10s. Disabled teacher in classroom	15	10
356	50s. Teacher and disabled children	70	50
357	200s. Blind person with guide dog	1·40	2·00
MS358	122×93 mm. Nos. 354/7	3·00	4·00

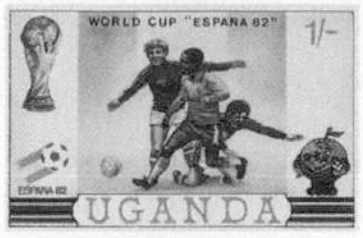

50 Footballers

1981. World Cup Football Championship, Spain (1982).

359	50	1s. multicoloured	10	10
360	-	10s. multicoloured	15	10
361	-	50s. multicoloured	55	50
362	-	200s. multicoloured	1·50	2·00
MS363		116×77 mm. 250s. multicol-oured	2·00	2·50

DESIGNS: Nos. 360/63, various football scenes.

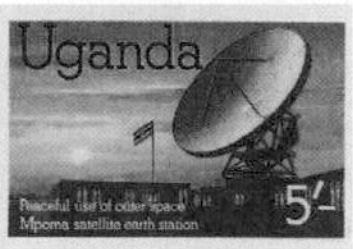

51 Mpoma Satellite Earth Station

1982. "Peaceful Use of Outer Space". Multicoloured.

364	5s. Type **51**	25	15
365	10s. "Pioneer II" (satellite)	35	35
366	50s. Space Shuttle	80	2·00
367	100s. "Voyager 2" (satellite)	1·10	4·00
MS368	118×89 mm. 150s. Space Shut-tle (different)	3·75	2·00

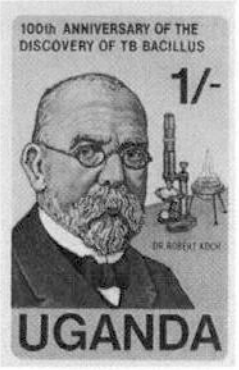

52 Dr. Robert Koch

1982. Centenary of Robert Koch's Discovery of Tubercle Bacillus. Multicoloured.

369	1s. Type **52**	25	10
370	10s. Microscope	70	40
371	50s. Ugandans receiving vac-cinations	1·75	2·50
372	100s. Tubercle virus	2·75	4·25
MS373	85×64 mm. 150s. Medical Col-lege classroom scence (horiz)	3·50	2·00

1982. 21st Birthday of Princess of Wales. Nos. 345/7 optd **21st BIRTHDAY HRH Princess of Wales JULY 1 1982.**

374	10s. Prince Charles and Lady Diana Spencer	20	10
375	50s. Type **45**	50	40
376	200s. Prince Charles at Balmoral	1·00	1·00
MS377	95×82 mm. 250s. Royal Mews	2·00	2·00

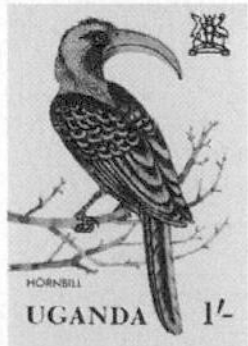

54 Yellow-billed Hornbill ("Hornbill")

1982. Birds. Multicoloured.

378	1s. Type **54**	15	10
379	20s. Superb starling	60	35
380	50s. Bateleur ("Bateleur Eagle")	1·25	1·75
381	100s. Saddle-bill stork	2·00	2·50
MS382	115×85 mm. 200s. Laughing dove	7·00	9·00

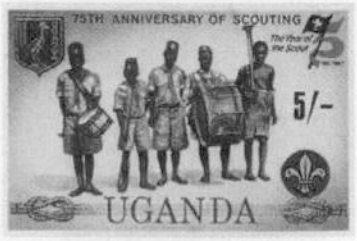

55 Scout Band

1982. 75th Anniv of Boy Scout Movement. Multicoloured.

383	5s. Type **55**	30	10
384	20s. Scout receiving Bata Shoe trophy	70	35
385	50s. Scouts with wheelchair patient	1·00	1·50
386	100s. First aid instruction	1·50	2·75
MS387	112×85 mm. 150s. Lord Baden-Powell	1·75	2·25

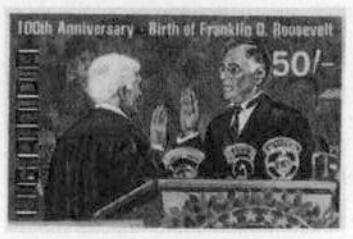

56 Swearing-in of Roosevelt

1982. 250th Birth Anniv of George Washington and Birth Centenary of Franklin D. Roosevelt. Multicoloured.

388	50s. Type **56**	30	30
389	200s. Swearing-in of Wash-ington	75	1·25
MS390	100×69 mm. 150s. Washington at Mt Vernon	1·00	1·25
MS391	100×70 mm. 150s. Roosevelt at Hyde Park Mansion	1·00	1·25

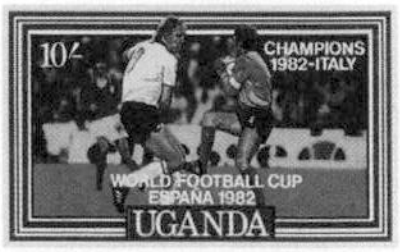

57 Italy v. West Germany

1982. World Cup Football Championship Winners. Multicoloured.

392	10s. Type **57**	25	25
393	200s. Victorious Italian team	1·00	2·75
MS394	97×117 mm. 250s. Espana '82 emblem with Spanish and Italian flags	1·00	1·50

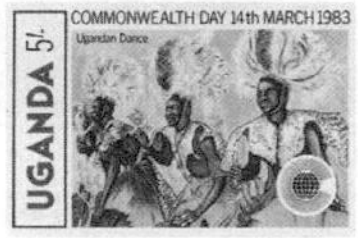

58 Dancers

1983. Commonwealth Day. Cultural Art. Multicoloured.

395	5s. Type **58**	10	10
396	20s. Traditional currency	15	20
397	50s. Homestead	35	55
398	100s. Drums	70	1·10

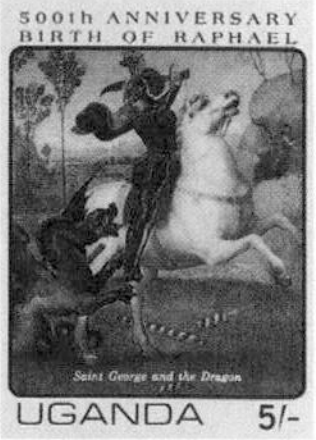

59 "St. George and the Dragon" (Raphael)

1983. 500th Birth Anniv of Raphael (painter). Multicoloured.

399	5s. Type **59**	10	10
400	20s. "St. George and the Dragon" (different)	25	20
401	50s. "Crossing the Red Sea" (detail)	50	60
402	200s. "The Expulsion of Heli-odorus" (detail)	90	3·00
MS403	126×101 mm. 250s. "The Meet-ing of Pope Leo the Great and Attila the Hun" (detail)	1·40	1·40

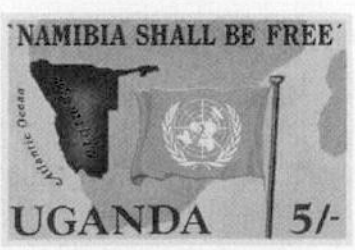

60 Map showing Namibia and U.N. Flag

1983. Commemorations. Multicoloured.

404	5s. Type **60**	10	10
405	200s. 7th Non-aligned Summit Conference logo	60	2·50

61 Elephants in Grassland

1983. Endangered Species (1st series). Multicoloured.
406	5s. Elephants in "Elephants' Graveyard"	1·50	50
407	10s. Type **61**	1·75	50
408	30s. Elephants at waterhole	3·00	2·50
409	70s. Elephants having dust bath	5·00	7·00
MS410	87×64 mm. 300s. Grevy's zebra drinking (vert)	4·75	3·25

See also No. 642 for the 10s. redrawn and Nos. 988/91 for these designs with different face values.

1983. Centenary of Boys' Brigade. Nos. 383/6 optd BOYS **BRIGADE CENTENARY 1883-1983** or surch also.
411	5s. Type **55**	10	10
412	20s. Scout receiving Bata Shoe trophy	15	15
413	50s. Scouts with wheelchair	20	30
414	400s. on 100s. First aid instruction	1·75	3·50
MS415	112×85 mm. 150s. Lord Baden-Powell	1·00	1·25

63 Mpoma Satellite Earth Station

1983. World Communications Year. Multicoloured.
416	20s. Type **63**	35	15
417	50s. Railroad computer and operator	70	85
418	70s. Cameraman filming lions	70	1·50
419	100s. Aircraft cockpit	80	2·25
MS420	128×103 mm. 300s. Communications satellite	1·00	1·75

1983. Nos. 303, 305/9 and 313 surch.
421	100s. on 10c. on 10c. Type **37**	1·25	80
422	135s. on 1s. on 1s. Type **38**	1·50	1·50
423	175s. on 30c. on 30c. Thomson's gazelle	1·75	2·00
424	200s. on 50c. on 50c. Lesser bushbaby	1·75	4·00
425	400s. on 80c. on 80c. Hunting dog	2·75	3·50
426	700s. on 5s. on 5s. Waterbuck	3·75	8·00
427	1000s. on 1s.50 on 1s.50 Gorilla	7·00	13·00

65 The Nativity

1983. Christmas. Multicoloured.
428	10s. Type **65**	10	10
429	50s. Shepherds and Angels	20	30
430	175s. Flight into Egypt	60	1·25
431	400s. Angels blowing trumpets	1·00	2·75
MS432	85×57 mm. 300s. The Three Kings	1·40	1·75

1983. As Nos. 308/12 and 315/16, but with face values in revalued currency.
433	100s. Type **38**	90	35
434	135s. Gorilla	1·25	50
435	175s. Common zebra	1·40	80
436	200s. Leopard with cub	1·75	1·50
437	400s. Black rhinoceros	3·00	3·75
438	700s. African elephant	5·00	8·50
439	1000s. Hippopotamus	9·00	12·00

66 Ploughing with Oxen

1984. World Food Day. Multicoloured.
| 440 | 10s. Type **66** | 15 | 10 |
| 441 | 300s. Harvesting bananas | 1·75 | 5·50 |

67 Ruth Kyalisiima, Sportsman of the Year 1983

1984. Olympic Games, Los Angeles. Multicoloured.
442	5s. Type **67**	10	10
443	115s. Javelin-throwing	55	1·00
444	155s. Wrestling	60	1·40
445	175s. Rowing	60	1·60
MS446	108×79 mm. 500s. Fund-raising walk (vert)	1·00	1·25

68 Entebbe Airport

1984. 40th Anniv of I.C.A.O. Multicoloured.
447	5s. Type **68**	15	10
448	115s. Loading cargo plane	1·50	1·75
449	155s. Uganda police helicopter	2·50	2·75
450	175s. East African Civil Flying School, Soroti	2·75	3·25
MS451	100×70 mm. 250s. Balloon race	2·00	1·75

69 "Charaxes druceanus"

1984. Butterflies. Multicoloured.
452	5s. Type **69**	30	10
453	115s. "Papilio lormieri"	1·75	2·00
454	155s. "Druryia antimachus"	2·10	2·50
455	175s. "Salamis temora"	2·50	3·25
MS456	127×90 mm. 250s. "Colotis protomedia"	4·50	2·50

70 Blue-finned notho

1985. Lake Fish. Multicoloured.
457	5s. Type **70**	30	40
458	10s. Semutundu	40	40
459	50s. Grey bichir	75	30
460	100s. Walking catfish	85	30
461	135s. Elephant-snout fish	1·25	1·00
462	175s. Blue-finned notho	1·00	1·00
463	205s. Brown's haplochromis	1·25	2·00
464	400s. Nile perch	1·25	2·25
465	700s. African lungfish	1·25	3·00
466	1000s. Radcliffe's barb	1·25	3·50
467	2500s. Electric catfish	1·50	4·50

71 The Last Supper

1985. Easter. Multicoloured.
468	5s. Type **71**	10	10
469	115s. Christ showing the nail marks to Thomas	1·40	1·40
470	155s. The raising of the Cross	1·60	2·25
471	175s. Pentecost	1·90	2·75
MS472	99×70 mm. 250s. The last prayer in the Garden	80	1·25

72 Breast Feeding

1985. UNICEF Child Survival Campaign. Multicoloured.
473	5s. Type **72**	10	10
474	115s. Growth monitoring	1·75	1·75
475	155s. Immunization	2·25	2·50
476	175s. Oral re-hydration therapy	2·50	3·00
MS477	77×55 mm. 500s. Pregnant woman preparing nourishing food	4·25	5·00

73 Queen Elizabeth the Queen Mother

1985. Life and Times of Queen Elizabeth the Queen Mother and Decade for Women. Multicoloured.
| 478 | **73** | 1000s. Type **73** | 1·40 | 2·10 |
| MS479 | | 57×81 mm. 1500s. The Queen Mother inspecting Kings African Rifles, Kampala | 2·25 | 3·50 |

74 Sedge Warbler

1985. Birth Bicentenary of John J. Audubon (ornithologist) (1st issue). Multicoloured.
480	115s. Type **74**	1·75	1·50
481	155s. Cattle egret	2·00	1·75
482	175s. Crested lark	2·00	2·25
483	500s. Tufted duck	2·25	4·50
MS484	99×69 mm. 1000s. Twany owl	11·00	10·00

See also Nos. 494/8.

1985. Olympic Gold Medal Winners, Los Angeles. Nos. 442/5 optd or surch also.
485	5s. Type **67** (optd GOLD MEDALIST BENITA BROWN-FITZGERALD USA)	10	10
486	115s. Javelin-throwing (optd GOLD MEDALIST ARTO HAERKOENEN FINLAND)	70	30
487	155s. Wrestling (optd GOLD MEDALIST ATSUJI MIYA-HARA JAPAN)	80	40
488	1000s. on 175s. on 175s. Rowing (surch GOLD MEDALIST WEST GERMANY)	3·00	2·00
MS489	108×79 mm. 250s. on 500s. Fund rasing walk (surch MEN'S HURDLES EDWIN MOSES USA)	2·25	2·50

On No. MS489 only the new value appears on the stamp the remainder of the surcharge is on the sheet margin.

76 Women carrying National Women's Day Banner

1985. Decade for Women. Multicoloured.
490	5s. Type **76**	10	10
491	115s. Girl Guides (horiz)	1·75	2·00
492	155s. Mother Teresa (Nobel Peace Prize winner, 1979)	3·00	3·25
MS493	85×59 mm. 1500s. As 115s.	4·00	4·00

No. 491 and MS493 also commemorates the 75th anniversary of Girl Guide movement.

76a Rock Ptarmigan

1985. Birth Bicentenary of John J. Audubon (ornithologist) (2nd issue). Multicoloured.
494	5s. Type **76a**	55	10
495	155s. Sage grouse	1·50	1·75
496	175s. Lesser yellowlegs	1·50	2·50
497	500s. Brown-headed cowbird	2·75	4·75
MS498	72×102 mm. 1000s. Whooping crane	7·50	9·50

77 Man beneath Tree laden with Produce (F.A.O.)

1986. 40th Anniv of U.N.O.
499	**77**	10s. multicoloured	10	10
500	-	180s. multicoloured	40	30
501	-	200s. blue, brown and green	40	35
502	-	250s. blue, black and red	40	40
503	-	2000s. multicoloured	1·25	5·00
MS504	69×69 mm. 2500s. multicoloured	1·75	2·75

DESIGNS—HORIZ: 180s. Soldier of U.N. Peace-keeping Force; 250s. Hands releasing peace dove. VERT: 200s. U.N. emblem; 2000s. Flags of U.N. and Uganda; 2500s. U.N. Building, New York, and Flags of member nations.

78 Goalkeeper catching Ball

1986. World Cup Football Championship, Mexico. Multicoloured.
505	10s. Type **78**	10	10
506	180s. Player with ball	60	55
507	250s. Two players competing for ball	70	65
508	2500s. Player running with ball	4·00	6·00
MS509	87×66 mm. 3000s. Player kicking ball (vert)	4·75	3·50

1986. Liberation by National Resistance Army. Nos. 462, 464/7 and MS493 optd NRA LIBERATION 1986.
510	175s. Lake Victoria squeaker	1·00	70
511	400s. Nile perch	1·75	1·25
512	700s. African lungfish	2·50	3·00
513	1000s. Radcliffe's barb	3·50	4·50
514	2500s. Electric catfish	4·50	7·50
MS514a	85×59 mm. 1500s. Girl Guides	6·50	3·50

1986. Appearance of Halley's Comet (1st issue). As T **191b** of Sierre Leone. Multicoloured.
515	50s. Tycho Brahe and Arecibo Radio Telescope, Puerto Rico	20	10
516	100s. Recovery of astronaut John Glenn from sea, 1962	35	15
517	140s. "The Star in the East" (painting by Giotto)	50	30
518	2500s. Death of Davy Crockett at the Alamo, 1835	3·75	6·00
MS519	102×70 mm. 3000s. Halley's Comet over Uganda	7·00	6·00

See also Nos. 544/8.

80 Niagara Falls

1986. "Ameripex '86" International Stamp Exhibition, Chicago. Multicoloured.
520	50s. Type **80**	15	10
521	100s. Jefferson Memorial, Washington D.C.	25	15
522	250s. Liberty Bell, Philadelphia	50	35
523	1000s. The Alamo, San Antonio, Texas	1·25	2·50
524	2500s. George Washington Bridge, New York–New Jersey	1·75	5·50
MS525	87×64 mm. 3000s. Grand Canyon	2·00	3·25

1986. 60th Birthday of Queen Elizabeth II. As T **191c** of Sierre Leone.
526	100s. black and yellow	85	30
527	140s. multicoloured	85	30
528	2500s. multicoloured	3·25	4·50
MS529	120×85 mm. 3000s. black and brown	4·00	4·00

DESIGNS: 100s. Princess Elizabeth at London Zoo; 140s. Queen Elizabeth at race meeting, 1970; 2500s. With Prince Philip at Sandringham, 1982; 3000s. Engagement photograph, 1947.

81 "Gloria" (Colombia)

1986. Centenary of Statue of Liberty. Cadet Sailing Ships. Multicoloured.
530	50s. Type **81**	70	20
531	100s. "Mircea" (Rumania)	1·10	30
532	140s. "Sagres II" (Portugal) (horiz)	1·75	1·00
533	2500s. "Gazela Primiero" (U.S.A.) (horiz)	7·00	12·00
MS534	113×82 mm. 3000s. Statue of Liberty	3·50	3·50

No. 533 is inscribed "Primero" in error.

1986. Royal Wedding. As T **192c** of Sierre Leone. Multicoloured.
| 535 | 50s. Prince Andrew and Miss Sarah Ferguson (horiz) | 10 | 10 |
| 536 | 140s. Prince Andrew with Princess Anne at shooting match (horiz) | 20 | 20 |

537	2500s. Prince Andrew and Miss Sarah Ferguson at Ascot (horiz)	2·75	4·00
MS538	88×88 mm. 3000s. Prince Andrew and Miss Sarah Ferguson (different)	3·00	3·25

1986. World Cup Football Championship Winners, Mexico. Nos. 505/8 optd **WINNERS Argentina 3 W.Germany 2** or surch also.

539	50s. on 10s. on 10s. Type **78**	10	10
540	180s. Player with ball	25	25
541	250s. Two players competing for ball	35	35
542	2500s. Player running with ball	2·75	4·50
MS543	87×66 mm. 3000s. Player kicking ball (vert)	4·75	3·25

1986. Appearance of Halley's Comet (2nd issue). Nos. 515/18 optd as T **198a** of Sierre Leone.

544	50s. Tycho Brahe and Arecibo Radio Telescope, Puerto Rico	20	15
545	100s. Recovery of astronaut John Glenn from sea, 1962	35	20
546	140s. "The Star in the East" (painting by Giotto)	55	40
547	2500s. Death of Davy Crockett at the Alamo, 1835	5·50	7·50
MS548	102×70 mm. 3000s. Halley's Comet over Uganda	6·00	5·00

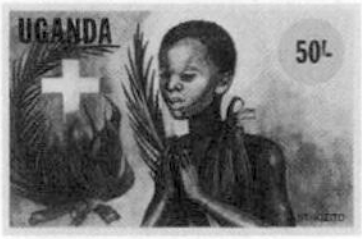

83 St. Kizito

1986. Christian Martyrs of Uganda. Multicoloured.

549	50s. Type **83**	20	10
550	150s. St. Kizito instructing converts	40	35
551	200s. Martyrdom of Bishop James Hannington, 1885	55	45
552	1000s. Burning of Bugandan Christians, 1886	2·25	4·00
MS553	89×59 mm. 1500s. King Mwanga of Buganda passing sentence on Christians	1·50	2·25

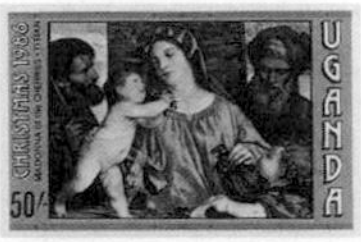

84 "Madonna of the Cherries" (Titian)

1986. Christmas. Religious Paintings. Multicoloured.

554	50s. Type **84**	25	15
555	150s. "Madonna and Child" (Durer) (vert)	60	30
556	200s. "Assumption of the Virgin" (Titian) (vert)	70	40
557	2500s. "Praying Hands" (Durer) (vert)	5·50	8·50
MS558	Two sheets, each 102×76 mm. (a) 3000s. "Presentation of the Virgin in the Temple" (Titian). (b) 3000s. "Adoration of the Magi" (Durer) Set of 2 sheets	8·50	10·00

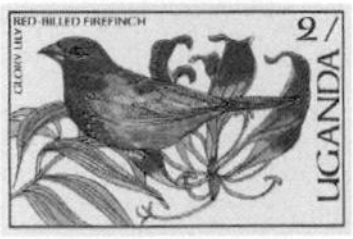

85 Red-billed Fire Finch and Glory Lily

1987. Flora and Fauna. Multicoloured.

559	2s. Type **85**	65	75
560	5s. African pygmy kingfisher and nandi flame	85	1·00
561	10s. Scarlet-chested sunbird and crown of thorns	95	1·00
562	25s. White rhinoceros and yellow-billed oxpecker	2·25	1·25
563	35s. Lion and elephant grass	1·25	1·25
564	45s. Cheetahs and doum palm	1·50	1·50
565	50s. Red-cheeked cordon-bleu and desert rose	2·25	2·25
566	100s. Giant eland and acacia	2·50	4·00
MS567	Two sheets, each 98×67 mm. (a) 150s. Carmine bee eaters and sausage tree. (b) 150s. Cattle egret and zebras Set of 2 sheets	11·00	9·50

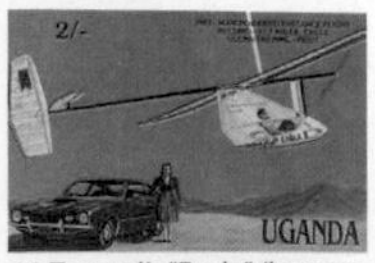

86 Tremml's "Eagle" (longest man-powered flight), 1987

1987. Milestones of Transportation. Multicoloured.

568	2s. Type **86**	40	70
569	3s. Junkers W.33 "Bremen" (first east-west transatlantic flight), 1928	40	70
570	5s. Lockheed Vega 5 "Winnie Mae" (Post's first solo round-the-world flight), 1933	50	70
571	10s. "Voyager" (first non-stop round-the-world flight), 1986	60	70
572	15s. Chanute biplane glider, 1896	75	85
573	25s. Airship N.1 "Norge" and polar bear (first transpolar flight), 1926	1·50	1·00
574	35s. Curtiss Golden Flyer biplane and U.S.S. "Pennsylvania" (battleship) (first take-off and landing from ship), 1911	1·75	1·25
575	45s. Shepard and "Freedom 7" spacecraft (first American in space), 1961	1·75	1·50
576	100s. Concorde (first supersonic passenger flight), 1976	7·50	7·50

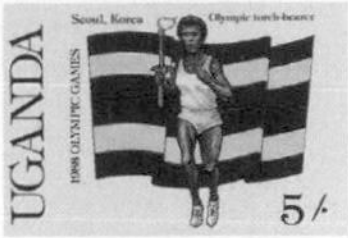

87 Olympic Torch-bearer

1987. Olympic Games, Seoul (1988) (1st issue). Multicoloured.

577	5s. Type **87**	10	10
578	10s. Swimming	20	25
579	50s. Cycling	1·00	1·25
580	100s. Gymnastics	2·00	2·50
MS581	100×775 mm. 150s. Boxing	2·00	3·50

See also Nos. 628/32.

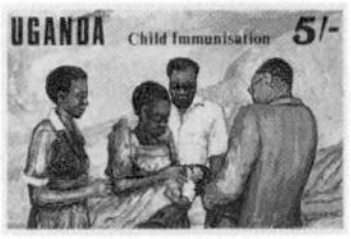

88 Child Immunization

1987. 25th Anniv of Independence.

582	88	5s. multicoloured	20	10
583	-	10s. multicoloured	35	25
584	-	25s. multicoloured	80	70
585	-	50s. multicoloured	1·50	1·50
MS586		90×70 mm. 100s. black, red and yellow	1·75	2·25

DESIGNS: 10s. Mulago Hospital, Kampala; 25s. Independence Mounument, Kampala City Park; 50s. High Court, Kampala; 100s. Stylized head of crested crane, "25" and Ugandan flag.

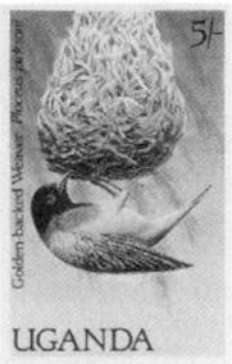

89 Eastern Golden-backed Weaver ("Golden-backed Weaver")

1987. Birds of Uganda. Multicoloured.

587	5s. Type **89**	1·25	80
588	10s. Hoopoe	2·25	1·25
589	15s. Red-throated bee eater	2·50	1·25
590	25s. Lilac-breasted roller	3·00	1·60
591	35s. African pygmy goose ("Pygmy Goose")	3·00	1·75
592	45s. Scarlet-chested sunbird	3·25	2·75
593	50s. South African crowned crane ("Crowned Crane")	3·25	2·75
594	100s. Long-tailed fiscal ("Long-tailed Fiscal Shrike")	5·00	5·50
MS595	Two sheets, each 80×60 mm. (a) 150s. African fish eagle. (B) 150s. Barn owl Set of 2 sheets	8·00	10·00

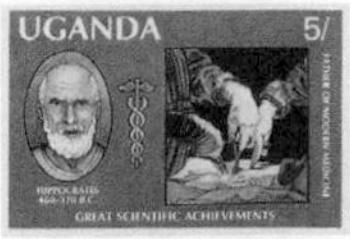

90 Hippocrates (physician) and Surgeons performing Operation

1987. Great Scientific Discoveries. Multicoloured.

596	5s. Type **90**	75	30
597	25s. Einstein and deep space (Theory of Relativity)	3·25	1·75
598	35s. Isaac Newton and diagram from "Opticks" (Theory of Colour and Light)	2·75	2·50
599	45s. Karl Benz and early Benz and modern Mercedes car	3·25	3·00
MS600	97×70 mm. 150s. "Challenger" (space shuttle) (vert)	4·25	4·00

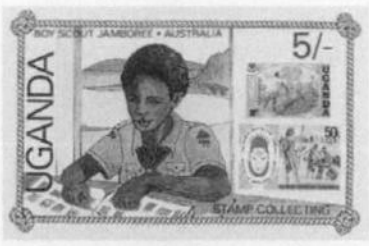

91 Scout with Stamp Album and Uganda Stamps

1987. World Scout Jamboree, Australia. Multicoloured.

601	5s. Type **91**	20	10
602	25s. Scouts planting tree	70	70
603	35s. Canoeing, Lake Victoria	1·00	85
604	45s. Hiking	1·50	1·10
MS605	95×65 mm. 150s. Jamboree and Uganda scout emblems	2·50	3·25

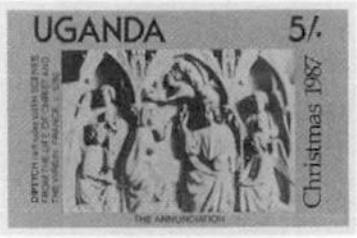

92 "The Annunciation"

1987. Christmas. Scenes from French diptych, c. 1250. Multicoloured.

606	5s. Type **92**	10	10
607	10s. "The Nativity"	20	25
608	50s. "Flight into Egypt"	1·00	1·25
609	100s. "The Adoration of the Magi"	2·00	2·50
MS610	76×105 mm. 150s. "Mystic Wine" (tapestry detail) (vert)	3·00	4·00

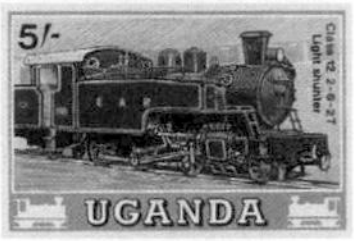

93 Class 12 Light Shunter Locomotive

1988. Locomotives of East Africa Railways. Multicoloured.

611	5s. Type **93**	60	35
612	10s. Class 92 diesel-electric	70	45
613	15s. Steam locomotive No. 2506	90	60
614	25s. Class 11 tank locomotive	1·25	85
615	35s. Class 24 steam locomotive	1·50	1·10
616	45s. Class 21 steam locomotive	1·75	1·40
617	50s. Class 59 Garratt steam locomotive, 1955	2·00	1·60
618	100s. Class 87 diesel-electric locomotive	3·00	2·40
MS619	Two sheets, each 100×74 mm. (a) 150s. Class 31 steam locomotive. (b) 150s. Class 59 Garratt steam locomotive Set of 2 sheets	9·50	7·50

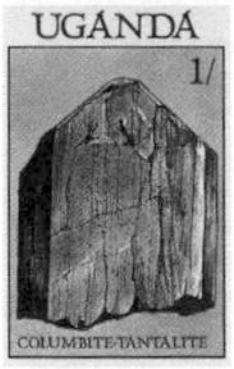

94 Columbite-Tantalite

1988. Minerals. Multicoloured.

620	1s. Type **94**	25	15
621	2s. Galena	30	20
622	5s. Malachite	50	35
623	10s. Cassiterite	70	55
624	35s. Ferberite	2·00	1·50
625	50s. Emerald	2·50	2·00
626	100s. Monazite	3·75	3·00
627	150s. Microcline	4·50	4·00

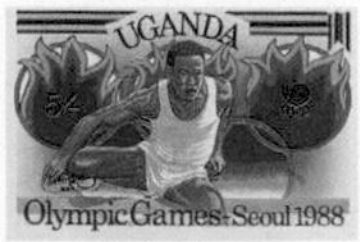

95 Hurdling

1988. Olympic Games, Seoul (2nd issue). Multicoloured.

628	5s. Type **95**	10	10
629	25s. High jumping	40	50
630	35s. Javelin throwing	45	55
631	45s. Long jumping	55	70
MS632	85×114 mm. 150s. Olympic medals	1·00	1·50

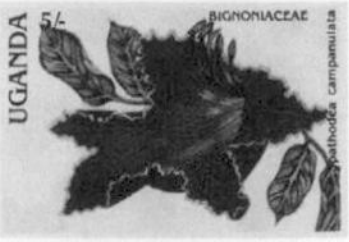

96 "Spathodea campanulata"

1988. Flowers. Multicoloured.

633	5s. Type **96**	15	15
634	10s. "Gloriosa simplex"	15	15
635	20s. "Thevetica peruviana" (vert)	20	20
636	25s. "Hibiscus schizopetalus"	20	25
637	35s. "Aframomum sceptrum"	20	30
638	45s. "Adenium obesum"	20	35
639	50s. "Kigelia africana" (vert)	25	40
640	100s. "Clappertonia ficifolia"	35	75
MS641	Two sheets, each 109×79 mm. (a) 150s. "Costus spectabilis". (b) 150s. "Canarina abyssinica" (vert) Set of 2 sheets	2·00	2·75

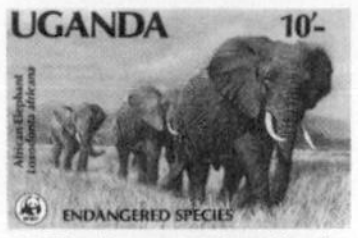

97 Elephants in Grassland (Type **61** redrawn)

1988. Endangered Species (2nd series).

642	**97**	10s. multicoloured	70·00	4·00

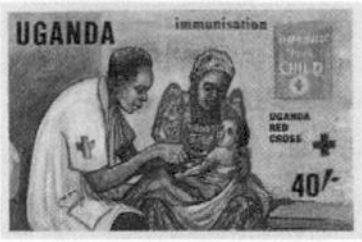

98 Red Cross Worker vaccinating Baby

1988. 125th Anniv of International Red Cross.

643	**98**	10s. red, yellow and black	25	15
644	-	40s. multicoloured	70	70
645	-	70s. multicoloured	1·50	2·00
646	-	90s. multicoloured	2·00	2·25
MS647		110×78 mm. 150s. multicoloured	1·00	1·60

DESIGNS—HORIZ: 10s. "AIDS" with test tube as "I"; 70s. Distributing food to refugees; 90s. Red Cross volunteers with accident victim. VERT: Henri Dunant (founder).

1988. 500th Birth Anniv of Titian (artist). As T **183a** of St. Vincent. Multicoloured.

648	10s. "Portrait of a Lady"	15	15
649	20s. "Portrait of a Man"	20	20
650	40s. "Isabella d'Este"	35	35
651	50s. "Vincenzo Mosti"	45	45
652	70s. "Pope Paul III Farnese"	50	60
653	90s. "Violante"	60	75
654	100s. "Titian's Daughter Lavinia"	70	85
655	250s. "Dr. Parma"	1·40	1·90
MS656	Two sheets, each 110×95 mm. (a) 350s. "The Speech of Alfonso D'Avalos" (detail). (b) 350s. "Cain and Abel" (detail) Set of 2 sheets	5·50	7·00

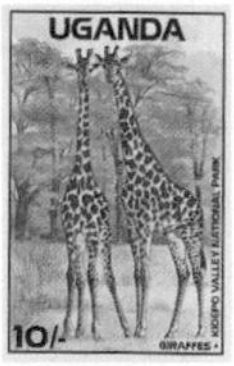

99 Giraffes, Kidepo Valley National Park

1988. National Parks of Uganda. Multicoloured.

657	10s. Type **99**	1·75	30
658	25s. Zebras, Lake Mburo National Park	2·00	30
659	100s. African buffalo, Murchison Falls National Park	2·50	2·50
660	250s. Eastern white pelicans, Queen Elizabeth National Park	8·00	7·00
MS661	97×68 mm. 350s. Roan antelopes, Lake Mburo National Park	2·50	2·75

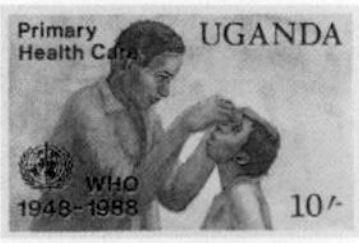

100 Doctor examining Child's Eyes

1988. 40th Anniv of W.H.O. Multicoloured.

662	10s. Type **100**	25	15
663	25s. Mental health therapist with patient	50	30

664	45s. Surgeon performing operation	70	60
665	100s. Dentist treating girl	1·40	1·50
666	200s. Doctor examining child	2·00	2·50
MS667	107×88 mm. 350s. Delegates approving Declaration of Alma-Ata, 1978	2·50	3·50

1988. Christmas. "Santa's Helpers". As T **219a** of Sierre Leone showing Walt Disney cartoon characters. Multicoloured.

668	50s. Father Christmas with list	1·25	1·00
669	50s. Goofy carrying presents	1·25	1·00
670	50s. Mickey Mouse on toy train	1·25	1·00
671	50s. Reindeer at window	1·25	1·00
672	50s. Donald Duck's nephew with building blocks	1·25	1·00
673	50s. Donald Duck holding sack	1·25	1·00
674	50s. Chip n' Dale on conveyor belt	1·25	1·00
675	50s. Donald Duck's nephew operating conveyor belt	1·25	1·00
MS676	Two sheets, each 127×102 mm. (a) 350s. Mickey Mouse loading sack of toys on sleigh (horiz). (b) 350s. Mickey Mouse and Chip n'Dale grooming reindeer. Set of 2 sheets	7·50	8·50

Nos. 668/75 were printed together, se-tenant, as a composite design.

1989. Olympic Gold Medal Winners, Seoul. Nos. 628/31 optd or surch.

677	5s. Type **95** (optd **110 M HURDLES R. KINGDOM USA**)	10	10
678	25s. High jumping (optd **HIGH JUMP G. AVDEENKO USSR**)	20	25
679	35s. Javelin throwing (optd **JAVELIN T. KORJUS FINLAND**)	25	30
680	300s. on 45s. Long jumping (optd **LONG JUMP C. LEWIS USA**)	2·50	3·00
MS681	85×114 mm. 350s. on 150s. Olympic medals with medal table optd on sheet margin	3·00	4·00

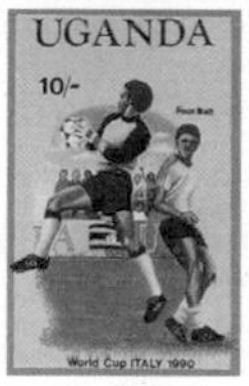

102 Goalkeeper

1989. World Cup Football Championship, Italy (1990) (1st issue). Multicoloured.

682	10s. Type **102**	25	15
683	25s. Player kicking ball (horiz)	55	40
684	75s. Heading ball towards net (horiz)	1·25	1·10
685	200s. Tackling	2·25	2·75
MS686	118×87 mm. 300s. Football and World Cup trophy (horiz)	2·50	3·25

See also Nos. 849/53.

1989. Japanese Art. Paintings by Hokusai. As T **188a** of St. Vincent. Multicoloured.

687	10s. "Fuji and the Great Wave off Kanagawa"	35	30
688	15s. "Fuji from Lake Suwa"	45	35
689	20s. "Fuji from Kajikazawa"	50	35
690	60s. "Fuji from Shichirigahama"	1·50	85
691	90s. "Fuji from Ejiri in Sunshu"	1·75	1·10
692	120s. "Fuji above Lightning"	2·00	1·25
693	200s. "Fuji from Lower Meguro in Edo"	2·75	2·00
694	250s. "Fuji from Edo"	3·00	2·25
MS695	Two sheets, each 102×76 mm. (a) 500s. "The Red Fuji from the Foot". (b) 500s. "Fuji from Umezawa" Set of 2 sheets	9·00	9·00

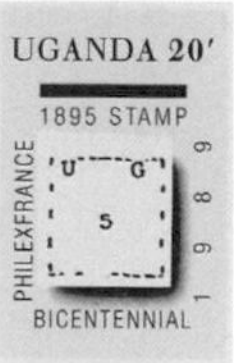

103 1895 5 Cowries Stamp

1989. "Philexfrance 89" International Stamp Exhibition, Paris.

696	**103**	20s. black, red and brown	60	35
697	-	70s. black, green and blue	1·75	1·00
698	-	100s. black, violet & pink	2·00	1·75
699	-	250s. black, yell & lt yell	3·00	4·25
MS700		176×131 mm. Nos. 696/9 (sold at 500s.)	6·50	8·00

DESIGNS: 70s. 1895 10 on 50 cowries stamp; 100s. 1896 25 cowries stamp; 250s. 1896 1 rupee stamp.

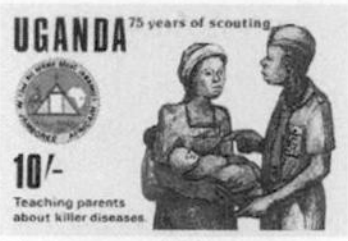

104 Scout advising on Immunization

1989. Second All African Scout Jamboree, Uganda, and 75th Anniv of Uganda Scout Movement. Multicoloured.

701	10s. Type **104**	40	15
702	70s. Poultry keeping	1·25	1·10
703	90s. Scout on crutches leading family to immunization centre	1·50	2·25
704	100s. Scouts making bricks	1·50	2·25
MS705	99×67 mm. 500s. Ugandan Scout logo (vert)	3·25	4·50

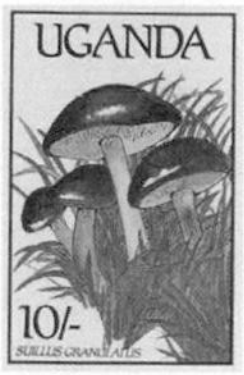

105 "Suillus granulatus"

1989. Fungi. Multicoloured.

706	10s. Type **105**	40	30
707	15s. "Omphalotus olearius"	55	40
708	45s. "Oudemansiella radicata"	1·25	1·00
709	50s. "Clitocybe nebularis"	1·25	1·10
710	60s. "Macrolepiota rhacodes"	1·40	1·25
711	75s. "Lepista nuda"	1·60	1·40
712	150s. "Suillus luteus"	2·75	3·00
713	200s. "Agaricus campestris"	3·00	3·25
MS714	Two sheets, each 100×68 mm. (a) 350s. "Bolbitius vitellinus" (b) 350s. "Schizophyllum commune" Set of 2 sheets	12·00	11·00

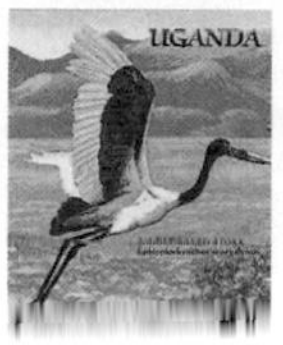

106 Saddle-bill Stork

1989. Wildlife at Waterhole. Multicoloured.

715	30s. Type **106**	90	75
716	30s. Eastern white pelican	90	75
717	30s. Marabou stork	90	75
718	30s. Egyptian vulture	90	75
719	30s. Bateleur	90	75
720	30s. African elephant	90	75
721	30s. Giraffe	90	75
722	30s. Goliath heron	90	75
723	30s. Black rhinoceros	90	75
724	30s. Common zebra and oribi	90	75
725	30s. African fish eagle	90	75
726	30s. Hippopotamus	90	75
727	30s. Black-backed jackal and eastern white pelican	90	75
728	30s. African buffalo	90	75
729	30s. Olive baboon	90	75
730	30s. Bohar reedbuck	90	75
731	30s. Lesser flamingo and serval	90	75
732	30s. Whale-headed stork ("Shoebill Stork")	90	75
733	30s. South African crowned crane	90	75
734	30s. Impala	90	75
MS735	Two sheets, each 99×68 mm. (a) 500s. Lion. (b) 500s. Long-crested eagle Set of 2 sheets	8·00	9·50

Nos. 715/34 were printed together, se-tenant, forming a composite design showing wildlife at a waterhole.

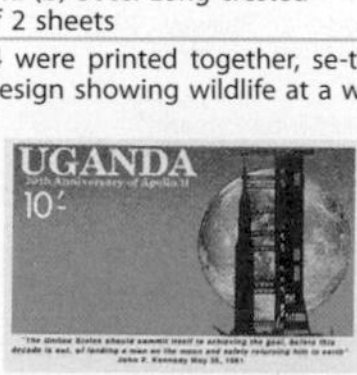

107 Rocket on Launch Pad

1989. 20th Anniv of First Manned Landing on Moon. Multicoloured.

736	10s. Type **107**	40	20
737	20s. Lunar module "Eagle" on Moon	55	30
738	30s. "Apollo 11" command module	65	40
739	50s. "Eagle" landing on Moon	1·00	60
740	70s. Astronaut Aldrin on Moon	1·25	85
741	250s. Neil Armstrong alighting from "Eagle" (vert)	4·25	2·75
742	300s. "Eagle" over Moon	4·25	3·00
743	350s. Astronaut Aldrin on Moon (vert)	4·25	3·25
MS744	Two sheets, each 77×104 mm. (a) 500s. "Saturn" rocket (vert). (b) 500s. "Apollo 11" capsule on parachutes (vert) Set of 2 sheets	7·50	8·50

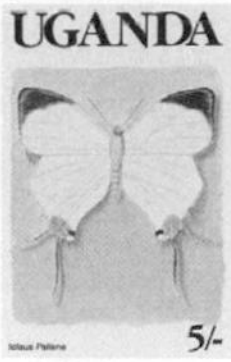

108 "Aphniolaus pallene"

1989. Butterflies. T **108** and similar vert designs showing "UGANDA" in black. Multicoloured.

745	5s. Type **108**	45	40
746	10s. "Hewitsonia boisduvali"	60	25
747	20s. "Euxanthe wakefieldi"	80	30
748	30s. "Papilio echerioides"	95	30
749	40s. "Acraea semivitrea"	1·00	40
750	50s. "Colotis antevippe"	1·00	40
751	70s. "Acraea perenna"	1·25	70
752	90s. "Charaxes cynthia"	1·25	70
753	100s. "Euphaedra neophron"	1·25	70
754	150s. "Cymothoe beckeri"	1·50	1·25
755	200s. "Vanessula milca"	1·50	1·25
756	400s. "Mimacraea marshalli"	1·75	3·25
757	500s. "Axiocerses amanga"	1·75	3·50
758	1000s. "Precis hierta"	2·75	6·50

For these, and similar designs showing "UGANDA" in blue, see Nos. 864/80.

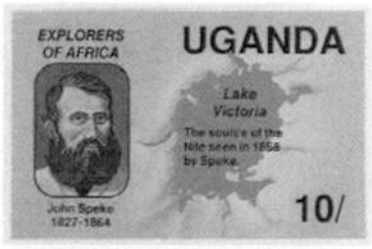

109 John Hanning Speke and Map of Lake Victoria

1989. Exploration of Africa. Multicoloured.

760	10s. Type **109**	1·00	35
761	25s. Sir Richard Burton and map of Lake Tanganyika	1·25	50
762	40s. Richard Lander and Bakota bronze	1·00	65
763	[illegible] Timbuktu	1·75	1·00
764	125s. Sir Samuel Baker and dorcas gazelle	1·75	1·75
765	150s. Pharaoh Necho and ancient Phoenician merchant ship	2·00	2·25
766	250s. Vasco da Gama and 15th-century caravel	4·00	3·75
767	300s. Sir Henry Morton Stanley and "Lady Alice" (sectional boat)	4·00	4·25
MS768	Two sheets, each 73×103 mm. (a) 500s. Dr. David Livingstone and steam launch "Ma Robert" (b) 500s. Mary Kingsley and map of Ogooue River Set of 2 sheets	8·50	9·50

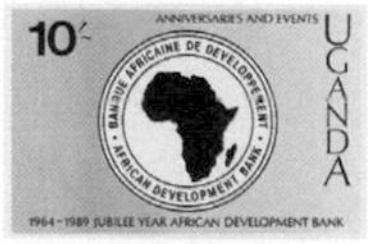

110 Logo (25th anniv of African Development Bank)

1989. Anniversaries. Multicoloured.

769	10s. Type **110**	25	15
770	20s. Arrows and dish aerials (World Telecommunication Day)	25	20
771	75s. Two portraits of Nehru (birth centenary)	4·00	1·75
772	90s. Pan Am Boeing 314A flying boat "Dixie Clipper" (50th anniv of first scheduled trans-Atlantic airmail flight)	2·50	1·75
773	100s. George Stephenson and "Locomotion", 1825 (175th anniv of first practical steam locomotive)	3·50	1·75
774	150s. Concorde cockpit (20th anniv of first test flight)	4·25	3·25
775	250s. "Wapen von Hamburg" and "Leopoldus Primus" (galleons) (800th anniv of Port of Hamburg)	3·50	4·25
776	300s. Concorde and cockpit interior (20th anniv of first test flight)	5·00	4·50
MS777	Two sheets (a) 91×87 mm. 500s. Revolutionary with musket and Bastille, Paris (bicentenary of French Revolution). (b) 110×82 mm. 500s. Emperor Frederick I Barbarossa and Hamburg charter (800th anniv of Port of Hamburg) Set of 2 sheets	10·00	11·00

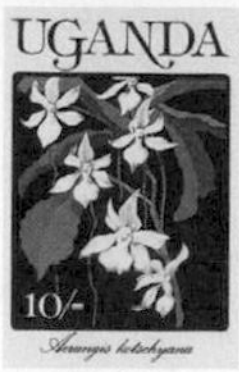

111 "Aerangis kotschyana"

1989. Orchids. Multicoloured.

778	10s. Type **111**	30	25
779	15s. "Angraecum infundibulare"	35	30
780	45s. "Cyrtorchis chailluana"	80	70
781	50s. "Aerangis rhodosticta"	85	75
782	100s. "Eulophia speciosa"	1·75	1·50
783	200s. "Calanthe sylvatica"	2·50	2·25
784	250s. "Vanilla imperialis"	2·75	2·40
785	350s. "Polystachya vulcanica"	3·25	2·75
MS786	Two sheets each 110×82 mm. (a) 500s. "Ansellia africana". (b) 500s. "Ancistrochilus rothschildianus" Set of 2 sheets	13·00	11·00

1989. Christmas. Paintings by Fra Angelico. As T **204a** of St. Vincent. Multicoloured.

787	10s. "Madonna and Child"	15	10
788	20s. "Adoration of the Magi"	20	15
789	40s. "Virgin and Child enthroned with Saints"	40	30
790	75s. "The Annunciation"	70	60
791	100s. "Virgin and Child" (detail, "St. Peter Martyr" triptych)	85	75
792	150s. "Virgin and Child enthroned with Saints" (different)	1·25	1·50
793	250s. "Virgin and Child enthroned"	1·75	2·25
794	350s. "Virgin and Child" (from Annalena altarpiece)	2·00	3·25
MS795	Two sheets, each 72×96 mm. (a) 500s. "Virgin and Child" (from Bosco ai Frati altarpiece). (b) 500s. "Madonna and Child with Twelve Angels" Set of 2 sheets	5·00	6·00

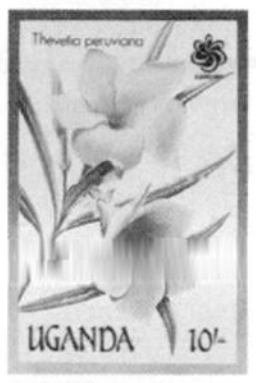

112 "Thevetia peruviana"

1990. "Expo '90" International Garden and Greenery Exhibition, Osaka (1st issue). Flowering Trees. Multicoloured.

796	10s. Type **112**	15	15
797	20s. "Acanthus eminens"	20	20
798	90s. "Gnidia glauca"	50	50
799	150s. "Oncoba spinosa"	70	70
800	175s. "Hibiscus rosa-sinensis"	75	75
801	400s. "Jacaranda mimosifolia"	1·25	1·75
802	500s. "Erythrina abyssinica"	1·40	1·90
803	700s. "Bauhinia purpurea"	1·60	2·25
MS804	Two sheets, each 93×85 mm. (a) 1000s. "Delonix regia". (b) 1000s. "Cassia didymobotrya" Set of 2 sheets	13·00	14·00

See also Nos. 820/8.

1990. 50th Anniv of Second World War. As T **206a** of St. Vincent. Multicoloured.

805	5s. Allied penetration of German West Wall, 1944	50	40
806	10s. Flags of the Allies, VE Day, 1945	70	40
807	20s. Capture of Okinawa, 1945	80	45
808	75s. Appointment of Gen. De Gaulle to command all Free French forces, 1944	1·25	60
809	100s. Invasion of Saipan, 1944	1·60	75
810	150s. Airborne landing, Operation Market Garden, 1944	2·25	1·75
811	200s. MacArthur's return to Philippines, 1944	2·50	1·75
812	300s. "Shoho" (Japanese aircraft carrier) under attack, Coral Sea, 1942	2·75	2·50
813	350s. First Battle of El Alamein, 1942	3·00	2·50
814	500s. Naval Battle of Guadalcanal, 1942	3·25	3·25
MS815	112×83 mm. 1000s. Battle of Britain, 1940 (vert)	4·50	5·50

1990. 90th Birthday of Queen Elizabeth the Queen Mother. As T **208a** of St. Vincent.

816	250s. black, mauve and blue	1·60	1·75
817	250s. black, mauve and blue	1·60	1·75
818	250s. black, mauve and blue	1·60	1·75
MS819	90×75 mm. 1000s. multicoloured	3·25	3·50

DESIGNS: No. 816, Queen Elizabeth with corgi; Nos. 817, **MS**819, Queen Elizabeth wearing feathered hat; No. 818, Queen Elizabeth at wartime inspection.

1990. "EXPO 90". International Garden and Greenery Exhibition, Osaka (2nd issue). Nos. 778/85 optd **EXPO '90** and emblem.

820	10s. Type **111**	90	40
821	15s. "Angraecum infundibulare"	90	40
822	45s. "Cyrtorchis chailluana"	1·40	45
823	50s. "Aerangis rhodosticta"	1·40	45
824	100s. "Eulophia speciosa"	2·25	80
825	200s. "Calanthe sylvatica"	3·00	2·75
826	250s. "Vanilla imperialis"	3·25	3·50
827	350s. "Polystachya vulcanica"	3·50	4·50
MS828	Two sheets, each 110×82 mm. (a) 500s. "Ansellia africana" (b) 500s. "Ancistrochilus rothschildianus" Set of 2 sheets	10·00	12·00

The overprint on No. **MS**828 occurs on the sheet margin and includes an additional inscription.

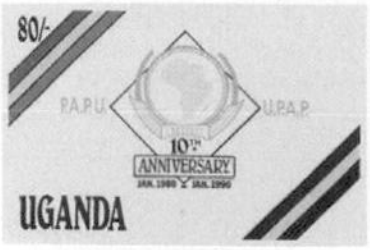

114 P.A.P.U. Emblem

1990. Tenth Anniv of Pan-African Postal Union.

829	**114** 80s. multicoloured	1·60	1·00
MS830	97×67 mm. 750s. black and blue	4·50	6·50

DESIGN: 750s. Clasped hands.

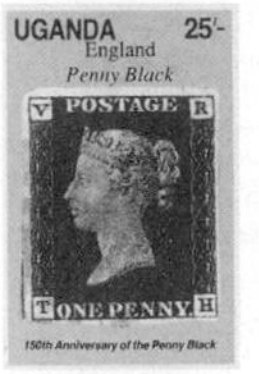

115 Unissued G. B. "V R" Penny Black

1990. 150th Anniv of the Penny Black.

831	**115**	25s. multicoloured	60	15
832	-	50s. red, black and green	80	25
833	-	100s. multicoloured	1·25	45
834	-	150s. multicoloured	1·75	1·25
835	-	200s. multicoloured	2·00	1·50
836	-	300s. multicoloured	2·25	2·00
837	-	500s. multicoloured	2·50	3·50
838	-	600s. multicoloured	2·50	3·50
MS839		Two sheets (a) 107×77 mm. 1000s. multicoloured. (b) 119×85 mm. 1000s. black and red Set of 2 sheets	10·00	12·00

DESIGNS: 50s. Canada 1858–59 3d. Beaver; 100s. Baden 1851 9k. on green error; 150s. Basel 1845 2½r. Dove; 200s. U.S.A. 1918 24c. Inverted "Jenny" error; 300s. Western Australia 1854 1d. Black Swan; 500s. Uganda 1895 20c. "narrow" typewritten stamp; 600s. G.B. Twopenny blue; 1000s. (No. **MS**839a), Uganda 1895 20c. "wide" typewritten stamp; 1000s. (No. **MS**839b), Sir Rowland Hill.

No. **MS**839 also commemorates "Stamp World London 90" International Stamp Exhibition.

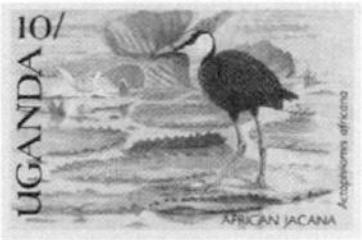

116 African Jacana

1990. Wild Birds of Uganda. Multicoloured.

840	10s. Type **116**	60	35
841	15s. Southern ground hornbill	60	35
842	45s. Kori bustard (vert)	85	50
843	50s. Secretary bird	85	50
844	100s. Egyptian geese	1·25	85
845	300s. Goliath heron (vert)	2·25	2·75
846	500s. Ostrich with chicks (vert)	2·75	3·50
847	650s. Saddle-bill stork (vert)	3·00	4·00
MS848	Two sheets, each 98×69 mm. (a) 1000s. Lesser flamingo (vert). (b) 1000s. Vulturine guineafowl (vert) Set of 2 sheets	9·50	10·00

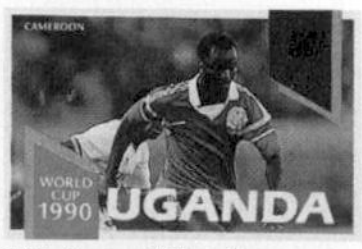

117 Roger Milla of Cameroon

1990. World Cup Football Championship, Italy (2nd issue). Multicoloured.

849	50s. Type **117**	35	25
850	100s. Ramzy of Egypt	55	45
851	250s. David O'Leary of Ireland	1·25	1·25
852	600s. Littbarsky of West Germany	1·75	2·50
MS853	Two sheets, each 75×90 mm. (a) 1000s. Ali McCoist of Scotland. (b) 1000s. Ekstrom of Sweden Set of 2 sheets	9·00	10·00

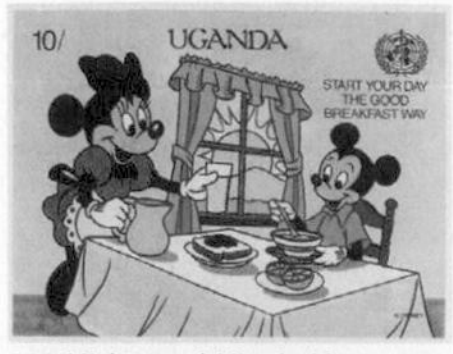

118 Mickey and Minnie Mouse at Breakfast

1990. Health and Safety Campaign. Designs showing Walt Disney cartoon characters. Multicoloured.

854	10s. Type **118**	35	10
855	20s. Donald Duck's nephews doing kerb drill	45	15
856	50s. Donald and Mickey stopping Big Pete smoking	80	35
857	90s. Mickey stopping Donald choking	1·40	40
858	100s. Mickey and Goofy using seat belts	1·50	45
859	250s. Mickey and Minnie dancing	2·50	2·25
860	500s. Donald Duck's fitness class	3·50	4·50
861	600s. Mickey's nephews showing lights at night	3·75	5·00
MS862	Two sheets, each 135×115 mm. (a) 1000s. Mickey weighing nephew (vert). (b) 1000s. Mickey and Pluto walking (vert) Set of 2 sheets	9·50	10·00

1990. As Nos. 746/55 and new values, showing butterflies, as T **108** with "UGANDA" in blue. Multicoloured.

A. Without imprint date

864A	10s. "Hewitsonia boisduvali"	30	15
865A	20s. "Euxanthe wakefieldi"	40	20
866A	30s. "Papilio echerioides"	40	20
867A	40s. "Acraea semivitrea"	40	20
869A	70s. "Acraea perenna"	50	30
870A	90s. "Charaxes cynthia"	60	30
871A	100s. "Euphaedra neophron"	60	40
872A	150s. "Cymothoe beckeri"	60	40
878A	3000s. "Euphaedra eusemoides"	6·00	9·50
879A	4000s. "Acraea natalica"	6·50	12·00
880A	5000s. "Euphaedra themis"	6·50	12·00

B. With imprint date

868B	50s. "Colotis antevippe"	60	30
873B	200s. "Vanessula milca"	1·25	60
874B	400s. "Mimacraea marshalli"	1·75	1·75
875B	500s. "Axiocerses amanga"	1·75	1·75
876B	1000s. "Precis hierta"	5·00	4·50
877B	2000s. "Precis hierta"	5·00	7·50

1990. Christmas. 350th Death Anniv of Rubens. As T **243** of Sierra Leone, but inscr "CHRISTMAS 1990". Multicoloured.

881	10s. "Baptism of Christ" (detail) (vert)	10	10
882	20s. "St. Gregory the Great and other Saints" (detail) (vert)	15	10
883	100s. "Saints Nereus, Domitilla and Achilleus" (detail) (vert)	65	35
884	150s. "St. Gregory the Great and other Saints" (different detail) (vert)	90	60
885	300s. "Saint Augustine" (detail) (vert)	1·50	1·75
886	400s. "St. Gregory the Great and other Saints" (different detail) (vert)	1·60	1·90
887	500s. "Baptism of Christ" (different detail) (vert)	1·75	2·00
888	600s. "St. Gregory the Great and other Saints" (different detail) (vert)	1·90	2·75
MS889	Two sheets, each 110×71 mm. (a) 1000s. "The Triumph of Faith" (detail). (b) 1000s. "The Victory of Eucharistic Truth over Heresy" (detail). Set of 2 sheets	12·00	14·00

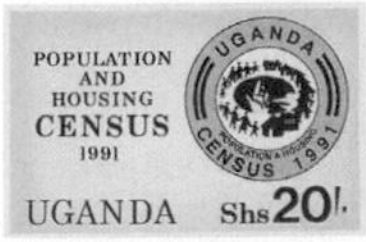

119 Census Emblem

1990. National Population and Housing Census. Multicoloured.

890	20s. Type **119**	65	50
MS891	105×73 mm. 1000s. Symbolic people and dwellings	5·50	6·50

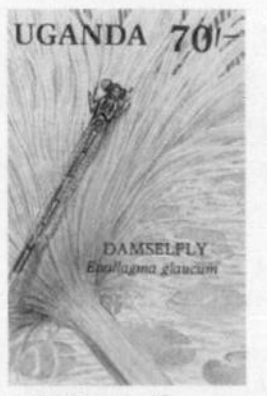

120 Damselfly

1991. Fauna of Uganda's Wetlands. Multicoloured.

892	70s. Type **120**	1·10	85
893	70s. Purple swamphen ("Gallinule")	1·10	85
894	70s. Sitatunga	1·10	85
895	70s. Western reef heron ("Purple heron")	1·10	85
896	70s. Bushpig	1·10	85
897	70s. Vervet monkey	1·10	85
898	70s. Long reed frog	1·10	85
899	70s. Malachite kingfisher	1·10	85
900	70s. Marsh mongoose	1·10	85
901	70s. Painted reed frog	1·10	85
902	70s. African jacana	1·10	85
903	70s. Charaxes butterfly	1·10	85
904	70s. Nile crocodile	1·10	85
905	70s. Herald snake	1·10	85
906	70s. Dragonfly	1·10	85
907	70s. Lungfish	1·10	85
MS908	118×78 mm. 1000s. Nile monitor (horiz)	6·50	7·50

Nos. 892/907 were printed together, se-tenant, forming a composite design.

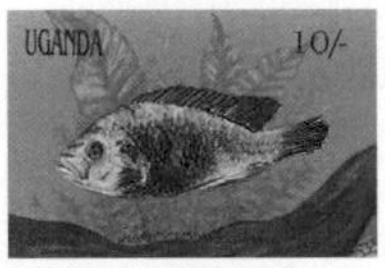

121 Slug Haplochromis

1991. Fish of Uganda. Multicoloured.

909	10s. Type **121**	20	10
910	20s. Palmquist's notho	30	15
911	40s. Silver distichodus	40	20
912	90s. Sauvege's haplochromis	70	40
913	100s. Blue calliurum	75	45
914	350s. Johnston's haplochromis	2·00	2·00
915	600s. Colour-tailed haplochromis	3·25	3·75
916	800s. Jewel cichlid	3·75	4·50
MS917	Two sheets, each 100×74 mm. (a) 1000s. Haplochromis. (b) 1000s. Striped panchax Set of 2 sheets	16·00	15·00

1991. Olympic Games, Barcelona (1992). As T **239a** of Sierra Leone. Multicoloured.

918	20s. Women's 100 metres hurdles	40	20
919	40s. Long jump	55	20
920	125s. Table tennis	1·40	1·25
921	250s. Football	2·00	2·00
922	500s. Men's 800 metres	2·75	3·75
MS923	Two sheets, each 110×71 mm. (a) 1200s. Opening Ceremony at Seoul Games (horiz). (b) 1200s. Women's 4×100 metres relay (horiz) Set of 2 sheets	10·00	12·00

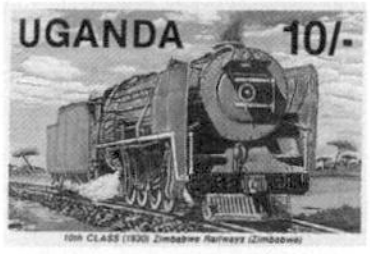

122 South African Railways Class 15f Steam Locomotive, 1938–48

1991. African Railway Locomotives. Multicoloured.

924	10s. Type **122**	1·00	40
925	20s. Rhodesian Railways 12th Class steam locomotive, 1900s	1·40	50
926	80s. Class "Tribal" steam locomotive, Tanzam Railway, 1951–56	2·50	80
927	200s. Steam locomotive, Egypt, 1905	3·50	1·50
928	300s. Mikado steam locomotive, Sudan, 1930	3·50	2·50
929	400s. East African Railways Class 59 Garratt steam locomotive, 1955	4·00	3·25
930	500s. East African Railways Mallet steam locomotive, 1900	4·00	3·25
931	1000s. Type 5 F 1 electric locomotive, South Africa, 1970	5·00	5·50
MS932	Four sheets, each 100×70 mm. (a) 1200s. Atlantic steam locomotive, Egypt, 1900s. (b) 1200s. Rhodesian Railways 12th Class steam locomotive, 1930. (c) 1200s. Benguela Railway Class 11 steam locomotive, Angola, 1920. (d) 1200s. Natal Govt Mallet steam locomotive, 1905–19 Set of 4 sheets	19·00	20·00

No. 924 is incorrectly captioned as a Rhodesia Railways 10th Class locomotive.

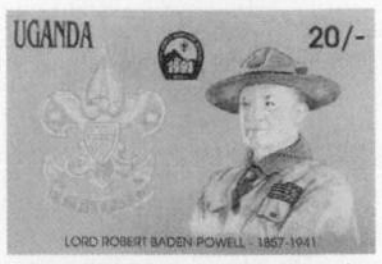

123 Lord Baden-Powell and Scout Emblem

1991. World Scout Jamboree, Mount Sorak, Korea.

933	**123**	20s. multicoloured	70	30
934	-	80s. multicoloured	1·10	65
935	-	100s. multicoloured	1·25	75
936	-	150s. black and green	1·75	1·00
937	-	300s. multicoloured	2·50	2·00
938	-	400s. multicoloured	2·50	2·75
939	-	500s. multicoloured	2·75	2·75
940	-	1000s. multicoloured	3·50	5·00
MS941		Two sheets. (a) 76×115 mm. 1200s. black and stone. (b) 115×76 mm. 1200s. black and blue Set of 2 sheets	14·00	14·00

DESIGNS: 80s. Scouts and Uganda 1982 100s. anniversary stamp; 100s. Scout encampment, New York World's Fair, 1939; 150s. Cover and illustration from "Scouting for Boys"; 300s. Cooking on campfire; 400s. Aldrin and Armstrong on Moon; 500s. Scout salutes; 1000s. Statue to the Unknown Scout, Gilwell Park; 1200s. (**MS**941a) Jamboree emblem; 1200s. (**MS**941b) Lord Baden-Powell, W. Boyce and Revd. L. Hadley.

1991. "Phila Nippon '91" International Stamp Exhibition, Tokyo. As T **221** of St. Vincent showing Walt Disney cartoon characters and Japanese traditions. Multicoloured.

942	10s. Uncle Scrooge celebrating Ga-No-Iwai	25	20
943	20s. Mickey Mouse removing shoes	35	20
944	70s. Goofy leading cart-horse	80	50
945	80s. Daisy Duck and Minnie Mouse exchanging gifts	90	60
946	300s. Minnie kneeling at doorway	2·25	2·00
947	400s. Donald Duck and Mickey taking a hot volcanic sand bath	2·50	2·25
948	500s. Clarabelle Cow burning incense	2·50	2·25
949	1000s. Mickey and Minnie writing New Year cards	3·25	3·50
MS950	Two sheets, each 127×112 mm. (a) 1200s. Mickey conducting (vert). (b) 1200s. Mickey in public bath (vert) Set of 2 sheets	13·00	13·00

1991. Death Cent (1990) of Vincent van Gogh (artist). As T **215a** of St. Vincent. Multicoloured.

951	10s. "Snowy Landscape with Arles"	60	30
952	20s. "Peasant Woman binding Sheaves" (vert)	70	30
953	60s. "The Drinkers"	1·00	50
954	80s. "View of Auvers"	1·25	65
955	200s. "Mourning Man" (vert)	2·25	1·25
956	400s. "Still Life: Vase with Roses"	2·75	2·50
957	800s. "The Raising of Lazarus"	4·00	4·50
958	1000s. "The Good Samaritan" (vert)	4·00	4·50
MS959	Two sheets, each 102×76 mm. (a) 1200s. "First Steps" (95×71 mm). (b) 1200s. "Village Street and Steps in Auvers" (95×71 mm). Imperf Set of 2 sheets	15·00	16·00

1991. 65th Birthday of Queen Elizabeth II. As T **220b** of St. Vincent. Multicoloured.

960	70s. Queen and Prince Charles after polo match	1·50	45
961	90s. Queen at Balmoral, 1976	1·50	55
962	500s. Queen with Princess Margaret, August 1980	3·00	2·25
963	600s. Queen and Queen Mother leaving St. George's Chapel, Windsor	3·25	2·75
MS964	68×90 mm. 1200s. Separate photographs of Queen and Prince Philip	5·50	5·00

1991. Tenth Wedding Anniv of Prince and Princess of Wales. As T **220b** of St. Vincent. Multicoloured.

965	20s. Prince and Princess of Wales in July 1986	70	15
966	100s. Separate photographs of Prince, Princess and sons	1·75	50
967	200s. Prince Henry and Prince William	1·90	1·00
968	1000s. Separate photographs of Prince and Princess in 1988	7·00	6·50
MS969	68×90 mm. 1200s. Princess William and Henry on Majorca and Prince and Princess of Wales in Cameroun	7·50	4·50

124 General
Charles de Gaulle

1991. Birth Centenary (1990) of Charles de Gaulle (French statesman). Multicoloured.

970	20s. Type **124**	30	20
971	70s. Liberation of Paris, 1944	65	45
972	90s. De Gaulle with King George VI, 1940	75	55
973	100s. Reviewing Free French troops, 1940 (horiz)	80	60
974	200s. Broadcasting to France, 1940 (horiz)	1·40	1·00
975	500s. De Gaulle in Normandy, 1944 (horiz)	2·25	2·00
976	600s. De Gaulle at Albert Hall, 1940 (horiz)	2·25	2·25
977	1000s. Inauguration as President, 1959	3·25	3·50

MS978 Two sheets. (a) 104×76 mm. 1200s. De Gaulle entering Paris, 1944. (b) 107×76 mm. 1200s. De Gaulle with Eisenhower, 1942 (horiz) Set of 2 sheets 12·00 12·00

125 "Volvariella bingensis"

1991. Fungi. Multicoloured.

979	20s. Type **125**	40	30
980	70s. "Agrocybe broadwayi"	70	55
981	90s. "Camarophyllus olidus"	80	65
982	140s. "Marasmius arborescens"	1·25	1·10
983	180s. "Marasmiellus subcinereus"	1·40	1·40
984	200s. "Agaricus campestris"	1·40	1·40
985	500s. "Chlorophyllum molybdites"	2·50	2·50
986	1000s. "Lepiota procera"	4·25	5·00

MS987 Two sheets, each 96×65 mm. (a) 1200s. "Leucocoprinus cepaestipes" (horiz). (b) 1200s. "Laccaria ohiensis" ("Laccaria lateritia") (horiz) Set of 2 sheets 9·00 9·50

1991. Endangered Species (3rd series). As Nos. 406/9, but with changed face value, and additional horiz designs as T **61**. Multicoloured.

988	100s. Elephants in "Elephants' Graveyard"	75	45
989	140s. Type **61**	95	75
990	200s. Elephants at waterhole	1·50	1·25
991	600s. Elephants having dust bath	3·00	4·25

MS992 Two sheets, each 102×74 mm. (a) 1200s. Giraffe. (b) 1200s. Rhinoceros and red-billed oxpecker Set of 2 sheets 25·00 18·00

126 "Anigozanthos manglesii"

1991. Botanical Gardens of the World. Multicoloured.

993– 1032	90s.×20, 100s.×20	25·00	26·00

MS1033 Two sheets, each 110×75 mm. (a) 1400s. The Pagoda, Kew. (b) 1400s. Temple of the Winds, Melbourne Set of 2 sheets 16·00 17·00

Nos. 993/1032 were issued together, se-tenant, as two sheetlets of 20 containing designs as Type **126**. The 90 s values show "Anigozanthos manglesii", "Banksia grandis", "Clianthus formosus", "Gossypium sturtianum", "Callistemon lanceolatus", "Saintpaulia ionantha", "Calodendrum capense", "Aloe ferox x arborescens", "Bolusanthus speciousus", "Lithops schwantesii", "Protea repens", "Plumbago capensis", "Clerodendrum thomsoniae", "Thunbergia alata", "Schotia latifolia", "Epacris impressa", "Acacia pycnantha", "Telopea speciosissima", "Wahlenbergia gloriosa", "Eucalyptus globulus" from Melbourne, and the 100s. "Cypripedium calceolus", "Rhododendron thomsonii", "Ginkgo biloba", "Magnolia campbellii", "Wisteria sinensis", "Clerodendrum ugandense", "Eulophia horsfallii", "Aerangis rhodosticta", "Abelmoschus moschatus", "Gloriosa superba", "Carissa edulis", "Ochna kirkii", "Canarina abyssinica", "Nymphaea caerulea", "Ceropegia succulenta", "Strelitzia reginae", "Strongylodon macrobotrys", "Victoria amazonica", "Orchis militaris" and "Sophora microphylla" from Kew.

1991. Nos. 573, 597 and 614 surch 20/-.

1034	20s. on 25s. on 25s. Airship N.1 "Norge" and polar bear (first transpolar flight), 1926		
1035	20s. on 25s. on 25s. Einstein and deep space (Theory of Relativity)		
1035a	20s. on 25s. on 25s. Tank locomotive No. 126		

1991. Christmas. Paintings by Piero della Francesca. As T **248a** of Sierra Leone. Multicoloured.

1036	20s. "Madonna with Child and Angels"	50	20
1037	50s. "The Baptism of Christ"	75	20
1038	80s. "Polyptych of Mercy"	1·00	40
1039	100s. "Polyptych of Mercy" (detail)	1·00	40
1040	200s. "The Annunciation" from "The Legend of the True Cross"	1·75	80
1041	500s. "Pregnant Madonna"	2·75	2·50
1042	1000s. "The Annunciation" from "Polyptych of St. Anthony"	4·00	4·50
1043	1500s. "The Nativity"	5·00	7·50

MS1044 Two sheets, each 102×127 mm. (a) 1800s. "The Brera Altarpiece". (b) 1800s. "Madonna and Child" from "Polyptych of St. Anthony" Set of 2 sheets 14·00 15·00

128 Boy Scout Monument, New York, and Ernest Thompson (first Chief Scout of U.S.A.)

1992. Anniversaries and Events. Multicoloured.

1045	20s. Type **128**	80	30
1046	50s. Treehouse design and Daniel Beard (vert)	85	40
1047	400s. Lilienthal's signature and "Flugzeug Nr. 8"	1·60	1·75
1048	500s. Demonstrator demolishing Berlin Wall	1·60	2·25
1049	700s. "The Magic Flute"	9·50	8·50

MS1050 Two sheets. (a) 114×85 mm. 1200s. Class VL8 electric locomotive leaving tunnel. (b) 117×89 mm. 1500s. Ugandan Boy Scout badge Set of 2 sheets 14·00 15·00

ANNIVERSARIES AND EVENTS: Nos. 1045/6, MS1050b, 50th death anniv of Lord Baden-Powell and World Scout Jamboree, Korea; No. 1047, Centenary of Lilienthal's first gliding experiments; No. 1048, Bicentenary of Brandenburg Gate, Berlin; No. 1049, Death bicentenary of Mozart; MS1050a, Centenary of Trans-Siberian Railway.

129 U.S.S. "Vestal" (repair ship) under Attack

1992. 50th Anniv of Japanese Attack on Pearl Harbor. Multicoloured.

1051	200s. Type **129**	1·75	1·50
1052	200s. Japanese Mitsubishi A6M Zero-Sen	1·75	1·50
1053	200s. U.S.S. "Arizona" (battleship) on fire	1·75	1·50
1054	200s. U.S.S. "Nevada" (battleship) passing burning ships	1·75	1·50
1055	200s. Japanese Aichi D3A "Val" bomber attacking		1·50
1056	200s. Douglas SBD Dauntless bombers attacking "Hiryu" (carrier) at Midway	1·75	1·50
1057	200s. Japanese Mitsubishi A6M Zero-Sen aircraft attacking Midway Island	1·75	1·50
1058	200s. U.S. Marine Brewster F2A Buffalo (fighter) defending Midway	1·75	1·50
1059	200s. American Grumman F6F Hellcat aircraft and carrier	1·75	1·50
1060	200s. U.S.S. "Yorktown" (carrier) torpedoed	1·75	1·50

130 Three Modern Hot Air Balloons

1992. 120th Anniv (1990) of Paris Balloon Post. Multicoloured.

1061	200s. Type **130**	1·50	1·50
1062	200s. Sport balloons and top of "Double Eagle II"	1·50	1·50
1063	200s. Pro Juventute balloon and top of Branson's "Virgin Otsuka Pacific Flyer"	1·50	1·50

1064	200s. Blanchard and Jeffries' balloon	1·50	1·50
1065	200s. Nadar's "Le Geant" and centre of "Double Eagle II"	1·50	1·50
1066	200s. Branson's "Virgin Otsuka Pacific Flyer"	1·50	1·50
1067	200s. Montgolfier balloon	1·50	1·50
1068	200s. "Double Eagle II" basket and Paris balloon of 1870	1·50	1·50
1069	200s. Henri Giffard's balloon "Le Grand Ballon Captif"	1·50	1·50

Nos. 1061/9 were printed together, se-tenant, forming a composite design.

1992. Mickey's World Tour. As T **250a** of Sierra Leone showing Walt Disney cartoon characters in different countries. Multicoloured.

1070	20s. Mickey Mouse and Goofy on African safari (horiz)	50	20
1071	50s. Mickey charming Pluto's tail, India (horiz)	70	20
1072	80s. Minnie Mouse, Donald and Daisy Duck as Caribbean calypso band (horiz)	1·00	25
1073	200s. Goofy pulling Donald and Daisy in rickshaw, China (horiz)	1·60	60
1074	500s. Mickey and Minnie on camel, Egypt (horiz)	2·25	1·75
1075	800s. Donald and Pete sumo wrestling, Japan (horiz)	2·50	2·75
1076	1000s. Goofy bullfighting, Spain (horiz)	2·50	2·75
1077	1500s. Mickey playing football, Italy (horiz)	3·00	4·00

MS1078 Two sheets, each 83×104 mm. (a) 2000s. Mickey as Cossack dancer, Russia. (b) 2000s. Daisy as Wagnerian diva, Germany Set of 2 sheets 12·00 13·00

1992. 40th Anniv of Queen Elizabeth II's Accession. As T **220b** of St. Vincent. Multicoloured.

1079	100s. Lake Victoria	80	25
1080	200s. Lake and mountains	1·25	60
1081	500s. Lakeside fields	2·75	2·25
1082	1000s. River Nile	4·00	4·25

MS1083 Two sheets, each 74×97 mm. (a) 1800s. Waterfalls. (b) 1800s. Owen Falls Dam Set of 2 sheets 13·00 11·00

131 "The Entry into Jerusalem" (detail) (Giotto)

1992. Prehistoric Animals. As T **229** of Sierra Leone. Multicoloured.

1084	50s. Kentrosaurus	50	30
1085	200s. Iguanodon	1·00	80
1086	250s. Hypsilophodon	1·10	90
1087	300s. Brachiosaurus	1·25	1·10
1088	400s. Peloneustes	1·40	1·40
1089	500s. Pteranodon	1·50	1·50
1090	800s. Tetralophodon	2·00	2·50
1091	1000s. Megalosaurus	2·00	2·50

MS1092 Two sheets, each 100×70 mm. (a) 2000s. As 250s. (b) 2000s. As 1000s. Set of 2 sheets 14·00 13·00

1992. Easter. Religious Paintings. Multicoloured.

1093	50s. Type **131**	75	20
1094	100s. "Pilate and the Watch" (Psalter of Robert de Lisle)	95	20
1095	200s. "The Kiss of Judas" (detail) (Giotto)	1·60	75
1096	250s. "Christ washing the Feet of the Disciples" (Vita Christi manuscript)	1·60	75
1097	300s. "Christ seized in the Garden" (Melissende Psalter)	1·75	85
1098	500s. "Doubting Thomas" (Vita Christi manuscript)	2·50	1·75
1099	1000s. "The Marys at the Tomb" (detail) (anon)	4·25	4·75
1100	2000s. "The Ascension" (Florentine manuscript)	6·50	8·50

MS1101 Two sheets, each 72×102 mm. (a) 2500s. "The Piercing of Christ's Side" (detail) (Limoges enamel). (b) 2500s. "Agony at Gethsemane" (detail) (Limoges enamel) Set of 2 sheets 18·00 19·00

132 Adungu

1992. Traditional Musical Instruments. Multicoloured.

1102	50s. Type **132**	60	20
1103	100s. Endingidi	80	35
1104	200s. Akogo	1·25	60
1105	250s. Nanga	1·40	70
1106	300s. Engoma	1·50	1·25
1107	400s. Amakondere	1·75	1·75
1108	500s. Akakyenkye	1·90	2·00
1109	1000s. Ennanga	3·50	5·50

133 Map of Known World, 1486

1992. 500th Anniv of Discovery of America by Columbus and "World Columbian Stamp Expo '92" Exhibition, Chicago. Multicoloured.

1110	50s. Type **133**	20	20
1111	100s. Map of Africa, 1508	30	30
1112	150s. Map of West Indies, 1500	50	50
1113	200s. "Nina" and astrolabe	60	60
1114	600s. "Pinta" and quadrant	1·50	1·50
1115	800s. Sand glass	1·60	1·60
1116	900s. 15th-century compass	1·75	1·75
1117	900s. Map of World, 1492	3·50	3·50

MS1118 Two sheets, each 95×75 mm. (a) 2500s. Sections of globe, 1492. (b) 2500s. Europe and Africa from map by Henricus Martellus, 1490 (vert) Set of 2 sheets 9·25 10·00

1992. Hummel Figurines. As T **215b** of St Vincent. Multicoloured.

1119	50s. Girl with washing	35	70
1120	100s. Girl feeding bird	60	50
1121	250s. Girl sweeping floor	90	60
1122	300s. Girl with baby	1·00	70
1123	600s. Boy mountaineer	2·25	2·00
1124	900s. Girl knitting	2·75	2·75
1125	1000s. Boy on stool	2·75	3·00
1126	1500s. Boy with telescope	3·25	3·50

MS1127 Two sheets, each 97×122 mm. (a) 500s. As No. 1119; 500s. As No. 1120; 500s. As No. 1121; 500s. As No. 1122. (b) 500s. As No. 1124; 500s. As No. 1123; 500s. As No. 1125; 500s. As No. 1126 Set of 2 sheets 12·00 13·00

134 Spotted Hyena

1992. Wildlife. Multicoloured.

1128	50s. Type **134**	50	20
1129	100s. Impala	60	25
1130	200s. Giant forest hog	85	45
1131	250s. Pangolin	95	65
1132	300s. Golden monkey	1·10	75
1133	800s. Serval	3·00	3·00
1134	1000s. Small-spotted genet ("Bush genet")	3·00	3·25
1135	3000s. Waterbuck	7·50	9·00

MS1136 Two sheets, each 100×70 mm. (a) 2500s. Gorilla. (b) 2500s. Hippopotamus Set of 2 sheets 10·00 12·00

1992. Olympic Games, Barcelona. As T **250d** of Sierra Leone. Multicoloured.

1137	50s. Men's javelin	40	20
1138	100s. Men's high jump (horiz)	55	30
1139	200s. Fencing (pentathlon)	80	45
1140	250s. Men's volleyball	85	60
1141	300s. Women's platform diving	90	60
1142	500s. Men's team cycling	5·00	2·50
1143	1000s. Women's tennis	5·50	6·00
1144	2000s. Boxing (horiz)	6·00	9·50

MS1145 Two sheets, each 100×70 mm. (a) 2500s. Men's basketball. (b) 2500s. Baseball Set of 2 sheets 18·00 18·00

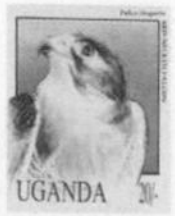

135 Red-headed Falcon

1992. Birds. Multicoloured.

1146	20s. Type **135**	55	40
1147	30s. Yellow-billed hornbill	65	40
1148	50s. Purple heron	70	30
1149	100s. Regal sunbird	90	30
1150	150s. White-browed robin chat	1·25	40
1151	200s. Shining-blue kingfisher	1·25	45
1152	250s. Great blue turaco	1·25	50
1153	300s. African emerald cuckoo	1·40	70
1154	500s. Abyssinian roller	1·75	1·25
1155	800s. South African crowned crane	2·50	2·00
1156	1000s. Doherty's bush shrike	3·00	2·50
1157	2000s. Splendid glossy starling	3·75	4·25
1158	3000s. Little bee eater	5·00	7·50
1159	4000s. Red-faced lovebird ("Red-headed Lovebird")	6·50	9·00

1992. Postage Stamp Mega Event, New York. Sheet 100×70 mm. containing vert design as T **240a** of St. Vincent. Multicoloured.

MS1160	2500s. United Nations Headquarters	3·75	4·50

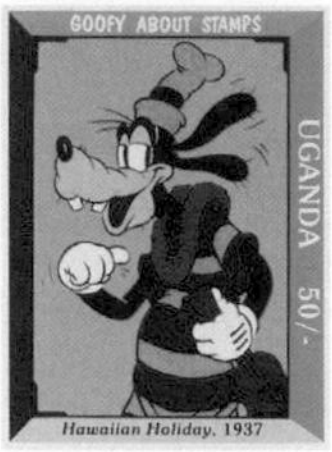

136 Goofy in "Hawaiian Holiday", 1937

1992. 60th Anniv of Goofy. Multicoloured.

1162	50s. Type **136**	30	20
1163	100s. Riding pennyfarthing cycle, 1941	40	20
1164	200s. Goofy and Mickey Mouse as firemen, 1935	60	35
1165	250s. Skiing, 1941 (horiz)	70	60
1166	300s. One man band, 1937 (horiz)	70	60
1167	1000s. Asleep against boat, 1938 (horiz)	2·25	2·50
1168	1500s. Ancient Olympic champion, 1942	3·25	3·75
1169	2000s. Pole vaulting, 1942	3·50	3·75
MS1170	Two sheets. (a) 105×115 mm. 3000s. Goofy and Wilbur the grasshopper, 1939 (horiz). (b) 92×116 mm. 3000s. Wyatt Goofy and Goofy today Set of 2 sheets	12·00	12·00

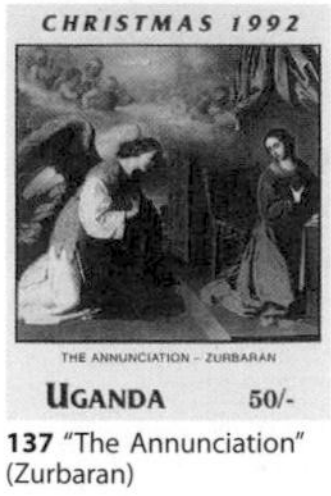

137 "The Annunciation" (Zurbaran)

1992. Christmas. Religious Paintings by Francisco Zurbaran. Multicoloured.

1171	50s. Type **137**	65	15
1172	200s. "The Annunciation" (different)	1·25	35
1173	250s. "The Virgin of the Immaculate Conception"	1·40	45
1174	300s. "The Virgin of the Immaculate Conception" (detail)	1·50	50
1175	800s. "Holy Family with Saints Anne, Joachim and John the Baptist"	3·50	3·50
1176	900s. "Holy Family with Saints Anne, Joachim and John the Baptist" (detail)	3·75	4·00
1177	1000s. "Adoration of the Magi"	3·75	4·00
1178	2000s. "Adoration of the Magi" (detail)	5·50	9·00
MS1179	Two sheets, each 76×102 mm. (a) 2500s. "The Virgin of the Immaculate Conception (different). (b) 2500s. "The Virgin of the Immaculate Conception" (different) Set of 2 sheets	19·00	20·00

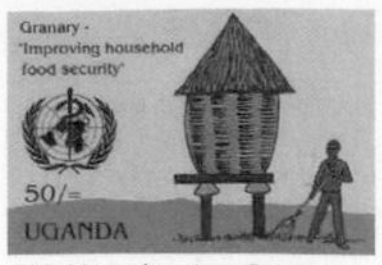

138 Man cleaning Granary

1992. Anniversaries and Events. Multicoloured.

1180	50s. Type **138**	20	15
1181	200s. Mother breast feeding	65	40
1182	250s. Mother feeding baby	70	50
1183	300s. Boy collecting water from pump	75	75
1184	300s. "Voyager 2" passing Jupiter	2·75	1·25
1185	800s. Mother and baby	2·00	2·75
1186	800s. Impala	2·00	2·75
1187	1000s. Mountain zebra	4·00	4·50
1188	1000s. Count Ferdinand von Zeppelin and airship	4·00	4·50
1189	2000s. "Voyager 2" passing Neptune	8·50	9·00
1190	3000s. Count Ferdinand von Zeppelin and Clement-Bayard airship "Fleurus"	9·00	11·00
MS1191	Four sheets, each 115×85 mm. (a) 2500s. "Voyager 2" and Jupiter. (b) 2500s. Warthog. (c) 2500s. Count Ferdinand von Zeppelin with Robert Brothers and Colin Hullin balloon. (d) 2500s. Doctor inoculating boy Set of 4 sheets	29·00	32·00

ANNIVERSARIES AND EVENTS: Nos. 1180/3, 1185, United Nations World Health Organization Projects; Nos. 1184, 1189, **MS**1191a, International Space Year; Nos. 1186/7, **MS**1191b, Earth Summit '92, Rio; Nos. 1188, 1190, **MS**1191c, 75th death anniv of Count Ferdinand von Zeppelin (airship pioneer); **MS**1191d, 75th anniv of International Association of Lions Clubs.

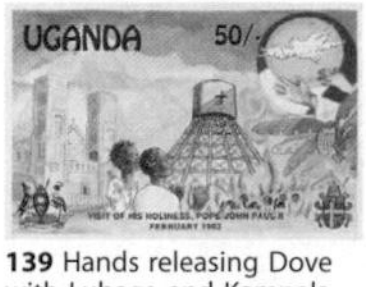

139 Hands releasing Dove with Lubaga and Kampala Catholic Cathedrals

1993. Visit of Pope John Paul II. Multicoloured.

1192	50s. Type **139**	75	10
1193	200s. Pope and Kampala Cathedral	1·25	30
1194	250s. Pope and Catholic worshipper	1·40	45
1195	300s. Ugandan bishops and Pope	1·60	60
1196	800s. Pope John Paul II waving	3·00	3·00
1197	900s. Pope and Kampala Cathedral (different)	3·00	3·00
1198	1000s. Pope, national flag and Kampala Cathedral	3·00	3·00
1199	2000s. Pope and national flag	5·50	6·00
MS1200	Two sheets, each 100×70 mm. (a) 3000s. Pope on aircraft steps (vert). (b) 3000s. Pope delivering blessing (vert) Set of 2 sheets	18·00	16·00

1993. Bicentenary of the Louvre, Paris. Paintings by Rembrandt. As T **254a** of St. Vincent. Multicoloured.

1201	500s. "Self Portrait at Easel"	1·10	1·10
1202	500s. "Birds of Paradise"	1·10	1·10
1203	500s. "The Carcass of Beef"	1·10	1·10
1204	500s. "The Supper at Emmaus"	1·10	1·10
1205	500s. "Hendrickje Stoffels"	1·10	1·10
1206	500s. "The Artist's Son, Titus"	1·10	1·10
1207	500s. "The Holy Family" (left detail)	1·10	1·10
1208	500s. "The Holy Family" (right detail)	1·10	1·10
MS1209	100×70 mm. 2500s. "The philosopher in Meditation" (89×57 mm)	4·50	5·00

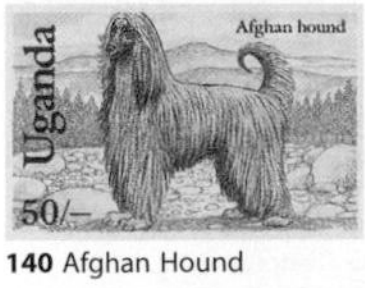

140 Afghan Hound

1993. Dogs of the World. Multicoloured.

1210	50s. Type **140**	1·00	40
1211	100s. Newfoundland	1·40	40
1212	200s. Siberian huskies	2·00	60
1213	250s. Briard	2·00	75
1214	300s. Saluki	2·00	1·00
1215	800s. Labrador guide-dog (vert)	3·50	3·50
1216	1000s. Greyhound	3·75	3·75
1217	1500s. Pointer	4·50	5·00
MS1218	Two sheets, each 103×80 mm. (a) 2500s. Cape hunting dog. (b) 2500s. Norwegian elkhound pup Set of 2 sheets	21·00	19·00

1993. 40th Anniv of Coronation. As T **256a** of St. Vincent. Multicoloured.

1219	50s. Queen Elizabeth II at Coronation (photograph by Cecil Beaton)	30	35
1220	200s. Orb and Sceptre	50	60
1221	500s. Queen Elizabeth during Coronation	90	1·10
1222	1500s. Queen Elizabeth II and Princess Margaret	2·25	2·50
MS1223	69×100 mm. 2500s. "The Crown" (detail) (Grace Wheatley) (28½×42½ mm)	5·00	5·50

1993. Asian International Stamp Exhibitions. As T **263** of St. Vincent, but vert. Multicoloured

(a) "Indopex '93", Surabaya, Indonesia. Javanese Wayang Puppets.

1224	600s. Bupati karma, Prince of Wangga	1·25	1·50
1225	600s. Rahwana	1·25	1·50
1226	600s. Sondjeng Sandjata	1·25	1·50
1227	600s. Raden Damar Wulan	1·25	1·50
1228	600s. Unidentified puppet	1·25	1·50
1229	600s. Hanaman	1·25	1·50
MS1230	135×105 mm. 2500s. Candi Mendut Temple, Java	6·00	7·00

(b) "Taipei '93", Taiwan. Funerary Pottery Figures.

1231	600s. Tomb guardian god in green armour	1·25	1·50
1232	600s. Civil official and shrine	1·25	1·50
1233	600s. Tomb guardian god in green and gold armour	1·25	1·50
1234	600s. Civil official in red robe	1·25	1·50
1235	600s. Chimera (tomb guardian)	1·25	1·50
1236	600s. Civil official in red and green robe	1·25	1·50
MS1237	135×105 mm. 2500s. Statue of the Sacred Mother, Taiyuan	6·00	7·00

(c) "Bangkok '93", Thailand. Sculptured Figures.

1238	600s. Standing Buddha in gilded red sandstone, 13th–15th century	1·25	1·50
1239	600s. Crowned Buddha in bronze, 13th century	1·25	1·50
1240	600s. Thepanom in stone, 15th century	1·25	1·50
1241	600s. Crowned Buddha in bronze, 12th century	1·25	1·50
1242	600s. Avalokitesvara in bronze, 9th century	1·25	1·50
1243	600s. Lop Buri standing Buddha in bronze, 13th century	1·25	1·50
MS1244	135×105 mm. 2500s. Buddha, Wat Mahathat	6·00	7·00

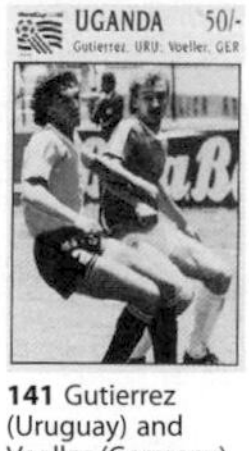

141 Gutierrez (Uruguay) and Voeller (Germany)

1993. World Cup Football Championship, U.S.A. (1994) (1st issue). Multicoloured.

1245	50s. Type **141**	60	20
1246	200s. Tomas Brolin (Sweden)	1·25	50
1247	250s. Gary Lineker (England)	1·50	50
1248	300s. Munoz and Butragueno (Spain)	1·50	65
1249	800s. Carlos Valderrama (Colombia)	2·75	3·00
1250	900s. Diego Maradona (Argentina)	2·75	3·00
1251	1000s. Pedro Troglio (Argentina)	2·75	3·00
1252	2000s. Enzo Scifo (Belgium)	4·00	5·50
MS1253	Two sheets, each 103×72 mm. (a) 2500s. Brazilians celebrating. (b) 2500s. De Napoli (Italy) and Skuhravy (Czechoslovakia) (horiz) Set of 2 sheets	13·00	14·00

See also Nos. 1322/8.

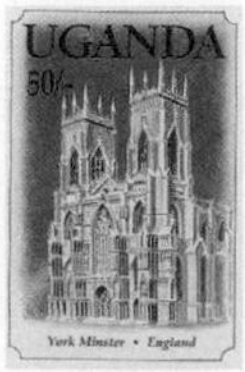

142 York Minster, England

1993. Cathedrals of the World. Multicoloured.

1254	50s. Type **142**	40	15
1255	100s. Notre Dame, Paris	55	20
1256	200s. Little Metropolis, Athens	85	40
1257	250s. St. Patrick's, New York	90	45
1258	300s. Ulm, Germany	95	50
1259	800s. St. Basil's, Moscow	2·50	2·75
1260	1000s. Roskilde, Denmark	2·50	2·75
1261	2000s. Seville, Spain	4·00	5·50
MS1262	Two sheets, each 70×100 mm. (a) 2500s. Namirembe, Uganda. (b) 2500s. St. Peter's, Vatican City Set of 2 sheets	13·00	14·00

1993. Christmas. Religious Paintings. As T **265a** of St. Vincent. Black, yellow and red (Nos. 1263, 1265, 1267, 1270 and **MS**1271a) or multicoloured (others).

1263	50s. "Virgin with Carthusian Monks" (detail) (Durer)	50	10
1264	100s. "Sacred Family" (detail) (Raphael)	75	10
1265	200s. "Virgin with Carthusian Monks" (different detail) (Durer)	1·10	30
1266	250s. "The Virgin of the Rose" (Raphael)	1·25	35
1267	300s. "Virgin with Carthusian Monks" (different detail) (Durer)	1·25	40
1268	800s. "Sacred Family" (different detail) (Raphael)	2·75	3·00
1269	1000s. "Virgin with Beardless Joseph" (Raphael)	2·75	3·00
1270	2000s. "Virgin with Carthusian Monks" (different detail) (Durer)	4·25	6·00
MS1271	Two sheets, each 102×127 mm. (a) 2500s. "Virgin with Carthusian Monks" (different detail) (Dürer). (b) 2500s. "Sacred Family" (different detail) (Raphael) Set of 2 sheets	15·00	13·00

Nos. **MS**1271 is inscribed "Canthusian Monks" in error.

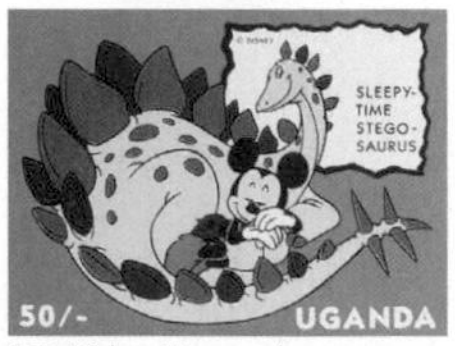

143 Mickey Mouse asleep on Stegosaurus

1993. Prehistoric Animals and Walt Disney Cartoon Characters. Multicoloured.

1272	50s. Type **143**	60	20
1273	100s. Minnie Mouse on pteranodon	70	20
1274	200s. Mickey being licked by mamenchisaurus	1·00	40
1275	250s. Mickey doing cave painting	1·10	45
1276	300s. Mickey wind-surfing on dinosaur	1·25	60
1277	500s. Mickey and Donald Duck sliding on diplodocus	1·90	1·40
1278	800s. Mamenchisaurus carrying Mickey	2·75	3·25
1279	1000s. Pluto on triceratops	2·75	3·25
MS1280	Two sheets, each 128×102 mm. (a) 2500s. Mickey and Minnie. (b) 2500s. Mickey feeding tyrannosaurus rex Set of 2 sheets	12·00	13·00

No. 1273 is inscribed "PTERANDOM" and No. 1278 "MAMENSHISAURUS", both in error.

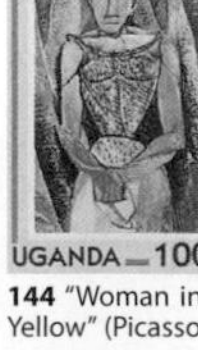

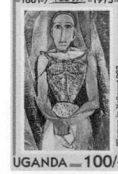

144 "Woman in Yellow" (Picasso)

1993. Anniversaries and Events. Multicoloured.

1281	100s. Type **144**	40	15
1282	200s. Head of cow and syringe	50	30
1283	250s. "Gertrude Stein" (Picasso)	60	35
1284	500s. Early telescope	3·50	1·50
1285	800s. "Creation" (S. Witkiewicz after J. Glogowski)	2·00	2·50
1286	1000s. Modern telescope	4·50	3·50
1287	1000s. "For the Right to Work" (A. Strumillo)	2·25	3·50
MS1288	Three sheets. (a) 75×105 mm. 2500s. "Woman by a Window" (detail) (Picasso). (b) 105×75 mm. 2500s. Copernicus. (c) 105×75 mm. 2500s. "Temptation of Saint Antony I" (detail) (S. Witkiewicz) (horiz) Set of 3 sheets	18·00	19·00

ANNIVERSARIES AND EVENTS: Nos. 1281, 1283, **MS**1288a, 20th death anniv of Picasso (artist); No. 1282, Pan African Rinderpest Campaign; Nos. 1284, 1286, **MS**1288b, 450th death anniv of Copernicus (astronomer); Nos. 1285, 1287, 1288c, "Polska '93" International Stamp Exhibition, Poznan.

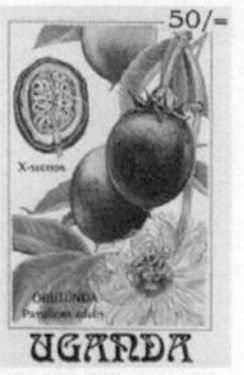

145 Passion Fruit

1994. Fruits and Crops. Multicoloured.

1289	50s. Type **145**	45	10
1290	100s. Sunflower	55	10
1291	150s. Bananas	75	25
1292	200s. Runner beans	85	30
1293	250s. Pineapple	90	55
1294	300s. Jackfruit	1·10	70
1295	500s. Sorghum	2·00	2·00
1296	800s. Maize	3·00	4·00
MS1297	Two sheets, each 101×71 mm. (a) 2000s. Sesame. (b) 2000s. Coffee (horiz) Set of 2 sheets	12·00	12·00

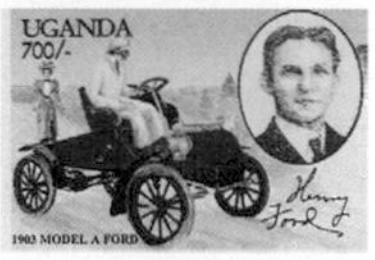

146 Ford Model "A", 1903

1994. Centenaries of Henry Ford's First Petrol Engine (Nos. 1298/1301, **MS**1306a) and Karl Benz's First Four-wheeled Car (others). Multicoloured.

1298	700s. Type **146**	1·25	1·50
1299	700s. Ford Model "T" snowmobile, 1932	1·25	1·50
1300	700s. Ford "Mustang"	1·25	1·50
1301	700s. Lotus-Ford racing car, 1965	1·25	1·50
1302	800s. Mercedes-Benz "S600" coupe, 1994	1·25	1·50
1303	800s. Mercedes-Benz "W196" racing car, 1955	1·25	1·50
1304	800s. Mercedes-Benz "W125" road speed record car, 1938	1·25	1·50
1305	800s. Benz "Viktoria", 1893	1·25	1·50
MS1306	Two sheets, each 85×85 mm. (a) 2500s. Henry Ford (vert). (b) 2500s. Karl Benz (vert) Set of 2 sheets	9·00	11·00

1994. "Hong Kong '94" International Stamp Exhibition (1st issue). As T **271a** of St. Vincent. Multicoloured.

1307	300s. Hong Kong 1980 60c. Catholic Cathedral stamp and religious shrines, Repulse Bay	80	1·00
1308	500s. Uganda 1993 2500s. Namirembe Cathedral stamp and religious shrines, Repulse Bay (different)	80	1·00

Nos. 1307/8 were printed together, se-tenant, forming a composite design.

1994. "Hong Kong '94" International Stamp Exhibition (2nd issue). Ching Dynasty Snuff Boxes. As T **271b** of St. Vincent, but vert. Multicoloured.

1309	200s. Glass box with pavilion design	60	70
1310	200s. Porcelain box with quail design	60	70
1311	200s. Porcelain box with floral design	60	70
1312	200s. Porcelain box with open-work design	60	70
1313	200s. Agate box with carved Lion-dogs	60	70
1314	200s. Agate box with man on donkey design	60	70

Captions for Nos. 1310/11 are transposed.

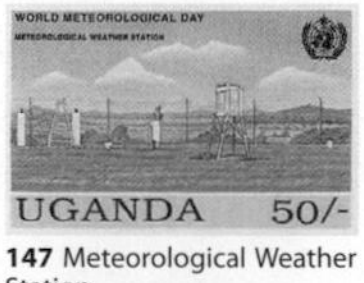

147 Meteorological Weather Station

1994. World Meteorological Day. Multicoloured.

1315	50s. Type **147**	70	15
1316	200s. Weather observatory at training school, Entebbe (vert)	1·50	55
1317	250s. Satellite link	1·50	70
1318	300s. Recording temperatures	1·75	1·00
1319	400s. Automatic weather station (vert)	2·00	2·25
1320	800s. Crops damaged by hailstones	3·00	5·00
MS1321	105×75 mm. 2500s. Barograph	8·00	9·00

1994. World Cup Football Championship, U.S.A. (2nd issue). As T **268** of Sierra Leone. Multicoloured.

1322	500s. Georges Grun (Belgium)	1·50	1·75
1323	500s. Oscar Ruggeri (Argentina)	1·50	1·75
1324	500s. Frank Rijkaard (Netherlands)	1·50	1·75
1325	500s. Magid "Tyson" Musisi (Uganda)	1·50	1·75
1326	500s. Ronald Koeman (Netherlands)	1·50	1·75
1327	500s. Igor Shalimov (Russia)	1·50	1·75
MS1328	Two sheets, each 70×100 mm. (a) 2500s. Ruud Gullit (Netherlands). (b) 2500s. Player and R.F.K. Stadium, Washington D.C. Set of 2 sheets	9·00	11·00

No. 1326 is inscribed "DONALD KOEMAN" in error.

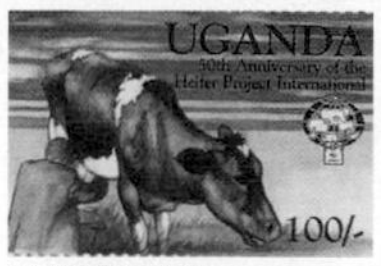

148 Milking Cow

1994. 50th Anniv of Heifer Project International.

1329	**148**	100s. multicoloured	1·75	1·00

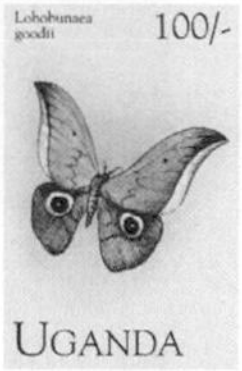

149 "Lobobunaea goodii"

1994. Moths. Multicoloured.

1330	100s. Type **149**	35	20
1331	200s. "Bunaeopsis hersilia"	65	40
1332	300s. "Rufoglanis rosea"	80	60
1333	350s. "Acherontia atropos"	85	75
1334	400s. "Rohaniella pygmaea"	95	95
1335	450s. "Euchloron megaera"	1·00	1·25
1336	500s. "Epiphora rectifascia"	1·10	1·25
1337	1000s. "Polyphychus coryndoni"	1·90	2·50
MS1338	Two sheets, each 117×88 mm. (a) 2500s. As Type **149**. (b) 2500s. "Lobobunaea goodii" (wings folded) Set of 2 sheets	9·50	10·00

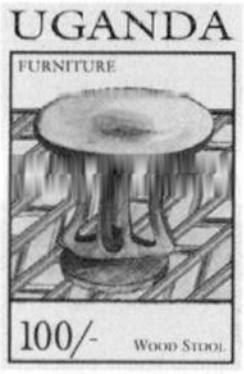

150 Wooden Stool

1994. Crafts. Multicoloured.

1339	100s. Type **150**	25	10
1340	200s. Wood and banana fibre chair	45	30
1341	250s. Raffia and palm leaves basket	50	35
1342	300s. Wool tapestry showing tree planting	55	45
1343	450s. Wool tapestry showing hair grooming	85	90
1344	500s. Wood sculpture of a drummer	95	1·10
1345	800s. Gourds	1·75	2·50
1346	1000s. Bark cloth handbag	2·00	3·25
MS1347	Two sheets, each 100×70 mm. (a) 2500s. Raffia baskets. (b) 2500s. Papyrus hats Set of 2 sheets	11·00	13·00

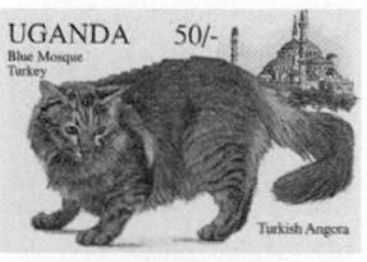

151 Turkish Angora Cat and Blue Mosque

1994. Cats. Multicoloured.

1348	50s. Type **151**	60	25
1349	100s. Japanese bobtail and Mt. Fuji	80	25
1350	200s. Norwegian forest cat and windmill, Holland	1·00	40
1351	300s. Egyptian mau and pyramids (vert)	1·40	75
1352	450s. Rex and Stonehenge, England (vert)	2·00	1·60
1353	500s. Chartreux and Eiffel Tower, France	2·25	1·75
1354	1000s. Burmese and Shwe Dagon Pagoda (vert)	3·25	3·75
1355	1500s. Maine coon and Pemaquid Point Lighthouse (vert)	5·50	6·00
MS1356	Two sheets, each 100×76 mm. (a) 2500s. Russian blue. (b) 2500s. Manx Set of 2 sheets	12·00	12·00

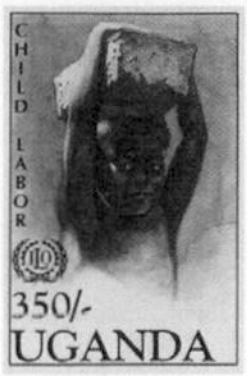

152 Child carrying Building Block

1994. 75th Anniv of I.L.O.

1357	**152**	350s. multicoloured	1·75	1·75

1994. 25th Anniv of First Manned Moon Landing. Astronauts. As Nos. 1977/89 of Antigua. Multicoloured.

1358	50s. Alan Shepard Jnr	1·10	1·10
1359	100s. M. Scott Carpenter	1·25	1·25
1360	200s. Virgil Grissom	1·50	1·50
1361	300s. L. Gordon Cooper Jnr	1·60	1·60
1362	400s. Walter Schirra Jnr	1·75	1·75
1363	500s. Donald Slayton	1·75	1·75
1364	600s. John Glenn Jnr	1·75	1·75
MS1365	88×91 mm. 3000s. "Apollo 11" anniversary emblem	7·00	7·50

1994. Centenary of International Olympic Committee. Gold Medal Winners. As T **285a** of St. Vincent. Multicoloured.

1366	350s. John Akll-Bua (Uganda) (400 metres hurdles), 1972 (horiz)	60	45
1367	900s. Heike Herkel (Germany) (high jump), 1992 (horiz)	1·25	1·75
MS1368	107×76 mm. 2500s. Aleski Urmanov (Russia) (figure skating), 1994	5·50	5·50

1994. 50th Anniv of D-Day. As T **284b** of St. Vincent. Multicoloured.

1369	300s. Mulberry Harbour pier	50	40
1370	1000s. Mulberry Harbour floating bridge	1·50	2·00
MS1371	105×76 mm. 2500s. Aerial view of Mulberry Harbour	6·00	6·50

1994. "Philakorea '94" International Stamp Exhibition, Seoul. As T **286a** of St. Vincent, but vert. Multicoloured.

1372	100s. Sari Pagoda, Paekyangsa	10	10
1373	350s. Ch'omsongdae	50	60
1374	1000s. Pulguksa Temple	1·40	2·75
MS1375	76×106 mm. 2500s. Bronze mural, Pagoda Park, Seoul	3·00	3·75

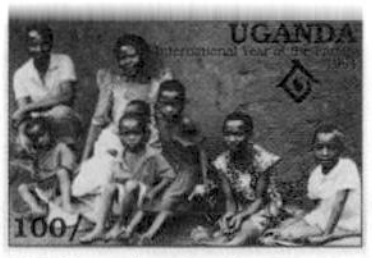

153 Ugandan family

1994. International Year of the Family.

1376	**153**	100s. multicoloured	40	20

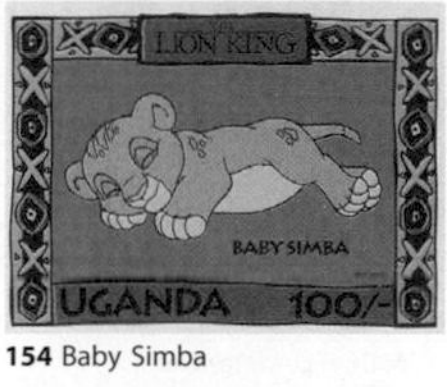

154 Baby Simba

1994. "The Lion King". Characters from Walt Disney's cartoon film. Multicoloured.

1377	100s. Type **154**	40	40
1378	100s. Mufasa, Simba and Sarabi	40	40
1379	100s. Young Simba and Nala	40	40
1380	100s. Timon	40	40
1381	100s. Rafiki	40	40
1382	100s. Pumbaa	40	40
1383	100s. The Hyenas	40	40
1384	100s. Scar	40	40
1385	100s. Zazu	40	40
1386	200s. Rafiki and Mufasa	40	40
1387	200s. Rafiki holding Simba with Mufasa and Sarabi	40	40
1388	200s. Rafiki holding Simba aloft	40	40
1389	200s. Scar and Zazu	40	40
1390	200s. Rafiki having vision	40	40
1391	200s. Simba and Scar	40	40
1392	200s. Simba and Nala	40	40
1393	200s. Simba with mane of leaves	40	40
1394	200s. Simba, Nala and Zazu	40	40
1395	250s. Scar and Simba	40	40
1396	250s. Mufasa rescues Simba	40	40
1397	250s. Scar killing Mufasa	40	40
1398	250s. Simba falling off cliff	40	40
1399	250s. Timon, Pumbaa and Simba at pool	40	40
1400	250s. Simba, Timon and Pumbaa	40	40
1401	250s. Rafiki with staff	40	40
1402	250s. Simba and Nala	40	40
1403	250s. Simba looking into pool	40	40
MS1404	Three sheets. (a) 127×94 mm. 2500s. Jungle animals. (b) 127×102 mm. 2500s. Simba and Timon on branch. (c) 127×94 mm. 2500s. Simba with parents and Rafiki (vert) Set of 3 sheets	13·00	14·00

1994. Centenary (1992) of Sierra Club (environmental protection society). Endangered Species. As T **276a** of Sierra Leone. Multicoloured

(a) Vert designs

1405	100s. Chimpanzee with arms folded	60	55
1406	200s. Head of chimpanzee	80	80
1407	250s. Head of African wild dog	80	80
1408	300s. Head of cheetah	80	90
1409	500s. Geleda baboon	90	1·00
1410	600s. Geleda baboon from back	1·00	1·10
1411	800s. Head of Grevy's zebra	1·10	1·25
1412	1000s. Geleda baboon sitting on rock	1·25	1·40

(b) Horiz designs.

1413	200s. Pair of cheetahs	80	90
1414	250s. Cheetah cubs	80	90
1415	300s. African wild dog at rest	90	1·00
1416	500s. Head of African wild dog	1·00	1·10
1417	600s. Grevy's zebra	1·10	1·25
1418	800s. Chimpanzee lying down	1·25	1·40
1419	1000s. Grevy's zebra feeding	1·40	1·50

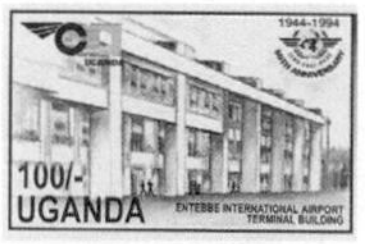

155 Terminal Building, Entebbe International Airport

1994. 50th Anniv of I.C.A.O. Multicoloured.

1420	100s. Type **155**	1·00	20
1421	250s. Control tower, Entebbe International Airport	1·75	1·25

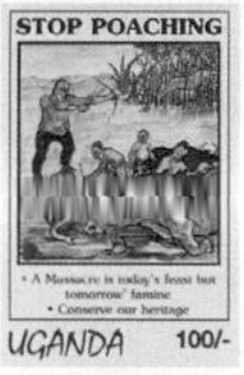

156 Game Poachers

1994. Ecology. Multicoloured.

1422	100s. Type **156**	50	10
1423	250s. Villagers at rubbish dump	90	45
1424	350s. Fishermen	1·25	1·25
1425	500s. Deforestation	1·90	2·25

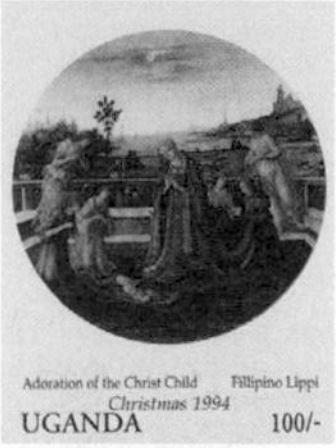

157 "Adoration of the Christ Child" (Filippino Lippi)

1994. Christmas. Religious Paintings. Multicoloured.

1426	100s. Type **157**	30	10
1427	200s. "The Holy Family rests on the Flight into Egypt" (Annibale Carracci)	50	30
1428	300s. "Madonna with Christ Child and St. John" (Piero di Cosimo)	70	40
1429	350s. "The Conestabile Madonna" (Raphael)	80	65
1430	450s. "Madonna and Child with Angels" (after Antonio Rossellino)	90	1·00
1431	500s. "Madonna and Child with St. John" (Raphael)	1·00	1·00
1432	900s. "Madonna and Child" (Luca Signorelli)	2·00	2·50
1433	1000s. "Madonna with the Child Jesus, St. John and an Angel" (pseudo Pier Francesco Fiorentino)	2·00	2·50
MS1434	Two sheets, each 115×95 mm. (a) 2500s. "The Madonna of the Magnificat" (detail) (Sandro Botticelli). (b) 2500s. "Adoration of the Magi" (detail) (Fra Angelico and Filippo Lippi) Set of 2 sheets	9·00	10·00

No. 1426 is inscribed "Fillipino" in error.

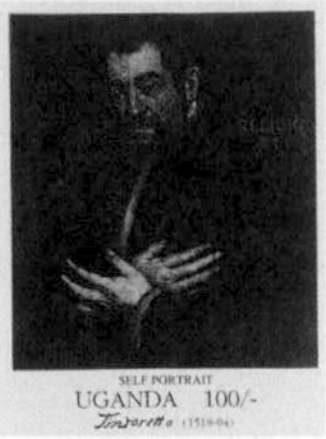

158 "Self-portrait" (Tintoretto)

1995. 400th Death Anniv (1994) of Jacopo Tintoretto (painter). Multicoloured.

1435	100s. Type **158**	40	10
1436	300s. "A Philosopher"	80	50
1437	400s. "The Creation of the Animals" (detail) (horiz)	1·00	90
1438	450s. "The Feast of Belshazzar" (detail) (horiz)	1·10	1·10
1439	500s. "The Raising of the Brazen Serpent"	1·25	1·25
1440	1000s. "Elijah fed by the Angel"	2·50	3·25
MS1441	Two sheets. (a) 114×124 mm. 2000s. "Moses striking Water from a Rock" (detail). (b) 124×114 mm. 200s. "Finding of Moses" (detail) Set of 2 sheets	8·50	9·50

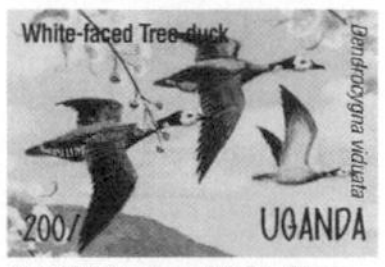

159 White-faced Whistling Duck ("White-faced Tree-duck")

1995. Waterfowl and Wetland Birds of Uganda. Multicoloured.

1442	200s. Type **159**	90	85
1443	200s. Common shoveler ("European Shoveler")	90	85
1444	200s. Hartlaub's duck	90	85
1445	200s. Verreaux's eagle owl ("Milky Eagle-owl")	90	85
1446	200s. Pied avocet ("Avocet")	90	85
1447	200s. African fish eagle	90	85
1448	200s. Spectacled weaver	90	85
1449	200s. Black-headed gonolek	90	85
1450	200s. Great crested grebe	90	85
1451	200s. Red-knobbed coot	90	85
1452	200s. Woodland kingfisher	90	85
1453	200s. Pintail	90	85
1454	200s. Squacco heron	90	85
1455	200s. Purple swamphen ("Purple Gallinule")	90	85
1456	200s. African darter	90	85
1457	200s. African jacana	90	85
MS1458	Two sheets, each 106×76 mm. (a) 2500s. African pygmy goose. (b) 2500s. Fulvous whistling duck ("Fulvous Tree-duck") Set of 2 sheets	9·00	10·00

Nos. 1442/57 were printed together, se-tenant, forming a composite design.

1995. 18th World Scout Jamboree, Netherlands. Nos. 701/4 optd or surch **18th World Scout Jamboree Mondial, Holland, August 1995.**

1459	100s. Scouts making bricks	25	10
1460	450s. on 70s. on 70s. Poultry keeping	95	55
1461	800s. on 90s. on 90s. Scout on crutches leading family to immunization centre	1·75	1·90
1462	1500s. on 10s. on 10s. Type **104**	3·00	3·50
MS1463	115×76 mm. 2500s. on 1200s. Lord Baden-Powell, W. Boyce and Revd. L. Hadley	4·25	5·00

1995. 50th Anniv of End of Second World War in Europe. As T **296a** of St. Vincent. Multicoloured.

1464	500s. Soviet artillery in action	1·40	1·25
1465	500s. Soviet tanks on the Moltke Bridge	1·40	1·25
1466	500s. Kaiser Wilhelm Memorial Church, Berlin	1·40	1·25
1467	500s. Soviet tanks and Brandenburg Gate	1·40	1·25
1468	500s. U.S. Boeing B-17 Flying Fortress	1·40	1·25
1469	500s. Soviet tanks enter Berlin	1·40	1·25
1470	500s. Ruins of the Chancellery	1·40	1·25
1471	500s. The Reichstag on fire	1·40	1·25
MS1472	104×74 mm. 2500s. Hoisting the Soviet flag on the Reichstag (57×42½ mm)	5·00	6·00

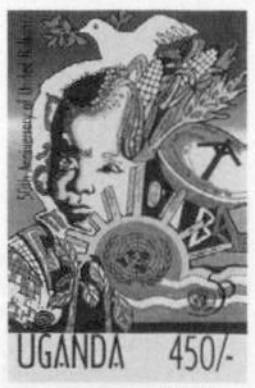

161 Dove, Child, Dish Aerial, Food and Emblem

1995. 50th Anniv of United Nations. Multicoloured.

1473	450s. Type **161**	70	50
1474	1000s. Hands releasing bird and insects	1·75	2·50
MS1475	100×70 mm. 2000s. Child's hand holding adult's finger (horiz)	2·75	3·50

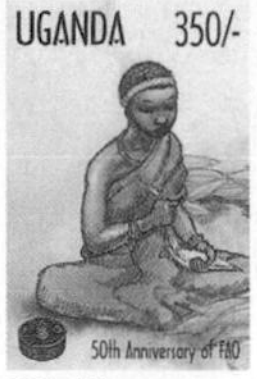

161a Woman peeling Maize

1995. 50th Anniv of F.A.O. Multicoloured.

1476	350s. Type **161a**	55	75
1477	500s. Woman and child with maize	65	85
1478	1000s. Woman and baby with maize	80	1·10
MS1479	100×70 mm. 2000s. Child and head of cow	2·50	3·25

Nos. 1476/8 were printed together, se-tenant, forming a composite design.

1995. 90th Anniv of Rotary International. As T **299** of St. Vincent, but vert. Multicoloured.

1480	2000s. Paul Harris (founder) and logo	2·00	2·75
MS1481	70×100 mm. 2000s. National flag and logo	2·25	3·00

1995. 95th Birthday of Queen Elizabeth the Queen Mother. As T **299a** of St. Vincent. Multicoloured.

1482	500s. brown, light brown and black	1·90	1·90
1483	500s. multicoloured	1·90	1·90
1484	500s. multicoloured	1·90	1·90
1485	500s. multicoloured	1·90	1·90
MS1486	102×127 mm. 2500s. multicoloured	5·50	5·50

DESIGNS: No. 1482, Queen Elizabeth the Queen Mother (pastel drawing); 1483, With bouquet of flowers; 1484, At desk (oil painting); 1485, Wearing turquoise-blue dress; **MS**1466, Wearing pale blue dress.

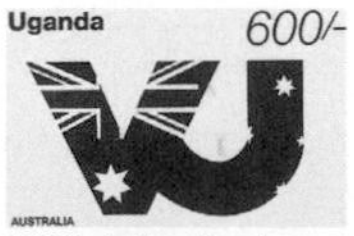

162 Australian Flag in Form of "VJ"

1995. 50th Anniv of End of Second World War in the Pacific. Designs showing national flags as "VJ".

1487	162	600s. red, violet and black	1·75	1·50
1488	-	600s. red, violet and black	1·75	1·50
1489	-	600s. red, violet and black	1·75	1·50
1490	-	600s. multicoloured	1·75	1·50
1491	-	600s. red, orange and black	1·75	1·50
1492	-	600s. red and black	1·75	1·50
MS1493		108×76 mm. 2500s. multicoloured	6·00	6·50

DESIGNS: No. 1488, Great Britain; 1489, New Zealand; 1490, United States of America; 1491, People's Republic of China; 1492, Canada; **MS**1493, American soldier and Flag.

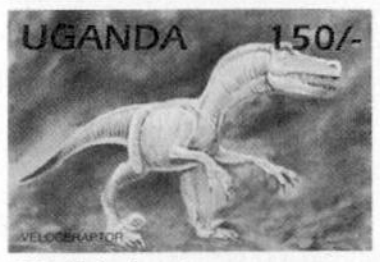

163 Velociraptor

1995. Prehistoric Animals. Multicoloured.

1494	150s. Type **163**	1·00	65
1495	200s. Head of psittacosaurus	1·00	65
1496	300s. Archaeopteryx (vert)	1·00	1·00
1497	300s. Quetzalcoatlus and volcano (vert)	1·00	1·00
1498	300s. Pteranodon and volcano (vert)	1·00	1·00
1499	300s. Brachiosaurus (vert)	1·00	1·00
1500	300s. Tsintaosaur (vert)	1·00	1·00
1501	300s. Allosaur (vert)	1·00	1·00
1502	300s. Tyrannosaurus (vert)	1·00	1·00
1503	300s. Apatosaur (vert)	1·00	1·00
1504	300s. Giant dragonfly (vert)	1·00	1·00
1505	300s. Dimorphodon (vert)	1·00	1·00
1506	300s. Triceratops (vert)	1·00	1·00
1507	300s. Compsognathus (vert)	1·00	1·00
1508	350s. Head of dilophosaurus	1·25	1·10
1509	400s. Kentrosaurus	1·40	1·25
1510	500s. Stegosaurus	1·60	1·40
1511	1500s. Pterodaustro	3·00	3·00
MS1512	Two sheets, each 106×75 mm. (a) 2000s. Head of parasaurolophus. (b) 2000s. Head of shunosaurus Set of 2 sheets	8·50	8·50
1601	350s. "Madonna" (Procaccini)	70	35

Nos. 1496/1507 were printed together, se-tenant, forming a composite design.

No. 1502 is inscribed "Tyranosaur" and No. 1506 "Tricreatops", both in error.

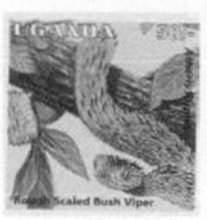

164 Rough-scaled Bush Viper

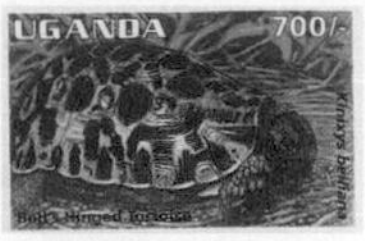

165 Bell's Hinged Tortoise

1995. Reptiles. Multicoloured.

1513	50s. Type **164**	25	10
1514	100s. Pygmy python	35	10
1515	150s. Three-horned chameleon	50	20
1516	200s. African rock python	60	20
1516a	300s. Armadillo girdled lizard	85	35
1517	350s. Nile monitor	85	35
1518	400s. Savannah monitor	1·00	40
1519	450s. Bush viper	1·00	55
1520	500s. Nile crocodile	1·00	55
1520a	600s. Spotted sandveld lizard	1·25	70
1521	700s. Type **165**	1·40	1·00
1521a	700s. Bell's hinged tortoise	1·40	1·00
1522	900s. Rhinoceros viper	1·75	1·25
1523	1000s. Gabon viper	1·75	1·40
1524	2000s. Spitting cobra	3·00	3·25
1525	3000s. Leopard tortoise	4·00	4·50
1526	4000s. Puff adder	5·00	6·00
1527	5000s. Common house gecko	6·50	7·50
1528	6000s. Dwarf chameleon	7·00	8·00
1529	10000s. Boomslang (snake)	11·00	13·00

SIZES—21×21 mm: 50, 100, 150, 200, 350, 400, 450, 500s.; 18×20 mm: 300, 600, 700s. (No. 1521a); 38½×24½ mm: 700s. (No. 1521), 900s. to 10000s.

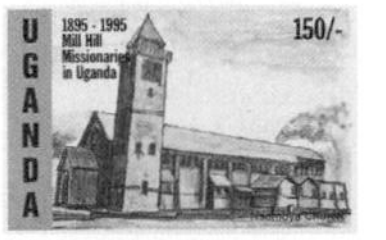

166 Nsambya Church

1995. Local Anniversaries. Multicoloured.

1530	150s. Type **166**	45	20
1531	450s. Namilyango College	90	70
1532	500s. Figures with symbolic wheel	95	75
1533	1000s. Volunteers with food sacks	1·75	2·50

ANNIVERSARIES: Nos. 1530/1, Centenary of Mill Hill Missionaries in Uganda; 1532, Centenary of International Co-operative Alliance; 1533, 25th anniv of U.N. volunteers.

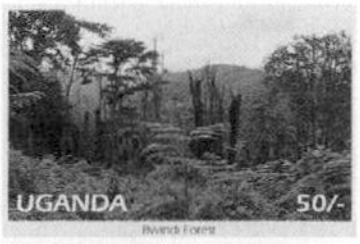

167 Bwindi Forest

1995. Landscapes. Multicoloured.

1534	50s. Type **167**	40	20
1535	100s. Karamoja	50	20
1536	450s. Sunset, Lake Mburo National Park	1·25	80
1537	500s. Sunset, Gulu District	1·25	80
1538	900s. Mist, Kabale District	2·00	2·75
1539	1000s. Ruwenzori Mountains	2·00	2·75

1995. Waterfalls. As T **167**. Multicoloured.

1540	50s. Sipi Falls (vert)	40	20
1541	100s. Murchison Falls	50	20
1542	450s. Bujagali Falls	1·25	80
1543	500s. The Two Falls at Murchison	1·25	80
1544	900s. Falls, Ruwenzori Mountains (vert)	2·00	2·75
1545	1000s. Falls, Ruwenzori Mountains (different) (vert)	2·00	2·75

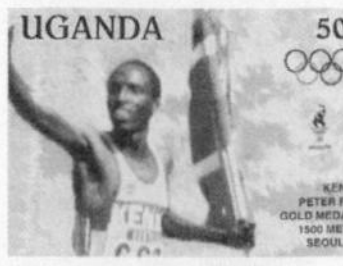

168 Peter Rono (1500 m), 1988

1995. Olympic Games, Atlanta (1996). Multicoloured.

1546	50s. Type **168**	20	10
1547	350s. Reiner Klimke (dressage), 1984	90	40
1548	450s. German team (cycling time trials), 1988	1·75	70
1549	500s. Grace Birungi (athlete)	90	70
1550	900s. Francis Ogola (athlete)	1·40	1·75
1551	1000s. Nyakana Godfrey (boxer)	1·50	1·75
MS1552	Two sheets, each 106×76 mm. (a) 2500s. Sebastian Coe (1500 metres), 1980 and 1984. (b) 2500s. Rolf Dannenberg (discus), 1984 (vert) Set of 2 sheets	7·00	8·00

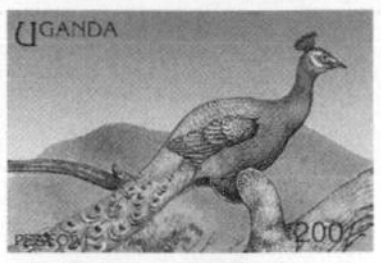

169 Common Peafowl ("Peafowl")

1995. Domestic Animals. Multicoloured.

1553	200s. Type **169**	80	70
1554	200s. Pouter pigeon	80	70
1555	200s. Feral rock dove ("Rock Doves")	80	70
1556	200s. Mallard ("Rouen Duck")	80	70
1557	200s. Guineafowl	80	70
1558	200s. Donkey	80	70
1559	200s. Shetland ponies	80	70
1560	200s. Palomino horse	80	70
1561	200s. Pigs	80	70
1562	200s. Border collie	80	70
1563	200s. Merino sheep	80	70
1564	200s. Milch goat	80	70
1565	200s. Black dutch rabbit	80	70
1566	200s. Lop rabbit	80	70
1567	200s. Somali cat	80	70
1568	200s. Asian cat	80	70
MS1569	Two sheets, each 106×76 mm. (a) 2500s. Saddle-bred horses. (b) 2500s. Oxen Set of 2 sheets	10·00	9·00

Nos. 1553/68 were printed together, se-tenant, forming a composite design.

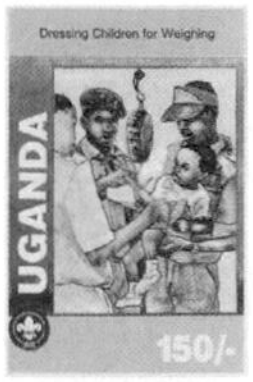

170 Scouts putting Child on Scales

1995. Uganda Boy Scouts in the Community. Multicoloured.

1570	150s. Type **170**	50	20
1571	350s. Scouts carrying children	85	45
1572	450s. Checking health cards (horiz)	95	70
1573	800s. Holding child for immunization (horiz)	1·75	2·00
1574	1000s. Weighing child before immunization	1·90	2·25

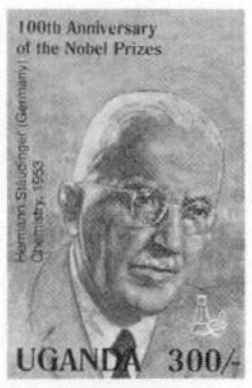

171 Hermann Staudinger (1953 Chemistry)

1995. Centenary of Nobel Prize Trust Fund. Multicoloured.

1575	300s. Type **171**	90	80
1576	300s. Fritz Haber (1918 Chemistry)	90	80
1577	300s. Bert Sakmann (1991 Medicine)	90	80
1578	300s. Adolf Windaus (1926 Chemistry)	90	80
1579	300s. Wilhelm Wien (1911 Physics)	90	80
1580	300s. Ernest Hemingway (1954 Literature)	90	80
1581	300s. Richard Willstatter (1915 Chemistry)	90	80

1582	300s. Stanley Cohen (1986 Medicine)	90	80
1583	300s. Hans Jensen (1963 Physics)	90	80
1584	300s. Otto Warburg (1931 Medicine)	90	80
1585	300s. Heinrich Wieland (1927 Chemistry)	90	80
1586	300s. Albrecht Kossel (1910 Medicine)	90	80
1587	300s. Hideki Yukawa (1949 Physics)	90	80
1588	300s. F. W. de Klerk (1993 Peace)	90	80
1589	300s. Nelson Mandela (1993 Peace)	90	80
1590	300s. Odysseus Elytis (1979 Literature)	90	80
1591	300s. Ferdinand Buisson (1927 Peace)	90	80
1592	300s. Lev Landau (1962 Physics)	90	80
1593	300s. Halldor Laxness (1955 Literature)	90	80
1594	300s. Wole Soyinka (1986 Literature)	90	80
1595	300s. Desmond Tutu (1984 Peace)	90	80
1596	300s. Susumu Tonegawa (1987 Medicine)	90	80
1597	300s. Louis de Broglie (1929 Physics)	90	80
1598	300s. George Seferis (1963 Literature)	90	80
MS1599	Two sheets, each 105×76 mm. (a) 2000s. Nelley Sachs (1966 Literature). (b) 2000s. Werner Forssmann (1956 Medicine) Set of 2 sheets	9·00	9·50

Nos. 1575/86 and 1587/98 respectively were printed together, se-tenant, forming composite designs.

1995. Christmas. Religious Paintings. As T **281a** of Sierra Leone. Multicoloured.

1600	150s. "The Virgin and Child" (Holbein the Younger)	40	20
1603	1000s. "Madonna and Child" (Crivelli)	1·75	2·00
1604	1500s. "The Nativity of the Virgin" (Le Nain)	2·25	3·00
MS1605	Two sheets, each 102×127 mm. (a) 2500s. "Madonna and Child" (detail) (Bellini). (b) 2500s. "The Holy Family" (detail) (Andrea del Sarto) Set of 2 sheets	8·50	8·50

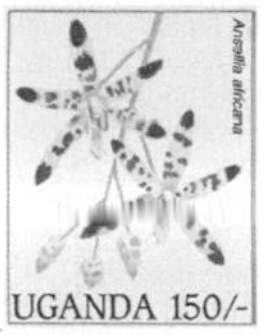

172 "Ansellia africana"

1995. Orchids. Multicoloured.

1606	150s. Type **172**	60	40
1607	350s. "Aerangis iuteoalba"	75	75
1608	350s. "Satyrium sacculatum"	75	75
1609	350s. "Bolusiella maudiae"	75	75
1610	350s. "Habenaria attenuata"	75	75
1611	350s. "Cyrtorchis arcuata"	75	75
1612	350s. "Eulophia angolensis"	75	75
1613	350s. "Tridactyle bicaudata"	75	75
1614	350s. "Eulophia horsfallii"	75	75
1615	350s. "Diaphananthe fragrantissima"	75	75
1616	450s. "Satyricum crassicaule"	85	85
1617	500s. "Polystachya cultriformis"	90	90
1618	800s. "Disa erubescens"	1·40	1·60
MS1619	Two sheets, each 66×76 mm. (a) 2500s. "Rangaeris amaniensis". (b) 2500s. "Diaphananthe pulchella" Set of 2 sheets	8·50	9·00

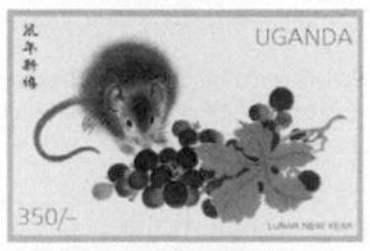

173 Rat and Purple Grapes

1996. Chinese New Year ("Year of the Rat"). Multicoloured.

1620	350s. Type **173**	60	65
1621	350s. Rat and radishes	60	65
1622	350s. Rat eating corn	60	65
1623	350s. Rat eating cucumber	60	65
MS1624	100×74 mm. Nos. 1620/3	1·25	1·60
MS1625	106×76 mm. 2000s. Rat and green grapes	3·00	3·50

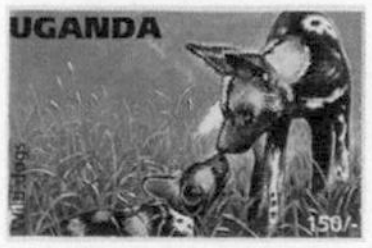

174 Wild Dog and Pup

1996. Wildlife of Uganda. Multicoloured.

(a) Horiz designs

1626	150s. Type **174**	55	55
1627	200s. African fish eagle	60	60
1628	250s. Hippopotamus	65	60
1629	350s. Leopard	60	60
1630	400s. Lion	65	65
1631	450s. Lioness	70	70
1632	500s. Meerkats	75	80
1633	550s. Pair of black rhinoceroses	1·00	1·00

(b) Vert designs.

1634	150s. Gorilla	50	50
1635	200s. Cheetah	50	55
1636	250s. African elephant	70	60
1637	350s. Thomson's gazelle	60	60
1638	400s. Crowned crane	80	80
1639	450s. Saddlebill	80	80
1640	500s. Vulture	80	80
1641	550s. Zebra	80	85
MS1642	Two sheets. (a) 72×102 mm. 200s. Grey heron (horiz). (b) 102×72 mm. 2000s. Giraffe Set of 2 sheets	7·00	8·00

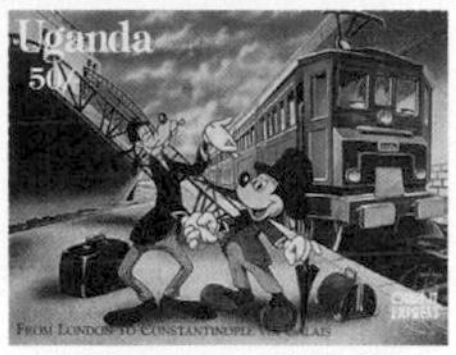

175 Mickey Mouse and Goofy on Platform at Calais

1996. Mickey's Orient Express. Walt Disney Cartoon Characters. Multicoloured.

1643	50s. Type **175**	35	30
1644	100s. Mickey and Goofy at Athens	45	30
1645	150s. Mickey showing Donald Duck his Pullman ticket	60	30
1646	200s. Daisy and Donald Duck in Pullman car	75	30
1647	250s. Mickey and Minnie Mouse in dining car	80	40
1648	300s. Goofy as guard assisting Mickey and Minnie	90	50
1649	600s. Mickey and Donald preparing for bed	1·75	2·00
1650	700s. Mickey and Minnie at Orient Express accident, Frankfurt, 1901	1·90	2·25
1651	800s. Mickey and Goofy building snowman and Orient Express in snowdrift, 1929	2·00	2·25
1652	900s. Disney characters filming "Murder on the Orient Express"	2·25	2·50
MS1653	Two sheets, each 132×106 mm. (a) 2500s. Donald driving Orient Express. (b) 2500s. Mickey, Minnie and Goofy on Observation platform Set of 2 sheets	9·50	11·00

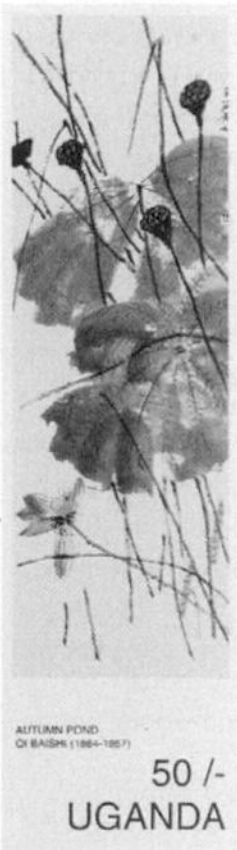

176 "Autumn Pond"

1996. "CHINA '96" Ninth Asian International Stamp Exhibition, Peking. Paintings by Qi Baishi. Multicoloured.

1654	50s. Type **176**	45	45
1655	100s. "Partridge and Smartweed"	60	60
1656	150s. "Begonias and Mynah"	70	70
1657	200s. "Chrysanthemums, Cocks and Hens"	70	70
1658	250s. "Crabs"	70	70
1659	300s. "Wisterias and Bee"	75	75
1660	350s. "Smartweed and Ink-drawn Butterflies"	80	80
1661	400s. "Lotus and Mandarin Ducks"	85	85
1662	450s. "Lichees and Locust"	90	90
1663	500s. "Millet and Praying Mantis"	95	95
MS1664	135×114 mm. 800s. "Morning Glories and Locust" (50×38 mm); 800s. "Shrimps" (50×38 mm)	7·50	7·50

The painting titles on 150s. and 200s. are transposed in error, with "CHRYSANTHEMUMS" shown as "RYSANTHEMUMS".

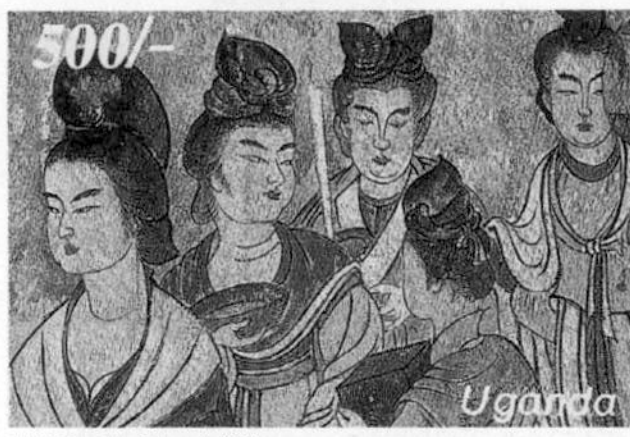

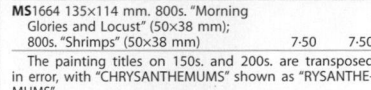

177 Tomb Mural, Xi'an

1996. "CHINA '96" Ninth Asian International Stamp Exhibition, Peking (2nd issue). Sheet 140×90 mm.

MS1664a	**177** 500s. multicoloured	2·25	2·25

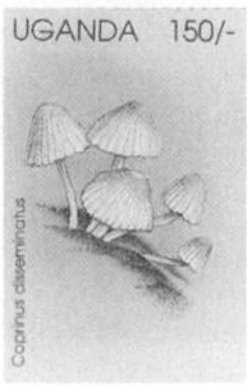

178 "Coprinus disseminatus"

1996. African Fungi. Multicoloured.

1665	150s. Type **178**	50	50
1666	300s. "Coprinus radians"	60	60
1667	350s. "Hygrophorus coccineus"	60	60
1668	400s. "Marasmius siccus"	70	70
1669	450s. "Cortinarius collinitus"	80	80
1670	500s. "Cortinarius cinnabarinus"	80	80
1671	550s. "Coltricia cinnamomea"	85	90
1672	1000s. "Mutinus elegans"	1·50	1·75
MS1673	Two sheets, each 110×80 mm. (a) 2500s. "Inocybe sororia". (b) 2500s. "Flammulina velutipes" Set of 2 sheets	6·50	7·00

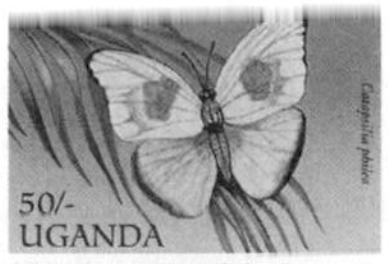

179 "Catopsilia philea"

1996. Butterflies. Multicoloured.

1674	50s. Type **179**	50	50
1675	100s. "Dione vanillae"	50	50
1676	150s. "Metamorpha dido"	65	65
1677	200s. "Papilio sesostris"	70	70
1678	250s. "Papilio neophilus"	75	75
1679	300s. "Papilio thoas"	75	75
1680	350s. "Diorina periander"	75	75
1681	400s. "Morpho cipris"	75	75
1682	450s. "Catonephele numilia"	80	80
1683	500s. "Heliconius doris"	80	80
1684	550s. "Prepona antimache"	80	80
1685	600s. "Eunica alcmena"	80	80
MS1686	Two sheets, each 100×70 mm. (a) 2500s. "Caligo martia" (b) 2500s. "Heliconius doris" (different) Set of 2 sheets	6·50	7·00

1996. 70th Birthday of Queen Elizabeth II. As T **323a** of St. Vincent. Different photographs. Multicoloured.

1687	500s. Queen Elizabeth II	1·40	1·40
1688	500s. In evening dress	1·40	1·40
1689	500s. Wearing red coat and hat	1·40	1·40
MS1690	125×103 mm. 2000s. Queen Elizabeth II	5·00	4·50

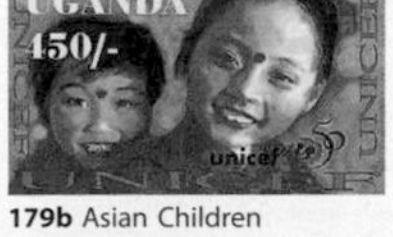

179b Asian Children

1996. 50th Anniv of UNICEF. Multicoloured.

1691	450s. Type **179b**	1·00	1·10
1692	500s. South American children	1·25	1·40
1693	550s. Boy holding pencil	1·40	1·60
MS1694	74×104 mm. 2000s. African mother and child	3·50	4·25

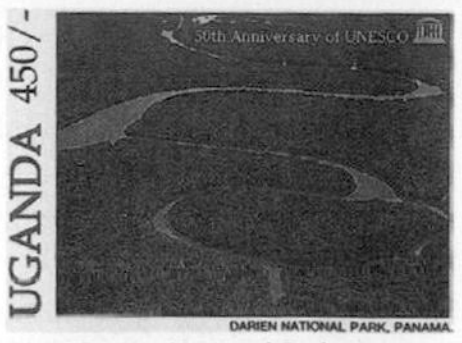

179c Darien National Park, Panama

1996. 50th Anniv of UNESCO. Multicoloured.

1695	450s. Type **179c**	1·40	1·40
1696	500s. Los Glaciares National Park, Argentina	1·50	1·50
1697	550s. Tubbatha Reef Marine Park, Philippines	1·60	1·60
MS1698	104×74 mm. 2500s. Ruwenzori Mountains National Park, Uganda	4·25	5·50

No. **MS**1698 is inscribed "RWENZORI" in error.

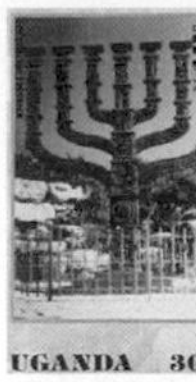

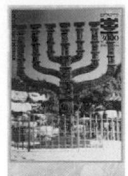

180 Statue of Menorah, Knesset

1996. 3000th Anniv of Jerusalem. T **180** and similar vert designs. Multicoloured.

MS1699	114×95 mm. 300s. Type **180**, 500s. Jerusalem Theatre. 1000s. Israel Museum	5·00	4·50
MS1700	104×74 mm. 2000s. Grotto of the Nativity	5·00	4·50

1996. Centenary of Radio. Entertainers. As T **326** of St. Vincent. Multicoloured.

1701	200s. Ella Fitzgerald	35	20
1702	300s. Bob Hope	90	40
1703	500s. Nat "King" Cole	90	70
1704	800s. George Burns and Gracie Allen	1·25	1·75
MS1705	74×104 mm. 2000s. Jimmy Durante	3·00	3·50

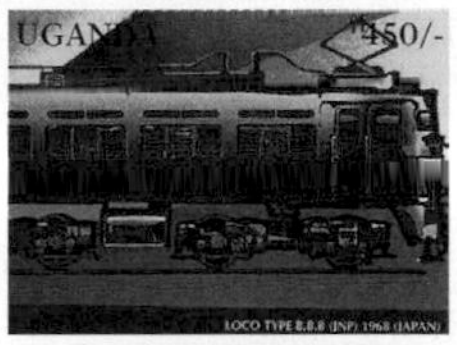

181 Electric Locomotive, 1968 (Japan)

1996. Railway Locomotives. Multicoloured.

1706	450s. Type **181**	1·00	1·00
1707	450s. Stephenson's "Rocket", 1829	1·00	1·00
1708	450s. William Norris's "Austria", 1843	1·00	1·00
1709	450s. Early American steam locomotive	1·00	1·00
1710	450s. Steam locomotive, 1947 (India)	1·00	1·00
1711	450s. Class 103 electric locomotive (Germany)	1·00	1·00
1712	550s. GWR steam locomotive "Lady of Lynn" (England)	1·00	1·00
1713	550s. Steam locomotive, 1930 (China)	1·00	1·00
1714	550s. Meyer-Kitson steam locomotive (Chile)	1·00	1·00
1715	550s. Union Pacific "Centennial" diesel locomotive No. 6900 (U.S.A.)	1·00	1·00
1716	550s. Type 581 diesel locomotive (Japan)	1·00	1·00
1717	550s. Class 120 electric locomotive (Germany)	1·00	1·00
MS1718	Two sheets, each 106×76 mm. (a) 2500s. Type 99 steam locomotive (Germany); (b) 2500s. LNER Class A4 steam locomotive "Mallard", Great Britain Set of 2 sheets	8·00	8·50

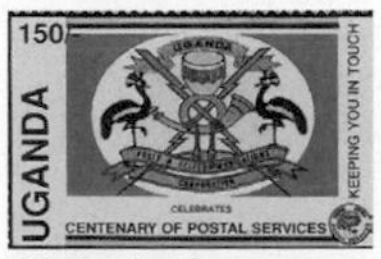

182 Postal and Telecommunications Corporation Emblem

1996. Centenary of Postal Services. Multicoloured.

1719	150s. Type **182**	25	20
1720	450s. Loading postbus	2·00	1·75
1721	500s. Modern postal transportation	2·25	2·00
1722	550s. 1896 25c. violet and 1r. black stamps	2·25	2·25

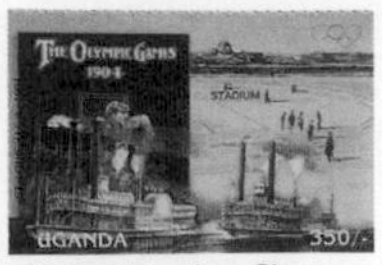

183 Two American River Steamers and 1904 Games, St. Louis

1996. Olympic Games, Atlanta (1st issue). Multicoloured.
1723 350s. Type **183** 90 45
1724 450s. George Finnegan (U.S.A.) (boxing), 1904 95 75
1725 500s. Chariot racing 1·10 95
1726 800s. John Flanagan (U.S.A.) (hammer), 1904 (vert) 1·75 3·00
See also Nos. 1764/81.

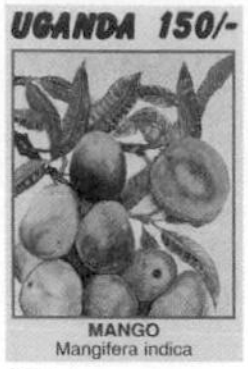

184 Mango

1996. Fruit. Multicoloured.
1727 150s. Type **184** 55 20
1728 350s. Orange 1·10 50
1729 450s. Pawpaw 1·25 1·10
1730 500s. Avocado 1·40 1·25
1731 550s. Watermelon (horiz) 1·75 2·50

1996. Christmas. Religious Paintings. As T **337** of St. Vincent. Multicoloured.
1732 150s. "Annunciation" (Lorenzo di Credi) 60 20
1733 350s. "Madonna of the Loggia" (detail) (Botticelli) 1·10 40
1734 400s. "Virgin in Glory with Child and Angels" (Lorenzetti) 1·25 75
1735 450s. "Adoration of the Child" (Lippi) 1·40 1·25
1736 500s. "Madonna of the Loggia" (Botticelli) 1·50 1·50
1737 550s. "The Strength" (Botticelli) 1·60 2·00
MS1738 Two sheets, each 106×76 mm. (a) 2500s. "Holy Allegory" (Bellini) (horiz); (b) 2500s. "The Virgin on the Throne with Child and the Saints" (ghirlandaio) (horiz) Set of 2 sheets 10·00 11·00

1996. 20th Anniv of "Rocky" (film). Sheet 143×182 mm, containing vert design as T **338** of St. Vincent. Multicoloured.
MS1739 800s.×3 Sylvester Stallone in "Rocky III" 4·00 5·00

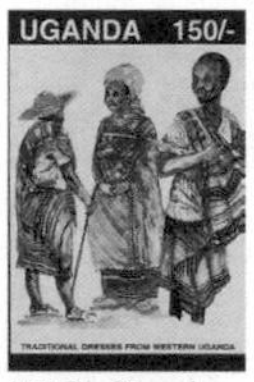

185 Traditional Costumes from Western Uganda

1997. Traditional Costumes. Multicoloured.
1740 150s. Type **185** 55 30
1741 300s. Acholi headdress 1·00 1·00
1742 300s. Alur headdress 1·00 1·00
1743 300s. Bwola dance headdress 1·00 1·00
1744 300s. Madi headdress 1·00 1·00
1745 300s. Karimojong headdress with plume 1·00 1·00
1746 300s. Karimojong headdress with two feathers 1·00 1·00
1747 350s. Karimojong women 1·00 1·00
1748 450s. Ganda traditional dress (horiz) 1·10 1·10
1749 500s. Acholi traditional dress (horiz) 1·25 1·50

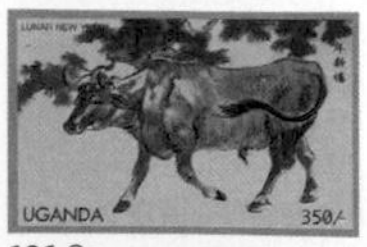

186 Ox

1997. Chinese New Year ("Year of the Ox"). Multicoloured.
1750 350s. Type **186** 1·00 1·00
1751 350s. Cow suckling calf 1·00 1·00
1752 350s. Cow and calf lying down 1·00 1·00
1753 350s. Ox lying down 1·00 1·00
MS1754 111×83 mm. Nos. 1750/3 3·50 3·75
MS1755 76×106 mm. 1500s. Young calf (vert) 3·50 3·75

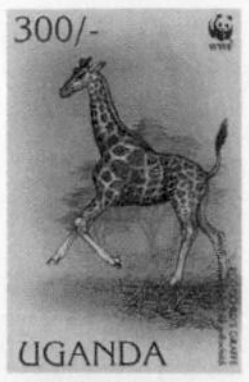

187 Giraffe running

1997. Endangered Species. Rothschild's Giraffe. Multicoloured.
1756 300s. Type **187** 90 90
1757 300s. Two adult giraffes 90 90
1758 300s. Head of giraffe 90 90
1759 300s. Giraffe with calf 90 90
MS1760 75×109 mm. 2500s. Head of giraffe (different) (horiz) 5·00 5·00

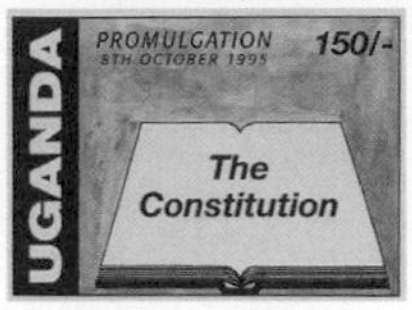

188 "The Constitution" on Open Book

1997. Promulgation of New Constitution (8 Oct 1995). Multicoloured.
1761 150s. Type **188** 50 20
1762 350s. "The Constitution" on scroll 85 60
1763 550s. "THE CONSTITUTION" on closed book (vert) 1·40 2·00

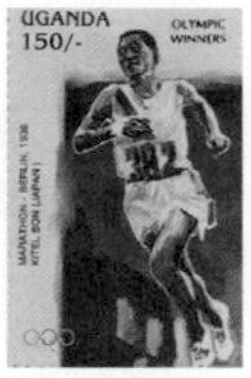

189 Kitel Son (Japan) (marathon), 1936

1997. Olympic Games, Atlanta (2nd issue). Previous Gold Medal Winners. Multicoloured.
1764 150s. Type **189** 60 70
1765 150s. Bob Hayes (U.S.A.) (100 m), 1964 60 70
1766 200s. Walter Davis (U.S.A.) (high jump), 1952 65 75
1767 200s. Rod Milburn (110 m hurdles), 1972 65 75
1768 250s. Matthes (swimming), 1968 70 80
1769 250s. Filbert Bayi (Tanzania) (athletics), 1976 70 80
1770 300s. Akii Bua (Uganda) (400 m hurdles), 1972 75 85
1771 300s. H. Kipchoge Keino (Kenya) (steeplechase), 1972 75 85
1772 350s. Nordwig (Germany) (pole vault), 1972 80 90
1773 350s. Ron Ray (U.S.A.) (athletics), 1976 80 90
1774 400s. Wilma Rudolph (U.S.A.) (100 m relay), 1960 80 90
1775 400s. Joe Frazer (U.S.A.) (boxing), 1976 80 90
1776 450s. Abebe Bikila (Ethiopia) (marathon), 1964 85 95
1777 450s. Carl Lewis (U.S.A.) (100 m), 1984 85 95
1778 500s. Edwin Moses (U.S.A.) (400 m hurdles), 1984 90 1·00
1779 500s. Gisela Mauermayer (Germany) (discus), 1936 90 1·00
1780 550s. Rady Williams (U.S.A.) (long jump), 1972 90 1·00
1781 550s. Dietmar Mogenburg (Germany) (high jump), 1984 90 1·00

Nos. 1764, 1766, 1768, 1770, 1772, 1774, 1776, 1778 and 1780 and 1765, 1767, 1769, 1771, 1773, 1775, 1777, 1779 and 1781 respectively were printed together, se-tenant, with the backgrounds forming composite designs.

No. 1769 is incorrectly inscribed "Eiilbert" and is dated "1976"; Filbert Bayi did not participate in the 1976 Games. No. 1779 is incorrectly inscribed "Mauemayer" and wrongly identifies the event as the shotput.

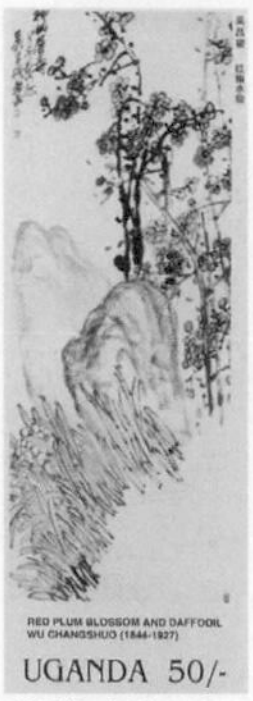

190 "Red Plum Blossom and Daffodil"

1997. "HONG KONG '97" International Stamp Exhibition. Paintings by Wu Changshuo. Multicoloured.
1782 50s. Type **190** 45 50
1783 100s. "Peony" 55 60
1784 150s. "Rosaceae" 60 65
1785 200s. "Pomegranate" 65 70
1786 250s. "Peach, Peony and Plum Blossom" 65 70
1787 300s. "Calyx Canthus" 65 70
1788 350s. "Chrysanthemum" 65 70
1789 400s. "Calabash" 70 75
1790 450s. "Chrysanthemum" (different) 70 75
1791 500s. "Cypress Tree" 70 75
MS1792 137×105 mm. 550s. "Litchi" (50×37 mm); 1000s. "Water Lily" (50×37 mm). 2·50 3·00

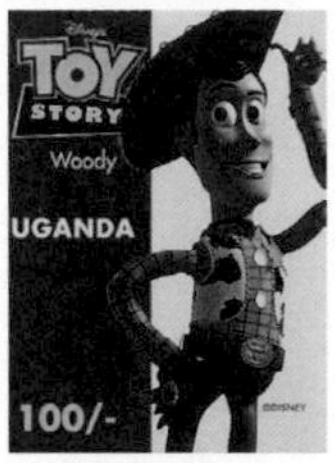

191 Woody

1997. Disney's "Toy Story" (cartoon film). Multicoloured.
1793 100s. Type **191** 55 55
1794 100s. Buzz Lightyear 55 55
1795 100s. Bo Peep 55 55
1796 100s. Hamm 55 55
1797 100s. Slinky 55 55
1798 100s. Rex 55 55
1799 150s. Woody on bed (horiz) 65 65
1800 150s. Woody at microphone (horiz) 65 65
1801 150s. Bo Peep (horiz) 65 65
1802 150s. Buzz Lightyear (horiz) 65 65
1803 150s. Slinky and Rex (horiz) 65 65
1804 150s. Woody hiding (horiz) 65 65
1805 150s. "Halt! Who goes there" (horiz) 65 65
1806 150s. Rex, Slinky and Buzz Lightyear (horiz) 65 65
1807 150s. "You're just an action figure!" (horiz) 65 65
1808 200s. "I'm the only sheriff in these parts" (horiz) 65 65
1809 200s. Green toy soldiers (horiz) 65 65
1810 200s. Woody and Buzz (horiz) 65 65
1811 200s. Woody pointing (horiz) 65 65
1812 200s. Buzz Lightyear (horiz) 65 65
1813 200s. Green aliens (horiz) 65 65
1814 200s. "This is an intergalactic emergency" (horiz) 65 65
1815 200s. Buzz and Woody argue (horiz) 65 65
1816 200s. Buzz and Woody in buggy (horiz) 65 65
MS1817 Three sheets, each 133×108 mm. (a) 133×108 mm. 2000s. Woody; (b) 108×133 mm. 2000s. Buzz Lightyear, Rex and other toys; (c) 2000s. Buzz Lightyear Set of 3 sheets 15·00 15·00

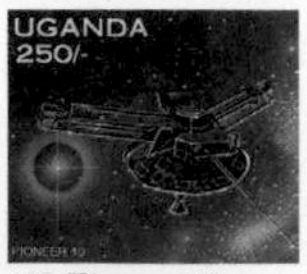

192 "Pioneer 10"

1997. Space Exploration. Multicoloured.
1818 250s. Type **192** 1·25 1·00
1819 250s. "Voyager 1" 1·25 1·00
1820 250s. "Viking Orbiter" 1·25 1·00
1821 250s. "Pioneer – Venus 1" 1·25 1·00
1822 250s. "Mariner 9" 1·25 1·00
1823 250s. "Galileo" Entry Probe 1·25 1·00
1824 250s. "Mariner 10" 1·25 1·00
1825 250s. "Voyager 2" 1·25 1·00
1826 300s. "Sputnik 1" 1·25 1·00
1827 300s. "Apollo" spacecraft 1·25 1·00
1828 300s. "Soyuz" spacecraft 1·25 1·00
1829 300s. "Intelsat 1" 1·25 1·00
1830 300s. Manned manoeuvring Unit 1·25 1·00
1831 300s. "Skylab" 1·25 1·00
1832 300s. "Telstar 1" 1·25 1·00
1833 300s. Hubble Telescope 1·25 1·00
MS1834 Two sheets, each 103×73 mm. (a) 2000s. Space Shuttle *Challenger* (35×61 mm). (b) 2000s. "Viking Lander" on Mars (61×35 mm) Set of 2 sheets 9·00 8·50

Nos. 1818/25 and 1826/33 respectively were printed together, se-tenant, with the backgrounds forming composite designs.

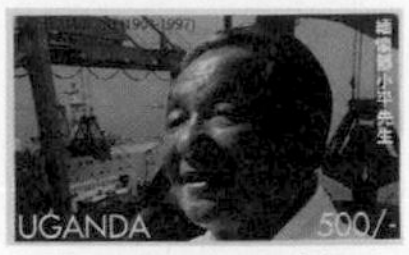

193 Deng Xiaoping and Port

1997. Deng Xiaoping (Chinese statesman) Commemoration.
1835 **193** 500s. multicoloured 1·25 1·25
1836 **193** 550s. multicoloured 1·25 1·25
1837 **193** 1000s. multicoloured 2·25 2·50
MS1838 100×70 mm. 200s. multicoloured (Deng Xiaoping and Shenzhen) 3·25 3·75

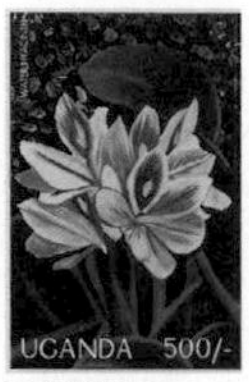

194 Water Hyacinth and Pebbles

1997. Environmental Protection. Multicoloured.
1839 500s. Water hyacinth and Lake Victoria (inscr at top left) 1·50 1·25
1840 500s. Water hyacinth and Lake Victoria (inscr at top right) 1·50 1·25
1841 500s. Type **194** 1·50 1·25
1842 500s. Larger clump of water hyacinth and pebbles 1·50 1·25
1843 550s. Buffalo 1·50 1·25
1844 550s. Uganda kob 1·50 1·25
1845 550s. Vulturine guineafowl ("Guinea Fowl") 1·50 1·25
1846 550s. Marabou stork 1·50 1·25
MS1847 106×76 mm. 2500s. Gorilla 6·00 5·50

Nos. 1839/42 and 1843/6 respectively were printed together, se-tenant, with the backgrounds forming composite designs.

No. 1845 is inscribed "GUINEA FOWEL" and No. 1846 "MALIBU STORK", both in error.

1997. Tenth Anniv of Chernobyl Nuclear Disaster. As T **347** of St. Vincent.
1848 500s. As Type **347** of St. Vincent 1·50 1·25
1849 700s. As No. 1848 but inscribed "CHABAD'S CHILDREN OF CHERNOBYL" at foot 2·25 2·25

1997. 50th Death Anniv of Paul Harris (founder of Rotary International). As T **347a** of St. Vincent. Multicoloured.
1850 1000s. Paul Harris and child drinking 2·50 3·00
MS1851 78×107 mm. 2500s. The first Rotarians 3·00 3·75

1997. Golden Wedding of Queen Elizabeth and Prince Philip. As T **347b** of St. Vincent. Multicoloured.
1852 200s. Queen Elizabeth II 1·10 1·25
1853 200s. Royal coat of arms 1·10 1·25
1854 200s. Queen Elizabeth and Prince Philip at reception 1·10 1·25
1855 200s. Queen Elizabeth and Prince Philip on royal visit 1·10 1·25
1856 200s. Buckingham Palace 1·10 1·25
1857 200s. Prince Philip in military uniform 1·10 1·25
MS1858 100×70 mm. 2000s. Princess Elizabeth in wedding dress 3·25 3·50

1997. "Pacific '97" International Stamp Exhibition, San Francisco. Death Centenary of Heinrich von Stephan (founder of the U.P.U.). As T **347c** of St. Vincent.
1859 800s. blue 1·10 1·25
1860 800s. brown 1·10 1·25
1861 800s. green 1·10 1·25
MS1862 82×119 mm. 2500s. deep blue and blue 3·25 3·75

DESIGNS: No. 1859, Chinese post boat; 1860, Von Stephan and Mercury; 1861, Russian post cart; **MS**1862, Von Stephan and French postman on stilts.

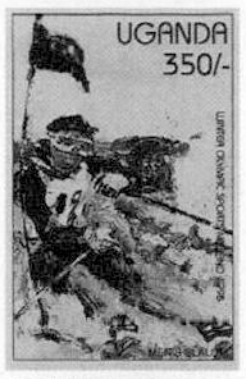

195 Men's Slalom

1997. Winter Olympic Games, Nagano, Japan (1998). Multicoloured.

1863	350s. Type **195**	50	35
1864	450s. Two-man bobsled	60	45
1865	500s. Ski jumping (horiz)	70	75
1866	500s. Giant slalom (horiz)	70	75
1867	500s. Cross-country skiing (horiz)	70	75
1868	500s. Ice hockey (horiz)	70	75
1869	500s. Pairs figure skating (man) (horiz)	70	75
1870	500s. Pairs figure skating (woman) (horiz)	70	75
1871	800s. Women's slalom (horiz)	1·10	1·25
1872	2000s. Men's speed skating (horiz)	2·25	3·00
MS1873	Two sheets, each 103×72 mm. (a) 2500s. Downhill skiing (horiz). (b) 2500s. Women's figure skating (horiz) Set of 2 sheets	6·50	7·50

Nos. 1865/70 were printed together, *se-tenant*, with the backgrounds forming a composite design.

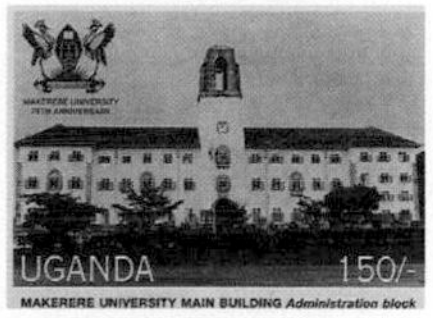

196 Main Building, Makerere University

1997. 75th Anniv of Makerere University. Multicoloured.

1874	150s. Type **196**	40	20
1875	450s. East African School of Librarianship building (vert)	80	90
1876	500s. Buyana Stock Farm, Makerere University	90	1·00
[illegible]	[illegible] of Architecture and Fine Arts	1·00	3·25

1997. World Cup Football Championship, France (1998). As T **351a** of St. Vincent. Multicoloured (except Nos. 1878, 1880, 1883 and 1886).

1878	200s. Fritz Walter, Germany (brown)	50	50
1879	250s. Paulo Rossi (horiz)	50	50
1880	250s. Mario Kempes (black) (horiz)	50	50
1881	250s. Gerd Muller (horiz)	50	50
1882	250s. Grzegorz Lato (horiz)	50	50
1883	250s. Joseph Gaetjens (black) (horiz)	50	50
1884	250s. Eusebio Ferreira da Silva (horiz)	50	50
1885	250s. Salvatore Schillaci (horiz)	50	50
1886	250s. Leonidas da Silva (black) (horiz)	50	50
1887	250s. Gary Lineker (horiz)	50	50
1888	250s. Argentine and West German player chasing ball (horiz)	50	50
1889	250s. Azteca Stadium (horiz)	50	50
1890	250s. Maradona holding World Cup (horiz)	50	50
1891	250s. Argentine and West German players with goalkeeper (horiz)	50	50
1892	250s. West German player tackling Argentine player (horiz)	50	50
1893	250s. Ball in back of net (horiz)	50	50
1894	250s. Argentine team (horiz)	50	50
1895	250s. Players competing to head ball (horiz)	50	50
1896	300s. Daniel Pasarella, Argentina	55	55
1897	450s. Dino Zoff, Italy	70	70
1898	500s. Bobby Moore, England	80	80
1899	550s. Franz Beckenbaur, West Germany	85	90
1900	600s. Diego Maradona, Argentina	90	1·10
MS1901	Two sheets. (a) 102×127 mm. 2000s. Celebrating West German players, 1990 (horiz). (b) 127×102 mm. 2000s. Bobby Moore, 1966 (horiz) Set of 2 sheets	5·50	7·50

No. 1883 is inscribed "ADEMIR" in error.

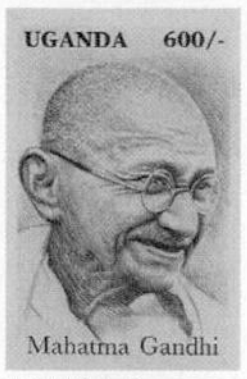

197 Mahatma Gandhi

1997. 50th Death Anniv of Mahatma Gandhi (1998) (1st issue).

1902	**197**	600s. brown and black	2·50	2·00
1903	-	700s. brown and black	2·50	2·00
MS1904		73×103 mm. 1000s. multicoloured	5·50	4·50

DESIGNS: 700s., 1000s. Different portait.

See also Nos. 2021/2.

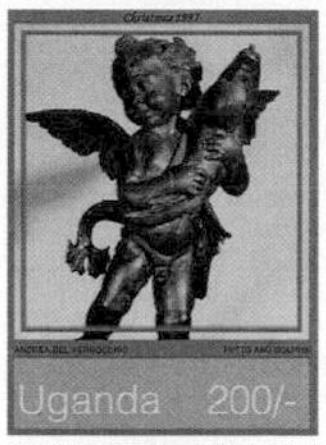

198 "Cupid and Dolphin" (Andrea del Verrocchio)

1997. Christmas. Paintings and Sculptures. Multicoloured.

1905	200s. Type **198**	50	20
1906	300s. "The Fall of the Rebel Angels" (Pieter Brueghel the Elder)	70	30
1907	400s. "The Immaculate Conception" (Bartolome Murillo)	85	50
1908	500s. "Music-making Angel" (Rosso Fiorentino)	90	80
1909	600s. "Cupid and Psyche" (Adolphe-William Bouguereau)	1·00	1·25
1910	700s. "Cupid and Psyche" (Antonio Canova)	1·25	1·75
MS1911	Two sheets, each 105×96 mm. (a) 2500s. Mary and Angels (detail, "The Assumption of the Virgin") (El Greco) (horiz). (b) 2500s. Angel holding baby (detail, "The Assumption of the Virgin") (El Greco) (horiz) Set of 2 sheets	6·00	8·00

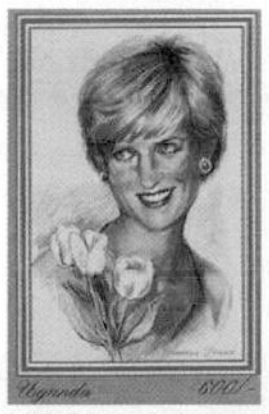

199 Diana, Princess of Wales

1997. Diana, Princess of Wales Commemoration.

1912	**199**	600s. multicoloured	1·25	1·40

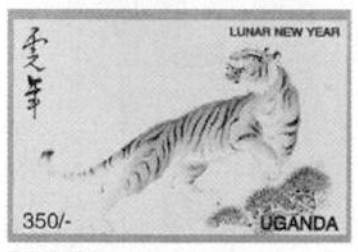

200 Tiger

1998. Chinese New Year ("Year of the Tiger"). Multicoloured.

1913	350s. Type **200**	75	75
1914	350s. Tiger leaping	75	75
1915	350s. Tiger resting	75	75
1916	350s. Tiger yawning	75	75
MS1917	106×76 mm. 1500s. Tiger	2·25	2·50

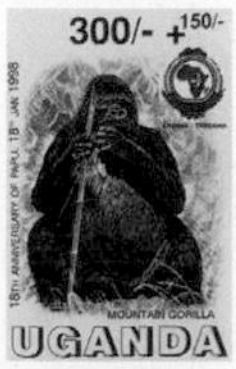

201 Mountain Gorilla

1998. 18th Anniv of Pan African Postal Union.

1918	**201**	300s.+150s. +150s. mult	2·50	3·00

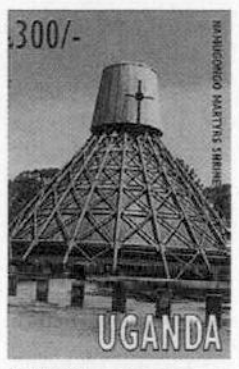

202 Namugongo Martyrs Shrine, Kampala

1998. Tourist Attractions. Multicoloured.

1919	300s. Type **202**	40	30
1920	400s. Kasubi Tombs, Kampala (horiz)	60	40
1921	500s. Tourist launch in Kazinga Channel, Queen Elizabeth Park (horiz)	1·00	80
1922	600s. Elephant, Queen Elizabeth Park (horiz)	1·50	1·50
1923	700s. Bujagali Falls, River Nile at Jinja (horiz)	1·50	2·00

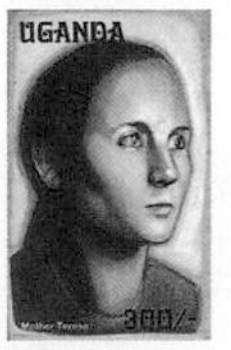

203 Mother Teresa, 1928

1998. Mother Teresa Commemoration. Multicoloured.

1924	300s. Type **203**	95	80
1925	300s. Holding child (56×42 mm)	95	80
1926	300s. Mother Teresa at United Nations, 1975 (56×42 mm)	95	80
1927	300s. Facing left	95	80
1928	300s. Full face portrait	95	80
1929	300s. With children (56×42 mm)	95	80
1930	300s. Mother Teresa rescuing child (56×42 mm)	95	80
1931	300s. Smiling	95	80
MS1932	95×81 mm. 2000s. Mother Teresa with Diana, Princess of Wales (50×37 mm)	7·00	6·00

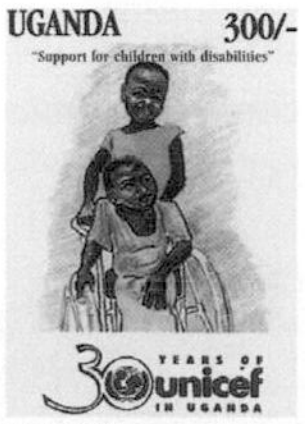

204 Child in Wheelchair

1998. 30th Anniv of UNICEF. Multicoloured.

1933	300s. Type **204**	80	30
1934	400s. Child receiving oral vaccination against polio	90	40
1935	600s. Children outside toilet	1·75	1·75
1936	700s. Children in class	1·90	2·25

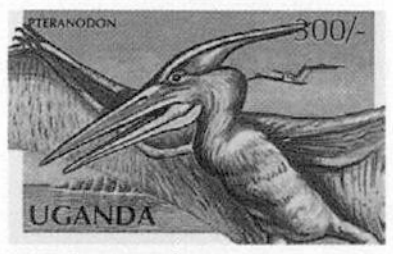

205 Pteranodon

1998. Prehistoric Animals. Multicoloured.

1937	300s. Type **205**	55	30
1938	400s. Diplodocus	65	45
1939	500s. Lambeosaurus	80	60
1940	600s. Centrosaurus	85	95
1941	600s. Cetiosaurus (vert)	1·50	1·50
1942	600s. Brontosaurus (vert)	1·50	1·50
1943	600s. Brachiosaurus (vert)	1·50	1·50
1944	600s. Deinonychus (vert)	1·50	1·50
1945	600s. Dimetrodon (vert)	1·50	1·50
1946	600s. Megalosaurus (vert)	1·50	1·50
1947	700s. Parasaurolophus	1·50	1·75
MS1948	Two sheets, each 73×103 mm. (a) 2500s. Tyrannosaurus rex (42×56 mm). (b) 2500s. Iguanodon (42×56 mm) Set of 2 sheets	9·50	11·00

Nos. 1941/6 were printed together, *se-tenant*, with the backgrounds forming a composite design.

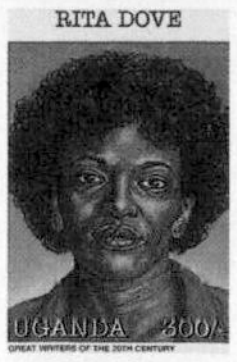

206 Rita Dove

1998. UNESCO. World Literacy Campaign. 20th-century Afro-American Writers. Multicoloured.

1949	300s. Type **206**	1·10	1·10
1950	300s. Mari Evans	1·10	1·10
1951	300s. Sterling A. Brown	1·10	1·10
1952	300s. June Jordan	1·10	1·10
1953	300s. Stephen Henderson	1·10	1·10
1954	300s. Zora Neale Hurston	1·10	1·10

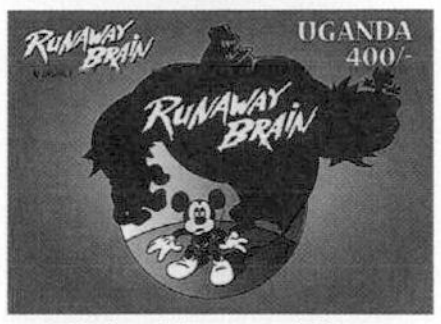

207 Mickey Mouse and Monster

1998. 70th Birthday of Mickey Mouse. Scenes from cartoon film "Runaway Brain". Multicoloured.

1955	400s. Type **207**	90	90
1956	400s. Mickey and Pluto with newspaper	90	90
1957	400s. Mickey and Pluto in front of television	90	90
1958	400s. Mickey and Minnie fleeing	90	90
1959	400s. Mickey on television screen	90	90
1960	400s. Monster and hostage Minnie Mouse clinging to skyscraper	90	90
1961	400s. Mickey Mouse throwing lasso	90	90
1962	400s. Mickey circling Monster on lasso	90	90
1963	400s. Mickey and Minnie on rope	90	90
MS1964	Two sheets, each 127×102 mm. (a) 3000s. Mickey and Minnie hugging on roof. (b) 3000s. Mickey and Minnie on liferaft (vert). Set of 2 sheets	11·00	11·00

1998. "Israel 98" International Stamp Exhibition, Tel-Aviv. Nos. **MS**1699/1700 optd with **98** and logo and each further optd **"ISRAEL 98 - WORLD STAMP EXHIBITION TEL-AVIV 13-21 MAY 1998"** on margin.

MS1965	114×95 mm. 300s. Type **180**; 500s. Jerusalem Theatre; 1000s. Israel Museum	3·25	3·25
MS1966	104×74 mm. 2000s. Grotto of the Nativity	3·25	3·25

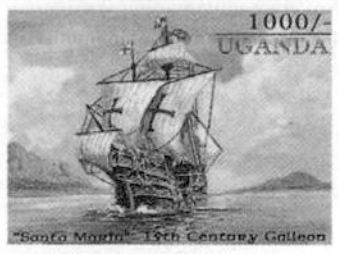

209 "Santa Maria" (Columbus)

1998. Ships of the World. Multicoloured.

1967	1000s. Type **209**	1·60	1·75
1968	1000s. "Mayflower" (Pilgrim Fathers)	1·60	1·75
1969	1000s. Barque	1·60	1·75
1970	1000s. Fishing schooner	1·60	1·75
1971	1000s. Chesapeake oyster boat	1·60	1·75
1972	1000s. Java Sea schooner	1·60	1·75
MS1973	Two sheets, each 100×70 mm. (a) 3000s. Thames barge (27×41 mm); (b) 3000s. Felucca (41×27 mm) Set of 2 sheets	8·00	8·50

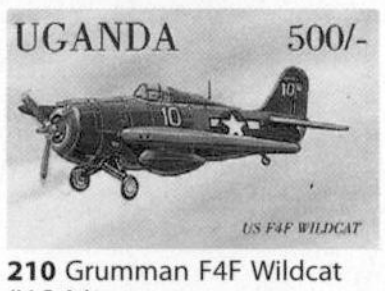

210 Grumman F4F Wildcat (U.S.A.)

1998. Aircraft. Multicoloured.

1974	500s. Type **210**	1·50	1·25
1975	500s. Mitsubishi A6M Zero-Sen (Japan)	1·50	1·25
1976	500s. Supermarine Seafire ("Spitfire") (Great Britain)	1·50	1·25
1977	500s. Hawker Siddeley Harrier (Great Britain)	1·50	1·25
1978	500s. S3A Viking (U.S.A.)	1·50	1·25
1979	500s. Corsair (U.S.A.)	1·50	1·25
1980	600s. Dornier Do-X (flying boat) (1929)	1·50	1·25

1981	600s. German Zucker mail rocket (1930)	1·50	1·25
1982	600s. North American X-15 rocket plane (1959)	1·50	1·25
1983	600s. Goddard's rocket (1930s)	1·50	1·25
1984	600s. Wright Brothers' "Flyer I" (1903)	1·50	1·25
1985	600s. 16 OR Sikorsky (first helicopter) (1939)	1·50	1·25
MS1986	Two sheets. (a) 85×110 mm. 2500s. P-40 Tomahawk (U.S.A.) (1940). (b) 110×85 mm. 2500s. SH-346 Seabat recovery helicopter (U.S.A.) Set of 2 sheets	8·50	8·50

Nos. 1974/9 and 1980/5 respectively were printed together, *se-tenant*, forming composite designs.

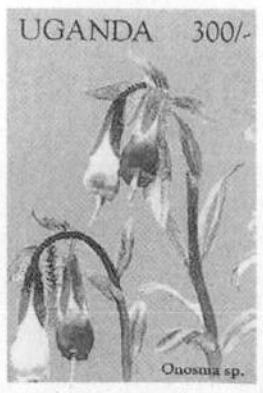
211 "Onosma" sp.

1998. Flowers of the Mediterranean. Multicoloured.

1987	300s. Type **211**	65	65
1988	300s. "Rhododendron luteum"	65	65
1989	300s. "Paeonia mascula"	65	65
1990	300s. "Geranium macrorrhizum"	65	65
1991	300s. "Cyclamen graecum"	65	65
1992	300s. "Lilium rhodopaedum"	65	65
1993	300s. "Narcissus pseudonarcissus"	65	65
1994	300s. "Paeonia rhodia"	65	65
1995	300s. "Aquilegia amaliae"	65	65
1996	600s. "Paeonia peregrina" (horiz)	80	80
1997	600s. "Muscari comutatum" (horiz)	80	80
1998	600s. "Sternbergia" sp. (horiz)	80	80
1999	600s. "Dianthus" sp. (horiz)	80	80
2000	600s. "Verbascum" sp. (horiz)	80	80
2001	600s. "Aubrieta gracilis" (horiz)	80	80
2002	600s. "Galanthus nivalis" (horiz)	80	80
2003	600s. "Campanula incurva" (horiz)	80	80
2004	600s. "Crocus sieberi" (horiz)	80	80
MS2005	Two sheets. (a) 70×100 mm. 2000s. "Paeonia parnassica" (b) 100×70 mm. 2000s. "Pancratium maritimum" Set of 2 sheets	7·50	8·50

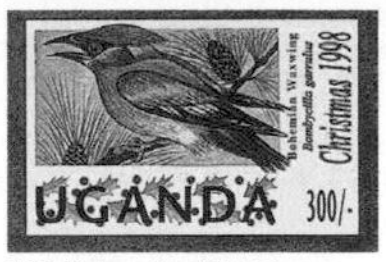
212 Bohemian Waxwing

1998. Christmas. Birds. Multicoloured.

2006	300s. Type **212**	65	30
2007	400s. House sparrow	75	40
2008	500s. Black-capped chickadee	85	50
2009	600s. Northern bullfinch ("Eurasian Bullfinch")	95	90
2010	700s. Painted bunting	1·10	1·25
2011	1000s. Common cardinal ("Northern Cardinal")	1·50	2·50
MS2012	Two sheets, each 70×97 mm. (a) 2500s. Winter wren (vert). (b) 2500s. Red-winged blackbird (vert) Set of 2 sheets	8·50	8·50

No. **MS**2012a is inscribed "Winter Wreu" in error.

1998. 25th Death Anniv of Pablo Picasso (painter). As T **373** of St. Vincent. Multicoloured.

2013	500s. "Woman Reading" (vert)	1·00	75
2014	600s. "Portrait of Dora Maar" (vert)	1·40	1·25
2015	700s. "Les Demoiselles d'Avignon"	1·60	1·75
MS2016	127×101 mm. 2500s. "Night Fishing at Antibes" (vert)	3·50	3·50

No. 2015 is inscribed "Des Moiselles D'Avignon" in error.

1998. 19th World Scout Jamboree, Chile. As T **373b** of St. Vincent. Multicoloured (except **MS**2020).

2017	700s. Cub Scouts greeting President Eisenhower, 1956	85	95
2018	700s. Scout with "Uncle Dan" Beard, 1940	85	95
2019	700s. Vice-President Hubert Humphrey as Scout leader, 1934	85	95
MS2020	70×100 mm. 2000s. Scout with pet beaver (purple, grey & brown)	3·00	3·25

1998. 50th Death Anniv of Mahatma Gandhi (2nd issue). As T **373c** of St. Vincent.

2021	600s. multicoloured	4·00	3·50
MS2022	98×58 mm. 2500s. brown, mauve and black	8·00	7·50

DESIGN—HORIZ: 600s. Gandhi as a young man. VERT: 2500s. Gandhi in Bombay law office.

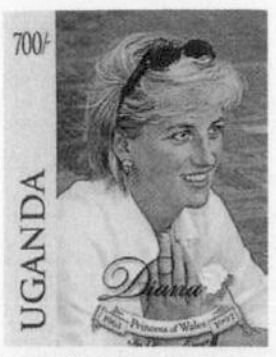
213 Diana, Princess of Wales

1998. First Death Anniv of Diana, Princess of Wales.

2023	**213**	700s. multicoloured	1·40	1·60

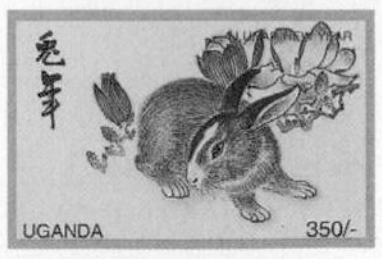
214 Rabbit

1999. Chinese New Year ("Year of the Rabbit"). Multicoloured.

2024	350s. White rabbit	75	80
2025	350s. Rabbit with carrot	75	80
2026	350s. Brown and white rabbit	75	80
2027	350s. Type **214**	75	80
MS2028	106×76 mm. 1500s. Rabbit	2·75	3·25

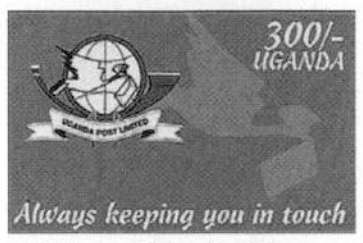
215 Post Office Emblem and Slogan

1999. Uganda Post Limited Commemoration.

2029	**215**	300s. multicoloured	1·50	65

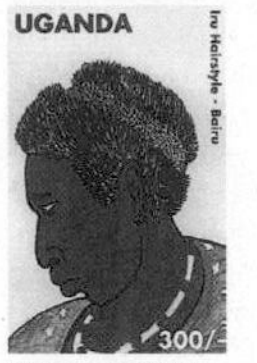
216 Iru Hairstyle

1999. Hairstyles. Multicoloured.

2030	300s. Type **216**	80	30
2031	500s. Enshunju hairstyle	1·10	75
2032	550s. Elemungole hairstyle	1·25	1·25
2033	600s. Lango hairstyle	1·25	1·50
2034	700s. Ekikuura hairstyle	1·40	1·75

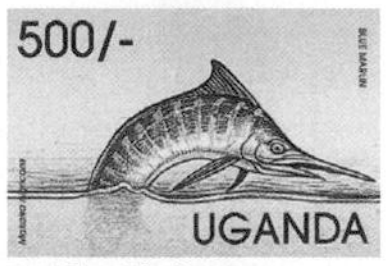
217 Blue Marlin

1999. International Year of the Ocean. Multicoloured.

2035	500s. Type **217**	95	85
2036	500s. Arctic tern	95	85
2037	500s. Common dolphin	95	85
2038	500s. Blacktip shark	95	85
2039	500s. Manta ray	95	85
2040	500s. Blackedge moray	95	85
2041	500s. Loggerhead turtle	95	85
2042	500s. Sail-finned tang	95	85
2043	500s. Two-spotted octopus	95	85
2044	500s. Atlantic wolffish	95	85
2045	500s. Equal sea star	95	85
2046	500s. Purple sea urchin	95	85
2047	500s. Mountain crab	95	85
MS2048	Two sheets, each 110×85 mm. (a) 2500s. Sea nettle jellyfish. (b) 2500s. "Decatopecten striatus" (scallop) Set of 2 sheets	7·50	8·00

Nos. 2035/43 and Nos. 2044/7 respectively were printed together, *se-tenant*, with the backgrounds forming a composite design.

No. 2036 is inscribed "ARTIC TERN" in error.

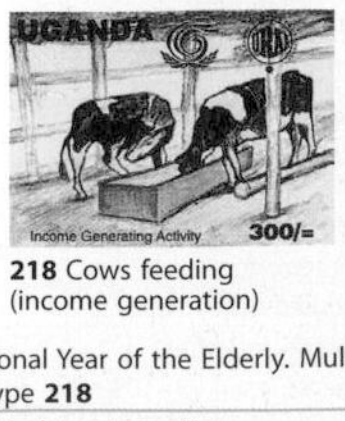
218 Cows feeding (income generation)

1999. International Year of the Elderly. Multicoloured.

2049	300s. Type **218**	80	30
2050	500s. Elderly man reading with child	1·25	75
2051	600s. Playing board game	1·40	1·75
2052	700s. Food distribution	1·50	2·25

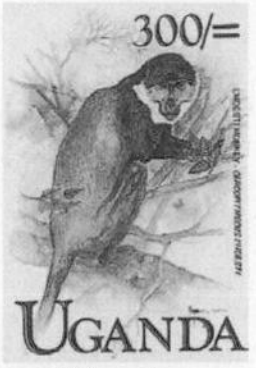
219 L'Hoest's Monkey

1999. Primates. Multicoloured.

2053	300s. Type **219**	80	30
2054	400s. Diademed monkey ("Sykes/Blue Monkey")	90	40
2055	500s. Patas monkey	1·10	70
2056	600s. Red-tailed monkey	1·25	1·40
2057	700s. Eastern black and white colobus	1·40	1·75
2058	1000s. Mountain gorilla	1·75	3·00
MS2059	73×54 mm. 2500s. Olive baboon (35×26 mm)	5·00	5·50

1999. 150th Death Anniv of Katsushika Hokusai (Japanese artist). As T **384b** of St. Lucia. Multicoloured.

2060	700s. "Dragon flying over Mount Fuji" (detail)	1·10	1·10
2061	700s. "Famous Poses from the Kabuki Theatre" (one woman)	1·10	1·10
2062	700s. "Kitsune No Yomeiri"	1·10	1·10
2063	700s. "Dragon flying over Mount Fuji" (complete picture)	1·10	1·10
2064	700s. "Famous Poses from the Kabuki Theatre" (man and woman)	1·10	1·10
2065	700s. "Girl holding Cloth"	1·10	1·10
MS2066	100×70 mm. 3000s. "Japanese Spaniel"	4·75	5·00

No. 2065 is inscribed "GIRL HOLDING CLOTHE" and No. **MS**2066 is inscribed 'Spainel' in error.

1999. "Queen Elizabeth the Queen Mother's Century". As T **386a** of St. Vincent.

2067	1200s. multicoloured	2·50	2·50
2068	1200s. black and gold	2·50	2·50
2069	1200s. black and gold	2·50	2·50
2070	1200s. multicoloured	2·50	2·50
MS2071	152×155 mm. 3000s. multicoloured	6·50	6·50

DESIGNS: No. 2067, Duchess of York wearing evening cape; 2068, Wedding of Duke and Duchess of York, 1923; 2069, Formal portrait of Queen Mother; 2070, Queen Mother at evening reception; **MS**2071, Queen Mother visiting Cambridge, 1961.

No. **MS**2071 also shows the Royal Arms embossed in gold.

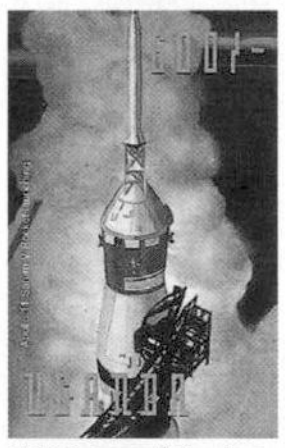
220 Saturn V Rocket Launch

1999. 30th Anniv of First Manned Landing on Moon. Multicoloured.

2072	600s. Type **220**	1·40	1·40
2073	600s. Command and service module "Columbia"	1·40	1·40
2074	600s. Edwin E. Aldrin descending ladder	1·40	1·40
2075	600s. Saturn V rocket on launch pad	1·40	1·40
2076	600s. Lunar module "Eagle"	1·40	1·40
2077	600s. Edwin E. Aldrin on Moon surface	1·40	1·40
2078	700s. Mercury mission "Freedom 7", 1961	1·40	1·40
2079	700s. "Gemini 4", 1965	1·40	1·40
2080	700s. "Apollo 11" command and service module "Columbia"	1·40	1·40
2081	700s. "Vostok 1", 1961	1·40	1·40
2082	700s. Saturn V rocket	1·40	1·40
2083	700s. "Apollo 11" lunar module "Eagle"	1·40	1·40
MS2084	Two sheets, each 76×106 mm. (a) 3000s. Edwin E. Aldrin with scientific experiment. (b) 3000s. "Apollo 11" command module re-entering Earth's atmosphere	15·00	15·00

Nos. 2078/83 were each printed together, se-tenant, with the backgrounds forming a composite design.

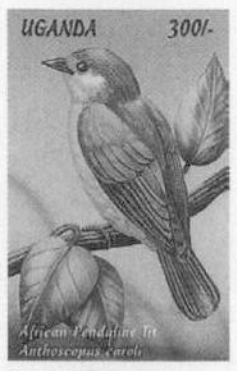
221 African Penduline Tit ("Penduline Tit")

1999. Birds of Uganda. Multicoloured.

2085	300s. Type **221**	1·50	60
2086	500s. Grey-headed kingfisher	1·75	1·40
2087	500s. Green-headed sunbird	1·75	1·40
2088	500s. Speckled pigeon	1·75	1·40
2089	500s. Grey parrot	1·75	1·40
2090	500s. Barn owl	1·75	1·40
2091	500s. South African crowned crane ("Grey Crowned Crane")	1·75	1·40
2092	500s. Whale-headed stork ("Shoebill")	1·75	1·40
2093	500s. Black heron	1·75	1·40
2094	600s. Scarlet-chested sunbird	1·75	1·40
2095	600s. Lesser honeyguide	1·75	1·40
2096	600s. African palm swift	1·75	1·40
2097	600s. Swamp flycatcher	1·75	1·40
2098	600s. Lizard buzzard	1·75	1·40
2099	600s. Osprey	1·75	1·40
2100	600s. Cardinal woodpecker	1·75	1·40
2101	600s. Pearl-spotted owlet	1·75	1·40
2102	700s. Speke's weaver ("Fox's Weaver")	1·75	1·40
2103	700s. Chin spot puff-backed flycatcher ("Chin-spot Flycatcher")	1·75	1·40
2104	700s. Blue swallow	1·75	1·40
2105	700s. Purple-breasted sunbird	1·75	1·40
2106	700s. Comb duck ("Knob-billed Duck")	1·75	1·40
2107	700s. Red-collared whydah ("Red-collared Widowbird")	1·75	1·40
2108	700s. Ruwenzori turaco	1·75	1·40
2109	700s. African cuckoo hawk	1·75	1·40
2110	1000s. Yellow-fronted tinkerbird	2·50	2·50
2111	1200s. Zebra waxbill	2·75	2·75
2112	1800s. Sooty chat ("Sooty Anteater Chat")	3·50	3·50
MS2113	Two sheets, each 76×106 mm. (a) 3000s. Four-banded sandgrouse. (b) 3000s. Paradise whydah Set of 2 sheets	16·00	16·00

Nos. 2086/93, 2094/2101 and 2102/9 were each printed together, *se-tenant*, with the backgrounds forming composite designs.

Nos. 2100/1 are inscribed "Cardinal Woopecker" or "Glaucidium periatum", both in error.

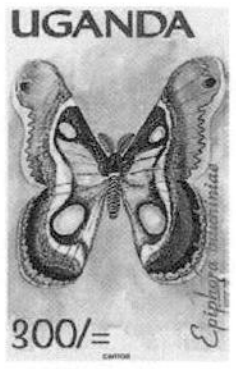
222 "Epiphora bauhiniae" (moth)

2000. Moths. Multicoloured.

2114	300s. Type **222**	80	30
2115	400s. "Phylloxiphia formosa" (horiz)	95	50
2116	500s. "Bunaea alcinoe"	1·25	70
2117	600s. "Euchloron megaera" (horiz)	1·40	1·25
2118	700s. "Argema mimosae"	1·50	1·60
2119	1800s. "Denephila nerii" (horiz)	3·75	6·00
MS2120	75×52 mm. 3000s. "Lobobunaea angasana" (horiz)	6·50	8·00

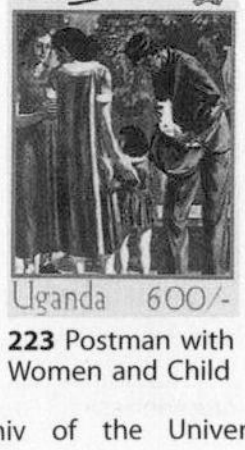
223 Postman with Women and Child

2000. 125th Anniv of the Universal Postal Union. Multicoloured.

2121	600s. Type **223**	1·25	1·00
2122	700s. American mother and child reading letter by post box	1·40	1·50
2123	1200s. Mail coach	3·50	4·75

Eulophia Paivenna

224 *Eulophia paivenna*

2000. Orchids. Multicoloured.

2124	600s. Type **224**	1·50	1·25
2125	600s. *Ansellia gigantea*	1·50	1·25
2126	600s. *Anglaecopsis gracillima*	1·50	1·25
2127	600s. *Bonatea steudneri*	1·50	1·25
2128	600s. *Bulbophyllum falcatum*	1·50	1·25
2129	600s. *Aerangis citrata*	1·50	1·25
2130	600s. *Eulophiella Elisabethae*	1·50	1·25
2131	600s. *Aerangis rhodosticta*	1·50	1·25
2132	600s. *Angraecum scottianum*	1·50	1·25
2133	600s. *Angraecum eichcerianum*	1·50	1·25
2134	600s. *Angraecum leonis*	1·50	1·25
2135	600s. *Arpophyllum giganteum*	1·50	1·25
2136	600s. *Bulbophyllum barbigerum*	1·50	1·25
2137	600s. *Angeraelum giryamae*	1·50	1·25
2138	600s. *Aeraungis ellisii*	1·50	1·25
2139	600s. *Disa uniflora*	1·50	1·25
2140	600s. *Eulophia alta*	1·50	1·25
2141	600s. *Ancistrochilius stylosa*	1·50	1·25
2142	700s. *Eulophia orthoplectra*	1·50	1·25
2143	700s. *Cirrhopetalum umbellatum*	1·50	1·25
2144	700s. *Eulophiella rolfei*	1·50	1·25
2145	700s. *Eulophia porphyroglossa*	1·50	1·25
2146	700s. *Eulophia petersii*	1·50	1·25
2147	700s. *Cyrtorchis arcuata*	1·50	1·25
2148	700s. *Eurychone rothschildiana*	1·50	1·25
2149	700s. *Eulophia quartiniana*	1·50	1·25
2150	700s. *Eulophia stenophylia* (single flower)	1·50	1·25
2151	700s. *Grammangis ellisii*	1·50	1·25
2152	700s. *Eulophia stenophylia* (several flowers)	1·50	1·25
2153	700s. *Oeoniella polystachys*	1·50	1·25
2154	700s. *Cymbidiella humblotii*	1·50	1·25
2155	700s. *Polystachya bella*	1·50	1·25
2156	700s. *Vanilla polycepis*	1·50	1·25
2157	700s. *Eulophiella roemplerana*	1·50	1·25
2158	700s. *Habenaria englerana*	1·50	1·25
2159	700s. *Ansella frallana*	1·50	1·25

MS2160 Four sheets, each 105×66 mm.
(a) 3000s. *Cymbidiella rhodochila* (horiz). (b) 3000s. *Calanthe corymbosa* (horiz). (c) 3000s. *Ancistrochilus rothschildianus* (horiz). (d) 3000s. *Polystachya tayloriana* (horiz) Set of 4 sheets ... 27·00 27·00

Nos. 2124/32, 2133/41, 2142/50 and 2151/9 were each printed together, *se-tenant*, with the backgrounds forming composite designs.

Antamartia hippomene

225 Short-tailed Admiral

2000. "The Stamp Show 2000" International Stamp Exhibition, London. Butterflies. Multicoloured.

2161	300s. Type **225**	1·50	40
2162	400s. Guineafowl	1·50	60
2163	500s. *Charaxes anticlea*	1·50	1·25
2164	500s. *Epitola posthumus*	1·50	1·25
2165	500s. Beautiful monarch	1·50	1·25
2166	500s. Blue-banded nymph	1·50	1·25
2167	500s. *Euxanthe crossleyi*	1·50	1·25
2168	500s. African map butterfly	1·50	1·25
2169	500s. Western blue charaxes	1·50	1·25
2170	500s. Noble butterfly	1·50	1·25
2171	600s. Green-veined charaxes	1·50	1·25
2172	600s. Ansorge's leaf butterfly	1·50	1·25
2173	600s. Crawshay's sapphire blue	1·50	1·25
2174	600s. *Palla ussheri*	1·50	1·25
2175	600s. Friar	1·50	1·25
2176	600s. Blood-red cymothoe	1·50	1·25
2177	600s. Mocker swallowtail	1·50	1·25
2178	600s. Green charaxes ("*Charaxes eupale*")	1·50	1·25
2179	700s. *Acraea pseudolycia*	1·50	1·25
2180	700s. *Colotis protomedia* ("Veined Yellow")	1·50	1·25
2181	700s. Buxton's hairstreak	1·50	1·25
2182	700s. *Iolaus isomenias*	1·50	1·25
2183	700s. Veined swallowtail	1·50	1·25
2184	700s. Fig-tree blue	1·50	1·25
2185	700s. Scarlet tip	1·50	1·25

2186	700s. Gaudy commodore ("*Precis octavia*")	1·50	1·25
2187	1200s. Club-tailed charaxes	2·50	2·50
2188	1800s. *Cymothoe egesta*	3·50	4·50

MS2189 Two sheets, each 63×69 mm. (a) 3000s. African monarch. (b) 3000s. Kigezi swordtail Set of 2 sheets ... 14·00 14·00

Nos. 2163/70, 2171/8 and 2179/86 were each printed together, *se-tenant*, with the backgrounds forming composite designs.

No. 2165 is inscribed "Danasus formosa", No. 2169 "Western Blue Caraxes" and No. 2183 "Graphium lionidas", all in error.

225a King Philip II of France, 1180–1223

2000. Monarchs of the Millennium.

2190	**225a** 900s. grey, brown and bistre	2·00	2·00
2191	– 900s. grey, brown and bistre	2·00	2·00
2192	– 900s. grey, brown and bistre	2·00	2·00
2193	– 900s. purple, brown and bistre	2·00	2·00
2194	– 900s. multicoloured	2·00	2·00
2195	– 900s. multicoloured	2·00	2·00
2196	– 900s. grey, brown and bistre	2·00	2·00
2197	– 900s. grey, brown and bistre	2·00	2·00
2198	– 900s. grey, brown and bistre	2·00	2·00

MS2199 Two sheets. (a) 117×137 mm. 3000s. multicoloured. (b) 116×136 mm. 3000s. multicoloured Set of 2 sheets ... 8·50 10·00

DESIGNS: No. 2191, King Richard I of England, 1189–99; 2192, King William I of England, 1066–87; 2193, Tsar Boris III of Bulgaria, 1918–43; 2194, Emperor Charles V of Holy Roman Empire, 1519–58; 2195, Emperor Pedro II of Brazil, 1831–89; 2196, Empress Elizabeth of Austria, 1854–98; 2197, Emperor Francis Joseph of Austria, 1848–1916; 2198, King Frederik of Bohemia, 1619–20; **MS**2199a, Kabaleega.

No. 2198 is inscribed "FREDRICH" in error.

225b Pope Agapitus II, 946–55

2000. Popes of the Millennium. Multicoloured (except MS2206).

2200	900s. Type **225b**	2·50	2·25
2201	900s. Alexander II, 1061–73	2·50	2·25
2202	900s. Anastasius IV, 1153–54	2·50	2·25
2203	900s. Benedict VIII, 1012–24	2·50	2·25
2204	900s. Benedict VII, 974–83	2·50	2·25
2205	900s. Callistus, 1119–24	2·50	2·25

MS2206 116×137 mm. 3000s. Celestine III, (grey, brown and buff) ... 8·50 8·50

225c Bow of Merchant Ship (opening of Japan to foreign trade, 1853)

2000. New Millennium. People and Events of Nineteenth Century (1850–1900). Multicoloured.

2207	300s. Type **225c**	1·50	1·50
2208	300s. First elevator, 1854	1·50	1·50
2209	300s. Ladle of molten steel (Bessemer Process, 1854)	1·50	1·50
2210	300s. Florence Nightingale (founder of nursing, 1854)	1·50	1·50
2211	300s. Louis Pasteur (French chemist, discovered bacteriology, 1856)	1·50	1·50

2212	300s. Oil gusher (first oil well, 1859)	1·50	1·50
2213	300s. Charles Darwin (*The Origin of Species*, 1859)	1·50	1·50
2214	300s. Gregor Mendel (law of heredity, 1866)	1·50	1·50
2215	300s. Alfred Nobel (invention of dynamite, 1867)	1·50	1·50
2216	300s. Modern freighter in Canal (opening of Suez Canal, 1869)	1·50	1·50
2217	300s. Early telephone (invented 1876)	1·50	1·50
2218	300s. Light bulb (invention of electric light, 1879)	1·50	1·50
2219	300s. Clocks (World's time zones established, 1884)	1·50	1·50
2220	300s. Electric motor (invented 1888)	1·50	1·50
2221	300s. Cinema projector (first motion pictures, 1895)	1·50	1·50
2222	300s. *Monitor* and *Merrimack* (ironclad warships) (American Civil War, 1861–65) (59×39 mm)	1·50	1·50
2223	300s. Olympic Torch and Rings (revival of Games, 1896)	1·50	1·50

226 Education in the Millennium

2000. Anniversaries and Events. Multicoloured.

2224	300s. Type **226**	80	30
2225	500s. Controlled and open borders (6th anniv of Comesa Treaty)	1·25	60
2226	600s. Flags of member countries (50th anniv of Commonwealth)	3·00	1·75
2227	600s. Aspects of the River Nile in the Millennium	1·75	1·75
2228	700s. Non-traditional exports in the Millennium	1·75	1·75
2229	1200s. World map (50th anniv of Commonwealth)	5·00	3·50
2230	1400s. People and exports crossing border (6th anniv of Comesa Treaty)	3·50	3·75
2231	1800s. Tourism in the Millennium	4·00	5·00

227 Kenya Railways Class A 60 Steam Locomotive

2000. African Railway Locomotives. Multicoloured.

2232	300s. Type **227**	85	25
2233	400s. Mozambique Railways Baldwin type	1·00	30
2234	600s. Uganda Railways Class 73 diesel locomotive	1·40	40
2235	700s. South Africa Railways Baby Garratt type	1·40	1·10
2236	700s. Uganda Railways Class 36 diesel locomotive (from back)	1·40	1·40
2237	700s. Rhodesian Railways 12th Class	1·40	1·40
2238	700s. Rhodesian Railways Garratt type	1·40	1·40
2239	700s. Uganda Railways Class 62 diesel locomotive	1·40	1·40
2240	700s. South African Railways Beyer-Garratt type	1·40	1·40
2241	700s. Sudan Railways oil-burning locomotive	1·40	1·40
2242	700s. Nigerian Railways coal train	1·40	1·40
2243	700s. South Africa Railways steam locomotive	1·40	1·40
2244	700s. Uganda Railways Class 36 diesel locomotive (from front)	1·40	1·40
2245	700s. South African Railways Class 19D	1·40	1·40
2246	700s. Algeria Railways Garratt type	1·40	1·40
2247	700s. Cameroon Railways locomotive No. 194	1·40	1·40
2248	700s. South African Railways electric freight locomotive	1·40	1·40
2249	700s. Rhodesian Railways Class 14A	1·40	1·40
2250	700s. Egyptian Railways British-built locomotive	1·40	1·40
2251	700s. Uganda Railways Class 73 diesel locomotive	1·40	1·40
2252	1200s. Uganda Railways Class 82 diesel locomotive	2·25	2·25
2253	1400s. East Africa Railways Beyer-Garratt type	2·50	2·50

2254	1800s. Rhodesian Railways Beyer-Garratt type	3·00	3·25
2255	2000s. East African Railways Garratt type	3·50	4·00

MS2256 Three sheets, each 106×76 mm. (a) 3500s. East Africa Railways steam locomotive (56×42 mm). (b) 3500s. Angola, Benguala Railway No. 402 (56×42 mm). (c) 3500s. Mozambique Railways Alco type (56×42 mm) Set of 3 sheets ... 16·00 18·00

No. 2237 also shows part of the inscription for No. 2236 in error.

228 "The Nativity" (Drateru Oliver)

2000. Christmas. Young People's Paintings. Multicoloured.

2257	300s. Type **228**	75	30
2258	400s. "Baby Jesus and Donkey" (Brenda Tumwebaze) (horiz)	80	35
2259	500s. "Angels" (Joseph Mukiibi)	95	45
2260	600s. "Holy Family in Stable" (Paul Serunjogi) (horiz)	1·10	50
2261	700s. "Holy Family with Oxon" (Edward Maswere) (horiz)	1·25	75
2262	1200s. "Children worshipping baby Jesus" (Ndeba Harriet) (horiz)	2·00	3·00
2263	1800s. "Madonna and Child with Shepherd" (Jude Kasagga)	3·00	4·50

MS2264 Two sheets, each 85×110 mm. (a) 3000s. "King with Gift and Christmas Tree" (Nicole Kwiringira). (b) 3000s. "Adoration of the Shepherds" (Michael Tinkamanyire) Set of 2 sheets ... 13·00 15·00

229 Snake

2001. Chinese New Year ("Year of the Snake") and "Hong Kong 2001" International Stamp Exhibition. Multicoloured.

2265	600s. Type **229**	1·75	1·75
2266	600s. Snake coiled around man	1·75	1·75
2267	600s. Snakes showing fangs	1·75	1·75
2268	600s. Snake on branch	1·75	1·75

MS2269 115×75 mm. 2500s. Cobra ... 10·00 10·00

230 Bongo

2001. Endangered Wildlife. Multicoloured.

2270	600s. Type **230**	2·75	2·75
2271	600s. Black rhinoceros	2·75	2·75
2272	600s. Leopard (vert)	2·75	2·75

MS2273 Two sheets. (a) 110×85 mm. 3000s. Mountain gorillas. (b) 85×110 mm. 3000s. Parrot (vert) Set of 2 sheets ... 15·00 15·00

231 Holy Family

2001. 2000th Birth Anniv of Jesus Christ. Multicoloured.

2274	300s. Type **231**	85	30
2275	700s. Madonna and child	1·75	1·50
2276	1200s. The Nativity (horiz)	3·00	4·00

232 East African School of Library and Information Science, Makerere

2001. East African Universities. Multicoloured.

2277	300s. Type **232**	85	30
2278	400s. Nairobi University	1·00	35

2279	1200s. Nkrumah Hall, University of Dar-es-Salaam	2·75	3·00
2280	1800s. Makerere, Kenyata and Open Universities (vert)	4·00	5·00

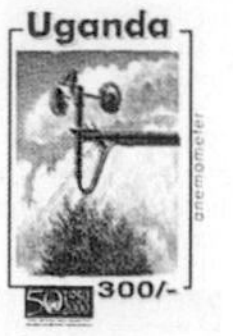

233
Anemometer

2001. 50th Anniv (2000) of World Meteorological Organization. Multicoloured.

2281	300s. Type **233**	1·25	50
2282	2000s. Tropical sun recorder (horiz)	4·50	5·50

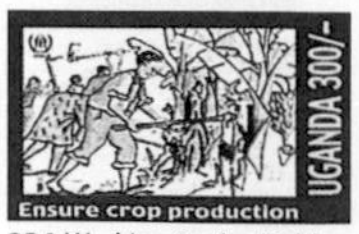

234 Working in the Fields

2001. 50th Anniv of United Nations High Commissioner for Refugees. Economic Development. Multicoloured.

2283	300s. Type **234**	80	30
2284	600s. Community building project	1·40	70
2285	1200s. Carpentry class	2·50	2·75
2286	1800s. New water supply	3·50	4·75

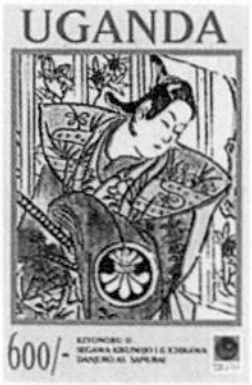

235 "Segawa Kikunojo and Ichikawa Danjuro as Samurai" (Kiyonobu II)

2001. "Philanippon '01" International Stamp Exhibition, Tokyo. Japanese Woodcuts. Multicoloured.

2287	600s. Type **235**	1·50	50
2288	700s. "Tchimura Kamezo as Warrior" (Kiyohiro)	1·60	65
2289	1000s. "Ichikawa Danjuro as Shirobei Tadanobu" (Kiyomitsu)	2·00	1·60
2290	1200s. "Actor Arashi Sangoro" (Shunsho)	2·25	2·25
2291	1400s. "Matsumoto Koshiro IV as Juro Sukenari" (Kiyonaga)	2·50	2·75
2292	2000s. "Pheasant on Pine Branch" (Kiyomasu II)	3·50	5·00
MS2293	68×105 mm 3500s. Depicts "Tale of Ise" (Eishi)	6·00	6·50

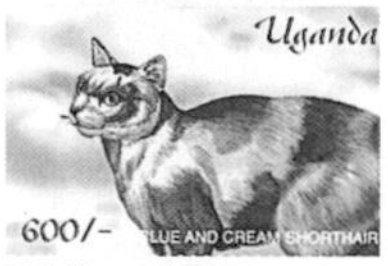

236 Blue and Cream Shorthair

2001. Cats and Dogs. Multicoloured.

2294	400s. Tabby British shorthair (vert)	1·75	50
2295	600s. Type **236**	2·25	2·25
2296	600s. Manx	2·25	2·25
2297	600s. Angora	2·25	2·25
2298	600s. Red and white British shorthair	2·25	2·25
2299	600s. Turkish cat	2·25	2·25
2300	600s. Egyptian mau	2·25	2·25
2301	700s. Rottweiler	2·25	2·25
2302	700s. Flat-coated retriever	2·25	2·25
2303	700s. Samoyed	2·25	2·25
2304	700s. Poodle	2·25	2·25
2305	700s. Maltese	2·25	2·25
2306	700s. Irish terrier	2·25	2·25
2307	900s. Turkish cat (vert)	2·25	2·25
2308	1100s. German shepherd (vert)	2·25	2·25
2309	1200s. Irish setter (vert)	2·25	2·25
2310	1300s. English sheepdog	2·25	2·25
2311	1300s. German shepherd	2·25	2·25
2312	1300s. Great Dane	2·25	2·25
2313	1300s. Boston terrier	2·25	2·25
2314	1300s. Bull terrier	2·25	2·25
2315	1300s. Australian terrier	2·25	2·25
2316	1400s. Red tabby shorthair	2·25	2·25
2317	1400s. Japanese bobtail	2·25	2·25
2318	1400s. Siamese	2·25	2·25
2319	1400s. Tabby Persian	2·25	2·25
2320	1400s. Black and white Persian	2·25	2·25
2321	1400s. Russian blue	2·25	2·25
MS2322	Four sheets. (a) 106×76 mm. 3500s. American calico shorthair (vert). (b) 76×106 mm. 3500s. Blue-eyed british shorthair (vert). (c) 106×76 mm. 3500s. Bloodhound (vert). (d) 106×76 mm. 3500s. Pointer Set of 4 sheets	32·00	32·00

2001. Death Centenary of Queen Victoria. As T **101** of St. Kitts. Multicoloured.

2323	1000s. Queen Victoria wearing brown	2·25	2·25
2324	1000s. Queen Victoria in white bonnet	2·25	2·25
2325	1000s. Wearing feathered hat	2·25	2·25
2326	1000s. In evening dress	2·25	2·25
2327	1000s. Queen Victoria wearing choker with pendant	2·25	2·25
2328	1000s. In black dress, looking down	2·25	2·25
MS2329	107×83 mm. 3500s. Queen Victoria in furred hat	6·50	7·50

2001. 75th Death Anniv of Claude-Oscar Monet (French painter). As T **103** of St. Kitts. Multicoloured.

2330	1200s. "Storm, Belle-Ile Coast"	2·50	2·50
2331	1200s. "Manneporte, Etretat"	2·50	2·50
2332	1200s. "Rocks at Low Tide, Pourville"	2·50	2·50
2333	1200s. "Wild Sea"	2·50	2·50
MS2334	137×109 mm. 3500s. "Sunflowers" (vert)	6·00	7·00

2001. 75th Birthday of Queen Elizabeth II. As T **104** of St. Kitts. Multicoloured.

2335	1000s. Princess Elizabeth as a baby, 1926	2·25	2·25
2336	1000s. Princess Elizabeth aged 5, 1931	2·25	2·25
2337	1000s. Princess Elizabeth in 1939	2·25	2·25
2338	1000s. Queen Elizabeth in 1955	2·25	2·25
2339	1000s. Queen Elizabeth wearing tiara, 1963	2·25	2·25
2340	1000s. Queen Elizabeth in 1999	2·25	2·25
MS2341	82×106 mm. 3500s. Queen Elizabeth in uniform for Trooping the Colour	6·00	7·00

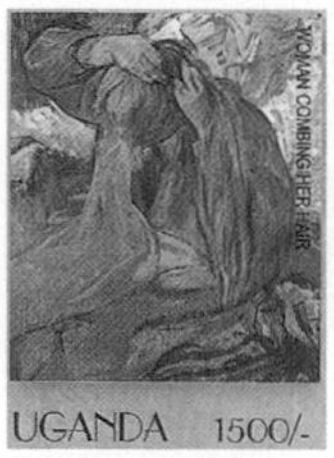

237 "Woman combing her Hair" (Toulouse-Lautrec)

2001. Death Centenary of Henri de Toulouse-Lautrec (French painter). Multicoloured.

2342	1500s. Type **237**	4·00	4·00
2343	1500s. "The Toilette"	4·00	4·00
2344	1500s. "English Girl at the Star Inn, Le Havre"	4·00	4·00
MS2345	74×109 mm. 3500s. "Aristide Bruant"	7·00	8·00

2001. Centenary of Royal Navy Submarine Service. As T **107** of St. Kitts. Multicoloured.

2346	1000s. H.M.S. *Tribune* (submarine) (vert)	4·00	3·25
2347	1000s. H.M.S. *Royal Oak* (battleship, launched 1914) (vert)	4·00	3·25
2348	1000s. H.M.S. *Invincible* (aircraft carrier) (vert)	4·00	3·25
2349	1000s. H.M.S. *Dreadnought* (nuclear submarine) (vert)	4·00	3·25
2350	1000s. H.M.S. *Ark Royal* (aircraft carrier, launched 1950) (vert)	4·00	3·25
2351	1000s. H.M.S. *Cardiff* (destroyer) (vert)	4·00	3·25
MS2352	70×57 mm. 3500s. H.M.S. Triad (submarine)	11·00	11·00

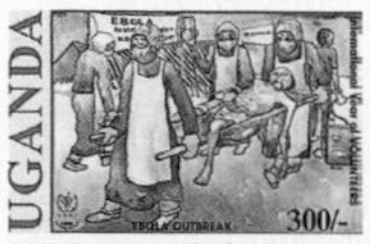

238 Carrying Ebola Victim on Stretcher

2001. U.N. Year of Dialogue among Civilizations (3000s.) and International Year of Volunteers (others). Multicoloured.

2353	300s. Type **238**	1·00	45
2354	700s. Blood donor session	1·75	80
2355	2000s. Provision of clean water	3·25	3·75
2356	3000s. Children encircling Globe (vert)	4·25	6·00

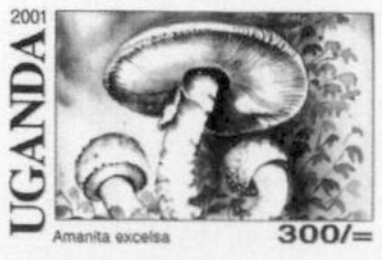

239 *Amanita excelsa*

2001. Fungi. Multicoloured.

2357	300s. Type **239**	1·00	30
2358	500s. *Coprinus cinereus*	1·50	50
2359	600s. *Scleroderma aurantium*	1·60	85
2360	700s. *Armillaria mellea*	1·75	1·40
2361	1200s. *Leopiota procera*	3·00	3·00
2362	2000s. *Flammulina velutipes*	5·00	6·00
MS2363	Two sheets, each 100×70 mm. (a) 3000s. *Amanita phalloides*. (b) 3000s. *Amanita fulva* Set of 2 sheets	18·00	17·00

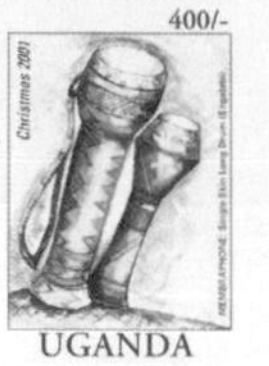

240 Long Drums

2001. Christmas. Musical Instruments. Multicoloured.

2364	400s. Type **240**	70	25
2365	800s. Animal horn trumpets (horiz)	1·25	65
2366	1000s. Bugisu clay drum	1·60	1·00
2367	1200s. Musical bows	1·75	1·75
2368	1400s. Pan pipes	1·90	2·25
2369	2000s. Two-man xylophone (horiz)	3·00	4·50
MS2370	Two sheets. (a) 85×110 mm. 3500s. Eight-stringed giant bow harp. (b) 110× 85 mm. 3500s. Nativity (horiz) Set of 2 sheets	14·00	15·00

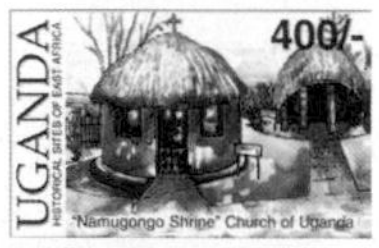

241 Namugongo Shrine, Uganda

2002. Historical Sites of East Africa. Multicoloured.

2371	400s. Type **241**	65	30
2372	800s. Maruhubi Palace ruins, Zanzibar	1·25	80
2373	1200s. Kings' Burial Grounds, Mparo, Hoima	1·75	2·00
2374	1400s. Old Law Courts, Mombasa (vert)	2·00	2·50

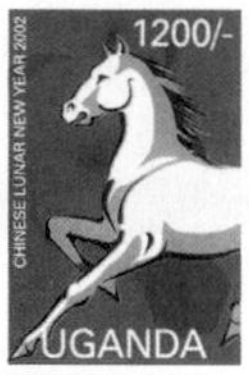

242 White Horse

2002. Chinese New Year ("Year of the Horse"). Multicoloured.

2375	1200s. Type **242**	2·25	2·25
2376	1200s. Piebald horse	2·25	2·25
2377	1200s. Dun horse	2·25	2·25
MS2378	75×105 mm. 3000s. Rearing horse	5·50	6·00

2002. Golden Jubilee. As T **110** of St. Kitts. Multicoloured.

2379	1500s. Young Queen Elizabeth looking to her left	3·00	3·00
2380	1500s. Queen Elizabeth in striped hat	3·00	3·00
2381	1500s. Queen Elizabeth in evening dress	3·00	3·00
2382	1500s. As No. 2379, but Queen Elizabeth looking to her right	3·00	3·00
MS2383	76×108 mm. 3500s. Queen Elizabeth wearing straw hat	6·50	7·50

2002. "United We Stand". Support for Victims of 11 September 2001 Terrorist Attacks. As T **179** of St. Kitts, but showing Ugandan flag.

2384	1500s. multicoloured	2·00	2·50

2002. International Year of Mountains. As T **115** of St. Kitts. Multicoloured.

2385	2000s. Mount Tateyama, Japan	3·00	3·00
2386	2000s. Mount Nikko Semdjoda-Hara, Japan	3·00	3·00
2387	2000s. Mount Hodaka, Japan	3·00	3·00
MS2388	70×55 mm. 3500s. Mount Fuji, Japan	6·00	7·00

2002. 20th World Scout Jamboree, Thailand. As T **116** of St. Kitts. Multicoloured.

2389	1400s. Scout from 1930s in forest	2·25	2·50
2390	1400s. Scout from 1930s saluting	2·25	2·50
2391	1400s. Two scouts with packs	2·25	2·50
2392	1400s. International Scouts symbol	2·25	2·50
MS2393	60×78 mm. 3500s. Lord Baden-Powell (vert)	7·50	8·50

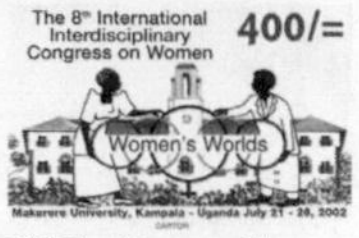

243 Two Women with Symbol and Makerere University

2002. Eighth International Interdisciplinary Congress on Women, Kampala. Multicoloured.

2394	400s. Type **243**	1·00	30
2395	1200s. Arms of Makerere University (vert)	2·50	3·00

2002. Winter Olympic Games, Salt Lake City. As T **111** of St. Kitts. Multicoloured.

2396	1200s. Cross-country skiing (vert)	2·50	2·75
2397	1200s. Ski-jumping (vert)	2·50	2·75
MS2398	82×113 mm. Nos. 2396/7	5·00	5·50

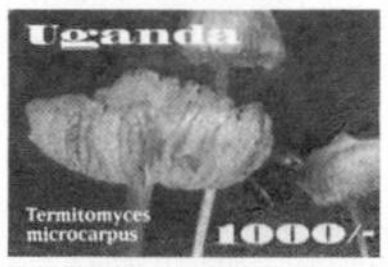

244 *Termitomyces microcarpus* (fungus)

2002. Flora and Fauna. Multicoloured.

2399	400s. White rhinoceros (vert)	2·25	1·00
2400	800s. *Macrotermes subhyalinus* (insect) (vert)	1·50	1·00
2401	1000s. Type **244**	2·25	2·25
2402	1000s. *Agaricus trisulphuratus*	2·25	2·25
2403	1000s. *Macrolepiota zeyheri*	2·25	2·25
2404	1000s. *Lentinus stupeus*	2·25	2·25
2405	1000s. *Lentinus sajor-caju*	2·25	2·25
2406	1000s. *Lentinus velutinus*	2·25	2·25
2407	1000s. *Nudaurelia cytherea* (caterpillar)	2·25	2·25
2408	1000s. *Locusta migratoria* (locust)	2·25	2·25
2409	1000s. *Anacridium aegyptium* (grasshopper)	2·25	2·25
2410	1000s. *Sternotomis bohemanni* (longhorn beetle)	2·25	2·25
2411	1000s. *Papilio dardanus* (butterfly)	2·25	2·25
2412	1000s. *Mantis polyspilota* (mantid)	2·25	2·25
2413	1200s. Uganda kob	2·25	2·25
2414	1200s. Hartebeest	2·25	2·25
2415	1200s. Topi	2·25	2·25
2416	1200s. Olive baboon	2·25	2·25
2417	1200s. Lion	2·25	2·25
2418	1200s. Common warthog	2·25	2·25
2419	1200s. *Canarina eminii*	2·25	2·25
2420	1200s. *Vigna unguiculata*	2·25	2·25
2421	1200s. *Gardenia ternifolia*	2·25	2·25
2422	1200s. *Canavalia rosea*	2·25	2·25
2423	1200s. *Hibiscus calyphyllus*	2·25	2·25
2424	1200s. *Nymphaea lotus*	2·25	2·25
2425	1200s. *Gloriosa superba* (flower) (vert)	2·25	2·25
2426	1400s. *Cyptotrama asprata* (fungus) (vert)	2·50	3·00
MS2427	Four sheets, each 95×70 mm. (a) 4000s. *Podoscypha parvula* (fungus). (b) 4000s. *Glossina austeni* (tsetse fly). (c) 4000s. Waterbuck (vert). (d) 4000s. *Abutilon grandiflorum* (flower) Set of 4 sheets	30·00	32·00

Nos. 2401/6 (fungi), 240712 (insects), 2423/28 (mammals) and 2419/24 (flowers) were each printed together, *se-tenant*, with the backgrounds forming composite designs.

For stamps previously listed as 2428/33, please see Nos. 1941/6.

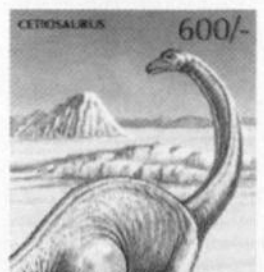

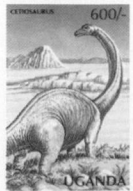

245 Cetiosaurus

2002. Prehistoric Animals. Multicoloured.

2428	600s. Type **245**	2·00	2·00
2429	600s. Brontosaurus	2·00	2·00

2430	600s. Brachiosaurus	2·00	2·00
2431	600s. Deinonychus	2·00	2·00
2432	600s. Dimetrodon	2·00	2·00
2433	600s. Megalosaurus	2·00	2·00

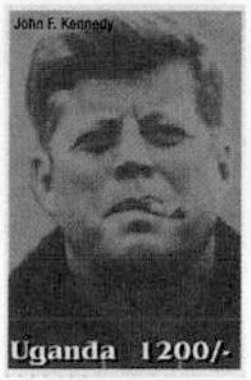

246 President John Kennedy

2002. Famous People of the Late 20th Century. Six miniature sheets containing T **246** and similar vert designs. Multicoloured (except No. **MS**2434/5)

(a) Life and Times of President John F. Kennedy. Two sheets containing portraits as T **246**.

MS2434 117×97 mm. 1200s. Type **246**; 1200s. In profile; 1200s. Facing right, speaking; 1200s. Smiling, facing forwards (all green and black)	9·00	10·00
MS2435 125×97 mm. 1400s. Wearing white jacket (brown and black); 1400s.Wearing brown jacket and white tie (light brown and black); 1400s. Wearing brown jacket and dark tie (brown and black); 1400s. Wearing brown jacket and dark tie (light brown and black)	10·00	11·00

(b) President Ronald Reagan. Two sheets, each containing four different portraits.

MS2436 138×115 mm. 1200s. Smiling with mouth open; 1200s. Looking down; 1200s. Smiling with mouth closed; 1200s. Facing forwards	9·00	10·00
MS2437 120×95 mm. 1400s. Wearing red necktie (facing right); 1400s. Wearing grey sweater; 1400s. Close up of face; 1400s. Wearing red tie (facing forwards)	10·00	11·00

(c) Fifth Death Anniv of Diana, Princess of Wales.

MS2438 125×150 mm. 1200s. Wearing red dress with white collar; 1200s. Wearing white jacket; 1200s. Wearing red and white jacket and hat; 1200s. Wearing evening dress and necklace	9·00	10·00
MS2439 140×115 mm. 2000s. Wearing white blouse; 2000s. Wearing lace blouse; 2000s. Wearing headscarf on visit to Middle East; 2000s. Wearing tiara and white jacket	13·00	15·00

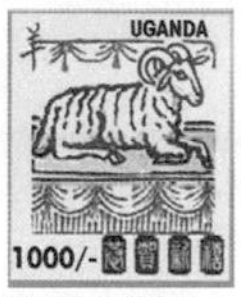

247 Ram (laying down)

2003. Chinese New Year ("Year of the Ram"). Sheet, 107×120 mm, containing T **247** and similar vert designs. Multicoloured.

MS2440 1000s. Type **247**; 1000s. Ram on hilltop; 1000s. Ram and six rams heads; 1000s. Six rams; 1000s. Ram (looking backwards); 1000s. Ram climbing mountain	11·00	12·00

2003. Paintings by Rembrandt. As T **466** of St. Vincent. Multicoloured.

2441	400s. "Jacob Blessing the Sons of Joseph" (detail)	80	40
2442	1000s. "A Young Woman in Profile with Fan"	2·00	1·50
2443	1200s. "The Apostle Peter (Kneeling)"	2·25	2·00
2444	1400s. "The Painter Hendrick Martensz Sorgh"	2·50	3·00
MS2445	185×175 mm. 1400s. "Portrait of Margaretha de Geer"; 1400s. "Portrait of a White Haired Man"; 1400s. "Portrait of Nicolaes Ruts"; 1400s. "Portrait of Catrina Hooghsaet"	11·00	12·00
MS2446	138×135 mm. 5000s. "Joseph accused by Potiphar's Wife" (detail)	10·00	11·00

2003. 20th Death Anniv of Joan Miro (artist). As T **282** of Turks and Caicos Islands. Multicoloured.

2447	400s. "Group of Personages in the Forest" (horiz)	80	40
2448	800s. "Nocturne" (horiz)	1·50	1·25
2449	1200s. "The Smile of a Tear" (horiz)	2·25	2·25
2450	1400s. "Personage before the Sun" (horiz)	2·50	3·00
MS2451	132×175 mm. 1400s. "Man's Head III"; 1400s. "Catalan Peasant by Moonlight"; 1400s. "Woman in the Night"; 1400s. "Seated Woman"	11·00	12·00
MS2452	Two sheets, each 102×82 mm. (a) 3500s. "Self Portrait II". Imperf. (b) 3500s. "Woman with Three Hairs, Birds, and Constellations". Imperf Set of 2 sheets	13·00	15·00

2003. Japanese Art. As T **467** of St. Vincent. Multicoloured.

2453	400s. "Beauty arranging her Hair" (Keisai Eisen)	80	40
2454	1000s. "Geishas" (detail) (Kitagawa Tsukimaro)	1·75	1·50
2455	1200s. "True Beauties" (Toyohara Chikanobu)	2·00	2·25
2456	1400s. "Geishas" (different detail) (Kitagawa Tsukimaro)	2·25	2·75
MS2457	150×148 mm. 1200s. "Scene in a Villa" (detail of two women and urn) (Toyohara Kunichika); 1200s. "Scene in a Villa" (detail of two women behind screen) (Toyohara Kunichika); 1200s. "Visiting a Flower Garden" (detail of two women in garden) (Utagawa Kunisada); 1200s. "Visiting a Flower Garden" (detail of woman picking flowers) (Utagawa Kunisada)	10·00	11·00
MS2458	90×152 mm. 5000s. "Woman and Children" (detail) (Chikakazu)	10·00	11·00

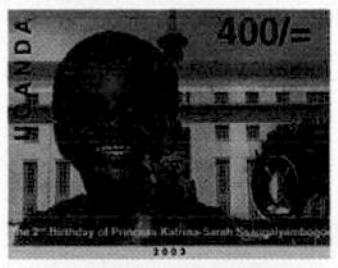

248 Princess Katrina-Sarah Ssangalyambogo and Bulange Building

2003. Second Birthday of Princess Katrina-Sarah Ssangalyambogo of Buganda. Multicoloured.

2459	400s. Type **248**	80	40
2460	1200s. Princess and Twekobe Palace, Mengo (vert)	2·25	2·50
2461	1400s. Princess and royal drum (vert)	2·50	2·75

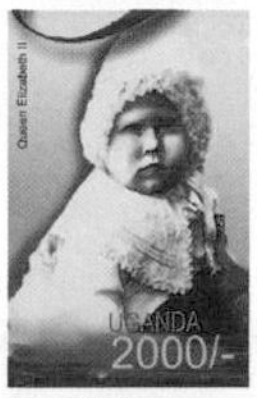

249 Princess Elizabeth as Baby

2003. 50th Anniv of Coronation. Multicoloured.

MS2462 143×77 mm. 2000s. Type **249**; 2000s. Princess Elizabeth; 2000s. Queen Elizabeth II in Garter robes	11·00	12·00
MS2463 105×75 mm. 3500s. Queen wearing Imperial State Crown	7·50	8·00

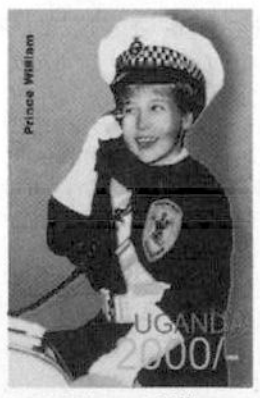

250 Prince William

2003. 21st Birthday of Prince William of Wales. Multicoloured.

MS2464 124×125 mm. 2000s. Type **250**; 2000s. Prince William as boy holding presents; 2000s. As teenager	11·00	12·00
MS2465 105×76 mm. 5000s. Prince William as adult	9·50	11·00

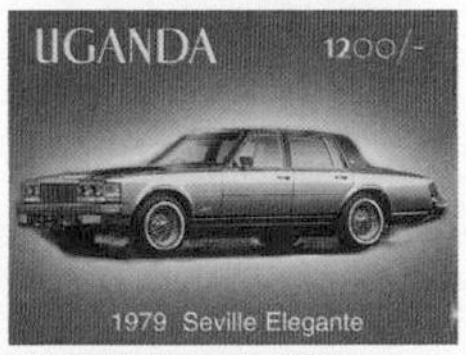

251 Seville Elegante (1979)

2003. Centenary of General Motors Cadillac. Multicoloured.

MS2466 118×167 mm. 1200s. Type **251**; 1200s. Eldorado Touring Coupe (1998); 1200s. Escalade (2002); 1200s. Seville Elegante (1983)	8·50	9·50
MS2467 89×126 mm. 3500s. Eldorado	6·00	7·00

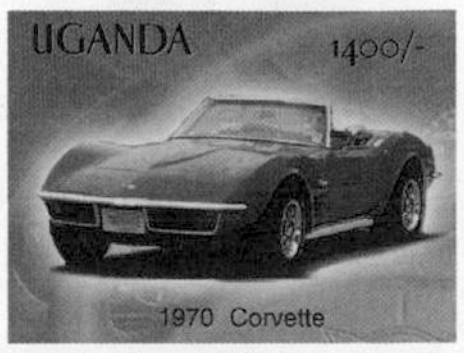

252 Corvette (1970)

2003. 50th Anniv of General Motors Chevrolet Corvette. Multicoloured.

MS2468 145×125 mm. 1400s. Type **252**; 1400s. Corvette (1972); 1400s. Collector Edition Corvette (1982); 1400s. Corvette (1977)	8·00	9·00
MS2469 125×90 mm. 3500s. Collector Edition Corvette (1982)	6·00	7·00

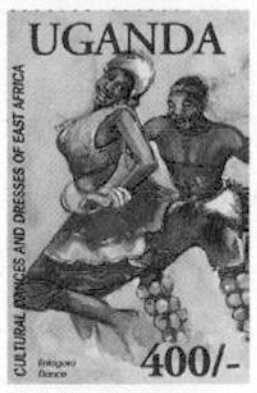

253 Endogoro Dance

2003. Cultural Dances and Dresses of East Africa. Multicoloured.

2470	400s. Type **253**	1·00	40
2471	800s. Karimojong dancers	1·75	1·40
2472	1400s. Dance from Teso	3·00	3·50
MS2473	70×105 mm. 1200s. Kiga; 1200s. Acholi; 1200s. Karimojong; 1200s. Ganda	11·00	12·00

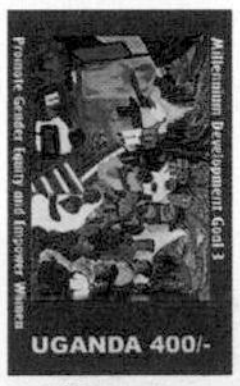

254 Women holding Meeting ("Promote Gender Equity and Empower Women")

2003. United Nations Millennium Development Goals. Multicoloured.

2474	400s. Type **254**	1·00	1·00
2475	400s. Men pushing bicycle for pregnant woman ("Improve Maternal Health")	1·00	1·00
2476	600s. Women fetching water ("Ensure Environmental Sustainability")	1·35	1·00
2477	1000s. Woman feeding children ("Reduce Child Mortality")	1·75	1·50
2478	1200s. Couple and storage hut ("Eradicate Extreme Poverty and Hunger")	1·90	1·90
2479	1200s. Family outside house ("Combat HIV/AIDS, Malaria and other diseases")	1·90	1·90
2480	1400s. Teacher and schoolchildren ("Achieve Universal Primary Education")	2·25	2·25
2481	2000s. Emblem ("Develop a Global Partnership for Development")	3·00	4·00

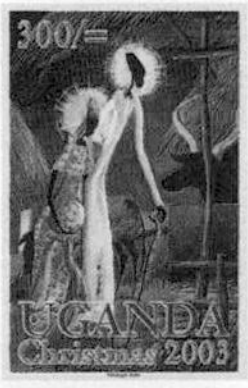

255 Mary and Joseph

2003. Christmas. Multicoloured.

2482	300s. Type **255**	75	25
2483	400s. Angels and Shepherds	90	30
2484	1200s. Nativity	2·25	2·50
2485	1400s. Three Wise Men	2·50	3·00
MS2486	105×70 mm. 3000s. Nativity (different)	7·00	8·00

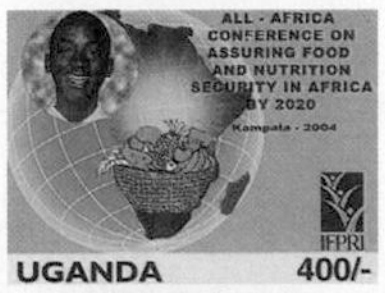

256 Outline of Africa, Boy and Basket of Food

2004. International Food Policy Research Institute. Conference on Sustainable Food and Nutrition, Kampala. Multicoloured.

2487	400s. Type **256**	1·00	50
2488	1400s. As No. 2487 but showing girl	3·00	3·50

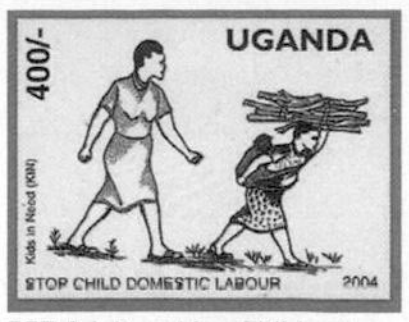

257 Adult making Child carry Baby and Bundle of Sticks

2004. Kids In Need. Prevention of Child Labour. Multicoloured.

2489	400s. Type **257**	1·00	40
2490	2000s. Speaker and people around blackboard	4·00	4·50

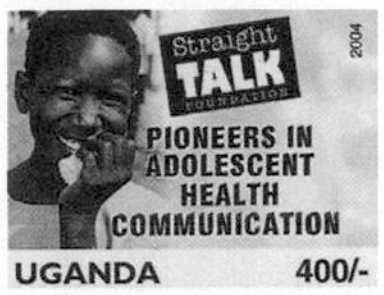

258 Child laughing

2004. Straight Talk Foundation. Adolescent Health. Multicoloured.

2491	400s. Type **258**	1·00	40
2492	1200s. Boy reading paper	2·50	3·00

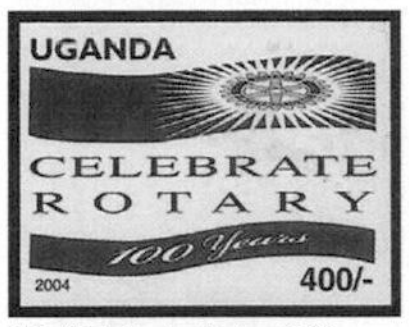

259 "Celebrate Rotary 100 Years"

2004. Centenary of Rotary International. Multicoloured.

2493	400s. Type **259**	1·00	40
2494	1200s. Rotary international emblem (vert)	2·50	3·00

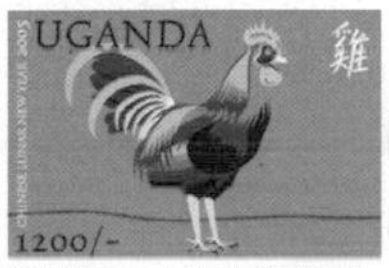

260 Blue and Black Cockerel

2005. Chinese New Year ("Year of the Rooster"). Multicoloured.

2495	1200s. Type **260**	2·25	2·25
2496	1200s. Brown and fawn cockerel	2·25	2·25
2497	1200s. Grey and white cockerel	2·25	2·25
2498	1200s. Pink and white cockerel	2·25	2·25
MS2499	105×75 mm. 5000s. Yellow cockerel	10·00	11·00

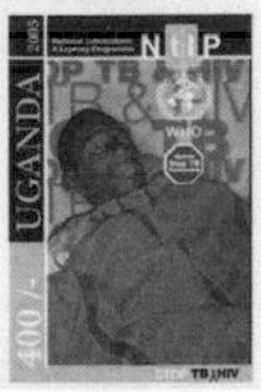

261 Sick Man under Blanket ("STOP TB×HIV")

2005. National Tuberculosis and Leprosy Programme. Multicoloured.

2500	400s. Type **261**	1·00	1·00
2501	400s. Woman holding baby ("STOP TB")	1·00	1·00
2502	400s. Baby ("STOP TB")	1·00	1·00
2503	400s. Man with artificial leg ("FOR A LEPROSY FREE WORLD")	1·00	1·00
2504	400s. Elderly man wearing blue T-shirt ("FOR A LEPROSY FREE WORLD")	1·00	1·00
2505	400s. Sick man (wearing white loin cloth) in hospital ("STOP TB×HIV")	1·00	1·00

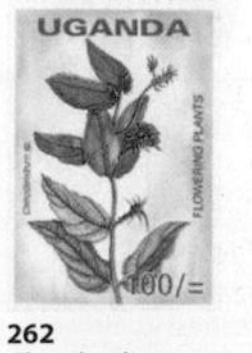

262 *Clerodendrum* sp.

2005. Flowering Plants of Uganda. Multicoloured.

2506	100s. Type **262**	10	15
2507	400s. *Calliandra haematocephala*	50	25

2508	600s. *Asteraceae compositae*	70	35
2509	850s. *Angraecumsp*	1·10	1·25
2510	900s. *Delonix regia*	1·10	1·25
2511	1100s. *Bidens grantii*	1·25	1·40
2512	1200s. *Musa sapientum*	1·40	1·50
2513	1400s. *Begonia coccinea*	1·75	1·90
2514	1600s. *Impatiens walleriana*	2·00	2·25
2515	2000s. *Strelitzia reginae*	2·25	2·40
2516	5000s. *Tecomaria capensis*	6·00	6·25
2517	6000s. *Ixora hybrida*	7·00	7·25
2518	10000s. *Datura suaveolens*	12·00	12·50
2519	20000s. *Cucurbita pepo*	24·00	25·00

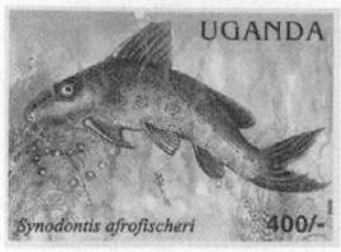
UGANDA
Synodontis afrofischeri 400/-

263 *Synodontis afrofischeri*

2005. Fish of Lake Victoria. Multicoloured.

2520	400s. Type **263**	90	45
2521	600s. *Protopterus aethiopicus*	1·50	60
2522	1100s. *Clarias gariepinus*	2·25	2·00
2523	1200s. *Rastrineobola argentea* (inscr "agentea")	2·25	2·00
2524	1600s. *Bagrus docmac*	2·75	3·25
2525	2000s. *Schilbe* (inscr "Schlbe") *mystus*	3·00	3·75
MS2526	97×77 mm. 1000s.×4, *Mormyrus kannume; Barbus jacksonni; Bagrus docmac; Labeo victorianus*	9·00	10·00

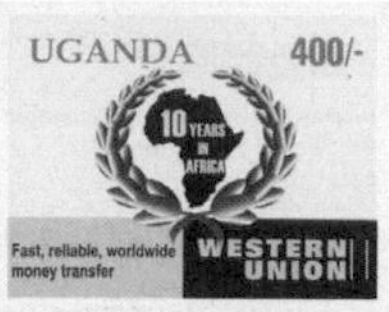
UGANDA 400/-
10 YEARS IN AFRICA
Fast, reliable, worldwide money transfer
WESTERN UNION

264 Map of Africa Emblem

2006. Tenth Anniv of Western Union in Africa. Multicoloured.

2527	400s. Type **264**	85	55
2528	1600s. Globe money transfer emblem	2·50	3·00
2529	2000s. Globe and national flags (vert)	2·75	3·50

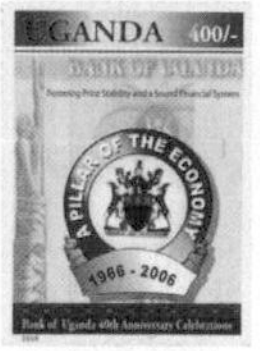
UGANDA 400/-
A PILLAR OF THE ECONOMY
1966 - 2006

265 Arms of Bank of Uganda

2006. 40th Anniv of the Bank of Uganda. Multicoloured.

2530	400s. Type **265**	85	55
2531	600s. Wildlife and city buildings	1·25	75
2532	1600s. *Tilapia nilotica* (fish)	2·50	3·00
2533	2000s. Mountain gorilla	3·00	3·75

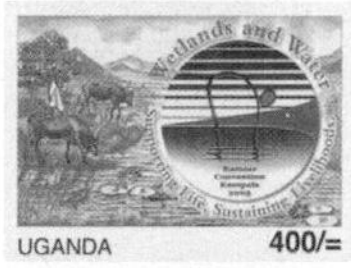
Wetlands and Water
UGANDA 400/=

266 Emblem of Ramsar Convention, Kampala, 2005 and Cattle in Marshland

2007. Wetlands. Multicoloured.

2534	400s. Type **266**	1·00	55
2535	1600s. River valley with crowned cranes and people observing birds	3·00	3·25
2536	2000s. Banana tree and fishermen in canoe, Lake George	3·25	3·75

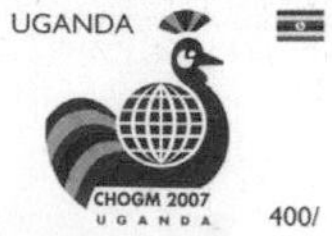
UGANDA
CHOGM 2007
UGANDA
400/

267 Emblem

2007. CHOGM (Commonwealth Heads of Government) Meeting, Kampala. Multicoloured.

2537	400s. Type **267**	75	55
2538	1600s. Boniface Kiprop winning 10,000 metres, Commonwealth Games, 2006	2·25	2·50
2539	2000s. Dorcas Inzikuru, gold medallist, 3000 metres steeplechase, Commonwealth Games, 2006	2·75	2·75
2540	5000s. Arms of Uganda (vert)	6·50	8·50

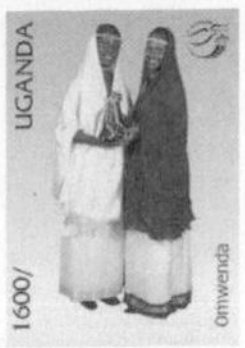
UGANDA
1600/-
Omwenda

268 Omwenda

2007. UPU Congress, Nairobi, Kenya. Costumes of Uganda. Multicoloured.

2541	1600s. Type **268**	2·50	2·50
2542	1600s. Ebibaraho	2·50	2·50
2543	1600s. Kikoyi	2·50	2·50
2544	1600s. Kanzu	2·50	2·50
2545	1600s. Gomesi	2·50	2·50
2546	1600s. Karimojong	2·50	2·50

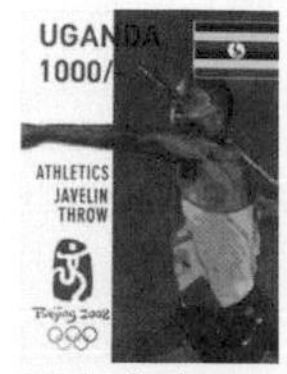
UGANDA
1000/-
ATHLETICS
JAVELIN
THROW

269 Javelin-thrower

2008. Olympic Games, Beijing. Multicoloured.

2547	1000s. Type **269**	2·00	2·00
2548	1000s. Athlete on starting block	2·00	2·00
2549	1000s. Boxer	2·00	2·00
2550	1000s. Swimmer	2·00	2·00

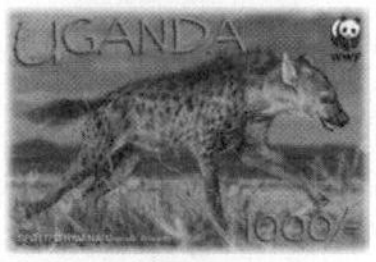
UGANDA
1000/-

270 Spotted Hyaena

2008. Endangered Species. Spotted Hyaena (*Crocuta crocuta*). Multicoloured.

2551	1000s. Type **270**	2·00	2·00
2552	1000s. Hyaenas around kill	2·00	2·00
2553	1000s. Female with pups	2·00	2·00
2554	1000s. Two young hyaenas	2·00	2·00
MS2555	113×165 mm. Nos. 2551/4, each ×2	12·00	13·00

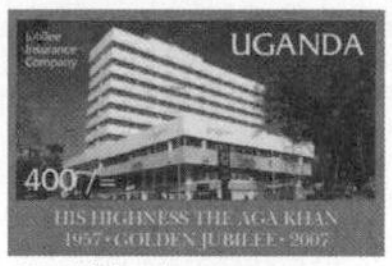
UGANDA
400/-
HIS HIGHNESS THE AGA KHAN
1957 • GOLDEN JUBILEE • 2007

271 Jubilee Insurance Company

2008. Golden Jubilee (2007) of the Aga Khan. Multicoloured.

2556	400s. Type **271**	1·00	1·00
2557	400s. Kampala Serena Hotel	1·00	1·00
2558	400s. Diamond Trust Bank Building	1·00	1·00
2559	1100s. Madrasa Programme	2·00	2·00
2560	1100s. The Ismaili Jamatkhana, Kampala	2·00	2·00
2561	1100s. Aga Khan HIgh School (Aga Khan Education Services)	2·00	2·00
2562	1100s. Air Uganda plane	2·00	2·00
2563	1100s. Bujagala Hydropower Project	2·00	2·00

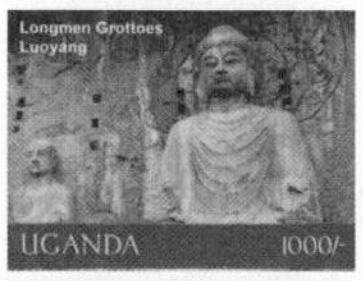
Longmen Grottoes
Luoyang
UGANDA 1000/-

272 Longmen Grottoes, Luoyang

2009. China 2009 World Stamp Exhibition, Luoyang (1st issue). Sites and Scenes of China. Sheet 101×147 mm containing T **272** and similar horiz designs. Multicoloured.

MS2564	Type **272**; Pearl River, Guangzhou; Twin Temples on Fir Lake, Guilin; Yi Yuan Garden, Shanghai	6·50	7·50

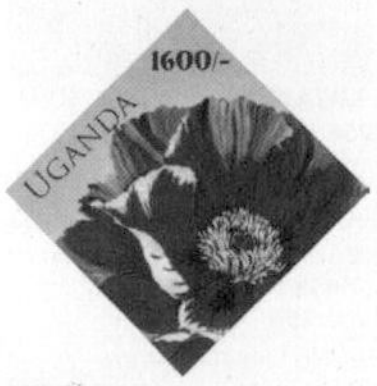
1600/-
UGANDA

273 Peony

2009. China 2009 World Stamp Exhibition, Luoyang (2nd issue). Peony.

2565	**273**	1600s. multicoloured	2·25	2·50

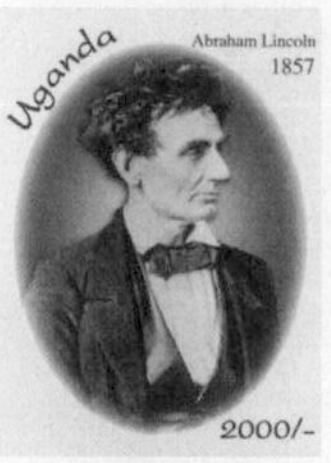
Uganda
Abraham Lincoln 1857
2000/-

274 Abraham Lincoln in 1857

2009. Birth Bicentenary of Abraham Lincoln. Sheet 181×142 mm containing T **274** and similar vert designs. Multicoloured.

MS2566	Type **274**; Abraham Lincoln in 1864; In profile, 1863; In 1857 (head and shoulders portrait)	10·00	11·00

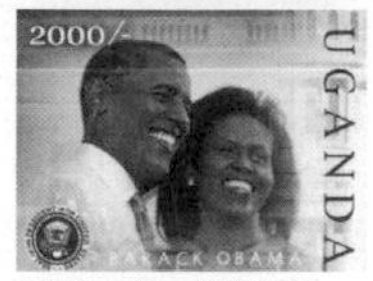
2000/-
UGANDA
BARACK OBAMA

275 Barack and Michelle Obama

2009. Inauguration of President Barack Obama. Sheet 151×151 mm containing T **275** and similar horiz designs. Multicoloured.

MS2567	Type **275**; Pres. Obama looking to right (window to his left); Pres. Obama facing camera; Pres. Obama looking to right; Pres. Obama facing camera (window with Christmas tree at top left); As Type **275** but different background (three large windows at top of stamp)	14·00	16·00

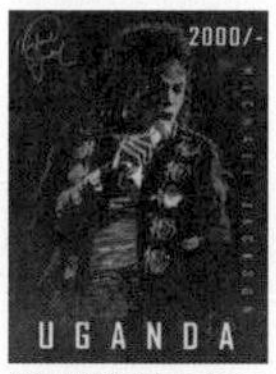
2000/-
UGANDA

276 Michael Jackson

2009. Michael Jackson Commemoration. Multicoloured.

MS2568	178×127 mm. 2000s.×4 Type **276**; Wearing white T-shirt and dark jacket (facing to left); Wearing white T-shirt and dark jacket (facing forward); Wearing jacket and white T-shirt both with glitter design	10·00	11·00
MS2569	178×127 mm. 2000s.×4 Michael Jackson as teenager: Wearing cream jacket and brown shirt (no tie); Wearing blue waistcoat and white shirt; Wearing pale blue jacket; Wearing brown shirt and cream jacket and tie	10·00	11·00

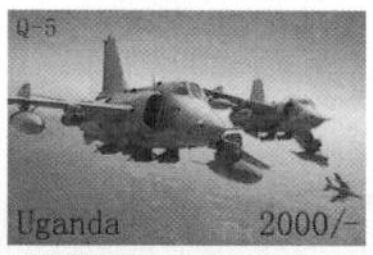
Q-5
Uganda 2000/-

277 Q-5

2009. Centenary of Chinese Aviation. Designs showing fighter planes. Multicoloured.

MS2570	145×95 mm. 2000s.×4 Type **277**; Q-5C; JH-7A; JH-7 (on ground)	11·00	12·00
MS2571	120×80 mm. 4000s. JH-7 taking off (50×38 mm)	7·50	8·50

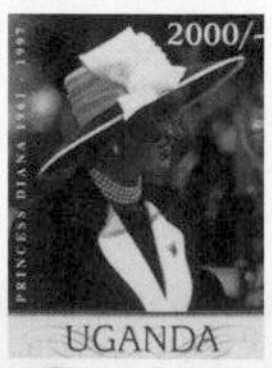
2000/-
PRINCESS DIANA
UGANDA

278 Diana, Princess of Wales

2010. Diana, Princess of Wales Commemoration. Multicoloured.

MS2572	2000s.×4 Type **278**; Wearing pink floral dress and pink hat; In close-up, wearing white; Carrying bouquet, wearing red jacket	10·00	11·00

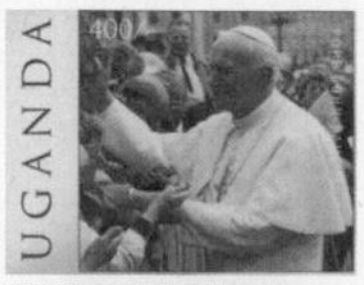
UGANDA
400

279 Pope John Paul II

2010. Fifth Death Anniv of Pope John Paul II . Multicoloured.

MS2573	400s. Type **279**; 1600s. With hands raised in blessing; 2000s. Smiling; 4000s. With hand on heart	13·00	13·00

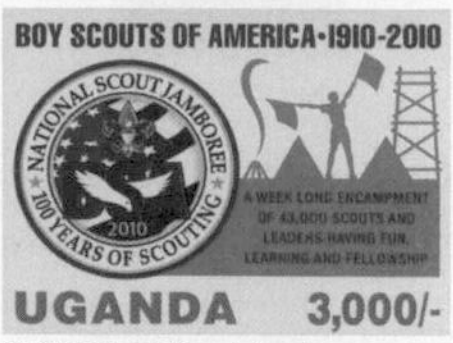
BOY SCOUTS OF AMERICA•1910-2010
NATIONAL SCOUT JAMBOREE
100 YEARS OF SCOUTING
2010
UGANDA 3,000/-

280 National Scout Jamboree Emblem and Scout Camp

2010. Centenary of the Boy Scouts of America. Multicoloured.

MS2574	3000s.×3 Type **280**; Philmont Scout Ranch, Cimarron, New Mexico emblem and horseman; Florida High Adventure Sea Base emblem, sailing dinghy and snorkeller	12·00	13·00

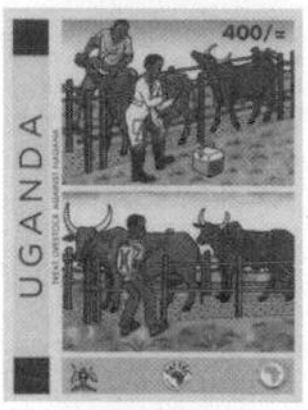
400/=
UGANDA

281 'Treat Livestock against Nagana'

2011. Campaign against Sleeping Sickness (Trypanosomiasis). Multicoloured.

2575	400s. Type **281**	75	30
2576	900s. 'Treat Humans against Sleeping Sickness' (horiz)	1·40	70
2577	1600s. 'War against Tsetse Flies in Uganda' (horiz)	2·50	2·50
2578	3000s. 'Empower Communities against Trypanosomiasis' (horiz)	4·00	4·50

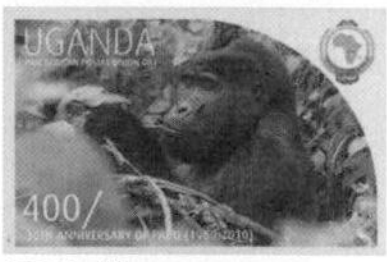
UGANDA
400/

282 Gorilla

2011. 30th Anniv of PAPU (Pan African Postal Union). Gorillas. Multicoloured.

2579	400s. Type **282**	75	75
2580	400s. Female carrying baby	75	75
2581	400s. Adult and baby	75	75
2582	400s. Head of gorilla, facing left	75	75
2583	400s. Male and female gorillas	75	75
2584	400s. Male gorilla seated	75	75
2585	400s. Close up of face	75	75
2586	400s. Male gorilla among bushes	75	75
2587	400s. Male gorilla feeding, facing right	75	75
2588	400s. Adult on all fours, two young gorillas in foreground	75	75
2589	1000s. Head of male gorilla, mouth open	1·50	1·50
2590	1000s. Gorilla sat in bushes	1·50	1·50
2591	1000s. Gorilla lying on back, mouth open	1·50	1·50
2592	1000s. Gorilla (half length photo)	1·50	1·50
2593	1000s. Head of gorilla (partly obscured by leaves)	1·50	1·50
2594	1600s. Head of gorilla, stalk in mouth	2·00	2·00
2595	1600s. Gorilla in tree	2·00	2·00
2596	1600s. Gorilla seen through vegetation	2·00	2·00
2597	1600s. Head of adult male gorilla, ferns at right	2·00	2·00
2598	1600s. Two young gorillas	2·00	2·00

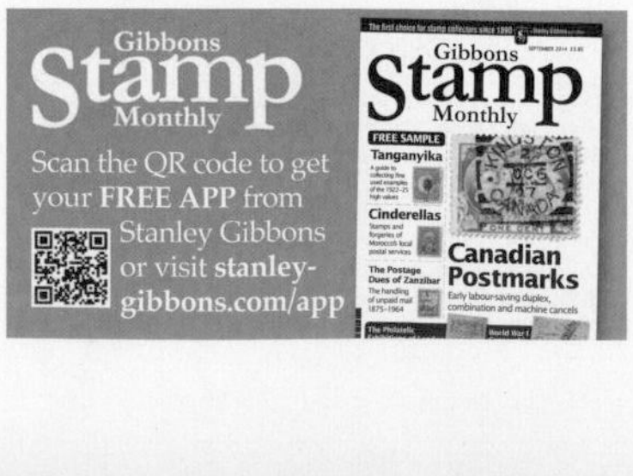
Gibbons Stamp Monthly
Scan the QR code to get your FREE APP from Stanley Gibbons or visit stanley-gibbons.com/app
Gibbons Stamp Monthly
Canadian Postmarks

POSTAGE DUE STAMPS

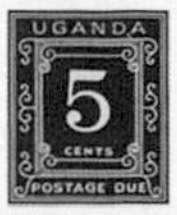

D1

1967

D10	**D1**	30c. brown	35	4·25
D11	**D1**	40c. purple	55	5·50
D17	**D1**	1s. orange	1·75	11·00

These stamps exist in limited quantities overprinted **UGANDA LIBERATED 1979**.

1979. Liberation. As Nos. D7/11 and D17 optd **LIBERATED 1979**.

D18	5c. red	15	40
D19	10c. green	15	40
D20	20c. blue	20	40
D21	30c. brown	20	60
D22	40c. purple	20	60
D23	1s. orange	20	60

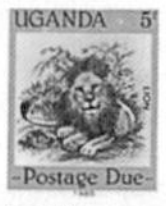

D3 Lion

1985. Animals.

D24	**D3**	5s. black and turquoise	15	1·00
D25	-	10s. black and lilac	15	1·00
D26	-	20s. black and orange	30	1·00
D27	-	40s. black and lilac	80	1·50
D28	-	50s. black and blue	80	1·50
D29	-	100s. black and mauve	1·40	3·00

DESIGNS: 10s. African buffalo; 20s. Kob; 40s. African elephant; 50s. Common zebra; 100s. Black rhinoceros.

Pt. 10

UKRAINE

A district of S.W. Russia, which issued stamps during its temporary independence after the Russian Revolution. In 1923 it became a constituent of the U.S.S.R.

In 1991 it became an independent republic.

1918. 100 shahiv = 1 hryvna (grivna); 2 hriven = 1 rouble.
1992. 100 kopeks = 1 rouble.
1992. Karbovanets (coupon currency).
1996. 100 kopiykas = 1 hryvna.

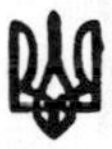

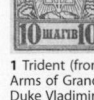

(L6)

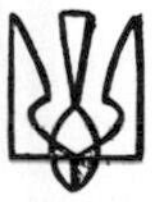

(L8)

1918. Arms types of Russia optd with Trident device in various types according to the district. Imperf or perf.

L51	**22**	1k. orange	25	30
L52	**22**	2k. green	25	30
L53	**22**	3k. red	25	30
L54	**23**	4k. red	25	30
L55	**22**	5k. red	25	30
L138	**22**	7k. blue	25	30
L57	**23**	10k. blue	25	30
L58	**22**	10k. on 7k. blue	30	40
L159	**9**	14k. red and blue	40	55
L60	**9**	15k. blue and purple	25	30
L61	**14**	20k. red and blue	25	30
L62	**9**	20k. on 14k. red and blue	25	30
L145	**9**	25k. mauve and green	40	95
L64	**9**	35k. green and purple	25	30
L65	**14**	50k. green and purple	25	30
L66	**9**	70k. orange and brown	25	30
L47	**15**	1r. orange and brown	40	45
L72	**11**	3r.50 grey and black	38·00	40·00
L212	**11**	3r.50 green and brown	95	1·30
L49	**20**	5r. blue and green	1·60	1·80
L14	**11**	7r. pink and green	3·75	4·00
L73	**11**	7r. yellow and black	21·00	25·00
L36	**20**	10r. grey, red and yellow	11·50	12·50

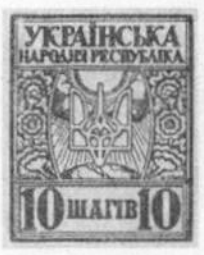

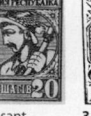

1 Trident (from Arms of Grand Duke Vladimir the Great)

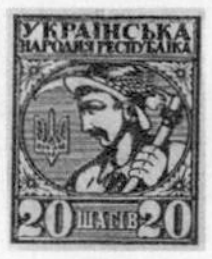

2 Peasant

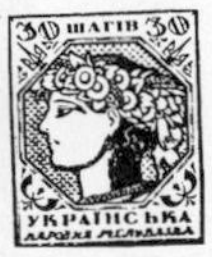

3 Ceres

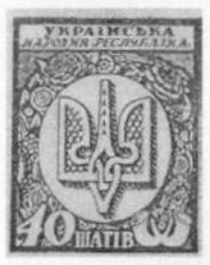

4 Trident

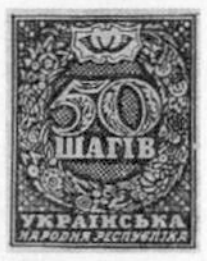

5

1918. Without inscription on back. Imperf.

1	**1**	10s. brown	40	1·90
2	**2**	20s. brown	40	1·90
3	**3**	30s. blue	40	1·90
4	**4**	40s. green	40	1·90
5	**5**	50s. red	40	1·90

1918. With trident and four lines of inscription on back.

6	**1**	10s. brown	5·00	8·75
7	**2**	20s. brown	5·00	8·75
8	**3**	30s. blue	5·00	8·75
9	**4**	40d. green	5·00	8·75
10	**5**	50s. red	5·00	8·75

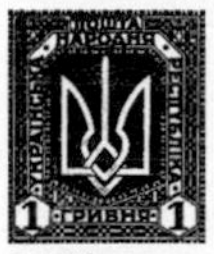

6a Trident

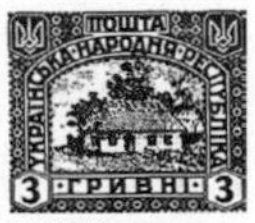

6b Parliament Building

Stamps of the above and similar designs were prepared for use but never used.

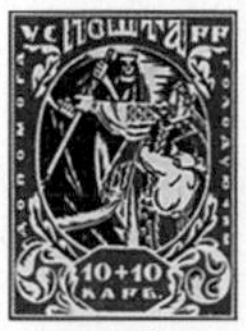

7 Spectre of Famine

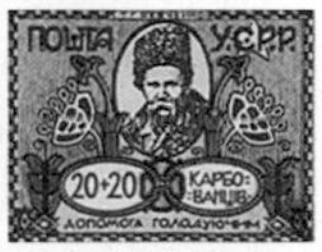

8 T. G. Shevchenko (Ukrainian poet)

1923. Charity.

12	**7**	10+10k. blue and black	1·50	6·25
13	**8**	20+20k. brown and orange	1·50	6·25
14	-	90+30k. black and bistre	3·00	10·50
15	-	150+50k. red and black	4·00	15·00

DESIGNS—VERT: 90k. "Death" and peasant; 150k. "Ukraine" (woman) distributing bread.

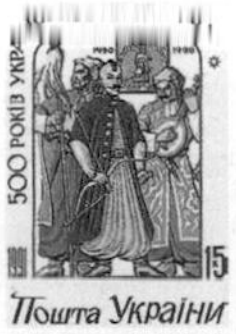

11 Cossack Chief with Musician and Standard Bearer

1992. 500th Anniv (1990) of Ukraine Cossacks.

20	**11**	15k. multicoloured	1·30	95

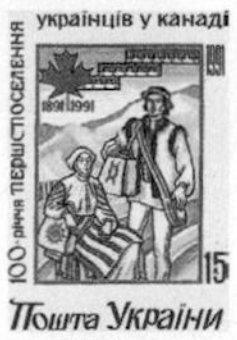

12 Galician Emigrant Couple

1992. Centenary (1991) of Ukrainian Emigration to Canada.

21	**12**	15k. multicoloured	1·30	95

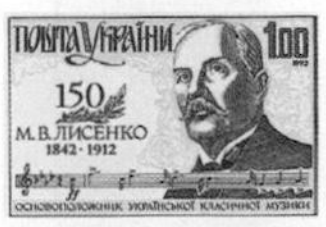

13 Mykola Lysenko and Score from "Taras Bulba"

1992. 150th Birth Anniv of Mykola Lysenko (composer).

22	**13**	1r. brown, red and bistre	1·30	95

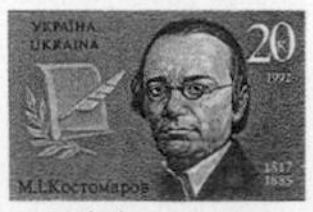

14 Mykola Kostomarov, Quill Pen and Scroll

1992. 175th Birth Anniv of Mykola Kostomarov (historian).

23	**14**	20k. brown and light brown	25	25

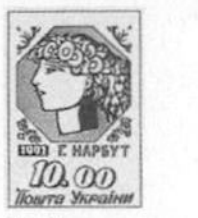

15 Ceres

1992

46	**15**	50k. blue	30	25
47	**15**	70k. brown	30	25
48	**15**	1r. green	30	25
49	**15**	2r. violet	30	25
50	**15**	5r. blue	40	35
51	**15**	10r. red	70	60
52	**15**	20r. green	3·50	3·00
53	**15**	50r. brown	4·25	3·50

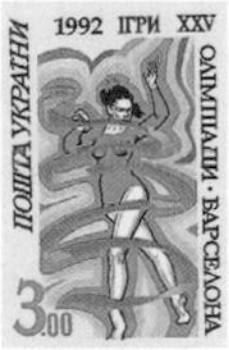

16 Rhythmic Gymnastics

1992. Olympic Games, Barcelona. Multicoloured.

54	3r. Type **16**	1·00	85
55	4r. Pole vaulting	1·10	95
56	5r. Type **16**	1·40	1·20

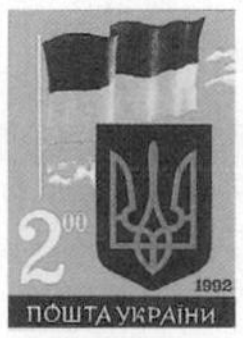

17 State Flag and Trident Symbol

1992. First Anniv of Regained Independence.

57	**17**	2r. multicoloured	1·40	1·20

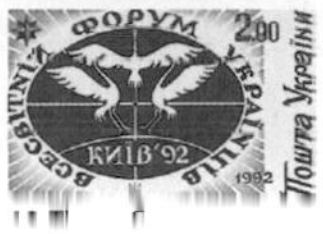

Globe

1992. World Congress of Ukrainians, Kyiv.

58	**18**	2r. multicoloured	1·40	1·20

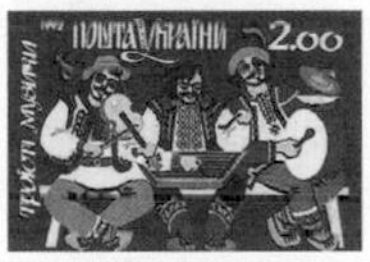

19 Folk Musicians

1992. 25th Anniv of Ukraine Philatelic Federation and First Stamp Exibition, Ivano—Frankivsk. Sheet 93×73 mm.

MS59 2r. multicoloured	2·10	2·00

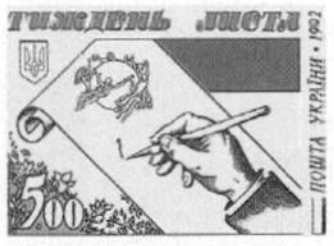

20 U.P.U. Emblem and Hand writing

1992. Correspondence Week.

60	**20**	5r. multicoloured	1·20	1·00

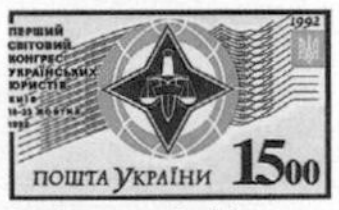

21 Congress Emblem

1992. World Congress of Ukrainian Jurists, Kyiv.

61	**21**	15r. multicoloured	2·30	2·00

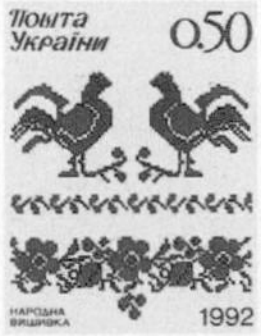

22 Embroidery

1992. Ukraine Folk Art.

62	**22**	0.50k. black and orange	60	50

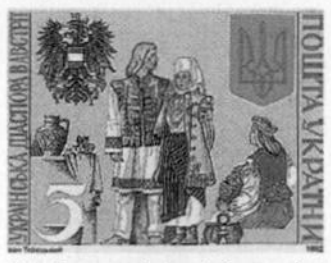

23 Arms of Austria and Ukraine with Traditional Costumes of Galicia and Bukovina

1992. Ukrainians in Austria.

63	**23**	5k. multicoloured	1·50	1·30

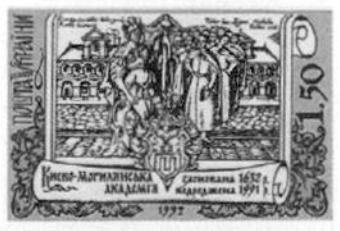

24 Students and Academy, 1632 (after I. Shyrsky)

1992. 360th Anniv of Mogilyanska's Academy, Kyiv.

64	**24**	1k.50 black, blue and brown	75	65

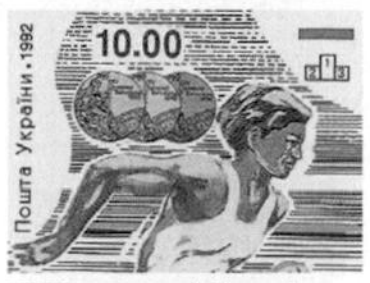

25 Runner and Olympic Medals

1992. Ukrain Medal Winners at Olympic Games, Barcelona. Sheet 90×70 mm.

MS65 **25** 10k. multicoloured	6·00	5·75

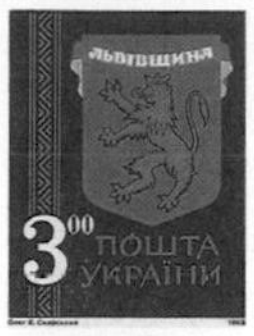

26 Lviv Arms

1993. Regional Arms.

66	**26**	3k. blue, deep blue and gold	1·50	1·30
67	-	5k. lake, gold and red	2·30	2·00

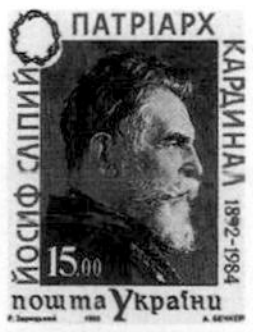

27 Cardinal Slipyj

1993. Birth Centenary (1992) of Cardinal Josyf Slipyj.

68	**27**	15k. multicoloured	3·00	2·50

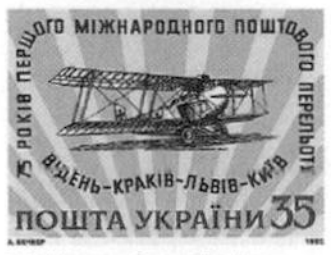

28 Hansa Brandenburg C-I

1993. 75th Anniv of First Vienna–Cracow–Lviv–Kyiv Flight.

69	**28**	35k. black, blue and mauve	2·30	2·00
70	-	50k. multicoloured	2·50	2·20

DESIGN: 50k. Airbus Industrie A300.

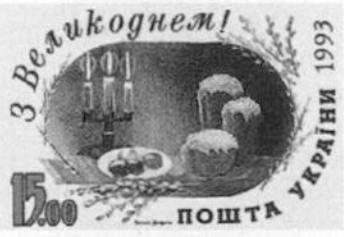

29 Candles and Traditional Foods

1993. Easter.

71	**29**	15k. multicoloured	1·80	1·60

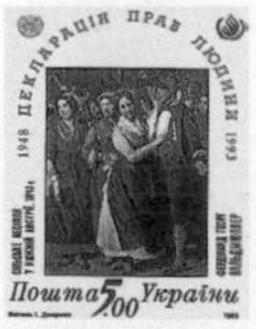

30 "Country Wedding in Lower Austria" (Ferdinand Georg Waldmuller)

1993. 45th Anniv of Declaration of Human Rights.
72 **30** 5k. multicoloured   2·50   2·20

31 National
Famine
Monument, Kyiv

1993. 60th Anniv of Famine Deaths.
73 **31** 75k. brown   1·20   1·00

32 1918 10sh. Stamp

1993. Stamp Day. 75th Anniv of First Ukrainian Postage Stamps.
74 **32** 100k. blue and brown   1·50   1·30

33 Kyiv

1993. 50th Anniv of Liberation of Kyiv.
75 **33** 75k. multicoloured   1·20   1·00

34
Mowing

1993. Agricultural Scenes.
76 **34** 50k. green   30   25
77 - 100k. blue   40   35
78 - 150k. red   45   40
79 - 200k. orange   55   45
80 - 300k. purple   60   50
81 - 500k. brown   75   65
DESIGNS: 100k. Laden bullock carts; 150, 300k. Shepherd and flock; 200, 500k. Women cutting corn.

35 Madonna and
Child (Albrecht
Durer)

1994. Ukrainian Health Fund.
82 **35** 150k.+20k. black, gold and red   1·10   90

36 St. Ahapit

1994. St. Ahapit (medieval doctor).
83 **36** 200k. black and red   90   80

37 Dog's-tooth
Violet
("Erythronium
denscanis")

1994. Red Book of Ukraine. Multicoloured.
84 **37** 200k. Type **37**   1·20   1·00
85 - 200k. Lady's slipper ("Cypripedium calceolus")   1·20   1·00

38 Laden
Bullock
Carts

1994. Agricultural Scenes. Value expressed by Cyrillic letter.
86 - A (5000k.) red   75   65
87 **38** V (10000k.) blue   1·50   1·30
DESIGN: A, Shepherd and flock.
The Cyrillic "V" on No. 87 resembles a "B".

39
Women
cutting
Corn

40 Cutting
Hay

1994. Agricultural Scenes. Value expressed by Cyrillic letter.
88 **39** B (100k.) brown   60   50
89 **40** G (250k.) green   75   65

41 Parliament Building and Map

1994. Independence Day. Sheet 68×90 mm. Imperf.
MS90 **41** 5000k. multicoloured   4·50   4·25

42 Kyiv University

1994. 160th Anniv of Kyiv University. Multicoloured.
91 10000k. Type **42**   1·50   1·30
MS92 100×80 mm. 25000k. Kyiv University (different) (40×28 mm)   4·50   4·25

43 Map and Airplanes
(Liberation of Ukraine)

1994. 50th Anniv of Liberation. Multicoloured.
93 500k. Map and rocket launchers (Russia)   60   50
94 500k. Type **43**   60   50
95 500k. Map, tank and soldiers (Byelorussia)   60   50

44
Ploughing

45 Fishing

1994. Agricultural Scenes. Value expressed by Cyrillic letter.
96 **44** E (100k.) mauve   30   25
97 **45** Zh (5300k.) blue   1·20   1·00

47 Potter
at Wheel

1994. Agricultural Scenes. Value expressed by Cyrillic letter.
98 **46** A (1800k.) brown   30   25
99 **47** E (17000k.) red   2·40   2·10

46 Bee-Keeping

48 Ceramics and
Map

1994. 100th Anniv of Excavation of Tripillya.
100 **48** 4000k. multicoloured   60   50

49 Reader and
Arms

1994. 500th Anniv of First Book printed in Ukrainian Language, "Book of Hours" by Sh. Fiol.
101 **49** 4000k. multicoloured   60   50

50 Repin and
Study of Soldier

1994. 150th Birth Anniv of Ilya Repin (painter).
102 **50** 4000k. multicoloured   60   50

51 Sofiyivka Park and
Statue

1994. Bicent of Sofiyivka Nature Park, Uman.
103 **51** 5000k. multicoloured   75   65

52 Uzhhorod Castle

1995. 1100th Anniv of Uzhhorod.
104 **52** 5000k. multicoloured   90   80

53 Ivan Franko (writer)

1995. Personalities. Multicoloured.
105 3000k. Type **53**   45   40
106 3000k. Ivan Pulyui (physicist) (vert)   45   40
107 3000k. Lesya Ukrainka (writer)   45   40

54 Peregrine
Falcon

1995. Red Book of Ukraine. Birds. Multicoloured.
108 5000k. Type **54**   75   65
109 10000k. Common crane   1·50   1·30

55 Rylskyi

1995. Birth Centenary of Maksym Rylskyi (writer).
110 **55** 50000k. multicoloured   3·75   3·25

56 Doves, Bell
Tower and River

1995. 50th Anniv of End of Second World War.
111 **56** 100000k. multicoloured   3·00   2·50

57 Figures around Globe
on Map of Ukraine

1995. 70th Anniv of Artek International Children's Holiday Camps, Crimea.
112 **57** 5000k. multicoloured   75   65

58 Ivan Kotlyarevski and
Scene from "Eneida"
(poem)

1995. Writers. Multicoloured.
113 1000k. Type **58**   30   25
114 3000k. Taras Shevchenko and cover of "Kobzar"   60   50

59 Siege of Theodosia

1995. 17th-century Hetmans. Petro Konashevich-Sahaidachnyi.
115 **59** 30000k. multicoloured   1·50   1·30

60 Lugansk

1995. Regional Arms.
116 **60** 10000k. multicoloured   75   65

61 Bell Tower of Domition
Church, National Museum
and Dominican Cathedral

1995. National Stamp Exhibition, Lviv.
117 **61** 50000k.+5000k. mult   2·30   2·00

62 St. Elias's Church, Subotov, and
Battle Scene

1995. 17th-century Hetmans. Bohdan Khimelnytskyi.
118 **62** 40000k. multicoloured   1·80   1·60

63 St. Michael's
Cathedral, Kyiv

1995. 17th-century Hetmans. Ivan Mazepa.
119 **63** 30000k. multicoloured   1·50   1·30

64 Part of
Rainbow and
White Stork

1995. European Nature Conservation Year.
120   **64**   50000k. multicoloured   2·30   2·00

1995. Regional Arms. As T **60**.
121   10000k. multicoloured   90   80
DESIGN: 10000k. Chernihiv.

65 Girl carrying
Water Pails

1995. International Children's Day.
122   **65**   50000k. multicoloured   1·50   1·30

66 Anniversary Emblem

1995. 50th Anniv of U.N.O.
123   **66**   50000k. blue, violet and
      black   1·50   1·30

67 Hrushevskyi

1995. 60th Death Anniv (1994) of Mykhailo Hrushevskyi
(first President).
124   **67**   50000k. multicoloured   1·50   1·30

68
Karpenko-Karyi

1995. 150th Birth Anniv of Ivan Karpenko-Karyi
(dramatist).
125   **68**   50000k. multicoloured   1·50   1·30

69 Shafaryk

1995. Birth Bicentenary of Pavel Shafaryk (historian and
philologist).
126   **69**   30000k. green   1·10   90

70 Trolleybus   **71** Tramcar   **72** Bus

1995. Transport. Value expressed by Cyrillic letter.
127   **70**   I (1000k.) blue   55   45
128   **71**   K (2000k.) green   1·20   1·00
129   **72**   Z (3000k.) pink   1·50   1·30

73 Oksana Bayul
(gold, ice-skating)

1996. Ukrainian Medal Winners at Winter Olympic Games,
Lillehammer. Sheet 90×70 mm containing T **73** and
similar vert designs. Multicoloured.
MS130 40000k. Valentia Tserbe (bronze,
      biathlon); 50000k. Type **73**   3·50   3·25

74 Research
Aids

1996. 150th Anniv of Observatory, Taras Shevchenko
University, Kyiv. Multicoloured.
131   20000k. Type **74**   60   50
132   30000k. Telescope   75   65
133   50000k. Sun over observatory
      buildings   1·20   1·00

75 Krymskyi

1996. 125th Birth Anniv of Ahatanhel Krymskyi (writer).
134   **75**   20000k. brown and
      ochre   75   65

76 Kozlovskyi

1996. Third Death Anniv of Ivan Kozlovskyi (tenor).
135   **76**   20000k. multicoloured   75   65

77 Animals

1996. Centenary of Kharkiv Zoo.
136   **77**   20000k. olive, green
      and blue   75   65

78 Dovshenko and
Birthplace

1996. Birth Centenary of Oleksandr Dovshenko (film
producer and set designer).
137   **78**   4000k. multicoloured   60   50

79 Lighted
Candle within
Tower

1996. Tenth Anniv of Chernobyl Nuclear Disaster.
138   **79**   20000k. multicoloured   75   65

80 Vasyl Fedorovych,
Volodymyr Levkovich
and Levko Platonovych
Symyrenko

1996. Symyrenko Family.
139   **80**   20000k. multicoloured   75   65
    Vasil was a sugar refiner; Volodimir and Levko fruit
growers and researchers.

81 Stefanik

1996. 60th Death Anniv of Vasyl Stefanik (writer and
politician).
140   **81**   20000k. multicoloured   75   65

82 Miklukho-Maklai

1996. 150th Birth Anniv of Mikola Mikolaiovich Miklukho-
Maklai (explorer and philologist).
141   **82**   40000k. multicoloured   1·50   1·30

83 Wrestling

1996. Olympic Games, Atlanta, U.S.A. Multicoloured.
142   20000k. Type **83**   75   65
143   40000k. Handball   1·50   1·30
MS144 40×70 mm. 100000k. Gymnast   2·30   2·00

84 "100" and Ancient
Greek Athletes

1996. Centenary of Modern Olympic Games.
145   **84**   40000k. bistre, turquoise
      and blue   1·50   1·30

85 Trident
Emblem and "V"
in National
Colours

1996. Fifth Anniv of Independence.
146   **85**   20000k. multicoloured   75   65

86 "Sich-1"

1996. First Ukrainian Satellite.
147   **86**   20000k. multicoloured   75   65

87 Series OD Steam
Locomotive

1996. Railway Locomotives. Multicoloured.
148   20000k. Type **87**   75   65
149   40000k. Class 2TE-116 diesel
      locomotive   1·50   1·30

88 Antonov

1996. 90th Birth Anniv of Oieh Antonov (aircraft
designer). Multicoloured.
150   20000k. Type **88**   55   45

151   20000k. Antonov An-2 biplane   55   45
152   40000k. Antonov An-124
      airliner   1·10   95
153   40000k. Antonov An-225 pig-
      gybacking airplane   1·10   95

89 Piddubnyi

1996. 125th Birth Anniv of Ivan Piddubnyi (weightlifting
world champion).
154   **89**   40k. multicoloured   1·10   95

90 Academician
Vernadskyi Antarctic
Station

1996. First Ukrainian Antarctic Expedition.
155   **90**   20k. multicoloured   1·20   1·10

91 Eidelwiess

1996. Protected Flowers. Multicoloured.
156   20k. Type **91**   55   45
157   40k. "Narcissus anqustifolius"   1·10   95

92 Emblem

1996. 50th Anniv of UNESCO.
158   **92**   20k. multicoloured   90   80

93 Kosenko

1996. Birth Centenary of W. S. Kosenko (composer).
159   **93**   20k. multicoloured   90   80

94 St. Sophia Cathedral,
Kyiv

1996. Churches. Multicoloured.
160   20k. Type **94**   90   80
161   20k. St. Elias's Church, Subotov   90   80
162   20k. St. George's Church,
      Drogobych   90   80
163   20k. Trinity Cathedral, Novo-
      moskovsk   90   80

95 Mohyla

1996. 400th Birth Anniv of Petro Mohyla (Metropolitan
of Kyiv).
164   **95**   20k. black and brown   90   80

96 Mother and Child
within Emblem

1996. 50th Anniv of UNICEF.
165 **96** 20k. multicoloured   90   80

97 Lynx

1997. Protected Animals. Multicoloured.
166   20k. Type **97**   90   80
167   20k. Brown bear   90   80

98 Cathedral of the Holy Cross, Poltava

1997. Religious Buildings. Multicoloured.
168   20k. Type **98**   90   80
169   20k. St. George's Cathedral, Lviv   90   80
170   20k. St. Mary's Church, Sythtsi   90   80

99 Kyiv and Schek

1997. Europa. Tails and Legends. The Founders of Kyvi. Sheet 100×80 mm containing T **99** and similar vert designs. Each green, yellow and brown.
MS171 40k. Type **99**; 40k. Khoryv and their sister Lybid   14·00   14·00

100 Taras Shevchenko Monument, Stamps and Exhibition Hall

1997. Fourth National Stamp Exhibition, Cherkasy.
172 **100** 10k. multicoloured   60   55

101 Kondratyuk and Diagram of Space Orbit

1997. Birth Centenary of Yury Kondratyuk (space pioneer).
173 **101** 20k. multicoloured   90   80

102 Arms, Map on Open Book and Assembly Building

1997. First Anniv of Constitution.
174 **102** 20k. multicoloured   90   80

103 Fire, Fern and Couple

1997. Midsummer Festival of Ivana Kupala.
175 **103** 20k. multicoloured   90   80

104 Princess Olga (regent of Kyiv, 945–55)

1997. Famous Women. Multicoloured.
176   40k. Type **104**   1·80   1·60
177   40k. Roxolana (wife of Sultan Suleiman II of Turkey)   1·80   1·60

105 Taras Shevchenko Monument, Buenos Aires

1997. Centenary of First Ukranian Emigration to Argentina.
178 **105** 20k. multicoloured   90   80

106 For Military Service for Ukraine

1997. Orders and Medals.
179 **106** 20k. multicoloured   90   80
180   -   20k. multicoloured   90   80
181   -   30k. grey, red and blue   1·10   95
182   -   40k. multicoloured   1·20   1·10
183   -   60k. multicoloured   1·80   1·60
MS184 100×80 mm. 60k. ×2, each slate, crimson and blue   7·00   6·50

DESIGNS: No. 180, For Meritorious Service; 181, For Valour; 182, Order of Bohdan Khemelnytskyi; 183, For Special Contributions. 34×43 mm—No. MS184, Order of Prince Yaroslav medal (profile in centre); badge (helmet in centre).

107 Dmytro Vyshnevetskyi Baida

1997. Hetmans. Multicoloured.
185   20k. Type **107**   90   80
186   20k. Stockholm, Pylyp Orlik and Thessalonika   90   80

108 KruschenInytska

1997. 125th Birth Anniv of Solomiya KruschenInytska (opera singer).
187 **108** 20k. multicoloured   90   80

109 Antonov An-74 TK-200

1997. Aircraft. Multicoloured.
188   20k. Type **109**   90   80
189   40k. Antonov An-38-100   1·80   1·60

110 "Zavetnyi" (torpedo boat), 1903

1997. Ships. Multicoloured.
190   20k. Type **110**   90   80
191   40k. "Akademik Sergei Korolov" (research ship), 1970   1·80   1·60

111 "Columbia" (space shuttle) and Flags

1997. Ukraine–U.S.A. Space Flight.
192 **111** 40k. multicoloured   2·10   1·90

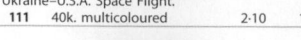

112 Krichevskyi

1997. 125th Birth Anniv of Vasyl Krichevskyi (painter and architect).
193 **112** 10k. stone, brown & black   55   45

113 "Nativity" (icon)

1997. Christmas.
194 **113** 20k. multicoloured   90   80

114 Painted Rooster, Dnipropetrovsk

1997. Folk Art. Multicoloured. Buff margins.
195   20k. Type **114**   90   80
196   20k. Fur-trimmed waistcoat, Chernivtsi   90   80
197   40k. Ceramic ram, Poltava   1·80   1·60
198   40k. Wooden plate, Ivano-Frankivsk   1·80   1·60
MS199 115×149 mm. As Nos. 195/8 but with white margins, each ×2.   10·50   10·00

115 Skovoroda

1997. 275th Birth Anniv of Grigorii Skovoroda (philosopher).
200 **115** 60k. multicoloured   2·10   1·90

116 Arms of Zakarpattskaya Oblast

1997. Regional Arms.
201 **116** 20k. multicoloured   90   80

117 Skylark

1997. Animals. Sheet 114×121 mm containing T **117** and similar vert designs. Multicoloured.
MS202 20k. Type **117**; 20k. Black stork; 20k. Garden dormouse; 40k. White-tailed eagle; 40k. Long-eared hedgehog; 40k. Wild boar   8·75   8·50

118 Sosyura

1998. Birth Centenary of Volodymyr Sosyura (poet).
203 **118** 20k. blue, black and brown   90   80

119 Figure Skating

1998. Winter Olympic Games, Nagano, Japan. Multicoloured.
204   20k. Type **119**   90   80
205   20k. Biathlon   90   80

120 City Walls

1998. 2500th Anniv of Bilhorod-Dnistrovskyi.
206 **120** 20k. multicoloured   90   80

121 "Hetman Sagaidachnyi" (frigate)

1998
207 **121** 30k. multicoloured   1·80   1·60

122 1 Million Karbovanets Coin showing Bohdan Khmelnytskyi

1998. Coins.
208 **122** 30k. black, green & purple   90   80
209   -   30k. black, green & purple   90   80
210   -   60k. brown, green and purple   1·80   1·60
211   -   60k. brown, green and purple   1·80   1·60
212   -   1h. brown, green & purple   4·50   4·00
213   -   1h. black, green and purple   4·50   4·00

DESIGNS: No. 209, 10 hryven coin showing Petro Mohila; 210, 500 hryven coin showing Virgin Mary; 211, 200 hryven coin showing Taras Shevchenko; 212, Gold coin of Vladymyr Svyatoslavich; 213, Silver coin of Vladymyr Svyatoslavich.

123 Festival of Ivana Kupala

1998. Europa. National Festivals.
214 **123** 40k. multicoloured   2·75   2·30

124 Red Deer

1998. Centenary of New Askaniya National Park. Sheet 100×800 mm containing T **124** and similar horiz designs. Multicoloured.
MS215 40k. Type **124**; 60k. Wild horses ... 5·25 ... 5·00

125 "Empress Maria Theresa" (J. E. Liotard)

1998. Paintings. Multicoloured.
216	20k. Type **125**	55	45
217	20k. "Man playing Cello" (G. Honthorst)	55	45
218	40k. "Madonna and Child" (icon)	90	80
MS219 93×73 mm. 1r.20 "Madonna and Child" ... 3·25 ... 2·75

126 University Campus

1998. Centenary of Kyvi Technical University (1st issue). Sheet 113×80 mm.
MS220 **126** 1h. multicoloured ... 2·75 ... 2·50
See also Nos. 232/6.

127 Askold and Dir

1998. First Rulers of Kyiv
221 **127** 3h. purple and bistre ... 5·25 ... 4·75

128 Armoured Rider and Swordsman

1998. 350th Anniv of Start of Campaign for Independence. Each brown, green and purple.
222	30k. Type **128**	90	80
223	30k. Warriors with staves and swordsman	90	80
224	40k. Stavesman, swordsman and archer	1·10	95
225	40k. Group of archers	1·10	95
226	60k. Rider	1·40	1·20
227	2h. Hetman Bohdan Khmelnytskyi	4·50	4·00
Nos. 222/7 were issued together, *se-tenant*, forming a composite design.

129 Crown of Prince Danylo Galitsky

1998. 1100th Anniv of the Town of Halich.
228 **129** 20k. multicoloured ... 90 ... 80

130 Anna Yaroslavna

1998. Anna Yaroslavna (daughter of King Yaroslav of Kyiv and wife of King Henri I of France).
229 **130** 40k. multicoloured ... 1·20 ... 1·10

131 Lisyansky

1998. 225th Birth Anniv of Yurii Fyodorovich Lisyansky (first Ukrainian to circumnavigate world).
230 **131** 40k. multicoloured ... 1·20 ... 1·10

132 Natalia Uzhvii

1998. Birth Centenary of Natalia Uzhvii (actress).
231 **132** 40k. brown and gold ... 1·20 ... 1·10

133 V. L. Kyrpychov (first Director)

1998. Centenary of Kyiv Technical University. Multicoloured.
232	10k. Type **133**	70	60
233	20k. E. Paton (metallurgist) and bridge in Kyiv	90	80
234	20k. Stefan Timoshenko (materials scientist) and formula	90	80
235	30k. Igor Sikorsky (aircraft designer) and test flight in Kyiv	1·10	95
236	40k. Sergei Korolev (space scientist) and spacecraft	1·20	1·10

134 Emblem and Posthorn on "Stamp"

1998. World Post Day.
237 **134** 10k. multicoloured ... 70 ... 60

135 Monk Nestor (early chronicler)

1998. Millenary of Book Production in Ukraine.
238 **135** 20k. multicoloured ... 90 ... 80

136 Cathedral of the Transfiguration, Chernigov

1998. Cathedrals. Multicoloured.
| 239 | 20k. Type **136** | 90 | 80 |
| 240 | 20k. Pokrovsky Cathedral, Kharkov | 90 | 80 |

137 Red-breasted Geese

1998. Endangered Species. The Red-breasted Goose. Multicoloured.
241	20k. Type **137**	90	80
242	30k. Goose	1·10	95
243	40k. Goose with chicks	1·20	1·10
244	60k. Geese with chicks	1·60	1·40
MS245 290×120 mm. Nos. 241/4, each ×2 ... 9·75 ... 9·25

138 Battle of Chyhyryn, Doroshenko and Volokolamsk

1998. Hetmans. Petro Doroshenko.
246 **138** 20k. multicoloured ... 90 ... 80

139 Antonov An-140

1998. Aircraft. Multicoloured.
| 247 | 20k. Type **139** | 90 | 80 |
| 248 | 40k. Antonov An-70 | 1·80 | 1·60 |

140 Hrinchenko and his Dictionary

1998. 135th Birth Anniv of B. Hrinchenko (philologist).
249 **140** 20k. multicoloured ... 70 ... 60

141 Folk Icon

1998. Christmas.
250 **141** 30k. multicoloured ... 90 ... 80

142 Map of Australia and Waratah

1998. 50th Anniv of Ukrainians in Australia.
251 **142** 40k. multicoloured ... 1·10 ... 95

143 "Flowers in Fog"

1998. 50th Anniv of Universal Declaration of Human Rights. Paintings by Kateryna Bilokur. Multicoloured.
| 252 | 30k. Type **143** | 55 | 45 |
| 253 | 50k. "Bouquet of Flowers" | 90 | 80 |

144 Meteorites striking Earth

1998. Illinetsk Meteorite Impact Site.
254 **144** 40k. multicoloured ... 1·10 ... 95

145 Paradzhanov

1999. 75th Birth Anniv of Sergei Paradzhanov (film director).
255 **145** 40k. multicoloured ... 1·20 ... 1·10

146 Ivasyuk

1999. 50th Birth Anniv of Volodymyr Ivasyuk (composer).
256 **146** 30k. multicoloured ... 55 ... 45

147 Quiver

1999. Scythian Gold. Multicoloured.
257	20k. Type **147**	35	30
258	40k. Statuette of boar	70	60
259	50k. Statuette of young elk	90	80
260	1h. Pectoral	1·40	1·20

148 Girls in Central Ukrainian National Costume

1999. Spring.
261 **148** 30k. multicoloured ... 55 ... 45

149 Lake and Carpathian Mountains

1999. Europa. Parks and Gardens. Synievyr Lake National Park. Multicoloured.
| 262 | 50k. Type **149** | 90 | 80 |
| 263 | 1h. Lake and European grayling | 1·80 | 1·60 |
Nos. 262/3 were issued together, *se-tenant*, forming a composite design.

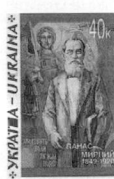

150 Mirny

1999. 150th Birth Anniv of Panas Mirny (writer).
264 **150** 40k. multicoloured ... 70 ... 60

151 Balzac

1999. Birth Bicentenary of Honore de Balzac (writer).
265 **151** 40k. black, gold and red ... 70 ... 60

152 Anniversary Emblem and Headquarters, Strasbourg

1999. 50th Anniv of Council of Europe.
266 **152** 40k. multicoloured ... 90 ... 80

153 Pushkin

1999. Birth Bicentenary of Aleksandr Sergyevich Pushkin (poet).
267 **153** 40k. multicoloured ... 90 ... 80

154 Baidak

1999. Traditional Warships. Multicoloured.
268	30k. Type **154**	70	60
269	30k. Chaika	70	60

155 Great Prince Yaroslav

1999. 800th Anniv of Accession of Prince Yaroslav (the Wise). Sheet 104×84 mm.
MS270 **155**	1h.20 multicoloured	3·50	3·25

156 St. George on Horseback (15th-century icon)

1999. Centenary of National Art Museum, Kyiv. Multicoloured.
271	30k. Type **156**	55	45
272	60k. "The Girl in the Red Hat" (O. O. Murashko)	1·10	95

157 Heraldic Lion (emblem of Lviv) and Armoured Knight

1999. 800th Anniv of Galitsian-Volynian State.
273	**157**	50k. multicoloured	90	80

158 Honey Bee on Flower

1999. Bee-keeping.
274	**158**	30k. multicoloured	90	80

159 Monument, Berne

1999. 125th Anniv of Universal Postal Union.
275	**159**	30k. multicoloured	90	80

160 Crest and Scroll

1999. 1100th Anniv of Poltava.
276	**160**	30k. multicoloured	90	80

161 Order of Princess Olga

1999. Order and Medals. Multicoloured.
277	30k. Type **161**	90	80

MS278 100×80 mm. 2h.50 For Service to the State (34×49 mm); 2h.50 Order of the Golden star (34×49 mm)
	10·50	10·00

162 Madonna and child (icon)

1999. International Year of The Elderly. Sheet115×90 mm.
MS279 **162**	1h.20+10k. multicoloured	5·25	5·00

163 Red Deer (Stuzhitsya Regional Landscape Park)

1999. Animals of the East Carpathian Mountains. Multicoloured.
280	1h.40 Type **163**	1·80	1·60
281	1h.40 Wild cat (Bieszczadzki National Park)	1·80	1·60

164 Bank Emblem

1999. 160th Anniv of National Bank.
282	**164**	3h. multicoloured	5·25	4·75

MS283 112×120 mm. **164** 5h. multicoloured
	8·00	7·75

165 Vyhovskyi and Battle of Konotop

1999. Hetmans. Ivan Vyhovskyi.
284	**165**	30k. multicoloured	90	80

166 Three Wise Men

1999. Christmas. Multicoloured.
285	30k. Type **166**	55	45
286	60k. Nativity	1·10	95

168 Space Rocket and Car on Moon (Ivan Kovalevskyi)

1999. Winning Entries in Children's Stamp Design Competition. Multicoloured.
287	10k. Type **168**	70	60
288	10k. Elephant wearing space helmet (Ivan Chuev)	70	60
289	10k. Aliens and space ship (Dmitro Verzhbyikyi)	70	60

169 Russian Desman

1999. Endangered Species. Multicoloured.
290	40k. Type **169**	70	60
291	40k. Stag beetle (*Lucanus cervus*)	70	60
292	60k. Griffon vulture	1·10	95

170 Angel and Church, Kyiv

1999. St. Andriya Pervozvannoho Commemoration.
293	**170**	60k. multicoloured	1·20	1·10

171 Boot-lace Fungus

1999. Fungi. Multicoloured.
294	30k. Type **171**	90	80
295	30k. Velvet-footed pax (*Paxillus atrotomentosus*)	90	80
296	30k. Oyster mushroom (*Pleurotus ostreatus*)	90	80
297	40k. Chanterelle (*Cantharellus cibarius*)	1·10	95
298	60k. Field mushroom (*Agaricus campestris*)	1·40	1·20

172 KRAZ-65032 Lorry

1999. Motor Vehicles. Multicoloured.
299	30k. Type **172**	90	80
300	30k. Tavriya car	90	80

173 Girl wearing New Year's Costume

1999. New Year.
301	**173**	50k. multicoloured	1·20	1·10

174 Ships, Polubotok and St. Petersburg

1999. Hetmans. Pavel Polubotok.
302	**174**	30k. multicoloured	90	80

175 "Pea Wild"

1999. Paintings by Mariya Primachenko. Multicoloured.
303	30k. Type **175**	90	80
304	30k. "Wild Boar"	90	80

176 Gulebichibna

1999. 425th Birth Anniv (2000) of Galshka Gulebichibna.
305	**176**	30k. multicoloured	90	80

177 Deer and Wild Cat

1999. Nature Reserves. Sheet 112×122 mm containing T **177** and similar horiz designs. Multicoloured.

MS306 10k. Type **177** (Karpatskyi Reserve); 30k. Owl ox and wolf (Poliskyi Reserve); 40k. Eagle catching fish (Kanivskyi Reserve); 60k. Deer and warthog (Trakhtemiriv Reserve); 1h. Goat and duck (Askaniya-Nova Reserve); 1h. Birds beside lake (Karadeazhskyi Reserve)
	7·00	6·50

178 Our Lady Oranta (mosaic), Sophia Cathedral, Kyiv

2000. Birth Bimillenary of Jesus Christ. Sheet 151×101 mm containing T **178** and similar vert designs. Multicoloured.

MS307 80k. Type **178**; 80k. Jesus Christ (fresco, Spaso-Preobrazhenskoi Church, Polotsk, Belarus); 80k. Our Lady Volodimirska (icon, National Tretyakov Gallery, Moscow)
	5·25	5·00

179 Moscow Bridge, 1976

2000. Bridges in Kyiv. Multicoloured.
308	10k. Type **179**	35	30
309	30k. Ye. O. Paton Bridge, 1953	45	40
310	40k. Pedestrian bridge, 1957	55	45
311	60k. Metro bridge, 1965	90	80

180 National Theatre, Kyiv

2000. Theatres. Sheet 92×135 mm containing T **180** and similar horiz designs. Multicoloured.

MS312 40k. Type **180**; 40k. State Theatre, Odessa; 40k. Mykoy Lysenka Theatre, Kharkov; 40k. Ivan Franka Theatre, Lviv
	8·75	8·50

181 Medieval Monk

2000. Peresoonytske Gospel (16th-century Ukranian translation). Sheet 121×85 mm.
MS313 **181**	1h.50 multicoloured	3·50	3·25

182 Petrusenko

2000. Birth Centenary of Oksana Petrusenko (singer). Multicoloured.
314	**182**	30k. multicoloured	90	80

183 Churai

2000. Marusia Churai (songwriter) Commemoration.
315 **183** 40k. multicoloured 1·10 95

184 Cossack Forces attacking
Derbent Fortress, Danylo Apostol
and Church

2000. Hetmans. Multicoloured.
316 30k. Type **184** 90 80
317 30k. Kozacha Dibrova (Cossack
council), Ivan Samoilovych
and Tobol'sk 90 80

185 Globe and
Emblem

2000. 50th Anniv of World Meteorological Organization.
318 **185** 30k. multicoloured 90 80

186 "Building
Europe"

2000. Europa.
319 **186** 3h. multicoloured 5·25 6·00

187 Podillia Region

2000. Easter. Sheet 103×137 containing T **187** and similar
horiz designs showing traditional egg decorations.
Multicoloured.
MS320 30k. Type **187**; 30k. Chernihiv
region; 30k. Kyiv; 30k. Odeska
region: 70k. Hutsulschyna region;
70k. Volynska region 6·25 6·00

188 Woman with Letter
and Austria 1850 2k. Stamp

2000. "WIPA 2000" International Stamp Exhibition,
Vienna. Sheet 160×46 mm containing T **188** and
similar horiz designs. Multicoloured.
MS321 80k. Type **188**; 80k. Man writing
letter and Great Britain Penny Black 3·50 3·25

189 Sunflower, Map and Emblem
(Donetsk)

2000. Regions. Multicoloured.
322 30k. Type **189** 90 80
323 30k. Statue, map and churches
(Kyiv) 90 80

190 Buildings and Emblem

2000. National Stamp Exhibition, Donetsk.
324 **190** 30k. multicoloured 90 80

191 Buildings

2000. 900th Anniv of Ostroh.
325 **191** 30k. multicoloured 90 80

192 High Jump

2000. Olympic Games, Sydney. Multicoloured.
326 30k. Type **192** 90 80
327 30k. Boxing 90 80
328 70k. Sailing 1·40 1·20
329 1h. Rhythmic gymnastics 2·10 1·90

193 Prokopovych

2000. 150th Death Anniv of Petro Prokopovych
(beekeeper).
330 **193** 30k. multicoloured 90 80

194 St. Paul (ship of the
line)

2000. Ships. Multicoloured.
331 40k. Type **194** 1·10 95
332 70k. St. Nicholas (frigate) 1·40 1·20

195 "Leafy Plants
with
Flowers–1950s
Series"

2000. Paintings by Tetiana Pata. Multicoloured.
333 40k. Type **195** 1·10 95
334 40k. "Viburnum Berries and
Bird" 1·10 95

196 Tower and
Arms

2000. 900th Anniv of Dubno.
335 **196** 30k. multicoloured 90 80

197 Women
harvesting

2000. Harvest Festival.
336 **197** 30k. multicoloured 90 80

198 Presidential Flag

2000. Official Presidential Symbols. Multicoloured.
337 60k. Type **198** 1·40 1·20
338 60k. Mace 1·40 1·20
339 60k. Seal 1·40 1·20
340 60k. Chain of office 1·40 1·20

199 Elk, Map and Arms

2000. Regions. Volynska.
341 **199** 30k. multicoloured 90 80

200 Kyiv General Post Office,
Anniversary Emblem and Figures

2000. 225th Anniv of Kyiv General Post Office.
342 **200** 30k. blue, green and
silver 90 80

201 Common Newts
(Trituris vulgaris)

2000. Endangered Amphibians. Multicoloured.
343 30k. Type **201** 90 80
344 70k. European fire salamander
(Salamandra salamandra) 1·40 1·20

202 Drogobych

2000. 250th Birth Anniv of Yuri Drogobych (Kotermack)
(first Ukrainian Doctor and author of the first book
printed in Slav).
345 **202** 30k. multicoloured 90 80

203 Mount Breskul

2000. Carpathian National Park. Sheet 90×60 mm
containing T **203** and similar vert designs.
Multicoloured.
MS346 80k. Type **203**; 80k. Mount
Hoberla 5·25 5·00

204 Marigolds

2000. Flora. Sheet 130×150 mm containing T **204** and
similar vert designs. Multicoloured.
MS347 30k. Type **204**; 30k. Camomile;
30k. Hollyhocks; 30k. Poppies; 30k.
Periwinkle; 30k. Cornflower; 30k.
Morning glory; 30k. Martagon lily;
30k. Peony; 30k. Bluebells 8·75 8·50

205 Grapes, Map and Lastivske
Hnizdo Castle

2000. Regions. Crimea.
348 **205** 30k. multicoloured 90 80

206 Young Boy and Witch
("Ivasyk-Telesky")

2000. Animated Children's Folk Tales. Multicoloured.
349 30k. Type **206** 90 80
350 30k. Elderly couple and duck
("Crooked Duck") 90 80
351 30k. Cat and rooster 90 80

207 Bridge joining Globes
and Father Frost carrying Tree

2000. New Year.
352 **207** 30k. multicoloured 90 80

208 St. Onufius
Church, Lviv

2000. Churches. Multicoloured.
353 30k. Type **208** 90 80
354 30k. Church of Christ's Birth,
Velyke 90 80
355 70k. Church of the Resurrection, Sumy 1·80 1·60

209 Prince Volodymyr
the Great

2000. 2000 Years of Christianity. Sheet 78×96 mm.
MS356 **209** 2h. multicoloured 5·25 5·00

210 Dymytryi Rostovskyi
and Icons

2001. 350th Birth Anniv of Dymytryi Rostovskyi.
357 **210** 75k. multicoloured 2·75 2·30

211 Basket of
Roses and Two
Doves

2001. St. Valentine's Day.
358 **211** 30k. multicoloured 90 80

212 Danylo Romanovich
and Flag

2001. 800th Birth Anniv of Prince Danylo Romanovich (ruler of Galicia and Volhynia (now in Poland and the Ukraine)). Sheet 86×106 mm.

MS359 **212** 3k. multicoloured   6·25   6·00

213 Turkish Prison, Yuryi Khmelnytskyi and Kamianets-Podilskyi Fortifications

2001. Hetmans. Multicoloured.
360   **30k.** Type **213**   70   60
361   50k. Ukraine and Polish armies, portrait and Mykhailo Khanenko relinquishing power to Ivan Samoilovych   1·20   1·10

214 1877 and Modern Telephones

2001. 125th Anniv of the Telephone.
362   **214** 70k. multicoloured   1·80   1·60

215 Girl with Yellow Hair (Alyna Nochvaj)

2001. Children's Paintings. Multicoloured.
363   10k. Type **215**   70   60
364   30k. Landscape (Olyia Pynych)   30   25
365   40k. Shopping (Dasha Chemberzhi)   40   30

216 Mallow Flowers

2001. Multicoloured
366   5k. Periwinkle   55   45
367   B (10k.) Type **216**   25   10
368   25k. Nasturtium   90   80
369   D (30k.) Carnation   90   80
369a   30k. Carnation   90   80
370   45k. Cornflower   1·40   1·20
371   65k. Sweetpea   1·80   1·60
372   70k. Water lily   1·20   1·10
373   E (71k.) Sunflower   90   80
374   C (80k.) Lilac   1·40   1·20
376   1h. Poppy   1·80   1·60
377   Nh. (1h.53) Sweet briar   2·75   2·30
378   Nh. (2h.55) Pansy   3·50   3·00
379   Zh. (2h.66) Viburnum berries   3·50   3·00
380   € (3h.65) Wheat   4·50   4·00
381   P (10h.84) Trident   10·50   9·25

217 Fox throwing Fish from Sled (Sister Fox and Brother Wolf)

2001. Folktales. Multicoloured.
382   30k. Type **217**   70   60
383   30k. Animals inside glove (Glove)   70   60
384   30k. Wolf with food and drink (Sirko)   70   60

218 *Twelve Apostles* (barque)

2001. Sailing Ships. Multicoloured.
385   20k. Type **218**   1·10   95

386   30k. *Three Saints* (barque)   1·40   1·20
See also Nos. 428/9 and 282/3.

219 Pebbles and Fish

2001. Europa. Water Resources.
387   1h. Type **219**   2·30   2·00
388   1h. Pebbles, fish and medusa (56×40 mm)   2·30   2·00
Nos. 387/8 were issued together, se-tenant, forming a composite design.

220 Holy Trinity enclosed in Flower Wreath

2001. Holy Trinity.
389   **220** 30k. multicoloured   90   80

221 Bee collecting Pollen

2001. Beekeeping. Sheet 185×144 mm containing T **221** and similar vert designs. Multicoloured.
MS390 50k. Type **221**; 50k. Honey and honey products; 50k. Worker bee on honeycomb; 50k. Queen; 50k. Hive; 50k. Drone   8·75   8·50

222 Uspensky Cathedral

2001. 950th Anniv of Kiec Pechersk Lavra (monastery). Sheet 112×113 mm.
MS391 **222** 1h.50 multicoloured   5·25   5·00

223 Pope John Paul II

2001. Visit of Pope John Paul II.
392   **223** 3h. multicoloured   4·50   4·00

224 Decorated Box, Flask, Map and Arms

2001. Regions. Zakarpatska.
393   **224** 30k. multicoloured   90   80

225 Virgin and Child

2001. Khaneko Museum of Art, Kiev. Sheet 130×78 mm containing T **225** and similar multicoloured designs.
MS394 20k. Type **225**; 30k. John the Baptist; 50k. St. Sergius and St. Bacchus (56×40 mm)   5·25   5·00

226 Red Kite (*Milvus milvus*)

2001. Endangered Species. Multicoloured.
395   1h. Type **226**   1·80   1·60
396   1h. Jerboa (*Scirtopoda telum*)   1·80   1·60

227 Dmitro Bortnjansky

2001. 250th Birth Anniv of Dmitro Bortnjansky (composer).
397   **227** 20k. multicoloured   55   45

228 Player and Ball

2001. Ukrainian Football.
398   **228** 50k. multicoloured   90   80

229 Ukrainian Flag held by Members of Parliament

2001. Tenth Anniv of Independence. Sheet 95×80 mm.
MS399 **229** 3h. multicoloured   8·75   8·50

230 Tractor, Map and Arms

2001. Regions. Kharkov.
400   **230** 30k. multicoloured   90   80

231 Church, Map and Arms

2001. Regions. Chernigov.
401   **231** 30k. multicoloured   90   80

232 Church, Map, Arms and Sunflowers

2001. Regions. Kirovograd.
402   **232** 30k. multicoloured   90   80

233 Messenger with Horn and Dnipropetrovsk

2001. Seventh National Philatelic Exhibition, Dnipropetrovsk.
403   **233** 30k. multicoloured   90   80

234 Children encircling Globe

2001. United Nations Year of Dialogue among Civilizations.
404   **234** 70k. multicoloured   1·40   1·20

235 Seahorses

2001. Fauna of the Black Sea. Sheet 115×90 mm containing T **235** and similar horiz design. Multicoloured.
MS405 30k. Type **235**; 70k. Dolphins   5·25   5·00

236 Children wearing Fancy Dress

2001. Christmas.
406   **236** 30k. multicoloured   90   80

237 St. Nikolas and Child

2001. St. Nikolas.
407   **237** 30k. multicoloured   90   80

238 Decorated Tree and Children

2001. New Year.
408   **238** 30k. multicoloured   90   80

239 Taras Chevtchenko

2001. Poets. Multicoloured.
409   40k. Type **239**   1·10   95
410   40k. Akakii Tsereteli   1·10   95
Nos. 399/400 were issued together, *se-tenant*, forming a composite design. Stamps of the same design were issued by Georgia.

240 Women wearing Traditional Costumes from Kiev

2001. Traditional Costumes (1st series). Multicoloured.
411   20k. Type **240**   70   60
412   20k. Musicians and woman, Chernigov   70   60
413   20k. Woman, child, bishop and clergy, Poltava   70   60
414   50k. Couple wearing coats, Kiev   1·10   95
415   50k. Couple and child, Chernigov   1·10   95
416   50k. Two girls, Poltava   1·10   95
MS417 100×140 mm. Nos. 411/6   7·00   6·75
See also Nos. 467/MS473, 518/MS524, 578/83, 636/MS642, 713/MS719 and 817/MS823.

241 Chorna Rada (red council), Ivan Bryukhovetsky and Death by Mob

2002. Hetmans. Multicoloured.
418	40k. Type **241**	90	80
419	40k. Election, Demiyan Mnogogreshnyi and Tobolsk, Siberia	90	80
420	40k. Moscow, Pavlo Teterya and stealing the war chest	90	80

242 Scythian Horseman

2002. History of Ukraine. (1st series).
421	**242**	40k. brown, blue and black	90	80
422	-	40k. brown, green and black	90	80
423	-	40k. brown, green and black	90	80
424	-	40k. brown, blue and black	90	80

DESIGNS: Type **242**; Warrior wearing armour; Young warrior and horseman; Horsewoman.
See also Nos. 478/81, 563/6, 626/9 and 701/4.

243 Zhanna Pintusevitsch (runner)

2002. Ukrainian Sportswomen. Multicoloured.
| 425 | 40k. Type **243** (100 metre gold medal, World Athletics Championship, 2001) | 80 | 70 |
| 426 | 40k. Jana Klotschkowa (swimmer) (2 gold and 2 silver medals, Olympic Games, 2000) | 80 | 70 |

244 War Memorial, Rye field and Arms

2002. Regions. Kiev.
| 427 | **244** | 40k. multicoloured | 80 | 70 |

2002. Sailing Ships. As T **218**. Multicoloured.
| 428 | 40k. *Sizopol* (frigate) | 80 | 70 |
| 429 | 40k. *Perseus* (brig) | 80 | 70 |

245 15k. Ukraine Stamp of 1992

2002. Tenth Anniv of First Modern Ukraine Stamp.
| 430 | **245** | 40k. multicoloured | 1·20 | 1·10 |

246 Leonid Glibov

2002. 175th Birth Anniv of Leonid Glibov (writer).
| 431 | **246** | 40k. multicoloured | 1·00 | 90 |

247 Knights and Chessboard

2002. 16th World Chess Championships, Moscow.
| 432 | **247** | 3h.50 multicoloured | 5·00 | 4·50 |

248 Tiger

2002. Europa. Circus. Sheet 106×71 mm containing T **248** and similar multicoloured design.
MS433 1h.75 ×2, Type **248**; Lion (vert) — 7·75 / 7·50

249 Hands holding Wreath

2002. Palm Sunday.
| 434 | **249** | 40k. multicoloured | 1·00 | 90 |

250 Leopard Snake

2002. Endangered Species. The Leopard Snake (Elaphe situla). Multicoloured.
435	40k. Type **250**	80	70
436	70k. Two snakes entwined	1·00	90
437	80k. Snake, branch and flowers	1·20	1·10
438	2h.50 Head, coils and beetle	3·00	2·75

Nos. 435/8 were issued together, forming a composite design.

251 Opera House, Donetsk

2002. Ukrainian Opera Houses. Sheet 108×80 mm. T **251**
MS439 1h.25 ×2, Type **251**; Opera house, Dnepropetrovsk — 5·75 / 5·50

252 Mary and Jesus (statue), Coastal Landscape and Arms

2002. Regions. Lugansk.
| 440 | **252** | 40k. multicoloured | 1·00 | 90 |

253 Shag (Phalacrocorax aristotelis)

2002. Endangered Species. Multicoloured.
| 441 | 70k. Type **253** | 1·40 | 1·20 |
| 442 | 70k. Harbour porpoise (Phocoena phocoena) | 1·40 | 1·20 |

254 Mikola Leontovich

2002. 125th Birth Anniv of Mikola Leontovich (composer).
| 443 | **254** | 40k. multicoloured | 1·00 | 90 |

255 Decorated Eggs, Buildings and Arms

2002. Regions. Chernovtsy.
| 444 | **255** | 40k. multicoloured | 1·00 | 90 |

255a Oyster Catcher (Haematopus ostralegos)

2002. Black Sea Nature Reserve. Sheet 96×100 mm containing T **255a** and similar multicoloured designs.
MS445 50k. ×5 Type **255**; Slender-billed gull (Larus genei); Iris pumila (22×26 mm); Western curlew (Numenius arquata) (26×22 mm); Kentish plover (Charadrius Alexandrinus) (26×22 mm) — 5·75 / 5·50

256 Fox and Kolobok (bun) (Kolobok)

2002. Folktales. Multicoloured.
446	40k. Type **256**	60	55
447	40k. Cat and porridge (Pan Kotski)	60	55
448	40k. Couple and chicken (Kurochka Raba)	60	55

257 Flowers (1963)

2002. Hanna Sobachko-Shostak (folk artist) Commemoration. Multicoloured.
449	45k. Type **257**	80	70
450	45k. Vase of flowers (1964)	80	70
451	45k. Flowers (different) (1964)	80	70

258 Yury Kondra

2002. Space Pioneers (1st series). Multicoloured.
452	40k. Type **258**	70	60
453	45k. Mikhail Jangel	80	70
454	50k. Nikolai Kibalchich	1·00	90
455	70k. Sergei Korlev	1·20	1·10

See also Nos. 488/91.

259 Caspian Seal (Phoca caspica)

2002. Endangered Species. Marine Animals. Multicoloured.
| 456 | 75k. Type **259** | 1·40 | 1·20 |
| 457 | 75k. *Huso huso ponticus* (fish) | 1·40 | 1·20 |

Stamps of the same design were issued by Kazakhstan.

260 Monument, Sea, Lighthouse and Arms

2002. Regions. Odessa.
| 458 | **260** | 45k. multicoloured | 1·00 | 90 |

261 Monument, Arms and Old Town Walls

2002. Millenary of Khotin.
| 459 | **261** | 40k. multicoloured | 90 | 80 |

262 Exhibition Emblem

2002. Odesafil 2002 Philatelic Exhibition.
| 460 | **262** | 45k. multicoloured | 1·00 | 90 |

263 Monument, Lake and Arms

2002. Regions. Cherkassy.
| 461 | **263** | 45k. multicoloured | 1·00 | 90 |

264 Church, Landscape and Arms

2002. Regions. Sumy.
| 462 | **264** | 45k. multicoloured | 1·00 | 90 |

265 "Askoldova Mogila"

2002. Paintings of Kiev (1st series). Taras Shevchenko (artist and poet) Commemoration.
463	45k. Type **265**	80	70
464	75k. "Kiev"	1·20	1·10
465	80k. "Saint Aleksandr Castle, Kiev"	1·30	1·10

See also Nos. 500/3, 542/5, 599/602, 670/3 and 760/3.

266 Father Christmas carrying Tree

2002. New Year.
| 466 | **266** | 45k. multicoloured | 1·00 | 90 |

2002. Traditional Costumes (2nd series). As T **240**. Multicoloured.
467	45k. Family, Vinnitsa	80	70
468	45k. Old man, women and child, Vinnitsa	80	70
469	45k. Young women dancing, Cherkassy	80	70
470	45k. Couple carrying pails, Cherkassy	80	70
471	45k. Bishop and family, Ternopol	80	70
472	45k. Women, child and young man, Ternopol	80	70
MS473	100×140 mm. Nos. 467/72	6·75	6·50

267 Goat on Bridge (Koza-Dereza)

2003. Folktales. Multicoloured.
474	45k. Type **267**	80	70
475	45k. Couple and bull (Straw Bull)	80	70
476	45k. Fox and crane (Fox and Crane)	80	70

Nos. 474/6 were issued together, se-tenant, forming a composite design.

268 Speed Skater

2003
| 477 | **268** | 65k. multicoloured | 1·40 | 1·20 |

2003. History of Ukraine (2nd series). As T **242**.

478	45k. brown, blue and black	80	70
479	45k. purple, bistre and black	80	70
480	45k. purple, bistre and black	80	70
481	45k. brown, blue and black	80	70

DESIGNS: No. 478 4th-century warrior; 479 5th-century bowman; 480 6th-century warrior with axe and shield; 481 6th-century spear thrower.

2003. Ships. T **218**. Multicoloured.

482	1h. *Grozny* (paddle steamer)	2·00	1·80
483	1h. *Odessa* (paddle steamer)	2·00	1·80

269 Mikola Arkas

2003. 150th Birth Anniv of Mikola Arkas (composer).

484 **269** 45k. multicoloured 1·00 90

270 Kingfisher (*Alcedo atthis*)

2003. Javorivsky National Park. Sheet 130×92 mm containing T **270** and similar multicoloured designs.

MS485 1h. Type **270**; 1h.50 Emperor moth (*Eudia pavonia*) (33×45 mm); 1h. *Cypripedium calceolus* (36×41 mm) 7·75 7·50

271 Mary holding Crane ("May it be to me as you have said")

2003. Europa. Poster Art. Multicoloured.

486	1h.75 Type **271**	3·50	3·25
487	1h.75 Angel holding atomic symbol ("You are highly favoured, the Lord is with you")	3·50	3·25

Nos. 486/7 were issued together, *se-tenant* forming a composite design.

272 Oleksandr Zasiadko

2003. Space Pioneers (2nd series).Multicoloured.

488	45k. Type **272**	80	70
489	65k. Kostiantyn Konstantynov	90	80
490	70k. Valetyn Hlushko	1·00	90
491	80k. Volodymyr Chelomei	1·10	95

273 Heart enclosing Figure

2003. Ukrainian Red Cross.

492 **273** 45k. gold, vermilion and black 1·00 90

274 Rocket, Bridge and Arms

2003. Regions. Dnipropetrovsk.

493 **274** 45k. multicoloured 1·00 90

275 Lion supporting Shield, Buildings and Arms

2003. Regions. Lviv.

494 **275** 45k. multicoloured 1·00 90

276 Crowd, Kirill Rozumovsky and Ruin

2003. Hetmans. Multicoloured.

495	45k. Type **276**	1·00	90
496	45k. Farm workers, Ivan Skoropadsky and his inauguration	1·00	90

277 Volodymyr Monomakh

2003. Volodymyr Monomakh (prince of Kyiv, 1113–25) Commemoration. Sheet 100×80 mm.

MS497 **277** 3h.50 multicoloured 6·75 6·50

278 Northern Eagle Owl (*Bubo bubo*)

2003. Owls. Sheet 135×131 mm containing T **278** and similar vert designs. Multicoloured.

MS498 45k ×12, Type **278**; Ural owl (*Strix uralensis*); Tawny owl (*Strix aluco*); Great grey owl (*Strix nebulosa*); Eurasian pygmy owl (*Glaucidium passerinum*); Tengmalm's owl (*Aegolius funereus*); Eurasian scops owl (*Otus scops*); Little owl (*Athene noctua*); Barn owl (*Tyto alba*); Long-eared owl (*Asio otus*); Short-eared owl (*Asio flammeus*); Hawk owl (*Surnia ulula*) 11·50 11·00

279 Oleksandr Myshuha

2003. 150th Birth Anniv of Oleksandr Myshuha (singer).

499 **279** 45k. multicoloured 1·00 90

2003. Paintings of Kiev (2nd series). As T **265**. Multicoloured.

500	45k. "Podil from Schekavytsia" (Mykhailo Sazhyn)	1·00	90
501	45k. "Ruins of St. Irene's Monastery" (Mykhailo Sazhyn)	1·00	90
502	45k. "Old Town from Yaroslaviv Val" (Vasyl Timm)	1·00	90
503	45k. "The Cathedral of the Assumption" (Vasyl Timm)	1·00	90

280 Flowers surrounding Church (Makovii)

2003. Holidays. Multicoloured.

504	45k. Type **280**	1·00	90
505	45k. Church and fruit (Spas)	1·00	90

281 Borys Hmyria

2003. Birth Centenary of Borys Romanovych Hmyria (singer).

506 **281** 45k. multicoloured 95 85

282 Maniava

2003. Monasteries. Sheet 116×85 mm containing T **282** and similar vert design. Multicoloured.

MS507 1h.25 ×2, Type **282**; Carpathian 4·75 4·50

283 Yachts and Mosque

2003. 2500th Anniv of Yevpatoria.

508 **283** 45k. multicoloured 95 85

284 Danish Coin and "Arrival of Scandinavian Seamen" (detail)

2003. Ancient Trade Route along Gulf of Finland and Dnieper River, Ukraine. Multicoloured.

509	80k. Type **284**	1·40	1·30
510	80k. 11th-century silver coin and Viking ship	1·40	1·30

Stamps of the same design were issued by Estonia.

285 Horse and Rider (statue), Walls and Arms

2003. Regions. Khmelnystsk.

511 **285** 45k. multicoloured 95 85

286 Sunflowers, Ships and Arms

2003. Regions. Mykolaiv.

512 **286** 45k. multicoloured 95 85

287 Statue, Power Station Dam and Arms

2003. Regions. Zaporizhia.

513 **287** 45k. multicoloured 95 85

288 Hryhorii Kvitka-Osnovianenko

2003. 225th Birth Anniv of Hryhorii Kvitka-Osnovianenko (writer).

514 **288** 45k. multicoloured 95 85

289 Cross surrounding Starving Woman

2003. 70th Anniv of 1932–33 Famine.

515 **289** 45k. multicoloured 1·10 95

290 The Nativity

2003. Christmas.

516 **290** 45k. multicoloured 95 85

291 Snow-covered House, Tree and Father Christmas

2003. New Year.

517 **291** 45k. multicoloured 95 85

2003. Traditional Costumes (3rd series). As T **240**. Multicoloured.

518	45k. Two women, Kharkia	95	85
519	45k. Child, woman and musician, Kharkia	95	85
520	45k. Young couple and matchmaker, Sumy	95	85
521	45k. Girl preparing for marriage, Sumy	95	85
522	45k. Woman, two men, child and toboggan, Donetsk	95	85
523	45k. Harvesting corn, Donetsk	95	85
MS524	100×140 mm. Nos. 518/23	7·25	7·00

292 Arms

2004. 85th Anniv of Unified State.

525 **292** 45k. multicoloured 95 85

293 Stanislav Liudkevych

2004. 125th Birth Anniv of Stanislav Liudkevych (composer).

526 **293** 45k. multicoloured 95 85

294 Flag

2004. Hetman Bohdan Khmelnytskyi's Regalia and Possessions. Sheet 120×131 mm containing T **294** and similar horiz designs. Multicoloured.

MS527 45k.×6, Type **294**; Mace; Embroidered hat; Chalice; Mug; Sabre 7·25 7·00

295 *Kriti Amber* (tanker)

2004. Ships. Sheet 115×110 mm containing T **295** and similar horiz designs.

MS528 1h. Type **295**; 2h.50 *Mykolaiv* (anti-submarine craft) (55×30 mm); 3h. *Admiral of the Fleet Kuznetsov* (aircraft carrier) (55×40 mm) 12·00 11·50

296 Turreted House, Arms, Map and Castle

2004. Regions. Ternopol.

529 **296** 45k. multicoloured 95 85

297 Emblem

2004. 50th Anniv of Membership of UNESCO.
530 **297** 45k. multicoloured 1·30 1·10

298 *Endromis versicolora*

2004. Butterflies. Sheet 130×110 mm containing T **298** and similar square designs. Multicoloured.
MS531 45k. Type **298**; 75k. *Smerinthus ocellatus*; 80k. *Catocala fraxini*; 2h.60 *Apatura ilia*; 3h.50 *Papilio machaon* 18·00 17·00
See also No. **MS587**.

299 Sergi Lifar

2004. Birth Centenary of Sergi (Serge) Lifar (dancer and choreographer).
532 **299** 45k. multicoloured 95 85

300 Rocket and Globe

2004. State Design Office.
533 **300** 45k. multicoloured 95 85

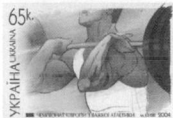

301 Weightlifter

2004. European Weightlifting Championship, Kiev.
534 **301** 65k. multicoloured 1·60 1·40

302
Lastochkino
Gnezdo Castle

2004. Europa. Holidays. Sheet 124×104 mm containing T **302** and similar multicoloured designs.
MS535 45k. Type **302**; 75k. River valley, Carpathian mountains; 2h.61 Khotyn Castle (29×33 mm); 3h.52 Kiev-Pechersk Lavra (40×28 mm) 16·00 15·00

303 Footballers

2004. Centenary of FIFA (Federation Internationale de Football Association). Multicoloured.
536 45k. Type **303** 95 85
537 75k. Player heading ball 1·60 1·40
538 80k. Supporter 1·90 1·70
539 2h.61 Women players 5·00 4·50

304 Players and
Anniversary
Emblem

2004. 50th Anniv of UEFA (Union of European Football Associations).
540 **304** 3h.52 multicoloured 8·00 7·00

305 Simon Petljura

2004. 125th Birth Anniv of Simon Petljura (socialist leader).
541 **305** 45k. multicoloured 95 85

2004. Paintings of Kiev (3rd series). As T **265**. Multicoloured.
542 45k. Andriivska Church 95 85
543 45k. "Fountain, Golden Gates" (Petro Levchenko) 95 85
544 45k. "Spring in Kurenivka" (Abram Manevych) 95 85
545 45k. "Mykhailivskyi Zolo-toverkhyi Cathedral" (Mykola Burachek) 95 85

306 Man in Water
and Cat (Cat)

2004. Folktales. Multicoloured.
546 45k. Type **306** 95 85
547 45k. [...] Telesyk) 95 85
548 45k. Man carrying club and dragon (Rolling Pea) 95 85
Nos. 546/8 were issued together, *se-tenant*, forming a composite design.

307 Charioteer

2004. Olympic Games, Athens.
549 **307** 2h.61 multicoloured 5·75 5·00

308 House, Arms, Map and Castle

2004. Regions. Rovno.
550 **308** 45k. multicoloured 95 85

309 Maria Zankovetska
(actress)

2004. Anniversaries. Multicoloured.
551 45k. Type **309** (150th birth anniv) 95 85
552 45k. Mykhailo Maksymovych (social historian) (birth bicentenary) 95 85

310 Engraving and Arms of Balaklava

2004. 2500th Anniv of Balaklava.
553 **310** 45k. multicoloured 95 85

311 Monument, Arms, Map and Combine Harvester

2004. Regions. Kherson.
554 **311** 45k. multicoloured 95 85

312 Skyline and Arms

2004. 350th Anniv of Kharkov.
555 **312** 45k. multicoloured 95 85

313 Inhul Bridge, Mykolaiv

2004. Bridges. Multicoloured.
556 45k. Type **313** 95 85
557 45k. Darnytsia bridge, Kiev 95 85
558 45k. B. M. Preobrazhenskyi bridge, Zaporizhia 95 85
559 45k. Pivdennyi Buh bridge, Mykolaiv 95 85

2004. 170th Anniv of Kiev University. No. MS92 surch 2004 2h.61.
MS560 2h.61 on 25000k. multicoloured 8·00 7·50

315 Arms, Landscape and Cannon

2004. 250th Anniv of Kirovograd.

316 Monument, Arms, Map, River and Castle

2004. Regions. Potava.
562 **316** 45k. multicoloured 95 85

2004. History of Ukraine (3rd series). As T **242**.
563 45k. brown, green and black 95 85
564 45k. purple, bistre and black 95 85
565 45k. purple, bistre and black 95 85
566 45k. brown, green and black 95 85
DESIGNS: No. 563, 10th-century warrior; 564, 11th-century national home guard; 565, 12th-century mounted bowman; 566, Armoured horse and rider.

317 Mute Swan (*Cygnus olor*)

2004. Danube Nature Reserve. Sheet 116×86 mm containing T **317** and similar diamond-shaped designs. Multicoloured.
MS567 45k. Type **317**; 75k. Pygmy cormorant (*Phalacrocorax pygmaeus*); 80k. Great egret (*Egretta alba*); 2h.61 Greylag goose (*Anser anser*); 3h.52 White spoonbill (*Platalea leucorodia*) 16·00 15·00

318 Spacecraft

2004. Space Exploration. Multicoloured.
568 45k. Type **318** 1·30 1·10
569 45k. 19th-century rocket image 1·30 1·10
See also No. 592/5.

319 Three Kings and Shepherds

2004. Christmas and New Year. Multicoloured.
570 45k. Type **319** 95 85
571 45k. The Nativity 95 85
572 45k. As No. 570 but with design reversed 95 85
573 45k. Santa Claus 95 85
574 45k. Decorated tree 95 85
575 45k. As No. 573 but with design reversed 95 85
Nos. 570, 571×2 and 572, and Nos. 573, 574×2 and 575, respectively, were issued in horizontal *se-tenant* strips of four stamps within the sheet, each strip forming a composite design of "2005" enclosing the designs.

320 Antonov-140

2004. Aircraft. Multicoloured.
576 80k. Type **320** 1·90 1·70
577 80k. Iran-140 1·90 1·70
Stamps of a similar design were issued by Iran.

2004. Traditional Costumes (3rd series). As T **240**. Multicoloured.
578 60k. Family with baby, Lvov 1·30 1·10
579 60k. Couple and girl, Lvov 1·30 1·10
580 60k. Musicians, Ivano-Frankovsk 1·30 1·10
581 60k. Dancers, Ivano-Frankovsk 1·30 1·10
582 60k. Couple and man carrying sheaf of corn, Gutsul 1·30 1·10
583 60k. Shepherds, mother and child, Gutsul 1·30 1·10
MS584 100×140 mm. Nos. 578/83 9·50 9·25

321 Protestors

2005. Maidan Nezalezhnosti (Independence Square) (political protest rally, November 2004).
585 **321** 45k. multicoloured 95 85

322 Pavlo Virskyi

2005. Birth Centenary of Pavlo Virskyi (ballet dancer).
586 **322** 45k. multicoloured 1·30 1·10

2005. Butterflies and Moths (2nd issue). Sheet 130×110 mm containing square designs as T **298**. Multicoloured.
MS587 45k. *Acherontia atropos*; 75k. *Catocala sponsa*; 80k. *Staurophora celsia*; 2h.61 *Marumba quercus*; 3h.50 *Saturnia pyri* 17·00 16·00

323 Statue, Arms, Map and Bridge

2005. Regions. Vinnytsia.
588 **323** 45k. multicoloured 1·10 1·00

324 "Seascape"

2005. Art. Paintings by Ivan Aivazovskyi. Multicoloured.
589 45k. Type **324** 95 85
590 45k. "Towers by Bosphorus" 95 85

325 "Shepherd"

2005. 75th Birth Anniv of Heorhiy Yakutovych (artist).
591 **325** 3h.52 slate and silver 8·00 7·00

2005. Space Exploration. As T **318**. Multicoloured.
592 45k. Rocket *Dnepr* 1·30 1·10
593 45k. Satellite *Kosmos-1* 1·30 1·10
594 45k. Rocket *Zenit-2* 1·30 1·10
595 45k. Rocket *Cyclone-3* 1·30 1·10

326 Flowers and Battle

2005. 60th Anniv of End of World War II. Multicoloured.
596 45k. Type **326** 1·30 1·10
MS597 82×57 mm. 80k. Returning
   soldier (40×40 mm) 2·50 2·20
   The stamp and margin of No. MS597 form a composite
design.

327 Coloured Rhombi and
Exhibition Emblem

2005. National Stamp Exhibition.
598 **327** 45k. multicoloured 1·30 1·10

2005. Paintings of Kiev (4th series). As T **265**.
Multicoloured.
599 45k. "New Street" (Sergei
   Shishko) 1·30 1·10
600 75k. "Winter Park" (Sergei
   Shishko) 1·80 1·50
601 80k. "Inviolable Sofia" (Yury
   Khimich) 1·90 1·70
602 1h. "Khreschatik" (Yury Khimich)
   (vert) 3·00 2·50

328 Ruslana (singer)
(winner—2004)

2005. Eurovision Song Contest, Kiev—2005.
Multicoloured.
603 45k. Type **328** 1·30 1·10
604 2h.50 Emblem (32×32 mm) 7·00 6·25

329 Borsch (beetroot soup)

2005. Europa. Gastronomy. Multicoloured.
605 2h.61 Type **329** 6·50 5·50
606 3h.52 Vegetables (ingredients) 8·00 7·00

330 "A" and Slavic
Ornament

2005. Slavic Writing.
607 **330** 45k. multicoloured 1·30 1·10

331 Monument, Arms, Map and
Ruins

2005. Regions. Svestapol.
608 **331** 45k. multicoloured 1·30 1·10

332 Volodymyr
Vynnychenko

2005. Birth Centenary of Volodymyr Vynnychenko (writer
and political activist).
609 **332** 45k. multicoloured 1·30 1·10

333 Building, Arms, Map and Snowy
Landscape

2005. Regions. Ivano-Frankivsk.
610 **333** 45k. multicoloured 1·10 1·00

334 Saker Falcon
(*Falco cherrug*)

2005. Karadag Nature Reserve. Sheet 130×83 mm
containing T **334** and similar multicoloured designs.
MS611 45k. Type **334**; 70k. *Ascalaphus
macaronius* (30×35 mm); 2h.50 Bottlenose dolphin (*Tursiops truncate*)
(33×33 mm); 3h.50 Beech marten
(*Martes foina*) (49×33 mm) 16·00 15·00
   The stamps and margin of No. MS611 form a composite design.

335 Emblem

2005. World Information Society Summit, Tunis.
612 **335** 2h.50 multicoloured 6·50 5·50

336 Locomotive OB 501

2005. Railways. Multicoloured.
613 70k. Type **336** 1·90 1·70
614 70k. Locomotive 1652 1·90 1·70
615 70k. Locomotive C11 1·90 1·70
616 70k. Locomotive 3619 1·90 1·70

337 Arms and Building

2005. 350th Anniv of Sumy.
617 **337** 45k. multicoloured 95 85

338 Statue, Arms, Map and River

2005. Regions. Zhytomyr.
618 **338** 70k. multicoloured 1·60 1·40

339 Novooleksandrivskyi
Carthorse

2005. Horses. Multicoloured.
619 70k. Type **339** 1·60 1·40
620 70k. Orlovskyi trotting-horse 1·60 1·40
621 70k. Ukrainian saddle-horse 1·60 1·40

622 70k. Thoroughbred saddle-
   horse 1·60 1·40

340 Child ("Say no to
Drugs")

2005. Child Awareness Campaign. Multicoloured.
623 70k. Type **340** 1·60 1·40
624 70k. Children on road crossing
   (road safety) 1·60 1·40
625 70k. Child holding candle (child
   homelessness) 1·60 1·40

2005. History of Ukraine (4th series). As T **242**.
626 70k. brown, blue and chocolate 1·60 1·40
627 70k. brown, green and
   chocolate 1·60 1·40
628 70k. brown, sage and chocolate 1·60 1·40
629 70k. brown, blue and chocolate 1·60 1·40
DESIGNS: No. 626 Voevoda Bobrok Volynets, Kulikovo
Field (1380); 627 14th-century armaments; 628 Knight
Ivanko Sushyk, Grunvald (1410); 629 Prince Konstantin
Ostrozkyi, Orsha (1512).

341 Dmitry Yavornytsky

2005. 150th Birth Anniv of Dmitry Yavornytsky.
630 **341** 70k. multicoloured 1·60 1·40

342 Angel

2005. Christmas and New Year. Multicoloured.
631 70k. Type **342** 1·60 1·40
632 70k. Snow covered village 1·60 1·40

343 Church
Facade

2006. St. Barbara's Church, Vienna.
633 **343** 75k. multicoloured 1·90 1·70

344 Archangel
Mikhail (icon)

2006. Centenary of National Museum, Lviv. Multicoloured.
634 70k. Type **344** 1·60 1·40
635 70k. "Dalmatinka" (Teofil
   Kopistinsky) 1·60 1·40

2005. Traditional Costumes (5th series). As T **240**.
Multicoloured.
636 70k. Family with dog, Zhytomyr 1·60 1·40
637 70k. Couple and beehives,
   Zhytomyr 1·60 1·40
638 70k. Horses, cattle and family,
   Rivne 1·60 1·40
639 70k. Musicians, Rivne 1·60 1·40
640 70k. Seed sowing, Volyn 1·60 1·40
641 70k. Couple and sleeping child,
   Volyn 1·60 1·40
MS642 100×140 mm. Nos. 636/412 9·50 9·25

345 Emblem
containing "50"

2006. 50th Anniv of Europa Stamps. Multicoloured.
643 1h.30 Type **345** 3·25 2·75
644 2h.50 Emblem containing
   "CEPT" 6·50 5·50
MS645 110×50 mm. Nos. 641/2 13·00 12·50

346 Oleg Antonov

2006. Birth Centenary of Oleg Konstantinovich Antonov
(aircraft designer).
646 **346** 70k. multicoloured 1·60 1·40

347 Woman seated (engraving)

2006. 120th Birth Anniv of Heorhiy Narbut (artist).
647 **347** 3h.33 olive and brown 8·00 7·00

348 The Ubrus and Fur Cap,
Kiev (11th—14th century)

2006. Headdresses. Multicoloured.
648 70k. Type **348** 1·60 1·40
649 70k. Kerchief, Kiev (19th—20th
   century) 1·60 1·40
650 70k. Namitka, Western Polissia
   (18th—20th century) 1·60 1·40
651 70k. Flowered headdress,
   Poltava (19th—20th century) 1·60 1·40
652 70k. Kerchief, Hutsul (19th—
   20th century) 1·60 1·40
653 70k. Koda, Bukovina (19th—
   20th century) 1·60 1·40
654 70k. Kerchief, Central Ukraine
   (20th century) 1·60 1·40
655 70k. Ochipok, Poltava (19th—
   20th century) 1·60 1·40
656 70k. Namitka, Hutsul (18th—
   19th century) 1·60 1·40
657 70k. Ochipok, Poltava (19th—
   20th century) 1·60 1·40
658 70k. Kerchief over Ochipok,
   Chernihiv (19th—20th
   century) 1·60 1·40
659 70k. Flowered headdress, Ivano-
   Frankovsk (20th century) 1·60 1·40

349 KORONAS-I International
Space Station

2006. Space Exploration. Multicoloured.
660 85k. Type **349** 2·20 2·00
661 85k. Astronauts repairing space
   station 2·20 2·00
662 85k. Halley's Comet 2·20 2·00

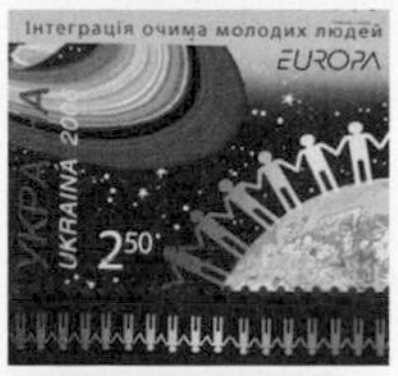

350 Saturn, Cut-out People and Earth

2006. Europa. Integration. Multicoloured.

663	2h.50 Type **350**	5·75	5·00
664	3h.50 Earth, cut-out people and Venus	8·00	7·00

Nos. 663/4 were issued together, se-tenant, forming a composite design.

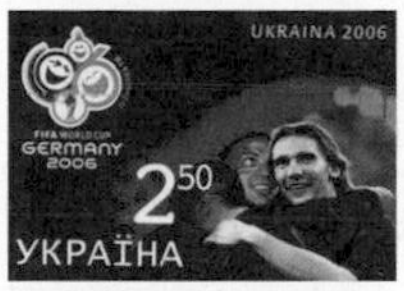

351 Emblem and Fans

2006. World Cup Football Championships, Germany. Multicoloured.

667	2h.50 Type **351**	5·75	5·00
668	3h.50 Football and emblem	8·00	7·00

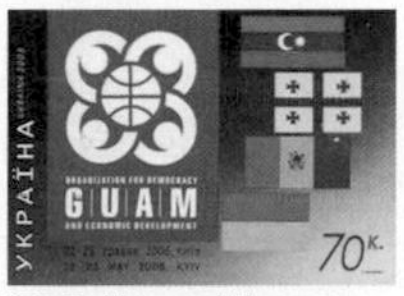

352 Emblem and Flags

2006. GUAM (Georgia, Ukraine, Armenia and Moldova) Summit, Kiev.

669	**352**	70k. multicoloured	1·90	1·70

2006. Paintings of Kiev (5th series). As T **265**. Multicoloured.

670	70k. "Zabroroskyi's Gate" (Boris Tulin)	1·90	1·70
671	70k. "Olha Basystiuk is singing" (Boris Tulin)	1·90	1·70
672	70k. "Kiev-Pechersk Lavra" [illegible]	[illegible]	1·70
673	70k. "Andriivskyi Uzviz" (Oleksandr Hubarev)	1·90	1·70

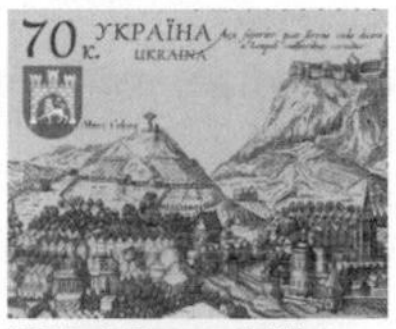

353 Early Town and Hills

2006. 750th Anniv of Lviv. Sheet 133×87 mm containing T **353** and similar horiz design. Multicoloured.

MS674 70k. Type **353**; 2h.50 Early town (69×31 mm) 8·00 7·50

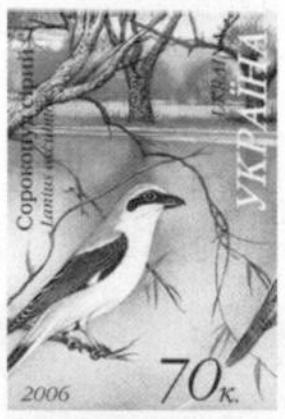

354 Great Grey Shrike (*Lanius excubitor*)

2006. Shatsk National Park. Sheet 130×83 mm containing T **354** and similar multicoloured designs.

MS675 70k.×5, Type **354**; Eurasian lynx (*Lynx lynx*) (33×35 mm); Eel (*Anguilla anguilla*) (42×29 mm); Natterjack toad (*Bufo calamita*) (28×29 mm); Ermine (*Mustela erminea*) (45×29 mm) 9·50 9·25

The stamps and margin of No. **MS**675 form a composite design.

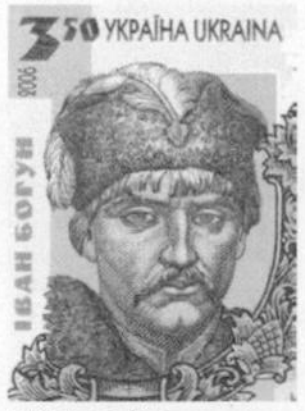

355 Ivan Bogun

2006. Ukrainian Cossacks. Sheet 133×123 mm containing T **355** and similar vert designs. Multicoloured.

MS676 3h.50×4, Type **355**; Ivan Pidkova; Ivan Gonta; Ivan Sirko 27·00 24·00

The stamps and margin of No. **MS**676 form a composite design.

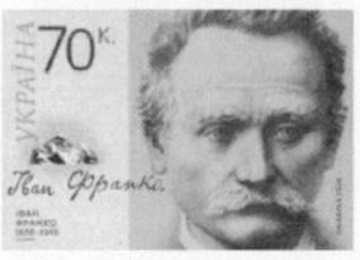

356 Ivan Franko

2006. 150th Birth Anniv of Ivan Franko (writer).

677	**356**	70k. multicoloured	1·90	1·70

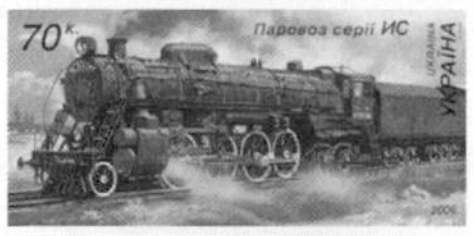

357 Steam locomotive IS 20-578

2006. Locomotives. Multicoloured.

678	70k. Type **357**	1·90	1·70
679	70k. Steam Locomotive L	1·90	1·70
680	70k. Steam locomotive SO No. 5307	1·90	1·70
681	70k. Steam locomotive FD17 2194	1·90	1·70

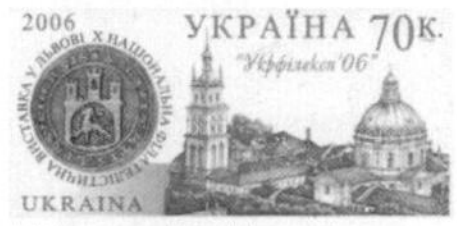

358 Lvov and Emblem

2006. Ukrphilexp'06, Tenth National Philatelic Exhibition, Lvov.

682	**358**	70k. multicoloured	2·20	2·00

2006. As T **216**. Multicoloured.

683	5k. As No. 366 (Periwinkle)	30	30
684	B (10k.) As Type **216** (Mallow)	30	30
685	10k. As Type **216** (Mallow)	30	30
686	25k. As No. 367c. (Nasturtium)	65	55
687	D (30k.) As No. 368 (Carnation)	95	85
688	30k. As No. 368a (Carnation)	95	85
689	45k. As No. 369 (Cornflower)	1·10	1·00
690	65k. As No. 370 (Sweet pea)	1·60	1·40
[illegible]	[illegible]	[illegible]	[illegible]
692	E (71k.) As No. 371 (Sunflower)	1·90	1·70
693	C (80k.) As No. 372 (Lilac)	2·10	1·80
694	1h. As No. 372b (Poppy)	2·50	2·20
695	N (1h.53) As No. 372c (Sweet briar)	3·75	3·25
696	L (2h.55) As No. 372d (Pansy)	4·50	4·00
697	Zh (2h.66) As No. 373 (Viburnum berries)	4·75	4·25
698	E (3h.65) As No. 374 (Wheat)	6·50	5·50
699	E (10h.84) As No. 375 (Trident)	16·00	14·00
700	P (10h.84) As No. 375a (Trident)	16·00	14·00

2006. History of Ukraine (5th series). As T **242**.

701	70k. lake, emerald and black	1·90	1·70
702	70k. ultramarine, bistre and black	1·90	1·70
703	70k. ultramarine, bistre and black	1·90	1·70
704	70k. lake, emerald and black	1·90	1·70

DESIGNS: No. 701 16th—17th century Cossack; 702 16th—18th century naval campaign; 703 17th-century national liberation battle; 704 18th-century national liberation fighters.

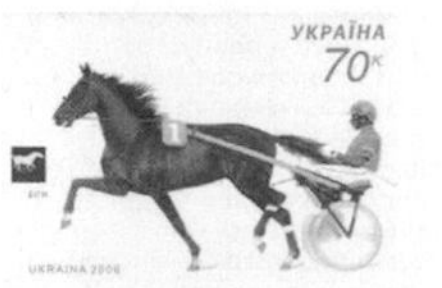

359 Harness Racing

2006. Equestrian Sports. Multicoloured.

705	70k. Type **359**	1·90	1·70
706	70k. Show-jumping	1·90	1·70
707	70k. Dressage	1·90	1·70
708	70k. Racing	1·90	1·70

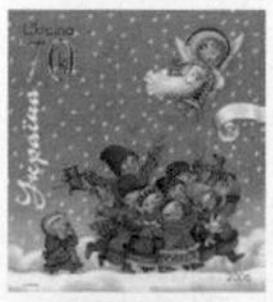

360 Children

2006. St Nicholas's Day. Multicoloured.

709	70k. Type **360**	1·90	1·70
710	70k. St Nicholas and angels	1·90	1·70

Nos. 709/10 were issued together, se-tenant, forming a composite design.

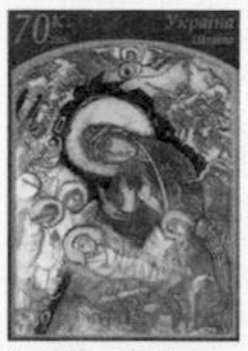

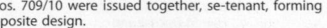

361 The Nativity

2006. Christmas.

711	**361**	70k. multicoloured	1·90	1·70

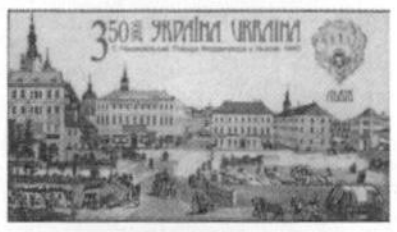

362 "Ferdinand Square" (T. Chyshkovskii)

2006. 750th Anniv of Lvov.

712	**362**	3k.50 multicoloured	9·50	9·25

A stamp of a similar design was issued by Austria.

2006. Traditional Costumes (6th series). As T **240**. Multicoloured.

713	70k. Four men, Zaporozhie	1·90	1·70
714	70k. Family and warrior, Zaporozhie	1·90	1·70
715	70k. Women spinning, Kherson	1·90	1·70
716	70k. Outdoor cooking, Kherson	1·90	1·70
717	70k. Musician, women and pig, Odessa	1·90	1·70
718	70k. Fisher folk, Odessa	1·90	1·70
MS719	100×140 mm. Nos. 713/18	9·50	9·25

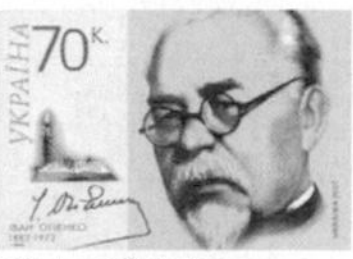

363 Ivan Ohienko

2007. Ivan Ohienko (Metropolitan of Chelm) Commemoration.

720	**363**	70k. multicoloured	1·90	1·70

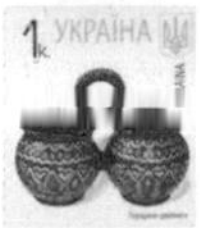

364 Double Pot with Handle

2007. Traditional Objects. Multicoloured.

721	1k. Type **364**	30	30
722	3k. Straw horse	30	30
723	5k. Clay whistle	30	30
724	10k. Glass Jug	50	40
724a	30k. Tobacco pipe	80	70
725	50k. Spinning wheel	1·10	1·00
726	60k. Straw covered flagon	1·30	1·10
727	70k. Kumanets (circular ceramic jar)	1·80	1·50
728	85k. Wooden ladle	2·20	2·00
729	1h. Decorated jug	2·50	2·20
730	1n. Candelabra	3·50	3·00
731	2h. Kumanets (ceramic jug with spout)	4·50	4·00
732	X Ceramic bull	4·75	4·25
733	E Ink well	6·50	5·50
734	R Glass jar	8·00	7·00
735	P Rag doll	13·00	11·00

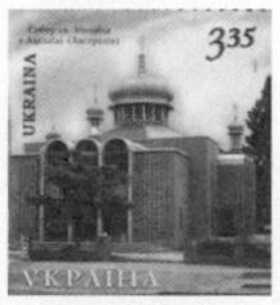

365 St. Michael's Cathedral, Adelaide, Australia

2007

750	**365**	3h.35 multicoloured	8·00	7·00

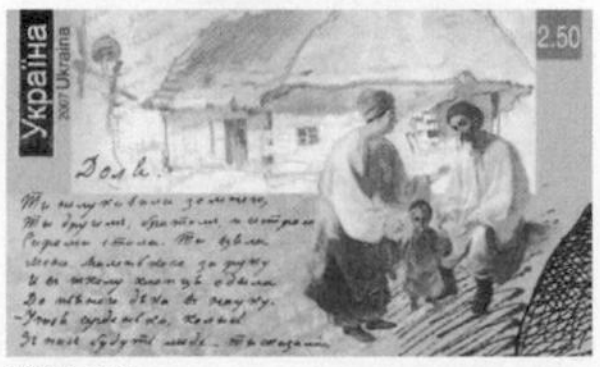

366 Script

2007. Birth Bicentenary of Taras Shevchenko (writer and artist). Sheet 130×80 mm containing T **366** and similar multicoloured design.

MS751 2h.50 Type **366**; 3h.35 Taras Shevchenko (36×40 mm) 14·50 14·00

The stamps and margin of **MS**751 form a composite design.

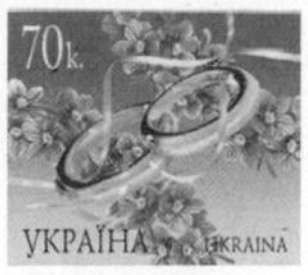

367 Wedding Rings

2007. Greetings Stamps.Multicoloured.

752	70k. Type **367**	6·50	5·50
753	70k. Flowers	6·50	5·50
754	70k. Kiev Pechersk Lavra Monastery	6·50	5·50
755	70k. Oranta the Victress	6·50	5·50

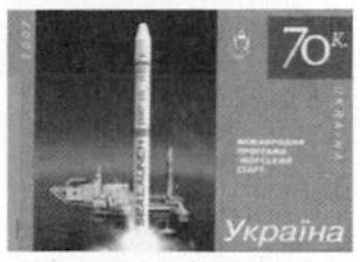

368 *Sea Launch* Craft

2007. Space Exploration. Multicoloured.

756	70k. Type **368**	1·60	1·40
757	70k. Leonid Kadeniuck (1st Ukrainian astronaut)	1·60	1·40

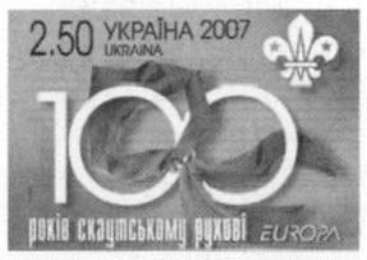

369 '100' and Neckerchief

2007. Europa. Centenary of Scouting. Multicoloured.

758	2h.50 Type **369**	6·50	5·50
759	3h.35 Ukrainian scouts c.1920	8·75	7·50

2007. Paintings of Kiev (6th series). As T **265**. Multicoloured.

760	70k. "Sunny Day" (Vitalii Petrovskyi)	1·90	1·70
761	70k. "Street of Recollections" [illegible]	[illegible]	[illegible]
762	70k. "Kyiv Wlk" (Yulia Kuznyetsova) (*vert*)	1·90	1·70
763	70k. "Snowing" (Maria Lashkevych)	1·90	1·70

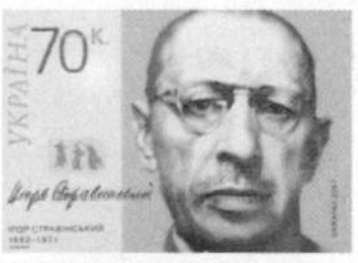

370 Igor Stravinsky

2007. 125th Birth Anniv of Igor Stravinsky (composer).

764	**370**	70k. multicoloured	1·90	1·70

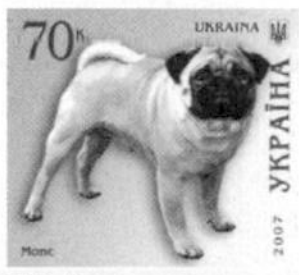

371 Pug

2007. Dogs and Cats. Multicoloured.

765	70k. Type **371**	1·90	1·70
766	70k. Irish setter	1·90	1·70
767	70k. Alaskan malamute	1·90	1·70
768	70k. Basset hound	1·90	1·70
769	70k. Bull mastiff	1·90	1·70
770	70k. American cocker spaniel	1·90	1·70
771	70k. American shorthair cat	1·90	1·70
772	70k. Sphynx	1·90	1·70
773	70k. Scottish fold	1·90	1·70
774	70k. Snowshoe	1·90	1·70
775	70k. Russian blue	1·90	1·70
776	70k. Somali	1·90	1·70

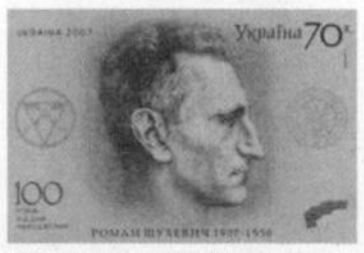

372 Roman Shukhevych

2007. Birth Centenary of Roman Shukhevych (politician and military leader).

777	**372**	70k. multicoloured	1·90	1·70

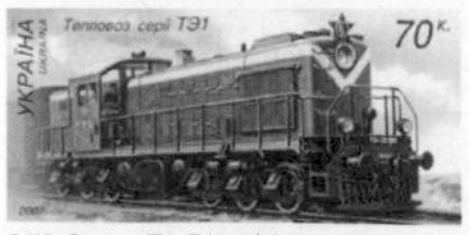
373 Series T1 Diesel Locomotive

2007. Locomotives. Multicoloured.

778	70k. Type **373**	1·90	1·70
779	70k. Series Tэ2 diesel locomotive	1·90	1·70
780	70k. Series Tэ3 diesel locomotive	1·90	1·70
781	70k. Series Tэ7 diesel locomotive	1·90	1·70

2007. Headdresses. As T **348**. Multicoloured.

782	70k. Garland with white train	1·90	1·70
783	70k. Headdress with bows, Polissya	1·90	1·70
784	70k. Garland with red train, Ivano-Frankivsk	1·90	1·70
785	70k. Headscarf with flowers and bows, Lviv	1·90	1·70
786	70k. Large flower covered bonnet, Kyiv	1·90	1·70
787	70k. Kerchief with metalled mesh band, Ivano Frankivsk	1·90	1·70
788	70k. Brimless raised flower covered hat, Lviv	1·90	1·70
789	70k. Man's hat with decorated bands and flowers, Ivano-Frankivsk	1·90	1·70
790	70k. Brimless pointed flower covered hat, Ternopil	1·90	1·70
791	70k. Man's tall hat with dark bands and flowers, Ternopil	1·90	1·70
792	70k. Flat garland with red band and train, Ivano-Frankivsk	1·90	1·70
793	70k. Man's wide brimmed hat with decorated band, Ternopil	1·90	1·70

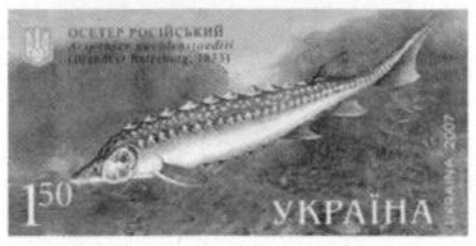
374 *Acipenser gueldenstaedtii*

2007. Fish. Multicoloured.

794	1h.50 Type **374**	4·25	3·75
795	2h.50 *Zinfgel zingel*	6·50	5·50

Stamps of a similar design were issued by Moldova.

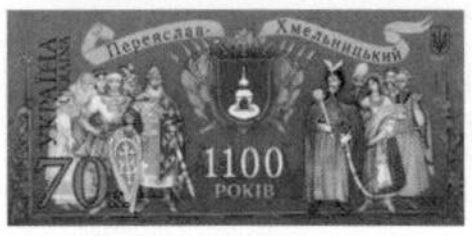
375 Arms

2007. 1100th Anniv of Pereyaslav-Khmelnytski.

796	**375**	70k. multicoloured	1·90	1·70

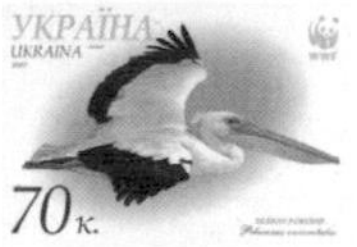
376 Great White Pelican

2007. Endangered Species. Great White Pelican (Pelekanus onocrotalus) Multicoloured.

797	70k. Type **376**	1·90	1·70
798	1h.50 Swimming	4·25	3·75
799	2h.50 Two pelicans	6·50	5·50
800	3h.50 Preening	8·75	7·50

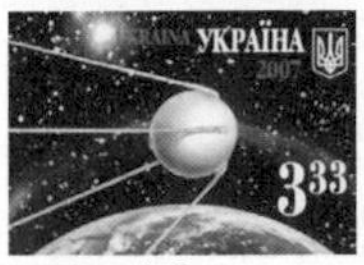
377 *Sputnik* (first man-made satellite)

2007. 50th Anniv of Space Exploration. Sheet 100×65 mm.

MS801	3h.33 multicoloured	8·25	8·00

The stamp and margins of No. **MS**801 form a composite design of *Sputnik* in flight and includes Sergei Korolev and Valentin Glushko (designers).

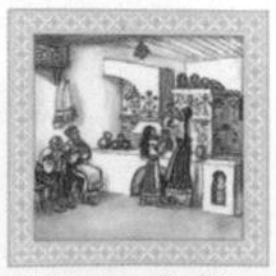
378 House, Podillya

2007. Folk Architecture. Peasant Houses Showing houses from different regions. Multicoloured.

802	70k. Type **378**	1·90	1·70
803	70k. Kyiv	1·90	1·70
804	70k. Lemkivshyna	1·90	1·70
805	70k. Hutsulschyna	1·90	1·70
806	70k. Volyn	1·90	1·70
807	70k. Slobozhanschyna	1·90	1·70
808	70k. Polissya	1·90	1·70
809	70k. Khorolschyna	1·90	1·70
810	70k. Bukovyna	1·90	1·70
811	70k. Bojkivschyna	1·90	1·70
812	70k. Poltava	1·90	1·70
813	70k. Dniepr	1·90	1·70

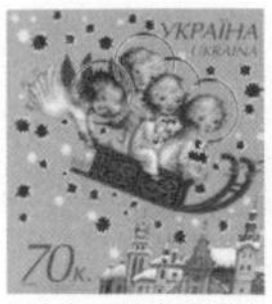
379 Angels in Sleigh

2007. Christmas and New Year. Multicoloured.

814	70k. Type **379**	1·90	1·70
815	70k. Angels and tree	1·90	1·70

Nos. 814/15 were issued together, *se-tenant*, forming a composite design.

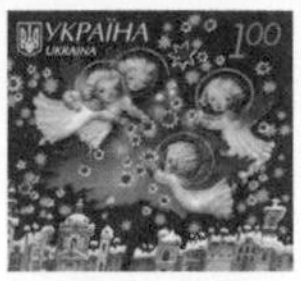
380 Angels and Tree

2007. Personal Stamp.

816	**380**	1h. multicoloured	9·50	8·50

2007. Traditional Costumes (7th series). As T **240**. Multicoloured.

817	70k. Christmas carollers, Khmelnytskyi	1·90	1·70
818	70k. Family dressed for St Simeon holiday, Khmelnytskyi	1·90	1·70
819	70k. Man and two women dressed for St. Ephrosinia holiday, Bukovyna	1·90	1·70
820	70k. Family dressed for Ascension, Bukovyna	1·90	1·70
821	70k. Men and anvil, Kuzma and Demyan holiday, Transcarpathia	1·90	1·70
822	70k. Man and two women, Radunytsa holiday, Transcarpathia	1·90	1·70
MS823	100×140 mm. Nos. 817/22	11·00	10·50

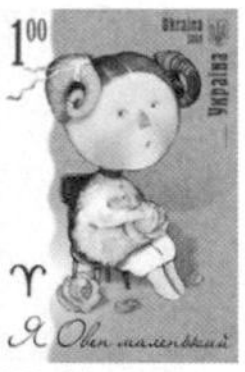
381 Aries

2008. Signs of the Western Zodiac. Designs showing children as Zodiac signs. Multicoloured.

824	1h. Type **381**	2·50	2·20
825	1h. Taurus	2·50	2·20
826	1h. Gemini	2·50	2·20
827	1h. Cancer	2·50	2·20
828	1h. Leo	2·50	2·20
829	1h. Virgo	2·50	2·20
830	1h. Libra	2·50	2·20
831	1h. Scorpio	2·50	2·20
832	1h. Sagittarius	2·50	2·20
833	1h. Capricorn	2·50	2·20
834	1h. Aquarius	2·50	2·20
835	1h. Pisces	2·50	2·20

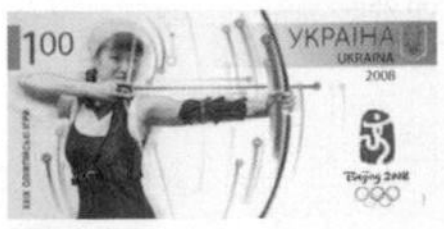
382 Archery

2008. Olympic Games, Beijing. Multicoloured.

836	1h. Type **832**	2·50	2·20
837	1h.30 Fencing	3·25	2·75
838	2h.47 Cycling	6·00	5·25
839	3h.33 Rowing	8·25	7·25

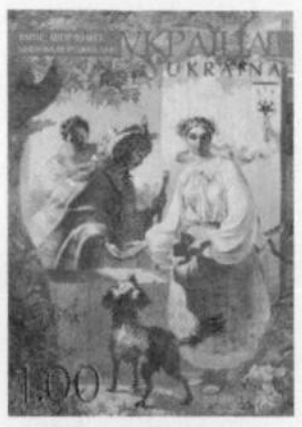
383 *Gypsy Fortune Teller*

2008. Birth Bicentenary of Taras Shevchenko (artist). Multicoloured.

840	1h. Type **383**	2·50	2·20
841	1h.52 *Kateryna*	3·75	3·25
842	2h.47 *Self Portrait*	6·50	5·50

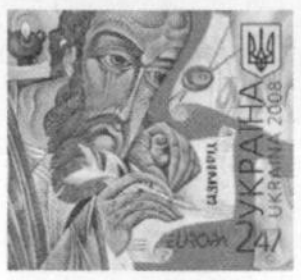
384 Scribe

2008. Europa. The Letter. Multicoloured.

843	2h.47 Type **384**	6·50	5·50
844	3h.33 Word processor	8·75	7·50

Nos. 843/4 were issued together, se-tenant, forming a composite design.

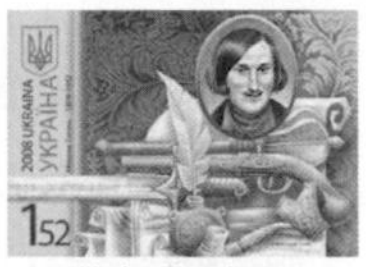
385 Nikolai Gogol

2008. Birth Bicentenary of Nikolai Gogol (Mykola Hohol) (Ukrainian writer, writing in Russian). Multicoloured.

845	1h.52 Type **385**	3·75	3·25
846	2h.47 Scene from *Taras Bulba*	10·00	9·00

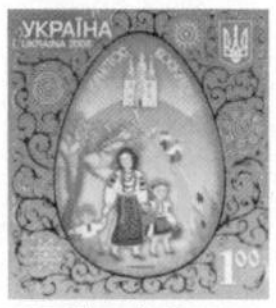
386 Church Goers

2008. Easter.

847	**386**	1h. multicoloured	2·50	2·20

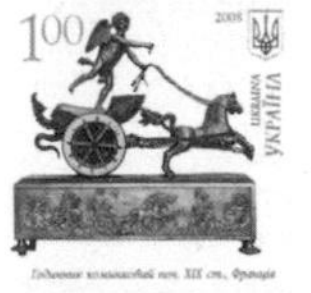
387 French 19th-century Mantle Clock

2008. Clocks. Sheet 123×166 mm containing T **387** and similar multicoloured designs.

MS848	1l.×9, Type **387**; Gold clock with ornate triangular case surmounted by cherubs (Russian 19th-century); Circular gold clock supported by two cherubs mounted on black goats (French 19th-century); Domed clock in green and gold case surmounted by cherub (French 19th-century) (33×45 mm); Black, red and gold cased clock with several legs surmounted by winged horses (French 18th-century) (33×45 mm); Porcelain clock decorated with figures and flower (German 18th-century) (33×45 mm); Black and gold cased clock with painted front panel (English 18th-century) (33×45 mm); Clock supported on lyre, surmounted by painted pediment supported by columns (Austrian 19th-century) (33×45 mm); Clock enclosed in goblet shaped case supported by large gold pedestal with cherubs and painted panel (French 19th-century) (33×45 mm)	22·00	21·00

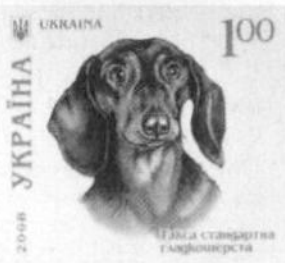
388 Standard Smooth Haired Dachshund

2008. Dogs and Cats. Two sheets, each 129×90 mm containing T **388** and similar square designs showing dogs (**MS**849) or cats (**MS**849a). Multicoloured.

MS849	1l.×6, Type **388**; American bulldog; Rottweiler; Chow; Standard Schnauzer; German Shepherd	15·00	14·00
MS849	1l.×6, Persian; Selkirk rex; Exotic shorthair; Burmese; Siamese; Kurile Island bobtail	15·00	14·00

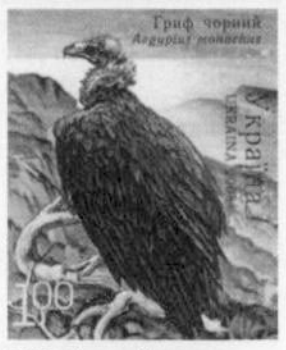
389 *Aegypius monachus* (Eurasian black vulture)

2008. Crimean Nature Reserve. Sheet 120×84 mm containing T **389** and similar multicoloured designs.

MS850	1l.×4, Type **389**; Egrets and swans (36×31 mm); *Cervus elaphus* (red deer) (47×31 mm); *Silene jailensis* (31×31 mm)	10·00	9·75

The stamps and margins of **MS**849 form a composite design.

No. 851 and Type **390** have been left for '90th Anniv of First Stamp', issued on 4 July 2008, not yet received.

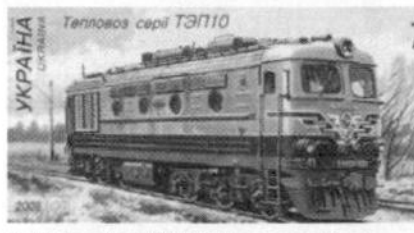
391 Series T**10 Locomotive

2008. Diesel Locomotives. Multicoloured. Phosphor markings.

852	1h. Type **391**	2·50	2·20
853	1h. Series 2TJE10JI	2·50	2·20
854	1h. Series M62	2·50	2·20
855	1h. Series TE109	2·50	2·20

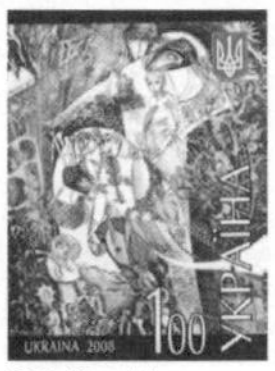
392 'Carols'

2008. Songs. Multicoloured.

856	1h. Type **392**	2·50	2·20
857	1h. Risen Christ ('Spring Songs')	2·50	2·20
858	1h. Ship ('Cossack Songs')	2·50	2·20
859	1h. Bull and flowers ('Chumak Songs')	2·50	2·20

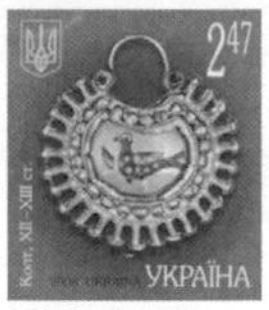
393 Earring (12th—13th century)

2008. Jewellery. Multicoloured.

860	2h.47 Type **393**	6·50	5·50
861	3h.33 Pendant (19th century)	8·75	7·50

Stamps of a similar design were issued by Azerbaijan.

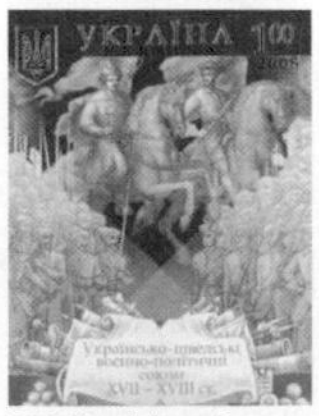
394 Swedish and Ukrainians

2008. Ukrainian - Swedish Military and Political Unions of 17th and 18th Centurie

862	**394**	1h. multicoloured	2·50	2·20

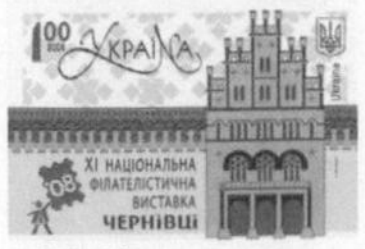
395 Emblem

2008. National Philatelic Exhibition, Chernivtsi.

863	**395**	1h. multicoloured	2·50	2·20

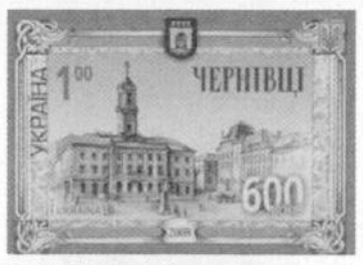

396 Central Square

2008. 600th Anniv of Chernivtsi.

864	**396**	1h. multicoloured	2·50	2·20

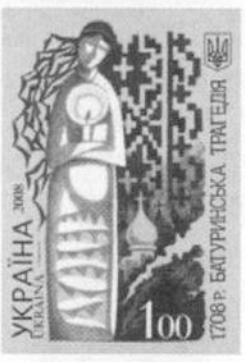

397 Woman holding Candle

2008. 300th Anniv of Baturyn Tragedy.

865	**397**	1h. multicoloured	2·50	2·20

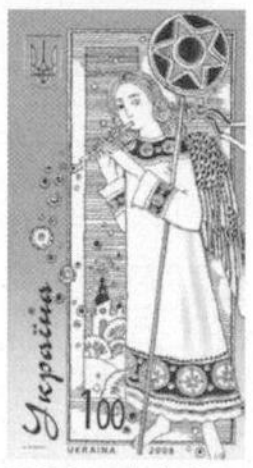

398 Angel playing Whistle

2008. Christmas and Happy New Year. Multicoloured.

866	1h. Type **398**	2·50	2·20
867	1h. Angel holding Horn of Plenty	2·50	2·20

Pt. 19

UMM AL QIWAIN

One of the Trucial States in the Persian Gulf. InJuly 1971 formed the United Arab Emirates with five other Gulf Sheikhdoms.

1964. 100 naye paise = 1 rupee.
1967. 100 dirhams = 1 riyal.

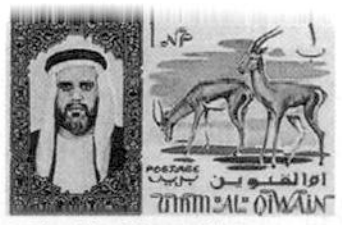

1 Shaikh Ahmed bin Rashid al Moalla and Mountain Gazelles

1964. Multicoloured. (a) Size as T **1**.

1	1n.p. Type **1**	25	25
2	2n.p. Snake	25	25
3	3n.p. Striped hyena	25	25
4	4n.p. Clown triggerfish	25	25
5	5n.p. Lionfish	25	25
6	10n.p. Diamond fingerfish	25	25
7	15n.p. Palace	25	25
8	20n.p. Town buildings	25	25
9	30n.p. Tower	35	25

(b) Size 42½×27 mm.

10	40n.p. Type **1**	35	30
11	50n.p. Snake	45	35
12	50n.p. Striped hyena	70	45
13	1r. Clown triggerfish	95	60
14	1r.50 Lionfish	1·20	70
15	2r. Diamond fingerfish	1·60	1·40

(c) Size 53½×33½ mm.

16	3r. Palace	3·00	2·30
17	5r. Town buildings	5·25	3·50
18	10r. Tower	8·25	6·50

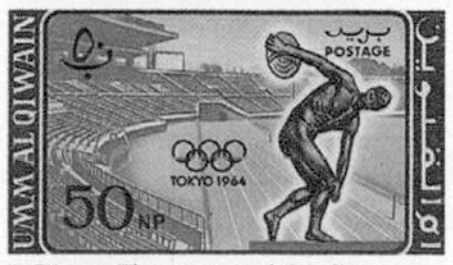

2 Discus Thrower and Stadium

1964. Olympic Games, Tokyo. Multicoloured.

19	50n.p. Type **2**	35	10
20	1r. Main stadium	95	25
21	1r.50 Swimming pool	1·40	45
22	2r. Main stadium	1·70	60
23	3r. Komazawa gymnasium	2·75	95
24	4r. Stadium entrance	3·50	1·20
25	5r. Type **2**	4·00	1·50
MS25a	145×115 mm. Nos. 22/5 but colours changed	13·00	3·50

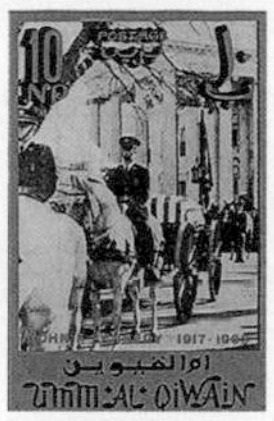

3 Cortege leaving White House

1965. Pres. Kennedy Commemoration. Each black and gold on coloured paper as given below.

26	**3**	10n.p. blue	10	10
27	-	15n.p. stone	10	10
28	-	50n.p. stone	35	20
29	-	1r. pink	70	25
30	-	2r. stone	1·20	35
31	-	3r. lilac	2·10	70
32	-	5r. blue	3·50	95
33	-	7r.50 buff	5·25	1·70
MS33a		115×70 mm. Nos. 32/3 but colours changed	11·50	8·75

DESIGNS—As T **3** (Funeral scenes): 15n.p. Coffin-bearers; 50n.p. Hearse; 1r. Presidents Eisenhower and Truman; 2r. Foreign dignitaries. 33×51 mm: 3r. Mrs. Kennedy and family at grave; 5r. Last salute; 7r.50, Pres. Kennedy.

1965. Air. Designs similar to Nos. 1/9 but inscr "AIR MAIL". Multicoloured. (a) Size 43×26½ mm.

34	15n.p. Type **1**	35	10
35	25n.p. Snake	60	10
36	35n.p. Striped hyena	65	15
37	50n.p. Clown triggerfish	95	20
38	75n.p. Lionfish	1·20	20
39	1r. Diamond fingerfish	1·50	25

(b) Size 53×34 mm.

40	2r. Palace	2·50	45
41	3r. Town buildings	3·75	80
42	5r. Tower	5·00	1·50

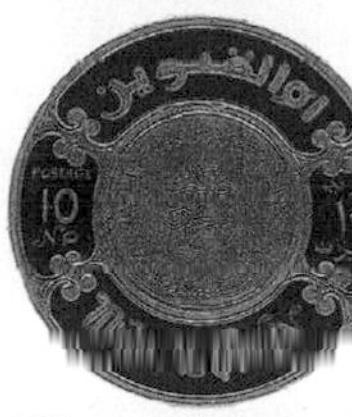

4 Tribute to Ruler (reverse of 10n.p. piece)

1965. Arabian Gulf Area Monetary Conf. Circular designs on silver foil, backed with paper inscr overall "Walsall Security Paper" in English and Arabic. Imperf. (a) Diameter 43 mm.

43	**4**	10n.p. purple and black	10	10
44	-	25n.p. blue and green	35	35

(b) Diameter 55½ mm.

45	**4**	1r. red and violet	95	95
46	-	2r. green and orange	2·00	2·00

(c) Diameter 64 mm.

47	**4**	3r. blue and mauve	3·00	3·00
48	-	5r. purple and blue	4·25	4·25

SILVER PIECES: Nos. 44, 46, 48 each show the obverse side (Shaikh Ahmed).

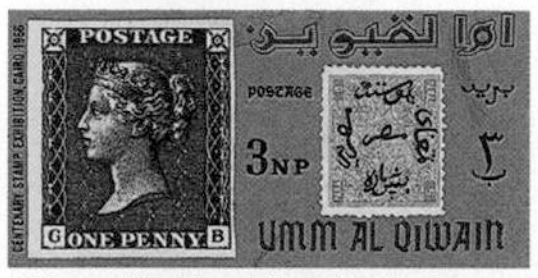

5 "Penny Black" and Egyptian 5p. Stamp of 1866

1966. Centenary Stamp Exhibition, Cairo.

49	**5**	3n.p. multicoloured	10	10
50	-	5n.p. multicoloured	10	10
51	-	7n.p. multicoloured	15	10
52	-	10n.p. multicoloured	15	10
53	-	15n.p. multicoloured	15	10
54	-	25n.p. multicoloured	25	15
55	-	50n.p. multicoloured	60	20
56	-	75n.p. multicoloured	80	25
57	-	1r. multicoloured	1·20	35
58	-	2r. multicoloured	2·30	80
MS58a		110×70 mm. 5r. multicoloured	4·75	2·30

DESIGNS: As Type **5** with Egyptian 5p. stamp: 7n.p. Brazil 30r. "Bull's-eye" of 1843; 15n.p. Mauritius "Post Office" One Penny of 1847; 50n.p. Belgium 10c. "Epaulettes" of 1849; 1r. New South Wales One Penny and Victoria One Penny of 1850. As Type **5**, but with Egyptian "Pyramid and Star" watermark of 1866: 5n.p. Basel 2½r. "Dove" of 1845, Geneva 5c.+5c. "Double Eagle" and Zurich 4r. "Numeral" of 1843; 10n.p. U.S. St. Louis "Bears" 5c., Baltimore 5c. and New York 5c. "Postmasters" stamps of 1845; 25n.p. France 20c. "Ceres" of 1849; 75n.p. Bavaria 1k. of 1850; 2r. Spain 6c. of 1850; 5r. Egyptian 5p. stamp of 1866.

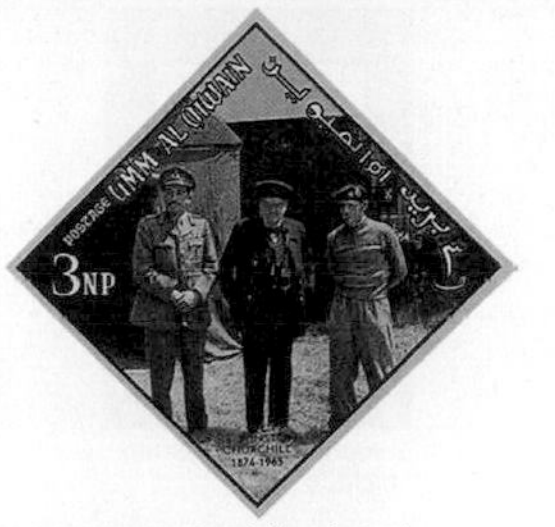

6 Sir Winston Churchill with Lord Alanbrooke and Field Marshal Montgomery

1966. Churchill Commemoration. Multicoloured designs each including Churchill.

59	3n.p. Type **6**	10	10
60	4n.p. With Roosevelt and Stalin at Yalta	10	10
61	5n.p. In garden at No. 10 Downing Street, London	10	10
62	10n.p. With Eisenhower	10	10
63	15n.p. With Lady Churchill in car	10	10
64	50n.p. Painting in Morocco	35	15
65	75n.p. Walking – on holiday	45	25
66	1r. Funeral cortege	60	35
67	3r. Lying-in-state, Westminster Hall	1·70	1·20
68	5r. Churchill giving "Victory" sign	3·50	1·70
MS69	100×100 mm. Nos. 67/8	8·25	8·25

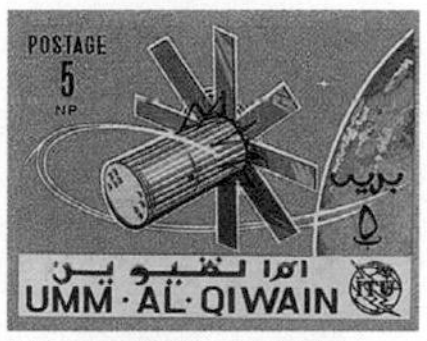

7 Communications Satellite

1966. Centenary (1965) of I.T.U. Communications Satellites. Multicoloured.

70	5n.p. Type **7**	10	10
71	10n.p. "Tiros"	25	10
72	25n.p. "Telstar"	35	15
73	50n.p. "Ariel"	60	25
74	75n.p. "Ranger"	80	35
[illegible]	[illegible]	[illegible]	[illegible]
76	2r. "Vanguard 1"	2·10	60
77	3r. "Explorer 10"	2·20	80
78	5r. "Early Bird"	3·50	1·50
MS79	120×79 mm. Nos. 75/6	5·75	3·00

NEW CURRENCY SURCHARGES. In 1967 various issues appeared surcharged in dirhams and riyals. The 1964 definitives, 1965 air stamps and officials with this surcharge are listed as there is evidence of their postal use. Nos. 19/33 and 49/68 also exist with these surcharges.

1967. Various issues with currency names changed by overprinting. (i) Nos. 1/18 (1964 Definitives).

80	1d. on 1n.p.	10	10
81	2d. on 2n.p.	10	10
82	3d. on 3n.p.	10	10
83	4d. on 4n.p.	10	10
84	5d. on 5n.p.	10	10
85	10d. on 10n.p.	10	10
86	15d. on 15n.p.	2·30	95
87	20d. on 20n.p.	2·30	95
88	30d. on 30n.p.	2·30	95
89	40d. on 40n.p.	35	25
90	50d. on 50n.p.	45	25
91	70d. on 70n.p.	70	30
92	1r. on 1r.	80	35
93	1r.50 on 1r.50	1·40	60
94	2r. on 2r.	1·70	70
95	3r. on 3r.	6·50	2·30
96	5r. on 5r.	8·75	3·75
97	10r. on 10r.	13·00	5·75

(ii) Nos. 34/42 (Airmails).

98	15d. on 15n.p.	25	10
99	25d. on 25n.p.	30	10
100	35d. on 35n.p.	60	25
101	50d. on 50n.p.	80	35
102	75d. on 75n.p.	1·40	60
103	1r. on 1r.	1·70	70
104	2r. on 2r.	4·00	1·60
105	3r. on 3r.	6·50	2·50
106	5r. on 5r.	10·50	4·25

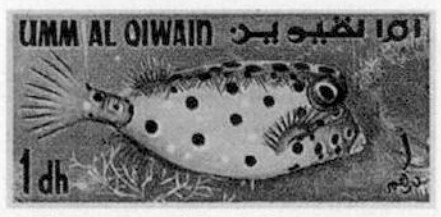

9 Blue-spotted Boxfish

1967. Fish of the Arabian Gulf. Multicoloured. (a) Postage. (i) Size 46×21 mm.

116	1d. Type **9**	10	10
117	2d. Parrotfish	10	10
118	3d. Striped sweetlips	10	10
119	4d. Black-wedged butterflyfish	10	10
120	5d. Japanese bonyhead	15	10
121	10d. Reticulate damselfish	25	10
122	15d. Picasso triggerfish	25	10
123	20d. Undulate triggerfish	35	10
124	30d. Black-saddled pufferfish	40	15

(ii) Size 56×26 mm.

125	40d. Type **9**	45	20
126	50d. As 2d.	60	25
127	70d. As 3d.	70	25
128	1r. As 4d.	80	30
129	1r.50 As 5d.	1·30	35
130	2r. As 10d.	1·50	45
131	3r. As 15d. (No. 122)	2·10	70
132	5r. As 20d.	3·50	1·20
133	10r. As 30d.	5·75	2·50

(b) Air. Size 70×35 mm.

134	15d. Type **9**	25	10
135	25d. As 2d.	35	15
136	35d. As 3d.	45	20
137	50d. As 4d.	60	25
138	75d. As 5d.	70	30
139	1r. As 10d.	80	35
140	2r. As 15d. (No. 122)	1·50	45
141	3r. As 20d.	2·10	70
142	5r. As 30d.	3·50	1·20

OFFICIAL STAMPS

1965. Designs similar to Nos. 1/9, additionally inscr "ON STATE'S SERVICE". Multicoloured. (a) Postage. Size 42½×27 mm.

O49	25n.p. Type **1**	35	10
O50	40n.p. Snake	45	15
O51	50n.p. Striped hyena	70	25
O52	75n.p. Clown triggerfish	1·00	30
O53	1r. Lionfish	1·30	35

(b) Air. (i) Size 42½×27 mm.

O54	75n.p. Diamond fingerfish	1·00	25

(ii) Size 53×34 mm.

O55	2r. Palace	2·50	80
O56	3r. Town buildings	3·75	1·20
O57	5r. Tower	5·25	1·70

1967. Nos. O49/57 with currency names changed by overprinting.

O107	25d. on 25n.p. (postage)	35	25
O108	40d. on 40n.p.	45	30
O109	50d. on 50n.p.	70	45
O110	75d. on 75n.p.	80	60
O111	1r. on 1r.	1·00	70
O112	75d. on 75d. (air)	80	60
O113	2r. on 2r.	2·30	1·70
O114	3r. on 3r.	3·00	1·70
O115	5r. on 5r.	5·00	3·00

For later issues see **UNITED ARAB EMIRATES**.

APPENDIX

The following stamps have either been issued in excess of postal needs or have not been available to the public in reasonable quantities at face value. Such stamps may later be given full listing if there is evidence of regular postal use.

1967

Self-portraits of Famous Painters. Postage 10, 15, 25, 50, 75d., 1, 1r.50; Air 1r.25, 2, 2r.50, 3, 5r.
Dogs. Postage 15, 25, 50, 75d., 1r.; Air 1r.25, 2r.50, 4r.
"Expo 67" World Fair, Montreal. Famous Paintings. 25, 50, 75d., 1, 1r.50, 2, 3r.

1968

Falcons. Postage 15, 25, 50, 75d., 1r.; Air 1r.50, 3, 5r.
Winter Olympic Games, Grenoble. Postage 10, 25, 75d., 1r.; Air 1r.50, 2, 3, 5r.
Famous Paintings. Postage 25, 50, 75d., 1, 1r.50, 2r.50; Air 1, 2, 3, 4, 5r.
Olympic Games, Mexico (1st issue). Optd on (a) 1964 Tokyo Olympic Games Issue. Postage 1r.50, 2, 4, 5r. (b) 1968 Winter Olympic Games issue. Air 1r.50, 2, 5r.
Robert Kennedy Memorial. Optd on 1965 Pres. Kennedy issue. Postage 3, 5, 7r.50.
Olympic Games, Mexico (2nd issue). Postage 10, 25, 50d., 1, 2r.; Air 2r.50, 3, 4, 5r.
Still Life Paintings. Postage 25, 50d., 1, 1r.50, 2r.; Air 1r.25, 2r.50, 3, 3r.50, 5r.
Mexico Olympic Medal Winners. Optd on Olympic Games, Mexico issue. Postage 10, 25, 50d., 1, 2r.; Air 2r.50, 3, 4, 5r.
Aviation History. Aircraft. Postage 25, 50d., 1, 1r.50, 2r.; Air 1r.25, 2r.50, 3, 5r.

1969

"Apollo 8" Moon Orbit. Optd on 1968 Aviation History issue. Postage 25, 50d., 1, 1r.50, 2r.; Air 1r.25, 2r.50, 3, 5r.
Horses (1st series). Postage 25, 50, 75d., 1, 2r.; Air 1r.50, 2r.50, 4, 5r.
Olympic Games, Munich, 1972 (1st issue). Optd on 1968 Olympic Games, Mexico issue. Postage 10, 25, 50d., 1, 2r.; Air 2r.50, 3, 4, 5r.

Winter Olympic Games, Sapporo 1972 (1st issue). Optd on 1968 Winter Olympics Grenoble issue. Postage 10, 25, 75d., 1r.; Air 1r.50, 2, 3, 5r.
Veteran and Vintage Cars. Postage 15d.×8, 25d.×8, 50d.×8, 75d.×8; Air 1r.×8, 2r.×8.
Famous Films. Postage 10, 15, 25, 50, 75d., 1r.; Air 1r.50, 2r.50, 3, 4, 5r.
"Apollo 12" Moon Landing. 10, 20, 30, 50, 75d., 1r.

1970

"Apollo 13" Astronauts. 10, 30, 50d.
"Expo 70" World Fair, Osaka, Japan. 5, 10, 20, 40d., 1, 1r.25.
150th Anniv of British Landing on Trucial Coast. Uniforms. 10, 20, 30, 50, 75d., 1r.

1971

Animals. Postage 10, 15, 20, 25d.; Air 5r.
Winter Olympic Games, Saporro, 1972 (2nd issue). Postage 5, 10, 15, 20, 25d.; Air 50, 75d., 1, 3, 5r.
Olympic Games, Munich, 1972 (2nd issue). Postage 5, 10, 15, 20, 25d.; Air 50, 75d., 1, 3, 5r.

1972

Durer's Religious Paintings. Postage 5, 10, 15, 20, 25d.; Air 3r.
Horses (2nd series). Postage 10, 15, 20, 25d.; Air 50d., 3r.
Locomotives (plastic surfaced). Postage 5, 10, 20, 40, 50d.; Air 6r.
Winter Olympic Games, Sapporo, 1972 (3rd issue) (plastic surfaced). Postage 5, 10, 20, 40, 50d.; Air 6r.
Easter, Religious Paintings. Postage 5, 10, 20, 50d.; Air 1, 3r.
Kennedy Brothers Memorial. Postage 5, 10, 15, 20d.; Air 1, 3r.
Winston Churchill Memorial. Postage 5, 10, 15, 20d.; Air 3r.
Arab Rulers. Postage 5d.×6, 10d.×6, 15d.×6, 20d.×6; Air 3r.×6.
13th World Jamboree, 1971 (plastic surfaced). Postage 5, 10, 20, 40, 50d.; Air 6r.
Fish. Postage 5, 10, 20, 40, 50d.; Air 6r.
International Airlines. Postage 5, 10, 15, 20, 25d.; Air 50d.
"Apollo 15" Moon Mission. Postage 5, 10, 15, 20, 25d.; Air 50, 75d., 1, 3, 5r.
Olympic Games, Munich, 1972 (3rd issue) (plastic surfaced). Postage 5, 10, 20, 40, 50d.; Air 6r.
2500th Anniv of Founding of Persian Empire. Postage 10, 20, 30, 40, 50, 60d.; Air 1r.
Portraits of Charles de Gaulle. 5, 10, 15, 20, 25d.
Paintings of Napoleon. Postage 5, 10, 15, 20, 25d.; Air 5r.
Butterflies. Postage 5, 10, 15, 20, 25d.; Air 3r.
Penguins. Postage 5, 10, 15, 20d.; Air 50d., 4r.
Cars. Postage 5, 10, 15, 20, 25d.; Air 3r.
Masks (1st series). Postage 5, 10, 15, 20, 25d.; Air 50d., 1, 3r.
Dogs and Cats. Postage 5, 5, 10, 10, 15, 15, 20, 20, 25, 25d.; Air 5, 5r.
Roses. Postage 10, 15, 20, 25d.; Air 50d., 5r.
Marine Fauna. Postage 5, 10, 15, 20, 25, 50d.; Air 1, 3r.
Masks (2nd series). Postage 5, 10, 15, 20, 25d.; Air 50d., 1, 3r.
Navigators. Postage 5, 10, 15, 20, 25, 50d.; Air 1, 3r.
Exotic Birds (1st series). Horiz and vert designs. Air 1r.×16.
Exotic Birds (2nd series). Horiz designs. Air 1r.×16.

In common with the other states of the United Arab Emirates the Umm al Qiwain stamp contract was terminated on 1 August 1972 and any further new issues released after that date were unauthorized.

Pt. 19

UNITED ARAB EMIRATES

Following the withdrawal of British forces from the Gulf and the ending of the Anglo-Trucial States treaties six of the states, Abu Dhabi, Ajman, Dubai, Fujeira, Sharjah and Umm al Qiwain, formed an independent union on 2 December 1971. The seventh state, Ras al Khaima, joined during February 1972. Each emirate continued to use its own stamps, pending the introduction of a unified currency. A Union Postal administration came into being on 1 August 1972 and the first stamps appeared on 1 January 1973.

For Abu Dhabi stamps optd U.A.E., etc, see under that heading.

100 fils = 1 dirham.

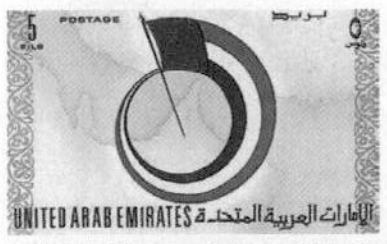

1 U.A.E. Flag and Map of Gulf

1973. Multicoloured. (a) Size 42×25 mm.

1	5f. Type **1**	10	10
2	10f. Type **1**	20	10
3	15f. Eagle emblem	55	10
4	35f. As 15f.	65	20

(b) Size 46×30 mm.

5	65f. Almaqta Bridge, Abu Dhabi	1·30	35
6	75f. Khor Fakkan, Sharjah	1·70	45
7	1d. Clock Tower, Dubai	1·90	55
8	1¼d. Buthnah Fort, Fujeira	5·50	2·75
9	2d. Alfalaj Fort, Umm al Qiwain	55·00	11·00
10	3d. Khor Khwair, Ras al Khaima	11·00	8·25
11	5d. Ruler's Palace, Ajman	13·50	8·75
12	10d. President Shaikh Zaid	28·00	17·00

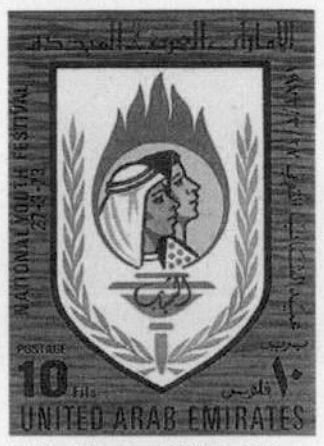

2 Youth and Girl within Shield

1973. National Youth Festival. Multicoloured.

13	10f. Type **2**	7·75	45
14	1d.25 Allegory of Youth	19·00	11·00

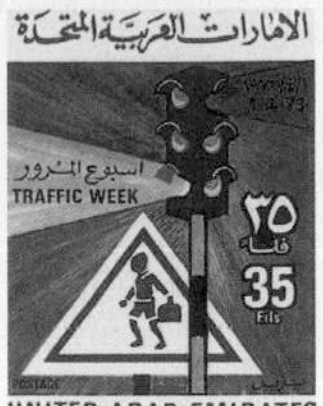

3 Traffic Lights and Road Sign

1973. Traffic Week. Multicoloured.

15	35f. Type **3**	4·00	1·90
16	75f. Pedestrian-crossing (horiz)	7·75	3·50
17	1d.25 Traffic policeman	13·50	5·25

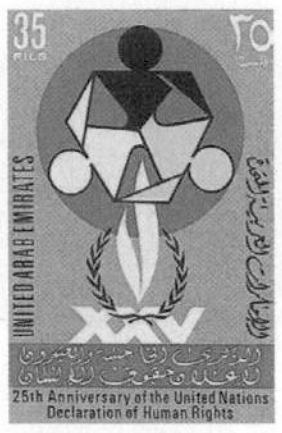

4 "Three Races of the World"

1973. 25th Anniv of Declaration of Human Rights.

18	4	35f. black, yellow and blue	2·20	90
19	4	65f. black, yellow and red	5·25	1·70
20	4	1¼d. black, yellow and green	8·25	4·50

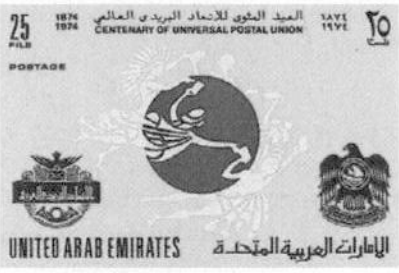

5 U.P.U. Emblem

1974. Centenary of Universal Postal Union.

21	5	25f. multicoloured	2·20	1·10
22	5	60f. multicoloured	3·25	1·70
23	5	1¼d. multicoloured	6·75	5·50

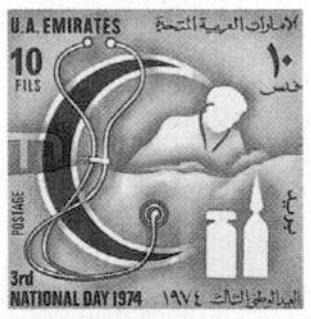

6 Medical Equipment (Health Service)

1974. Third National Day.

24	6	10f. red, brown and lilac	1·30	35
25	-	35f. gold, green and blue	2·75	1·10
26	-	65f. brown, sepia and blue	3·50	1·70
27	-	1¼d. multicoloured	7·75	4·50

DESIGNS—49×30 mm: 35f. Children reading (Education); 65f. Tools and buildings (Construction); 1¼d. U.A.E. flag with emblems of U.N. and Arab League.

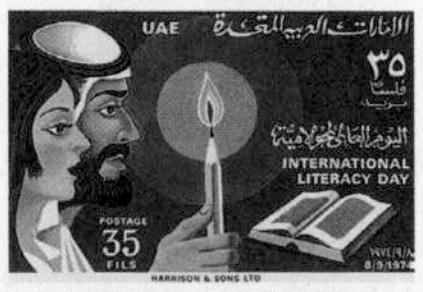

7 Arab Couple with Candle and Book

1974. International Literacy Day.

28	7	35f. multicoloured	3·25	65
29	-	65f. black, blue and brown	3·50	1·30
30	-	1d.25 black, blue and brown	6·75	2·75

DESIGN—VERT: 65f., 1f.25, Arab couple with book.

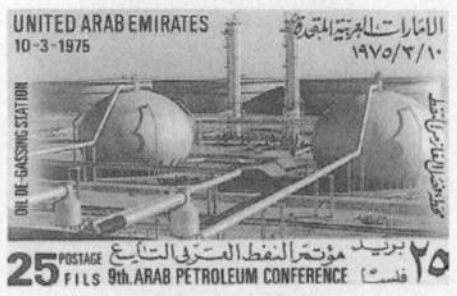

8 Oil De-gassing Installation

1975. Ninth Arab Oil Conference. Multicoloured.

31	25f. Type **8**	1·60	55
32	50f. "Al Ittiad" (offshore oil drilling platform)	3·25	1·00
33	100f. Underwater storage tank	8·25	2·50
34	125f. Marine oil production platform	11·00	2·75
MS35	168×122 mm. Nos. 31/4	33·00	22·00

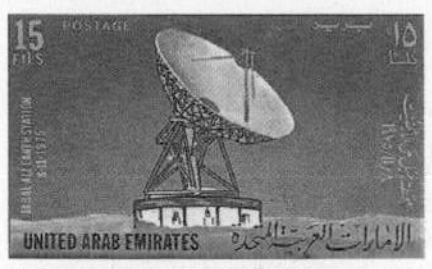

9 Station and Dish Aerial

1975. Inauguration of Jabal Ali Satellite Earth Station. Multicoloured.

36	15f. Type **9**	1·30	45
37	35f. Satellite beaming information to Earth	3·00	65
38	65f. As 35f.	5·00	1·10
39	2d. Type **9**	10·00	5·25

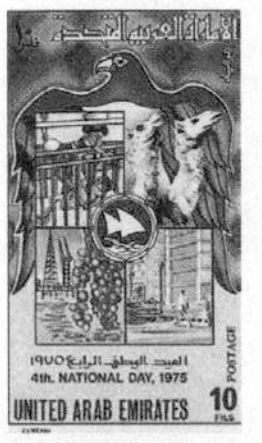

10 "Snapshots" within Eagle Emblem

1975. Fourth National Day. Multicoloured.

40	10f. Type **10**	80	25
41	35f. Shaikh Mohamed bin Hamad al Sharqi of Fujeira	2·30	1·30
42	60f. Shaikh Rashid bin Humaid al Naimi of Ajman	3·50	2·50
43	80f. Shaikh Ahmed bin Rashid al Moalla of Umm al Qiwain	4·75	3·25
44	90f. Shaikh Sultan bin Mohammed al Qasimi of Sharjah	5·25	3·25
45	1d. Shaikh Saqr bin Mohammed al Qasimi of Ras al Khaima	5·75	3·75
46	1d.40 Shaikh Rashid bin Said of Dubai	8·25	5·00
47	5d. Shaikh Zaid bin Sultan al Nahayyan of Abu Dhabi, President of U.A.E	35·00	19·00

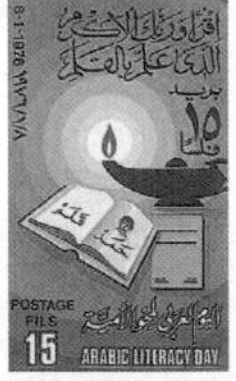

11 Symbols of Learning

1976. Arab Literacy Day. Multicoloured.

48	15f. Type **11**	60	40
49	50f. Arabs seeking enlightenment	2·30	90
50	3d. As 50f.	11·50	8·25

1976. No. 6 surch 50 in English and Arabic.

50a	50f. on 75f. multicoloured	60·00	19·00

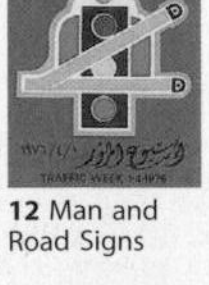

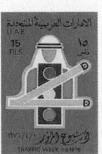

12 Man and Road Signs

1976. Traffic Week. Multicoloured.

51	15f. Type **12**	2·00	1·10
52	80f. Example of dangerous driving and road signals (horiz)	9·25	5·25
53	140f. Children on road crossing (horiz)	17·00	10·00

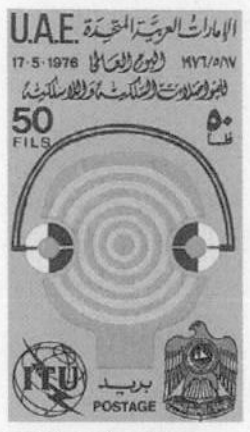

13 Headphones

1976. International Telecommunications Day.

54	13	50f. multicoloured	1·40	65
55	13	80f. multicoloured	3·25	1·30
56	13	2d. multicoloured	7·00	3·75

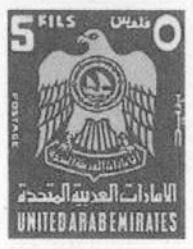

14 U.A.E. Crest

1976

57	14	5f. red	10	10
58	14	10f. brown	15	15
59	14	15f. pink	25	20
60	14	35f. brown	60	25
61	14	50f. violet	1·20	55
62	14	60f. bistre	1·40	65
63	14	80f. green	1·70	70
64	14	90f. blue	2·30	75
65	14	1d. blue	2·75	90
66	14	140f. green	3·00	1·40
67	14	150f. violet	5·75	2·00
68	14	2d. grey	6·00	2·30
69	14	5d. blue	13·00	6·25
70	14	10d. mauve	23·00	15·00

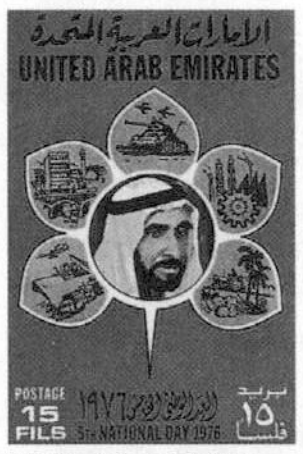

15 President Shaikh Zaid

1976. Fifth National Day.

71	15	15f. multicoloured	3·50	65
72	15	140f. multicoloured	11·50	5·00

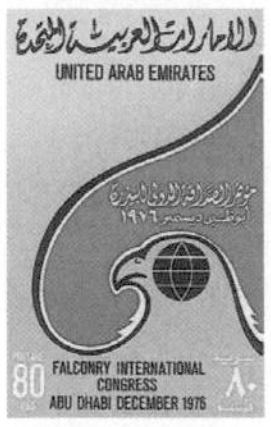

16 Falcon's Head and Gulf

1976. International Falconry Congress, Abu Dhabi.

73	16	80f. multicoloured	3·00	1·90
74	16	2d. multicoloured	7·50	3·75

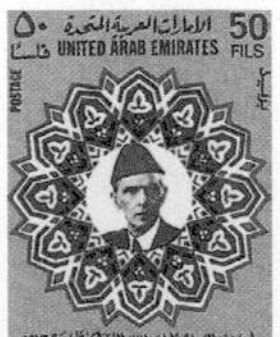

17 Mohammed Ali Jinnah (Quaid-i-Azam)

1976. Birth Centenary of Mohammed Ali Jinnah (founder of Pakistan).

75	17	50f. multicoloured	5·25	1·50
76	17	80f. multicoloured	7·50	3·25

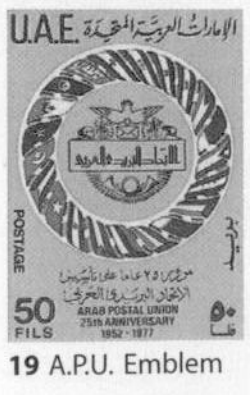

19 A.P.U. Emblem

1977. 25th Anniv of Arab Postal Union.

78	19	50f. multicoloured	4·00	1·50
79	19	80f. multicoloured	6·50	2·75

20 U.A.E. Crest

1977

80	20	5f. red and black	35	40
81	20	10f. brown and black	40	45
82	20	15f. pink and black	60	50
83	20	35f. brown and black	1·00	50
84	20	50f. mauve and black	1·60	50
85	20	60f. bistre and black	2·75	1·00
86	20	80f. green and black	3·00	65
87	20	90f. blue and black	3·25	40
88	20	1d. blue and black	4·50	75
89	20	1d.40 green and black	5·75	2·00
90	20	1d.50 violet and black	7·00	2·10
91	20	2d. grey and black	8·75	3·00
92	20	5d. blue and black	21·00	7·50
93	20	10d. purple and black	35·00	15·00

21 Arab Scholar and Emblems

1977. International Literacy Day.

94	21	50f. multicoloured	3·00	1·50
95	21	3d. multicoloured	11·50	7·50

22 Armoured Cars

1977. Sixth National Day. Multicoloured.

96		15f. Type **22**		
97		50f. Anti-aircraft missiles		
98		150f. Soldiers marching		

Nos. 96/8 were withdrawn from sale on day of issue as the date in Arabic was wrongly inscribed backwards.

23 Posthorn Dhow

1979. Second Gulf Postal Organization Conf, Dubai.

99	23	50f. multicoloured	1·30	90
100	23	5d. multicoloured	8·25	7·00

24 Koran on Map of World

1980. The Arabs.

101	24	50f. multicoloured	95	65
102	24	1d.40 multicoloured	2·30	1·80
103	24	3d. multicoloured	5·00	3·75

25 Dassault Mirage III Jet Fighters and Sud Aviation Alouette III Helicopter

1980. Ninth National Day.

104	25	15f. multicoloured	60	40
105	25	50f. multicoloured	1·70	65
106	25	80f. multicoloured	2·30	1·50
107	25	150f. multicoloured	3·50	2·50
MS108		120×85 mm. **25** 3d. multi-coloured	14·00	14·00

26 Family on Graph

1980. Population Census.

109	26	15f. blue and pink	80	40
110	-	80f. brown and grey	2·50	1·30
111	-	90f. brown and buff	3·00	1·50
112	26	2d. blue and cobalt	7·50	7·00

DESIGN: 80, 90f. Figure standing in doorway.

27 Mosque and Kaaba, Mecca

1980. 1400th Anniv of Hejira.

113	27	15f. multicoloured	60	25
114	27	80f. multicoloured	1·70	90
115	27	90f. multicoloured	2·00	1·30
116	27	140f. multicoloured	5·00	3·25
MS117		90×120 mm. **27** 2d. multicoloured (36×57 mm)	11·50	11·50

28 Figures supporting O.P.E.C. Emblem

1980. 20th Anniv of Organization of Petroleum Exporting Countries. Multicoloured.

118	28	50f. Type **28**	1·00	65
119	28	80f. Type **28**	1·90	1·00
120		90f. O.P.E.C. emblem and globe	2·30	1·40
121		140f. As No. 120	4·00	3·25
MS122		120×90 mm. 3d. As No. 120 (68×52 mm)	15·00	15·00

29 Policeman helping Child across Road

1981. Traffic Week. Multicoloured.

123	29	15f. Type **29**	80	25
124		50f. Policeman and traffic signs (21×31 mm)	1·70	90
125	29	80f. Type **29**	2·50	1·50
126		5d. As No. 124	9·25	8·25

30 Symbols of Industry

1981. Tenth National Day.

127	30	25f. blue and black	1·20	50
128	-	150f. multicoloured	4·00	2·00
129	-	2d. red, green and black	5·75	3·75

DESIGNS: 150f. Soldiers; 2d. Flag and U.N. and U.A.E emblems.

31 Helping the Disabled (pictogram) and I.Y.D.P. Emblem

1981. Int Year of Disabled Persons. Multicoloured.

130		25f. Type **31**	80	40

131		45f. Disabled person in wheel-chair (pictogram) (vert)	1·70	90
132		150f. As No. 131	5·25	2·50
133		2d. Type **31**	6·50	3·75

32 U.A.E. Crest

1982. Multicoloured. Background colour given. (a) Size 17×21 mm.

134	32	5f. pink	10	10
135	32	10f. green	15	10
136	32	15f. violet	25	10
137	32	25f. brown	35	15
138	32	35f. brown	45	25
139	32	50f. blue	4·00	2·10
140	32	75f. yellow	1·20	75
141	32	100f. grey	1·40	1·00
142	32	110f. green	1·50	1·10
143	32	125f. mauve	1·70	1·40
144	32	150f. blue	2·30	1·60
145	32	175f. blue	2·50	1·80

(b) Size 23×27 mm.

146		2d. green	3·00	1·90
147		250f. pink	3·75	1·90
148		3d. blue	3·50	2·50
149		5d. yellow	5·75	3·25
150		10d. brown	10·50	6·25
151		20d. silver	20·00	14·00
151c		50d. purple	44·00	22·00

33 Flags of Competing Countries and Emblem

1982. Sixth Arab Gulf Football Championships. Multicoloured.

152		25f. Type **33**	80	65
153		75f. American bald eagle holding ball over stadium (vert)	2·50	1·80
154		125f. Footballers (vert)	3·50	3·00
155		150f. As Type **33**	3·25	2·00

34 Figure breaking Gun

1982. Second U.N. Disarmament Conference.

156	34	25f. multicoloured	25	25
157	34	75f. multicoloured	1·70	1·30
158	34	125f. multicoloured	3·00	2·50
159	34	150f. multicoloured	3·50	3·25

35 National Emblems

1982. 11th National Day. Multicoloured.

160	35	25f. Type **35**	60	40
161		75f. Dove and flag (vert)	1·90	1·30
162		125f. As 75f.	3·00	2·10
163		150f. Type **35**	3·50	3·25

36 Arab writing

1983. Arab Literacy Day.

164	-	25f. multicoloured	41·00	60·00
165	36	35f. brown, violet and black	1·50	90
166	-	75f. yellow, black & mauve	41·00	60·00
167	36	3d. brown, yellow and black	11·50	5·00

DESIGN: 25, 75f. Koran and lamp.

37 W.C.Y. Emblem

1983. World Communications Year.

168	37	25f. multicoloured	1·30	25
169	37	75f. multicoloured	3·75	1·90
170	37	2d. multicoloured	4·50	2·50
171	37	3d. multicoloured	6·25	3·75

38 Satellite Orbit within "20"

1984. 20th Anniv of International Tele-communications Satellite Consortium.

172	38	2d. blue, purple & deep blue	5·75	5·00
173	38	2½d. blue, purple and green	8·25	7·50

39 Shaikh Hamad bin Mohamed al Sharqi and Buthnah Fort, Fujeira

1984. 13th National Day. Multicoloured.

174	39	1d. Type **39**	3·25	1·90
175		1d. Shaikh Rashid bin Ahmed al Moalla and Alfalaj Fort, Umm al Qiwain	3·25	1·90
176		1d. Shaikh Humaid bin Rashid al Naimi and Palace, Ajman	3·25	1·90
177		1d. Shaikh Saqr bin Moham-med al-Qasimi and harbour, Ras al Khaima	3·25	1·90
178		1d. Shaikh Zaid bin Sultan al Nahayyan and refinery, Abu Dhabi	3·25	1·90
179		1d. Shaikh Sultan bin Moham-med al Qasimi, oil well and mosque, Sharjah	3·25	1·90
180		1d. Shaikh Rashid bin Said and building, Dubai	3·25	1·90

40 Pictograms of Refuse Collection

1985. Tidy Week.

181	40	5d. orange and black	11·50	9·50

41 Globe and Knights

1985. World Junior Chess Championship, Sharjah.

182	41	2d. multicoloured	5·75	3·25
183	41	250f. multicoloured	8·25	5·00

42 Map and Hand holding Flag

1985. 14th National Day.

184	42	50f. multicoloured	75	65
185	42	3d. multicoloured	5·75	3·25

43 Stylized People and Map

1985. Population Census.

186	**43**	50f. multicoloured	1·00	65
187	**43**	1d. multicoloured	2·40	1·30
188	**43**	3d. multicoloured	6·00	3·75

44 Profiles looking at Sapling

1985. International Youth Year. Multicoloured.

189	50f. Type **44**		90	65
190	175f. Open book, flame and people between hemispheres (horiz)		3·25	1·50
191	2d. Youth carrying globe on back		3·75	2·10

45 Emblem

1986. Arabic Woman and Family Day.

192	**45**	1d. multicoloured	1·90	1·40
193	**45**	3d. multicoloured	5·75	4·25

46 Globe, Map and Posthorn

1986. First Anniv of General Postal Authority. Multicoloured.

194	50f. Type **46**		75	65
195	1d. Banner around globe (vert)		1·60	90
196	2d. As No. 195		3·25	2·50
197	250f. Type **46**		3·75	3·25

47 Sakar Falcon

1986

198	**47**	50f. gold, blue and green	90	90
199	**47**	75f. gold, blue and mauve	1·40	1·40
200	**47**	125f. gold, blue and grey	2·40	2·40

48 Container Ship in Dock

1986. Tenth Anniv of United Arab Shipping Company. Multicoloured.

201	2d. Type **48**		4·75	2·75
202	3d. Container ship at sea (vert)		5·75	4·25

49 Dawn, Satellite, Emblem and Dish Aerials

1986. Tenth Anniv of Emirates Telecommunications Corporation.

203	250f. Type **49**		4·00	2·75
204	3d. As Type **49** but with sun behind emblem		5·00	3·75

50 Emblem, Boeing 737 Airliner and Camel Rider

1986. First Anniv of Emirates Airlines. Multicoloured.

205	50f. Type **50**		1·40	1·00
206	175f. Boeing 737, emblem and national colours		4·75	4·25

51 Emblem and Member States' Crests

1986. Seventh Supreme Council Session of Gulf Co-operation Council, Abu Dhabi.

207	50f. Type **51**		90	65
208	1d.75 Emblem beneath tree		3·25	2·75
209	3d. As No. 208		5·25	5·25

The face value of No. 208 is wrongly shown as "1.75 FILS".

52 Dubai Trade Centre

1986. 27th Chess Olympiad, Dubai. Multicoloured.

210	50f. Type **52**		1·30	90
211	2d. Chess players (miniature from King Alfonso X's "Book of Chess, Dice and Tablings") (horiz)		5·75	4·50
212	250f. Chess players (miniature) (different) (horiz)		7·00	5·75
MS213	154×90 mm. Nos. 210/12. Perf or imperf		16·00	16·00

53 Dhow, Oil Rig, Tower Block and Sun's Rays

1986. 15th National Day. Multicoloured.

214	50f. Type **53**		1·10	50
215	1d. Type **53**		2·10	1·00
216	175f. Flag and hands holding Arabic "15" (vert)		3·75	2·75
217	2d. As No. 216		4·50	3·75

54 Emblem

1986. Arab Police Day.

218	**54**	50f. multicoloured	1·30	90
219	**54**	1d. multicoloured	2·50	2·10

55 Emblem on Landscape

1987. Municipalities and Environment Week.

220	**55**	50f. multicoloured	1·40	1·00
221	**55**	1d. multicoloured	2·40	2·10

56 Boeing 737 Airliner and Map

1987. First Anniv of United Arab Emirates Flight Information Region.

222	**56**	200f. multicoloured	3·75	3·75
223	**56**	250f. multicoloured	4·50	4·50

57 Flower in Droplet

1987. "Save Energy". Multicoloured.

224	50f. Type **57**		90	90
225	2d. Globe as sun over oil derrick		9·50	9·50

58 University Emblem

1987. Tenth Anniv of U.A.E. University.

226	**58**	1d. multicoloured	1·50	1·50
227	**58**	3d. multicoloured	4·50	4·50

59 Oil Rig

1987. 25th Anniv of First Crude Oil Shipment from Abu Dhabi.

228	**59**	50f. multicoloured	90	90
229	-	1d. light blue, black and blue	1·60	1·60
230	-	175f. grey, black and blue	3·25	3·25
231	-	2d. multicoloured	3·75	3·75

DESIGNS:—VERT: 1d. Aerial view of drilling platform; 175f. Rig workers with drill head. HORIZ: 2d. Oil tanker at sea.

60 Trees and Dates in Arched Window

1987. Arab Palm Tree and Dates Day. Multicoloured.

232	50f. Type **60**		90	50
233	1d. Trees and fruit		1·60	1·00

61 Graph and Woman holding Baby

1987. U.N.I.C.E.F Child Survival Campaign.

234	**61**	50f. multicoloured	65	50
235	-	1d. blue, black and pink	1·30	1·00
236	-	175f. black, green & emer	2·30	1·90
237	-	2d. multicoloured	2·75	2·30

DESIGNS:—VERT: 1d. Vaccinating baby; 175f. Oral rehydration therapy. HORIZ: 2d. Mother breastfeeding.

62 Emblem on Man's Head and Globe

1987. International Year of Shelter for the Homeless.

238	**62**	2d. multicoloured	3·25	3·00
239	**62**	250f. multicoloured	4·50	3·75

63 Salim bin Ali al-Owais

1987. Birth Centenary of Salim bin Ali al-Owais (poet).

240	**63**	1d. multicoloured	2·10	2·10
241	**63**	2d. multicoloured	4·50	4·50

64 Lockheed TriStar 500 and Terminal Building

1987. Sixth Anniv of Abu Dhabi Int Airport. Multicoloured.

242	50f. Type **64**		90	90
243	50f. Reception area		90	90
244	100f. Lockheed TriStar 500 over air traffic control centre		2·40	2·40
245	100f. Lockheed TriStar 500 and Boeing 737 at gangways		2·40	2·40

65 Writing in Sand, Black-lip Pearl Oyster and Pearls

1988. National Arts Festival.

246	**65**	50f. multicoloured	1·10	1·10
247	**65**	250f. multicoloured	4·50	4·50

66 Fisherman on Shore (Layla Mohammed Khalfan)

1988. Children's Paintings. Multicoloured.

248	50f. Type **66**		90	50
249	1d. Woman and flowers (Zeinab Nasir Mohammed) (vert)		1·50	1·30
250	1d.75 Flowers with girls' faces (Fatma Ali Abdullah) (vert)		2·50	2·10
251	2d. Teddy bear, cat and girls playing (Saaly Mohammed Jowda)		2·75	2·40

67 Masked Youth

1988. Palestinian "Intifida" Movement.

252	**67**	2d. multicoloured	3·25	1·90
253	**67**	250f. multicoloured	3·75	2·30

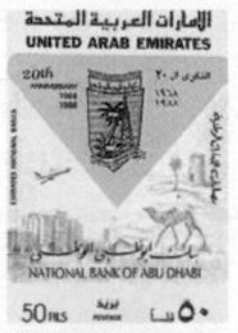

68 Emblem and Urban and Desert Scenes

1988. National Banking Anniversaries. Multicoloured.

254	50f. Type **68** (20th anniv of National Bank of Abu Dhabi)	1·90	1·90
255	50f. Emblem (25th anniv of National Bank of Dubai Ltd)	1·90	1·90

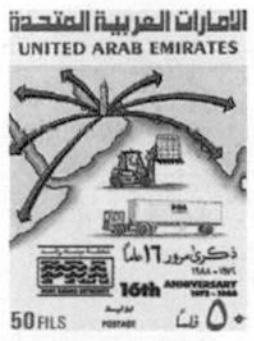

69 Map, Fork-lift Truck and Container Lorry

1988. 16th Anniv of Port Rashid. Multicoloured.

256	50f. Type **69**	65	65
257	1d. Container ship and view of port	1·30	1·30
258	175f. Ro-ro ferry and small boats at anchorages	2·40	2·40
259	2d. Container ship at dockside	3·00	3·00

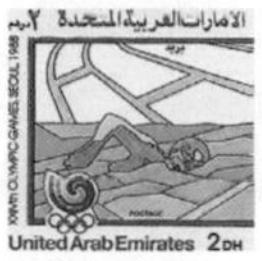

70 Swimming

1988. Olympic Games, Seoul. Multicoloured.

260	2d. Type **70**	2·75	2·75
261	250f. Cycling	3·50	3·50

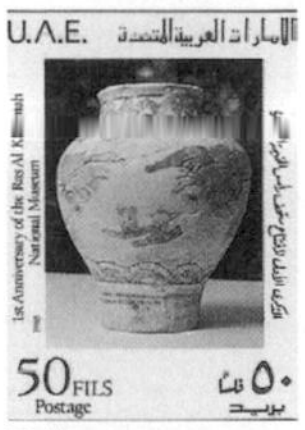

71 Vase

1988. First Anniv of Ras al Khaimah National Museum. Multicoloured.

262	50f. Type **71**	65	50
263	3d. Gold ornament (horiz)	3·75	3·25

72 Emblem

1988. 18th Arab Scouts Conference, Abu Dhabi.

264	**72**	1d. multicoloured	1·90	1·00

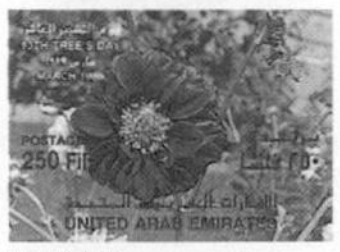

73 Dahlia

1989. Tenth Tree Day. Multicoloured.

265	50f. Ghaf tree	65	50
266	100f. Palm tree	1·30	1·00
267	250f. Type **73**	3·25	2·50

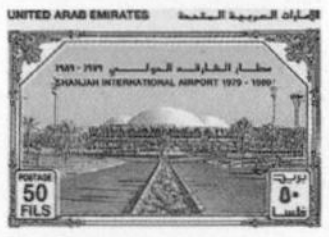

74 Airport

1989. Tenth Anniv of Sharjah International Airport.

268	**74**	50f. multicoloured	90	90
269	**74**	100f. multicoloured	1·90	1·90

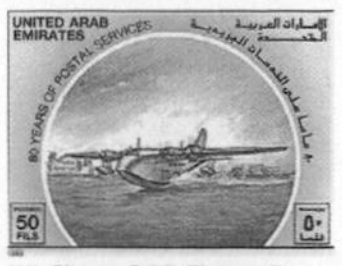

75 Short S.23 Flying Boat

1989. 80th Anniv of Gulf Postal Services. Multicoloured.

270	50f. Type **75**	1·30	1·30
271	3d. "Bombala" (freighter)	6·25	6·25

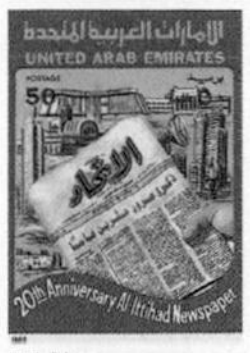

76 Newspaper

1989. 20th Anniv of "Al-Ittihad" (newspaper). Multicoloured.

272	50f. Type **76**	75	75
273	1d. Newspaper offices	1·50	1·50

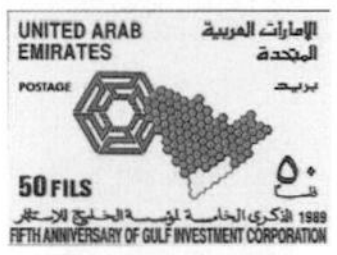

77 Emblem and Map

1989. Fifth Anniv of Gulf Investment Corporation.

274	**77**	50f. multicoloured	65	65
275	**77**	2d. multicoloured	2·50	2·50

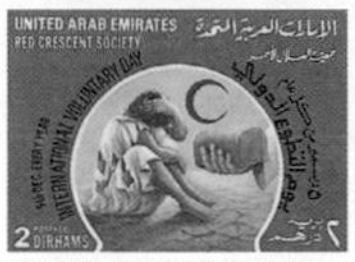

78 Offering Leaf to Child

1989. International Volunteer Day. U.A.E. Red Crescent Society. Multicoloured.

276	2d. Type **78**	2·50	2·50
277	250f. Crippled child in open hands (vert)	3·00	3·00

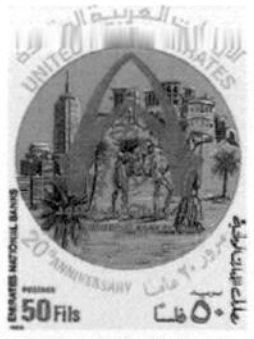

79 Bank Emblem and Buildings

1989. 20th Anniv of Commercial Bank of Dubai. Multicoloured.

278	50f. Type **79**	75	75
279	1d. Bank building	1·50	1·50

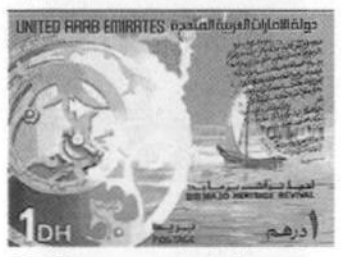

80 Compass and Dhow

1989. Bin Majid (15th-century navigator) Heritage Revival. Multicoloured.

280	1d. Type **80**	1·40	1·40
281	3d. Dhow (vert)	4·00	4·00

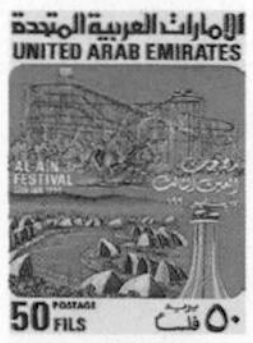

81 Festival Sites

1990. Third National Arts Festival, Al-Ain.

282	**81**	50f. multicoloured	50	75
283	**81**	1d. multicoloured	1·50	1·50

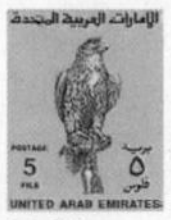

82 Saker Falcon

1990. Multicoloured, background colour given. (a) Size 18×23 mm.

284	**82**	5f. blue	20	20
285	**82**	20f. mauve	20	20
286	**82**	25f. pink	25	25
287	**82**	50f. brown	50	30
288	**82**	100f. bistre	1·00	65
288b	**82**	125f. bistre	1·30	1·30
289	**82**	150f. green	1·60	90
290	**82**	175f. green	1·90	1·00

(b) Size 21×26 mm.

291	2d. lilac	2·10	1·30
291a	225f. mauve	1·40	90
292	250f. blue	2·75	1·50
292b	275f. blue	2·75	2·75
293	3d. pink	3·25	1·90
293b	325f. pink	3·75	3·75
293d	375f. orange	5·00	5·00
293f	4d. grey	1·20	1·10
294	5d. orange	5·25	3·25
294b	6d. white	6·25	6·25
295	10d. yellow	10·50	6·25
296	20d. green	21·00	12·50
297	50d. green	55·00	31·00

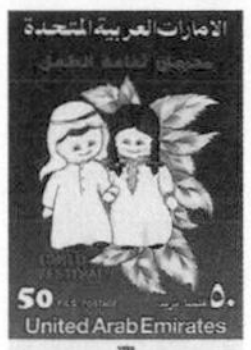

83 Children and Leaves

1990. Children's Culture Festival.

301	**83**	50f. multicoloured	65	65
302	**83**	250f. multicoloured	2·75	2·75

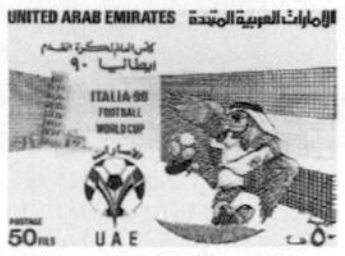

84 Leaning Tower of Pisa, Flag and U.A.E. Mascot

1990. World Cup Football Championship, Italy. Multicoloured.

303	50f. Type **84**	75	75
304	1d. Desert, flag and mascot (vert)	1·50	1·50
305	2d. Mascot on ball (vert)	2·75	2·75
306	250f. Flags around mascot	3·50	3·50
MS307	82×60 mm. 3d. Mascot and world map (vert)	5·75	5·75

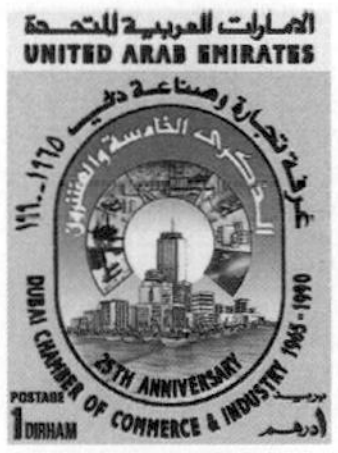

85 Projects and Buildings

1990. 25th Anniv of Dubai Chamber of Commerce and Industry. Multicoloured.

308	**85**	50f. multicoloured	65	65
309	**85**	1d. multicoloured	1·10	1·10

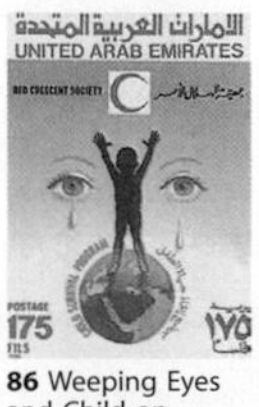

86 Weeping Eyes and Child on Globe

1990. Child Survival Programme. Multicoloured.

310	175f. Type **86**	1·80	1·80
311	2d. Emaciated child and newspapers	2·00	2·00

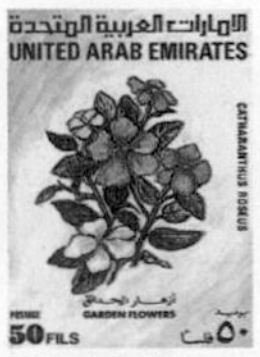

87 Periwinkle ("Catharanthus roseus")

1990. Flowers. Multicoloured.

312	50f. "Centavrea pseudo sinaica"	1·00	1·00
313	50f. Ushar bush ("Calotropis procera")	1·00	1·00
314	50f. "Argyrolobeum roseum"	1·00	1·00
315	50f. "Lamranthus roseus"	1·00	1·00
316	50f. "Hibiscus rosa sinensis"	1·00	1·00
317	50f. "Nerium oleander"	1·00	1·00
318	50f. Type **87**	1·00	1·00
319	50f. "Bougainvillaea glabra" (wrongly inscr "Bogainvillea")	1·00	1·00
MS320	Two sheets, each 90×120 mm. (a) Nos. 312/15; (b) Nos. 316/19	8·75	8·75

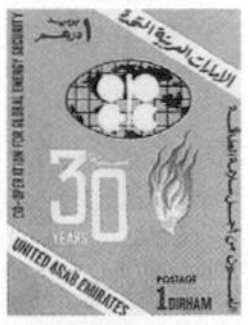

88 O.P.E.C. Emblem and Flame

1990. 30th Anniv of Organization of Petroleum Exporting Countries. Multicoloured.

321	50f. Emblem, flames, hands and oil rigs	90	50
322	1d. Type **88**	1·60	1·10
323	175f. Emblem and droplet	2·50	1·90

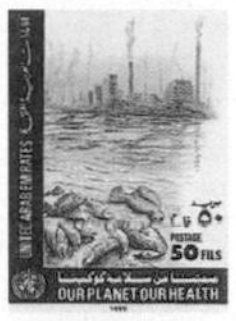

89 Industrial Pollution and Dead Animals

1990. "Our Planet Our Health". Multicoloured.

324	50f. Type **89**	50	50
325	3d. Industrial and vehicle pollution covering globe	3·25	3·25

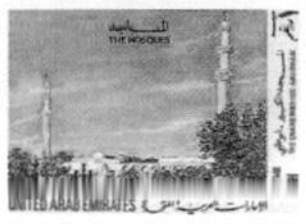

90 Grand Mosque, Abu Dhabi

1990. Mosques. Multicoloured.

326	1d. Type **90**	1·00	1·00
327	2d. Al-Jumeirah Mosque, Dubai (vert)	2·10	2·10

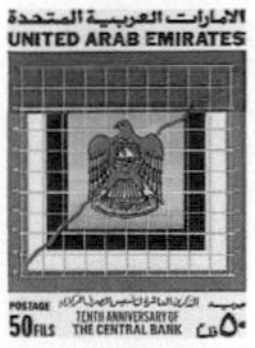

91 U.A.E. Crest and Graph

1990. Tenth Anniv of Central Bank. Multicoloured.

328	50f. Type **91**	65	65
329	175f. Banknotes and building (horiz)	2·50	2·50

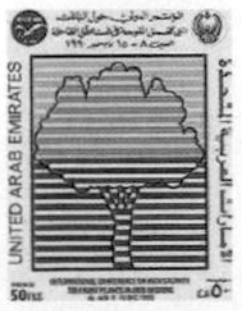

92 Tree

1990. International Conference on High-salinity Tolerant Plants, Al-Ain. Multicoloured.

330	50f. Type **92**	75	75
331	250f. Trees along shoreline	2·50	2·50

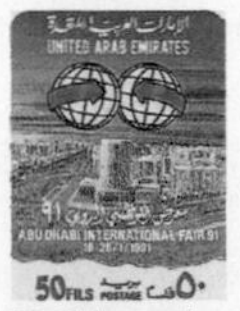

93 Globes and Buildings

1991. Abu Dhabi International Fair.

332	**93**	50f. multicoloured	75	50
333	**93**	2d. multicoloured	2·50	2·10

94 Emblem

1991. World Telecommunications Day. "Telecommunications and Safety of Human Life".

334	**94**	2d. multicoloured	2·75	2·10
335	**94**	3d. multicoloured	4·00	3·25

95 Shaikh Saqr Mosque, Ras al Khaimah

1991. Mosques. Multicoloured.

336		1d. Type **95**	1·00	1·00
337		2d. King Faisal Mosque, Sharjah	2·30	2·30

See also Nos. 371/2 and 411/12.

96 "Native Games" (Robba Mohamed Sofian)

1991. Children's Paintings. Multicoloured.

338		50f. Type **96**	50	50
339		1d. "National Day" (Yasmin Mohamed al-Rahim)	1·30	1·00
340		175f. "Blind Man's Buff" (Amal Ibrahim Mohamed)	2·30	1·90
341		250f. "Native Dance" (Amina Ali Hassan)	2·75	2·50

97 Yellow-banded Angelfish

1991. Fish. Multicoloured.

342		50f. Type **97**	75	75
343		50f. Hump-backed snapper	75	75
344		50f. Golden trevally	75	75
345		50f. Two-banded seabream ("Porgy")	75	75
346		1d. Yellow-finned seabream ("Black Bream")	1·00	1·00
347		1d. Three-banded grunt	1·00	1·00
348		1d. Convict ("Greasy") grouper	1·00	1·00
349		1d. Rabbitfish	1·00	1·00
MS350		121×152 mm. Nos. 342/9	7·50	7·50

98 Shaikh Rashid and Abu Dhabi Airport

1991. First Death Anniv of Shaikh Rashid bin Said al-Maktoum (ruler of Dubai). Multicoloured.

351		50f. Type **98**	65	50
352		1d. Shaikh Rashid and modern and old buildings (horiz)	1·30	1·00
353		175f. Shaikh Rashid and sea-front hotels	2·00	2·00
354		2d. Jebel Ali container port, Shaikh Rashid and dish aerial (horiz)	2·10	2·10

99 Fire Fighting

1991. Civil Defence Day.

355	**99**	50f. multicoloured	75	75
356	**99**	1d. multicoloured	1·60	1·60

100 Panavia Tornado F Mk 3 Jet Fighter over Dubai Airport

1991. Int Aerospace Exhibition, Dubai. Multicoloured.

357		175f. Type **100**	1·90	1·90
358		2d. View of under-side of Panavia Tornado over Dubai airport	2·10	2·10

101 Flags and Emblem

1991. Tenth Anniv of Gulf Co-operation Council.

359	**101**	50f. multicoloured	50	50
360	**101**	3d. multicoloured	3·25	3·25

102 Shaikh Zaid bin Sultan al Nahayyan of Abu Dhabi (President of U.A.E.)

1991. 20th National Day. Multicoloured.

361		75f. Type **102**	1·10	1·10
362		75f. Shaikh Humaid bin Rashid al Naimi of Ajman and fort (to right of stamp) with cannon	1·10	1·10
363		75f. Shaikh Maktoum bin Rashid al-Maktoum of Dubai and fort (to left of stamp) with cannon	1·10	1·10
364		75f. Shaikh Hamad bin Mohamed al Sharqi of Fujeira and fort on hillock	1·10	1·10
365		75f. Shaikh Saqr bin Mohamed al-Qasimi of Ras al Khaima and fort (tower and tree in foreground)	1·10	1·10
366		75f. Shaikh Sultan bin Mohamed al Qasimi of Sharjah and fort (to left of stamp with Arabs in doorway)	1·10	1·10
367		75f. Shaikh Rashid bin Ahmed al Moalla of Umm al Qiwain and fort (to right of stamp with trees growing over walls)	1·10	1·10
MS368		70×90 mm. 3d. Shaikh Zaid of Abu Dhabi and parade of army and tanks. Imperf	5·25	5·25

103 Derrick

1992. 20th Anniv of Abu Dhabi National Oil Company.

369	**103**	175f. multicoloured	2·00	2·00
370	**103**	250f. multicoloured	2·50	2·50

1992. Mosques. As T **95**. Multicoloured.

371		50f. Shaikh Rashid bin Humaid al Naimi Mosque, Ajman	75	75
372		1d. Shaikh Ahmed bin Rashid al Moalla Mosque, Umm al Qiwain	1·50	1·50

104 Fort Jahili, Al Ain

1992. "Expo '92" World's Fair, Seville.

373	**104**	2d. multicoloured	2·10	2·10
374	**104**	250f. multicoloured	65·00	65·00

105 Emblem and Family

1992. Deaf Child Week. Multicoloured.

375		1d. Type **105**	1·50	1·00
376		3d. Hearing aid in ear	3·75	3·25

106 Aerial View of Port

1992. 20th Anniv of Zayed Sea Port, Abu Dhabi. Multicoloured.

377		50f. Type **106**	50	50
378		1d. Cranes on dockside	1·00	1·00
379		175f. Loading container ship	1·90	1·90
380		2d. Map showing routes from port	2·40	2·40

107 Yachting

1992. Olympic Games, Barcelona. Multicoloured.

381		50f. Type **107**	50	50
382		1d. Running	1·00	1·00
383		175f. Swimming	2·00	2·00
384		250f. Cycling	2·75	2·75
MS385		60×90 mm. 3d. Show jumping	3·75	3·75

108 Football Match (Najla Saif Mohamed Harib)

1992. Children's Paintings. Multicoloured.

386		50f. Type **108**	55	55
387		1d. Children in park (Anoud Adnan Ali Mohamed)	1·10	1·10
388		2d. Family at playground (Ahlam Ibrahim Ahmed)	2·30	2·30
389		250f. Children playing amongst trees (Dallal Ali Salih)	3·00	3·00

109 Bank Building

1992. 15th Anniv of Emirates Bank International.

390	**109**	50f. multicoloured	55	55
391	-	175f. gold, brown and red	2·00	2·00

DESIGN—33×40 mm: 175f. Bank emblem.

110 Tambourah

1992. Musical Instruments. Multicoloured.

392		50f. Type **110**	65	65
393		50f. Oud (stringed instrument)	65	65
394		50f. Rababah (stringed instrument with bow)	65	65
395		1d. Mizmar (wind instrument) and shindo (drum) (horiz)	1·20	1·20
396		1d. Marwas and duff (hand-held drums) (horiz)	1·20	1·20
397		1d. Tabel (drum) and hibban (bagpipe) (horiz)	1·20	1·20
MS398		Two sheets. (a) 75×95 mm. Nos. 392/4; (b) 95×75 mm. Nos. 395/7	6·50	6·50

111 Emblem

1992. 13th Supreme Council Session of Gulf Co-operation Council, Abu Dhabi.

399	**111**	50f. multicoloured	55	55
400	**111**	2d. multicoloured	2·40	2·40

112 Camel Race

1992. The Dromedary. Multicoloured.

401		50f. Type **112**	55	55
402		1d. Camel riders and mother with young (vert)	1·20	1·20
403		175f. Camels at well and mother with young	2·10	2·10
404		2d. Camels (vert)	2·40	2·40

113 Golf

1993. Tourism. Multicoloured.

405		50f. Type **113**	80	80
406		1d. Fishing (vert)	1·20	1·20
407		2d. Sailing	2·40	2·40
408		250f. Sight-seeing by car	3·00	3·00

114 Club Building

1993. Dubai Creek Golf and Yacht Club. Multicoloured.

409		2d. Type **114**	2·50	2·50
410		250f. Club building and sea shore	3·00	3·00

1993. Mosques. As T **95**. Multicoloured.

411		50f. Thabit bin Khalid Mosque, Fujeira	85	85
412		1d. Sharq al Morabbah Mosque, Al-Ain	1·70	1·70

115 National Crest and Sports

1993. National Youth Festival. Multicoloured.

413		50f. Type **115**	70	70
414		3d. National crest and sciences	4·50	4·50

116 Textile Cone

1993. Sea Shells. Multicoloured.

415		25f. Type **116**	40	40
416		50f. Atlantic pearl oyster	55	55
417		100f. Woodcock murex	1·20	1·20
418		150f. "Natica pulicaris"	1·80	1·80
419		175f. Giant spider conch	2·10	2·10
420		200f. "Cardita bicolor"	2·50	2·50
421		250f. Gray's cowrie	3·00	3·00
422		300f. "Cymatium trilineatum"	3·50	3·50

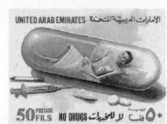

117 Addict within Capsule

1993. Anti-drugs Campaign. Multicoloured.
423	50f. Type **117**	85	85
424	1d. Family on skull, globe and drugs (vert)	1·40	1·40

118 Commercial Buildings

1993. 25th Anniv of Abu Dhabi National Bank. Multicoloured.
425	50f. Type **118**	55	55
426	1d. Bank emblem	1·20	1·20
427	175f. Bank building and emblem	2·20	2·20
428	2d. Commercial buildings within shield	2·50	2·50

119 Aerial View of Port

1993. Dubai Ports Authority. Multicoloured.
429	50f. Type **119**	55	55
430	1d. Cranes loading containers	1·20	1·20
431	2d. Aerial view of port (different)	2·50	2·50
432	250f. Different view of port (horiz)	2·99	2·99

120 Soldiers on Parade (Mouza Musabah al-Mazroui)

1993. National Day. Children's Paintings. Multicoloured.
433	50f. Type **120**	55	55
434	1d. Woman and children (Shreen Naeem Hassan Radwan) (vert)	1·20	1·20
435	175f. Flag and dhow (Samiha Mohamad Sultan)	2·40	2·40
436	2d. Decorations and fireworks (Omer Abdulla Rabia Thani)	2·75	2·75

121 Hili Tomb

1993. Archaeological Finds from Al-Ain. Multicoloured.
437	50f. Type **121**	55	55
438	1d. Hili decorative tile	1·20	1·20
439	175f. Qattarah figure	2·20	2·20
440	250f. Hili bowl	3·50	3·50

122 Horse rearing

1994. Arab Horses. Multicoloured.
441	50f. Type **122**	55	55
442	1d. Grey (horiz)	1·20	1·20
443	175f. Bay with white blaze	2·20	2·20
444	250f. Piebald (horiz)	3·50	3·50

123 Children with Flags and Balloons

1994. Tenth Children's Festival, Sharjah. Children's Paintings. Multicoloured.
445	50f. Type **123**	85	85
446	1d. Children in forest	1·70	1·70
447	175f. Children with balloons and child painting	2·75	2·75
448	2d. Children in garden	3·00	3·00

124 Dubai, Map and Emblems

1994. Tenth Arab Towns Organization Congress, Dubai. Multicoloured.
449	50f. Type **124**	55	55
450	1d. Different view of Dubai, map and emblems (horiz)	1·20	1·20

125 Holy Kaaba and Globe

1994. Pilgrimage to Mecca. Multicoloured.
451	50f. Type **125**	85	85
452	2d. Crowds around Holy Kaaba	3·25	3·25

126 Homes (Arab Housing Day)

1994. Anniversaries and Events. Multicoloured.
453	1d. Type **126**	1·40	1·40
454	1d. Children playing and couple (International Year of the Family) (horiz)	1·40	1·40
455	1d. National Olympic Committee emblem, rings and sports (cent of Int Olympic Committee) (horiz)	1·40	1·40
456	1d. Paper, pen-nib and dove (10th anniv of Emirates Writers' Association)	1·40	1·40

127 Covered Vessel

1994. Archaeological Finds from Al-Qusais, Dubai. Multicoloured.
457	50f. Type **127**	70	70
458	1d. Jug (horiz)	1·40	1·40
459	175f. Jug (different) (horiz)	2·40	2·40
460	250f. Bowl (horiz)	3·50	3·50

128 Arabian Leopard

1994. Environmental Protection. The Cat Family. Multicoloured.
461	50f. Type **128**	70	70
462	1d. Gordon's wildcat	1·40	1·40
463	2d. Caracal	2·75	2·75
464	250f. Sandcat	4·25	4·25

129 Little Green Bee Eaters

1994. Birds. Multicoloured.
465	50f. Type **129**	70	70
466	175f. White-collared kingfishers	2·20	2·20
467	2d. Crab plovers	2·75	2·75
468	250f. Indian rollers	4·25	4·25
MS469	90×60 mm. 3d. Greater flamingos (29×40 mm)	4·50	4·50

130 Championship Emblem

1994. 12th Arab Gulf Football Championship, Abu Dhabi. Multicoloured.
470	50f. Type **130**	55	55
471	3d. Match scene (horiz)	3·50	3·50

131 Horse's Head

1995. Archaeological Finds from Mulaiha, Sharjah. Multicoloured.
472	50f. Type **131**	55	55
473	175f. Coin	2·20	2·20
474	2d. Ancient writing on leather	2·50	2·50
475	250f. Stone tablet (horiz)	2·75	2·75

132 Al-Naashat

1995. National Dances. Multicoloured.
476	50f. Type **132**	55	55
477	175f. Al-Ayaalah	2·20	2·20
478	2d. Al-Shahhoh	2·50	2·50

133 Helicopters

1995. International Defence Exhibition and Conference, Abu Dhabi. Multicoloured.
479	50f. Type **133**	55	55
480	1d. Exhibition emblem	1·10	1·10
481	175f. Missile corvettes (horiz)	1·90	1·90
482	2d. Artillery (horiz)	2·20	2·20

134 Arab League

1995. 50th Anniversaries. Anniversary Emblems. Multicoloured.
483	1d. Type **134**	1·10	1·10
484	2d. F.A.O.	2·20	2·20
485	250f. U.N.O.	2·75	2·75

135 Symbols of Postal Services

1995. Tenth Anniv of General Postal Authority.
486	**135** 50f. multicoloured	70	70

136 Exhibition Emblem

1995. First Gulf Co-operation Council Stamp Exhibition, Abu Dhabi.
487	**136** 50f. multicoloured	70	70

137 Bowling Hoop

1995. National Games. Multicoloured.
488	50f. Type **137**	45	45
489	175f. Swinging	1·70	1·70
490	2d. Sticks in stone square game	1·80	1·80
491	250f. Stone game	2·30	2·30

138 Lesser Kestrel

1995. Birds. Multicoloured.
492	50f. Type **138**	60	60
493	175f. Socotra cormorant	2·30	2·30
494	2d. Cream-coloured courser	2·50	2·50
495	250f. Hoopoe	3·00	3·00

139 Figures and Tower Block

1995. Population and Housing Census. Multicoloured.
496	50f. Type **139**	45	45
497	250f. City and stylized family	2·30	2·30

140 "Folklore Show" (Ibtisam Mussa)

1995. National Day. Children's Paintings. Multicoloured.
498	50f. Type **140**	45	45
499	175f. "Children dancing" (Shimaa Mohamed Abdullah Khoury)	1·70	1·70
500	2d. "Children holding balloons" (Khoula Ibrahim)	1·80	1·80
501	250f. "Car festival" (Fatima Jumaa)	2·30	2·30

141 Dugongs

1996. Environmental Protection. Sea Mammals. Multicoloured.
502	50f. Type **141**	45	45
503	2d. Common dolphins	2·00	2·00

504	3d. Humpback whales	3·00	3·00
MS505	90×70 mm. Nos. 502/4	5·25	5·25

142 Competitor

1996. Hobie Cat 16 World Championships. Multicoloured.
506	50f. Type **142**	45	45
507	3d. Hobie 1b catamaran and building	3·00	3·00

143 Earthenware Urn (Bathna-Fujaira)

1996. Archaeological Finds. Multicoloured.
508	50f. Type **143**	45	45
509	175f. Earthenware pot with handles (Bidya-Fujaira)	1·70	1·70
510	250f. Bronze bangle (Qidfa-Fujaira)	2·50	2·50
511	3d. Bronze ring (Dibba-Fujaira) (horiz)	3·00	3·00

144 Shooting

1996. Olympic Games, Atlanta. Multicoloured.
512	50f. Type **144**	45	45
513	1d. Cycling (vert)	90	90
514	250f. Running (vert)	2·40	2·40
515	350f. Swimming	3·00	3·00

145 Emblem

1996. 21st Anniv of Women's Union. Multicoloured.
516	50f. Type **145**	45	45
517	3d. Woman's hands and emblem (horiz)	3·00	3·00

146 Emblem, Landmarks and Players

1996. 11th Asian Football Cup Championship. Multicoloured.
518	1d. Type **146**	1·10	1·10
519	250f. Player with ball	2·75	2·75

147 "Drug" Snake crushing weeping Globe

1996. Anti-drugs Campaign. Multicoloured.
520	50f. Type **147**	90	90
521	3d. Healthy man and drug-wrecked skull	2·40	2·40

148 Shaikh Said and House

1996. Centenary of Shaikh Said al Maktoum House (museum). Multicoloured.
522	50f. Type **148**	45	45
523	250f. Shaikh Said and close-up view of House	2·40	2·40
524	350f. House at sunset	3·25	3·25

149 Chestnut-bellied Sandgrouse

1996. Birds. Multicoloured.
525	50f. Type **149**	30	30
526	150f. Striated scops owl	1·50	1·50
527	250f. Grey hypocolius	2·30	2·30
528	3d. White-throated robin	3·00	3·00
529	350f. Sooty falcon	3·25	3·25

150 Head forming Waterfall (Abdullah Muhammed Abdullah al-Sharhan)

1996. Children's Paintings. Multicoloured.
530	50f. Type **150**	30	30
531	1d. Dhows (Hamda Muhammed Abdullah) (horiz)	90	90
532	250f. Flowers (Hind Muhammed bin Dhahi)	2·30	2·30
533	350f. Girl and tent (Lin Atta Yaghi)	3·00	3·00

151 Emirates Rulers

1996. 25th National Day. Multicoloured.
534	50f. Type **151**	45	45
535	1d. Emirates crest and flag	75	75
536	150f. Type **151**	1·20	1·20
537	3d. As No. 535	2·40	2·40
MS538	70×90 mm. 5d. Score of national anthem. Imperf	4·75	4·75

152 U.A.E. Crest   **153** Shaikh and Trees

1996. 30th Anniv of Accession of Shaikh Zaid ibn Sultan al Nahayyan of Abu Dhabi and 25th Anniv of United Arab Emirates. (a) Type **152**.
539	**152**	50f. multicoloured	45	45
540	**152**	1d. multicoloured	1·10	1·10

(b) As T **153**. Multicoloured.
541	50f. Type **153**	45	45
542	1d. Shaikh and dates	90	90
543	250f. Type **153**	2·40	2·40
544	3d. As No. 542	3·00	3·00
MS545	90×70 mm. 5d. Shaikh on horseback. Imperf	4·75	4·75

154 Loew's Blue

1997. Butterflies. Multicoloured.
546	50f. Type **154**	45	45
547	1d. Swallowtail	1·20	1·20
548	150f. Blue argus	1·80	1·80
549	250f. African monarch	3·25	3·25

155 Festival Poster

1997. Shopping Festival, Dubai. Multicoloured.
550	50f. Type **155**	45	45
551	250f. Emblem (vert)	2·10	2·10

156 Helicopter lifting Vehicle

1997. International Defence Exhibition and Conference, Abu Dhabi. Multicoloured.
552	50f. Type **156**	45	45
553	1d. Exhibition emblem	75	75
554	250f. Weapons demonstration	2·10	2·10
555	350f. Frigates and submarine	3·00	3·00

157 Sky and Anniversary Emblem

1997. 20th Anniv of Emirates Bank Group. Multicoloured.
556	50f. Type **157**	45	45
557	1d. Anniversary emblem	1·10	1·10

158 "TEND" and Emblem

1997. Technological, Education and National Development. Multicoloured.
559	50f. Type **158**	45	45
560	250f. Emblem	2·10	2·10

159 Silver Coins spilling from Pot

1997. Sharjah Heritage. Multicoloured.
561	50f. Type **159**	45	45
562	3d. Courtyard and minarets	2·75	2·75

160 Stamps and Magnifying Glass

1997. Emirates Philatelic Association. Multicoloured.
563	50f. Type **160**	45	45
564	250f. Magnifying glass, tweezers and "river" of stamps (horiz)	2·30	2·30

161 Cats and Kittens

1997. Children's Paintings. Multicoloured.
565	50f. Type **161**	45	45
566	1d. Fashion parade	90	90
567	250f. Group of children (vert)	2·40	2·40
568	3d. Abstract	3·00	3·00

162 Cliffs

1997. Fine Arts. Multicoloured.
569	50f. Type **162**	60	60
570	50f. Still-life (vert)	60	60
571	50f. Modern painting in blues and yellows	60	60
572	50f. Couple (vert)	60	60
573	50f. Waterfall and rocks	60	60
574	50f. Coral hind (fish) (vert)	60	60
MS575	149×105 mm. 5d. Architecture. Imperf	5·25	5·25

163 Jet Fighter over Airport

1997. International Aerospace Exhibition, Dubai. Multicoloured.
576	250f. Type **163**	2·40	2·40
577	3d. Buildings, airplane and oil rig	3·00	3·00

164 Park

1997. 26th National Day. Environmental Protection. Multicoloured.
578	50f. Type **164**	45	45
579	1d. Mountains and forest	90	90
580	150f. Mountains and river	1·40	1·40
581	250f. Landscaped road verge	2·50	2·50

165 Emblems and Venue

1997. Third Afro–Arab Trade Fair, Sharjah. Multicoloured.
582	150f. Type **165**	1·50	1·50
583	350f. Organization of African Unity and Arab League emblems' handclasp over Fair emblem (horiz)	3·25	3·25

166 "Blepharopsis mendica" (praying mantis)

1998. Insects. Multicoloured.
584	50f. Type **166**	45	45
585	150f. "Galeodes" sp. (spider)	1·40	1·40
586	250f. "Crocothemis arythraea" (darter)	2·40	2·40
587	350f. "Xylocopa aestuans" (carpenter bee)	3·25	3·25

167 Laser
Dinghies

1998. World Sailing Championships, Dubai.
Multicoloured.
588	50f. Type **167**	45	45
589	1d. Racing yachts (horiz)	90	90
590	250f. High-performance 2-man dinghies (horiz)	2·40	2·40
591	3d. Catamarans	3·00	3·00

168 Military Personnel

1998. Triple International Defence Exhibition and
Conference, Abu Dhabi. Multicoloured.
592	50f. Type **168**	60	60
593	1d. Exhibition emblem and city (vert)	1·10	1·10
594	150f. Radar equipment (vert)	1·70	1·70
595	350f. Rocket launcher and communications equipment (vert)	4·00	4·00

169 Emblem and
City Landmarks

1998. Sharjah, Arab Cultural Capital. Multicoloured.
596	50f. Type **169**	45	45
597	3d. Emblem and tower	3·00	3·00

170 Oryx on
Hillside

1998. Protection of the Environment. Multicoloured.
598	1d. Type **170**	90	90
599	350f. Palm tree and sun	3·25	3·25

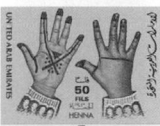

171 Decorated Hands

1998. Henna.
600	**171**	50f. multicoloured	45	45
601	-	1d. multicoloured	90	90
602	-	150f. multicoloured	1·40	1·40
603	-	2d. multicoloured	2·00	2·00
604	-	250f. multicoloured	2·40	2·40
605	-	3d. multicoloured	3·00	3·00

DESIGNS: 1d. to 3d. Different hand decorations.

172 Underwater Scene
(Rashid al Shayaa)

1998. Paintings. Multicoloured.
606	50f. Type **172**	45	45
607	1d. Woman and cradle (Nadia Othman al Baroot)	90	90
608	250f. Village scene (Mahmoud Hassan) (vert)	2·30	2·30
609	350f. Rural still life (Shaikha Saeed)	3·25	3·25

173 Mountain Road

1998. 27th National Day. Tourism. Multicoloured.
610	50f. Type **173**	45	45
611	350f. Dubai Harbour	3·25	3·25

174 "Indigofera
arabica"

1998. Wild Flowers. Multicoloured.
612	25f. Type **174**	15	15
613	50f. "Centaureum pulchellum"	45	45
614	75f. "Lavandula citriodora"	60	60
615	1d. "Taverniera glabra"	90	90
616	150f. "Convolvulus deserti"	1·40	1·40
617	2d. "Capparis spinosa"	1·80	1·80
618	250f. "Rumex vesicrius"	2·40	2·40
619	3d. "Anagallis arvensis"	3·00	3·00
620	350f. "Tribulus arabicus"	3·25	3·25
621	5d. "Reichardia tinitana"	4·75	4·75

175 "Anthia
duodecimguttata"
(ground beetle)

1999. Insects and Arachnids. Multicoloured.
622	50f. Type **175**	60	60
623	150f. Oleander hawk moth	1·70	1·70
624	250f. Acrolypia glaucopsis	3·00	3·00
625	350f. "Androctonus crassicauda"	4·00	4·00

176 Emblem

1999. International Monuments Day. Multicoloured.
626	150f. Type **176**	1·40	1·40
627	250f. Al Faheidi fort, Dubai	2·40	2·40

177 U.P.U. Emblem

1999. 125th Anniv of Universal Postal Union.
Multicoloured.
628	50f. Type **177**	1·70	1·70
629	250f. U.P.U. emblem and "125"	4·00	4·00
MS630	90×70 mm. 5d. Hemispheres, UPU emblem and "125". Imperf	5·50	5·50

178 Jellyfish

1999. Protection of the Environment. Multicoloured.
631	50f. Feather star	45	45
632	150f. Type **178**	1·70	1·70
633	250f. Spanish dancer	3·00	3·00
634	3d. Sponge	3·25	3·25

179 Woman
braiding

1999. Crafts. Multicoloured.
635	50f. Type **179**	45	45
636	1d. Braided trousers	1·10	1·10
637	250f. Weaving palm leaves	3·00	3·00
638	350f. Woven palm leaf products	4·00	4·00

180
Championship
Emblem

1999. 14th World Tenpin Bowling Championship, Abu
Dhabi. Multicoloured.
639	50f. Type **180**	60	60
640	250f. Competitor	3·00	3·00

181 Couple outside House

1999. Children's Paintings. Multicoloured.
641	50f. Type **181**	45	45
642	1d. Pattern	1·10	1·10
643	150f. Underwater scene	1·70	1·70
644	250f. Family having picnic	3·00	3·00

182 "2000" and
Dove

1999. Year 2000.
645	**182**	50f. black and silver	45	45
646		250f. blue and gold	3·00	3·00

DESIGN: 250f. "2000" and dove (different).

183 Dubai Port

2000. Centenary of Dubai Ports and Customs.
Multicoloured.
647	50f. Type **183**	60	60
648	3d. Dubai Customs House	4·00	4·00

184 Conference
Emblem

2000. Int Conference on Desertification, Dubai.
649	**184**	250f. multicoloured	3·00	3·00

185 River

2000. Environmental Protection. Multicoloured.
650	50f. Type **185**	55	55
651	250f. Beach	2·75	2·75

186 Swimming

2000. Olympic Games, Sydney. Multicoloured.
652	50f. Type **186**	70	70
653	2d. Athletics	2·75	2·75
654	350f. Shooting	4·75	4·75

187 Ribbon and
Award

2000. International Holy Koran Award. Multicoloured.
655	50f. Type **187**	70	70
656	250f. Pres. Shaikh Zaid ibn Sultan al Nahayyan (recipient of award)	3·50	3·50

188 Map of United
Arab Emirates and
Barometer

2000. 50th Anniv of World Meteorological Organization.
Multicoloured.
657	50f. Type **188**	70	70
658	250f. Old map of Gulf region and sun dial	3·50	3·50

189 Airplanes

2000. Expansion of Dubai International Airport.
659	**189**	50f. multicoloured	70	70
660	**189**	350f. multicoloured	4·75	4·75

190 White
Crescent forming
Smile

2001. Development and Environment.
661	**190**	50f. green	70	70
662	-	2d.50 green and deep green	3·00	3·00
663	-	3d. green, light green and deep green	3·50	3·50
664	-	3d.50 light green, green and deep green	4·50	4·50

DESIGNS: 250f. White flower casting shadow; 3d. Heart-shaped leaf; 350f. Heart-shaped world map.

191 "Dubai Millennium"
(race horse)

2001. "Dubai Millennium", Dubai World Cup Horse Race
Winner. Multicoloured.
665	3d. Type **191**	4·00	4·00
666	350f. In paddock	4·50	4·50

192 Calligraph

2001. Sultan Bin Ali Al Owais (poet) Commemoration. Multicoloured.

667	50f. Type **192**	85	85
668	1d. Sultan bin Ali Al Owais	1·70	1·70

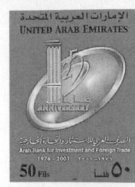

193 Anniversary Emblem and Plate

2001. 25th Anniv of Arab Investment and Foreign Trade Bank. Multicoloured.

669	50f. Type **193**	70	70
670	1d. Emblem and ribbon	1·50	1·50

194 Al Shahoof

2001. Traditional Craft. Multicoloured.

671	50f. Type **194**	70	70
672	250f. Al Bagarah	3·25	3·25
673	3d. Al Sam'aa	4·00	4·00
674	350f. Al Jahboot	4·50	4·50

195 Three birds ("Changing")

2001. Emirates Post. Multicoloured.

675	50f. Type **195**	85	85
676	250f. Corporate emblem ("Growing")	4·25	4·25
677	3d. Emblem ("Achieving")	4·75	4·75

196 Stylized Stamp

2001. Seventh GCC (Arab Gulf States Co-operation Council) Stamp Exhibition, Dubai.

678	**196**	50f. vermilion, green and black	95	95

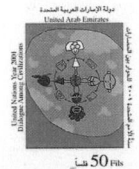

197 Children encircling Globe

2001. United Nations Year of Dialogue among Civilizations. Multicoloured.

679	50f. Type **197**	85	85
680	250f. Leaves	4·25	4·25

198 Mosque

2001. Children's Paintings. Multicoloured.

681	1d. Type **198**	1·40	1·40
682	250f. Boat building	3·50	3·50
683	3d. Man pouring coffee (vert)	4·25	4·25
684	350f. Falconry	4·75	4·75

199 Emblem, Fighter Plane and Ship

2001. 25th Anniv of Unification of Armed Forces.

685	**199**	1d. multicoloured	1·80	1·80

200 Conference Emblem

2002. International Conference on Water Resources, Dubai.

686	**200**	50f. multicoloured	95	95

201 Emblem

2002. 25th Anniv of United Arab Emirates University. Multicoloured.

687	50f. Type **201**	85	85
688	1d. As No. 687	1·70	1·70

202 Saluki and Sand Storm

2002. Hunting Dogs. Saluki. Multicoloured.

689	50f. Type **202**	85	85
690	150f. Facing left	2·50	2·50
691	250f. Five hounds	4·25	4·25
692	3d. Facing right	5·00	5·00

203 "1"

2002. First Anniv of UAE Postal Corporation.

693	**203**	50f. blue	85	85

MS694 81×120 mm. 3d. multicoloured (45×120 mm) — 15·00 — 15·00

DESIGN: 3d. Corporation emblem and "1".

204 Open Book

2002. Rashid Bin Al Suwadi (Al Khadhar) (poet) Commemoration. Multicoloured.

695	50f. Type **204**	1·00	1·00
696	250f. Al Khadhar	5·00	5·00

205 Sun, Antelope's Head and Yacht

2002. Children's Paintings. Multicoloured.

697	50f. Type **205**	65	65
698	1d. Figures with raised arms	1·10	1·10
699	2d. Globe with arms	2·30	2·30

700	250f. Fish	2·75	2·75
701	3d. Child holding heart	3·50	3·50
702	350f. Stick children	4·00	4·00
703	5d. Arabic script	5·75	5·75

206 Sand Dunes and Emblem

2002. Sheikh Hamdan Bin Rashid Al Maktoum Award for Medical Science. Multicoloured.

704	50f. Type **206**	65	65
705	250f. Emblem and map of UAE	3·25	3·25

207 Ajman

2002. 31st National Day. Showing landmarks of Emirate named. Multicoloured.

706	50f. Type **207**	50	50
707	50f. Sharjah	50	50
708	50f. Dubai	50	50
709	50f. Abu Dhabi	50	50
710	50f. Ras Al-Khaimah	50	50
711	50f. Fujairah	50	50
712	50f. Umm al Quwain	50	50

MS713 175×117 mm. Nos. 706/12. (Imperf) — 8·75 — 8·75

208 View of Earth from Space

2003. Thuraya Telecommunications Satellite.

714	**208**	25f. multicoloured	25	25
715	**208**	250f. multicoloured	2·50	2·50

209 Pottery Jar with Geometric Designs

2003. Al Ain National Museum. Multicoloured.

716	50f. Type **209**	50	50
717	275f. Pottery vase with animal designs	2·75	2·75
718	4d. Iron Age bronze axe	3·75	3·75
719	6d. Soap stone mortar	5·75	5·75

210 Buildings and Emblem

2003. 40th Anniv of National Bank of Dubai.

720	**210**	50f. multicoloured	50	50
721	**210**	4d. multicoloured	3·75	3·75
722	**210**	6d. multicoloured	5·75	5·75

211 Arabian Leopard

2003. Animals. Multicoloured.

723	50f. Type **211**	50	50
724	50f. Blanford's fox	50	50
725	50f. Caracal	50	50
726	50f. Cheetah	50	50
727	50f. Gordon's wild cat	50	50
728	50f. Striped hyena	50	50

729	50f. Jackal	50	50
730	50f. White-tailed mongoose	50	50
731	50f. Ruppell's fox	50	50
732	50f. Sand cat	50	50
733	50f. Small spotted genet	50	50
734	50f. Arabian wolf	50	50

212 Dirham, Al Walid Bin Abdul Malik Caliphate

2003. Arab Coins. Multicoloured.

735	50f. Type **212**	50	50
736	125f. Dirham, Abdul Malik Bin Marwan caliphate	1·30	1·30
737	275f. Dinar showing Al Mustansir Billah Al Fatimi	2·75	2·75
738	375f. Dinar, Abdul Malik Bin Marwan caliphate	3·75	3·75

MS739 106×73 mm. 5d. Dirham, Muhammed Al Ameen caliphate. Imperf — 21·00 — 21·00

213 Sheikh Zayed Bin Sultan Al Nahyan and Camel

2003. 37th Anniv of Accession of Sheikh Zayed Bin Sultan Al Nahyan, President of United Arab Emirates. Multicoloured.

740	50f. Type **213**	50	50
741	175f. Sheikh and high-rise buildings	1·80	1·80

214 Championship Emblem

2003. FIFA World Youth Football Championships, United Arab Emirates 2003.

742	**214**	375f. multicoloured	3·75	3·75

215 Emirates Towers, Dubai

2003. IMF and World Bank Group Meetings, Dubai. Dubai 2003 Expo. Multicoloured.

743	50f. Type **215**	50	50
744	175f. Falcon	1·80	1·80
745	275f. Domes (horiz)	2·75	2·75
746	375f. Traditional boat	3·75	3·75

MS747 118×74 mm. 5d. Emblem. Imperf — 8·75 — 8·75

216 Archway with Zakharaf (design)

2003. Peace Message. Multicoloured.

748	50f. Type **216**	50	50
749	225f. Traditional house with barjeel (wind tower)	2·30	2·30
750	275f. Traditional merchant's house with decorative columns	2·75	2·75
751	325f. Abras (traditional boats)	3·25	3·25

217 Al Areesh (palm frond) House

2003. Traditional Houses. Multicoloured.
752	50f. Type **217**	50	50
753	175f. Al Teen (mud)	1·80	1·80
754	275f. Al Saf (pebbles)	2·75	2·75
755	325f. Al Shaar (tent)	3·25	3·25

218 Peregrine Falcon

2003. Falcons. Multicoloured.
756	50f. Type **218**	50	50
757	125f. Gyr-peregrine	1·30	1·30
758	275f. Gyrfalcon	2·75	2·75
759	375f. Saker	3·75	3·75

219 Script

2003. Saeed Bin Ateej al Hamli (poet) Commemoration. Multicoloured.
760	125f. Type **219**	1·30	1·30
761	175f. Script (different)	1·80	1·80

220 Mohammed Bin Saeed Bin Ghubash

2004. 35th Death Anniv of Mohammed Bin Saeed Bin Ghubash (scholar). Multicoloured.
762	50f. Type **220**	50	50
763	175f. Books	1·80	1·80

221 Clasped Hands enclosed in Heart

2004. Fourth Family Meeting. Multicoloured.
764	3d.75 Type **221**	3·75	3·75
765	4d. Clasped hands (different)	4·00	4·00

222 Emblem

2004. Centenary of FIFA (Federation Internationale de Football Association).
766	**222**	375f. multicoloured	3·75	3·75

223 Decorated Pot

2004. Handicrafts. Multicoloured.
767	50f. Type **223**	60	60
768	125f. Flowers (painting)	1·50	1·50
769	275f. Twig collage	3·25	3·25
770	5d. Plaque	6·00	6·00

224 Running

2004. Olympic Games, Athens 2004. Multicoloured.
771	50f. Type **224**	60	60
772	125f. Shooting	1·50	1·50
773	275f. Swimming	3·25	3·25
774	375f. Runner holding Olympic torch	4·50	4·50

225 Black Fin-less Porpoise

2004. Endangered Species. Multicoloured.
775	50f. Type **225**	55	55
776	175f. Serranidae	1·90	1·90
777	275f. Whale shark	3·00	3·00
778	375f. Dugongidae	4·00	4·00

226 Removing Mine

2004. Mine Clearance in South Lebanon. Multicoloured.
779	275f. Type **226**	3·00	3·00
780	275f. Wounded (horiz)	3·00	3·00

227 Sheikh Bin Mohammed Al Qassimi

2004
781	**227**	50f. multicoloured	55	55
782	**227**	125f. multicoloured	1·40	1·40
783	**227**	275f. multicoloured	3·00	3·00
784	**227**	4d. multicoloured	4·25	4·25

228 Al Serwal

2004. Women's Clothes. Multicoloured.
785	50f. Type **228**	55	55
786	125f. Al Thob	1·40	1·40
787	175f. Al Abaiah	1·90	1·90
788	225f. Al Kandoura	2·50	2·50
789	275f. Al Shailah	3·00	3·00
790	375f. Al Burga	4·25	4·25

229 Anniversary Emblem and Buildings

2005. 25th Anniv of Dubai Aluminium Company.
791	50f. Type **229**	55	55
792	275f. Sheikh Hamdan bin Rashid Al Maktoum and emblem	3·00	3·00
793	375f. As No. 792	4·25	4·25

230 Festival Emblem

2005. Tenth Dubai Shopping Festival. Multicoloured.
794	50f. Type **230**	55	55
795	125f. Emblem (different)	1·40	1·40
796	275f. "10" enclosing emblem	3·00	3·00
797	375f. "10" enclosing emblem (different)	4·25	4·25

231 Emblem

2005. Emirates Scout Association Gathering, Sharjah. Multicoloured.
798	50f. Type **231**	55	55
799	375f. Sultan bin Mohammed Al Qassimi	4·25	4·25

232 "Mother of the Nation" (in script)

2005. Shaikha Fatima Bint Mubarak (wife of the late H.H. Sheikh Zayed bin Sultan Al Nahyan and president of UAE Women's Association). Multicoloured.
800	50f. Type **232**	55	55

233 Furrows

2005. Al Majedi Bin Dhaher (poet) Commemoration. Multicoloured.
801	50f. Type **233**	55	55
802	175f. Dry stone wall	1·80	1·80

234 Agama

2005. Reptiles. Multicoloured.
803	50f. Type **234**	55	55
804	125f. Desert monitor	1·40	1·40
805	225f. Sand lizard	2·50	2·50
806	275f. Dune sand gecko	3·00	3·00
807	375f. Spiny tailed lizard	4·25	4·25
808	5d. Sand skink	5·50	5·50

235 Sheikh Khalifa Bin Zayed Al Nahyan and as Child in Father's Arms

2005. First Anniv of Accession of Sheikh Khalifa Bin Zayed Al Nahyan to Presidency of UAE. Designs showing Sheikh Khalifa Bin Zayed Al Nahyan. Multicoloured.
809	50f. Type **235**	55	55
810	175f. Seated wearing dark clothes	1·80	1·80
811	275f. Seated wearing white clothes	3·00	3·00
812	375f. Embracing	4·25	4·25
MS813	150×140 mm. Nos. 809/12. Sold at 10d	10·50	10·50

236 Emblem

2005. Census. Multicoloured.
814	50f. Type **236**	55	55
815	375f. As No. 814 (horiz)	4·25	4·25

237 *Leptadenia pyrotechnica*

2005. Desert Plants. Multicoloured.
816	50f. Type **237**	55	55
817	125f. *Lycium shawii*	1·40	1·40
818	225f. *Calotropis procera*	2·50	2·50
819	275f. *Prosopis cineraria*	3·00	3·00
820	325f. *Zizyphus spina-christi*	3·50	3·50
821	375f. *Acacia tortilis*	4·25	4·25

238 Flower of Script (Shaimaa Mohammed Al Halabi)

2005. 34th National Day. Winning Designs in Children's Painting Competition. Multicoloured.
822	50f. Type **238**	55	55
823	125f. Circle of children (Muaz Jamal Ahmed Hassan) (horiz)	1·40	1·40
824	275f. Hands (Rithani Srinidhi)	3·00	3·00
825	375f. Dhow carrying flag (Omar Abu Baker Mukhtar) (horiz)	4·25	4·25

239 F'ttam (nose clip)

2005. Pearl Diving Tools. Multicoloured.
826	50f. Type **239**	55	55
827	125f. Al Khabet (finger guards)	1·40	1·40
828	175f. Al Dayeen (basket)	1·90	1·90
829	175f. Diving weight	3·00	3·00
830	375f. Diving clothes	4·25	4·25

240 Emblem

2006. Gulf Cooperation Council Day for Autistic Children.
831	**240**	4d. multicoloured	4·25	4·25

241 Hamad Bin Khalifa Abu Shehab

2006. Hamad Bin Khalifa Abu Shehab (poet) Commemoration. Sheet 71×111 mm containing T **241** and similar vert design. Multicoloured.
MS832	1d. Type **241**; 2d. Hand holding pen	3·25	3·25

The stamps and margins of **MS**832 form composite design of Hamad Bin Khalifa Abu Shehab writing.

242 Flag

2006. 25th Anniv of Gulf Co-operation Council. Multicoloured.

833	1d. Type **242**	1·10	1·10

MS834 165×105 mm. 500f. Flags of member states. Imperf 5·50 5·50

Stamps of similar designs were issued by Kuwait, Oman, Qatar, Saudi Arabia and Bahrain.

243 Emblems and Building

2006. 50th Anniv of Dubai Police Force.

835	**243**	1d. multicoloured	1·10	1·10

244 Tower

2005. 19th Asian Stamp Exhibition, Dubai. Each rosine, black and gold.

836	1d. Type **244**	1·10	1·10
837	4d. Four towers	4·50	4·50

245 Script and "10"

2006. Tenth Anniv of Dubai International Koran Awards.

838	**245**	1d. multicoloured	1·10	1·10

246 Al Raha Beach

2005. Al Raha Beach. Multicoloured.

839	1d. Type **246**	1·10	1·10
840	2d. Marina	2·10	2·10
841	3d.50 Skyline at night (horiz)	3·75	3·75
842	4d. Marina (different) (horiz)	4·25	4·25

247 Arrows

2005. UPU Strategy Conference, Dubai. Each green, blue and purple.

843	1d. Type **247**	1·10	1·10
844	4d. Curved arrows	4·50	4·50

248 '12'

2006. 12th Gulf Cooperation Council Postage Stamp Exhibition.

845	**248**	1d. multicoloured	1·10	1·10

249 Tahr

2006. Gazelles. Multicoloured.

846	1d. Type **249**	1·10	1·10
847	2d. Sand gazelle	2·20	2·20
848	3d. Mountain gazelle	3·25	3·25
849	3d.50 Arabian Oryx	4·00	4·00

MS850 155×125 mm. Nos. 846/9 17·00 17·00

The stamps of **MS**850 and with the margins form a composite design of a desert scene.

250 '35'

2006. 35th National Day.

851	**250**	1d. multicoloured	1·10	1·10

MS852 70×110 mm. **250** 1d. multi-coloured 10·50 10·50

251 Sheikh Mohamed Bin Rashid Al Maktoum

2006. Sheikh Mohamed Bin Rashid Al Maktoum. Multicoloured. Self-adhesive.

853	1d. Type **251**	1·10	1·10
854	4d. On horseback (43×53 mm)	4·50	4·50

252 Dispensing Aid

2006. International Volunteering Day. Red Crescent. Multicoloured.

855	2d. Type **252**	2·20	2·20
856	4d. Volunteer and children	4·50	4·50

253 Mariya um Alnairat

2006. Jewellery. Multicoloured.

857	1d. Type **253**	1·10	1·10
858	1d.50 Mortasha	1·70	1·70
859	2d. Shaghab bu Shouk	2·20	2·20
860	3d. Shahid ring	3·25	3·25
861	3d.50 Bushuq (bracelet)	4·00	4·00
862	4d. Tassah (headdress)	4·50	4·50

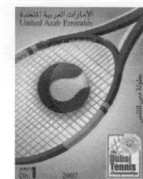

254 Falcon

2007

863	254	1d. multicoloured	1·20	1·20
864	254	1d.50 multicoloured	1·80	1·80
865	254	2d. multicoloured	2·40	2·40
866	254	3d. multicoloured	3·75	3·75
867	254	3d.50 multicoloured	4·25	4·25
868	254	4d. multicoloured	4·75	4·75
869	254	5d. multicoloured	6·00	6·00

Numbers have been left for possible additions to this series.

255 Racquet and Ball

2007. Dubai Tennis Championships.

900	255	1d. multicoloured	1·20	1·20
901	255	3d. multicoloured	3·75	3·75

256 Arms grasping Trophy

2007. Arabian Gulf Cup, Abu Dhabi 2007.

902	256	1d. multicoloured	1·20	1·20
903	256	3d. multicoloured	3·75	3·75

MS904 186×120 mm. Nos. 902/3 13·50 13·50

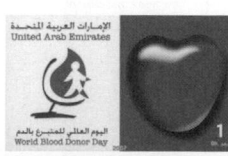

257 Emblem

2007. 300th Anniv of Etisalat.

905	257	1d. multicoloured	1·20	1·20
906	257	3d. multicoloured	3·75	3·75
907	257	3d.50 multicoloured	4·25	4·25
908	257	4d. multicoloured	4·75	4·75

The centres of Nos. 903/6 have been removed to give irregular triangular holes.

258 Emblem and Heart-shaped Blood Droplet

2007. World Blood Donor Day. Sheet 116×78 mm containing T **258** and similar horiz design.

MS909 1d. Type **258**; 3d. Emblem and blood droplet 5·25 5·25

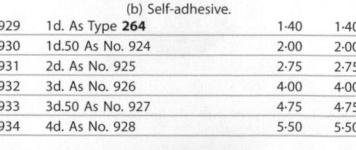

259 Ahmed Mohamed Al Maktoum

2007. Ahmed Mohamed Al Maktoum–Men's Double Trap Olympic Gold Medallist, Athens 2004.

910	259	3d. multicoloured	3·75	3·75

260 Emblem and '30'

2007. 30th Anniv of Emirates Bank. Multicoloured.

911	1d. Type **260**	1·20	1·20
912	1d.50 Emblem and '30' (41×35 mm (triangular))	1·80	1·80
913	3d. As Type **260**	3·75	3·75
914	3d.50 As No. 912 (41×35 mm (triangular))	4·25	4·25

MS915 165×120 mm. Nos. 911/14 15·00 15·00

261 Emblem

2007. 25th Anniv of Emirates Banks' Association.

916	261	1d. multicoloured	1·40	1·40

262 Anniversary Emblem

2007. Tenth Anniv of Abu Dhabi Islamic Bank.

917	262	1d. multicoloured	1·40	1·40
918	262	1d.50 multicoloured	2·00	2·00
919	262	2d. multicoloured	2·75	2·75
920	262	3d. multicoloured	4·00	4·00

MS921 143×112 mm. Nos. 918/20 17·00 17·00

263 Anniversary Emblem

2007. 50th Anniv of Abu Dhabi Police Force.

922	263	1d. multicoloured	1·40	1·40

264 Man supporting Woman and Elderly Man

2007. Children's Paintings. Multicoloured. (a) Ordinary gum.

923	1d. Type **264**	1·40	1·40
924	1d.50 Woman receiving gift (vert)	2·00	2·00
925	2d. Mosque and boys	2·75	2·75
926	3d. Hands supporting woman and child (vert)	4·00	4·00
927	3d.50 Boy leading elderly man across road	4·75	4·75
928	4d. Able bodied and disabled boys (vert)	5·50	5·50

(b) Self-adhesive.

929	1d. As Type **264**	1·40	1·40
930	1d.50 As No. 924	2·00	2·00
931	2d. As No. 925	2·75	2·75
932	3d. As No. 926	4·00	4·00
933	3d.50 As No. 927	4·75	4·75
934	4d. As No. 928	5·50	5·50

265 Sheikh Al Khazraji

2007. Sheikh Mohammed Al Khazraji (Chief Justice) Commemoration. Sheet 140×85 mm containing T **265** and similar vert design. Multicoloured.
MS935 1d. Type **265**; 3d. Facing front   6·00   6·00

266 Emblems

2007. 40th Anniv of Al Abbas Group.
936	**266**	1d. multicoloured	1·40	1·40
937	**266**	1d.50 multicoloured	2·00	2·00
938	**266**	2d. multicoloured	2·75	2·75
939	**266**	3d. multicoloured	4·00	4·00

267 Anniversary Emblem

2007. 50th Anniv of Al Rostamani Group.
| 940 | **267** | 1d. multicoloured | 1·40 | 1·40 |
| 941 | **267** | 1d.50 multicoloured | 2·00 | 2·00 |

268 Company Emblem

2007. 20th Anniv of Union Properties. Multicoloured.
942		1d. Type **268**	1·40	1·40
943		1d.50 F1 Theme Park (horiz)	2·00	2·00
944		2d. Uptown building	2·75	2·75
945		3d. Green Community (horiz)	4·00	4·00

A miniature sheet containing Nos. 942/5 was on sale f 1 d l

269 Building Facade

2008. Federal National Council.
| 946 | **269** | 1d. multicoloured | 1·40 | 1·40 |

270 '40 Years'

2008. 40th Anniv of National Bank of Abu Dhabi. Multicoloured.
947		1d. Type **270**	1·40	1·40
948		1d.50 As Type **270**	2·00	2·00
949		2d.25 40	3·00	3·00
950		4d. As No. 949	5·50	5·50

A miniature sheet containing Nos. 947/50 was on sale for 15d.

271 Emblem

2008. Municipality and Planning Department, Ajman. Multicoloured.
951		1d. Type **271**	1·40	1·40
952		1d.50 Emblem (Ajman Urban Planning Conference)	2·00	2·00
953		2d. e	3·00	3·00
954		4d. GIS	5·50	5·50

A miniature sheet containing Nos. 951/4 was on sale for 15d.

272 Spice Souk, Dubai

2008. Souks. Multicoloured.
955		1d. Type **272**	1·40	1·40
956		1d.50 Al Arsa Souk, Sharjah	2·00	2·00
957		2d. Gold Souk, Dubai	2·75	2·75
958		3d. Old Souk, Abu Dhabi	4·00	4·00

A miniature sheet containing Nos. 955/8 was on sale for 15d.

273 Emblem

2008. Hamdan bin Rashid Al Maktoum Award for Distinguished Academic Performance. Sheet 132×96 mm containing T **273** and similar horiz design. Multicoloured.
MS959 1d. Type **273**; 2d. Hamdan bin
Rashid Al Maktoum   4·25   4·25

274 Emblem

2008. 25th Anniv of Drydocks World, Dubai. Multicoloured.
| 960 | | 1d. Type **274** | 1·40 | 1·40 |
| 961 | | 4d. Emblem (horiz) | 5·50 | 5·50 |

275 Anniversary Emblem

2008. 75th Anniv of Sharjah Airport.
| 962 | **275** | 1d. multicoloured | 1·40 | 1·40 |

276 Olympic Emblem and Stylized Sportsmen

2008. Olympic Games, Bejing. Multicoloured.
963		1d. Type **276**	1·40	1·40
964		4d. Olympic flame (vert)	5·50	5·50
965		4d.75 As No. 964 (vert)	6·75	6·75
966		5d.50 As Type **276**	7·75	7·75
MS967 120×120 mm. As Nos. 963/6.
Imperf   21·00   21·00

277 'Gulf News'

2008. 30th Anniv of Gulf News.
968	**277**	1d. blue	1·50	1·50
969	**277**	1d.50 deep claret	2·10	2·10
970	**277**	2d.25 yellow-orange	2·75	2·75
MS971 150×150 mm. Nos. 968/70   6·50   6·50

278 Pigeon

2008. Arab Post Day. Sheet 170×60 mm containing T **278** and similar horiz design. Multicoloured.
MS972 1d. Type **278**; 2d.25 Caravan
of camels   1·50   1·50

The stamps and margins of MS972 form a composite design.

279 Abumaan

2008. Dates. Two sheets, each 141×141 mm, containing T **279** and similar multicoloured designs showing dates.
MS973 1d.×3, Type **279**; Jash Hammad;
Msalli   4·50   4·50
MS974 1d.×4. Farth; Mirzaban;
Abukibal; Salani. All vert   6·00   6·60
Nos. 975/81 are vacant.

280 National Centre for Documentation and Research

2008. 40th Anniv of National Centre for Documentation and Research. Multicoloured. (a) Ordinary gum.
| 982 | | 1d. Type **280** | 1·50 | 1·50 |
| 983 | | 4d. Opening ceremony | 6·00 | 6·00 |

(b) Size 35×50 mm. Self-adhesive.
| 984 | | 10d. Leaders | 15·00 | 15·00 |
No. 984, when tilted, shows a diferent leader of UNAE.

281 Trophy

2008. Tenth Anniv of Sheikh Hamdan Bin Rashid Al Maktoum Award for Medical Sciences. Multicoloured.
985		1d. Type **281**	1·50	1·50
986		2d. Trophy (different)	2·75	2·75
987		3d. Sheikh Hamdan Bin Rashid Al Maktoum	3·25	3·25
988		4d. Anniversary emblem	6·00	6·00
MS989 123×123 mm (circular). Nos.
985/8. Sold at 15d.   13·00   13·00

282 Hennaed Hands holding Banknotes (Al Eidiya)

2008. Eid Al Adha (Festival of Sacrifice). Multicoloured.
| 990 | | 1d. Type **282** | 1·50 | 1·50 |
| 991 | | 3d. Mecca (Eid prayers) | 4·50 | 4·50 |
MS992 82×102 mm. Nos. 990/1. Sold
at 6d.   6·00   6·00

283 Annivesary Emblem

2008. 25th Anniv of Duty Free Dubai. Multicoloured.
993		1d. Type **283**	1·50	1·50
994		2d. As Type **283**	2·75	2·75
995		3d. Palm tree in shopping mall	4·50	4·50
996		4d. Escalator in shopping mall	6·00	6·00
MS997 100×181 mm. Nos. 993/6. Sold
at 10d.   15·00   15·00

284 Profile and Globe

2008. 60th Anniv of Universal Declaration of Human Rights.
| 998 | **284** | 1d. multicoloured | 1·50 | 1·50 |
| 999 | **284** | 4d. multicoloured | 6·00 | 6·00 |
MS1000 112×112 mm. Nos. 998/9.
Sold at 6d.   7·50   7·50

285 Emblem

2009. Second Arab Stamp Exhibition, Dubai
| 1001 | **285** | 1d. gold and black | 1·50 | 1·50 |

286 ECSSR Publications

2009. 15th Anniv of Emirates Centre for Strategic Studies and Research. Multicoloured.
1002		1d. Type **286**	1·50	1·50
1003		1d.50 UAE Federation Library	2·00	2·00
1004		2d. Media monitoring room	2·75	2·75
1005		4d. ECSSR building	6·00	6·00
MS1006 112×122 mm. Nos. 1002/5.
Sold at 10d.   12·00   12·00

287 Rashid Bin Tannaf

2009. Rashid Bin Tannaf (poet) Commemoration. Multicoloured.
| 1007 | | 1d. Type **287** | 1·50 | 1·50 |
| 1008 | | 4d. With shaven head and arm raised | 6·00 | 6·00 |

288 Circular Tomb

2009. 50th Anniv of Discovery of Umm an-Nar Culture
1009	**288**	1d. multicoloured	1·50	1·50
1010	**288**	1d.50 multicoloured	2·00	2·00
1011	**288**	4d. multicoloured	6·00	6·00

289 Emblem

2009. Al Quds–Capital of Arab Culture
| 1012 | **289** | 2d. multicoloured | 2·75 | 2·75 |

290 Envelopes with Indian Stamps overprinted 'Pakistan'

2009. Centenary of Postal Services. Multicoloured.
1013		1d. Type **290**	1·50	1·50
1014		1d.50 With Trucial States and GB stamps	2·00	2·00
1015		4d. With UAE, Sharjah and Dubai stamps	6·00	6·00
1016		5d. Envelope with multiple stamps and Dubai postmark	7·50	7·50
MS1017 140×80 mm. 10d. Envelopes
with Indian stamps   14·00   14·00

291 Emblem

2009. 38th Anniv of National Day
1018 **291** 1d. bright emerald, bright scarlet-vermilion and black ... 1·50 1·50

292 Embem

2009. FIFA Club World Cup, 2009–Abu Dhabi
1019 1d. Type **292** ... 1·50 1·50
MS1020 120×120 mm. (circular). 10d. Emblem and flag as streamer (40×40 mm) ... 14·00 14·00

293 Mirrored Globe

2010. Tenth Anniv of Securities and Commodities Authority. Multicoloured.
1021 1d. Type **293** ... 1·50 1·50
1022 2d. Graph ... 2·75 2·75
1023 3d. Stock information screen ... 4·50 4·50
1024 5d. Falcon ... 7·50 7·50

294 Emblem

2010. Emirates Aluminium (emal). Multicoloured.
1025 1d. Type **294** ... 1·50 1·50
1026 2d. Dunes and hand holding photograph of highway ... 2·75 2·75
1027 3d. Saker falcon and Arab horse's head ... 4·50 4·50
1028 5d. Flag ... 7·50 7·50
1029 120×150mm. Nos. 1025/8. Sold at 15d. ... 16·00 16·00

295 UAE Pavilion

2010. Expo 2010, Shanghai. Multicoloured.
1030 1d. Type **295** ... 1·50 1·50
1031 5d.50 Aerial view of UAE pavilion at night ... 7·50 7·50

296 Barjeel, Traditional Air-conditioning Tower, UAE

2010. 30th Anniv of United Arab Emirates–Korea Diplomatic Relations. Multicoloured.
1032 1d. Type **296** ... 1·50 1·50
1033 5d.50 Chimney of Mt. Amisan in Gyeongbokgung Palace, Korea ... 7·50 7·50
MS1034 141×140 mm. Nos. 1032/3

297 Jebel Ali

2010. Jebel Ali Free Zone (Jafza) (free economic zone located in the Jebel Ali area at the far western end of Dubai). Multicoloured.
1035 1d. Type **297** ... 1·50 1·50
1036 2d. As Type **297** ... 2·75 2·75
1037 3d. As Type **297** ... 4·50 4·50
1038 4d. Anniversary emblem ... 6·00 6·00

298 Torch

2010. Youth Olympic Games, Singapore
MS1039 **298** 4d.75 multicoloured ... 7·00 7·00

299 Sheikh Zayed Grand Mosque

2010. Sheikh Zayed Grand Mosque
1040 1d. Type **299** ... 1·50 1·50
1041 5d. Sheikh Zayed Grand Mosque, central gate and side façades (horiz) ... 7·50 7·50
MS1042 120×140 mm. 25d. Central gate. Imperf ... 22·00 22·00

300 Pupils, Al Nehyania School

2010. Old Schools in United Arab Emirates. Multicoloured.
1043 1d. Type **300** ... 1·50 1·50
1044 1d.50 Teacher and pupils, Al Ahmadiyah School ... 2·00 2·00
1045 4d. Seats, Al Eslah School ... 6·00 6·00
MS1046 120×116mm. Nos. 1043/5 ... 9·50 9·50

301 Anniversary Emblem

2010. 50th Anniv of Organization of the Petroleum Exporting Countries (OPEC)
1047 **301** 1d. multicoloured ... 1·50 1·50

302 Dove carrying envelope

2010. World Post Day. Multicoloured.
1048 1d. Type **302** ... 1·50 1·50
1049 5d.50 UPU emblem ... 7·50 7·50

303 Black-headed Gull

2010. Seabirds of the United Arab Emirates. Multicoloured.
MS1050 1d. Type **303**; 1d.50 Crab plover; 2d. Grey heron (inscr 'Grey Heron Ardea'); 3d. Sooty gull; 4d.50 Socotra cormorant; 5d.50 Caspian gull ... 19·00 19·00

304 Crane and Container Ship

2010. DP World (operator of marine ports). Multicoloured.
1051 1d. Type **304** ... 1·50 1·50
1052 2d. Base of crane, dockside and trucks ... 2·75 2·75
1053 3d. Terminal at night, viewed from sea ... 4·50 4·50
1054 4d. Terminal at night, viewed from above ... 6·00 6·00

305 Race Car

2010. Yas Marina Race Circuit, Abu Dhabi. Multicoloured.
1055 1d. Type **305** ... 1·50 1·50
1056 5d.50 Stands ... 7·50 7·50

306 Finger Prints

2010. Watani (National Identity Program). Multicoloured.
1057 1d. Type **306** ... 1·50 1·50
1058 1d.50 Finger prints as map of UAE (vert) ... 2·00 2·00

307 Cars

2010. 39th National Day through the Eyes of Children. Multicoloured.

(a) Ordinary gum
1059 1d. Type **307** ... 1·50 1·50
1060 1d. Cooking and women waving flags ... 1·50 1·50
1061 1d. National flag bisected by Khalifa Tower ... 1·50 1·50
1062 1d. Skyscrapers, woman and children ... 1·50 1·50
1063 1d. Children wearing national colours ... 1·50 1·50
1064 1d. 2 December ... 1·50 1·50

(b) Size 33×24 mm. Booklet Stamps. Self-adhesive
1065 1d. As Type **307** ... 1·50 1·50
1066 1d. Cooking and women waving flags ... 1·50 1·50
1067 1d. National flag bisected by Khalifa Tower ... 1·50 1·50
1068 1d. Skyscrapers, woman and children ... 1·50 1·50
1069 1d. Children wearing national colours ... 1·50 1·50
1070 1d. 2 December ... 1·50 1·50

Pt. 22; Pt. 8; Pt. 2

UNITED NATIONS

A. NEW YORK HEADQUARTERS.
100 cents = 1 dollar.

B. GENEVA HEADQUARTERS.
100 centimes = 1 Swiss franc.

C. VIENNA HEADQUARTERS.
1979. 100 groschen = 1 schilling.
2002. 100 cents = 1 euro.

A. NEW YORK HEADQUARTERS

For use on mail posted at the Post Office at U.N. Headquarters, New York.

NOTE: Similar designs, but in different colours and values in Swiss Francs (F.S.) are issues of the Geneva office. Those with face values in Austrian Schillings are issues of the Vienna office. These are listed after the New York issues.

1 "Peoples of the World"

3 U.N. Emblem

1951
1	**1**	1c. mauve	10	10
2	-	1½c. green	10	10
3	**3**	2c. violet	20	20
4	-	3c. blue and purple	25	25
5	-	5c. blue	35	35
6	**1**	10c. brown	55	55
7	-	15c. blue and violet	75	75
8	-	20c. brown	90	90
9	-	25c. blue and black	1·00	1·00
10	-	50c. blue	4·50	4·50
11	**3**	$1 red	2·30	2·30

DESIGNS—VERT: 1½, 50c. U.N. Headquarters, New York; 5c. Clasped hands. HORIZ: 3, 15, 25c. U.N. flag; 20c. Hemispheres and U.N. emblem.

A7 Seagull and Airplane

1951. Air.
A12	**A7**	6c. red	25	25
A13	**A7**	10c. green	45	45
A14	-	15c. blue	65	65
A15	-	25c. black	90	90

DESIGN: 15, 25c. Swallows and U.N. emblem.

7 Veterans' War Memorial Building, San Francisco

1952. Seventh Anniv of Signing of U.N. Charter.
12 **7** 5c. blue ... 65 55

8 "Flame of Freedom"

1952. Human Rights Day.
13 **8** 3c. green ... 35 35
14 **8** 5c. blue ... 75 75

9 Homeless Family

1953. Protection for Refugees.
15 **9** 3c. brown ... 35 35
16 **9** 5c. blue ... 1·30 1·30

10 "Universal Postal Union"

1953. Universal Postal Union.

17	10	3c. sepia	45	45
18	10	5c. blue	1·40	1·40

11 Gearwheels and U.N. Emblem

1953. Technical Assistance for Underdeveloped Areas.

19	11	3c. grey	20	20
20	11	5c. green	1·50	1·50

12 "Flame of Freedom"

1953. Human Rights Day.

21	12	3c. blue	45	45
22	12	5c. red	1·80	1·60

13 F.A.O. Symbol

1954. Food and Agriculture Organization.

23	13	3c. yellow and green	45	45
24	13	8c. yellow and blue	1·80	1·60

...... In the .... the majority of the values unillustrated have the .... initials in another language.

14 U.N. Emblem and Anvil

1954. International Labour Organization.

25	14	3c. brown	45	45
26	14	8c. mauve	2·75	2·75

15 U.N. European Office, Geneva

1954. United Nations Day.

27	15	3c. violet	3·75	2·75
28	15	8c. red	90	90

16 Mother and Child

1954. Human Rights Day.

29	16	3c. orange	13·50	4·50
30	16	8c. green	1·80	1·80

17 "Flight"

1955. International Civil Aviation Organization.

31	17	3c. blue	3·75	3·25
32	17	8c. red	1·80	1·40

18 UNESCO Symbol

1955. U.N. Educational, Scientific and Cultural Organization.

33	18	3c. mauve	1·20	90
34	18	8c. blue	45	45

19 U.N. Charter

19a (image scaled to 44% of original size)

1955. Tenth Anniv of U.N.

35	19	3c. red	2·75	1·80
36	19	4c. green	90	90
37	19	8c. black	75	75
MS38	19a	83×100 mm. Nos. 35/7. Imperf	£140	45·00

20 "Flame of Freedom"

1955. Human Rights Day.

39	20	3c. blue	20	20
40	20	8c. green	90	90

21 "Telecommunication"

1956. International Telecommunication Union.

41	21	3c. blue	45	45
42	21	8c. red	65	65

22 Staff of Aesculapius

1956. World Health Organization.

43	22	3c. blue	20	20
44	22	8c. brown	90	90

23 General Assembly

1956. United Nations Day.

45	23	3c. slate	20	20
46	23	8c. olive	25	25

24 "Flame of Freedom"

1956. Human Rights Day.

47	24	3c. purple	20	20
48	24	8c. blue	25	25

25 Weather Balloon

1957. World Meteorological Organization.

49	25	3c. blue	20	20
50	25	8c. red	25	25

26 U.N.E.F. Badge

1957. United Nations Emergency Force.

51	26	3c. blue	20	20
52	26	8c. red	25	25

A26 "Flight"

1957. Air.

A51	A 26	4c. brown	20	20
A52	A 26	5c. red	25	25
A53	–	7c. blue	35	35

DESIGNS—HORIZ: 7c. U.N. flag and Douglas DC-8-60 airplane.

On the 5c. value inscriptions are redrawn larger than those on Type A **26**.

27 U.N. Emblem over Globe

1957. U.N. Security Council.

55	27	3c. brown	20	20
56	27	8c. green	25	25

28 "Flames of Freedom"

1957. Human Rights Day.

57	28	3c. brown	20	20
58	28	8c. black	25	25

29 Atomic Symbol

1958. International Atomic Energy Agency.

59	29	3c. olive	20	20
60	29	8c. blue	25	25

30 Central Hall, Westminster (site of first General Assembly)

1958. U.N. General Assembly Buildings.

61	30	3c. blue	20	20
62	30	8c. purple	25	25

See also Nos. 69/70, 77/8 and 123/4.

31 U.N. Seal

1958

63	31	4c. orange	20	20
64	31	8c. blue	25	25

32 Cogwheels

1958. Economic and Social Council.

65	32	4c. turquoise	20	20
66	32	8c. red	25	25

33 Hands holding Globe

1958. Human Rights Day.

67	33	4c. green	20	20
68	33	8c. brown	25	25

34 New York City Building, Flushing Meadows (1946–50)

1959. U.N. General Assembly Buildings.

69	34	4c. mauve	20	20
70	34	8c. turquoise	25	25

35 Emblems of U.N. Industry and Agriculture

1959. U.N. Economic Commission for Europe.

71	35	4c. blue	20	20
72	35	8c. red	25	25

36 "The Age of Bronze" (Rodin)

1959. U.N. Trusteeship Council.

73	36	4c. red	20	20
74	36	8c. green	25	25

37 "Protection for Refugees"

1959. World Refugee Year.

75	37	4c. red and bistre	20	20
76	37	8c. blue and bistre	25	25

38 Palais de Chaillot, Paris (1948, 1951)

1960. U.N. General Assembly Buildings.

77	**38**	4c. blue and purple	20	20
78	**38**	8c. brown and green	25	25

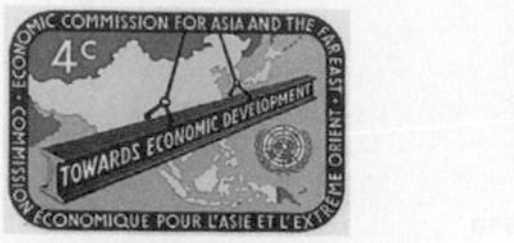

39 Steel Girder and Map

1960. U.N. Economic Commission for Asia and the Far East ("ECAFE").

79	**39**	4c. purple, buff and turquoise	20	20
80	**39**	8c. green, pink and blue	25	25

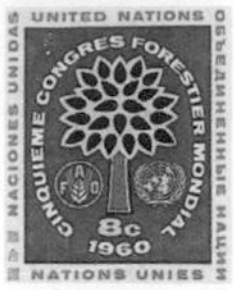

40 Tree and Emblems

1960. Fifth World Forestry Congress, Seattle.

81	**40**	4c. multicoloured	20	20
82	**40**	8c. multicoloured	25	25

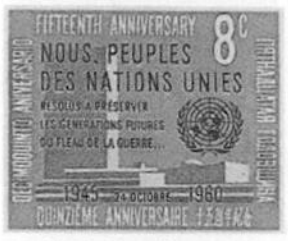

41 U.N. Headquarters and Emblem

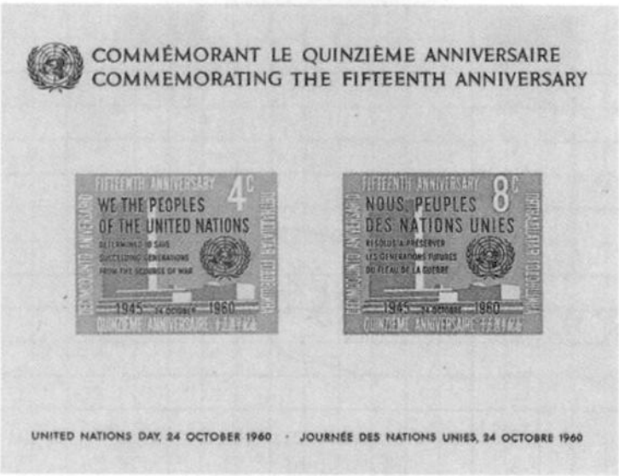

41a (image scaled to 52% of original size)

1960. 15th Anniv of U.N.

83	**41**	4c. blue	20	20
84	**41**	8c. black	25	25
MS85	**41a**	92×70 mm. Nos. 83/4. Imperf	2·30	2·30

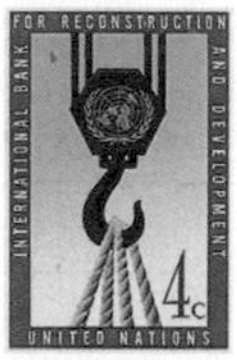

42 Double Block and Hook

1960. International Bank for Reconstruction and Development ("World Bank").

86	**42**	4c. multicoloured	20	20
87	**42**	8c. multicoloured	25	25

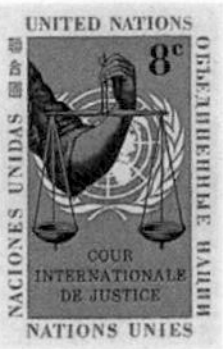

43 Scales of Justice

1961. International Court of Justice.

88	**43**	4c. black, brown and yellow	20	20
89	**43**	8c. black, green and yellow	25	25

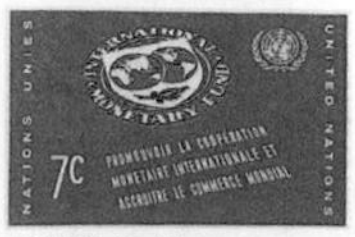

44 I.M.F. Emblem

1961. International Monetary Fund.

90	**44**	4c. blue	20	20
91	**44**	7c. brown and yellow	25	25

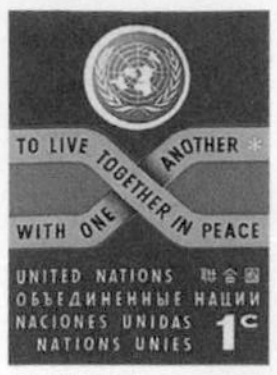

45 "Peace"

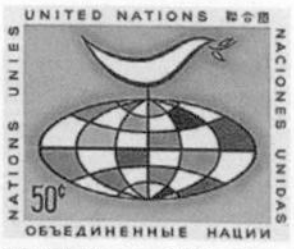

53 Globe and Weather Vane

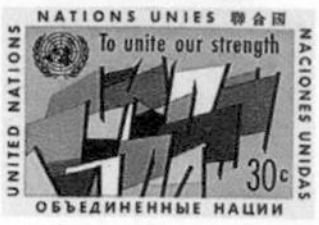

52 Flags

1961

92	**45**	1c. multicoloured	20	20
93	-	2c. multicoloured	20	20
94	-	3c. multicoloured	20	20
95	-	5c. red	20	20
96	-	7c. brown, black and blue	25	25
97	-	10c. black, green and blue	30	30
98	-	11c. gold, light blue and blue	55	55
99	**52**	30c. multicoloured	65	65
100	**53**	50c. multicoloured	1·10	1·10

DESIGNS—HORIZ: 32×23 mm: 2c. Map of the World; 10c. Three figures on globe ("Races United"). 30½×23½ mm: 3c. U.N. Flag. 36½×23½ mm: 5c. Hands supporting "UN" and globe. 37½×22½ mm: 11c. U.N. emblem across globe. VERT—21×26 mm: 7c. U.N. emblem as flowering plant.

For 1c. in same design, but smaller, see No. 146 and for 5c. multicoloured see No. 165.

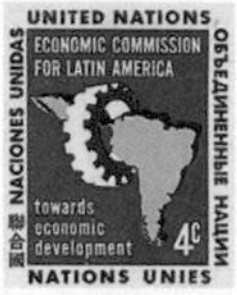

54 Cogwheel and Map of S. America

1961. Economic Commission for Latin America.

101	**54**	4c. red, olive and blue	20	20
102	**54**	11c. purple, red and green	45	45

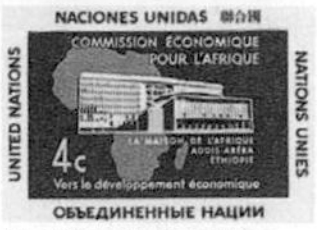

55 Africa Hall, Addis Ababa

1961. Economic Commission for Africa.

103	**55**	4c. multicoloured	20	20
104	**55**	11c. multicoloured	45	45

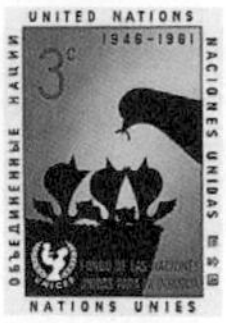

56 Bird feeding Young

1961. 15th Anniv of UNICEF.

105	**56**	3c. multicoloured	15	15
106	**56**	4c. multicoloured	20	20
107	**56**	13c. multicoloured	25	25

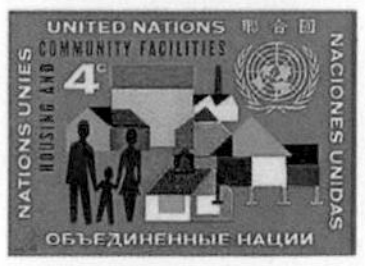

57 "Housing and Community Facilities"

1962. U.N. Housing and Related Community Facilities Programme.

108	**57**	4c. multicoloured	20	20
109	**57**	7c. multicoloured	35	35

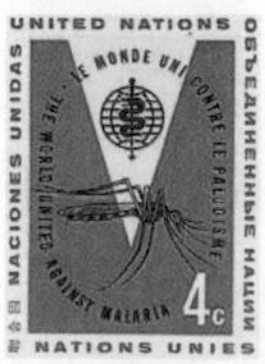

58 Mosquito and W.H.O. Emblem

1962. Malaria Eradication.

110	**58**	4c. multicoloured	20	20
111	**58**	11c. multicoloured	35	35

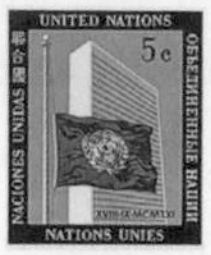

59 U.N. Flag at Half-mast

1962. Dag Hammarskjold (U.N. Secretary-General, 1953–61) Memorial Issue.

112	**59**	5c. indigo, blue and black	20	20
113	**59**	15c. blue, grey and black	55	55

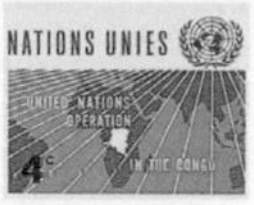

60 Congo on World Map

1962. U.N. Congo Operation.

114	**60**	4c. multicoloured	20	20
115	**60**	11c. multicoloured	55	55

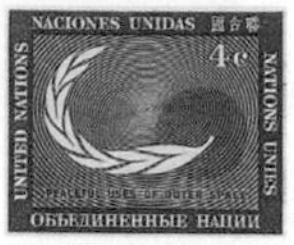

61 "Peace in Space"

1962. U.N. Committee on Peaceful Uses of Outer Space.

116	**61**	4c. blue	20	20
117	**61**	11c. mauve	25	25

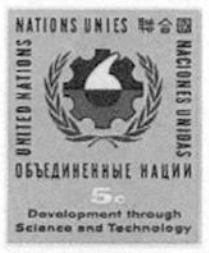

62 Conference Emblem

1963. Science and Technology Conf, Geneva.

118	**62**	5c. multicoloured	20	20
119	**62**	11c. multicoloured	25	25

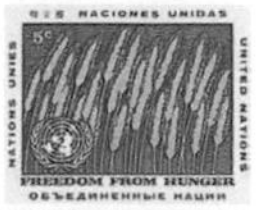

63 Wheat

1963. Freedom from Hunger.

120	**63**	5c. yellow, green and orange	20	20
121	**63**	11c. yellow, red and orange	25	25

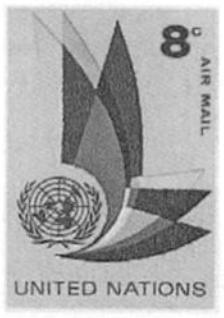

A65 "Flight"

1963. Air. Multicoloured.

A122		6c. "Space"	20	20
A123		8c. Type A **65**	20	20
A124		13c. "Bird"	35	35
A125		15c. "Birds in Flight"	55	55
A126		25c. Douglas DC-8 and airmail envelope	75	75

SIZES—HORIZ: 6c. As Type A **65**; 13, 25c. 30½×23 mm. VERT: 15c. 23×30½ mm.

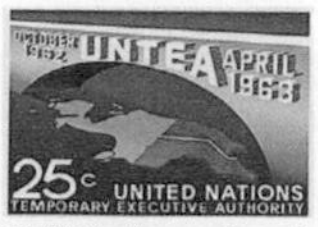

64 "Bridge" over Map of West New Guinea

1963. United Nations Temporary Executive Authority (UNTEA) in West New Guinea.

122	**64**	25c. green, blue and drab	75	75

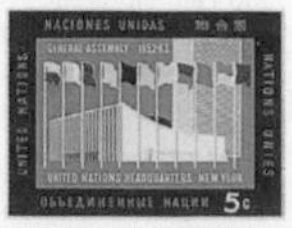

65 General Assembly Building and Flags

1963. U.N. General Assembly Buildings.

123	**65**	5c. multicoloured	20	20
124	**65**	11c. multicoloured	25	25

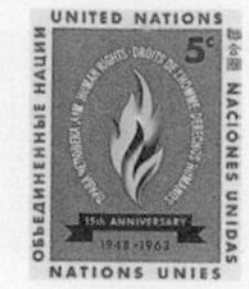

66 "Flame of Freedom"

1963. 15th Anniv of Declaration of Human Rights.

125	**66**	5c. multicoloured	20	20
126	**66**	11c. multicoloured	25	25

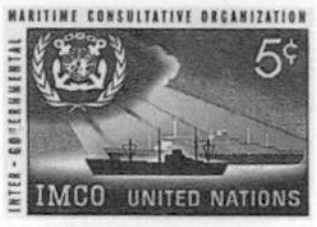

67 Ships at Sea

1964. Inter-Governmental Maritime Consultative Organization (I.M.C.O.).

127	**67**	5c. multicoloured	20	20
128	**67**	11c. multicoloured	25	25

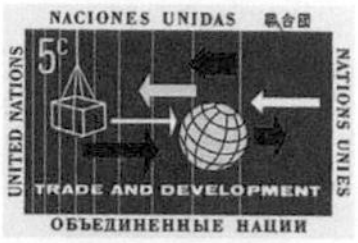

68 "Trade and Development"

1964. U.N. Trade and Development Conf, Geneva.

129	**68**	5c. yellow, black and red	20	20
130	**68**	11c. yellow, black and bistre	25	25

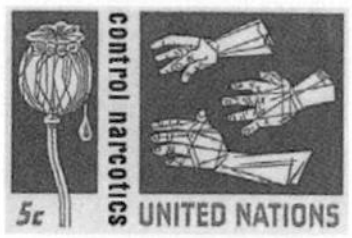

69 Opium Poppy and Reaching Hands

1964. Narcotics Control.

131	**69**	5c. red and black	20	20
132	**69**	11c. green and black	25	25

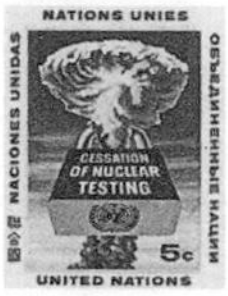

70 Atomic Explosion and Padlock

1964. Cessation of Nuclear Testing.

133	**70**	5c. sepia and brown	20	20

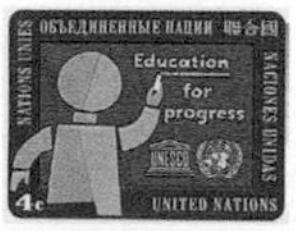

71 "Teaching"

1964. "Education for Progress".

134	**71**	4c. multicoloured	15	15
135	**71**	5c. multicoloured	20	20
136	**71**	11c. multicoloured	25	25

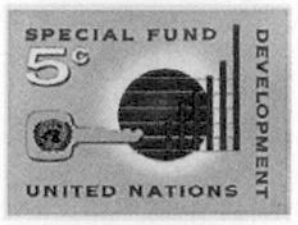

72 Key, Globe and "Graph"

1965. U.N. Special Fund.

137	**72**	5c. multicoloured	20	20
138	**72**	11c. multicoloured	25	25

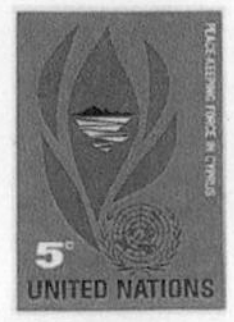

73 Cyprus "Leaves" and U.N. Emblem

1965. Peace-keeping Force in Cyprus.
139	73	5c. olive, black and orange	20	20
140	73	11c. green, black & lt green	25	25

74 "From Semaphore to Satellite"

1965. I.T.U. Centenary.
141	74	5c. multicoloured	20	20
142	74	11c. multicoloured	25	25

75 I.C.Y. Emblem

75a (image scaled to 52% of original size)

1965. 20th Anniv of United Nations and International Co-operation Year.
143	75	5c. blue	20	20
144	75	15c. mauve	35	35
MS145	75a	92×70 mm. Nos. 143/4	90	1·10

76 "Peace"

1965
146	76	1c. multicoloured	10	10
147	-	15c. multicoloured	25	25
148	-	20c. multicoloured	45	45
149	-	25c. ultramarine and blue	90	90
150	-	$1 blue and turquoise	2·30	2·30

DESIGNS—24½×30 mm: 15c. Opening words, U.N. Charter. 22×32 mm: 20c. U.N. emblem and Headquarters. 24×24 mm: 25c. U.N. emblem. 33×23 mm: $1 U.N. emblem encircled.

81 "Expanding Population"

1965. Population Trends and Development.
151	81	4c. multicoloured	20	20
152	81	5c. multicoloured	20	20
153	81	11c. multicoloured	30	30

82 Globe and Flags

1966. World Federation of United Nations Assns. (W.F.U.N.A.).
154	82	5c. multicoloured	20	20
155	82	15c. multicoloured	35	35

83 W.H.O. Building

1966. Inaug of W.H.O. Headquarters, Geneva.
156	83	5c. multicoloured	20	20
157	83	11c. multicoloured	25	25

84 Coffee

1966. International Coffee Agreement of 1962.
158	84	5c. multicoloured	20	20
159	84	11c. multicoloured	25	25

85 Military Observer

1966. U.N. Military Observers.
160	85	15c. multicoloured	45	45

86 Children in Closed Railway Wagon

1966. 20th Anniv of UNICEF. Multicoloured.
161		4c. Type 86	15	15
162		5c. Children in locomotive and tender	20	20
163		11c. Children in open railway wagon	25	25

89 U.N. Headquarters and World Map
91 "UN" and Emblem

(1967)
164	89	1½c. multicoloured	25	25
165	-	5c. multicoloured	20	20
166	-	6c. multicoloured	20	20
167	91	13c. blue, gold and black	25	25

DESIGNS—HORIZ: 5c. As No. 95. 23×34 mm: 6c. Aerial view of U.N. Headquarters.

92 "Progress through Development"

1967. U.N. Development Programme.
168	92	5c. multicoloured	20	20
169	92	11c. multicoloured	25	25

93 U.N. Emblem and Fireworks

1967. New Independent Nations Commem.
170	93	5c. multicoloured	20	20
171	93	11c. multicoloured	25	25

94 "Peace"

1967. "Expo 67", World Fair, Montreal.
172	94	4c. brown and red	20	20
173	-	5c. brown and blue	20	20
174	-	8c. multicoloured	20	20
175	-	10c. brown and green	30	30
176	-	15c. chestnut and brown	45	45

DESIGNS—VERT: 5c. "Justice"; 10c. "Fraternity"; 15c. "Truth". HORIZ (32×23½ mm): 8c. Facade of U.N. Pavilion.

The above stamps are expressed in Canadian currency and were valid for postage only from the U.N. Pavilion at the World Fair.

99 Baggage Labels

1967. International Tourist Year.
177	99	5c. multicoloured	20	20
178	99	15c. multicoloured	45	45

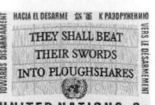
100 "Towards Disarmament"

1967. Disarmament Campaign.
179	100	6c. multicoloured	20	20
180	100	13c. multicoloured	25	25

101 "The Kiss of Peace" (part of Chagall's stained glass window)

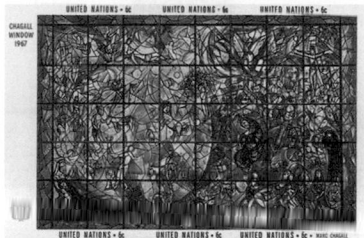
102 (image scaled to 38% of original size)

1967. United Nations Art (1st issue). Chagall's Memorial Window in U.N. Secretariat Building.
181	101	6c. multicoloured	20	20
MS182		123×81 mm. 6c. ×6, multicoloured	1·60	1·60

The miniature sheet is divisible into six 6c. stamps size 41×46 mm, 24×46 mm, 41½×33½ mm, 29×33½ mm and 41½×47 mm.
See also Nos. 185/6, 201/2, 203/4, 236/7 and 251/2.

103 Globe and Diagram of U.N. Organs

1968. U.N. Secretariat.
183	103	6c. multicoloured	20	20
184	103	13c. multicoloured	25	25

104 Starcke's Statue

1968. United Nations Art (2nd issue). Henrik Starcke's Statue in U.N. Trusteeship Council Chamber.
185	104	6c. multicoloured	20	20
186	104	75c. multicoloured	2·10	1·80

105 Industrial Skyline

1968. U.N. Industrial Development Organization (U.N.I.D.O.).
187	105	6c. multicoloured	20	20
188	105	13c. multicoloured	25	25

A106 "Winged Envelopes"

A107 Aircraft and U.N. Emblem

1968. Air.
A189	A106	10c. multicoloured	25	25
A190	A107	20c. multicoloured	45	45

106 Radar Scanner

1968. World Weather Watch.
189	106	6c. multicoloured	20	20
190	106	20c. multicoloured	45	45

107 Human Rights Emblem

1968. Human Rights Year.
191	107	6c. gold, ultramarine & bl	20	20
192	107	13c. gold, red and pink	35	35

108 Textbooks

1969. United Nations Institute for Training and Research (U.N.I.T.A.R.).
193	108	6c. multicoloured	20	20
194	108	13c. multicoloured	25	25

In the 13c. the name and value panel is at foot of stamp.

109 U.N. Building, Santiago

1969. U.N. Building, Santiago, Chile.
195	109	6c. blue, light blue & green	20	20
196	109	15c. purple, red and buff	35	35

110 "Peace Through International Law"

1969. 20th Anniv of Session of U.N. Int Law Commission.
197	110	6c. multicoloured	20	20
198	110	13c. multicoloured	30	30

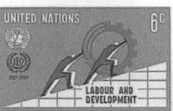
111 "Labour and Development"

1969. 50th Anniv of I.L.O.
199	111	6c. multicoloured	20	20
200	111	20c. multicoloured	45	45

112 "Ostrich"

1969. United Nations Art (3rd issue). 3rd-century A.D. Tunisian Mosaic, Delegates' North Lounge. Multicoloured.

201	6c. Type **112**		20	20
202	13c. "Ring-necked Pheasant"		35	35

114 Peace Bell

1970. United Nations Art (4th issue). Japanese Peace Bell.

203	**114**	6c. multicoloured	20	20
204	**114**	25c. multicoloured	45	45

115 River, Power Lines and Map

1970. Lower Mekong Basin Development Project.

205	**115**	6c. multicoloured	20	20
206	**115**	13c. multicoloured	30	30

116 "Fight Cancer"

1970. Tenth Int Cancer Congress, Houston, Texas.

207	**116**	6c. black and blue	20	20
208	**116**	13c. black and olive	30	30

117 Laurel Branch

119 (image scaled to 50% of original size)

1970. 25th Anniv of United Nations.

209	**117**	6c. multicoloured	20	20
210	**117**	13c. multicoloured	30	30
211	-	25c. gold, light blue & blue	45	45

MS212 96×78 mm. **119** Nos. 209/11.

	Imperf		90	90

DESIGN—VERT: 25c. U.N. emblem.
On No. 210 the inscription is in French.

120 Scales and Olive-branch

1970. "Peace, Justice and Progress" (Aims of the United Nations).

213	**120**	6c. multicoloured	20	20
214	**120**	13c. multicoloured	35	35

121 U.N. Emblem on Sea-bed

1971. Peaceful Uses of the Sea-bed.

215	**121**	6c. multicoloured	20	20

122 "Refugees" (sculpture, Kaare Nygaard)

1971. U.N. Work with Refugees.

216	**122**	6c. black, yellow & brown	20	20
217	**122**	13c. black, turq & blue	30	30

123 Wheatsheaf on Globe

1971. World Food Programme.

218	**123**	13c. multicoloured	35	35

124 New U.P.U. H.Q. Building

1971. Opening of New U.P.U. Headquarters Building, Berne.

219	**124**	20c. multicoloured	45	45

125 Four-leafed Clover

1971. Racial Equality Year. Multicoloured.

220	8c. Type **125**		20	20
221	13c. Linked globes (horiz)		30	30

127 U.N. H.Q., New York

1971. Multicoloured.. Multicoloured..

222	8c. Type **127**		20	20
223	60c. U.N. emblem and flags		1·10	1·10
224	95c. "Letter changing Hands"		1·80	1·80

130 "Maia" (Picasso)

1971. U.N. International Schools.

225	**130**	8c. multicoloured	20	20
226	**130**	21c. multicoloured	45	45

131 "X" over Atomic Explosion

1972. Non-proliferation of Nuclear Weapons.

227	**131**	8c. blue, black and pink	20	20

132 "Proportions of Man" (Leonardo da Vinci)

1972. World Health Day.

228	**132**	15c. multicoloured	35	35

A134 Birds in Flight

1972. Air.

A229	-	9c. multicoloured	15	15
A230	**A134**	11c. multicoloured	20	20
A231	-	17c. orange, yellow and red	35	35
A232	-	21c. multicoloured	45	45

DESIGNS—23×31 mm: 9c. "Contemporary Flight". 38×23 mm: 17c. Clouds. 33×23 mm: 21c. "U.N." jetstream.

137 Environmental Emblem

1972. U.N. Environmental Conservation Conf, Stockholm.

233	**137**	8c. multicoloured	20	20
234	**137**	15c. multicoloured	35	35

138 Europe "Flower"

1972. Economic Commission for Europe (E.C.E.).

235	**138**	21c. multicoloured	45	45

139 "World United" (detail, Sert mural, Geneva)

1972. United Nations Art (5th issue).

236	**139**	8c. brown, gold & lt brown	20	20
237	**139**	15c. brown, gold and green	45	45

140 Laurel and Broken Sword

1973. Disarmament Decade.

238	**140**	8c. multicoloured	20	20
239	**140**	15c. multicoloured	45	45

141 Skull on Poppy

1973. "Stop Drug Abuse" Campaign.

240	**141**	8c. multicoloured	20	20
241	**141**	15c. multicoloured	45	45

142 Emblems within Honeycomb

1973. U.N. Volunteers Programme.

242	**142**	8c. multicoloured	20	20
243	**142**	21c. multicoloured	55	55

143 Namibia on Map of Africa

1973. U.N. Resolution on Namibia (South West Africa).

244	**143**	8c. multicoloured	20	20
245	**143**	15c. multicoloured	45	45

144 Human Rights Flame

1973. 25th Anniv of Declaration of Human Rights.

246	**144**	8c. multicoloured	20	20
247	**144**	21c. multicoloured	55	55

145 H.Q. Building

1973. Inauguration of New I.L.O. Headquarters Building, Geneva.

248	**145**	10c. multicoloured	25	25
249	**145**	21c. multicoloured	55	55

146 Globe within Posthorn

1974. Centenary of U.P.U.

250	**146**	10c. multicoloured	35	35

147 "Children's Choir" (mural detail, C. Portinari)

1974. United Nations Art (6th issue). Brazilian Peace Mural, Delegates' Lobby.

251	**147**	10c. multicoloured	25	25
252	**147**	18c. multicoloured	55	55

148 Peace Dove

1974

253	**148**	2c. blue and ultramarine	20	20
254	-	10c. multicoloured	25	25
255	-	18c. multicoloured	45	45

DESIGNS—VERT: 10c. U.N. Headquarters, New York; 18c. Globe over U.N. emblem and flags.

A151 Globe and Jet Aircraft

1974. Air. Multicoloured.

A256	13c. Type **A 151**		20	20
A257	18c. "Channels of Communication" (38×23 mm)		25	25
A258	26c. Dove in flight and U.N. Headquarters		45	45

154 Young Children with Globe

1974. World Population Year.

259	**154**	10c. multicoloured	25	25
260	**154**	18c. multicoloured	55	55

155 Ship and Fish

1974. U.N. Conference on "Law of the Sea".
261	**155**	10c. multicoloured	25	25
262	**155**	26c. multicoloured	65	65

156 Satellite, Globe and Symbols

1975. Peaceful Uses of Outer Space.
263	**156**	10c. multicoloured	25	25
264	**156**	26c. multicoloured	65	65

157 "Sex Equality"

1975. International Women's Year.
265	**157**	10c. multicoloured	20	20
266	**157**	18c. multicoloured	55	55

158 "The Hope of Mankind"

159 (image scaled to 53% of original size)

1975. 30th Anniv of U.N.O.
267	**158**	10c. multicoloured	25	25
268	**158**	26c. multicoloured	75	75
MS269	88×70 mm. **159** Nos. 267/8.			
	Imperf		90	90

160 Cupped Hand

1975. "Namibia—United Nations Direct Responsibility".
270	**160**	10c. multicoloured	20	20
271	**160**	18c. multicoloured	45	45

161 Wild Rose and Barbed Wire

1975. U.N. Peace-keeping Operations.
272	**161**	13c. blue	20	20
273	**161**	26c. mauve	65	65

162 "Bird of Peace"

1976. Multicoloured.. Multicoloured..
274		3c. Type **162**	15	15
275		4c. "Gathering of Peoples" (39×23 mm)	20	20
276		30c. U.N. flag (23×39 mm)	55	55
277		50c. "Universal Peace" (Dove and rainbow) (23×39 mm)	75	75

166 Linked Ribbons

1976. World Federation of U.N. Associations.
278	**166**	13c. multicoloured	25	25
279	**166**	26c. multicoloured	55	55

167 Globe and Crate

1976. U.N. Conf on Trade and Development.
280	**167**	13c. multicoloured	25	25
281	**167**	31c. multicoloured	65	65

168 Houses bordering Globe

1976. U.N. Conf on Human Settlements.
282	**168**	13c. multicoloured	25	25
283	**168**	25c. multicoloured	55	55

169 Magnifying Glass and Emblem

1976. 25th Anniv of U.N. Postal Administration.
284	**169**	13c. multicoloured	45	45
285	**169**	31c. multicoloured	2·50	2·50

170 Stylized Ear of Wheat

1976. World Food Council.
286	**170**	13c. multicoloured	35	35

171 U.N. Emblem

1976
287	**171**	9c. multicoloured	25	25

172 W.I.P.O. Headquarters Building

1977. World Intellectual Property Organization Headquarters.
288	**172**	13c. multicoloured	25	25
289	**172**	31c. multicoloured	65	65

173 Rain Drops and Funnel

1977. United Nations Water Conference.
290	**173**	13c. multicoloured	25	25
291	**173**	25c. multicoloured	55	55

174 Severed Fuse

1977. Security Council.
292	**174**	13c. multicoloured	25	25
293	**174**	31c. multicoloured	65	65

175 Winged Airmail Letter

1977. Air. Multicoloured.
A294		25c. Type **175**	25	25
A295		31c. multicoloured		

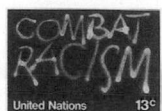

177 "Combat Racism"

1977. Campaign Against Racial Discrimination.
296	**177**	13c. black and yellow	25	25
297	**177**	25c. black and red	55	55

178 Atomic Symbol and Produce

1977. Peaceful Uses of Atomic Energy.
298	**178**	13c. multicoloured	25	25
299	**178**	18c. multicoloured	45	45

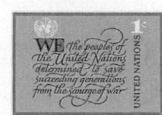

179 U.N. Charter

1978. Multicoloured.. Multicoloured..
300		1c. Type **179**	10	10
301		25c. Knotted flags	45	45
302		$1 Multi-racial group	1·60	1·60

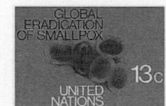

182 Smallpox Bacilli

1978. Global Eradication of Smallpox.
303	**182**	13c. black and red	25	25
304	**182**	31c. black and blue	55	55

183 Broken Manacle

1978. "Namibia: Liberation, Justice, Co-operation".
305	**183**	13c. multicoloured	25	25
306	**183**	18c. multicoloured	45	45

184 Clouds within Ribbon

1978. International Civil Aviation Organization—Safety in the Air.
307	**184**	13c. multicoloured	25	25
308	**184**	25c. multicoloured	50	50

185 General Assembly

1978. General Assembly.
309	**185**	13c. multicoloured	25	25
310	**185**	18c. multicoloured	50	50

186 Hemispheres within Cogwheels

1978. Technical Co-operation among Developing Countries.
311	**186**	13c. multicoloured	25	25
312	**186**	31c. multicoloured	55	55

187 Hand holding Olive Branch

1979. Multicoloured
313		5c. Type **187**	10	10
314		14c. Multiple "tree"	25	25
315		15c. Globe and peace dove	35	35
316		20c. Doves crossing globe	40	40

191 Fire and Flood

1979. U.N. Disaster Relief Co-ordinator.
317	**191**	15c. multicoloured	25	25
318	**191**	20c. multicoloured	45	45

192 Child's Drawing

1979. International Year of the Child.
319	**192**	15c. multicoloured	25	25
320	**192**	31c. multicoloured	65	65

193 Olive Branch and Map of Namibia

1979. "For a Free and Independent Namibia".

321	**193**	15c. multicoloured	20	20
322	**193**	31c. multicoloured	65	65

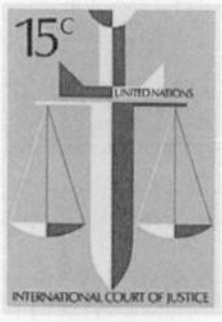

194 Sword and Scales of Justice

1979. International Court of Justice.

323	**194**	15c. olive, green and black	25	25
324	**194**	20c. blue, lt blue & black	45	45

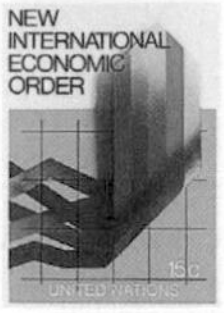

195 Graph

1980. New International Economic Order. Multicoloured.

325	15c. Type **195**	25	25
326	31c. Key	55	55

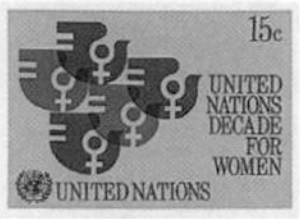

197 Doves

1980. U.N. Decade for Women.

327	**197**	15c. multicoloured	25	25
328	**197**	20c. multicoloured	55	55

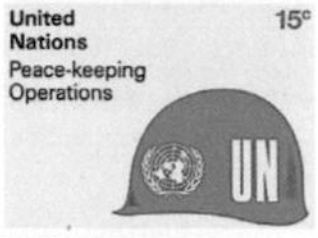

198 Helmet

1980. Peace-keeping Operations.

329	**198**	15c. blue and black	25	25
330	-	31c. multicoloured	55	55

DESIGN: 31c. "Peace-keeping".

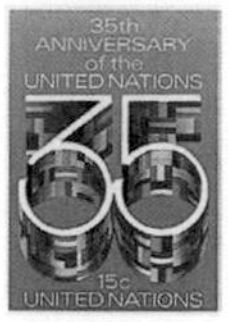

200 "35" composed of Flags

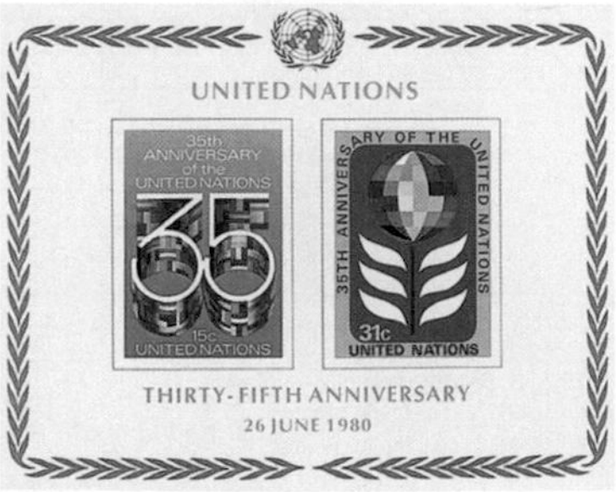

202 (image scaled to 52% of original size)

1980. 35th Anniv of United Nations. Multicoloured.

331	15c. Type **200**	25	25
332	31c. Stylized flower	55	55
MS333	92×73 mm. **202** Nos. 331/2. Imperf	90	90

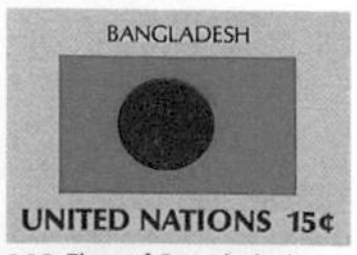

203 Flag of Bangladesh

1980. Flags of Member Nations (1st series). Multicoloured.

334	15c. Type **203**	20	20
335	15c. Guinea	20	20
336	15c. Mali	20	20
337	15c. Surinam	20	20
338	15c. Cameroun	20	20
339	15c. Hungary	20	20
340	15c. Madagascar	20	20
341	15c. Rwanda	20	20
342	15c. El Salvador	20	20
343	15c. France	20	20
344	15c. Venezuela	20	20
345	15c. Yugoslavia	20	20
346	15c. Fiji	20	20
347	15c. Luxembourg	20	20
348	15c. Turkey	20	20
349	15c. Vietnam	20	20

See also Nos. 359/74, 383/98, 408/23, 434/9, 458/74, 486/501, 508/23, 537/52, 563/78, 710/17, 744/51, 785/92, 849/56 and 990/3.

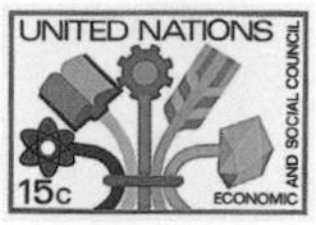

204 Various Emblems forming Bunch of Flowers

1980. Economic and Social Council. Multicoloured.

350	15c. Type **204**	25	25
351	20c. Economic and social emblems	45	45

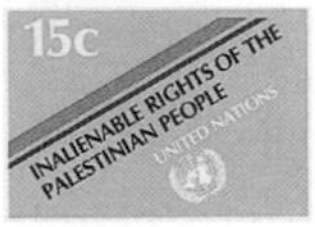

206 Text and U.N. Emblem

1981. Inalienable Rights of the Palestinian People.

352	**206**	15c. multicoloured	35	35

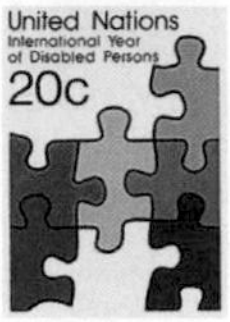

207 Jigsaw

1981. International Year of Disabled Persons.

353	**207**	20c. multicoloured	35	35
354	-	35c. black and orange	55	55

DESIGN: 35c. Disabled person.

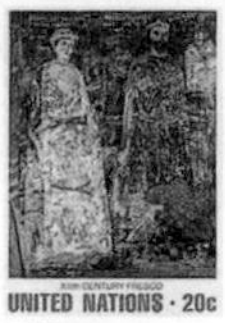

209 "Sebastocrator Kaloyan and his Wife Desislava" (13th-cent Bulgarian fresco)

1981. Art.

355	**209**	20c. multicoloured	35	35
356	**209**	31c. multicoloured	65	65

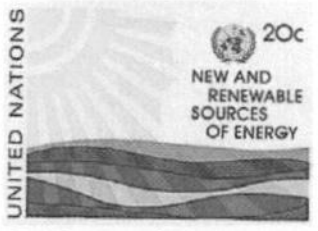

210 Sun and Sea

1981. New and Renewable Sources of Energy.

357	**210**	20c. multicoloured	35	35
358	-	40c. gold and blue	60	60

DESIGN: 40c. U.N. energy conference emblem.

1981. Flags of Member Nations (2nd series). As T **203**. Multicoloured.

359	20c. Djibouti	25	25
360	20c. Sri Lanka	25	25
361	20c. Bolivia	25	25
362	20c. Equatorial Guinea	25	25
363	20c. Malta	25	25
364	20c. Czechoslovakia	25	25
365	20c. Thailand	25	25
366	20c. Trinidad and Tobago	25	25
367	20c. Ukrainian S.S.R.	25	25
368	20c. Kuwait	25	25
369	20c. Sudan	25	25
370	20c. Egypt	25	25
371	20c. United States	25	25
372	20c. Singapore	25	25
373	20c. Panama	25	25
374	20c. Costa Rica	25	25

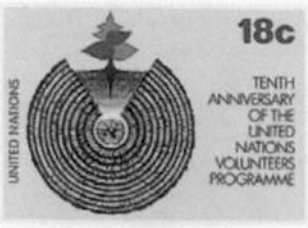

212 Grafted Plant

1981. Tenth Anniv of U.N. Volunteers Programme. Multicoloured.

375	18c. Type **212**	25	25
376	28c. "10" enclosing symbols of services	45	45

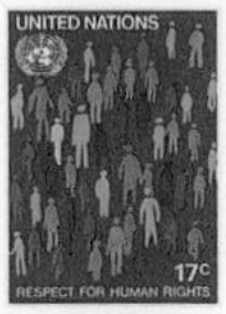

214 "Respect for Human Rights"

1982. Multicoloured.

377	17c. Type **214**	25	25
378	28c. "Granting of Independence to Colonial Countries and Peoples"	45	45
379	40c. "Second Disarmament Decade"	75	75

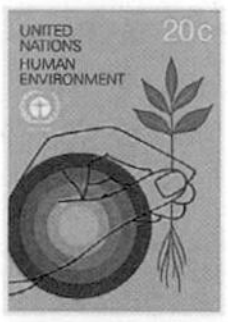

217 Hand holding Seedling

1982. Human Environment. Multicoloured.

380	20c. Type **217**	25	25
381	40c. Symbols of the environment	75	75

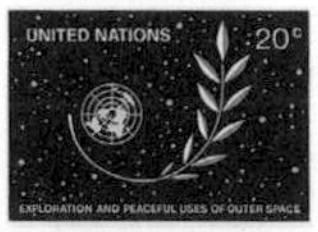

219 Olive Branch and U.N. Emblem

1982. Second United Nations Conference on Exploration and Peaceful Uses of Outer Space.

382	**219**	20c. ultramarine, blue and green	45	45

1982. Flags of Member Nations (3rd series). As T **203**. Multicoloured.

383	20c. Austria	25	25
384	20c. Malaysia	25	25
385	20c. Seychelles	25	25
386	20c. Ireland	25	25
387	20c. Mozambique	25	25
388	20c. Albania	25	25
389	20c. Dominica	25	25
390	20c. Solomon Islands	25	25
391	20c. Philippines	25	25
392	20c. Swaziland	55	55
393	20c. Nicaragua	25	25
394	20c. Burma	25	25
395	20c. Cape Verde	25	25
396	20c. Guyana	25	25
397	20c. Belgium	25	25
398	20c. Nigeria	25	25

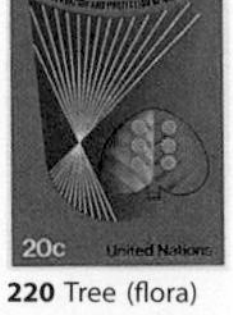

220 Tree (flora)

1982. Conservation and Protection of Nature. Multicoloured.

399	20c. Type **220**	35	35
400	28c. Butterfly (insects)	55	55

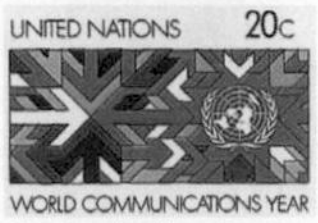

222 Interlocking Arrows

1983. World Communications Year. Multicoloured.

401	20c. Type **222**	25	25
402	40c. Cable network	75	75

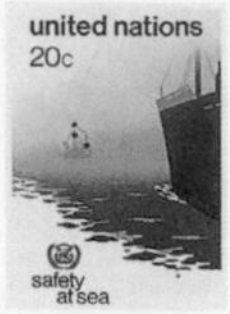

224 Ship and Buoy

1983. Safety at Sea: International Maritime Organization. Multicoloured.

403	20c. Type **224**	25	25
404	37c. Stylized liner	65	65

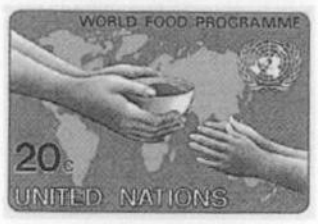

226 Giving Food

1983. World Food Programme.

405	**226**	20c. red	35	35

227 Coins and Cogwheels

1983. Trade and Development. Multicoloured.

406	20c. Type **227**	35	35
407	28c. Emblems of trade	55	55

1983. Flags of Member Nations (4th series). As T **203**. Multicoloured.

408	20c. United Kingdom	35	35
409	20c. Barbados	35	35
410	20c. Nepal	35	35
411	20c. Israel	35	35
412	20c. Malawi	35	35
413	20c. Byelorussian S.S.R.	35	35
414	20c. Jamaica	35	35
415	20c. Kenya	35	35
416	20c. China	35	35
417	20c. Peru	35	35
418	20c. Bulgaria	35	35
419	20c. Canada	35	35
420	20c. Somalia	35	35
421	20c. Senegal	35	35
422	20c. Brazil	35	35
423	20c. Sweden	35	35

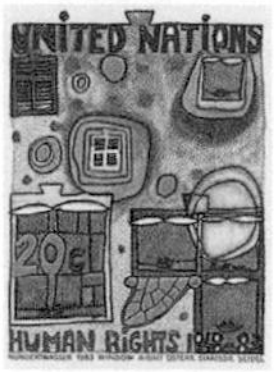

229 "Window Right"

1983. 35th Anniv of Declaration of Human Rights. Multicoloured.

424	20c. Type **229**	55	55
425	40c. "Treaty with Nature"	1·10	1·10

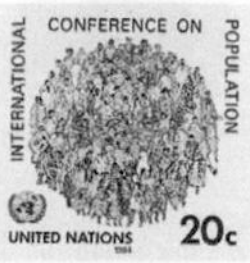

231 World Population

1984. International Conference on Population, Mexico.

426	**231**	20c. multicoloured	35	35
427	**231**	40c. multicoloured	75	75

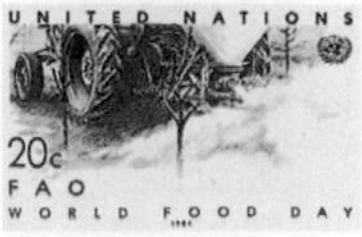

232 Fertilizing Crops

1984. World Food Day. Multicoloured.

428	20c. Type **232**	35	35
429	40c. Planting rice	75	75

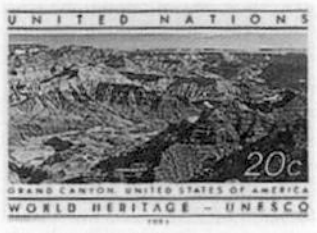

234 Grand Canyon, U.S.A

1984. World Heritage—U.N. Educational, Scientific and Cultural Organization. Multicoloured.

430		20c. Type **234**	35	35
431		50c. Polonnaruwa, Sri Lanka	90	90

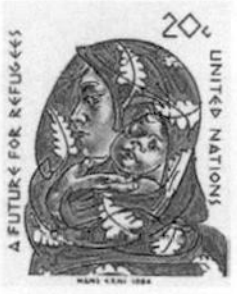

236 Mother with Baby

1984. Future for Refugees.

432	**236**	20c. brown and black	35	35
433	-	50c. black and blue	90	90

DESIGN: 50c. Mother with child.

1984. Flags of Member Nations (5th series). As T **203**. Multicoloured.

434	20c. Burundi	45	45
435	20c. Pakistan	45	45
436	20c. Benin	45	45
437	20c. Italy	45	45
438	20c. Poland	45	45
439	20c. Papua New Guinea	45	45
440	20c. Uruguay	45	45
441	20c. Chile	45	45
442	20c. Paraguay	45	45
443	20c. Bhutan	45	45
444	20c. Central African Republic	45	45
445	20c. Australia	45	45
446	20c. Tanzania	45	45
447	20c. United Arab Emirates	45	45
448	20c. Ecuador	45	45
449	20c. Bahamas	45	45

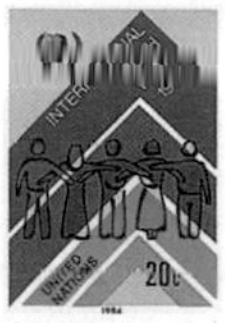

238 Emblem and Figures linking Arms

1984. International Youth Year.

450	**238**	20c. multicoloured	35	35
451	**238**	35c. multicoloured	75	75

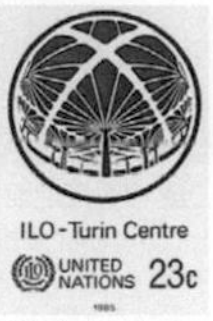

239 Turin Centre Emblem

1985. 20th Anniv of Turin Centre of International Labour Organization.

452	**239**	23c. blue	45	45

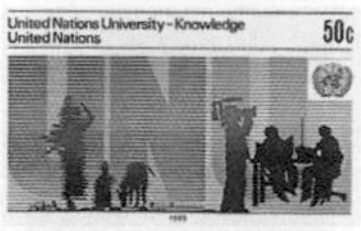

240 Farming and Mediums of Communication

1985. Tenth Anniv of United Nations University, Tokyo.

453	**240**	50c. multicoloured	1·10	1·10

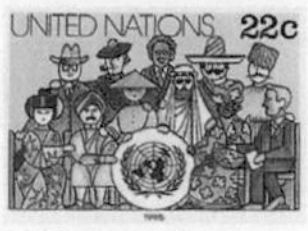

241 People of Various Nations

1985. Multicoloured.. Multicoloured..

454	22c. Type **241**	45	45
455	$3 Paintbrush and emblem	5·00	5·00

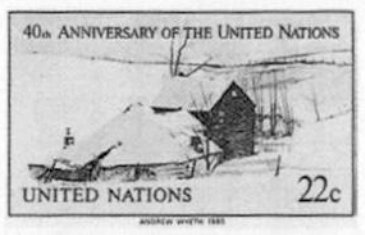

243 "Snow Scene" (Andrew Wyeth)

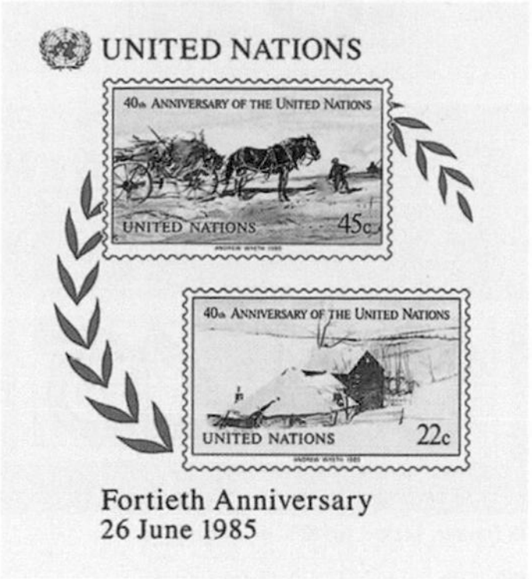

245

1985. 40th Anniv of U.N.O. Multicoloured.

456	22c. Type **243**	45	45
457	45c. "Harvest Scene" (Andrew Wyeth)	90	90

MS458 76×82 mm. **245** Nos. 456/7. Imperf 1·60 1·60

1985. Flags of Member Nations (6th series). As T **203**. Multicoloured.

459	22c. Grenada	45	45
460	22c. Federal Republic of Germany	45	45
461	22c. Saudi Arabia	45	45
462	22c. Mexico	45	45
463	22c. Liberia	45	45
464	22c. Mauritius	45	45
465	22c. Chad	45	45
466	22c. Dominican Republic	45	45
467	22c. Oman	45	45
468	22c. Ghana	45	45
469	22c. Sierra Leone	45	45
470	22c. Finland	45	45
471	22c. Uganda	45	45
472	22c. St. Thomas and Prince Islands	45	45
473	22c. U.S.S.R.	45	45
474	22c. India	45	45

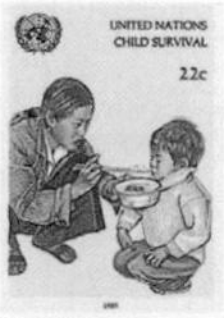

246 Woman feeding Child

1985. UNICEF Child Survival Campaign. Multicoloured.

475	32c. Type **246**	45	45
476	33c. Mother breast-feeding child	75	75

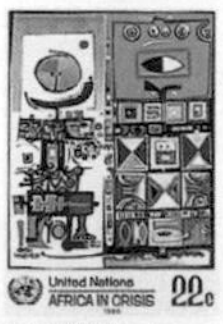

248 "Africa in Crisis"

1986. Africa in Crisis.

477	**248**	22c. multicoloured	55	55

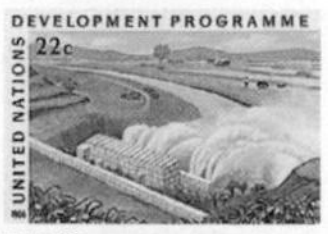

249 Dam

1986. Development Programme. Water Resources. Multicoloured.

478	22c. Type **249**	1·40	1·40
479	22c. Working in the fields	1·40	1·40
480	22c. Girls at waterhole	1·40	1·40
481	22c. Women at well	1·40	1·40

Nos. 478/81 were printed together, se-tenant, forming a composite design.

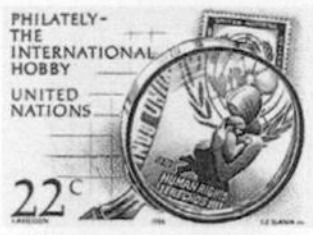

253 Magnifying Glass and Stamp

1986. Philately: The International Hobby.

482	**253**	22c. lilac and blue	55	55
483	-	44c. brown and green	90	90

DESIGN: 44c. Engraver.

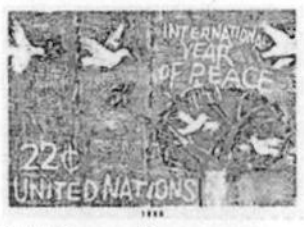

255 Peace Doves

1986. International Peace Year.

484	**255**	22c. multicoloured	45	45
485	-	33c. multicoloured	90	90

DESIGN: 33c. Words for "Peace" around U.N. emblem.

1986. Flags of Member Nations (7th series). As T **203**. Multicoloured.

486	22c. New Zealand	55	55
487	22c. Laos	55	55
488	22c. Burkina Faso	55	55
489	22c. Gambia	55	55
490	22c. Maldives	55	55
491	22c. Ethiopia	55	55
492	22c. Jordan	55	55
493	22c. Zambia	55	55
494	22c. Iceland	55	55
495	22c. Antigua and Barbuda	55	55
496	22c. Angola	55	55
497	22c. Botswana	55	55
498	22c. Rumania	55	55
499	22c. Togo	55	55
500	22c. Mauritania	55	55
501	22c. Colombia	55	55

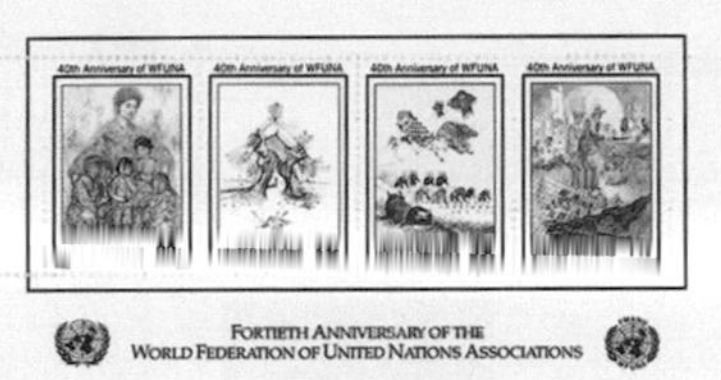

257 (image scaled to 40% of original size)

1986. 40th Anniv of World Federation of United Nations Associations. Sheets 120×65 mm. Multicoloured.

MS502 22c. Woman and children (Edna Hibel); 33c. Clasped hands (Slavador Dali); 39c. Kites, people planting and oxen (Don Kingman); 44c. Refugees (Chaim Gross) 4·00 4·00

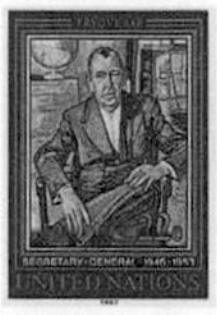

258 Trygve Lie (after Harald Dal)

1987. Ninth Death Anniv of Trygve Lie (first U.N. Secretary-General).

503	**258**	22c. multicoloured	55	55

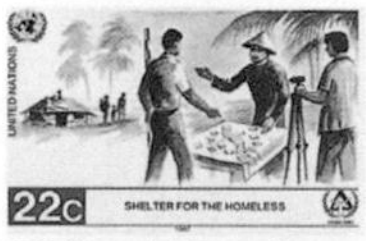

259 Men with Surveying Equipment and Blueprints

1987. International Year of Shelter for the Homeless.

504	**259**	22c. deep brown, brown and black	55	55
505	-	44c. multicoloured	1·10	1·10

DESIGN: 44c. Cutting bamboo.

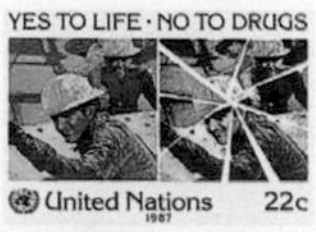

261 Construction Workers

1987. Anti-drugs Campaign. Multicoloured.

506	22c. Type **261**	55	55
507	33c. University graduates	80	80

1987. Flags of Member Nations (8th series). As T **203**. Multicoloured.

508	22c. Comoros	55	55
509	22c. People's Democratic Republic of Yemen	55	55
510	22c. Mongolia	55	55
511	22c. Vanuatu	55	55
512	22c. Japan	55	55
513	22c. Gabon	55	55
514	22c. Zimbabwe	55	55
515	22c. Iraq	55	55
516	22c. Argentina	55	55
517	22c. Congo	55	55
518	22c. Niger	55	55
519	22c. St. Lucia	55	55
520	22c. Bahrain	55	55
521	22c. Haiti	55	55
522	22c. Afghanistan	55	55
523	22c. Greece	55	55

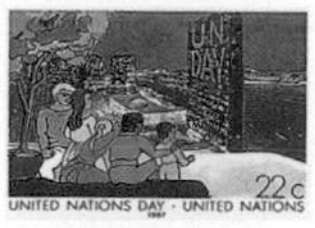

263 Family and U.N. Building, New York

1987. United Nations Day. Multicoloured.

524	22c. Type **263**	55	55
525	39c. Dancers	80	80

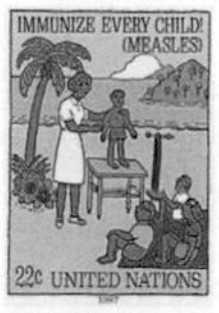

265 Measles

1987. "Immunize Every Child". Multicoloured.

526	22c. Type **265**	75	75
527	44c. Tetanus	1·40	1·40

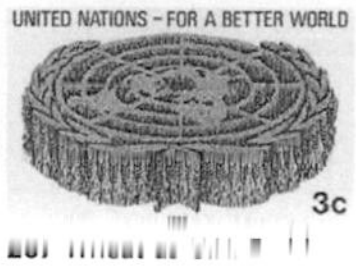

1988. "For a Better World".

528	**267**	3c. yellow, brown and black	20	20

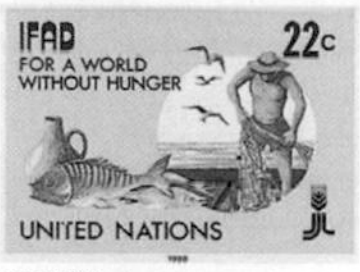

268 Fisherman

1988. International Fund for Agricultural Development "For a World Without Hunger" Campaign. Multicoloured.

529	22c. Type **268**	55	55
530	33c. Farmers ploughing with oxen	1·10	1·10

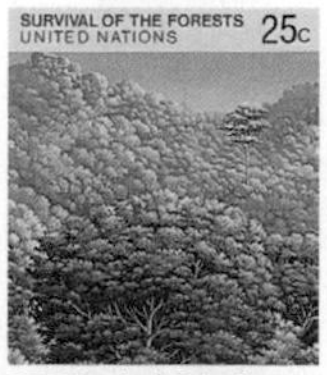

270 Tropical Rain Forest Canopy

1988. "Survival of the Forests". Multicoloured.

531	25c. Type **270**	1·40	1·40
532	44c. Tropical rain forest floor	2·75	2·75

Nos. 531/2 were printed together, *se-tenant*, forming a composite design.

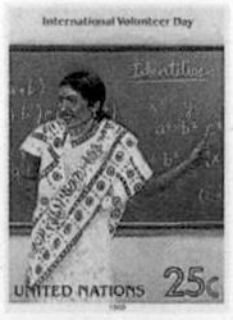

272 Teacher at Blackboard

1988. International Volunteer Day. Multicoloured.

533	25c. Type **272**	55	55
534	50c. Teaching basketry (horiz)	90	90

274 Cycling

1988. "Health in Sports". Multicoloured.

535	25c. Type **274**	45	45
536	38c. Marathon (horiz)	1·00	1·00

1988. Flags of Member Nations (9th series). As T **203**. Multicoloured.

537	25c. Spain	55	55
538	25c. St. Vincent and Grenadines	55	55
539	25c. Ivory Coast	55	55
540	25c. Lebanon	55	55
541	25c. Yemen	55	55
542	25c. Cuba	55	55
543	25c. Denmark	55	55
544	25c. Libya	55	55
545	25c. Qatar	55	55
546	25c. Zaire	55	55
547	25c. Norway	55	55
548	25c. German Democratic Republic	55	55
549	25c. Iran	55	55
550	25c. Tunisia	55	55
551	25c. Samoa	55	55
552	25c. Belize	55	55

276 Flame

277 (image scaled to 40% of original size)

1988. 40th Anniv of Declaration of Human Rights.

553	**276**	25c. multicoloured	45	45
MS554 120×79 mm. **277** $1 multicoloured			1·80	1·80

278 Electricity Production

1989. World Bank. Multicoloured.

555	25c. Type **278**	75	75
556	45c. Planting rice	1·30	1·30

280 "Blue Helmet" Soldier

1989. Award of Nobel Peace Prize to United Nations Peace-keeping Forces.

557	**280**	25c. multicoloured	75	75

281 U.N. Headquarters, New York

1989

558	**281**	45c. multicoloured	90	90

282 Satellite Image of Storm over Chesapeake Bay Area

1989. 25th Anniv of World Weather Watch. Multicoloured.

559	25c. Type **282**	90	90
560	36c. Typhoon Abby approaching China	1·80	1·80

284 Band

1989. Tenth Anniv of United Nations Vienna International Centre. Multicoloured.

561	25c. Type **284**	2·30	2·30
562	90c. Mountain and butterfly as tree	1·40	1·40

1989. Flags of Member Nations (10th series). As T **203**. Multicoloured.

563	25c. Indonesia	55	55
564	25c. Lesotho	55	55
565	25c. Guatemala	55	55
566	25c. Netherlands	55	55
567	25c. Algeria	55	55
568	25c. Brunei	55	55
569	25c. St. Kitts and Nevis	55	55
570	25c. United Nations	55	55
571	25c. Honduras	55	55
572	25c. Kampuchea	55	55
573	25c. Guinea-Bissau	55	55
574	25c. Cyprus	55	55
575	25c. South Africa	55	55
576	25c. Portugal	55	55
577	25c. Morocco	55	55
578	25c. Syria	55	55

286 "Table of Universal Brotherhood" (Jose Clemente Orozco) (Article 1)

1989. Declaration of Human Rights (1st series). Multicoloured.

579	25c. Type **286**	35	35
580	45c. "Composition II" (V. Kandinsky) (Article 2)	75	75

See also Nos. 592/3, 609/10, 626/7 and 637/8.

288 Port Activities

1990. International Trade Centre.

581	**288**	25c. multicoloured	1·40	1·40

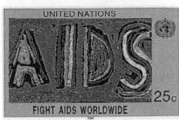

289 "AIDS"

1990. Anti-AIDS Campaign. Multicoloured.

582	25c. Type **289**	65	65
583	40c. Group at risk	1·00	1·00

291 Madagascar Periwinkle

1990. Medicinal Plants. Multicoloured.

584	25c. Type **291**	45	45
585	90c. American ginseng	1·80	1·80

293 Ribbons forming "45"

295 (image scaled to 48% of original size)

1990. 45th Anniv of U.N.O. Multicoloured.

586	25c. Type **293**	90	90
587	45c. "45" and U.N. Emblem	2·30	2·30
MS588 100×73 mm. **295** Nos. 586/7		5·00	5·00

296 Youth waylaying Elderly Man

1990. Crime Prevention. Multicoloured.

590	25c. Type **296**	90	90
591	36c. Burglars leaving burning building	1·80	1·80

1990. Universal Declaration of Human Rights (2nd series). As T **286**. Multicoloured.

592	25c. Sarcophagus of Plotinus (detail) (Article 7)	40	40
593	45c. "Combined Chambers of High Court of Appeal" (Charles Paul Renouard, from "The Dreyfus Case") (Article 8)	80	80

300/303 Alpine Lake and Wildlife

1991. Economic Commission for Europe. "For a Better Environment".

594	**300**	30c. multicoloured	1·00	1·00
595	**301**	30c. multicoloured	1·00	1·00
596	**302**	30c. multicoloured	1·00	1·00
597	**303**	30c. multicoloured	1·00	1·00

Nos. 594/7 were printed together, *se-tenant*, forming the composite design illustrated.

304 Desert

1991. First Anniv of Namibian Independence. Multicoloured.

598	30c. Type **304**	75	75
599	50c. Open grassland	1·40	1·40

306 U.N. Building

1991

600	**306**	$2 blue	3·25	2·75

307 Children around Globe (Nicole Delia Legnani)

1991. 30th Anniv (1989) of U.N. Declaration on the Rights of the Child and 1990 World Summit on Children, New York. Children's Drawings. Multicoloured.

601	30c. Type **307**	90	90
602	70c. Dove, rainbow and houses (Alissa Duffy)	1·80	1·80

309 Bubbles of Toxin approaching City

1991. Banning of Chemical Weapons. Multicoloured.

603	30c. Type **309**	90	90
604	90c. Hand pushing back barrels of toxins	2·75	2·75

311 U.N. Flag

1991. Multicoloured.. Multicoloured..

605	30c. Type **311**	65	65
606	50c. "The Golden Rule" (mosaic, Norman Rockwell) (vert)	1·60	1·60

313 1951 1c. Stamp

1991. 40th Anniv of United Nations Postal Administration.

607	**313**	30c. red on cream	80	80
608	-	40c. purple on cream	1·20	1·20

DESIGN: 40c. 1951 2c. stamp.

1991. Declaration of Human Rights (3rd series). As T **286**. Multicoloured.

609	30c. "The Last of England" (Ford Maddox Brown) (Article 13)	45	45
610	50c. "The Emigration to the East" (Tito Salas) (Article 14)	1·00	1·00

317 Uluru National Park, Australia

1992. 20th Anniv of UNESCO World Heritage Convention. Multicoloured.

611	30c. Type **317**	90	90
612	50c. Great Wall of China	1·10	1·10

319/320 Sea Life

1992. "Clean Oceans".

613	**319**	29c. multicoloured	60	60
614	**320**	29c. multicoloured	60	60

Nos. 613/14 were issued together, *se-tenant*, forming the composite design illustrated.

321/324 Planet Earth

1992. Second U.N. Conference on Environment and Development, Rio de Janeiro.

615	**321**	29c. multicoloured	60	60
616	**322**	29c. multicoloured	60	60
617	**323**	29c. multicoloured	60	60
618	**324**	29c. multicoloured	60	60

Nos. 615/18 were issued together, se-tenant, forming the composite design illustrated.

325/326 "Mission Planet Earth"

1992. International Space Year. Roul.

619	**325**	29c. multicoloured	2·30	2·30
620	**326**	29c. multicoloured	2·30	2·30

Nos. 619/20 were issued together, se-tenant, forming the composite design illustrated.

327 Winged Man with V.D.U.

1992. Commission on Science and Technology for Development Multicoloured.

621		29c. Type **327**	45	45
622		50c. Man sitting in crocodile's mouth	1·10	1·10

329 Aerial View of Building

1992. United Nations University, Tokyo. Multicoloured.

623		4c. Type **329**	20	20
624		40c. Front elevation of building	75	75

331 U.N. Headquarters, New York

1992.

625	**331**	29c. multicoloured	55	55

1992. Universal Declaration of Human Rights (4th series). As T **286**. Multicoloured.

626		29c. "Lady writing a letter with her Maid" (Johannes Vermeer) (Article 19)	65	65
627		50c. "The Meeting"(Ester Almqvist) (Article 20)	90	90

334 Family Life

1993. "Ageing: Dignity and Participation". Tenth Anniv (1992) of International Plan of Action on Ageing. Multicoloured.

628		29c. Type **334**	75	75
629		52c. Health and nutrition	1·50	1·50

336 Queensland Hairy-nosed Wombat

1993. Endangered Species (1st series). Multicoloured.

630		29c. Type **336**	55	55
631		29c. Whooping crane ("Grus americana")	55	55
632		29c. Giant clams ("Tridacnidae")	55	55
633		29c. Sable antelope ("Hippotragus niger")	55	55

See also Nos. 649/52, 667/70, 694/7, 720/3, 755/8, 803/6, 819/22, 841/4, 875/8, 905/8, 921/4 and 966/9.

340 "United Nations"

1993.

634	**340**	5c. multicoloured	20	20

341 Personal Environment

1993. 45th Anniv of W.H.O. Multicoloured.

635		29c. Type **341**	65	65
636		50c. Family environment	1·10	1·10

1993. Declaration of Human Rights (5th series). As T **286**. Multicoloured.

637		29c. "Shocking Corn" (Thomas Hart Benton) (Article 25)	55	55
638		35c. "The Library" (Jacob Lawrence) (Article 26)	80	80

345/348 Peace

1993. International Peace Day. Roul.

639	**345**	29c. multicoloured	1·60	1·60
640	**346**	29c. multicoloured	1·60	1·60
641	**347**	29c. multicoloured	1·60	1·60
642	**348**	29c. multicoloured	1·60	1·60

Nos. 639/42 were issued together, se-tenant, forming the composite design illustrated.

349 Chameleon

1993. The Environment—Climate. Multicoloured.

643		29c. Type **349**	75	75
644		29c. Storm	75	75
645		29c. Antelopes fleeing from flood	75	75
646		29c. Lesser bird of paradise	75	75

Nos. 643/6 were issued together, se-tenant, forming a composite design.

353 Equality across Generations

1994. Int Year of the Family. Multicoloured.

647		29c. Type **353**	90	90
648		45c. Poor family	1·40	1·40

1994. Endangered Species (2nd series). As T **336**. Multicoloured.

649		29c. Chimpanzees ("Pan troglodytes")	75	75
650		29c. St. Lucia amazon ("Amazona versicolor")	75	75
651		29c. American crocodile ("Crocodylus acutus")	75	75
652		29c. Addra gazelles ("Gazelle dama")	75	75

359 "Dove of Peace" (mosaic)

1994

653	**359**	10c. multicoloured	20	20
654	-	19c. multicoloured	35	35
655	-	$1 brown	2·30	2·30

DESIGNS: 19c. "Sleeping Child" (stained-glass window after drawing by Stanislaw Wyspianski); $1 "Mourning Owl" (Vanessa Isitt).

362 Refugee crossing Bridge of Hands

1994. United Nations High Commissioner for Refugees.

656	**362**	50c. multicoloured	1·30	1·30

363/366 Shattered Globe and "Warning"

1994. International Decade for Natural Disaster Reduction.

657	**363**	29c. multicoloured	1·40	1·40
658	**364**	29c. multicoloured	1·40	1·40
659	**365**	29c. multicoloured	1·40	1·40
660	**366**	29c. multicoloured	1·40	1·40

Nos. 657/60 were issued together, se-tenant, forming the composite design illustrated.

367 Children Playing (health and family planning)

1994. International Population and Development Conference, Cairo. Multicoloured.

661		29c. Type **367**	45	45
662		52c. Family unit (demographic changes)	1·40	1·40

369 Map and Looped Ribbon

1994. 30th Anniv of United Nations Conference on Trade and Development. Multicoloured.

663		29c. Type **369**	45	45
664		50c. Map and coiled ribbon	1·30	1·30

371 Anniversary Emblem

1995. 50th Anniv of U.N.O. (1st issue).

665	**371**	32c. multicoloured	1·00	1·00

See also Nos. 673/4 and 679/90.

372 "Social Summit 1995"

1995. World Summit for Social Development, Copenhagen.

666	**372**	50c. multicoloured	1·40	1·40

1995. Endangered Species (3rd series). As T **336**. Multicoloured.

667		32c. Giant armadillo ("Priodontes maximus")	75	75
668		32c. American bald eagle ("Haliaeetus leucocephalus")	75	75
669		32c. Fijian banded iguana ("Brachylophus fasciatus")	75	75
670		32c. Giant panda ("Ailuropoda melanoleuca")	75	75

377 Man looking out to Sea

1995. "Youth: Our Future". 10th Anniv of International Youth Year. Multicoloured.

671		32c. Type **377**	75	75
672		55c. Family cycling	1·20	1·20

379 Signing U.N. Charter

381 (image scaled to 52% of original size)

1995. 50th Anniv of U.N.O. (2nd issue).

673	**379**	32c. black	75	75
674	-	50c. purple	1·40	1·40
MS675	92×70 mm. **381** Nos. 673/4. Imperf		2·50	2·50

DESIGN: 50c. Veterans' Memorial Hall and Opera House, San Francisco (venue for signing of Charter).

382 Mother and Child

1995. Fourth World Conference on Women, Peking.

676		32c. Type **382**	75	75
677		40c. Harpist and cranes	90	90

384 U.N. Headquarters, New York

1995.

678	**384**	20c. multicoloured	45	45

385/387

388/390

391/393

394/396

1995. 50th Anniv of U.N.O. (3rd issue).

679	**385**	32c. multicoloured	90	90
680	**386**	32c. multicoloured	90	90
681	**387**	32c. multicoloured	90	90
682	**388**	32c. multicoloured	90	90
683	**389**	32c. multicoloured	90	90
684	**390**	32c. multicoloured	90	90
685	**391**	32c. multicoloured	90	90
686	**392**	32c. multicoloured	90	90
687	**393**	32c. multicoloured	90	90
688	**394**	32c. multicoloured	90	90
689	**395**	32c. multicoloured	90	90
690	**396**	32c. multicoloured	90	90

Nos. 679/81 and 682/4 form the left and right halves respectively of a composite design, and Nos. 685/7 and 688/90 another composite design.

397 Rainbow and Faces within "Sun"

1996. 50th Anniv of World Federation of United Nations Associations.

691	**397**	32c. multicoloured	55	55

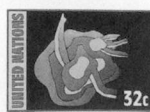

398 Mural

1996. Murals by Fernand Leger in General Assembly, U.N. Headquarters. Multicoloured.

692	32c. Type **398**	55	55
693	60c. Mural (different)	1·40	1·40

1996. Endangered Species (4th series). As T **336**. Multicoloured.

694	32c. "Masdevallia veitchiana"	75	75

695	32c. Saguaro ("Carnegiea gigantea")	75	75
696	32c. West Australian pitcher plant ("Cephalotus follicularis")	75	75
697	32c. "Encephalartos horridus"	75	75

404 Deer under Tree

1996. "Habitat II" Second United Nations Conference on Human Settlements, Istanbul, Turkey. Multicoloured.

698	32c. Type **404**	80	80
699	32c. City and countryside	80	80
700	32c. Walking in city park	80	80
701	32c. City and village	80	80
702	32c. Village and parrot	80	80

Nos. 698/702 were issued together, se-tenant, forming a composite design.

409 Basketball

411 (image scaled to 55% of original size)

1996. Sport and the Environment. Multicoloured.

703	32c. Type **409**	75	75
704	50c. Volleyball	1·40	1·40
MS705	88×78 mm. **411** Nos. 703/4	2·30	2·30

412 Two Birds

1996. "A Plea for Peace". Winners of China Youth Design Competition. Multicoloured.

706	32c. Type **412**	55	55
707	60c. Peace dove	1·10	1·10

414 "Yeh-Shen" (Chinese tale)

1996. 50th Anniv of UNICEF. Children's Stories.

708	32c. Type **414**	55	55
709	60c. "The Ugly Duckling" (Hans Christian Andersen)	1·10	1·10

1997. Flags of Member Nations (11th series). As T **203**. Multicoloured.

710	32c. Liechtenstein	75	75
711	32c. Republic of Korea	75	75
712	32c. Kazakhstan	75	75
713	32c. Latvia	75	75
714	32c. Tajikistan	75	75
715	32c. Georgia	75	75
716	32c. Armenia	75	75
717	32c. Namibia	75	75

416 Cherry Tree

1997. Multicoloured.

718	8c. Type **416**	35	35
719	55c. Rose "Peace" (horiz)	90	90

1997. Endangered Species (5th series). As T **336**. Multicoloured.

720	32c. African elephant ("Loxodonta africana")	55	55
721	32c. Major Mitchell's cockatoo ("Cacatua leadbeateri")	55	55
722	32c. Black-footed ferret ("Mustela nigripes")	55	55
723	32c. Puma ("Felis concolor")	55	55

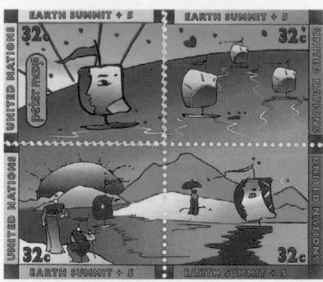

422/425 Ocean Scene

426 (image scaled to 54% of original size)

1997. "Earth Summit + 5". Fifth Anniv of United Nations Conference on Environment and Development.

724	**422**	32c. multicoloured	85	85
725	**423**	32c. multicoloured	85	85
726	**424**	32c. multicoloured	85	85
727	**425**	32c. multicoloured	85	85
MS728	Two sheets, each 90×75 mm. (a) **426** $1 multicoloured. Imperf; (b) No. **MS**728a optd for "Pacific 97" in bottom margin		13·00	13·00

Nos. 724/7 were issued together, se-tenant, forming the composite design illustrated.

427 Clipper

1997. 50th Anniversaries of Economic Commission for Europe and Economic and Social Commission for Asia and the Pacific. Multicoloured.

729	32c. Type **427**	1·20	1·20
730	32c. Sail/steam ship	1·20	1·20
731	32c. Liner	1·20	1·20
732	32c. Hovercraft	1·20	1·20
733	32c. Hydrofoil	1·20	1·20

Nos. 729/33 were issued together, se-tenant, forming a composite design.

432 1986 22c. Philately Stamp

1997. "Tribute to Philately". Multicoloured.

734	32c. Type **432**	1·00	1·00
735	50c. 1986 44c. Philately stamp	1·90	1·90

434 Kneeling Warrior

1997. 25th Anniv of World Heritage Convention. Terracotta Warriors from Emperor Qin Shi Huang's Tomb, Xian, China. Multicoloured.

736	8c. Type **434**	55	55
737	8c. Ranks of armoured warriors	55	55
738	8c. Head	55	55
739	8c. Group in wrap-over tunics	55	55
740	8c. Head and shoulders	55	55
741	8c. Group in armour	55	55
742	32c. Type **434**	80	80
743	60c. As No. 737	1·60	1·60

1998. Flags of Member Nations (12th series). As T **203**.

744	32c. blue, grey and black	85	85
745	32c. multicoloured	85	85
746	32c. multicoloured	85	85
747	32c. multicoloured	85	85
748	32c. multicoloured	85	85
749	32c. red, grey and black	85	85
750	32c. multicoloured	85	85
751	32c. black, blue and grey	85	85

FLAGS: No. 744, Micronesia; 745, Slovakia; 746, Democratic People's Republic of Korea; 747, Azerbaijan; 748, Uzbekistan; 749, Monaco; 750, Czech Republic; 751, Estonia.

440 Boy holding Dove

1998. Multicoloured.. Multicoloured..

752	1c. Type **440**	10	10
753	2c. Birds	10	10
754	21c. Dancing around U.N. emblem (vert)	35	35

1998. Endangered Species (6th series). As T **366**. Multicoloured.

755	32c. Lesser bushbaby ("Galago senegalensis")	65	65
756	32c. Hawaiian goose ("Branta sandvicensis")	65	65
757	32c. Golden birdwing ("Troides aeacus")	65	65
758	32c. Sun bear ("Helarctos malayanus")	65	65

447 Turtles

1998. International Year of the Ocean. Multicoloured.

759	32c. Type **447**	65	65
760	32c. Rays	65	65
761	32c. Sunfishes	65	65
762	32c. Head of whale	65	65
763	32c. Dugongs	65	65
764	32c. Striped fishes	65	65
765	32c. Dolphin (fish) and orca	65	65
766	32c. Jellyfish and seahorse	65	65
767	32c. Sealions, seahorse and fishes	65	65
768	32c. Dolphins, octopus and diver's head	65	65
769	32c. Submersible	65	65
770	32c. Sharks	65	65

448 Jaguar

449 (image scaled to 59% of original size)

1998. Rainforest Preservation.

771	**448**	32c. multicoloured	65	65
MS772	82×70 mm. **449** $2 multicoloured		4·25	4·25

450 Soldier holding
Binoculars

1998. 50 Years of United Nations Peacekeeping.
Multicoloured.

773	33c. Type **450**	65	65
774	40c. Soldiers sitting on tank	85	85

452 Man carrying
Flag

1998. 50th Anniv of Universal Declaration of Human
Rights. Multicoloured.

775	32c. Type **452**	75	75
776	55c. Walking pens	1·20	1·20

454 Blue and White
Vase (Mirror Room)

1998. World Heritage Site. Schonbrunn Palace, Vienna.
Multicoloured.

777	11c. Type **454**	45	45
778	11c. Detail of wall hanging (Johann Wenzl Bergl)	45	45
779	11c. Porcelain stove	45	45
780	16c. Palace facade (horiz)	55	55
781	15c. Great Palm House (horiz)	55	55
782	15c. Gloriette (horiz)	55	55
783	33c. As No. 782	65	65
784	60c. As No. 778	1·30	1·30

1999. Flags of Member Nations (13th series). As T **203**.
Multicoloured.

785	33c. Lithuania	75	75
786	33c. San Marino	75	75
787	33c. Turkmenistan	75	75
788	33c. Marshall Islands	75	75
789	33c. Moldova	75	75
790	33c. Kyrgyzstan	75	75
791	33c. Bosnia and Herzegovina	75	75
792	33c. Eritrea	75	75

460 Man putting
Banner of Flags
around Globe

1999. Multicoloured.. Multicoloured..

793	33c. Type **460**	85	85
794	$5 Roses	8·75	8·75

462 Tasmanian Wilderness

1999. World Heritage Sites in Australia. Multicoloured.

795	5c. Type **462**	25	25
796	5c. Wet Tropics, Queensland	25	25
797	5c. Great Barrier Reef	25	25
798	15c. Uluru-Kata Tjuta National Park	65	65
799	15c. Kakadu National Park	65	65
800	15c. Willandra Lakes Region	65	65
801	33c. As No. 800	65	65
802	60c. As No. 796	1·50	1·50

1999. Endangered Species (7th series). As T **336**.
Multicoloured.

803	33c. Tiger ("Panthera tigris")	65	65

804	33c. Secretary bird ("Sagittarius serpentarius")	65	65
805	33c. Green tree python ("Chondropython viridis")	65	65
806	33c. Long-tailed chinchilla ("Chinchilla lanigera")	65	65

472/473 International Planetary Exploration

474 (image scaled to 54% of original size)

1999. Third Conference on Exploration and Peaceful Uses
of Outer Space, Vienna.

807	**472**	33c. multicoloured	85	85
808	**473**	33c. multicoloured	85	85
MS809	90×75 mm. **474** $2 multicoloured		4·25	4·25

Nos. 807/8 were issued together, *se-tenant*, forming
the composite design illustrated.

475/478 19th-century Mail Transport

1999. 125th Anniv of Universal Postal Union.

810	**475**	33c. multicoloured	75	75
811	**476**	33c. multicoloured	75	75
812	**477**	33c. multicoloured	75	75
813	**478**	33c. multicoloured	75	75

Nos. 810/13 were issued together, *se-tenant*, forming
the composite design illustrated.

479 U.N.
Headquarters, New
York

480 (image scaled to 54% of original size)

1999. "In Memoriam: Fallen in the Cause of Peace".

814	**479**	37c. multicoloured	1·10	1·10
MS815	90×75 mm. **480** $1 multicoloured		2·75	2·75

481 Couple with Books

1999. Education: Keystone to the 21st Century.
Multicoloured.

816	33c. Type **481**	75	75
817	60c. Heart and open book	1·40	1·40

483 Glory Window
(Gabrielle Loire),
Chapel of
Thanksgiving, Dallas

2000. International Year of Thanksgiving.

818	**483** 33c. multicoloured	85	85

2000. Endangered Species (8th series). As T **336**.
Multicoloured.

819	33c. Brown bear (*Ursus arctos*)	85	85
820	33c. Black-bellied bustard (*Lissotis melanogaster*)	85	85
821	33c. Chinese crocodile lizard (*Shinisaurus crocodilurus*)	85	85
822	33c. Pygmy chimpanzee (*Pan paniscis*)	85	85

488 "Crawling Toward the
Millennium" (Sam Yeates)

2000. "Our World 2000" International Art Exhibition, New
York. Entries in Millennium Painting Competition.
Multicoloured.

823	33c.	75	75
824	60c. "Crossing" (Masakazu Takahata) (vert)	1·50	1·50

2000. "Anaheim 2000" International Stamp Exhibition,
California. No. MS809 optd **WORLD STAMP EXPO
2000 ANAHEIM, CALIFORNIA U.S.A. 7 – 16 JULY
2000** in the margin.

MS825	90×75 mm. **474** $2 multicoloured	7·75	7·75

491 Auditorium,
General Assembly
Building, 1956

2000. 55th Anniv of the United Nations and 50th Anniv
of Opening of U.N. Headquarters, New York.

826	**491** 33c. blue, green and ochre	75	75
827	- 55c. blue, green and ochre	1·40	1·40
MS828	67×86 mm. Nos. 826/7	2·40	2·40

DESIGN: 55c. Headquarters, 1951.

493 Globe, Sun and
Olympic Rings (Mateja
Prunk)

2000. Winning Entry in "International Flag of Peace"
Children's Design Competition.

829	**493** 33c. multicoloured	75	75

494 Workers in Rice Field

495 (image scaled to 34% of original size)

2000. "The United Nations in the 21st Century". Sheet
141×161 containing T **494** and similar horiz designs,
forming the overall design T **495**. Multicoloured.

MS830 33c. Type **494**; 33c. Loading
Machinery and supplies; 33c. Posting
votes; 33. Mother holding child
receiving vaccination; 33c. Sack
of grain and women using water
pump. 33c. Men building house   6·00   6·00

496 Granada

2000. World Heritage Sites in Spain. Multicoloured.

831	5c. Type **496**	35	35
832	5c. Cliff-top Houses, Cuence	35	35
833	5c. Roman Aqueduct, Segovia	35	35
834	15c. Archaeological Site, Merida	55	55
835	15c. Toledo	55	55
836	15c. Guell Park, Barcelona	55	55
837	33c. As No. 831	65	65
838	60c. As No. 834	1·50	1·50

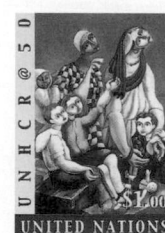

502 Family of Refugees

503 (image scaled to 40% of original size)

2000. 50th Anniv of United Nations High Commissioner
for Refugees.

839	**502** 33c. multicoloured	85	85
MS840	121×82 mm. **503** $1 multicoloured	2·75	2·75

2001. Endangered Species (9th series). As T **336**.
Multicoloured.

841	34c. Spotted phalanger (*Phalanger maculatus*)	85	85
842	34c. Resplendent quetzal (*Pharomachrus mocinno*)	85	85
843	34c. Gila monster (*Heloderma suspectum*)	85	85
844	34c. Eastern black and white colobus (*Colobus guereza*)	85	85

508 Landscape and Silhouette (Jose Zaragoza)

2001. United Nations International Year of Volunteers. Multicoloured.

845		34c. Type **508**	1·10	1·10
846		80c. Piano keys, hands and music score (John Terry)	2·20	2·20

510 Sunflower

2001. Multicoloured.

847		7c. Type **510**	20	20
848		34c. Rose	85	85

2001. Flags of Member Nations (14th series). As T **203**. Multicoloured.

849		34c. Slovenia	85	85
850		34c. Palau	85	85
851		34c. Tonga	85	85
852		34c. Croatia	85	85
853		34c. Macedonia	85	85
854		34c. Kiribati	85	85
855		34c. Andorra	85	85
856		34c. Nauru	85	85

512 Pagoda, Kyoto

2001. World Heritage Sites in Japan. Multicoloured.

857		5c. Type **512**	20	20
858		5c. Imperial Palace, Nara	20	20
859		5c. Himeji Castle	20	20
860		20c. Shirakawa-go and Gokayama Villages	65	65
861		20c. Itsukushima Shinto Shrine	65	65
862		20c. Temple, Nikko	65	65
863		34c. As No. 857	85	85
864		70c. As No. 860	1·90	1·90

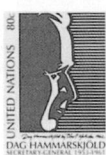

518 Hammarskjold

2001. 40th Death Anniv of Dag Hammarskjold (United Nations Secretary General, 1953–61).

865	**518**	80c. blue	2·20	2·20

519 "Stamps" and Ribbons

2001. 50th Anniv of United Nations Postal Administration.

866	**519**	34c. multicoloured	85	85
867		80c. multicoloured	2·20	2·20
MS868		102×102 mm. $1 ×2, cobalt and blue	5·50	5·50

DESIGNS: 80c. Presents; $1 Emblem.

522 Landscape, Butterfly and Goose

2001. Climate Change. Multicoloured.

869		34c. Type **522**	1·00	1·00
870		34c. Penguin and tomato plant	1·00	1·00
871		34c. Palm tree and solar panel	1·00	1·00
872		34c. Hand planting sapling	1·00	1·00

Nos. 869/72 were issued together, *se-tenant*, forming a composite design.

526 United Nations Flag

2001. Kofi Annan, Winner of Nobel Peace Prize, 2001.

873	**526**	34c. multicoloured	1·10	1·10

527 Children carrying Stamps

2002

874	**527**	80c. multicoloured	2·00	2·00

2002. Endangered Species (10th series). As T **336**. Multicoloured.

875		34c. Hoffmann's two-toed sloth (*Choloepus hoffmanni*)	1·00	1·00
876		34c. American bighorn (*Ovis canadensis*)	1·00	1·00
877		34c. Cheetah (*Acinonyx jubatus*)	1·00	1·00
878		34c. San Esteban Island chuck-walla (*Sauromalus varius*)	1·00	1·00

532 Wooden Mask, Dili

2002. East Timor Independence. Multicoloured.

879		34c. Type **532**	85	85
880		57c. Traditional wooden door panels	1·50	1·50

534 Khan-Tengri, Kyrgyzstan

2002. International Year of Mountains. Multicoloured.

881		34c. Type **534**	85	85
882		34c. Kilimanjaro, Tanzania	85	85
883		80c. Mt. Foraker, U.S.A	1·90	1·90
884		80c. Paine Grande, Chile	1·90	1·90

538 Sun, Earth and Planets

2002. World Summit on Sustainable Development, Johannesburg. Multicoloured.

885		37c. Type **538**	85	85
886		37c. Women's profile	85	85
887		60c. Yacht	1·30	1·30
888		60c. Figures wearing fashionable dress	1·30	1·30

542 Duomo di Sant'Andrea, Amalfi Coast

2002. World Heritage Sites in Italy. Multicoloured.

889		5c. Type **542**	20	20

890		5c. View across Islands, Aeolian Islands	20	20
891		5c. Del Moro Fountain, Rome	20	20
892		15c. Santa Maria del Fiore, Florence	55	55
893		15c. Leaning Tower, Pisa	55	55
894		15c. The Forum, Pompeii	55	55
895		37c. As No. 892	1·00	1·00
896		70c. As No. 889	1·70	1·70

548 AIDS Symbol on U.N. Secretariat Building, New York

549 (image scaled to 60% of original size)

2002. AIDS Awareness Campaign. Multicoloured.

897		70c. Type **548**	1·90	1·90
MS898		80×80 mm. 37c.+6c. **549**	2·00	2·00

The premium was for AIDS charities.

550 Artefacts (image scaled to 40% of original size)

2003. Indigenous Art (1st series). Sheet 121×97 mm. Multicoloured.

MS899 37c. Paracas (detail), Peru; 37c. Sinu pendant, Colombia; 37c. Hicholi embroidery, Mexico; 37c. Rigpaktsa back ornament, Brazil; 37c. Woollen textile, Santiago, Chile; 37c. Huari hat, Bolivia ... 5·50 ... 5·50

See also No. **MS925** and **MS965**.

551 Interlocking Hands and "peace"

2003

900	**551**	23c. multicoloured	55	55

552 United Nations Emblem

2003

901	**552**	37c. gold and blue	75	75

553 Bi-plane Propeller

2003. Centenary of Powered Flight. Multicoloured.

902		23c. Type **553**	55	55
903		70c. As No. 902	1·60	1·60

Nos. 902/3 were issued in tête-bêche pairs forming a composite design of a propeller.

554 United Nations Headquarters, New York

2003. Greetings from the United Nations.

904	**554**	70c. multicoloured	1·40	1·40

555 Great Hornbill

2003. Endangered Species (11th series). 30th Anniv of Convention on International Trade in Endangered Species (CITES). Multicoloured.

905		37c. Type **555**	85	85
906		37c. Scarlet ibis	85	85
907		37c. Knob-billed goose	85	85
908		37c. White-faced whistling duck	85	85

559 Animals and Freshwater

2003. International Year of Freshwater. Multicoloured.

909		23c. Type **559**	55	55
910		37c. Decay	75	75

Nos. 909/10 were issued together, *se-tenant*, forming a composite design.

561 Ralph Bunche

2003. Ralph Bunche (politician) Commemoration.

911	**561**	37c. multicoloured	75	75

562 Yosemite National Park

2003. World Heritage Sites in USA. Showing USA National Parks. Multicoloured.

912		10c. Type **562**	35	35
913		10c. Smoky Mountains	35	35
914		10c. Olympic National Park	35	35
915		20c. Hawaii Volcanoes	55	55
916		20c. Everglades	55	55
917		20c. Yellowstone National Park	55	55
918		37c. As No. 912	85	85
919		60c. As No. 915	1·70	1·70

Nos. 912/19 have blue bands at top and bottom edges.

568 Flag at
Half-mast

2003. In Memoriam. Support for United Nations Staff
Killed or Injured in Terrorist Attacks.
920 **568** 60c. multicoloured 1·50 1·50

569 Black Bear (*Ursus
americanus*)

2004. Endangered Species (12th series). Multicoloured.
921 37c. Type **569** 75 75
922 37c. Musk deer (*Moschus*) 75 75
923 37c. Golden snub-nose monkey
(*Pygathrix roxellana*) 75 75
924 37c. Wild yak (*Bos mutus*) 75 75

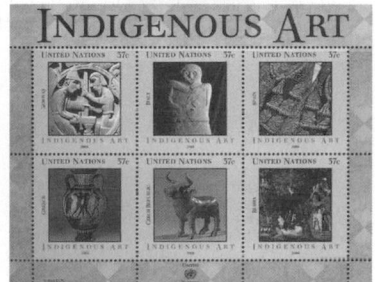

573 Artefacts (image scaled to 39% of original size)

2004. Indigenous Art (2nd series). Sheet 125×96 mm.
Multicoloured.
MS925 37c.×6, Viking wood carving,
Norway; Stele, Lunigiana, Italy;
Amphora, Greece; Bronze bull, Byci
Skala, Czech Republic; Illustration by
D. Butorin from "On the Seashore"
(Alexander Pushkin), lacquer box,
Russia 4·50 4·50

574 Traffic Signs on Car
(traffic sign awareness
campaign)

2004. Road Safety Campaign. Multicoloured.
926 37c. Type **574** 70 70
927 70c. Hand Raising Car (courtesy
to other road users) (vert) 1·50 1·50

576 Peace Bell, United Nations
Headquarters, New York

2004. 50th Anniv of Japanese Peace Bell.
928 **576** 80c. multicoloured 1·60 1·60

577 Ruins, Delphi

2004. World Heritage Sites in Greece. Multicoloured.
929 23c. Type **577** 50 50
930 23c. Pythagoreion and Heraion,
Samos 50 50
931 23c. Tunnel, Olympia 50 50
932 23c. Relief, Mycenae and Tiryns 50 50
933 37c. Acropolis, Athens 70 70
934 37c. Lions, Delos 70 70
935 37c. As No. 933 70 70
936 60c. As No. 934 1·30 1·30

583 Children riding
on Dove and Carpet
of Flags (Sittichok
Pariyaket)

2004. Winning Designs in Children's Painting
Competition "My Dream of Peace". Multicoloured.
937 37c. Type **583** 80 80
938 80c. Hand as dove (Bayan Fais
Abu Blal) 1·70 1·70

585 Prisoners, Men,
Woman and Blue Roses

2004. International Decade of Human Rights' Education.
Multicoloured.
939 37c. Type **585** 70 70
940 70c. Scales, fallen man and
woman holding child 1·50 1·50
The stamps of United Nations Headquarters in New
York, Geneva and Vienna form a composite design.

587 Figure enclosing
Rifle and "Books not
Guns"

2004. Disarmament.
941 **587** 37c. multicoloured 1·00 1·00

588 General Assembly

2005. 60th Anniv of United Nations.
942 **588** 80c. multicoloured 1·50 1·50
MS943 100×80 mm. **588** $1 multicol-
oured. Imperf 8·00 8·00
Nos. 942/MS943 have ultramarine borders.

589 *Vanda coerulea*

2005. Endangered Species (13th series). Multicoloured.
944 37c. Type **589** 70 70
945 37c. Cycnoche 70 70
946 37c. Cattleya trianae 70 70
947 37c. Aerangis modesta 70 70

593 Ice Climber, Norway

2005. EXPO 2005 World Exhibition, Aichi, Japan.
Multicoloured.
948 37c. Type **593** 50 50
949 80c. Egret, Japan 1·50 1·50

595 Sailing

2005. International Year of Sport. Multicoloured.
950 37c. Type **596** 50 50
951 70c. Running 1·50 1·50

597 Sphinx, Necropolis, Memphis

2005. World Heritage. Egypt. Multicoloured.
952 23c. Type **597** 50 50
953 23c. Castle, Philae 50 50
954 23c. Abu Mena 50 50
955 37c. Head, Necropolis, Thebes 70 70
956 37c. Mosque, Cairo 70 70
957 37c. Saint Catherine Monastery 70 70
958 37c. Type **597** 70 70
959 80c. Head, Necropolis, Thebes 1·50 1·50

603 Candle of Flags
(Vittoria
Sansebastiano)

2005. My Dream of Peace One Day. Winning Designs in
Children's Painting Competition. Multicoloured.
960 37c. Type **603** 70 70
961 80c. Dove as Light Bulb and
Globe (Jordan Harris) 1·50 1·50

605 Father and Child

2005. Food for Life.
962 **605** 37c. black, ultramarine
and blue 70 70
963 – 80c. black, ultramarine
and blue 1·50 1·50
DESIGN: 80c. Starving mother and child, ears of corn and
well-fed mother and child.

607 Hands enclosing Flags
as Heart

2006
964 **607** 25c. multicoloured 40 40

608 Musical Instruments (image scaled to 38% of
original size)

2006. Indigenous Art (3rd series). Sheet 125×96 mm.
Multicoloured.
MS965 37c.×6, Anthropomorphic drum,
Ivory Coast; Drum, Tunisia; Guinbri,
Morocco; Drums and swords, Sudan;
Carved figures, Cameroon; Stringed
instrument (harp), Congo 4·50 4·50

609 Golden Mantella

2006. Endangered Species (14th series). Multicoloured.
966 39c. Type **609** 70 70
967 39c. Panther chameleon 70 70
968 39c. Peruvian rainbow boa 70 70
969 39c. Dyeing poison frog 70 70

613 Families gathering
Grapes

2006. International Day of Families. Multicoloured.
970 39c. Type **613** 70 70
971 84c. Children floating Boats 1·50 1·50

615 Banks of the Seine

2006. World Heritage. France. Multicoloured.
972 24c. Type **615** 50 50
973 24c. Provins 50 50
974 24c. Carcassonne 50 50
975 39c. Roman Aqueduct 70 70
976 39c. Mont Saint Michel 70 70
977 39c. Chateau de Chambord 70 70
978 39c. Type **615** 70 70
979 84c. Roman Aqueduct 1·50 1·50

621 Dove (Cheuk Tat
Li)

2006. My Dream of Peace One Day. Winning Designs in
Children's Painting Competition. Multicoloured.
980 39c. Type **621** 70 70
981 84c. Multicoured Nautilus (Kos-
sapan Paitoon) 1·50 1·50

623 China

2006. Coins and Flags of Member Countries (1st series).
Multicoloured.
982 39c. Type **623** 70 70
983 39c. Australia 70 70
984 39c. Russian Federation 70 70
985 39c. Mexico 70 70
986 39c. Ghana 70 70
987 39c. Israel 70 70
988 39c. Japan 70 70
989 39c. Cambodia 70 70
See also Nos. 998/1005.

2007. Flags of Member Nations (15th series). As T **203**.
Multicoloured.
990 39c. Tuvalu 70 70
991 39c. Switzerland 70 70
992 39c. East Timor 70 70
993 39c. Montenegro 70 70

631 Drill (*Mandrillus
leucophaeus*)

2007. Endangered Species (15th series).
994 39c. Type **631** 70 70

995	39c. Common squirrel monkey (*Saimiri sciureus*)	70	70
996	39c. Ring-tailed lemur (*Lemur catta*)	70	70
997	39c. Collared magabey (*Cercocebus torquatus*)	70	70

2007. Coins and Flags of Member Countries (2nd series). As T **623**. Multicoloured.

998	39c. Brazil	60	60
999	39c. Thailand	60	60
1000	39c. India	60	60
1001	39c. South Africa	60	60
1002	39c. Vietnam	60	60
1003	39c. Ecuador	60	60
1004	39c. Barbados	60	60
1005	39c. Republic of Korea	60	60

643 Family

2007. Peaceful Visions. Multicoloured.

1006	39c. Type **643**	60	60
1007	84c. Three Women	1·40	1·40

645 Rapa Nui, Chile

2007. World Heritage Sites. South America. Multicoloured.

1008	26c. Type **645**	40	40
1009	26c. Cueva de las Manos, Argentina	40	40
1010	26c. Machu Pichu, Peru	40	40
1011	41c. Tiwanaku, Bolivia	60	60
1012	41c. Iguacu, Brazil	60	60
1013	41c. Galapagos Islands	60	60
1014	90c. Type **645**	1·40	1·40

651 Peace Keeper's Helmet

2007

1015	**651** 90c. multicoloured	1·50	1·50

652 Flying Postman and Hands

2007. Humanitarian Mail.

1016	**652** 90c. multicoloured	1·50	1·50

653 Shuttle Spacecraft

2007. 50th Anniv of Space Exploration. Multicoloured.

1017	41c. Type **653**	60	60
1018	90c. Space Walk	1·50	1·50
MS1019	100×80 mm. $1 Satellite	1·60	1·60

656 Barbed Wire becoming Flowers

2008. International Holocaust Remembrance Day.

1020	**656** 41c. multicoloured	60	60

A stamp of a similar design was issued by Israel.

657 Cape Fur Seal (*Arctocephalus pusillus*)

2008. Endangered Species (16th series). Multicoloured.

1021	41c. Type **657**	65	65
1022	41c. Orange cup coral (*Tubastraea coccinea*)	65	65
1023	41c. Longsnout seahorse (*Hippocampus reidi*)	65	65
1024	41c. Grey whale (*Eschrichtius robustus*)	65	65

661 United Kingdom

2008. Flags and Coins of Member Countries (3rd series). Multicoloured.

1025	41c. Type **661**	65	65
1026	41c. Singapore	65	65
1027	41c. Philipines	65	65
1028	41c. Indonesia	65	65
1029	41c. Colombia	65	65
1030	41c. Sri Lanka	65	65
1031	41c. United Arab Emirates	65	65
1032	41c. Libya	65	65

669 Accessibility

2008. Convention on the Rights of People with Disablities. Multicoloured.

1033	42c. Type **669**	75	75
1034	94c. Braille	1·50	1·50

671 Track Race

2008. Olympic Games, Beijing. Multicoloured.

1035	42c. Type **671**	85	85
1036	94c. Hurdle race	1·70	1·70
MS1037	92×83 mm. $1.25 As Type **671**	2·40	2·40

673 People of Many Nations (Grace Tsang)

2008. We Can End Poverty. Winning Designs in Children's Painting Competition. Multicoloured.

1038	42c. Type **673**	80	80
1039	94c. Mothers and Children (Bryan Jevoncia) (vert)	1·70	1·70

675a/d Coral Reef (image scaled to 49% of original size)

676a/d Ice Floes (image scaled to 49% of original size)

677a/d Pollution (image scaled to 49% of original size)

678a/d Desert (image scaled to 49% of original size)

679a/d Polar Bear (image scaled to 49% of original size)

680a/d Deforestation

2008. Action on Climate Change. Phosphor markings.

1040	27c. Type **675a**	55	55
1041	27c. Type **675b**	55	55
1042	27c. Type **675c**	55	55
1043	27c. Type **675d**	55	55
1044	27c. Type **676a**	55	55
1045	27c. Type **676b**	55	55
1046	27c. Type **676c**	55	55
1047	27c. Type **676d**	55	55
1048	27c. Type **677a**	55	55
1049	27c. Type **677b**	55	55
1050	27c. Type **677c**	55	55
1051	27c. Type **677d**	55	55
1052	42c. Type **678a**	85	85
1053	42c. Type **678b**	85	85
1054	42c. Type **678c**	85	85
1055	42c. Type **678d**	85	85
1056	42c. Type **679a**	85	85
1057	42c. Type **679b**	85	85
1058	42c. Type **679c**	85	85
1059	42c. Type **679d**	85	85
1060	42c. Type **680a**	85	85
1061	42c. Type **680b**	85	85
1062	42c. Type **680c**	85	85
1063	42c. Type **680d**	85	85

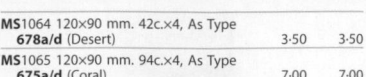

MS1064	120×90 mm. 42c.×4, As Type **678a/d** (Desert)	3·50	3·50
MS1065	120×90 mm. 94c.×4, As Type **675a/d** (Coral)	7·00	7·00

681 Cielo rosado

2009. Roses (paintings by Jaime Arredondo). Multicoloured.

1066	1c. Type **681**	15	15
1067	9c. *Rosa de sangre* multicoloured	30	30
1068	10c. *Espiritu de mujer*	30	30

684 U Thant

2009. Birth Centenary of U Thant (United Nations Secretary General 1961–1971).

1069	**684** 94c. multicoloured	2·00	2·00

685 *Anax imperator* (Emperor dragonfly)

686 *Formica rufa* (Southern wood ant)

687 *Rosalia alpina* (longhorn beetle)

688 *Parnassius apollo* (Apollo butterfly)

2009. Endangered Species (17th series).

1070	**685** 42c. multicoloured	90	90
1071	**686** 42c. multicoloured	90	90
1072	**687** 42c. multicoloured	90	90
1073	**688** 42c. multicoloured	90	90

689 Town Hall and Roland on the Marketplace of Bremen

2009. World Heritage Sites. Germany. Multicoloured.

1074	27c. Type **689**	70	70
1075	27c. Wartburg Castle	70	70
1076	27c. Palaces and Parks of Potsdam and Berlin	70	70
1077	42c. Aachen Cathedral	1·00	1·00
1078	42c. Monastic Island of Reichenau	1·00	1·00
1079	42c. Luther Memorials in Eisleben and Wittenberg	1·00	1·00
1080	44c. As No. 1074	1·00	1·00
1081	98c. As No. 1077	2·30	2·30

695 Woman carrying Bucket (Water and sanitation)

2009. United Nations Economic and Social Council (ECOSOC). Multicoloured.

1082	44c. Type **695**	85	85
1083	98c. Herbalist (Traditional medicines)	2·00	2·00

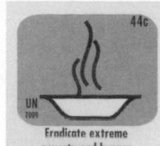

697 Bowl of Food
(Eradicate extreme
poverty and hunger)

2009. Millennium Development Goals.
1084	697	44c. chrome-yellow, black and new blue	1·00	1·00
1085	-	44c. bright yellow-green, black and new blue	1·00	1·00
1086	-	44c. orange-red, black and new blue	1·00	1·00
1087	-	44c. pale turquoise-blue, black and new blue	1·00	1·00
1088	-	44c. pale bright rose, black and new blue	1·00	1·00
1089	-	44c. scarlet-vermilion, black and new blue	1·00	1·00
1090	-	44c. apple-green, black and new blue	1·00	1·00
1091	-	44c. blue, black and new blue	1·00	1·00

DESIGNS: No.1085, Pencil (Achieve universal primary education); 1086, Female symbol (Promote gender equality and empower women); Teddy bear (Reduce child mortality); 1088, Female figure enclosing Heart (Improve maternal health); 1089, Medicine jar (Combat HIV/AIDS, malaria and other diseases); 1090, Stylized tree (Ensure environmental sustainability); 1091, Stylized figures (Develop a global partnership for development).

705 Mahatma
Gandhi

2009. International Day of Non-Violence.
1092	705	$1 multicoloured	1·00	1·00

706 Seychelles

2009. Indigenous Peoples. Multicoloured
1093	44c. Type **706**	1·00	1·00
1094	44c. Malaysia	1·00	1·00
1095	44c. Australia	1·00	1·00
1096	44c. Thailand	1·00	1·00
1097	44c. Indonesia	1·00	1·00
1098	44c. United Republic of Tanzania	1·00	1·00

712 Bahamas

2010. Coins and Flags of Member Countries (4th series). Multicoloured.
1099	44c. Type **712**	1·00	1·00
1100	44c. Jamaica	1·00	1·00
1101	44c. Panama	1·00	1·00
1102	44c. Guatemala	1·00	1·00
1103	44c. Honduras	1·00	1·00
1104	44c. Kuwait	1·00	1·00
1105	44c. Saint Lucia	1·00	1·00
1106	44c. Yemen	1·00	1·00

720 *Araucaria araucana*
(Monkey Puzzle Tree)
721 *Aloe dichotoma*
(Quiver Tree)

722 *Pinus longaeva*
(Bristlecone Pine Tree)
723 *Parodia haselbergii*
(Scarlet Bell Cactus)

2010. Endangered Species (18th series)
1107	**720**	44c. multicoloured	1·10	85
1108	**721**	44c. multicoloured	1·10	85
1109	**722**	44c. multicoloured	1·10	85
1110	**723**	44c. multicoloured	1·10	85

725-728 Turtle, Eel, Fish and Coral (image scaled to 49% of original size)

737-740 Dolphin, Fish and Turtle (image scaled to 49% of original size)

729-732 Dolphins, Shark and Fish (image scaled to 49% of original size)

741-744 Two Dolphins, Shark, Ray and Turtle (image scaled to 49% of original size)

733-736 Turtle, Hammerhead Shark and Coral (image scaled to 49% of original size)

745-748 Dolphin Pod, Shark, Ray and Coral (image scaled to 49% of original size)

2010. One Planet, One Ocean. 50th Anniv of Intergovernmental Oceanographic Commission. Multicoloured.
1111	**725**	28c. multicoloured	65	45
1112	**726**	28c. multicoloured	65	45
1113	**727**	28c. multicoloured	65	45
1114	**728**	28c. multicoloured	65	45
1115	**729**	28c. multicoloured	65	45
1116	**730**	28c. multicoloured	65	45
1117	**731**	28c. multicoloured	65	45
1118	**732**	28c. multicoloured	65	45
1119	**733**	28c. multicoloured	65	45
1120	**734**	28c. multicoloured	65	45
1121	**735**	28c. multicoloured	65	45
1122	**736**	28c. multicoloured	65	45
1123	**737**	44c. multicoloured	1·10	85
1124	**738**	44c. multicoloured	1·10	85
1125	**739**	44c. multicoloured	1·10	85
1126	**740**	44c. multicoloured	1·10	85
1127	**741**	44c. multicoloured	1·10	85
1128	**742**	44c. multicoloured	1·10	85
1129	**743**	44c. multicoloured	1·10	85
1130	**744**	44c. multicoloured	1·10	85
1131	**745**	44c. multicoloured	1·10	85
1132	**746**	44c. multicoloured	1·10	85
1133	**747**	44c. multicoloured	1·10	85
1134	**748**	44c. multicoloured	1·10	85
MS1135	180×110 mm. 44c.×4, As Types 725/728		6·00	6·00
MS1136	180×110 mm. 98c.×4, As Types 729/732		8·00	8·00

749 People of Many
Nationalities
750 People of Many
Nations as
Skyscrapers

2010. New York - Multicultural City
1137	**749**	3c. multicoloured	30	30
1138	**750**	4c. multicoloured	40	40

751 '65'

2010. 65th Anniv of United Nations
1139	**751**	98c. azure and gold	2·00	2·00
MS1140	80×80 mm. 98c.×2, As Type 751×2, bluish violet and gold		5·00	5·00

752 Twin-hulled
Cruiser
753 Stern of
Passenger Boat with
Awning

754 Peacekeepers in
dinghy
755 Small Patrol
Boat

756 Large gunboat

2010. United Nations Transport - Sea
1141	**752**	44c. multicoloured	1·10	85
1142	**753**	44c. multicoloured	1·10	85
1143	**754**	44c. multicoloured	1·10	85
1144	**755**	44c. multicoloured	1·10	85
1145	**756**	44c. multicoloured	1·10	85

757 Hummingbird
758 Liverwort

2010. International Year of Biodiversity. Art from Nature by Ernst Heinrich
1146	**757**	15c. multicoloured	50	50
1147	**758**	$1.50 multicoloured	2·50	2·25

760 French
Polynesia
761 Papua New
Guinea

762 French Polynesia
763 Australia

764 Australia

2010. Indigenous Peoples
1148	**759**	44c. multicoloured	1·10	85
1149	**760**	44c. multicoloured	1·10	85
1150	**761**	44c. multicoloured	1·10	85
1151	**762**	44c. multicoloured	1·10	85
1152	**763**	44c. multicoloured	1·10	85
1153	**764**	44c. multicoloured	1·10	85

765 Aerial View of UN
Building
766 Building and
Flags of Member
Countries

2011. UN Building
1154	**765**	11c. multicoloured	50	45
1155	**766**	$5 multicoloured	12·00	10·00

767 Mauritius
768 Guyana

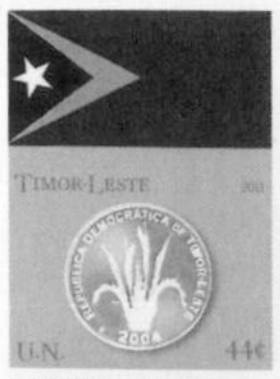
769 Timor-Leste

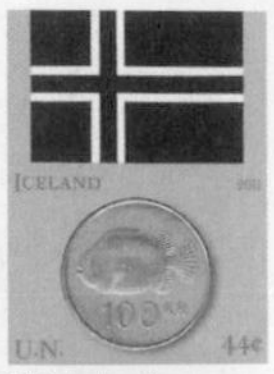
770 Iceland

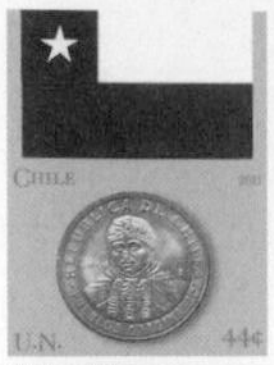
771 Chile

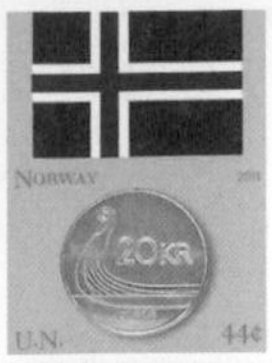
772 Norway

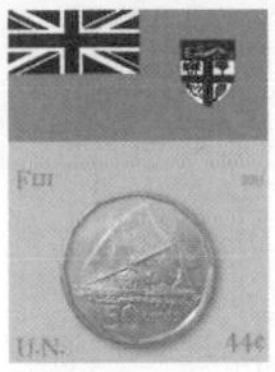
773 Fiji

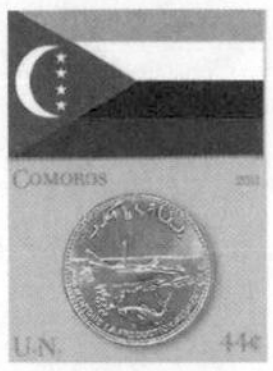
774 Comoros

2011. Coins and Flags of Member Countries (5th series)

1156	**767**	44c. multicoloured	1·10	85
1157	**768**	44c. multicoloured	1·10	85
1158	**769**	44c. multicoloured	1·10	85
1159	**770**	44c. multicoloured	1·10	85
1160	**771**	44c. multicoloured	1·10	85
1161	**772**	44c. multicoloured	1·10	85
1162	**773**	44c. multicoloured	1·10	85
1163	**774**	44c. multicoloured	1·10	85

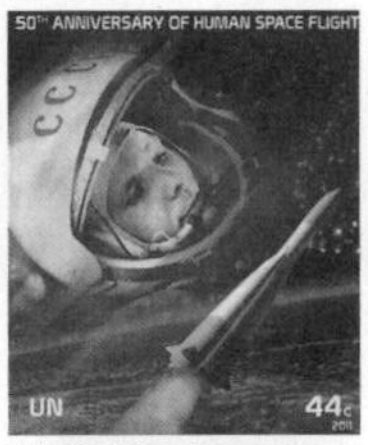
775 Yuri Gagarin

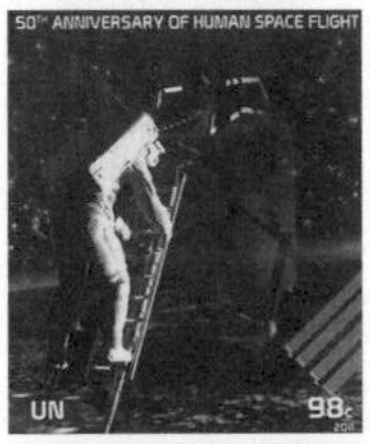
776 Astronaut on Ladder

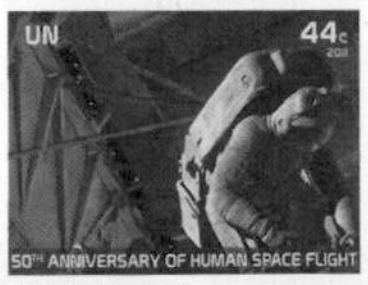
777 Astronaut

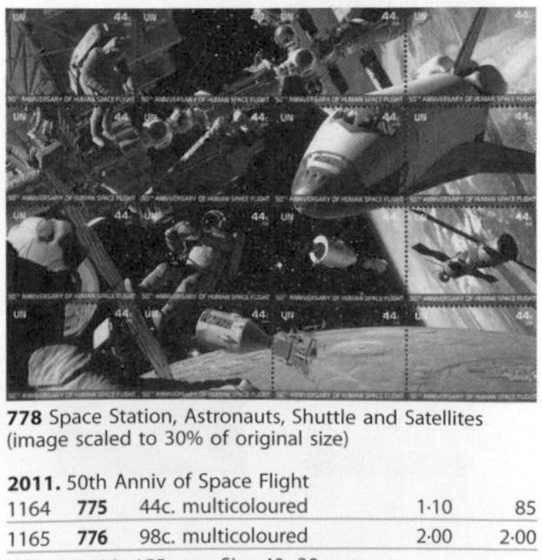
778 Space Station, Astronauts, Shuttle and Satellites (image scaled to 30% of original size)

2011. 50th Anniv of Space Flight

1164	**775**	44c. multicoloured	1·10	85
1165	**776**	98c. multicoloured	2·00	2·00

MS1166 180×155 mm. Size 40×30 mm. 44c.×16, Type **777** and 15 other horiz designs forming the overall design Type **778** 35·00 35·00

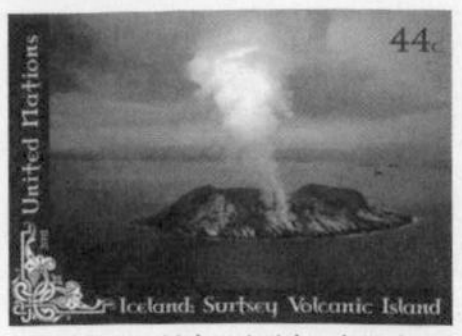
779 Surtsey Volcanic Island, Iceland

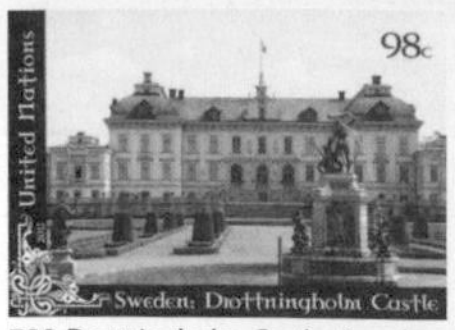
780 Drottringholm Castle, Sweden

2011. World Heritage Sites - Nordic Countries

1167	**779**	44c. multicoloured	1·10	85
1168	**780**	98c. multicoloured	2·00	2·00

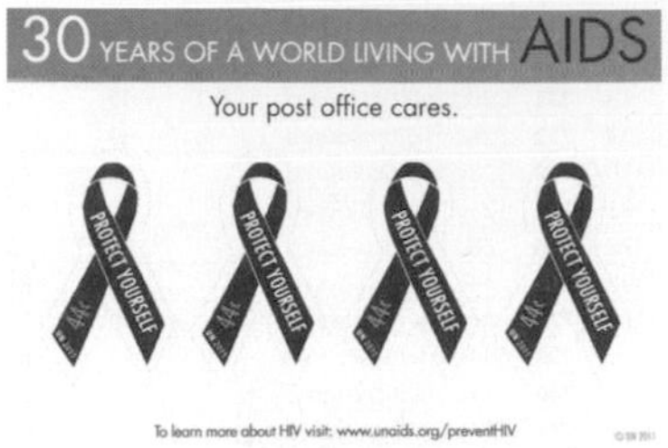

781 AIDS Ribbon (image scaled to 45% of original size)

2011. '30 Years of a World living with AIDS'

1169	**781**	44c. scarlet and azure	1·10	85

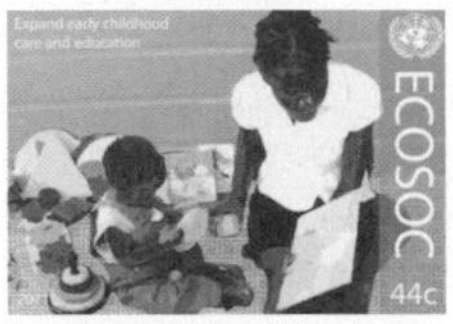
782 'Expand early childhood care and education'

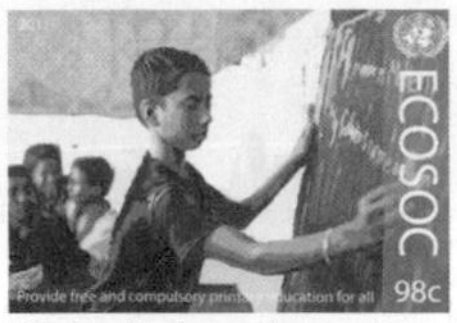
783 'Provide free and compulsory primary education for all'

2011. ECOSOC (Economic and Social Council) - Education

1170	**782**	44c. multicoloured	1·10	85
1171	**783**	98c. multicoloured	2·00	2·00

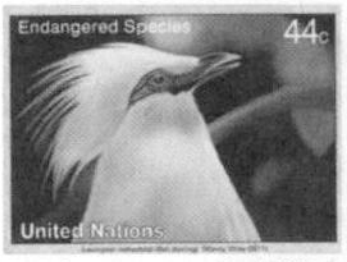
784 *Leucopsar rothschildi* (Bali Starling)

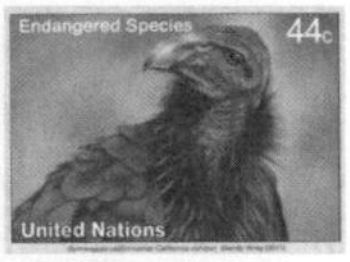
785 *Gymnogyps californianus* (California Condor)

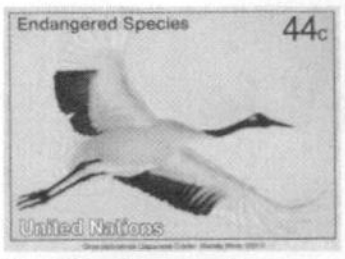
786 *Grus japonensis* (Japanese Crane)

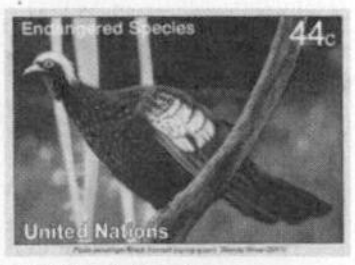
787 *Pipile jacutinga* (Black-fronted Piping Guan)

2011. Endangered Species (19th series)

1172	**784**	44c. multicoloured	1·10	85
1173	**785**	44c. multicoloured	1·10	85
1174	**786**	44c. multicoloured	1·10	85
1175	**787**	44c. multicoloured	1·10	85

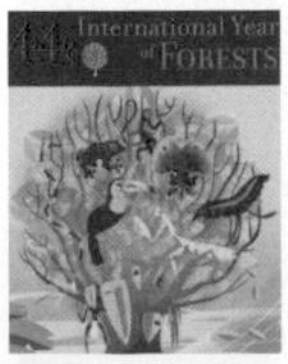
788 Tree enclosing Wildlife and Masks

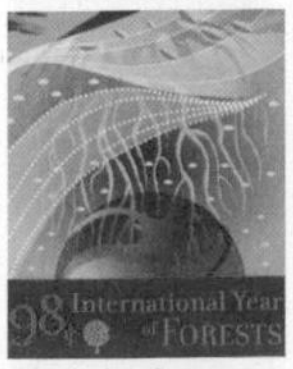
789 Stylised stream and tree roots

2011. International Year of Forests

1176	**788**	44c. multicoloured	1·10	85
1177	**789**	98c. multicoloured	2·00	2·00

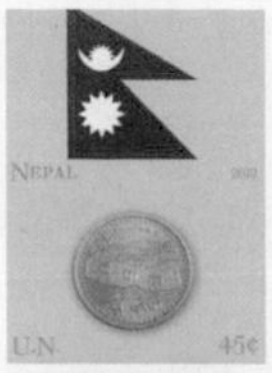
790 Nepal

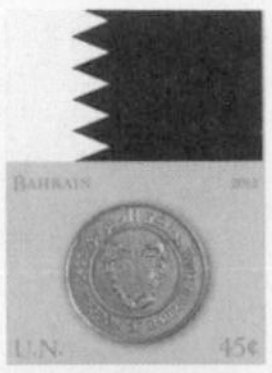
791 Bahrain

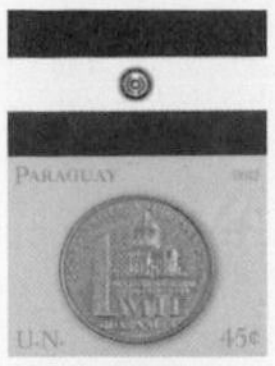
792 Paraguay

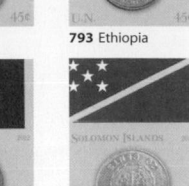

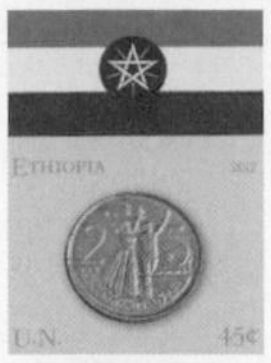
793 Ethiopia

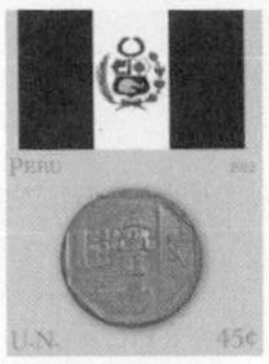
794 Peru

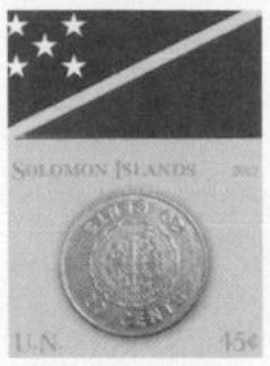
795 Solomon Islands

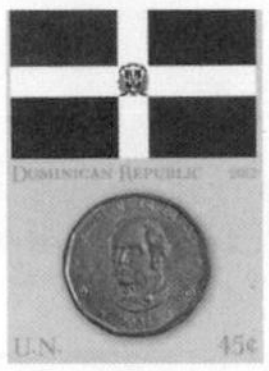
796 Dominican Republic

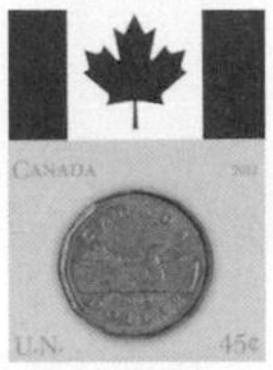
797 Canada

2012. Coins and Flags of Member Countries (6th series)

1178	**790**	45c. multicoloured	1·20	95
1179	**791**	45c. multicoloured	1·20	95
1180	**792**	45c. multicoloured	1·20	95
1181	**793**	45c. multicoloured	1·20	95
1182	**794**	45c. multicoloured	1·20	95
1183	**795**	45c. multicoloured	1·20	95
1184	**796**	45c. multicoloured	1·20	95
1185	**797**	45c. multicoloured	1·20	95

B. GENEVA HEADQUARTERS

For use on mail posted at the United Nations Geneva Headquarters. Before 1969 the Swiss PTT issued stamps for use at the Palais des Nations; these are listed at the end of Switzerland.

NOTE: References to numbers and types in this section. other than to those with a "G" prefix are to the United Nations (New York Office) listing. Designs adapted for the Geneva issue are inscribed in French and have face values in francs.

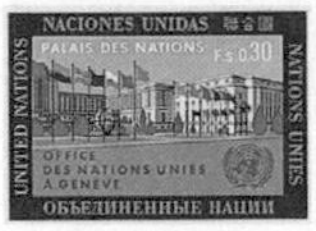
G4 Palais des Nations, Geneva

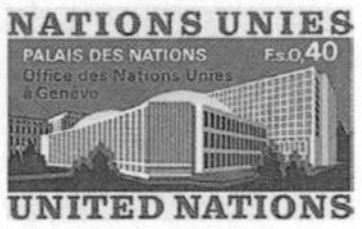
G5 Palais des Nations, Geneva

1969. Existing United Nations (New York) designs adapted with new colours and values in Swiss francs (F.S.). 30 and 40c. new designs. Multicoloured unless otherwise stated.

G1	-	5c. (As No. 164)	15	15
G2	-	10c. (As No. 94)	20	20
G3	-	20c. (As No. 97)	25	25
G4	**G4**	30c. multicoloured	30	30
G5	**G5**	40c. multicoloured	65	65
G6	-	50c. (As No. 147, but scroll inscr in French)	65	65
G7	-	60c. gold, red and brown (As No. 98)	65	65
G8	-	70c. red, gold and black (As No. 167)	65	65
G9	-	75c. (As No. A125)	70	70
G10	-	80c. (As No. 148)	75	75
G11	**52**	90c. (Inscr in French)	90	90
G12	-	1f. deep green and green (As No. 149)	1·00	1·00
G13	**53**	2f. multicoloured	2·10	2·10
G14	**104**	3f. multicoloured	3·00	3·00
G15	**3**	10f. blue	8·75	8·75

1971. Peaceful Uses of the Sea-bed.

G16	**121**	30c. multicoloured	65	65

1971. United Nations Work with Refugees.

G17	**122**	50c. black, orange and red	1·00	1·00

1971. World Food Programme.

G18	**123**	50c. multicoloured	1·00	1·00

1971. Opening of New Universal Postal Union Headquarters Building, Berne.

G19	**124**	75c. multicoloured	1·30	1·30

1971. Racial Equality Year. Designs as Nos. 220/1, with background colours changed.

G20		30c. Type **125**	50	50
G21		50c. Linked globes (horiz)	75	75

1971. U.N. International Schools.

G22	**130**	1f.10 multicoloured	1·50	1·50

1972. Non-proliferation of Nuclear Weapons.

G23	**131**	40c. multicoloured	1·00	1·00

1972. World Health Day.

G24	**132**	80c. multicoloured	1·30	1·30

1972. United Nations Environmental Conservation Conference, Stockholm.

G25	**137**	40c. multicoloured	65	65
G26	**137**	80c. multicoloured	1·30	1·30

1972. Economic Commission for Europe (ECE).

G27	**138**	1f.10 multicoloured	2·10	2·10

1972. United Nations Art.

G28	**139**	40c. multicoloured	65	65
G29	**139**	80c. multicoloured	1·30	1·30

1973. Disarmament Decade.

G30	**140**	60c. multicoloured	75	75
G31	**140**	1f.10 multicoloured	1·40	1·40

1973. "No Drugs" Campaign.

G32	**141**	60c. multicoloured	1·00	1·00

1973. U.N. Volunteers Programme.

G33	**142**	80c. multicoloured	1·30	1·30

1973. "Namibia" (South West Africa).

G34	**143**	60c. multicoloured	1·00	1·00

1973. 25th Anniv of Declaration of Human Rights.

G35	**144**	40c. multicoloured	50	50
G36	**144**	80c. multicoloured	1·00	1·00

1973. Inauguration of New I.L.O. Headquarters, Geneva.

G37	**145**	60c. multicoloured	90	90
G38	**145**	80c. multicoloured	1·00	1·00

1973. Centenary of Universal Postal Union.

G39	**146**	30c. multicoloured	50	50
G40	**146**	60c. multicoloured	1·00	1·00

1974. Brazilian Peace Mural.

G41	**147**	60c. multicoloured	75	75
G42	**147**	1f. multicoloured	1·30	1·30

1974. World Population Year.

G43	**154**	60c. multicoloured	75	75
G44	**154**	80c. multicoloured	1·00	1·00

1974. U.N. Conference on "Law of the Sea".

G45	**155**	1f.30 multicoloured	1·50	1·50

1975. Peaceful Uses of Outer Space.

G46	**156**	60c. multicoloured	75	75
G47	**156**	90c. multicoloured	1·00	1·00

1975. International Women's Year.

G48	**157**	60c. multicoloured	75	75
G49	**157**	90c. multicoloured	1·00	1·00

1975. 30th Anniv of U.N.O.

G50	**158**	60c. multicoloured	75	75
G51	**158**	90c. multicoloured	1·10	1·10
MSG52		92×70 mm. Nos. G50/1. Imperf	1·90	1·90

1975. "Namibia—U.N. Direct Responsibility".

G53	**160**	50c. multicoloured	55	55
G54	**160**	1f.30 multicoloured	1·40	1·40

1975. U.N. Peace Keeping Operations.

G55	**161**	60c. blue	70	70
G56	**161**	70c. violet	90	90

1976. World Federation of U.N. Associations.

G57	**166**	90c. multicoloured	1·00	1·00

1976. U.N. Conf on Trade and Development.

G58	**167**	1f.10 multicoloured	1·30	1·30

1976. U.N. Conf on Human Settlements.

G59	**168**	40c. multicoloured	45	45
G60	**168**	1f.50 multicoloured	1·60	1·60

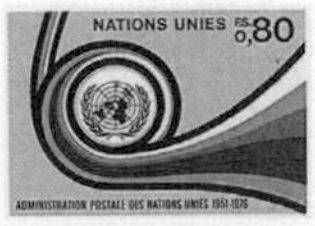
G46 U.N. Emblem within Posthorn

1976. 25th Anniv of U.N. Postal Administration.

G61	**G46**	80c. multicoloured	2·30	2·30
G62	**G46**	1f.10 multicoloured	2·75	2·75

1976. World Food Council Publicity.

G63	**170**	70c. multicoloured	1·00	1·00

1977. World Intellectual Property Organization Publicity.
G64 172 80c. multicoloured   1·00 1·00

G49 Rain Drop and Globe

1977. U.N. Water Conference.
G65 **G49** 80c. multicoloured   1·00 1·00
G66 **G49** 1f.10 multicoloured   1·40 1·40

G50 Protective Hands

1977. Security Council Commemoration.
G67 **G50** 80c. multicoloured   1·00 1·00
G68 **G50** 1f.10 multicoloured   1·40 1·40

G51 "Intertwining of Races"

1977. "Combat Racism".
G69 **G51** 40c. multicoloured   50 50
G70 **G51** 1f.10 multicoloured   1·40 1·40

G52 Atoms and Laurel Leaf

1977. "Peaceful Uses for Atomic Energy".
G71 **G52** 80c. multicoloured   90 90
G72 **G52** 1f.10 multicoloured   1·40 1·40

G53 Tree and Birds

1978
G73 **G53** 35c. multicoloured   65 65

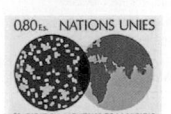

G54 Smallpox Bacilli and Globe

1978. Global Eradication of Smallpox.
G74 **G54** 80c. multicoloured   1·00 1·00
G75 **G54** 1f.10 multicoloured   1·40 1·40

1978. "Namibia: Liberation, Justice, Co-operation".
G76 183 80c. multicoloured   1·00 1·00

G56 Aircraft Flightpaths

1978. International Civil Aviation Organization—Safety in the Air.
G77 **G56** 70c. multicoloured   90 90
G78 **G56** 80c. multicoloured   1·00 1·00

G57 Globe, Flags and General Assembly Interior

1978. General Assembly.
G79 **G57** 70c. multicoloured   90 90
G80 **G57** 1f.10 multicoloured   1·40 1·40

1978. Technical Co-operation among Developing Countries.
G81 186 80c. multicoloured   1·00 1·00

G59 "Disaster"

1979. United Nations Disaster Relief Co-ordinator.
G82 **G59** 80c. multicoloured   1·00 1·00
G83 **G59** 1f.50 multicoloured   1·80 1·80

G60 Children and Rainbow

1979. International Year of the Child.
G84 **G60** 80c. multicoloured   1·00 1·00
G85 **G60** 1f.10 multicoloured   1·40 1·40

1979. "For a Free and Independent Namibia".
G86 193 1f.10 multicoloured   1·40 1·40

G62 Int Court of Justice and Scales

1979. International Court of Justice.
G87 **G62** 80c. multicoloured   1·00 1·00
G88 **G62** 1f.10 multicoloured   1·40 1·40

G63 Key symbolizing Unity of Action

1980. New International Economic Order.
G89 **G63** 80c. multicoloured   1·00 1·00

G64 Emblem

1980. U.N. Decade for Women.
G90 **G64** 40c. multicoloured   50 50
G91 **G64** 70c. multicoloured   90 90

1980. Peace Keeping Operations.
G92 198 1f.10 blue and green   · 1·40 1·40

1980. 35th Anniv of United Nations.
G93 -   40c. black and blue   50 50
G94 200 70c. multicoloured   90 90
MSG95 92×73 mm. Nos. G93/4. Imperf   1·50 1·50
DESIGN: 40c. Dove and "35".

1980. Economic and Social Council.
G96 204 40c. multicoloured   50 50
G97 -   70c. blue, red and black   90 90
DESIGN: 70c. Human figures ascending graph.

1981. Inalienable Rights of the Palestinian People.
G98 206 80c. multicoloured   1·00 1·00

G71 Disabled Person

1981. International Year of Disabled Persons.
G99 **G71** 40c. black and blue   50 50
G100 -   1f.50 black and red   1·90 1·90
DESIGN: 1f.50, Knot pattern.

1981. Art.
G101 209 80c. multicoloured   1·00 1·00

1981. New and Renewable Sources of Energy.
G102 210 1f.10 multicoloured   1·40 1·40

1981. Tenth Anniv of U.N. Volunteers Programme. Multicoloured.
G103 40c. Type **212**   50 50
G104 70c. Emblems of science, agriculture and industry 90 90

G77 "Anti-apartheid"

1982. Multicoloured
G105 30c. Type G **77**   40 40
G106 1f. Flags   1·30 1·30

1982. Human Environment. Multicoloured.
G107 40c. Leaves   50 50
G108 1f.20 Type **217**   1·50 1·50

1982. Second United Nations Conference on Exploration and Peaceful Uses of Outer Space.
G109 219 80c. violet, pink & green   1·00 1·00
G110 -   1f. multicoloured   1·30 1·30
DESIGN: 1f. Satellite and emblems.

G83 Bird

1982. Conservation and Protection of Nature. Multicoloured.
G111 40c. Type G **83**   50 50
G112 1f.50 Snake (reptiles)   1·90 1·90

G85 Cable Network

1983. World Communications Year.
G113 **G85** 1f.20 multicoloured   1·50 1·50

1983. Safety at Sea: International Maritime Organization. Multicoloured.
G114 40c. Type **224**   50 50
G115 80c. Radar screen within lifebelt   1·00 1·00

1983. World Food Programme.
G116 226 1f.50 blue   1·90 1·90

1983. Trade and Development. Multicoloured.
G117 80c. Type **227**   1·00 1·00
G118 1f.10 Exports   1·40 1·40

G91 "Homo Humus Humanitas"

1983. 35th Anniv of Universal Declaration of Human Rights. Multicoloured.
G119 40c. Type G **91**   65 65
G120 1f.20 "Droit de Creer"   1·60 1·60

G93 World Housing

1984. International Conference on Population, Mexico City.
G121 **G93** 1f.20 multicoloured   1·50 1·50

G94 Fishing

1984. World Food Day. Multicoloured.
G122 50c. Type G **94**   65 65
G123 80c. Planting saplings   1·10 1·10

G96 Fort St. Angelo, Malta (wrongly inscr "Valetta")

1984. World Heritage—UNESCO. Multicoloured.
G124 50c. Type G **96**   75 75
G125 70c. Los Glaciares, Argentina   1·00 1·00

G98 Man and Woman

1984. Future for Refugees.
G126 **G98** 35c. black and green   50 50
G127 -   1f.50 black and brown   2·00 2·00
DESIGN: 1f.50, Head of woman.

G100 Heads

1984. International Youth Year.
G128 **G100** 1f.20 multicoloured   1·80 1·80

1985. 20th Anniv of Turin Centre of International Labour Organization.
G129 239 80c. red   1·10 1·10
G130 045 1f.20 green   1·60 1·60

G103 Ploughing and Group of People

1985. Tenth Anniv of U.N. University, Tokyo.
G131 **G103** 50c. multicoloured   75 75
G132 **G103** 80c. multicoloured   1·10 1·10

G104 Postman

1985
G133 **G104** 20c. multicoloured   30 30
G134 -   1f.20 blue and black   1·50 1·50
DESIGN: 1f.20, Doves.

1985. 40th Anniv of United Nations Organization. Multicoloured.
G135 50c. Type **243**   75 75
G136 70c. "Harvest Scene" (Andrew Wyeth) 1·00 1·00
MSG137 76×81 mm. Nos. G135/6. Imperf   2·50 2·50

G108 Children

1985. UNICEF. Child Survival Campaign. Multicoloured.
G138 50c. Type G **108**   65 65
G139 1f.20 Child drinking   1·50 1·50

G110 Children raising Empty Bowls to weeping Mother

1986. Africa in Crisis.
G140   **G110**   1f.40 multicoloured   1·90   1·90

G111 Herring Gulls

1986
G141   **G111**   5c. multicoloured   40   40

G112 Tents in Clearing

1986. Development Programme. Timber Production. Multicoloured.
G142   35c. Type **G112**   2·75   2·75
G143   35c. Felling tree   2·75   2·75
G144   35c. Logs on lorries   2·75   2·75
G145   35c. Girls with sapling   2·75   2·75
    Nos. G142/5 were printed together, *se-tenant*, forming a composite design.

1986. Philately: The International Hobby.
G146   **253**   50c. green and red   75   75
G147   -   80c. black and orange   1·40   1·40
DESIGN: 80c. United Nations stamps (as Type V **56**).

G118 Ribbon forming Dove

1986. International Peace Year. Multicoloured.
G148   45c. Type G **118**   65   65
G149   1f.40 "Paix" and olive branch   2·10   2·10

G120 (image scaled to 40% of original size)

1986. 40th Anniv of World Federation of United Nations associations. Sheet 120×65 mm. Multicoloured.
MSG150 35c. Birds (Benigno Gomez); 45c. Circle and prisms (Alexander Calder); 50c. "Eye" (Joan Miro); 70c. Done and musical instruments (Ole Hamann)   10·00   10·00

1987. Ninth Death Anniv of Trygve Lie (first U.N. Secretary-General).
G151   **258**   1f.40 multicoloured   1·90   1·90

G122 Abstract

1987. Multicoloured.. Multicoloured..
G152   90c. Type **G122**   1·10   1·10
G153   1f.40 Armillary Sphere, Geneva Centre (30×30 mm)   1·80   1·80

G124 Mixing Cement and Carrying Bricks

1987. International Year of Shelter for the Homeless.
G154   **G124**   50c. green and black   1·00   1·00
G155   -   90c. blue, turquoise and black   1·50   1·50
DESIGN: 90c. Fitting windows and painting.

G126 Mother and Baby

1987. Anti-drugs Campaign. Multicoloured.
G156   80c. Type **G126**   1·30   1·30
G157   1f.20 Workers in paddy field   1·90   1·90

G128 People in Boat and Palais des Nations, Geneva

1987. United Nations Day. Multicoloured.
G158   35c. Type **G128**   75   75
G159   50c. Dancers   1·30   1·30

G130 Whooping Cough

1987. "Immunize Every Child". Multicoloured.
G160   90c. Type **G130**   1·50   1·50
G161   1f.70 Tuberculosis   2·50   2·50

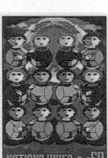

G132 Goatherd

1988. International Fund for Agricultural Development "For a World Without Hunger" Campaign. Multicoloured.
G162   35c. Type **G132**   70   70
G163   1f.40 Women and baskets of fruit   2·10   2·10

G134 People

1988
G164   **G134**   50c. multicoloured   90   90

G135 Mountains and Pine Forest

1988. "Survival of the Forests". Multicoloured.
G165   50c. Type **G135**   5·75   5·75
G166   1f.10 Pine forest and lake shore   5·75   5·75
    Nos. G165/6 were printed together, *se-tenant*, forming a composite design.

G137 Instruction in Fruit Growing

1988. International Volunteer Day. Multicoloured.
G167   80c. Type **G137**   1·30   1·30
G168   90c. Teaching animal husbandary (horiz)   1·60   1·60

G139 Football

1988. "Health in Sports". Multicoloured.
G169   50f. Type **G139**   75   75
G170   1f.40 Swimming   2·00   2·00

1988. 40th Anniv of Declaration of Human Rights.
G171   **276**   90c. multicoloured   1·30   1·30
MSG172 120×79 mm. 2f. multicoloured   3·75   3·75

G142 Communications

1989. World Bank. Multicoloured.
G173   80c. Type **G142**   1·30   1·30
G174   1f.40 Industry   1·90   1·90

1989. Award of Nobel Peace Prize to United Nations Peace-keeping Forces.
G175   **280**   90c. multicoloured   1·50   1·50

G145 Cold Arctic Air over Europe

1989. 25th Anniv of World Weather Watch.
G176   90c. Type **G145**   1·60   1·60
G177   1f.10 Surface temperatures of Kattegat   2·10   2·10

G147 Tree and Birds

1989. Tenth Anniv of United Nations Vienna International Centre.
G178   50c. Type **G147**   90   90
G179   2f. Woman and flower   3·50   3·50

G149 "Young Mother sewing" (Mary Cassatt) (Article 3)

1989. Universal Declaration of Human Rights (1st series). Multicoloured.
G180   35f. Type **G149**   65   65
G181   80f. "Runaway Slave" (Albert Mangones) (Article 4)   1·10   1·10
    See also Nos. G193/4, G209/10, G224/5 and G234/5.

1990. International Trade Centre.
G182   **288**   1f.50 multicoloured   2·40   2·40

G152 Palais des Nations

1990
G183   **G152**   5f. multicoloured   6·25   6·25

1990. Anti-AIDS Campaign. Multicoloured.
G184   50c. Type **289**   1·00   1·00
G185   80c. "Man" (Leonardo da Vinci)   1·50   1·50

G155 Frangipani

1990. Medicinal Plants. Multicoloured.
G186   90c. Type **G155**   1·30   1·30
G187   1f.40 "Cinchona officinalis"   1·90   1·90

G157 Projects forming "45"

1990. 45th Anniv of U.N.O. Multicoloured.
G188   90c. Type **G157**   1·60   1·60
G189   1f.10 Dove and "45"   2·10   2·10
MSG190 100×73 mm. Nos. G188/9   5·75   5·75

G159 Men making Deal over Painting

1990. Crime Prevention. Multicoloured.
G191   50c. Type B**159**   90   90
G192   2f. Man spilling waste from cart   3·25   3·25

1990. Universal Declaration of Human Rights (2nd series). As Type **G149**
G193   35c. multicoloured   65   65
G194   90c. black and flesh   1·50   1·50
DESIGNS: 35c. "Prison Courtyard" (Vincent van Gogh) (Article 9); 90c. "Katho's Son Redeems the Evil Doer from Execution" (Albrecht Durer) (Article 10).

G163/166 Lake

1991. Economic Commission for Europe. "For a Better Environment".
G195   **G163**   90c. multicoloured   2·50   2·50
G196   **G164**   90c. multicoloured   2·50   2·50
G197   **G165**   90c. multicoloured   2·50   2·50
G198   **G166**   90c. multicoloured   2·50   2·50
    Nos. G195/8 were issued together, *se-tenant*, forming the composite design illustrated.

G167 Mountains

1991. First Anniv of Namibian Independence. Multicoloured.
G199   70c. Type **G167**   1·30   1·30
G200   90c. Baobab   1·90   1·90

G169 Papers and Ballot Box

1991. Multicoloured.. Multicoloured..
G201   80c. Type **G169**   1·30   1·30
G202   1f.50 U.N. emblem   2·00   2·00

G171 Baby in Open Hands (Ryuta Nakajima)

1991. 30th Anniv (1989) of U.N. Declaration of the Rights of the Child and 1990 World Summit on Children, New York. Children's Drawings. Multicoloured.

G203 80c. Type **G171** 1·50 1·50
G204 1f.10 Children playing amongst flowers (David Popper) 2·00 2·00

G173 Bubble of Toxin, City and Drums

1991. Banning of Chemical Weapons. Multicoloured.

G205 80c. Type **G173** 1·50 1·50
G206 1f.40 Hand pushing back gas mask 2·50 2·50

G175 U.N. (New York) 1951 15c. Stamp

1991. 40th Anniv of United Nations Postal Administration.

G207 **G175** 50c. blue and lilac on cream 90 90
G208 - 1f.60 blue on cream 2·75 2·75

DESIGN: 1f.60, U.N. (New York) 1951 50c. stamp.

1991. Declaration of Human Rights (3rd series). As Type **G149**. Multicoloured.

G209 50c. "Early Morning in Ro, 1925" (Paul Klee) (Article 15) 90 90
G210 90c. "The Marriage of Arnolfini" (Jan van Eyck) (Article 16) 1·60 1·60

G179 Sagarmatha National Park, Nepal

1992. 20th Anniv of UNESCO World Heritage Convention. Multicoloured.

G211 50c. Type **G179** 1·10 1·10
G212 1f.10 Stonehenge, United Kingdom 2·40 2·40

G181 U.N. Headquarters, New York

1992

G213 **G181** 3f. multicoloured 4·50 4·50

G182/183 Sea Life

1992. "Clean Oceans".

G214 **G182** 80c. multicoloured 1·60 1·60
G215 **G183** 80c. multicoloured 1·60 1·60

Nos. G214/15 were issued together, *se-tenant*, forming the composite design illustrated.

G184/187 Planet Earth

1992. Second U.N. Conference on Environment and Development, Rio de Janeiro.

G216 **G184** 75c. multicoloured 1·60 1·60
G217 **G185** 75c. multicoloured 1·60 1·60
G218 **G186** 75c. multicoloured 1·60 1·60
G219 **G187** 75c. multicoloured 1·60 1·60

Nos. G216/19 were issued together, *se-tenant*, forming the composite design illustrated.

G188/189 "Mission Planet Earth"

1992. International Space Year. Roul.

G220 **G188** 1f.10 multicoloured 1·90 1·90
G221 **G189** 1f.10 multicoloured 1·90 1·90

Nos. G220/1 were issued together, *se-tenant*, forming the composite design illustrated.

G190 Women in Science and Technology

1992. Commission on Science and Technology for Development. Multicoloured.

G222 90c. Type **G190** 1·50 1·50
G223 1f.60 Graduate using V.D.U. 3·00 3·00

1992. Universal Declaration of Human Rights (4th series). As Type **G149**. Multicoloured.

[illegible]
Court" (Jacques Louis David) (Article 21) 90 90
G225 90c. "Rocking Chair I" (Henry Moore) (Article 22) 1·60 1·60

G194 Voluntary Work

1993. "Ageing: Dignity and Participation". Tenth Anniv (1992) of International Plan of Action on Ageing. Multicoloured.

G226 50c. Type **G194** 90 90
G227 1f.60 Security of employment 3·00 3·00

G196 Gorilla

1993. Endangered Species (1st series). Multicoloured.

G228 80c. Type **G196** 1·30 1·30
G229 80c. Peregrine falcon ("Falco peregrinus") 1·30 1·30
G230 80c. Amazon manatee ("Tricheous inunguis") 1·30 1·30
G231 80c. Snow leopard ("Panthera uncia") 1·30 1·30

See also Nos. G246/9, G264/7, G290/3, G308/11, G333/6, G372/5, G389/92, G409/12, G433/6, G460/3, G476/9, G498/501, G520/3 and G544/7.

G200 Neighbourhood and Community Environment

1993. 45th Anniv of W.H.O. Multicoloured.

G232 60c. Type **G200** 1·30 1·30
G233 1f. Urban environment 2·30 2·30

1993. Declaration of Human Rights (5th series). As Type **G149**. Multicoloured.

G234 50c. "Three Musicians" (Pablo Picasso) (Article 27) 90 90
G235 90c. "Voice of Space" (Rene Magritte) (Article 28) 1·60 1·60

G204/207 Peace

1993. International Peace Day. Roul.

G236 **G204** 60c. multicoloured 1·30 1·30
G237 **G205** 60c. multicoloured 1·30 1·30
G238 **G206** 60c. multicoloured 1·30 1·30
G239 **G207** 60c. multicoloured 1·30 1·30

Nos. G236/9 were issued together, *se-tenant*, forming the composite design illustrated.

G208 Polar Bears

1993. The Environment—Climate. Multicoloured.

G240 1f.10 Type **G208** 2·10 2·10
G241 1f.10 Whale in melting ice 2·10 2·10
G242 1f.10 Elephant seal 2·10 2·10
G243 1f.10 Adelie penguins 2·10 2·10

Nos. G240/3 were issued together, *se-tenant*, forming a composite design.

G212 Father calling Child

1994. International Year of the Family. Multicoloured.

G244 80c. Type **G212** 1·50 1·50
G245 1f. Three generations 2·30 2·30

1994. Endangered Species (2nd series). As Type **G196**. Multicoloured.

G246 80c. Mexican prairie dogs ("Cynomys mexicanus") 1·30 1·30
G247 80c. Jabiru ("Jabiru mycteria") 1·30 1·30
G248 80c. Blue whale ("Balaenoptera musculus") 1·30 1·30
G249 80c. Golden lion tamarin ("Leontopithecus rosalia") 1·30 1·30

G218 Hand delivering Refugee to New Country

1994. U.N. High Commissioner for Refugees.

G250 **G218** 1f.20 multicoloured 2·75 2·75

G219/222 Shattered Globe and "Evaluation"

1994. International Decade for Natural Disaster Reduction.

G251 **G219** 60c. multicoloured 1·90 1·90
G252 **G220** 60c. multicoloured 1·90 1·90
G253 **G221** 60c. multicoloured 1·90 1·90
G254 **G222** 60c. multicoloured 1·90 1·90

Nos. G251/4 were issued together, *se-tenant*, forming the composite design illustrated.

G223 Mobilization of Resources in Developing Countries

1994. International Population and Development Conference, Cairo. Multicoloured.

G255 60c. Type **G223** 1·30 1·30
G256 80c. Internal migration of population 1·80 1·80

G225 Palais des Nations, Geneva

1994. Multicoloured.

G257 60c. Type **G225** 1·00 1·00
G258 80c. "Creation of the World" (detail of tapestry, Oili Maki) 1·30 1·30
G259 1f.80 Palais des Nations 2·75 2·75

G228 Map and Linked Ribbons

1994. 30th Anniv of United Nations Conference on Trade and Development.

G260 80c. Type **G228** 1·50 1·50
G261 1f. Map and ribbons 2·00 2·00

1995. 50th Anniv of U.N.O. (1st issue).

G262 **371** 80c. multicoloured 1·50 1·50

See also Nos. G270/1 and G275/86.

G231 "Social Summit 1995"

1995. World Summit for Social Development, Copenhagen.

G263 **G231** 1f. multicoloured 2·75 2·75

1995. Endangered Species (3rd series). As Type **G196**. Multicoloured.

G264 80c. Crowned lemur ("Lemur coronatus") 1·30 1·30
G265 80c. Giant scops owl ("Otus gurneyi") 1·30 1·30
G266 80c. Painted frog ("Atelopus varius zeteki") 1·30 1·30
G267 80c. American wood bison ("Bison bison athabascae") 1·30 1·30

G236 Field in Summer

1995. "Youth: Our Future". 10th Anniv of International Youth Year. Multicoloured.

G268 80c. Type **G236** 1·90 1·90
G269 1f. Field in winter 2·50 2·50

1995. 50th Anniv of U.N.O. (2nd issue).

G270 **379** 60c. purple 1·30 1·30
G271 - 1f.80 green 3·25 3·25
MSG272 92×70 mm. Nos. G270/1. Imperf 4·50 4·50

DESIGN: 1f.80, Veteran's Memorial Hall and Opera House, San Francisco (venue for signing of Charter).

G240 Woman and Cranes

1995. Fourth World Conference on Women, Peking. Multicoloured.

G273	60c. Type G **240**	1·30	1·30
G274	1f. Women worshipping (30×49 mm)	2·30	2·30

1995. 50th Anniv of U.N.O. (3rd issue).

G275	**385**	30c. multicoloured	65	65
G276	**386**	30c. multicoloured	65	65
G277	**387**	30c. multicoloured	65	65
G278	**388**	30c. multicoloured	65	65
G279	**389**	30c. multicoloured	65	65
G280	**390**	30c. multicoloured	65	65
G281	**391**	30c. multicoloured	65	65
G282	**392**	30c. multicoloured	65	65
G283	**393**	30c. multicoloured	65	65
G284	**394**	30c. multicoloured	65	65
G285	**395**	30c. multicoloured	65	65
G286	**396**	30c. multicoloured	65	65

Nos. G275/80 and G281/6 respectively were issued together, *se-tenant*, forming two composite designs.

G254 Catching Fish

1996. 50th Anniv of World Federation of United Nations Associations.

G287	**G254**	80c. multicoloured	1·60	1·60

G255 "Galloping Horse treading on a Flying Swallow" (Chinese bronze sculpture, Han Dynasty)

1996. Multicoloured.

G288	40c. Type **G255**	75	75
G289	70c. Palais des Nations, Geneva	1·50	1·50

1996. Endangered Species (4th series). As Type **G196**. Multicoloured.

G290	80c. "Paphiopedilum delenatii"	1·30	1·30
G291	80c. "Pachypodium baronii"	1·30	1·30
G292	80c. Yellow amaryllis ("Sternbergia lutea")	1·30	1·30
G293	80c. Cobra plant ("Darlingtonia californica")	1·30	1·30

G261 Family on Verandah of House

1996. "Habitat II" Second United Nations Conference on Human Settlements, Istanbul, Turkey. Multicoloured.

G294	70c. Type **G261**	1·50	1·50
G295	70c. Women in traditional dress in gardens	1·50	1·50
G296	70c. Produce seller and city	1·50	1·50
G297	70c. Boys playing on riverside	1·50	1·50
G298	70c. Elderly couple reading newspaper	1·50	1·50

Nos. G294/8 were issued together, *se-tenant*, forming a composite design.

G266 Cycling

1996. Sport and the Environment. Multicoloured.

G299	70c. Type **G266**	1·30	1·30
G300	1f.10 Running (horiz)	2·30	2·30
MSG301	88×78 mm. Nos. G299/300	3·75	3·75

G268 Birds in Treetop

1996. "A Plea for Peace". Winning Entries in China Youth Design Competition. Multicoloured.

G302	90c. Type **G268**	1·80	1·80
G303	1f.10 Flowers growing from bomb	2·30	2·30

G270 "The Sun and the Moon" (South American legend)

1996. 50th Anniv of UNICEF. Multicoloured.

G304	70c. Type **G270**	1·10	1·10
G305	1f.80 "Ananse" (African spider tale)	3·00	3·00

G272 U.N. Flag

1997

G306	10c. Type **G272**	25	25
G307	1f.10 "Building Palais des Nations" (detail of fresco, Massimo Campigli)	2·00	2·00

1997. Endangered Species (5th series). As Type **G196**. Multicoloured.

G308	80f. Polar bear ("Ursus maritimus")	1·30	1·30
G309	80f. Blue crowned pigeon ("Goura cristata")	1·30	1·30
G310	80f. Marine iguana ("Amblyrhynchus cristatus")	1·30	1·30
G311	80f. Guanaco ("Lama guanicoe")	1·30	1·30

G278/281 Sunrise over Mountains

1997. "Earth Summit + 5". Fifth Anniv of United Nations Conference on Environment and Development.

G312	**G278**	45f. multicoloured	1·00	1·00
G313	**G279**	45f. multicoloured	1·00	1·00
G314	**G280**	45f. multicoloured	1·00	1·00
G315	**G281**	45f. multicoloured	1·00	1·00
MSG316	90×75 mm. 1f.10 Motifs as Nos. G312/15. Imperf		2·50	2·50

Nos. G312/15 were issued together, *se-tenant*, forming the composite design illustrated.

G282 Fokker F.7 Trimotor and Airship

1997. 50th Anniversaries of Economic Commission for Europe and Economic and Social Commission for Asia and the Pacific. Multicoloured.

G317	70f. Type **G282**	1·50	1·50
G318	70f. Lockheed Constellation and Boeing 314 flying boat	1·50	1·50
G319	70f. De Havilland D.H.106 Comet and Boeing 747 jetliners	1·50	1·50
G320	70f. Ilyushin and Boeing 747 jetliners	1·50	1·50
G321	70f. Concorde Supersonic jetliner	1·50	1·50

Nos. 317/21 were issued together, *se-tenant*, forming a composite design.

1997. "Tribute to Philately". Multicoloured.

G322	70c. Type **G287**	1·30	1·30
G323	1f.10 1986 80c. philately stamp (as Type V **227**)	1·60	1·60

1997. 25th Anniv of World Heritage Convention. Terracotta Warriors from Emperor Qin Shi Huang's Tomb, Xian, China. Multicoloured.

G324	10c. As Type **434**	50	50
G325	10c. As No. 737	50	50
G326	10c. As No. 738	50	50
G327	10c. As No. 739	50	50
G328	10c. As No. 740	50	50
G329	10c. As No. 741	50	50
G330	45c. As No. 738	75	75
G331	70c. As No. 739	1·50	1·50

G295 Palais des Nations, Geneva

1998

G332	**G295**	2f. multicoloured	3·50	3·50

1998. Endangered Species (6th series). As Type **G196**. Multicoloured.

G333	80c. Tibetan stump-tailed macaques ("Macaca thibetana")	1·30	1·30
G334	80c. Greater flamingoes ("Phoenicopterus ruber")	1·30	1·30
G335	80c. Queen Alexandra's birdwings ("Ornithoptera alexandrae")	1·30	1·30
G336	80c. Fallow deer ("Cervus dama")	1·30	1·30

G300 Bull Seal

1998. International Year of the Ocean. Multicoloured.

G337	45c. Type **G300**	75	75
G338	45c. Polar bears	75	75
G339	45c. Polar bear, musk oxen, king penguins and seal on ice	75	75
G340	45c. Diver	75	75
G341	45c. Seals	75	75
G342	45c. Narwhal	75	75
G343	45c. Fishes and shark	75	75
G344	45c. Shark's tail, seal and horned puffin	75	75
G345	45c. Fishes and Gentoo penguin's back	75	75
G346	45c. Fish and jellyfishes	75	75
G347	45c. Seal, Gentoo penguin and squid	75	75
G348	45c. Gentoo penguin hunting fishes	75	75

G301 Orang-utan with Young

1998. Rainforest Preservation.

G349	**G301**	70c. multicoloured	1·30	1·30
MSG350	82×70 mm. G **301** 3f. multicoloured		5·25	5·25

G302 Soldier with Children

1998. 50 Years of United Nations Peacekeeping. Multicoloured.

G351	70c. Type **G302**	1·30	1·30
G352	90c. Soldier holding baby	1·50	1·50

G304 Birds

1998. 50th Anniv of Universal Declaration of Human Rights. Multicoloured.

G353	90c. Type **G304**	1·60	1·60
G354	1f.80 Hand releasing birds	3·25	3·25

1998. World Heritage Site. Schonbrunn Palace, Vienna. Multicoloured.

G355	10c. As No. 780	40	40
G356	10c. As No. 781	40	40
G357	10c. As No. 782	40	40
G358	30c. As Type **454**	90	90
G359	30c. As No. 778	90	90
G360	30c. As No. 779	90	90
G361	70c. As No. 781	1·30	1·30
G362	1f.10 As Type **454**	1·90	1·90

G312 Palais Wilson, Geneva

1999. Headquarters of United Nations High Commissioner for Human Rights.

G363	**G312**	1f.70 red	2·75	2·75

1999. World Heritage Sites in Australia. Multicoloured.

G364	10c. As Type **462**	40	40
G365	10c. As No. 796	40	40
G366	10c. As No. 797	40	40
G367	20c. As No. 798	75	75
G368	20c. As No. 799	75	75
G369	20c. As No. 800	75	75
G370	90c. As No. 801	1·50	1·50
G371	1f.10 As No. 802	2·00	2·00

1999. Endangered Species (7th series). As Type **G196**. Multicoloured.

G372	90c. Asiatic wild ass ("Equus hemionus")	1·60	1·60
G373	90c. Hyacinth macaw ("Anodorhynchus hyacinthinus")	1·60	1·60
G374	90c. Jamaican boa ("Epicrates subflavus")	1·60	1·60
G375	90c. Bennett's tree kangaroo ("Dendrolagus bennettianus")	1·60	1·60

G323/324 Satellite-aided Agriculture

1999. Third Conference on Exploration and Peaceful Uses of Outer Space, Vienna.

G376	**G323**	45c. multicoloured	75	75
G377	**G324**	45c. multicoloured	75	75
MSG378	90×75 mm. 2f. Combined design as Nos. G376/7 (71×29 mm)		3·75	3·75
MSG379	90×75 mm. 2f. As No. **MS**G378 but additionally inscr "PHILEXFRANCE 99 LE MONDIAL DU TIMBRE PARIS 2 AU 11 JUILLET 1999" in bottom margin		5·00	5·00

Nos. G376/7 were issued together, *se-tenant*, forming the composite design illustrated.

G325/328 Early 20th-century Mail Transport

1999. 125th Anniv of Universal Postal Union.

G380	**G325**	70c. multicoloured	1·30	1·30
G381	**G326**	70c. multicoloured	1·30	1·30
G382	**G327**	70c. multicoloured	1·30	1·30
G383	**G328**	70c. multicoloured	1·30	1·30

Nos. G380/3 were issued together, *se-tenant*, forming the composite design illustrated.

G329 Palais des Nations, Geneva

1999. "In Memoriam: Fallen in the Cause of Peace".

G384	**G329**	1f.10 multicoloured	1·90	1·90
MSG385	90×75 mm. 2f. multicoloured		3·75	3·75

G331 Couple on Globe

1999. Education: Keystone to the 21st Century.

G386	90c. Type **G331**	1·60	1·60
G387	1f.80 "Environment"	3·25	3·25

2000. International Year of Thanksgiving. Multicoloured.

G388	90c. As Type **483**	1·60	1·60

2000. Endangered Species (8th series). As Type **G196**. Multicoloured.

G389	90c. Hippopotamus (*Hippopotamus amphibius*)	1·60	1·60
G390	90c. Coscoroba swan (*Coscoroba coscoroba*)	1·60	1·60
G391	90c. Emerald monitor (*Varanus prasinus*)	1·60	1·60
G392	90c. Sea otter (*Enhydra lutris*)	1·60	1·60

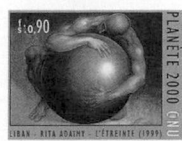

G338 "The Embrace" (Rita Adaimy)

2000. "Our World 2000" International Art Exhibition, New York. Entries in Millennium Painting Competition. Multicoloured.

G393	90c. Type **G338**	1·60	1·60
G394	1f.10 "Living Single" (Richard Kimanthi) (vert)	1·90	1·90

G340 Corner Stone Dedication, 1949

2000. 55th Anniv of the United Nations and 50th Anniv of Opening of U.N. Headquarters, New York.

G395	**G340**	90c. red, blue and ochre	1·60	1·60
G396	–	1f.40 red, blue and ochre	2·40	2·40
MSG397	67×86 mm. Nos. G395/6		4·00	4·00

DESIGN: 1f.40, Window cleaner, Secretariat Building, 1951.

G342 Two Women

G343 (image scaled to 34% of original size)

2000. "The United Nations of the 21st century". Sheet 141×165 mm containing Type **G342** and similar horiz designs, forming the overall design Type **G343**. Multicoloured.

MSG398	50c. Type **G342**; 50c. Man carrying bricks on head; 50c. Soldier and villagers; 50c. Dam and doves; 50c. Men digging; 50c. Men damming irrigation channel		6·25	6·25

2000. World Heritage Sites in Spain. Multicoloured.

G399	10c. As Type **496**	30	30
G400	10c. As No. 832	30	30
G401	10c. As No. 833	30	30
G402	20c. As No. 834	65	65
G403	20c. As No. 835	65	65
G404	20c. As No. 836	65	65
G405	1f. As No. 837	1·80	1·80
G406	1f.20 As No. 838	2·30	2·30

G350 Family of Refugees

2000. 50th Anniv of United Nations High Commissioner for Refugees.

G407	**G350**	80c. multicoloured	1·50	1·50
MSG408	121×82 mm. 1f.80 multicoloured		3·75	3·75

2001. Endangered Species (9th series). As Type **G196**. Multicoloured.

G409	90c. Lynx (*Felis lynx canadensis*)	1·60	1·60
G410	90c. Green peafowl (*Pavo muticus*)	1·60	1·60
G411	90c. Galapagos tortoise (*Geochelone elephantopus*)	1·60	1·60
G412	90c. Lemur (*Lepilemur* sp.)	1·60	1·60

G356 Hands forming Heart (Ernest Pignon-Ernest)

2001. United Nations International Year of Volunteers. Multicoloured.

G413	**G356**	90c. multicoloured	1·60	1·60
G414	1f.30 Woman's head and white dove (Paul Siche)		2·50	2·50

2001. World Heritage Sites in Japan. Multicoloured.

G415	10c. As Type **512**	25	25
G416	10c. As No. 858	25	25
G417	10c. As No. 859	25	25
G418	30c. As No. 860	65	65
G419	30c. As No. 861	65	65
G420	30c. As No. 862	65	65
G421	1f.10 As No. 858	1·90	1·90
G422	1f.30 As No. 861	2·10	2·10

2001. 40th Death Anniv of Dag Hammarskjold (United Nations Secretary General, 1953–61).

G423	**518**	2f. red	3·50	3·50

G365 Postman and "Stamps"

2001. 50th Anniv of United Nations Postal Administration.

G424	**G365**	90c. multicoloured	1·50	1·50
G425	–	1f.30 multicoloured	2·30	2·30
MS426	102×102 mm. 1f.30, 1f.80 cobalt and carmine		5·25	5·25

DESIGNS: G425, Trumpets and "Stamps"; **MS**426, Emblem.

G368 Flowers and Coastline

2001. Climate Change. Multicoloured.

G427	90c. Type **G368**	1·80	1·80
G428	90c. Wind-powered generators and brick making	1·80	1·80
G429	90c. Power station inside glass dome	1·80	1·80
G430	90c. Couple sitting beside lake	1·80	1·80

Nos. G427/30 were issued together, *se-tenant*, forming a composite design.

2001. Kofi Annan, Winner of Nobel Peace Prize, 2001.

G431	**526**	90c. multicoloured	1·60	1·60

G373 Armillary Sphere, Ariana Park

2002

G432	**G373**	1f.30 multicoloured	2·30	2·30

2002. Endangered Species (10th series). As Type **G196**. Multicoloured.

G433	90c. Bald uakari (*Cacajao calvus*)	1·60	1·60
G434	90c. Ratel (*Mellivora capensis*)	1·60	1·60
G435	90c. Pallas's cat (*Otocolobus manul*)	1·60	1·60
G436	90c. Savannah monitor (*Varanus exanthematicus*)	1·60	1·60

2002. East Timor Independence. As T **532**. Multicoloured.

G437	90c. Wooden statue	1·60	1·60
G438	1f.30 Carved wooden container	2·40	2·40

2002. International Year of Mountains. As T **534**. Multicoloured.

G439	70c. Type Weisshorn, Switzerland	1·10	1·10
G440	70c. Mount Fuji, Japan	1·10	1·10
G441	1f.20 Vinson Massif, Antarctica	2·00	2·00
G442	1f.20 Kamet, India	2·00	2·00

G384 Sun, Water, Birds and Flowers

2002. World Summit on Sustainable Development, Johannesburg. Multicoloured.

G443	90c. Type **G384**	1·60	1·60
G444	90c. Figure's wearing fashionable dress	1·60	1·60
G445	1f.80 Women's profile	3·25	3·25
G446	1f.80 Yacht	3·25	3·25

2002. World Heritage Sites in Italy. As T **547**. Multicoloured.

G447	10c. Duomo di Sant'Andrea, Amalfi Coast	40	40
G448	10c. View across Islands, Aeolian Islands	40	40
G449	10c. Del Moro Fountain, Rome	40	40
G450	20c. Santa Maria del Fiore, Florence	75	75
G451	20c. Leaning Tower, Pisa	75	75
G452	20c. The Forum, Pompeii	75	75
G453	90c. As No. G451	1·60	1·60
G454	1f.30 As No. G448	2·75	2·75

2002. AIDS Awareness Campaign. As T **548**.

G455	1f.30 AIDS Symbol on UN Secretariat Building, New York	2·50	2·50
MSG456	80×80 mm. 90c.+30c. AIDS symbol on UN Secretariat Building, New York at night	2·50	2·50

The premium was for AIDS charities.

G396 Doves

2002

G457	**G396**	3f. multicoloured	5·25	5·25

2003. Indigenous Art (1st series). Sheet 121×97 mm. As T **550**. Multicoloured.

MSG458	90c. Inca poncho, Peru; 90c. Bahia statue, Brazil; 90c. Blanket, Ecuador; 90c. Mayan stone sculpture, Xunantunich, Belize; 90c. Embroidered fabric, Guatemala; 90c. Colima terracotta sculpture, Mexico		10·00	10·00

See also Nos. **MS**G480 and **MS**G518.

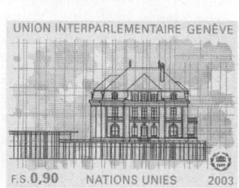

G398 Headquarters Building

2003. Inauguration of New Inter-Parliamentary Union Headquarters, Geneva.

G459	**G398**	90c. multicoloured	1·80	1·80

2003. Endangered Species (11th series). 30th Anniv of Convention on International Trade in Endangered Species (CITES). As Type **G196**. Multicoloured.

G460	90c. Red-breasted goose (*Branta ruficollis*)	1·60	1·60
G461	90c. Bald ibis (*Geronticus calvus*)	1·60	1·60
G462	90c. Fulvous whistling duck (*Dendrocygna bicolour*)	1·60	1·60
G463	90c. Channel-billed toucan (*Ramphastos vitellinus*)	1·60	1·60

2003. International Year of Freshwater. As T **559**. Multicoloured.

G464	70c. Autumnal trees and stream	1·30	1·30
G465	1f.30 Depleted lake	2·30	2·30

Nos. G464/5 were issued together, *se-tenant*, forming a composite design.

2003. Ralph Bunche (politician) Commemoration. As T **561**. Multicoloured.

G466	1f.80 Ralph Bunche	3·25	3·25

2003. World Heritage Sites in USA. As T **562**. Showing USA National Parks. Multicoloured.

G467	10c. Yosemite National Park	25	25
G468	10c. Smoky Mountains	25	25
G469	10c. Olympic National Park	25	25
G470	30c. Hawaii Volcanoes	75	75
G471	30c. Everglades	75	75
G472	30c. Yellowstone National Park	75	75
G473	90c. As G471	1·60	1·60
G474	1f.30 As G472	2·40	2·40

Nos. G467/74 have chestnut bands top and bottom.

2003. In Memoriam. Support for United Nations Staff Killed or Injured in Terrorist Attacks. As T **568**. Multicoloured.

G475	85c. Flag at half-mast	1·60	1·60

2004. Endangered Species (12th series). As Type **G196**. Multicoloured.

G476	1f. Asiatic Black Bear (*Ursus thibetanus*)	1·60	1·60
G477	1f. Northern Andean Deer (*Hippocamelus antisensis*)	1·60	1·60
G478	1f. Lion-tailed Macaque (*Macaca silenus*)	1·60	1·60
G479	1f. Guar (*Bos Gaurus*)	1·60	1·60

2004. Indigenous Art (2nd series). Sheet 125×96 mm. As T **550**. Multicoloured.

MSG480	1f.×6, Cow's decorative headgear, Switzerland; Seated woman (sculpture), Cirna Woda, Romania; Butter pats, France; Herald's embroidered tabard, United Kingdom; Medieval woodcut, Cologne; Mother and child (sculpture), Serbia & Montenegro		10·00	10·00

G418 Hand enclosing Pedestrian (pedestrians awareness campaign)

2004. Road Safety Campaign. Multicoloured.

G481	85c. Type **G418**	1·40	1·40
G482	1f. Seatbelt enclosing Body as Map (seatbelt campaign) (vert)	1·80	1·80

2004. 50th Anniv of Japanese Peace Bell. As Type **567**. Multicoloured.

G483	1f.30 Peace Bell, United Nations Headquarters, New York	2·30	2·30

2004. World Heritage Sites in Greece. As T **577**. Multicoloured.

G484	20c. Acropolis, Athens	50	50
G485	20c. Ruins, Delphi	50	50
G486	20c. Tunnel, Olympia	50	50
G487	50c. Lions, Delos	1·10	1·10
G488	50c. Pythagoreion and Heraion, Samos	1·10	1·10
G489	50c. Relief, Mycenae and Tiryns	1·10	1·10
G490	1f. As No. G485	1·80	1·80
G491	1f.30 As No. G488	2·30	2·30

Nos. G484/G491 have lake bands at left and bottom edges.

G427 Globe as Face enclosed in Dove and Hands (Anggun Sita Rustinya)

2004. Winning Designs in Children's Painting Competition "My Dream of Peace". Multicoloured.

G492	85c. Type **G427**	1·50	1·50

G493	1f.20 Woman with hair of doves (Amanda Nunez)	2·00	2·00

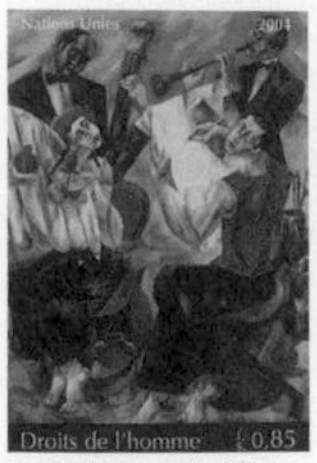

G429 Woman holding Blue Rose and Musicians

2004. International Decade of Human Rights' Education. Multicoloured.

G494	85c. Type **G429**	1·50	1·50
G495	1f.30 Family and large blue rose	2·30	2·30

The stamps of United Nations Headquarters in New York, Geneva and Vienna form a composite design.

2005. 60th Anniv of United Nations. As T **588**.

G496	**588** 1f.30 multicoloured	2·30	2·30
MSG497	100×80 mm. **588** 3f. multicoloured. Imperf	6·00	6·00

Nos. G496/**MS**G497 have lilac borders.

2005. Endangered Species (13th series). As T **589**. Multicoloured.

G498	1f. *Laelia milleri*	1·80	1·80
G499	1f. *Psygmorchis pusilla*	1·80	1·80
G500	1f. *Dendrobium cruentum*	1·80	1·80
G501	1f. *Orchis purpurea*	1·80	1·80

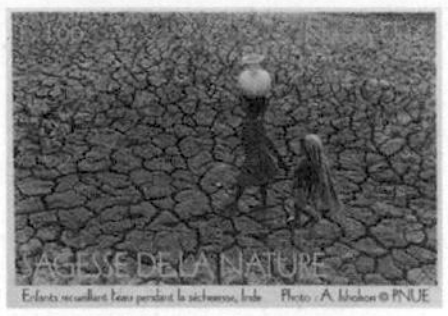
G436 Children collecting Water, India

2005. EXPO 2005 World Exhibition, Aichi, Japan. Multicoloured.

G502	**G436** 1f. Type G 436	1·90	1·90
G503	**G436** 1f.30 *Ophioderma rubicundum*, Bahamas	2·40	2·40

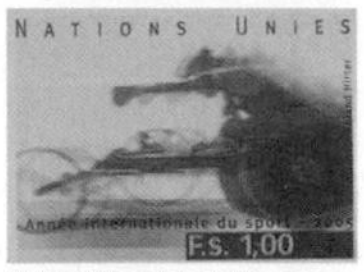

G438 Wheelchair Racer

2005. International Year of Sport. Multicoloured.

G504	1f. Type **G438**	1·90	1·90
G505	1f.30 Cyclists	2·40	2·40

2005. World Heritage. Egypt. As T **577**. Multicoloured.

G506	20c. Sphinx, Necropolis, Memphis	40	40
G507	20c. Castle, Philae	40	40
G508	20c. Abu Mena	40	40
G509	50c. Head, Necropolis, Thebes	95	95
G510	50c. Mosque, Cairo	95	95
G511	50c. Saint Catherine Monastery	95	95
G512	1f. Castle, Philae	1·90	1·90
G513	1f.30 Mosque, Cairo	2·40	2·40

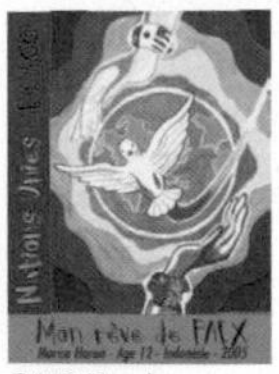

G446 Hands enclosing Globe and Dove (Marisa Harun)

2005. My Dream of Peace One Day. Winning Designs in Children's Painting Competition. Multicoloured.

G514	1f. Type **G446**	1·80	1·80
G515	1f.30 Globe and flags as dream-catcher (Carlos Teixido)	2·30	2·30

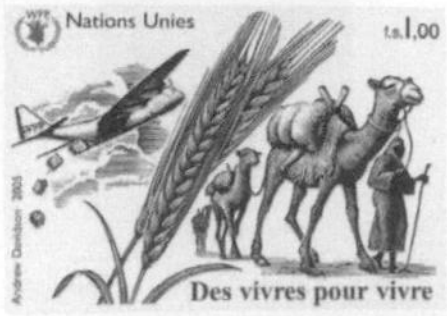

G448 Food Aid Delivery by Aircraft and Camels

2005. Food for Life.

G516	**G448** 1f. black, red and blue	1·80	1·80
G517	- 1f.30 black, red and blue	2·30	2·30

DESIGN: Women and lorries carrying food.

2006. Indigenous Art (3rd series). Musical Instruments. Sheet 125×96 mm. As T **550**. Multicoloured

MSG518	1f.20×6, Horse head bell, Benin; Drum, Swaziland; Stringed instrument (Sanza), Congo; Stringed instruments (Cavaquinho and Cimbo), Cape Verde; Gourd Caixixi, Ghana; General De Gaulle shaped bells, Central African Republic	12·00	12·00

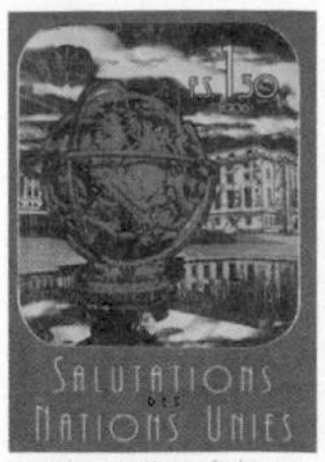

G451 Armillary Sphere, Geneva Headquarters

2006

G519	**G451** 1f.30 multicoloured	2·40	2·40

2006. Endangered Species (14th series). As T **589**. Multicoloured.

G520	1f. Tomato frog	1·80	1·80
G521	1f. Flap-necked chameleon	1·80	1·80
G522	1f. Emerald tree boa	1·80	1·80
G523	1f. Golfodulcean poison frog	1·80	1·80

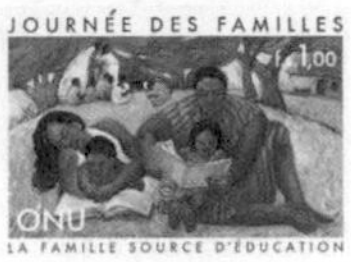

G456 Family reading

2006. International Day of Families. Multicoloured.

G524	1f. Type **G456**	1·80	1·80
G525	1f.30 Family riding Motor Scooter	2·30	2·30

2006. World Heritage. France. As T **615**.

G526	20c. Banks of the Seine	40	40
G527	20c. Provins	40	40
G528	20c. Carcassonne	40	40
G530	50c. Mont Saint Michel	95	95
G531	50c. Chateau de Chambord	95	95
G532	1f. Provins	1·80	1·80
G533	1f.30 Mont Saint Michel	2·30	2·30
G529	50c. Roman Aqueduct	95	95

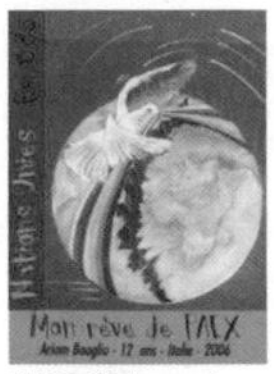

G464 Globe and Dove (Ariam Boaglio)

2006. My Dream of Peace One Day. Winning Designs in Children's Painting Competition. Multicoloured.

G534	85c. Type **G464**	1·60	1·60
G535	1f.20 Dove with Flag covered Chicks (Sierra Spicer)	2·20	2·20

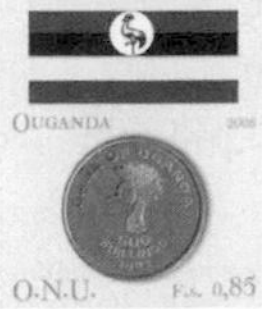

G466 Uganda

2006. Coins and Flags of Member Countries (1st series). Multicoloured.

G536	85c. Type **G466**	1·50	1·50
G537	85c. Luxembourg	1·50	1·50
G538	85c. Italy	1·50	1·50
G539	85c. New Zealand	1·50	1·50
G540	85c. Cape Verde	1·50	1·50
G541	85c. Belgium	1·50	1·50
G542	85c. Switzerland	1·50	1·50
G543	85c. Lebanon	1·50	1·50

See also Nos. G548/55.

2006. Endangered Species (15th series). As T **589**. Multicoloured.

G544	1f. Gelada baboon (*Theropithecus gelada*)	1·80	1·80
G545	1f. De Brazza's monkey (*Cercopithecus neglectus*)	1·80	1·80
G546	1f. Ruffed lemur (*Varecia varigata*)	1·80	1·80
G547	1f. Javan gibbon (*Hylobates moloch*)	1·80	1·80

2007. Coins and Flags of Member Countries (2nd series). As Type **G466**. Multicoloured.

G548	85c. Burkina Faso	1·50	1·50
G549	85c. France	1·50	1·50
G550	85c. Bolivia	1·50	1·50
G551	85c. Myanmar	1·50	1·50
G552	85c. Moldova	1·50	1·50
G553	85c. Papua New Guinea	1·50	1·50
G554	85c. Mali	1·50	1·50
G555	85c. Tunisia	1·50	1·50

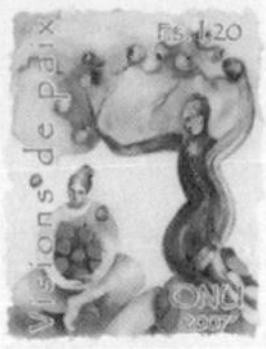
G486 Women with Apples

2007. Peaceful Visions. Multicoloured.

G556	1f.20 Type **G486**	2·00	2·00
G557	1f.80 Women with Doves	3·00	3·00

2007. World Heritage Sites. South America. As T **645**. Multicoloured.

G558	20c. Tiwanaku, Bolivia	40	40
G559	20c. Iguacu, Brazil	40	40
G560	20c. Galapagos Islands	40	40
G561	50c. Rapa Nui, Chile	95	95
G562	50c. Cueva de las Manos, Argentina	95	95
G563	50c. Machu Pichu, Peru	95	95
G564	1f. Tiwanaku, Bolivia	1·80	1·80
G565	1f.80 Machu Pichu, Peru	3·00	3·00

2007. Humanitarian Mail. As T **652**. Mulricoloured.

G566	1f.80 Flying postman and hands	3·00	3·00

2007. 50th Anniv of Space Exploration. As T **653**. Multicoloured.

G567	1f. Astronaut	1·80	1·80
G568	1f.80 Jupiter and spacecraft	3·00	3·00
MSG569	100×80 mm. 3f. Space walk	5·00	5·00

2008. International Holocaust Remembrance Day. As T **656**. Multicoloured.

G570	85c. Barbed wire becoming flowers	1·50	1·50

A stamp of a similar design was issued by Israel.

2008. Endangered Species (16th series). As T **589**. Multicoloured.

G571	1f. Pacific walrus (*Odobenus rosmarus*)	1·80	1·80
G572	1f. Brain coral (*Platygyra daedalea*)	1·80	1·80
G573	1f. Pygmy seahorse (*Hippocampus bargibanti*)	1·80	1·80
G574	1f. Beluga whale (*Delphinapterus leucas*)	1·80	1·80

2008. Coins and Flags of Member Countries (3rd series). As T **G466**. Multicoloured.

G575	85c. Madagascar	1·50	1·50
G576	85c. Rwanda	1·50	1·50
G577	85c. Nambia	1·50	1·50
G578	85c. Maldives	1·50	1·50
G579	85c. Benin	1·50	1·50
G580	85c. Iran	1·50	1·50
G581	85c. Albania	1·50	1·50
G582	85c. Turkey	1·50	1·50

2008. Convention on the Rights of People with Disablities. As T **669**. Multicoloured.

G583	1f. Rein a Notre Sujet Sans	2·10	2·10
G584	1f.80 Rein a Notre Sujet Sans	3·75	3·75

2008. Olympic Games, Beijing. As T **671**. Multicoloured.

G585	1f. Gymnastics	2·10	2·10
G586	1f.80 Tennis	3·75	3·75
MSG587	92×83 mm. As No 1035	6·00	6·00

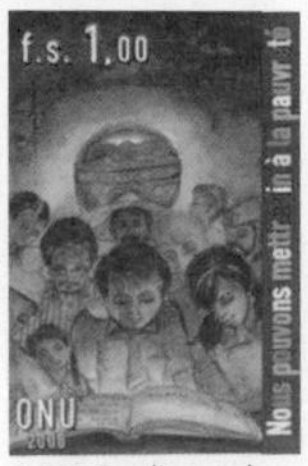

G 515 Reading and Education (Ranajoy Banerjee)

2008. We Can End Poverty. Winning Designs in Children's Painting Competition. Multicoloured.

G588	1f. Type **G515**	2·10	2·10
G589	1f.80 Children sharing (Elizabeth Elaine Chun Ning Au)	3·75	3·75

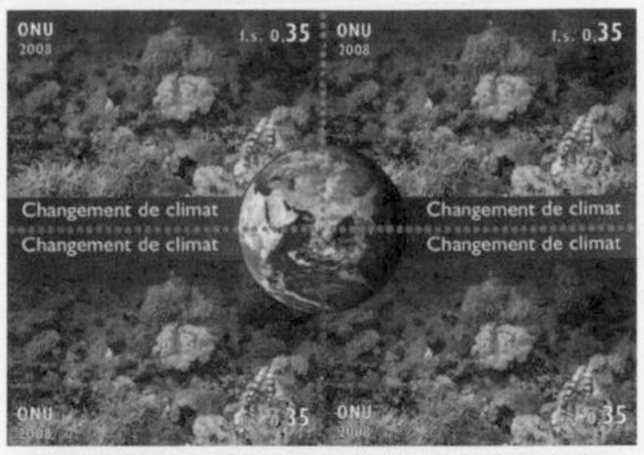

G 517a/d Coral Reef (image scaled to 49% of original size)

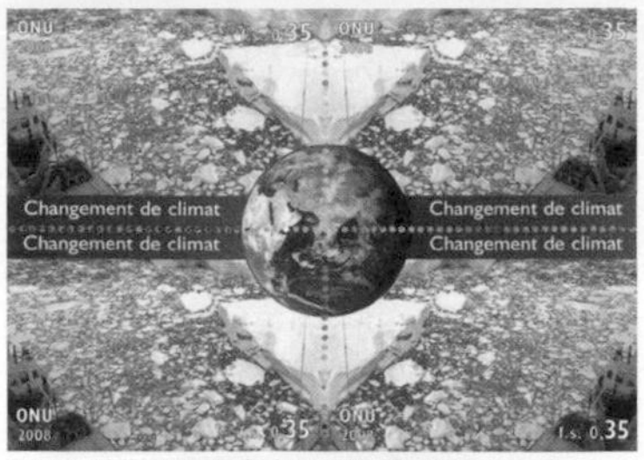

G 518a/d (image scaled to 49% of original size)

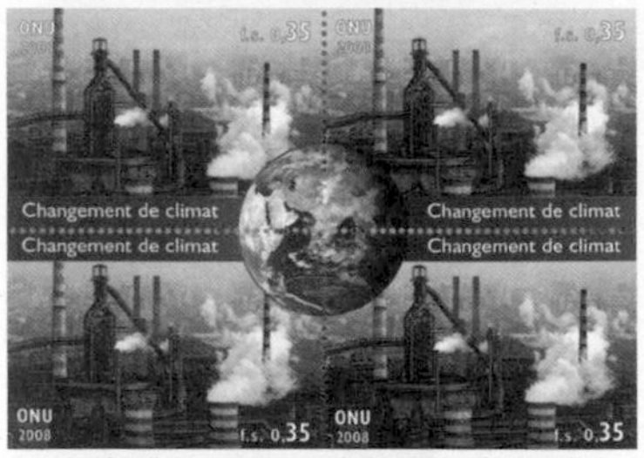

G 519a/d Pollution (image scaled to 49% of original size)

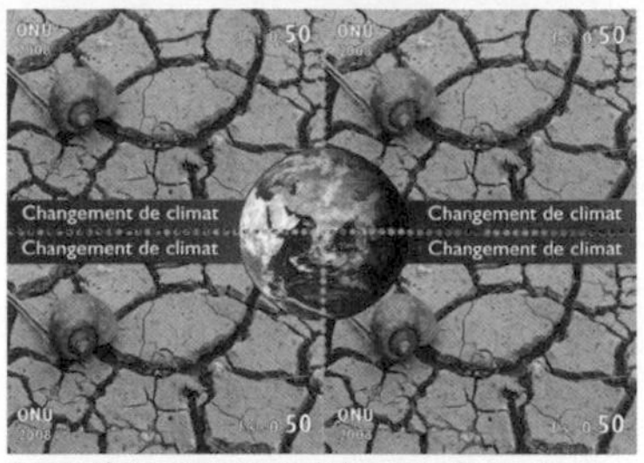

G 520a/d Desert (image scaled to 49% of original size)

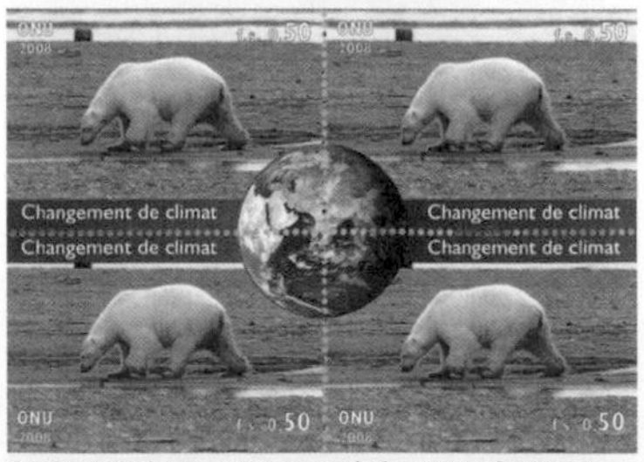

G 521a/d Polar Bear (image scaled to 49% of original size)

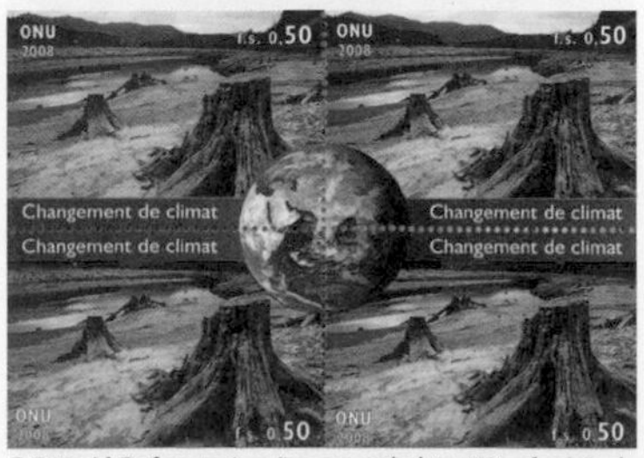

G 522a/d Deforestation (image scaled to 49% of original size)

2008. Action on Climate Change.

G590	**G517a** 35c. multicoloured	85	85
G591	**G517b** 35c. Ice Floes	85	85
G592	**G517c** 35c. multicoloured	85	85
G593	**G517d** 35c. multicoloured	85	85
G594	**G518a** 35c. multicoloured	85	85
G595	**G518b** 35c. multicoloured	85	85

G596	**G518c**	35c. multicoloured	85	85
G597	**G518d**	35c. multicoloured	85	85
G598	**G519a**	35c. multicoloured	85	85
G599	**G519b**	35c. multicoloured	85	85
G600	**G519c**	35c. multicoloured	85	85
G601	**G519d**	35c. multicoloured	85	85
G602	**G520a**	50c. multicoloured	1·00	1·00
G603	**G520b**	50c. multicoloured	1·00	1·00
G604	**G520c**	50c. multicoloured	1·00	1·00
G605	**G520d**	50c. multicoloured	1·00	1·00
G606	**G521a**	50c. multicoloured	1·00	1·00
G607	**G521b**	50c. multicoloured	1·00	1·00
G608	**G521c**	50c. multicoloured	1·00	1·00
G609	**G521d**	50c. multicoloured	1·00	1·00
G610	**G522a**	50c. multicoloured	1·00	1·00
G611	**G522b**	50c. multicoloured	1·00	1·00
G612	**G522c**	50c. multicoloured	1·00	1·00
G613	**G522d**	50c. multicoloured	1·00	1·00
MSG614		120×90 mm. 1f.20×4, As Type **G 521a/d** (Polar bear)	10·50	10·50
MSG615		120×90 mm. 1f.80×4, As Type **G 518a/d** (Ice floes)	15·00	15·00

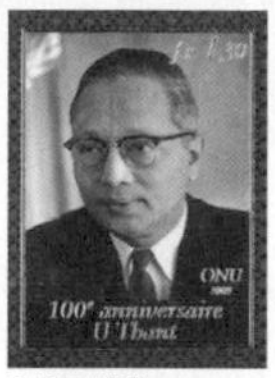

G 523 U Thant

2009. Birth Centenary of U Thant (United Nations Secretary General 1961–1971).

G616	**G 523**	1f.30 multicoloured	3·50	3·50

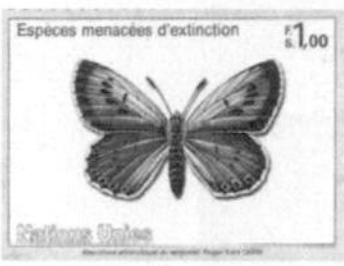

G 524 *Maculinea arion* (Large blue butterfly)

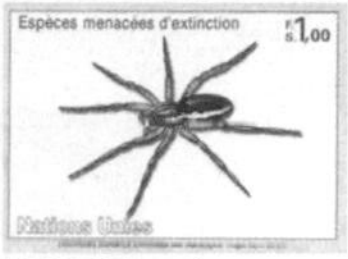

G 525 *Dolomedes plantarius* (Fen raft spider)

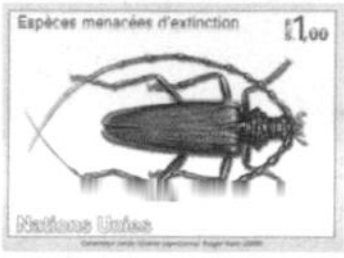

G 526 *Cerambyx cerdo* (Great Capricorn beetle)

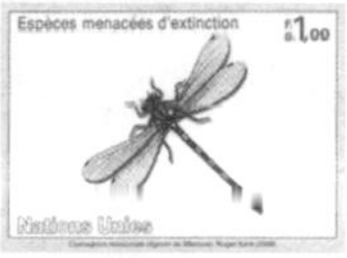

G 527 *Coenagrion mercuriale* (Southern damselfly)

2009. Endangered Species (17th series).

G617	**G524**	1f. multicoloured	2·10	2·10
G618	**G525**	1f. multicoloured	2·10	2·10
G619	**G526**	1f. multicoloured	2·10	2·10
G620	**G527**	1f. multicoloured	2·10	2·10

2009. World Heritage Sites. Germany. As T **689**. Multicoloured.

G621	30c. Town Hall and Roland on the Marketplace of Bremen	85	85
G622	30c. Wartburg Castle	85	85
G623	30c. Palaces and Parks of Potsdam and Berlin	85	85
G624	50c. Aachen Cathedral (Cathedrale d'Aix-la-Chapelle)	1·20	1·20
G625	50c. Monastic Island of Reichenau	1·20	1·20
G626	50c. Luther Memorials in Eisleben and Wittenberg	1·20	1·20
G627	1f. As N0. G622	2·30	2·30
G628	1f.30 As No. G625	3·00	3·00

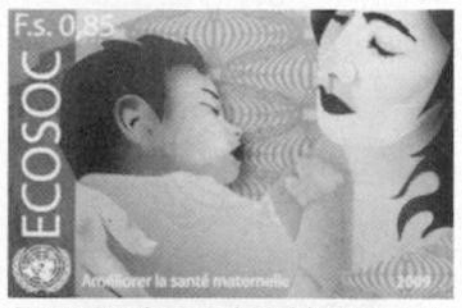

G 534 Mother and Child (Maternal health)

2009. United Nations Economic and Social Council (ECOSOC). Multicoloured.

G629	85c. Type **G534**	1·80	1·80
G630	1f.80 Vaccination (Access to essential medicines)	4·00	4·00

2009. Millennium Development Goals. As Type **697**.

G631	1f.30 chrome-yellow, black and red	2·50	2·50
G632	1f.30 bright yellow-green, black and red	2·50	2·50
G633	1f.30 orange-red, black and red	2·50	2·50
G634	1f.30 pale turquoise-blue, black and red	2·50	2·50
G635	1f.30 pale bright rose, black and red	2·50	2·50
G636	1f.30 scarlet-vermilion, black and red	2·50	2·50
G637	1f.30 apple-green, black and red	2·50	2·50
G638	1f.30 blue, black and red	2·50	2·50

DESIGNS: No. G631, Bowl of food (Eradicate extreme poverty and hunger), No. G631, Pencil (Achieve universal primary education), G632, Pencil (Achieve universal primary education); No. G633; Female symbol (Promote gender equality and empower women), No. G634, Teddy bear (Reduce child mortality); No. G635, Female figure enclosing heart (Improve maternal health); No. G636, Medicine jar (Combat HIV/AIDS, malaria and other diseases); No. G637, Stylized Tree (Ensure environmental sustainability); No. G638, Stylized figures (Develop a global partnership for development).

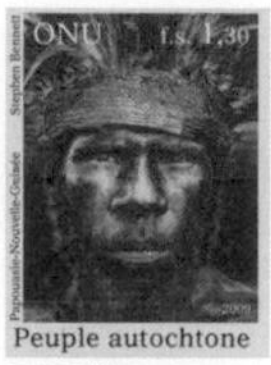

G 544 New Caledonia

2009. Indigenous Peoples. Mmulticoloured.

G639	1f.30 Type **G544**	3·00	3·00
G640	1f.30 Namibia	3·00	3·00
G641	1f.30 Namibia (different)	3·00	3·00
G642	1f.30 United Republic of Tanzania	3·00	3·00
G643	1f.30 Thailand	3·00	3·00
G644	1f.30 French Polynesia	3·00	3·00

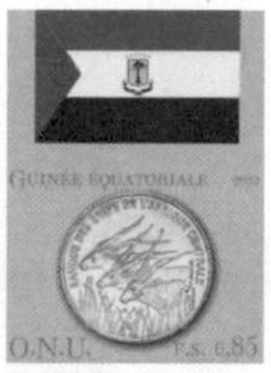

G 550 Equatorial Guinea

2010. Coins and Flags of Member Countries (4th series). Multicoloured.

G645		85c. Type **G550**	1·80	1·80
G646		85c. Laos	1·80	1·80
G647		85c. Argentine	1·80	1·80
G648		85c. Morocco	1·80	1·80
G649		85c. Seychelles	1·80	1·80
G650		85c. Mauritania	1·80	1·80
G651		85c. Sudan	1·80	1·80
G652		85c. Brunei Darussalam	1·80	1·80

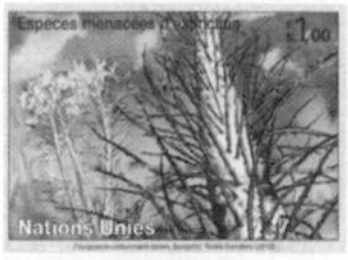

G557 *Fourquieria columnaris* (Boojum Tree)

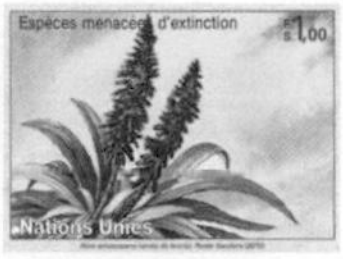

G558 *Aloe arborescens* (Krantz Aloe)

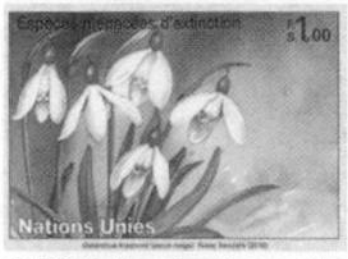

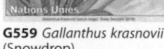

G559 *Gallanthus krasnovii* (Snowdrop)

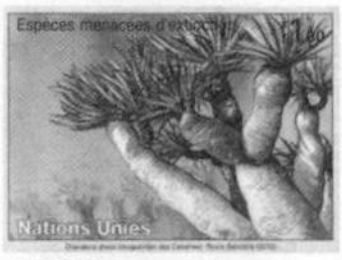

G560 *Dracaena draco* (Dragon Tree)

2010. Endangered Species (18th series)

G653	**G557**	1f. multicoloured	2·00	2·00
G654	**G558**	1f. multicoloured	2·00	2·00
G655	**G559**	1f. multicoloured	2·00	2·00
G656	**G560**	1f. multicoloured	2·00	2·00

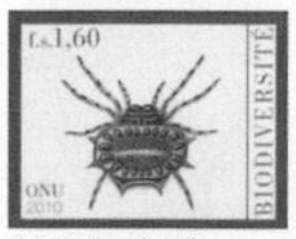

G561 Arachnid

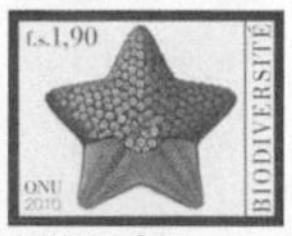

G562 Starfish

2010. International Year of Biodiversity. Art from Nature by Ernst Heinrich. Multicoloured.

G657	**G561**	1f.60 multicoloured	2·50	2·25
G658	**G562**	1f.90 multicoloured	2·50	2·25

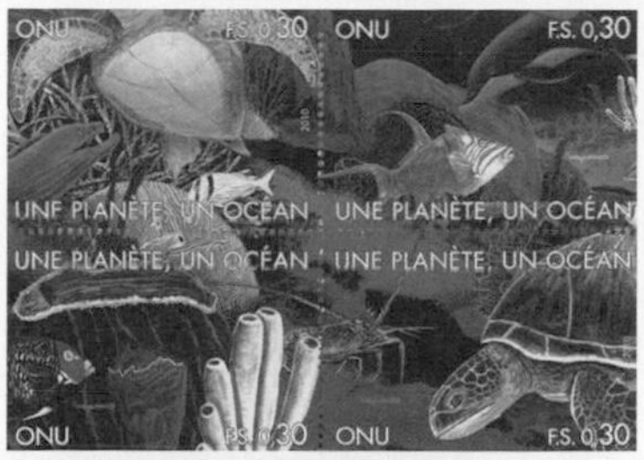

G563 - G566 Turtle, Eel, Fish and Coral (image scaled to 49% of original size)

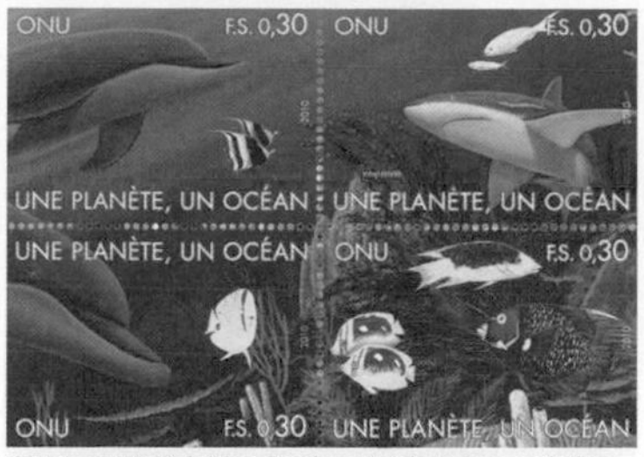

G567 - G570 Dolphins, Shark and Fish (image scaled to 49% of original size)

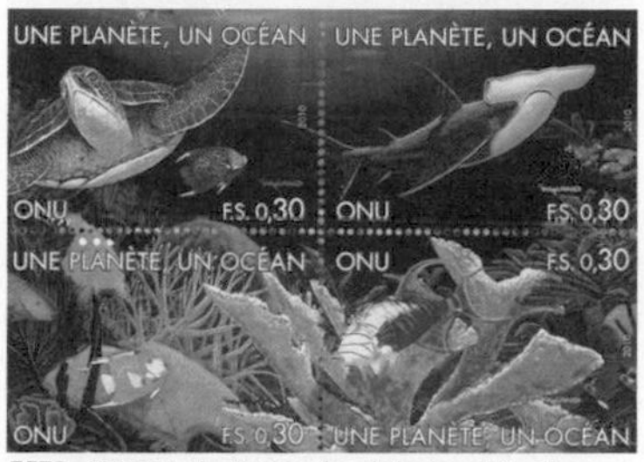

G571 - G574 Turtle, Hammerhead shark and Coral (image scaled to 49% of original size)

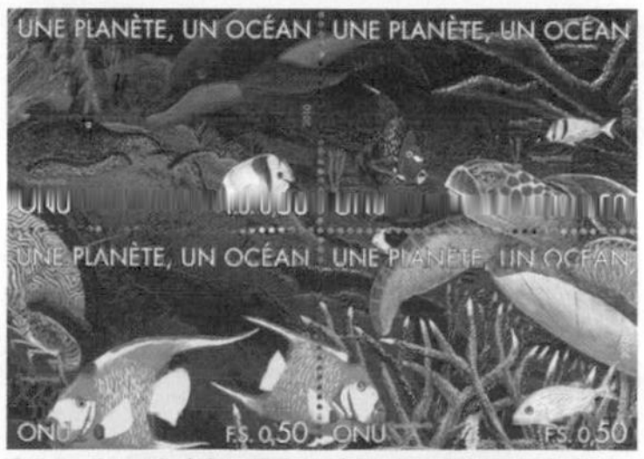

G575 - G578 Dolphin, Fish and Turtle (image scaled to 49% of original size)

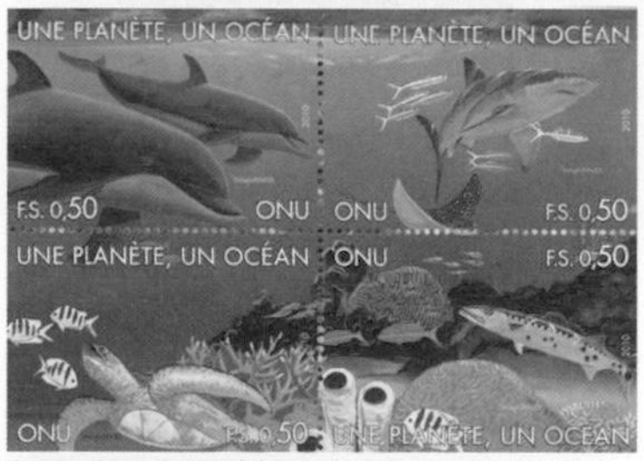

G579 - G582 Two Dolphins, Shark, Ray and Turtle (image scaled to 49% of original size)

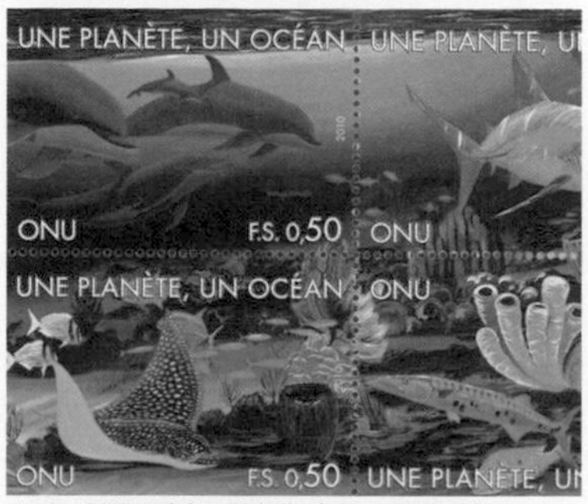

G583 - G586 Dolphin Pod, Shark, Ray and Coral

2010. One Planet, One Ocean. 50th Anniv of Intergovernmental Oceanographic Commission. Multicoloured.

G659	**G563**	30c. multicoloured	70	50
G660	**G564**	30c. multicoloured	70	50
G661	**G565**	30c. multicoloured	70	50
G662	**G566**	30c. multicoloured	70	50
G663	**G567**	30c. multicoloured	70	50
G664	**G568**	30c. multicoloured	70	50
G665	**G569**	30c. multicoloured	70	50
G666	**G570**	30c. multicoloured	70	50
G667	**G571**	30c. multicoloured	70	50
G668	**G572**	30c. multicoloured	70	50
G669	**G573**	30c. multicoloured	70	50
G670	**G574**	30c. multicoloured	70	50
G671	**G575**	50c. multicoloured	1·50	1·35
G672	**G576**	50c. multicoloured	1·50	1·35
G673	**G577**	50c. multicoloured	1·50	1·35
G674	**G578**	50c. multicoloured	1·50	1·35
G675	**G579**	50c. multicoloured	1·50	1·35
G676	**G580**	50c. multicoloured	1·50	1·35
G677	**G581**	50c. multicoloured	1·50	1·35
G678	**G582**	50c. multicoloured	1·50	1·35
G679	**G583**	50c. multicoloured	1·50	1·35
G680	**G584**	50c. multicoloured	1·50	1·35
G681	**G585**	50c. multicoloured	1·50	1·35
G682	**G586**	50c. multicoloured	1·50	1·35
MSG683		180×110 mm. 85c.×4, As Types **G579/G582**	10·00	10·00
MSG684		180×110 mm. 1f.×4, As Type **G583/G586**	12·00	12·00

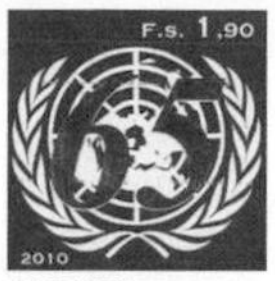

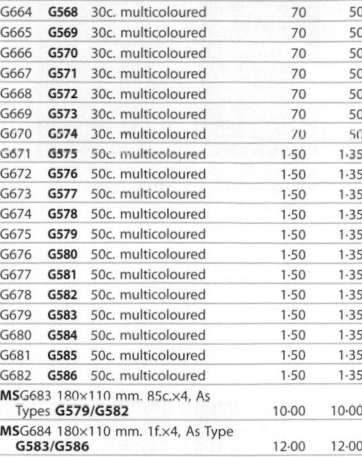

G587 '65'

2010. 65th Anniv of United Nations

G685	**G587**	1f.90 bright scarlet and gold	2·50	2·25
MSG686		80×80 mm. 1f.90×2, Type **G587**×2	12·00	12·00

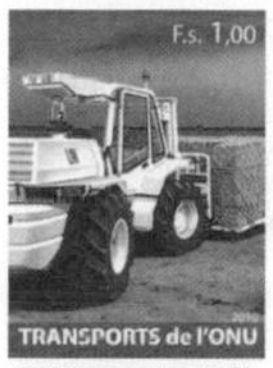

G588 Large Forklift Truck

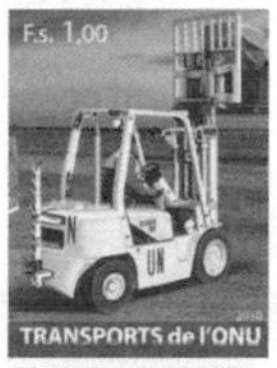

G589 Small forklift truck

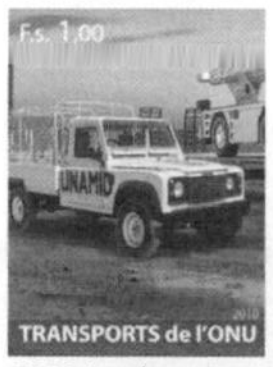

G590 Landrover with truck back

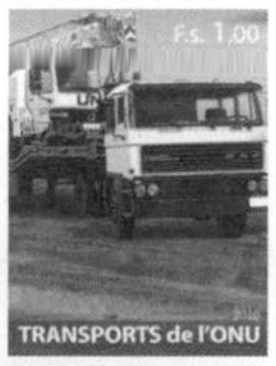

G591 Flat bed truck carrying crane

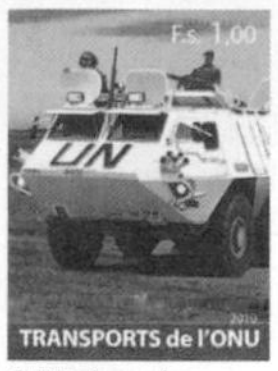

G592 Armed personnel carrier

2010. United Nations Transport - Land. Multicoloured.

G687	**G588**	1f. multicoloured	2·00	2·00
G688	**G589**	1f. multicoloured	2·00	2·00
G689	**G590**	1f. multicoloured	2·00	2·00
G690	**G591**	1f. multicoloured	2·00	2·00
G691	**G592**	1f. multicoloured	2·00	2·00

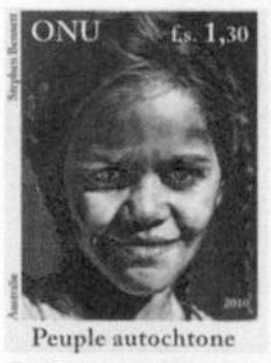

G593 Australia

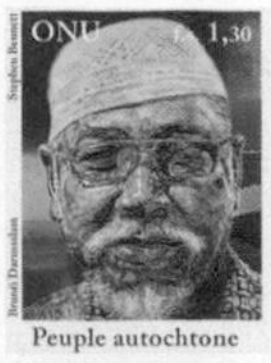

G594 Brunei

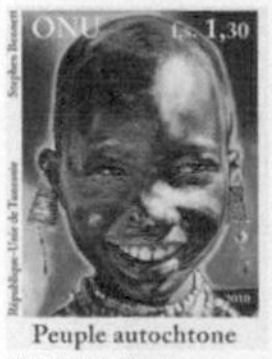

G595 United Republic of Tanzania

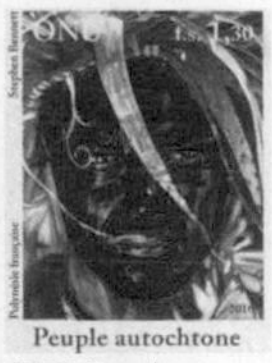

G596 French Polynesia

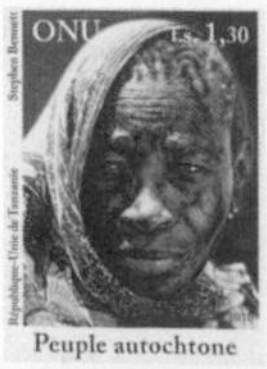

G597 United Republic of Tanzania

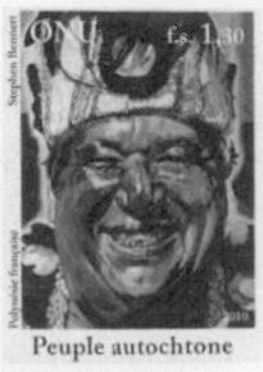

G598 French Polynesia

2010. Indigenous Peoples

G692	**G593**	1f.30 multicoloured	2·05	1·85
G693	**G594**	1f.30 multicoloured	2·05	1·85
G694	**G595**	1f.30 multicoloured	2·05	1·85
G695	**G596**	1f.30 multicoloured	2·05	1·85
G696	**G597**	1f.30 multicoloured	2·05	1·85
G697	**G598**	1f.30 multicoloured	2·05	1·85

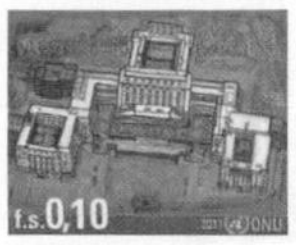

G599 Aerial View of UN Headquarters Geneva

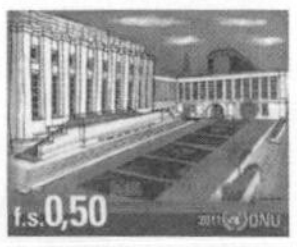

G600 UN headquarters Geneva building façade

2011. UN Building

G698	**G599**	10c. multicoloured	65	45
G699	**G600**	50c. multicoloured	1·20	95

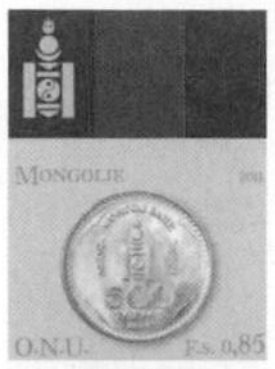

G601 Mongolia

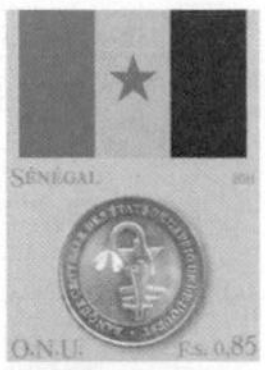

G602 Senegal

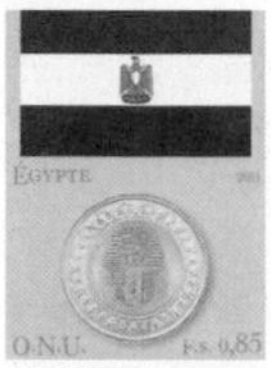

G603 Egypt

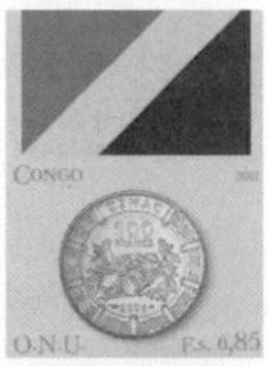

G604 Republic of the Congo

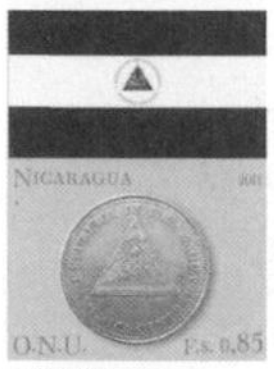

G605 Nicaragua

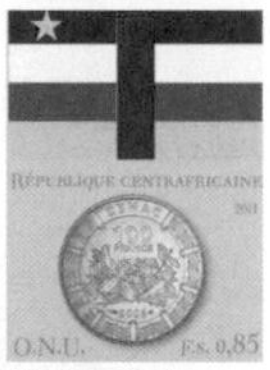

G606 Central African Republic

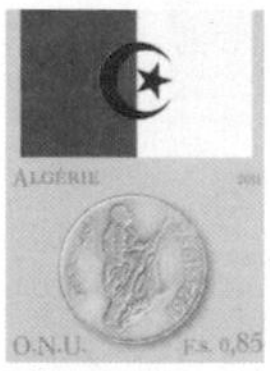

G607 Algeria

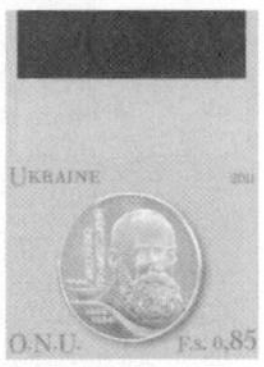

G608 Ukraine

2011. Coins and Flags of Member Countries (5th series). Multicoloured.

G700	**G601**	85c. multicoloured	1·85	1·65
G701	**G602**	85c. multicoloured	1·85	1·65
G702	**G603**	85c. multicoloured	1·85	1·65
G703	**G604**	85c. multicoloured	1·85	1·65
G704	**G605**	85c. multicoloured	1·85	1·65
G705	**G606**	85c. multicoloured	1·85	1·65
G706	**G607**	85c. multicoloured	1·85	1·65
G707	**G608**	85c. multicoloured	1·85	1·65

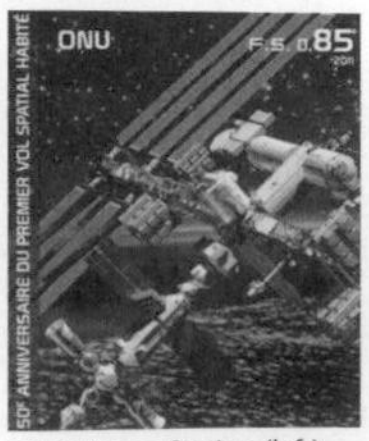

G609 Space Station (left)

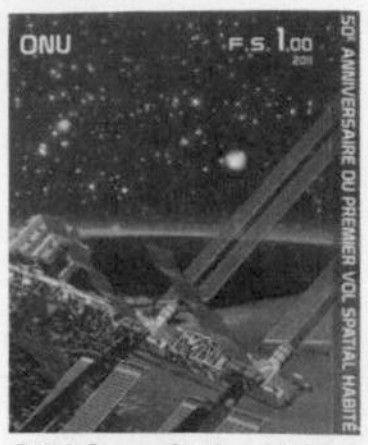

G610 Space Station (right)

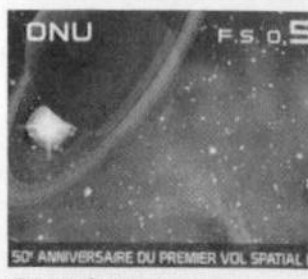

G611 Saturn

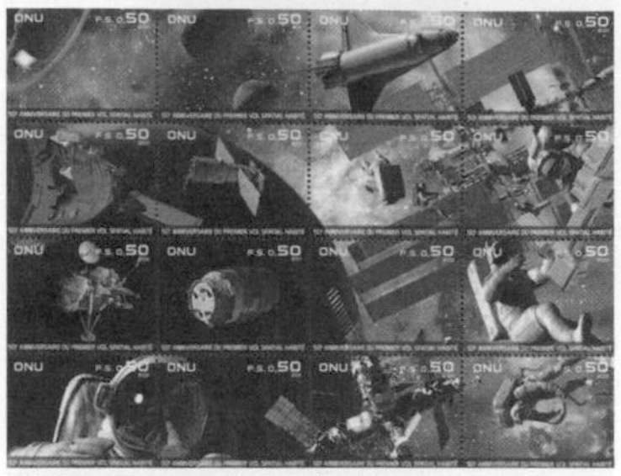

G612 Shuttle, Space Station, Satellites and Astronauts (image scaled to 30% of original size)

2011. 50th Anniv of Space Flight

G708	**G609**	85c. multicoloured	1·85	1·65
G709	**G610**	1f. multicoloured	2·00	2·00

MSG710 180×155 mm. Size 40×30 mm. 50c.×16, Type **G611** and 15 other horiz designs forming the overall design Type **G612** 25·00 25·00

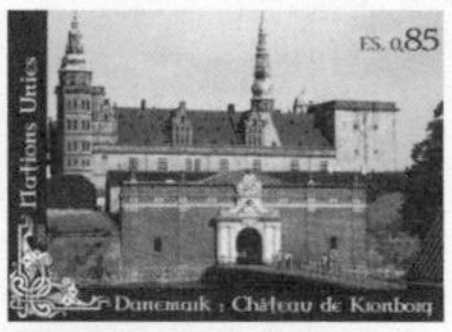

G613 Kronborg Castle, Denmark

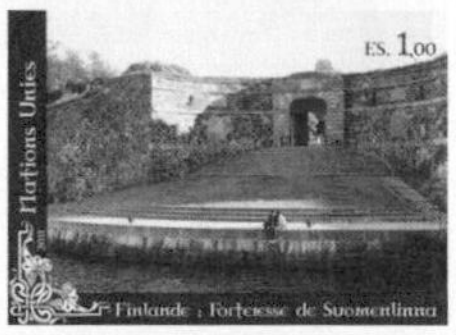

G614 Suomenlinna Fortress, Finland

2011. World Heritage Sites - Nordic Countries

G711	**G613**	85c. multicoloured	1·85	1·65
G712	**G614**	1f. multicoloured	2·00	2·00

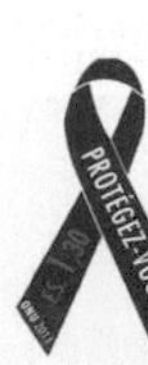

G615 AIDS Ribbon

2011. '30 Years of a World living with AIDS'

G713	**G615**	1f.30 scarlet and orange	2·50	2·25

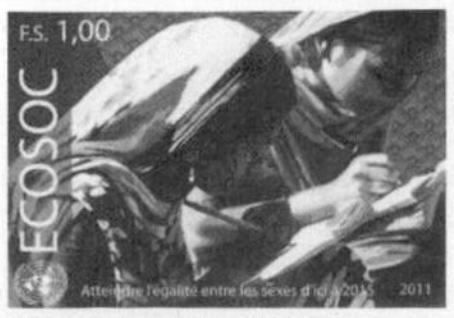

G616 Girls writing ('Achieve equality by 2015')

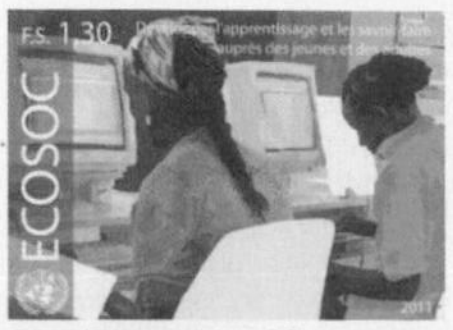

G617 Women using PCs ('Developing earning and knowledge among young people and adults')

2011. ECOSOC (Economic and Social Council) - Education

G714	**G616**	1f. multicoloured	2·00	2·00
G715	**G617**	1f.30 multicoloured	2·50	2·25

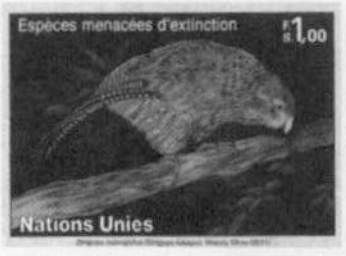

G618 *Strigops habroptilus* (Kakapo)

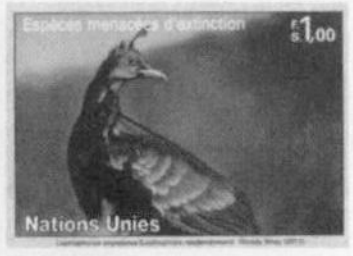

G619 *Lophophorus impejanus* (Himalayan Monal)

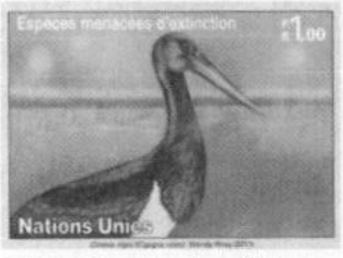

G620 *Ciconia nigra* (Black Stork)

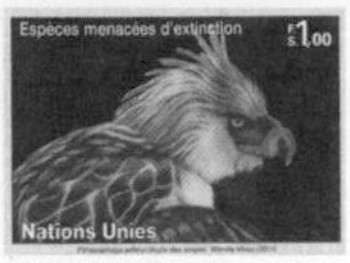

G621 *Pithecophaga jefferyi* (Philippine Eagle)

2011. Endangered Species (19th series)

G716	**G618**	1f. multicoloured	2·00	2·00
G717	**G619**	1f. multicoloured	2·00	2·00
G718	**G620**	1f. multicoloured	2·00	2·00
G719	**G621**	1f. multicoloured	2·00	2·00

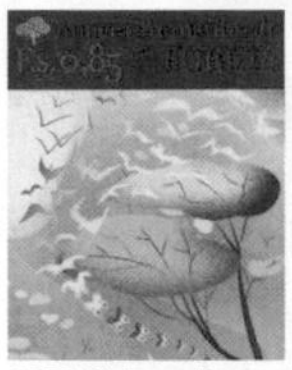

G622 Birds and Butterflies in Flight and Tree Canopy

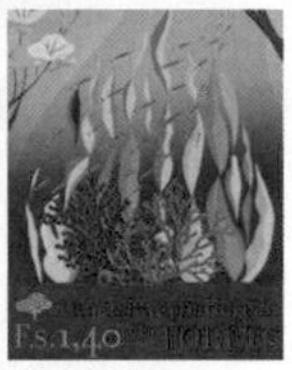

G623 Under-sea 'forest'

2011. International Year of Forests. Multicoloured.

G720	**G622**	85c. multicoloured	1·85	1·65
G721	**G623**	1f.40 multicoloured	2·50	2·25

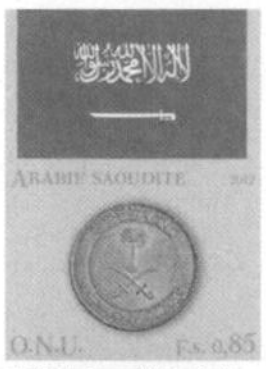

G624 Saudi Arabia

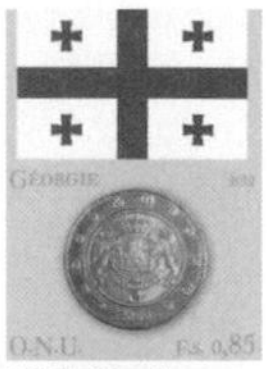

G625 Georgia

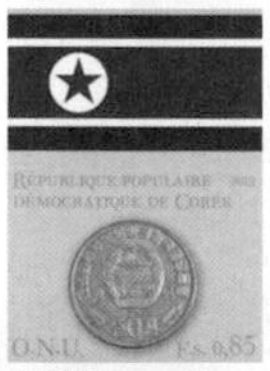

G626 Democratic People's Republic of Korea

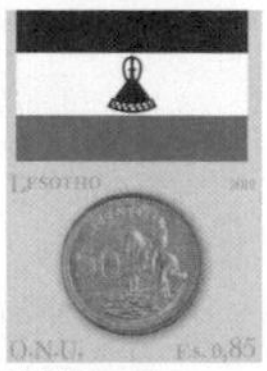

G627 Lesotho

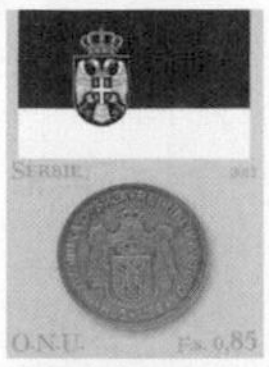

G628 Serbia

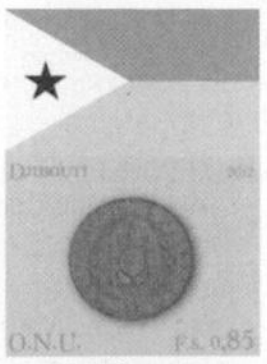

G629 Djibouti

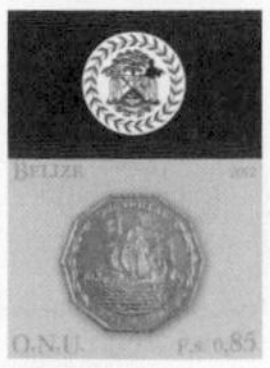

G630 Belize

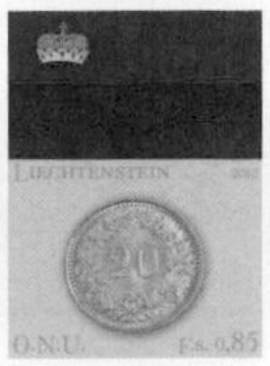

G631 Liechtenstein

2012. Coins and Flags of Member Countries (6th series). Multicoloured.

G722	**G624**	85c. multicoloured	1·50	1·50
G723	**G625**	85c. multicoloured	1·50	1·50
G724	**G626**	85c. multicoloured	1·50	1·50
G725	**G627**	85c. multicoloured	1·50	1·50
G726	**G628**	85c. multicoloured	1·50	1·50
G727	**G629**	85c. multicoloured	1·50	1·50
G728	**G630**	85c. multicoloured	1·50	1·50
G729	**G631**	85c. multicoloured	1·50	1·50

C. VIENNA HEADQUARTERS.

For use on mail posted at the United Nations Vienna International Centre and by the International Atomic Energy Agency.

NOTE. Reference to numbers and types in this section, other than those with a "V" prefix, are to the United Nations (New York or Geneva) Headquarters listing. Designs adapted for the Vienna issues are inscribed in Austrian and have face values in schillings.

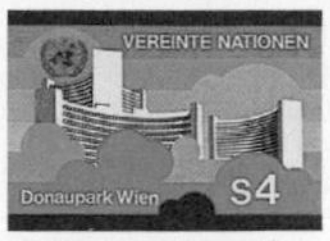

V4 Donaupark Complex

1979. Some designs adapted from issues of New York or Geneva Headquarters. Multicoloured.

V1	50g. Type **G53**	10	10
V2	1s. As No. 94	20	20
V3	2s.50 Type **162**	40	40
V3a	3s. "... for a better world"	45	45
V4	4s. Type **V4**	55	55
V5	5s. Birds in flight	55	55
V6	6s. Aerial view of Donaupark (vert)	65	65
V7	10s. As Type **52**, but without frame	1·10	1·10

1980. New International Economic Order.

V8	**195**	4s. multicoloured	85	85

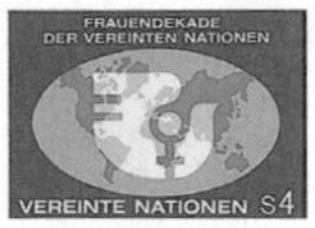

V9 Dove and World Map

1980. U.N. Decade for Women.

V9	**V9**	4s. multicoloured	55	45
V10	**V9**	6s. multicoloured	75	75

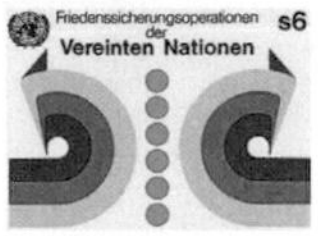

V10 "Peace-keeping"

1980. Peace-keeping Operations.

V11	**V10**	6s. multicoloured	85	85

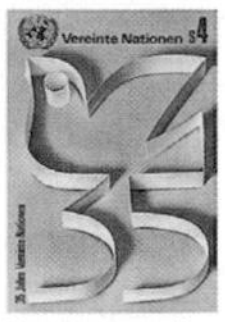

V11 Dove and "35"

1980. 35th Anniv of U.N.O.

V12	**V11**	4s. black and red	55	55
V13	-	6s. multicoloured	85	85

MSV14 92×73 mm. Nos. V12/13. Imperf 1·40 1·40

DESIGN: 6s. Stylized flower.

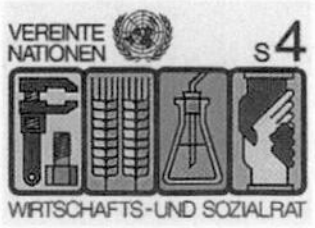

V13 Economic and Social Emblems

1980. Economic and Social Council. Multicoloured.

V15	**V13**	4s. multicoloured	55	55
V16	-	6s. green, red and black	85	85

DESIGN: 6s. Figures ascending graph.

1981. "Inalienable Rights of the Palestinian People".

V17	**206**	4s. multicoloured	55	55

1981. International Year of Disabled Persons.

V18	**207**	4s. multicoloured	55	55
V19	-	6s. orange and black	75	75

DESIGN: 6s. Knot pattern.

1981. Art.

V20	**209**	6s. multicoloured	75	75

V19 U.N. Energy Conference Emblem

1981. New and Renewable Sources of Energy.

| V21 | **V19** | 7s.50 gold and mauve | 85 | 85 |

V20 Symbols of Services

1981. Tenth Anniv of U.N. Volunteers Programme. Multicoloured.

| V22 | | 5s. Type **V20** | 55 | 55 |
| V23 | | 7s. Emblems of science, agriculture and industry | 85 | 85 |

V22 Symbols of the Environment

1982. Human Environment. Multicoloured.

| V24 | | 5s. Type Multicoloured.**22** | 55 | 55 |
| V25 | | 7s. Leaves | 85 | 85 |

V24 Satellite and Emblems

1982. Second United Nations Conference on Exploration and Peaceful Uses of Outer Space.

| V26 | **V24** | 5s. multicoloured | 75 | 75 |

V25 Fish

1982. Conservation and Protection of Nature. Multicoloured.

| V27 | | 5s. Type **V25** | 55 | 55 |
| V28 | | 7s. Elephant (mammals) | 85 | 85 |

1983. World Communications Year.

| V29 | **222** | 4s. multicoloured | 55 | 55 |

V28 Radar Screen within Lifebelt

1983. Safety at Sea: International Maritime Organization. Multicoloured.

| V30 | | 4s. Type **V28** | 55 | 55 |
| V31 | | 6s. Stylized liner | 75 | 75 |

1983. World Food Programme.

| V32 | **226** | 5s. green | 55 | 55 |
| V33 | **226** | 7s. brown | 85 | 85 |

V31 Exports

1983. Trade and Development. Multicoloured.

| V34 | | 5s. Type **V31** | 55 | 55 |
| V35 | | 8s.50 Emblems of trade | 1·10 | 1·10 |

V33 "Die Zweite Haut"

1983. 35th Anniv of Declaration of Human Rights. Multicoloured.

| V36 | | 5s. Type **V33** | 85 | 85 |
| V37 | | 7s. "Recht auf Traume" | 1·10 | 1·10 |

V35 World Agriculture

1984. International Conference on Population, Mexico City.

| V38 | **V35** | 7s. multicoloured | 1·10 | 1·10 |

V36 Irrigation

1984. World Food Day. Multicoloured.

| V39 | | 4s.50 Type **V36** | 65 | 65 |
| V40 | | 6s. Combine harvesters | 85 | 85 |

V38 Serengeti National Park, Tanzania

1984. World Heritage—UNESCO. Multicoloured.

| V41 | | 3s.50 Type **V38** | 55 | 55 |
| V42 | | 15s. Schibam, Yemen | 1·70 | 1·70 |

V40 Woman with Child

1984. Future for Refugees.

| V43 | **V40** | 4s.50 black and brown | 65 | 65 |
| V44 | - | 8s.50 black and yellow | 1·10 | 1·10 |

DESIGN: 8s.50, Woman.

V42 Stylized Figures

1984. International Youth Year.

| V45 | **V42** | 3s.50 multicoloured | 45 | 45 |
| V46 | **V42** | 6s.50 multicoloured | 95 | 95 |

V43 U Thant Pavilion

1985. 20th Anniv of Turin Centre of International Labour Organization.

| V47a | **V43** | 7s.50 violet | 95 | 95 |

V44 Rural Scene and Researcher with Microscope

1985. Tenth Anniv of United Nations University, Tokyo.

| V48 | **V44** | 8s.50 multicoloured | 1·10 | 1·10 |

V45 "Boat"

1985. Multicoloured.. Multicoloured..

| V49 | | 4s.50 Type **V45** | 55 | 55 |
| V50 | | 15s. Sheltering under U.N. umbrella | 1·60 | 1·60 |

1985. 40th Anniv of United Nations Organization. Multicoloured.

V51		6s.50 Type **243**	85	85
V52		8s.50 "Harvest Scene" (Andrew Wyeth)	1·10	1·10
MSV53		8s.50 76×82 mm. Nos. V51/2. Imperf	2·50	2·50

V49 Oral Immunization

1985. UNICEF. Child Survival Campaign. Multicoloured.

| V54 | | 4s. Type **V49** | 75 | 75 |
| V55 | | 6s. Mother and baby | 95 | 95 |

V51 "Africa in Crisis"

1986. "Africa in Crisis".

| V56 | **V51** | 8s. multicoloured | 1·10 | 1·10 |

V52 Growing Crops

1986. Development Programme. Village Scene. Multicoloured.

V57		4s.50 Type **V52**	1·10	1·10
V58		4s.50 Villagers with livestock	1·10	1·10
V59		4s.50 Woodwork instructor	1·10	1·10
V60		4s.50 Nutrition instructor	1·10	1·10

Nos. V57/60 were issued together, *se-tenant*, forming a composite design.

V56 United Nations Stamps

1986. Philately: The International Hobby.

| V61 | **V56** | 3s.50 blue and brown | 65 | 65 |
| V62 | - | 6s.50 blue and red | 1·10 | 1·10 |

DESIGN: 6s.50, Engraver.

V58 Olive Branch and Rainbow

1986. International Peace Year. Multicoloured.

| V63 | | 5s. Type **V58** | 75 | 75 |
| V64 | | 6s. Doves on U.N. emblem | 85 | 85 |

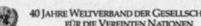

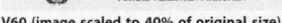

V60 (image scaled to 40% of original size)

1986. 40th Anniv of World Federation of United Nations Associations Sheet 120×65 mm. Multicoloured.

MSV65 **V60** 4s. Horse's head (Elisabeth von Janota-Bzowski); 5s. Horse rider carved from rock face (Ernst Fuchs); 6s. Abstract (Victor Vassrely); 7s. Couple (Wofgang Hutter) 4·00 4·00

1986. 9th Death Anniv of Trygve Lie (first U.N. Secretary-General).

| V66 | **259** | 8s. multicoloured | 1·30 | 1·30 |

V62 Family looking at New Houses

1987. International Year of Shelter for the Homeless.

| V67 | **V62** | 4s. orange, blk & yell | 65 | 65 |
| V68 | - | 9s.50 orange and black | 1·50 | 1·50 |

DESIGN: 9s.50, Family entering door of new house.

V64 Footballers

1987. Anti-drugs Campaign. Multicoloured.

| V69 | | 5s. Type **V64** | 85 | 85 |
| V70 | | 8s. Family | 1·30 | 1·30 |

V66 U.N. Centre, Vienna

1987. Multicoloured.. Multicoloured..

| V71 | | 2s. Type **V66** | 30 | 30 |
| V72 | | 17s. Wreath of olive leaves and doves around globe | 1·80 | 1·80 |

V68 Dancers and Vienna Headquarters

1987. United Nations Day. Multicoloured.

| V73 | | 5s. Type **V68** | 75 | 75 |
| V74 | | 6s. Dancers | 85 | 85 |

V70 Poliomyelitis

1987. "Immunize Every Child". Multicoloured.

| V75 | | 4s. Type **V70** | 75 | 75 |
| V76 | | 9s.50 Diphtheria | 1·60 | 1·60 |

V72 Woman planting

1987. International Fund for Agricultural Development "For a World without Hunger" Campaign. Multicoloured.

| V77 | | 4s. Type **V72** | 75 | 75 |
| V78 | | 6s. Women and foodstuffs | 1·10 | 1·10 |

V74 Hills and Forest in Autumn

1988. "Survival of the Forests". Multicoloured.

| V79 | | 4s. Type **V74** | 2·75 | 2·75 |
| V80 | | 5s. Forest in autumn | 3·25 | 3·25 |

Nos. V79/80 were issued together, *se-tenant*, forming a composite design.

V76 Testing
Blood Pressure

1988. International Volunteer Day. Multicoloured.
| V81 | 6s. Type **V76** | 85 | 85 |
| V82 | 7s.50 Building houses (horiz) | 1·30 | 1·30 |

V78 Skiing

1988. "Health in Sports". Multicoloured.
| V83 | 6s. Type **V78** | 85 | 85 |
| V84 | 8s. Tennis (horiz) | 1·30 | 1·30 |

1988. 40th Anniv of Declaration of Human Rights.
| V85 | **276** 5s. multicoloured | 85 | 85 |
| MSV86 | 120×79 mm. 11s. multicoloured | 2·20 | 2·20 |

V81 Transport

1989. World Bank. Multicoloured.
| V87 | 5s.50 Type **V81** | 85 | 85 |
| V88 | 8s. Health and education | 1·50 | 1·50 |

1989. Award of Nobel Peace Prize to United Nations
Peace-keeping Forces.
| V89 | **280** 6s. multicoloured | 85 | 85 |

V84 Depression
over Italy

1989. 25th Anniv of World Weather Watch.
| V90 | 4s. Type **V84** | 75 | 75 |
| V91 | 9s.50 Short-range rainfall forecast for Tokyo | 1·70 | 1·70 |

V86 Man in
Winter Clothes

1989. Tenth Anniv of United Nations Vienna International
Centre. Multicoloured.
| V92 | 5s. Type **V86** | 85 | 85 |
| V93 | 7s.50 Abstract | 1·30 | 1·30 |

V88 "Prisoners" (Kathe
Kollwitz) (Article 5)

1989. Universal Declaration of Human Rights (1st series).
| V94 | **V88** 4s. black | 65 | 65 |
| V95 | – 6s. multicoloured | 85 | 85 |
DESIGN: 6s. "Jurisprudence" (Raphael) (Article 6).
    See also Nos. V107/8, V122/3, V138/9 and V149/150.

1990. International Trade Centre.
| V96 | **287** 12s. multicoloured | 1·70 | 1·70 |

V91 "Earth" (painting by
Kurt Regschek in I.A.E.A.
Building)

1990
| V97 | **V91** 1s.50 multicoloured | 40 | 40 |

1990. Anti-AIDS Campaign. Multicoloured.
| V98 | 5s. Type **289** | 85 | 85 |
| V99 | 11s. Attacking infected blood | 1·80 | 1·80 |

V94 Annatto

1990. Medicinal Plants. Multicoloured.
| V100 | 4s.50 Type **94** | 85 | 85 |
| V101 | 9s.50 Cundeamor | 1·70 | 1·70 |

V96 "45"

1990. 45th Anniv of U.N.O. Multicoloured.
V102	7s. Type **V96**	1·20	1·20
V103	9s. "45" (different)	1·50	1·50
MSV104	100×73 mm. Nos. V102/3	3·75	3·75

V98 Men fighting

1990. Crime Prevention. Multicoloured.
| V105 | 6s. Type **V98** | 1·10 | 1·10 |
| V106 | 8s. Masked man damaging painting | 1·50 | 1·50 |

1990. Universal Declaration of Human Rights (2nd series).
As Type **V88**. Multicoloured.
| V107 | 4s.50 "Before the Judge" (Sandor Bihari) (Article 11) | 75 | 75 |
| V108 | 7s. "Young Man greeted by Woman writing Poem" (Suzuki Harunobu) (Article 12) | 1·10 | 1·10 |

V102/105 Mediterranean Coastline and Wildlife

1991. Economic Commission for Europe. "For a Better
Environment".
V109	**V102** 5s. multicoloured	95	95
V110	**V103** 5s. multicoloured	95	95
V111	**V104** 5s. multicoloured	95	95
V112	**V105** 5s. multicoloured	95	95
Nos. V109/12 were issued together, *se-tenant*, forming
the composite design illustrated.

V106 Scrubland

1991. First Anniv of Namibian Independence.
Multicoloured.
| V113 | 6s. Type **V106** | 1·10 | 1·10 |
| V114 | 9s.50 Sand dune | 1·70 | 1·70 |

V108 Different
Races

1991
| V115 | **V108** 20s. multicoloured | 2·75 | 2·75 |

V109 Boy and Girl (Anna
Harmer)

1991. 30th Anniv (1989) of U.N. Declaration of the Rights
of the Child and 1990 World Summit on Children,
New York. Children's Drawings. Multicoloured.
| V116 | 7s. Type **V109** | 1·20 | 1·20 |
| V117 | 9s. Child's world (Emiko Takegawa) | 1·60 | 1·60 |

V111 City, Bubbles of Toxin
and Gas Mask

1991. Banning of Chemical Weapons. Multicoloured.
| V118 | 5s. Type **V111** | 85 | 85 |
| V119 | 10s. Hand pushing back cloud of toxin sprayed from airplane | 1·80 | 1·80 |

V113 U.N. (New York)
1951 20c. Stamp

1991. 40th Anniv of United Nations Postal
Administration.
| V120 | **V113** 5s. brown on cream | 85 | 85 |
| V121 | – 8s. blue on cream | 1·30 | 1·30 |
DESIGN: 8s. U.N. (New York) 1951 5c. stamp.

1991. Declaration of Human Rights (3rd series). As Type
V88. Multicoloured.
| V122 | 4s.50 Ancient Mexican pottery (Article 17) | 85 | 85 |
| V123 | 7s. "Windows, 1912" (Robert Delaunay) (Article 18) | 1·30 | 1·30 |

V117 Iguacu National
Park, Brazil

1992. 20th Anniv of UNESCO. World Heritage Convention.
Multicoloured.
| V124 | 5s. Type **V117** | 95 | 95 |
| V125 | 9s. Abu Simbel, Egypt | 1·70 | 1·70 |

V119/120 Sea Life

1992. "Clean Oceans".
| V126 | **V119** 7s. multicoloured | 1·20 | 1·20 |
| V127 | **V120** 7s. multicoloured | 1·20 | 1·20 |
Nos. V126/7 were issued together, *se-tenant*, forming
the composite design illustrated.

V121/124 Planet Earth

1992. Second U.N. Conference on Environment and
Development, Rio de Janeiro.
V128	**V121** 5s.50 multicoloured	1·20	1·20
V129	**V122** 5s.50 multicoloured	1·20	1·20
V130	**V123** 5s.50 multicoloured	1·20	1·20
V131	**V124** 5s.50 multicoloured	1·20	1·20
Nos. V128/131 were issued together, *se-tenant*, forming
the composite design illustrated.

V125/126 "Mission Planet Earth"

1992. International Space Year.
| V132 | **V125** 10s. multicoloured | 1·90 | 1·90 |
| V133 | **V126** 10s. multicoloured | 1·90 | 1·90 |
Nos. V132/3 were printed together, *se-tenant*, forming
the composite design illustrated.

V127 Woman with Book
emerging from V.D.U.

1992. Commission on Science and Technology for
Development. Multicoloured.
| V134 | 5s.50 Type **V127** | 1·10 | 1·10 |
| V135 | 7s. Flowers growing from thumb | 1·30 | 1·30 |

V129 Woman's
Profile, Birds,
Butterfly and
Rose

1992. Painting. Multicoloured.
| V136 | 5s.50 Type **V129** | 85 | 85 |
| V137 | 7s. Vienna International Centre (horiz) | 1·30 | 1·30 |

1992. Universal Declaration of Human Rights (4th series).
As Type **V88**. Multicoloured.
| V138 | 6s. "The Builders" (Fernand Leger) (Article 23) | 1·20 | 1·20 |
| V139 | 10s. "Sunday Afternoon on the Island of La Grande Jatte" (Georges Seurat) (Article 24) | 1·60 | 1·60 |

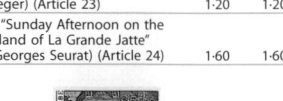

V133 Housing
and Environment

1993. "Ageing: Dignity and Participation". Tenth Anniv
(1992) of International Plan of Action on Ageing.
Multicoloured.
| V140 | 5s.50 Type **V133** | 1·20 | 1·20 |
| V141 | 7s. Education | 1·50 | 1·50 |

V135 Grevy's Zebra

1993. Endangered Species (1st series). Multicoloured.
| V142 | 7s. Type **V135** | 1·20 | 1·20 |
| V143 | 7s. Humboldt penguin ("Spheniscus humboldti") | 1·20 | 1·20 |

V144	7s. Desert monitor ("Varanus griseus")	1·20	1·20
V145	7s. Wolf ("Canis lupus")	1·20	1·20

See also Nos. V161/4, V179/82, V205/8, V223/6, V249/52, V288/91, V304/7, V324/7, V353/6, V398/401 and V442/5.

V139 Globe, Doves and U.N. Emblem

1993

V146	**V139**	13s. multicoloured	2·20	2·20

V140 Regional and National Environment

1993. 45th Anniv of W.H.O. Multicoloured.

V147	6s. Type **V140**	1·10	1·10
V148	10s. Continental and global environment	1·60	1·60

1993. Declaration of Human Rights (5th series). As Type **V88**. Multicoloured.

V149	5s. "Lower Austrian Peasants' Wedding" (Ferdinand Waldmuller) (Article 29)	1·10	1·10
V150	6s. "Outback" (Sally Morgan) (Article 30)	1·30	1·30

V144/147 Peace

1993. International Peace Day. Roul.

V151	**V144**	5s.50 multicoloured	95	95
V152	**V145**	5s.50 multicoloured	95	95
V153	**V146**	5s.50 multicoloured	95	95
V154	**V147**	5s.50 multicoloured	95	95

Nos V151/4 were issued together, *se-tenant*, forming the composite design illustrated.

V148 Monkeys

1993. The Environment—Climate. Multicoloured.

V155	7s. Type **V148**	1·40	1·40
V156	7s. Eastern bluebird and factory chimneys	1·40	1·40
V157	7s. Volcano, smokestacks and tree stumps	1·40	1·40
V158	7s. Great horned owl in desert	1·40	1·40

Nos. V155/8 were issued together, *se-tenant*, forming a composite design.

V152 Family holding Hands

1994. International Year of the Family. Multicoloured.

V159	5s.50 Type **V152**	1·10	1·10
V160	8s. Family at work	1·60	1·60

1994. Endangered Species (2nd series). As Type **V135**. Multicoloured.

V161	7s. Ocelot ("Felis pardalis")	1·20	1·20
V162	7s. White-crested white eye ("Zosterups albogularis")	1·20	1·20
V163	7s. Mediterranean monk seals ("Monachus monachus")	1·20	1·20
V164	7s. Indian elephant ("Elephas maximus")	1·20	1·20

V158 Tree and Doves

1994. Peace. Multicoloured.

V165	50g. Type **V158**	20	20
V166	4s. Herring gulls	75	75
V167	30s. Globe and dove	5·50	5·50

V161 Hands ready to help Refugees

1994. United Nations High Commissioner for Refugees.

V168	**V161**	12s. multicoloured	2·40	2·40

V162/165 Shattered Globe and "Preparation"

1994. International Decade for Natural Disaster Reduction.

V169	**V162**	6s. multicoloured	1·40	1·40
V170	**V163**	6s. multicoloured	1·40	1·40
V171	**V164**	6s. multicoloured	1·40	1·40
V172	**V165**	6s. multicoloured	1·40	1·40

Nos. V169/72 were issued together, *se-tenant*, forming the composite design illustrated.

V166 Enhancing Role of Women

1994. International Population and Development Conference, Cairo. Multicoloured.

V173	5s.50 Type **V166**	1·20	1·20
V174	7s. Relationship of population and environment	1·50	1·50

V168 Map and Crossed Ribbons

1994. 30th Anniv of United Nations Conference on Trade and Development. Multicoloured.

V175	6s. Type **V168**	1·30	1·30
V176	7s. Map and ribbons forming star	1·50	1·50

1995. 50th Anniv of U.N.O. (1st issue).

V177	**371**	7s. multicoloured	1·50	1·50

See also Nos. V185/6 and V190/201.

V171 "Social Summit 1995"

1995. World Summit for Social Development, Copenhagen.

V178	**V171**	14s. multicoloured	3·25	3·25

1995. Endangered Species (3rd series). As Type **V135**. Multicoloured.

V179	7s. Black rhinoceros ("Diceros bicornis")	1·20	1·20
V180	7s. Golden conure ("Aratinga guarouba")	1·20	1·20
V181	7s. Variegated langur ("Pygathrix nemaeus")	1·20	1·20
V182	7s. Arabian oryx ("Oryx leucoryx")	1·20	1·20

V176 Village in Winter

1995. "Youth: Our Future". 10th Anniv of International Youth Year. Multicoloured.

V183	6s. Type **V176**	1·40	1·40
V184	7s. Wheat stacks in field	1·60	1·60

1995. 50th Anniv of U.N.O. (2nd issue).

V185	**379**	7s. green	1·50	1·50
V186	-	10s. black	1·90	1·90
MSV187		92×70 mm. Nos. V185/6. Imperf	4·25	4·25

DESIGN: 10s. Veterans' Memorial Hall and Opera House, San Francisco (venue for signing of U.N. Charter).

V180 Women in Jungle

1995. Fourth World Conference on Women, Peking. Multicoloured.

V188	5s.50 Type **V180**	1·40	1·40
V189	6s. Woman reading book (28×48 mm)	1·50	1·50

1995. 50th Anniv of U.N.O. (3rd issue).

V190	**385**	3s. multicoloured	75	75
V191	**386**	3s. multicoloured	75	75
V192	**387**	3s. multicoloured	75	75
V193	**388**	3s. multicoloured	75	75
V194	**389**	3s. multicoloured	75	75
V195	**390**	3s. multicoloured	75	75
V196	**391**	3s. multicoloured	75	75
V197	**392**	3s. multicoloured	75	75
V198	**393**	3s. multicoloured	75	75
V199	**394**	3s. multicoloured	75	75
V200	**395**	3s. multicoloured	75	75
V201	**396**	3s. multicoloured	75	75

Nos. V190/201 were issued together, *se-tenant*, forming two composite designs.

V194 Jester holding Dove

1996. 50th Anniv of World Federation of United Nations Associations. Multicoloured.

V202	**V194**	7s. multicoloured	1·30	1·30

V195 U.N. Flag

1996. U.N. Flag. Multicoloured.

V203	1s. Type **V195**	20	20
V204	10s. Abstract painting (Karl Korab)	1·80	1·80

1996. Endangered Species (4th series). As Type **V135**. Multicoloured.

V205	7s. Venus slipper orchid ("Cypripedium calceolus")	1·20	1·20
V206	7s. "Aztekium ritteri"	1·20	1·20
V207	7s. "Euphorbia cremersii"	1·20	1·20
V208	7s. "Dracula bella"	1·20	1·20

V201 Family with Agricultural Products

1996. "Habitat II" Second U.N. Conf on Human Settlements, Istanbul, Turkey. Multicoloured.

V209	6s. Type **V201**	1·20	1·20
V210	6s. Women with sacks of grain	1·20	1·20
V211	6s. Woman and city	1·20	1·20
V212	6s. Ploughing with oxen	1·20	1·20
V213	6s. Villlage and elephant	1·20	1·20

Nos. V209/13 were issued together, *se-tenant*, forming a composite design.

V206 Gymnastics

1996. Sport and the Environment. Multicoloured.

V214	6s. Type **V206**	1·20	1·20
V215	7s. Hurdling	1·60	1·60
MSV216	88×78 mm. Nos. V214/15	3·25	3·25

V208 Dove and Butterflies

1996. "A Plea for Peace". Winners of China Youth Design Competition. Multicoloured.

V217	7s. Type **V208**	1·40	1·40
V218	10s. Children and flowers in dove	2·20	2·20

V210 "Hansel and Gretel" (Brothers Grimm)

1996. 50th Anniv of UNICEF. Children's Stories.. Multicoloured.

V219	5s.50 Type **V210**	1·10	1·10
V220	8s. "How Maui Stole Fire from the Gods" (Pacific Islands myth)	1·40	1·40

1997. Details of "Phoenixes flying Down" by Sagenji Yoshida. Multicoloured.

V221	5s. Type **V212**	95	95
V222	6s. Green phoenix	1·20	1·20

V212 Red Phoenix

1997. Endangered Species (5th series). As Type **V135**. Multicoloured.

V223	7s. Barbary ape ("Macaca sylvanus")	1·30	1·30
V224	7s. Stanley crane ("Anthropoides paradisea")	1·30	1·30
V225	7s. Przewalski's horse ("Equus przewalskii")	1·30	1·30
V226	7s. Giant anteater ("Myrmecophaga tridactyla")	1·30	1·30

V218/221 River Scene

1997. "Earth Summit + 5". Fifth Anniv of United Nations Conference on Environment and Development.

V227	**V218**	3s.50 multicoloured	85	85
V228	**V219**	3s.50 multicoloured	85	85
V229	**V220**	3s.50 multicoloured	85	85
V230	**V221**	3s.50 multicoloured	85	85
MSV231	V **231**	90×75 mm. 11s. Motifs as Nos. V227/30. Imperf	3·50	3·50

Nos. V227/30 were issued together, *se-tenant*, forming the composite design illustrated.

V222 Stephenson's Locomotive "Rocket" and Darraque Motor Car (1901)

1997. 50th Anniversaries of Economic Commission for Europe and Economic and Social Commission for Asia and the Pacific. Multicoloured.

V232	7s. Type **V222**	1·30	1·30
V233	7s. Russian steam locomotive and American streetcar	1·30	1·30
V234	7s. Diesel train and British double-decker bus	1·30	1·30
V235	7s. Diesel locomotive and articulated trailer lorry	1·30	1·30
V236	7s. High speed electric train and electric-powered car	1·30	1·30

Nos. V232/6 were issued together, *se-tenant*, forming a composite design.

V227 1986 3s.50 Philately Stamp

1997. "Tribute to Philately". Multicoloured.

V237	6s.50 Type **V227**	1·10	1·10
V238	7s. 1986 6s.50 Philately stamp	1·30	1·30

1997. 25th Anniv of World Heritage Convention. Terracotta Warriors from Emperor Qin Shi Huang's Tomb, Xian, China. Multicoloured.

V239	1s. As Type **434**	45	45
V240	1s. As No. 737	45	45
V241	1s. As No. 738	45	45
V242	1s. As No. 739	45	45
V243	1s. As No. 740	45	45
V244	1s. As No. 741	45	45
V245	3s. As No. 740	85	85
V246	6s. As No. 741	1·50	1·50

V235 Japanese Peace Bell, Vienna

1998. Architecture. Multicoloured.

V247	6s.50 Type **V235**	1·10	1·10
V248	9s. Underground train passing Vienna Centre	1·60	1·60

1998. Endangered Species (6th series). As Type **V135**. Multicoloured.

V249	7s. Green turtle ("Chelonia mydas")	1·20	1·20
V250	7s. Burrowing owl ("Speotyto cunicularia")	1·20	1·20
V251	7s. Raja Brooke's birdwing ("Trogonoptera brookiana")	1·20	1·20
V252	7s. Lesser panda ("Ailurus fulgens")	1·20	1·20

V241 Shark

1998. International Year of the Ocean. Multicoloured.

V253	3s.50 Type **V241**	75	75
V254	3s.50 Diver and submersible	75	75
V255	3s.50 Diver and dolphins	75	75
V256	3s.50 School of fishes above diver and submersible	75	75
V257	3s.50 Sealions	75	75
V258	3s.50 Diver and underwater camera	75	75
V259	3s.50 Angelfishes	75	75
V260	3s.50 Fishes and diver	75	75
V261	3s.50 Turtle	75	75
V262	3s.50 Butterflyfishes	75	75
V263	3s.50 Anemonefish, other fishes and starfish	75	75
V264	3s.50 Starfish and butterfly-fishes	75	75

V242 Ocelot

1998. Rainforest Preservation.

V265	**V242** 6s.50 multicoloured	1·40	1·40
MSV266	82×70 mm. 22s. multicoloured	5·50	5·50

V243 Soldier distributing Supplies

1998. 50 Years of United Nations Peacekeeping. Multicoloured.

V267	4s. Type **V243**	85	85
V268	7s.50 Voters	1·50	1·50

V245 Open Head

1998. 50th Anniv of Universal Declaration of Human Rights. Multicoloured.

V269	4s.50 Type **V245**	1·10	1·10
V270	7s. Cogwheels	1·50	1·50

1998. World Heritage Site. Schonbrunn Palace, Vienna. Multicoloured.

V271	1s. As Type **454**	65	65
V272	1s. As No. 778	65	65
V273	1s. As No. 779	65	65
V274	2s. As No. 780	85	85
V275	2s. As No. 781	85	85
V276	2s. As No. 782	85	85
V277	3s.50 As No. 780	1·10	1·10
V278	7s. As No. 779	2·40	2·40

V253 "Volcanic Landscape" (detail, Peter Pongratz)

1999

V279	**V253** 8s. multicoloured	1·40	1·40

1999. World Heritage Sites in Australia. Multicoloured.

V280	1s. As Type **462**	45	45
V281	1s. As No. 796	45	45
V282	1s. As No. 797	45	45
V283	2s. As No. 798	65	65
V284	2s. As No. 799	65	65
V285	2s. As No. 800	65	65
V286	4s.50 As No. 801	95	95
V287	6s.50 As No. 802	1·40	1·40

1999. Endangered Species (7th series). As Type **V135**. Multicoloured.

V288	7s. Orang-utan ("Pongo pygmaeus")	1·20	1·20
V289	7s. Dalmatian pelican ("Pelecanus crispus")	1·20	1·20
V290	7s. Yellow anaconda ("Eunectes notaeus")	1·20	1·20
V291	7s. Caracal ("Caracal caracal")	1·20	1·20

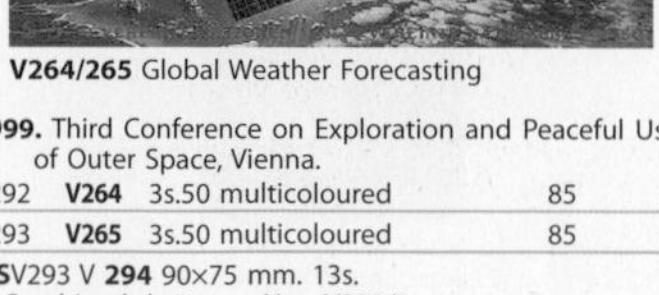

V264/265 Global Weather Forecasting

1999. Third Conference on Exploration and Peaceful Uses of Outer Space, Vienna.

V292	**V264** 3s.50 multicoloured	85	85
V293	**V265** 3s.50 multicoloured	85	85
MSV293	V **294** 90×75 mm. 13s. Combined design as Nos. V292/3 (71×29 mm)	3·00	3·00

Nos. V292/3 were issued together, *se-tenant*, forming the composite design illustrated.

V266/269 Modern Communications

1999. 125th Anniv of Universal Postal Union.

V295	**V266** 33c. multicoloured	1·20	1·20
V296	**V267** 33c. multicoloured	1·20	1·20
V297	**V268** 33c. multicoloured	1·20	1·20
V298	**V269** 33c. multicoloured	1·20	1·20

Nos. V295/8 were issued together, *se-tenant*, forming the composite design illustrated.

V270 U.N. Centre, Vienna

1999. "In Memoriam: Fallen in the Cause of Peace".

V299	**V270** 6s.50 multicoloured	1·40	1·40
MSV300	90×75 mm. 14s. multicoloured	3·00	3·00

V272 Couple leaping over Open Book

1999. Education: Keystone to the 21st Century.

V301	7s. Type **V272**	1·30	1·30
V302	13s. Group of readers	2·40	2·40

DENOMINATION. From Nos. V303 to V346, United Nations Vienna Centre stamps are denominated both in Austrian schillings and in euros. As no cash for the latter was in circulation the catalogue uses the schilling value.

2000. International Year of Thanksgiving.

V303	**483** 7s. multicoloured	1·40	1·40

2000. Endangered Species (8th series). As Type **V135**. Multicoloured.

V304	7s. Leopard (*Panthera pardus*)	1·20	1·20
V305	7s. White spoonbill (*Platalea leucorodia*)	1·20	1·20
V306	7s. Chilean guemal (*Hippocamelus bisulcus*)	1·20	1·20
V307	7s. Killer whale (*Orcinus orca*)	1·20	1·20

V279 "Tomorrow's Dream" (Voltaire Perez)

2000. "Our World 2000" International Art Exhibition, New York. Entries in Millennium Painting Competition. Multicoloured.

V308	7s. Type **279**	1·20	1·20
V309	8s. "Remembrance" (Dimitris Nalbandis)	1·40	1·40

V281 Dome of General Assembly Hall, 1951

2000. 55th Anniv of the United Nations and 50th Anniv of Opening of U.N. Headquarters, New York.

V310	**V281** 7s. green, yellow and ochre	1·30	1·30
V311	- 9s. green, yellow and ochre	1·60	1·60
MSV312	67×86 mm. Nos. V310/11	3·50	3·50

DESIGN: 9s. Ceremony to mark completion of steel framework of Secretariat Building, 1949.

V283 Agriculture

V284 (image scaled to 34% of original size)

2000. "The United Nations in the 21st Century" Sheet 141×165 mm containing Type **V283** and similar horiz designs, forming the overall design Type **V284**. Multicoloured.

MSV313	3s.50 Type V **283**; 3s.50 Soldiers with children; 3s.50 Women working; 3s.50 Soldiers using landmine detectors; 3s.50 Detectors; 3s.50 Scientist in laboratory; 3s.50 Disabled athletes	4·75	4·75

2000. World Heritage Sites in Spain. Multicoloured.

V314	1s. As Type **496**	45	45
V315	1s. As No. 832	45	45
V316	1s. As No. 833	45	45
V317	2s. As No. 834	65	65
V318	2s. As No. 835	65	65
V319	2s. As No. 836	65	65
V320	4s.50 As No. 837	95	95
V321	6s.50 As No. 838	1·40	1·40

V291 Family of Refugees

2000. 50th Anniv of United Nations Commissioner for Refugees.

V322	**V291** 7s. multicoloured	1·40	1·40
MSV323	121×82 mm. 25s. multicoloured	4·75	4·75

2001. Endangered Species (9th series). As Type **V135**. Multicoloured.

V324	7s. Spectacled bear (*Tremarctos ornatus*)	1·20	1·20
V325	7s. Laysan duck (*Anas laysanensis*)	1·20	1·20
V326	7s. Aardwolf (*Proteles cristatus*)	1·20	1·20
V327	7s. Silver langur (*Trachypithecus cristatus*)	1·20	1·20

V297 Couple (Nguyen Thanh Chuong)

2001. United Nations International Year of Volunteers. Multicoloured.

V328	10s. Type **V297**	1·60	1·60
V329	12s. Hands and heart (Ikko Tanaka)	2·00	2·00

2001. World Heritage Sites in Japan. Multicoloured.

V330	1s. As Type **512**	30	30
V331	1s. As No. 858	30	30
V332	1s. As No. 859	30	30
V333	2s. As No. 860	65	65
V334	2s. As No. 861	65	65
V335	2s. As No. 862	65	65
V336	7s. As No. 859	1·30	1·30
V337	15s. As No. 862	2·75	2·75

2001. 40th Death Anniv of Dag Hammarskjold (United Nations Secretary General, 1953–61).

V338	**518**	7s. green	1·40	1·40

V306 Balloons

2001. 50th Anniv of United Nations Postal Administration.

V339	**V306**	7s. multicoloured	1·40	1·40
V340	-	8s. multicoloured	1·50	1·50
MSV341		102×102 mm. 21s. ×2 cobalt and green	5·00	5·00

DESIGNS: V340, Cake; **MS**V341, Emblem.

V309 Futuristic Electric Car and Solar Panels

2001. Climate Change. Multicoloured.

V342	7s. Type **V309**	1·50	1·50
V343	7s. Airship, cyclists and horse rider	1·50	1·50
V344	7s. Couple walking, balloon and coastline	1·50	1·50
V345	7s. Train and traffic signs in glass dome	1·50	1·50

Nos. V342/5 were issued together, *se-tenant*, forming a composite design.

2001. Kofi Annan, Winner of Nobel Peace Prize, 2001.

V346	**526**	7s. multicoloured	1·70	1·70

V314 Semmering Railway

2002. World Heritage Sites in Austria. Multicoloured.

V347	7c. Type **V314**	30	30
V348	51c. Pferdeschwemme, Salzburg	1·30	1·30
V349	58c. Aggstein Ruin	1·40	1·40
V350	73c. Hallstatt	1·70	1·70
V351	87c. Melk Abbey	2·00	2·00
V352	€2.03 Kapitelschwemme, Salzburg	4·50	4·50

2002. Endangered Species (10th series). As Type **V135**. Multicoloured.

V353	51c. Siamang gibbon (*Hylobates syndactylus*)	1·20	1·20
V354	51c. Jackass penguin (*Spheniscus demersus*)	1·20	1·20
V355	51c. Banded linsang (*Prionodon linsang*)	1·20	1·20
V356	51c. Sonoran green toad (*Bufo retiformis*)	1·20	1·20

2002. East Timor Independence. As T **532**. Multicoloured.

V357	51c. Carved deer horn container	1·30	1·30
V358	€1.09 Weaving loom	2·75	2·75

2002. International Year of Mountains. As T **534**. Multicoloured.

V359	22c. Mt. Cook, New Zealand	65	65
V360	22c. Mt. Robson, Canada	65	65
V361	51c. Rakaposhi, Pakistan	1·20	1·20
V362	51c. Sagarmatha, Nepal	1·20	1·20

V330 Rainbow

2002. World Summit on Sustainable Development, Johannesburg. Multicoloured.

V363	51c. Type **V330**	1·20	1·20
V364	51c. Women's profiles	1·20	1·20
V365	58c. Figures wearing fashionable dress	1·50	1·50
V366	58c. Wave and doves	1·50	1·50

2002. World Heritage Sites in Italy. As T **542**. Multicoloured.

V367	7c. Duomo di Sant'Andrea, Amalfi Coast	30	30
V368	7c. View across Islands, Aeolian Islands	30	30
V369	7c. Del Moro Fountain, Rome	30	30
V370	15c. Santa Maria del Fiore, Florence	65	65
V371	15c. Leaning Tower, Pisa	65	65
V372	15c. The Forum, Pompeii	65	65
V373	51c. As No. 372	1·30	1·30
V374	58c. As No. 369	1·50	1·50

2002. AIDS Awareness Campaign. As T **549**. Multicoloured.

V375	€1.53 AIDS Symbol on UN Secretariat Building, New York	4·00	4·00
MSV376	80×80 mm. 51c.+25c. AIDS Symbol on UN Secretariat Building, New York at night	2·40	2·40

The premium was for AIDS charities.

2003. Indigenous Art (1st series). Sheet 121×97 mm. As T **550**. Multicoloured.

MSV377	51c. Mola, Panama; 51c. Mochican vessel, Peru; 51c. Tarabuco cloth, Bolivia; 51c. Masks, Cuba; 51c. Aztec headdress, Mexico; 51c. Bird-shaped staff head, Colombia	8·00	8·00

See also No. **MS**V402 and **MS**V441.

V343 Kunsthistorisches Museum, Vienna

2003. Architecture. Multicoloured.

V378	25c. Type **V343**	65	65
V379	€1 Belevedere Palace, Vienna	2·30	2·30

2003. Endangered Species. (11th series). 30th Anniv of Convention on International Trade in Endangered Species (CITES). As Type **V135**. Multicoloured.

V380	51c. Baikal teal (*Anas Formosa*)	1·20	1·20
V381	51c. Hagedash ibis (*Bostrychia hagedash*)	1·20	1·20
V382	51c. Toco toucan (*Ramphostos toco*)	1·20	1·20
V383	51c. Egyptian goose (*Alopochen aegyptiacus*)	1·20	1·20

2003. International Year of Freshwater. As T **559**. Multicoloured.

V384	55c. Snow scene with bridge	1·20	1·20
V385	75c. Snow scene with horse	1·70	1·70

Nos. V384/5 were issued together, *se-tenant*, forming a composite design.

V351 Schloss Eggenberg, Graz

2003

V386	**V351**	4c. multicoloured	30	30

2003. Ralph Bunche (politician) Commemoration. As T **561**. Multicoloured.

V387	€2.10 Ralph Bunche	5·00	5·00

2003. World Heritage Sites in USA. As T **562**. Showing USA National Parks. Multicoloured.

V388	15c. Yosemite National Park	55	55
V389	15c. Smoky Mountains	55	55
V390	15c. Olympic National Park	55	55
V391	20c. Hawaii Volcanoes	65	65
V392	20c. Everglades	65	65
V393	20c. Yellowstone National Park	65	65
V394	55c. As No. V390	1·40	1·40
V395	55c. As No. V392	2·00	2·00

V388/95 have olive bands at top and bottom edges.

2003. In Memoriam. Support for United Nations Staff Killed or Injured in Terrorist Attacks. As T **568**. Multicoloured.

V396	€2.10 Flag at half-mast	5·00	5·00

V360 Schonbrunn Schloss, Vienna

2004

V397	**V364**	55c. multicoloured	1·20	1·20

2004. Endangered Species (12th series). As T **V135**. Multicoloured.

V398	55c. Sloth Bear (*Melursus ursinus*)	1·20	1·20
V399	55c. Eld's Deer (*Cervus eldi*)	1·20	1·20
V400	55c. Cherry-crowned Mangabey (*Cercocebus torquatus*)	1·20	1·20
V401	55c. Water Buffalo (*Bubalus arnee*)	1·20	1·20

2004. Indigenous Art (2nd series). Sheet 125×96 mm. As T **550**. Multicoloured.

MSV402	55c.×6, Illuminated writing, Book of Kells, United Kingdom; Decorated eggs, Ukraine; Venus of Willendorf (statue), Austria; Carved Flatatunga panel, Iceland; Seated figure (statue), Szegvar-Tuzcoves, Hungary; Illuminated writing enclosing woman, Portugal	8·00	8·00

V366 Car and Bottles (don't drink and drive campaign)

2004. Road Safety Campaign. Multicoloured.

V403	55c. Type **V366**	1·30	1·30
V404	75c. Narrowing Road (speed control campaign) (vert)	1·90	1·90

2004. 50th Anniv of Japanese Peace Bell. As T **576**. Multicoloured.

V405	€2.10 Peace Bell, United Nations Headquarters, New York	5·25	5·25

2004. World Heritage Sites in Greece. As T **577**. Multicoloured.

V406	25c. Acropolis, Athens	65	65
V407	25c. Lions, Delos	65	65
V408	25c. Ruins, Delphi	65	65
V409	30c. Pythagoreion and Heraion, Samos	75	75
V410	30c. Tunnel, Olympia	75	75
V411	30c. Relief, Mycenae and Tiryns	75	75
V412	55c. As No. V411	1·30	1·30
V413	75c. As No. V410	1·90	1·90

Nos. V406/13 have olive bands at left and bottom edges.

V375 Child sleeping during Battle and in Field (Henry Ulfe Rentería)

2004. Winning Designs in Children's Painting Competition "My Dream of Peace". Multicoloured.

V414	55c. Type **V375**	1·20	1·20
V415	€1 Candle, doves and woman (Michelle Fortaliza)	2·40	2·40

V377 Two Families and Blue Roses

2004. International Decade of Human Rights' Education. Multicoloured.

V416	55c. Type **V377**	1·20	1·20
V417	€1.25 Dove, three couples and blue roses	3·00	3·00

The stamps of United Nations Headquarters in New York, Geneva and Vienna form a composite design.

2005. 60th Anniv of United Nations.

V418	**588**	55c. multicoloured	1·40	1·40
MSV419	100×80 mm. **588**	€2.10 multicoloured. Imperf	5·00	5·00

Nos. V418/**MS**V419 have green borders.

V380 United Nations International Centre, Vienna

2005. Greetings from the United Nations.

V420	**V380**	75c. multicoloured	1·90	1·90

2005. Endangered Species (13th series). As T **589**. Multicoloured.

V421	55c. *Ansellia Africana*	1·20	1·20
V422	55c. *Phragmipedium kovachi*	1·20	1·20
V423	55c. *Cymbidium ensifolium*	1·20	1·20
V424	55c. *Renanthera imschootiana*	1·20	1·20

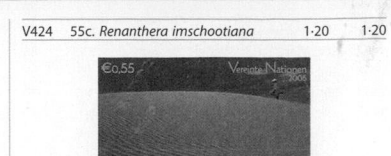

V385 Desert, China

2005. EXPO 2005 World Exhibition, Aichi, Japan. Multicoloured.

V425	55c. Type **V385**	1·30	1·30
V426	75c. Cheetahs, Africa	1·80	1·80

V387 Show Jumping

2005. International Year of Sport. Multicoloured.

V427	37c. Type **V387**	1·40	1·40
V428	70c. Football	2·75	2·75

2005. World Heritage. Egypt. As T **577**. Multicoloured.

V429	25c. Sphinx, Necropolis, Memphis	70	70
V430	25c. Castle, Philae	70	70
V431	25c. Abu Mena	70	70
V432	30c. Head, Necropolis, Thebes	85	85
V433	30c. Mosque, Cairo	85	85
V434	30c. Saint Catherine Monastery	85	85
V435	55c. Abu Mena	1·40	1·40
V436	75c. Saint Catherine Monastery	2·20	2·20

V395 Globe as Person Holding Umbrella of Flags (Lee Min Gi)

2005. My Dream of Peace One Day. Winning Designs in Children's Painting Competition. Multicoloured.

V437	55c. Type **V395**	1·40	1·40
V438	€1 People of Many Nations holding Flags as Torch (Natalie Chan)	2·40	2·40

V397 Starving Children and School Lesson

2005. Food for Life.

V439	**V397**	55c. black, green and blue	1·30	1·30
V440	-	1f.25 black, green and blue	3·00	3·00

DESIGN: 1f.25 Food aid delivery.

2006. Indigenous Art (3rd series). Musical Instruments. As T **550**. Sheet 125×96 mm. Multicoloured.

MSV441	55c.×6, Wooden drum, Republic of Guinea; Carved whistle, Congo; Figure shaped horn, Botswana; Drums, Burundi; Fang harp, Gabon; Double bell, Nigeria	7·50	7·50

2006. Endangered Species (13th series). As Type **V135**. Multicoloured.

V442	55c. Red and blue poison frog	1·20	1·20
V443	55c. Carpet chameleon	1·20	1·20
V444	55c. Amazon tree boa	1·20	1·20
V445	55c. Yellow-banded poison frog	1·20	1·20

V404 Children at Waterpipe

2006. International Day of Families. Multicoloured.

V446	55c. Type **V404**	1·30	1·30
V447	1f.25 Pounding Grain	3·00	3·00

2006. World Heritage. France. As T **615**. Multicoloured.

V448	25c. Banks of the Seine	70	70
V449	25c. Provins	70	70
V450	25c. Carcassonne	70	70

V451	30c. Roman Aqueduct	85	85
V452	30c. Mont Saint Michel	85	85
V453	30c. Chateau de Chambord	85	85
V454	55c. Carcassonne	1·30	1·30
V455	75c. Chateau de Chambord	1·80	1·80

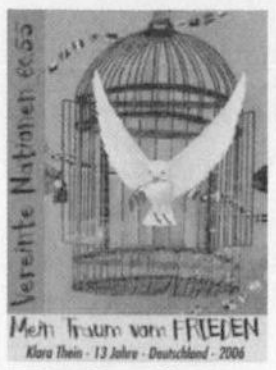

V412 Dove flying from Cage (Klara Thein)

2006. My Dream of Peace One Day. Winning Designs in Children's Painting Competition. Multicoloured.

V456	55c. Type **V412**	1·30	1·30
V457	€1 Doves and Stylized Figures rising from Globe of Flags (Laurensi Levina)	2·40	2·40

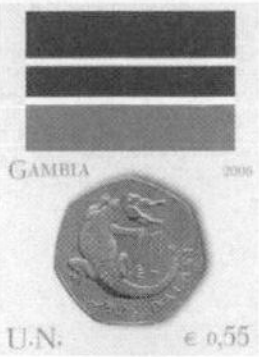

V414 Gambia

2006. Flags and Coins of Member Countries (1st series). Multicoloured.

V458	55c. Type **414**	1·30	1·30
V459	55c. Pakistan	1·30	1·30
V460	55c. Germany	1·30	1·30
V461	55c. Haiti	1·30	1·30
V462	55c. Afghanistan	1·30	1·30
V463	55c. Austria	1·30	1·30
V464	55c. Denmark	1·30	1·30
V465	55c. Netherlands	1·30	1·30

See also Nos. V470/7.

2006. Endangered Species (15h series). As T **589**. Multicoloured.

V466	55c. Savanna monkey (*Chlorocebus aethiops*)	1·30	1·30
V467	55c. Long-nosed monkey (*Nasalis larvatus*)	1·30	1·30
V468	55c. Chacma baboon (*Papio hamadryas ursinus*)	1·30	1·30
V469	55c. Patas monkey (*Erythrocebus patas*)	1·30	1·30

2007. Flags and Coins of Member Countries (2nd series). As Type **V414**. Multicoloured.

V470	55c. Trinidad and Tobago	1·30	1·30
V471	55c. Sierra Leone	1·30	1·30
V472	55c. Hungary	1·30	1·30
V473	55c. San Marino	1·30	1·30
V474	55c. Croatia	1·30	1·30
V475	55c. Spain	1·30	1·30
V476	55c. Kazakhstan	1·30	1·30
V477	55c. Eire	1·30	1·30

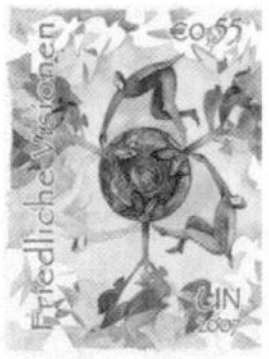

V434 Trees and Figures encircling Globe

2007. Peaceful Visions. Multicoloured.

V478	55c. Type **V434**	1·30	1·30
V479	€1.25 Couple and doves	3·00	3·00

2007. World Heritage Sites. South America. As T **645**. Multicoloured.

V480	25c. Rapa Nui, Chile	60	60
V481	25c. Cueva de las Manos, Argentina	60	60
V482	25c. Machu Pichu, Peru	60	60
V483	30c. Tiwanaku, Bolivia	70	70
V484	30c. Iguacu, Brazil	70	70
V485	30c. Galapagos Islands	70	70
V486	55c. Cueva de las Manos, Argentina	1·30	1·30
V487	75c. Iguacu, Brazil	1·80	1·80

2007. Humanitarian Mail. As T **652**. Multicoloured.

V488	75c. Flying postman and hands	1·80	1·80

2007. 50th Anniv of Space Exploration. As T **653**. Multicoloured.

V489	65c. Satellite	1·50	1·50
V490	€1.15 Satellite (different)	2·50	2·50
MSV491	100×80 mm. $2.10 Jupiter and spacecraft	4·75	4·75

2008. International Holocaust Remembrance Day. As T **656**. Multicoloured.

V492	65c. Barbed wire becoming flowers	1·50	1·50

A stamp of a similar design was issued by Israel.

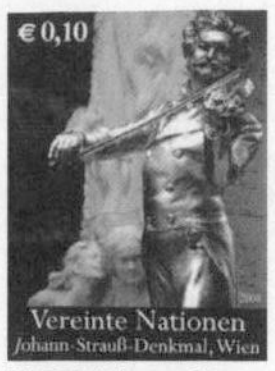

V 447 Johann Straus Memorial, Stadtpark, Vienna

2008. Tourism. Each black.

V493	10c. Type **V447**	45	45
V494	15c. Pallas Athene Fountain, Parliament Square, Vienna (horiz)	55	55
V495	65c. Pegasus Fountain, Mirabelle Palace Gardens, Salzburg (horiz)	1·70	1·70
V496	€1.40 Statue, Belevedere Palace Gardens, Vienna (horiz)	3·75	3·75

2008. Endangered Species (16th series). As T **589**. Multicoloured.

V497	65c. Northern elephant seal (*Mirounga angustirostris*)	1·60	1·60
V498	65c. Fire coral (*Millepora alcicornis*)	1·60	1·60
V499	65c. Thorny seahorse (*Hippocampus histrix*)	1·60	1·60
V500	65c. Grey whale (*Eschrichtius robustus*)	1·60	1·60

2008. Flages and Coins of Member Countries (3rd series). As T **V414**. Multicoloured.

V501	65c. Poland	1·60	1·60
V502	65c. Latvia	1·60	1·60
V503	65c. Sweden	1·60	1·60
V504	65c. Cyprus	1·60	1·60
V505	65c. Portugal	1·60	1·60
V506	65c. Armenia	1·60	1·60
V507	65c. Slovakia	1·60	1·60
V508	65c. Qatar	1·60	1·60

2008. Convention on the Rights of People with Disablities. As T **670**. Multicoloured.

V509	55c. Bildung	1·40	1·40
V510	€1.40 Bildung	3·75	3·75

2008. Olympic Games, Beijing. As T **671**. Multicoloured.

V511	- 65c. Gymnastics	1·80	1·80
V512	**V 463** €1.30 Swimming	3·75	3·75
MSV513	92×83 mm. As No. 1035	6·00	6·00

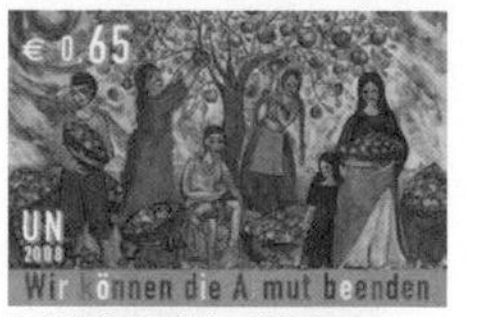

V 464 Fruit picking (Mariam Marukian)

2008. We Can End Poverty. Winning Designs in Children's Painting Competition. Multicoloured.

V514	65c. Type **V464**	2·00	2·00
V515	75c. Shelter, Health, Food and Education (Rufaro Duri)	2·20	2·20

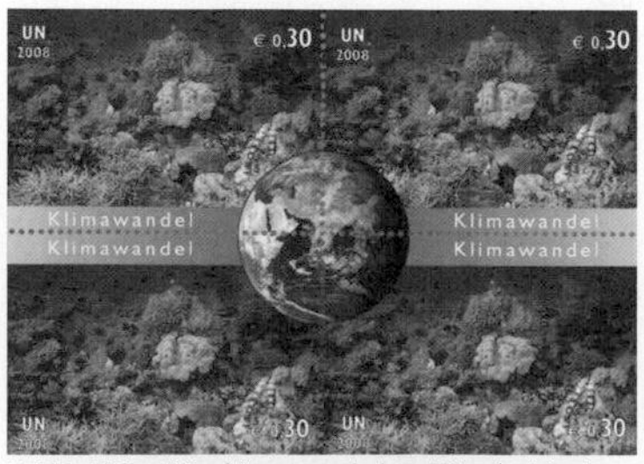

V 466a/d Coral Reef (image scaled to 49% of original size)

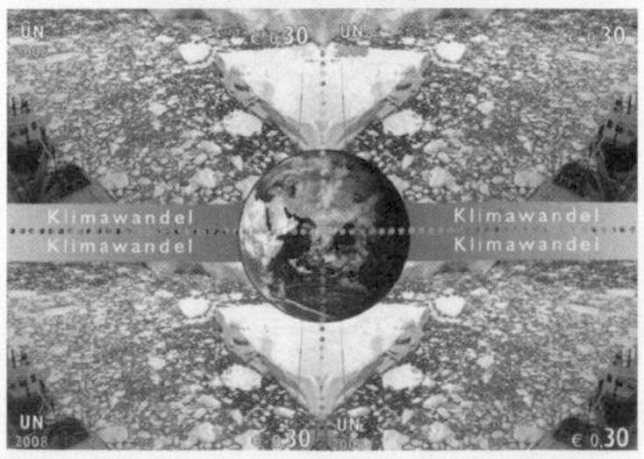

V 467a/d Ice Floes (image scaled to 49% of original size)

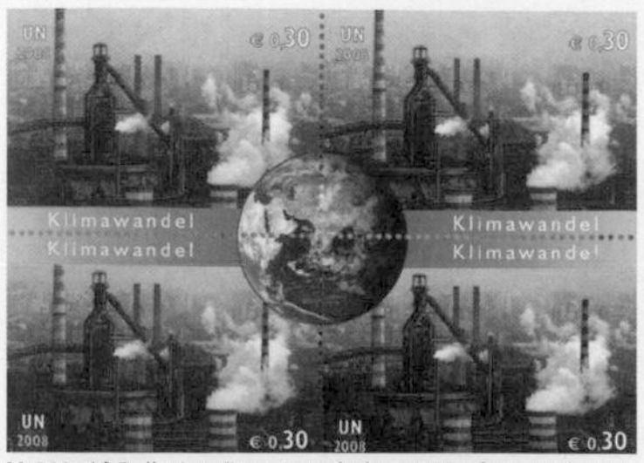

V 468a/d Pollution (image scaled to 49% of original size)

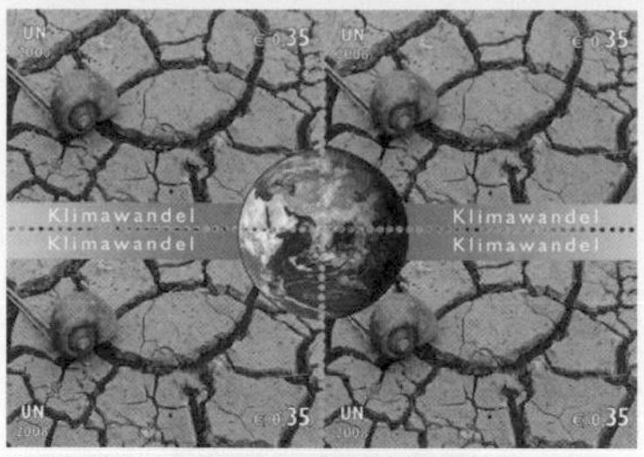

V 469a/d Desert (image scaled to 49% of original size)

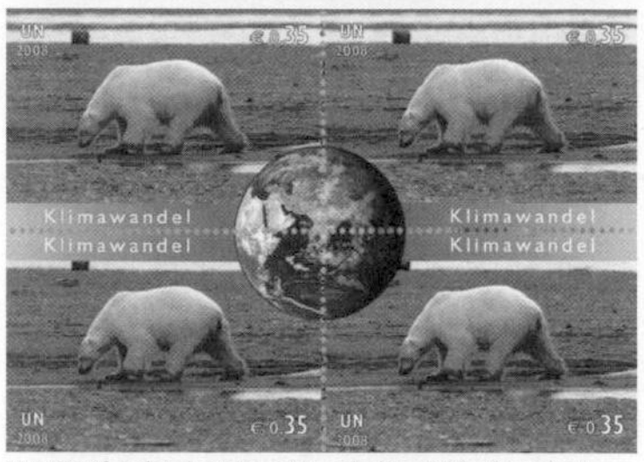

V 470a/d Polar Bear (image scaled to 49% of original size)

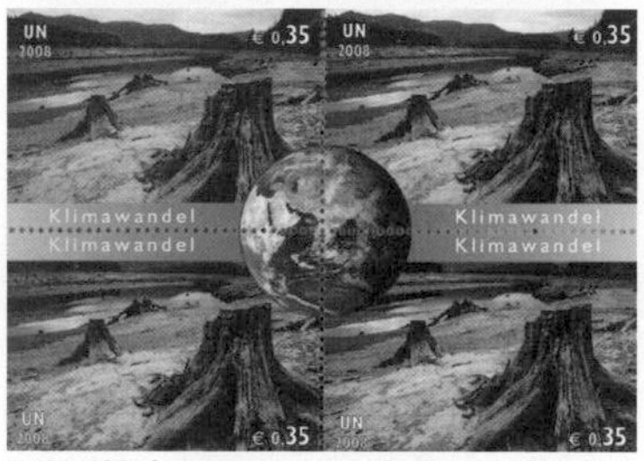

V 471a/d Deforestation (image scaled to 49% of original size)

2008. Action on Climate Change. Multicoloured.

V516	30c. Type **V466a**	95	95
V517	30c. Type **V466b**	95	95
V518	30c. Type **V466c**	95	95
V519	30c. Type **V466d**	95	95
V520	30c. Type **V467a**	95	95
V521	30c. Type **V467b**	95	95
V522	30c. Type **V467c**	95	95
V523	30c. Type **V467d**	95	95
V524	30c. Type **V468a**	95	95
V525	30c. Type **V468b**	95	95
V526	30c. Type **V468c**	95	95
V527	30c. Type **V468d**	95	95
V528	35c. Type **V469a**	95	95
V529	35c. Type **V469b**	95	95
V530	35c. Type **V469c**	95	95
V531	35c. Type **V469d**	95	95
V532	35c. Type **V470a**	95	95
V533	35c. Type **V470b**	95	95
V534	35c. Type **V470c**	95	95
V535	35c. Type **V470d**	95	95
V536	35c. Type **V471a**	95	95
V537	35c. Type **V471b**	95	95
V538	35c. Type **V471c**	95	95
V539	35c. Type **V471d**	95	95
MSV540	120×90 mm. 65c.×4, As Type **V468a/d** (Pollution)	8·50	8·50
MSV541	120×90 mm. €1.15×4, As Type **V471a/d** (Deforestation)	15·00	15·00

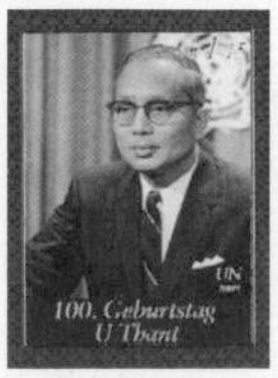

V 472 U Thant

2009. Birth Centenary of U Thant (United Nations Secretary General 1961–1971).

V542	**V472** €1.15 multicoloured	3·75	3·75

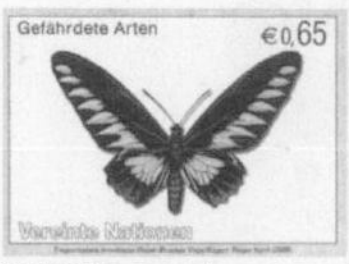

V 473 *Trogonoptera brookiana* (Rajah Brooke's Birdwing)

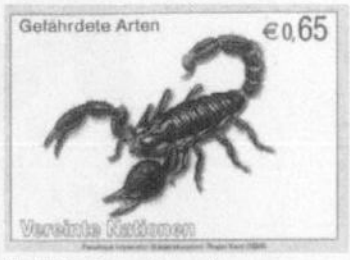

V 474 *Pandinus imperator* (Emperor Scorpion)

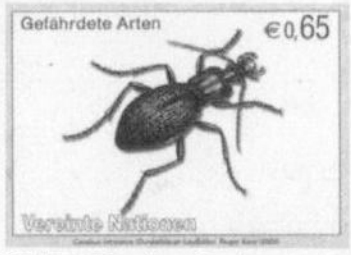

V 475 *Carabus intricatus* (Blue Ground Beetle)

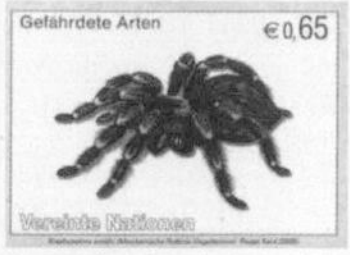

V 476 *Brachypelma smithi* (Mexican Red Knee Tarantula)

2009. Endangered Species (17th series).

V543	**V473** 65c. multicoloured	1·80	1·80
V544	**V474** 65c. multicoloured	1·80	1·80
V545	**V475** 65c. multicoloured	1·80	1·80
V546	**V476** 65c. multicoloured	1·80	1·80

2009. World Heritage Sites. Germany. As T **689**. Multicoloured.

V547	30c. Town Hall and Roland on the Marketplace of Bremen	90	90
V548	30c. Wartburg Castle	90	90
V549	30c. Palaces and Parks of Potsdam and Berlin	90	90
V550	35c. Aachen Cathedral	95	95
V551	35c. Monastic Island of Reichenau	95	95
V552	35c. Luther Memorials in Eisleben and Wittenberg	95	95
V553	65c. As No. V552	1·80	1·80
V554	€1.40 As No. 549	3·75	3·75

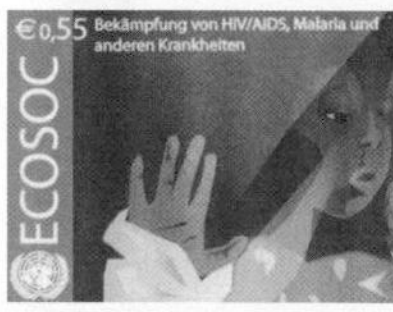

V 483 Child behind Mosquito Netting (prevention of HIV/AIDS, malaria and other diseases)

2009. United Nations Economic and Social Council (ECOSOC). Multicoloured.

V555	55c. Type **V483**	1·50	1·50
V556	65c. Children (Reduction of child mortality)	1·80	1·80

2009. Millennium Development Goals. As T **697**. Multicoloured.

V557	65c. chrome-yellow, black and green	1·80	1·80
V558	65c. bright yellow-green, black and green	1·80	1·80
V559	65c. orange-red, black and green	1·80	1·80
V560	65c. pale turquoise-blue, black and new blue	1·80	1·80
V561	65c. pale bright rose, black and green	1·80	1·80
V562	65c. scarlet-vermilion, black and green	1·80	1·80
V563	65c. apple-green, black and green	1·80	1·80
V564	65c. blue, black and green	1·80	1·80

DESIGNS: No. V557, Bowl of food (Eradicate extreme poverty and hunger); No.V558, Pencil (Achieve universal primary education); No. V559, Female Symbol (Promote gender equality and empower women); No. V560, Teddy bear (Reduce child mortality); No. V561, Female figure enclosing Heart (Improve maternal health); No. V562, Medicine jar (Combat HIV/AIDS, malaria and other diseases); No. V623, Stylized tree (Ensure environmental sustainability); No. V564, Stylized figures (Develop a global partnership for development).

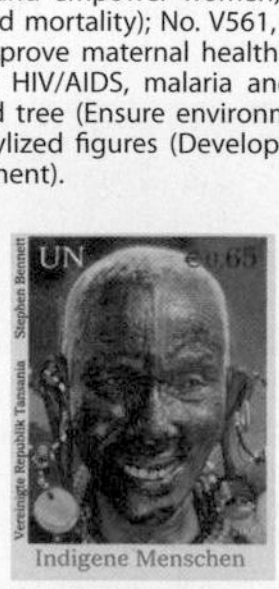

V 493 United Republic of Tanzania

2009. Indigenous Peoples. Multicoloured.

V565	65c. Type **V493**	1·80	1·80
V566	65c. Australia	1·80	1·80
V567	65c. Namibia	1·80	1·80
V568	65c. Indonesia	1·80	1·80
V569	65c. Namibia (different)	1·80	1·80
V570	65c. United Arab Emirates	1·80	1·80

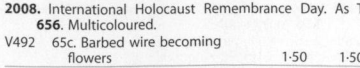

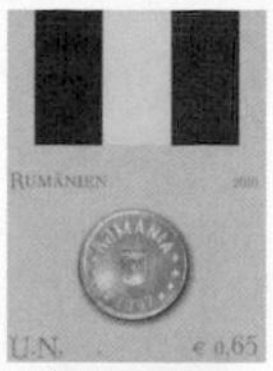

V 499 Romania

2010. Coins and Flags of Member Countries (3rd series). Multicoloured.

V571	65c. Type V**499**	1·80	1·80
V572	65c. Slovenia	1·80	1·80
V573	65c. Belarus	1·80	1·80
V574	65c. Malta	1·80	1·80
V575	65c. Azerbaijan	1·80	1·80
V576	65c. Bangladesh	1·80	1·80
V577	65c. Swaziland	1·80	1·80
V578	65c. Jordan	1·80	1·80

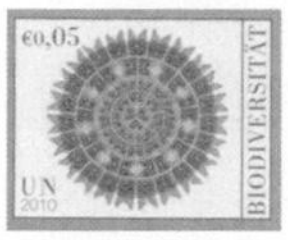

V507 Colonial Algae

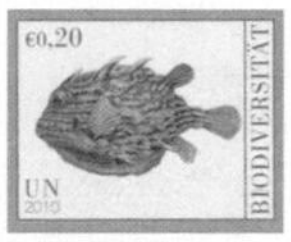

V508 Boxfish

2010. International Year of Biodiversity. Art from Nature by Ernst Heinrich. Multicoloured.

V579	**V507**	5c. multicoloured	40	40
V580	**V508**	20c. multicoloured	65	45

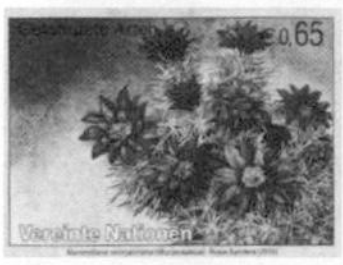

V509 *Mammillaria zeilmanniana* (Pincushion Cactus)

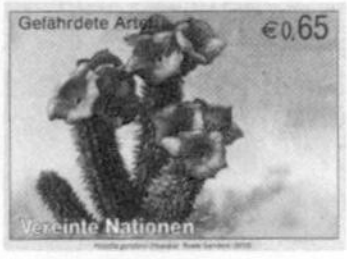

V510 *Hoodia gordonii*

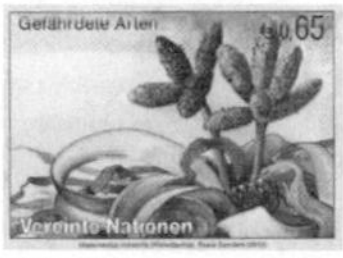

V511 *Welwitschia mirabilis*

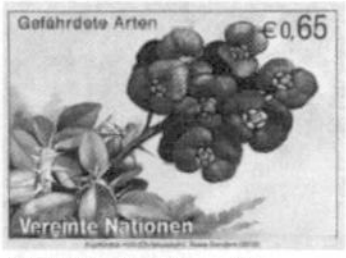

V512 *Euphorbia milii* (Crown of Thorns)

2010. Endangered Species (18th series). Multicoloured.

V581	**V509**	65c. multicoloured	1·50	1·35
V582	**V510**	65c. multicoloured	1·50	1·35
V583	**V511**	65c. multicoloured	1·50	1·35
V584	**V512**	65c. multicoloured	1·50	1·35

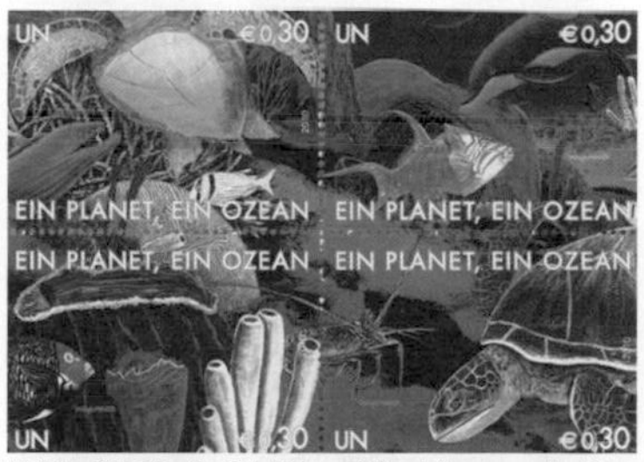

V513 - V516 Turtle, Eel, Fish and Coral (image scaled to 49% of original size)

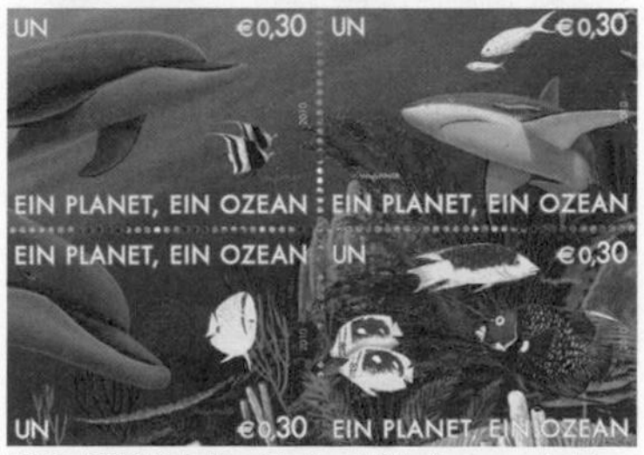

V517 - V520 Dolphins, Shark and Fish (image scaled to 49% of original size)

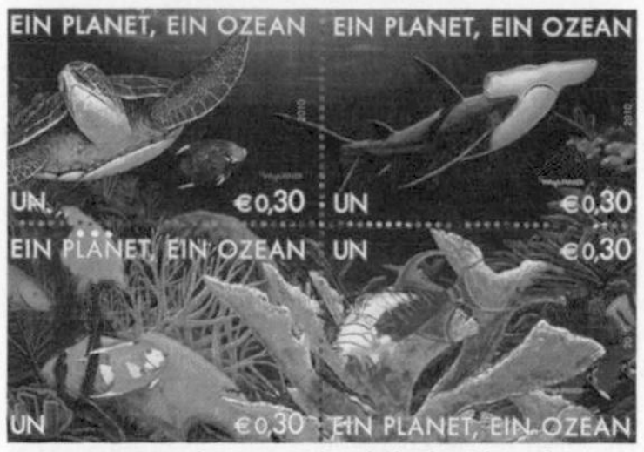

V521 - V524 Turtle, Hammerhead Shark and Coral (image scaled to 49% of original size)

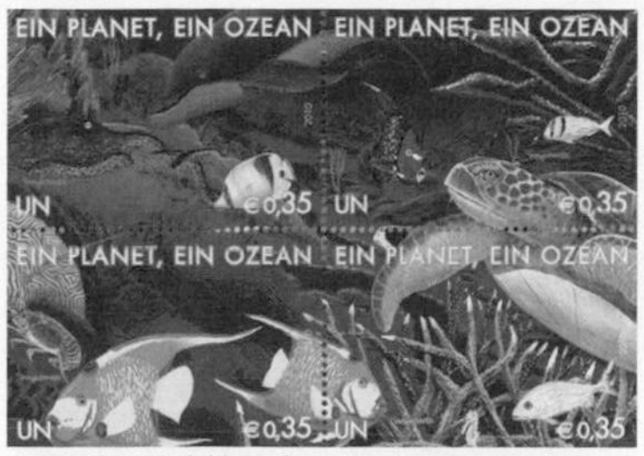

V525 - V528 Dolphin, Fish and Turtle (image scaled to 49% of original size)

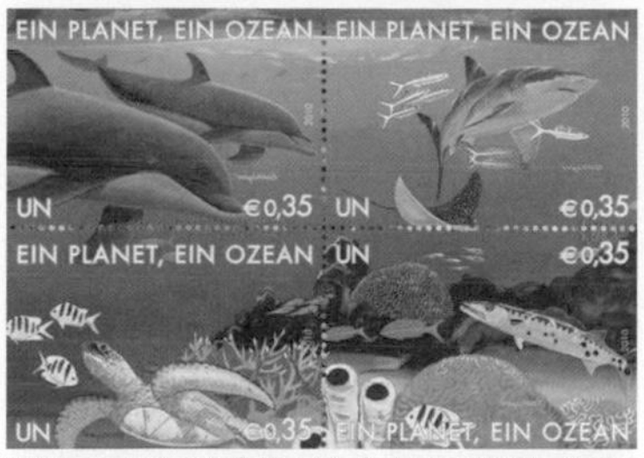

V529 - V532 Two Dolphins, Shark, Ray and Turtle (image scaled to 49% of original size)

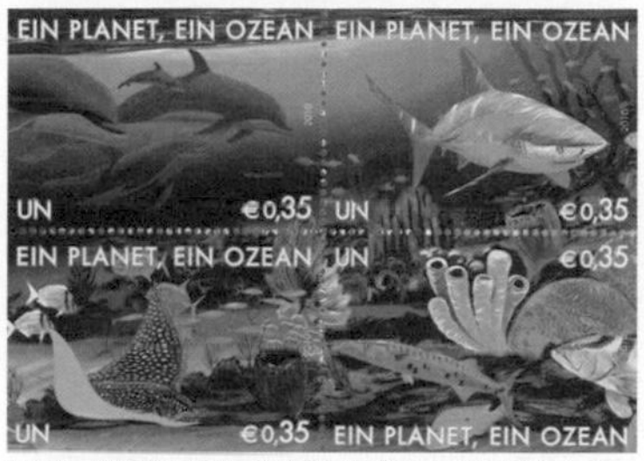

V533 - V536 Dolphin Pod, Shark, Ray and Coral (image scaled to 49% of original size)

2010. One Planet, One Ocean. 50th Anniv of Intergovernmental Oceanographic Commission

V585	**V513**	30c. multicoloured	70	50
V586	**V514**	30c. multicoloured	70	50
V587	**V515**	30c. multicoloured	70	50
[illegible]	[illegible]	[illegible]	70	50
V589	**V517**	30c. multicoloured	70	50
V590	**V518**	30c. multicoloured	70	50
V591	**V519**	30c. multicoloured	70	50
V592	**V520**	30c. multicoloured	70	50
V593	**V521**	30c. multicoloured	70	50
V594	**V522**	30c. multicoloured	70	50
V595	**V523**	30c. multicoloured	70	50
V596	**V524**	30c. multicoloured	70	50
V597	**V525**	35c. multicoloured	1·50	1·35
V598	**V526**	35c. multicoloured	1·50	1·35
V599	**V527**	35c. multicoloured	1·50	1·35
V600	**V528**	35c. multicoloured	1·50	1·35
V601	**V529**	35c. multicoloured	1·50	1·35
V602	**V530**	35c. multicoloured	1·50	1·35
V603	**V531**	35c. multicoloured	1·50	1·35
V604	**V532**	35c. multicoloured	1·50	1·35
V605	**V533**	35c. multicoloured	1·50	1·35
V606	**V534**	35c. multicoloured	1·50	1·35
V607	**V535**	35c. multicoloured	1·50	1·35
V608	**V536**	35c. multicoloured	1·50	1·35
MSV609		180×110 mm. 55c.×4, As Types **V517/520**	10·00	10·00
MSV610		180×110 mm. 65c.×4, As Type **V529/532**	12·00	12·00

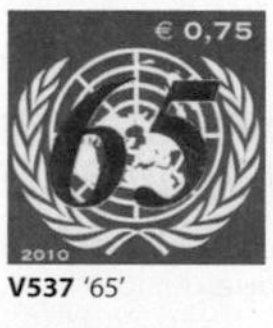

V537 '65'

2010. 65th Anniv of United Nations

V611	**V537**	75c. bright myrtle green and gold	1·85	1·65
MSV612		80×80 mm. 75c.×2, Type **V537**×2	12·00	12·00

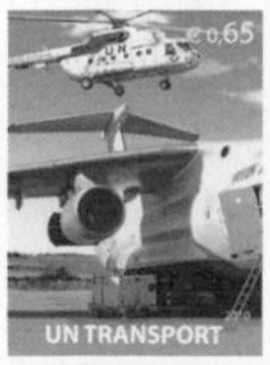

V538 Helicopter and Aircraft Wing

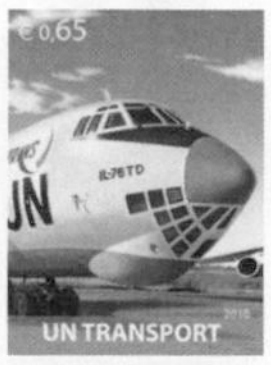

V539 Cockpit of ILyushin 1l-76TD

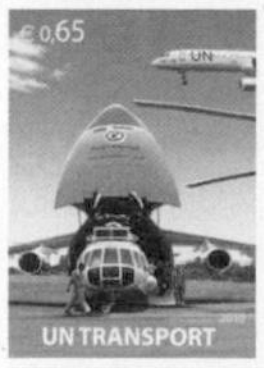

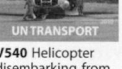

V540 Helicopter disembarking from carrier

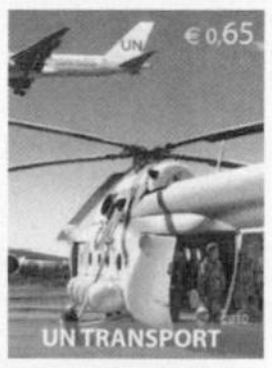

V541 Peacekeepers loading Mil Mi-8 Helicopter

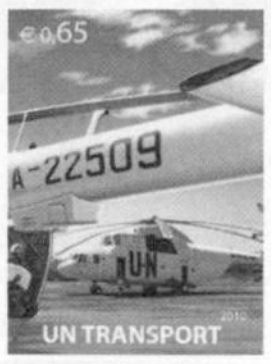

V542 Tail of Mil Mi-8 helicopter

2010. United Nations Transport - Air

V613	**V538**	65c. multicoloured	1·50	1·35
V614	**V539**	65c. multicoloured	1·50	1·35
V615	**V540**	65c. multicoloured	1·50	1·35
V616	**V541**	65c. multicoloured	1·50	1·35
V617	**V542**	65c. multicoloured	1·50	1·35

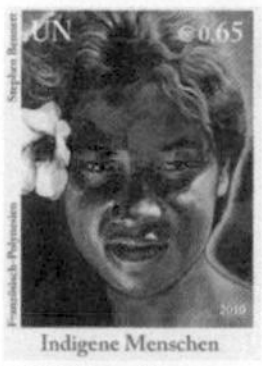

V543 French Polynesia

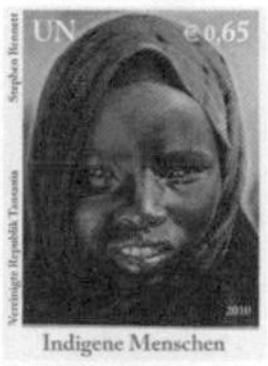

V544 United Republic of Tanzania

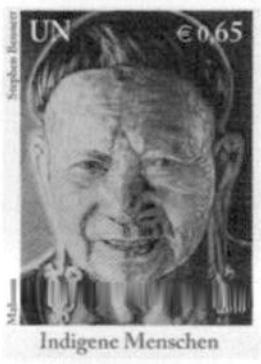

V545 Malaysia

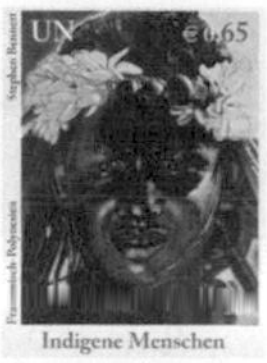

V546 French Polynesia

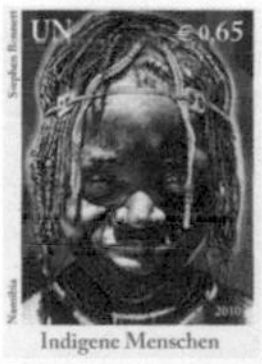

V547 Namibia

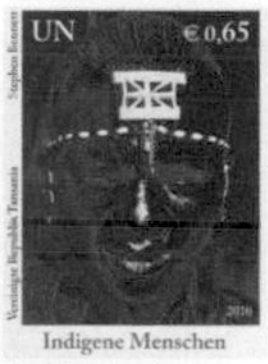

V548 United Republic of Tanzania

2010. Indigenous Peoples

V618	**V543**	65c. multicoloured	1·50	1·35
V619	**V544**	65c. multicoloured	1·50	1·35
V620	**V545**	65c. multicoloured	1·50	1·35
V621	**V546**	65c. multicoloured	1·50	1·35
V622	**V547**	65c. multicoloured	1·50	1·35
V623	**V548**	65c. multicoloured	1·50	1·35

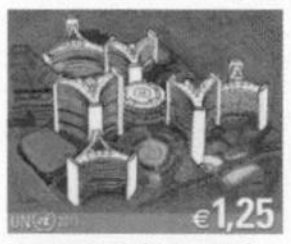

V549 Aerial View of UN Headquarters Vienna

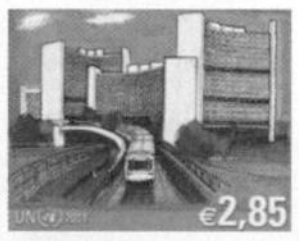

V550 UN Headquarters Vienna Building Façade

2011. UN Building. Multicoloured.

V624	**V549**	€1.25 multicoloured	2·50	2·50
V625	**V550**	€2.85 multicoloured	4·50	4·50

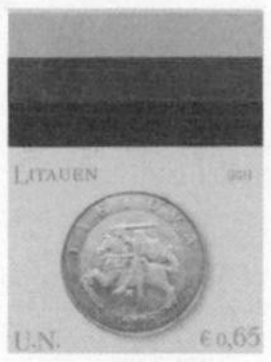

V551 Lithuania

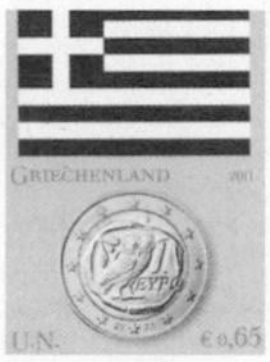

V552 Greece

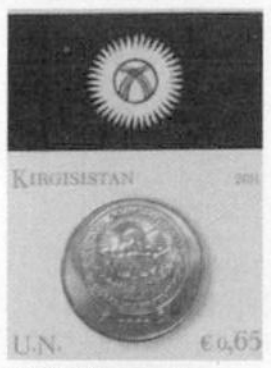

V553 Kyrgyzstan

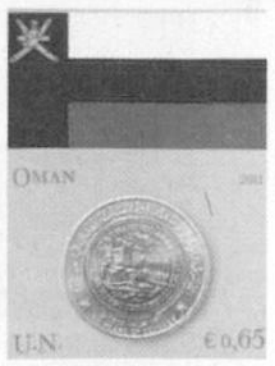

V554 Oman

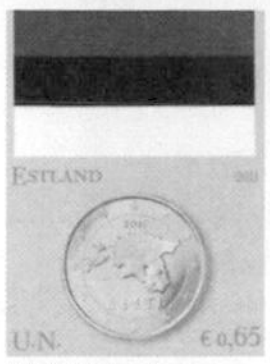

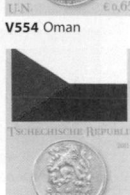

V555 Estonia

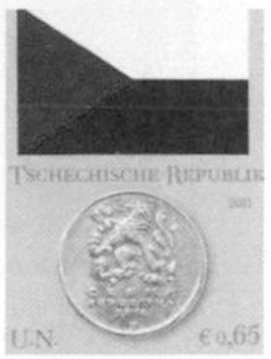

V556 Czech Republic

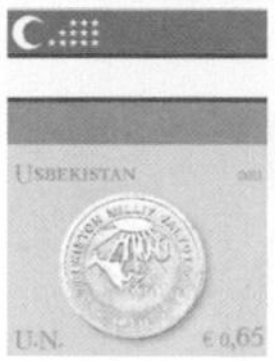

V557 Uzbekistan

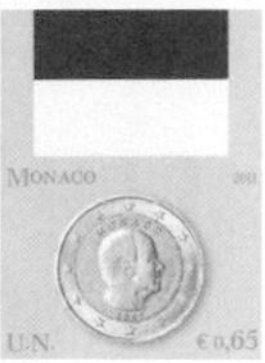

V558 Monaco

2011. Coins and Flags of Member Countries (5th series). Multicoloured.

V626	**V551**	65c. multicoloured	1·50	1·35
V627	**V552**	65c. multicoloured	1·50	1·35
V628	**V553**	65c. multicoloured	1·50	1·35
V629	**V554**	65c. multicoloured	1·50	1·35
V630	**V555**	65c. multicoloured	1·50	1·35
V631	**V556**	65c. multicoloured	1·50	1·35
V632	**V557**	65c. multicoloured	1·50	1·35
V633	**V558**	65c. multicoloured	1·50	1·35

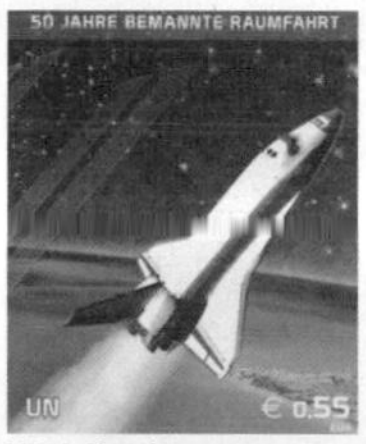

V559 Shuttle

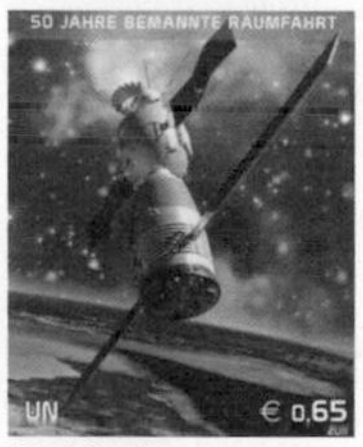

V560 Satellite

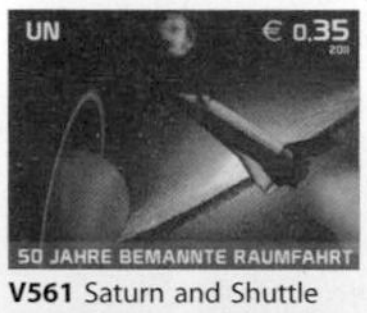

V561 Saturn and Shuttle

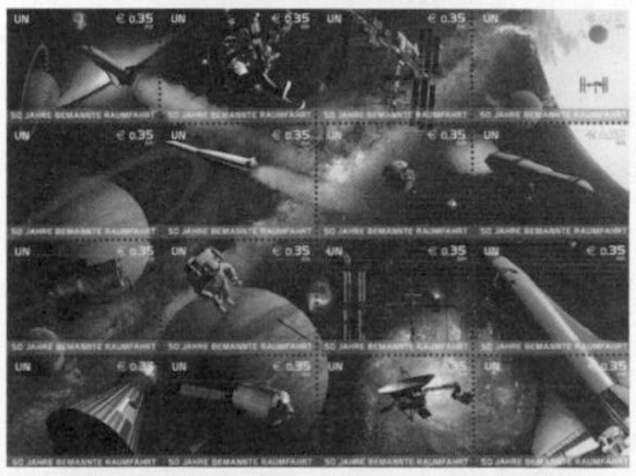
V562 Planets, Astronauts, Satellites and Shuttles (image scaled to 30% of original size)

2011. 50th Anniv of Space Flight

V634	**V559**	55c. multicoloured	1·50	1·35
V635	**V560**	65c. multicoloured	1·50	1·35
MSV636		180×155 mm. Size 40×30 mm. 35c.×16, Type **V561** and 15 other horiz designs forming the overall design Type **V562**	25·00	25·00

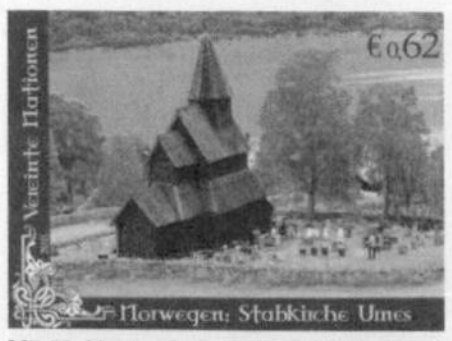

V563 Urnes Stave Church, Norway

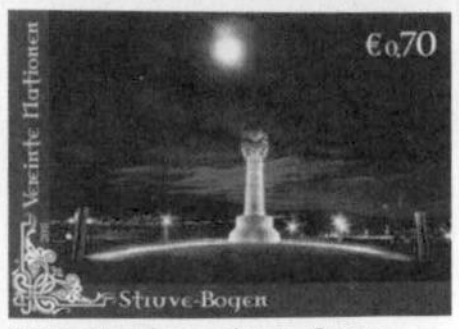

V564 Meridian column, Struve Geodetic Arc, Hammerfest, Norway

2011. World Heritage Sites - Nordic Countries

V637	**V563**	62c. multicoloured	1·50	1·35
V638	**V564**	70c. multicoloured	1·50	1·35

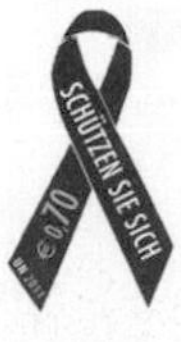

V565 AIDS Ribbon

2011. '30 Years of a World living with AIDS'

V639	**V565**	70c. scarlet and apple-green	1·50	1·35

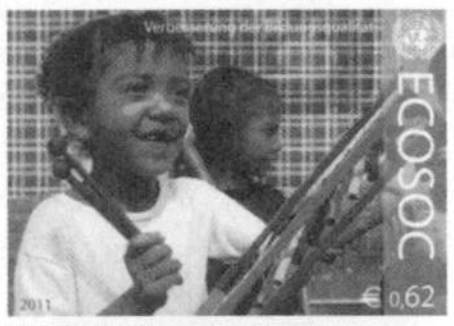

V566 Children playing Music ('Improvement in education quality')

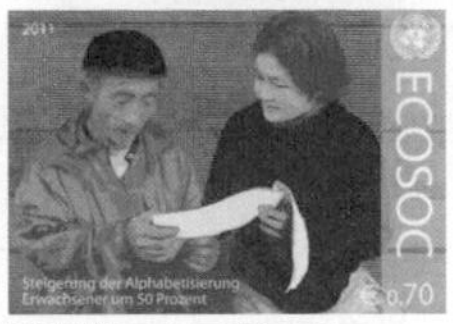

V567 Woman teaching man ('Increase adult literacy by 50%')

2011. ECOSOC (Economic and Social Council) - Education

V640	**V566**	62c. multicoloured	1·00	1·00
V641	**V567**	70c. multicoloured	1·50	1·35

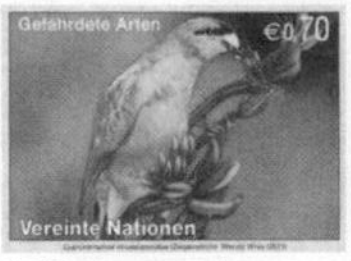

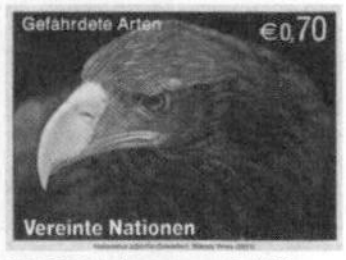

V568 *Cyanoramphus novaezelandiae* (Red-fronted Parakeet)

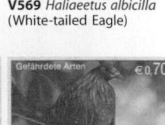

V569 *Haliaeetus albicilla* (White-tailed Eagle)

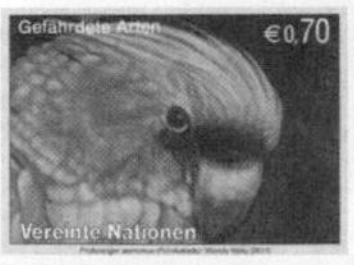

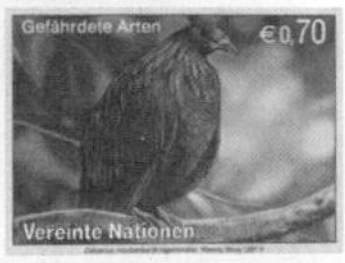

V570 *Probosciger aterrimus* (Black Palm Cockatoo)

V571 *Caloenas nicobarica* (Nicobar Pigeon)

2011. Endangered Species (19th series)

V642	**V568**	70c. multicoloured	1·50	1·35
V643	**V569**	70c. multicoloured	1·50	1·35
V644	**V570**	70c. multicoloured	1·50	1·35
V645	**V571**	70c. multicoloured	1·50	1·35

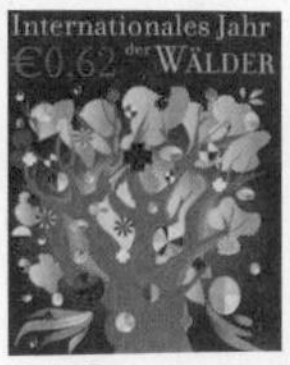

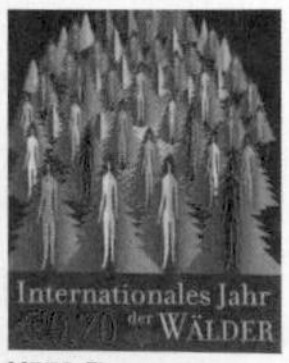

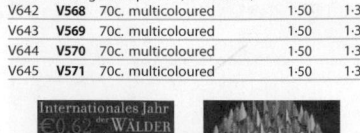

V572 Tree

V573 Figures as Forest

2011. International Year of Forests

V646	**V572**	62c. multicoloured	1·00	1·00
V647	**V573**	70c. multicoloured	1·50	1·35

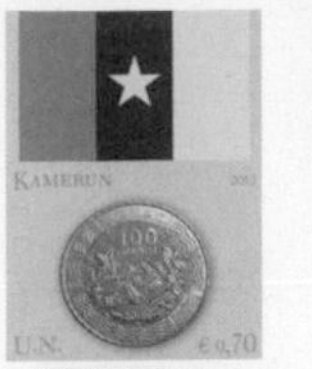

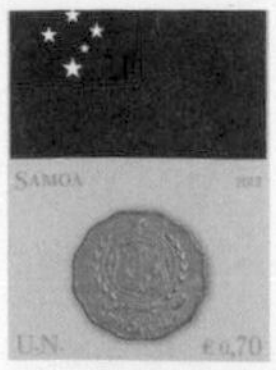

V574 Cameroun

V575 Samoa

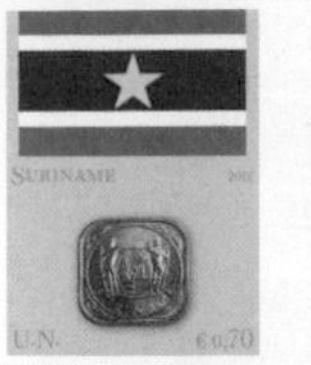

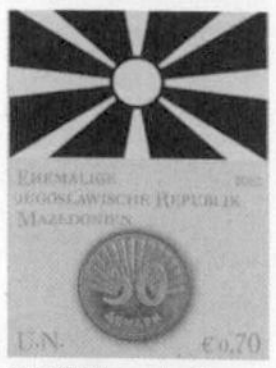

V576 Suriname

V577 Macedonia

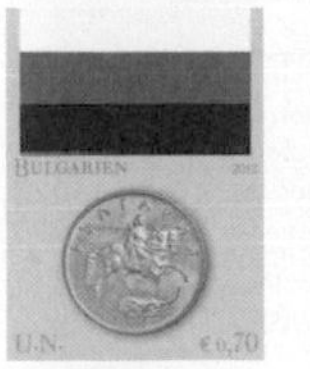

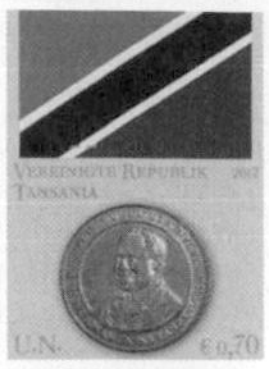

V578 Bulgaria

V579 Tanzania

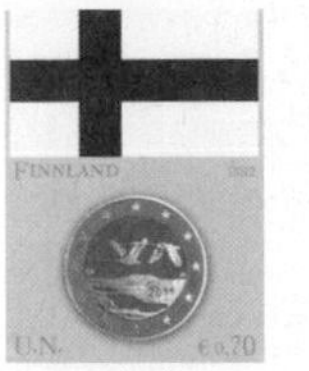

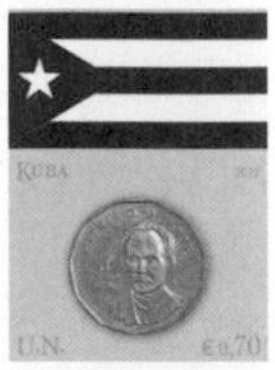

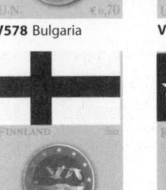

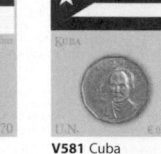

V580 Finland

V581 Cuba

2012. Coins and Flags of Member Countries (6th series)

V648	**V574**	70c. multicoloured	1·80	1·80
V649	**V575**	70c. multicoloured	1·80	1·80
V650	**V576**	70c. multicoloured	1·80	1·80
V651	**V577**	70c. multicoloured	1·80	1·80
V652	**V578**	70c. multicoloured	1·80	1·80
V653	**V579**	70c. multicoloured	1·80	1·80
V654	**V580**	70c. multicoloured	1·80	1·80
V655	**V581**	70c. multicoloured	1·80	1·80

F. Kosovo

United Nations Interim Administration Mission

The following stamps were issued by the United Nations Interim Administration Mission (U.N.M.I.K.) and the Post & Telecommunications of Kosovo for postal purposes in Kosovo. They were for local use only for the first two months with international use commencing in May 2000.

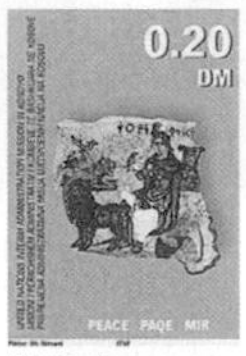

K1 Orpheus (mosaic, 5–6th century, Podujeve)

2000. Artefacts. Multicoloured.

K1	20pf. Type K **1**	50	50
K2	30pf. "Dardanian idol", 3500 B.C.	95	95
K3	50pf. Obverse and reverse of 4th-century B.C. silver coin, Damastion	1·50	1·50
K4	1m. Mother Teresa (statue, Prizren)	2·40	2·40
K5	2m. Map of Kosovo showing various sites	4·25	4·25

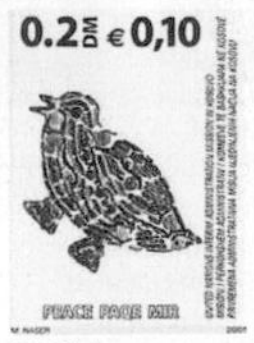

K2 Bird

2001. Art. Multicoloured

K6	20pf. Type K **2**	50	50
K7	30pf. Musician	95	95
K8	50pf. Butterfly and pear (horiz)	1·50	1·50
K9	1m. Children and stars	2·40	2·40
K10	2m. Handprints surrounding globe	4·25	4·25

Nos. K6/10 have the face values shown in deutsche Marks and euros.

K11/15 and Type K **3** are left for Freedom in Kosovo (euro) issued on 2 May 2002, not yet received.

K16/17 and Type K **4** are left for Christmas issued on 20 December 2003, not yet received.

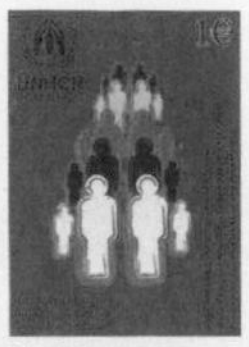

K5 Returnees (return of refugees)

2009. Fifth Anniv of United Nations Support for Kosovo

K18	€1 Type K **5**		5·50	5·50
K19	€2 '5' of flags on map		15·00	15·00

K20/21 and Type K **6** are left for Instruments issued on 20 August 2004, not yet received.

K22/5 and Type K **7** are left for Costumes issued on 28 October 2004, not yet received.

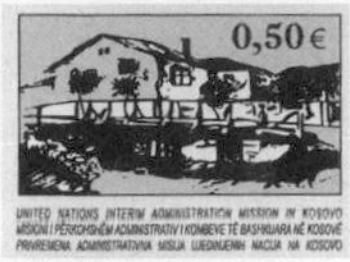

K8 Bridge and Houses (ink drawing)

2009. Art

K26	**K8**	50c. multicoloured	2·50	2·50

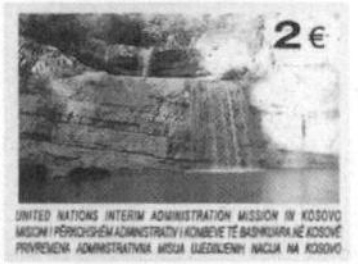

K9 Mirusha Waterfall

2009. Kosovo Landscape

K27	**K9**	€2 multicoloured	15·00	15·00

NOTE: Numbers are left for the following issues that are known, but have not been received.

Nos. K28/30 and Type **K10** for Flora issued on 29 June 2005.

Nos. K31/2 and Type **K11** for Crafts issued on 15 July 2005.

Nos. K33/5 and Type **K12** for Settlements issued on 15 September 2005.

Nos. K36/9 and Type **K13** for Archeology issued on 2 November 2005.

Nos. K40 and Type **K14** for Minerals issued on 10 December 2005.

Nos. K41/2 and Type **K15** for Europa, Integration issued on 9 May 2006.

Nos. K43/7 and Type **K16** for Fauna issued on 23 May 2006.

Nos. K48/51 and Type **K17** for Children issued on 30 June 2006.

Nos. K52/5 and Type **K18** for Tourism issued on 1 September 2006.

Nos. K56 and Type **K19** for Day of Peace issued on 21 September 2006.

Nos. K57/60 and Type **K20** for Coins issued on 1 November 2006.

Nos. K61 and Type **K21** for Art issued on 1 December 2006.

Nos. K62/5 and Type **K22** for Convention on Rights of Disabled issued on 23 April 2007.

Nos. K66/7 and Type **K23** for Europa, Centenary of Scouting issued on 12 May 2007.

Nos. K68/71 and Type **K24** for Children's Day issued on 1 June 2007.

Nos. K72/6 and Type **K25** for Costumes issued on 7 July 2007.

Nos. K77/80 and Type **K26** for Masks issued on 11 September 2007.

Nos. K81/3 and Type **K27** for Sport issued on 2 October 2007.

Nos. K84/7 and Type **K28** for Architecture issued on 6 November 2007.

Nos. K88/9 and Type **K29** for Railways issued on 7 December 2007.

Nos. K90 and Type **K30** for Skanderberg issued on 17 January 2008.

Republic of Kosovo declared independence on 17 February 2008.

For issues for Republic of Kosovo see Kosovo

Pt. 22

UNITED STATES OF AMERICA

A Federal Republic in N. America, consisting of 50 states and one federal district.

100 cents = 1 dollar.

PRICES. On the issues before 1890 the gum is rarely complete and the unused prices quoted are for stamps with part original gum.

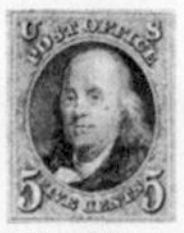

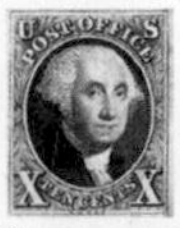

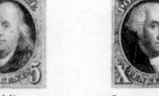

1 Franklin (after drawings by James B. Longacre)

2 Washington (after painting by Stuart)

1847. Imperf.

1	1	5c. brown	£6000	£550
2	2	10c. black	£32000	£1400

The 5c. blue and 10c. orange, both imperf, come from miniature sheets isssued in 1947 to commemorate the Centenary Philatelic Exhibition, New York.

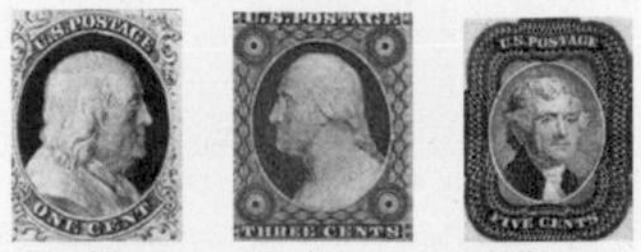

3 Franklin (after bust by Caffieri) **4** Washington (after bust by Houdon) **5** Jefferson

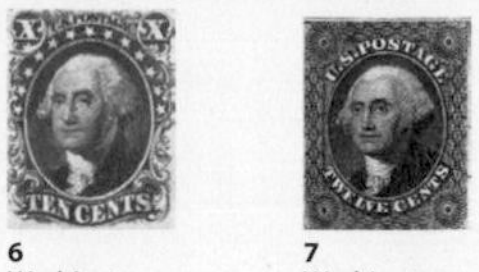

6 Washington **7** Washington

1851. Imperf.

11	3	1c. blue	£600	£110
13a	4	3c. red	£400	13·50
14	5	5c. brown	£23000	£1100
16	6	10c. green	£4500	£180
19	7	12c. black	£5500	£275

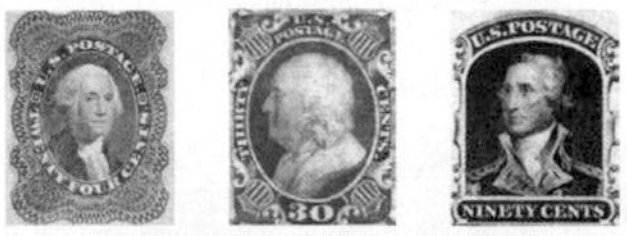

8 Washington **9** Franklin (after bust by Caffieri) **10** Washington (after Trumbull painting)

1857. Perf.

26	**3**	1c. blue	£140	41·00
28	**4**	3c. red	70·00	8·25
33	**5**	5c. brown	£2000	£275
39	**6**	10c. green	£225	60·00
40c	**7**	12c. black	£750	£325
41	**8**	24c. lilac	£1500	£375
42	**9**	30c. orange	£2250	£450
43	**10**	90c. blue	£3250	£9000

DESIGNS: Types **5**, **6**, **7** and **8** are after paintings by Stuart.

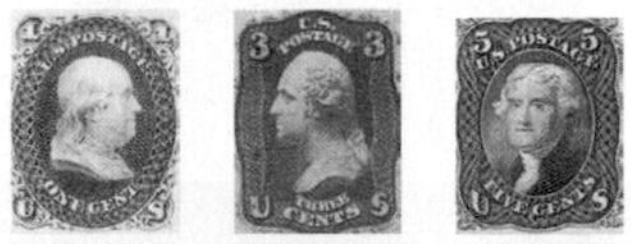

11 Franklin **12** Washington **13** Jefferson

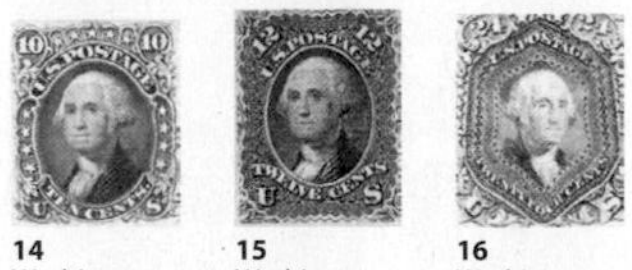

14 Washington **15** Washington **16** Washington

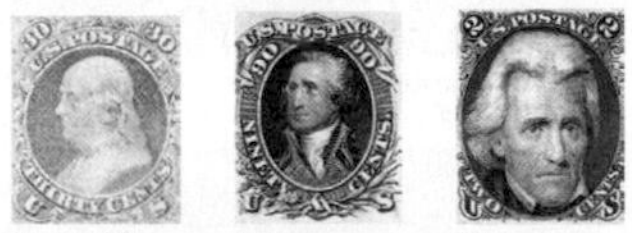

17 Franklin **18** Washington **19** Andrew Jackson (after miniature by J. W. Dodge)

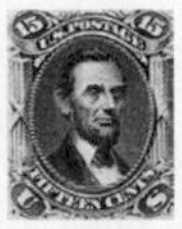

20 Lincoln (from a photograph)

1861

60b	**11**	1c. blue	£300	45·00
69	**19**	2c. black	£350	65·00
62	**12**	3c. red	£110	2·75
63	**13**	5c. yellow	£25000	£1100
64	**14**	10c. green	£1000	55·00
72	**13**	5c. brown	£1500	£140
65	**15**	12c. black	£1800	£120
73	**20**	15c. black	£4000	£200
66c	**16**	24c. blue	£15000	£800
74	**16**	24c. lilac	£2500	£325
74b	**16**	24c. grey	£2750	£275
67	**17**	30c. orange	£2250	£180
68a	**18**	90c. blue	£3000	£600

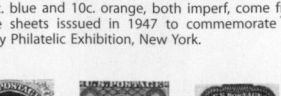

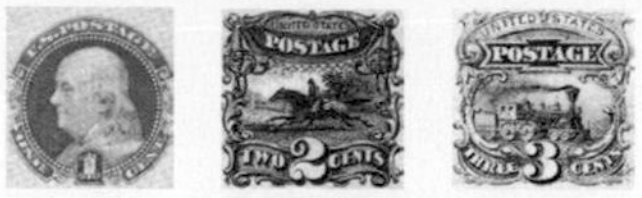

21 Franklin (after Houdon bust) **22** Post Rider **23** Baldwin Steam Locomotive

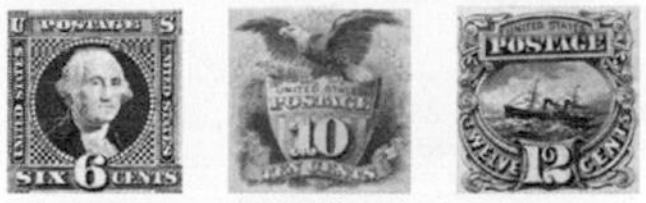

24 Washington (after Stuart) **25** Shield and Eagle **26** Paddle-steamer "Adriatic" (after C. Parsons)

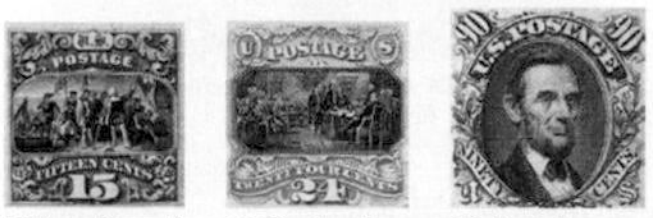

27 Landing of Columbus (after Vanderlyn) **28** Declaration of Independence (after Trumbull) **30** Lincoln (from a photograph)

1869

114	**21**	1c. brown	£700	£160
115	**22**	2c. brown	£650	90·00
116	**23**	3c. blue	£250	18·00
117	**24**	6c. blue	£2500	£225
118	**25**	10c. orange	£2000	£140
119	**26**	12c. green	£2250	£180
121	**27**	15c. blue and brown	£3250	£250
122	**28**	24c. purple and green	£8000	£700
123	**25**	30c. red and blue	£6500	£500
124	**30**	90c. black and red	£12000	£2250

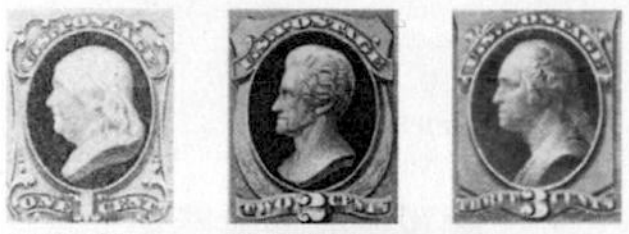

31 Franklin **32** Jackson **33** Washington

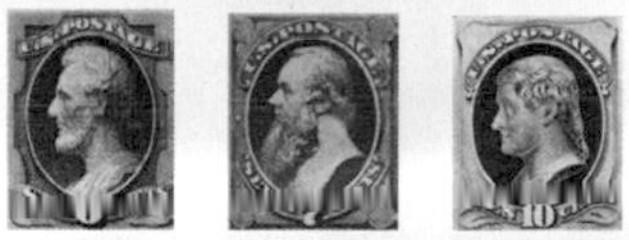

34 Lincoln **35** Stanton **36** Jefferson

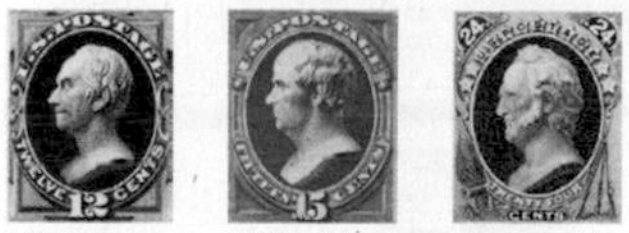

37 Henry Clay **38** Daniel Webster **39** General Winfield Scott

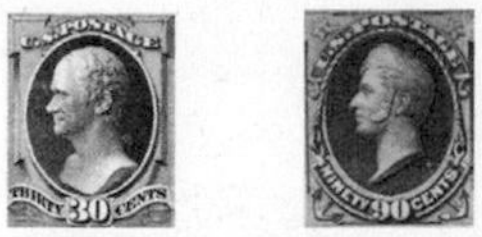

40 Alexander Hamilton **41** Commodore Perry

1870

207	**31**	1c. blue	75·00	90
148	**32**	2c. brown	£325	18·00
185	**32**	2c. red	£100	4·50
208	**33**	3c. green	75·00	75
219	**33**	3c. red	60·00	60·00
161	**34**	6c. red	£375	18·00
151	**35**	7c. red	£1000	90·00
210	**36**	10c. brown	£160	5·50
153	**37**	12c. purple	£2500	£200
191	**38**	15c. orange	£250	25·00
155	**39**	24c. violet	£1800	£200
192	**40**	30c. black	£850	90·00
222	**40**	30c. brown	£350	£120
193	**41**	90c. red	£2000	£350
223	**41**	90c. violet	£900	£250

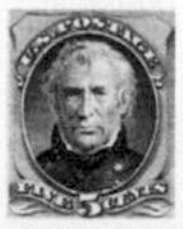

42 General Zachary Taylor (from a daguerreotype)

1875

181	**42**	5c. blue	£700	23·00

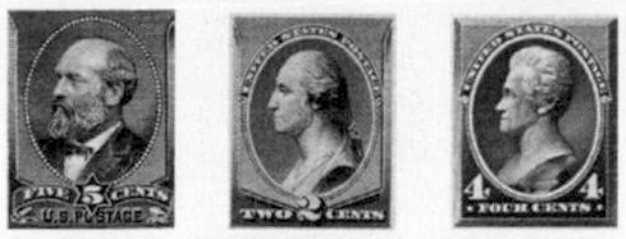

43 Garfield (from a photograph) **44** Washington (after bust by Houdon) **45** Jackson (after bust by Powers)

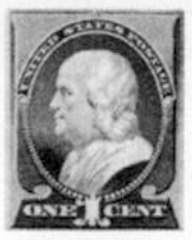

46 Franklin

1882

217	**46**	1c. blue	90·00	2·30
213	**44**	2c. brown	39·00	70
218	**44**	2c. green	41·00	55
214	**45**	4c. green	£275	25·00
220	**45**	4c. red	£200	25·00
211	**43**	5c. brown	£250	11·00
221	**43**	5c. blue	£225	16·00

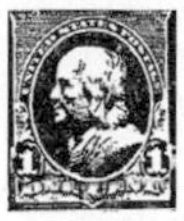

47 Franklin

1890. No triangles in upper corners.

224	**47**	1c. blue (Franklin)	23·00	70
225a	-	2c. red (Washington)	20·00	65
226	-	3c. violet (Jackson)	70·00	8·25
227	-	4c. sepia (Lincoln)	90·00	4·00
228	-	5c. brown (Grant)	75·00	4·00
229	-	6c. red (Garfield)	70·00	23·00
230	-	8c. purple (Sherman)	55·00	15·00
231	-	10c. green (Webster)	£170	3·75
232	-	15c. blue (Clay)	£225	25·00
233	-	30c. black (Jefferson)	£375	39·00
234	-	90c. orange (Perry)	£500	£150

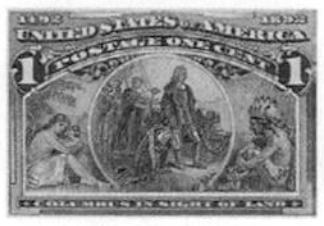

58 Columbus in Sight of Land

1893. Columbian Exposition, Chicago.

235	**58**	1c. blue	23·00	45
236	-	2c. purple	20·00	45
237	-	3c. green	60·00	14·50
238	-	4c. blue	90·00	8·25
239	-	5c. brown	85·00	8·75
240	-	6c. violet	75·00	23·00
241	-	8c. red	75·00	11·00
242	-	10c. sepia	£130	8·25
243	-	15c. green	£200	75·00
244	-	30c. orange	£300	90·00
245	-	50c. slate	£475	£180
246	-	$1 red	£1400	£650
247	-	$2 lake	£1500	£650
248	-	$3 green	£2000	£900
249	-	$4 red	£3000	£1200
250	-	$5 black	£3250	£1400

DESIGNS: 2c. Landing of Columbus; 3c. "Santa Maria", flag-ship of Columbus; 4c. Fleet of Columbus; 5c. Columbus soliciting aid of Isabella; 6c. Columbus welcomed at Barcelona, Ferdinand (left) and Balboa (right); 8c. Columbus restored to favour; 10c. Columbus presenting natives; 15c. Columbus announcing his discovery; 30c. Columbus at La Rabida; 50c. Recall of Columbus; $1 Isabella pledging her jewels; $2 Columbus in chains; $3 Columbus describing his third voyage; $4 Isabella and Columbus; $5 Columbus, America and Liberty.

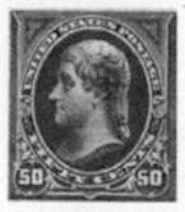

83 Jefferson

1894. Triangles in upper corners as T **83**. Same portraits as issue of 1890, except dollar values.

267		1c. blue	5·50	55
283	-	1c. green	8·25	45
270		2c. red	5·00	45
271		3c. violet	34·00	2·00
285	-	4c. brown	27·00	3·25
273		5c. brown	32·00	3·25
286	-	5c. blue	30·00	2·00
274		6c. brown	£110	7·75
287a	-	6c. purple	41·00	6·00
275		8c. brown	65·00	2·50
276		10c. green	85·00	2·00
289	-	10c. brown	£140	5·00
277		15c. blue	£200	16·00
290	-	15c. green	£150	12·00
278	**83**	50c. orange	£250	36·00
279	-	$1 black (Perry)	£600	£100
281a	-	$2 blue (Madison)	£900	£400
282	-	$5 green (Marshall)	£2000	£600

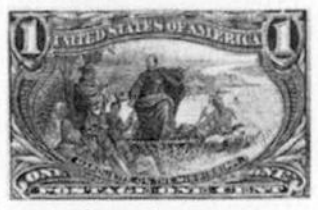

88 Father Marquette on the Mississippi

1898. Trans-Mississippi Exposition, Omaha.

291	**88**	1c. green	28·00	6·25
292	-	2c. red	28·00	2·50
293	-	4c. orange	£140	25·00
294	-	5c. blue	£140	23·00
295	-	8c. purple	£200	45·00
296	-	10c. violet	£180	32·00
297	-	50c. green	£700	£190
298	-	$1 black	£1300	£600
299	-	$2 brown	£2250	£950

DESIGNS: 2c. Farming in the West; 4c. Indian hunting American bison; 5c. Fremont on Rocky Mountains; 8c. Troops guarding emigrant train; 10c. Hardships of emigration; 50c. Western mining prospector; $1 Western cattle in storm; $2 Eads Bridge over Mississippi at St. Louis and paddle-steamer "Grey Eagle".

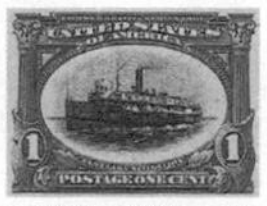

97 "City of Alpena" (Great Lakes steamer)

1901. Pan-American Exposition, Buffalo. Inscr "COMMEMORATIVE SERIES, 1901.".

300	**97**	1c. black and green	20·00	2·75
301	-	2c. black and red	19·00	90
302	-	4c. black and brown	85·00	17·00
303	-	5c. black and blue	90·00	16·00
304	-	8c. black and brown	£110	50·00
305	-	10c. black and brown	£150	30·00

DESIGNS: 2c. "Empire State Express"; 4c. Automobile; 5c. Railway bridge below Niagara Falls; 8c. Canal locks at Sault Sainte Marie; 10c. "Saint Paul" (liner).

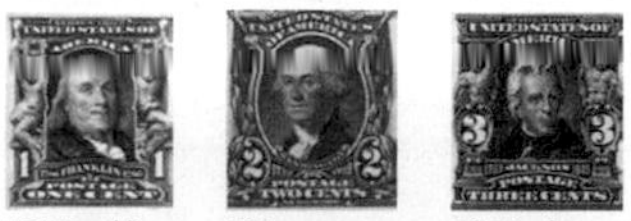

103 Franklin **104** Washington **105** Jackson

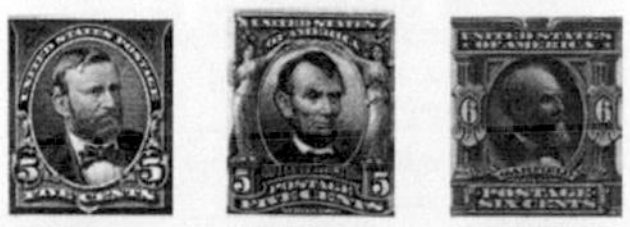

106 Grant **107** Lincoln **108** Garfield

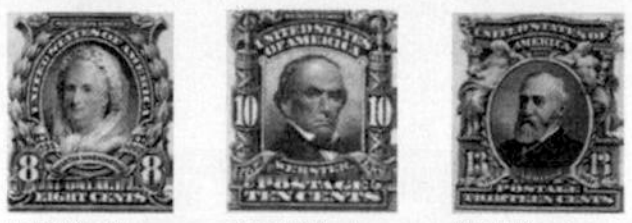

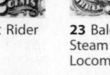

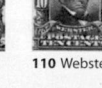

109 Martha Washington **110** Webster **111** Harrison

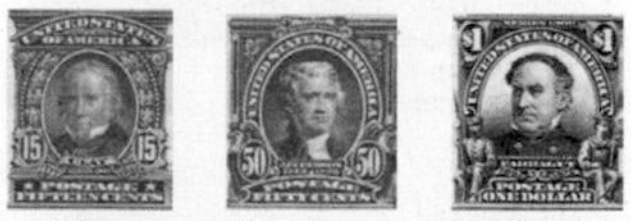

112 Clay **113** Jefferson **114** Farragut

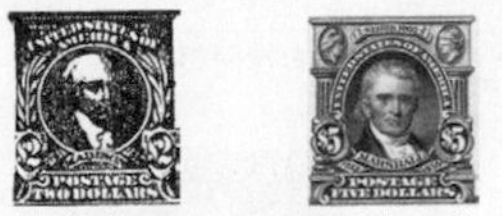

115 Madison **116** Marshall

1902. Inscr "SERIES 1902". 1, 4 and 5c. perf or imperf.

306	**103**	1c. green	13·50	45
307	**104**	2c. red	18·00	45
308a	**105**	3c. violet	65·00	3·75
309a	**106**	4c. brown	70·00	2·30
310	**107**	5c. blue	70·00	2·00
311	**108**	6c. lake	70·00	5·25
312	**109**	8c. violet	45·00	3·25
313	**110**	10c. brown	70·00	3·00
314	**111**	13c. purple	45·00	10·00
315	**112**	15c. olive	£225	13·50
316	**113**	50c. orange	£475	32·00
317	**114**	$1 black	£800	80·00
485	**115**	$2 blue	£250	48·00
486	**116**	$5 green	£200	45·00

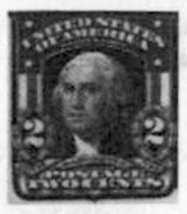

117 Washington (after Stuart)

1903. Perf or imperf.

326	**117**	2c. red	11·50	45

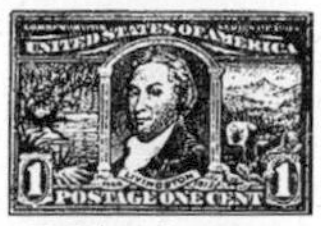

118 Robert R. Livingston (after Stuart)

1904. International Exposition, St. Louis, and Louisiana Purchase. Inscr "COMMEMO- RATIVE SERIES OF 1904".

330	**118**	1c. green	28·00	4·50
331	-	2c. red	25·00	1·80
332	-	3c. violet	85·00	27·00
333	-	5c. blue	90·00	23·00
334	-	10c. brown	£160	27·00

DESIGNS: 2c. Thomas Jefferson; 3c. James Monroe (after Vanderlyn); 5c. William McKinley; 10c. Map of Louisiana Purchase.

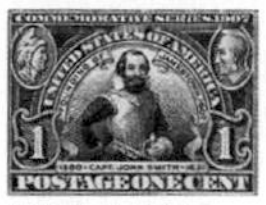

123 Capt. John Smith, Pocahontas and Powhatan (after painting)

1907. Jamestown Exposition.

335	**123**	1c. green	28·00	4·50
336	-	2c. red	34·00	4·00
337	-	5c. blue	£140	30·00

DESIGN: 2c. Founding of Jamestown, 1607; 5c. Princess Pocahontas.

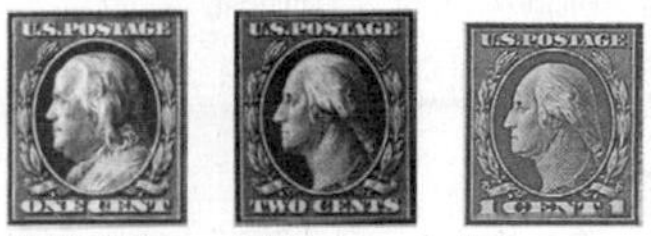

126 Franklin **127** **128**

1908. 1 to 5c. perf or imperf.

390	**126**	1c. green	2·75	2·75
497	**128**	1c. green	70	55
433	**127**	2c. red	2·50	25
506a	**128**	2c. red	40	30
537a	**128**	3c. violet	2·30	35
510a	**128**	4c. brown	11·50	45
503	**128**	5c. blue	4·50	2·30
513	**128**	6c. orange	15·00	45
514	**128**	7c. black	32·00	1·40
344a	**128**	8c. green	50·00	2·75
345	**128**	10c. yellow	75·00	1·80
346	**128**	13c. green	43·00	17·00
347	**128**	15c. blue	75·00	6·00
348	**128**	50c. violet	£350	18·00
349	**128**	$1 black	£550	90·00

DESIGNS: Types **127** and **128**, Washington (after Houdon bust).

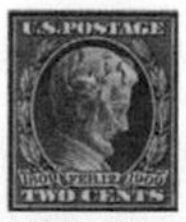

129 Lincoln (detail of statue by Saint Gaudens in Grant Park, Chicago)

1909. Birth Centenary of Abraham Lincoln. Perf or imperf.

374	**129**	2c. red	5·75	1·80

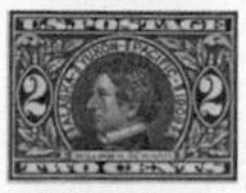

130 Wm. H. Seward

1909. Alaska–Yukon–Pacific Exposition. Perf or imperf.

377	**130**	2c. red	8·50	2·00

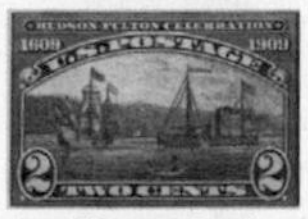

131 "Clermont" and "Half Moon" on Hudson River

1909. Hudson–Fulton Celebration. Perf or imperf.

379	**131**	2c. red	11·50	4·25

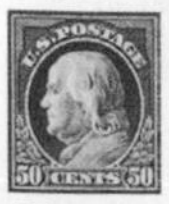
133 Franklin (after Caffieri bust)

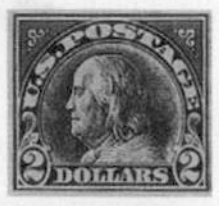
138 Franklin (after Caffieri bust)

1912

515	**133**	8c. olive	13·50	75
516	**133**	9c. pink	16·00	2·30
517	**133**	10c. yellow	20·00	35
518	**133**	11c. green	10·00	3·50
519	**133**	12c. brown	10·00	60
520	**133**	13c. green	12·50	6·75
521	**133**	15c. grey	40·00	1·70
522	**133**	20c. blue	65·00	55
523	**133**	30c. orange	45·00	1·70
524	**133**	50c. lilac	85·00	1·10
525	**133**	$1 black	80·00	2·30
526	**138**	$2 black and orange	£700	£250
527	**138**	$2 black and red	£200	45·00
528	**138**	$5 black and green	£275	45·00

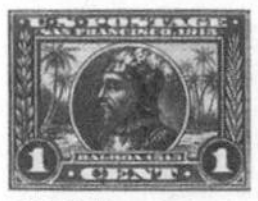
134 Balboa

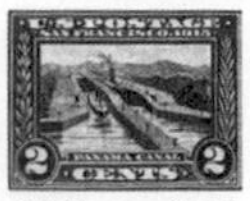
135 Panama Canal (after model of Pedro Miguel Locks)

1913. Panama–Pacific Exposition. Inscr "SAN FRANCISCO 1915".

423	**134**	1c. green	19·00	1·80
424	**135**	2c. red	20·00	90
425	-	5c. blue	80·00	9·00
426	-	10c. yellow	£140	20·00

DESIGNS: 5c. Golden Gate, San Francisco; 10c. Discovery of San Francisco Bay (after painting by Mathew).

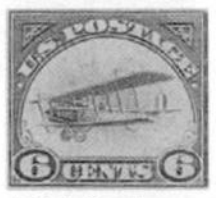
A139 Curtiss JN-4 "Jenny"

1918. Air.

A546	**A139**	6c. orange	75·00	34·00
A547	**A139**	16c. green	95·00	40·00
A548	**A139**	24c. blue and red	95·00	40·00

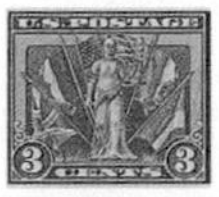
139 Liberty and Allies' Flags

1919. Victory.

546	**139**	3c. violet	11·50	3·75

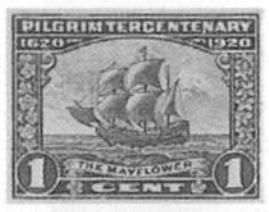
140 The "Mayflower"

1920. Tercentenary of Landing of Pilgrim Fathers. Inscr as in T **140**.

556	**140**	1c. green	5·75	3·50
557	-	2c. red	6·75	2·30
558	-	5c. blue	45·00	16·00

DESIGNS: 2c. Landing of the Pilgrims (after drawing by White); 5c. Signing the Compact.

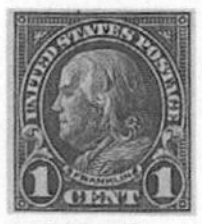
144 Franklin

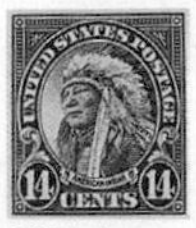
157 Indian Chief

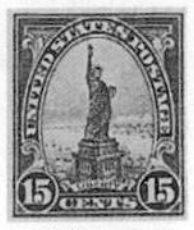
158 Statue of Liberty

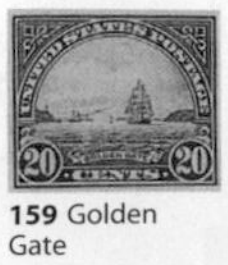
159 Golden Gate

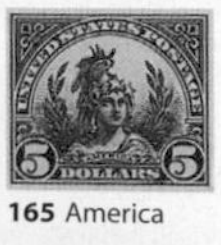
165 America

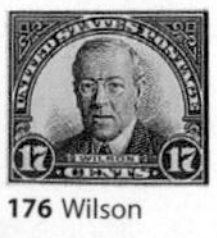
176 Wilson

1922. Perf or imperf (1, 1½, 2c.).

559		½c. brown (Hale)	30	25
632	**144**	1c. green	30	25
612	-	1½c. brown (Harding)	45	25
634	-	2c. red (Washington)	25	25
636a	-	3c. violet (Lincoln)	35	25
637	-	4c. brown (Martha Washington)	2·75	25
608	-	5c. blue (T. Roosevelt)	2·20	25
639	-	6c. orange (Garfield)	2·40	25
640	-	7c. black (McKinley)	2·40	25
641	-	8c. green (Grant)	2·40	30
642	-	9c. pink (Jefferson)	2·40	25
610	-	10c. orange (Monroe)	4·00	25
571a		11c. blue (Hayes)	1·70	70
571b		11c. green (Hayes)	1·70	70
693	-	12c. violet (Cleveland)	5·75	25
694	-	13c. green (B. Harrison)	2·50	30
695	**157**	14c. blue	4·50	70
696	**158**	15c. grey	8·75	30
697	**176**	17c. black	5·50	30
698	**159**	20c. red	8·75	30
699	-	25c. green (Niagara)	9·00	30
700	-	30c. brown (American bison)	15·00	30
701	-	50c. lilac (Arlington Amphitheatre and Unknown Soldier's Tomb)	34·00	30
579		$1 brown (Lincoln Memorial)	43·00	75
580		$2 blue (Capitol, Washington)	90·00	10·00
581	**165**	$5 blue and red	£150	17·00

The 25c. to $2 are horiz designs as T **159**, the remainder vert as T **144**.

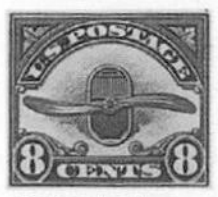
A166 Airplane Radiator and Propeller

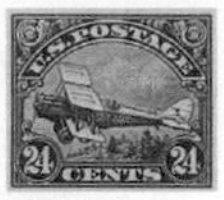
A168 de Havilland DH.4M "Liberty"

1923. Air.

A614	**A166**	8c. green	24·00	16·00
A615	-	16c. blue	90·00	34·00
A616	**A 168**	24c. red	95·00	34·00

DESIGN: 16c. Air mail service insignia.

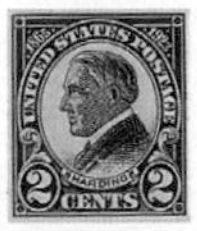
166 Harding

1923. President Harding Memorial.

614	**166**	2c. black	65	30

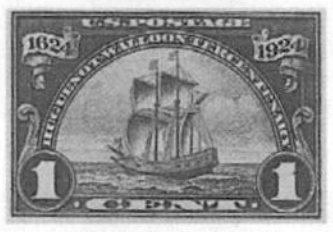
167 "Nieu Nederland" (emigrant ship)

1924. Huguenot–Walloon Tercentenary.

618	**167**	1c. green	3·25	3·75
619	-	2c. red	5·50	2·75
620	-	5c. blue	25·00	15·00

DESIGNS: 2c. Landing at Fort Orange; 5c. Ribault Memorial, Mayport, Florida.

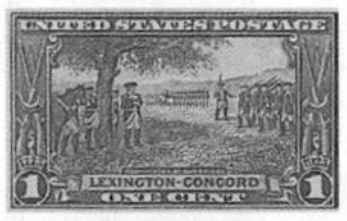
170 Washington at Cambridge

1925. 150th Anniv of Battle of Lexington and Concord.

621	**170**	1c. green	3·25	3·50
622	-	2c. red	4·50	5·75
623	-	5c. blue	28·00	16·00

DESIGNS: 2c. Battle of Lexington-Concord; 5c. Statue of "Minute Man".

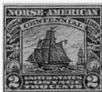

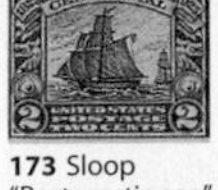
173 Sloop "Restaurationen"

1925. Norse-American Centennial. Dated "1825 1925".

624	**173**	2c. black and red	4·50	3·50
625	-	5c. black and blue	16·00	13·50

DESIGN: 5c. "Raven" (replica Viking longship).

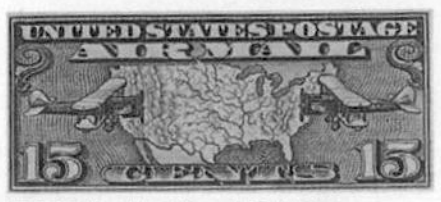
A177 De Havilland D.H.4M Biplanes and Relief Map of U.S.A.

1926. Air.

A628	**A177**	10c. blue	2·75	40
A629	**A177**	15c. brown	4·00	2·75
A630	**A177**	20c. green	8·50	2·30

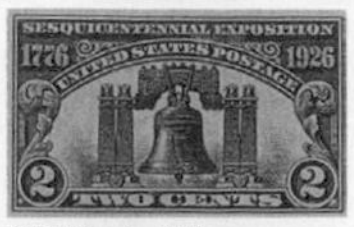
177 Liberty Bell

1926. 150th Anniv of Independence and Sesquicentennial Exhibition.

628	**177**	2c. red	3·25	70

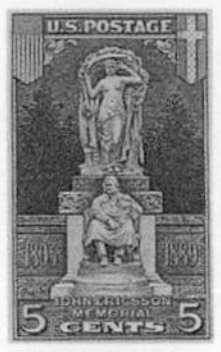
178 Ericsson Memorial (J. E. Fraser) In Washington, D.C.

1926. John Ericsson Commemoration.

629	**178**	5c. violet	6·75	4·00

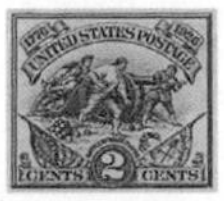
179 Alexander Hamilton's Battery (after painting by E. F. Ward)

1926. 150th Anniv of Battle of White Plains.

644	**179**	2c. red	2·30	1·90

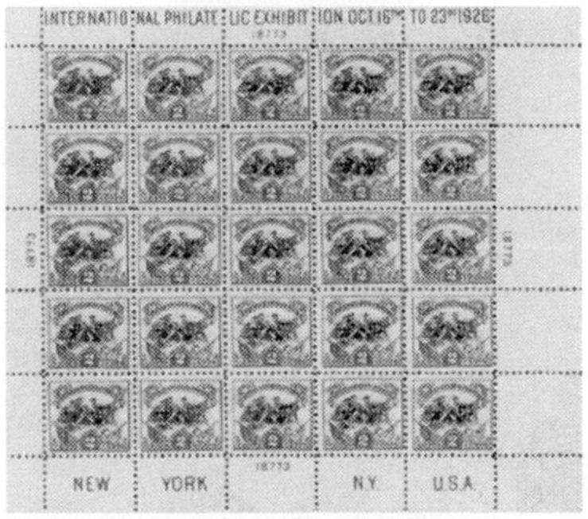
180 (image scaled to 30% of original size)

1926. International Philatelic Exhibition, New York. Sheet 161×149 mm containing No. 644 in block of 25.

MS645	**180**	2c. (×25) carmine	£425	£500

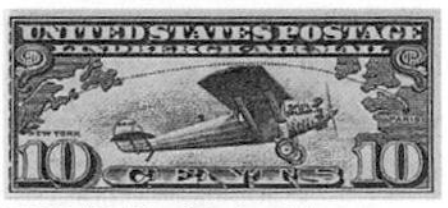
A180 "Spirit of St. Louis"

1927. Air. Lindbergh's Transatlantic Flight.

A646	**A180**	10c. blue	9·00	3·25

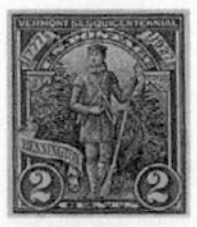
181 Green Mountain Boy

1927. 150th Anniv of Independence of Vermont and Battle of Bennington.

646	**181**	2c. red	1·60	90

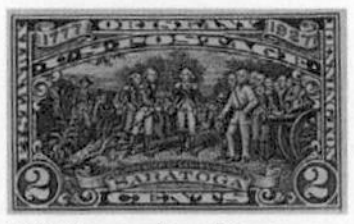
182 Surrender of Gen. Burgoyne (after painting by Trumbull)

1927. 150th Anniv of Burgoyne Campaign.

647	**182**	2c. red	4·00	2·40

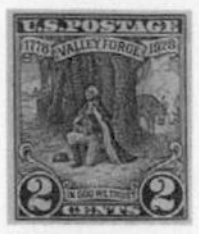
183 Washington at Valley Forge (after engraving by J. C. McRae)

1928. 150th Anniv of Valley Forge.

648	**183**	2c. red	1·10	55

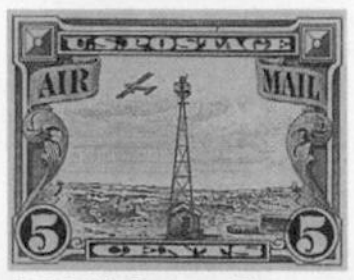
A184 Air Beacon, Sherman Hill, Rocky Mountains

1928. Air.

A649	**A184**	5c. blue and red	5·75	85

1928. 150th Anniv of Discovery of Hawaii. Optd **HAWAII 1778 - 1928**.

649	2c. red (No. 634)	5·00	4·50
650	5c. blue (No. 608)	13·50	14·00

1928. 150th Anniv of Battle of Monmouth. Optd **MOLLY PITCHER**.

651	2c. red (No. 634)	1·30	1·10

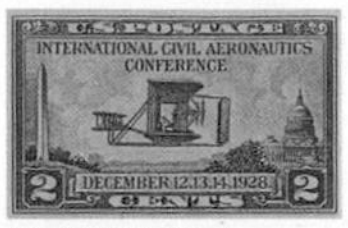
186 Wright Flyer I

1928. Civil Aeronautics Conference and 25th Anniv of Wright Brothers' First Flight.

652	**186**	2c. red	1·30	90
653	-	5c. blue	5·75	3·75

DESIGN: 5c. Globe and Ryan B-5 Brougham biplane.

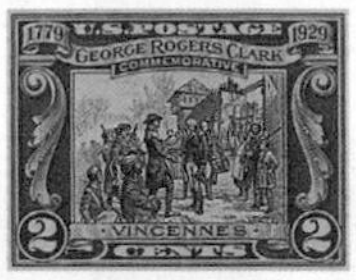
188 George Rogers Clark at Vincennes (from painting by F. C. Yohn)

1929. 150th Anniv of Surrender of Fort Sackville.

654	**188**	2c. black and red	80	55

1929. Stamps of 1922 optd. (a) **Kans.**

655	**144**	1c. green	2·75	2·30
656	**166**	1½c. brown	4·50	3·50
657	-	2c. red	4·75	1·30
658	-	3c. violet	23·00	16·00
659	-	4c. brown	22·00	10·00
660	-	5c. blue	15·00	11·00
661	-	6c. orange	33·00	20·00
662	-	7c. black	33·00	28·00
663	-	8c. olive	£100	80·00
664	-	9c. red	16·00	13·00
665	-	10c. yellow	26·00	14·00

(b) **Nebr.**

666	**144**	1c. green	3·75	2·50
667	**166**	1½c. brown	3·75	2·75
668	-	2c. red	3·75	1·80
669	-	3c. violet	15·00	13·50
670	-	4c. brown	23·00	17·00
671	-	5c. blue	22·00	17·00
672	-	6c. orange	47·00	27·00
673	-	7c. black	25·00	20·00
674	-	8c. olive	40·00	28·00
675	-	9c. red	45·00	31·00
676	-	10c. yellow	£140	26·00

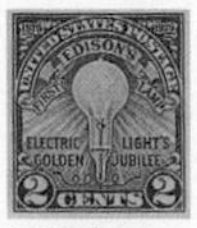
191 Edison's Original Lamp

1929. 50th Anniv of Edison's First Electric Lamp.

678	**191**	2c. red	70	30

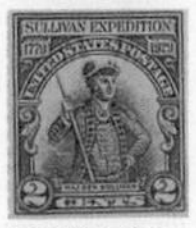
192 Maj.-Gen. Sullivan

1929. 150th Anniv of Maj.-Gen. Sullivan's Western Campaign.

680	**192**	2c. red	90	70

193 Gen. Wayne Memorial in Fallen Timbers Park, by E. W. Laville

1929. 135th Anniv of Battle of Fallen Timbers.

681	**193**	2c. red	1·00	80

194 Ohio River Lock No. 5, Monongahela R.

1929. Completion of Ohio River Canalization.

682	**194**	2c. red	75	70

A195 Air Mail Pilot's Badge

1930. Air.

A684	**A195**	5c. violet	5·75	70
A685	**A195**	6c. orange	4·00	30
A686	**A195**	8c. green	2·50	45

195 Seal of the Colony

1930. Massachusetts Bay Colony Tercentenary.

683	**195**	2c. red	70	55

196 Governor and Indian

1930. 250th Anniv of Original Settlement near Charleston.

684	**196**	2c. red	1·40	1·30

A197 Over the Atlantic

1930. Air. Airship "Graf Zeppelin" Europe–Pan-American Flight.

A687	**A197**	65c. green	£250	£170
A688	–	$1.30 brown	£550	£400
A689	–	$2.60 blue	£800	£650

DESIGNS: $1.30, Between continents; $2.60, Over the globe.

197 Harding

1930

685	**197**	1½c. brown	45	25
686	–	4c. brown	1·30	30

DESIGN: 4c. Taft.

199 George Washington (after statue by F. Vittor in Braddock, Pa.)

1930. 175th Anniv of Battle of Braddock's Field.

689	**199**	2c. red	1·30	95

200 Gen. Wilhelm von Steuben (from medallion by Karl Dautert)

1930. Birth Bicentenary of Gen. von Steuben.

690	**200**	2c. red	60	55

201 Gen. Casimir Pulaski (from etching by H. B. Hall)

1931. 150th Death Anniv of Gen. Pulaski.

691	**201**	2c. red	35	30

202 Red Cross Nurse (from poster "The World's Greatest Mother")

1931. 50th Anniv of American Red Cross Society.

702	**202**	2c. black and red	30	25

203 Rochambeau, Washington, De Grasse (Washington, after painting by Trumbull, others from ...)

1931. 150th Anniv of Surrender of Cornwallis at Yorktown.

703	**203**	2c. black and red	40	30

204 George Washington   **205** George Washington

1932. Birth Bicentenary of George Washington. Portraits dated "1732 1932".

704	**204**	½c. sepia	35	35
705	**205**	1c. green	35	35
706	–	1½c. brown	55	35
707	–	2c. red	35	35
708	–	3c. violet	80	35
709	–	4c. brown	45	35
710	–	5c. blue	1·90	35
711	–	6c. orange	4·50	35
712	–	7c. black	55	35
713	–	8c. olive	3·25	55
714	–	9c. red	2·75	35
715	–	10c. yellow	12·50	35

For 3c. as No. 707, see No. 720.

216 Skiing

1932. Winter Olympic Games, Lake Placid.

716	**216**	2c. red	45	35

217 Tree-planting

1932. 60th Anniv of Establishment of Arbor Day.

717	**217**	2c. red	30	25

218 Sprinter   **219** Discus Thrower

1932. Summer Olympic Games, Los Angeles.

718	**218**	3c. violet	1·70	25
719	**219**	5c. blue	2·75	25

1932. As No. 707, but without date.

720		3c. violet	35	25

221 Wm. Penn

1932. 250th Anniv of Penn's Arrival in America.

723	**221**	3c. violet	50	25

222 Webster

1932. 150th Birth Anniv of Daniel Webster.

724	**222**	3c. violet	55	30

223 Gen. Oglethorpe

1933. Bicentenary of Founding of Georgia.

725	**223**	3c. violet	50	25

224 Washington's H.Q.

1933. 150th Anniv of Proclamation of Peace after War of Independence.

726	**224**	3c. violet	30	25

225 Fort Dearbon (after painting by Dwight Benton)   **226** Federal Building

1933. "Centenary of Progress" International Exhibition, Chicago.

727	**225**	1c. green	30	25
728	**226**	3c. violet	35	25

227 Agriculture, Commerce and Industry

1933. National Recovery Act.

729	**227**	3c. violet	30	25

228 (image scaled to 36% of original size)

229 (image scaled to 36% of original size)

1933. American Philatelic Society Convention and Exhibition, Chicago. Two sheets, each 134×120 mm containing Nos. 727/8 in blocks of 25. Imperf. No gum.

MS730	**228**	1c. (pane of 25) green	31·00	31·00
MS731	**229**	3c. (pane of 25) violet	28·00	28·00

A230 Chicago Federal Building, "Graf Zeppelin" and Friedrichshafen Hangar

1933. Air. "Graf Zeppelin" Chicago Flight.

A732	**A230**	50c. green	£100	75·00

230 Routes of various Admiral Byrd Flights

1933. Byrd Antarctic Expedition.

732	**230**	3c. blue	80	55

231 Gen. Kosciuszko (from statue in Lafayette Park, Washington)

1933. 150th Anniv of Naturalization of Kosciuszko.

733	**231**	5c. blue	70	30

232 (image scaled to 55% of original size)

1934. National Stamp Exhibition, New York. Sheet 87×93 mm containing T **230** in block of six. Imperf. No gum.

MS734	**232**	3c. (pane of 6) blue	23·00	16·00

233 The "Ark" and the "Dove" (from drawing by E. Tunis)

1934. Maryland Tercentenary.

735	**233**	3c. red	35	25

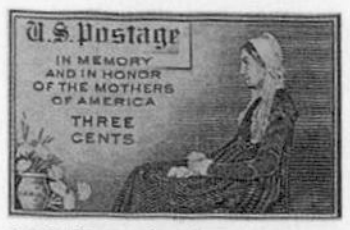

234 "Portrait of my Mother" by Whistler

1934. Mothers' Day. Perf or imperf.

736	**234**	3c. violet	35	25

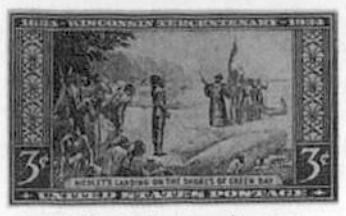

235 Nicolet's Landing at Green Bay (after painting by E. W. Deming)

1934. Tercentenary of Wisconsin.

738	**235**	3c. violet	35	25

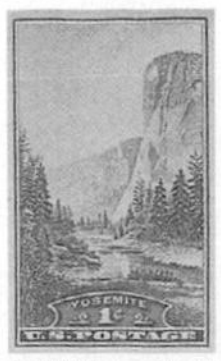

236 "El Capitan", Yosemite

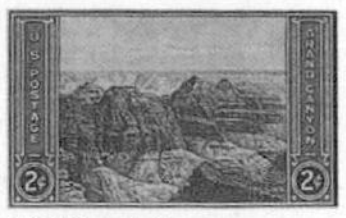

237 Grand Canyon

1934. National Parks.

739	**236**	1c. green	30	15
740	**237**	2c. red	30	15
741	-	3c. violet	40	25
742	-	4c. brown	50	45
743	-	5c. blue	85	75
744	-	6c. blue	1·30	95
745	-	7c. black	85	85
746	-	8c. green	2·30	1·70
747	-	9c. red	2·00	75
748	-	10c. grey	3·50	1·40

DESIGNS—VERT: 5c. "Old Faithful" geyser, Yellowstone; 8c. Great White Throne, Zion; 10c. Mount le Conte, Smoky Mountain. HORIZ: 3c. Mirror Lake, Mt. Rainier; 4c. Cliff dwellings, Mesa Verde; 6c. Crater Lake and Wizard Is; 7c. Great Head, Acadia; 9c. Mt. Rockwell and Two Medicine Lake Glacier.

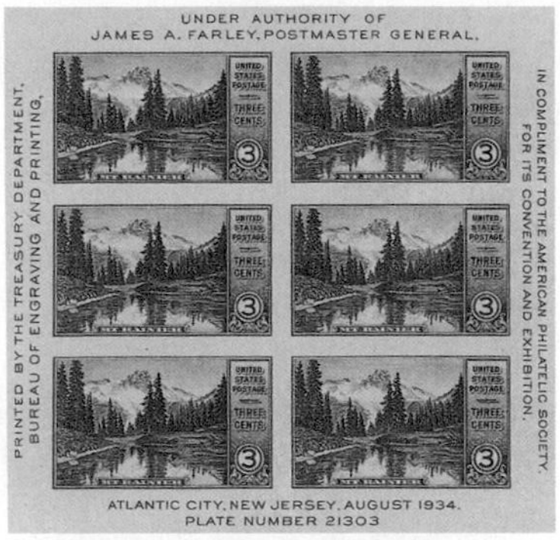

246 (image scaled to 49% of original size)

1934. American Philatelic Society Convention and Exhibition, Atlantic City. Sheet 97×99 mm containing T **238** in block of 6. Imperf.

MS749 **246**	3c. (pane of 6) violet	40·00	34·00

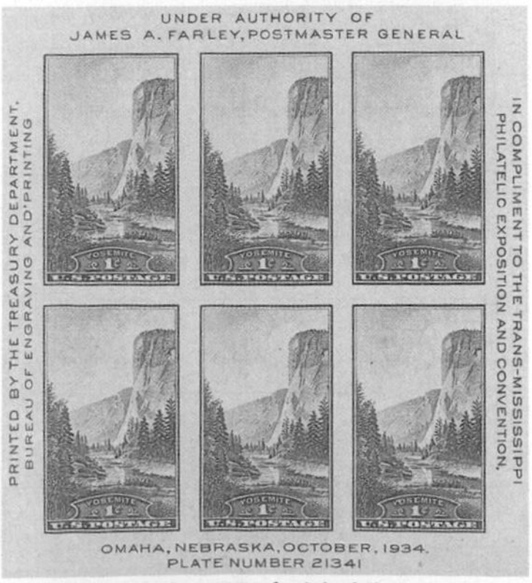

247 (image scaled to 51% of original size)

1934. Trans-Mississippi Philatelic Exhibition and Convention, Omaha. Sheet 94×99 mm containing T **236** in block of 6. Imperf.

MS750 **247**	1c. (pane of 6) green	16·00	16·00

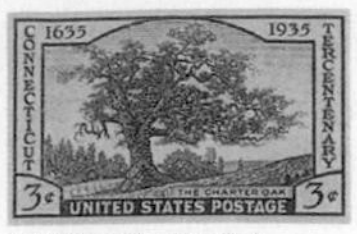

248 The Charter Oak

1935. Connecticut Tercentenary.

771	**248**	3c. purple	35	25

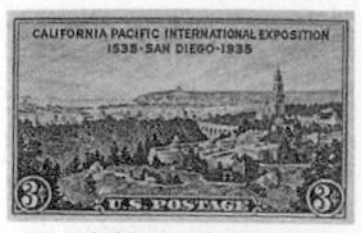

249 Exhibition Grounds, Point Loma and San Diego Bay

1935. California Pacific Int Exn, San Diego.

772	**249**	3c. violet	35	25

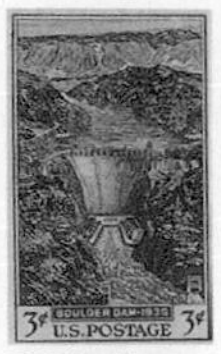

250 Boulder Dam, Nevada

1935. Dedication of Boulder Dam.

773	**250**	3c. violet	35	25

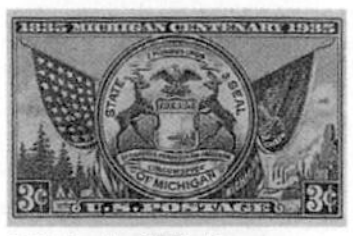

251 Seal of Michigan

1935. Michigan Centenary.

774	**251**	3c. violet	35	25

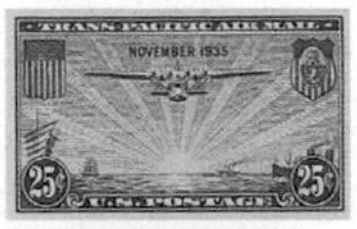

A253 Martin M-130 Flying Boat

1935. Air. Trans-Pacific Air Mail.

A775	-	20c. green	12·50	2·00
A776	**A 253**	25c. blue	1·60	1·10
A777	-	50c. red	12·50	5·75

Nos. A775 and A777 are as Type A **253** but without the date.

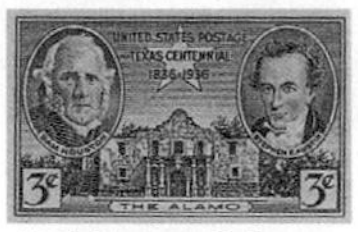

252 S. Houston, S. F. Austin, and the Alamo

1936. Centenary of Declaration of Texan Independence.

775	**252**	3c. violet	35	25

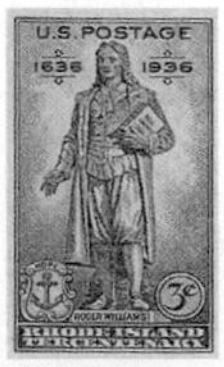

253 Roger Williams (from statue in Roger Williams Park, Providence, R. I.)

1936. Rhode Island Tercentenary.

776	**253**	3c. violet	40	25

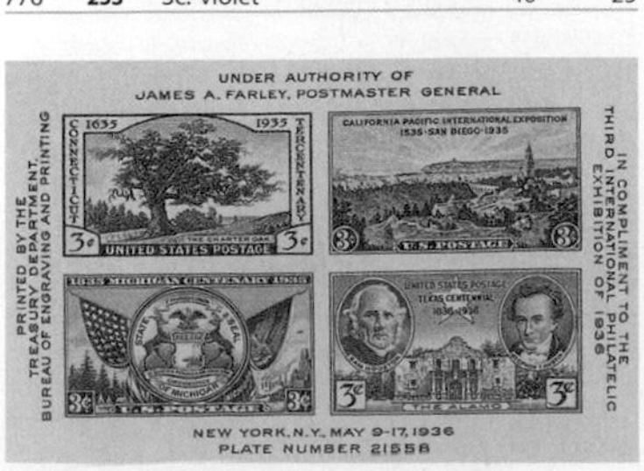

254 (image scaled to 49% of original size)

1936. Third International Philatelic Exhibition, New York. Sheet containing Nos. 771/2 and 774/5 in block of 4, each in purple. Imperf.

MS777 **254**	98×66 mm	2·75	2·75

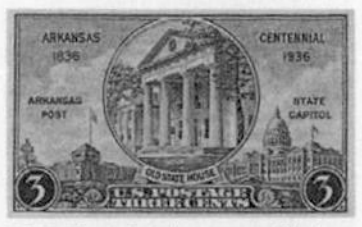

255 First Settlement, Old State House and Capitol

1936. Centenary of Arkansas.

778	**255**	3c. violet	35	25

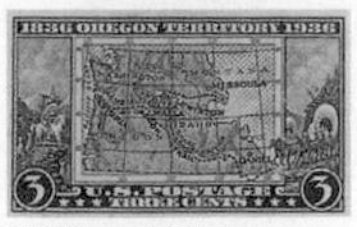

256 Map of Old Oregon Territory

1936. Centenary of Oregon.

779	**256**	3c. violet	30	25

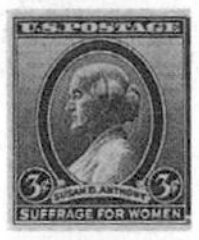

257 Susan B. Anthony (detail from statue by Adelaide Johnson in Capitol)

1936. 16th Anniv of Women's Suffrage.

780	**257**	3c. purple	30	25

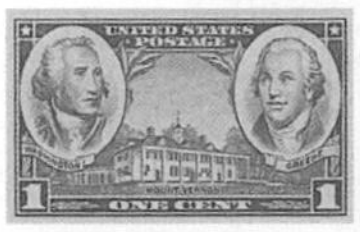

258 Washington and Greene, Mt. Vernon in background

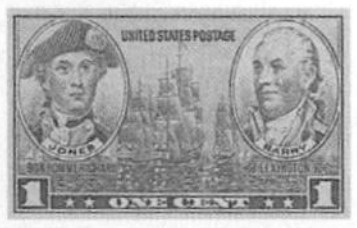

263 Jones, Barry and Battle of Flamborough Head

1936. Army and Navy Heroes. (a) Army.

781	**258**	1c. green	35	25
782	-	2c. red	35	25
783	-	3c. purple	45	25
784	-	4c. blue	55	35
785	-	5c. blue	70	35

DESIGNS: 2c. Jackson, Scott and the Hermitage; 3c. Sherman, Grant and Sheridan; 4c. Lee, Jackson and Stratford Hall; 5c. West Point Military Acadamy.

(b) Navy.

786	**263**	1c. green	35	25
787	-	2c. red	35	25
788	-	3c. purple	45	25
789	-	4c. blue	55	35
790	-	5c. blue	70	35

DESIGNS: 2c. Decatur, MacDonough and U.S.S. "United States" (frigate); 3c. Farragut, Porter and U.S.S. "Hartford" (steam frigate); 4c. Sampson, Dewey and Schley; 5c. Seal of Naval Academy and cadets.

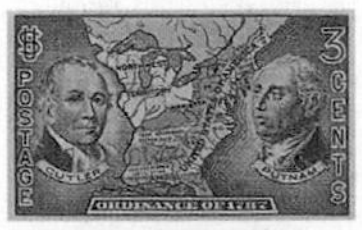

268 Cutler, Putnam and Map of N. W. Territory

1937. 150th Anniv of Enactment of North West Territory Ordinance.

791	**268**	3c. violet	35	25

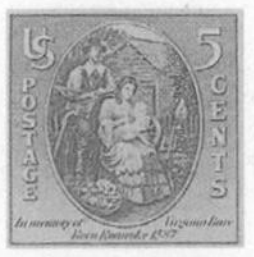

269 Virginia Dare

1937. 350th Birth Anniv of Virginia Dare.

792	**269**	5c. blue	40	30

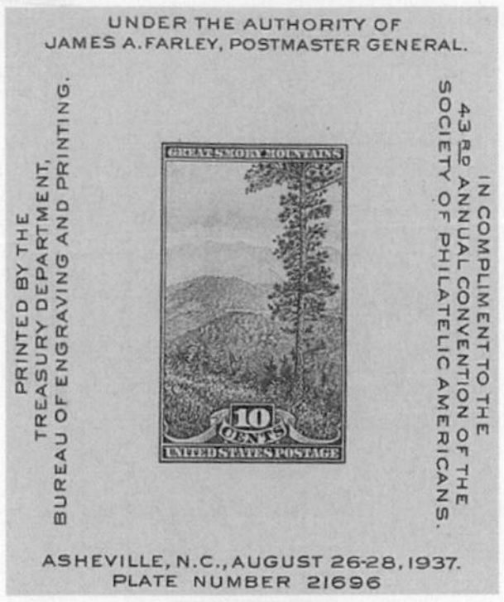

270

1937. 43rd Annual Convention of the Society of Philatelic Americans. Sheets containing stamp as No. 748 but printed in new colour. Imperf.

MS793 **270**	67×78 mm. 10c. green	90	80

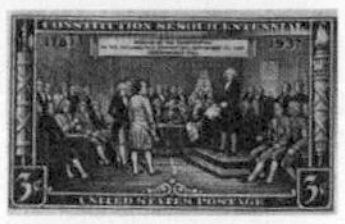

271 Signing the Constitution (after painting by J. B. Stearns)

1937. 150th Anniv of U.S. Constitution.

794	**271**	3c. mauve	45	25

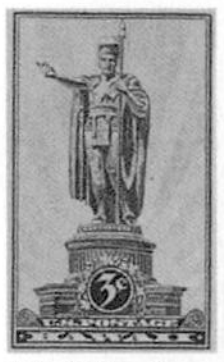

272 Statue to Kamehameha I, Honolulu

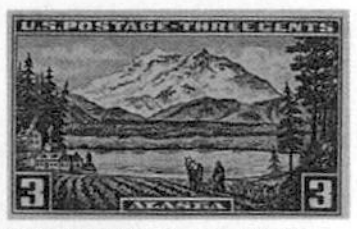

273 Mt. McKinley, Alaska

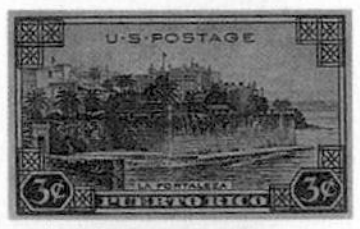

274 Fortaleza Castle, Puerto Rico

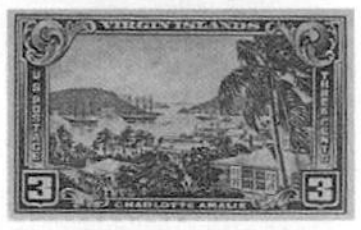

275 Charlotte Amalie (St. Thomas), Virgin Islands

1937. Territorial Issue.

795	**272**	3c. violet	40	25
796	**273**	3c. violet	40	25
797	**274**	3c. violet	40	25
798	**275**	3c. mauve	40	25

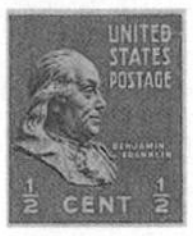

276 Benjamin Franklin

1938. Presidential Series.

799	**276**	½c. orange	35	25
800	-	1c. green	35	25
801	-	1½c. brown	35	25
802	-	2c. red	35	25
803	-	3c. violet	35	2·30
804	-	4c. purple	85	25
805	-	4½c. grey	35	25
806	-	5c. blue	35	25
807	-	6c. red	35	25
808	-	7c. brown	45	25
809	-	8c. green	45	25
810	-	9c. pink	45	25
811	-	10c. red	45	25
812	-	11c. blue	85	25
813	-	12c. mauve	1·10	25
814	-	13c. green	1·60	30
815	-	14c. blue	1·10	25
816	-	15c. slate	70	25
817	-	16c. black	1·40	50
818	-	17c. red	1·10	25
819	-	18c. purple	2·50	25
820	-	19c. mauve	1·60	65
821	-	20c. green	1·10	25
822	-	21c. blue	1·60	30

823	-	22c. red	1·50	70
824	-	24c. black	4·00	35
825	-	25c. mauve	1·00	25
826	-	30c. blue	4·50	25
827	-	50c. lilac	5·75	25
828	-	$1 black and purple	8·00	25
830	-	$2 black and green	22·00	5·50
831	-	$5 black and red	£100	5·75

DESIGNS: 1c. Washington; 1½c. Martha Washington; 2c. John Adams; 3c. Jefferson; 4c. Madison; 4½c. White House; 5c. James Monroe; 6c. John Quincy Adams; 7c. Jackson; 8c. Martin van Buren; 9c. Wm. Henry Harrison; 10c. John Tyler; 11c. James K. Polk; 12c. Zachary Taylor; 13c. Millard Fillmore; 14c. Franklin Pierce; 15c. James Buchanan; 16c. Lincoln; 17c. Johnson; 18c. Grant; 19c. Rutherford B. Hayes; 20c. James A. Garfield; 21c. Chester A. Arthur; 22c. Grover Cleveland; 24c. Benjamin Harrison; 25c. William McKinley; 30c. Theodore Roosevelt; 50c. Taft; $1 Woodrow Wilson; $2 Harding; $5 Coolidge.

A308 American Bald Eagle and Shield

1938. Air.

A845	**A308**	6c. red and blue	55	25

308 Colonial Court House

1938. 150th Anniv of Ratification of U.S. Constitution.

845	**308**	3c. violet	50	25

309 Landing of the Swedes and Finns from "Calmare Nyckel" (after S. Arthurs)

1938. Tercentenary of Scandinavian Settlement in America.

846	**309**	3c. mauve	40	25

310 Colonization of the West (from statue by G. Borglum at Marietta, Ohio)

1938. North West Territory Sesquicentennial.

847	**310**	3c. violet	35	25

311 Old Capitol Building, Iowa

1938. Iowa Territory Centennial.

848	**311**	3c. violet	40	25

312 Tower of the Sun

1939. Golden Gate Int Exn, San Francisco.

849	**312**	3c. purple	35	25

313 Trylon and Perisphere

1939. New York World's Fair.

850	**313**	3c. violet	35	25

314 Inauguration of Washington

1939. 150th Anniv of Election of Washington as First President.

851	**314**	3c. purple	65	25

A315 Winged Globe

1939. Air.

A852	**A315**	30c. blue	13·50	1·70

315 Baseball

1939. Baseball Centenary.

852	**315**	3c. violet	2·00	25

316 T. Roosevelt, Goethals and "Andrea F. Luckenbach" (freighter) in Gaillard Cut

1939. 25th Anniv of Opening of Panama Canal.

853	**316**	3c. purple	40	25

317 Stephen Daye Press (from sketch by G. F. Trenholm)

1939. Tercent of Printing in Colonial America.

854	**317**	3c. violet	30	25

318 Washington, Montana, N. and S. Dakota

1939. 50th Anniv of Statehood of Washington, Montana and N. and S. Dakota.

855	**318**	3c. mauve	40	25

319 Washington Irving   **324** Henry W. Longfellow    **329** Horace Mann

334 John James Audubon   **339** Stephen Collins Foster    **344** Gilbert Charles Stuart

349 Eli Whitney

1940. Famous Americans. (a) Authors.

856	**319**	1c. green	25	20
857	-	2c. red	25	20
858	-	3c. purple	30	20
859	-	5c. blue	40	25
860	-	10c. brown	2·00	1·50

PORTRAITS: 2c. J. Fenimore Cooper; 3c. Ralph Waldo Emerson; 5c. Louisa May Alcott; 10c. Samuel L. Clemens ("Mark Twain").

(b) Poets.

861	**324**	1c. green	25	20
862	-	2c. red	25	20
863	-	3c. purple	30	20
864	-	5c. blue	55	30
865	-	10c. brown	2·00	1·70

PORTRAITS: 2c. John Greenleaf Whittier; 3c. James Russell Lowell; 5c. Walt Whitman; 10c. James Whitcomb Riley.

(c) Educationalists.

866	**329**	1c. green	25	20
867	-	2c. red	25	20
868	-	3c. purple	30	20
869	-	5c. blue	55	25
870	-	10c. brown	2·50	1·40

PORTRAITS: 2c. Mark Hopkins; 3c. Charles W. Eliot; 5c. Frances E. Willard; 10c. Booker T. Washington.

(d) Scientists.

871	**334**	1c. green	25	20
872	-	2c. red	25	20
873	-	3c. purple	30	20
874	-	5c. blue	55	25
875	-	10c. brown	1·70	1·30

PORTRAITS: 2c. Dr. Crawford W. Long; 3c. Luther Burbank; 5c. Dr. Walter Reed; 10c. Jane Addams.

(e) Composers.

876	**339**	1c. green	25	20
877	-	2c. red	25	20
878	-	3c. purple	30	20
879	-	5c. blue	55	30
880	-	10c. brown	4·25	1·60

PORTRAITS: 2c. John Philip Sousa; 3c. Victor Herbert; 5c. Edward A. MacDowell; 10c. Ethelbert Nevin.

(f) Artists.

881	**344**	1c. green	25	20
882	-	2c. red	25	20
883	-	3c. purple	35	20
884	-	5c. blue	55	25
885	-	10c. brown	2·00	1·60

PORTRAITS: 2c. James A. McNeill Whistler; 3c. Augustus Saint-Gaudens; 5c. Daniel Chester French; 10c. Frederic Remington.

(g) Inventors.

886	**349**	1c. green	30	20
887	-	2c. red	35	20
888	-	3c. purple	35	20
889	-	5c. blue	1·30	45
890	-	10c. brown	12·50	2·75

PORTRAITS: 2c. Samuel F. B. Morse; 3c. Cyrus Hall McCormick; 5c. Elias Howe; 10c. Alexander Graham Bell.

354 "Pony Express"

1940. 80th Anniv of Inauguration of Pony Express.

891	**354**	3c. red	55	25

355 "The Three Graces" (after Botticelli's "Spring")

1940. 50th Anniv of Pan-American Union.

892	**355**	3c. mauve	35	25

356 State Capitol, Boise

1940. 50th Anniv of Idaho.

893	**356**	3c. violet	40	25

357 Wyoming State Seal

1940. 50th Anniv of Wyoming.

894	**357**	3c. purple	35	25

358 Coronado and His Captains (after painting by Gerald Cassidy)

1940. 400th Anniv of Coronado Expedition.

895	**358**	3c. violet	35	25

360 Anti-aircraft Gun

1940. National Defence.

896	-	1c. green	25	20
897	**360**	2c. red	25	20
898	-	3c. violet	25	20

DESIGNS: 1c. Statue of Liberty; 3c. Hand holding torch.

362 Emancipation (Freedom Group statue by Thomas Ball, Lincoln Park, Washington)

1940. 75th Anniv of Abolition of Slavery.

899	**362**	3c. violet	35	25

363 State Capitol Building, Montpelier

1941. 150th Anniv of Vermont.

900	**363**	3c. violet	45	25

A364 Mail Plane

1941. Air.

A901	**A364**	6c. red	30	25
A902	**A364**	8c. green	30	25
A903	**A364**	10c. violet	1·40	25
A904	**A364**	15c. red	2·50	40
A905	**A364**	20c. green	2·50	35
A906	**A364**	30c. blue	2·50	40
A907	**A364**	50c. orange	12·50	3·75

364 Daniel Boone and Companions viewing Kentucky (from mural by Gilbert White in State Capitol, Frankfort)

1942. 150th Anniv of Kentucky.

901	**364**	3c. violet	25	25

365
Symbolical of
Victory

1942. Independence Day.
902   **365**   3c. violet   25   20

366 Lincoln and Sun
Yat-sen

1942. Chinese War Effort.
903   **366**   5c. blue   1·60   30

367 Allegory
of Victory

1943. Allied Nations.
904   **367**   2c. red   25   20

368 Liberty
holding Torch of
Freedom and
Enlightenment

1943. Four Freedoms.
905   **368**   1c. green   25   20

369 Flag of Poland

1943. Flags of Oppressed Nations. Frames in violet, flags
in national colours.
906   5c. Type **369**   30   20
907   5c. Czechoslovakia   30   20
908   5c. Norway   30   20
909   5c. Luxembourg   30   20
910   5c. Netherlands   30   20
911   5c. Belgium   30   20
912   5c. France   30   20
913   5c. Greece   55   40
914   5c. Yugoslavia   45   35
915   5c. Albania   30   20
916   5c. Austria   35   20
917   5c. Denmark   35   20
918   5c. Korea   30   20

382 "Golden Spike
Ceremony" (mural, John
McQuarrie)

1944. 75th Anniv of First Transcontinental Railway.
919   **382**   3c. violet   30   20

383 Paddle-steamer
"Savannah"

1944. 125th Anniv of Transatlantic Crossing of "Savannah".
920   **383**   3c. violet   35   20

384 "What Hath God
Wrought"

1944. Centenary of First Telegraph Message.
921   **384**   3c. mauve   30   20

385 View of Corregidor

1944. Defence of Corregidor.
922   **385**   3c. violet   25   20

386 Open-air Cinema

1944. 50th Anniv of Motion Pictures.
923   **386**   3c. violet   35   25

387 Gates of St. Augustine,
State Seal and Capitol

1945. Centenary of Statehood of Florida.
924   **387**   3c. purple   35   20

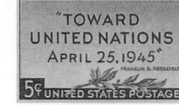

388 "Toward United
Nations"

1945. San Francisco Conference.
925   **388**   5c. blue   35   20

389 Franklin D. Roosevelt
and Hyde Park

1945. Pres. Roosevelt Commemoration. Inscr "1882 1945".
926   **389**   1c. green   35   20
927   -   2c. red   35   20
928   -   3c. violet   35   20
929   -   5c. blue   35   20
DESIGNS: 2c. "Little White House", Warm Springs, Georgia;
3c. "White House", Washington; 5c. Western Hemisphere
and Four Freedoms.

393 Raising
U.S.A. Flag at Iwo
Jima

1945. U.S. Marines.
930   **393**   3c. green   35   20

394 U.S. Troops marching
through Paris

1945. U.S. Army.
931   **394**   3c. olive   30   20

395 U.S. Sailors

1945. U.S. Navy.
932   **395**   3c. blue   30   20

396 "Arthur Middleton"
(supply ship) and
Coastguard Landing Craft)

1945. U.S. Coastguard.
933   **396**   3c. green   30   20

397 Alfred E.
Smith

1945. Alfred E. Smith (Governor of New York)
Commemoration.
934   **397**   3c. violet   30   20

398 Flags of U.S.A. and
Texas

1945. Centenary of Texas Statehood.
935   **398**   3c. blue   30   20

399 "Liberty" type
Freighter unloading Cargo

1946. U.S. Mercantile Marine.
936   **399**   3c. green   30   20

400
Honourable
Discharge
Emblem

1946. Honourable Discharged Veterans of Second World
War.
937   **400**   3c. violet   30   20

401 Andrew Jackson, John
Sevier and Tennessee State
Capitol

1946. 150th Anniv of Tennessee Statehood.
938   **401**   3c. violet   30   20

402 Iowa State Flag and
Map

1946. Centenary of Iowa Statehood.
939   **402**   3c. blue   30   20

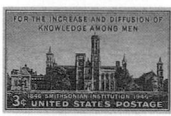

403 Smithsonian
Institution

1946. Centenary of Smithsonian Institution.
940   **403**   3c. purple   30   20

A404 Douglas DC-4

1946. Air.
A941   **A404**   5c. red   30   20

404 Entry into Santa Fe
(after painting by Kenneth
M. Chapman)

1946. Centenary of Entry of Stephen Watts Kearny
Expedition into Santa Fe.
941   **404**   3c. purple   30   20

405 Thomas A.
Edison

1947. Birth Cent of Thomas Edison (scientist).
942   **405**   3c. violet   30   20

A406 Douglas
DC-4

1947. Air.
A943   **A406**   5c. red   30   20
A944   **A406**   6c. red   30   20

406 Joseph Pulitzer (from
portrait by J. S. Sargent)

1947. Birth Centenary of Joseph Pulitzer (journalist and
newspaper publisher).
943   **406**   3c. violet   35   20

407 Washington, Franklin
and Evolution of Postal
Transport

1947. U.S. Postage Stamp Centenary.
944   **407**   3c. blue   35   20

408 Franklin and Washington (reproductions of T **1** and
2) (image scaled to 46% of original size)

1947. Centenary of First U.S. Postage Stamps and
Centenary of First International Philatelic Exhibition, New
York. Imperf.
MS945   **408**   103×67 mm. 5c.+10c   1·10   1·10

409 "The Doctor" (after
painting by Sir Luke Fildes)

1947. Medical Profession.
946   **409**   3c. purple   35   20

410 Pioneer Caravan

1947. Centenary of Utah.
947   **410**   3c. violet   35   20

A411 Pan-American Union
Building, Washington

1947. Air.
A948   **A411**   10c. black   45   20
A949   -   15c. green   55   20
A950   -   25c. blue   1·30   20
DESIGNS: 15c. Statue of Liberty and New York City; 25c.
San Francisco–Oakland Bay Suspension Bridge.

411 U.S.S. "Constitution"

1947. 150th Anniv of Launching of Frigate U.S.S. "Constitution" ("Old Ironsides").
948 411 3c. green 35 20

412 Great Blue Heron and Map of Florida

1947. Dedication of Everglades National Park, Florida.
949 412 3c. green 35 20

413 George Washington Carver

1948. Fifth Death Anniv of George Washington Carver (scientist).
950 413 3c. violet 35 20

414 Sutter's Mill, Coloma

1948. Cent of Discovery of Gold in California.
951 414 3c. violet 35 20

415 Gov. Winthrop Sargent, Map and Seal of Mississippi Territory (from portrait by Gilbert Stuart)

1948. 150th Anniv of Mississippi Territory.
952 415 3c. purple 35 20

416 Four Chaplains and Liner "Dorchester"

1948. Fifth Death Anniv of George Fox, Clark Poling, John Washington and Alexander Goode (who gave up life-jackets).
953 416 3c. black 35 20

417 Scroll and State Capitol, Madison

1948. Centenary of Statehood of Wisconsin.
954 417 3c. violet 35 20

418 Pioneer and Covered Wagon

1948. Centenary of Swedish Pioneers in Middle West.
955 418 5c. blue 35 20

419 Elizabeth Stanton, Carrie C. Catt, and Lucretia Mott

1948. Progress of American Women.
956 419 3c. violet 35 20

A420 Map of New York, Ring and Planes (from Poster by G. A. Lorimer)

1948. Air. Golden Anniv of New York City Council.
A957 A420 5c. red 35 20

420 William Allen White

1948. Honouring W. A. White (editor and author).
957 420 3c. purple 35 20

421 Niagara Railway Suspension Bridge (from print by H. Peters)

1948. Centenary of Friendship between United States and Canada.
958 421 3c. blue 35 20

422 Francis Scott Key

1948. Honouring F. S. Key (author of "Star Spangled Banner").
959 422 3c. red 35 20

423 Boy and Girl Students

1948. Salute to Youth.
960 423 3c. blue 35 20

424 John McLoughlin, Jason Lee and Covered Wagon

1948. Oregon Territory Centennial.
961 424 3c. red 35 20

425 Harlan Fiske Stone

1948. Honouring Chief Justice H. F. Stone.
962 425 3c. purple 35 20

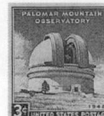

426 Palomar Mountain Observatory

1948. Dedication of Palomar Observatory.
963 426 3c. blue 35 20

427 Clara Barton and Cross

1948. Honouring Clara Barton (founder of American Red Cross).
964 427 3c. red 35 20

428 Light Brahma Rooster

1948. Centenary of American Poultry Industry.
965 428 3c. brown 35 20

429 Star and Palm Branch

1948. Honouring Bereaved Mothers.
966 429 3c. yellow 35 20

430 Fort Kearny and Pioneers (Pioneer group from sculpture on Nebraska State Capitol)

1948. Centenary of Fort Kearny, Nebraska.
967 430 3c. violet 35 20

431 Peter Stuyvesant and Fire Engines (from painting in Library of Congress)

1948. Tercentenary of Volunteer Firemen.

432 Indian Seals and Map of Oklahoma

1948. Centenary of Five Civilized Indian Tribes of Oklahoma.
969 432 3c. brown 35 20

433 Statue of Capt. William Owen "Bucky" O'Neill, Prescott, Arizona (S. H. Borglum)

1948. 50th Anniv of Organization of Rough Riders.
970 433 3c. purple 35 20

434 Juliette Gordon Low

1948. Honouring Juliette Gordon Low (founder of U.S.A. Girl Scouts).
971 434 3c. green 35 20

435 Will Rogers

1948. Honouring Will Rogers (political commentator).
972 435 3c. purple 35 20

436 Rocket Testing

1948. Centenary of Fort Bliss.
973 436 3c. red 35 20

437 Moina Michael and Poppies

1948. Honouring Moina Michael (founder of Memorial Poppy).
974 437 3c. red 35 20

438 Abraham Lincoln (from statue by D. C. French at Lincoln, Neb.)

1948. 85th Anniv of Gettysburg Address.
975 438 3c. blue 35 20

439 Torch and Emblem

1948. Centenary of American Turners' Society.
976 439 3c. red 35 20

440 Joel Chandler Harris

1948. Birth Centenary of J. C. Harris (author).
977 440 3c. purple 35 20

441 Pioneer and Red River Ox Cart

1949. Cent of Territorial Status of Minnesota.
978 441 3c. green 35 20

442 Washington, Lee and University Building

1949. Bicentenary of Washington and Lee University, Lexington, Virginia.
979 442 3c. blue 35 20

443 Puerto Rican, Cogwheel and Ballot Box

1949. First Gubernatorial Election in Puerto Rico.
980 443 3c. green 35 20

A444 Wings, Seal, Carlyle House and Gadsby's Tavern

1949. Air. Bicentenary of Alexandria, Virginia.
A981 A444 6c. red 35 20

444 Map, "Het Vergulde Vsanker" (sailing barge) and Shield

1949. Tercentenary of Annapolis, Maryland.
981   **444**   3c. green   35   20

445 Young and Old Soldiers

1949. Final National Encampment of the Grand Army of the Republic.
982   **445**   3c. red   35   20
For similar stamp see No. 995.

446 Edgar Allan Poe

1949. Death Centenary of Edgar Allan Poe (poet and author).
983   **446**   3c. purple   35   20

A447 U.P.U. Monument, Berne and P.O. Department, Washington

1949. Air. 75th Anniv of U.P.U.
A984   **A447**   10c. violet   35   20
A985   -   15c. blue   55   50
A986   -   25c. red   90   65
DESIGNS: 15c. Globe and birds; 25c. Globe and Boeing 377 Stratocruiser.

A450 Wright Brothers and Wright Flyer I

1949. Air. 46th Anniv of Wright Brothers' First Flight.
A987   **A450**   6c. purple   35   20

447 Symbolic of Investments

1950. 75th Anniv of American Bankers' Assn.
984   **447**   3c. green   35   20

448 Samuel Gompers

1950. Birth Centenary of Samuel Gompers (labour leader).
985   **448**   3c. purple   35   20

449 Statue of Freedom (by Crawford) on Capitol Dome

450 The White House

1950. National Capital Sesquicentennial.
986   **449**   3c. blue   35   20
987   **450**   3c. green   35   20
988   -   3c. violet   35   20
989   -   3c. purple   35   20

DESIGNS—HORIZ: No. 988, U.S. Supreme Court building; 989, Capitol, Washington.

453 Casey Jones, Locomotive No. 382 and "Rocket" Diesel Train

1950. Honouring Railway Engineers.
990   **453**   3c. purple   35   20

454 Kansas City in 1850 and 1950

1950. Centenary of Kansas City.
991   **454**   3c. violet   35   20

455 Scouts and Badge

1950. American Boy Scouts.
992   **455**   3c. brown   35   20

456 First Capitol and W. H. Harrison

1950. Sesquicentennial of Indiana.
993   **456**   3c. blue   35   20

457 Pioneers

1950. Centenary of California.
994   **457**   3c. yellow   35   20

1951. Final Reunion of United Confederate Veterans. As T **445**, but initials at left and in hat badge changed to "UCV".
995   **445**   3c. grey   35   20

458 Log Cabin

1951. Centenary of Nevada.
996   **458**   3c. olive   35   20

459 Cadillac Disembarking

1951. 250th Anniv of Landing of Cadillac at Detroit.
997   **459**   3c. blue   35   20

460 Mount of the Holy Cross, State Seal and Capitol

1951. 75th Anniv of Colorado.
998   **460**   3c. violet   35   20

461 Emblem and Chemical Plant

1951. 75th Anniv of American Chemical Society.
999   **461**   3c. purple   35   20

462 Washington at Brooklyn

1951. 175th Anniv of Battle of Brooklyn.
1000   **462**   3c. violet   35   20

463 Betsy Ross and Flag

1952. Birth Bicentenary of Betsy Ross (maker of First American flag).
1001   **463**   3c. red   35   20

464 Emblem and Young Club Members

1952. 50th Anniv of 4-H Clubs.
1002   **464**   3c. green   35   20

465 Horse-drawn "Pioneer" Coach, "Tom Thumb" (1829) and Diesel Locomotive

1952. 125th Anniv of Baltimore and Ohio Railway.
1003   **465**   3c. blue   35   20

466 Cars of 1902 and 1952

1952. 50th Anniv of American Automobile Assn.
1004   **466**   3c. blue   35   20

467 "Torch of Freedom"

1952. Third Anniv of N.A.T.O.
1005   **467**   3c. violet   35   20

A467 Diamond Head, Oahu, Honolulu

1952. Air.
A1005   **A467**   80c. purple   6·75   1·70

468 Grand Coulee Dam

1952. 50th Anniv of Columbia Basin Reclamation.
1006   **468**   3c. green   35   20

469 Lafayette and Flags

1952. 175th Anniv of Lafayette's Arrival in America.
1007   **469**   3c. blue   35   20

470 Mt. Rushmore National Memorial

1952. 25th Anniv of Mt. Rushmore National Memorial.
1008   **470**   3c. green   35   20

471 Bridges in 1852 and 1952

1952. Centenary of American Society of Civil Engineers.
1009   **471**   3c. blue   35   20

472 Women in Uniform

1952. Women's Services Commemoration.
1010   **472**   3c. blue   35   20

473 Gutenberg and Elector of Mainz (after Edward Laning)

1952. 500th Anniv of Printing of First Book from Movable Type.
1011   **473**   3c. violet   35   20

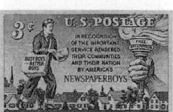

474 Newspaperboy and Torch of Free Enterprise

1952. Newspaperboys Commemoration.
1012   **474**   3c. violet   35   20

475 Red Cross and Globe

1952. International Red Cross.
1013   **475**   3c. blue and red   35   20

476 Guardsman and Amphibious Landing

1953. National Guard.
1014   **476**   3c. blue   35   20

477 Map and Seal of Ohio

1953. 150th Anniv of Ohio.
1015   **477**   3c. sepia   35   20

478 Seal of Washington Territory and Settlers

1953. Centenary of Washington Territory.
1016   **478**   3c. green   35   20

479 Monroe, Livingston and Marbois signing Transfer (from sculpture plaque by Karl Bitter)

1953. 150th Anniv of Louisiana Purchase.
| 1017 | **479** | 3c. purple | 35 | 20 |

A480 Wright Flyer I and Boeing 377 Stratocruiser

1953. Air. 50th Anniv of Aviation.
| A1018 | **A 480** | 6c. red | 35 | 20 |

480 Commodore Perry and U.S.S. "Susquehanna" and "Mississippi" (paddle-gunboats) in Tokyo Bay

1953. Centenary of Opening of Japan to Foreign Trade.
| 1018 | **480** | 5c. turquoise | 35 | 20 |

481 "Wisdom", "Justice and Divine Inspiration" and "Truth"

1953. 75th Anniv of American Bar Association.
| 1019 | **481** | 3c. violet | 35 | 20 |

482 "Sagamore Hill"

1953. Opening of Theodore Roosevelt's Home.
| 1020 | **482** | 3c. green | 35 | 20 |

483 Young Farmer and Landscape

1953. 25th Anniv of "Future Farmers of America".
| 1021 | **483** | 3c. blue | 35 | 20 |

484 Truck and Distant City

1953. 50th Anniv of Trucking Industry.
| 1022 | **484** | 3c. violet | 35 | 20 |

485 Gen. Patton and Tanks in Action

1953. Gen. George Patton and U.S. Armoured Forces.
| 1023 | **485** | 3c. violet | 35 | 20 |

486 New York in 1653 and 1953

1953. Tercent of Foundation of New York City.
| 1024 | **486** | 3c. purple | 35 | 20 |

487 Pioneer Family

1953. Centenary of Gadsden Purchase.
| 1025 | **487** | 3c. chestnut | 35 | 20 |

488 Low Memorial Library

1954. Bicentenary of Columbia University.
| 1026 | **488** | 3c. blue | 35 | 20 |

490 Washington (after Stuart) **492** Mount Vernon **501** Statue of Liberty

1954. Liberty Issue.
1027	-	½c. red	35	20
1028	**490**	1c. green	35	20
1029	-	1¼c. turquoise	35	20
1030	**492**	1½c. lake	35	20
1031	-	2c. red	35	20
1032	-	2½c. blue	35	20
1033	**501**	3c. violet	35	20
1034	-	4c. mauve	35	20
1035	-	4½c. green	35	20
1036	-	5c. blue	35	20
1037	-	6c. red	45	20
1038	-	7c. red	45	20
1039	**501**	8c. red and blue	45	20
1040	-	8c. red and blue	45	20
1041	-	8c. brown	45	20
1042	-	9c. purple	55	20
1043	-	10c. red	45	20
1044	-	11c. blue and red	55	20
1045	-	12c. red	70	20
1046	-	15c. red	1·10	30
1047	-	20c. blue	80	30
1048	-	25c. turquoise	1·10	30
1049	-	30c. black	2·00	55
1050	-	40c. lake	2·50	35
1051	-	50c. violet	2·30	35
1052	-	$1 violet	6·75	55
1053	-	$5 black	80·00	7·75

DESIGNS—As Type **490**: ½c. Benjamin Franklin; 2c. Jefferson; 4c. Lincoln; 5c. Monroe; 6c. Theodore Roosevelt; 7c. Woodrow Wilson; 8c. (No. 1040), As Type **501** but torch flame below "P"; 8c. (No. 1041), Gen. John J. Pershing; 11c. As No. 1040; 12c. Benjamin Harrison; 15c. John Jay; 25c. Paul Revere; 30c. Robert F. Lee; 40c. John Marshall; 50c. Susan B. Anthony; $1 Patrick Henry; $5 Alexander Hamilton. As Type **492**—VERT: 2½c. Bunker Hill Monument and Massachusetts flag. HORIZ: 1¼c. Palace of the Governors, Santa Fe; 4½c. The Hermitage; 9c. The Alamo; 10c. Independence Hall; 20c. Monticello, Thomas Jefferson's home.

516 "The Sower" and Mitchell Pass (from statue on Capitol, Lincoln, Neb)

1954. Centenary of Nebraska Territory.
| 1062 | **516** | 3c. violet | 35 | 20 |

517 Pioneers and Cornfield

1954. Centenary of Kansas Territory.
| 1063 | **517** | 3c. salmon | 35 | 20 |

518 George Eastman

1954. Birth Centenary of Eastman (inventor).
| 1064 | **518** | 3c. purple | 35 | 20 |

519 Landing on Riverbank, Missouri

1954. 150th Anniv of Lewis and Clark Expedition.
| 1065 | **519** | 3c. purple | 35 | 20 |

A520 American Bald Eagle in Flight

1954. Air.
| A1066 | **A520** | 4c. blue | 35 | 20 |
| A1067 | **A520** | 5c. red | 35 | 20 |

520 "Peale in his Museum" (self-portrait)

1955. 150th Anniv of Pennsylvania Academy of Fine Arts.
| 1066 | **520** | 3c. purple | 35 | 20 |

521 Open Book and Symbols of Subjects taught

1955. Centenary of First Land-Grant Colleges.
| 1067 | **521** | 3c. green | 35 | 20 |

522 Torch, Globe and Rotary Emblem

1955. 50th Anniv of Rotary International.
| 1068 | **522** | 8c. blue | 55 | 35 |

523 Marine, Coastguard, Soldier, Sailor and Airman

1955. Armed Forces Reserve.
| 1069 | **523** | 3c. purple | 35 | 20 |

524 "The Old Man of the Mountains"

1955. 150th Anniv of Discovery of "The Old Man of the Mountains" (New Hampshire landmark).
| 1070 | **524** | 3c. turquoise | 35 | 20 |

525 The Great Lakes and "Altadoc" (freighter)

1955. Soo Locks Centenary.
| 1071 | **525** | 3c. blue | 35 | 20 |

526

527 Plan of Fort, Ethan Allen and Artillery

1955. Bicentenary of Fort Ticonderoga.
| 1073 | **527** | 3c. brown | 35 | 20 |

528 Mellon (after Edward Birley)

1955. Birth Centenary of Andrew W. Mellon (philanthropist).
| 1074 | **528** | 3c. red | 35 | 20 |

529 Benjamin Franklin (after painting by Benjamin West)

1956. 250th Birth Anniv of Franklin.
| 1075 | **529** | 3c. red | 35 | 20 |

530 Log Cabin

1956. Birth Centenary of Booker T. Washington.
| 1076 | **530** | 3c. blue | 35 | 20 |

1955. "Atoms for Peace".
| 1072 | **526** | 3c. blue | 35 | 20 |

531 Statue of Liberty (reproductions of No. 1033 and T **501**) (image scaled to 44% of original size)

1956. Fifth International Philatelic Exhibition, New York. Sheet 108×73 mm. Imperf
| MS1077 | **531** | 3c.+8c. multicoloured | 2·75 | 2·75 |

532 New York Coliseum and Columbus Monument

1956. Fifth International Philatelic Exn, New York.
| 1078 | **532** | 3c. violet | 35 | 20 |

533 Pronghorns

1956. Wild Life Conservation.
1079	**533**	3c. purple	35	20
1080	-	3c. sepia	35	20
1081	-	3c. green	35	20

DESIGNS: No. 1080, Common Turkey; 1081, Chinook "king" salmon.

536 H. W. Wiley

1956. 50th Anniv of Pure Food and Drug Laws.
1082   **536**   3c. green   35   20

537 Wheatland

1956. Home of James Buchanan.
1083   **537**   3c. sepia   35   20

538 Mosaic by L. M. Winter, A.F.L.-C.I.O. Headquarters

1956. Labour Day.
1084   **538**   3c. blue   35   20

539 Nassau Hall (contemporary engraving by Dawkins)

1956. Bicentenary of Nassau Hall.
1085   **539**   3c. black on orange   35   20

540 Devils Tower

1956. 50th Anniv of Devils Tower National Monument.
1086   **540**   3c. violet   35   20

541 "The Key to World Peace"

1956. Children's Friendship.
1087   **541**   3c. blue   35   20

542 Alexander Hamilton and Federal Hall, New York

1957. Birth Bicentenary of Alexander Hamilton.
1088   **542**   3c. red   35   20

543 Women, Children and Shield

1957. Infantile Paralysis Relief Campaign.
1089   **543**   3c. mauve   35   20

544 Survey Flag and Coastguard Vessels "Pathfinder", "Explorer" and "Surveyor"

1957. 150th Anniv of Coast and Geodetic Survey.
1090   **544**   3c. blue   35   20

545 Ancient and Modern Capitals

1957. Cent of American Institute of Architects.
1091   **545**   3c. mauve   35   20

546 Eagle and Ladle

1957. Centenary of American Steel Industry.
1092   **546**   3c. blue   35   20

547 Festival Emblem and Aircraft Carrier U.S.S. "Forrestal"

1957. Jamestown Festival and Int Naval Review.
1093   **547**   3c. green   35   20

548 Arrow piercing Atomic Symbol

1957. 50th Anniv of Oklahoma Statehood.
1094   **548**   3c. blue   35   20

549 Teacher with Pupils

1957. Teachers of America Commemoration.
1095   **549**   3c. red   35   20

550 U.S. Flag

1957. Flag Issue.
1096   **550**   4c. red and blue   35   20

A551 Boeing B-52 Stratofortress and Lockheed F-104 Starfighters

1957. Air. 50th Anniv of U.S. Air Force.
A1097   **A551**   6c. blue   35   20

551 "Virginia of Sagadahock" (shallop) and Arms of Maine

1957. 350th Anniv of American Shipbuilding.
1097   **551**   3c. violet   35   20

552 Pres. Magsaysay of the Philippines (medallion)

1953. Pres. Magsaysay Commemoration.
1098   **552**   8c. ochre, blue and red   35   20

553 Marquis de Lafayette (portrait by Court in Versailles Museum)

1957. Birth Bicentenary of Marquis de Lafayette.
1099   **553**   3c. red   35   20

554 Whooping Cranes

1957. Wild Life Conservation.
1100   **554**   3c. blue, orange and green   35   20

555 "Religious Freedom"

1957. Tercentenary of Flushing Remonstrance.
1101   **555**   3c. black   35   20

556 "Abundance"

1958. Gardening and Horticulture Commem.
1102   **556**   3c. green   35   20

557 U.S. Pavilion

1958. Brussels International Exhibition.
1103   **557**   3c. purple   35   20

558 James Monroe (portrait by Stuart)

1958. Birth Bicentenary of Pres. James Monroe.
1104   **558**   3c. violet   35   20

559 Lake in Minnesota

1958. Centenary of Minnesota Statehood.
1105   **559**   3c. green   35   20

560 Sun's Surface and Hands (after Michelangelo's "The Creation of Adam")

1958. I.G.Y.
1106   **560**   3c. red and black   35   20

561 Gunston Hall (after drawing by Rene Clarke)

1958. Bicentenary of Gunston Hall, Virginia (home of George Mason, patriot).
1107   **561**   3c. green   35   20

562 Mackinac Bridge

1958. Mackinac Bridge Commemoration.
1108   **562**   3c. turquoise   35   20

563 Simon Bolivar (after painting by Ricardo Arcevedo-Bernal)

1958. Bolivar Commemoration.
1109   **563**   4c. ochre   35   20
1110   **563**   8c. brown, blue and red   35   20

See also Nos. 1116/17, 1124/5, 1135/6, 1146/7. 1158/9, 1164/5, 1167/8 and 1173/4.

A564 Silhouette of Jet Airliner

1958. Air.
A1111   **A564**   7c. blue   35   20
A1112   **A564**   7c. red   35   20

564 Globe, Neptune and Mermaid

1958. Centenary of Inaug of Atlantic Cable.
1111   **564**   4c. purple   35   20

565 Abraham Lincoln (from painting by G. Healy)

1958. 150th Birth Anniv of Lincoln.
1112   **565**   1c. green   35   20
1113   -   3c. red   35   20
1114   -   4c. brown   35   20
1115   -   4c. blue   35   20

DESIGNS: No. 1113, Bust of Lincoln; 1114, Addressing Electorate; 1115, Lincoln Statue, Washington.

1958. Lajos Kossuth Commemoration. Medallion portrait as T **563**.
1116   4c. green   35   20
1117   8c. brown, blue and red   40   20

570 Hand with Quill Pen and Printing Press

1958. Freedom of the Press.
1118　**570**　4c. black　35　20

571 Mail Coach under Attack

1958. Overland Mail Centenary.
1119　**571**　4c. red　35　20

572 Noah Webster (engraving by G. Parker after painting by James Herring)

1958. Birth Bicentenary of Noah Webster (lexicographer).
1120　**572**　4c. red　35　20

573 Forest Pines

1958. Forest Conservation.
1121　**573**　4c. yellow, green & brown　35　20

574 British Forces occupying Fort Duquesne (from etching by T. B. Smith)

1958. Bicentenary of Fort Duquesne.
1122　**574**　4c. blue　35　20

A575 Stars on Alaskan Map

1959. Air. Alaska Statehood.
A1123　**A575**　7c. blue　45　30

575 Covered Wagon and Mt. Hood

1959. Centenary of Oregon Statehood.
1123　**575**　4c. green　35　20

1959. San Martin Commemoration. Medallion portrait as T **563**.
1124　4c. blue　35　20
1125　8c. ochre, red and blue　35　20

577 N.A.T.O. Emblem

1959. Tenth Anniv of N.A.T.O.
1126　**577**　4c. blue　35　20

578 Peary with Dog-team and Submarine U.S.S. "Nautilus"

1959. Arctic Explorations by Robert Peary (50th anniv of reaching North Pole) and U.S.S. "Nautilus".
1127　**578**　4c. blue　35　20

579

1959. World Peace through World Trade.
1128　**579**　8c. red　45　30

580 Discovery of Silver at Mt. Davidson, Nevada (from a print)

1959. Cent of Discovery of Silver in Nevada.
1129　**580**　4c. black　35　20

581 Maple Leaf linked with American Eagle

1959. Opening of St. Lawrence Seaway.
1130　**581**　4c. blue and red　35　20

582 New U.S. Flag (with 49 stars)

1959. Inauguration of New United States Flag.
1131　**581**　4c. red, blue and orange　35　20

A583 John Wise's Balloon "Jupiter"

1959. Air. Centenary of Balloon "Jupiter's" Mail-carrying Flight.
A1132　**A583**　7c. red and blue　45　20

A584 Hawaiian Warrior, Map and Star

1959. Air. Hawaii Statehood.
A1133　**A584**　7c. red　35　20

583 "The Good Earth"

1959. Soil Conservation.
1132　**583**　4c. green, brown and blue　35　20

584 Oil Derrick

1959. Centenary of First Oil-well at Titusville, Pennsylvania.
1133　**584**　4c. brown　35　20

A585 Runner with Olympic Torch

1959. Air. Third Pan-American Games, Chicago.
A1134　**A585**　10c. red and blue　45　30

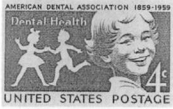

585 "Happy Children with Healthy Teeth"

1959. Dental Health. Centenary of American Dental Association.
1134　**585**　4c. green　35　20

1959. Ernst Reuter Commemoration. Medallion portrait as T **563**.
1135　4c. grey　35　20
1136　8c. ochre, red and blue　35　20

A588 Statue of Liberty

1959. Air.
A1137　-　10c. black and green　1·70　90
A1138　-　13c. black and red　45　20
A1139　**A588**　15c. black & orge (A)　55　20
A1140　**A588**　15c. black & orge (B)　55　20
A1141　-　25c. black and brown　80　20

Types as A585/8, plus 25c. Abraham Lincoln, double frame-line (A) or single frame-line (B); 25c. Abraham Lincoln.

587 Dr. E. McDowell (from painting)

1959. 150th Anniv of First Recorded Successful Abdominal Operation.
1137　**587**　4c. purple　35　20

588

1960. "American Credo" series.
1138　**588**　4c. red and blue　35　20
1139　-　4c. green and bistre　35　20
1140　-　4c. red and grey　35　20
1141　-　4c. blue and red　35　20
1142　-　4c. green and purple　35　20
1143　-　4c. brown and green　35　20

INSCRIPTIONS: No. 1139, "Fear to do ill, and you need fear Nought else" (Franklin); 1140, "I have sworn … Hostility against every form of TYRANNY over the mind of man" (Jefferson); 1141, "And this be our Motto in GOD is our TRUST" (Francis Scott Key); 1142, "Those who Deny freedom to others Deserve it not for Themselves" (Lincoln); 1143, "Give me LIBERTY or give me DEATH" (P. Henry).

594 Scout Saluting

1960. 50th Anniv of American Boy Scout Movement.
1144　**594**　4c. ochre, red and blue　35　20

595 Olympic Rings and Snow Crystal

1960. Winter Olympic Games.
1145　**595**　4c. blue　35　20

1960. Thomas Masaryk Commemoration. Medallion portrait as T **563**.
1146　4c. blue　35　20
1147　8c. ochre, red and blue　35　20

597 "Towards the Light"

1960. World Refuge Year.
1148　**597**　4c. black　35　20

598 "Irrigation"

1960. Water Conservation Campaign.
1149　**598**　4c. green, brown and blue　35　20

599 S.E.A.T.O. Emblem

1960. S.E.A.T.O. Conference.
1150　**599**　4c. blue　35　20

600 Mother and Child

1960. American Womanhood Commemoration.
1151　**600**　4c. violet　35　20

601 New U.S. Flag (with 50 stars)

1960. New United States Flag (50 stars).
1152　**601**　4c. red and blue　35　20

602 Pony Express

1960. Centenary of Pony Express.
1153　**602**　4c. brown　35　20

603 Cripple operating Press

1960. Employment of the Handicapped Campaign.
1154　**603**　4c. blue　35　20

604 Congress
Seal

1960. Fifth World Forestry Congress, Seattle.
1155   **604**   4c. green   35   20

605 Dolores Bell
(Mexico)

1960. 150th Anniv of Mexican Independence.
1156   **605**   4c. red and green   35   20

606 Washington
Monument and
Cherry Blossom

1960. Centenary of U.S.–Japan Treaty.
1157   **606**   4c. red and turquoise   35   20

1960. Jan Paderewski Commemoration. Medallion
portrait as T **563**.
1158   4c. blue   35   20
1159   8c. ochre, red and blue   35   20

608 Robert A.
Taft

1960. Robert A. Taft Memorial Issue.
1160   **608**   4c. violet   35   20

609 Steering Wheel, Motor
Transport and Globes

1960. "Wheels of Freedom" (Motor Industry).
1161   **609**   4c. blue   35   20

610 Boy

1960. Cent of Boys' Clubs of America Movement.
1162   **610**   4c. red, black and indigo   35   20

611 New P.O. Building

1960. Inauguration of First U.S. Automated P.O.,
Providence, Rhode Island.
1163   **611**   4c. blue and red   35   20

1960. Marshal Mannerheim Commem. Medallion portrait
as T **563**.
1164   4c. blue   35   20
1165   8c. ochre, red and blue   35   20

613 Camp Fire
Girls Emblem

1960. 50th Anniv of Camp Fire Girls Movement.
1166   **613**   4c. red and blue   40   20

1960. Garibaldi Commem. Medallion portrait as T **563**.
1167   4c. green   35   20
1168   8c. ochre, red and blue   35   20

615 George

1960. Senator Walter F. George Memorial Issue.
1169   **615**   4c. violet   35   20

616 Andrew
Carnegie

1960. Andrew Carnegie.
1170   **616**   4c. red   35   20

617 Dulles

1960. John Foster Dulles Memorial Issue.
1171   **617**   4c. violet   35   20

618 "Echo I"
Communications Satellite

1960. "Communications for Peace".
1172   **618**   4c. violet   35   20

1961. Mahatma Gandhi Commemoration. Medallion
portrait as T **563**.
1173   4c. red on orange   35   20
1174   8c. ochre, red and blue   35   20

620 Trail Boss and Prairie

1961. Range Conservation.
1175   **620**   4c. black, orange and
blue   35   20

621 Horace
Greeley (from
steel engraving
by A. H. Ritchie)

1961. Horace Greeley (editor).
1176   **621**   4c. violet   35   20

622 Sea Coast Gun

1961. Civil War Centennial. Battles.
1177   **622**   4c. green   50   20
1178   –   4c. black on pink   40   20
1179   –   5c. indigo and blue   40   20
1180   –   5c. black and red   40   20
1181   –   5c. black and blue   60   20

DESIGNS—HORIZ: No. 1178, Rifleman (Shiloh); 1179,
Armed combat (Gettysburg); 1180, Artillery crew (Wilderness). VERT: No. 1181, Soldier and rifles (Appomattox).

627 Sunflower and Pioneers

1961. Centenary of Kansas Statehood.
1182   **627**   4c. red, green and brown
on yellow   35   20

628 Senator G. W. Norris

1961. Birth Centenary of George W. Norris.
1183   **628**   4c. green   35   20

629 Curtiss A-1 Seaplane,
1911 (Navy's first plane)

1961. 50th Anniv of U.S. Naval Aviation.
1184   **629**   4c. blue   35   20

630 "Balanced
Judgement"

1961. 150th Anniv of Workmen's Compensation Law.
1185   **630**   4c. blue   35   20

631 "The Smoke
Signal" (after
Remington)

1961. Birth Centenary of Frederic Remington (painter).
1186   **631**   4c. multicoloured   35   20

632 Dr. Sun
Yat-sen

1961. 50th Anniv of Republic of China.
1187   **632**   4c. blue   35   20

633 Basketball

1961. Birth Centenary of Dr. James A. Naismith (inventor
of basketball).
1188   **633**   4c. brown   35   20

634 Nurse
lighting Candle
of Dedication

1961. Nursing.
1189   **634**   4c. multicoloured   35   20

635 Ship Rock, New Mexico

1962. 50th Anniv of Statehood of New Mexico.
1190   **635**   4c. lake, ochre & turq   35   20

636 Saguaro
Cactus and
Flowers

1962. 50th Anniv of Arizona Statehood.
1191   **636**   4c. blue, green and red   35   20

637 "U.S. Man in Space"

1962. Project Mercury. Colonel John Glenn's Space Flight.
1192   **637**   4c. blue and yellow   35   20

638 U.S. and Campaign
Emblems

1962. Malaria Eradication.
1193   **638**   4c. ochre and blue   35   20

639 C. E. Hughes

1962. Birth Centenary of Chief Justice Hughes.
1194   **639**   4c. black on buff   35   20

640 Space
Needle and
Monorail

1962. "Century 21" Exn ("World's Fair"), Seattle.
1195   **640**   4c. blue and red   35   20

641 Mississippi Sternwheel
Steamer

1962. 150th Anniv of Lousiana Statehood.
1196   **641**   4c. myrtle, red and blue   35   20

642 Settlers' Homestead

1962. Centenary of Homestead Act.
1197   **642**   4c. grey   35   20

643 Girl Scout and Flag

1962. 50th Anniv of U.S. Girl Scouts.
1198 **643** 4c. red 35 20

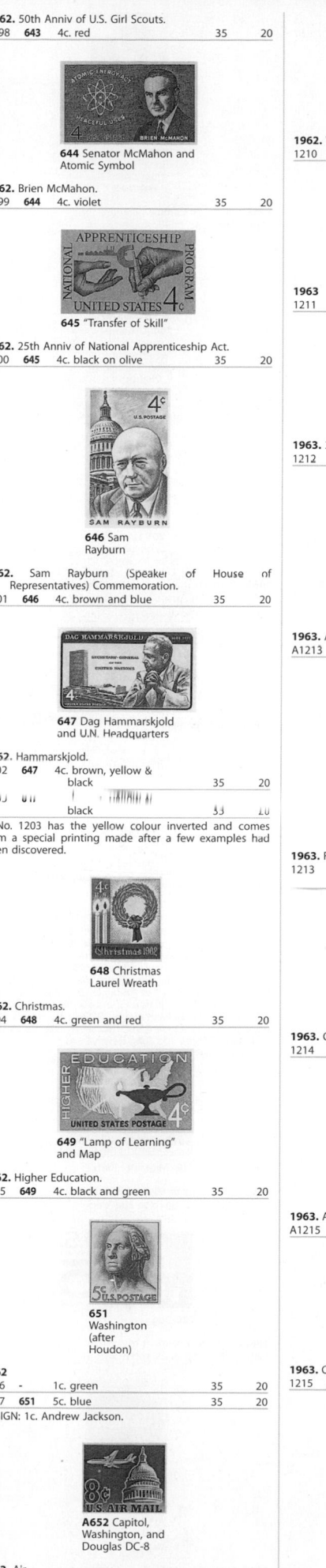

644 Senator McMahon and Atomic Symbol

1962. Brien McMahon.
1199 **644** 4c. violet 35 20

1962. 25th Anniv of National Apprenticeship Act.
1200 **645** 4c. black on olive 35 20

645 "Transfer of Skill"

1962. Sam Rayburn (Speaker of House of Representatives) Commemoration.
1201 **646** 4c. brown and blue 35 20

646 Sam Rayburn

1962. Hammarskjold.
1202 **647** 4c. brown, yellow & black 35 20
1203 **647** 4c. brown, yellow & black 35 20

647 Dag Hammarskjold and U.N. Headquarters

No. 1203 has the yellow colour inverted and comes from a special printing made after a few examples had been discovered.

648 Christmas Laurel Wreath

1962. Christmas.
1204 **648** 4c. green and red 35 20

649 "Lamp of Learning" and Map

1962. Higher Education.
1205 **649** 4c. black and green 35 20

651 Washington (after Houdon)

1962
1206 - 1c. green 35 20
1207 **651** 5c. blue 35 20
DESIGN: 1c. Andrew Jackson.

A652 Capitol, Washington, and Douglas DC-8

1962. Air.
A1210 **A652** 8c. red 35 20

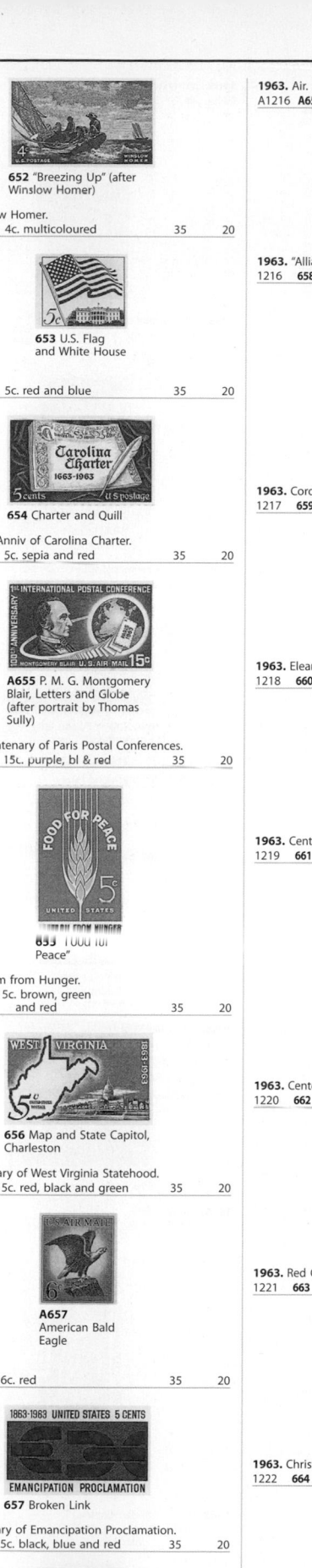

652 "Breezing Up" (after Winslow Homer)

1962. Winslow Homer.
1210 **652** 4c. multicoloured 35 20

653 U.S. Flag and White House

1963
1211 **653** 5c. red and blue 35 20

654 Charter and Quill

1963. 300th Anniv of Carolina Charter.
1212 **654** 5c. sepia and red 35 20

A655 P. M. G. Montgomery Blair, Letters and Globe (after portrait by Thomas Sully)

1963. Air. Centenary of Paris Postal Conferences.
A1213 **A655** 15c. purple, bl & red 35 20

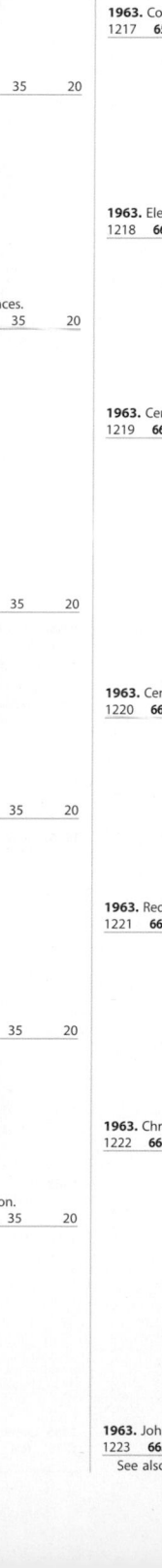

655 "Food for Peace"

1963. Freedom from Hunger.
1213 **655** 5c. brown, green and red 35 20

656 Map and State Capitol, Charleston

1963. Centenary of West Virginia Statehood.
1214 **656** 5c. red, black and green 35 20

A657 American Bald Eagle

1963. Air.
A1215 **A657** 6c. red 35 20

657 Broken Link

1963. Centenary of Emancipation Proclamation.
1215 **657** 5c. black, blue and red 35 20

A658 Amelia Earhart and Lockheed "Electra"

1963. Air. Amelia Earhart Commemoration.
A1216 **A658** 8c. purple and red 35 20

658 Torch of Progress

1963. "Alliance for Progress".
1216 **658** 5c. green and blue 35 20

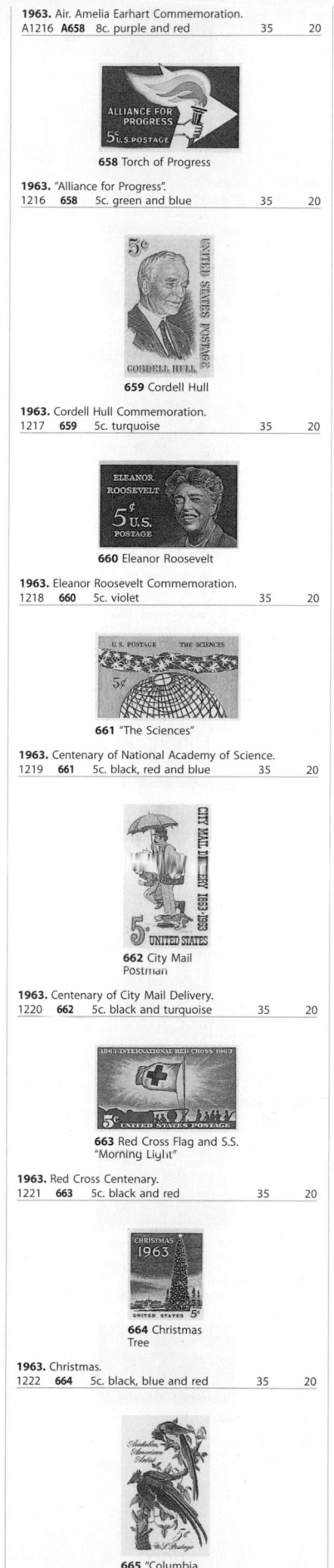

659 Cordell Hull

1963. Cordell Hull Commemoration.
1217 **659** 5c. turquoise 35 20

660 Eleanor Roosevelt

1963. Eleanor Roosevelt Commemoration.
1218 **660** 5c. violet 35 20

661 "The Sciences"

1963. Centenary of National Academy of Science.
1219 **661** 5c. black, red and blue 35 20

662 City Mail Postman

1963. Centenary of City Mail Delivery.
1220 **662** 5c. black and turquoise 35 20

663 Red Cross Flag and S.S. "Morning Light"

1963. Red Cross Centenary.
1221 **663** 5c. black and red 35 20

664 Christmas Tree

1963. Christmas.
1222 **664** 5c. black, blue and red 35 20

665 "Columbia Jays" (print) (actually Collie's Magpie-jays)

1963. John James Audubon Commemoration.
1223 **665** 5c. multicoloured 35 20
See also No. A1304.

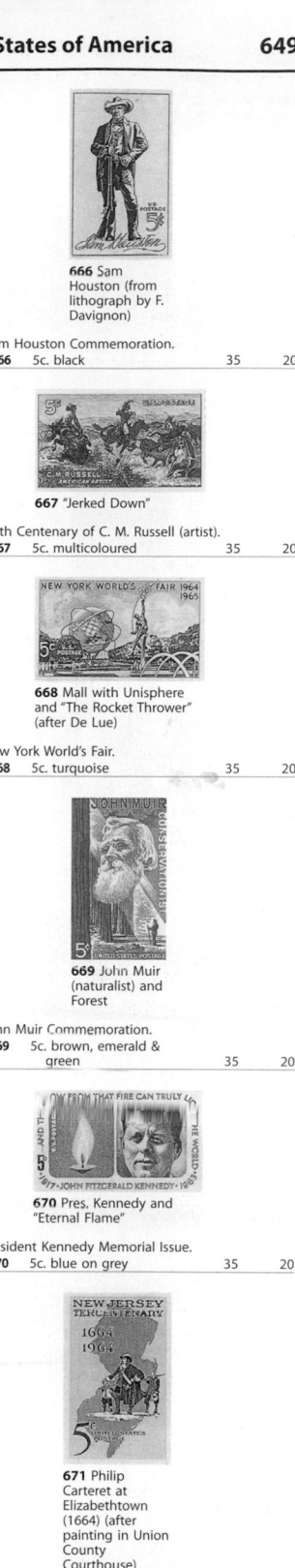

666 Sam Houston (from lithograph by F. Davignon)

1964. Sam Houston Commemoration.
1224 **666** 5c. black 35 20

667 "Jerked Down"

1964. Birth Centenary of C. M. Russell (artist).
1225 **667** 5c. multicoloured 35 20

668 Mall with Unisphere and "The Rocket Thrower" (after De Lue)

1964. New York World's Fair.
1226 **668** 5c. turquoise 35 20

669 John Muir (naturalist) and Forest

1964. John Muir Commemoration.
1227 **669** 5c. brown, emerald & green 35 20

670 Pres. Kennedy and "Eternal Flame"

1964. President Kennedy Memorial Issue.
1228 **670** 5c. blue on grey 35 20

671 Philip Carteret at Elizabethtown (1664) (after painting in Union County Courthouse)

1964. Tercentenary of New Jersey.
1229 **671** 5c. blue 35 20

672 Virginia City in 19th Century

1964. Centenary of Nevada Statehood.
1230 **672** 5c. multicoloured 35 20

673 U.S. Flag

1964. "Register and Vote" Campaign.
1231   **673**   5c. red and blue   35   20

674 Shakespeare

1964. 400th Birth Anniv of William Shakespeare.
1232   **674**   5c. sepia on buff   35   20

675 Drs. William and Charles Mayo (after J. E. Fraser)

1964. Mayo Brothers (founders of Mayo Clinic) Commemoration.
1233   **675**   5c. green   35   20

A676 R. H. Goddard, "Atlas" Rocket and Launching Tower

1964. Air. Robert H. Goddard Commem.
A1234   **A676**   8c. blue, red & yellow   50   30

676 Lute, Horn and Music Score

1964. American Music.
1234   **676**   5c. black, red and blue on light blue   35   20

677 Sampler

1964. "Homemakers" Commemoration.
1235   **677**   5c. multicoloured   35   20

678 Holly

1964. Christmas. Each red, green and black.
1236   5c. Type **678**   35   20
1237   5c. Mistletoe   35   20
1238   5c. Poinsettia   35   20
1239   5c. Pine cone   35   20

682 Verrazano-Narrows Bridge

1964. Opening of Verrazano-Narrows Bridge, New York.
1240   **682**   5c. green   35   20

683 "Abstract Art" (from lithograph by S. Davis)

1964. "To the Fine Arts".
1241   **683**   5c. red, black and blue   35   20

684 Radio Waves

1964. Amateur Radio.
1242   **684**   5c. purple   35   20

685 General Jackson leading Troops into Battle

1965. 150th Anniv of Battle of New Orleans.
1243   **685**   5c. red, blue and black   35   20

686 Discus-thrower (Washington statue)

1965. Centenary of Sokol Physical Fitness Organization in the U.S.A.
1244   **686**   5c. blue and lake   35   20

687 Microscope and Stethoscope

1965. Crusade Against Cancer.
1245   **687**   5c. black, violet and red   35   20

688 Sir Winston Churchill (from photo by Karsh)

1965. Churchill Commemoration.
1246   **688**   5c. black   35   20

689 Procession of Barons, and King John's Crown

1965. 750th Anniv of Magna Carta.
1247   **689**   5c. black, yellow & violet   35   20

690 I.C.Y. Emblem

1965. International Co-operation Year.
1248   **690**   5c. black and blue   35   20

691 "One hundred years of service"

1965. Centenary of Salvation Army.
1249   **691**   5c. black, red and blue   35   20

692 Dante

1965. 700th Anniv of Dante's Birth.
1250   **692**   5c. red on flesh   35   20

693 Herbert Hoover

1965. Hoover Commemoration.
1251   **693**   5c. red   35   20

694 Robert Fulton (after Houdon) and "Clermont"

1965. Birth Bicent of Robert Fulton (inventor).
1252   **694**   5c. black and blue   35   20

695 Spanish Knight and Banners

1965. 400th Anniv of Florida Settlement.
1253   **695**   5c. black, red and yellow   35   20

696 Traffic Signal

1965. Traffic Safety.
1254   **696**   5c. red, black and green   35   20

697 Elizabeth Clarke Copley (from "The Copley Family" by John S. Copley)

1965. John Singleton Copley.
1255   **697**   5c. brown, drab and black   35   20

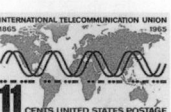

698 Radio "Waves" on World Map (based on Galt projection)

1965. Centenary of I.T.U.
1256   **698**   11c. red, black and brown   45   30

699 Adlai Stevenson (from photo by P. Halsman)

1965. Stevenson Commemoration.
1257   **699**   5c. multicoloured   35   20

700 Archangel Gabriel (weathervane) (after painting by L. Chabot)

1965. Christmas.
1258   **700**   5c. green, ochre and red   35   20

705 Lincoln (after photo by M. Brady)

1965. Prominent Americans (1st series).
1259   -   1c. green   35   20
1260   -   1¼c. green   35   20
1261   -   2c. blue   35   20
1262   -   3c. violet   35   20
1263   **705**   4c. black   35   20
1265   -   5c. blue   35   20
1266   -   6c. brown   35   20
1282   -   6c. brown   35   20
1267   -   8c. violet   35   20
1268   -   10c. purple   35   20
1269   -   12c. black   40   20
1270   -   13c. brown   45   20
1271   -   15c. red   45   20
1272   -   20c. green   55   20
1273   -   25c. red   75   20
1274   -   30c. purple   85   20
1275   -   40c. blue   1·00   20
1276   -   50c. purple   1·30   20
1283   - $1 purple   3·25   45
1278   - $5 black   11·50   2·50

DESIGNS—VERT: 1c. Thomas Jefferson (after Rembrandt Peale); 1¼c. Albert Gallatin; 2c. Frank Lloyd Wright and Guggenheim Museum, New York; 5c. Washington (after Rembrandt Peale); 6c. (No. 1282) Franklin D. Roosevelt; 8c. Albert Einstein; 10c. Andrew Jackson (after T. Sully); 13c. John F. Kennedy; 15c. Justice Wendell Holmes; 20c. George C. Marshall; 25c. Frederick Douglass; 40c. Tom Paine (after John W. Jarvis); 50c. Lucy Stone; $1 Eugene O'Neill; $5 John Bassett Moore. HORIZ: 3c. Francis Parkman; 6c. (No. 1266) Franklin D. Roosevelt; 12c. Henry Ford and Model "T" car; 30c. John Dewey.
    See also Nos. 1383/9.

719 "Migratory Birds"

1966. 50th Anniv of Migratory Bird Treaty.
1286   **719**   5c. red, blue and black   35   20

720 Dog

1966. Humane Treatment of Animals.
1287   **720**   5c. black and brown   35   20

721 Seal, Emblem and Map

1966. 150th Anniv of Indiana Statehood.
1288   **721**   5c. blue, brown & yellow   35   20

722 Lou Jacobs
(clown)

1966. The American Circus.
1289 **722** 5c. multicoloured   35   20

723 SIPEX "Letter"

1966. 6th Int Philatelic Exn, Washington (SIPEX).
1290 **723** 5c. multicoloured   35   20

724 (image scaled to 44% of original size)

1966. Sixth International Philatelic Exhibition, Washington (SIPEX). Sheet 109x73½ mm. Imperf.
MS1291 **724** 5c. multicoloured   55   45

725 "Freedom" opposing "Tyranny"

1966. 175th Anniv of Bill of Rights.
1292 **725** 5c. red, indigo and blue   35   20

726 Polish Eagle

1966. Polish Millennium.
1293 **726** 5c. red   35   20

727 N.P.S. Emblem

1966. 50th Anniv of National Park Service.
1294 **727** 5c. black, green & yellow   35   20

728 Marines Past and Present

1966. 50th Anniv of Marine Corps Reserve.
1295 **728** 5c. multicoloured   35   20

729 Women of 1891 and 1966

1966. 75th Anniv of General Federation of Women's Clubs.
1296 **729** 5c. black, pink and blue   35   20

730 Johnny Appleseed and Apple

1966. Johnny Appleseed.
1297 **730** 5c. black, red and green   35   20

731 Jefferson Memorial, Washington

1966. "Beautification of America" Campaign.
1298 **731** 5c. black, green and pink   35   20

732 Map of Great River Road

1966. Opening of Great River Road.
1299 **732** 5c. red, yellow and blue   35   20

733 Statue of Liberty and U.S. Flag (after photo by B. Noble)

1966. 25th Anniv of U.S. Savings Bond Programme and Tribute to U.S. Servicemen.
1300 **733** 5c. multicoloured   35   20

734 "Madonna and Child" (after Memling)

1966. Christmas.
1301 **734** 5c. multicoloured   35   20

735 "The Boating Party" (after Mary Cassatt)

1966. Mary Cassatt.
1302 **735** 5c. multicoloured   35   20

A736 Tlingit Totem, Southern Alaska

1967. Air. Centenary of Alaska Purchase.
A1303 **A736** 8c. brown   40   20

736 Recruiting Poster

1967. Centenary of National Grange (farmers' organization).
1303 **736** 5c. multicoloured   35   20

A737 "Columbia Jays" by Audubon

1967. Air.
A1304 **A737** 20c. multicoloured   1·30   35
See also No. 1223.

737 Canadian Landscape

1967. Canadian Centennial.
1304 **737** 5c. multicoloured   35   20

738 Canal Barge

1967. 150th Anniv of Erie Canal.
1305 **738** 5c. multicoloured   35   20

739 Peace Dove Emblem

1967. "Search for Peace" (Lions Int essay theme).
1306 **739** 5c. black, red and blue   35   20

740 H. D. Thoreau

1967. 150th Birth Anniv of Henry Thoreau (writer).
1307 **740** 5c. black, red and green   35   20

741 Hereford Bull

1967. Centenary of Nebraska Statehood.
1308 **741** 5c. multicoloured   35   20

742 Radio Tower and "Waves"

1967. "Voice of America". 25th Anniv of Radio Branch of United States Information Agency.
1309 **742** 5c. black, red and blue   35   20

743 Davy Crockett and Pine

1967. Davy Crockett Commemoration.
1310 **743** 5c. black, green & yellow   35   20

744 Astronaut in Space

1967. U.S. Space Achievements. Multicoloured.
1311 5c. Type **744**   70   55
1312 5c. "Gemini 4" over Earth   70   55
Nos. 1311/12 were issued together se-tenant, forming a composite design.

746 "Planned City"

1967. Urban Planning.
1313 **746** 5c. ultramarine, black & blue   35   20

747 Arms of Finland

1967. 50th Anniv of Finnish Independence.
1314 **747** 5c. blue   35   20

748 "The Biglin Brothers racing" (Eakins)

1967. Thomas Eakins.
1315 **748** 5c. multicoloured   35   20

749 "Madonna and Child with Angels" (Memling)

1967. Christmas.
1316 **749** 5c. multicoloured   35   20

750 Magnolia

1967. 150th Anniv of Mississippi Statehood.
1317 **750** 5c. brown, green and turquoise   35   20

A751 "Fifty Stars"

1968. Air.
A1318 **A751** 10c. red   45   35

751 U.S. Flag and The White House

1968. Flag Issue.

| 1318 | **751** | 6c. multicoloured | 35 | 20 |
| 1320 | **751** | 8c. multicoloured | 35 | 20 |

752 Homestead and Cornfield

1968. 150th Anniv of Illinois Statehood.

| 1323 | **752** | 6c. multicoloured | 35 | 20 |

753 Map of the Americas

1968. "HemisFair '68" Exn, San Antonio.

| 1324 | **753** | 6c. blue, pink and white | 35 | 20 |

754 Eagle with Pennant (after late 19th-century wood carving)

1968. "Airlift".

| 1325 | **754** | $1 brown, blue and buff | 3·50 | 2·75 |

No. 1325 was issued primarily for a special reduced-rate parcels service to forces personnel overseas and in Alaska, Hawaii and Puerto Rico.

755 Boys and Girls

1968. Youth Programme of Elks Benevolent Society.

| 1326 | **755** | 6c. blue and red | 35 | 20 |

A756 Curtiss JN-4 "Jenny"

1968. Air. 50th Anniv of Scheduled Airmail Services.

| A1327 | **A756** | 10c. black, red & blue | 35 | 20 |

756 Policeman with Small Boy

1968. "Law and Order".

| 1328 | **756** | 6c. blue, red and black | 35 | 20 |

757 Eagle Weathervane

1968. "Register and Vote".

| 1329 | **757** | 6c. yellow, orange & black | 35 | 20 |

758 Fort Moultrie, 1776

1968. Historic Flags.

1330	**758**	6c. blue	45	35
1331	-	6c. red and blue	45	35
1332	-	6c. green and blue	45	35
1333	-	6c. red and blue	45	35
1334	-	6c. blue, yellow and red	45	35
1335	-	6c. red and blue	45	35
1336	-	6c. blue, red and green	45	35
1337	-	6c. red and blue	45	35
1338	-	6c. blue, red and yellow	45	35
1339	-	6c. red, yellow and blue	45	35

FLAGS: No. 1331, U.S. (Fort McHenry), 1795–1818; 1332, Washington's Cruisers, 1775; 1333, Bennington, 1777; 1334, Rhode Island, 1775; 1335, First Stars and Stripes, 1777; 1336, Bunker Hill, 1775; 1337, Grand Union, 1776; 1338, Philadelphia Light Horse, 1775; 1339, First Navy Jack, 1775.

768 Walt Disney (after portrait by P. E. Wenzel)

1968. Walt Disney Commemoration.

| 1340 | **768** | 6c. multicoloured | 70 | 25 |

769 Father Jacques Marquette (explorer) with Jolliet and Indians Canoeing

1968. Marquette Commemoration.

| 1341 | **769** | 6c. multicoloured | 35 | 20 |

770 Rifle, Tomahawk, Powder-horn and Knife

1968. Daniel Boone Commemoration.

| 1342 | **770** | 6c. multicoloured | 35 | 20 |

771 Ship's Wheel and River Tanker

1968. Arkansas River Navigation Project.

| 1343 | **771** | 6c. black, blue & lt blue | 35 | 20 |

772 "Leif Erikson" (statue by Stirling Calder, Reykjavik, Iceland)

1968. Leif Erikson Commemoration.

| 1344 | **772** | 6c. sepia and brown | 35 | 20 |

773 Pioneers racing to Cherokee Strip

1968. 75th Anniv of Opening of Cherokee Strip to Settlers.

| 1345 | **773** | 6c. brown | 35 | 20 |

774 "Battle of Bunker's Hill (detail) (after John Trumbull)

1968. John Trumbull.

| 1346 | **774** | 6c. multicoloured | 35 | 20 |

775 Wood Ducks

1968. Waterfowl Conservation.

| 1347 | **775** | 6c. multicoloured | 35 | 20 |

776 "The Annunciation" (Jan van Eyck)

1968. Christmas.

| 1348 | **776** | 6c. multicoloured | 35 | 20 |

777 "Chief Joseph" (after C. Hall)

1968. "The American Indian".

| 1349 | **777** | 6c. multicoloured | 35 | 20 |

A778 "U.S.A." and Jet Aircraft

1968. Air.

| A1350 | **A778** | 20c. red, blue & blk | 70 | 25 |
| A1351 | **A778** | 21c. blue, red & blk | 70 | 25 |

778 Capitol and Flowers ("Cities")

1969. "Beautification of America" Campaign.

1352	**778**	6c. multicoloured	50	25
1353	-	6c. multicoloured	50	25
1354	-	6c. multicoloured	50	25
1355	-	6c. multicoloured	50	25

DESIGNS: No. 1353, Potomac River and flowers ("Parks"); 1354, Motorway and flowers ("Highways"); 1355, Road and trees ("Streets").

782 "Eagle" (U.S. Seal)

1969. 50th Anniv of American Legion.

| 1356 | **782** | 6c. black, blue and red | 35 | 20 |

783 "July Fourth"

1969. Grandma Moses (Mrs. A. M. R. Moses).

| 1357 | **783** | 6c. multicoloured | 35 | 20 |

784 Earth and Moon's Surface (from an astronaut's photograph)

1969. Moon Flight of "Apollo 8".

| 1358 | **784** | 6c. ochre, blue and black | 35 | 20 |

785 W. C. Handy (statue, Memphis)

1969. Handy (composer) Commemoration.

| 1359 | **785** | 6c. mauve, blue and violet | 40 | 20 |

786 Belfry, Carmel Mission

1969. Bicentenary of California.

| 1360 | **786** | 6c. multicoloured | 35 | 20 |

787 Powell exploring Colorado River

1969. John Wesley Powell (geologist). Centenary of Colorado River Exploration.

| 1361 | **787** | 6c. multicoloured | 35 | 20 |

788 Camellia and Common Flicker

1969. 150th Anniv of Alabama Statehood.

| 1362 | **788** | 6c. multicoloured | 35 | 20 |

791 Ocotillo

1969. 11th International Botanical Congress, Seattle. Multicoloured.

1363		6c. Douglas fir	70	35
1364		6c. Lady's slipper	70	35
1365		6c. Type **791**	70	35
1366		6c. Franklinia	70	35

A793 Astronaut setting foot on Moon

1969. Air. First Man on the Moon.

| A1367 | **A793** | 10c. multicoloured | 35 | 20 |

793 Daniel
Webster and
Dartmouth Hall

1969. 150th Anniv of Dartmouth College Legal Case.
1368 **793** 6c. green   35 20

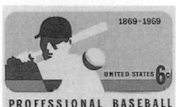

794 Striker

1969. Centenary of Professional Baseball.
1369 **794** 6c. multicoloured   85 25

795 Footballer and Coach

1969. Centenary of Intercollegiate Football.
1370 **795** 6c. green and red   50 20

796 Dwight D.
Eisenhower (from
photograph by B.
Noble)

1969. Eisenhower Commemoration.
1371 **796** 6c. black, blue and lake 35 20

797 "Winter Sunday in
Norway, Maine" (unknown
artist)

1969. Christmas.
1372 **797** 6c. multicoloured   35 20

798
Rehabilitated
Child

1969. Rehabilitation of the Handicapped.
1373 **798** 6c. multicoloured   35 20
No. 1373 also commemorates the 50th anniv of the
National Society for Crippled Children and Adults.

800 "Old Models"
(William Harnett)

1969. William M. Harnett.
1376 **800** 6c. multicoloured   35 20

THE AGE OF REPTILES
804 Prehistoric Creatures (from
mural by R. Zallinger in Yale's
Peabody Museum)

1970. Natural History. Centenary of American Natural
History Museum. Multicoloured.
1377 6c. American bald eagle   35 25
1378 6c. African elephant herd 35 25
1379 6c. Haida ceremonial canoe 35 25
1380 6c. Type **804**   35 25

805 "The Lighthouse at
Two Lights" (painting by
Edward Hopper in
Metropolitan Museum of
Art, New York)

1970. Maine Statehood Sesquicentennial.
1381 **805** 6c. multicoloured   35 20

806 American Bison

1970. Wildlife Conservation.
1382 **806** 6c. black on brown   35 20

807 Dwight   **809** Benjamin
D. Eisenhower   Franklin

1970. Prominent Americans (2nd series).
1383 **807** 6c. blue   35 20
1384 **809** 7c. blue   35 20
1390 **807** 8c. black, blue and red 35 20
1392 **807** 8c. maroon   35 20
1386 -   14c. black   45 25
1387 -   16c. brown   80 35
1388 -   18c. violet   70 25
1389 -   21c. green   70 25
DESIGNS: VFRT: 14c. F. H. La Guardia; 16c. Ernest T. Pyle;
18c. Dr. Elizabeth Blackwell; 21c. Amadeo P. Giannini (after painting by J. Kozlowski).

822 Edgar Lee
Masters

1970. Edgar Lee Masters (poet) Commem.
1401 **822** 6c. black and bistre   35 20

823 Suffragettes, 1920, and
Woman operating Voting
Machine

1970. 50th Anniv of Women's Suffrage.
1402 **823** 6c. blue   35 20

824 Symbols of South
Carolina

1970. 300th Anniv of South Carolina.
1403 **824** 6c. multicoloured   35 20

825 Stone Mountain
Memorial

1970. Dedication of Stone Mountain Confederate
Memorial.
1404 **825** 6c. black   35 20

826 Fort Snelling and Keel
Boat

1970. 150th Anniv of Fort Snelling, Minnesota.
1405 **826** 6c. multicoloured   35 20

828 City Park

1970. Prevention of Pollution.
1406 6c. Wheat   40 25
1407 6c. Type **828**   40 25
1408 6c. Blue-gilled sunfish 40 25
1409 6c. Western gull   40 25

832 Toy Steam Locomotive
(after drawing by C.
Hemming)

1970. Christmas. Multicoloured.
1410 6c. "The Nativity" (L. Lotto)
              (vert)   35 20
1411 6c. Type **832**   45 30
1412 6c. Toy horse on wheels   45 30
1413 6c. Mechanized tricycle   45 30
1414 6c. Doll's pram   45 30
Nos. 1412/14 are taken from "Golden Age of Toys" by
Fondin and Remise.

836 "U.N." and Emblem

1970. 25th Anniv of U.N.O.
1415 **836** 6c. red, blue and black   35 20

837 "Mayflower"
and Pilgrims

1970. 350th Anniv of Landing of the Pilgrim Fathers in
America.
1416 **837** 6c. multicoloured   35 20

838 Disabled
American
Veterans
Emblem

1970. 50th Anniv of Disabled American Veterans
Organization, and Armed Forces Commemoration.
1417 **838** 6c. multicoloured   35 20
1418 -   6c. black, blue and red   35 20
DESIGN: No. 1418, Inscriptions—"Prisoners of War", "Missing and Killed in Action".

840 Ewe and
Lamb

1970. 450th Anniv of Introduction of Sheep into North
America.
1419 **840** 6c. multicoloured   35 20

841 General
Douglas
MacArthur

1971. 91st Birth Anniv of General Douglas MacArthur.
1420 **841** 6c. black, blue and red   35 20

842 "Giving Blood Saves
Lives"

1971. Salute to Blood Donors.
1421 **842** 6c. deep blue, red
              & blue   35 20

A844 Jet   **A845** Winged
Aircraft   Letter

1971. Air.
A1422 -   9c. red   35 20
A1423 **A 844** 11c. red   35 20
A1424 **A 845** 13c. red   45 20
DESIGN—HORIZ: 9c. Delta-wing plane.

846 "Settlers and Indians"
(after mural "Independence
and the Opening of the
West" by Thomas H.
Benton)

1971. 150th Anniv of Missouri Statehood.
1427 **846** 8c. multicoloured   35 20

847 Rainbow Trout

1971. Wildlife Conservation. Multicoloured.
1428 **847** 8c. Type **847**   45 25
1429 8c. Alligator   45 25
1430 8c. Polar bear and cubs 45 25
1431 8c. California condor   45 25

851 Antarctic Map Emblem

1971. Tenth Anniv of Antarctic Treaty.
1432 **851** 8c. blue and red   35 20

852 Postal
Service
Emblem

1971. Reorganization of U.S. Post Office as U.S. Postal
Service.
1433 **852** 8c. multicoloured   35 20

853 Bicentennial
Emblem

1971. American Revolution Bicent. Bicentennial Commisssion Emblem.

| 1434 | 853 | 8c. multicoloured | 35 | 20 |

A854 Head of Statue of Liberty

1971. Air.

| A1435 | A854 | 17c. blue, red & grn | 55 | 25 |

855 "The Wake of the Ferry" (John Sloan)

1971. Birth Centenary of John Sloan (artist).

| 1436 | 855 | 8c. multicoloured | 35 | 20 |

856 Landing Module on Moon

1971. Decade of U.S. Space Achievements. Multicoloured.

| 1437 | | 8c. Type **856** | 35 | 20 |
| 1438 | | 8c. Astronauts in lunar rover | 35 | 20 |

Nos. 1437/8 were issued together, *se-tenant*, forming a composite design.

858 Emily Dickinson

1971. 85th Death Anniv of Emily Dickinson (poet).

| 1439 | 858 | 8c. multicoloured on green | 35 | 20 |

859 Watch-tower, El Morro, San Juan

1971. 450th Anniv of San Juan, Puerto Rico.

| 1440 | 859 | 8c. multicoloured | 35 | 20 |

860 Drug Victim

1971. Drug Abuse Prevention Week.

| 1441 | 860 | 8c. black, lt blue & blue | 35 | 20 |

861 Hands reaching to "CARE"

1971. 25th Anniv of "CARE" (Co-operative for American Relief Everywhere).

| 1442 | 861 | 8c. multicoloured | 35 | 20 |

862 Decatur House, Washington D.C.

1971. Historic Preservation.

1443	862	8c. black & flesh on cream	35	20
1444	-	8c. black & flesh on cream	35	25
1445	-	8c. black & flesh on cream	35	20
1446	-	8c. black & flesh on cream	35	20

DESIGNS: No. 1444, Whaling ship "Charles W. Morgan", Mystic, Conn; 1445, San Francisco cable car; 1446, San Xavier del Bac Mission, Tucson, Arizona.

866 "Adoration of the Shepherds" (Giorgione)

1971. Christmas. Multicoloured.

| 1447 | | 8c. Type **866** | 35 | 20 |
| 1448 | | 8c. "Partridge in a Pear Tree" | 35 | 20 |

868 Sidney Lanier

1972. 90th Death Anniv (1971) of Sidney Lanier (poet).

| 1449 | 868 | 8c. black, brown and blue | 35 | 20 |

869 Peace Corps Poster (D. Battle)

1972. Peace Corps.

| 1450 | 869 | 8c. red, light blue & blue | 35 | 20 |

870/873 Cape Hatteras National Seashore

875 "Old Faithful", Yellowstone Park

A877 Statue and Temple, City of Refuge, Hawaii

1972. Centenary of National Parks.

1451	870	2c. multicoloured (postage)	25	20
1452	871	2c. multicoloured	25	20
1453	872	2c. multicoloured	25	20
1454	873	2c. multicoloured	25	20
1455	-	6c. multicoloured	35	20
1456	875	8c. multicoloured	35	20
1457	-	15c. multicoloured	55	35
A1458	A 877	11c. mult (air)	45	25

DESIGNS—HORIZ (As Type A **877**): 6c. Theatre at night, Wolf Trap Farm, Virginia; 15c. Mt. McKinley, Alaska.

878 American Family

1972. Family Planning.

| 1459 | 878 | 8c. multicoloured | 35 | 20 |

879 Glassblower

1972. Bicentenary of American Revolution. American Colonial Craftsmen.

1460	879	8c. brown on yellow	35	20
1461	-	8c. brown on yellow	35	20
1462	-	8c. brown on yellow	35	20
1463	-	8c. brown on yellow	35	20

DESIGNS: No. 1461, Silversmith; 1462, Wigmaker; 1463, Hatter.

883 Cycling

1972. Olympic Games, Munich and Sapporo, Japan. Multicoloured.

1464		6c. Type **883** (postage)	35	20
1465		8c. Bobsleighing	35	20
1466		15c. Running	55	35
A1467		11c. Skiing (air)	45	25

887 Classroom Blackboard

1972. 75th Anniv of Parent Teacher Association.

| 1468 | 887 | 8c. black and yellow | 35 | 20 |

888 Northern Fur Seals

1972. Wildlife Conservation. Multicoloured.

1469		8c. Type **888**	35	20
1470		8c. Common cardinal (bird)	35	20
1471		8c. Brown pelicans	35	20
1472		8c. American bighorn	35	20

892 19th-century Country Post Office and Store

1972. Centenary of Mail Order Business.

| 1473 | 892 | 8c. multicoloured | 35 | 20 |

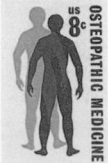

893 "Quest for Health"

1972. 75th Anniv of American Osteopaths.

| 1474 | 893 | 8c. multicoloured | 35 | 20 |

894 "Tom Sawyer" (N. Rockwell)

1972. "The Adventures of Tom Sawyer" by Mark Twain.

| 1475 | 894 | 8c. multicoloured | 35 | 20 |

895 "Angels" (detail, "Mary, Queen of Heaven" by Master of the St. Lucy Legend)

1972. Christmas. Multicoloured.

| 1476 | | 8c. Type **895** | 35 | 20 |
| 1477 | | 8c. Santa Claus | 35 | 20 |

897 Pharmaceutical Equipment

1972. 120th Anniv of American Pharmaceutical Association.

| 1478 | 897 | 8c. multicoloured | 35 | 20 |

898 Five Cent Stamp of 1847 under Magnifier

1972. 125th Anniv of 1st U.S. Stamp, and Stamp Collecting Promotion.

| 1479 | 898 | 8c. brown, black & green | 35 | 20 |

899 "LOVE"

1973. Greetings Stamp.

| 1480 | 899 | 8c. red, green and blue | 35 | 20 |

900 Pamphleteers with Press

1973. American Revolution Bicentennial. Colonial Communications.

1481	900	8c. green, blue and red	35	20
1482	-	8c. black, red and blue	35	20
1483	-	8c. multicoloured	35	20
1484	-	8c. multicoloured	35	20

DESIGNS: No. 1482, Posting a broadside; 1483, Post-rider; 1484, Drummer.

904 George Gershwin (composer) and Scene from "Porgy and Bess"

1973. American Arts Commemoration. Multicoloured.

1485		8c. Type **904**	35	20
1486		8c. Robinson Jeffers (poet) and people of Carmel	35	20
1487		8c. Henry Tanner (painter) and palette	35	20
1488		8c. Willa Cather (novelist) and pioneer family	35	20

908 Nicolas
Copernicus
(after 18th-cent
engraving)

1973. 500th Birth Anniv of Copernicus (astronomer).
1489 **908** 8c. black and yellow 35 20

909 Counter
Clerk

1973. Postal Service Employees. Multicoloured.
1490 8c. Type **909** 35 20
1491 8c. Collecting mail 35 20
1492 8c. Sorting on conveyor belt 35 20
1493 8c. Sorting parcels 35 20
1494 8c. Cancelling letters 35 20
1495 8c. Sorting letters by hand 35 20
1496 8c. Coding desks 35 20
1497 8c. Loading mail-van 35 20
1498 8c. City postman 35 20
1499 8c. Rural postman 35 20

919 Harry S. Truman

1973. Pres. Harry Truman Commemoration.
1500 **919** 8c. black, red and blue 45 20

920/923 Boston Tea Party

1973. American Revolution Bicentennial. The Boston Tea
Party.
1501 **920** 8c. multicoloured 40 20
1502 **921** 8c. multicoloured 40 20
1503 **922** 8c. multicoloured 40 20
1504 **923** 8c. multicoloured 40 20

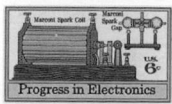

924 Marconi's Spark Coil
and Gap (1901)

1973. Progress in Electronics. Multicoloured.
1505 6c. Type **924** (postage) 40 20
1506 8c. Modern transistor circuit 40 20
1507 15c. Early microphone and
radio speaker, radio and T.V.
camera tubes 65 40
A1508 11c. DeForest audions (1915)
(air) 50 30

928 Lyndon B.
Johnson (from
painting by
Elizabeth
Shoumatoff)

1973. Pres. Lyndon B. Johnson Commem.
1509 **928** 8c. multicoloured 40 2·00

929 Angus and Longhorn
Cattle (painting by F. C.
Murphy)

1973. "Rural America" Centenaries.
1510 8c. Type **929** 40 20
1511 10c. Institute marquee 40 20
1512 10c. Steam train crossing
wheatfield 40 20
CENTENARIES: No. 1510, Introduction of Aberdeen Angus
cattle into United States; 1511, Foundation of Chautau-
qua Institution (adult education organization); 1512, Introduction of hard winter wheat into Kansas.

932 "Small
Cowper
Madonna"
(Raphael)

933 Christmas
Tree in
Needlepoint

1973. Christmas.
1513 **932** 8c. multicoloured 40 20
1514 **933** 8c. multicoloured 40 20

934 U.S. Flags
of 1777 and
1973

935 Jefferson
Memorial

936 "Mail
Transport"
(from poster
by R.
McDougall)

937 Liberty
Bell

1973
1515 **934** 10c. red and blue 40 20
1516 **935** 10c. blue 40 20
1517 **936** 10c. multicoloured 40 20
1519 **937** 6.3c. red 40 20

A938 Statue of Liberty

1974. Air.
A1521 **A 938** 18c. black, red & bl 75 50
A1522 - 26c. black, bl & red 90 30
DESIGN: 26c. Mt. Rushmore National Memorial.

940 "VFW" and Emblem

1974. 75th Anniv of Veterans of Foreign Wars
Organization.
1523 **940** 10c. red and blue 40 20

941 Robert Frost

1974. Birth Centenary of Robert Frost (poet).
1524 **941** 10c. black 40 20

942 "Cosmic Jumper" and
"Smiling Sage" ("Preserve
the Environment" theme)

1974. "Expo 74" World Fair, Spokane.
1525 **942** 10c. multicoloured 40 20

943 Horse-racing

1974. Centenary of Kentucky Derby
1526 **943** 10c. multicoloured 40 20

944 "Skylab" in Orbit

1974. "Skylab" Space Project.
1527 **944** 10c. multicoloured 40 20

945 "Michelangelo"
(detail from "School
of Athens" by
Raphael)

1974. Centenary of U.P.U. Multicoloured.
1528 10c. Type **945** 45 25
1529 10c. "Five Feminine Virtues"
(Hokusai) 45 25
1530 10c. "Old Scraps" (J. F. Peto) 45 25
1531 10c. "The Lovely Reader" (J.
Liotard) 45 25
1532 10c. "The Lady Writing Letter"
(G. Terborch) 45 25
1533 10c. "Inkwell and Quill" (detail
from "Young Boy with Top"
by J. Chardin) 45 25
1534 10c. "Mrs. John Douglas" (T.
Gainsborough) 45 25
1535 10c. "Don Antonio Noriega"
(F. Goya) 45 25

955 Amethyst

1974. Mineral Heritage. Multicoloured.
1536 10c. Petrified wood 45 25
1537 10c. Tourmaline 45 25
1538 10c. Type **955** 45 25
1539 10c. Rhodochrosite 45 25

957 Covered
Wagon at Fort
Harrod

1974. Bicentenary of Fort Harrod, First Settlement in
Kentucky.
1540 **957** 10c. multicoloured 35 20

959 "We ask but for peace
..." (First Continental
Congress)

1974. American Revolution Bicentennial. First Continental
Congress.
1541 - 10c. blue and red 45 25
1542 **959** 10c. grey, blue and red 45 25
1543 - 10c. grey, red and blue 45 25
1544 - 10c. red and blue 45 25
DESIGNS: No. 1541, Carpenters' Hall, Philadelphia; 1543,
"Deriving their just powers …" (Declaration of Independence); 1544, Independence Hall, Philadelphia.

962 Slogan,
Molecules and
Petrol Drops

1974. Energy Conservation.
1545 **962** 10c. multicoloured 35 20

963 "The Headless
Horseman"

1974. Washington Irving's "Legend of Sleepy Hollow".
1546 **963** 10c. multicoloured 35 20

964 Child
clasping Hand

1974. Help for Retarded Children.
1547 **964** 10c. lake and brown 35 20

966 "The Road — Winter"
(from a Currier and Ives
print, drawn by O. Knirsch)

1974. Christmas. Multicoloured.
1548 10c. "Angel" (detail, Perussis
altarpiece) (vert) 35 20
1549 10c. Type **966** 35 20
1550 10c. Dove weathervane, Mount
Vernon 40 25
No. 1550 has self-adhesive gum.

968 "Benjamin
West"
(self-portrait)

1975. Benjamin West (painter) Commem.
1551 **968** 10c. multicoloured 35 20

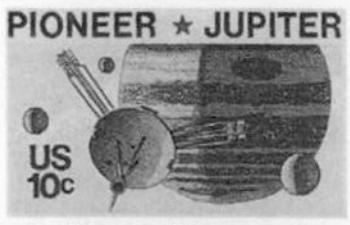

969 "Pioneer" Spacecraft passing Jupiter

1975. U.S. Unmanned Space Missions. Multicoloured.

1552	10c. Type **969**	35	20
1553	10c. "Mariner 10", Venus and Mercury	35	20

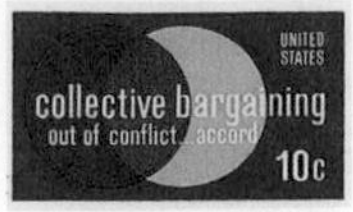

971 Overlapping Circles

1975. Collective Bargaining in Labour Relations.

1554	**971**	10c. multicoloured	35	20

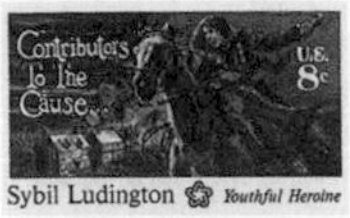

972 Sybil Ludington on Horseback

1975. American Revolution Bicent. Contributors to the Cause.

1555	**972**	8c. multicoloured	35	20
1556	-	10c. multicoloured	35	20
1557	-	10c. multicoloured	35	20
1558	-	18c. multicoloured	60	35

DESIGNS: No. 1556, Salem Poor loading musket; 1557, Haym Salomon writing in ledger; 1558, Peter Francisco carrying cannon.

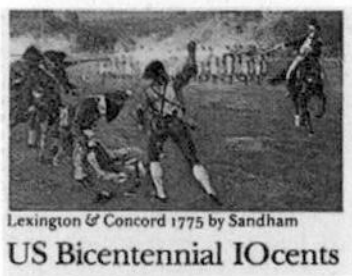

976 "Lexington" (from painting "Birth of Liberty" by H. Sandham)

1975. American Revolution Bicentennial. Battles of Lexington and Concord.

1559	**976**	10c. multicoloured	35	20

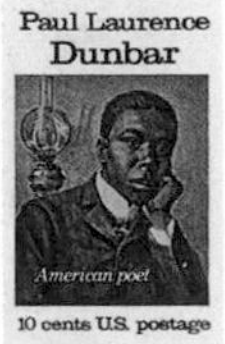

977 Paul Laurence Dunbar (poet)

1975. Dunbar Commemoration.

1560	**977**	10c. multicoloured	35	20

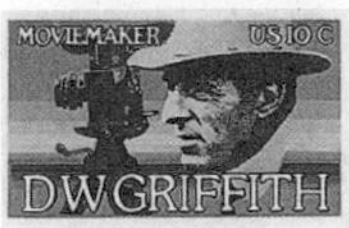

978 D. W. Griffith (film producer)

1975. Griffith Commemoration.

1561	**978**	10c. multicoloured	35	20

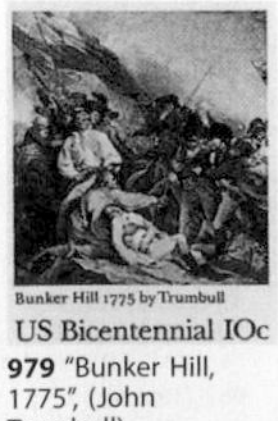

979 "Bunker Hill, 1775", (John Trumbull)

1975. Bicentenary of American Revolution. Battle of Bunker Hill.

1562	**979**	10c. multicoloured	35	20

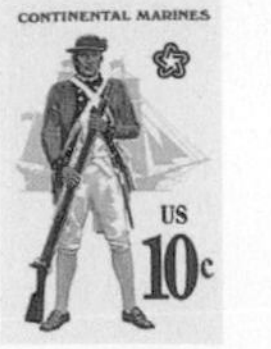

980 Marine with Musket

1975. American Revolution Bicentennial. U.S. Military Services. Multicoloured.

1563	10c. Type **980**	40	25
1564	10c. Militiaman with musket	40	25
1565	10c. Soldier with flintlock	40	25
1566	10c. Sailor with grappling-iron	40	25

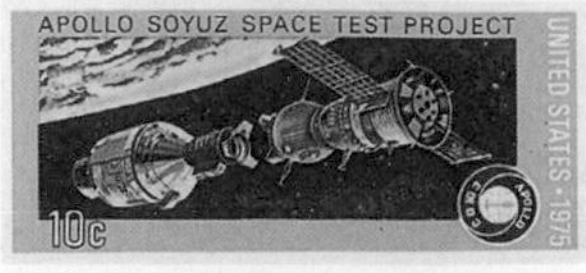

984 Docking Manoeuvre

1975. "Apollo–Soyuz" Space Test Project. Multicoloured.

1567	10c. Type **984**	35	25
1568	10c. Spacecraft docked	35	25

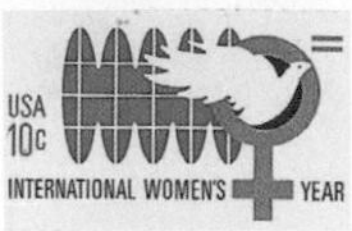

986 "Worldwide Equality"

1975. International Women's Year.

1569	**986**	10c. multicoloured	35	20

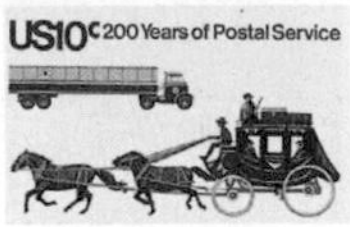

987 Stagecoach and Modern Lorry

1975. Bicentenary of Postal Services. Multicoloured.

1571	10c. Type **987**	40	25
1572	10c. Early steam and modern diesel locomotives	40	25
1573	10c. Curtiss JN-4 "Jenny" and Boeing 747-100 jetliner	40	25
1574	10c. Telecommunications satellite	40	25

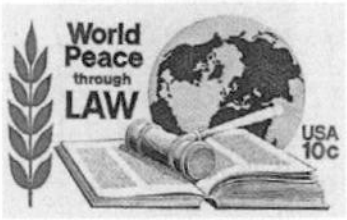

991 Law Book, Gavel and Globe

1975. "World Peace through Law".

1575	**991**	10c. brown, blue & green	35	25

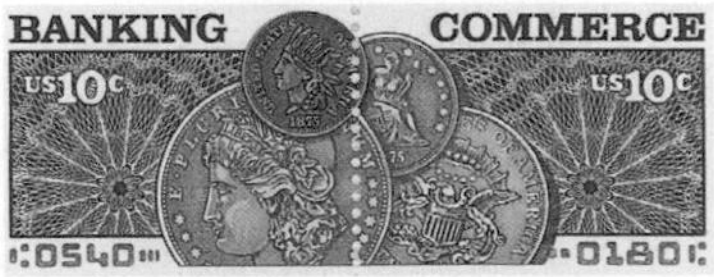

992/993 Coins and Engine-turned Motif

1975. "Banking and Commerce".

1576	**992**	10c. multicoloured	45	25
1577	**993**	10c. multicoloured	45	25

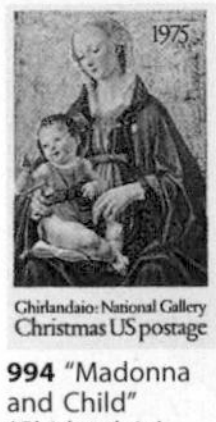

994 "Madonna and Child" (Ghirlandaio)

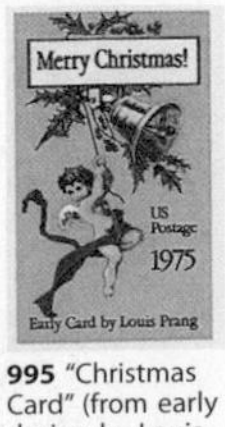

995 "Christmas Card" (from early design by Louis Prang)

1975. Christmas.

1578	**994**	(10c.) multicoloured	35	25
1579	**995**	(10c.) multicoloured	45	25

Nos. 1578/9 were each sold at 10c. Because of an imminent increase in the postage rates the two designs were issued without face values.

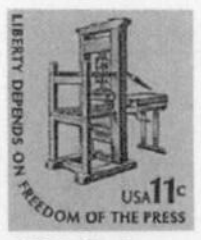

1002 Early Printing Press

1975

1580	-	1c. deep blue on grey	35	20
1581	-	2c. red on cream	35	20
1582	-	3c. olive on green	35	20
1597b	-	3.1c. lake on yellow	35	25
1598	-	3.5c. lilac on yellow	35	25
1582a	-	4c. red on cream	35	20
1599	-	7.7c. brown on yellow	35	25
1600	-	7.9c. red on yellow	40	25
1601	-	8.4c. blue on yellow	45	25
1583	-	9c. green on grey	35	20
1584	-	9c. green	60	25
1585	-	10c. purple on grey	35	25
1585a	**1002**	11c. orange on grey	45	25
1585b	-	12c. brown on cream	45	35
1586	-	13c. brown on cream	45	25
1595	-	13c. multicoloured	45	25
1596	-	15c. blue, red and black	45	20
1605	-	16c. blue	60	35
1589	-	24c. red on blue	90	35
1589a	-	28c. brown on blue	90	35
1590	-	29c. blue on light blue	90	45
1591	-	30c. green on turquoise	90	25
1592	-	50c. black, red & brn	1·40	35
1593	-	$1 multicoloured	3·00	35
1594	-	$2 multicoloured	6·25	1·10
1594a	-	$5 multicoloured	12·50	2·75

DESIGNS: 1c. Inkwell and quill; 2c. Speaker's stand; 3c. Ballot box; 3.1c. Guitar; 3.5c. Weaver violins; 4c. Books, spectacles and bookmark; 7.7c. Saxhorns; 7.9c. Drum; 8.4c. Grand piano; 9c. (both) Dome of Capitol; 10c. "Contemplation of Justice" (statue, J. E. Fraser); 12c. Statue of Liberty torch; 13c. (No. 1586) Liberty Bell; 13c. (No. 1595) Eagle and shield; 15c. Fort McHenry flag; 16c. Statue of Liberty; 24c. Old North Church, Boston; 28c. Fort Nisqually, Washington; 29c. Sandy Hook Lighthouse, N.J.; 30c. Morris Township School; 50c. Iron "Betty" lamp; $1 Rush lamp and candle holder; $2 Kerosene lamp; $5 Railway conductor's lantern.

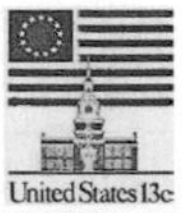

1020 Flag over Independence Hall

1975

1606	**1020**	13c. red and blue	45	25
1606c	-	13c. red and blue	45	35

DESIGN: No. 1606c, Flag over Capitol, Washington.

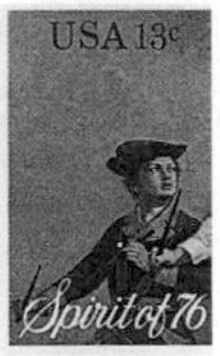

1021 Drummer Boy (after A. M. Willard)

1976. American Revolution Bicentennial. "The Spirit of '76". Multicoloured.

1607	13c. Type **1021**	45	25
1608	13c. Old drummer	45	25
1609	13c. Fifer	45	25

Nos. 1607/9 were issued together, *se-tenant*, forming a composite design.

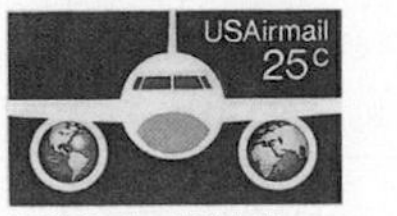

1024 Boeing 737 Jetliner

1976. Air.

A1610	**1024**	25c. black, blue & red	80	35
A1611	-	31c. black, blue & red	1·00	35

DESIGN: 31c. As 25c. but with background of U.S. flag.

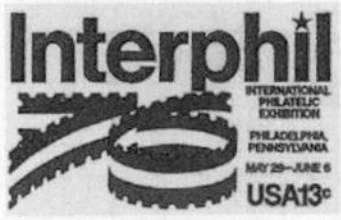

1026 "Interphil 76"

1976. "Interphil 76" International Stamp Exhibition, Philadelphia.

1612	**1026**	13c. red and blue	45	25

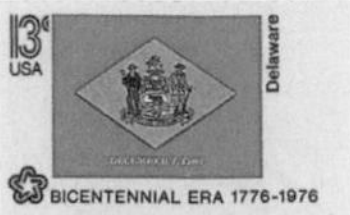

1027 Delaware Flag

1976. Bicentenary of American Revolution. State Flags. Multicoloured.

1613	13c. Type **1027**	60	35
1614	13c. Pennsylvania	60	35
1615	13c. New Jersey	60	35
1616	13c. Georgia	60	35
1617	13c. Connecticut	60	35
1618	13c. Massachusetts	60	35
1619	13c. Maryland	60	35
1620	13c. South Carolina	60	35
1621	13c. New Hampshire	60	35
1622	13c. Virginia	60	35
1623	13c. New York	60	35
1624	13c. North Carolina	60	35
1625	13c. Rhode Island	60	35
1626	13c. Vermont	60	35
1627	13c. Kentucky	60	35
1628	13c. Tennessee	60	35
1629	13c. Ohio	60	35
1630	13c. Louisiana	60	35
1631	13c. Indiana	60	35
1632	13c. Mississippi	60	35
1633	13c. Illinois	60	35
1634	13c. Alabama	60	35
1635	13c. Maine	60	35
1636	13c. Missouri	60	35
1637	13c. Arkansas	60	35
1638	13c. Michigan	60	35
1639	13c. Florida	60	35
1640	13c. Texas	60	35
1641	13c. Iowa	60	35
1642	13c. Wisconsin	60	35
1643	13c. California	60	35
1644	13c. Minnesota	60	35
1645	13c. Oregon	60	35
1646	13c. Kansas	60	35
1647	13c. West Virginia	60	35
1648	13c. Nevada	60	35
1649	13c. Nebraska	60	35
1650	13c. Colorado	60	35
1651	13c. North Dakota	60	35
1652	13c. South Dakota	60	35
1653	13c. Montana	60	35
1654	13c. Washington	60	35
1655	13c. Idaho	60	35
1656	13c. Wyoming	60	35
1657	13c. Utah	60	35
1658	13c. Oklahoma	60	35
1659	13c. New Mexico	60	35
1660	13c. Arizona	60	35
1661	13c. Alaska	60	35
1662	13c. Hawaii	60	35

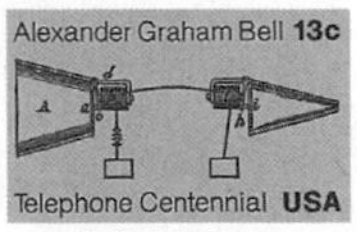

1028 Bell's Telephone

1976. Telephone Centenary.

1663	**1028**	13c. violet, black and red on brown	45	25

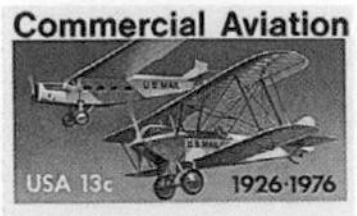

1029 Stout Air Pullman and Laird Swallow Biplane

1976. Commercial Aviation.

1664	**1029**	13c. multicoloured	45	25

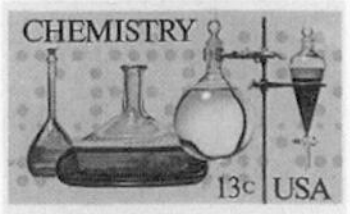

1030 Laboratory Equipment

1976. Centenary of American Chemical Society.

1665	**1030**	13c. multicoloured	45	25

1031 "Surrender of Cornwallis at Yorktown" (John Turnbull) (image scaled to 23% of original size)

1976. American Revolution Bicentennial. "Interphil '76" issue. Four sheets, each 204×153 mm. Invisible gum.

MS1666a	**1031**	13c. ×5 multicoloured	5·25	5·25
MS1666b	–	18c. ×5 multicoloured	6·25	6·25
MS1666c	–	24c. ×5 multicoloured	9·25	9·25
MS1666d	–	31c. ×5 multicoloured	11·50	11·50

DESIGNS: MS1666a, Type **1031**; MS1666b, "Declaration of Independence" (John Turnbull); MS1666c, "Washington crossing the Delaware" (Leutze/Johnson); MS1666d, "Washington reviewing his Ragged Army at Valley Forge" (William T. Trego).

1035 Benjamin Franklin and 1776 Map of North America

1976. American Revolution Bicentennial.

1667	**1035**	13c. multicoloured	50	25

1036/1039 "Signing the Declaration of Independence" (John Turnbull) (image scaled to 49% of original size)

1976. American Revolution Bicentennial.

1668	**1036**	13c. multicoloured	50	25
1669	**1037**	13c. multicoloured	50	25
1670	**1038**	13c. multicoloured	50	25
1671	**1039**	13c. multicoloured	50	25

Nos. 1668/71 were issued together, se-tenant, forming the composite design illustrated.

1040 Diving

1976. Olympic Games, Innsbruck and Montreal. Multicoloured.

1672		13c. Type **1040**	45	25
1673		13c. Skiing	45	25
1674		13c. Running	45	25
1675		13c. Skating	45	25

1044 Clara Maass

1976. Birth Centenary of Clara Maass (martyr to yellow fever).

1676	**1044**	13c. multicoloured	45	25

1045 A. S. Ochs

1976. Adolph S. Ochs (publisher of "New York Times") Commemoration.

1677	**1045**	13c. black	45	25

1046 "Winter Pastime" (N. Currier)

1976. Christmas. Multicoloured.

1678		13c. Type **1046**	45	25
1679		13c. "Nativity" (John S. Copley)	45	25

1048 "Washington at Princeton" (Peale)

1977. American Revolution Bicentennial.

1680	**1048**	13c. multicoloured	45	25

1049 Early Gramophone

1977. Centenary of Sound Recording.. Multicoloured.

1681	**1049**	13c. multicoloured	45	25

1050 Zia Pot

1977. American Folk Art. Pueblo Art. Multicoloured.

1682		13c. Type **1050**	45	25
1683		13c. San Ildefonso pot	45	25
1684		13c. Hopi pot	45	25
1685		13c. Acoma pot	45	25

1054 "Spirit of St. Louis"

1977. 50th Anniv of Lindbergh's Transatlantic Flight.

1686	**1054**	13c. multicoloured	45	25

1055 Columbine and Rocky Mountains

1977. Centenary (1976) of Colorado Statehood.

1687	**1055**	13c. multicoloured	45	25

1056 American Swallowtail

1977. Butterflies. Multicoloured.

1688		13c. Type **1056**	45	25
1689		13c. Checkerspot	45	25
1690		13c. Dogface	45	25
1691		13c. Falcate orange-tip	45	25

1060 Marquis de Lafayette

1977. American Revolution Bicent. Bicentenary of Lafayette's Landing on Coast of South Carolina.

1692	**1060**	13c. black, blue and red	45	25

1061 Seamstress

1977. American Revolution Bicentenary. "Skilled Hands for Independence". Multicoloured.

1693		13c. Type **1061**	45	25
1694		13c. Blacksmith	45	25
1695		13c. Wheelwright	45	25
1696		13c. Leatherworker	45	25

1065 Peace Bridge and Dove

1977. 50th Anniv of Opening of Peace Bridge.

1697	**1065**	13c. blue	45	25

1066 "Herkimer at Oriskany" (F. Yohn)

1977. American Revolution Bicent. Bicentenary of Battle of Oriskany.

1698	**1066**	13c. multicoloured	45	25

1067 Farmhouses, Fl Pueblo

1977. Bicentenary of First Civil Settlement in Alta California.

1699	**1067**	13c. multicoloured	45	25

1068 Members of the Continental Congress

1977. Bicentenary of Drafting of the Articles of Constitution.

1700	**1068**	13c. brown and red	45	25

1069 "Vitaphone" Projector and Sound Equipment

1977. 50th Anniv of Talking Pictures.

1701	**1069**	13c. multicoloured	45	25

1070 "Surrender of Burgoyne at Saratoga" (J. Trumbull)

1977. American Revolution Bicent. Surrender of General Burgoyne.

1702	**1070**	13c. multicoloured	45	25

1071 "Conservation"

1977. Energy Conservation and Development.

1703	**1071**	13c. multicoloured	45	25
1704	–	13c. multicoloured	45	25

DESIGN: No. 1704, "Development".

1073 Washington at Valley Forge (after Leyendecker)

1977. Christmas.

1705	**1073**	13c. multicoloured	45	25
1706	–	13c. multicoloured	45	25

DESIGN: No. 1706, Rural mailbox.

1075 Carl Sandburg

1978. Birth Centenary of Carl Sandburg (poet and biographer).

1707	**1075**	13c. black and brown	45	25

1076 Indian Head Penny

1978

1708	**1076**	13c. brown & blue on buff	45	25

1077 Captain James Cook (with Hula Dance)

1978. Bicentenary of Capt. Cook's Visits to Hawaii and Alaska.

1709	**1077**	13c. blue	45	25
1710	–	13c. green	45	25

DESIGN—HORIZ: No. 1710, H.M.S. "Resolution" and H.M.S. "Discovery" at Hawaii (after John Webber).

1079 Harriet Tubman and Slaves

1978. Black Heritage. Harriet Tubman (organizer of slave "underground railway").

1711	**1079**	13c. multicoloured	45	25

1082 Quilt Design

1978. American Folk Art. Quilts.

1712	–	13c. brown and grey	45	25
1713	–	13c. red and grey	45	25
1714	**1082**	13c. multicoloured	45	25
1715	–	13c. multicoloured	45	25

DESIGNS: No. 1712, Chequered; 1713, Dotted; 1715, Striped.

1084 Ballet

1978. American Dance.

1716	**1084**	13c. blue, mauve & black	45	25
1717	-	13c. orange, red & black	45	25
1718	-	13c. green, yellow & black	45	25
1719	-	13c. blue, ultram & black	45	25

DESIGNS: No. 1717, Theatre; 1718, Folk dance; 1719, Modern.

1088 "Louis XVI and Benjamin Franklin" (statuette, C. G. Sauvage)

1978. Bicentenary of French Alliance.

1720	**1088**	13c. black, blue and red	45	25

1089 Dr. Papanicolaou

1978. Dr. George Papanicolaou (developer of Pap (cancer detection) test) Commemoration.

1721	**1089**	13c. brown	45	25

1090 American Eagle

1978. No value expressed.

1722	**1090**	(15c.) orange	60	25

For "B" stamp see No. 1843, for "C" stamp Nos. 1909/10 and for "D" stamp Nos. 2137/8.

1091 Jimmie Rodgers

1978. Performing Arts and Artists. Jimmie Rodgers, "Father of Country Music".

1725	**1091**	13c. multicoloured	45	25

1092 Common Cardinal, Mallard, Canada Goose, Blue Jay Elk, Least Chipmunk, Red Fox and Common Racoon (image scaled to 44% of original size)

1978. "CAPEX 78" International Stamp Exhibition, Toronto. Wildlife of U.S.–Canadian Border. Sheet 108×73 mm.

MS1726	**1092**	13c. ×8 multicoloured	4·00	4·00

1093 Camera and Accessories

1978. Photography.

1727	**1093**	15c. multicoloured	60	25

1094 George M. Cohan

1978. Performing Arts. Birth Centenary of George M. Cohan (actor and playwright).

1728	**1094**	15c. multicoloured	60	25

1095 "Red Masterpiece" and "Medallion" Roses

1978. Roses.

1729	**1095**	15c. red, orange & grn	45	25

1096 "Viking 1" Lander scooping Soil from Mars

1978. Second Anniv of "Viking 1" Landing on Mars.

1730	**1096**	15c. multicoloured	60	25

1097 Great Grey Owl

1978. Wildlife Conservation. American Owls. Multicoloured.

1731	15c. Type **1097**	60	25
1732	15c. Saw-whet owl	60	25
1733	15c. Barred owl	60	25
1734	15c. Great horned owl	60	25

1101 Wright Brothers and Wright Flyer I

1978. Air. 75th Anniv of First Powered Flight. Multicoloured.

A1735	31c. Type **1101**	1·00	35
A1736	31c. Wright Flyer I and Wright Brothers (in bowler hats)	1·00	35

1103 White Pine

1978. American Trees. Multicoloured.

1737	15c. Type **1103**	60	25
1738	15c. Giant sequoia	60	25
1739	15c. Grey birch	60	25
1740	15c. White oak	60	25

1107 "Madonna and Child with Cherubim" (Andrea della Robbia)

1978. Christmas. Multicoloured.

1741	15c. Type **1107**	60	25
1742	15c. Child on rocking horse	60	25

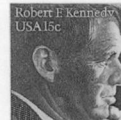

1109 Robert F. Kennedy

1979. Robert F. Kennedy Commemoration.

1743	**1109**	15c. blue	60	25

1110 Martin Luther King

1979. Black Heritage. Martin Luther King (Civil Rights leader).

1744	**1110**	15c. multicoloured	60	25

1111 Children of Different Races

1979. International Year of the Child.

1745	**1111**	15c. red	60	25

1112 John Steinbeck

1979. Literary Arts. John Steinbeck (novelist).

1746	**1112**	15c. blue	60	25

1113 Einstein

1979. Birth Cent of Albert Einstein (physicist).

1747	**1113**	15c. brown	60	25

1114 Chanute and Glider

1979. Air. Aviation Pioneers. Octave Chanute. Multicoloured.

A1748	21c. Type **1114**	90	70
A1749	21c. Chanute and glider (different)	90	70

1116 Coffee Pot

1979. American Folk Art. Pennsylvania Toleware. Multicoloured.

1750	15c. Type **1116**	60	25
1751	15c. Tea caddy	60	25
1752	15c. Sugar bowl with lid	60	25
1753	15c. Coffee pot with gooseneck spout	60	25

1120 Virginia Rotunda (Thomas Jefferson)

1979. American Architecture. Each black and red.

1754	15c. Type **1120**	60	25
1755	15c. Baltimore Cathedral (Benjamin Latrobe)	60	25
1756	15c. Boston State House (Charles Bulfinch)	60	25
1757	15c. Philadelphia Exchange (William Strickland)	60	25

1124 Persistent Trillium

1979. Endangered Flora. Multicoloured.

1758	15c. Type **1124**	60	25
1759	15c. Hawaiian wild broadbean	60	25
1760	15c. Contra costa wallflower	60	25
1761	15c. Antioch dunes evening primrose	60	25

1128 Guide Dog

1979. 50th Anniv of First U.S. Guide Dog Programme.

1762	**1128**	15c. multicoloured	60	25

1129 Child with Medal

1979. Special Olympic Games for the Handicapped.

1763	**1129**	15c. multicoloured	60	25

1130 Throwing the Javelin (Decathlon)

1979. Olympic Games, Moscow (1980). Multicoloured.

1764	10c. Type **1130** (postage)	45	25
1765	15c. Running (horiz)	60	25
1766	15c. Swimming (horiz)	60	25
1767	15c. Rowing (horiz)	60	25
1768	15c. Show jumping (horiz)	60	25
A1769	31c. High jumping (horiz) (air)	1·00	45

1136 John Paul Jones (after Peale)

1979. American Revolution Bicentennial. John Paul Jones (naval commander).

1770	**1136**	15c. multicoloured	60	25

1137 "Rest on the Flight to Egypt" (G. David)

1979. Christmas. Multicoloured.
1771		15c. Type **1137**	60	25
1772		15c. Santa Claus tree ornament	60	25

1139 Will Rogers

1979. Performing Arts and Artists. Will Rogers (cowboy philosopher).
1773	**1139**	15c. multicoloured	60	25

1140 Vietnam Service Medal Ribbon

1979. Vietnam Veterans.
1774	**1140**	15c. multicoloured	70	25

1141 Wiley Post

1979. Air. Aviation Pioneers. Wiley Post. Multicoloured.
A1775		25c. Type **1141**	1·50	1·10
A1776		25c. Wiley Post and Lockheed Vega "Winnie Mae"	1·50	1·10

1143 W. C. Fields

1980. Performing Arts and Artists. W. C. Fields (comedian).
1777	**1143**	15c. multicoloured	60	25

1144 Speed Skating

1980. Winter Olympic Games, Lake Placid. Multicoloured.
1778		15c. Type **1144**	60	25
1779		15c. Downhill skiing	60	25
1780		15c. Ski jumping	60	25
1781		15c. Ice hockey	60	25

1148 Robertson Windmill, Williamsburg, Va.

1980. Windmills.
1782	**1148**	15c. brown on yellow	60	25
1783	-	15c. brown on yellow	60	25
1784	-	15c. brown on yellow	60	25
1785	-	15c. brown on yellow	60	25
1786	-	15c. brown on yellow	60	25

DESIGNS: No. 1783, Replica of old windmill, Portsmouth, R.I.; 1784, Cape Cod windmill, Eastham, Mass.; 1785, Dutch mill, Fabyan Park Forest Preserve, Ill.; 1786, Southwestern windmill, Texas.

1153 Benjamin Banneker

1980. Black Heritage. Benjamin Banneker (astronomer and mathematician).
1787	**1153**	15c. multicoloured	60	25

1154 Photograph and Envelope

1157 "P.S. Write Soon"

1980. National Letter Writing Week.
1788	**1154**	15c. multicoloured	60	25
1789	**1157**	15c. multicoloured (purple background)	60	25
1790	-	15c. multicoloured	60	25
1791	**1157**	15c. multicoloured (green background)	60	25
1792	-	15c. multicoloured	60	25
1793	**1157**	15c. blue, black and red	60	25

DESIGNS—As T **1154**: No. 1790, Flowers and envelope; 1792, Capitol and envelope.

1158 Frances Perkins

1980. Frances Perkins (first woman Cabinet member) Commemoration.
1794	**1158**	15c. blue	60	25

1159 Dolley Madison (after Stuart)

1980
1795	**1159**	15c. dp brown & brown	60	25

1160 Emily Bissell

1980. Emily Bissell (crusader against tuberculosis) Commemoration.
1796	**1160**	15c. black and red	60	25

1161 Helen Keller and Anne Sullivan

1980. Birth Centenary of Helen Keller.
1797	**1161**	15c. multicoloured	60	25

1162 Veterans Administration Emblem

1980. 50th Anniv of Veterans Administration.
1798	**1162**	15c. red and blue	60	25

1163 Statue of Gen. Galvez, Mobile

1980. General Bernardo de Galvez (leader of Spanish forces in Louisiana during American Revolution) Commemoration.
1799	**1163**	15c. multicoloured	60	25

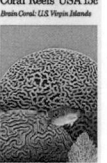

1164 Brain Corals

1980. Coral Reefs. Multicoloured.
1800		15c. Type **1164**	60	25
1801		15c. Elkhorn coral	60	25
1802		15c. Chalice coral	60	25
1803		15c. Finger coral	60	25

1168 American Bald Eagle

1980. Organized Labour.
1804	**1168**	15c. multicoloured	60	25

1169 Edith Wharton

1980. Literary Arts. Edith Wharton (novelist).
1805	**1169**	15c. violet	60	25

1170 "Homage to the Square: Glow" (J. Albers)

1980. American Education.
1806	**1170**	15c. multicoloured	60	25

1171 Heiltsuk, Bella Bella

1980. American Folk Art, Indian Masks. Multicoloured.
1807	**1171**	15c. Type **1171**	60	25
1808		15c. Chilkat Tlingit	60	25
1809		15c. Tlingit	60	25
1810		15c. Bella Coola	60	25

1175 Smithsonian Institution, Washington (James Renwick)

1980. American Architecture.
1811	**1175**	15c. black and red	60	25
1812	-	15c. black and red	60	25
1813	-	15c. black and red	60	25
1814	-	15c. black and red	60	25

DESIGNS: No. 1812, Trinity Church, Boston (Henry Hobson Richardson); 1813, Penn Academy, Philadelphia (Frank Furness); 1814, Lyndhurst, Tarrytown, New York (Alexander Jackson Davis).

1179 Philip Mazzei

1980. Air. 250th Birth Anniv of Philip Mazzei (patriot).
A1815	**1179**	40c. multicoloured	1·30	35

1180 "Madonna and Child" (Epiphany Window, Washington Cathedral)

1181 Antique Toys

1980. Christmas.
1816	**1180**	15c. multicoloured	60	25
1817	**1181**	15c. multicoloured	60	25

1191 Sequoyah (Cherokee scholar) (after C. B. Wilson)

1980. Great Americans. With "c" after face value.
1818	-	1c. black	25	20
1819	-	2c. black	30	20
1820	-	3c. green	35	20
1821	-	4c. violet	35	25
1822	-	5c. red	35	25
1823	-	10c. blue	45	25
1824	-	13c. red	60	25
1825	-	17c. green	70	25
1826	-	18c. blue	70	25
1827	**1191**	19c. brown	70	35
1828	-	20c. purple	70	35
1829	-	20c. green	80	35
1830	-	20c. black	80	35
1831	-	30c. green	90	65
1832	-	35c. black	1·20	55
1833	-	37c. blue	1·20	55
1834	-	40c. brown	1·40	80

DESIGNS: 1c. Dorothea Dix (social pioneer); 2c. Igor Stravinsky (composer); 3c. Henry Clay (politician); 4c. Carl Schurz (reformer); 5c. Pearl Buck (author) (after F. Elliot); 10c. Richard Russell (politician); 13c. Crazy Horse (Sioux chief) (after K. Ziolkowski); 17c. Rachel Carson (scientist); 18c. George Mason (patriot); 20c. (No. 1828), Ralph Bunche (U.N. Secretariat member); 20c. (No. 1829), Thomas H. Gallaudet (educator of the deaf); 20c. (No. 1830), Pres. Harry S. Truman; 30c. Frank C. Laubach (literacy educator); 35c. Charles R. Drew (surgeon); 37c. Robert Millikan (physicist); 40c. Lillian M. Gilbreth (engineer).

For similar designs without "c", see Nos. 2108/36.

1203 Blanche Stuart Scott and Curtiss Golden Flyer

1980. Air. Aviation Pioneers. Multicoloured.

A1839	28c. Type **1203**	90	35
A1840	35c. Glenn Curtiss and Curtiss "June Bug"	1·00	45

1205 Everett Dirksen

1981. Senator Everett Dirksen Commemoration.

1841	**1205**	15c. grey	60	25

1206 Whitney Moore Young

1981. Black Heritage. Whitney Moore Young (civil rights leader).

1842	**1206**	15c. multicoloured	60	25

1981. Non-denominational "B" stamp. As T **1090**.

1843	(18c.) lilac	5·75	25

1207 Rose

1981. Flowers. Multicoloured.

1846	18c. Type **1207**	70	30
1847	18c. Camellia	70	30
1848	18c. Dahlia	70	30
1849	18c. Lily	70	30

1211 ". . . for amber waves of grain"

1212 Stars

1981

1851	**1212**	6c. blue and red	1·00	50
1850	**1211**	18c. brown, red and blue	70	30
1852	-	18c. lilac, red and blue	60	35
1853	-	18c. brown, blue and red	70	40

DESIGNS—As T **1211**: No. 1852, "... for purple mountain majesties"; 1853, "... from sea to shining sea".

1215 Nurse and Child

1981. Centenary of American Red Cross.

1854	**1215**	18c. multicoloured	70	30

1216 Money Box

1981. 150th Anniv of First Savings and Loans Association.

1855	**1216**	18c. multicoloured	70	30

1217 American Bighorn

1981. Wildlife.

1856	**1217**	18c. brown	80	30
1857	-	18c. brown	80	30
1858	-	18c. brown	80	30
1859	-	18c. brown	80	30
1860	-	18c. brown	80	30
1861	-	18c. brown	80	30
1862	-	18c. brown	80	30
1863	-	18c. brown	80	30
1864	-	18c. brown	80	30
1865	-	18c. brown	80	30

DESIGNS: No. 1857, Puma; 1858, Common seal; 1859, American bison; 1860, Brown bear; 1861, Polar bear; 1862, Red deer; 1863, Elk; 1864, White-tailed deer; 1865, Pronghorn.

1238 Detroit Electric Auto, 1917

1981. Transport. With "c" after face value.

1866		1c. violet	25	20
1867		2c. black	25	20
1868		3c. green	30	20
1869		4c. brown	30	20
1870		5c. green	35	20
1871		5.2c. red	35	25
1872		5.9c. blue	35	25
1873		7.4c. brown	45	30
1874		9.3c. red	45	35
1875		10.9c. mauve	60	40
1876		11c. red	45	40
1877	**1238**	17c. blue	70	40
1878	-	18c. brown	60	30
1879	-	20c. red	70	30

DESIGNS: 1c. Omnibus, 1880s; 2c. Steam locomotive, 1870s; 3c. Railway handcar, 1880s; 4c. Concord stagecoach, 1890s; 5c. Pope motor-cycle, 1913; 5.2c. Sleigh, 1880s; 5.9c. Bicycle, 1870s; 7.4c. Baby buggy, 1880s; 9.3c. Mail wagon, 1880s; 10.9c. Hansom cab, 1890s; 11c. Railway caboose, 1890s; 18c. Surrey, 1890s; 20c. Amoskeag fire pumper, 1860s.

For similar designs without "c", see Nos. 2150/74 and 2477/82.

1247 Exploring the Moon ("Apollo" mission)

1981. Space Achievements.

1886	**1247**	18c. multicoloured	70	35
1887	-	18c. multicoloured	70	35
1888	-	18c. multicoloured	70	35
1889	-	18c. multicoloured	70	35
1890	-	18c. multicoloured	70	35
1891	-	18c. multicoloured	70	35
1892	-	18c. multicoloured	70	35
1893	-	18c. multicoloured	70	35

DESIGNS: No. 1887, Space Shuttle loosing boosters; 1888, Space Shuttle performing experiment; 1889, Understanding the Sun ("Skylab"); 1890, Probing the Planets ("Pioneer II"); 1891, Space Shuttle launch; 1892, Space Shuttle landing; 1893, Comprehending the Universe (space telescope).

Nos. 1886/93 were issued together in se-tenant blocks of eight, each block forming a composite design.

1255 Joseph Wharton (founder of Wharton School)

1981. Cent of Professional Management Education.

1894	**1255**	18c. blue and black	70	30

1256 Great Blue Heron

1981. Wildlife Habitats.

1895	**1256**	18c. multicoloured	70	30
1896	-	18c. multicoloured	70	30
1897	-	18c. multicoloured	70	30
1898	-	18c. multicoloured	70	30

DESIGNS: No. 1896, American badger; 1897, Brown bear; 1898, Ruffed grouse.

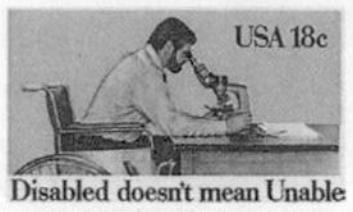

1260 Disabled Man using Microscope

1981. International Year of Disabled Persons.

1899	**1260**	18c. multicoloured	70	30

1261 Edna St. Vincent Millay

1981. Edna St. Vincent Millay (poet) Commem.

1900	**1261**	18c. multicoloured	70	30

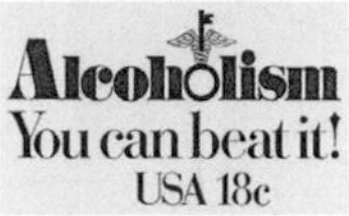

1262 "Alcoholism. You can beat it!"

1981. Anti-alcoholism Campaign.

1901	**1262**	18c. blue and black	70	30

1263 New York University Library (Stanford White)

1981. American Architecture (3rd series).

1902	**1263**	18c. black and brown	70	30
1903	-	18c. black and brown	70	30
1904	-	18c. black and brown	70	30
1905	-	18c. black and brown	70	30

DESIGNS: No. 1903, Biltmore House, Asheville, North Carolina (Richard Morris Hunt); 1904, Palace of Arts, San Francisco (Bernard Maybeck); 1905, Bank, Owatonna, Minnesota (Louis Sullivan).

1267 Bobby Jones (golfer)

1981. American Sports Personalities.

1906	**1267**	18c. green	1·20	60
1907	-	18c. red	80	40

DESIGN: No. 1907, Babe Zaharias (golfer and athlete).

1269 "Coming through the Rye"

1981. Frederic Remington (sculptor) Commem.

1908	**1269**	18c. brown, green and light brown	70	30

1981. Non-denominational "C" stamp. As T **1090** but inscribed "Domestic Mail".

1909	(20c.) brown (19×22 mm)	70	30
1910	(20c.) brown (15×18½ mm)	70	30

1271 James Hoban and White House

1981. 150th Death Anniv of James Hoban (architect).

1912	**1271**	18c. multicoloured	70	30
1913	**1271**	20c. multicoloured	70	30

1272 Map of Yorktown Peninsula

1981. Bicentenary of Battles of Yorktown and Virginia Capes. Multicoloured.

1914	18c. Type **1272**	80	50
1915	18c. French ships blocking Chesapeake Bay	80	50

1274 "Madonna and Child" (Botticelli)

1981. Christmas. No value expressed. Multicoloured.

1916	(20c.) Type **1274**	70	30
1917	(20c.) Teddy bear on sleigh	70	30

1276 John Hanson

1981. John Hanson (American revolutionary leader) Commemoration.

1918	**1276**	20c. multicoloured	70	30

1277 Barrel Cactus

1981. Desert Plants. Multicoloured.

1919	20c. Type **1277**	70	30
1920	20c. Agave (horiz)	70	30
1921	20c. Saguaro	70	30
1922	20c. Beavertail cactus (horiz)	70	30

1281 Flag over Supreme Court

1981

1923c	**1281**	20c. black, red and blue	70	30

1282 American Bighorn

1982

1926	**1282**	20c. blue	70	30

1283 Franklin D. Roosevelt

1982. Birth Centenary of President Franklin D. Roosevelt.

1927	**1283**	20c. blue	70	30

1284 Flowers spelling "Love"

1982. Greetings Stamp.
1928	**1284**	20c. multicoloured	70	30

1285 George Washington

1982. 250th Birth Anniv of George Washington.
1929	**1285**	20c. multicoloured	70	30

1286 Common Flicker (inscr "Yellow-hammer") and Camellia (Alabama)

1982. State Birds and Flowers. Multicoloured.
1930	20c. Type **1286**	90	40
1931	20c. Willow grouse (inscr "Ptarmigan") and forget-me-not (Alaska)	90	40
1932	20c. Cactus wren and saguaro cactus blossom (Arizona)	90	40
1933	20c. Northern mockingbird and apple blossom (Arkansas)	90	40
1934	20c. California quail and California poppy (California)	90	40
1935	20c. Lark bunting and Rocky Mountain columbine (Colorado)	90	40
1936	20c. American robin and mountain laurel (Connecticut)	90	40
1937	20c. Blue hen chicken and peach blossom (Delaware)	90	40
1938	20c. Northern mockingbird and orange blossom (Florida)	90	40
1939	20c. Brown thrasher and Cherokee rose (Georgia)	90	40
1940	20c. Hawaiian goose and hibiscus (Hawaii)	90	40
1941	20c. Mountain bluebird and syringa (Idaho)	90	40
1942	20c. Common cardinal and violet (Illinois)	90	40
1943	20c. Common cardinal and peony (Indiana)	90	40
1944	20c. American (inscr "Eastern") goldfinch and wild rose (Iowa)	90	40
1945	20c. Western meadowlark and sunflower (Kansas)	90	40
1946	20c. Common cardinal and goldenrod (Kentucky)	90	40
1947	20c. Brown pelican and magnolia (Louisiana)	90	40
1948	20c. Black-capped chickadee, white pine cone and tassel (Maine)	90	40
1949	20c. Northern (inscr "Baltimore") oriole and black-eyed susan (Maryland)	90	40
1950	20c. Black-capped chickadee and mayflower (Massachusetts)	90	40
1951	20c. American robin and apple blossom (Michigan)	90	40
1952	20c. Great northern diver (inscr "Common Loon") and showy lady slipper (Minnesota)	90	40
1953	20c. Northern mockingbird and magnolia (Mississippi)	90	40
1954	20c. Eastern bluebird and red hawthorn (Missouri)	90	40
1955	20c. Western meadowlark and bitterroot (Montana)	90	40
1956	20c. Western meadowlark and goldenrod (Nebraska)	90	40
1957	20c. Mountain bluebird and sagebrush (Nevada)	90	40
1958	20c. Purple finch and lilac (New Hampshire)	90	40
1959	20c. American goldfinch and violet (New Jersey)	90	40
1960	20c. Road-runner and yucca flower (New Mexico)	90	40

1961	20c. Eastern bluebird and rose (New York)	90	40
1962	20c. Common cardinal and flowering dogwood (North Carolina)	90	40
1963	20c. Western meadowlark, and wild prairie rose (North Dakota)	90	40
1964	20c. Common cardinal and red carnation (Ohio)	90	40
1965	20c. Scissor-tailed flycatcher and mistletoe (Oklahoma)	90	40
1966	20c. Western meadowlark and Oregon grape (Oregon)	90	40
1967	20c. Ruffed grouse and mountain laurel (Pennsylvania)	90	40
1968	20c. Rhode Island red and violet (Rhode Island)	90	40
1969	20c. Carolina wren and Carolina jessamine (South Carolina)	90	40
1970	20c. Common pheasant ("Ring-necked Pheasant") and pasque flower (South Dakota)	90	40
1971	20c. Northern mockingbird and iris (Tennessee)	90	40
1972	20c. Northern mockingbird and bluebonnet (Texas)	90	40
1973	20c. California gull and sego lily (Utah)	90	40
1974	20c. Hermit thrush and red clover (Vermont)	90	40
1975	20c. Common cardinal and flowering dogwood (Virginia)	90	40
1976	20c. American goldfinch and rhododendron (Washington)	90	40
1977	20c. Common cardinal ("Cardinal") and "Rhododendron maximum" (West Virginia)	90	40
1978	20c. American robin and wood violet (Wisconsin)	90	40
1979	20c. Western meadowlark and Indian paint bush (Wyoming)	90	40

1287 Stripes in National Colours

1982. Bicent of U.S.A.–Netherlands Diplomatic Relations.
1980	**1287**	20c. red, blue and black	70	30

1288 Library of Congress

1982. Library of Congress.
1981	**1288**	20c. black and red	70	30

1289 Garment Tag

1982. Consumer Education.
1982	**1289**	20c. blue	1·00	40

1290 Solar Energy

1982. Knoxville World's Fair.
1983	**1290**	20c. multicoloured	80	40
1984	-	20c. multicoloured	80	40
1985	-	20c. blue, light blue and black	80	40
1986	-	20c. blue, black and brown	80	40

DESIGNS: No. 1984, Synthetic fuels; 1985, Breeder reactor; 1986, Fossil fuels.

1294 Frontispiece from "Ragged Dick"

1982. 150th Birth Anniv of Horatio Alger (novelist).
1987	**1294**	20c. black and red on buff	70	30

1295 Family Group

1982. Ageing together.
1988	**1295**	20c. red	70	30

1296 John, Ethel and Lionel Barrymore

1982. Performing Arts and Artists. The Barrymores (theatrical family).
1989	**1296**	20c. multicoloured	70	30

1297 Dr. Mary Walker

1982. Dr. Mary Walker (army surgeon) Commem.
1990	**1297**	20c. multicoloured	70	30

1298 Maple Leaf and Rose

1982. 50th Anniv of International Peace Garden (on U.S.A.–Canada border).
1991	**1298**	20c. multicoloured	70	30

1299 Typographic Design

1982. America's Libraries.
1992	**1299**	20c. red and black	70	30

1300 Jackie Robinson

1982. Black Heritage. Jackie Robinson (baseball player).
1993	**1300**	20c. multicoloured	1·50	40

1301 Touro Synagogue

1982. Touro Synagogue, Newport, Rhode Island.
1994	**1301**	20c. multicoloured	70	30

1302 Open Air Theatre

1982. Wolf Trap Farm Park, Vienna, Virginia.
1995	**1302**	20c. multicoloured	70	30

Architecture USA 20c

1303 Fallingwater, Mill Run, Pennsylvania (Frank Lloyd Wright)

1982. American Architecture.
1996	**1303**	20c. black and brown	80	50
1997	-	20c. black and brown	80	50
1998	-	20c. black and brown	80	50
1999	-	20c. black and brown	80	50

DESIGNS: No. 1997, Illinois Institute of Technology, Chicago (Mies van der Rohe); 1998, Gropius House, Lincoln, Massachusetts (Walter Gropius); 1999, Dulles Airport, Washington D.C. (Eero Saarinen).

1307 St. Francis and Doves

1982. 800th Birth Anniv of St. Francis of Assisi.
2000	**1307**	20c. multicoloured	70	35

1308 Ponce de Leon and Map of Florida

1982. Ponce de Leon (explorer) Commemoration.
2001	**1308**	20c. multicoloured	70	35

1309 "Madonna and Child" (Tiepolo)

1982. Christmas. Multicoloured.
2002	20c. Type **1309**	70	35
2003	20c. Building a snowman (horiz)	80	45
2004	20c. Sledging (horiz)	80	45
2005	20c. Decorating a Christmas tree (horiz)	80	45
2006	20c. Skating (horiz)	80	45

1314 Puppy and Kitten

1982
2007	**1314**	13c. multicoloured	45	25

1316 Industrial Complex

1983. Science and Industry.
2015	**1316**	20c. multicoloured	70	35

1317 Benjamin Franklin and Great Seal of Sweden

1983. Bicentenary of Sweden–U.S.A. Treaty of Amity and Commerce.
2016	**1317**	20c. indigo, brown and black	70	35

1319/1320 Hot Air Ballooning

1983. Bicentenary of Manned Flight. Multicoloured.

2017		20c. "Intrepid", 1861 (vert)	70	35
2018		20c. Type **1319**	70	35
2019		20c. Type **1320**	70	35
2020		20c. Stratosphere balloon "Explorer II", 1935 (vert)	70	35

1322 C.C.C. Workers repairing Trail

1983. 50th Anniv of Civilian Conservation Corps.

2021	**1322**	20c. multicoloured	70	35

1323 Shot Putting

1983. Air. Olympic Games, Los Angeles (1984) (1st issue). Multicoloured.

A2022	40c. Type **1323**		1·40	55
A2023	40c. Gymnastics		1·40	55
A2024	40c. Swimming		1·40	55
A2025	40c. Weightlifting		1·40	55

See also Nos. A2034/7, 2040/3, A2058/61 and 2079/82.

1327 Joseph Priestley (after G. Stuart)

1983. 250th Birth Anniv of Joseph Priestley (discoverer of oxygen).

2026	**1327**	20c. multicoloured	70	35

1328 Reaching Hands

1983. Voluntary Work.

2027	**1328**	20c. black and red	70	35

1329 "Concord"

1983. 300th Anniv of First German Settlers in America.

2028	**1329**	20c. brown	70	35

1330 Joggers and Electrocardiograph Trace

1983. Physical Fitness.

2029	**1330**	20c. multicoloured	70	35

1331 Brooklyn Bridge, New York

1983. Centenary of Brooklyn Bridge.

2030	**1331**	20c. blue	70	35

1332 Norris Hydro-electric Dam

1983. 50th Anniv of Tennessee Valley Authority.

2031	**1332**	20c. multicoloured	70	35

1333 Army, Air Force and Navy Medals of Honour

1983. Medal of Honour.

2032	**1333**	20c. multicoloured	70	35

1334 Scott Joplin

1983. Black Heritage. Scott Joplin (ragtime composer).

2033	**1334**	20c. multicoloured	70	35

1335 Gymnastics

1983. Air. Olympic Games, Los Angeles (1984) (2nd issue). Multicoloured.

A2034	28c. Type **1335**		1·50	55
A2035	28c. Hurdling		1·50	55
A2036	28c. Basketball		1·50	55
A2037	28c. Football		1·50	55

1339 Babe Ruth

1983. American Sports Personalities. Babe Ruth (baseball player).

2038	**1339**	20c. blue	1·80	55

1340 Hawthorne (after C. G. Thompson)

1983. Literary Arts. Nathaniel Hawthorne (writer).

2039	**1340**	20c. multicoloured	70	35

1341 Discus

1983. Olympic Games, Los Angeles (1984) (3rd issue). Multicoloured.

2040		13c. Type **1341**	60	25
2041		13c. High jump	60	25
2042		13c. Archery	60	25
2043		13c. Boxing	60	25

1345 American Bald Eagle and Moon

1983

2044	**1345**	$9.35 multicoloured	29·00	20·00

1346 Signing the Treaty of Paris (after Benjamin West)

1983. Bicentenary of Treaty of Paris.

2045	**1346**	20c. multicoloured	70	35

1347 Text in Early and Modern Type

1983. Centenary of Civil Service.

2046	**1347**	20c. stone, red and black	70	35

1348 Part of Proscenium and Modern Facade

1983. Centenary of Metropolitan Opera, New York.

2047	**1348**	20c. yellow and purple	70	35

1349 Charles Steinmetz and Graph

1983. American Inventors.

2048	**1349**	20c. pink and black	80	45
2049	-	20c. pink and black	80	45
2050	-	20c. pink and black	80	45
2051	-	20c. pink and black	80	45

DESIGNS: No. 2049, Edwin Armstrong and frequency modulator; 2050, Nikola Tesla and induction motor; 2051, Philo T. Farnsworth and television camera.

1353 "John Mason" Streetcar, New York City, 1832

1983. Streetcars. Multicoloured.

2052		20c. Type **1353**	80	45
2053		20c. Electric streetcar, Montgomery, Alabama, 1886	80	45
2054		20c. "Bobtail" horsecar, Sulphur Rock, Arkansas, 1926	80	45
2055		20c. St. Charles streetcar, New Orleans, 1923	80	45

1357 "Madonna and Child" (Raphael)

1358 Santa Claus

1983. Christmas.

2056	**1357**	20c. multicoloured	70	35
2057	**1358**	20c. multicoloured	70	35

1359 Fencing

1983. Air. Olympic Games, Los Angeles (1984) (4th issue). Multicoloured.

A2058	35c. Type **1359**		1·70	90
A2059	35c. Cycling		1·70	90
A2060	35c. Volleyball		1·70	90
A2061	35c. Pole vault		1·70	90

1363 Martin Luther

1983. 500th Birth Anniv of Martin Luther.

2062	**1363**	20c. multicoloured	70	35

1364 Reindeer and Pipeline

1984. 25th Anniv of Alaska Statehood.

2063	**1364**	20c. multicoloured	70	35

1365 Ice Dancing

1984. Winter Olympic Games, Sarajevo. Multicoloured.

2064		20c. Type **1365**	80	45
2065		20c. Downhill skiing	80	45
2066		20c. Cross-country skiing	80	45
2067		20c. Ice hockey	80	45

1369 Column and "$" Sign

1984. 50th Anniv of Federal Deposit Insurance Corporation.

2068	**1369**	20c. multicoloured	70	35

1370 "Love"

1984. Greetings Stamp.

2069	**1370**	20c. multicoloured	70	35

1371 Carter G. Woodson

1984. Black Heritage. Carter G. Woodson (historian).

2070	**1371**	20c. multicoloured	70	35

1372 Hand holding Plant

1984. 50th Anniv of Soil and Water Conservation Movement.

| 2071 | **1372** | 20c. multicoloured | 70 | 35 |

1373 Coin and "$" Sign

1984. 50th Anniv of Credit Union Act.

| 2072 | **1373** | 20c. multicoloured | 70 | 35 |

1374 Wild Pink

1984. Orchids. Multicoloured.

2073	20c. Type **1374**	80	45
2074	20c. Yellow lady's slipper	80	45
2075	20c. Spreading pogonia	80	45
2076	20c. Pacific calypso	80	45

1378 Eastern Polynesian Canoe and Pacific Golden Plover

1984. 25th Anniv of Hawaii Statehood.

| 2077 | **1378** | 20c. multicoloured | 70 | 35 |

1379 Silhouettes of Lincoln and Washington

1984. 50th Anniv of National Archives.

| 2078 | **1379** | 20c. black, olive and red | 70 | 35 |

1380 Diving

1984. Olympic Games, Los Angeles (5th issue). Multicoloured.

2079	20c. Type **1380**	90	45
2080	20c. Long jump	90	45
2081	20c. Wrestling	90	45
2082	20c. Canoeing	90	45

1384 Bayou Wildlife

1984. Louisiana World Exposition, New Orleans.

| 2083 | **1384** | 20c. multicoloured | 90 | 35 |

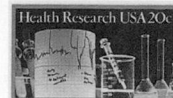

1385 Laboratory Equipment

1984. Health Research.

| 2084 | **1385** | 20c. multicoloured | 70 | 35 |

1386 Fairbanks in Film Roles

1984. Performing Arts and Artists. Douglas Fairbanks (film actor).

| 2085 | **1386** | 20c. multicoloured | 70 | 35 |

1387 Jim Thorpe

1984. American Sports Personalities. Jim Thorpe (athlete, footballer and baseball player).

| 2086 | **1387** | 20c. brown | 70 | 35 |

1388 John McCormack

1984. Performing Arts and Artists. John McCormack (singer).

| 2087 | **1388** | 20c. multicoloured | 70 | 35 |

1389 St. Lawrence Seaway

1984. 25th Anniv of St. Lawrence Seaway.

| 2088 | **1389** | 20c. multicoloured | 70 | 35 |

1390 "Mallards dropping In" (Jay Norwood Darling)

1984. 50th Anniv of Migratory Bird Hunting and Conservation Stamp Act.

| 2089 | **1390** | 20c. blue | 80 | 45 |

1391 Galleon "Elizabeth"

1984. Explorers. 400th Anniv of First Raleigh Expedition to Roanoke Island, North Carolina.

| 2090 | **1391** | 20c. multicoloured | 70 | 35 |

1392 Melville (after J. O. Eaton)

1984. Literary Arts. Herman Melville (novelist).

| 2091 | **1392** | 20c. green | 70 | 35 |

1393 Horace Moses

1984. Horace Moses (founder of Junior Achievement (training organization) Commem.

| 2092 | **1393** | 20c. orange and black | 70 | 35 |

1394 Smokey Bear and American Black Bear Cub clinging to burnt Tree

1984. Smokey Bear (symbol of forest fire prevention campaign).

| 2093 | **1394** | 20c. multicoloured | 70 | 35 |

1395 Clemente and Flag of Puerto Rico

1984. American Sports Personalities. Roberto Clemente (baseball player).

| 2094 | **1395** | 20c. multicoloured | 2·50 | 55 |

1396 Beagle and Boston Terrier

1984. Centenary of American Kennel Club. Multicoloured.

2095	20c. Type **1396**	80	45
2096	20c. Chesapeake Bay retriever and cocker spaniel	80	45
2097	20c. Alaskan malamute and collie	80	45
2098	20c. Black and tan coonhound and American foxhound	80	45

1400 McGruff (campaign character)

1984. National Crime Prevention Month.

| 2099 | **1400** | 20c. multicoloured | 70 | 35 |

1401 "Family Unity"

1984. National Stamp Collecting Month.

| 2100 | **1401** | 20c. black, red and blue | 70 | 35 |

1402 Eleanor Roosevelt

1984. Eleanor Roosevelt Commemoration.

| 2101 | **1402** | 20c. blue | 70 | 35 |

1403 Abraham Lincoln reading to his Son, Tad

1984. "Nation of Readers".

| 2102 | **1403** | 20c. brown and red | 70 | 35 |

1404 "Madonna and Child (Fra Filippo Lippi)

1984. Christmas. Multicoloured.

| 2103 | 20c. Type **1404** | 70 | 35 |
| 2104 | 20c. Santa Claus | 70 | 35 |

1406 Uniformed Group and Flag

1984. Hispanic Americans.

| 2105 | **1406** | 20c. Multicoloured | 70 | 35 |

1407 Memorial (Maya Ying Lin)

1984. Vietnam Veterans Memorial, Washington, D.C.

| 2106 | **1407** | 20c. black, green and deep green | 80 | 35 |

1408 Kern

1985. Performing Arts and Artists. Birth Centenary of Jerome Kern (composer).

| 2107 | **1408** | 22c. multicoloured | 80 | 35 |

1409 Margaret Mitchell (writer)

1985. Great Americans. Without "c" after face value.

2108	**1409**	1c. brown	25	15
2109	-	2c. blue	25	15
2110	-	3c. blue	35	15
2111	-	4c. blue	35	15
2112	-	5c. green	35	15
2113	-	6c. red	35	20
2114	-	7c. red	35	20
2115	-	8c. brown	35	20
2116	-	9c. green	45	20
2117	-	10c. red	45	20
2118	-	11c. blue	45	20
2119	-	14c. green	60	20
2120	-	14c. red	45	20

2121	-	15c. purple	60	30
2122	-	17c. green	70	30
2123	-	21c. purple	80	35
2124	-	22c. blue	80	30
2125	-	23c. violet	80	30
2126	-	25c. blue	80	30
2127	-	28c. green	90	35
2128	-	39c. mauve	1·40	40
2129	-	45c. blue	1·40	40
2130a	-	50c. brown	1·50	65
2131	-	56c. red	1·70	35
2132	-	65c. blue	1·70	35
2133	-	$1 green	3·50	50
2134a	-	$1 blue	3·25	1·80
2135	-	$2 violet	5·25	90
2136	-	$5 brown	11·50	2·75

DESIGNS: 2c. Mary Lyon (educator); 3c. Paul Dudley White (cardiologist); 4c. Father Flanagan (founder of Boys Town); 5c. Hugo L. Black (Supreme Court Justice); 6c. Walter Lippmann (journalist); 7c. Abraham Baldwin (politician); 8c. General Henry Knox; 9c. Sylvanus Thayer (military educator) (after R. Weir); 10c. Red Cloud (Oglala Sioux chief); 11c. Alden Partridge (educationist); 14c. (No. 2119) Sinclair Lewis (writer) (after S. Melik); 14c. (No. 2120) Julia Ward Howe (author of "Battle Hymn of the Republic") (after J. Elliott); 15c. Buffalo Bill Cody (showman); 17c. Belva Ann Lockwood (women's rights campaigner); 21c. Chester Carlson (inventor of photocopying); 22c. J. J. Audubon (ornithologist); 23c. Mary Cassatt (artist); 25c. Jack London (writer); 28c. Sitting Bull (Hunkpapa Sioux chief); 39c. Grenville Clark (peace activist); 45c. Dr. Harvey Cushing (neurosurgeon); 50c. Admiral Chester W. Nimitz; 56c. John Harvard (philanthropist) (after D. C. French); 65c. Gen. Henry Harley "Hap" Arnold; $1 (No. 2133) Bernard Revel (scholar); $1 (No. 2134) Johns Hopkins (philanthropist); $2 William Jennings Bryan (politician); $5 Bret Harte (writer).

1985. Non-denominational "D" stamp. As T **1090** but inscribed "Domestic Mail".

2137	(22c.) green (18×21 mm)	80	25
2138	(22c.) green (15×18 mm)	90	25

1438 Alfred V. Verville and Verville-Sperry R-3

1985. Air. Aviation Pioneers. Multicoloured.

A2142	33c. Type **1438**	90	25
A2143	39c. Lawrence and Elmer Sperry and Curtiss F flying boat	1·20	35

1440 Loading Mail into "China Clipper"

1985. Air. 50th Anniv of Martin M-130 Flying Boat, First Transpacific Airmail Flight.

A2144	**1440** 44c. multicoloured	1·20	35

1441 Mary McLeod Bethune

1985. Black Heritage. Mary McLeod Bethune (social activist).

2145	**1441** 22c. multicoloured	80	25

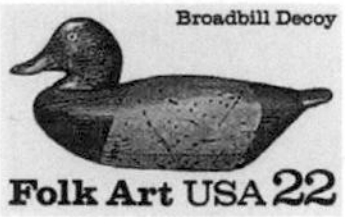

1442 Lesser Scaup ("Broadbill") Decoy, 1890 (Ben Holmes)

1985. American Folk Art. Duck Decoys. Multicoloured.

2146	22c. Type **1442**	1·60	30
2147	22c. Mallard decoy, 1900 (Percy Grant)	1·60	30
2148	22c. Canvasback decoy, 1929 (Bob McGraw)	1·60	30
2149	22c. Redhead decoy, 1925 (Keyes Chadwick)	1·60	30

1446 Omnibus, 1880s

1985. Transport. Without "c" after face value.

2150	**1446**	1c. violet	25	15
2151	-	2c. black	35	15
2152	-	3c. purple	35	15
2153	-	3.4c. green	35	20
2154	-	4.9c. black	35	20
2155	-	5c. black	35	20
2156	-	5.3 black	35	20
2157	-	5.5c. red	35	20
2158	-	6c. brown	35	20
2159	-	7.1c. red	35	20
2160	-	7.6c. brown	35	20
2161	-	8.3c. green	35	20
2162	-	8.4c. purple	35	20
2163	-	8.5c. green	40	20
2163a	-	10c. blue	45	20
2164	-	10.1c. grey	45	20
2165	-	11c. black	45	20
2166	-	12c. blue	45	20
2167	-	12.5c. green	45	20
2167b	-	13c. black	60	20
2168	-	13.2c. green	60	20
2169	-	14c. blue	60	20
2170	-	15c. violet	60	20
2170b	-	16.7c. red	60	20
2171	-	17c. blue	70	25
2172	-	17.5c. violet	70	25
2172b	-	20c. purple	70	30
2172c	-	20.5c. red	90	35
2172d	-	21c. green	80	40
2173	-	24.1c. blue	90	40
2174	-	25c. brown	90	20

DESIGNS: 2c. Steam locomotive, 1870s; 3c. Conestoga wagon, 1800s; 3.4c. School bus, 1920s; 4.9c. Buckboard, 1880s; 5c. Milk wagon, 1900s; 5.3c. Lift, 1900s; 5.5c. Star Route truck, 1910s; 6c. Tricycle, 1880s; 7.1c. Tractor, 1920s; 7.6c. Carreta, 1770s; 8.3c. "McKean" ambulance, 1860s; 8.4c. Wheelchair, 1920s; 8.5c. Tow truck, 1920s; 10c. Canal barge, 1880s; 10.1c. Oil wagon, 1890s; 11c. Stutz "Bearcat", 1933; 12c. Stanley "Steamer", 1909; 12.5c. Pushcart, 1880s; 13c. Police patrol wagon, 1880s; 13.2c. Coal wagon, 1870s; 14c. Iceboat, 1880s; 15c. Tug, 1900s; 16.7c. Popcorn wagon, 1902; 17c. Dog sledge, 1920s; 17.5c. Marmon "Wasp", 1911; 20c. Cable car, 1880s; 20.5c. Ahrens-Fox fire engine, 1900s; 21c. Railway mail van, 1920s; 24.1c. Pope tandem, 1890s; 25c. Bread wagon, 1880s.

The 5.3, 7.6, 8.4, 13, 13.2, 16.7, 21 and 24.1c. were only issued with precancelled inscription of the type of service in red and the 20.5c. in black. Prices in the unused column are for stamps with full gum.

1471 Ice Skating, Skiing and Emblem

1985. Winter Special Olympic Games, Park City, Utah.

2175	**1471** 22c. multicoloured	80	25

1472 Flag over Capitol, Washington

1985

2176	**1472** 22c. black, red and blue	80	20
2178	- 22c. black, red and blue	80	20

DESIGN—40×22 mm: No. 2178, Flag over Capitol, Washington, and inscription "Of the People By the People For the People".

1474 Frilled Dogwinkle

1985. Sea Shells.

2179	**1474**	22c. red and black	70	20
2180	-	22c. red, purple and black	70	20
2181	-	22c. red and black	70	20
2182	-	22c. purple and black	70	20
2183	-	22c. red, purple and black	70	20

DESIGNS: No. 2180, Reticulated cowrie helmet; 2181, New England neptune; 2182, Calico scallop; 2183, Lightning whelk.

1479 Coloured Lines and "Love"

1985. Greetings Stamp.

2184	**1479** 22c. multicoloured	80	25

1480 American Bald Eagle and Moon

1985

2185	**1480** $10.75 multicoloured	30·00	6·50

1481 Electricity Pole and Rural Landscape

1985. 50th Anniv of Rural Electrification Administration.

2186	**1481** 22c. multicoloured	80	25

1482 1c. Franklin Stamp, 1870

1985. "Ameripex 86" International Stamp Exhibition, Chicago.

2187	**1482** 22c. multicoloured	80	25

1483 Abigail Adams

1985. Abigail Adams (wife of Pres. John Adams and writer) Commemoration.

2188	**1483** 22c. multicoloured	80	25

1484 Bartholdi (after J. Frappa) and Statue of Liberty)

1985. Frederic Auguste Bartholdi (sculptor of Statue of Liberty) Commemoration.

2189	**1484** 22c. multicoloured	80	25

1485 Troops in Mountain Pass

1985. Korean War Veterans.

2190	**1485** 22c. green and red	80	25

1486 Disabled and Needy People

1985. 50th Anniv of Social Security Act.

2191	**1486** 22c. blue and deep blue	80	25

1487 Junipero Serra and Mission San Gabriel

1985. Air. Death Bicentenary (1984) of Father Junipero Serra (missionary).

A2192	**1487** 44c. multicoloured	1·70	45

1488 "Battle of the Marne" (Harvey Dunn)

1985. World War I Veterans.

2193	**1488** 22c. green and red	80	25

1489 Quarter Horse

1985. Horses. Multicoloured.

2194	22c. Type **1489**	2·30	85
2195	22c. Morgan horse	2·30	85
2196	22c. Saddlebred horse	2·30	85
2197	22c. Appaloosa	2·30	85

1493 Alphabet, Spectacles, Quill and Apple

1985. Public Education.

2198	**1493** 22c. multicoloured	90	25

1494 Y.M.C.A. Youth Camping (centenary)

1985. International Youth Year. Multicoloured.

2199	22c. Type **1494**	1·20	25
2200	22c. Boy Scouts of America (75th anniv)	1·20	25
2201	22c. Big Brothers and Big Sisters	1·20	25
2202	22c. Camp Fire Inc. (75th anniv)	1·20	25

1498 Hungry Faces

1985. "Help End Hunger".

2203	**1498** 22c. multicoloured	80	25

1499 Envelopes

1985

2204	**1499** 21.1c. multicoloured	80	30

No. 2204 exists both with and without precancel "ZIP + 4".

1500 "Genoa Madonna" (Luca della Robbia)

1985. Christmas.

2205	**1500**	22c. multicoloured	80	25
2206	-	22c. red, green and black	80	25

DESIGN—HORIZ: No. 2206, Poinsettias.

1502 George
Washington
(after Stuart)
and
Washington
Monument

1985

2207	**1502**	18c. multicoloured	60	35

No. 2207 exists both with and without precancel "PRE-SORTED FIRST-CLASS".

1503 Old State House,
Little Rock

1986. 150th Anniv of Arkansas State.

2208	**1503**	22c. multicoloured	80	35

1504 Sheet of Stamps,
Handstamp and
Magnifying Glass

1986. "Ameripex 86" International Stamp Exhibition, Chicago. Stamp Collecting. Mult.

2209	22c. Type **1504**	80	40
2210	22c. Boy holding stamp in tweezers	80	40
2211	22c. Mounted stamps and 3c. U.S. stamp under glass	80	40
2212	22c. "Ameripex" miniature sheet on cover and handstamp	80	40

1508 Puppy

1986. Greetings Stamp.

2213	**1508**	22c. multicoloured	80	35

1509 Sojourner
Truth

1986. Black Heritage. Sojourner Truth (human rights activist).

2214	**1509**	22c. multicoloured	80	35

1510 Texan
Flag and Santa
Anna's Spur

1986. 150th Anniv of Battle of San Jacinto.

2215	**1510**	22c. red, blue and black	80	35

1511 Muskellunge

1986. Fish. Multicoloured.

2216	22c. Type **1511**	1·20	40
2217	22c. Atlantic cod	1·20	40
2218	22c. Large-mouthed black bass	1·20	40
2219	22c. Blue-finned tuna	1·20	40
2220	22c. Bullhead catfish	1·20	40

1516 Modern Hospital

1986. Public Hospitals. 250th Anniv of Bellevue Hospital Centre, New York.

2221	**1516**	22c. multicoloured	80	35

1517 Ellington

1986. Performing Arts and Artists. Duke Ellington (jazz musician).

2222	**1517**	22c. multicoloured	90	40

1518 Presidents (image scaled to 40% of original size)

1986. "Ameripex 86" International Stamp Exhibition, Chicago (2nd issue). U.S. Presidents. Four sheets, each 120×205 mm, as T **1518**.

MS2223 Four sheets. (a) 22c. ×9, each royal blue, ochre and bright scarlet: George Washington, John Adams, Thomas Jefferson, James Madison, James Monroe, John Quincy Adams, Andrew Jackson, Martin van Buren, William Henry Harrison. (b) 22c. ×9, each bottle green, ochre and bright scarlet: John Tyler, James K. Polk, Zachary Taylor, Millard Fillmore, Franklin Pierce, James Buchanan, Abraham Lincoln, Andrew Johnson. (c) 22c. ×9, each chocolate, ochre and bright scarlet: Rutherford B. Hayes, James A. Garfield, Chester A. Arthur, Grover Cleveland, Benjamin Harrison, William McKinley, Theodore Roosevelt, William H. Taft, Woodrow Wilson. (d) 22c. ×9, each blue-black, ochre and bright scarlet: William G. Harding, Calvin Coolidge, Herbert C. Hoover, Franklin D. Roosevelt, White House, Harry S. Truman, Dwight D. Eisenhower, John F. Kennedy, Lyndon B. Johnson Set of 4 sheets | 35·00 | 35·00 |

1519 Elisha Kent Kane and
Polar Brig "Advance"

1986. Polar Explorers. Multicoloured.

2224	22c. Type **1519**	1·00	40
2225	22c. Adolphus W. Greely	1·00	40
2226	22c. Vilhjalmur Stefansson	1·00	40
2227	22c. Robert E. Peary and Matthew Henson	1·00	40

1523 Head of
Statue

1986. Centenary of Statue of Liberty.

2228	**1523**	22c. blue and red	80	35

1524 Blanket
Design
1525 Blanket
Design
1526 Blanket
Design

1527 Blanket
Design

1986. American Folk Art. Navajo Blankets.

2229	**1524**	22c. multicoloured	1·00	40
2230	**1525**	22c. multicoloured	1·00	40
2231	**1526**	22c. multicoloured	1·00	40
2232	**1527**	22c. multicoloured	1·00	40

1528 T.S. Eliot

1986. Literary Arts. Thomas Stearns Eliot (poet).

2233	**1528**	22c. red	80	35

1529
Highlander
Figure
(tobacconist)

1986. American Folk Art. Carved Wooden Figures. Multicoloured.

2234	**1529**	22c. Type **1529**	90	40
2235		22c. Ship's figurehead	90	40
2236		22c. Nautical figure (nautical instrument maker)	90	40
2237		22c. Indian (cigar store)	90	40

1533
"Madonna" (Il
Perugino)

1986. Christmas. Multicoloured.

2238	22c. Type **1533**	80	35
2239	22c. Winter village	80	35

1535 White
Pine and Lake
Huron

1987. 150th Anniv of Michigan Statehood.

2240	**1535**	22c. multicoloured	80	35

1536 Stylized Runner

1986. Tenth Pan-American Games, Indianapolis.

2241	**1536**	22c. multicoloured	80	35

1537 Heart

1987. Greetings Stamp.

2242	**1537**	22c. multicoloured	80	35

1538 Du Sable

1987. Black Heritage. Jean Baptiste Pointe du Sable (founder of Chicago).

2243	**1538**	22c. multicoloured	80	35

1539 Caruso as
Duke of Mantua
in "Rigoletto"

1987. Performing Arts and Artists. Enrico Caruso (operatic tenor).

2244	**1539**	22c. multicoloured	80	35

1540 Badges

1987. 75th Anniv of Girl Scouts of America.

2245	**1540**	22c. multicoloured	80	35

1541 "Congratulations!"

1987. Greetings Stamps. Multicoloured.

2246	22c. Type **1541**	1·20	50
2247	22c. "Get Well!" (18×33 mm)	1·20	50
2248	22c. "Thank You!" (18×33 mm)	1·20	50
2249	22c. "Love You, Dad!"	1·20	50
2250	22c. "Best Wishes!" (18×21 mm)	1·20	50
2251	22c. "Happy Birthday!" (18×21 mm)	1·20	50
2252	22c. "Love You, Mother!"	1·20	50
2253	22c. "Keep in Touch!" (18×21 mm)	1·20	50

1549 Ethnic Faces

1987. Centenary of United Way Volunteer Organization.

2254	**1549**	22c. multicoloured	80	35

1550 Flag
and
Fireworks

1987

2255	**1550**	22c. multicoloured	80	35

1551 Barn Swallows

1987. "Capex '87" International Stamp Exhibition, Toronto. North American Wildlife. Multicoloured.

2256	22c. Type **1551**	1·40	80
2257	22c. Monarch butterflies on field thistle	1·40	80
2258	22c. Bighorn sheep	1·40	80
2259	22c. Broad-tailed hummingbird on Colorado columbine	1·40	80
2260	22c. Rabbit and red clover	1·40	80
2261	22c. Osprey	1·40	80
2262	22c. Mountain lion	1·40	80
2263	22c. Luna moth on trumpet honeysuckle	1·40	80
2264	22c. Mule deer	1·40	80
2265	22c. Grey squirrel on red oak	1·40	80
2266	22c. Armadillo and Texas prickly pear	1·40	80
2267	22c. Eastern chipmunk and European white birch	1·40	80
2268	22c. Moose	1·40	80
2269	22c. Black bear	1·40	80
2270	22c. Tiger swallowtail butterflies on orange milkweed	1·40	80
2271	22c. Northern bobwhite ("Bobwhite") and purple coneflower	1·40	80
2272	22c. Ringtail and Cape marigold	1·40	80
2273	22c. Red-winged blackbird on common cattail	1·40	80
2274	22c. American lobster	1·40	80
2275	22c. Black-tailed hare and beavertail	1·40	80
2276	22c. Scarlet tanager and American basswood	1·40	80
2277	22c. Woodchuck and dandelion	1·40	80
2278	22c. Roseate spoonbill and red mangrove	1·40	80
2279	22c. American bald eagle	1·40	80
2280	22c. Alaskan brown bear	1·40	80
2281	22c. Iiwi on "Ohia lehua"	1·40	80
2282	22c. Badger	1·40	80
2283	22c. Pronghorns	1·40	80
2284	22c. River otter	1·40	80
2285	22c. Ladybird on rose	1·40	80
2286	22c. Beaver, maple and quaking aspen	1·40	80
2287	22c. White-tailed deer	1·40	80
2288	22c. Blue jays on Table Mountain pine	1·40	80
2289	22c. Pikas	1·40	80
2290	22c. Bison	1·40	80
2291	22c. Snowy egret	1·40	80
2292	22c. Grey wolf	1·40	80
2293	22c. Mountain goat	1·40	80
2294	22c. Deer mouse	1·40	80
2295	22c. Black-tailed prairie dog	1·40	80
2296	22c. Box turtle and Virginia creeper	1·40	80
2297	22c. Wolverine	1·40	80
2298	22c. American elk	1·40	80
2299	22c. California sea-lion	1·40	80
2300	22c. Northern mockingbird on royal poinciana	1·40	80
2301	22c. Racoon	1·40	80
2302	22c. Bobcat	1·40	80
2303	22c. Black-footed ferret	1·40	80
2304	22c. Canada goose	1·40	80
2305	22c. Red fox and red maple	1·40	80

1552 State Seal

1987. Bicentenary of Delaware Statehood.

2306	**1552** 22c. multicoloured	90	35

1553 Arabesque from Door, Dar Batha Palace, Fez

1554 Faulkner (after M. L. Goldsborough)

1987. Bicentenary of Diplomatic Relations with Morocco.

2307	**1553** 22c. red and black	75	30

1987. Literary Arts. 25th Death Anniv of William Faulkner (novelist).

2308	**1554** 22c. green	75	30

1555 Squash Blossoms (Ruth Maxwell)

1556 Floral Design (Mary McPeek)

1557 Floral Design (Leslie Saari)

1558 Dogwood Blossoms (Trenna Ruffner)

1987. American Folk Art. Lacemaking.

2309	**1555** 22c. white, blue and ultramarine	75	30
2310	**1556** 22c. white, blue and ultramarine	75	30
2311	**1557** 22c. white, blue and ultramarine	75	30
2312	**1558** 22c. white, blue and ultramarine	75	30

1559 Independence Hall

1987. Bicentenary of Pennsylvania Statehood.

2313	**1559** 22c. multicoloured	85	30

1560 "The Bicentennial …"

1987. Bicentenary of United States Constitution (1st issue). Multicoloured.

2314	22c. Type **1560**	95	30
2315	22c. "We the people …"	95	30
2316	22c. "Establish justice …"	95	30
2317	22c. "And secure …"	95	30
2318	22c. "Do ordain …"	95	30

See also No. 2320.

1565 Farmer with Basket of Produce

1987. Bicentenary of New Jersey Statehood.

2319	**1565** 22c. multicoloured	90	30

1566 First Page of Constitution and Hand holding Quill Pen

1567 Ledger Page and Pen Nib

1987. Centenary of American Institute of Certified Public Accountants.

2321	**1567** 22c. multicoloured	2·50	20

1568 "Stourbridge Lion", 1829

1987. Steam Railway Locomotives. Multicoloured.

2322	22c. Type **1568**	90	35
2323	22c. "Best Friend of Charleston", 1830	90	35
2324	22c. "John Bull", 1831	90	35
2325	22c. "Brother Jonathan", 1832	90	35
2326	22c. "Gowan and Marx", 1839	90	35

1573 "A Gentleman in Adoration before the Madonna" (detail, Giovanni Battista Moroni)

1987. Christmas. Multicoloured.

2327	22c. Type **1573**	80	30
2328	22c. Baubles on tree (horiz)	80	30

1575 Oak Tree

1988. Bicentenary of Georgia Statehood.

2329	**1575** 22c. multicoloured	90	30

1576 "Charles W. Morgan" (whaling ship) and Mystic Town

1988. Bicentenary of Connecticut Statehood.

2330	**1576** 22c. multicoloured	90	30

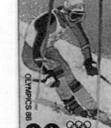

1577 Slalom

1988. Winter Olympic Games, Calgary.

2331	**1577** 22c. multicoloured	80	20

1578 Koala and American Bald Eagle

1579 Johnson and Music Score

1988. Black Heritage. James Weldon Johnson (writer, lyricist and diplomat).

2333	**1579** 22c. multicoloured	90	20

1580 Siamese and Exotic Shorthair Cats

1988. Cats. Multicoloured.

2334	22c. Type **1580**	90	30
2335	22c. Abyssinian and Himalayan cats	90	30
2336	22c. Maine coon and Burmese cats	90	30
2337	22c. American shorthair and Persian cats	90	30

1987. Bicentenary of United States Constitution (2nd issue).

2320	**1566** 22c. multicoloured	90	30

1988. Bicentenary of Australian Settlement.

2332	**1578** 22c. multicoloured	80	20

1584 "A Southwest View of the Statehouse, Boston" (S. Hill)

1988. Bicentenary of Massachusetts Statehood.

2338	**1584** 22c. blue, black and red	90	30

1585 St. Anne's Church, "Clarence Crockett" (yacht) and Statehouse, Annapolis

1988. Bicentenary of Maryland Statehood.

2339	**1585** 22c. multicoloured	90	30

1586 Rockne

1988. American Sports Personalities. Birth Centenary of Knute Rockne (football player and coach).

2340	**1586** 22c. multicoloured	90	20

1587 Earth

1988. No value expressed.

2341	**1587** (25c.) multicoloured	80	20

A1588 Map, Settlers, Indians, "Calmare Nyckel" and "Fagel Grip"

1988. Air. 350th Anniv of Founding of New Sweden (settlement in America).

A2345	**A1588** 44c. multicoloured	1·70	70

1589 Common Pheasant

1988
2346	**1589**	25c. multicoloured	80	20

1590 Flag and Clouds

1988
2347	**1590**	25c. multicoloured	90	30

1591 "Aerodrome No. 5" and Langley

1988. Air. Aviation Pioneers. Samuel Pierpont Langley.
A2348	**1591**	45c. multicoloured	1·40	30

1593 Flag over Half Dome, Yosemite National Park

1988
2352	**1593**	25c. blue, red and green	90	20

1594 Palmetto Trees and Sea Grass

1988. Bicentenary of South Carolina Statehood.
2353	**1594**	25c. multicoloured	90	20

1595 Rose-breasted Grosbeak on Dogwood

1988. Multicoloured
2354	25c. Type **1595**		90	20
2355	25c. Saw-whet owl on Eastern hemlock		90	20

1597 Ouimet

1988. American Sports Personalities. 75th Anniv of Francis Ouimet's Open Golf Championship Victory.
2356	**1597**	25c. multicoloured	1·10	20

1598 Old Man of the Mountain

1988. Bicentenary of New Hampshire Statehood.
2357	**1598**	25c. multicoloured	1·10	20

1599 Sikorsky and Vought Sikorsky VS-300 Helicopter Prototype

1988. Air. Aviation Pioneers. Igor Sikorsky.
A2358	**1599**	36c. multicoloured	1·20	45

1600 Carriage and Capitol Building, Williamsburg

1988. Bicentenary of Virginia Statehood.
2359	**1600**	25c. multicoloured	1·10	20

1601 Rose

1988. Greetings Stamp.
2360	**1601**	25c. multicoloured	95	20

1602 Trinity Church, Wall Street and Federal Hall, New York City

1988. Bicentenary of New York Statehood.
2361	**1602**	25c. multicoloured	1·10	20

1603 Roses

1988. Greetings Stamp.
2362	**1603**	45c. multicoloured	1·40	60

1604 Gymnast

1988. Olympic Games, Seoul.
2363	**1604**	25c. multicoloured	95	20

1605 Locomobile, 1928

1988. Classic Cars. Multicoloured.
2364	25c. Type **1605**		1·50	45
2365	25c. Pierce-Arrow, 1929		1·50	45
2366	25c. Cord, 1931		1·50	45
2367	25c. Packard, 1932		1·50	45
2368	25c. Duesenberg, 1935		1·50	45

1610 Honey Bee on Clover

1988
2369	**1610**	25c. multicoloured	95	20

1611 Nathaniel Palmer (after Samuel Waldo) and "Hero"

1988. Antarctic Explorers. Multicoloured.
2370	25c. Type **1611**		1·10	30
2371	25c. Charles Wilkes (after Samuel Bell Waugh) and "Polar Star"		1·10	30
2372	25c. Richard E. Byrd and Ford Trimotor "Floyd Bennett"		1·10	30
2373	25c. Lincoln Ellsworth and Northrop Gamma "Polar Star"		1·10	30

1615 Buck (Gustav Dentzel)

1988. American Folk Art. Carousel Animals. Multicoloured.
2374	25c. Type **1615**		1·10	25
2375	25c. Armoured horse (Daniel C. Muller)		1·10	25
2376	25c. Camel (Charles Looff)		1·10	25
2377	25c. Goat (Charles Looff)		1·10	25

1619 American Bald Eagle and Moon

1988
2378	**1619**	$8.75 multicoloured	24·00	12·00

1620 "Madonna and Child" (detail, Sandro Botticelli)

1988. Christmas. Multicoloured.
2379	25c. Type **1620**		85	20
2380	25c. "White Christmas" (horiz)		85	20

1622 "Happy Birthday"

1988. Greetings Stamps. Multicoloured.
2381	25c. Type **1622**		1·10	30
2382	25c. "Thinking of you"		1·10	30
2383	25c. "Love you"		1·10	30
2384	25c. "Best Wishes"		1·10	30

1626 "C.M. Russell and Friends" (Charles M. Russell)

1989. Centenary of Montana Statehood.
2385	**1626**	25c. multicoloured	95	25

1627 A. Philip Randolph

1989. Black Heritage. A. Philip Randolph (trade union activist).
2386	**1627**	25c. multicoloured	95	25

1628 Grain Elevator and Buckboard

1989. Centenary of North Dakota Statehood.
2387	**1628**	25c. multicoloured	95	25

1629 Mt. Rainer and Canoe on Reflection Lake

1989. Centenary of Washington Statehood.
2388	**1629**	25c. multicoloured	95	25

1630 "Experiment", 1788–90

1989. Paddle-steamers. Multicoloured.
2389	25c. Type **1630**		95	40
2390	25c. "Phoenix", 1809		95	40
2391	25c. "New Orleans", 1812		95	40
2392	25c. "Washington", 1816		95	40
2393	25c. "Walk in the Water", 1818		95	40

1635 Cancelled 1869 90c. Lincoln Stamp

1989. "World Stamp Expo'89" International Stamp Exhibition, Washington D.C.
2394	**1635**	25c. red, black & brown	95	25

1636 Toscanini

1989. Performing Arts and Artists. Arturo Toscanini (conductor).
2395	**1636**	25c. multicoloured	95	25

1637 "Car of History" Clock (Carlo Franzoni)

1989. Bicentenary of House of Representatives.
2396	**1637**	25c. multicoloured	95	25

1638 Eagle and Shield over Vice-President's Chair

1989. Bicentenary of Senate.
2397	**1638**	25c. multicoloured	95	25

BICENTENNIAL
EXECUTIVE BRANCH
USA
25

1639 George Washington (statue, J. Q. A. Ward)

1989. Bicentenary of Executive Branch.

2398	**1639**	25c. multicoloured	95	25

South Dakota 1889
USA25

1640 Pasque Flowers, Pioneer Woman and House

1989. Centenary of South Dakota Statehood.

2399	**1640**	25c. multicoloured	95	25

Lou Gehrig
USA
25

1641 Gehrig

1989. American Sports Personalities. Lou Gehrig (baseball player).

2400	**1641**	25c. multicoloured	95	25

1789
French Revolution · USAirmail 45

1642 Liberty, Equality and Fraternity

1989. Air. Bicentenary of French Revolution.

A2401	**1642**	45c. multicoloured	1·40	40

Hemingway
USA25

1643 Hemingway

1989. Literary Arts. Ernest Hemingway (novelist).

2402	**1643**	25c. multicoloured	95	25

USA
$2.40

1644 Astronauts planting Flag on Moon

1989. 20th Anniv of First Manned Moon Landing.

2403	**1644**	$2.40 multicoloured	7·00	3·50

25
USA
November 21, 1789
North Carolina

1645 Dogwood Blossoms

1989. Bicentenary of North Carolina Statehood.

2404	**1645**	25c. multicoloured	95	25

Letter Carriers: We Deliver! USA
25

1646 Letter Carriers

1989. Centenary of National Association of Letter Carriers.

2405	**1646**	25c. multicoloured	95	25

Bill of Rights
USA
25

1647 Eagle and Flag as Shield

1989. Bicentenary of Bill of Rights.

2406	**1647**	25c. black, red and blue	95	25

USA
25
Tyrannosaurus

1648 Tyrannosaurus Rex

1989. Prehistoric Animals. Multicoloured.

2407	25c. Type **1648**	1·20	40
2408	25c. Pteranodon	1·20	40
2409	25c. Stegosaurus	1·20	40
2410	25c. Brontosaurus	1·20	40

25
USA
AMERICA

1652 Mimbres Ritual Figure

1989. America. Pre-Columbian Carvings. Multicoloured.

2411	25c. Type **1652** (postage)	95	25
A2412	45c. Calusa "Key Marco cat" (air)	1·40	40

CHRISTMAS
USA25
Carracci, National Gallery

1654 "Dream of St. Catherine of Alexandria" (detail, Ludovico Carracci)

1989. Christmas. Multicoloured.

2413	25c. Type **1654**	95	25
2415	25c. Gifts on sleigh (horiz)	95	25

USA 25

1656 Eagle and Shield

1989. Self-adhesive. Imperf.

2416	**1656**	25c. multicoloured	95	40

WORLD STAMP EXPO'89
The classic 1869 U.S. Abraham Lincoln stamp is reborn in these four larger versions commemorating World Stamp Expo'89, held in Washington, D.C. during the 20th Universal Postal Congress of the UPU. These stamps show the issued colors and three of the trial proof color combinations.

1657 1869 90c. Lincoln Stamp in Issued and Proof Colours (image scaled to 44% of original size)

1989. "World Stamp Expo '89" International Stamp Exhibition, Washington D.C. (2nd issue). Sheet 108×83 mm. Imperf.

MS2417 **1657**	90c. black and scarlet; 90c. brown and blue; 90c. ultramarine and green; 90c. ultramarine and orange	18·00	18·00

USA
25
20th Universal Postal Congress

1658 Western Stagecoach

20th Universal Postal Congress
A review of historical methods of delivering the mail in the United States is the theme of these four stamps issued in commemoration of the convening of the 20th Universal Postal Congress in Washington, D.C. from November 13 through December 14, 1989. The United States, as host nation to the Congress for the first time in ninety-two years, welcomed more than 1,000 delegates from most of the member nations of the Universal Postal Union to the major international event.

1662 (image scaled to 47% of original size)

1989. 20th U.P.U. Congress, Washington D.C. (1st issue). Classic Mail Transport. Multicoloured.

2418	25c. Type **1658**	1·10	40
2419	25c. "Chesapeake" (Mississippi river steamer)	1·10	40
2420	25c. Curtiss JN-4 "Jenny" biplane	1·10	40
2421	25c. Motor car	1·10	40
MS2422	101×83 mm. **1662** Nos. 2418/21. Imperf	6·25	6·25

See also Nos. 2423/**MS**2427.

USAirmail
45
20th Universal Postal Congress

A1663 Hypersonic Airliner

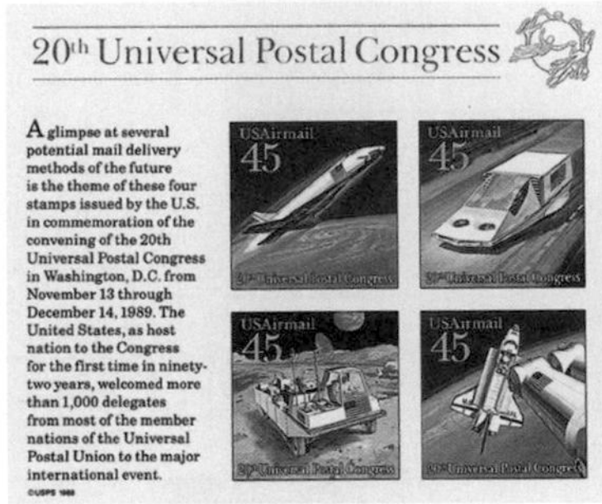
20th Universal Postal Congress
A glimpse at several potential mail delivery methods of the future is the theme of these four stamps issued by the U.S. in commemoration of the convening of the 20th Universal Postal Congress in Washington, D.C. from November 13 through December 14, 1989. The United States, as host nation to the Congress for the first time in ninety-two years, welcomed more than 1,000 delegates from most of the member nations of the Universal Postal Union to the major international event.

1667 (image scaled to 48% of original size)

1989. Air. 20th Universal Postal Union Congress, Washington D.C. (2nd issue). Mail Transport of the Future. Multicoloured.

A2423	45c. Type **A1663**	1·40	40
A2424	45c. Hovercar	1·40	40
A2425	45c. Rover vehicle delivering mail to space colony	1·40	40
A2426	45c. Space shuttle delivering mail to space station	1·40	40
MS2427	101×83 mm. **A1667** Nos. 2423/6	7·50	7·00

IDAHO
USA 25 1890

1668 Mountain Bluebird

1990. Centenary of Idaho Statehood.

2428	**1668**	25c. multicoloured	95	25

LOVE
USA
25

1669 Lovebirds

1990. Greetings Stamp.

2429	**1669**	25c. multicoloured	95	25

Ida B. Wells
25
Black Heritage USA

1670 Ida Wells

1990. Black Heritage. Ida B. Wells (civil rights activist).

2431	**1670**	25c. multicoloured	95	25

BICENTENNIAL
U.S. SUPREME COURT
USA
25
Chief Justice John Marshall

1671 John Marshall

1990. Bicentenary of Supreme Court.

2432	**1671**	25c. multicoloured	95	25

USA
15

1672 Beach Umbrella

1990

2433	**1672**	15c. multicoloured	45	25

Luis Muñoz Marín
USA
05
Governor, Puerto Rico

1674 Luis Munoz Marin

1990. Great Americans. (a) Ordinary gum.

2435	**1674**	5c. red	35	15
2437	-	20c. red	70	25
2439	-	29c. blue	95	30
2440	-	29c. black	95	30
2442	-	32c. brown	1·00	40
2443	-	32c. green	1·00	45
2444	-	32c. red	1·00	45
2445	-	32c. blue	1·00	45
2448	-	35c. black	1·10	55
2450	-	40c. blue	1·20	60
2452	-	46c. red	1·40	75
2454	-	52c. lilac	1·50	95
2456	-	55c. green	1·50	95
2458	-	75c. red	2·40	1·40
2460a	-	78c. violet	2·50	1·50

(b) Self-adhesive gum.

2464	55c. black	1·70	75
2466	77c. blue	2·10	95

DESIGNS: 20c. Virginia Apgar; 29c. (No. 2439) Earl Warren; 29c. (No. 2440) Thomas Jefferson (President, 1801–09); 32c. (No. 2442) Milton S. Hershey; 32c. (No. 2443) Cal Farley; 32c. (No. 2444) Henry Luce; 32c. (No. 2445) Lila and DeWitt Wallace (after Paul Calle); 35c. Dennis Chavez; 40c. Lt-Gen. Claire Chennault; 46c. Ruth Benedict; 52c. Hubert Humphrey (Vice-president, 1965–69); 55c. (No. 2456) Dr. Alice Hamilton; 55c. (No. 2464) Justin Morrill; 75c. Wendell Wilkie; 77c. Mary Breckinridge; 78c. Alice Paul.

1890
USA
Wyoming 25

1710 "High Mountain Meadows" (Conrad Schwiering)

1990. Centenary of Wyoming Statehood.

2471	**1710**	25c. multicoloured	95	25

The WIZARD OF Oz
USA
25

1711 Judy Garland ("The Wizard of Oz")

1990. Classic Films. Multicoloured.

2472	25c. Type **1711**	1·70	55
2473	25c. Clark Gable and Vivien Leigh ("Gone with the Wind")	1·70	55

| 2474 | | 25c. Gary Cooper ("Beau Geste") | 1·70 | 55 |
| 2475 | | 25c. John Wayne ("Stagecoach") | 1·70 | 55 |

1715 Marianne Moore

1990. Literary Arts. Marianne Moore (poet).
| 2476 | **1715** | 25c. multicoloured | 95 | 25 |

1717 Circus Wagon, 1900s ("05")

1990. Transport.
2477	-	4c. purple	35	20
2478	**1717**	5c. red	35	25
2484	-	5c. red	35	25
2485	-	5c. brown	35	25
2487	-	5c. red	35	25
2486	-	10c. green	45	25
2479	-	20c. green	60	30
2480	-	23c. blue	85	40
2481	-	32c. blue	95	40
2482	-	$1 blue and red	3·50	1·50

DESIGNS: 4c. Richard Dudgeon steam carriage, 1866; 5c. (Nos. 2485, 2487) Birch bark canoe, 1800s; 5c. (No. 2484) Circus wagon 1900s ("5c."); 10c. Tractor trailer, 1930s; 20c. Mt. Washington Cog Railway, 1870s; 23c. Lunch wagon, 1890s; 32c. Ferryboat, 1900s; $1 Benoist Type XIV flying boat.

1755 Admiralty Head, Nugent Sound

1990. Lighthouses. Multicoloured.
2516	**1755**	25c. Type	1·80	40
2517		25c. Cape Hatteras	1·80	40
2518		25c. West Quoddy Head	1·80	40
2519		25c. American Shoals	1·80	40
2520		25c. Sandy Hook, New York Harbour	1·80	40

1760 Stars and Stripes

1990. Self-adhesive. Imperf.
| 2521 | **1760** | 25c. red and blue | 1·10 | 75 |

1761 Slater Mill

1990. Bicentenary of Rhode Island Statehood.
| 2522 | **1761** | 25c. multicoloured | 95 | 25 |

1763 Bobcat

1990. Wildlife.
| 2523 | **1763** | $2 multicoloured | 4·75 | 1·90 |

1769 Jesse Owens

1990. American Olympic Medal Winners. Multicoloured.
2530		25c. Type **1769**	1·10	35
2531		25c. Ray Ewry	1·10	35
2532		25c. Hazel Wightman	1·10	35
2533		25c. Eddie Eagan	1·10	35
2534		25c. Helene Madison	1·10	35

1774 Assiniboine

1990. American Folk Art. Indian Headdresses. Multicoloured.
2535		25c. Type **1774**	1·20	35
2536		25c. Cheyenne	1·20	35
2537		25c. Comanche	1·20	35
2538		25c. Flathead	1·20	35
2539		25c. Shoshone	1·20	35

1779 Micronesian Outrigger Canoe and Flag

1990. Fourth Anniv of Ratification of Marshall Islands and Micronesia Compacts of Free Association. Multicoloured.
| 2540 | | 25c. Type **1779** | 95 | 25 |
| 2541 | | 25c. Marshallese stick chart, outrigger canoe and flag | 95 | 25 |

1781 Killer Whales

1990. Marine Mammals. Multicoloured.
2542		25c. Type **1781**	95	35
2543		25c. Northern sea lions	95	35
2544		25c. Sea otter	95	35
2545		25c. Common dolphin	95	35

1785 Grand Canyon

1990. America. Natural World. Multicoloured.
| 2546 | | 25c. Type **1785** (postage) | 95 | 25 |
| A2547 | | 45c. Tropical island coastline (air) | 1·40 | 50 |

1787 Eisenhower and Soldiers

1990. Birth Cent of Dwight David Eisenhower (President, 1953–61).
| 2548 | **1787** | 25c. multicoloured | 1·10 | 25 |

1788 "Madonna and Child" (Antonello da Messina)

1990. Christmas. Multicoloured.
| 2549 | | 25c. Type **1788** | 95 | 25 |
| 2551 | | 25c. Christmas tree | 95 | 25 |

1790 Tulip

1991. No value expressed.
| 2552 | **1790** | (29c.) multicoloured | 1·10 | 25 |

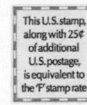

1791

1991. No value expressed. Make-up rate stamp.
| 2556 | **1791** | (4c.) red and brown | 35 | 20 |

1792 Stars and Stripes

1991. No value expressed. Self-adhesive. Imperf.
| 2557 | **1792** | (29c.) red, blue and black | 1·10 | 60 |

1794 Federal Palace, Berne, and Capitol, Washington

1991. 700th Anniv of Swiss Confederation.
| 2559 | **1794** | 50c. multicoloured | 1·70 | 85 |

1795 Farm

1991. Bicentenary of Vermont Statehood.
| 2560 | **1795** | 29c. multicoloured | 1·10 | 25 |

1796 Fawn

1991.
| 2561 | **1796** | 19c. multicoloured | 60 | 25 |

1797 Flag over Mt. Rushmore

1991.
| 2562 | **1797** | 29c. red, brown & black | 95 | 25 |

1798 Tulip

1991.
| 2564 | **1798** | 29c. multicoloured | 95 | 25 |

1799 Wood Duck

1991. (a) Inscriptions in black.
| 2565 | **1799** | 29c. multicoloured | 95 | 25 |

(b) Inscriptions in red.
| 2567 | | 29c. multicoloured | 95 | 25 |

1800 Flag and Olympic Rings

1991.
| 2569 | **1800** | 29c. multicoloured | 95 | 25 |

1801 Quimby and Bleriot XI Airplane

1991. Air. Aviation Pioneers. Harriet Quimby (first American woman pilot).
| A2570 | **1801** | 50c. multicoloured | 1·80 | 50 |

1802 American Bald Eagle

1991. 50th Anniv of "E Series" Defence Bonds.
| 2571 | **1802** | 29c. multicoloured | 95 | 25 |

1803 Heart-shaped Globe

1991. Greetings Stamps. Multicoloured.
| 2572 | | 29c. Type **1803** | 95 | 25 |
| 2574 | | 52c. Fischer's lovebirds (21×35 mm) | 1·40 | 45 |

1805 Hot-air Balloon

1991.
| 2575 | **1805** | 19c. multicoloured | 70 | 45 |

1806 Piper and Piper J-3 Cub

1991. Air. Aviation Pioneers. William Piper.
| A2576 | **1806** | 40c. multicoloured | 1·40 | 45 |

1807 Saroyan

1991. Literary Arts. 10th Death Anniv of William Saroyan (dramatist and novelist).
| 2578 | **1807** | 29c. multicoloured | 95 | 25 |

1808 Flags on Parade

1991. 125th Anniv of Memorial Day.
| 2579 | **1808** | 29c. multicoloured | 95 | 25 |

1809 Royal Wulff

1991. Fishing Flies. Multicoloured.
2580		29c. Type **1809**	1·80	45
2581		29c. Jock Scott	1·80	45
2582		29c. Apte tarpon fly	1·80	45
2583		29c. Lefty's deceiver	1·80	45
2584		29c. Muddler minnow	1·80	45

1814 Porter and Score

1991. Performing Arts and Artists. Birth Centenary of Cole Porter (composer).

2585	**1814**	29c. multicoloured	95	25

1815 American Bald Eagle

1991. U.S. Olympic Festival.

2586	**1815**	$9.95 multicoloured	28·00	10·50

A1816 U.S.S. "Glacier" (ice-breaker) near Palmer Station

1991. Air. 30th Anniv of Antarctic Treaty.

A2587	**A1816**	50c. multicoloured	1·70	60

1817 American Kestrel

1991. Birds. Multicoloured.

2588	1c. Type **1817**	25	15
2589	3c. Eastern bluebird	25	15
2590	30c. Common cardinal ("Cardinal")	95	35

For Nos. 2588/9 and 2c. but with face value expressed as "1c" etc see No. 3023 etc.

1823 Liberty Torch

1991. Self-adhesive. Imperf.

2591	**1823**	29c. green, gold & black	1·10	45

1824 South-West Asia Service Medal

1991. Operations Desert Shield and Desert Storm (liberation of Kuwait).

2592	**1824**	29c. multicoloured	95	25

1825 American Bald Eagle

1991.

2594	**1825**	$2.90 multicoloured	9·50	3·50

1826 Pole Vaulting

1991. Olympic Games, Barcelona (1992). Multicoloured.

2595	29c. Type **1826**	95	35
2596	29c. Throwing the discus	95	35
2597	29c. Running	95	35
2598	29c. Throwing the javelin	95	35
2599	29c. Hurdling	95	35

1831 Rowing Boat

1991

2600	**1831**	19c. multicoloured	70	35

1832 Coins and Banknotes

1991. Cent Convention of American Numismatic Association.

2603	**1832**	29c. multicoloured	1·10	35

1833 Shot at Goal

1991. Centenary of Basketball.

2604	**1833**	29c. multicoloured	1·10	35

1834 Stan Laurel and Oliver Hardy

1991

2605	**1834**	29c. black, violet and red	1·20	35
2606	-	29c. black, red and violet	1·20	35
2607	-	29c. black, violet and red	1·20	35
2608	-	29c. black, violet and red	1·20	35
2609	-	29c. black, red and violet	1·20	35

DESIGNS: No. 2606, Edgar Bergen and Charlie McCarthy; 2607, Jack Benny; 2608, Fanny Brice; 2609, Bud Abbott and Lou Costello.

1839 American Bald Eagle

1991

2610	**1839**	$14 multicoloured	33·00	17·00

1840 Burma Road Convoy

1991. 50th Anniv of America's Entry into Second World War. Multicoloured.

2611	29c. Type **1840**	95	70
2612	29c. America's first peacetime draft	95	70
2613	29c. Lend-Lease Act	95	70
2614	29c. Roosevelt and Churchill (Atlantic Charter)	95	70
2615	29c. Munitions factory	95	70
2616	29c. Sinking of "Reuben James" (destroyer)	95	70
2617	29c. Gas mask (Civil Defence)	95	70
2618	29c. Delivery of "Patrick Henry" (first "Liberty" freighter)	95	70
2619	29c. U.S.S. "West Virginia" and U.S.S. "Tennessee" ablaze, Pearl Harbor	95	70
2620	29c. US Declaration of War on Japan	95	70

1850 Pennsylvania Avenue, 1903

1991. Bicentenary of District of Columbia.

2621	**1850**	29c. multicoloured	1·10	35

1851 Matzeliger

1991. Black Heritage. Jan Ernst Matzeliger (inventor of shoe lasting machine).

2622	**1851**	29c. multicoloured	1·10	35

1852 Flag

1991

2623	**1852**	23c. blue, red and black	85	50

1853 Postal Service Emblem and Olympic Rings

1991

2624	**1853**	$1 multicoloured	3·50	1·70

1854 "Mariner 10" and Mercury

1991. Space Exploration. Multicoloured.

2625	29c. Type **1854**	1·30	50
2626	29c. Venus and "Mariner 2"	1·30	50
2627	29c. Earth and "Landsat"	1·30	50
2628	29c. Moon and Lunar Orbiter	1·30	50
2629	29c. "Viking" Orbiter and Mars	1·30	50
2630	29c. Jupiter and "Pioneer 11"	1·30	50
2631	29c. "Voyager 2" and Saturn	1·30	50
2632	29c. Uranus and "Voyager 2"	1·30	50
2633	29c. Neptune and "Voyager 2"	1·30	50
2634	29c. Pluto	1·30	50

1864 Early Explorers from Asia

1991. Air. America. Voyages of Discovery.

A2635	**1864**	50c. multicoloured	1·80	85

1865 "Madonna and Child with Donor" (detail, Antoniazzo Romano)

1991. Christmas. No value expressed. Multicoloured.

2636	(29c.) Type **1865**	95	45
2637	(29c.) Santa Claus in chimney (horiz)	95	45
2639	(29c.) Santa Claus checking list (horiz)	95	25
2640	(29c.) Santa Clause leaving by chimney (horiz)	95	25
2642	(29c.) Santa Claus on sleigh (horiz)	95	25

1871 Eagle and Shield

1991. Inscr "Bulk Rate USA".

2644	**1871**	(10c.) multicoloured	35	25

For design T **1871** but inscribed "USA Bulk Rate" see Nos. 2800/1.

1872 Ice Hockey

1992. Winter Olympic Games, Albertville. Multicoloured.

2645	29c. Type **1872**	95	25
2646	29c. Figure skating	95	25
2647	29c. Speed skating	95	25
2648	29c. Skiing	95	25
2649	29c. Two-man bobsleigh	95	25

1877 1869 15c. Columbus Stamp

1992. "World Columbian Stamp Expo '92", Chicago.

2650	**1877**	29c. multicoloured	95	35

1878 Du Bois

1992. Black Heritage. William Edward Burghardt Du Bois (founder of Niagara Movement (precursor of National Association for Advancement of Colored People)).

2651	**1878**	29c. multicoloured	95	35

1879 Heart in Envelope

1992. Greetings Stamp.

2652	**1879**	29c. multicoloured	95	35

1880 Catcher and Baserunner

1992. Addition of Baseball to Olympic Games.

2653	**1880**	29c. multicoloured	1·10	45

1881 Flag over White House

1992. Bicentenary of White House.

2654	**1881**	29c. red and blue	95	35

1882 Seeking Queen Isabella's Support

1992. 500th Anniv of Discovery of America by Columbus. Multicoloured.

2655	29c. Type **1882**	1·10	35
2656	29c. Crossing the Atlantic	1·10	35
2657	29c. Approaching land	1·10	35
2658	29c. Coming ashore	1·10	35

1886 Exchange Facade and Trading Floor

1992. Bicentenary of New York Stock Exchange.

2659	**1886**	29c. green, black and red	95	35

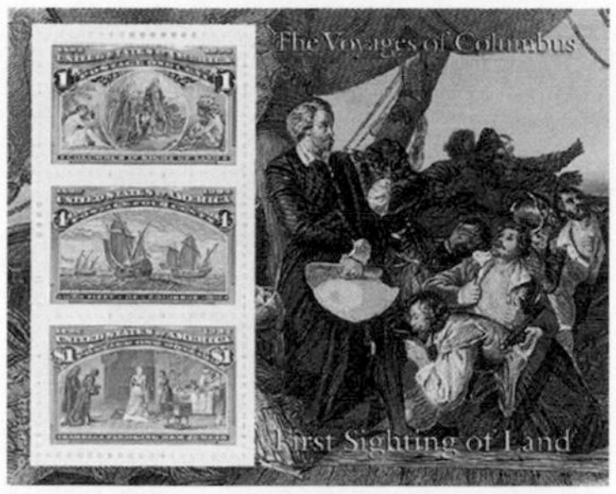

1887 First Sighting of Land (image scaled to 43% of original size)

1992. "World Columbian Stamp Expo '92", Chicago (2nd issue). Six sheets, each 111×90 mm containing reproductions of 1893 Columbian Exposition issue.

MS2660a/f	**1887**	1c. deep blue, 4c. blue, $1 vermilion; 2c. brown, 3c. green, $4 red; 5c. brown, 30c. red, 50c. slate; 6c. lilac, 8c. crimson, $3 green; 10c. black, 15c. green, $2 claret; $5 black	47·00	47·00

DESIGNS: No. **MS**2660a, Type **1887**; **MS**2660b, Claiming a New World; **MS**2660c, Seeking Royal Support; **MS**2660d, Royal Favour Restored; **MS**2660e, Reporting Discoveries; **MS**2660f, Christopher Columbus.

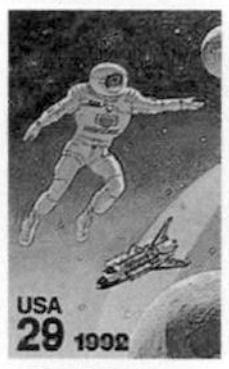

1893 Russian Cosmonaut and Space Shuttle

1992. International Space Year. Multicoloured.

2661	29c. Type **1893**	1·10	35
2662	29c. American astronaut and "Mir" space station	1·10	35
2663	29c. "Apollo" and "Vostok" spacecraft and Sputnik	1·10	35
2664	29c. "Soyuz", "Mercury" and "Gemini" spacecraft	1·10	35

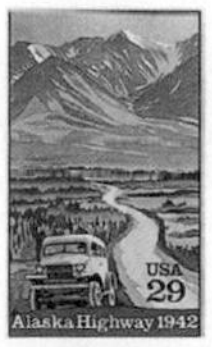

1897 Army Lorry using New Highway

1992. 50th Anniv of Alaska Highway.

2665	**1897**	29c. multicoloured	95	35

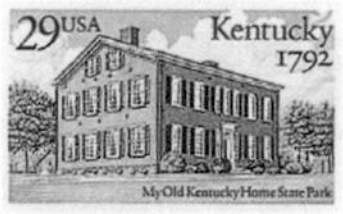

1898 My Old Kentucky Home State Park, Bardstown

1992. Bicentenary of Kentucky Statehood.

2666	**1898**	29c. multicoloured	95	35

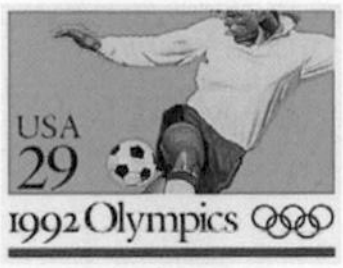

1899 Football

1992. Olympic Games, Barcelona. Multicoloured.

2667	29c. Type **1899**	95	35
2668	29c. Gymnastics	95	35
2669	29c. Volleyball	95	35
2670	29c. Boxing	95	35
2671	29c. Swimming	95	35

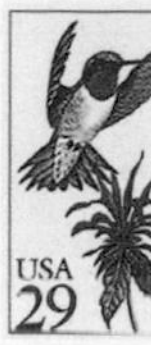

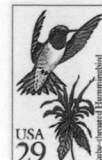

1904 Ruby-throated Hummingbird

1992. Hummingbirds. Multicoloured.

2672	29c. Type **1904**	1·10	35
2673	29c. Broad-billed hummingbird	1·10	35
2674	29c. Costa's hummingbird	1·10	35
2675	29c. Rufous hummingbird	1·10	35
2676	29c. Calliope hummingbird	1·10	35

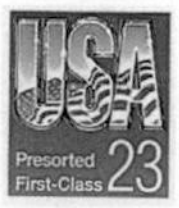

1909 Flag in "USA"

1992. Presorted First Class stamp.

2678	**1909**	23c. multicoloured	85	50

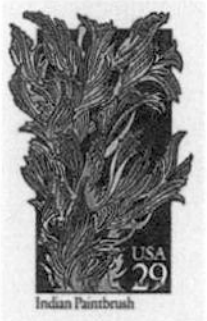

1910 Indian Paintbrush

1992. Wild Flowers. Multicoloured.

2680	29c. Type **1910**	95	50
2681	29c. Fragrant water lily	95	50
2682	29c. Meadow beauty	95	50
2683	29c. Jack-in-the-pulpit	95	50
2684	29c. California poppy	95	50
2685	29c. Large-flowered trillium	95	50
2686	29c. Tickseed	95	50
2687	29c. Shooting star	95	50
2688	29c. Stream violet	95	50
2689	29c. Bluets	95	50
2690	29c. Herb Robert	95	50
2691	29c. Marsh marigold	95	50
2692	29c. Sweet white violet	95	50
2693	29c. Claret cup cactus	95	50
2694	29c. White mountain avens	95	50
2695	29c. Sessile bellwort	95	50
2696	29c. Blue flag	95	50
2697	29c. Harlequin lupine	95	50
2698	29c. Twinflower	95	50
2699	29c. Common sunflower	95	50
2700	29c. Sego lily	95	50
2701	29c. Virginia bluebells	95	50
2702	29c. Ohi'a lehua	95	50
2703	29c. Rosebud orchid	95	50
2704	29c. Showy evening primrose	95	50
2705	29c. Fringed gentian	95	50
2706	29c. Yellow lady's slipper	95	50
2707	29c. Passionflower	95	50
2708	29c. Bunchberry	95	50
2709	29c. Pasqueflower	95	50
2710	29c. Round-lobed hepatica	95	50
2711	29c. Wild columbine	95	50
2712	29c. Fireweed	95	50
2713	29c. Indian pond lily	95	50
2714	29c. Turk's cap lily	95	50
2715	29c. Dutchman's breeches	95	50
2716	29c. Trumpet honeysuckle	95	50
2717	29c. Jacob's ladder	95	50
2718	29c. Plains prickly pear	95	50
2719	29c. Moss campion	95	50
2720	29c. Bearberry	95	50
2721	29c. Mexican hat	95	50
2722	29c. Harebell	95	50
2723	29c. Desert five spot	95	50
2724	29c. Smooth Solomon's seal	95	50
2725	29c. Red maids	95	50
2726	29c. Yellow skunk cabbage	95	50
2727	29c. Rue anemone	95	50
2728	29c. Standing cypress	95	50
2729	29c. Wild flax	95	50

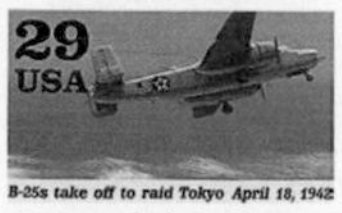

1911 Doolittle Raid on Tokyo

1992. United States Participation in Second World War. Multicoloured.

2730	29c. Type **1911**	95	75
2731	29c. Ration stamps	95	75
2732	29c. Douglas SBD-3 Dauntless on aircraft carrier (Battle of Coral Sea)	95	75
2733	29c. Japanese occupation of Corregidor	95	75
2734	29c. Japanese invasion of Aleutian Islands	95	75
2735	29c. Allies decipher enemy codes	95	75
2736	29c. U.S.S. "Yorktown" ablaze (Battle of Midway)	95	75
2737	29c. Woman engaged in war effort	95	75
2738	29c. Marines landing at Guadalcanal	95	75
2739	29c. Allied tanks in North Africa	95	75

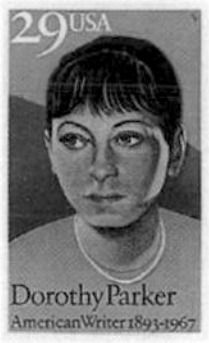

1921 Dorothy Parker

1992. Literary Arts. Dorothy Parker (short story writer, poet and critic).

2740	**1921**	29c. multicoloured	95	35

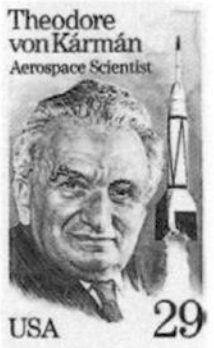

1922 Von Karman and Rocket

1992. Theodore von Karman (space pioneer).

2741	**1922**	29c. multicoloured	95	35

1923 Flag and "I pledge allegiance ..."

1992. Centenary of Pledge of Allegiance.

2742	**1923**	29c. mult (value in blk)	95	35
2743	**1923**	29c. mult (value in red)	2·40	70

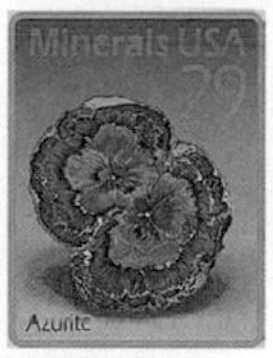

1924 Azurite

1992. Minerals. Multicoloured.

2744	29c. Type **1924**	95	35
2745	29c. Copper	95	35
2746	29c. Variscite	95	35
2747	29c. Wulfenite	95	35

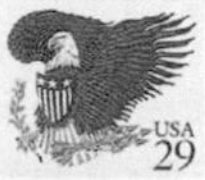

1928 Eagle and Shield

1992. Self-adhesive. Imperf.

2748	**1928**	29c. mult (inscr in red)	95	45
2749	**1928**	29c. mult (inscr in grn)	95	45
2750	**1928**	29c. mult (inscr in brn)	95	45

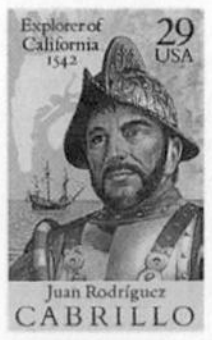

1929 Spanish Galleon, Map and Cabrillo

1992. 450th Anniv of Discovery of California by Juan Rodriguez Cabrillo.

2751	**1929**	29c. multicoloured	95	35

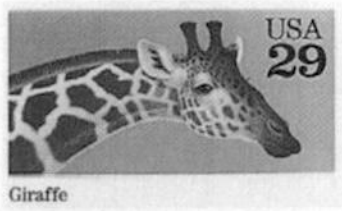

1930 Giraffe

1992. Wild Animals. Multicoloured.

2752	29c. Type **1930**	95	35
2753	29c. Giant panda	95	35
2754	29c. Greater flamingo ("Flamingo")	95	35
2755	29c. King penguins	95	35
2756	29c. White Bengal tiger	95	35

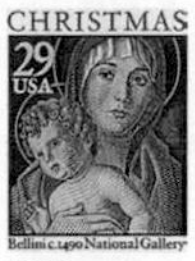

1935 "Madonna and Child with Saints" (Giovanni Bellini)

1992. Christmas. Multicoloured.

2757	29c. Type **1935**	95	35
2758	29c. Wheeled racing horse (horiz)	95	35
2759	29c. Toy steam locomotive (horiz)	95	35
2760	29c. Toy steam engine (horiz)	95	35
2761	29c. Toy steamer (horiz)	95	35

No. 2759 also comes imperf and self adhesive.

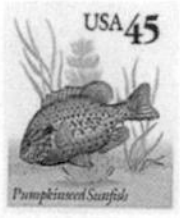

1940 Pumpkinseed

1992

2767	**1940**	45c. multicoloured	1·40	45

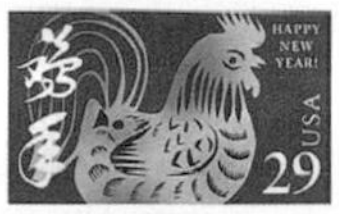

1941 Rooster

1992. New Year

2768	**1941**	29c. multicoloured	1·10	35

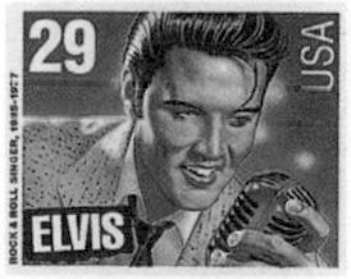

1942 Elvis Presley

1993. Elvis Presley (rock singer and actor).

2769	**1942**	29c. multicoloured	1·10	35

For similar design but inscr "ELVIS PRESLEY" see Type **1987**.

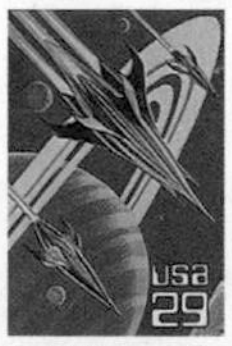

1943 Spacecraft and Ringed-planet

1993. Space Fantasy. Multicoloured.

2770	29c. Type **1943**	95	35
2771	29c. Space capsules	95	35
2772	29c. Astronauts	95	35
2773	29c. Spaceship	95	35
2774	29c. Spacecraft and planet	95	35

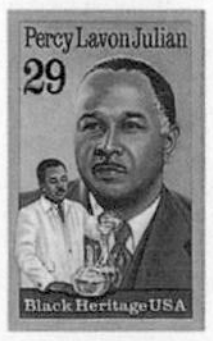

1948 Julian

1993. Black Heritage. Percy Lavon Julian (research chemist).

2775	**1948**	29c. multicoloured	95	35

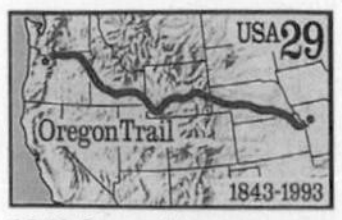

1949 Route Map

1993. 150th Anniv of Oregon Trail.

2776	**1949**	29c. multicoloured	95	35

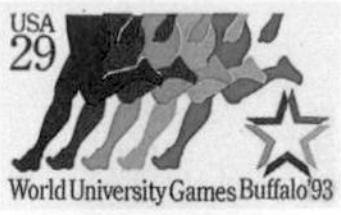

1950 Athletes

1993. World University Games, Buffalo.

2777	**1950**	29c. multicoloured	95	35

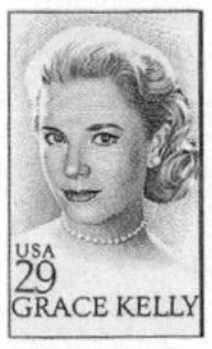

1951 Princess Grace

1993. Tenth Death Anniv of Princess Grace of Monaco (former Grace Kelly).

2778	**1951**	29c. blue	95	35

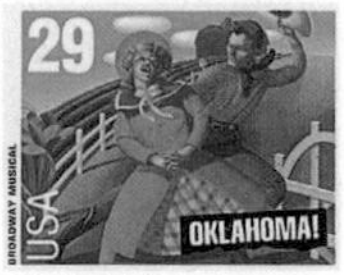

1952 "Oklahoma"

1993. Broadway Musicals. Multicoloured. (a) No frame. Size 36×28 mm.

2779	29c. Type **1952**	95	35

(b) With frame. Size 35×27 mm.

2780	29c. "Show Boat"	95	35
2781	29c. "Porgy and Bess"	95	35
2782	29c. Type **1952**	95	35
2783	29c. "My Fair Lady"	95	35

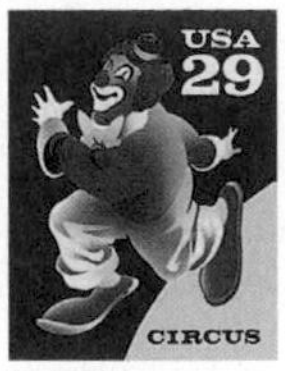

1956 Clown

1993. Bicentenary of First Circus Performance in America. Multicoloured.

2784	29c. Type **1956**	95	35
2785	29c. Ringmaster	95	35
2786	29c. Trapeze artiste	95	35
2787	29c. Elephant	95	35

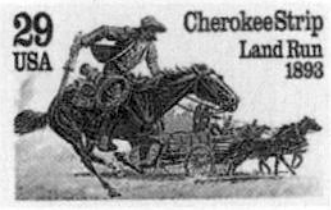

1960 Pioneers racing to Cherokee Strip

1993. Centenary of Cherokee Strip Land Run.

2789	**1960**	29c. multicoloured	95	35

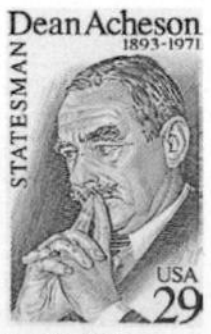

1961 Acheson

1993. Birth Centenary of Dean Acheson (Secretary of State, 1949–53).

2790	**1961**	29c. green	95	35

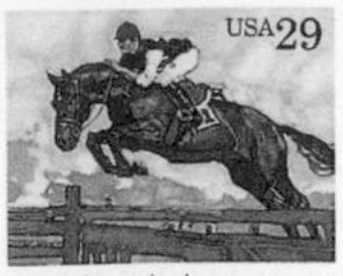

1962 Steeplechase

1993. Equestrian Sports. Multicoloured.

2791	29c. Type **1962**	95	35
2792	29c. Thoroughbred racing	95	35
2793	29c. Harness racing	95	35
2794	29c. Polo	95	35

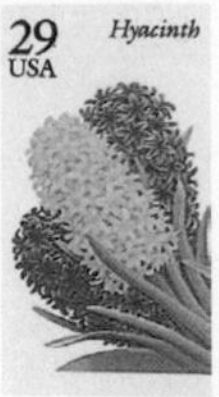

1966 Hyacinths

1993. Garden Flowers. Multicoloured.

2795	29c. Type **1966**	95	35
2796	29c. Daffodils	95	35
2797	29c. Tulips	95	35
2798	29c. Irises	95	35
2799	29c. Lilac	95	35

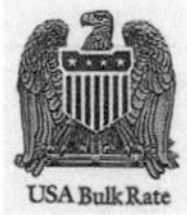

1971 Eagle and Shield

1993. Coil stamps. Inscr "USA Bulk Rate". Multicoloured, colours of eagle given.

2800	**1971**	(10c.) yellow and brown	35	25
2801	**1971**	(10c.) gold and brown	35	25

No. 2802 exists with both ordinary gum and self-adhesive gum.

For design as Type **1971** but inscr "Bulk Rate USA" see No. 2644.

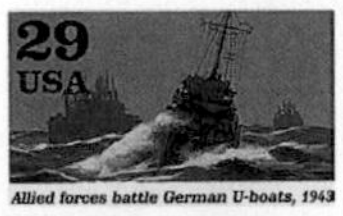

1972 Atlantic Convoy

1993. United States Participation in Second World War. Multicoloured.

2803	29c. Type **1972**	95	80
2804	29c. Treating the wounded	95	80
2805	29c. Allied attack on Sicily	95	80
2806	29c. Consolidated B-24 Liberators bombing Ploesti refineries	95	80
2807	29c. G.I.s with mail from home	95	80
2808	29c. Allied invasion of Italy	95	80
2809	29c. War Savings stamps and bonds	95	80
2810	29c. Willie and Joe (cartoon characters)	95	80
2811	29c. Gold Star emblem	95	80
2812	29c. Marine assault on Tarawa, Gilbert Islands	95	80

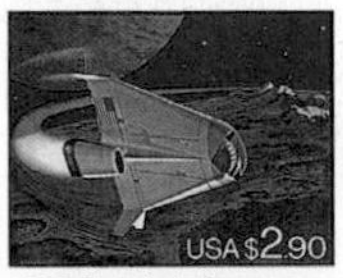

1982 Futuristic Space Shuttle

1993

2813	**1982**	$2.90 multicoloured	8·25	3·50

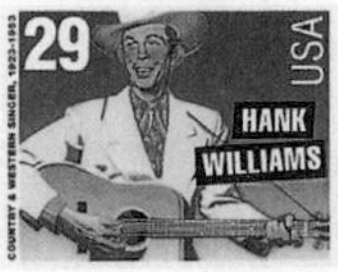

1983 Hank Williams

1993. Country Music. Multicoloured. (a) No frame.

2815	29c. Type **1983**	1·10	50
2816	29c. Patsy Cline	1·10	50
2817	29c. Carter Family	1·10	50
2818	29c. Bob Wills	1·10	50

(b) With frame.

2819	29c. Type **1983**	95	35
2820	29c. Carter Family	95	35
2821	29c. Patsy Cline	95	35
2822	29c. Bob Wills	95	35

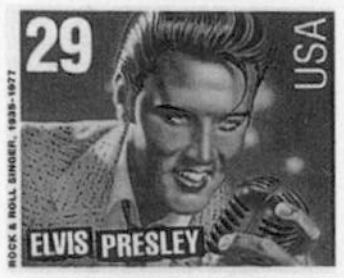

1987 Elvis Presley

1993. Rock and Rhythm and Blues Music. Multicoloured. (a) No frame.

2823	29c. Type **1987**	1·20	45
2824	29c. Buddy Holly	1·20	45
2825	29c. Ritchie Valens	1·20	45
2826	29c. Bill Haley	1·20	45
2827	29c. Dinah Washington	1·20	45
2828	29c. Otis Redding	1·20	45
2829	29c. Clyde McPhatter	1·20	45

(b) With frame.

2830	29c. Type **1987**	1·10	35
2831	29c. Bill Haley	1·10	35
2832	29c. Clyde McPhatter	1·10	35
2833	29c. Ritchie Valens	1·10	35
2834	29c. Otis Redding	1·10	35
2835	29c. Buddy Holly	1·10	35
2836	29c. Dinah Washington	1·10	35

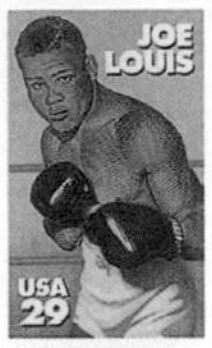

1994 Louis

1993. Joe Louis (boxer).

2837	**1994**	29c. multicoloured	95	35

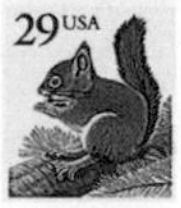

1995 Red Squirrel

1993. Self-adhesive. Imperf.

2838	**1995**	29c. multicoloured	95	35

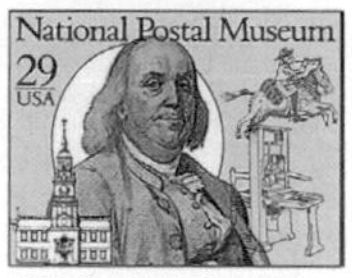

1996 Benjamin Franklin, Liberty Hall, Philadelphia, Post Rider and Printing Press

1993. Inauguration of National Postal Museum, Washington. Multicoloured.

2839	29c. Type **1996**	95	35
2840	29c. Pony Express rider, Civil War soldier and stagecoach	95	35
2841	29c. Curtiss JN-4 "Jenny" biplane, pilot, railway mail/ baggage car and mail truck	95	35
2842	29c. Gold rush miner's letter and stamps	95	35

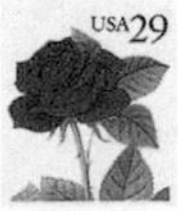

2000 Red Rose

1993. Self-adhesive. (a) Pink rose. Imperf (29c.) or roul (32c.).

2843	**2000**	29c. multicoloured	95	35
3047	**2000**	32c. multicoloured	95	45

(b) Yellow rose. Roul.

3266	32c. multicoloured	1·10	55

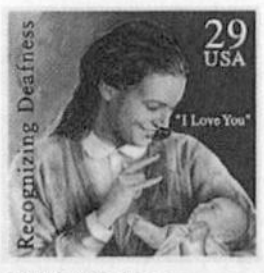

2001 Mother signing "I Love You"

1993. Deaf Communication. Multicoloured.

2845	29c. Type **2001**	95	35
2846	29c. "I Love You" in sign language	95	35

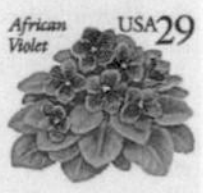

2003 African Violet

1993

2847	**2003**	29c. multicoloured	95	35

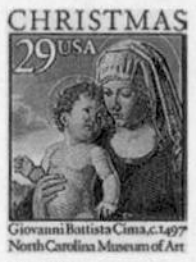

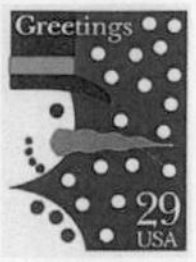

2004 "Madonna and Child in a Landscape" (Giovanni Battista Cima de Conegliano)

2005 Snowman

1993. Christmas. (a) Type **2004**.

2848	29c. multicoloured	95	35

(b) As T **2005**. Multicoloured. Perf or imperf (self-adhesive).

2849	29c. Type **2005**	95	35
2850	29c. Toy soldier	95	35
2851	29c. Jack-in-the-box	95	35
2852	29c. Reindeer	95	35

All designs come in more than one version, which differ slightly in size.

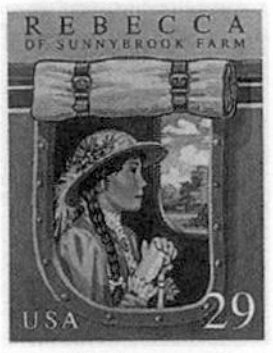

2009 "Rebecca of Sunnybrook Farm" (Kate Douglas Wiggin)

1993. Classic Children's Books. Multicoloured.

2863	29c. Type **2009**	95	35
2864	29c. "Little House on the Prairie" (Laura Ingalls Wilder)	95	35
2865	29c. "The Adventures of Huckleberry Finn" (Mark Twain)	95	35
2866	29c. "Little Women" (Louisa May Alcott)	95	35

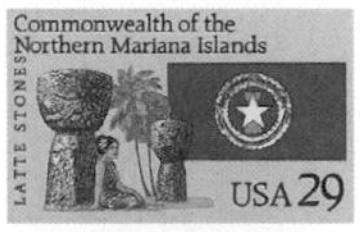

2013 Latte Stones and Flag

1993. 15th Anniv of Commonwealth of Northern Mariana Islands.

2867	**2013**	29c. multicoloured	95	35

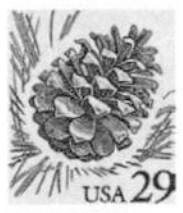

2014 Pine Cone

1993. Self-adhesive. Imperf.

2868	**2014**	29c. red, green and black	95	45

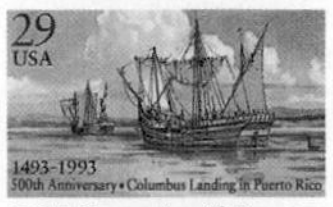

2015 Caravels off Puerto Rico

1993. 500th Anniv of Columbus's Landing at Puerto Rico.

2869	**2015**	29c. multicoloured	95	35

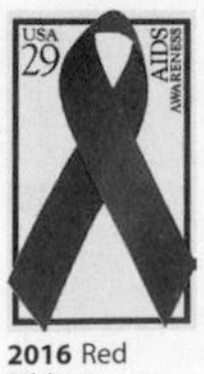

2016 Red Ribbon

1993. World AIDS Day.

2870	**2016**	29c. red and black	95	35

2017 Skiing

1994. Winter Olympic Games. Lillehammer. Multicoloured.

2872	29c. Type **2017**		95	45
2873	29c. Luge		95	45
2874	29c. Ice dancing		95	45
2875	29c. Cross-country skiing		95	45
2876	29c. Ice hockey		95	45

2022 Murrow

1994. 29th Death Anniv of Edward Murrow (radio and television journalist).

2877	**2022**	29c. brown	95	35

2023 Heart-shaped Sun

1994. Greetings Stamp. Self-adhesive. Imperf.

2878	**2023**	29c. multicoloured	95	35

2024 Davis

1994. Black Heritage. Dr. Allison Davis (educationist).

2879	**2024**	29c. sepia and brown	95	45

2025 American Bald Eagle

1994. Self-adhesive. Imperf.

2880	**2025**	29c. multicoloured	95	35

2026 Pekingese

1994. New Year.

2881	**2026**	29c. multicoloured	1·30	50

2027 Dove on Heart-shaped Bouquet of Roses

1994. Greetings Stamps. Multicoloured.

2882	29c. Type **2027** (16×24½ mm)		95	35
2883	29c. Type **2027** (18×27 mm)		1·10	35
2884	52c. Doves on flower arrangement		1·40	70

2029 Troopers on Western Frontier

1994. "Buffalo Soldiers" (U.S. Army black regiments).

2885	**2029**	29c. multicoloured	1·10	45

2030 Rudolph Valentino

1994. Silent Screen Stars.

2886	**2030**	29c. black, violet and red	1·10	50
2887	-	29c. black, violet and red	1·10	50
2888	-	29c. black, red and violet	1·10	50
2889	-	29c. black, red and violet	1·10	50
2890	-	29c. black, violet and red	1·10	50
2891	-	29c. black, red and violet	1·10	50
2892	-	29c. black, violet and red	1·10	50
2893	-	29c. black, violet and red	1·10	50
2894	-	29c. black, red and violet	1·10	50
2895	-	29c. black, red and violet	1·10	50

DESIGNS: No. 2887, Clara Bow; 2888, Charlie Chaplin; 2889, Lon Chaney; 2890, John Gilbert; 2891, Zasu Pitts; 2892, Harold Lloyd; 2893, Keystone Cops; 2894, Theda Bara; 2895, Buster Keaton.

2040 Lilies

1994. Garden Flowers. Multicoloured.

2896	29c. Type **2040**		95	45
2897	29c. Zinnias		95	45
2898	29c. Gladioli		95	45
2899	29c. Marigolds		95	45
2900	29c. Roses		95	45

2045 Surrender at Saratoga (after John Trumbull)

1994

2901	**2045**	$1 blue	3·00	1·30

2046 U.S.A. Player kicking Ball

2049 (image scaled to 36% of original size)

1994. World Cup Football Championship, U.S.A. Multicoloured.

2902	29c. Type **2046**		95	45
2903	40c. Controlling the ball		1·40	60
2904	50c. Heading the ball		1·80	85
MS2905	134×89 mm. **2049** Nos. 2902/4		5·25	4·25

2050 Liberating New Guinea

1994. United States Participation in Second World War. Multicoloured.

2906	29c. Type **2050**		1·80	1·30

2907	29c. P-51 escorting B-17 bombers		1·80	1·30
2908	29c. Normandy Landings		1·80	1·30
2909	29c. Glider and paratroops		1·80	1·30
2910	29c. Submarine crew		1·80	1·30
2911	29c. Liberating Rome		1·80	1·30
2912	29c. Troops clearing Saipan bunkers		1·80	1·30
2913	29c. Red Ball Express truck		1·80	1·30
2914	29c. U.S.S. "Pennsylvania" (battleship) (Battle of Leyte Gulf)		1·80	1·30
2915	29c. Battle of the Bulge		1·80	1·30

2060 Statue of Liberty

1994. Self-adhesive. Imperf.

2918	**2060**	29c. multicoloured	95	70
3273	**2060**	32c. multicoloured	1·10	45

2061 "Triple Self-portrait"

2062 "The Four Freedoms" (image scaled to 36% of original size)

1994. Birth Centenary of Norman Rockwell (illustrator).

2919	**2061**	29c. multicoloured	95	50
MS2920	135×89 mm. **2062** 50c. ×4, multicoloured		6·50	5·25

2063 Astronauts planting Flag on Moon

2064 Planting Flag (image scaled to 33% of original size)

1994. 25th Anniv of First Manned Moon Landing.

2921	**2063**	$9.95 multicoloured	28·00	21·00
MS2922	147×195 mm. **2064** 29c. ×12, multicoloured		14·00	11·00

2065 William Hudson's "General", 1855

1994. Locomotives. Multicoloured.

2923	29c. Type **2065**		95	45
2924	29c. Walter McQueen's "Jupiter", 1868		95	45
2925	29c. Wilson Eddy's No. 242, 1874		95	45
2926	29c. Theodore Ely's No. 10, 1881		95	45
2927	29c. William Buchanan's No. 999, 1893		95	45

2070 Meany

1994. Birth Centenary of George Meany (trades unionist).

2928	**2070**	29c. blue	95	45

2071 Presidents Washington and Jackson

1994

2929	**2071**	$5 green	14·00	7·00

2072 Al Jolson

1994. Popular Music. Multicoloured.

2930	29c. Type **2072**		1·10	50
2931	29c. Bing Crosby		1·10	50
2932	29c. Ethel Waters		1·10	50
2933	29c. Nat "King" Cole		1·10	50
2934	29c. Ethel Merman		1·10	50

2077 "Male Type (eastern seaboard)"

1994. Literary Arts. Birth Centenary of James Thurber (writer and cartoonist).

2935	**2077**	29c. multicoloured	95	45

2078 Bessie Smith

1994. Jazz and Blues Music. Multicoloured.

2936	29c. Type **2078**		1·50	50
2937	29c. Muddy Waters		1·50	50
2938	29c. Billie Holiday		1·50	50
2939	29c. Robert Johnson		1·50	50
2940	29c. Jimmy Rushing		1·50	50
2941	29c. "Ma" Rainey		1·50	50
2942	29c. Mildred Bailey		1·50	50
2943	29c. Howlin' Wolf		1·50	50

2086/2089 Sea Life

1994. Wonders of the Seas.

2944	**2086**	29c. multicoloured	95	35
2945	**2087**	29c. multicoloured	95	35
2946	**2088**	29c. multicoloured	95	35
2947	**2089**	29c. multicoloured	95	35

Nos. 2944/7 were issued together, se-tenant, forming the composite design illustrated.

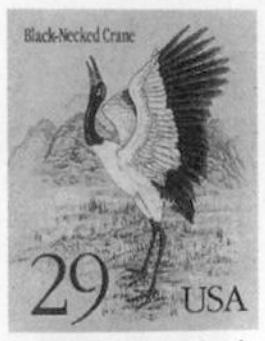

2090 Black-necked Crane

1994. Cranes. Multicoloured.

2948	29c. Type **2090**	1·20	50
2949	29c. Whooping crane	1·20	50

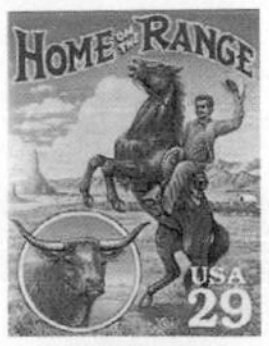

2092 Home on the Range

1994. Legends of the West. Multicoloured.

2950	29c. Type **2092**	1·10	80
2951	29c. Buffalo Bill (William Cody)	1·10	80
2952	29c. Jim Bridger	1·10	80
2953	29c. Annie Oakley	1·10	80
2954	29c. Native American culture	1·10	80
2955	29c. Chief Joseph	1·10	80
2956	29c. Bill Pickett	1·10	80
2957	29c. Bat Masterson	1·10	80
2958	29c. John Fremont	1·10	80
2959	29c. Wyatt Earp	1·10	80
2960	29c. Nellie Cashman	1·10	80
2961	29c. Charles Goodnight	1·10	80
2962	29c. Geronimo	1·10	80
2963	29c. Kit Carson	1·10	80
2964	29c. Wild Bill Hickok	1·10	80
2965	29c. Western wildlife	1·10	80
2966	29c. Jim Beckwourth	1·10	80
2967	29c. Bill Tilghman	1·10	80
2968	29c. Sacagawea	1·10	80
2969	29c. Overland mail	1·10	80

Each stamp is inscribed on the back, under the gum, with a brief history of the subject depicted.

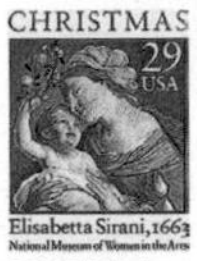

2097 "Virgin and Child" (Elisabetta Sirani)

2100 Common Cardinal

1994. Christmas. Multicoloured. (a) Perf.

2970	29c. Type **2097**	95	35
2972	29c. Stocking	95	35

(b) Self-adhesive. Imperf.

2973	29c. Santa Claus	1·10	50
2974	29c. Type **2100**	1·10	50

Nos. 2972/3 are as Type **2097** in size.

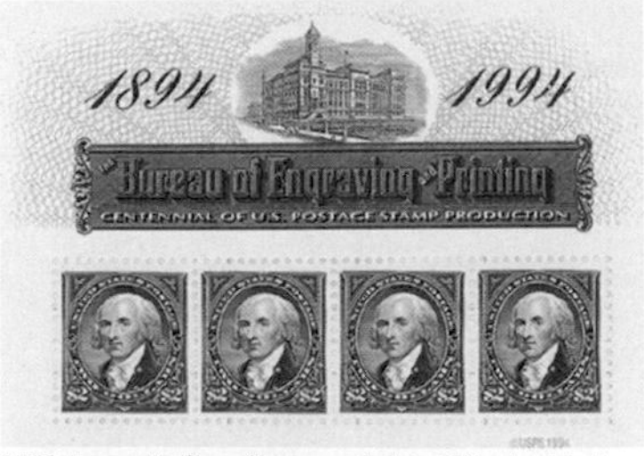

2101 James Madison (image scaled to 45% of original size)

1994. Centenary of Bureau of Engraving and Printing. Sheet 107×75 mm containing reproductions of 1894 issue.

MS2975 **2101**	$2 ×4 blue	26·00	26·00

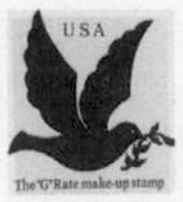

2102 Dove with Olive Branch

1994. Make-up Rate stamp. No value expressed.

2976	**2102**	(3c.) blue, brn & red	35	15

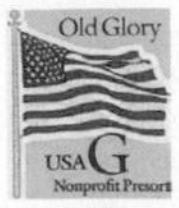

2103 Old Glory

1994. With service indicator. (a) Nonprofit Presort. Green background.

2978	**2103**	(5c.) multicoloured	45	35

(b) Postcard rate. Yellow background.

2979	(20c.) mult (black "G")	85	35
2980	(20c.) mult (red "G")	95	35

(c) First-Class Presort. Blue background.

2981	(25c.) multicoloured	95	60

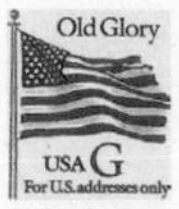

2104 Old Glory

1994. No value expressed. Perf (Nos. 2982, 2984); perf or imperf (self-adhesive) (No. 2986).

2982	**2104**	(32c.) mult (red "G")	1·50	70
2984	**2104**	(32c.) mult (blue "G")	95	35
2986	**2104**	(32c.) mult (black "G")	1·50	35

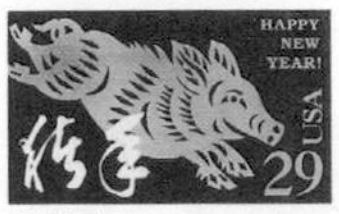

2106 Boar

1994. New Year.

2991	**2106**	29c. multicoloured	1·30	85

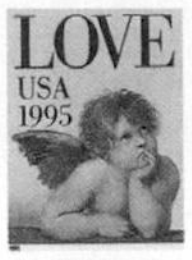

2107 Cherub (detail from "Sistine Madonna" by Raphael)

1995. Greetings Stamp. No value expressed. (a) Size 20×26 mm.

2992	**2107**	(32c.) multicoloured	95	35

(b) Size 18×22 mm. Self-adhesive. Imperf.

2993	(32c.) multicoloured	1·10	45

For Type **2107** but with face value "32", see No. 3035.

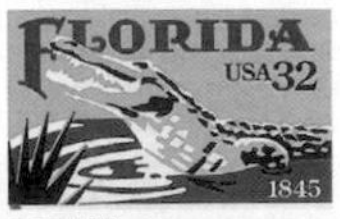

2108 Alligator

1995. 150th Anniv of Florida Statehood.

2994	**2108**	32c. multicoloured	95	45

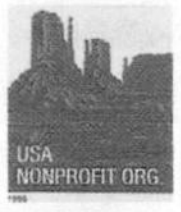

2109 Butte

1995. Non-profit Organizations Stamp. Ordinary or self-adhesive gum.

2995	**2109**	(5c.) orange, blue and yellow	35	15

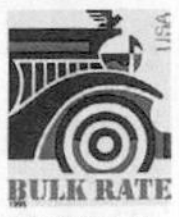

2110 Front of Motor Car

1995. Bulk Rate Stamp. Ordinary or self-adhesive gum.

2997	**2110**	(10c.) vermilion, black and red	45	25

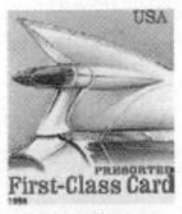

2111 Motor Car Tail Fin

1995. Presorted First Class Postcard Stamp. Ordinary or self-adhesive gum.

2999	**2111**	(15c.) multicoloured	60	35

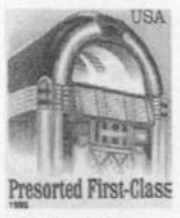

2112 Juke Box

1995. Presorted First Class Stamp. Ordinary or self-adhesive gum.

3003	**2112**	(25c.) multicoloured	1·20	85

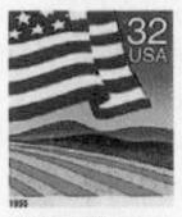

2113 Flag over Field

1995. Self-adhesive. Imperf.

3007	**2113**	32c. multicoloured	1·10	50

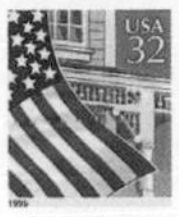

2114 Flag over Porch

1995. Perf or imperf (self-adhesive).

3008	**2114**	32c. multicoloured	1·10	50

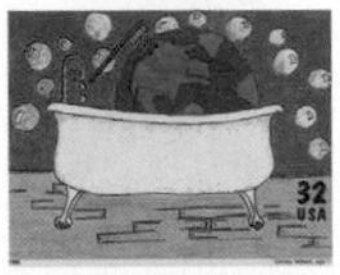

2115 Flag over Porch

1995. 25th Anniv of Earth Day. Multicoloured.

3017	32c. Type **2115**	1·10	50
3018	32c. Solar energy (Jennifer Michalove)	1·10	50
3019	32c. Youth planting tree (Brian Hailes)	1·10	50
3020	32c. Family cleaning up beach (Melody Kiper)	1·10	50

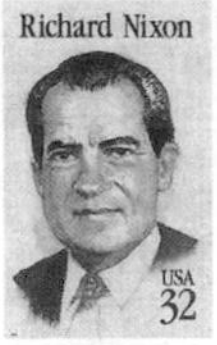

2119 Nixon

1995. First Death Anniv of Richard Nixon (President, 1968–74).

3021	**2119**	32c. multicoloured	95	45

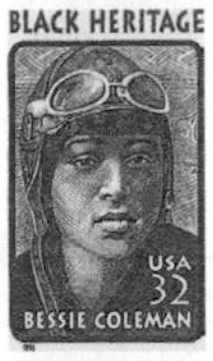

2120 Bessie Coleman

1995. Black Heritage. Bessie Coleman (aviator).

3022	**2120**	32c. black and red	95	45

1995. Birds. Value expressed as "1c" etc. Multicoloured.

3023	1c. As T **1817**	25	15
3024	2c. Red-headed woodpecker	25	15
3025	3c. As No. 2589	25	15

No. 3023 also comes self-adhesive.

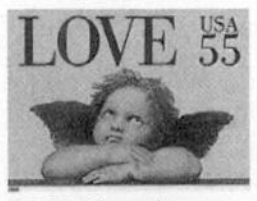

2125 Cherub

1995. Greetings Stamps. Details from "Sistine Madonna" by Raphael. Ordinary or self-adhesive gum Nos. 3035/6.

3035	**2107**	32c. multicoloured (19½×27 mm)	95	45
3036	**2125**	55c. multicoloured (27×20½ mm)	1·70	85
3038	**2107**	32c. multicoloured (18½×22 mm)	95	50
3039	**2125**	55c. multicoloured (21½×19 mm)	1·50	70

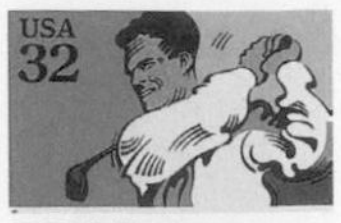

2126 Golf

1995. Sports. Multicoloured.

3040	32c. Type **2126**	1·10	50
3041	32c. Volleyball	1·10	50
3042	32c. Baseball	1·10	50
3043	32c. Bowls	1·10	50
3044	32c. Tennis	1·10	50

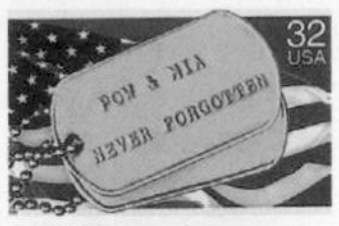

2131 Flag and Identification Tags

1995. Memorial Day.

3045	**2131**	32c. multicoloured	95	50

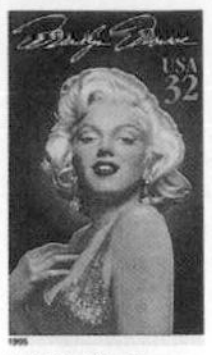

2132 Marilyn Monroe

1995. Legends of Hollywood.

3046	**2132**	32c. multicoloured	1·20	50

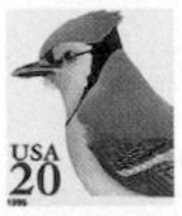

2133 Blue Jay

1995. Ordinary or self-adhesive gum.

3048	**2133**	20c. multicoloured	60	35

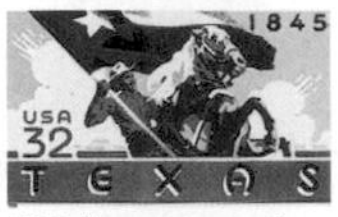

2134 Horseman carrying Flag

1995. 150th Anniv of Texas Statehood.

3051	**2134**	32c. multicoloured	1·00	50

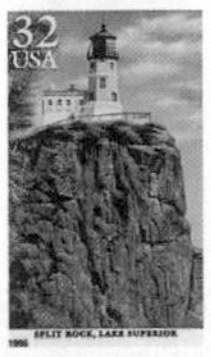

2135 Split Rock, Lake Superior

1995. Great Lakes Lighthouses. Multicoloured.

3052	32c. Type **2135**	1·00	50
3053	32c. St. Joseph, Lake Michigan	1·00	50
3054	32c. Spectacle Reef, Lake Huron	1·00	50
3055	32c. Marblehead, Lake Erie	1·00	50
3056	32c. Thirty Mile Point, Lake Ontario	1·00	50

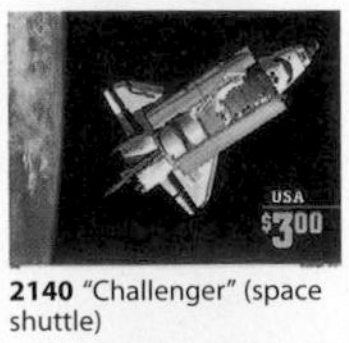

2140 "Challenger" (space shuttle)

1995

3057	**2140**	$3 multicoloured	9·25	4·25

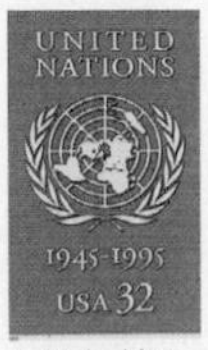

2141 Emblem

1995. 50th Anniv of U.N.O.

3058	**2141**	32c. blue	1·00	50

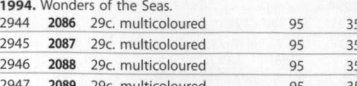

2142 U.S.S. "Monitor" and C.S.S. "Virginia" (ironclads) in Battle

1995. 130th Anniv of End of American Civil War. Multicoloured.

3059	32c. Type **2142**	1·20	80
3060	32c. Gen. Robert E. Lee (Confederate)	1·20	80
3061	32c. Clara Barton (Union nurse)	1·20	80
3062	32c. Gen. Ulysses Grant (Union)	1·20	80
3063	32c. Battle of Shiloh	1·20	80
3064	32c. Jefferson Davis (Confederate President)	1·20	80
3065	32c. Vice-Admiral David Farragut (Union)	1·20	80
3066	32c. Frederick Douglass (journalist and diplomat)	1·20	80
3067	32c. Rear-Admiral Raphael Semmes (Confederate)	1·20	80
3068	32c. Abraham Lincoln (U.S. President, 1861–65)	1·20	80
3069	32c. Harriet Tubman (black rights campaigner)	1·20	80
3070	32c. Brig.-Gen. Stand Watie (Confederate)	1·20	80
3071	32c. Gen. Joseph Johnston (Confederate)	1·20	80
3072	32c. Major-Gen. Winfield Hancock (Union)	1·20	80
3073	32c. Mary Chesnut (Confederate diarist)	1·20	80
3074	32c. Battle of Chancellorsville	1·20	80
3075	32c. Major-Gen. William Sherman (Union)	1·20	80
3076	32c. Phoebe Pember (Confederate nurse)	1·20	80
3077	32c. Lt.-Gen. Thomas "Stonewall" Jackson (Confederate)	1·20	80
3078	32c. Battle of Gettysburg	1·20	80

Each stamp is inscribed on the back, under the gum, with a brief history of the subject depicted.

2147 Peaches

1995. Multicoloured. Ordinary or self-adhesive gum.

3079	32c. Type **2147**	1·10	60
3080	32c. Pear	1·10	60

2149 King Horse, 1910 (Stein and Goldstein)

2150 Indian Pony, 1905 (Daniel Muller)

2151 Armoured Horse, 1912 (Stein and Goldstein)

2152 Lillie Belle, 1917 (C. W. Parker Co)

1995. Carousel Horses.

3085	**2149**	32c. multicoloured	1·10	50
3086	**2150**	32c. multicoloured	1·10	50
3087	**2151**	32c. multicoloured	1·10	50
3088	**2152**	32c. multicoloured	1·10	50

2153 Launch of Space Shuttle "Endeavour"

1995

3089	**2153**	$10.75 multicoloured	27·00	14·50

2154 1913 and 1976 Women's Rights Marches

1995. 75th Anniv of Ratification of 19th Amendment (giving women the right to vote).

3090	**2154**	32c. multicoloured	1·00	50

2155 Coleman Hawkins

1995. Jazz Musicians. Multicoloured. (a) With value in white.

3091	32c. Louis Armstrong	1·10	50

(b) With value in black.

3092	32c. Type **2155**	1·40	70
3093	32c. Louis Armstrong	1·40	70
3094	32c. James Johnson	1·40	70
3095	32c. Jelly Roll Morton	1·40	70
3096	32c. Charlie Parker	1·40	70
3097	32c. Eubie Blake	1·40	70
3098	32c. Charles Mingus	1·40	70
3099	32c. Thelonious Monk	1·40	70
3100	32c. John Coltrane	1·40	70
3101	32c. Erroll Garner	1·40	70

2165 Marines raising Flag on Iwo Jima

1995. United States Participation in Second World War. Multicoloured.

3102	32c. Type **2165**	1·00	80
3103	32c. Liberation of Manila	1·00	80
3104	32c. Troops advancing on Okinawa	1·00	80
3105	32c. Bridge across River Elbe	1·00	80
3106	32c. Liberation of concentration camp survivors	1·00	80
3107	32c. German Surrender at Reims	1·00	80
3108	32c. Refugees	1·00	80
3109	32c. President Truman announcing Japanese surrender	1·00	80
3110	32c. News of victory reaches America	1·00	80
3111	32c. Honouring returned service personnel	1·00	80

2175 Asters

1995. Garden Flowers. Multicoloured.

3112	32c. Type **2175**	1·00	50
3113	32c. Chrysanthemums	1·00	50
3114	32c. Dahlias	1·00	50
3115	32c. Hydrangea	1·00	50
3116	32c. Rudbeckias	1·00	50

2180 Rickenbacker

1995. Aviation Pioneers. Eddie Rickenbacker (fighter pilot).

3117	**2180**	60c. multicoloured	1·80	70

2181 Racoon Butterflyfish, Soldierfish, Shell and Palau Flag

1995. First Anniv of Independence of Palau.

3118	**2181**	32c. multicoloured	1·00	50

2182 Santa Claus on Rooftop

1995. Christmas (1st issue). Victorian Designs from writing tablet (T **2182**) or postcards (others). Ordinary or self-adhesive gum.

3119	32c. Type **2182**	1·10	45
3120	32c. Boy holding jumping jack	1·10	45
3121	32c. Boy holding tree	1·10	45
3122	32c. Santa Claus making toy sleigh	1·10	45

See also Nos. 3153/7.

2186 The Yellow Kid

1995. Centenary of Comic Strips. Multicoloured.

3131	32c. Type **2186**	1·10	70
3132	32c. Katzenjammer Kids	1·10	70
3133	32c. Little Nemo in Slumberland	1·10	70
3134	32c. Bringing Up Father	1·10	70
3135	32c. Krazy Kat	1·10	70
3136	32c. Rube Goldberg's Inventions	1·10	70
3137	32c. Toonerville Folks	1·10	70
3138	32c. Gasoline Alley	1·10	70
3139	32c. Barney Google	1·10	70
3140	32c. Little Orphan Annie	1·10	70
3141	32c. Popeye	1·10	70
3142	32c. Blondie	1·10	70
3143	32c. Dick Tracy	1·10	70
3144	32c. Alley Oop	1·10	70
3145	32c. Nancy	1·10	70
3146	32c. Flash Gordon	1·10	70
3147	32c. Li'l Abner	1·10	70
3148	32c. Terry and the Pirates	1·10	70
3149	32c. Prince Valiant	1·10	70
3150	32c. Brenda Starr, Reporter	1·10	70

Each stamp is inscribed on the back, under the gum, with a brief history of the subject depicted.

2187 "Swift" (racing sloop) and Academy Chapel

1995. 150th Anniv of Naval Academy, Annapolis.

3151	**2187**	32c. multicoloured	1·00	50

2188 Williams and Streetcars

1995. Literary Arts. Tennessee Williams (dramatist).

3152	**2188**	32c. multicoloured	1·00	50

2189 "Enthroned Madonna and Child" (Giotto)

2190 Midnight Angel (after Ellen Clapsaddle)

2191 Children Sledding

1995. Christmas (2nd issue). (a) Ordinary gum. Perf.

3153	**2189**	32c. multicoloured	1·00	35

(b) Self-adhesive. Roul (No. 3137) or imperf (No. 3187).

3155	**2190**	32c. multicoloured	1·00	50
3157	**2191**	32c. multicoloured	1·10	50

2192 Polk

1995. Birth Bicentenary of James K. Polk (President, 1844–49).

3158	**2192**	32c. brown	1·00	45

2193 Columbia Battery-powered Car, 1898

1996. Veteran Cars. Multicoloured.

3159	32c. Type **2193**	1·10	65
3160	32c. Winton Car, 1899	1·10	65
3161	32c. White Steam-powered Car, 1901	1·10	65
3162	32c. Duryea Car, 1893	1·10	65
3163	32c. Haynes Car, 1894	1·10	65

2198 Delicate Arch, Arches National Park

1996. Centenary of Utah Statehood.

3164	**2198**	32c. multicoloured	1·00	55

2199 Crocus

1996. Garden Flowers. Multicoloured.

3165	32c. Type **2199**	1·10	65
3166	32c. Winter aconites	1·10	65
3167	32c. Pansies	1·10	65
3168	32c. Snowdrops	1·10	65
3169	32c. Anemones	1·10	65

2204 Just

1996. Black Heritage. Ernest Just (marine biologist).

3170	**2204**	32c. multicoloured	1·00	55

2205 The Castle (first Smithsonian building)

1996. 150th Anniv of Smithsonian Institution.

3171	**2205**	32c. multicoloured	1·00	55

2206 Rat

1996. New Year.

3172	**2206**	32c. multicoloured	1·40	75

2207 Frederic Ives (halftone process)

1996. Pioneers of Communication. Multicoloured.

3173	32c. Type **2207**	1·10	65
3174	32c. William Dickson (motion pictures)	1·10	65
3175	32c. Eadweard Muybridge (photography)	1·10	65
3176	32c. Ottmar Mergenthaler (linotype)	1·10	65

2211 Face,
Map and
Compass

1996. 50th Anniv of Fulbright Scholarships (international educational exchange programme).
3177 **2211** 32c. multicoloured 1·00 55

2212 Jacqueline
Cochran

1996. Aviation Pioneers. Jacqueline Cochran (first woman to fly faster than speed of sound).
3178 **2212** 50c. multicoloured 1·50 90

2213
Mountains

1996. Non-profit Organizations. No value expressed. Ordinary or self-adhesive gum.
3179 **2213** (5c.) multicoloured 35 20

2214 Runners

1996. 100th Boston Marathon.
3183 **2214** 32c. multicoloured 1·00 55

2215 Decathlon

1996. Olympic Games, Atlanta. Multicoloured.
3184 32c. Type **2215** 1·10 75
3185 32c. Men's canoeing 1·10 75
3186 32c. Women's running 1·10 75
3187 32c. Women's diving 1·10 75
3188 32c. Men's cycling 1·10 75
3189 32c. Freestyle wrestling 1·10 75
3190 32c. Women's gymnastics 1·10 75
3191 32c. Women's sailboarding 1·10 75
3192 32c. Men's putting the shot 1·10 75
3193 32c. Women's football 1·10 75
3194 32c. Beach volleyball 1·10 75
3195 32c. Men's rowing 1·10 75
3196 32c. Men's sprinting 1·10 75
3197 32c. Women's swimming 1·10 75
3198 32c. Women's softball 1·10 75
3199 32c. Men's hurdling 1·10 75
3200 32c. Men's swimming 1·10 75
3201 32c. Men's gymnastics 1·10 75
3202 32c. Show jumping 1·10 75
3203 32c. Men's basketball 1·10 75

2216 "Red Poppy"

1996. Tenth Death Anniv of Georgia O'Keeffe (painter).
3204 **2216** 32c. multicoloured 1·00 55

2217 State
Capitol,
Nashville

1996. Bicentenary of Tennessee. Ordinary or self-adhesive gum.
3205 **2217** 32c. multicoloured 1·20 80

2218 Fancy
Dance

1996. Traditional Amerindian Dances.
3207 32c. Type **2218** 1·10 65
3208 32c. Butterfly dance 1·10 65
3209 32c. Traditional dance 1·10 65
3210 32c. Raven dance 1·10 65
3211 32c. Hoop dance 1·10 65

2223 Mastodon

1996. Prehistoric Animals.
3212 32c. Type **2223** 1·10 65
3213 32c. Sabre-tooth tiger 1·10 65
3214 32c. Eohippus 1·10 65
3215 32c. Woolly mammoth 1·10 65

2227 Woman
and Ribbon

1996. Breast Cancer Awareness Campaign.
3216 **2227** 32c. multicoloured 1·00 55

2228 James
Dean

1996. Legends of Hollywood.
3217 **2228** 32c. multicoloured 1·00 55

2229 Mighty
Casey

1996. Folk Heroes. Multicoloured.
3218 32c. Type **2229** 1·10 65
3219 32c. Paul Bunyan 1·10 65
3220 32c. John Henry 1·10 65
3221 32c. Pecos Bill 1·10 65

2233 "The
Discus
Thrower"
(Miron)

1996. Centenary of Modern Olympic Games.
3222 **2233** 32c. brown 1·20 75

2234 "Young
Corn" (Grant
Wood)

1996. 150th Anniv of Iowa Statehood. Ordinary or self-adhesive gum.
3223 **2234** 32c. multicoloured 1·20 75

2235 Early Postal Carrier
and Horse-drawn Mail
Wagon

1996. Centenary of Free Rural Postal Deliveries.
3225 **2235** 32c. multicoloured 1·00 55

2236 "Robert E. Lee"

1996. 19th-century Paddle-steamers. Multicoloured. Self-adhesive.
3226 32c. Type **2236** 1·00 55
3227 32c. "Sylvan Dell" 1·00 55
3228 32c. "Far West" 1·00 55
3229 32c. "Rebecca Everingham" 1·00 55
3230 32c. "Bailey Gatzert" 1·00 55

2241 Count Basie

1996. Big Band Leaders (Nos. 3231/4) and Songwriters (Nos. 3235/8). Multicoloured.
3231 32c. Type **2241** 1·10 65
3232 32c. Tommy and Jimmy Dorsey 1·10 65
3233 32c. Glenn Miller 1·10 65
3234 32c. Benny Goodman 1·10 65
3235 32c. Harold Arlen 1·10 65
3236 32c. Johnny Mercer 1·10 65
3237 32c. Dorothy Fields 1·10 65
3238 32c. Hoagy Carmichael 1·10 65

2249 Fitzgerald

1996. Birth Centenary of Francis Scott Fitzgerald (writer).
3239 **2249** 23c. multicoloured 75 45

2250 Black-footed Ferret

1996. Endangered Species. Multicoloured.
3240 32c. Type **2250** 1·00 75
3241 32c. Thick-billed parrot 1·00 75
3242 32c. Hawaiian monk seal 1·00 75
3243 32c. American crocodile 1·00 75
3244 32c. Ocelot 1·00 75
3245 32c. Schaus swallowtail 1·00 75
3246 32c. Wyoming toad 1·00 75
3247 32c. Brown pelican 1·00 75
3248 32c. California condor 1·00 75
3249 32c. Gila trout 1·00 75
3250 32c. San Francisco garter snake 1·00 75
3251 32c. Woodland caribou 1·00 75
3252 32c. Florida panther 1·00 75
3253 32c. Piping plover 1·00 75
3254 32c. Florida manatee 1·00 75

2251 Circuit Boards
covering Brain

1996. Computer Technology. 50th Anniv of ENIAC (Army computer system).
3255 **2251** 32c. multicoloured 1·00 55

2252 Family
at Fireside

2256 Ice
Skaters

1996. Christmas (1st issue). Multicoloured. Ordinary or self-adhesive gum (Nos. 3256/9), self-adhesive (No. 3264).
3256 32c. Type **2252** 1·00 35
3257 32c. Decorating Christmas tree 1·00 35
3258 32c. Santa Claus in chimney and child sleeping 1·00 35
3259 32c. Mother and child carrying gifts 1·00 35
3264 32c. Type **2256** 1·10 75
See also No. 3268.

2257 Lighted Candles

1996. Festival of Hanukkah. Self-adhesive.
3265 **2257** 32c. multicoloured 1·00 55
3693 **2257** 33c. multicoloured 1·00 55

2258
Madonna and
Child (detail
from
"Adoration of
the
Shepherds",
Paolo de
Matteis)

1996. Christmas (2nd issue). Ordinary or self-adhesive gum.
3268 **2258** 32c. multicoloured 1·00 35

2259 Cycling (image scaled to 36% of original size)

1996. Professional Cycling. Sheet 133×89 mm.
MS3270 **2259** 50c. multicoloured; 50c.
multicoloured 3·25 3·00

2260 Ox

1997. New Year.
3271 **2260** 32c. multicoloured 1·00 55

2261 Davis on
Inspection Tour
in France, 1944

1997. Black Heritage. Brigadier-General Benjamin Davis. Self-adhesive.

3272	**2261**	32c. blk, lt grey & grey	1·00	55

2262 Mute Swans

1997. Greetings Stamps. Multicoloured. Self-adhesive.

3274	32c. Type **2262**	1·00	55
3275	55c. Mute swans (horiz)	1·70	75

2264 Adult and Child with Book

1997. Helping Children Learn. Self-adhesive.

3276	**2264**	32c. multicoloured	1·00	55

2265 Beetle, Moth and Lava on Citron

1997. 350th Birth Anniv of Maria Sibylla Merian (painter). Multicoloured. Self-adhesive. (a) Size 18½×24½ mm.

3277	32c. Type **2265**	1·10	55
3278	32c. Cockroaches on flowering pineapple	1·10	55

(b) Size 19½×27½ mm.

3279	32c. Type **2265**	1·50	90
3280	32c. As No. 3278	1·50	90

2267 U.S. Mail Coach

1997. "Pacific 97" International Stamp Exhibition, San Francisco.

3281	**2267**	32c. red	1·10	75
3282	-	32c. blue	1·10	75

DESIGN: No. 3282, "Richard S. Ely" (clipper).

2269 Wilder (after Michael Deas)

1997. Literary Arts. Birth Centenary of Thornton Wilder (novelist, playwright and essayist).

3283	**2269**	32c. multicoloured	1·00	55

2270 Holocaust Survivors and Wallenberg

1997. Raoul Wallenberg (Swedish diplomat) Commemoration.

3284	**2270**	32c. multicoloured	1·00	55

2271 Ceratosaurus

1997. Prehistoric Animals. Multicoloured.

3285	32c. Type **2271**	1·00	80
3286	32c. Camptosaurus (38½×30 mm)	1·00	80
3287	32c. Camarasaurus (38½×30 mm)	1·00	80
3288	32c. Brachiosaurus (30×38 mm)	1·00	80
3289	32c. Stegosaurus (38½×30 mm)	1·00	80
3290	32c. Allosaurus (38½×30 mm)	1·00	80
3291	32c. Goniopholis	1·00	80
3292	32c. Opisthias	1·00	80
3293	32c. Parasaurolophus	1·00	80
3294	32c. Edmontonia (38½×30 mm)	1·00	80
3295	32c. Einiosaurus (38½×30 mm)	1·00	80
3296	32c. Daspletosaurus (30×38½ mm)	1·00	80
3297	32c. Corythosaurus (38½×30 mm)	1·00	80
3298	32c. Ornithomimus (38½×30 mm)	1·00	80
3299	32c. Palaeosaniwa	1·00	80

Nos. 3285/99 were issued together, *se-tenant*, forming two composite designs.

2272 Bugs Bunny

1997. Bugs Bunny (cartoon character). Self-adhesive.

3300	**2272**	32c. multicoloured	1·10	80
MS3301		87×130 mm. No. 3300	1·50	55

2273 Benjamin Franklin (image scaled to 27% of original size)

1997. "Pacific 97" International Stamp Exhibition, San Francisco (2nd issue). 150th Anniv of First United States Postage Stamps. Two sheets, each 176×117 mm, as T **2273**.

MS3302	Two sheets. (a) 12 ×50c. blue (Franklin); (b) 12 ×60c. carmine (George Washington)	37·00	37·00

2274 Map of Europe and General George Marshall

1997. 50th Anniv of European Recovery Program ("Marshall Plan").

3303	**2274**	32c. multicoloured	1·00	55

2275 North American P-51 Mustang Fighter

1997. American Aircraft. Multicoloured.

3304	32c. Type **2275**	1·00	75
3305	32c. Wright Model B biplane	1·00	75
3306	32c. Piper J-3 Cub light airplane	1·00	75
3307	32c. Lockheed Vega	1·00	75
3308	32c. Northrop Alpha	1·00	75
3309	32c. Martin B-10 bomber	1·00	75
3310	32c. Vought Corsair fighter	1·00	75
3311	32c. Boeing B-47 Stratojet	1·00	75
3312	32c. Gee Bee	1·00	75
3313	32c. Beech Staggerwing	1·00	75
3314	32c. Boeing B-17 Flying Fortress bomber	1·00	75
3315	32c. Stearman PT-13 biplane	1·00	75
3316	32c. Lockheed Constellation	1·00	75
3317	32c. Lockheed P-38 Lightning fighter	1·00	75
3318	32c. Boeing P-26 "Peashooter" fighter	1·00	75
3319	32c. Ford Trimotor "Tin Goose"	1·00	75
3320	32c. Douglas DC-3	1·00	75
3321	32c. Boeing 314 Clipper flying boat	1·00	75
3322	32c. Curtiss JN-4 "Jenny" trainer	1·00	75
3323	32c. Grumman F4F Wildcat fighter	1·00	75

Each stamp is inscribed on the back, under the gum, with a description of the airplane depicted.

2276 Bear Bryant

1997. Football Coaches. Multicoloured. (a) With red line above coach's name.

3324	32c. Type **2276**	1·00	45
3325	32c. Pop Warner	1·00	45
3326	32c. Vince Lombardi	1·00	45
3327	32c. George Halas	1·00	45

(b) Without red line.

3328	32c. Type **2276**	1·00	65
3329	32c. As No. 3325	1·00	65
3330	32c. As No. 3326	1·00	65
3331	32c. As No. 3327	1·00	65

2280 "Alabama Baby" (Ella Smith) and Cloth Doll by Martha Chase

1997. American Dolls. Multicoloured.

3332	32c. Type **2280**	1·00	75
3333	32c. "The Columbian Doll" (Emma Adams and Marietta Adams Ratta)	1·00	75
3334	32c. "Raggedy Ann" (John Gruelle)	1·00	75
3335	32c. Cloth doll by Martha Chase	1·00	75
3336	32c. "American Child" (Dwees Cochran)	1·00	75
3337	32c. "Baby Coos"	1·00	75
3338	32c. Plains Indian doll	1·00	75
3339	32c. Moulded doll by Izannah Walker	1·00	75
3340	32c. "Babyland Rag"	1·00	75
3341	32c. "Scootles" (Rose O'Neill)	1·00	75
3342	32c. Doll with papier-mache head, cloth body and leather arms by Ludwig Greiner	1·00	75
3343	32c. "Betsy McCall"	1·00	75
3344	32c. "Skippy"	1·00	75
3345	32c. "Maggie Mix-up"	1·00	75
3346	32c. Wooden moveable dolls by Albert Schoenut	1·00	75

2281 Humphrey Bogart

1997. Legends of Hollywood.

3347	**2281**	32c. multicoloured	1·00	55

2282 Flag and Bandsmen

1997. Centenary of "The Stars and Stripes Forever" by John Philip Sousa.

3348	**2282**	32c. multicoloured	1·00	55

2283 Lily Pons as Rosina in "The Barber of Seville" and as Lucia in "Lucia di Lammermoor"

1997. Opera Singers. Multicoloured.

3349	32c. Type **2283**	1·00	65
3350	32c. Richard Tucker as the Duke in "Rigoletto" and in "Carmen"	1·00	65
3351	32c. Lawrence Tibbet as the Toreador in "Carmen"	1·00	65
3352	32c. Rosa Ponselle in "Norma"	1·00	65

2287 Leopold Stokowski (Philadelphia Symphony Orchestra)

1997. Classical Conductors (Nos. 3353/6) and Composers (Nos. 3357/60). Multicoloured.

3353	32c. Type **2287**	1·10	65
3354	32c. Arthur Fiedler (Boston Pops Orchestra)	1·10	65
3355	32c. George Szell (Cleveland Orchestra)	1·10	65
3356	32c. Eugene Ormandy (Philadelphia Symphony Orchestra)	1·10	65
3357	32c. Samuel Barber	1·10	65
3358	32c. Ferde Grofe	1·10	65
3359	32c. Charles Ives	1·10	65
3360	32c. Louis Moreau Gottschalk	1·10	65

2295 Varela

1997. Father Felix Varela (social reformer).

3361	**2295**	32c. violet	1·00	55

2296 U.S.A.F. Thunderbirds flying in Formation

1997. 50th Anniv of United States Air Force.

3362	**2296**	32c. multicoloured	1·00	55

2297 Lon Chaney as The Phantom of the Opera

1997. Movie Monsters. Multicoloured.

3363	32c. Type **2297**	1·00	65
3364	32c. Bela Lugosi as Dracula	1·00	65
3365	32c. Boris Karloff in "Frankenstein"	1·00	65
3366	32c. Boris Karloff as The Mummy	1·00	65
3367	32c. Lon Chaney Jr. as The Wolf Man	1·00	65

2302 Bell XS-1 Rocket Airplane

1997. 50th Anniv of First Supersonic Flight (by Charles Yeager). Self-adhesive.

3368	**2302**	32c. multicoloured	1·00	55

2303 Uniformed Women

1997. Women in Military Service.

3369	**2303**	32c. multicoloured	1·00	55

2304 Family

1997. Kwanzaa Festival. Self-adhesive.

3370	**2304**	32c. multicoloured	1·00	55
3694	**2304**	33c. multicoloured	1·00	55

2305
"Madonna
and Child
with Saints
and Angels"
(Sano di
Pietro)

1997. Christmas (1st issue). Self-adhesive.
3371 **2305** 32c. multicoloured 1·00 55

2306 Holly

1997. Christmas (2nd issue). Self-adhesive.
3372 **2306** 32c. multicoloured 1·00 55

2307 *Sojourner* (roving vehicle) (image scaled to 33% of original size)

1997. Mars "Pathfinder" Mission. Sheet 145×82 mm.
MS3373 **2307** $3 multicoloured 8·50 8·25

2308 Tiger

1998. New Year.
3374 **2308** 32c. multicoloured 1·00 55

2309 Skier

1998. Alpine Skiing.
3375 **2309** 32c. multicoloured 1·00 55

2310 Madam
Walker

1998. Black Heritage. Madam C. J. Walker (designer of cosmetics for black women). Self-adhesive.
3376 **2310** 32c. brown, grey and black 1·00 55

2311 Model T Ford   **2312** Charlie Chaplin as the Little Tramp

1998. The Twentieth Century (1st series). (a) The 1900s. Red (No. 3389) or multicoloured (others).
3377 32c. Type **2311** 1·00 75
3378 32c. President Theodore Roosevelt 1·00 75
3379 32c. Film frame from "The Great Train Robbery", 1903 1·00 75
3380 32c. Box of Crayola crayons, 1903 1·00 75
3381 32c. Children with ice cream cones, St. Louis World's Fair, 1904 1·00 75
3382 32c. Advertisement for "unfailing" elixir (Pure Food and Drugs Act, 1904) 1·00 75

3383 32c. Wright Brothers' Flyer I (first powered flight, Kitty Hawk, 1903) 1·00 75
3384 32c. "Stag at Sharkey's" (detail, George Bellows) (Ash Can Painters) 1·00 75
3385 32c. Immigrants arriving at Ellis Island 1·00 75
3386 32c. John Muir (preservationist) and mountains 1·00 75
3387 32c. Teddy bear (created 1902) 1·00 75
3388 32c. W. E. B. Du Bois (civil rights activist) 1·00 75
3389 32c. Gibson Girl (fashionable "look" created by Charles Gibson) 1·00 75
3390 32c. Baseball player (first World Series championship, 1903) 1·00 75
3391 32c. Robie House (Frank Lloyd Wright), Chicago 1·00 75

(b) The 1910s. Blue (No. 3397) or multicoloured (others).
3392 32c. Type **2312** 1·00 75
3393 32c. Eagle (Federal Reserve System (regulation of financial institutions), 1913) 1·00 75
3394 32c. George Washington Carver (botanist) and microscope (increased commercial use of peanuts and sweet potatoes) 1·00 75
3395 32c. Couple viewing "Nude Descending a Staircase, No. 2" (Marcel Duchamp) (Armory Show of avant-garde art, 1913) 1·00 75
3396 32c. Linesmen and flag (first transcontinental telephone line, 1914) 1·00 75
3397 32c. Freighter in lock (opening of Panama Canal, 1914) 1·00 75
3398 32c. Jim Thorpe (gold medal winner in pentathlon and decathlon at Olympic Games, Stockholm, 1912) 1·00 75
3399 32c. Grand Canyon (designation as National Park, 1919) 1·00 75
3400 32c. First World War recruitment poster 1·00 75
3401 32c. Scouts and camp (formation of Boy Scouts of America (1910) and Girl Scouts (1912)) 1·00 75
3402 32c. President Woodrow Wilson (Nobel Peace Prize, 1919) 1·00 75
3403 32c. Grids and hand holding pencil (first crossword puzzle created by Arthur Wynne, 1913) 1·00 75
3404 32c. Jack Dempsey (World heavyweight boxing champion, 1919–25) 1·00 75
3405 32c. Boy with construction toys 1·00 75
3406 32c. Girl beside loom (child labour reform) 1·00 75

See also Nos. 3421/35, 3496/3510, 3550/64, 3606/20, 3652/66, 3705/19, 3726/40 and 3763/77.

2313 U.S.S. "Maine"

1998. Centenary of Sinking of the "Maine" (battleship) (cause of Spanish–American War).
3407 **2313** 32c. black and red 1·00 55

2314 Southern Magnolia

1998. Flowers and Fruits. Self-adhesive. Multicoloured.
3408 32c. Type **2314** 1·00 65
3409 32c. Blue paloverde 1·00 65
3410 32c. Yellow poplar 1·00 65
3411 32c. Prairie crab apple 1·00 65
3412 32c. Pacific dogwood 1·00 65

2319 "Black Cascade, 13 Verticals"

1998. Birth Centenary of Alexander Calder (sculptor).
3413 **2319** 32c. black, grey and red 1·00 65
3414 - 32c. multicoloured 1·00 65
3415 - 32c. black, grey and red 1·00 65

3416 - 32c. multicoloured 1·00 65
3417 - 32c. black, red and grey 1·00 65
DESIGNS: No. 3414, "Untitled"; 3415, "Rearing Stallion"; 3416, "Portrait of a Young Man"; 3417, "Un Effet du Japonais".

2324 Dancers in Traditional Costumes

1998. Cinco de Mayo Festival. Self-adhesive.
3418 **2324** 32c. multicoloured 1·00 55
3594 **2324** 33c. multicoloured 1·00 55

2325 Sylvester and Tweety

1998. Sylvester and Tweety (cartoon characters). Self-adhesive.
3419 **2325** 32c. multicoloured 1·10 75
MS3420 86×130 mm. No. 3419 1·20 90

2326 Babe Ruth (baseball player)

1998. The Twentieth Century (2nd series). The 1920s. Brown (Nos. 3432/3) or mult (others).
3421 32c. Type **2326** 1·00 75
3422 32c. The Gatsby style ("The Great Gatsby" by F. Scott Fitzgerald, 1925) 1·00 75
3423 32c. Federal agents pouring away wine (after Ben Shahn) (prohibition) 1·00 75
3424 32c. Electric model steam train 1·00 75
3425 32c. Woman voter (19th Amendment, 1920) 1·00 75
3426 32c. Dinner plate and cutlery (Emily Post's writings on etiquette) 1·00 75
3427 32c. Margaret Mead (anthropologist) 1·00 75
3428 32c. Flapper doing the Charleston (after John Held jr.) 1·00 75
3429 32c. Radio 1·00 75
3430 32c. Chrysler Building, New York (Art Deco style) 1·00 75
3431 32c. Jazz trombonists 1·00 75
3432 32c. Notre Dame's Four Horsemen (college football players) 1·00 75
3433 32c. Charles Lindbergh and "Spirit of St. Louis" (first non-stop solo trans-Atlantic flight) 1·00 75
3434 32c. "Automat" (detail, Edward Hopper) (American Realism) 1·00 75
3435 32c. Torn banknote (Stock Market crash, 1929) 1·00 75

2327 Wisconsin

1998. 150th Anniv of Wisconsin Statehood.
3436 **2327** 32c. multicoloured 1·00 55

2328 Diner

1998. Presorted First-Class Mail coil stamp. Ordinary or self-adhesive gum.
3437 **2328** (25c.) multicoloured 75 55

2329 Wetlands

1998. With service indication. Ordinary or self-adhesive gum.
3439 **2329** (5c.) multicoloured 35 35

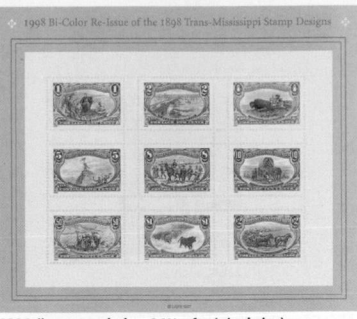

1998 Bi-Color Re-issue of the 1898 Trans-Mississippi Stamp Designs

2330 (image scaled to 26% of original size)

1998. Centenary of Trans-Mississippi Exposition, Omaha. Two sheets, each 188×161 mm, as T **2330** containing Nos. 291/299.
MS3441 No. 298, $1 ×9, black and scarlet 18·00 18·00
MS3442 No. 291, 1c. black and green; 299, 2c. black and red; 293, 4c. black and orange; 294, 5c. black and ultramarine; 294, 8c. black and chocolate; 296, 10c. black and lilac; 297, 50c. black and green; 298, $1 black and scarlet; 292, $2 black and brown (inscr changed to "Harvesting in the West") 31·00 31·00

2331 Family watching Douglas C-54 Transport

1998. 50th Anniv of Berlin Airlift (relief during Soviet blockade).
3443 **2331** 32c. multicoloured 1·00 55

2332 Leadbelly

1998. Folk Music. Multicoloured.
3444 32c. Type **2332** 1·10 75
3445 32c. Woody Guthrie 1·10 75
3446 32c. Sonny Terry 1·10 75
3447 32c. Josh White 1·10 75

2336 Mission of San Miguel

1998. 400th Anniv of Spanish Settlement at San Gabriel.
3448 **2336** 32c. multicoloured 1·00 55

2337 Mahalia Jackson

1998. Gospel Music. Multicoloured.
3449 32c. Type **2337** 1·10 75
3450 32c. Roberta Martin 1·10 75
3451 32c. Clara Ward 1·10 75
3452 32c. Sister Rosetta 1·10 75

2341 Benet

1998. Literary Arts. Birth Centenary of Stephen Vincent Benet (poet).
3453 **2341** 32c. multicoloured 1·00 55

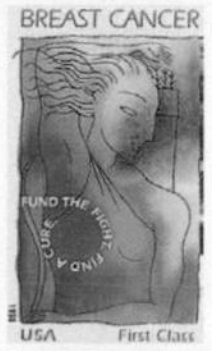

2342 Diana, The Huntress

1998. Breast Cancer Awareness Campaign. Inscr "First Class". Self-adhesive.

3454	**2342**	(32c.+8c.) mult	1·20	90

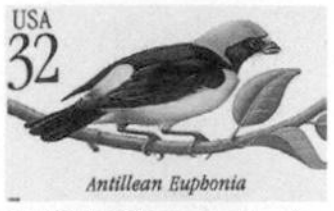

2343 Antillean Euphonia

1998. Tropical Birds. Multicoloured.

3455	32c. Type **2343**	1·00	65
3456	32c. Green-throated carib	1·00	65
3457	32c. Crested honeycreeper	1·00	65
3458	32c. Cardinal honeyeater	1·00	65

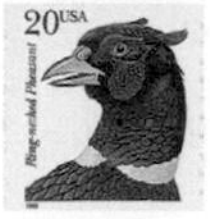

2347 Common Pheasant ("Ringed-necked Pheasant")

1998. Self-adhesive.

3459	**2347**	20c. multicoloured	60	45

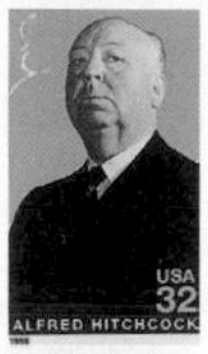

2348 Alfred Hitchcock (director)

1998. Legends of Hollywood.

3465	**2348**	32c. black and silver	1·10	55

No. 3465 includes a cut-out of Hitchcock's trademark caricature above his right shoulder.

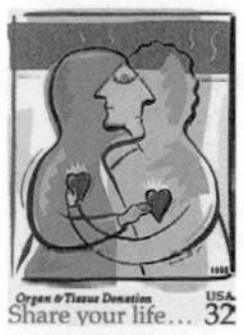

2349 Couple swapping Hearts

1998. Organ and Tissue Donation Campaign. Self-adhesive.

3466	**2349**	32c. multicoloured	1·00	55

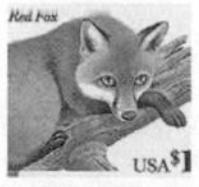

2350 Red Fox

1998. Self-adhesive.

3467	**2350**	$1 multicoloured	3·00	1·40

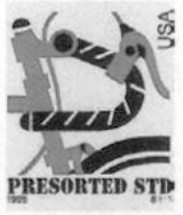

2351 Bicycle Handlebars

1998. Ordinary or self-adhesive gum.

3468	**2351**	(10c.) black, grn & vio	35	25

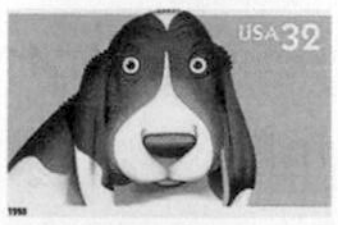

2352 Dog

1998. "Bright Eyes". Multicoloured. Self-adhesive.

3470	32c. Type **2352**	1·00	65
3471	32c. Cat	1·00	65
3472	32c. Hamster	1·00	65
3473	32c. Goldfish	1·00	65
3474	32c. Parakeet	1·00	65

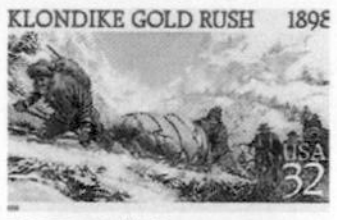

2357 Gold Prospectors

1998. Centenary of Klondike Gold Rush.

3475	**2357**	32c. multicoloured	1·00	55

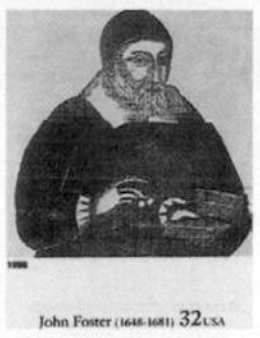

2358 "Portrait of Richard Mather" (John Foster)

1998. American Art. Multicoloured.

3476	32c. Type **2358**	1·10	80
3477	32c. "Mrs. Elizabeth Freake and Baby Mary" (The Freake Limner)	1·10	80
3478	32c. "Girl in Red Dress with Cat and Dog" (Ammi Phillips)	1·10	80
3479	32c. "Rubens Peale with Geranium" (Rembrandt Peale)	1·10	80
3480	32c. "Long-billed Curlew, Numenius longrostris" (John James Audubon)	1·10	80
3481	32c. "Boatmen on the Missouri" (George Caleb Bingham)	1·10	80
3482	32c. "Kindred Spirits" (Asher B. Durand)	1·10	80
3483	32c. "Westwood Children" (Joshua Johnson)	1·10	80
3484	32c. "Music and Literature" (William Harnett)	1·10	80
3485	32c. "Fog Warning" (Winslow Homer)	1·10	80
3486	32c. "White Cloud, Head Chief of the Iowas" (George Catlin)	1·10	80
3487	32c. "Cliffs of Green River" (Thomas Moran)	1·10	80
3488	32c. "Last of the Buffalo" (Albert Bierstadt)	1·10	80
3489	32c. "Niagara" (Frederic Edwin Church)	1·10	80
3490	32c. "Breakfast in Bed" (Mary Cassatt)	1·10	80
3491	32c. "Nighthawks" (Edward Hopper)	1·10	80
3492	32c. "American Gothic" (Grant Wood)	1·10	80
3493	32c. "Two against the White" (Charles Sheeler)	1·10	80
3494	32c. "Mahoning" (Franz Kline)	1·10	80
3495	32c. "No. 12" (Mark Rothko)	1·10	80

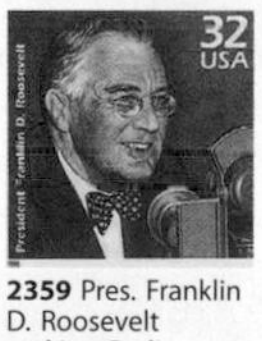

2359 Pres. Franklin D. Roosevelt making Radio Broadcast

1998. The Twentieth Century (3rd series). The 1930s. Blue (No. 3497) or multicoloured (others).

3496	32c. Type **2359**	1·00	75
3497	32c. Empire State Building (completed 1931)	1·00	75
3498	32c. Front cover of "Life" magazine's first issue, 1936	1·00	75
3499	32c. Eleanor Roosevelt (First Lady) and child	1·00	75
3500	32c. New Deal economic recovery plan	1·00	75
3501	32c. Superman (first comic book super hero, 1938)	1·00	75
3502	32c. Electric food mixer (household conveniences)	1·00	75
3503	32c. "Snow White and the Seven Dwarfs" (first feature-length animated film, 1937)	1·00	75
3504	32c. "Gone with the Wind" (novel by Margaret Mitchell) (published 1936)	1·00	75
3505	32c. Jesse Owens (athlete)	1·00	75
3506	32c. "New 20th Century Limited" (streamlined steam train)	1·00	75
3507	32c. Inauguration of Golden Gate Bridge, San Francisco, 1937	1·00	75
3508	32c. Florence Owens Thompson (photograph by Dorothea Lange, 1936) (Great Depression)	1·00	75
3509	32c. Bobby Jones (golfer) (only person to win Grand Slam, 1930)	1·00	75
3510	32c. Monopoly board (first produced commercially, 1933)	1·00	75

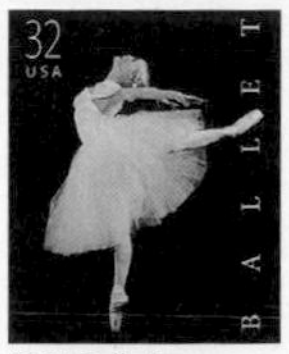

2360 Ballerina

1998. 50th Anniv of New York City Ballet.

3511	**2360**	32c. multicoloured	1·00	55

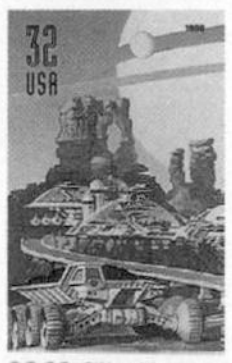

2361 City Domes and Vehicle

1998. Future of Space Travel. Multicoloured.

3512	32c. Type **2361**	1·00	75
3513	32c. Capsule preparing to land	1·00	75
3514	32c. Space pioneer on rock	1·00	75
3515	32c. Capsule taking off and pioneer with vehicle	1·00	75
3516	32c. Dome and bridge over canyon	1·00	75

Nos. 3512/16 were issued together, *se-tenant*, forming a composite design.

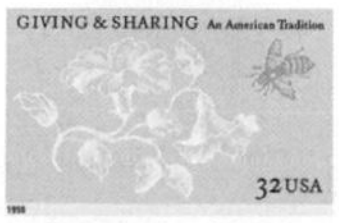

2366 Flower and Bee

1998. "Giving and Sharing". Self-adhesive.

3517	**2366**	32c. multicoloured	1·00	55

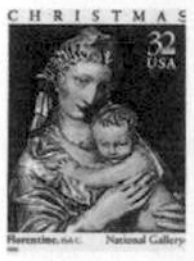

2367 "Florentine Madonna and Child" (sculpture, anon)

2368 Evergreen Wreath

1998. Christmas. Multicoloured. Self-adhesive. (a) Size 19½×26½ mm.

3518	32c. Type **2367**	1·10	55
3519	32c. Type **2368**	1·10	65
3520	32c. Victorian wreath	1·10	65
3521	32c. Chilli wreath	1·10	65
3522	32c. Tropical wreath	1·10	65

(b) Size 17×22 mm.

3523	32c. Type **2368**	1·10	65
3524	32c. As No. 3520	1·10	65
3525	32c. As No. 3521	1·10	65
3526	32c. As No. 3522	1·10	65

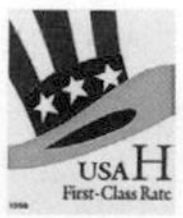

2372 Uncle Sam's Hat

1998. First-Class Rate stamps. No value expressed. Ordinary or self-adhesive gum.

3527	**2372**	(33c.) multicoloured	1·10	55

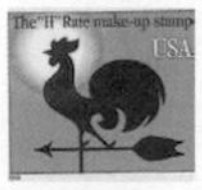

2373 Rooster Weathervane

1998. No value expressed. Make-up Rate stamps.

3533	**2373**	(1c.) multicoloured (blue imprint date) (21×17¾ mm)	50	20
3534	**2373**	(1c.) multicoloured (black imprint date) (21×18¾ mm)	50	20

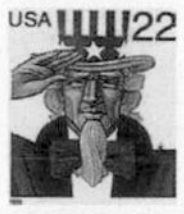

2374 Uncle Sam

1998. Self-adhesive.

3535	**2374**	22c. multicoloured	85	35

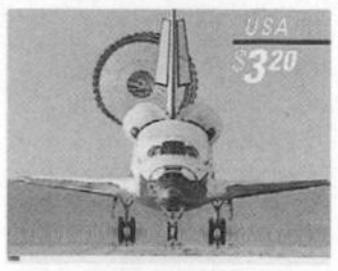

2375 Space Shuttle landing

1998. Multicoloured. Self-adhesive.

3538	$3.20 Type **2375**	8·50	5·50
3539	$11.75 Space shuttle on transport plane	31·00	18·00

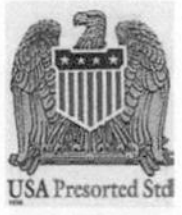

2377 Eagle and Shield

1998. Presorted coil stamp. Ordinary or self-adhesive gum.

3540	**2377**	(10c.) multicoloured	50	20

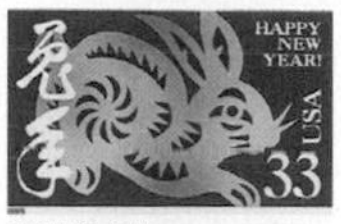

2378 Rabbit

1999. Chinese New Year.

3545	**2378**	33c. multicoloured	1·10	55

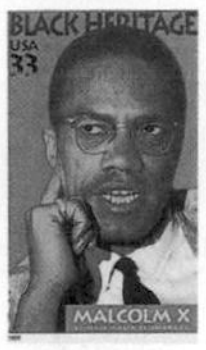

2379 Malcolm X

1999. Black Heritage. Malcolm X (el-Hajj Malik el-Shabazz) (black nationalist leader). Self-adhesive.

3546	**2379**	33c. green, grey and black	1·10	55

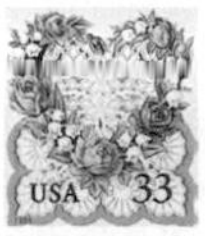

2380 Heart of Pink Roses

1999. Greetings Stamps. Multicoloured. Self-adhesive.

3547	33c. Type **2380**	1·10	55
3548	55c. Heart of red roses	1·60	1·10

Nos. 3547/8 are die-cut to shape around the design.

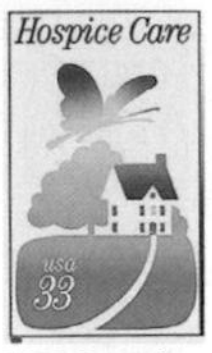

2382 Butterfly and Hospice

1999. Hospice Care. Self-adhesive.

3549	**2382**	33c. multicoloured	1·10	55

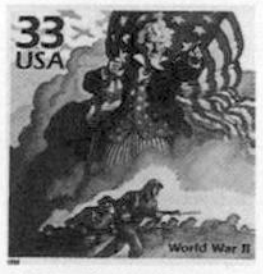

2383 Uncle Sam and Soldiers (World War II)

1999. The Twentieth Century (4th series). The 1940s. Brown (No. 3560) or multicoloured (others).

3550	33c. Type **2383**	1·00	75
3551	33c. Penicillin (development of antibiotics)	1·00	75
3552	33c. Jackie Robinson (baseball player)	1·00	75
3553	33c. President Harry Truman	1·00	75
3554	33c. Women's War Effort poster ("We Can Do It")	1·00	75
3555	33c. Filming of television programme	1·00	75
3556	33c. Couple jitterbugging	1·00	75
3557	33c. Jackson Pollock at work (Abstract Expressionism)	1·00	75

3558	33c. Soldier studying (Service-men's Readjustment Act (GI Bill), 1944)	1·00	75
3559	33c. Big Band music	1·00	75
3560	33c. United Nations building, New York (International Style of architecture)	1·00	75
3561	33c. Postwar baby boom (front cover of "The Saturday Evening Post", 2 November 1946)	1·00	75
3562	33c. Slinky (coiled wire toy)	1·00	75
3563	33c. Poster for Broadway production of "A Streetcar Named Desire" (Tennessee Williams), 1947	1·00	75
3564	33c. Scene from Orson Welles's "Citizen Kane" (film), 1941	1·00	75

A brief description of the subject is printed under the gum on the back of each stamp.

2384 Flag and Skyscrapers

1999. Ordinary or self-adhesive gum.

| 3565 | **2384** | 33c. multicoloured | 1·00 | 55 |

2385 Irish Immigration Ship

1999. Irish Immigration.

| 3570 | **2385** | 33c. multicoloured | 1·00 | 55 |

2386 Alfred Lunt and Lynn Fontanne (actors)

1999. Preforming Arts and Artists.

| 3571 | **2386** | 33c. multicoloured | 1·00 | 55 |

2387 Arctic Hare

1999. Arctic Animals. Multicoloured.

3572	33c. Type **2387**	1·00	65
3573	33c. Arctic fox	1·00	65
3574	33c. Snowy owl	1·00	65
3575	33c. Polar bear	1·00	65
3576	33c. Grey wolf	1·00	65

2392 Flag and Alphabet on Board

1999. Automatic Teller Machine stamp.

| 3577 | **2392** | 33c. multicoloured | 1·00 | 55 |

2393 Saguaro

SONORAN DESERT

2394 Sonoran Desert (image scaled to 21% of original size)

1999. Nature of America (1st issue). Sheet 232×172 mm containing T **2393** and similar multicoloured designs, forming the overall design T **2394**.

MS3578 33c. Type **2393**; 33c. White-winged doves (horiz); 33c. Desert mule deers; 33c. Gila woodpecker; 33c. Cactus wren; 33c. Desert tortoise; 33c. Gambel's quail and chicks (horiz); 33c. Desert cottontail; 33c. Gila monster (horiz); 33c. Cactus mouse and western diamondback rattlesnake (horiz)   9·00   9·00

The back of the sheet has a description of the desert and a key to the flora and fauna in the design.
See also Nos. **MS**3748, **MS**3975, **MS**4089, **MS**4305, **MS**4339, **MS**4417, **MS**4661 and **MS**4783.

2395 Blueberries

1999. Berries. Self-adhesive. Multicoloured.

3579	33c. Type **2395**	1·10	65
3580	33c. Raspberries	1·10	65
3581	33c. Strawberries	1·10	65
3582	33c. Blackberries	1·10	65

2399 Daffy Duck

1999. Daffy Duck (cartoon character). Self-adhesive.

| 3591 | **2399** | 33c. multicoloured | 1·10 | 80 |
| MS3592 | 174×130 mm. No. 3591 | | 1·80 | 1·80 |

2400 Ayn Rand

1999. Literary Arts. Ayn Rand (novelist).

| 3593 | **2400** | 33c. multicoloured | 1·00 | 55 |

2401 Bird-of-Paradise Flower

1999. Tropical Flowers. Self-adhesive. Multicoloured.

3595	33c. Type **2401**	1·10	75
3596	33c. Royal poinciana	1·10	75
3597	33c. Gloriosa lily	1·10	75
3598	33c. Chinese hibiscus	1·10	75

A2405 Rio Grande

1999. Air. Self-adhesive. Multicoloured.

A3599	40c. Type **A2405**	1·20	75
A3600	48c. Niagara Falls	1·50	90
A3600a	80c. Mt. Mckinley, Alaska	2·20	1·40
A3601	60c. Grand Canyon	1·80	1·10
A3602	60c. Acadia National Park, Maine	1·70	1·10
A3603	70c. Nine-mile Piairie, Nebraska	2·00	1·20

2410 "Franklinia alatamaha" (after William Bartram)

1999. 300th Birth Anniv of John and 260th Birth Anniv of William Bartram (botanists). Self-adhesive.

| 3605 | **2410** | 33c. multicoloured | 1·00 | 55 |

2411 Polio Vaccination

1999. The Twentieth Century (5th series). The 1950s. Red (No. 3606) or multicoloured (others).

3606	33c. Type **2411**	1·00	75
3607	33c. Teen fashions	1·00	75
3608	33c. Baseball (The "Shot Heard 'Round the World")	1·00	75
3609	33c. Rocket launch, 1958	1·00	75
3610	33c. U.S. soldiers in snow (Korean War, 1950–53)	1·00	75
3611	33c. Desegregation of state ("public") schools	1·00	75
3612	33c. Tailfin of car ("Tail Fins and Chrome")	1·00	75
3613	33c. "The Cat in the Hat" (reading primer by Theodor Seuss, 1957)	1·00	75
3614	33c. Drive-in movies	1·00	75
3615	33c. Stadium and badges for New York Yankees and Brooklyn Dodgers baseball teams (World Series Rivals)	1·00	75
3616	33c. Rocky Marciano (world heavyweight boxing cham-pion, 1952–56)	1·00	75
3617	33c. Lucille Ball and Desi Arnaz in "I Love Lucy" (television series)	1·00	75
3618	33c. Singer/guitarist and jivers (Rock 'n' Roll)	1·00	75
3619	33c. Stock car race	1·00	75
3620	33c. Audience at 3-D movie	1·00	75

A brief description of the subject is printed under the gum on the back of each stamp.

2412 Male Gender Sign

1999. Prostate Cancer Awareness Campaign. Self-adhesive.

| 3621 | **2412** | 33c. multicoloured | 1·00 | 55 |

2413 Prospectors

1999. 150th Anniv of California Gold Rush.

| 3622 | **2413** | 33c. multicoloured | 1·00 | 55 |

2414 Long-horned Cowfish, Black-tailed Damselfish, Cleaner Shrimp and Flame Hawkfish

2415 Copper-band Butterflyfish, Mushroom Polyps and Blue Starfish

2416 Powder-blue Surgeonfish and Long-spined Sea Urchin   **2417** Clown Anemonefish and Red Hermit Crab

1999. Aquarium Fish. Self-adhesive.

3623	**2414**	33c. multicoloured	1·00	55
3624	**2415**	33c. multicoloured	1·00	55
3625	**2416**	33c. multicoloured	1·00	55
3626	**2417**	33c. multicoloured	1·00	55

Nos. 3623/6 were issued together, *se-tenant*, forming a composite design.

2418 Skateboarding

1999. "Xtreme" Sports. Self-adhesive. Multicoloured.

3627	33c. Type **2418**	1·00	55
3628	33c. BMX biking	1·00	55
3629	33c. Snowboarding	1·00	55
3630	33c. Inline skating	1·00	55

2422 Free-blown Glass

1999. American Glass. Multicoloured.

3631	33c. Type **2422**	1·00	55
3632	33c. Mould-blown glass	1·00	55
3633	33c. Pressed glass	1·00	55
3634	33c. Art glass	1·00	55

2426 James Cagney

1999. Legends of Hollywood.

| 3635 | **2426** | 33c. multicoloured | 1·00 | 55 |

2427 Mitchell and SPAD XVI Biplane

1999. 120th Birth Anniv of Billy Mitchell (aviation pioneer). Self-adhesive.

| 3636 | **2427** | 55c. multicoloured | 1·70 | 1·00 |

2428 Rose

1999. Self-adhesive.

| 3637 | **2428** | 33c. multicoloured | 1·00 | 55 |

2429 Flag

1999. "Honoring Those Who Served". Self-adhesive.

| 3638 | **2429** | 33c. red, blue and black | 1·00 | 55 |

2430 Stars

1999. 125th Anniv of Universal Postal Union.

| 3639 | **2430** | 45c. blue and red | 1·40 | 90 |

2431 "Daylight"

1999. Trains. Multicoloured.

| 3640 | 33c. Type **2431** | 1·00 | 75 |
| 3641 | 33c. "20th Century Limited" | 1·00 | 75 |

3642	33c. "Super Chief"	1·00	75
3643	33c. "Congressional"	1·00	75
3644	33c. "Hiawatha"	1·00	75

Details of the trains are printed under the gum on the back of each stamp.

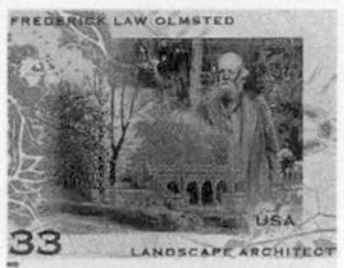

2436 Olmsted (after John Singer Sargent) and Central Park, New York

1999. 77th Birth Anniv of Frederick Law Olmsted (landscaper).

3645	**2436**	33c. multicoloured	1·00	55

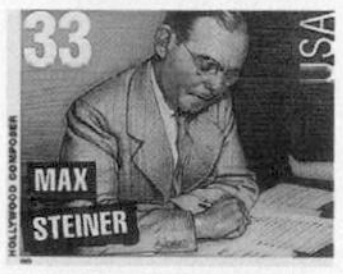

2437 Max Steiner

1999. Hollywood Composers. Multicoloured.

3646	33c. Type **2437**	1·20	75
3647	33c. Dimitri Tiomkin	1·20	75
3648	33c. Bernard Herrmann	1·20	75
3649	33c. Franz Waxman	1·20	75
3650	33c. Alfred Newman	1·20	75
3651	33c. Erich Wolfgang Korngold	1·20	75

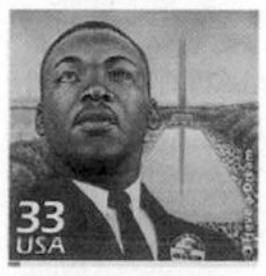

2443 Martin Luther King (Civil Rights leader)

1999. The Twentieth Century (6th series). The 1960s. Black (No. 3654) or multicoloured.(others).

3652	33c. Type **2443**	1·00	75
3653	33c. Bird on guitar neck (Woodstock Music Festival, 1969)	1·00	75
3654	33c. Footprint (first manned moon landing, 1969)	1·00	75
3655	33c. Members of Green Bay Packers football team	1·00	75
3656	33c. Starship "Enterprise" (television series "Star Trek")	1·00	75
3657	33c. Peace Corps volunteers	1·00	75
3658	33c. Troops disembarking from helicopter (Vietnam War)	1·00	75
3659	33c. Ford Mustang sportscar	1·00	75
3660	33c. Barbie doll	1·00	75
3661	33c. Integrated circuit	1·00	75
3662	33c. Lasers	1·00	75
3663	33c. Ticket to football match (Super Bowl I)	1·00	75
3664	33c. Peace symbol	1·00	75
3665	33c. Roger Maris (baseball player)	1·00	75
3666	33c. Yellow submarine (The Beatles pop group)	1·00	75

A brief description of the subject is printed under the gum on the back of each stamp.

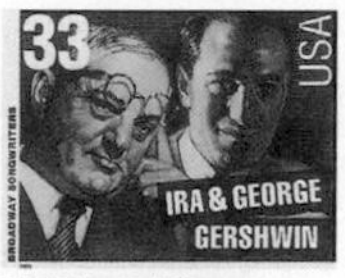

2444 Ira and George Gershwin

1999. Broadway Songwriters. Multicoloured.

3667	33c. Type **2444**	1·00	75
3668	33c. Alan Jay Lerner and Frederick Loewe	1·00	75
3669	33c. Lorenz Hart	1·00	75
3670	33c. Richard Rodgers and Oscar Hammerstein II	1·00	75
3671	33c. Meredith Willson	1·00	75
3672	33c. Frank Loesser	1·00	75

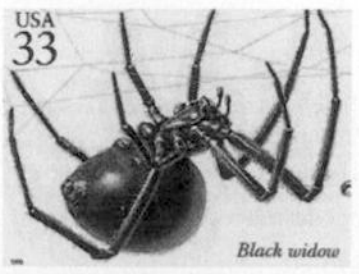

2450 Black Widow

1999. Insects and Spiders. Multicoloured.

3673	33c. Type **2450**	1·00	75
3674	33c. Elderberry longhorn	1·00	75
3675	33c. Ladybird ("Lady beetle")	1·00	75
3676	33c. Yellow garden spider	1·00	75
3677	33c. Dogbane beetle	1·00	75
3678	33c. Flower fly	1·00	75
3679	33c. Assassin bug	1·00	75
3680	33c. Ebony jewelwing	1·00	75
3681	33c. Velvet ant	1·00	75
3682	33c. Monarch (caterpillar)	1·00	75
3683	33c. Monarch (butterfly)	1·00	75
3684	33c. Eastern Hercules beetle	1·00	75
3685	33c. Bombadier beetle	1·00	75
3686	33c. Dung beetle	1·00	75
3687	33c. Spotted water beetle	1·00	75
3688	33c. True katydid	1·00	75
3689	33c. Spiny-backed spider	1·00	75
3690	33c. Periodical cicada	1·00	75
3691	33c. Scorpionfly	1·00	75
3692	33c. Jumping spider	1·00	75

Descriptions of the subject are printed under the gum on the back of each stamp.

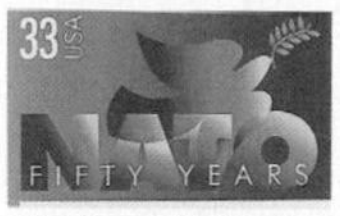

2451 Dove with Laurel

1999. 50th Anniv of North Atlantic Treaty Organization.

3695	**2451**	33c. multicoloured	1·00	55

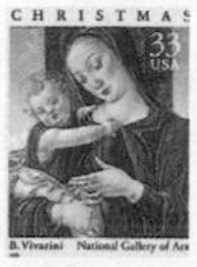

2452 "Madonna and Child" (Bartolomeo Vivarini)

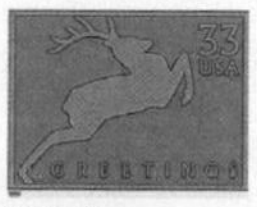

2453 Stag

1999. Christmas. Self-adhesive. (a) Size 20×27 mm.

3696	**2452**	33c. multicoloured	1·20	90

(b) Size 27×20½ mm.

3697	33c. gold and red	1·10	65
3698	33c. gold and blue	1·10	65
3699	33c. gold and violet	1·10	65
3700	33c. gold and green	1·10	65

(c) Size 21½×19½ mm.

3701	**2453**	33c. gold and red	2·20	90
3702	**2453**	33c. gold and blue	2·20	90
3703	**2453**	33c. gold and violet	2·20	90
3704	**2453**	33c. gold and green	2·20	90

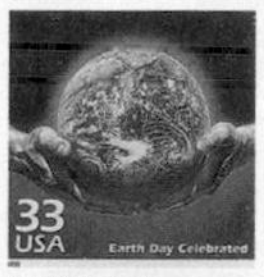

2454 Hands holding Globe (first Earth Day, 1970)

1999. The Twentieth Century (7th series). The 1970s. Blue (Nos. 3712, 3714) or multicoloured (others).

3705	33c. Type **2454**	1·00	75
3706	33c. Scene from "All in the Family" (television series)	1·00	75
3707	33c. Big Bird (character from children's television series "Sesame Street")	1·00	75
3708	33c. Disco dancers	1·00	75
3709	33c. American football helmet (winning of four Super Bowls by Pittsburgh Steelers)	1·00	75
3710	33c. Statue of Liberty and fireworks (bicentenary of United States, 1976)	1·00	75
3711	33c. Secretariat (racehorse) (winner of Triple Crown, 1973)	1·00	75
3712	33c. Video cassette recorder	1·00	75
3713	33c. "Pioneer 10" (launch of Jupiter space probe, 1972)	1·00	75
3714	33c. Emblem of Women's Rights Movement	1·00	75
3715	33c. 1970s fashion	1·00	75
3716	33c. Cameraman filming American football match (television series "Monday Night Football")	1·00	75
3717	33c. "Smiley face" badges	1·00	75
3718	33c. Girl gazing at Boeing jumbo jet	1·00	75
3719	33c. Scan of skull ("Medical imaging")	1·00	75

A brief description of the subject is printed under the gum on the back of each stamp.

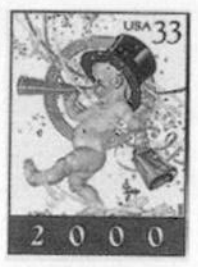

2455 New Year Baby

1999. Year 2000. Self-adhesive.

3720	**2455**	33c. multicoloured	1·00	55

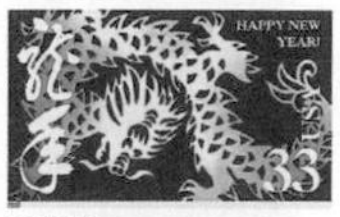

2456 Dragon

2000. New Year.

3725	**2456**	33c. multicoloured	1·00	55

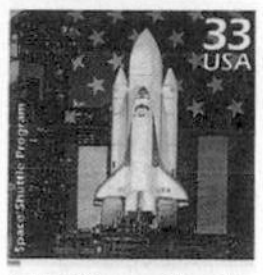

2457 Space Shuttle "Columbia"

2000. The Twentieth Century (8th series). The 1980s. Multicoloured.

3726	33c. Type **2457**	1·00	75
3727	33c. Poster for "Cats" (stage musical)	1·00	75
3728	33c. San Francisco 49ers (American football team)	1·00	75
3729	33c. Welcome in Washington for homecoming of hostages held in siege of U.S. Embassy, Teheran	1·00	75
3730	33c. Figure skater	1·00	75
3731	33c. Dish aerials (cable TV)	1·00	75
3732	33c. Vietnam Veterans Memorial	1·00	75
3733	33c. Compact disc	1·00	75
3734	33c. Cabbage Patch doll	1·00	75
3735	33c. Opening shot of "The Cosby Show" (television comedy series)	1·00	75
3736	33c. Fall of the Berlin Wall	1·00	75
3737	33c. Children playing video game	1·00	75
3738	33c. "E.T." the Extra-Terrestrial (film)	1·00	75
3739	33c. Personal computer	1·00	75
3740	33c. Hip-hop culture	1·00	75

A brief description of the subject is printed under the gum on the back of each stamp.

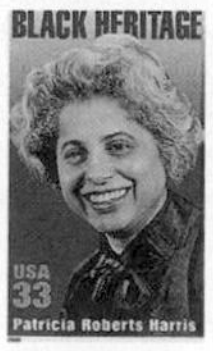

2458 Patricia Harris

2000. Black Heritage. Patricia Roberts Harris (diplomat). Self-adhesive.

3741	**2458**	33c. multicoloured	1·00	55

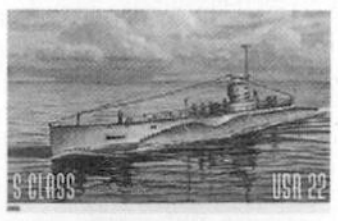

2459 S-Class Submarine

2000. Centenary of United States Navy Submarine Fleet. Multicoloured.

3743	22c. Type **2459**	1·80	1·10
3744	33c. Los Angeles Class	1·80	1·10
3745	55c. Ohio Class	3·75	2·75
3746	60c. U.S.S. *Holland I*, 1900	5·00	3·75
3747	$3.20 Gato Class (77×22 mm)	14·50	11·00

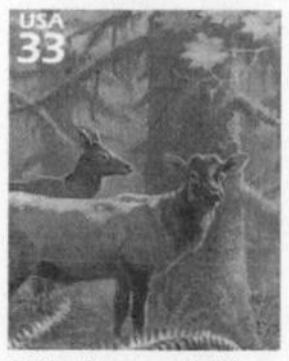

2464 Roosevelt Elk

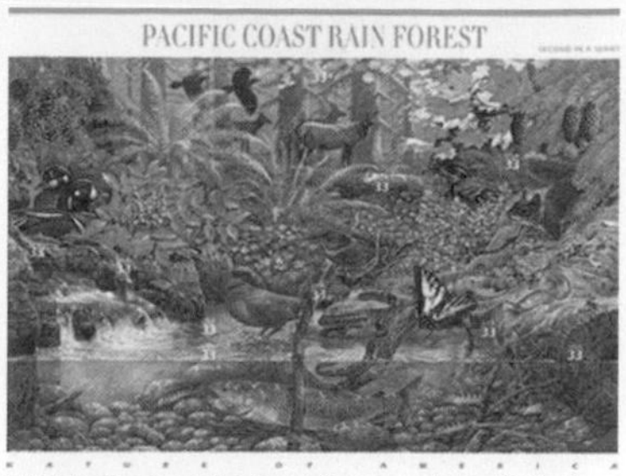

2465 Pacific Coast Rainforest (image scaled to 21% of original size)

2000. Nature of America (2nd issue). Sheet 232×172 mm containing T **2464** and similar multicoloured designs forming the overall design T **2465**.

MS3748	33c. Type **2464**; 33c. Harlequin duck; 33c. Dwarf oregongrape and snail-eating ground beetle; 33c. Winter wren; 33c. Douglas squirrel; 33c. American dipper; 33c. Pacific giant salamander; 33c. Western tiger swallowtail; 33c. Banana slug and tailed frog; 33c. Cut-throat trout	9·25	9·25

The back of the sheet has a description of the rainforest and a key to the flora and fauna in the design.

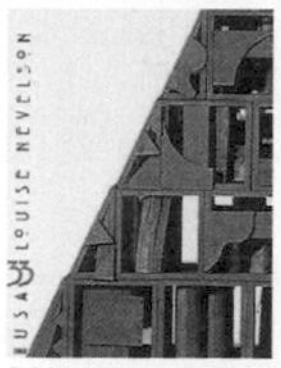

2466 "Silent Music I"

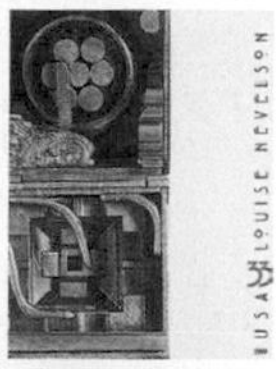

2467 "Royal Tide I"

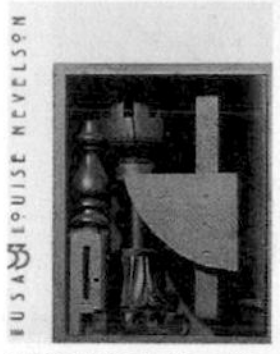

2468 "Black Chord"

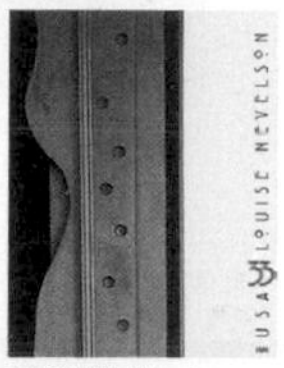

2469 "Nightsphere-Light"

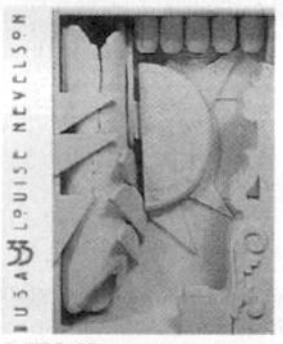

2470 "Dawn's Wedding Chapel I"

2000. Birth Centenary of Louise Nevelson (sculptress).

3749	**2466**	33c. multicoloured	1·00	75
3750	**2467**	33c. multicoloured	1·00	75
3751	**2468**	33c. multicoloured	1·00	75
3752	**2469**	33c. multicoloured	1·00	75
3753	**2470**	33c. multicoloured	1·00	75

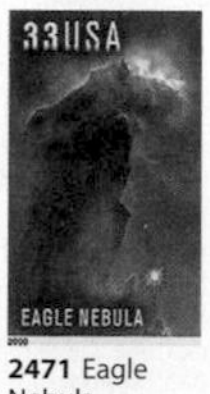

2471 Eagle Nebula

2000. Tenth Anniv of Hubble Space Telescope. Multicoloured.

3754	33c. Type **2471**	1·00	75
3755	33c. Ring Nebula	1·00	75
3756	33c. Lagoon Nebula	1·00	75
3757	33c. Egg Nebula	1·00	75
3758	33c. Galaxy NGC 1316	1·00	75

A brief description of the subject is printed under the gum on the back of each stamp.

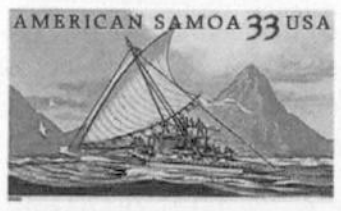

2476 Sunuitao Peak, Ofu Island and Alia (fishing catamaran)

2000. Centenary of Samoa's Status as an Unorganized United States Territory.

3759	**2476**	33c. multicoloured	1·00	55

2477 Main Reading Room, Thomas Jefferson Building, Library of Congress

2000. Bicentenary of Library of Congress, Washington, D.C.

3760	**2477**	33c. multicoloured	1·00	65

2478 Road Runner and Wile E. Coyote

2000. Wile E. Coyote and Road Runner (cartoon characters). Self-adhesive.

3761	**2478**	33c. multicoloured	1·10	75
MS3762	85×130 mm. No. 3761		3·75	3·75

2479 Baseball and Newspaper Headline

2000. The Twentieth Century (9th series). The 1990s. Multicoloured.

3763	33c. Type **2479**		1·00	75
3764	33c. Soldier and Chinook helicopters (Iraqi invasion of Kuwait, 1990)		1·00	75
3765	33c. Set from *Seinfeld* (television comedy show)		1·00	75
3766	33c. Snowboarder (increased popularity in extreme sports)		1·00	75
3767	33c. Child writing (improvement in quality of education)		1·00	75
3768	33c. Hand and butterfly (computer generated art)		1·00	75
3769	33c. Peregrine falcon (recovery of endangered species)		1·00	75
3770	33c. Space shuttle *Discovery* (John Glenn's (first American to orbit Earth) return to space, 1998)		1·00	75
3771	33c. Olympic gold medal (30th anniv of special Olympics, 1998)		1·00	75
3772	33c. Man using virtual reality game		1·00	75
3773	33c. Tyrannosaurus rex (*Jurassic Park* (film), 1993)		1·00	75
3774	33c. Poster for *Titanic* (film), 1997		1·00	75
3775	33c. Increase in popularity of off-road vehicles		1·00	75
3776	33c. Computer keyboard (introduction of the Internet and the World Wide Web)		1·00	75
3777	33c. Man using mobile phone (increase in use of cellular phones)		1·00	75

A brief description of the subject is printed under the gum on the back of each stamp.

2480 John L. Hines and 4th Division Insignia (Distinguished Service Cross and Medal)

2000. Distinguished Soldiers. Multicoloured.

3778	33c. Type **2480**		1·00	75
3779	33c. Omar N. Bradley and First Army Insignia (Army Chief of Staffs)		1·00	75
3780	33c. Alvin C. York and 82nd Division Insignia (Medal of Honor)		1·00	75
3781	33c. Audie L. Murphy and 3rd Infantry Division Insignia (Medal of Honor)		1·00	75

2484 Athletes

2000. Summer Sports. Lilac Bloomsday Run, Washington.

3782	**2484**	33c. multicoloured	1·00	55

2485 Stylized Man and Woman

2000. Adoption Awareness. Self-adhesive.

3783	**2485**	33c. multicoloured	1·10	55

2486 Basketball

2000. Youth Team Sports.

3784	33c. Type **2486**		1·00	75
3785	33c. American football		1·00	75
3786	33c. Soccer		1·00	75
3787	33c. Baseball		1·00	75

2490 Sons of Liberty Flag, 1775

2000. History of the American Flag.

3788	**2490**	33c. red and black	1·00	75
3789	-	33c. multicoloured	1·00	75
3790	-	33c. red and black	1·00	75
3791	-	33c. red, blue and black	1·00	75
3792	-	33c. red, blue and black	1·00	75
3793	-	33c. red and black	1·00	75
3794	-	33c. red, blue and black	1·00	75
3795	-	33c. red, blue and black	1·00	75
3796	-	33c. red, blue and black	1·00	75
3797	-	33c. blue, red and black	1·00	75
3798	-	33c. red, blue and black	1·00	75
3799	-	33c. red, blue and black	1·00	75
3800	-	33c. red, blue and black	1·00	75
3801	-	33c. red, blue and black	1·00	75
3802	-	33c. red, blue and black	1·00	75
3803	-	33c. red, blue and black	1·00	75
3804	-	33c. red, blue and black	1·00	75
3805	-	33c. red, blue and black	1·00	75
3806	-	33c. red, blue and black	1·00	75
3807	-	33c. red, blue and black	1·00	75

DESIGNS: No. 3789, New England flag, 1775; 3790, Forster flag, 1775; 3791, Continental Colors, 1776; 3792, Francis Hopkinson flag, 1777; 3793, Brandywine flag, 1777; 3794, John Paul Jones flag, 1779; 3795, Pierre L'Enfant flag, 1783; 3796, Indian Peace flag, 1803; 3797, Easton flag, 1814; 3798, Star-Spangled Banner, 1814; 3799, Bennington flag, 1820; 3800, Great Star flag, 1837; 3801, 29-Star flag, 1847; 3802, Fort Sumter flag, 1861; 3803, Centennial flag, 1876; 3804, 38-Star flag, 1877; 3805, Peace flag, 1891; 3806, 48-Star flag, 1912; 3807, 50-Star flag, 1960.

A brief history of the subject is printed under the gum on the back of each stamp.

2491 Blackberries

2000. Berries. Self-adhesive. Multicoloured.

3808	33c. Type **2491**		1·40	75
3809	33c. Raspberries		1·40	75
3810	33c. Blueberries		1·40	75
3811	33c. Strawberries		1·40	75

2495 Jackie Robinson

2000. Legends of Baseball. Self-adhesive. Multicoloured.

3812	33c. Type **2495**		1·00	75
3813	33c. Eddie Collins		1·00	75
3814	33c. Christy Mathewson		1·00	75
3815	33c. Ty Cobb		1·00	75
3816	33c. George Sisler		1·00	75
3817	33c. Rogers Hornsby		1·00	75
3818	33c. Mickey Cochrane		1·00	75
3819	33c. Babe Ruth		1·00	75
3820	33c. Walter Johnson		1·00	75
3821	33c. Roberto Clemente		1·00	75
3822	33c. Lefty Grove		1·00	75
3823	33c. Tris Speaker		1·00	75
3824	33c. Cy Young		1·00	75
3825	33c. Jimmie Foxx		1·00	75
3826	33c. Pie Traynor		1·00	75
3827	33c. Satchel Paige		1·00	75
3828	33c. Honus Wagner		1·00	75
3829	33c. Josh Gibson		1·00	75
3830	33c. Dizzy Dean		1·00	75
3831	33c. Lou Gehrig		1·00	75

2496 (image scaled to 26% of original size)

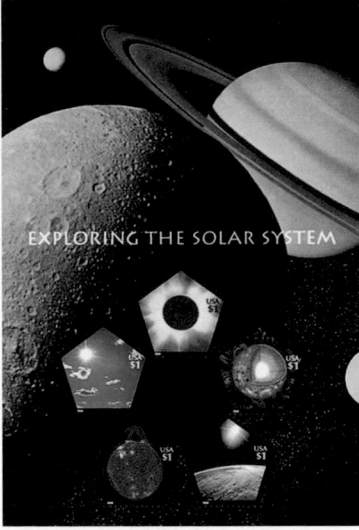

2497 (image scaled to 38% of original size)

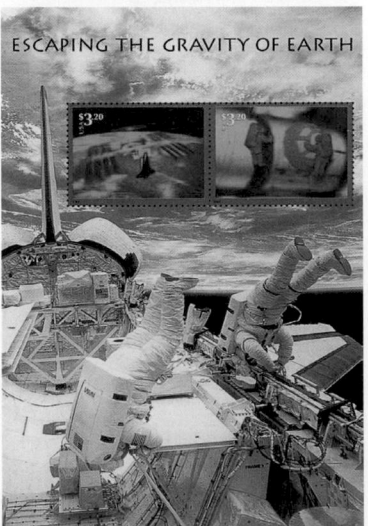

2498 (image scaled to 38% of original size)

2499 (image scaled to 26% of original size)

2500 (image scaled to 52% of original size)

2000. "World Expo 2000" International Stamp Exhibition, Anaheim, California. Five sheets.

MS3832a 184×127 mm. **2496** 60c. Hubble Space Telescope; 60c. Radio interferometers, New Mexico; 60c. Two 10-metre optical and infrared telescopes, Keck Observatory, Hawaii; 60c. Optical telescopes, Inter-American Observatory, Chile; 60c. 1000-inch optical telescope, Mount Wilson Observatory, California; 60c. 305-metre radio telescope, Arecibo Observatory, Puerto Rico ... 15·00 15·00

MS3832b 127×184 mm. **2497** $1 Solar Eclipse; $1 Sun in blue sky; $1 Illustrated cross-section of sun; $1 Solar eruption; $1 Sunrise from space ... 20·00 20·00

MS3832c 127×184 mm. **2498** $3.20, Space Shuttle docking with Space Station; $3.20, Astronauts entering station ... 22·00 22·00

MS3832d 184×127 mm. **2499** $11.75, Probe landing on Lunar surface ... 37·00 37·00

MS3832e 92×92 mm. **2500** $11.75, Earth ... 37·00 37·00

2501 "Astronauts" (Zachary Canter)

2000. "Stampin' the Future". Winning Entries in Children's International Painting Competition. Self-adhesive. Multicoloured.

3833	33c. Type **2501**		1·00	75
3834	33c. "Children" (Sarah Lipsey)		1·00	75
3835	33c. "Rocket" (Morgan Hill)		1·00	75
3836	33c. "Dog" (Ashley Young)		1·00	75

2507 Joseph W. Stillwell

2000. Great Americans. (a) Ordinary gum.

3839	**2507**	10c. black and rosine	35	25
3840	-	33c. black and rosine	1·00	55

(ii) Self-adhesive.

3841	23c. black and scarlet		60	45
3849a	58c. black and scarlet		1·10	70
3849b	63c. black and scarlet		80	45
3846	75c. black and scarlet		90	50
3850	76c. black and scarlet		2·20	1·40
3847	83c. black and scarlet		2·20	1·50
3855	87c. black and scarlet		2·20	1·50

DESIGNS: 23c. Wilma Rudolph; 33c. Claude Pepper; 58c. Magaret Chase Smith (senator); 63c. Jonas Silk; 75c. Harriet Beecher Stowe (writer); 76c. Hattie W. Caraway; 83c. Edna Ferber; 87c. Albert Sabin.

2538 Coastline

2000. 150th Anniv of Californian Statehood.
3870 **2538** 33c. multicoloured 1·00 55

2539 Edward
G. Robinson

2000. Legends of Hollywood.
3871 **2539** 33c. multicoloured 1·00 55

2540 Fanfin Anglerfish

2000. Deep Sea Creatures. Multicoloured.
3872 33c. Type **2540** 1·00 75
3873 33c. Sea cucumber 1·00 75
3874 33c. Fangtooth 1·00 75
3875 33c. Amphipod 1·00 75
3876 33c. Medusa 1·00 75

2545 Thomas Wolfe

2000. Birth Centenary of Thomas Wolfe (writer).
3877 **2545** 33c. multicoloured 1·00 55

2546 North Facade

2000. Bicentenary of The White House as President's Residence. Self-adhesive.
3878 **2546** 33c. multicoloured 1·20 55

2547 Lion
Statue, New
York Public
Library

2000. Presorted coil stamp. Self-adhesive or ordinary gum.
3879 **2547** (10c.) multicoloured 35 25

2548 Farm
and Flag

2000. Ordinary or self-adhesive gum.
3880 **2548** (34c.) multicoloured 85 65

2549 Statue
of Liberty   **2550** Statue of
Liberty

2000. First-Class Rate stamps. (a) Ordinary or self-adhesive gum.
3883 **2549** (34c.) multicoloured 1·10 55

(b) Self-adhesive gum.
3885 **2550** (34c.) multicoloured 1·10 55

2551 Lily   **2552** Freesia   **2553** Lily

2554 Orchid

2000. Flowers. Self-adhesive.
3890 **2551** (34c.) multicoloured 1·10 45
3891 **2552** (34c.) multicoloured 1·10 45
3892 **2553** (34c.) multicoloured 1·10 45
3893 **2554** (34c.) multicoloured 1·10 45

2555 Statue
of Liberty   **2556** Statue of
Liberty

2001. (a) Ordinary or Self-adhesive gum.
3894 **2555** 34c. multicoloured 1·10 55

(b) Self-adhesive.
3895 **2556** 34c. multicoloured 1·10 55

2557 Red
Rose and
"LOVE"

2001. Greeting Stamps. First-Class Rate stamp. Self-adhesive.
3897 **2557** (34c.) multicoloured 1·10 55

2558 Snake

2001. New Year.
3898 **2558** 34c. multicoloured 1·00 55

2559 Roy
Wilkins

2001. Black Heritage. Roy Wilkins (civil rights pioneer). Self-adhesive.
3899 **2559** 34c. blue and black 1·00 55

2560 Capitol,
Washington

2001. Self-adhesive. Multicoloured.
3900 $3.50 Type **2560** 9·75 8·25
3901 $12.25 Washington Monument 31·00 27·00

Nos. 3900/1 each incorporate an additional hidden inscription "PRIORITY MAIL" (No. 3900) or "EXPRESS MAIL" (No. 3901) visible only under a special decoder.

No. 3900 was intended mainly for Priority mail and No. 3901 for Express Mail Service but they could be used on other mail as well.

2562 "First in the
Fight, Always
Faithful"
(recruitment
poster, James
Montgomery
Flagg)

2001. American Illustrators. Black (No. 3918) or multicoloured (others). Self-adhesive.
3902 34c. Type **2562** 1·00 75
3903 34c. "Interlude (The Lute Players)" (mural, Maxfield Parrish) 1·00 75
3904 34c. Couple dancing (advertisement, Joseph Christian Leyendecker) 1·00 75
3905 34c. Man sawing ice (advertisement, Robert Fawcett) 1·00 75
3906 34c. Couple in car (advertisement, Coles Philips) 1·00 75
3907 34c. Woman combing hair ("How I Make a Picture") (Al Parker) 1·00 75
3908 34c. Br'er Rabbit (Arthur Burdett Frost) 1·00 75
3909 34c. "An Attack on a Galleon" (illustration, Howard Pyle) 1·00 75
3910 34c. Kewpies (Rose O'Neill) 1·00 75
3911 34c. Steam boat (magazine cover illustration, Dean Cornwell) 1·00 75
3912 34c. "Galahad's Departure" (detail of mural, Edwin Austin Abbey) 1·00 75
3913 34c. "The First Lesson" (magazine cover illustration, Jessie Willcox Smith) 1·00 75
3914 34c. Woman holding artist's palette (magazine cover illustration, Neysa McMein) 1·00 75
3915 34c. "Back Home for Keeps" (advertisement, Jon Whitcomb) 1·00 75
3916 34c. "Something for Supper" (Harvey Dunn) 1·00 75
3917 34c. "A Dash for the Timber" (Frederic Remington) 1·00 75
3918 34c. Scene from *Moby Dick* (book illustration, Rockwell Kent) 1·00 75
3919 34c. "Captain Bill Bones" (book illustration, Newell Convers Wyeth) 1·00 75
3920 34c. Doctor and child (magazine cover illustration, Norman Rockwell) 1·00 75
3921 34c. "The Girl He Left Behind" (John Held Jr.) 60 60

A brief biography of the artist is printed on the backing paper on the back of each stamp.

2563 Farm
and Flag

2001. Ordinary or Self-adhesive gum.
3922 **2563** 34c. multicoloured 1·00 55

2564 Lily   **2565** Freesia   **2566** Lily

2567 Orchid

2001. Flowers. Self-adhesive.
3930 **2564** 34c. multicoloured 1·10 55
3931 **2565** 34c. multicoloured 1·10 55
3932 **2566** 34c. multicoloured 1·10 55
3933 **2567** 34c. multicoloured 1·10 55

2568 Rose
and "LOVE"   **2569** Rose and
"LOVE"

2001. Greetings Stamps. Self-adhesive.
3938 **2568** 34c. multicoloured 1·00 55
3939 **2569** 55c. multicoloured 1·70 1·10
3940 **2569** 57c. multicoloured 1·70 1·10

2570 George
Washington

2001. Self-adhesive.
3941 **2570** 20c. red 85 45
3942 **2570** 23c. green 1·50 90
3942 also comes with ordinary gum.

2571 Bison

2001. Ordinary or Self-adhesive gum.
3951 **2571** 21c. multicoloured 75 45

2572 Art
Deco Eagle

2001. Self-adhesive.
3960 **2572** 55c. multicoloured 1·60 1·00
3961 **2572** 57c. multicoloured 1·60 1·00

2573 Apple

2001. Fruit. Self-adhesive. Multicoloured.
3965 34c. Type **2573** 1·00 55
3966 34c. Orange 1·00 55

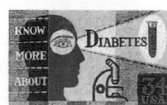

2576 Head, Test-tube
and Microscope

2001. Diabetes Awareness Campaign. Self-adhesive.
3969 **2576** 34c. multicoloured 1·10 55

2577 Obverse of Medals
and Alfred Nobel
(founder)

2001. Centenary of Nobel Prizes.
3970 **2577** 34c. yell, lt brn & brn 1·10 55

2578 1c. Stamp
with Inverted
Centre   **2581** Exposition
Emblem

2001. Centenary of Pan-American Exposition.
3971 **2578** 1c. black and green 1·10 80
3972 — 2c. black and red 1·10 80
3973 — 4c. black and brown 1·10 80
3974 **2581** 80c. red and blue 2·20 1·60

DESIGNS: No. 3972, 2c. stamp with inverted centre; 3973, 4c. stamp with inverted centre.

2583 Great Plains Prairie (image scaled to 21% of original size)

10

2001. Nature of America. (3rd series). Sheet 233×172 mm. Forming the overall design T **2583**. Multicoloured. Self-adhesive.

MS3975 34c. Canada geese and Pronghorn deer; 34c. Bison, burrowing owls and buffalo grass; 34c. Bison, wild alfalfa and prairie dogs (horiz); 34c. Black-tailed prairie dog; 34c. Painted lady butterfly, coneflower and wild rose (horiz); 34c., Camel cricket and western meadow lark; 34c. Badger and buffalo grass; 34c. Eastern short-horned lizard and plains pocket gopher; 34c. Plains spadefoot and dung beetle (horiz); 34c. Two-striped grasshopper and Ord's kangaroo rat .... 9·25   9·25

The back of the sheet has a description of the plains prairie and a key to the flora and fauna in the design.

2584 Snoopy as World War I Flying Ace (Charles M. Schultz)

2001. "Peanuts" (comic strip). Self-adhesive.
3976   **2584**   34c. multicoloured   1·10   55

2585 Flag

2001. "Honoring Veterans". Self-adhesive.
3977   **2585**   34c. multicoloured   1·10   55

2586 Kahlo

2001. Frida Kahlo (artist) Commemoration.
3978   **2586**   34c. multicoloured   1·10   55

2587 Ebbets Field, Brooklyn

2001. Baseball Fields. Multicoloured. Self-adhesive.
3979   34c. Type **2587**   1·10   75
3980   34c. Tiger Stadium, Detroit   1·10   75
3981   34c. Crosley Field, Cincinnati   1·10   75
3982   34c. Yankee Stadium, New York City   1·10   75
3983   34c. Polo Grounds, New York City   1·10   75
3984   34c. Forbes Field, Pittsburgh   1·10   75
3985   34c. Fenway Park, Boston   1·10   75
3986   34c. Comiskey Park, Chicago   1·10   75
3987   34c. Shibe Park, Philadelphia   1·10   75
3988   34c. Wrigley Field, Chicago   1·10   75

A brief description of the stadium is included on the backing paper of each stamp.

2588 Atlas (statue), Rockefeller Centre, New York City

2001. Presorted coil stamp. Multicoloured. Self-adhesive.
3989   **2588**   (10c.) multicoloured   35   25

2589 Leonard Bernstein (composer)

2001
3990   **2589**   34c. black   1·10   55

2590 Car

2001. Presorted First-Class Card coil stamp. Self-adhesive.
3991   **2590**   (15c.) multicoloured   50   25

2591 Lucille Ball

2001. Legends of Hollywood. Self-adhesive.
3992   **2591**   34c. multicoloured   1·20   55

2592 Diamond in Square   **2593** Lone Star

2594 Sunshine and Shadow   **2595** Double Ninepatch

2001. Amish Quilts. Self-adhesive.
3993   **2592**   34c. multicoloured   1·10   75
3994   **2593**   34c. multicoloured   1·10   75
3995   **2594**   34c. multicoloured   1·10   75
3996   **2595**   34c. multicoloured   1·10   75

2596 Venus Flytrap

2001. Carnivorous Plants. Multicoloured. Self-adhesive.
3997   34c. Type **2596**   1·10   75
3998   34c. Yellow trumpet   1·10   75
3999   34c. Cobra lily   1·10   75
4000   34c. English sundew   1·10   75

2600 Calligraphy

2001. Eid al-Fitr and Eid al-Adha (Islamic festivals). Self-adhesive.
4001   **2600**   34c. gold, blue and brown   1·10   55

2601 Fermi

2001. Birth Centenary of Enrico Fermi (nuclear physicist).
4002   **2601**   34c. multicoloured   1·10   55

2602 Porky Pig delivering Letter

2001. Porky Pig (cartoon character). Self-adhesive.
4003   **2603**   34c. multicoloured   1·10   55
MS4004 87×130 mm. No. 4003   5·00   5·00

2603 "Virgin and Child" (Lorenzo Costa)

2001. Christmas. (1st issue). Self-adhesive gum.
4005   34c. multicoloured   1·10   55

2604 Santa Claus with Armful of Presents

2001. Christmas (2nd issue). Multicoloured. Self-adhesive.
(a) Size 18×25 mm.
4006   34c. Type **2604**   1·10   55
4007   34c. Wearing blue outfit   1·10   55
4008   34c. Wearing red outfit with fur collar   1·10   55
4009   34c. Wearing holly wreath   1·10   55

(b) Size 18×21 mm.
4010   34c. As T **2604**   1·10   55
4011   34c. As No. 4007   1·10   55
4012   34c. As No. 4008   1·10   55
4013   34c. As No. 4009   1·10   55

2608 Madison

2001. 250th Birth Anniv of James Madison (fourth president of United States).
4018   **2608**   34c. green and black   1·10   55

2609 Cornucopia

2001. Thanksgiving Festival. Self-adhesive.
4019   **2609**   34c. multicoloured   1·10   55

2001. Hanukkah and Kawanzaa Festivals. As Nos. 3265 and 3370 but with face values changed. Self-adhesive.
4020   **2257**   34c. multicoloured   1·10   55
4021   **2304**   34c. multicoloured   1·10   55
See also Nos. 3693/4.

2610 Flag

2001. "United We Stand". Self-adhesive.
4022   **2610**   34c. multicoloured   1·10   55

2611 Snowboarding

2002. Winter Sports. Multicoloured. Self-adhesive.
4030   34c. Type **2611**   1·10   55
4031   34c. Ice hockey   1·10   55
4032   34c. Figure skating   1·10   55
4033   34c. Ski jumping   1·10   55

2615 Man and Boy

2002. Mentoring a Child. Self-adhesive.
4034   **2615**   34c. multicoloured   1·10   55

2616 Langston Hughes

2002. 25th Anniv of Black Heritage Stamps. Langston Hughes (writer) Self-adhesive.
4035   **2616**   34c. multicoloured   1·10   55

2617 "HAPPY BIRTHDAY"

2002. Greetings Stamp. Self-adhesive.
4036   **2617**   34c. multicoloured   1·10   55

2618 Horse

2002. New Year. Year of the Horse. Self-adhesive.
4037   **2618**   34c. multicoloured   1·10   55

2619 Academy Arms

2002. Centenary of West Point Military Academy. Self-adhesive.
4038   **2619**   34c. multicoloured   1·10   55

2620 Alabama

2002. Greetings from America (1st issue). Multicoloured. Self-adhesive.
4039   34c. Type **2620**   1·00   75
4040   34c. Alaska   1·00   75
4041   34c. Arizona   1·00   75
4042   34c. Arkansas   1·00   75
4043   34c. California   1·00   75
4044   34c. Colorado   1·00   75
4045   34c. Connecticut   1·00   75
4046   34c. Delaware   1·00   75
4047   34c. Florida   1·00   75
4048   34c. Georgia   1·00   75
4049   34c. Hawaii   1·00   75
4050   34c. Idaho   1·00   75
4051   34c. Illinois   1·00   75
4052   34c. Indiana   1·00   75
4053   34c. Iowa   1·00   75
4054   34c. Kansas   1·00   75
4055   34c. Kentucky   1·00   75
4056   34c. Louisiana   1·00   75
4057   34c. Maine   1·00   75
4058   34c. Maryland   1·00   75
4059   34c. Massachusetts   1·00   75
4060   34c. Michigan   1·00   75
4061   34c. Minnesota   1·00   75
4062   34c. Mississippi   1·00   75
4063   34c. Missouri   1·00   75
4064   34c. Montana   1·00   75
4065   34c. Nebraska   1·00   75
4066   34c. Nevada   1·00   75
4067   34c. New Hampshire   1·00   75
4068   34c. New Jersey   1·00   75
4069   34c. New Mexico   1·00   75
4070   34c. New York   1·00   75
4071   34c. North Carolina   1·00   75

4072	34c. North Dakota	1·00	75
4073	34c. Ohio	1·00	75
4074	34c. Oklahoma	1·00	75
4075	34c. Oregon	1·00	75
4076	34c. Pennsylvania	1·00	75
4077	34c. Rhode Island	1·00	75
4078	34c. South Carolina	1·00	75
4079	34c. South Dakota	1·00	75
4080	34c. Tennessee	1·00	75
4081	34c. Texas	1·00	75
4082	34c. Utah	1·00	75
4083	34c. Vermont	1·00	75
4084	34c. Virginia	1·00	75
4085	34c. Washington	1·00	75
4086	34c. West Virginia	1·00	75
4087	34c. Wisconsin	1·00	75
4088	34c. Wyoming	1·00	75

Nos. 4039/88 were issued in *se-tenant* sheets of 50 stamps, with list of bird, flower, tree, capital and statehood printed on the backing paper of each stamp.

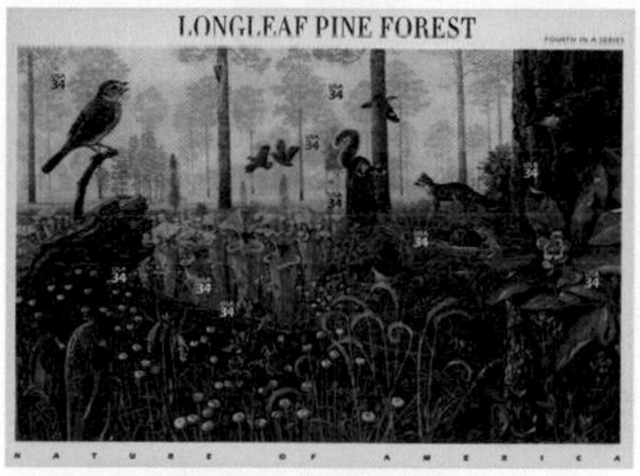

2621 Longleaf Pine Forest (image scaled to 21% of original size)

2002. Nature of America (4th series). Sheet 233×172 mm forming the overall design T **2621**. Multicoloured. Self-adhesive.

MS4089	34c. Bachman's sparrow; 34c. Northern bobwhites; 34c. Fox squirrel and red-bellied woodpecker; 34c. Grey fox (horiz); 34c. Brown-headed nuthatch; 34c. Broad-headed skink; 34c. Rosebud orchid; 34c. Grass-pink orchid (horiz); 34c. Eastern towhee; 34c. Sweetbay and pine woods treefrog	9·25	9·25

The backing paper of the sheet has a description of the pine of forest and a key to the flora and fauna in the design.

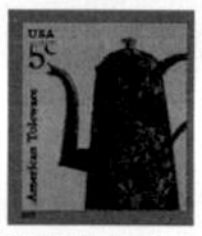

2622 Toleware Coffee Pot

2002. Arts and Crafts. Multicoloured.

(a) Ordinary gum. Coil stamps. Imperf×10

(ai) Litho Banknote Corporation of America Inc, Browns Summit, North Carolina

4090	1c. Tiffany lamp (7 June 2008)	25	20
4090a	2c. Navajo jewellery (12 February 2011)	25	20

(aii) Photo American Packaging Corporation, Columbus, Wisconsin

4091	1c. Tiffany lamp (16 March 2007)	25	20
4091b	3c. Silver coffee pot (16 September 2005)	25	20
4091c	4c. Chippendale chair (19 July 2007)	25	20
4091d	5c. Type **2622** (31 May 2002)	25	20
4091e	10c. Early American clock (4 August 2006)	25	20

(b) Self-adhesive.

(bi) Litho Ashton Potter (USA) Ltd, Williamsville, New York

(bia) Die-cut perf 11½×11

4091f	1c. Tiffany Lamp (16 March 2007)	25	20
4092	2c. Navajo jewellery (8 December 2005)	25	20
4093	10c. Early American clock (24 January 2004)	25	20

(bib) Die-cut perf 11×10½

4094	4c. Chippendale chair (5 March 2004)	25	20

(bii) Photo American Packaging Corporation, Columbus, Wisconsin. Die-cut perf 11½

4095	2c. Navajo jewellery (8 December 2005)	25	20
4096	5c. As Type **2622** (25 June 2004)	25	20

(biii) Litho Banknote Corporation of America Inc, Browns Summit, North Carolina. Die-cut perf perf 11½×11

4097	3c. Silver coffee pot (16 March 2007)	25	20

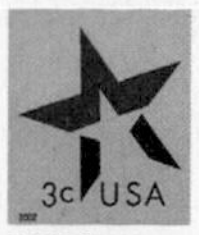

2623 Star

2002. Make-up Rate Stamps. Ordinary or Self-adhesive gum.

4100	**2623**	3c. red, ultramarine and black	25	20

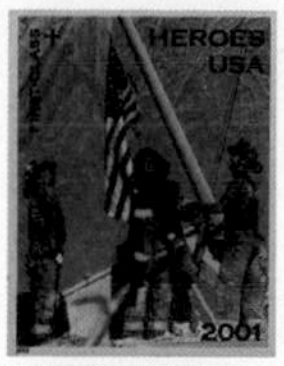

2624 Fire-fighters raising Flag

2002. Heroes of America. Self-adhesive.

4110	**2624**	(34c.+11c.) multicoloured	1·40	1·00

The premium was for assistance to families of those killed or disabled in the line of duty on September 11th. The face value became 37c.+8c. on 30 June 2002.

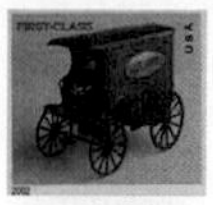

2625 Mail Van

2002. Antique Toys. Multicoloured. Self-adhesive.

4111	(37c.) Type **2625**	1·00	55
4112	(37c.) Steam locomotive	1·00	55
4113	(37c.) Taxi	1·00	55
4114	(37c.) Fire pump	1·00	55

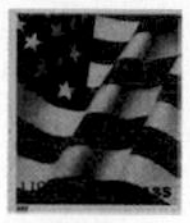

2629 Flag

2002. First Class Stamps. Ordinary or Self-adhesive gum.

4115	**2629**	(37c.) multicoloured	1·10	55

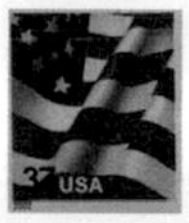

2630 Flag

2002. Self-adhesive or ordinary gum.

4123	**2630**	37c. multicoloured	1·10	55

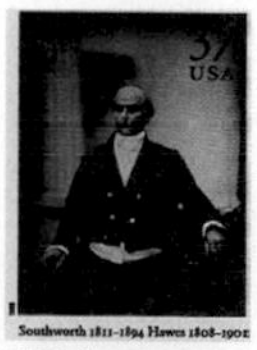

2631 Senator Daniel Webster (c. 1850, A. S. Southworth and J. J. Hawes)

2002. American Photographers. Showing works by photographers. Each black. Self-adhesive.

4132	37c. Type **2631**	1·10	75
4133	37c. General U. S. Grant and officers (1864, T. H. O'Sullivan)	1·10	75
4134	37c. Columbia river (1867, C. E. Watkins)	1·10	75
4135	37c. Agnes Rand Lee and Peggy (1899, Gertrude Kasebier)	1·10	75
4136	37c. Ellis Island (1905, L. W. Hine)	1·10	75
4137	37c. Aerial view of Madison Square Park (1912, A. L. Coburn)	1·10	75
4138	37c. Lotus flower (1915, E. Steichen)	1·10	75
4139	37c. Hands (1920, A. Stieglitz)	1·10	75
4140	37c. "Rayograph" (1923, Man Ray)	1·10	75
4141	37c. "Two shells" (1927, E. Weston)	1·10	75
4142	37c. Woman with corsage (1931, J. VanDerZee)	1·10	75
4143	37c. Man in vehicle (1935, Dorothea Lange)	1·10	75
4144	37c. Sharecropper's kitchen (1936, W. Evans)	1·10	75
4145	37c. Soldiers (1944, W. E. Smith)	1·10	75
4146	37c. Church steeple (1946, P. Strand)	1·10	75
4147	37c. Sand dunes (1948, A. Adams)	1·10	75
4148	37c. Ida C. Pabst (1958, Imogen Cunningham)	1·10	75
4149	37c. New York skyline (A. Kertesz)	1·10	75
4150	37c. Woman walking (1965, G. Winogrand)	1·10	75
4151	37c. Snow scene (1971, M. White)	1·10	75

Nos. 4132/51 were issued in *se-tenant* sheetlets of 20 stamps. The backing paper of the sheet has a description of the photograph and a short biography of the photographer.

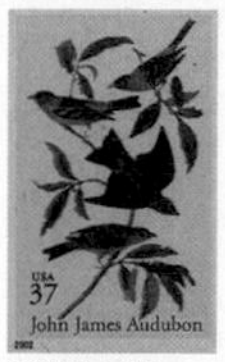

2632 Louisiana and Scarlet Tanagers

2002. John James Audubon Commemoration. Self-adhesive.

4152	**2632**	37c. multicoloured	1·10	55

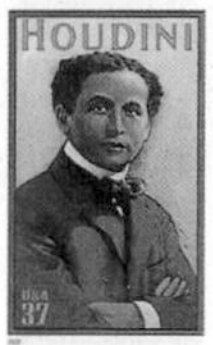

2633 Harry Houdini (escape artist)

2002. Self-adhesive.

4153	**2633**	37c. multicoloured	1·00	55

No. 4153 incorporates an additional hidden design of chains across the figure visible only under a special decoder.

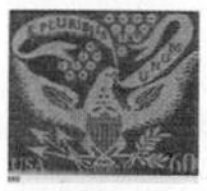

2634 Eagle (detail, woven coverlet)

2002. Self-adhesive.

4154	**2634**	60c. multicoloured	1·60	1·10

2002. Antique Toys. As Nos. 4111/14, but with value expressed. Self-adhesive.

4155	37c. multicoloured	1·10	75
4156	37c. multicoloured	1·10	75
4157	37c. multicoloured	1·10	75
4158	37c. multicoloured	1·10	75

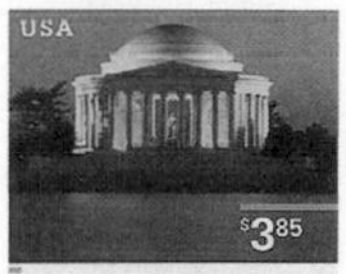

2635 Jefferson Memorial

2002. Self-adhesive.

4163	**2635**	$3.85 multicoloured	9·25	8·25
4164	**2560**	$13.65 multicoloured	34·00	30·00

Nos. 4163/4 each incorporate additional hidden designs, Jefferson's signature at lower left (No. 4164) or Union flag at top right (No. 4165) visible only under a special decoder.

No. 4163 was intended mainly for Priority mail and No. 4164 for Express Mail Service but they could be used on other mail as well.

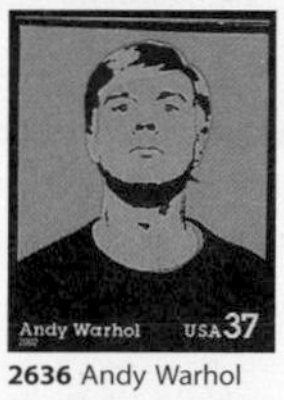

2636 Andy Warhol

2002. Andy Warhol (artist) Commemoration. Self-adhesive.

4165	**2636**	37c. multicoloured	1·00	55

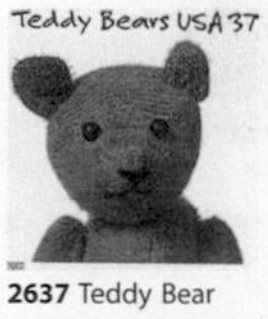

2637 Teddy Bear

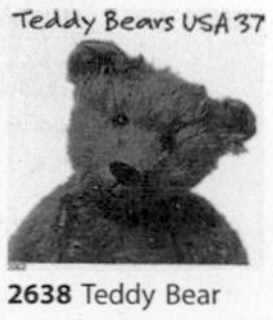

2638 Teddy Bear

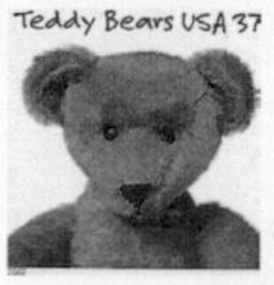

2639 Teddy Bear

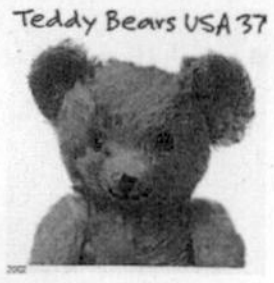

2640 Teddy Bear

2002. Centenary of the Teddy Bear. Self-adhesive.

4166	**2637**	37c. multicoloured	1·00	75
4167	**2638**	37c. multicoloured	1·00	75
4168	**2639**	37c. multicoloured	1·00	75
4169	**2640**	37c. multicoloured	1·00	75

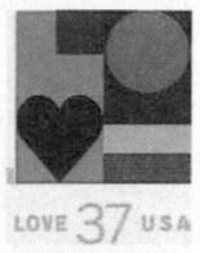

2641 'Love'

2002. Multicoloured. Self-adhesive.

4170	37c. Type **2641**	1·10	55
4171	60c. Love	1·60	1·20

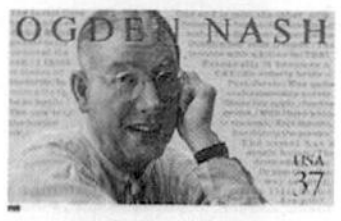

2643 Ogden Nash

2002. Birth Centenary of Frederick Ogden Nash (writer). Self-adhesive.

4172	**2643**	37c. multicoloured	1·00	55

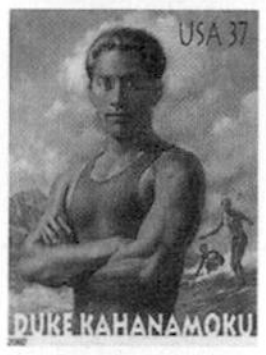

2644 Duke Kahanamoku (swimmer and surfer)

2002. Duke Paoa Kahanamoku Commemoration. Self-adhesive.

4173	**2644**	37c. multicoloured	1·00	55

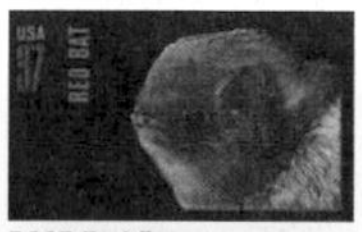

2645 Red Bat

2002. National Stamp Collecting Month. Bats. Multicoloured. Self-adhesive.

4174	37c. Type **2645**	1·00	75
4175	37c. Leaf-nosed bat	1·00	75
4176	37c. Pallid bat	1·00	75
4177	37c. Spotted bat	1·00	75

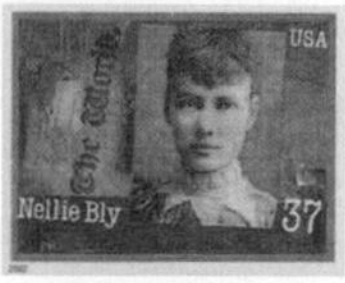

2649 Nellie Bly

2002. Women Journalists. Multicoloured. Self-adhesive.

4178	37c. Type **2649**	1·00	75
4179	37c. Ida M. Tarbell	1·00	75
4180	37c. Ethel L. Payne	1·00	75
4181	37c. Marguerite Higgins	1·00	75

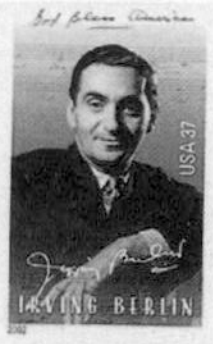

2653 Irving Berlin (composer)

2002. Self-adhesive.

4182	**2653**	37c. multicoloured	1·00	55

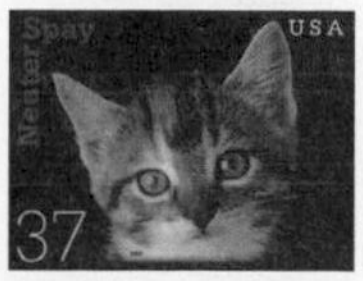

2654 Kitten

2002. Animal Population Control Campaign. Multicoloured. Self-adhesive.

4183	37c. Type **2654**	1·00	65
4184	37c. Puppy	1·00	65

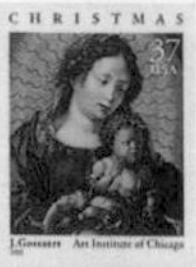

2656 "Virgin and Child" (Jan Gossaert)

2002. Christmas. (1st issue). Self-adhesive.

4185	**2656**	37c. multicoloured	1·00	55

See also No. 4323.

2002. Hanukkah, Kwanzaa and Eid Festivals. As Nos. 3265, 3370 and 4001 but with face values changed.

4186	**2257**	37c. multicoloured	1·00	55
4187	**2304**	37c. multicoloured	1·00	55
4188	**2600**	37c. gold, blue and brown	1·00	55

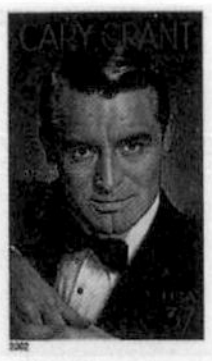

2657 Cary Grant (actor)

2002. Legends of Hollywood. Self-adhesive.

4189	**2657**	37c. multicoloured	1·00	55

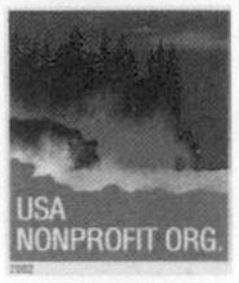

2658 Sea Coast

2002. Non-profit Organisations. Ordinary or self-adhesive gum.

4190	**2658**	(5c.) multicoloured	35	25

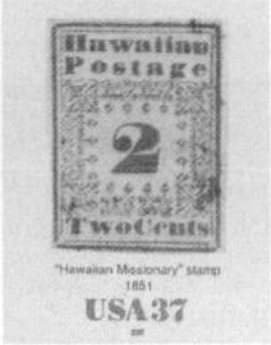

2659 1851 Hawaiian 2 cent Postage Stamp

2002. Hawaiian Missionary Stamps. Sheet 147×157 mm containing T **2659** and similar vert designs. Multicoloured.

MS4193	37c. Type **2659**; 37c. 1851 5 cent stamp; 37c. 1851 13 cent stamp; 37c. 1852 13 cent stamp	5·50	5·50

2002. Greetings stamp. As No. 4036 but with face value changed. Self-adhesive.

4194	**2617**	37c. multicoloured	1·00	55

2002. Greetings from America (2nd issue). As T 2620. Multicoloured. Self-adhesive.

4195	37c. As No. 4039	1·00	75
4196	37c. As No. 4040	1·00	75
4197	37c. As No. 4041	1·00	75
4198	37c. As No. 4042	1·00	75
4199	37c. As No. 4043	1·00	75
4200	37c. As No. 4044	1·00	75
4201	37c. As No. 4045	1·00	75
4202	37c. As No. 4046	1·00	75
4203	37c. As No. 4047	1·00	75
4204	37c. As No. 4048	1·00	75
4205	37c. As No. 4049	1·00	75
4206	37c. As No. 4050	1·00	75
4207	37c. As No. 4051	1·00	75
4208	37c. As No. 4052	1·00	75
4209	37c. As No. 4053	1·00	75
4210	37c. As No. 4054	1·00	75
4211	37c. As No. 4055	1·00	75
4212	37c. As No. 4056	1·00	75
4213	37c. As No. 4057	1·00	75
4214	37c. As No. 4058	1·00	75
4215	37c. As No. 4059	1·00	75
4216	37c. As No. 4060	1·00	75
4217	37c. As No. 4061	1·00	75
4218	37c. As No. 4062	1·00	75
4219	37c. As No. 4063	1·00	75
4220	37c. As No. 4064	1·00	75
4221	37c. As No. 4065	1·00	75
4222	37c. As No. 4066	1·00	75
4223	37c. As No. 4067	1·00	75
4224	37c. As No. 4068	1·00	75
4225	37c. As No. 4069	1·00	75
4226	37c. As No. 4070	1·00	75
4227	37c. As No. 4071	1·00	75
4228	37c. As No. 4072	1·00	75
4229	37c. As No. 4073	1·00	75
4230	37c. As No. 4074	1·00	75
4231	37c. As No. 4075	1·00	75
4232	37c. As No. 4076	1·00	75
4233	37c. As No. 4077	1·00	75
4234	37c. As No. 4078	1·00	75
4235	37c. As No. 4079	1·00	75
4236	37c. As No. 4080	1·00	75
4237	37c. As No. 4081	1·00	75
4238	37c. As No. 4082	1·00	75
4239	37c. As No. 4083	1·00	75
4240	37c. As No. 4084	1·00	75
4241	37c. As No. 4085	1·00	75
4242	37c. As No. 4086	1·00	75
4243	37c. As No. 4087	1·00	75
4244	37c. As No. 4088	1·00	75

Nos. 4195/244 were issued in *se-tenant* sheets of 50 stamps, with list of bird, flower, tree, capital and statehood printed on the backing paper of each stamp.

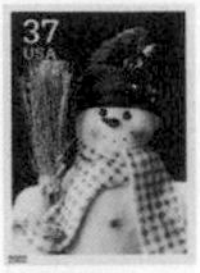

2660 Snowman wearing Check Scarf

2002. Christmas Holiday Snowmen. Multicoloured. Self-adhesive. (a) 19×27 mm.

4245	37c. Type **2660**	1·00	55
4246	37c. Snowman wearing tartan scarf	1·00	55
4247	37c. Snowman wearing top hat	1·00	55
4248	37c. Snowman with pipe	1·00	55

(b) Size 18×21 mm.

4249	37c. As No. 4245	1·00	55
4250	37c. As No. 4246	1·00	55
4251	37c. As No. 4247	1·00	55
4252	37c. As No. 4248	1·00	55

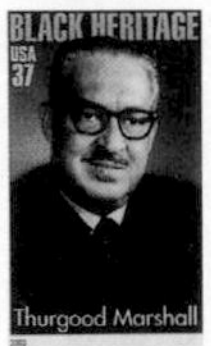

2664 Thurgood Marshall

2003. Black Heritage. Thurgood Marshall (first black Supreme Court judge). Self-adhesive.

4261	**2664**	37c. black	1·00	55

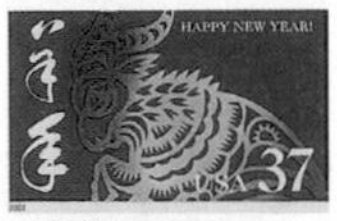

2665 Goat

2003. New Year. Year of the Goat. Self-adhesive.

4262	**2665**	37c. multicoloured	1·00	55

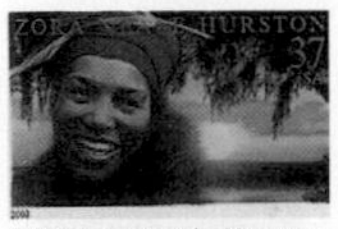

2666 Zora Neale Hurston

2003. Zora Neale Hurston (writer) Commemoration. Self-adhesive.

4263	**2666**	37c. multicoloured	1·00	55

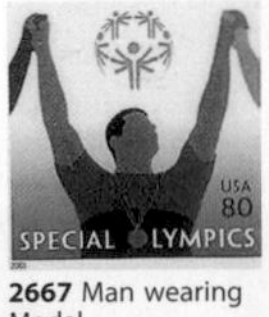

2667 Man wearing Medal

2002. Special Olympics Programme (disabled sports). Self-adhesive.

4264	**2667**	80c. multicoloured	2·20	1·30

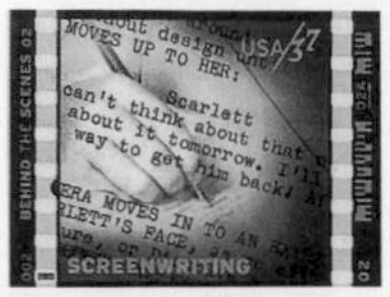

2668 Script for "Gone with the Wind" (film)

2003. American Film Making. Multicoloured. Self-adhesive.

4265	37c. Type **2668** (screenwriting)	1·00	65
4266	37c. Perry Ferguson and scenery design (art direction)	1·00	65
4267	37c. John Cassavetes (directing)	1·00	65
4268	37c. Camera and cameraman (cinematography)	1·00	65
4269	37c. Edith Head and dress design (costume design)	1·00	65
4270	37c. Hands, scissors and film (film editing)	1·00	65
4271	37c. Musical notation and hand holding pencil (music)	1·00	65
4272	37c. Model of E.T. (film character) (special effects)	1·00	65
4273	37c. Boris Karloff as Frankenstein (make up)	1·00	65
4274	37c. Hand and sound mixing board	1·00	65

The backing paper of the sheet has a brief description of the stamp.

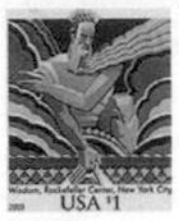

2669 Wisdom (Rockefeller Centre, New York)

2003. Self-adhesive.

4275	**2669**	$1 multicoloured	2·50	1·30

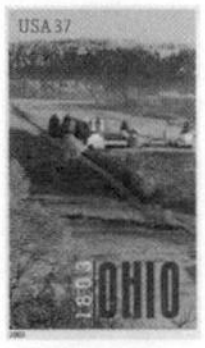

2670 Farm in Landscape

2003. Bicentenary of Ohio State. Self-adhesive.

4276	**2670**	37c. multicoloured	1·00	55

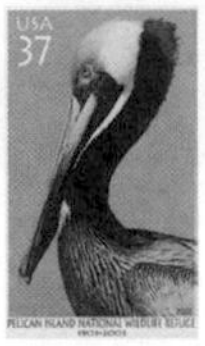

2671 Brown Pelican

2003. Centenary of Pelican Island Wildlife Refuge, Florida. Self-adhesive.

4277	**2671**	37c. multicoloured	1·00	55

A brief description of the Wildlife Refuge is printed on the back of the stamp.

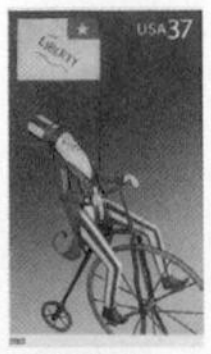

2672 Uncle Sam riding Penny-farthing Bicycle

2003. "Old Glory". Multicoloured. Self-adhesive.

4278	37c. Type **2672**	1·00	65
4279	37c. Benjamin Harrison presidential campaign badge	1·00	65
4280	37c. Silk bookmark (c.1893)	1·00	65
4281	37c. Modern fan showing flag	1·00	65
4282	37c. Woman holding flag (statue) (19th-century)	1·00	65

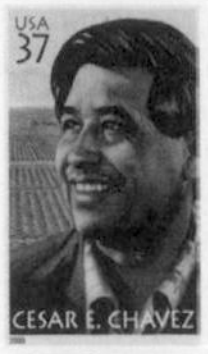

2673 Cesar Chavez

2003. Tenth Death Anniv of Cesar Chavez (workers rights activist). Self-adhesive.

4283	**2673**	37c. multicoloured	1·00	55

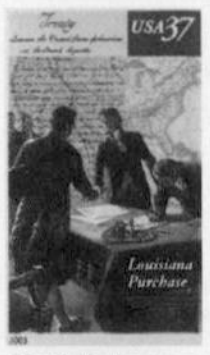

2674 Robert Livingston and Francois de Barbe-Marbois shaking Hands and James Monroe Signing Treaty

2003. Bicentenary of Treaty purchasing Louisiana Territory from France. Self-adhesive.

4284	**2674**	37c. multicoloured	1·00	55

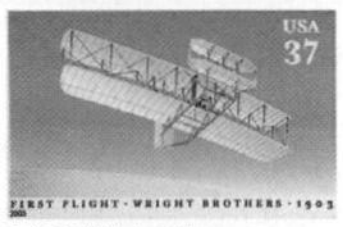

2675 Wright Flyer

2003. Centenary of Powered Flight. Self-adhesive.

4285	**2675**	37c. multicoloured	1·10	55
MS4286		130×87 mm. No. 4235	2·50	2·50

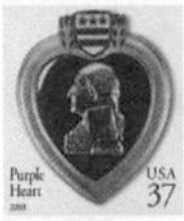

2676 Purple Heart (military medal)

2003

4287	**2676**	37c. multicoloured	1·00	55

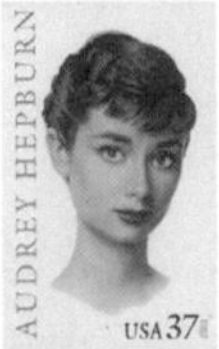

2677 Audrey Hepburn

2003. Legends of Hollywood. Self-adhesive.

4289	**2677**	37c. multicoloured	1·00	55

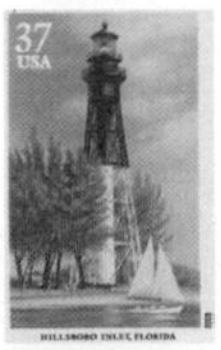

2678 Hillsboro Inlet, Florida

2003. South Eastern Lighthouses. Multicoloured. Self-adhesive.

4290	37c. Type **2678**	1·00	65
4291	37c. Old Cape Henry, Virginia	1·00	65
4292	37c. Cape Lookout, North Carolina	1·00	65
4293	37c. Morris Island, South Carolina	1·00	65
4294	37c. Tybee Island, Georgia	1·00	65

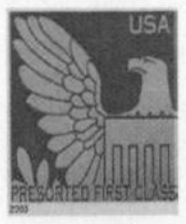

2683 Eagle

2003. Pre-sorted First Class Mail Coil Stamps. Self-adhesive.

4295	**2683**	25c. buff and blue	60	45
4296	**2683**	25c. blue and buff	60	45
4297	**2683**	25c. buff and emerald	60	45

4298	2683	25c. slate and buff	60	45
4299	2683	25c. blue and buff	60	45
4300	2683	25c. blue and buff	60	45
4301	2683	25c. buff and vermilion	60	45
4302	2683	25c. emerald and buff	60	45
4303	2683	25c. buff and slate	60	45
4304	2683	25c. vermilion and buff	60	45

2684 Raven

2685 Arctic Tundra (image scaled to 21% of original size)

2003. Nature of America (5th series). Sheet 233×172 mm containing T **2684** and forming the overall design T **2685**. Multicoloured. Self-adhesive.

MS4305 37c. Type **2684**; 37c. Bison; 37c. Caribou (horiz); 37c. Gyrfalcon (horiz); 37c. Grey wolf; 37c. Grizzly bear (horiz); 37c. Arctic ground squirrel (horiz); 37c. Singing vole (horiz); 37 c.Willow ptarmigan (horiz); 37c. Arctic grayling (horiz)   9·25   9·25

The backing paper of the sheet has a description of the tundra and a key to the flora and fauna in the design.

2686 Korean War Veterans' Memorial, Washington, DC

2003. 50th Anniv of End of Korean War. Self-adhesive.

4306	2686	37c. black, blue and vermilion	1·00	45

2687 "Young Mother"

2003. Mary Cassatt (artist) Commemoration. Multicoloured. Self-adhesive.

4307	37c. Type **2687**	1·00	55
4308	37c. "Children playing on Beach"	1·00	55
4309	37c. "On Balcony"	1·00	55
4310	37c. "Child in Straw Hat"	1·00	55

2691 Bronko Nagurski

2003. Early Football Players. Multicoloured. Self-adhesive.

4311	37c. Type **2691**	1·00	55
4312	37c. Walter Camp	1·00	55
4313	37c. Ernie Nevers	1·00	55
4314	37c. Red Grange	1·00	55

2695 Roy Acuff

2003. Birth Centenary of Roy Acuff (singer). Self-adhesive.

4315	2695	37c. black, scarlet and lemon	1·00	55

2696 Images of Washington, DC

2003. Washington, District of Columbia. Self-adhesive.

4316	2696	37c. multicoloured	1·00	55

2697 Scarlet King Snake

2003. Reptiles. Multicoloured. Self-adhesive.

4317	37c. Type **2697**	1·00	65
4318	37c. Blue-spotted salamander	1·00	65
4319	37c. Reticulate collared lizard	1·00	65
4320	37c. Ornate chorus frog	1·00	65
4321	37c. Ornate box turtle	1·00	65

2702 Crying Child

2003. Family Violence Campaign. Self-adhesive.

4322	2702	(45c.) multicoloured	1·20	80

2003. "Virgin and Child" (Jan Gossaert) (2nd issue). Self-adhesive.

4323	2656	37c. multicoloured	1·10	65

2703 Deer and Panpipes

2003. Christmas. Music Makers. (a) 20×27 mm. Self-adhesive.

4324	37c. Type **2703**	1·00	65
4325	37c. Father Christmas and drum	1·00	65
4326	37c. Father Christmas and trumpet	1·00	65
4327	37c. Deer and horn	1·00	65

(b) Size 18×21 mm.

4332	37c. As Type **2703**	1·00	65
4333	37c. As No. 4325	1·00	65
4334	37c. As No. 4236	1·00	65
4335	37c. As No. 4237	1·00	65

2707 Snowy Egret

2003. Self-adhesive.

4336	2707	37c. multicoloured	1·00	55

2708 Humphead Wrasse

2709 Pacific Coral Reef (image scaled to 21% of original size)

2004. Nature of America (6th series). Sheet 233×172 mm containing T **2708** and forming the overall design T **2709**. Multicoloured. Self-adhesive.

MS4339 37c.×10, Type **2708**; Bump-head parrotfish (vert); Emperor angelfish (vert); Black-spotted puffer; Hawksbill turtle; Magnificent sea anemone and Pink anemonefish (vert); Snowflake moray eel and Spanish dancer; Lionfish (vert); Triton's trumpet; Oriental sweetlips, Bluestreak cleaner wrasse and Mushroom coral   9·25   9·25

The backing paper of the sheet has a description of the coral reef and a key to the flora and fauna in the design.

2710 Monkey

2004. New Year. Year of the Monkey. Self-adhesive.

4340	2710	37c. multicoloured	1·00	55

2711 Heart-shaped Sweets

2004. Greetings Stamps. Love. Self-adhesive.

4341	2711	37c. multicoloured	1·00	55

2712 Paul Robeson

2004. Black Heritage. Paul Robeson (singer). Self-adhesive.

4342	2712	37c. black	1·00	55

2713 Theodor Geisel

2004. Birth Centenary of Theodor Seuss Geisel (Dr. Seuss) (writer). Self-adhesive.

4343	2713	37c. multicoloured	1·00	55

2714 Bouquet

2004. Greetings Stamps. Multicoloured. Self-adhesive.

4344	37c. Type **2714**	1·00	55
4345	60c. Bouquet	1·40	90

2716 Cadets' Chapel

2004. 50th Anniv of Air Force Academy. Self-adhesive.

4346	2716	37c. multicoloured	1·00	55

2717 Henry Mancini

2004. 80th Birth Anniv of Henry Mancini (composer and conductor). Self-adhesive.

4347	2717	37c. multicoloured	1·00	55

2718 Martha Graham

2004. American Choreographers. Multicoloured. Self-adhesive.

4348	37c. Type **2718**	1·00	55
4349	37c. Alvin Ailey	1·00	55
4350	37c. Agnes de Mille	1·00	55
4351	37c. George Ballantine	1·00	55

2004. Pre-sorted First Class Mail Coil Stamps. Ordinary gum.

4352	2683	25c. buff and blue	60	45
4353	2683	25c. blue and buff	60	45
4354	2683	25c. buff and emerald	60	45
4355	2683	25c. slate and buff	60	45
4356	2683	25c. blue and buff	60	45
4357	2683	25c. blue and buff	60	45
4358	2683	25c. buff and vermilion	60	45
4359	2683	25c. emerald and buff	60	45
4360	2683	25c. buff and slate	60	45
4361	2683	25c. vermilion and buff	60	45

2722 Lewis and Clark

2004. Bicentenary of Meriwether Lewis and William Clark's Expedition to Explore the West Coast of America. Self-adhesive.

4362	2722	37c. multicoloured	1·00	65

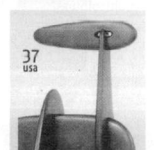

2723 "Figure" (detail)

2004. Birth Centenary of Isamu Noguchi (sculptor). Each black. Self-adhesive.

4363	37c. Type **2723**	1·00	55
4364	37c. "Akari 25N" (lamp)	1·00	55
4365	37c. "Margaret La Farge Osborn"	1·00	55
4366	37c. "Black Sun"	1·00	55
4367	37c. "Mother and Child"	1·00	55

2728 National World War II Memorial, Washington

2004. Self-adhesive.

4368	2728	37c. multicoloured	1·00	55

2729 Early Greek Athlete

2004. Olympic Games, Athens. Self-adhesive.

4369	2729	37c. multicoloured	1·00	55

2730 Mickey Mouse, Goofy and Donald Duck

2004. Disney Cartoon Characters. Multicoloured. Self-adhesive.

4370	37c. Type **2730**	1·00	55

2006. Greetings Stamps. Wedding. Self-adhesive.

4540	**2855**	39c. lilac	90	55
4541	-	63c. green	1·40	1·00

DESIGN: 63c. Dove.

2857 Common Buckeye

2006. Butterfly. Ordinary or self-adhesive Gum.

4542	**2857**	24c. multicoloured	70	35

2858 Sunflower

2006. Crop Plants. Multicoloured. Self-adhesive.

4545	39c. Type **2858**	90	55
4546	39c. Squash	90	55
4547	39c. Corn	90	55
4548	39c. Peppers	90	55
4549	39c. Beans	90	55

2863 In Flight

2006. X-Planes. Multicoloured. Self-adhesive.

4560	$4.05 Type **2863**	8·00	7·25
4561	$14.40 Passing through grid	28·00	18·00

No. 4560 was for use on priority mail and No. 4561 was for use on express mail.

2865 Sugar Ray Robinson (boxer)

2006. Self-adhesive.

4562	**2865**	39c. blue and vermilion	90	55

2866 Benjamin Franklin as Printer

2006. 300th Birth Anniv of Benjamin Franklin. Multicoloured. Self-adhesive.

4563	39c. Type **2866**	90	55
4564	39c. As postmaster	90	55
4565	39c. As statesman	90	55
4566	39c. As scientist	90	55

Nos. 4563/6 were issued with a brief description of the stamp on the backing sheet.

2870 Mickey and Minnie Mouse

2006. Disney Cartoon Characters. Multicoloured. Self-adhesive.

4567	39c. Type **2870**	90	55
4568	39c. Cinderella and Prince Charming	90	55
4569	39c. Beauty and the Beast	90	55
4570	39c. Lady and the Tramp	90	55

2874 Love Birds

2006. Greetings Stamp. True Blue. Self-adhesive.

4571	**2874**	39c. multicoloured	90	55

See also No. 4525.

2875 Katherine Anne Porter and Ship ("Ship of Fools" (novel))

2006. Katherine Anne Porter (writer) Commemoration. Self-adhesive.

4572	**2875**	39c. multicoloured	90	55

2876 Mother and Child

2006. Amber Alert (America's Missing. Broadcast Emergency Response). Self-adhesive.

4573	**2876**	39c. multicoloured	90	55

No. 4573 has a brief description of the service inscribed on the backing paper of the stamp.

2877 Purple Heart (military medal)

2006

4574	**2877**	39c. multicoloured	90	55

See also Nos. 4237/8.

2878 American Alligator

2006. Wonders of America. Multicoloured. Self-adhesive.

4575	39c. Type **2878**	90	55
4576	39c. Moloka'i	90	55
4577	39c. Saguro	90	55
4578	39c. Bering glacier	90	55
4579	39c. Great Sand Dunes	90	55
4580	39c. Chesapeake Bay	90	55
4581	39c. Cliff Palace	90	55
4582	39c. Crater Lake	90	55
4583	39c. American bison	90	55
4584	39c. Florida Keys	90	55
4585	39c. Pacific Crest Trail	90	55
4586	39c. Gateway Arch	90	55
4587	39c. Appalachians	90	55
4588	39c. American lotus	90	55
4589	39c. Lake Superior	90	55
4590	39c. Pronghorn deer	90	55
4591	39c. Bristlecone pines	90	55
4592	39c. Yosemite Falls	90	55
4593	39c. Great Basin	90	55
4594	39c. Verrazano—Narrows bridge	90	55
4595	39c. Mount Washington	90	55
4596	39c. Grand Canyon	90	55
4597	39c. American bullfrog	90	55
4598	39c. Oroville Dam	90	55
4599	39c. Peregrine falcon	90	55
4600	39c. Mississippi river delta	90	55
4601	39c. Steamboat geyser	90	55
4602	39c. Rainbow bridge	90	55
4603	39c. White sturgeon	90	55
4604	39c. Rocky Mountains	90	55
4605	39c. Redwoods	90	55
4606	39c. American beaver	90	55
4607	39c. Mississippi—Missouri river	90	55
4608	39c. Mount Wai'ale'ale	90	55
4609	39c. Kilauea	90	55
4610	39c. Mammoth cave	90	55
4611	39c. Blue whale	90	55
4612	39c. Death Valley	90	55
4613	39c. Cornish—Windsor bridge	90	55
4614	39c. Quaking Aspen	90	55

Nos. 4575/614 were issued with a brief description on the backing paper of each stamp.

2879 Champlain's Ship

2006. 400th Anniv of Samuel de Champlain's Survey of East Coast of North America. (a) Self-adhesive sheet stamps.

4615	39c. Type **2879**	90	55

A stamp in the same design and an identical miniature sheet were also issued by Canada, the Canada miniature sheet has a barcode at lower left, the USA sheet does not.

(b) Miniature sheet. Ordinary gum.

MS4616 204×146 mm. 39c.×2, As Type **2879**, 51c.×2, As Type **854** of Canada (40×40 mm)	3·75	3·75

2880 Robert D Murphy

Distinguished American Diplomats

2881 Diplomats (image scaled to 32% of original size)

2006. Diplomats. Sheet 146×84 mm containing T 2880 and forming the overall design as T **2881**. Multicoloured. Self-adhesive.

MS4617 39c.×6, Type **2881**; Frances E. Willis; Hiram Bingham; Philip C. Habib; Charles Bohlen; Clifton R. Wharton Sr	5·00	5·00

The stamps of **MS**4617 form a composite background design.

2882 As No. 579

2883 Washington 2006 (image scaled to 54% of original size)

2006. Washington 2006 International Stamp Exhibition. Sheet 89×83 mm containing T **2882** and forming the overall design as T **2883**. Multicoloured.

MS4618 $1 brown; $2 blue; $5 blue and carmine	15·00	14·50

DESIGNS: Type **2882**; $2 As Type **164**; $5 As Type **165**

2884 Judy Garland

2006. Legends of Hollywood. Self-adhesive.

4619	**2884**	39c. multicoloured	90	55

2885 Ronald Reagan

2006. Ronald Reagan (president 1981—1989) Commemoration. Self-adhesive.

4620	**2885**	39c. multicoloured	90	55

See also No. 4414.

2886 "HAPPY BIRTHDAY"

2006. Greetings Stamp.

4621	**2886**	39c. multicoloured	90	55

See also No. 4036.

2887 Roy Campanella

2006. Baseball Sluggers. Multicoloured. Self-adhesive.

4622	39c. Type **2887**	90	55
4623	39c. Hank Greenberg	90	55
4624	39c. Mel Ott	90	55
4625	39c. Mickey Mantle	90	55

Nos. 4622/5 were issued with a brief description on the backing paper of each stamp.

2891 Superman

2006. Comic Book Superheroes. Multicoloured. Self-adhesive.

4626	39c. Type **2891**	90	55
4627	39c. Green Lantern	90	55
4628	39c. Wonder Woman	90	55
4629	39c. Green Arrow	90	55
4630	39c. Batman	90	55
4631	39c. The Flash	90	55
4632	39c. Plastic Man	90	55
4633	39c. Aquaman	90	55
4634	39c. Supergirl	90	55
4635	39c. Hawkman	90	55
4636	39c. Superman Comic Cover	90	55
4637	39c. Green Lantern Cover	90	55
4638	39c. Wonder Woman Cover	90	55
4639	39c. Green Arrow Cover	90	55
4640	39c. Batman Cover	90	55
4641	39c. The Flash Cover	90	55
4642	39c. Plastic Man Cover	90	55
4643	39c. Aquaman Cover	90	55
4644	39c. Supergirl Cover	90	55
4645	39c. Hawkman Cover	90	55

Nos. 4626/45 were issued with a brief description on the backing paper of each stamp.

2911 Chopper (1970)

2006. Motorcycles. Multicoloured. Self-adhesive.

4646	39c. Type **2911**	90	55
4647	39c. Harley-Davidson (1965)	90	55
4648	39c. Indian (1940)	90	55
4649	39c. Cleveland (1918)	90	55

Nos. 4646/9 were issued with a brief description on the backing paper of each stamp.

2915 Quilt

2916 Quilt

2917 Quilt

2918 Quilt

2919 Quilt

2920 Quilt

2921 Quilt

2922 Quilt

2923 Quilt

2924 Quilt

2006. American Quilts from Gee's Bend, Alabama. Self-adhesive.

4650	**2915**	39c. multicoloured	1·00	65
4651	**2916**	39c. multicoloured	1·00	65
4652	**2917**	39c. multicoloured	1·00	65
4653	**2918**	39c. multicoloured	1·00	65
4654	**2919**	39c. multicoloured	1·00	65
4655	**2920**	39c. multicoloured	1·00	65
4656	**2921**	39c. multicoloured	1·00	65
4657	**2922**	39c. multicoloured	1·00	65
4658	**2923**	39c. multicoloured	1·00	65
4659	**2924**	39c. multicoloured	1·00	65

2925 Snail Kite

2926 Southern Florida Wetland (image scaled to 21% of original size)

2006. Nature of America (8th series). Sheet 233×172 mm containing T **2925** and forming the overall design T **2926**. Multicoloured. Self-adhesive.

MS4661 39c.×10, Type **2925**; Wood stork; Red mangrove and Florida panther; Bald eagle (horiz); American crocodile (horiz); Roseate spoonbill (horiz); Everglades mink; American alligator (horiz); White ibis; Cape Sable seaside sparrow (horiz) 9·00 9·00

The backing paper of the sheet has a description of the forest and a key to the flora and fauna in the design.

2927 Snowflake

2928 Snowflake

2929 Snowflake

2930 Snowflake

2006. Christmas (1st issue). Snowflakes. Self-adhesive.

4662	**2927**	39c. multicoloured	90	55
4663	**2928**	39c. multicoloured	90	55
4664	**2929**	39c. multicoloured	90	55
4665	**2930**	39c. multicoloured	90	55

See also No. 4681.

(b) Size 22×24 mm.

4670	**2927**	39c. multicoloured	90	55
4671	**2928**	39c. multicoloured	90	55
4672	**2929**	39c. multicoloured	90	55
4673	**2930**	39c. multicoloured	90	55

2006. Eid al-Fitr and Eid al-Adha (Islamic festivals). Self-adhesive.

4678	**2600**	39c. gold, blue and brown	90	55

2006. Hanukkah Festival. Self-adhesive.

4679	**2758**	39c. multicoloured	90	55

2006. Kwanzaa Festival. Self-adhesive.

4680	**2759**	39c. multicoloured	90	55

2931 "Madonna and Child" (I. Chacon)

2006. Christmas (2nd issue). Self-adhesive.

4681	**2931**	39c. multicoloured	90	55

2932 Ella Fitzgerald

2007. Black Heritage. Ella Fitzgerald (singer) Commemoration. Self-adhesive.

4682	**2932**	39c. multicoloured	90	55

2933 *Dawn over the Cimarron* (Mike Larson)

2007. Centenary of Oklahoma Statehood. Self-adhesive.

4683	**2933**	39c. multicoloured	90	55

2934 Hershey's Chocolate Kiss

2007. Love and Kisses. Centenary of Hershey's Chocolate Kiss (confectionary). Self-adhesive.

4684	**2934**	39c. multicoloured	90	55

2935 Aurora Borealis

2007. International Polar Year. Sheet 108×70 mm containing T **2935** and forming the overall design. Multicoloured. Self-adhesive.

MS4685 84c.×2, Type **2935**; Aurora Australis; International Polar Year 3·50 3·50

2937 Henry Longfellow and Horseman (*Paul Revere's Ride* (poem))

2007. Birth Bicentenary of Henry Wadsworth Longfellow (writer). Self-adhesive.

4686	**2937**	39c. multicoloured	90	55

2938 Liberty Bell

2007. Forever. First Class Self-adhesive.

4687	**2938**	(41c.) multicoloured	90	55

2939 Flag

2007. First Class Stamps. No value expressed

(a) Litho Ashton-Potter (USA) Ltd, Williamsville, New York

(i) Sheet Stamps

(ia) Ordinary gum

4692	**2939**	(41c.) multicoloured	90	55

(ib) Self-adhesive

4693	**2939**	(41c.) multicoloured	90	55

(ii) Coil Stamps

(iia) Ordinary gum

4694	**2939**	(41c.) multicoloured	90	55

(iib) Self-adhesive

4695	**2939**	(41c.) multicoloured (October 2007)	90	55

(iii) Booklet stamps

4696	**2939**	(41c.) multicoloured	90	55

(b) Litho Banknote Corporation of America Inc, Browns Summit, North Carolina

(i) Coil Stamps

(ia) Ordinary gum

4697	**2939**	(41c.) multicoloured	90	55

(ib) Self-adhesive

4698	**2939**	(41c.) multicoloured	90	55

(ii) Booklet stamps

4699	**2939**	(41c.) multicoloured	90	55

(c) Photo Avery Dennison, Clinton, South Carolina

(i) Coil Stamps. Self-adhesive

(ia)

4700	**2939**	(41c.) multicoloured	90	55

(ib)

4701	**2939**	(41c.) multicoloured	90	55

2940 *Susan Constant, Godspeed* and *Discovery* (ships carrying settlers)

2007. 400th Anniv of Settlement of Jamestown, Virginia. Self-adhesive.

4705	**2940**	41c. multicoloured	90	55

2941 Florida Panther

2007. Wildlife. Ordinary or self-adhesive gum.

4706	**2941**	26c. multicoloured	45	35

2942 Bighorn Sheep

2007. Wildlife. Self-adhesive.

4710	**2942**	17c. multicoloured	35	25

2943 Darth Vader

2007. 30th Anniv of Stars Wars (film) Premiere. Sheet 233×172 mm containing T **2943** and forming the overall design. Multicoloured. Self-adhesive.

MS4712 41c.×15, Type **2943**; *Millennium Falcon* (47×25 mm); Emperor Palpatine (41×26 mm); Anakin Skywalker and Obi-Wan Kenobi (41×33 mm); Luke Skywalker (31×41 mm); Princess Leia and R2-D2 (41×33 mm); C3-PO (21×65 mm); Queen Padme Amidala (26×48 mm); Obi-Wan Kenobi (31×48 mm); Boba Fett (32×40 mm); Darth Maul (26×41 mm); Chewbacca and Hans Solo (48×31 mm); X-wing Starfighter (41×26 mm); Yoda (31×48 mm); Stormtroopers (41×31 mm) 11·50 10·50

The backing paper of the sheet has a description of the stamps.

A2945 Okefenoke Swamp, Georgia and Florida

2007. Air. Self-adhesive. Multicoloured.

A4713	69c. Type A **2945**	1·30	90
A4714	90c. Hagatna Bay, Guam	1·60	1·10

See also Nos. A3599/603 and A4537/9.

2947 *Air Force One*

2007. Presidential Aircraft. Multicoloured.

4715	$4.60 Type **2974**	8·00	7·25
4716	$16.25 *Marine One*	28·00	20·00

No. 4715 was for use on Priority Mail and No. 4716 was for use on Express Mail.

2949 Grays Harbour, Washington

2007. Pacific Lighthouses. Self-adhesive. Multicoloured.

4717	41c. Type **2949**	80	55
4718	41c. Umpqua River, Oregon	80	55
4719	41c. St George Reef, California	80	55
4720	41c. Diamond Head, Hawai	80	55
4721	41c. Five Finger, Alaska	80	55

2954 Heart

2007. Greetings Stamps. Multicoloured. Self-adhesive.

4723	41c. Type **2954**	80	55
4724	58c. Heart	1·10	80

2956 Purple Nightshade and Morrison's Bumble Bee

2007. Pollination. Self-adhesive. Multicoloured.

4725	41c. Type **2956**	80	55
4726	41c. Caliope hummingbird and hummingbird trumpet	80	55
4727	41c. Saguro and lesser long-nosed bat	80	55
4728	41c. Southern dogface and butterfly prairie ironweed	80	55

Nos. 4725/8, were arranged in *se-tenant* blocks of four stamps. The arrangement of the blocks alternate, one showing a composite design with the pollinators central (No. 4725 at top left), the other showing a composite design with the flowers central (No. 4728 at top left).

2960 Stars and Stripes

2007. Pre-sorted First Class Mail. Self-adhesive.

| 4729 | 2960 | (10c.) ultramarine, scarlet and gold | 35 | 25 |

2961 Spiderman

2007. Comic Book Superheroes. Multicoloured. Self-adhesive.

4731	41c. Type **2961**	80	55
4732	41c. The Hulk	80	55
4733	41c. Sub-Mariner	80	55
4734	41c. The Thing	80	55
4735	41c. Captain America	80	55
4736	41c. Silver Surfer	80	55
4737	41c. Spider Woman	80	55
4738	41c. Iron Man	80	55
4739	41c. Elektra	80	55
4740	41c. Wolverine	80	55
4741	41c. Spiderman Comic Cover	80	55
4742	41c. The Hulk Cover	80	55
4743	41c. Sub-Mariner Cover	80	55
4744	41c. Fantastic Four Cover	80	55
4745	41c. Captain America Cover	80	55
4746	41c. Silver Surfer Cover	80	55
4747	41c. Spiderwoman Cover	80	55
4748	41c. Iron Man Cover	80	55
4749	41c. Elektra cover	80	55
4750	41c. X-men Cover	80	55

Nos. 4631/50 were issued in *se-tenant* sheets of 20 stamps, with a brief description on the backing paper of each stamp.

2981 Hutchinson Brothers Launch (1915)

2007. Vintage Mahogany Speedboats. Multicoloured. Self-adhesive.

4751	41c. Type **2981**	80	55
4752	41c. Chris-Craft Racing Runabout (1954)	80	55
4753	41c. Hacker-Craft (1939)	80	55
4754	41c. Gar Wood Runabout (1931)	80	55

2985 Purple Heart (military medal)

2007

| 4755 | 2985 | 41c. multicoloured | 80 | 55 |

2986 Magnolia and Irises (stained glass window by Louis Tiffany)

2007. Self-adhesive.

| 4756 | 2986 | 41c. multicoloured | 80 | 55 |

2987 Chrysanthemum

2007. Flowers. Multicoloured. Self-adhesive.

4757	41c. Type **2987**	80	55
4758	41c. Orange gerbera	80	55
4759	41c. Iris	80	55
4760	41c. Dahlia	80	55
4761	41c. Pink magnolia	80	55
4762	41c. Red gerbera	80	55
4763	41c. Water lily	80	55
4764	41c. Poppy	80	55
4765	41c. Cone flower	80	55
4766	41c. Tulip	80	55

2996a Flag

2007. First Class Stamps. With face value

(a) Litho Ashton-Potter (USA) Ltd, Williamsville, New York

(ai) Coil Stamp

| 4776a | 2996a | 41c. multicoloured (October 2007) | 90 | 55 |

(aii) Booklet Stamp

| 4776b | 2996a | 41c. multicoloured | 90 | 55 |

(b) Litho Banknote Corporation of America Inc, Browns Summit, North Carolina

(i) Coil Stamp

| 4776c | 2996a | 41c. multicoloured (November 2007) | 90 | 55 |

(ii) Booklet Stamp

| 4776d | 2996a | 41c. multicoloured | 90 | 55 |

(c) Photo Avery Dennison, Clinton, South Carolina

(i)

| 4776e | 2996a | 41c. multicoloured | 90 | 55 |

(ii)

| 4776f | 2996a | 41c. multicoloured | 90 | 55 |

2997 Peter Pan and Tinkerbelle

2007. Disney Cartoon Characters. Multicoloured. Self-adhesive.

4777	41c. Type **3001** 'Celebrate'	80	55
4778	41c. Mickey Mouse	80	55
4779	41c. Aladdin and Genie	80	55
4780	41c. Dumbo and Timothy	80	55

3001 'Celebrate'

2007. Greeting Stamp.

| 4781 | 3001 | 41c. multicoloured | 80 | 55 |

3002 James Stewart

2007. Legends of Hollywood. Self-adhesive.

| 4782 | 3002 | 41c. multicoloured | 80 | 55 |

3003 Golden Eagle

3004 Alpine Tundra (image scaled to 21% of original size)

2007. Nature of America (9th series). Sheet 233×172 mm containing T **3003** and forming the overall design T **3004**. Multicoloured. Self-adhesive.

| MS4783 | 41c.×10, Type **3003**; Elk (vert); Yellow-bellied marmot (vert); American pika (vert); Bighorn sheep (vert); White-tailed ptarmigan (vert); Magdalena alpine butterfly (vert); Rocky Mountain Parnassian butterfly (vert); Melissa Arctic butterfly; Brown-capped rosy finch | 8·00 | 8·00 |

The backing paper of the sheet has a description of the forest and a key to the flora and fauna in the design.

3005 Gerald Ford

2007. Gerald Ford (president 1974–1977) Commemoration. Self-adhesive.

| 4784 | 3005 | 41c. multicoloured | 80 | 55 |

3006 Jurors

2007. Jury Duty. Self-adhesive.

| 4785 | 3006 | 41c. multicoloured | 80 | 55 |

3007 Looking towards Light

2007. 60th Anniv of Mendez v.Westminster (successful anti-segregation lawsuit). Self-adhesive.

| 4786 | 3007 | 41c. multicoloured | 80 | 55 |

2007. Eid al-Fitr and Eid al-Adha (Islamic festivals). Self-adhesive.

| 4787 | 2600 | 41c. gold, blue and brown | 80 | 55 |

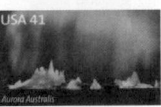

3008 Aurora Australis

2007. Polar Lights. Multicoloured. Self-adhesive.

| 4788 | 41c. Type **3008** | 80 | 55 |
| 4789 | 41c. Aurora Borealis | 80 | 55 |

3010 Yoda

2007. Stars Wars Characters. Self-adhesive.

| 4790 | 3010 | 41c. multicoloured | 80 | 55 |

3011 Reindeer

2007. Christmas (1st issue). Holiday Knits. Self-adhesive.

(i).

4791	41c. Type **3011**	80	55
4792	41c. Christmas tree	80	55
4793	41c. Snowman	80	55
4794	41c. Bear	80	55

(ii) Size 22×25 mm.

4795	41c. As Type **3011**	80	55
4796	41c. As No. 4792	80	55
4797	41c. As No. 4793	80	55
4798	41c. As No. 4794	80	55

(b) Size 22×24 mm.

4799	41c. As Type **3011**	80	55
4800	41c. As No. 4792	80	55
4801	41c. As No. 4793	80	
4802	41c. As No, 4794	80	55

3015 Madonna of the Carnation (Bernardino Luini)

2007. Christmas (2nd issue). Self-adhesive.

| 4803 | 3015 | 41c. multicoloured | 80 | 55 |

2007. Hanukkah Festival. Self-adhesive.

| 4804 | 2758 | 41c. multicoloured | 80 | 55 |

2007. Kwanzaa Festival. Self-adhesive.

| 4805 | 2759 | 41c. multicoloured | 80 | 55 |

3016 Lantern, Rat and Script

2008. New Year. Year of the Rat. Self-adhesive.

| 4806 | 3016 | 41c. multicoloured | 80 | 55 |

No. 4806 was issued in sheets of 12 stamps with an enlarged illustrated border and a brief description of the Chinese lunar calender on the backing paper.

3017 Charles Chesnutt

2008. Black Heritage. 150th Birth Anniv of Charles Waddell Chesnutt (writer). Self-adhesive.

| 4807 | 3017 | 41c. multicoloured | 80 | 55 |

3018 Marjorie Rawlings and Scene from *The Yearling*

2008. Marjorie Kinnan Rawlings (writer) Commemoration. Self-adhesive.

| 4808 | 3018 | 41c. multicoloured | 80 | 55 |

3019 Gerty Cori (biochemist)

2008. American Scientists. Multicoloured. Self-adhesive.

4809	41c. Type **3019**	80	55
4810	41c. Linus Pauling (chemist)	80	55
4811	41c. Edwin Hubble (astronomer)	80	55
4812	41c. John Bardeen (physicist)	80	55

Nos. 4809/12 were issued in horizontal *se-tenant* strips of four stamps, each strip forming a composite design.

3023 Flag at Sunrise **3024** Flag at Midday **3025** Flag in Afternoon

3026 Flag at Sunset

2008. Flags 24/7. (a) Ordinary gum. Size 22×25 mm.

4813	3023	42c. multicoloured	80	55
4814	3024	42c. multicoloured	80	55
4815	3025	42c. multicoloured	80	55
4816	3026	42c. multicoloured	80	55

(b) Self-adhesive gum. Size 21×25 mm.

4817	3023	42c. multicoloured	80	55
4818	3024	42c. multicoloured	80	55
4819	3025	42c. multicoloured	80	55
4820	3026	42c. multicoloured	80	55

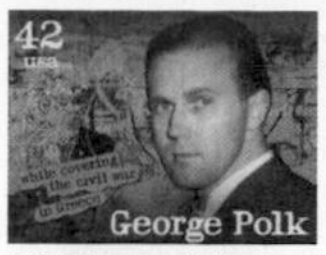

3027 George Polk

2008. American Journalists. Multicoloured. Self-adhesive.

4833	42c. Type **3027**	80	55
4834	42c. Ruben Salazar	80	55
4835	42c. Eric Sevareid	80	55
4836	42c. Martha Gellhorn	80	55
4837	42c. John Hersey	80	55

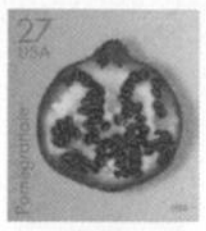

3032 Pomegranate

2008. Tropical Fruit. Multicoloured. Self-adhesive.

4838	27c. Type **3032**	55	40
4839	27c. Star Fruit	55	40
4840	27c. Kiwi	55	40
4841	27c. Papaya	55	40
4842	27c. Guava	55	40

Nos. 4838/42 were issued in horizontal *se-tenant* strips of five stamps, each strip forming a composite design.

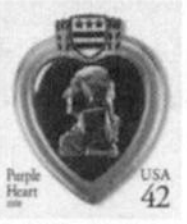

3037 Purple Heart

2008. Ordinary or self-adhesive gum.

4848	**3037** 42c. multicoloured	80	55

See also Nos. 4237/8, 4574 and 4755.

2008. Forever. First Class Self-adhesive.

4850	**2938** (42c.) multicoloured	80	55

See also No. 4689.

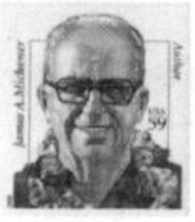

3038 James Michener (writer)

2008. Great Americans. Multicoloured. Self-adhesive.

4851	59c. Type **3038**	1·10	80
4852	76c. Edward Trudeau (phthisiologist (specialist in tuberculosis))	1·40	1·00

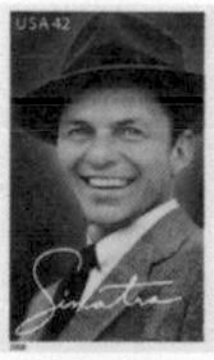

3040 Frank Sinatra

2008. Tenth Death Anniv of Frank Sinatra (singer and actor). Self-adhesive.

4853	**3040** 42c. multicoloured	80	55

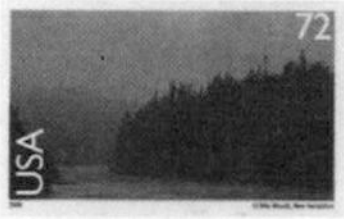

A 3041 13 Mile Woods, New Hampshire

2008. Air. Self-adhesive.

A4854	72c. Type A **3041**	1·00	1·00
A4855	94c. Trunk Bay, St John, Virgin Islands	1·20	1·20

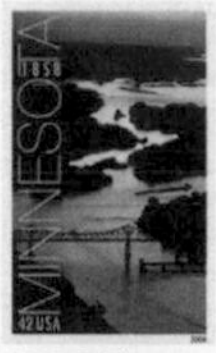

3043 Bridge over Mississippi River, Winona

2008. 150th Anniv of Minnesota Statehood. Self-adhesive.

4856	**3043** 42c. multicoloured	80	55

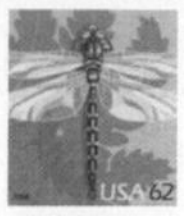

3044 Dragonfly

2008. Self-adhesive.

4857	**3044** 62c. multicoloured	1·10	80

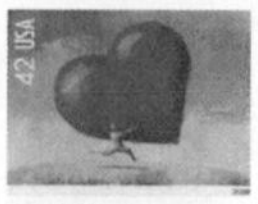

3045 Man carrying Heart

2008. Love. Self-adhesive.

4858	**3045** 42c. multicoloured	80	55

2008. Greetings Stamps. Multicoloured. Self-adhesive.

4859	42c. Type **2954** multicoloured	80	55
4860	59c. Heart	1·10	80

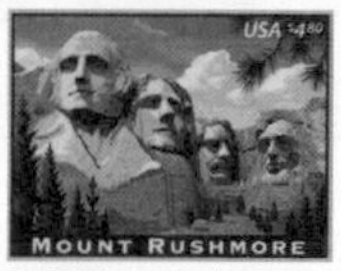

3046 Mount Rushmore

2008. American Landmarks. Self-adhesive. Multicoloured.

4861	$4.80 Type **3046**	9·00	8·25
4862	$16.50 Hoover Dam	32·00	25·00

No. 4861 was for use on Priority Mail and No. 4862 was for use on Express Mail.

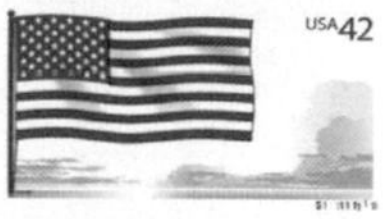

3048 USA

2008. Flags of the Nation. Multicoloured. Self-adhesive.

4863	42c. Type **3048**	80	55
4864	42c. Alabama	80	55
4865	42c. Alaska	80	55
4866	42c. American Samoa	80	55
4867	42c. Arizona	80	55
4868	42c. Arkansas	80	55
4869	42c. California	80	55
4870	42c. Colorado	80	55
4871	42c. Connecticut	80	55
4872	42c. Delaware	80	55

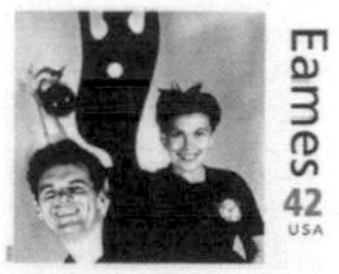

3058 Charles and Ray Eames

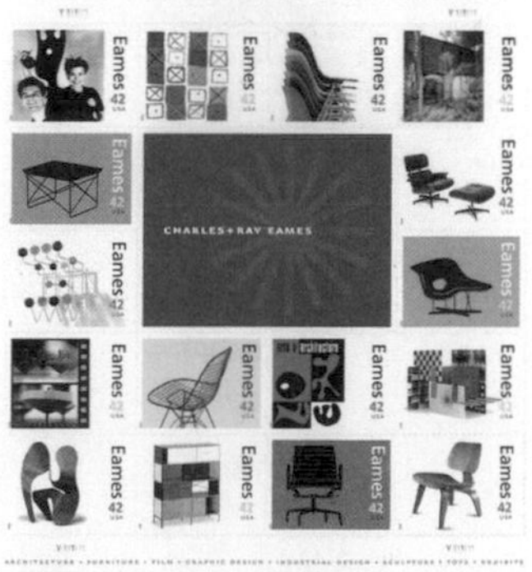

3059 (image scaled to 26% of original size)

2008. 30th Death Anniv of Charles and 20th Death Anniv of Ray Eames (designers). Sheet 184×182 mm containing T **3058** and forming the overall design T **3059**. Multicoloured. Self-adhesive.

MS4873	42c.×16, Type **3058**; *Cross-patch* fabric design; Stacking chairs; Case Study House; Wire base table; Lounge chair and ottoman; Hang-It-All; *La Chaise*; Scene from film *Tops*; Wire mesh chair; Magazine cover; House of Cards; Moulded plywood sculptures; Storage unit; Aluminium Group chair; Moulded plywood chair	12·50	12·50

The backing paper of the sheet has a brief description of the stamps.

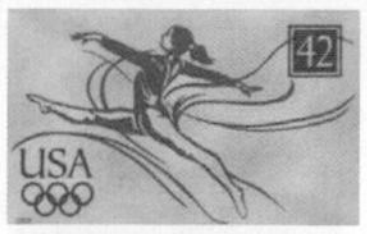

3060 Gymnast

2008. Olympic Games, Beijing. Self-adhesive.

4874	**3060** 42c. multicoloured	80	55

2008. Greeting Stamp. Celebrate

4875	42c. As Type **3001**	80	55

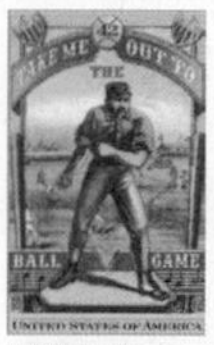

3061 Early Baseball Player

2008. Centenary of Take Me Out to the Ball Game (song).

4876	**3061** 42c. multicoloured	80	55

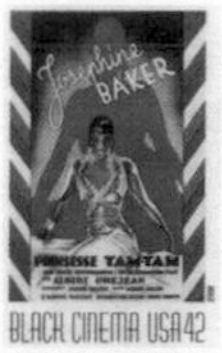

3062 Josephine Baker in *Princess Tam-Tam*

2008. Vintage Black Cinema. Multicoloured.

4877	42c. Type **3062**	80	55
4878	42c. Louis Jordan in *Caldonia*	80	55
4879	42c. Poster for *Hallelujah!*	80	55
4880	42c. Poster for *Black and Tan*	80	55
4881	42c. Poster for *Sport of the Gods*	80	55

The backing paper of the sheet has a brief description of the stamps.

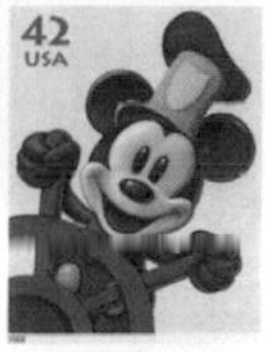

3067 Mickey Mouse as Steamboat Willie

2008. Disney Cartoon Characters. Multicoloured. Self-adhesive.

4882	42c. Type **3067**	80	55
4883	42c. Pongo and pup	80	55
4884	42c. Mowgli and Baloo	80	55
4885	42c. Princess Aurora and Flora, Fauna and Merryweather	80	55

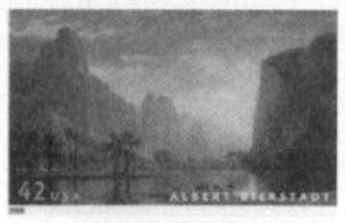

3071 *Valley of the Yosemite*

2008. Albert Bierstadt (artist) Commemoration. Self-adhesive.

4886	**3071** 42c. multicoloured	80	55

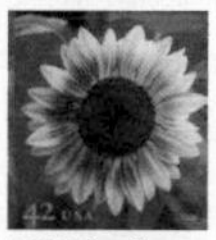

3072 Sunflower

2008. Self-adhesive.

4887	**3072** 42c. multicoloured	80	55

2008. Forever. First Class Self-adhesive.

4888	**2938** (42c.) multicoloured	80	55

2008. Flags of the Nation. As T **3048**. Multicoloured. Self-adhesive.

4890	42c. District of Columbia	80	55
4891	42c. Florida	80	55
4892	42c. Georgia	80	55
4893	42c. Guam	80	55
4894	42c. Hawaii	80	55
4895	42c. Idaho	80	55
4896	42c. Illinois	80	55
4897	42c. Indiana	80	55
4898	42c. Iowa	80	55
4899	42c. Kansas	80	55

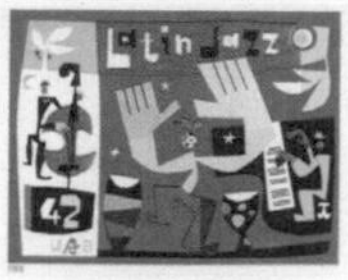

3083 Stylized Musicians

2008. Latin Jazz.

4900	**3083** 42c. multicoloured	80	55

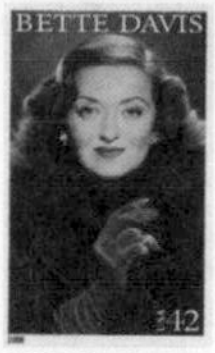

3084 Bette Davis

2008. Legends of Hollywood.

4901	**3084** 42c. multicoloured	80	55

2008. Eid al-Fitr and Eid al-Adha (Islamic festivals). As Type **2600**. Self-adhesive.

4902	42c. gold, deep blue and grey-brown	80	55

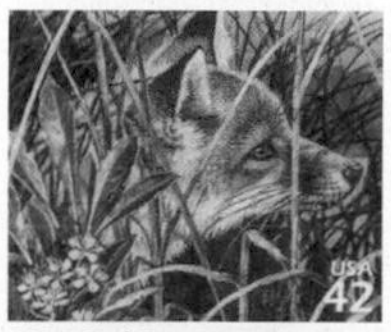

3085 Red Fox

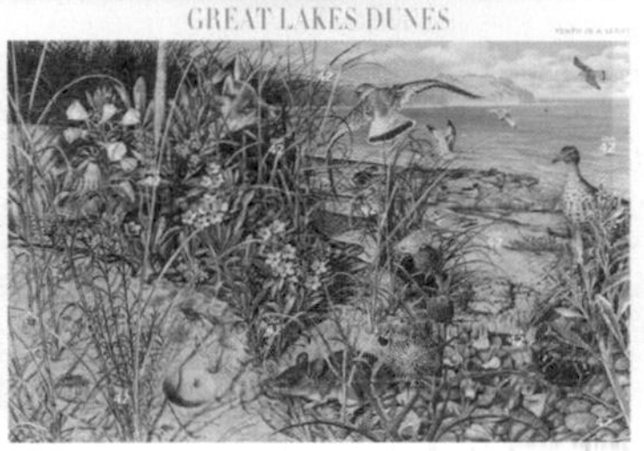

3086 Great Lake Dunes (image scaled to 21% of original size)

2008. Nature of America (10th series). Sheet 233×172 mm containing T **3085** and forming the overall design T **3086**. Multicoloured. Self-adhesive.

MS4903	42c.×10, Type **3085**; Piping plover (horiz); Vesper sparrow (horiz); Eastern hognose snake (horiz); Common merganser and plover (horiz); Spotted sandpiper; Piping plover nestlings (horiz); Tiger beetle; White-footed mouse; Red Admiral butterfly	8·50	8·50

The backing paper of the sheet has a description of the forest and a key to the flora and fauna in the design.

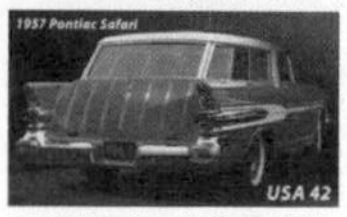

3087 Pontiac Safari, 1957

2008. Cars of the 1950's. Multicoloured. Self-adhesive.

4904	42c. Type **3087**	80	55
4905	42c. Lincoln Premiere, 1957	80	55
4906	42c. Chrysler 300c, 1957	80	55
4907	42c. Cadillac Eldorado, 1959	80	55
4908	42c. Studebaker Golden Hawk, 1957	80	55

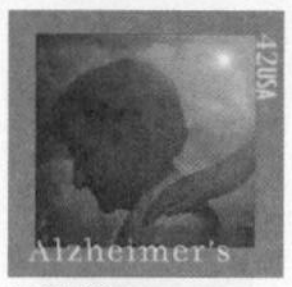

3092 Woman

2008. Alzheimer's Disease Awareness Campaign. Self-adhesive.

4909	**3092** 42c. multicoloured	80	55

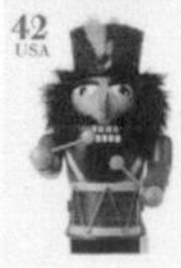

3093 Nutcracker

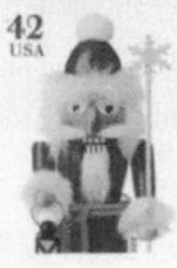

3094 Nutcracker

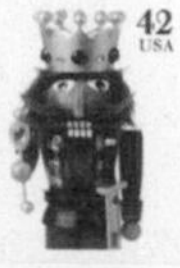

3095 Nutcracker

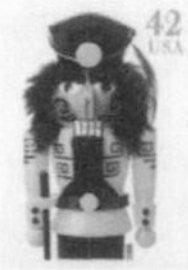

3096 Nutcracker

2008. Christmas (1st issue). Nutcrackers. Self-adhesive

4910	**3093**	42c. multicoloured	80	55
4911	**3094**	42c. multicoloured	80	55
4912	**3095**	42c. multicoloured	80	55
4913	**3096**	42c. multicoloured	80	55

(ii) Size 22×25 mm.

4914	**3093**	42c. multicoloured	80	55
4915	**3094**	42c. multicoloured	80	55
4916	**3095**	42c. multicoloured	80	55
4917	**3096**	42c. multicoloured	80	55

(b) Size 22×24 mm.

4918	**3093**	42c. multicoloured	80	55
4919	**3094**	42c. multicoloured	80	55
4920	**3095**	42c. multicoloured	80	55
4921	**3096**	42c. multicoloured	80	55

Nos. 4910/13, each×5 were issued in double-sided booklets of 20 (6×2, 4×2).

Nos. 4914/17, each×5 were issued in folded vending booklets of 20 (10×2).

Nos. 4918×5, 4919×5, 4920×4, 4921×4 were issued in panes of 18 (6×3) from automatic teller machines.

All types of booklet have outer edges imperforate.

Single stamps may be die-cut all round or show one side or two adjacent sides imperforate.

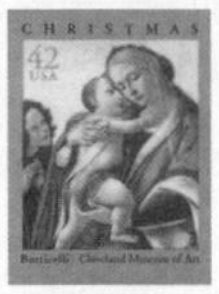

3097 *Madonna and Child and John the Baptist* (Sandro Botticelli)

2008. Christmas (2nd issue). Self-adhesive.

4922	**3097**	42c. multicoloured	80	55

No. 4922 was issued in unfolded double-sided booklets of 20 (12×2, 4×2).

2008. Hanukkah Festival. As Type **2758**. Self-adhesive.

4923	42c. multicoloured	80	55

2008. Kwanza Festival. As Type **2759**. Self-adhesive.

4924	42c. multicoloured	80	55

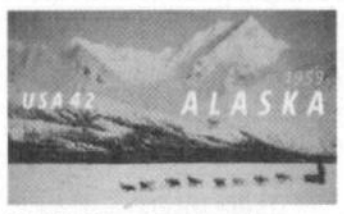

3098 Snow-covered Mountains and Dog Sled Team

2009. 50th Anniv of Alaska Statehood. Self-adhesive.

4925	**3098**	42c. multicoloured	80	55

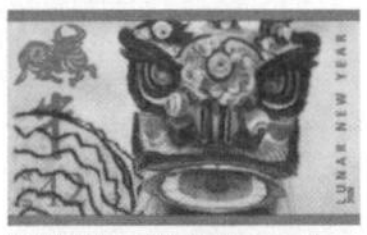

3099 Lion Mask, Ox and Script

2009. Chinese New Year. Year of the Ox. Self-adhesive.

4926	**3099**	42c. multicoloured	80	55

No. 4926 was issued in sheets of 12 stamps with an enlarged illustrated border and a brief description of the Chinese lunar calender on the backing paper.

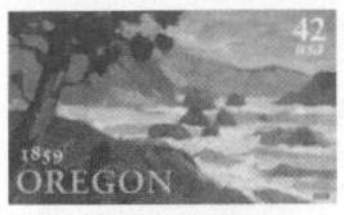

3100 Shoreline

2009. 150th Anniv of Oregon Statehood. Self-adhesive.

4927	**3100**	42c. multicoloured	80	55

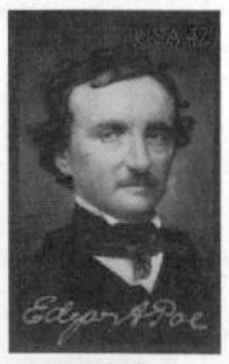

3101 Edgar Allan Poe

2009. Birth Bicentenary of Edgar Allan Poe (writer). Self-adhesive.

4928	**3101**	42c. multicoloured	80	55

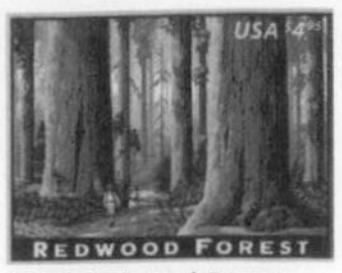

3102 Redwood Forest

2009. American Landmarks. Self-adhesive.. Multicoloured.

4929	$4.95 Type **3102**	11·50	9·50
4930	$17.50 Old Faithful (geyser)	38·00	29·00

No. 4929 was for use on Priority mail and No. 4930 was for use on Express mail.

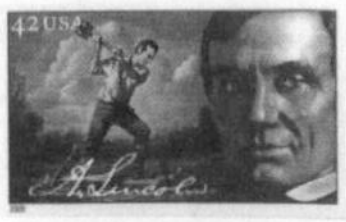

3104 As Young Man working as Rail Splitter

2009. Birth Bicentenary of Abraham Lincoln (president 1861–180.65). Multicoloured. Self-adhesive.

4931	42c. Type **3104**	80	55
4932	42c. As Lawyer	80	55
4933	42c. As Politician addressing crowd	80	55
4934	42c. As President in conference	80	55

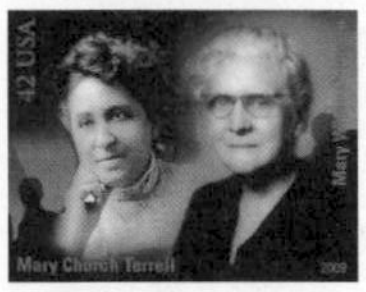

3108 Mary Church Terrell and Mary White Ovington

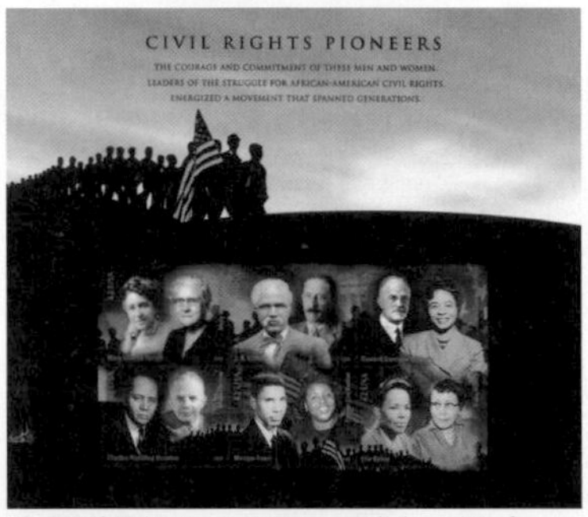

3109 Civil Rights Pioneers (image scaled to 26% of original size)

2009. Civil Rights Pioneers. Sheet 184×159 mm containing T **3108** and forming the overall design T **3109**. Multicoloured. Self-adhesive.

MS4935	42c.×6, Type **3108**; J. R. Clifford and Joel Elias Spingarn; Oswald Garrison Villard and Daisy Gatson Bates; Charles Hamilton Houston and Walter White; Medgar Evers and Fannie Lou Hamer; Ella Baker and Ruby Hurley	5·25	5·00

The backing paper of the sheet has a brief description of the personalities shown in the design.

2009. Stars and Stripes. Pre-sorted First Class mail coil stamp. Ordinary gum. As Type **2960**.

4937	(10c.) multicoloured	30	30

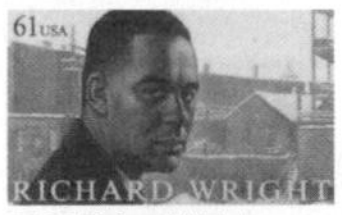

3110 Richard Wright

2009. Richard Wright (writer) Commemoration. Self-adhesive.

4938	**3110**	61c. multicoloured	1·30	90

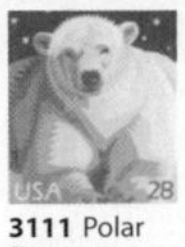

3111 Polar Bear

2009. Wildlife. Self-adhesive.

4939	**3111**	28c. multicoloured	55	40

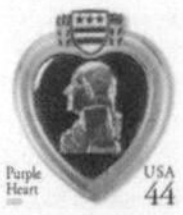

3112 Purple Heart (military medal)

2009. Self-adhesive.

4941	**3112**	44c. multicoloured	55	40

See also Nos. 4237/8, 4574, 4755 and 4848/9.

3113 Flag

2009. Flag. (a) Ordinary gum.

4945	**3113**	44c. multicoloured	85	55

(b) Self-adhesive.

4946	44c. multicoloured	85	55

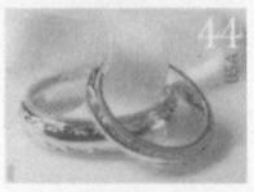

3114 Rings

2009. Greetings Stamps. Weddings. Multicloured. Self-adhesive.

4950	44c. Type **3114**	85	55
4951	61c. Wedding cake	1·30	90

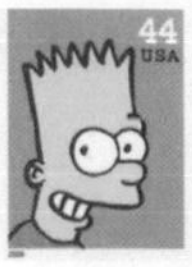

3116 Bart

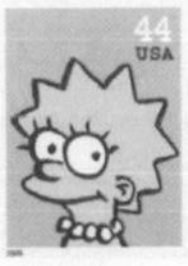

3117 Lisa

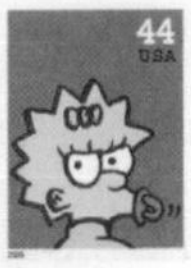

3118 Maggie

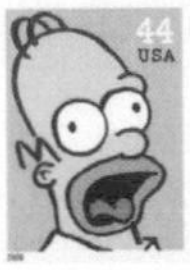

3119 Homer

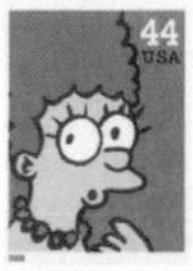

3120 Marge

2009. The Simpsons (television cartoon created by Matt Groening). Self-adhesive.

4952	**3116**	44c. multicoloured	85	55
4953	**3117**	44c. multicoloured	85	55
4954	**3118**	44c. multicoloured	85	55
4955	**3119**	44c. multicoloured	85	55
4956	**3120**	44c. multicoloured	85	55

Nos. 4952/6, each×4 was issued in single sided booklets of 20 (5×4) with straight outer edges. Single stamps may be die-cut all round or show one side or two adjacent sides imperforate.

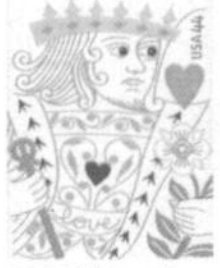

3121 King of Hearts

2009. Love. Booklet Stamps. Self-adhesive. Multicoloured.

4957	**3121**	44c. Type **3121**	85	55
4957a	**3121**	44c. Queen of Hearts	85	55

Nos. 4957/a were printed in single sided booklets of 20 stamps.

Nos. 4957/a were perforated on two, three or four sides depending on position.

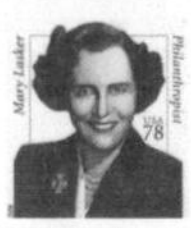

3121ba Mary Lasker

2010. Great Americans

4957b	**3121ba**	78c. multicoloured	2·10	1·40

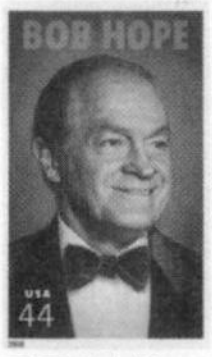

3122 Bob Hope

2009. Bob Hope (entertainer) Commemoration. Self-adhesive.

4958	**3122**	44c. multicoloured	85	55

No. 4958 has a brief discription of Bob Hope on the backing paper.

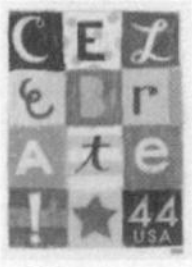

3123 'Celebrate'

2009. Greetings Stamp. Self-adhesive.

4959	**3123**	44c. multicoloured	85	55

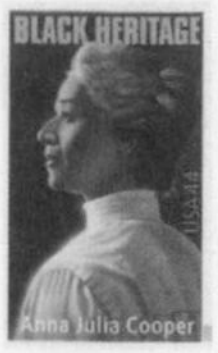

3124 Anna Julia Cooper

2009. Black Heritage. Anna Julia Cooper (educator) Commemoration. Self-adhesive.

4960	**3124**	44c. multicoloured	85	55

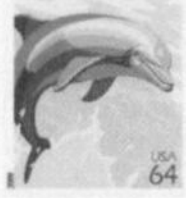

3125 Bottlenose Dolphin

2009. Wildlife. Self-adhesive.

4961	**3125**	64c. multicoloured	1·50	1·00

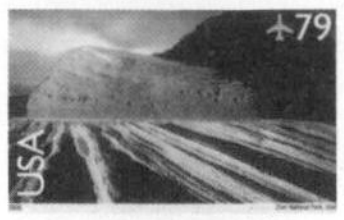

A3126 Zion National Park, Utah

2009. Air. Multicoloured. Self-adhesive.

A4962	79c. Type **A3126**	1·70	1·10
A4963	98c. Grand Teton National Park, Wyoming	2·10	1·40

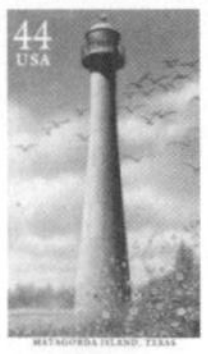

3128 Matagorda Island, Texas

2009. Gulf Coast Lighthouses. Multicoloured. Self-adhesive.

4964	44c. Type **3128**	85	55
4965	44c. Sabine Pass, Louisana	85	55
4966	44c. Biloxi, Mississippi	85	55
4967	44c. Sand Island, Alabama	85	55
4968	44c. Fort Jefferson, Florida	85	55

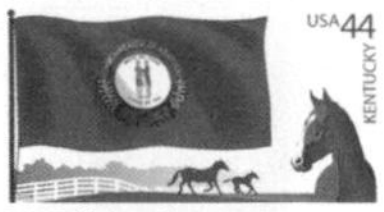

3133 Kentucky

2009. Flags of the Nation. Multicoloured. Self-adhesive.

4969	44c. Type **3133**	95	65
4970	44c. Louisiana	95	65
4971	44c. Maine	95	65
4972	44c. Maryland	95	65
4973	44c. Massachusetts	95	65
4974	44c. Michigan	95	65
4975	44c. Minniesota	95	65
4976	44c. Mississippi	95	65
4977	44c. Missouri	95	65
4978	44c. USA	95	65

Nos. 4969/78 were issued in coils of 50 stamps with the designs alternating.

2009. Forever. First Class Booklet Stamps. Self-adhesive.

4978a	**2938**	(44c.) multicoloured	95	65

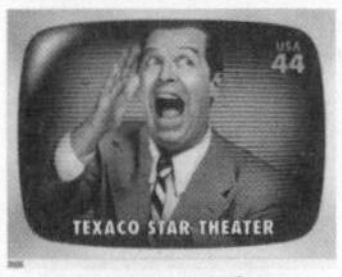

3143 *Texaco Star Theatre*

2009. Early TV Memories. Multicoloured. Self-adhesive.

4979	44c. Type **3143**	95	65
4980	44c. *I Love Lucy*	95	65
4981	44c. *Red Skelton Show*	95	65
4982	44c. *Howdy Doody*	95	65
4983	44c. *Dragnet*	95	65
4984	44c. *Lassie*	95	65
4985	44c. *Hopalong Cassidy*	95	65
4986	44c. *You Bet Your Life*	95	65
4987	44c. *Dinah Shore Show*	95	65

4988	44c. *Ed Sullivan Show*	95	65
4989	44c. *Kukla, Fran and Ollie*	95	65
4990	44c. *Phil Silvers Show*	95	65
4991	44c. *Lone Ranger*	95	65
4992	44c. *Perry Mason*	95	65
4993	44c. *Alfred Hitchcock Presents*	95	65
4994	44c. *Burns and Allen*	95	65
4995	44c. *Ozzzie and Harriet*	95	65
4996	44c. *Tonight Show*	95	65
4997	44c. *Twlight Zone*	95	65
4998	44c. *Honeymooners*	95	65

The backing paper of the sheet has a brief description of the television shows shown in the design.

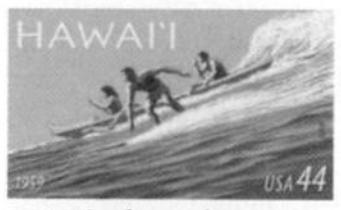

3163 Surfer and Outrigger Canoe

2009. Hawaii Statehood. Self-adhesive.

4999	**3163**	44c. multicoloured	95	65

2009. Eid al-Fitr and Eid al-Adha (Islamic festivals). As Type **2600**. Self-adhesive.

4999a	44c. gold, deep blue and grey-brown	95	65

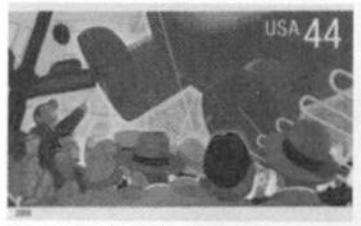

3163a Thanksgiving Parade

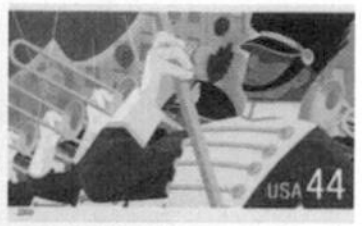

3163b Thanksgiving Parade

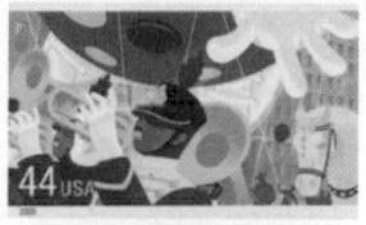

3163c Thanksgiving Parade

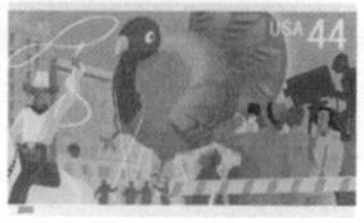

3163d Thanksgiving Parade

2009. Thanksgiving Parade. Self-adhesive.

4999b	**3163a**	44c. multicoloured	95	65
4999c	**3163b**	44c. multicoloured	95	65
4999d	**3163c**	44c. multicoloured	95	65
4999e	**3163d**	44c. multicoloured	95	65

Nos. 4999b/e were printed, se-tenant, in horizontal strips, each strip forming a composite design of a parade.

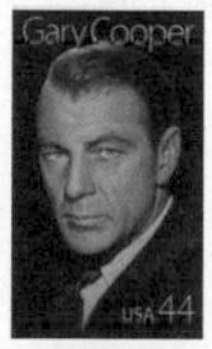

3163e Gary Cooper

2009. Legends of Hollywood. Gary Cooper

4999f	**3163e**	44c. multicoloured	95	65

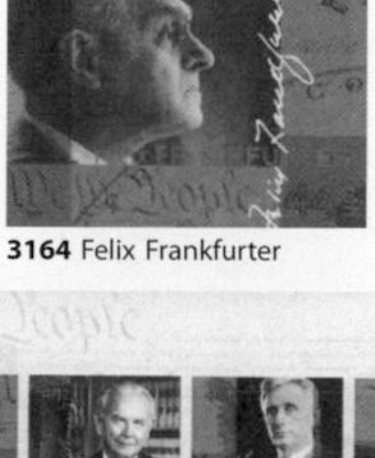

3164 Felix Frankfurter

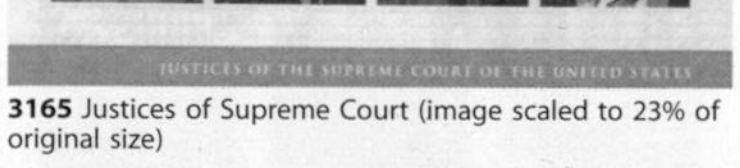

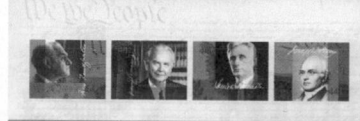

3165 Justices of Supreme Court (image scaled to 23% of original size)

2009. Justices of Supreme Court. Sheet 213×86 mm containing T **3164** and forming the overall design T **3165**. Multicoloured. Self-adhesive.

MS5000 44c.×4, Type **3164**; William Brennan; Louis Brendeis; Joseph Story	4·00	3·25

The backing paper of the sheet has a brief description of the personalities shown in the design.

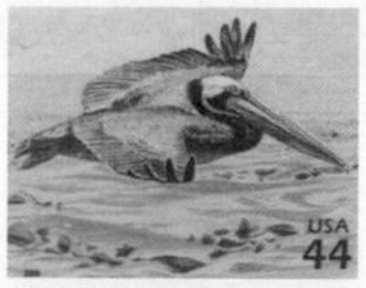

3166 Brown Pelican

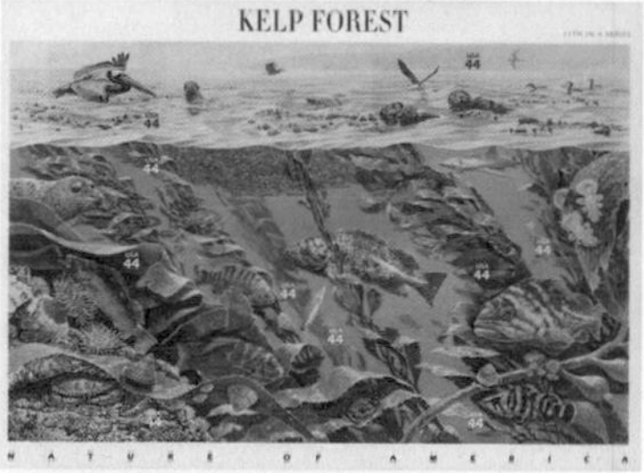

3167 Kelp Forest (image scaled to 21% of original size)

2009. Nature of America (11th series). Sheet 233×172 mm containing T **3166** and forming the overall design T **3167**. Multicoloured. Self-adhesive.

MS5001 44c.×10, Type **3166**; Southern sea otter and red sea urchin; Harbour seal; Lion's mane nudibranch (vert); Vermilion rockfish; Yellowtail rockfish; Copper rockfish; Pacific rock crab; Northern kelp crab (vert); Treefish	10·00	9·50

The backing paper of the sheet has a description of the kelp forest and a key to the flora and fauna in the design.

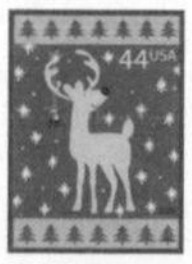

3168 Reindeer

2009. Christmas (1st issue). Winter Holidays. Multicoloured. Self-adhesive.

5002	44c. Type **3168**	95	65
5003	44c. Snowman	95	65
5004	44c. Gingerbread man	95	65
5005	44c. Nutcracker	95	65

Size 22×24 mm.

5006	44c. Type **3168**	95	65
5007	44c. Snowman	95	65
5008	44c. Gingerbread man	95	65
5009	44c. Nutcracker	95	65

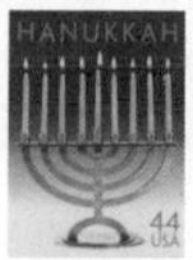

3172 Menorah

2009. Hanukkah Festival. Self-adhesive.

5010	**3172**	44c. multicoloured	95	65

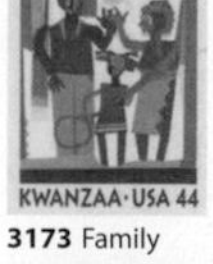

3173 Family

2009. Kwanza Festival. Self-adhesive.

5011	**3173**	44c. multicoloured	95	65

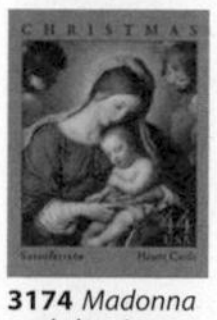

3174 *Madonna and sleeping Child* (Sassoferato)

2009. Christmas (2nd issue). Booklet Stamp. Self-adhesive.

5012	**3174**	44c. multicoloured	95	65

No. 5012 was issued in double-sided booklets of 20 (6×2, 4×2).

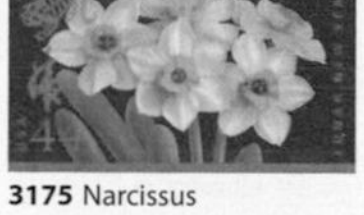

3175 Narcissus

2010. Chinese New Year

5013	**3175**	44c. multicoloured	95	65

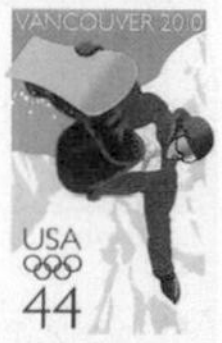

3176 Snowboarder

2010. Winter Olympic Games, Vancouver

5014	**3176**	multicoloured	95	65

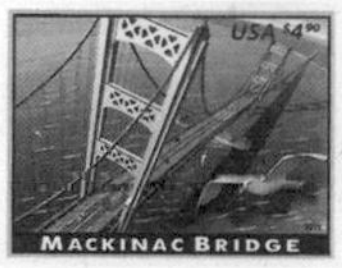

3177 Mackinac Bridge

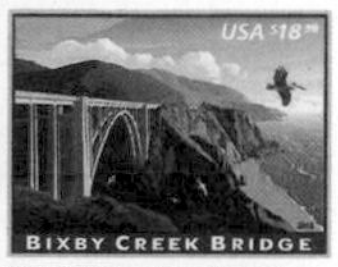

3178 Bixby Creek Bridge

2010. Landmarks

5015	**3177**	$4.90 multicoloured	10·00	6·00
5016	**3178**	$18.30 multicoloured	38·00	23·00

No. 5015 was for use on Priority Mail and No. 5016 was for use on Express Mail.

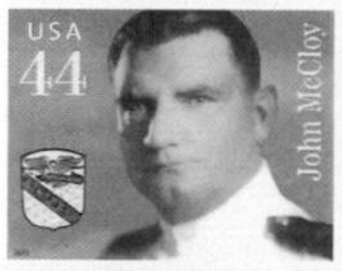

3179 Lieutenant Commander John McCloy

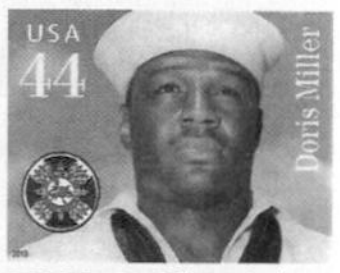

3180 Petty Officer 3rd Class Doris Miller

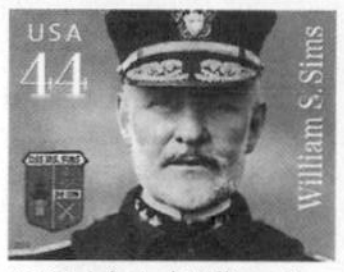

3181 Admiral William S. Sims

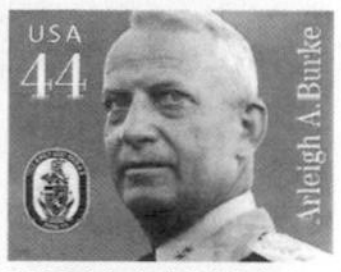

3182 Admiral Arleigh A. Burke

2010. Distinguished Sailors

5017	**3179**	44c. multicoloured	95	65
5018	**3180**	44c. multicoloured	95	65
5019	**3181**	44c. multicoloured	95	65
5020	**3182**	44c. multicoloured	95	65

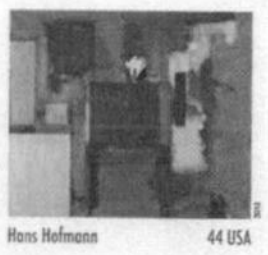

3183 The Golden Wall (Hans Hofmann)

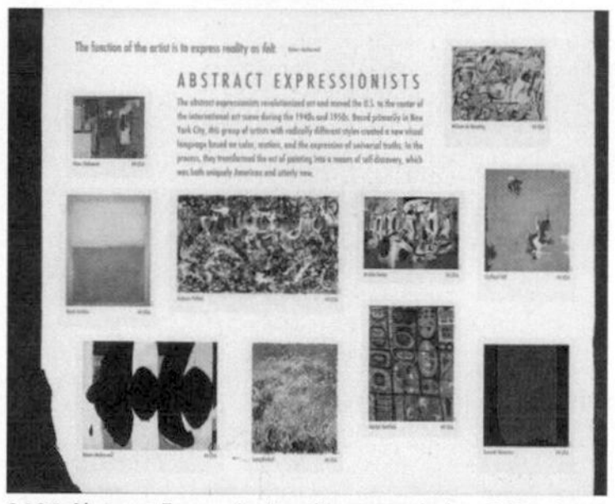

3184 Abstract Expressionists (image scaled to 22% of original size)

2010. Abstract Expressionists. Multicoloured.

MS5021 44c.×10, Type **3183**; *Asheville* (Willem de Kooning) (38×38mm); *Orange and Yellow* (Mark Rothko) (35×49mm); *Convergence* (Jackson Pollock) (63×43 mm); *The Liver is the Cock's Comb* (Arshile Gorky) (39×32 mm); *1948-C* (Clyfford Still) (35×49 mm); *Elegy to the Spanish Republic No. 34* (Robert Motherwell) (54×49 mm); *La Grand Vallée* (Joan Mitchell) (35×49 mm); *Romanesque Façade* (Adolph Gottilieb) (35×49 mm); *Achilles* (Barnett Newman) (35×49 mm)	9·50	9·50

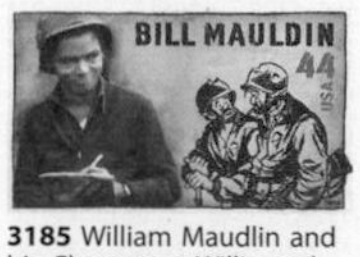

3185 William Maudlin and his Characters, Willie and Joe

William Henry 'Bill' Mauldin (cartoonist) Commemoration

5022	**3185**	44c. multicoloured	95	65

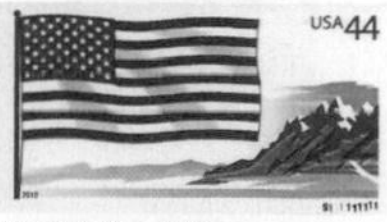

3186 National Flag

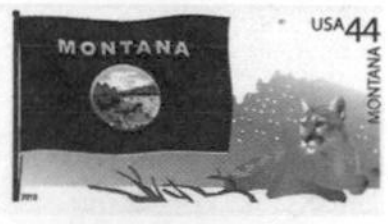

3187 Montana

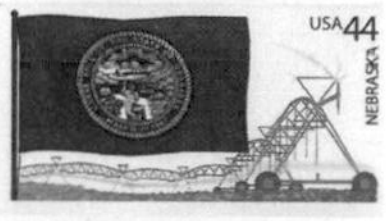

3188 Nebraska

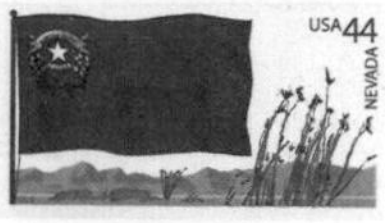

3189 Nevada

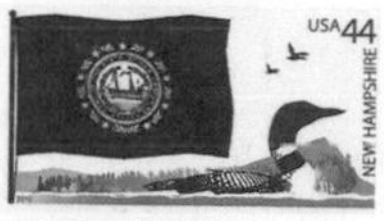

3190 New Hampshire

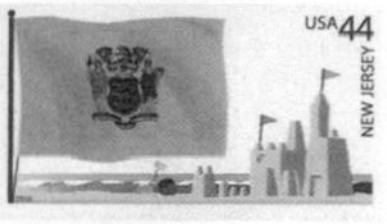

3191 New Jersey

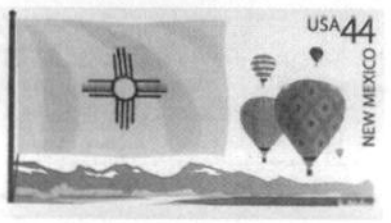

3192 New Mexico

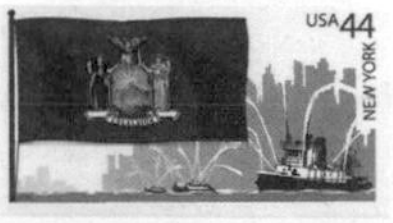

3193 New York

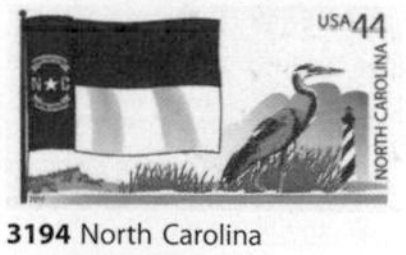

3194 North Carolina

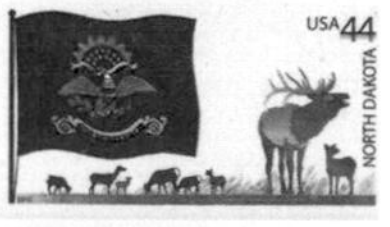

3195 North Dakota

2010. Flags of the Nation

5023	**3186**	44c. multicoloured	95	65
5024	**3187**	44c. multicoloured	95	65
5025	**3188**	44c. multicoloured	95	65
5026	**3189**	44c. multicoloured	95	65
5027	**3190**	44c. multicoloured	95	65
5028	**3191**	44c. multicoloured	95	65
5029	**3192**	44c. multicoloured	95	65
5030	**3193**	44c. multicoloured	95	65
5031	**3194**	44c. multicoloured	95	65
5032	**3195**	44c. multicoloured	95	65

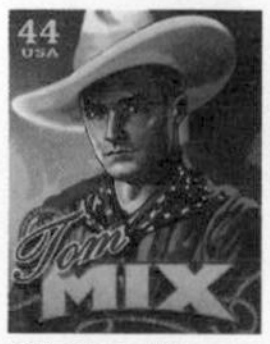

3197 Tom Mix

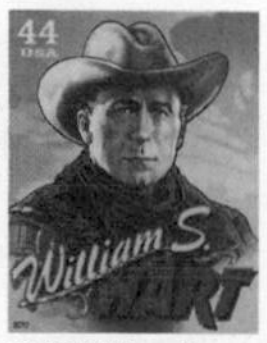

3198 William S. Hart

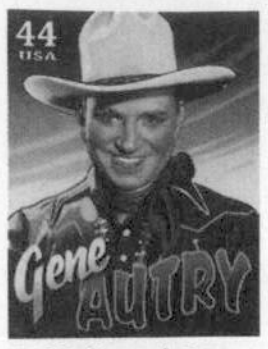

3199 Gene Autry

2010. Cowboys of the Silver Screen

5033	**3196**	44c. multicoloured	1·00	70
5034	**3197**	44c. multicoloured	1·00	70
5035	**3198**	44c. multicoloured	1·00	70
5036	**3199**	44c. multicoloured	1·00	70

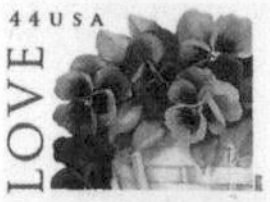

3200 Pansies

2010. Love

5037	**3200**	44c. multicoloured	4·00	2·50

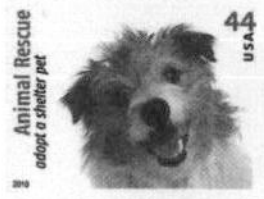
3201 Rough-coated Jack Russell Terrier

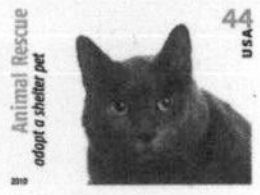
3202 Grey Cat

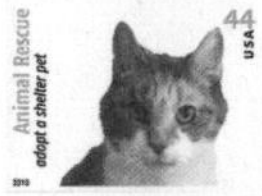
3203 Tortoiseshell and White Cat

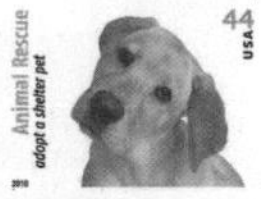
3204 Labrador-type Dog

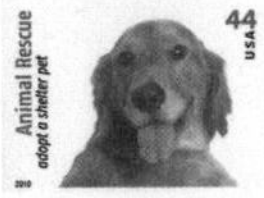
3205 Golden Retriever

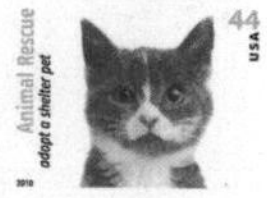
3206 Tortoiseshell, Grey and White Cat

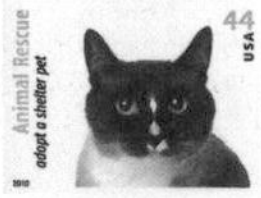
3207 Buremese-type Black, Brown and White Cat

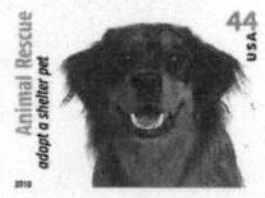
3208 Australian Shepherd

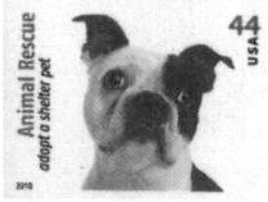
3209 Boston Terrier

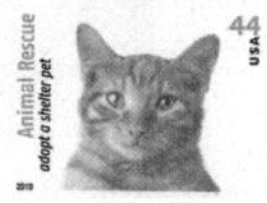
3210 Ginger Cat

2010. Animal Rescue

5038	**3201**	44c. multicoloured	1·00	70
5039	**32002**	44c. multicoloured	1·00	70
5040	**3203**	44c. multicoloured	1·00	70
5041	**3204**	44c. multicoloured	1·00	70
5042	**3205**	44c. multicoloured	1·00	70
5043	**3206**	44c. multicoloured	1·00	70
5044	**3207**	44c. multicoloured	1·00	70
5045	**3208**	44c. multicoloured	1·00	70
5046	**3209**	44c. multicoloured	1·00	70
5047	**3210**	44c. multicoloured	1·00	70

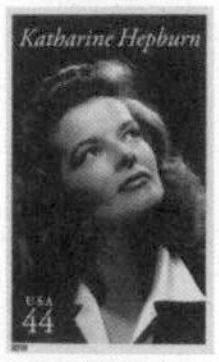

3211 Katherine Hepburn

2010. Legends of Hollywood. Katherine Hepburn

5049	**3211**	44c. black	70	25

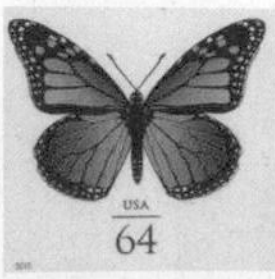

3212 Monarch Butterfly

2010. Butterfly

5050	**3212**	64c. multicoloured	90	25

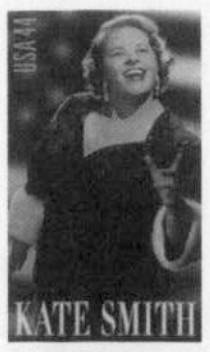

3213 Kate Smith

2010. Kate Smith (singer) Commemoration

5051	**3213**	44c. mutlicoloured	60	25

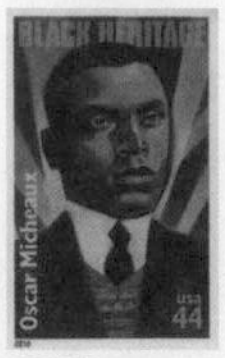

3214 Oscar Micheaux

2010. Black Heritage. Oscar Micheaux (writer and film director) Commemoration

5052	**3214**	44c. multicoloured	60	25

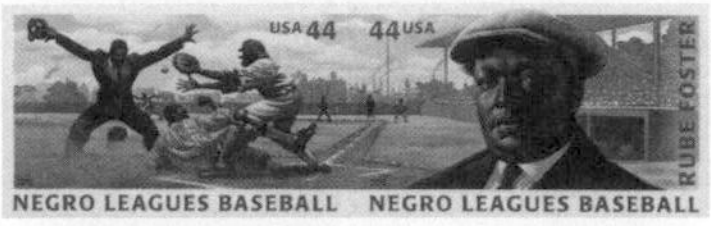

3215/3216 Players and Andrew 'Rube' Foster (founder of Negro National League)

2010. Baseball

5053	**3215**	44c. multicoloured	60	25
5054	**3216**	44c. multicoloured	60	25

Nos. 5053/4 were printed, *se-tenant*, in horizontal pairs within the sheet, each pair forming a composite design.

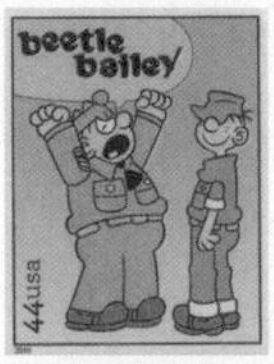

3217 'beetle bailey'

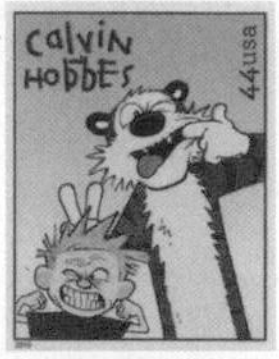

3218 'Calvin and Hobbs'

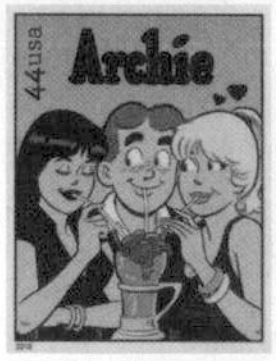

3219 'Archie'

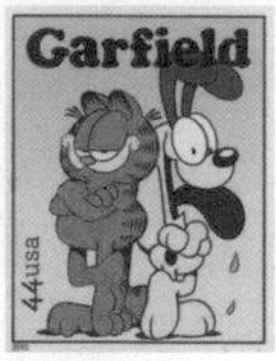

3220 'Garfield'

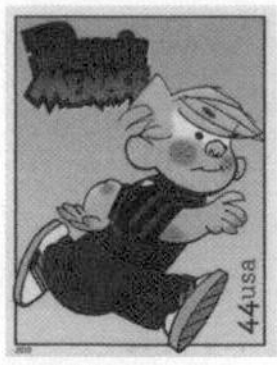
3221 'Dennis the Menace'

2010. Cartoons. Sunday Funnies

5055	**3217**	44c. multicoloured	60	25
5056	**3218**	44c. multicoloured	60	25
5057	**3219**	44c. multicoloured	60	25
5058	**3220**	44c. multicoloured	60	25
5059	**3221**	44c. multicoloured	60	25

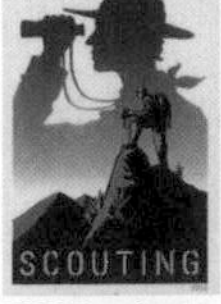

3222 Boy Scout

2010. Centenary of Boy Scouts of America

5060	**3222**	44c. multicoloured	60	23

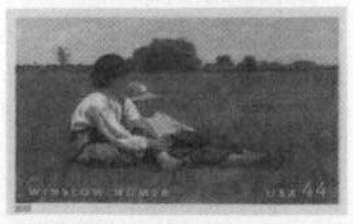
3223 *Boys in Pasture*

2010. Death Centenary of Winslow Homer (artist)

5061	**3223**	44c. multicoloured	60	25

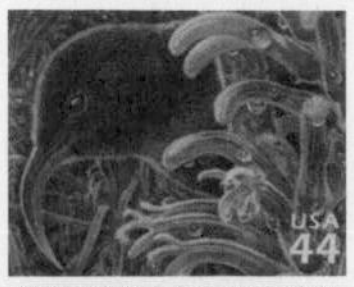
3224 Ohi'a lehua (myrtle) and Hawai'i 'Amakihi (finch)

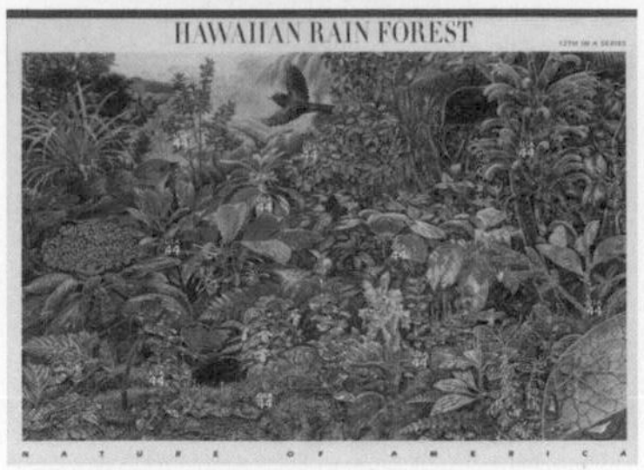

3225 Hawaiian Rain Forest (image scaled to 21% of original size)

2010. Nature of America (12th series). Hawaiian Rain Forest. Multicoloured.

MS5062 44c.×10, Type **3224**; Akepa (finch) and Hawaiian hoary bat (vert); I'iwi (scarlet honeycreeper); Oma'o (Hawaiian thrush) (vert); Ohelo kau la'au (vaccinium) and Oha (clermontia) (vert); Pulelehua (Kamehameha butterfly); Koele mountain damselfly (vert); Apapane (finch) (vert); Jewel orchid (vert); Ala'ala wai nui (black pepper) and Happyface spider (vert)		10·00	9·50

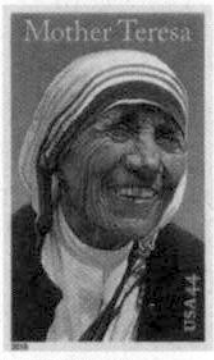

3226 Mother Teresa

2010. Birth Centenary of Mother Teresa (Agnes Gonxha Bojaxhiu) (founder of Missionaries of Charity in Calcutta)

5063	**3226**	44c. multicoloured	60	25

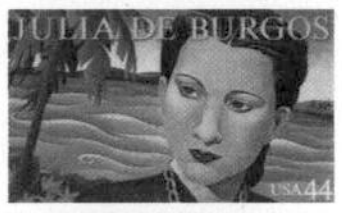

3227 Julia de Burgos

2010. Julia de Burgos (poet) Commemoration

5064	**3227**	44c. multicoloured	60	25

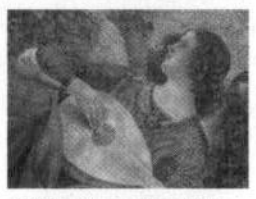
3228 Angel with Lute (detail, fresco by Melozzo da Forli)

2010. Christmas (1st issue)

5065	**3228**	44c. multicoloured	60	25

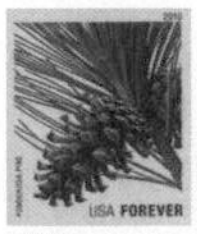
3229 Ponderosa Pine

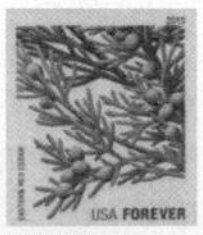
3230 Eastern Red Cedar

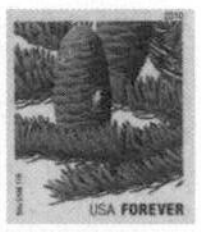
3231 Balsam Fir

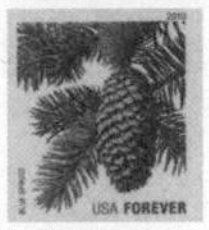
3232 Blue Spruce

2010. Christmas (2nd issue). Holiday Evergreens

(a) Booklet Stamps

5066	**3229**	(44c.) multicoloured	60	25
5067	**3230**	(44c.) multicoloured	60	25
5068	**3231**	(44c.) multicoloured	60	25
5069	**3232**	(44c.) multicoloured	60	25

(b) Size 22×24 mm. Automatic Teller Machine Stamps

5070	**3229**	(44c.) multicoloured	60	25
5071	**3230**	(44c.) multicoloured	60	25
5072	**3231**	(44c.) multicoloured	60	25
5073	**3232**	(44c.) multicoloured	60	25

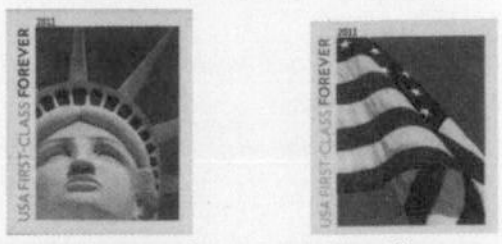
3233 Statue of Liberty **3234** Flag

2010. Lady Liberty and Flag

(a) Coil Stamps

5074	**3233**	(44c.) multicoloured	60	25
5075	**3234**	(44c.) multicoloured	60	25

(b) Coil Stamps

5076	**3233**	(44c.) multicoloured	60	25
5077	**3234**	(44c.) multicoloured	60	25

(c) Coil Stamps

5078	**3233**	(44c.) multicoloured	60	25
5079	**3234**	(44c.) multicoloured	60	25

(d) Automatic Teller Machine Stamps

5080	**3233**	(44c.) multicoloured (8 April 2011)	60	25
5081	**3234**	(44c.) multicoloured (8 April 2011)	60	25

Numbers are left for additions to this series.

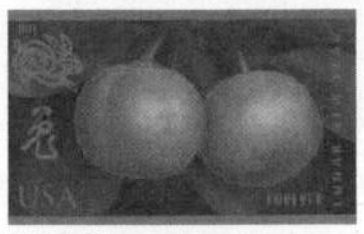
3236 Clementines

2011. Chinese New Year. Year of the Rabbit

5091	**3236**	(44c.) multicoloured	60	25

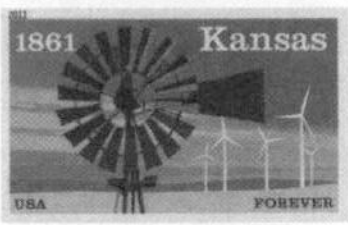

3237 Windmill and Wind Turbines

2011. 150th Anniv of Kansas Statehood

5092	**3237**	(44c.) multicoloured	60	25

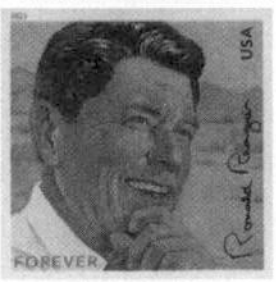
3238 Ronald Reagan

2011. Birth Centenary of Ronald Wilson Reagan (president 1981 - 1989)

5093	**3238**	(44c.) multicoloured	60	25

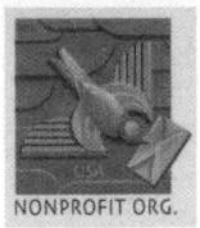

3239 Art Deco Bird carrying Envelope

2011. Non-profit Organisations. Coil stamp

5094	**3239**	5c. multicoloured	25	25

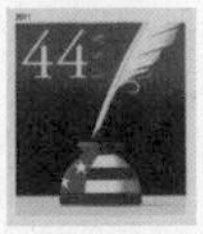

3240 Inkwell and Quill Pen

2011. Patriotic Inkwell and Quill Pen. Coil Stamp

5095	**3240**	44c. multicoloured	60	25

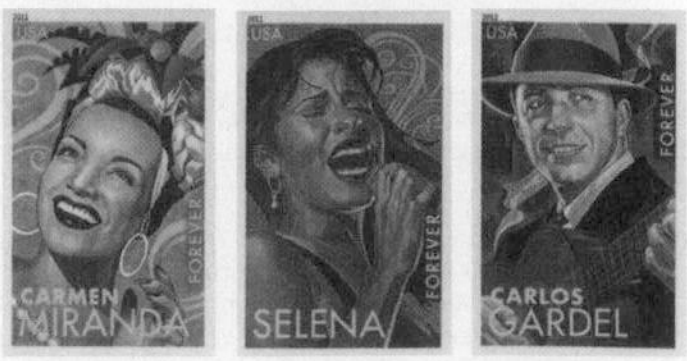

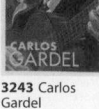

3241 Carmen Miranda **3242** Selena (Selena Quintanilla-Pérez) **3243** Carlos Gardel

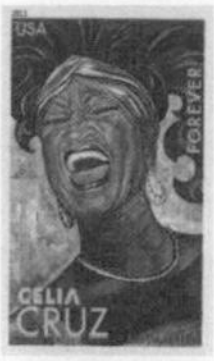

3244 Celia Cruz

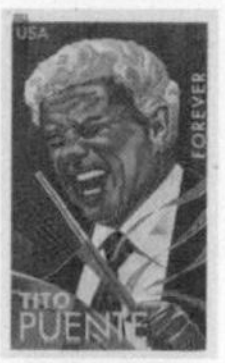

3245 Tito Puente

2011. Latin Music Legends

5096	**3241**	(44c.) multicoloured	60	25
5097	**3242**	(44c.) multicoloured	60	25
5098	**3243**	(44c.) multicoloured	60	25
5099	**3244**	(44c.) multicoloured	60	25
5100	**3245**	(44c.) multicoloured	60	25

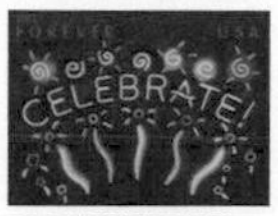

3246 'CELEBRATE'

2011. Greeting Stamp. Celebrate

5101	**3246**	(44c.) multicoloured	60	25

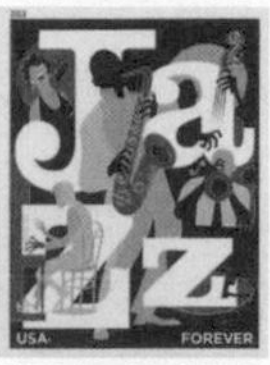

3247 Jazz Musicians

2011. Jazz

5102	**3247**	(44c.) multicoloured	60	25

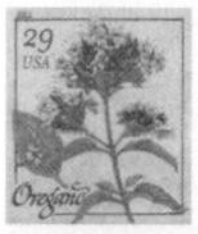

3248 Oregano

3249 Flax

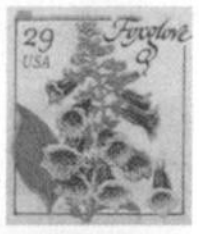

3250 Foxglove

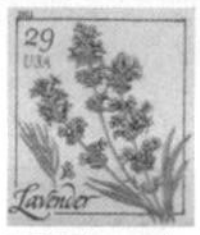

3251 Lavender

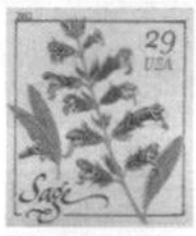

3252 Sage

2011. Herbs

(a) Sheet Stamps

5103	**3248**	29c. multicoloured	45	25
5104	**3249**	29c. multicoloured	45	25
5105	**3250**	29c. multicoloured	45	25
5106	**3251**	29c. multicoloured	45	25
5107	**3252**	29c. multicoloured	45	25

(b) Coil Stamps

5108	**3248**	29c. multicoloured	45	25
5109	**3249**	29c. multicoloured	45	9·25
5110	**3250**	29c. multicoloured	45	25
5111	**3251**	29c. multicoloured	45	25
5112	**3252**	29c. multicoloured	45	25

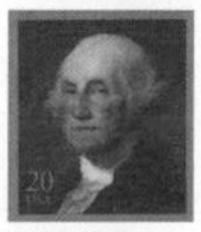

3253 *George Washington* (Gilbert Stuart)

2011. George Washington

(a) Sheet Stamps

5113	**3253**	20c. multicoloured	25	25

(b) Coil Stamps

5114	**3253**	20c. multicoloured	25	25

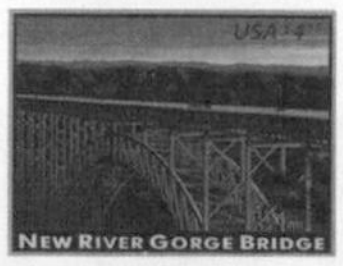

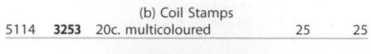

3254 New River Gorge Bridge

2011. Landmarks

5115	**3254**	$4.95 multicoloured	7·00	7·00

No. 5115 was for use on Priority Mail.

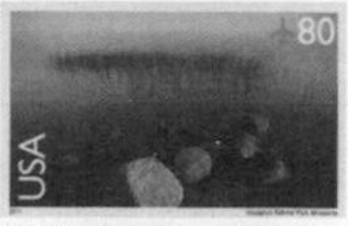

A3255 Voyageurs National Park, Minnesota

2011. AIR

A5116	**A3255**	80c. multicoloured	1·30	60

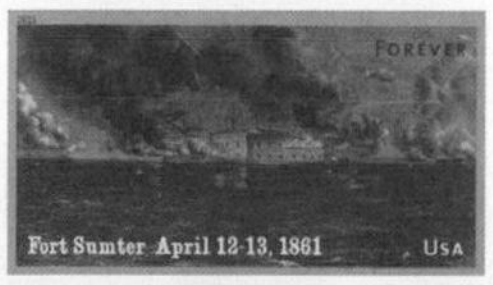

3256 Fort Sumter, April 12 – 13, 1861

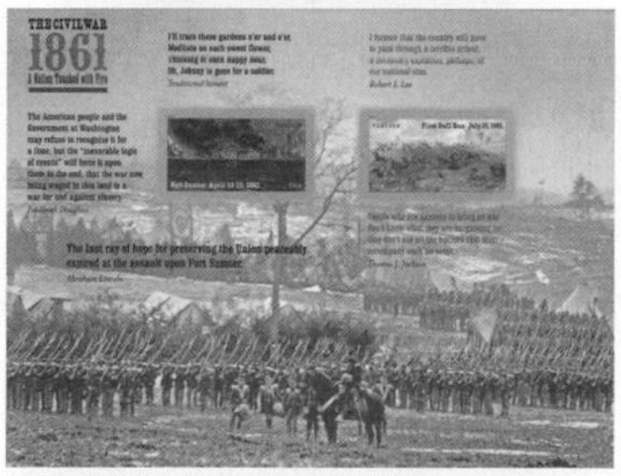

3257a 'A Nation Touched with Fire' (image scaled to 21% of original size)

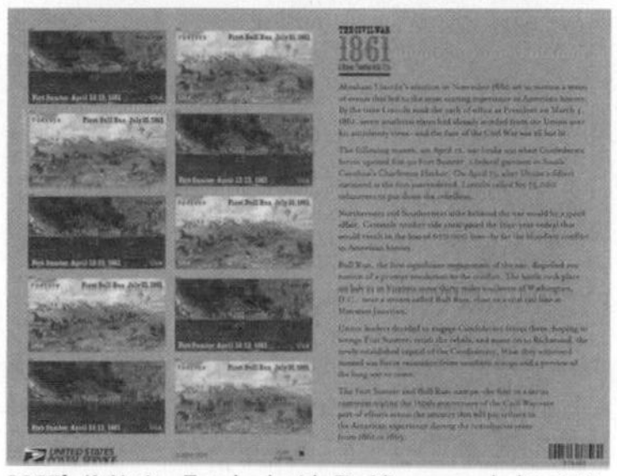

3257b 'A Nation Touched with Fire' (image scaled to 21% of original size)

2011. 150th Anniv of Civil War. 'A Nation Touched with Fire'

MS5117	Side (a), (44c.)×2, Type **3256**; First Bull Run, July 21, 1861. Side (b), (44c.)×10, Type **3256**×5; First Bull Run, July 21, 1861×5	16·00	16·00

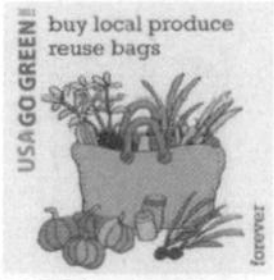

3258 'buy local produce, reuse bags'

2011. Go Green. Sheet 153×152 mm containing T **3258** and similar vert designs showing 'green' strategies, title given. Multicoloured.

MS5118	(44c.)×16, Type **3258**; 'fix water leaks'; 'share rides'; 'turn off lights not in use'; 'choose to walk'; 'GO GREEN reduce our environmental footprint usa'; 'compost'; 'let nature do the work'; 'recycle more'; 'ride a bike'; 'plant trees'; 'insulate the home'; 'use public transportation'; 'use efficient light bulbs'; 'adjust the thermostat'; 'maintain tire pressure'	10·00	10·00

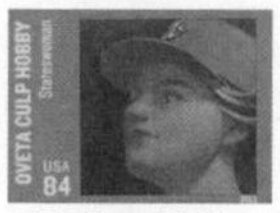

3259 Oveta Hobby

2011. Distinguished Americans. Oveta Culp Hobby (first Health, Education and Welfare Department Secretary)

5119	**3259**	84c. multicoloured	1·20	35

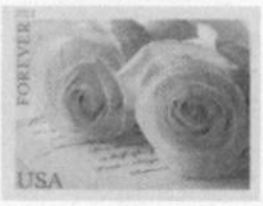

3260 Roses

2011. Greetings Stamp. Wedding Roses

5120	**3260**	(44c.) multicoloured	60	25

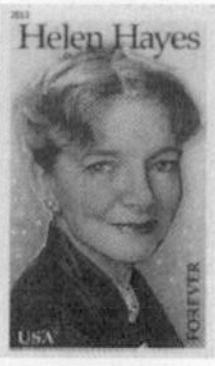

3261 Helen Hayes

2011. Helen Hayes (actress) Commemoration

5121	**3261**	(44c.) multicoloured	60	25

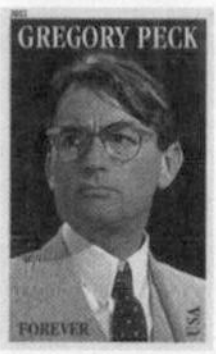

3262 Gregory Peck

2011. Legends of Hollywood. Gregory Peck

5122	**3262**	(44c.) black	60	25

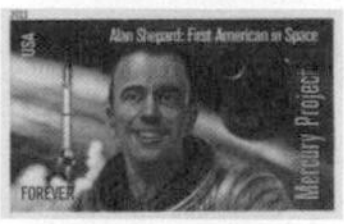

3263 Alan Shepard (first American in space)

2011. Space Firsts. Multicoloured.

5123	(44c.) Type **3263**	60	25
5124	(44c.) *Messenger* (first spacecraft to orbit Mercury)	60	25

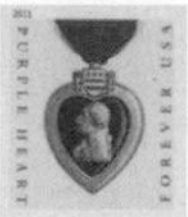

3264 Purple Heart and Ribbon

2011. Purple Heart (military medal)

5125	**3264**	(44c.) multicoloured	60	25

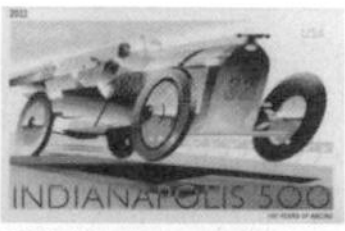

3265 Ray Harroun driving Marmon *Wasp*

2011. Centenary of Indianapolis 500 Mile Race

5126	**3265**	(44c.) multicoloured	60	25

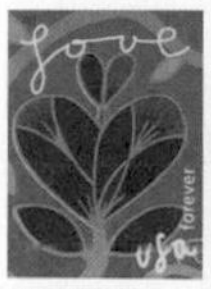

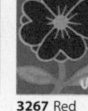

3266 Pink Flower

3267 Red Flower with Yellow Edging

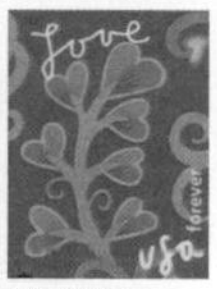

3268 Blue Flowers

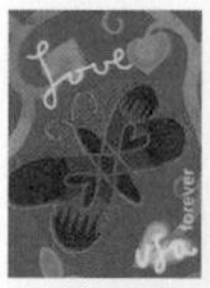

3269 Butterfly

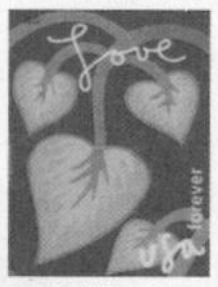

3270 Vine Leaves

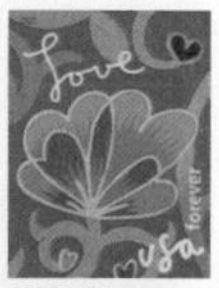

3271 Blue Flower

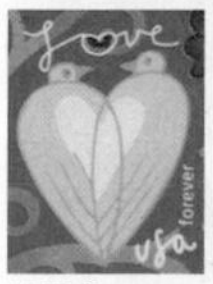

3272 Two Doves

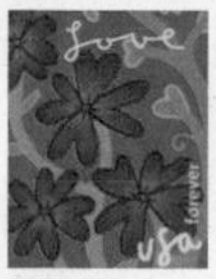

3273 Orange Flowers

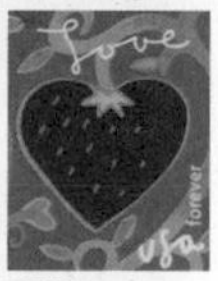

3274 Heart-shaped Strawberry

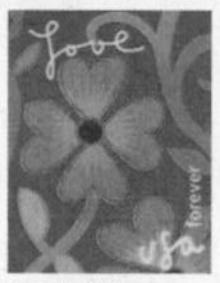

3275 Yellow Flowers

2011. Love. Garden of Love

5127	**3266**	(44c.) multicoloured	60	25
5128	**3267**	(44c.) multicoloured	60	25
5129	**3568**	(44c.) multicoloured	60	25
5130	**3569**	(44c.) multicoloured	60	25
5131	**3570**	(44c.) multicoloured	60	25
5132	**3571**	(44c.) multicoloured	60	25
5133	**3272**	(44c.) multicoloured	60	25
5134	**3273**	(44c.) multicoloured	60	25
5135	**3274**	(44c.) multicoloured	60	25
5136	**3275**	(44c.) multicoloured	60	25

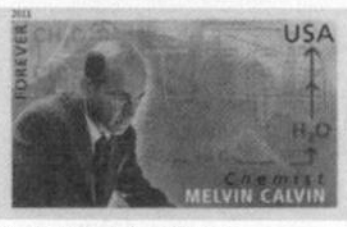

3276 Melvin Calvin (chemist)

2011. Scientists. Multicoloured.

5137	(44c.) Type **3276**	60	25
5138	(44c.) Asa Gray (botanist)	60	25
5139	(44c.) Maria Goeppert Mayer (physicist)	60	25
5140	(44c.) Severo Ochoa (biochemist)	60	25

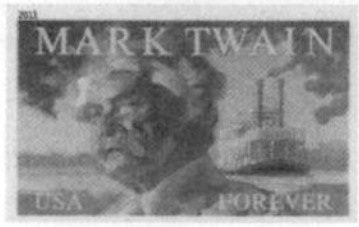

3277 Mark Twain

2011. Samuel Langhorne Clemens (Mark Twain) (writer) Commemoration

5141	**3277**	(44c.) multicoloured	60	25

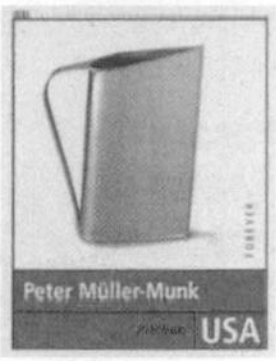

3278 Normandie Pitcher (Peter Müller-Munk)

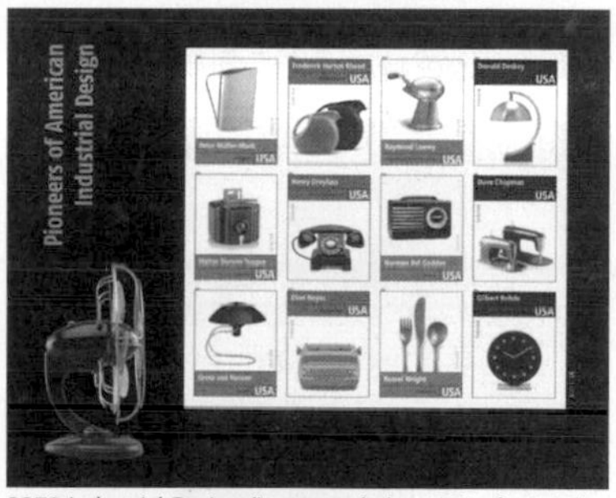

3279 Industrial Design (image scaled to 24% of original size)

2011. Pioneers of Industrial Design. Multicoloured.

MS5142	(44c.)×12, Type **3278**; Fiesta dinnerware (Frederick Hurten Rhead); Pencil sharpener (Raymond Loewy); Steel table lamp (Donald Deskey); Kodak 'Baby Brownie' camera (Walter Dorwin Teague); Bell Model 302 telephone (Henry Frefuss); Emerson 'Patriot' radio (Norman Bel Geddes); Sewing machines (Dave Chapman); 'Anywhere' lamp (Greta von Nessen); IBM 'Selectric' typewriter (Eliot Noyes); 'Highlight/Pinch' tableware (Russel Wright); Herman Miller electric clock (Gilbert Rohde)	7·50	7·50

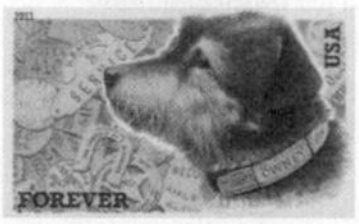

3280 Owney and his Medals and Tags

2011. Owney (stray mixed breed terrier adopted as first official postal mascot by Railway Mail Service and Albany, New York, 1888) Commemoration

5143	**3280**	(44c.) multicoloured	60	25

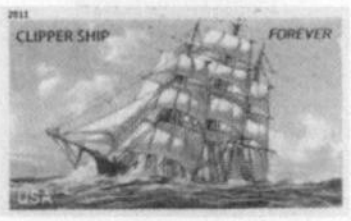

3281 Clipper Ship

2011. United States Merchant Marine. Multicoloured.

5144	(44c.) Type **3281**	60	25

5145	(44c.) Auxilliary steam ship		60	25
5146	(44c.) Liberty ship		60	25
5147	(44c.) Container ship		60	25

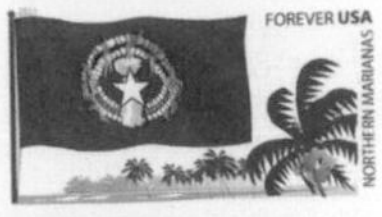
3282 Northern Marianas

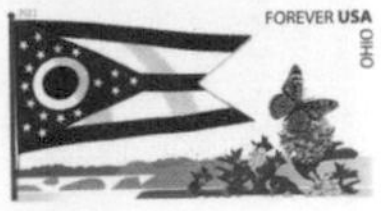
3283 Ohio

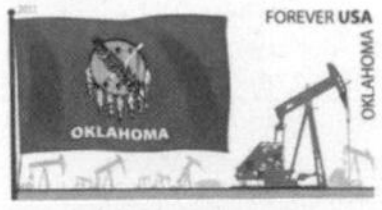
3284 Oklahoma

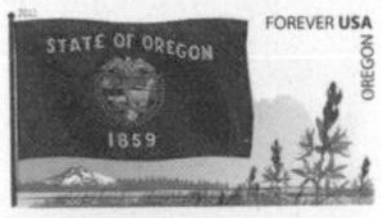
3285 Oregon

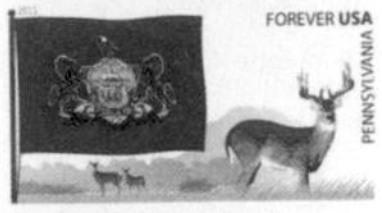
3286 Pennsylvania

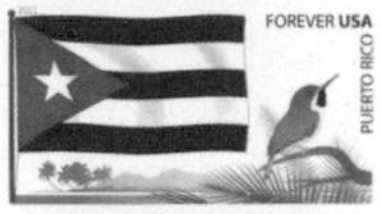
3287 Puerto Rico

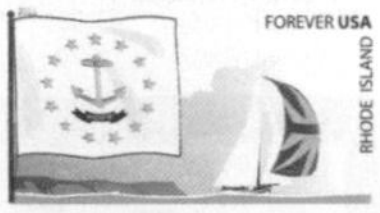
3288 Rhode Island

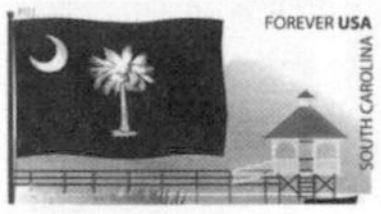
3289 South Carolina

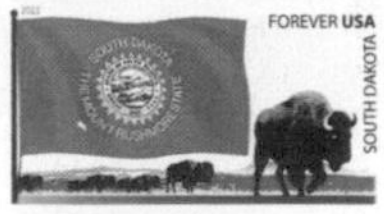
3290 South Dakota

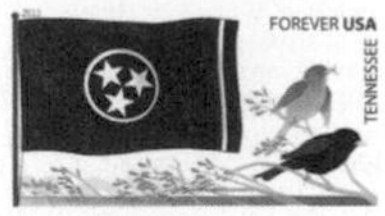
3291 Tennessee

2011. Flags of the Nation

5148	**3282**	(44c.) multicoloured	60	25
5149	**3283**	(44c.) multicoloured	60	25
5150	**3284**	(44c.) multicoloured	60	25
5151	**3285**	(44c.) multicoloured	60	25
5152	**3286**	(44c.) multicoloured	60	25
5153	**3287**	(44c.) multicoloured	60	25
5154	**3288**	(44c.) multicoloured	60	25
5155	**3289**	(44c.) multicoloured	60	25
5156	**3290**	(44c.) multicoloured	60	25
5157	**3291**	(44c.) multicoloured	60	25

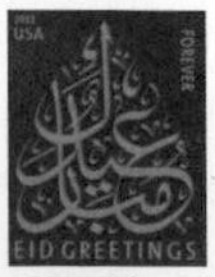
3291a Eid Mubarack

2011. Eid al-Fitr and Eid al-Adha (Islamic festivals). Multicoloured.

5158	(44c.) As Type **3291a**		60	25

As Type **3291a**

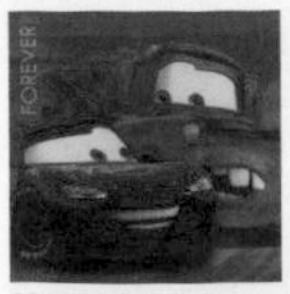
3292 Lightening McQueen and Mater from *Cars*

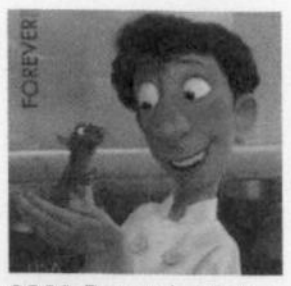
3293 Remy the Rat and Linguini from *Ratatouile*

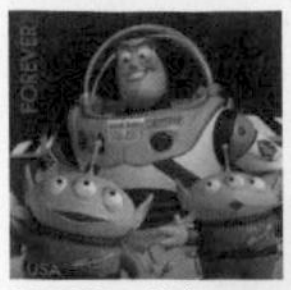
3294 Buzz Lightyear and Aliens from *Toy Story*

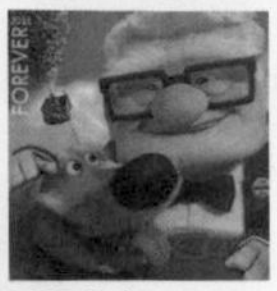
3295 Carl Fredricksen and Dug the Dog from *Up*

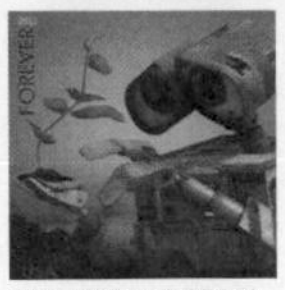
3296 WALL-E FROM *WALL-E*

2011. Greetings Stamps. Characters from Disney-Pixar Films

5159	**3292**	(44c.) multicoloured	60	25
5160	**3293**	(44c.) multicoloured	60	25
5161	**3294**	(44c.) multicoloured	60	25
5162	**3295**	(44c.) multicoloured	60	25
5163	**3296**	(44c.) multicoloured	60	25

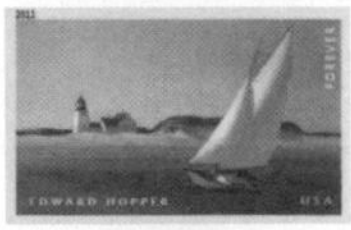
3297 *The Long Leg*

2011. Edward Hopper (artist) Commemoration

5164	**3297**	(44c.) multicoloured	60	25

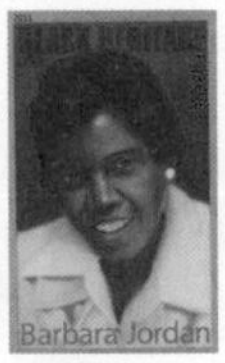
3298 Barbara Jordan

2011. Black Heritage. Barbara Jordan (congresswoman) Commemoration

5165	**3298**	(44c.) multicoloured	60	25

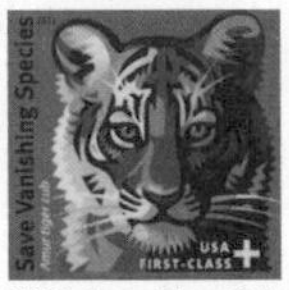
3299 Amur Tiger Cub

2011. Endangered Species

5166	**3299**	(44c.+11c.) multicoloured	80	35

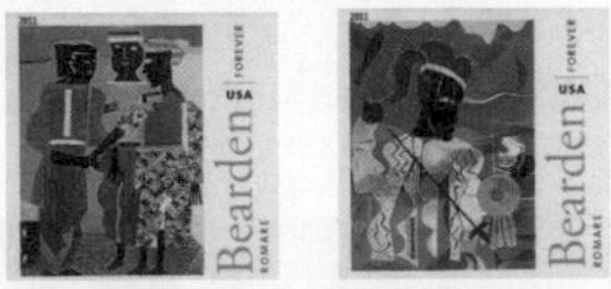
3300 *Conjunction* **3301** *Odysseus: Poseidon*

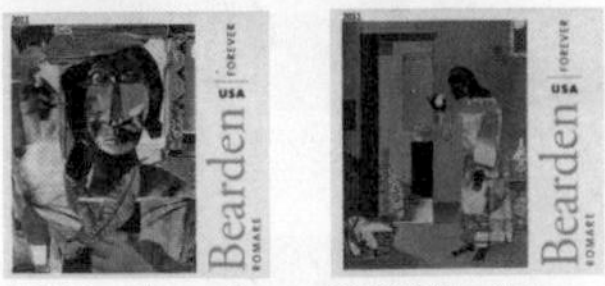
3302 *Prevalence of Ritual: Conjur* **3303** *Falling Star*

2011. Birth Centenary of Romare Bearden (artist)

5167	**3300**	(44c.) multicoloured	60	25
5168	**3301**	(44c.) multicoloured	60	25
5169	**3302**	(44c.) multicoloured	60	25
5170	**3303**	(44c.) multicoloured	60	25

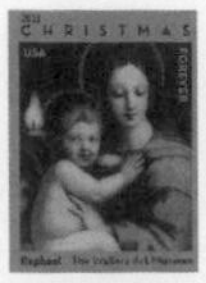
3304 *Madonna of the Candelabra* (Raphael)

2011. Christmas (1st issue)

5171	**3304**	44c. multicoloured	1·10	85

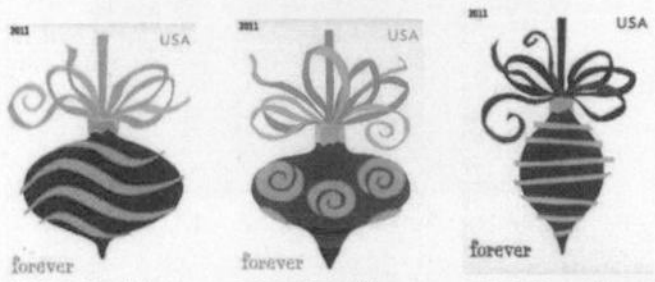
3305 Bauble **3306** Bauble **3307** Bauble

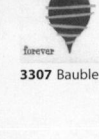

3308 Bauble

2011. Christmas (2nd issue). Baubles

(a) Booklet Stamps

5172	**3305**	(44c.) multicoloured	1·10	85
5173	**3306**	(44c.) multicoloured	1·10	85
5174	**3307**	(44c.) multicoloured	1·10	85
5175	**3308**	(44c.) multicoloured	1·10	85

(b) Booklet Stamps

5176	**3305**	(44c.) multicoloured	1·10	85
5177	**3306**	(44c.) multicoloured	1·10	85
5178	**3307**	(44c.) multicoloured	1·10	85
5179	**3308**	(44c.) multicoloured	1·10	85

(c) Size 22×24 mm. Automatic Teller Machine Stamps

5180	**3305**	(44c.) multicoloured	1·10	85
5181	**3306**	(44c.) multicoloured	1·10	85
5182	**3307**	(44c.) multicoloured	1·10	85
5183	**3308**	(44c.) multicoloured	1·10	85

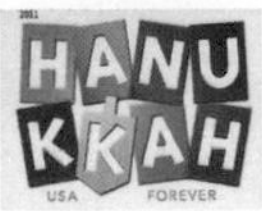
3309 'HANUKKAH'

2010. Hanukkah Festival

5184	**3309**	(44c.) multicoloured	1·10	85

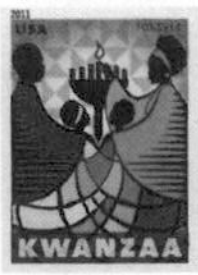
3310 Family

2011. Kwanza Festival

5185	**3310**	(44c.) multicoloured	1·10	85

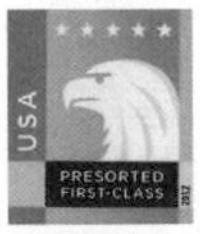
3311 Eagle

2012. Pre-sorted First Class Mail. Coil Stamps

5186	**3311**	(25c.) multicoloured (orange)	65	45
5187	**3311**	(25c.) multicoloured (yellow)	65	45
5188	**3311**	(25c.) multicoloured (green)	65	45
5189	**3311**	(25c.) multicoloured (turquoise)	65	45
5190	**3311**	(25c.) multicoloured (blue)	65	45
5191	**3311**	(25c.) multicoloured (magenta)	65	45

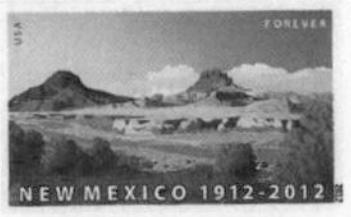
3312 *Sanctuary II* (Doug West)

2012. Centenary of New Mexico Statehood

5192	**3312**	(44c.) multicoloured	1·10	85

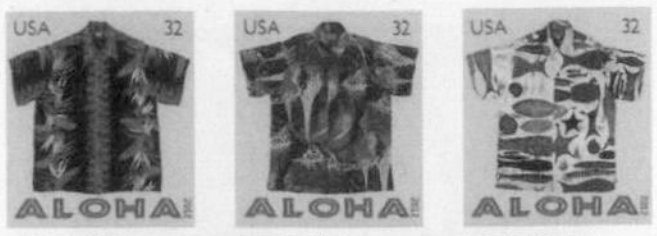
3313 Shirt **3314** Shirt **3315** Shirt

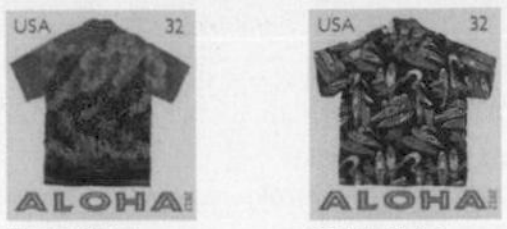
3316 Shirt **3317** Shirt

2012. Aloha Shirts

(a) Sheet Stamps

5193	**3313**	32c. multicoloured	70	50
5194	**3314**	32c. multicoloured	70	50
5195	**3315**	32c. multicoloured	70	50
5196	**3316**	32c. multicoloured	70	50
5197	**3317**	32c. multicoloured	70	50

(b) Size 22×24 mm. Coil Stamps. Multicoloured

5198	32c. As Type **3313**		70	50
5199	32c. As Type **3314**		70	50
5200	32c. As Type **3315**		70	50
5201	32c. As Type **3316**		70	50
5202	32c. As Type **3317**		70	50

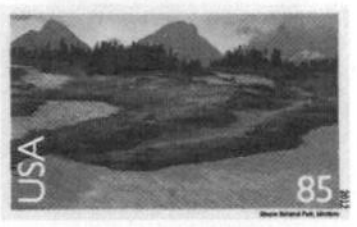
3318 Glacier National Park, Montana

2012. AIR

A5203	**3318**	85c. multicoloured	1·85	1·65

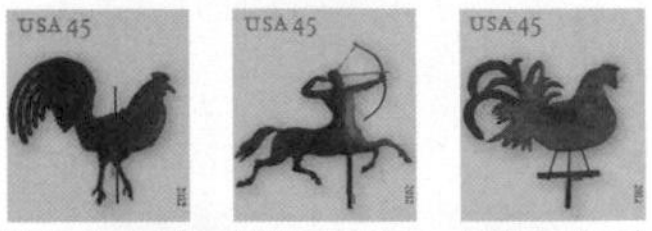
3319 Cockerel **3320** Centaur **3321** Cockerel on Perch

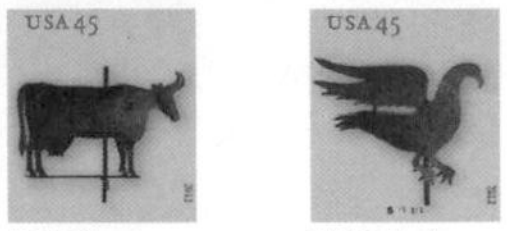
3322 Cow **3323** Eagle

2012. Weather Vanes

5204	**3319**	45c. multicoloured	1·20	95
5205	**3320**	45c. multicoloured	1·20	95
5206	**3321**	45c. multicoloured	1·20	95
5207	**3322**	45c. multicoloured	1·20	95
5208	**3323**	45c. multicoloured	1·20	95

No. 5209 is vacant.

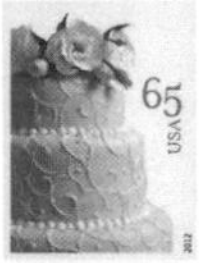
3324 Wedding Cake

2012. Greetings Stamp. Wedding Cake

5210	**3324**	65c. multicoloured	1·50	1·35

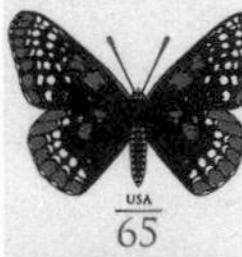
3325 Baltimore Checkerspot Butterfly

2011. Butterfly

5211	**3325**	65c. multicoloured	1·50	1·35

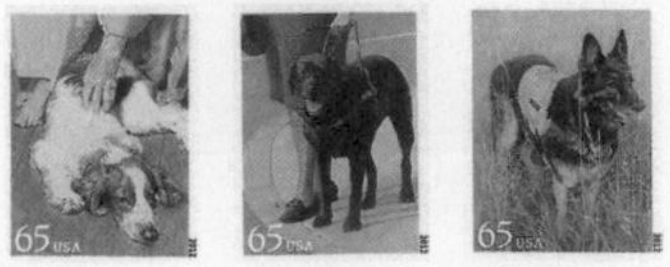
3326 Spaniel (Therapy Dog) **3327** Black Labrador (Guide Dog) **3328** German Shepherd (Rescue Dog)

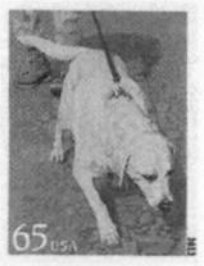

3329 Yellow Labrador (Military Dog)

2012. Working Dogs

5212	**3326**	65c. multicoloured	1·50	1·35
5213	**3327**	65c. multicoloured	1·50	1·35
5214	**3328**	65c. multicoloured	1·50	1·35
5215	**3329**	65c. multicoloured	1·50	1·35

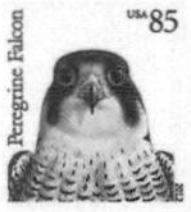

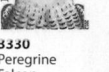

3330 Peregrine Falcon

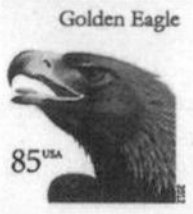

3331 Golden Eagle

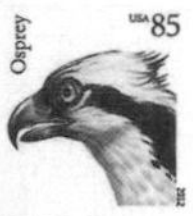

3332 Osprey

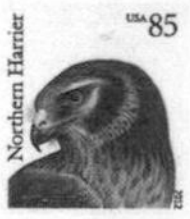

3333 Northern Harrier

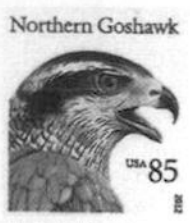

3334 Northern Goshawk

2012. Birds of Prey

5216	**3330**	85c. multicoloured	1·85	1·65
5217	**3331**	85c. multicoloured	1·85	1·65
5218	**3332**	85c. multicoloured	1·85	1·65
5219	**3333**	85c. multicoloured	1·85	1·65
5220	**3334**	85c. multicoloured	1·85	1·65

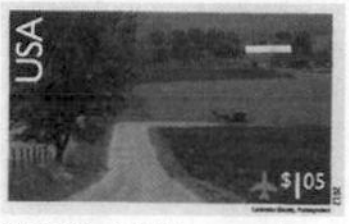

3335 Amish Horse and Buggy, Lancaster County, Pennsylvania

2012. AIR

A5221	**3335**	$1.05 multicoloured	1·85	1·65

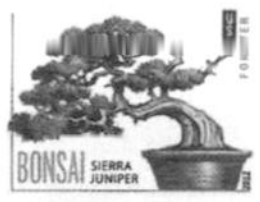

3336 Sierra Juniper

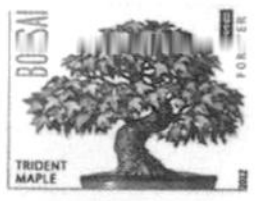

3337 Trident Maple

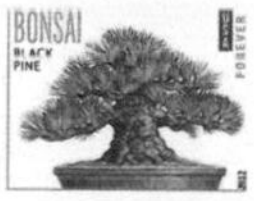

3338 Black Pine

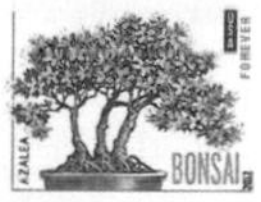

3339 Azalea

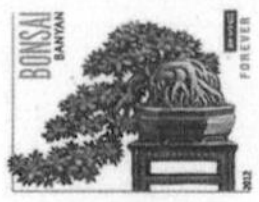

3340 Banyan

2012. Bonsai Trees. Booklet Stamps

5222	**3336**	(45c.) multicoloured	1·20	95
5223	**3337**	(45c.) multicoloured	1·20	95
5224	**3338**	(45c.) multicoloured	1·20	95
5225	**3339**	(45c.) multicoloured	1·20	95
5226	**3340**	(45c.) multicoloured	1·20	95

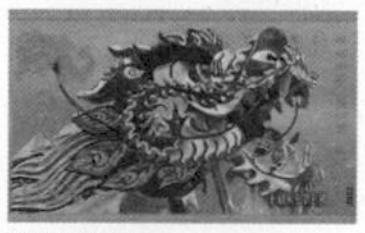

3341 Dragon

2012. Chinese New Year. Year of the Dragon

5227	**3341**	(45c.) multicoloured	1·20	95

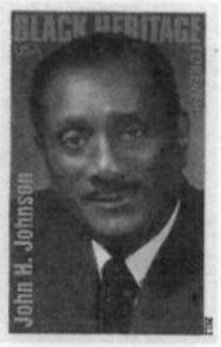

3342 John H. Johnson

2012. Black Heritage. John H. Johnson (magazine publisher) Commemoration

5228	**3342**	(45c.) multicoloured	1·20	95

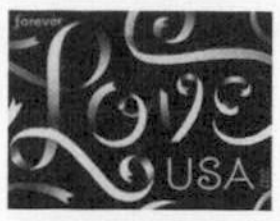

3343 'Love'

2012. Love

5229	**3343**	(45c.) multicoloured	1·20	95

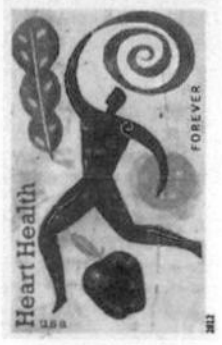

3344 Leaf, Male Figure, Sun and Apple

2012. Heart Health

5230	**3344**	(45c.) multicoloured	1·20	95

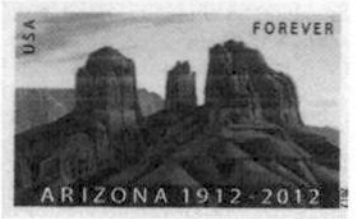

3345 Cathedral Rock

2012. Centenary of Arizona Statehood

5231	**3345**	(45c.) multicoloured	1·20	95

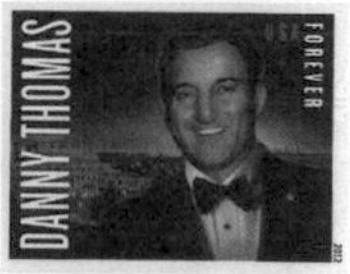

3346 Danny Thomas

2012. Danny Thomas (comedian) Commemoration

5232	**3346**	(45c.) multicoloured	1·20	95

3347 Freedom

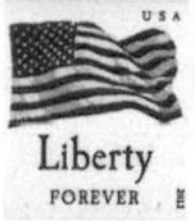

3348 'Liberty'

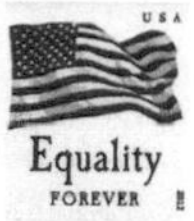

3349 'Equality'

3350 'Justice'

2012. Freedom, Liberty, Equality and Justice (1st issue)

(a) Coil Stamps

5233	**3347**	(45c.) multicoloured	1·20	95
5234	**3348**	(45c.) multicoloured	1·20	95
5235	**3349**	(45c.) multicoloured	1·20	95
5236	**3350**	(45c.) multicoloured	1·20	95

(b) Coil Stamps

5237	**3347**	(45c.) multicoloured	1·20	95
5238	**3348**	(45c.) multicoloured	1·20	95
5239	**3349**	(45c.) multicoloured	1·20	95
5240	**3350**	(45c.) multicoloured	1·20	95

(c) Coil Stamps

5241	**3347**	(45c.) multicoloured	1·20	95
5242	**3348**	(45c.) multicoloured	1·20	95
5243	**3349**	(45c.) multicoloured	1·20	95
5244	**3350**	(45c.) multicoloured	1·20	95

(d) Booklet Stamps. With darker shading and duller phosphor

5245	**3347**	(45c.) multicoloured	1·20	95
5246	**3348**	(45c.) multicoloured	1·20	95
5247	**3349**	(45c.) multicoloured	1·20	95
5248	**3350**	(45c.) multicoloured	1·20	95

(e) Booklet Stamps. With lighter shading and brighter phosphor

5249	**3347**	(45c.) multicoloured	1·20	95
5250	**3348**	(45c.) multicoloured	1·20	95
5251	**3349**	(45c.) multicoloured	1·20	95
5252	**3350**	(45c.) multicoloured	1·20	95

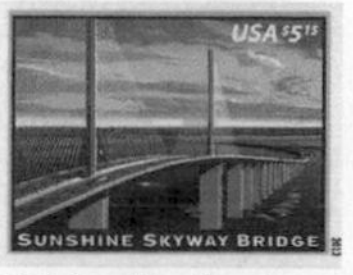

3351 Sunshine Skyway Bridge, Florida

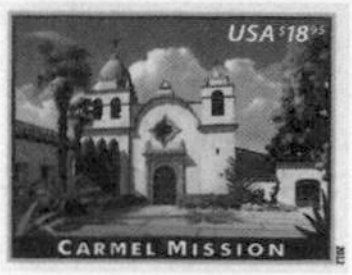

3352 Carmel Mission, Carmel

2012. Landmarks

5253	**3351**	$5.15 multicoloured	12·50	10·50
5254	**3352**	$18.95 multicoloured	39·00	36·00

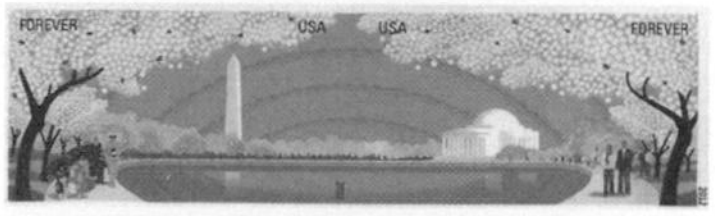

3353-3354 Cherry Blossom and Washington Monument, Cherry Blossom and Jefferson Memorial

2012. Centenary of USA - Japan Friendship. Cherry Blossom Centennial

5255	**3353**	(45c.) multicoloured	1·20	95
5256	**3354**	(45c.) multicoloured	1·20	95

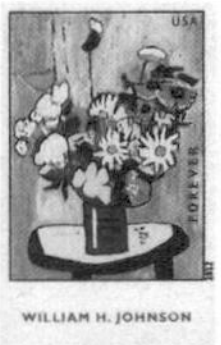

3355 Bouquet

2012. William H. Johnson (artist) Commemoration

5257	**3355**	(45c.) multicoloured	1·20	95

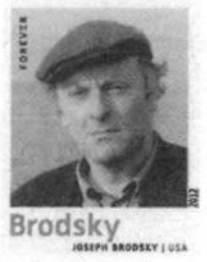

3356 Joseph Brodsky

2012. Twentieth Century Poets. Multicoloured.

5258	(45c.) Type **3356**	1·20	95
5259	(45c.) Gwendolyn Brooks	1·20	95
5260	(45c.) William Carlos Williams	1·20	95
5261	(45c.) Robert Hayden	1·20	95
5262	(45c.) Sylvia Plath	1·20	95
5263	(45c.) Elizabeth Bishop	1·20	95
5264	(45c.) Wallace Stevens	1·20	95
5265	(45c.) Denise Levertov	1·20	95
5266	(45c.) E. E. Cummings	1·20	95
5267	(45c.) Theodore Roethke	1·20	95

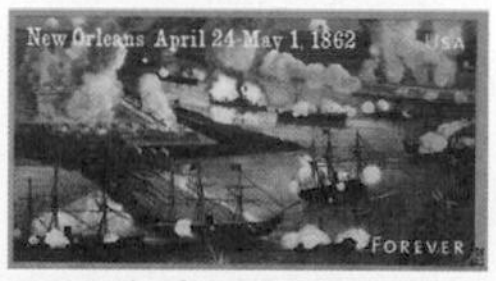

3357 Battle of New Orleans

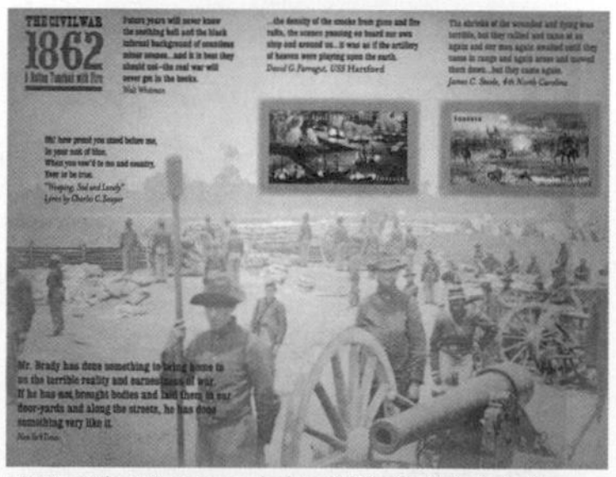

3357a Side 1 (image scaled to 22% of original size)

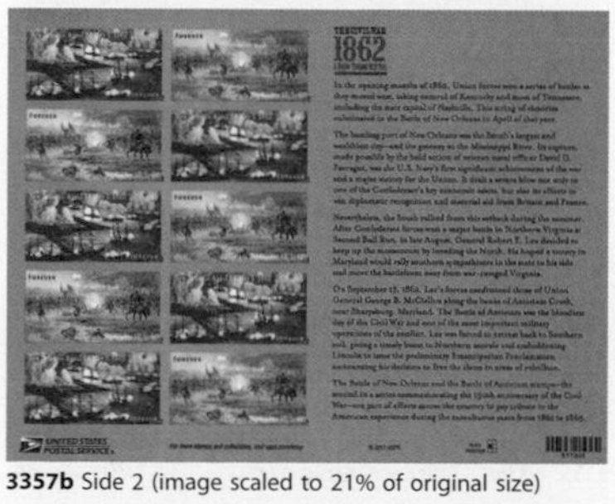

3357b Side 2 (image scaled to 21% of original size)

2012. 150th Anniv of Civil War. Battles of 1862

MS5117	Side (a), (45c.)×2, Type **3357**; Battle of Antietam. Side (b), (45c.)×10, Type **3357**×5; Battle of Antietam, 1861×5	16·00	16·00

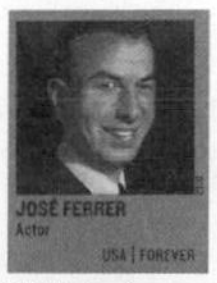

3358 José Ferrer

2012. Distinguished Americans. José Ferrer (actor, director and musician)

5269	**3358**	(45c.) multicoloured	1·20	95

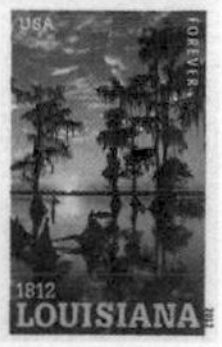

3359 Sunset over Flat Lake, Atchafalaya Basin

2012. Bicentenary of Louisiana Statehood

5270	**3359**	(45c.) multicoloured	1·20	95

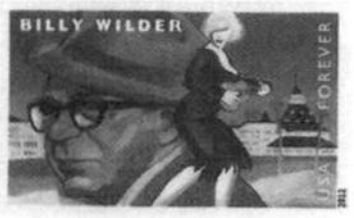

3360 Billy Wilder and Scene from *Some like it Hot*

2012. Film Directors. Multicoloured.

5271	(45c.) Type **3360**	1·20	95
5272	(45c.) John Huston and scene from *Maltese Falcon*	1·20	95
5273	(45c.) John Ford and scene from *The Searchers*	1·20	95
5274	(45c.) Frank Capra and scene from *It happened One Night*	1·20	95

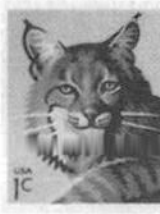

3361 Bobcat

2012. Wildlife. Coil Stamp

5275	**3361**	1c. multicoloured	25	25

2012. Freedom, Liberty, Equality and Justice. Booklet Stamps

5276	**3347**	(45c.) multicoloured	1·20	95
5277	**3348**	(45c.) multicoloured	1·20	95
5278	**3349**	(45c.) multicoloured	1·20	95
5279	**3350**	(45c.) multicoloured	1·20	95

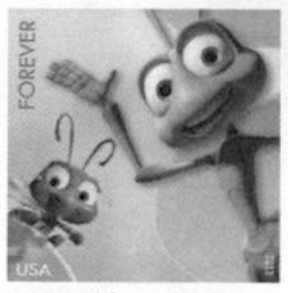

3362 Flik and Dot from *A Bug's Life*

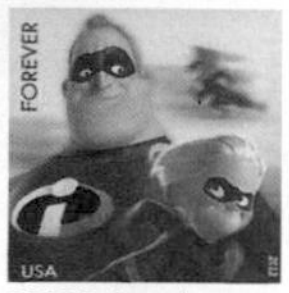

3363 Bob and Dashiell Parr from *The Incredibles*

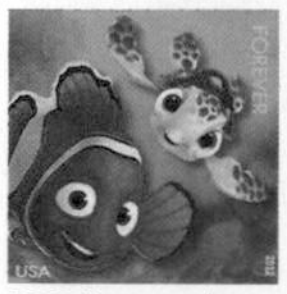

3364 Nemo and Squirt from *Finding Nemo*

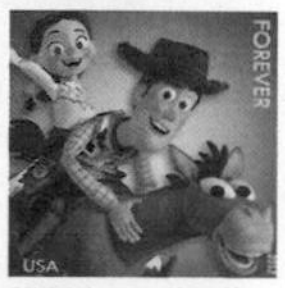

3365 Jessie, Woody and Bullseye from *Toy Story 2*

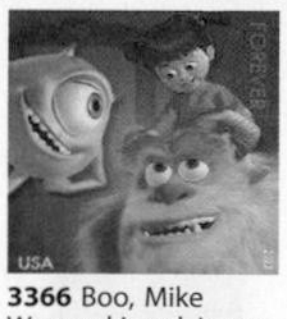

3366 Boo, Mike Wazowski and James P. 'Sulley' Sullivan from *Monsters Inc.*

2012. Animated Cartoons by Pixar

5280	**3362**	(45c.) multicoloured	1·20	95
5281	**3363**	(45c.) multicoloured	1·20	95
5282	**3364**	(45c.) multicoloured	1·20	95
5283	**3365**	(45c.) multicoloured	1·20	95
5284	**3366**	(45c.) multicoloured	1·20	95

2012. Aloha Shirts. Booklet Stamps. Multicoloured.

5285	32c. As Type **3315**	70	50
5286	32c. As Type **3316**	70	50
5287	32c. As Type **3317**	70	50
5288	32c. As Type **3313**	70	50
5289	32c. As Type **3314**	70	50

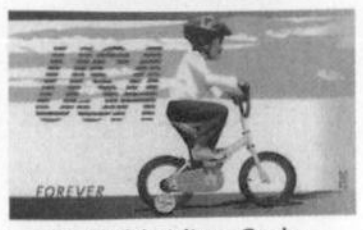

3367 Child riding Cycle with Training Wheels

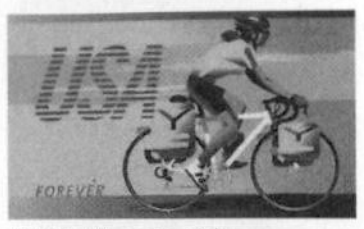

3368 Woman riding Touring Cycle

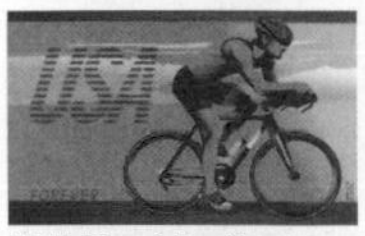

3369 Man riding Sports Cycle

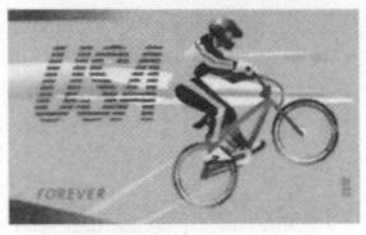

3370 BMX Rider

2012. Cycling

5290	**3367**	(45c.) multicoloured	1·20	95
5291	**3368**	(45c.) multicoloured	1·20	95
5292	**3369**	(45c.) multicoloured	1·20	95
5293	**3370**	(45c.) multicoloured	1·20	95

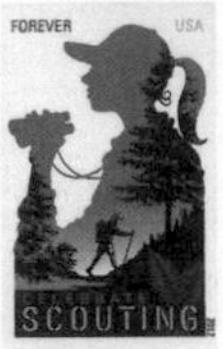

3371 Girl Scouts

2012. Centenary of Girl Scouts of America

5294	**3371**	(45c.) multicoloured	1·20	95

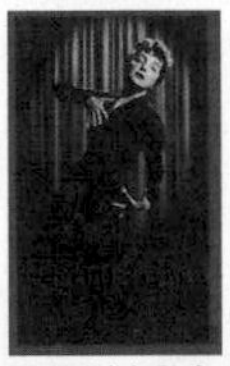
3372 Edith Piaf

2012. Musicians of USA and France. Multicoloured.

5295	(45c.) Type **3372**	1·20	95
5296	(45c.) Miles Davis	1·20	95

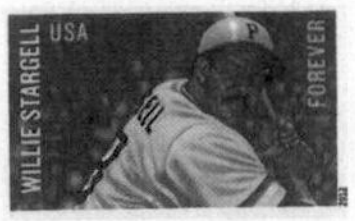

3373 Willie Stargell

2012. Baseball All Stars. Multicoloured.

5297	(45c.) Type **3373**	1·20	95
5298	(45c.) Joe Dimaggio	1·20	95
5299	(45c.) Ted Williams	1·20	95
5300	(45c.) Larry Doby	1·20	95

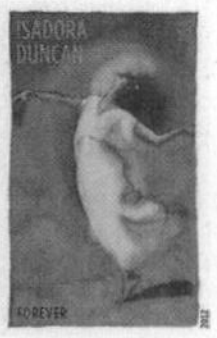

3374 Isadora Duncan

2012. Choreographers. Multicoloured.

5301	(45c.) Type **3374**	1·20	95
5302	(45c.) José Limon	1·20	95
5303	(45c.) Katherine Dunham	1·20	95
5304	(45c.) Bob Fosse	1·20	95

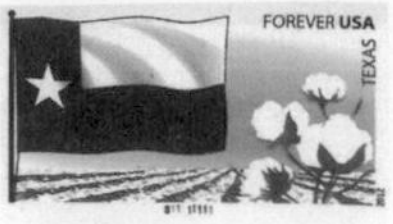

3375 Texas

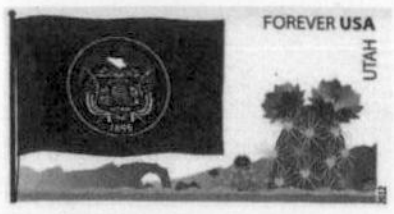

3376 Utah

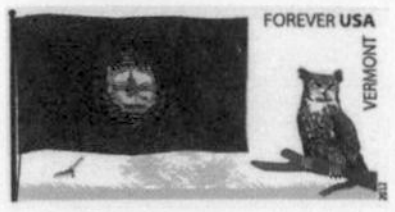

3377 Vermont

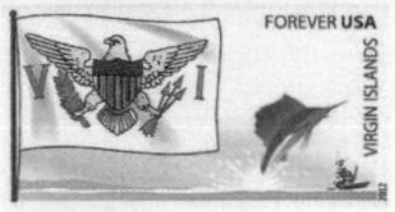

3378 Virgin Islands

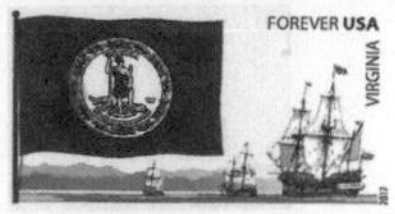

3379 Virginia

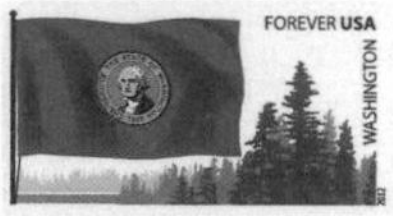

3380 Washington

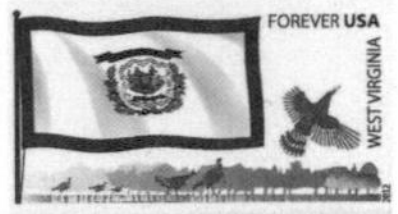

3381 West Virginia

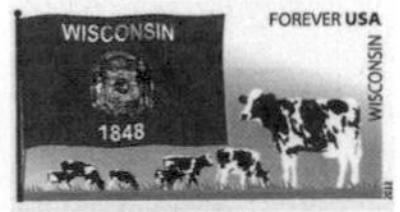

3382 Wisconsin

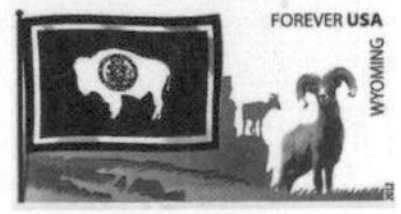

3383 Wyoming

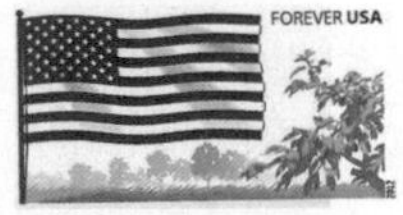

3384 National Flag

2012. Flags of the Nation. Coil Stamps

5305	**3375**	(45c.) multicoloured	1·20	95
5306	**3376**	(45c.) multicoloured	1·20	95
5307	**3377**	(45c.) multicoloured	1·20	95
5308	**3378**	(45c.) multicoloured	1·20	95
5309	**3379**	(45c.) multicoloured	1·20	95
5310	**3380**	(45c.) multicoloured	1·20	95
5311	**3381**	(45c.) multicoloured	1·20	95
5312	**3382**	(45c.) multicoloured	1·20	95
5313	**3383**	(45c.) multicoloured	1·20	95
5314	**3384**	(45c.) multicoloured	1·20	95

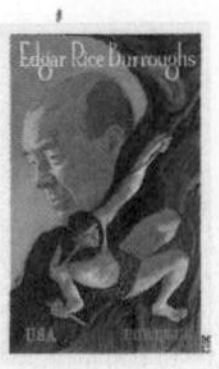

3385 Edgar Rice Burroughs and Scene from *Tarzan*

2012. Edgar Rice Burroughs (writer) Commemoration

5315	**3385**	(45c.) multicoloured	1·20	95

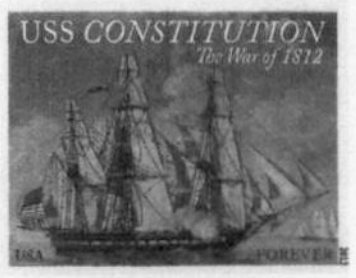

3386 USS *Constitution*

2012. Bicentenary of The War of 1812

5316	**3386**	(45c.) multicoloured	1·20	95

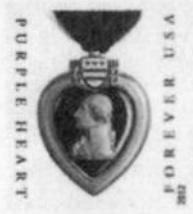

3387 Purple Heart

2012. Purple Heart (military medal)

5317	**3387**	(45c.) multicoloured	1·20	95

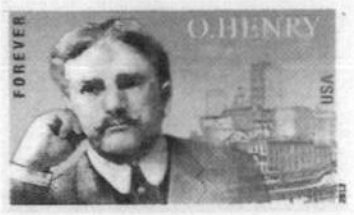

3388 O. Henry

2012. O. Henry (William S. Porter) (writer) Commemoration

5318	**3388**	(45c.) multicoloured	1·20	95

2012. Freedom, Liberty, Equality and Justice. Size 22×24 mm. Automatic Teller Machine Stamps

5319	**3347**	(45c.) multicoloured	1·20	95
5320	**3348**	(45c.) multicoloured	1·20	95
5321	**3349**	(45c.) multicoloured	1·20	95
5322	**3350**	(45c.) multicoloured	1·20	95

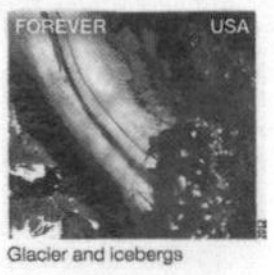

3389 Glaciers and Icebergs

2012. Earthscapes. Multicoloured.

5323	(45c.) Type **3389**	1·20	95
5324	(45c.) Volcanic crater	1·20	95
5325	(45c.) Geothermal spring	1·20	95
5326	(45c.) Butte in early morning fog	1·20	95
5327	(45c.) Inland marsh	1·20	95
5328	(45c.) Salt evaporation ponds	1·20	95
5329	(45c.) Log rafts on way to sawmill	1·20	95
5330	(45c.) Centre-pivot irrigation	1·20	95
5331	(45c.) Cherry orchard	1·20	95
5332	(45c.) Cranberry harvest	1·20	95
5333	(45c.) Residential subdivision	1·20	95
5334	(45c.) 'Barge fleeting'	1·20	95
5335	(45c.) 'Railroad roundhouse'	1·20	95
5336	(45c.) Skyscraper apartments	1·20	95
5337	(45c.) Highway interchange	1·20	95

Nos. 5323/37 were printed in sheets of 15 stamps with an enlarged upper margin and with a brief description on the backing paper.

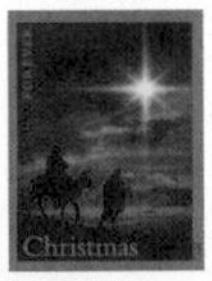

3390 Holy Family

2012. Christmas (1st issue). Booklet Stamp

5338	**3390**	(45c.) multicoloured	1·20	95

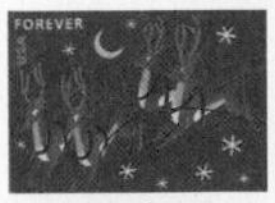

3391 Reindeer

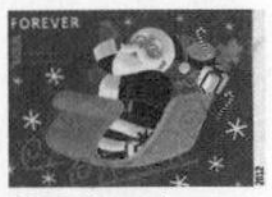

3392 Santa in Sleigh

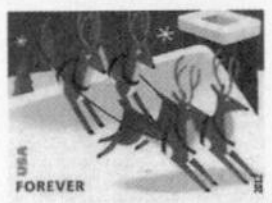

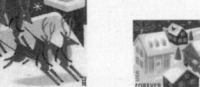

3393 Reindeer landing on Roof

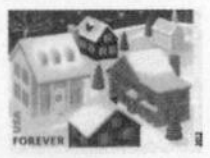

3394 Houses Below

2012. Christmas (2nd issue). Santa. Booklet Stamps

5339	**3391**	(45c.) multicoloured	1·20	95
5340	**3392**	(45c.) multicoloured	1·20	95
5341	**3393**	(45c.) multicoloured	1·20	95
5342	**3394**	(45c.) multicoloured	1·20	95

CERTIFIED MAIL

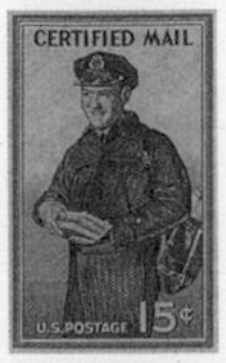

C524 Postman

1955

C1070	**C524**	15c. red	70	55

NEWSPAPER STAMPS

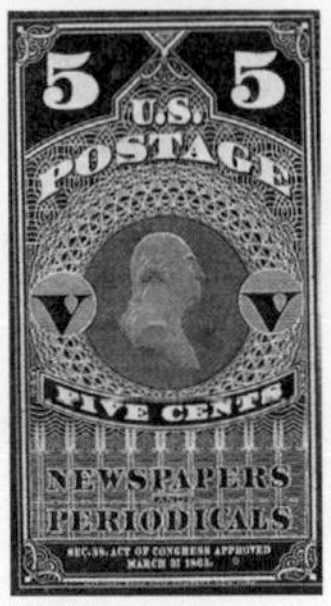

N21 Washington

1865. 5c. with coloured or white border.

N78	**N21**	5c. blue	£300
N80	-	10c. green	£225
N81	-	25c. red	£225

DESIGNS: 10c. Franklin; 20c. Lincoln.

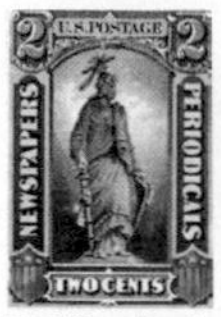

N42 "Freedom"

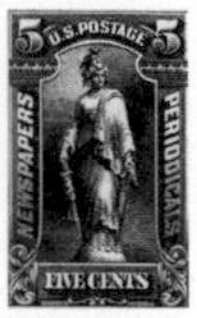

N87 "Freedom"

1875. Different Frames.

N252	**N42**	1c. black	75·00	7·75
N291	**N87**	1c. black	7·25	23·00
N228	**N42**	2c. black	45·00	7·75
N292	**N87**	2c. black	7·25	23·00
N229	**N42**	3c. black	55·00	9·50
N230	**N42**	4c. black	55·00	9·50
N293	**N87**	5c. black	12·00	36·00
N231	**N42**	6c. black	95·00	19·00
N232	**N42**	8c. black	£100	19·00
N185	**N42**	9c. black	£425	85·00
N233	**N42**	10c. black	£100	19·00
N294	**N87**	10c. black	12·00	23·00
N253	**A**	12c. red	£160	18·00
N254	**A**	24c. red	£160	20·00
N295	**A**	25c. red	18·00	60·00
N255	**A**	36c. red	£250	34·00
N256	**A**	48c. red	£375	50·00
N296	**A**	50c. red	23·00	70·00
N191	**A**	60c. red	£1100	£100
N258	**A**	72c. red	£475	75·00
N240	**A**	84c. red	£1100	£200
N241	**A**	96c. red	£1100	£150
N242	-	$1.92 brown	£500	£120
N297	-	$2 red	27·00	£100
N243	-	$3 red	£550	£140
N298	-	$5 blue	36·00	£150
N244	-	$6 blue	£950	£200
N245	-	$9 orange	£750	£150
N299	-	$10 green	39·00	£150
N246	-	$12 green	£750	£190
N300	-	$20 black	41·00	£160
N247	-	$24 purple	£750	£225
N248	-	$36 red	£750	£250
N249	-	$48 brown	£800	£350
N301	-	$50 red	70·00	£200
N250	-	$60 violet	£750	£325
N302	-	$100 violet	60·00	£225

DESIGNS: A, Astraea or "Justice"; $1.92, Ceres; $2, $3 "Victory"; $5, $6 Clio; $9 Minerva; $10, $12 Vesta; $20, $24 "Peace"; $36, $50 "Commerce"; $48 Hebe; $60, $100 Minnehaha.

OFFICIAL STAMPS

For list of stamps used on correspondence from individual Government Departments, between 1873 and 1879, see the Stanley Gibbons Part 22 (U.S.A.) Catalogue.

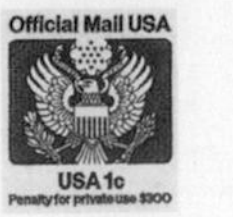

O1315 Eagle

1983

O2008	**O1315**	1c. blue, red & blk	35	20
O2009	**O1315**	4c. blue, red & blk	35	20
O2010	**O1315**	13c. blue, red & blk	60	55
O2011	**O1315**	14c. blue, red & blk	60	45
O2012	**O1315**	17c. blue, red & blk	80	65
O2015	**O1315**	20c. blue, red & blk	1·70	1·80
O2016	**O1315**	22c. blue, red & blk	1·20	1·80
O2013	**O1315**	$1 blue, red & blk	3·25	1·40
O2014	**O1315**	$5 blue, red & blk	14·00	11·00

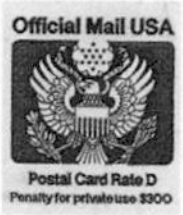

O1438

1985. No value expressed. (a) Inscr "Postal Card Rate D".

O2140 **O 1438**	(14c.) bl, red & blk	4·50	4·00

(b) Inscr "Domestic Letter Rate D".

O2141	(22c.) blue, red and black	4·50	3·50

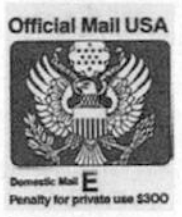

O1588

1988. No value expressed.

O2344 **O 1588**	(25c.) bl, blk & red	1·50	1·20

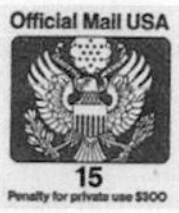

O1592

1988

O2348	**O1592**	1c. blue, black & red	25	30
O2349	**O1592**	4c. blue, black & red	35	30
O2350	**O1592**	15c. blue, blk & red	70	60
O2352	**O1592**	19c. blue, blk & red	55	70
O2353	**O1592**	20c. blue, blk & red	70	70
O2351	**O1592**	23c. blue, blk & red	80	70
O2354	**O1592**	25c. blue, blk & red	90	95
O2355	**O1592**	29c. blue, blk & red	1·00	1·10

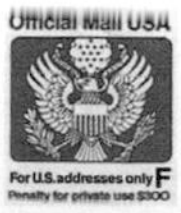

O1793

1991. Value expressed as "F".

O2558 **O 1793**	(29c.) blue, blk & red	1·50	1·10

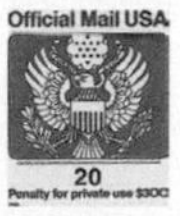

O2001

1993

O2844	**O2001**	1c. blue, blk & red	35	25
O2845	**O2001**	10c. blue, blk & red	60	50
O2846	**O2001**	20c. blue, blk & red	85	60
O2847	**O2001**	23c. blue, blk & red	95	70
O2849	**O2001**	32c. blue, blk & red	1·70	1·20
O2850	**O2001**	33c. blue, blk & red	1·10	80
O2851	**O2001**	34c. blue, blk & red	1·20	85
O2852	**O2001**	37c. blue, blk & red	1·10	80
O2848	**O2001**	$1 blue, blk & red	4·25	3·00

No. O2844 has the face value expressed as "1c".

The line above the face value consists of "USA" and the year date repeated several times.

1994. Value expressed as "G".

O2990 **O 1793**	(32c.) blue, black and red	85	90

1995. As Type **O1592**.

O3022a 1c. ultramarine, black and rosine	10	10
O3022b 20c. ultramarine, black and rosine	30	10
O3022c 23c. ultramarine, black and rosine	35	10

1999. As Type **O1592**.

O3692a33c. ultramarine, black and rosine	45	10

2001. As Type **O1592**.

O3962 34c. l ultramarine, black and rosine	45	10

2002. As Type **O1592**.

O4164a37c. ultramarine, black and rosine	55	10

2006. As Type **O1592**.

O4544a39c. ultramarine, black and rosine

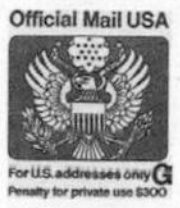

O2105

2006

O4660 **O2105** $1 ultramarine, black and rosine	2·30	1·60

2007. As Type **O1592**.

O4722 41c. ultramarine, black and rosine	80	55

PARCEL POST STAMPS

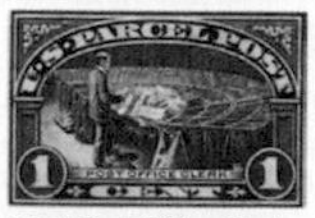

P134 Post Office Clerk

1912

P423	**P134**	1c. red	6·00	1·60
P424	-	2c. red	6·75	1·30
P425	-	3c. red	13·50	6·00
P426	-	4c. red	40·00	3·25
P427	-	5c. red	34·00	2·30
P428	-	10c. red	55·00	3·25
P429	-	15c. red	70·00	13·50
P430	-	20c. red	£150	27·00
P431	-	25c. red	70·00	7·75
P432	-	50c. red	£325	45·00
P433	-	75c. red	£110	36·00
P434	-	$1 red	£375	41·00

DESIGNS: 2c. City carrier; 3c. Railway postal clerk; 4c. Rural carrier; 5c. Steam mail train; 10c. "Kronprinz Wilhelm" (liner) and mail tender; 15c. Automobile service; 20c. Wright Type A biplane carrying mail; 25c. Manufacturing (Pullman works); 50c. Dairying; 75c. Harvesting; $1 Fruit growing.

PARCEL POST POSTAGE DUE STAMPS

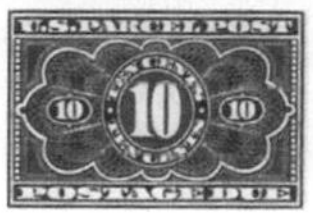

PD 134

1912

PD423	**PD134**	1c. green	11·00	4·00
PD424	**PD134**	2c. green	85·00	18·00
PD425	**PD134**	5c. green	14·00	5·00
PD426	**PD134**	10c. green	£170	43·00
PD427	**PD134**	25c. green	95·00	4·50

POSTAGE DUE STAMPS

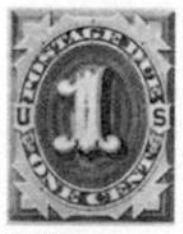
D43

1879

D207	**D43**	1c. brown	85·00	12·50
D222	**D43**	2c. brown	80·00	5·50
D209	**D43**	3c. brown	95·00	5·50
D224	**D43**	5c. brown	£550	41·00
D225	**D43**	10c. brown	£550	32·00
D226	**D43**	30c. brown	£200	55·00
D213	**D43**	50c. brown	£600	80·00

1891

D235	**D43**	1c. red	32·00	1·80
D236	**D43**	2c. red	34·00	1·80
D237	**D43**	3c. red	70·00	14·50
D238	**D43**	5c. red	£100	14·50
D239	**D43**	10c. red	£160	27·00
D240	**D43**	30c. red	£600	£200
D241	**D43**	50c. red	£650	£190

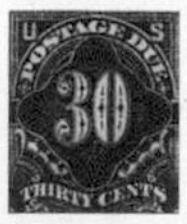

D87

1917

D529	**D87**	½c. red	1·10	30
D530	**D87**	1c. red	3·50	30
D531	**D87**	2c. red	3·50	30
D532	**D87**	3c. red	17·00	90
D533	**D87**	5c. red	14·00	90
D534	**D87**	10c. red	28·00	1·10
D535a	**D87**	30c. red	£100	2·30
D536	**D87**	50c. red	£170	1·10

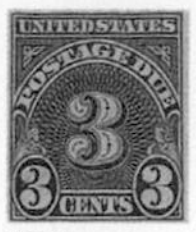

D201

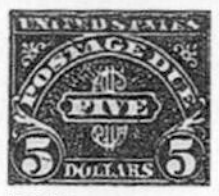

D202

1930

D702	**D 201**	½c. red	1·30	15
D703	**D 201**	1c. red	25	15
D704	**D 201**	2c. red	25	15
D705	**D 201**	3c. red	40	15
D706	**D 201**	5c. red	65	15
D707	**D 201**	10c. red	1·60	15
D708	**D 201**	30c. red	8·50	30
D709	**D 201**	50c. red	12·50	30
D699a	**D 202**	$1 red	34·00	40
D700a	**D 202**	$5 red	40·00	40

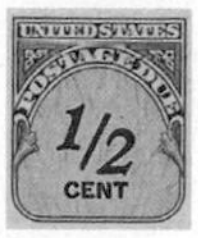

D581

1959. Centres in black.

D1130	**D 581**	½c. red	1·70	1·20
D1131	**D 581**	1c. red	35	20
D1132	**D 581**	2c. red	35	20
D1133	**D 581**	3c. red	35	20
D1134	**D 581**	4c. red	35	20
D1135	**D 581**	5c. red	35	20
D1136	**D 581**	6c. red	35	20
D1137	**D 581**	7c. red	35	20
D1138	**D 581**	8c. red	35	20
D1139	**D 581**	10c. red	40	25
D1140	**D 581**	11c. red	45	35
D1141	**D 581**	13c. red	55	45
D1142	**D 581**	17c. red	80	60
D1143	**D 581**	30c. red	90	20
D1144	**D 581**	50c. red	1·30	35
D1145	**D 581**	$1 red	2·30	35
D1146	**D 581**	$5 red	10·00	1·00

In the dollar values the numerals are double-lined and vertical.

REGISTERED LETTER STAMP

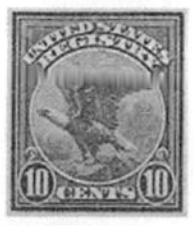
R 133 American Bald Eagle

1911

R404	**R133**	10c. blue	90·00	12·00

SPECIAL DELIVERY AIR STAMPS

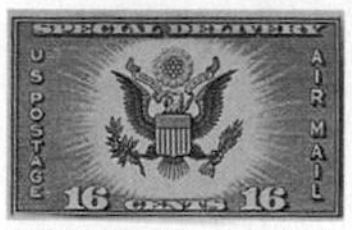

AE247 Great Seal of U.S.A.

1934

AE750	**AE247**	16c. blue	90	80
AE751	**AE247**	16c. blue and red	55	30

SPECIAL DELIVERY STAMPS

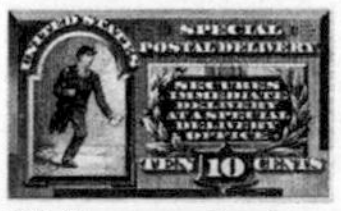

E46 Messenger Running

1885. Inscr "AT A SPECIAL DELIVERY OFFICE".

E217	**E46**	10c. blue	£500	70·00

1888. Inscr "AT ANY POST OFFICE".

E251	10c. orange	£275	41·00
E283	10c. blue	£190	9·00

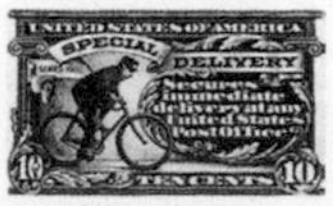

E117 Messenger on Bicycle

1917

E529	**E117**	10c. blue	23·00	85

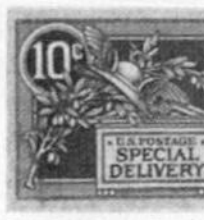

E129 Hat of Mercury and Olive-branch

1908

E374	**E129**	10c. green	80·00	41·00

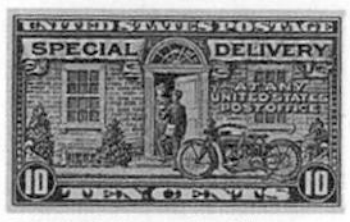

E143 Delivery by Motor Cycle

1922

E648	**E143**	10c. blue	75	30
E648a	**E143**	10c. violet	75	30
E649	**E143**	13c. blue	70	25
E650	**E143**	15c. orange	80	30
E651	**E143**	17c. yellow	4·00	2·75

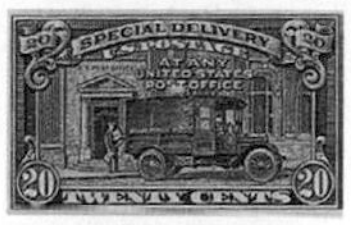

E144 Delivery by Van

1925

E652	**E144**	20c. black	1·70	25

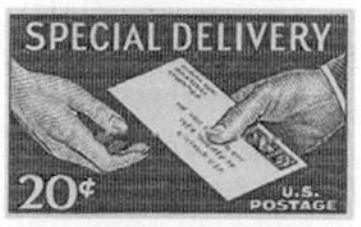

E520 Delivery by Hand

1954

E1066	**E520**	20c. blue	70	30
E1067	**E520**	30c. lake	90	35

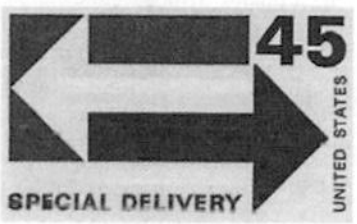

E799 Arrows

1969

E1374	**E799**	45c. red and blue	1·60	45
E1375	**E799**	60c. blue and red	1·80	45

SPECIAL HANDLING STAMPS

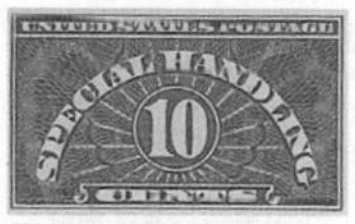

SH173

1925

SH624	**SH173**	10c. green	2·30	1·10
SH625	**SH173**	15c. green	2·50	1·00
SH626	**SH173**	20c. green	4·25	1·70
SH628	**SH173**	25c. green	23·00	17·00

Pt. 17

UNITED STATES POSTAL AGENCY IN SHANGHAI

These stamps were valid for use on mail despatched from the U.S. Postal Agency in Shanghai to addresses in the United States. This agency was closed on 31 December 1922.

100 cents = 1 dollar (Chinese).

1919. United States stamps of 1908–12 surch **SHANGHAI CHINA** and new value.

1	**128**	2c. on 1c. green	28·00	40·00
17	**128**	2Cts. on 1c. green	£150	£140
2	**128**	4c. on 2c. pink	30·00	41·00
18	**128**	4Cts. on 2c. red	£130	£110
3	**128**	6c. on 3c. violet	55·00	80·00
4	**128**	8c. on 4c. brown	65·00	80·00
5	**128**	10c. on 5c. blue	70·00	85·00
6	**128**	12c. on 6c. orange	85·00	£140
7	**128**	14c. on 7c. black	90·00	£140
8a	**133**	16c. on 8c. olive	70·00	£130
9	**133**	18c. on 9c. orange	70·00	£100
10	**133**	20c. on 10c. yellow	65·00	80·00
11	**133**	24c. on 12c. red	70·00	95·00
12	**133**	30c. on 15c. grey	90·00	£160
13	**133**	40c. on 20c. blue	£140	£250
14	**133**	60c. on 30c. red	£130	£180
15	**133**	$1 on 50c. lilac	£550	£700
16	**133**	$2 on $1 black	£450	£650

Pt. 6

UPPER SENEGAL AND NIGER

A French Colony in W. Africa, E. of Senegal, formerly called Senegambia and Niger, and became part of French Sudan in 1920.

100 centimes = 1 franc.

1906. "Faidherbe", "Palms" and "Balay" key-types inscr "HT-SENEGAL-NIGER" in blue (10, 40c., 5f.) or red (others).

35	I	1c. grey	1·70	1·70
36	I	2c. brown	2·00	1·70
37	I	4c. brown on blue	2·75	2·10
38	I	5c. green	5·50	2·75
39	I	10c. red	6·50	1·80
40	I	15c. violet	5·50	10·00
41	J	20c. black on blue	3·00	3·75
42	J	25c. blue	11·00	3·25
43	J	30c. brown on pink	3·50	12·00
44	J	35c. black on yellow	1·80	2·75
45	J	40c. red on blue	6·00	14·00
46	J	45c. brown on green	6·50	21·00
47	J	50c. violet	6·00	8·25
48	J	75c. green on orange	5·50	27·00
49	K	1f. black on blue	21·00	55·00
50	K	2f. blue on red	39·00	75·00
51	K	5f. red on yellow	£100	£130

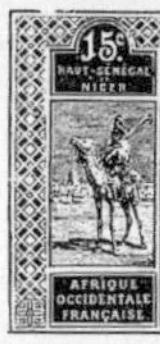

7 Touareg

1914

59	7	1c. violet and purple	35	2·30
60	7	2c. purple and grey	20	1·80
61	7	4c. blue and black	1·80	2·00
62	7	5c. green and light green	75	1·00
63	7	10c. carmine and red	1·40	3·25
64	7	15c. yellow and brown	1·90	3·00
65	7	20c. black and purple	4·25	7·00
66	7	25c. blue and ultramarine	2·50	3·25
67	7	30c. chocolate and brown	3·25	8·00
68	7	35c. violet and red	3·50	7·75
69	7	40c. red and grey	2·75	7·25
70	7	45c. brown and blue	2·75	7·75
71	7	50c. green and black	3·75	6·75
72	7	75c. brown and yellow	4·50	8·00
73	7	1f. purple and brown	7·25	11·50
74	7	2f. blue and green	3·50	11·00
75	7	5f. black and violet	26·00	30·00

1915. Red Cross. Surch **5c** and red cross.

76	10c.+5c. carmine and red	3·25	4·50

POSTAGE DUE STAMPS

1906. "Natives" key-type inscr "HT-SENEGAL-NIGER".

D52	L	5c. green and red	1·70	1·80
D53	L	10c. purple and blue	3·75	3·75
D54	L	15c. blue and red on blue	3·75	14·50
D55	L	20c. black & red on yellow	5·50	8·25
D56	L	50c. violet and red	17·00	46·00
D57	L	60c. black and red on buff	14·00	50·00
D58	L	1f. black and red on flesh	30·00	65·00

1915. "Figures" key-type inscr "HT. SENEGAL-NIGER".

D77	M	5c. green	1·30	3·50
D78	M	10c. red	1·50	3·50
D79	M	15c. grey	1·30	7·25
D80	M	20c. brown	1·30	4·00
D81	M	30c. blue	2·40	11·00
D82	M	50c. black	2·00	10·00
D83	M	60c. orange	6·50	21·00
D84	M	1f. violet	3·75	17·00

For later issues see **FRENCH SUDAN.**

Pt. 7

UPPER SILESIA

Stamps issued during a plebiscite held in 1921 to decide the future of the district. After the plebiscite it was divided between Germany and Poland.

100 pfennig = 1 mark.

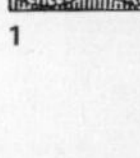

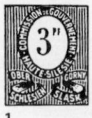

1

1920

1	1	2½pf. grey	55	1·10
2	1	3pf. brown	55	1·70
3	1	5pf. green	35	1·10
4	1	10pf. brown	55	1·80
5	1	15pf. violet	35	1·10
6	1	20pf. blue	35	1·10
7	1	50pf. purple	6·25	11·50
8	1	1m. pink	6·75	16·00
9	1	5m. orange	6·50	16·00

1920. Surch.

11	5pf. on 15pf. violet	£225	£750
12	5pf. on 20pf. blue	1·60	4·50
14	10pf. on 20pf. blue	1·70	5·00
17	50pf. on 5m. orange	46·00	80·00

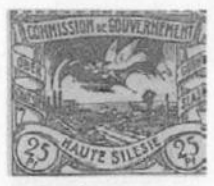

9 Coal-mine in Silesia

1920

19	9	2½pf. grey	45	1·10
20	9	3pf. purple	65	1·10
21	9	5pf. green	45	1·10
22	9	10pf. red	65	1·10
23	9	15pf. violet	65	1·10
24	9	20pf. blue	1·10	2·75
25	9	25pf. brown	65	1·10
26	9	30pf. yellow	80	1·10
27	9	40pf. green	80	1·50

Same design, but larger.

28	50pf. grey	90	1·10
29	60pf. blue	70	2·30
30	75pf. green	1·80	2·75
31	80pf. purple	1·80	1·50
32	1m. mauve	1·80	1·10
33	2m. brown	1·70	1·10
34	3m. violet	1·60	1·10
35	5m. orange	5·00	6·25

1921. Optd **Plebiscite 20 mars 1921**.

36	10pf. red	5·75	13·50
37	15pf. violet	5·75	13·50
38	20pf. blue	8·00	19·00
39	25pf. brown	17·00	46·00
40	30pf. yellow	15·00	28·00
41	40pf. green	15·00	28·00
42	50pf. grey	15·00	40·00
43	60pf. blue	17·00	34·00
44	75pf. green	17·00	40·00
45	80pf. purple	28·00	50·00
46	1m. mauve	34·00	90·00

1922. Type **9** in new colours and surch.

47	4m. on 60pf. green	1·10	2·75
48	10m. on 75pf. red	1·70	4·00
49	20m. on 80pf. orange	9·00	23·00

OFFICIAL STAMPS

1920. Stamps of Germany optd **C.I.H.S.** within a circle.
(a) Stamps of 1902 and 1916.

O1	24	2pf. grey		£3500
O2	24	2½pf. grey	£2500	£1000
O3	10	3pf. brown		£950
O4	10	5pf. green	35	2·20
O5	24	7½pf. orange	£2500	£1100
O6	10	10pf. red	£900	£425
O7	24	15pf. violet	£900	£350
O8	10	20pf. blue	£900	£425
O9	10	25pf. black & red on yell		£2500
O10	10	30pf. blk & orge on pink	£1600	£375
O11	24	35pf. brown	£1600	£350
O12	10	40pf. black and red	£1000	£350
O13	10	50pf. black & pur on pink	£1000	£350
O14	10	60pf. purple	£1600	£350
O15	10	75pf. black and green	£900	£350
O16	10	80pf. black and red on red		£4000
O17	12	1m. red	£2500	£1000
O18	13	2m. blue		£3250

(b) War Charity. Nos. 105/6.

O19	10	10+5pf. red		
O20	24	15+5pf. violet		

(c) National Assembly at Weimar. Nos. 107/10.

O21	26	10pf. red	£1700	£1400
O22	27	15pf. blue and brown		£1400
O23	28	25pf. red and green		£4000
O24	28	30pf. red and purple	£1700	£1800

1920. Official stamps of Germany optd **C.G.H.S.** (a) As Types **O31** and **O32** (with figures "21").

O25	5pf. green	45	1·80
O26	10pf. red	45	1·80
O27	15pf. brown	45	1·80
O28	20pf. blue	45	1·80
O29	30pf. orange on buff	45	1·80
O30	50pf. violet on buff	1·10	3·50
O31	1m. red on buff	9·00	18·00

(b) As Types **O31** and **O32** but without figures.

O32	5pf. green	1·10	10·50
O33	10pf. red	35	2·20
O34	15pf. purple	35	2·75
O35	20pf. blue	35	2·20
O36	30pf. orange on buff	35	2·20
O37	40pf. red	35	2·20
O38	50pf. violet on buff	35	2·20
O39	60pf. brown	35	2·20
O40	1m. red on buff	35	2·20
O41	1m.25 blue on yellow	11·50	13·50
O43	2m. blue	35	3·50
O44	5m. brown on yellow	35	3·50

Pt. 6, Pt. 14

UPPER VOLTA

Formerly part of Upper Senegal and Niger, Upper Volta was created a separate colony in 1919. In 1932 it was divided among French Sudan, Ivory Coast and Niger but was reconstituted as a separate territory in 1947 from when it used the stamps of French West Africa.

In 1958 it became an autonomous republic within the French Community and attained full independence in 1960.

In 1984 the name of the state was changed to Burkina Faso.

100 centimes = 1 franc.

1920. Stamps of Upper Senegal and Niger optd **HAUTE-VOLTA**.

1	7	1c. violet and purple	20	3·25
2	7	2c. purple and grey	20	5·00
3	7	4c. blue and black	30	3·75
4	7	5c. green and light green	1·30	6·50
18	7	5c. chocolate and brown	20	4·50
5	7	10c. carmine and red	1·60	6·75
19	7	10c. green and light green	35	6·00
20	7	10c. blue and mauve	35	2·75
6	7	15c. yellow and brown	45	4·00
7	7	20c. black and purple	90	5·75
8	7	25c. blue and ultramarine	5·00	5·50
21	7	25c. green and black	80	3·25
9	7	30c. chocolate and brown	4·00	9·50
22	7	30c. carmine and red	1·60	8·25
23	7	30c. red and violet	60	5·25
23a	7	30c. turquoise and green	2·30	8·75
10	7	35c. violet and red	1·10	4·25
11	7	40c. red and grey	45	4·25
12	7	45c. brown and blue	85	5·25
13	7	50c. green and black	5·75	20·00
24	7	50c. blue and ultramarine	2·30	7·75
25	7	50c. blue and orange	1·00	2·75
26	7	60c. red	1·10	4·75
26a	7	65c. blue and brown	2·75	10·00
14	7	75c. brown and yellow	2·50	8·00
15	7	1f. purple and brown	1·80	5·50
16	7	2f. blue and green	3·00	5·75
17	7	5f. black and violet	3·75	11·00

1922. Surch in figures and bars.

27	0,01 on 15c. yellow & brown	1·70	7·00
28	0,02 on 15c. yellow & brown	80	9·50
29	0,05 on 15c. yellow & brown	45	9·00
30	25c. on 2f. blue and green	1·30	9·75
31	25c. on 5f. black and violet	1·60	9·50
32	60 on 75c. violet on pink	55	4·50
33	65 on 45c. brown and blue	1·40	8·25
34	85 on 45c. brown and yellow	1·80	7·00
35	90c. on 75c. pink and red	1·90	10·50
36	1f.25 on 1f. lt blue & blue	1·10	9·50
37	1f.50 on 1f. ultram & bl	2·50	4·25
37a	3f. on 5f. brown and pink	3·00	18·00
38	10f. on 5f. pink and green	12·00	55·00
39	20f. on 5f. violet and brown	13·00	70·00

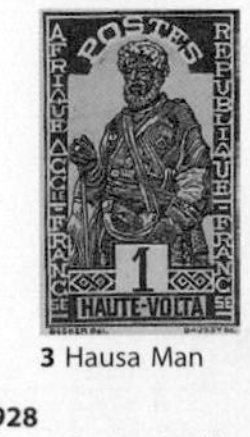

3 Hausa Man

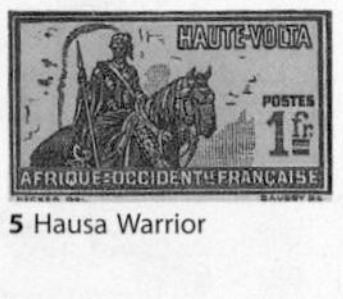

5 Hausa Warrior

1928

40	3	1c. blue and green	40	3·25
41	3	2c. brown and mauve	65	6·50
42	3	4c. black and yellow	35	5·25
43	3	5c. indigo and blue	55	3·25
44	3	10c. blue and pink	85	3·75
45	3	15c. brown and blue	1·50	8·00
46	3	20c. brown and green	1·40	7·25
47	-	25c. brown and yellow	2·50	2·75
48	-	30c. deep green and green	2·00	7·50
49	-	40c. black and pink	2·50	3·00
50	-	45c. brown and blue	2·75	9·50
51	-	50c. black and green	2·75	1·80
52	-	65c. indigo and blue	2·75	12·00
53	-	75c. black and mauve	3·50	11·00
54	-	90c. red and mauve	3·25	9·75
55	5	1f. brown and green	4·25	12·50
56	5	1f.10 blue and mauve	3·50	11·00
57	5	1f.50 blue	4·25	12·00
58	5	2f. black and blue	6·25	19·00
59	5	3f. brown and yellow	6·25	18·00
60	5	5f. brown and mauve	6·75	22·00
61	5	10f. black and green	20·00	60·00
62	5	20f. black and pink	30·00	75·00

DESIGN—VERT: 25c. to 90c. Hausa woman.

1931. "Colonial Exhibition" key-types inscr "HAUTE-VOLTA".

63	E	40c. green and black	4·75	8·25
64	F	50c. mauve and black	4·00	8·50
65	G	90c. red and black	2·00	11·50
66	B	1f.50 blue and black	2·75	10·00

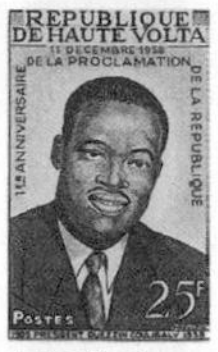

6 President Coulibaly

1959. First Anniv of Republic.

67	6	25f. purple and black	65	45

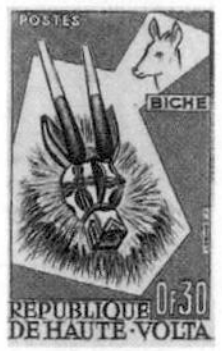

7 Antelope Mask

1960. Animal Masks.

68	7	30c. violet and red	20	10
69	7	40c. purple and ochre	20	10
70	7	50c. olive and turquoise	20	10
71	-	1f. black, brown and red	20	10
72	-	2f. multicoloured	20	10
73	-	4f. black, violet and blue	20	10
74	-	5f. red, brown and bistre	20	10
75	-	6f. purple and turquoise	20	10
76	-	8f. brown and red	35	20
77	-	10f. purple and green	35	35
78	-	15f. blue, brown and red	55	40
79	-	20f. green and blue	65	45
80	-	25f. purple, green and blue	75	45
81	-	30f. black, brown & turquoise	1·10	45
82	-	40f. black, red and blue	1·40	65
83	-	50f. brown, green and mauve	1·80	75
84	-	60f. blue and brown	2·00	1·00
85	-	85f. blue and turquoise	2·75	1·50

MASKS: 1f. to 4f. Wart-hog; 5f. to 8f. Monkey; 10f. to 20f. Buffalo; 25f. Antelope; 30f. to 50f. Elephant; 60f., 85f. Secretary bird.

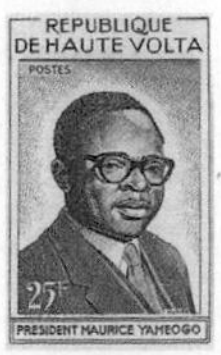

8 President Yameogo

1960

86	8	25f. purple and grey	75	35

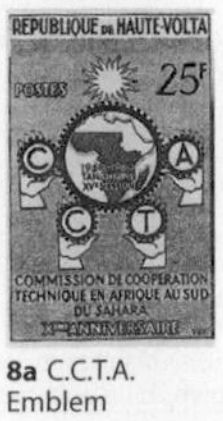

8a C.C.T.A. Emblem

1960. Tenth Anniv of African Technical Co-operation Commission.
87   **8a**   25f. indigo and blue   1·00   55

8b Conseil de l'Entente Emblem

1960. First Anniv of Conseil de l'Entente.
88   **8b**   25f. multicoloured   90   55

9

1960. Proclamation of Independence.
89   **9**   25f. brown, red and black   65   50

10 Holste Broussard Airplane and Map

1961. Air.
90   **10**   100f. blue, green and red   2·20   1·00
91   —   200f. brown, red and green   6·00   1·90
92   —   500f. multicoloured   14·50   6·00
DESIGNS: 200f. Scene at Ouagadougou Airport; 500f. Aerial view of Champs Elysees, Ouagadougou.

11 W.M.O. Emblem, Sun and Meteorological Instruments

1961. First World Meteorological Day.
93   **11**   25f. red, blue and black   85   50

12 Arms of Republic

1961. Independence Festival.
94   **12**   25f. multicoloured   60   45

1962. Air. "Air Afrique" Airline. As T **47a** of Senegal.
95   25f. mauve, green and purple   80   45

13 W.M.O. Emblem, Weather Station and Crops

1962. World Meteorological Day.
96   **13**   25f. blue, green and black   80   50

1962. Malaria Eradication. As T **47b** of Senegal.
97   25f.+5f. red   1·00   1·00

14 Nurse and Hospital

1962. Establishment of Red Cross in Upper Volta.
98   **14**   25f. brown, blue and red   95   60

15 African Buffalo at Water-hole

1962. Hunting and Tourism.
99   **15**   5f. green, blue and sepia   45   25
100   —   10f. green, yellow & brown   60   40
101   —   15f. green, yellow & brown   1·70   70
102   —   25f. green, blue and mauve   1·10   75
103   —   50f. green, blue and mauve   2·20   1·80
104   —   85f. green, blue and brown   5·00   2·50
DESIGNS—VERT: 15f. Waterbuck; 85f. Kob. HORIZ: 10f. Lion and lioness; 25f. Arly Camp; 50f. Diapaga Camp.

15a Football

1962. Abidjan Games, 1961. Multicoloured.
105   20f. Type **15a**   60   40
106   25f. Cycling   95   60
107   85f. Boating   1·80   1·00

1962. First Anniv of Union of African and Malagasy States. As T **47c** of Senegal.
108   30f. multicoloured   1·70   90

16 Flag and U.N. Emblem

1962. Air. Second Anniv of Admission to U.N.
109   **16**   50f. multicoloured   90   45
110   **16**   100f. multicoloured   1·80   85

17 G.P.O., Ouagadougou

1962. Air. Opening of Ouagadougou P.O.
111   **17**   100f. multicoloured   1·80   80

1963. Freedom from Hunger. As T **47d** of Senegal.
112   25f.+5f. blue, brn & myrtle   1·00   1·00

18 Rainfall Map

1963. World Meteorological Day.
113   **18**   70c. multicoloured   1·40   85

19 Basketball

1963. Dakar Games. Centres in black and red.
114   **19**   20f. violet   45   25
115   —   25f. ochre (Discus)   60   25
116   —   50f. blue (Judo)   1·30   55

20 "Argyreia nervosa"

1963. Flowers. Multicoloured.
117   50c. "Hibiscus rosa-sinensis"   10   10
118   1f. "Oldenlandia grandiflora"   10   10
119   1f.50 "Portulaca grandiflora"   10   10

120   2f. "Nicotiana tabacum"   20   10
121   4f. "Ipomaea stolonifera"   30   10
122   5f. "Striga senegalensis"   30   20
123   6f. "Vigna"   35   20
124   8f. "Lepidagathis heudelotiana"   40   25
125   10f. "Euphorbia splendens"   40   25
126   15f. "Hippeastrum equestre"   50   40
127   25f. Type **20**   80   45
128   30f. "Quisqualis indica"   1·00   40
129   40f. "Nymphea lotus"   1·70   70
130   50f. "Plumeria alba"   1·80   70
131   60f. "Crotalaria retusa"   2·50   1·10
132   85f. "Hibiscus esculentus"   3·50   1·50
The 50c. to 10f. are vert.

21 Douglas DC-8 in Flight

1963. Air. First Jet-flight, Ouagadougou–Paris.
133   **21**   200f. multicoloured   5·25   2·75

1963. Air. African and Malagasy Posts and Telecommunications Union. As T **5a** of Rwanda.
134   85f. multicoloured   1·60   85

22 Centenary Emblem and Globe

1963. Red Cross Centenary.
135   **22**   25f. multicoloured   1·00   75

1963. Air. First Anniv of "Air Afrique". Surch **AIR AFRIQUE 19-11-63 50F.**
136   **21**   50f. on 200f. multicoloured   1·50   85

24 "Declaration universelle. . ."

1963. 15th Anniv of Declaration of Human Rights.
137   **24**   25f. multicoloured   85   55

25 "Europafrique"

1964. Air. "Europafrique".
138   **25**   50f. multicoloured   1·70   95

26 "Telecommunications"

1964. Admission of Upper Volta to I.T.U.
139   **26**   25f. multicoloured   60   35

27 Rameses II, Abu Simbel

1964. Air. Nubian Monuments Preservation.
140   **27**   25f. purple and green   85   60
141   **27**   100f. brown and blue   2·75   2·30

28 Barograph, Landscape and W.M.O. Emblem

1964. World Meteorological Day.
142   **28**   50f. mauve, blue and green   1·10   75

29 Dove and Letters

1964. First Anniv of Admission to U.P.U.
143   **29**   25f. sepia and blue   75   45
144   —   60f. sepia and orange   1·20   80
DESIGN: 60f. Jet airliner and letters.

30 Head of Athlete (bronze)

1964. Air. Olympic Games, Tokyo.
145   **30**   15f. green, red and sepia   55   25
146   —   25f. green, red and sepia   75   45
147   —   85f. green, red and brown   1·50   95
148   —   100f. chocolate, red & brn   2·20   1·10
MS148a 100×145 mm. Nos. 145/8   12·50   12·00
DESIGNS: 25f. Seated athlete (bronze), 85f. "Victorious athlete" (bronze); 100f. Venus de Milo.

31 Symbols of Solar Research

1964. International Quiet Sun Years.
149   **31**   30f. red, ochre and green   90   60

32 Grey Woodpecker

1964. Air.
150   **32**   250f. multicoloured   11·50   5·00

1964. French, African and Malagasy Co-operation. As T **60a** of Senegal.
151   70f. brown, red and blue   1·30   75

33 President Kennedy

1964. Air. Pres. Kennedy Commemoration.
152   **33**   100f. multicoloured   2·30   1·50
MS152a 90×130 mm. No. 152 in block of four   6·00   4·00

1969. Agricultural Produce.

274	**88**	15f. brown, green and yellow (postage)	55	25
275	-	30f. blue and mauve	95	45
276	-	100f. brown and violet (air)	1·70	55
277	-	200f. green and red	3·50	1·10

DESIGNS: 30f. Cotton. LARGER—48×27 mm: 100f. Ground-nuts; 200f. Rice.

89 Stylized Tree

1969. Air. Europafrique.

278	**89**	100f. multicoloured	1·30	80

1969. Tenth Anniv of Aerial Navigation Security Agency for Africa and Madagascar (A.S.E.C.N.A.). As T **112** of Senegal.

279		100f. brown	1·70	1·00

90 "Niadale"

1970. Figurines and Masks in National Museum.

280	**90**	10f. brown, orange and red	35	10
281	-	30f. brown, blue and violet	55	25
282	-	45f. brown, blue and green	1·00	55
283	-	80f. brown, purple, & violet	1·80	85

DESIGNS: 30f. "Niaga"; 45f. "Iliu bara"; 80f. "Karan Weeba".

91 Lenin

1970. Air. Birth Centenary of Lenin.

284	**91**	20f. brown and ochre	1·00	45
285	-	100f. red, blue and green	2·10	1·20

DESIGN—HORIZ: 100f. "Lenin addressing workers" (A. Serov).

92 African Huts and City Buildings

1970. Linked Cities' Day.

286	**92**	30f. brown, blue and red	80	45

93 Cauris Dancers

1970. Upper Volta Dances. Multicoloured.

287		5f. Mask of Nebwa Gnomo dance (horiz)	45	20
288		8f. Type **93**	60	20
289		20f. Gourmantches dancers	85	25
290		30f. Larlle dancers (horiz)	1·10	35

94 "Pupils", Sun and Emblem of Education Year

1970. Int Education Year. Multicoloured.

291		40f. Type **94**	60	25
292		90f. Visual aids and emblem	1·40	60

95 New U.P.U. Headquarters Building, U.P.U. Monument and Abraham Lincoln

1970. New U.P.U. Headquarters Building.

293	**95**	30f. grey, red and brown	75	25
294	**95**	60f. purple, green & brown	1·40	55

96 Footballers and Cup

1970. Air. World Cup Football Championship, Mexico.

295	**96**	40f. lake, green and brown	75	45
296	-	100f. brown, purple & green	1·60	80

DESIGN: 100f. Goalkeeper saving ball, Globe and footballers.

97 Franklin D. Roosevelt

1970. Air. 25th Anniv of Roosevelt's Death.

297	**97**	10f. brown, black and green	30	25
298	-	200f. red, violet and grey	2·40	1·00

DESIGN—HORIZ: 200f. Roosevelt with his stamp collection.

98 Naval Construction

1970. Hanover Fair.

299	**98**	15f. multicoloured	1·00	45
300		45f. green, blue and black	1·00	45
301		80f. purple, brown & black	2·00	60

DESIGNS: 45f. Test-tubes and retorts ("Chemistry"); 80f. Power transmission lines and pylons ("Electro-techniques").

99 Inoculating Cattle

1970. National Veterinary School.

302	**99**	30f. multicoloured	1·00	50

100 "Manchurian Cranes and Seashore" and Expo Monorail Coach

1970. Air. World Fair "EXPO 70" Osaka, Japan.

303	**100**	50f. Type **100**	2·20	75
304		150f. "Geisha", rocket and satellite	2·30	1·20

101 Nurse attending Patient

1970. Upper Volta Red Cross.

305	**101**	30f. brown, red and green	1·00	50

102 "Nurse and Child" (F. Hals)

1970. "Europafrique". Multicoloured.

306	**102**	25f. Type **102**	1·10	35
307		30f. "Courtyard in Delft" (Hoogh)	1·40	45
308		150f. "Christina of Denmark" (Holbein)	4·25	1·20
309		250f. "Hofburg Courtyard, Innsbruck" (Durer)	6·50	1·90

103 U.N. Emblem and Dove

1970. Air. 25th Anniv of U.N.O.

310	**103**	60f. ultramarine, bl & grn	75	45
311		250f. violet, brown & grn	3·50	1·40

DESIGNS—HORIZ: 250f. U.N. emblem and two doves.

104 Front of Car

1970. Paris Motor Show.

312	**104**	25f. green, lake and brown	1·40	55
313	-	40f. blue, purple and green	1·80	90

DESIGN: 40f. Old and new cars.

105 "Holy Family"

1970. Christmas.

314	**105**	300f. silver	10·00	10·00
315	**105**	1000f. gold	25·00	25·00

106 Centre Buildings

1970. Inauguration of Austro-Voltaic Centre.

316	**106**	50f. orange, green and red	80	45

107 Arms and Stork

1970. Tenth Anniv of Independence.

317	**107**	30f. multicoloured (postage)	45	25
318	-	500f. blk, red & gold (air)	7·50	3·75

DESIGN—27×37 mm: 500f. Family and flag. No. 318 is embossed on gold foil.

108 U.N. "Key" and Split Globe

1970. Tenth Anniv of U.N. Declaration on Colonies.

319	**108**	40f. red, blue and brown	1·00	50
320	-	50f. multicoloured	80	45

DESIGN: 50f. Two maps of Africa showing former colonies.

109 Pres. Nasser

1971. Air. Pres. Nasser Commemoration.

321	**109**	100f. multicoloured	1·30	55

110 Beingolo Hunting Horn

1971. Musical Instruments.

322	**110**	5f. brown, red and blue	40	25
323	-	15f. brown, red and green	80	25
324	-	20f. red, grey and blue	1·60	25
325	-	25f. drab, green and red	1·80	55

INSTRUMENTS—VERT: 15f. Mossi "guitar"; 20f. Gurunssi "flutes". HORIZ: 25f. Lunga "drum".

111 Heads of Different Races

1971. Racial Equality Year.

326	**111**	50f. brown, red & turq	1·50	65

112 "The Purple Herons" (Egypt, 1354)

1971. Air. Muslim Miniatures. Multicoloured.

327	**112**	100f. Type **112**	1·80	85
328		250f. Page from the Koran (Egypt, c. 1368–88) (vert)	4·00	2·00

113 Telephone and Hemispheres

1971. World Telecommunications Day.

329	**113**	50f. violet, grey and brown	1·00	45

114 Olympic Rings and Events

1971. Air. "Pre-Olympic Year".

330	**114**	150f. red, violet and blue	3·75	1·80

115 Cutting
Cane and Sugar
Factory, Banfora

1971. Local Industries. Multicoloured.
331	10f. Type **115**		30	10
332	35f. Cotton-plant and textiles ("Voltex" project)		50	30

116 "Gonimbrasia hecate"

1971. Butterflies. Multicoloured.
333	1f. Type **116**	25	10
334	2f. "Hamanumida daedalus"	50	10
335	3f. "Ophideres materna"	55	10
336	5f. "Danaus chrysippus"	1·30	45
337	40f. "Hypolimnas misippus"	7·25	1·80
338	45f. "Danaus petiverana"	9·75	2·20

117 Scout and
Pagodas

1971. Air. 13th World Scout Jamboree, Asagari (Japan).
339	**117**	45f. multicoloured	1·10	55

118 Actor with
Fan

1971. "Philatokyo" Stamp Exn, Tokyo. Multicoloured.
340	25f. Type **118**	50	25
341	40f. Actor within mask	75	45

119 African
with
Seed-packet

1971. National Seed-protection Campaign. Multicoloured.
342	35f. Grading seeds (horiz)	55	25
343	75f. Type **119**	95	50
344	100f. Harvesting crops (horiz)	1·20	55

1971. Tenth Anniv of Volta Red Cross. Surch **Xe ANNIVERSAIRE** and new value.
345	**101**	100f. on 30f. brown, red and purple	1·80	85

121 Teacher and Class

1971. "Women's Access to Education". Multicoloured.
346	35f. Type **121**	65	25
347	50f. Family learning alphabet	95	50

122 Soldier and
Tractors

1971. Dakiri Project. Military Aid for Agriculture. Multicoloured.
348	15f. Type **122**	60	25
349	40f. Soldiers harvesting (horiz)	1·00	55

123 General De Gaulle and Map

1971. Air. De Gaulle Commemoration.
350	**123**	40f. multicoloured	95	55
351	-	500f. gold and green	14·00	12·50

DESIGN—VERT (30×40 mm): 500f. De Gaulle.
No. 351 is embossed on gold foil.

1971. Air. Tenth Anniv of African and Malagasy Posts and Telecommunications Union. As No. 432 of Rwanda. Multicoloured.
352	100f. U.A.M.P.T. H.Q. and Mossi dancer	1·60	75

124 "Simulium
damnosum" and
Preventive Measures

1971. Regional Anti-onchocerciasis Campaign.
353	**124**	40f. multicoloured	95	50

125 Pres. Lamizana

1971
354	**125**	35f. multicoloured	1·00	55

126 Children
acclaiming
Emblem

1971. 25th Anniv of UNICEF.
355	**126**	45f. multicoloured	80	50

127 Peulh Straw Hut

1971. Traditional Housing (1st series). Multicoloured.
356	10f. Type **127**	30	10
357	20f. Gourounsi house	50	30
358	35f. Mossi huts	70	50

See also Nos. 370/2.

128 Town Halls of
Bobo-Dioulasso and
Chalons-sur-Marne, France

1971. "Twin Cities" Co-operation.
359	**128** 40f. multicoloured	1·00	55

129 Ice-hockey

1972. Air. Winter Olympic Games, Sapporo, Japan.
360	**129**	150f. purple, blue and red	2·75	1·40

1972. Air. UNESCO "Save Venice" Campaign. As T **145** of Senegal. Multicoloured.
361	100f. "La Musica" (P. Longhi) (vert)	2·75	1·30
362	150f. "Panorama da Ponte della Marina" (detail, Caffi) (horiz)	4·00	1·60

130 Running

1972. Air. Olympic Games, Munich.
363	**130**	65f. brown, blue and green	75	60
364	-	200f. brown and blue	2·50	1·60
MS365	130×100 mm. No. 363/4		4·25	4·00

DESIGN: 200f. Throwing the discus.

131 Louis Armstrong

1972. Famous Negro Musicians. Multicoloured.
366	45f. Type **131** (postage)	4·50	1·30
367	500f. Jimmy Smith (air)	9·25	5·75

132 Globe and Emblems

1972. World Red Cross Day.
368	**132** 40f. multicoloured (postage)	75	25
369	**132** 100f. multicoloured (air)	1·50	60

133 Bobo House

1972. Traditional Housing (2nd series). Multicoloured.
370	45f. Type **133**	85	30
371	50f. Dagari house	95	45
372	90f. Interior of Bango house (horiz)	1·90	75

134 Hair Style

1972. Upper Volta Hair Styles.
373	**134** 25f. multicoloured	45	25
374	- 35f. multicoloured	75	25
375	- 75f. multicoloured	1·50	65

DESIGNS: 35, 75f. Similar hair styles.

135 "Teaching"

1972. Second National Development Plan.
376	**135**	10f. mauve, green and turquoise (postage)	10	10
377	-	15f. brown, orange & green	30	25
378	-	20f. brown, green and blue	45	25
379	-	35f. brown, blue and green	85	25
380	-	40f. brown, green & purple	85	45
381	-	85f. black, red & blue (air)	1·20	80

DESIGNS: 15f. Doctor and patient ("Health"); 20f. Factory and silos ("Industry"); 35f. Cattle ("Cattle-raising"); 40f. Rice-planting ("Agriculture"); 85f. Road-making machine ("Infrastructure").

1972. Tenth Anniv of West African Monetary Union. As T **156** of Senegal.
382	40f. grey, blue and mauve	60	25

136 Lottery Building

1972. Fifth Anniv of National Lottery.
383	**136**	35f. multicoloured	80	30

137 Presidents Pompidou and
Lamizana

1972. Air. Visit of Pres, Pompidou to Upper Volta.
384	**137** 40f. multicoloured	2·20	2·10
385	- 250f. multicoloured	8·25	7·75

DESIGN: 250f. As T **137** but frame differs and portraits are embossed on gold.

138 Mary Peters
(pentathlon)

1972. Air. Gold Medal-winners, Olympic Games, Munich. Multicoloured.
386	40f. Type **138**	45	25
387	65f. Ragno-Lonzi (fencing)	80	45
388	85f. Touritcheva (gymnastics)	1·20	55
389	200f. Maury (sailing)	2·20	90
390	300f. Meyfarth (high-jumping)	3·50	1·40
MS391	80×105 mm. 500f. King (diving)	9·50	5·50

139 Donkeys

1972. Animals. Multicoloured.
392	5f. Type **139**	25	10
393	10f. Spur-winged geese	70	20
394	30f. Goat	1·30	35
395	50f. Bull	1·60	50
396	65f. Dromedaries	2·20	80

140 "The Nativity" (Della Notte)

1972. Air. Christmas. Religious Paintings. Multicoloured.
397	100f. Type **140**	1·50	90
398	200f. "The Adoration of the Magi" (Durer)	3·00	2·00

141 Mossi Hair-style and Village

1973. Air.
399	**141**	5f. multicoloured	10	10
400	**141**	40f. multicoloured	80	30

1973. 25th Anniv of W.H.O. No. 353 surch **O. M. S. 25 Anniversaire 45F.**
401	**124**	45f. on 40f. multicoloured	80	45

1973. 12th Anniv of African and Malagasy Posts and Telecommunications Union. As T **170** of Senegal.
402		100f. purple, red and yellow	1·40	80

1974. 15th Anniv of Council of Accord. As T **176** of Togo.
403		40f. multicoloured	80	50

143 Map and Harvester

1974. Kou Valley Project.
404	**143**	35f. multicoloured	80	50

144 Woman, Globe and I.W.Y. Emblem

1975. International Women's Year.
405	**144**	65f. multicoloured	95	60

145 Mgr. Joanny Thevenoud and Cathedral

1975. 75th Anniv of Evangelization of Upper Volta.
406	**145**	55f. black, brown & green	95	40
407	–	65f. black, brown & green	1·00	60

DESIGN: 65f. Father Guillaume Templier and Cathedral.

146 Farmer's Hat, Hoe and Emblem

1975. Development of the Volta Valleys.
408	**146**	15f. multicoloured	40	10
409	**146**	50f. multicoloured	85	35

147 Diseased People

1976. Campaign against Onchocerciasis (round-worm).
410	**147**	75f. mauve, orange & grn	1·20	45
411	**147**	250f. sepia, orange & brn	3·50	1·40

148 Globe and Emblem

1976. Non-aligned Countries' Summit Conference, Colombo, Sri Lanka. Multicoloured.
412	55f. Type **148**	55	25
413	100f. Globe, dove and emblem	1·40	65

149 Washington at Trenton

1976. "Interphil '76" International Stamp Exhibition, Philadelphia. Multicoloured.
414	60f. Type **149** (postage)	75	25
415	90f. Seat of Government, Pennsylvania	95	25
416	100f. Siege of Yorktown (air)	1·20	45
417	200f. Battle of Cape St. Vincent	2·00	80
418	300f. Peter Francisco's act of bravery	3·50	1·20
MS419	116×79 mm. 500f. Surrender of the Hessians	6·75	2·20

150 U.P.U. and U.N. Emblems

1976. 25th Anniv of U.N. Postal Administration.
420	**150** 200f. blue, bronze and red	2·30	1·30

151 Tenkodogo Commune

1977. Arms. Multicoloured.
421	10f. Type **151**	15	10
422	20f. Ouagadougou	30	10
423	55f. Type **151**	75	25
424	100f. As 20f.	95	40

152 Bronze Statuette

1977
425	**152**	55f. multicoloured	65	35
426	–	65f. multicoloured	1·00	55

DESIGN: 65f. Bronze statuette of woman with bowl.

153 Samo Granary

1977. Millet Granaries. Multicoloured.
427	5f. Type **153**	40	10
428	35f. Boromo	45	25
429	45f. Banfora	60	25
430	55f. Mossi	75	45

154 Gouin Basket

1977. Local Handicrafts. Baskets and Bags. Multicoloured.
431	30f. Type **154**	40	10
432	40f. Bissa	45	25
433	60f. Lobi	60	25
434	70f. Mossi	95	45

155 "Crinum ornatum"

1977. Fruits and Flowers. Multicoloured.
435	2f. "Cordia myxa"	20	35
436	3f. "Opilia celtidifolia"	25	10
437	15f. Type **155**	50	25
438	25f. "Haemanthus multiflorus"	55	10
439	50f. "Hannoa undulata"	95	45
440	90f. "Cochlospermum planchonii"	1·50	50
441	125f. "Clitoria ternatea"	3·00	75
442	150f. "Cassia alata"	2·00	1·20
443	175f. "Nauclea latifolia" (horiz)	2·30	1·30
444	300f. "Bombax costatum" (horiz)	3·50	1·40
445	400f. "Eulophia cucullata"	6·00	2·10

156 General De Gaulle

1977. Personalities. Multicoloured.
446	100f. Type **156**	3·25	1·00
447	200f. King Baudouin	2·20	75

157 Queen Elizabeth II

1977. Silver Jubilee of Queen Elizabeth II. Multicoloured.
448	200f. Type **157**	2·20	75
449	300f. Queen Elizabeth II taking salute at Trooping the Colour	3·25	1·00
MS450	103×78 mm. 500f. Elizabeth II in Coronation robes	5·00	2·10

158 Cars on "Road" of Banknotes

1977. Tenth Anniv of National Lottery.
451	**158** 55f. multicoloured	75	50

159 Selma Lagerlof and Bean Geese

1977. Nobel Prize Winners. Multicoloured.
452	55f. Type **159** (Literature, 1909)	95	35
453	65f. Guglielmo Marconi and early transmitter (Physics, 1909)	55	55
454	125f. Bertrand Russell, laurel, book and dove (Literature, 1950)	1·20	55
455	200f. L. C. Pauling, formula and atomic explosion (Chemistry, 1954)	2·00	75
456	300f. Robert Koch, slide and X-ray plate (Medicine, 1905)	3·50	95
MS457	121×84 mm. 500f. Albert Schweitzer (Peace, 1952)	7·00	2·10

160 "The Three Graces"

1977. 400th Birth Anniv of Rubens. Multicoloured.
458	55f. "Heads of Four Negroes" (horiz)	55	10
459	65f. Type **160**	75	25
460	85f. "Bathsheba at the Fountain"	95	30
461	150f. "The Drunken Silenus"	1·70	55
462	200f. "The Story of Maria de Medici" (detail)	2·30	75
463	300f. "The Story of Maria de Medici" (different detail)	3·75	90
MS464	87×108 mm. 500f. "Virgin and Child"	5·25	2·00

161 Lenin

1977. 60th Anniv of Russian Revolution. Multicoloured.
465	10f. Type **161**	30	25
466	85f. Lenin Monument and Kremlin	1·30	45
467	200f. Lenin with children (horiz)	3·00	1·40
468	500f. Lenin and Pres. Brezhnev (horiz)	6·50	3·00

162 Stadium and Brazil 5cr.80 Stamp of 1950

1978. World Cup Football Championship, Argentina. Multicoloured.
469	55f. Type **162**	45	10
470	55f. Brazil 1969 Pele stamp	55	15
471	125f. G.B. 1966 England winners stamp	1·20	45
472	200f. Chile 1962 World Cup stamp	2·00	55
473	300f. Switzerland 1954 World Cup stamp	2·75	85
MS474	119×81 mm. 500f. West German 40pf. World Cup stamp, 1974	5·25	2·10

163 Jean Mermoz

1978. Aviation History. Multicoloured.
475	65f. Type **163**	75	25
476	75f. Anthony Fokker	75	25
477	85f. Wiley Post	95	35
478	90f. Otto Lilienthal (vert)	1·20	30
479	100f. Concorde	1·40	80
MS480	92×117 mm. 500f. Charles Lindbergh and Ryan NYP Special "Spirit of St. Louis"	6·00	2·10

164 "Crateva religiosa"

1978. Trees of Upper Volta. Multicoloured.
481	55f. Type **164**	75	45
482	75f. "Ficus sp."	95	60

165 Microwave Antennae

1978. World Telecommunications Day.
483   **165**   65f. multicoloured   75   50

166 Bobo Fetish Portals

1978. Sacred Objects. Multicoloured.
484   55f. Type **166**   75   40
485   65f. Mossi fetish   95   55

167 I.P.U. Emblem over Globe

1978. Air. Centenary of Paris Postal Congress.
486   **167**   350f. multicoloured   3·75   2·20

168 Capt. Cook and H.M.S. "Endeavour"

1978. 250th Birth Anniv of Captain James Cook. Multicoloured.
487   **168**   65f. Type **168**   75   25
488   85f. Death of Captain Cook   95   45
489   250f. Cook and navigation instruments   2·40   90
490   350f. Cook and H.M.S. "Resolution"   3·50   1·30

169 Yuri Gagarin and Spacecraft

1978. "Conquest of Space". Multicoloured.
491   **169**   50f. Type **169**   55   25
492   60f. Jules Verne, "Apollo 11" badge and Neil Armstrong in space-suit   60   45
493   100f. Montgolfier medallion and balloon, Bleriot XI and Concorde   1·30   55

170 I.A.Y. Emblem

1978. Air. Anti-Apartheid Year.
494   **170**   100f. multicoloured   1·00   60

1978. 25th Anniv of Coronation of Queen Elizabeth II. Nos. 448/MS450 optd **ANNIVERSAIRE DU COURONNEMENT 1953-1978.**
495   **157**   200f. multicoloured   2·00   1·20
496   –   300f. multicoloured   3·00   1·80
MS497 103×78 mm. 500f. multicoloured   5·00   4·50

1978. Air. "Philexafrique" Stamp Exhibition, Libreville (Gabon), and Int Stamp Fair, Essen, West Germany (1st series). As T **237a** of Senegal. Multicoloured.
498   100f. River kingfisher and Hanover 1850 1ggr. stamp   2·75   2·00
499   100f. Hippopotamus and 1964 250f. Grey woodpecker stamp   2·75   2·00
See also Nos. 518/19.

172 "Trent Castle"

1978. 450th Death Anniv of Albrecht Durer. Multicoloured.
500   65f. Type **172**   95   30
501   150f. "Virgin and Child" (vert)   1·60   55
502   250f. "Saints George and Eustace" (vert)   2·75   85
503   350f. "H. Holzschuher" (vert)   3·75   1·20

173 Horus

1978. Air. UNESCO Campaign: "Save the Philae Temples". Multicoloured.
504   200f. Type **173**   1·80   90
505   300f. Stylized falcon   2·75   1·30

174 Jules Verne

1978. 150th Birth Anniv of Jules Verne (author).
506   **174**   20f. purple, blue and green   2·75   1·30

175 Human Rights Flame

1978. 30th Anniv of Declaration of Human Rights.
507   **175**   55f. multicoloured   75   45

1979. World Cup Football Championship Winners. Nos. 469/MS474 optd.
508   **162**   55f. multicoloured   55   30
509   –   65f. multicoloured   75   60
510   –   125f. multicoloured   1·30   80
511   –   200f. multicoloured   1·80   1·10
512   –   300f. multicoloured   3·00   1·50
MS513 119×81 mm.   5·50   4·50

OPTS: 55f. **VAINQUEURS 1950 URUGUAY 1978 ARGENTINE**; 65f. **VAINQUEURS 1970 BRESIL 1978 ARGENTINE**; 125f. **VAINQUEURS 1966 GRANDE BRETAGNE 1978 ARGENTINE**; 200f. **VAINQUEURS 1962 BRESIL 1978 ARGENTINE**; 300f. **VAINQUEURS 1954 ALLEMAGNE (RFA) 1978 ARGENTINE**; 500f. **VAINQUEURS 1974 ALLEMAGNE (RFA)/1978 ARGENTINE.**

177 Radio Station

1979. Tenth Anniv of Posts and Telecommunications Organization. Multicoloured.
514   55f. Type **177**   50   25
515   65f. Loading mail aboard Beech A100 King Air monoplane   75   45

178 Children listening to Story

1979. International Year of the Child.
516   **178**   75f. multicoloured   1·20   60

179 Wave Pattern and Human Figures

1979. World Telecommunications Day.
517   **179**   70f. multicoloured   75   45

180 Basket Weaving and Upper Volta 50c. Stamp of 1963

1979. "Philexafrique" Exhibition, Libreville, Gabon (2nd series). Multicoloured.
518   100f. Type **180**   3·25   2·50
519   100f. Concorde, van, shouting man and U.P.U. emblem   3·25   2·50

181 Volta Squeaker

1979. Freshwater Fish. Multicoloured.
520   20f. Type **181**   50   25
521   50f. Como tetra   1·60   65
522   85f. Airbreathing catfish   2·10   1·00

182 Class 241-P Steam Locomotive, France

1979. Death Centenary of Sir Rowland Hill. Multicoloured.
523   65f. Type **182**   75   45
524   165f. Class 215 diesel locomotive, Germany   1·90   55
525   200f. Class "Warship" diesel locomotive, Great Britain   2·20   90
526   300f. French TGV express train   3·75   90
MS527 120×81 mm. 500f. Steam train USA (different)   6·00   2·10

183 Kob

1979. Endangered Animals. Multicoloured.
528   30f. Type **183**   65   10
529   40f. Roan antelope   1·00   10
530   60f. Caracal   1·70   10
531   100f. African elephant   2·50   55
532   175f. Hartebeest   4·25   75
533   250f. Leopard   8·75   95

184 Teacher and Class

1979. World Literacy Day. Multicoloured.
534   55f. Farmer reading book (vert)   65   50
535   250f. Type **184**   2·75   1·60

185 Telecommunications

1979. Third World Telecommunications Exhibition, Geneva.
536   **185**   200f. multicoloured   2·00   1·00

186 King Vulture

1979. Protected Birds. Multicoloured.
537   5f. Type **186**   55   15
538   10f. Hoopoe   65   15
539   15f. Ruppell's griffon   75   20
540   25f. Intermediate egret   1·20   30
541   35f. Ostrich   1·80   35
542   45f. Crowned crane   2·20   45
543   125f. Cassin's hawk eagle   5·00   1·40

187 Airport

1979. 20th Anniv of A.S.E.C.N.A. (Air Navigation Security Agency).
544   **187**   65f. multicoloured   95   60

188 Headquarters Building

1979. Opening of West African Savings Bank Building, Dakar, Senegal.
545   **188**   55f. multicoloured   75   45

189 Jamot, Map and Tsetse Fly

1979. Birth Centenary of Eugené Jamot (discoverer of cure for sleeping sickness).
546   **189**   55f. multicoloured   2·00   75

190 Stamp under Magnifying Glass

1980. Stamp Day.
547   **190**   55f. multicoloured   80   45

191 Electric Locomotives

1980. 25th Anniv of World Locomotive Speed Record.
548   **191**   75f. multicoloured   1·60   55
549   **191**   100f. multicoloured   2·40   1·20

192 Pope John
Paul II

1980. Papal Visit. Multicoloured.
550   55f. Pres. Lamizana, Pope and
      Cardinal Pau Zoungrana
      (horiz)   2·50   80
551   100f. Type **192**   2·75   1·30

193 Telephone

1980. World Telecommunications Day.
552   **193**   50f. multicoloured   65   35

194 Mountains
and Statue

1980. Solar Energy. Multicoloured.
553   65f. Sun and Earth   75   25
554   100f. Type **194**   1·00   55

195 Downhill Skiing (L. Stock)

1980. Winter Olympic Games Winners. Multicoloured.
555   65f. Type **195**   55   25
556   100f. Women's downhill skiing
      (A. Moser-Proell)   1·00   45
557   200f. Figure skating (A.
      Poetzsch)   2·00   55
558   350f. Slalom (I. Stenmark) (vert)   3·50   95
MS559 112×86 mm. 500f. Speed skat-
    ing (E. Heiden)   5·50   1·90

196 Map of Europe
and Africa

1980. Europafrique.
560   **196**   100f. red, black and
      green   1·30   60

197 Hand
pushing back
Sand Dune

1980. Operation "Green Sahara". Multicoloured.
561   50f. Type **197**   75   25
562   55f. Hands planting saplings   1·00   45

198 Cyclists

1980. Air. Olympic Games, Moscow. Cycling.
563   **198**   65f. multicoloured   75   25

564   -   150f. multicoloured (vert)   1·50   55
565   -   250f. multicoloured   3·00   80
566   -   350f. multicoloured   3·50   1·10
MS567 108×82 mm. 500f. mult   6·75   2·10
DESIGNS: 150f. to 500f. Different cyclists.

199 Installation of Chief

1980. National History. Multicoloured.
568   30f. Type **199**   55   35
569   55f. Moro Naba, Emperor of
      Mossis   75   45
570   65f. Princess Guimbe Ouattara
      (vert)   1·10   45

200 Gourounsi
Mask

1980. World Tourism Conference, Manila.
571   **200**   65f. multicoloured   80   35

201 Tractor, Cattle
and Grain
(Agriculture)

1980. Fifth Anniv of West African Economic Council.
Multicoloured.
572   55f. Type **201**   45   10
573   65f. "Communications"   55   30
574   75f. Dam and highway   75   45
575   100f. "Industry"   1·20   55

1980. Air. Olympic Winners. Nos. **MS**564 optd.
576   **198**   65f. multicoloured   1·00   45
577   -   150f. multicoloured   1·80   1·20
578   -   250f. multicoloured   3·25   1·60
579   -   350f. multicoloured   4·00   2·10
MS580 108×82 mm. 500f. multicol-
    oured   7·00   4·25
OVERPRINTS: 65f. **SOUKHOROUCHENKOV (URSS)**; 150f.
HESSLICH (RDA); 250f. **LANG (POL)**; 350f. **DILL-BUNDI
(SUISSE)**; 500f. **BONDUE (FRANCE)**.

203 Coat of Arms and Map

1980. 20th Anniv of Independence.
581   **203**   500f. multicoloured   6·00   3·50

204 "Sistine
Madonna" (detail)

1980. Christmas. Multicoloured.
582   60f. Type **204**   50   25
583   150f. "Virgin de l'Impannata"   1·50   50
584   250f. "Alba Madonna"   2·50   80

1980.   Fifth   Anniv   of   African   Post   and
Telecommunications. As T **272a** of Togo.
585   55f. multicoloured   80   45

205 "Scarabaeus sacer"

1981. Insects. Multicoloured.
586   5f. Type **205**   40   10
587   10f. "Gryllus campestris"   40   10
588   15f. Termites   80   25
589   20f. "Mantis religiosa" (vert)   1·60   30
590   55f. "Nyctaon pyri"   2·75   45
591   65f. "Locusta migratorius" (vert)   2·75   40

206 Bobo Mask,
Hounde

1981. Masks. Multicoloured.
592   45f. Type **206**   55   20
593   55f. Bwa mask   65   30
594   85f. Kouroumba mask   1·00   50
595   105f. Gourounsi mask   1·30   60

207 College Emblem

1981. 25th Anniv of Notre-Dame College, Kologh'naba.
596   **207**   55f. multicoloured   60   25

208 Von Stephan and U.P.U. Emblem

1981.   150th Birth Anniv of Heinrich von Stephan
(founder of U.P.U.).
597   **208**   65f. multicoloured   1·00   60

209 Ribbons
forming Caduceus,
I.T.U. and W.H.O.
Emblems

1981. World Telecommunications Day.
598   **209**   90f. multicoloured   1·00   50

210 Series ZE
Diesel-electric Train

1981. Abidjan–Niger Railway. Multicoloured.
599   25f. Type **210**   45   25
600   30f. "La Gazelle" express train   75   25
601   40f. "Le Belier" express train   85   40

211 Group of Trees

1981. Tree Month.
602   **211**   70f. multicoloured   1·20   50

212 Nurse and Doctor
with Medical Equipment

1981. 25th Anniv of Upper Volta Red Cross.
603   **212**   70f. multicoloured   1·00   60

213
Handicapped
Sculptor

1981. International Year of Disabled People.
604   **213**   70f. multicoloured   1·00   45

214 Koudougou

1981. Landscapes. Multicoloured.
605   35f. Type **214**   45   25
606   45f. Toma   55   25
607   85f. Volta Noire   1·00   45

215 Agricultural Scenes within
Map

1981. World Food Day.
608   **215**   90f. multicoloured   1·20   65

216 Topi

1981. Wildlife Protection. Multicoloured.
609   5f. Type **216**   55   25
610   15f. Waterbuck   80   35
611   40f. Roan antelopes   1·30   35
612   60f. Dorcas gazelle   2·75   80
613   70f. African elephant   2·75   95

217 Campaign
Emblem

1981. Anti-Apartheid Campaign.
614   **217**   90f. red   1·00   50

218 Papaya

1981. Fruit and Vegetables. Multicoloured.
615   20f. Type **218**   45   10
616   35f. Fruit and vegetables   55   30
617   75f. Mangoes (vert)   90   50
618   90f. Melons   1·00   60

219 Donkey

1981. Stock Breeding. Multicoloured.
619   10f. Type **219**   20   10
620   25f. Pig   35   10
621   70f. Cow   90   25
622   90f. Helmeted guineafowl (vert)   1·10   45
623   250f. Rabbit   2·75   1·20
MS624 90×70 mm. 300f. Shepherd
and flock   5·50   5·00

220 Women
carrying Rice

1981. Tenth Anniv of West African Rice Development
Association.
625	**220**	90f. multicoloured	1·30	55

221 Father and
Son

1982. 20th Anniv of World Food Programme.
626	**221**	50f. multicoloured	60	25

222 Morhonaba
Palace,
Ouagadougou

1982. Traditional Houses. Multicoloured.
627	30f. Type **222**		30	20
628	70f. Bobo (horiz)		75	25
629	100f. Gourounsi (horiz)		1·20	55
630	200f. Peulh (horiz)		2·00	90
631	250f. Dagari (horiz)		2·75	90

223 Hexagonal Pattern

1982. World Telecommunications Day.
632	**223**	90f. multicoloured	1·30	60

224 Symbols of National
Life

1982. National Life.
633	**224**	90f. multicoloured	1·00	40

225 Passing Ball

1982. Air. World Cup Football Championship, Spain.
Multicoloured.
634	70f. Type **225**		75	25
635	90f. Tackle		95	40
636	150f. Running with ball		1·50	75
637	300f. Receiving ball		2·50	1·10
MS638	120×98 mm. 500f. Goalkeeper		5·50	4·25

226 Water Lily

1982. Flowers. Multicoloured.
639	25f. Type **226**	35	10
640	40f. Kapoka	65	35
641	70f. Frangipani	95	45
642	90f. "Cochlospermum plan-
chonii"	1·30	60
643	100f. Cotton	1·40	75

227 Symbols of
Communication on Map
of Africa

1982. African Post and Telecommunications Union.
644	**227**	70f. multicoloured	60	25
645	**227**	90f. multicoloured	1·00	50

228 Children
holding Torch

1982. 25th Anniv of Cultural Aid Fund.
646	**228**	70f. multicoloured	80	45

229 Hairstyle

1983
647	**229**	90f. multicoloured	95	25
648	**229**	120f. multicoloured	1·50	45
649	**229**	170f. multicoloured	2·00	75

230 Audience watching
Film

1983. Eighth Film Festival, Ouagadougou. Multicoloured.
650	90f. Type **230**	1·50	75
651	500f. Oumarou Ganda	7·50	3·25

231 Joseph Montgolfier
and First
Demonstration of
Hot-air Balloon, 1783

1983. Bicentenary of Manned Flight. Multicoloured.
652	15f. Type **231** (postage)	10	10
653	25f. Jean-Francois Pilatre de
Rozier and first manned
flight, 1783	30	10
654	70f. Jacques Charles and
hydrogen balloon "The
Globe", 1783	75	25
655	90f. John Jeffries and first
Channel crossing, 1785	95	35
656	100f. Wilhelmine Reichardt and
ascent on a horse, 1798 (air)	1·30	45
657	250f. Salomon Andree and
Spitzbergen–Expedition,
1897	2·50	75
MS658	80×100 mm. 300f. Auguste
Piccard and stratospheric balloon
"F.N.R.S.", 1931 (37×46 mm)	4·00	1·40

232 Campaign
Emblem and River

1983. International Drinking Water Decade.
Multicoloured.
659	60f. Type **232**	55	25
660	70f. Woman carrying water	95	50

233 Man reading
Letter

1983. World Communications Year. Multicoloured.
661	30f. Type **233**	30	25
662	35f. Type **233**	55	25
663	45f. Canoe and Boeing 727
airliner	75	25
664	90f. Woman on telephone	95	45

234 Space Shuttle "Challenger"

1983. Air. World Events. Multicoloured.
665	90f. Type **234**	95	25
666	120f. World Cup football final	1·20	55
667	300f. World Cup football final
(different)	2·75	1·00
668	450f. Royal wedding	4·00	1·50
MS669	116×90 mm. 500f. Prince and
Princess of Wales	3·00	1·70

235 Gambian Squeaker

1983. Fishery Resources. Multicoloured.
670	20f. Type **235**	50	25
671	30f. Gunther's krib	65	25
672	40f. Line fishing (vert)	75	30
673	50f. Net fishing	95	40
674	75f. Trap fishing	1·40	45

236 Soling Class Yacht

1983. Air. Pre-Olympic Year. Multicoloured.
675	90f. Type **236**	95	25
676	120f. Type **236** yacht	1·40	55
677	300f. Windsurfing	3·00	80
678	400f. Windsurfing (different)	3·75	1·10
MS679	104×77 mm. 500f. Soling yacht
and windsurfers (horiz)	7·00	2·10

237 Planting a Sapling

1983. Campaign for Control of the Desert. Multicoloured.
680	10f. Type **237**	30	10
681	50f. Plantation	55	25
682	100f. Control of forest fires	1·20	45
683	150f. Woman cooking	2·00	90
684	200f. Control of timber trade
(vert)	2·40	1·10

238 Arms of Upper Volta

1983. 25th Anniv of Republic. Multicoloured.
685	90f. Type **238**	75	45
686	500f. Family with flag	4·50	1·70

239 "Self-portrait"
(Picasso)

1983. Celebrities' Anniversaries. Multicoloured.
687	120f. Type **239**	1·80	45
688	185f. "Self-portrait with a Pal-
ette" (Manet (1832–1883))	2·00	60
689	300f. Fresco detail (Raphael
(1483–1520)) (horiz)	3·00	75
690	350f. Fresco detail (Raphael
(different) (horiz)	3·25	1·10
691	500f. J. W. Goethe (1749–1832)
(portrait by Georg Oswald)	5·00	1·50

240 "Adoration of the
Shepherds"

1983. Air. Christmas. Multicoloured.
692	120f. Type **240**	1·20	45
693	350f. "Virgin of the Garland"	3·25	90
694	500f. "Adoration of the Magi"	4·50	1·30

242 Handball

1984. Air. Olympic Games, Los Angeles. Multicoloured.
695	90f. Type **242**	95	30
696	120f. Volleyball	1·20	45
697	150f. Handball (horiz)	1·50	55
698	250f. Basketball (horiz)	2·40	75
699	300f. Football (horiz)	3·00	90
MS700	102×78 mm. 500f. Volleyball
(horiz)	5·50	1·90

243 Greater Flamingo

1984. Air. Birds. Multicoloured.
701	90f. Type **243**	1·40	50
702	185f. Kori bustard (vert)	2·50	1·00
703	200f. Red-billed oxpecker (vert)	2·75	1·20
704	300f. Southern ground hornbill	3·50	1·80

244 Pres. Houari Boumedienne of
Algeria

1984. Air. Celebrities. Multicoloured.
705	5f. Type **244**	10	10
706	125f. Gottlieb Daimler (automo-
bile designer) and car	1·30	45

707	250f. Louis Bleriot (aviator) and Bleriot XI airplane	2·50	75
708	300f. Pres. Abraham Lincoln of U.S.A. and White House	3·00	80
709	400f. Henry Dunant (founder of Red Cross), red cross and battle of Solferino	3·75	90
710	450f. Auguste Piccard and bathyscape "Trieste"	4·25	1·20
711	500f. Robert Baden-Powell (founder of Boy Scout movement) and scouts	4·50	1·30
712	600f. Anatole Karpov, 1978 world chess champion	5·50	1·60
MS713	71×87 mm. 1000f. Paul Harris (Rotary International founder)	9·00	1·80

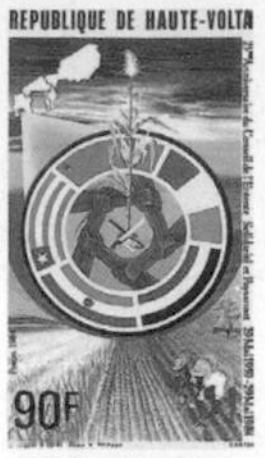

245 Seedling and Clasped Hands within Circle of Flags

1984. 25th Anniv of Council of Unity.

714	**245**	90f. multicoloured	95	40
715	**245**	100f. multicoloured	1·20	45

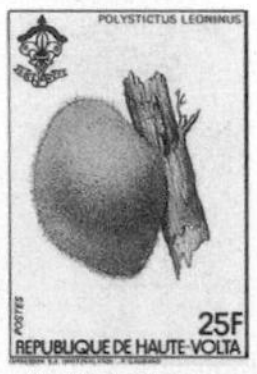

246 "Polystictus leoninus"

1984. Fungi and Flowers. Multicoloured.

716	25f. Type **246** (postage)	35	10
717	185f. "Pterocarpus lucens"	2·30	60
718	200f. "Phlebopus colossus sudanicus"	2·75	60
719	250f. "Cosmos suplhureus"	3·75	90
720	300f. "Trametes versicolour" (air)	3·25	75
721	400f. "Ganoderma lucidum"	5·25	1·00
MS722	63×92 mm. 600f. "Leucocoprinus cepaestipes"	8·25	2·40

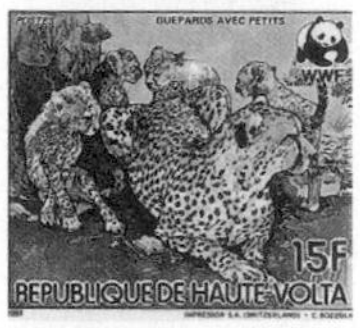

247 Cheetah with Cubs

1984. Protected Animals. Multicoloured.

723	15f. Type **247** (postage)	30	10
724	35f. Two cheetahs	60	35
725	90f. Cheetah	1·40	50
726	120f. Cheetah with cubs (different)	1·60	70
727	300f. Baboons (air)	3·50	1·00
728	400f. Marabou stork and African white-backed vulture	5·00	1·00
MS729	79×68 mm. 1000f. Roan antelope	10·00	2·40

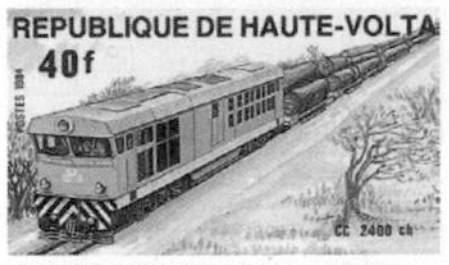

248 CC 2400 Diesel Locomotive and Lumber Train

1984. Transport. Multicoloured. (a) Locomotives.

730	40f. Type **248**	45	10
731	100f. Steam locomotive No. 1806	1·00	25
732	145f. Steam locomotive "Livingstone"	1·50	60
733	450f. Class C51 steam locomotive, Japan	4·50	1·10

(b) Ships.

734	20f. "Maiden Queen"	30	10
735	60f. "Scawfell"	70	10
736	120f. "Harbinger"	1·50	45
737	400f. "True Briton"	4·50	1·50

For later issues see **BURKINA FASO**.

OFFICIAL STAMPS

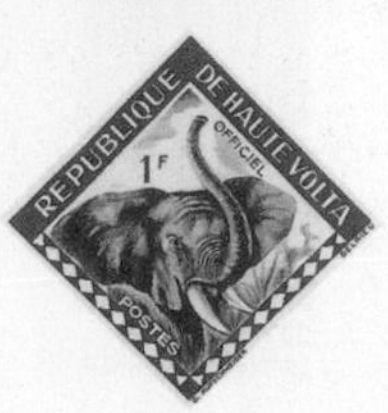

O18 African Elephant

1963

O112	**O18**	1f. sepia and brown	10	10
O113	**O18**	5f. sepia and green	20	25
O114	**O18**	10f. sepia and violet	30	25
O115	**O18**	15f. sepia and orange	45	40
O116	**O18**	25f. sepia and purple	95	90
O117	**O18**	50f. sepia and green	1·40	1·30
O118	**O18**	60f. sepia and red	1·50	1·40
O119	**O18**	85f. sepia and myrtle	2·20	2·10
O120	**O18**	100f. sepia and blue	3·50	3·50
O121	**O18**	200f. sepia and mauve	5·00	4·75

POSTAGE DUE STAMPS

1920. Postage Due stamps of Upper Senegal and Niger, "Figures" Key-type, optd **HAUTE-VOLTA**.

D18	**M**	5c. green	45	8·00
D19	**M**	10c. red	45	8·00
D20	**M**	15c. grey	45	8·00
D21	**M**	20c. brown	45	8·25
D22	**M**	30c. blue	55	9·25
D23	**M**	50c. black	85	11·00
D24	**M**	60c. orange	70	10·50
D25	**M**	1f. violet	75	12·00

1927. Surch.

D40	2f. on 1f. mauve	2·00	23·00
D41	3f. on 1f. brown	2·50	25·00

1928. "Figures" key-type inscr "HAUTE-VOLTA".

D63	5c. green	70	8·75
D64	10c. red	1·50	8·75
D65	15c. grey	2·00	9·50
D66	20c. brown	1·40	9·50
D67	30c. blue	2·50	10·50
D68	50c. black	2·30	20·00
D69	60c. orange	2·75	26·00
D70	1f. violet	5·00	40·00
D71	2f. purple	10·50	60·00
D72	3f. brown	8·25	60·00

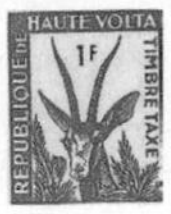

D13 Red-fronted Gazelle

1962. Figures of value in black.

D95	**D13**	1f. blue	10	10
D96	**D13**	2f. orange	10	10
D97	**D13**	5f. blue	30	25
D98	**D13**	10f. purple	45	40
D99	**D13**	20f. green	70	70
D100	**D13**	50f. red	1·70	1·60

APPENDIX

The following stamps have either been issued in excess of postal needs or have not been available to the public in reasonable quantities at face value. Such stamps may later be given full listing if there is evidence of regular postal use.

1973

Gold Medal Winners, Munich Olympic Games (2nd series). Air 50, 60, 90, 150, 350f.
Christmas 1972. Paintings of the Madonna and Child. Air 50, 75, 100, 125, 150f.
Moon Mission of "Apollo 17". Air 50, 65, 100, 150, 200f.
Gold Medal Winners, Munich Olympic Games (3rd series). Air 35, 45, 75, 250, 400f.
Exploration of the Moon. Air 50, 65, 100, 150, 200f.
Wild Animals. Air 100, 150, 200, 250, 500f.
10th Anniv of Organization of African Unity. Air 45f.
Europafrique. European Paintings. Air 50, 65, 100, 150, 200f.
Historic Railway Locomotives, French Railway Museum, Mulhouse. Air 10, 40, 50, 150, 250f.
Upper Volta Boy Scouts. Postage 20f.; Air 40, 75, 150, 200f.
Pan-African Drought Relief. Surch on values of 1973 Europafrique issue. Air 100f. on 65f., 200f. on 150f.
10th Death Anniv of President John Kennedy. Rockets. Postage 5, 10, 30f.; Air 200, 300f.
50th Anniv of International Police Organization (Interpol). 50, 65, 70, 150f.
Tourism. Postage 35, 40f.; Air 100f.
Religious Buildings. Postage 35, 40f.; Air 200f.
Folk-dancers. Postage 35, 40f.; Air 100, 225f.
Famous Men. 5, 10, 20, 25, 30, 50, 60, 75, 100, 175, 200, 250f.

1974

World Cup Football Championship, Munich (1st issue). Postage 5, 40f.; Air 75, 100, 250f.
Pres. De Gaulle Commemoration. Postage 35, 40, 60f.; Air 300f.
World Cup Football Championship (2nd issue). Postage 10, 20, 50f.; Air 150, 300f.
Centenary of Universal Postal Union. Postage 35, 40, 85f.; Air 100, 200, 300f.
World Cup Football Championship (3rd issue). Previous Finals. Postage 10, 25, 50f.; Air 150, 200, 250f.
Centenary of Berne Convention. 1974 U.P.U. issue optd. Postage 35, 40, 85f., Air 100, 200, 300f.
Bouquets of Flowers. Postage 5, 10, 30, 50f.; Air 300f.

1975

Birth Centenary of Sir Winston Churchill. 50, 75, 100, 125, 300f.
Bicentenary of American Revolution (1st issue). 35, 40, 75, 100, 200, 300f.
Railway Locomotives. Postage 15, 25, 50f.; Air 100, 200f.
Vintage and Veteran Cars. Postage 10, 30, 35f.; Air 150, 200f.
Bicent of American Revolution (2nd issue). Postage 30, 40, 50f.; Air 200, 300f.
Birth Cent of Dr Albert Schweitzer. Postage 5, 15f.; Air 150, 175, 200f.
"Apollo–Soyuz" Joint Space Test Project. Postage 40, 50f.; Air 100, 200, 300f.
Paintings by Picasso. Postage 50, 60, 90f.; Air 150, 350f.
"Expo '75" Exhibition, Okinawa, Japan. Postage 15, 25, 45, 50, 60f.; Air 150f.
Winter Olympic Games, Innsbruck. Postage 35, 45, 85f.; Air 100, 200f.

1976

Olympic Games, Montreal (1st issue). "Pre-Olympic Year" (1975). Postage 40, 50, 100f.; Air 125, 150f.
Olympic Games, Montreal (2nd issue). Postage 30, 55, 75f.; Air 150, 200f.
Zeppelin Airships. Postage 10, 40, 50f.; Air 100, 200, 300f.
"Viking" Space Flight. Postage 30, 55, 75f.; Air 200, 300f.

1977

Olympic Games Medal Winners, 1976 Olympic Games issue optd. Postage 30, 55, 75f.; Air 150, 200f.

1983

Bicentenary of Manned Flight. Air 1500f.

Pt. 19

UPPER YAFA

A Sultanate of South Arabia, formerly part of the Western Aden Protectorate. Independent from September to December 1967 and then part of the People's Democratic Republic of Yemen.

1000 fils = 1 dinar.

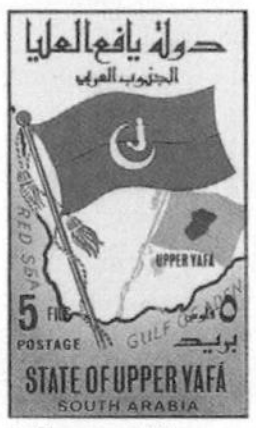

1 Flag and Map

1967

UY1	1	5f. mult (postage)	25	25
UY2	1	10f. multicoloured	25	25
UY3	1	20f. multicoloured	30	30
UY4	1	25f. multicoloured	40	30
UY5	1	40f. multicoloured	60	40
UY6	1	50f. multicoloured	75	50
UY7	-	75f. multicoloured (air)	90	75
UY8	-	100f. multicoloured	1·30	85
UY9	-	250f. multicoloured	3·00	3·00
UY10	-	500f. multicoloured	3·75	5·00

DESIGNS: UY7/10, Arms of Sultanate.

APPENDIX

The following stamps have either been issued in excess of postal needs or have not been available to the public in reasonable quantities at face value. Such stamps may later be given full listing if there is evidence of regular postal use.

1967

Olympic Games, Mexico (1968). Postage 15, 25, 50, 75f.; Air 150f.
Sculptures. Postage 10, 30, 60, 75f.; Air 150f.
Paintings from the Louvre. Postage 50f.; Air 100, 150, 200, 250f.
World Cup Football Championship, England (1966). Postage 5, 10, 50f.; Air 100f.
Paintings by Old Masters. Postage 10, 15, 20, 25, 30, 40, 50, 60, 75f.; Air 150f.
Human Rights Year and 5th Death Anniv of J. F. Kennedy. Postage 5, 10, 50, 75f.; Air 125f.
Persian Miniatures. 10, 20, 30, 40, 50f.
Ballet Paintings. 20, 30, 40, 50, 60f.
Portraits by Old Masters. Postage 25, 50, 75f.; Air 100, 125, 150, 175, 200, 225, 250f.
Winter Olympic Games, Grenoble (1968). 1967 World Cup issue optd. Postage 5f.×2, 10f.×2, 50f.×2; Air 100f.×2.
20th Anniv of UNICEF. Paintings. Postage 50, 75f.; Air 100, 125, 250f.
Flower Paintings. Postage 5, 10, 50f.; Air 100, 150f.

Pt. 20

URUGUAY

A republic in S. America, bordering on the Atlantic Ocean, independent since 1828.

1856. 120 centavos = 1 real.
1859. 1000 milesimos = 100 centesimos = 1 peso.

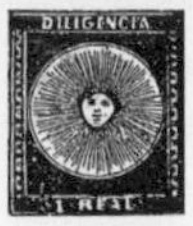

1

1856. Imperf.

1	1	60c. blue	£325	
2	1	80c. green	£300	
3	1	1r. red	£275	

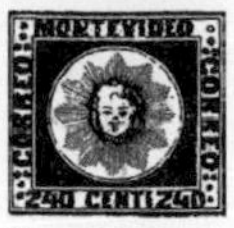

3

1858. Imperf.

5	3	120c. blue	£600	£600
6	3	180c. green	70·00	£130
7	3	240c. red	£100	£750

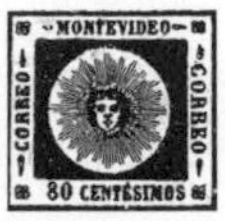

4

1859. Imperf.

15	4	60c. purple	23·00	13·00
16	4	80c. yellow	29·00	21·00
17	4	100c. red	60·00	35·00
18	4	120c. blue	33·00	20·00
12	4	180c. green	23·00	26·00
13	4	240c. red	95·00	95·00

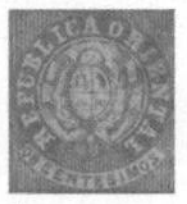

6

1864. Imperf.

20a	6	6c. red	9·50	8·00
21	6	8c. green	23·00	22·00
22	6	10c. yellow	32·00	26·00
23	6	12c. blue	16·00	12·00

1866. Surch in figures. Imperf.

24	5c. on 12c. blue	28·00	55·00
25	10c. on 8c. green	17·00	35·00
26	15c. on 10c. yellow	28·00	85·00
27a	20c. on 6c. red	37·00	90·00

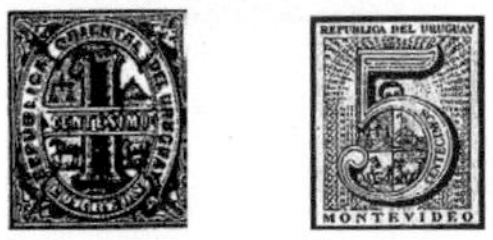

8 **9**

1866. Imperf.

28	8	1c. black	5·25	8·25
29	9	5c. blue	5·25	25·00
30	9	10c. green	21·00	8·00
31	9	15c. yellow	28·00	11·50
32	9	20c. red	32·00	11·50

1866. Perf.

37	8	1c. black	6·25	6·00
33		5c. blue	5·25	7·50
34		10c. green	18·00	6·00
35		15c. yellow	9·75	3·75
36		20c. red	15·00	5·50

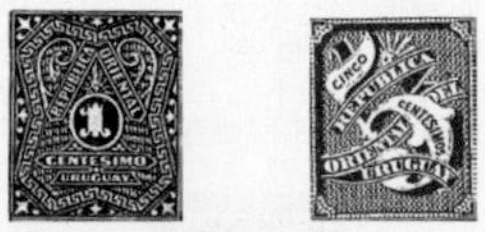

10 **11**

1877. Roul. Various frames.

42	10	1c. brown	75	50
43	11	5c. green	75	50
44	10	10c. red	75	40
45	10	20c. bistre	80	40
46	10	50c. black	6·00	2·50
47	10	1p. blue	30·00	15·00

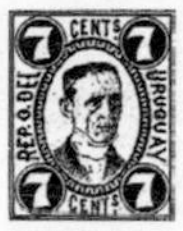
15 J. Suarez

1881. Perf.

60a	**15**	7c. blue	2·30	2·30

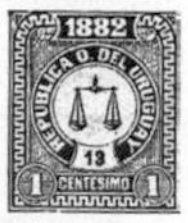
16

1882

62	**16**	1c. green	1·60	1·50
63	-	2c. red	80	65

The central device on the 2c. shows a mountain.

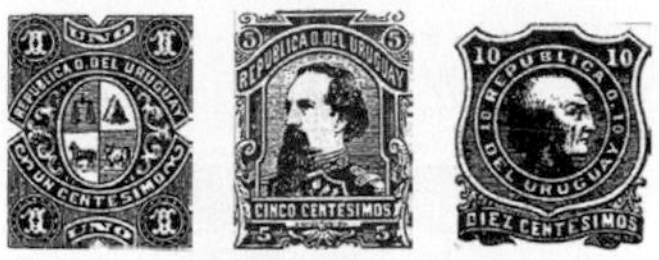
18 Arms **20** Gen. Maximo Santos **21** General Artigas

1883

66	**18**	1c. green	1·00	70
67	**18**	2c. red	2·00	1·50
68	**20**	5c. blue	2·00	1·20
69	**21**	10c. brown	2·40	1·60

1883. Optd **1883 Provisorio.** Roul.

75	**11**	5c. green	1·30	90

1884. Optd **PROVISORIO 1884** or surch **1 CENTESIMO** also.

76	**10**	1c. on 10c. red	40	40
77	-	2c. red (No. 63)	60	60

26

1884

79	**26**	5c. blue	3·50	1·00

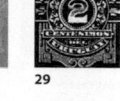

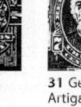

28 **29** **31** Gen. Artigas

32 M. Santos **33** **34**

1884. Roul.

83a	**28**	1c. grey	70	40
100	**28**	1c. green	65	15
101	**29**	2c. red	55	15
85a	**28**	5c. blue	70	25
86	**28**	5c. lilac	35	15
87	**31**	7c. brown	1·50	60
103	**31**	7c. orange	2·50	90
88	**32**	10c. brown	55	20
89	**33**	20c. mauve	1·60	65
105	**33**	20c. brown	2·10	70
90	**34**	25c. lilac	3·25	1·20
106	**34**	25c. red	4·75	1·70

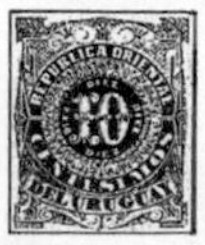
35

1887. Roul.

99	**35**	10c. mauve	3·25	1·50

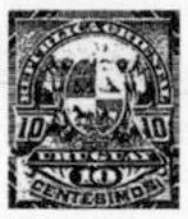
36

1888. Roul.

104	**36**	10c. violet	65	20

1889. Optd **Provisorio.** Roul.

114	**28**	5c. lilac	50	50

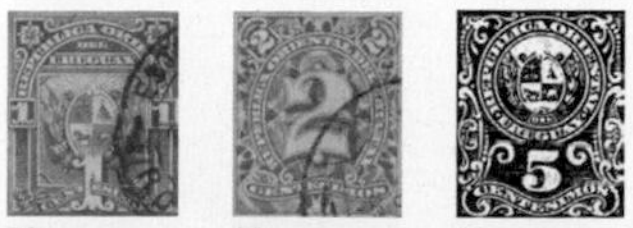
38 **39** **40**

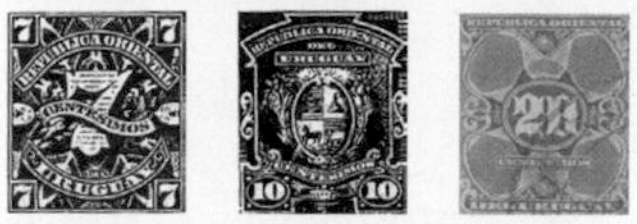
41 **42** **43**

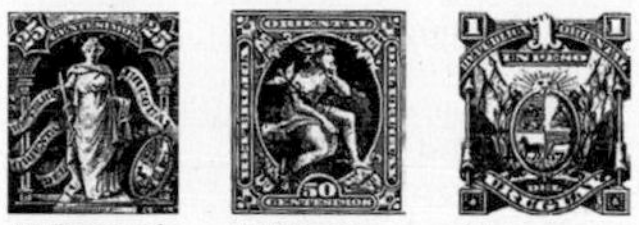
44 Figure of Justice **45** Mercury **46**

1889. Perf.

115	**38**	1c. green	65	15
116	**39**	2c. red	65	15
117	**40**	5c. blue	65	15
118	**41**	7c. brown	1·30	40
119	**42**	10c. green	4·75	1·10
120	**43**	20c. orange	3·25	70
121	**44**	20c. brown	4·25	1·10
122	**45**	50c. blue	9·00	3·25
123	**46**	1p. violet	23·00	5·50

See also Nos. 142/52, 220, 222, 224 and 236/7.

1891. Optd **Provisorio 1891.** Roul.

133	**28**	5c. lilac	20	15

1892. Optd **Provisorio 1892** or surch also in words.

135		1c. green	55	50
137	**43**	1c. on 20c. orange	55	15
136	**41**	5c. on 7c. brown	55	15

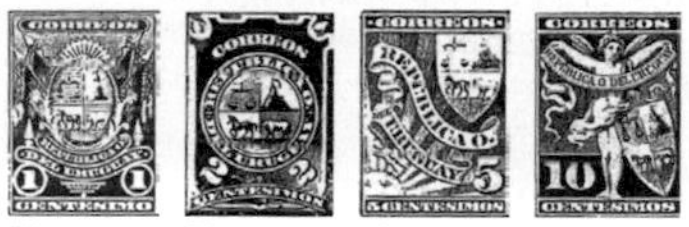
50 **51** **52** **53**

1892. Perf.

138	**50**	1c. green	65	15
139	**51**	2c. red	65	15
140	**52**	5c. blue	65	15
141	**53**	10c. orange	2·75	1·10

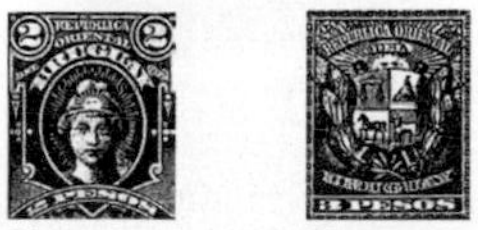
54 **55**

1894

142	**38**	1c. blue	40	15
143	**39**	2c. brown	45	25
144	**40**	5c. red	45	15
145	**41**	7c. green	4·00	2·20
146	**42**	10c. orange	3·00	45
147	**43**	20c. brown	4·00	1·40
148	**44**	25c. red	5·75	3·00
149	**45**	50c. purple	9·50	4·75
150	**46**	1p. blue	20·00	5·75
151	**54**	2p. red	24·00	14·00
152	**55**	3p. purple	24·00	14·00

56 Gaucho **57** Solis Theatre **58** Steam Locomotive

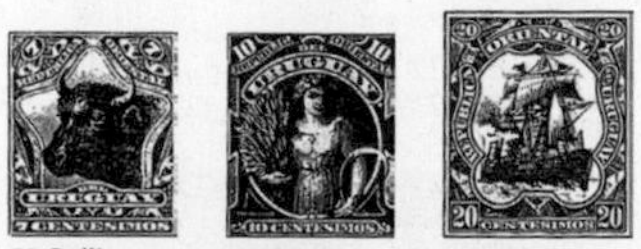
59 Bull's Head **60** Ceres **61** Steamer "Elbe"

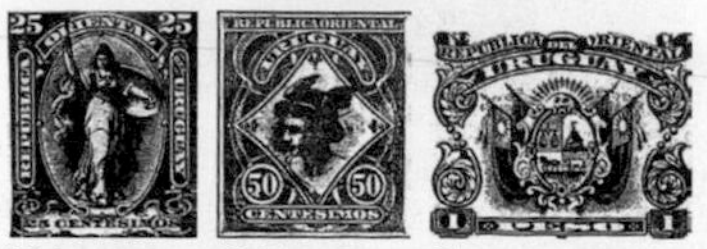
62 Amazon **63** Mercury **64**

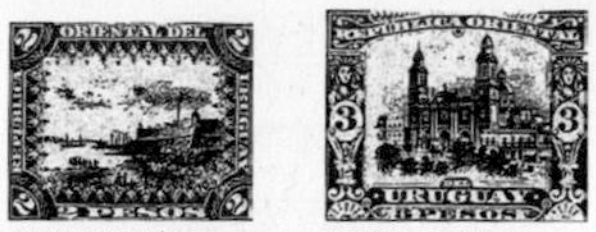
65 Montevideo Fortress **66** Montevideo Cathedral

1895

153	**56**	1c. bistre	65	15
154	**57**	2c. blue	65	15
155	**58**	5c. red	2·30	15
156	**59**	7c. green	10·50	3·00
157	**60**	10c. brown	2·75	60
158	**61**	20c. black and green	9·50	1·10
159	**62**	25c. black and brown	4·75	1·60
160	**63**	50c. black and blue	9·50	4·50
161	**64**	1p. black and brown	20·00	7·25
162	**65**	2p. green and violet	43·00	26·00
163	**66**	3p. blue and red	43·00	26·00

For further stamps in these types, see Nos. 183/93 and 221.

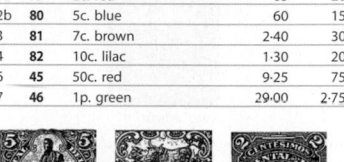

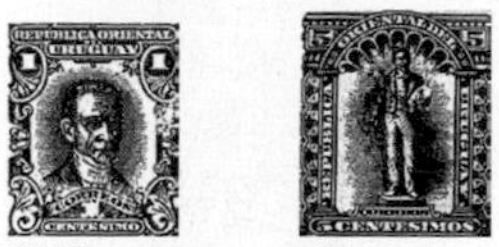
67 J. Suarez **68** J. Suarez Monument

1896. Unveiling of President Joaquin Suarez Monument.

177	**67**	1c. black and red	35	20
178	**68**	5c. black and blue	40	25
179	-	10c. black and lake	1·30	65

DESIGN: 10c. Larger stamp showing whole Suarez Monument.

1897. Optd **PROVISORIO 1897.**

180	**67**	1c. black and red	55	50
181	**68**	5c. black and blue	65	50
182	-	10c. black and lake	1·30	70

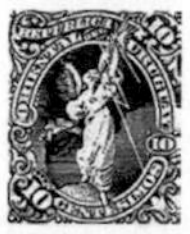
72

1897

183	**56**	1c. blue	40	15
184	**57**	2c. purple	40	15
185	**58**	5c. green	1·30	15
186	**59**	7c. orange	3·00	95
187	**72**	10c. red	1·60	35
188	**61**	20c. black and mauve	4·00	45
189	**62**	25c. blue and red	3·00	45
190	**63**	50c. brown and green	4·25	1·00
191	**64**	1p. blue and brown	8·00	2·50
192	**65**	2p. red and yellow	8·00	1·60
193	**66**	3p. red and lilac	10·50	1·90

See also No. 223.

1897. End of Civil War. Optd with palm leaf and **PAZ 1897.**

197	**56**	1c. blue	1·10	70
198	**57**	2c. purple	1·60	1·60
199	**58**	5c. green	2·30	2·00
200	**72**	10c. red	3·75	3·50

1898. Surch **PROVISIONAL ½ CENTESIMO.**

209	**38**	½c. on 1c. blue	30	30
210	**56**	½c. on 1c. bistre	30	30
211	**67**	½c. on 1c. black and red	30	30
212	**57**	½c. on 2c. blue	30	30
213	**68**	½c. on 5c. black and blue	30	30
214	**59**	½c. on 7c. green	30	30

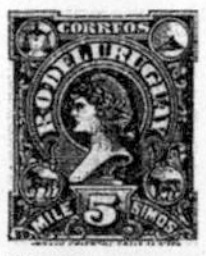
75 Liberty

1898

215	**75**	5m. red	20	20
216	**75**	5m. violet	25	25

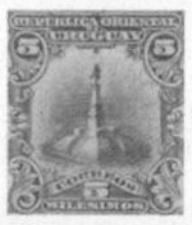
76 Monument to Gen. Artigas

1899

217	**76**	5m. blue	20	15
218	**76**	5m. orange	65	15
220	**39**	2c. orange	65	40
221a	**58**	5c. blue	1·10	15
222	**41**	7c. red	5·50	2·10
223	**72**	10c. purple	1·00	65
224	**43**	20c. blue	3·75	55

1900. No. 182 surch **1900 5 CENTESIMOS** and bar.

229	5c. on 10c. black and lake	65	30

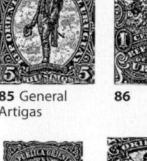

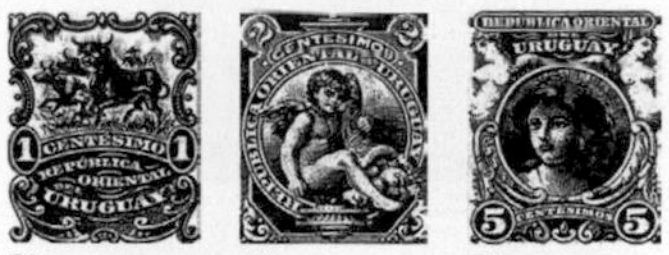
78 **79** **80**

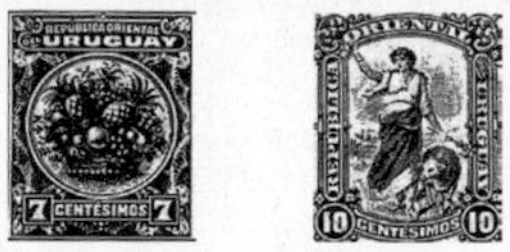
81 **82**

1900

230	**78**	1c. green	55	20
231a	**79**	2c. red	65	20
232b	**80**	5c. blue	60	15
233	**81**	7c. brown	2·40	30
234	**82**	10c. lilac	1·30	20
236	**45**	50c. red	9·25	75
237	**46**	1p. green	29·00	2·75

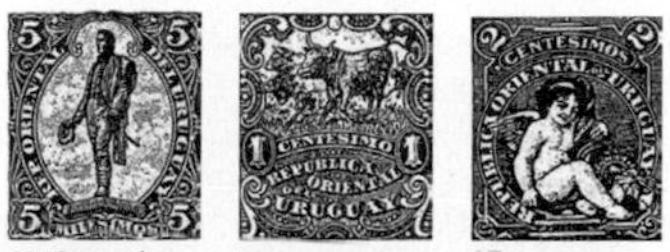
85 General Artigas **86** **87**

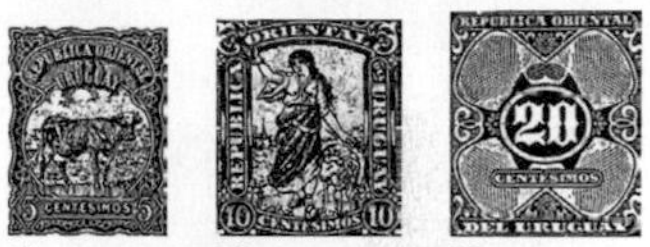
88 **89** **90**

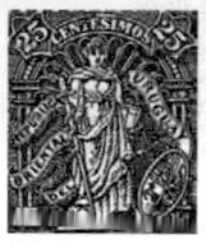
91

1904

251	**85**	5m. yellow	55	20
252	**86**	1c. green	65	20
253a	**87**	2c. orange	20	20
254b	**88**	5c. blue	1·10	20
255	**89**	10c. lilac	65	20
256	**90**	20c. green	3·25	65
257	**91**	25c. bistre	4·50	1·10

1904. End of the Civil War. Optd **Paz-1904.**

258	**86**	1c. green	55	55
259	**87**	2c. orange	90	85
260	**88**	5c. blue	1·10	55

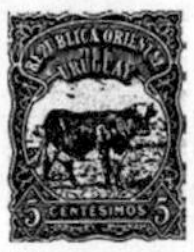
95

1906

268	**95**	5c. blue	1·40	20

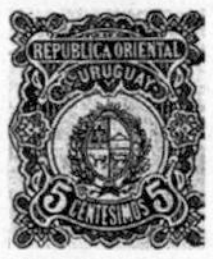
96

1906

269	**96**	5c. blue	20	20
270	**96**	7c. brown	65	30
271	**96**	50c. red	6·00	1·10

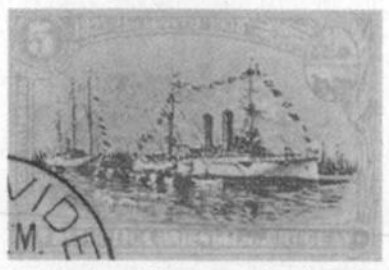
98 Cruiser "Montevideo" and Cadet Ship "Diez-y-Ocho de Julio"

1908. 83rd Anniv of Revolt of the "Immortal 33" under Levalleja. Roul.

279	**98**	1c. green and red	2·20	1·60
280	**98**	2c. green	2·20	1·60
281	**98**	5c. green and orange	2·20	1·60

99 Montevideo Port

1909. Opening of the Port of Montevideo.

282	**99**	2c. black and brown	1·70	1·60
283	**99**	5c. black and red	1·70	1·60

1909. Surch **Provisorio** and value.

284	**82**	8c. on 10c. violet	1·10	20
285	**44**	23c. on 25c. brown	2·20	75

103 Centaur

1910. Centenary of 1810 Argentine Revolution.

286	**103**	2c. red	75	55
287	**103**	5c. blue	75	55

1910. Surch **PROVISORIO 5 MILESIMOS** (or **CENTESIMOS**) **1910.**

294	**78**	5m. on 1c. green	20	20
295	**45**	5c. on 50c. red	55	20
296	**96**	5c. on 50c. red	1·10	20

107 Artigas

108

1910

297	**107**	5m. purple	20	10
298	**107**	1c. green	20	10
299	**107**	2c. red	20	10
324	**107**	2c. pink	20	20
319	**107**	4c. yellow	20	20
300	**107**	5c. blue	20	10
301	**107**	8c. black	55	10
327	**107**	8c. blue	65	20
302	**107**	20c. brown	75	10
303	**108**	23c. blue	3·75	55
330	**108**	50c. orange	5·00	1·30
331	**108**	1p. red	14·50	1·60

109

1911. First Pan-American Postal Congress.

306	**109**	5c. black and red	1·10	75

1911. Centenary of Battle of Las Piedras. Surch **ARTIGAS**, value and **1811-1911.**

314	**81**	2c. on 7c. brown	55	55
315	**81**	5c. on 7c. brown	55	20

1913. Centenary of 1813 Conference. Optd **CENTENARIO DE LAS INSTRUCCIONES DEL ANO XIII.**

332	**107**	2c. brown	1·20	65
333	**107**	4c. yellow	1·20	65
334	**107**	5c. blue	1·20	65

114 Liberty offering Peace to Uruguay

1918. Promulgation of New Constitution.

347	**114**	2c. brown and green	1·10	65
348	**114**	5c. blue and brown	1·10	65

115 Montevideo Harbour

1919

349	**115**	5m. grey and violet	10	10
350	**115**	1c. grey and green	10	10
351	**115**	2c. grey and red	10	10
352	**115**	4c. grey and orange	45	10
353	**115**	5c. grey and blue	55	10
354	**115**	8c. brown and blue	65	20
355	**115**	20c. grey and brown	2·20	45
356	**115**	23c. brown and green	3·75	85
357	**115**	50c. blue and brown	7·25	2·75
358	**115**	1p. blue and red	14·50	5·25

116 Statue of Liberty, New York

1919. Peace Commemoration.

359	**116**	2c. brown and red	75	20
360	**116**	4c. brown and orange	75	20
361	**116**	5c. brown and blue	1·10	55
362	**116**	8c. blue and brown	1·10	55
363	**116**	20c. black and bistre	2·75	1·10
364	**116**	23c. black and green	5·50	1·70

118 J. E. Rodo

1920. Honouring J. E. Rodo (writer).

372	**118**	2c. black and lake	75	55
373	**118**	4c. blue and orange	90	65
374	**118**	5c. brown and blue	1·00	75

1921. Air. Optd with airplane and **CORREO AEREO.**

377	**44**	25c. brown	7·25	5·25

120 Mercury

1921

378	**120**	5m. mauve	20	10
410	**120**	5m. black	20	20
380	**120**	1c. green	20	10
411	**120**	1c. mauve	20	20
411a	**120**	1c. violet	20	20
412	**120**	2c. orange	35	20
412a	**120**	2c. red	55	20
384	**120**	3c. green	55	10
385	**120**	4c. yellow	55	10
386	**120**	5c. blue	65	20
413	**120**	5c. brown	90	20
414	**120**	8c. red	1·40	1·30
388	**120**	12c. blue	3·25	75
389	**120**	36c. olive	11·00	3·75

122 Damaso A. Larranaga

1921. 150th Birth Anniv of D. A. Larranaga.

390	**122**	5c. slate	1·70	1·30

127 Artigas Monument

1923. Unveiling of Monument to Artigas.

418	**127**	2c. brown and red	55	30
419	**127**	5c. brown and violet	55	30
420	**127**	12c. brown and blue	55	30

128 Southern Lapwing

1923. Various sizes.

450	**128**	5m. grey	20	10
422	**128**	1c. yellow	20	10
451	**128**	1c. pink	20	10
477	**128**	1c. purple	1·70	30
528	**128**	1c. violet	55	30
423	**128**	2c. mauve	20	10
529	**128**	2c. red	55	30
453	**128**	3c. green	35	10
454	**128**	5c. blue	35	10
455	**128**	8c. red	65	10
456	**128**	10c. green	55	10
457	**128**	12c. blue	65	10
458	**128**	15c. mauve	65	10
459	**128**	20c. brown	1·00	10
429	**128**	36c. green	5·50	2·30
460	**128**	36c. red	3·50	1·60
430	**128**	50c. orange	9·25	3·75
461	**128**	50c. olive	5·50	2·10
431	**128**	1p. red	46·00	27·00
462	**128**	1p. buff	17·00	5·25
432	**128**	2p. green	65·00	27·00
463	**128**	2p. lilac	29·00	14·00

130

1923. Centenary of Battle of Sarandi.

433	**130**	2c. green	75	55
434	**130**	5c. red	75	55
435	**130**	12c. blue	90	55

131 Biplane

1924. Air.

436	**131**	6c. blue	2·10	2·00
437	**131**	10c. red	2·75	2·75
438	**131**	20c. green	5·00	5·00

134 "Victory" of Samothrace

1924. Uruguayan Football Victory in Olympic Games.

464	**134**	2c. red	22·00	14·00
465	**134**	5c. purple	22·00	14·00
466	**134**	12c. blue	22·00	14·00

135 Landing of Lavalleja

1925. Centenary of Rising against Brazilian Rule.

467	**135**	2c. grey and red	1·90	1·10
468	**135**	5c. grey and mauve	1·90	1·10
469	**135**	12c. grey and blue	1·90	1·10

136 Parliament House

1925. Inauguration of Parliament House.

470	**136**	5c. black and violet	1·70	85
471	**136**	12c. black and blue	1·70	85

137 White-necked Heron

1925. Air. Centenary of Assembly of Florida. (a) Inscr "MONTEVIDEO".

472	**137**	14c. black and blue	33·00	15·00

(b) Inscr "FLORIDA".

473	14c. black and blue	33·00	15·00

138 Gen. F. Rivera

139 Gaucho Cavalryman at Rincon

1925. Centenary of Battle of Rincon.

474	**138**	5c. pink (postage)	65	55
475	**139**	45c. green (air)		16·00

140 Battle of Sarandi

1925. Centenary of Battle of Sarandi.

482	**140**	2c. green	1·70	1·30
483	**140**	5c. mauve	1·70	1·30
484	**140**	12c. blue	1·70	1·30

141 Albatross

1926. Air. Imperf.

495	**141**	6c. blue	1·70	1·60
496	**141**	10c. red	2·20	2·10
497	**141**	20c. green	3·25	3·25
498	**141**	25c. violet	3·25	3·25

See also Nos. 569/80.

145 New G.P.O., Montevideo

1927. Philatelic Exhibition, Montevideo. Imperf.

534	**145**	2c. green	6·50	4·75
535	**145**	5c. red	6·50	4·75
536	**145**	8c. blue	6·50	4·75

1928. Opening of San Carlos–Rocha Railway. Surch **Inauguracion Ferrocarril SAN CARLOS a ROCHA 14/1/928** and value.

537	**128**	2c. on 12c. blue	2·75	2·75
538	**128**	5c. on 12c. blue	2·75	2·75
539	**128**	10c. on 12c. blue	2·75	2·75
540	**128**	15c. on 12c. blue	2·75	2·75

147 Gen. F. Rivera (after M. Bucasso)

1928. Centenary of Conquest of Las Misiones.

541	**147**	5c. red	65	45

148 Artigas

149 Artigas Statue, Paysandu

1928

542	**148**	5m. black	10	10
762	**148**	5m. brown	10	10
868	**148**	5m. orange	20	10
543	**148**	1c. violet	10	10
544	**148**	1c. purple	10	10
869	**148**	1c. blue	20	10

687	148	15m. black	35	20
545	148	2c. green	10	10
764	148	2c. brown	15	10
870	148	2c. red	20	10
546	148	3c. bistre	10	10
871	148	3c. green	20	10
548	148	5c. red	10	10
549	148	5c. olive	20	10
766	148	5c. blue	15	10
767	148	5c. turquoise	15	10
872	148	5c. violet	20	10
550	148	7c. red	20	10
551	148	8c. blue	20	10
552	148	8c. brown	35	10
553	148	10c. orange	35	10
768	148	12c. blue	55	20
556	148	15c. blue	45	10
557	148	17c. violet	1·10	20
558	148	20c. brown	90	10
757	148	20c. buff	2·00	65
770	148	20c. red	1·10	55
771	148	20c. violet	1·30	55
560	148	24c. red	1·20	45
561	148	24c. yellow	1·10	55
562	148	36c. olive	1·90	85
563	148	50c. grey	2·20	1·10
564	148	50c. black	4·75	2·10
772	148	50c. sepia	4·50	1·10
566	148	1p. green	6·50	4·75
567	149	2p. brown and blue	22·00	10·50
568	149	3p. black and red	33·00	16·00

1928. Air. Re-issue of T **141**. Perf.

634	141	4c. brown	3·75	3·75
569	141	10c. green	2·75	2·10
570	141	20c. orange	4·50	3·25
571	141	30c. blue	4·50	3·25
572	141	38c. green	7·75	6·50
573	141	40c. yellow	8·75	6·50
574	141	50c. violet	10·00	7·50
575	141	76c. orange	19·00	16·00
576	141	1p. red	22·00	19·00
577	141	1p.14 blue	46·00	43·00
578	141	1p.52 yellow	75·00	70·00
579	141	1p.90 violet	£100	80·00
580	141	3p.80 red	£250	£170

150 Goal Posts

1928. Uruguayan Football Victories in 1924 and 1928 Olympic Games.

581	150	2c. purple	17·00	13·00
582	150	5c. red	17·00	13·00
583	150	8c. blue	17·00	13·00

151 General Garzon

1928. Unveiling of Monument to Gen. Garzon. Imperf.

584	151	2c. red	1·90	1·80
585	151	5c. green	1·90	1·80
586	151	8c. blue	1·90	1·80

154 Artigas

1929

759	154	1p. brown	12·00	3·75
596	154	2p. green	24·00	13·00
597	154	2p. red	28·00	21·00
760	154	2p. blue	20·00	16·00
598	154	3p. blue	35·00	23·00
761	154	3p. black	29·00	21·00
600	154	4p. violet	40·00	23·00
601	154	4p. green	33·00	27·00
602	154	5p. red	46·00	32·00
603	154	5p. orange	44·00	27·00
604	154	10p. blue	£130	95·00
605	154	10p. red	£130	95·00

156 Pegasus

1929. Air. Size 34½×23½ mm.

617	156	1c. mauve	45	45
659	156	1c. blue	45	45
618	156	2c. yellow	45	45
660	156	2c. olive	45	45
619	156	4c. blue	75	65
661	156	4c. lake	75	65
620	156	6c. violet	75	65
662	156	6c. brown	85	65
621	156	8c. orange	3·50	3·00
663	156	8c. grey	4·75	3·25
664	156	8c. green	55	55
622	156	16c. blue	2·75	2·30
665	156	16c. red	3·50	3·25
623	156	24c. purple	3·00	2·50
666	156	24c. violet	4·75	3·75
624	156	30c. brown	3·25	3·00
667	156	30c. green	2·20	1·10
625	156	40c. brown	6·00	5·25
668	156	40c. orange	6·50	5·75
626	156	60c. blue	5·50	3·50
669	156	60c. green	9·25	7·50
670	156	60c. red	3·25	2·10
627	156	80c. blue	9·25	8·00
671	156	80c. green	17·00	13·00
628	156	90c. blue	9·25	7·00
672	156	90c. olive	17·00	13·00
629	156	1p. red	11·00	8·00
630	156	1p.20 olive	24·00	21·00
673	156	1p.20 red	33·00	28·00
631	156	1p.50 purple	28·00	21·00
674	156	1p.50 sepia	22·00	16·00
632	156	3p. red	44·00	37·00
675	156	3p. blue	33·00	27·00
633	156	4p.50 black	85·00	60·00
676	156	4p.50 lilac	50·00	37·00
677	156	10p. blue	19·00	17·00

For stamps as Type **156**, but smaller, see Nos. 725/44.

1931. Philatelic Exhibition, Montevideo. Miniature sheets each comprising block of four stamps as T **1**. Imperf.

MS678 2c. blue; 5c. green; 8c. scarlet; 15c. slate Set of 4 sheets 75·00 75·00

157 Rio Negro Railway Bridge

159 "Peace"

1930. Independence Centenary.

639	157	5m. black	20	10
640	-	1c. sepia	20	10
641	159	2c. lake	20	10
642	-	3c. green	35	20
643	-	5c. blue	35	20
644	-	8c. red	45	20
645	-	10c. violet	65	45
646	-	15c. green	90	65
647	-	20c. blue	1·10	85
648	-	24c. lake	1·50	85
649	-	50c. red	4·50	2·75
650	-	1p. black	8·25	3·75
651	-	2p. blue	20·00	11·50
652	-	3p. red	29·00	19·00
653	-	4p. orange	33·00	26·00
654	-	5p. lilac	50·00	30·00

DESIGNS—HORIZ: 1c. Gaucho horse-breaker; 5c. Head of Liberty and Uruguayan flag; 10c. "Artigas", from picture by Blanes; 15c. Seascape; 20c. Montevideo harbour, 1830; 24c. Head of Liberty and Arms of Uruguay; 50c. Montevideo Harbour, 1930. VERT: 3c. Montevideo; 8c. Allegorical figure with torch; 1p. to 5p. Artigas Monument.

161

1930. Fund for Old People.

655	161	1c.+1c. violet	20	20
656	161	2c.+2c. green	20	20
657	161	5c.+5c. red	55	55
658	161	8c.+8c. blue	55	55

163 J. Zorrilla de San Martin

1932

679	163	1½c. purple	20	20
680	163	3c. green	20	20
681	163	7c. blue	20	20
682	163	12c. blue	55	20
683	163	1p. brown	29·00	18·00

1932. Surch.

684	161	1½c. on 2c.+2c. green	45	45

167 J. Zorrilla de San Martin

1933. Various portraits.

689	-	15m. red (Lavalleja)	20	10
690	-	3c. green (Rivera)	20	10
691	167	7c. grey	20	10

168 Flag of the Race

1933. 441st Anniv of Columbus' Departure from Palos.

692	168	3c. green	65	30
693	168	5c. pink	65	30
694	168	7c. blue	65	30
695	168	8c. red	1·40	75
696	168	12c. blue	90	30
697	168	17c. violet	2·40	1·10
698	168	20c. brown	5·00	2·10
699	168	24c. bistre	5·00	2·30
700	168	36c. red	7·25	3·25
701	168	50c. brown	7·75	4·25
702	168	1p. brown	19·00	8·50

169 Sower

1933. Opening of the Third National Assembly.

703	169	3c. green	35	20
704	169	5c. violet	55	30
705	169	7c. blue	55	30
706	169	8c. red	1·10	65
707	169	12c. blue	1·70	1·10

170 Map and Albatross

1933. Seventh Pan-American Conference, Montevideo.

708	170	3c. green, brown and black	3·75	2·75
709	170	7c. blue, black and brown	2·20	1·10
710	170	12c. blue, red and grey	3·25	2·10
711	170	17c. red, blue and grey	7·25	3·75
712	170	20c. yellow, green and blue	8·25	4·75
713	170	36c. red, yellow and black	11·00	7·50

1934. Air. Closure of the Seventh Pan-American Conference. Optd **SERVICIO POSTAL AEREO 1-1-34** in circle.

714	17c. red, blue and grey	22·00	16·00
715	36c. red, yellow and black	22·00	16·00

172

1934. First Anniv of Third Republic.

716	172	3c. green	75	55
717	172	7c. red	75	55
718	172	12c. blue	2·20	1·10
719	172	17c. brown and pink	2·75	1·60
720	172	20c. yellow and grey	3·25	2·10
721	172	36c. violet and green	3·25	2·10
722	172	50c. grey and blue	8·25	4·25
723	172	1p. red and mauve	20·00	9·00

1935. Air. As T **156**, but size 31½×21½ mm.

725	15c. yellow	2·75	2·10
726	22c. red	1·70	1·40
727	30c. purple	2·75	2·10
728	37c. purple	1·40	1·10
729	40c. red	2·20	1·40
730	47c. red	4·50	3·50
731	50c. blue	1·40	85
732	52c. blue	4·50	3·75
733	57c. blue	2·20	1·90
734	62c. green	2·00	85
735	87c. green	5·50	4·25
736	1p. olive	4·00	2·40
737	1p.12 brown	4·00	2·30
738	1p.20 brown	17·00	13·00
739	1p.27 brown	17·00	14·00
740	1p.62 red	11·00	9·50
741	2p. lake	19·00	15·00
742	2p.12 grey	19·00	15·00
743	3p. blue	17·00	14·00
744	5p. orange	65·00	65·00

173 Friendship of Uruguay and Brazil

1935. Visit of President Vargas of Brazil.

747	173	5m. brown	1·10	55
748	173	15m. black	55	20
749	173	3c. green	55	20
750	173	7c. orange	55	20
751	173	12c. blue	1·10	75
752	173	50c. brown	5·50	3·25

174 Florencio Sanchez

1935. 25th Death Anniv of F. Sanchez (dramatist).

753	174	3c. green	20	20
754	174	7c. brown	20	20
755	174	12c. blue	75	45

176 Rio Negro Dam

1937

780	176	1c. violet (postage)	35	10
781	176	10c. blue	65	20
782	176	15c. red	1·70	85
783	176	1p. brown	8·75	3·25
793	176	8c. green (air)	65	55
794	176	20c. green	2·00	45
785	176	35c. brown	8·75	7·00
786	176	62c. green	90	30
787	176	68c. orange	2·20	1·60
788	176	68c. brown	1·90	75
789	176	75c. violet	8·25	8·00
790	176	1p. red	2·75	1·80
791	176	1p.38 red	28·00	21·00
792	176	3p. blue	19·00	13·00

178 Artigas

1939. (a) Plain background.

806	178	5m. orange	10	10
807	178	1c. blue	10	10
808	178	2c. violet	10	10
809	178	5c. brown	20	10
810	178	8c. red	35	10
811	178	10c. green	65	10
812	178	15c. blue	1·80	75
813	178	1p. brown	3·25	1·30
1008	178	1p. purple	2·20	75

814	178	2p. lilac	10·00	4·25
815	178	4p. orange	13·00	5·25
816	178	5p. red	20·00	8·00

Nos. 806/12 are size 16×19 mm. No. 1008 is 18×22 mm. and Nos. 813/6 are 24×29½ mm.

(b) Lined background. (i) Size 17×22 mm.

835		5m. orange	10	10
848		5m. black	10	10
849		5m. blue	20	10
836		1c. blue	10	10
837		1c. purple	10	10
838		2c. violet	10	10
839		2c. orange	10	10
840a		2c. brown	10	10
1152		2c. grey	10	10
841		3c. green	10	10
842		5c. brown	10	10
843b		7c. blue	20	10
844		8c. red	20	10
845		10c. green	55	10
851		10c. brown	20	10
852		12c. blue	65	10
853		20c. mauve	65	20
846		50c. bistre	8·75	2·30
847		50c. green	6·50	2·30
1153		50c. brown	55	10

(ii) Size 23½×29½ mm.

1024		2p. brown	20·00	10·50

180 Airplane over "La Carreta" (sculpture, Jose Bellini)

1939. Air.

817	180	20c. blue	55	45
818	180	20c. violet	90	85
820	180	35c. red	1·10	85
821	180	50c. orange	1·10	30
822	180	75c. pink	1·20	20
823	180	1p. blue	3·50	65
824	180	1p.38 violet	6·00	2·30
825	180	1p.38 orange	5·50	4·25
826a	180	2p. blue	8·25	1·20
827	180	5p. lilac	11·00	2·30
828	180	5p. green	17·00	7·50
829	180	10p. red	£110	70·00

181 Congress of Montevideo

1939. 50th Anniv of 1st International Juridical Congress, Montevideo.

830	181	1c. red	20	10
831	181	2c. green	35	20
832	181	5c. red	35	20
833	181	12c. blue	90	55
834	181	50c. violet	3·50	1·80

183 Juan Manuel Blanes (artist)

1941. 40th Death Anniv of Blanes.

855	183	5m. brown	35	20
856	183	1c. brown	35	20
857	183	2c. green	35	20
858	183	5c. red	75	20
859	183	12c. blue	1·80	75
860	183	50c. violet	6·50	4·50

185 Francisco Acuna de Figueroa

1942. 80th Death Anniv of Figueroa (author of words of National Anthem).

863	185	1c. brown	20	20
864	185	2c. green	20	20
865	185	5c. red	35	20
866	185	12c. blue	1·20	55
867	185	50c. violet	4·75	3·50

1943. Surch **Valor $ 0.005**.

873	178	5m. on 1c. blue	20	20

187

1943

874	187	1c. on 2c. brown	20	20
875	187	2c. on 2c. brown	20	20

189 Clio

1943. Centenary of Historical and Geographical Institute. Montevideo.

878	189	5m. violet	20	20
879	189	1c. blue	20	20
880	189	2c. red	65	20
881	189	5c. brown	65	20

191

1944. 75th Anniv of Founding of Swiss Colony.

889	191	1c. on 3c. green	10	10
890	191	5c. on 7c. brown	20	20
891	191	10c. on 12c. blue	90	30

192 Emblems of Y.M.C.A.

1944. Centenary of Young Men's Christian Assn.

892	192	5c. blue	20	10

1944. Air. Air stamps of 1935, Nos. 730, etc, surch.

893		40c. on 47c. red	65	55
894		40c. on 57c. blue	75	55
895		74c. on 1p.12 brown	75	55
896		79c. on 87c. green	4·00	2·75
897		79c. on 1p.27 brown	6·00	4·25
898		1p.20 on 1p.62 red	3·25	2·10
899		1p.43 on 2p.12 grey	3·25	2·75

194 Legislative Palace

1945. Air.

900	194	2p. blue	6·50	2·30

195 Book

198 Statue

1945. Birth Centenary of Jose Pedro Varela (writer).

901	195	5m. green	20	20
902	-	1c. brown (Varela)	20	20
903	-	2c. red (Statue)	20	20
904a	198	5c. blue	35	10

Nos. 902/3 are vert.

205 Eduardo Acevedo (statesman)

200 Jose Pedro Varela (writer)

1945

905	-	5m. violet	10	10
911	-	1c. brown	10	10
912	205	2c. purple	20	10
945	-	3c. green	20	20
906	200	5c. red	10	10
907	-	10c. blue	55	20
946	-	20c. brown and green	1·70	65

PORTRAITS: 5m. Santiago Vazquez (statesman); 1c. Sylvestre Blanco (statesman); 3c. Bruno Mauricio de Zabala (founder of Montevideo); 10c. Jose Ellauri (President, 1873–75); 20c. Col. Luis de Larrobla (first Postmaster).

206 Full-rigged Ship "La Eolo"

1945. Air.

913	206	8c. green	1·70	55

1945. Air. Victory. Surch with figure as "Victory of Samothrace", 1945 and new value. No. 908 optd **VICTORIA** also.

914	180	14c. on 50c. orange	1·30	55
915	180	23c. on 50c. orange	1·30	55
916	180	23c. on 1p.38 orange	1·40	55
908	156	44c. on 75c. brown	1·70	75
917	180	1p. on 1p. 38 orange	5·50	2·75

1946. Inaug of Rio Negro Hydro-electric Power Plant. Optd **INAUGURACION DICIEMBRE, 1945**, No. 918 also surch **CORREO 20 CENTS**.

918	176	20c. on 68c. brown (postage)	1·70	75
919	176	62c. green (air)	1·30	1·10

1946. As T 187. (a) Postage. Optd **CORREOS** and **Caduceus**.

920	187	5m. orange	10	10
921	187	2c. brown	20	10
922	187	3c. green	20	10
923	187	5c. blue	20	10
924	187	10c. brown	45	10
925	187	20c. green	90	30
926	187	50c. brown	2·75	1·30
927	187	3p. red	10·50	6·50

(b) Air. Optd **SERVICIO AEREO** and an airplane.

928		8c. red	20	10
929		50c. brown	75	20
930		1p. blue	1·70	55
931		2p. olive	4·50	2·75
932		3p. red	7·25	2·75
933		5p. red	13·00	8·00

215 National Airport

217 Douglas DC-4

1947. Air.

947	217	3c. brown	20	10
948	217	8c. red	35	20
949	217	10c. black	20	10
950	217	10c. red	20	10
951	217	14c. blue	65	45
952	217	15c. brown	35	20
953	217	20c. purple	45	30
954	217	21c. lilac	55	30
955	217	23c. green	65	55
956	217	27c. green	55	20
957	217	31c. brown	75	30
958	217	36c. blue	55	20
959	217	36c. black	55	20
960	217	50c. turquoise	90	65
961	217	50c. blue	65	20
962	217	62c. blue	1·00	65
963	217	65c. red	1·00	65
964	217	84c. orange	1·40	95
941	215	1p. brown and red	1·50	50
965	217	1p.08 plum	2·20	1·10
966	217	2p. blue	3·50	1·90
942	215	3p. brown and blue	3·75	1·90
967	217	3p. orange	4·50	2·30
943	215	5p. brown and green	7·75	3·75
968	217	5p. green	9·25	5·25
969	217	5p. grey	5·00	3·50
944	215	10p. brown and purple	8·75	5·25
970	217	10p. green	24·00	17·00

1947. As T **187** but surch in figures above shield and wavy lines.

976		2c. on 5c. blue	20	10
977		3c. on 5c. blue	35	10

219 "Ariel"

221 Bas-reliefs

1948. Unveiling of Monument to J. E. Rodo (writer).

978	219	1c. brown and olive	10	10
979	-	2c. brown and violet	20	10
980	221	3c. brown and green	20	10
981	221	5c. brown and mauve	35	20
982	221	10c. brown and red	45	20
983	221	12c. brown and blue	55	20
984	219	20c. brown and purple	1·10	65
985	-	50c. brown and red	3·75	1·90

DESIGN: 2, 50c. Bust of J. E. Rodo.

The 5c. and 12c. are as Type **221** but inscr "UN GRAN AMOR ES EL ALMA MISMA DE QUIEN AMA".

1948. Air. As T **187**, optd **AVIACION** and airplane.

986		12c. blue	20	15
987		24c. green	65	30
988		36c. grey	75	55

223 Paysandu

1948. Industrial and Agricultural Exhibitions, Paysandu.

989	223	3c. green	35	20
990	-	7c. blue	55	30

DESIGN—HORIZ: 7c. Livestock, sower and arms of Paysandu.

225 River Santa Lucia Railway Bridge

1948. Uruguayan–Brazilian Friendship.

991	225	10c. blue	1·10	20
992	225	50c. green	3·25	1·30

226 Ploughing

1949. Fourth American Labour Conference.

993	226	3c. green	20	10
994	-	7c. blue	55	10

DESIGN—HORIZ: 7c. Horseman herding cattle.

227 Medical Faculty

1949. Air. Centenary of Montevideo University.

995		15c. red	20	20
996	227	27c. brown	20	20
997	-	31c. blue	55	20
998	-	36c. green	75	55

DESIGNS: 15c. Architectural faculty; 31c. Engineering faculty; 36c. View of University.

228 Cannon and Buildings

1950. Bicentenary of Cordon (district of Montevideo).

1003	228	1c. mauve	35	20
1004	228	3c. green	35	20
1005	228	7c. blue	35	20

229 Kicking Football

1951. Fourth World Football Championship.

1006	229	3c. green	1·40	30
1007	229	7c. blue	3·00	1·10

230 Gen. Artigas

231 Emigration from Eastern Provinces

1952. Death Cent of Artigas. Dated "1950".

1009	**230**	5m. blue	20	10
1010	-	1c. black and blue	20	10
1011	-	2c. brown and violet	20	10
1012	**231**	3c. sepia and green	20	10
1013	-	5c. black and orange	20	10
1014	**231**	7c. black and olive	35	10
1015	-	8c. black and red	45	10
1016	-	10c. red, blue and brown	45	10
1017	-	14c. blue	45	10
1018	-	20c. red, blue and yellow	1·10	10
1019	-	50c. olive and brown	2·20	55
1020	-	1p. olive and blue	4·50	1·60

DESIGNS (all show Artigas except 10c. and 20c.)—As Type **230**: 1c. at Las Huerfanas; 2c. at Battle of Las Piedras; 5c. in Cerrito; 14c. at Ciudadela; 20c. Arms; 50c. in Paraguay; 1p. Bust. As Type **231**: 7c. Dictating instructions; 8c. in Congress; 10c. Flag.

232 Boeing 377 Stratocruiser over Mail Coach

1952. 75th Anniv of U.P.U. (1949).

1021	**232**	3c. green	20	10
1022	**232**	7c. black	20	20
1023	**232**	12c. blue	35	30

234 Franklin D. Roosevelt

1953. Fifth Postal Congress of the Americas and Spain.

1025	**234**	3c. green	20	10
1026	**234**	7c. blue	35	10
1027	**234**	12c. brown	55	30

235 Ceibo (National Flower)

236 Ombu Tree

237 Parliament House

1954

1028	**235**	5m. multicoloured	10	10
1029	-	1c. black and red	10	10
1030	**236**	2c. green and brown	10	10
1031	-	3c. multicoloured	20	10
1032	**237**	5c. brown and lilac	20	10
1033	-	7c. green and brown	20	10
1034	-	8c. blue and red	55	10
1035	**236**	10c. green and orange	45	10
1036	-	12c. sepia and blue	35	10
1037	-	14c. black and purple	35	10
1038	**235**	20c. multicoloured	1·00	10
1039	-	50c. multicoloured	2·75	10
1040	**237**	1p. brown and red	3·50	1·30
1041	-	2p. sepia and red	5·50	2·10
1042	-	3p. green and lilac	6·50	2·75
1043	-	4p. blue and brown	19·00	7·00
1044	**236**	5p. green and blue	14·50	5·25

DESIGNS—As T **235**: 3c., 50c. Passion flower. As T **236**—HORIZ: 1c., 14c. Gaucho breaking-in horse. VERT: 7c., 3p. Montevideo Citadel. As T **237**—VERT: 8c., 4p. Isla de Lobos lighthouse and southern sealions. HORIZ: 12c., 2p. Outer Gateway of Montevideo, 1836.

239 Exhibition Entrance

1956. First National Production Exhibition.

1050	**239**	3c. green (postage)	35	20
1051	**239**	7c. blue	35	20
1052	-	20c. blue (air)	65	55
1053	-	31c. green	75	30
1054	-	36c. red	1·20	55

DESIGN—HORIZ: Nos. 1052/4, Exhibition symbol and two airliners.

241 Uruguay's First Stamp and "Diligencia"

1956. Air. Centenary of First Uruguay Stamps. Stamp in blue.

1055	**241**	20c. green and yellow	75	55
1056	**241**	31c. brown and blue	90	55
1057	**241**	36c. red and pink	1·70	55

242 Pres. Jose Batlle y Ordonez

1956. Birth Centenary of Jose Batlle y Ordonez (President, 1903–07 and 1911–15).

1058	**242**	3c. red (postage)	20	10
1059	-	7c. sepia	20	10
1060	-	10c. mauve (air)	55	20
1061	**242**	20c. slate	55	20
1062	-	31c. brown	55	55
1063	-	36c. green	1·10	75

PORTRAIT OF PRESIDENT—VERT: 7c. Wearing overcoat; 10c. Similar to Type **242**; 36c. Profile, facing right. HORIZ: 31c. Seated at desk.

1957. Surch **5** or **10 Cts.**

1071	**242**	5c. on 3c. red	20	10
1072	-	10c. on 7c. sepia (No. 1059)	35	10

248 High Diver

1958. 14th S. American Swimming Championships, Montevideo. Inscr as in T **248**.

1073	**248**	5c. green	35	20
1074	-	10c. blue	65	30

DESIGN—HORIZ: 10c. Diving.

249 Dr. E. Acevedo

1958. Birth Centenary of Dr. Eduardo Acevedo (lawyer).

1075	**249**	5c. black and green	20	10
1076	**249**	10c. black and blue	35	20

250 Flags

1958. Air. Day of the Americas.

1077	**250**	23c. black and blue	55	20
1078	**250**	34c. black and green	75	30
1079	**250**	44c. black and mauve	90	55

251 Baygorria Dam

1958. Inauguration of Baygorria Hydro-electric Power Station.

1080	**251**	5c. black and green	10	10
1081	**251**	10c. black and brown	10	10
1082	-	1p. black and blue	90	30
1083	-	2p. black and mauve	1·70	75

DESIGN: 1, 2p. Aerial view of dam.

252 "Flame of Freedom"

1958. Air. Tenth Anniv of Declaration of Human Rights.

1084	**252**	23c. black and blue	45	20
1085	**252**	34c. black and green	65	30
1086	**252**	44c. black and red	1·10	65

1958. Nos. 1028, 1031 and 1033 surch with **Caduceus** and value.

1087		5c. on 3c. multicoloured	20	10
1088		10c. on 7c. green and brown	20	20
1089		20c. on 5m. multicoloured	35	10

254 Statue on Capt. Boiso Lanza Monument

1959. Air. Centres in black.

1090	**254**	3c. brown	35	20
1091	**254**	8c. mauve	35	20
1092	**254**	38c. black	35	20
1093	**254**	50c. yellow	35	20
1094	**254**	60c. violet	35	30
1095	**254**	90c. olive	45	30
1096	**254**	1p. blue	55	30
1097	**254**	2p. orange	1·90	75
1098	**254**	3p. green	2·20	1·30
1099	**254**	5p. purple	2·75	2·10
1100	**254**	10p. red	10·00	6·50

See also Type **266**.

255 Santos-Dumont and his Biplane "14 bis"

1959. Air. Santos-Dumont Commemoration.

1101	**255**	31c. multicoloured	35	20
1102	**255**	36c. multicoloured	35	20

257 "Tourism in Uruguay"

1959. Air. Tourist Publicity and 50th Anniv of Punta del Este.

1103	**257**	10c. blue and ochre	10	10
1104	-	38c. buff and green	20	10
1105	-	60c. buff and violet	55	10
1106	**257**	90c. green and red	65	30
1107	-	1p.05 buff and blue	1·10	75

DESIGN: 38, 60c., 1p.05, Beach and compass.

258 Gabriela Mistral (poet)

1959. Second Death Anniv of Gabriela Mistral.

1108	**258**	5c. green	20	10
1109	**258**	10c. blue	20	10
1110	**258**	20c. red	35	10

259 Dr. Vaz Ferreira

1959. Honouring Dr. Carlos Vaz Ferreira (philosopher).

1111	**259**	5c. black and blue	35	20
1112	**259**	10c. black and ochre	35	20
1113	**259**	20c. black and red	35	20
1114	**259**	50c. black and violet	45	30
1115	**259**	1p. black and green	75	30

260 Emblem of Y.M.C.A.

1959. Air. 50th Anniv of Y.M.C.A. in Uruguay.

1116	**260**	38c. black, grey and green	55	30
1117	**260**	50c. black, grey and blue	55	20
1118	**260**	60c. black, grey and red	75	65

261 Boy and Dam

1959. National Recovery.

1119	**261**	5c.+10c. green and orange (postage)	10	10
1120	**261**	10c.+10c. blue & orange	10	10
1121	**261**	1p.+10c. violet & orange	65	65
1122	**261**	38c.+10c. brown and orange (air)	35	30
1123	**261**	60c.+10c. green & orge	55	55

262 Artigas and Washington

1960. Air. Visit of President Eisenhower.

1124	**262**	38c. black and red	20	20
1125	**262**	50c. black and blue	35	20
1126	**262**	60c. black and green	65	20

1960. Air. Surch with **caduceus** and **20 c**.

1128	**217**	20c. on 27c. green	35	20

265 Martinez

1960. Birth Centenary of Dr. Martin C. Martinez.

1129	**265**	3c. black and purple	10	10
1130	**265**	5c. black and violet	10	10
1131	**265**	10c. black and blue	20	10
1132	**265**	20c. black and brown	35	10
1133	**265**	1p. black and grey	55	10
1134	**265**	2p. black and orange	1·40	10
1135	**265**	3p. black and olive	2·20	55
1136	**265**	4p. black and brown	2·75	1·10
1137	**265**	5p. black and red	3·25	1·10

266 Statue on Lanza Monument

1960. Air.

1138	**266**	3c. black and lilac	10	10
1139	**266**	20c. black and red	10	10

1140	266	38c. black and blue	10	10
1141	266	50c. black and buff	10	10
1142	266	60c. black and green	10	10
1143	266	90c. black and red	35	10
1144	266	1p. black and grey	35	20
1145	266	2p. black and green	65	45
1146	266	3p. black and purple	1·10	85
1147	266	5p. black and salmon	1·70	1·60
1148	266	10p. black and yellow	3·75	2·75
1149	266	20p. black and blue	8·25	5·25

267 Refugees

1960. World Refugee Year.

1150	-	10c. black & bl (postage)	20	20
1151	267	60c. black and mauve (air)	55	30

DESIGN: 10c. "Uprooted tree".

268 Scene of Revolution

1960. 150th Anniv of Argentine May Revolution.

1154	268	5c. black & blue (postage)	20	20
1155	268	10c. brown and blue	20	20
1156	268	38c. olive and blue (air)	20	20
1157	268	50c. red and blue	20	20
1158	268	60c. violet and blue	55	20

269 Pres. M. Oribe

1961. 104th Death Anniv of Manuel Oribe (President, 1835–38).

1159	269	10c. black and blue	20	10
1160	269	20c. black and brown	20	10
1161	269	40c. black and green	35	20

270 Pres. Gronchi

1961. Air. Visit of President of Italy.

1162	270	90c. multicoloured	35	20
1163	270	1p.20 multicoloured	55	30
1164	270	1p.40 multicoloured	65	65

271 Carrasco Airport Building

1961. Air. Carrasco National Airport.

1165	271	1p. grey and violet	35	20
1166	271	2p. grey and olive	75	10
1167	271	3p. grey and yellow	1·30	65
1168	271	4p. grey and purple	1·70	75
1169	271	5p. grey and turquoise	2·20	1·10
1170	271	10p. grey and blue	4·50	1·80
1171	271	20p. grey and red	6·50	3·75

272 "Charging Horsemen" (by C. M. Herrera)

1961. 150th Anniv of 28 February Revolution.

1172	272	20c. black and blue	20	10
1173	272	40c. black and green	55	20

273 Welfare, Justice and Education

1961. Latin-American Economic Commission Conference, Punta del Este. (a) Postage. Centres in bistre.

1174	273	2c. violet	45	20
1175	273	5c. orange	45	20
1176	273	10c. red	45	20
1177	273	20c. green	45	20
1178	273	50c. lilac	45	20
1179	273	1p. blue	55	20
1180	273	2p. yellow	1·40	30
1181	273	3p. grey	2·00	85
1182	273	4p. blue	3·25	1·10
1183	273	5p. brown	3·50	1·60

(b) Air. Centres in black.

1184	20c. orange	45	20
1185	45c. green	45	20
1186	50c. purple	45	20
1187	90c. violet	45	20
1188	1p. red	55	20
1189	1p.40 lilac	65	20
1190	2p. ochre	75	30
1191	3p. blue	1·20	45
1192	4p. yellow	1·70	75
1193	5p. blue	2·20	1·20
1194	10p. green	4·00	2·10
1195	20p. mauve	8·25	3·75

274 Gen. Rivera

1962. Honouring Gen. Fructuoso Rivera (1st President, 1830–35).

1196	274	10c. black and red	20	20
1197	274	20c. black and ochre	20	20
1198	274	40c. black and green	20	20

275 Symbols of Swiss Settlers

1962. Centenary of First Swiss Settlers.

1199	275	10c. red, black and blue (postage)	20	10
1200	275	20c. red, black and green	20	10
1201	-	90c. black, red and orange (air)	35	20
1202	-	1p.40 black, red and blue	55	55

DESIGN—HORIZ: 90c., 1p.40, Wheatsheaf, harvester and Swiss flag.

276 B. P. Berro

1962. Bernardo Prudencio Berro (President, 1860–64).

1203	276	10c. black and blue	20	20
1204	276	20c. black and brown	35	30

277 Red-crested Cardinal

1962. Birds.

1205	-	2c. brown, pink and black (postage)	20	10
1206	-	50c. brown and black	90	20
1207	-	1p. brown and black	2·20	20
1208	-	2p. black, brown and grey	4·50	1·10
1209	277	20c. red, black and grey (air)	35	20
1210	-	45c. red, blue and black	65	30
1211	-	90c. brown, black and red	1·30	20
1212	-	1p. blue, black and brown	90	30
1213	-	1p.20 multicoloured	1·80	30
1214	-	1p.40 brown, black and blue	2·75	45
1215	-	2p. yellow, black & brown	1·80	45
1216	-	3p. black, yellow & brown	2·75	75
1217	-	5p. black, blue and green	4·50	1·10
1218	-	10p. multicoloured	8·75	1·90
1219	-	20p. orange, black and grey	22·00	11·50

BIRDS—HORIZ: 2c. Rufous-bellied thrush; 45c. Diademed tanager; 50c. Rufous hornero; 1p. (1207), Chalk-browed mockingbird; 1p. (1212), Shiny-headed cowbird; 1p.20, Great kiskadee; 2p. (1208), Rufous-collared sparrow; 2p. (1215), Yellow cardinal; 3p. Hooded siskin; 5p. Sayaca tanager; 10p. Blue and yellow tanager; 20p. Scarlet-headed blackbird. VERT: 90c. Vermilion flycatcher; 1p.40, Fork-tailed flycatcher.

Nos. 1208, 1210, 1212 and 1215 have no frame; Nos. 1206 and 1214 have a thin frame line; the others are as Type **277**.

278 D. A. Larranaga

1963. 85th Death Anniv of Damaso Antonio Larranaga (founder of National Library).

1220	278	20c. sepia and turquoise	20	20
1221	278	40c. sepia and drab	35	30

279 U.P.A.E. Emblem

1963. 50th Anniv of Postal Union of the Americas and Spain.

1222	279	20c. blue & black (postage)	20	20
1223	279	45c. green and black (air)	20	20
1224	279	90c. red and black	45	30

280 Campaign Emblem

1963. Freedom from Hunger.

1225	280	10c. yell & grn (postage)	10	10
1226	280	20c. yellow and brown	10	10
1227	280	90c. yellow and red (air)	35	30
1228	280	1p.40 yellow and violet	65	65

281 Anchors

1963. World Voyage of "Alferez Campora".

1229	281	10c. vio & orge (postage)	10	10
1230	281	20c. grey and red	10	10
1231	-	90c. green & orange (air)	45	20
1232	-	1p.40 blue and yellow	1·00	65

DESIGN: 90c., 1p.40, Sailing ship "Alferez Campora".

282 Large Intestine Congress Emblem

1963. First Uruguayan Proctological Congress, Punta del Este.

1233	282	10c. red, black and green	20	20
1234	282	20c. red, black and ochre	35	30

283 Centenary Emblem

1964. Red Cross Centenary.

1235	283	20c. red and blue	20	20
1236	283	40c. red and grey	35	30

284 L. A. de Herrera

1964. Fifth Death Anniv of Luis A. de Herrera (statesman).

1237	284	20c. black, green and blue	10	10
1238	284	40c. black, lt blue & blue	10	10
1239	284	80c. black, yellow & blue	20	20
1240	284	1p. black, lilac and blue	55	30
1241	284	2p. black, slate and blue	75	65

285 Pres. De Gaulle

1964. Air. Visit of President of France. Multicoloured.

1242	1p.50 Type **285**	55	30
1243	2p.40 Flags of France and Uruguay	1·30	55

286 Reliefs from Abu Simbel

1964. Nubian Monuments Preservation. Multicoloured.

1244	20c. Type **286** (postage)	20	20
1245	1p.30 Sphinx, Sebua (air)	35	30
1246	2p. Rameses II, Abu Simbel	1·30	75
MS1247	110×131 mm. Nos. 1244/6. Imperf. No gum	2·75	2·75

Nos. 1245/6 are vert.

292 Arms

1965. Air.

1248	-	50p. blue, yellow and grey	9·25	5·25
1261	292	20p. multicoloured	2·75	1·60

DESIGN—HORIZ (38×27 mm) 50p. National flag.

288 Pres. Kennedy

1965. Pres. Kennedy Commemoration. Frame and laurel in gold.

1249	288	20c. blk & grn (postage)	20	20
1250	288	40c. black and brown	35	30
1251	288	1p.50 black and lilac (air)	35	30
1252	288	2p.40 black and blue	75	75

289 "Tete-beche" Pair of Uruguayan 8c. Stamps of 1864

290 6c. "Arms-type" of 1964

1965. First River Plate Stamp Exn, Montevideo. (a) Postage. T **289**.
| 1253 | 40c. green and black | 35 | 30 |

(b) Air. As T **290** showing Arms-type stamps of 1864 (values in brackets).
1254A	1p. black and blue (12c.)	35	30
1255A	1p. black and orange (T **290**)	35	30
1256A	1p. black and green (8c.)	35	30
1257A	1p. black and bistre (10c.)	35	30
1258A	1p. black and red (6c.)	35	30

Nos. 1254/8 were issued together in sheets of 10 (5×2), each design arranged in a vertical pair with "URUGUAY" either at top or bottom.

291 B. Nardone

1965. First Death Anniv of Benito Nardone (statesman).
| 1259 | **291** | 20c. black and green | 20 | 20 |
| 1260 | - | 40c. black and green | 35 | 30 |

DESIGN—VERT: 40c. Portrait as Type **291**, but Nardone with microphone.

293 Part of Artigas' Speech before the 1813 Congress

1965. Birth Bicent (1964) of Gen. Jose Artigas.
1262	**293**	20c. red, blue and yellow (postage)	10	10
1263	-	40c. olive, black and blue	10	10
1264	-	80c. multicoloured	20	18
1265	-	1p. multicoloured (air)	20	20
1266	-	1p.50 multicoloured	55	30
1267	**293**	2p.40 multicoloured	1·00	75

DESIGNS—HORIZ: 40c. Bust of Artigas; 80c. Artigas and his army flag; 1p.50, Bust, flag and exodus of his followers to Argentina. VERT: 1p. Artigas' statue.

295 Football

1965. Olympic Games, Tokyo (1964).
1269	**295**	20c. orange, black and green (postage)	10	10
1270	-	40c. olive, black & brown	10	10
1271	-	80c. red, black and drab	10	10
1272	-	1p. green, black and blue	10	10
1273	-	1p. grey, black & red (air)	10	10
1274	-	1p.50 blue, black & grn	20	20
1275	-	2p. blue, black and red	55	30
1276	-	2p.40 orange, black & bl	75	55
1277	-	3p. yellow, black and lilac	1·10	85
1278	-	20p. pink, blue & indigo	1·80	1·30
MS1279	70×125 mm. 5p. blue, buff and black (as T **134**) and 10p. red, blue and black (as T **150**)		3·25	3·25

DESIGNS: 40c. Basketball; 80c. Cycling; 1p. (No. 1272) Swimming; 1p. (No. 1273) Boxing; 1p.50, Running; 2p. Fencing; 2p.40, Sculling; 3p. Pistol-shooting; 20p. Olympic "Rings".

1965. Surch with **caduceus** and value.
| 1280 | **178** | 10c. on 7c. blue | 35 | 20 |

1966. 50th Anniv of Uruguay Architects' Assn. Surch **CINCUENTENARIO Sociedad Arquitectos del Uruguay** and value.
| 1281 | **261** | 4c. on 5c.+10c. green and orange | 20 | 20 |

298 I.T.U. Emblem and Satellite

1966. Air. Centenary of I.T.U.
| 1282 | **298** | 1p. deep blue, red & blue | 35 | 30 |

299 Sir Winston Churchill

1966. Churchill Commemoration.
| 1283 | **299** | 40c. brown, red and blue (postage) | 20 | 20 |
| 1284 | - | 2p. brn, red & gold (air) | 45 | 20 |

DESIGN—VERT: 2p. Churchill-full-face portrait and signed quotation.

300 Arms and View of Rio de Janeiro

1966. 400th Anniv of Rio de Janeiro.
| 1285 | **300** | 40c. grn & brn (postage) | 20 | 20 |
| 1286 | **300** | 80c. red and brown (air) | 20 | 20 |

301 I.C.Y. Emblem

1966. Air. I.C.Y.
| 1287 | **301** | 1p. black and green | 35 | 20 |

302 Army Engineer

1966. 50th Anniv of Army Engineers.
| 1288 | **302** | 20c. multicoloured | 20 | 20 |

304 Pres. Shazar

1966. Air. Visit of President of Israel.
| 1291 | **304** | 7p. multicoloured | 75 | 45 |

305 Crested Screamer

1966. Air.
| 1292 | **305** | 100p. multicoloured | 11·00 | 3·25 |

306 Jules Rimet Cup, Ball and Globe

1966. Air. World Cup Football Championship.
| 1293 | **306** | 10p. yellow and violet | 1·10 | 45 |

307 Hereford Bull

1966. Air. Cattle-breeding.
1294	**307**	4p. brown, chest & sepia	20	10
1295	-	6p. black, green & turq	20	10
1296	-	10p. mauve, green & turq	75	30
1297	-	15p. black, red and orange	1·30	55

1298	-	20p. brown, yell & grey	2·40	85
1299	-	30p. brown and yellow	3·25	1·30
1300	-	50p. brown, grey & green	5·50	2·10

DESIGNS (Cattle breeds): 6p. Dutch; 10p. Shorthorn; 15p. Aberdeen Angus; 20p. Norman; 30p. Jersey; 50p. Charolais.

308 L. Batlle Berres (1947–51 and 1955–56)

1966. Former Uruguayan Presidents.
1301	**308**	20c. black and red	35	20
1302	-	20c. black and blue	35	20
1303	-	20c. brown and blue	35	20

PRESIDENTS: No. 1302, Daniel Fernandez Crespo (1963–64); 1303, Dr. Washington Beltran (1965–66).

309 Gutenberg Press

1966. 50th Anniv of State Printing Works.
| 1304 | **309** | 20c. sepia, green & brown | 20 | 20 |

310 Capt. Boiso Lanza

1966. Air. Honouring Boiso Lanza (pioneer military aviator).
| 1305 | **310** | 25c. black, blue & ultram | 1·30 | 75 |

311 Fireman

1966. 50th Anniv of Firemen's Corps.
| 1306 | **311** | 20c. black and red | 55 | 30 |

1966. Second River Plate Stamp Exn, Montevideo. (a) Postage. No. 1253 optd **Segunda Muestra y Jornadas Rioplatenses**, etc.
| 1307 | **187** | 40c. green and black | 20 | 20 |

(b) Air. Nos. 1254/8 optd **CENTENARIO DEL SELLO ESCUDITO RESELLADO**, etc.
1308A	1p. blue	35	30
1309A	1p. orange	35	30
1310A	1p. green	35	30
1311A	1p. bistre	35	30
1312A	1p. red	35	30

Nos. 1308/12 commemorate the centenary of Uruguay's first surcharged stamps.

313 General J. A. Lavalleja

1966. Heroes of War of Independence.
1313	**313**	20c. brown, red and blue	35	20
1314	-	20c. blue, black and grey	35	20
1315	-	20c. black and blue	35	20

DESIGNS—VERT: No. 1314, Gen. L. Gomez. HORIZ: 1315, Gen. A. Saravia on horseback.

1966. Air. 40th Anniv of Uruguayan Philatelic Club. No. 1036 surch **40 ANIVERSARIO Club Filatelico del Uruguay $ 1.00 aereo**.
| 1316 | 1p. on 12p. sepia and blue | 35 | 20 |

315 Dante

1966. Air. 700th Birth Anniv (1965) of Dante (writer).
| 1317 | **315** | 50c. brown and sepia | 20 | 20 |

316 Sunflower

1967. 20th Anniv of Young Farmers' Movement.
| 1318 | **316** | 40c. sepia, yellow & brn | 55 | 30 |

317 Planetarium

1967. Tenth Anniv of Montevideo Planetarium.
| 1319 | **317** | 40c. blk & mve (postage) | 55 | 30 |
| 1320 | - | 5p. black and blue (air) | 75 | 45 |

DESIGN: 5p. Planetarium projector.

318 Pres. Makarios

1967. Air. Visit of President of Cyprus.
| 1321 | **318** | 6p.60 black and mauve | 35 | 20 |

319 Dr. Schweitzer

1967. Air. Schweitzer Commemoration.
| 1322 | **319** | 6p. multicoloured | 75 | 75 |

320 Corriedale Ram

1967. Air. Uruguayan Sheep-breeding.
1323	**320**	3p. black, bistre and red	1·90	20
1324	-	4p. black, bistre and green	1·90	20
1325	-	5p. black, bistre and blue	1·90	20
1326	-	10p. black, bistre & yellow	1·90	75

DESIGNS (sheep breeds): 4p. "Ideal"; 5p. Romney Marsh; 10p. Australian merino.

321 Uruguayan Flag and Globe

1967. Air. Heads of State Meeting, Punta del Este.
| 1327 | **321** | 10p. gold, blue and black | 55 | 30 |

322 Church, San Carlos

1967. Bicentenary of San Carlos.
| 1328 | **322** | 40c. black, red and blue | 55 | 30 |

385 "Mother and Son" (statue, E. Prati)

1970. "Homage to Mothers".
1440 **385** 10p. black and green 65 55

386 Flags of Member Countries

1970. Air. Tenth Anniv of Founding of Latin-American Association for Free Trade by the Montevideo Treaty.
1441 **386** 22p. multicoloured 55 30

387 "Stamp" Emblem

1970. "URUEXPO 70" Stamp Exn, Montevideo.
1442 **387** 15p. violet, blue & brown 55 30

388 "Playing Ring-o-Roses" (Ana Gaye)

1970. International Education Year. Children's Drawings. Multicoloured.
1443 10p. Type **388** 35 30
1444 10p. "Two Girls" (Andrea Burca-tovsky) (vert) 35 30
1445 10p. "Boy at Desk" (Humberto Abel Garcia) (vert) 35 30
1446 10p. "Spaceman" (Aquiles Vaxelaire) 35 30

389 Dr. Alfonso Espinola

1971. 125th Birth Anniv (1970) of Dr. Alfonso Espinola (physician and philanthropist).
1447 **389** 5p. black and orange 20 15

391 "Stamps" and Poster

1971. "EFU 71" Stamp Exn, Montevideo.
1449 **391** 15p. multicoloured 35 20

392 5c. Coin of 1840 (obverse)

1971. Numismatics Day.
1450 **392** 25p. black, brown & blue 75 75
1451 – 25p. black, brown & blue 75 75
DESIGN: No. 1451, Reverse of coin showing "Sun" emblem.

393 Dr. Domingo Arena (from caricature by A. Sifredi)

1971. Birth Centenary (1970) of Arena (lawyer and statesman).
1452 **393** 5p. lake 20 10

394 Opening Bars of Anthem

1971. National Anthem Commemoration.
1453 **394** 15p. black, blue and gold 55 30

395 Dr. Jose Arias

1971. First Death Anniv of Dr Jose Arias (statesman).
1454 **395** 5p. brown 20 10

396 "Yellow Fever" (J. M. Blanes)

1971. Air. 70th Death Anniv of Juan Blanes (artist).
1455 **396** 50p. multicoloured 90 55

397 Eduardo Fabini

1971. 21st Death Anniv of Eduardo Fabini (composer).
1456 **397** 5p. black and red 55 20

398 "Two Races"

1971. Air. Racial Equality Year.
1457 **398** 27p. black, pink and gold 55 30

399 Congress Emblem

1971. Air. 12th Pan-American Gastro-enterological Congress, Punta del Este.
1458 **399** 58p. orange, black & grn 75 65

400 J. E. Rodo and U.P.A.E. Emblem

1971. Birth Centenary of Jose E. Rodo (writer and first delegate to U.P.A.E.).
1459 **400** 15p. black and blue 35 20

401 Old Water-cart and Tap

1971. Centenary of Montevideo's Water Supply.
1460 **401** 5p. multicoloured 20 20

402 Sheep and Roll of Cloth

1971. Wool Production.
1461 **402** 5p. green, grey & lt green 20 20
1462 – 15p. grey, violet and blue 35 20
DESIGN: 15p. Sheep, and loading bales of cloth.

403 Dr. Jose Elorza and Sheep

1971. 12th Death Anniv of Dr. Jose Elorza (sheep-breeder).
1463 **403** 5p. black, green and blue 20 20

404 Creole Horse

1971. Uruguayan Horse-breeding.
1464 **404** 5p. black, blue and orange 20 20

405 Bull, Sheep and Ears of Corn

1971. Cent of Uruguayan Rural Association.
1465 **405** 20p. multicoloured 55 30

406 Police Emblem

1971. Honouring Police Heroes.
1466 **406** 10p. blue, black and grey 20 10
1467 – 20p. multicoloured 55 30
DESIGN: 20p. Policeman and flag.

407 1896 10 Peso Banknote (obverse)

1971. 75th Anniv of Uruguayan State Bank.
1468 **407** 25p. green, black and gold 55 55
1469 – 25p. green, black and gold 55 55
DESIGN: No. 1469 Reverse of banknote showing rural scene.

408 Labourer and Arms

1971. 150th Anniv of Town of Durazno.
1470 **408** 20p. multicoloured 35 20

409 Shield and Laurel

1971. Uruguay's Victory in Liberators' Cup Football Championships.
1471 **409** 10p. gold, red and blue 20 20

411 Voter and Ballot-box

1971. General Election.
1473 **411** 10p. black and blue 20 20
1474 – 20p. black and blue 35 30
DESIGN—HORIZ: 20p. Voters in line.

412 C.I.M.E. Emblem and Globe

1971. Air. 20th Anniv of Inter-Governmental Committee for European Migration (C.I.M.E.).
1475 **412** 30p. multicoloured 55 30

413 Exhibition Emblem and Map of Uruguay

1971. "EXPO LITORAL" Industrial Exhibition, Paysandu.
1476 **413** 20p. purple and blue 55 20

414 Juan Lindolfo Cuestas (1897–1903)

1971. Uruguayan Presidents. Each brown and blue.
1477 10p. Type **414** 20 20
1478 10p. J. Herrara y Obes (1890–94) 15 15
1479 10p. Claudio Williman (1907–11) 20 20
1480 10p. Jose Serrato (1923–27) 20 20
1481 10p. Andres Martinez Trueba (1951–55) 20 20

415 Llama Emblem

1971. Air. "EXFILIMA" Stamp Exn, Lima, Peru.
1482 **415** 37p. multicoloured 70 65

416 1858 Mail Coach Stamp Design

1972. Stamp Day (1971). Sheet 99×69 mm. Imperf.
MS1483 **416** 120p. blue 1·10 1·10

417 Olympic Symbols

1972. Air. Olympic Games, Munich (1st issue).

1484	**417**	50p. black, red and yellow	45	20
1485	-	100p. multicoloured	75	55
1486	-	500p. grey, red and blue	4·00	2·75

DESIGNS: 100p. Athlete and torch; 500p. Discus-thrower. See also Nos. 1493/4.

418 Chemical Jar

1972. Air. 50th Anniv of Discovery of Insulin.

1487	**418**	27p. multicoloured	20	20

419 Bartolome Hidalgo

1972. 150th Death Anniv (1973) of Bartolome Hidalgo (Gaucho poet).

1488	**419**	5p. black, red and brown	20	20

420 "Flagship"

1972. Air. American Stamp Day.

1489	**420**	37p. multicoloured	45	30

1972. 15th Anniv of Uruguay–Germany Air Service by Lufthansa. No. MS1403 optd **JUEGOS OLIMPICOS MUNICH 1972/15 ANIVERSARIO VUELO INAUGURAL / LUFTHANSA / Uruguay–Alemania / 1957–15 ABRIL–1972.**

MS1490	60p. blue; 80p. green; 100p. red	35·00	34·00

421 "Face" on Beethoven Score

1972. 12th Eastern Uruguay Choral Festival.

1491	**421**	20p. black, green & purple	20	20

422 Dove supporting Wounded Bird (after Maria Mullin)

1972. Dionisio Diaz (9 year-old hero) Commemoration.

1492	**422**	10p. multicoloured	20	20

423 Footballer and 1928 Gold Medal

1972. Air. Olympic Games, Munich. Multicoloured.

1493	100p. Type **423**	90	85
1494	300p. Olympic flag (vert)	2·40	1·80

424 Columbus Monument, Colon

1972. Centenary of Colon (suburb of Montevideo).

1495	**424**	20p. black, blue and red	55	20

1972. Uruguay's Victory in Intercontinental Football Cup Championships. No. 1471 surch **COPA INTER CONTINENTAL 1971,** football cup and **50.**

1496	**409**	50p. on 10p. gold, red and blue	20	20

426 Sapling and Spade

1972. Tree Planting Campaign.

1497	**426**	20p. black, myrtle & grn	20	20

427 Cross of Remembrance

1972. Air. Second Death Anniv of Dan Mitrione (U.S. police instructor assassinated by terrorists in Uruguay).

1498	**427**	37p. violet and gold	20	20

428 U.N.C.T.A.D. Emblem

1972. Air. Third United Nations Conference on Trade and Development (U.N.C.T.A.D.), Santiago, Chile.

1499	**428**	30p. multicoloured	20	20

429 Brazilian "Bull's-Eye" Stamp of 1843

1972. Air. "EXFILBRA 72" Stamp Exhibition, Rio de Janeiro.

1500	**429**	50p. multicoloured	35	20

430 Compass Rose and Map of South America

1972. Air. Campaign for Extension of Territorial Waters to 200 Mile Limit.

1501	**430**	37p. multicoloured	20	20

431 "Birds' Nests in Tree"

1972. National Building Project for Communal Dwellings.

1502	**431**	10p. multicoloured	20	10

432 Amethyst

1972. Uruguayan Mineralogy. Rocks and Gems

1503	**432**	5p. multicoloured	20	10
1504	-	9p. multicoloured	35	10
1505	-	15p. green, brown & blk	55	30

DESIGNS: 9p. Agate; 15p. Chalcedony.

433 "The Three Holy Kings" (R. Barradas)

1972. Air. Christmas

1506	**433**	20p. multicoloured	55	30

435 Infantry Uniform of 1830

1972. Military Uniforms. Multicoloured.

1509	10p. Type **435**	20	20
1510	20p. Artigas cavalry regiment uniform	45	45

436 Red Cross over Map

1972. 75th Anniv of Uruguayan Red Cross.

1511	**436**	30p. multicoloured	45	45

437 Arms Stamp Design of 1864

1972. Stamp Day. Two sheets, each 100×70 mm containing designs as T **437.** Imperf.

MS1512	(a) 60p. orange; 60p. red; 80p. green (b) 100p. orange; 120p. blue Set of 2 sheets	2·40	2·30

438 Open Book

1972. 25th Anniv of Full Civil Rights for Uruguayan Women.

1513	**438**	10p. gold, blue & lt blue	20	20

439 General Jose Artigas

1972

1514	**439**	5p. yellow	10	10
1515	**439**	10p. brown	10	10
1516	**439**	15p. green	10	10
1517	**439**	20p. lilac	10	10
1518	**439**	30p. blue	10	10
1519	**439**	40p. orange	10	10
1520	**439**	50p. red	10	10
1521	**439**	75p. green	20	10
1522	**439**	100p. green	35	20
1523	**439**	150p. brown	55	20
1524	**439**	200p. blue	75	30
1525	**439**	250p. violet	90	55
1526	**439**	500p. grey	1·70	85
1527	**439**	1000p. blue	3·25	2·10

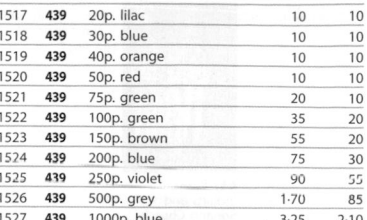

440 Cup and Ear of Wheat on Map

1973. 30th Anniv of Inter-American Institute for Agricultural Sciences.

1531	**440**	30p. black, yellow and red	20	10

441 E. Fernandez and J. P. Varela (founders)

1973. Centenary (1968) of Friends of Popular Education Society.

1532	**441**	10p. black, green & brn	20	20

442 Columbus and Map

1973. American Tourist Year.

1533	**442**	50p. purple	20	20

443 Carlos Ramirez

1973. Eminent Uruguayan Jurists. Each black, brown and bistre.

1534	10p. Type **443**	20	10
1535	10p. Justino Jimenez de Arechaga	20	10
1536	10p. Juan Ramirez	20	10
1537	10p. Justino E. Jimenez de Arechaga	20	10

444 Departmental Map

1973. Uruguayan Departments.

1538	**444**	20p. multicoloured	35	20

See also No. 1844.

1973. 400th Anniv of Cordoba, Argentine Republic. No. MS1342 surch **HOMENA JEAL 4°CENTENARIO DE CORDOBA.ARGENTINA.1973.**

MS1539	**328**	100p. on 5p. blue-green, deep blue and yellow	1·30	1·30

446 Francisco de los Santos and Artigas

1973. Francisco de los Santos (courier) Commem.

1540	**446**	20p. emerald, black and green	35	30

1976. 23rd South American Swimming, Diving and Water-polo Championships, Maldonado.

| 1631 | **503** | 30c. multicoloured | 35 | 20 |

504 Telephone Receiver

1976. Telephone Centenary.

| 1632 | **504** | 83c. multicoloured | 75 | 55 |

505 Dornier Wal Flying Boat "Plus Ultra"

1976. 50th Anniv of "Plus Ultra" Spain–South America Flight.

| 1633 | **505** | 63c. multicoloured | 75 | 55 |

506 Dornier Wal Flying Boat and Airliner rising around Hour-glass

1976. 50th Anniv of Lufthansa Airline.

| 1634 | **506** | 83c. multicoloured | 75 | 55 |

507 Louis Braille and word "Braille"

1976. 150th Anniv of Braille System for the Blind.

| 1635 | **507** | 60c. black and brown | 65 | 55 |

508 Signing of Declaration of Independence

1976. Bicentenary of American Revolution.

| 1636 | **508** | 1p.50 multicoloured | 3·25 | 2·30 |

509 "Candombe" (Pedro Figari)

1976. 150th Anniv of Abolition of Slavery.

| 1637 | **509** | 30c. multicoloured | 55 | 30 |

510 Rivera Monument

1976. Dedication of General Rivera Monument.

| 1638 | **510** | 5p. on 10p. multicoloured | 5·00 | 2·30 |

511 Southern Lapwing

1976

1639	**511**	1c. violet	20	10
1640	-	5c. green	20	10
1641	-	15c. red	20	10
1642	-	20c. black	20	10
1643	-	30c. grey	20	10
1644	-	45c. blue	20	10
1645	-	50c. green	55	20
1646	-	1p. brown	75	30
1646b	-	1p. yellow	20	20
1647	-	1p.75 green	55	20
1648	-	1p.95 grey	55	20
1649	-	2p. green	55	30
1649a	-	2p. mauve	55	55
1650	-	2p.65 violet	55	55
1651	-	5p. blue	2·75	2·75
1651a	-	10p. brown	8·25	2·75

DESIGNS—VERT: 5c. Passion flower; 15c. National flower; 20c. Indian lance-head; 30c. Indian statue; 45c., 1p. (No. 1646b), 1p.75, 1p.95, 2p. (both), 2p.65, 5, 10p., Artigas; 1p. (No. 1646), "At Dawn" (J. M. Blanes). HORIZ: 50c. "Branding Cattle" (J. M. Blanes).

513 Office Building and Reverse of First Uruguayan Coin of 1840

1976. 150th Anniv of State Accounting Office.

| 1652 | **513** | 30c. black, brown & blue | 35 | 20 |

514 Hand-pump within Flames

1976. Centenary of Fire Service.

| 1653 | **514** | 20c. black and red | 20 | 20 |

515 Uruguay 60c. Stamp of 1856 and "Commemorative Postmark"

1976. 50th Anniv of Uruguay Philatelic Club.

| 1654 | **515** | 30c. red, blue and bistre | 35 | 20 |

516 Championship Emblem

1976. Fifth World Universities' Football Championships, Montevideo.

| 1655 | **516** | 83c. multicoloured | 1·30 | 75 |

517 Human Eye and Spectrum

1976. Prevention of Blindness.

| 1656 | **517** | 20c. multicoloured | 55 | 20 |

518 Map of Montevideo

1976. 250th Anniv of Montevideo. Multicoloured.

1657	30c. Type **518**		20	10
1658	45c. Montevideo panorama, 1842		35	20
1659	70c. First settlers, 1726		55	30
1660	80c. Montevideo coin (vert)		90	30
1661	1p.15 Montevideo's first arms (vert)		1·30	65

519 "VARIG" Emblem

1977. 50th Anniv of VARIG Airline.

| 1662 | **519** | 80c. multicoloured | 90 | 85 |

520 Artigas Mausoleum

1977. Mausoleum of General Jose Artigas.

| 1663 | **520** | 45c. multicoloured | 55 | 20 |

521 Arch on Map

1977. Cent of Salesian Education in Uruguay.

| 1664 | **521** | 45c. multicoloured | 55 | 20 |

522 Globe and Emblems

1977. Air. 150th Anniv of Uruguayan Postal Services.

| 1665 | **522** | 8p. multicoloured | 14·50 | 14·00 |

523 Children

1977. 50th Anniv of Inter-American Children's Institute.

| 1667 | **523** | 45c. multicoloured | 65 | 65 |

524 "Windmills"

1977. Hispanidad Day.

| 1668 | **524** | 70c. red, yellow and black | 55 | 20 |

525 Sun on "Stamp" and Stripes of Uruguayan Flag

1977. Stamp Day.

| 1669 | **525** | 45c. multicoloured | 20 | 10 |

526 "Sans" (R. P. Barradas) (left-hand section of painting)

1977. Espamer 77 International Stamp Exhibition, Barcelona. Sheet 109×85 mm containing T **526** and similar vert design, forming a composite design. Multicoloured.

| MS1669 | 5p. Type **526**; 5p. Right-hand section of painting | | 7·25 | 7·00 |

527 Globe and Aircraft

1977. 30th Anniv of International Civil Aviation Organization.

| 1670 | **527** | 45c. multicoloured | 20 | 20 |

528 "The Holy Family"

1977. Christmas.

| 1671 | **528** | 45c. multicoloured | 20 | 20 |
| 1672 | - | 70c. red, yellow and black | 35 | 20 |

DESIGN—HORIZ: (45×26 mm): 70c. "Santa Claus".

529 Arms, Map and Products

1977. Rio Negro Department.

| 1673 | **529** | 45c. multicoloured | 20 | 20 |

530 Postman clearing Mail-box

1977. 150th Anniv of National Mail Service. Multicoloured.

1674	50c. Type **530**		20	20
1675	50c. Loading mail-van		20	20
1676	50c. Post Office counter, Montevideo G.P.O		20	20
1677	50c. Post-boxes area		20	20
1678	50c. Sorting mail		20	20
1679	50c. Postal sorters		20	20
1680	50c. Postmen sorting "walks"		20	20
1681	50c. Postman on rounds		20	20
1682	50c. Postmen on motor-scooters		20	20
1683	50c. Postal counter, Carrasco Airport		20	20

531 Edison's First "Phonograph"

1977. Centenary of Sound Recording.

| 1684 | **531** | 50c. purple and yellow | 20 | 20 |

532 "R" and Spectrum

1977. World Rheumatism Year.
1685 **532** 50c. multicoloured 20 20

533 Emblem, Diploma, Sword and Flag

1978. 50th Anniv of Military College.
1686 **533** 50c. multicoloured 20 20

534 Arms and Map

1978. Department of Artigas.
1687 **534** 45c. multicoloured 55 20

535 "Papilio thoas"

1978. Urexpo 78 National Stamp Exhibition. Sheet 96×106 mm containing T **535** and similar horiz designs. Multicoloured.
MS1688 2p. Type **535**; 4p. Flag (Centenary of Parva Domus social club); 4p. Commemorative coins (World Cup Football Championship, Argentina); 5p. Model "T" Ford (75th Anniv of Ford Motor Company) 19·00 18·00

1978. Air. "Riccione" and "Europhil 78" Stamp Exhibitions, Italy and Urphila Stamp Exhibition, Uruguay. Optd **EUROPA 1978 ITALIA Riccione 78 urphila 78.**
1689 **522** 8p. multicoloured 8·25 3·75

537 "Wandering Angels" (detail)

1978. National Artists. Luis A. Solari. Multicoloured.
1690 1p.50 Type **537** 55 30
1691 1p.50 "Wandering Angels" (horiz 38×30 mm) 55 30
1692 1p.50 "Wandering Angels" (detail) 55 30

538 Bernardo O'Higgins

1978. Birth Bicentenary of Bernardo O'Higgins (national hero of Chile).
1693 **538** 1p. multicoloured 35 20

539 Telephone Dials and "Antel" Emblem

1978. Telephone Automation.
1694 **539** 50c. multicoloured 20 20

1978. Birth Bicentenary of General Jose de San Martin.
1695 **540** 1p. multicoloured 35 20

541 Spanish Tiles

1978. Hispanidad.
1696 **541** 1p. blue, yellow and black 35 20

542 Corners of "Stamps"

1978. Stamp Day.
1697 **542** 50c. multicoloured 20 20

543 Boeing 727 in Flight

1978. PLUNA Airline Inaugural Boeing 727 Flight.
1698 **543** 50c. multicoloured 75 20

544 Angel blowing Trumpet

1978. Christmas.
1699 **544** 50c. green, orange & black 20 20
1700 **544** 1p. blue, red and black 55 20

545 Flag Monument, Montevideo

1978. Homage to the National Flag.
1701 **545** 1p. multicoloured 35 20

546 Horacio Quiroga

1978. Birth Centenary of Horacio Quiroga (playwright).
1702 **546** 1p. black, yellow and red 35 20

547 Arms and Map of Paysandu

1979. Department of Paysandu.
1703 **547** 45c. multicoloured 20 20

548 Olympic Rings and Ciudadela

1979. Olympic Games, Moscow (1980) and Winter Olympics, Lake Placid (1980). Multicoloured.
1704 **548** 5p. Type **548** 2·40 1·30
1705 7p. Lake Placid emblem 2·75 1·40
See also Nos. 1728/9.

549 Arms and Map of Salto

1979. Department of Salto.
1706 **549** 45c. multicoloured 20 20

550 Artilleryman, 1830

1979. Uruguayan Military Uniforms. Multicoloured.
1707 **550** 5p. Type **550** 1·90 85
1708 5p. Sapper, 1837 1·90 85

551 Arms and Map of Maldonado

1979. Department of Maldonado.
1709 **551** 45c. multicoloured 20 20

552 Salto Grande Dam

1979. Salto Grande Dam.
1710 **552** 2p. multicoloured 75 30

553 Centenary Symbol and Branch

1979. Centenary of Crandon Uruguayan–American High School.
1711 **553** 1p. blue and violet 20 20

554 Kites

1979. International Year of the Child (1st issue).
1712 **554** 2p. multicoloured 55 30
See also Nos. 1715, 1718 amd 1720.

555 Arms and Map of Cerro Largo

1979. Department of Cerro Largo.
1713 **555** 45c. multicoloured 20 10

556 Arms and Map of Trienta y Tres

1979. Department of Trienta y Tres.
1714 **556** 50c. multicoloured 20 20

557 Cinderella

1979. International Year of the Child (2nd issue).
1715 **557** 2p. multicoloured 55 30

558 National Coat of Arms

1979. 150th Anniv of First National Coat of Arms.
1716 **558** 8p. multicoloured 3·50 2·10

559 U.P.U. Emblem and Arrow

1979. 18th U.P.U. Congress, Rio de Janeiro.
1717 **559** 5p. multicoloured 1·40 1·10

560 "Chico Carlo" (Juana de Ibarbourou)

1979. International Year of the Child (3rd issue).
1718 **560** 1p. multicoloured 55 20

561 Drawing by J. M. Torres-Garcia

1979. 31st Death Anniv of Joaquin Torres-Garcia (artist).
1719 **561** 10p. yellow and black 4·00 2·30

562 Madonna and Child

1979. Christmas and International Year of the Child (4th issue).
1720 **562** 10p. multicoloured 2·75 1·60

563 Arms and Map of Durazno

619 Fabini

1983. Birth Centenary of Edouardo Fabini (composer).
1812	619	3p. deep brown & brown	90	30

620 2nd Cavalry
Regiment, 1885

1983. Army Day. Multicoloured.
1813		3p. Type **620**	90	30
1814		3p. Military College, 1885	90	30

621 "Santa Maria"
on Globe

1983. Visit of King and Queen of Spain. Multicoloured.
1815		3p. Type **621**	1·10	55
1816		7p. Royal couple and Uruguayan and Spanish flags (44×31 mm)	2·40	1·10

622 Headquarters
Building

1983. Inauguration of Postal Union of the Americas and Spain H.Q., Montevideo.
1817	622	3p. black, blue and brown	75	20

623 Exhibition
Emblem

1983. "Brasiliana 83" International Stamp Exhibition, Rio de Janeiro.
1818	623	3p. multicoloured	75	20

624 Space Shuttle
"Columbia"

1983. First Flight of Space Shuttle "Columbia".
1819	624	7p. multicoloured	1·70	75

625 "Delin 1900"
Car

1983. First Imported Car.
1820	625	3p. blue and black	75	20

626 Goethe and Scene
from "Faust"

1983. 150th Death Anniv (1982) of Johann Wolfgang von Goethe (writer).
1821	626	7p. blue and black	1·70	75

627 "Moonlit
Landscape"

1983. Sixth Death Anniv of Jose Cuneo (artist).
1822	627	3p. multicoloured	1·10	30

628 Statue of
Lavelleja

1983. Bicentenary of Minas City.
1823	628	3p. multicoloured	1·10	20

629 W.C.Y. Emblem

1983. World Communications Year.
1824	629	3p. multicoloured	45	20

630 Garibaldi

1983. Death Centenary (1982) of Guiseppe Garibaldi (Italian revolutionary).
1825	630	7p. multicoloured	1·20	55

631 "Graf Zeppelin"

1983. Zeppelin Flight over Montevideo (1934).
1826	631	7p. black, blue and mauve	2·20	75

632 Footballers, World Cup
and Italian Team Badge

1983. Italy's Victory in World Cup Football Championship (1982).
1827	632	7p. multicoloured	1·70	75

633 Virgin, Child and Star

1983. Christmas.
1828	633	4p.50 multicoloured	90	20

634 "50" on Telephone Dial

1984. 50th Anniv of Automatic Telephone Dialling.
1829	634	4p.50 multicoloured	75	20

635 Leandro
Gomez

1984. General Leandro Gomez Commemoration.
1830	635	4p.50 blue, light blue and black	65	30

636 Emblem,
Map, Flag and
Tanker

1984. 25th Anniv (1983) of International Maritime Organization.
1831	636	4p.50 multicoloured	65	30

637 Flags and
Emblem

1984. American Women's Day.
1832	637	4p.50 multicoloured	65	30

638 Map of Uruguay
and Bank Emblem

1984. 25th Annual Meeting of Governors of International Development Bank, Punta del Este.
1833	638	10p. blue, gold and black	1·70	75

639 Simon Bolivar

1984. Birth Bicentenary (1983) of Simon Bolivar.
1834	639	4p.50 lt brown & brown	1·70	55

640 Club Emblem and
Radio Waves

1984. 50th Anniv (1983) of Uruguay Radio Club.
1835	640	7p. multicoloured	1·10	55

641 Monument

1984. 1930 World Cup Football Championship Monument.
1836	641	4p.50 multicoloured	65	30

642 National Emblem
wlthin "200"

1984. Bicentenary (1983) of San Jose de Mayo.
1837	642	4p.50 multicoloured	65	30

643 Emblem

1984. 50th Anniv of Tourist Organization.
1838	643	4p.50 gold, violet and blue	65	30

644 Artillery
Uniform, 1895

1984. Army Day. Multicoloured.
1839		4p.50 Type **644**	65	20
1840		4p.50 2nd Battalion Cazadores uniform, 1894	65	20

645 Artigas on
Horseback

1984
1841	645	4p.50 black and blue	65	30
1842	645	8p.50 brown and blue	1·30	65

646 Trophy

1984. Penarol Athletic Club. Winners of European–South American Football Cup, 1982.
1843	646	4p.50 black, yellow and deep yellow	75	30

1984. Uruguayan Departments.
1844	444	4p.50 multicoloured	75	30

647 Child holding Flower
and "50 ANOS"

1984. 50th Anniv of Children's Council.
1845	647	4p.50 multicoloured	65	30

648 Christmas Tree with Candles

1984. Christmas.
1846   **648**   6p. multicoloured   90   45

649 Pelota Player and Flags

1985. First Junior Pelota World Championship.
1847   **649**   4p.50 multicoloured   65   30

650 Bruno Mauricio de Zabala

1985. 300th Birth Anniv (1983) of Don Bruno Mauricio de Zabala (Governor of Buenos Aires and founder of Montevideo).
1848   **650**   4p.50 multicoloured   55   20

651 Emblems of Los Angeles and Sarajevo Games and Olympic Rings

1985. 90th Anniv of International Olympic Committee.
1849   **651**   12p. multicoloured   1·30   65

652 Carlos Gardel

1985. 50th Death Anniv of Carlos Gardel (entertainer).
1850   **652**   6p. grey, blue and brown   55   20

653 Emblem and Flags of Member States

1985. 25th Anniv of American Air Forces' Co-operation System.
1851   **653**   12p. multicoloured   55   20

654 Icarus

1985. 40th Anniv of I.C.A.O.
1852   **654**   4p.50 deep blue, green and blue   35   20

655 Stylized Factory and "50"

1985. 50th Anniv of FUNSA Tyre Factory.
1853   **655**   6p. multicoloured   35   20

656 Cross and Clasped Hands

1985. Centenary of Catholic Workers Circle.
1854   **656**   6p. multicoloured   20   20

657 I.Y.Y. Emblem

1985. International Youth Year.
1855   **657**   12p. red and black   55   20

658 Peace Dove and Sun

1985. "Return to Democracy".
1856   **658**   20p. blue, yellow and violet   1·10   55

659 Books forming "8"

1985. Eighth International Book Exhibition.
1857   **659**   20p. multicoloured   1·10   55

660 Emblem

1985. Centenary of Military School.
1858   **660**   10p. multicoloured   55   20

661 Map and Arms

1985. Centenary of Flores Department.
1859   **661**   6p. multicoloured   20   20

662 Father Christmas

1985. Christmas.
1860   **662**   10p. multicoloured   55   20
1861   **662**   22p. multicoloured   90   55

663 Monument to Isabel the Catholic

1985. Hispanidad Day.
1862   **663**   12p. black, red and brown   55   20

664 Emblem and Meeting Logo

1986. Third Inter-American Agriculture Co-operation Institute Meeting.
1863   **664**   12p. yellow, red and black   55   20

665 Emblem and Flag

1986. World Post Day.
1864   **665**   15p.50 multicoloured   75   45

666 Map and Symbolic House

1986. Sixth Population and Fourth Housing Census (1985).
1865   **666**   10p. black, blue and yellow   45   20

667 Emblem

1986. 50th Anniv (1985) of Conaprole Milk and Cattle Co-operative.
1866   **667**   10p. gold, blue and light blue   45   20

668 U.N. Emblem and Population Diagram

1986. 40th Anniv (1985) of U.N.O.
1867   **668**   20p. multicoloured   75   30

669 Emblem

1986. 50th Anniv (1985) of National Brokers and Auctioneers Association.
1868   **669**   10p. black, deep blue and blue   20   20

670 Manuel Oribe

1986. Liberation Heroes.
1869   **670**   1p. green (postage)   20   20
1870   **670**   2p. red   20   10
1871   **A**   3p. blue   20   10
1872   **A**   5p. blue   20   10

No.	Type	Description		
1872a	670	5p. blue	10	10
1873	670	7p. brown	20	20
1874	B	10p. mauve	35	30
1875	C	10p. green	20	20
1875a	670	10p. green	20	10
1876	670	15p. blue	20	10
1877	B	17p. blue	35	20
1877a	670	20p. brown	20	10
1877b	A	25p. orange	55	20
1878	B	26p. brown	55	20
1879	C	30p. orange	55	30
1879a	A	30p. blue	55	30
1879b	B	45p. red	55	20
1880	C	50p. ochre	1·10	75
1880a	B	50p. mauve	90	75
1881	C	60p. grey	1·30	75
1881a	A	60p. orange	20	10
1881b	B	60p. mauve	65	45
1881c	B	75p. red	55	30
1881d	B	90p. red	1·10	55
1882	C	100p. red	1·90	1·10
1882a	B	100p. brown	1·90	1·10
1882b	C	150p. green	1·00	65
1883	C	200p. green	2·75	1·30
1883a	C	300p. blue	1·80	1·40
1883b	C	500p. red	2·75	1·30
1883c	C	1000p. red	6·00	3·75
1884	B	22p. violet (air)	55	20

DESIGNS: A, Lavalleja; B, Jose Fructuoso Rivera; C, Jose Gervasio Artigas.

671 Mosaic in National Colours

1986. Italian Chamber of Commerce in Uruguay.
1885   **671**   20p. multicoloured   55   20

672 Armenian Flag and Monument

1986. 71st Anniv of Armenian Genocide.
1886   **672**   10p. black, red and blue   20   20

673 Emblem and Footballer

1986. World Cup Football Championship, Mexico.
1887   **673**   20p. multicoloured   75   45

674 Newspaper Page

1986. Centenary of "El Dia".
1888   **674**   10p. gold, black and red   20   20

675 Alan Garcia

1986. Visit of President of Peru.
1889   **675**   20p. brown, red and blue   55   20

676 Map, Gen. Sucre and Simon Bolivar

1986. Visit of Pres. Jaime Lusinchi of Venezuela.
1890　676　20p. multicoloured　　75　30

677 Jose Sarney

1986. Visit of President of Brazil.
1891　677　20p. multicoloured　　55　20

678 Michelini

1986. Tenth Death Anniv of Zelmar Michelini (senator).
1892　678　10p. blue and red　　20　20

679 Menorah and "50"

1986. 50th Anniv of B'nai B'rith in Uruguay.
1893　679　10p. brown, gold and red　　35　20

680 Handshake across "GATT"

1986. General Agreement on Tariffs and Trade Assembly, Punta del Este.
1894　680　10p. multicoloured　　20　20

681 Dr. Raul Alfonsin

1986. Visit of President of Argentina.
1895　681　20p. orange, black & blue　　55　20

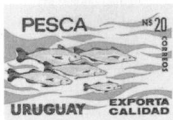

682 Fishes in Sea

1986. Quality Exports. Multicoloured.
1896　20p. Type **682**　　55　20
1897　20p. Lambs　　55　20

683 Flags and Dr. Blanco

1986. Visit of Dr. Salvador Jorge Blanco, President of Dominican Republic.
1898　683　20p. multicoloured　　35　20

684 Dr. Pertini

1986. Visit of Dr. Sandro Pertini, President of Italy.
1899　684　20p. yellow and green　　35　30

685 Douglas DC-10 and DC-3 Aircraft and Flags

1986. 40th Anniv of First Scheduled Spain-Uruguay Flight.
1900　685　20p. multicoloured　　55　20

686 Statue of Sts. Philip and John and Montevideo Cathedral

1987. Hispanidad Day.
1901　686　10p. red and black　　20　20

687 Emblem

1987. 50th Anniv (1986) of Juventus Catholic Cultural Organization.
1902　687　10p. yellow, black and blue　　20　20

688 Ruiz

1987. Tenth Death Anniv (1986) of Hector Gutierrez Ruiz (Chamber of Deputies member).
1903　688　10p. brown and red　　20　20

689 Emblem

1987. International Science and Technology Symposium, Montevideo and Punta del Este (1986).
1904　689　20p. multicoloured　　35　30

690 "Arrowhead" of Flying Doves

1987. Visit of Pope John Paul II.
1905　690　50p. orange and grey　　1·10　55

691 Dr. Arias and Emblem

1987. Birth Centenary of Dr. Jose F. Arias (founder of Uruguay Trades University).
1906　691　10p. multicoloured　　20　20

692 "70" and Menorah

1987. 70th Anniv of Uruguayan Jewish Community.
1907　692　10p. blue, orange & black　　35　20

693 De Havilland Dragon Fly

1987. 50th Anniv (1986) of Pluna National Airline. Multicoloured.
1908　10p. Type **693**　　20　10
1909　20p. Douglas DC-3　　35　20
1910　25p. Vickers Viscount 810　　55　20
1911　30p. Boeing 707　　75　30

694 Artigas Antarctic Base

1987
1912　694　20p. multicoloured　　35　20

695 Sun, Symbolic House and "75"

1987. 75th Anniv of Uruguayan Mortgage Bank.
1913　695　26p. multicoloured　　55　20

696 Dairy Products

1987. Uruguayan Quality Exports. Multicoloured.
1914　51p. Type **696**　　90　55
1915　51p. Map and cattle　　90　55

697 "Holy Family"

1987. Christmas. Stained Glass Windows. Multicoloured.
1916　17p. Type **697**　　55　20
1917　66p. "Angels"　　1·10　65

698 Pres. Duarte

1988. Visit of Pres. Jose Napoleon Duarte of El Salvador.
1918　698　20p. blue and yellow　　35　20

699 Airplane and Globe forming "60"

1988. 60th Anniv (1987) of VARIG (airline).
1919　699　66p. blue, yellow & black　　1·20　1·10

700 Emblem and Globe

1988. International Peace Year (1986).
1920　700　10p. multicoloured　　20　10

701 Flags and Beret

1988. 75th Anniv (1987) of Basque Immigration.
1921　701　66p. multicoloured　　90　55

702 Farman "Shorthorn" within Airplane Wing

1988. 75th Anniv of Air Force.
1922　702　17p. multicoloured　　35　20

703 Lantern and "75"

1988. 75th Anniv (1987) of UTE (hydro-electric dam programme).
1923　703　17p. multicoloured　　20　10
1924　-　17p. black, blue and green　　20　10
1925　-　51p. black and blue　　75　30
1926　-　51p. black, blue and red　　75　30
1927　-　66p. blue, black & yellow　　1·10　55

DESIGNS: No. 1924, Baygorria Dam; 1925, Dr. Gabriel Terra Dam; 1926, Constitucion Dam; 1927, Map showing dam sites on River Negro.

704 Flag and Globe

1988. 75th Anniv (1986) of Postal Union of the Americas and Spain.
1928　704　66p. multicoloured　　90　55

705 Menorah in "40"

1988. 40th Anniv of Israel.
1929　705　66p. blue and black　　90　55

706 Airmail Envelope and Postman

1988. "Post, Messenger of Peace".
1930　706　66p. multicoloured　　90　55

707 Emblem on Map

1988. 60th Anniv of Inter-American Institute for the Child.
| 1931 | **707** | 30p. lt green, green & blk | 55 | 20 |

708 Matos Rodriguez

1988. Gerardo H. Matos Rodriguez (composer) Commemoration.
| 1932 | **708** | 17p. black and violet | 55 | 20 |
| 1933 | - | 51p. brown on lt brown | 1·70 | 75 |

DESIGN: 51p. Matos Rodriguez and score of "La Cumparsita".

709 Col. Pablo Banales (founder)

1988. Centenary (1987) of Fire Service. Multicoloured.
1934	**709**	17p. Type **709**	35	20
1935		26p. Fireman, 1900	45	30
1936		34p. Emblem (horiz)	55	45
1937		51p. Merryweather fire engine, 1907 (horiz)	90	65
1938		66p. 8-man hand pump, 1888 (horiz)	1·30	85
1939		100p. Magirus mechanical ladder, 1921 (44×25 mm)	2·00	1·50

710 Route Map and "Capitan Miranda"

1988. First World Voyage of "Capitan Miranda".
| 1940 | **710** | 30p. multicoloured | 55 | 20 |

711 Citrus Fruits

1988. Exports. Multicoloured.
1941	**711**	30p. Type **711**	35	20
1942		45p. Rice	65	30
1943		55p. Shoes	75	30
1944		55p. Clothes	75	30

712 "Toxodon platensis" (mammal bone)

1988. 150th Anniv of National Natural History Museum, Montevideo.
| 1945 | - | 30p. brown, yellow & blk | 55 | 30 |
| 1946 | **712** | 90p. brown, blue & black | 1·30 | 75 |

DESIGN: 30p. "Usnea densirostra" (moss).

713 Bird posting Letter

1988. Postal Officers' Day. Unissued stamp surch.
| 1947 | **713** | 30p. on 10p.+5p. yellow, black and blue | 35 | 20 |

714 Abstract

1988. 150th Anniv (1986) of Battle of Carpinteria.
| 1948 | **714** | 30p. multicoloured | 35 | 20 |

715 Virgin and Child

1988. Christmas.
| 1949 | **715** | 115p. multicoloured | 1·30 | 1·30 |

716 "Self-portrait" (Joaquin Torres Garcia)

1988. Uruguayan Painters. Multicoloured.
1950	**716**	115p. Type **716**	1·30	75
1951		115p. Poster for Pedro Figari exhibition, Montevideo	1·30	75
1952		115p. "Squares and Rectangles LXXVIII" (Jose P. Costigliolo)	1·30	75
1953		115p. "Manolita Pina, 1920" (Joaquin Torres Garcia)	1·30	75

717 "Santa Maria"

1989. Hispanidad Day.
| 1954 | **717** | 90p. multicoloured | 90 | 55 |
| 1955 | | 115p. multicoloured | 1·30 | 65 |

718 Emblem

1989. Cent of Armenian Organization Hnchakian.
| 1956 | **718** | 210p. blue, yellow and red | 1·90 | 75 |

719 Plumb Line suspended on Frame

1989. Bicentenary of French Revolution. Each black, red and blue.
1957	**719**	50p. Type **719**	35	20
1958		50p. Tree of Liberty	35	20
1959		210p. Eye in centre of sunburst	1·70	75
1960		210p. "Liberty", "Equality", "Fraternity" around phrygian cap	1·70	75

720 Map

1989. "Use the Post Code". Each black and red.
| 1961 | **720** | 50p. Type **720** | 35 | 10 |
| 1962 | | 210p. Map showing numbered zones (vert) | 1·40 | 55 |

721 Map, Cow, Factory and Baby

1989. Third Pan-American Milk Congress.
| 1963 | **721** | 170p. deep blue and blue | 1·30 | 55 |

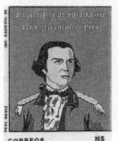

722 "Tiradentes"

1989. Birth Bicentenary of Joaquin Jose da Silver Xavier.
| 1964 | **722** | 170p. multicoloured | 1·10 | 30 |

723 Emblem and Flag

1989. Interparliamentary Union Centenary Conference, London.
| 1965 | **723** | 210p. red, blue and black | 1·30 | 55 |

724 F.A.O. Emblem, Map and Fruit Slices

1989. Eighth Intergovernmental Group on Citrus Fruits Meeting.
| 1966 | **724** | 180p. multicoloured | 1·10 | 55 |

725 Flower, Hand and Emblem

1989. U.N. Decade for Disabled People. Multicoloured.
| 1967 | **725** | 50p. Type **725** | 35 | 10 |
| 1968 | | 210p. Disabled people and emblem | 1·30 | 55 |

726 Nacurutu Artefact

1989. America. Pre-Columbian Culture.
| 1969 | **726** | 60p. multicoloured | 75 | 20 |
| 1970 | **726** | 180p. multicoloured | 2·00 | 75 |

727 Virgin of the Thirty Three

1989. Christmas. Multicoloured.
| 1971 | **727** | 70p. Type **727** | 55 | 20 |
| 1972 | | 210p. "Adoration of the Animals" (Barradas) (horiz) | 1·70 | 75 |

728 Old and Modern Buildings

1989. Bicentenary of Pando.
| 1973 | **728** | 60p. multicoloured | 35 | 20 |

729 Hospital Building

1990. Bicentenary of Charity Hospital.
| 1974 | **729** | 60p. flesh, black & brown | 1·00 | 95 |

730 Map and Arms of Soriano

1990. Departments. Multicoloured.
1975	**730**	70p. Type **730**	45	45
1976		70p. Florida (vert)	55	55
1977		90p. San Jose (vert)	65	65
1978		90p. Canelones	65	65
1979		90p. Lavalleja (vert)	65	65
1980		90p. Rivera	65	65

731 Luisa Luisi

1990. Writers. Multicoloured.
1981	**731**	60p. Type **731**	35	30
1982		60p. Javier de Viana	35	30
1983		75p. J. Zorilla de San Martin	45	35
1984		75p. Dekmira Agustini	45	35
1985		170p. Julio Casal	1·00	95
1986		170p. Alfonsina Storni	1·00	95
1987		210p. Juana de Ibarbourou	1·30	1·30
1988		210p. Carlos Roxlo	1·30	1·30

732 Mercedes Church

1990. Bicentenary of Mercedes.
| 1989 | **732** | 70p. multicoloured | 55 | 55 |

733 Ear of Wheat and Tractor

1990. Tenth Anniv of International Agricultural Fund.
1990	**733**	210p. multicoloured	1·70	1·60

734 Glass and Smashed Car

1990. Road Safety. Multicoloured.
1991		70p. Type **734**	45	45
1992		70p. Traffic waiting at red light	45	45
1993		70p. Road signs	45	45
1994		70p. Children crossing road at green light	45	45

735 Sculpture of Artigas

1990. Artigas Day.
1995	**735**	60p. blue and red	55	55

736 Woman

1990. International Women's Day.
1996	**736**	70p. multicoloured	45	45

737 Gonzalo Ramirez

1990. Centenary of First International Juridical Congress, Montevideo.
1997	**737**	60p. black, yellow & mve	50	45
1998	-	60p. black, blue & mauve	50	45
1999	-	60p. multicoloured	50	45
2000	-	60p. multicoloured	50	45

DESIGNS: No. 1998, Ildefonso Garcia; 1999, Flags and left half of 50th anniversary memorial; 2000, Flags and right half of memorial.

738 Microphone and Radio Mast

1990. The Media. Multicoloured.
2001		70p. Type **738**	65	60
2002		70p. Newpaper vendor	65	60
2003		70p. Television screen, camera and aerial	65	60
2004		70p. Books and type	65	60

739 Burning Trees

1990. Fire Prevention.
2005	**739**	70p. black, yellow and red	2·40	2·10

740 American Deer

1990. America. The Natural World. Multicoloured.
2006		120p. Type **740**	1·00	90
2007		360p. "Peltophorum dubium" (vert)	2·75	2·40

741 "Nativity" (Juan B. Maino)

1990. Christmas.
2008	**741**	170p. multicoloured	1·40	1·20
2009	**741**	830p. multicoloured	7·00	6·00

742 Carlos Federico Saez

1990. Artists. Multicoloured.
2010		90p. Type **742**	75	65
2011		90p. Pedro Blanes Viale	75	65
2012		210p. Edmundo Prati	1·90	1·70
2013		210p. Jose L. Zorrilla de San Martin	1·90	1·70

743 Mechanical Digger

1991. 75th Anniv of Army Engineers Division.
2014	**743**	170p. multicoloured	1·40	1·20

744 Drum and Masks

1991. Carnival.
2015	**744**	170p. multicoloured	1·40	1·20

745 Campaign Emblem

1991. Campaign against AIDS.
2016	**745**	170p. multicoloured	1·40	1·20
2017	**745**	830p. multicoloured	7·00	6·00

746 Anniversary Emblem

1991. Centenary of Organization of American States.
2018	**746**	830p. yellow, blue & blk	7·00	6·00

747 Textiles

1991. Uruguayan Quality Exports. Multicoloured.
2019		120p. Type **747**	50	45
2020		120p. Clothes (vert)	65	20

2021		400p. Semi-precious stones and granite	1·90	1·70

748 Flint Axe and Stone Monument

1991. Education. Multicoloured.
2022		120p. Type **748**	50	45
2023		120p. Wheel and pyramids	50	45
2024		330p. Printing press and diagram of planetary orbits	1·50	1·30
2025		330p. Space probe and computer diagram	1·50	1·30

749 Sword piercing Crab

1991. Anti-cancer Day.
2026	**749**	360p. red and black	1·50	1·30

750 College Arms

1991. Centenary of Holy Family College.
2027	**750**	360p. multicoloured	1·50	1·30

751 College Building

1991. Centenary of Immaculate Heart of Mary College.
2028	**751**	1370p. multicoloured	5·75	5·00

752 Emblem

1991. Seventh Pan-American Maccabiah Games.
2029	**752**	1490p. multicoloured	5·75	5·00

753 World Map and Dornier Wal Flying Boat "Plus Ultra"

1991. "Espamer '91" Spain–Latin America Stamp Exhibition, Buenos Aires.
2030	**753**	1510p. multicoloured	7·00	6·00

754 "Oath of the Constitution" (P. Blanes Viale)

1991. 1830 Constitution.
2031	**754**	360p. multicoloured	1·50	1·30

755 Gateway, Sacramento

1991
2032	**755**	360p. brown and yellow	1·50	90
2033	-	540p. grey and blue	2·10	1·30
2034	**755**	600p. brown, yellow & blk	1·50	1·20
2035	-	825p. grey, blue and black	2·10	1·70
2036	-	1510p. brown and green	7·00	4·00
2037	-	2500p. brown, grn & blk	5·75	4·50

DESIGNS: 540, 825p. First locomotive in Uruguay, 1869; 1510, 2500p. Horse tram.
For 800p. as Type **755** see No. 2103.

756 "William Tell" (statue) and Flags

1991. 700th Anniv of Swiss Confederation.
2038	**756**	1510p. multicoloured	8·75	7·75
MS2039	**756**	3000p. multicoloured	18·00	18·00

757 Yacht

1991. Whitbread Regatta.
2040	**757**	1510p. multicoloured	5·75	5·00

758 Emblem

1991. 50th Anniv of Uruguayan Society of Actors.
2041	**758**	450p. black and red	1·80	1·50

759 Camera and Photograph

1991. 150th Anniv of First Photograph in Rio de la Plata.
2042	**759**	1370p. multicoloured	5·25	4·75

760 Anniversary Emblem

1991. 25th Anniv of CREA (livestock organization).
2043	**760**	450p. multicoloured	1·80	1·50

761 Margarita Xirgu

1991. 22nd Death Anniv of Margarita Xirgu (actress).
2044	**761**	360p. brown, light brown and yellow	1·40	1·20

762 "General Rivera" (gunboat)

1991. Centre for Study of Naval and Maritime History. Multicoloured.

2045	**762**	450p. Type **762**	1·80	1·50
2046		450p. "Salto" (coastguard patrol boat)	1·80	1·50
2047		1570p. "Uruguay" (cruiser)	5·25	4·75
2048		1570p. "Pte. Oribe" (tanker)	5·25	4·75

763 "Rio de la Plata, 1602" (woodcut)

1991. America. Voyages of Discovery.

2049	**763**	450p. brown and yellow	1·80	1·50
2050	-	1740p. green and brown	6·25	5·50

DESIGN—HORIZ: 1740p. Amerigo Vespucci.

764 "The Tree is the Fountain of Life"

1991. World Food Day.

2051	**764**	1740p. multicoloured	5·75	5·00

765 "The Table" (Zoma Baitler)

1991

2052	**765**	360p. multicoloured	1·40	1·20

766 Gladiator, 1902

1991. Old Cars. Multicoloured.

2053		360p. Type **766**	1·40	1·20
2054		1370p. E.M.F., 1909	5·25	4·75
2055		1490p. Renault, 1912	5·25	4·75
2056		1510p. Clement-Bayard, 1903 (vert)	5·75	5·00

767 Emblem

1991. 60th General Assembly of Interpol, Punta del Este.

2057	**767**	1740p. multicoloured	5·75	5·00

768 Club Badge and Trophy

1991. National Football Club, Winners of World Cup Football Cup, 1988, and the Toyota Cup. Multicoloured.

2058		450p. Type **768**	1·80	1·50

2059		450p. Trophies on football pitch (horiz)	1·80	1·50

769 School and Pupils

1991. Centenary of Maria Auxiliadora Institute.

2060	**769**	450p. blue, black and red	1·80	1·50

770 "LATU"

1991. 25th Anniv of Uruguay Technological Laboratory.

2061	**770**	1570p. blue and deep blue	4·50	3·75

771 Emblem and Couple

1991. World AIDS Day.

2062	**771**	550p. black, yellow & bl	1·50	1·30
2063	**771**	2040p. black, lilac & grn	5·75	5·00

772 Theodolite and Measuring Rod on Map of Uruguay

1991. 160th Anniv of Topographic Survey.

2064	**772**	550p. multicoloured	1·50	1·30

773 Angel

1991. Christmas. Multicoloured.

2065		550p. Type **773**	1·50	1·30
2066		2040p. "Adoration of the Angels"	5·75	5·00

774 Anibal Troilo

1992. Musicians.

2067	**774**	450p. black, mauve & bl	1·30	1·10
2068	-	450p. black, orange & red	1·30	1·10
2069	-	450p. black, light green and green	1·30	1·10
2070	-	450p. black, blue & mve	1·30	1·10

DESIGNS: No. 2068, Francisco Canaro; 2069, Pintin Castellanos; 2070, Juan de Dios Filiberto.

775 Worker and Factory Building

2071	**775**	120p. multicoloured	25	15

1992. Quality Exports.

776 Pres. Aylwin

1992. Visit of President Patricio Aylwin of Chile.

2072	**776**	550p. multicoloured	1·40	1·20

777 Trophy

1992. Penarol F.C., Three-times World Club Football Champions.

2073	**777**	600p. black and yellow	1·50	1·30
MS2074	90×70 mm. **777** 3000p. black and yellow		7·50	7·50

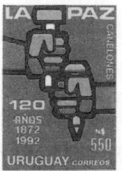

778 Hands holding Hammer and Chisel

1992. 120th Anniv of La Paz.

2075	**778**	550p. multicoloured	1·40	1·20

779 No Smoking Emblem

1992. World No Smoking Day.

2076	**779**	2500p. red, black & brn	5·75	5·00

780 Heart and Emblems

1992. World Health Day. "Health in Rhythm with the Heart".

2077	**780**	2500p. ultramarine, blue and red	5·75	5·00

781 Map of South America and Food Products

1992. Mercosur (South American economic organization).

2078	**781**	2500p. multicoloured	5·75	5·00

782 Stamp

1992. "Olymphilex 92" International Olympic Stamps Exhibition, Barcelona.

2079	**782**	2900p. multicoloured	7·00	6·00

783 Emblems

1992. 22nd Latin American–Caribbean Regional Conference of Food and Agricultural Organization.

2080	**783**	2500p. multicoloured	5·00	4·50

784 Children with Basket of Food

1992. International Nutrition Conference, Rome.

2081	**784**	2900p. multicoloured	5·75	5·00

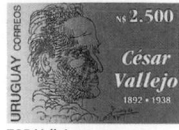

785 Vallejo

1992. Birth Centenary of Cesar Vallejo (painter and poet).

2082	**785**	2500p. brown & lt brown	5·00	4·50

786 Monument and Route Map

1992. Centenary of Christopher Columbus Monument, Durazno.

2083	**786**	700p. black, blue & green	1·40	1·20

787 Ruins of Sacramento and Lighthouse

1992. 500th Anniv of Discovery of America by Columbus.

2084	**787**	700p. multicoloured	1·40	1·20

788 Caravel

1992. America. 500th Anniv of Discovery of America by Columbus. Multicoloured.

2085		700p. Type **788**	1·40	1·20
2086		2900p. Globe showing Americas and old map (horiz)	5·75	5·00

789 Emblem

1992. Centenary of Christopher Columbus Philanthropic Society.

2087	**789**	700p. black, mauve and magenta	1·40	1·20

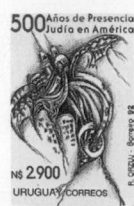

790 Emblem

1992. 500th Anniv of Presence of Jews in America.
| 2088 | **790** | 2900p. multicoloured | 5·75 | 5·00 |

791 Arms

1992. 50th Anniv of Jose Pedro Varela Teachers' College.
| 2089 | **791** | 700p. multicoloured | 1·40 | 1·20 |

792 Cambadu Building

1992. Centenary of Chamber of Wholesale and Retail Traders.
| 2090 | **792** | 700p. grey, black and red | 1·40 | 1·20 |

793 Emblem

1992. 50th Anniv of Lebanon Club of Uruguay.
| 2091 | **793** | 2900p. multicoloured | 5·75 | 5·00 |

794 Nativity

1992. Christmas. Multicoloured.
| 2092 | | 800p. Type **794** | 1·50 | 1·30 |
| 2093 | | 3200p. Star | 5·75 | 5·00 |

795 Map and Emblem

1992. 22nd Latin American and Carribean Lions Clubs Forum.
| 2094 | **795** | 2700p. multicoloured | 5·00 | 4·50 |

796 Immigrant

1992. Immigrants Day.
| 2095 | **796** | 800p. green and black | 1·50 | 1·30 |

797 Oribe

1992. Birth Bicentenary of Manuel Oribe (Liberation hero). Multicoloured.
| 2096 | | 800p. Type **797** | 1·50 | 1·30 |
| 2097 | | 800p. Oribe (founder) and Eastern University (horiz) | 1·50 | 1·30 |

798 Anniversary Emblem

1992. 90th Anniv of Pan-American Health Organization.
| 2098 | **798** | 3200p. multicoloured | 5·75 | 5·00 |

799 Anniversary Emblem

1992. 50th Anniv of Jose H. Molaguero S.A.
| 2099 | **799** | 800p. brown and stone | 1·50 | 1·30 |

800 Satellite and Map

1992. 70th Anniv of ANDEBU (association of broadcasting stations).
| 2100 | **800** | 2700p. multicoloured | 5·00 | 4·50 |

801 Emblem and Shanty Town

1992. 30th Anniv of Caritas Uruguaya.
| 2101 | **801** | 3200p. multicoloured | 5·75 | 5·00 |

802 Gonzalez Pecotche (founder) and Emblem

1992. 60th Anniv of Logosofia.
| 2102 | **802** | 800p. yellow and blue | 1·50 | 1·30 |

1993. Size 35×24 mm.
| 2103 | **755** | 800p. olive and green | 1·50 | 1·30 |

803 Wilson Ferreira Aldunate

1993
| 2104 | **803** | 80c. red, black and grey | 1·40 | 1·20 |

804 Post Car

1993
| 2105 | **804** | 1p. blue and yellow | 1·80 | 1·50 |

805 Graph and Personal Computer

1993. Centenary of Economic Sciences and Accountancy College.
| 2106 | **805** | 1p. multicoloured | 1·80 | 1·50 |

806 Lech Walesa (Polish President)

1993. Polska 93 International Stamp Exhibition, Posnan. Sheet 90×70 mm containing T **806** and similar vert design. Multicoloured.
| **MS**2107 | 2p. Type **806**; 2p. Pope John Paul II | 7·50 | 7·50 |

807 Magirus Deutz Fire Engine, 1958

1993. 50th Anniv of National Fire Service.
| 2108 | **807** | 1p. multicoloured | 1·60 | 1·40 |

808 Earth

1993. 15th Congress of Postal Union of the Americas, Spain and Portugal.
| 2109 | **808** | 3p.50 multicoloured | 5·75 | 5·00 |

809 Schooner and Pedro Campbell (first Navy General)

1993. 175th Anniv (1992) of Uruguayan Navy.
| 2110 | **809** | 1p. multicoloured | 1·60 | 1·40 |

810 Emblem

1993. 25th Anniv of International University Circles.
| 2111 | **810** | 1p. multicoloured | 1·60 | 1·40 |

811 Hupmobile, 1910

1993. 75th Anniv of Uruguay Automobile Club.
| 2112 | **811** | 3p.50 multicoloured | 5·75 | 5·00 |

812 Uruguay (winner 1930, 1950)

1993. World Cup Football Championship, USA (1994). Sheet 92×72 mm containing T **812** and similar vert design. Multicoloured.
| **MS**2113 | 2p.50 Type **812**; 2p.50 Brazil (winner, 1958, 1962, 1970) | 12·50 | 12·50 |

No. **MS**2113 also commemorates "Brasiliana 90" International Stamp Exhibition, Rio de Janeiro and 150th Anniv of first Brazilian stamp.

813 Bird

1993. No value expressed.
2114	**813**	(1p.20) blue and azure	1·40	1·20
2115	**813**	(1p.40) emerald and green	1·50	1·30
2147	**813**	(1p.60) red and pink	2·00	1·80
2148	**813**	(1p.80) brown and pink	2·00	1·80
2186	**813**	(2p.) grey	2·10	1·90
2207	**813**	(2p.30) violet	2·50	2·20

These were sold at the current inland letter rate.

814 Armadillo

1993
| 2116 | **814** | 1p.20 brown and green | 2·00 | 1·80 |

815 Village and Soldier

1993. Uruguayan Battalion of Peace-keeping Force in Cambodia.
| 2117 | **815** | 1p. multicoloured | 1·60 | 1·40 |

816 Dish Aerials and Studio

1993. 30th Anniv of National Television Channel 5.
| 2118 | **816** | 1p.20 multicoloured | 2·00 | 1·80 |

817 "The Tree of Life" (detail, Pablo Serrano)

1993. 60th Anniv of Anda.
| 2119 | **817** | 1p.20 multicoloured | 2·00 | 1·80 |

818 Arms and Officers

1993. 50th Anniv of Juan Carlos Gomez Folle National Police School.
| 2120 | **818** | 1p.20 multicoloured | 2·00 | 1·80 |

819 Graphics

1993. 75th Anniv of "Diario El Pais" (newspaper).
| 2121 | **819** | 1p.20 multicoloured | 2·00 | 1·80 |

820 Broad-nosed Caiman

1993. America. Endangered Animals. Multicoloured.
| 2122 | | 1p.20 Type **820** | 2·00 | 1·80 |
| 2123 | | 3p.50 Burrowing owl (vert) | 5·75 | 5·00 |

821 Power Lines supplying
Illuminated Building

1993. 14th Latin American Conference on Rural Electrification.

| 2124 | **821** | 3p.50 multicoloured | 5·75 | 5·00 |

822 Emblem

1993. 150th Anniv of B'nai B'rith (Jewish cultural and social organization).

| 2125 | **822** | 3p.70 multicoloured | 5·75 | 5·00 |

823
Red-legged
Seriema

1993. Natural World.

2126	**823**	20c. brown and pink	75	20
2127	-	30c. yellow and violet	1·00	35
2128	-	50c. brown and pink	1·80	55

DESIGNS—VERT: 30c. Saffron-cowled blackbird. HORIZ: 50c. Two-toed anteater.

824 "Uruguay
Natural"

1993. Whitbread Round-the-World Yacht Race. Sheet 90×70 mm.

| MS2129 | **824** | 5p. multicoloured | 7·00 | 7·00 |

825 Crucifix,
Mother Francisca
and Nuns with
Sick People

1993. Beatification of Mother Francisca Rubatto.

| 2130 | **825** | 1p.20 multicoloured | 1·80 | 1·50 |

826 Amerindian

1993. International Year of Indigenous Peoples.

| 2131 | **826** | 3p.50 multicoloured | 5·00 | 4·50 |

827 Emblem on
Map

1993. 75th Anniv of Montevideo Rotary Club.

| 2132 | **827** | 3p.50 blue and gold | 5·00 | 4·50 |

828 Private Swiss Air and
Basel 1845 2r. Stamps

1993. Uruguay 94 National Stamp Exhibition. Two sheets containing multicoloured designs as T **828**.

MS2133 Two sheets (a) 98×89 mm. 1p. Type **828** (150th anniv of Swiss stamps); 1p. Germany 1928 4r. and Uruguay 1977 Zeppelin stamps (125th birth anniv of Hugo Eckener (aeronautical engineer)); 1p. Uruguay 1970 200p. and USA 1969 10c. space stamps (25th anniv of Apollo 11 flight); 1p. Uruguay 1965 and USA 1983 28c. Olympic stamps (World Cup Football Championship, USA). (b) 89×98 mm. 2p.50 Zurich 1843 4 and 6r. stamps; 2p.50 Switzerland 1908 140c. 60c. stamp (150th anniv of Swiss stamps)

| | | | 30·00 | 30·00 |

829 Phoenician Cargo Ship
(carving)

1993. 50th Anniv of Independence of Lebanon.

| 2134 | **829** | 3p.70 brown, deep brown and green | 5·00 | 4·50 |

830 Haedo

1993. Eduardo Victor Haedo.

| 2135 | **830** | 1p.20 multicoloured | 1·80 | 1·50 |

831 Ribbon

1993. Anti-AIDS Campaign.

| 2136 | **831** | 1p.40 multicoloured | 1·90 | 1·70 |

832 Adoration of
the Wise Men

1993. Christmas. Multicoloured.

| 2137 | | 1p.40 Type **832** | 1·80 | 1·50 |
| 2138 | | 4p. Adoration of the Shepherds | 5·75 | 5·00 |

833 Adult with Chick
and Eggs

1993. The Greater Rhea. Multicoloured.

2139		20c. Type **833**	40	20
2140		20c. Adults sitting and standing	40	20
2141		50c. Close-up of head	90	55
2142		50c. Adults feeding	90	55

834 Child's view of life
(Alejandro Cuende)

1994. Children's Rights Day.

| 2143 | **834** | 1p.40 multicoloured | 1·90 | 1·70 |

835 Emblem

1994. National Postal Directorate.

| 2144 | **835** | 1p.40 blue and yellow | 1·40 | 65 |

836 Torch Carrier

1994. Fifth World Sports Congress, Punta del Este.

| 2145 | **836** | 4p. multicoloured | 5·75 | 5·00 |

837 Frigate

1994. 17th Inter-American Naval Conference.

| 2146 | **837** | 3p.70 multicoloured | 5·00 | 4·50 |

838 Emblem

1994. Seventh Iberian–American Youth Organization Conference.

| 2149 | **838** | 3p.90 multicoloured | 5·00 | 4·50 |

839 Sheep

1994. Fourth International Merino Sheep Conference.

| 2150 | **839** | 4p.30 multicoloured | 5·75 | 5·00 |

840 Anniversary
Emblem

1994. 75th Anniv of I.L.O.

| 2151 | **840** | 4p.30 multicoloured | 5·75 | 5·00 |

841 Katja Seizinger (skiing,
gold)

1994. Uruguay 94 National Stamp Exhibition (2nd issue). Winter Olympic Medal Winners. Sheet 99×95 mm containing T **841** and similar horiz designs. Multicoloured.

MS2152 1p.25 Type **841**; 1p.25 Markus Wasmeier (skiing, gold); 1p.25 Vreni Schneider (slalom, gold); 1p.25 Gustav Weder (four-man bobsleigh, silver)

| | | | 12·50 | 12·50 |

842 Uruguay and Brazil
Flags

1994. World Cup Football Championship, USA (2nd issue). Sheet 100×95 mm containing T **842** and similar horiz designs showing World Cup winners. Multicoloured.

MS2153 1p.25 Type **842**; 1p.25 Italy and Argentina flags; 1p.25 German Federal Republic and United Kingdom flags; 1p.25 Olympic flag (Uruguay, Olympic Champions)

| | | | 12·50 | 12·50 |

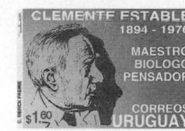

843 Estable

1994. Birth Centenary of Clemente Estable (biologist).

| 2154 | **843** | 1p.60 green and black | 2·00 | 1·80 |

844 Dove flying
from Ballot Box

1994. 75th Anniv of Electoral Court.

| 2155 | **844** | 1p.60 multicoloured | 2·00 | 1·80 |

845 Hand pulling Worm
from Dog's Mouth

1994. National Commission on Eradication of Tapeworms.

| 2156 | **845** | 1p.60 multicoloured | 2·00 | 1·80 |

846 Gen. Cesareo
Berisso (first pilot
to land at airport)

1994. 50th Anniv of Carrasco National Airport. Sheet 90×70 mm.

| MS2157 | **846** | 5p. multicoloured | 5·75 | 5·75 |

847 First Co-operative
Headquarters, Rochdale,
England

1994. 150th Anniv of Co-operative Movement.

| 2158 | **847** | 4p.30 multicoloured | 5·00 | 4·50 |

848 National Flags
on Plugs

1994. 30th Anniv of Commission for Regional Integration of Electricity.

| 2159 | **848** | 1p.60 multicoloured | 1·90 | 1·70 |

849 Astronaut standing on
Moon

1994. 25th Anniv of First Manned Moon Landing.

| 2160 | **849** | 3p. multicoloured | 3·25 | 2·75 |

850 Family

1994. International Year of the Family.
2161 **850** 4p.80 multicoloured   5·75   5·00

851 Fr. Pierre (founder)

1994. 45th Anniv of Emmaus Movement (social welfare organization).
2162 **851** 4p.80 multicoloured   5·75   5·00

852 Pillar-box

1994. 150th Anniv of Neighbourhood Pillar Boxes.
2163 **852** 50c. yellow and green   40   35
2164 **852** 1p. yellow and brown   50   45
2165 **852** 1p.80 yellow and blue   2·10   1·90
2166 **852** 2p.60 yellow and brown   2·50   2·20
2168 **852** 7p.50 yellow and violet   5·75   5·00

853 "The Man of Lugano"

1994. 50th Death Anniv of Goffredo Sommavilla (painter).
2169 **853** 4p.80 multicoloured   5·75   5·00

854 Swimmer

1994. Centenary of International Olympic Committee.
2170 **854** 4p.80 multicoloured   5·75   5·00

855 Fernandez and Pupils with National Flag

1994. 125th Anniv of Elbio Fernandez School.
2171 **855** 1p.80 multicoloured   2·00   1·80

856 Saravia

1994. 90th Death Anniv of Gen. Aparicio Saravia.
2172 **856** 1p.80 blue, turquoise and deep blue   2·00   1·80

857 Statuette

1994. 65th Anniv of General Association of Uruguayan Writers.
2173 **857** 1p.80 multicoloured   2·00   1·80

858 Town Plan

1994. Sixth Latin American Town Planning Congress.
2174 **858** 4p.80 multicoloured   5·00   4·50

860 Mail Coach

1994. America. Postal Transport. Multicoloured.
2176   1p.80 Type **860**   1·90   1·70
2177   4p.80 "Eolo" (paddle- steamer)   5·75   5·00

861 Plan

1994. First International Seminar on Provision of Roads in Uruguay, Punte del Este.
2178 **861** 2p. multicoloured   2·10   1·90

862 Facade

1994. 150th Anniv of National Mint. Sheet 100×96 mm containing T **862** and similar horiz designs. Multicoloured.
MS2179 1p.50 Type **862**; 1p.50 1844 gold coin; 1p.50 Obverse of 1844 one peso fuerte coin; 1p.50 Reverse of 1844 one peso fuerte coin   6·25   6·25

863 Computer Terminal and Reporter

1994. 50th Anniv of Uruguay Press Association.
2180 **863** 2p. multicoloured   2·10   1·90

864 Statuette

1994. 50th Anniv of Uruguay Marketing Association.
2181 **864** 2p. multicoloured   2·10   1·90

865 "Uruguay" and "Artigas" (destroyers)

1994. 177th Anniv of Navy. Ships. Sheet 101×90 mm containing T **865** and similar horiz designs. Multicoloured.
MS2182 1p.50 Type **865**; 1p.50 "Fortuna" (minesweeper); 1p.50 "Uruguay" (frigate); 1p.50 "Commandante" (frigate); 1p.50 "Commandante Pedro Campbell" (ice patrol ship)   6·25   6·25

866 Dove over Latin America

1994. 25th Anniv of Latin American Movement "Long Live the People".
2183 **866** 4p.30 multicoloured   4·50   3·75

867 Draw Balls

1994. 55th Anniv of Lottery.
2184 **867** 2p. multicoloured   2·10   1·90

868 Footballers

1994. 85th Anniv of Young Men's Christian Association.
2185 **868** 2p. multicoloured   2·10   1·90

869 Tree

1994. Christmas. Multicoloured.
2187   2p. Type **869**   2·10   1·90
2188   5p.50 Star over village   5·75   5·00

870 Emblem and Venue

1994. Fourth Assembly of Latin American and Caribbean Organization of Higher Fiscal Entities, Montevideo.
2189 **870** 5p.50 multicoloured   5·75   5·00

871 Cross and Crescent on Globe

1994. 75th Anniv of International Federation of Red Cross and Red Crescent Societies.
2190 **871** 5p. multicoloured   5·00   4·50

872 Chuy Post Office

1995
2191 **872** 20c. green   50   45
2192 **872** 10p. brown   3·75   3·50
2195 **872** 10p. mauve and black   4·50   3·75

873 CANT 18 Flying Boat

1995. 70th Anniv of Naval Aviation.
2198 **873** 2p. multicoloured   2·10   1·90

874 Swimming Park

1995. 20th Anniv of World Tourism Organization. Multicoloured.
2199   5p. Type **874**   5·00   4·50
2200   5p. Deer and greater rhea   5·00   4·50
2201   5p. Ranch   5·00   4·50
2202   5p. Beach resort   5·00   4·50

875 Lifeboat

1995. 17th World Lifeguards' Conference.
2203 **875** 5p. multicoloured   5·00   4·50

876 Globe and Emblem forming "90"

1995. 90th Anniv of Rotary International.
2204 **876** 5p. ultramarine, blue and gold   5·00   4·50

877 Anniversary Emblem and Airplane

1995. 50th Anniv of International Civil Aviation Organization.
2205 **877** 5p. ultramarine, orange and blue   5·00   4·50

878 Mascagni and Set from "Cavalleria Rusticana" (opera)

1995. 50th Death Anniv of Piero Mascagni (composer).
2206 **878** 5p. multicoloured   5·00   4·50

879 Cimarron

1995
2208 **879** 2p.30 multicoloured   2·50   2·20

880 "Phoebis neocypris"

1995. Butterflies and Moths. Sheet 100×80 mm containing T **880** and similar horiz designs. Multicoloured.
MS2209 5p. Type **880**; 5p. "Diogas erippus"; 5p. "Euryades duponcheli"; 5p. "Automeris coresus"   20·00   20·00

881 Paysandu Players

1995. America Cup Football Championship, Uruguay. Multicoloured.
2210   2p.30 Type **881**   2·00   1·80
2211   2p.30 Rivera players   2·00   1·80
2212   2p.30 Ball in net   2·00   1·80
2213   2p.30 Montevideo players   2·00   1·80
2214   2p.30 Maldonado players   2·00   1·80
Nos. 2210/14 were issued together, se-tenant, forming a composite design of a match.

882 Orange
incorporating Globe

1995. 50th Anniv of F.A.O.
2215 **882** 5p.50 multicoloured 5·00 4·50

883 U.N. Soldier and Detail
of World Map

1995. Participation in United Nations Peace-keeping
Forces.
2216 **883** 2p.30 multicoloured 2·50 2·20

884 Italian National
Colours on Map of Italy

1995. Visit of President Scalfaro of Italy.
2217 **884** 5p.50 multicoloured 5·00 4·50

885 People walking
Hand in Hand
towards Gateway

1995. Latin American Integration Day.
2218 **885** 5p. multicoloured 4·50 3·75

886 "Zidona dufresnei"

1995. Sea Shells. Sheet 100×80 mm containing T **886**
and similar horiz designs. Multicoloured.
MS2219 5p. Type **886**; 5p. "Boccinan-
ops duartei"; 5p. "Dorsanum monil-
iferum"; 5p. "Olivancillaria uretai" 20·00 20·00

887 Postal
Symbol

1995. No Value Expressed.
2220 **887** (2p.60) yellow & green 2·50 2·20
2221 **887** (2p.90) yellow and blue 2·50 2·20
2222 **887** (3p.20) pink and red 5·25 4·75
2223 **887** (3p.50) brown & purple 1·80 1·50

888 Carlos Gardel
(entertainer)

1995
2226 **888** 5p.50 multicoloured 5·00 4·50

889 "Notocactus
roseinflorus"

1995. Flowers. Multicoloured.
2227 3p. Type **889** 2·75 2·40
2228 3p. "Verbena chamaedryfolia" 2·75 2·40
2229 3p. "Bauhinia candicans" 2·75 2·40
2230 3p. "Tillandsia aeranthos" 2·75 2·40
2231 3p. "Eichhornia crassipes" 2·75 2·40

890 Varela

1995. 150th Birth Anniv of Jose Verela (educationalist).
2232 **890** 2p.60 multicoloured 2·50 2·20

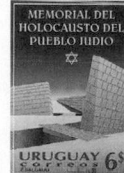

891 Monument

1995. Holocaust Monument, Pueblo Judio.
2233 **891** 6p. multicoloured 5·25 4·75

892 "Dirksonia
sellowiana"

1995. America. Environmental Protection. Multicoloured.
2234 3p. Type **892** 2·75 2·40
2235 6p. Maned wolf (horiz) 5·25 4·75

893 Albatross

1995. Tenth Anniv of Artigas Antarctic Scientific Base.
Sheet 101×90 mm containing T **893** and similar
horiz designs. Multicoloured.
MS2236 2p.50 Type **893**; 2p.50 Tracked
vehicle; 4p. Fairchild FAU-572 airplane; 4p. "Vanguardua" (ship) 12·00 12·00

894 Anniversary
Emblem over
Globe

1995. 50th Anniv of U.N.O.
2237 **894** 6p. multicoloured 5·25 4·75

895 Beyer Peacock, 1876

1995. Steam Railway Locomotives. Multicoloured.
2238 3p. Type **895** 2·75 2·40
2239 3p. Criollo, 1895 2·75 2·40
2240 3p. Beyer Peacock, 1910 2·75 2·40

896 Brigantine (privateer of
Artigas)

1995. 178th Anniv of Naval Service. Multicoloured.
2241 3p. Type **896** 2·75 2·40

2242 3p. "Montevideo" (training
frigate) 2·75 2·40
2243 3p. "Pte. Rivera" (tanker) 2·75 2·40

897 Crib

1995. Christmas. Multicoloured.
2244 2p.90 Type **897** 2·50 2·20
2245 6p.50 Beam of light and rose
window 5·75 5·00

898 Lumiere Brothers and
Film Reel

1995. Centenary of Motion Pictures.
2246 **898** 6p. violet, deep mauve
and mauve 5·25 4·75

899 Dressage Rider
(Atlanta, 1996)

1996. Latin American Stamp Exhibition (1st issue) and
Centenary of Modern Olympic Games. Sheet 100×90
mm containing T **899** and similar horiz designs.
Multicoloured.
MS2247 2p.50 Type **899**; 2p.50 Skier
(Nagano, 1998); 2p.50 Torch bearer
and Opera House (Sydney, 2000);
2p.50 Skier (Salt Lake City, 2002) 16·00 16·00

900 Rosa Luna (dancer)

1996. Carnival. Multicoloured.
2248 2p.90 Type **900** 2·50 2·20
2249 2p.90 Santiago Luz (clarinettist) 2·50 2·20
2250 2p.90 Pepino (clown) 2·50 2·20

901 Cantegril Country Club

1996. Golf. Multicoloured.
2251 2p.90 Type **901** 2·50 2·20
2252 2p.90 Cerro Golf Club 2·50 2·20
2253 2p.90 Fay Crocker and trophy 2·50 2·20
2254 2p.90 Lago Golf Club 2·50 2·20
2255 2p.90 Uruguay Golf Club 2·50 2·20

902 Solis Theatre

1996. Montevideo, Latin American Cultural Capital.
2256 **902** 2p.90 multicoloured 2·50 2·20

903 Cardinal Barbieri and
Our Lady of the
Foundation (statue)

1996. Tenth Anniv of Broadcasting by Stamp Academy
of "Stamp of the Day" on Sodre Television. Sheet
100×90 mm containing T **903** and similar horiz
designs. Multicoloured.
MS2257 2p.50 Type **903**; 2p.50
Yitzhak Rabin (Prime Minister of
Israel, 1974–77 and 1992–95); 2p.50
Belgium–USA football match, 1930
(first World Cup game); 2p.50 Score
and Robert Stolz (composer, 20th
death anniv) 11·50 11·50

904 Zitarrosa

1996. 60th Birth Anniv of Alfredo Zitarrosa (musician).
2258 **904** 3p. multicoloured 2·50 2·20

905 Footballer and Jules
Rimet Cup

1996. Latin American Stamp Exhibition (2nd issue) and
World Cup Football Championship, France (1998).
Sheet 100×90 mm containing T **905** and similar
horiz designs. Multicoloured.
MS2259 2p.50 Type **905**; 2p.50 World
Cup and footballer; 2p.50 Footballers
and 50th anniv of UNICEF emblem;
2p.50 Olympic rings and footballers 12·50 12·50

906 Skeletons

1996. Archaeological Congress.
2260 **906** 3p.20 multicoloured 2·50 2·20

907 "Glyptodon claripes"

1996. Prehistoric Animals. Multicoloured.
2261 3p.20 Type **907** 2·75 2·30
2262 3p.20 "Macrauchenia pata-
chonica" 2·75 2·30
2263 3p.20 "Toxodon platensis" 2·75 2·30
2264 3p.20 "Glossotherium robostum" 2·75 2·30
2265 3p.20 "Titanosaurus" 2·75 2·30

908 People-Houses

1996. Population and Housing Censuses.
2266 **908** 3p.20 multicoloured 2·50 2·20

909 Dion-Button
Double-deck Bus, 1912

1996. Old Vehicles. Multicoloured.
2267 3p.20 Type **909** 2·75 2·30
2268 3p.20 Ford Model "A" patrol
car, 1928 2·75 2·30
2269 3p.20 Raleigh bicycle, 1940 2·75 2·30
2270 3p.20 Magirus fire-engine, 1926 2·75 2·30
2271 3p.20 Hotchkiss ambulance,
1917 2·75 2·30

910 Knot (Calidris canutus)

1996. Capex 96 International Stamp Exhibition, Toronto. Sheet 90×90 mm.

MS2272	12p. multicoloured	8·75	8·75

911 Children and Globe holding Hands (Soraya Campanella)

1996. "Care for Our Planet: Everyone's Mission".

2273	911	3p.20 multicoloured	2·50	2·20

912 New Postal Administration Emblem

1996. Postal Emblems.

2273a	912	5p. yellow and blue	3·75	3·25
2274	912	7p. yellow and blue	5·00	4·50

914 "Nuestra Senora de la Encina" (caravel), 1726

1996. Sailing Ships. Multicoloured.

2276		3p.20 Type **914**	2·75	2·30
2277		3p.20 "San Francisco" (ship of the line), 1729	2·75	2·30
2278		3p.20 Etienne Moreau's fleet, 1720	2·75	2·30
2279		3p.20 "Atrevida" (corvette), 1789–94	2·75	2·30
2280		3p.20 "Nuestra Senora de la Luz" (brig), 1752	2·75	2·30

915 "Flores Landscape" (Carmelo de Arzadun)

1996

2281	915	3p.50 multicoloured	2·75	2·30

916 Old Jewish Quarter

1996. 80th Anniv of Jewish Community in Uruguay.

2282	916	7p.50 red, yellow and purple	5·75	5·00

917 Dr. Victor Bertullo (veterinary researcher)

1996. Scientists. Multicoloured.

2283		3p.50 Type **917**	2·75	2·30
2284		3p.50 Tomas Beno Hirschfeld (chemical engineer) (horiz)	2·75	2·30
2285		3p.50 Enrique Legrand (astronomer and physicist)	2·75	2·30
2286		3p.50 Dr. Miguel C. Rubino (veterinary researcher) (horiz)	2·75	2·30

919 Aristotle (philosopher)

1996. Scientists. Multicoloured.

2288		7p.50 Type **919**	5·75	5·00
2289		7p.50 Sir Isaac Newton (mathematician)	5·75	5·00
2290		7p.50 Albert Einstein (physicist)	5·75	5·00

920 500 Peso Note

1996. Centenary of Republica Oriental Bank. Multicoloured.

2291		3p.50 Type **920**	2·75	2·30
2292		3p.50 Ten peso note	2·75	2·30

921 Narbona Chapel

1996. National Heritage Day. Multicoloured.

2293		3p.50 Type **921**	2·75	2·30
2294		3p.50 Map of Gorriti Island showing sites of Spanish fortifications	2·75	2·30

922 "125" and Emblem

1996. 125th Anniv of Uruguay Rural Association.

2295	922	3p.50 multicoloured	2·75	2·30

923 Great White Sark ("Carchardon barcharias")

1996. Istanbul 96 International Stamp Exhibition. Sharks. Sheet 100×80 mm containing T **923** and similar horiz designs. Multicoloured.

MS2296	3p.50 Type **923**; 3p.50 Fox shark ("Alopias vulpinus"); 3p.50 Spotted cow shark ("Notorhynchus cepedianus"); 3p.50 Atlantic angel shark ("Squatina dumerili")	10·50	10·50

924 Angel Rodriguez (South American boxing champion, 1917)

1996. Sports Personalities. Multicoloured.

2297		3p.50 Type **924**	2·75	2·40
2298		3p.50 Leandro Noli (winner of first Uruguayan cycling race, 1939)	2·75	2·40
2299		3p.50 Eduardo G. Risso (Olympic rowing medallist, 1948)	2·75	2·40
2300		3p.50 Estrella Puente (South American javelin champion, 1949)	2·75	2·40
2301		3p.50 Oscar Moglia (Olympic basketball medallist, 1956)	2·75	2·40

925 Gaucho

1996. America. Traditional Costumes. Multicoloured.

2302		3p.50 Type **925**	2·75	2·30
2303		3p.50 Countrywoman	5·75	5·00

926 Rat

1996. Taipei 96 International Stamp Exhibition, Taiwan. Sheet 110×100 mm.

MS2304	926	7p.+3p. multicoloured	7·50	7·50

927 Satellite

1996. Third Space Conference of the Americas.

2305	927	3p.50 multicoloured	2·75	2·30

928 "Football Match" (Julio Suarez)

1996. Centenary of Comics. Museum of Humour and Anecdotes, Minas.

2306	928	4p. multicoloured	3·25	2·75

929 Institute Building

1996. Centenary of Hygiene Institute.

2307	929	4p. multicoloured	3·25	2·75

930 De Azara

1996. 175th Death Anniv of Felix de Azara (naturalist).

2308	930	4p. multicoloured	3·25	2·75

931 Angels blowing Trumpets over Globe

1996. Centenary of Seventh Day Adventist Church in Uruguay.

2309	931	3p.50 multicoloured	2·75	2·30

932 Hands fingering Frets and Lyre (National Folklore Festival, Durazno)

1997. Festivals. Multicoloured. Self-adhesive and imperf (2315) or ordinary (others) gum.

2310		4p. Type **932**	3·25	2·75
2311		4p. Man smoking cigar (Festival of Gaucho Traditions, Tacuarembo) (vert)	3·25	2·75
2312		5p. Stage (Beer Week, Paysandu)	3·75	3·25
2313		5p. Ruben Lena and bridge over river (Olimar River Festival, Treinta y Tres) (vert)	3·75	3·25
2314		5p. Guitar and horseman (Minas y Abril Festival, Lavelleja)	3·75	3·25
2315		5p. Man mounted on blindfolded horse tied to post (Criolla Parque Roosevelt, Canelones)	3·75	3·25

933 Naked Mushroom ("Tricholoma nudum")

1997. Fungi. Multicoloured.

2316		4p. Type **933**	3·25	2·75
2317		4p. Yellow stainer ("Agaricus xanthodermus")	3·25	2·75

2318		4p. "Russula sardonia"	3·25	2·75
2319		4p. Girl hugging dog and "Microsporum canis"	3·25	2·75
2320		4p. "Polyporus versicolor"	3·25	2·75

934 Black-finned Pearlfish

1997. Fish. Multicoloured. Self-adhesive. Imperf.

2321		4p. Type **934**	3·25	2·75
2322		4p. Uruguayan pearlfish ("Cynolebia viarius")	3·25	2·75

935 Buceo

1997. Yachting Harbours. Multicoloured. Self-adhesive. Imperf.

2323		4p. Type **935**	3·25	2·75
2324		4p. Colonia	3·25	2·75
2325		4p. Punta del Este	3·25	2·75
2326		4p. Santiago Vazquez	3·25	2·75

936 Artigas and Lancer

1997. Bicentenary of Artigas's Lancers (Presidential escort).

2327	936	4p. multicoloured	3·25	2·75

937 Cadet

1997. 50th Anniv of General Artigas Military Academy.

2328	937	4p. multicoloured	3·25	2·75

938 Ambulance

1997. 18th Anniv of United Coronary Mobile (first mobile medical emergency unit in the world). Self-adhesive. Imperf.

2329	938	5p. multicoloured	4·00	3·50

939 Toy holding Box

1997. 50th Anniv (1996) of UNICEF. Self-adhesive. Imperf.

2330	939	5p. multicoloured	4·00	3·50

940 Anchorena, 1920

1997. Lighthouses. Multicoloured. Self-adhesive. Imperf.

2331		5p. Type **940**	4·00	3·50
2332		5p. Farallon, 1870	4·00	3·50
2333		5p. Jose Ignacio, 1877	4·00	3·50
2334		5p. Santa Maria, 1874	4·00	3·50
2335		5p. Vigia, 18th-century	4·00	3·50

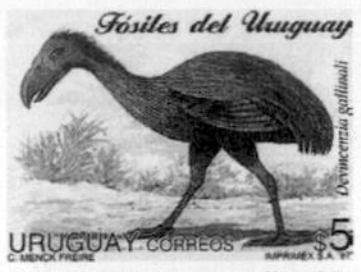

941 "Devincenzia gallinali"

1997. Prehistoric Animals. Multicoloured. Self-adhesive. Imperf.

2336	5p. Type **941**		4·00	3·50
2337	5p. "Smilodon populator"		4·00	3·50
2338	5p. "Mesosaurus tenuidens"		4·00	3·50
2339	5p. "Doedicurus clavicaudatus"		4·00	3·50
2340	5p. "Artigasia magna"		4·00	3·50

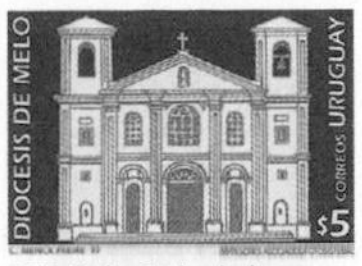

942 Melo Cathedral

1997. Dioceses. Multicoloured.

2341	5p. Type **942**	4·00	3·50
2342	5p. Monsignor Mariano Soler (first archbishop of Archdiocese of Montevideo)	4·00	3·50
2343	5p. Monsignor Jacinto Vera (first bishop of Archdiocese of Montevideo)	4·00	3·50
2344	5p. Salto Cathedral	4·00	3·50

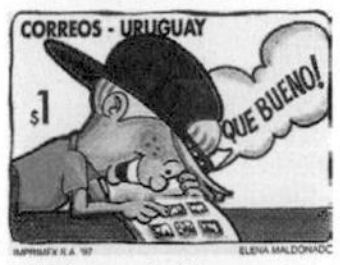

943 Boy admiring Stamps in Album

1997. Youth Philately. Multicoloured.

2345	1p. Type **943**	1·30	1·20
2346	1p. Winking boy with tweezers and magnifying glass	1·30	1·20
2347	2p. Boy thinking "MMMM... FILATELIA?"	1·30	1·20
2348	2p. Boy thinking of stamps	1·30	1·20
2349	2p. Boy rejecting friend's offer of football game	1·30	1·20

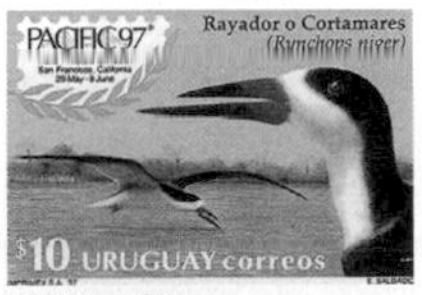

944 Black Skimmers

1997. "Pacific 97" International Stamp Exhibition, San Francisco, U.S.A.

2350	**944** 10p. multicoloured	8·00	8·00

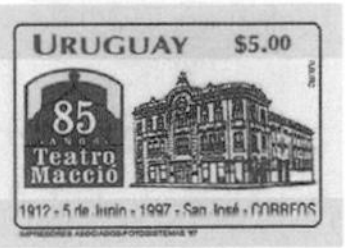

945 Theatre

1997. 85th Anniv of Teatro Maccio, San Jose.

2351	**945** 5p. black, red and stone	4·00	3·50

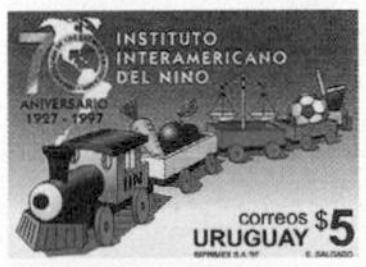

946 Toy Steam Train

1997. 70th Anniv of Inter-American Institute for the Child.

2352	**946** 5p. multicoloured	4·00	3·50

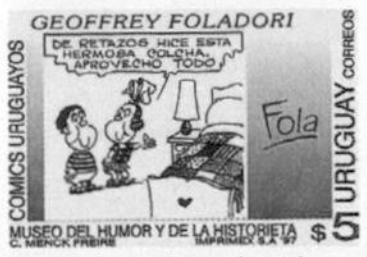

947 Fola and Boy beside Bed (Geoffrey Foladori)

1997. Comic Strip Characters. Multicoloured.

2353	5p. Type **947**	3·25	3·00
2354	5p. Peloduro running for goal (Julio Suarez)	3·25	3·00

948 Sun, Birds and Waves

1997. 90th Anniv of Punta del Este.

2355	**948** 5p. multicoloured	4·00	3·50

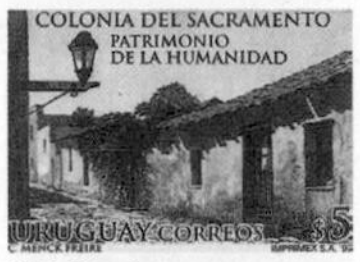

949 Street

1997. World Heritage Site. Colonia del Sacramento.

2356	**949** 5p. multicoloured	4·00	3·50

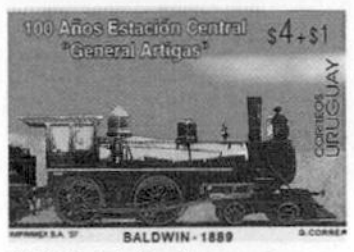

950 Baldwin Steam Locomotive, 1889

1997. Centenary of General Artigas Central Station, Montevideo. Multicoloured.

2357	4p.+1p. Type **950**	3·25	3·00
2358	4p.+1p. Hudswell Clarke steam locomotive, 1895	3·25	3·00
2359	4p.+1p. Station facade and Luis Andreoni	3·25	3·00
2360	4p.+1p. Hawthorn Leslie steam locomotive, 1914	3·25	3·00
2361	4p.+1p. General Electric diesel shunting locomotive, 1954	3·25	3·00

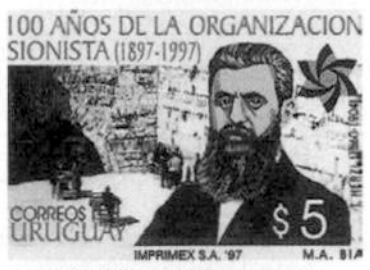

951 Wailing Wall (Jerusalem) and Theodor Herzl (founder)

1997. Centenary of Zionist Congress, Basel.

2362	**951** 5p. multicoloured	3·25	3·00

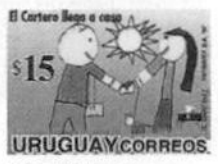

952 Woman giving Letter to Postman

1997. Collection at Sender's Address Service. Self-adhesive. Imperf.

2363	**952**	15p. multicoloured	17·00	15·00
2363a	**952**	20p. multicoloured	9·25	8·25
2364	-	25p. green, yell & blk	29·00	26·00
2364a	-	32p. green, yell & blk	14·50	13·00
2364b	-	80p. green, yell & blk	37·00	33·00

DESIGNS: Nos. 2364/64b Black-chested buzzard eagle (*Geranoaetus melanoleucus*).

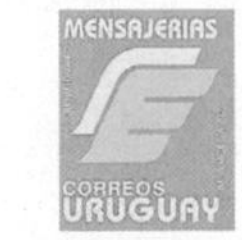

953 Postal Symbol

1997. No Value Expressed.

2365	**953**	(4p.) yellow and brown	1·90	1·70
2367	**953**	(–) blue	1·60	1·40
2368	**953**	(–) blue and violet	1·90	1·70
2369	**953**	(–) green and grey	1·30	1·20

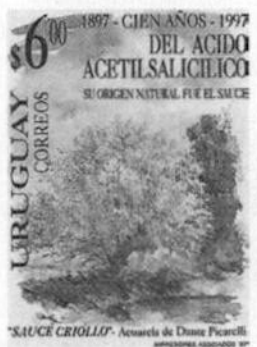

954 "Creole Willow" (Dante Picarelli)

1997. Centenary of Discovery of Acetylsalycylic Acid (aspirin) by Dr. Felix Hoffman.

2371	**954** 6p. multicoloured	2·75	2·40

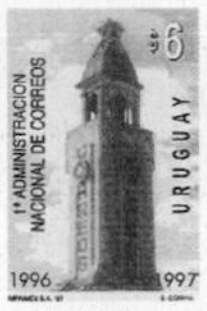

955 Clock Tower

1997. First National Administration of Posts.

2372	**955** 6p. blue and black	2·75	2·40

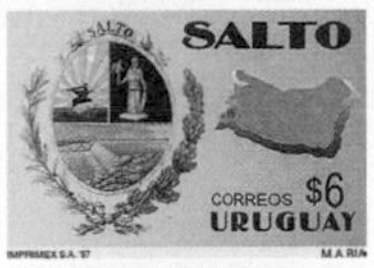

956 Arms and Map

1997. Department of Salto.

2373	**956** 6p. multicoloured	2·75	2·40

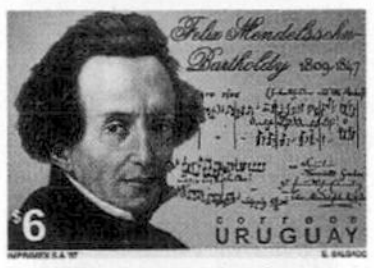

957 Felix Mendelssohn-Bartholdy and Score

1997. Composers' Death Anniversaries. Multicoloured.

2374	6p. Type **957** (150th anniv)	2·75	2·40
2375	6p. Johannes Brahms and score (centenary)	2·75	2·40

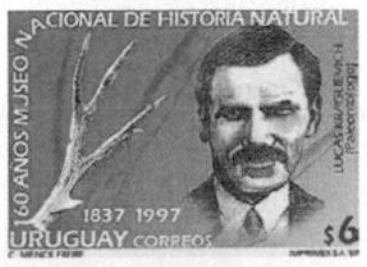

958 Antler and Lucas Kraglievich (palaeontologist)

1997. 160th Anniv of National Natural History Museum, Montevideo. Multicoloured.

2376	6p. Type **958**	2·75	2·40
2377	6p. Plant and Jose Arechavaleta (botanist)	2·75	2·40
2378	6p. Left-eyed flounder and Garibaldi Devincenzi (zoologist)	2·75	2·40
2379	6p. Flint axe head and Antonio Iadel (archaeologist)	2·75	2·40

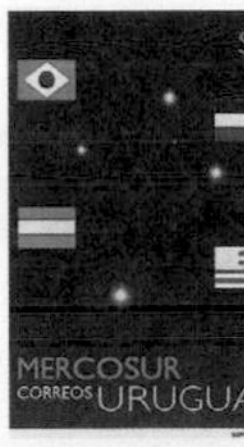

959 Members' Flags and Southern Cross

1997. Mercosur (South American Common Market). Multicoloured.

2380	11p. Type **959** (6th anniv)	4·75	4·25
MS2381	90×70 mm. 15p. Passion flower ("Passiflora coerulea") (first Mercosur Stamp Exhibition, Asuncion, Paraguay) (26×38 mm)	6·25	6·25

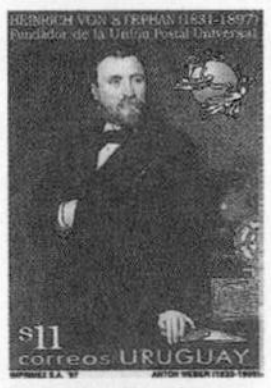

960 Von Stephan (after Anton Weber)

1997. Death Centenary of Heinrich von Stephan (founder of Universal Postal Union).

2382	**960** 11p. multicoloured	4·75	4·25

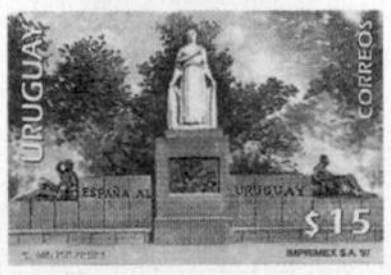

961 Monument

1997. "Centenary of 1898 Generation of Spanish Writer's Stamp Exhibition. Sheet 90×70 mm.

MS2383	**961** 15p. multicoloured	6·25	6·25

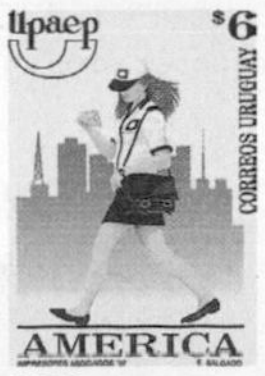

962 Postwoman

1997. America. Postal Delivery. Multicoloured.

2384	6p. Type **962**	3·00	2·50
2385	11p. Woman receiving letters from postman	5·50	5·00

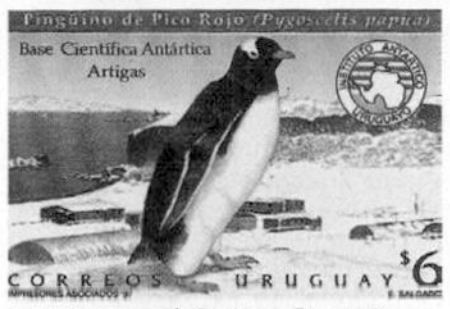

963 Base and Gentoo Penguin

1997. Artigas Scientific Base, Antarctica.

2386	**963** 6p. multicoloured	2·75	2·40

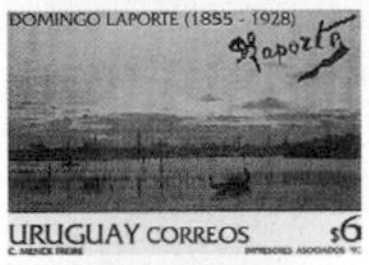

964 River Scene

1997. 70th Death Anniv (1998) of Domingo Laporte (artist).

2387	**964** 6p. multicoloured	2·75	2·40

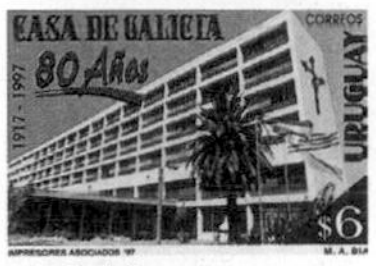

965 Building

1997. 80th Anniv of Casa de Galicia.

2388	**965** 6p. multicoloured	2·75	2·40

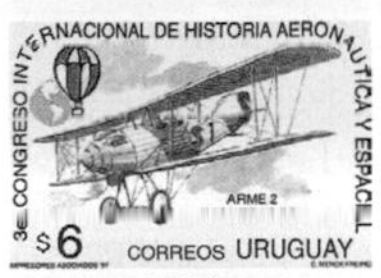

966 Arme 2 Biplane "Montevideo"

1997. Third International Aeronautical and Space History Congress.

2389	**966** 6p. multicoloured	2·75	2·40

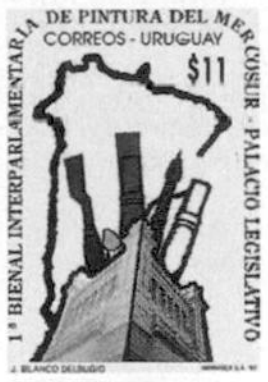

967 Map, Painting Materials and Legislative Palace Tower

1997. First Interparliamentary Mercosur Paintings Biennale, Montevideo.

2390	**967** 11p. multicoloured	4·75	4·25

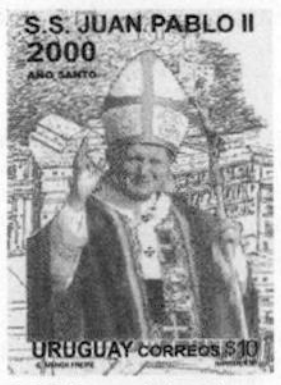

968 Pope John II (Holy Year 2000)

1997. Third International Assembly, Punta del Este and Centenary of Arrival of First Polish Colonists at River Plate. Sheet 90×70 mm. Multicoloured.

MS2391	**968** 10p. multicoloured	8·75	8·75

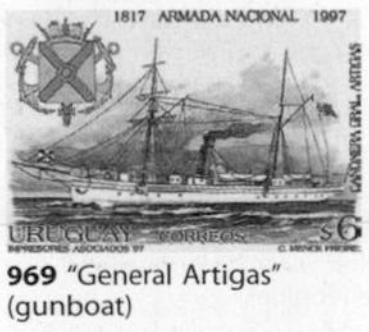

969 "General Artigas" (gunboat)

1997. 180th Anniv of Navy.

2392 | **969** | 6p. multicoloured | 2·75 | 2·40

970 Obverse and Reverse
of 1 Peso Coin

1997. Shanghai 97 International Stamp and Coin Exhibition. Two sheets, each 103×113 mm containing horiz designs as T **970**.

MS2393 Two sheets (a) 3p.50 Type **970**; 3p.50 Central business District and junk (return of Hong Kong to China); 4p. Michael Schumacher and car (world Formula 1 motor racing champion); 4p. "Sojouner" (roving vehicle) and planet surface (Mars "pathfinder" mission); (b) 3p.50 Martina Hingis (1997 Wimbledon Ladies' Champion; 3p.50 Jan Ullrich (1997 Tour de France winner); 4p. Footballers (World Cup Football Championship, France (1998)); 4p. Ski jumper (Winter Olympic Games, Nagano, Japan (1998)) | 16·00 | 16·00

971 Three Kings

1997. Christmas. Multicoloured.

2394 | 6p. Type **971** | 2·40 | 2·10
2395 | 11p. Madonna and Child | 4·25 | 3·75

972 Adesio Lambardo and
Bronze Medal (Olympic
Games, Helsinki, 1952)

1997. Sportsmen. Multicoloured.

2396 | 6p. Type **972** | 2·75 | 2·40
2397 | 6p. Guillermo Douglas (single sculls) and bronze medal (Olympic Games, Rome, 1932) | 2·75 | 2·40
2398 | 6p. Obdulio Varela (footballer) and World Cup Trophy (Uruguay, 1950 World Cup champion) | 2·75 | 2·40
2399 | 6p. Atilio Francois (cyclist) and silver medal (World Cycling Championships, Paris, 1947) | 2·75 | 2·40
2400 | 6p. Juan Lopez Testa (South American 100 metres champion, Buenos Aires, 1947) | 2·75 | 2·40

973 Silhouette and Personal
Computer

1997. "Mevifil '97" First International Exhibition of Philatelic Audio-Visual and Computer Systems.

2401 | **973** | 11p. multicoloured | 4·75 | 4·25

974 Land Rover

1997. "INDEPEX 97" International Stamp Exhbition, New Delhi. Transport Anniversaries. Multicoloured.

2402 | 6p. Type **974** (50th anniv) | 2·75 | 2·40
2403 | 6p. Henry Ford (50th death anniv) and motor car | 2·75 | 2·40
2404 | 6p. Robert Bosch (centenary of electric motor) | 2·75 | 2·40
2405 | 6p. Rudolf Diesel (centenary of diesel engine) | 2·75 | 2·40

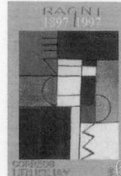

975 Academy Flag and
Officer

1997. 90th Anniv of Naval Academy.

2406 | **975** | 6p. multicoloured | 2·75 | 2·40

976 Courthouse

1997. 90th Anniv of Uruguay Supreme Court.

2407 | **976** | 6p. multicoloured | 2·75 | 2·40

977 Postal Transport
and Stone Relief

1997. 170th Anniv of Uruguay Post Office.

2408 | **977** | 6p. multicoloured | 2·75 | 2·40

978 Houses and Dr. Gallinal
(founder)

1997. 30th Anniv of Movement for the Eradication of Insanitary Rural Housing.

2409 | **978** | 6p. multicoloured | 2·75 | 2·40

979 Preparing Materials

1997. Construction. Multicoloured.

2410 | 6p. Type **979** | 2·75 | 2·40
2411 | 6p. Planning | 2·75 | 2·40
2412 | 6p. Construction in progress | 2·75 | 2·40

Nos. 2410/12 were issued together, se-tenant, forming a composite design.

980 Antonia "Chiquito"
Saravia and Diego Lamas

1997. Centenary of 1897 Uprising. Sheet 90×71 mm.

MS2413 **980** 15p. multicoloured | 6·25 | 6·25

981 Princess
Diana with African
Boy

1998. Death Commemoration of Diana, Princess of Wales. Multicoloured.

2414 | 2p.+1p. Type **981** | 2·40 | 2·10
2415 | 2p.+1p. Wearing protective mask | 2·40 | 2·10

MS2416 90×70 mm. 12p.+3p. Diana with Indian children (34×49 mm) | 20·00 | 20·00

982 Constructivist
Painting

1998. Birth Centenary (1997) of Hector Ragni (artist).

2417 | **982** | 6p. multicoloured | 2·75 | 2·40

983 Naval Station,
Montevideo

1998. 220th Anniv (1996) of Establishment of First Spanish Naval Station in America.

2418 | **983** | 6p. multicoloured | 2·75 | 2·40

984 Cartoon by
Oscar Abmn

1998. Cartoonists. Multicoloured.

2419 | 6p. Type **984** | 2·75 | 2·40
2420 | 6p. Cartoon by Emilio Cortinas | 2·75 | 2·40

985 Ferreira

1998. Tenth Death Anniv of Wilson Ferreira Aldunate (politician).

2421 | **985** | 6p. multicoloured | 2·75 | 2·40

986 Butia Palm

1998. Trees. Multicoloured.

2422 | 6p. Type **986** | 2·75 | 2·40
2423 | 6p. Butia palms by stream | 2·75 | 2·40
2424 | 6p. Ombu grove | 2·75 | 2·40
2425 | 6p. Ombu ("Phytolacca dioica"), leaf and fruit | 2·75 | 2·40

987 "Testudinites sellowi"

1998. Prehistoric Animals. Fossilised remains found in Uruguay. Multicoloured.

2426 | 6p. Type **987** | 2·75 | 2·40
2427 | 6p. "Proborhyaena gigantea" | 2·75 | 2·40
2428 | 6p. "Propachyrucos schiaffinos" | 2·75 | 2·40
2429 | 6p. "Stegomastodon platensis" | 2·75 | 2·40

988 "Sabbath" (Nelson
Romero)

1998. 50th Anniv of State of Israel.

2430 | **988** | 12p. multicoloured | 5·50 | 5·00

989 Map of
Americas and Sun

1998. 50th Anniv of Organization of American States.

2431 | **989** | 12p. blue, yellow & silver | 5·50 | 5·00

990 Athlete

1998. 61st World Congress of Sports Journalism.

2432 | **990** | 6p. multicoloured | 2·75 | 2·40

991 Farmhouses

1998. 50th Anniv of Land Settlement Institute.

2433 | **991** | 6p. multicoloured | 2·75 | 2·40

992 Common Caracara

1998. Birds. Multicoloured.

2434 | 6p. Type **992** | 2·75 | 2·40
2435 | 6p. Black-necked swan ("Cygnus melancoryphus") | 2·75 | 2·40
2436 | 6p. Roseate spoonbill ("Platalea ajaja") | 2·75 | 2·40
2437 | 6p. Buff-necked ibis ("Theristicus caudatus") | 2·75 | 2·40

993 Switerland 1850 5r.
and Uruguay 1856 60c.
Stamp

1998. 150th Anniv of Swiss Confederation and Uruguyuan–Swiss Thematic Stamps Exhibition, Nueva Helvecia. Sheet 100×110 mm containing T **993** and similar horiz designs. Multicoloured.

MS2438 3p.50 Type **993**; 3p.50 1 euro cent coin; 4p. Olympic rings (Swiss candidature for Winter Olympic Games, 2006); 4p. Proposed NASA International Space Station | 10·00 | 10·00

994 Fin Whale

1998. Ambiente 98 Thematic Stamp Exhibition (Maia, Portugal). International Year of the Ocean and Expo 98 World's Fair (Lisbon). Whales. Sheet 100×110 mm containing T **994** and similar horiz designs. Multicoloured.

| MS2439 | 3p.50 Type **994**; 3p.50 Minke whale ("Balaenoptera acutorostrata"); 4p. Humpback whale ("Megaptera novaeangliae"); 4p. Southern right whale ("Eubalaena australis") | 6·75 | 6·75 |

995 Demonstration outside Parliament, 1983

1998. Labour Day.

| 2440 | **995** | 6p. brown and black | 2·75 | 2·40 |

996 Electric Tramcar, 1906

1998. 50th Anniv of Circle for Studies on Public Transport. Trams of Montevideo. Multicoloured.

2441		6p. Type **996**	2·75	2·40
2442		6p. German Transatlantica tramcar, 1907	2·75	2·40
2443		6p. German Transatlantica tramcar, 1908	2·75	2·40
2444		6p. Transatlantica double-deck tramcar, 1916	2·75	2·40

997 Pampas Cat

1998. Big Cats. Multicoloured.

2445		6p. Type **997**	2·75	2·40
2446		6p. Ocelot ("Felis pardalis")	2·75	2·40
2447		6p. Tree-ocelot ("Felis wiedii")	2·75	2·40
2448		6p. Jaguar ("Panthera onca")	2·75	2·40

998 "Sirius" (schooner)

1998. Ships. Multicoloured.

2449		6p. Type **998**	2·75	2·40
2450		6p. "18 de Julio" (sail/steam gunboat)	2·75	2·40
2451		6p. "Maldonado" (transport paddle-steamer)	2·75	2·40
2452		6p. "Instituto de Pesca No. 1" (fishery research vessel)	2·75	2·40

999 Chapel, Orphans Lime-quarry, Colonia

1998. Mercosur. Jesuit Missions.

| 2453 | **999** | 12p. multicoloured | 5·50 | 5·00 |

1000 Monument (Juan Ferrari)

1998. 125th Anniv of Monument to the Peace of 6 April 1872.

| 2454 | **1000** | 6p. multicoloured | 2·75 | 2·40 |

1001 Headquarters and Obus 155 mm. M114 A-2 Gun

1998. Centenary of Fifth Artillery Batallion.

| 2455 | **1001** | 6p. multicoloured | 2·75 | 2·40 |

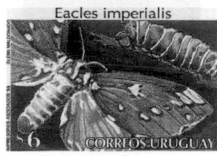

1002 Imperial Moth

1998. Moths. Multicoloured.

| 2456 | | 6p. Type **1002** | 2·75 | 2·40 |
| 2457 | | 6p. Protoparce lucetius | 2·75 | 2·40 |

1003 Artigas Monument

1998. Centenary of First Artigas Monument, San Jose.

| 2458 | **1003** | 6p. multicoloured | 2·75 | 2·40 |

1004 Lomba and Porcupine

1998. 80th Birth Anniv of Dr. Mauricio Lopez Lomba (doctor and philanthropist).

| 2459 | **1004** | 6p. multicoloured | 2·75 | 2·40 |

1005 Conservatory Emblem

1998. Centenary of Falleri-Balzo Music Conservatory, Montevideo.

| 2460 | **1005** | 6p. multicoloured | 2·75 | 2·40 |

1006 Jose Fernandez Vergara (founder)

1998. 95th Anniv of Pueblo Vergara (town).

| 2461 | **1006** | 6p. multicoloured | 2·75 | 2·40 |

1007 Front Page of First Edition

1998. 80th Anniv of "El Pais" (newspaper). Sheet 90×70 mm.

| MS2462 | **1007** | 12p. multicoloured | 5·50 | 5·50 |

1008 Institution Building

1998. 145th Anniv of Spanish Association of Primary Mutual Assistance (medical organization).

| 2463 | **1008** | 6p. multicoloured | 2·75 | 2·40 |

1009 La Princesa (frigate) and Emblem

1998. "Espamer'98" Iberian–Latin American Stamp Exhibition, Buenos Aires. 230th Anniv of First Montevideo–La Coruna Maritime Mail Service.

| 2464 | **1009** | 12p. multicoloured | 5·50 | 5·00 |

1010 Students with Banners

1998. 15th Anniv of School and University Students' Demonstration, Montevideo.

| 2465 | **1010** | 6p. brown and black | 2·75 | 2·40 |

1011 Junkers J52

1998. "IBEROAMERICANA'98" Iberian–American Stamp Exhibition, Maia, Portugal. Aircraft. Multicoloured.

2466		6p. Type **1011**	2·75	2·40
2467		6p. SPAD VII	2·75	2·40
2468		6p. Ansaldo SVA-10	2·75	2·40
2469		6p. Neybar	2·75	2·40

1012 Allende

1998. 25th Death Anniv of Salvador Allende (Chilean President, 1970–73).

| 2470 | **1012** | 12p. multicoloured | 5·50 | 5·00 |

1013 Fabregat (teacher and writer)

1998. 50th Anniv of Enrique Rodriguez Fabregat's Participation in United Nations Conciliation Commission.

| 2471 | **1013** | 6p. multicoloured | 2·75 | 2·40 |

1014 Microphone, Emblem and Station Headquarters, Montevideo and Emblem

1998. 70th Anniv of Radio Carve.

| 2472 | **1014** | 6p. multicoloured | 2·75 | 2·40 |

1015 Iulia Guarino (architect)

1998. America. Famous Women. Multicoloured.

| 2473 | | 6p. Type **1015** | 2·75 | 2·40 |
| 2474 | | 12p. Paulina Luisi (doctor) | 5·50 | 5·00 |

1016 Universal Postal Union Emblem and Stars

1998. World Post Day. "ILSAPEX '98" International Stamp Exhibition, Johannesburg, South Africa.

| 2475 | **1016** | 12p. multicoloured | 5·50 | 5·00 |

1017 Emblem and Equipment

1998. 50th Anniv of Association of Pharmacies.

| 2476 | **1017** | 6p. multicoloured | 2·75 | 2·40 |

1018 Globe and Postal Services

1998. Small Packets Service. Self-adhesive.

| 2477 | **1018** | 25p multicoloured | 11·50 | 10·00 |

1019 Lancia Fire Engine, 1930

1998. "Italia 98" International Stamp Exhibition, Milan, Italy. Motor Vehicles. Multicoloured.

2478		6p. Type **1019**	2·75	2·40
2479		6p. Maserati "San Remo", 1946	2·75	2·40
2480		6p. Alfa Romeo trolleybus, 1954	2·75	2·40
2481		6p. Fiat "500" Topolino, 1936	2·75	2·40

1020 Hector Maria Artola (musician) and Score

1998. Personalities. Multicoloured.

2482		6p. Type **1020**	2·75	2·40
2483		6p. Serafin J. Garcia (writer)	2·75	2·40
2484		6p. Nerses Ounanian (sculptor) (horiz)	2·75	2·40

1021 "Play in order to help" (Melissa Migliozzi)

1998. "Juvenalia'98" Youth Exhibition, Montevideo. Winning Entry in Children's Stamp Design Competition.

| 2485 | **1021** | 6p. multicoloured | 2·75 | 2·40 |

1076 "Bearded Drinker" (Nelson Romero)

1999. 20th Anniv of Juanico Wine Cellar. Winning Designs in "Art and Wine" Competition. Multicoloured.

| 2587 | **1076** | 9p. Type **1076** | 4·25 | 3·75 |
| 2588 | | 9p. "Carport of the Old Wine Cellar" (Nelson Ramos) | 4·25 | 3·75 |

1077 Council Offices

1999. Inauguration of Maldonado Department Council Building.

| 2589 | **1077** | 9p. multicoloured | 4·25 | 3·75 |

1078 Stylized Sun (Carlos Paez Vilaro)

2000. Contemporary Art.

| 2590 | **1078** | 9p. multicoloured | 4·25 | 3·75 |

1080 Cattleya corcovado

2000. Orchids. Multicoloured.

2592	**1080**	4p. Type **1080**	1·70	1·50
2593		4p. Cattleya sp. hybrid	1·70	1·50
2594		5p. Laelia purpurata	2·30	2·00
2595		5p. Laelia tenebrosa	2·30	2·00

1081 Punta del Este Lighthouse

2000. Lighthouses. Multicoloured.

2596	**1081**	4p. Type **1081**	1·70	1·50
2597		4p. Cabo Polonio	1·70	1·50
2598		5p. Flores Island	2·30	2·00
2599		5p. Punta Brava	2·30	2·00

1082 Quijano

2000. Birth Centenary of Carlos Quijano (journalist).

| 2600 | **1082** | 9p. multicoloured | 4·00 | 3·50 |

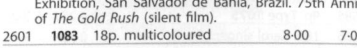

1083 Charlie Chaplin (leading actor)

2000. "LUBRAPEX 2000" Brazilian–Portuguese Stamp Exhibition, San Salvador de Bahia, Brazil. 75th Anniv of The Gold Rush (silent film).

| 2601 | **1083** | 18p. multicoloured | 8·00 | 7·00 |

1084 Chapel

2000. 250th Anniv of El Cordon, Montevideo.

| 2602 | **1084** | 9p. multicoloured | 4·00 | 3·50 |

1085 Mural (right-hand detail)

2000. Indigenous Flora Mural, Luis Koster Stadium, Mercedes City. Multicoloured.

| 2603 | **1085** | 4p. Type **1085** | 1·70 | 1·50 |
| 2604 | | 5p. Mural (left-hand detail) | 2·30 | 2·00 |

Nos. 2603/4 were issued together, se-tenant, forming a composite design of a portion of the mural.

1086 Garcia

2000. 144th Birth Anniv of Francisco Garcia y Santos (Director General of Posts and Telegraphs, 1901–17).

| 2605 | **1086** | 9p. multicoloured | 4·00 | 3·50 |

1087 Emblem

2000. 125th Anniv of Association of Uruguayan Notaries.

| 2606 | **1087** | 9p. multicoloured | 4·00 | 3·50 |

1088 Emblem

2000. International Museums Day.

| 2607 | **1088** | 9p. multicoloured | 4·00 | 3·50 |

1089 Skyscrapers (Maria Pia Pereyra)

2000. "Stampin' the Future". Winning Entries in Children's International Painting Competition. Multicoloured.

2608	**1089**	4p. Type **1089**	1·70	1·50
2609		4p. "2000", fish and national colours (Virginia Regueiro)	1·70	1·50
2610		5p. People building globe (Helena Perez Acevedo)	2·30	2·00
2611		5p. Letters between postman and computer (Blanca Esther Lima)	2·30	2·00

1090 Emblem

2000. 90th Anniv of Club Soriano (cultural and sports association).

| 2612 | **1090** | 9p. multicoloured | 4·00 | 3·50 |

1091 Antonio Rupenian (founder)

2000. 65th Anniv of Radio Armenia (Armenian community radio service).

| 2613 | **1091** | 18p. multicoloured | 8·00 | 7·00 |

1092 Woman reading

2000. Centenary of The 1900 Generation (Uruguayan writers).

| 2614 | **1092** | 9p. multicoloured | 4·00 | 3·50 |

1093 Echinopsis multiplex

2000. Cacti. Multicoloured.

| 2615 | **1093** | 4p. Type **1093** | 2·00 | 1·80 |
| 2616 | | 5p. Thorn ball (Notocactus ottonis) | 2·40 | 2·10 |

1094 Team (Olympic Champion, Amsterdam, 1928)

2000. Centenary of Uruguay Football Association. Multicoloured.

2617	**1094**	4p. Type **1094**	2·00	1·80
2618		4p. Stadium (first World Cup Football Champion, Uruguay, 1930)	2·00	1·80
2619		5p. Team (Olympic Champion, Paris, 1924)	2·40	2·10
2620		5p. Player scoring goal (World Cup Football Champion, Brazil, 1950)	2·40	2·10

1095 Georges Bizet (composer) and Scene from Carmen

2000. Opera Anniversaries. Multicoloured.

| 2621 | **1095** | 9p. Type **1095** (125th anniv of first performance) | 4·00 | 3·50 |
| 2622 | | 9p. Giacomo Puccini (composer) and scene from Tosca (centenary of first performance) | 4·00 | 3·50 |

1096 Emblem

2000. 20th Anniv of Latin American Association of Integration.

| 2623 | **1096** | 18p. multicoloured | 8·00 | 7·00 |

1097 Vought Sikorsky OS2U Kingfisher (seaplane)

2000. 75th Anniv of Uruguay Naval Aviation.

| 2624 | **1097** | 9p. multicoloured | 4·00 | 3·50 |

1098 Fingerprints and Emblem

2000. 120th Anniv of O.R.T. (educational organization).

| 2625 | **1098** | 9p. multicoloured | 4·75 | 4·25 |

1099 De La Robla

2000. Luis de la Robla (first Postmaster General in Uruguay) Commemoration.

| 2626 | **1099** | 9p. multicoloured | 4·75 | 4·25 |

1100 Rodriguez and Racing Car

2000. First Death Anniv of Gonzalo Rodriguez (racing driver). Multicoloured.

| 2627 | **1100** | 9p. Type **1100** | 4·75 | 4·25 |
| 2628 | | 9p. Racing car and Rodriguez with trophy | 4·75 | 4·25 |

1101 Map and Artigas

2000. 150th Death Anniv of Jose Artigas.

| 2629 | **1101** | 9p. multicoloured | 4·75 | 4·25 |

1102 Common Miner (Geositta cunicularia)

2000. "Espana 2000" World Stamp Exhibition, Madrid. Birds. Multicoloured.

2630	**1102**	4p. Type **1102**	2·10	1·90
2631		4p. Freckle-breasted thornbird (Phacellodomus striaticollis)	2·10	1·90
2632		5p. Long-tailed reed finch (Donacospiza albifrons)	2·50	2·20
2633		5p. Golden-winged cacique (Cacicus chrysopterus)	2·50	2·20

1103 T. Makiguchi, J. Toda and Emblem

2000. 25th Anniv of Soka Gakkai International (Buddhist organization).

| 2634 | **1103** | 18p. multicoloured | 9·25 | 8·25 |

1104 Noughts and Crosses

2000. America. A.I.D.S. Awareness. Multicoloured.

| 2635 | **1104** | 9p. Type **1104** | 4·75 | 4·25 |
| 2636 | | 18p. A.I.D.S. ribbon and needle | 9·25 | 8·25 |

1105 Emblem

2000. Mercosur. Cultural Heritage Day.
2637 **1105** 18p. multicoloured 9·25 8·25

1106 "Dragon"

2000. 105th Birth Anniv of Luis Mazzey (artist).
2638 **1106** 9p. multicoloured 4·75 4·25

1107 Firemen on Roof

2000. Firemen. Multicoloured.
2639 9p. Type **1107** 4·75 4·25
2640 9p. Firemen attending motor vehicle fire (horiz) 4·75 4·25

1108 Prof. Julio Ricaldoni (engineer)

2000. 50th Anniv of and 29th South American Conference on Structural Engineering, Punta Del Este.
2641 **1108** 9p. multicoloured 4·75 4·25

1109 Capitan Miranda

2000. 70th Anniv Capitan Miranda (cadet ship).
2642 **1109** 9p. multicoloured 4·75 4·25

1110 Charles V and Map

2000. 500th Birth Anniv of Charles V, Holy Roman Emperor.
2643 **1110** 22p. multicoloured 9·25 8·25

1111 Fireworks

2000. Christmas. Multicoloured.
2644 11p. Type **1111** 4·75 4·25
2645 22p. Holy Family (crib figures) 9·25 8·25

1112 Emblem

2000. 125th Anniv of Sarandi Del Yi, Montevideo.
2646 **1112** 11p. multicoloured 5·00 4·50

1113 Emblem

2001. Forest Fire Prevention Campaign.
2647 **1113** 11p. multicoloured 5·00 4·50

1114 Little Monkey Frog (Phyllomedusa iheringii)

2001. Amphibians and Reptiles. Multicoloured.
2648 11p. Type **1114** 5·00 4·50
2649 11p. Black spine-necked swamp turtle (Acanthochelys spixii) 5·00 4·50
2650 11p. Hilaire's side-necked turtle (Phrynops hilarii) 5·00 4·50
2651 11p. Striped snouted treefrog (Scinax squalirostris) 5·00 4·50

1115 Clubhouse, River and Emblem

2001. Centenary of Paysandu Rowing Club.
2652 **1115** 11p. multicoloured 5·00 4·50

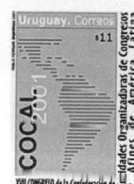

1116 Map of South America and Emblem

2001. 18th Congress of Latin American Confederation of Organizers of Congresses and Similar Events (COCAL) and 17th Congress of International Convention and Congress Association, Montevideo.
2653 **1116** 11p. multicoloured 5·00 4·50

1117 Building Facade

2001. Bicentenary of Belen.
2654 **1117** 11p. multicoloured 5·00 4·50

1118 Crow's Gorge

2001. Natural Sights. Multicoloured. Self-adhesive gum.
2655 2p. Waterfall, Salto del Penitente 95 85
2658 11p. Type **1118** 5·00 4·50
2661 20p. Palace Cave (vert) 9·25 8·25
2664 100p. Hill of Shells 35·00 31·00

1119 "David"

2001. 500th Anniv of "David" (sculpture, Michelangelo).
2665 **1119** 22p. black, yellow and red 10·00 8·75

1120 Musicians and Emblem

2001. 50th Anniv of Uruguayan Society of Performers (S.U.D.E.I.).
2666 **1120** 11p. multicoloured 5·00 4·50

1121 Figure and Emblem

2001. 75th Anniv of Casal Catala (Catalan cultural organization).
2667 **1121** 11p. multicoloured 5·00 4·50

1122 Emblem

2001. 85th Anniv of Engineering School, Montevideo.
2668 **1122** 11p. blue 5·00 4·50

1123 Talice

2001. Second Death Anniv of Rudolfo Talice (biologist).
2669 **1123** 11p. multicoloured 5·00 4·50

1124 Anniversary Emblem

2001. 50th Anniv of Lion's Club, Montevideo.
2670 **1124** 11p. multicoloured 5·00 4·50

1125 Early Telephone and Alexander Graham Bell

2001. 125th Anniv of the Telephone.
2671 **1125** 22p. multicoloured 10·00 8·75

1126 Urtutu Pit Viper (Bothrops alternatus)

2001. Snakes. Multicoloured.
2672 11p. Philodyras olfersii 5·00 4·50
2673 11p. Type **1126** 5·00 4·50

1127 "Two Ways" (detail, oil painting)

2001. Death Centenary of Juan Manuel Blanes (artist).
2674 **1127** 11p. multicoloured 5·00 4·50

1128 Dr. Morquio

2001. Centenary of Appointment of Dr. Luis Morquio as Professor of Paediatrics at Uruguay University.
2675 **1128** 11p. multicoloured 5·00 4·50

1129 "Rheingold"

2001. 125th Anniv of First Performance of Richard Wagner's Ring of the Nibelungs. Scenes from the operas. Multicoloured.
2676 11p. Type **1129** 5·00 4·50
2677 11p. Valkyrie 5·00 4·50
2678 11p. Siegfried 5·00 4·50
2679 11p. Decline of the Gods and Wagner 5·00 4·50

1130 Emblem

2001. 50th Anniv of International Organization for Migration.
2680 **1130** 22p. blue and black 10·00 8·75

1131 Edison

2001. 75th Death Anniv of Thomas Alva Edison (inventor).
2681 **1131** 22p. multicoloured 10·00 8·75

1132 Container Ship

2001. Centenary of Montevideo Port.
2682 **1132** 11p. multicoloured 5·00 4·50

1133 New Hampshire

2001. Domestic Chickens. Designs showing pairs of each breed. Multicoloured.
2683 11p. Type **1133** 5·00 4·50
2684 11p. Buff Orpingtons 5·00 4·50
2685 11p. Araucanas 5·00 4·50
2686 11p. Light brown leghorns 5·00 4·50

1134 Moby Dick and Whalers

2001. 150th Anniv of Publication of Moby Dick (novel by Herman Melville).
2687 **1134** 22p. multicoloured 10·00 8·75

1135 Flags, Globe and Gonzalez Pecotche

2001. Birth Centenary of Carlos Bernado Gonzalez Pecotche (founder of Logosophy self-development).
2688	**1135**	11p. multicoloured	5·00	4·50

1136 Concorde

2001. 25th Anniv of First Flight of Concorde.
2689	**1136**	22p. multicoloured	10·00	8·75

1137 "Louis Philippe"

2001. Roses. Multicoloured.
2690	**1137**	11p. Type **1137**	5·00	4·50
2691		11p. "Souvenir de Mme Leonie Viennot"	5·00	4·50
2692		11p. "Kronenbourg"	5·00	4·50
2693		11p. "Lady Hillingdon"	5·00	4·50

1138 Bee-keepers

2001. Bee-keeping. Multicoloured.
2694	**1138**	12p. Type **1138**	5·00	4·50
2695		12p. Honey bee on flower	5·00	4·50

Nos. 2694/5 were issued together, *se-tenant*, forming a composite design.

1139 Bicentenary Emblem

2001. Bicentenary of Dolores (village), Soriano Department.
2696	**1139**	12p. multicoloured	5·00	4·50

1140 Girl and Flowers

2001. 80th Anniv of Uruguay–Japan Diplomatic Relations.
2697	**1140**	24p. multicoloured	10·50	9·25

1141 Stylized Sun with Face

2001. 75th Anniv of Uruguay Philatelic Club. Multicoloured.
2698	**1141**	12p. Type **1141**	5·25	4·75
2699		12p. Square sun	5·25	4·75

1142 Basilica of the Blessed Sacrament, Colonia Family, Sauce

2001. America. World Heritage. Multicoloured.
2700		12p. Type **1142**	5·25	4·75
2701		24p. San Benito Chapel, Colonia	10·50	9·25

1143 "Experience" (Carlos Amoretti)

2001. "50 Years in Art" Exhibition by Carlos Amoretti.
2702	**1143**	12p. multicoloured	5·25	4·75

1144 Altarpiece, Temple of the Sacred

2001. 150th Anniv of Sauce, Canelones.
2703	**1144**	12p. multicoloured	5·25	4·75

1145 "Life and Health" (Mariana Tarigo)

2001. Anti-drugs Campaign. Winning Entry in Stamp Design Competition.
2704	**1145**	12p. multicoloured	5·25	4·75

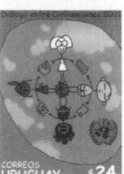

1146 Children encircling Globe

2001. United Nations Year of Dialogue among Civilizations.
2705	**1146**	24p. multicoloured	10·50	9·25

1147 Family flying Kite

2001. Honorary Anti-Cancer Campaign Committee.
2706	**1147**	12p. multicoloured	5·25	4·75

1148 Newspapers on Conveyor-belt

2001. 20th Anniv of Ultimas Noticias (newspaper).
2707	**1148**	12p. multicoloured	5·25	4·75

1149 Emblem, Basket and Ball

2001. 50th Anniv of Sauce Basketball Club.
2708	**1149**	12p. multicoloured	5·25	4·75

1150 Blood Droplet Figure

2001. Voluntary Blood Donation Day.
2709		12p. multicoloured	5·50	5·00

1151 San Martin Portrait overlaid with Grid Pattern

2001. 70th Death Anniv of Juan Zorrilla de San Martin (writer).
2710	**1151**	12p. multicoloured	5·50	5·00

1152 Oyarvide (survey ship)

2001
2711	**1152**	12p. multicoloured	5·50	5·00

1153 Mr. and Mrs. King

2001. Visit to Uruguay of Mr. Richard King (president of Rotary Club International).
2712	**1153**	24p. multicoloured	10·50	9·25

1154 Emblems

2001. 110th Anniv of Penarol Athletics Club.
2713	**1154**	12p. multicoloured	5·50	5·00

1155 Sosa

2001. 75th Birth Anniv of Julio Sosa (singer).
2714	**1155**	12p. black and violet	5·50	5·00

1156 Nasazzi

2001. Birth Cent of Jose Nasazzi (footballer).
2715	**1156**	12p. multicoloured	5·50	5·00

1157 "Adoration of the Shepherds" (Jose Ribera)

2001. Christmas. Multicoloured.
2716		12p. Type **1157**	5·50	5·00
2717		24p. "Adoration of the Shepherds" (Anton Raphael Mengs)	10·50	9·25

1158 Bell Tower

2001. Bicentenary of San Carlos Church.
2718	**1158**	12p. multicoloured	5·50	5·00

1159 "Cosmic Monument" (Joaquiin Torres Garcia)

2001. 90th Anniv of National Museum of Visual Arts.
2719	**1159**	12p. multicoloured	5·50	5·00

1160 Building Facade

2001. 90th Anniv of State Insurance Bank.
2720	**1160**	12p. multicoloured	5·50	5·00

1161 *Guettarda uruguensis*

2001. Mercosur.
2721	**1161**	24p. multicoloured	10·50	9·25

1162 Josemaria Escriva

2002. Birth Centenary of Josemaria Escriva de Balaguer (founder of Opus Dei religious order). Multicoloured.
2722		12p. Type **1162**	5·50	5·00
2723		12p. Facing front	5·50	5·00
2724		12p. Facing left	5·50	5·00
2725		12p. With mother and baby	5·50	5·00

2002. Flowers. As T **1025**. Multicoloured. Self-adhesive gum.
2726		1p. *Oxalis pudica*	55	50
2727		5p. As No. 2726 but with colour changed	2·20	2·00
2728		10p. *Aechmea recurvata*	4·75	4·25

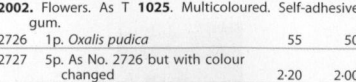
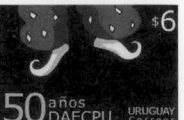

1163 Legs

2002. 50th Anniv of DAECPU (carnival directors).

2742	1163	6p. black and blue	2·75	2·40
2743	-	6p. black and magenta	2·75	2·40
2744	-	12p. black	5·50	5·00

DESIGNS: Type **1163**; 6p.Cane, legs and top hat; 12p. Legs (different).

1164 Church

2002. 1700th Anniv of Christianity in Armenia.

2745	1164	12p. multicoloured	5·50	5·00

1165 Hoof Print

2002. Year of the Horse.

2746	1165	24p. blue, black and magenta	10·50	9·25

1166 Winners' Flags and Football

2002. World Cup Football Championship, Japan and South Korea. Multicoloured.

2747		12p. Type **1166**	5·25	4·75
2748		12p. Footballer	5·25	4·75

1167 "N"

2002. Book Day.

2749	1167	12p. multicoloured	5·25	4·75

1168 Stylized Children

2002. 75th Anniv of Inter-America Children's Institute.

2750	1168	12p. multicoloured	5·25	4·75

1169 Bernabe Rivera and Arms

2002. 165th Anniv of the Foundation of Tacuarembo.

2751	1169	12p. multicoloured	5·25	4·75

1170 Lighthouse Building

2002. Bicentenary of Cerro de Montevideo Lighthouse. Multicoloured.

2752	1170	12p. Type **1170**	5·25	4·75
2753		24p. Entrance to lighthouse (vert)	10·50	9·25

1171 Building Façade

2002. 150th Anniv of Villa Constitucion, Salto Department.

2754	1171	12p. multicoloured	5·25	4·75

1172 Jose Leandro Andrade (footballer)

2002. Sportsmen. Multicoloured.

2755		12p. Type **1172**	5·25	4·75
2756		12p. Cesar Gallardo (fencer, rower and basketball player)	5·25	4·75
2757		12p. Alvaro Gestido (footballer)	5·25	4·75
2758		12p. Pedro Petrone (footballer)	5·25	4·75
2759		12p. Lorenzo Fernandez (footballer)	5·25	4·75

1173 Figures enclosing Globe

2002. "United We Stand". 175th Anniv of Postal Service. Sheet 100×80 mm containing T **1173** and similar horiz designs. Multicoloured.

MS2760	6p. ×3 Type **1172** ×3	8·25	8·25

1174 Tourism Emblem

2002. Tourism.

2761	1174	24p. blue and yellow	10·50	9·25

1175 Museum Building and *Erthrina crista-galli*

2002. Centenary of Montevideo Botanical Museum. Multicoloured.

2762		12p. Type **1175**	5·25	4·75
2763		12p. Oxblood lily (*Rhodophiala bifida*)	5·25	4·75
2764		12p. Atilio Lombardo (founder) and *Tillandsia arequitae*	5·25	4·75
2765		12p. *Heteroterys dumetorum*	5·25	4·75

1176 Man carrying Cane

2002. Centenary of Montevideo Wanderers Football Club.

2766	1176	12p. black	5·25	4·75

1177 Elvis Presley

2002. 25th Death Anniv of Elvis Presley (entertainer).

2767	1177	24p. multicoloured	10·50	9·25

1178 Agustin Bisio

2002. 50th Death Anniv of Agustin Bisio (writer). Self-adhesive gum.

2768	1178	12p. multicoloured	5·25	4·75

1179 Obelisk to the Heroes of 1825

2002. 150th Anniv of Foundation of Artigas City. Self-adhesive.

2769	1179	12p. multicoloured	5·25	4·75

1180 Early and Modern Buses

2002. 65th Anniv of CUTSA (society of bus services).

2770	1180	12p. multicoloured	5·25	4·75

1181 Sigmund Freud

2002. Latin-American Psychoanalysis Conference, Montevideo.

2771	1181	12p. multicoloured	5·25	4·75

1182 Horacio Arredondo and San Miguel Fort

2002. 35th Death Anniv of Horacio Arredondo (historian). National Heritage Day.

2772	1182	12p. multicoloured	5·25	4·75

1183 1905 Lieutenant Colonel's Uniform and Barracks Building

2002. Paso del Rey Barrack, Sarandi del Yi.

2773	1183	12p. multicoloured	5·25	4·75

1184 Bathers (Patrica Torres and Patricia Molina)

2002. International Year of Ecotourism. Winning Entry in Design a Stamp Competition.

2774	1184	12p. multicoloured	5·25	4·75

1185 Post Office Building

2002. 175th Anniv of Uruguay Post Office. Multicoloured.

2775		12p. Type **1185**	5·25	4·75
MS2776	100×90 mm. 12p. Post box. Imperf	5·50	5·50

1186 Brigadier General Juan Antonio Lavalleja on Horseback (statue) (Juan Manuel Ferrari)

2002. Centenary of Erection of First Equestrian Statue.

2777	1186	12p. multicoloured	5·25	4·75

1187 Letters

2002. America. Literacy Campaign. Multicoloured.

2778		12p. Type **1187**	5·25	4·75
2779		24p. Alphabet soup	10·50	9·25

1188 Wreath

2002. Christmas.

2780	1188	12p. multicoloured	5·25	4·75

1189 Pharmacy Centre Building

2002. 65th Anniv of Pharmacy Centre.

2781	1189	12p. multicoloured	5·25	4·75

1190 Wine Bottle

2002. 125th Anniv of Tannat Wine Producers.

2782	1190	12p. multicoloured	5·25	4·75

1191 *Maldonado* (hydrographic ship)

2002. 185th Anniv of Uruguay Navy.

2783	1191	12p. multicoloured	5·25	4·75

1192 Jigsaw Puzzle Piece and Emblem

2002. 24th Anniv of National Organs and Tissue Bank. National Organ Donation Day.
2784 **1192** 12p. multicoloured 5·25 4·75

1193 Early and Modern Taxis

2002. Centenary of Taxi Service.
2785 **1193** 12p. multicoloured 5·25 4·75

1194 Brigadier General Manuel Oribe

2002. 145th Birth Anniv of Brigadier General Manuel Oribe (politician).
2786 **1194** 12p. multicoloured 5·25 4·75

1195 Guitar Neck wrapped in Black Ribbon

2002. First Death Anniv of George Harrison (musician).
2787 **1195** 24p. multicoloured 10·50 9·25

1196 Baby in Womb

2002. Centenary of Pan American Health Organization.
2788 **1196** 12p. multicoloured 5·25 4·75

1197 Emblems, Map and Soldiers

2002. 50th Anniv of Uruguay Army's Participation in United Nations Peace Keeping Force.
2789 **1197** 12p. multicoloured 5·25 4·75

1198 "Costa Azul" (Alfredo Testoni)

2002. Alfredo Testoni (artist).
2790 **1198** 12p. multicoloured 5·25 4·75

1199 Coast and Ship at Night

2002. Mercosur. Tourism. Multicoloured.
2791 12p. Type **1199** 5·25 4·75
2792 24p. Beach 10·50 9·25

1200 Village Square and School Building

2002. 130th Anniv of Juanico.
2793 **1200** 12p. multicoloured 5·25 4·75

1201 Ships under Fire

2002. 175th Anniv of Juncal Sea Battle.
2794 **1201** 12p. multicoloured 5·25 4·75

1202 Cavalry Charge

2002. 175th Anniv of Ituzaingo Battle.
2795 **1202** 12p. multicoloured 5·25 4·75

1203 Globe and Compass

2003. International Relations.
2796 **1203** 12p. multicoloured 5·25 4·75

1204 Typewriter

2003. 30th Anniv of Busqueda.
2797 **1204** 12p. multicoloured 5·25 4·75

1205 Imanja (sea goddess)

2003
2798 **1205** 12p. multicoloured 5·25 4·75

1206 National Symbols

2003. 15th Anniv of Uruguay–China Diplomatic Relations.
2799 **1206** 12p. multicoloured 5·25 4·75

1207 Goat

2003. New Year. Year of the Goat.
2800 **1207** 5p. multicoloured 2·20 2·00

1208 Christopher Columbus (500th anniv of fourth visit (2002))

2003. Navigators. Multicoloured.
2801 12p. Type **1208** 5·25 4·75
2802 12p. Juan Diaz de Solis 5·25 4·75
2803 12p. Sebastian Cabot (Sebastiano Gaboto) 5·25 4·75
2804 12p. Hernando Arias de Saavedra (Hernandarias) 5·25 4·75

1209 Symbols of Communication

2003. 20th Anniv of URSEC (Unidad Reguladora de Servicios de Comunicaciones) (regulating unit of communication services).
2805 **1209** 12p. multicoloured 5·25 4·75

1210 Flower and Outline of Woman

2003. International Women's Day.
2806 **1210** 12p. multicoloured 5·25 4·75

1211 Monument

2003. 150th Anniv of Treinta y Tres.
2807 **1211** 12p. multicoloured 5·25 4·75

1212 *Heliconius erato*

2003. Butterflies. Multicoloured.
2808 12p. Type **1212** 5·25 4·75
2809 12p. *Junonia evarete* 5·25 4·75
2810 12p. *Dryadula phaetusa* 5·25 4·75
2811 12p. *Parides perrhebus* 5·25 4·75
Nos. 2808/11 were issued together, *se-tenant*, forming a composite design.

1213 Jose Batalle y Ordonez

2003. Centenary of First President—Jose Batalle y Ordonez. Designs showing President Batalle y Ordonez. Multicoloured.
2812 12p. Type **1213** 5·25 4·75
2813 12p. As younger man 5·25 4·75
2814 12p. With head resting on hand 5·25 4·75
2815 12p. Facing right 5·25 4·75

1214 Basket weaving

2003. Rural Craftswomen. Multicoloured.
2816 12p. Type **1214** 5·25 4·75
2817 12p. Knitting 5·25 4·75
2818 12p. Pottery 5·25 4·75
2819 12p. Jam making 5·25 4·75
2820 12p. Jewellery 5·25 4·75

1215 Capilla de Farruco

2003
2821 **1215** 12p. multicoloured 5·25 4·75

1216 Cow

2003. Natural Food.
2822 **1216** 12p. multicoloured 5·25 4·75

1217 *Caiman latirostris*

2003. Endangered Species. "Cerros Azules" Caiman Breeding Farm. Self-adhesive.
2823 **1217** 12p. multicoloured 5·25 4·75

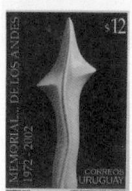

1218 Los Andes Memorial

2003. 30th Anniv of Cordillera de Los Andes Aircraft Crash (2002).
2824 **1218** 12p. multicoloured 5·25 4·75

1219 Building Facade

2003. Centenary of Military Centre.
2825 **1219** 12p. multicoloured 5·25 4·75

1220 Museum Building (painting)

2003. Cultural Heritage. 150th Anniv of "18 de Mayo 1811" Military Museum, Montevideo.
2826 **1220** 12p. multicoloured 5·25 4·75

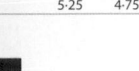

1221 Buildings

2003. Cultural Heritage. Casa Ximenez, Las Bovedas.
2827 **1221** 14p. multicoloured 5·50 5·00

1222 Wilson Ferreira
Aldunate

2003. 15th Death Anniv of Wilson Ferreira Aldunate (politician). Designs showing Wilson Ferreira Aldunate, Multicoloured.
2828 14p. Type **1222** 5·50 5·00
2829 14p. Facing left 5·50 5·00
2830 14p. With arms raised 5·50 5·00
2831 14p. Wearing shirt 5·50 5·00

1223 Winning Team

2003. 75th Anniv of Uruguay Football Team winning Gold at Olympic Games, Amsterdam.
2832 **1223** 14p. multicoloured 5·50 5·00

1224 Arms

2003. 70th Anniv of Richard Anderson College.
2833 **1224** 14p. multicoloured 5·50 5·00

1225 "100"

2003. Centenary of Santa Isabel Paso de Los Toros, Tacuarembo.
2834 **1225** 14p. multicoloured 5·50 5·00

1226 "70" and Emblem

2003. 70th Anniv of ANDA.
2835 **1226** 14p. multicoloured 5·50 5·00

1227 "50" and Emblem

2003. 50th Anniv of Jesus Maria College.
2836 **1227** 14p. multicoloured 5·50 5·00

1228 Juan Carlos Onetti (writer)

2003. National Philatelic Academy. Juan Carlos Onetti (writer) Commemoration.
2837 **1228** 14p. multicoloured 5·50 5·00

1229 Palacio Heber (Gaucho and Currency Museum)

2003. Historic Neighbourhoods.
2838 **1229** 14p. multicoloured 5·50 5·00

1230 Musician (statue)

2003. 125th Anniv of Parva Domus Magna Quies.
2839 **1230** 14p. multicoloured 5·50 5·00

1231 Emblem

2003. Fourth Anniv of Neighbourhood Security Commission.
2840 **1231** 14p. black and blue 5·50 5·00

1232 Team Members

2003. Centenary of National Football Team's First International Triumph.
2841 **1232** 14p. multicoloured 5·50 5·00

1233 Lauro Ayestaran

2003. Cultural Heritage. Lauro Ayestaran (musician) Commemoration.
2842 **1233** 14p. multicoloured 5·50 5·00

1234 Building Facade

2003. 150th Anniv of Spanish Mutual Aid Association.
2843 **1234** 14p. multicoloured 5·50 5·00

1235 Hospital Building

2003. 50th Anniv of Manuel Quintela Clinical Hospital.
2844 **1235** 14p. multicoloured 5·50 5·00

1236 Elbio Fernandez

1237 Emblem

2003. 135th Anniv of Friends of Popular Education Society.
2845 **1236** 14p. multicoloured 5·50 5·00

2003. 45th Anniv of Photo Journalists' Association.
2846 **1237** 14p. multicoloured 5·50 5·00

1238 General Rivera

2003. Brigadier General Fructuoso Rivera (first constitutional president) Commemoration.
2847 **1238** 14p. multicoloured 5·50 5·00

1239 Emblem and Yacht

2003. 75th Anniv of Club Naval.
2848 **1239** 14p. multicoloured 5·50 5·00

1240 Radio

2003. Malos Pensamientos (radio programme).
2849 **1240** 14p. multicoloured 5·50 5·00

1241 Cyclists

2003. Milton Wynants—Olympic Silver Medal and Pan American Gold Medal Cyclist.
2850 **1241** 14p. multicoloured 5·50 5·00

1242 Emblem

2003. 50th Anniv of ANAS (National Social Assistance).
2851 **1242** 14p. vermilion, blue and black 5·50 5·00

1243 Emblem

2003. Centenary of Cardona City, Soriano.
2852 **1243** 14p. multicoloured 5·50 5·00

1244 Buildings

2003. 84th Anniv of Construction Industry Integration.
2853 **1244** 14p. multicoloured 5·50 5·00

1245 Building Facade

2003. 25th Anniv of Maria Tsakos Foundation (Greek association).
2854 **1245** 14p. multicoloured 5·50 5·00

1246 Prosopis affinis

2003. America. Flora and Fauna. Multicoloured.
2855 14p. Type **1246** 5·50 5·00
2856 36p. Agouti paca paca 14·00 12·00

1247 Cedar of Lebanon

2003. 60th Anniv of Lebanon Independence.
2857 **1247** 14p. vermilion and green 5·50 5·00

1248 Masonic Emblem

2003. 147th Anniv of Masonic Activity in Uruguay. Sheet 90×71 mm.
MS2858 **1248** 14p. multicoloured 5·75 5·75

1249 "30"

2003. 30th Anniv of Cacho Bochinche (television programme).
2859 **1249** 14p. multicoloured 5·50 5·00

1250 Carnival Procession

2003. 50th Anniv of Morenada (carnival dance). Juan Angel Silva (folklorist) Commemoration.
2860 **1250** 14p. multicoloured 5·50 5·00

1251 Juan Antonio
Lavalleja

2003. 150th Death Anniv of Juan Antonio Lavalleja (soldier). T **1252** and similar vert design. Multicoloured.
MS2862 12p.×2, Type **1252**; Arms and
    map (10th anniv of USOPAL)   11·00   11·00
    The stamps and margins of **MS**2862 form a composite design.

1253 J. A. Schiaffino

2003. World Cup Football Championship, Germany—2006. Sheet 90×70 mm containing T **1253** and similar vert design. Multicoloured.
MS2863 12p.×2, Type **1253**; Fritz Walter   11·00   11·00
    The stamps and margins of **MS**2863 form a composite design.

1254 The Nativity

2003. Christmas.
2864   **1254**   14p. multicoloured   5·50   5·00

1255 Emblem

2003. 120th Anniv of Italian Chamber of Commerce.
2865   **1255**   14p. multicoloured   5·50   5·00

1256 President Manuel Fraga
Iribarne

2003. Visit of Manuel Fraga Iribarne (president of Galicia).
2866   **1256**   14p. multicoloured   5·50   5·00

1257 Emblems

2003. 150th Anniv of San Gregorio de Polanco, Tacuarembo.
2867   **1257**   14p. multicoloured   5·50   5·00

1258 Page

2003. Bicentenary of Bible Society.
2868   **1258**   14p. multicoloured   5·50   5·00

1259 Paysandu

2003. National Navy.
2869   **1259**   14p. multicoloured   5·50   5·00

1260 Bookshelves

2003. 35th Anniv of Cultural University.
2870   **1260**   14p. multicoloured   5·50   5·00

1261 Lockheed F-80 C
Shooting Star

2003. 50th Anniv of Air Force.
2871   **1261**   14p. multicoloured   5·50   5·00

1262 Italian Colours
and Map

2003. Visit of Mirko Tremaglia (Italian minister).
2872   **1262**   14p. multicoloured   5·50   5·00

1263 Horn

2003. Mercosur. Crafts. Multicoloured.
2873   14p. Type **1263**   5·50   5·00
2874   36p. Decorated stirrup   14·00   12·00

1264 Wright Flyer, Orville
and Wilbur Wright

2003. Centenary of Powered Flight.
2875   **1264**   14p. multicoloured   5·50   5·00

2004. No. 2116 surch.
2876   1p. on 1p.20 chocolate and
    green   55   50

2004. No. 2166 surch.
2878   2p. on 2p.60 yellow and blue   85   75

1268 Puffinus gravis

2004. Sea Birds. Multicoloured.
2879   14p. Type **1268**   5·50   5·00
2880   14p. Macronectes halli   5·50   5·00
2881   14p. Daption capense   5·50   5·00
2882   14p. Diomedea (inscr "Diame-
    dea") melanophrys   5·50   5·00
    Nos. 2879/82 were issued together, se-tenant, forming a composite design.

1269 Isla de Flores

2004. Lighthouses. Multicoloured.
2883   10p. Type **1269**   4·75   4·25
2884   10p. Farallon   4·75   4·25
2885   10p. La Panela   4·75   4·25
2886   10p. Ponton Banco Ingles   4·75   4·25
2887   14p. Isla de Lobos   5·50   5·00

1270 Building
Facade

2004. Tenth Anniv of Abitab.
2888   **1270**   14p. multicoloured   5·50   5·00

2004. No. 2037 surch.
2889   5p. on 2500p. brown, green
    and black   2·20   2·00
2890   10p. on 360p. sepia and lemon   4·75   4·25

1273 Prefectura

2004. 175th Anniv of National Navy.
2891   **1273**   14p. multicoloured   5·50   5·00

1274 Mate Cup
(Mate de Calabaza)

2004. Cultural Heritage. Designs showing mate cups. Multicoloured.
2892   5p. Type **1274**   2·20   2·00
2893   5p. Mate de Caliz   2·20   2·00
2894   5p. Mate de Plata Colonial   2·20   2·00

1275 Armoured Personnel
Carrier (O. T.-64 M-93 B)

2004. Centenary of 1 MEC No. 10 Battalion (33 Orientales).
2895   **1275**   14p. multicoloured   5·50   5·00

2004. No. 2035 surch.
2896   50p. on 825p. grey, blue and
    black   21·00   18·00

1277 Spilt Water

2004. World Water Day.
2897   **1277**   14p. multicoloured   5·50   5·00

1278 Pylons and
Power Lines

2004. 40th Anniv of Regional Energy Integration.
2898   **1278**   14p. multicoloured   5·50   5·00

1279 Guardsman

2004. 80th Anniv of Grenadier Guards.
2899   **1279**   14p. multicoloured   5·50   5·00

1280 Refinery

2004. Inauguration of Extension of La Teja Oil Refinery.
2900   **1280**   14p. multicoloured   5·50   5·00

1281 Soldier and Building

2004. 175th Anniv of Florida Infantry Battalion.
2901   **1281**   14p. multicoloured   5·50   5·00

1282 Soldiers

2004. Loyal Service.
2902   **1282**   14p. multicoloured   5·50   5·00

1283 Malva sylvestris

2004. Medicinal Plants. Multicoloured.
2903   36p. Type **1283**   14·00   12·00
2904   36p. Achyrocline satureoides
    (inscr "satureiodes")   14·00   12·00
2905   36p. Baccharis trimera   14·00   12·00
2906   36p. Mentha piperita   14·00   12·00

1284 Map and Arms

2004. Montevideo.
2907   **1284**   14p. multicoloured   5·50   5·00

1285 Carlos Gardel

2004. Carlos Gardel (singer) Commemoration.
2908 **1285** 14p. multicoloured 5·50 5·00

1286 Para-glider above Globe (Sofia Garcia Dovat)

2004. Say No to Drugs. Winning Design in Children's Painting Competition.
2909 **1286** 14p. multicoloured 5·50 5·00

1287 Renan Rodriguez

2004. Renan Rodriguez (politician) Commemoration.
2910 **1287** 14p. multicoloured 5·50 5·00

1288 Maimonides

2004. 800th Death Anniv of Moses ben Maimon (Maimonides).
2911 **1288** 16p. multicoloured 5·75 5·25

1289 Couple wearing Traditional Dress and Building Façade

2004. 125th Anniv of Galician Centre, Montevideo.
2912 **1289** 16p. multicoloured 5·75 5·25

1290 Battle of Illescas

2004. Death Centenary of General Aparicio Saravia. Designs showing battles. Multicoloured.
2913 10p. Type **1290** 4·75 4·25
2914 10p. Fray-Marcos 4·75 4·25
2915 10p. Paso del Parque 4·75 4·25
2916 10p. Masoller 4·75 4·25

1291 Helicopter, Motorcycle and Policeman

2004. 50th Anniv of Traffic Police.
2917 **1291** 16p. multicoloured 5·75 5·25

1292 Abstract

2004. Cultural Heritage. Joaquin Torres Garcia (artist) Commemoration.
2918 **1292** 16p. multicoloured 5·75 5·25

1293 Lighted Building

2004. 75th Anniv of Magisterial Cooperative.
2919 **1293** 16p. multicoloured 5·75 5·25

1294 Emblem

2004. Centenary of Army Quartermaster Service.
2920 **1294** 16p. multicoloured 5·75 5·25

1295 Emblem and Stadium

2004. Centenary of Federation Internationale de Football (FIFA).
2921 **1295** 37p. multicoloured 14·00 12·00

1296 *Geranoaetus melanoleucus*

2004. Self-adhesive.
2922 **1296** 100p. multicoloured 37·00 33·00

1297 Tango and Talchumnori (dances)

2004. 40th Anniv of Uruguay—Korea Diplomatic Relations.
2923 **1297** 16p. multicoloured 5·75 5·25

1298 Cathedral Facade

2004. Bicentenary of Montevideo Cathedral.
2924 **1298** 16p. multicoloured 5·75 5·25

1299 Cabildo de Montevideo

2004. Historic Neighbourhoods. Multicoloured.
2925 16p. Type **1299** 5·75 5·25
2926 16p. Tomas Toribo's house (vert) 5·75 5·25

1300 Dirty and Clean Water

2004. America. Water Conservation. Multicoloured.
2927 16p. Type **1300** 5·75 5·25
2928 37p. Oil covered and healthy egret 14·00 12·00

1301 Tank

2004. Centenary of Blindado No. 13 Infantry Division.
2929 **1301** 16p. multicoloured 5·75 5·25

1302 Almacen del Hacha

2004
2930 **1302** 16p. multicoloured 5·75 5·25

1303 Early Adding Machine

2004. 85th Anniv of Price Waterhouse Coopers (accountants).
2931 **1303** 16p. multicoloured 5·75 5·25

1304 Frontispiece

2004. Centenary of Public Notaries' Magazine.
2932 **1304** 16p. multicoloured 5·75 5·25

1305 "Adoration of Shepherds" (E. Murillo)

2004. Christmas.
2933 **1305** 16p. multicoloured 5·75 5·25

1306 Water and Cracked Earth

2004. Mercosur. Water Conservation Campaign.
2934 **1306** 37p. multicoloured 14·00 12·00

1307 Hotel

2004. Tourism. Punta del Este.
MS2935 **1307** 16p. multicoloured 6·25 6·25

1308 Orenstein & Kopell Steam Locomotive (1912)

2004. Self-adhesive.
2936 **1308** 30p. multicoloured 13·00 11·50

1309 Emblem

2005. Centenary of Rotary International.
2937 **1309** 37p. blue, gold and green 14·00 12·00

1313 Monument

2005. 90th Anniv of Armenian Genocide.
2944 **1313** 16p. multicoloured 5·75 5·25

2005. No. 2163 surch.
2946 2p. on 50c. yellow and olive 85 75

1316 Botanical Garden Fountain

2005. Fountains. Multicoloured.
2947 10p. Type **1316** 4·75 4·25
2948 10p. Athletes Fountain, Rodo Park 4·75 4·25
2949 10p. Constitution Plaza 4·75 4·25
2950 37p. Cordier Fountain, Prado (horiz) 14·00 12·00

1317 Pope John Paul II Sanatorium

2005. 120th Anniv of Catholic Circle.
2951 **1317** 16p. multicoloured 5·75 5·25

1318 Girl

2005. 45th Anniv of SOS Children's Villages.
2952 **1318** 16p. multicoloured 5·75 5·25

1319 Building Facade and Statue

2005. 75th Anniv of St. John the Baptist College.
2953 **1319** 16p. multicoloured 5·75 5·25

1320 Monument to Pope John Paul II

2005. Pope John Paul II Commemoration and Inauguration of Pope Benedict XVI. 1320 and similar vert design. Multicoloured.

MS2954 100×90 mm. 10p.×2, Type 1320; Pope Benedict XVI 10·50 10·50

1321 Emblem

2005. 75th Anniv of Medical Association Assistance Centre. Each blue and vermilion.

| 2955 | 16p. Type **1321** | 5·75 | 5·25 |
| 2956 | 16p. As No. 2955 but with additional inscription | 5·75 | 5·25 |

1322 Ignatius Loyola

2005. 125th Anniv of Seminary College. Multicoloured.

| 2957 | 16p. Type **1322** | 5·75 | 5·25 |
| 2958 | 16p. Aerial view | 5·75 | 5·25 |

1323 Liber Seregni

2005. 90th Birth Anniv of Liber Seregni (soldier and politician). Multicoloured.

2959	16p. Type **1323**	5·75	5·25
2960	16p. With raised arms	5·75	5·25
2961	16p. With megaphone	5·75	5·25
2962	16p. Facing right	5·75	5·25

1325 "Paisaje" and 1964 Spain 5p stamp (No. 1675)

2005. 50th Anniv of First Europa Stamps. Paintings by C. de Arzadun. Multicoloured.

| 2964 | 16p. Type **1325** | 5·75 | 5·25 |
| 2965 | 37p. "Los Nandues" and 1962 Spain 5p. (No. 1510) (vert) | 14·00 | 12·00 |

1326 Building Facade

2005. Urutem 2005 Philatelic Exhibition.

| 2966 | **1326** | 16p. multicoloured | 5·75 | 5·25 |

1327 Atrium

2005. 80th Anniv of Legislative Palace.

| 2967 | **1327** | 16p. multicoloured | 5·75 | 5·25 |

1328 "75" (Sofia Arca)

2005. 75th Anniv of Centenary Stadium. Winning Designs in Children's Painting Competition. Multicoloured.

| 2968 | 16p. Type **1328** | 5·75 | 5·25 |
| 2969 | 16p. Stadium (Jonatan Belon) | 5·75 | 5·25 |

1329 Carlos Sole

2005. Cultural Heritage. Carlos Sole (writer).

| 2970 | **1329** | 16p. multicoloured | 5·75 | 5·25 |

1330 Presentation of First World Cup Trophy to Uruguay (1930)

2005. World Cup Football Championships, Germany. 75th Anniv of World Cup. Multicoloured.

2971	16p. Type **1330**	5·75	5·25
2972	16p. Shaking hands	5·75	5·25
2973	16p. Entering the stadium	5·75	5·25
2974	37p.20 06 championship emblem	14·00	12·00

2005. Self-adhesive. As Type **1296**.

| 2975 | 25p. multicoloured | 10·50 | 9·25 |

1331 Sun, Fish and Tower

2005. World ICCA Congress, Montevideo. Multicoloured.

| 2976 | 8p. Type **1331** | 4·25 | 3·75 |
| 2977 | 8p. Mountains and ICCA emblem | 4·25 | 3·75 |

Nos. 2976/7 were issued together, se-tenant, forming a composite design.

1332 Rhamdia sapo

2005. Uruguay River Fish. Multicoloured.

2978	16p. Type **1332**	5·75	5·25
2979	16p. Odontesthes bonariensis	5·75	5·25
2980	16p. Hoplias malabaricus	5·75	5·25
2981	16p. Pygocentrus nattereri	5·75	5·25

Nos. 2978/81 were issued together, se-tenant, forming a composite design.

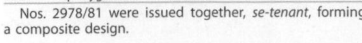

1333 "50 Anos" and Student (Adrian Makowski)

2005. 50th Anniv of "El Scolar" (the student) Magazine.

| 2982 | **1333** | 16p. multicoloured | 5·75 | 5·25 |

1334 Emblem and Map

2005. 70th Anniv of Custom Workers' Association.

| 2983 | **1334** | 16p. multicoloured | 5·75 | 5·25 |

1335 "Office" (fragment) (mural) (Julio Alpuy)

2005. Art.

| 2984 | **1335** | 16p. multicoloured | 5·75 | 5·25 |

1336 Juan Zorrilla de San Martin

2005. Mercosur. Writers. Multicoloured.

| 2985 | 16p. Type **1336** | 5·75 | 5·25 |
| 2986 | 37p. "La Hormiguita viajera" (Constancio C. Vigil) | 14·00 | 12·00 |

1337 Luis Rijo, Rodriguez Andrade and Juan Lopez

2005. Centenary of Central Espanol Football Club.

| 2987 | **1337** | 16p. multicoloured | 5·75 | 5·25 |

1338 Poinsettia Leaves

2005. Christmas.

| 2988 | **1338** | 16p. multicoloured | 5·75 | 5·25 |

1339 Building Facade

2005. Centenary of Commercial and Industrial Centre, Salto.

| 2989 | **1339** | 16p. multicoloured | 5·75 | 5·25 |

1340 Statue and Building Facade

2005. Centenary (2008) of Atenio de Montevideo (cultural centre).

| 2990 | **1340** | 16p. multicoloured | 5·75 | 5·25 |

1341 Juan Pedro Cea

2005. Olympic Footballers. Multicoloured.

2991	16p. Type **1341**	5·75	5·25
2992	16p. Andreas Mazali	5·75	5·25
2993	16p. Alfredo Ghierra	5·75	5·25
2994	37p. Vase with medallion showing footballers (vert)	14·00	12·00

1342 School Children (education)

2005. America. Struggle against Poverty. Multicoloured.

| 2995 | 16p. Type **1342** | 5·75 | 5·25 |
| 2996 | 37p. Men holding spade (work) | 14·00 | 12·00 |

1343 Capitan Miranda (1930)

2005. 75th Anniv of Capitan Miranda (hydro graphic ship). Multicoloured.

2997	16p. Type **1343**	5·75	5·25
2998	16p. Capitan Miranda (2005)	5·75	5·25
2999	16p. Francisco Miranda (hydrographer)	5·75	5·25
3000	16p. Emblems of Cadiz, Capitan Miranda and Montevideo	5·75	5·25

1344 San Fernado Cathedral

2006. 250th Anniv of Foundation of Madonado. Multicoloured.

| 3001 | 16p. Type **1344** | 5·75 | 5·25 |
| 3002 | 16p. Dragoons' quarters | 5·75 | 5·25 |

1345 Alfred Zitarrosa

2006. Alfred Zitarrosa (musician) Commemoration. Multicoloured.

| 3003 | 16p. Type **1345** | 5·75 | 5·25 |
| 3004 | 16p. Alfred Zitarrosa (vert) | 5·75 | 5·25 |

1346 Building Facade

2006. 150th Anniv of Solis Theatre.

| 3005 | **1346** | 16p. multicoloured | 5·75 | 5·25 |

1347 Manuel Magarinos

2006. Centenary of Espanol Newspaper.
3006 **1347** 16p. multicoloured ... 5·75 5·25

1348 Symbols of Industry

2006. State Company Day.
3007 **1348** 16p. black ... 5·75 5·25

1349 Zelmar Michelini

2006. 30th Death Anniv of Murdered Politicians. Multicoloured.
3008 16p. Type **1349** ... 5·75 5·25
3009 16p. Hector Gutierrez Ruiz ... 5·75 5·25
3010 16p. Zelmar Michelini and Hector Gutierrez Ruiz ... 5·75 5·25

1350 Lamberto Baldi (conductor)

2006. 75th Anniv of Ossodre Orchestra.
3011 **1350** 16p. agate and black ... 5·75 5·25

1351 Emblem

2006. 150th Anniv of Masons in Uruguay.
3012 **1351** 16p. multicoloured ... 5·75 5·25

1352 Appaloosa

2006. Horses. Multicoloured.
3013 16p. Type **1352** ... 5·75 5·25
3014 16p. Percheron ... 5·75 5·25
3015 16p. Belgian ... 5·75 5·25
3016 16p. Criollo ... 5·75 5·25

1353 Stage Coach

2006. 150th Anniv of First Stamp.
3017 **1353** 16p. multicoloured ... 5·75 5·25

1354 Crowd and Banners

2006. 40th Anniv of Congreso Unification Sindical. Multicoloured.
3018 16p. Type **1354** ... 5·75 5·25
3019 16p. Delegates ... 5·75 5·25

1355 Eladio Dieste

2006. Eladio Dieste (engineer) Commemoration.
3020 **1355** 16p. multicoloured ... 5·75 5·25

1356 Building Facade

2006. 40th Anniv of Diplomatic Relations with Sovereign Order of Malta.
3021 **1356** 16p. multicoloured ... 5·75 5·25

1357 Plaza de Paysandu (Francisco Vincent)

2006. 250th Anniv of Foundation of Paysandu.
3022 **1357** 16p. multicoloured ... 5·75 5·25

1358 Quebrada de Los Cuervos

2006. Landscapes. Multicoloured.
3023 10p. Type **1358** ... 4·75 4·25
3024 20p. Gruta del Palacio (vert) ... 6·25 5·50

1359 Washington Beltrán

2006. Washington Beltrán (president 1965–6) Commemoration.
3025 **1359** 16p. multicoloured ... 5·75 5·25

1360 Dandelion

2006. Latin American Summit—Migrations and Development.
3026 **1360** 37p. multicoloured ... 14·00 12·00

1361 Park

2006. 250th Anniv of Salto City.
3027 **1361** 16p. multicoloured ... 5·75 5·25

1362 Transmitter

2006. 50th Anniv of Channel 10 Television Station.
3028 **1362** 16p. multicoloured ... 5·75 5·25

1363 Low Energy Light Bulbs

2006. America. Energy Conservation. Multicoloured.
3029 16p. Type **1363** ... 5·75 5·25
3030 37p. Solar panels ... 14·00 12·00

1364 Tennis

2006. Sport. Multicoloured.
3031 16p. Type **1364** ... 5·75 5·25
3032 16p. Handball (Antonio Valeta created El balon (precursor of handball)) ... 5·75 5·25
3033 16p. Rugby ... 5·75 5·25
3034 16p. Futsal ... 5·75 5·25

1365 Red-legged Seriema

2006
3035 **1365** 5p. multicoloured ... 2·20 2·00

1366 The Nativity

2006. Christmas.
3036 **1366** 37p. multicoloured ... 14·00 12·00

1367 Guitar

2006. Mercosur. Musical Instruments. Multicoloured.
3037 15p. Type **1367** ... 5·50 5·00
3038 37p. El Tamboril (horiz) ... 14·00 12·00

1368 Queen Mary2, Montevideo Port

2006. Ports and Cruise Ships. Multicoloured.
3039 37p. Type **1368** ... 14·00 12·00
3040 37p. Costa Fortuna, Montevideo ... 14·00 12·00
3041 37p. Zuiderman, Montevideo ... 14·00 12·00
3042 37p. Star Princess, Punta del Este ... 14·00 12·00

1369 Mother and Children

2006. 150th Anniv of National Lottery.
3043 **1369** 15p. multicoloured ... 5·50 5·00

1370 Yacht

2006. Optimist World's—2006 (dinghy championship).
3044 **1370** 37p. multicoloured ... 14·00 12·00

1371 Emblem

2006. Postal Services Logo. Self-adhesive.
3045 **1371** 15p. ultramarine and lemon ... 5·50 5·00

2007. No. 2116 and No. 2165 surch.
3046 1p. on 50c. chocolate and green ... 55 50
3047 2p. on 1p.80 yellow and ultramarine ... 85 75

1372 Punta del Este

2007. Centenary of Punta del Este.
3048 **1372** 37p. multicoloured ... 14·00 12·00

1373 Boy and Jose Nasazzi

2007. Jose Nasazzi Cup International Football Competition (for those born in 1993).
3049 **1373** 15p. multicoloured ... 5·50 5·00

1374 Julia Arévalo

2007. Julia Arevalo de Roche (senator) Commemoration.
3050 **1374** 15p. multicoloured ... 5·50 5·00

1375 Road laying

2007. Centenary of Ministry of Transport and Public Works. Sheet 110×100 mm containing T **1375** and similar horiz designs. Multicoloured.
MS3051 5p. Type **1375**; 10p. Aircraft; 15p. Bridge ... 13·50 13·50

1376 Player

2007. Centenary of Colon Football Club.
3052 **1376** 15p. multicoloured ... 5·50 5·00

1377 Emblem

2007. Denge Awareness Campaign. Self-adhesive.
3053 **1377** 15p. blue and scarlet ... 5·50 5·00

1378 Early Document and Map

2009. Spiders. Multicoloured.
3156 12p. Type **1434** 5·50 5·00
3157 12p. *Argiope argentata* 5·50 5·00

1435 *Acipenser gueldenstaedtii*

2009. Mercosur. Exports. Black River Caviar.
3158 **1435** 37p. multicoloured 15·00 13·00

1436 Emblem

2009. 90th Anniv of Working for Social Justice.
3159 **1436** 37p. multicoloured 15·00 13·00

1437 *Hamadryas amphione*

2009. Birds and Butterflies. Multicoloured.
3160 12p. Type **1437** 5·50 5·00
3161 12p. *Anartia amathea* 5·50 5·00
3162 12p. *Tachuris rubrigasta* (many-coloured rush-tyrant) 5·50 5·00
3163 12p. *Colaptes melanochloros* (green-barred woodpecker) 5·50 5·00

1438 Hand holding Rock

2009. America. Traditional Games. The Taba. Multicoloured.
3164 12p. Type **1438** 5·50 5·00
3165 37p. *The Taba* (Juan Manuel Blanes) 15·00 13·00

1439 Government House

2009. Tenth Anniv of Government House Museum.
3166 **1439** 12p. multicoloured 5·50 5·00

1440 Nacimiento (Edgardo Ribeiro)

2009. Christmas
3167 **1440** 12p. multicoloured 5·50 5·00

1441 Tomatoes and Lemons

2009. Exports. Multicoloured.
3168 10p. Type **1441** 5·00 4·50
3169 25p. Avocados, grapes, bananas and apples 11·00 13·00

1442 Globe as Eye

2009. 50th Anniv of Inter-American Development Bank.
3170 **1442** 37p. multicoloured 15·00 13·00

1443 Figure and Emblem

2009. Centenary of YMCA.
3171 **1443** 12p. multicoloured 5·50 5·00

2009. Professions. Design as T **1389**. Self-adhesive.
3172 8p. Greengrocer 3·25 2·75

1444 Building and Early Car and Driver

2009. Centenary of Drivers' Insurance of Montevideo
3173 **1444** 12p. multicoloured 5·50 5·00

1445 HMS Ajax

2009. 70th Anniv of Battle of River Plate. Sheet 112×80 mm containing T **1445** and similar horiz designs. Multicoloured.
MS3174 10p. Type **1445**; 12p. *HMSNZ Achilles*; 15p. *HMS Exeter* 15·00 13·00

1446 Violin and Ballet Dancer

2009. 80th Anniv of SODRE (official broadcasting service and diffusion of performances)
3175 **1446** 37p. multicoloured 15·00 13·00

1447 Alba Roballo

2010. Alba Roballo (lawyer and politician) Commemoration
3176 **1447** 12p. multicoloured 5·50 5·00

1448 Gran Hotel Concordia de Salto

2010. Historic Hotels. Multicoloured.
3177 12p. Type **1448** 5·50 5·00
3178 12p. Grand Hotel Colon de Piriapolis 5·50 5·00

2010. Professions. Multicoloured.
3179 5p. Seller of trinkets (vert) 2·75 2·50
3180 10p. Shoemaker (vert) 5·00 4·50

1449 Flag, Arms and Ship

2010. 150th Anniv of First Russians in Uruguay
3181 **1449** 37p. multicoloured 15·00 13·00

1450 Emblem

2010. Mercosur. Decade of Peace
3182 **1450** 12p. multicoloured 5·50 5·00

1451 Symbols of Uruguay and Romania

2010. 75th Anniv of Uruguay - Romania Diplomatic Relations
3183 **1451** 37p. multicoloured 15·00 13·00

2010. Professions
3184 17p. El Cuarteador (vert) 7·50 7·00
3185 25p. Fishmonger (vert) 11·00 10·00
3186 30p. Ice cream seller 14·00 13·00

1452 Pouring Wine

2010. Centenary of Casa de Asturias (Asturian Centre)
3187 **1452** 37p. multicoloured 15·00 13·00

1453 Darwin Piñeyrúa

2010. Centenary of Uruguay Sporting Club
3188 **1453** 12p. multicoloured 5·50 5·00

1454 Parthenon and Legislative Palace

2010. 135th Anniv of Uruguay - Greece Diplomatic Relations
3189 **1454** 37p. multicoloured 15·00 13·00

1455 Frederic Chopin

2010. Birth Bicentenary of Frédéric François Chopin. Multicoloured.
MS3190 12p. Type **1455**; 37p. Piano 24·00 23·00

1456 Florencio Sánchez

2010. Heritage Day. Theatre in Uruguay. Birth Centenary of Florencio Sánchez (playwright)
3191 **1456** 12p. multicoloured 5·50 5·00

1457 *Libertad* (sculpture by Jose Luis Zorrilla de San Martin)

2010. 25th Anniv of Return to Democracy
3192 **1457** 12p. multicoloured 5·50 5·00

1458 Mario Benedetti

2010. 90th Birth Anniv of Mario Benedetti (writer). Multicoloured.
3193 12p. Type **1458** 5·50 5·00
3194 12p. With head in hands 5·50 5·00

1459 *Passiflora coerulea*

2010. Flora and Fauna. Multicoloured.
3195 12p. Type **1459** 5·50 5·00
3196 12p. *Guira guira* (Guira Cuckoo) 5·50 5·00
3197 12p. *Furnarius rufus* (Rufous Hornero) 5·50 5·00
3198 12p. *Bauhina forficata* 5·50 5·00

1460 Building and Chinstrap Penguin (*Pygoscelis antarcticus*)

2010. 25th Anniv of Uruguay as Consultative Member of Antarctic Treaty
3199 **1460** 37p. multicoloured 15·00 14·00

2010. Professions
3200 7p. Caramel maker 4·00 3·75

1461 La Pastoral de los ninos (Carmelo de Arzadun)

2010. Christmas
3201 **1461** 12p. multicoloured 5·50 5·00

1462 Flag and National Hymn

2010. America. National Symbols. Multicoloured.
3202 12p. Type **1462** 5·50 5·00
3203 37p. Flag and National Arms 15·00 14·00

1463 Early Team

2010. Centenary of 'Blue Shirts' (National Football Team). Multicoloured.

3202	**1463**	12p. Type **1463**	5·50	5·00
3203		12p. Current team (84×30 mm)	5·50	5·00

1464 MSC Lirica, Punte del Este

2010. Tourism. Cruise Ships. Multicoloured.

3206	**1464**	37p. Type **1464**	15·00	14·00
3207		37p. *Veendam*, Montevideo	15·00	14·00
3208		37p. *Silver Whisper*, Punta del Este	15·00	14·00
3209		37p. *Splendour of the Seas*, Punta del Este	15·00	14·00

1465 Armand Prevost (first flight in Uruguay)

2010. Centenary of First Flight in Uruguay. Multicoloured.

MS3211 37p.×2, Type **1465**; Bartolomeo Cattaneo (first official international air transport) 31·00 30·00

1466 El Telégrapho Building

2010. Centenary of *El Telegrafo de Paysandu* Newspaper

3212	**1466**	12p. multicoloured	5·50	5·00

1467 Fist and Scarlet Flowers

2010. Centenary of the Uruguayan Socialist Party

3213	**1467**	12p. multicoloured	5·50	5·00

1468 *Gato con Botas* (Eduardo Vernazza)

2010. Uruguayan Painters

3214	**1468**	12p. Type **1468**	5·50	5·00
3215		12p. Female dancer, Chinese Opera (Eduardo Vernazza)	5·50	5·00
3216		12p. *Couronnes I*, 1948 (Carmelo Arden Quin) (horiz)	5·50	5·00
3217		12p. *Dualité - Periode indienne*, 1947(Carmelo Arden Quin) (horiz)	5·50	5·00

1469 Emblem

2011. Bicentenary of Uruguay

3218	**1469**	1p. multicoloured	45	35

1470 Thistle and Cattail

2011. Crafts. Basketwork

3219	**1470**	2p. multicoloured	90	70

1471 Spurs and Gaucho

2011. Bicentenary of Uruguay (1st issue). 25th Feast of Gaucho the Homeland. Multicoloured.

3220	**1471**	12p. Type **1471**	5·50	5·00
3221		12p. Cauldron and grill	5·50	5·00
3222		12p. Bolas and gaucho	5·50	5·00

1472 Rabindranath Tagore

2011. 150th Birth Anniv of Rabindranath Tagore. Indipex 2011 International Stamp Exhibition, New Delhi

3223	**1472**	37p. multicoloured	15·00	14·00

1473 Postbox, Plaza Independencia

2011. America. Mailboxes

3224	**1473**	37p. multicoloured	15·00	14·00

1474 *Batalla de Las Piedras* (detail) (Juan Luis and Juan Manuel Blanes)

2011. Bicentenary of Uruguay (2nd issue). Bicentenary of Uruguayan Forces

3225	**1474**	12p. multicoloured	5·50	5·00

1475 Swords

2011. Bicentenary of Uruguay (3rd issue). Bicentenary of Grito de Asencio (start of the Artigas's Revolution). Multicoloured.

3226	**1475**	12p. Type **1475**	5·50	5·00
3227		37p. Revolutionaries	15·00	14·00

1476 Leandro Gomez

2011. Birth Bicentenary of General Leandro Gomez

3228	**1476**	12p. multicoloured	5·50	5·00

1477 *Las Llamadas*

2011. Personalities. Carlos Paez Vilaro (artist). Sheet 110×90 mm

MS3229 **1477** 37p. multicoloured 15·00 14·00

1478 Josefa Oribe

2011. Bicentenary of Uruguay (4th issue). Famous Women. Multicoloured.

3230	**1478**	12p. Type **1478**	5·50	5·00
3231		12p. Petrona Rosende	5·50	5·00

2011. Crafts. Multicoloured.

3232		10p. Woven woollen bag	4·75	4·25
3233		37p. Ceramic pot	14·00	12·00

1479 1911 5cent Stamp

2011. Centenary of UPAEP. Century of Culture

3234	**1479**	37p. multicoloured	14·00	12·00

1480 Planeta Building, 1937

2011. Centenary of Atlántida

3235	**1480**	12p. multicoloured	5·25	4·75

2011. Crafts. Multicoloured.

3236		12p. Wooden sheep	5·25	4·75
3237		20p. Silver vase	6·25	5·50
3238		200p. Woven leather bag	20·00	20·00

1481 'TE AMO MAMA' (Rodrigo Piriz Gómez)

2011. Mother's Day. Winning Design in a Children's Competition

3239	**1481**	12p. multicoloured	5·50	5·00

1482 Symbols of Broadcasting

2011. 50th Anniv of Channel 4 Monte Carlo TV

3240	**1482**	12p. multicoloured	5·50	5·00

1483 Battle

2011. Bicentenary of Uruguay (5th issue). Battle of Las Piedras

3241	**1483**	12p. multicoloured	5·50	5·00

2011. Crafts. Multicoloured.

3242		44p. Wire mobile (27×19 mm)	16·00	15·00

1484 Flags of Competing Countries and Uruguay Player

2011. Copa America 2011, Argentina

3243	**1484**	37p. multicoloured	14·00	12·00

1485 *Aitona* (Ignacio Iturria)

2011. Centenary of Centro Euskaro (Euskaro Basque Club)

3244	**1485**	12p. multicoloured	5·50	5·00

1486 '3' and AIDS Ribbon forming 30

2011. 30th Anniv of AIDS Prevention Campaign

3245	**1486**	12p. scarlet-vermilion and black	5·50	5·00

1487 Athletes

2011. Centenary of National Physical Education Commission

3246	**1487**	12p. multicoloured	5·50	5·00

1488 Cristian Rodriguez

2011. Champions of America. Multicoloured.

3247	**1488**	6p. Type **1488**	3·00	2·75
3248		6p. Alvaro Pereira	3·00	2·75
3249		6p. Abel Hernandez	3·00	2·75
3250		6p. Luis Suarez	3·00	2·75
3251		6p. Nicolas Lodeiro	3·00	2·75
3252		6p. Sebastian Abreu	3·00	2·75
3253		6p. Diego Perez	3·00	2·75
3254		6p. Fernando Muslera	3·00	2·75
3255		6p. Diego Forlan	3·00	2·75
3256		6p. Washington Tabarez	3·00	2·75
3257		6p. Edinson Cavani	3·00	2·75
3258		6p. Sebastian Eguren	3·00	2·75
3259		6p. Martin Caceres	3·00	2·75
3260		6p. Diego Godin	3·00	2·75
3261		6p. Egidio Arevalo	3·00	2·75
3262		6p. Alvaro Gonzalez	3·00	2·75
3263		6p. Maximiliano Pereira	3·00	2·75
3264		6p. Juan Castillo	3·00	2·75
3265		6p. Diego Lugano	3·00	2·75
3266		6p. Walter Gargano	3·00	2·75
3267		6p. Mauricio Victorino	3·00	2·75
3268		6p. Andres Scotti	3·00	2·75
3269		6p. Martin Silva	3·00	2·75
3270		6p. Sebastian Coates	3·00	2·75

1489 *Acacia caven* Trees

2011. International Year of Forests

3271	**1489**	12p. multicoloured	5·50	5·00

1490 Post Box, 18 de Julio Avenue

2011. America. Mailboxes (2nd issue)
3272	**1490**	12p. multicoloured	5·50	5·00

1491 Castillo Himezi

2011. 90th Anniv of Uruguay - Japan Diplomatic Relations
3273	**1491**	37p. multicoloured	15·00	12·00

1492 Exodo del Pueblo Oriental (Guillermo C. Rodriguez)

2011. Bicentenary of Uruguay (6th issue). Heritage Day. La Redota (Exodus East)
3274	**1492**	12p. multicoloured	5·50	5·00

1493 China Zorrilla

2011. Mercosur. National Actors. Sheet 110×87 mm
MS3275	**1493**	37p. multicoloured	16·00	14·00

1494 Southern Right Whale's Tail and Whale Watchers

2011. Whale Watching. *Eubalaena australis* (Southern Right Whale). Multicoloured.
3276	**1494**	12p. Type **1494**	5·50	5·00
3277		12p. Swimming underwater	5·50	5·00
3278		37p. Swimming near surface, island in background	15·00	13·00
3279		37p. Diving	15·00	13·00

1495 *Egretta thula, Larus dominicanus Haematopus*, Isla de Flores

2011. National Parks. Coastal Islands National Park
3280	**1495**	12p. multicoloured	5·50	5·00

1496 de Havilland DH90 Churrinche and Bombardier CRJ900

2011. 75th Anniv of Pluna Aviation
3281	**1496**	12p. multicoloured	5·50	5·00

1497 J. Batlle y Ordóñez and Thermal Generation Centre

2011. Tourism. Cruise Ships. Multicoloured.
3282		37p. Type **1497**	15·00	13·00
3283		37p. J. Torres Garcia and Telecommunications Tower Complex	15·00	13·00
3284		37p. Montevideo Port	15·00	13·00
3285		37p. Montevideo Hill	15·00	13·00

1498 Cesar Zagnoli

2011. Cultural Heritage of Humanity. Tango. Personalities. Multicoloured.
3286		12p. Type **1498**	5·50	5·00
3287		12p. Juan D'Arienzo	5·50	5·00
3288		12p. Donato Racciatti	5·50	5·00

1499 The Nativity (M. de los Ángeles Martinez)

2011. Christmas
3289	**1499**	12p. multicoloured	5·50	5·00

1500 Quartz SiO2, Amethyst and Agate

2011. International Year of Chemistry. Sheet 90×70 mm
MS3290	**1500**	37p. multicoloured	15·50	14·00

1501 Arms and Old Town Astronomical Clock, Prague

2011. 90th Anniv of Royal Decree with Czechoslovakia
3291	**1501**	37p. multicoloured	15·00	13·00

2011. Crafts. Multicoloured.
3292		10p. Toy car (metal work)	5·00	4·50
3293		22p. Canes and cane work	11·00	10·00

1502 Crepúsculo (Vicente Martin)

2011. Uruguayan Painters
3294		12p. Type **1502**	5·00
3295		12p. Dama con Mandolina (Vicente Martin)	5·00
3296		12p. Composición 17 Julio - 1968 (Maria Freire)	5·00
3297		12p. Formas (Maria Freire) (horiz)	5·00

1503 La Lancera

2011. International Year of African Descendents. Paintings by Mary Porto Casas
3299		12p. Type **1503**	5·50	5·00
3300		37p. Mandela (horiz)	15·00	13·00

1504 National History Museum (Former Headquarters)

2011. Centenary of the State Insurance Bank
3301	**1504**	12p. multicoloured	5·50	5·00

1505 Indigenous Fighter

2011. Bicentenary of Uruguay (7th issue). Revolutionaries of African and Indigenous Descent. Multicoloured.
3302		12p. Type **1505**	5·50	5·00
3303		12p. African fighter	5·50	5·00

2012. Crafts. Multicoloured.
3304		1p. Wooden and woollen cows (Carlos Cavelli)	55	50
3305		1p. Woollen poncho (Siv Göransson)	55	50
3306		1p. Leather pot and lid (Albertina Morelli)	55	50
3307		1p. Silver and wooden pendant (Nilda Echenique)	55	50
3308		1p. Wirework ball (Gustavo Genta)	55	50

1506 'A'

2012. Sign Language
3309	**1506**	5p. multicoloured	2·20	2·00

2012. Sign Language. Multicoloured.
3310		10p. 'M'	4·75	4·25

1507 Woman and 'TAMBIÉN HICIMOS PATRIA'

2012. International Woman's Day
3311	**1507**	12p. multicoloured	5·50	5·00

1508 Gandós Palace (Current Headquarters)

2012. BID2012CII Annual Meeting of Board of Governors, Montevideo
3312	**1508**	37p. multicoloured	15·00	13·00

1509 Enrique V. Iglesias

2012. Personalities. Enrique V. Iglesias
3313	**1509**	37p. multicoloured	15·00	13·00

1510 Footballer and the Orbit, Olympic Park

2012. Olympic Games, London. Multicoloured.
3314		15p. Type **1510**	6·00	5·50
3315		15p. Cyclist and St Paul's Cathedral	6·00	5·50
3316		15p. Sailor and Tower Bridge	6·00	5·50
3317		15p. Hurdler, Big Ben and Parliament	6·00	5·50

2012. Sign Language. Multicoloured.
3318		12p. 'O'	5·50	5·00
3319		50p. 'G'	21·00	18·00
3320		60p. 'I' (27×19 mm)	24·00	22·00

1511 Dancers of Uruguay and Ukraine

2012. 20th Anniv of Uruguay - Ukraine Diplomatic Relations
3321	**1511**	37p. multicoloured	14·00	12·00

1512 Anniversary Emblem, Cow and Dairy Produce

2012. 150th Anniv of Nueva Helvecia Swiss Colony
3322	**1512**	12p. multicoloured	5·50	5·00

No. 3323 is vacant.

2012. Sign Language. Multicoloured.
3324		20p. 'S'	6·50	5·50

1513 Zesta-Punta (variety of Pelota) and Casa de Juntas de Guernika

2012. Centenary of Euskal Erria
3325	**1513**	37p. multicoloured	15·00	13·00

1514 Blood Droplet

2012. International Day of Blood Donation
3326	**1514**	12p. multicoloured	5·50	5·00

EXPRESS MAIL STAMPS

1921. Overprinted **MENSAJERIAS**.
E389	**120**	2c. orange	75	20

E126 Caduceus

1923

E415	**E126**	2c. red	55	20
E416	**E126**	2c. blue	55	20

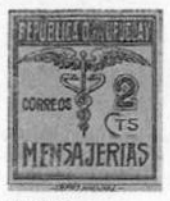

E153 Caduceus

1928

E591	**E153**	2c. black on green	20	20
E635a	**E153**	2c. green	20	20
E636	**E153**	2c. blue	20	20
E637	**E153**	2c. pink	35	20
E638	**E153**	2c. brown	20	10

1957. Surch **$ 0.05.**

E1065	5c. on 2c. brown	20	20

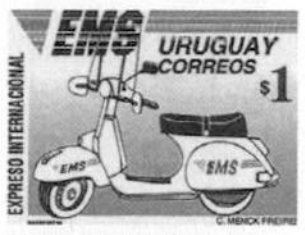

E859 Motor Scooter

1994. International Service.

E2170	**E859**	1p. orange and blue	55	50

E913

1996

E2275	**E913**	8p. yellow and blue	5·75	5·00

LATE FEE STAMPS

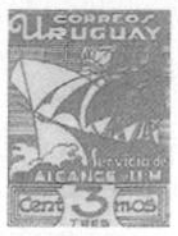
L175

1936

L774	**L175**	3c. green	15	15
L775	**L175**	5c. violet	15	15
L776	**L175**	6c. green	15	15
L777	**L175**	7c. brown	15	15
L778	**L175**	8c. red	25	25
L779	**L175**	12c. blue	35	35

NEWSPAPER STAMPS

1922. Optd **PRENSA** (= Printed Matter) or surch also.

N519	**128**	3c. olive (imperf)	1·10	30
N447	**118**	3c. on 2c. black and lake (perf)	55	55
N403	**120**	3c. on 4c. yellow (perf)	55	55
N448	**118**	6c. on 4c. blue and orange (perf)	55	55
N449	**118**	9c. on 5c. brown and blue (perf)	55	55
N520	**128**	9c. on 10c. green (imperf)	1·30	55
N521	**128**	15c. mauve (imperf)	1·70	65

OFFICIAL STAMPS

1880. Optd **OFICIAL**. Perf.

O51	**9**	15c. yellow	3·50	3·00

1880. Optd **OFICIAL**. Roul.

O48	**10**	1c. brown	3·75	6·50
O49	**11**	5c. green	1·30	1·10
O61	**15**	7c. blue (perf)	4·75	3·50
O50	**10**	10c. red	1·40	1·20
O52	**10**	20c. bistre	2·10	1·90
O53	**10**	50c. black	23·00	23·00
O55	**10**	1p. blue	23·00	23·00

1883. Optd **OFICIAL**.

O64	**16**	1c. green	7·00	6·50
O65	-	2c. red (No. 63)	10·00	9·75

1883. Optd **OFICIAL**.

O70	**18**	1c. green	38·00	33·00
O71	**18**	2c. red	13·00	10·00
O72	**20**	5c. blue	4·00	4·00
O73	**21**	10c. brown	7·00	6·75

1884. Optd **FRANCO** in frame.

O74	**18**	1c. green	38·00	32·00

1884. Optd **OFICIAL**.

O80	**10**	1c. on 10c. (No. 76)	2·00	1·60
O81	-	2c. red (No. 77)	4·00	3·75
O82	**26**	5c. blue	6·50	2·00

1884. Optd **OFICIAL**. Roul.

O91	**28**	1c. green	3·50	1·60
O91a	**28**	1c. grey	7·50	3·25
O92	**29**	2c. red	1·00	60
O93a	**28**	5c. blue	2·30	1·20
O94	**28**	5c. lilac	7·00	3·25
O95	**31**	7c. brown	3·50	1·60
O110	**31**	7c. orange	3·50	2·30
O96	**32**	10c. brown	2·10	90
O111	**36**	10c. violet	17·00	9·75
O97	**33**	20c. mauve	3·25	1·60
O112	**33**	20c. brown	17·00	7·25
O98	**34**	25c. lilac	3·50	1·60
O113	**34**	25c. red	17·00	7·25

1890. Optd **OFICIAL**. Perf.

O124	**38**	1c. green	1·10	15
O125	**39**	2c. red	1·10	15
O126	**40**	5c. blue	2·30	1·70
O127	**41**	7c. brown	1·60	1·00
O128	**42**	10c. green	1·60	1·00
O129	**43**	20c. orange	1·60	1·00
O130	**44**	25c. brown	1·60	1·50
O131	**45**	50c. blue	6·25	6·25
O132	**46**	1p. violet	8·00	7·25

1891. Optd **OFICIAL**.

O134	**28**	5c. lilac (No. 133)	2·10	1·50

1895. Optd **OFICIAL**.

O164	**38**	1c. blue	1·40	1·30
O165	**39**	2c. brown	1·70	1·60
O166	**40**	5c. red	2·50	2·40
O167	**45**	50c. purple	4·25	4·25

1895. Optd **OFICIAL**.

O168	**56**	1c. bistre	30	30
O169	**57**	2c. blue	30	30
O170	**58**	5c. red	1·10	70
O171	**59**	7c. green	65	60
O172	**60**	10c. brown	65	60
O173	**61**	20c. black and green	1·10	1·00
O174	**62**	25c. black and brown	1·10	1·00
O175	**63**	50c. black and blue	1·30	1·20
O176	**64**	1p. black and brown	6·50	6·00

1897. Nos. 180/2 optd **OFICIAL**.

O194	**67**	1c. black and red	1·60	1·00
O195	**68**	5c. black and blue	1·60	1·00
O196	-	10c. black and lake	2·10	1·20

1897. Optd **OFICIAL**.

O201	**56**	1c. blue	1·10	50
O202	**57**	2c. purple	1·60	70
O203	**58**	5c. green	1·60	70
O204	**72**	10c. red	5·25	2·75
O205	**61**	20c. black and mauve	6·50	3·00
O206	**62**	25c. blue and red	6·50	3·00
O207	**63**	50c. brown and green	8·00	3·50
O208	**64**	1p. blue and brown	13·00	7·75

1899. Optd **OFICIAL**.

O226	**39**	2c. orange	1·10	1·10
O227	**58**	5c. blue	1·30	1·30
O228	**72**	10c. purple	2·75	2·75
O243	**43**	20c. blue	11·00	5·25

1901. Optd **OFICIAL**.

O238	**78**	1c. green	65	20
O239	**79**	2c. red	90	20
O240	**80**	5c. blue	90	20
O241	**81**	7c. brown	1·20	65
O242	**82**	10c. lilac	1·30	75
O245	**46**	1p. green	14·50	8·00

1904. Optd **OFICIAL**.

O272	**86**	1c. green	35	20
O262	**87**	2c. orange	65	20
O263	**88**	5c. blue	65	20
O275	**89**	10c. lilac	35	20
O276	**90**	20c. green	55	45
O277	**91**	25c. bistre	65	55

1907. Optd **OFICIAL**.

O273	**96**	5c. blue	35	20
O274	**96**	7c. brown	35	20
O278	**96**	50c. red	1·30	95

1910. Optd **OFICIAL 1910.**

O288	**79**	2c. red	12·00	5·25
O289	**80**	5c. blue	7·25	4·25
O290	**82**	10c. lilac	3·50	1·60
O291	**43**	20c. green	3·50	1·60
O292	**44**	25c. brown	6·00	3·25
O293	**96**	50c. red	8·25	3·25

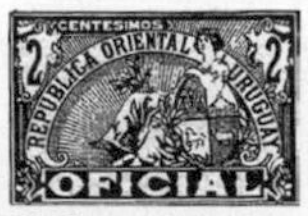

O110

1911

O307	**O110**	2c. brown	55	30
O308	**O110**	5c. blue	55	55
O309	**O110**	8c. slate	55	85
O310	**O110**	20c. brown	75	1·30
O311	**O110**	23c. red	1·10	1·30
O312	**O110**	50c. orange	2·20	1·60
O313	**O110**	1p. red	5·50	2·10

1915. Optd **Oficial**.

O340	**107**	2c. pink	75	55
O341	**107**	5c. blue	75	55
O342	**107**	8c. blue	75	55
O343	**107**	20c. brown	1·70	65
O344	**108**	23c. blue	5·50	4·75
O345	**108**	50c. orange	8·25	4·75
O346	**108**	1p. red	11·00	4·75

1919. Optd **Oficial**.

O365	**115**	2c. grey and red	1·10	55
O366	**115**	5c. grey and blue	1·30	55
O367	**115**	8c. brown and blue	1·30	55
O368	**115**	20c. grey and brown	2·75	1·10
O369	**115**	23c. brown and green	2·75	1·10
O370	**115**	50c. blue and brown	5·50	2·75
O371	**115**	1p. blue and red	13·00	4·25

1924. Optd **OFICIAL** in frame. (a) Perf.

O439	**128**	2c. mauve	20	10
O440	**128**	5c. blue	20	10
O593	**128**	8c. red	2·20	65
O594	**128**	10c. green	2·75	65
O441	**128**	12c. blue	45	10
O442	**128**	20c. brown	55	20
O443	**128**	36c. green	2·40	1·70
O444	**128**	50c. orange	5·00	3·50
O445	**128**	1p. red	8·75	7·00
O446	**128**	2p. green	14·50	11·50

(b) Imperf.

O499	2c. mauve	55	20
O500	5c. blue	90	20
O501	8c. red	1·10	20
O502	12c. blue	1·30	20
O503	20c. brown	2·75	55
O504	36c. pink	4·50	1·30

PARCEL POST STAMPS

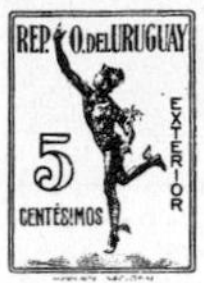

P123

1922. (a) Inscr "EXTERIOR".

P391	**P123**	5c. green on buff	15	15
P516	**P123**	5c. black on yellow	20	15
P392	**P123**	10c. green on blue	20	15
P517	**P123**	10c. black on blue	30	15
P393	**P123**	20c. green on rose	1·10	30
P518	**P123**	20c. black on pink	75	15
P394	**P123**	30c. green on green	1·00	15
P395	**P123**	50c. green on blue	1·80	15
P396	**P123**	1p. green on orange	3·25	70

(b) Inscr "INTERIOR".

P397	5c. green on buff	15	15
P512	5c. black on yellow	20	15
P398	10c. green on blue	15	15
P513	10c. black on blue	20	15
P399	20c. green on pink	45	15
P514	20c. black on pink	40	15
P400	30c. green on green	75	15
P515	30c. black on green	75	15
P401	50c. green on blue	1·10	15
P402	1p. green on orange	3·50	70

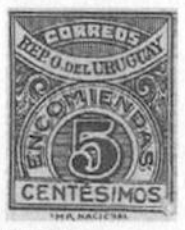

P144

1927

P522	**P144**	1c. blue	15	15
P606	**P144**	1c. violet	15	15
P523	**P144**	2c. green	15	15
P524	**P144**	4c. violet	15	15
P609a	**P144**	5c. red	15	15
P526	**P144**	10c. brown	20	15
P527	**P144**	20c. orange	25	15

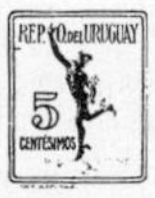

P152

1928

P587	**P152**	5c. black on yellow	20	20
P588	**P152**	10c. black on blue	20	20
P589	**P152**	20c. black on red	35	20
P590	**P152**	30c. black on green	55	20

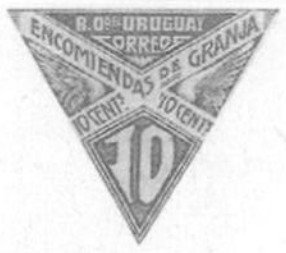

P155

1929. Agricultural Parcels.

P610	**P155**	10c. orange	35	35
P611	**P155**	15c. blue	35	35
P612	**P155**	20c. brown	35	35
P613	**P155**	25c. red	70	35
P614	**P155**	50c. grey	1·40	70
P615	**P155**	75c. violet	5·50	4·00
P616	**P155**	1p. olive	5·25	2·00

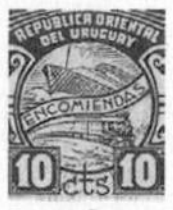

P177 Sea and Rail Transport

1938

P971	**P177**	5c. orange	20	20
P801	**P177**	10c. red	55	20
P972	**P177**	10c. purple	35	20
P1066	**P177**	10c. green	20	20
P973	**P177**	20c. red	55	20
P1067	**P177**	20c. blue	20	20
P974	**P177**	30c. blue	75	20
P1068	**P177**	30c. purple	35	30
P1069	**P177**	50c. green	35	55
P805	**P177**	1p. red	3·50	20
P975	**P177**	1p. blue	55	55
P1070	**P177**	1p. green	65	65

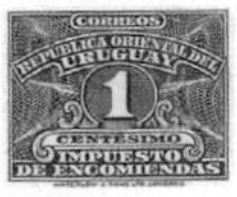

P188

1943

P876	**P188**	1c. red	20	20
P877	**P188**	2c. green	20	20

1944. Optd **ANO 1943.**

P882	**P155**	10c. orange	35	10
P883	**P155**	15c. blue	35	30
P884	**P155**	20c. brown	55	30
P885	**P155**	25c. red	90	45
P886	**P155**	50c. grey	1·90	85
P887	**P155**	75c. violet	3·50	2·50
P888	**P155**	1p. olive	4·75	3·50

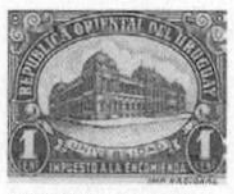
P204 University

1945

P909	**A**	1c. green	10	10
P999	**P204**	1c. red	20	10
P910	**P204**	2c. violet	10	10
P1000	**A**	2c. blue	20	10
P1045	**B**	5c. brown	20	10
P1047	**B**	5c. grey	55	10
P1001	**A**	10c. turqoise	20	10
P1002	**A**	10c. olive	20	10
P1048	**C**	20c. yellow	20	10
P1049	**C**	20c. brown	20	10
P1290	**D**	1p. brown	20	20
P1046	**D**	1p. blue	2·75	2·10

DESIGNS—HORIZ: A, Bank. VERT: B, Customs House; C. Solis Theatre; D. Montevideo Railway Station.

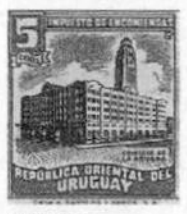
P211 Customs House

1946

P934	**P211**	5c. blue and brown	20	10

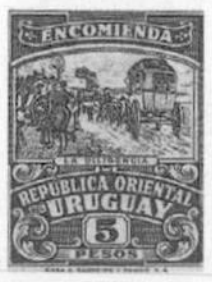

P212 Mail Coach (Guillermo Rodriguez)

1946

P935	**P212**	5p. brown and red	17·00	5·25

1946. Armorial type as T **187** obliterated by arrow-head device. (a) Optd **IMPUESTO** and **ENCOMIENDAS**.

P936	1c. mauve	10	10
P937	2c. brown	10	10
P938	5c. blue	10	10

(b) Optd **ENCOMIENDAS** only.

P939	1p. blue	1·30	30
P940	5p. red	5·50	2·30

1957. No. P1047 surch **$ 0.30**.

P1064	30c. on 5c. grey	20	20

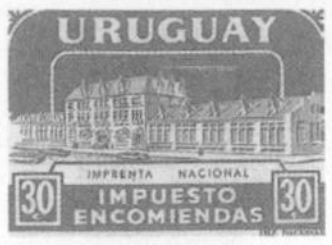

P263 National Printing Works

1960

P1127	**P263**	30c. green	20	20

1965. Surch with **caduceus** and **$ 5.00 ENCOMIENDAS**.

P1268	**217**	5p. on 84c. orange	45	20

1966. No. 1092 surch with **caduceus** and **ENCOMIENDAS 1.00 PESO.**

P1289	**254**	1p. on 38c. black	20	20

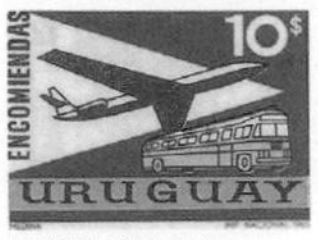

P355 Sud Aviation Caravelle and Motor-coach

1969

P1397	**P355**	10p. black, red & grn	20	20
P1398	-	20p. yellow, blk & bl	55	20

DESIGN: 20p. Side views of Sud Aviation Caravelle and motor-coach.

1971. No. 1121 surch **Encomiendas $ 0.60**.

P1448	**261**	60c. on 1p.+10c. violet and orange	1·10	75

1971. No. 1380 surch **IMPUESTOS A ENCOMIENDAS $0.60** and diesel locomotive.

P1472	60c. on 6p. black and green	55	30

1972. Nos. 1401/2 surch **$1 IMPUESTO A ENCOMIENDAS** and **caduceus**.

P1507	**358**	1p. on 6p. black, red and blue	2·00	75
P1508	-	1p. on 6p. black, red and blue	2·00	75

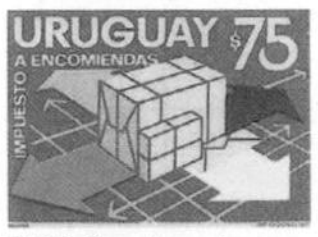

P460 Parcels and Arrows

1974

P1555	**P460**	75p. multicoloured	20	10

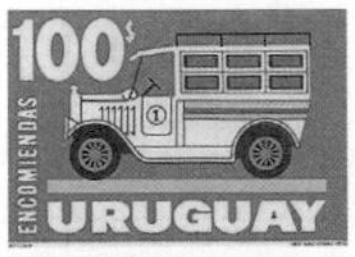

P461 Mail-van

1974. Old-time Mail Transport.

P1556	**P461**	100p. multicoloured	55	30
P1557	-	150p. multicoloured	1·30	1·30
P1558	-	300p. black, bl & orge	1·20	75
P1559	-	500p. multicoloured	2·00	1·10

DESIGNS: 150p. Steam locomotive; 300p. Paddle-steamer; 500p. Monoplane.

POSTAGE DUE STAMPS

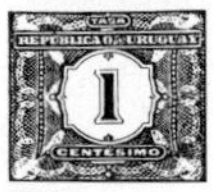

D84

1902

D795	**D84**	1c. green	10	10
D405	**D84**	2c. red	35	20
D796	**D84**	2c. brown	10	10
D491	**D84**	3c. brown	55	20
D797	**D84**	3c. red	20	10
D798	**D84**	4c. violet	20	10
D799	**D84**	5c. blue	20	10
D746	**D84**	5c. red	55	30
D494	**D84**	6c. brown	55	55
D800	**D84**	8c. red	20	15
D249	**D84**	10c. blue	1·30	20
D409a	**D84**	10c. green	45	20
D250	**D84**	20c. orange	2·20	1·10

1904. Surch **PROVISORIO UN cent'mo.**

D267	1c. on 10c. blue	1·10	1·10

Pt. 10

UZBEKISTAN

Formerly a constituent republic of the Soviet Union, Uzbekistan became independent in 1991.

1992. 100 kopeks = 1 rouble.
1994. (June) Sum (temporary coupon currency).
1994. (Sept) 100 tyin = 1 sum.

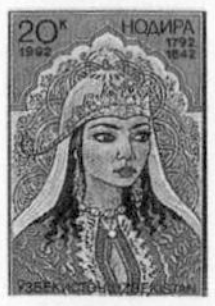

1 Princess Nadira (from portrait by Sh. Khasanov)

1992. Birth Bicentenary of Princess Nadira (poetess).

1	**1**	20k. multicoloured	1·10	85

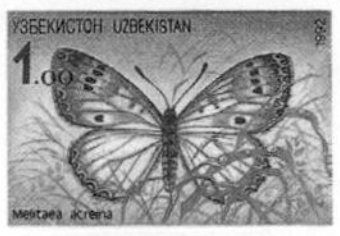

2 "Melitaea acreina" (butterfly)

1992. Nature Protection.

2	**2**	1r. multicoloured	1·10	85

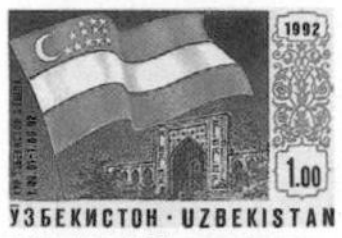

3 National Flag and Kukeldash Mosque, Tashkent

1992. First Anniv of Independence.

3	**3**	1r. multicoloured	1·10	85

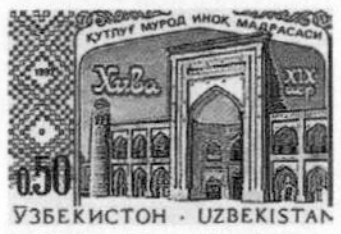

4 Kutlug-Murad-inak Mosque, Khiva

1992. Uzbek Architecture.

4	**4**	50k. multicoloured	90	70

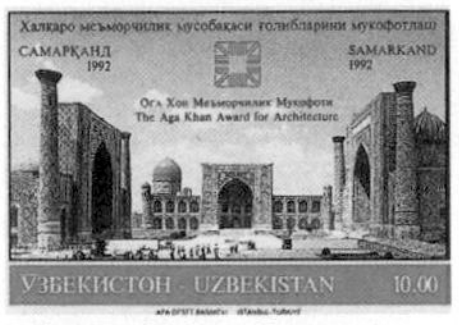

5 Mosque, Registan Square, Samarkand

1992. Award of Aga Khan Prize for Architecture to Samarkand.

5	**5**	10r. multicoloured	1·30	1·00

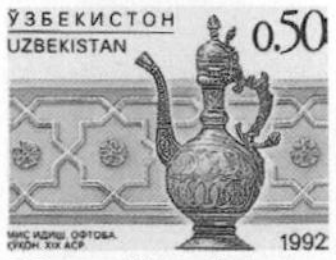

6 Copper Water Pot, Kokand, and Sculptured Relief

1992. Uzbek Handicrafts.

6	**6**	50k. multicoloured	1·10	85

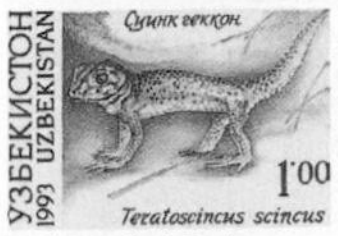

7 Plate-tailed Gecko

1993. Animals. Multicoloured.

7	1r. Type **7**	20	15
8	2r. Cobra	45	35
9	2r. Muskrat (vert)	45	35
10	3r. Osprey (vert)	55	45
11	5r. Penduline tit (vert)	65	50
12	10r. Forest dormouse (vert)	1·10	85
13	15r. Desert monitor	1·80	1·40
MS14	90×60 mm. 20r. Red deer	3·25	3·00

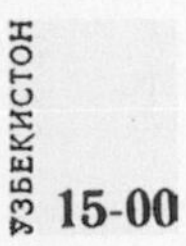

(8)

1993. Stamps of Russia surch as T **8**.

15	2r. on 1k. brown (No. 5940)	90	70
16	8r. on 4k. red (No. 4672)	1·10	85
17	15r. on 2k. mauve (No. 4670)	4·50	3·50
18	15r. on 2k. brown (No. 6073)	4·50	3·50
19	15r. on 3k. green (No. 5941)	4·50	3·50
20	15r. on 4k. red (No. 4672)	4·50	3·50
21	15r. on 4k. blue (No. 6075)	4·50	3·50
22	15r. on 5k. red (No. 6076)	4·50	3·50
23	15r. on 6k. blue (No. 4673)	4·50	3·50
24	15r. on 7k. blue (No. 6077)	4·50	3·50
25	15r. on 10k. brown (No. 6078)	4·50	3·50
26	15r. on 15k. blue (No. 6081)	4·50	3·50
27	20r. on 4k. red (No. 4672)	1·80	1·00
28	30r. on 3k. red (No. 4671)	1·50	1·20
29	100r. on 1k. green (No. 4533)	2·75	2·00
30	500r. on 1k. green (No. 4533)	8·75	6·75

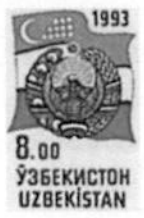

9 Arms and Flag

1993

31	**9**	8r. multicoloured	95	85
32	**9**	15r. multicoloured	1·10	1·00
33	**9**	50r. mult (19×27 mm)	2·20	2·00
34	**9**	100r. multicoloured	4·00	3·50

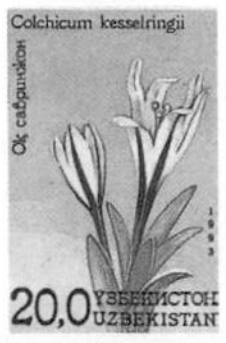

10 "Colchicum kesselringii"

1993. Flowers. Multicoloured.

35	20r. Type **10**	55	50
36	20r. "Dianthus uzbekistanicus"	55	50
37	25r. "Crocus alatavicus"	70	65
38	25r. "Salvia bucharica"	70	65
39	30r. "Tulipa kaufmanniana"	80	70
40	30r. "Tulipa greigii"	80	70
MS41	61×90 mm. 50r. Tulip	1·90	1·80

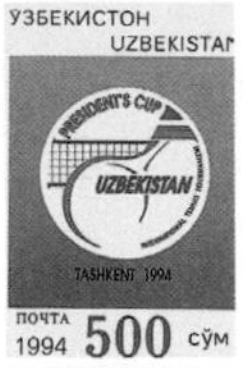

11 Tournament Emblem

1994. President's Cup Tennis Championships, Tashkent. Sheet 91×66 mm.

MS42	**11**	500s. multicoloured	2·30	2·20

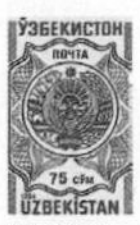

12 Arms

1994

43	**12**	75s. red	60	55

See also Nos. 58/60 and 103/7. For a similar design inscr "O'ZBEKISTON" see Nos. 160/5.

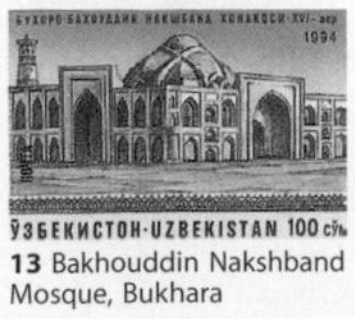

13 Bakhouddin Nakshband Mosque, Bukhara

1994. 675th Birth Anniv of Sheikh Bakhouddin Nakshband.

44	**13**	100s. multicoloured	90	80

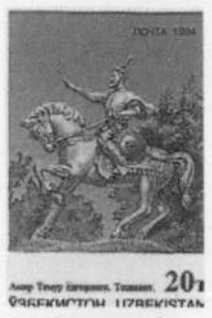

14 Statue of Timur, Tashkent

1994

45	**14**	20t. multicoloured	55	50

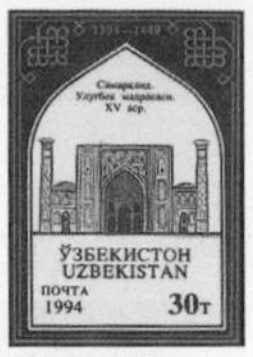

15 Ulugh Beg Mosque, Samarkand

1994. 600th Birth Anniv of Ulugh Beg (central Asian ruler).

46	30t. Type **15**	45	40
47	35t. Ulugh Beg Mosque, Bukhara	55	50
48	40t. Astronomical equipment	60	55
49	45t. Statue, Tashkent	70	65
MS50	70×90 mm. 60t. Ulugh Beg	1·10	95

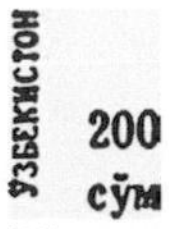

(16)

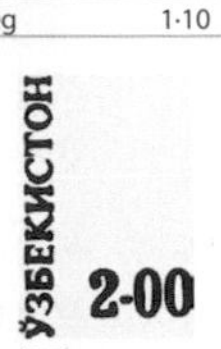

(17)

1995. Stamps of Russia surch. (a) With T **16** in coupon currency.

51	200s. on 2k. brown (No. 6073)	2·75	2·40
52	200s. on 2k. brown (imperf) (No. 6073)	2·75	2·40
53	200s. on 4k. blue (No. 6075)	2·75	2·40
54	200s. on 5k. blue (No. 5061)	2·75	2·40
55	200s. on 15k. blue (No. 6081)	2·75	2·40

(b) With T **17** in permanent currency.

56	2s. on 1k. green (No. 4533)	2·75	2·40
57	2s. on 3k. turquoise (No. 5941)	2·75	2·40

1995. As T **12** but value expressed as "1.00" etc. (a) Size 14×22 mm.

58	1s. green	70	65

(b) Size 22×33 mm.

59	3s. red	90	80
60	6s. blue	1·80	1·60

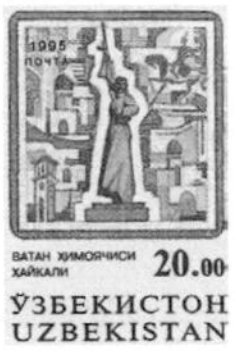

18 Statue, Tashkent

1995. 50th Anniv of End of Second World War. Sheet 100×68 mm.

MS61	**18**	20s. multicoloured	5·25	5·00

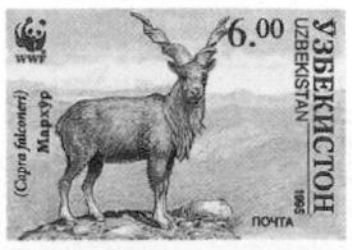

19 Markhor

1995. Endangered Species. The Markhor. Multicoloured.

62	6s. Type **19**	2·30	1·40
63	10s. Three markhors on rocks	3·75	2·10
64	10s. Head	3·75	2·10
65	15s. Lying down	5·25	2·75

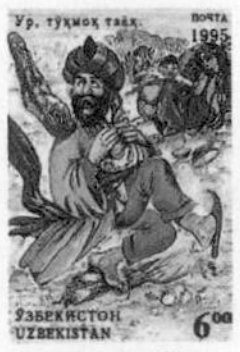

20 "The Fool"

1995. Folk Tales. Multicoloured.

66	6s. Type **20**	1·50	1·40
67	10s. "The Golden Melon"	2·30	2·10

68	10s. Man and white stork on nest ("Are you Stupid?")	2·30	2·10
69	10s. Woman and monster bird ("Thousand Plaits")	2·30	2·10
70	15s. "Story of the Parrot"	3·00	2·75

21 Player and Emblem

1995. Second President's Cup Tennis Championships.

71	**21**	10s. multicoloured	1·80	1·70

22 Gur Amir Mausoleum, Samarkand

1995. Architecture of the Silk Road (1st series). Multicoloured.

72	6s. Type **22**	2·30	2·10
73	10s. Mausoleum, Shakhrisabz	3·00	2·75
74	10s. Mosque, Bukhara	3·00	2·75
75	15s. Kaltaminor Minaret, Khiva	4·50	4·25
MS76	91×71 mm. 20s. Camel, Kaltaminor Minaret and map of Silk Road	6·00	6·25

See also No. 155/MS159.

23 Emblem

1995. First Anniv of Membership of Univeral postal Union. Sheet 91×71 mm.

MS77	**23**	20s. yellow, blue and deep blue	3·75	3·50

24 "Karanasa abramovi"

1995. Butterflies and Moths. Multicoloured.

78	6s. Type **24**	2·30	2·10
79	10s. "Colias romanovi"	3·25	3·00
80	10s. "Parnassius delphius"	3·25	3·00
81	10s. "Chasara staudingeri"	3·25	3·00
82	10s. "Colias wiskotti"	3·25	3·00
83	10s. "Neohipparchia fatua"	3·25	3·00
84	15s. "Parnassius tianschanicus"	4·25	3·75
MS85	90×70 mm. 20s. "Colias christophi"	5·25	5·00

25 Lisunov Li-2 Airliner

1995. Aircraft. Multicoloured.

86	6s. Type **25**	1·50	1·40
87	10s. Kamov Ka-22 helicopter	2·30	2·10
88	10s. Antonov An-8 transport	2·30	2·10
89	10s. Antonov An-12 transport	2·30	2·10
90	10s. Antonov An-22 Anteus jet transport	2·30	2·10
91	10s. Ilyushin Il-76 jet transport	2·30	2·10
92	15s. Ilyushin Il-114	3·00	2·75
MS93	91×71 mm. 20s. As No. 92 (51×36 mm)	4·50	4·25

26 "Madjnun and Laila"

1995. 540th Birth Anniv of Kemal ad-Din Behsad (Persian miniaturist).

94	**26**	15s. multicoloured	3·75	3·50

27 Bactrian Camel

1995. Tashkent Zoo. Multicoloured.

95	6s. Type **27**	1·50	1·40
96	10s. Brown bear	2·30	2·10
97	10s. Cinereous vulture	2·30	2·10
98	10s. Rhesus macaque	2·30	2·10
99	10s. Dalmatian pelican	2·30	2·10
100	10s. Zebra	2·30	2·10
101	15s. African elephant	3·00	2·75
MS102	91×70 mm. 20s. Makhor	5·25	5·00

1995. As T **12.** Value expressed as "2 SUM" etc. (a) Size 14×22½ mm.

103	**12**	2s. green	75	70
104	**12**	6s. green	4·50	4·25

(b) Size 20×32 mm.

105	3s. mauve	75	70
106	6s. mauve	1·50	1·40
107	15s. blue	3·75	3·50

28 Argali

1996. Mammals. Multicoloured.

108	10s. Type **28**	1·50	1·40
109	15s. Argali ("Ovis ammon cycloceros")	2·30	2·10
110	15s. Argali ("Ovis ammon severtzov")	2·30	2·10
111	15s. Argali ("Ovis ammon karelini")	2·30	2·10
112	15s. Red deer ("Cervus elaphas")	2·30	2·10
113	15s. Siberian ibex ("Capra sibirica")	2·30	2·10
114	20s. Saiga ("Saiga tatarica")	3·75	3·50
MS115	90×70 mm. 25s. Goitred gazelle	6·00	5·50

29 Pike Asp

1996. "Save the Aral Sea". Sheet 128×108 mm containing T **29** and similar horiz designs. Multicoloured.

MS116	15s. Caracal; 15s. Aral trout; 20s. Striped hyena; 20s. Kaufmann's shovelnose; 25s. Type **29**	9·00	8·50

30 Football

1996. Olympic Games, Atlanta, U.S.A. Multicoloured.

117	6s. Type **30**	1·50	1·40
118	10s. Show jumping	2·30	2·10
119	15s. Boxing	3·00	2·75
120	20s. Cycling	3·75	3·50

31 Timur

1996. 660th Anniv of Timur (Tamerlane) Sheet 70×90 mm. (a) Wrongly dated "1336—1401".

MS121	**31**	20s. multicoloured	11·50	10·50

(b) Correctly dated "1336—1405".

MS122	**31**	20s. multicoloured	5·25	5·00

32 State Arms and Flag

1996. Fifth Anniv of Independence. Sheet 90×90 mm.

MS123	**32**	20s. multicoloured	4·50	4·25

33 Trophy

1996. Third President's Cup Tennis Championships.

124	**33**	12s. green and grey	12·00	11·00

34 Zhuzhaev

1996. Birth Centenary of Faizulla Zhuzhaev (politician).

125	**34**	15s. black and green	6·00	5·50

35 Fitrat

1996. 110th Birth Anniv of Abdurauf Fitrat (writer).

126	**35**	15s. black and brown	6·00	5·50

36 Spacecraft

1997. Fantasy Spacecraft. Multicoloured.

127	9s. Type **36**	1·50	1·40
128	15s. Spacecraft landing on planet	2·30	2·10
129	15s. Spacecraft with external "wings" and "probes"	2·30	2·10
130	15s. Spacecraft and sun's rays (horiz)	2·30	2·10
131	15s. Spacecraft passing sun (horiz)	2·30	2·10
132	15s. Spacecraft passing Saturn's rings (horiz)	2·30	2·10
133	25s. Two cosmonauts in spacecraft	3·75	3·50
MS134	90×70 mm. 30s. Two spacecraft (39×49 mm)	6·00	5·50

37 Bird of Paradise

1997. Folk Tales. Multicoloured.

135	15s. Type **37**	2·10	1·60
136	15s. Jinn	2·10	1·60
137	20s. Queen looking in mirror	2·75	2·20
138	20s. Man riding on monkey	2·75	2·20
139	25s. Eagle and deer	3·50	3·25
140	25s. Monster and horse	3·50	3·25
141	30s. Two men kneeling before throne	4·25	3·75
MS142	70×90 mm. 35s. Horse rider	7·00	6·50

38 Leopard

1997. The Leopard. Multicoloured.

143	9s. Type **38**	1·10	95
144	15s. Leopard yawning	2·10	1·90
145	15s. Leopard stretching	2·10	1·90
146	25s. Leopard on prowl	3·50	3·25
MS147	90×70 mm. 30s. Head of leopard (29×39 mm)	4·50	4·00

39 Cho'lpon

1997. Birth Centenary of Abdulhamid Sulaymon Cho'lpon.

148	**39**	6s. black and mauve	3·50	3·25

40 Trophy

1997. Fourth President's Cup Tennis Championships. Each green and blue.

149	6s. Type **40**	4·50	4·00
150	6s. Woman player	4·50	4·00
151	6s. Camel and ball	4·50	4·00

41 Tico

1997. Uz-Daewoo Automobile Works. Multicoloured.

152	9s. Type **41**	1·80	1·60
153	12s. Damas	2·75	2·40
154	15s. Nexia	3·50	3·25

42 Ismail Samani Mausoleum, Bukhara

1997. Architecture of the Silk Road (2nd series). Multicoloured.

155	15s. Type **42**	3·50	3·25
156	15s. Citadel, Bukhara (horiz)	3·50	3·25
157	15s. Minaret, Khiva	3·50	3·25
158	15s. Gateway, Khiva (horiz)	3·50	3·25
MS159	Two sheets, each 90×70 mm. (a) 30s. Mosque, Bukhara (29×39 mm); (b) 30s. Mosque, Khiva (39×29 mm)	10·50	10·00

1998. As T **12** (value expressed as "2-00" etc.) but inscr "O'ZBEKISTON".

160	2s. green	35	30

2002. Ozone Protection.
| 419 | **77** | 40s. multicoloured | 2·40 | 2·20 |

78 Monument

2002. 2700th Anniv of Shakhrisabz. Sheet 90×70 mm.
MS420 **78** 30s. multicoloured   2·20   2·00

79 Polo ("Chavgon")

2002. Sports. Multicoloured.
421	45s. Type **79**	1·00	95
422	50s. Horse racing ("Poyga")	1·10	1·00
423	60s. Mounted archery ("Kamondan otish")	1·20	1·10
424	70s. Mounted couple racing ("Qiz quvmoq")	1·40	1·30
425	85s. Picking kerchiefs ("Ro'molcha olish")	1·70	1·60
426	90s. Wrestling ("Kurash")	1·80	1·70
427	145s. Riders ("Uloq")	2·75	2·50

MS428 90×70 mm. 175s. Rider picking up scarf ("Ro'molcha olish")   5·50   5·25

80 Inscr "Yevkratid"

2002. Ancient Coins. Multicoloured.
429	30s. Type **80**	80	75
430	45s. Reverse of "Yevkratid"	1·00	95
431	60s. Inscr "Evtedem tangalargia o'xshatma"	1·20	1·10
432	90s. Reverse of "Evtedem tangalargia o'xshatma"	2·20	2·00
433	125s. Inscr "Amir Temur Ko'ragonly va Suyurg'atmishxon"	3·00	2·75
434	160s. Reverse of "Amir Temur Ko'ragonly va Suyurg'atmishxon"	4·00	3·75

81 Inscr "Qoraqum"

2002. Irises. Multicoloured.
435	15s. Type **81**	60	55
436	30s. Inscr "Solnechniy zaichik"	80	75
437	45s. Inscr "Simfoniya"	1·20	1·10
438	50s. Inscr "Chimyon"	1·40	1·30
439	60s. Inscr "Ikar"	1·60	1·50
440	90s. Inscr "Babye leto"	2·40	2·20
441	125s. Inscr "Toshkent"	3·00	2·75

MS442 70×90 mm. 160s. Inscr "Askiya"   5·50   5·25

82 Emblem

2002. 70th Anniv of Nukus.
| 443 | **82** | 100s. multicoloured | 2·75 | 2·50 |

83 G'afur G'ulom

2003. Birth Centenary of G'afur G'ulom (writer).
| 444 | **83** | 1000s. brown | 12·00 | 11·00 |

84 Komil Yormatov (film maker)

2003. Personalities. Each brown.
| 445 | 125s. Type **84** | 3·00 | 2·75 |
| 446 | 500s. Jo'raxon Sultonov | 6·50 | 6·00 |

85 Ciconia nigra

2003. Wading Birds. Multicoloured.
447	100s. Type **85**	2·40	2·20
448	100s. *Ciconia ciconia asiatica*	2·40	2·20
449	125s. *Platalea leucorodia*	3·00	2·75
450	125s. *Phoenicopterus rubber*	3·00	2·75

86 Man's Skull-cap

2003. Traditional Headdresses. Multicoloured.
451	100s. Type **86**	2·00	1·80
452	100s. Kula-tung (cap), Shakhrisabz	2·00	1·80
453	100s. Scull-cap, Khorazm	2·00	1·80
454	125s. Women's skull-cap, Khiva	2·50	2·30
455	125s. Women's skull-cap, Kokand	2·50	2·30
456	155s. Children's skull-cap, Samarkand	3·25	3·00
457	155s. Man's skull-cap, Samarkand	3·25	3·00

87 "Morning Motherhood" (R. Ahmedov) (1962)

2003. Paintings. Multicoloured.
| 458 | 970s. Type **87** | 12·50 | 11·50 |
| 459 | 970s. "Happiness" (S. Ayitbaev) (1966) | 12·50 | 11·50 |

Stamps of similar designs were issued by Kazakhstan

88 Monuments

2003. 900th Anniv of Abduxoliq G'ijduvoniy.
| 460 | **88** | 125s. multicoloured | 3·75 | 3·50 |

89 Emblems

2004. Olympic Games, Athens. Sheet 70×90 mm.
MS461 **89** 205s. multicoloured   7·50   7·25

90 Qora kaltak

2004. Grapes. Multicoloured.
462	60s. Type **90**	1·30	1·20
463	100s. Kattaqo'rg'on	2·30	2·10
464	100s. Oq husayni	2·30	2·10
465	125s. Qizil Xurmoni	3·00	2·75
466	125s. Echkemar	3·00	2·75
467	155s. Qora Andijon	3·50	3·25
468	210s. Parkent	4·75	4·25

91 Ma'murjon Uzoqov (birth centenary)

2004. Personalities. Each green and black.
| 469 | 100s. Type **91** | 3·50 | 3·25 |
| 470 | 125s. Abdulla Qodiriy (110th birth anniv) | 4·00 | 3·75 |

92 Pendant, Samarkand

2004. Jewellery. Multicoloured.
471	60s. Type **92**	1·30	1·20
472	100s. Pendant with coins, Qo'qon	2·30	2·10
473	100s. Earrings, Tashkent	2·30	2·10
474	125s. Triangular pendant and tasselled earrings, Tashkent	3·00	2·75
475	125s. Rectangular pendant, Buxoro	3·00	2·75
476	155s. Rectangular pendant with curved top, Buxoro	3·50	3·25
477	210s. Triangular pendant with coins and beads, Buxoro	4·75	4·25

93 Mountains

2004. Kitab State Geological Reserve.
| 478 | **93** | 100s. multicoloured | 3·50 | 3·25 |

94 Oybek

2005. Birth Centenary of Muso Toshmuhamedov (Oybek) (writer).
| 479 | **94** | 125s. multicoloured | 3·00 | 2·75 |

95 Veterans

2005. 60th Anniv of End of World War II. Sheet 150×168 mm containing T **95** and similar vert designs. Multicoloured.
MS480 60s.×2, Type **95**; Child holding balloon; 100s.×2, War memorial; Child reading war memorial; 125s.×2, Aircraft and veterans; Modern soldiers with female veteran; 155s.×2, Soldier on guard at memorial; Veteran and photo album   14·00   13·50

96 University Building

2005. 50th Anniv of Tashkent University.
| 481 | **96** | 125s. multicoloured | 3·75 | 3·50 |

97 Emblem

2005. 2700th Anniv of Karshi.
| 482 | **97** | 125s. multicoloured | 3·25 | 3·00 |

98 Qorgon-chinni

2005. Pigeons. Two sheets containing T **98** and similar horiz designs. Multicoloured.
MS483 196×94 mm 85s.×2, Type **98**; Ruyun; 100s.×2, Novvosti; Og kaptor; 125s.×2, Juk; Chelkar; 155s.×2, Udi; Gulsor   19·00   18·00
MS484 70×90 mm 210s. Buxara kaptari   5·50   5·25

99 Teapot

2005. Toreutic (decorated metal) Teapots. Sheet 168×130 mm containing T **99** and similar horiz designs. Multicoloured.
MS485 60s.×2, Type **99**; With medallion; 100s. With chased body and squared spout; 125s. With decorated handle and slender squared spout; 155s. Polished with pierced base; 340s. With squared body and lid   12·50   12·00

100 Emblem

2005. Ma'mun Academy Millenary.
| 486 | **100** | 430s. multicoloured | 7·00 | 6·50 |

101 "Osuda kun" (B. Boboyev)

2006. Paintings. Multicoloured.
487	200s. Type **101**	2·50	2·30
488	200s. "Lake" (V. I. Enin) (horiz)	2·50	2·30
489	250s. "Samarkand, Navruz" (G. Abdurakhmanov)	3·00	2·75
490	250s. "Chaihana in Kokand" (Z. Umarbekov)	3·00	2·75
491	300s. "Oktosh" (R. Ahmedov)	3·75	3·50
492	300s. "Summer" (E. P. Melnikov)	3·75	3·50
493	350s. "Autumn" (N. Kuziboev)	4·25	4·00

2006. As Nos. 160/5.
494	**12**	35s. emerald	50	45
495	**12**	65s. emerald	75	70
496	**12**	200s. red	2·00	1·80
497	**12**	250s. blue	2·30	2·10

498	12	290s. red	2·50	2·30
499	12	350s. blue	3·25	3·00
500	12	430s. red	3·75	3·50
501	12	2500s. red	20·00	18·00
502	12	3700s. blue	28·00	25·00

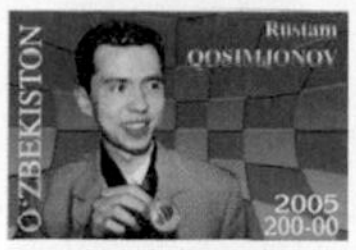

102 Rustam Qosimjonov

2006. Rustam Qosimjonov (Kasimdzhanov)—World Chess Champion.

503	102	200s. multicoloured	3·75	3·50

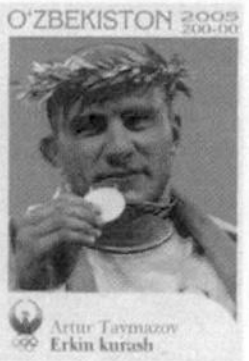

103 Artur Taymazov (wrestling)

2006. Olympic Medallists. Multicoloured.

504	200s. Type **101**	3·50	3·25
505	200s. Aleksandr Doxturushvili (wrestling)	3·50	3·25
506	250s. Magomed Ibragimov (wrestling)	4·00	3·75
507	350s. O'tkir Haydarov and Bahodir Sultonov (boxing) (horiz)	5·00	4·50

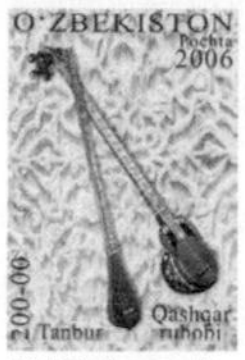

104 Tanbur and Qashqar Rubobi

2006. Traditional Musical Instruments. Multicoloured.

508	200s. Type **104**	2·40	2·20
509	250s. Surnay and Tor	3·00	2·75
510	290s. Surnay and Diora	3·50	3·25
511	350s. Nay and Dutor	4·25	3·75
512	410s. G'ijak	4·75	4·50
513	430s. Nog'ora	5·00	4·75
514	580s. Tanbur and Chang	7·00	6·25

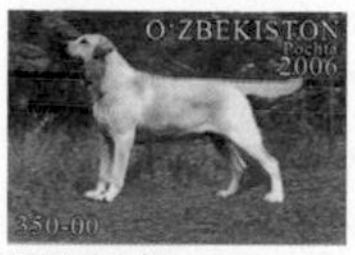

105 Labrador

2006. Dogs. Multicoloured.

515	350s. Type **105**	4·00	3·50
516	540s. Spaniel	5·00	4·75
517	600s. German shepherd	5·75	5·25
518	780s. Asiatic shepherd	7·75	7·25
MS519	89×70 mm. 1150s. Collie and German shepherd	12·00	11·50

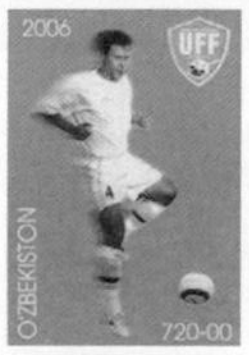

106 Player

2006. World Cup Football Championship, Germany. Sheet 70×89 mm.

MS520	**106**	720s. multicoloured	8·75	8·50

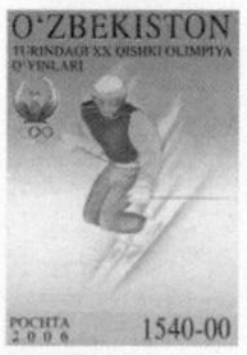

107 Skier

2006. Winter Olympic Games, Turin. Multicoloured.

521	1540s. Type **107**	15·00	14·00
522	2155s. Ice skaters	21·00	19·00

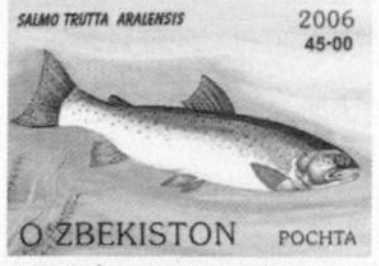

108 *Salmo trutta aralensis*

2006. Fish. Two sheets containing T **108** and similar horiz designs. Multicoloured.

MS523	(a) 125×107 mm. 45s. Type **108**; 90s. *Acipenser nudiventris*; 250s. *Pseudoscaphirhynchus kaufmanni*; 300s. *Barbus brachycephalus*. (b) 90×70 mm. 1010s. *Aspiolucius escocinus*	19·00	18·00

The stamps and margins of **MS**523a/b each form a composite design.

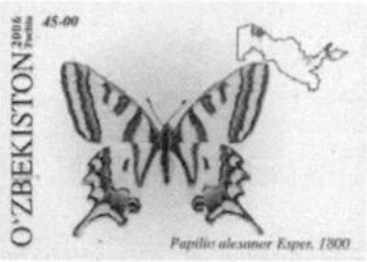

109 *Papilio alexanor*

2006. Butterflies. Multicoloured.

524	45s. Type **109**	80	75
525	90s. *Parnassius mnemosyne*	1·60	1·50
526	200s. *Parnassius apollonius*	2·75	2·75
527	250s. *Parnassius maximinus*	3·50	3·50
528	300s. *Parnassius honrathi*	4·00	3·75
529	350s. *Parnassius charltonius*	4·75	4·50
530	350s. *Hypermnestra helios*	4·75	4·50
MS531	80×100 mm. 1010s. *Parnassius actius*	14·00	13·50

The stamp and margin of **MS**531 form a composite design.

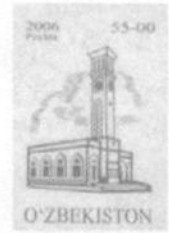
110 Chime of Tashkent

2006. Architecture.

532		55s. emerald	2·00	1·90
533		90s. light green (horiz)	2·75	2·75

DESIGNS: 55s. Type **110**; 90s. Alisher Navoli State Academic Theatre.

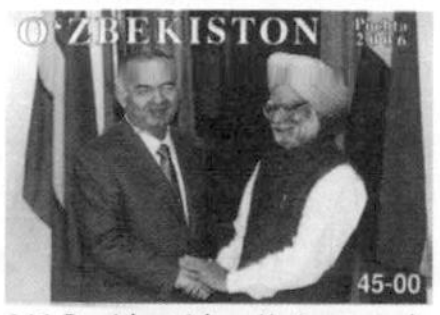

111 President Islam Karimov and Manmohan Singh (Prime Minister of India)

2006. 15th Anniv of Independence (1st issue). International Relations. Designs showing President Karimov with international dignatories. Multicoloured.

534	45s. Type **111**	80	75
535	55s. With Saied Sirajuddin Djamallail (King of Malaysia)	1·20	1·10
536	100s. With Saied Akhmad	1·60	1·50
537	200s. With Vaira Vike-Freiberg (president of Latvia)	3·25	3·00
538	200s. With Hu Tzintao (Chinese Chairman)	3·25	3·00
539	250s. With Janez Drnovsek (President of Slovenia)	4·00	3·75
539a	250s. Presidents		
540	290s. With Vladimir Putin (President of Russia)	4·75	4·50
541	350s. With Mo Mu Khon	5·25	5·00
542	410s. With labour veteran	6·75	6·50
543	580s. With academics from Vaseda University	9·50	9·00

2006. 15th Anniv of Independence (2nd issue). Democracy. As T **111**. Multicoloured.

544	90s. Parliament	1·60	1·50
545	250s. Delegates at Shanghai Cooperation Organization meeting, Tashkent	4·00	3·75
546	410s. Delegates of Eurasian Economic Community's Interstate Council	6·50	6·00

2006. 15th Anniv of Independence (3rd issue). Textile Industry. As T **111**. Multicoloured.

547	90s. Tashkent—2005 Cotton Fair emblem	1·60	1·50
MS548	115×85 mm. 250s. Machinery; 410s. Women and loom; 580s. Women holding spools	20·00	19·00

2006. 15th Anniv of Independence (4th issue). Industry. As T **111**. Multicoloured.

549	45s. Almalik quarry	80	75
550	55s. Bronze smelting	1·20	1·10
551	200s. Qungirot Soda factory	3·25	3·00
552	250s. Qizilqummsement factory (vert)	4·00	3·75
553	350s. Angren coal mine (vert)	5·25	5·00

2006. 15th Anniv of Independence (5th issue). Architecture. As T **111**. Multicoloured.

554	45s. Academy of Science	80	75
555	45s. Lyceum	80	75
556	95s. Humanism Arch	2·00	1·90
557	290s. Medical College	4·75	4·50
558	430s. Senate, Tashkent	7·25	6·75
559	720s. Senate	12·00	11·50
560	1010s. Independence and Humanism Monument (vert)	16·00	15·00

2006. 15th Anniv of Independence (6th issue). Agriculture. As T **111**. Multicoloured.

561	90s. President Karimov and farmers	1·60	1·50
562	200s. President Karimov and women farmers	3·25	3·00
563	250s. President Karimov and cotton collectors	4·00	3·75

2006. 15th Anniv of Independence (7th issue). Infrastructure. As T **111**. Multicoloured.

564	290s. Railway	4·75	4·50
MS565	115×85 mm. 55s. Ring road; 90s. Kamchik Pass; 180s. Road construction	6·00	5·75

2006. 15th Anniv of Independence (8th issue). Cars. As T **111**. Multicoloured.

566	200s. Daewoo Damas II	3·25	3·00
567	290s. Daewoo Nexia	4·75	4·50

2006. 15th Anniv of Independence (9th issue). Culture. As T **111**. Multicoloured.

568	55s. Dancers and carpets	1·20	1·10
569	90s. Dancers	1·60	1·50

2006. 15th Anniv of Independence (10th issue). Armed Forces. As T **111**. Multicoloured.

MS570	115×85 mm. 100s. Student pilots; 250s. Radio operators; 410s. Russian and Uzbekistan soldiers on anti-terrorist exercise	12·00	11·50

2006. 15th Anniv of Independence (11th issue). Medals and Orders. As T **111**. Multicoloured.

571	410s. International Kurash Association (IKA) Gold Order	6·75	6·50
572	580s. International Federation of Associated Wrestling Styles (FILA) Medal	9·50	9·00
573	720s. Association of National Olympic Committees (ANOC) Gold Order	11·50	11·00

2006. 15th Anniv of Independence (12th issue). Sport. Kurash (jacket wrestling). Vert designs as T **111**. Multicoloured.

574	90s. Combatants	1·60	1·50
575	100s. Winner	1·80	1·70
576	430s. Wrestler jumping	6·75	6·50

2006. 15th Anniv of Independence (13th issue). Sport. Umid nihollari—2006 Schools Sports Competition. As T **111**. Multicoloured.

MS577	171×126 mm. Horiz. 45s. Arena; 55s. Indoor swimming pool; 90s. Medal winners; 100s. Synchronised swimming; 200s. Karate combatants; 250s. Football; 290s. Show jumping; 580s. President Karimov and young sportsmen	26·00	25·00

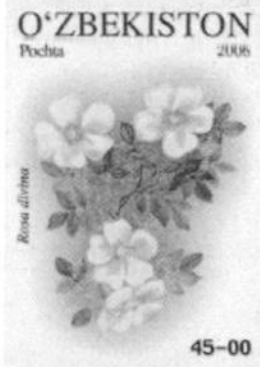

112 *Rosa divina*

2006. Roses. Multicoloured.

578	45s. Type **112**	1·20	1·10
579	90s. *Rosa maracandica*	1·60	1·50
580	250s. *Rosa persica*	4·00	3·75
581	350s. *Rosa vassilczencoi*	5·25	5·00
MS582	70×90 mm. 600s. *Rosa divina F. Plena*	9·50	9·25

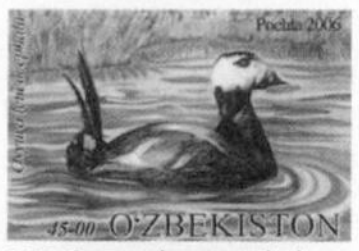

113 *Oxyura leucocephala* (white-headed duck)

2006. Birds. Sheet 125×95 mm containing T **113** and similar horiz designs. Multicoloured.

MS583	45s. Type **113**; 250s. *Haliaeetus albicilla* (white-tailed eagle); 350s. *Phalacrocorax pygmaeus* (pygmy cormorant); 350s. *Marmaronetta angustirostris* (marbled duck)	15·00	14·50

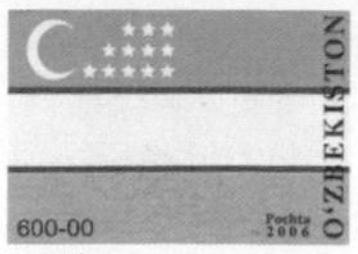

114 Flag

2006. 15th Anniv of National Flag.

584	114	600s. multicoloured	9·50	9·25

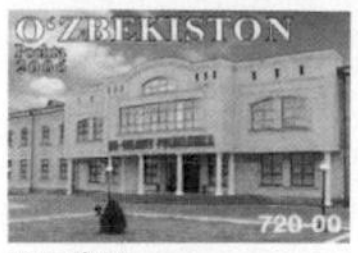

115 Clinic

2006. Year of Medical and Charity Workers. Sheet 90×70 mm.

MS585	**115**	720s. multicoloured	10·00	9·75

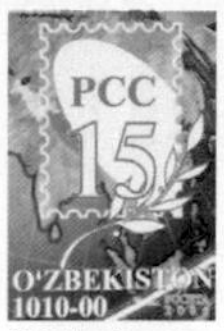

116 Anniversary Emblem

2006. 15th Anniv of Regional Communications Community. Sheet 90×70 mm.

MS586	**116**	1010s. multicoloured	16·00	15·00

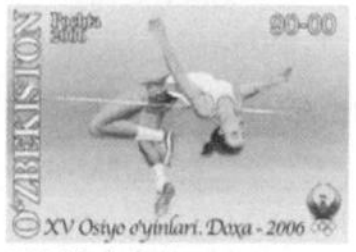

117 High Jump

2006. Doha—2006 Sports Competition. Multicoloured.

587	90s. Type **117**	1·60	1·50
588	250s. Tennis	4·00	3·75
589	350s. Football	5·25	5·00
590	350s. Basketball	5·25	5·00

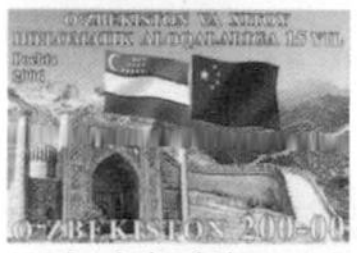
118 Symbols of China and Uzbekistan

2006. 15th Anniv of Uzbekistan—China Diplomatic Relations.

591	118	200s. multicoloured	3·25	3·00

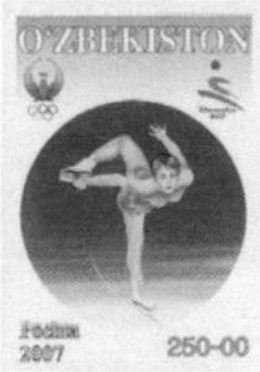

119 Skater

2007. Asian Winter Games, Changchun. Multicoloured.

592	250s. Type **119**	4·00	3·75
593	350s. Skier	5·25	5·00

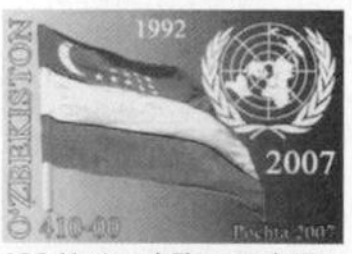

120 National Flag and UN Emblem

2007. 15th Anniv of United Nations Membership.

594	120	410s. multicoloured	6·00	5·75

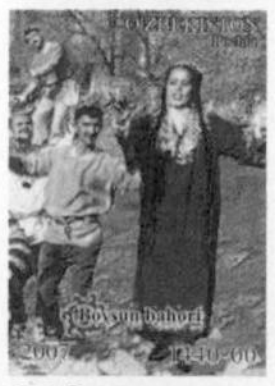
121 Dancers

2007. Boysun bahori (Spring Holiday). Sheet 69×90 mm.

MS595	**121**	1440s. multicoloured	20·00	19·00

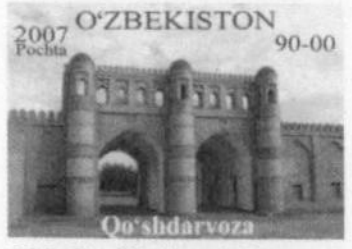

122 City Wall and Gates

2007. Architecture. Four sheets containing T **122** and similar multicoloured designs.

MS596	95×70 mm. (a) 90s. Type **122**; 250s. Medrese Mukhamed Rahim; 1010s. Mausoleum Pakhvalan Makhmud. (b) 200s. Medrese Norbo-tabij; 410s. Mausoleum Dakhma-i-Shokhon; 430s. Palace of Hudoyar-khan. (c) 250s. Medrese Modarikson; 420s. Medrese Miri-Arab; 430s. Mausoleum Char-Bakr	46·00	45·00
MS597	70×95 mm. Vert. 300s. Mausoleum Junus-khan; 350s. Medrese Barak-khan; 720s. Medrese Abulgosim	20·00	19·00

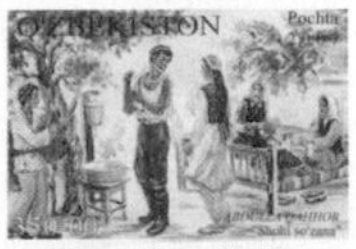
123 Scene from *Shohi so'zana*

2007. Birth Centenary of Abdullah Qahhar (writer). Multicoloured.

598	350s. Type **123**	5·25	5·00
599	420s. Abdullah Qahhar	6·00	5·75

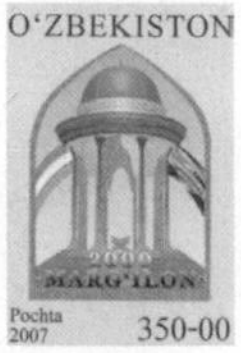

124 Anniversary Emblem

2007. 2000th Anniv of Marg'ilon

600	**124**	350s. multicoloured	4·75	4·50

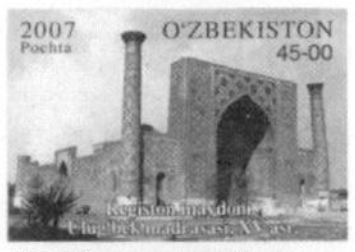

125 Medrese Ulug'bek

2007. Architecture. 2750th Anniversary of Samarqand. Two sheets containing T **125** and similar multicoloured designs.

MS601	188×128 mm. 45s. Type **125**; 55s. Medrese Sherdor; 100s. Medrese Tillakori; 180s. Amir Temur Mosque; 200s. Bibixonim Mosque; 250s. Ruhobod Mosque; 490s. Umumiy Mosque; 720s. Qo'shgumbazli Mosque	29·00	28·00
MS602	128×188 mm. Vert. 90s. Imom al-Moturidiy Mosque; 100s. Imom Buxoriy Mosque; 180s. Amir Temur Mosque courtyard; 200s. Amir Temur monument; 410s. Bibixonim Mosque entrance; 680s. Shohizinda Mosque; 700s. Bibixonim Mosque tower; 1150s. Shohizinda Mosque entrance	48·00	47·00

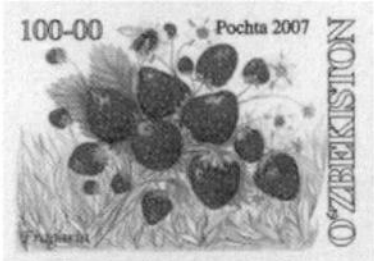

126 *Fragaria* (strawberry)

2007. Berries. Multicoloured.

603	100s. Type **126**	1·60	1·50
604	250s. *Ribes nigrum* (blackcurrant)	3·50	3·50
605	580s. *Rubus idaeus* (raspberry)	8·00	7·50
606	720s. *Grossularia rechnata* (gooseberry)	10·00	9·50

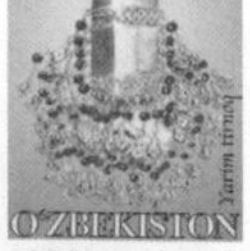

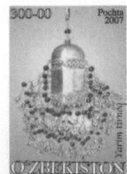

127 'Yarim tirnoq'

2007. Jewellery. Designs showing jewellery, inscriptions given. Multicoloured.

607	300s. Type **127**	4·50	4·25
608	350s. Ko	4·75	4·50
609	670s. Shovkala	9·25	8·75
610	720s. Bodomoy	10·00	9·50

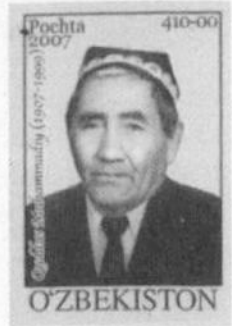

128 Quddus Mukhammadiy

2007. Birth Centenary of Quddus Muhammadiy.

611	**128**	410s. multicoloured	5·50	5·25

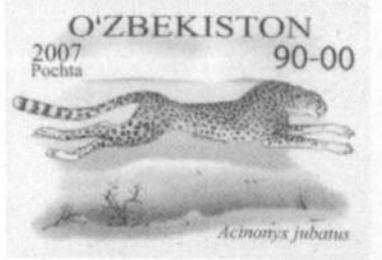

129 Cheetah

2007. Cheetah (Acinonyx jubatus). Multicoloured.

612	90s. Type **129**	1·20	1·10
613	490s. Lying down	6·50	6·00
614	680s. Prowling	8·75	8·25
615	780s. Facing left	10·00	9·50
MS616	89×70 mm. Size 30×42 mm. 1440s. Mother and cub	18·00	17·00

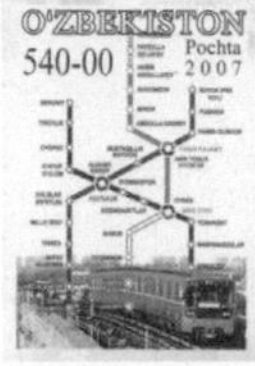

130 Locomotive and Map of Line

2007. 30th Anniv of Tashkent Metro. Sheet 82×89 mm containing T **130** and similar vert design. Multicoloured.

MS617	540s. Type **130**; 780s. Station entrance	18·00	17·00

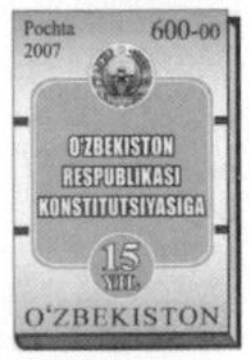

131 National Arms and Emblem

2007. 15th Anniv of Constitution.

618	**131**	600s. multicoloured	8·00	7·50

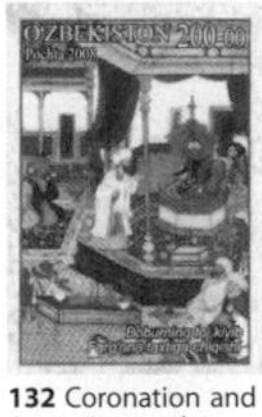
132 Coronation and Accession to the Throne of Ferghana

2008. 525th Birth Anniversary of Zakhiriddin Mukhamad Babur (poet, historian and founder of the dynasty and empire of Timurids). Sheet 120×156 mm containing T **132** and similar vert designs. Multicoloured.

MS619	200s. Type **132**; 250s. Inhabitants of Samarqand welcoming Babur; 350s. At Sultan Husein's House, Herat; 350s. Receiving Ambassador of Bengalia; 350s. Zakhiriddin Mukhammad Babur; 410s. Relieving Kabul Fortress from mutiny; 490s. Surveying Mausoleum, Delhi; 540s. At Khodja Seyaran spring near Kabul; 680s. Surveying the Palaces of Man Singh and Bikramajit	44·00	43·00

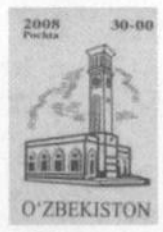

133 Building with Clock Tower

2008. Architecture.

620	30s. emerald	80	75
621	75s. emerald (horiz)	1·20	1·10
622	85s. emerald	1·60	1·50
623	100s. pale rose-red (horiz)	1·80	1·70
624	150s. emerald (horiz)	2·00	1·90
625	160s. emerald	2·40	2·30
626	200s. pale rose-red (horiz)	3·25	3·00
627	250s. new blue (horiz)	4·00	3·75
628	310s. emerald (horiz)	4·75	4·50
629	350s. new blue (horiz)	5·50	5·25

DESIGNS: 30s., 85s. and 160s. Type **133**; 75s., 100s., 200s. and 350s. Theatre; 150s., 250s., and 310s. Opera and ballet theatre

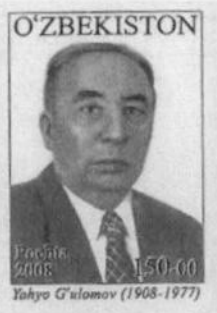

134 Yahyo G'ulomov

2008. Birth Centenary of Yahyo G'ulomov (scientist)

630	**136**	150s. multicoloured	2·40	2·30

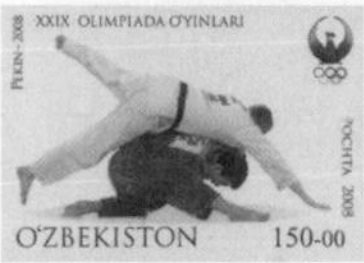

135 Judo

2008. Olympic Games, Beijing. Multicoloured.

631	150s. Type **135**	3·25	3·00
632	200s. Boxing	4·00	3·75
633	250s. Athletics	4·75	4·50
634	310s. Gynastics (vert)	6·00	5·75

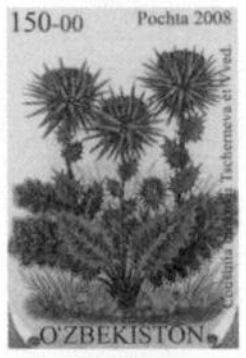

137 *Cousinia butkovii*

2008. Flora. Multicoloured.

635	150s. Type **137**	2·00	1·90
636	200s. *Cousinia dshisakensis*	2·75	2·75
637	250s. *Cousinia adenophora*	3·25	3·00
638	310s. *Cousinia angereni*		

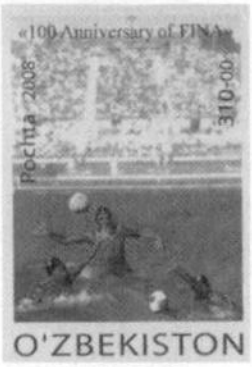

138 Water Polo

2008. Centenary of FINA (Fédération Internationale de Natation). Multicoloured.

639	310s. Type **138**	4·00	3·75
640	450s. Synchronised swimming	6·00	5·75
641	620s. Diving	8·00	7·50
642	750s. Swimming	10·00	9·50

DESIGNS: 620s. Type **140**; 750s. Mirzakalon Ismoiliy

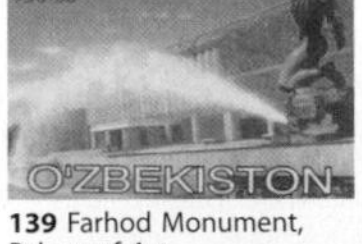

139 Farhod Monument, Palace of Art

2008. 50th Anniv of Navoi Metallurgical Combine. Sheet 100×120 mm containing T **139** and similar horiz design. Multicoloured.

MS643	930s. Type **139**; 1250s. Gold bars	28·00	27·00

No. 644 is vacant.

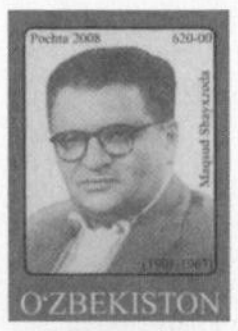

140 Maqsud Shayxzoda

2008. Writers Birth Centenaries.

645	620s. pale brown-olive and black	8·00	7·50
646	750s. brown and black	10·00	9·50

Designs: 620s. Type **140**; 750s. Mirzakalon Ismoily.

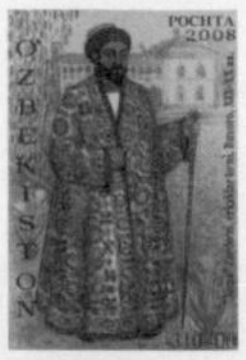

141 Joma, Buhara 19th–20th century

2008. Traditional Men's Costume. Multicoloured.

647	310s. Type **141**	4·00	3·75
648	350s. Yaktak, Buhara 20th century	4·75	4·50
649	750s. Buhara 19th century	10·00	9·50
650	1250s. Joma, Buhara 19th–20th century (different)	16·00	15·00

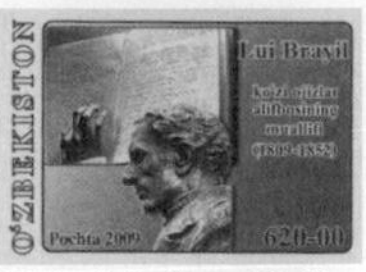

142 Louis Braille and Braille Book

2009. Birth Bicentenary of Louis Braille (inventor of Braille writing for the blind).

651	**142**	620s. red-brown and black	8·00	7·50

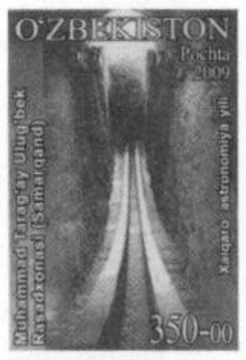

143 Ulugbek Observatory, Samarkand

2009. International Year of Astronomy. Multicoloured.

652	350s. Type **143**	4·50	4·25
653	750s. Muhammad Taragay Ulugbek (astronomer) monument, Tashkent	11·50	11·00

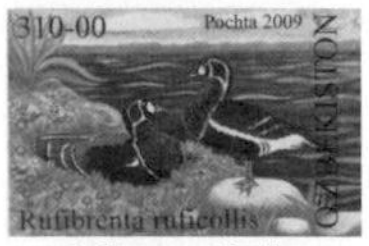

144 *Rufibrenta ruficollis* (Red-breasted Goose)

2009. Water Birds. Multicoloured.

654	310s. Type **144**	4·00	3·75
655	350s. *Cygnus cygnus* (Whooper Swan)	4·50	4·25
656	620s. *Aythya nyroca* (Ferruginous Duck)	8·00	7·50
657	750s. *Anser erythropus* (Lesser White-fronted Goose)	9·50	9·00

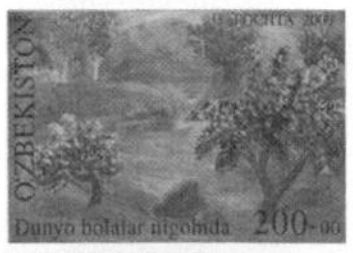

145 Flowering Trees

2009. Children's Paintings. Multicoloured.

658	200s. Type **145**	2·40	2·30
659	200s. Lion	2·40	2·30
660	200s. Dove and flowers (vert)	2·40	2·30
661	200s. Dancer and drummer (vert)	2·40	2·30
662	200s. Stork on nest (vert)	2·40	2·30
663	200s. Elderly man and school boy	2·40	2·30

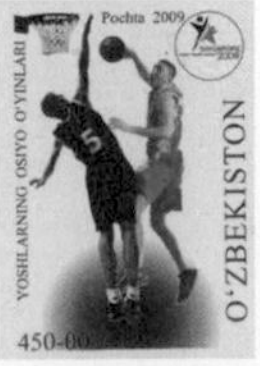

146 Basketball

2009. Singapore 2009–Youth Games. Multicoloured.

664	450s. Type **146**	6·00	5·75
665	750s. Football (horiz)	9·50	9·00

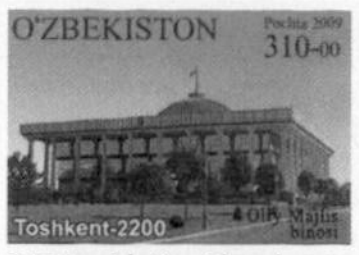

147 Legislative Chamber

2009. 2200th Anniv of Tashkent. Sheet 133×70 mm containing T **147** and similar horiz designs. Multicoloured.

MS666 310s. Type **147**; 310s. Senate; 350s. International Business Centre; 350s. History Museum; 620s. Turkiston Palace; 620s. Medrese; 750s. Museum of Victims of Repression; 750s. Map of the Great Silk Road 50·00 49·00

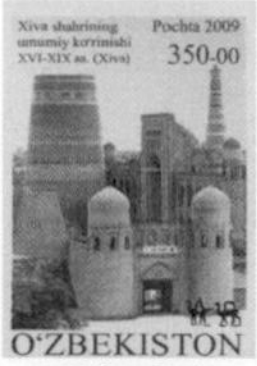

148 Walls of Itchan Kala, Khiva (Xiva)

2009. Architecture of Silk Road. Multicoloured.

667	350s. Type **148**	4·50	4·25
668	750s. Suyudji-khan Madrassah	9·50	9·00
MS669	90×70 mm. 1250s. Old City Gate, Buchara	16·00	15·00

2009. Architecture

670	450s. red	6·00	5·75
671	600s. new blue	8·00	7·50

Designs: 450s. Opera and Ballet theatre; 600s. Theatre.

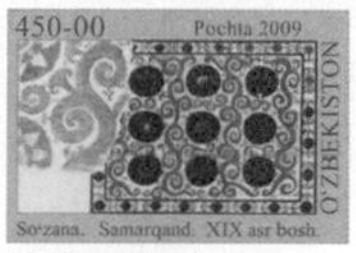

149 Samarkand

2009. Syuzane Carpets. Multicoloured.

672	450s. Type **149**	6·00	5·75
673	600s. Bukhara	8·00	7·50
674	1000s. Tashkent	14·00	13·00
675	1200s. Andijan	16·00	15·00

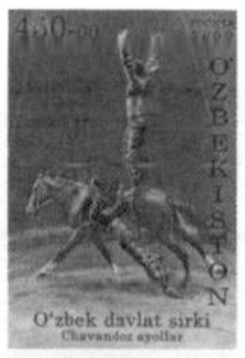

150 Two Artistes

2009. Uzbek Circus. Multicoloured.

676	450s. Type **150**	6·00	5·75
677	600s. Two horses and three artistes in tower formation	8·00	7·50
678	1200s. One horse and three artistes	16·00	15·00

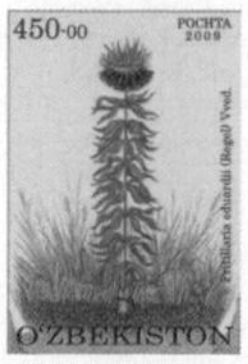

151 *Fritillaria eduardii*

2010. Endangered Flora. Multicoloured.

679	450s. Type **151**	6·00	5·75
680	1200s. *Iridodictyum winklerii*	16·00	15·00

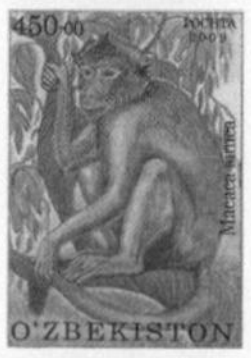

152 *Macaca sinica* (toque macaque)

2010. Tashkent Zoo. Multicoloured.

681	450s. Type **152**	6·00	5·75
682	800s. *Macaca fascicularis* (crab-eating macaque)	10·00	9·50
683	1000s. *Macaca sphinx* (mandrill baboon)	14·00	13·00
MS684	70×90 mm. 1650s. *Lemur catta*	22·00	21·00

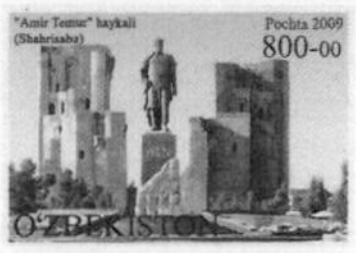

153 Amir Temir Monument, Shahrisabz

2010. Regions of Uzbekistan. Multicoloured.

685	800s. Type **153**	10·00	9·50
686	1200s. Railway Station, Karshi	14·00	13·00

2010. Architecture. Each emerald.

687	25s. As Type **133**	40	40
688	100s. Theatre (horiz)	1·20	1·10
689	110s. As Type **133**	1·40	1·30
690	125s. Theatre (horiz)	1·60	1·50
691	200s. Theatre (horiz)	2·40	2·30

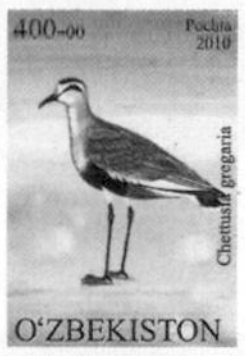

154 *Chettusia gregaria* (Sociable Lapwing)

2010. Birds. Multicoloured.

693	400s. Type **154**	4·75	4·50
694	800s. *Myophonus caeruleus* (inscr '*Myophonus coeruleus*') (Blue Whistling Thrush)	9·50	9·00
695	1000s. *Tichodroma muraria* (Wall Creeper)	12·00	11·50
696	1200s. *Grus leucogeranus* (Siberian Crane)	14·00	13·00
MS697	90×70 mm. 1900s. *Cygnus olor* (Mute Swan)	23·00	22·00

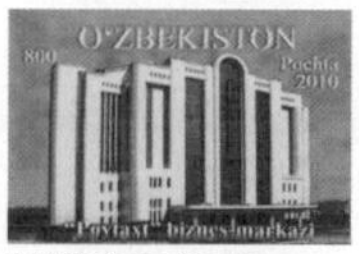

155 Business Centre

2010. 43rd Annual Meeting of Governors of Asian Development Bank, Tashkent. Multicoloured.

698	800s. Type **155**	11·00	10·00
699	800s. Senate building	11·00	10·00
700	800s. Olij Majlis building	11·00	10·00
701	800s. Bank Association building	11·00	10·00
702	800s. Archway	11·00	10·00
703	800s. Palace of Sitorai Mohi Xosa	11·00	10·00
704	800s. Oil refining plant in Bukhora	11·00	10·00
705	800s. Truck	11·00	10·00
706	800s. Combine harvester	11·00	10·00
707	900s. Motorway flyover	12·00	11·50
708	900s. Motorway multi junction	12·00	11·50
709	900s. Nurse and incubator	12·00	11·50
710	900s. Waterpolo match	12·00	11·50
711	900s. Women wearing traditional dress sewing	12·00	11·50
712	900s. Couple wearing traditional dress	12·00	11·50
713	1000s. Oil refining plant in Fergana	13·00	12·50
714	1000s. UZ-Daewoo plant	13·00	12·50
715	1000s. Building construction vehicles	13·00	12·50
716	1000s. Students in laboratory	13·00	12·50
717	1000s. Channel	13·00	12·50
718	1000s. National flag	13·00	12·50
719	1100s. Bridge	14·00	13·00
720	1100s. Two lane sunken underpass	14·00	13·00
721	1200s. State Arms	15·00	14·00
722	1200s. Uzbekistan Palace	15·00	14·00
723	1200s. Ok Saroi building	15·00	14·00
724	1200s. Conservatory	15·00	14·00
725	1200s. Central Bank	15·00	14·00
726	1200s. Business district, Tashkent	15·00	14·00
727	1200s. Hazrati Imam complex	15·00	14·00
728	1200s. Tractor plant	15·00	14·00
729	1200s. Locomotive	15·00	14·00
730	1200s. Railway bridge over river	15·00	14·00
731	1200s. Operating theatre, operation in progress	15·00	14·00
732	1200s. Pupils using computers	15·00	14·00
733	1200s. Parade in sports complex	15·00	14·00
734	1200s. Potter decorating pots	15·00	14·00
735	1200s. Family wearing traditional dress	15·00	14·00

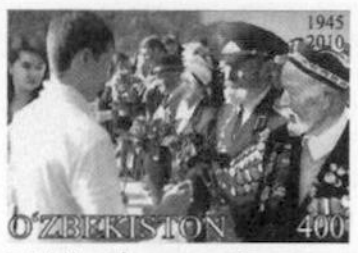

156 Youth presenting Flowers to Veterans

2010. 65th Anniv of End of World War II. Multicoloured.

MS736 400s. Type **156**; 800s. Monument; 1000s. Returning soldier; 1200s. Parade of soldiers and veterans 44·00 43·00

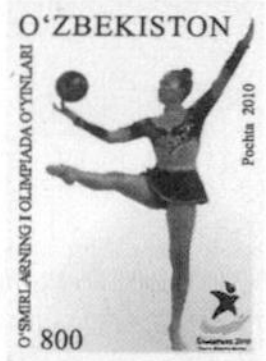

157 Gymnast

2010. Youth Olympic Games Singapore 2010

737	**157** 800s. multicoloured	10·00	9·50

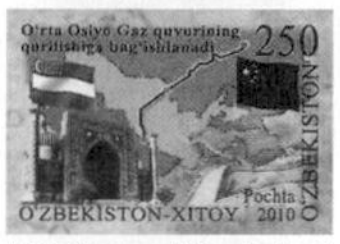

158 Flags and Symbols of Uzbekistan and China and Map of Route

2010. Uzbekistan-China Gas Main

738	**158** 250s. multicoloured	3·50	3·50

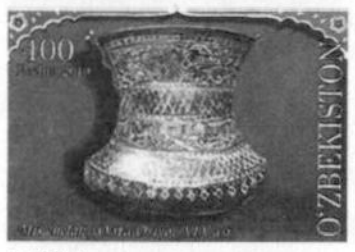

159 Vase

2010. Copperware. Multicoloured.

MS739 400s. Type **159**; 800s. Bowl and jug; 1000s. Coffee pot and lamp bowl; 1200s. Tray and coffee pot 44·00 43·00

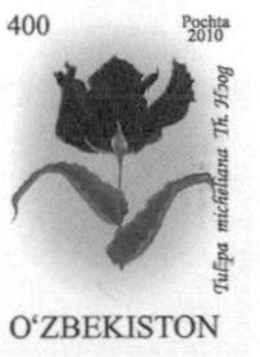

160 *Tulipa biflorimis*

2010. Tulips. Multicoloured.

740	400s. Type **160**	6·00	5·75
741	800s. *Tulipa micheliana*	10·00	9·50
742	1000s. *Tulipa lehmaniana*	12·00	11·50
743	1200s. *Tulipa dasystemon*	16·00	15·00
MS744	99×77 mm. 1000s. *Tulipa dasystemon* in alpine pature; 1900s. *Tulipa dasystemon* against rocks	36·00	35·00

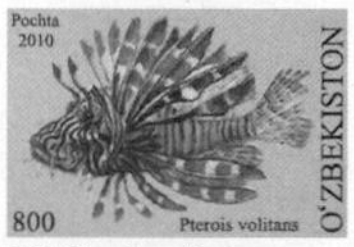

161 *Pterois volitans*

2010. Auarium Fish. Multicoloured.

745	800s. Type **161**	10·00	9·50
746	1000s. *Trichogaster leeri*	12·00	11·50
747	1200s. *Carassius auratus*	16·00	15·00
MS748	92×70 mm. 1000s. *Pterophyllum scalare*; 1900s. *Trichogaster leeri* amongst seaweeds	36·00	35·00

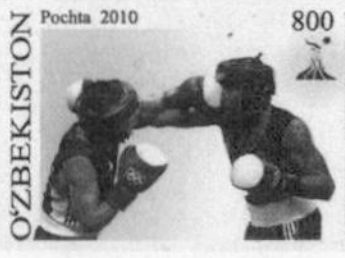

162 Boxers

2010. Asian Games

749	**162** 800s. multicoloured	10·00	9·50

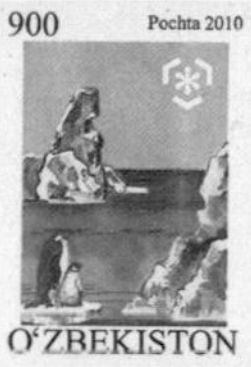

163 Retreating Ice and Penguins on Ice Flow

2010. Preserve Polar Regions and Glaciers

750	**163** 900s. multicoloured	11·00	10·50

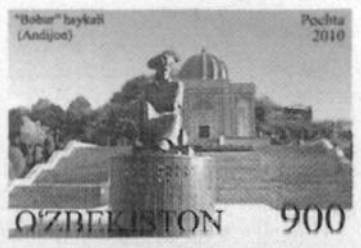

164 Bobur Monument

2010. Regions of Uzbekistan. Multicoloured.

751	900s. Type **164**	11·00	10·50
752	1200s. Olympic Athletic College	16·00	15·00

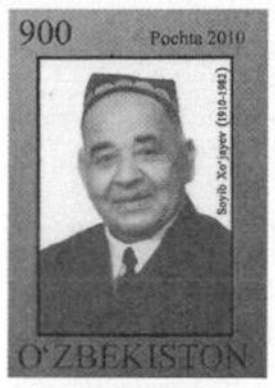

165 Saylb Hodzhaev

2010. Birth Centenary of Sayib Hodzhaev (actor)

753	**165** 900s. multicoloured	11·00	10·50

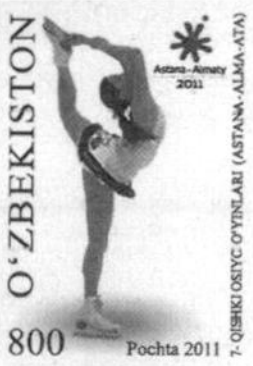

166 Figure Skating

2011. Asiatic Winter Games. Multicoloured.

754	800s. Type **166**	10·00	9·50
755	900s. Freestyle ski jump	11·00	10·50

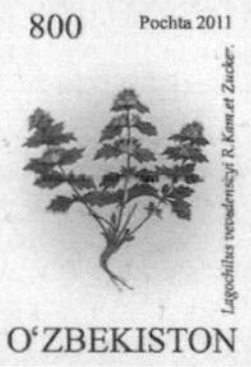

167 *Lagochilus vevedenskyi*

2010. Flowers. Multicoloured.

756	800s. Type **167**	10·00	9·50
757	900s. *Echinops babatagensis*	11·00	10·50
758	1000s. *Saxifraga hirculus*	13·00	12·00
759	1200s. *Nathaliella alaica*	16·00	14·50
MS760	100×80 mm. 1000s. *Eremurus korolkovii*; 1900s. *Eremurus korolkovii* (larger)	36·00	35·00

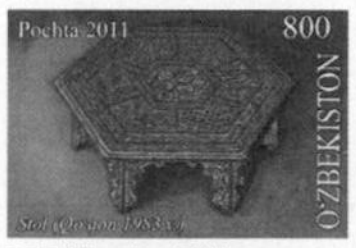

168 Wooden Table

2011. Cultural Heritage. Multicoloured.

MS761 800s. Type **168**; 900s. Circular casket; 1000s. Folding stool; 1200s. Decorated gourd 75·00 70·00

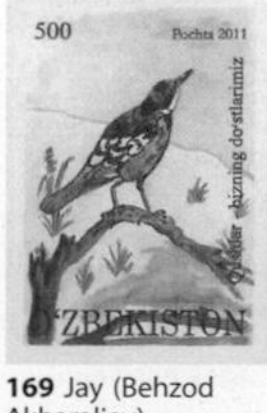

169 Jay (Behzod Akbaraliev)

2011. Birds. Children's Drawings. Multicoloured.
762 500s. Type **169** 7·25 6·75
763 500s. Hoopoe (Catherina Melyukova) 7·25 6·75
764 500s. Pheasant (blue) (Adele Sharapova) (horiz) 7·25 6·75
765 500s. Birds in flight (Abdulhamid Vakilov) (horiz) 7·25 6·75

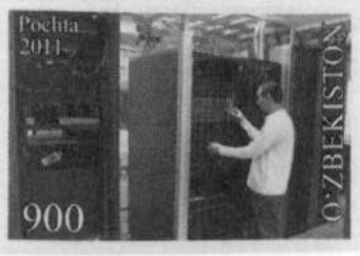

170 Working

2011. 20th Anniv of Independence (1st issue). Communications. Multicoloured.
766 900s. Type **170** 11·00 10·50
767 1200s. Man seated at computer array, Uztelekom Control Centre 16·00 14·50

2011. 20th Anniv of Independence (2nd issue). Sport. Multicoloured.
768 800s. High Jump 10·00 9·50
769 1200s. Judo 16·00 14·50

2011. 20th Anniv of Independence (3rd issue). Health. Multicoloured.
770 900s. Nurse, Regional Perinatal Centre, Syrdarya 11·00 10·50
771 1200s. Central Hospital Medical Centre, Surkhanarya 16·00 14·50

2011. 20th Anniv of Independence (4th issue). Fauna, Hisar State Reserve Park. Multicoloured.
772 900s. Pelicans 11·00 10·50
773 1200s. Eagle 16·00 14·50

2011. 20th Anniv of Independence (5th issue). Landscape. Multicoloured.
774 900s. Par region in winter 11·00 10·50
775 1200s. Spring in the mountains 16·00 14·50

2011. 20th Anniv of Independence (6th issue). Culture. Multicoloured.
776 800s. Independence celebration 10·00 9·50
777 1000s. Eski Machit folk ensemble 13·00 12·00
778 1200s. State Boldhoi Theatre 16·00 14·50
779 1200s. Karny Par musicians 16·00 14·50

2011. 20th Anniv of Independence (7th issue). Transport. Multicoloured.
780 800s. Clover leaf road junction and flyover 10·00 9·50
781 1000s. Badamzar Metro Station 13·00 12·00
782 1200s. Road bridge 16·00 14·50
783 1200s. Tashguzar Boysun Kumkurgan railway bridge 16·00 14·50

2011. 20th Anniv of Independence (8th issue). Industry. Multicoloured.
784 800s. Navioyazot OJSC plant (vert) 10·00 9·50
785 800s. Daewoo vehicle plant 10·00 9·50
786 900s. Zarafshan gold mining plant (vert) 11·00 10·50
787 900s. Talimarzhdanstaya TPS station 11·00 10·50
788 900s. Textile mill, Bokhara 11·00 10·50
789 900s. Buhkungradsky soda plant 11·00 10·50
790 1000s. Isuzu vehicle plant 13·00 12·00
791 1200s. Maxam Chirchiq plant (vert) 16·00 14·50
792 1200s. Daewoo cars 16·00 14·50
793 1200s. Bekabad steel making plant 16·00 14·50
794 1200s. Sogdiana substation 16·00 14·50
795 1200s. Textile mill, Gulistan 16·00 14·50
796 1200s. Shurtangaz chemical complex 16·00 14·50
797 1200s. Isuzu truck 16·00 14·50

2011. 20th Anniv of Independence (9th issue). Architecture. Multicoloured.
798 800s. Central Square, Urgench 10·00 9·50
799 800s. Jokargy Kenes Building, Nukus 10·00 9·50
800 800s. Wedding Palace, Termez 10·00 9·50
801 800s. Barkamol Avlod sports complex, Namangan 10·00 9·50
802 800s. Theatre, Bokhara 10·00 9·50
803 900s. Youth Centre, Andijan 11·00 10·50
804 900s. Wedding House, Samarkand 11·00 10·50
805 900s. Karsi State University Academy Lyceum 11·00 10·50
806 900s. Istikol Street, Kokland 11·00 10·50
807 1000s. Forum Palace 13·00 12·00
808 1000s. Al Xorani Monument, Urgench 13·00 12·00
809 1200s. National Museum, Nukus 16·00 14·50
810 1200s. Archaeological Museum, Termez 16·00 14·50
811 1200s. Alokabank Building, Namangan 16·00 14·50
812 1200s. Ancient and Eternal monument, Bokhara 16·00 14·50
813 1200s. College of Light Industry, Andijan 16·00 14·50
814 1200s. Concert Hall 16·00 14·50
815 1200s. TUIT Fergana Branch 16·00 14·50
816 1200s. Ozodlik prospect, Kokland 16·00 14·50
817 1200s. Education Centre 16·00 14·50

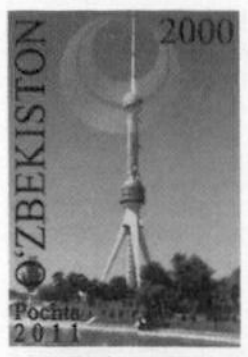

171 Taskent TV Tower

2011. 20th Anniv of Regional Communication Community (RCC). Sheet 90×70 mm
MS818 **171** 2000s. multicoloured 26·00 25·00

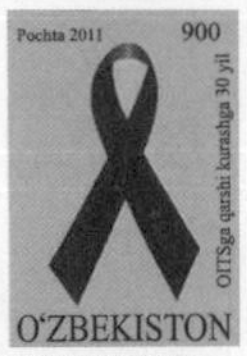

172 AIDS Ribbon

2011. AIDS Awareness Campaign
819 **172** 900s. multicoloured 11·00 10·50

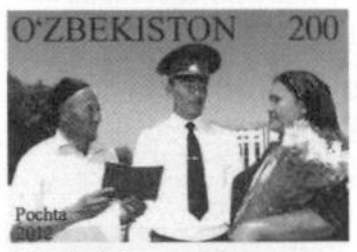

173 Soldier and Parents

2012. 20th Anniv of Uzbekistan Armed Forces. Multicoloured.
MS820 200s. Type **173**; 550s. Taking the oath; 700s. Serviceman with family; 900s. Combat helicopter over mountains; 1000s. Firing mortar; 1200s. Parade; 1900s. Students at Military Academy in class; 2150s. Tank 28·00 27·00

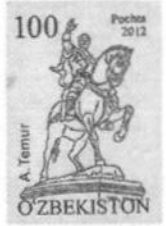

174 Statue

2012. Monuments. Each emerald.
821 100s. Type **174** 1·20 1·10
822 150s. Berbaq 2·00 1·90
823 170s. Berbaq 2·40 2·30
824 250s. Al-Khorezmiy (horiz) 4·00 3·75
825 300s. Al-Khorezmiy (horiz) 4·75 4·50
826 450s. A. Temur 6·00 5·75
827 600s. A. Temur 7·25 6·75

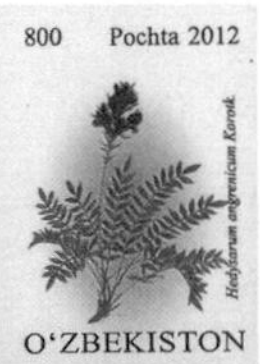

175 *Hedysarum angrenicum*

2012. Endangered Species. Flora. Multicoloured.
828 800s. Type **175** 10·00 9·50
829 900s. *Cousinia glabriseta* 11·00 10·50
830 1000s. *Oxytropis pseudoleptophysa* 13·00 12·00
831 1200s. *Phlomoides tschimganica* 16·00 14·50
MS831a 110×80 mm. 1000s. *Scorzonera bungei*; 1900s. *Spirostegia bucharica* 10·00 10·00

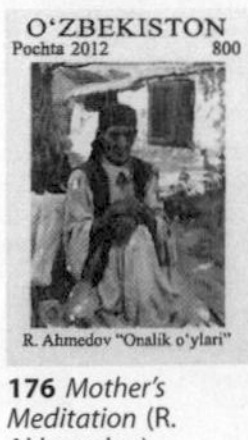

176 *Mother's Meditation* (R. Akhmedov)

2012. Art of Uzbekistan. Multicoloured.
832 800s. Type **176** 10·00 9·50
833 900s. *Lagan o'yini* (J. Umarbekov) 11·00 10·50
834 1000s. *Bog 'da* (S. Shoahmedov) 13·00 12·00
835 1200s. *Chavgon o'yini* (S. Shoahmedov) 16·00 14·50

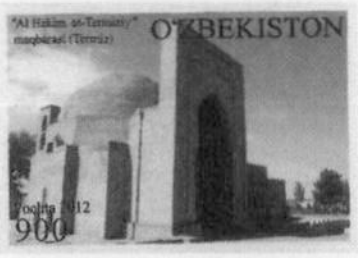

177 Al-hakim at-Termezi Mausoleum

2012. Regions of Uzbekistan. Surhardar. Multicoloured.
836 900s. Type **177** 11·00 10·50
837 1200s. Ulok-kupkari (horse back game) 16·00 14·50

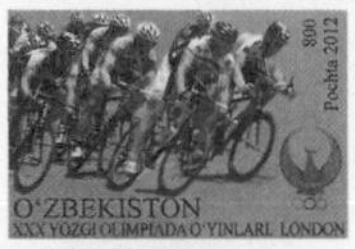

178 Cyclists

2012. Olympic Games - 2012, London
838 **178** 800s. multicoloured 10·00 9·50

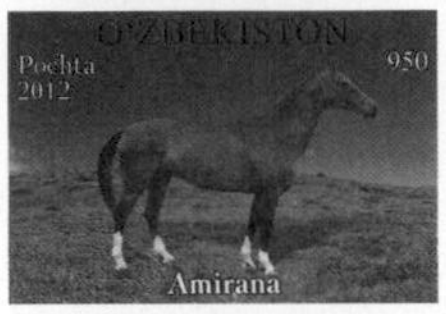

180 Amirana

2012. Akhal-Teke Horses of Uzbekistan. Multicoloured.
MS844 950s.×3, Type **180**; G'ayrat; Asmanbek; 1050s.×3, Go'zalli; Ayg'ir; Gallas; 2200s.×3, Geldi Botir; Xon; Potmagul £120 £120

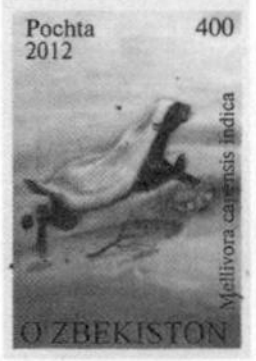

179 *Mellivora capensis* (Honey Badger)

2012. Endangered Species. Fauna. Multicoloured.
839 400s. Type **179** 1·25 1·00
840 800s. *Falco pelegrinoides* (Barbary Falcon) 1·40 1·00
841 1000s. *Hemiechinus hypomelas* (Brandt's Hedgehog) 2·75 2·00
842 1200s. *Lutra lutra* (Otter) 3·75 2·75
MS843 90×70 mm. 1000s. *Lynx lynx* (Lynx) 5·00 5·00

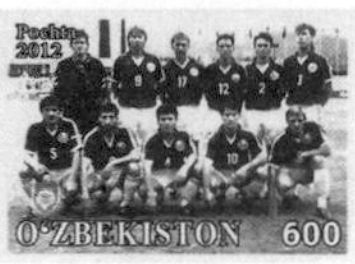

181 Team Members

2012. Centenary of Uzbek Football. Multicoloured.
MS845 600s. Type **181**; 650s. No. 9 Uzbek player with ball; 950s. Modern team (wearing white); 1050s. No. 19 Uzbek player with ball; 1150s. Extended team members wearing training jackets; 1300s. No. 5 Uzbek player with ball; 2200s. Modern team (wearing blue); 2500s. Early team members wearing traditional dress 15·00 15·00

Pt. 1

VANUATU

The New Hebrides became the Republic of Vanuatu on 30 July 1980.

1980. 100 centimes = 1 franc (Vanuatu).
1981. Vatus.

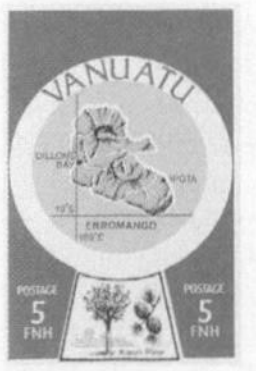

99 Island of Erromango and Kauri Pine

1980. As Nos. 242/54 of New Hebrides but inscr "VANUATU" and without royal and republican cyphers. (a) Inscr in English.
287E 5f. Type **99** 15 25
288E 10f. Territory map and copra making 15 25
289E 15f. Espiritu Santo and cattle 20 30
290E 20f. Efate and Vila P.O. 20 40
291E 25f. Malakula and headdresses 25 40
292E 30f. Aoba, Maewo and pigs' tusks 35 55
293E 35f. Pentecost and land diver 40 60
294E 40f. Tanna and John Frum cross 40 70
295E 50f. Shepherd Is. and outrigger canoe 45 80
296E 70f. Banks Is. and custom dancers 50 1·75
297E 100f. Ambrym and idols 50 80
298E 200f. Aneityum and baskets 60 1·40
299E 500f. Torres Is. and archer fisherman 75 3·00

(b) Inscr in French.
287F 5f. Type **99** 35 15
288F 10f. Territory map and copra making 40 15
289F 15f. Espiritu Santo and cattle 45 25
290F 20f. Efate and Vila P.O. 50 30
291F 25f. Malakula and headdresses 55 40
292F 30f. Aoba, Maewo and pigs' tusks 55 55
293F 35f. Pentecost and land diver 60 60
294F 40f. Tanna and John Frum cross 75 60
295F 50f. Shepherd Is. and outrigger canoe 80 80
296F 70f. Banks Is. and custom dancers 1·00 1·50
297F 100f. Ambrym and idols 1·25 1·10
298F 200f. Aneityum and baskets 1·50 1·75
299F 500f. Torres Is. and archer fisherman 1·75 3·50

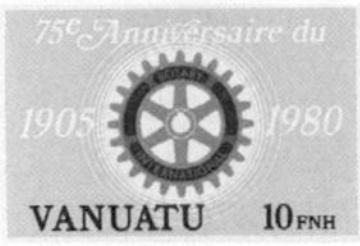

100 Rotary International

1980. 75th Anniv of Rotary International. Multicoloured. (a) Inscr in English.
300E 10f. Type **100** 10 10
301E 40f. Rotary emblem (vert) 30 30

(b) Inscr in French.
300F 10f. Type **100** 15 15
301F 40f. Rotary emblem (vert) 45 45

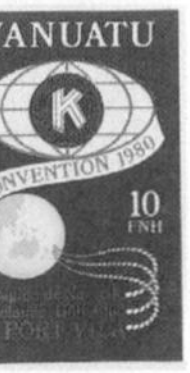

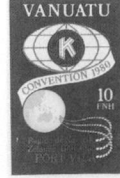

101 Kiwanis Emblem and Globe

1980. Kiwanis International (service club), New Zealand District Convention, Port Vila. (a) Inscr in English.
302E **101** 10f. gold, blue and brown 10 20
303E - 40f. green and blue 30 80

(b) Inscr in French.
302F **101** 10f. gold, blue and brown 40 65
303F - 40f. green and blue 85 1·10
DESIGN: 40f. Kiwanis and Convention emblems.

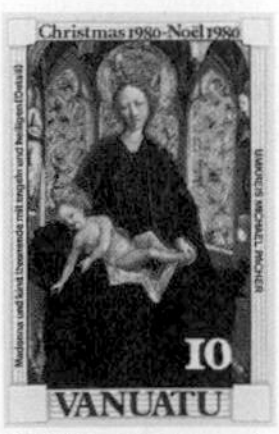

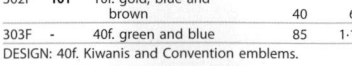

102 "The Virgin and Child enthroned with Saints and Angels" (Umkreis Michael Pacher)

1980. Christmas. Details from Paintings. Multicoloured.
304 10f. Type **102** 10 10
305 15f. "The Virgin and Child with Saints, Angels and Donors" (Hans Memling) 10 10
306 30f. "The Rest on the Flight to Egypt" (Adriaen van der Werff) 20 20

103 Blue-faced
Parrot Finch

1981. Birds (1st series). Multicoloured.
307	10f. Type **103**	35	25
308	20f. Emerald dove	40	45
309	30f. Golden whistler	45	80
310	40f. Silver-shouldered fruit dove	50	1·00

See also Nos. 327/30.

104 Tribesman
with Portrait of
Prince Philip

1981. 60th Birthday of Prince Philip, Duke of Edinburgh.
Multicoloured.
311	15v. Type **104**	10	15
312	25v. Prince Philip in casual dress	15	20
313	35v. Queen and Prince Philip with Princess Anne and Master Peter Phillips	15	25
314	45v. Prince Philip in ceremonial dress	20	35

105 Prince Charles
with his Dog,
Harvey

1981. Royal Wedding. Multicoloured.
315	15v. Wedding bouquet from Vanuatu	10	10
316	45v. Type **105**	20	15
317	75v. Prince Charles and Lady Diana Spencer	35	45

106 National Flag
and Map of
Vanuatu

1981. First Anniv of Independence.
318	**106**	15v. multicoloured	15	15
319	-	25v. multicoloured	15	15
320	-	45v. yellow and brown	20	20
321	-	75v. multicoloured	35	70

DESIGNS—HORIZ: 25v. Vanuatu emblem; 45v. Vanuatu national anthem. VERT: 75v. Vanuatu coat of arms.

107 Three Shepherds

1981. Christmas. Children's Paintings. Multicoloured.
322	15v. Type **107**	10	10
323	25v. Vanuatu girl with lamb (vert)	15	15
324	35v. Angel as butterfly	15	20
325	45v. Boy carrying torch and gifts (vert)	25	30
MS326	133×94 mm. Nos. 322/5	80	1·25

108 New Caledonian
Myiagra Flycatchers

1982. Birds (2nd series). Multicoloured.
327	15v. Type **108**	30	20
328	20v. Rainbow lorys	40	30
329	25v. Buff-bellied flycatchers	45	35
330	45v. Collared grey fantails	50	65

109 "Flickingeria
comata"

1982. Orchids. Multicoloured.
331	1v. Type **109**	10	50
332	2v. "Calanthe triplicata"	10	50
333	10v. "Dendrobium sladei"	15	30
334	15v. "Dendrobium mohlianum"	20	20
335	20v. "Dendrobium macrophyllum"	25	30
336	25v. "Dendrobium purpureum"	30	35
337	30v. "Robiquetia mimus"	35	40
338	35v. "Dendrobium mooreanum" (horiz)	50	50
339	45v. "Spathoglottis plicata" (horiz)	55	70
340	50v. "Dendrobium seemannii" (horiz)	60	80
341	75v. "Dendrobium conanthum" (horiz)	1·00	1·50
342	100v. "Dendrobium macranthum"	1·25	1·50
343	200v. "Coelogyne lamellata"	1·50	2·75
344	500v. "Bulbophyllum longioscapum"	2·00	6·50

110 Scouts round Campfire

1982. 75th Anniv of Boy Scout Movement. Multicoloured.
345	15v. Type **110**	20	20
346	20v. First aid	25	20
347	25v. Constructing tower	25	25
348	45v. Constructing raft	30	35
349	57v. Scout saluting	35	70

111 Baby Jesus

1982. Christmas. Nativity Scenes. Multicoloured.
350	15v. Type **111**	30	35
351	25v. Mary and Joseph	50	45
352	35v. Shepherds (vert)	60	1·00
353	45v. Kings bearing gifts (vert)	65	1·40
MS354	132×92 mm. As Nos. 350/3 but without yellow borders	1·50	2·25

112 "Euploea sylvester"

1983. Butterflies. Multicoloured.
355	15v. Type **112**	45	65
356	15v. "Hypolimnas octocula"	45	65
357	45v. "Papilio canopus"	45	80
358	20v. "Polyura sacco"	45	80
359	25v. "Luthrodes cleotas"	50	80
360	25v. "Danaus pumila"	50	80

113 President Afi George
Sokomanu

1983. Commonwealth Day. Multicoloured.
361	15v. Type **113**	15	10
362	20v. Fisherman and liner "Oriana"	20	15
363	25v. Herdsman and cattle	25	15
364	75v. World map showing position of Vanuatu with Commonwealth and Vanuatu flags	50	70

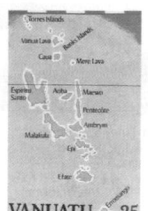

114 Map of Northern
Vanuatu

1983. Economic Zone. Sheet 120×120 mm, containing T **114** and similar vert designs. Multicoloured.
MS365	25v.×6 Yellow-finned tuna; Type **114**; Map of Matthew Island; Map of Hunter Island; Cornet grouper; Skipjack tuna	2·75	2·75

115 Montgolfier
Balloon of De Rozier
and D'Arlandes,
1783

1983. Bicentenary of Manned Flight. Multicoloured.
366	15v. Type **115**	15	15
367	20v. J. A. C. Charles hydrogen balloon (first use of hydrogen, 1783)	20	25
368	25v. Blanchard and Jeffries crossing English Channel, 1785	20	30
369	35v. Giffard's steam-powered dirigible airship, 1852 (horiz)	30	40
370	40v. "La France" (airship of Renard and Krebs), 1884 (horiz)	35	45
371	45v. "Graf Zeppelin" (first aerial circumnavigation, 1929) (horiz)	40	55

116 Mail at Bauerfield
Airport

1983. World Communications Year. Multicoloured.
372	15v. Type **116**	20	25
373	20v. Switchboard operator	30	35
374	25v. Telex operator	35	40
375	45v. Satellite earth station	65	70
MS376	138×95 mm. Nos. 372/5	2·00	2·75

117 "Cymatoderma
elegans var.
lamellatum"

1984. Fungi. Multicoloured.
377	15v. Type **117**	35	35
378	25v. "Lignosus rhinocerus"	50	70
379	35v. "Stereum ostrea" (horiz)	65	1·50
380	45v. "Ganoderma boninense"	75	1·60

118 Port Vila

1984. 250th Anniv of "Lloyd's List" (newspaper). Multicoloured.
381	15v. Type **118**	20	25
382	20v. "Induna" (container ship)	30	35
383	25v. Air Vanuatu Boeing 737 aircraft	35	40
384	45v. "Brahman Express" (container ship)	65	70

1984. Universal Postal Union Congress, Hamburg. As No. 371 but inscr "UPU CONGRESS HAMBURG" and U.P.U. logo.
385	45v. multicoloured	80	80

119 Charolais

1984. Cattle. Multicoloured.
386	15v. Type **119**	15	20
387	25v. Charolais-afrikander	20	30
388	45v. Friesian	40	55
389	75v. Charolais-brahman	60	1·00

120 "Makambo"

1984. "Ausipex" International Stamp Exn, Melbourne. Inter-island Freighters. Multicoloured.
390	25v. Type **120**	60	50
391	45v. "Rockton"	80	90
392	100v. "Waroonga"	1·25	3·50
MS393	140×70 mm. Nos. 390/2	3·00	5·00

121 Father Christmas in
Children's Ward

1984. Christmas. Multicoloured.
394	25v. Type **121**	45	40
395	45v. Nativity play	80	70
396	75v. Father Christmas distributing presents	1·40	1·25

1985. No. 331 surch.
397	5v. on 1v. Type **109**	65	50

123 Ambrym
Island Ceremonial
Dance

1985. Traditional Costumes. Multicoloured.
398	20v. Type **123**	35	35
399	25v. Pentecost Island marriage ceremony	40	40
400	45v. Women's grade ceremony, South West Malakula	75	70
401	75v. Ceremonial dance, South West Malakula	1·10	1·25

124 Peregrine
Falcon diving

1985. Birth Bicentenary of John J. Audubon (ornithologist). Peregrine Falcon. Multicoloured.
402	20v. Type **124**	50	35
403	35v. Peregrine falcon in flight	60	50

1993. 50th Anniv of Outbreak of the Pacific War (2nd issue). As T **162**. Multicoloured.

623	20v. Grumman F6F Hellcat	2·25	1·10
624	55v. Lockheed P-38F Lightning	3·25	2·00
625	65v. Grumman TBF Avenger	3·25	2·00
626	80v. U.S.S. "Essex" (aircraft carrier)	3·50	3·25
MS627	82×58 mm. 200v. Douglas C-47 Skytrain	11·00	10·00

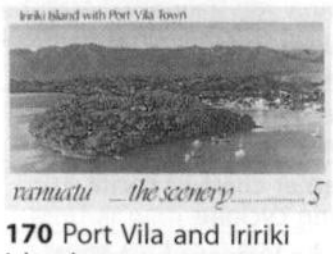

170 Port Vila and Iririki Island

1993. Local Scenery. Multicoloured.

628	5v. Type **170**	20	75
629	10v. Yachts and Iririki Island	30	60
630	15v. Court House, Port Vila	40	70
631	20v. Two girls, Pentecost Island	40	80
632	25v. Women dancers, Tanna Island	45	30
633	30v. Market, Port Vila	50	35
634	45v. Man in canoe, Erakor Island (vert)	60	45
635	50v. Coconut trees, Champagne Beach	60	50
636	55v. Coconut trees, North Efate Islands	70	55
637	60v. Underwater shoal of fishes, Banks Group	75	60
638	70v. Sea fan, Tongoa Island (vert)	1·00	90
639	75v. Santo Island	1·00	95
640	80v. Sunset, Port Vila harbour (vert)	1·25	1·00
641	100v. Mele Waterfall (vert)	2·25	1·50
642	300v. Yasur Volcano, Tanna Island (vert)	4·00	6·00
643	500v. Aerial view of Erakor Island	5·50	10·00

For miniature sheet containing Nos. 629, 636/7 and 639 see **MS**673.

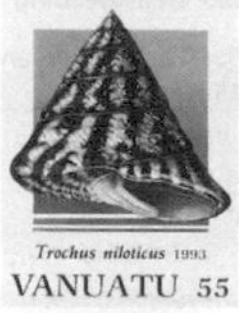

171 Commercial Trochus

1993. Shells (1st series). Multicoloured.

644	55v. Type **171**	1·10	85
645	65v. Camp pitar venus	1·25	95
646	80v. Tapestry turban	1·60	1·75
647	150v. Trapezium horse conch	2·75	4·25

See also Nos. 665/8 and 692/5.

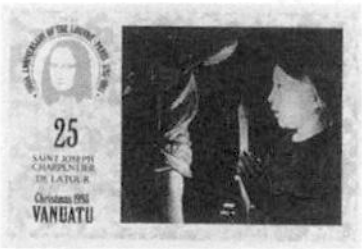

172 "St. Joseph the Carpenter" (detail) (De la Tour)

1993. Christmas. Bicentenary of the Louvre, Paris. Religious Paintings by Georges de la Tour. Multicoloured.

648	25v. Type **172**	45	30
649	55v. "Holy Child" (detail)	80	65
650	80v. "Adoration of the Shepherds" (detail)	1·00	1·00
651	150v. "Adoration of the Shepherds" (different detail)	1·75	3·00

1993. South Pacific Mini Games, Port Vila. Nos. 602, 604, 631 and 633 surch **SOUTH PACIFIC MINI GAMES PORT VILA DECEMBER 1993** and value.

652	15v. on 20v. Two girls, Pentecost Island	30	40
653	25v. on 30v. Market, Port Vila	45	50
654	55v. on 65v. Melanesian Cup Final, 1990	85	80
655	70v. on 80v. Mary Estelle Kapalu (400, 400 hurdles and 800 m)	95	1·60

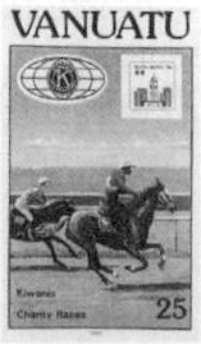

174 Charity Horse Race and Kiwanis Emblem

1994. "Hong Kong '94" International Stamp Exhibition. Charitable Organizations. Multicoloured.

656	25v. Type **174**	50	30
657	60v. Twin Otter airplane and Lions Club emblem (horiz)	80	75
658	75v. Mosquito and Rotary International emblem	90	1·00
659	150v. Blood donor service ambulance and Red Cross emblem (horiz)	1·60	2·75
MS660	126×96 mm. 200v. Charity emblems (horiz)	2·00	3·00

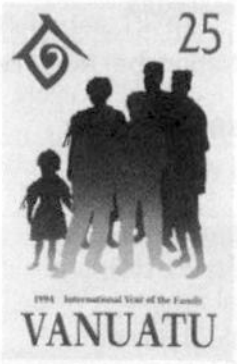

175 Silhouetted Family

1994. International Year of the Family.

661	**175**	25v. brown and violet	35	30
662	**175**	60v. green and red	70	75
663	**175**	90v. brown and green	1·00	1·10
664	**175**	150v. violet and brown	1·60	2·75

1994. Shells (2nd series). As T **171**. Multicoloured.

665	60v. Eyed cowrie	2·25	1·00
666	70v. Marble cone	2·25	1·25
667	85v. Chiragra spider conch	2·50	2·25
668	155v. Adusta murex	3·75	6·00

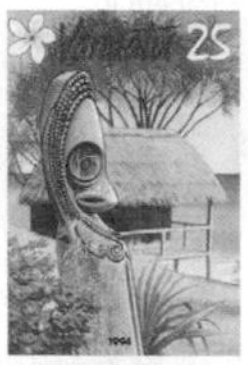

176 Traditional Sculpture and Hut

1994. Tourism. Multicoloured.

669	25v. Type **176**	90	90
670	75v. Outrigger canoe and inflatable dinghy	1·60	1·60
671	90v. Yachts, airliner and parrot	2·50	2·50
672	200v. Helicopter and local woman with fruit	4·00	4·25

Nos. 669/72 were printed together, *se-tenant*, forming a composite design.

1994. "Philakorea '94" International Stamp Exhibition. Sheet 130×68 mm, containing Nos. 629, 636/7 and 639. Multicoloured.

MS673	10v. Yachts and Iririki Island; 55v. Coconut trees, North Efate Islands; 60v. Underwater shoal of fishes, Banks Group; 75v. Santo Island	2·50	3·50

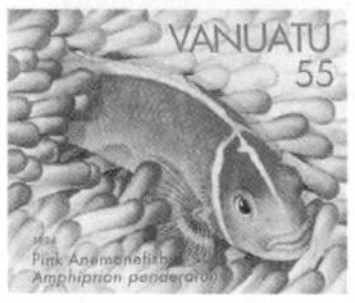

177 Pink Anemonefish

1994. Anemonefish. Multicoloured.

674	55v. Type **177**	2·25	80
675	70v. Yellow-tailed anemonefish	2·50	1·25
676	80v. Fire anemonefish	2·75	2·00
677	140v. Orange-finned anemonefish	4·75	6·50
MS678	80×60 mm. No. 677	5·00	6·00

No. **MS**678 shows the "Philakorea '94" International stamp Exhibition logo on the sheet margin.

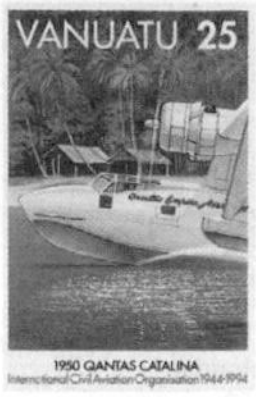

178 Consolidated PBY-5 Catalina Flying Boat

1994. 50th Anniv of I.C.A.O. Multicoloured.

679	25v. Type **178**	75	50
680	60v. Douglas DC-3	1·25	1·00
681	75v. De Havilland D.H.A.3 Drover	1·40	1·60
682	90v. Boeing 737 on runway	1·60	2·25

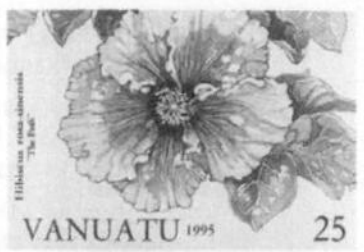

179 "Hibiscus rosa-sinensis" "The Path"

1995. Hibiscus Flowers (2nd issue). Multicoloured.

683	25v. Type **179**	60	45
684	60v. "Hibiscus rosa-sinensis" "Old Frankie"	1·10	1·00
685	90v. "Hibiscus sinensis" "Fijian White"	1·60	1·75
686	200v. "Hibiscus rosa-sinensis" "Surfrider"	3·25	4·50

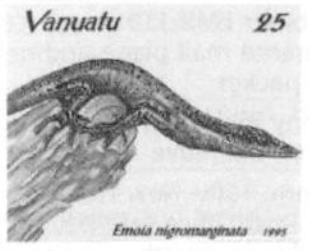

180 "Emoia nigromarginata"

1995. Lizards. Multicoloured.

687	25v. Type **180**	80	45
688	55v. "Nactus multicarinatus"	1·50	1·00
689	70v. "Lepidodactylus"	1·60	1·50
690	80v. "Emoia caeruleocauda"	1·75	1·60
691	140v. "Emoia sanfordi"	2·75	4·25

1995. Shells (3rd series). As T **171**. Multicoloured.

692	25v. "Epitonium scalare"	60	50
693	55v. "Strombus latissimus"	1·25	1·25
694	90v. "Conus bullatus"	1·75	1·75
695	200v. "Pteryntotus pinnatus"	3·50	4·50

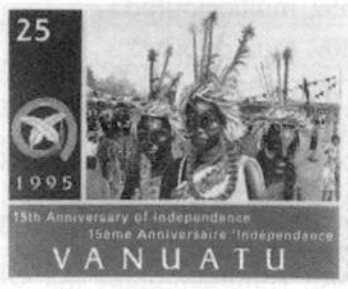

181 "Tanna Girls" (A. Toni)

1995. 15th Anniv of Independence. Multicoloured.

696	25v. Type **181**	45	40
697	55v. "Black Coral Dancers" (sculpture, E. Watt) (vert)	90	90
698	75v. Erromango tapestry by Juliet Peta (vert)	1·25	1·25
699	90v. "Parade Day" (H. Di-Donna)	1·40	1·75
700	140v. "Banks Dancers" (J. John)	2·00	3·00
MS701	100×75 mm. No. 699	3·50	5·00

No. **MS**701 also includes the "Singapore '95" International Stamp Exhibition logo on the sheet margin.

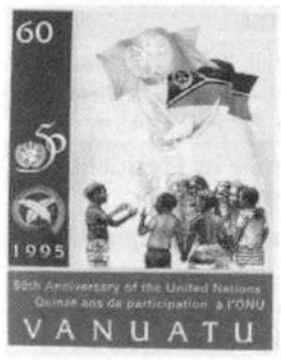

182 Children with Doves and Flags

1995. 50th Anniv of United Nations.

702	**182**	60v. multicoloured	1·25	1·00

1995. 50th Anniv of End of Second World War in the Pacific. As T **162** showing aircraft. Multicoloured.

703	60v. Curtiss SB2C Helldiver	2·75	1·75
704	70v. Supermarine Spitfire Mk VIII	2·75	1·90
705	75v. Chance Vought F4U-1A Corsair	2·75	2·00
706	80v. Lockheed PV-1 Ventura	2·75	2·00
MS707	94×68 mm. 140v. Japanese delegation at signing of Unconditional Surrender, Tokyo Bay	4·25	5·50

No. **MS**707 also includes the "Singapore '95" International Stamp Exhibition logo on the sheet margin.

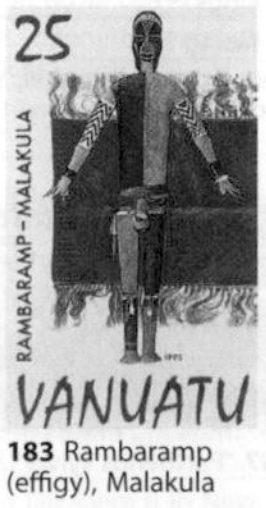

183 Rambaramp (effigy), Malakula

1995. Vanuatu Culture (1st series). Opening of New National Museum. Artefacts. Multicoloured.

708	25v. Type **183**	35	30
709	60v. Pot from Wusi, Espiritu Santo	75	75
710	75v. Slit gong from Mele, Efate	90	1·10
711	90v. Tapa cloth, Erromango	1·25	1·75

See also Nos. 772/6.

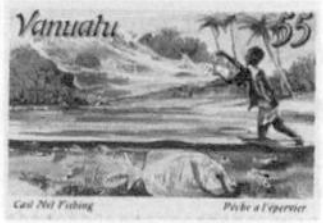

184 Boy throwing Cast Net

1996. Fishing. Multicoloured.

712	55v. Type **184**	85	65
713	75v. Fishing canoes	1·10	90
714	80v. "Etelis" (fishing boat) and deep water fish (vert)	1·25	1·10
715	140v. Game fisherman catching sailfish (vert)	2·50	4·00

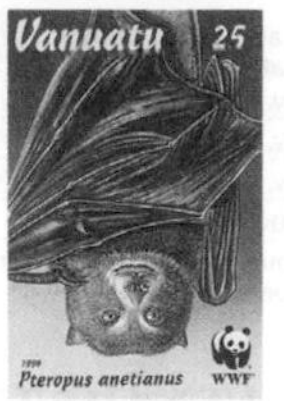

185 "Pteropus anetianus"

1996. Endangered Species. Flying Foxes. Multicoloured.

716	25v. Type **185**	40	55
717	25v. "Notopteris macdonaldi" upside down eating fruit (horiz)	40	55
718	25v. "Pteropus anetianus" hanging on branch	40	55
719	25v. "Notopteris macdonaldi" on branch (horiz)	40	55

1996. "CHINA '96" Ninth Asian International Stamp Exhibition, Peking.

MS720	75×85 mm. No. 711	2·00	2·25
MS721	75×85 mm. 90v. "Pteropus tonganus" (flying fox); 140v. "Pteropus tonganus" (different)	5·00	6·00

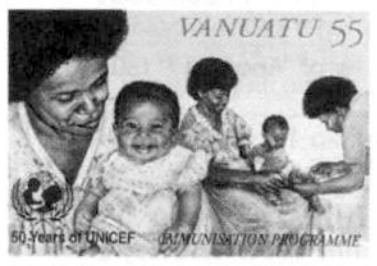

186 Immunization Programme

1996. 50th Anniv of UNICEF. Multicoloured.

722	55v. Type **186**	1·50	1·00
723	60v. Breast-feeding programme	1·50	1·00

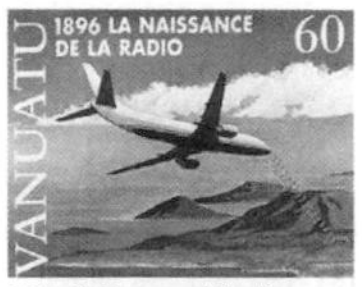

187 Airliner and Radio Waves

1996. Centenary of Radio. Multicoloured.

724	60v. Type **187**	90	1·25
725	75v. Radio Vanuatu broadcaster	1·10	1·40
726	80v. Guglielmo Marconi	1·25	1·50
727	90v. Cruise liner and radio waves	1·40	1·60

Nos. 724/7 were issued together, *se-tenant*, forming a composite aerial view of Port Vila.

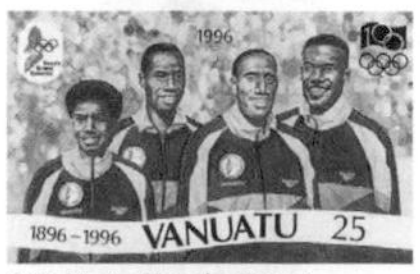

188 Marie Kapalu, Tawai Keiruan, Baptiste Firiam and Tava Kalo

1996. Centenary of Modern Olympics Games. Multicoloured.

728	25v. Type **188**	35	30
729	70v. Athletes training	95	95
730	75v. Athletes from 1950s	1·00	1·00
731	200v. Athletes in 1896	2·75	4·00

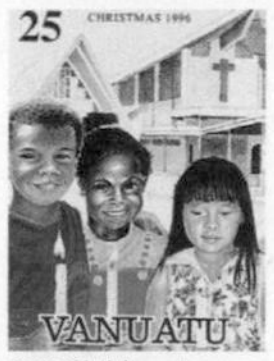

189 Children in Front of Presbyterian Church and Roman Catholic Cathedral

1996. Christmas. Religious Buildings. Multicoloured.

732	25v. Type **189**	45	30
733	60v. Children and Church of Christ	90	80
734	75v. Children and Seventh Day Adventist and Apostolic churches	95	1·00
735	90v. Children and Anglican church	1·25	1·60

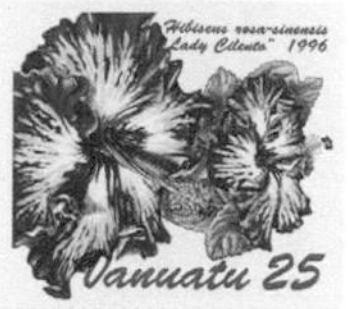

190 "Hibiscus rosa-sinensis" "Lady Cilento"

1996. Hibiscus Flowers (3rd issue). Multicoloured.

736	25v. Type **190**	40	30
737	60v. "Hibiscus rosa-sinensis" "Kinchen's Yellow"	90	70
738	90v. "Hibiscus rosa-sinensis" "D. J. O'Brien"	1·25	1·25
739	200v. "Hibiscus rosa-sinensis" "Cuban Variety"	3·00	4·25

For miniature sheet containing Nos. 736 and 739 see No. **MS**745.

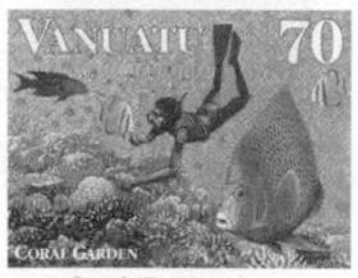

191 Coral Garden

1997. Diving. Multicoloured.

740	70v. Type **191**	90	90
741	75v. Carving on the "President Coolidge"	95	85
742	90v. "Boris" (Giant grouper)	1·25	1·25
743	140v. Wreck of the "President Coolidge"	2·25	3·75
MS744	124×75 mm. Nos. 740/3	7·00	7·50

For further miniature sheet containing Nos. 741 and 743 see No. **MS**750.

1997. "HONG KONG '97" International Stamp Exhibition. Sheet 100×85 mm, containing Nos. 736 and 739. Multicoloured.

MS745	25v. Type **190**; 200v. "Hibiscus rosasinensis" "Cuban Variety"	3·50	5·00

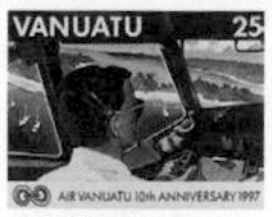

192 View from Cockpit

1997. Tenth Anniv of Air Vanuatu. Multicoloured.

746	25v. Type **192**	55	40
747	60v. Boeing 737-400 airliner being serviced, Bauerfield International Airport, Port Vila (81×31 mm)	1·00	75
748	90v. Air stewardess serving drinks	1·50	1·40
749	200v. Passengers disembarking	2·50	4·75

1997. "Pacific '97" International Philatelic Exhibition, San Francisco. Sheet 100×86 mm, containing Nos. 741 and 743. Multicoloured.

MS750	75v. Carving on the "President Coolidge"; 140v. Wreck of the "President Coolidge"	4·50	5·00

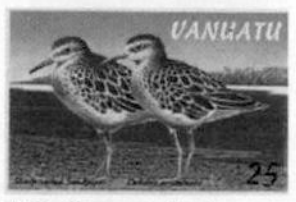

193 Sharp-tailed Sandpiper

1997. Birds (1st series). Coastal Birds. Multicoloured.

751	25v. Type **193**	45	45
752	55v. Greater crested tern ("Crested Tern")	80	70
753	60v. Little pied cormorant	85	75
754	75v. Brown booby	1·00	1·10
755	80v. Reef heron (vert)	1·10	1·40
756	90v. Red-tailed tropic bird (vert)	1·25	1·60

See also Nos. 804/7 and 848/52.

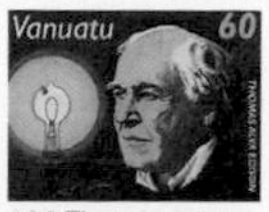

194 Thomas Edison and Light Bulb

1997. 150th Birth Anniv of Thomas Edison (inventor). Multicoloured.

757	60v. Type **194**	1·50	1·50
758	70v. Hydro-electric dam, Espiritu Santo	1·50	1·50
759	200v. Port Vila at dusk (80×29 mm)	3·00	4·00

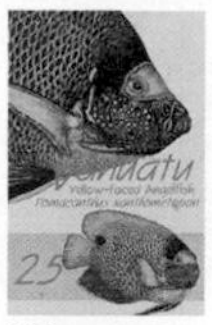

195 Yellow-faced Angelfish

1997. Angelfish. Multicoloured.

760	25v. Type **195**	40	30
761	55v. Flame angelfish	85	70
762	60v. Lemonpeel angelfish	90	80
763	70v. Emperor angelfish	1·10	1·00
764	140v. Multi-barred angelfish	2·25	3·00

1998. No. 638 surch **5.**

765	5v. on 70v. Sea fan, Tongoa Island (vert)	3·00	3·00

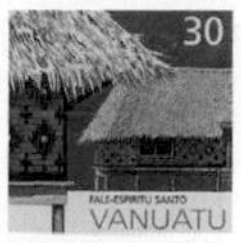

197 Fale, Espiritu Santo

1998. Local Architecture. Multicoloured.

766	30v. Type **197**	35	35
767	65v. National Cultural Centre	80	80
768	80v. University of South Pacific	95	95
769	200v. Chiefs' Nakamal	1·90	3·25

1998. Diana, Princess of Wales Commemoration. As T **62a** of Tokelau. Multicoloured.

770	95v. Wearing black jacket, 1997	1·00	1·10
MS771	145×70 mm. 75v. Wearing green jacket, 1987; 85v. Wearing cream jacket and hat, 1991; 95v. No. 769; 145v. Wearing red dress, 1992 (sold at 400v. + 50v. charity premium)	2·25	3·75

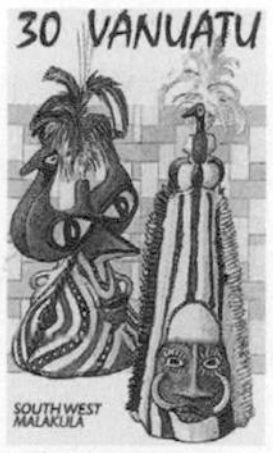

198 Nalawan Headdresses from South West Bay, Malakula

1998. Vanuatu Culture (2nd series). Masks. Multicoloured.

772	30v. Type **198**	50	35
773	65v. Rom mask from North Ambrym	75	65
774	75v. Tamate mask from Gaua Island	85	85
775	85v. Banglulu headdress from Uripiv Island, north-east Malakula	95	1·10
776	95v. Chubwan masks from Vao Island, Malakula, and from Pentecost	1·10	1·50

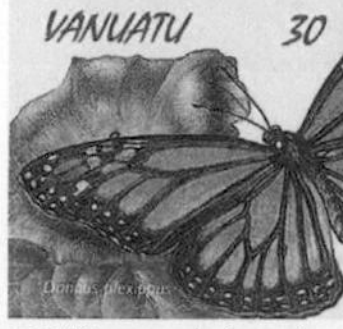

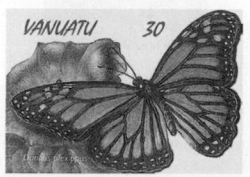

199 "Danaus plexippus"

1998. Butterflies. Self-adhesive. Multicoloured.

777	30v. Type **199**	60	50
778	60v. "Hypolimnas bolina"	90	80
779	65v. "Eurema hecabe"	95	85
780	75v. "Nymphalidae" sp.	1·10	90
781	95v. "Precis villida"	1·40	1·40
782	205v. "Tirumala hamata"	2·50	4·00
MS783	105×79 mm. No. 782	3·25	4·00

No. **MS**783 also commemorates "SINGPEX '98" International Stamp Exhibition, Singapore.

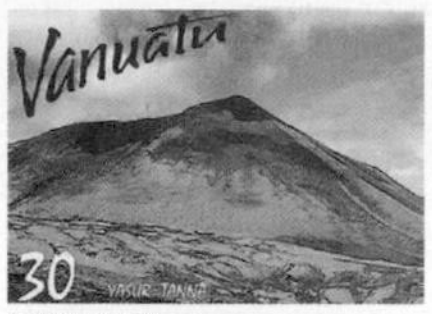

200 Yasur, Tanna

1998. Volcanoes in Vanuatu. Multicoloured.

784	30v. Type **200**	45	40
785	60v. Marum and Benbow, Ambrym	65	60
786	75v. Mount Garet, Gaua	85	85
787	80v. Lopevi	90	90
788	145v. Lake Manaro Voui, Ambae	1·40	2·75

1998. Nos. 631, 634, 636/42 surch.

789	1v. on 100v. Mele Waterfall (vert)	70	1·75
790	2v. on 45v. Man in canoe, Erakor Island (vert)	3·00	3·50
791	2v. on 55v. Coconut trees, North Efate Islands	70	1·25
792	3v. on 60v. Underwater shoal of fishes, Banks Group	70	1·25
793	3v. on 75v. Santo Island	3·25	3·25
794	4v. on 45v. Man in canoe, Erakor Island (vert)	1·75	2·50
795	5v. on 70v. Sea fan, Tongoa Island (vert)	11·00	11·00
796a	34v. on 20v. Two girls, Pentecost Island	1·75	2·00
796b	67v. on 300v. Yasur Volcano, Tanna Island (vert)	3·00	3·25
797	73v. on 80v. Sunset, Port Vila harbour (vert)	2·00	2·50

Nos. 789/97 were produced as a result of the addition of VAT at 13% to postal rates from 14 September 1998.

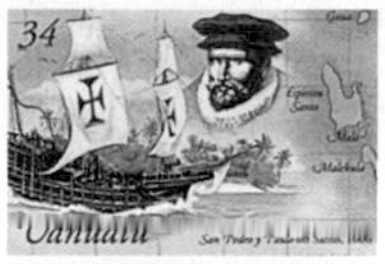

204 De Quiros and "San Pedro y Paulo"

1999. Early Explorers. Multicoloured.

798	34v. Type **204**	90	50
799	73v. De Bougainville and "La Boudeuse"	1·40	1·00
800	84v. Cook and H.M.S. "Resolution"	1·60	1·75
801	90v. La Perouse and "L'Astrolabe"	1·75	2·00
802	96v. Dumont d'Urville and "L'Astrolabe"	1·90	2·75

No. 802 is inscribed "1788" in error.

1999. "Australia '99" World Stamp Exhibition, Melbourne. Multicoloured.

MS803	95×82 mm. Nos. 800/2	2·50	3·00

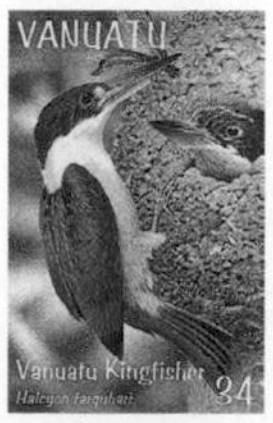

205 Chestnut-bellied Kingfisher ("Vanuatu Kingfisher")

1999. Birds (2nd series). Bush and Lowland Birds. Multicoloured.

804	34v. Type **205**	70	50
805	67v. Golden-bronze cuckoo ("Shining Cuckoo")	1·00	90
806	73v. Peregrine falcon	1·10	1·10
807	107v. Rainbow lorikeet	1·60	2·75
MS808	111×95 mm. No. 807 (sold at 214v.)	2·75	3·25

No. **MS**808 has the frame, series inscription and artist's signature shown in gold die-stamping on sheet margins.

1999. "PhilexFrance '99" International Stamp Exhibition, Paris. Multicoloured.

MS809	105×82 mm. Nos. 799 and 801/2	3·50	4·25

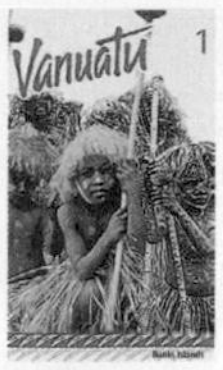

206 Banks Islands Dancers

1999. Vanuatu Dances. Multicoloured.

810	1v. Type **206**	10	50
811	2v. Small Nambas, Lamap-Malakula	10	50
812	3v. Small Nambas, Malakula	10	50
813	5v. Smol Bag Theatre	15	50
814	35v. Snake Dance, Banks Island (horiz)	70	40
815	100v. Toka Dance, Tanna (horiz)	1·90	1·10
816	107v. South West Bay, Malakula	2·00	1·50
817	200v. Big Nambas, Malakula	3·75	3·00
818	300v. Rom Dance, Ambrym (horiz)	5·00	5·50
819	500v. Pentecost Island	8·50	11·00
820	1000v. Brasive Dance, Futuna (horiz)	15·00	21·00

1999. "China '99" International Stamp Exhibition, Beijing. Sheet as No. **MS**808, but 100×80 mm, without gold die-stamped features, with "China '99" logo added to the margin in carmine.

MS822	107v. No. 807	1·25	1·75

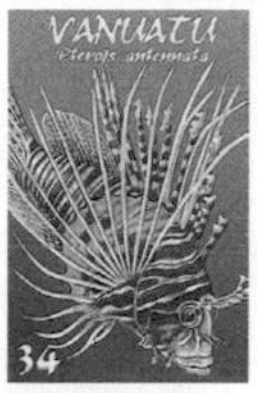

207 "Pterois antennata"

1999. Lionfish. Multicoloured.

823	34v. Type **207**	60	40
824	84v. Head of "Pterois antennata"	1·25	1·10
825	90v. "Pterois volitans"	1·40	1·40
826	96v. Head of "Pterois volitans"	1·50	2·25

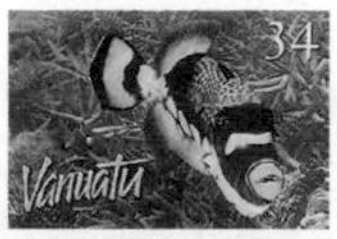

208 Clown Triggerfish

1999. New Millennium. Sheet 165×75 mm, containing T **208** and similar multicoloured designs.

MS827	165×75 mm. 34v. Type **208**; 68v. Young girl and Pentecost Island land diver (vert); 84v. Statue and pig's tusk (vert); 90c. Vanuatu kingfisher; 96v. Tanna islander blowing Triton shell and Yasur volcano	4·50	5·50

2000. "The Stamp Show 2000" International Stamp Exhibition, London. Queen Elizabeth the Queen Mother's 100th Birthday. Sheet 105×70 mm, containing vert designs as T **274** of Tonga. Multicoloured.

MS828	100v. Queen Elizabeth the Queen Mother holding bouquet; 107v. Lady Elizabeth Bowes-Lyon as young girl	5·00	5·00

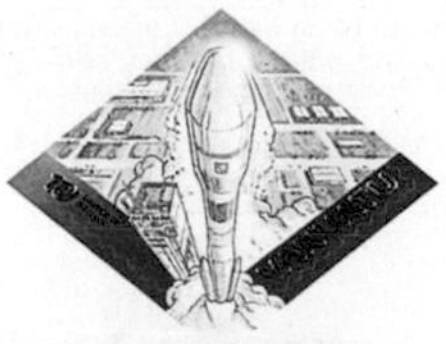

209 Launch of "Intelsat" Satellite

2000. "EXPO 2000" World Stamp Exhibition, Anaheim, U.S.A. Satellite Communications. Multicoloured. Self-adhesive.

829	10v. Type **209**	30	30
830	34v. Port Villa Ground Station	60	40
831	100v. "Intelsat" satellite in orbit over Vanuatu	1·40	1·40
832	225v. Tam Tam drum and Intelsat satellite	2·50	4·00
MS833	122×97 mm. Nos. 830 and 832	3·75	4·50

210 Abstract Painting (Sero Kuautonga)

2000. 20th Anniv of Independence. Local Art. Multicoloured.

834	34v. Type **210**	90	40
835	67v. Tapa cloth art (Moses Pita)	1·40	70
836	73v. Tapestry (Juliet Pita)	1·40	1·00
837	84v. Carving (Emmanuel Watt)	1·50	1·75
838	90v. "Tree of Peace" (watercolour) (Joseph John)	1·75	2·25

211 Running

2000. Olympic Games, Sydney. Each including the Olympic Torch. Multicoloured.

839	56v. Type **211**	75	75
840	67v. Weightlifting	85	85
841	90v. High-jumping	1·10	1·10
842	96v. Boxing	1·25	1·75

212 Common Dolphin

2000. Dolphins. Multicoloured.

843	34v. Type **212**	80	50
844	73v. Spotted dolphin	1·25	90
845	84v. Spinner dolphin	1·40	1·40
846	107v. Bottlenose dolphin	1·75	2·50
MS847	Circular, 100 mm diameter. Nos. 845/6	3·00	3·50

No. **MS**847 includes the "HONG KONG 2001" Stamp Exhibition logo on the sheet margin.

213 Cardinal Honeyeater

2001. Birds (3rd series). Highland Birds. Multicoloured.

848	35v. Type **213**	1·00	55
849	60v. Yellow-fronted white-eye ("Vanuatu White-eye")	1·50	65
850	90v. Mountain starling ("Santo Mountain Starling")	2·25	1·50
851	100v. Red-headed parrotfinch ("Royal Parrot finch")	2·50	3·00
852	110v. White-billed honeyeater ("Vanuatu Mountain Honeyeater")	2·50	3·00

In addition to being available in separate sheets Nos. 848/52 were also printed together, se-tenant, with the backgrounds forming a composite design.

214 Vanilla

2001. Food Exports. Multicoloured.

853	35v. Type **214**	70	40
854	75v. Cacao	1·10	80
855	90v. Coffee	1·25	1·25
856	110v. Copra	1·40	2·25

215 Sperm Whales

2001. Whales. Joint Issue with New Caledonia. Multicoloured.

857	60v. Type **215**	1·00	1·00
858	80v. Humpback whales (vert)	1·25	1·25
859	90v. Blue whales	1·40	1·40
MS860	220×90 mm. Nos. 857/9	3·25	3·25

No. **MS**860 is in the shape of a pair of Humpback whales.

216 Lyre-shaped Sand Drawing

2001. Sand Drawings. Multicoloured.

861	60v. Type **216**	75	75
862	90v. Interwoven scroll design	1·25	1·25
863	110v. Drawing of turtle	1·40	1·75
864	135v. Drawing of fish	1·60	2·00

217 Vanuatan, Yasur Volcano and Pentecost Island Land Diver

2002. U.N. Year of Eco Tourism. Multicoloured.

865	35v. Type **217**	60	40
866	60v. Making kava and dancers	75	60
867	75v. Siri Falls and birds (vert)	1·50	1·25
868	110v. Tourist kayaks and scuba diving (vert)	1·75	2·25
869	135v. Tourist village	2·00	3·00
MS870	170×76 mm. Nos. 865/9	6·00	7·00

218 Horse pulling Plough

2002. Local Horses. Multicoloured.

871	35v. Type **218**	75	40
872	60v. Cattle round-up	95	65
873	75v. Horse racing	1·10	1·00
874	80v. Pony trekking on beach	1·25	1·10
875	200v. Wild horse from Tanna	3·00	4·00
MS876	180×90 mm. Nos. 8875	3·00	4·00
MS876	180×90 mm. Nos. 8875	3·00	4·00

219 Children's Football

2002. Vanuatu Football Federation. Multicoloured.

877	35v. Type **219**	65	40
878	80v. Under 17's football	1·10	80
879	110v. Women's football	1·60	2·00
880	135v. International football	1·90	2·75

220 Young Girl holding Breadfruit Plant

2002. Year of Reforestation. Multicoloured. Self-adhesive.

881	35v. Type **220**	65	65
882	60v. Man and boy planting seedling (*Endospermum medullosum*)	1·00	1·10

883	90v. Man hollowing out canoe	1·40	1·75
884	110v. Woman and boy eating fruit	1·75	2·25

2002. "Philakorea 2002" International Stamp Exhibition, Seoul. Multicoloured.

MS885	115×90 mm. No. 875	2·75	3·25

221 Adult Dugong with Calf

2002. Dugong. Multicoloured.

886	35v. Type **221**	65	50
887	75v. Adult and calf swimming	1·00	1·00
888	80v. Adult Dugong	1·10	1·00
889	135v. Dugong feeding	1·75	2·50
MS890	133×112 mm. Nos. 888/9	5·50	5·50

222 *Dendrobium gouldii*

2002. Orchids. Multicoloured.

891	35v. Type **222**	75	50
892	60v. *Dendrobium polysema*	95	60
893	90v. *Dendrobium spectabile*	1·40	1·40
894	110v. *Flickingeria comata*	1·75	2·50

223 Limousin Cattle

2003. "Year Blong Buluk". Beef Production in Vanuatu. Multicoloured.

895	35v. Type **223**	90	50
896	80v. Charolais cattle	1·40	80
897	110v. Simmental cattle	1·75	2·00
898	135v. Red Brahman cattle	2·25	2·50

224 Land Diver on Platform

2003. Pentecost Island Land Diving. Multicoloured.

899	35v. Type **224**	1·00	55
900	80v. Islander making dive	1·75	1·10
901	110v. Diving tower and dancers	2·00	2·25
902	200v. Land diver jumping from tower (33×89 mm)	3·75	4·50
MS903	90×110 mm. No. 902	3·50	4·00

225 Snorkeller and Butterflyfish

2003. Snorkelling. Multicoloured.

904	35v. Type **225**	50	40
905	80v. Snorkeller over coral (vert)	90	80
906	90v. Two snorkellers over coral (vert)	1·00	95
907	110v. Snorkellers underwater and at surface	1·25	1·50
908	135v. Snorkeller and fish of three species	1·50	2·25
MS909	175×80 mm. Nos. 904/8	5·25	6·00

226 Planting Natanggura Palm

2003. Natanggura Palm. Multicoloured.

910	35v. Type **226**	50	40
911	80v. Thatching roof with leaves	90	80
912	90v. Carving seeds	1·00	85
913	135v. Carved fish and seahorse	1·50	2·50

227 Diver taking Letter to Underwater Post Office

2003. Underwater Post Office, Hideaway Island (1st series).

914	**227** 90v. multicoloured	1·75	1·50

See also Nos. 923/**MS**927.

228 *Hippocampus kuda*

2003. Seahorses. Multicoloured.

915	60v. Type **228**	1·00	60
916	90v. *Hippocampus histrix*	1·50	90
917	200v. *Hippocampus bargibanti*	3·75	4·75
MS918	105×70 mm. No. 917	3·75	4·75

229 *Daphnis hypothous*

2003. Moths. Multicoloured.

919	35v. Type **229**	60	50
920	90v. *Hippotion celerio*	1·00	90
921	110v. *Euchromia creusa*	1·25	1·60
922	135v. *Eudocima salaminia*	1·50	2·25

230 Diver collecting Mail

2004. Underwater Post Office, Hideaway Island (2nd series). Multicoloured.

923	35v. Type **230**	70	45
924	80v. Diver putting letter in underwater postbox	1·25	1·00
925	110v. Diver above reef, diver at Underwater Post Office and postbox	1·60	1·60
926	220v. Underwater Post Office and diver at postbox	2·75	3·50
MS927	92×71 mm. 220v. No. 926	2·75	3·50

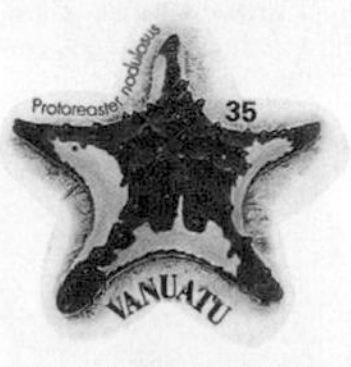

231 *Protoreaster nodulosus*

2004. Starfish. Multicoloured. Self-adhesive.

928	35v. Type **231**	65	55
929	60v. *Linckia laevigata*	1·00	75
930	90v. *Fromia monilis*	1·40	1·10
931	250v. *Echinaster callosus*	3·25	5·00

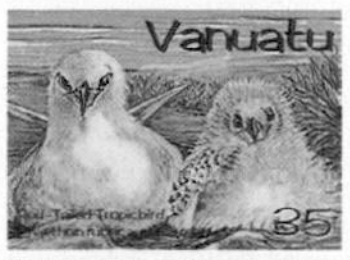

232 Red-tailed Tropic Birds

2004. Red-tailed Tropic Birds. Multicoloured.

932	35v. Type **232**	70	50
933	50v. Bird feeding chick (vert)	90	70
934	75v. Chick and adult bird flying (vert)	1·40	1·25
935	135v. Bird in flight	2·00	2·00
936	200v. Adult feeding juvenile bird	3·00	4·00
MS937	175×80 mm. Nos. 932/6	9·00	9·00

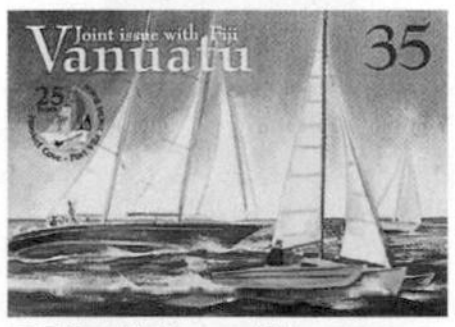

233 Two Yachts and Trimaran

2004. 25th Anniv of the Musket Cove—Port Vila Yacht Race. Multicoloured.

938	35v. Type **233**	75	50
939	80v. Sailing with spinnakers raised (vert)	1·60	1·50
940	90v. Sailors at helm and yachts racing alongside	1·60	1·50
941	200v. Racing along the coast	3·75	4·50
MS942	100×70 mm. 200v. As No. 941	3·75	4·50

Stamps of a similar design were issued by Fiji.

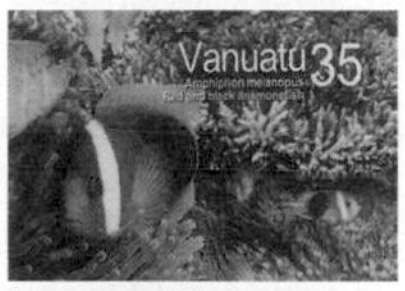

234 Red and Black Anemonefish

2004. Tropical Marine Life. Sheet 187×140 mm containing T **234** and similar horiz designs. Multicoloured. Self-adhesive.

MS943	35v. ×12, Type **234**; Longfin bannerfish; Goldman's sweetlips; Green turtle; Clark's anemonefish; Harlequin sweetlips; Yellowtail coris; Emperor angelfish; Hairy red hermit crab; Spotfin lionfish; Yellow-lipped sea krait; Clam	7·00	8·00

No. **MS**943 was issued together, *se-tenant*, forming a composite design.

235 Star

2004. Christmas. Self-adhesive.

944	**235**	80v. multicoloured	2·00	1·75

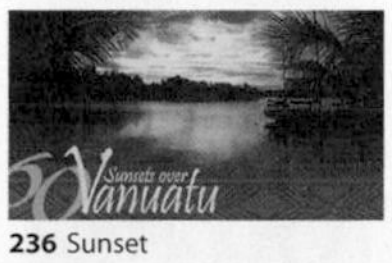

236 Sunset

2005. Sunsets. Multicoloured.

945	60v. Type **236**	1·25	80
946	80v. Boy holding stick (vert)	1·60	1·50
947	90v. Yachts in Port Vila (vert)	1·60	1·50
948	135v. Native blowing into conch shell	2·75	4·00

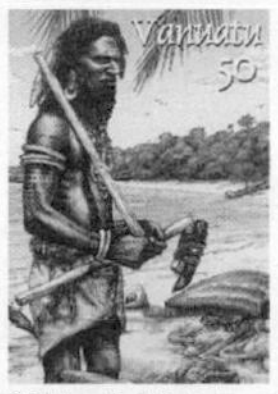

237 Lapita Man

2005. Pacific Explorer World Stamp Exhibition, Sydney. Lapita People. Sheet, 196×83 mm, containing T **237** and similar multicoloured designs.

MS949	50v. Type **237**; 70v. Preparing fish (horiz); 110v. Carrying wild boar and children watching (horiz); 200v. Woman holding child and basket weaving	7·00	8·00

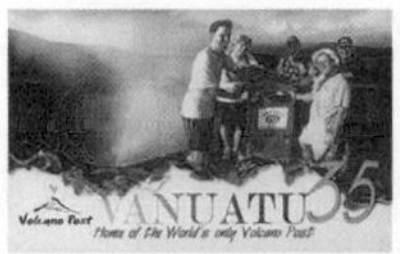

238 Postbox on Rim of Mount Yasur

2005. Volcano Post. Multicoloured.

950	35v. Type **238**	70	35
951	80v. Native by post box	1·50	1·10
952	100v. Three people in matching shirts by post box	1·75	1·60
953	250v. Man with open post box	4·00	5·00
MS954	109×54 mm. 250v. As No. 953	4·50	5·50

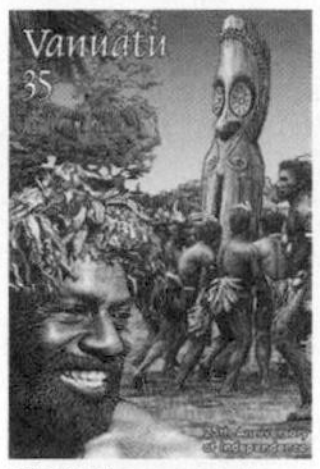

239 Natives around Totem

2005. 25th Anniv of Independence. Sheet, 150×81 mm, containing T **239** and similar vert designs. Multicoloured.

MS955	35v. Type **239**; 50v. Procession with flags; 400v. Children with ferns and flags	8·75	9·50

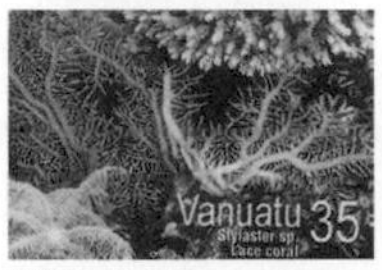

240 Lace Coral

2005. Coral Gardens. Sheet, 188×140 mm, containing T **240** and similar horiz designs. Multicoloured. Self-adhesive.

MS956	35v.×12, Type **240**; Star coral; Sun coral (*Tubastraea* sp.); Plate coral; Brown anthelia; Bubble coral; Flowerpot coral; Cup coral; Daisy coral; Sun coral (*Tubastraea diaphana*); Mushroom leather coral; Sun coral (*Tubastraea micrantha*)	9·00	9·50

The stamps in No. **MS**956 form a composite design.

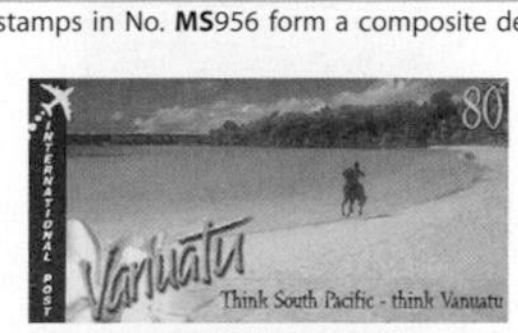

241 Horse and Rider on Beach

2005. Tourism. Multicoloured.

957	80v. Type **241**	1·60	1·10
958	90v. Coconut palms at sunset	1·60	1·50
959	110v. Waterfalls	2·25	2·50
960	135v. Harbour with yachts	2·50	3·25

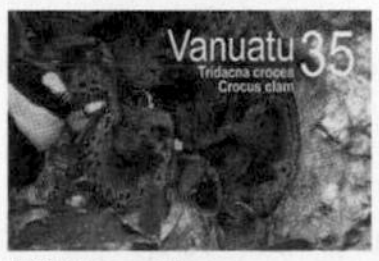

242 Crocus Clam

2006. Reef Shells of Vanuatu. Multicoloured. Self-adhesive.

MS961	188×140 mm. 35v.×12, Type **242**; Pearl oyster; Gold-ringer cowrie; Cock's-comb oyster; Tiger cowrie; Textile cone; Marlinspike; Vibex bonnet; Erosa cowrie; . Scorpion conch; 35v. Honey cowrie; 35v. Umbilical ovula	8·00	9·00

The stamps and margins of No. **MS**961 form a composite background design showing a coral reef.

2006. 80th Birthday of Queen Elizabeth II. As T **237** of St. Helena. Multicoloured.

962	50v. Princess Elizabeth in uniform, c. 1944	1·00	80
963	100v. Queen Elizabeth, c. 1958	2·25	2·00
964	110v. Wearing blue hat	2·25	2·25
965	200v. Wearing yellow hat	3·75	4·25
MS966	144×75 mm. 110v. As No. 963; 200v. As No. 964	6·00	7·00

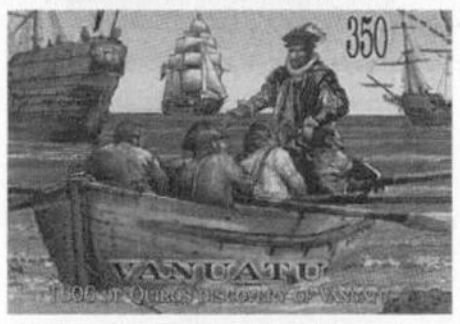

243 De Quiros rowing ashore at Big Bay, Espiritu Santo

2006. 400th Anniv of Discovery of Vanuatu by PedroFernando de Quiros (Portuguese navigator). Sheet 147×73 mm.

MS967	**243** 350v. multicoloured	10·00	11·00

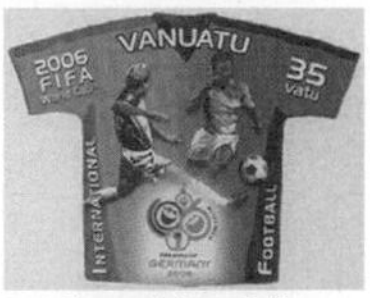

244 Player kicking Ball

2006. World Cup Football Championship, Germany. Designs, each showing two players. Multicoloured. Self-adhesive.

968	35v. Type **244**	90	80
969	80v. Heading ball	1·90	1·75
970	110v. Two players pursuing ball	2·50	2·75
971	135v. Goalkeeper reaching for ball	3·25	3·75
MS972	Circular 98×98 mm. Nos. 968/71	7·75	8·50

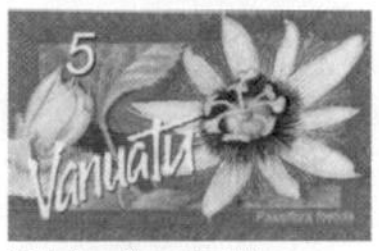

245 *Passiflora foetida*

2006. Flowers. Multicoloured. Self-adhesive.

973	5v. Type **245**	30	50
974	10v. *Hibiscus rosa-sinensis* "Powder Puff"	40	50
975	20v. *Cereus undatus*	65	40
976	40v. *Strelitzia reginae*	1·00	60
977	50v. *Spathodea campanulata*	1·10	70
978	70v. *Delonix regia*	1·40	1·00
979	100v. *Nymphaea* sp.	1·90	1·50
980	150v. *Plumeria obtusa*	2·75	3·00
981	500v. *Allamanda cathartica*	8·50	9·50
982	1000v. *Thunbergia grandiflora*	15·00	20·00

(b) International Post.

982a	5v. Type **245**	30	50
982b	10v. *Hibiscus rosa-sinensis* 'Powder Puff'	40	50
982c	20v. *Cerus undatus*	65	40
982d	50v. *Spathodea campanulata*	1·10	70
982e	90v. *Hibiscus tiliaceus*	1·90	1·50
982f	100v. *Nymphaea* sp.	1·90	1·50
982g	500v. *Allamanda cathartica*	8·50	9·50
982h	1000v. *Thunbergia grandiflora*	15·00	20·00

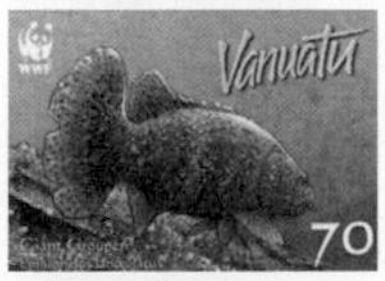

246 Giant Grouper

2006. Endangered Species. Giant Grouper (Epinephelus lanceolatus). Sheet 199×135 mm containing T **246** and similar horiz designs. Multicoloured.

MS983	70v.×2 Type **246**; 90v.×2 Giant grouper (front view with mouth open); 100v.×2 Two juvenile giant groupers; 150v.×2 Giant grouper swimming with other fish	14·00	16·00

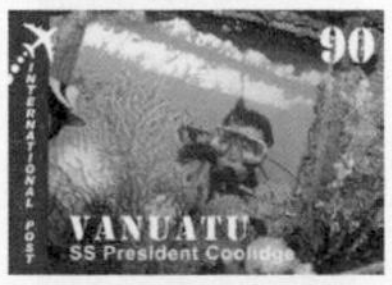

247 Diver looking through Porthole and Coral

2006. Vanuatu Dive Sites (1st series). Wreck of SS President Coolidge (liner/transport ship). Multicoloured.

984	90v. Type **247**	1·90	1·50
985	100v. Two divers on wreck	2·00	1·75
986	130v. *President Coolidge* on side on sea floor	2·50	2·75
987	150v. Troops abandoning grounded *President Coolidge* (84×29 mm)	2·75	3·00
MS988	197×112 mm. As Nos. 984/7	8·00	8·50

Nos. 984/7 are inscribed "INTERNATIONAL POST". Stamps from **MS**988 are without the "INTERNATIONAL POST" inscription and panel and also differ from the sheet stamps in having the face values at top left.

See also Nos. 995/1003.

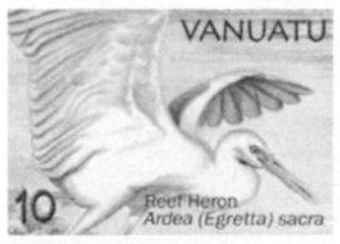

248 Reef Heron

2007. Reef Herons (Ardea (Egretta) sacra). Multicoloured.

989	10v. Type **248**	45	50
990	20v. Reef heron standing on rock (vert)	80	75
991	50v. With fish catch (vert)	1·50	1·25
992	70v. Close-up of head	1·60	1·40
993	250v. Nestlings	4·50	5·00
MS994	158×86 mm. Nos. 989/93	8·00	8·50

The stamps and margins of **MS**994 form a composite design showing reef herons on the seashore.

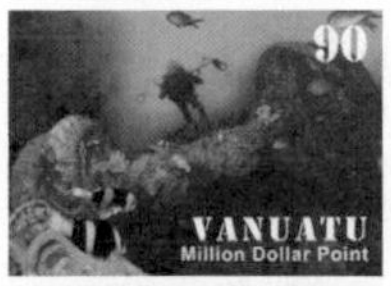

249 Wheelbase of Vehicle, Fish and Diver

2007. Vanuatu Dive Sites (2nd issue). Million Dollar Point. Multicoloured. (i) Postage.

995	90v. Type **249**	1·75	1·60
996	100v. Tyres and other wreckage, fish and diver (42×60 mm)	1·90	1·90
997	130v. Wreckage and diver	2·40	2·75
998	150v. Diver and lionfish	2·75	3·25
MS999	174×113 mm. Nos. 995/8	8·00	8·50

(ii) International Post.

1000	90v. As Type **249**	2·00	1·60
1001	100v. As No. 996 (42×60 mm)	2·25	2·00
1002	130v. As No. 997	2·75	3·00
1003	150v. As No. 998	3·00	3·50

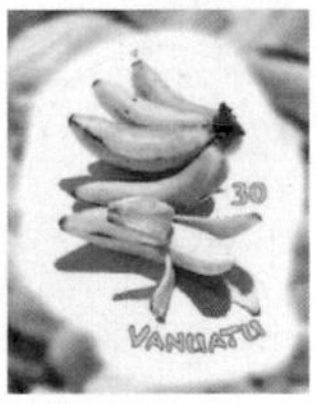

250 Bananas

2007. Tropical Fruits. Multicoloured. Self-adhesive.

1004	30v. Type **250**	75	75
1005	40v. Melon	80	80
1006	70v. Limes	1·60	1·60
1007	100v. Mangoes	2·00	2·00
1008	250v. Coconuts	3·75	4·50

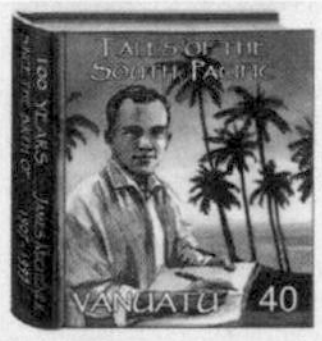

251 James Michener writing in Book

2007. Birth Centenary of James Michener (author). Designs showing the author on book covers. Multicoloured.

1009	40v. Type **251**	85	80
1010	90v. James Michener typing and troops coming ashore	1·75	1·75
1011	130v. James Michener, Vanuatu tribesmen and volcano eruption	2·50	2·50
1012	350v. James Michener holding book *Tales of the South Pacific* and seashore at sunset	6·00	7·00

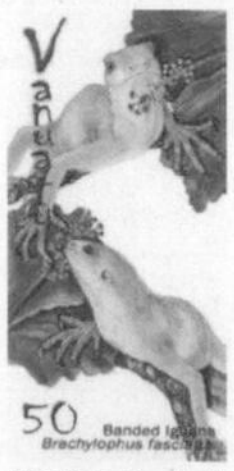

252 Two Banded Iguanas

2007. Banded Iguana (Brachylophus fasciatus). Multicoloured. Self-adhesive.

1013	50v. Type **252**	1·40	1·40
1014	70v. Iguana on thin branches	1·60	1·60
1015	100v. Iguana on leaf, seen from above	2·25	2·25
1016	250v. Iguana on fruit	3·75	4·50
MS1017	156×92 mm. Nos. 1015/16	6·00	6·50

No. **MS**1017 is cut around the miniature sheet design and forms an irregular semi-circular shape.

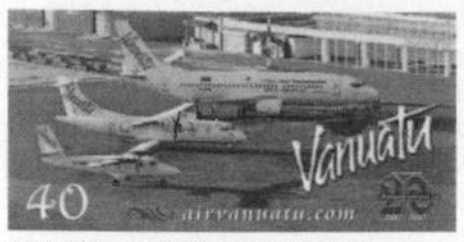

253 Three Air Vanuatu Planes

2007. 20th Anniv of Air Vanuatu. Multicoloured. Self-adhesive.

1018	40v. Type **253**	1·00	80
1019	130v. Boeing 737-300	3·00	2·75
1020	180v. Twin Otter	3·50	3·75
1021	250v. ATR 42	4·50	5·00

2008. Arrival of New Air Vanuatu Boeing 737-800. As T **253**. Self-adhesive. International Post.

1022	90v. Boeing 737-800 in flight over Vanuatu	2·25	1·75

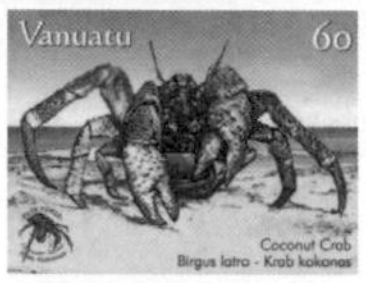

254 Coconut Crab on Shore

2008. Coconut Crabs (Birgus latro) of Vanuatu. Multicoloured.

1023	60v. Type **254**	1·50	1·50
1024	500v. Crab climbing tree (vert)	8·50	10·00
MS1025	115×75 mm. Nos. 1023/4	10·00	11·00

255 Archery

2008. Olympic Games, Beijing. Sheet 151×95 mm containing T **255** and similar vert designs. Multicoloured.

MS1026 10v. Type **255**; 40v. Athletics; 60v. Table tennis; 90v. Weightlifting 3·50 4·00

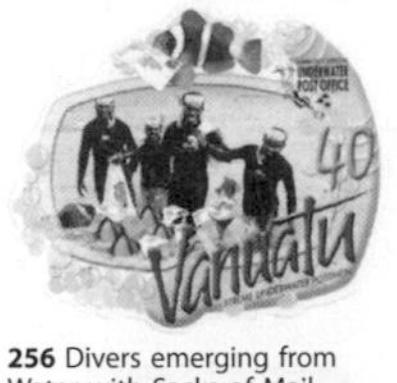

256 Divers emerging from Water with Sacks of Mail

2008. Xtreme Postmen of the Underwater Post Office, Hideaway Island. Multicoloured. Self-adhesive.

1027	40v. Type **256**	80	80
1028	80v. Diver with school of fish carrying mail	1·50	1·50
1029	100v. Two divers on inflatable and school of fish carrying mail	2·00	2·25
1030	200v. Diver at Underwater Post Office and fish carrying mail	3·75	4·75

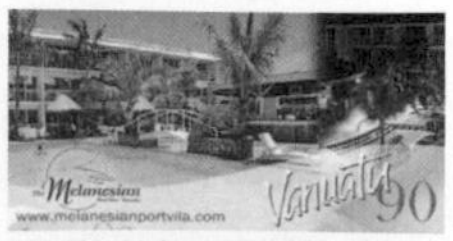

257 The Melanesian Hotel, Port Vila

2008. 'Resorts in Paradise'. Multicoloured.

1031	90v. Type **257**	1·75	1·75
1032	90v. Le Meridien Port Vila Resort, Spa and Casino	1·75	1·75
1033	90v. Le Lagon Resort	1·75	1·75
1034	90v. Iririki Island Resort and Spa	1·75	1·75
1035	90v. The Sebel Hotel, Port Vila	1·75	1·75
1036	90v. Breakas Beach Resort and Villas	1·75	1·75
1037	90v. Frangipani flowers and beach, Vanuatu	1·75	1·75

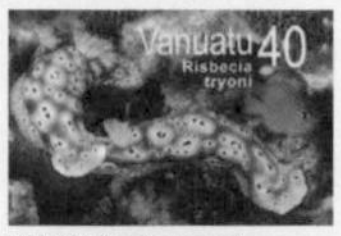

258 *Risbecia tryoni*

2008. Nudibranchs of Vanuatu. Sheet 169×126 mm containing T **258** and similar horiz designs. Multicoloured. Self-adhesive.

MS1038 40v.×12 Type **258**; *Phyllidia coelestis; Flabellina rubrolineata; Chromodoris lochi; Chromodoris elisabethina; Jorunna funebris; Glossodoris rufomarginata; Phyllidiaocellata; Chromodoris geometrica; Phyllidia madangensis; Hexabranchussanguineus; Glossodoris atromarginata* 11·00 11·00

The stamps and margins of No. **MS**1038 form a composite design showing nudibranchs on a coral reef.

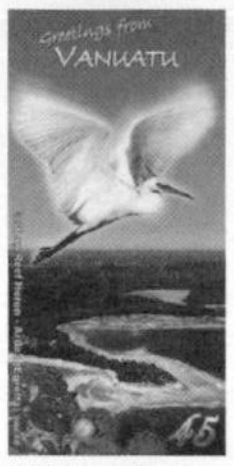

259 Inscr 'Eastern Reef Heron'

2008. 'Greetings from Vanuatu'. Designs showing sea birds and flamboyant (Delonix regia) flowers. Multicoloured.

1039	45v. Type **259**	85	90
1040	100v. Great crested tern	2·00	2·10
1041	130v. White-tailed tropicbird	2·75	2·75
1042	250v. Fairy tern	4·25	4·75
MS1043	100×70 mm. No. 1042	4·25	4·75

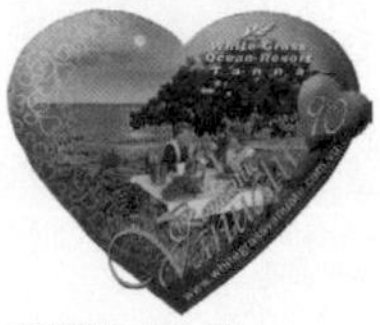

260 White Grass Ocean Resort, Tanna

2009. Tourism. 'Romantic Vanuatu'. Multicoloured. Self-adhesive.

1044	90v. Type **260**	1·75	2·00
1045	90v. Bride and groom on beach with champagne	1·75	2·00
1046	90v. Bride and groom under palm tree	1·75	2·00
1047	90v. Couple on sun loungers, Breakas Beach Resort	1·75	2·00
1048	90v. Couple on beach	1·75	2·00

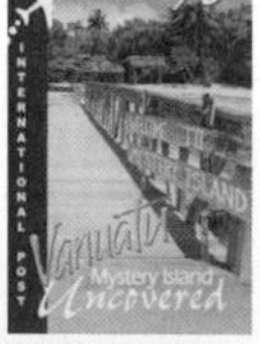

261 Boardwalk

2009. Tourism. 'Vanuatu Uncovered' (1st series). Mystery Island. Multicoloured. (i) International Post.

1049	90v. Type **261**	1·75	1·25
1050	100v. Couple snorkelling (horiz)	2·00	1·50
1051	130v. Yacht offshore (horiz)	2·50	2·50
1052	200v. Couple sat on outrigger canoe on beach	4·00	5·00

(ii) Domestic Mail

MS1053	195×83 mm. As Nos. 1049/52	11·00	11·00

Stamps from No. **MS**1053 omit the 'International Post' inscriptions. The miniature sheet and its margins form a composite design showing a beach scene.

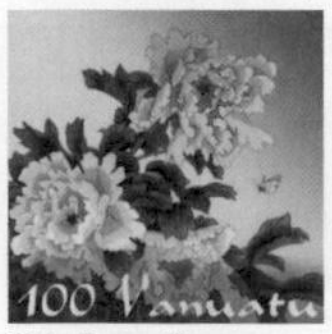

261a Peony Flowers

2009. China 2009 World Stamp Exhibition and Peony Festival, Luoyang

1053a	**261a**	100v. multicoloured	2·00	2·10

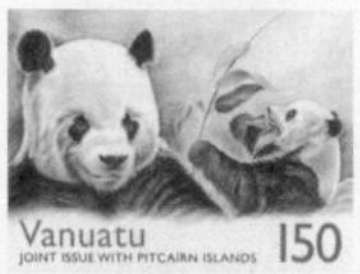

262 Two Giant Pandas

2009. 23rd Asian International Stamp Exhibition, Hong Kong. Sheet 135×95 mm containing T **206** of Pitcairn Islands and T **262**. Multicoloured.

MS1054 $2.50 Type **206** of Pitcairn Islands; 150v. Type **262** (sold at 310v.) 7·00 7·50

No. **MS**1054 is identical to **MS**783 of Pitcairn Islands, which was also issued on 14 May 2009.

263 Deep Pink Frangipani

2009. Frangipani (Pllumeria). Multicoloured.

1055	90v. Type **263**	2·25	1·25
1056	100v. White frangipani with yellow centre	2·50	1·75
1057	130v. Pale pink frangipani	3·00	3·25
1058	150v. Yellow and white frangipani	3·25	3·75

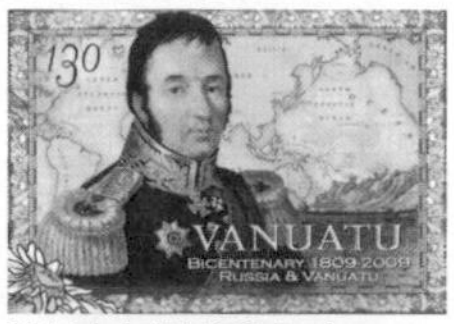

264 Admiral V. M. Golovnin

2009. Bicentenary of First Contact between Russia and Vanuatu. Oval sheet 128×89 mm containing T **264** and similar horiz design. Multicoloured.

MS1059 130v. Type **264**; 350v. *Diana* (sloop) 8·00 9·00

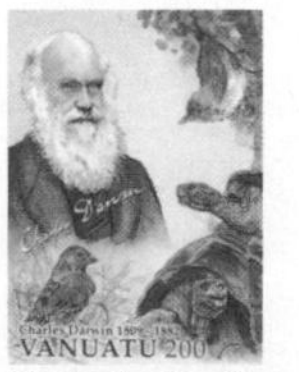

265 Charles Darwin, Galapagos Tortoises and Birds

2009. Birth Bicentenary of Charles Darwin (naturalist and evolutionary theorist). Multicoloured.

1060	200v. Type **265**	4·00	4·50
1061	200v. Charles Darwin, iguanas and birds	4·00	4·50

Nos. 1060/1 were printed together, se-tenant, in horizontal pairs with a central label showing book *The Origin of Species* and animals, the whole forming a composite design.

No. 1062, Type **266** are vacant.

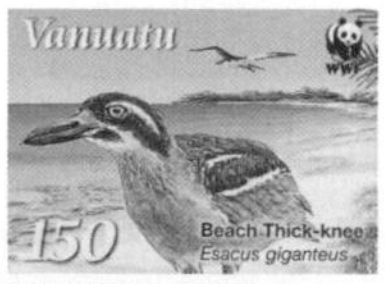

267 Adult on beach

2009. Endangered Species. Beach Thick-knee (*Esacus giganteus*). Sheet 194×115 mm containing T **267** and similar horiz designs. Multicoloured.

MS1063 50s. Beach thick-knee on nest×2; 90s. Adult with fledgeling×2; 130s. Pair at water's edge×2; 150s. Type **267**×2 10·00 10·00

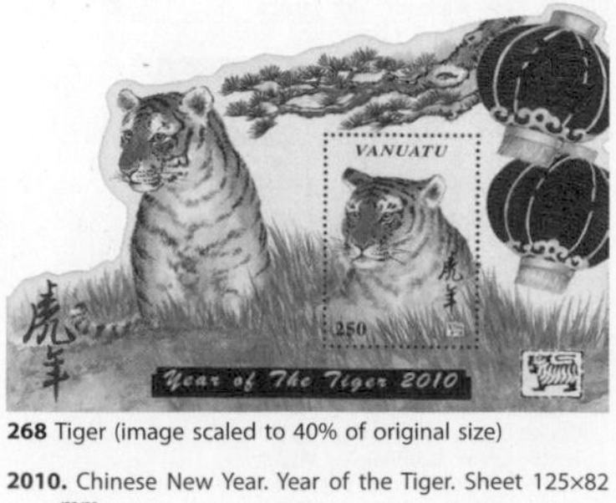

268 Tiger (image scaled to 40% of original size)

2010. Chinese New Year. Year of the Tiger. Sheet 125×82 mm.

MS1064	**268**	250v. multicoloured	5·50	6·00

The top portion of No. **MS**1064 is irregularly shaped, being cut around the shape of a tiger, pine tree branches and two red lanterns.

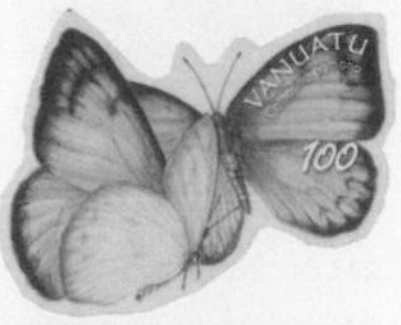

269 *Catopsilia pomona* (common emigrant or lemon emigrant)

2010. Butterflies of Vanuatu. Sheet 181×162 mm containing T **269** and similar horiz designs. Multicoloured. Self-adhesive.

MS1065 100v.×6 Type **269**; *Papilio godeffroyi* (swallowtail); *Hypolimnas octocula* (eight-spot butterfly); *Doleschallia bisaltide* (leafwing or autumnleaf); *Acraea andromacha* (glasswing or small greasy); *Danaus affinis* (black and white tiger or swamp butterfly) 12·00 13·00

The top portion of **MS**1065 is cut around in the shape of a butterfly and flowers. The stamps within **MS**1065 form a composite background design of flowers and foliage.

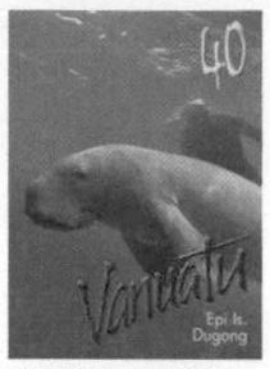

270 Dugong, Epi Island

2010. World Stamp Expo 2010, Shanghai, China. Multicoloured.

(a) Domestic mail

1066	40v. Type **270**	1·25	50

(b) International Post

1067	140v. Banks Islands snake dance (horiz)	3·00	2·75
1068	160v. Iririki Resort, Efate Island	3·50	3·50
1069	190v. Eruption of Mt. Yasur volcano, Tanna Island (horiz)	4·25	4·75
MS1070	125×185 mm. Nos. 1066/9	11·00	11·00

Nos. 1066/9, Type **270** are left for World Expo 2010, China, issued 30 April 2010, not yet received.

Nos. 1066/9, Type **270** are left for World Expo 2010, China, issued 30 April 2010, not yet received.

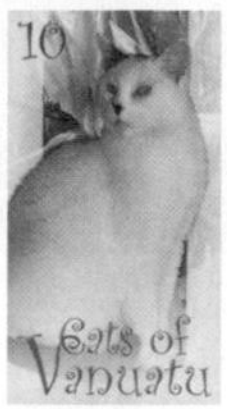

271 White Cat

2010. Cats of Vanuatu. Multicoloured.

1071	10v. Type **271**	45	70
1072	100v. 'Boots' (black and white cat) ringing ship's bell	3·00	2·25
1073	160v. Ginger cat	4·00	4·00
1074	190v. Tabby and white cat	4·50	4·75

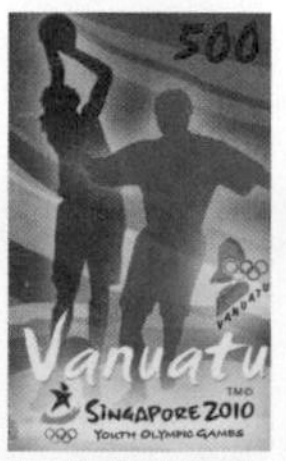

272 Footballer and Basketball Player

2010. Youth Olympic Games, Singapore. Sheet 150×82 mm

MS1075	**272**	500v. multicoloured	11·00	12·00

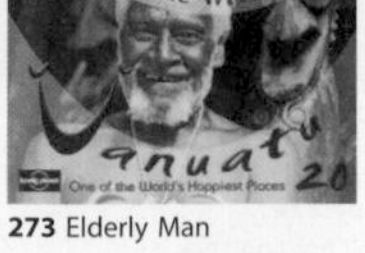

273 Elderly Man

2010. 'Smile with Us'. Multicoloured.

1076	20v. Type **273**	75	90
1077	20v. Dugong	75	90

1078	20v. Two women	75	90
1079	20v. Anemonefish	75	90
1080	20v. Three boys	75	90
1081	100v. Airliner	2·50	2·75
1082	100v. Atoll	2·50	2·75
1083	100v. Dolphin	2·50	2·75
1084	100v. Woman with painted face wearing headdress	2·50	2·75
1085	100v. Underwater post office	2·50	2·75

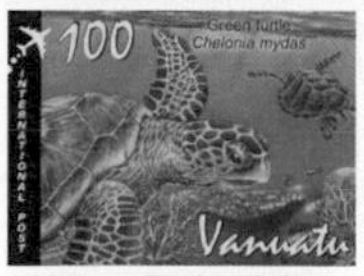

274 Green Turtle (*Chelonia mydas*)

2011. Turtles of Vanuatu. Multicoloured.

1086	100v. Type **274**	3·50	3·50
1087	100v. Green turtle (swimming to left)	3·50	3·50
1088	100v. Hawksbill turtle (*Eretmochelys imbricata*) (swimming to right)	3·50	3·50
1089	100v. Hawksbill turtle (swimming to left)	3·50	3·50

Nos. 1086/9 were printed together, *se-tenant*, each pair forming a composite background design.

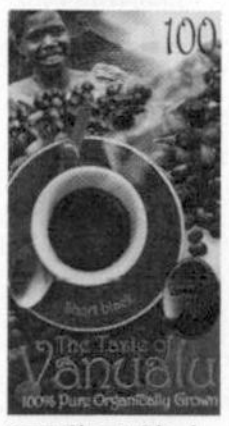

275 Short Black Coffee

2011. Tanna Coffee. Multicoloured.

1090	100v. Type **275**	2·50	2·50
1091	100v. Long black coffee	2·50	2·50
1092	140v. Latte	3·25	3·50
1093	160v. Cappuccino	3·50	4·00

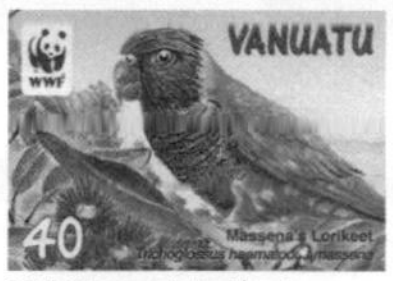

276 Massena's Lorikeet

2011. Endangered Species. Massena's Lorikeet (*Trichoglossus haematodus massena*). Multicoloured.

1094	40v. Type **276**	1·75	1·75
1095	60v. Lorikeet perched on branch	2·00	2·00
1096	140v. Pair of lorikeets	3·50	3·50
1097	160v. Lorikeet perched on palm frond	4·00	4·00
MS1098	200×140 mm. Nos. 1094/7, each ×2	18·00	18·00

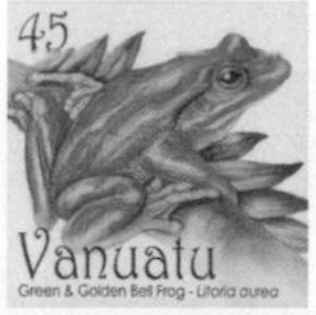

277 Green and Golden Bell Frog

2011. Green and Golden Bell Frog (*Litoria aurea*). Multicoloured.

1099	45v. Type **277**	1·50	65
1100	70v. Frog on flower	2·00	1·40
1101	140v. Three frogs in flower	3·25	3·50
1102	200v. Frog on branch	4·75	5·50
MS1103	97×90 mm. Nos. 1101/2	8·00	9·00

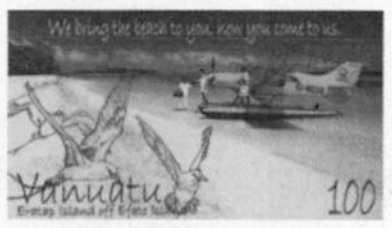

278 Eratap Island off Efate Island

2011. Vanuatu Beaches. Multicoloured.

1104	100v. Type **278**	2·75	2·75
1105	100v. Near Champagne Beach, Espiritu Santo Island	2·75	2·75
1106	140v. Havannah Harbour, Efate Island	3·50	3·75
1107	160v. Pele Island, off Efate Island	4·50	5·00

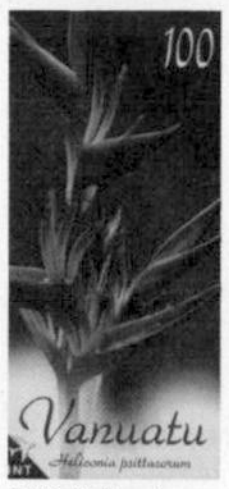

279 *Heliconia psittacorum*

2011. 'Colours in Bloom' (*Strelitzia* and *Heliconia* flowers). Multicoloured.

1108	100v. Type **279**	3·50	3·00
1109	100v. *Heliconia rostrata*	3·50	3·00
1110	140v. *Strelitzia reginae*	3·75	4·00
1111	180v. *Heliconia caribaea* var.	6·50	7·50

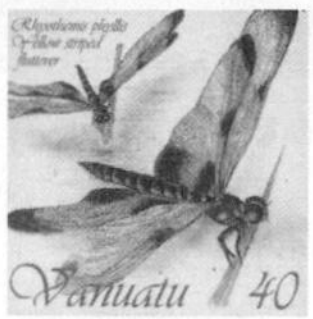

280 Yellow Striped Flutterer (*Rhyothemis phyllis*)

2012. Dragonflies of Vanuatu. Multicoloured.

1112	40v. Type **280**	75	50
1113	90v. Globe skimmer (*Lantala flavescens*)	2·00	1·25
1114	140v. Fiery skimmer (*Orthetrum villosovittatum*)	3·75	3·75
1115	250v. Painted grasshawk (*Neurothemis stigmatizens*)	7·00	8·00
MS1116	133×90 mm. Nos. 1113 and 1115	9·00	10·00

No. **MS**1116 is cut around in the shape of a dragonfly.

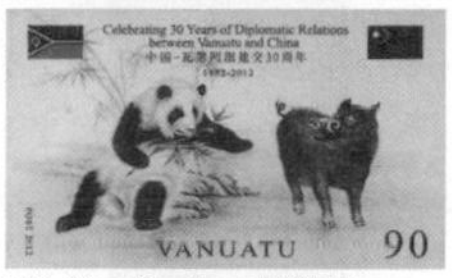

281 Giant Panda and Wild Boar

2012. 30th Anniv of Diplomatic Relations between Vanuatu and People's Republic of China

1117	**281** 90v. multicoloured	2·00	2·10

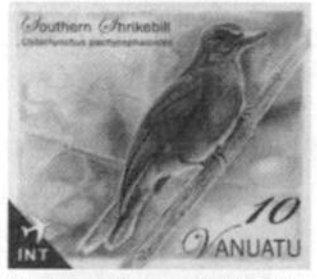

282 Southern Shrikebill (*Clytorhynchus pachycephaloides*)

2012. Birds of Vanuatu. Multicoloured.

1118	10v. Type **282**	25	35
1119	20v. Silvereye (*Zosterops lateralis*)	40	40
1120	40v. Red-bellied fruit dove (*Ptilinopus greyii*)	60	45
1121	50v. Pacific imperial pigeon (*Ducula pacifica*)	70	50
1122	70v. Long-tailed triller (*Lalage leucopyga simillima*)	90	60
1123	90v. Vanuatu scrubfowl (*Megapodius layardi*)	1·25	70
1124	100v. Streaked fantail (*Rhipidura verreauxi*)	1·40	1·00
1125	140v. Dark-brown honeyeater (*Lichmera incana*)	2·00	1·75
1126	160v. Vanuatu petrel (*Pterodroma occulta*)	2·25	2·25
1127	400v. Ruddy turnstone (*Arenaria interpres*)	5·50	6·50
1128	500v. Purple swamphen (*Porphyrio porhyrio*)	6·00	7·00
1129	1000v. Striated mangrove heron (*Butorides striata solomonensis*)	10·00	12·00
MS1130	164×164 mm. Nos. 1118/29	28·00	30·00

Nos. 1120 and 1122 have the blue International Post marker omitted, and Nos. 1123 and 1127/9 have it at bottom right.

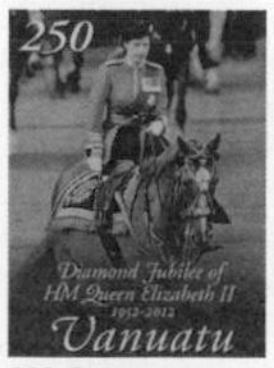

283 Queen Elizabeth II at Trooping the Colour

2012. Diamond Jubilee. Multicoloured.

1131	250v. Type **283**	4·50	5·00
1132	300v. Queen Elizabeth II, c. 2005	5·00	5·50

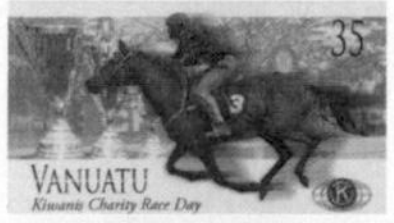

284 Racehorse and Trophies

2012. Kiwanis Charity Race Day, Port Vila. Multicoloured.

1133	35v. Type **284**	90	55
1134	50v. Two horses racing and horses parading before race	1·40	95
1135	150v. Two horses racing and band	4·25	4·00
1136	250v. Racehorses going around bend	7·50	8·50

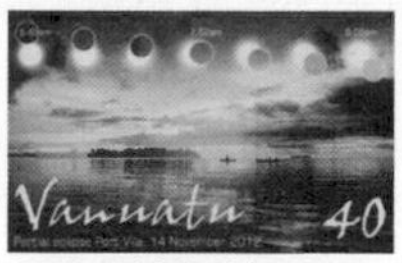

285 Partial Solar Eclipse over Vanuatu

2012. Partial Solar Eclipse over Vanuatu, 14 November 2012. Multicoloured.

1137	40v. Type **285**	70	45
1138	60v. Partial solar eclipse over four people in outrigger	95	70
1139	160v. Partial solar eclipse over man in canoe	2·75	3·25
1140	180v. Partial solar eclipse over Vanuatu with man paddling canoe offshore	3·00	3·50

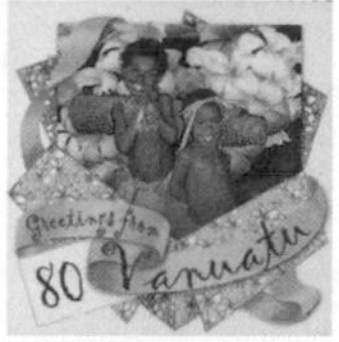

286 Children and Frangipani Flowers

2012. Greetings from Vanuatu. Multicoloured.

1141	80v. Type **286**	1·25	1·00
1142	100v. Diver and coral reef	1·50	1·25
1143	140v. Volcanic eruption	2·00	2·25
1144	160v. Aerial view of atolls	2·25	2·75

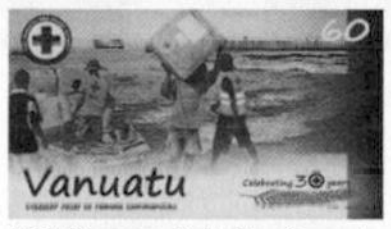

287 Disaster Relief to Remote Communities

2012. 30th Anniv of the Vanuatu Red Cross. Multicoloured.

1145	60v. Type **287**	1·25	1·00
1146	100v. Tap ('Sustainable access to water year round')	2·00	2·25

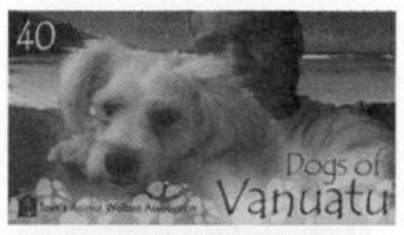

288 Man with White Dog

2013. Dogs of Vanuatu. Sam's Animal Welfare Association. Multicoloured.

(i) Domestic Mail

1147	40v. Type **288**	1·50	65
1148	60v. Man with black and tan dog	2·00	1·25

(ii) International Post

1149	160v. Man on beach with five dogs	5·00	4·50
1150	200v. Elderly woman on beach with seven dogs	7·00	7·50
MS1151	121×85 mm. Nos. 1149/50	14·00	14·00

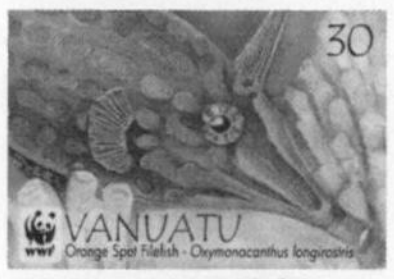

289 Orange Spot Filefish

2013. Endangered Species. Orange Spot Filefish (*Oxymonacanthus longirostris*). Multicoloured.

MS1152	30v. Type **289**×2; 70v. Orange Spot Filefish (different)×2; 100v. Two Orange Spot Filefish×2; 200v. Heads of two Orange Spot Filefish×2	16·00	17·00

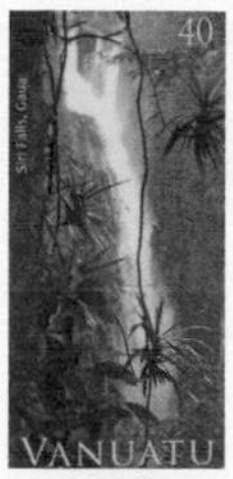

290 Siri Falls, Gaua

2013. Waterfalls. Multicoloured.

1153	40v. Type **290**	70	45
1154	100v. 'Big Wota', Northern Maewo	1·60	1·25
1155	140v. Sasar Twin Falls, Vanua Lava	2·25	2·25
1156	160v. Cascades, Mele, Efate	2·75	3·25

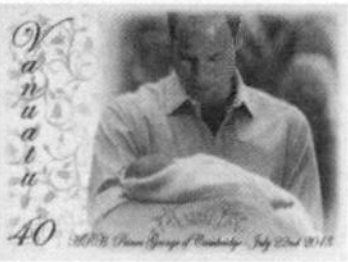

291 Prince William holding Prince George

2013. Birth of Prince George of Cambridge. Multicoloured.

1157	40v. Type **291**	70	45
1158	60v. Duchess of Cambridge holding Prince George	95	70
1159	100v. Duke and Duchess of Cambridge with Prince George	1·60	1·25
1160	250v. Prince George	4·00	4·50

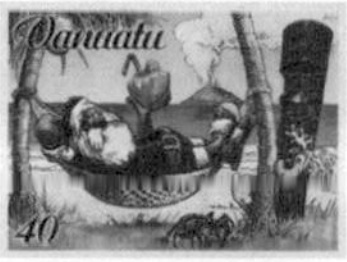

292 Santa in Hammock

2013. Christmas. Multicoloured.

1161	40v. Type **292**	70	45
1162	100v. Scuba diving Santa posting letter in Underwater Post Office (vert)	1·60	1·25
1163	160v. Santa's sleigh over Vanuatu (vert)	2·75	3·25
1164	250v. Santa with postcard at Vanuatu post office	4·00	4·50

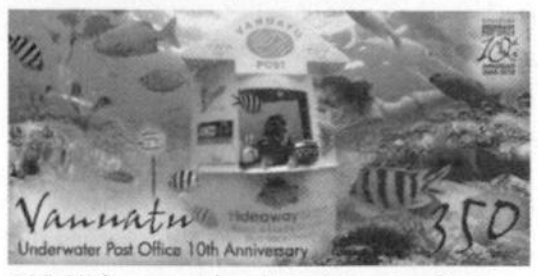

293 Hideaway Island Underwater Post Office

2013. Tenth Anniv of Vanuatu's Underwater Post Office. Sheet 140×96 mm

MS1165	**293** 350v. multicoloured	5·50	6·00

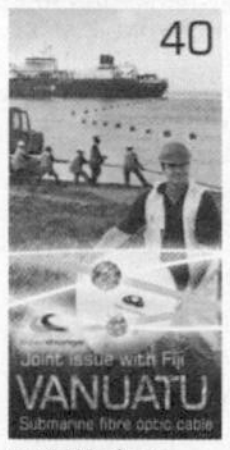

294 Workers handling Cable and *Isle de Re* (cable laying ship)

2014. Submarine Cable System linking Vanuatu and Fiji. Multicoloured.

1166	40v. Type **294**	70	45
1167	130v. Divers laying cable	2·00	2·00
1168	190v. Cables connected to computer	3·25	3·75

Nos. 1166/8 were inscr Joint issue with Fiji'.

Pt. 6

VATHY

A town on the island of Samos, where there was a French Post Office which closed in 1914.

25 centimes = 1 piastre.

EXPRESS LETTER STAMPS

1893. Stamps of France optd **Vathy** or surch also.

81	10	5c. green	14·00	8·25
84	10	10c. black and lilac	16·00	36·00
86	10	15c. blue	14·00	9·25
87	10	1pi. on 25c. black on pink	10·50	9·25
88	10	2pi. on 50c. pink	42·00	42·00
89	10	4pi. on 1f. green	33·00	18·00
90	10	8pi. on 2f. brown on blue	90·00	£100
91	10	20pi. on 5f. mauve	£120	£120

Pt. 8

VATICAN CITY

A small area in Rome under the independent sovereignty of the Pope since 1929.

1929. 100 centesimi = 1 lira.
2002. 100 cents = 1 euro.

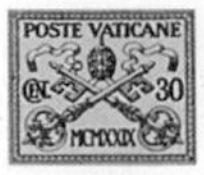

1 Papal Tiara and St. Peter's Keys

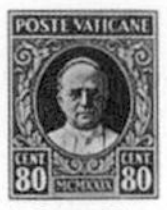

2 Pope Pius XI

1929

1	1	5c. brown on pink	40	35
2	1	10c. green on green	70	65
3	1	20c. violet on lilac	1·60	90
4	1	25c. blue on blue	1·80	1·10
5	1	30c. black on yellow	2·30	1·20
6	1	50c. black on orange	2·50	1·30
7	1	75c. red on grey	4·00	2·40
8	2	80c. red	3·50	1·20
9	2	1l.25 blue	5·75	3·00
10	2	2l. brown	8·75	3·50
11	2	2l.50 red	8·75	6·00
12	2	5l. green	11·50	17·00
13	2	10l. black	20·00	29·00

1931. Surch **C. 25** and bars.

14	1	25c. on 30c. black on yellow	5·25	2·75

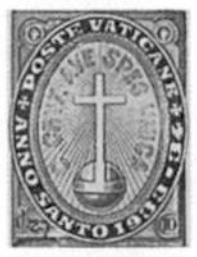

4

1933. "Holy Year" (1933–1934).

15	4	25c.+10c. green	8·00	7·50
16	4	75c.+15c. red	15·00	25·00
17	4	80c.+20c. brown	50·00	35·00
18	4	1l.25+25c. blue	17·00	25·00

The 80c. and 1l.25 have inscriptions and frame differently arranged.

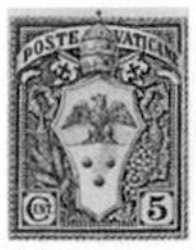

6 Arms of Pope Pius XI

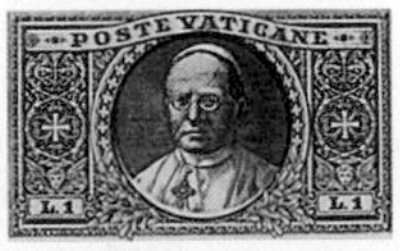

9 Pope Pius XI

1933

19	6	5c. red	25	25
20	-	10c. black and brown	25	25
21	-	12½c. black and green	25	25
22	-	20c. black and orange	25	25
23	-	25c. black and green	25	25
24	-	30c. brown and black	25	25
25	-	50c. brown and purple	25	25
26	-	75c. brown and red	25	25
27	-	80c. brown and pink	25	25
28	9	1l. black and violet	5·75	5·50
29	9	1l.25 black and blue	17·00	14·00
30	9	2l. black and brown	60·00	50·00
31	9	2l.75 black and purple	£110	£100
32	-	5l. green and brown	30	60
33	-	10l. green and blue	30	1·20
34	-	20l. green and black	60	1·20

DESIGNS—As Type **6**: 10c. to 25c. Wing of Vatican Palace; 30c. to 80c. Vatican Gardens and Dome of St. Peter's. As Type **9**: 5l. to 20l. St. Peter's Basilica.

1934. Surch.

35	2	40c. on 80c. red	11·50	8·00
36	2	1l.30 on 1l.25 blue	£160	70·00
37	2	2l.05 on 2l. brown	£375	27·00
38	2	2l.55 on 2l.50 red	£225	£300
39	2	3l.05 on 5l. green	£550	£600
40	2	3l.70 on 10l. black	£600	£700

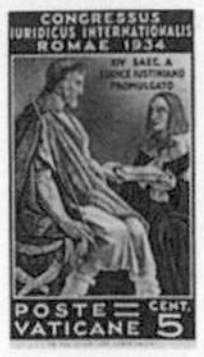

13 Tribonian presenting Pandects to Justinian

1935. International Juridical Congress, Rome. Frescoes by Raphael.

41	13	5c. orange	3·00	2·30
42	13	10c. violet	3·50	2·30
43	13	25c. green	40·00	18·00
44	-	75c. red	90·00	70·00
45	-	80c. brown	70·00	46·00
46	-	1l.25 blue	90·00	50·00

DESIGN: 75c. to 1l.25, Pope Julius II (wrongly inscribed as representing Pope Gregory IX).

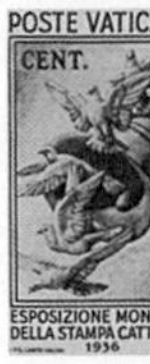

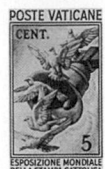

15 Doves and Bell

1936. Catholic Press Exhibition, Rome.

47	15	5c. green	2·30	2·30
48	-	10c. black	2·30	2·30
49	-	25c. green	75·00	23·00
50	15	50c. purple	2·30	2·30
51	-	75c. red	50·00	90·00
52	-	80c. brown	4·50	4·50
53	-	1l.25 blue	4·50	4·50
54	-	5l. brown	5·75	12·50

DESIGNS: 10, 75c. Church and Bible; 25, 80c. St. John Bosco; 1l.25, 5l. St. Francis of Sales.

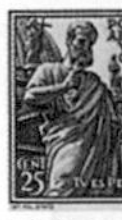

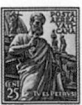

16 Statue of St. Peter

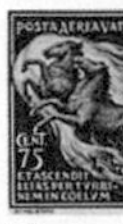

17 Ascension of Elijah

1938. Air.

55	16	25c. brown	20	25
56	-	50c. green	20	25
57	17	75c. red	25	30
58	-	80c. blue	25	55
59	16	1l. violet	60	75
60	-	2l. blue	85	1·20
61	17	5l. black	2·10	3·00
62	-	10l. purple	2·40	3·50

DESIGNS: 50c., 2l. Dove with olive branch and St. Peter's Square; 80c., 10l. Transportation of the Holy House.

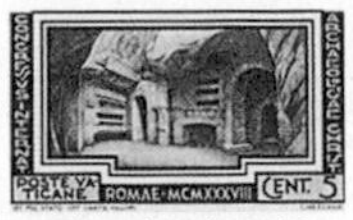

18 Crypt of Basilica of St. Cecilia

1938. International Christian Archaeological Congress. Inscr "CONGRESSVS INTERNAT. ARCHAEOLOGIAE CHRIST".

63	18	5c. brown	35	60
64	18	10c. red	35	60
65	18	25c. green	50	85
66	-	75c. red	10·00	14·50
67	-	80c. violet	38·00	31·00
68	-	1l.25 blue	43·00	43·00

DESIGN: 75, 80c. and 1l.25, Basilica of Saints Nereus and Achilles in the Catacombs of Domitilla.

1939. Death of Pope Pius XI. Optd **SEDE VACANTE MCMXXXIX.**

69	1	5c. brown on pink	60·00	16·00
70	1	10c. green on green	1·20	30
71	1	20c. violet on lilac	1·20	30
72	1	25c. blue on blue	1·20	8·75
73	1	30c. black on yellow	1·20	60
74	1	50c. black on orange	1·20	60
75	1	75c. red on grey	1·20	60

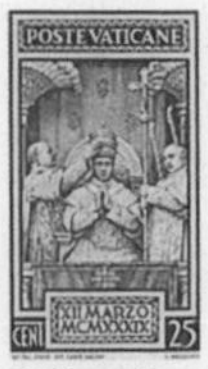

20 Coronation

1939. Coronation of Pope Pius XII.

76	20	25c. green	1·50	1·00
77	20	75c. red	50	1·00
78	20	80c. violet	5·50	5·50
79	20	1l.25 blue	50	1·20

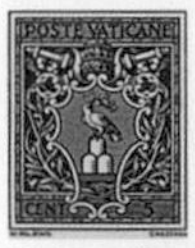

21 Arms of Pope Pius XII

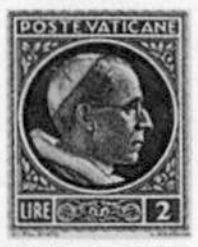

22 Pope Pius XII

1940. First Anniv of Coronation of Pope Pius XII.

80	21	5c. red	30	30
81	22	1l. black and violet	30	30
82	-	1l.25 black and blue	35	30
83	22	2l. black and brown	1·20	1·90
84	-	2l.75 black and purple	2·75	4·00
99	21	5c. grey	20	20
100	21	30c. brown	20	20
101	21	50c. green	20	20
102	-	1l. black and brown	20	25
103	-	1l.50 black and red	20	25
104	-	2l.50 black and blue	20	25
105	22	5l. black and lilac	50	45
106	22	20l. black and green	1·00	75

DESIGN: 1l. (No. 102), 1l.25, 1l.50, 2l.50, and 2l.75, as Type **22** but with portrait of Pope facing left.

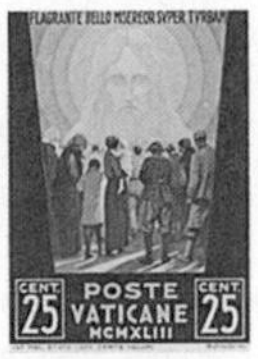

23

1942. Prisoners of War Relief Fund (1st series). Inscr "MCMXLII".

85	23	25c. green	20	25
86	23	80c. brown	20	25
87	23	1l.25 blue	20	25

See also Nos. 92/4 and 107/9.

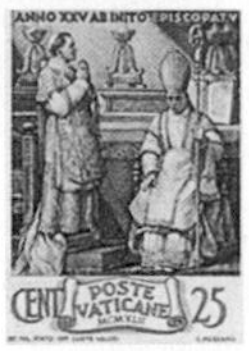

24 Consecration of Archbishop Pacelli

1943. Pope's Episcopal Silver Jubilee.

88	24	25c. turquoise and green	20	25
89	24	80c. chocolate and brown	20	25
90	24	1l.25 blue and ultramarine	20	25
91	24	5l. blue and black	25	60

1944. Prisoners of War Relief Fund (2nd series). Inscr "MCMXLIII".

92	23	25c. green	10	20
93	23	80c. brown	10	20
94	23	1l.25 blue	10	55

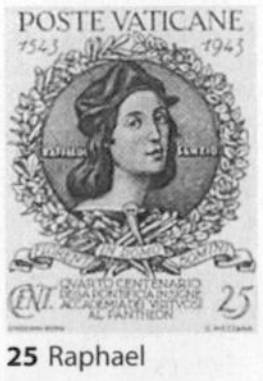

25 Raphael

1944. Fourth Centenary of Pontifical Academy of the Virtuosi of the Pantheon.

95	25	25c. olive and green	25	25
96	-	80c. violet and lilac	25	60
97	-	1l.25 blue and violet	60	60
98	-	10l. bistre and yellow	2·00	2·75

PORTRAITS: 80c. Antonio da Sangallo (architect); 1l.25, Carlo Maratti (painter) (after Francesco Maratta); 10l. Antonio Canova (sculptor, self-portrait).

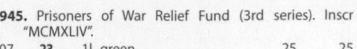

1945. Prisoners of War Relief Fund (3rd series). Inscr "MCMXLIV".

107	23	1l. green	25	25
108	23	3l. red	25	25
109	23	5l. blue	35	30

1946. Surch in figures between bars.

110	21	20c. on 5c. grey	25	20
111	21	25c. on 30c. brown	25	20
112	21	1l. on 50c. green	25	20
113	-	1l.50 on 1l. black and brown (No. 102)	50	25
114	-	3l. on 1l.50 black and red (No. 103)	60	25
115	-	5l. on 2l.50 black and blue (No. 104)	60	25
116	22	10l. on 5l. black and lilac	4·25	85
117	22	30l. on 20l. black and green	6·25	4·00

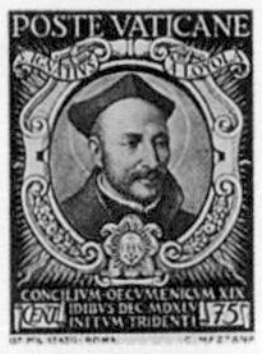

27 St. Ignatius of Loyola

1946. 400th Anniv of Inauguration of Council of Trent.

118	-	5c. brown and bistre	30	30
119	-	25c. brown and violet	30	30
120	-	50c. sepia and brown	30	30
121	27	75c. brown and black	30	30
122	-	1l. brown and purple	30	30
123	-	1l.50 brown and red	30	30
124	-	2l. brown and green	30	30
125	-	2l.50 brown and blue	30	30
126	-	3l. brown and red	30	30
127	-	4l. brown and bistre	35	30
128	-	5l. brown and blue	60	30
129	-	10l. brown and red	1·20	35

DESIGNS: 5c. Trent Cathedral; 25c. St. Angela Merici; 50c. St. Anthony Maria Zaccaria; 1l. St. Cajetan of Thiene; 1l.50, St. John Fisher, Bishop of Rochester; 2l. Cristoforo Madrussi, Bishop of Trent; 2l.50, Reginald Pole, Archbishop of Canterbury; 3l. Marcello Cervini; 4l. Giovanni Maria Del Monte; 5l. Emperor Charles V; 10l. Pope Paul III Farnese.

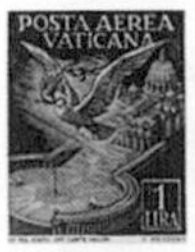

28 Dove with Olive Branch over St. Peter's Forecourt

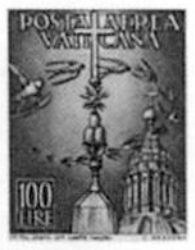

29 Barn Swallows circling Spire of St. Peter's Basilica

1947. Air.

130	28	1l. red	30	30
131	-	4l. brown	30	30
132	28	5l. blue	60	30
133	29	15l. violet	1·90	1·70
134	-	25l. green	8·00	3·50
135	29	50l. black	10·00	7·00
136	29	100l. orange	43·00	13·00

DESIGN—As Type **28**: 4l., 25l. Transportation of the Holy House.

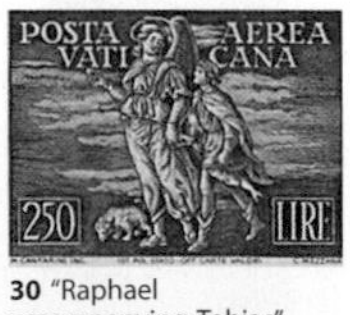

30 "Raphael accompanying Tobias" (after Botticelli)

1948. Air.

137	30	250l. black	70·00	6·25
138	30	500l. blue	£1000	£700

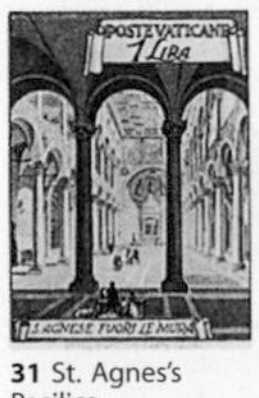

31 St. Agnes's Basilica

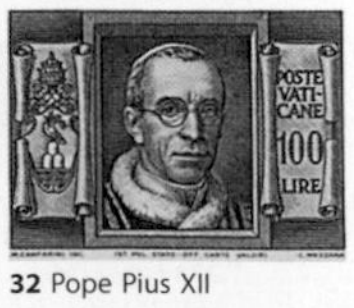

32 Pope Pius XII

1949

139A	31	1l. brown	25	25
140A	-	3l. violet	25	25
141A	-	5l. orange	25	25
142A	-	8l. green	1·00	30
143A	-	13l. green	7·50	5·50
144A	-	16l. grey	60	60

145A	-	25l. red	20·00	1·60
146A	-	35l. mauve	55·00	27·00
147B	-	40l. blue	95	30
148A	32	100l. black	10·00	6·50

DESIGNS (Basilicas)—VERT: 3l. St. Clement; 5l. St. Praxedes; 8l. St. Mary in Cosmedin. HORIZ: 13l. Holy Cross; 16l. St. Sebastian; 25l. St. Laurence's; 35l. St. Paul's; 40l. Sta. Maria Maggiore.

33 Angels over Globe

1949. Air. 75th Anniv of U.P.U.

149	33	300l. blue	43·00	19·00
150	33	1000l. green	£200	£150

34 "I Will Give You the Keys of the Kingdom"

1949. "Holy Year".

151	34	5l. brown and light brown	20	20
152	-	6l. brown and black	20	20
153	-	8l. green and blue	1·50	85
154	-	10l. blue and green	35	25
155	34	20l. brown and green	2·50	60
156	-	25l. blue and brown	1·60	60
157	-	30l. purple and green	3·75	2·10
158	-	60l. red and brown	2·40	1·90

DESIGNS: 6, 25l. Four Basilicas; 8, 30l. Pope Boniface VIII; 10, 60l. Pope Pius XII opening the Holy Door.

35 Guards Marching

1950. Centenary of Papal Guard.

159	35	25l. brown	10·00	6·75
160	35	35l. green	5·00	5·00
161	35	55l. brown	3·00	5·50

36 Pope Proclaiming Dogma

1951. Proclamation of Dogma of the Assumption.

162	36	25l. purple	18·00	2·50
163	36	55l. blue	8·75	18·00

DESIGN: 55l. Angels over St. Peter's.

37 Pope Pius X

1951. Beatification of Pope Pius X.

164	37	6l. gold and violet	60	60
165	37	10l. gold and green	2·50	60
166	-	60l. gold and blue	17·00	10·00
167	-	115l. gold and brown	41·00	32·00

DESIGN: 60, 115l. Pope looking left.

38 Final Session of Council (fresco)

1951. 1500th Anniv of Council of Chalcedon.

168	38	5l. grey	60	60
169	-	25l. red	6·25	3·75
170	38	35l. red	19·00	8·00
171	-	60l. blue	40·00	21·00
172	38	100l. brown	90·00	55·00

DESIGN: 25, 60l. "Pope Leo I meeting Attila" (Raphael).

39 Gratian

1951. Air. 800th Anniv of Decree of Gratian.

173	39	300l. purple	£475	£300
174	39	500l. blue	75·00	37·00

1952. No. 143 surch **L. 12** and bars.

175		12l. on 13l. green	3·25	2·20

41 Mail Coach and First Stamp

1952. Centenary of First Papal States' Stamp.

176	41	50l. black & blue on cream	6·75	6·25
MS176a		112×121 mm. No. 176 (block of four)	£450	£275

42 St. Maria Goretti

1953. 50th Anniv of Martyrdom of St. Maria Goretti.

177	42	15l. violet and brown	6·75	4·25
178	42	25l. brown and red	3·75	4·25

43 St. Peter and Inscription

1953. St. Peter's Basilica. Medallions in black.

179	43	3l. red	20	20
180	-	5l. grey	20	20
181	-	10l. green	20	20
182	-	12l. brown	20	20
183	-	20l. violet	25	20
184	-	25l. brown	25	20
185	-	35l. red	25	20
186	-	45l. brown	25	30
187	-	60l. blue	25	25
188	-	65l. red	60	30
189	-	100l. purple	45	25

DESIGNS: 5l. Pius XII and Roman sepulchre; 10l. St. Peter's tomb; 12l. St. Sylvester I and Constantine's basilica (previous building); 20l. Julius II and Bramante's design; 25l. Paul III and apse; 35l. Sixtus V and cupola; 45l. Paul V and facade; 60l. Urban VIII and baldaquin; 65l. Alexander VII and colonnade; 100l. Pius VI and sacristy.

44 Dome of St. Peter's

1953. Air.

190	44	500l. brown & deep brown	43·00	13·50
190a	44	500l. green and turquoise	11·00	8·75
191	44	1000l. blue and deep blue	£150	35·00
191a	44	1000l. red and lake	1·20	1·20

45 St. Clare of Assisi (after Giotto)

1953. 700th Death Anniv of St. Clare (founder of Poor Clares Order).

192	45	25l. dp brown, brown & bl	5·00	2·50
193	45	35l. brown, lt brown & red	27·00	24·00

46 "St. Bernard" (after Lippi)

1953. 800th Death Anniv of St. Bernard of Clairvaux.

194	46	20l. purple and green	1·20	1·20
195	46	60l. green and blue	12·50	10·00

47 Lombard's Episcopal Seal

1953. 800th Anniv of "Libri Sententiarum" (theological treatise by Peter Lombard, Bishop of Paris).

196	47	100l. yellow, blue and red	75·00	50·00

48 Pope Pius XI and Vatican City

1954. 25th Anniv of Lateran Treaty.

197	48	25l. red, brown and blue	1·90	1·20
198	48	60l. blue, grey and brown	5·50	5·00

49 Pope Pius XII

1954. Marian Year and Centenary of Dogma of the Immaculate Conception.

199	-	3l. violet	20	20
200	49	4l. red	20	20
201	-	6l. red	20	20
202	49	12l. green	2·10	1·90
203	-	20l. brown	1·40	1·10
204	49	35l. blue	3·00	2·75

DESIGN: 3, 6, 20l. Pope Pius IX facing right with different inscr and dates "1854–1954".

50 St. Pius X

1954. Canonization of Pope Pius X.

205	50	10l. yellow, red and brown	60	30
206	50	25l. yellow, red and violet	3·75	3·00
207	50	35l. yellow, red and black	7·50	6·25

51 Basilica of St. Francis of Assisi

1954. Bicentenary of Elevation of Basilica of St. Francis of Assisi to Papal Chapel.

208	51	20l. black and cream	2·75	2·20
209	51	35l. brown and cream	2·10	2·50

52 "St. Augustine" (after Botticelli)

1954. 1600th Birth Anniv of St. Augustine.

210	52	35l. green	1·40	1·10
211	52	50l. brown	2·75	2·50

53 Madonna of Ostra Brama, Vilna

1954. Termination of Marian Year.

212	53	20l. multicoloured	3·75	1·20
213	53	35l. multicoloured	15·00	11·00
214	53	60l. multicoloured	25·00	22·00

54 St. Boniface and Fulda Cathedral

1955. 1200th Anniv of Martyrdom of St. Boniface.

215	54	10l. green	25	10
216	54	35l. violet	85	60
217	54	60l. green	1·50	1·20

55 "Pope Sixtus II and St. Lawrence" (fresco, Niccolina Chapel)

1955. 500th Death Anniv of Fra Giovanni da Fiesole, "Fra Angelico" (painter).

218	55	50l. red and blue	6·25	4·25
219	55	100l. blue and flesh	3·75	3·75

56 Pope Nicholas V

1955. Fifth Death Centenary of Pope Nicholas V.

220	56	20l. brown and blue	25	20
221	56	35l. brown and pink	60	35
222	56	60l. brown and green	1·20	75

57 St. Bartholomew

1955. 900th Death Anniv of St. Bartholomew the Young.

223	57	10l. black and brown	25	10
224	57	25l. black and red	75	60
225	57	100l. black and green	2·75	2·50

58 "Annunciation"
(Melozzo da Forli)

1956. Air.

226	58	5l. black	20	10
227	A	10l. green	20	10
228	B	15l. orange	25	20
229	58	25l. red	25	20
230	A	35l. red	75	60
231	B	50l. brown	50	25
232	58	60l. blue	6·75	4·25
233	A	100l. brown	35	30
234	B	300l. violet	1·20	85

PAINTINGS: A, "Annunciation" (P. Cavallini); B, "Annunciation" (Leonardo da Vinci).

59 Corporal of the Guard

1956. 450th Anniv of Swiss Guard. Inscr 'GUARDIA SVIZZERA PONTIFICIA'.

235	-	4l. red	20	10
236	59	6l. orange	20	10
237	-	10l. blue	20	10
238	-	35l. brown	75	45
239	59	50l. violet	1·40	1·10
240	-	60l. green	1·90	1·60

DESIGNS: 4, 35l. Captain Roust; 10, 60l. Two drummers.

60 St. Rita

1956. Fifth Death Centenary of St. Rita at Cascia.

241	60	10l. grey	25	20
242	60	25l. brown	85	75
243	60	35l. blue	50	35

61 St. Ignatius presenting Jesuit Constitution to Pope Paul III

1956. Fourth Death Centenary of St. Ignatius of Loyola.

244	61	35l. brown	60	55
245	61	60l. grey	1·20	1·00

62 St. John of Capistrano

1956. Fifth Death Centenary of St. John of Capistrano.

246	62	25l. green and black	2·75	2·40
247	62	35l. brown and purple	1·20	95

63 Madonna and Child

1956. "Black Madonna" of Czestochowa Commemoration.

248	63	35l. black and blue	50	35
249	63	60l. blue and green	60	55
250	63	100l. purple and brown	1·20	1·10

64 St. Domenico Savio

1957. Death Centenary of St. Domenico Savio.

251	64	4l. brown	20	10
252	-	6l. red	25	20
253	64	25l. green	50	35
254	-	60l. blue	1·20	95

DESIGN: 6, 60l. St. Domenico Savio and St. John Bosco.

65 Cardinal D. Capranica (founder) and Capranica College

1957. Fifth Centenary of Capranica College.

255	65	5l. red	25	20
256	-	10l. brown	25	20
257	65	35l. grey	25	20
258	-	100l. blue	75	60

DESIGNS: 10, 100l. Pope Pius XII and plaque.

66 Pontifical Academy of Science

1957. 20th Anniv of the Pontifical Academy of Science.

259	66	35l. green and blue	65	65
260	66	60l. blue and brown	1·10	1·10

67 Mariazell Basilica

1957. Eighth Centenary of Mariazell Basilica.

261	67	5l. green	35	25
262	-	15l. black	45	40
263	67	60l. blue	1·50	1·30
264	-	100l. violet	2·10	2·00

DESIGN: 15, 100l. Statue of the Virgin of Mariazell within Sanctuary.

68 Apparition of the Virgin Mary

1958. Centenary of Apparition of the Virgin Mary at Lourdes.

265	68	5l. blue	25	20
266	-	10l. green	25	20
267	-	15l. brown	25	20
268	68	25l. red	25	20
269	-	35l. brown	25	20
270	-	100l. violet	25	20

DESIGNS: 10, 35l. Invalid at Lourdes; 15, 100l. St. Bernadette.

69 "Civitas Dei" ("City of God" at Exhibition)

1958. Brussels International Exhibition.

271		35l. purple	40	25
272	69	60l. red	1·10	95
273	69	100l. violet	4·00	3·25
274	-	300l. blue	2·00	1·70

70 Pope Clement XIII (from sculpture by A. Canova)

MS274a 91×149 mm. Nos. 271/4   55·00   55·00
DESIGN: 35, 300l. Pope Pius XII.

1958. Birth Bicentenary of Antonio Canova (sculptor).

275	70	5l. brown	25	20
276	-	10l. red	35	25
277	-	35l. green	40	35
278	-	100l. blue	80	75

SCULPTURES: 10l. Pope Clement XIV; 35l. Pope Pius VI; 100l. Pope Pius VII.

71 St. Peter's Keys

1958. "Vacant See".

279	71	15l. brown on yellow	2·75	2·40
280	71	25l. brown	55	35
281	71	60l. brown on lilac	55	35

72 Pope John XXIII

1959. Coronation of Pope John XXIII. Inscr "IV-XI MCMLVIII".

282	72	25l. multicoloured	25	20
283	-	35l. multicoloured	25	20
284	72	60l. multicoloured	25	20
285	-	100l. multicoloured	35	25

DESIGN: 35, 100l. Arms of Pope John XXIII.

73 St. Lawrence

1959. 1700th Death Annivs (15 to 100l. in 1958) of Martyrs under Valerian.

286	73	15l. brown, yellow and red	20	20
287	-	25l. brown, yellow and lilac	30	20
288	-	50l. multicoloured	40	25
289	-	60l. brown, yellow & green	40	40
290	-	100l. brown, yellow & pur	50	45
291	-	300l. sepia and brown	65	60

PORTRAITS: 25l. Pope Sixtus II; 50l. St. Agapitus; 60l. St. Filisissimus; 100l. St. Cyprian; 300l. St. Fructuosus.

74 Pope Pius XI

1959. 30th Anniv of Lateran Treaty.

292	74	30l. brown	30	20
293	74	100l. blue	40	35

75 Radio Mast

1959. Second Anniv of St. Maria di Galeria Radio Station Vatican City.

294	75	25l. pink, yellow and black	30	20
295	75	60l. yellow, red and blue	40	35

76 Obelisk and St. John Lateran Basilica

1959. Air. Roman Obelisks.

296	76	5l. violet	20	15
297	-	10l. green	20	15
298	-	15l. brown	20	15
299	-	25l. green	20	15
300	-	35l. blue	20	15
301	76	50l. green	20	15
302	-	60l. red	20	15
303	-	100l. blue	20	15
304	-	200l. brown	55	35
305	-	500l. brown	1·00	65

DESIGNS: 10, 50l. Obelisk and Church of Sta. Maria Maggiore; 15, 100l. Vatican Obelisk and Apostolic Palace; 25, 200l. Obelisk and Churches of St. Mary in Montesanto and St. Mary of the Miracles, Piazza del Popolo; 35, 500l. Sallustian Obelisk and Trinita dei Monti Church.

77 St. Casimir, Vilna Palace and Cathedral

1959. 500th Birth Anniv of St. Casimir (patron saint of Lithuania).

306	77	50l. brown	30	20
307	77	100l. green	35	25

78 "Christ Adored by the Magi" (after Raphael)

1959. Christmas.

308	78	15l. black	20	15
309	78	25l. red	30	20
310	78	60l. blue	40	25

79 "St. Antoninus" (after Dupre)

1960. 500th Death Anniv of St. Antoninus of Florence.

311	79	15l. blue	15	15
312	-	25l. green	20	20
313	79	60l. brown	55	40
314	-	110l. purple	1·10	85

DESIGN: 25, 110l. "St. Antoninus preaching sermon" (after Portigiani).

80 Transept of St. John Lateran Basilica

1960. Roman Diocesan Synod.

315	80	15l. brown	30	20
316	80	60l. black	40	25

81 "The Flight Into Egypt" (after Beato Angelico)

1960. World Refugee Year.

317	81	5l. green	15	15
318	-	10l. brown	20	15
319	-	25l. red	30	20
320	81	60l. violet	35	25
321	-	100l. blue	3·25	2·75
322	-	300l. green	1·80	1·30

DESIGNS: 10, 100l. "St. Peter giving Alms" (Masaccio); 25, 300l. "Madonna of Mercy" (Piero della Francesca).

82 Cardinal Sarto (Pius X) leaving Venice for Conclave in Rome

1960. First Anniv of Transfer of Relics of Pope Pius X from Rome to Venice.

323	82	15l. brown	40	25
324	-	35l. red	4·25	2·75
325	-	60l. green	2·10	1·70

DESIGNS: 35l. Pope John XXIII kneeling before relics of Pope Pius X; 60l. Relics in procession across St. Mark's Square, Venice.

83 "Feeding the Hungry"

1960. "Corporal Works of Mercy". Della Robbia paintings. Centres in brown.

326	83	5l. brown	20	15
327	-	10l. green	20	15
328	-	15l. black	20	15
329	-	20l. red	20	15
330	-	30l. violet	20	15
331	-	35l. brown	20	15
332	-	40l. orange	20	15
333	-	70l. stone	20	15

DESIGNS: 10l. "Giving drinks to the thirsty"; 15l. "Clothing the naked"; 20l. "Sheltering the homeless"; 30l. "Visiting the sick"; 35l. "Visiting the imprisoned"; 40l. "Burying the dead"; 70l. Pope John XXIII between "Faith" and "Charity".

84 "The Nativity" after Gerard Honthorst (Gherardo delle Notte)

1960. Christmas.

334	84	10l. black and green	20	15
335	84	15l. deep brown and brown	30	15
336	84	70l. blue and turquoise	35	25

85 St. Vincent de Paul

1960. Death Tercentenaries of St. Vincent de Paul and St. Louise de Marillac.

337	85	40l. violet	30	20
338	-	70l. black	50	35
339	-	100l. brown	1·30	95

DESIGNS: 70l. St. Louise de Marillac; 100l. St. Vincent giving child to care of St. Louise.

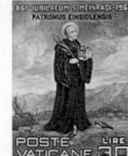

86 St. Meinrad

1961. 11th Death Centenary of St. Meinrad.

340	86	30l. black	70	55
341	-	40l. lilac	2·30	95
342	-	100l. brown	2·75	2·40

DESIGNS—VERT: 40l. The "Black Madonna", Einsiedeln Abbey. HORIZ: 100l. Einsiedeln Abbey, Switzerland.

87 "Pope Leo I meeting Attila" (Algardi)

1961. 15th Death Centenary of Pope Leo I.

343	87	15l. red	30	20
344	87	70l. green	1·10	65
345	87	300l. brown	3·00	2·50

88 Route of St. Paul's Journey to Rome

1961. 1900th Anniv of St. Paul's Arrival in Rome.

346	88	10l. green	20	15
347	-	15l. black and brown	20	15
348	-	20l. black and red	30	20
349	88	30l. blue	40	35
350	-	75l. black and brown	1·10	60
351	-	200l. black and blue	2·50	2·10

DESIGNS: 15, 75l. St. Paul's arrival in Rome (after sculpture by Maraini); 20, 200l. Basilica of St. Paul-outside-the-Walls, Rome.

89 "l'Osservatore Romano", 1861 and 1961

1961. Centenary of "L'Osservatore Romano" (Vatican newspaper).

352	89	40l. black and brown	30	20
353	-	70l. black and blue	1·00	75
354	-	250l. black and yellow	3·50	2·75

DESIGNS: 70l. "L'Osservatore Romano" offices; 250l. Printing machine.

90 St. Patrick (ancient sculpture)

1961. 15th Death Centenary of St. Patrick.

355	90	10l. green and buff	20	15
356	-	15l. brown and blue	20	15
357	90	40l. green and yellow	20	15
358	-	150l. brown and blue	85	75

DESIGN: 15, 150l. St. Patrick's Sanctuary, Lough Derg.

91 Arms of Roncalli Family

1961. Pope John XXIII's 80th Birthday.

359	91	10l. brown and black	20	15
360	-	25l. green and brown	30	20
361	-	30l. violet and blue	30	20
362	-	40l. blue and violet	30	20

363	-	70l. brown and grey	35	25
364	-	115l. black and brown	85	65

DESIGNS: 25l. Church of St. Mary, Sotto il Monte; 30l. Church of St. Mary, Monte Santo; 40l. Church of Saints Ambrose and Charles, Rome; 70l. St. Peter's Chair, Vatican Basilica; 115l. Pope John XXIII.

92 "The Nativity"

1961. Christmas. Centres multicoloured.

365	92	15l. green	20	15
366	92	40l. black	25	20
367	92	70l. purple	30	25

93 "Annunciation" (after F. Valle)

1962. Air.

368	93	1000l. brown	2·10	1·70
369	93	1500l. blue	2·75	2·10

94 "Land Reclamation" Medal of 1588

1962. Malaria Eradication.

370	94	15l. violet	15	15
371	-	40l. red	25	20
372	94	70l. brown	30	25
373	-	300l. green	70	55

DESIGN: 40, 300l. Map of Pontine Marshes reclamation project (at time of Pope Pius VI).

95 "The Good Shepherd" (statue, Lateran Museum)

1962. Religious Vocations.

374	95	10l. black and violet	15	15
375	-	15l. brown and blue	20	15
376	95	70l. black and green	40	35
377	-	115l. brown and red	3·00	2·10
378	95	200l. black and brown	1·70	1·30

DESIGN: 15, 115l. Wheatfield ready for harvest.

96 St. Catherine (after Il Sodoma (Bazzi))

1962. Fifth Centenary of St. Catherine of Siena's Canonization.

379	96	15l. brown	30	15
380	96	60l. violet	40	25
381	96	100l. blue	90	80

97 Paulina M. Jaricot

1962. Death Centenary of Paulina M. Jaricot (founder of Society for the Propagation of the Faith). Multicoloured centres.

382	97	10l. lilac	20	15
383	97	50l. green	30	20
384	97	150l. grey	70	60

98 St. Peter and St. Paul (from graffito on child's tomb)

1962. Sixth International Christian Archaeology Congress, Ravenna.

385	98	20l. brown and violet	15	15
386	-	40l. green and brown	20	15
387	98	70l. brown and turquoise	30	25
388	-	100l. green and red	35	35

DESIGN: 40, 100l. "The Passion" (from bas relief on tomb in Domitilla cemetery, near Rome).

99 "Faith" (after Raphael)

1962. Ecumenical Council.

389	99	10l. brown and green	20	15
390	-	...	...	...
391	-	15l. brown and red	20	15
392	-	25l. grey and red	20	15
393	-	30l. black and mauve	20	15
394	-	40l. brown and red	30	15
395	-	60l. brown and green	20	15
396	-	115l. red	35	25

DESIGNS—Divine Virtues: 10l. "Hope"; 15l. "Charity" (both after Raphael); 25l. Arms of Pope John XXIII and symbols of Evangelists (frontispiece of "Humanae Salutis" by Arrigo Bravi); 30l. Central Nave, St. Peter's (council venue); 40l. Pope John XXIII; 60l. "St. Peter" (bronze in Vatican Basilica); 115l. The Holy Ghost in form of dove.

100 "The Nativity"

1962. Christmas. Centres multicoloured.

397	100	10l. grey	15	15
398	100	15l. drab	20	15
399	100	90l. green	30	20

101 "Miracle of the Loaves and Fishes" (after Murillo)

1963. Freedom from Hunger.

400	101	15l. sepia and brown	15	15
401	-	40l. green and red	15	15
402	101	100l. brown and blue	20	15
403	-	200l. green and turquoise	30	20

DESIGN: 40, 200l. "Miracle of the Fishes" (after Raphael).

102 Pope John XXIII

1963. Award of Balzan Peace Prize to Pope John XXIII.

404	**102**	15l. brown	30	20
405	**102**	160l. black	40	35

103 St. Peter's Keys

1963. "Vacant See".

406	**103**	10l. brown	15	15
407	**103**	40l. brown on yellow	20	15
408	**103**	100l. brown on violet	30	20

104 Pope Paul VI

1963. Coronation of Pope Paul VI.

409	**104**	15l. black	15	15
410	-	40l. red	15	15
411	**104**	115l. brown	20	15
412	-	200l. grey	50	40

DESIGN: 40, 200l. Arms of Pope Paul VI.

105 "The Nativity" (African terracotta statuette)

1963. Christmas.

413	**105**	10l. brown and light brown	15	15
414	**105**	40l. brown and blue	15	15
415	**105**	100l. brown and green	20	15

106 St. Cyril

1963. 1100th Anniv of Conversion of Slavs by Saints Cyril and Methodius.

416	**106**	30l. purple	20	15
417	**106**	70l. brown	20	15
418	-	150l. purple	35	25

DESIGNS: 70l. Map of Moravia; 150l. St. Methodius.

107 Pope Paul VI

1964. Pope Paul's Visit to the Holy Land.

419	**107**	15l. black	15	15
420	-	25l. red	15	15
421	-	70l. sepia	20	15
422	-	160l. blue	30	20

DESIGNS: 25l. Church of the Nativity, Bethlehem; 70l. Church of the Holy Sepulchre, Jerusalem; 160l. Well of the Virgin Mary, Nazareth.

108 St. Peter, Pharaoh's Tomb, Wadi-es-Sebua

1964. Nubian Monuments Preservation.

423	**108**	10l. brown and blue	15	15
424	-	20l. multicoloured	15	15
425	**108**	70l. brown and light brown	20	15
426	-	200l. multicoloured	30	20

DESIGN: 20, 200l. Philae Temple.

109 Pope Paul VI

1964. Vatican City's Participation in New York World's Fair.

427	**109**	15l. blue	15	15
428	-	50l. brown	15	15
429	**109**	100l. blue	20	15
430	-	250l. brown	30	25

DESIGNS: 50l. Michelangelo's "Pieta"; 250l. Detail of Madonna's head from "Pieta".

110 Michelangelo

1964. 400th Death Anniv of Michelangelo. Paintings in the Sistine Chapel.

431	**110**	10l. black	15	15
432	-	25l. purple	15	15
433	-	30l. green	15	15
434	-	40l. violet	15	15
435	-	150l. green	30	20

PAINTINGS: 25l. Prophet Isaiah; 30l. Delphic Sibyl; 40l. Prophet Jeremiah; 150l. Prophet Joel.

111 "The Good Samaritan" (after Emilio Greco)

1964. Red Cross Centenary (1963). Cross in red.

436	**111**	10l. brown	20	15
437	**111**	30l. blue	20	15
438	**111**	300l. brown	35	25

112 "Christmas Scene" (after Kimiko Koseki)

1964. Christmas.

439	**112**	10l. multicoloured	20	15
440	**112**	15l. multicoloured	20	15
441	**112**	135l. multicoloured	30	20

113 Cues's Birthplace

1964. 500th Death Anniv of Nicholas Cues (Cardinal Cusanus).

442	**113**	40l. green	20	15
443	-	200l. red	30	25

DESIGN: 200l. Cardinal Cusanus's sepulchre, St. Peter's (relief by A. Bregno).

114 Pope Paul at prayer

1964. Pope Paul's Visit to India.

444	**114**	15l. purple	15	15
445	-	25l. green	15	15
446	-	60l. brown	20	15
447	-	200l. purple	30	25

DESIGN—HORIZ: 25l. Public altar, "The Oval", Bombay; 60l. "Gateway to India", Bombay. VERT: 200l. Pope Paul walking across map of India.

115 Sts. Mbaga Tuzinde, Carolus Lwanga and Kizito

1965. Ugandan Martyrs.

448		15l. turquoise	15	15
449	**115**	20l. brown	15	15
450	-	30l. blue	15	15
451	-	75l. black	15	15
452	-	100l. red	20	15
453	-	160l. violet	30	25

DESIGNS: 15l. St. Joseph Mukasa and six other martyrs; 30l. Sts. Matthias Mulumba, Noe Mawagalli and Lucas Banabakintu; 75l. Sts. Gonzaga Gonza, Athanasius Bazzekuketta, Pontianus Ngondwe and Bruno Serunkuma; 100l. Sts. Anatolius Kiriggwajjo, Andreas Kaggwa and Adulphus Mukasa; 160l. Sts. Mukasa Kiriwananvu and Gyavira.

116 Dante (after Raphael)

1965. 700th Anniv of Dante's Birth.

454	**116**	10l. brown and light brown	15	15
455	-	40l. brown and red	15	15
456	-	70l. brown and green	15	15
457	-	200l. brown and blue	30	25

DESIGNS—After drawings by Botticelli: 40l. "Inferno"; 70l. "Purgatory"; 200l. "Paradise".

117 St. Benedict (after Perugino)

1965. Declaration of St. Benedict as Patron Saint of Europe.

458	**117**	40l. brown	20	15
459	-	300l. green	55	55

DESIGN: 300l. Montecassino Abbey.

118 Pope Paul

1965. Pope Paul's Visit to the U.N., New York.

460	**118**	20l. brown	15	15
461	-	30l. blue	15	15
462	-	150l. green	30	20
463	**118**	300l. purple	40	35

DESIGN: 30, 150l. U.N.O. Headquarters, New York.

119 "The Nativity" (Peruvian setting)

1965. Christmas.

464	**119**	20l. red	15	15
465	**119**	40l. brown	15	15
466	**119**	200l. green	30	25

120 Pope Paul

1966

467	**120**	5l. brown	15	15
468	-	10l. violet	15	15
469	-	15l. brown	15	15
470	-	20l. green	15	15
471	-	30l. brown	15	15
472	-	40l. turquoise	15	15
473	-	55l. blue	15	15
474	-	75l. purple	15	15
475	-	90l. mauve	15	15
476	-	130l. green	30	20

DESIGNS (SCULPTURES): 10l. "Music"; 15l. "Science"; 20l. "Painting"; 30l. "Sculpture"; 40l. "Building"; 55l. "Carpentry"; 75l. "Agriculture"; 90l. "Metallurgy"; 130l. "Learning".

121 Queen Dabrowka and King Mieszko I

1966. Poland's Christian Millennium.

477	**121**	15l. black	15	15
478	-	25l. violet	15	15
479	-	40l. red	15	15
480	-	50l. red	15	15
481	-	150l. grey	20	15
482	-	220l. brown	30	25

DESIGNS: 25l. St. Adalbert (Wojciech) and Wroclaw and Gniezno Cathedrals; 40l. St. Stanislas, Skalka Cathedral and Wawel Royal Palace, Cracow; 50l. Queen Jadwiga (Hedwig); Ostra Brama Gate with Mater Misericordiae, Wilno, and Jagellon University Library, Cracow; 150l. "Black Madonna", Jasna Gora Monastery (Czestochowa) and St. John's Cathedral, Warsaw; 220l. Pope Paul VI greeting Poles.

122 Pope John XXIII and St. Peter's, Rome

1966. Fourth Anniv of Opening of Ecumenical Council.

483	**122**	10l. black and red	15	10
484	-	15l. green and brown	15	15
485	-	55l. mauve and brown	15	15
486	-	90l. black and green	15	15
487	-	100l. yellow and green	20	15
488	-	130l. sepia and brown	30	25

DESIGNS: 15l. Book of Prayer, St. Peter's; 55l. Mass; 90l. Pope Paul with Patriarch Athenagoras; 100l. Episcopal ring; 130l. Pope Paul at closing ceremony (12.10.65).

123 "The Nativity" (after sculpture by Scorzelli)

1966. Christmas.

489	**123**	20l. purple	15	15
490	**123**	55l. green	15	15
491	**123**	225l. brown	30	25

124 Jetliner over St. Peter's

1967. Air.

492	**124**	20l. violet	15	15
493	-	40l. lilac and pink	15	15
494	-	90l. blue and grey	15	15
495	**124**	100l. black and red	20	15
496	-	200l. lilac and grey	35	25
497	-	500l. brown & light brown	70	55

DESIGNS: 40, 200l. Radio mast and St. Gabriel's statue; 90, 500l. Aerial view of St. Peter's.

125 St. Peter

1967. 1900th Anniv of Martyrdom of Saints Peter and Paul. Multicoloured.

498		15l. Type **125**	15	15
499		20l. St. Paul	15	15
500		55l. The two Saints	15	15
501		90l. Bernini's baldachin, St. Peter's	20	15
502		220l. Arnolfo di Cambio's tabernacle, St. Paul's Basilica	30	25

126 "The Three Shepherd Children" (sculpture)

1967. 50th Anniv of Fatima Apparitions. Multicoloured.

503		30l. Type **126**	15	15
504		50l. Basilica of Fatima	15	15
505		200l. Pope Paul VI praying before Virgin's statue at Fatima	30	25

127 Congress Emblem

1967. Third World Apostolic Laity Congress, Rome.

506	**127**	40l. red	20	20
507	**127**	130l. blue	35	25

128 "The Nativity" (Byzantine carving)

1967. Christmas.

508	**128**	25l. multicoloured	15	15
509	**128**	55l. multicoloured	15	15
510	**128**	180l. multicoloured	30	25

129 "Angel Gabriel" (detail from "The Annunciation" by Fra Angelico)

130 Pope Paul VI

1968. Air.

511	**129**	1000l. red on cream	2·10	1·60
512	**129**	1500l. black on cream	2·50	2·30

1968. Pope Paul's Visit to Colombia.

513	**130**	25l. brown and black	15	15
514	-	55l. brown, grey and black	15	15
515	-	220l. brown, blue & black	35	25

DESIGNS: 55l. Monstrance (Raphael's "Disputa"); 220l. Map of South America.

131 "The Holy Child of Prague"

1968. Christmas.

516	**131**	25l. purple and red	15	15
517	**131**	50l. violet and lilac	15	15
518	**131**	250l. blue and light blue	40	40

132 "The Resurrection" (Fra Angelico)

1969. Easter.

519	**132**	20l. red and buff	15	15
520	**132**	90l. green and buff	15	15
521	**132**	180l. blue and buff	30	20

133 Colonnade

1969. Europa.

522	**133**	50l. brown and grey	20	20
523	**133**	90l. brown and red	30	20
524	**133**	130l. brown and green	40	35

134 Pope with Young Africans

1969. Pope Paul's Visit to Uganda.

525	**134**	25l. brown and ochre	15	15
526	-	55l. brown and red	15	15
527	-	250l. multicoloured	30	25

DESIGNS: 55l. Pope with African bishops; 250l. Map of Africa and olive branch.

135 Pope Pius IX

1969. Centenary of St. Peter's Circle Society.

528	**135**	30l. brown	15	15
529	-	50l. grey	15	15
530	-	220l. purple	30	25

DESIGNS: 50l. Monogram of Society; 220l. Pope Paul VI.

136 "Expo 70" Emblem

1970. "Expo 70" World's Fair, Osaka. Multicoloured.

531		25l. Type **136**	15	15
532		40l. Osaka Castle	15	15
533		55l. "Madonna and Child" (Domoto)	15	15
534		90l. Vatican pavilion	20	15
535		110l. Mt. Fuji	30	20

137 Commemorative Medal of Pius IX

1970. Centenary of First Vatican Council.

536	**137**	20l. brown and orange	15	15
537	-	50l. multicoloured	15	15
538	-	180l. purple and red	30	25

DESIGNS: 50l. Arms of Pius IX; 180l. Council souvenir medal.

138 "Christ" (Simone Martini)

1970. 50th Anniv of Pope Paul's Ordination as Priest. Multicoloured.

539		15l. Type **138**	15	15
540		25l. "Christ" (R. v. d. Weyden)	15	15
541		50l. "Christ" (Durer)	15	15
542		90l. "Christ" (El Greco)	15	15
543		100l. Pope Paul VI	30	25

139 "Adam" (Michelangelo)

1970. 25th Anniv of United Nations.

544		20l. Type **139**	15	15
545		90l. "Eve" (Michelangelo)	15	15
546		220l. Olive branch	30	25

140 Pope Paul VI

1970. Pope Paul's Visit to Asia and Oceania. Multicoloured.

547		25l. Type **140**	15	15
548		55l. "Holy Child of Cebu" (Philippines)	15	15
549		100l. "Madonna and Child", Darwin Cathedral (G. Hamori)	20	15
550		130l. Manila Cathedral	30	25
551		220l. Sydney Cathedral	35	35

141 "Angel with Lectern"

1971. Racial Equality Year. Multicoloured.

552		20l. Type **141**	15	15
553		40l. "Christ Crucified, and Doves"	15	15
554		50l. Type **141**	15	15
555		130l. As 40l.	30	20

142 "Madonna and Child" (F. Gnissi)

1971. Easter. Religious Paintings. Multicoloured.

556		25l. Type **142**	15	15
557		40l. "Madonna and Child" ("Sassetta", S. di Giovanni)	15	15
558		55l. "Madonna and Child" (C. Crivelli)	15	15
559		90l. "Madonna and Child" (C. Maratta)	15	15
560		180l. "The Holy Family" (G. Ceracchini)	30	25

143 "St. Dominic Guzman" (Sienese School)

1971. 800th Birth Anniv of St. Dominic Guzman (founder of Preaching Friars Order). Mult.

561		25l. Type **143**	15	15
562		55l. Portrait by Fra Angelico	15	15
563		90l. Portrait by Titian	20	15
564		180l. Portrait by El Greco	30	25

144 "St. Matthew"

1971. Air.

565	**144**	200l. black and green	30	25
566	-	300l. black and brown	50	40
567	-	500l. black and pink	90	65
568	-	1000l. black and mauve	1·70	1·30

DESIGNS—"The Four Evangelists" (ceiling frescoes by Fra Angelico in the Niccolina Chapel, Vatican City): 300l. "St. Mark"; 500l. "St. Luke"; 1000l. "St. John".

145 "St. Stephen" (from chasuble, Szekesfehervar Church, Hungary)

1971. Millennium of St. Stephen, King of Hungary.

569	**145**	50l. multicoloured	15	15
570	-	180l. black and yellow	30	20

DESIGN: 180l. "Madonna, Patroness of Hungary", (sculpture, circa 1511).

146 Bramante's Design for Cupola, St. Peter's

1972. Bramante Celebrations.

571	**146**	25l. black and yellow	15	15
572	-	90l. black and yellow	20	15
573	-	130l. black and yellow	30	25

DESIGNS: 90l. Donato Bramante (architect) from medal; 130l. Spiral staircase, Innocent VIII's Belvedere, Vatican.

147 "St. Mark at Sea" (mosaic)

1972. UNESCO "Save Venice" Campaign. Multicoloured.
574	25l. Type **147**		35	35
575	50l. Venice (top left-hand section)		25	20
576	50l. Venice (top right-hand section)		25	20
577	50l. Venice (bottom left-hand section)		25	20
578	50l. Venice (bottom right-hand section)		25	20
579	180l. St. Mark's Basilica		90	85
MS580	113×161 mm. Nos. 574/9		3·25	3·00

Nos. 575/8 are smaller 39×28 mm and were issued together, *se-tenant*, forming a composite design of a 1581 fresco showing a panoramic map of Venice.

148 Gospel of St. Mark (from codex "Biblia dell'Aracoeli")

1972. International Book Year. Illuminated Manuscripts. Multicoloured.
581	30l. Type **148**		15	25
582	50l. Gospel of St. Luke ("Biblia dell'Aracoeli")		15	15
583	90l. 2nd Epistle of St. John (Bologna codex)		15	15
584	100l. Revelation of St. John (Bologna codex)		20	15
585	130l. Epistle of St. Paul to the Romans (Italian codex)		30	25

149 Luigi Orione (founder of "Caritas")

1972. Birth Centenaries. Multicoloured.
586	50l. Type **149**		20	15
587	180l. Lorenzo Perosi (composer)		35	25

150 Cardinal Bassarione (Roselli fresco, Sistine Chapel)

1972. 500th Death Anniv of Cardinal Bassarione.
588	-	40l. green	15	15
589	**150**	90l. red	15	15
590	-	130l. black	35	30

DESIGNS: 40l. "Reading of Bull of Union" (relief); 130l. Arms of Cardinal Bassarione.

151 Congress Emblem

1973. Int Eucharistic Congress. Melbourne. Multicoloured.
591	25l. Type **151**		15	15
592	75l. Michelangelo's "Pieta"		15	15
593	300l. Melbourne Cathedral		40	35

152 St. Theresa's Birthplace

1973. Birth Centenary of St. Theresa of Lisieux.
594	**152**	25l. black and red	15	15
595	-	55l. black and yellow	15	15
596	-	220l. black and blue	30	25

DESIGNS: 55l. St. Theresa; 220l. Basilica of Lisieux.

153 Torun (birthplace)

1973. 500th Birth Anniv of Copernicus.
597	**153**	20l. green	15	15
598	-	50l. brown	15	15
599	**153**	100l. purple	20	15
600	-	130l. blue	30	20

DESIGN: 50, 130l. Copernicus.

154 "St. Wenceslas"

1973. Millenary of Prague Diocese. Multicoloured.
601	20l. Type **154**		15	15
602	90l. Arms of Prague Diocese		15	15
603	150l. Tower of Prague Cathedral		30	20
604	220l. "St. Adalbert"		40	35

155 Church of St. Hripsime

1973. 800th Death Anniv of St. Narsete Shnorali (Armenian patriarch).
605	**155**	25l. brown and ochre	15	15
606	-	90l. black and lilac	15	15
607	-	180l. purple and green	30	20

DESIGNS: 90l. Armenian "khatchkar" (stone stele) inscribed "Victory"; 180l. St. Narsete Shnorali.

156 "Angel" (porch of St. Mark's, Venice)

1974. Air.
608	**156**	2500l. multicoloured	4·00	3·25

157 "And there was Light"

1974. International Book Year (1973). "The Bible". Biblical Texts. Multicoloured.
609	15l. Type **157**		15	15
610	25l. "Noah entrusts himself to God" (horiz)		15	15
611	50l. "The Annunciation"		15	15
612	90l. "The Nativity"		15	15
613	180l. "The Lord feeds His People" (horiz)		30	25

158 Noah's Ark and Dove

1974. Centenary of U.P.U. Mosaics. Multicoloured.
614	50l. Type **158**		20	15
615	90l. Sheep in landscape		30	25

159 Pupils

1974. 700th Death Anniv of St. Thomas Aquinas (founder of Fra Angelico School). "The School of St. Thomas" (painting, St. Mark's Convent, Florence). Each brown and gold.
616	50l. Type **159**		15	15
617	90l. St. Thomas and pupils (24×40 mm)		20	20
618	220l. Pupils (different)		30	25

Nos. 616/18 were issued together, *se-tenant*, forming a composite design.

160 "Civita" (medieval quarter), Bagnoregio

1974. 700th Death Anniv of St. Bonaventura of Bagnoregio. Wood-carvings. Multicoloured.
619	40l. Type **160**		15	15
620	90l. "Tree of Life" (13th-century motif)		20	15
621	220l. "St. Bonaventura (B. Gozzoli)		35	25

161 Christus Victor

1974. Holy Year (1975). Multicoloured.
622	10l. Type **161**		15	15
623	25l. Christ		15	15
624	30l. Christ (different)		15	15
625	40l. Cross and dove		15	15
626	50l. Christ enthroned		15	15
627	55l. St. Peter		15	15
628	90l. St. Paul		15	15
629	100l. St. Peter		15	15
630	130l. St. Paul		20	15
631	220l. Arms of Pope Paul VI		30	25
632	250l. Pope Paul VI giving blessing		35	35

162 Fountain, St. Peter's Square

1975. European Architectural Heritage Year. Fountains.
633	**162**	20l. black and brown	15	15
634	-	40l. black and lilac	15	15
635	-	50l. black and pink	15	15
636	-	90l. black and green	15	15
637	-	100l. black and green	20	15
638	-	200l. black and blue	30	25

FOUNTAINS: 40l. Piazza St. Martha; 50l. Del Forno; 90l. Belvedere courtyard; 100l. Academy of Sciences; 200l. Galley fountain.

163 "Pentecost" (El Greco)

1975. Pentecost.
639	**163**	300l. orange and red	70	55

164 "Miracle of Loaves and Fishes" (gilt glass)

1975. Ninth International Christian Archaeological Congress. Fourth-century Art. Multicoloured.
640	30l. Type **164**		15	15
641	150l. Christ (painting)		20	15
642	200l. Raising of Lazarus (gilt glass)		35	30

165 Pope Sixtus IV investing Bartolomeo Sacchi as First Librarian (fresco)

1975. 500th Anniv of Apostolic Library.
643	**165**	70l. red and violet	15	15
644	-	100l. green and light green	20	15
645	-	250l. red and blue	35	30

DESIGNS—VERT: 100l. Pope Sixtus IV (codex). HORIZ: 250l. Pope Sixtus IV visiting library (fresco).

166 Passionists' House, Argentario

1975. Death Bicentenary of St. Paul of the Cross (founder of Passionist religious order). Multicoloured.
646	50l. Type **166**		15	15
647	150l. "St. Paul" (D. della Porta) (26×31 mm)		30	25
648	300l. Basilica of Saints John and Paul		50	40

167 Detail from Painting

1975. International Women's Year. Painting by Fra Angelico. Multicoloured.
649	100l. Type **167**		30	20
650	200l. Detail from painting (different)		45	40

168 "The Last Judgement" (detail)

1976. Air.
651	**168**	500l. brown and blue	1·20	1·10
652	-	1000l. brown and blue	1·60	1·50
653	-	2500l. brown and blue	3·50	3·00

DESIGNS: 1000l., 2500l. Different motifs from Michelangelo's "The Last Judgement".

169 "Madonna in Glory with the Child Jesus and Six Saints" (detail)

1976. 400th Death Anniv of Titian. Details from "The Madonna in Glory with the Child Jesus and Six Saints".

| 654 | **169** | 100l. red | 35 | 35 |
| 655 | - | 300l. red | 60 | 55 |

170 Eucharist Ear of Wheat and Globe

1976. 41st Int Eucharist Congress, Philadelphia.

656	**170**	150l. multicoloured	20	20
657	-	200l. gold and blue	35	30
658	-	400l. gold and green	80	75

DESIGNS: 200l. Eucharist within protective hands; 400l. Adoration of the Eucharist.

171 "Transfiguration" (detail)

1976. Details of Raphael's "Transfiguration". Multicoloured.

659	**171**	30l. Type 171 ("Moses")	15	15
660	-	40l. "Christ Transfigured"	15	15
661	-	50l. "Prophet Elijah"	15	15
662	-	100l. "Two Apostles"	15	15
663	-	150l. "The Relatives"	20	15
664	-	200l. "Landscape"	30	25

172 St. John's Tower and Fountain

1976. Architecture.

665	**172**	50l. brown and lilac	15	15
666	-	100l. sepia and brown	15	15
667	-	120l. black and green	30	25
668	-	180l. black and grey	35	35
669	-	250l. brown and stone	45	40
670	-	300l. purple	60	55

DESIGNS: 100l. Fountain of the Sacrament; 120l. Fountain at entrance to Gardens; 180l. Cupola of St. Peter's and Sacristy Basilica; 250l. Borgia Tower, Sistine Chapel and Via della Fondamenta; 300l. Apostolic Palace, Courtyard of St. Damasius.

173 "Canticles of Brother Sun" (detail)

1977. 750th Death Anniv of St. Francis of Assisi. Details from "Canticles of Brother Sun" by D. Cambellotti. Multicoloured.

671	**173**	50l. Type 173 ("The Lord's Creatures")	15	15
672	-	70l. "Brother Sun"	15	15
673	-	100l. "Sister Moon and Stars"	15	15
674	-	130l. "Sister Water"	15	15
675	-	170l. "Praise in Infirmities and Tribulations"	30	25
676	-	200l. "Praise for Bodily Death"	45	35

174 Detail from Fresco

1977. 600th Anniv of Return of Pope Gregory from Avignon. Fresco by G. Vasari. Multicoloured.

| 677 | **174** | 170l. Type 174 | 35 | 35 |
| 678 | | 350l. Detail from fresco (different) | 60 | 55 |

175 "Death of the Virgin"

1977. Festival of Assumption. Miniatures from Apostolic Library. Multicoloured.

| 679 | | 200l. Type 175 | 45 | 35 |
| 680 | | 400l. "Assumption of Virgin into Heaven" | 75 | 65 |

176 "God of the Nile"

1977. Classical Sculpture in Vatican Museums (1st series). Statues. Multicoloured.

681		50l. Type 176	15	15
682		120l. "Pericles"	15	15
683		130l. "Husband and Wife with joined Hands"	30	25
684		150l. "Belvedere Apollo"	30	25
685		170l. "Laocoon"	35	30
686		350l. "Belvedere Torso"	60	55

See also Nos. 687/92.

177 "Creation of the Human Race"

1977. Classical Sculpture in Vatican Museums (2nd series). Paleo-Christian Sarcophagi Carvings. Multicoloured.

687		50l. Type 177	15	15
688		70l. "Three Youths in the Fiery Furnace"	15	15
689		100l. "Adoration of the Magi"	20	15
690		130l. "Christ raising Lazarus from the Dead"	30	25
691		200l. "The Good Shepherd"	30	25
692		400l. "Resurrection"	65	60

178 "Madonna with the Parrot" (detail)

1977. 400th Birth Anniv of Rubens.

| 693 | **178** | 350l. multicoloured | 75 | 65 |

179 "The Face of Christ"

1978. 80th Birthday of Pope Paul VI. Multicoloured.

| 694 | | 350l. Type 179 | 65 | 60 |
| 695 | | 400l. "Pope Paul VI" (drawing by L. B. Barriviera) | 75 | 65 |

180 Arms of Pope Pius IX

1978. Death Cent of Pope Pius IX. Multicoloured.

696		130l. Type 180	20	15
697		170l. Seal of Pius IX	30	20
698		200l. Portrait of Pius IX	35	25

181 Microwave Antenna and Radio Vatican Emblem

1978. Air. Tenth World Telecommunications Day.

699	**181**	1000l. multicoloured	1·50	1·30
700	**181**	2000l. multicoloured	3·00	2·75
701	**181**	3000l. multicoloured	4·25	4·00

182 St. Peter's Keys

1978. "Vacant See".

702	**182**	120l. blue and violet	25	20
703	**182**	150l. pink and violet	30	25
704	**182**	250l. yellow and violet	35	30

183 St. Peter's Keys

1978. "Vacant See".

705	**183**	120l. yellow, blue & black	25	20
706	**183**	200l. yellow, red and black	30	25
707	**183**	250l. multicoloured	35	30

184 Pope John Paul I on Throne

1978. Pope John Paul I Commem. Multicoloured.

708		70l. Type 184	15	15
709		120l. The Pope smiling	20	15
710		250l. The Pope in Vatican Gardens	45	40
711		350l. The Pope giving blessing (horiz)	75	65

185 Arms of Pope John Paul II

1979. Inauguration of Pontificate of Pope John Paul II. Multicoloured.

712		170l. Type 185	30	25
713		250l. The Pope giving his blessing	45	40
714		400l. "Christ handing the keys to St. Peter" (relief, A. Buonvicino)	85	80

186 The Martyrdom (14th-century Latin codex)

1979. 900th Death Anniv of St. Stanislaus. Multicoloured.

715		120l. Type 186	30	25
716		150l. St. Stanislaus appears to the people (14th century Latin codex)	30	25
717		250l. Gold reliquary	45	40
718		500l. Cracow Cathedral	85	80

187 Meteorograph

1979. Death Centenary of Angelo Secchi (astronomer). Multicoloured.

719		180l. Type 187	30	25
720		220l. Spectroscope	45	40
721		300l. Telescope	60	55

188 St. Basil and Vignette "Handing Monastic Laws to a Hermit"

1979. 160th Death Anniv of St. Basil the Great. Multicoloured.

| 722 | | 150l. Type 188 | 45 | 40 |
| 723 | | 520l. St. Basil and vignette "Caring for the Sick" | 1·00 | 95 |

189 Aerial View of Vatican City

1979. 50th Anniv of Vatican City State.

724	**189**	50l. brown, black and pink	15	15
725	-	70l. multicoloured	15	15
726	-	120l. multicoloured	15	15
727	-	150l. multicoloured	30	20
728	-	170l. multicoloured	30	25
729	-	250l. multicoloured	45	40
730	-	450l. multicoloured	95	65

DESIGNS—POPES AND ARMS: 70l. Pius XI; 120l. Pius XII; 150l. John XXIII; 170l. Paul VI; 250l. John Paul I; 450l. John Paul II.

190 Child in Swaddling Clothes (relief, Foundling Hospital, Florence)

1979. International Year of the Child. Sculptures by Della Robbia.

731	**190**	50l. multicoloured	20	15
732	-	120l. multicoloured	30	20
733	-	200l. multicoloured	35	35
734	-	350l. multicoloured	60	55

DESIGNS: 120l. to 350l. Similar sculptures.

191 Abbot Desiderius offering Codices to St. Benedict

1980. 1500th Birth Anniv of St. Benedict of Nursia (founder of Benedictine Order). Multicoloured.

735	80l. Type **191**	15	15
736	100l. St. Benedict composing rules of the Order	20	15
737	150l. Page of St. Benedict's Rules	30	25
738	220l. Death of St. Benedict	35	35
739	450l. Montecassino Abbey (after Paul Bril)	75	55

192 Hands reaching out to Pope and Arms of Santo Domingo

1980. Air. Pope John Paul II's Journeys (1st series). Different coats of arms.

740	**192**	200l. multicoloured	35	25
741	-	300l. multicoloured	50	40
742	-	500l. violet, red and black	85	80
743	-	1000l. multicoloured	1·60	1·30
744	-	1500l. multicoloured	2·50	2·00
745	-	2000l. red, blue and black	3·75	3·00
746	-	3000l. black, red and blue	5·00	4·50

COATS OF ARMS: 300l. Mexico; 500l. Poland; 1000l. Ireland; 1500l. United States; 2000l. United Nations; 3000l. Pope John Paul II, Archbishop Dimitrios and arms of Turkey.

See also Nos. 768/78, 814/25, 862/9, 886/93, 912/16, 940/4, 963/6, 992/6, 1019/22, 1049/51, 1076/80, 1113/14, 1136/41, 1174/9, 1206/11, 1236/40, 1284/8 and 1312/16.

193 Bernini (self-portrait) and Medallion showing Baldacchino, St. Peter's

1980. 300th Death Anniv of Gian Lorenzo Bernini (artist and architect). Multicoloured.

747	80l. Type **193**	15	15
748	170l. Bernini and medallion showing his plan for St. Peter's	30	25
749	250l. Bernini, medallion of bronze chair and group "Doctors of the Church", St. Peter's	45	40
750	350l. Bernini and medallion of Apostolic Palace stairway	65	45

194 St. Albertus on Mission of Peace

1980. 700th Death Anniv of St. Albertus Magnus. Multicoloured.

| 751 | 300l. Type **194** | 60 | 45 |
| 752 | 400l. St. Albertus as Bishop | 75 | 60 |

195 Communion of the Saints

1980. Feast of All Saints. Multicoloured.

| 753 | 250l. Type **195** | 50 | 45 |
| 754 | 500l. Christ and saints | 95 | 75 |

196 Marconi, Pope Pius XI and Radio Emblem

1981. 50th Anniv of Vatican Radio. Multicoloured.

755	100l. Type **196**	20	20
756	150l. Microphone	35	30
757	200l. Antenna of Santa Maria di Galeria Radio Centre and statue of Archangel Gabriel	45	40
758	600l. Pope John Paul II	85	80

197 Virgil and his Writing-desk

1981. Death Bimillenary of Virgil (Roman poet). Multicoloured.

| 759 | 350l. Type **197** | 60 | 45 |
| 760 | 600l. As Type **197** but inscr "P. VERGILI MARONIS AENEIDOS LIBRI" | 1·00 | 85 |

198 Congress Emblem and Apparition of Virgin to St. Bernadette

1981. 42nd International Eucharistic Congress, Lourdes. Multicoloured.

761	80l. Congress emblem	20	20
762	150l. Type **198**	30	25
763	200l. Emblem and pilgrims going to Lourdes	35	30
764	500l. Emblem and Bishop with faithful venerating Virgin	80	65

199 Jan van Ruusbroec writing Treatise

1981. 600th Death Anniv of Jan van Ruusbroec (Flemish mystic). Multicoloured.

| 765 | 200l. Type **199** | 35 | 30 |
| 766 | 300l. Ruusbroec | 60 | 45 |

200 Turin Shroud and I.Y.D.P. Emblem

1981. International Year of Disabled Persons.

| 767 | **200** | 600l. multicoloured | 1·10 | 95 |

201 Arms of John Paul II

1981. Pope John Paul II's Journeys (2nd series). Multicoloured.

768	50l. Type **201**	15	15
769	100l. Crucifix and map of Africa	15	15
770	120l. Hands holding crucifix	20	20
771	150l. Pope performing baptism	30	25
772	200l. Pope embracing African bishop	35	30
773	250l. Pope blessing sick man	50	40
774	300l. Notre-Dame Cathedral, Paris	50	45
775	400l. Pope addressing UNESCO, Paris	65	55
776	600l. "Christ of the Andes", Rio de Janeiro	1·00	80
777	700l. Cologne Cathedral	1·20	1·00
778	900l. Pope giving blessing	1·70	1·60

202 Agnes handing Church to Grand Master of the Crosiers of the Red Star

1982. 700th Death Anniv of Blessed Agnes of Prague. Multicoloured.

| 779 | 700l. Type **202** | 1·30 | 1·10 |
| 780 | 900l. Agnes receiving letter from St. Clare | 1·60 | 1·50 |

203 "Pueri Cantores" (left panel)

1982. 500th Death Anniv of Luca della Robbia (sculptor).

781	**203**	1000l. green and blue	1·50	1·30
782	-	1000l. multicoloured	1·50	1·30
783	-	1000l. green and blue	1·50	1·30

DESIGNS—As T **203**: No. 783, "Pueri Cantores" (right panel). 44×36 mm: No. 782, "Virgin Mary in Prayer".

204 Virgin Mary and St. Joseph clothe St. Theresa

1982. 400th Death Anniv of St. Theresa of Avila.

784	**204**	200l. orange, grey and red	45	40
785	-	600l. grey, orange and blue	1·00	95
786	-	1000l. grey, orange and mauve	1·70	1·60

DESIGNS: 600l. Ecstasy of St. Theresa; 1000l. St. Theresa writing "The Interior Castle".

205 Examining Globe

1982. 400th Anniv of Gregorian Calendar. Details from Pope Gregory XIII's tomb.

787	**205**	200l. green	35	35
788	-	300l. black	60	55
789	-	700l. mauve	1·30	1·20
MS790	159×109 mm. Nos. 787/9		3·00	2·75

DESIGNS: 300l. Presenting proposals to Pope Gregory XIII; 700l. Kneeling figures.

206 "Nativity" (Veit Stoss)

1982. Christmas.

| 791 | **206** | 300l. stone, brown & gold | 60 | 55 |
| 792 | - | 450l. lilac, purple and silver | 80 | 65 |

DESIGN: 450l. "Nativity with Pope John Paul II" (Enrico Manfrini).

208 Greek Vase

1983. "The Vatican Collections: The Papacy and Art—U.S.A. 1983" Exhibition (1st issue). Sheet 125×170 mm containing T **208** and similar vert designs. Multicoloured.

| **MS**797 | 100l. Type **208**, 200l. Italiante vase; 250l. Terracotta female bust; 300l. Bust of Emperor Marcus Aurelius; 350l. Bird (fresco fragment); 400l. Sacred vestment of Pope Clement VIII | 8·00 | 7·25 |

See also Nos. **MS**802 and **MS**803.

209 "Theology"

1983. 500th Birth Anniv of Raphael (artist).

798	**209**	50l. blue and ultramarine	15	15
799	-	400l. purple and mauve	65	55
800	-	500l. brown and chestnut	85	65
801	-	1200l. green and turquoise	2·20	1·70

DESIGNS—Allegories on the Segnatura Room ceiling: 400l. "Poetry"; 500l. "Justice"; 1200l. "Philosophy".

1983. "The Vatican Collections: The Papacy and Art—U.S.A. 1983" Exhibition (2nd issue). Sheet 124×171 mm containing vert designs as T **208**. Multicoloured.

| **MS**802 | 100l. Etruscan terracotta horse's head; 200l. Greek relief of horseman; 300l. Etruscan head of man; 400l. Head of Apollo Belvedere; 500l. Fresco of Moses; 1000l. "Madonna and Child" (Bernardo Daddi) | 4·25 | 4·00 |

1983. "The Vatican Collections: The Papacy and Art—U.S.A. 1983" Exhibition (3rd issue). Sheet 124×171 mm containing vert designs as T **208**. Multicoloured.

| **MS**803 | 150l. Oedipus and Sphinx (Greek cup); 200l. Votive statue of child (Etruscan bronze); 350l. Statue of Emperor Augustus; 400l. Statue of Good Shepherd; 500l. "St. Nicholas saving ship" (Gentile Fabriano); 1200l. "The Holy Face" (Georges Rouault) | 5·00 | 4·75 |

210 "Moses explaining the Law to the People" (Luca Signorelli)

1983. Air. World Communications Year. Multicoloured.

| 804 | 2000l. Type **210** | 3·25 | 3·00 |
| 805 | 5000l. "St. Paul preaching in Athens" (Raphael) | 8·50 | 7·25 |

211 Mendel and Hybrid Experiment

1984. Death Centenary of Gregor Johan Mendel (geneticist).

| 806 | **211** | 450l. multicoloured | 85 | 75 |
| 807 | **211** | 1500l. multicoloured | 3·00 | 2·00 |

212 St. Casimir and Vilna Cathedral and Castle

1984. 500th Death Anniv of St. Casimir (patron saint of Lithuania).

| 808 | **212** | 550l. multicoloured | 95 | 80 |
| 809 | **212** | 1200l. multicoloured | 2·20 | 1·90 |

213 Pontifical Academy of Sciences

1984. Cultural and Scientific Institutions.

810	**213**	150l. yellow and brown	35	30
811	-	450l. multicoloured	75	60
812	-	550l. yellow and violet	1·20	95
813	-	1500l. yellow and blue	3·00	2·40

DESIGNS: 450l. Seals and document from Vatican Secret Archives; 550l. Entrance to Vatican Apostolic Library; 1500l. Vatican Observatory, Castelgandolfo.

214 Pope in Karachi

1984. Pope John Paul II's Journeys (3rd series). Multicoloured.

814	50l. Type **214**	15	15
815	100l. Pope and image of Our Lady of Penafrancia, Philippines	15	15
816	150l. Pope with crucifix (Guam)	30	25
817	250l. Pope and Tokyo Cathedral	45	35
818	300l. Pope at Anchorage, Alaska	50	40
819	400l. Crucifix, crowd and map of Africa	65	45
820	450l. Pope and image of Our Lady of Fatima (Portugal)	80	60
821	550l. Pope, Archbishop of Westminster and Canterbury Cathedral	1·00	65
822	1000l. Pope and image of Our Lady of Lujan (Argentina)	1·70	1·30
823	1500l. Pope, Lake Leman and Geneva	3·00	2·00
824	2500l. Pope and Mount Titano (San Marino)	5·75	3·25
825	4000l. Pope and Santiago de Compostela Cathedral (Spain)	10·00	6·50

215 Damascus and Sepulchre of Sts. Marcellinus and Peter

1984. 1600th Death Anniv of Pope St. Damasus. Multicoloured.

826	200l. Type **215**	35	35
827	500l. Damasus and epigraph from St. Januarius's tomb	1·00	80
828	2000l. Damasus and basilica ruins	3·75	3·00

216 More (after Holbein) and Map

1985. 450th Death Anniv of Saint Thomas More. Multicoloured.

829	250l. Type **216**	45	25
830	400l. St. Thomas More and title page of "Utopia"	75	55
831	2000l. St. Thomas More and title page of "Life of Thomas More" by Domenico Regi	3·75	3·00

217 St. Methodius holding Religious Paintings

1985. 1100th Death Anniv of Saint Methodius. Multicoloured.

832	500l. Type **217**	85	65
833	600l. Saints Cyril and Methodius with Pope Clement I's body	1·00	95
834	1700l. Saints Benedict, Cyril and Methodius	3·00	2·40

218 Cross on Map of Africa

1985. 43rd International Eucharistic Congress, Nairobi. Multicoloured.

835	100l. Type **218**	20	20
836	400l. Assembly of bishops	65	55
837	600l. Chalice	1·00	80
838	2300l. Family gazing at cross	4·00	3·25

219 Eagle (from Door, St. Paul's Basilica, Rome)

1985. 900th Death Anniv of Pope Gregory VII. Multicoloured.

839	150l. Type **219**	30	30
840	450l. Pope Gregory VII	85	65
841	2500l. Pope Gregory's former sarcophagus (horiz)	4·25	3·25

220 Mosaic Map of Italy and Symbol of Holy See

1985. Ratification of Modification of 1929 Lateran Concordat.

842	**220**	400l. multicoloured	80	65

221 Carriage

1985. "Italia '85" Int Stamp Exn, Rome.

843	**221**	450l. red and blue	75	60
844	-	1500l. blue and mauve	2·30	1·90
MS845	161×108 mm. Nos. 843/4		4·00	3·75

DESIGN: 1500l. Carriage (different).

222 "Nation shall not Lift up Sword against Nation. . ."

1986. International Peace Year. Multicoloured.

846	50l. Type **222**	15	15
847	350l. Messenger's feet ("How beautiful … are the feet …")	60	40
848	450l. Profiles and olive branch ("Blessed are the peace-makers …")	85	75
849	650l. Dove and sun ("Glory to God in the highest …")	1·20	1·10
850	2000l. Pope's hand releasing dove over rainbow ("Peace is a value with no frontiers …")	3·25	2·75

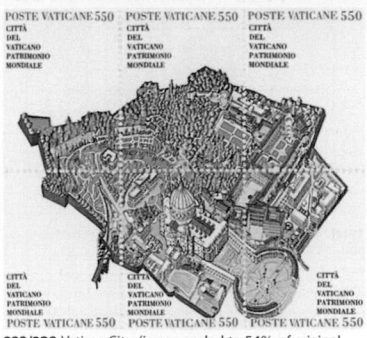

223/228 Vatican City (image scaled to 54% of original size)

1986. World Heritage. Vatican City. Multicoloured.

851	**223**	550l. multicoloured	1·20	95
852	**224**	550l. multicoloured	1·20	95
853	**225**	550l. multicoloured	1·20	95
854	**226**	550l. multicoloured	1·20	95
855	**227**	550l. multicoloured	1·20	95
856	**228**	550l. multicoloured	1·20	95

Nos. 851/6 were printed together, *se-tenant*, forming the composite design illustrated.

229 St. Camillus saving Invalid from Flood (after Pierre Subleyras)

1986. Centenary of Proclamation of St. Camillus de Lellis and St. John of God as Patron Saints of Hospitals and the Sick.

857	**229**	700l. green, violet and red	1·20	1·00
858	-	700l. blue, green and red	1·20	1·00
859	-	2000l. multicoloured	3·50	3·00

DESIGNS: No. 858, St. John supporting the sick (after Gomez Moreno); 859, Emblems of Ministers of the Sick and Brothers Hospitallers, and Pope John Paul II talking to patient.

230 "The Philosophers"

1986. 50th Anniv of Pontifical Academy of Sciences. Details from fresco "School of Athens" by Raphael. Multicoloured.

860	1500l. Type **230**	2·50	2·20
861	2500l. "The Scientists"	4·25	3·75

231 Pope and Young People (Central America)

1986. Air. Pope John Paul II's Journeys (4th series). Multicoloured.

862	350l. Type **231**	60	50
863	450l. Pope in prayer, Warsaw Cathedral and Our Lady of Czestochowa (Poland)	75	65
864	700l. Pope kneeling and crowd at Lourdes (France)	1·20	1·00
865	1000l. Sanctuary of Mariazell and St. Stephen's Cathedral, Vienna (Austria)	1·70	1·50
866	1500l. Pope and representatives of nations visited (Alaska, Asia and Pacific Islands)	2·50	2·30
867	2000l. Image of St. Nicholas of Flue, Basilica of Einsiedeln and Pope (Switzerland)	3·50	3·00
868	2500l. Crosses, Notre Dame Cathedral, Quebec, and Pope (Canada)	4·25	3·75
869	5000l. Pope, bishop and young people with cross (Spain, Dominican Republic and Puerto Rico)	8·75	7·75

232 "St. Augustine reading St. Paul's Epistles" (fresco, Benozzo Gozzoli)

1987. 1600th Anniv of Conversion and Baptism of St. Augustine. Multicoloured.

870	300l. Type **232**	50	45
871	400l. "Baptism of St. Augustine" (Bartolomeo di Gentile)	65	60
872	500l. "Ecstasy of St. Augustine" (fresco, Benozzo Gozzoli)	85	75
873	2200l. "Dispute of the Sacrament" (detail of fresco, Raphael)	3·75	3·25

233 Statue of Christ, Lithuanian Chapel, Vatican Crypt

1987. 600th Anniv of Conversion to Christianity of Lithuania. Multicoloured.

874	200l. Type **233**	35	25
875	700l. Statue of Virgin Mary with body of Christ and two angels	1·20	1·00
876	3000l. Lithuanian shrine	5·00	4·00

234 Chapter of Riga Church Seal

1987. 800th Anniv of Conversion to Christianity of Latvia. Multicoloured.

877	700l. Type **234**	1·50	1·30
878	2400l. Basilica of the Assumption, Aglona	4·75	4·00

235 Judge

1987. "Olymphilex '87" Olympic Stamps Exhibition, Rome. Figures from Caracalla Baths floor mosaic. Multicoloured.

879	400l. Type **235**	65	50
880	500l. Runner	80	65
881	600l. Discus-thrower	1·00	75
882	2000l. Athlete	3·75	3·25
MS883	151×100 mm. As Nos. 879/82 but with Greek key borders	5·75	5·25

236 Stamp Room and 1929 5c. Stamp

1987. Inauguration of Philatelic and Numismatic Museum. Multicoloured.

884	400l. Type **236**	75	75
885	3500l. Coin room and reverse of 1000l. 1986 coin	5·75	4·50

1987. Pope John Paul II's Journeys (5th series). As T **231**. Multicoloured.

886	50l. Youths, Pope and Machu Picchu (Venezuela, Ecuador, Peru, Trinidad and Tobago)	20	20
887	250l. Antwerp Cathedral, smoke stacks and Pope (Netherlands, Luxembourg and Belgium)	45	40

888	400l. People, buildings and Pope (Togo, Ivory Coast, Cameroun, Central African Republic, Zaire, Kenya and Morocco)	75	65
889	500l. Pope holding Cross and youths (Liechtenstein)	85	75
890	600l. Pope, Indians and Delhi Mosque (India)	1·10	90
891	700l. Pope, people, ceramic and Bogota Cathedral (Colombia and St. Lucia)	1·30	1·00
892	2500l. Pope, Cure d'Ars and Lyon Cathedral (France)	7·25	5·25
893	4000l. Hands releasing dove and symbols of countries visited (Bangladesh, Singapore, Fiji, New Zealand, Australia and Seychelles)	11·50	7·75

237 Arrival of Relics

1987. 900th Anniv of Transfer of St. Nicholas's Relics from Myra to Bari. Multicoloured.

894	500l. Type **237**	2·00	1·30
895	700l. St. Nicholas giving purses of gold to save from dishonour the three daughters of a poor man	3·00	1·90
896	3000l. St. Nicholas saving a ship	13·00	9·50

238 Children and Sister of Institute of the Daughters of Mary Help of Christians

1988. Death Centenary of St. John Bosco (founder of Salesian Brothers). Multicoloured.

897	500l. Type **238**	85	65
898	1000l. Bosco and children	1·50	1·20
899	2000l. Children and Salesian lay brother	3·00	2·50

Nos. 897/9 were printed together, se-tenant, forming a composite design.

239 The Annunciation

1988. Marian Year. Multicoloured.

900	50l. Type **239**	20	20
901	300l. Nativity	50	40
902	500l. Pentecost	75	65
903	750l. The Assumption	1·20	90
904	1000l. Mother of the Church	1·70	1·30
905	2400l. Refuge of Sinners	3·75	2·75

240 Prince Vladimir the Great (15th-century icon)

1988. Millenary of Conversion to Christianity of Rus of Kiev. Multicoloured.

906	450l. Type **240**	75	65
907	650l. St. Sophia's Cathedral, Kiev	1·00	90
908	2500l. "Mother of God in Prayer" (mosaic, St. Sophia's Cathedral)	4·00	3·25

241 "Marriage at Cana" (detail)

1988. 400th Death Anniv of Paolo Veronese (painter).

909	241	550l. blue and red	85	75
910	-	650l. multicoloured	1·00	90
911	-	3000l. red and brown	4·75	4·25

DESIGNS—HORIZ: 650l. "Self-portrait". VERT: 3000l. "Marriage at Cana" (different detail).

1988. Air. Pope John Paul II's Journeys (6th series). As T **231**. Multicoloured.

912	450l. Hands releasing dove, St. Peter's, Rome, Santiago Cathedral and Sanctuary of Our Lady, Lujan (Uruguay, Chile and Argentina)	75	65
913	650l. Pope in act of blessing, Speyer Cathedral and youths (German Federal Republic)	1·20	90
914	1000l. Hands releasing dove, Gdansk altar and intertwined flowers and thorns (Poland)	1·70	1·30
915	2500l. Skyscrapers and Pope blessing youths (U.S.A.)	3·00	3·25
916	5000l. Hands releasing dove, tepee at Fort Simpson and American Indians (Canada)	8·00	6·50

242 Angel with Olive Branch

1988. Christmas. Multicoloured.

917	50l. Type **242**	20	20
918	400l. Angel holding olive branch in both hands	65	50
919	500l. Angel with olive branch (flying from right)	85	65
920	550l. Shepherds	95	75
921	850l. Nativity	1·50	1·20
922	1500l. Wise Men	2·40	2·10
MS923	120×140 mm. As Nos. 917/22 but with gold backgrounds	7·00	6·00

243 Head of Apis

1989. 150th Anniv of Gregorian Egyptian Museum. Sheet 140×100 mm containing T **243** and similar vert designs. Multicoloured.

MS924	400l. Type **243**; 650l. Double-headed statue of Isis and Apis; 750l. Headless statue of physician Ugiahorresne, 2400l. Phoraoh Mentuhotep	7·25	6·50

244 The Annunciation

1989. 600th Anniv of Feast of Visitation of Virgin Mary. Illuminated Initials. Multicoloured.

925	550l. Type **244**	85	75
926	750l. Virgin Mary and St. Elizabeth	1·20	1·00
927	2500l. Virgin Mary and St. Elizabeth with Jesus and John the Baptist as babies	3·75	3·25

245 Purple-naped Lory ("Parrot")

1989. Birds featured in "Histoire Naturelle des Oiseaux" by Eleazar Albin. Multicoloured.

928	100l. Type **245**	20	20
929	150l. Green woodpecker	30	30
930	200l. Goldcrest ("Crested wren") and winter ("Common") wren	35	40
931	350l. River kingfisher	60	60
932	500l. Common cardinal ("Red Groas Beak of Virginia")	80	65
933	700l. Northern bullfinch ("Bullfinch")	1·10	90
934	1500l. Northern lapwing ("Lapwing Plover")	2·50	1·90
935	3000l. Green-winged ("French") teal	5·00	3·75

246 Broken Bread (Congress emblem)

1989. 44th International Eucharistic Congress, Seoul.

936	246	550l. red and green	85	75
937	-	850l. multicoloured	1·30	1·20
938	-	1000l. multicoloured	1·90	1·30
939	-	2500l. green, pink and violet	4·00	3·25

DESIGNS: 850l. Cross; 1000l. Cross and fishes; 2500l. Small cross on wafer.

247 Pope's Arms, Map of South America and Pope

1989. Pope John Paul II's Journeys (7th series). Multicoloured.

940	50l. Type **247**	30	20
941	550l. Austria	95	75
942	800l. Southern Africa	1·50	1·20
943	1000l. France	1·70	1·40
944	4000l. Italy	7·25	5·75

248 Basilica of the Assumption, Baltimore

1989. Bicentenary of First Catholic Diocese in U.S.A. Each agate and brown.

945	450l. Type **248**	75	65
946	1350l. John Carroll (first Archbishop of Baltimore)	2·20	1·90
947	2400l. Cathedral of Mary Our Queen, Baltimore (after Martin Barry)	4·25	3·25

249 Vision of Ursulines on Mystical Stair

1990. 450th Death Anniv of St. Angela Merici (founder of Company of St. Ursula). Multicoloured.

948	700l. Type **249**	1·20	1·10
949	800l. St. Angela teaching Ursulines	1·50	1·30
950	2800l. Ursulines	5·00	4·00

250 Ordination and Arrival in Frisia

1990. 1300th Anniv of Beginning of St. Willibrord's Missions. Multicoloured.

951	300l. Type **250**	50	40
952	700l. St. Willibrord in Antwerp, creation as bishop by Pope Sergius I and gift of part of Echternach by Abbess of Euren	1·10	90
953	3000l. Gift of Echternach by King Pepin and St. Willibrord's death	5·00	3·75

251 Abraham

1990. 40th Anniv of Caritas Internationalis. Details of mosaic from Basilica of Sta. Maria Maggiore, Rome. Multicoloured.

954	450l. Type **251**	95	75
955	650l. Three visitors	1·40	1·20
956	800l. Sarah making bread	1·70	1·50
957	2000l. Visitors seated at Abraham's table	4·25	3·50
MS958	100×135 mm. As Nos. 954/7 but without gold frame	10·50	9·50

252 Fishermen on Lake Peking

1990. 300th Anniv of Peking–Nanking Diocese. Details of two enamelled bronze vases given by Peking Apostolic Delegate to Pope Pius IX. Multicoloured.

959	500l. Type **252**	75	65
960	750l. Church of the Immaculate Conception (first Peking church, 1650)	1·20	1·00
961	1500l. Lake Peking	2·30	2·10
962	2000l. Church of the Redeemer, Peking, 1703	3·25	2·75

253 Pope and African Landscape

1990. Air. Pope John Paul II's Journeys (8th series). Multicoloured.

963	500l. Type **253**	95	65
964	1000l. Northern European landscape (Scandinavia)	2·00	1·40
965	3000l. Cathedral (Santiago de Compostela, Spain)	5·75	5·25
966	5000l. Oriental landscape (Korea, Indonesia and Mauritius)	9·50	7·00

254 Choir of Angels

1990. Christmas. Details of painting by Sebastiano Mainardi. Multicoloured.

967	50l. Type **254**	20	20
968	200l. St. Joseph	50	30
969	650l. Holy Child	1·50	1·00
970	750l. Virgin Mary	1·70	1·30
971	2500l. "Nativity" (complete picture) (vert)	6·25	5·25

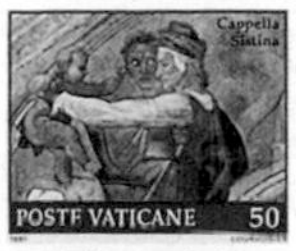

255 "Eleazar" (left half)

1991. Restoration of Sistine Chapel. Details of Lunettes of the Ancestors of Christ by Michelangelo. Multicoloured.

972	50l. Type **255**	20	20
973	100l. "Eleazar" (right half)	20	20
974	150l. "Jacob" (left half)	30	25
975	250l. "Jacob" (right half)	45	30
976	350l. "Josiah" (left half)	60	45
977	400l. "Josiah" (right half)	75	60
978	500l. "Asa" (left half)	85	65
979	650l. "Asa" (right half)	1·20	90
980	800l. "Zerubbabel" (left half)	1·50	1·30
981	1000l. "Zerubbabel" (right half)	1·70	1·50
982	2000l. "Azor" (left half)	3·50	3·00
983	3000l. "Azor" (right half)	5·25	4·00

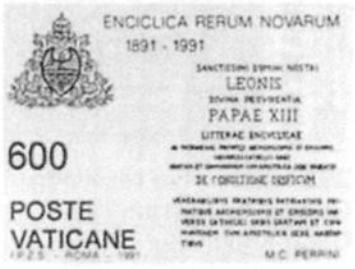

256 Title Page and Pope Leo XIII's Arms

1991. Centenary of "Rerum Novarum" (encyclical on workers' rights).

984	**256**	600l. blue and green	1·10	95
985	-	750l. green and brown	1·40	1·20
986	-	3500l. purple and black	6·25	5·50

DESIGNS: 750l. Allegory of Church, workers and employers (from Leo XIII's 15th Anniv medal, 1892); 3500l. Profile of Pope Leo XIII (from same medal).

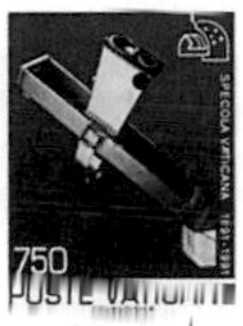

257 Astrograph (astronomical camera)

1991. Centenary of Vatican Observatory. Multicoloured.

987	750l. Type **257**	1·50	1·40
988	1000l. Castelgandolfo observatory (horiz)	2·00	1·80
989	3000l. Vatican Observatory telescope, Mount Graham, Tucson, U.S.A.	6·00	5·25

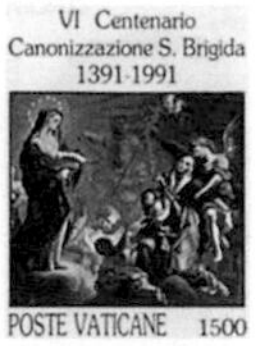

258 "Apparition of Virgin Mary" (Biagio Puccini)

1991. 600th Anniv of Canonization of St. Bridget (founder of Order of the Holy Saviour). Multicoloured.

990	1500l. Type **258**	3·50	3·00
991	2000l. "Revelation of Christ" (Biagio Puccini)	4·75	4·00

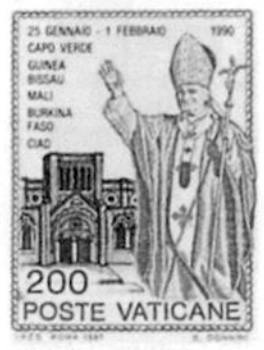

259 Cathedral of the Immaculate Conception, Ouagadougou

1991. Pope John Paul II's Journeys (9th series). Multicoloured.

992	200l. Type **259** (Cape Verde, Guinea-Bissau, Mali, Burkina Faso and Chad)	45	40
993	550l. St. Vitus's Cathedral, Prague (Czechoslovakia)	1·20	1·10
994	750l. Basilica of Our Lady of Guadaloupe (Mexico and Curacao)	1·80	1·60
995	1500l. Ta'Pinu Sanctuary, Gozo (Malta)	3·50	3·25
996	3500l. Cathedral of Christ the King, Giteca (Tanzania, Burundi, Rwanda and Ivory Coast)	8·50	7·50

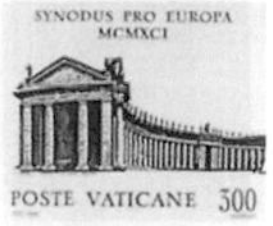

260 Colonnade of St. Peter's Cathedral, Rome

1991. Synod of Bishops' Special Assembly for Europe. Each black and brown.

997	300l. Type **260**	60	55
998	500l. St. Peter's Cathedral and square	1·10	95
999	4000l. Apostolic Palace and colonnade	8·50	7·50

Nos. 997/9 were issued together, *se-tenant*, forming a composite design.

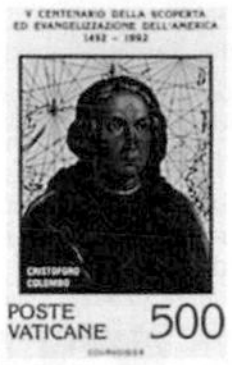

261 Christopher Columbus

1992. 500th Anniv of Discovery of America by Columbus. Multicoloured.

1000	500l. Type **261**	90	80
1001	600l. St. Pedro Claver	1·10	95
1002	850l. "Virgin of the Catholic Kings"	1·50	1·40
1003	1000l. Bortolome de las Casas	2·00	1·80
1004	2000l. Junipero Serra	3·75	3·50
MS1005	138×95 mm. 1500l. Details of nautical chart from atlas of Battista Agnese	10·00	9·50

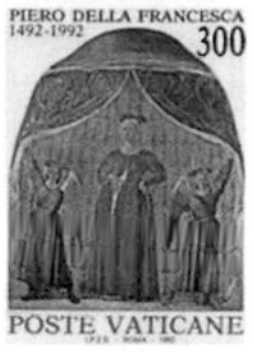

262 "Our Lady of Childbirth"

1992. 500th Death Anniv of Piero della Francesca (painter). Multicoloured.

1006	300l. Type **262**	90	80
1007	750l. "Our Lady of Childbirth" (detail)	1·80	1·60
1008	1000l. "The Resurrection"	2·50	2·20
1009	3000l. "The Resurrection" (detail)	7·25	6·50

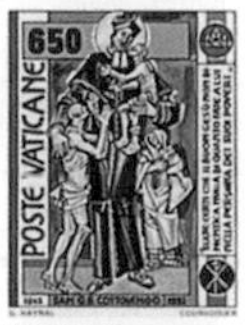

263 St. Giuseppe comforting the Sick

1992. 150th Death Anniv of St. Giuseppe Benedetto Cottolengo. Multicoloured.

1010	650l. Type **263**	1·80	1·60
1011	850l. St. Giuseppe holding Piccolo Casa della Divina Provvidenza (infirmary), Turin	2·30	2·10

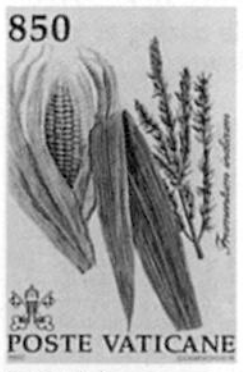

264 Maize

1992. Plants of the New World. Illustrations from the 18th-century "Phytanthoza Iconographia". Multicoloured.

1012	850l. Type **264**	1·70	1·50
1013	850l. Tomatoes ("Solanum pomiferum")	1·70	1·50
1014	850l. Cactus ("Opuntia")	1·70	1·50
1015	850l. Cacao ("Cacaos, Cacavifera")	1·70	1·50
1016	850l. Peppers ("Solanum tuberosum")	1·70	1·50
1017	850l. Pineapple ("Ananas sagitae")	1·70	1·50

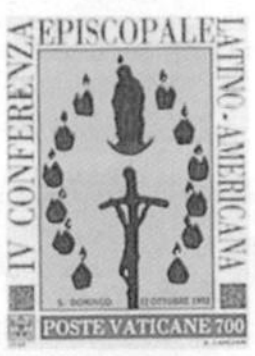

265 Our Lady of Guadalupe, Crucifix and Mitres

1992. Fourth Latin American Episcopal Conference, Santo Domingo.

1018	**265**	700l. gold, emerald and green	2·00	1·80

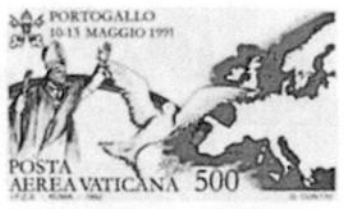

266 Pope, Dove and Map of Europe

1992. Air. Pope John Paul II's Journeys (10th series). Multicoloured.

1019	500l. Type **266** (Portugal)	1·10	95
1020	1000l. Map of Europe highlighting Poland	2·00	1·80
1021	4000l. Our Lady of Czestochowa and map highlighting Poland and Hungary	8·50	7·50
1022	6000l. Map of South America highlighting Brazil	13·00	11·50

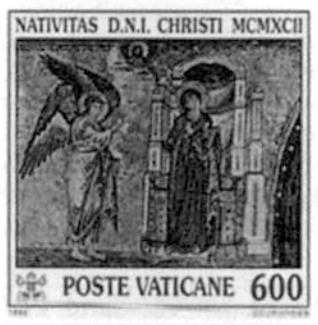

267 "The Annunciation"

1992. Christmas. Mosaics in Church of Sta.Maria Maggiore, Rome. Multicoloured.

1023	600l. Type **267**	1·70	1·50
1024	700l. "Nativity"	1·90	1·70
1025	1000l. "Adoration of the Kings"	2·75	2·50
1026	1500l. "Presentation in the Temple"	4·50	4·00

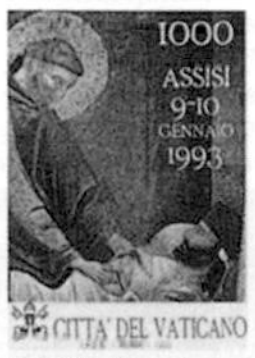

268 "St. Francis healing the Man from Ilerda" (fresco by Giotto in Upper Church, Assisi)

1993. "Peace in Europe" Prayer Meeting, Assisi.

1027	**268**	1000l. multicoloured	2·50	2·30

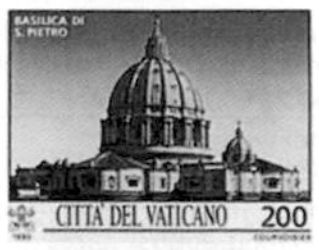

269 Dome of St. Peter's Cathedral

1993. Architectural Treasures of Rome and the Vatican. Multicoloured.

1028	200l. Type **269**	40	35
1029	300l. St. John Lateran's Basilica	60	55
1030	350l. Basilica of Sta. Maria Maggiore	70	60
1031	500l. St. Paul's Basilica	1·00	90
1032	600l. Apostolic Palace, Vatican	1·20	1·00
1033	700l. Apostolic Palace, Lateran	1·40	1·20
1034	850l. Papal Palace, Castelgandolfo	1·80	1·60
1035	1000l. Chancery Palace	2·30	2·10
1036	2000l. Palace of Propagation of the Faith	4·50	4·00
1037	3000l. San Calisto Palace	6·50	5·75

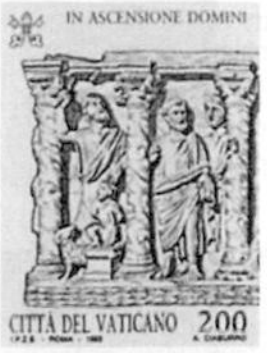

270 "The Sacrifice of Isaac"

1993. Ascension Day. Multicoloured.

1038	200l. Type **270**	45	40
1039	750l. Jesus handing New Law to St. Peter	1·70	1·50
1040	3000l. Christ watching servant washing Pilate's hands	6·50	5·75

Nos. 1038/40 were issued together, *se-tenant*, forming a composite design of the bas-relief "Traditio Legis" from 4th-century sarcophagus.

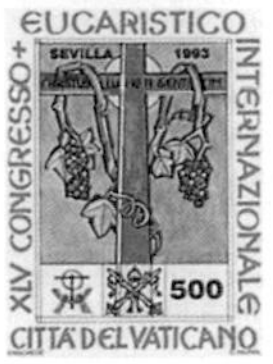

271 Cross and Grape Vines

1993. 45th Int Eucharistic Congress, Seville. Multicoloured.

1041	500l. Type **271**	1·00	90
1042	700l. Cross and hands offering broken bread	1·40	1·20
1043	1500l. Hands holding chalice	3·00	2·75
1044	2500l. Cross, banner and ears of wheat	5·00	4·50

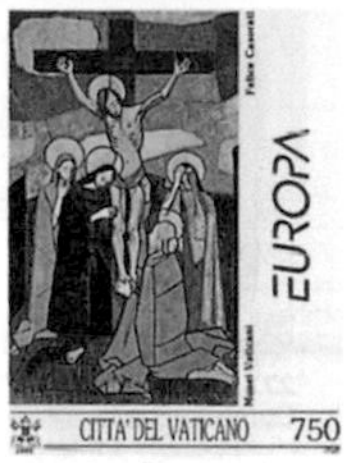

272 "Crucifixion" (Felice Casorati)

1993. Europa. Contemporary Art. Multicoloured.

1045	750l. Type **272**	1·50	1·40
1046	850l. "Rouen Cathedral" (Maurice Utrillo)	1·80	1·60

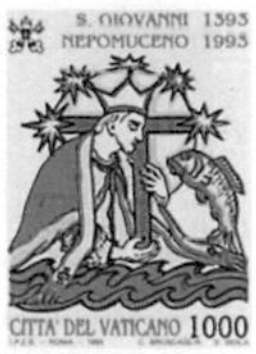

273 St. John, Cross, Carp and Moldava River

1993. 600th Death Anniv of St. John of Nepomuk (patron saint of Bohemia). Multicoloured.

1047	1000l. Type **273**	2·20	1·90
1048	2000l. Charles Bridge, Prague	4·00	3·50

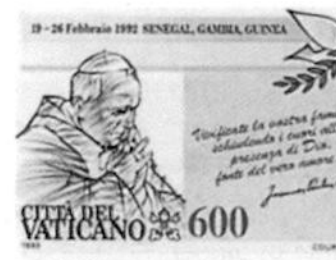

274 Pope praying

1993. Pope John Paul II's Journeys (11th series). Multicoloured.

1049	600l. Type **274** (Senegal, Gambia and Guinea)	1·70	1·50
1050	1000l. Pope with Pastoral Staff (Angola and St. Thomas and Prince Islands)	3·00	2·75
1051	5000l. Pope with hands clasped in prayer (Dominican Republic)	12·00	10·50

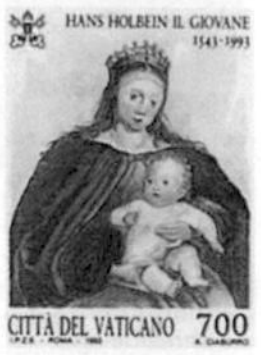

275 "Madonna of Solothurn" (detail)

MS1205	106×130 mm. 600l. Peter's Denial; 900l. Praying woman; 1000l. Christ with the Cross and two Apostles	9·75	9·50

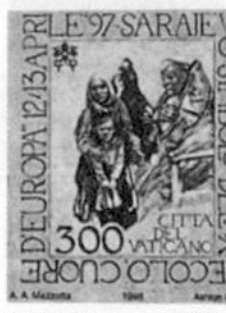

318 Pope and War Refugees

1998. Pope John Paul II's Journeys (16th series). Multicoloured.

1206	300l. Type **318** (Bosnia and Herzegovina)	60	55
1207	600l. Kneeling in front of statue of Jesus (Czech Republic)	1·20	1·00
1208	800l. With girls (Lebanon)	1·50	1·40
1209	900l. Welcome by garlanded girls (Poland)	1·70	1·50
1210	1300l. With young people (France)	2·50	2·30
1211	5000l. With children (Brazil)	10·50	9·50

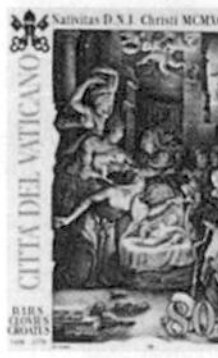

319 "Nativity" (Giulio Clovio)

1998. Christmas.

1212	**319**	800l. multicoloured	3·00	2·75

1999. Popes and their Holy Years (2nd series). As T **311**. Multicoloured.

1213	300l. Julius III (1550)	1·70	1·50
1214	600l. Gregory XIII (1575)	3·50	3·00
1215	800l. Clement VIII (1600)	5·00	4·50
1216	900l. Urban VIII (1625)	5·50	4·75
1217	1000l. Innocent X (1650)	5·75	5·25
1218	1300l. Clement X (1675)	8·00	7·00
1219	1500l. Innocent XII (1700)	9·75	8·50
1220	2000l. Benedict XIII (1725)	15·00	13·50

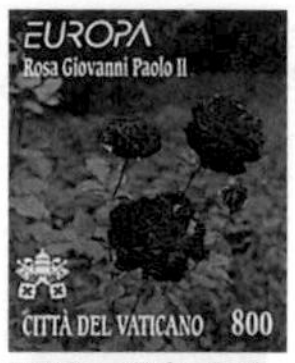

320 Rose "John Paul II"

1999. Europa. Parks and Gardens. Multicoloured.

1221	800l. Type **320**	3·00	2·75
1222	900l. Water lilies (Fountain of the Frogs, Vatican Gardens)	3·75	3·50

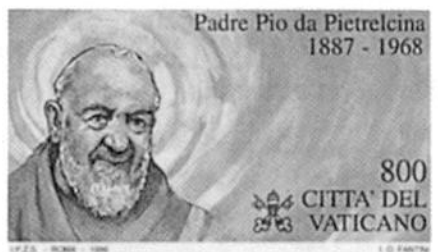

321 Father Pio

1999. Beatification of Father Pio da Pietrelcina (Capuchin friar who bore the stigmata). Multicoloured.

1223	800l. Type **321**	1·50	1·40
MS1224	86×115 mm. 300l. Monastery Church, San Giovanni Rotondo (29×39 mm); 600l. San Giovanni Rotondo new church (29×39 mm); 900l. Type **321** (59×39 mm)	3·25	3·00

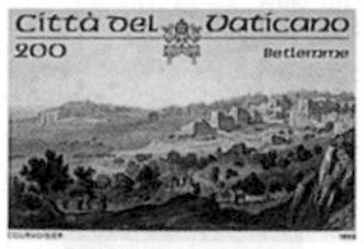

322 Bethlehem

1999. Sacred Places in the Holy Land. Illustrations from "The Holy Land" by I. Messmer. Multicoloured.

1225	200l. Type **322**	30	25
1226	500l. Nazareth	1·00	90
1227	800l. Lake Tiberius	1·50	1·40
1228	900l. Jerusalem	1·80	1·60
1229	1300l. Mount Tabor	2·50	2·30
MS1230	110×86 mm. 1000l. ×4, composite design of map of the Holy Land (from 17th-century Geographia Blaviana) (each 50×38 mm)	17·00	16·00

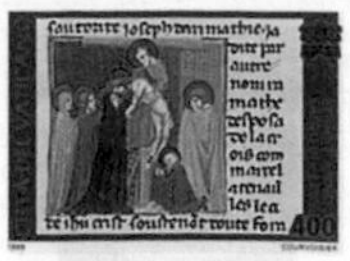

323 Deposition from the Cross

1999. Holy Year 2000 (5th issue). Illustrations from illuminated New Testament in Vatican Apostolic Library. Multicoloured.

1231	400l. Type **323**	75	70
1232	700l. The Resurrection	1·20	1·10
1233	1300l. Pentecost	2·50	2·20
1234	3000l. The Last Judgement	5·75	5·25

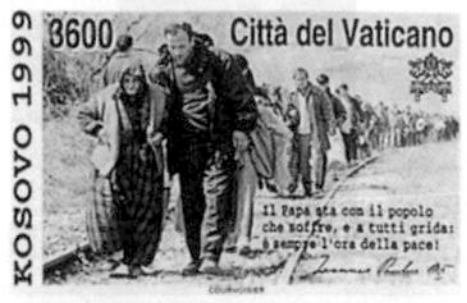

324 Refugees

1999. Kosovo Relief Fund.

1235	**324**	3600l. black	6·25	5·50

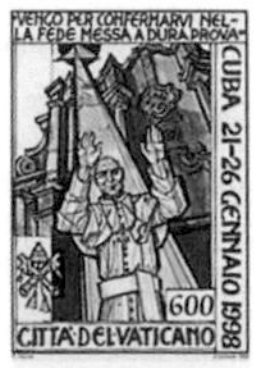

325 Visit to Cuba

1999. Pope John Paul II's Journeys (17th series). Multicoloured.

1236	600l. Type **325**	1·70	1·50
1237	800l. Stole over hands and staff (Nigeria)	2·20	1·90
1238	900l. Dove, cathedral and disabled people (Austria)	2·50	2·20
1239	1300l. With crucifix and statue (Croatia)	3·50	3·25
1240	2000l. Quirinal Palace, Rome (Italy)	5·50	5·00

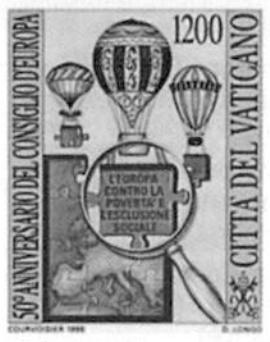

326 Hot Air Balloons, Jigsaw Puzzle of Europe and Magnifying Glass

1999. 50th Anniv of Council of Europe.

1241	**326**	1200l. multicoloured	2·30	2·10

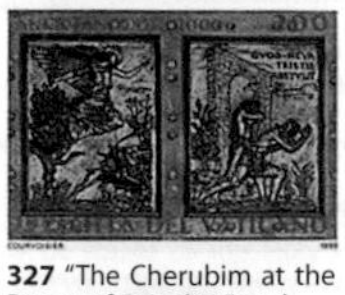

327 "The Cherubim at the Doors of Paradise" and "The Banishment from the Garden of Eden"

1999. Holy Year 2000 (6th issue). Opening of Holy Door, St. Peter's Basilica. Door panels. Multicoloured.

1242	200l. Type **327**	45	40
1243	300l. "The Annunciation" and "Angel"	75	70
1244	400l. "Baptism of Christ" and "Straying Sheep"	1·00	90
1245	500l. "The Merciful Father" and "Curing Paralysed Man"	1·20	1·10
1246	600l. "The Penitent Woman" and "The Obligation to Forgive"	1·50	1·30
1247	800l. "Peter's Denial" and "A Thief in Paradise"	2·00	1·80
1248	1000l. "Jesus appears to Thomas" and "Jesus appears to the Eleven"	2·50	2·20
1249	1200l. "Jesus appears to Saul" and "Opening of the Holy Door"	3·00	2·50
MS1250	106×142 mm. As Nos. 1242/9	12·50	11·50

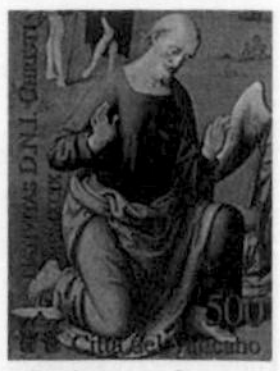

328 St. Joseph (detail)

1999. Christmas. "St. Joseph, the Virgin Mary and the Holy Child" (Giovanni di Petro). Multicoloured.

1251	500l. Type **328**	1·20	1·10
1252	800l. Holy Child (detail)	2·00	1·80
1253	900l. Virgin Mary (detail)	2·30	2·10
1254	1200l. Complete painting	3·50	3·00

2000. Popes and their Holy Years (3rd series). As T **311**. Multicoloured.

1255	300l. Benedict XIV (1750)	1·50	1·40
1256	400l. Pius VI (1775)	2·20	1·90
1257	500l. Leo XII (1825)	2·50	2·30
1258	600l. Pius IX (1875)	3·00	2·75
1259	700l. Leo XIII (1900)	3·75	3·50
1260	800l. Pius XI (1925)	4·50	4·00
1261	1200l. Pius XII (1950)	6·75	6·00
1262	1500l. Paul VI (1975)	8·50	7·50
1263	2000l. John Paul II (2000)	13·00	11·50
MS1264	137×103 mm. 2000l. John Paul II resting face on hand	5·50	5·00

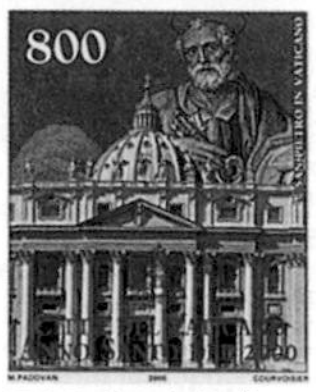

329 St. Peter's Basilica

2000. Holy Year 2000 (7th issue). Multicoloured.

1265	800l. Type **329**	1·80	1·60
1266	1000l. St. John Lateran Basilica	2·30	2·10
1267	1200l. St. Mary Major Basilica	3·00	2·50
1268	2000l. St. Paul-outside-the-Walls Basilica	4·75	4·25

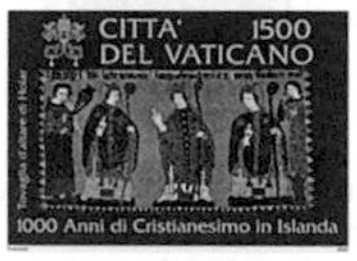

330 Embroidered Altar Frontal, Holar Cathedral

2000. Millenary of Christianity in Iceland.

1269	**330**	1500l. multicoloured	5·50	4·75

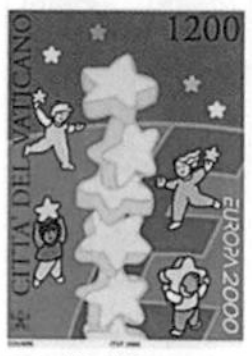

331 "Building Europe"

2000. Europa.

1270	**331**	1200l. multicoloured	4·50	4·00

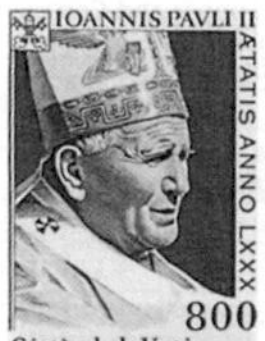

332 Pope John Paul II

2000. 80th Birthday of Pope John Paul II.

1271	**332**	800l. lilac	1·80	1·60
1272	-	1200l. blue	3·00	2·75
1273	-	2000l. green	5·50	4·75

DESIGNS: 1200l. Black Madonna of Czestochowa; 2000l. Pastoral Staff.

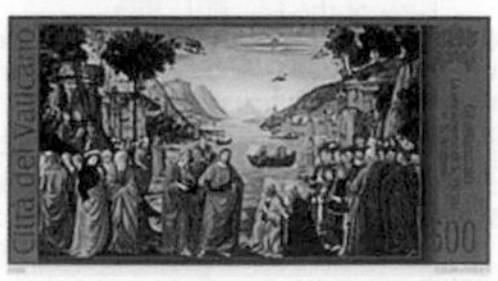

333 "The Calling of St. Peter and St. Andrew" (Domenico Ghirlandaio)

2000. Restoration of the Sistine Chapel (1st series). Multicoloured.

1274	500l. Type **333**	1·50	1·40
1275	1000l. "The Trials of Moses" (Sandro Botticelli)	2·30	2·10
1276	1500l. "The Donation of the Keys" (Pietro Perugino)	3·00	2·75
1277	3000l. "The Worship of the Golden Calf" (Cosimo Rosselli)	7·00	6·25

See also Nos. 1294/7 and 1339/42.

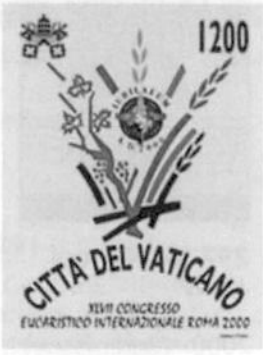

334 Congress Emblem

2000. 47th International Eucharistic Congress, Rome.

1278	**334**	1200l. multicoloured	3·00	2·75

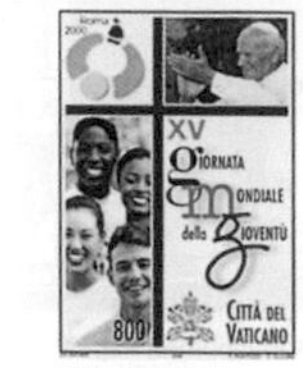

335 Pope John Paul II and Youths' Faces

2000. 15th World Youth Day, Rome. Multicoloured. (a) Ordinary gum.

1279	800l. Type **335**	1·80	1·60
1280	1000l. Girl waving flag	2·30	2·10
1281	1200l. Youths' cheering	3·00	2·75
1282	2000l. Youth waving flag	4·50	4·00

(b) Self-adhesive.

1283	1000l. As No. 1280	3·00	2·75

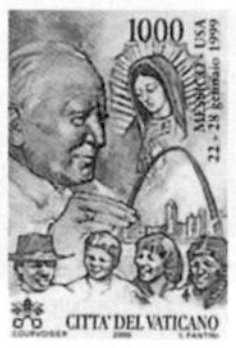

336 Pope and Children

2000. Pope John Paul II's Journeys (18th series). Multicoloured.

1284	1000l. Type **336** (Mexico and United States of America)	2·30	2·10
1285	1000l. Pope praying, building and children waving (Rumania)	2·30	2·10
1286	1000l. Holding Pastoral Staff (Poland)	2·30	2·10
1287	1000l. Pope and Bishop Anton Martin Slomsek (Slovenia)	2·30	2·10
1288	1000l. Pope, churches and crowd (India and Georgia)	2·30	2·10

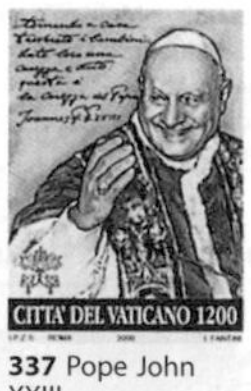

337 Pope John XXIII

2000. Beatification of Pope John XXIII.

1289	**337**	1200l. multicoloured	3·00	2·75

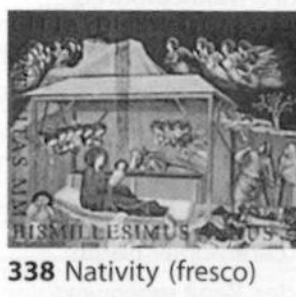

338 Nativity (fresco)

2000. Christmas. Designs showing Fresco by Giotto from St. Francis Basilica. Multicoloured.

1290	800l. Type **338**	2·30	2·10
1291	1200l. Baby Jesus (detail)	3·25	3·00
1292	1500l. Mary (detail)	4·25	3·75
1293	2000l. Joseph (detail)	6·00	5·25

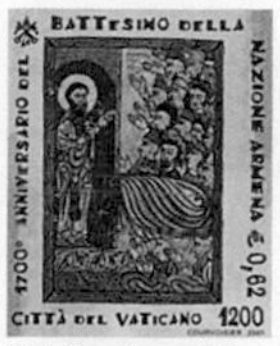

339 Freedom of St. Gregory

2001. Restoration of the Sistine Chapel (2nd series). As T **333**. Multicoloured.

1294	800l. "The Baptism of Christ" (Pietro Perugino)	1·80	1·60
1295	1200l. "The Passage through the Red Sea" (Biagio d'Antonio)	2·75	2·50
1296	1500l. "The Punishment of Core, Datan and Abiron" (Botticelli)	3·75	3·50
1297	4000l. "The Sermon on the Mount" (Cosimo Rosselli)	8·50	7·50

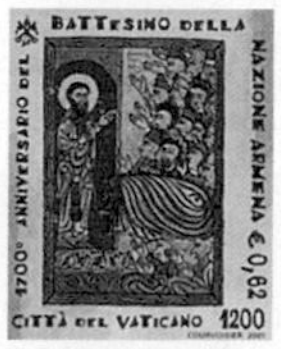

339 Freedom of St. Gregory

2001. 1700th Anniv of the Adoption of Christianity in Armenia. Multicoloured.

1298	1200l. Type **339**	3·00	2·75
1299	1500l. St. Gregory making Agatangel write	3·75	3·50
1300	2000l. St. Gregory and King Tirade meet Emperor Constantine and Pope Sylvester I	4·50	4·00

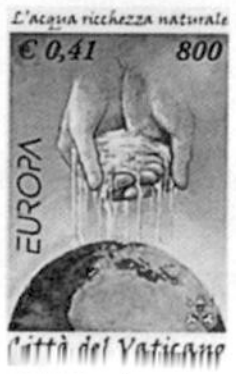

340 Hands holding Water and Globe

2001. Europa. Water Resources. Multicoloured.

1301	800l. Type **340**	2·30	2·10
1302	1200l. Hand and catching rain water	4·25	3·75

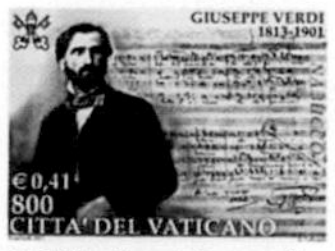

341 Verdi and Score of *Nabucco*

2001. Death Centenary of Giuseppe Verdi (composer). Multicoloured.

1303	800l. Type **341**	2·30	2·10
1304	1500l. Verdi and character from *Aida*	3·75	3·50
1305	2000l. Verdi and scene from *Otello*	5·50	4·75

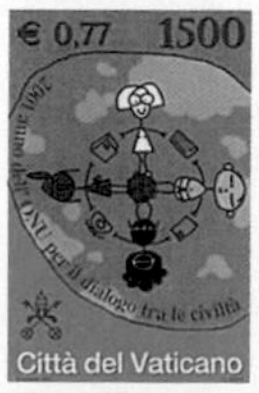

342 Children encircling Globe

2001. U.N. Year of Dialogue between Civilizations.

1306	**342**	1500l. multicoloured	4·25	3·75

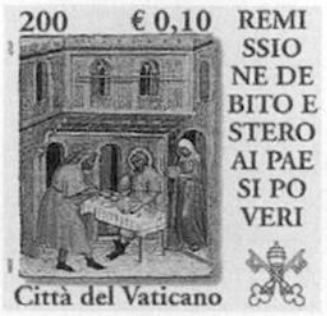

343 Couple feeding Poor Man

2001. Cancellation of Foreign Debt of Poor Countries. Showing illustrations from "Works of Corporal Mercy" (15th-century panels by Carlo di Camerino). Multicoloured.

1307	200l. Type **343**	45	40
1308	400l. Giving alms	1·10	95
1309	800l. Giving clothing	1·80	1·60
1310	1000l. Women caring for sick man	2·30	2·10
1311	1500l. Man visiting prisoner	4·50	4·00

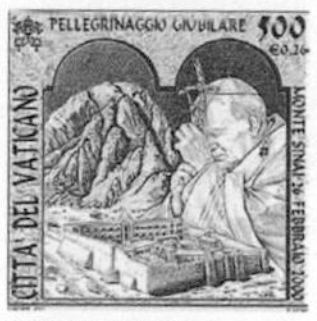

344 Mount Sinai, Monastery of Holy Catherine and Pope

2001. Pope John Paul II's Journeys (19th series). The Holy Land. Multicoloured.

1312	500l. Type **344**	1·50	1·40
1313	800l. Pope before Crucifix, Mount Nebo	2·30	2·10
1314	1200l. Pope celebrating Mass	3·75	3·50
1315	1500l. Pope at prayer Holy Sepulchre	4·50	4·00
1316	5000l. Pope praying at Shrine of Fatima	11·00	9·50
MS1317	85×115 mm. 3000l. Pope at Western Wall, Jerusalem (35×27 mm)	7·75	7·50

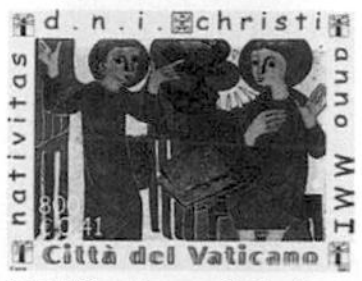

345 "The Annunciation"

2001. Christmas. Designs showing scenes from "Life of Christ" (enamel, Egino G. Weinert). Multicoloured.

1318	800l. Type **345**	2·50	2·20
1319	1200l. "The Nativity"	3·00	2·75
1320	1500l. "Adoration of the Magi"	4·50	4·00

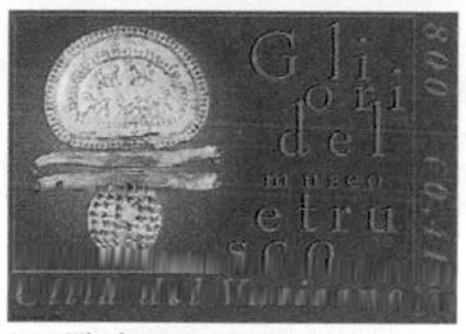

346 Fibula, 675–650 B.C.

2001. Etruscan Museum Exhibits. Multicoloured.

1321	800l. Type **346**	1·80	1·60
1322	1200l. 6th-century earrings	2·75	2·40
1323	1500l. Embossed Greek stud, 425–400 B.C	3·75	3·50
1324	2000l. 3rd-century Greek head of Medusa	5·50	4·75

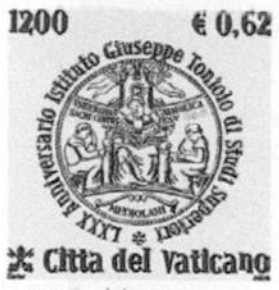

347 Emblem

2001. 80th Anniv of Guiseppe Toniolo Institute for Higher Studies and the Catholic University of the Sacred Heart.

1325	**347**	1200l. blue and red	3·50	3·25

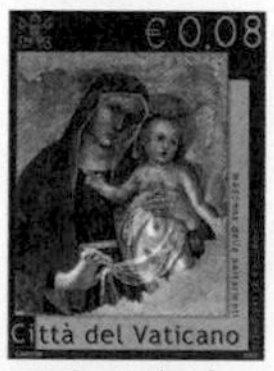

348 Our Lady of Women in Labour (14th-century fresco)

2002. Our Lady in the Vatican Basilica. Multicoloured.

1326	8c. Type **348**	30	25
1327	15c. Our Lady with people praying (mosaic)	55	50
1328	23c. Our Lady at the Tomb of Pius XII (15th-century fresco)	90	80
1329	31c. Our Lady of the Fever (13th-century)	1·20	1·10
1330	41c. Our Lady of the Slap	1·70	1·50
1331	52c. Mary Immaculate (mosaic)	2·10	1·80
1332	62c. Our Lady of Christians	2·50	2·20
1333	77c. The Virgin of the Deesis	3·75	3·50
1334	€1.03 L'Addolorata (painting, Lippo Memmi)	4·50	4·00
1335	€1.55 Presentation of Mary at the Temple (mosaic)	7·75	6·75

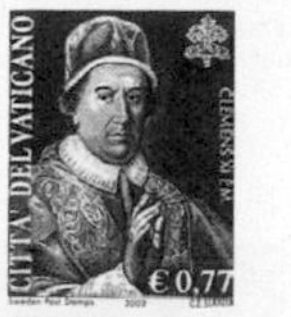

349 Pope Clement XI

2002. 300th Anniv of Pontifical Ecclesiastical Academy, Rome.

1336	**349**	77c. purple	3·00	2·75
1337	-	77c. green (46×33 mm)	3·00	2·75
1338	-	77c. purple	3·00	2·75

DESIGNS: No. 1337 Facade of Piazza della Minerva Institute, Rome; 1338 Pope John Paul II.

2002. Restoration of the Sistine Chapel (3rd series). As T **333**. Multicoloured.

1339	26c. "The Temptation of Christ" (Botticelli)	1·20	1·10
1340	41c. "The Last Supper" (Cosimo Rosselli)	1·80	1·60
1341	77c. "Moses' Journey into Egypt" (Pietro Perugino)	3·50	3·00
1342	€1.55 "The Last Days of Moses" (Luca Signorelli)	7·00	6·25

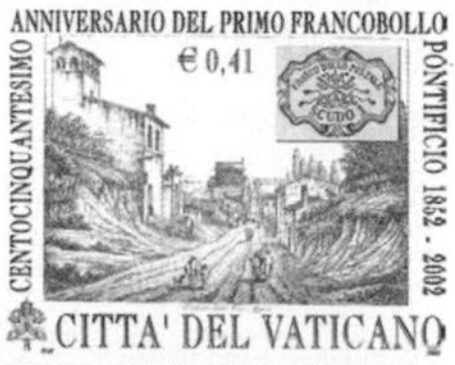

350 Regina Viarum (Appian Way) and 1852 Papal States Stamp

2002. Centenary of Pontifical Stamps.

1343	**350**	41c. deep brown, purple and brown	1·70	1·50
1344	-	52c. multicoloured	2·30	2·10
1345	-	€1.03 blue, indigo and green	4·75	4·25
MS1346		104×83 mm. €1.55 brown, buff and purple	7·00	6·50

DESIGNS: No. 1344, Cassian Way and 1868 80ch. Papal States stamp; 1345, Porta Angelica, Vatican and 1929 Vatican City State 10ch. stamp. 30×30 mm (circular)—**MS**1346, Courtyard, Palazzo Madama, Rome.

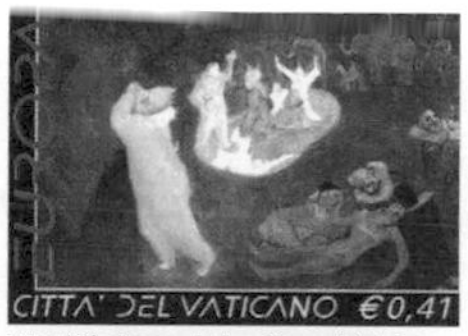

351 "Christ and the Circus" (Aldo Carpi)

2002. Europa. Circus. Multicoloured.

1347	41c. Type **351**	1·80	1·60
1348	62c. Christ with clown (detail of "Christ and the Circus")	3·00	2·75

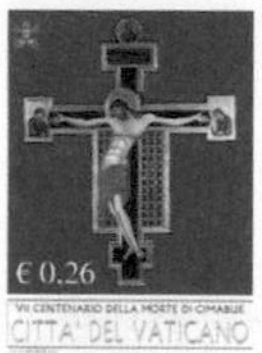

352 Crucifix, St. Dominic Church, Arezzo

2002. 700th Death Anniv of Cenni di Pepo (Cimabue) (artist). Showing the Crucifix and details thereof. Multicoloured.

1349	41c. Type **352**	1·20	1·10
1350	62c. Jesus	2·75	2·40
1351	77c. Mary	3·50	3·00
1352	€1.03 John the Baptist	4·50	4·00

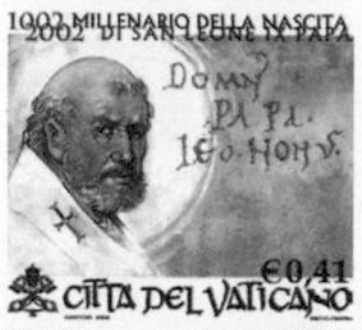

353 Pope Leo IX and Wall Inscription

2002. Birth Millenary of Pope Leo IX. Multicoloured.

1353	41c. Type **353**	1·80	1·60
1354	62c. Arrival in Rome as pilgrim and coronation as Pope	2·75	2·40
1355	€1.29 Leo IX in chains	5·50	5·00

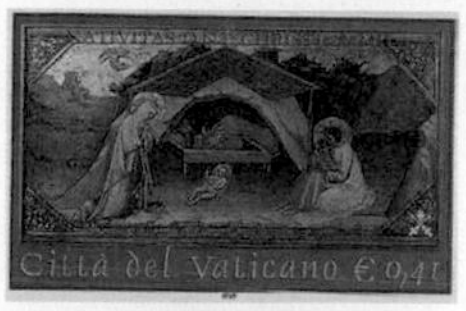

354 "The Nativity" (15th-century painting in style of Di Baldese) (⅔-size illustration)

2002. Christmas.

1356	**354**	41c. multicoloured	5·50	4·75

A stamp of a similar design was issued by New Zealand.

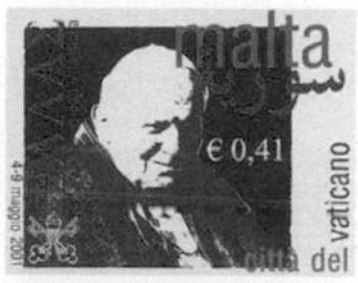

355 Pope John Paul II (Malta)

2002. Journeys of Pope John Paul II in 2001. Multicoloured.

1357	41c. Type **355**	1·80	1·60
1358	62c. Praying (Ukraine)	2·75	2·50
1359	€1.55 Wearing mitre (Kazakhstan)	6·75	6·00

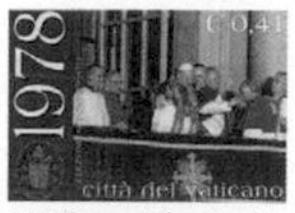

356 Pope John Paul II on Balcony of St. Peter's Basilica, 1978

2003. 25th Anniv of the Pontificate of Pope John Paul II (1st issue). Multicoloured.

1360	41c. Type **356**	1·50	1·40
1361	41c. Celebrating mass, Victory Square, Warsaw, 1979	1·50	1·40
1362	41c. Addressing young people, Parc des Princes Stadium, Paris, 1980	1·50	1·40
1363	41c. Assassination attempt, St. Peter Square, 1981	1·50	1·40
1364	41c. Giving homily surrounded by flowers, Portugal, 1982	1·50	1·40
1365	41c. Kneeling in front of Holy Doors, start of Holy Year of Redemption, 1983	1·50	1·40
1366	41c. Meeting Sandro Pertini, President of Italy, 1984	1·50	1·40
1367	41c. International Youth Day, Rome, 1985	1·50	1·40
1368	41c. First visit of Pope to Synagogue, 1986	1·50	1·40
1369	41c. Inaugurating Year of Mary, 1987	1·50	1·40
1370	41c. Visiting European Parliament, Strasbourg, 1988	1·50	1·40
1371	41c. Meeting President Mikhail Gorbachev, Soviet Union, 1989	1·50	1·40
1372	41c. Visiting lepers in Guinea-Bissau, 1990	1·50	1·40
1373	41c. Addressing Bishop's Synod, 1991	1·50	1·40
1374	41c. Pronouncing the Catechism, 1992	1·50	1·40
1375	41c. Enthroned, Assissi, 1993	1·50	1·40
1376	41c. Celebrating Mass in the Sistine Chapel, 1994	1·50	1·40
1377	41c. Addressing the United Nations, 1995	1·50	1·40
1378	41c. Walking through the Brandenburg Gate with Chancellor Helmut Kohl, 1996	1·50	1·40
1379	41c. Celebrating Mass in Sarajevo, 1997	1·50	1·40
1380	41c. With Fidel Castro, Cuba, 1998	1·50	1·40
1381	41c. Opening door, Christmas, 1999	1·50	1·40
1382	41c. With young people, World Youth Day, Rome, 2000	1·50	1·40
1383	41c. Closing door of St. Peter's Basilica, 2001	1·50	1·40
1384	41c. Visiting the Italian Parliament, 2002	1·50	1·40

Stamps of the same design were issued by Poland.

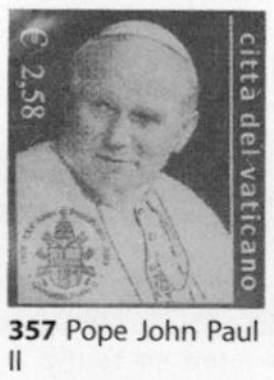

357 Pope John Paul II

2003. 25th Anniv of the Pontificate of Pope John Paul II (2nd issue). Self-adhesive.

1385 357 €2.58 silver 13·00 11·50

A stamp of the same design was issued by Poland.

358 Dove (Holy Year 1975)

2003. Europa. Poster Art. Multicoloured.

| 1386 | 41c. Type **358** | 1·80 | 1·60 |
| 1387 | 62c. St. Cyril and St. Methodius | 3·00 | 2·75 |

359 St. Sixtus ordaining St. Lawrence

2003. Paintings from the Niccolina Chapel by Friar Giovanni da Fiesole (Beato Angelico). Multicoloured.

1388	41c. Type **359**	1·70	1·50
1389	62c. St. Stephen preaching	2·50	2·30
1390	77c. St. Lawrence on trial	3·25	2·75
1391	€1.03 Stoning of St. Stephen	4·50	4·00

360 St. George slaying Dragon

2003. 1700th Anniv of Death of St. George.

1392 360 62c. multicoloured 3·50 3·00

361 Dragon

2003. Animal Paintings from the Vatican Basilica. Multicoloured.

1393	21c. Type **361**	85	75
1394	31c. Camel	1·50	1·40
1395	77c. Horse	3·25	2·75
1396	€1.03 Leopard	4·50	4·00

362 Mother Teresa

2003. Beatification of Mother Teresa (humanitarian worker).

1397 362 41c. multicoloured 2·30 2·10

363 "Blessed are the Pure in Heart" (Paul Gauguin)

2003. Artists' Anniversaries. Multicoloured.

| 1398 | 41c. Type **363** (death centenary) | 2·00 | 1·80 |
| 1399 | 62c. "The Pieta" (Vincent van Gogh) (150th birth anniv) | 3·00 | 2·75 |

364 Josemaria Escriva

2003. Birth Centenary (2002) of Josemaria Escriva De Balaguer (founder of Opus Dei (religious organization)).

1400 364 41c. multicoloured 1·80 1·60

365 The Nativity

2003. Christmas. 25th Death Anniv of Pope Paul VI (MS1402).

| 1401 | 365 | 41c. multicoloured | 2·20 | 1·90 |
| MS1402 | 106×83 mm. **365** 41c. multicoloured | | 5·50 | 5·25 |

366 Orthodox Priests and Pope John Paul II (Bulgaria and Azerbaijan)

2003. Journeys of Pope John Paul II in 2002. Multicoloured.

1403	62c. Type **366**	2·50	2·20
1404	77c. Pope John Paul II and World Youth Day emblem (Canada, Guatemala and Mexico City)	3·00	2·75
1405	€2.55 With raised hand (Poland)	8·25	7·50

367 Pope Pius V (detail, altarpiece) (Grazio Cossoli)

2004. 500th Birth Anniv of Pope Pius V. Multicoloured.

| 1406 | 4c. Type **367** | 30 | 25 |
| 1407 | €2 Our Lady of the Rosary (detail, altarpiece) (Grazio Cossoli) | 8·75 | 7·75 |

368 Pope John Paul II

2004. Pope John Paul II visits to Poland, 1979—2002. Two sheets, each 115×185 mm containing T **368** and similar vert designs. Multicoloured.

| MS1408 | (a) 45c.×4, Type **368** (1979); At prayer (1983); Holding reliquary (1987); Resting head against staff (1991). (b) 62c.×4, Holding staff (1991); With raised hand (1997); Seated facing right (1999); Seated facing left (2002) | 25·00 | 23·00 |

Stamps of the same design were issued by Poland.

369 Pope John Paul II (Spain)

2004. Journeys of Pope John Paul II in 2003. Multicoloured.

1409	60c. Type **369**	4·50	4·00
1410	62c. With head in hand (Bosnia and Herzegovina)	4·75	4·25
1411	80c. Holding staff (Croatia)	6·25	5·50
1412	€1.40 Wearing stole and zucchetto (Slovakia)	11·00	9·50

Nos. 1409/10 were issued with a se-tenant label inscribed "Priority Mail".

370 Austrian Flag and Coin

2004. The Euro. Showing country flag and coin. Multicoloured.

1413	4c. Type **370**	30	25
1414	8c. Belgium	45	40
1415	15c. Finland	75	70
1416	25c. France	1·20	1·10
1417	30c. Germany	1·40	1·20
1418	40c. Greece	1·50	1·40
1419	45c. Vatican City	1·80	1·60
1420	60c. Eire	2·30	2·10
1421	62c. Italy	2·50	2·20
1422	70c. Luxembourg	2·75	2·50
1423	80c. Monaco	3·25	2·75
1424	€1 Netherlands	4·00	3·50
1425	€1.40 Portugal	5·50	5·00
1426	€2 San Marino	9·25	8·25
1427	€2.80 Spain	11·50	10·50

371 Children

2004. AIDS Awareness Campaign.

1428 371 45c. multicoloured 2·50 2·30

372 Horse Riding

2004. Europa. Holidays. Multicoloured.

| 1429 | 45c. Type **372** | 3·00 | 2·75 |
| 1430 | 62c. Walking in French-style garden | 3·75 | 3·50 |

373 "Still Life with Bottles" (Giorgio Morandi)

2004. Modern Art. Multicoloured.

1431	45c. Type **373**	2·10	1·80
1432	60c. "Falling Angel" (Marino Marini)	2·75	2·50
1433	80c. "Landscape with Houses" (Ezio Pastorio)	3·75	3·50
1434	85c. "Tuscan Dunes" (Giulio Ceasare Vinzio)	4·25	3·75

374 Eucharist

2004. 48th International Eucharist Congress, Guadalajara, Mexico. Multicoloured.

| 1435 | 45c. Type **374** | 2·20 | 2·00 |
| 1436 | 65c. Hands | 3·00 | 2·75 |

375 Petrarch and Script

2004. 700th Birth Anniv of Petrarch (Francesco Petrarca) (poet).

1437 375 60c. multicoloured 3·25 3·00

376 Nativity

2004. Christmas.

| 1438 | 376 | 80c. brown, green and black | 4·00 | 3·75 |

377 Emblems, Manuscript and Pen

2005. 20th Anniv of Ratification Italy—Vatican Concordat (abolishing Catholicism as state religion). Multicoloured.

| 1448 | 45c. Type **377** | 2·20 | 1·90 |
| 1449 | €2.80 Emblems and map | 12·00 | 11·00 |

Stamps of the same design were issued by Italy.

378 Man Sleeping

2005. "Resurrection of Christ" by Pietro Vannucci (Perugino). Details of the painting. Multicoloured.

1450	60c. Type **378**	3·25	3·00
1451	62c. Sleeping soldier	3·25	3·00
1452	80c. With head in hand	3·75	3·50
1453	€1 With raised eyes	4·75	4·25
MS1454	80×120 mm. €2.80 Risen Christ (29×60 mm)	12·00	11·00

Nos. 1441/4, respectively, were each issued with a se-tenant label inscribed "priority mail".

379 Apostolic Camera Arms (Carlo Malli)

2005. "Vacant See".

1439	379	60c. multicoloured	3·25	3·00
1440	379	62c. multicoloured	3·50	3·25
1441	379	80c. multicoloured	3·75	3·50

380 Pope Benedict XVI

2005. Enthronement of Pontificate of Pope Benedict XVI. Multicoloured.

1442	45c. Type **380**	2·20	1·90
1443	62c. With clasped hands	3·25	3·00
1444	80c. With raised hands	3·75	3·50

381 Cross and Globe

2005. World Youth Day.

1445 381 62c. multicoloured 2·75 2·50

A stamp of the same design was issued by Germany.

382 Ceramic Plate (Pablo Picasso)

2005. Europa. Gastronomy. Multicoloured.

| 1446 | 62c. Type **382** | 2·75 | 2·20 |
| 1447 | 80c. Ceramic plate (Pablo Picasso) (different) | 3·75 | 3·50 |

383 Pope John Paul II
(Bern, Switzerland)

2005. Journeys of Pope John Paul II in 2004. Multicoloured.

1455	45c. Type **383**	2·20	1·90
1456	80c. Facing right (Lourdes)	4·25	3·75
1457	€2 With raised arms (Loreto, Italy)	9·75	8·75

384 "Dinner at Emmaus"
(Primo Conti)

2005. Ordinary General Assembly of Bishops' Synod.

1458	**384** 62c. multicoloured	3·50	3·25

385 "The Annunciation"

2005. Art. "The Annunciation" by Raffello Sanzio (Raphael). Multicoloured.

1459	62c. Type **385**	2·75	2·50
1460	€1 "The Annunciation" (different)	4·75	4·25
MS1461	131×86 mm. €1.40×2, As Type **385**; As No. 1460	12·50	12·00

Stamps of a similar design were issued by France.

386 Child with
Doves

2005. Christmas. "Adoration of Shepherds" by Francois le Moyne. Showing details from the painting. Multicoloured.

1462	45c. Type **386**	2·20	1·90
1463	62c. Angel	3·25	3·00
1464	80c. Mary and Jesus	3·75	3·50

387 Swiss Papal Guard

2005. 500th Anniv of Swiss Papal Guard. Multicoloured.

1465	62c. Type **387**	2·75	2·50
1466	80c. Three guards facing left	3·75	3·50

Stamps of a similar design were issued by Switzerland.

388 Pierre Favre (500th
birth anniv)

2006. Saints' Anniversaries.

1467	**388** 45c. multicoloured	2·10	1·90
1468	- 62c. blue	2·75	2·40
1469	- €2 multicoloured	9·00	8·00

DESIGNS: 45c. Type **388**; 60c. Ignatius Loyola (450th death anniv); €2 Francis Xavier (500th birth anniv).

389 Madonna and Child

2006. 500th Death Centenary of Andrea Mantegna (artist). Designs showing details of San Zeno Polyptych, Verona. Multicoloured.

1470	60c. Type **389**	2·75	2·40
1471	85c. Saint John the Baptist	3·75	3·50
1472	€1 Saints Peter and Paul	4·75	4·50
MS1473	96×116 mm. Size 21×37 mm. €1.40×2, Saints Peter and Paul; Saints John the Baptist and Gregory	12·50	12·00

390 Places of Worship and
Hands

2006. Europa. Integration. Multicoloured.

1474	62c. Type **390**	3·25	3·00
1475	80c. Children in classrooms	4·75	4·25

391 Figure and
Building

2006. 500th Anniv of Saint Peter's Basilica. Medallions. Multicoloured.

1476	45c. Type **391**	2·75	2·40
1477	45c. Donato Bramante	2·75	2·40
1478	60c. Pope Julius II	3·50	3·25
1479	60c. Basilica	3·50	3·25

Nos. 1476/7 and 1478/9 were issued together, se-tenant, forming a composite design.

392 Pope Benedict
XVI (National
Eucharistic Congress,
Bari)

2006. Apostolic Journeys of Pope Benedict XVI in 2005. Multicoloured.

1480	62c. Type **392**	2·75	2·50
1481	€1.40 World Youth Day, Cologne	6·50	5·75

Nos. 1480/1 each have a label inscribed "Posta Prioritaria" attached at foot.

393 Mozart

2006. 250th Birth Anniv of Wolfgang Amadeus Mozart (composer).

1482	**393** 80c. multicoloured	4·00	3·50

394 Shepherds

2006. Christmas. Multicoloured.

1483	60c. Type **394**	3·00	2·75
1484	65c. Holy Family	3·25	3·00
1485	85c. Three Kings	4·25	3·75

395 Antiphantes

2006. 500th Anniv of Vatican Museums. Multicoloured.

1486	60c. Type **395**	2·75	2·50

1487	65c. Laocoon	3·00	2·75
1488	€1.40 Thymbraeus	6·75	6·00
MS1489	81×95 mm. €2.80 Laocoon (81×30 mm)	13·50	13·00

396 Child and Parched Earth

2006. International Year of Deserts and Desertification. Multicoloured.

1490	62c. Type **396**	2·75	2·50
1491	€1 Child and oxen	4·50	4·00

397 Singapore
Merlion and St.
Peter's Basilica,
Rome

2006. 25th Anniv of Diplomatic Relations between Singapore and Vatican City. Multicoloured.

1492	85c. Type **397**	3·75	3·50
1493	€2 Flags of Singapore and Vatican City	9·00	8·00

398 Francesco di Paola

2007. 500th Death Anniv of Francesco di Paola (St Francis of Paola) (founder of the Order of Minims). Each black and cobalt.

1494	60c. Type **398**	2·75	2·40
1495	€1 Angel	4·50	4·00

399 Pope Benedict
XVI

2007. 80th Birth Anniv of Pope Benedict XVI. Multicoloured.

1496	60c. Type **399**	2·75	2·40
1497	65c. Giving blessing	3·25	2·75
1498	85c. Wearing mitre	4·00	3·75

400 Scouts

2007. Europa. Centenary of Scouting. Multicoloured.

1499	60c. Type **400**	2·75	2·40
1500	65c. Campfire	3·00	2·75

401 Carlo Goldoni, Actors
and Rialto Bridge, Venice

2007. 300th Birth Anniv of Carlo Goldoni (playwright). Multicoloured.

1501	60c. Type **401**	2·75	2·40
1502	85c. Carlo Goldoni, actors and Notre Dame, France	3·75	3·50
MS1503	285×110 mm. €2.80 Carlo Goldoni	12·50	12·00

No. **MS**1503 was divided into five parts, the whole forming a composite design.

402 Gilded Glass and
Silver Vase

2007. 250th Anniv of Christian Museum. Multicoloured.

1504	85c. Type **402**	3·75	3·50
1505	€2 Bronze lamp and silver bottle	9·00	8·00

403 Atomium, Brussels

2007. 50th Anniv of Treaties of Rome. Designs showing original members. Multicoloured.

1506	15c. Type **403**	70	65
1507	30c. Eiffel Tower, Paris	1·30	1·20
1508	60c. Brandenburg Gate, Berlin	2·75	2·40
1509	65c. The Capitol, Rome	3·00	2·75
1510	€1 Vianden Castle, Luxembourg	4·50	4·00
1511	€4 Old Town, Amsterdam	18·00	16·00
MS1512	115×85 mm. €2.80 Mother and child (41×37 mm)	12·50	12·00

The stamp of **MS**1512 is placed in the top right corner and together with the margins forms a composite design.

404 Papal Stamps

2007. Inauguration of Philatelic and Numismatic Museum. Multicoloured.

1513	60c. Type **404**	2·50	2·30
1514	60c. Papal coins	2·50	2·30

405 Poland

2007. Journeys of Benedict XVI. Multicoloured. (a) Ordinary gum.

1515	60c. Type **405**	2·75	2·40
1516	65c. Valencia	3·00	2·75
1517	85c. Germany	3·75	3·50
1518	€1.40 With Bartholomew I (Ecumenical Patriarch of Constantinople), Turkey	6·25	5·75

(b) Self-adhesive.

1519	85c. As No. 1517	3·75	3·50

406 Madonna and Child

2007. Christmas. Designs showing details from painting The Nativity by Giuseppe Cali, St. Andrew's Parish Church, Luqa. Multicoloured.

1520	60c. Type **406**	2·75	2·50
1521	65c. Holy Family, women and child	3·00	2·75
1522	85c. Infant Christ and child	4·00	3·75

Stamps of a similar design were issued by Malta.

407 St Elizabeth
tending the Sick

2007. 800th Birth Anniv of St Elizabeth von Thuringen.

1523	**407** 65c. multicoloured	3·25	3·00

408 'libica' (Libyan Sibyl)

2008. 500th Anniv of Sistine Chapel. Multicoloured.

1524	5c. Type **408**	20	15
1525	10c. 'eritrea' (Eritrean Sibyl)	40	35
1526	25c. 'delfica' (Delphic Sibyl)	95	85
1527	60c. 'cumana' (Cumean Sibyl)	2·75	2·50
1528	65c. 'daniele' (Daniel)	3·00	2·75
1529	85c. 'giona' (Jonah)	4·00	3·50
1530	€2 'ezechiele' (Ezikiel)	9·25	8·50
1531	€5 'zaccaria' (Zacheriah)	23·00	21·00

409 Postmarks

2008. Europa. The Letter. Multicoloured.

| 1532 | 60c. Type **409** | 2·75 | 2·50 |
| 1533 | 85c. Pope Benedict XVI writing | 4·00 | 3·75 |

410 Wedding at Cana, Washing Christ's Feet and The Last Supper

2008. 49th International Eucharistic Congress, Quebec. Multicoloured.

| 1534 | 60c. Type **410** | 2·75 | 2·50 |
| 1535 | 85c. Crucifixion, Resurrection and Disciples | 4·00 | 3·75 |

411 Lourdes

2008. 150th Anniv of Apparition at Lourdes. Multicoloured.

| 1536 | 65c. Type **411** | 6·50 | 6·00 |
| 1537 | 85c. Apparition | 8·50 | 7·75 |

412 Map and Crowd

2008. World Youth Day 2008, Sydney.

| 1538 | **412** | €1 multicoloured | 4·75 | 4·25 |

413 UN Emblem and Pope Benedict XVI

2008. Pope Benedict XVI's visit to United Nations to Celebrate 60th Anniv of Universal Declaration of Human Rights.

| 1539 | **413** | €1.40 multicoloured | 6·50 | 6·00 |

414 Conversion on Road to Damascus

2008. Pauline Year. Designs showing scenes from the life of St. Paul. Multicoloured.

1540	60c. Type **414**	3·50	3·25
1541	65c. Preaching	4·00	3·50
1542	85c. In prison	5·00	4·75

415 Pope Benedict XVI (Brazil)

2008. Apostolic Journeys of Pope Benedict XVI in 2007. Multicoloured.

| 1543 | 65c. Type **415** | 4·00 | 3·50 |
| 1544 | 85c. Pope Benedict XVI (Austria) | 5·00 | 4·75 |

416 Adoration of the Magi (Raphael (Raffaello Sanzio))

2008. Christmas. Multicoloured.

(a) Ordinary gum

| 1545 | 60c. Type **416** | 3·50 | 3·25 |
| 1546 | 65c. Birth of Christ (Albrecht Durer) (vert) | 4·00 | 3·50 |

(b) Self-adhesive.

| 1546a | 60c. As Type **416** | 3·50 | 3·25 |

417 Villa Rotonda

2008. 500th Birth Anniv of Andrea Palladio (architect). Multicoloured.

1547	65c. Type **417**	4·00	3·75
1548	85c. San Giorgio Maggiore Church	5·00	5·00
MS1549	88×115 mm. €2.80 Andrea Palladio	17·00	16·00

418 Arms of Vatican and Order of Malta

2008. Vatican City–Order of Malta Postal Convention.

| 1550 | **418** | €2.50 multicoloured | 15·00 | 14·50 |

419 Pope Pius XI

2009. 80th Anniv of Vatican City State. Multicoloured.

1551	65c. Type **419**	4·00	3·75
1552	65c. Pius XII	4·00	3·75
1553	65c. John XXIII	4·00	3·75
1554	65c. Paul VI	4·00	3·75
1555	65c. John Paul I	4·00	3·75
1556	65c. John Paul II	4·00	3·75
1557	65c. Benedict XVI	4·00	3·75
MS1558	88×115 mm. €2.80 Map of Vatican City (detail) (P. Isola, P. Di Sciuillo and G. Greco)	17·00	16·00

420 Virgin and Child (shrine of Our Lady of Europe at Europa Point, Gibraltar)

2009. 700th Anniv of Our Lady of Europe.

| 1559 | **420** | 85c. multicoloured | 5·00 | 5·00 |

Stamps of a similar design were issued by Gibraltar.

421 Codex Vaticanus

2009. World Book and Copyright Day.

| 1560 | **421** | 60c. multicoloured | 3·50 | 3·50 |

422 Astronomical Observations–The Sun (Donato Creti)

2009. Europa. Astronomy. Multicoloured.

| 1561 | 60c. Type **422** | 3·50 | 3·50 |
| 1562 | 65c. Astronomical Observations– Saturn (Donato Creti) | 4·00 | 3·75 |

423 Scholar

2009. Centenary of Pontifical Biblical Institute.

| 1563 | **423** | 85c. multicoloured | 5·00 | 5·00 |

424 Healing of Poor Man with Injured Arm

2009. 400th Anniv of Canonization of St. Francisca Romana. Design showing frescoes from Tor de' Specchi Convent. Multicoloured.

| 1564 | 85c. Type **424** | 5·00 | 5·00 |
| 1565 | €1 Miracle of the Grapes | 6·00 | 5·75 |

425 Vatican Library

2009. International Federation of Library Associations and Institutions General Conference, Milan.

| 1566 | **425** | €1.40 multicoloured | 8·50 | 8·25 |

426 Cardinal Massaia

2009. Birth Bicentenary of Cardinal Guglielmo Massaia.

| 1567 | **426** | 60c. multicoloured | 3·50 | 3·25 |

427 Disputation of the Holy Sacrament (detail)

2009. 500th Anniv of Disputation of the Holy Sacrament (frescoes, Stanza della Segnatura (Raphael)). Designs showing details from the frescoes. Multicoloured.

1568	65c. Type **427**	4·00	3·75
1569	65c. Speaker with arm raised (detail, lower central right)	4·00	3·75
1570	65c. Friar, woman and two men examining book (detail, lower front left)	4·00	3·75
MS1571	110×80 mm. €3.30 Detail, showing upper and lower central	19·00	19·00

428 Pope Benedict XVI praying at Lourdes (France)

2009. Apostolic Journeys of Pope Benedict XVI in 2008. Multicoloured.

1572	65c. Type **428**	4·00	3·75
1573	85c. Pope Benedict XVI (USA)	5·00	4·75
1574	€1 Pope Benedict XVI (Australia)	6·00	5·75

429 Dante and Virgil and Three Wild Beasts (from 15th-century Codex Urbinate Latino 365, Vatican Apostolic Library)

2009. Italia 2009 International Stamp Exhibition, Rome. Italian Language.

| 1575 | **429** | 60c. multicoloured | 3·50 | 3·25 |

A stamp of a similar design was issued by Italy.

430 George Friedrich Handel (250th death anniv)

2009. Composers' Anniversaries. Multicoloured.

1576	65c. Type **430**	4·00	3·75
1577	85c. Franz Joseph Haydn (death bicentenary)	5·00	4·75
1578	€5 Felix Mendelssohn-Bartholdy (birth bicentenary)	30·00	29·00

431 Bronze Panel, Door of Good and Evil, St. Peter's Basilica (Luciano Minguzzi)

2009. 50th Anniv of Convocation of Second Vatican Council.

| 1579 | **431** | 60c. multicoloured | 3·50 | 3·25 |

432 Madonna and Child enthroned with two Angels and Saints Joachim and Anne (Francesco Melanzio) (detail)

2009. Christmas. Multicoloured.

| 1580 | 60c. Type **432** | 3·50 | 3·25 |
| 1581 | 65c. Madonna and Child enthroned with two Angels and Saints Joachim and Anne | 4·00 | 3·75 |

433 Louis Braille

2009. Birth Bicentenary of Louis Braille (inventor of Braille writing for the blind).
| 1582 | **433** | 65c. multicoloured | 4·00 | 3·75 |

434 Two Women (Three Temptations of Christ)

2010. 500th Death Anniv of Sandro Botticelli (artist). Multicoloured.
1583		60c. Type **434**	3·50	3·25
1584		85c. Woman (*The Life of Moses: Trials and Calling of Moses*)	5·00	4·75
1585		145c. Woman carrying basket (*The Life of Moses: Trials and Calling of Moses*)	8·75	8·50

435 Anàstasis from 4th-century Sarcophagus

2010. Easter
| 1586 | **435** | 65c. multicoloured | 4·00 | 3·75 |

436 Shrine of Our Lady of Mentorella

2010. 1500th Anniv of Shrine of Our Lady of Mentorella
| 1587 | **436** | 65c.+20c. multicoloured | 5·00 | 5·00 |
The premium was for aid to victims of the Haiti earthquake.

437 Father Ricci on and Xu Guangqi (court official)

2010. 400th Death Anniv of Father Matteo Ricci (pioneer of missions to China). Multicoloured.
| 1588 | | 5c. Type **437** | 45 | 30 |
| 1589 | | €3.30 Father Ricci | 20·00 | 19·00 |

Nos. 1590/1 and Type **438** are left for Europa. Children's Books issued on 22 June 2010, not yet received.
No. 1592 and Type **439** are left for 400th Death Anniv of Caravaggio, issued on 22 June 2010, not yet received.

440 St. John Vianney

2010. 150th Death Anniv of St Jean-Marie Vianney. Multicoloured.
| 1593 | | €1.40 Type **440** | 8·50 | 8·25 |
| 1594 | | €1.50 As shepherd with sheep | 9·00 | 8·75 |

441 Pope Leo XIII

2010. Birth Bicentenary of Vincenzo Gioacchino Pecci (Pope Leo XIII)
| 1595 | **441** | 65c. multicoloured | 4·00 | 3·75 |

442 Christ Crucified

2010. Re-opening of Vatican Apostolic Library. Multicoloured.

(a) Ordinary gum
| 1596 | | 65c. Type **442** | 4·00 | 3·75 |
| 1597 | | 85c. St. Cosmas and St. Damian | 5·00 | 4·75 |

(b) Self-adhesive
| 1598 | | €3.90 Pope Sixtus V (vert) | 23·00 | 23·00 |

443 Fryderyk Franciszek Chopin

2010. Composers' Birth Bicentenaries. Multicoloured.
1599		65c. Type **443**	4·00	3·75
1600		€1 Robert Alexander Schumann	6·00	5·75
MS1601	65×100 mm. €4.40 Score of *Nocturne Opus 9 No. 2.* Imperf	26·00	25·00

444 Parish of Saint Anthony, Luanda

2010. Apostolic Journeys of Pope Benedict XVI in 2008. Multicoloured.
1602		10c. Type **444**	75	60
1603		65c. Garden of Gethsemane, Israel	4·00	3·75
1604		85c. St. Vitus Cathedral, Prague	5·00	4·75

445 *The Birth of Jesus* (Gheorghe Tattarascu)

2010. Christmas. Multicoloured.

(a) Sheet stamps. Ordinary gum
| 1605 | | 60c. Type **445** | 3·50 | 3·25 |
| 1606 | | 65c. *The Nativity and Adoration of the Shepherds* (school of Murillo) | 4·00 | 3·75 |

(b) Booklet stamps. Self-adhesive
| 1607 | | 60c. As Type **445** | 3·50 | 3·25 |
| 1608 | | 65c. As No. 1606 | 4·00 | 3·75 |

446 Chekhov seated on Stage as Spectator viewing *Three Sisters* and *The Cherry Orchard*

2010. Writers' Anniversaries. Multicoloured.
| 1609 | | 60c. Type **446** (150th birth anniv) | 3·50 | 3·25 |
| 1610 | | 65c. Tolstoy as character in *War and Peace*, observed by Anna Karenina (death centenary) | 4·00 | 3·75 |

447 St. Francis (Giunta Pisano)

2010. 800th Anniv of Papal Approval of Franciscan Rule
| 1611 | **447** | 65c. multicoloured | 4·00 | 3·75 |

448 1852 15c. Stamp (As No. 4) and Modena Cathedral

2011. 150th Anniv of Italian Unification. Multicoloured.
1612		60c. Type **448**	3·50	3·25
1613		60c. 1852 25 centes Stamp (As No.7) and Parma Cathedral	3·50	3·25
1614		60c. 1859 2g. Stamp (As No. 3) and Sicilian Landscape	3·50	3·25
1615		60c. 1850 45 centes Stamp and Milan Cathedral	3·50	3·25
1616		60c. 1851 20 centes Stamp (As No. 4) and Equestrian Statue of Emanuel Filbert, Piazza San Carlo, Turin	3·50	3·25
1617		60c. 1851 1q. Stamp (As Type 1) and Palazzo Vecchio, Florence	3·50	3·25
MS1618	96×80 mm. Palazzo Montecitorio, Rome and Palazzo Carignano, Turin, Flaminio Obelisk, Santa Maria dei Miracoli Church and Santa Maria in Montesanto Church, Piazza del Popolo, Rome (48×40 mm)	9·00	8·75

449 The Resurrection (detail of fresco) (Hendrick van den Broeck), Sistine Chapel

2011. Easter
| 1619 | **449** | 75c. multicoloured | 4·50 | 4·25 |

450 Father Kino on Horseback

2011. 300th Death Anniv of Father Eusebio Francisco Kino (missionary and Jesuit explorer)
| 1620 | **450** | €1.60 blackish brown and reddish brown | 9·50 | 9·25 |

451 Pope John Paul II

2011. Beatification of Pope John Paul II
| 1621 | **451** | 75c. multicoloured | 4·50 | 4·25 |

452 Ordination as Priest, 29 June 1951 and Shell of St. Augustine

2011. 60th Anniv of Ordination of Pope Benedict XVI (Joseph Aloisius Ratzinger). Multicoloured.
1622		75c. Type **452**	4·50	4·25
1623		75c. Consecration as Bishop, 28 May 1977 and bear of St. Corbinian, Bishop of Freising	4·50	4·25
1624		75c. Created Cardinal, 27 June 1977 and Moor's Head (emblem of Munich and Freising)	4·50	4·25
1625		75c. Elected Pope, 19 April 2005 and complete coat of arms	4·50	4·25

453 *The Journey of Moses into Egypt* (detail) (Perugino)

2011. Europa. Forests. Multicoloured.
| 1626 | | 60c. Type **453** | 3·50 | 3·25 |
| 1627 | | 75c. *The Journey of Moses into Egypt* (detail) (right) | 4·50 | 4·25 |
Nos. 1626/7 were printed, *se-tenant*, each pair forming a composite design.

454 Emblem

2011. World Youth Day's, Madrid
| 1628 | **454** | 75c. vermilion, black and yellow | 4·50 | 4·25 |

455 Leo XII

2011. 150th Anniv of *L'Osservatore Romano* (Vatican daily newspaper). Multicoloured.
1629		60c. Type **455**	3·50	3·25
1630		60c. Pius X	3·50	3·25
1631		60c. Benedict XV	3·50	3·25
1632		60c. Pius XI	3·50	3·25
1633		60c. Pius XII	3·50	3·25
1634		60c. John XXIII	3·50	3·25
1635		60c. Paul VI	3·50	3·25
1636		60c. John Paul I	3·50	3·25
1637		60c. John Paul II	3·50	3·25
1638		60c. Benedict XVI	3·50	3·25

456 Pope John XXIII

2011. 50th Anniv *Mater et Magistra* (encyclical letter) by Pope John XXIII
| 1639 | **456** | 60c. multicoloured | 3·50 | 3·50 |

457 Pope Julius II carried on Litter (detail lower left from *Expulsion of Heliodorus from the Temple*)

2011. Room of Heliodorus (from Stanze di Raffaello). Frescoes by Raphael. Multicoloured.
| 1640 | | 75c. Type **457** | 4·50 | 4·25 |
| 1641 | | €1.60 Horseman fighting Heliodorus (detail lower right from *Expulsion of Heliodorus from the Temple*) | 9·50 | 9·25 |

458 Ruđer Bošković (inscr 'Rugerius Boscovich') (portrait by R. E. Pine)

2011. 300th Birth Anniv of Ruđer Bošković (inscr 'Rugerius Boscovich') (scientist)
| 1642 | **458** | €3.30 bronze and black | 19·00 | 19·00 |

459 The Nativity
(painting from
Vatican Pinacoteca
Art Gallery)

2011. Christmas

(a) Sheet stamps. Ordinary gum
| 1643 | 60c. Type **459** | 3·50 | 3·25 |
| 1644 | 75c. The Nativity (detail) | 4·50 | 4·25 |

(b) Booklet stamp. Self-adhesive
| 1644a | 75c. As No. 1644 | 4·50 | 4·25 |

460 Mgarr Parish Church
Façade and St Paul, Malta

2011. Apostolic Journeys of Pope Benedict XVI in 2010.
Multicoloured.
1645	60c. Type **460**	3·50	3·25
1646	75c. Shrine of Our Lady of Fatima, Portugal	4·50	4·25
1647	€1.40 Orthodox Church, Cyprus	8·50	8·25
1648	€1.60 Canterbury Cathedral, United Kingdom	9·50	9·25
1649	€2 Santiago de Compostela, Spain	12·00	11·50

461 Franz Liszt

2011. Anniversaries. Composers. Multicoloured.
| 1650 | 75c. Type **461** (birth bicentenary) | 4·50 | 4·25 |
| 1651 | €1.60 Gustav Mahler (death centenary) | 9·50 | 9·25 |

462 Madonna of
Foligno (painting from
Vatican Pinacoteca
Art Gallery)

2012. 500th Anniv of Sistine Madonna and Madonna of
Foligno (by Raphael). Multicoloured.
1652	60c. Type **462**	3·50	3·25
1653	75c. Sistine Madonna	4·50	4·25
MS1653a	87×135 mm. €1.40 As Type **462**	14·50	14·00
MS1653b	98×134 mm. €2.40 As No. 1653	8·50	8·25

463 Risen Christ
from the Breviary of
Matthias Corvinus

2012. Easter
| 1654 | **463** | 75c. multicoloured | 4·50 | 4·25 |

464 Father Christopher
Clavius

2012. 400th Death Anniv of Father Christopher Clavius
| 1655 | **464** | €1.60 multicoloured | 9·50 | 9·25 |

465 Joan of Arc
(detail from
miniature c.
1485)

2012. 600th Birth Anniv of Joan of Arc
| 1656 | **465** | 75c. multicoloured | 4·50 | 4·25 |

466 Dome of St.
Peter's Basilica

2012. Europa. Visit Vatican City. Multicoloured.
| 1657 | 75c. Type **466** | 4·50 | 4·25 |
| 1658 | 75c. Dove in window above the Altar of the Chair in St. Peter's Basilica | 4·50 | 4·25 |

467 Celtic Cross, Rock of
Cashel, Tipperary

2012. 50th International Eucharistic Congress, Dublin.
Multicoloured.
| 1659 | 75c. Type **467** | 4·50 | 4·25 |
| 1660 | €1 Ardagh Chalice found in West Limerick | 6·00 | 5·75 |

468 Family

2012. Seventh World Meeting of Families, Milan
| 1661 | **468** | €1.50 multicoloured | 9·00 | 8·75 |

469 Pope John Paul
I

2012. Birth Centenary of Pope John Paul I
| 1662 | **469** | 75c. multicoloured | 2·40 | 2·20 |

470 Pope
Benedict XVI

2012. 400th Anniv of Vatican Secret Archives. Multicoloured.
1663	75c. Type **470**	4·50	4·25
1664	75c. Seal	4·50	4·25
1665	75c. Pope Paul V	4·50	4·25

471 Battle against Maxentius at the Milvian Bridge (Giulio
Romano) (image scaled to 48% of original size)

2012. 1700th Anniv of Battle of Ponte Milvio. Sheet
100×75 mm
| MS1666 | **471** | €4.40 multicoloured | 26·00 | 25·00 |

472 Croatia

2012. Apostolic Journeys of Pope Benedict XVI in 2011.
Multicoloured.
1667	60c. Type **472**	3·50	3·25
1668	75c. San Marino	4·50	4·25
1669	€1.40 Spain	8·50	8·25
1670	€1.60 Germany	9·50	9·25
1671	€2 Benin	12·00	11·50

473 The
Annunciation of
Mary (detail)

2012. Christmas. Paintings by János Hajnal.
Multicoloured.
| 1672 | 60c. Type **473** | 3·50 | 3·25 |
| 1673 | 75c. The Nativity | 4·50 | 4·25 |

Nos. 1674/6 and Type **474** are left for Year of Faith, not
yet received.

No. 1677 and Type **475** are left for Easter, not yet received.

476 Mass of Bolsena (detail)
(Raffaello Sanzio)

2013. 750th Anniv of Miracle of Bolsena. Sheet 110×55
mm
| MS1678 | **476** | €4.80 multicoloured | 29·00 | 28·00 |

477 Apostolic
Camera Arms
(Daniela Longo)

2013. Vacant See
1679	**477**	70c. multicoloured	4·25	4·00
1680	85c. multicoloured	5·00	5·00
1681	€2 multicoloured	12·00	11·50
1682	€2.50 multicoloured	15·00	14·50

478 Post Van and St.
Peter's Basilica

2013. Europa. Postal Transport. Multicoloured.
| 1683 | 70c. Type **478** | 4·25 | 4·00 |
| 1684 | 85c. Post van and globe | 5·00 | 5·00 |

479 Pope Francis

2013. Enthronement of Pontificate of Pope Francis.
Multicoloured.
1685	70c. Type **478**	4·25	4·00
1686	85c. Wearing zucchetto, head bowed	5·00	5·00
1687	€2 Wearing zucchetto, giving blessing	12·00	11·50
1688	€2.50 Enthroned wearing mitre and holding staff	15·00	14·50

480 Christ the
Redeemer, Rio de
Janeiro

2013. World Youth Day, Rio de Janeiro
| 1689 | **480** | €1.90 multicoloured | 11·00 | 11·00 |

481 Giuseppe Belli

2013. 150th Death Anniv of Giuseppe Francesco
Antonio Maria Gioachino Raimondo Belli (Giuseppe
Gioachino Belli) (poet). Multicoloured.
| 1690 | **481** | €1 multicoloured | 6·00 | 5·75 |

482 Pope Sylvester
baptising Emperor
Constantine

2013. 1700th Anniv of Edict of Milan
1691	70c. Type **482**	4·25	4·00
1692	85c. Pope Sylvester enthroned greeting Emperor Constantine	5·00	5·00
1693	€2.50 Pope Sylvester mounted and Emperor Constantine	15·00	14·50
MS1694	100×72 mm. €1.90 Pope Sylvester 'curing' Emperor Constantine of leprosy	12·00	11·50

483 Pope John XXIII

2013. 50th Death Anniv of Pope John XXIII
| 1695 | **483** | 85c. multicoloured | 5·00 | 5·00 |

484 St. Cyril and St.
Methodius, Jesus Christ and
Angels

2013. 1150th Anniv of Arrival of Saints Cyril and
Methodius to Great Moravia. Sheet 115×156 mm
| MS1696 | **484** | €1.90 multicoloured | 12·00 | 11·50 |

EXPRESS LETTER STAMPS

E3

1929
| E14 | **E3** | 2l. red | 35·00 | 25·00 |
| E15 | **E3** | 2l.50 blue | 25·00 | 32·00 |

1933
E35	**E12**	2l. brown and red	45	90
E36	**E12**	2l.50 brown and blue	1·30	2·50
E107	**E12**	3l.50 blue and red	75	80
E108	**E12**	5l. green and blue	1·20	1·40

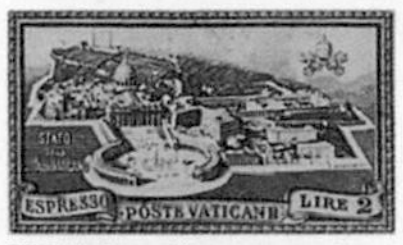

E12 Vatican City

1945. Surch in figures over bars.

E118	6l. on 3l.50 blue & red	9·25	4·25
E119	12l. on 5l. green & blue	9·25	4·25

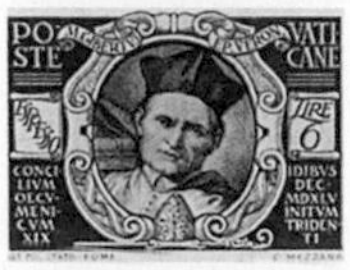

E28 Matthew Giberti, Bishop of Verona

1946. 400th Anniv of Council of Trent.

E130	**E28**	6l. brown and green	85	70
E131	-	12l. sepia and brown	1·10	1·00

DESIGN: 12l. Cardinal Gaspare Contarini, Bishop of Belluno.

1949. As Nos. 139/48 (Basilicas), but inscr "ESPRESSO".

E149	40l. grey	31·00	10·00
E150	80l. brown	60·00	46·00

DESIGNS—HORIZ: 40l. St. Peter's; 80l. St. John's.

1953. Designs as Nos. 179/89, but inscr "ESPRESSO".

E190	50l. brown and turquoise	45	30
F191	85l. brown and orange	60	55

DESIGNS: 50l. St. Peter and tomb; 85l. Pius XII and sepulchre.

1960. Designs as Nos. 326/33 (Works of Mercy), but inscr "ESPRESSO". Centres in brown.

E334	75l. red	20	15
E335	100l. blue	20	15

DESIGN: 75, 100l. Arms of Pope John XXIII between "Justice" and "Hope".

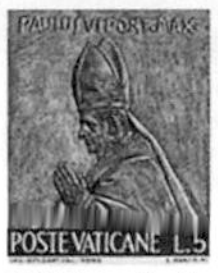

120 Pope Paul

1966. Designs as Nos. 467/76, but inscr "ESPRESSO".

E477	-	150l. brown	30	20
E478	**120**	180l. brown	30	20

DESIGN: 150l. Arms of Pope Paul VI.

PARCEL POST STAMPS

1931. Optd **PER PACCHI.**

P15	**1**	5c. brown on pink	45	90
P16	**1**	10c. green on green	45	90
P17	**1**	20c. violet on lilac	5·25	4·75
P18	**1**	25c. blue on blue	11·00	12·00
P19	**1**	30c. black on yellow	10·50	9·50
P20	**1**	50c. black on orange	15·00	10·50
P21	**1**	75c. red on grey	2·40	5·25
P22	**2**	80c. red	2·00	5·25
P23	**2**	1l.25 blue	3·00	6·00
P24	**2**	2l. brown	1·80	4·75
P25	**2**	2l.50 red	3·00	7·75
P26	**2**	5l. green	4·50	8·25
P27	**2**	10l. black	3·00	7·25

PARCEL POST EXPRESS STAMPS

1931. Optd **PER PACCHI.**

PE15	**E3**	2l. red	3·75	7·75
PE16	**E3**	2l.50 blue	6·25	8·25

POSTAGE DUE STAMPS

1931. Optd **SEGNATASSE** and cross or surch also.

D15	**1**	5c. brown on pink	60	90
D16	**1**	10c. green on green	60	90
D17	**1**	20c. violet on lilac	3·50	4·75
D18	**1**	40c. on 30c. black on yell	4·50	9·50
D19	**2**	60c. on 2l. brown	70·00	44·00
D20	**2**	1l.10 on 2l.50 red	27·00	32·00

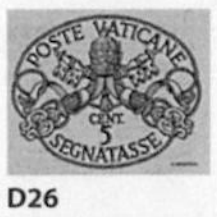

D26

1945. Coloured network shown in brackets.

D107	**D26**	5c. black (yellow)	25	20
D108	**D26**	20c. black (violet)	25	20
D109	**D26**	80c. black (red)	25	25
D110	**D26**	1l. black (green)	25	25
D111	**D26**	2l. black (blue)	35	30
D112	**D26**	5l. black (grey)	35	35

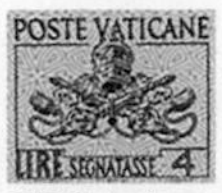

D49 State Arms

1954. Coloured network shown in brackets.

D199	**D49**	4l. black (red)	25	20
D200	**D49**	6l. black (green)	35	30
D201	**D49**	10l. black (yellow)	25	20
D202	**D49**	20l. black (blue)	75	70
D203	**D49**	50l. black (brown)	25	20
D204	**D49**	70l. black (brown)	25	20

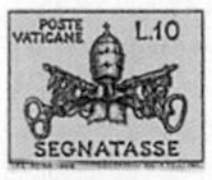

D130

1968

D513	**D130**	10l. black on grey	15	15
D514	**D130**	20l. black on blue	15	15
D515	**D130**	50l. black on pink	15	15
D516	**D130**	60l. black on green	15	15
D517	**D130**	100l. black on buff	15	15
D518	**D130**	180l. black on mauve	15	15

Pt. 8

VEGLIA

During the period of D'Annunzio's Italian Regency of Carnaro (Fiume), separate issues were made for the island of Veglia (now Krk).

100 centesimi = 1 lira.

1920. Nos. 148 etc. of Fiume optd **VEGLIA**.

1B	5c. green	19·00	19·00
2B	10c. red	31·00	31·00
3B	20c. bistre	75·00	44·00
4B	25c. blue	44·00	44·00
5	50 on 20c. bistre	80·00	44·00
6	55 on 5c. green	80·00	44·00

EXPRESS LETTER STAMPS

1920. Nos. E163/4 of Fiume optd **VEGLIA**.

E7	30c. on [illegible]	£250	£140
E8	50 on 5c. green	£190	£140

Pt. 1

VENDA

The Republic of Venda was established on 13 September 1979, being constructed from tribal areas formerly part of the Republic of South Africa. This independence did not receive international political recognition, but the stamps were accepted as valid on international mail.

Venda was reincorporated into South Africa on 27 April 1994.

100 cents = 1 rand.

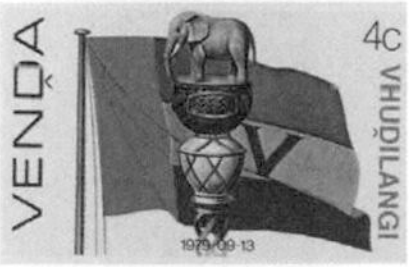

1 Flag and Mace

1979. Independence. Multicoloured.

1	4c. Type **1**	20	20
2	15c. Government Buildings, Thohoyandou	25	40
3	20c. Chief Minister P. R. Mphephu	30	60
4	25c. Coat of arms	45	90

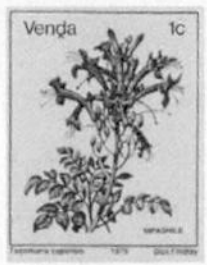

2 "Tecomaria capensis"

1979. Flowers. Multicoloured.

5	1c. Type **2**	40	10
6a	2c. "Catophractes alexandri"	20	15
7	3c. "Tricliceras longipedunculatum"	30	10
8	4c. "Dissotis princeps"	30	10
9a	5c. "Gerbera jamesonii"	30	10
10	6c. "Hibiscus mastersianus"	15	10
11	7c. "Nymphaea caerulea"	20	10
12a	8c. "Crinum lugardiae"	30	15
13	9c. "Xerophyta retinervis"	20	15
14a	10c. "Hypoxis angustifolia"	1·25	15
14b	11c. "Combretum microphyllum"	55	15
14c	12c. "Clivia caulescens"	30	15
15	15c. "Pycnostachys urticifolia"	30	15
16	20c. "Zantedeschia jucunda"	75	15
17a	25c. "Leonotis mollis"	50	40
18	30c. "Littonia modesta"	40	30
19	50c. "Protea caffra"	40	40
20	1r. "Adenium multiflorum"	75	85
21	2r. "Strelitzia caudata"	1·25	2·00

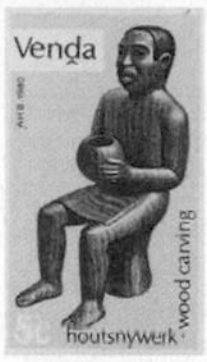

3 Man drinking Beer

1980. Wood Carving. Multicoloured.

22	5c. Type **3**	15	15
23	10c. Frying mealies in gourd	25	25
24	15c. King Nebuchadnezzar (horiz)	40	40
25	20c. Python squeezing woman to death (horiz)	50	60

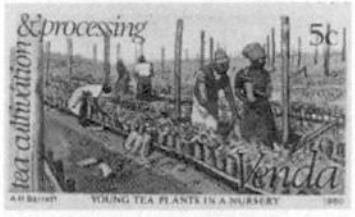

4 Tea Plants in Nursery

1980. Tea Cultivation. Multicoloured.

26	5c. Type **4**	15	10
27	10c. Tea pluckers	20	20
28	15c. Withering in the factory	35	35
29	20c. Cut, twist, curl unit	40	45

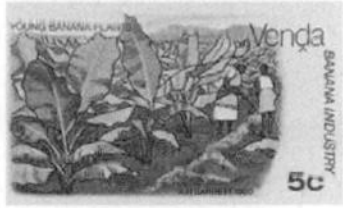

5 Young Banana Plants

[illegible] Cultivation. Multicoloured.

30	5c. Type **5**	15	10
31	10c. Cutting "hands"	25	25
32	15c. Sorting and dividing into clusters	30	30
33	20c. Packing	40	45

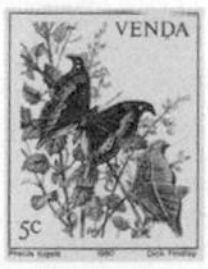

6 "Precis tugela"

1980. Butterflies. Multicoloured.

34	5c. Type **6**	20	15
35	10c. "Charaxes bohemani"	30	40
36	15c. "Catacroptera cloanthe"	40	55
37	20c. "Papilio dardanus"	50	70

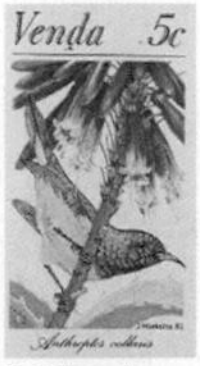

7 Collared Sunbird

1981. Sunbirds. Multicoloured.

38	5c. Type **7**	20	15
39	15c. Mariqua sunbird	30	40
40	20c. Southern white-bellied sunbird	35	45
41	25c. Scarlet-chested sunbird	35	55

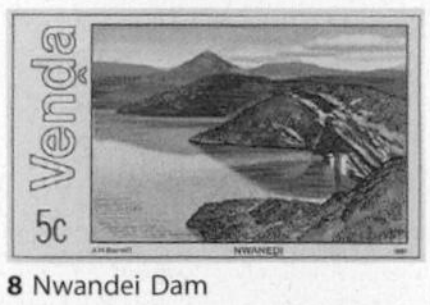

8 Nwandei Dam

1981. Lakes and Waterfalls. Multicoloured.

42	5c. Type **8**	15	10
43	15c. Mahovhohovho Falls	30	30
44	20c. Phiphidi Falls	35	35
45	25c. Lake Fundudzi	35	40

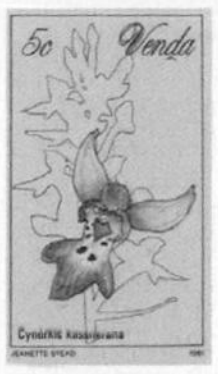

9 "Cynorkis kassnerana"

1981. Orchids. Multicoloured.

46	5c. Type **9**	15	10
47	15c. "Eulophia fridericii"	30	35
48	20c. "Bonatea densiflora"	35	45
49	25c. "Mystacidium brayboniae"	35	55
MS50	96×120 mm. Nos. 46/9	1·25	1·40

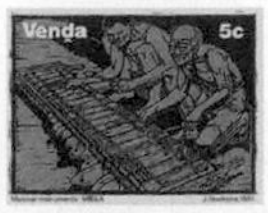

10 Mbila

1981. Musical Instruments.

51	**10**	5c. orange and black	10	10
52	-	15c. orange and black	25	25
53	-	20c. brown and black	30	35
54	-	25c. brown and black	30	35

DESIGNS: 15c. Phalaphala; 20c. Tshizambi; 25c. Ngoma.

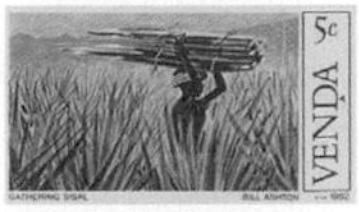

11 Gathering Sisal

1982. Sisal Cultivation. Multicoloured.

55	5c. Type **11**	10	10
56	10c. Drying	20	20
57	20c. Grading	30	35
58	25c. Baling	30	40

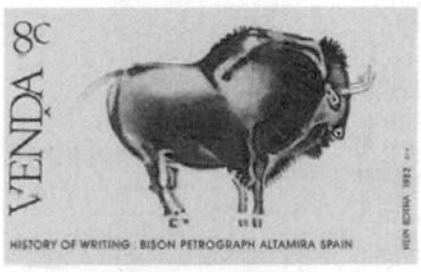

12 Bison Petrograph, Altamira, Spain

1982. History of Writing (1st series). Multicoloured.

59	8c. Type **12**	15	10
60	15c. Petroglyph, Eastern California	30	30
61	20c. Pictograph script (Sumerian tablet)	40	40
62	25c. Bushman burial stone, Humansdorp	45	45

No. 59 is inscr "AHAMIRA" in error.

See also Nos. 75/8, 87/90, 107/10, 139/42, 171/4 and 203/6.

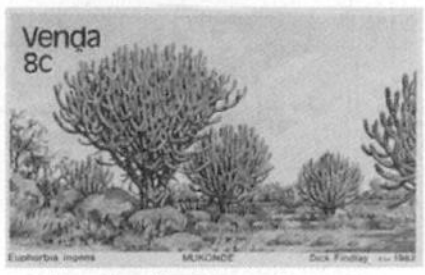

13 "Euphorbia ingens"

1982. Indigenous Trees (1st series). Multicoloured.

63	8c. Type **13**	15	10
64	15c. "Pterocarpus angolensis"	25	30
65	20c. "Ficus ingens"	30	40
66	25c. "Andansonia digitata"	40	55

See also Nos. 79/82, 95/8 and 227/30.

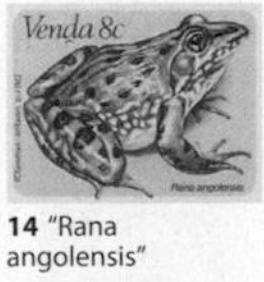

14 "Rana angolensis"

1982. Frogs. Multicoloured.

67	8c. Type **14**	15	10
68	15c. "Chiromantis xerampelina"	25	30
69	20c. "Leptopelis sp"	30	40
70	25c. "Ptychadena anchietae"	40	55

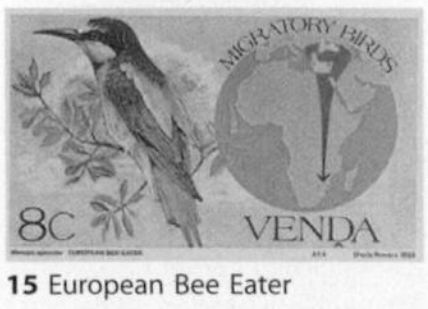

15 European Bee Eater

1983. Migratory Birds (1st series). Multicoloured.

71	8c. Type **15**	25	15

72	20c. Tawny eagle ("Steppe Eagle")	50	65
73	25c. Violet starling ("Plum-coloured Starling")	60	75
74	40c. Abdim's stork ("White-bellied Stork")	90	1·50

See also Nos. 91/4.

1983. History of Writing (2nd series). As T **12**. Multicoloured.

75	10c. Indus Valley script	15	10
76	20c. Sumerian cuneiform	20	25
77	25c. Egyptian hieroglyphics	25	30
78	40c. Chinese handscroll	50	70

1983. Indigenous Trees (2nd series). As T **13**. Multicoloured.

79	10c. "Gardenia spatulifolia"	15	10
80	20c. "Hyphaene natalensis"	25	30
81	25c. "Albizia adianthifolia"	30	40
82	40c. "Sesamothamnus lugardii"	40	60

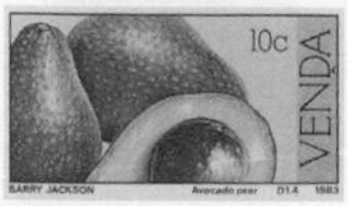

16 Avocado

1983. Subtropical Fruit. Multicoloured.

83	10c. Type **16**	15	10
84	20c. Mango	25	30
85	25c. Papaya	30	40
86	40c. Litchi	40	60

1983. History of Writing (3rd series). As T **12**. Multicoloured.

87	10c. Evolution of cuneiform sign	15	10
88	20c. Evolution of Chinese character	25	30
89	25c. Development of Cretan hieroglyphics	30	40
90	40c. Development of Egyptian hieroglyphics	40	60

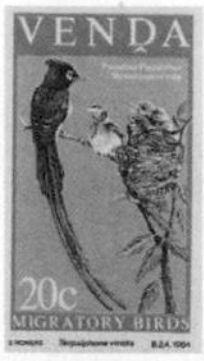

17 African Paradise Flycatcher ("Paradise Flycatcher")

1984. Migratory Birds (2nd series). Multicoloured.

91	11c. White stork	30	20
92	20c. Type **17**	50	50
93	25c. Black kite ("Yellow-billed kite")	60	60
94	30c. Wood sandpiper	70	85

1984. Indigenous Trees (3rd series). As T **13**. Multicoloured.

95	11c. "Afzelia quanzensis"	15	10
96	20c. "Peltophorum africanum"	25	30
97	25c. "Gyrocarpus americanus"	30	40
98	30c. "Acacia sieberana"	40	55

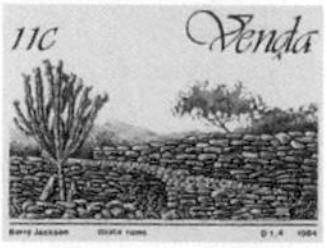

18 Dzata Ruins, Nzhelele Valley

1984. Fifth Anniv of Independence. Multicoloured.

99	11c. Type **18**	15	10
100	25c. Traditional hut	25	30
101	30c. Sub-economical house	30	35
102	45c. Modern home	45	65

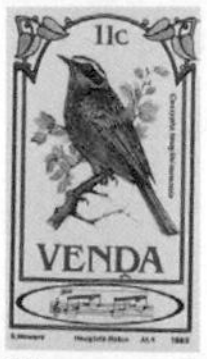

19 White-browed Robin Chat

1985. Songbirds. Multicoloured.

103	11c. Type **19** (inscr "Heuglin's Robin")	25	20
104	25c. Black-collared barbet	35	40
105	30c. African black-headed oriole ("Black-headed Oriole")	40	50
106	50c. Kurrichane thrush	60	80

1985. History of Writing (4th series). As T **12**. Multicoloured.

107	11c. Southern Arabic characters	15	10
108	25c. Phoenician characters	25	30
109	30c. Aramaic characters	30	40
110	50c. Canaanite characters	50	75

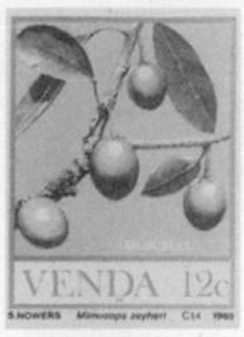

20 Transvaal Red Milkwood

1985. Food from the Veld (1st series). Multicoloured.

111	12c. Type **20**	15	10
112	25c. Buffalo thorn	25	30
113	30c. Wild water melon	30	35
114	50c. Brown ivory	40	60

See also Nos. 163/6.

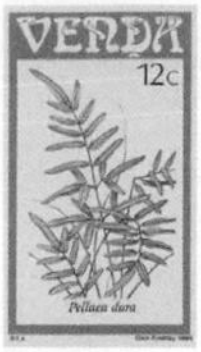

21 "Pellaea dura"

1985. Ferns. Multicoloured.

115	12c. Type **21**	15	10
116	25c. "Actiniopteris radiata"	25	25
117	30c. "Adiantum hispidulum"	30	35
118	50c. "Polypodium polypodioides"	40	65

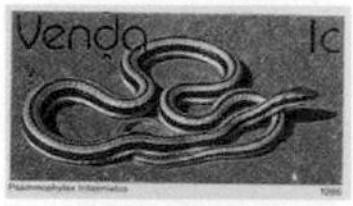

22 Three-lined Grass Snake

1986. Reptiles. Multicoloured.

119	1c. Type **22**	10	10
120	2c. Mole snake	10	10
121	3c. Ornate scrub lizard	10	10
122	4c. Puff adder	10	10
123	5c. Three-lined skink	10	10
124	6c. Egyptian cobra	15	10
125	7c. Blue-tailed kopje skink	15	10
126	8c. Spotted bush snake	20	20
127	9c. Yellow-throated plated lizard	20	20
128	10c. Northern lined shovelsnout	20	20
129	14c. Transvaal flat lizard	1·25	20
130	15c. Soutpansberg lizard	30	20
131	16c. Iguana water leguan	60	20
132	18c. Black mamba	75	20
133	20c. Transvaal flat gecko	30	20
133b	21c. Flap-necked chameleon	75	20
134	25c. Longtailed garter snake	40	30
135	30c. Tigroid thick-toed gecko	40	35
136	50c. Cape file snake	40	50
137	1r. Soutpansberg girdled lizard	55	1·00
138	2r. African python	70	2·00

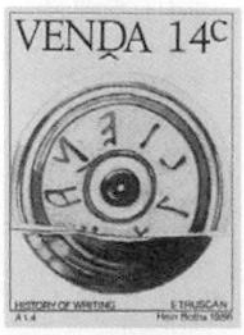

23 Etruscan Dish

1986. History of Writing (5th series). Multicoloured.

139	14c. Type **23**	15	10
140	20c. Greek inscription, A.D. 70	30	30
141	25c. Roman inscription	40	40
142	30c. Cyrllic inscription (Byzantine mosaic)	55	60

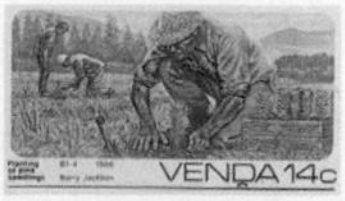

24 Planting Pine Seedlings

1986. Forestry. Multicoloured.

143	14c. Type **24**	20	15
144	20c. Mule hauling logs	30	30
145	25c. Off-loading logs at sawmill	40	40
146	30c. Using timber in construction	55	60

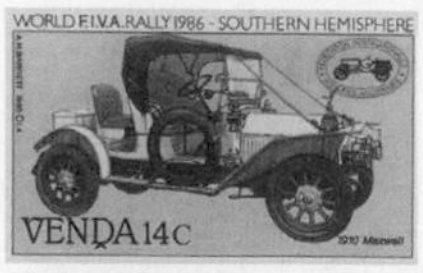

25 Maxwell, 1910

1986. FIVA International Veteran Car Rally. Multicoloured.

147	14c. Type **25**	20	15
148	20c. Bentley 4½ litre, 1929	30	30
149	25c. Plymouth Coupe, 1933	40	40
150	30c. Mercedes Benz 220, 1958	55	60

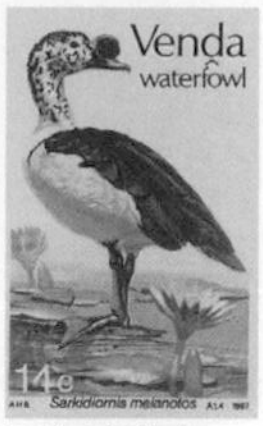

26 Comb Duck

1987. Waterfowl. Multicoloured.

151	14c. Type **26**	1·00	40
152	20c. White-faced whistling duck	1·10	70
153	25c. Spur-winged goose (horiz)	1·25	90
154	30c. Egyptian goose (horiz)	1·40	1·25

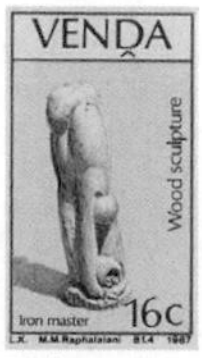

27 "Iron Master"

1987. Wood Sculptures by Meshack Matamela Raphalalani. Multicoloured.

155	16c. Type **27**	15	15
156	20c. "Distant Drums"	25	25
157	25c. "Sunrise"	30	30
158	30c. "Obedience"	40	40

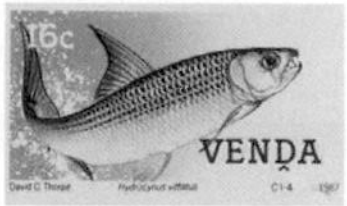

28 Tigerfish

1987. Freshwater Fish. Multicoloured.

159	16c. Type **28**	25	20
160	20c. Barred minnow	35	35
161	25c. Mozambique mouthbrooder	45	45
162	30c. Sharp-toothed catfish	55	60

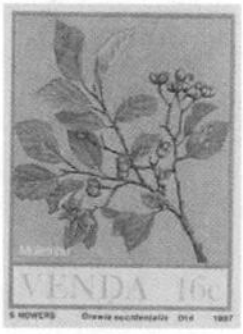

29 Cross-berry

1987. Food from the Veld (2nd series). Multicoloured.

163	16c. Type **29**	20	15
164	30c. Wild date palm	30	30
165	40c. Tree fuchsia	40	40
166	50c. Wild cucumber	50	55

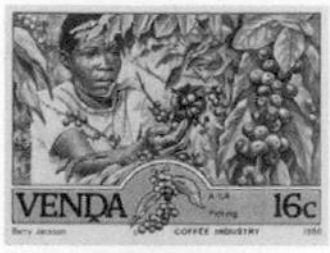

30 Picking Berries

1988. Coffee Industry. Multicoloured.

167	16c. Type **30**	20	20
168	30c. Weighing bags of berries	30	30
169	40c. Drying beans in sun	35	35
170	50c. Roasting graded beans	45	45

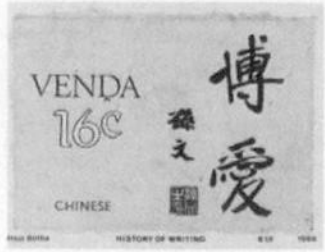

31 "Universal Love" in Chinese

1988. History of Writing (6th series).

171	**31**	16c. stone, black and red	20	20
172	-	30c. stone, black and red	25	35
173	-	40c. stone, black and red	35	45
174	-	50c. black and gold	45	60

DESIGNS: 30c. "Picture of a lion on a stone" in Devanagari (Indian script); 40c. "Information" in Russian; 50c. "Peace be upon you" in Thuluth (Arabic script).

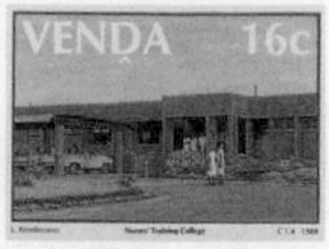

32 College

1988. Fifth Anniv of Shayandima Nurses' Training College. Multicoloured.

175	16c. Type **32**	20	15
176	30c. Students using microscope	30	35
177	40c. Anatomy class	35	40
178	50c. Clinical training	40	50

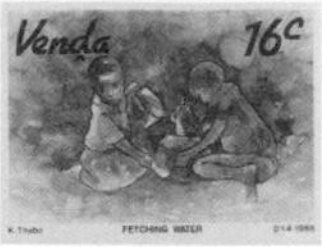

33 "Fetching Water"

1988. Watercolours by Kenneth Thabo. Multicoloured.

179	16c. Type **33**	20	15
180	30c. "Grinding Maize"	30	35
181	40c. "Offering Food"	35	40
182	50c. "Kindling the Fire"	40	50

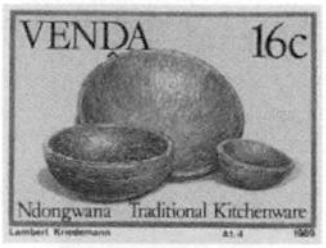

34 Ndongwana (clay bowls)

1989. Traditional Kitchenware. Multicoloured.

183	16c. Type **34**	15	20
184	30c. Ndilo (wooden porridge bowls)	25	30
185	40c. Mufaro (basket with lid)	30	40
186	50c. Muthatha (dish woven from ilala palm)	40	45

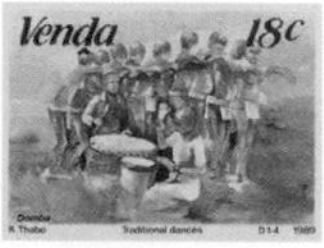

35 Domba

1989. Traditional Dances. Multicoloured.

187	18c. Type **35**	15	20
188	30c. Tshinzerere	25	30
189	40c. Malende	30	40
190	50c. Malombo	40	45

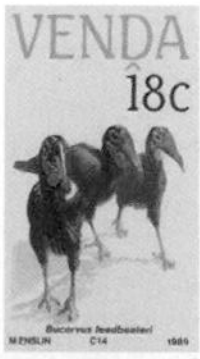

36 Southern Ground Hornbill

1989. Endangered Birds. Multicoloured.

191	18c. Type **36**	80	30
192	30c. Lappet-faced vulture	1·10	70
193	40c. Bateleur	1·40	90
194	50c. Martial eagle	1·60	1·25

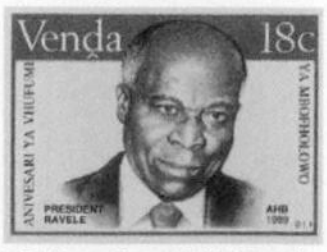

37 Pres. Gota F. N. Ravele

1989. Tenth Anniv of Independence. Multicoloured.

195	18c. Type **37**	20	20
196	30c. Presidential offices	30	30
197	40c. President's residence	40	40
198	50c. Thohoyandou Sports Stadium	45	45

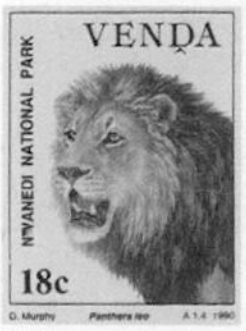
38 Lion

1990. Nwanedi National Park. Multicoloured.

199	18c. Type **38**	40	25
200	30c. Common zebra	70	55
201	40c. Cheetah	75	65
202	50c. White rhinoceros	1·50	1·25

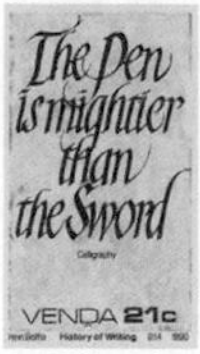
39 Calligraphy

1990. History of Writing (7th series).

203	**39**	21c. black and grey	20	15
204	-	30c. black and brown	40	40
205	-	40c. black and green	50	50
206	-	50c. deep blue, blue & black	60	65

DESIGNS: 30c. Part of score for Beethoven's "Moonlight Sonata"; 40c. Characters from personal computer; 50c. Television picture of message transmitted into outer space from Arecibo 1000 radio telescope.

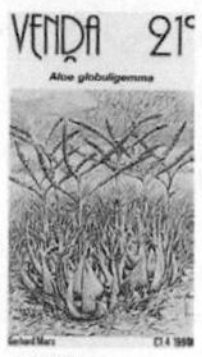
40 "Aloe globuligemma"

1990. Aloes. Multicoloured.

207	21c. Type **40**	30	25
208	35c. "Aloe aculeata"	50	50
209	40c. "Aloe lutescens"	60	70
210	50c. "Aloe angelica"	70	90

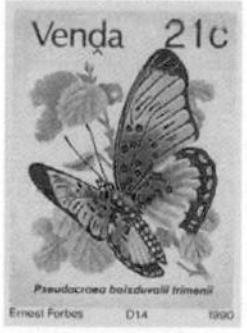
41 "Pseudacraea boisduvalii"

1990. Butterflies. Multicoloured.

211	21c. Type **41**	70	40
212	35c. "Papilio nireus"	1·00	75
213	40c. "Charaxes jasius"	1·10	1·00
214	50c. "Aeropetes tulbaghia"	1·25	1·25

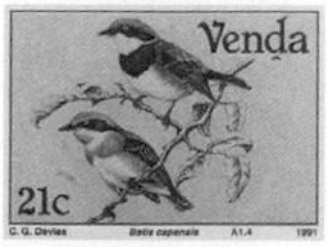
42 Cape Puff-back Flycatchers

1991. Birds. Paintings by Claude Finch-Davies. Multicoloured.

215	21c. Type **42**	50	40
216	35c. Red-capped robin chat	75	80
217	40c. Collared sunbirds	85	1·00
218	50c. Yellow-streaked greenbul	1·10	1·40

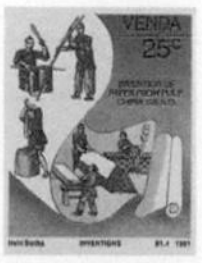
43 Paper made from Pulp

1991. Inventions (1st series). Multicoloured.

219	25c. Type **43**	55	35
220	40c. Magnetic compass	1·00	75
221	50c. Abacus	1·10	1·00
222	60c. Gunpowder	1·75	1·25

See also Nos. 239/42 and 260/3.

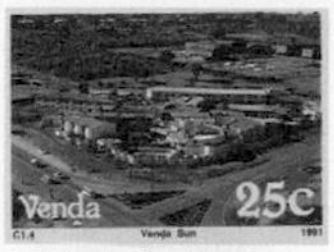
44 Venda Sun Hotel Complex, Thohoyandou

1991. Tourism. Multicoloured.

223	25c. Type **44**	55	35
224	40c. Mphephu resort	85	75
225	50c. Sagole Spa	95	95
226	60c. Luphephe-Nwanedi resort	1·00	1·25

1991. Indigenous Trees (4th series). As T **13**. Multicoloured.

227	27c. Fever tree	60	35
228	45c. Transvaal beech	1·00	75
229	65c. Transvaal wild banana	1·10	1·10
230	85c. Sausage tree	1·40	1·50

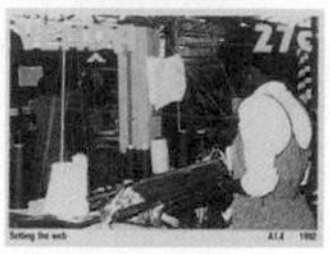
45 Setting the Web

1992. Clothing Factory. Multicoloured.

231	27c. Type **45**	45	25
232	45c. Knitting	60	55
233	65c. Making up garment	90	1·00
234	85c. Inspection of finished product	1·25	1·50

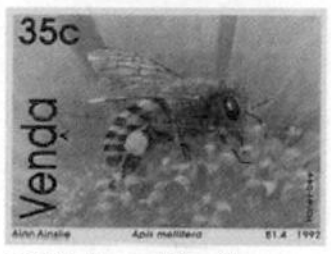
46 "Apis mellifera"

1992. Bees. Multicoloured.

235	35c. Type **46**	70	40
236	70c. "Anthidium cordiforme"	1·10	90
237	90c. "Megachile frontalis"	1·50	1·25
238	1r.05 "Xylocopa caffra"	1·60	1·40

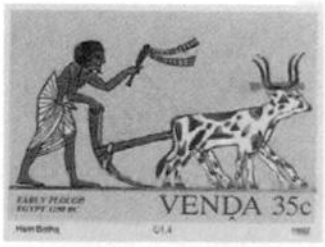
47 Egyptian Plough

1992. Inventions (2nd series). Multicoloured.

239	35c. Type **47**	60	40
240	70c. Early wheel, Mesopotamia	1·00	90
241	90c. Making bricks, Egypt	1·40	1·25
242	1r.05 Early Egyptian sailing ship	1·50	1·40

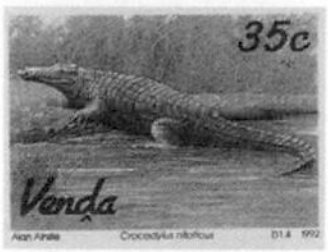
48 Nile Crocodile

1992. Crocodile Farming. Multicoloured.

243	35c. Type **48**	85	40
244	70c. Egg laying	1·40	1·00
245	90c. Eggs hatching	1·60	1·60
246	1r.05 Mother carrying young	1·75	1·90

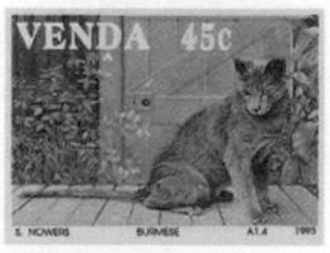
49 Burmese

1993. Domestic Cats. Multicoloured.

247	45c. Type **49**	1·00	45
248	65c. Tabby	1·40	1·00
249	85c. Siamese	1·60	1·40
250	1r.05 Persian	1·75	1·75

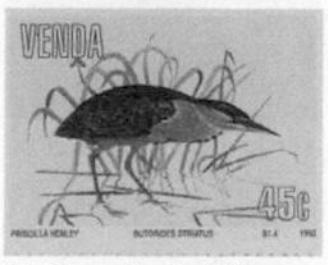
50 Green-backed Heron

1993. Herons. Multicoloured.

251	45c. Type **50**	80	50
252	65c. Black-crowned night heron	1·10	95
253	85c. Purple heron	1·40	1·40
254	1r.05 Black-headed heron	1·60	1·90
MS255	86×132 mm. Nos. 251/4	4·50	4·75

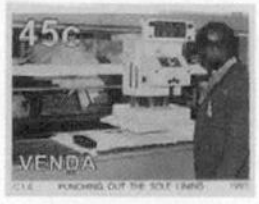
51 Punching-out Sole Lining

1993. Shoe Factory. Multicoloured.

256	45c. Type **51**	25	20
257	65c. Shaping heel	45	50
258	85c. Joining the upper to inner sole	60	75
259	1r.05 Forming sole	70	1·25

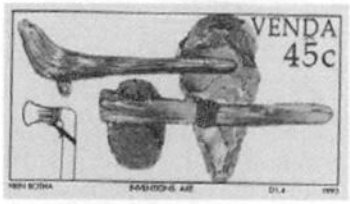
52 Axes

1993. Inventions (3rd series). Multicoloured.

260	45c. Type **52**	25	20
261	65c. Armour	40	50
262	85c. Arches	60	75
263	1r.05 Pont du Gard aqueduct	70	1·25

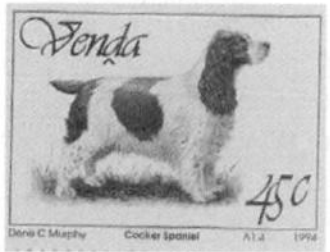
53 Cocker Spaniel

1994. Dogs. Multicoloured.

264	45c. Type **53**	90	50
265	65c. Maltese	1·25	1·00
266	85c. Scottish terrier	1·50	1·50
267	1r.05 Miniature schnauzer	1·90	2·00

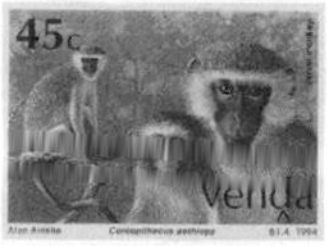
54 Savanna Monkey

1994. Monkeys. Multicoloured.

268	45c. Type **54**	75	55
269	65c. Lesser bushbaby	1·00	1·00
270	85c. Diademed monkey	1·25	1·50
271	1r.05 Thick-tailed bushbaby	1·50	2·00
MS272	119×70 mm. Nos. 268/71	4·00	4·50

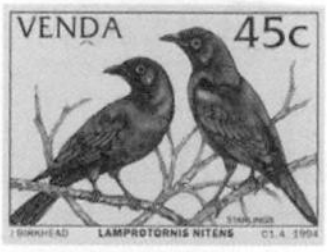
55 Red-shouldered Glossy Starlings

1994. Starlings. Multicoloured.

273	45c. Type **55**	1·00	65
274	70c. Violet starlings	1·50	1·50
275	95c. African red-winged starlings	1·75	1·90
276	1r.15 Wattled starlings	2·00	2·25

Pt. 3

VENEZIA GIULIA AND ISTRIA

Formerly part of Italy. Stamps issued during the Allied occupation, 1945-7. The Peace Treaty of 1947 established the Free Territory of Trieste (q.v.) and gave the rest of the territory to Yugoslavia.

For stamps of Austria overprinted Venezia Giulia see AUSTRIAN TERRITORIES ACQUIRED BY ITALY, in Volume 1 of Stamps of the World.

100 centesimi = 1 lira.

A. YUGOSLAV OCCUPATION PROVISIONAL ISSUES
Issues for Trieste.

1945. Stamps of Italian Social Republic 1944, surch **1.V.1945 TRIESTE TRST**, five-pointed star and value.

4	-	20c.+1l. on 5c. brn (No. 106)	55	2·20
5	**13**	+1l. on 25c. green	55	2·20
6	-	+1l. on 30c. brown (No. 110)	55	2·20
7	-	+1l. on 50c. violet (No. 111)	55	2·20
8	-	+1l. on 1l. violet (No. 113)	55	2·20
9	-	+2l. on 1l.25 blue (No. 114)	55	2·20
2	**12**	2+2l. on 25c. green	55	2·20
10	-	+2l. on 3l. green (No. 115)	55	2·20
11	-	5+5l. on 1l. violet (No. 113)	55	2·20
12	-	10+10l. on 30c. brn (No. 110)	3·25	9·00
13	-	20+20l. on 5c. brn (No. 106)	11·00	17·00

Issue for Istria

In 1945 various stamps of Italy were overprinted "ISTRA" and further surcharged for use in Istria and Pola but they were not issued. However, four of these were further surcharged and issued later.

1945. Stamps of Italy (No. 14) or Italian Social Republic (others) surch **ISTRA** with new value and bars obliterating old surch.

14	**99**	4l. on 2l. on 1l. (No. 249) violet	1·10	1·70
15	-	6l. on 1,50l. on 75c. (No. 112) red	4·50	9·00
16	-	10l. on 0,10l. on 5c. (No. 106) brown	39·00	30·00
17	**103**	20l. on 1l. on 50c. (No. 247) violet	5·50	11·00

Issues for Fiume

1945. Stamps of Italian Social Republic 1944, surch **3-V-1945 FIUME RIJEKA**, five-pointed star over rising sun and new value.

18	**12**	2l. on 25c. green	1·10	1·70
20	-	4l. on 1l. violet (No. 113)	1·10	1·70
21	-	5l. on 10c. brn (No. 107)	1·10	1·70
22	-	6l. on 10c. brn (No. 107)	1·10	1·70
23	**13**	10l. on 25c. green	1·10	1·70
24	-	16l. on 75c. red (No. 112)	£200	£325
25	**E16**	20l. on 1l.25c. green	3·25	9·00

B. ALLIED MILITARY GOVERNMENT

1945. Stamps of Italy optd **A.M.G. V.G.** in two lines. (a) Imperial Series.

26	-	10c. brown (No. 241)	25	60
27	-	10c. brown (No. 633)	25	60
28	**99**	20c. red (No. 243)	25	2·30
29	**99**	20c. red (No. 640)	35	1·20
31	-	60c. red (No. 636)	30	1·20
32	**103**	60c. green (No. 641)	25	60
33	**99**	1l. violet (No. 637)	60	45
34	-	2l. red (No. 638)	65	60
35	**98**	5l. red (No. 645)	95	60
36	-	10l. violet (No. 646)	1·20	65
37	**99**	20l. green (No. 257)	3·00	4·00

(b) Stamps of 1945-48.

38	-	25c. blue (No. 649)	35	1·20
39	-	2l. brown (No. 656)	95	65
40	-	3l. red (No. 657)	65	45
41	-	4l. red (No. 658)	95	60
42	**195**	6l. violet (No. 660)	3·00	3·50
43	-	20l. purple (No. 665)	70·00	5·00
44	**196**	25l. green (No. 666)	7·00	8·25
45	**196**	50l. purple (No. 668)	7·00	13·00
46	**197**	100l. red (No. 669)	41·00	70·00

1945. Air stamps of Italy, optd as above.

47	**110**	50c. brown (No. 271)	80	80
48	**198**	1l. grey (No. 670)	95	4·00
49	-	2l. blue (No. 671)	95	3·00
50	-	5l. green (No. 673)	4·75	3·00
51	**198**	10l. red (No. 674)	4·75	3·00
52	-	25l. blue (No. 675)	4·75	3·00
53	-	25l. brown (No. 676)	32·00	34·00
54	**198**	50l. green (No. 677)	8·75	11·50

EXPRESS LETTER STAMPS

1946. Express Letter Stamps of Italy optd **A.M.G. V.G.** in two lines.

E55	-	10l. blue (No. E680)	7·75	4·00
E56	**E200**	30l. violet (No. E683)	16·00	24·00

C. YUGOSLAV MILITARY GOVERNMENT

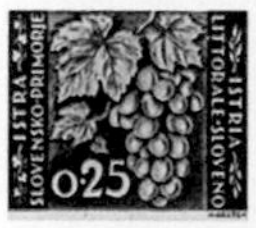
6 Grapes

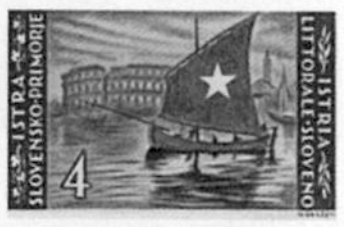
7 Roman Amphitheatre, Pula, and Istrian Fishing Vessel

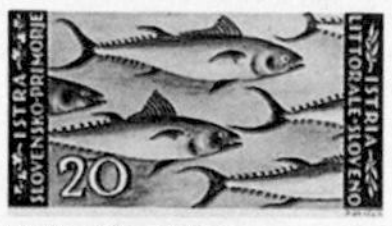
8 Blue-finned Tuna

1945. Inscr "ISTRA SLOVENSKO PRIMORJE – ISTRIA LITTORALE SLOVENO".

74	**6**	0.25l. green	80	80
58	-	0.50l. brown	70	80
59	-	1l. red	70	80

76	-	1l. green	1·20	80
77	-	1.50l. green	80	80
78	-	2l. green	80	80
100	-	3l. red	8·25	4·00
62	7	4l. blue	70	80
79	7	4l. red	80	80
80	-	5l. black	1·20	1·20
101	7	6l. blue	11·50	10·50
81	-	10l. brown	1·70	1·20
65	8	20l. purple	17·00	17·00
82	8	20l. blue	8·25	10·50
83	-	30l. mauve	7·00	7·00

DESIGNS—As Type **6**: 0.50l. Donkey and view; 1l. Rebuilding damaged homes; 1.50l. Olive branch; 2, 3l. Duino Castle near Trieste. As Type **7**: 5l. Birthplace of Vladimir Gortan, Piran; 10l. Ploughing. As Type **8**: 30l. Viaduct over River Solkan.

1946. Nos. 82 and 66 surch.

96	8	1 on 20l. blue	3·00	2·75
97	-	2 on 30l. mauve	3·00	2·75

1947. As Nos. 514 and O540 of Yugoslavia with colours changed, surch **VOJNA UPRAVA JUGOSLAVENSKE ARMIJE** and new value.

102	1l. on 9d. pink	1·20	1·20
103	1.50l. on 0.50d. blue	1·20	1·20
104	2l. on 9d. pink	1·20	1·20
105	3l. on 0.50d. blue	1·20	1·20
106	5l. on 9d. pink	1·20	1·20
107	6l. on 0.50d. blue	1·20	1·20
108	10l. on 9d. pink	1·20	1·20
109	15l. on 0.50d. blue	1·20	1·20
110	35l. on 9d. pink	1·20	1·70
111	50l. on 0.50d. blue	1·20	1·70

POSTAGE DUE STAMPS

1945. Stamps of 1945 surch **PORTO** and value in Lit.

D72	8	0.50 on 20l. purple	5·75	4·75
D67	6	1l. on 0.25l. green	35·00	11·50
D73	-	2l. on 30l. mauve	13·00	9·25
D68	-	4l. on 0.50l. brown	9·25	3·50
D69	-	8l. on 0.50l. brown	11·50	4·75
D70	-	10l. on 0.50l. brown	17·00	9·25
D71	-	20l. on 0.50l. brown	23·00	14·00

1946. Stamps of 1945 surch **PORTO** and value expressed in Lira.

D90	6	1l. on 0.25l. green	1·20	1·20
D84		1l. on 1l. green (No. 76)	1·20	1·20
D91	6	2l. on 0.25l. green	2·30	2·30
D85		2l. on 1l. green (No. 76)	1·20	1·20
D92	6	4l. on 0.25l. green	2·30	2·30
D86		4l. on 1l. green (No. 76)	1·20	1·20
D93	8	10l. on 20l. blue	10·50	10·50
D87		10l. on 30l. mauve (No. 66)	11·50	9·25
D94	8	20l. on 20l. blue	15·00	15·00
D88		20l. on 30l. mauve (No. 66)	17·00	14·00
D95	8	30l. on 20l. blue	16·00	16·00
D89		30l. on 30l. mauve (No. 66)	17·00	14·00

1947. No. D528 of Yugoslavia with colour changed and surch **Vojna Uprava Jugoslavenske Armije** and value.

D112	1l. on 1d. green	1·70	1·70
D113	2l. on 1d. green	1·70	1·70
D114	6l. on 1d. green	1·70	1·70
D115	10l. on 1d. green	1·70	1·70
D116	30l. on 1d. green	1·70	1·70

Pt. 20

VENEZUELA

A republic in the N. of S. America, independent since 1811.

1859. 100 centavos = 8 reales = 1 peso.
1879. 100 centesimos = 1 venezolano.
1880. 100 centimos = 1 bolivar.

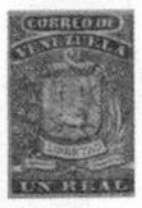

1

1859. Imperf.

7	1	½r. orange	17·00	5·25
8	1	1r. blue	24·00	12·00
9	1	2r. red	90·00	45

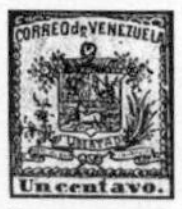

2

1862. Imperf.

13	2	¼c. green	28·00	£150
14	2	½c. lilac	31·00	£190
15	2	1c. brown	60·00	£325

3

1863. Imperf.

16	3	½c. red	55·00	£120
17a	3	1c. grey	60·00	£150
21	3	½r. yellow	6·75	60·00
19	3	1r. blue	24·00	11·50
20	3	2r. green	24·00	20·00

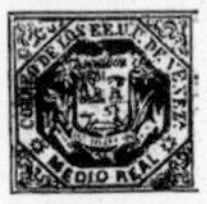

4

1866. Imperf.

22	4	½c. green	£200	£190
23	4	1c. green	£200	£190
24	4	½r. red	13·00	2·75
26	4	1r. red	60·00	21·00
27a	4	2r. yellow	£225	£110

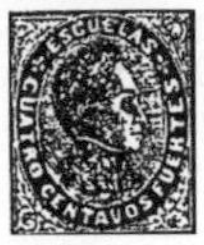

5 Bolivar

1871. Optd with inscription in very small letters. Imperf.

58	5	1c. yellow	1·00	30
59d	5	2c. yellow	1·00	30
60	5	3c. yellow	1·60	35
61	5	4c. yellow	3·25	85
62b	5	5c. yellow	2·10	60
63b	5	1r. red	2·10	30
64a	5	2r. red	8·50	1·70
65a	5	3r. red	2·75	55
66a	5	5r. red	4·25	70
52a	5	7r. red	4·50	1·80
53a	5	9r. green	19·00	3·25
54	5	15r. green	35·00	4·25
68	5	20r. green	95·00	22·00
56	5	30r. green	£450	£450
70	5	50r. green	£1300	£325

1873. Optd with inscription in very small letters. Imperf.

74a	4	1c. lilac	4·50	11·50
75a	4	2c. green	28·00	34·00
76a	4	½r. pink	21·00	2·75
77a	4	1r. red	25·00	6·00
78a	4	2r. yellow	75·00	34·00

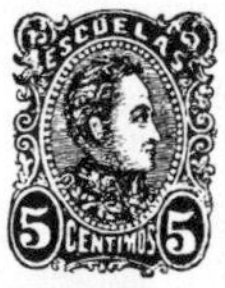

7 Bolivar

1879. New Currency. Optd with inscription in small letters. Imperf.

83	7	1c. yellow	1·80	55
84	7	5c. yellow	1·80	50
85	7	10c. blue	3·50	35
86	7	30c. blue	4·50	70
87	7	50c. blue	5·25	70
88	7	90c. blue	21·00	4·25
89	7	1v. red	46·00	6·00
90	7	3v. red	75·00	24·00
91	7	5v. red	£130	44·00

1880. New Currency. Without opt. Perf.

92	5c. yellow	90	15
93	10c. yellow	90	15
94	25c. yellow	1·20	15
95	50c. yellow	2·50	20
96	1b. blue	6·25	50
97	2b. blue	9·75	55
98	5b. blue	23·00	50
99	10b. red	£110	35·00
100	20b. red	£700	£110
101	25b. red	£3000	£350

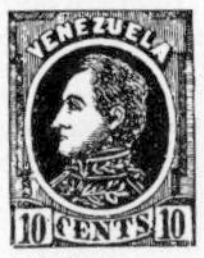

8 Bolivar

1880

107	8	5c. blue	21·00	10·00
108	8	10c. red	29·00	17·00
109	8	25c. yellow	21·00	10·00
110	8	50c. brown	£275	55·00
106	8	1b. green	£200	65·00

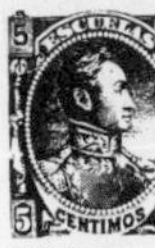

9 Bolivar

1882. Various frames. Perf or roul.

111	9	5c. green	15	15
112	9	10c. brown	15	15
113	9	25c. orange	15	15
114	9	50c. blue	15	15
115	9	1b. red	15	15
116	9	3b. violet	15	15
117	9	10b. brown	35	35
118	9	20b. purple	45	45

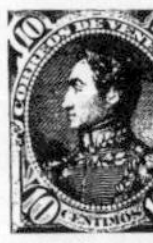

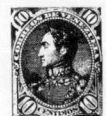

10 Bolivar

1882. Various frames. Perf or roul.

119	10	5c. blue	1·00	45
120	10	10c. brown	1·00	45
121	10	25c. brown	1·50	55
122	10	50c. green	3·25	95
123	10	1b. violet	6·00	2·30

1892. Surch **RESOLUCION DE 10 DE OCTUBRE DE 1892** and value in circle.

134	9	25c. on 5c. green	7·00	4·00
138	10	25c. on 5c. blue	28·00	27·00
135	9	25c. on 10c. brown	7·00	4·00
139	10	25c. on 10c. brown	11·00	11·00
136	9	1b. on 25c. orange	8·75	2·75
140	10	1b. on 25c. brown	11·00	11·00
137	9	1b. on 50c. blue	12·50	2·75
141	10	1b. on 50c. green	14·00	13·50

1893. Optd with coat of arms and diagonal shading.

142	9	5c. green	15	15
150	10	5c. blue	35	15
143	9	10c. brown	15	15
151	10	10c. brown	45	45
144	9	25c. orange	15	15
152	10	25c. brown	35	15
145	9	50c. blue	15	15
153	10	50c. green	45	25
146	9	1b. red	30	15
154	10	1b. violet	1·10	40
147	9	3b. violet	40	20
148	9	10b. brown	1·20	1·00
149	9	20b. purple	1·10	1·00

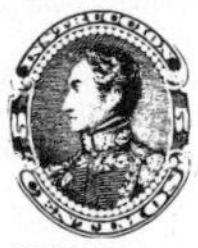

13 Bolivar

1893. Schools Tax stamps.

155	13	5c. grey	15	15
156	13	10c. green	15	15
157	13	25c. blue	15	15
158	13	50c. orange	15	15
159	13	1b. purple	15	15
160	13	3b. red	25	15
161	13	10b. violet	45	35
162	13	20b. brown	1·40	1·20

See also Nos. 227/35.

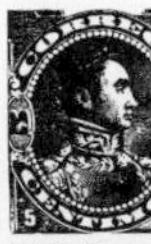

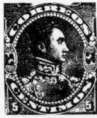

14 Bolivar

1893

163	14	5c. brown	40	15
164	14	10c. blue	1·80	40
165	14	25c. mauve	8·50	25
166	14	50c. purple	1·80	25
167	14	1b. green	2·30	40

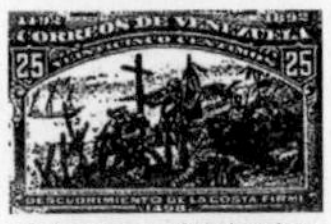

15 Landing of Columbus

1893. Columbian Exposition, Chicago, and 400th Anniv of Discovery of America by Columbus.

168	15	25c. purple	15·00	85

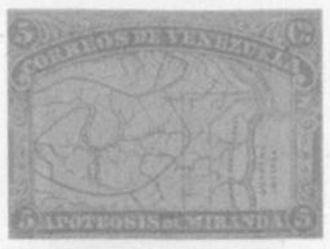

16 Map of Venezuela

1896. 80th Death Anniv of Gen. Miranda.

169	16	5c. green	4·50	3·75
170	16	10c. blue	5·50	4·00
171	16	25c. yellow	5·50	7·50
172	16	50c. red	75·00	37·00
173	16	1b. mauve	75·00	50·00

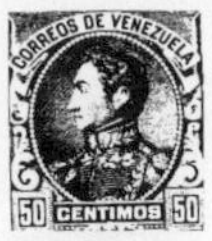

18 Bolivar

1899

179	18	5c. green	1·40	30
180	18	10c. red	1·90	55
181	18	25c. blue	2·20	75
182	18	50c. black	2·75	1·30
183	18	50c. orange	2·20	65
184	18	1b. green	46·00	20·00
185	18	2b. yellow	£550	£325

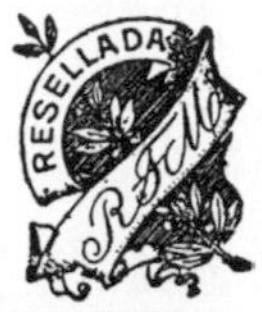

(21) "R.T.M." = Ramon Tellos Mendoza, Minister of Interior

1900. Stamps of 1893 optd with T **21**.

191	13	5c. grey	20	20
192	13	10c. green	20	20
193	13	25c. blue	20	20
194	13	50c. orange	20	20
195	13	1b. purple	35	20
196	13	3b. red	55	20
197	13	10b. violet	1·30	85
198	13	20b. brown	8·25	8·00

1900. Stamps of 1899 optd with T **21**.

199	18	5c. green	1·70	55
200	18	10c. red	1·70	55
201	18	25c. blue	11·00	1·60
202	18	50c. black	5·50	75
203	18	1b. green	2·40	1·10
204	18	2b. yellow	4·00	2·75

1900. Stamps of 1893 optd **1900**. Colours changed.

206	13	5c. orange	20	20
207	13	10c. blue	20	20
208	13	25c. purple	20	20
209	13	50c. green	1·20	20
210	13	1b. black	11·00	1·90
211	13	3b. brown	2·40	1·20
212	13	10b. red	14·50	3·75
213	13	20b. violet	22·00	5·75

1900. Stamps of 1899 optd **1900**.

214	18	5c. green	£1100	£1100
215	18	10c. red	£1100	£1100
216	18	25c. blue	£850	£800
217	18	50c. orange	33·00	2·10
218	18	1b. black	1·90	1·40

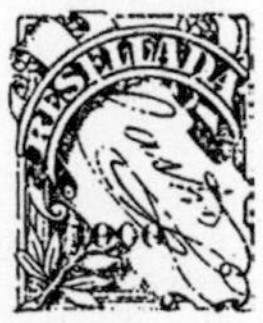

(23)

1900. Stamps of 1899 optd with T **23**.

219	5c. green	11·00	75
220	10c. red	10·00	1·30
221	25c. blue	11·00	1·30

1901. Re-issue of T **13** in new colours.

227	13	5c. orange	10	10
228	13	10c. red	10	10
229	13	10c. blue	10	10
231	13	50c. green	10	10
232	13	1b. black	11·00	2·75
233	13	3b. brown	20	10
234	13	10b. red	55	45
235	13	20b. violet	1·30	75

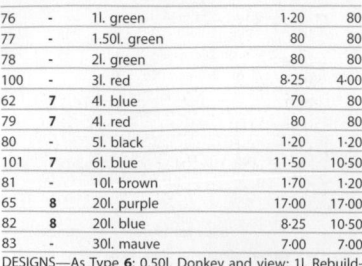

1902. Stamp of 1901 optd **1901**.

236	1b. black	90	55

1904. No. 231 surch **CORREOS Vale B 0,05 1904**.

310	5c. on 50c. green	1·10	85

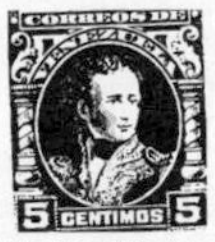
38 General Sucre

1904

311	**38**	5c. green	65	20
312	**38**	10c. red	75	20
313	**38**	15c. violet	1·30	55
314	**38**	25c. blue	9·25	55
315	**38**	50c. red	1·30	65
316	**38**	1b. red	1·70	65

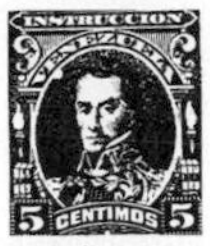
39 Bolivar

1904

317	**39**	5c. green	10	10
318	**39**	10c. grey	10	10
319	**39**	25c. red	20	20
320	**39**	50c. yellow	20	20
321	**39**	1b. red	3·75	55
322	**39**	3b. blue	65	20
323	**39**	10b. violet	90	65
324	**39**	20b. red	2·20	65

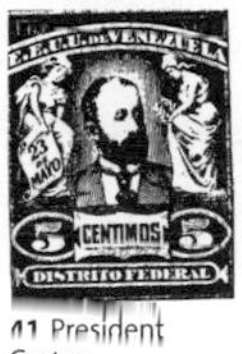
41 President Castro

1905. Sixth Anniv of General Castro's Revolt.

330	**41**	5c. red	4·75	4·50
331a	**41**	10c. blue	7·75	5·75
332a	**41**	25c. yellow	2·75	1·80

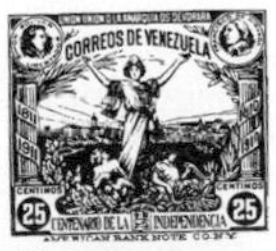
42 Liberty

1910. Independence Centenary.

333	**42**	25c. blue	19·00	95

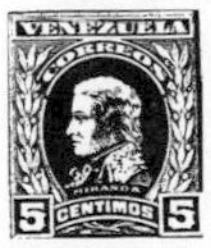
43 F. de Miranda

1911. Portraits as T **43**.

340	**43**	5c. green	65	20
341	**43**	10c. red	65	20
342	-	15c. grey (Urdaneta)	4·75	3·25
343	-	25c. blue (Urdaneta)	2·75	85
344	-	50c. violet (Bolivar)	2·75	85
339	-	1b. orange (Bolivar)	5·00	2·10

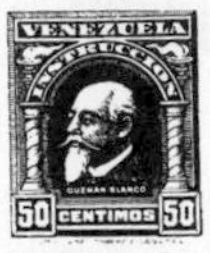
44

1911. Portraits as T **44**.

345		5c. blue (Vargas)	10	10
346		10c. yellow (Avila)	10	10
347		25c. grey (Sanz)	10	10
348	**44**	50c. red (Blanco)	10	10
349	-	1b. green (Bello)	10	10
350	-	2b. brown (Sanabria)	1·10	65
351	-	3b. violet (Paez)	1·10	45
352	-	10b. purple (Sucre)	2·20	95
353	-	20b. blue (Bolivar)	2·20	1·40

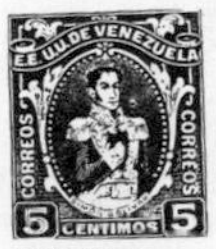
46 Bolivar

1914

359	**46**	5c. green	55·00	75
360	**46**	10c. red	50·00	65
361	**46**	25c. blue	8·25	30

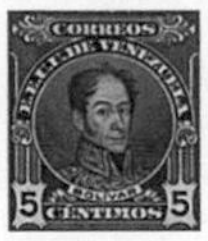
47 Bolivar

1915. Various Frames.

362a	**47**	5c. green	6·00	55
379	**47**	5c. brown	75	25
570	**47**	7½c. green	1·70	55
380	**47**	10c. green	35	25
571	**47**	10c. red	4·50	30
381	**47**	15c. olive	3·25	65
382	**47**	15c. brown	45	25
383	**47**	25c. blue	3·25	25
384	**47**	25c. red	35	25
368	**47**	40c. green	33·00	16·00
385	**47**	40c. blue	75	30
369	**47**	50c. violet	9·25	1·10
386	**47**	50c. blue	75	30
371	**47**	75c. turquoise	85·00	32·00
387	**47**	1b. black	75	45
388	**47**	3b. orange	2·40	1·30
389	**47**	5b. violet	22·00	11·50

See also Nos. 414/5.

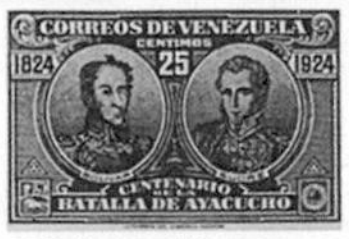
48 Bolivar and Sucre

1924. Centenary of Battle of Ayacucho.

390	**48**	25c. blue	4·00	75

1926. Fiscal stamps surch **CORREOS VALE 1926** and value.

392	0,05b. on 1b. olive	90	55
393	0,25b. on 5c. brown	90	55

DESIGNS: No. 392, Portrait of Sucre; No. 393, Numeral.

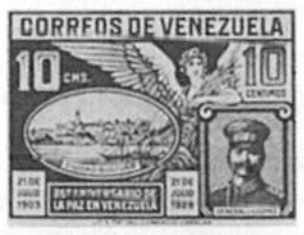
50 General J. V. Gomez and Ciudad Bolivar

1928. 25th Anniv of Capture of Ciudad Bolivar and Peace in Venezuela.

394	**50**	10c. green	1·30	85

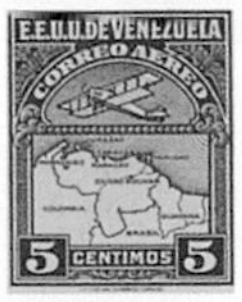
51 Biplane and Venezuela

1930. Air.

395	**51**	5c. brown	10	10
575	**51**	5c. green	35	20
396	**51**	10c. yellow	10	10
576	**51**	10c. orange	75	20
577	**51**	12½c. purple	1·70	1·20
397	**51**	15c. grey	10	10
578	**51**	15c. blue	1·30	20
398	**51**	25c. violet	10	10
579	**51**	25c. brown	1·70	20
399	**51**	40c. green	20	10
581	**51**	70c. red	28·00	10·50
400	**51**	75c. red	45	20
401	**51**	1b. blue	65	20
402	**51**	1b.20 green	1·00	45
403	**51**	1b.70 blue	1·30	65
404	**51**	1b.90 green	1·50	75
405	**51**	2b.10 blue	2·40	95
406	**51**	2b.30 red	2·40	75
407	**51**	2b.50 blue	2·40	75
408	**51**	3b.70 green	2·40	1·30
409	**51**	10b. purple	6·00	3·00
410	**51**	20b. green	10·50	6·50

See also Nos. 426/49.

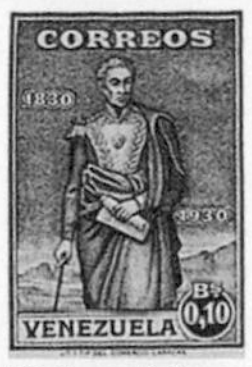
52 Simon Bolivar

1930. Death Centenary of Bolivar.

411	**52**	5c. yellow	1·30	45
412	**52**	10c. blue	1·30	30
413	**52**	25c. red	1·30	30

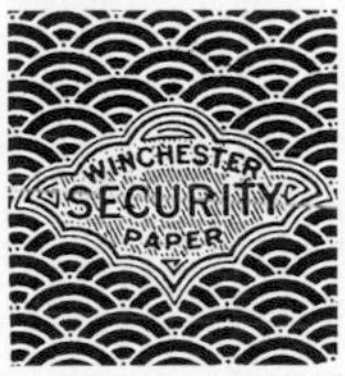
53

1932. Stamps of 1915 on paper printed with pattern as T **53**.

414	**47**	5c. violet	65	20
415	**47**	7½c. green	1·50	55
416	**47**	10c. green	90	20
417	**47**	15c. yellow	2·10	30
418	**47**	22½c. red	5·00	65
419	**47**	25c. red	1·80	20
420	**47**	37½c. blue	6·50	2·75
421	**47**	40c. blue	6·50	30
422	**47**	50c. olive	6·50	20
423	**47**	1b. blue	8·75	95
424	**47**	3b. brown	65·00	18·00
425	**47**	5b. brown	90·00	23·00

1932. Air. Air stamps as 1930 on paper printed with pattern as T **53**.

426	**51**	5c. brown	55	20
427	**51**	10c. yellow	55	20
428	**51**	15c. grey	55	20
429	**51**	25c. blue	55	20
430	**51**	40c. green	1·10	20
431	**51**	70c. red	75	20
432	**51**	75c. orange	1·40	20
433	**51**	1b. slate	1·50	20
434	**51**	1b.20 green	3·25	1·20
435	**51**	1b.70 brown	6·50	75
436	**51**	1b.80 blue	3·25	45
437	**51**	1b.90 green	8·25	5·00
438	**51**	1b.95 blue	9·25	3·75
439	**51**	2b. brown	5·50	3·25
440	**51**	2b.10 blue	13·00	8·00
441	**51**	2b.30 red	5·50	3·25
442	**51**	2b.50 blue	8·25	1·90
443	**51**	3b. violet	8·25	1·20
444	**51**	3b.70 green	11·00	8·00
445	**51**	4b. orange	8·25	1·90
446	**51**	5b. black	9·25	3·25
447	**51**	8b. red	19·00	6·50
448	**51**	10b. violet	39·00	10·50
449	**51**	20b. green	85·00	28·00

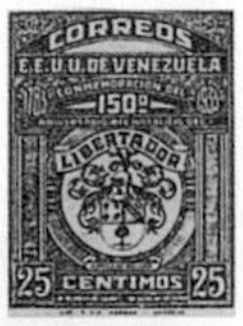
54 Arms of Bolivar

1933. 150th Birth Anniv of Bolivar.

450	**54**	25c. red	3·75	3·25

1934. Surch **1933** and figures of value and old value blocked out.

451	**47**	7½ on 10c. green (380)	65	30
452	**47**	22½ on 25c. red (419)	2·75	1·20
453	**47**	22½ on 25c. red (384)	2·20	2·10
454	**47**	37½ on 40c. blue (385)	2·75	1·30

1937. Air. Air stamps of 1932 surch **1937 VALE POR** and new value.

455	**51**	5c. on 1b.70 brown	17·00	9·50
456	**51**	10c. on 3b.70 green	18·00	9·50
457	**51**	15c. on 4b. orange	7·25	4·75
458	**51**	25c. on 5b. black	7·25	4·75
459	**51**	1b. on 8b. red	5·50	4·75
460	**51**	2b. on 2b.10 blue	44·00	32·00

1937. Surch **1937 VALE POR** and value.

461	**47**	25c. on 40c. (No. 421)	11·00	1·30

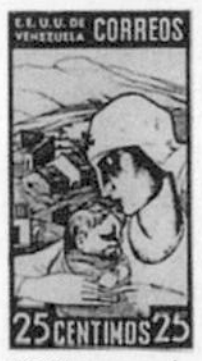
59 Nurse and Child

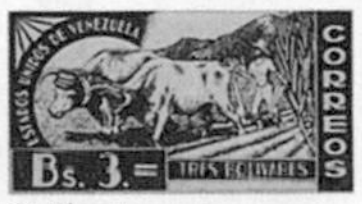
60 Ploughing

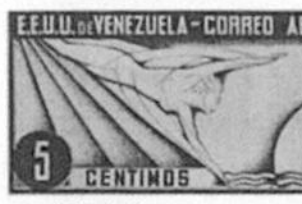
61 "Flight"

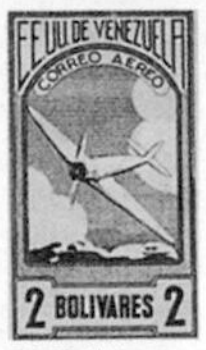
64 Caribbean Coast

1937. (a) Postage.

463	**59**	5c. violet	75	45
464	-	10c. green	75	20
465	-	15c. brown	1·40	75
466	**59**	25c. red	1·40	45
467	-	50c. green	9·25	5·75
468	**60**	3b. red	17·00	10·50
469	**59**	5b. brown	33·00	21·00

DESIGNS—VERT: 10c. Sailing barges on Orinoco; 15c. Women gathering cocoa-beans. HORIZ: 50c. Rounding up cattle.

(b) Air.

470	**61**	5c. brown	45	55
471	-	10c. orange	35	10
472	-	15c. black	90	55
473	**64**	25c. violet	90	55
474	-	40c. green	1·70	75
475	**61**	70c. red	1·70	55
476	-	75c. bistre	3·50	1·80
477	**61**	1b. grey	2·20	75
478	-	1b.20 green	9·25	5·75
479	**61**	1b.80 blue	4·75	2·75
480	-	1b.95 blue	14·50	10·50
481	**64**	2b. brown	6·00	3·75
482	**64**	2b.50 blue	17·00	16·00
483	-	3b. lilac	9·25	6·50
484	**64**	3b.70 red	17·00	21·00
485	-	10b. purple	35·00	21·00
486	**61**	20b. black	44·00	32·00

DESIGNS—HORIZ: 10, [illegible] 1b.20, 3b. Puerto Cabello; 15, 75c., 1b.95, 10b. Caracas.

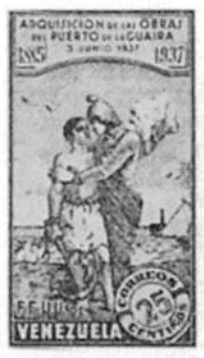
65 "Venezuela" welcoming La Guaira

1937. Acquisition of La Guaira Harbour.

487	**65**	25c. blue (postage)	1·80	65
488	-	70c. green (air)	2·00	75
489	-	1b.80 blue	3·00	1·40

DESIGN: 70c., 1b.80, Statue of Bolivar and La Guaira Harbour.

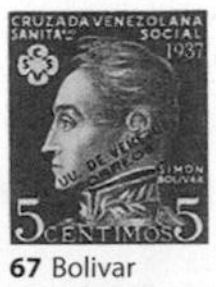
67 Bolivar

1937. Red Cross Fund.

490	**67**	5c. green	2·40	75

1937. Stamps of 1937 optd **RESELLADO 1937-1938**.

491	**59**	5c. violet (postage)	8·25	4·50
492	-	10c. green	2·75	1·10
493	**59**	25c. red	1·70	75
494	**60**	3b. red	£300	£130
495	-	10c. orange (air)	1·30	95
496	**64**	25c. violet	2·75	1·30
497	-	40c. green	2·75	1·90
498	**61**	70c. red	2·20	1·30
499	**61**	1b. grey	2·75	1·90
500	-	1b.20 green	44·00	27·00
501	**61**	1b.80 blue	8·25	3·25
502	-	1b.95 blue	11·00	5·75
503	**64**	2b. brown	70·00	32·00
504	**64**	2b.50 blue	70·00	27·00
505	-	3b. lilac	44·00	16·00
506	-	10b. purple	£100	55·00
507	**61**	20b. black	£110	65·00

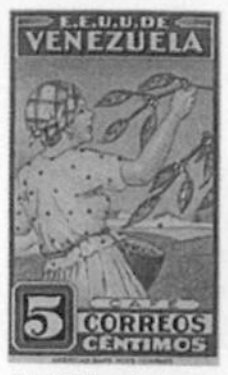

69 Gathering Coffee Beans

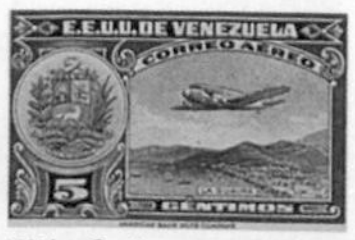

72 La Guaira

1938. (a) Postage. As T **69**.

508	**69**	5c. green	55	10
509	**A**	10c. red	1·00	10
510	**B**	15c. violet	2·00	30
544	**B**	15c. green	1·20	30
511	**A**	25c. blue	55	10
546	**A**	37½c. blue	4·00	1·20
513	**B**	40c. sepia	29·00	10·50
547	**B**	40c. black	13·00	1·20
514	**69**	50c. olive	40·00	10·50
548	**69**	50c. violet	17·00	7·50
515	**A**	1b. brown	17·00	7·50
516	**69**	3b. orange	£130	75·00
517	**B**	5b. black	22·00	10·50
750	**B**	5b. orange	£100	45·00
751	**B**	5b. brown	28·00	9·00

DESIGNS: A, Bolivar; B, G.P.O., Caracas.

(b) Air. As T **72**.

550	**72**	5c. green	20	20
551	**C**	10c. red	20	20
552	**72**	12½c. violet	90	75
520	**D**	15c. violet	4·50	1·70
553	**D**	15c. blue	1·20	20
521	**72**	25c. blue	4·50	1·70
554	**72**	25c. brown	35	20
555	**D**	30c. violet	2·75	20
522	**C**	40c. violet	5·00	1·60
556	**C**	40c. brown	3·50	20
557	**72**	45c. green	1·40	20
558	**C**	50c. blue	1·80	20
523	**D**	70c. red	1·20	30
524	**72**	75c. brown	8·75	2·75
559	**72**	75c. green	2·00	20
560	**D**	90c. red	1·40	20
525	**C**	1b. green	10·00	3·75
561	**C**	1b. violet	1·80	20
526	**D**	1b.20 orange	29·00	8·00
562	**D**	1b.20 green	2·75	75
527	**72**	1b.80 blue	2·75	75
528	**C**	1b.90 black	7·75	3·75
529	**D**	1b.95 blue	6·00	3·50
530	**72**	2b. green	65·00	21·00
563	**72**	2b. red	2·40	95
531	**C**	2b.50 brown	65·00	27·00
564	**C**	2b.50 orange	14·50	3·50
565	**D**	3b. green	7·75	2·75
533	**72**	3b.70 black	11·00	7·50
566	**D**	5b. red	11·00	2·75
771	**D**	5b. green	13·00	4·50
534	**C**	10b. purple	29·00	3·25
773	**C**	10b. yellow	17·00	6·50
535	**D**	20b. orange	85·00	34·00

DESIGNS: C, National Pantheon; D, Oil Wells.

1938. Surch **VALE Bs. 0,40 1938.**

536	**59**	40c. on 5b. brown	12·00	6·50

1938. Air. Postage stamps surch **1938 VALE** and value in words.

537	**61**	5c. on 1b.80 blue	1·20	85
538	**64**	10c. on 2b.50 blue	4·00	1·90
539	**64**	15c. on 2b. brown	2·00	1·60
540	-	25c. on 40c. green (No. 474)	2·20	1·90
541	**64**	40c. on 3b.70 red	5·00	4·50

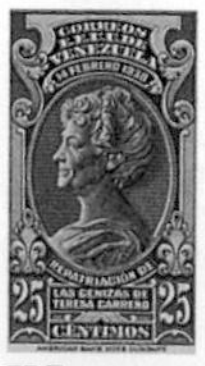

77 Teresa Carreno

1938. Repatriation of Ashes of Teresa Carreno (concert pianist).

567	**77**	25c. blue	8·25	85

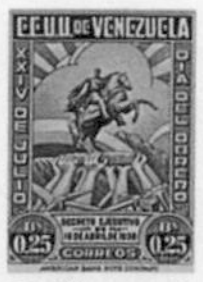

78 Allegory of Labour and Statue of Bolivar

1938. Labour Day.

568	**78**	25c. blue	9·25	85

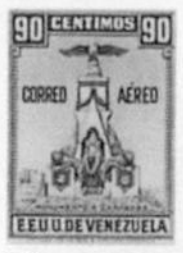

80 Monument at Carabobo

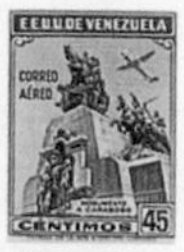

81 Monument at Carabobo

1938. Air. Independence Issue.

583	-	20c. brown	55	30
584	**80**	30c. violet	75	30
585	**81**	45c. blue	1·10	20
586	-	50c. blue	1·00	20
587	**81**	70c. red	18·00	9·50
588	**80**	90c. orange	1·70	65
589	**81**	1b.35 black	2·00	95
590	-	1b.40 slate	8·25	3·25
591	**80**	2b.25 green	4·00	2·10

DESIGN: 20, 50c., 1b.40, Airplane over Sucre Monument.

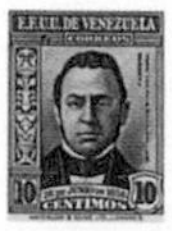

82 Gen. J. I. Paz Castillo

1939. 80th Anniv of Venezuelan Posts.

592	**82**	10c. red	3·50	95

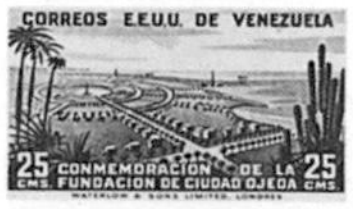

83 View of Ojeda

1939. Founding of Ojeda.

593	**83**	25c. blue	13·00	1·10

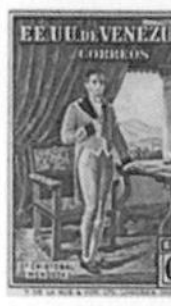

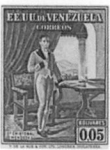

84 Dr. Cristobal Mendoza

1939. Centenary of Death of Dr. Mendoza.

594	**84**	5c. green	55	20
595	**84**	10c. red	55	20
596	**84**	15c. violet	1·40	45
597	**84**	25c. blue	1·10	20
598	**84**	37½c. blue	22·00	10·50
599	**84**	50c. olive	22·00	7·00
600	**84**	1b. brown	8·75	5·75

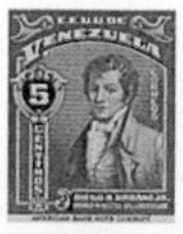

85 Diego B. Urbaneja

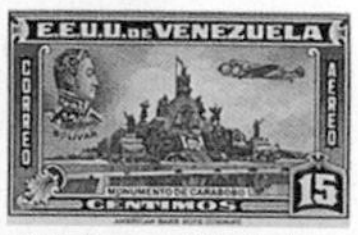

86 Bolivar and Carabobo Monument

1940. Independence Issue.

601	**85**	5c. green (postage)	75	20
602	**85**	7½c. green	1·10	30
603	**85**	15c. olive	1·30	30
604	**85**	37½c. blue	2·00	1·10
605	**85**	40c. blue	1·70	55
745	**85**	40c. mauve	1·30	30
746	**85**	40c. orange	1·10	30
606	**85**	50c. violet	9·25	2·30
607	**85**	1b. brown	4·75	1·30
748	**85**	1b. blue	3·25	30
608	**85**	3b. red	13·00	5·75
749	**85**	3b. grey	6·50	1·30
609	**86**	15c. blue (air)	75	20
610	**86**	20c. olive	75	10
611	**86**	25c. brown	3·25	55
612	**86**	40c. brown	2·75	20
613	**86**	1b. lilac	6·00	75
614	**86**	2b. red	13·00	1·80

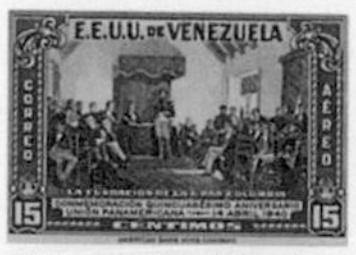

87 Foundation of Greater Colombia

1940. Air. 50th Anniv of Pan-American Union.

615	**87**	15c. brown	1·30	65

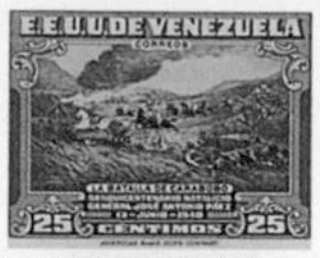

88 Battle of Carabobo

1940. 150th Birth Anniv of Gen. Paez.

616	**88**	25c. blue	9·25	75

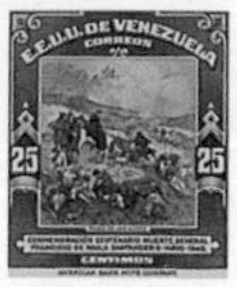

89 "The Crossing of the Andes" (after Salas)

1940. Death Centenary of Gen. Santander.

617	**89**	25c. blue	9·25	75

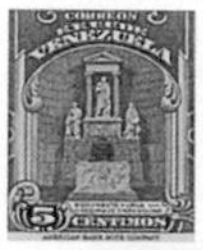

90 Monument and Urn

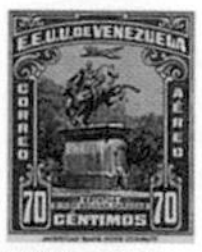

91 Statue of Bolivar at Caracas

1940. 110th Anniv of Death of Simon Bolivar. (a) Postage.

738	**90**	5c. green	10	10
739	**90**	5c. blue	20	10
619	-	10c. pink	35	10
620	-	15c. green	90	20
741	-	15c. red	1·10	10
621	-	20c. blue	1·50	10
622	-	25c. blue	90	10
742	-	25c. violet	75	10
623	-	30c. mauve	2·20	30
743	-	30c. black	2·00	1·10
744	-	30c. purple	1·10	20
624	-	37½c. blue	4·50	1·50
625	-	50c. violet	2·75	65
747	-	50c. green	1·70	30

DESIGNS—VERT: 15c. Bolivar's baptism; 25c. Simon Bolivar on horseback. HORIZ: 10c. Bolivar's bed; 20c. House where Bolivar was born; 30c. Courtyard and Bolivar's baptismal font; 37½c. Courtyard of house where Bolivar was born; 50c. "Rebellion of 1812".

(b) Air.

626	**91**	5c. green	35	10
752	**91**	5c. orange	10	10
627	**91**	10c. red	35	10
753	**91**	10c. green	10	10
628	**91**	12½c. violet	1·10	45
754	**91**	12½c. brown	75	75
629	**91**	15c. blue	65	10
755	**91**	15c. grey	20	10
630	**91**	20c. brown	65	10
756	**91**	20c. violet	35	10
631	**91**	25c. brown	65	10
757	**91**	25c. green	20	10
632	**91**	30c. violet	65	10
758	**91**	30c. blue	75	20
633	**91**	40c. brown	90	10
759	**91**	40c. green	55	20
634	**91**	45c. green	90	10
760	**91**	45c. red	1·10	20
635	**91**	50c. blue	90	10
761	**91**	50c. claret	55	20
636	**91**	70c. pink	2·75	45
762	**91**	70c. red	1·90	1·10
637	**91**	75c. olive	11·00	2·10
763	**91**	75c. orange	9·25	5·75
764	**91**	75c. violet	1·90	1·10
638	**91**	90c. orange	1·80	45
765	**91**	90c. black	1·70	65
639	**91**	1b. mauve	90	10
766	**91**	1b. blue	1·30	30
640	**91**	1b.20 green	3·25	1·10
767	**91**	1b.20 brown	2·75	1·30
641	**91**	1b.35 black	14·50	6·50
642	**91**	2b. red	2·75	20
643	**91**	3b. black	4·50	1·10
768	**91**	3b. brown	28·00	8·00
769	**91**	3b. blue	4·50	1·20
644	**91**	4b. black	3·50	1·10
645	**91**	5b. brown	29·00	10·50

1941. No. 622 surch **HABILITADO 1941 VALE BS. 0.20.**

646	20c. on 25c. blue	90	20

1941. Optd **HABILITADO 1940.**

647	**59**	5c. violet	2·75	65
648	-	10c. green (No. 464)	1·50	45

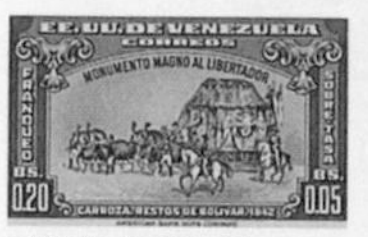

94 Bolivar's Funeral

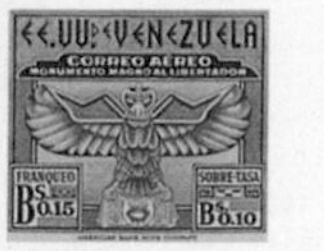

95 Condor

1941. Centenary of Arrival of Bolivar's Ashes at Caracas and Liberator's Monument Fund.

649	**94**	20c.+5c. blue (postage)	7·25	65
650	**95**	15c.+10c. brown (air)	2·75	1·10
651	**95**	30c.+5c. violet	7·75	1·30

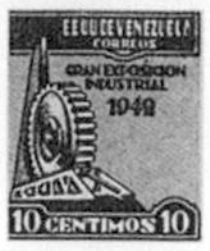

96 Symbolical of Industry

1942. National Industrial Exhibition.

652	**96**	10c. red	1·50	30

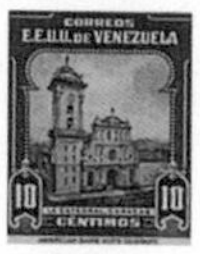

97 Caracas Cathedral

1943

653	**97**	10c. red	35	10
740	**97**	10c. orange	1·10	20

1943. Surch **Habilitado Vale Bs. 0.20.**

654	**59**	20c. on 25c. red	39·00	37·00
655	**65**	20c. on 25c. blue	£110	£110
656	**77**	20c. on 25c. blue	22·00	21·00
657	**78**	20c. on 25c. blue	22·00	21·00

1943. Optd **Resellado 1943.**

658	**59**	5c. violet	22·00	13·00
659	-	10c. green (No. 464)	8·25	5·25
660	-	50c. green (No. 467)	11·00	5·25
661	**60**	3b. red	65·00	29·00

1943. Air. Optd **Resellado 1943.**

662	-	10c. orange (No. 471)	1·80	1·10
663	**64**	25c. violet	1·80	1·30
664	-	40c. green (No. 474)	2·20	1·30
665	**61**	70c. red	1·80	1·30
666	-	70c. green (No. 488)	2·20	1·30
667	-	75c. bistre (No. 476)	2·40	1·60
668	**61**	1b. grey	2·75	1·90
669	-	1b.20 green (No. 478)	3·50	1·90
670	**61**	1b.80 blue	3·00	1·60
671	-	1b.80 blue (No. 489)	4·50	2·10
672	-	1b.95 blue (No. 480)	5·00	2·30
673	**64**	2b. brown	5·00	3·75
674	**64**	2b.50 blue	6·00	3·75
675	-	3b. lilac (No. 483)	7·25	4·25
676	**64**	3b.70 red	85·00	60·00
677	-	10b. purple (No. 485)	29·00	17·00
678	**61**	20b. black	46·00	34·00

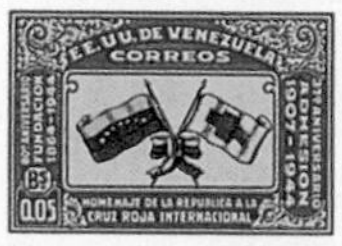

99

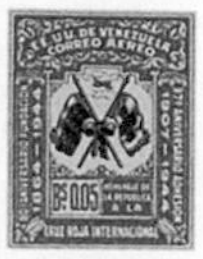

100 National and Red Cross Flags

1944. Air. 80th Anniv of Int Red Cross and 37th Anniv of Adherence of Venezuela.

MS679 **99** 5c. green; 10c. red; 20c. blue; 1b. claret (104×115 mm) (postage) 46·00 46·00

680	**100**	5c. green (air)	20	10
681	**100**	10c. mauve	20	10
682	**100**	20c. blue	20	10
683	**100**	30c. blue	55	10
684	**100**	40c. brown	75	20
685	**100**	45c. green	2·40	1·30
686	**100**	90c. orange	2·20	85
687	**100**	1b. black	3·25	75

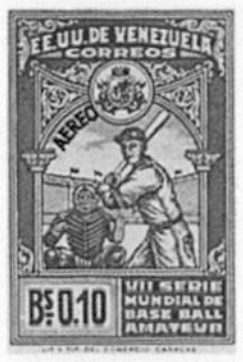

101 Baseball Players

1944. Air. Seventh World Amateur Baseball Championship Games, Caracas. Optd **AEREO**.

688	**101**	5c. brown	55	20
689	**101**	10c. green	55	20
690	**101**	20c. blue	75	30
691	**101**	30c. red	1·10	55
692	**101**	45c. purple	2·20	95
693	**101**	90c. orange	5·00	1·90
694	**101**	1b. grey	5·50	1·90
695	**101**	1b.20 green	13·00	10·00
696	**101**	1b.80 yellow	18·00	13·00

1944. Air. No. 590 surch **Habilitado 1944 VALE Bs. 0.30**.

697	30c. on 1b.40c. slate	75	75

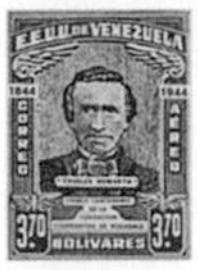

103 Charles Howarth

1944. Air. Cent of Rochdale Co-operative Society.

698	**103**	5c. black	20	20
699	**103**	10c. violet	20	20
700	**103**	20c. brown	55	30
701	**103**	30c. green	75	30
702	**103**	1b.20 brown	3·50	3·25
703	**103**	1b.80 blue	6·00	3·75
704	**103**	3b.70 red	8·25	6·50

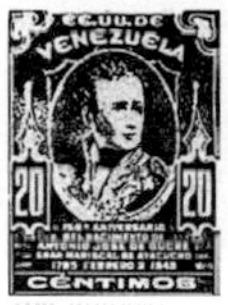

104 Antonio José de Sucre

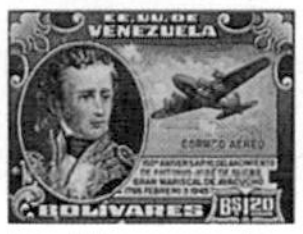

105 Antonio José de Sucre and Douglas DC-4

1945. 150th Anniv of Birth of Gen. Sucre.

705	**104**	5c. yellow (postage)	3·25	1·10
706	**104**	10c. blue	4·50	2·10
707	**104**	20c. red	5·50	3·25
708	**105**	5c. orange (air)	55	45
709	**105**	10c. purple	55	65
710	**105**	20c. black	1·10	65
711	**105**	30c. green	1·70	1·30
712	**105**	40c. olive	2·75	2·10
713	**105**	45c. brown	3·75	2·10
714	**105**	90c. brown	6·50	2·75
715	**105**	1b. mauve	5·00	2·10
716	**105**	1b.20 black	12·00	11·50
717	**105**	2b. yellow	17·00	11·50

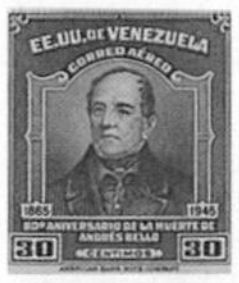

106 Andres Bello

1946. 80th Death Anniv of A. Bello (educationalist).

718	**106**	20c. blue (postage)	1·40	55
719	**106**	30c. green (air)	1·30	55

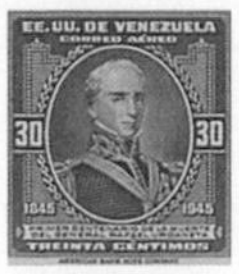

107 Gen. Rafael Urdaneta

1946. Death Centenary of Gen. R. Urdaneta.

720	**107**	20c. blue (postage)	1·40	55
721	**107**	30c. green (air)	1·30	55

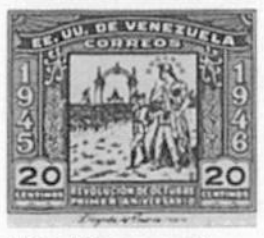

108 Allegory of Republic

1946. First Anniv of Revolution.

722	**108**	20c. blue (postage)	1·30	55
723	-	15c. blue (air)	75	55
724	-	20c. bistre	75	55
725	-	30c. violet	1·10	75
726	-	1b. red	7·25	5·75

Nos. 723/6 are as Type **108**, but vert.

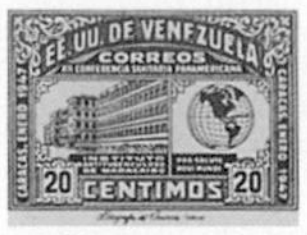

110 Western Hemisphere and Anti-tuberculosis Inst, Maracaibo

1947. 12th Pan-American Health Conf, Caracas.

727	**110**	20c. yellow & bl (postage)	1·30	55
728	-	15c. yellow and blue (air)	1·10	75
729	-	20c. yellow and brown	1·10	65
730	-	30c. yellow and violet	1·10	75
731	-	1b. yellow and red	9·25	8·00

Nos. 728/31 are as Type **110** but vert.

1947. Surch **J. R. G. CORREOS Vale Bs.0.15 1946**.

732	**85**	15c. on 1b. brown	1·30	55

1947. Air. Surch **J. R. G. AEREO Vale Bs.**, new value, and **1946**.

733	**47**	10c. on 22½c. red (No. 418)	35	20
734	-	15c. on 25c. blue (No. 622)	65	30
735	**91**	20c. on 50c. blue	65	30
736	**85**	70c. on 1b. brown	1·40	65
737	-	20b. on 20b. orange (No. 535)	50·00	19·00

1947. Nos. 743 and 624 surch **CORREOS Vale Bs.**, new value, and **1947**. (a) Postage.

776	5c. on 30c. black	75	10
777	5c. on 37½c. blue	90	10

(b) Air. No. 621 with **AEREO** instead of CORREOS.

778	5c. on 20c. blue	45	25
779	10c. on 20c. blue	45	25

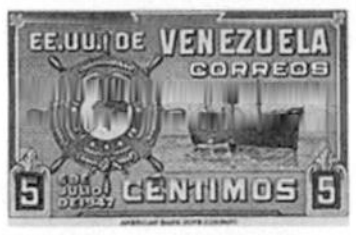

116 Freighter "Republica de Venezuela" and Ship's Wheel

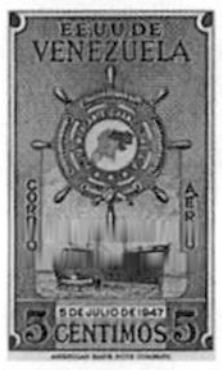

117 Freighter "Republica de Venezuela" and Ship's Wheel

1948. First Anniv of Greater Colombia Merchant Marine. Frame size 37½×22½ mm or 22½×37½ mm. Inscr "AMERICAN BANK NOTE COMPANY" at foot.

780	**116**	5c. blue (postage)	20	10
781	**116**	7½c. red	1·10	55
782	**116**	10c. red	75	10
783	**116**	15c. grey	1·20	20
784	**116**	20c. sepia	65	10
785	**116**	25c. violet	1·20	30
786	**116**	30c. yellow	8·25	3·25
787	**116**	37½c. brown	3·25	2·10
788	**116**	40c. olive	5·00	2·75
789	**116**	50c. mauve	1·30	30
790	**116**	1b. green	2·20	75
791	**117**	5c. brown (air)	10	10
792	**117**	10c. green	10	10
793	**117**	15c. buff	20	10
794	**117**	20c. purple	35	10
795	**117**	25c. grey	35	10
796	**117**	30c. olive	55	20
797	**117**	45c. blue	90	30
798	**117**	50c. black	1·30	55
799	**117**	70c. orange	2·75	55
800	**117**	75c. blue	5·00	75
801	**117**	90c. red	2·75	1·60
802	**117**	1b. violet	3·25	1·10
803	**117**	2b. slate	3·75	1·60
804	**117**	3b. green	13·00	5·25
805	**117**	4b. blue	6·50	5·25
806	**117**	5b. red	28·00	9·00

For stamps as T **116/17** in larger size and inscribed "COURVOISIER S.A." at foot, see Nos. 1012/7.

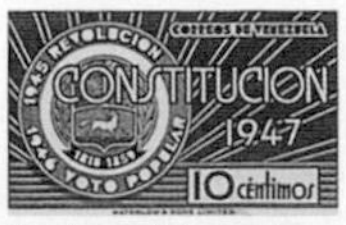

118 Arms of Venezuela

1948. New Constitution Promulgation.

807	**118**	5c. blue	2·75	1·30
808	**118**	10c. red	3·25	1·50

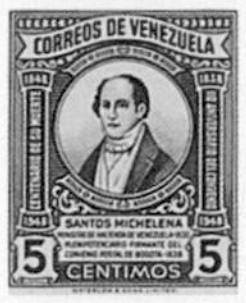

120 Santos Michelena

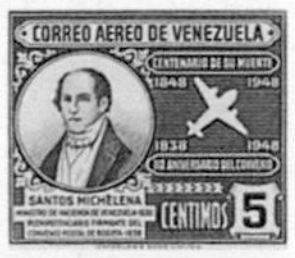

121 Santos Michelena and Silhouette of Douglas DC-3

1949. 110th Anniv of First International Postal Convention, Bogota.

810	**120**	5c. blue (postage)	35	20
811	**120**	10c. red	75	20
812	**120**	20c. sepia	3·25	1·10
813	**120**	1b. green	11·00	4·75
814	**121**	5c. brown (air)	35	20
815	**121**	10c. grey	35	20
816	**121**	15c. orange	1·10	65
817	**121**	25c. green	2·00	1·10
818	**121**	30c. purple	2·00	1·10
819	**121**	1b. violet	11·00	3·75

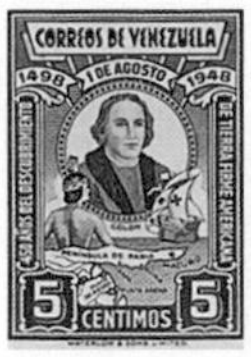

122 Columbus, Indian, "Santa Maria" and Map

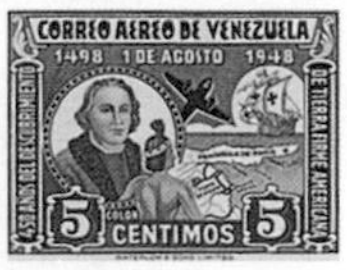

123 Columbus, Indian, "Santa Maria" and Map

1949. 450th Anniv of Columbus's Discovery of America.

820	**122**	5c. blue (postage)	75	20
821	**122**	10c. red	3·25	75
822	**122**	20c. sepia	3·75	1·10
823	**122**	1b. green	8·75	3·75
824	**123**	5c. brown (air)	75	10
825	**123**	10c. grey	75	30
826	**123**	15c. orange	1·30	30
827	**123**	25c. green	2·40	75
828	**123**	30c. mauve	3·25	1·10
829	**123**	1b. violet	12·00	3·25

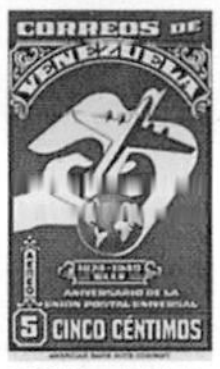

124 Hand, Bird, Airplane and Globe

1950. Air. 75th Anniv of U.P.U.

830	**124**	5c. lake	20	10
831	**124**	10c. green	10	10
832	**124**	15c. brown	20	10
833	**124**	25c. grey	90	65
834	**124**	30c. olive	1·30	75
835	**124**	50c. black	75	30
836	**124**	60c. blue	2·75	1·40
837	**124**	90c. red	4·00	1·60
838	**124**	1b. violet	4·00	1·40

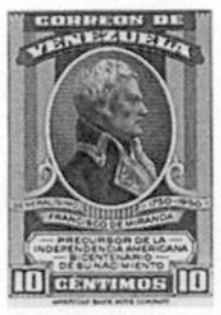

125 Francisco de Miranda

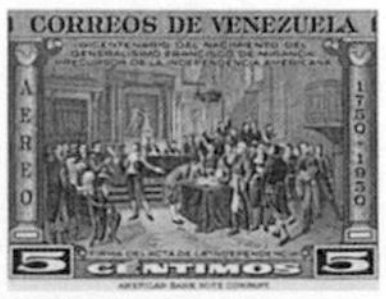

126 Declaration of Independence

1950. Birth Bicentenary of Miranda.

839	**125**	5c. blue (postage)	35	10
840	**125**	10c. green	75	20
841	**125**	20c. brown	1·70	75
842	**125**	1b. red	8·25	3·75
843	**126**	5c. red (air)	55	25
844	**126**	10c. brown	55	25
845	**126**	15c. violet	1·10	55
846	**126**	30c. blue	1·70	85
847	**126**	1b. green	8·25	3·75

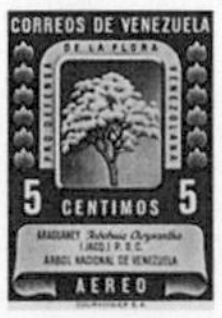

127 Tabebuia (National Tree)

1950. Air. Protection of Flora. Centres in yellow.

848	**127**	5c. brown	2·20	30
849	**127**	10c. green	2·20	30
850	**127**	15c. mauve	4·50	30
851	**127**	25c. green	28·00	2·10
852	**127**	30c. orange	30·00	2·75
853	**127**	50c. grey	18·00	65
854	**127**	60c. blue	28·00	1·40
855	**127**	90c. red	44·00	2·75
856	**127**	1b. violet	65·00	3·50

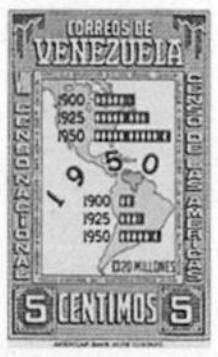

128 Map and Statistics

1950. Census of the Americas.

857	**128**	5c. blue (postage)	35	10
858	**128**	10c. grey	35	10
859	**128**	15c. sepia	55	10
860	**128**	25c. green	75	20
861	**128**	30c. red	1·10	30
862	**128**	50c. violet	2·20	75
863	**128**	1b. brown	6·00	2·30
864	**128**	5c. grey (air)	20	10
865	**128**	10c. green	10	10
866	**128**	15c. olive	55	10
867	**128**	25c. black	75	75
868	**128**	30c. orange	1·30	75
869	**128**	50c. brown	75	30
870	**128**	60c. blue	75	55
871	**128**	90c. red	3·25	1·30
872	**128**	1b. violet	5·00	3·75

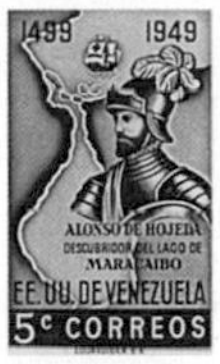

129 Alonso de Ojeda

1950. 450th Anniv of Discovery of Lake Maracaibo.

873	**129**	5c. blue (postage)	35	20
874	**129**	10c. red	55	20
875	**129**	15c. grey	65	30
876	**129**	20c. blue	2·75	1·10
877	**129**	1b. green	11·00	5·25
878	**129**	5c. brown (air)	35	10
879	**129**	10c. red	55	20
880	**129**	15c. sepia	90	30
881	**129**	25c. purple	1·30	65
882	**129**	30c. orange	2·75	1·10
883	**129**	1b. green	11·00	5·25

1951. Surch **RESELLADO** and new value.

884	**116**	5c. on 7½c. red	45	25
885	**116**	10c. on 37½c. brown	45	25

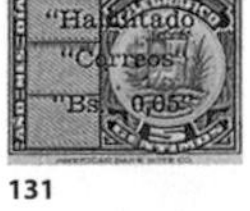

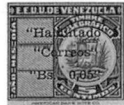

131

1951. Telegraph stamps surch as in T **131**.

886	5c. on 5c. brown	20	10
887	10c. on 10c. green	55	10
888	20c. on 1b. black	1·10	20
889	25c. on 25c. red	1·30	55
890	30c. on 2b. olive	2·00	1·60

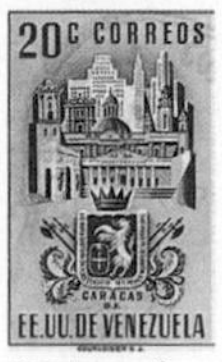

132 Arms of Caracas and View

1951. Arms issue. Federal District of Caracas.

891	**132**	5c. green (postage)	1·10	30
892	**132**	10c. red	3·25	30
893	**132**	15c. brown	5·50	65
894	**132**	20c. blue	17·00	65
895	**132**	25c. brown	17·00	1·30
896	**132**	30c. blue	17·00	1·60
897	**132**	35c. violet	£170	34·00

898	132	5c. turquoise (air)	3·25	30
899	132	7½c. green	2·20	1·30
900	132	10c. red	55	30
901	132	15c. brown	17·00	1·10
902	132	20c. blue	8·25	1·10
903	132	30c. blue	22·00	2·10
904	132	45c. purple	3·75	1·10
905	132	60c. green	33·00	2·10
906	132	90c. red	17·00	9·00

See also Nos. 922/37, 938/53, 954/69, 970/85, 991/1006, 1018/33, 1034/49, 1050/65, 1066/81, 1082/97, 1098/113, 1137/52, 1153/68, 1169/84, 1185/1200, 1201/16, 1217/32, 1258/73, 1274/89, 1290/1305, 1306/21, 1322/37, and 1338/53.

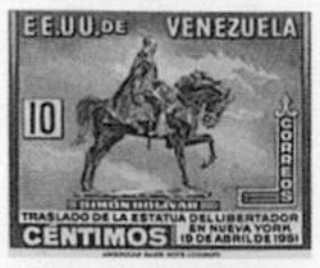

133 Statue of Bolivar, New York

1951. Transfer of Statue of Bolivar to Central Park, New York.

907	133	5c. green (postage)	55	10
908	133	10c. red	1·10	30
909	133	20c. blue	1·10	30
910	133	30c. grey	1·30	65
911	133	40c. green	1·70	65
912	133	50c. brown	4·75	1·30
913	133	1b. black	13·00	6·50
914	133	5c. violet (air)	65	20
915	133	10c. green	75	20
916	133	20c. grey	75	20
917	133	25c. olive	1·10	20
918	133	30c. red	1·30	75
919	133	40c. brown	1·30	75
920	133	50c. slate	4·75	1·60
921	133	70c. orange	7·75	5·75

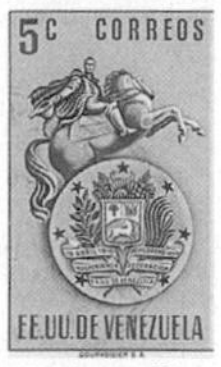

134 Arms of Venezuela and Bolivar Statue

1951. Arms issue. National Arms of Venezuela.

922	134	5c. green (postage)	1·10	30
923	134	10c. red	1·70	30
924	134	15c. brown	33·00	75
925	134	20c. blue	4·50	55
926	134	25c. brown	17·00	1·50
927	134	30c. blue	11·00	1·50
928	134	35c. violet	£110	27·00
929	134	5c. turquoise (air)	1·10	30
930	134	7½c. green	4·50	1·20
931	134	10c. red	55	30
932	134	15c. brown	4·50	1·20
933	134	20c. blue	8·25	85
934	134	30c. blue	28·00	1·90
935	134	45c. purple	4·50	75
936	134	60c. green	28·00	3·75
937	134	90c. red	22·00	9·00

1951. Arms issue. State of Tachira. As T **132** showing Arms of Tachira and agricultural products.

938	5c. green (postage)	55	30
939	10c. red	2·20	30
940	15c. brown	2·75	45
941	20c. blue	4·50	85
942	50c. orange	£375	26·00
943	1b. green	4·50	1·20
944	5b. purple	8·25	4·50
945	5c. turquoise (air)	55	30
946	10c. red	55	30
947	15c. brown	2·20	30
948	30c. blue	44·00	2·00
949	60c. green	33·00	2·00
950	1b.20 lake	55·00	9·00
951	3b. green	2·20	1·70
952	5b. purple	4·50	3·75
953	10b. violet	17·00	7·50

1951. Arms issue. State of Zulia. As T **132** showing Arms of Zulia and Oil Well.

954	5c. green (postage)	55	30
955	10c. red	55	30
956	15c. brown	1·70	55
957	20c. blue	2·20	75
958	50c. orange	44·00	7·00
959	1b. green	2·20	1·20
960	5b. purple	5·50	4·50
961	5c. turquoise (air)	2·20	30
962	10c. red	55	30
963	15c. brown	2·20	30
964	30c. blue	22·00	2·40
965	60c. green	5·50	75
966	1b.20 lake	33·00	9·50
967	3b. green	2·20	1·60
968	5b. purple	7·75	3·75
969	10b. violet	11·00	7·50

1951. Arms issue. State of Carabobo. As T **132** showing Arms of Carabobo and agricultural produce.

970	5c. green (postage)	55	30
971	10c. red	55	30
972	15c. brown	1·10	30
973	20c. blue	1·10	30
974	25c. brown	1·70	30
975	30c. blue	3·25	65
976	35c. violet	28·00	5·00
977	5c. turquoise (air)	55	30
978	7½c. green	55	55
979	10c. red	55	30
980	15c. brown	1·70	30
981	20c. blue	2·20	30
982	30c. blue	11·00	45
983	45c. purple	1·10	45
984	60c. green	4·50	95
985	90c. red	8·25	3·25

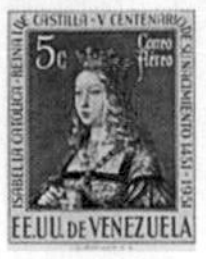

138 Isabella the Catholic

1951. Air. 500th Birth Anniv of Isabella the Catholic.

986	138	5c. green and light green	1·00	30
987	138	10c. red and yellow	1·00	30
988	138	20c. blue and grey	1·70	45
989	138	30c. blue and grey	1·70	30
MS990		80×100 mm. Nos. 986/9	19·00	19·00

1951. Arms issue. State of Anzoategui. As T **132** showing Arms of Anzoategui and globe.

991	5c. green (postage)	55	30
992	10c. red	55	30
993	15c. brown	2·20	55
994	20c. blue	2·20	30
995	40c. orange	13·00	2·00
996	45c. purple	33·00	7·00
997	3b. blue	11·00	2·30
998	5c. turquoise (air)	55	30
999	10c. red	55	30
1000	15c. brown	90	30
1001	25c. black	90	30
1002	30c. blue	7·75	1·50
1003	50c. orange	4·50	75
1004	60c. green	3·25	45
1005	1b. violet	4·50	1·50
1006	2b. violet	13·00	3·25

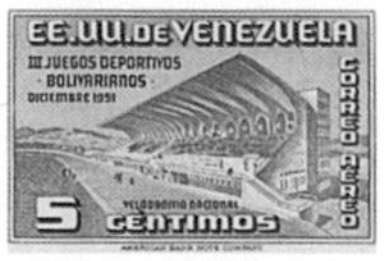

140 National Stadium

1951. Air. Third Bolivarian Games, Caracas.

1007	140	5c. green	1·70	30
1008	140	10c. red	1·70	30
1009	140	20c. brown	1·80	55
1010	140	30c. blue	2·20	75
MS1011		190×150 mm. Nos. 1007/10	33·00	33·00

1951. As Nos. 780/806 but frame size 38×23½ mm or 23½×38 mm. Inscr "COURVOISIER S.A." at foot.

1012	116	5c. green (postage)	1·90	30
1013	116	10c. red	3·25	30
1014	116	15c. slate	11·00	30
1015	117	5c. brown (air)	2·75	30
1016	117	10c. brown	4·00	30
1017	117	15c. olive	5·50	30

1952. Arms issue. State of Aragua. As T **132** showing Arms of Aragua and Stylized Farm.

1018	5c. green (postage)	55	30
1019	10c. red	1·10	30
1020	15c. brown	2·75	30
1021	20c. blue	1·30	30
1022	25c. brown	2·00	45
1023	30c. blue	2·00	75
1024	35c. violet	33·00	7·00
1025	5c. turquoise (air)	3·25	30
1026	7½c. green	55	55
1027	10c. red	55	30
1028	15c. brown	2·00	45
1029	20c. blue	2·00	45
1030	30c. blue	8·75	55
1031	45c. purple	2·20	45
1032	60c. green	5·50	75
1033	90c. red	£110	15·00

1952. Arms issue. State of Bolivar. As T **132** showing Arms of Bolivar and Iron Foundry.

1034	5c. green (postage)	55	30
1035	10c. red	1·80	30
1036	15c. brown	2·75	30
1037	20c. blue	4·50	30
1038	40c. orange	11·00	1·80
1039	45c. purple	39·00	8·50
1040	3b. blue	4·50	3·75
1041	5c. turquoise (air)	11·00	75
1042	10c. red	55	30
1043	15c. brown		
1044	25c. black	55	65
1045	30c. blue	11·00	1·70
1046	50c. red	2·75	75
1047	60c. green	5·50	95
1048	1b. violet	4·50	75
1049	2b. violet	22·00	3·25

1952. Arms issue. State of Lara. As T **132** showing Arms of Lara and Sisal Industry.

1050	5c. green (postage)	55	30
1051	10c. red	55	30
1052	15c. brown	75	30
1053	20c. blue	1·10	30
1054	25c. brown	1·70	85
1055	30c. blue	2·75	75
1056	35c. violet	33·00	7·00
1057	5c. turquoise (air)	1·70	30
1058	7½c. green	55	55
1059	10c. red	55	30
1060	15c. brown	1·10	30
1061	20c. blue	3·75	30
1062	30c. blue	11·00	75
1063	45c. purple	1·30	65
1064	60c. green	5·50	1·20
1065	90c. red	85·00	18·00

1952. Arms issue. State of Miranda. As T **132** showing Arms of Miranda and Agricultural Products.

1066	5c. green (postage)	55	30
1067	10c. red	2·20	30
1068	15c. brown	90	30
1069	20c. blue	2·20	30
1070	25c. brown	2·75	65
1071	30c. blue	4·50	1·10
1072	35c. violet	39·00	2·75
1073	5c. turquoise (air)	2·20	30
1074	7½c. green	55	55
1075	10c. red	55	30
1076	15c. brown	90	30
1077	20c. blue	1·70	45
1078	30c. blue	2·20	30
1079	45c. purple	1·50	75
1080	60c. green	3·75	95
1081	90c. red	50·00	15·00

1952. Arms issue. State of Sucre. As T **132** showing Arms of Sucre, Palms and Seascape.

1082	5c. green (postage)	55	30
1083	10c. red	55	30
1084	15c. brown	90	30
1085	20c. blue	90	30
1086	40c. orange	7·75	2·75
1087	45c. purple	28·00	4·75
1088	3b. blue	2·75	2·10
1089	5c. turquoise (air)	55	30
1090	10c. red	55	30
1091	15c. brown	75	30
1092	25c. black	75	55
1093	30c. blue	8·75	2·10
1094	50c. red	1·40	75
1095	60c. green	4·50	1·30
1096	1b. violet	3·75	1·30
1097	2b. violet	15·00	3·50

1952. Arms issue. State of Trujillo. As T **132** showing Arms of Trujillo and Stylised Coffee Plant.

1098	5c. green (postage)	55	30
1099	10c. red	75	30
1100	15c. brown	2·00	30
1101	20c. blue	2·00	30
1102	50c. orange	33·00	5·25
1103	1b. green	1·50	95
1104	5b. purple	10·00	3·50
1105	5c. turquoise (air)	13·00	65
1106	10c. red	55	30
1107	15c. brown	8·25	30
1108	30c. blue	22·00	1·90
1109	60c. green	17·00	1·80
1110	1b.20 lake	11·00	4·25
1111	3b. green	2·20	1·80
1112	5b. purple	10·00	3·25
1113	10b. violet	11·00	7·00

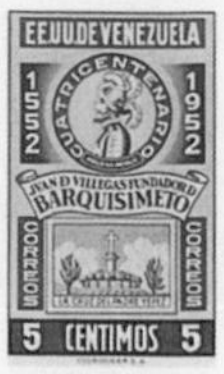

147 Juan de Villegas

1952. Fourth Centenary of Barquisimeto.

1114	147	5c. green (postage)	55	10
1115	147	10c. red	1·10	10
1116	147	20c. slate	1·70	55
1117	147	40c. orange	8·25	3·75
1118	147	50c. brown	4·00	2·10
1119	147	1b. violet	8·25	2·75
1120	147	5c. turquoise (air)	55	15
1121	147	10c. red	20	15
1122	147	20c. blue	75	20
1123	147	25c. black	1·10	30
1124	147	30c. blue	1·30	20
1125	147	40c. orange	9·25	4·50
1126	147	50c. bronze	2·75	1·10
1127	147	1b. purple	11·00	5·25

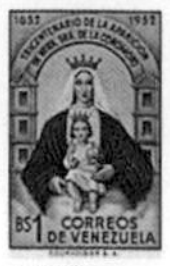

148 Our Lady of Coromoto

1952. 300th Anniv of Apparition of Our Lady of Coromoto.

1128	148	1b. red (17×26½ mm)	14·50	2·30
1129	148	1b. red (26½×41 mm)	11·00	2·30
1130	148	1b. red (36×65 mm)	5·00	1·80

1952. National Objective Exn. Telegraph stamps as T **131** surch **Correos Exposicion Objetiva Nacional 1948 - 1952** and new value.

1131	5c. on 25c. red	55	20
1132	10c. on 1b. black	55	20

1952. Telegraph stamps as T **131** surch **CORREOS HABILITADO 1952** and new value.

1133	20c. on 25c. red	75	20
1134	30c. on 2b. olive	4·75	2·75
1135	40c. on 1b. black	1·70	85
1136	50c. on 3b. orange	6·00	3·25

1953. Arms issue. State of Merida. As T **132** showing Arms of Merida and Church.

1137	5c. green (postage)	55	30
1138	10c. red	55	30
1139	15c. brown	55	30
1140	20c. blue	5·50	30
1141	50c. orange	22·00	2·30
1142	1b. green	2·20	95
1143	5b. purple	11·00	2·75
1144	5c. turquoise (air)	2·20	30
1145	10c. red	55	30
1146	15c. brown	1·70	30
1147	30c. blue	26·00	1·50
1148	60c. green	7·75	75
1149	1b.20 lake	7·75	3·75
1150	3b. green	2·20	1·50
1151	5b. purple	15·00	3·75
1152	10b. violet	17·00	5·75

1953. Arms issue. State of Monagas. As T **132** showing Arms of Monagas and Horses.

1153	5c. green (postage)	75	30
1154	10c. red	55	30
1155	15c. brown	1·30	30
1156	20c. blue	1·30	55
1157	40c. orange	11·00	1·60
1158	45c. purple	42·00	7·00
1159	3b. blue	3·75	4·50
1160	5c. turquoise (air)	1·30	30
1161	10c. red	55	30
1162	15c. brown	1·00	30
1163	25c. black	1·00	30
1164	30c. blue	22·00	1·70
1165	50c. red	3·25	75
1166	60c. green	3·25	75
1167	1b. violet	6·00	95
1168	2b. violet	6·50	2·75

1953. Arms issue. State of Portuguesa. As T **132** showing Arms of Portuguesa and Woodland.

1169	5c. green (postage)	55	30
1170	10c. red	55	30
1171	15c. brown	2·00	30
1172	20c. blue	2·00	30
1173	50c. orange	8·75	3·25
1174	1b. green	1·70	55
1175	5b. purple	7·75	3·75

1176	5c. turquoise (air)	6·50	65
1177	10c. red	55	30
1178	15c. brown	3·25	30
1179	30c. blue	22·00	5·25
1180	60c. green	8·75	1·10
1181	1b.20 lake	39·00	8·00
1182	3b. green	2·20	2·10
1183	5b. purple	8·75	3·75
1184	10b. violet	11·00	8·50

1953. Arms issue. Federal Territory of Delta Amacuro. As T **132** showing Arms of Delta Amacuro and map.

1185	5c. green (postage)	55	30
1186	10c. red	55	30
1187	15c. brown	75	30
1188	20c. blue	1·50	30
1189	40c. orange	7·75	1·90
1190	45c. purple	39·00	8·50
1191	3b. blue	2·20	2·75
1192	5c. turquoise (air)	55	30
1193	10c. red	55	30
1194	15c. brown	55	30
1195	25c. black	1·10	1·50
1196	30c. blue	11·00	75
1197	50c. red	2·20	3·75
1198	60c. green	5·00	1·50
1199	1b. violet	7·75	3·75
1200	2b. violet	22·00	5·75

1953. Arms issue. State of Falcon. As T **132** showing Arms of Falcon and Stylised Oil Refinery.

1201	5c. green (postage)	55	30
1202	10c. red	55	30
1203	15c. brown	1·10	30
1204	20c. blue	2·75	30
1205	50c. orange	22·00	1·80
1206	1b. green	2·00	1·40
1207	5b. purple	7·25	3·50
1208	5c. turquoise (air)	2·75	30
1209	10c. red	55	30
1210	15c. brown	55	30
1211	30c. blue	17·00	1·60
1212	60c. green	6·50	1·30
1213	1b.20 lake	6·00	5·25
1214	3b. green	2·00	3·50
1215	5b. purple	7·75	7·00
1216	10b. violet	13·00	9·50

1953. Arms issue. State of Guarico. As T **132** showing Arms of Guarico and Factory.

1217	5c. green (postage)	55	30
1218	10c. red	55	30
1219	15c. brown	90	30
1220	20c. blue	90	30
1221	40c. orange	7·75	2·75
1222	45c. purple	28·00	4·75
1223	3b. blue	2·75	2·10
1224	5c. turquoise (air)	55	30
1225	10c. red	55	30
1226	15c. brown	75	30
1227	25c. black	75	55
1228	30c. blue	8·75	2·10
1229	50c. red	1·40	75
1230	60c. green	4·50	1·30
1231	1b. violet	3·75	1·30
1232	2b. violet	15·00	3·50

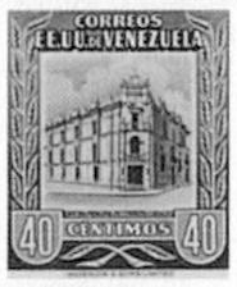

157 G.P.O., Caracas

1953. Inscr "EE. UU. DE VENEZUELA".

1233	**157**	5c. green (postage)	35	30
1234	**157**	7½c. green	65	45
1235	**157**	10c. red	55	30
1236	**157**	15c. black	65	30
1237	**157**	20c. blue	45	30
1238	**157**	25c. mauve	65	30
1239	**157**	30c. blue	3·50	45
1240	**157**	35c. mauve	1·50	45
1241	**157**	40c. orange	2·20	65
1242	**157**	45c. violet	3·50	1·30
1243	**157**	50c. orange	2·20	65
1244	**157**	5c. orange (air)	35	30
1245	**157**	7½c. green	35	30
1246	**157**	15c. purple	35	30
1247	**157**	20c. slate	35	30
1248	**157**	25c. sepia	65	30
1249	**157**	30c. brown	3·50	1·80
1250	**157**	40c. red	65	30
1251	**157**	45c. purple	65	30
1252	**157**	50c. red	1·00	30
1253	**157**	60c. red	3·50	55
1254	**157**	70c. myrtle	2·00	95
1255	**157**	75c. blue	7·25	1·80
1256	**157**	90c. brown	1·70	75
1257	**157**	1b. violet	1·70	75

See also Nos. 1365/82.

1953. Arms issue. State of Cojedes. As T **132** showing Arms of Cojedes and Cattle.

1258	5c. green (postage)	55	30
1259	10c. red	55	30
1260	15c. brown	55	30
1261	20c. blue	2·20	30
1262	25c. brown	2·20	45
1263	30c. blue	7·75	65
1264	35c. violet	4·50	1·90
1265	5c. turquoise (air)	5·50	75
1266	7½c. green	1·00	75
1267	10c. red	55	30
1268	15c. brown	55	30
1269	20c. blue	2·75	30
1270	30c. blue	8·75	1·10
1271	45c. purple	1·70	65
1272	60c. green	3·25	95
1273	90c. red	7·75	3·75

1954. Arms issue. Federal Territory of Amazonas. As T **132** showing Arms of Amazonas and Orchid.

1274	5c. green (postage)	1·10	30
1275	10c. red	2·20	30
1276	15c. brown	5·50	30
1277	20c. blue	40·00	75
1278	40c. orange	15·00	2·10
1279	45c. purple	11·00	5·75
1280	3b. blue	33·00	6·50
1281	5c. turquoise (air)	5·50	30
1282	10c. red	55	30
1283	15c. brown	7·25	30
1284	25c. black	11·00	30
1285	30c. blue	25·00	75
1286	50c. red	28·00	1·60
1287	60c. green	28·00	1·60
1288	1b. violet	£375	5·25
1289	2b. violet	75·00	5·25

1954. Arms issue. State of Apure. As T **132** showing Arms of Apure, Horse and Bird.

1290	5c. green (postage)	55	30
1291	10c. red	55	30
1292	15c. brown	1·10	30
1293	20c. blue	39·00	30
1294	50c. orange	6·00	3·25
1295	1b. green	1·00	1·30
1296	5b. purple	10·00	5·25
1297	5c. turquoise (air)	6·50	30
1298	10c. red	55	30
1299	15c. brown	75	30
1300	30c. blue	11·00	1·40
1301	60c. green	3·00	65
1302	1b.20 lake	5·50	3·50
1303	3b. green	1·90	1·50
1304	5b. purple	15·00	2·75
1305	10b. violet	11·00	7·00

1954. Arms issue. State of Barinas. As T **132** showing Arms of Barinas, Cow and Horse.

1306	5c. green (postage)	55	30
1307	10c. red	55	30
1308	15c. brown	55	30
1309	20c. blue	4·50	55
1310	50c. orange	7·25	2·10
1311	1b. green	75	55
1312	5b. purple	1·30	3·75
1313	5c. turquoise (air)	2·00	30
1314	10c. red	55	30
1315	15c. brown	1·40	30
1316	30c. blue	8·75	2·10
1317	60c. green	5·50	1·10
1318	1b.20 lake	3·75	3·75
1319	3b. green	2·75	2·10
1320	5b. purple	8·75	2·10
1321	10b. violet	13·00	7·00

1954. Arms issue. State of Nueva Esparta. As T **132** showing Arms of Nueva Esparta and Fish.

1322	5c. green (postage)	1·10	30
1323	10c. red	55	30
1324	15c. brown	65	30
1325	20c. blue	3·75	30
1326	40c. orange	6·50	1·60
1327	45c. purple	22·00	6·50
1328	3b. blue	28·00	3·75
1329	5c. turquoise (air)	2·20	30
1330	10c. red	55	30
1331	15c. brown	1·30	30
1332	25c. black	1·30	45
1333	30c. blue	7·25	1·10
1334	50c. red	3·25	1·10
1335	60c. green	3·25	55
1336	1b. violet	5·50	1·30
1337	2b. violet	15·00	4·75

1954. Arms issue. State of Yaracuy. As T **132** showing Arms of Yaracuy and Tropical Foliage.

1338	5c. green (postage)	55	30
1339	10c. red	55	30
1340	15c. brown	90	30
1341	20c. blue	1·10	45
1342	25c. brown	1·30	65
1343	30c. blue	2·20	55
1344	35c. violet	3·75	2·30
1345	5c. turquoise (air)	1·10	30
1346	7½c. green	28·00	10·50
1347	10c. red	55	30
1348	15c. brown	55	30
1349	20c. blue	2·20	30
1350	30c. blue	3·75	1·10
1351	45c. purple	1·70	65
1352	60c. green	2·75	1·10
1353	90c. red	5·50	5·25

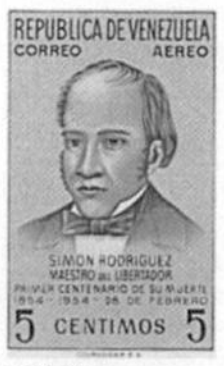

164 Simon Rodriguez

1954. Air. Death Cent of Rodriguez (Bolivar's tutor).

1354	**164**	5c. turquoise	45	30
1355	**164**	10c. red	65	30
1356	**164**	20c. blue	90	30
1357	**164**	45c. purple	1·30	55
1358	**164**	65c. green	4·50	1·80

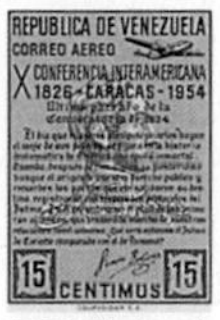

165 Bolivar and 1824 Edict

1954. Air. Tenth Pan-American Conf, Caracas.

1359	**165**	15c. black and brown	35	30
1360	**165**	25c. brown and grey	1·30	30
1361	**165**	40c. brown and orange	90	30
1362	**165**	65c. black and blue	2·20	1·40
1363	**165**	80c. brown and red	1·70	85
1364	**165**	1b. violet and mauve	3·50	65

1954. As T **157** but inscr "REPUBLICA DE VENEZUELA".

1365	5c. green (postage)	35	30
1366	10c. red	35	30
1367	15c. black	35	30
1368	20c. blue	55	30
1369	30c. blue	1·70	75
1370	35c. mauve	1·70	45
1371	40c. orange	2·40	55
1372	45c. violet	2·40	1·10
1373	5c. yellow (air)	45	45
1374	10c. bistre	45	45
1375	15c. purple	45	45
1376	20c. slate	55	45
1377	30c. brown	55	45
1378	40c. red	1·50	55
1379	45c. purple	1·50	65
1380	70c. green	3·75	1·80
1381	75c. blue	2·40	1·10
1382	90c. brown	1·70	55

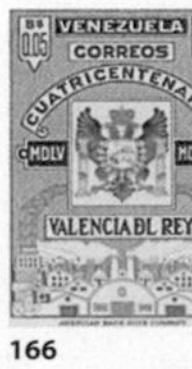

166

1955. 400th Anniv of Valencia Del Rey.

1383	**166**	5c. green (postage)	35	30
1384	**166**	20c. blue	45	30
1385	**166**	25c. brown	1·20	30
1386	**166**	50c. orange	1·90	55
1387	**166**	5c. turquoise (air)	35	30
1388	**166**	10c. red	35	30
1389	**166**	20c. blue	35	30
1390	**166**	25c. black	35	30
1391	**166**	40c. violet	90	55
1392	**166**	50c. red	90	55
1393	**166**	60c. olive	1·80	55

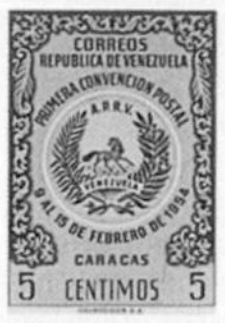

167

1955. First Postal Convention, Caracas.

1394	**167**	5c. green (postage)	75	15
1395	**167**	20c. blue	1·30	15
1396	**167**	25c. lake	2·20	15
1397	**167**	50c. orange	2·40	15
1398	**167**	5c. yellow (air)	20	10
1399	**167**	15c. brown	55	15
1400	**167**	25c. black	55	15
1401	**167**	40c. red	75	20
1402	**167**	50c. orange	1·10	30
1403	**167**	60c. red	2·75	75

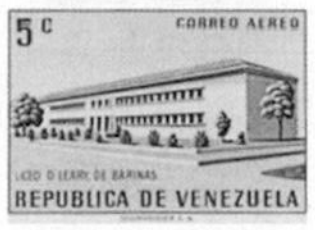

168 O'Leary College, Barinas

1956. Air. Public Works.

1404	**168**	5c. yellow	45	30
1405	**168**	10c. sepia	45	30
1406	**168**	15c. brown	45	30
1407	**A**	20c. blue	45	30
1408	**A**	25c. black	45	30
1409	**A**	30c. brown	55	30
1410	**B**	40c. red	75	35
1411	**B**	45c. brown	55	35
1412	**B**	50c. orange	1·00	35
1413	**C**	60c. olive	65	35
1414	**C**	65c. blue	1·90	45
1415	**168**	70c. green	1·90	45
1416	**C**	75c. blue	1·90	65
1417	**A**	80c. red	2·10	30
1418	**B**	1b. purple	1·30	45
1419	**C**	2b. red	2·50	1·30

DESIGNS—HORIZ: A, University Hospital, Caracas; B, Caracas–La Guaira Highway; C, Simon Bolivar Centre.

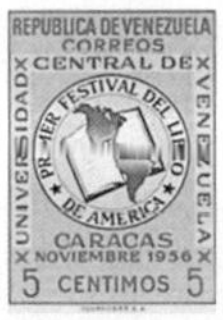

169

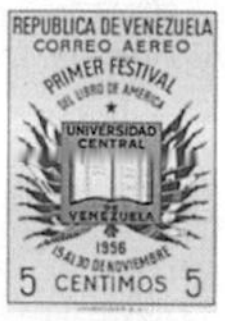

170

1956. First American Book Festival, Caracas.

1420	**169**	5c. turq & grn (postage)	20	10
1421	**169**	10c. purple and red	20	10
1422	**169**	20c. blue and ultramarine	35	20
1423	**169**	25c. grey and green	55	20
1424	**169**	30c. blue and light blue	55	20
1425	**169**	40c. sepia and brown	75	30
1426	**169**	50c. brown and red	1·30	55
1427	**169**	1b. slate and violet	2·20	1·10
1428	**170**	5c. brown and orange (air)	10	10
1429	**170**	10c. sepia and brown	20	10
1430	**170**	20c. blue and turquoise	20	10
1431	**170**	25c. slate and violet	55	20
1432	**170**	40c. purple and red	75	20
1433	**170**	45c. brown and chocolate	1·10	20
1434	**170**	60c. grey and olive	2·75	1·10

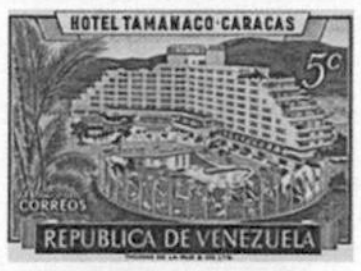

171 Tamanaco Hotel, Caracas

1957. Tamanaco Hotel, Caracas Commem.

1435	**171**	5c. green (postage)	45	30
1436	**171**	10c. red	45	30
1437	**171**	15c. black	65	30
1438	**171**	20c. blue	65	30
1439	**171**	25c. purple	65	30
1440	**171**	30c. blue	1·20	30
1441	**171**	35c. lilac	65	30
1442	**171**	40c. orange	90	30
1443	**171**	45c. purple	1·20	30
1444	**171**	50c. yellow	1·70	55
1445	**171**	1b. myrtle	2·20	65
1446	**171**	5c. yellow (air)	45	30
1447	**171**	10c. brown	45	30

1448	**171**	15c. brown	45	30
1449	**171**	20c. slate	55	30
1450	**171**	25c. brown	45	30
1451	**171**	30c. blue	45	30
1452	**171**	40c. red	55	30
1453	**171**	45c. brown	65	30
1454	**171**	50c. orange	65	30
1455	**171**	60c. green	1·30	30
1456	**171**	65c. orange	3·50	1·30
1457	**171**	70c. black	1·90	65
1458	**171**	75c. turquoise	2·10	75
1459	**171**	1b. purple	2·10	75
1460	**171**	2b. black	3·50	95

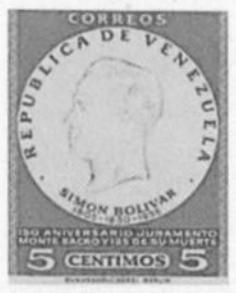

172 Simon Bolivar

1957. 150th Anniv of Oath of Monte Sacro and 125th Anniv of Death of Bolivar.

1461	**172**	5c. green (postage)	35	30
1462	**172**	10c. red	35	30
1463	**172**	20c. blue	75	30
1464	**172**	25c. red	75	30
1465	**172**	30c. blue	1·10	30
1466	**172**	40c. orange	1·70	30
1467	**172**	50c. yellow	2·00	1·10
1468	**172**	5c. orange (air)	35	30
1469	**172**	10c. brown	35	30
1470	**172**	20c. blue	1·10	30
1471	**172**	25c. purple	1·20	30
1472	**172**	40c. red	1·10	30
1473	**172**	45c. purple	1·30	55
1474	**172**	65c. brown	2·20	75

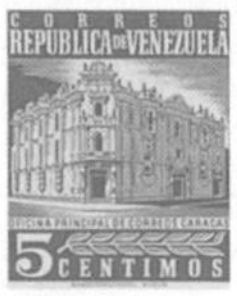

173 G.P.O., Caracas

1958

1475	**173**	5c. green (postage)	10	10
1476	**173**	10c. red	10	10
1477	**173**	15c. grey	10	10
1478	**173**	20c. blue	20	10
1479	**173**	25c. yellow	20	10
1480	**173**	30c. grey	35	10
1481	**173**	35c. purple	35	10
1482	**173**	40c. red	75	20
1483	**173**	45c. violet	3·25	1·80
1484	**173**	50c. yellow	75	20
1485	**173**	1b. olive	1·90	75
1486	**173**	5c. yellow (air)	10	10
1487	**173**	10c. brown	10	10
1488	**173**	15c. brown	10	10
1489	**173**	20c. blue	10	10
1490	**173**	25c. grey	20	10
1491	**173**	30c. blue	20	10
1492	**173**	35c. olive	35	15
1493	**173**	40c. green	35	15
1494	**173**	50c. red	35	20
1495	**173**	55c. olive	55	30
1496	**173**	60c. mauve	55	30
1497	**173**	65c. red	65	30
1498	**173**	70c. green	90	30
1499	**173**	75c. brown	1·30	30
1500	**173**	80c. brown	1·30	55
1501	**173**	85c. red	1·90	75
1502	**173**	90c. violet	1·30	55
1503	**173**	95c. purple	1·70	75
1504	**173**	1b. mauve	1·70	55
1505	**173**	1b.20 brown	19·00	10·50

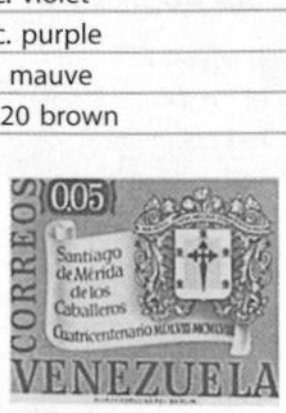

174 Arms of Santiago de Merida

1958. 400th Anniv of Santiago de Merida de los Caballeros.

1506	**174**	5c. green (postage)	10	10
1507	**174**	10c. red	10	10
1508	**174**	15c. grey	10	10
1509	**174**	20c. blue	35	10
1510	**174**	25c. purple	1·10	10
1511	**174**	30c. violet	55	20
1512	**174**	35c. violet	65	20
1513	**174**	40c. orange	1·70	55
1514	**174**	45c. purple	75	20
1515	**174**	50c. yellow	1·30	55
1516	**174**	1b. grey	4·00	1·30
1517	**174**	5c. ochre (air)	10	10
1518	**174**	10c. brown	10	10
1519	**174**	15c. brown	20	10
1520	**174**	20c. blue	20	10
1521	**174**	25c. olive	65	20
1522	**174**	30c. blue	55	10
1523	**174**	40c. red	75	20
1524	**174**	45c. purple	75	30
1525	**174**	50c. orange	1·10	55
1526	**174**	60c. olive	75	30
1527	**174**	65c. brown	2·75	1·10
1528	**174**	70c. black	1·70	75
1529	**174**	75c. blue	3·25	1·60
1530	**174**	80c. violet	1·90	75
1531	**174**	90c. green	1·90	85
1532	**174**	1b. lilac	2·20	1·10

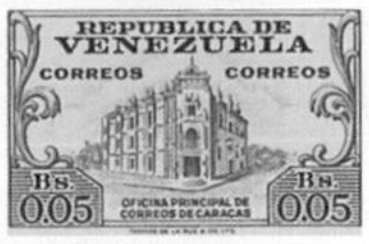

175 G.P.O., Caracas

1958

1533	**175**	5c. green (postage)	55	10
1534	**175**	10c. red	75	10
1535	**175**	15c. black	1·10	10
1536	**175**	5c. yellow (air)	55	10
1537	**175**	10c. brown	75	10
1538	**175**	15c. brown	1·10	10

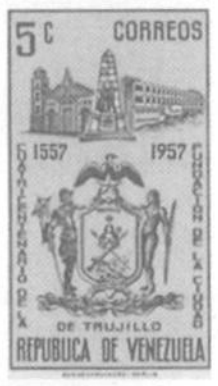

176 Arms of Trujillo and Bolivar Monument

1958. 400th Anniv of Trujillo.

1539	**176**	5c. green (postage)	10	10
1540	**176**	10c. red	10	10
1541	**176**	15c. grey	10	10
1542	**176**	20c. blue	20	10
1543	**176**	25c. mauve	55	20
1544	**176**	30c. blue	75	30
1545	**176**	35c. lilac	90	30
1546	**176**	45c. purple	1·20	55
1547	**176**	50c. yellow	1·20	30
1548	**176**	1b. olive	3·25	1·30
1549	**176**	5c. buff (air)	10	10
1550	**176**	10c. brown	10	10
1551	**176**	15c. brown	35	20
1552	**176**	20c. blue	55	20
1553	**176**	25c. grey	65	25
1554	**176**	30c. blue	65	25
1555	**176**	40c. green	1·10	30
1556	**176**	50c. orange	1·10	55
1557	**176**	60c. mauve	1·70	65
1558	**176**	65c. red	5·00	1·80
1559	**176**	1b. violet	3·25	75

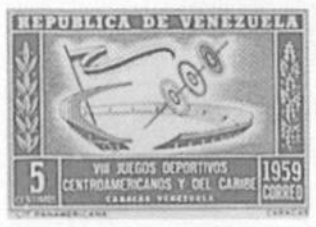

177 Caracas Stadium

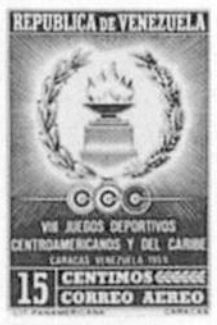

178 "Eternal Flame"

1959. Eighth Central American and Caribbean Games.

1560	**177**	5c. green (postage)	55	10
1561	**177**	10c. mauve	55	10
1562	**177**	20c. blue	1·30	55
1563	**177**	30c. blue	1·30	65
1564	**177**	50c. lilac	2·40	55
1565	**178**	5c. yellow (air)	20	10
1566	**178**	10c. brown	55	20
1567	**178**	15c. orange	75	30
1568	**178**	30c. slate	1·70	65
1569	**178**	50c. green	2·20	75

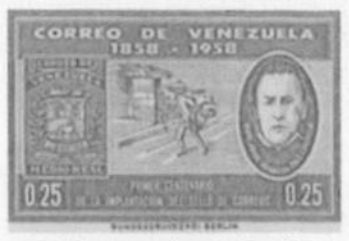

179 Venezuelan ½ Real Stamp of 1859, Gen. J. I. Paz Castillo and Postman

1959. Cent of First Venezuelan Postage Stamps.

1570	**179**	25c. ochre (postage)	1·90	25
1571	-	50c. blue	2·75	55
1572	-	1b. red	3·75	1·10
1573	**179**	25c. ochre (air)	1·90	25
1574	-	50c. blue	2·75	55
1575	-	1b. red	3·75	1·10

DESIGNS: 50c. (2), 1 real stamp of 1859, Don Jacinto Gutierrez and postman on mule; 1b. (2), 2 reales stamp of 1859, Don Miguel Herrera, steam mail train and Douglas DC-6 airliner.

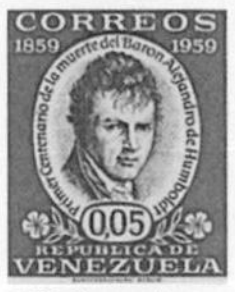

180 Alexander von Humboldt

1960. Death Centenary of Von Humboldt (naturalist).

1576	**180**	5c. olive & grn (postage)	65	30
1577	**180**	30c. violet and blue	1·90	30
1578	**180**	40c. brown and orange	2·20	75
1579	**180**	5c. brown and bistre (air)	65	30
1580	**180**	20c. turquoise and blue	1·90	30
1581	**180**	40c. bronze and olive	2·75	75

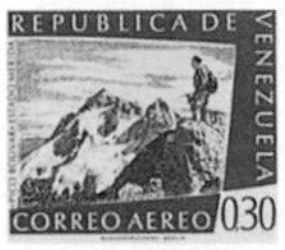

181 Bolivar Peak, Merida

1960. Tourist issue.

1582	**181**	5c. green and emerald (postage)	1·50	1·50
1583	-	15c. grey and purple	5·00	4·75
1584	-	35c. purple and light purple	4·50	4·25
1585	**181**	30c. blue and deep blue (air)	3·75	3·75
1586	-	50c. brown and orange	3·75	3·75
1587	-	65c. brown and orange	3·75	3·75

DESIGNS: 15, 50c. Caroni Falls, Bolivar; 35, 65c. Cuachara Caves, Monagas.

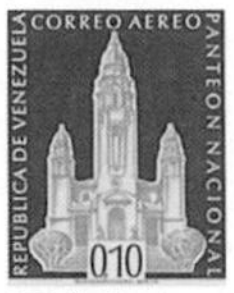

182 National Pantheon, Caracas

1960. Pantheon in olive.

1588	**182**	5c. green (postage)	10	10
1589	**182**	20c. blue	75	20
1590	**182**	25c. olive	1·20	30
1591	**182**	30c. grey	1·30	30
1592	**182**	40c. brown	2·40	75
1593	**182**	45c. violet	1·70	75
1594	**182**	5c. bistre (air)	10	10
1595	**182**	10c. brown	35	10
1596	**182**	15c. brown	55	10
1597	**182**	20c. blue	75	20
1598	**182**	25c. grey	4·50	55
1599	**182**	30c. violet	4·50	85
1600	**182**	40c. green	75	20
1601	**182**	45c. violet	1·20	30
1602	**182**	60c. mauve	1·70	65
1603	**182**	65c. red	1·70	65
1604	**182**	70c. grey	2·40	85
1605	**182**	75c. blue	6·50	1·60
1606	**182**	80c. blue	3·25	1·30
1607	**182**	1b.20 yellow	4·00	1·80

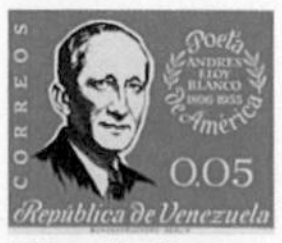

183 A. Eloy Blanco

1960. Fifth Death Anniv of Blanco (poet). Portrait in black.

1608	**183**	5c. green (postage)	35	30
1609	**183**	30c. grey	55	30
1610	**183**	50c. yellow	1·20	45
1611	**183**	20c. blue (air)	75	30
1612	**183**	75c. turquoise	2·40	55
1613	**183**	90c. violet	2·20	55

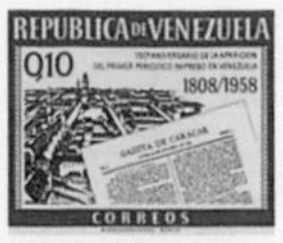

184 1808 Newspaper and Caracas, 1958

1960. 150th Anniv of "Gazeta de Caracas". Centres in black.

1614	**184**	10c. red (postage)	75	20
1615	**184**	20c. blue	1·30	30
1616	**184**	35c. violet	1·90	1·40
1617	**184**	5c. yellow (air)	3·25	1·60
1618	**184**	15c. brown	2·20	75
1619	**184**	65c. orange	2·75	1·10

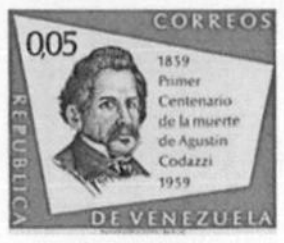

185 A. Codazzi

1960. Death Centenary of Codazzi (geographer).

1620	**185**	5c. deep green and light green (postage)	10	10
1621	**185**	15c. black and grey	90	20
1622	**185**	20c. blue and light blue	95	20
1623	**185**	45c. purple and lilac	1·10	55
1624	**185**	5c. brown and orange (air)	20	10
1625	**185**	10c. sepia and brown	55	10
1626	**185**	25c. black and grey	75	15
1627	**185**	30c. deep blue and blue	1·70	20
1628	**185**	50c. brown and light brown	2·75	65
1629	**185**	70c. black and brown	4·50	1·10

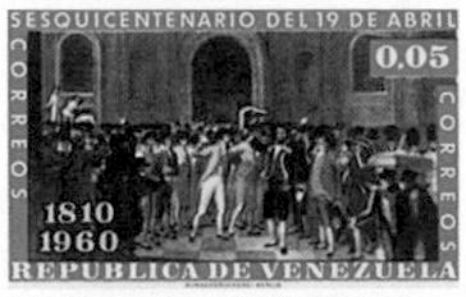

186 Declaration of Independence

1960. 150th Anniv of Independence. Centres multicoloured.

1630	**186**	5c. green (postage)	90	20
1631	**186**	20c. blue	1·70	30
1632	**186**	30c. blue	2·40	55
1633	**186**	50c. orange (air)	1·10	55
1634	**186**	75c. turquoise	2·75	85
1635	**186**	90c. violet	2·20	1·10

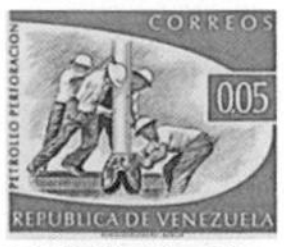

187 Drilling for Oil

1960. Oil Industry.

1636	**187**	5c. myrtle and turquoise (postage)	2·75	1·10
1637	**187**	10c. brown and red	1·10	30
1638	**187**	15c. mauve and purple	1·40	55
1639	-	30c. indigo and blue (air)	2·00	55
1640	-	40c. olive and green	2·20	65
1641	-	50c. brown and orange	2·50	85

DESIGN: Nos. 1639/41, Oil refinery.

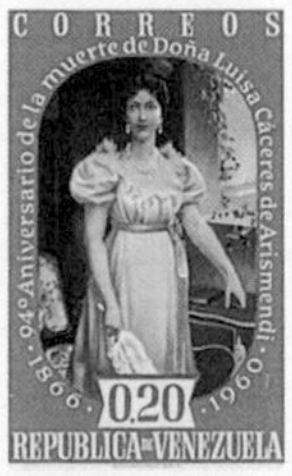

188 L. Caceres de Arismendi

1960. 94th Death Anniv of Luisa Caceres de Arismendi. Centres multicoloured.

1642	**188**	20c. blue (postage)	2·10	55
1643	**188**	25c. yellow	1·70	55
1644	**188**	30c. blue	2·20	75
1645	**188**	5c. bistre (air)	1·50	55
1646	**188**	10c. brown	2·10	85
1647	**188**	60c. red	3·75	1·10

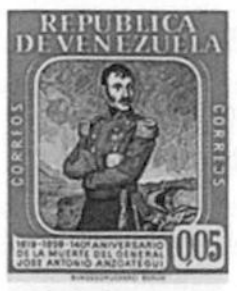

189 Gen. J. A. Anzoategui

1960. 140th Death Anniv of Gen. Anzoategui.

1648	**189**	5c. olive & grn (postage)	55	20
1649	**189**	15c. purple and brown	75	25
1650	**189**	20c. deep blue and blue	1·10	30
1651	**189**	25c. brown and grey (air)	90	30
1652	**189**	40c. olive and yellow	1·70	45
1653	**189**	45c. purple and mauve	1·80	65

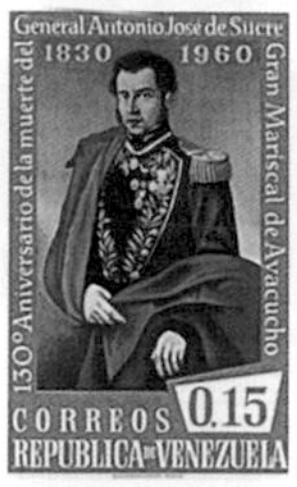

190 Gen. A. J. de Sucre

1960. 130th Death Anniv of Gen. A. J. de Sucre.

1654	**190**	10c. mult (postage)	65	20
1655	**190**	15c. multicoloured	75	30
1656	**190**	20c. multicoloured	1·30	55
1657	**190**	25c. multicoloured (air)	1·30	55
1658	**190**	30c. multicoloured	1·90	75
1659	**190**	50c. multicoloured	2·40	1·10

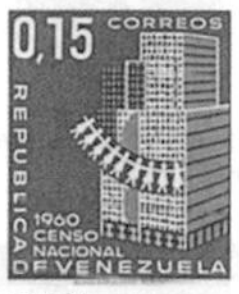

191 Skyscraper

1961. National Census. Skyscraper in orange.

1660	**191**	5c. green	10	10
1661	**191**	10c. red	15	10
1662	**191**	15c. grey	20	10
1663	**191**	20c. blue	30	10
1664	**191**	25c. brown	45	15
1665	**191**	30c. blue	50	15
1666	**191**	35c. purple	55	20
1667	**191**	40c. brown	75	30
1668	**191**	45c. violet	1·10	55
1669	**191**	50c. yellow	75	30

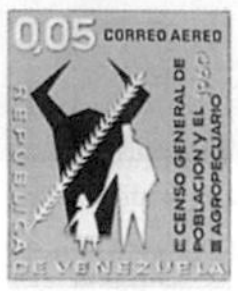

192 "Population and Farming"

1961. Air. Ninth Population Census and 3rd Farming Census. Animal's head and inscr in black.

1670	**192**	5c. yellow	10	10
1671	**192**	10c. brown	15	10
1672	**192**	15c. orange	20	10
1673	**192**	20c. blue	30	15
1674	**192**	25c. grey	35	15
1675	**192**	30c. blue	40	20
1676	**192**	40c. green	55	25
1677	**192**	45c. violet	55	30
1678	**192**	50c. orange	65	45
1679	**192**	60c. mauve	90	50
1680	**192**	65c. red	1·10	55
1681	**192**	70c. grey	1·70	75
1682	**192**	75c. turquoise	1·40	65
1683	**192**	80c. violet	1·50	55
1684	**192**	90c. violet	2·20	1·10

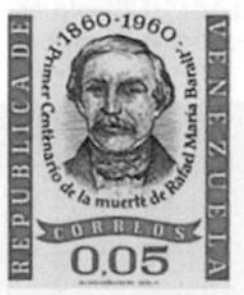

193 R. M. Baralt

1961. Death Centenary of R. M. Baralt (writer).

1685	**193**	5c. turq & grn (postage)	20	10
1686	**193**	15c. brown and grey	65	20
1687	**193**	35c. violet and mauve	1·10	30
1688	**193**	25c. sepia and grey (air)	1·20	55
1689	**193**	30c. violet and blue	1·30	65
1690	**193**	40c. bronze and green	1·80	75

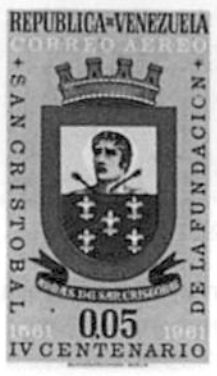

195 Arms of San Cristobal

1961. Air. Fourth Centenary of San Cristobal. Arms in red, yellow and blue.

1692	**195**	5c. sepia and orange	20	10
1693	**195**	55c. black and green	1·20	45

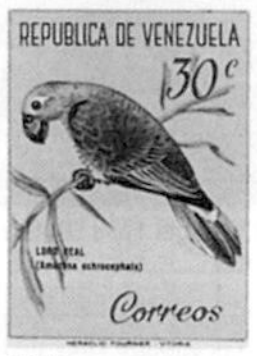

196 Yellow-crowned Amazon

1961. Birds. Multicoloured.

1694	30c. Type **196** (postage)	1·30	65
1695	40c. Snowy egret	2·00	75
1696	50c. Scarlet ibis	3·25	1·20
1697	5c. Troupial (air)	3·25	1·70
1698	10c. Guianan cock of the rock	1·30	85
1699	15c. Tropical mockingbird	2·00	1·10

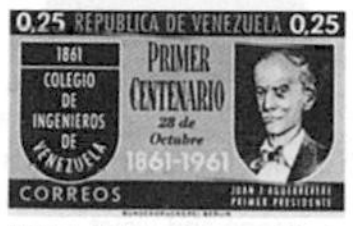

197 J. J. Aguerrevere (first College President)

1961. Engineering College Centenary.

1700	**197**	25c. blue	55	20
MS1701 100×65 mm No. 1700. Imperf. (sold at 1b.)			6·50	6·50

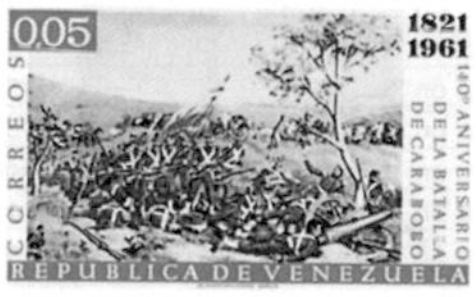

198 Battle Scene

1961. 140th Anniv of Battle of Carabobo. Centres multicoloured.

1702	**198**	5c. green (postage)	20	10
1703	**198**	40c. brown	90	30
1704	-	50c. blue (air)	90	20
1705	-	1b.05 orange	2·00	85
1706	-	1b.50 mauve	2·20	95
1707	-	1b.90 violet	2·75	1·80
1708	-	2b. sepia	3·25	1·90
1709	-	3b. blue	5·50	2·10

DESIGN: 50c. to 3b. Cavalry charge.

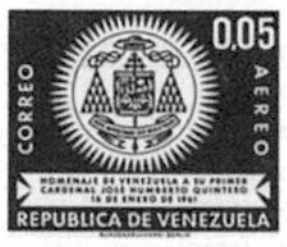

199 Cardinal's Arms

1962. Air. Elevation to Cardinal of Jose Humberto Quintero.

1710	**199**	5c. mauve	20	10
MS1711 100×75 mm No. 1710. Imperf. (sold at 1b.)			2·75	2·75

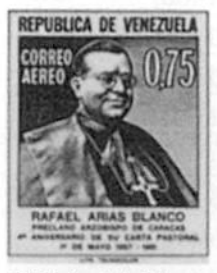

200 Archbishop Blanco

1962. Air. Fourth Anniv of Archbishop Blanco's Pastoral Letter.

1712	**200**	75c. mauve	1·10	45

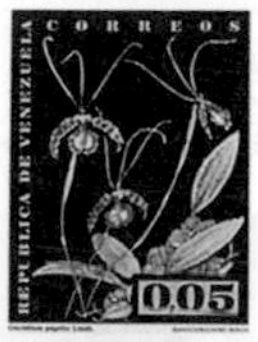

201 "Oncidium papilio Lindl"

1962. Orchids. Multicoloured.

1713	5c. Type **201** (postage)	10	10
1714	10c. "Caularthron bilamellatum (Rchb. f.) R.E. Schultes"	20	10
1715	20c. "Stanhopea Wardii Lodd. ex Lindl"	65	15
1716	25c. "Catasetum pileatum Rchb f."	90	15
1717	30c. "Masdevallia tovarensis Rchb f."	1·10	20
1718	35c. "Epidendrum Stamfordianum Batem" (horiz)	1·20	30
1719	50c. "Epidendrum atropurpureum Willd"	1·30	55
1720	3b. "Oncidium falcipetalum Lindl."	8·25	4·50
1721	5c. "Oncidium volvox Rchb f." (air)	10	10
1722	20c. "Cycnoches chlorochilon Kl."	35	15
1723	25c. "Cattleya Gaskelliana Rchb f.var. alba"	90	20
1724	30c. "Epidendrum difforme Jacq." (horiz)	75	20
1725	40c. "Catasetum callosum Lindl" (horiz)	90	25
1726	50c. "Oncidium bicolor Lindl"	1·30	55
1727	1b. "Brassavola nodosa Lindl" (horiz)	1·80	85
1728	1b.05 "Epidendrum lividum Lindl"	5·50	2·75
1729	1b.50 "Schomburgkia undulata Lindl"	6·00	3·25
1730	2b. "Oncidium zebrinum Rchb f."	7·25	3·75

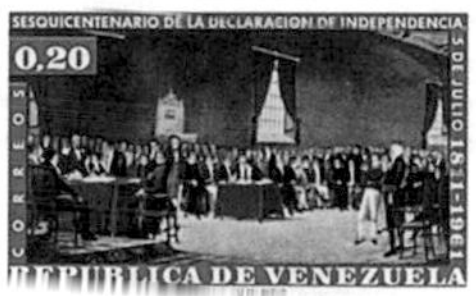

202 Signing of Independence

1962. 150th Anniv of Declaration of Independence. Multicoloured centres; frame colours given.

1731	**202**	5c. green (postage)	35	15
1732	**202**	20c. blue	75	20
1733	**202**	25c. orange	1·10	55
MS1734 140×140 mm. Nos. 1731/3. Imperf			5·50	5·50
1735		55c. green (air)	90	30
1736		1b.05 mauve	2·75	1·20
1737		1b.50 violet	2·40	1·10
MS1738 140×140 mm. Nos. 1735/7. Imperf. (sold at 4b.10)			8·75	8·75

1962. Air. Bicentenary of Upata. Surch **BICENTENARIO DE UPATA 1762 - 1962 RESELLADO AEREO VALOR Bs 2,00.**

1739	**173**	2b. on 1b. olive	3·50	1·70

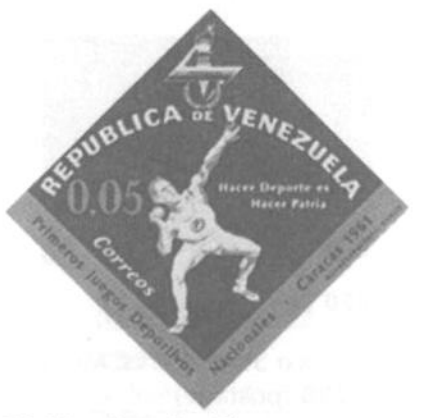

204 Putting the Shot

1962. First National Games, Caracas, 1961.

1740	**204**	5c. green (postage)	10	10
1741	-	10c. mauve	20	15
1742	-	25c. blue	45	20
MS1743 165×110 mm. Nos. 1740/2. Imperf. (sold at 1b.40)			5·00	5·00
1744		40c. grey (air)	65	35
1745		75c. brown	1·30	55
1746		85c. red	2·75	1·30
MS1747 165×110 mm. Nos. 1744/6 (sold at 3b.). Imperf			6·50	6·50

SPORTS: 10c. Football; 25c. Swimming; 40c. Cycling; 75c. Baseball; 85c. Gymnastics.

Each value is arranged in blocks of 4 within the sheet, with the top corners of each stamp converging to the centre of the block.

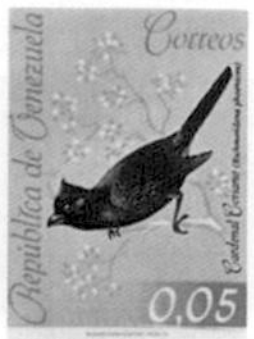

205 Vermilion Cardinal

1962. Birds. Multicoloured.

1748	5c. Type **205** (postage)	10	10
1749	10c. Great kiskadee	20	15
1750	20c. Glossy-black thrush	75	20
1751	25c. Collared trogons	90	35
1752	30c. Swallow tanager	1·10	45
1753	40c. Long-tailed sylph	1·40	55
1754	3b. Black-necked stilts	8·25	6·00
1755	5c. American kestrel (air)	35	10
1756	20c. Red-billed whistling duck (horiz)	75	20
1757	25c. Amazon kingfisher	90	35
1758	30c. Rufous-vented chachalaca	1·10	45
1759	50c. Oriole blackbird	1·70	65
1760	55c. Common pauraque	2·75	1·10
1761	2b.30 Red-crowned woodpecker	8·75	5·00
1762	2b.50 Lined quail dove	8·75	5·50

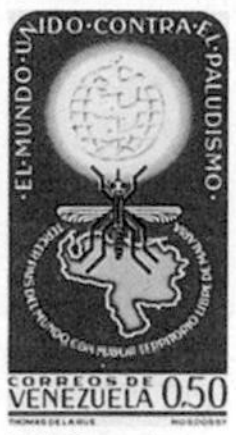

206 Campaign Emblem and Map

1962. Malaria Eradication.

1763	**206**	50c. brn & blk (postage)	1·10	45
1764	-	30c. green and black (air)	1·00	45
MS1765 90×108 mm. Nos. 1763/4 (sold at 2b.) Imperf			5·50	5·50

DESIGN: As T **206** but size 26×36 mm.

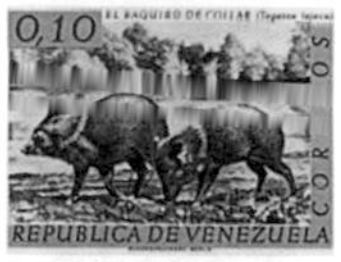

207 Collared Peccary

1963. Venezuelan Wild Life. Multicoloured.

1766	5c. White-tailed deer (postage)	10	10
1767	10c. Type **207**	15	10
1768	35c. Widow monkey	35	20
1769	50c. Giant otter	90	35
1770	1b. Puma	5·00	2·75
1771	3b. Capybara	10·00	6·50
1772	5c. Spectacled bear (vert) (air)	20	10
1773	40c. Paca	90	35
1774	50c. Pale-throated sloth	1·30	55
1775	55c. Giant anteater	1·70	65
1776	1b.50 Brazilian tapir	5·00	2·75
1777	2b. Jaguar	8·25	4·50

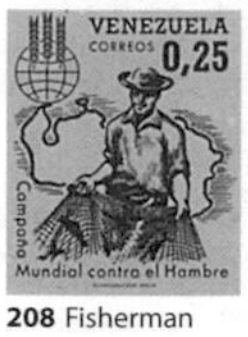

208 Fisherman

1963. Freedom from Hunger.

1778	**208**	25c. bl on pink (postage)	35	20
1779	-	40c. red on green (air)	90	55
1780	-	75c. sepia on yellow	1·10	90

DESIGNS: 40c. Farmer with lambs; 75c. Harvester.

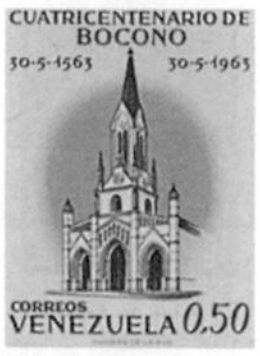

209 Bocono Cathedral

1963. 400th Anniv of Bocono.

1781	**209**	50c. mult on buff (postage)	1·00	35
1782	-	1b. mult on buff (air)	2·75	90

1994	60c. Constellations over Caracas (horiz)	90	45
1995	65c. Arms of Caracas	1·20	55
1996	70c. Federal Legislative Building (horiz)	1·20	45
1997	75c. University City (horiz)	1·30	55
1998	85c. El Pulpo road junction (horiz)	1·40	60
1999	90c. Map of Caracas (horiz)	1·50	65
2000	1b. Plaza Mayor, Caracas c. 1800 (horiz)	1·70	70
2001	2b. Avenida Libertador (horiz)	4·00	1·70

MS2002 Two sheets each 80×120 mm. Nos. 1990/1. Imperf. (sold at 1b. each) 90·00 90·00

259 Francisco Esteban Gomez

1967. Air. 150th Anniv of Battle of Matasiete.
2003 **259** 90c. multicoloured 1·70 75

260 J. V. Gonzalez

1967. Air. Death Centenary of Juan Gonzalez (journalist).
2016 **260** 80c. black and yellow 1·70 65

261 Child with Toy Windmill

1967. Air. Children's Festival.
2017 **261** 45c. multicoloured 90 35
2018 **261** 75c. multicoloured 1·20 45
2019 **261** 90c. multicoloured 1·50 65

262 "The Madonna of the Rosary" (Lochner)

1967. Air. Christmas.
2020 **262** 1b. multicoloured 2·20 1·10

263 Dr. J. M. Nunez Ponte (educator)

1968. Air. Third Death Anniv of Dr. Jose Manuel Nunez Ponte.
2021 **263** 65c. multicoloured 1·00 45

264 General Miranda and Printing Press

1968. Air. 150th Death Anniv of General Francisco de Miranda. Multicoloured.
2022 20c. Type **264** 45 30

2023	35c. Portrait and Houses of Parliament, London	75	35
2024	45c. Portrait and Arc de Triomphe, Paris	1·50	45
2025	70c. Portrait (vert)	1·80	55
2026	80c. Bust and Venezuelan flags (vert)	2·10	75

265 Title Page and Printing Press

1968. 150th Anniv of Newspaper "Correo del Orinoco".
2027 **265** 1b.50 multicoloured 2·75 1·10

266 "Spodoptera frugiperda"

1968. Insects. Multicoloured.
2028 20c. Type **266** (postage) 55 20
2029 75c. "Anthonomus grandis" 1·70 35
2030 90c. "Manduca sexta" 2·40 55
2031 5c. "Atta sextens" (air) 45 20
2032 15c. "Aeneolamia varia" 65 30
2033 90c. "Systena sp." 1·00 35
The 20 (air), 75 and 90c. are horiz.

267 Keys

1968. Air. 30th Anniv of Office of Controller-General.
2034 **267** 95c. multicoloured 1·90 65

268 Pistol-shooting

1968. Air. Olympic Games, Mexico. Multicoloured.
2035 5c. Type **268** 20 10
2036 15c. Running (horiz) 55 15
2037 30c. Fencing (horiz) 75 20
2038 75c. Boxing (horiz) 1·80 55
2039 5b. Sailing 8·75 3·25

269 Guayana Sub-station

1968. Rural Electrification. Multicoloured.
2040 15c. Type **269** 35 20
2041 45c. Encantado Dam 1·00 35
2042 50c. Macagua Dam 1·40 45
2043 80c. Guri Dam 2·10 90
The 45 and 50c. are horiz.

270 "The Holy Family" (F. J. de Lerma)

1968. Air. Christmas.
2044 **270** 40c. multicoloured 1·00 35

271 House and Savings Bank

1968. National Savings System.
2045 **271** 45c. multicoloured 1·10 45

272 Children and Star

1968. Air. Children's Festival.
2046 **272** 80c. orange and violet 1·40 45

273 Planting a Tree

1968. Conservation of Natural Resources. Multicoloured designs each incorporating central motif as in T **273**.
2047 15c. Type **273** (postage) 45 30
2048 20c. Plantation 55 35
2049 30c. Waterfall 65 40
2050 45c. Logs 90 45
2051 55c. Cultivated land 1·90 55
2052 75c. Palambra (fish) 1·30 45
2053 15c. Marbled wood quails (air) 45 30
2054 20c. Scarlet ibis, jabiru, great blue heron and red-billed whistling duck 55 35
2055 30c. Wood-carving 65 40
2056 90c. Brown trout 1·90 55
2057 95c. Mountain highway 3·00 90
2058 1b. Red-eyed vireo and shiny-headed cowbird (young) 2·20 65
The 15c. (both), 20c. (air), 30c. (both) and 55c. are vert, the remainder are horiz.

274 Colorada Beach, Sucre

1969. Tourism. Multicoloured.
2059 15c. Type **274** (postage) 35 10
2060 45c. San Francisco de Yare Church, Miranda 1·00 35
2061 90c. Houses on stilts, Zulia 1·40 90
2062 15c. Desert landscape, Falcon (air) 45 10
2063 30c. Humboldt Hotel, Caracas 50 20
2064 40c. Mountain cable-car, Merida 75 35
MS2065 120×80 mm. Nos. 2060 and 2063. Imperf 4·00 4·00

275 Bolivar addressing Congress

1969. 150th Anniv of Angostura Congress.
2066 **275** 45c. multicoloured 1·10 35

276 Dr. Martin Luther King

1969. First Death Anniv of Martin Luther King (American Civil Rights leader).
2067 **276** 1b. multicoloured 1·40 45

277 "Tabebuia pentaphylla"

1969. Nature Conservation. Trees. Multicoloured.
2068 50c. Type **277** (postage) 1·00 35
2069 65c. "Erythrina poeppigiana" 1·30 45
2070 90c. "Platymiscium sp." 2·10 80
2071 5c. "Cassia grandis" (air) 45 35
2072 55c. "Triplaris caracasana" 55 40
2073 25c. "Samanea saman" 65 45

278 "On the Balcony" (C. Rojas)

1969. Paintings by Cristobal Rojas. Multicoloured.
2074 25c. Type **278** 45 25
2075 35c. "The Pheasant" 75 35
2076 45c. "The Christening" 1·10 40
2077 50c. "The Empty Place" 1·40 45
2078 60c. "The Tavern" 1·80 70
2079 1b. "The Arm" (27×55 mm) 2·75 1·10
Nos. 2075/8 are horiz.

279 I.L.O. Emblem

1969. 50th Anniv of I.L.O.
2080 **279** 2b.50 black and brown 3·50 2·75

280 Charter and Arms of Guayana

1969. Industrial Development. Multicoloured.
2081 45c. Type **280** 1·10 35
2082 1b. SIDOR steel-works 1·80 70

281 Arcade, Casa del Balcon

1969. 400th Anniv of Carora. Multicoloured.
2083 20c. Type **281** 35 10
2084 25c. Ruins of La Pastora Church 45 25
2085 55c. Chapel of the Cross 1·30 55
2086 65c. Museum and library building 1·70 70

282 "Alexander von Humboldt" (J. Stieler)

1969. Air. Birth Bicent of Alexander von Humboldt (German naturalist).

2087	**282**	50c. multicoloured	1·10	35

283 A. Alfinger, A. Pacheco and P. Maldonado (founders)

1969. Air. 400th Anniv of Maracaibo. Multicoloured.

2088	20c. Type **283**		45	25
2089	25c. Map of Maracaibo, 1562		55	30
2090	40c. City coat-of-arms		65	35
2091	70c. University Hospital		1·30	55
2092	75c. Cacique Mara Monument		1·70	70
2093	1b. Baralt Plaza		2·00	80

Nos. 2089/92 are vert.

284 "Bolivar's Wedding" (T. Salas)

1969. "Bolivar in Spain".

2094	**284**	10c. multicoloured	20	10
2095	–	15c. black and red	45	15
2096	–	35c. multicoloured	75	25

MS2097 80×120 mm. Nos. 2095/6. Imperf. (sold at 75c.) — 3·50 — 3·50

DESIGNS—VERT: 15c. "Bolivar as a Student" (artist unknown); 35c. Bolivar's statue, Madrid.

285 Astronauts and Moon Landing

1969. Air. First Man on the Moon.

2098	**285**	90c. multicoloured	2·20	90

MS2099 119×80 mm. No. 2098. Imperf (sold at 1b.) — 4·50 — 4·50

286 "Virgin of the Rosary" (17th-cent Venetian School)

1969. Air. Christmas. Multicoloured.

2100	75c. Type **286**		1·30	55
2101	80c. "The Holy Family" (Landaeta School, Caracas, 18th cent)		1·70	70

287 "Children and Birds"

1969. Children's Day. Multicoloured.

2102	5c. Type **287**		20	10
2103	45c. "Children's Camp"		1·10	55

288 Map of Greater Colombia

1969. 150th Anniv of Greater Colombia Federation.

2104	**288**	45c. multicoloured	1·00	35

289 San Antonio Church, Clarines

1970. Architecture of the Colonial Era. Multicoloured.

2105	10c. Type **289**		20	10
2106	30c. Church of the Conception, Caroni		45	25
2107	40c. San Miguel Church, Burbusay		1·00	35
2108	45c. San Antonio Church, Maturin		1·30	55
2109	75c. San Nicolas Church, Moruy		1·80	70
2110	1b. Coro Cathedral		2·00	80

MS2111 100×60 mm. No. 2108. Imperf. (sold at 75c.) — 2·75 — 2·75

290 Seven Hills of Valera

1970. 150th Anniv of Valera.

2112	**290**	95c. multicoloured	1·80	70

291 "Simon Bolivar" (M. N. Bate)

1970. Air. Portraits of Bolivar. Stamps in brown on buff; inscriptions in green; colours of country name and value given below.

2113	**291**	15c. brown	35	10
2114	**291**	45c. blue	55	25
2115	**291**	55c. orange	75	35
2116	–	65c. brown	85	40
2117	–	70c. blue	90	55
2118	–	75c. orange	1·20	70
2119	–	85c. brown	1·30	75
2120	–	90c. blue	1·40	80
2121	–	95c. orange	1·70	85
2122	–	1b. brown	1·80	90
2123	–	1b.50 blue	2·00	90
2124	–	2b. orange	4·00	2·75

PORTRAITS BY: 65, 70, 75c. F. Roulin; 85, 90, 95c. J. M. Espinoza (1828); 1, 1b.50, 2b. J. M. Espinoza (1830).

292 Gen. A. Guzman Blanco and Dr. M. J. Sanabria

1970. Air. Centenary of Free Compulsory Education in Venezuela.

2125	**292**	75c. black, green & brown	1·10	55

293 Map of Venezuela

1970. States of Venezuela. Maps and Arms of the various States. Multicoloured.

2126	5c. Federal District (postage)		20	10
2127	15c. Monagas		20	10
2128	20c. Nueva Esparta		35	15
2129	25c. Portuguesa (vert)		40	20
2130	45c. Sucre		55	25
2131	55c. Tachira (vert)		65	35
2132	65c. Trujillo		75	45
2133	75c. Yaracuy		1·00	50
2134	85c. Zulia (vert)		1·30	55
2135	90c. Amazonas Federal Territory (vert)		2·50	70
2136	1b. Federal Island Dependencies		3·00	1·10
2137	5c. Type **293** (air)		20	10
2138	15c. Apure		35	10
2139	20c. Aragua		45	15
2140	20c. Anzoategui		50	25
2141	25c. Barinas		55	30
2142	25c. Bolivar		55	30
2143	45c. Carabobo		90	35
2144	55c. Cojedes (vert)		1·00	40
2145	65c. Falcon		1·10	45
2146	75c. Guarico		1·30	55
2147	85c. Lara		1·50	75
2148	90c. Merida (vert)		1·70	80
2149	1b. Miranda		1·80	90
2150	2b. Delta Amacuro Federal Territory		4·00	1·80

294 "Monochaetum humboldtianum"

1970. Flowers of Venezuela. Multicoloured.

2151	20c. Type **294** (postage)	55	10
2152	25c. "Symbolanthus vasculosus"	1·10	20
2153	45c. "Cavendishia splendens"	1·30	55
2154	1b. "Befaria glauca"	1·80	80
2155	20c. "Epidendrum secundum (air)	45	10
2156	25c. "Oyedaea verbesinoides"	55	20
2157	45c. "Heliconia villosa"	1·30	55
2158	1b. "Macleania nitida"	1·80	80

295 "The Battle of Boyaca" (M. Tovar y Tovar)

1970. 150th Anniv (1969) of Battle of Boyaca.

2159	**295** 30c. multicoloured	65	25

296 Archiepiscopal Cross

1970. Religious Art. Multicoloured.

2160	35c. Type **296**	75	25
2161	40c. "Our Lady of the Valley"	1·00	35
2162	60c. "Our Lady of Belen de San Mateo"	1·40	55
2163	90c. "The Virgin of Chiquin-quira"	1·80	80
2164	1b. "Our Lady of Socorro de Valencia"	2·20	90

MS2165 102×62 mm. No. 2162. Imperf. (sold at 75c.) — 2·40 — 2·40

297 "Caracciolo Parra Olmedo" (T. Salas)

1970. Air. 150th Birth Anniv of Caracciola Parra Olmedo (lawyer).

2166	**297** 20c. multicoloured	45	20

298 National Flags and Exhibition Emblem

1970. "EXFILCA 70" Philatelic Exhibition, Caracas. Multicoloured.

2167	20c. Type **298**	45	25
2168	25c. 1871 1c. stamp and emblem (horiz)	65	30
2169	70c. 1930 2b.50 air stamp and emblem	1·30	55

MS2170 101×87 mm. (hexagonal). No. 2169. Imperf. (sold at 85c.) — 2·40 — 2·40

299 "Guardian Angel" (J. P. Lopez)

1970. Christmas.

2171	**299** 45c. multicoloured	1·00	45

300 Caudron G-3 Biplane and Dassault Mirage III

1970. 50th Anniv of Venezuelan Air Force.

2172	**300** 5c. multicoloured	20	10

301 People In Question Mark

1971. National Census.

2173	**301** 30c. black, green and red (postage)	1·20	55
2174	– 70c. multicoloured (air)	1·40	70

DESIGN: 70c. National flag and "pin-men".

302 Battle Scene

1971. 150th Anniv of Battle of Carabobo.

2175	**302** 2b. multicoloured	2·75	1·70

303 "Cattleya percivaliana"

1971. Air. Venezuelan Orchids. Multicoloured.

2176	20c. Type **303**	75	25
2177	25c. "Cattleya gaskelliana" (horiz)	1·10	35
2178	75c. "Cattleya mossiae"	1·90	70
2179	90c. "Cattleya violacea o superba" (horiz)	2·75	1·10
2180	1b. "Cattleya lawrenceana" (horiz)	2·75	1·30

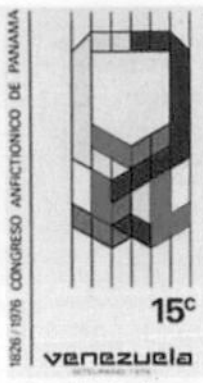

350 "Unity" Emblem

1976. 150th Anniv of Panama Amphictyonic Congress.

2335	**350**	15c. multicoloured	20	10
2336	-	45c. multicoloured	45	20
2337	-	1b.25 multicoloured	1·00	70

DESIGN: 45c., 1b.25, As Type **275**, but with different "Unity" emblems.

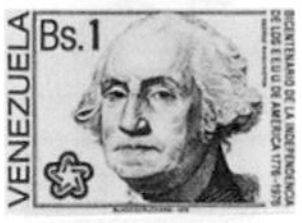

351 George Washington

1976. Bicentenary of American Revolution.

2338	**351**	1b. black and brown	1·00	55
2339	-	1b. black and green	1·00	55
2340	-	1b. black and purple	1·00	55
2341	-	1b. black and blue	1·00	55
2342	-	1b. black and brown	1·00	55

DESIGNS: No. 2339, Thomas Jefferson; No. 2340, Abraham Lincoln; No. 2341, Franklin D. Roosevelt; No. 2342, John F. Kennedy.

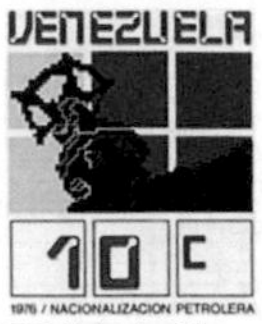

352 Valve in Oil Pipeline

1976. Oil Nationalization.

2343	**352**	10c. multicoloured	10	10
2344	-	30c. multicoloured	20	10
2345	-	35c. multicoloured	30	15
2346	-	40c. multicoloured	35	20
2347	-	55c. multicoloured	45	25
2348	-	90c. multicoloured	75	35

DESIGNS: 30c. to 90c. Various computer drawings of valves and pipelines.

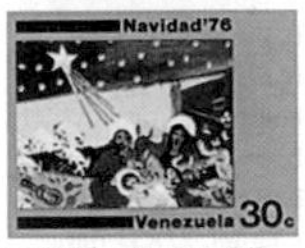

353 "The Nativity" (B. Rivas)

1976. Christmas.

2349	**353**	30c. multicoloured	65	15

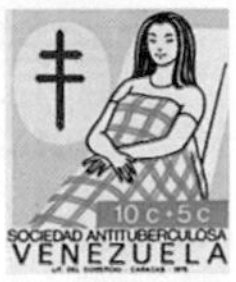

354 Patient

1976. Anti-tuberculosis Society Fund.

2350	**354**	10c.+5c. multicoloured	20	10
2351	**354**	30c.+10c. multicoloured	35	25

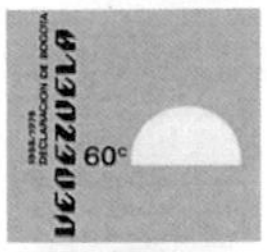

355 Declaration Emblem

1976. Tenth Anniv of Bogota Declaration.

2352	**355**	60c. black and yellow	65	25

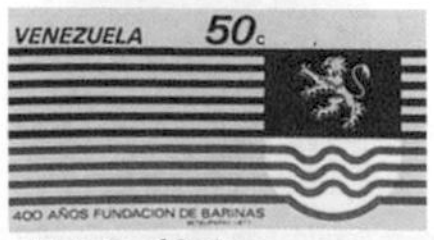

356 Arms of Barinas

1977. 400th Anniv of Barinas.

2353	**356**	50c. multicoloured	65	25

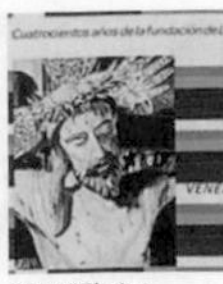

357 "Christ Crucified"

1977. 400th Anniv (1976) of La Grita.

2354	**357**	30c. multicoloured	35	10

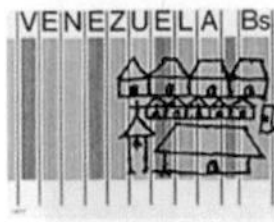

358 Coro Settlement

1977. 450th Anniv of Coro.

2355	**358**	1b. multicoloured	90	45

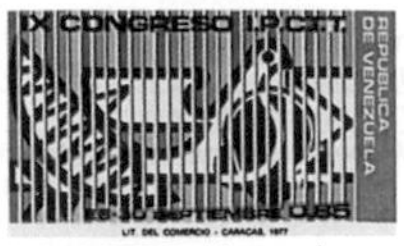

359 I.P.C.T.T. Emblem and Stylized Dove

1977. Ninth Inter-American Postal and Telecommunications Staff Congress, Caracas.

2356	**359**	85c. multicoloured	90	25

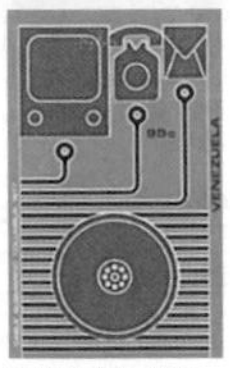

360 Cable Links to Domestic Equipment

1977. Inauguration of "Columbus" Submarine Cable.

2357	**360**	95c. grey, blue and green	95	25

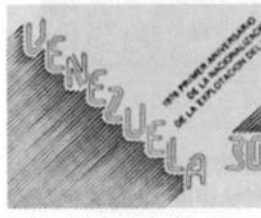

361 "VENEZUELA" and Value as Rolled Steel

1977. First Anniv of Nationalization and Exploitation of Steel.

2358	**361**	30c. black and yellow	35	20
2359	-	50c. black and orange	45	25
2360	-	80c. black and grey	75	35
2361	-	1b.05 black and red	1·00	45
2362	-	1b.25 black and yellow	1·10	50
2363	-	1b.50 black and grey	1·40	55

DESIGNS: 50c. to 1b.50, Similar to Type **361** but each differently arranged.

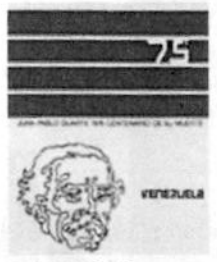

362 J. P. Duarte

1977. Death Cent (1976) of Juan Pablo Duarte.

2364	**362**	75c. black and mauve	75	25

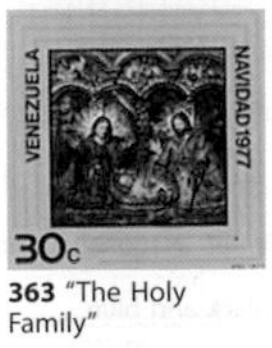

363 "The Holy Family"

1977. Christmas.

2365	**363**	30c. multicoloured	45	35

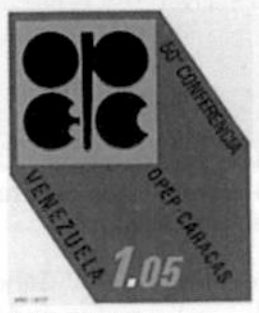

364 O.P.E.C. Emblem

1977. 50th O.P.E.C. Conference, Caracas.

2366	**364**	1b.05 black and blue	90	25

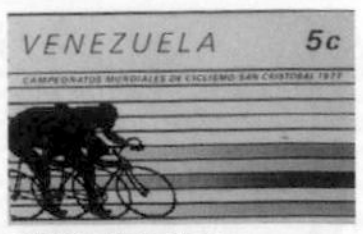

365 Cyclists Racing

1978. World Cycling Championships, San Cristobal, Tachira. Multicoloured.

2367	5c. Type **365**	20	10
2368	1b.25 Cyclist racing	1·10	35

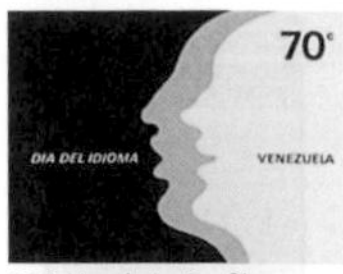

366 Heads in Profile

1978. Language Day.

2369	**366**	70c. black, grey & mauve	55	25

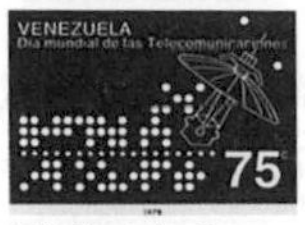

367 Computer Tape and Satellite

1978. Tenth World Telecommunications Day.

2370	**367**	75c. blue	65	35

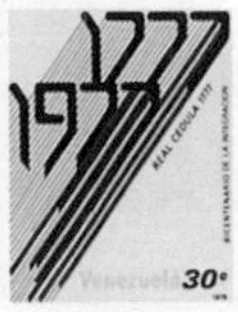

368 "1777–1977"

1978. Bicentenary of Venezuelan Unification. Multicoloured.

2381	30c. Type **368**	30	20
2382	1b. Computer print of Goya's "Carlos III"	90	30

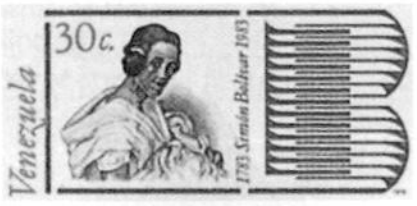

369 Bolivar in Nurse Hipolita's Arms

1978. Birth Bicent (1983) of Simon Bolivar (1st issue).

2383	**369**	30c. black, brown & grn	20	10
2384	-	1b. black, brown and blue	90	45

MS2384a 154×130 mm. 50c.×5 multicoloured 55·00 55·00

See also Nos. 2399/**MS**2401, 2408/**MS**2410, 2422/**MS**2424, 2431/**MS**2433, 2467/**MS**2469, 2480/**MS**2482, 2483/**MS**2485, 2494/**MS**2496, 2498/**MS**250, 2518/**MS**2520 and 2521/**MS**2523.

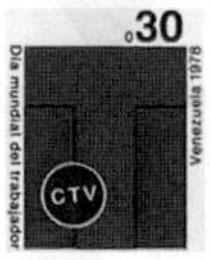

370 "T" ("Trabajadors")

1978. Workers' Day.

2385	**370**	30c. red and black	20	10
2386	-	30c. blue and black	20	10
2387	-	30c. yellow, blue & black	20	10
2388	-	30c. red, blue and black	20	10
2389	-	30c. red and black	20	10
2390	-	95c. black and red	45	30
2391	-	95c. grey and blue	45	30
2392	-	95c. black and red	45	30
2393	-	95c. blue and black	45	30
2394	-	95c. multicoloured	45	30

DESIGNS: Nos. 2386/94 based on the letter "T", also inscribed "CTV".

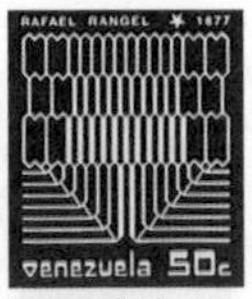

371 Medical Abstract

1978. Birth Centenary (1977) of Rafael Rangel (physician and scientist).

2395	**371**	50c. brown	90	45

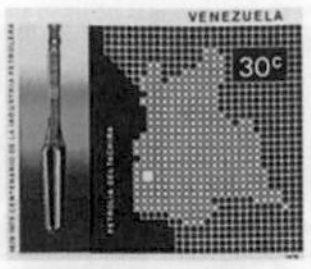

372 Drill Head and Map of Tachira Oilfield

1978. Centenary of Venezuelan Oil Industry. Multicoloured.

2396	30c. Type **372**	20	10
2397	1b.05 Letter "P" as pipeline	90	45

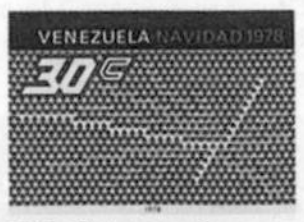

373 Christmas Star

1978. Christmas.

2398	**373**	30c. multicoloured	35	10

1978. Birth Bicentenary (1983) of Simon Bolivar (2nd Issue). As T **369**.

2399	30c. black, brown and purple	35	15
2400	1b. black, grey and red	55	35

MS2401 130×155 mm. 50c.×5 multicoloured 33·00 33·00

DESIGNS: 30c. Bolivar at 25 (after M. N. Bate); 1b. Simon Rodriguez (Bolivar's tutor). Each 20×24 mm—No. **MS**2401, "The Oath on Monte Sacro" (Tito Salas) (composite design).

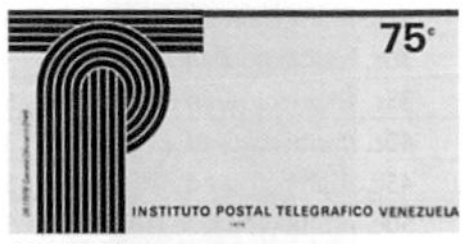

374 "P T"

1979. Creation of Postal and Telegraph Institute.

2402	**374**	75c. blk & red on cream	45	20

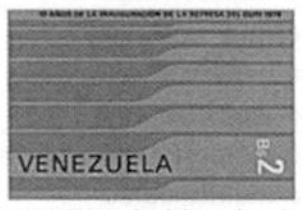

375 Dam holding back Water

1979. Tenth Anniv of Guri Dam.

2403	**375**	2b. silver, grey and black	1·20	55

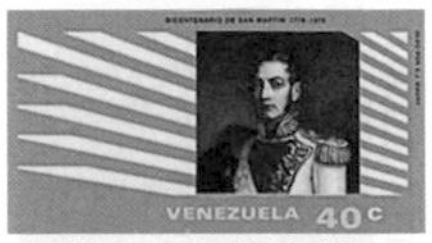

376 "General San Martin" (E. J. Maury)

1979. Birth Bicentenary of General Jose de San Martin. Multicoloured.

2404	40c. Type **376**	30	20
2405	60c. Portrait by Mercedes San Martin	45	25
2406	70c. San Martin Monument, Guayaquil	50	30
2407	75c. San Martin's signature	55	35

1979. Birth Bicentenary (1983) of Simon Bolivar (3rd series). As T **369**.

2408	30c. black, violet and red	20	10
2409	1b. black, orange and red	55	25

MS2410 155×130 mm. 50c.×5 multicoloured 5·50 5·50

DESIGNS: 30c. Alexandre Sabes Petion (President of Haiti); 1b. Bolivar's signature. No. **MS**2410: 25×19 mm—(a) Map Showing Kingston, Jamaica. (b) Map showing Portland, Jamaica. 19×25 mm—(c) Luis Brion. (e) Petion.

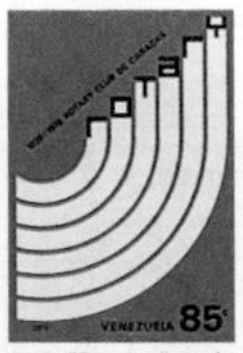

377 "Rotary" and Curves

1979. 50th Anniv of Rotary Club of Caracas.

2411	**377**	85c. black and gold	55	25

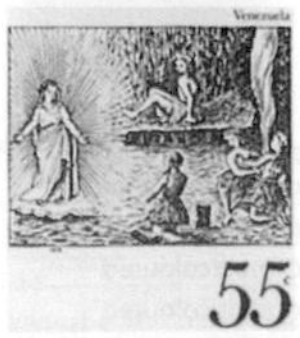

378 Statue of Virgin working Miracles, 1654

1979. 25th Anniv of Canonization of Virgin of Coromoto.
2412 **378** 55c. black and red 35 10

379 Miranda, London Residence and Arms

1979. Acquisition by Venezuela of Francisco de Miranda's House in London.
2413 **379** 50c. multicoloured 35 10

380 O'Leary and Maps

1979. 125th Death Anniv of Daniel O'Leary (publisher of Bolivar's memoirs).
2414 **380** 30c. multicoloured 20 10

381 Boy with Nest

1979. International Year of the Child.
2415 **381** 70c. black and blue 35 10
2416 - 80c. multicoloured 55 25
DESIGN: 80c. Boys playing in sea.

382 Candle

1979. Christmas.
2417 **382** 30c. multicoloured 35 10

383 Caudron G-3 Biplane

1979. "Exfilve 79" National Stamp Exhibition and 59th Anniv of Air Force. Multicoloured.
2418 75c. Type **383** 45 30
2419 75c. Stearman Kaydett biplane 45 30
2420 75c. Bell Iroquois helicopter 45 30
2421 75c. Dassault Mirage IIIC jet fighter 45 30

1979. Birth Bicentenary (1983) of Simon Bolivar (4th series). As T **369**.
2422 30c. black, red and turquoise 20 10
2423 1b. black, blue and red 55 30
MS2424 130×156 mm. 50c.×5 multi-coloured 8·75 8·75
DESIGNS: 30c. Bolivar; 1b. Slave. **MS**2424; each 22×28 mm—"Freeing of the Slaves" (Tito Salas) (composite design).

384 Emblem and World Map

1979. Introduction of New Emblem for Postal and Telegraph Institute.
2425 **384** 75c. multicoloured 45 25

385 Queen Victoria and Hill

1980. Death Centenary of Sir Rowland Hill (1979).
2426 **385** 55c. multicoloured 35 10

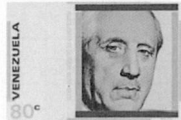

386 Augusto Pi Suner

1980. Birth Centenary (1979) of Dr. Augusto Pi Suner (physiologist).
2427 **386** 80c. multicoloured 55 25

387 "Cotyledon hIspanica"

1980. 250th Birth Anniv of Pedro Loefling (Swedish botanist).
2428 **387** 50c. multicoloured 35 10

388 Lovera (self-portrait)

1980. Birth Bicentenary (1978) of Juan Lovera (artist).
2429 **388** 60c. blue and red 35 75
2430 **388** 75c. violet and orange 45 30

1980. Birth Bicentenary (1983) of Simon Bolivar (5th issue). As T **369**.
2431 30c. black, green and purple 20 10
2432 1b. black, dp brown & brown 55 35
MS2433 156×129 mm. 50c.×5 multi-coloured 5·50 5·50
DESIGNS: 30c. Signing document; 1b. Congress House, Angostura. No. **MS**2433, 25×19 mm or 19×25 mm—"Angostura Congress" (Tito Salas) (composite design).

389 "Self-portrait with Children" (detail)

1980. 25th Death Anniv (1979) of Armando Reveron (artist). Multicoloured.
2434 50c. Type **389** 20 10
2435 65c. "Self-portrait" (26×41 mm) 75 45

390 Bernardo O'Higgins

1980. 204th Birth Anniv of Bernardo O'Higgins.
2436 **390** 85c. black, red and blue 1·00 45

391 Frigate "Mariscal Sucre"

1980. Venezuelan Navy. Multicoloured.
2437 1b.50 Type **391** 1·40 55
2438 1b.50 Submarine "Picua" 1·40 55
2439 1b.50 Naval School 1·40 55
2440 1b.50 Cadet barque "Simon Bolivar" (33×52 mm) 1·40 55

392 Figures supporting O.P.E.C. Emblem

1980. 20th Anniv of Organization of Petroleum Exporting Countries. Multicoloured.
2441 1b.50 Type **392** 90 45

2442 1b.50 O.P.E.C. emblem and globe 90 45

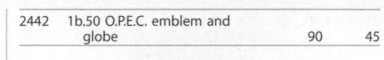

393 "The Death of Bolivar" (Antonio Herrera Toro)

1980. 150th Death Anniv of Simon Bolivar.
2443 **393** 2b. multicoloured 2·20 70

394 Antonio Jose de Sucre

1980. 150th Death Anniv of Marshal Antonio Jose de Sucre.
2444 **394** 2b. multicoloured 1·20 55

395 "The Adoration of the Shepherds" (Rubens)

1980. Christmas.
2445 **395** 1b. multicoloured 65 35

396 Helen Keller's Initials in Braille and Print

1981. Birth Centenary (1980) of Helen Keller.
2446 **396** 1b.50 grey, orange & blk 75 45

397 Gateway, San Felipe

1981. 250th Anniv of San Felipe.
2447 **397** 3b. blue, grey and red 1·30 70

398 Jean Baptiste de la Salle (founder)

1981. 300th Anniv (1980) of Brothers of Christian Schools.
2448 **398** 1b.25 silver, red & black 65 35

399 Municipal Theatre

1981. Centenary of Caracas Municipal Theatre.
2449 **399** 1b.25 pink, black & lilac 2·40 45

400 U.P.U. Emblem, Map of Venezuela and Envelope

1981. Centenary of Admission to Universal Postal Union.
2450 **400** 2b. multicoloured 75 35

401 People on Map

1981. 11th National Population and Housing Census.
2451 **401** 1b. lilac, violet, and black 55 25

402 Games Emblem

1981. Ninth Bolivarian Games, Barquismeto.
2452 **402** 95c. multicoloured 55 25

403 "Penny-farthing" Bicycle

1981. Transport History (1st series). Multicoloured.
2453 1b. Type **403** 70 45
2454 1b.05 Steam locomotive, 1926 75 50
2455 1b.25 Buick car, 1937 1·10 55
2456 1b.50 Horse-drawn cab 1·30 70
See also Nos. 2490/3 and 2514/7.

404 Musicians

1981. Christmas.
2457 **404** 1b. multicoloured 45 25

405 Mt. Autana

1982. 50th Anniv of Venezuelan Natural Sciences Society. Multicoloured.
2458 1b. Type **405** 55 25
2459 1b.50 Sarisarinama 75 35
2460 2b. Guacharo Cave 1·10 55

406 Calligraphic Script and Arms

1982. 20th Anniv of Constitution.
2461 **406** 1b.85 gold and black 1·10 35

407 "Landscape"

1982. 20th Anniv of Agricultural Reform.
| 2462 | 407 | 3b. multicoloured | 1·70 | 70 |

408 Jules Verne

1982. Jules Verne (writer) Commemoration.
| 2463 | 408 | 1b. deep blue and blue | 55 | 25 |

409 Bars of National Anthem

1982. Centenary of National Anthem (1981).
| 2464 | 409 | 1b. multicoloured | 55 | 25 |

410 Rose

1982. 1300th Anniv of Bulgarian State.
| 2465 | 410 | 65c. multicoloured | 35 | 10 |

411 Flags

1982. Sixth National Plan.
| 2466 | 411 | 2b. multicoloured | 55 | 25 |

1982. Birth Bicentenary (1983) of Simon Bolivar (6th issue). As T **369**.
2467		30c. black, brown and orange	20	10
2468		1b. black, brown and green	35	25
MS2469 156×131 mm. 50c.×5 multicoloured			5·00	5·00

DESIGNS: 30c. Col. Rondon; 1b. Gen. Anzoategui. No. **MS**2469, 26×19 mm or 19×26 mm—"Battle of Boyaca" (Martin Tovar y Tovar) (composite design).

412 Cecilio Acosta

1982. Death Centenary (1981) of Cecilio Acosta (statesman).
| 2470 | 412 | 3b. black, blue and violet | 75 | 35 |

413 "Fourcroya humboldtiana"

1982. Flora and Fauna. Multicoloured.
2471		1b.05 Type **413**	90	25
2472		2b.55 Turtle ("Podocnemis expansa")	2·30	35
2473		2b.75 "Oyedaea verbesinoides"	2·50	40
2474		3b. Oilbird	2·75	45

414 Andres Bello and Initials

1982. Birth Bicentenary of Andres Bello (1981).
2475	414	1b.05 light blue, blue and black	55	25
2476	414	2b.55 yellow, violet and black	1·00	45
2477	414	2b.75 blue, deep blue and black	1·10	55

| 2478 | 414 | 3b. olive, deep olive and black | 1·30 | 70 |

415 "Nativity"

1982. Christmas.
| 2479 | 415 | 1b. multicoloured | 35 | 10 |

1982. Birth Bicentenary (1983) of Simon Bolivar (7th issue). As T **369**.
2480		30c. black, grey and red	35	20
2481		1b. black, grey and red	65	30
MS2482 155×132 mm. 50c.×5 multicoloured			6·50	6·50

DESIGNS: 30c. Carabobo Monument; 1b. Gen. Jose Antonio Peaz. No. **MS**2482, each 19×25 mm—"Battle of Carabobo" (detail, Martin Tovar y Tovar) (composite design).

1982. Birth Bicentenary (1983) of Simon Bolivar (8th issue). As T **369**.
2483		30c. black, blue and deep blue	35	20
2484		1b. black, violet and red	65	30
MS2485 155×130 mm. 50c.×5 multicoloured			6·50	6·50

DESIGNS: 30c. Commemorative plaque to the meeting at Guayaquil; 1b. San Martin (detail of monument). No. **MS**2485, each 22×28 mm—Monument to the Meeting at Guayaquil (composite design).

416 Bermudez

1982. Birth Bicentenary of General Jose Francisco Bermudez (statesman).
| 2486 | 416 | 3b. multicoloured | 1·70 | 55 |

417 Briceno

1982. Birth Bicentenary of Antonio Nicolas Briceno (liberation hero).
| 2487 | 417 | 3b. multicoloured | 1·70 | 55 |

418 Rejoicing Crowd and Flag

1983. 25th Anniv of 1958 Reforms.
| 2488 | 418 | 3b. multicoloured | 1·70 | 55 |

419 Police Badge

1983. 25th Anniv of Judicial Police Technical Department.
| 2489 | 419 | 4b. red and green | 2·00 | 70 |

1983. Transport History (2nd series). As T **403**. Multicoloured.
2490		75c. Lincoln touring car, 1923	1·30	50
2491		80c. Steam locomotive No. 129, 1889	1·40	55
2492		85c. Willys truck, 1927	1·50	65
2493		95c. Cleveland motorcycle, 1920	1·70	70

1983. Birth Bicentenary of Simon Bolivar (9th issue). As T **369**.
2494		30c. black, red and blue	35	10
2495		1b. black, gold and blue	65	30
MS2496 155×130 mm. 50c.×5 multicoloured			65	6·50

DESIGNS: 30c. Gen. Antonio Sucre; 1b. Sword hilt. No. **MS**2496, 29×15 mm or 10×25 mm—"Ayacucho" (Martin Tovar y Tovar) (composite design).

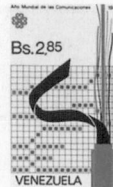
420 Cable and Computer Circuitboard

1983. World Communications Year.
| 2497 | 420 | 2b.85 multicoloured | 75 | 55 |

1983. Birth Bicentenary of Simon Bolivar (10th issue). As T **369**.
2498		30c. multicoloured	20	10
2499		1b. black, yellow and blue	65	30
MS2500 130×154 mm. 50c.×5 multicoloured			6·50	6·50

DESIGNS: 30c. Flag; 1b. "Ascent of Postosi". No. **MS**2500, each 19×25 mm—"The Liberator on Potosi" (detail, Tito Salas) (composite design).

421 Map of the Americas

1983. Ninth Pan-American Games, Caracas. Multicoloured.
2501		2b. Type **421**	55	25
2502		2b. Swimming	55	25
2503		2b.70 Cycling	65	55
2504		2b.70 Fencing	65	55
2505		2b.85 Weightlifting	75	70
2506		2b.85 Running	75	70
MS2507 168×121 mm. 1b.×5 scarlet, yellow and black			22·00	22·00

DESIGNS: 27×43 mm—No. **MS**2507, (a) Tennis ball; (b) Bicycle wheel; (c) Boxing glove; (d) Football; (e) Archery target.

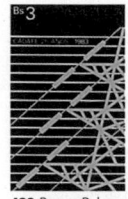
422 Power Pylon

1983. 25th Anniv of State Electricity Authority.
| 2508 | 422 | 3b. blue, silver and red | 1·70 | 80 |

423 Nativity

1983. Christmas.
| 2509 | 423 | 1b. multicoloured | 45 | 10 |

424 Erecting a Tent

1983. 75th Anniv (1982) of Scout Movement. Multicoloured.
2510		2b.25 Type **424**	65	30
2511		2b.55 Nature watch	70	35
2512		2b.75 Mountaineering	75	40
2513		3b. Camp at night	85	45

1983. Transport History (3rd series). Caracas Underground Railway. As T **403**. Multicoloured.
2514		55c. black, orange and silver	75	45
2515		75c. black, yellow and silver	90	55
2516		95c. black, green and silver	1·00	70
2517		2b. black, blue and silver	2·00	80

DESIGNS: 55c. Central computer building; 75c. Maintenance bay; 95c. Train on elevated section; 2b. Train at Cano Amarillo station.

1984. Birth Bicentenary of Simon Bolivar (11th issue). As T **369**.
| 2518 | | 30c. black, red and brown | 20 | 10 |
| 2519 | | 1b. black, green and blue | 45 | 20 |

| **MS**2520 131×156 mm. 50c.×5 multicoloured | | | 6·50 | 6·50 |

DESIGNS: 30c. Open volume of "Opere de Raimondo Montecuccoli"; 1b. Dr. Jose Maria Vargas (President, 1835–36); **MS**2520, each 19×29 mm—"Arts, Science and Education" (detail, of fresco by Hector Poleo in Caracas University) (composite design).

1984. Birth Bicentenary of Simon Bolivar (12th issue). As T **369**.
2521		30c. black, red and lilac	35	10
2522		1b. black, green and orange	45	20
MS2523 131×155 mm. 50c.×5 multicoloured			6·50	6·50

DESIGNS: 30c. Pedro Gaul (President, 1859 and 1861; 1b. Jose Faustino Sanchez; **MS**2523, each 26×18 or 18×26 mm—Map of central and South America, 1829 (composite design).

425 Radio Mast and Waves

1984. 50th Anniv of Venezuela Radio Club.
| 2524 | 425 | 2b.70 multicoloured | 65 | 35 |

426 Doves and Hands covering Eyes

1984. "Intelligentsia for Peace". Multicoloured.
2525		1b. Type **426**	35	10
2526		2b.70 Profile head	65	30
2527		2b.85 Profile head, flower and hexagonal nut	75	35

427 Romulo Gallegos

1984. Birth Centenary of Romulo Gallegos (writer and President, 1948). Multicoloured.
2528	427	1b.70 multicoloured	75	35
2529	-	1b.70 multicoloured	75	35
2530	-	1b.70 green, grey and black	75	35
2531	-	1b.70 deep green, green and black	75	35

DESIGNS: Nos. 2529/31, Different portraits of Gallegos.

428 Emblem and Digital Eight

1984. 18th Pan-American Union of Engineering Associations Convention.
| 2532 | 428 | 2b.55 buff and blue | 90 | 35 |

429 "Nativity" (Maria Candelaria de Ramirez)

1984. Christmas.
| 2533 | 429 | 1b. multicoloured | 35 | 10 |

430 Pope and "Virgin of Coromoto"

1985. Visit of Pope John Paul II (1st issue).

2534	430	1b. multicoloured	55	35

See also Nos. 2628/33.

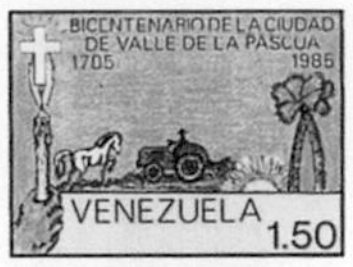

431 Cross, Hand holding Candle and Agricultural Scene

1985. Bicentenary of Valle de la Pascua City.

2535	431	1b.50 multicoloured	65	45

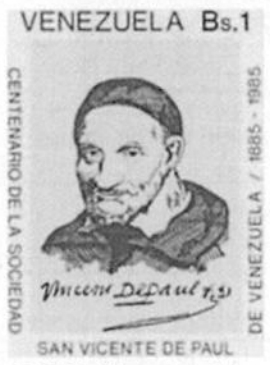

432 St. Vincent de Paul

1985. Centenary of Venezuelan Society of St. Vincent de Paul.

2536	432	1b. brown, yellow and red	45	10

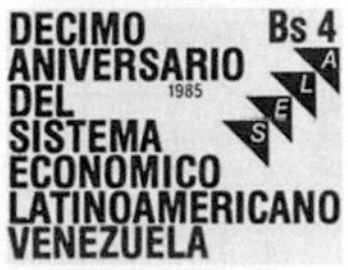

433 Text and "SELA"

1985. Tenth Anniv of Latin American Economic System.

2537	433	4b. black and red	2·40	1·10

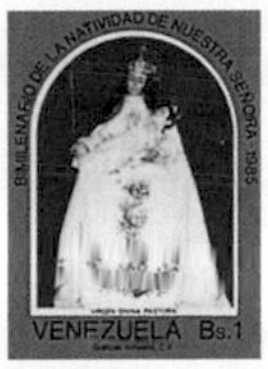

434 "Divine Shepherdess"

1985. 2000th Birth Anniv of Virgin Mary. Multicoloured.

2538	1b. Type **434**	75	30
2539	1b. "Virgin of Chiquinquira"	75	30
2540	1b. "Virgin of Coromoto"	75	30
2541	1b. "Virgin of the Valley"	75	30
2542	1b. "Virgin of Perpetual Succour"	75	30
2543	1b. "Virgin of Peace"	75	30
2544	1b. "Virgin of the Immaculate Conception"	75	30
2545	1b. "Virgin of Solitude"	75	30
2546	1b. "Virgin of Consolation"	75	30
2547	1b. "Virgin of the Snow"	75	30

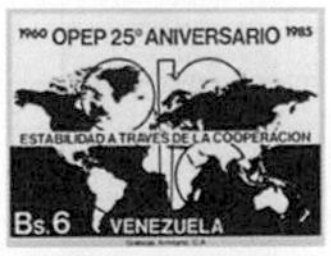

435 Map and Emblem

1985. 25th Anniv of Organization of Petroleum Exporting Countries.

2548	435	6b. black, blue and light blue	1·90	1·10

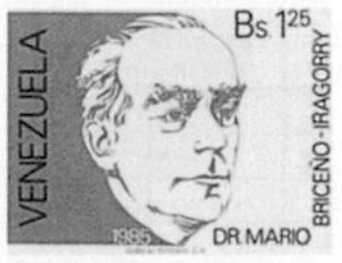

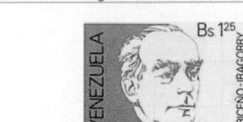

436 Dr Briceno-Iragorry

1985. 27th Death Anniv of Dr. Mario Briceno-Iragorry (politician).

2549	436	1b.25 silver and red	55	35

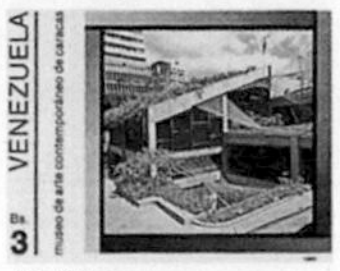

437 Museum

1985. Tenth Anniv (1983) of Museum of Modern Art, Caracas.

2550	437	3b. multicoloured	1·00	55

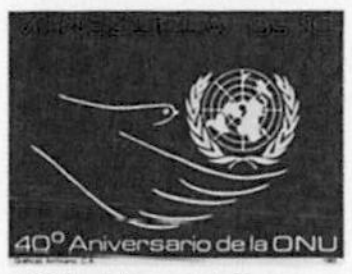

438 Emblem and Dove as Hand

1985. 40th Anniv of U.N.O.

2551	438	10b. blue and red	2·75	1·70

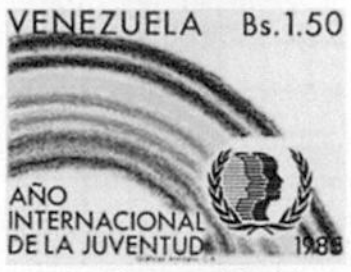

439 Rainbow and Emblem

1985. International Youth Year.

2552	439	1b.50 multicoloured	55	35

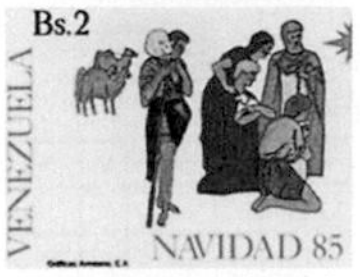

440 Shepherds and Camels

1985. Christmas. Multicoloured.

2553	2b. Type **440**	1·10	35
2554	2b. Holy Family and the Three Kings	1·10	35

Nos. 2553/4 were printed together, se-tenant, forming a composite design of the Nativity.

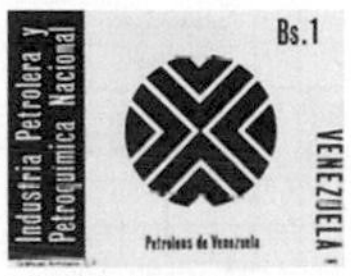

441 Petroleos de Venezuela Emblem

1985. Tenth Anniv of National Petrochemical Industry.

2555	441	1b. blue and black	35	20
2556	-	1b. multicoloured	35	20
2557	-	2b. multicoloured	75	35
2558	-	2b. multicoloured	75	35
2559	-	3b. multicoloured	1·30	45
2560	-	3b. multicoloured	1·30	45
2561	-	4b. multicoloured	1·70	55
2562	-	4b. multicoloured	1·70	55
2563	-	5b. multicoloured	2·10	70
2564	-	5b. multicoloured	2·10	70

DESIGNS: No. 2556, Refinery and Isla S.A. emblem; 2557, Bariven oil terminal; 2558, Pequiven storage tank; 2559, Corpoven drilling site; 2560, Support vessel, oil rig and Maraven emblem; 2561, Meneven refinery; 2562, Intervep scientist; 2563, "Nodding Donkey"; 2564, Lagoven refinery.

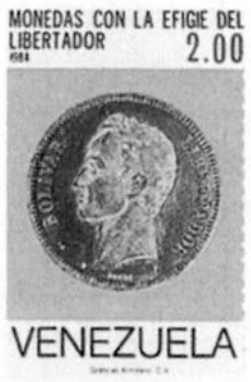

442 Five Reales Silver Coin, 1873

1985. Coins with Portrait of Simon Bolivar. Multicoloured.

2565	2b. Type **442**	65	45
2566	2b.70 Five bolivares gold coin, 1886	90	55
2567	3b. Birth bicentenary gold proof coin, 1983	1·00	70

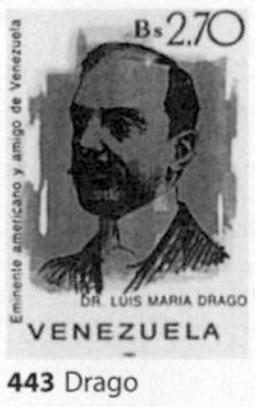

443 Drago

1985. 125th Birth Anniv (1984) of Dr. Luis Maria Drago (Argentine politician).

2568	443	2b.70 black, orge & red	90	55

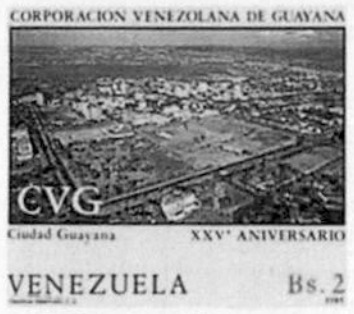

444 Guayana City

1985. 25th Anniv of Guayana Development Corporation. Multicoloured.

2569	2b. Type **444**	65	45
2570	3b. Orinoco steel mill	1·00	70
2571	5b. Raul Leoni-Guri dam	1·70	1·10

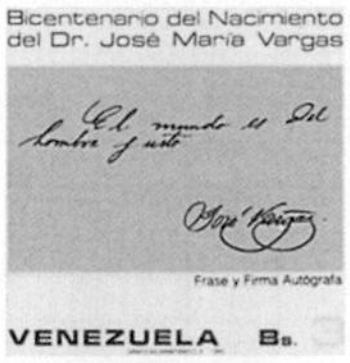

445 Signature

1985. Birth Bicentenary of Dr. Jose Maria Vargas (President, 1835–36). Multicoloured.

2572	3b. Type **445**	75	55
2573	3b. "Vargas" (Martin Tovar y Tovar) (vert)	75	55
2574	3b. Statue at Palace of Academies (vert)	75	55
2575	3b. "Exfilbo '86" National Stamp Exhibition emblem and flags	75	55
2576	3b. Facade of Vargas Hospital, Caracas	75	55
2577	3b. Title page of Vargas's "Manual and Compendium of Surgery" (vert)	75	55
2578	3b. "Vargas" (Alirio Palacios) (vert)	75	55
2579	3b. "Gesneria vargasii" (flower)	75	55
2580	3b. Portraits of Vargas and Bolivar on Sixth Venezuelan Congress of Medical Sciences medal	75	55
2581	3b. "Vargas" (anonymous) (vert)	75	55
MS2582	97×65 mm. 15b. Vargas; 15b. Bolivar (each 28×38 mm). Imperf	17·00	17·00

No. **MS**2582 is inscribed with the emblem and title of "Exfilbo 86" Bolivarian Stamp Exhibition, Caracas.

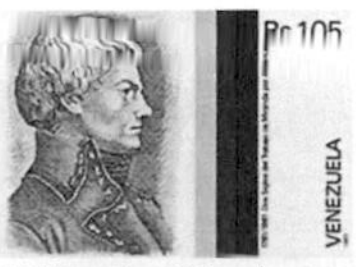

446 Francisco Miranda

1986. Bicentenary (1981) of Francisco Miranda's Work for Latin American Liberation.

2583	446	1b.05 multicoloured	35	15

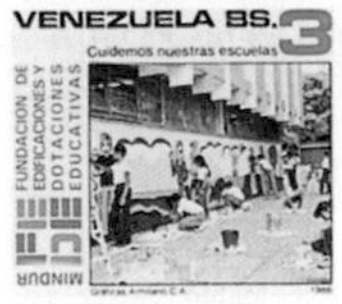

447 Children painting Wall

1986. Foundation for Educational Buildings and Equipment. Multicoloured.

2584	3b. Type **447**	90	35
2585	5b. Boys at woodwork class	1·50	45

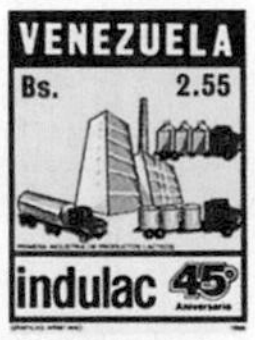

448 Lorries and Processing Plant

1986. 45th Anniv of Venezuelan Dairy Industry Corporation. Multicoloured.

2586	2b.55 Type **448**	45	25
2587	2b.70 Map and milk containers	55	30
2588	3b.70 Processing plant Machiques, Edo Zulia (horiz)	65	35

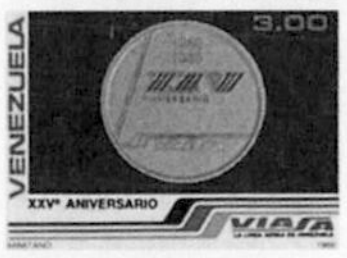

449 Emblem

1986. 25th Anniv of VIASA (airline). Multicoloured.

2507	3b.25 Douglas DC-9 flying over mountains	35	20
2589	3b. Type **449**	65	45
2590	3b. Douglas DC-8 in flight	65	45
2591	3b. Douglas DC-8 on ground	65	45
2592	3b. Boeing 747 flying out to sea	65	45
2593	3b. Tail fins of Douglas DC-10s	65	45
2594	3b.25 Hemispheres	75	50
2595	3b.25 Douglas DC-10 flying through cloud	75	50
2596	3b.25 Douglas DC-8 and DC-10 on ground	75	50
2598	3b.25 Manned flight deck	75	50

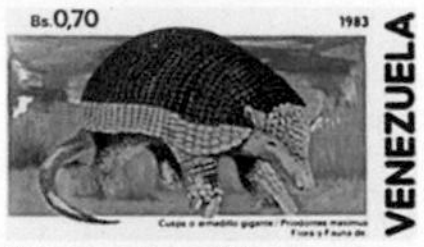

450 Giant Armadillo

1986. Flora and Fauna. Dated "1983". Multicoloured.

2599	70c. Type **450**	75	55
2600	85c. "Espeletia angustifolia"	85	75
2601	2b.70 Orinoco crocodile	90	80
2602	3b. Mountain rose	1·10	90

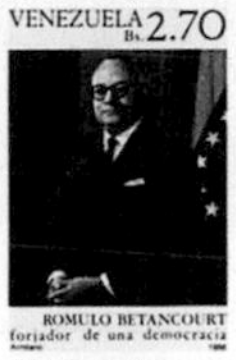

451 Romulo Betancourt

1986. Fifth Death Anniv of Romulo Betancourt (President, 1959–64). Each black, deep brown and brown.

2603	2b.70 Type **451**	55	30
2604	2b.70 Betancourt in armchair	55	30
2605	2b.70 Betancourt and inscription	55	30
2606	2b.70 Betancourt wearing sash	55	30
2607	2b.70 Betancourt working	55	30
2608	3b. As No. 2606	65	45
2609	3b. As No. 2607	65	45
2610	3b. As No. 2605	65	45
2611	3b. Type **451**	65	45
2612	3b. As No. [illegible]	65	45

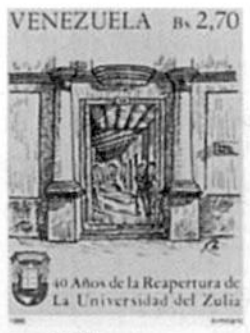

452 Library Entrance

1986. 40th Anniv of Re-opening of Zulia University. Each grey, black and blue.

2624	2b.70 Type **452**	55	45
2625	2b.70 University building	55	45

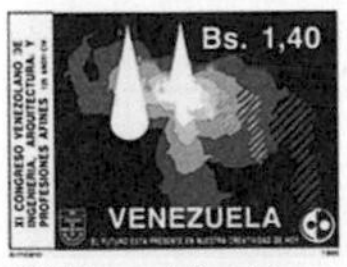

453 Map and Droplets

1986. 11th Venezuelan Engineers, Architects and Affiliated Professions Congress.

2626	453	1b.40 blue, black & yell	35	25
2627	453	1b.55 multicoloured	35	25

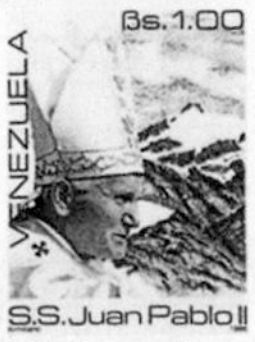

454 Pope and Andes

1986. Visit of Pope John Paul II (1985) (2nd issue). Multicoloured.

2628	1b. Type **454**	35	20
2629	1b. Pope and Maracaibo bridge	45	25
2630	3b. Pope kissing ground	65	35
2631	3b. Pope and "Virgin of Coromoto"	65	35
2632	4b. Pope holding crucifix, Caracas	1·00	40
2633	5b.25 Pope and waterfall	1·30	45

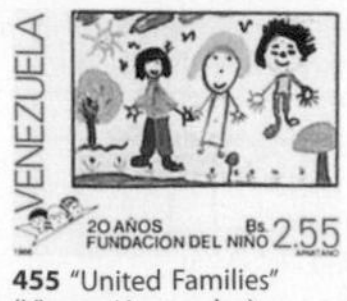

455 "United Families" (Vianny Hernandez)

1986. 20th Anniv of Childrens' Paintings. Multicoloured.

2634	2b.55 Type **455**	65	35
2635	2b.55 "Love and Peace" (Yuraima L. Jimenez)	65	35
2636	2b.55 "Woodland Animals" (Maria Valentina Arias)	65	35
2637	2b.55 "Noah's Ark" (Andreina Acero)	65	35
2638	2b.55 "House on Hillside" (Yenelsa)	65	35
2639	2b.70 "Flowers on Table" (Yenny Jimenez)	70	40
2640	2b.70 "Peace Lover" (Ramon Briceno)	70	40
2641	2b.70 "Children for World Peace" (Blanca Yesenia Hernandez)	70	40
2642	2b.70 "Lighthouse and Cable Railway" (Julio V. Hernandez)	70	40
2643	2b.70 "Flowers of a Thousand Colours" (with butterfly) (Maryolin Rodriguez Ortega)	70	40

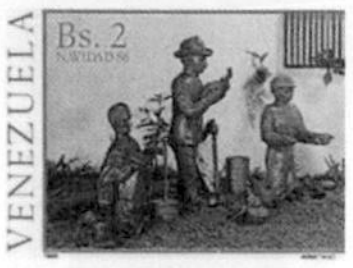

456 Three Kings

1986. Christmas. Crib figures modelled by Eliecer Alvarez. Multicoloured.

2644	2b. Type **456**	45	25
2645	2b. Nativity	45	25

Nos. 2644/5 were printed together, se-tenant, forming a composite design.

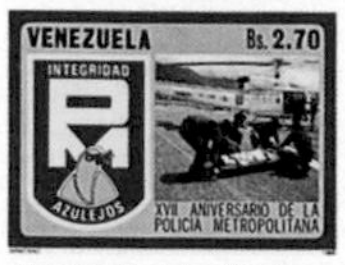

457 Treating Accident Victim

1986. 17th Anniv of Caracas City Police. Multicoloured.

2646	2b.70 Type **457**	65	25
2647	2b.70 On duty at sporting event	65	25
2648	2b.70 Computer identification bar code	65	25
2649	2b.70 Cadets on parade	65	25
2650	2b.70 Motor cycle police	65	25

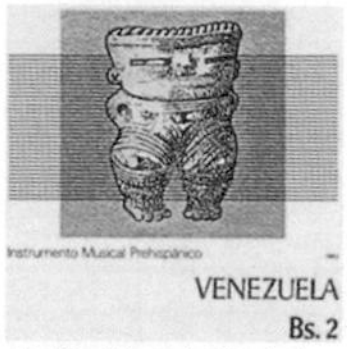

458 Prehispanic Musical Instrument

1987. Native Art. Multicoloured.

2651	2b. Type **458**	45	25
2652	2b. Woven fabric	45	25
2653	3b. Prehispanic ceramic bottle	65	35
2654	3b. Basket design	65	35

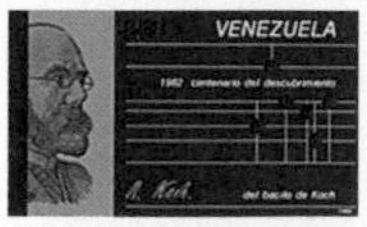

459 Robert Koch (discoverer) and Bacillus Symbol

1987. Centenary (1982) of Discovery of Tubercle Bacillus.

2655	**459**	2b.55 multicoloured	1·00	35

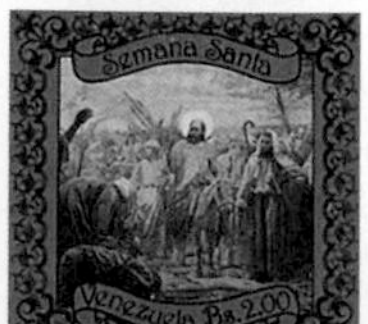

460 "Entry of Jesus into Jerusalem" (Antonio Herrera Toro)

1987. Holy Week. Multicoloured.

2656	2b. Type **460**	55	30
2657	2b. "Christ at the Pillar" (statue, Jose Francisco Rodriguez)	55	30
2658	2b. "Jesus of Nazareth" (wood carving, School of Seville)	55	30
2659	2b. "Descent from the Cross" (Jose Rivadefrecha, El Campeche)	55	30
2660	2b. "Virgin of Solitude" (sculpture)	55	30
2661	2b.25 "The Last Supper" (Arturo Michelena)	55	30
2662	2b.25 "Ecce Homo" (sculpture)	55	30
2663	2b.25 "The Crucifixion" (sculpture, Gregorio de Leon Quintana)	55	30
2664	2b.25 "Holy Sepulchre" (sculpture, Sebastian de Ochoa Montes)	55	30
2665	2b.25 "The Resurrection" (attr. Peter Paul Rubens)	55	30

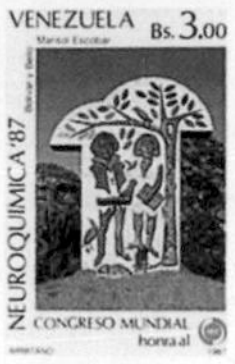

461 "Bolivar and Bello"(Marisol Escobar)

1987. World Neurochemical Congress. Multicoloured.

2666	3b. Type **461**	75	35
2667	4b.25 Retinal cells	1·10	45

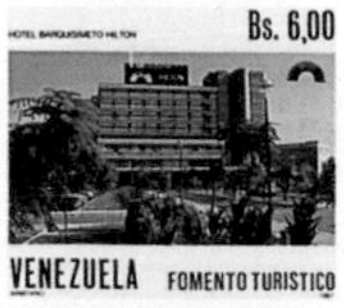

462 Barquisimeto Hilton Hotel

1987. Tourism Development. Multicoloured.

2668	6b. Type **462**	90	35
2669	6b. Lake Hotel Intercontinental, Maracaibo	90	35
2670	6b. Macuto Sheraton Hotel, Caraballeda	90	35
2671	6b. Melia Caribe Hotel, Caraballeda	90	35
2672	6b. Melia Hotel, Puerto la Cruz	90	35
2673	6b.50 Pool, Barquisimeto Hilton Hotel	90	35
2674	6b.50 Lake Hotel Intercontinental, Maracaibo, at night	90	35
2675	6b.50 Macuto Sheraton Hotel, Caraballeda, and marina	90	35
2676	6b.50 Melia Caribe Hotel, Caraballeda (different)	90	35
2677	6b.50 Melia Hotel, Puerto la Cruz (different)	90	35

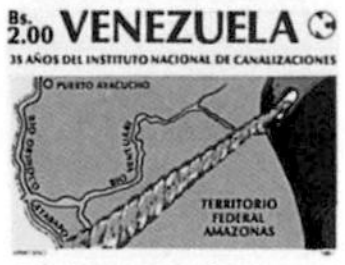

463 Amazon Federal Terrritory Map and Ship's Bow

1987. 35th Anniv of National Canals Institute. Multicoloured.

2678	2b. Type **463**	35	10
2679	4b.25 Map of River Orinoco and buoy	65	45

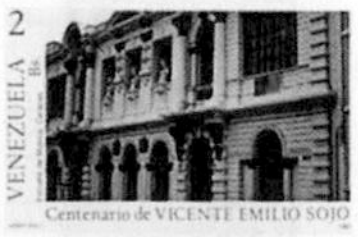

464 Music School, Caracas

1987. Birth Centenary of Vicente Emilio Sojo (composer). Each deep brown and brown.

2680	2b. Type **464**	35	10
2681	4b. Conducting choir	55	30
2682	5b. Score of "Hymn to Bolivar"	65	35
2683	6b. Standing beside blackboard	90	45
2684	7b. Sojo and signature	1·10	55

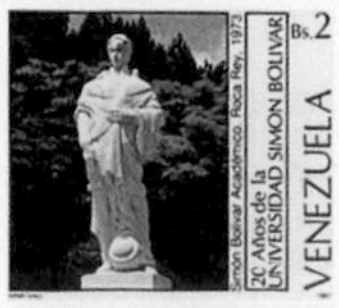

465 "Simon Bolivar, Academician" (Roca Rey)

1987. 20th Anniv of Simon Bolivar University. Multicoloured.

2685	2b. Type **465**	20	10
2686	3b. "Solar Delta" (sculpture, Alejandro Otero)	35	15
2687	4b. Rector's residence	55	30
2688	5b. Laser beam	65	35
2689	6b. Owl sculpture	75	45

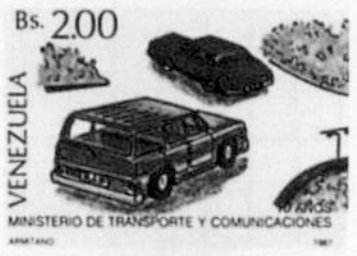

466 Motor Vehicles

1987. Tenth Anniv of Ministry of Transport and Communications. Multicoloured.

2690	2b. Type **466**	35	25
2691	2b. Bulk carrier and crane	35	25
2692	2b. Local electric train	35	25
2693	2b. Envelopes and telegraph key	35	25
2694	2b. Transmission masts and globe	35	25
2695	2b.25 Motorway interchange system	40	30
2696	2b.25 Boeing 737 airliner	40	30
2697	2b.25 Mainline diesel train	40	30
2698	2b.25 Dish aerial	40	30
2699	2b.25 Globe and communications satellite	40	30

Nos. 2690/9 were printed together, *se-tenant*, each horizontal pair forming a composite design.

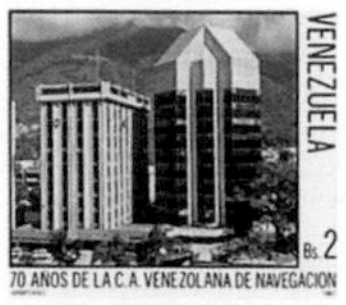

467 Administration Building, Caracas

1987. 70th Anniv of Venezuelan Navigation Company. Multicoloured.

2700	2b. Type **467**	20	10
2701	2b. Containers being loaded	20	10
2702	3b. Company emblem on ship's funnel	35	15
2703	3b. Ship's engine-room	35	15
2704	4b. "Zulia" (freighter) at sea	55	30
2705	4b. "Guarico" (freighter) off Venezuelan coast	55	30
2706	5b. "Cerro Bolivar" (bulk carrier)	65	35
2707	5b. Ship's bridge	65	35
2708	6b. Map	75	40
2709	6b. Containers being loaded onto Ro-Ro ferry	75	40

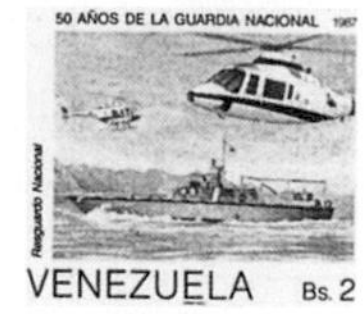

468 Air-sea Rescue

1987. 50th Anniv of National Guard. Multicoloured.

2710	2b. Type **468**	35	25
2711	2b. Traffic patrol	35	25
2712	2b. Guard on horseback	35	25
2713	2b. Guard with children	35	25
2714	2b. Armed guard on industrial site	35	25
2715	4b. As No. 2714	65	35
2716	4b. As No. 2713	65	35
2717	4b. As No. 2712	65	35
2718	4b. As No. 2711	65	35
2719	4b. Type **468**	65	35

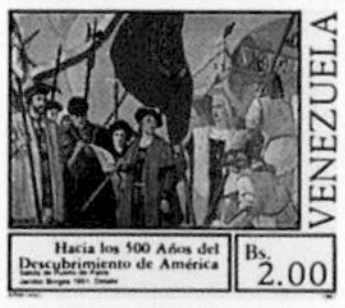

469 "Departure from Puerto Palos" (detail, Jacobo Borges)

1987. 500th Anniv (1992) of Discovery of America by Columbus. Multicoloured.

2720	2b. Type **469**	35	25
2721	7b. "Discovery of America" (Tito Salas)	1·00	45
2722	11b.50 "Fr. de las Casas, Protector of the Indians" (detail, Tito Salas)	1·80	90
2723	12b. "Trade in Venezuela during the Time of the Conquest" (detail, Tito Salas)	1·90	95
2724	12b.50 "Rout of Guaicaipuro" (Jacobo Borges)	2·00	1·00

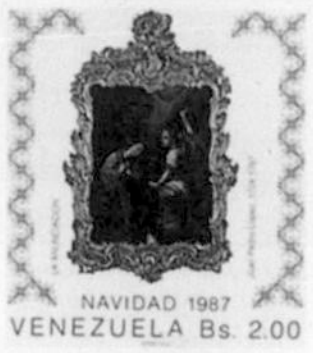

470 "Annunciation" (Juan Pedro Lopez)

1987. Christmas. Multicoloured.

2725	2b. Type **470**	35	25
2726	3b. "Nativity" (Jose Francisco Rodriguez)	45	35
2727	5b.50 "Adoration of the Kings" (anon)	90	40
2728	6b. "Flight into Egypt" (Juan Pedro Lopez)	1·00	45

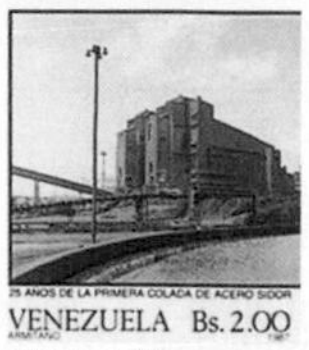

471 Steel Plant Building

1987. 25th Anniv of Steel Production by National SIDOR Mills.

2729	**471**	2b. multicoloured	35	25
2730	-	2b. multicoloured	35	25
2731	-	6b. multicoloured	1·00	45
2732	-	6b. multicoloured	1·00	45
2733	-	7b. multicoloured	1·20	55
2734	-	7b. multicoloured	1·20	55
2735	-	11b.50 multicoloured	2·00	90
2736	-	11b.50 multicoloured	2·00	90
2737	-	12b. black	2·10	1·10
2738	-	12b. multicoloured	2·10	1·10

DESIGNS: No. 2730, Rolling strip; 2731, Walkways and towers of plant; 2732, Drawing steel bars; 2733, Walkway, towers and buildings; 2734, Slab mill; 2735, Building and towers; 2736, Steel bar production; 2737, Company emblem; 2738, Anniversary emblem.

Nos. 2729/38 were printed together, *se-tenant*, Nos. 2729, 2731, 2733 and 2735 forming a composite design of the SIDOR steel plant.

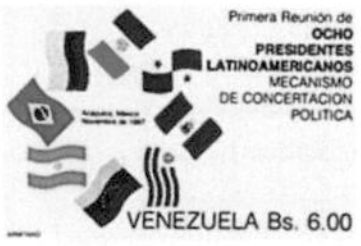

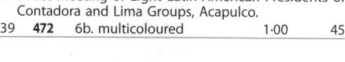

472 Flags

1987. First Meeting of Eight Latin-American Presidents of Contadora and Lima Groups, Acapulco.

2739	**472**	6b. multicoloured	1·00	45

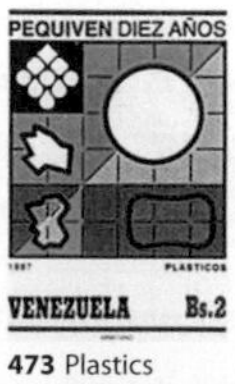

473 Plastics

1987. Tenth Anniv of Petro-Chemical Company of Venezuela. Multicoloured.

2740	2b. Type **473**	35	25
2741	6b. Formulae (oil refining)	1·00	45
2742	7b. Leaves (fertilizers)	1·20	55
2743	11b.50 Pipes (installations)	2·00	90
2744	12b. Expansion	2·10	1·10

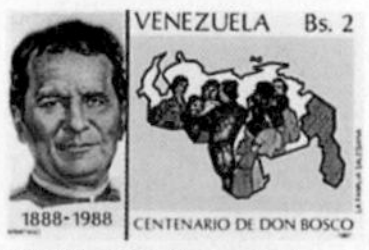

474 St. John Bosco and People on Map

1987. Birth Centenary of St. John Bosco (founder of Salesian Brothers). Multicoloured.

2745	2b. Type **474**	35	25
2746	3b. National Temple, Caracas	45	35
2747	4b. Vocational training	65	40
2748	5b. Church of Maria Auxiliadora	75	45
2749	6b. Missionary work	1·10	50

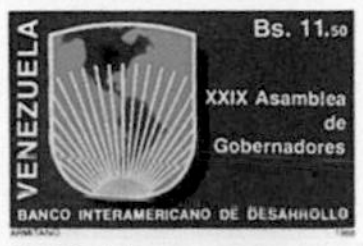

475 Emblem

1988. 29th Governors' Meeting of Inter-American Development Bank.

2750	**475**	11b.50 multicoloured	1·80	90

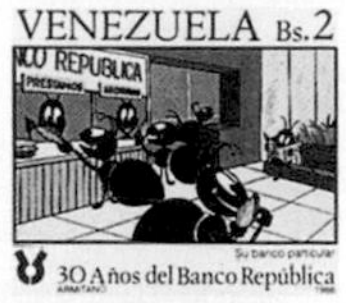

476 Bank Branch

1988. 30th Anniv of Banco Republica. Multicoloured.

2751	2b. Type **476**	35	25
2752	2b. Pottery (small business finance)	35	25
2753	2b. Factory and security guards (industrial finance)	35	25
2754	2b. Laboratory workers (technology finance)	35	25
2755	2b. Quay-side scene (exports and imports)	35	25
2756	6b. Farm workers (agricultural finance)	90	45
2757	6b. Fishing boat (fisheries finance)	90	45
2758	6b. Milk production (livestock development)	90	45
2759	6b. Building site (construction finance)	90	45
2760	6b. Tourist bus (tourism development)	90	45

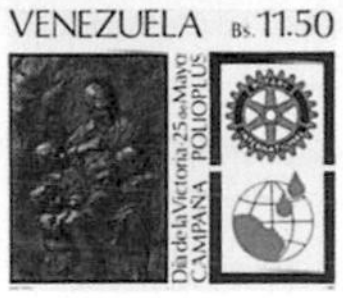

477 "Mother and Children" and Emblems

1988. Rotary International Anti-polio Campaign Victory Day.

2761	**477**	11b.50 multicoloured	1·70	80

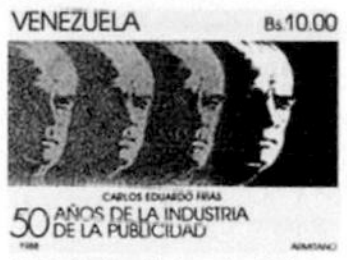

478 Carlos Eduardo Frias (publicist)

1989. 50th Anniv of Publicity Industry. Multicoloured.

2762	4b. Three profiles of Frias	55	35
2763	10b. Type **478**	1·40	80

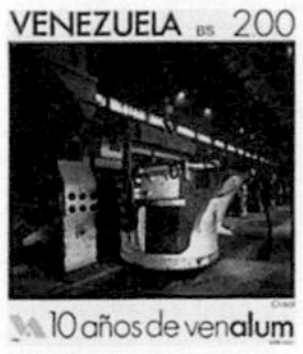

479 Smelter

1988. Tenth Anniv of Venalum (aluminium company).

2764	**479**	2b. multicoloured	35	25
2765	-	6b. black	90	45
2766	-	7b. multicoloured	1·00	50
2767	-	11b.50 multicoloured	1·70	1·00
2768	-	12b. multicoloured	1·80	1·10

DESIGNS: 6b. Plan of electrolytic cell; 7b. Aluminium pipes; 11b.50, Loading ship with aluminium for export; 12b. Workers playing football.

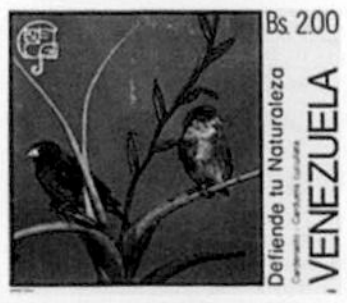

480 Red Siskins

1988. Endangered Birds. Multicoloured.

2769	2b. Type **480**	45	15
2770	6b. Scarlet ibis	1·10	35
2771	11b.50 Harpy eagle	2·00	80
2772	12b. Greater flamingoes	2·10	85
2773	12b.50 Helmeted curassow	2·20	90

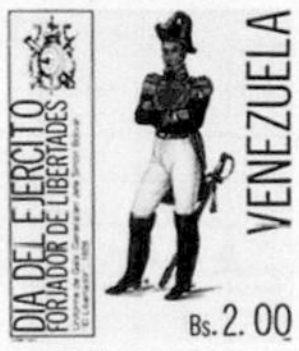

481 Bolivar in Dress Uniform, 1828

1988. Army Day. Multicoloured.

2774	2b. Type **481**	35	15
2775	2b. Lieutenant in ceremonial uniform, 1988	35	15
2776	6b. Gen. Jose Antonio Paez in dress uniform, 1821	90	35
2777	6b. Major-General in No. 1 dress, 1988	90	35
2778	7b. Major-General, 1820	1·00	45
2779	7b. Line infantryman, 1820	1·00	45
2780	11b.50 Brigadier-General, 1820	1·70	80
2781	11b.50 Garrison infantryman, 1820	1·70	80
2782	12b. Artilleryman, 1836	1·80	85
2783	12b. Light cavalryman, 1820	1·80	85

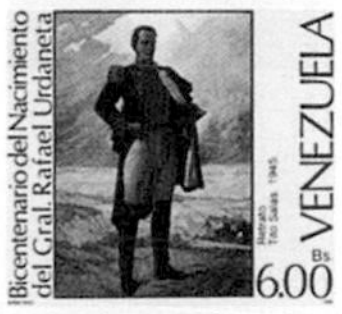

482 Urdaneta (after Salas)

1988. Birth Bicentenary of General Rafael Urdaneta. Multicoloured.

2784	2b. Sword and scabbard	35	15
2785	4b.75 "Wedding of the General" (Tito Salas)	65	35
2786	6b. Type **482**	75	40
2787	7b. "Siege of Valencia" (Tito Salas)	1·00	45
2788	12b. "Retreat from San Carlos" (Tito Salas)	1·80	80

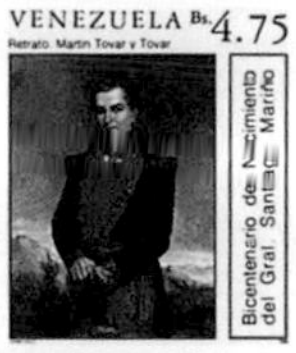

483 Marino (after Martin Tovar y Tovar)

1988. Birth Bicentenary of General Santiago Marino.

2789	**483**	4b.75 multicoloured	65	35

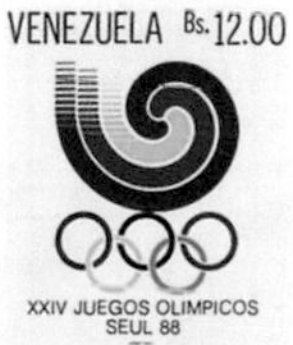

484 Games Emblem

1988. Olympic Games, Seoul.

2790	**484**	12b. multicoloured	1·70	80

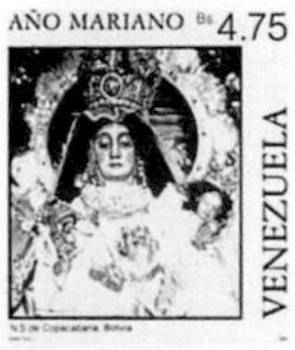

485 "Virgin of Copacabana" (Bolivia)

1988. Marian Year. Multicoloured.

2791	4b.75 Type **485**	55	35
2792	4b.75 "Virgin of Chiquinquira" (Colombia)	55	35
2793	4b.75 "Virgin of Coromoto" (Venezuela)	55	35
2794	4b.75 "Virgin of the Cloud" (Ecuador)	55	35
2795	4b.75 "Virgin of Antigua" (Panama)	55	35
2796	6b. "Virgin of Evangelisation" (Peru)	65	45
2797	6b. "Virgin of Lujan" (Argentina)	65	45
2798	6b. "Virgin of Altagracia" (Dominican Republic)	65	45
2799	6b. "Virgin of Aparecida" (Brazil)	65	45
2800	6b. "Virgin of Guadelupe" (Mexico)	65	45

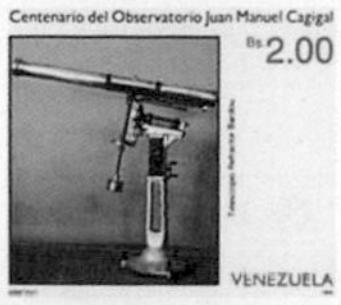

486 Bardou Refracting Telescope

1988. Centenary of Juan Manuel Cagigal Observatory. Multicoloured.

2801	2b. Type **486**	35	15
2802	4b.75 Universal "AUZ-27" theodolite	75	35
2803	6b. Bust of Cagigal	1·10	45
2804	11b.50 Boulton Cupola and night sky over Caracas in September	1·90	90
2805	12b. Satellite photographing Hurricane Allen	2·00	1·00

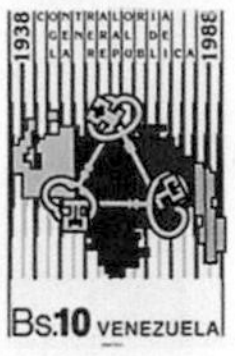

487 Keys

1988. 50th Anniv of Controller-General's Office.

2806	**487**	10b. multicoloured	1·30	70

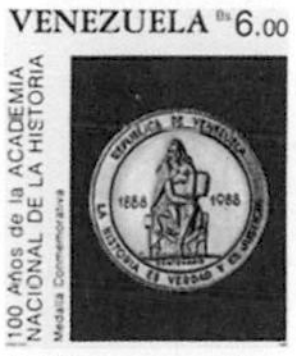

488 Commemorative Medal

1988. Cent of National Historical Museum. Multicoloured.

2807	6b. Type **488**	75	45
2808	6b.50 Juan Pablo Rojas Paul (founder) (after Cristobal Rojas)	90	50

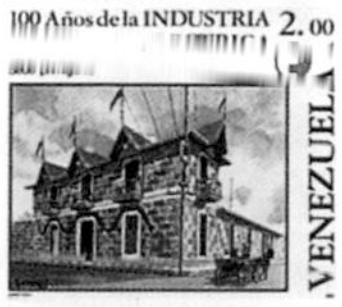

489 First Headquarters

1988. Centenary of Electricity Industry. Multicoloured.

2809	2b. Type **489**	35	15
2810	4b.75 "Electrical Plant, 1888" (Jaime Carrillo)	65	35
2811	10b. Plaza Bolivar, 1888	1·30	70
2812	11b.50 Baralt Theatre, 1888	1·50	80
2813	12b.50 Ramon Laguna Central Thermo-electricity Station	1·70	85

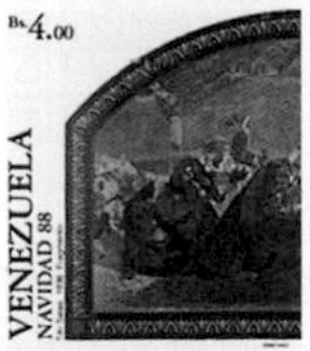

490 "Nativity" (Tito Salas, left-hand detail)

1988. Christmas. Multicoloured.

2814	4b. Type **490**	55	25
2815	6b. "Christ Child" (anonymous)	75	35
2816	15b. "Nativity" (Salas, right-hand detail)	2·10	1·00

Nos. 2814 and 2816 form a composite design.

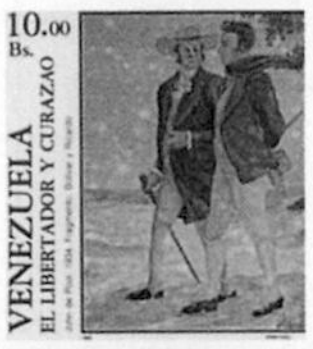

491 "Bolivar and Ricardo" (John de Pool)

1989. "The Liberator at Curacao". Multicoloured.

2817	10b. Type **491**	1·30	70
2818	10b. "The Octagon" (John de Pool)	1·30	70
2819	11b.50 "Doctor Mordechay Ricardo"	1·80	90

Nos. 2817/19 were printed together, *se-tenant*, Nos. 2817/18 forming a composite design.

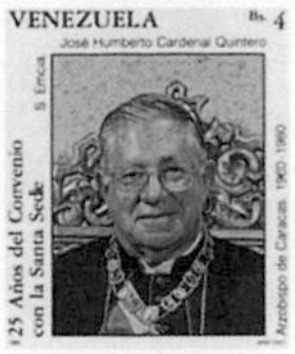

492 Cardinal Quintero (Archbishop of Caracas, 1960–80)

1989. 25th Anniv of Convention with Holy See. Multicoloured.

2820	4b. Type **492**	35	25
2821	4b. Dr. Raul Leoni (President, 1964–69)	35	25
2822	12b. Arms of Luciano Storero (Papal Nuncio)	1·50	1·00
2823	12b. Arms of Cardinal Lebrun (Archbishop of Caracas)	1·50	1·00
2824	16b. Pope Paul VI	1·90	1·50

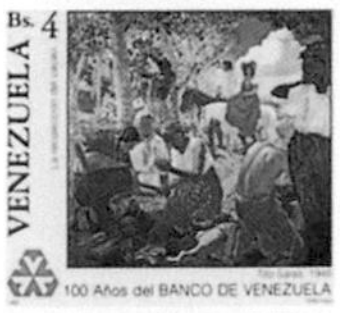

493 "Cacao Harvest" (Tito Salas)

1989. Centenary of Bank of Venezuela. Multicoloured.

2825	4b. Type **493**	55	35
2826	4b. "Teaching Sowing Time of Coffee" (Tito Salas)	55	35
2827	4b. Head Office, Caracas	55	35
2828	4b. Archive of the Liberator, Caracas	55	35
2829	4b. Tree-planting programme	55	35
2830	4b. Family planting tree	55	35
2831	8b. Left-hand side of 50b. banknote	1·10	70
2832	8b. Right-hand side of 50b. banknote	1·10	70
2833	8b. Portrait of Bolivar on left-hand side of 500b. banknote	1·10	70
2834	8b. Right-hand side of 500b. banknote	1·10	70

Nos. 2825/34 were printed together, *se-tenant*, Nos. 2831/2 and 2833/4 forming composite designs.

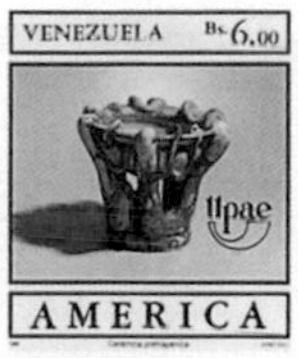

494 Dish

1989. America. Pre-Columbian Artefacts. Multicoloured.

2835	6b. Type **494**	1·10	55
2836	24b. Figure	5·50	2·75

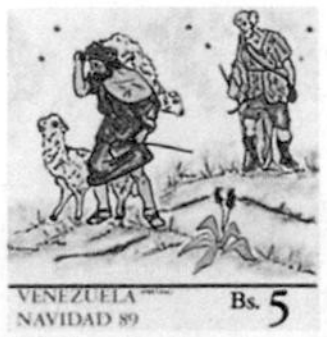

495 Shepherds and Sheep

1989. Christmas. Multicoloured.

2837	5b. As Type **495** but inscr at top	65	30
2838	5b. Type **495**	65	30
2839	6b. Angel and shepherds (inscr at top)	75	35
2840	6b. As No. 2839 but inscr at bottom	75	35
2841	6b. Nativity (inscr at top)	75	35
2842	6b. As No. 2841 but inscr at bottom	75	35
2843	12b. Shepherds (inscr at top)	1·80	90
2844	12b. As No. 2843 but inscr at bottom	1·80	90
2845	15b. Adoration of the Magi (inscr at top)	2·10	1·10
2846	15b. As No. 2845 but inscr at bottom	2·10	1·10

Nos. 2837/46 were printed together, each horizontal strip forming a composite design.

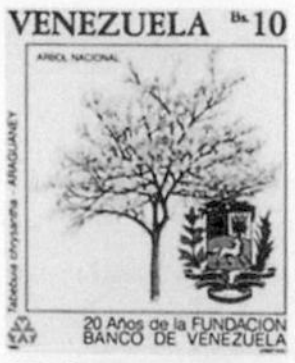

496 Araguaney Tree and State Arms

1990. 20th Anniv of Bank of Venezuela Foundation. Multicoloured.

2847	10b. Type **496**	1·10	80
2848	10b. Silk-cotton tree and Federal District arms	1·10	80
2849	10b. "Myrospermum frutescens" and Anzoategui State arms	1·10	80
2850	10b. "Pithecellobium saman" and Aragua State arms	1·10	80
2851	10b. West Indian cedar and Barinas State arms	1·10	80
2852	10b. "Dipteryx punctata" and Bolivar State arms	1·10	80
2853	10b. Pink trumpet tree and Cojedes State arms	1·10	80
2854	10b. "Prosopis juliflora" and Falcon State arms	1·10	80
2855	10b. "Copernicia tectorum" and Guarico State arms	1·10	80
2856	10b. Mountain immortelle and Merida State arms	1·10	80
2857	10b. "Brawnea leucantha" and Miranda State arms	1·10	80
2858	10b. "Mauritia flexuosa" and Monagas State arms	1·10	80
2859	10b. Mahogany and Portuguesa State arms	1·10	80
2860	10b. "Platymiscium diadelphum" and Sucre State arms	1·10	80
2861	10b. "Prumnopitys montana de Laub" and Tachira State arms	1·10	80
2862	10b. "Roystonea venezuelana" and Yaracuy State arms	1·10	80
2863	10b. Coconut palm and Zulia State arms	1·10	80
2864	10b. "Hevea benthamiana" and Amazonas Federal Territory arms	1·10	80
2865	40b. "Licania pyrofolia" and Apure State arms	3·75	2·75
2866	40b. "Malpighia glabra" and Lara State arms	3·75	2·75
2867	40b. "Erythrina fusca" and Trujillo State arms	3·75	2·75
2868	50b. "Sterculia apetala" and Carabobo State arms	4·50	3·50
2869	50b. "Lignum vitae" and Nueva Esparta State arms	4·50	3·50
2870	50b. Mangrove and Amacuro Federal Territory arms	4·50	3·50

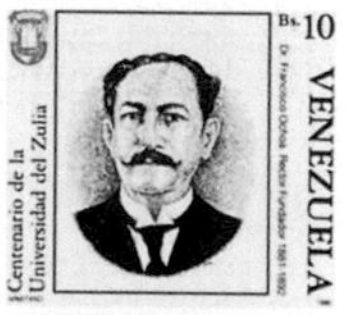

497 Dr. Francisco Ochoa (founder)

1990. Centenary of Zulia University.

2871	**497**	10b. black and blue	95	55
2872	-	10b. black and blue	95	55
2873	-	15b. multicoloured	1·40	75
2874	-	15b. multicoloured	1·40	75
2875	-	20b. multicoloured	2·00	90

DESIGNS: No. 2872, Dr. Jesus E. Lossada (Rector, 1946–47); 2873, Research into acid soils; 2874, Petroleum research; 2875, Transplant surgery.

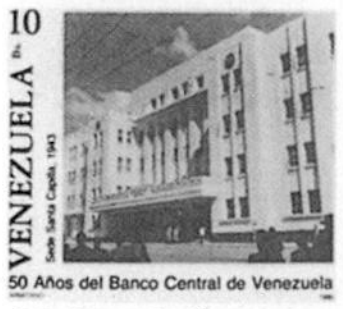

498 Santa Capilla, 1943

1990. 50th Anniv of Central Bank. Multicoloured.

2876	10b. Type **498**	1·10	55
2877	10b. Headquarters, 1967	1·10	55
2878	10b. Left half of 1940 500b. note	1·10	55
2879	10b. Right half of 1940 500b. note	1·10	55
2880	10b. "Sun of Peru" decoration, 1825	1·10	55
2881	10b. Medals	1·10	55
2882	15b. Peruvian sword, 1825	1·40	70
2883	15b. Cross, Bucaramanga, 1830	1·40	70
2884	40b. Medallion of George Washington, 1826	3·75	2·10
2885	50b. Gen. O'Leary (enamel portrait)	4·50	2·30

Nos. 2876/85 were printed together, *se-tenant*, Nos. 2878/9 forming a composite design.

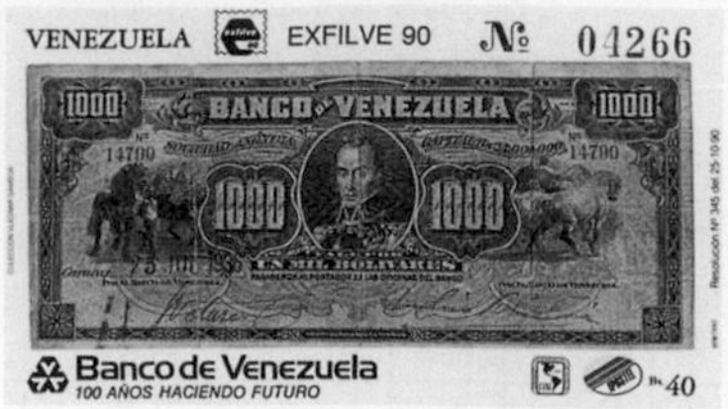

499 Bank of Venezuela 1000b. Note (image scaled to 50% of original size)

1990. Exfilve 90 National Stamp Exhibition. Bank Centenaries. Multicoloured.

MS2886 Two sheets each 100×55 mm. (a) 40b. Type **499**; (b) 50b. Bank of Caracas 100b. note 10·50 10·50

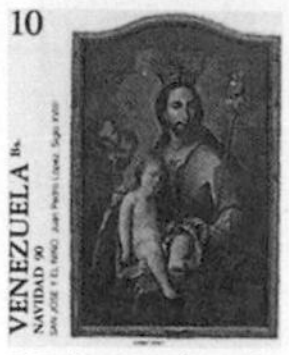

500 "St. Joseph and the Child" (Juan Pedro Lopez)

1990. Christmas. Multicoloured.

2887	10b. Type **500**	1·10	55
2888	10b. "Nativity" (Juan Pedro Lopez)	1·10	55
2889	10b. "Return from Egypt" (Matheo Moreno)	1·10	55
2890	20b. "Holy Family" (anon)	2·00	90
2891	20b. "Nativity" (Juan Pedro Lopez) (different)	2·00	90

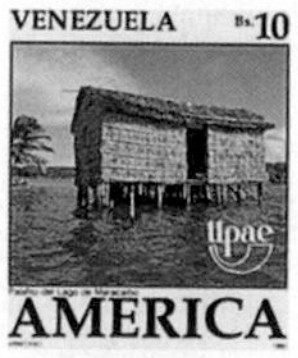

501 Lake House, Maracaibo

1990. America. The Natural World. Multicoloured.

2892	10b. Type **501**	1·10	55
2893	40b. East Venezuelan shore	3·75	2·10

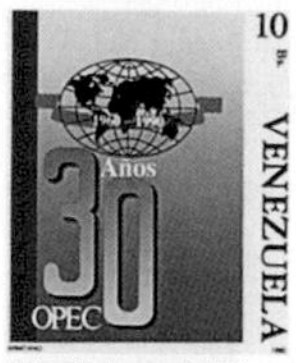

502 Globe and "30"

1990. 30th Anniv of O.P.E.C. Multicoloured.

2894	10b. Type **502**	95	55
2895	10b. O.P.E.C. emblem	95	55
2896	20b. Anniversary emblem	2·00	90
2897	30b. O.P.E.C. emblem and dates	3·00	1·40
2898	40b. Members' flags around O.P.E.C. emblem	3·75	1·90

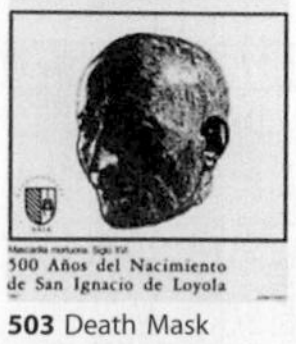

503 Death Mask

1991. 500th Birth Anniv of St. Ignatius de Loyola (founder of Society of Jesus). Multicoloured.

2899	12b. Type **503**	1·10	55
2900	12b. St. Ignatius de Loyola College, Caracas	1·10	55
2901	40b. Silver statue of Loyola by Francisco de Vergara	3·75	1·70
2902	50b. "Our Lady of Montserrat" (wooden statue)	4·50	1·90

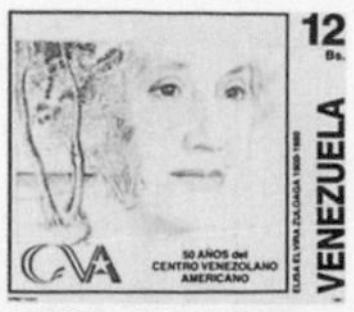

504 Elisa Elvira Zuloaga (painter and engraver)

1991. 50th Anniv of American–Venezuelan Cultural Centre. Designs showing Centre directors.

2903	**504**	12b. green and black	1·10	55
2904	-	12b. violet and black	1·10	55
2905	-	12b. red and black	1·10	55
2906	-	40b. blue and black	3·75	1·80
2907	-	50b. brown and black	4·25	1·90

DESIGNS: No. 2904, Gloria Stolk (writer); 2905, Caroline Lloyd (composer); 2906, Jules Waldman (linguist and journalist); 2907, William Coles (entrepreneur).

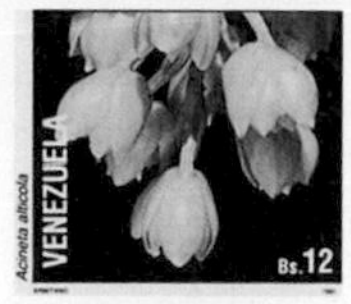

505 "Acineta alticola"

1991. Orchids. Multicoloured.

2908	12b. Type **505**	1·10	55
2909	12b. "Brassavola nodosa"	1·10	55
2910	12b. "Brachionidium brevicaudatum"	1·10	55
2911	12b. "Bifrenaria maguirei"	1·10	55
2912	12b. "Odontoglossum spectatissimum"	1·10	55
2913	12b. "Catasetum macrocarpum"	1·10	65
2914	40b. "Mendocella jorisiana"	3·50	2·00
2915	40b. "Cochleanthes discolor"	3·50	2·00
2916	50b. "Maxillaria splendens"	4·75	2·75
2917	50b. "Pleurothallis dunstervillei"	4·75	2·75

MS2918 93×100 mm. 50b. "Cattleya violacea" (41×36 mm) 11·50 11·50

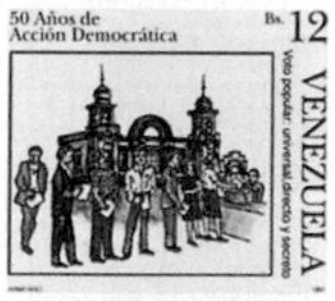

506 Voters at Ballot Box

1991. 50th Anniv of Democratic Action Party.

2919	**506**	12b. multicoloured	1·10	65
2920	-	12b. multicoloured	1·10	65
2921	-	12b. multicoloured	1·10	65
2922	-	12b. black and blue	1·10	65

DESIGNS: No. 2920, Agrarian reform; 2921, Education; 2922, Nationalization of petroleum industry.

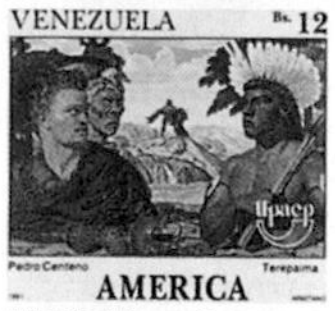

507 Rodrigues Suarez and Terepaima Chieftain

1991. America. Voyages of Discovery. Showing paintings by Pedro Centeno. Multicoloured.

2923	12b. Type **507**	1·10	65
2924	40b. Paramaconi chieftain and Garcia Gonzalez	4·00	2·40

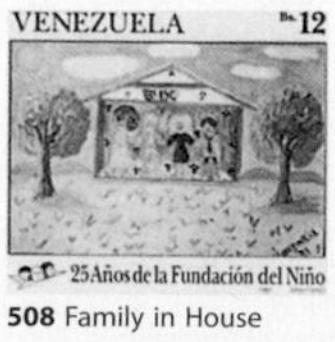

508 Family in House

1991. 25th Anniv of Children's Foundation. Multicoloured.

2925	12b. Type **508**	85	50
2926	12b. Children's playground	85	50
2927	12b. Fairground	85	50
2928	12b. Mother and daughter	85	50
2929	12b. Boy in hospital	85	50
2930	12b. Children and tree	85	50
2931	40b. Girls at home	2·75	1·70
2932	40b. Children in classroom	2·75	1·70
2933	50b. Children acting in play	3·50	2·20
2934	50b. Children playing ring-a-ring of roses	3·50	2·20

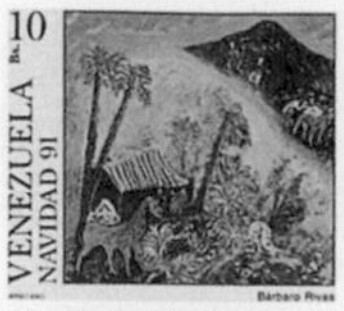

509 "Stable" (Barbaro Rivas)

1991. Christmas. Multicoloured.

2935	10b. Type **509**	70	55
2936	12b. "Nativity" (Elsa Morales)	85	70
2937	20b. "Nativity" (model, Glenda Mendoza)	1·40	1·10
2938	25b. "Shepherds watching flock (Maritza Marin)	1·70	1·40
2939	30b. "Nativity" (Antonia Azuaje)	2·10	1·70

1991. Nos. 2613/15 surch **RESELLADO** and value.

2940	**347**	5b. on 25c. red	45	25
2941	**347**	5b. on 75c. mauve	45	25
2942	**347**	10b. on 25c. red	85	35
2943	**347**	10b. on 75c. mauve	85	35
2944	**347**	12b. on 50c. blue	1·10	45
2945	**347**	12b. on 75c. mauve	1·10	45
2946	**347**	20b. on 50c. blue	1·80	70
2947	**347**	20b. on 75c. mauve	1·80	70
2948	**347**	40b. on 50c. blue	3·75	1·50
2949	**347**	40b. on 75c. mauve	3·75	1·50
2950	**347**	50b. on 50c. blue	4·50	1·80
2951	**347**	50b. on 75c. mauve	4·50	1·80

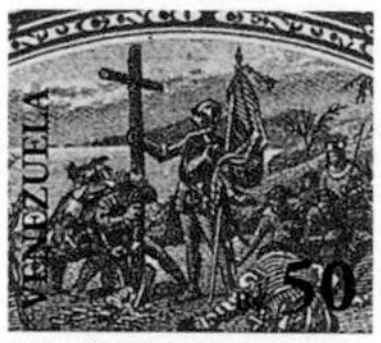

511 1893 Columbus 25c. Stamp

1991. "Exfilve 91" National Stamp Exhibition. Sheet 91×76 mm.

MS2952 **511** 50b. lilac, cream and black 5·00 5·00

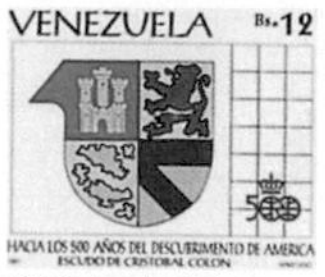

512 Columbus's Arms

1991. 500th Anniv (1992) of Discovery of America by Columbus.

2953	**512**	12b. multicoloured	70	55
2954	-	12b. black, blue & orange	70	55
2955	-	12b. multicoloured	70	55
2956	-	40b. black, brown & orge	2·30	1·80
2957	-	50b. black and orange	2·75	2·30

DESIGNS: No. 2954, "Santa Maria"; 2955, Juan de la Cosa's map; 2956, Sighting land; 2957, Columbus before King Ferdinand and Queen Isabella the Catholic.

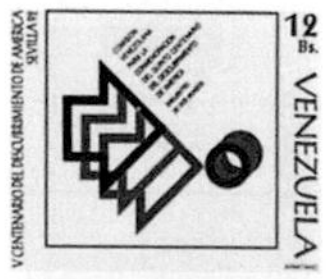

513 Anniversary Emblem

1992. "Expo 92" World's Fair, Seville. 500th Anniv of Discovery of America by Columbus.

2958	**513**	12b. black, red and blue	55	45
2959	-	12b. multicoloured	55	45
2960	-	12b. multicoloured	55	45
2961	-	12b. multicoloured	55	45
2962	-	12b. multicoloured	55	45
2963	-	12b. multicoloured	55	45
2964	-	40b. multicoloured	2·00	1·60
2965	-	40b. multicoloured	2·00	1·60
2966	-	50b. multicoloured	2·40	1·90
2967	-	50b. black and brown	2·40	1·90

MS2968 85×99 mm. 50b. multicoloured 5·00 5·00

DESIGNS: No. 2959, Venezuelan pavilion at "Expo 92"; 2960, Landmarks and map of southern Spain; 2961, Columbus; 2962, "Encounters"; 2963, "0x500 America"; 2964, "Imago-Mundi"; 2965, "The Grand Voyage"; 2966, "Golden Beach"; 2967, Idols; **MS**2968, "Untitled" (Muaricio Sanchez).

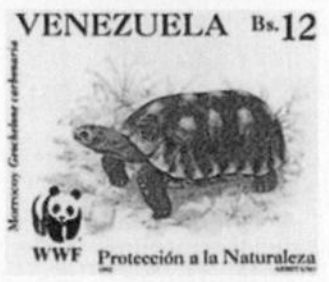

514 Red-footed Tortoise

1992. Tortoises. Multicoloured.

2969	12b. Type **514**	2·10	1·70
2970	12b. "Red-footed tortoise ("Geochelone carbonaria") (different)	2·10	1·70
2971	12b. South American river turtle ("Podocnemis expansa") (on land)	2·10	1·70
2972	12b. South American river turtle (swimming)	2·10	1·70

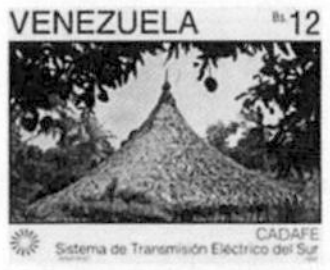

515 Native Hut

1992. Electricity Distribution in the South.

2973	**515**	12b. multicoloured	55	45
2974	-	12b. black and blue	55	45
2975	-	12b. multicoloured	55	45
2976	-	40b. multicoloured	1·80	1·50
2977	-	50b. multicoloured	2·30	1·80

DESIGNS: No. 2974, Pylons; 2975, Horses galloping through water; 2976, Engineers working on pylon; 2977, Traditional baskets beside lake.

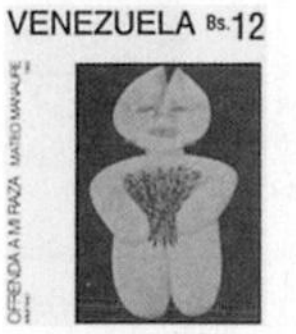

516 Figure holding Sheaf of Wheat

1992. "Offering to My Race" (Mateo Manaure). Designs showing various "mother" figures. Multicoloured.

2978	12b. Type **516**	55	45
2979	12b. Orange figure	55	45
2980	12b. Yellow figure	55	45
2981	12b. Pink figure	55	45
2982	40b. Brown figure	2·00	1·60
2983	40b. Purple and orange figures	2·00	1·60
2984	50b. Three-quarter length figure	2·40	1·90
2985	50b. Head and shoulders	2·40	1·90

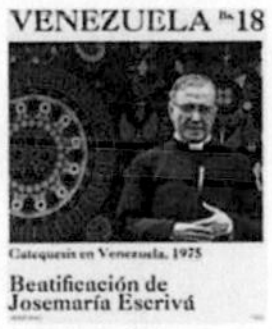

517 Catechism in Venezuela, 1975

1992. Beatification of Josemaria Escriva (founder of Opus Dei).

2986	**517**	18b. multicoloured	1·00	80
2987	-	18b. multicoloured	1·00	80
2988	-	18b. multicoloired	1·00	80
2989	-	18b. black and yellow	1·00	80
2990	-	18b. multicoloured	1·00	80
2991	-	18b. multicoloured	1·00	80
2992	-	60b. multicoloured	3·50	2·50
2993	-	60b. multicoloured	3·50	2·50
2994	-	75b. multicoloured	4·50	3·25
2995	-	75b. multicoloured	4·50	3·25

DESIGNS: No. 2987, Celebrating mass; 2988, Jose Escriva and Dolores Albas (parents); 2989, Text and autograph; 2990, With statuette of Madonna and Child; 2991, Commemorative medal; 2992, With Pope Paul VI, 1964; 2993, Writing at desk; Portrait; 2995, Portrait in St. Peter's Square, 17 May 1992.

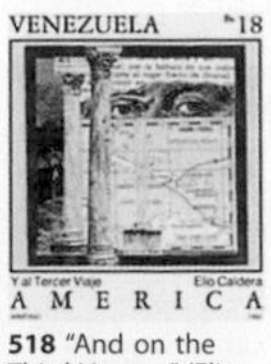

518 "And on the Third Voyage" (Elio Caldera)

1992. America. 500th Anniv of Discovery of America by Columbus. Multicoloured.

2996	18b. Type **518**	1·10	90
2997	60b. "Descontextura" (Juan Pablo Nascimiento)	3·50	2·75

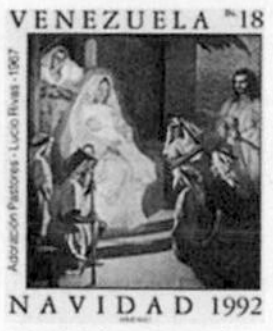

519 "Adoration of the Shepherds"

1992. Christmas. Paintings by Lucio Rivas. Multicoloured.

2998	18b. Type **519**	1·10	90
2999	75b. "Adoration of the Magi"	3·50	2·75
MS3000	86×93 mm. 100b. "Flight into Egypt" (41×36 mm)	6·50	6·50

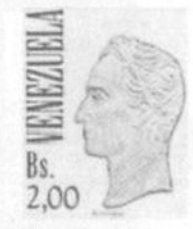

520 Simon Bolivar

1993. Portraits and Monuments.

3001	**520**	1b. silver	30	25
3002	**520**	2b. blue	35	30
3005	-	5b. red	45	35
3006	-	10b. purple	55	45
3007	-	20b. green	1·00	80
3008	-	25b. orange	1·30	1·00
3009	-	35b. green	1·40	1·10
3010	-	40b. blue	1·60	1·30
3011	-	50b. orange	2·75	1·50
3012	-	50b. mauve	2·10	1·70
3013	-	100b. brown	5·75	2·75
3014	-	100b. blue	3·75	3·00
3015	-	200b. orange	7·75	6·25

DESIGNS: 5b. National Pantheon, Caracas; 10b. War of Independence Memorial, Carabobo; 20b. General Jose Antonio de Paez (President, 1830–35, 1837–43 and 1861–63); 25b. Luisa Caceres de Arismendi; 35b. General Ezequiel Zamora (politician); 40b. Cristobal Mendoza (jurist and provincial governor); 50b. (3011) National Library; 50b. (3012) Jose Felix, Ribas (independence fighter); 100b. (3013), 200. Bolivar (different); 100b. (3014) General Manuel Piar.

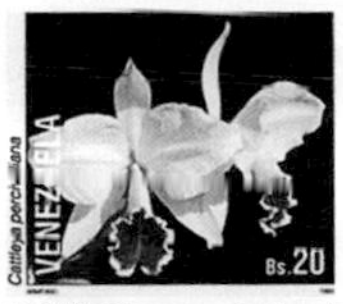

521 "Cattleya percivaliana"

1993. Orchids. Multicoloured.

3016	20b. Type **521**	70	55
3017	20b. "Anguloa ruckeri"	70	55
3018	20b. "Chondrorhyncha flaveola"	70	55
3019	20b. "Stenia pallida"	70	55
3020	20b. "Zygosepalum lindeniae"	70	55
3021	20b. "Maxillaria triloris"	70	55
3022	80b. "Stanhopea wardii"	2·40	1·90
3023	80b. "Oncidium papilio"	2·40	1·90
3024	100b. "Oncidium hastilabium"	2·75	2·30
3025	100b. "Sobralia cattleya"	2·75	2·30
MS3026	93×100 mm. 150b. "Polycycnis muscifera" (41×36 mm)	11·50	11·50

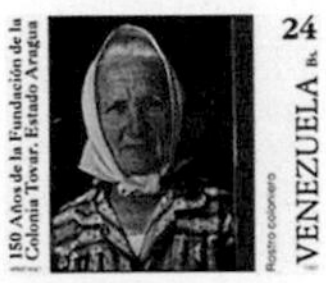

522 Woman

1993. 150th Anniv of Tovar Colony, Aragua State. Multicoloured.

3027	24b. Type **522**	70	55
3028	24b. Children	70	55
3029	24b. Catholic church	70	55
3030	24b. St. Martin of Tours (patron saint)	70	55
3031	24b. Vegetables and fruit	70	55
3032	24b. School	70	55
3033	80b. House of Augustin Codazzi (founder)	2·40	1·90
3034	80b. House of Alexander Benitz	2·40	1·90
3035	100b. Breidenbach mill	2·75	2·30
3036	100b. Procession of Jokili (carnival group)	2·75	2·30

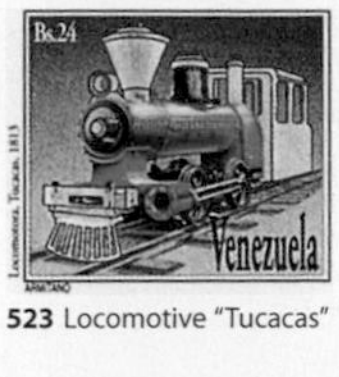

523 Locomotive "Tucacas"

1993. 19th Pan-American Railways Congress. Multicoloured.

3037	24b. Type **523**	85	70
3038	24b. Locomotive "Halcon" heading "El Encanto" on Las Mostazas bridge	85	70
3039	24b. Locomotive "Maracaibo"	85	70
3040	24b. Tender and carriages in Palo Grande station	85	70
3041	24b. Fiat diesel railcar, 1957	85	70
3042	24b. GP-9-L diesel locomotive, 1957	85	70
3043	80b. GP-15-L diesel locomotive, 1982	2·50	2·10
3044	80b. Underground train, Caracas	2·50	2·10
3045	100b. Electric multiple unit set (left half)	3·50	2·75
3046	100b. Electric multiple unit set (right half)	3·50	2·75

Nos. 3037/46 were issued together, *se-tenant*, Nos. 3039/40 and 3043/4 forming composite designs.

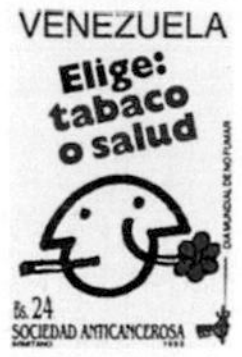

524 Smoker and Non-Smoker

1993. World No Smoking Day. Each black, blue and red.

3047	24b. Type **524**	70	55
3048	80b. No smoking sign	2·40	1·90

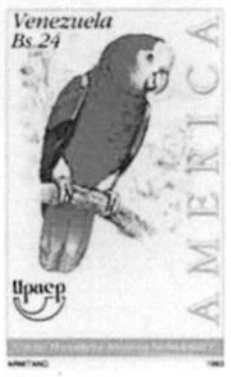

525 Yellow-shouldered Amazon

1993. America. Endangered Animals. Multicoloured.

3049	24b. Type **525**	85	70
3050	80b. Scarlet macaw	3·50	2·75

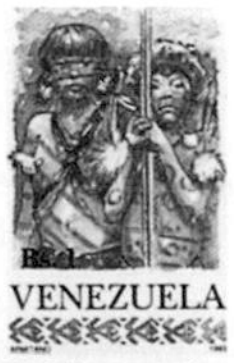

526 Yanomami Boys

1993. Amerindians (1st series). Multicoloured.

3051	1b. Type **526**	30	10
3052	1b. Yanomami woman preparing casabe	30	10
3053	40b. Panare children in Katyay-into ceremony	1·60	1·30
3054	40b. Taurepan man paddling canoe	1·60	1·30
3055	40b. Piaroa mother holding child	1·60	1·30
3056	40b. Panare man playing nose flute	1·60	1·30
3057	40b. Taurepan woman weaving	1·60	1·30
3058	40b. Masked Piaroa dancers in Warime ceremony	1·60	1·30
3059	100b. Hoti man with blowpipe	4·00	3·25
3060	100b. Hoti woman carrying child and fruit	4·00	3·25
MS3061	101×90 mm. 150b. Panare child with pan-pipes	7·00	7·00

See also No. 3170/**MS**3180, 3266/**MS**76, 3392/**MS**3402 and 3568/**MS**78.

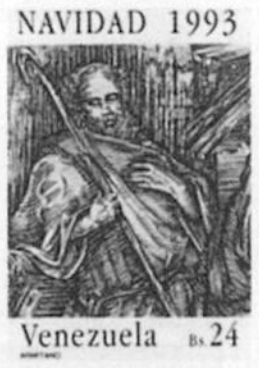

527 Joseph

1993. Christmas. (a) Each cream, brown and black.

3062	24b. Type **527**	1·00	80
3063	24b. Madonna and Child	1·00	80
3064	24b. Shepherd girl, wise man and sheep	1·00	80
3065	80b. Wise man and shepherd girl	3·00	2·50
3066	100b. Wise man and shepherd girl	4·25	3·50

(b) Each cream, purple and black.

3067	24b. Type **527**	1·00	80
3068	24b. As No. 3063	1·00	80
3069	24b. As No. 3064	1·00	80
3070	80b. As No. 3065	3·00	2·50
3071	100b. As No. 3066	4·25	3·50

Nos. 3062/71 were issued together, *se-tenant*, each horizontal strip forming a composite design of the Nativity.

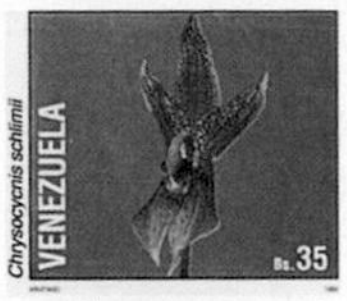

528 "Chrysocycnis schlimii"

1994. Orchids. Multicoloured.

3072	35b. Type **528**	1·30	1·00
3073	35b. "Galeandra minax"	1·30	1·00
3074	35b. "Oncidium falcipetalum"	1·30	1·00
3075	35b. "Oncidium lanceanum"	1·30	1·00
3076	40b. "Sobralia violacea"	1·40	1·10
3077	40b. "Sobralia infundibuligera"	1·40	1·10
3078	80b. "Mendoncella burkei"	2·75	2·30
3079	80b. "Phragmipedium caudatum"	2·75	2·30
3080	100b. "Phragmipedium kaieteurum"	5·75	4·50
3081	200b. "Stanhopea grandiflora"	7·00	5·75
MS3082	96×100 mm. 150b. "Epidendrum elongatum" (41×36 mm)	6·50	6·50

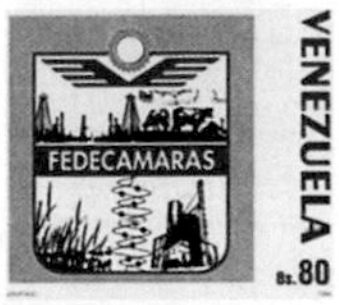

529 Federation Emblem

1994. 50th Anniv of Federation of Chambers of Industry and Commerce.

3083	-	35b. blue, gold and black	1·30	1·00
3084	-	35b. black and brown	1·30	1·00
3085	**529**	35b. blue and black	1·30	1·00
3086	**529**	80b. blue and black	3·00	2·50
3087	-	80b. black, brown and blue	3·00	2·50
3088	-	80b. blue, gold and black	3·00	2·50

DESIGNS: Nos. 3083, 3088, "50" on text; 3084, 3087, Luis Gonzalo Marturet (first Federation President).

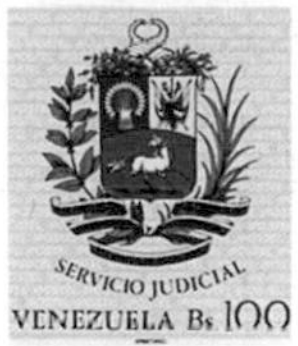

530 State Arms

1994. Judicial Service.

3089	**530**	100b. multicoloured	3·25	2·75

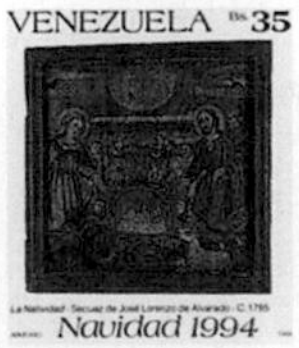

531 "Nativity" (School of Jose Lorenzo de Alvarado)

1994. Christmas. Multicoloured.

3090	35b. Type **531**	1·30	1·00
3091	35b. "Nativity"	1·30	1·00
3092	35b. "Nativity" (School of Jose Lorenzo de Alvarado)	1·30	1·00
3093	35b. Holy Family (inscr "Adoracion de los Pastores")	1·30	1·00
3094	35b. "Nativity" (School of Tocuyo)	1·30	1·00
3095	80b. As No. 3094	3·00	2·50
3096	80b. Type **531**	3·00	2·50
3097	80b. As No. 3091	3·00	2·50
3098	80b. As No. 3092	3·00	2·50
3099	80b. As No. 3093 but inscr "El Nacimiento"	3·00	2·50

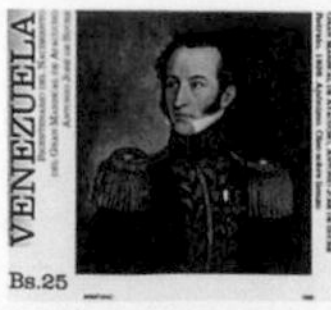

532 Sucre (anonymous portrait)

1995. Birth Bicentenary of Antonio Jose de Sucre (President of Bolivia, 1825–29). Multicoloured.

3100	25b. Type **532**	1·00	80
3101	25b. Mariana Carcelen y Larrea, Marquesa de Solanda (Sucre's wife) (after Juan Pinto Ortiz)	1·00	80
3102	35b. Equestrian statue of Sucre (Turini Verana), Cumana	1·30	1·00
3103	35b. Base of statue	1·30	1·00
3104	40b. "Battle of Pichincha" (top detail) (Victor Mideros Almeida)	1·60	1·30
3105	40b. "Battle of Pichincha" (bottom detail)	1·60	1·30
3106	80b. "Battle of Ayacucho" (left detail) (Antonio Herrera Toro)	3·00	2·50
3107	80b. "Battle of Ayacucho" (right detail)	3·00	2·50
3108	100b. "Capitulation of Ayacucho" (left detail) (Daniel Hernandez)	3·75	3·00
3109	100b. "Capitulation of Ayacucho" (right detail)	3·75	3·00
MS3110	206×119 mm. 150b. "Venezuela" (detail of mural by Pedro Centeno Vallenilla in Carabobo Hall of Honour, Caracas) (41×37 mm)	5·75	5·75

Nos. 3100/9 were issued together, *se-tenant*, the 35, 40, 80 and 100b. values forming four composite designs.

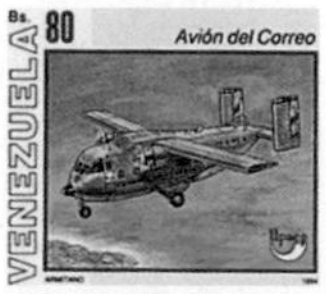

533 Short S.7 Skyvan Mail Plane

1995. America (1994). Postal Transport. Multicoloured.

3111	35b. Mobile post office	1·00	80
3112	80b. Type **533**	2·40	1·90

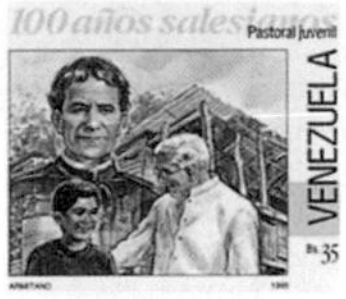

534 St. John Bosco (founder) and Boy with Salesian

1995. Centenary of Salesian Brothers in Venezuela. Multicoloured.

3113	35b. Type **534**	1·00	80
3114	35b. Boy sitting in street and Virgin and Child	1·00	80
3115	35b. Men working machinery	1·00	80
3116	35b. Youths working on radio	1·00	80
3117	35b. Boys playing baseball	1·00	80
3118	35b. Youths playing basketball	1·00	80
3119	80b. Men planting saplings	2·40	1·90
3120	80b. Youth and boxes of produce	2·40	1·90
3121	100b. Salesian and Amerindian boys	3·00	2·50
3122	100b. Amerindian youth	3·00	2·50

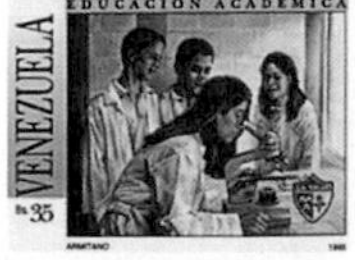

535 Laboratory Technicians

1995. 50th Anniv of Christian Brothers' La Colina School, Caracas. Multicoloured.

3123	35b. As T **535** but country inscr at right	1·00	80
3124	35b. Young people camping (country inscr at left)	1·00	80
3125	35b. Youths playing football (country inscr at right)	1·00	80
3126	35b. Type **535**	1·00	80
3127	35b. As No. 3124 but country inscr at right	1·00	80
3128	35b. As No. 3125 but country inscr at left	1·00	80
3129	80b. School building (country inscr at left)	2·40	1·90
3130	80b. As No. 3129 but country inscr at right	2·40	1·90
3131	100b. Jean Baptiste de la Salle (founder of Order) (country inscr at right)	3·00	2·50
3132	100b. As No. 3131 but country inscr at left	3·00	2·50

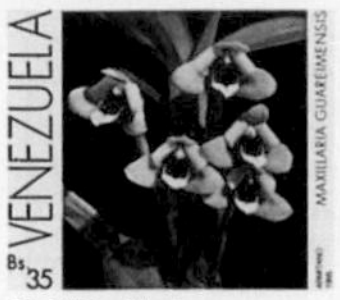

536 "Maxillaria guareimensis"

1995. Orchids. Multicoloured.

3133	35b. Type **536**	1·00	80
3134	35b. "Paphinia lindeniana"	1·00	80
3135	35b. "Coryanthes biflora"	1·00	80
3136	35b. "Catasetum pileatum"	1·00	80
3137	35b. "Mormodes convolutum"	1·00	80
3138	35b. "Huntleya lucida"	1·00	80
3139	50b. "Catasetum longifolium"	1·70	1·40
3140	50b. "Anguloa clowesii"	1·70	1·40
3141	80b. "Maxillaria histrionica"	2·40	1·90
3142	80b. "Sobralia ruckeri"	2·40	1·90
MS3143	133×124 mm. 150b. "Catasetum barbatum" (41×36 mm)	5·00	5·00

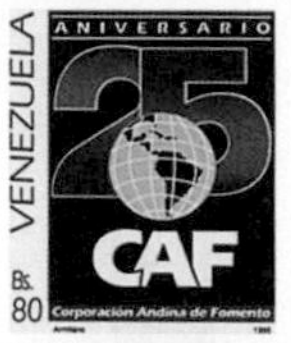

537 Anniversary Emblem

1995. 25th Anniv of Andean Pact (international co-operation group).

3144	**537** 80b. multicoloured	2·40	1·90

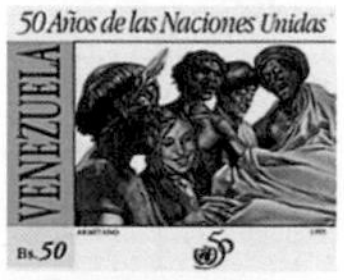

538 People of Different Races

1995. 50th Anniv of U.N.O. Multicoloured.

3145	50b. Type **538**	1·60	1·30
3146	50b. U.N. flag	1·60	1·30

Nos. 3145/6 were issued together, *se-tenant*, forming a composite design.

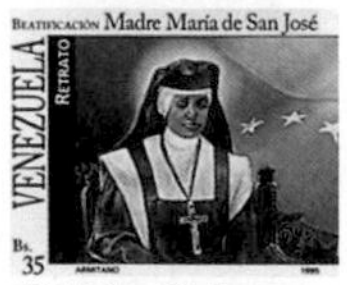

539 Mother Maria

1995. Beatification of Mother Maria de San Jose. Multicoloured.

3147	35b. Type **539**	1·00	80
3148	35b. Pope John Paul II	1·00	80
3149	35b. Handing out books to girls	1·00	80
3150	35b. Embroidering	1·00	80
3151	35b. Statue of Virgin Mary and altar	1·00	80
3152	35b. Mother Maria in prayer before altar	1·00	80
3153	80b. Mother Maria and three nuns in hospital ward	2·40	1·90
3154	80b. Nun beside hospital beds	2·40	1·90
3155	100b. Nuns with poor children	3·00	2·50
3156	100b. Nun giving alms to beggar	3·00	2·50

Nos. 3147/56 were issued together, *se-tenant*, each horizontal pair forming a composite design.

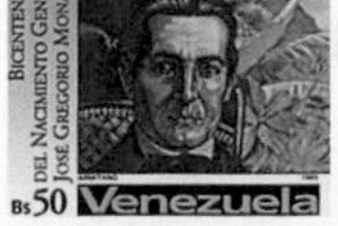

540 Monagas

1995. Birth Bicentenary of Jose Gregorio Monagas (anti-slavery campaigner and President 1851–55). Multicoloured.

3157	50b. Type **540**	1·40	1·10
3158	50b. Freed slaves	1·40	1·10

Nos. 3157/8 were issued together, *se-tenant*, forming a composite design.

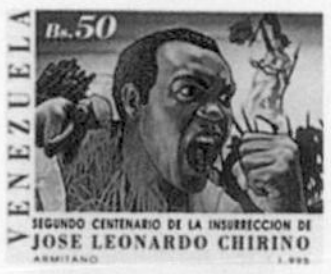

541 Chirino

1995. Bicentenary of Jose Chirino's Insurrection. Multicoloured.

3159	50b. Type **541**	1·40	1·10
3160	50b. Insurrectionists	1·40	1·10

Nos. 3159/60 were issued together, *se-tenant*, forming a composite design.

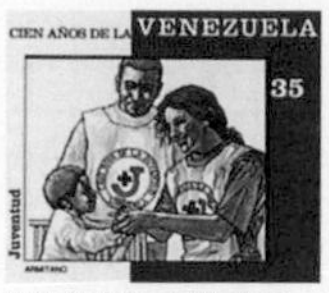

542 Red Cross Workers and Child

1995. Centenary of Venezuelan Red Cross. Multicoloured.

3161	35b. Type **542**	1·00	80
3162	35b. Volunteers carrying injured man on stretcher	1·00	80
3163	35b. Operating theatre	1·00	80
3164	80b. Carlos J. Bello Hospital	2·40	1·90
3165	100b. Red Cross flag	2·75	2·30

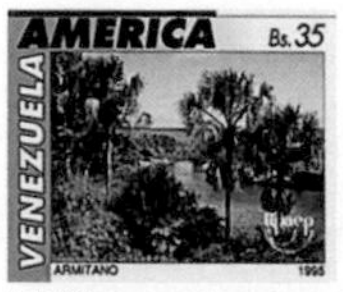

543 River

1995. America. Environmental Protection. Multicoloured.

(a) With thin frame line over face value.

3166	35b. Type **543**	1·00	80
3167	80b. Hillside	2·30	1·80

(b) Without thin frame line over face value.

3168	35b. Type **543**	1·00	80
3169	80b. As No. 3167	2·30	1·80

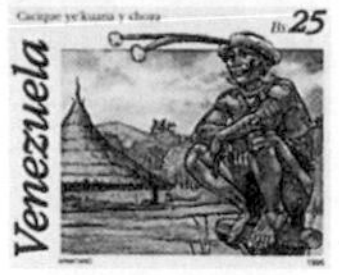

544 Ye'kuana Chief

1995. Amerindians (2nd series). Multicoloured.

3170	25b. Type **544**	70	55
3171	25b. Ye'kuana woman making manioc cake	70	55
3172	35b. Guahibo musicians	1·00	80
3173	35b. Guahibo shaman treating boy	1·00	80
3174	50b. Uruak fisherman	1·40	1·10
3175	50b. Uruak woman cooking	1·40	1·10
3176	80b. Warao woman making thread	2·30	1·80
3177	80b. Warao couple transporting belongings in sailing canoe	2·30	1·80
3178	100b. Bari men hunting	2·75	2·30
3179	100b. Bari man making fire	2·75	2·30
MS3180	151×126 mm. 150b. Boy with macaw on shoulder (41×36 mm)	5·75	5·75

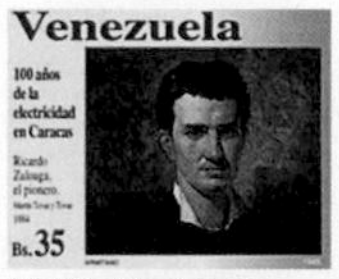

545 Ricardo Zuloaga (pioneer)

1995. Centenary of Electricity in Caracas. Multicoloured.

3181	35b. Type **545**	1·00	80
3182	35b. El Encantado Plant	1·00	80
3183	35b. Caracas sub-station	1·00	80
3184	35b. Electric tram	1·00	80
3185	35b. Streetlamps outside Congress building	1·00	80
3186	35b. Streetlamps, Plaza Bolivar	1·00	80
3187	80b. Engineer repairing streetlamp	2·40	1·90
3188	80b. Avila Cross	2·40	1·90
3189	100b. Teresa Carreno Cultural Centre	3·00	2·50
3190	100b. Ricardo Zuloaga power station	3·00	2·50

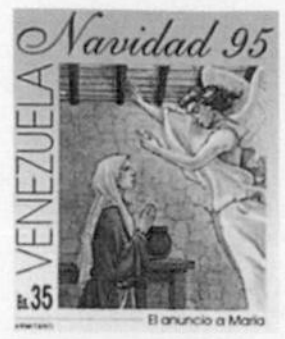

546 The Annunciation

1995. Christmas. Multicoloured.

3191	35b. Type **546**	1·00	80
3192	35b. Mary and Joseph turned away from the inn	1·00	80
3193	35b. Archangel Gabriel visits shepherds	1·00	80
3194	35b. Three wise men bearing gifts	1·00	80
3195	40b. Family gathering	1·10	90
3196	40b. Children on rollerskates	1·10	90
3197	40b. Women and girl preparing food	1·10	90
3198	40b. Woman and children preparing food	1·10	90
3199	100b. Mary and Joseph holding Child Jesus	3·00	2·50
3200	100b. Box of toys	3·00	2·50

Nos. 3191/3200 were issued together, *se-tenant*, Nos. 3195/6 and 3197/8 forming composite designs.

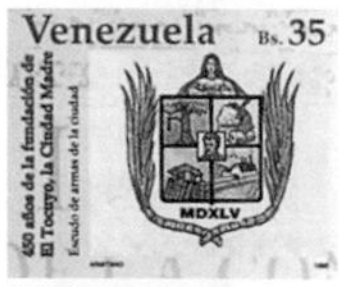

547 Arms

1995. 450th Anniv of El Tocuyo. Multicoloured.

3201	35b. Type **547**	1·00	80
3202	35b. Cutting sugar cane	1·00	80
3203	35b. Church of Our Lady of the Immaculate Conception	1·00	80
3204	35b. "Our Lady of the Immaculate Conception" (statue)	1·00	80
3205	35b. Ruins of Santo Domingo Temple	1·00	80
3206	35b. Cultural centre	1·00	80
3207	80b. Natural vegetation	2·40	1·90
3208	80b. Cactus	2·40	1·90
3209	100b. Sword dance	3·00	2·50
3210	100b. Man playing guitar	3·00	2·50

Nos. 3201/10 were issued together, *se-tenant*, Nos. 3209/10 forming a composite design.

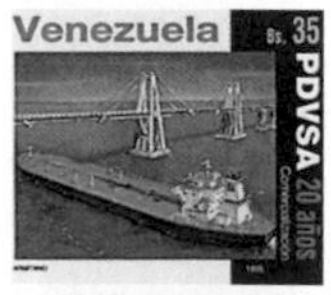

548 Oil Tanker

1995. 20th Anniv of PDVSA National Fossil Fuels Association. Multicoloured.

3211	35b. Type **548**	1·00	80
3212	35b. Orimulsion storage tanks	1·00	80
3213	35b. Coal	1·00	80
3214	35b. Lorry carrying sacks	1·00	80
3215	35b. Petrol station	1·00	80
3216	35b. Gas storage cylinders	1·00	80
3217	80b. Drilling for oil	2·40	1·90
3218	80b. Refinery	2·40	1·90
3219	100b. Emblems ("Lagoven" at top)	3·00	2·50
3220	100b. Emblems ("bitor" at top)	3·00	2·50

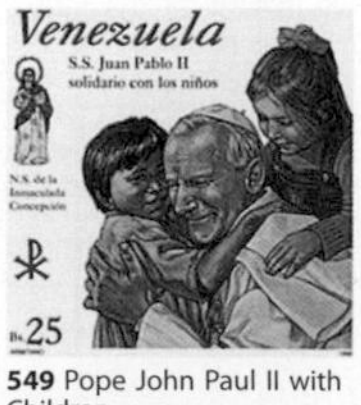

549 Pope John Paul II with Children

1996. Papal Visit. Multicoloured.

3221	25b. Type **549**	55	45
3222	25b. Pope with young couple	55	45
3223	40b. Pope with family	1·00	80
3224	40b. Pope with elderly man	1·00	80
3225	50b. Pope with mother and son	1·10	90
3226	50b. Pope with patient	1·10	90
3227	60b. Pope with prisoner	1·40	1·10
3228	60b. Pope with workman	1·40	1·10
3229	100b. Pope giving speech to workers	2·40	1·90
3230	100b. Pope with priest and nuns	2·40	1·90
MS3231	204×120 mm. 200b. Pope holding crucifix (41×36 mm)	5·00	5·00

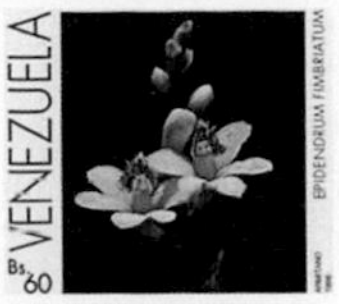

550 "Epidendrum fimbriatum"

1996. Orchids. Multicoloured.

3232	60b. Type **550**	1·40	1·10
3233	60b. "Myoxanthus reymondii"	1·40	1·10
3234	60b. "Catasetum pileatum"	1·40	1·10
3235	60b. "Ponthieva maculata"	1·40	1·10
3236	60b. "Maxillaria triloris"	1·40	1·10
3237	60b. "Scaphosepalum breve"	1·40	1·10
3238	60b. "Cleistes rosea"	1·40	1·10
3239	60b. "Maxillaria sophronitis"	1·40	1·10
3240	60b. "Catasetum discolor"	1·40	1·10
3241	60b. "Oncidium ampliatum"	1·40	1·10
MS3242	133×124 mm. 200b. "Odontoglossum naevium" (41×36 mm)	5·00	5·00

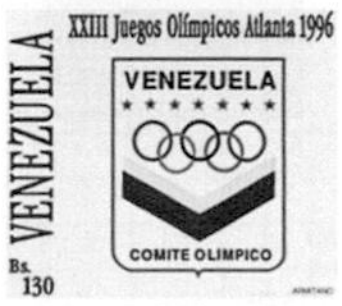

551 National Olympic Committee Emblem

1996. Olympic Games, Atlanta. Multicoloured.

3243	130b. Type **551**	2·75	2·30
3244	130b. Swimming	2·75	2·30
3245	130b. Boxing	2·75	2·30
3246	130b. Cycling	2·75	2·30
3247	130b. Medal winners on podium	2·75	2·30

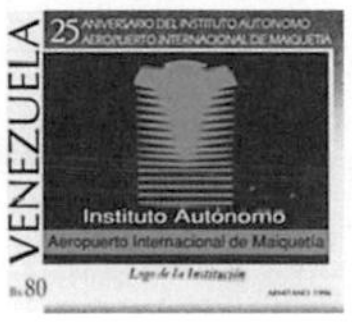

552 Emblem

1996. 25th Anniv of Liberator Simon Bolivar International Airport, Maiquetia, as Autonomous Company. Multicoloured.

3248	80b. Type **552**	2·00	1·60
3249	80b. Flight paths into airport	2·00	1·60
3250	80b. La Guaira Aerodrome, 1929	2·00	1·60
3251	80b. Maiquetia Airport, 1944	2·00	1·60
3252	80b. Liberator Simon Bolivar Airport, 1972	2·00	1·60
3253	80b. Airport interior by Carlos Cruz Diez	2·00	1·60
3254	80b. Control tower and airport police	2·00	1·60
3255	80b. Fire tender	2·00	1·60
3256	80b. Airplanes at terminal building	2·00	1·60
3257	80b. Boeing 747 airliner and terminal buildings	2·00	1·60

Nos. 3248/57 were issued together, *se-tenant*, Nos. 3256/7 forming a composite design.

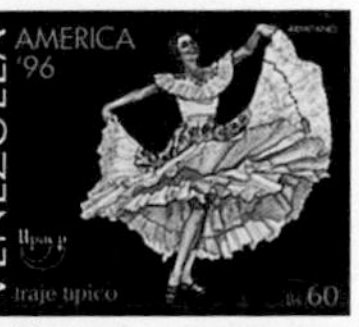

553 Woman

1996. America. Traditional Costume. Multicoloured.

3258	60b. Type **553**	1·40	1·10
3259	130b. Man	3·00	2·50

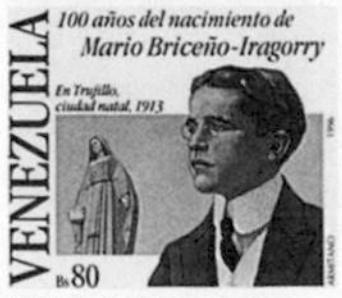

554 As Child in Trujillo, 1913

1996. Birth Centenary (1997) of Dr. Mario Briceno-Iragorry (politician). Designs showing different periods of his life. Multicoloured.

3260	80b. Type **554**	2·00	1·60
3261	80b. Student at Merida University, 1919	2·00	1·60
3262	80b. Politician making speech, 1944	2·00	1·60
3263	80b. Writer, 1947	2·00	1·60
3264	80b. Historian of Caracas, 1952	2·00	1·60

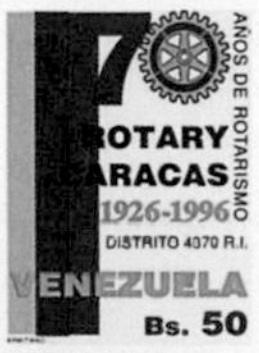

555 Emblem

1996. 70th Anniv of Rotary International in Caracas.

3265	**555** 50b. multicoloured	1·10	90

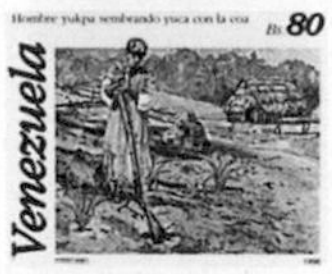

556 Man planting Yucca

1996. Amerindians (3rd series). Multicoloured.

3266	80b. Type **556**	2·00	1·60
3267	80b. Child gathering fruits	2·00	1·60
3268	80b. Women harvesting reed-mace	2·00	1·60
3269	80b. Youth gathering bananas	2·00	1·60
3270	80b. Mother carrying child	2·00	1·60
3271	100b. Guajiros indians	2·40	1·90
3272	100b. Man carrying bundle	2·40	1·90
3273	100b. Man fishing with bow and arrow	2·40	1·90
3274	100b. Couple grinding maize	2·40	1·90
3275	100b. Weaver	2·40	1·90
MS3276	149×126 mm. 200b. Woman breast-feeding (41×36 mm)	5·25	5·25

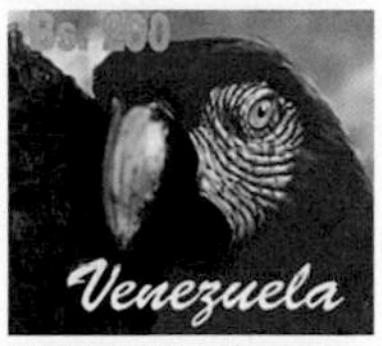

557 Green-winged Macaw

1996. Tenth Asian International Stamp Exhibition, Taipeh. Sheet 152×127 mm.

MS3277	**557** 200b. multicoloured	12·00	12·00

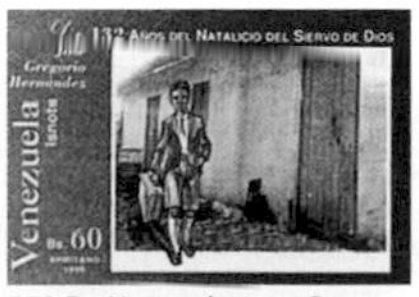

558 Dr. Hernandez as a Boy

1996. 132nd Birth Anniv of Dr. Jose Hernandez (physician). Designs representing different aspects of his life. Multicoloured.

3278	60b. Type **558**	1·00	80
3279	60b. Student	1·00	80
3280	60b. Kneeling in prayer and statue of the Madonna	1·00	80
3281	60b. Dining and distributing food to the needy	1·00	80
3282	60b. Research scientist examining test tube	1·00	80
3283	60b. University professor teaching students	1·00	80
3284	60b. Administering to patient	1·00	80
3285	60b. Meeting room of Academy of Numbers	1·00	80
3286	60b. Portrait and statue of Hernandez and Vargas hospital	1·00	80
3287	60b. Dr. Jose Gregorio Hernandez hospital and statue	1·00	80
MS3288	150×125 mm. 200b. Portrait of Hernandez (41×36 mm)	4·00	4·00

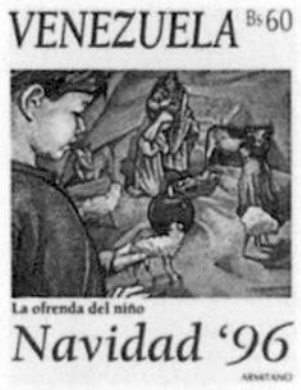

559 Child and Nativity figures

1996. Christmas. Multicoloured.

3289	60b. Type **559**	90	75
3290	60b. Guitar players and percussionist	90	75
3291	60b. Crowing cockerel and musicians	90	75
3292	60b. Traditional dancers	90	75
3293	60b. Drummers, maracas player and guitarist	90	75
3294	80b. Woman and girl exchanging traditional food	1·20	1·00
3295	80b. Family meal	1·20	1·00
3296	80b. Child in hammock and gifts	1·20	1·00
3297	80b. Couple with child	1·20	1·00
3298	80b. Mother kissing baby's foot	1·20	1·00

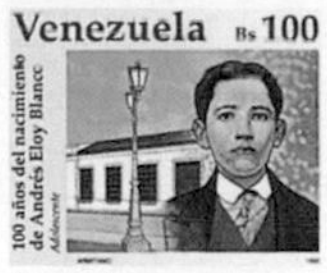

560 As Boy

1997. Birth Centenary of Andres Eloy Blanco (writer and politician). Multicoloured.

3299	100b. Type **560**	1·50	1·20
3300	100b. Councillor for Caracas	1·50	1·20
3301	100b. With family	1·50	1·20
3302	100b. With two men	1·50	1·20
3303	100b. Politician	1·50	1·20
3304	100b. President of Constitutional Assembly	1·50	1·20
3305	100b. Poet and Juan Bimba (character from poem)	1·50	1·20
3306	100b. Chancellor of the Republic and Lincoln Memorial	1·50	1·20
3307	100b. Eloy Blanco and "Santa Maria" ("Canto a Espana")	1·50	1·20
3308	100b. "Pinto" and "Nina" and Don Quixote ("Canto a Espana")	1·50	1·20

Nos. 3299/3308 were issued together, *se-tenant*, Nos. 3307/8 forming a composite design.

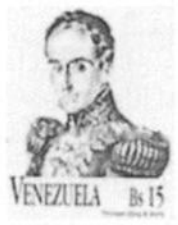

561 Simon Bolivar (after Jose Maria Espinoza)

1997

3311	**561**	15b. green	15	10
3312	**561**	20b. orange	30	25
3313	**561**	40b. brown	45	35
3314	**561**	50b. red	75	60
3315	**561**	70b. purple	1·00	85
3316	**561**	90b. blue	1·50	1·20
3317	**561**	200b. blue	3·00	2·40
3318	**561**	300b. green	4·75	3·75
3319	**561**	400b. grey	6·25	5·00
3320	**561**	500b. drab	7·50	5·50
3321	**561**	600b. brown	9·75	7·25
3322	**561**	800b. brown	12·50	9·25
3323	**561**	900b. blue	14·00	9·75
3324	**561**	1000b. copper	15·00	10·00
3325	**561**	2000b. green	30·00	18·00

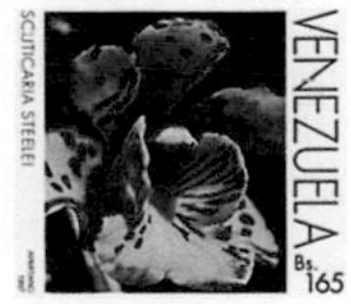

562 "Scuticaria steelei"

1997. Orchids. Multicoloured.

3330	165b. "Phragmipedium lindleyanum"	2·50	2·10
3331	165b. "Zygosepalum labiosum"	2·50	2·10
3332	165b. "Acacallis cyanea"	2·50	2·10
3333	165b. "Maxillaria camaridii"	2·50	2·10
3334	165b. Type **562**	2·50	2·10
3335	165b. "Aspasia variegata"	2·50	2·10
3336	165b. "Comparettia falcata"	2·50	2·10
3337	165b. "Scaphyglottis stellata"	2·50	2·10
3338	165b. "Maxillaria rufescens"	2·50	2·10
3339	165b. "Vanilla pompona"	2·50	2·10
MS3340	140×122 mm. 250b. "Rodriguezia lanceolata" (40×35 mm)	4·00	4·00

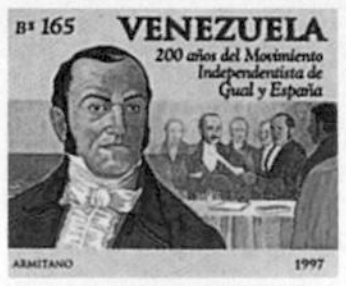

563 Espana and Meeting of Conspirators

1997. Bicentenary of Independence Movement of Manuel Gual and Jose Maria Espana. Multicoloured.

3341	165b. Type **563**	2·50	2·10
3342	165b. Soldiers escorting Espana to his execution	2·50	2·10
3343	165b. Gual, conspirators and soldiers with bayonets	2·50	2·10
3344	165b. Gual in exile on Trinidad	2·50	2·10
3345	165b. Flag	2·50	2·10

Nos. 3341/5 were issued together, se-tenant, each horiz pair forming a composite design.

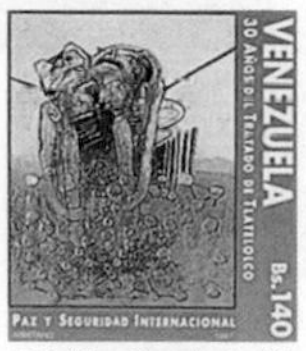

564 "The People boil"

1997. 30th Anniv of Tlatelolco Treaty (Latin American and Caribbean treaty banning nuclear weapons). Paintings by Alirio Rodriguez from his "Hiroshima" sequence. Multicoloured.

3346	140b. Type **564**	2·20	1·80
3347	140b. "An empty Epicentre where Once even a Whisper Sounded" (white and black disc)	2·20	1·80
3348	140b. "Darkness like the high Horizon" (red disc on black panel)	2·20	1·80
3349	140b. "My God! In the Shell, Emptiness" (red and black "shelves")	2·20	1·80
3350	140b. "Devil. Perverse geometry" (yellow atomic model)	2·20	1·80
3351	140b. "At the Heart of the Area the Bareness of the Disaster" (four blue discs)	2·20	1·80
3352	140b. "Without Thought, only Grief in living Flesh" (figure within atomic model)	2·20	1·80
3353	140b. "Thus in order to Reveal" (red panel)	2·20	1·80
3354	140b. "Calvary of multiple Symbiosis" (drab atomic model)	2·20	1·80
3355	140b. "Released Energy which attempts to Silence the Scream" (screaming head with legs)	2·20	1·80

Distinguishing parts of the design are given in brackets to aid identification.

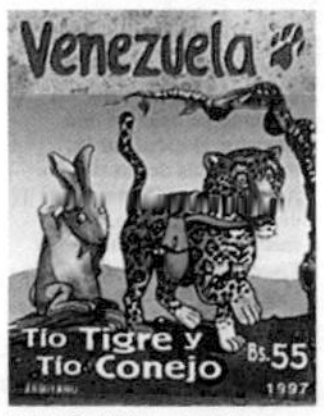

565 Rabbit watching Jaguar

1997. Children's Stories (1st series). "Uncle Jaguar and Uncle Rabbit". Multicoloured.

3356	55b. Type **565**	90	75
3357	55b. Rabbit listening to conversation between Jaguar and Anteater	90	75
3358	55b. Jaguar catching Turtle	90	75
3359	55b. Rabbit going to help Turtle	90	75
3360	55b. Rabbit freeing Anteater from net	90	75
3361	55b. Anteater telling Jaguar that his vegetables have been stolen	90	75
3362	55b. Anteater and Rabbit looking at wasps' nest in tree	90	75
3363	55b. Rabbit releasing Turtle from Jaguar's bag and replacing him with wasps' nest	90	75
3364	55b. Jaguar returning from fruitless pursuit	90	75
3365	55b. Jaguar opening bag and being stung by wasps	90	75
MS3366	151×126 mm. 250b. Rabbit and jaguar (41×36 mm)	4·00	4·00

A number and the relevant portion of the story is printed on the back of each stamp over the gum.

See also Nos. 3537/46.

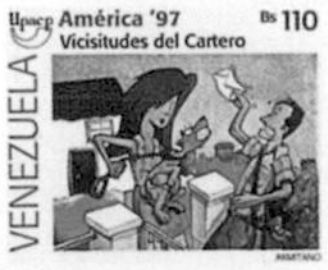

566 Dog growling at Postman

1997. America. The Postman. Multicoloured.

3367	110b. Type **566**	2·20	1·80
3368	280b. Postman's moped punctured in rain	5·25	4·25

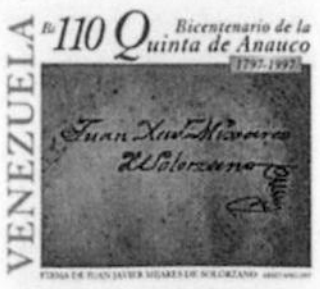

567 Signature of Juan Xavier Misares de Solorzano (first owner)

1997. Bicentenary of Quinta de Anauco (historic house). Multicoloured.

3369	110b. Type **567**	1·60	1·30
3370	110b. Principal facade	1·60	1·30
3371	110b. Entrance passage	1·60	1·30
3372	110b. Inner courtyard	1·60	1·30
3373	110b. Passageway to kitchen	1·60	1·30
3374	110b. Kitchen	1·60	1·30
3375	110b. Living quarters	1·60	1·30
3376	110b. Coach house with fountain	1·60	1·30
3377	110b. Cart in stable	1·60	1·30
3378	110b. Water trough and stable	1·60	1·30

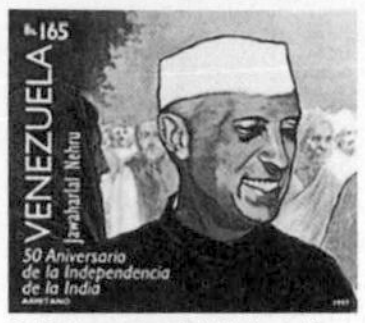

568 Jarwaharlal Nehru (first Prime Minister)

1997. 50th Anniv of Independence of India. Multicoloured.

3379	165b. Type **568**	2·50	2·10
3380	165b. Congress building, New Delhi	2·50	2·10
3381	165b. Ritual cleansing in River Ganges	2·50	2·10
3382	165b. Actress and film camera-man	2·50	2·10
3383	165b. "INSAT-1B" meteorological satellite orbiting Earth	2·50	2·10
3384	200b. Sardar Patel (politician) and flag	3·00	2·40
3385	200b. Mahatma Gandhi	3·00	2·40
3386	200b. Rabindranath Tagore (poet and philosopher)	3·00	2·40
3387	200b. Musician playing traditional instrument	3·00	2·40
3388	200b. Woman at computer	3·00	2·40
MS3389	111×124 mm. 250b. Minarets, Taj Mahal, Agra (41×36 mm)	4·00	4·00

Nos. 3379/88 were issued together, *se-tenant*, forming a composite design.

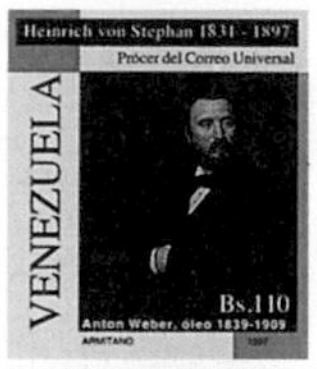

569 Von Stephan (after Anton Weber)

1997. Death Centenary of Heinrich von Stephan (founder of U.P.U.). Multicoloured.

3390	110b. Type **569**	1·80	1·50
3391	280b. U.P.U. monument, Berne	4·25	3·50

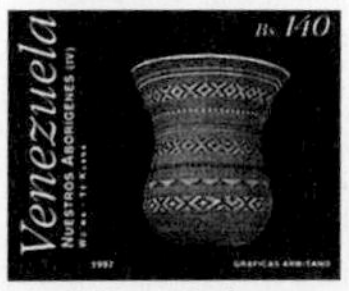

570 Ye'Kuana Basket

1997. Amerindians (4th series). Basketwork. Multicoloured.

3392	140b. Type **570**	2·20	1·80
3393	140b. Ye'Kuana basket with handle	2·20	1·80
3394	140b. Ye'Kuana lidded jar with bird decoration	2·20	1·80
3395	140b. Panare round dish	2·20	1·80
3396	140b. Pemon baby carrier	2·20	1·80
3397	140b. Yanomani basket with strap	2·20	1·80
3398	140b. Ye'Kuana lidded jar	2·20	1·80
3399	140b. Ye'Kuana dish	2·20	1·80
3400	140b. Panare oval dish	2·20	1·80
3401	140b. Warao fluted basket	2·20	1·80
MS3402	150×125 mm. 250b. Lid of Ye'Kuana basket-box (41×36 mm)	4·00	4·00

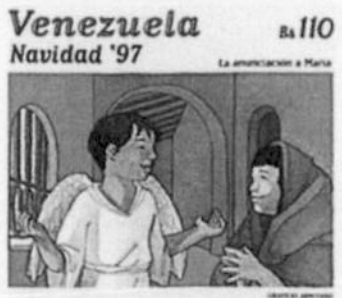

571 The Annunciation

1997. Christmas. Multicoloured.

3403	110b. Type **571**	1·60	1·30
3404	110b. Mary visits St. Isabel	1·60	1·30
3405	110b. Mary and Joseph arrive at Bethlehem	1·60	1·30
3406	110b. The Nativity	1·60	1·30
3407	110b. Angel and shepherds	1·60	1·30
3408	110b. Adoration of the Shepherds	1·60	1·30
3409	110b. Wise Men following star	1·60	1·30
3410	110b. Wise Men offer gifts	1·60	1·30
3411	110b. Presentation in the Temple	1·60	1·30
3412	110b. Flight into Egypt	1·60	1·30

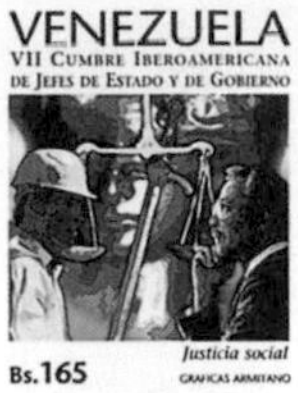

572 Workers and Scales of Justice (social justice)

1997. Seventh Summit of Latin American Heads of State, Isla de Margarita. Multicoloured.

3413	165b. Type **572**	2·50	2·10
3414	165b. Voting box (open elections)	2·50	2·10
3415	165b. Summit emblem	2·50	2·10
3416	165b. Broadcaster (true information)	2·50	2·10
3417	165b. Constitution and people (human rights)	2·50	2·10
3418	200b. As No. 3417	3·00	2·40
3419	200b. As No. 3416	3·00	2·40
3420	200b. As No. 3415	3·00	2·40
3421	200b. As No. 3414	3·00	2·40
3422	200b. As No. 3413	3·00	2·40

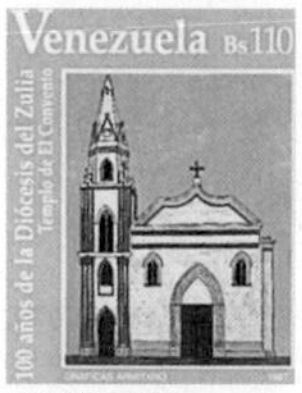

573 Monastery Church, Puerta de Agua

1997. Centenary of Diocese of Zulia. Multicoloured.

3423	110b. Type **573**	1·60	1·30
3424	110b. St. Anne's Church	1·60	1·30
3425	110b. Reliquary of the Virgin of the Rosary, Chiquinquira	1·60	1·30
3426	110b. Basilica of St. John of God, Chiquinquira	1·60	1·30
3427	110b. Santo Cristo de Aranza church	1·60	1·30
3428	110b. Maracaibo cathedral	1·60	1·30
3429	110b. Machiques cathedral	1·60	1·30
3430	110b. Arms of Archbishop Ovidio Perez Morales	1·60	1·30
3431	110b. Cabimas cathedral	1·60	1·30
3432	110b. Cathedral of El Vigia and San Carlos del Zulia	1·60	1·30

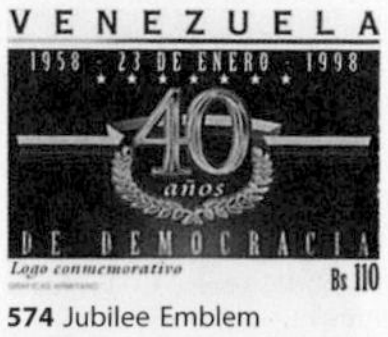

574 Jubilee Emblem

1998. "40 Years of Democracy". Multicoloured.

3433	110b. Type **574**	1·60	1·30
3434	110b. People voting	1·60	1·30
3435	110b. Child studying globe	1·60	1·30
3436	110b. Underground train	1·60	1·30
3437	110b. Man making speech (freedom of expression)	1·60	1·30
3438	110b. Senate and Constitution	1·60	1·30
3439	110b. Orchestra	1·60	1·30
3440	110b. Children and Scales of Justice	1·60	1·30
3441	110b. Brown bear and El Avila National Park (protection of environment)	1·60	1·30
3442	110b. Adult education	1·60	1·30

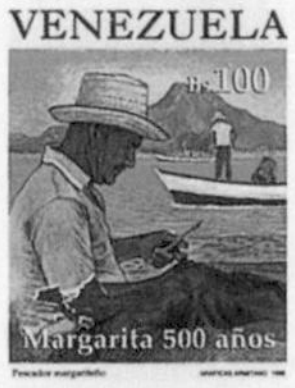

575 Fishermen

1998. 500th Anniv of Discovery of Margarita Island. Multicoloured.

3443	100b. Type **575**	1·50	1·20
3444	100b. Petronila Mata (freedom fighter)	1·50	1·20
3445	100b. Yellow-shouldered amazon	1·50	1·20
3446	200b. Angel Rock	3·00	2·40
3447	200b. Simon Bolivar	3·00	2·40
3448	200b. Pearl diver	3·00	2·40
3449	200b. General Santiago Marino	3·00	2·40
3450	200b. General Juan Bautista Arismendi	3·00	2·40
3451	265b. Christopher Columbus	4·00	3·25
3452	265b. "Our Lady the Virgin of the Valley" and church	4·00	3·25
MS3453	205×125 mm. 250b. Grieving women (41×36 mm)	4·00	4·00

Nos. 3443/52 were issued together, *se-tenant*, Nos. 3446 with 3451 and Nos. 3448/52 forming composite designs.

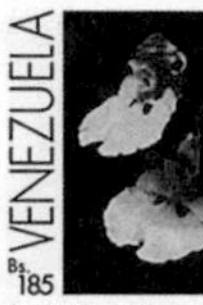

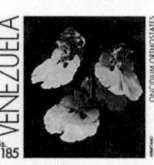

576 "Oncidium orthostates"

1998. Orchids. Multicoloured.

3454	185b. Type **576**	2·75	2·20
3455	185b. "Epidendrum praetervisum"	2·75	2·20
3456	185b. "Odontoglossum schilleranum"	2·75	2·20
3457	185b. "Bletia lansbergii"	2·75	2·20
3458	185b. "Caularthron bicornutum"	2·75	2·20
3459	185b. "Darwiniera bergoldii"	2·75	2·20
3460	185b. "Houlletia tigrina"	2·75	2·20
3461	185b. "Pleurothallis acuminata"	2·75	2·20
3462	185b. "Elleanthus lupulinus"	2·75	2·20
3463	185b. "Epidendrum ferrugineum"	2·75	2·20
MS3464	143×127 mm. 250b. "Pleurithallis immerse"	4·00	4·00

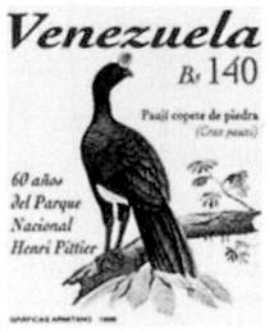

577 Helmeted Curassow

1998. 60th Anniv of Henri Pittier National Park. Multicoloured.

3465	140b. Type **577**	2·10	1·70
3466	140b. Swallow tanager ("Tersina virdis")	2·10	1·70
3467	150b. Ornate hawk eagle ("Spizaetus ornatus")	2·20	1·80
3468	150b. Leaf frog ("Phyllomedusa trinitatis")	2·20	1·80
3469	200b. Lilac-tailed parrotlet ("Touit collaris")	3·00	2·40
3470	200b. Collared trogon ("Trogon collaris")	3·00	2·40
3471	200b. Emperor ("Morpho peleides")	3·00	2·40
3472	200b. Longhorn beetle ("Acrocinus longimanus")	3·00	2·40
3473	350b. Green jay ("Cyanocorax yncas")	5·25	4·25
3474	350b. Hercules beetle ("Dynastes hercules")	5·25	4·25

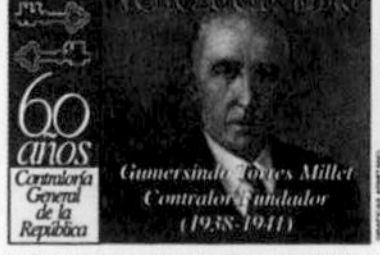

578 Gumersindo Torres Millet (first Comptroller)

1998. 60th Anniv of Office of Comptroller General. Black, red and blue (Nos. 3477, 3479) or multicoloured (others).

3475	140b. Type **578**	1·90	1·60
3476	140b. Luis Antonio Pieri Yepez (comptroller, 1958–69)	1·90	1·60
3477	140b. Congress building	1·90	1·60
3478	140b. Flag	1·90	1·60
3479	200b. Banknotes and coins	2·75	2·30
3480	200b. Numbers	2·75	2·30
3481	350b. Newspapers	4·75	4·00
3482	350b. Scales of Justice	4·75	4·00
3483	350b. Code of Ethics	4·75	4·00
3484	350b. Emblem of Seventh Assembly of Latin American and Caribbean Organization of Higher Fiscal Bodies	4·75	4·00
MS3485	191×127 mm. 480b. As No. 3484 (38×33 mm)	4·50	4·50

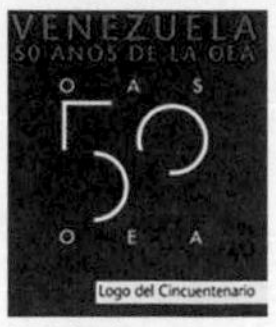

579 Anniversary Emblem

1998. 50th Anniv of Organization of American States. Multicoloured.

3486	140b. Type **579**	1·90	1·60
3487	140b. Institutional emblem	1·90	1·60
3488	150b. Soldier uncovering landmine	2·10	1·70
3489	150b. Official with prisoner (Defence of Human Rights)	2·10	1·70
3490	200b. Simon Bolivar	2·75	2·30
3491	200b. Scroll commemorating 50th anniv of American Declaration of Human Rights	2·75	2·30
3492	200b. Map of the Americas on road sign	2·75	2·30
3493	200b. Three rock climbers (anti-drugs co-operation)	2·75	2·30
3494	350b. Members' flags including Brazil and U.S.A. forming double helix	4·75	4·00
3495	350b. Members' flags including Jamaica and Venezuela forming a double helix	4·75	4·00

Nos. 3486/7, 3492/3 and 3494/5 were issued together, *se-tenant*, forming composite designs.

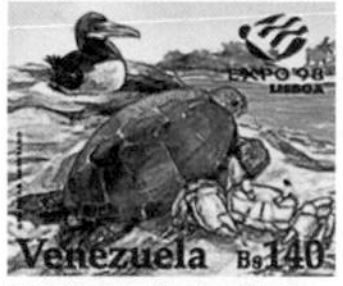

580 Brown Booby, Turtle and Crab

1998. "Expo '98" World's Fair, Lisbon. Multicoloured.

3496	140b. Type **580**	1·90	1·60
3497	140b. Fishermen in boat	1·90	1·60
3498	150b. Shells, baby turtle and jellyfish	2·10	1·70
3499	150b. Yellow-finned tuna and snapper	2·10	1·70
3500	200b. Great barracuda and underwater vegetation (value at top)	2·75	2·30
3501	200b. Octopus, fishes and underwater vegetation (value at foot)	2·75	2·30
3502	200b. Horse rider	2·75	2·30
3503	200b. Cattle in water and common squirrel-monkey	2·75	2·30
3504	350b. Great egret and scarlet ibis	4·75	4·00
3505	350b. Red howler (monkey), waterfall and plants	4·75	4·00

Nos. 3496/3505 were issued together, *se-tenant*, forming a composite design.

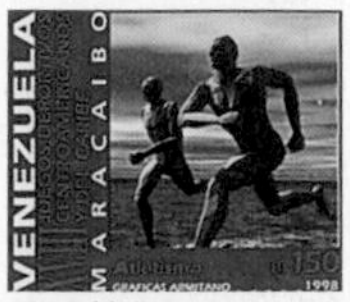

581 Athletics

1998. 18th Central American and Caribbean Games, Maracaibo. Multicoloured.

3506	150b. Type **581**	2·10	1·70
3507	150b. Ten-pin bowling	2·10	1·70
3508	150b. Cycling	2·10	1·70
3509	150b. Gymnastics	2·10	1·70
3510	150b. Swimming	2·10	1·70
3511	200b. Basketball	2·75	2·30
3512	200b. Boxing	2·75	2·30
3513	200b. Fencing	2·75	2·30
3514	200b. Weightlifting	2·75	2·30
3515	200b. Tennis	2·75	2·30

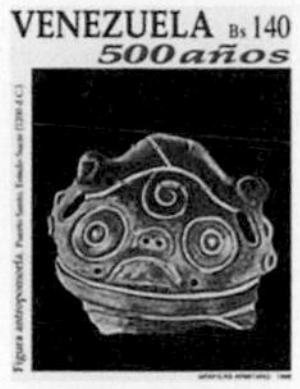

582 Anthropomorphic Vessel

1998. 500th Anniv of Discovery of Venezuela. Multicoloured.

3516	140b. Type **582**	1·90	1·60
3517	140b. "Catholic Royal Couple" (wood carving, Manuel Cabrera)	1·90	1·60
3518	150b. Three women of different races	2·10	1·70
3519	150b. Mixed-race people	2·10	1·70
3520	200b. Lake houses on stilts	2·75	2·30
3521	200b. Modern city	2·75	2·30
3522	200b. Juan de la Cosa and 1499 map	2·75	2·30
3523	200b. Detail of 1599 map by Jodocus Hondius	2·75	2·30
3524	350b. Christopher Columbus	4·75	4·00
3525	350b. Alonso de Ojeda	4·75	4·00

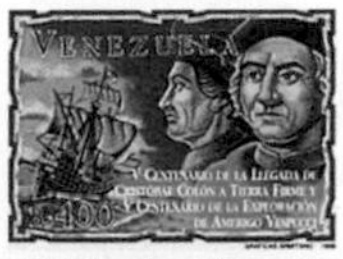

583 Columbus, Vespucci and Galleon

1998. 500th Anniversaries of Christopher Columbus's Discovery of America and Amerigo Vespucci's Exploration of Venezuela.

3526	**583** 400b. multicoloured	5·75	4·75

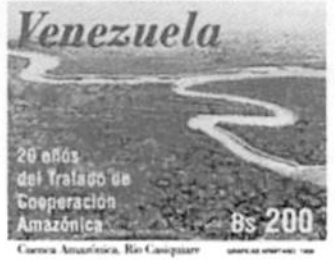

584 River Casiquiare, Amazon Basin

1998. 20th Anniv of Amazon Co-operation Treaty. Multicoloured.

3527	200b. Type **584**	3·00	2·40
3528	200b. River Casiquiare, Amazon Basin (right-hand detail)	3·00	2·40
3529	200b. Berries of "Bactris gasipaes"	3·00	2·40
3530	200b. "Neblinaria celiae" (plant)	3·00	2·40
3531	200b. Cardinal tetra ("Paracheidon axelrodi")	3·00	2·40
3532	200b. Yellow-banded poison-arrow frogs ("Dendrobates leucomelas")	3·00	2·40
3533	200b. Nocturnal curassows ("Nocthocrax urumatum")	3·00	2·40
3534	200b. Bush dogs ("Speothos venaticus")	3·00	2·40
3535	200b. Cocuy Stone	3·00	2·40
3536	200b. Neblina Ridge	3·00	2·40

Nos. 3527/8 were issued together, *se-tenant*, forming a composite design.

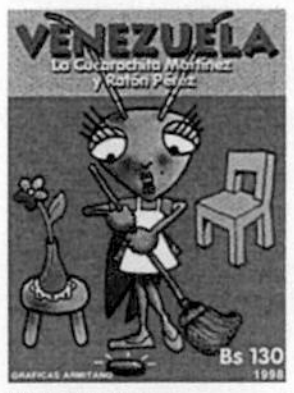

585 Martinez Cockroach cleaning

1998. Children's Stories (2nd series). "Martinez Cockroach and Perez Rat" from "Uncle Jaguar and Uncle Rabbit" by Antonio Arraiz. Multicoloured.

3537	130b. Type **585**	1·60	1·30
3538	130b. Doctor Ass writing on pad	1·60	1·30
3539	130b. Parakeet in dress	1·60	1·30
3540	130b. Photographer and reporter	1·60	1·30
3541	130b. Piojo (cat)	1·60	1·30
3542	130b. Martinez Cockroach and pig	1·60	1·30
3543	130b. Chivo (goat)	1·60	1·30
3544	130b. Martinez Cockroach and Perez Rat gazing at moon	1·60	1·30
3545	130b. Perez Rat sniffing cauldron in which he later drowned	1·60	1·30
3546	130b. Guinea-hen and Misia Rata reviving Martinez Cockroach	1·60	1·30
MS3547	150×124 mm. 350b. Martinez Cockroach (41×36 mm)	5·25	4·25

A number and the relevant portion of the story is printed on the back of each stamp over the gum.

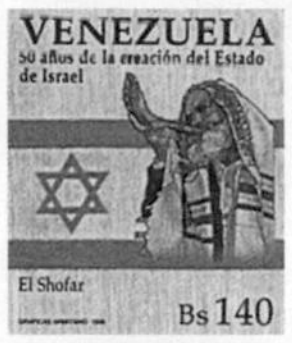

586 Ram's-horn Blower

1998. 50th Anniv of State of Israel. Multicoloured.

3548	140b. Type **586**	2·20	1·80
3549	140b. Book Museum	2·20	1·80
3550	200b. King David	2·75	2·30
3551	200b. Knesset building, Jerusalem	2·75	2·30
3552	200b. Dr. Theodor Herzl (founder of World Zionist Movement)	2·75	2·30
3553	200b. David Ben Gurion (first Israeli Prime Minister)	2·75	2·30
3554	350b. Moses holding Ten Commandments	4·75	4·00
3555	350b. Man at Wailing Wall	4·75	4·00
3556	350b. Menorah	4·75	4·00
3557	350b. Torah	4·75	4·00

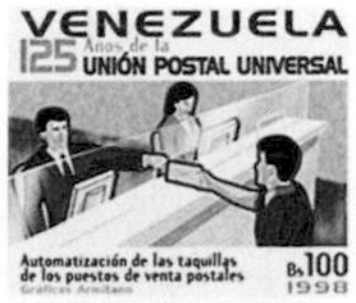

587 Handing Letter over Post Office Counter

1998. 125th Anniv of Universal Postal Union. Multicoloured.

3558	100b. Type **587**	80	65
3559	100b. Checking barcode on envelope	80	65
3560	100b. Computer operators using e-mail	80	65
3561	100b. Woman holding computer disc	80	65
3562	100b. Arrows and binary code, offices and factory	80	65
3563	300b. As Type **587** but design reversed	2·40	1·90
3564	300b. As No. 3559 but design reversed	2·40	1·90
3565	300b. As No. 3560 but design reversed	2·40	1·90
3566	300b. As No. 3561 but design reversed	2·40	1·90
3567	300b. As No. 3562 but design reversed	2·40	1·90

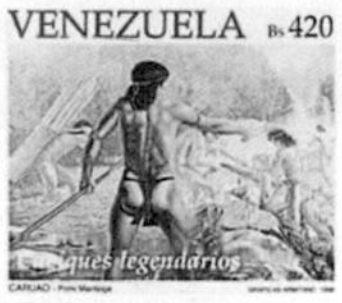

588 Caruao

1998. Amerindians (5th series). Paintings of Indian Chiefs by Primi Manteiga. Multicoloured.

3568	420b. Type **588**	3·50	2·75
3569	420b. Manaure	3·50	2·75
3570	420b. Guacamayo	3·50	2·75
3571	420b. Tapiaracay	3·50	2·75
3572	420b. Mamacuri	3·50	2·75
3573	420b. Maniacuare	3·50	2·75
3574	420b. Mara	3·50	2·75
3575	420b. Chacao	3·50	2·75
3576	420b. Tamanaco	3·50	2·75
3577	420b. Tiuna	3·50	2·75
MS3578	206×126 mm. 500b. Guaicaipuro (41×36 mm)	4·75	4·75

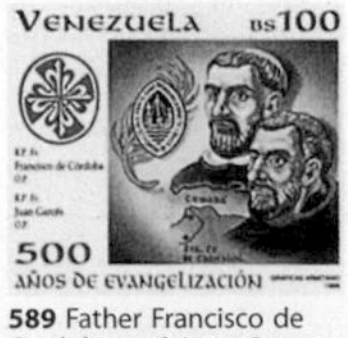

589 Father Francisco de Cordoba and Juan Garces

1998. 500th Anniv of First Christian Missions to Venezuela. Multicoloured.

3579	100b. Type **589**	80	65
3580	100b. Father Matias Ruiz Blanco	80	65
3581	100b. Father Vicente de Requejada	80	65
3582	100b. Jose Gumilla	80	65
3583	100b. Antonio Gonzalez de Acuna	80	65
3584	300b. Father Pedro de Cordoba	2·50	2·10
3585	300b. Father Francisco de Pamplona	2·50	2·10
3586	300b. Father Bartolome Diaz	2·50	2·10
3587	300b. Felipe Salvador Gilij	2·50	2·10
3588	300b. Mariano Marti	2·50	2·10
MS3589	204×127 mm. 350b. Arms of Papal Nuncio (38×33 mm)	3·50	3·50

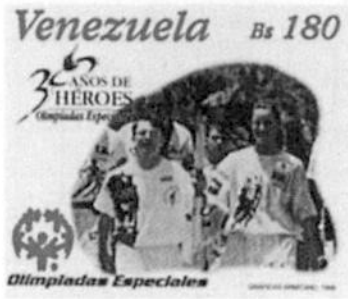

590 Opening Parade

1998. 30th Anniv of First Special Olympics. Multicoloured.

3590	180b. Type **590**	1·60	1·30
3591	180b. Two people hugging	1·60	1·30
3592	180b. Football	1·60	1·30
3593	180b. Medal winner	1·60	1·30
3594	180b. Gymnastics	1·60	1·30
3595	420b. Swimming	3·50	2·75
3596	420b. Athletes and officials walking on track	3·50	2·75
3597	420b. Volleyball	3·50	2·75
3598	420b. Cheering medal winners	3·50	2·75
3599	420b. Baseball	3·50	2·75

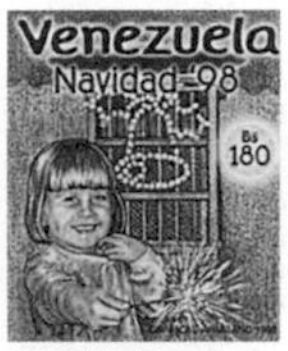

591 Girl with Sparkler

1998. Christmas. Multicoloured.

3600	180b. Type **591**	1·60	1·30
3601	180b. Boy with figurine and paintbrush	1·60	1·30
3602	180b. Girl with kite	1·60	1·30
3603	180b. Boy with toy windmill	1·60	1·30
3604	180b. Girls with tambourine and drum	1·60	1·30
3605	420b. Boy in go-cart	3·50	2·75
3606	420b. Girl with yo-yo and rag doll	3·50	2·75
3607	420b. Boy with bell	3·50	2·75
3608	420b. Girl in hat with spinning toy	3·50	2·75
3609	420b. Boy on skateboard	3·50	2·75

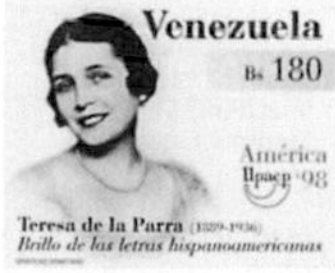

592 Teresa de la Parra (writer)

1998. America. Famous Women. Multicoloured.

3610	180b. Type **592**	1·60	1·30
3611	420b. Teresa Carreno (pianist)	3·50	2·75

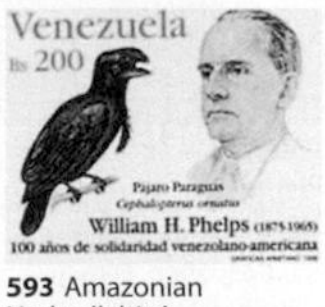

593 Amazonian Umbrellabird

1998. 100 Years of Venezuela–United States Solidarity. Each showing a portrait of William Phelps (ornithologist and entrepreneur). Multicoloured.

3612	200b. Type **593**	1·90	1·60
3613	200b. Crimson topaz ("Topaza pella")	1·90	1·60
3614	200b. Great antpitta ("Grallaria excelsa")	1·90	1·60
3615	200b. Ruby-throated hummingbird ("Chrysolampis mosquitus")	1·90	1·60
3616	200b. Yellow-bellied tanager ("Tangara xanthogastra")	1·90	1·60
3617	300b. Radio microphone (founder of Broadcasting Caracas)	2·75	2·20
3618	300b. Phelps Peak	2·75	2·20
3619	300b. Baseball in glove	2·75	2·20
3620	300b. Phelps Library, San Antonio de Maturin	2·75	2·20
3621	300b. Cash register	2·75	2·20

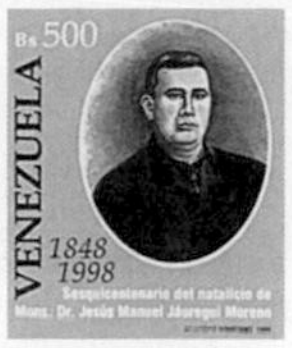

594 Jauregui

1999. Monseigneur Jesus Manuel Jauregui Moreno. Multicoloured.

3622	500b. Type **594**	4·00	3·50
3623	500b. Crucifix	4·00	3·50
3624	500b. Church of Our Lady of the Angels, La Grita	4·00	3·50
3625	500b. Our Lady of the Angels (statue)	4·00	3·50
3626	500b. Jauregui in Cardinal's robes	4·00	3·50

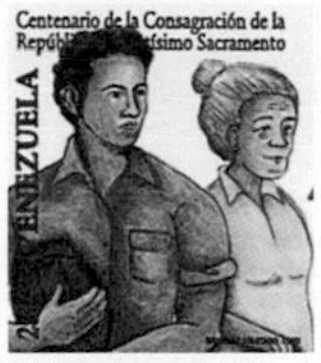

595 Worker and Old Lady

1999. Centenary of Consecration of Church of the Blessed Sacrament, Caracas. Multicoloured.

3627	250b. Type **595**	2·00	1·70
3628	250b. Priest	2·00	1·70
3629	250b. Reliquary	2·00	1·70
3630	250b. Boy and girl	2·00	1·70
3631	250b. Family	2·00	1·70
3632	250b. Doctor	2·00	1·70
3633	250b. Woman with flower in hair	2·00	1·70
3634	250b. Angels beside base of reliquary	2·00	1·70
3635	250b. Soldier	2·00	1·70
3636	250b. Boy with spear	2·00	1·70
MS3637	205×120 mm. 500b. Wafer (41×36 mm)	4·75	4·75

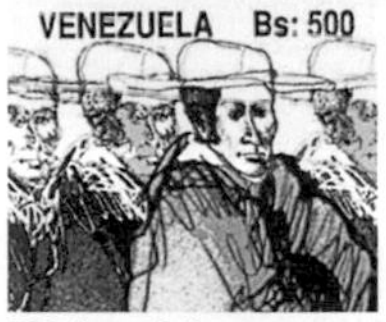

596 Simon Bolivar

1999. 20th Anniv of Andean Parliament.

MS3638	207×126 mm. **596** 500b. multicoloured	4·75	4·75

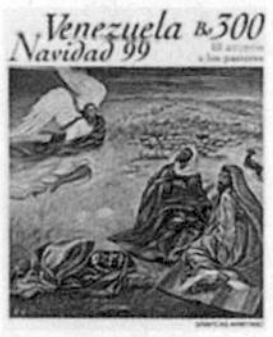

597 Angel appearing to Wise Men

1999. Christmas. Multicoloured.

3639	300b. Type **597**	2·50	2·10
3640	300b. Wise men on camels	2·50	2·10
3641	300b. Wise men presenting gifts	2·50	2·10
3642	300b. Flight into Egypt	2·50	2·10
3643	300b. Roman soldier chasing Mary and Baby Jesus	2·50	2·10
3644	500b. Mary and Joseph	4·00	3·50
3645	500b. Mary and Archangel Gabriel	4·00	3·50
3646	500b. Women talking	4·00	3·50
3647	500b. Joseph with Mary on donkey	4·00	3·50
3648	500b. Mary, Baby Jesus and old man	4·00	3·50

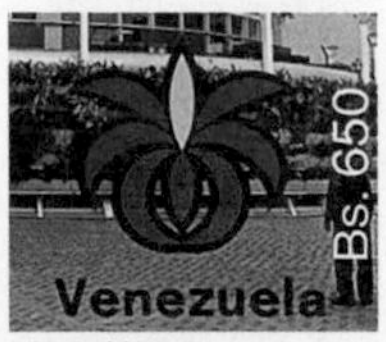

598 Emblem

2000. EXPO 2000 World's Fair, Hanover, Germany. Sheet 206×120 mm.

MS3649	**598** 650b. multicoloured	7·00	7·00

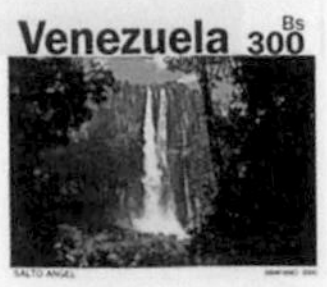

599 Angel Falls

2000. Organization of Petroleum Exporting Countries Conference, Caracas. Multicoloured.

3650	300b. Type **599**	3·25	2·50
3651	300b. View over Forest	3·25	2·50
3652	300b. Waterfall	3·25	2·50
3653	300b. Aerial view of swamp	3·25	2·50
3654	300b. Auyantipuy Peak from Rio Carrao	3·25	2·50
3655	400b. Lake Maracaibo	4·50	3·75
3656	400b. Humboldt Peak	4·50	3·75
3657	400b. Aerial view of swamp	4·50	3·75
3658	400b. Rio Morichal swamp	4·50	3·75
3659	400b. Auyantepuy Peak	4·50	3·75
3660	550b. Emblem of "Riyadh, Cultural Capital of Arab World, 2000", Saudi Arabia	6·25	5·25
3661	550b. "Mohammed Racim" (painting, detail), Algeria	6·25	5·25
3662	550b. Dubai, United Arab Emirates	6·25	5·25
3663	550b. Greater bird of paradise, Indonesia	6·25	5·25
3664	550b. Figure from relief depicting Assyrian War, Iraq	6·25	5·25
3665	550b. Procession, Tehran, Iran	6·25	5·25
3666	550b. National emblem, Kuwait	6·25	5·25
3667	550b. "The Great Artificial River" project emblem, Libya	6·25	5·25
3668	550b. Bronze mask, Nigeria	6·25	5·25
3669	550b. Al-Zubarah Fort, Qatar	6·25	5·25

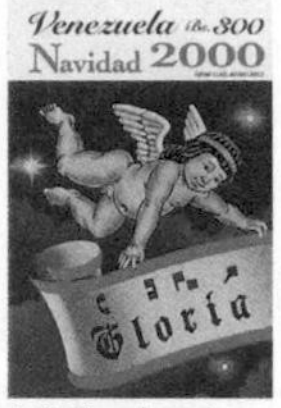

600 Cherub and "Gloria"

2000. Christmas. Multicoloured.

3670	300b. Type **600**	3·00	2·50
3671	300b. Cherub and "a"	3·00	2·50
3672	300b. Cherub and "en los"	3·00	2·50
3673	300b. Cherub and "Tielos"	3·00	2·50
3674	300b. Shepherd carrying lamb	3·00	2·50
3675	300b. Woman carrying jug	3·00	2·50
3676	550b. Joseph	5·75	4·75
3677	550b. Mary	5·75	4·75
3678	650b. Cherub and "Dios"	6·50	5·50
3679	650b. Baby Jesus	6·50	5·50

Nos. 3670/9 were issued together, *se-tenant*, with the whole forming a composite design.

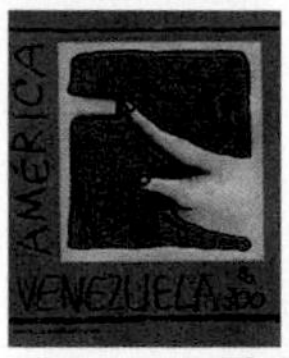

601 Finger over Rifle End

2000. America. Millennium without Arms. Multicoloured.

3680	300b. Type **601**	3·25	2·50
3681	650b. Seated man holding lyre	6·25	5·25

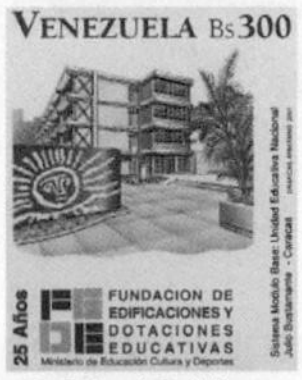

602 School Buildings, Caracas

2001. Educational Building and Endowment Foundation. Multicoloured.

3682	300b. Type **602**	3·00	2·50
3683	300b. Las Salinas, Vargas	3·00	2·50
3684	300b. Las Matas "Education for All" centre, Portuguesa	3·00	2·50
3685	400b. Santo Domingo school, Merida	4·00	3·25
3686	400b. Miguel Flores school, Yaracuy	4·00	3·25

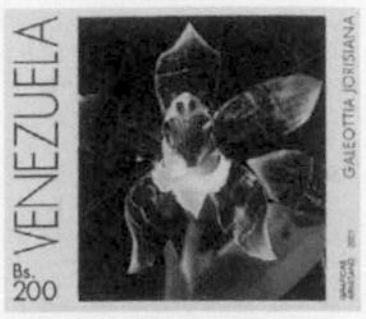

603 *Galeottia jorisiana*

2001. Orchids. Two sheets. Multicoloured.

MS3687 (a) 136×210 mm. 200b. ×2, Type **603**; *Lycaste longipetala*; 300b. ×2, *Coryanthes albertinae*; *Hexisea bidentata*; 400b. ×2, *Lycaste macrophylla*; *Masdevalliamaculate*; 550b. ×4, *Ada aurantiaca*; *Kefersteinia graminea*; *Sobralia liliastrum*; Gongora maculata (b) 146×120 mm. 650b. *Masdevallia tovarensis*. Set of 2 sheets — 43·00 43·00

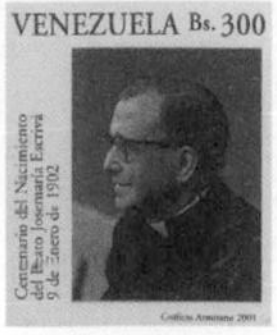

604 Josemaria Escriva

2001. Birth Centenary of Josemaria Escriva de Balaguer (founder of Opus Dei (religious organization)). Sheet 192×115 mm containing T **604** and similar vert designs. Multicoloured.

MS3688 300b. ×6, Type **604**; Bells, Opus Dei foundation, Madrid; Infant Jesus; With men from five continents; Commemorative plaque, Caracas Cathedral; Crowds, St. Peter's Square, Vatican; 550b. ×4, With women from many nations; Receiving honorary doctorate, Navarra University; With children, Venezuela; Josemaria Escriva (different) — 38·00 38·00

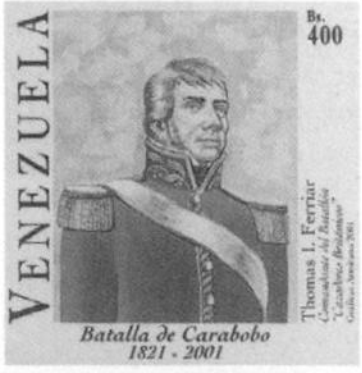

605 Thomas Ferriar

2001. 180th Anniv of Battle of Carabobo. Sheet 252×126 mm containing T **605** and similar vert designs showing paintings. Multicoloured.

MS3689 400b. ×5, Type **605** (battalion commander); "Bolivar in Buenavista" (Martin Tovar y Tovar); Letter (detail) (Simon Bolivar (leading general, War of Independence)); Commemorative column; Pedro Camejo (cavalry lieutenant, War of Independence); 600b. ×5, "Jose Antonio Paez" (post-Independence president) (Martin Tovar y Tovar); "General Santiago Marino" (Martin Tovar y Tovar); "Simon Bolivar" (M. Eberstein); "Manuel Cedeno" (Tito Salas); "Ambrosio Plaza" (Tito Salas) — 43·00 43·00

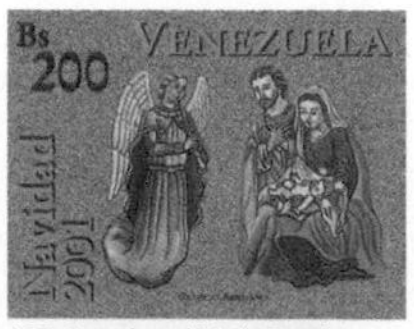

606 Angel and Holy Family

2001. Christmas. Sheet 133×210 mm containing T **606** and similar horiz designs. Multicoloured.

MS3690 200b. Type **606**; 200b. Family and angel playing guitar; 220b. Family and angel playing lute; 220b. Family and angel playing trumpet; 280b. Family and angel playing violin; 280b. Family and angel playing harp; 400b. Family and angel playing bagpipes; 400b. Family and angel playing panpipes; 500b. Family and angel playing drum; 500b. Family and angel playing bowed instrument — 28·00 28·00

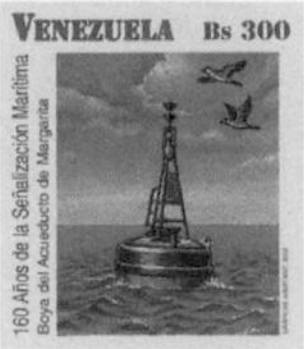

607 South Cardinal Buoy, Acueducto de Margarita

2002. 160th Anniv of Maritime Signalling. Sheet 210×120 mm containing T **607** and similar vert designs showing buoys (300b.) or lighthouses (others). Multicoloured.

MS3691 300b. ×2, Type **607**; North Cardinal buoy; 450b. ×4, Lighthouses, Punta Brava; Punta Macolla; Los Roques; Redonda Island; 500b. ×4, Punta Faagoza; Punta Ballena; Punta Tigre; Recalada de Guiria — 23·00 23·00

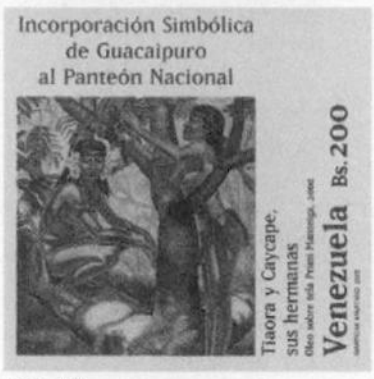

608 Women

2002. Guacaipuro (aboriginal resistance fighter). Sheet 124×250 mm containing T **608** and similar square designs. Multicoloured.

MS3692 200b. Type **608**; 300b. Attacking horseman; 300b. Scout leading Spanish soldiers; 300b. Carrying spear and dead soldiers; 300b. Killing Spanish soldier; 300b. Running from fire; 300b. Spaniards killing Guacaipuro; 350b. Woman; 400b. Carrying spear by stream; 500b. Seated — 17·00 17·00

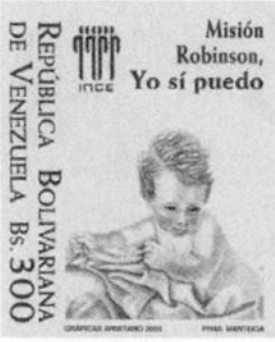

609 Toddler

2003. Mission Robinson (educational initiative). Sheet 97×228 mm containing T **609** and similar vert designs. Multicoloured.

MS3693 300b. ×4, Type **609**; Boy reading; Simon Bolivar and torch; Simon "Robinson" Rodriguez (Bolivar's teacher); 400b. ×2, Rodriguez and Eiffel Tower, Paris; Bolivar and flag; 500b. ×4, Bolivar and Rodriguez reading; Rodriguez seated and Bolivar standing; Rodriguez and reading class; Natives reading — 10·00 10·00

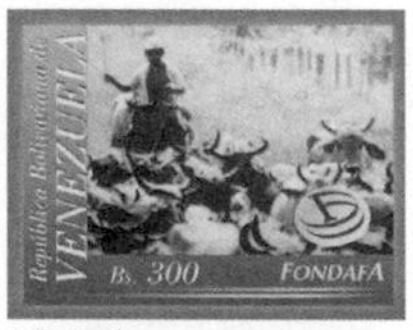

610 Cattle

2003. Fourth Anniv of FONDAFA (Agricultural, fisheries and forestry fund). Sheet 135×210 mm containing T **610** and similar horiz designs. Multicoloured.

MS3694 300b. ×6, Type **610**; Ploughing with cattle; Tractors; Farmer holding beet; Maize; FONDAFA boats; 400b. ×2, Corn cob; Farmer driving tractor; 500b. ×2, Cacao pods; Cacao beans — 9·25 9·25

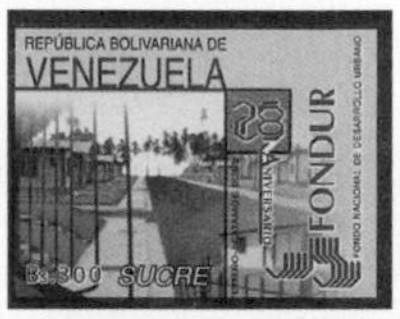

611 Sucre

2003. 28th Anniv of FONDUR (National urban development fund). Sheet 136×210 mm containing T **611** and similar horiz designs showing urban areas. Multicoloured.

MS3695 300b. ×6, Type **611**; Trujillo; Carabobo; Miranda; Barinas; Portuguesa; 400b. ×2, Tachira; Vargas; 500b. ×2, Emblem; Lara — 9·25 9·25

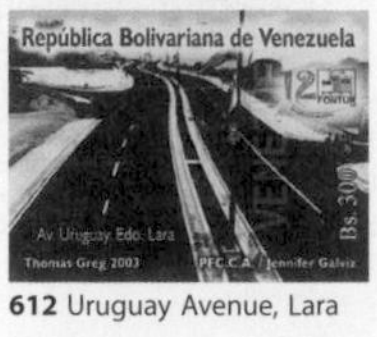

612 Uruguay Avenue, Lara

2003. 12th Anniv of FONTUR (National urban transportation fund). Sheet 135×210 mm containing T **612** and similar horiz designs. Multicoloured.

MS3696 300b. ×3, Type **612**; Parama highway, Merida; Gumana Avenue, Sucre; 400b. ×3, Santa Lucia—Jocoa highway, Barinas; Francisco Fajardo freeway, Caracas; Students; 500b. ×4, El Paraiso tunnel, Caracas; Vivex monitoring station; Trucks financed by FONTUR; Cruz Paredes Avenue, Barinas — 10·50 10·50

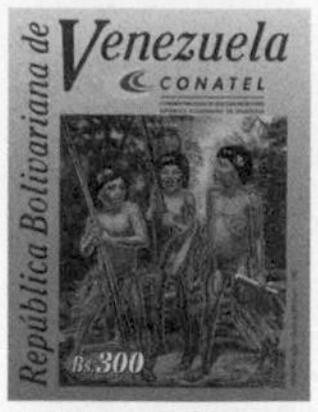

613 Native Children

2003. 12th Anniv of CONATEL (National telecommunications commission). Sheet 210×135 mm containing T **613** and similar vert designs. Multicoloured.

MS3697 300b. ×4, Type **613**; Children, hammock and dogs; Mountains; Caracas city; 400b. ×2, Child holding bow standing in boat; Beach; 500b. ×2, Children firing arrows; Angel Falls; 600b. ×2, Children making baskets; Sand and palms — 11·00 11·00

No. **MS**3697 has a brief description of each stamp printed in the margin.

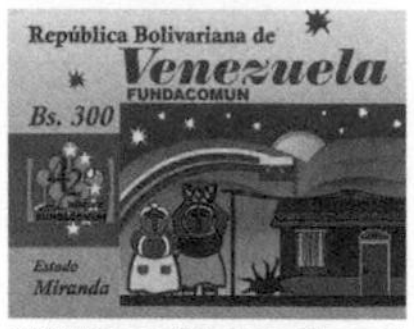

614 Women, Rainbow, Flag and Sun

2004. 42nd Anniv of FUNDCOMUN (Community and municipal reconstruction development fund). Sheet 135×209 mm containing T **614** and similar horiz designs. Multicoloured.

MS3698 300b. ×3, Type **614** (Miranda); House and kites (Trujillo); Mountains, house and couple (Merida); 400b. ×3, Sun, sand and buildings (Falcon); House, boy, beach ball and fish (Vargas); Yachts, rainbow and church (Esparta); 500b. ×4, Houses, rainbow, woman and children (Caracas); Children in playground (Caracas); Maracas, moon and houses (Barinas); Temple, children, sun and houses (Lara) — 10·50 10·50

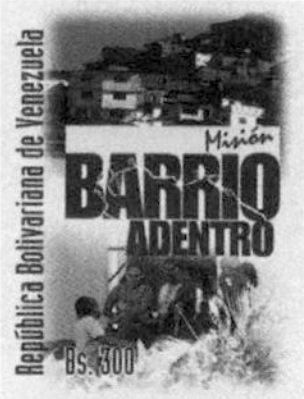

615 Houses and People in Doorway

2004. Mission Barrio Adentro (health initiative). Two sheets containing T **615** and similar vert designs. Multicoloured.

MS3699 (a) 210×134 mm. 300b. ×2, Type **615**; Smiling woman and street scene; 500b. ×4, Men pushing barrows and woman holding child; Family and children; Boys playing baseball and boat; Fence, people and man wearing cap; 750b. Man and sand dunes; 1500b. ×2, Man holding guitar and cattle; Mountain and girl; 1700b. Aboriginals and river (b) 205×120 mm. 1000b. Men pushing barrows. Set of 2 sheets — 21·00 21·00

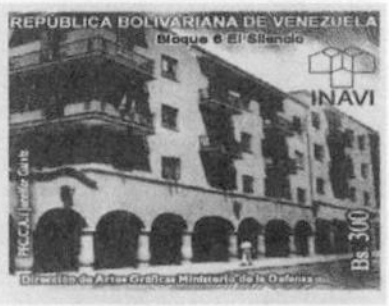

616 El Silencio, Caracas

2004. INAVI (National Housing Institute). Sheet 133×211 mm containing T **616** and similar horiz designs.

MS3700 300b. black; 300b. multicoloured; 300b. black; 400b. multicoloured; 400b. black; 400b. multicoloured; 500b. black; 500b. multicoloured; 500b. black; 500b. multicoloured — 19·00 19·00

DESIGNS: Type **616**; 300b. Building facades, El Pillar, Merido; 300b. Doorway, El Silencio; 400b. Bungalow with blue door, La Quiborena, Lara; 400b. Building with balconies, El Silencio; 400b. Bungalows with shuttered windows, Santa Ana, Nueva Esparta; 500b.Arches and multi-storey building, El Silencio; 500b.Four-storied building, La Quircacha, Tachira; 500b. Building plans; 500b. Los Peregrinos, Bolivar.

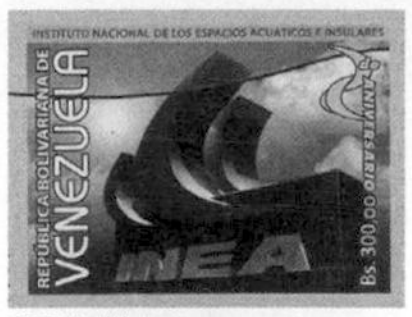

617 Emblem

2004. INEA (National Institute of Water Bodies). Sheet 133×207 mm containing T **617** and similar horiz designs. Multicoloured.

MS3701 300b. Type **617**; 300b. Emblem and building; 500b. Marine fire-fighters; 500b. Marine fire-fighter moving barrel; 500b. Sinking of tug-boat *Gran Roche*; 500b. *Gran Roche* from underwater; 600b. Tugboats; 1000b. Merchant shipping; 1500b. Our Lady of Valle Ante Dios (patron saint of sailors); 1700b. Boats and birds 18·00 18·00

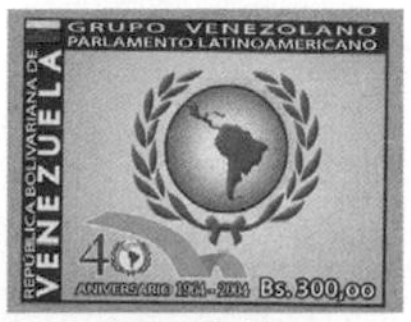

618 Parliament Emblem

2004. 40th Anniv of Latin American Parliament. Two sheets containing T **618** and similar horiz designs. Multicoloured.

MS3702 (a) 134×208 mm. 300b. Type **618**; 300b. Anniversary emblem; 300b. Parliamentary flag; 450b. Members flags; 450b. Andres Townsend Escurraz (co-founder); 500b. Luis Beltran Prieto Figueroa (co-founder); 500b. Nelson Carneiro (co-founder); 1500b. Assembly, Venezuela headquarters; 1500b. Assembly, Sao Paulo, Brasil; 1700b. Headquarters, Brasil. (b) 208×134 mm. 300b. Emblem (35×45 mm); 300b. Mountain and flags (35×45 mm); 300b. Anniversary emblem (35×45 mm); 450b. Children (35×45 mm); 450b. Map of Latin America and flags (35×45 mm); 500b. "Tierra de Integracion" (35×45 mm); 500b. Map of Central America (35×45 mm); 1500b. Dove (35×45 mm); 1500b. Simon Bolivar (35×45 mm); 1700b. Laurel wreath of flags (35×45 mm) 35·00 35·00

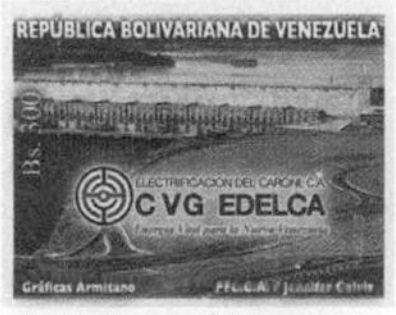

619 Emblem and Dam

2004. CVG EDELCA (electricity providers). Two sheets containing T **619** and similar horiz designs. Multicoloured.

MS3703 (a) 133×208 mm. 300b. Type **619**; 300b. Pylons and cables; 400b. Power station; 500b. Power station interior; 500b. Children; 500b. Dam and water-shoot; 500b. Dam (different); 600b. Solar panels; 1000b. Water and buildings (Eco-museum); 1500b. Gran Sabana mountains. (b) 205×119 mm. 1000b. Dam and water-shoot (as 500b.) (42×37 mm) 17·00 17·00

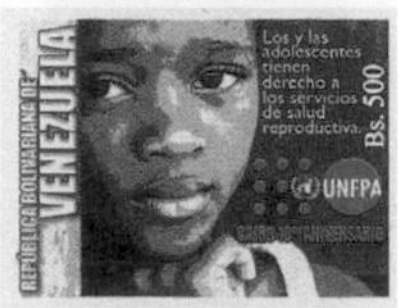

620 Child's Face

2004. Tenth Anniv of International Conference on Population and Development, Cairo. UNFPA (United Nations Population Fund). Sheet 134×210 mm containing T **620** and similar horiz designs. Multicoloured.

MS3704 500b. Type **620**; 500b. Men seated; 500b. Two girls; 500b. Boys; 1000b. Smiling woman; 1000b. Two children; 1000b. Mothers and children; 1000b. Children and adults; 1000b. Woman's face; 1000b. Many faces and AIDS sufferers 19·00 19·00

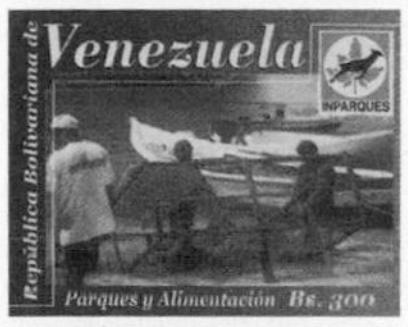

621 Fishermen

2004. National Parks. Sheet 135×210 mm containing T **621** and similar horiz designs. Multicoloured.

MS3705 300b. Type **621**; 300b. Teacher and students; 400b. Children; 500b. Waterfall and rapids; 500b. Mountains and lake; 500b. Waterfall and lake; 500b. Bird flying over mountains; 600b. Tower and waterfall; 1000b. Cable car and mountain; 1500b. Child holding bird 15·00 15·00

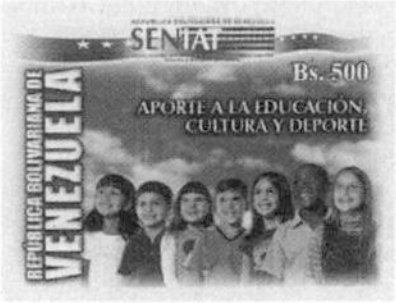

622 Children

2004. SENIAT (National Integrated Services Administration). Sheet 135×211 mm containing T **622** and similar horiz designs. Multicoloured.

MS3706 500b. Type **622**; 500b. Doctor and child; 500b. Customs officers; 500b. Skyscrapers; 1000b. Baseball players; 1000b. Customs headquarters building; 1000b. Buses; 1000b. School child, train and roadway; 1000b. Traditional building; 1000b. Modern building 19·00 19·00

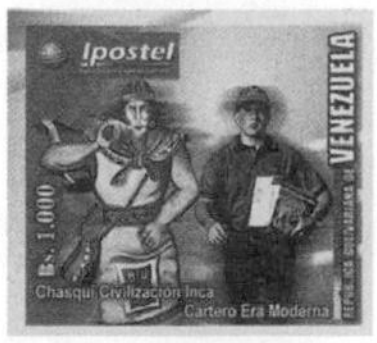

623 Inca and Modern Messenger

2004. World Post Day. Sheet [illegible] mm

MS3707 **623** 1000b. multicoloured 2·40 2·40

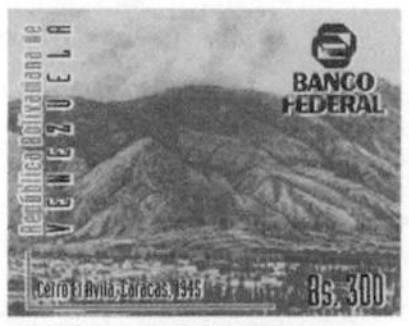

624 Cerro El Avila, Caracas, 1945

2004. Banco Federal. Two sheets, each 182×211 mm containing T **624** and similar horiz designs. Multicoloured.

MS3708 (a) 300b. Type **624**; 300b. New Circus, Caracas, 1970; 300b. Venezuela Plaza, Caracas, 1943; 300b. Couple (sculpture) (Francisco Narvaez), 1943; 300b. Baralt Theatre, Maracaibo, 1883; 400b. Race car, Caracas, 1956; 400b. El Paraiso racecourse, Caracas, 1908; 400b. Luis Sanchez Olivares (bullfighter), Caracas, 1950; 600b. Cable car, Merida, 1954; 600b. Men and women, Salto Angel, Bolivar, 1937; 750b. Emblem; 750b. Banco Federal building; 1000b. Virgen de Coromoto; 1700b. El Silencio, Caracas, 1945. (b) 300b. San Fernando de Apure church; 300b. Caracas Cathedral; 300b. Coro Cathedral; 300b. Santa Ines de Cumana Cathedral; 300b. Our Lady of Chiquinquira Basilica; 400b. Our Lady of Coromoto Basilica; 400b. Santa Rosa de Lima de Ortiz church; 400b. Merida Cathedral; 600b. Our Lady of Asuncion Cathedral; 600b. San Cristobal Cathedral; 750b. Emblem; 750b. Banco Federal building (different); 1000b. Virgen de Coromoto (different); 1700b. Valencia Cathedral 38·00 38·00

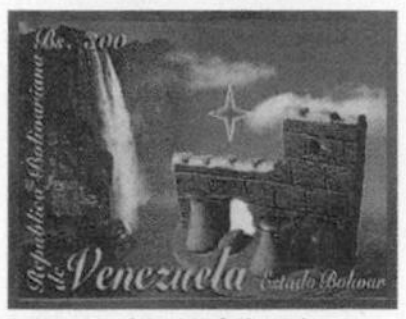

625 Angel Waterfall and Nativity (Bolivar)

2004. Christmas. Sheet 127×210 mm containing T **625** and similar horiz designs. Multicoloured.

MS3709 300b. Type **625**; 300b. Church and Nativity (Falcon); 400b. Nativity and cable car (Merida); 400b. Beach and Nativity (Aragua); 600b. Building and Nativity (Miranda); 750b. Mountains and Nativity (Miranda); 750b. Sand dunes and Nativity (Falcon); 1000b. Nativity and bridge (Zulia); 1000b. Mountains and angel (Bolivar); 1700b. Tree, Mary and Joseph (Trujillo) 18·00 18·00

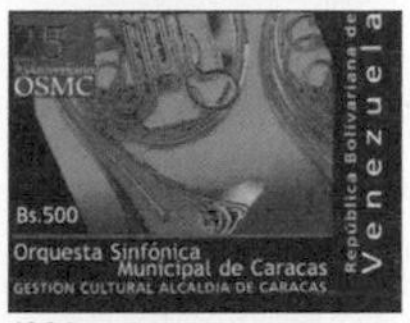

626 French Horn

2005. 25th Anniv of Caracas Municipal Orchestra. Sheet 130×210 mm containing T **626** and similar horiz designs. Multicoloured.

MS3710 500b. Type **626**; 500b. Cello; 500b. Violin; 500b. Xylophone; 1000b. Drums; 1000b. Clarinets; 1000b. Flutes; 1000b. Oboes; 2000b. Trumpets; 2000b. Trombone 48·00 48·00

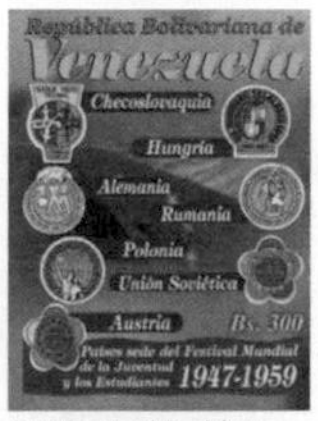

627 Festival Emblems 1947–1959

2005. World Youth and Student Festival. Two sheets containing T **627** and similar multicoloured designs.

MS3711 210×136 mm. 300b. Type **627**; 300b. Festival emblems 1962–2005; 300b. Hands grasping arms; 300b. 'Simon Bolivar...' and emblem; 500b. Simon Bolivar and signature; 500b. Broken chain; 500b. Simon Bolivar, head and shoulders; 500b. Dove; 500b. Dove and hands supporting globe; 1500b. Festival emblem [illegible]

MS3712 212×125 mm. 1000b. Simon Bolivar with arm outstretched (42×37 mm) 8·00 8·00

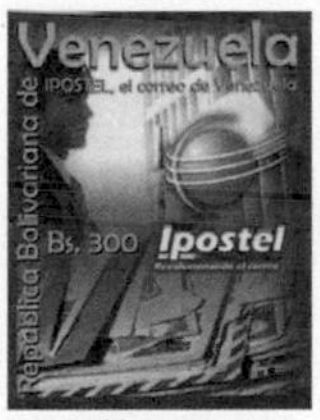

628 Emblem, Postman and Envelopes

2005. IRPOSTEL Postal Services. Sheet 210×132 mm containing T **628** and similar vert designs. Multicoloured.

MS3713 300b. Type **628**; 300b. Postal worker and mail sacks; 400b. Mail on conveyor belt; 400b. Postmen and parcels; 600b. Postal workers sorting mail; 600b. Seated postal workers, Ribas Mission; 1700b. Mail sacks; 1700b. Doctor and medical equipment, Barrio Adentro Mission; 1700b. Postal worker and machinery; 2000b. Fork lift truck and Mercal emblem 45·00 45·00

It is reported that another miniature sheet was released for this issue.

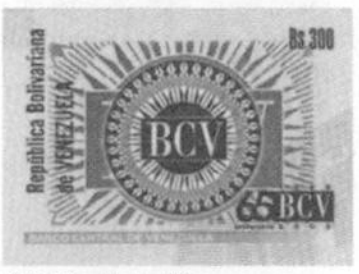

629 Bank Emblem

2005. 65th Anniv of Central Bank. Sheet 210×132 mm containing T **629** and similar horiz designs. Multicoloured.

MS3714 300b. Type **629**; 300b. Caracas branch; 400b. Maracaibo branch; 400b. National mint; 600b. Children's hands (Children's economic educational programme); 600b. Numismatic museum; 1500b. Plaza Juan Pedro Lopez; 1500b. Gold bars; 1700b. Bank notes and printing plates; 1700b. Coins 45·00 45·00

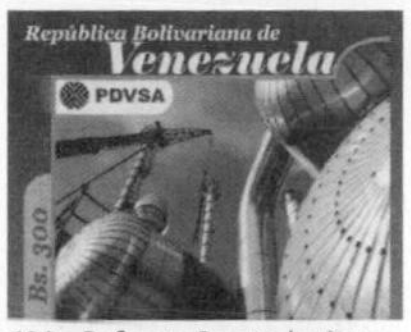

629a Refinery, Puerto La Cruz

2005. PDVSA–Petroleum in Venezuela. Sheet 135×210 mm. containing T **629a** and similar horiz designs. Multicoloured.

MS3714a 300s. Type **629a**; 300s. Refinery (different); 450s. Aerial view of refinery; 450s. Pipes, Musca complex; 500s. Drilling rig, Morichal; 500s. Holding tanks; 600s. Oilfield, Morichal; 600s. Fractionation plant and despatch, Jose; 750s. Storage terminal and shipment of crude oil, Jose; 1000s. Marine terminal, Guarguao 45·00 45·00

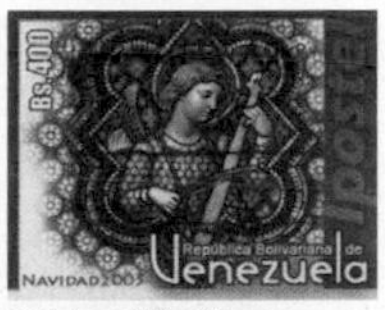

630 Angel Musician

2005. Christmas. Sheet 135×210 mm containing T **630** and similar horiz designs. Multicoloured.

MS3715 400b. Type **630**; 400b. Angel with lute; 400b. Angel with harp; 600b. Angel with maracas; 600b. Angel with bowed instrument; 600b. Angel playing serpent; 1000b. Angel with maracas; 1000b. Angel musician; 1500b. Angel with bowed instrument; 2000b. Angel with lute 38·00 38·00

No. 3716 and Type **631** have been left for 'National Guard', issued on 23 February 2006, not yet received.

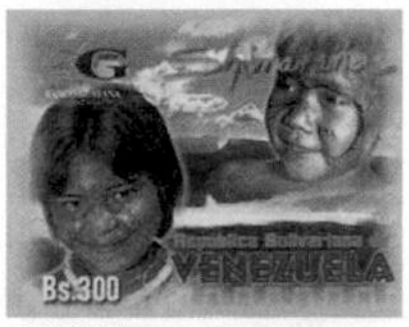

632 Children

2006. 50th Anniv of Guayana Bank. Shimarana Tribal Nation. Sheet 135×210 mm containing T **632** and similar horiz designs. Multicoloured.

MS3717 300b. Type **632**; 300b. [illegible]ers; 500b. Canoeists; 300b. Grass skirted women; 500b. Woman's face and canoeist; 500b. Children; 1700b. Archers in canoes; 1700b. Man and child; 2000b. Small child; 2000b. Women, river and dancers 16·00 16·00

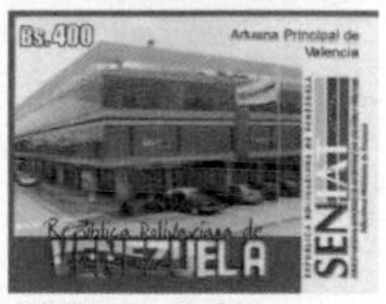

633 Customs Building, Valencia

2006. National Tax and Customs Administration. Sheet 131×206 mm containing T **633** and similar horiz designs showing Customs buildings. Multicoloured.

MS3718 400b. Type **633** ; 400b. Puerto Cabello; 500b. Paraguachon; 500b. Santa Elena de Uairen; 700b. Maiquetia; 700b. Maiquetia (different); 1000b. Urena; 1000b. San Antonio del Tachira; 2000b. Barcelona; 2000b. La Guaira 18·00 18·00

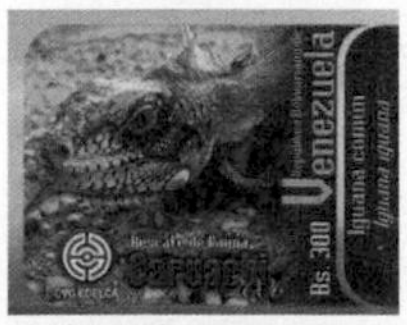

634 *Iguana iguana*

2006. Carauchi Hydroelectric Dam Project. Two sheets containing T **634** and similar horiz designs . Multicoloured.

MS3719 136×210 mm. 300b. Type **634** ; 300b. *Caluromys philander* (bare-tailed woolly opossum); 1000b. *Paleosuchus palpebrosus* (Cuvier's dwarf caiman); 1000b. *Geochelone carbonaria* (red-footed tortoise); 1000b. *Cebus olivaceus* (weeper capuchin) ; 1000b. *Choloepus didactylus* (two-toed sloth); 1500b. *Tupinambis teguixin* (common tegu); 1500b. *Oxybelis fulgidus* (green vine snake); 2000b. *Coendou prehensilis* (Brazilian porcupine); 2000b. *Tamandua tetradactyla* (lesser anteater) 35·00 35·00

MS3720 208×123 mm. 1000b. Dam (42×36 mm) 8·00 8·00

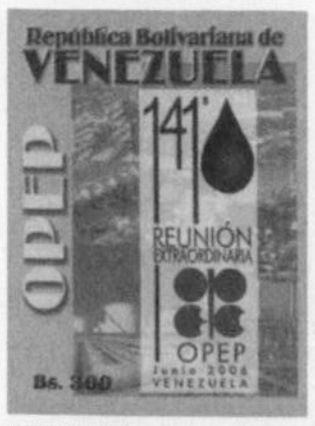

635 Emblem

2006. OPEC Extraordinary Meeting, Venezuela. Sheet 245×135 mm containing T **635** and similar vert designs showing oil refineries and flags of member countries. Multicoloured.

MS3721 300b. Type **635** ; 300b. United Arab Emirates; 500b. Lybia; 500b. Iraq; 500b. Saudi Arabia; 500b. Indonesia; 500b. Nigeria; 500b. Algeria; 1500b. Iran; 1500b. Qatar; 2000b. Venezuela; 2000b. Kuwait 48·00 48·00

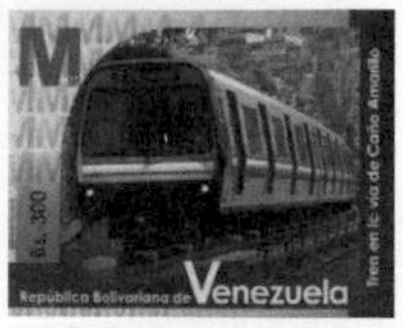

636 Train

2006. Caracas Mass Transit (Metro). Sheet 135×210 mm containing T **636** and similar horiz designs. Multicoloured.

MS3722 300b. Type **636** ; 300b. Yellow Line Station; 500b. Plaza Venezuela Station; 500b. Three trains; 1500b. Points; 1500b. Line 4 tunnel; 2000b. Metro bus; 2000b. Control room; 2000b. Construction of Line 4 Nuevo Circo Station; 2000b. *Cubo virtual azul y progresion amarilla* (Jesus Soto), Chacaito Station 48·00 48·00

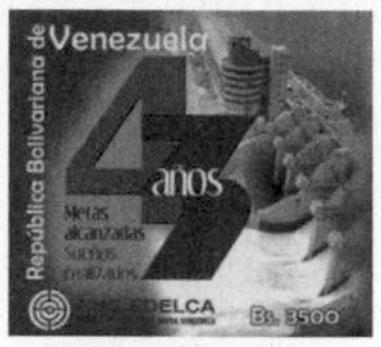

637 '43' and Power Plant

2006. 43rd Anniv of CVG EDELCA (electricity providers). Sheet 211×124 mm.

MS3723 multicoloured 34·00 34·00

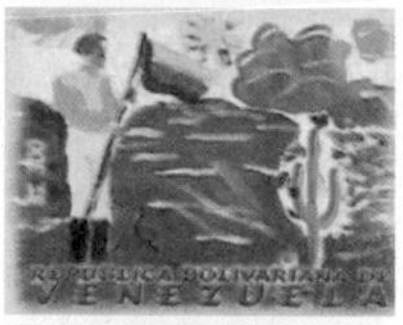

638 Francisco de Miranda and Flag of Liberty (Elimar Sanchez)

2006. Francisco de Miranda University. Three sheets containing T **638** and similar multicoloured designs.

MS3724 134×208 mm. 300b. Type **638** ; 300b. Francisco de Miranda and broken chain (Gabriel Solano); 300b. Francisco de Miranda and Catalina (Elikarina Sanchez); 300b. G clef (Josmelys Diaz); 500b. Child riding hobby horse (Nasser Sultan); 500b. Francisco de Miranda (Cynthia Urbina); 1500b. Flag (Janem Sultan); 1500b. Francisco de Miranda (Luis Miguel Martinez); 2000b. Family (Vianny Gonella); 2000b. Diary (Jose A Martinez) 27·00 27·00

MS3725 219×133 mm. Size 35×45 mm. 300b. Francisco de Miranda on horseback; 300b. Francisco de Miranda (head) facing left; 300b. Face (*Untitled* (Filipe Herrera)); 300b. Francisco de Miranda (statue); 500b. Francisco de Miranda holding flag; 500b. Francisco de Miranda at signing of independence treaty; 1500b. Francisco de Miranda (head and shoulders) facing left; 1500b. Two statues; 2000b. Francisco de Miranda (head) facing right; 2000b. Francisco de Miranda seated 27·00 27·00

MS3726 219×125 mm. 1500b. Francisco de Miranda seated 11·00 11·00

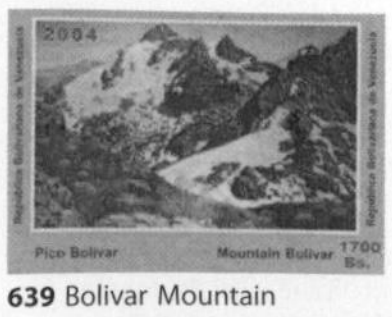

639 Bolivar Mountain

2006. Mountains. Multicoloured.

3727 1700b. Type **639** 16·00 16·00

3728 1700b. Damavand Mountain, Iran 16·00 16·00

No. 3727 is overprinted with 'REPUBLICA BOLIVARIANA DE VENEZUELA' in black. it is reported that No. 3727 also exists without the overprint.

Stamps of a similar design were issued by Iran.

Nos. 3727/8 are imprinted 2004.

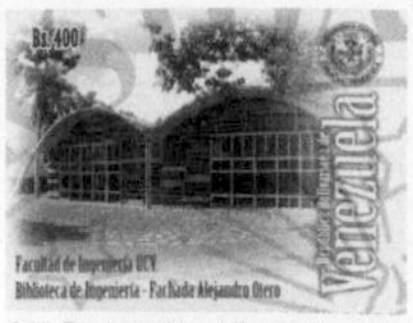

640 Engineering Library Façade

2006. Engineering Faculty, Central University, Caracas. Sheet 136×210 mm containing T **640** and similar horiz designs. Multicoloured.

MS3729 400b. Type **640**; 400b. Engineering Library interior; 400b. School of Electrical Engineering; 400b. Metallurgical and Engineering School of Materials Science; 600b. School of Civil Engineering; 600b. School of Chemical Engineering and Petroleum Geology; 3000b. Basic Cycle Engineering; 3000b. Institute of Materials and Structural Models; 5000b. Institute of Fluid Mechanics; 5000b. Auditorium 32·00 32·00

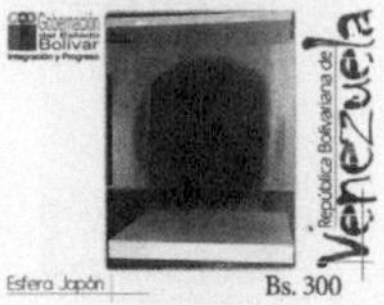

641 *Esfera Japon*

2006. Jesus Raphael Soto Commemoration. Two sheets containing T **641** and similar horiz designs. Multicoloured.

MS3730 136×210 mm. 300b. Type **641**; 300b. *Biface Naranja*; 500b. *Repeticion y progresión*; 500b. *Repeticion optica*; 500b. *Composicion dinámica*; 500b. *Muro optico*; 1000b. *Pardelas interferentes*; 1000b. *Espiral*; 1000b. *Ambivalencia diciembre*; 1000b. *Estructura cinetica* 48·00 48·00

MS3731 113×116 mm. 1500b. *Espiral* 11·00 11·00

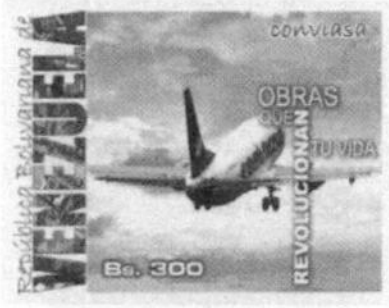

642 Conviasa Aircraft

2006. Infrastructure. Sheet 136×245 mm containing T **642** and similar horiz designs. Multicoloured.

MS3732 300b. Type **642**; 300b. Simon Bolivar Airport; 300b. Gran Mariscal de Ayacucho highway; 300b. Barquisimeto north ring road; 300b. José Antonio Paez highway; 300b. Caracas—La Guaira viaduct; 300b. Line 3, Caracas Metro; 2000b. Line 4, Caracas Metro; 2000b. Maracaibo Metro; 2000b. Los Teques Metro; 3000b. Valencia Metro; 3000b. Caracas—Tuy Medio railway 35·00 35·00

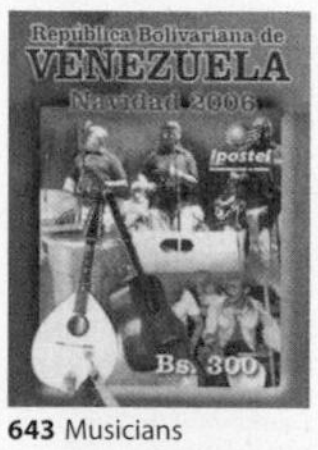

643 Musicians

2006. Christmas. Two sheets containing T **643** and similar multicoloured designs.

MS3733 210×134 mm. 300b. Type **643**; 300b. Cup and ball; 450b. Spinning top; 450b. Christmas table; 550b. Stuffed leaves; 550b. Christmas note; 1000b. Crucifix in lights; 1000b. Yoyo; 2000b. Toys; 3000b. Envelope enclosing Nativity 45·00 45·00

MS3734 210×126 mm. Size 42×37 mm. 300b. Nativity; 300b. Stuffed leaves; 1000b. Christmas note; 2000b. Nativity enclosed in postal emblem 29·00 29·00

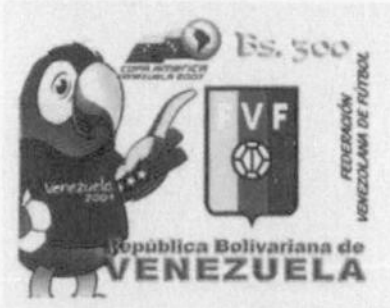

644 Guaky and Federacion Venezolana de Futbol Emblem

2007. Copa America Football Championship, Venezuela. Three sheets containing T **644** and similar horiz designs showing Guaky (championship mascot) (**MS**3736a), Guaky and Football Federation emblems (**MS**3735) or stadiums (**MS**3736b). Multicoloured.

MS3735 135×245 mm. 300b. Type **644**; 300b. Confederacion Brasilera de Futbol; 300b. Asociacion del Futbol Argentino; 300b. Federacion Mexicana de Futbol Asociacion; 400b. Federacion Colombiana de Futbol; 400b. Federacion de Futbol de Chile; 400b. Federacion Peruana de Futbol; 400b. Asocicion Uruguaya de Futbol; 2000b. Federacion Ecuatoriana de Futbol; 2000b. Federacion Boliviana de Futbol; 3000b. Asociacion Paraguaya de Futbol; 5000b. US Soccer Federation 55·00 55·00

MS3736 135×210 mm. (a) 300b. Guaky as player; 300b. As referee; 400b. As fireman; 400b. As doctor; 400b. As footballer; 400b. As construction worker; 2000b. As gardener; 2000b. As soldier; 3000b. As policeman; 5000b. As player kicking ball. (b) 300b. Guaky; 300b. University Olympic Stadium, Caracas; 400b. Estadio Jose Pachencho Romero, Maracaibo; 400b. Estadio Metropolitano de Futbol de Lara, Barquisimeto; 400b. Estadio Agustin Tovar (La Carolina), Barinas; 400b. Estadio General JA Anzoátegui, Puerto La Cruz; 2000b. Centro Total de Entretenimiento Cachamay; 2000b. Estadio Metropolitano, Merida; 3000b. Estadio Monumental, Maturin; 5000b. Estadio Polideportivo de Pueblo Nuevo, San Cristobal 55·00 55·00

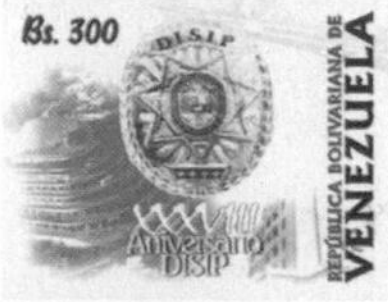

645 Emblem

2007. 38th Anniv of Intelligence and Prevention Service. Two sheets containing T **645** and similar horiz designs showing 'El Helicoide' Service Headquarters designed by Jorge Romero Gutiérrez. Multicoloured.

MS3737 135×210 mm. 300b. Type **645**; 300b. Model viewed from above; 300b. Model viewed from side; 300b. Construction; 300b. Cupola exterior; 300b. Cupola interior; 2000b. Aerial view showing cupola; 2000b. Aerial view showing entrance; 3000b. Garden; 5000b. Plaza Bolivar 45·00 45·00

MS3738 212×122 mm. Size 42×37 mm. 3500b. Aerial view of 'El Helicoide' 32·00 32·00

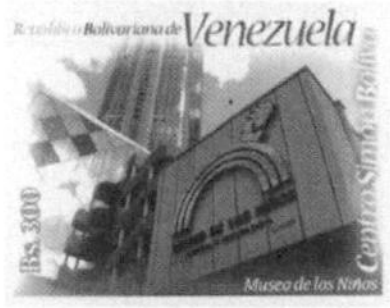

646 Museo de los Ninos

2007. Simon Bolivar Centre, Caracab. Sheet 135×210 mm containing T **646** and similar horiz designs. Multicoloured.

MS3739 300b. Type **646**; 300b. John Paul II building; 300b. Torres del Silencio (towers of silence); 300b. Palaicio de Justica; 450b. Parque Central; 450b. Museo de Arte Contemporaneo de Caracas; 2000b. Avenida Bolivar; 2000b. Paseo Vargas; 3000b. Teatro Teresa Carreno; 5000b. Cristobal Rojas 38·00 38·00

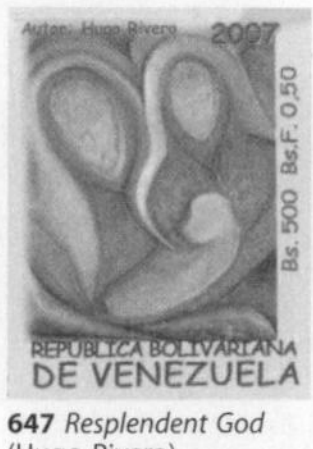

647 *Resplendent God* (Hugo Rivero)

2007. Christmas. Art. Sheet 210×134 mm containing T **647** and similar vert designs. Multicoloured.

MS3740 500b. Type **647**; 500b. *Creole Christmas* (Vidalia Gonzalez); 500b. *Christmas Door* (Socorro Perraza); 500b. *Nativity* (Orlando Campos); 1000b. *Nativity* (Tomás Flores); 1000b. *Christmas Wish* (Alberto Allup); 1000b. *St Joseph, Virgin and Child* (Baldomero Higuera); 1000b. *Nativity* (Edgar Vegas); 1500b. *Holy Family* (Margarita Perez de Lamanna); 1500b. *Merry Christmas* (Ana Teresa Peesce) 35·00 35·00

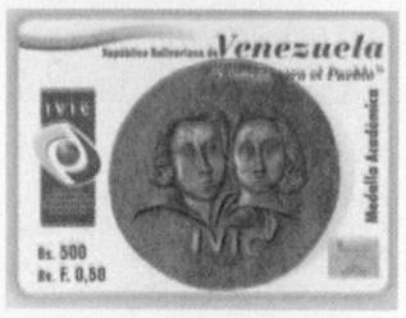

648 Academic Medal

2007. 50th Anniv (2005) of Institute of Scientific Investigation (IVIC). Two sheets containing T **648** and similar multicoloured designs.

MS3741 135×210 mm. 500b. Type **648**; 500b. Gargoyle; 500b. Plant producing blood derivatives; 500b. Beatriz de Roche children's education center ; 1000b. Molecular structure of myosin (motor proteins); 1000b. Laboratory; 1000b. Graduates from the Centre of Advanced Studies; 1000b. Bolivar y Bello Plaza; 2000b. Marcel Roche Library; 2000b. Samuel Robinson student residence 40·00 40·00

MS3742 201×121 mm. Size 42×37 mm. 500b. Abstract (Linda Morales); 500b. Waterfall (Alberto Allup); 500b. Landscape (Freddy Simonza); 500b. Figures (Orlando Campos) 16·00 16·00

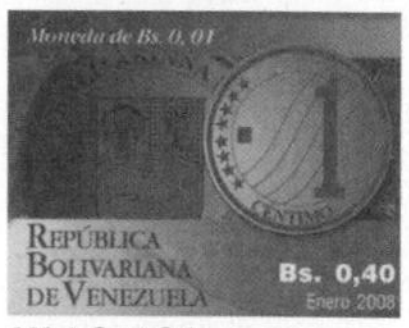

649 1 Cent Coin

2008. Currency Change. Sheet 135×280 mm. containing T **649** and similar horiz designs. Multicoloured.

MS3743 40c. Type **649**; 40c. New banknotes and coins; 40c. 10 cent coin; 40c. 5 cent coin; 50c. 25 cent coin; 50c. 12 cent coin; 60c. 1 bolivar coin; 60c. 50 cent coin; 1bf. Pedro Camejo (5 bolivar fuerte banknote); 1bf. Francisco de Miranda (2 bolivar fuerte banknote); 1bf.50 Luisa Caceres de Arismendi (20 bolivar fuerte banknote); 1bf. 50 Guaicaipuro (10 bolivar fuerte banknote); 2bf. Simon Bolivar (100 bolivar fuerte banknote); 2bf. Simon Rodriguez (50 bolivar fuerte banknote) 17·00 17·00

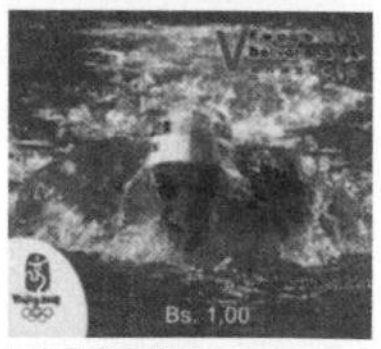

650 Swimming

2008. Olympic Games, Beijing. Sheet 200×120 mm containing T **650** and similar horiz designs. Multicoloured.

MS3744 1bf.×4, Type **650**; Weightlifting; Women wrestlers; Fencing 1·70 1·70

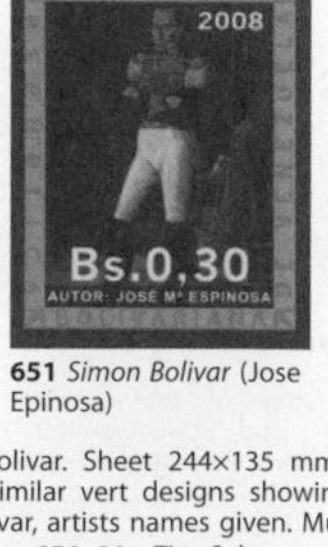

651 *Simon Bolivar* (Jose Epinosa)

2008. Simon Bolivar. Sheet 244×135 mm. containing T **651** and similar vert designs showing paintings of Simon Bolivar, artists names given. Multicoloured.

MS3745 30c. Type **651**; 30c. Tito Salas; 30c. Pierre Colf; 30c. Jose Gil de Castro; 50c. Angel Zeballos; 50c. Tito Salas; 50c. Jose Gil de Castro; 1bf.50 Juan Lovera; 1bf.50 Anonymous; 1bf. 50 Tito Salas; 3bf. Tito Salas; 10bf. Daniel Hernandez 3·50 3·50

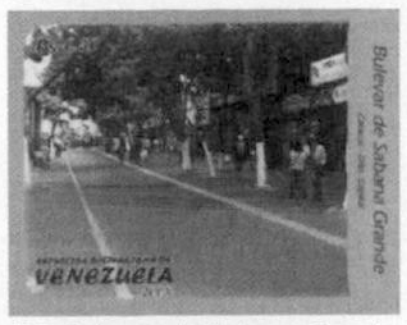

652 Bulevar de Sabana Grande

2008. Reconstruction of Caracas. Two sheets containing T **652** and similar horiz designs. Multicoloured.

MS3746 135×211 mm. 30c. Type **652**; 30c. Palacio de las Academias; 40c. El Venezolano Plaza; 40c. Abra Solar; 60c. Correo de Carmelitas; 60c. Plaza O'Leary ; 1bf.50 Paseo Monumental los Proceres; 1bf.50 Palacio Municipal; 5bf. Casona Anauco Arriba; 10bf. Plaza Bolivar 6·40 6·40

MS3747 223×125 mm. 3bf. Paseo Monumental los Proceres (different) 4·50 4·50

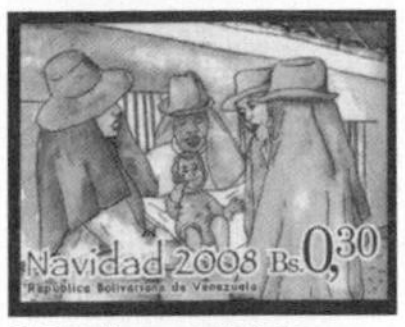

653 Indigenous Nativity

2008. Christmas. Sheet 135×210 mm containing T **653** and similar horiz designs. Multicoloured.

MS3748 30c. Type **653**; 30c. Children and Christ child in manger; 30c. Woman wrapping presents; 40c. Family meal; 40c. Girl and boy with toys; 1bf. Boys with kites; 1bf. Choir; 2bf. Children and creche; 3bf. Musicians; 5bf. Young people 4·75 4·75

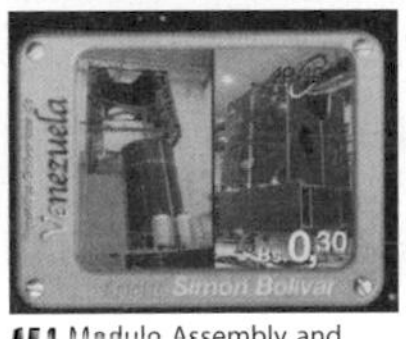

654 Modulo Assembly and Communication Platform

2009. Satellite Simon Bolivar. Sheet 137×210 mm containing T **654** and similar horiz designs. Multicoloured.

MS3749 30c. Type **654**; 30c. Operation assembly; 60c. Test deployment of antenna; 60c. Test deployment of solar north wing; 1bf. LM-3B rocket launcher; 1bf. Satellite control station; 2bf. launch, 28 October 2008; 3bf. Aerial view of the station monitoring and controling satellite, Bamari; 3bf. Inside monitoring station; 8bf. *Simon Bolivar* 17·00 17·00

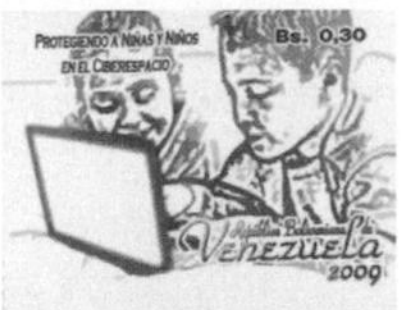

655 Children

2009. Protection for Children using the Internet. Sheet 136×210 mm containing T **655** and similar horiz designs showing children and computers. Multicoloured.

MS3750 30c. Type **655**; 30c. Children using PCs; 50c. Boy and PC; 50c. Two boys, one with head resting in hands watching PC; 50c. Two boys, one using PC, one writing; 50c. Boy and teacher in front of PC; 2bf. Indigenous children, teacher and laptops; 2bf. Boy with eyes raised in front of screen; 4bf. Young couple using laptop outside; 6bf.50 Children on laptop screen 17·00 17·00

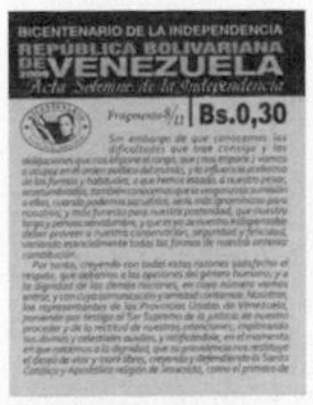

656 Act of Independence, Fragment 8/11

2009. Bicentenary of Independence (1st issue). Sheet 247×136 mm containing T **656** and similar horiz designs extracts from Act of Independence, fragment number given. Multicoloured.

MS3751 30c. Type **656**; 30c. Fragment 7/11; 30c. Fragment 9/11; 50c. Fragment 4/11; 50c. Fragment 6/11; 50c. Fragment 5/11; 1bf. Fragment 2/11; 1bf. Fragment 3/11; 2bf. Signatures, fragment 10/11; 2bf. Fragment 1/11; 3bf.50 Signatures, fragment 11/11; 9bf.50 Simon Bolivar 10·75 10·75

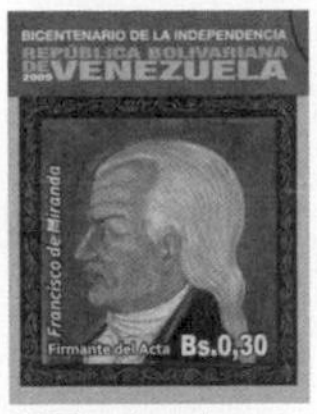

657 Francisco de Miranda

2009. Bicentenary of Independence (2nd issue). Multicoloured.

MS3752 246×136 mm. 30c. Type **657**; 30c. Salvador Delgado; 30c. Francisco Hernandez; 50c. Juan Antonio Diaz Argote; 50c. Felipe Fermin Paul; 50c. Juan José de Maya; 1bf. Manuel Vicente Maya; 1bf. Juan Toro; 2bf. Francisco Policarpo Ortiz; 2bf. Gabriel Perez de Pagola; 3bf.50 José Maria Ramirez; 9bf.50 Fernando Toro 12·00 12·00

MS3753 210×135 mm. 30c. Mariano de la Cova; 30c. Juan Bermudez; 50c. Francisco Isnardi; 50c. Manuel Placido Maneiro; 1bf. Juan Pablo Pacheo; 1bf. José Luis Cabrera; 2bf. Manuel Palacio; 2bf. Juan Nepomuceno Quintana; 3bf.50 Luis José de Cazorla; 9bf.50 Francisco Javier de Mayz 9·00 9·00

MS3754 210×135 mm. 30c. Juan German Roscio; 30c. Fernando Penalver; 50c. Martin Tovar Ponte; 1bf. Ignacio Fernandez; 1bf. José Angel Alamo; 1bf. Luis Ignacio Mendoza; 2bf. Nicolas de Castro; 2bf. Ignacio Ramon Briceno; 3bf.50 Francisco Javier Yanes; 9bf.50 Gabriel de Alcala 12·00 12·00

MS3755 210×135 mm. 30c. Gabriel de Ponte; 50c. Ramon Ignacio Mendéz; 50c.Lino de Clemente; 1bf. Isidoro Antonio Lopez Mendéz; 1bf. Francisco Javier Ustariz; 1bf. Marques del Toro; 2bf. Juan Antonio Rodriguez Dominguez; 2bf. José de Sata y Busy; 3bf.50 José Vicente de Unda; 9bf.50 Antonio Nicolas Briceno 12·00 12·00

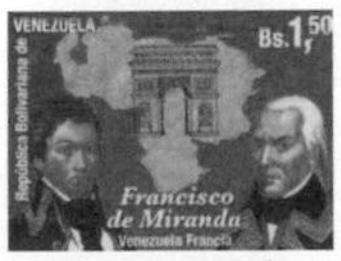

658 Francisco Miranda

2009. Sebastián Francisco de Miranda y Rodríguez (Francisco Miranda) (revolutionary) Commemoration

3756 1bf.50 multicoloured 85 85

A stamp of a similar design was issued by France.

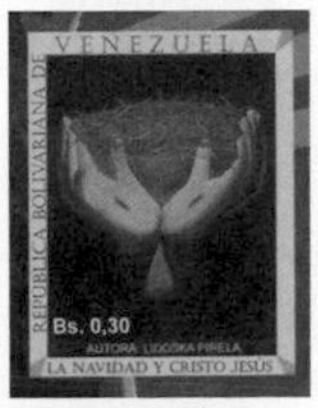

659 Hands holding Crown of Thorns (Lidoska Pirela)

2009. Christmas. Multicoloured.

MS3757 30c. Type **659**; 30c. Stylized crucifixion amongst clouds (Miguel Marsan); 30c. Headless torso on cross (Thays Artega); 30c. Christ as monk with bleeding heart (Gustavo Martinez); 50c. Stylized crucified Christ (Orlando Campos); 50c. Christ and chalice (Daniel Sanseviero); 50c. Head of Christ (Hugo Rivero); 3bf.10 Christ as stained glass window and three women (Edgar Vegas); 4bf.20 Symbols of crucifixion (Liliana Benitez); 6bf.50 Risen Christ, waterfall and forest (Alberto Allup) 12·00 12·00

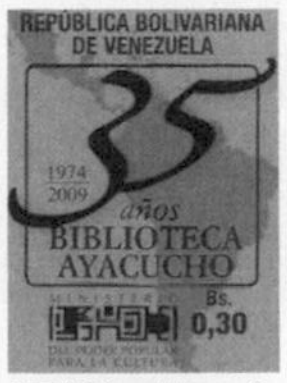

660 '35' and Map of South America

2009. 35th Anniv of Ayacucho Library. Multicoloured, background colour given.

MS3758 30c. Type **660**; 30c. Type **660** (green); 30c. Type **660** (blue); 30c. Type **660** (pale purple); 2bf. Type **660** (grey-brown); 2bf. Type **660** (pale blue); 3bf.50 Type **660** (gold); 3bf.50 Type **660** (pale yellow-olive); 4bf. Type **660** (pale pinkish brown); 4bf. Type **660** (pale olive-grey) 9·00 9·00

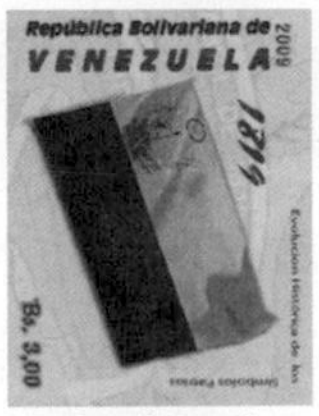

661 Flag of Manuel Gual y José Maria Espana, 1797

2009. Patriotic Symbols. Multicoloured.

MS3759 40c. Type **661**; 40c. Flag of Francisco de Miranda, 1800; 50c. Naval flag of Francisco de Miranda, 1806; 60c. Tricolour flag of Francisco de Miranda, 1806; 1bf. Flag of revolutionaries created to defend the rights of King Ferdinand VII, 1810; 1bf. Flag of Independence and first republic, 1811; 2bf. Flag of Congress of Cariaco, 1817; 2bf. Venezuelan flag created by Simon Bolivar ; 3bf. Provisional flag of Gran Colombia, 1819; 3bf. Constitutional congress flag of Gran Colombia, 1821 11·00 11·00

MS3760 40c. Constitional congress flag of Gran Colombia, 1821 (different); 40c. Constitutional congress flag of Gran Colombia, 1830; 50c. National flag of Gran Colombia, 1836 ; 60c. Provisional government federal flag, 1859; 1bf. Federal flag of General Ezequiel Zamora, 1859; 1bf. National flag of General Juan Crisostomo Falcon, 1863; 2bf. National flag of General Cipriano Castro, 1905; 2bf. Congress of United States of Venezuela flag, 1930; 3bf. Flag of republic decreed by National congress during government of General Marcos Perez Jimenez, 1954; 3bf. National flag of Bolivarian Republic of Venezuela sanctioned during the government of President Hugo Chavez Frias, 2006 11·00 11·00

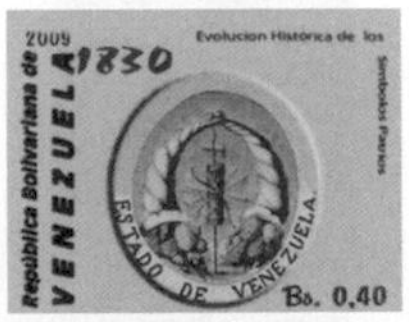

662 Constitutional Congress Arms of Republic, 1830

2009. Patriotic Symbols. Multicoloured.

MS3762 40c. Arms of city of Santiago de Leon, capital of province of Venezuela, granted by King Felipe II, according to royal decree, 1591; 40c. Oldest known arms of Republic of Venezuela from *El Publicista de Venezuela*, 1811; 50c. Seal type arms from cover of Federal Constitution for States of Venezuela, 1811; 60c. One of coats of arms of Republic of Venezuela used during the first republic, 1811; 1bf. Seal type arms from front-page of Federal Constitution for States of Venezuela, 1812; 1bf. Constitional congress arms of Confederation of Venezuela, 1812; 2bf. Provisionally decreed arms of Gran Colombia, 1819; 2bf. Constitional congress arms (Villa de Rosario de Cucuta) of Gran Colombia, 1821; 3bf. Constitional congress arms (Villa de Rosario de Cucuta) of Gran Colombia, 1821 (different); 3bf. Constitional congress arms (Guayaquil) of Gran Colombia, 1822 12·00 12·00

MS3763 40c. Type **662**; 40c. Chamber of Senate draft arms of Republic, 1834; 50c. Sir Robert Ker Porter arms of Republic, 1836; 60c. Arms of Republic, during government of General Jefe José Tadeo Monagas, 1856; 1bf. Federal arms of General Juan Crisostomo Falcon, 1863; 1bf. Arms of Congress of United States of Venezuela during government of General Antonio Guzman Blanco, 1871; 2bf. Arms of Congress of United States of Venezuela during government of General Cipriano Castro, 1905; 2bf. Arms of Congress of United States of Venezuela during government of General Juan Vicente Gomez, 1930; 3bf. Arms of Congress of United States of Venezuela during government of General Marcos Perez Jimenez, 1954; 3bf. Arms of Bolivarian Republic of Venezuela Naional sanctioned during the government of President Hugo Chavez Frias, 2006 13·00 13·00

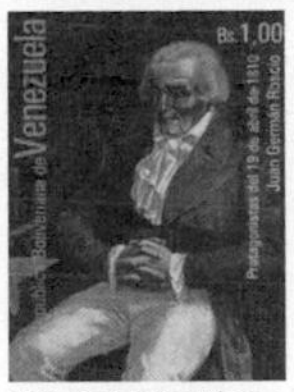

663 José Félix Ribas

2010. Bicentenary of 19 April 1810, establishment of First Republic of Venezuela. Multicoloured.

MS3764 1bf. Type **663**; 1bf. Juan German Roscio; 2bf.50 Juan Félix Sosa; 2bf.50 Lino de Clemente; 2bf.50 Isidoro Lopez Mendéz; 2bf.50 Francisco Espejo; 4bf. Francisco Salias; 4bf. Francisco Javier Ustariz; 4bf. Martin Tovar Ponte; 12bf. José Cortés de Madariaga 9·00 9·00

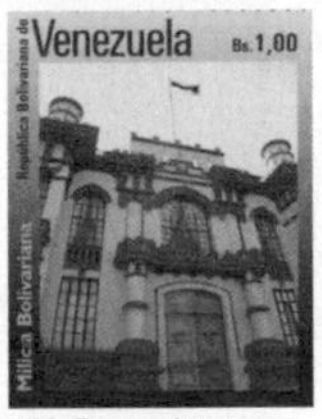

664 Principal Entrance

2010. Bolivarian Militia Building. Multicoloured.

MS3765 1bf. Type **664**; 1bf. Internal façade; 1bf. Main tower; 2bf. Square tower; 2bf. Semicircular arches; 2bf. Tower and arches; 4bf.50 Militiamen; 4bf.50 Courtyard; 6bf. Main building façade, right; 10bf.50 Main building façade, left 9·00 9·00

No. **MS**3765 form composite designs of the buiding.

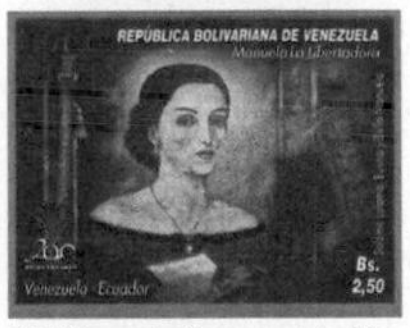

665 Manuela Saenz painted by Salome Lalama entitled *Buena y Bella Manuela*

2010. Doña Manuela Saenz (revolutionary hero) Commemoration

3766 **665** 2bf.50 multicoloured 1·70 1·70

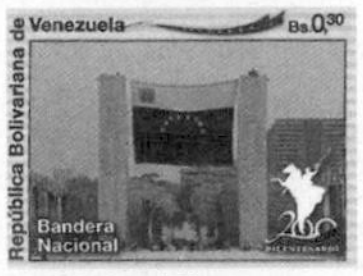

666 National Flag

2010. Bicentenary of Independence. Military Parade. Multicoloured.

3767	30c. Type **666**	20	20
3768	30c. '1810, Arms, 2010'	20	
3769	30c. Women dancers wearing green and yellow	20	20
3770	30c. Male dancers wearing masks	20	20
3771	30c. Women dancers wearing multicoloured skirts	20	20
3772	30c. Idigenous people with spears	20	20
3773	30c. FANB (Fuerza Armada Bolivariana de Venezuela) standard bearers	20	20
3774	30c. Horse carrying replica of Sword of Freedom led by two guards	20	20
3775	30c. Military Academy students in uniform	20	20
3776	30c. Naval students in uniform	20	20

3777	30c. Miltary Aviation students in uniform	20	20
3778	30c. National Guard (EFOFAC)	20	20
3779	30c. Military Technical students in uniform	20	20
3780	30c. Bolivar militia, men	20	20
3781	30c. Bolivar militia, women	20	20
3782	30c. Peasants millitia, wearing grey uniforms	20	20
3783	30c. AMX-30 tank	20	20
3784	30c. C-90 Scorpion tank	20	20
3785	30c. Dragon 300 armoured vehicle	20	20
3786	30c. EE-11 Urutu armoured personnel carrier	20	20
3787	30c. National guard Otta Melara gun vehicle	20	20
3788	30c. Sultan tank	20	20
3789	30c. AMX-13 tank	20	20
3790	30c. Mechanised infantry tank	20	20
3791	1bf. Brazil delegation	35	35
3792	1bf. Cuba delegation	35	35
3793	1bf. Bolivia delegation	35	35
3794	1bf. Nicaragua delegation	35	35
3795	1bf. Argentine delegation	35	35
3796	1bf. Ecuador delegation	35	35
3797	1bf. Belarus delegation	35	35
3798	1bf. Dominican Republic delegation	35	35
3799	1bf. Paratroop battalion	35	35
3800	1bf. Caribbean battalion	35	35
3801	1bf. Forest (Selva) battalion	35	35
3802	1bf. Special Forces, wearing hooded and fringed camouflage	35	35
3803	1bf. Special Forces, wearing green camouflage	35	35
3804	1bf. Special Forces, wearing black camouflage	35	35
3805	1bf. Special Forces, wearing berets, facing left	35	35
3806	1bf. Special Forces, with white gazebo roof in background	35	35
3807	1bf. Sukhoi 30MK2 aircraft	35	35
3809	1bf. F-16 aircraft	35	35
3810	1bf. K-8 aircraft	35	35
3811	1bf. MI-26T helicopter	35	35
3812	1bf. MI-35M helicopter	35	35
3813	1bf. MI-17V5 helicopter	35	35
3814	1bf. Sikorsky AS-61D	35	35
3815	1bf. Cavalry squadron	35	35

667 *Sembradores* (Ender Cepeda)

2010. 50th Anniv of OPEC. Paintings (**MS**3815). Multicoloured.
MS3815a 210×135 mm. 30c. Type **667**; 30c. *Y Por Fin Nos Toco un Chorrito de Petróleo* (Socorro Salinas); 30c. *Cartografia Soberana* (Saul Huetra); 50c. *Serie Atardecer en Campos Petroleros* (Ernesto Leon); 50c. *Como Caido del Cielo* (Rosa Contreras); 3bf. *Marea* (Morella Jurado); 3bf. *Julio* (Omar Carreño); 8bf. *Del Reventón al Barril Dorado* (Gabriel Bracho); 10bf. *Petróleo Nuestro de Cada Dia* (Manuel Qintana Castillo); 10bf. *El Pozo y las Ocho Estrellas* (Paúl del Rio)   9·00   9·00
MS3816 200×121 mm. 12bf. '50' (anniversary emblem) (42×37 mm)   9·50   9·50

668 *Venezuela* (Armando Reverón)

2010. Central Bank of Venezuela Art Collection Exhibits. Multicoloured.
MS3817 30c. Type **668**; 30c. *Formas en Equilibro N-1* (Angel Hurtado); 5bf. *Bananeros* (Camille Pissarro); 8bf. *La pareja* (Armando Barrios); 12bf. *El Avila visto desde el Country Club* (detail, left) (Manuel Cabre); 12bf. *El Avila visto desde el Country Club* (detail, right)   13·00   13·00

669 The Nativity

2010. Christmas. Multicoloured.
MS3818 30c. Type **669**; 30c. Satellite and Three Wise Men; 30c. Musicians; 60c. Cable car, children and hilltop homes; 60c. Woman buying ham; 4bf.50 Fireworks, mother and children; 4bf.50. Children, computers and teacher; 6bf.50 Father and son opening presents; 10bf. Father and son eating chocolates outside sweet shop; 10bf. Four adults holding four corners of sheet containing child   13·00   13·00

670 Shrinking Iceberg (global warming)

2010. Venezuelan Antarctic Programme. Ministery of Popular Science, Technology and Intermediate Industries. Multicoloured.
MS3819 30c. First Expedition Team Members, 2008; 30c. Researchers and monitoring euipment; 40c. Third expedition team members, 2010; 40c. Team members walking through snow storm; 60c. Type **670**; 60c. Base camp buildings (cooperation with South American base); 6bf.50 Second expedition team members, 2009; 8bf.50 Giant petrel; 8bf.50 Penguins and moored research ship, Barrientos Island; 13bf.50 Minke whale fin and island (endangered species)   13·00   13·00

671 Symbols of Bicentenary of Independence

2011. America. Bicentenary of Independence
3820	**671**	2bf. multicoloured	70	70

672 *Batallón Bravos de Apure*

2011. Army Day. Military Uniforms. Multicoloured.
MS3821 30c. Type **672**; 30c. Guardia de Honor del Libertador; 40c. Soldado Lanero; 40c. Batallón de Rifles; 40c. Batallón Tiradores de la Guardia; 1bf.50 Cazadores Británicos; 1bf.50 Drogones de la Guardia; 6bf.50 Húsares de Páez; 10bf. General de División Patriota; 15bf.60 Campaña del Libertador   16·00   16·00

673 Conversation

2011. Bicentenary of Independence. Paintings. Multicoloured.
MS3822 210×135 mm. 30c. Type **673**; 30c. Speaker at podium, three men seated on bench and three men standing behind; 30c. Three workers seated on floor, man wearing wig seated on bench and six men standing behind and to side of bench; 60c., Woman wearing green and cream dress, man standing leaning left and three men seated at table; 60c.As Type **673**; 1bf.50 Three workers seated on floor, man wearing wig seated on bench and six men standing behind and to side of bench; 8bf.50, Two men seated on bench, five men standing behind, one man facing right, one man leaning on bench, facing left and and left edge of podium; 8bf.50 Woman wearing green and cream dress, man standing leaning left and three men seated at table; 12bf.50 Speaker at podium, three men seated on bench and three men standing behind; 12bf.50 wo men seated on bench, five men standing behind, one man facing right, one man leaning on bench, facing left and and left edge of podium   24·00   24·00
MS3823 207×123 mm. 18bf. Simon Bolivar and leaders of the independence (horiz)   9·50   9·50

674 1975 1000 bolivares (Venezuela), Reverse

2011. Central Bank of Venezuela. Numismatic Collection Exhibits. Multicoloured.
MS3824 40c. Type **674**; 60c. 1886 100 bolivares (Pachano), reverse; 1851 $20 (Morocola) (USA), obverse; 5bf.50 1851 $20 (Morocola) (USA), reverse; 5bf.50 1886 100 bolivares (Pachano), obverse; 13bf. 20bf. 1975 1000 bolivares (Venezuela), obverse   11·00   11·00

EXPRESS LETTER STAMPS

E119

1949
E809	**E119**	30c. lake	90	45

E194

1961
E1691	**E194**	30c. orange	75	30

OFFICIAL STAMPS

O17

1898
O174	**O17**	5c. black and green	1·10	75
O175	**O17**	10c. black and red	1·30	1·40
O176	**O17**	25c. black and blue	2·20	1·70
O177	**O17**	50c. black and yellow	3·50	3·50
O178	**O17**	1b. black and mauve	4·00	3·50

1899. Surch **1899** and new value.
O187		5c. on 50c. blk & yell	6·50	6·50
O188		5c. on 1b. blk & mve	28·00	27·00
O189		25c. on 50c. blk & yell	28·00	27·00
O190		25c. on 1b. blk & mve	17·00	16·00

1900. Optd **1900** in upper corners.
O222		5c. black and green	55	55
O223		10c. black and red	75	75
O224		25c. black and blue	75	75
O225		50c. black and yellow	75	75
O226		1b. black and mauve	90	85

O40 With Stars

1904
O325	**O40**	5c. black and green	35	30
O326	**O40**	10c. black and red	90	85
O327	**O40**	25c. black and blue	90	85
O328	**O40**	50c. black and red	6·00	5·75
O329	**O40**	1b. black and lake	3·00	2·75

O45 Without Stars

1912
O354	**O45**	5c. black and green	75	45
O355	**O45**	10c. black and red	75	45
O356	**O45**	25c. black and blue	75	45
O357	**O45**	50c. black and violet	75	55
O358	**O45**	1b. black and yellow	1·90	1·10

REGISTRATION STAMPS

R19 Bolivar

1899
R186	**R19**	25c. brown	4·75	3·75

1899. Optd with T **21**.
R205		25c. brown	2·75	2·75

Pt. 1

VICTORIA

The south-eastern state of the Australian Commonwealth, whose stamps it now uses.

12 pence = 1 shilling; 20 shillings = 1 pound.

1 Queen Victoria ("half length")

1850. Imperf.
28	**1**	1d. red to brown	£1300	48·00
10	**1**	2d. lilac to grey	£7500	£200
17	**1**	2d. brown	£3250	£170
31c	**1**	3d. blue	£1400	48·00

2 Queen on Throne

1852
21	**2**	2d. brown to lilac	£425	32·00

3

1854. Imperf.
25	**3**	1s. blue	£900	35·00

4

1854. Imperf
32a	**4**	6d. orange	£500	19·00
34	**6**	1s. red and blue	£3250	£190

7 Queen on Throne

1856. Imperf.

No.	Type	Description	Un	Used
40	7	1d. green	£250	38·00

8 Emblems in Corners

1857. Imperf.

No.	Type	Description	Un	Used
41	8	1d. green	£200	24·00
45	8	2d. lilac	£600	11·00
43	8	4d. red	£350	8·00

1857. Rouletted.

No.	Type	Description	Un	Used
72	8	1d. green	£475	35·00
69	8	2d. lilac	£250	9·00
48	1	3d. blue	£2750	£250
71c	8	4d. red	£250	3·75
53a	4	6d. orange	—	60·00
54	3	1s. blue		£110
56	4	2s. green on yellow	£7500	£600

1858. Rouletted.

No.	Type	Description	Un	Used
73	7	6d. blue	£425	18·00

1859. Perf.

No.	Type	Description	Un	Used
98	8	1d. green	£120	7·00
100	8	2d. grey	£190	6·00
101b	8	2d. lilac	£225	26·00
78	1	3d. blue	£2000	£130
87	1	4d. red	£250	7·50
102	4	6d. black	£350	65·00
81	3	1s. blue	£300	15·00
82	4	2s. green on yellow	£550	50·00
129b	4	2s. blue on green	£350	6·50

1860. Perf

No.	Type	Description	Un	Used
90	9	3d. blue	£250	7·00
91	9	3d. purple	£300	30·00
92d	9	4d. red	£150	4·75
93	9	6d. orange	£7000	£425
94	9	6d. black	£350	8·00

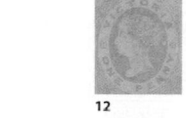

12

1861

No.	Type	Description	Un	Used
104b	12	1d. green	£110	14·00

13

1862

No.	Type	Description	Un	Used
107	13	6d. black	£150	6·50

14   **15**   **16**

18

1863

No.	Type	Description	Un	Used
131g	14	1d. green	95·00	3·25
132b	14	2d. lilac	90·00	3·25
118	15	3d. lilac	£225	48·00
378	15	3d. orange	15·00	4·50
135d	14	4d. pink	£110	3·50
136c	16	4d. blue	75·00	5·00
380	16	6d. green	12·00	14·00
112	14	8d. orange	£650	£100
146	16	8d. brown on pink	£170	20·00
119	16	10d. grey	£900	£140
123	16	10d. brown on pink	£225	7·50
124	17	1s. blue	£130	4·25
139	18	5s. blue on yellow	£3250	£425
148	18	5s. blue and red	£500	15·00

No.	Type	Description	Un	Used
383	18	5s. red and blue	55·00	75·00

For designs additionally inscribed "POSTAGE" see Nos. 399 etc.

20

1870

No.	Type	Description	Un	Used
169a	20	2d. lilac	85·00	1·00

1871. Surch in figures and words.

No.	Type	Description	Un	Used
174	14	½d. on 1d. green	80·00	18·00
171	16	9d. on 10d. brown on pink	£700	12·00

22   **23**   **24**

25   **26**   **27**

1873

No.	Type	Description	Un	Used
176b	22	½d. red	27·00	2·50
195	22	½d. red on pink	75·00	38·00
376	22	½d. green	2·00	3·00
177b	23	1d. green	70·00	2·00
196	23	1d. green on yellow	£130	28·00
197	23	1d. green on grey	£225	65·00
179	24	2d. mauve	80·00	1·25
198	24	2d. mauve on lilac		£800
199	24	2d. mauve on green	£300	35·00
200	24	2d. mauve on brown	£275	35·00
172a	25	9d. brown on pink	£160	32·00
319	25	9d. green	30·00	15·00
366	25	9d. red	20·00	3·25
180	26	1s. blue on blue	£130	4·50
381	26	1s. yellow	75·00	48·00
190	27	2s. blue on green	£225	22·00
382	27	2s. blue on pink	47·00	70·00

For designs additionally inscribed "POSTAGE" see Nos. 399 etc.

1876. Surch **8d.. 8d.. EIGHTPENCE.**

No.	Type	Description	Un	Used
191	25	8d. on 9d. brown on pink	£450	30·00

30   **31**

1880. Frame differs in 4d.

No.	Type	Description	Un	Used
209b	30	1d. green	60·00	2·75
202d	31	2d. brown	50·00	1·50
377	31	2d. mauve	13·00	4·25
213	31	4d. red	£100	15·00
379	31	4d. yellow	25·00	27·00

For designs additionally inscribed "POSTAGE" see Nos. 416 etc.

34   **35**   **36**

1884. "Inscr "STAMP STATUTE"". Frames differ

No.	Type	Description	Un	Used
220	34	3d. green	£100	65·00
221	34	3d. mauve	£1600	£500
222	-	4d. pink	£1100	£425
223a	-	6d. blue	£140	32·00
224c	-	1s. blue on blue	£160	42·00
225	35	2s. blue on green	£275	£100

37

No.	Type	Description	Un	Used
232	36	2s.6d. yellow	£1500	£275
227	-	5s. blue on yellow	£600	£110
228	-	10s. brown on pink	£2000	£375
229ba	-	£1 violet on yellow	£2250	£375
230	37	£5 black and green	£16000	£1800

DESIGNS. As Type **34/36**: 1d., 6d., 1s., 5s. to £1, Uncrowned portrait of Queen Victoria in centre; 4d. Obverse and reverse of fourpenny coin.

1884. No. 220 surch **½d. HALF.**

No.	Type	Description	Un	Used
234	37	½d. on 1d. green	£110	£100

39   **40**   **44**

52   **56**

58

61

1884. Inscr "STAMP DUTY". Frames differ.

No.	Type	Description	Un	Used
253	39	1d. green	£110	50·00
254	40	1d. bistre	60·00	10·00
255	-	6d. blue	£160	28·00
256	-	1s. blue on blue	£190	7·00
257	-	1s. blue on yellow	£225	29·00
267	-	1s.6d. red to pink	£250	32·00
258c	44	2s. blue on green	£300	42·00
259	-	3s. purple on blue	£600	60·00
345	-	3s. drab	£100	29·00
371	-	3s. green	£200	42·00
269	-	4s. red to orange	£120	16·00
260	-	5s. purple on yellow	£100	7·00
347	-	5s. red	£150	24·00
348	-	6s. green	£170	35·00
240	-	10s. brown on pink	£1400	£110
349a	-	10s. green	£650	26·00
241	-	15s. mauve	£5000	£450
350	-	15s. brown	£750	85·00
262b	-	£1 orange	£800	60·00
274	52	£1 5s. pink	£4250	£160
275	-	£1 10s. green	£4250	£140
245	-	35s. violet	£13000	
276a	-	£2 blue	£1300	£130
247	44	45s. lilac	£8500	£475
248	56	£5 red	£12000	£1500
249	58	£6 blue on pink		£1500
250	58	£7 violet on blue		£1500
251	-	£8 red on yellow		£1700
252	-	£9 green on green		£1700
279	61	£10 mauve	£13000	£200

DESIGNS—As T **39/52**: 6d. to 1s.6d., 4s. to £1, £1 10s., £2, Various arms; 35s. "V R STAMP DUTY". As T **56/8**: £8, Crown; £9, Arms.

62

1884

No.	Type	Description	Un	Used
351	62	£25 green		£325
352	62	£50 mauve		£475
291	62	£100 red		£800

63

1884

No.	Type	Description	Un	Used
292a	63	2s.6d. yellow	£120	13·00

64   **65**   **66**

67   **68**

1884. Inscr "STAMP DUTY".

No.	Type	Description	Un	Used
296	64	½d. red	28·00	2·50
297	65	1d. green	28·00	3·00
298	66	2d. mauve	42·00	1·75
361	65	3d. buff	7·50	7·50
362	65	3d. green	38·00	20·00
300	65	4d. mauve	£100	6·00
301b	65	6d. blue	£110	4·25
293	68	8d. red on pink	45·00	9·50
294	68	1s. blue on yellow	£160	16·00
303	68	2s. green on green	50·00	6·50
304a	68	2s. green on white	20·00	25·00

1885. Optd **STAMP DUTY.**

No.	Type	Description	Un	Used
308	15	3d. orange	65·00	50·00
309	31	4d. blue on blue	55·00	75·00
306	26	1s. blue on blue	£130	47·00
307	27	2s. blue on green	£170	18·00

70   **71**   **72**

73   **74**   **75**

76   **77**   **78**

79   **80**

1886. Inscr "STAMP DUTY".

No.	Type	Description	Un	Used
310	70	½d. grey	35·00	11·00
330a	70	½d. red	9·00	2·75
356	70	½d. green	5·00	3·00
312	71	1d. red	18·00	3·25
329	72	1d. brown on pink	15·00	4·00
332a	72	1d. brown	10·00	10
357a	72	1d. red	5·50	10
358	72	1d. green	12·00	4·00
333	81	1½d. green	3·00	7·50
355	81	1½d. red on yellow	4·25	5·50
314d	73	2d. purple	12·00	30
315b	74	2½d. red on yellow	23·00	70
335	74	2½d. blue	21·00	24·00
363	76	4d. red	25·00	7·50
317a	76	5d. brown	13·00	3·25
365	77	6d. blue	30·00	5·00
341	78	1s. red	30·00	4·50
322	79	1s.6d. blue	£170	75·00
323a	79	1s.6d. orange	32·00	13·00
324	80	£5 blue and purple	£8000	£150
325	80	£6 yellow and green	£9000	£170
326	80	£7 red and black	£9500	£200
327	80	£8 mauve and orange	£10000	£250

328	80	£9 green and red	£11000	£275

For designs additionally inscribed "POSTAGE" see Nos. 416 etc.

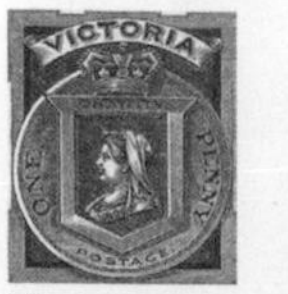

83

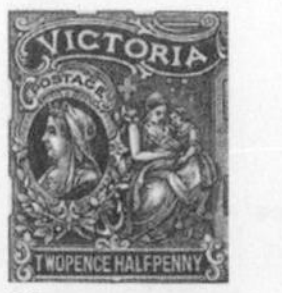

84

1897. Hospital Charity Fund.

353	**83**	1d. (1s.) blue	20·00	23·00
354	**84**	2½d. (2s.6d.) brown	£130	80·00

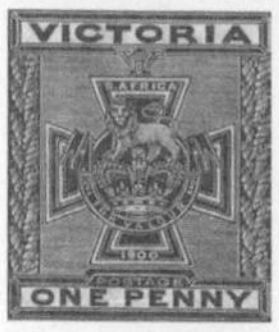

86

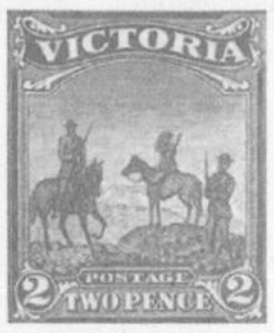

87

1900. Empire Patriotic Fund.

374	**86**	1d. (1s.) brown	£150	85·00
375	**87**	2d. (2s.) green	£275	£225

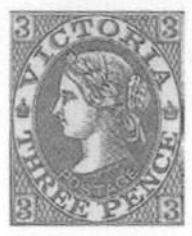

93

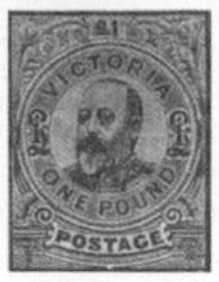

101

1901. As previous types but inscr "POSTAGE" instead of "STAMP DUTY" or with "POSTAGE" added to design, and new designs.

416	**22**	½d. green	4·00	1·25
417*a*	**30**	1d. red	2·00	10
386*b*	**81**	1½d. brown on yellow	2·75	55
418*c*	**31**	2d. mauve	5·50	1·25
419*a*	**74**	2½d. blue	3·00	40
389*a*	**93**	3d. brown	17·00	1·00
390	**31**	4d. yellow	9·50	1·00
391*a*	**76**	5d. brown	13·00	1·50
392	**16**	6d. green	12·00	1·00
424*d*	**25**	9d. red	12·00	2·25
425	**26**	1s. orange	10·00	2·00
395	**27**	2s. blue on pink	29·00	2·00
398	**18**	5s. red and blue	60·00	23·00
399	**101**	£1 pink	£300	£130
400	-	£2 blue	£650	£300

DESIGN: £2, as Type **101** but different frame.

1912. Surch **ONE PENNY**.

456	**31**	1d. on 2d. mauve (No. 387)	1·00	60

POSTAGE DUE STAMPS

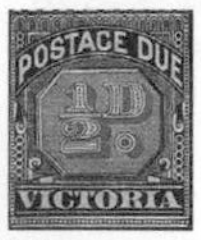

D1

1890

D1*a*	**D 1**	½d. blue and red	6·00	6·50
D2	**D 1**	1d. blue and red	7·00	2·25
D3	**D 1**	2d. blue and red	14·00	2·25
D4	**D 1**	4d. blue and red	28·00	5·00
D5	**D 1**	5d. blue and red	27·00	3·50
D6	**D 1**	6d. blue and red	22·00	8·50
D7	**D 1**	10d. blue and red	75·00	55·00
D8	**D 1**	1s. blue and red	50·00	11·00
D9	**D 1**	2s. blue and red	£130	70·00
D10	**D 1**	5s. blue and red	£180	£110

1895

D11a	½d. red and green	5·00	3·50
D12a	1d. red and green	6·00	2·75
D13a	2d. red and green	25·00	1·50
D14a	4d. red and green	10·00	2·50
D15a	5d. red and green	18·00	20·00
D25	6d. red and green	15·00	7·00
D17	10d. red and green	45·00	10·00
D18	1s. red and green	24·00	3·50
D19	2s. red and green	90·00	24·00
D20	5s. red and green	£140	40·00

REGISTRATION STAMPS

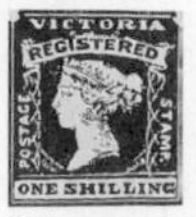

6

1854. Imperf.

34	**6**	1s. red and blue	£3250	£190

1857. Roul.

55		1s. red and blue	£8500	£375

TOO LATE STAMP

1855. As T **6** but inscr "TOO LATE". Imperf.

Pt. 1

VICTORIA LAND

Stamps issued in connection with Capt. Scott's Antarctic Expedition.

12 pence = 1 shilling.

1911. Scott Expedition. Stamps of New Zealand optd **VICTORIA LAND.**

A2	**51**	½d. green	£750	£850
A3	**53**	1d. red	55·00	£120

Pt. 21

VIETNAM

The Democratic Republic was proclaimed by the Viet Minh Nationalists on 2 September 1945 and recognised by France on 6 March 1946 as a free state within the Indo-China Federation. It consisted of Tongking, Annam and Cochin-China.

A. Democratic Republic.
1945. 100 cents = 1 piastre.
1945. 100 xu = 10 hao = 1 dong.

B. Independent State.
100 cents = 1 piastre.

C. South Vietnam.
100 cents = 1 piastre.

D. National Front for the Liberation of South Vietnam.
1963. 100 xu = 1 dong.

E. North Vietnam.
1946. 100 cents = 1 dong.
1959. 100 xu = 1 dong.

F. Socialist Republic of Vietnam.
100 xu = 1 dong.

A. DEMOCRATIC REPUBLIC

Stamps of Indo-China overprinted.
("DAN-CHU CONG-HOA" = Democratic Republic; "DOC-LAP TU-DO HANH-PHUC = Independence, Freedom, Happiness; "BUU-CHINH" = Postage.)

VIET-NAM
DAN-CHU CONG-HOA
DOC-LAP
TU-DO HANH-PHUC
BUU-CHINH III

(1)

1945. Independence. Variously optd as T 1 (all with **DOC-LAP TU-DO HANH-PHUC** in opt).

1	**53**	1c. brown	2·50	2·75
2	-	2c. mauve (No. 315)	2·50	2·75
3	-	3c. brown (Courbet)	2·50	2·75
4	-	4c. brown (No. 316)	2·50	2·75
5	-	5c. sepia (De Genouilly)	2·50	2·75
6	-	6c. red (No. 304)	2·50	2·75
7	-	6c. red (No. 305)	4·50	4·75
8	-	10c. green (No. 307)	3·75	4·00
9	-	10c. green (No. 322)	6·25	20·00
10	-	20c. red (No. 309)	6·25	20·00
11	**64**	40c. blue	6·25	20·00
12	-	$1 green (No. 311)	12·50	33·00

Nos. 3 and 5 were not issued without opt and are as Nos. 304 and 305 of Indo-China respectively.

1945. Variously optd. (a) **VIET-NAM DAN-CHU CONG-HOA.**

13	**69**	10c. purple and yellow	10·00	13·50
14	-	15c. purple (No. 292)	3·75	5·25
15	-	30c. brown (No. 294)	3·75	4·00
16	**69**	50c. red	25·00	33·00
17	-	$1 green (No. 295)	3·75	6·75

(b) **VIET-NAM DAN-CHU CONG-HOA BUU-CHINH.**

18	**53**	3c. brown	3·75	4·00
19	-	4c. yellow (No. 317)	3·75	4·00
20	**53**	6c. red	3·75	4·00
21	**53**	10c. green	6·25	6·75
22	-	10c. green (No. 320)	6·25	8·00
23	-	20c. red (Pavie)	3·75	4·00
24	**53**	40c. blue	6·25	13·50
25	**53**	40c. grey	12·50	27·00

No. 23 was not issued without opt and is as No. 320 of Indo-China.

VIET-NAM
DAN-CHU
3$00 CONG-HOA
CUU-DOI

2 "CUU-DOI" = Famine Relief

1945. Famine Relief. Surch as T **2**.

26	**70**	"2$00" on 15c.+60c. purple	31·00	33·00
27	**70**	"3$00" on 40c.+$1.10c. blue	31·00	33·00

1945. War Wounded. Surch as T **2** but with **Binh-si Bi-nan** (= Fund for War Wounded).

28	"5$00" on 15c.+60c. purple	50·00	55·00

1945. Surch in new currency and variously optd as before (except Nos. 43/7). (a) **VIET-NAM DAN-CHU CONG-HOA BUU-CHINH.**

29	**64**	30x. on 1c. brown	3·75	4·75
30	-	30x. on 15c. purple (Garnier)	2·50	4·00
31	**67**	50x. on 1c. brown	5·00	6·75
32	-	60x. on 1c. brown (No. 313)	6·25	6·75
33	-	1d. on 5c. brown (No. 303)	10·00	10·50
34	-	1d.60x. on 10c. green (No. 319)	3·75	5·25
35	**64**	3d. on 15c. purple	5·00	8·00
36	**67**	3d. on 15c. purple	7·50	9·25
37	-	4d. on 1c. brown (No. 302)	5·00	8·00
38	-	5d. on 1c. brown (No. 301)	7·50	9·25

(b) **VIET-NAM DAN-CHU CONG-HOA.**

39		1d. on 5c. purple (No. 318)	3·75	5·25
40	**49**	2d. on 3c. brown	55·00	60·00
41	-	2d. on 10c. green (No. 321)	5·00	6·75
42	**49**	4d. on 6c. red	55·00	60·00

(c) Surch only.

43	**56**	50x. on 1c. brown	6·25	8·00
44	**56**	2d. on 6c. red	38·00	40·00
45	**48**	5d. on 1c. orange	55·00	60·00
46	**48**	10d. on 6c. violet	60·00	65·00
47	**48**	15d. on 25c. blue	60·00	65·00

No. 30 was not issued without opt and is as No. 301 of Indo-China.

OVERPRINT. Nos. 48/55 are all optd **VIET-NAM DAN-CHU CONG-HOA** with varying additional words as noted in headings.

1945. National Defence (**Quoc-Phong**).

48	**49**	"+5d." on 3c. brown	10·00	13·50
49	**49**	"+10d." on 6c. red	10·00	16·00

1946. People's Livelihood. (**DAN SINH**).

50	**57**	"30xu.+3d." on 6c. red	2·50	4·00
51	**55**	"30xu.+3d." on 6c. red	3·25	4·00

1946. Campaign against Illiteracy (**Chong nan mu chu**).

52	**59**	"+4dong" on 6c. red	12·50	13·50

1946. New Life Movement (**Doi song moi**).

53	**66**	"+4dong" on 6c. red	6·25	8·00

1946. Child Welfare (**Bao-Anh**).

54	"+2dong" on 6c. red (No. 290)	6·25	9·25

1946. War Wounded (**Binh si bi nan**).

55	"+3dong" on 20c. red (No. 293)	11·50	12·00

Definitive issues.

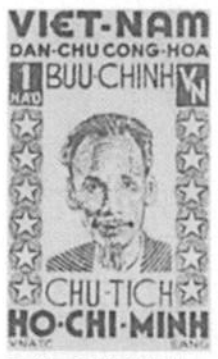

3 Ho Chi Minh

1946

56	**3**	1h. green	1·30	1·50
57	**3**	3h. red	1·30	1·50
58	**3**	9h. yellow	1·30	1·50

1946. National Defence.

59	4+6h. blue	3·25	6·75
60	6+9h. brown	3·25	6·75

The Viet-Minh Government was at war with the French from 19 December 1946 until July 1954, and the stamps issued by the Democratic Republic in this period are listed as North Vietnam Nos. N1/13, NO1/9 and ND1/4.

B. INDEPENDENT STATE

On 14 June 1949, Vietnam, comprising Tongking, Annam and Cochin-China, became an independent state within the French Union under Emperor Bao-Dai. Until the 1951 issue Indo-Chinese stamps continued in use.

By the Geneva Declaration of 21 July 1954, Vietnam was partitioned near the 17th Parallel, and all authority of Bao-Dai's Government north of that line ended. Later issues are therefore those of SOUTH VIETNAM and NORTH VIETNAM.

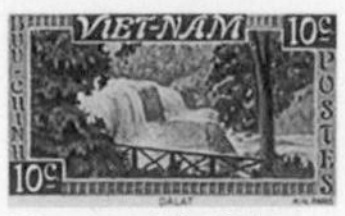

4 Bongour Falls, Dalat

1951

61	**4**	10c. bronze	65	25
62	-	20c. purple	1·90	30
63	-	30c. blue	1·90	45
64	-	50c. red	3·50	25
65	**4**	60c. sepia	1·90	25
66	-	1p. brown	1·90	25
67	-	1p.20 brown	12·50	3·50
68	-	2p. violet	3·50	25
69	-	3p. blue	12·50	25
70	**4**	5p. green	9·50	80
71	-	10p. red	23·00	1·10
72	-	15p. brown	75·00	6·75
73	-	30p. green	£180	8·00

DESIGNS—HORIZ: 20c., 2p., 10p. Imperial Palace, Hue; 30c., 15p. Small Lake, Hanoi; 50c., 1p. Temple of Remembrance, Saigon. VERT: 1p.20, 3p., 30p. Emperor Bao Dai.

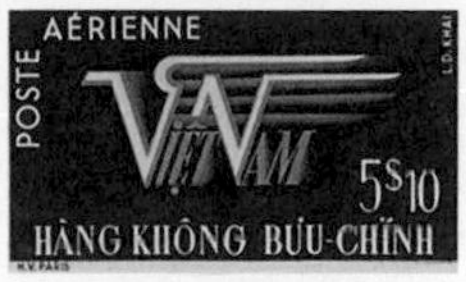

9

1952. Air.

74	**9**	3p.30 green and lake	1·40	90
75	**9**	4p. yellow and brown	1·90	55
76	**9**	5p.10 pink and blue	1·90	1·20
77	-	6p.30 red and yellow (symbolic of airlines)	2·00	1·50

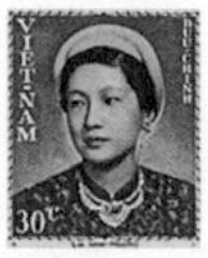

10 Empress Nam Phuong

1952

78	**10**	30c. brown, yellow & purple	1·90	45
79	**10**	50c. brown, yellow and blue	2·50	75
80	**10**	1p.50 brown, yellow & olive	5·75	45

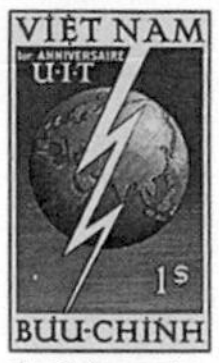

11 Globe and Lightning

1952. First Anniv of Admission of Vietnam into I.T.U.

81	**11**	1p. blue	11·50	2·00

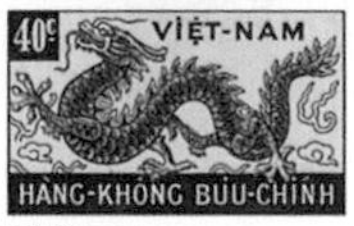

12 Dragon

1952. Air. Day of Wandering Souls.

82	**12**	40c. red	2·50	45
83	**12**	70c. green	3·25	55
84	**12**	80c. blue	3·25	55
85	**12**	90c. brown	3·25	55
86	-	3p.70 purple	7·00	90

DESIGN—VERT: 3p.70, Fish dragon.

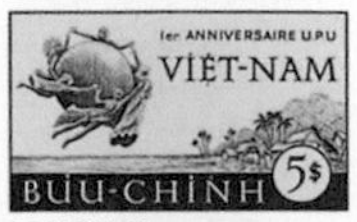

13 U.P.U. Monument, Berne, and Coastline

1952. First Anniv of Admission of Vietnam into U.P.U.

87	**13**	5p. brown	5·75	2·30

1952. Red Cross. T **10** surch with red cross and **+50c.**

88	**10**	1p.50+50c. brn, yell & bl	12·50	4·00

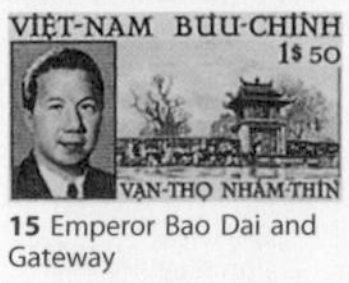

15 Emperor Bao Dai and Gateway

1952. 40th Birthday of Emperor.

89	**15**	1p.50 purple	6·25	1·70

16 Sabres and Flag

1952. Wounded Soldiers' Relief Fund.
90	16	3p.30+1p.70 lake	4·50	3·50

17 Crown Prince Bao Long

1959
91	17	40c. turquoise	65	55
92	17	70c. lake	65	55
93	17	80c. sepia	65	55
94	-	90c. green	1·90	1·70
95	-	20p. red	2·50	2·30
96	-	50p. violet	8·75	8·00
97	17	100p. blue	28·00	25·00

PORTRAIT: 90c. to 50p. Crown Prince in uniform.

POSTAGE DUE STAMPS

D10 Dragon

1952
D78	D10	10c. green and red	75	75
D79	D10	20c. yellow and green	75	75
D80	D10	30c. orange and violet	75	75
D81	D10	40c. pink and green	75	75
D82	D10	50c. grey and lake	75	75
D83	D10	1p. silver and blue	1·50	1·50

C. SOUTH VIETNAM

INDEPENDENT STATE
(Within the French Union)

1 Turtle

1955. First Anniv of Govt of Ngo Dinh Diem.
S1	1	30c. purple	2·75	90
S2	1	50c. green	7·25	2·75
S3	1	1p.50 blue	6·75	2·30

2 Phoenix

1955. Air.
S4	2	4p. mauve and violet	4·50	3·50

3 Refugees

1955. First Anniv of Arrival of Refugees from North Vietnam.
S5	3	70c. red	2·00	1·70
S6	3	80c. purple	5·25	4·50
S7	3	10p. blue	10·00	8·00
S8	3	20p. brown, orange & violet	27·00	20·00
S9	3	35p. sepia, yellow and blue	55·00	39·00
S10	3	100p. purple, orange & green	£120	90·00

No. S9 is inscribed "CHIEN-DICH-HUYNE-DE" in margin at foot.
See also No. S26.

REPUBLIC
(from 26th October, 1955)

4 G.P.O., Saigon

1956. Fifth Anniv of Entry of Vietnam into U.P.U.
S11	4	60c. green	3·25	2·30
S12	4	90c. violet	6·00	2·75
S13	4	3p. brown	11·50	5·75

5 Pres. Ngo Dinh Diem

1956
S14	5	20c. brown	65	45
S15	5	30c. purple	1·30	55
S16	5	50c. red	65	55
S17	5	1p. violet	1·30	70
S18	5	1p.50 violet	2·00	80
S19	5	3p. sepia	3·25	90
S20	5	4p. blue	4·75	1·00
S21	5	5p. brown	5·25	1·10
S22	5	10p. blue	6·75	1·80
S23	5	20p. black	14·50	3·50
S24	5	35p. green	33·00	5·75
S25	5	100p. brown	75·00	28·00

1956. No. S9 with bottom marginal inscription obliterated by bar.
S26	3	35p. sepia, yellow and blue	20·00	13·50

1956. Optd **Cong-thu Buu-dien** (= "Government Postal Building").
S27	4	60c. green	3·00	1·40
S28	4	90c. violet	4·00	1·40
S29	4	3p. brown	6·00	2·30

7 Bamboo

1956. First Anniv of Republic.
S30	7	50c. red	1·60	1·40
S31	7	1p.50 purple	2·00	1·70
S32	7	2p. green	2·75	2·30
S33	7	4p. blue	6·75	5·75

8 Refugee Children

1956. United Nations "Operation Brotherhood".
S34	8	1p. mauve	1·10	55
S35	8	2p. turquoise	1·70	90
S36	8	6p. violet	2·75	1·10
S37	8	35p. blue	16·00	4·50

9 Hunters on Elephants

1957. Third Anniv of Govt of Ngo Dinh Diem.
S38	9	20c. purple and green	1·70	70
S39	9	30c. red and bistre	2·00	80
S40	-	90c. sepia and green	2·30	90
S41	-	2p. blue and green	3·25	1·00
S42	-	3p. brown and violet	4·00	1·80

DESIGN—VERT: 90c. to 3p. Mountain hut.

10 Ship's Cargo being offloaded at Saigon

1957. Ninth Colombo Plan Conference, Saigon.
S43	10	20c. purple	55	50
S44	10	40c. olive	65	65
S45	10	50c. red	80	70
S46	10	2p. blue	2·10	75
S47	10	3p. green	3·00	1·30

11 Torch and Constitution

1957. Inauguration of National Assembly.
S48	11	50c. salmon, green & black	40	40
S49	11	80c. purple, blue and black	55	45
S50	11	1p. red, green and black	65	55
S51	11	4p. brown, myrtle and black	1·10	75
S52	11	5p. olive, turquoise & black	1·30	90
S53	11	10p. brown, blue and black	2·75	1·50

12 Youth felling Tree

1958. Better Living Standards.
S54	12	50c. green	65	40
S55	12	1p. violet	1·10	55
S56	12	2p. blue	1·70	65
S57	12	10p. red	3·25	1·30

13 Young Girl with Chinese Lantern

1958. Children's Festival.
S58	13	30c. lemon	55	40
S59	13	50c. red	65	55
S60	13	2p. red	1·10	65
S61	13	3p. green	2·00	80
S62	13	4p. olive	2·40	95

14 Emblem

1958. United Nations Day.
S63	14	1p. light brown	65	40
S64	14	2p. turquoise	1·30	55
S65	14	4p. red	2·00	80
S66	14	5p. purple	2·75	1·00

15 UNESCO Emblem and Building

1958. Inauguration of UNESCO Headquarters Building, Paris.
S67	15	50c. blue	75	45
S68	15	2p. red	1·10	60
S69	15	3p. purple	1·90	75
S70	15	6p. violet	2·50	1·20

16 U.N. Emblem and "Torch of Freedom"

1958. Tenth Anniv of Declaration of Human Rights.
S71	16	50c. blue	55	45
S72	16	1p. lake	85	60
S73	16	2p. green	1·10	75
S74	16	6p. purple	2·50	1·20

17 Phu-Cam Cathedral **18** Saigon Museum

1958
S75	17	10c. slate	70	60
S76	-	30c. green	1·50	1·00
S77	18	40c. green	1·20	1·20
S78	-	50c. green	1·50	1·50
S79	-	2p. blue	3·75	3·00
S80	-	4p. lilac	4·50	3·75
S81	18	5p. red	5·25	4·00
S82	17	6p. brown	5·75	4·50

DESIGNS—HORIZ: 30c., 4p. Thien Mu Pagoda; 50c., 2p. Palace of Independence, Saigon.

19 Trung Sisters (national heroines) on Elephants

1959. Trung Sisters Commemoration.
S83	19	50c. multicoloured	2·10	1·50
S84	19	2p. multicoloured	2·75	2·20
S85	19	3p. multicoloured	4·75	3·00
S86	19	6p. multicoloured	9·75	4·50

20

1959. Agricultural Reform.
S87	20	70c. purple	70	45
S88	20	2p. green and blue	1·10	60
S89	20	3p. olive	2·10	75
S90	20	6p. red and deep red	4·25	2·20

21 Diesel Train

1959. Re-opening of Trans-Vietnam Railway. Centres in green.
S91	21	1p. violet	2·75	1·50
S92	21	2p. grey	4·25	2·20
S93	21	3p. blue	5·50	3·00
S94	21	4p. lake	8·25	4·50

22 Tilling the Land

1959. Fourth Anniv of Republic.
S95	22	1p. brown, green and blue	1·40	65
S96	22	2p. violet, green and orange	2·10	95
S97	22	4p. indigo, blue and bistre	4·25	1·30
S98	22	5p. brown, olive and light brown	4·75	1·90

25 Scout climbing Mountain

1959. First National Scout Jamboree, Trang Bom.

S99	25	3p. green	95	50
S100	25	4p. mauve	2·20	65
S101	25	8p. mauve and purple	3·75	1·30
S102	25	20p. dp turquoise & turq	7·50	2·40

26 "Family Code"

1960. First Anniv of Family Code.

S103	26	20c. green	1·70	1·60
S104	26	30c. blue	2·10	1·90
S105	26	2p. red and orange	3·25	3·00
S106	26	6p. violet and red	4·00	3·75

27 Refugee Family in Flight

1960. World Refugee Year.

S107	27	50c. mauve	70	50
S108	27	3p. green	95	65
S109	27	4p. red	1·10	80
S110	27	5p. violet	2·10	1·30

28 Henri Dunant

1960. Red Cross Day. Cross in red.

S111	28	1p. blue	1·70	65
S112	28	3p. green	2·75	85
S113	28	4p. red	3·50	1·20
S114	28	6p. mauve	4·25	1·70

29 Co-operative Farm

1960. Establishment of Co-operative Rice Farming.

S115	29	50c. blue	95	50
S116	29	1p. green	1·10	65
S117	29	3p. orange	2·10	85
S118	29	7p. mauve	3·50	1·30

30 X-ray Camera and Patient

1960. National T.B. Relief Campaign Day.

S119	30	3p.+50c. green and red	2·50	2·30

31 Flag and Map

1960. Fifth Anniv of Republic. Flag and map in red and yellow.

S120	31	50c. turquoise	85	60
S121	31	1p. blue	1·20	75
S122	31	3p. violet	2·10	95
S123	31	7p. green	3·50	1·50

32 Woman with Rice

1960. F.A.O. Regional Conference, Saigon.

S124	32	2p. turquoise and green	2·10	95
S125	32	4p. ultramarine and blue	2·75	1·50

33 Crane carrying Letter

1960. Air.

S126	33	1p. green	1·40	1·20
S127	33	4p. blue and turquoise	3·50	1·50
S128	33	5p. violet and brown	4·75	2·10
S129	33	10p. mauve	7·00	3·00

34 Farm Tractor

1961. Agricultural Development and Pres. Diem's 60th Birthday.

S130	34	50c. brown	85	50
S131	34	70c. mauve	1·20	65
S132	34	80c. red	1·40	85
S133	34	10p. mauve	7·00	2·20

35 Child and Plant

1961. Child Welfare.

S134	35	70c. blue	85	50
S135	35	80c. blue	95	65
S136	35	4p. bistre	1·40	1·00
S137	35	7p. green and turquoise	2·50	1·50

36 Pres. Ngo Dinh Diem

1961. Second Term of President.

S138	36	50c. blue	1·90	1·20
S139	36	1p. red	2·50	1·70
S140	36	2p. purple	3·25	2·20
S141	36	4p. violet	5·00	3·25

37 Young People and Torch

1961. Sports and Youth.

S142	37	50c. red	50	50
S143	37	70c. mauve	90	65
S144	37	80c. mauve and red	1·10	85
S145	37	8p. purple and red	3·25	1·70

38 Bridge over Mekong

1961. Inaug of Saigon–Bien Hoa Motor Highway.

S146	38	50c. green	1·00	50
S147	38	1p. brown	1·30	65
S148	38	2p. blue	2·10	85
S149	38	5p. purple	3·75	1·00

39 Alexander of Rhodes

1961. Death Tercent of Alexander of Rhodes.

S150	39	50c. red	65	50
S151	39	1p. purple	90	65
S152	39	3p. bistre	1·00	85
S153	39	6p. green	2·50	1·30

40 Vietnamese with Torch

1961. Youth Moral Rearmament.

S154	40	50c. red	65	50
S155	40	1p. green	1·00	65
S156	40	3p. red	1·30	85
S157	40	8p. brown and purple	3·50	1·70

41 Gateway of Van Mieu Temple, Hanoi

1961. 15th Anniv of UNESCO.

S158	41	1p. green	65	50
S159	41	2p. red	1·30	65
S160	41	5p. olive	3·25	1·00

42 Tractor and Cottages

1961. Rural Reform.

S161	42	50c. green	1·40	50
S162	42	1p. lake and blue	2·10	65
S163	42	2p. brown and green	2·75	85
S164	42	10p. turquoise	7·00	1·70

43 Attack on Mosquito

1962. Malaria Eradication.

S165	43	50c. mauve	65	50
S166	43	1p. orange	90	65
S167	43	2p. green	1·30	90
S168	43	6p. blue	2·50	1·30

44 Postal Cheque Building, Saigon

1962. Inauguration of Postal Cheques Service.

S169	44	70c. green	55	50
S170	44	80c. brown	75	65
S171	44	4p. purple	1·50	85
S172	44	7p. red	3·75	1·70

45 St. Mary of La Vang

1962. St. Mary of La Vang Commemoration.

S173	45	50c. red and violet	65	50
S174	45	1p. blue and brown	1·00	65
S175	45	2p. lake and brown	1·50	85
S176	45	8p. blue and turquoise	5·00	1·30

46 Armed Guards and Fortified Village

1962. Strategic Villages.

S177	46	50c. red	1·00	50
S178	46	1p. bronze	1·50	65
S179	46	1p.50 purple	1·90	85
S180	46	7p. blue	5·00	1·70

47 Gougah Waterfalls, Dalat

1963. Pres. Ngo Dinh Diem's 62nd Birthday and Spring Festival.

S181	47	60c. red	1·90	65
S182	47	1p. blue	3·25	1·00

48 Trung Sisters Monument

1963. Women's Day.

S183	48	50c. green	50	35
S184	48	1p. red	85	65
S185	48	3p. purple	1·30	1·00
S186	48	8p. blue	2·50	1·30

49 Harvester

1963. Freedom from Hunger.

S187	49	50c. red	85	50
S188	49	1p. red	1·00	65
S189	49	3p. purple	1·30	1·00
S190	49	5p. violet	2·20	1·50

50 Sword and Fortress

1963. Communal Defence and Ninth Anniv of Inaug of Pres. Diem.

S191	50	30c. bistre	1·10	40
S192	50	50c. mauve	1·50	50
S193	50	3p. green	2·00	65
S194	50	8p. red	3·00	1·30

51 Soldier and Emblem

1963. Republican Combatants.

S195	51	50c. red	90	50
S196	51	1p. green	1·20	65
S197	51	4p. violet	2·30	85
S198	51	5p. orange	4·00	1·70

52 Centenary Emblem and Globe

1963. Red Cross Centenary. Cross in red.

S199	52	50c. blue	75	50
S200	52	1p. red	1·50	65
S201	52	3p. orange	2·75	85
S202	52	6p. brown	5·25	1·30

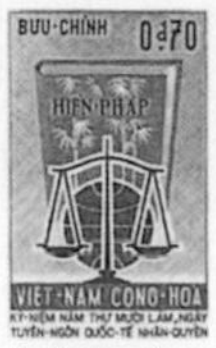

53 Scales of Justice and Book

1963. 15th Anniv of Declaration of Human Rights.

S203	**53**	70c. orange	60	50
S204	**53**	1p. mauve	90	65
S205	**53**	3p. green	1·40	85
S206	**53**	8p. ochre	2·40	1·30

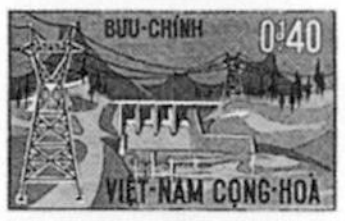

54 Danhim Hydro-electric Station

1964. Inauguration of Danhim Hydro-electric Station.

S207	**54**	40c. red	90	50
S208	**54**	1p. brown	1·20	65
S209	**54**	3p. violet	1·80	85
S210	**54**	8p. green	3·50	1·30

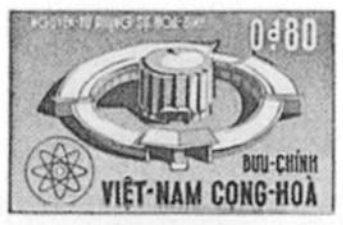

55 Atomic Reactor

1964. Peaceful Uses of Atomic Energy.

S211	**55**	80c. olive	90	50
S212	**55**	1p.50 brown	1·40	65
S213	**55**	3p. brown	2·30	1·00
S214	**55**	7p. blue	3·75	1·50

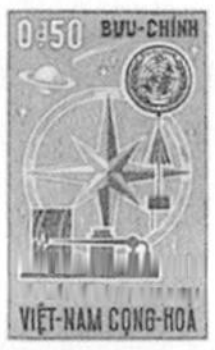

56 "Meteorology"

1964. World Meteorological Day.

S215	**56**	50c. ochre	60	50
S216	**56**	1p. red	75	65
S217	**56**	1p.50 lake	90	85
S218	**56**	10p. green	2·50	1·30

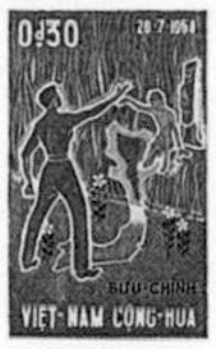

57 "Unification"

1964. Tenth Anniv of Partition of Vietnam.

S219	**57**	30c. blue and green	2·00	50
S220	**57**	50c. blue, red and yellow	2·30	65
S221	**57**	1p.50 indigo, blue & orange	3·00	1·30

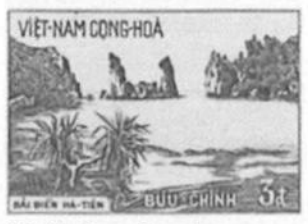

58 Hatien Beach

1964

S222	**58**	20c. blue	1·50	50
S223	**58**	3p. green	3·00	85

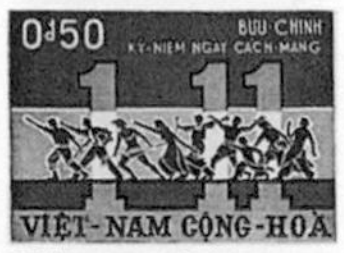

59 "Support of the People"

1964. First Anniv of Revolution of 1 November 1963.

S224	**59**	50c. blue and purple	75	50
S225	-	80c. brown and lilac	1·20	65
S226	-	3p. brown and blue	2·10	1·20

DESIGNS—HORIZ: 80c. Soldier breaking chain. VERT: 3p. Allegory of Revolution.

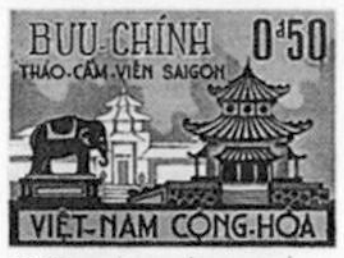

60 Temple and Monument, Botanic Gardens, Saigon

1964. Monuments and Views.

S227	**60**	50c. brown, green and blue	75	50
S228	-	1p. slate and bistre	1·50	65
S229	-	1p.50 green and drab	2·30	85
S230	-	3p. red, green and violet	4·50	1·30

DESIGNS: 1p. Tomb of Minh Mang, Hue; 1p.50, Phan Thiet waterfront; 3p. General Le Van Duyet Temple, Gia Dinh.

For 1p. in smaller size, see No. S352.

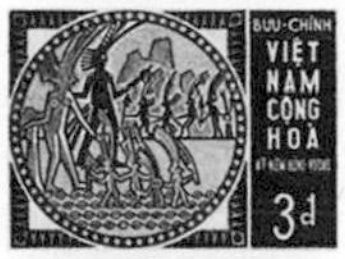

61 Face of Bronze Drum

1965. Hung Vuong (legendary founder of Vietnam, 2000 B.C.).

S231	**61**	3p. orange and lake	4·50	1·00
S232	**61**	100p. violet and purple	33·00	14·00

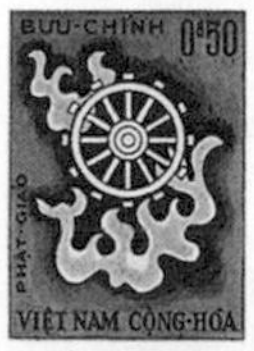

62 Dharmachakra and "Fire of Clemency"

1965. Buddhism.

S233	**62**	50c. red	2·30	50
S234	-	1p.50 orange, blue and deep blue	3·00	65
S235	-	3p. deep brown, sepia and brown	3·75	1·00

DESIGNS—HORIZ: 1p.50, Dharmachakra, lotus and globe. VERT: 3p. Dharmachakra and flag.

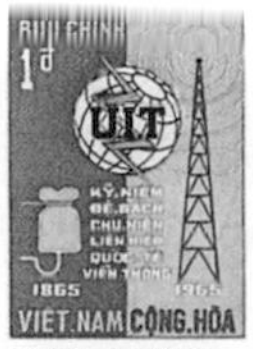

63 I.T.U. Emblem and Symbols

1965. I.T.U. Centenary.

S236	**63**	1p. red and bistre	1·10	65
S237	**63**	3p. red, mauve and brown	2·75	1·30

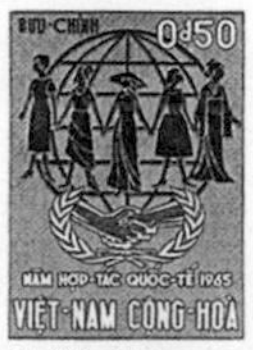

64 "World Solidarity"

1965. International Co-operation Year.

S238	**64**	50c. blue and brown	1·40	50
S239	**64**	1p. sepia and brown	2·10	65
S240	**64**	1p.50 red and grey	3·25	1·00

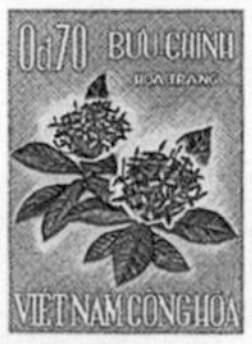

65 Ixora

1965. Mid-Autumn Festival.

S241	**65**	70c. red, green & dp green	60	50
S242	-	80c. purple, green & mve	90	65
S243	-	1p. yellow, blue and deep blue	1·10	85
S244	-	1p.50 green and olive	1·50	1·00
S245	-	3p. orange and green	3·00	1·70

FLOWERS—VERT: 80c. Orchid; 1p. Chrysanthemum; 3p. "Ochna harmandii". HORIZ: 1p.50, Nenuphar.

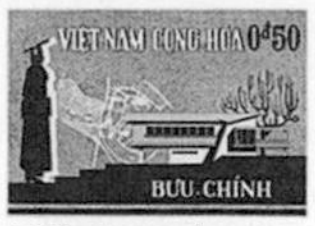

66 Student and University Building

1965. Re-opening of Vietnam University.

S246	**66**	50c. brown	45	35
S247	**66**	1p. green	75	50
S248	**66**	3p. red	1·40	65
S249	**66**	7p. violet	2·75	1·20

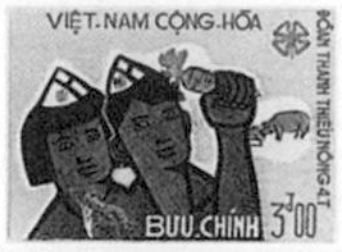

67 Young Farmers

1965. Tenth Anniv of "4-T" Rural Youth Clubs.

S250	**67**	3p. red and green	2·30	50
S251	-	4p. violet, blue and purple	3·75	85

DESIGN: 4p. Young farmer and club banner.

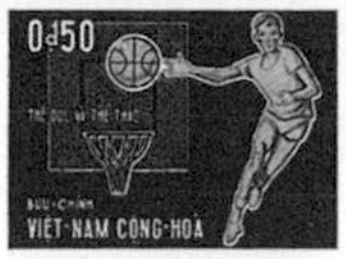

68 Basketball

1965. Third S.E. Asia Peninsular Games, Kuala Lumpur (Malaysia).

S252	**68**	50c. bistre, brown and red	90	50
S253	-	1p. red and brown	1·40	65
S254	-	1p.50 green	2·00	85
S255	-	10p. lake and purple	4·75	1·30

DESIGNS: 1p. Throwing the javelin; 1p.50, "Physical Culture" (gymnasts and Olympic Games' symbols); 10p. Pole-vaulting.

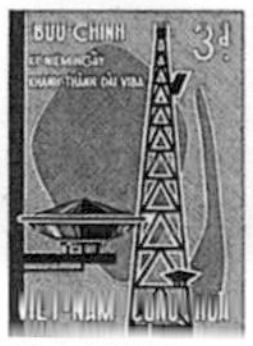

69 Aerial Mast and Equipment

1966. First Anniv of Saigon Microwave Station.

S256	**69**	3p. sepia, blue and brown	75	65
S257	-	4p. purple, red and green	1·10	85

DESIGN: 4p. Aerial mast, telephone dial and map.

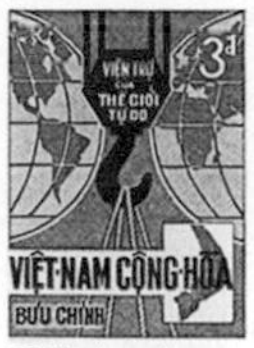

70 Hook and Hemispheres

1966. "Free World's Aid to Vietnam".

S258	**70**	3p. red and grey	60	50
S259	**70**	4p. violet and brown	90	65
S260	**70**	6p. blue and green	1·50	85

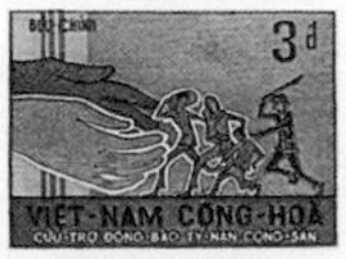

71 Help for Refugees

1966. Refugee Aid.

S261	**71**	3p. olive, mauve & brown	75	50
S262	**71**	7p. violet, brown & mauve	1·80	65

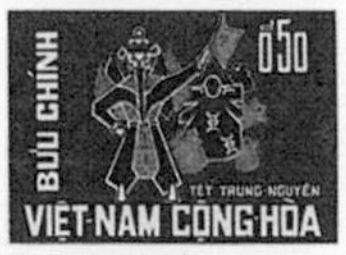

72 Paper "Soldiers"

1966. Wandering Souls' Festival.

S263	**72**	50c. bistre, brown and red	1·20	50
S264	-	1p.50 red, green & brown	1·80	65
S265	-	3p. vermilion, crim & red	2·50	85
S266	-	5p. brown, ochre and deep brown	3·75	1·30

DESIGNS: 1p.50, Obeisance; 3p. Pool of candles; 5p. Votive offering.

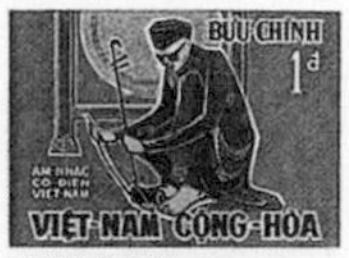

73 "Violinist"

1966. Ancient Musical Instruments.

S267	**73**	1p. deep brown, mauve and brown	1·40	55
S268	-	3p. violet and purple	1·50	70
S269	-	4p. brown and red	2·40	90
S270	-	7p. deep blue and blue	5·25	1·40

DESIGNS: 3p. "Harpist"; 4p. Small band; 7p. "Flautists".

For 3p. in smaller size, see No. S302.

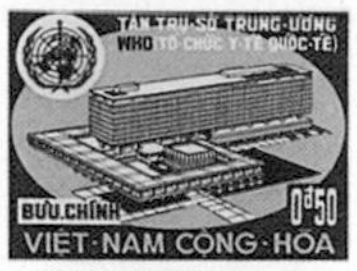

74 W.H.O. Building

1966. Inaug of W.H.O. Headquarters, Geneva.

S271	**74**	50c. purple, violet and red	1·10	55
S272	-	1p.50 black, blue and lake	1·20	70
S273	-	8p. blue, sepia & turquoise	3·00	1·80

DESIGNS—VERT: 1p.50, W.H.O. Building and flag; 8p. U.N. flag and W.H.O. Building.

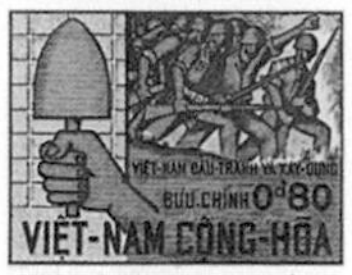

75 Spade in Hand, and Soldiers

1966. Third Anniv of Overthrow of Diem Government.

S274	**75**	80c. brown and bistre	75	55
S275	-	1p.50 purple, red & yell	1·50	70
S276	-	3p. green, brown & chest	3·00	90
S277	-	4p. lake, black and purple	3·75	1·40

DESIGNS—HORIZ: 1p.50, Agricultural workers, soldier and flag. VERT: 3p. Soldier, tractor and labourers; 4p. Soldier and horseman.

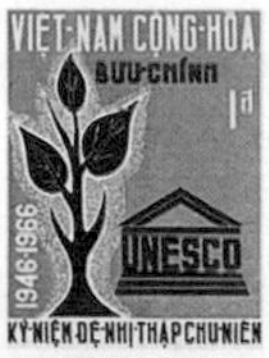

76 UNESCO Emblem and Tree

1966. 20th Anniv of UNESCO.

S278	**76**	1p. brown and lake	1·50	55
S279	-	3p. brown, turquoise & blue	2·30	70
S280	-	7p. blue, turquoise and red	3·75	1·20

DESIGNS—VERT: 3p. Globe and laurel sprigs. HORIZ: 7p. Pagoda.

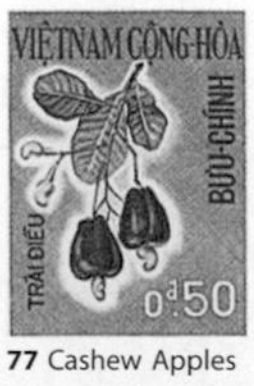

77 Cashew Apples

1967. Exotic Fruit.

S281	**77**	50c. red, green and blue	2·30	55
S282	-	1p.50 orange, green & brown	3·00	70
S283	-	3p. brown, green & choc	3·75	90
S284	-	20p. olive, green and lake	8·25	2·75

FRUITS—HORIZ: 1p.50, Bitter "cucumbers"; 3p. Cinnamon apples; 20p. Areca-nuts.

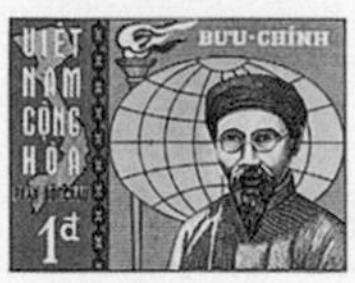

78 Phan Boi Chau

1967. Vietnamese Patriots.

S285	**78**	1p. purple, brown and red	1·10	55
S286	-	20p. black, violet & green	5·75	1·80

DESIGN: 20p. Phan Chau-Trinh (portrait and making speech).

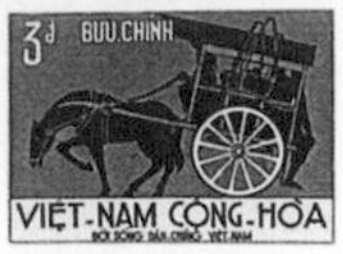

79 Horse-cab

1967. Life of the People.

S287		50c. ultramarine, blue & green	60	55
S288		1p. violet, green & myrtle	75	70
S289	**79**	3p. lake and red	1·10	90
S290	-	8p. violet and red	2·10	1·60

DESIGNS: 50c. Itinerant merchant; 1p. Market-place; 8p. Pastoral activities.

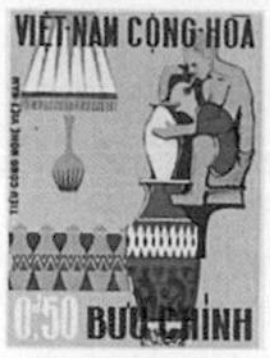

80 Pottery-making

1967. Arts and Crafts. Multicoloured.

S291	50c. Type **80**	60	55
S292	1p.50 Wicker basket and vase	1·10	70
S293	3p. Weavers and potters	2·30	90
S294	35p. Baskets and pottery	6·75	3·25

The 3p. is a horiz design.

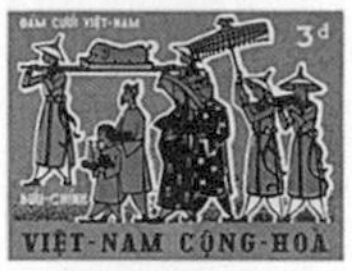

81 Wedding Procession

1967. Vietnamese Wedding.

S295	**81**	3p. red, violet and purple	2·75	1·10

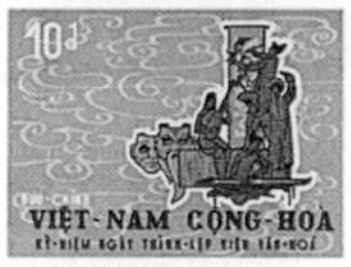

82 "Culture"

1967. Foundation of Vietnamese Cultural Institute.

S296	**82**	10p. multicoloured	4·50	1·20

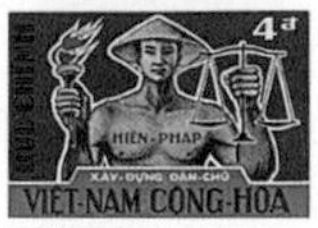

83 "Freedom and Justice"

1967. Democratic Elections. Multicoloured.

S297	4p. Type **83**	1·50	75
S298	5p. Vietnamese and hands casting votes	2·30	1·00
S299	30p. Two Vietnamese with Constitution and flaming torch	4·50	2·00

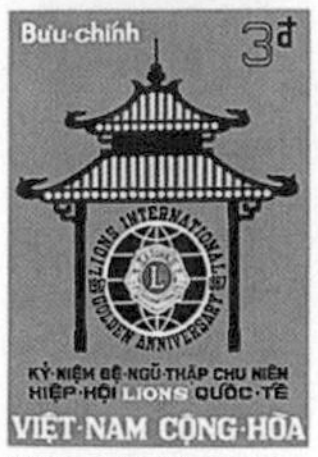

84 Lions Emblem and Pagoda

1967. 50th Anniv of Lions International.

S300	**84**	3p. multicoloured	4·00	3·00

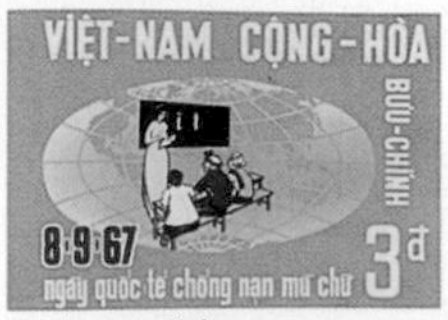

85 Class on Globe

1967. World Literacy Day (8 Sept).

S301	**85**	3p. multicoloured	4·00	2·00

1967. Mobile Post Office Inaug. As No. S268 but smaller, size 23×17 mm.

S302	3p. violet and purple	23·00	18·00

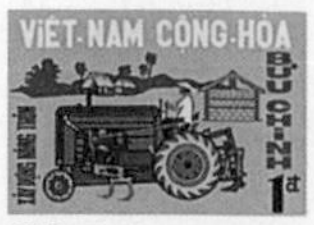

87 Tractor

1968. Rural Development. Multicoloured.

S303	1p. Type **87**	45	50
S304	9p. Bulldozer	1·80	75
S305	10p. Workers with wheel-barrow and tractor	2·30	1·00
S306	20p. Building construction	3·50	1·50

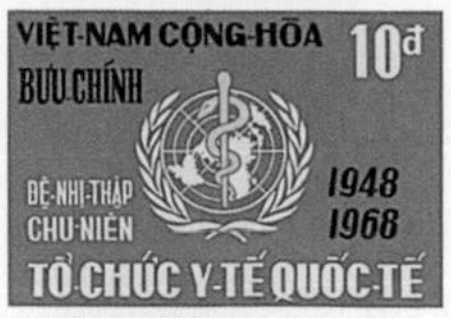

88 W.H.O. Emblem

1968. 20th Anniv of W.H.O.

S307	**88**	10p. yellow, black & green	3·00	2·50

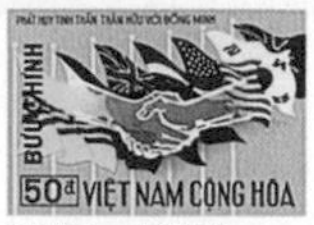

89 Flags of Allied Nations

1968. Thanks for International Aid. Multicoloured.

S308	1p. Handclasp, flags and soldiers	1·10	75
S309	1p.50 S.E.A.T.O. emblem and flags	2·10	1·00
S310	3p. Handclasp and flags	4·00	1·30
S311	50p. Type **89**	12·00	3·25

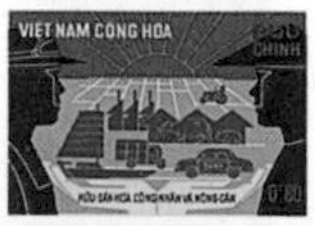

92 Farmers, Farm, Factory and Transport

1968. Development of Private Ownership. Multicoloured.

S318	80c. Type **92**	60	75
S319	2p. Motor vehicles and labourers	75	1·00
S320	10p. Tractor and tri-car	1·80	1·30
S321	30p. Motor vehicles and labourers	5·50	3·25

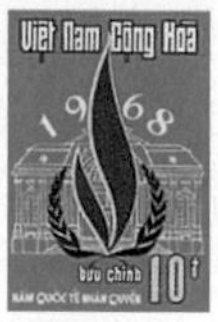

93 Human Rights Emblem

1968. Human Rights Year. Multicoloured.

S322	10p. Type **93**	1·20	75
S323	16p. Men of all races acclaiming Human Rights Emblem	2·50	1·30

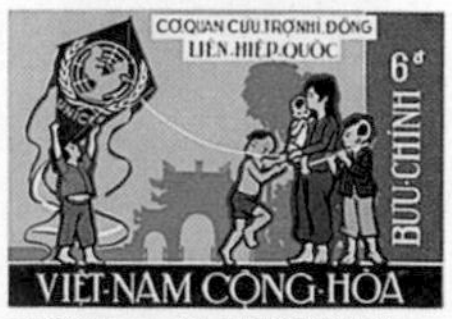

94 Children with UNICEF "Kite"

1968. UNICEF Day. Multicoloured.

S324	6p. Type **94**	3·00	1·30
S325	16p. Mother and child	3·75	1·80

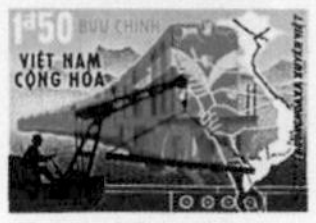

95 Diesel Train, Map and Mechanical Loader

1968. Re-opening of Trans-Vietnam Railway. Multicoloured.

S326	1p.50 Type **95**	2·00	75
S327	3p. Type **95**	2·50	1·00
S328	9p. Diesel train and permanent-way workers	3·00	1·30
S329	20p. As No. S328	6·00	3·00

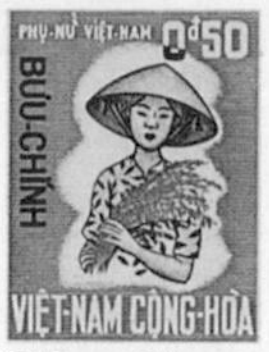

97 Peasant Woman

1969. Vietnamese Women.

S331	**97**	50c. violet, ochre and blue	85	75
S332	-	1p. brown and green	1·10	1·00
S333	-	3p. black, blue and sepia	1·50	1·30
S334	-	20p. multicoloured	3·50	2·50

DESIGNS—VERT: 1p. Tradeswoman; 20p. "Ladies of fashion". HORIZ: 3p. Nurse.

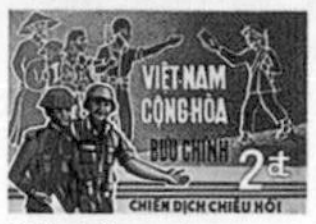

98 Soldier and Militiaman

1969. "Open-arms" National Unity Campaign. Multicoloured.

S335	2p. Type **98**	90	85
S336	50p. Family welcoming soldier	4·50	3·25

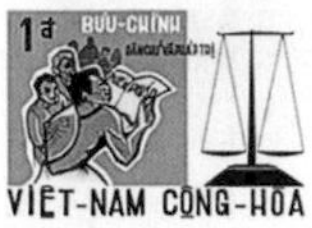

99 Vietnamese and Scales of Justice

1969. First Anniv of New Constitution. Multicoloured.

S337	1p. Type **99**	85	75
S338	20p. Voters at polling station	4·25	2·50

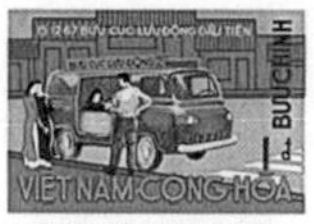

100 Mobile Post Office Van in Street

1969. Vietnamese Mobile Post Offices System. Multicoloured.

S339	1p. Type **100**	85	75
S340	3p. Clerk serving customers	1·20	1·00
S341	4p. Child with letter, and mobile post office	1·50	1·50
S342	20p. Queue at mobile post office, and postmark	2·75	2·50

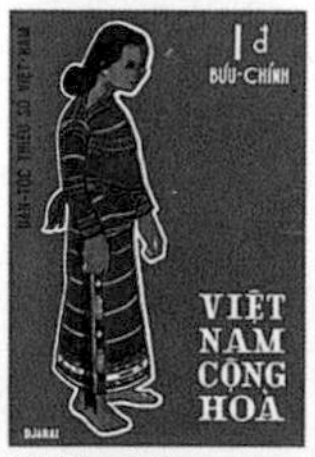

101 Djarai Woman

1969. Second Anniv of Ethnic Minorities Statute. Multicoloured.

S343	1p. Type **101**	1·50	1·30
S344	6p. Mnong-gar woman	3·75	2·00
S345	50p. Bahnar man	15·00	3·00

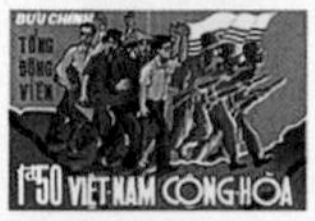

102 "Civilians to Soldiers"

1969. General Mobilization.

S346	**102**	1p.50 multicoloured	1·20	75
S347	-	3p. multicoloured	2·75	1·00
S348	-	5p. brown, red and yellow	3·75	1·30
S349	-	10p. multicoloured	5·25	2·00

DESIGNS: 3p. Bayonet practice; 5p. Recruits arriving at depot; 10p. Happy conscripts.

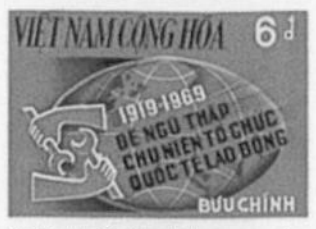

103 I.L.O. Emblem and Globe

1969. 50th Anniv of I.L.O.

S350	**103**	6p. black, grey and green	1·50	1·00
S351	**103**	20p. black, grey and red	3·00	1·50

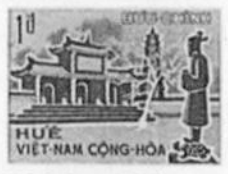

104 Imperial Palace, Hue

1970. Reconstruction of Hue.

S352	**104**	1p. blue and brown	21·00	18·00

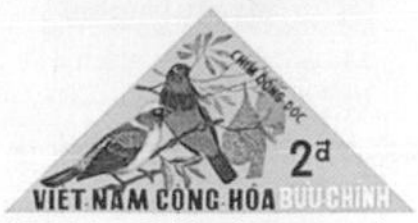

105 Asian Golden Weaver and Baya Weaver

1970. Birds of Vietnam. Multicoloured.

S353	2p. Type **105**	3·00	1·30
S354	6p. Chestnut mannikin	4·50	1·80
S355	7p. Great Indian hornbill	6·00	2·50
S356	30p. Eurasian tree sparrow	17·00	5·25

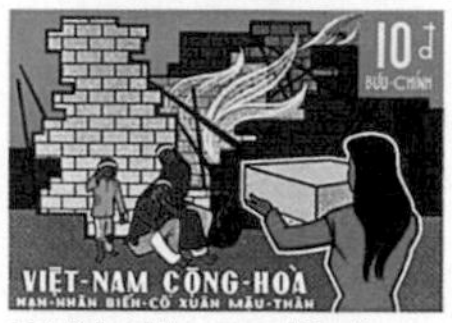

106 Ruined House and Family

1970. Aid for Victims of Communist Tet Offensive. Multicoloured.

S357	10p. Type **106**	2·30	75
S358	20p. Refugee family, and First Aid	3·75	1·80

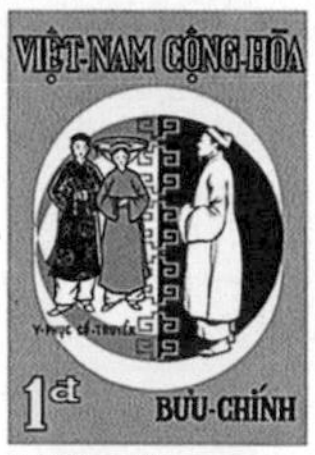

107 Man, Woman and Priest in Traditional Costume

1970. Vietnamese Traditional Costumes. Multicoloured.

S359	1p. Type **107**	75	65
S360	2p. Seated woman (horiz)	85	75
S361	3p. Three women with carved lion (horiz)	1·00	90
S362	100p. Man and woman (horiz)	9·75	5·00

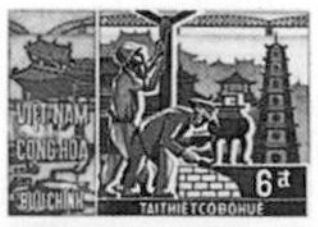

108 Builders and Pagoda

1970. Reconstruction of Hue. Multicoloured.

S363	6p. Type **108**	1·50	1·00
S364	20p. Mixing cement	2·75	1·30

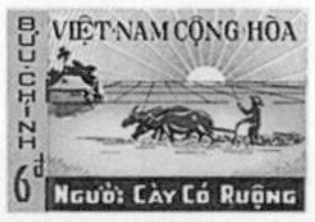

109 Ploughing Paddyfield

1970. "Land to the Tiller". Agrarian Reform Law.

S365	**109**	6p. black, green & brown	2·20	1·30

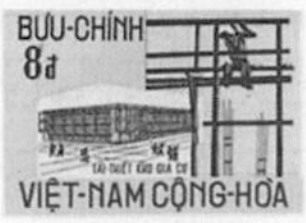

110 Scaffolding and New Building

1970. Reconstruction after Tet Offensive. Multicoloured.
| S366 | 8p. Type **110** | 1·60 | 85 |
| S367 | 16p. Construction workers | 3·50 | 2·00 |

111 A.P.Y. Symbol

1970. Asian Productivity Year.
| S368 | **111** | 10p. multicoloured | 1·90 | 1·10 |

112 Nguyen Dinh Chieu
and Poems

1970. Nguyen Dinh Chieu (poet) Commem.
| S369 | **112** | 6p. brown, red and violet | 1·30 | 85 |
| S370 | **112** | 10p. brown, red & green | 2·50 | 1·30 |

113 I.E.Y.
Emblem

1970. International Education Year.
| S371 | **113** | 10p. black, yellow & brown | 2·10 | 1·10 |

114 Senate House

1970. Ninth Council Meeting and Sixth General Assembly of Asian Interparliamentary Union, Saigon. Multicoloured.
| S372 | 6p. Type **114** | 90 | 85 |
| S373 | 10p. House of Representatives | 1·70 | 1·30 |

115 Two
Dancers

1971. Vietnamese Traditional Dances.
S374	**115**	2p. multicoloured	1·10	85
S375	-	6p. brown, blue & green	3·00	1·10
S376	-	7p. red, blue and brown	3·50	1·30
S377	-	10p. multicoloured	4·00	1·50

DESIGNS—HORIZ: 6p. Drum dance; 7p. Drum dancers in various positions. VERT: 10p. Flower dance.

116 Paddyfield,
Peasants and Agrarian
Law

1971. First Anniv of "Land to the Tiller" Agrarian Reform Law. Multicoloured.
S378	2p. Type **116** (dated "26.3.1971")	80	65
S378a	2p. Type **116** (dated "26.3.1970")	50·00	
S379	3p. Tractor and Law	1·00	85
S380	16p. Peasants ringing Law	4·50	1·30

117 Postal Courier

1971. History of Vietnam Postal Service. Multicoloured.
| S381 | 2p. Type **117** | 1·20 | 85 |
| S382 | 6p. Mounted courier with banner | 3·25 | 1·30 |

118 Armed Forces on Map of
Vietnam

1971. Armed Forces Day.
| S383 | **118** | 3p. multicoloured | 1·90 | 1·30 |
| S384 | **118** | 40p. multicoloured | 6·50 | 2·75 |

119 Hog-deer

1971. Vietnamese Fauna. Multicoloured.
| S385 | 9p. Type **119** | 2·30 | 1·10 |
| S386 | 30p. Tiger | 5·25 | 3·00 |

120 Rice Harvesters

1971. "The Rice Harvest".
S387	**120**	1p. multicoloured	1·20	85
S388	-	30p. lilac, black and red	3·75	2·20
S389	-	40p. brown, yellow & blue	4·75	2·40

DESIGNS: 30p. Threshing and winnowing rice; 40p. Harvesters in paddyfield.

121 New H.Q. Building

1971. New U.P.U. Headquarters Building, Berne.
| S390 | **121** | 20p. multicoloured | 3·75 | 1·50 |

122 Percoid fish

1971. Vietnam Fish. Multicoloured.
S391	2p. Type **122**	2·40	85
S392	10p. Striped scat (horiz)	3·75	1·30
S393	100p. Freshwater angelfish (horiz)	24·00	11·00

123 "Local Delivery"

1971. Development of Rural Post System. Multicoloured.
S394	5p. Type **123**	1·20	85
S395	10p. Symbolic crane	2·40	1·30
S396	20p. Cycle postman delivering letter	3·75	1·70

124 Fishermen in Boat,
and Modern Trawler

1972. Vietnamese Fishing Industry. Multicoloured.
S397	4p. Type **124**	1·20	65
S398	7p. Fishermen hauling net	2·20	85
S399	50p. Trawl net	7·25	2·20

125 Emperor
Quang Trung

1972. Emperor Quang Trung (victor of Dong Da) Commemoration.
| S400 | **125** | 6p. multicoloured | 1·20 | 1·10 |
| S401 | **125** | 20p. multicoloured | 3·75 | 3·25 |

126 Community
Workers

1972. Community Development Projects.
| S403 | **126** | 3p. multicoloured | 85 | 60 |
| S404 | **126** | 8p. multicoloured | 1·60 | 1·00 |

127 Harvesting Rice

1972. Farmers' Day.
| S405 | 1p. Type **127** | 60 | 50 |
| S406 | 10p. Sowing rice | 2·10 | 85 |

128 Boeing 727 over
Dalat

1972. 20th Anniv of Viet-Nam Airlines. Multicoloured.
S407	10p. Type **128**	3·00	1·20
S408	10p. Boeing 727 over Ha Tien	3·00	1·20
S409	10p. Boeing 727 over Hue	3·00	1·20
S410	10p. Boeing 727 over Saigon	3·00	1·20
S411	25p. Type **128**	5·50	2·50
S412	25p. As No. S408	5·50	2·50
S413	25p. As No. S409	5·50	2·50
S414	25p. As No. S410	5·50	2·50

129 Vietnamese Scholar

1972. Vietnamese Scholars. Multicoloured.
S415	5p. Type **129**	1·20	75
S416	20p. Scholar with pupils	2·75	1·20
S417	50p. Scholar with scroll	6·50	2·50

130 Sentry

1972. Civilian Self-defence Force. Multicoloured.
S418	2p. Type **130**	1·60	85
S419	6p. Young volunteer and badge (horiz)	2·40	1·20
S420	20p. Volunteers at rifle practice	3·25	1·30

131 Hands supporting
Savings Bank

1972. Treasury Bonds Savings Scheme.
| S421 | **131** | 10p. multicoloured | 2·10 | 75 |
| S422 | **131** | 25p. multicoloured | 4·25 | 1·50 |

132 Three Guards with
Horse

1972. Traditional Vietnamese Frontier Guards. Multicoloured.
S423	10p. Type **132**	1·20	75
S424	30p. Pikeman (vert)	2·75	1·30
S425	40p. Guards on parade	4·00	1·70

133 Wounded
Soldier

1972. Vietnamese War Veterans. Multicoloured.
S426	9p. Type **133**	1·80	75
S427	16p. Soldier on crutches	2·40	1·00
S428	100p. Veterans' memorial	9·00	4·25

134 Soldiers on Tank,
and Memorial

1972. Victory at Binh Long. Multicoloured.
| S429 | 5p. Type **134** | 9·75 | 65 |
| S430 | 10p. Soldiers on map of An Loc (vert) | 14·50 | 1·00 |

135 "Books for
Everyone"

1972. International Book Year. Multicoloured.
S431	2p. Type **135**	1·20	60
S432	4p. Book Year emblems encircling globe	1·80	75
S433	5p. Emblem, books and globe	2·40	1·00

136 "200,000th
Returnees"

1973. 200,000th Returnees under "Open Arms" National Unity Campaign.
| S434 | **136** | 10p. multicoloured | 3·25 | 2·50 |

137 Soldiers
raising Flag

1973. Victory at Quang Tri. Multicoloured.
| S435 | 3p. Type **137** | 1·80 | 85 |
| S436 | 10p. Map and defenders | 3·00 | 1·70 |

138 Satellite and
Globe

1973. World Meteorological Day.
| S437 | **138** | 1p. multicoloured | 1·60 | 1·30 |

139 Programme
Emblem and
Farm-workers

1973. Five-Year Agricultural Development Programme. Multicoloured.
S438	2p. Type **139**	2·40	50
S439	5p. Ploughing in paddy-field	3·75	1·00
S439a	10p. As T **149** but dated "26-03-1973" (34×54 mm)	£150	50·00

140 Emblem and H.Q.
Paris

1973. 50th Anniv of International Criminal Police Organization (Interpol). Multicoloured.

S440	1p. Type **140**	75	50
S441	2p. "INTERPOL 1923 1973"	1·10	65
S442	25p. Emblem and view of head-quarters (different)	4·75	1·00

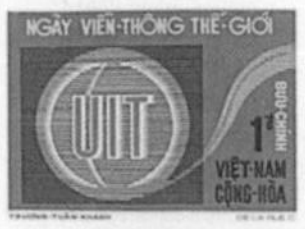

141 I.T.U. Emblem

1973. World Telecommunications Day.

S443	**141**	1p. multicoloured	60	50
S444	-	2p. black and blue	85	65
S445	-	3p. multicoloured	1·70	1·00

DESIGNS: 2p. Globe; 3p. I.T.U. emblem in frame.

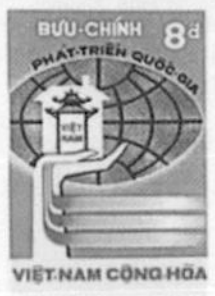

142 Lamp in Hand

1973. National Development.

S446	**142**	8p. multicoloured	1·20	50
S447	-	10p. blue, black & brown	1·80	65
S448	-	15p. multicoloured	2·40	1·00

DESIGNS: 10p. "Agriculture, Industry and Fisheries"; 15p. Workers on power pylon.

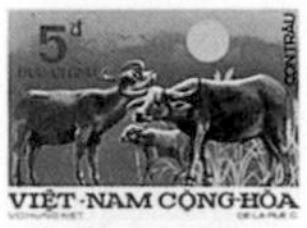

143 Water Buffaloes

1973. "Year of the Buffalo". Multicoloured.

S449	5p. Type **143**	2·40	85
S450	10p. Water buffalo	4·75	1·30

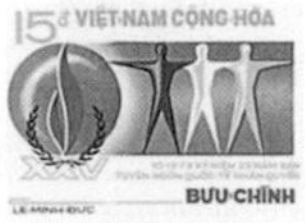

144 Flame Emblem and "Races of the World"

1973. 25th Anniv of Declaration of Human Rights. Multicoloured.

S451	15p. Type **144**	1·20	85
S452	100p. Flame emblem and scales of justice (vert)	4·00	1·20

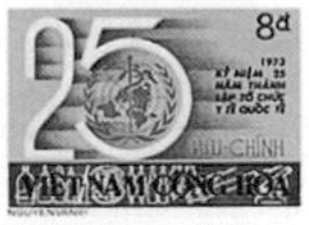

145 Emblem within "25"

1973. 25th Anniv of W.H.O.

S453	**145**	8p. multicoloured	1·20	65
S454	-	15p. blue, red and brown	1·80	1·00

DESIGN: 15p. W.H.O. emblem and inscription.

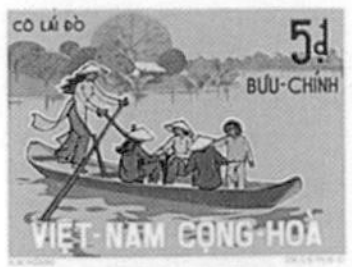

146 Sampan crossing River

1974. Vietnamese Sampan Women. Multicoloured.

S455	5p. Type **146**	2·40	65
S456	10p. Sampan and passengers	3·75	1·20

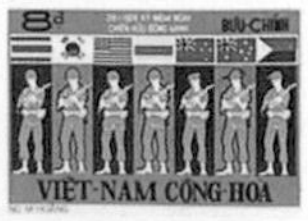

147 Flags and Soldiers of Allies

1974. Allies Day. Multicoloured.

S457	8p. Type **147**	80	50
S458	15p. Soldiers and flags	1·70	85
S459	15p. Allied Nations Monument	1·70	85
S460	60p. Raising South Vietnamese flag, and map (vert)	4·75	1·70

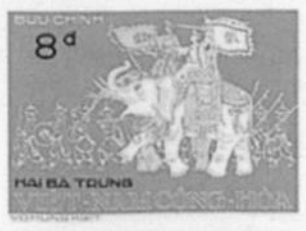

148 Trung Sisters on Elephant

1974. Trung Sisters' Festival.

S461	**148**	8p. green, yellow & black	1·80	65
S462	**148**	15p. red, yellow and black	2·40	85
S463	**148**	80p. blue, pink and black	4·25	1·20

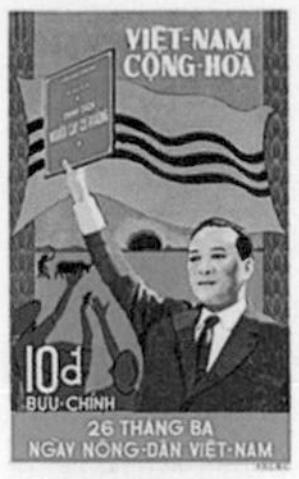

149 Pres. Thieu holding Agrarian Reform Law

1974. Farmers' Day. Multicoloured.

S464	10p. Type **149**	1·20	65
S465	20p. Farm-workers (32×22 mm)	2·40	1·00
S466	70p. Girl harvesting rice (22×32 mm)	48·00	65·00

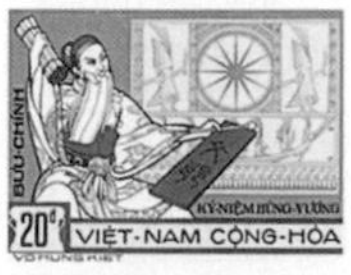

150 King Hung Vuong

1974. King Hung Vuong (first Vietnamese monarch) Commemoration. Multicoloured.

S467	20p. Type **150**	2·40	85
S468	100p. Banner inscribed "Hung Vuong, National Founder"	6·00	1·70

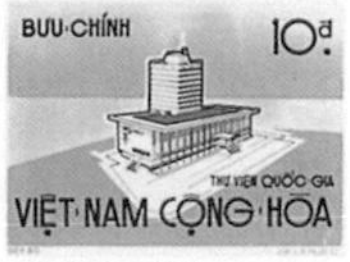

151 National Library

1974. New National Library Building. Multicoloured.

S469	10p. Type **151**	2·40	1·70
S470	15p. Library and Phoenix bas-relief	3·75	2·50

1974. Surch.

S470a	**142**	10p. on 8p. mult	36·00	33·00
S470b	**145**	10p. on 8p. mult	30·00	28·00
S470c	**120**	25p. on 1p. mult	12·00	11·50
S470d	**140**	25p. on 1p. mult	12·00	11·50
S470e	**138**	25p. on 1p. mult	12·00	11·50
S470f	**141**	25p. on 1p. mult	18·00	17·00
S470g	-	25p. on 7p. red, blue and brown (No. S376)		
S470h	**147**	25p. on 8p. mult	17·00	15·00
S470i	-	25p. on 16p. mult (No. S427)	14·50	4·50
S470j	-	25p. on 16p. mult (No. S380)	14·50	4·50

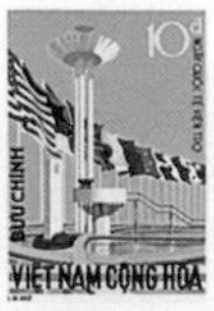

152 Allied Nations Memorial, Saigon

1974. International Aid Day. Multicoloured.

S471	10p. Type **152**	1·10	85
S472	20p. Flags on crane (horiz)	2·20	1·00
S473	60p. Crate on hoist	6·00	1·70

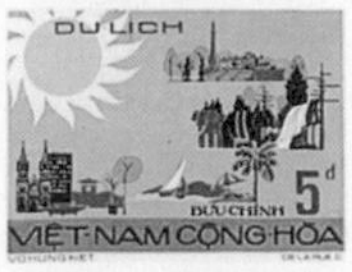

153 "Tourist Attractions"

1974. Tourism. Multicoloured.

S474	5p. Type **153**	1·80	85
S475	10p. Xom Bong Bridge Nhatrang	2·40	1·30
S476	15p. Thien Mu Pagoda, Hue (vert)	3·00	2·20

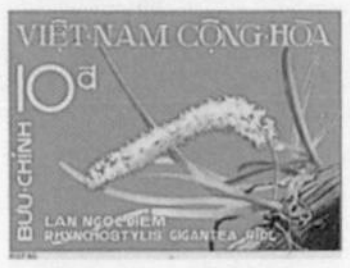

154 "Rhynchostylis gigantea"

1974. Orchids. Multicoloured.

S477	10p. Type **154**	75	85
S478	20p. "Cypripedium callosum" (vert)	1·10	1·00
S479	200p. "Dendrobium nobile"	7·75	2·30

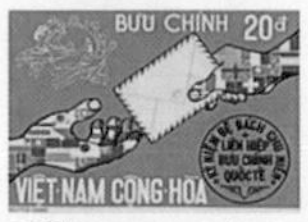

155 "International Exchange of Mail"

1974. Centenary of U.P.U. Multicoloured.

S480	20p. Type **155**	60	65
S481	30p. "U.P.U. letter" and Hemi-spheres	1·20	1·00
S482	300p. U.P.U. emblem and Vietnamese girl (vert)	5·25	2·50

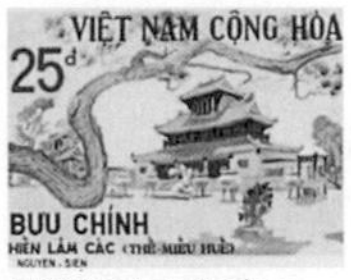

156 Hien Lam Pavilion, Hue

1975. Historical Sites. Multicoloured.

S483	25p. Type **156**	1·80	1·70
S484	30p. Throne Room, Imperial Palace, Hue	2·75	2·20
S485	60p. Tu Duc's Pavilion, Hue	3·25	3·25

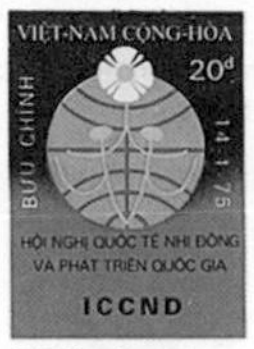

157 Conference Emblem

1975. International Conference on Children and National Development, Saigon. Multicoloured.

S486	20p. Type **157**	3·75	85
S487	70p. Vietnamese family (32×22 mm)	4·75	85

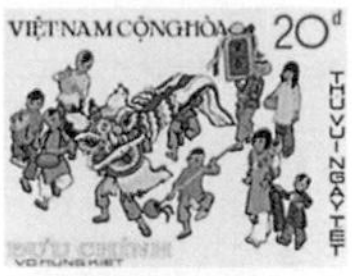

158 Unicorn Dance

1975. Vietnamese New Year Festival. Multicoloured.

S488	20p. Type **158**	3·00	85
S489	30p. Letting-off fire-crackers (vert)	3·75	1·20
S490	100p. New Year greeting custom (vert)	8·50	2·20

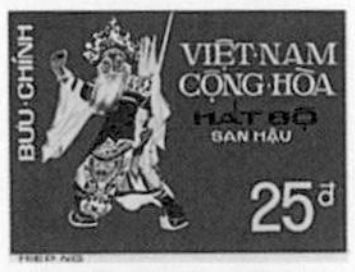

159 Military Mandarin ("San Hau" play)

1975. "Hat Bo" Vietnamese Traditional Theatre. Multicoloured.

S491	25p. Type **159**	1·80	85
S492	40p. Two characters from "Tam Ha Nam Duong" (vert)	3·00	1·20
S493	100p. Heroine "Luu Kim Giai Gia Tho Chau" (vert)	9·75	2·20

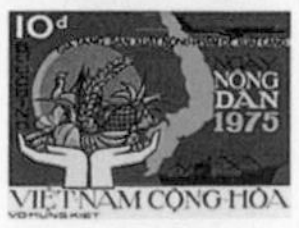

160 Produce for Export and Map

1975. Farmers' Day. Multicoloured.

S494	10p. Type **160**	2·40	1·70
S495	50p. Ancient and modern irrigation	6·25	2·50

MILITARY FRANK STAMPS

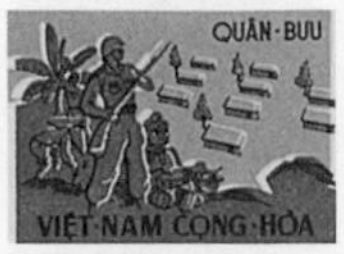

MF29 Soldier and Barracks

1961. No value indicated. Roul.

SMF115	**MF29**	(–) yellow, brown, green and black	39·00	30·00
SMF116	**MF29**	(–) yellow, brown and green	39·00	30·00

POSTAGE DUE STAMPS

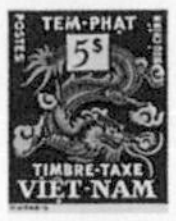

D1 Dragon

1955

SD1	**D1**	2p. yellow and mauve	1·00	1·00
SD2	**D1**	3p. turquoise and violet	1·10	1·10
SD3	**D1**	5p. yellow and violet	1·60	1·60
SD4	**D1**	10p. red and green	2·30	2·30
SD14	-	20p. green and red	6·75	2·30
SD15	-	30p. yellow and green	10·00	3·50
SD16	-	50p. yellow and brown	17·00	6·75
SD17	-	100p. yellow and violet	29·00	13·50

The 20p. to 100p. are inscribed "BUU-CHINH" instead of "TIMBRE TAXE".

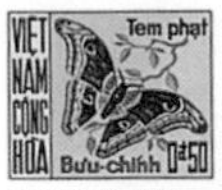

D90 Butterfly

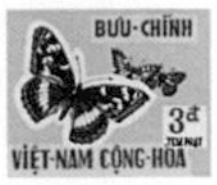

D91 Butterflies

1968

SD312	**D90**	50c. multicoloured	3·75	3·00
SD313	**D90**	1p. multicoloured	4·50	3·50
SD314	**D90**	2p. multicoloured	7·50	6·75
SD315	**D91**	3p. multicoloured	10·50	8·75
SD316	**D91**	5p. multicoloured	17·00	15·00
SD317	**D91**	10p. multicoloured	27·00	20·00

1974. Surch.

SD470k	**D91**	5p. on 3p. mult	6·00	5·00
SD470l	**D90**	10p. on 50c. mult	6·00	5·00
SD470m	**D90**	40p. on 1p. mult	6·00	5·00
SD470n	**D90**	60p. on 2p. mult	6·00	5·00

D. NATIONAL FRONT FOR THE LIBERATION OF SOUTH VIETNAM

The National Front for the Liberation of South Vietnam was formed by the Communists, known as the Vietcong, in December 1960. With the support of troops from North Vietnam and Vietcong gradually gained control of more and more territory within South Vietnam until the surrender of the last South Vietnamese Republican forces in May 1975 enabled them to take control of the entire country. The following stamps were used in those areas controlled by the National Liberation Front.

The value of the N.L.F. dong fluctuated considerably and was not on parity with the North Vietnamese currency.

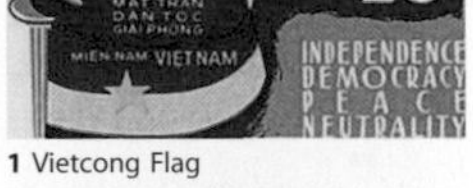

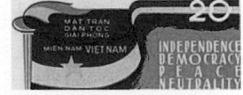

1 Vietcong Flag

1963. Third Anniv of National Liberation Front.

NLF1	**1**	20x. multicoloured (English inscr)	6·75	7·25
NLF2	**1**	20x. multicoloured (French inscr)	6·75	7·25
NLF3	**1**	20x. multicoloured (Spanish inscr)	6·75	7·25

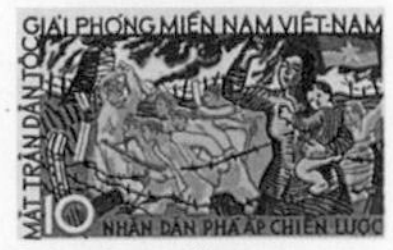

2 Attack on Village

1963. Third Anniv of Revolutionary Struggle in South Vietnam. Multicoloured.

NLF4	10x. Type **2**	13·50	14·50
NLF5	10x. Attack on U.S. helicopter	13·50	14·50

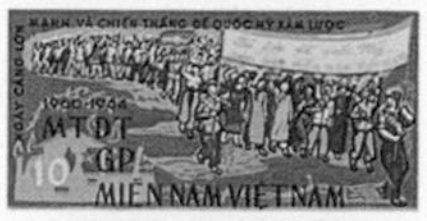

3 Demonstrators with Banner

1964. Fourth Anniv of National Liberation Front.

NLF6	10x. Type **3**		5·25	5·75
NLF7	20x. multicoloured		6·00	6·50
NLF8	30x. green and blue		6·75	7·25

DESIGNS: 20x. Harvesting rice; 30x. Sinking of U.S.S. "Card" (destroyer).

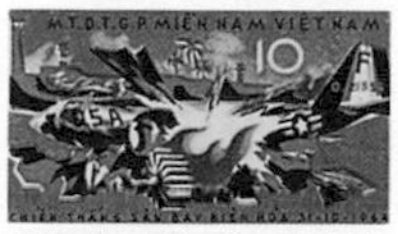

4 Attack on Bien Hoa Airfield

1965. Fifth Anniv of National Liberation Front.

NLF9	**4**	10x. multicoloured	6·00	6·50
NLF10	-	20x. black, grey and red	6·75	7·25
NLF11	-	40x. multicoloured	8·00	8·75

DESIGNS: 20x. Nguyen Van Troi facing firing squad; 40x. Vietcong flags.

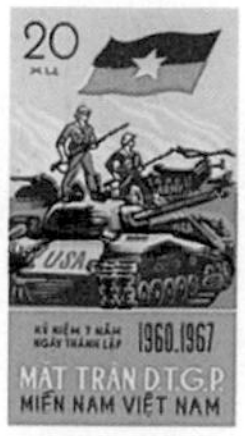

5 Vietcong Soldiers on U.S. Tanks

1967. Seventh Anniv of National Liberation Front. Multicoloured.

NLF12	20x. Type **5**	6·00	6·50
NLF13	20x. Vietcong guerrillas (horiz)	6·00	6·50
NLF14	30x. Crowd with banners	6·75	7·25

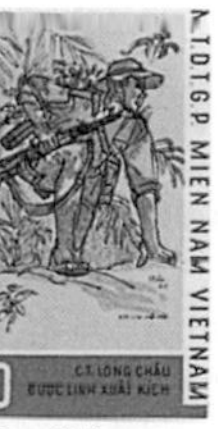

6 "Guerrilla"

1968. "The Struggle For Freedom". Paintings. Multicoloured.

NLF15	10x. Type **6**	6·00	6·50
NLF16	20x. "Jungle Patrol" (horiz)	6·75	7·25
NLF17	30x. "Woman Soldier"	7·25	8·00
NLF18	40x. "Towards the Future" (horiz)	8·00	8·75

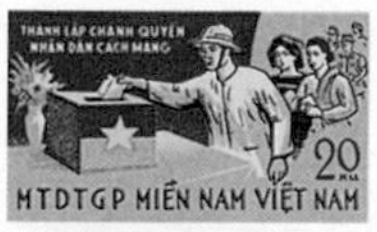

7 Casting Votes

1968. Eighth Anniv of National Liberation Front. Multicoloured.

NLF19	20x. Type **7**	6·75	7·25
NLF20	20x. Bazooka crew and burning airplane	6·75	7·25
NLF21	30x. Vietcong flag and crowd (French inscr)	8·00	8·75
NLF22	30x. Vietcong flag and crowd (English inscr)	8·00	8·75

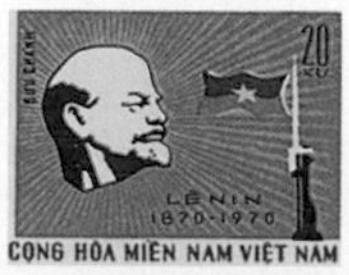

8 Lenin and Vietcong Flag

1970. Birth Centenary of Lenin.

NLF23	**8**	20x. multicoloured	6·00	6·50
NLF24	**8**	30x. multicoloured	6·75	7·25
NLF25	**8**	50x. multicoloured	8·00	8·75
NLF26	**8**	2d. multicoloured	10·00	11·00

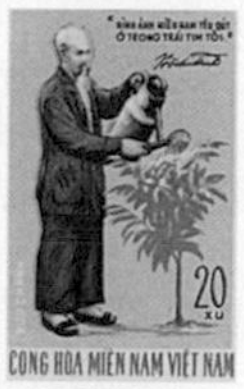

9 Ho Chi Minh watering Kainito Plant

1970. 80th Birth Anniv of Ho Chi Minh.

NLF27	**9**	20x. multicoloured	6·00	6·50
NLF28	**9**	30x. multicoloured	6·75	7·25
NLF29	**9**	50x. multicoloured	8·00	8·75
NLF30	**9**	2d. multicoloured	10·00	11·00

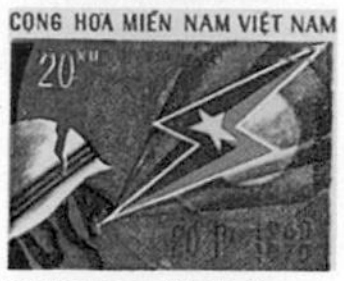

10 Vietcong "Lightning Flash"

1970. Tenth Anniv of National Liberation Front.

NLF31	**10**	20x. multicoloured	65	75
NLF32	**10**	30x. multicoloured	1·30	1·50
NLF33	**10**	50x. multicoloured	2·00	2·20
NLF34	**10**	3d. multicoloured	6·75	7·25

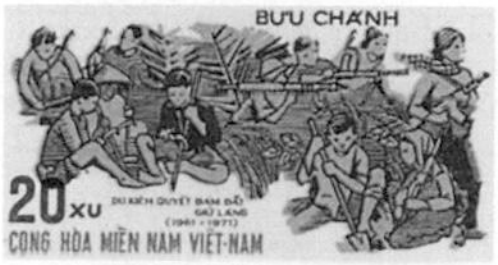

11 Home Guards defending Village

1971. Tenth Anniv of People's Liberation Armed Forces. Multicoloured.

NLF35	20x. Type **11**	6·00	6·50
NLF36	30x. Surrender of U.S. tank	6·75	7·25
NLF37	50x. Agricultural workers	8·00	8·75
NLF38	1d. Vietcong ambush	10·00	11·00

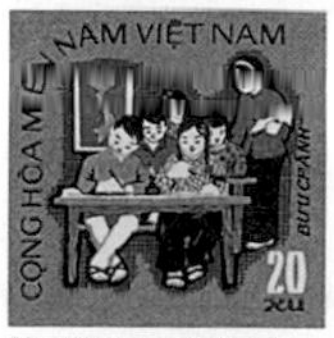

12 Children in School

1971. Second Anniv of Provisional Government. Life in Liberated Areas. Multicoloured.

NLF39	20x. Type **12**	1·30	1·50
NLF40	30x. Women sewing Vietcong flag	2·75	3·00
NLF41	40x. Fortifying village	4·00	4·50
NLF42	50x. Medical clinic	5·25	5·75
NLF43	1d. Harvesting	8·00	8·75

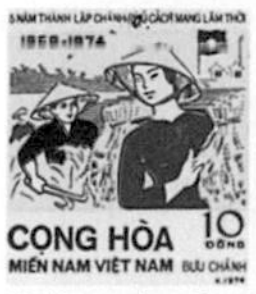

13 Harvesting Rice

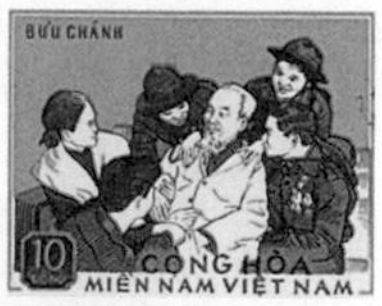

14 Ho Chi Minh with Vietcong Soldiers

1974. Fifth Anniv of Provisional Government. Multicoloured.

NLF44	10d. Type **13**	3·25	3·75
NLF45	10d. Demonstrators with banner	3·25	3·75
NLF46	10d. Schoolchildren	3·25	3·75
NLF47	10d. Women home guards	3·25	3·75
NLF48	10d. Vietcong conference delegate	3·25	3·75
NLF49	10d. Soldiers and tanks	3·25	3·75
NLF50	10d. Type **14**	1·60	1·80
NLF51	20d. Type **14**	2·75	3·00

For other values as Type **14**, see Nos. NLF57/60.

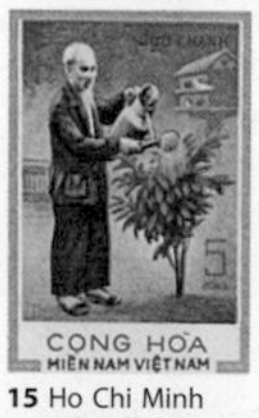

15 Ho Chi Minh watering Kainito Plant

1975. 85th Birth Anniv of Ho Chi Minh (1st issue).

NLF52	**15**	5d. multicoloured	65	75
NLF53	**15**	10d. multicoloured	1·30	1·50
NLF54	**15**	30d. mult (mve frame)	6·75	7·25
NLF54a	**15**	30d. mult (grn frame)	6·75	7·25

1975. 15th Anniv of National Front for Liberation of South Vietnam. As T **14** but 35½×26 mm.

NLF55	**14**	15d. black and green	1·30	1·50
NLF56	**14**	30d. black and red	2·75	3·00
NLF57	**14**	60d. black and blue	4·00	4·50
NLF58	**14**	300d. black and yellow	13·50	14·50

1975. 85th Birth Anniv of Ho Chi Minh (2nd issue). As T **284** of North Vietnam, but inscr "MIEN NAM VIET NAM".

NLF59	30d. multicoloured	2·00	2·20
NLF60	60d. multicoloured	4·00	4·50

1976. Various stamps surch in South Vietnamese currency.

NLF61	-	10p. on 1d. multicoloured (No. NLF38)		
NLF62	-	20p. on 6x. yellow and red (No. NLF75)		
NLF63	-	20p. on 20x. multicoloured (No. NLF27)		
NLF64	-	20p. on 40x. multicoloured (No. NLF11)		
NLF65	**9**	20p. on 2d. multicoloured (No. NLF30)		
NLF66	**15**	20p. on 5d. multicoloured (No. NLF52)		
NLF67	**14**	20p. on 10d. multicoloured (No. NLF50)		
NLF68	**15**	20p. on 10d. multicoloured (No. NLF53)		
NLF69	**15**	20p. on 30d. multicoloured (No. NLF54)		
NLF70	**15**	20p. on 30d. mult (No. NLF54a)		

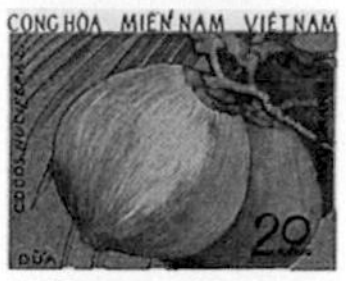

17 "Cocos nucifera"

1976. Fruit. Multicoloured.

NLF71	20d. Type **17**	4·00	4·50
NLF72	30d. "Garcinia mangostana"	6·75	7·25
NLF73	60d. "Mangifera indica"	12·50	14·00

1976. First Elections to Unified National Assembly. As Nos. N858/60 of North Vietnam, but inscr "MIEN NAM VIET NAM".

NLF74	6x. red and blue (as No. N858)	65	75
NLF75	6x. yellow and red (as No. N859)	65	75
NLF76	12x. red and green (as No. N860)	2·00	1·50

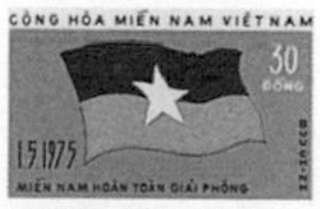

18 Flag of Provisional Revolutionary Government

1976. First Anniv of Liberation of South Vietnam.

NLF77	**18**	30d. multicoloured	2·30	2·20

1976. First Session of Unified National Assembly. As Nos. N861/2 of North Vietnam, but inscr "MIEN NAM VIET NAM".

NLF78	6x. brown, red and yellow	65	75
NLF79	12x. turquoise, red & yell	2·00	1·50

The unified National Assembly proclaimed the reunification of Vietnam on 2 July 1976 and the united country was then known as the Socialist Republic of Vietnam.

E. NORTH VIETNAM.

(Vietnam Democratic Republic)

I. TONGKING

Issues before April 1954 were made in Tongking and Central Annam, in areas under Viet Minh control. From 21 July 1954 French troops withdrew from north of the 17th Parallel and the Ho Chi Minh Government assumed complete control.

GUM. All stamps were issued without gum unless otherwise stated.

1946. No. 190 of Indo-China optd **V VIET-NAM N DAN-CHU CONG-HOA BUU CHINH**.

N1	25c. blue	90·00	£130

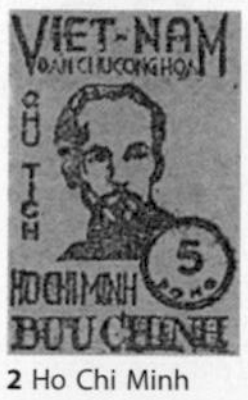

2 Ho Chi Minh

1948

N2a	**2**	2d. brown	10·50	£100
N3a	**2**	5d. red	10·50	£100

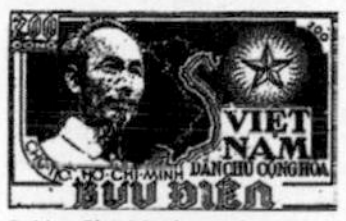

3 Ho Chi Minh and Vietnam Map

1951. Imperf or perf.

N4	**3**	100d. green	36·00	42·00
N5	**3**	100d. brown	36·00	42·00
N6	**3**	200d. red	50·00	65·00

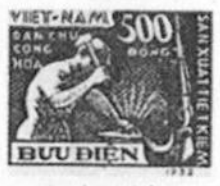

5 Blacksmith

1953. Production Campaign.

N11	**5**	100d. violet	8·25	4·25
N12	**5**	500d. brown	12·50	6·25

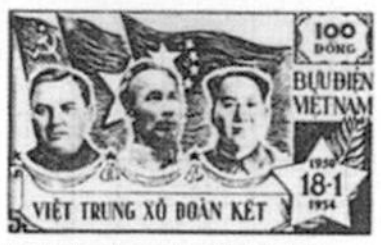

7 Malenkov, Ho Chi Minh, Mao Tse-tung and Flags

1954. Friendship Month.

N13	**7**	100d. red	26·00	21·00

II. CENTRAL ANNAM

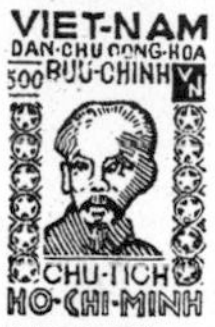

NA1 Ho Chi Minh

1950. Imperf. (a) Figures of value in white.

NA1	**NA1**	1d. violet		
NA2	**NA1**	1d. green		
NA3	**NA1**	5d. green		
NA4	**NA1**	15d. brown		

(b) Figures coloured.

NA7	300d. blue	£500	£550
NA8	500d. red	£950	£1000

1952. Surch in figures. Imperf. (a) Figures in white.

NA5	30d. on 5d. green	£400	£475
NA6	60d. on 1d. violet	£425	£500
NA8a	90d. on 3d. red		

(b) Figures coloured.

NA8b	5d. on 10d. mauve		
NA8c	100d. on 300d. blue		

III. GENERAL ISSUES

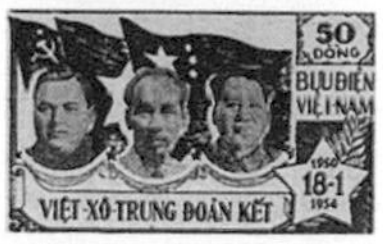

8 Malenkov, Ho Chi Minh and Mao Tse-tung

1954

N14	**8**	50d. brown and red	28·00	27·00
N15	**8**	100d. red and yellow	34·00	33·00

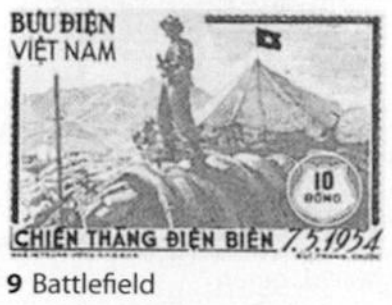

9 Battlefield

1954. Dien Bien Phu Victory. Imperf or perf.

N16a	**9**	10d. bistre and red	23·00	22·00
N17a	**9**	50d. ochre and red	23·00	8·25
N18d	**9**	150d. blue and brown	23·00	11·00

See also No. NO24.

1954. (a) Handstamped 10 dNH.

N19	**3**	10d. on 100d. green	28·00	27·00
N20	**3**	10d. on 100d. brown	28·00	27·00
N21	**3**	20d. on 200d. red	28·00	27·00

(b) Handstamped 10d.

N22	10d. on 100d. green	28·00	27·00
N25	10d. on 100d. brown	28·00	27·00
N28	20d. on 200d. red	70·00	80·00

See also Nos. N46/9.

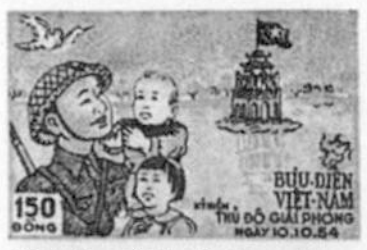

12 Lake of the Returned Sword, Hanoi

1954. Proclamation of Hanoi as Capital.

N30	**12**	10d. blue	9·00	4·25
N31	**12**	50d. green	11·50	5·50
N32	**12**	150d. red	13·50	6·50

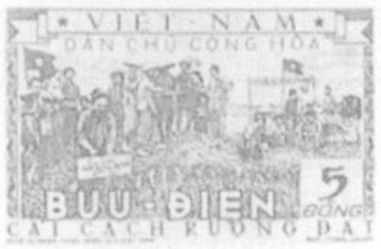

13 Distribution of Title Deeds

1955. Land Reform.

N33	**13**	5d. green	11·50	6·50
N34	**13**	10d. grey	13·50	7·50
N35	**13**	20d. orange	17·00	8·25
N36	**13**	50d. mauve	28·00	9·75
N37	**13**	100d. brown	34·00	13·00

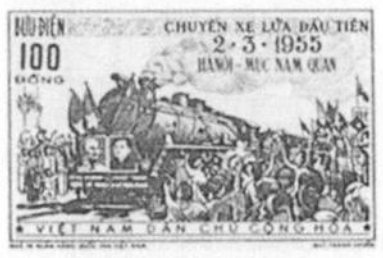

14 Crowd welcoming Steam Train

1956. Hanoi–China Railway Re-opening.

N38	**14**	100d. blue	28·00	8·25
N39	**14**	200d. turquoise	34·00	8·75
N40	**14**	300d. violet	55·00	11·00
N41	**14**	500d. brown	70·00	13·00

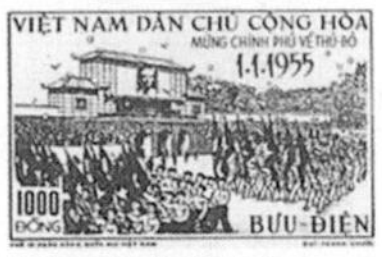

15 Parade, Ba Dinh Square, Hanoi

1956. Return of Govt to Hanoi.

N42	**15**	1000d. violet	70·00	16·00
N43	**15**	1500d. blue	90·00	22·00
N44	**15**	2000d. turquoise	£110	27·00
N45	**15**	3000d. turquoise	£150	33·00

1956. Surch **10 d** or **20 d** in frame.

N46	**3**	10d. on 100d. green	34·00	55·00
N48	**3**	10d. on 100d. brown	34·00	55·00
N49	**3**	20d. on 200d. red	28·00	49·00

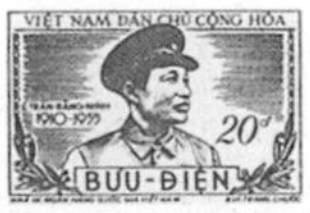

17 Tran Dang Ninh

1956. First Death Anniv of Tran Dang Ninh (patriot).

N50	**17**	5d. green	5·75	2·50
N51	**17**	10d. red	6·25	2·75
N52	**17**	20d. brown	8·00	3·75
N53	**17**	100d. blue	9·00	5·00

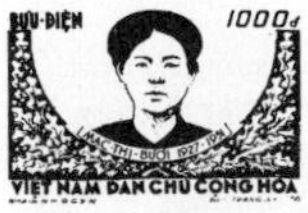

18 Mac Thi Buoi

1956. Fifth Death Anniv of Mac Thi Buoi (guerilla heroine).

N54	**18**	1000d. red	70·00	22·00
N55	**18**	2000d. brown	£140	33·00
N56	**18**	4000d. green	£250	49·00
N57	**18**	5000d. blue	£325	80·00

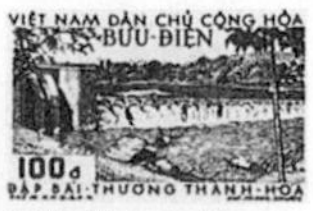

19 Bai Thuong Dam

1956. Reconstruction of Bai Thuong Dam.

N58	**19**	100d. violet and brown	12·50	8·75
N59	**19**	200d. red and black	16·00	11·00
N60a	**19**	300d. red and lake	19·00	15·00

1956. Surch **50 DONG**.

N61	**2**	50d. on 5d. red	£110	£130

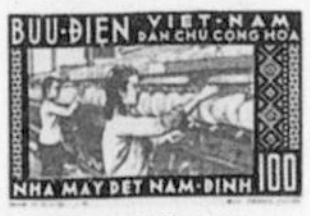

21 Cotton Mill

1957. First Anniv of Opening of Nam Dinh Mill.

N62	**21**	100d. brown and red	9·00	8·75
N63	**21**	200d. grey and blue	11·50	11·00
N64	**21**	300d. light green and green	13·50	13·00

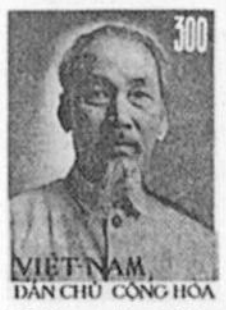

22 Pres. Ho Chi Minh

1957. President's 67th Birthday.

N65	**22**	20d. green	4·50	1·60
N66	**22**	60d. bistre	5·25	1·90
N67	**22**	100d. blue	6·75	2·75
N68	**22**	300d. brown	11·50	5·00

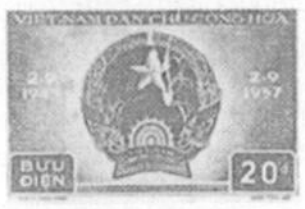

23 Arms of Republic

1957. 12th Anniv of Democratic Republic.

N69	**23**	20d. green	3·50	2·20
N70	**23**	100d. red	8·00	5·50

24 Congress Emblem

1957. Fourth World T.U. Congress, Leipzig.

N71	**24**	300d. purple	11·50	7·50

See also Nos. NO69/72.

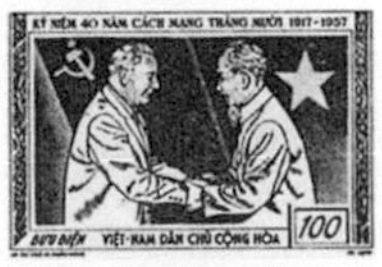

25 Presidents Voroshilov and Ho Chi Minh

1957. 40th Anniv of Russian Revolution.

N72	**25**	100d. red	11·50	8·75
N73	**25**	500d. brown	17·00	13·00
N74	**25**	1000d. orange	28·00	22·00

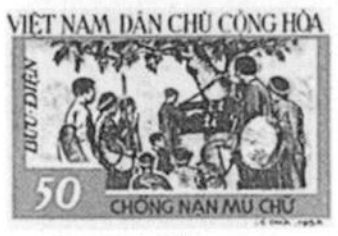

26 Open-air Class

1958. Education Campaign.

N75	**26**	50d. blue	6·75	4·25
N76	**26**	150d. red	8·50	5·50
N77	**26**	1000d. brown	20·00	9·75

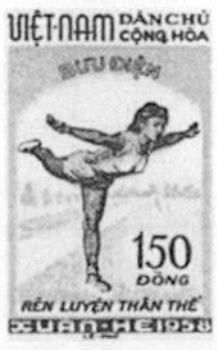

27 Girl Gymnast

1958. Physical Education.

N78	**27**	150d. brown and blue	12·50	3·25
N79	**27**	500d. brown and rose	20·00	5·50

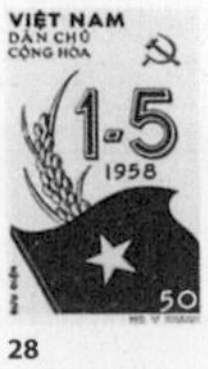

28

1958. Labour Day.

N80	**28**	50d. yellow and red	5·75	1·60
N81	**28**	150d. red and yellow	6·75	2·20

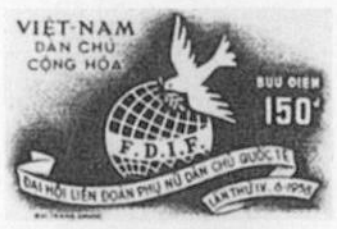

29 Congress Emblem

1958. Fourth International Congress of Democratic Women, Vienna.

N82	**29**	150d. blue	11·50	4·25

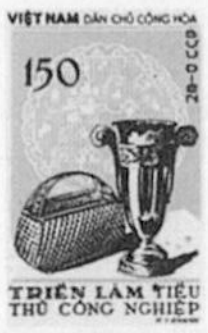

30 Cup, Basket and Lace

1958. Arts and Crafts Fair, Hanoi.

N83	**30**	150d. sepia and turquoise	4·50	2·20
N84	**30**	2000d. black and lilac	32·00	8·75

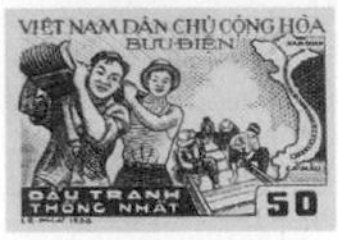

31 Hanoi–Saigon Railway Reconstruction

1958. Re-unification of Vietnam Propaganda.

N85	**31**	50d. blue	4·50	1·10
N86	**31**	150d. brown	6·75	1·40

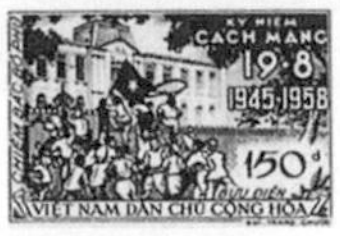

32 Revolution in Hanoi

1958. 13th Anniv of Vietnamese Revolution.

N87	**32**	150d. red	4·00	1·00
N88	**32**	500d. blue	6·25	1·10

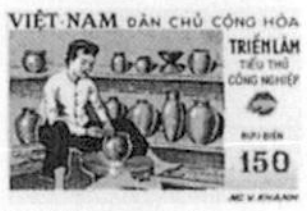

33 Woman Potter

1958. Handicrafts Exhibition.

N89	**33**	150d. lake and red	3·50	1·10
N90	**33**	1000d. brown and ochre	8·00	1·60

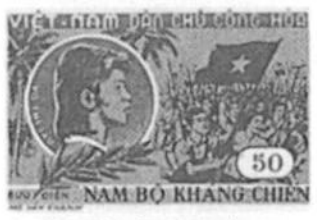

34 Vo Thi Sau and Crowd

1958. 13th Anniv of South Vietnam Resistance Movement.

N91	**34**	50d. green and buff	5·00	85
N92	**34**	150d. red and orange	7·25	1·20

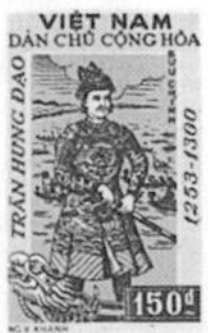

35 Tran Hung Dao

1958. 658th Death Anniv of Tran Hung Dao.

N93	**35**	150d. grey and blue	3·50	75

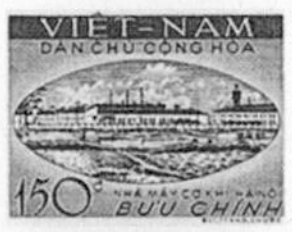

36 Hanoi Factories

1958. Hanoi Mechanical Engineering Plant.

N94	**36**	150d. sepia	4·00	1·10

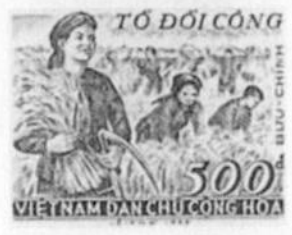

37 Harvesting Rice

1958. Mutual Aid Teams.

N95	**37**	150d. lake	4·50	2·20
N96	**37**	500d. brown	9·00	2·50

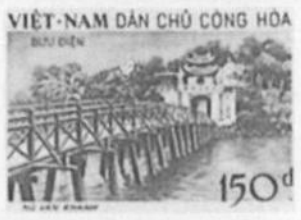

38 Temple of Jade, Hanoi

1958

N97	**38**	150d. green	5·75	2·75
N98	-	150d. blue	3·50	1·10
N99	-	350d. brown	5·75	2·20
N100	**38**	2000d. green	28·00	8·75

DESIGNS—HORIZ: 150d. blue; 350d. Bay of Halong.

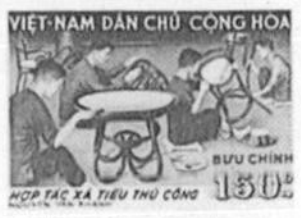

39 Furniture-makers

1958. Furniture Co-operatives.

N101	**39**	150d. blue	4·00	1·30

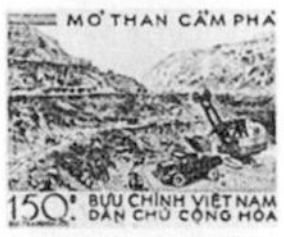

40 Cam Pha Coal Mines

1959

N102	**40**	150d. blue	11·50	1·10

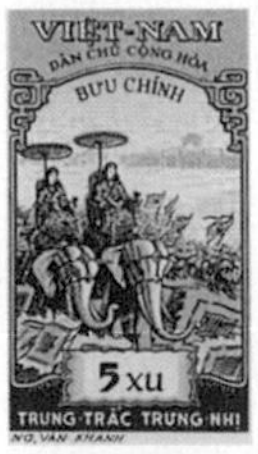

41 The Trung Sisters

1959. Trung Sisters Commemoration.

N103	**41**	5x. red and yellow	3·50	1·10
N104	**41**	8x. deep brown and brown	6·75	1·60

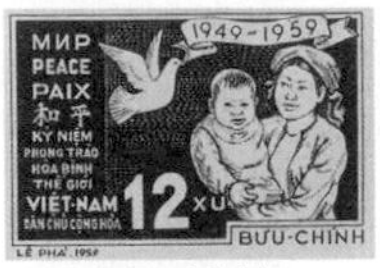

42 Mother and Child

1959. Tenth Anniv of World Peace Movement.

N105	**42**	12x. violet	1·70	1·10

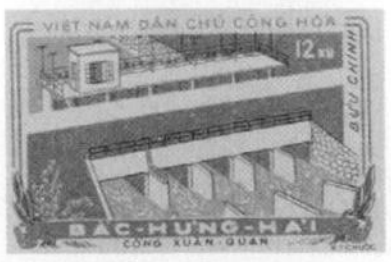

43 Xuan Quan Dam

1959. Bac Hung Hai Irrigation Project.

N106	**43**	6x. yellow, green & violet	2·30	85
N107	**43**	12x. ochre, blue and grey	6·75	1·30

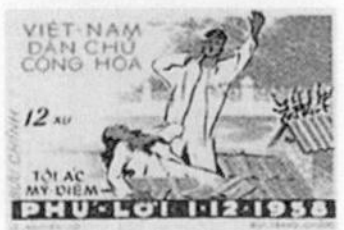

44 Victims in Phu Loi Concentration Camp

1959. The Phu Loi Massacre on 1 December 1958.

N108	**44**	12x. salmon, olive & black	2·75	1·00
N109	**44**	20x. ochre, grey and black	5·75	1·40

45 Radio Mast

1959. Me Tri Radio Station.
| N110 | 45 | 3x. green and orange | 2·30 | 55 |
| N111 | 45 | 12x. sepia and blue | 3·50 | 1·10 |

46 Hien Luong Railway Bridge

1959. Vietnam Day.
| N112 | 46 | 12x. red and black | 3·50 | 1·30 |

47 Rifle-shooting

1959. Sports.
N113	47	1x. deep blue and blue	1·70	55
N114	–	6x. olive and red	2·75	1·00
N115	–	12x. red and rose	5·00	1·60
DESIGNS. 6x. Swimming; 12x. Wrestling.

48 Balloons

1959. Tenth Anniv of Chinese People's Republic.
| N116 | 48 | 12x. red, yellow and green | 6·25 | 1·10 |

49 Coconuts

1959. Fruit. Multicoloured.
N117		3x. Type 49	1·10	55
N118		12x. Bananas	2·75	1·00
N119		30x. Pineapple	5·00	1·60

50 Convair CV 340

1959. Air.
| N120 | 50 | 20x. black and blue | 11·50 | 5·50 |

51 Soldiers

1959. 15th Anniv of N. Vietnam People's Army.
| N121 | 51 | 12x. yellow, brown & blue | 3·50 | 1·10 |

52 Sailing Ship

1959. 30th Anniv of N. Vietnam Workers' Party.
| N122 | 52 | 2x. multicoloured | 1·70 | 55 |
| N123 | 52 | 12x. multicoloured | 4·50 | 1·30 |

53 Girl in "F-De" Costume

1960. National Costumes.
N124	53	2x. red, blue and purple	1·70	75
N125	–	10x. blue, orange & green	2·30	1·10
N126	–	12x. blue and brown	4·00	1·60
N127	–	12x. blue and buff	4·00	1·60
COSTUMES: No. N125, "Meo"; N126, "Thai"; N127, "Tay".

54 Women of Vietnam

1960. National Census.
| N128 | 54 | 1x. green | 90 | 65 |
| N129 | – | 12x. brown and red | 4·50 | 2·00 |
DESIGN: 12x. Workers and factories.

55 Emblem and Women

1960. 50th Anniv of International Women's Day.
| N130 | 55 | 12x. multicoloured | 3·25 | 1·30 |

56 Hung Vuong Temple

1960. Hung Vuong Anniversary Day.
| N131 | 56 | 12x. green and buff | 6·25 | 2·75 |
| N132 | 56 | 4d. brown and blue | 70·00 | 37·00 |

57 Lenin

1960. 90th Birth Anniv of Lenin.
| N133 | 57 | 5x. red and blue | 1·90 | 65 |
| N134 | 57 | 12x. blue and buff | 6·25 | 1·30 |
MSN134a 50×77 mm. **57** 5x. blue and brown. Imperf £120 £120

58 Ballot Box

1960. Second Election of Parliamentary Deputies.
| N135 | 58 | 12x. multicoloured | 2·50 | 80 |

59 Red Cross Nurse

1960. International Red Cross Commemoration.
| N136 | 59 | 8x. blue, red and bistre | 2·75 | 65 |
| N137 | 59 | 12x. green, red and grey | 4·25 | 1·30 |

60 Pres. Ho Chi Minh

1960. President Ho Chi Minh's 70th Birthday.
N138	60	4x. lilac and green	2·50	65
N139	60	12x. purple and rose	3·75	1·10
N140	–	12x. multicoloured	3·75	1·10
MSN140a Two sheets, 60×85 mm and 58×78 mm. 10x. brown and ochre (as N139) and 10x. multicoloured (as N140). Imperf 38·00 39·00
DESIGN—24½×39 mm: No. N140, Ho Chi Minh and children.

61 "New Constitution"

1960. Opening of Second National Assembly.
| N141 | 61 | 12x. sepia and ochre | 3·75 | 2·00 |

62 Pres. Ho Chi Minh at Microphone

1960. 15th Anniv of Vietnam Democratic Republic.
N142	62	4x. multicoloured	3·75	65
N143	62	12x. multicoloured	5·50	1·60
N144		12x. deep blue and blue	5·50	1·60
N145	–	12x. green and yellow	5·50	1·60
N146	–	12x. blue and brown	5·50	1·60
DESIGNS: No. N144, Ploughing; N145, Electricity Works, Vietri; N146, Classroom.

63 Workers and Flags

1960. Third Vietnam Workers' Party Congress.
| N147 | 63 | 1x. multicoloured | 3·75 | 65 |
| N148 | 63 | 12x. multicoloured | 4·50 | 1·10 |

64 Handclasp of Three Races

1960. 15th Anniv of W.F.T.U.
| N149 | 64 | 12x. black and red | 7·50 | 2·75 |

65 Dragon

1960. 950th Anniv of Hanoi.
| N150 | 65 | 8x. yellow, brown & turquoise | 4·50 | 1·60 |
| N151 | 65 | 12x. yellow, brown & blue | 6·25 | 1·60 |
MSN151a 98×67 mm. No. N151. Imperf 25·00 20·00

66 Exhibition Entrance

1960. "Fifteen Years of Republic" Exhibition.
| N152 | 66 | 2x. grey and red | 1·90 | 65 |
| N153 | 66 | 12x. green and red | 3·25 | 95 |

67 Badge, Dove and Flag

68 Emblem of Vietnamese Trade Unions

1960. 15th Anniv of World Federation of Democratic Youth.
| N154 | 67 | 12x. multicoloured | 4·50 | 1·60 |

1961. Second National Congress of Trade Unions.
| N155 | 68 | 12x. red, blue and yellow | 3·25 | 1·30 |

69 Woman, Globe and Dove

1961. Third National Congress of Women.
| N156 | 69 | 6x. green and blue | 3·25 | 1·30 |
| N157 | 69 | 12x. green and salmon | 4·50 | 1·60 |

IMPERF STAMPS. Many issues from here onwards also exist imperf.

70 Sambar

1961. Vietnamese Fauna.
N158	70	12x. buff, black and olive	5·00	2·00
N159		20x. multicoloured	7·50	2·75
N160	–	50x. grey, black and green	11·50	3·25
N161	–	1d. black, grey and green	15·00	4·00
DESIGNS: 20x. Sun bear; 50x. Indian elephant; 1d. Crested gibbon.

71 Ly Tu Trong (revolutionary)

1961. Third Congress of Vietnam Labour Youth Union.
| N162 | 71 | 2x. olive and blue | 1·50 | 80 |
| N163 | 71 | 12x. olive and salmon | 3·25 | 1·30 |

72 Bugler and Drummer

1961. 20th Anniv of Vietnam Youth Pioneers.
| N164 | 72 | 1x. multicoloured | 1·90 | 1·10 |
| N165 | 72 | 12x. multicoloured | 4·50 | 2·40 |

73 Disabled Soldier learning to use Crutches

1961. 101st Anniv of Proposal for Int Red Cross.
| N166 | 73 | 6x. multicoloured | 3·75 | 1·90 |
| N167 | 73 | 12x. multicoloured | 6·25 | 3·00 |

74 Nurse weighing Baby

1961. International Children's Day.
| N168 | 74 | 4x. green, black and red | 2·50 | 80 |

N169	**74**	12x. yellow, black and red	5·00	1·30

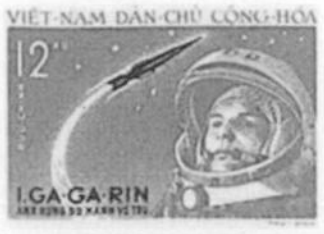

75 Major Yuri Gagarin

1961. World's First Manned Space Flight.

N170	**75**	6x. red and violet	11·50	4·00
N171	**75**	12x. red and green	15·00	5·25

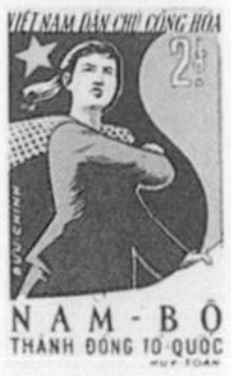

76

1961. Vietnam Reunification Campaign.

N172	**76**	12x. multicoloured	1·30	95
N173	**76**	2d. multicoloured	11·50	1·60

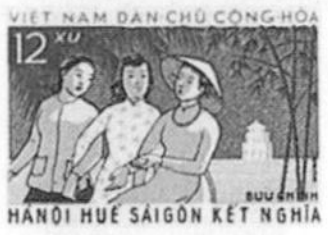

77 Women

1961. Tripling of Hanoi, Hue and Saigon.

N174	**77**	12x. multicoloured	5·00	95
N175	**77**	3d. brown, myrtle and green	20·00	9·25

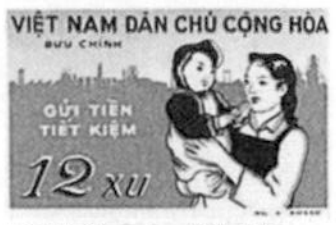

78 Mother and Child

1961. National Savings Campaign.

N176	**78**	3x. multicoloured	1·90	65
N177	**78**	12x. multicoloured	3·75	1·10

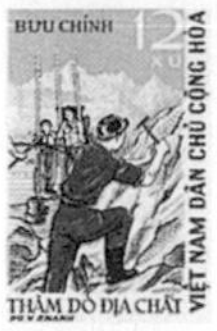

79 Prospecting Team

1961. Geological Research.

N178	**79**	2x. green, blue and purple	1·90	65
N179	**79**	12x. brown, black & turquoise	5·75	1·60

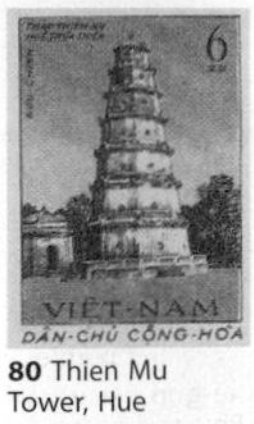

80 Thien Mu Tower, Hue

1961. Ancient Towers.

N180	**80**	6x. brown and chestnut	1·90	1·10
N181	-	10x. olive and buff	3·25	1·50
N182	-	12x. olive and green	3·75	1·70
N183	-	12x. brown and blue	3·75	1·70

TOWERS: No. N181, Pen Brush, Bac Ninh; N182, Binh Son, Vinh Phuc; N183, Cham, Phan Rang.

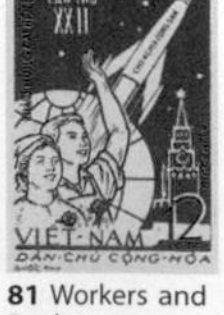

81 Workers and Rocket

1961. 22nd Communist Party Congress, Moscow.

N184	**81**	12x. red and black	4·50	1·30

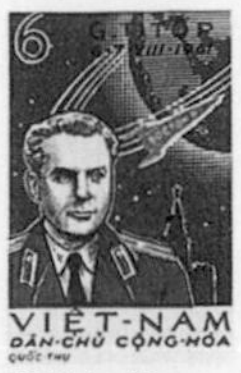

82 Major Titov and Rocket

1961. Second Manned Space Flight.

N185	**82**	6x. multicoloured	3·75	1·10
N186	**82**	12x. multicoloured	6·25	1·60

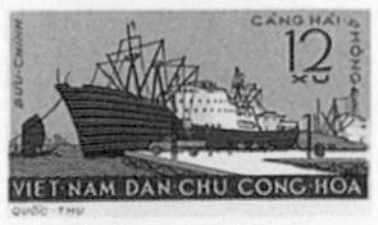

83 Freighter at Haiphong

1961. Haiphong Port Commemoration.

N187	**83**	5x. grey, green and myrtle	3·75	65
N188	**83**	12x. brown, light brown and sepia	10·00	2·00

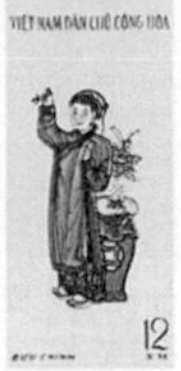

84 Cymbalist

1961. Third Writers and Artists Congress. Multicoloured.

N189	12x. Type **84**	2·50	80
N190	12x. Flautist	2·50	80
N191	30x. Fan dancer	6·25	1·50
N192	50x. Guitarist	8·75	2·00
MSN192a	136×102 mm. Nos. N189/92 in strip of four	75·00	75·00

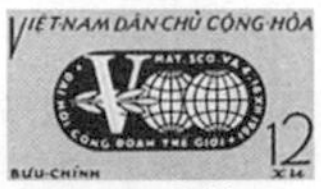

85 Congress Emblem

1961. Fifth W.F.T.U. Congress, Moscow.

N193	**85**	12x. mauve and drab	2·50	80

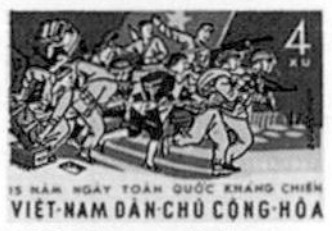

86 Resistance Fighters

1961. 15th Anniv of National Resistance.

N194	**86**	4x. multicoloured	1·30	40
N195	**86**	12x. multicoloured	1·90	65

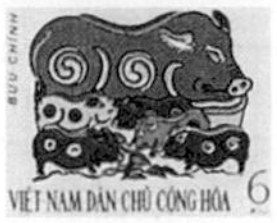

87 "Pigs"

1962. New Year.

N196	**87**	6x. multicoloured	4·50	1·10
N197	-	12x. multicoloured	5·00	1·60

DESIGN: 12x. "Poultry".

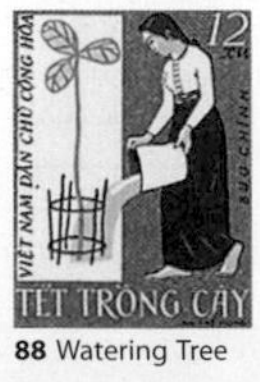

88 Watering Tree

1962. Tree-planting Festival.

N198	**88**	12x. multicoloured	3·25	1·10
N199	**88**	40x. multicoloured	5·75	1·70

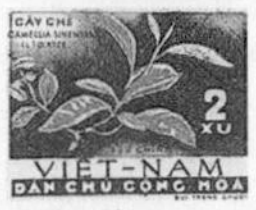

89 Tea Plant

1962. Multicoloured.. Multicoloured..

N200	2x. Type **89**	1·50	80
N201	6x. Aniseed	1·90	1·10
N202	12x. Coffee	7·00	1·60
N203	12x. Castor-oil	7·00	1·60
N204	30x. Lacquer-tree	12·50	3·25

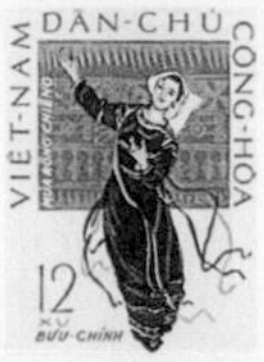

90 Gong Dance

1962. Folk-dancing. Multicoloured.

N205	12x. Type **90**	3·75	95
N206	12x. Bamboo dance	3·75	95
N207	30x. Hat dance	6·25	1·30
N208	50x. Parasol dance	11·50	2·00
MSN208a	67×91 mm. 30x. As Type **90**	25·00	25·00

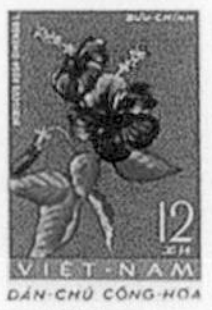

91 Hibiscus

1962. Flowers. Multicoloured.

N209	12x. Type **91**	3·75	1·30
N210	12x. Frangipani	3·75	1·30
N211	20x. Chrysanthemum	5·00	1·60
N212	30x. Lotus	7·50	1·90
N213	50x. Ipomoea	12·50	2·75
MSN213a	64×87 mm. No. N212	19·00	19·00

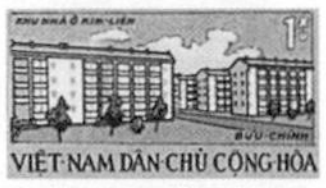

92 Kim Lien Flats, Hanoi

1962. First Five-Year Plan (1st issue).

N214	**92**	1x. blue, black and grey	65	40
N215	-	3x. multicoloured	1·50	65
N216	-	8x. violet, black and stone	2·30	1·10

DESIGNS: 3x. State agricultural farm; 8x. Institute of Hydraulic and Electro-Dynamic Studies.

See also Nos. N245/8, N251/2, N270/1 and N294/6.

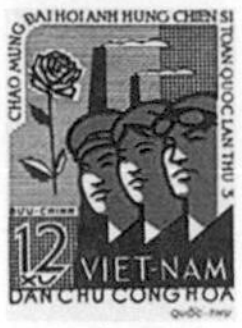

93 Workers and Rose

1962. Third National "Heroes of Labour" Congress.

N217	**93**	12x. orange, olive and red	3·75	1·30

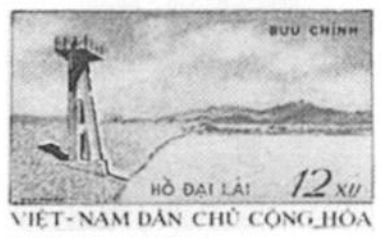

94 Dai Lai Lake

1962

N218	**94**	12x. turquoise and brown	3·25	95

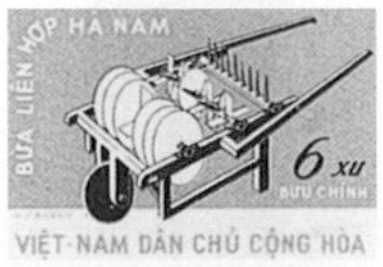

95 "Plough of Perfection"

1962

N219	**95**	6x. black and turquoise	1·90	65

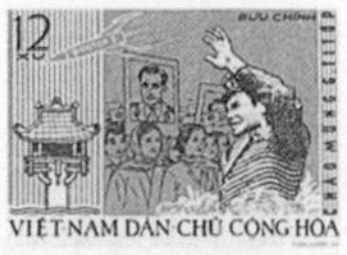

96 Titov greeting Children

1962. Visit of Major Titov.

N220	**96**	12x. sepia and blue	1·90	65
N221	-	20x. sepia and salmon	3·25	95
N222	-	30x. sepia and green	5·00	1·50

DESIGNS: 20x. Pres. Ho Chi Minh pinning medal on Titov; 30x. Titov in space-suit.

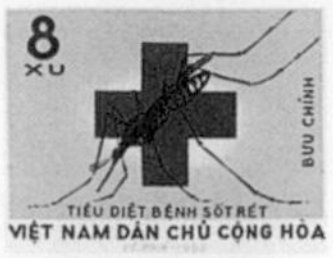

97 Mosquito and Red Cross

1962. Malaria Eradication.

N223	**97**	8x. red, black and blue	2·50	95
N224	**97**	12x. red, black and violet	3·00	1·20
N225	**97**	20x. red, black and purple	5·25	1·60

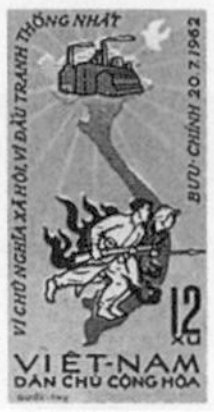

98 Factory and Soldiers

1962. Eighth Anniv of Geneva Vietnamese Agreements.

N226	**98**	12x. multicoloured	3·75	95

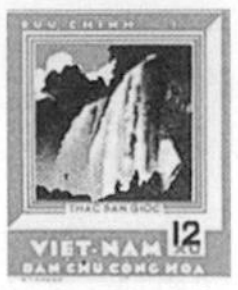

99 Ban Gioc Falls

1962. Vietnamese Scenery.

N227	-	12x. purple and blue	2·50	1·10
N228	**99**	12x. sepia and turquoise	2·50	1·10

DESIGN—HORIZ: (32½×23 mm): No. N227, Ba Be Lake.

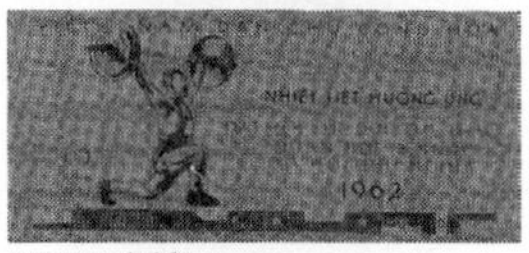

99a Weightlifting

1962. Int Military Sports Festival of Socialist States, Prague.

N228a	**99a**	12x. multicoloured	£160	£200

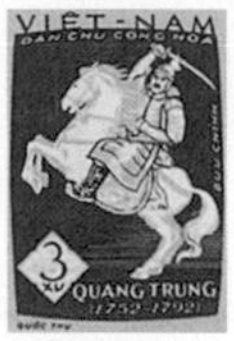

100 Quang Trung

1962. National Heroes.

N229	**100**	3x. yellow, brown & grey	1·30	65
N230	-	3x. orange, blk & ochre	1·30	65
N231	**100**	12x. yellow, green & grey	3·25	95
N232	-	12x. orange, blk & grey	3·25	95

PORTRAIT: Nos. N230, N232, Nguyen Trai.

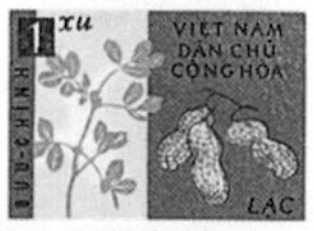

101 Groundnuts

1962. Multicoloured.

N233	1x. Type **101**	65	55
N234	4x. Haricot beans	1·10	65
N235	6x. Sweet potatoes	1·50	80
N236	12x. Maize	3·50	1·70
N237	30x. Manioc	8·25	4·25

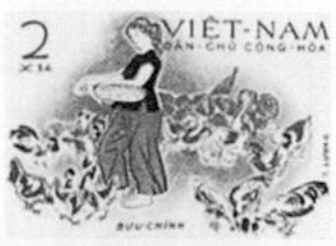

102 Girl feeding Poultry

1962. Farm Stock-breeding.

N238	**102**	2x. red, grey and blue	75	65
N239	-	12x. ochre, turquoise and blue	2·50	1·10
N240	-	12x. brown, green and deep green	2·50	1·10
N241	-	12x. buff, mauve and sepia	2·50	1·10

DESIGNS: No. N239, Woman tending pigs; N240, Herdgirl with oxen; N241, Boy feeding buffalo.

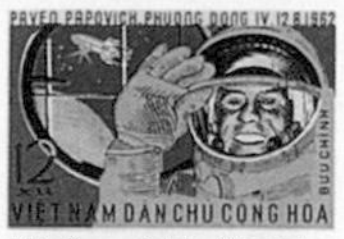

103 Popovich in "Vostok 4"

1962. First "Team" Manned Space Flights.

N242	**103**	12x. multicoloured	1·90	65
N243	-	20x. ochre, blue & black	2·50	1·10
N244	-	30x. red, blue and black	3·75	1·50

DESIGNS—HORIZ: 20x. Nikolaev in "Vostok 3". VERT: 30x. "Vostoks 3 and 4".

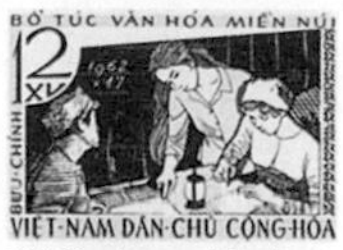

104 Teacher and Students

1962. First Five-Year Plan (2nd issue). Higher Education and Land Cultivation.

N245	**104**	12x. black and yellow	1·90	65
N246	-	12x. black, brown & buff	4·50	1·10

DESIGN: No. N246, Tree felling.

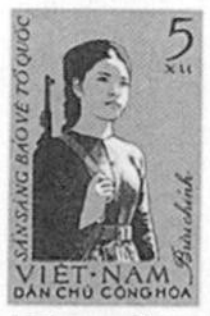

105 Guerrilla Fighter

1963. First Five-Year Plan (3rd issue). National Defence.

N247	**105**	5x. green and grey	1·50	40
N248	**105**	12x. brown and buff	2·30	80

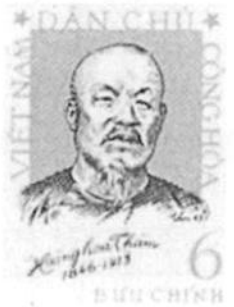

106 Hoang Hoa Tham

1963. 50th Death Anniv of Hoang Hoa Tham (freedom fighter).

N249	**106**	6x. myrtle and blue	1·50	65
N250	**106**	12x. black and brown	2·30	95

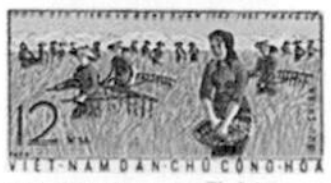

107 Workers in Field

1963. First Five-Year Plan (4th issue). Agricultural and Chemical Manufacture.

N251	**107**	12x. multicoloured	2·50	95
N252	-	12x. red, mauve and black	1·90	65

DESIGN: No. N252, Lam Thao Fertilizer Factory.

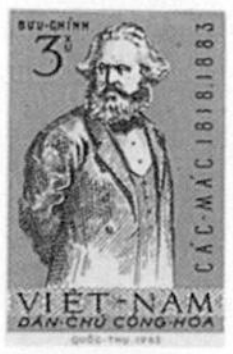

108 Karl Marx

1963. 80th Death Anniv of Karl Marx.

N253	**108**	3x. black and green	1·30	65
N254	**108**	12x. black and drab on pink	3·75	1·10

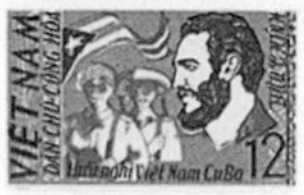

109 Castro and Vietnamese Soldiers

1963. Vietnamese–Cuban Friendship.

N255	**109**	12x. multicoloured	2·75	95

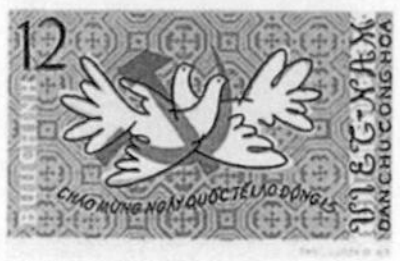

110 Doves and Labour Emblem

1963. Labour Day.

N256	**110**	12x. orange, black & bl	2·75	95

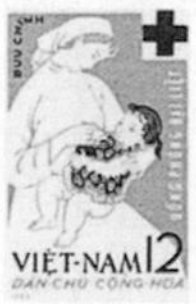

111 Nurse tending Child

1963. Red Cross Centenary.

N257	**111**	12x. red, black and blue	2·50	80
N258	-	12x. red, grey & turq	2·50	80
N259	-	20x. red, grey and yellow	3·75	1·10

DESIGNS: No. N258, Child and syringe inscr "BCG". 25×42 mm: 20x. Centenary emblem.

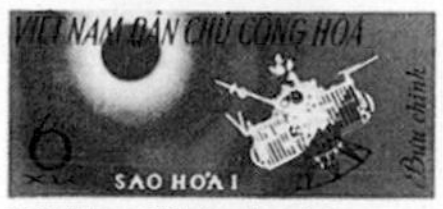

112 "Mars 1" Interplanetary Station

1963. Launching of Soviet Rocket "Mars 1". Multicoloured.

N260	6x. Type **112**	1·30	65
N261	12x. Type **112**	1·90	80
N262	12x. "Mars 1" in space (vert)	2·50	95
N263	20x. "Mars 1" in space (vert)	3·75	1·10

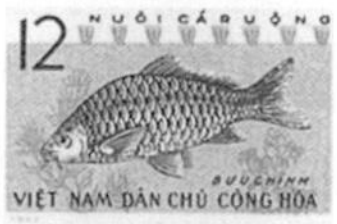

113 Common Carp

1963. Fishing Industry. Multicoloured.

N264	12x. Type **113**	7·00	2·00
N265	12x. Fishes and trawler	7·00	2·00

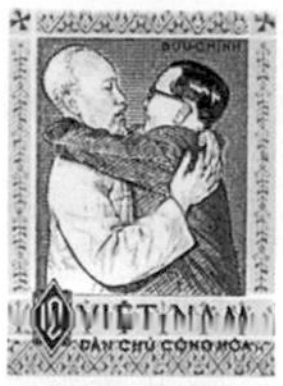

114 Pres. Ho Chi Minh embracing Prof. Nguyen Van Hien of South Vietnam

1963. Campaign for Reunification of Vietnam.

N266	**114**	12x. black, blue & turq	3·25	1·00

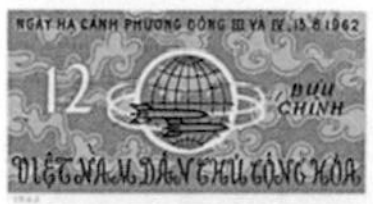

115 Globe and "Vostoks 3 and 4"

1963. First Anniv of "Team" Manned Space Flights.

N267	**115**	12x. black, brown & yellow	1·30	65
N268	-	20x. black, blue & green	2·50	1·10
N269	-	30x. black, violet & blue	5·00	1·50

DESIGNS: 20x. Nikolaev and "eagle" motif; 30x. Popovich and "phoenix" motif.

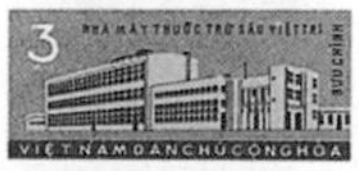

116 Viet Tri Insecticide Factory

1963. First Five-Year Plan (5th issue).

N270	**116**	3x. buff, brown and blue	1·00	40
N271	-	12x. pink, brown and bistre	2·75	95

DESIGN: 12x. Viet Tri chemical factory.

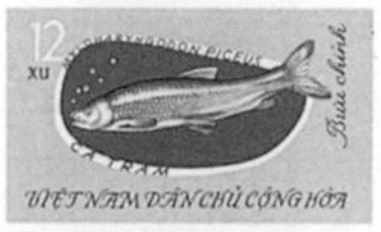

117 Black Carp

1963. Freshwater Fish Culture. Multicoloured.

N272	12x. Type **117**	2·75	1·20
N273	12x. Common carp ("Cyprinus carpio")	2·75	1·20
N274	12x. Silver carp ("Hypophthalmichthys molitrix)	2·75	1·20
N275	20x. Asiatic snakehead	7·00	2·10
N276	30x. Mozambique mouthbrooder	8·75	3·25

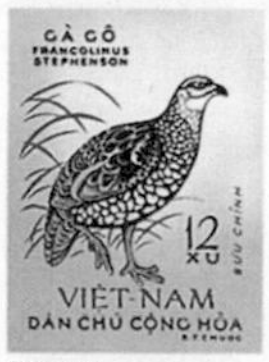

118 Chinese Francolin

1963. Birds. Multicoloured.

N277	12x. Type **118**	3·75	1·30
N278	12x. Chinese jungle mynah	3·75	1·30
N279	12x. White-throated kingfisher	3·75	1·30
N280	20x. Siamese fireback pheasant (horiz)	7·50	2·00
N281	30x. Eastern reef heron	11·50	2·75
N282	40x. Slaty-headed parakeet	15·00	3·25
MSN282a	64×93 mm. 50x. (as 30x.)	£110	£110

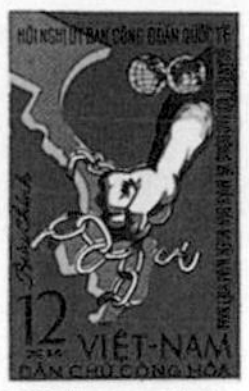

119 Broken Chain and Map

1963. W.F.T.U. Assembly, Hanoi.

N283	**119**	12x. multicoloured	2·50	95

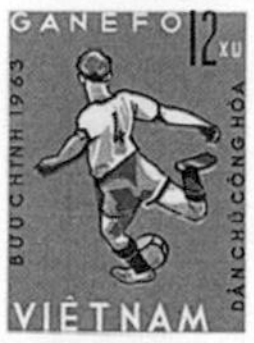

120 Football

1963. "GANEFO" Athletic Games, Jakarta.

N284	**120**	12x. black, grey & ochre	1·30	65
N285	-	12x. black, grey & orange	1·30	65
N286	-	12x. black, grey and blue	1·30	65
N287	-	30x. black, grey & mag	2·50	95

DESIGNS—VERT: No. N285, Volleyball. HORIZ: No. N286, Swimming; N287, High-jumping.

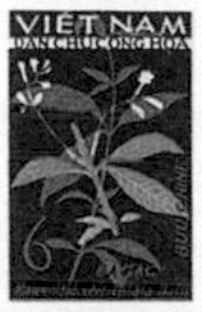

121 "Rauwolfia verticillata"

1963. Medicinal Plants. Multicoloured.

N288	6x. Type **121**	1·30	65
N289	12x. "Chenopodium ambrosioides"	1·50	80
N290	12x. "Sophora japonica"	1·50	80
N291	12x. "Fibraurea tinctoria"	1·50	80
N292	20x. "Momordica cochinchinensis"	3·75	1·30

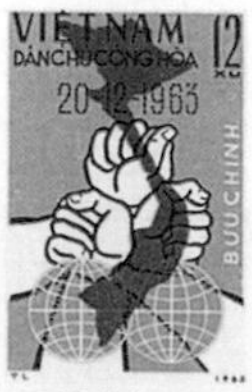

122 "Solidarity"

1963. Third Anniv of South Vietnam National Liberation Front.

N293	**122**	12x. black, brn & ochre	3·25	1·20

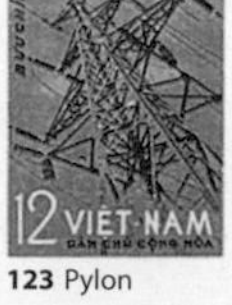

123 Pylon

1964. First Five-Year Plan (6th issue).

N294	-	6x. black, red and purple	90	65
N295	-	12x. multicoloured	2·50	1·10
N296	**123**	12x. black, grey & orange	2·50	1·10

DESIGNS—HORIZ: (40×22½ mm): 6x. Tapping cast-iron; No. N295, Thai Ngyuen Iron and Steel Works.

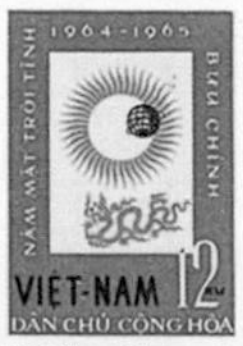

124 Sun, Globe and Dragon

1964. International Quiet Sun Years.

N297	**124**	12x. orange, black & green	1·90	65
N298	**124**	50x. drab, black & pur	4·50	1·30

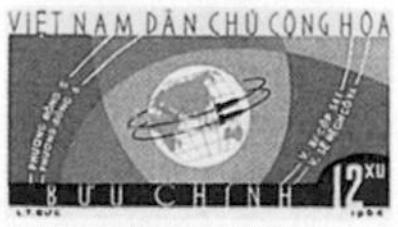

125 Twin Space Flights

1964. Space Flights of Bykovsky and Tereshkova. Multicoloured.

N299	12x. Type **125**	1·90	65
N300	12x. Bykovsky and "Vostok 5"	1·90	65
N301	30x. Tereshkova and "Vostok 6"	5·00	2·00

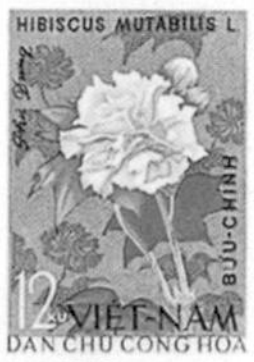

126 "Hibiscus mutabilis"

1964. Flowers. Multicoloured.

N302	12x. Type **126**	1·50	65
N303	12x. "Persica vulgaris"	1·50	65
N304	12x. "Saraca dives"	1·50	65
N305	12x. "Passiflora hispida"	1·50	65
N306	20x. "Michelia champaca"	4·50	1·60
N307	30x. "Camellia amplexicaulis"	7·50	2·75

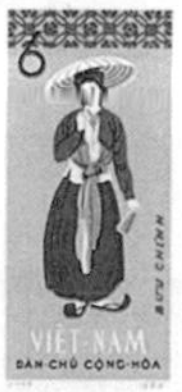

127 Rural Costume

1964. National Costumes. Multicoloured.

N308	6x. Type **127**	1·40	65
N309	12x. "Ceremonial"	2·75	95
N310	12x. "Everyday"	2·75	95

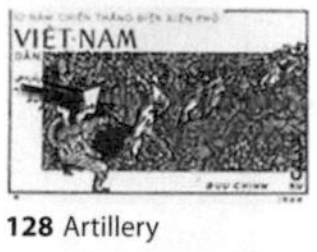

128 Artillery

1964. Tenth Anniv of Battle of Dien Bien Phu.

N311	**128**	3x. black and red	1·30	65
N312	-	6x. black and blue	2·00	80
N313	-	12x. black and yellow	3·25	95
N314	-	12x. black and purple	3·25	95

DESIGNS: 6x. Machine-gun post; No. N313, Bomb-disposal; N314, Dien Bien Phu and tractor.

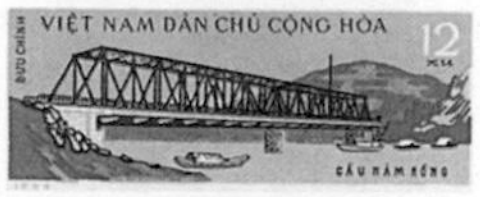

129 Ham Rong Railway Bridge

1964. Inaug of Reconstructed Ham Rong Bridge.

N315	**129**	12x. multicoloured	3·25	1·30

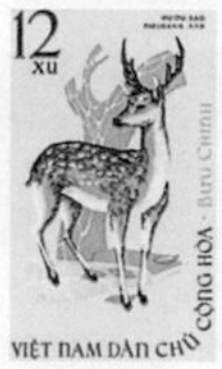

130 Spotted Deer

1964. Wild Animals. Multicoloured.

N316	12x. Type **130**	1·50	65
N317	12x. Malayan tapir (horiz)	1·50	65
N318	12x. Tiger	1·50	65
N319	20x. Water buffalo (horiz)	3·75	95
N320	30x. Sumatran rhinoceros (horiz)	5·75	1·20
N321	40x. Banteng (horiz)	7·50	1·70

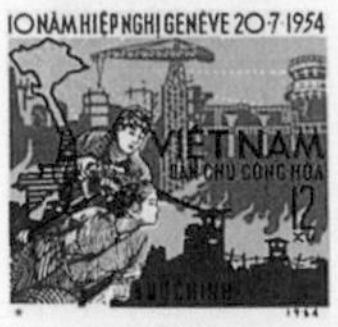

131 Women Fighters, Map, Industrial Scene and Watch-towers

1964. Tenth Anniv of Geneva Agreements on Vietnam.

N322	**131**	12x. multicoloured	1·90	65
N323	-	12x. multicoloured	1·90	65

DESIGN—VERT: (23×45 mm): No. N323, Map of Vietnam, T.U. emblem and flag, inscr ("NHAN DAN MIEN NAM") etc.

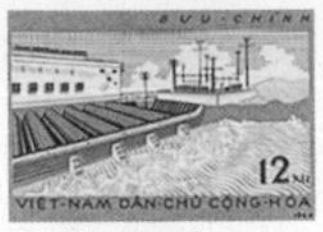

132 Nhu Quynh Pumping Station

1964. Irrigation for Agriculture.

N324	**132**	12x. slate and black	2·50	1·10

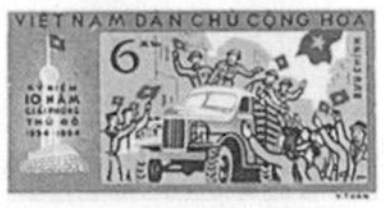

133 Populace Greeting Soldiers

1964. Tenth Anniv of Liberation of Hanoi. Multicoloured.

N325	6x. Type **133**	1·90	65
N326	12x. Building construction	3·25	1·10

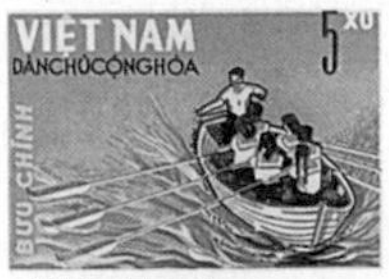

134 Naval Longboat

1964. "National Defence" Games.

N327	**134**	5x. black, grey and blue	1·30	65
N328	-	12x. black, grey & yellow	2·50	1·10
N329	-	12x. black, brown & blue	2·50	1·10
N330	-	12x. multicoloured	2·50	1·10

DESIGNS—HORIZ: No. N328, Pistol-shooting. VERT: No. N329, Gliding; N330, Parachuting.

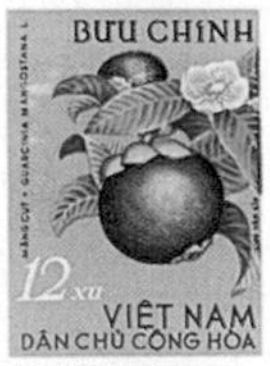

135 "Guarcinia mangostana"

1964. Tropical Fruit. Multicoloured.

N331	12x. Type **135**	1·50	65
N332	12x. "Mangifera indica"	1·50	65
N333	12x. "Nephelium litchi"	1·50	65
N334	20x. "Anona squamosa"	3·75	1·20
N335	50x. "Citrus medica"	8·25	2·75

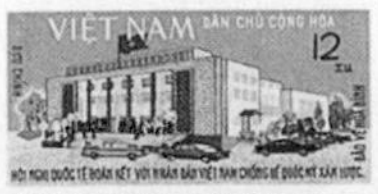

136 Conference Building

1964. World Solidarity Conf, Hanoi. Multicoloured.

N336	12x. Type **136**	1·90	65
N337	12x. Soldier greeting workers	1·90	65
N338	12x. Clenched fist, ships and Boeing B-52 Stratofortress	1·90	65

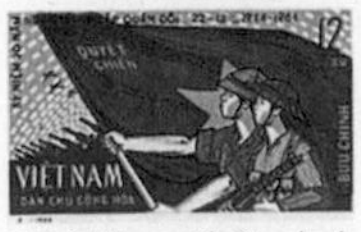

137 Soldiers with Standard

1964. 20th Anniv of Vietnamese People's Army. Multicoloured.

N339	12x. Type **137**	1·90	65
N340	12x. Coastguards	1·90	65
N341	12x. Frontier guards (vert)	1·90	65

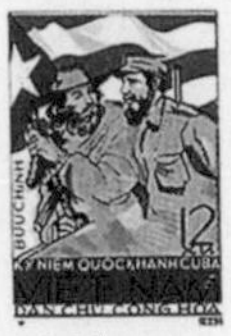

138 Cuban Revolutionaries

1965. Sixth Anniv of Cuban Republic.

N342	**138**	12x. black, red and blue	2·50	1·10
N343	-	12x. multicoloured	2·50	1·10

DESIGN: No. N343, Flags of Cuba and North Vietnam.

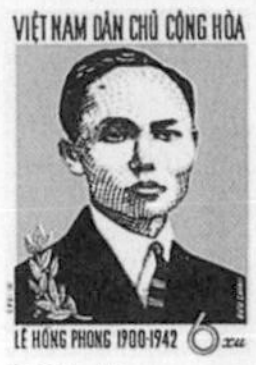

139 Le Hong Phong

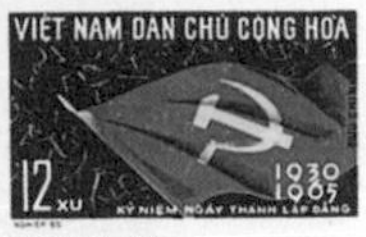

140 Party Flag

1965. 35th Anniv of Vietnamese Workers' Party. (a) As T **139**. Portraits and inscr purple-brown; background colours given.

N344	**139**	6x. grey	75	65
N345	-	6x. bistre	75	65
N346	-	6x. drab	75	65
N347	-	6x. brown	75	65
N348	-	6x. lilac	75	65

DESIGNS: No. N345, Tran Phu; N346, Hoang Van Thu; N347, Hgo Gia Tu; N348, Nguyen van Cu (Party leaders).

(b) As T **140**.

N349	**140**	12x. yellow, red and mauve	1·90	1·30
N350	-	12x. mauve, yellow and red	1·90	1·30

DESIGN: No. N350, Foundryman and guerilla fighter.

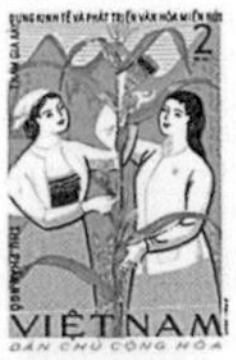

141 Women tending Maize

1965. Populating Mountain Settlements.

N351	**141**	2x. multicoloured	75	60
N352	**141**	3x. multicoloured	1·30	65
N353	-	12x. indigo, orange and blue	1·90	80

DESIGN: 12x. Young girls going to school.

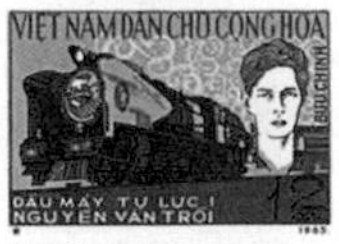

142 Steam Locomotive and Nguyen Van Troi (patriot)

1965. Transport Ministers' Congress, Hanoi.

N354	**142**	12x. blue and red	3·25	80
N355	-	30x. black and green	6·25	1·30

DESIGN: 30x. As Type **142** but position of locomotive, portrait and value transposed.

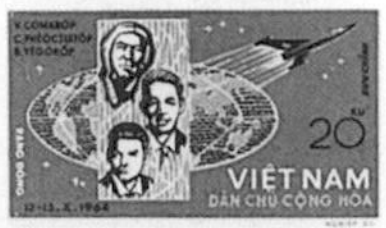

143 Cosmonauts Komarov, Feoktistov, Yegorov, and "Voskhod I"

1965. Three-manned Space Flight.

N356	**143**	20x. violet, green & blue	2·50	65
N357	-	1d. violet, red & mauve	8·75	1·90

DESIGN: 1d. "Voskhod I" and cosmonauts.

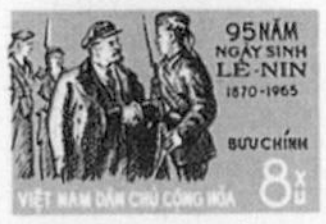

144 Lenin with Red Guards

1965. Lenin's 95th Birth Anniv.

N358	**144**	8x. purple and buff	1·90	65
N359	**144**	12x. purple and grey	1·90	65

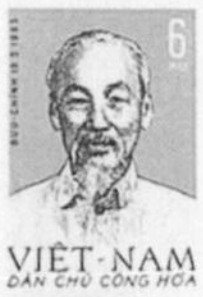

145 Pres. Ho Chi Minh

1965. Pres. Ho Chi Minh's 75th Birthday.

N360	**145**	6x. violet, yellow & green	1·30	55
N361	**145**	12x. violet, yellow & buff	1·90	65

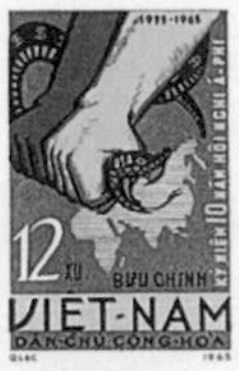

146 Hands clasping Serpent

1965. Tenth Anniv of Afro-Asian Conf, Bandung.

N362	**146**	12x. multicoloured	3·25	1·10

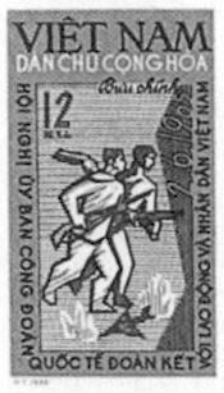

147 Two Soldiers advancing

1965. Trade Union Conference, Hanoi.

N363	**147**	12x. blue and purple	1·90	65
N364	-	12x. multicoloured	1·90	65
N365	-	12x. red, black and green	1·90	65

DESIGNS—HORIZ: No. N364, Sea battle; N365, "Peoples of the World" on Globe, and soldiers.

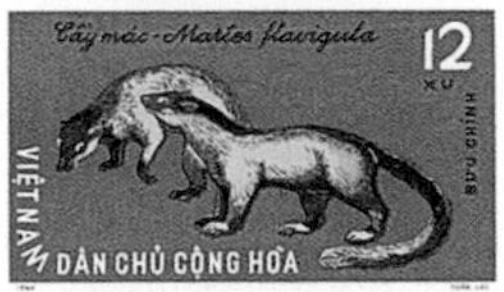

148 Yellow-throated Marten

1965. Fauna Protection. Multicoloured.

N366	12x. Type **148**	1·90	65
N367	12x. Owston's palm civet	1·90	65
N368	12x. Chinese pangolin	1·90	65
N369	12x. Francois' monkey (vert)	1·90	65
N370	20x. Red giant flying squirrel	5·00	1·30
N371	50x. Lesser slow loris (vert)	8·75	2·00

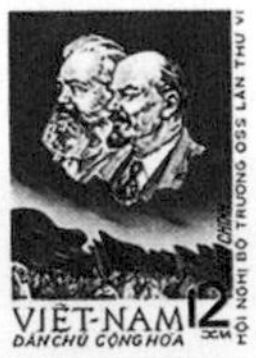

149 Marx and Lenin

1965. Postal Ministers Congress, Peking.

N372	**149**	12x. multicoloured	5·00	1·10

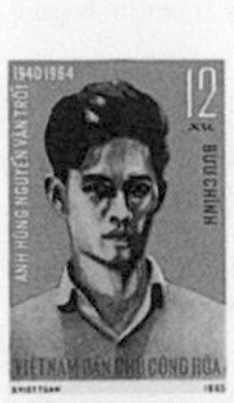

150 Nguyen Van Troi (patriot)

1965. Nguyen Van Troi Commemoration.

N373	**150**	12x. sepia, brown & green	1·30	55
N374	**150**	50x. sepia, brn & ochre	2·50	80
N375	**150**	4d. sepia and red	7·50	2·75

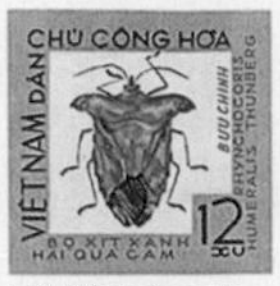

151 "Rhynchocoris humeralis"

1965. Noxious Insects. Multicoloured.

N376	12x. Type **151**	1·90	65
N377	12x. "Tessaratoma papillosa"	1·90	65
N378	12x. "Poeciliocoris latus"	1·90	65
N379	12x. "Tosena melanoptera"	1·90	65
N380	20x. "Cicada sp."	4·50	1·30
N381	30x. "Fulgora candelaria"	5·75	2·00

Nos. N379/81 are vert, 20½×38 mm.

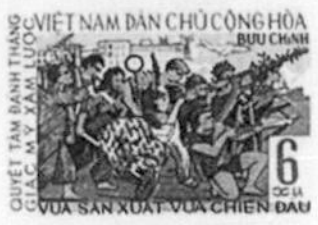

152 Revolutionaries

1965. 20th Anniv of August Revolution.

N382	**152**	6x. brown, black & blue	1·30	55
N383	**152**	12x. black and red	2·50	1·10

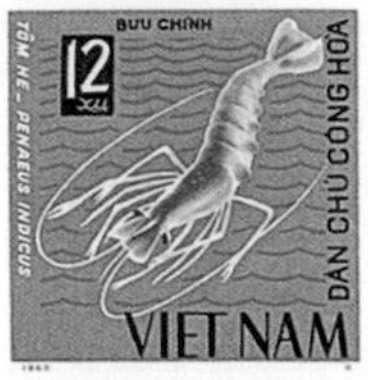

153 Prawn

1965. Marine Life. Multicoloured.

N384	12x. Type **153**	2·50	1·10
N385	12x. Shrimp	2·50	1·10
N386	12x. Swimming crab	2·50	1·10
N387	12x. Serrate swimming crab	2·50	1·10
N388	20x. Spiny lobster	5·00	1·30
N389	50x. Fiddler crab	10·00	2·30

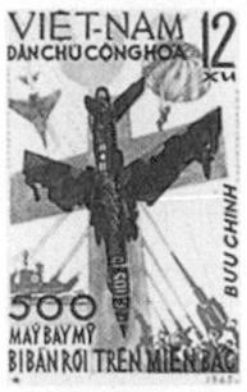

154 Air Battle

1965. "500th U.S. Aircraft Brought Down over North Vietnam".

N390	**154**	12x. green and lilac	9·50	7·25

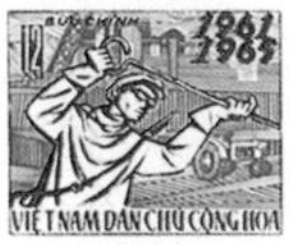

155 Foundryman ("Heavy Industries")

1965. 20th Anniv of Republic and Completion of First Five-Year Plan.

N391	**155**	12x. black and orange	1·50	95
N392	-	12x. black and green	1·50	95
N393	-	12x. black and purple	1·50	95

DESIGNS: No. N392, Irrigation, pylon and power station ("Hydro-electric Power"); N393, Nurse examining child ("Social Medicine").

See also Nos. N417/19.

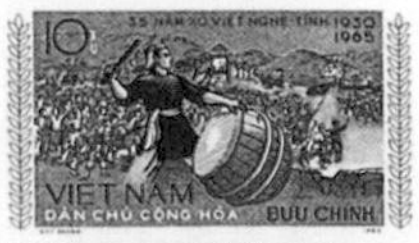

156 Drummer and Peasants

1965. 35th Anniv of Movement of Nghe An and Ha Tinh Soviet Peasants.

N394	**156**	10x. multicoloured	1·80	55
N395	**156**	12x. multicoloured	2·00	65

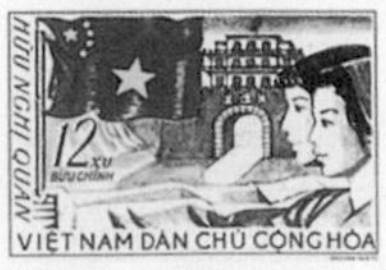

157 Girls and Flags

1965. 16th Anniv of Friendship between China and Vietnam. Multicoloured.

N396	12x. Type **157**	6·25	1·30

N397	12x. Vietnamese and Chinese girls with flags (vert)	6·25	1·30

158 Tsiolkovsky and "Sputnik 1"

1965. Space Flight of "Voskhod 2".

N398	158	12x. blue and purple	1·30	65
N399	–	12x. ochre and blue	1·30	65
N400	–	50x. blue and green	3·75	2·00
N401	–	50x. blue and turquoise	3·75	2·00

DESIGNS: No. N399, Leonov, Belyaev and "Voskhod 2"; N400, Gagarin; N401, Leonov in space.

159 Red Lacewing

1965. Butterflies. Multicoloured.

N402	12x. Type **159**	3·25	95
N403	12x. Leopard lacewing	3·25	95
N404	12x. Blue triangle	3·25	95
N405	12x. Indian purple emperor	3·25	95
N406	20x. Paris peacock	6·25	1·60
N407	30x. Common rose	8·75	2·30

160 Norman R. Morrison and Demonstrators

1965. Homage to Norman R. Morrison (American Quaker who immolated himself).

N408	160	12x. black and red	3·75	1·30

161 Birthplace of Nguyen Du (poet)

1965. Nguyen Du Commem. Multicoloured.

N409	161	12x. Type **161**	1·30	55
N410		12x. Nguyen Du Museum	1·30	55
N411		20x. "Kieu" (volume of poems)	1·90	65
N412		1d. Scene from "Kieu"	3·25	95

162 Pres. Ho Chi Minh

1965. Engels' 145th Birth Anniv. Multicoloured.

N413	162	12x. Type **162**	1·30	55
N414		12x. Marx	1·30	55
N415		12x. Lenin	1·30	55
N416		50x. Engels	3·75	95

163 Rice-field and Insecticide-sprayer ("Agriculture")

1965. Completion of First Five-Year Plan (2nd issue).

N417	163	12x. orange and green	1·50	60

N418	–	12x. blue and red	1·50	60
N419	–	12x. orange and blue	1·50	60

DESIGNS: No. N418, Factory-worker ("Light Industries"); N419, Children at play and students ("Social Education").

164 Soldier and Demonstrators

1965. Fifth Anniv of South Vietnam National Liberation Front.

N420	164	12x. violet and lilac	3·25	95

165 Casting Votes

1966. 20th Anniv of First Vietnamese General Elections.

N421	165	12x. black and red	3·25	1·10

166 "Dendrobium moschatum"

1966. Orchids. Multicoloured.

N422	12x. Type **166**	1·90	65
N423	12x. "Vanda teres"	1·90	65
N424	12x. "Dendrobium crystallinum"	1·90	65
N425	12x. "Dendrobium nobile"	1·90	65
N426	20x. "Vandopsis gigantea"	3·25	95
N427	30x. "Dendrobium"	4·50	1·60

167 Child on Rocking-horse

1966. New Year.

N428	167	12x. multicoloured	3·25	1·10

168 "Physignathus cocincinus"

1966. Protection of Nature—Reptiles. Multicoloured.

N429	12x. Type **168**	1·90	65
N430	12x. "Trionyx sinensis"	1·90	65
N431	12x. Gecko (inscr "GEKKO GECKO")	1·90	65
N432	12x. "Testudo elongata"	1·90	65
N433	20x. "Varanus salvator"	2·50	95
N434	40x. "Eretmochelys imbricata"	5·00	1·30

169 Wrestling

1966. National Games.

N435	169	12x. multicoloured	2·10	75
N436	–	12x. multicoloured	2·10	75
N437	–	12x. multicoloured	2·10	75

GAMES: No. N436, Archery (with crossbow); N437, "Fencing".

170 Ly Tu Trong (revolutionary), Badge and Banner

1966. 35th Anniv of Labour Youth Union.

N438	170	12x. multicoloured	2·50	1·10

171 Republic Thunderchief in Flames

1966. "1,000th U.S. Aircraft Brought Down over North Vietnam".

N439	171	12x. multicoloured	9·50	6·75

172 Worker and Rifle

1966. Labour Day.

N440	172	6x. black, red and salmon	2·50	95

173 Battle Scene on Con Co Island

1966. Defence of Con Co ("Steel Island").

N441	173	12x. multicoloured	4·50	1·30

174 Children and Banners

1966. 25th Anniv of Vietnam Youth Pioneers.

N442	174	12x. black and red	2·50	95

175 View of Dien An (Yenan)

1966. 45th Anniv of Chinese Communist Party. Multicoloured.

N443	175	3x. Type **175**	2·50	95
N444		12x. Ho Chi Minh and Mao Tse-tung	2·50	95

176 "Luna 9" in Space

1966. "Luna 9" Space Flight. Multicoloured. Inscr "MAT TRANG 9".

N445		12x. Type **176**	2·50	1·30
N446		50x. "Luna 9" on Moon	6·25	1·70

177 Airplane in Flames

1966. "1,500th U.S. Aircraft Brought Down over North Vietnam".

N447	177	12x. multicoloured	12·50	4·75
N448	177	12x. mult (optd **NGAY** 14.10.1966)	19·00	5·25

178 Liberation Fighter

1966. Victories of Liberation Army. Inscr "1965–1966".

N449	178	1x. purple	2·10	80
N450	178	12x. multicoloured	2·50	95
N451	–	12x. multicoloured	2·50	95

DESIGN: No. N451, Soldier escorting prisoners-of-war. See also No. 646.

179 Women from different Regions, and Child

1966. 20th Anniv of Vietnamese Women's Union.

N452	179	12x. black and salmon	1·40	65

180 Moluccan Pittas

1966. Birds. Multicoloured.

N453	12x. Type **180**	1·50	65
N454	12x. Black-naped orioles	1·50	65
N455	12x. River kingfisher	1·50	65
N456	12x. Long-tailed broadbill	1·50	65
N457	20x. Hoopoe	2·75	95
N458	30x. Maroon orioles	3·75	1·20

Nos. N454/5 and N457 are vert.

181 Football

1966. Ganefo Games. Multicoloured.

N459	12x. Type **181**	1·90	65
N460	12x. Rifle-shooting	1·90	65
N461	30x. Swimming	2·50	95
N462	30x. Running	2·50	95

182 Harvesting Rice

1967. Agricultural Production.

N463	182	12x. multicoloured	1·90	65

183 Ho Chi Minh Text and Fighters

1967. Ho Chi Minh's Appeal.
N464 **183** 12x. purple and red — 1·90 — 65
N465 - 12x. purple and red — 1·90 — 65
DESIGN: No. N465, Ho-Chi-Minh text and marchers with banners.
See also Nos. 519/22.

184 Bamboo ("Arundinaria rolleana")

1967. Bamboo. Multicoloured.
N466 12x. Type **184** — 1·90 — 65
N467 12x. "Arundinaria racemosa" — 1·90 — 65
N468 12x. "Bambusa bingami" — 1·90 — 65
N469 12x. "Bambusa arundinaceu" — 1·90 — 65
N470 30x. "Bambusa nutans" — 2·75 — 95
N471 50x. "Dendrocalamus patellaris" — 3·75 — 1·20

185 Dhole

1967. Wild Animals. Multicoloured.
N472 12x. Type **185** — 1·90 — 65
N473 12x. Binturong — 1·90 — 65
N474 12x. Hog-badger — 1·90 — 65
N475 20x. Large Indian civet — 2·50 — 1·00
N476 40x. Bear macaque — 3·75 — 1·30
N477 50x. Clouded leopard — 5·00 — 2·00

186 Captured Pilot

1967. "2,000th U.S. Aircraft Brought Down over North Vietnam".
N478 **186** 6x. black and red on pink — 5·75 — 2·75
N479 **186** 12x. black & red on grn — 6·25 — 3·00

187 Rocket Launching and Agricultural Scene

1967. Launching of First Chinese Rocket. Multicoloured.
N480 12x. Type **187** — 3·25 — 2·00
N481 30x. Rocket launching, and Gate of Heavenly Peace, Peking — 5·75 — 2·75

188 Belted Bearded Grunt

1967. Vietnamese Fish. Multicoloured.
N482 12x. Type **188** — 1·40 — 65
N483 12x. Japanese mackerel ("Scomberomus niphonius") — 1·40 — 65
N484 12x. Thread-finned lizardfish ("Saurida filamentosa") — 1·40 — 65
N485 20x. Adjutant emperor — 2·50 — 95
N486 30x. Black pomfret — 3·75 — 1·20
N487 50x. Blood snapper — 5·00 — 1·50

189 Lenin and Revolutionary Soldiers

1967. 50th Anniv of October Revolution. Multicoloured.
N488 6x. Type **189** — 75 — 55
N489 12x. Lenin and revolutionaries — 1·40 — 65
N490 12x. Lenin, Marx and Vietnamese soldiers — 1·40 — 65
N491 20x. Cruiser "Aurora" — 2·00 — 80

190 Air Battle

1967. "2,500th U.S. Aircraft Brought Down over North Vietnam".
N492 **190** 12x. black, red and green — 5·75 — 3·25
N493 - 12x. black, red and blue — 5·75 — 3·25
DESIGN—VERT: No. N493, Boeing B-52 Stratofortress falling in flames.

191 Atomic Symbol and Gate of Heavenly Peace, Peking

1967. First Chinese "H"-Bomb Test. Multicoloured.
N494 12x. Type **191** — 2·50 — 1·30
N495 20x. Chinese lantern, atomic symbol & dove (30×35 mm) — 3·75 — 1·60

192 Factory Anti-aircraft Unit

1967. Anti-aircraft Defences. Multicoloured.
N496 12x. Type **192** — 1·00 — 65
N497 12x. Rifle-fire from trenches — 1·00 — 65
N498 12x. Seaborne gun-crew — 1·00 — 65
N499 12x. Militiawoman with captured U.S. pilot — 1·00 — 65
N500 20x. Air battle — 1·50 — 85
N501 30x. Military anti-aircraft post — 3·00 — 1·20

193 Chickens

1968. Domestic Fowl. Multicoloured designs showing cocks and hens.
N502 12x. Type **193** — 1·30 — 65
N503 12x. Inscr "Ga ri" — 1·30 — 65
N504 12x. Inscr "Ga trong thien ri" — 1·30 — 65
N505 12x. Inscr "Ga den chanchi" — 1·30 — 65
N506 20x. Junglefowl — 1·90 — 95
N507 30x. Hen — 2·50 — 1·10
N508 40x. Hen and chicks — 3·75 — 1·50
N509 50x. Two hens — 4·50 — 1·70

194 Gorky

1968. Birth Centenary of Maxim Gorky.
N510 **194** 12x. black and brown — 2·50 — 95

195 Burning Village

1968. Victories of 1966–67.
N511 **195** 12x. brown and red — 1·30 — 1·10
N512 - 12x. brown and red — 1·30 — 1·10

N513 - 12x. brown and red — 1·30 — 1·10
N514 - 12x. brown and red — 1·30 — 1·10
N515 - 12x. black and violet — 1·30 — 1·10
N516 - 12x. black and violet — 1·30 — 1·10
N517 - 12x. black and violet — 1·30 — 1·10
N518 - 12x. black and violet — 1·30 — 1·10
DESIGNS: No. N512, Firing mortars; N513, Attacking tanks with rocket-gun; N514, Sniping; N515, Attacking gun-site; N516, Escorting prisoners; N517, Interrogating refugees; N518, Civilians demonstrating.

197 Ho Chi Minh Text and Fighters

1968. Intensification of Production.
N519 **197** 6x. blue on yellow — 1·30 — 40
N520 **197** 12x. blue — 1·90 — 65
N521 **197** 12x. purple — 1·90 — 65
N522 **197** 12x. red — 1·90 — 65

198 Hong boch Rose

1968. Roses. Multicoloured.
N523 12x. Type **198** — 1·30 — 65
N524 12x. Hong canh sap — 1·30 — 65
N525 12x. Hong leo — 1·30 — 65
N526 20x. Hong vang — 2·50 — 1·10
N527 30x. Hong nhung — 3·75 — 1·30
N528 40x. Hong canh tim — 5·00 — 2·00

199 Ho Chi Minh and Flag

1968. Ho Chi Minh's New Year Message.
N529 **199** 12x. brown and violet — 2·50 — 80

200 Karl Marx

1968. 150th Birth Anniv of Karl Marx.
N530 **200** 12x. black and green — 2·50 — 65

201 Anti-aircraft Machine-gun Crew

1968. "3,000th U.S. Aircraft Brought Down over North Vietnam". Multicoloured.
N531 12x. Type **201** — 2·50 — 2·00
N532 12x. Women manning anti-aircraft gun — 2·50 — 2·00
N533 40x. Aerial dogfight — 6·25 — 3·00
N534 40x. Anti-aircraft missile — 6·25 — 3·00

202 Rattan-cane Work

1968. Arts and Crafts. Multicoloured.
N535 6x. Type **202** — 65 — 55
N536 12x. Bamboo work — 75 — 65
N537 12x. Pottery — 75 — 65
N538 20x. Ivory carving — 1·30 — 80
N539 30x. Lacquer work — 1·90 — 95
N540 40x. Silverware — 2·50 — 1·30

203 Quarter-staff Contest

1968. Traditional Sports. Multicoloured.
N541 12x. Type **203** — 1·00 — 55
N542 12x. Dagger fighting — 1·00 — 55
N543 12x. Duel with sabres — 1·00 — 55
N544 30x. Unarmed combat — 2·50 — 65
N545 40x. Scimitar fighting — 3·25 — 95
N546 50x. Sword and buckler — 3·75 — 1·60

205 Temple, Khue

1968. Vietnamese Architecture. Multicoloured.
N548 12x. Type **205** — 75 — 55
N549 12x. Bell tower, Keo Pagoda — 75 — 55
N550 20x. Bridge, Bonze Pagoda (horiz) — 1·00 — 65
N551 30x. Mot Cot Pagoda, Hanoi — 1·30 — 80
N552 40x. Gateway, Ninh Phuc Pagoda (horiz) — 2·00 — 1·10
N553 50x. Tay Phuong Pagoda (horiz) — 2·50 — 1·30

206 Vietnamese Militia

1968. Cuban–North Vietnamese Friendship. Mult. With gum.
N554 12x. Type **206** — 1·30 — 1·10
N555 12x. Cuban revolutionary (vert) — 1·30 — 1·10
N556 20x. "Revolutionary Solidarity" (vert) — 2·50 — 1·90

207 "Ploughman with Rifle"

1968. "The War Effort". Paintings. With gum.
N557 **207** 12x. black, blue & yellow — 65 — 55
N558 - 12x. multicoloured — 65 — 55
N559 - 30x. brown, blue and turquoise — 1·50 — 1·30
N560 - 40x. multicoloured — 2·30 — 2·00
DESIGNS—HORIZ: No. N558, "Defending the Mines"; N559, "Repairing Railway Track"; N560, "Crashed Aircraft".

208 Nam Ngai shooting down Aircraft

1969. Lunar New Year. Victories of the National Liberation Front. Multicoloured.
N561 12x. Type **208** — 65 — 55
N562 12x. Tay Nguyen throwing grenade — 65 — 55
N563 12x. Gun crews, Tri Thien — 65 — 55
N564 40x. Insurgents, Tay Ninh — 1·90 — 1·10
N565 50x. Home Guards — 3·75 — 1·60

209 Loading Timber Lorries

1969. North Vietnamese Timber Industry. Multicoloured.
N566 6x. Type **209** — 75 — 55
N567 12x. Log raft on river — 1·40 — 65
N568 12x. Tug towing "log train" — 1·40 — 65
N569 12x. Elephant hauling logs — 1·40 — 65

N570	12x. Insecticide spraying	1·40	65
N571	20x. Buffalo hauling log	1·90	95
N572	30x. Logs on overhead cable	3·25	1·60

210 "Young Guerrilla" (Co Tan Long Chau)

1969. "South Vietnam—Land and People". Paintings. Multicoloured.

N573	12x. Type **210**	75	55
N574	12x. "Scout on Patrol" (Co Tan Long Chau)	75	55
N575	20x. "Woman Guerrilla" (Le Van Chuong) (vert)	1·30	65
N576	30x. "Halt at a Relay Station" (Co Tan Long Chau)	1·60	80
N577	40x. "After a Skirmish" (Co Tan Long Chau)	2·50	1·10
N578	50x. "Liberated Hamlet" (Huynh Phuong Dong)	3·75	1·60

211 Woman Soldier, Ben Tre

1969. Victories in Tet Offensive (1968).

N579	**211**	8x. black, green and pink	65	55
N580	**211**	12x. black, emer & green	1·00	80
N581	-	12x. multicoloured	1·00	80
N582	-	12x. multicoloured	1·00	80
N583	-	12x. multicoloured	1·00	80

DESIGNS—VERT: No. N581, Urban guerilla and attack on U.S. Embassy, Saigon; N582, Two soldiers with flag, Hue; N583, Mortar crew, Khe Sanh.

212 Soldier with Flame-thrower

1969. 15th Anniv of Liberation of Hanoi.

| N584 | **212** | 12x. black and red | 3·25 | 1·30 |
| N585 | - | 12x. multicoloured | 3·25 | 1·30 |

DESIGN: No. N585, Children with construction toy.

213 Grapefruit

1969. Fruit. Multicoloured.

N586	12x. Type **213**	50	25
N587	12x. Pawpaw	50	25
N588	20x. Tangerines	65	40
N589	30x. Oranges	1·00	65
N590	40x. Lychees	1·90	1·10
N591	50x. Persimmons	3·25	2·00

See also Nos. N617/21 and N633/6.

214 Tribunal Emblem and Falling Airplane

1969. International War Crimes Tribunal, Stockholm and Roskilde.

| N592 | **214** | 12x. black, red & brown | 3·25 | 1·10 |

215 Ho Chi Minh in 1924

1970. 40th Anniv of Vietnamese Workers' Party. Multicoloured.

N593	12x. Type **215**	1·30	1·10
N594	12x. Ho Chi Minh in 1969	1·30	1·10
N595	12x. Le Hong Phong	1·30	1·10
N596	12x. Tran Phu	1·30	1·10
N597	12x. Nguyne Van Cu	1·30	1·10

Nos. N595/7 are smaller, size 40×24 mm.

216 Playtime in Nursery School

1970. Children's Activities. Multicoloured.

N598	12x. Type **216**	50	55
N599	12x. Playing with toys	50	55
N600	20x. Watering plants	90	65
N601	20x. Pasturing buffalo	90	65
N602	30x. Feeding chickens	1·00	75
N603	40x. Making music	1·30	95
N604	50x. Flying model airplane	1·90	1·30
N605	60x. Going to school	2·50	1·60

217 Lenin and Red Flag

1970. Birth Centenary of Lenin.

| N606 | **217** | 12x. multicoloured | 50 | 55 |
| N607 | - | 1d. purple, red & yellow | 5·00 | 2·00 |

DESIGN: 1d. Portrait of Lenin.

218 Great Green Turban

1970. Sea-shells. Multicoloured.

N608	12x. Type **218**	1·30	65
N609	12x. Indian volute	1·30	65
N610	20x. Tiger cowrie	1·90	1·10
N611	1d. Trumpet triton	4·50	2·00

219 Ho Chi Minh in 1930

1970. Ho Chi Minh's 80th Birth Anniv.

N612	**219**	12x. black, brn & flesh	65	55
N613	-	12x. black, blue & green	65	55
N614	-	2d. black, ochre & yell	5·00	2·40

MSN615 Two sheets 134×93 mm, each containing Nos. N612/14.
(a) Background in pale orange (b) Background in mauve. Imperf ... 20·00 | 20·00

PORTRAITS: No. N613, In 1945 with microphone; N614, In 1969.

220 Vietcong Flag

1970. First Anniv of National Liberation Front Provisional Government in South Vietnam.

| N616 | **220** | 12x. multicoloured | 1·90 | 65 |

221 Water-melon

1970. Fruit. Multicoloured.

N617	12x. Type **221**	65	55
N618	12x. Pumpkin	65	55
N619	20x. Cucumber	1·00	65
N620	50x. Courgette	1·90	1·10
N621	1d. Charantais melon	3·75	1·60

222 Power Linesman

1970. North Vietnamese Industries.

N622	**222**	12x. blue and red	1·10	80
N623	-	12x. red, yellow and blue	1·10	80
N624	-	12x. black, orange & blue	1·10	80
N625	-	12x. yellow, purple & green	1·10	80

DESIGNS—VFRT: No. N623, Hands winding thread on bobbin ("Textiles"); N624, Stoker and power station ("Electric Power"); N625, Workers and lorry ("More coal for the Fatherland").

223 Peasant Girl with Pigs

1970. North Vietnamese Agriculture.

| N626 | **223** | 12x. multicoloured | 2·50 | 65 |

224 Ho Chi Minh proclaiming Republic, 1945

1970. 25th Anniv of Democratic Republic of Vietnam.

N627	**224**	12x. black, brown & red	50	55
N628	-	12x. deep brown, brown and green	71	80
N629	-	12x. brown, grey and red	50	55
N630	-	12x. deep brown, brown and green	50	55
N631	-	20x. brown, red & bistre	90	65
N632	-	1d. brown, drab and chestnut	3·25	1·10

DESIGNS. No. N628, Vo Thi Sau facing firing-squad; N629, Nguyen Van Troi and captors; N630, Phan Dinh Giot attacking pill-box; N631, Nguyen Viet Xuan encouraging troops; N632, Nguyen Van Be attacking tank.

225 Chuoi Tieu Bananas

1970. Bananas. Multicoloured.

N633	12x. Type **225**	1·00	65
N634	12x. Chuoi Tay	1·00	65
N635	50x. Chuoi Ngu	2·30	1·10
N636	1d. Chuoi Mat	3·25	1·60

226 Flags, and Bayonets in Helmet

1970. Indo-Chinese People's Summit Conference.

| N637 | **226** | 12x. multicoloured | 3·25 | 95 |

227 Engels and Signature

1970. 150th Birth Anniv of Friedrich Engels.

| N638 | **227** | 12x. black, brown & red | 1·30 | 65 |
| N639 | **227** | 1d. black, brown & grn | 2·50 | 1·10 |

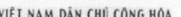

228 "Akistrodon ciatus"

1970. Snakes. Multicoloured.

N640	12x. Type **228**	1·10	65
N641	20x. "Calliophis macclellandii"	1·60	95
N642	50x. "Bungarus faciatus"	2·00	1·20
N643	1d. "Trimeresurus gramineus"	3·50	1·70

229 Mother and Child with Flag

1970. Tenth Anniv of National Front for Liberation of South Vietnam. Multicoloured.

| N644 | 6x. Type **229** | 1·30 | 65 |
| N645 | 12x. Vietcong flag and torch (horiz) | 2·50 | 1·10 |

1971. Victories of Liberation Army. As No. N449, but value and colours changed.

| N646 | **178** | 2x. black and orange | 2·50 | 1·10 |

232 Satellite in Earth Orbit

1971. First Anniv of Launching of Chinese Satellite.

| N649 | **232** | 12x. multicoloured | 2·50 | 1·20 |
| N650 | **232** | 50x. multicoloured | 3·25 | 1·70 |

234 Ho Chi Minh Medal

1971. 81st Birth Anniv of Pres. Ho Chi Minh.

N652	**234**	1x. multicoloured	50	40
N653	**234**	3x. multicoloured	65	55
N654	**234**	10x. multicoloured	90	80
N655	**234**	12x. multicoloured	1·00	95
MSN656	90×130 mm. **234** 12x. multi-coloured (53×52 mm). Imperf	9·50	9·25

235 Emperor Quang Trung liberating Hanoi

1971. Bicentenary of Tay Son Rising.

| N657 | **235** | 6x. multicoloured | 1·30 | 65 |
| N658 | **235** | 12x. multicoloured | 2·50 | 1·20 |

236 Karl Marx and Music of the "Internationale"

1971. Centenary of Paris Commune.

| N659 | **236** | 12x. black, red and pink | 1·90 | 65 |

237 Hai Thuong Lan Ong

1971. 250th Birth Anniv of Hai Thuong Lan Ong (physician).

| N660 | **237** | 12x. black, green & brn | 1·90 | 65 |
| N661 | **237** | 50x. multicoloured | 2·50 | 1·20 |

238 "Kapimala"

1971. Folk Sculptures in Tay Phuong Pagoda. Multicoloured.

N662	12x. Type **238**	75	65
N663	12x. "Sangkayasheta"	75	65
N664	12x. "Vasumitri"	75	65
N665	12x. "Dhikaca"	75	65
N666	30x. "Bouddha Nandi"	1·60	80
N667	40x. "Rahulata"	1·90	1·10
N668	50x. "Sangha Nandi"	3·25	1·50
N669	1d. "Cakyamuni"	4·25	2·10

239 Ho Chi Minh, Banner and Young Workers

1971. 40th Anniv of Ho Chi Minh Working Youth Union.

N670	**239**	12x. multicoloured	1·90	65

240 "Luna 16" on Moon

1971. Moon Flight of "Luna 16".

N671	-	12x. multicoloured	1·30	65
N672	-	12x. multicoloured	1·30	65
N673	**240**	1d. brown, blue & turq	3·75	1·90

DESIGNS: No. N671, Flight to Moon; N672, Return to Earth.

Nos. N671/2 were issued together horizontally, se-tenant, each pair forming a composite design.

241 "Luna 17" landing on Moon

1971. Moon Flight of "Luna 17".

N674	**241**	12x. red, blue and green	1·30	65
N675	-	12x. pink, green & myrtle	1·30	65
N676	**240**	1d. pink, brown & green	3·75	1·60

DESIGNS—HORIZ: No. N675, "Luna 17" on Moon; N676, "Lunokhod 1" crossing Moon crevasse.

243 "White Tiger"

1971. "The Five Tigers" (folk-art paintings). Multicoloured.

N679	12x. Type **243**	65	55
N680	12x. "Yellow Tiger"	65	55
N681	12x. "Red Tiger"	65	55
N682	40x. "Green Tiger"	2·50	1·10
N683	50x. "Grey Tiger"	3·25	1·60

N684	1d. "Five Tigers"	4·50	2·10
MS685	90×120 mm. 1d. As No. N684 but size 47×63 mm. Imperf	18·00	18·00

244 Flags and Gate of Heavenly Peace, Peking

1971. 50th Anniv of Chinese Communist Party.

N686	**244**	12x. multicoloured	2·00	95

245 Mongolian Emblem

1971. 50th Anniv of Mongolian People's Republic.

N687	**245**	12x. multicoloured	2·00	95

246 Drum Procession

1972. Dong Ho Folk Engravings.

N688	**246**	12x. pink, brown & blk	1·30	1·10
N689	-	12x. pink and black	1·30	1·10
N690	-	12x. multicoloured	1·30	1·10
N691	-	12x. multicoloured	1·30	1·10
N692	-	40x. multicoloured	3·25	1·60
N693	-	50x. multicoloured	4·50	2·40

DESIGNS—HORIZ: No. N689, "Traditional Wrestling"; N692, "Wedding of Mice"; N693, "The Toads' School". VERT: No. N690, "Jealous Attack"; N691, "Gathering Coconuts".

247 Workers

1972. Third Vietnamese Trade Unions Congress.

N694	**247**	1x. black and blue	90	40
N695	-	12x. black and orange	1·30	65

DESIGN: 12x. As Type **247**, but design reversed.

248 Planting Rice

1972. 25th Anniv of National Resistance.

N696	**248**	12x. multicoloured	1·00	65
N697	-	12x. multicoloured	1·00	65
N698	-	12x. multicoloured	1·00	65
N699	-	12x. turq, red & pink	1·00	65

DESIGNS: No. N697, Munitions worker; N698, Soldier with flame-thrower; N699, Text of Ho Chi Minh's Appeal.

249 Ho Chi Minh's Birthplace

1972. 82nd Birth Anniv of Ho Chi Minh.

N700	**249**	12x. black, drab & ochre	1·90	95
N701	-	12x. black, green & pink	1·90	95

DESIGN: No. N701, Ho Chi Minh's house, Hanoi.

250 Captured Pilot and Falling Airplane

1972. "3,500th U.S. Aircraft Brought Down over North Vietnam".

N702	**250**	12x. green and red	3·25	2·00
N703	**250**	12x. black and red	3·25	2·00

No. N703 has the inscription amended to record the actual date on which the 3,500th aircraft was brought down: 20.4.1972.

251 Georgi Dimitrov

1972. 90th Birth Anniv of Georgi Dimitrov (Bulgarian statesman).

N704	**251**	12x. brown and green	1·60	65
N705	-	12x. black and pink	1·60	65

DESIGN: No. N705, Dimitrov at Leipzig Court, 1933.

252 Falcated Teal

1972. Vietnamese Birds. Multicoloured.

N706	12x. Type **252**	90	60
N707	12x. Red-wattled lapwing	90	60
N708	30x. Cattle egret	1·50	75
N709	40x. Water cock	2·10	1·00
N710	50x. Purple swamphen	3·25	1·20
N711	1d. Greater adjutant stork	7·00	2·30

253 Anti-aircraft Gunner

1972. "4,000th U.S. Aircraft Brought Down over North Vietnam".

N712	**253**	12x. black, mauve and pink	4·50	1·60
N713	-	12x. green, black and red	4·50	1·60

DESIGN: No. N713, Anti-aircraft gunner with shell.

254 Umbrella Dance

1972. Tay Nguyen Folk Dances. Multicoloured.

N714	12x. Type **254**	65	55
N715	12x. Drum dance	65	55
N716	12x. Shield dance	65	55
N717	20x. Horse dance	1·00	65
N718	30x. Ka-Dong dance	1·30	80
N719	40x. Grinding-rice dance	1·50	95
N720	50x. Gong dance	2·50	1·30
N721	1d. Cham Rong dance	4·50	2·00

255 "Soyuz 11" Spacecraft and "Salyut" Space Laboratory

1972. Space Flight of "Soyuz 11".

N722	**255**	12x. blue and lilac	1·30	65
N723	-	1d. brown and flesh	3·25	1·60

DESIGN: 1d. "Soyuz 11" astronauts.

256 Dhole

1973. Wild Animals (1st series). Multicoloured.

N724	12x. Type **256**	90	60
N725	30x. Leopard	1·50	65
N726	50x. Leopard cat	3·25	1·30
N727	1d. European otter	4·50	2·00

See also Nos. N736/9.

257 Copernicus and Globe

1973. 500th Birth Anniv of Copernicus (astronomer).

N728	**257**	12x. black, red & brown	1·60	1·10
N729	-	12x. black, red & brown	1·60	1·10
N730	-	30x. black and brown	2·50	1·30

DESIGNS—HORIZ: No. N729, Copernicus and sun. VERT: 30x. Copernicus and facsimile signature.

258 "Drummers"

1973. Engravings from Ngoc Lu Bronze Drums. Each yellow and green.

N731	12x. Type **258**	1·00	65
N732	12x. "Pounding rice"	1·00	65
N733	12x. "Folk-dancing"	1·00	65
N734	12x. "War canoe"	1·00	65
N735	12x. "Birds and beasts"	1·00	65

259 Lesser Malay Chevrotain

1973. Wild Animals (2nd series). Multicoloured.

N736	12x. Type **259**	65	55
N737	30x. Mainland serow	1·30	65
N738	50x. Wild boar	1·90	95
N739	1d. Siberian musk deer	2·50	1·20

260 Striated Canegrass Warblers

1973. Birds useful to Agriculture. Multicoloured.

N740	12x. Type **260**	65	55
N741	12x. Red-whiskered bulbuls	65	55
N742	20x. Magpie robin	1·30	65
N743	40x. White-browed fantails	1·90	95
N744	50x. Great tits	2·50	1·20
N745	1d. Japanese white-eyes	3·25	1·60

262 "Ready to Learn"

1973. "Three Readies" Youth Movement.

N748	**262**	12x. brown and green	1·10	65
N749	-	12x. violet and blue	1·10	65
N750	-	12x. green and mauve	1·10	65

DESIGNS: No. N749, Soldiers on the march ("Ready to Fight"); N750, Road construction ("Ready to Work").

263 Flags of North Vietnam and North Korea

1973. 25th Anniv of People's Republic of Korea.

N751	**263**	12x. multicoloured	1·90	80

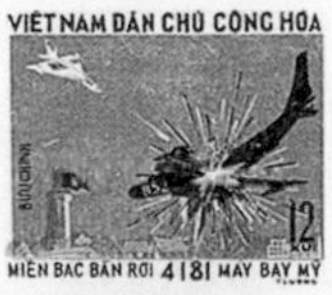

264 Dogfight over Hanoi

1973. Victory over U.S. Air Force.

N752	**264**	12x. multicoloured	1·90	80
N753	-	12x. multicoloured	1·90	80
N754	-	12x. multicoloured	1·90	80
N755	-	1d. black and red	5·00	2·10

DESIGNS: No. N753, Boeing B-52 Stratofortress exploding over Haiphong; N754, Anti-aircraft gun; N755, Aircraft wreckage in China Sea.

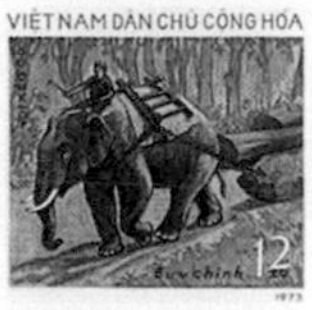

266 Elephant hauling Logs

1974. Vietnamese Elephants. Multicoloured.

N758	12x. Type **266**	65	55
N759	12x. War elephant	65	55
N760	40x. Elephant rolling logs	1·90	65
N761	50x. Circus elephant	2·00	80
N762	1d. Elephant carrying war supplies	3·75	1·60

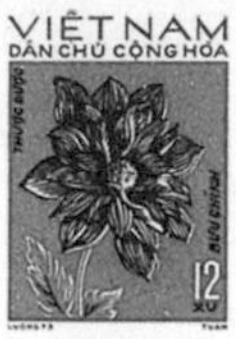

267 Dahlia

1974. Flowers.

N763	**267**	12x. red, lake and green	1·10	65
N764	-	12x. red, lake and green	1·10	65
N765	-	12x. yellow, green & blue	1·10	65
N766	-	12x. multicoloured	1·50	80
N767	-	12x. multicoloured	1·50	80

FLOWERS: No. N764, Rose; N765, Chrysanthemum; N766, Bach Mi; N767, Dai Doa.

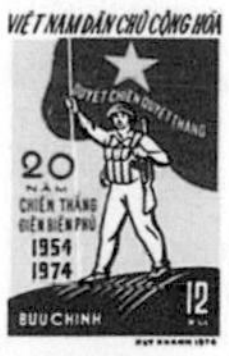

268 Soldier planting Flag

1974. 20th Anniv of Victory at Dien Bien Phu.

N768	12x. Type **268**	1·60	80
N769	12x. Victory badge	1·60	80

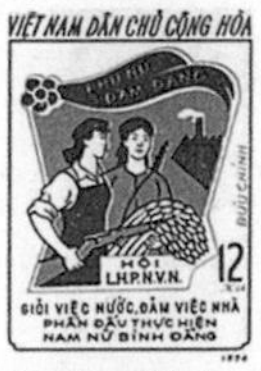

269 Armed Worker and Peasant

1974. "Three Responsibilities" Women's Movement.

N770	**269**	12x. blue and pink	1·60	80
N771	-	12x. blue and pink	1·60	80

DESIGN: No. N771, Woman operating loom.

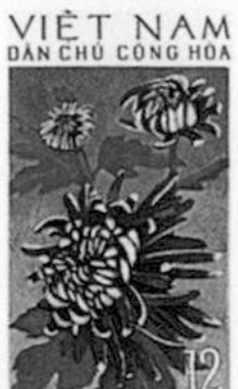

270 Cuc Nau Chrysanthemum

1974. Vietnamese Chrysanthemums. Multicoloured.

N772	12x. Type **270**	65	40
N773	12x. Cuc Vang	65	40
N774	20x. Cuc Ngoc Khong Tuoc	75	45
N775	30x. Cuc Trang	1·00	55
N776	40x. Kim Cuc	1·30	80
N777	50x. Cuc Hong Mi	1·50	95
N778	60x. Cuc Gam	1·90	1·10
N779	1d. Cuc Tim	2·50	1·90

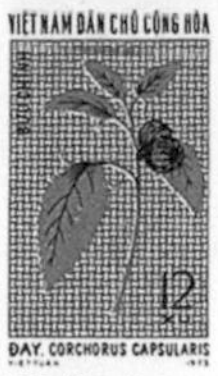

271 "Corchorus capsularis"

1974. Textile Plants.

N780	**271**	12x. brown, green and olive	1·90	65
N781	-	12x. brown, grn & pink	1·90	65
N782	-	30x. brown, green & yellow	2·50	1·20

DESIGNS: No. N781, "Cyperus tojet jormis"; N782, "Morus alba".

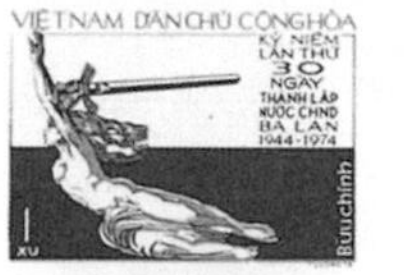

272 Nike Statue, Warsaw

1974. 30th Anniv of People's Republic of Poland.

N783	**272**	1x. purple, pink and red	65	55
N784	**272**	2x. red, pink and red	75	60
N785	**272**	3x. brown, pink and red	90	65
N786	**272**	12x. light red, pink & red	1·50	1·10

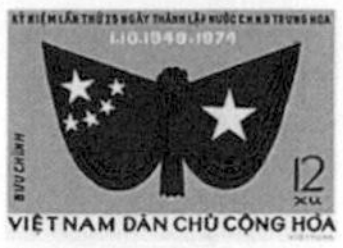

273 Flags of China and Vietnam

1974. 25th Anniv of People's Republic of China.

N787	**273**	12x. multicoloured	1·50	65

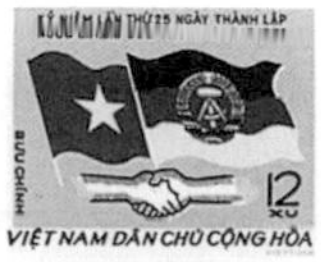

274 Handclasp with Vietnamese and East German Flags

1974. 25th Anniv of German Democratic Republic.

N788	**274**	12x. multicoloured	1·90	80

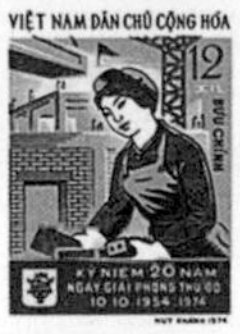

275 Woman Bricklayer

1974. 20th Anniv of Liberation of Hanoi. Multicoloured.

N789	12x. Type **275**	1·50	65
N790	12x. Soldier with child	1·50	65

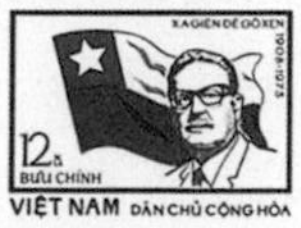

276 Pres. Allende with Chilean Flag

1974. First Death Annivs of Salvador Allende (President of Chile) and Pablo Neruda (Chilean poet).

N791	**276**	12x. blue and red	1·50	65
N792	-	12x. blue (Pablo Neruda)	1·50	65

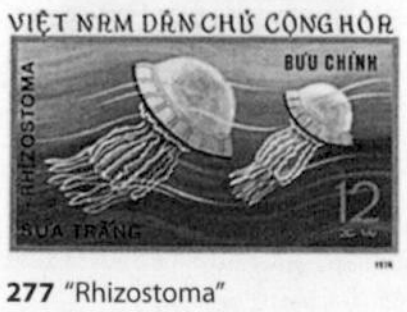

277 "Rhizostoma"

1974. Marine Life. Multicoloured.

N793	12x. Type **277**	65	25
N794	12x. "Loligo"	65	25
N795	30x. Variously coloured abalone	1·30	40
N796	40x. Japanese pearl oyster	1·50	55
N797	50x. Common cuttlefish	2·30	80
N798	1d. "Palinurus japonicus"	3·25	1·70

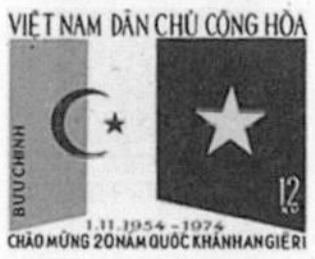

278 Flags of Algeria and Vietnam

1974. 20th Anniv of Algerian War of Liberation.

N799	**278**	12x. multicoloured	1·50	80

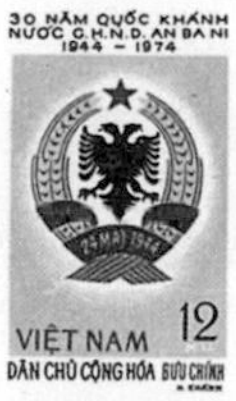

279 Albanian Emblem

1974. 30th Anniv of People's Republic of Albania. Multicoloured.

N800	12x. Type **279**	1·30	65
N801	12x. Girls from Albania and North Vietnam	1·30	65

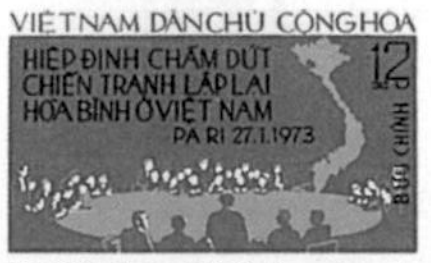

280 Signing of Paris Agreement

1975. Second Anniv of Paris Agreement on Vietnam.

N802	**280**	12x. black, green & emerald	1·60	75
N803	-	12x. black, blue and grey	1·60	75

DESIGN: No. N803, International Conference in session.

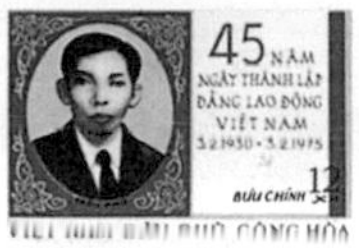

281 Tran Phu

1975. 45th Anniv of Vietnamese Workers' Party.

N804	**281**	12x. brown, red and pink	65	45
N805	-	12x. brown, red and pink	65	45
N806	-	12x. brown, red and pink	65	45
N807	-	12x. brown, red and pink	65	45
N808	-	60x. brown, chestnut and pink	1·50	80

PORTRAITS—HORIZ: No. N805, Nguyen Van Cu; N806, Le Hong Phong; N807, Ngo Gia Tu. VERT: No. N808, Ho Chi Minh in 1924.

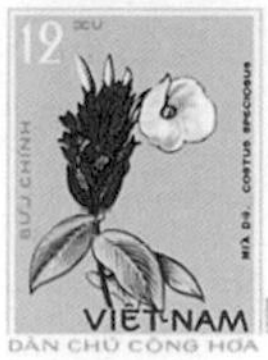

282 "Costus speciosus"

1975. Medicinal Plants. Multicoloured.

N809	12x. Type **282**	65	55
N810	12x. "Rosa laevigata"	65	55
N811	12x. "Curcuma zedoaria"	65	55
N812	30x. "Erythrina indica"	1·00	65
N813	40x. "Lilium brownii"	1·30	80
N814	50x. "Hibiscus sagittifolius"	1·50	95
N815	60x. "Papaver somniferum"	1·60	1·00
N816	1d. "Belamcanda chinensis"	3·75	1·60

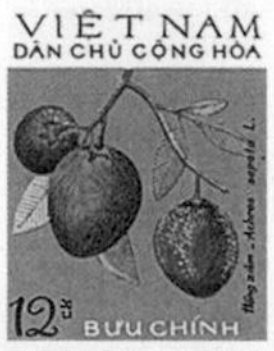

283 "Achras sapota"

1975. Fruit. Multicoloured.

N817	12x. Type **283**	65	55
N818	12x. "Persica vulgaris"	65	55
N819	20x. "Eugenia jambos"	90	65
N820	30x. "Chrysophyllum cainito"	1·00	65
N821	40x. "Lucuma mamosa"	1·10	75
N822	50x. "Prunica granitum"	1·30	1·10
N823	60x. "Durio ziberthinus"	1·90	1·30
N824	1d. "Prunus salicina"	3·25	1·90

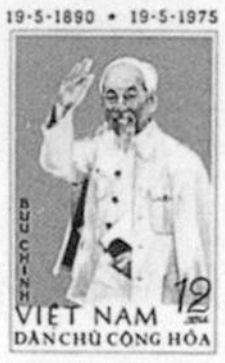

284 Ho Chi Minh

1975. 85th Birth Anniv of Ho Chi Minh.

N825	**284**	12x. multicoloured	1·30	65
N826	**284**	60x. multicoloured	3·25	1·30

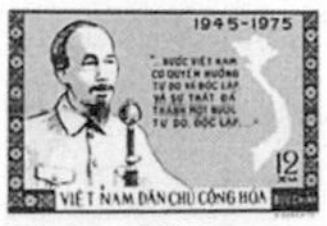

285 Ho Chi Minh proclaiming Independence, 1945

1975. 30th Anniv of Democratic Republic of Vietnam. Multicoloured.

N827	12x. Type **285**	1·50	75
N828	12x. Democratic Republic emblem	1·50	75
N829	12x. Democratic Republic flag	1·50	75
MSN829	130×100 mm. 20x. Type **285** (45×30 mm). Imperf	11·50	11·50

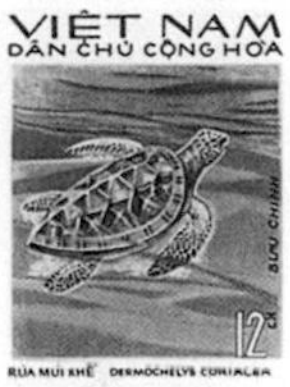

286 "Dermochelys coriacea"

1975. Reptiles. Multicoloured.

N831	12x. Type **286**	65	55
N832	12x. "Physignathus cocincinus"	65	55
N833	20x. "Hydrophis brookii"	1·00	65
N834	30x. "Platysternum megacephalum"	1·30	80
N835	40x. "Leiolepis belliana"	1·50	85
N836	50x. "Python molurus"	1·80	95
N837	60x. "Naja hannah"	2·00	1·00
N838	1d. "Draco maculatus"	2·50	1·30

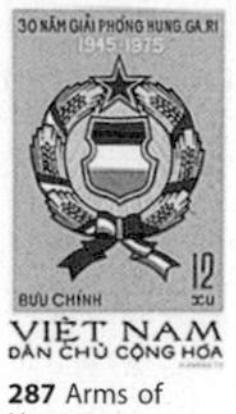

287 Arms of Hungary

1975. 30th Anniv of Liberation of Hungary.

N839	**287**	12x. multicoloured	1·50	75

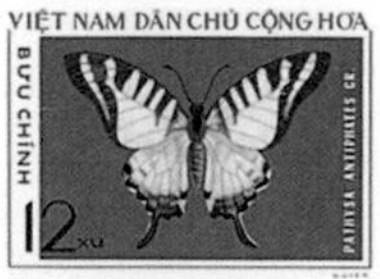

288 "Pathysa antiphates"

1976. Butterflies. Multicoloured.

N840	12x. Type **288**	65	55
N841	12x. "Danaus plexippus"	65	55
N842	20x. "Gynautocera papilionaria"	1·30	80
N843	30x. "Maenas salaminia"	1·40	80
N844	40x. "Papilio machaon"	1·50	85
N845	50x. "Ixias pyrene"	1·80	95
N846	60x. "Eusemia vetula"	2·00	1·00
N847	1d. "Eriboea sp."	2·50	1·30

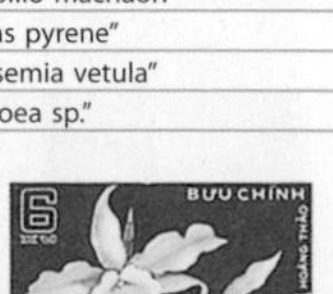

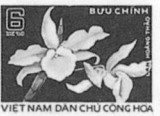

289 Hoang Thao Orchid

1976. Lunar New Year.

N848	**289**	6x. yellow, green & blue	2·30	1·30
N849	**289**	12x. yellow, green & red	2·50	1·60

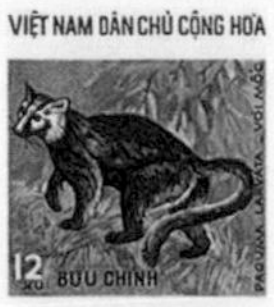
VIỆT NAM DÂN CHỦ CỘNG HÒA
BƯU CHÍNH

290 Masked Palm Civet

1976. Wild Animals. Multicoloured.

N850	12x. Type **290**		90	25
N851	12x. Belly-banded squirrel		90	25
N852	20x. Rhesus macaque		1·00	35
N853	30x. Chinese porcupine		1·00	40
N854	40x. Racoon-dog		1·10	45
N855	50x. Asiatic black bear		1·30	55
N856	60x. Leopard		1·50	80
N857	1d. Malayan flying lemur		2·30	1·10

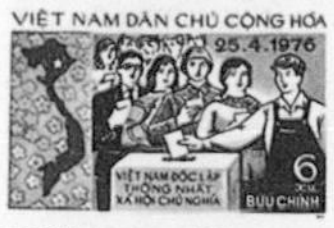
VIỆT NAM DÂN CHỦ CỘNG HÒA
25.4.1976
BƯU CHÍNH

291 Voters and Map

1976. First Elections Unified National Assembly.

N858	**291**	6x. red and sepia	1·00	65
N859	-	6x. yellow and red	1·00	65
N860	**291**	12x. red and blue	2·50	1·30

DESIGN:—35×24 mm: No. N859, Map and ballot box.

See also Nos. NLF64/6 of National Front for the Liberation of South Vietnam.

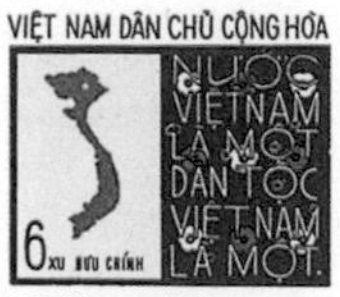
VIỆT NAM DÂN CHỦ CỘNG HÒA
NƯỚC VIỆT NAM LÀ MỘT DÂN TỘC VIỆT NAM LÀ MỘT
BƯU CHÍNH

292 Map and Text

1976. First Session of Unified National Assembly.

N861	**292**	6x. purple, red & yellow	1·30	65
N862	**292**	12x. turquoise, red & yellow	1·90	1·10
N863	-	12x. bistre, red & yellow	1·90	1·10

DESIGN—VERT (27×42 mm): No. N863, Vietnam map and design from Ngoc Lu Drum. No. N862 shows different text from Type **292**.

See also Nos. NLF68/9 of National Front for the Liberation of South Vietnam.

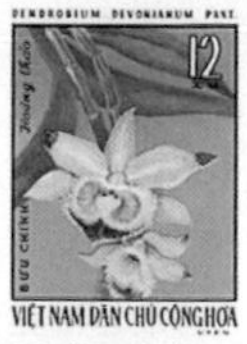
VIỆT NAM DÂN CHỦ CỘNG HÒA

293 "Dendrobium devonianum"

1976. Orchids. Multicoloured.

N864	12x. Type **293**		75	25
N865	12x. "Habenaria rhodocheila"		75	25
N866	20x. "Dendrobium tortile"		1·00	35
N867	30x. "Doritis pulcherima"		1·10	40
N868	40x. "Dendrobium farmeri"		1·30	55
N869	50x. "Dendrobium aggregatum"		1·50	65
N870	60x. "Eria pannae"		1·90	95
N871	1d. "Paphiopedilum concolor"		3·25	1·30

FRANK STAMPS

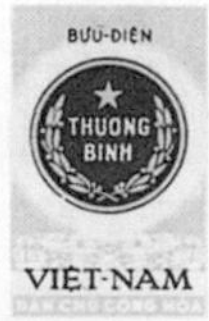
BƯU-ĐIỆN
THƯƠNG BINH
VIỆT-NAM

F29

1958. No value indicated.

NF82	**F29**	(–) red, yellow and green	17·00	6·50

Issued to war-disabled persons for private correspondence.

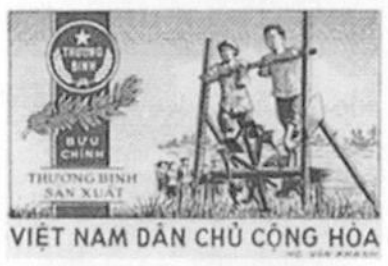
VIỆT NAM DÂN CHỦ CỘNG HÒA

F42 Invalids in Rice-field

1959. No value indicated.

NF105	**F42**	(–) brown	1·70	1·10
NF106	**F42**	(–) olive and blue	2·30	85

Issued to invalids in agriculture for private correspondence.

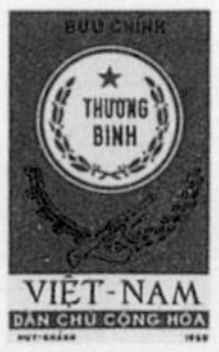
THƯƠNG BINH
VIỆT-NAM
DÂN CHỦ CỘNG HÒA

F230 Invalid's Badge

1971. No value indicated.

NF647	**F230**	(–) brown and red	1·90	2·00

Issued to disabled ex-servicemen for private correspondence.

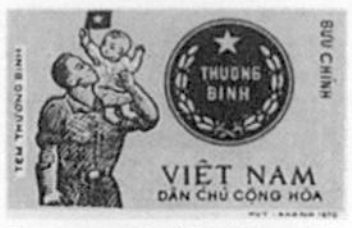
THƯƠNG BINH
VIỆT NAM
DÂN CHỦ CỘNG HÒA

F233 Disabled Soldier with Baby

1971. No value indicated.

NF651	**F233**	(–) brn, red & yell	2·00	2·00

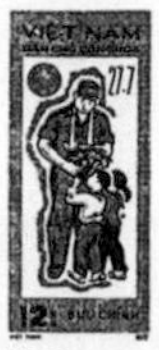

F261 "Returning Home"

1973

NF746	**F261**	12x. black and red	65	65
NF747	-	12x. black and blue	65	65

DESIGN—22×33 mm: No. NF747, Disabled soldier with drill.

Issued to disabled veterans for private correspondence.

MILITARY FRANK STAMPS

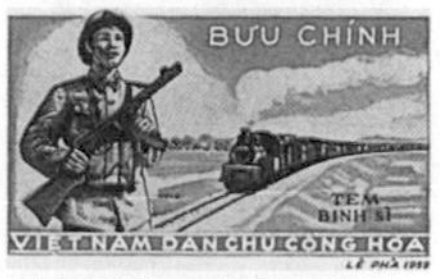
BƯU CHÍNH
VIỆT NAM DÂN CHỦ CỘNG HÒA

MF46 Soldier and Steam Train

1959. No value indicated.

NMF112	**MF46**	(–) black & green	5·75	3·25

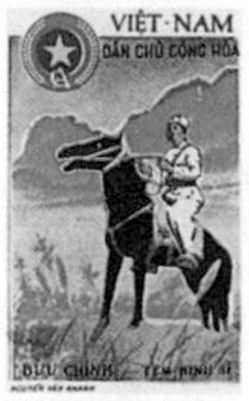
VIỆT-NAM
DÂN CHỦ CỘNG HÒA

MF68 Mounted Frontier Guard

1961. No value indicated.

NMF154	**MF68**	(–) mult	21·00	16·00

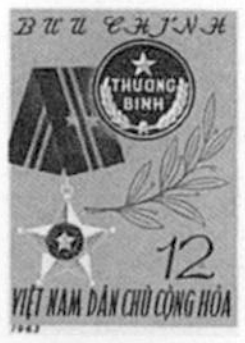
THƯƠNG BINH
12
VIỆT NAM DÂN CHỦ CỘNG HÒA

MF118 Military Medal and Invalid's Badge

1963

NMF277	**MF118**	12x. mult	6·25	6·75

For use on disabled soldiers' mail.

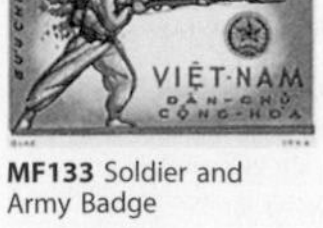
VIỆT-NAM

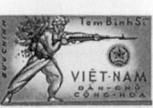

MF133 Soldier and Army Badge

1964. No value indicated.

NMF325	**MF133**	(–) green, black and orge	6·25	6·75

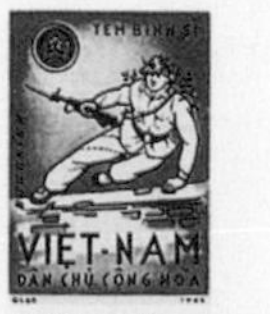
VIỆT-NAM
DÂN CHỦ CỘNG HÒA

MF150 Soldier in Action

1965. No value indicated.

NMF373	**MF150**	(–) black and red	6·25	6·75
NMF374	**MF150**	(–) black & green	6·25	6·75

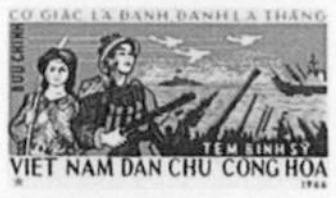
VIỆT NAM DÂN CHỦ CỘNG HÒA

MF177 Soldiers and Weapons

1966. No value indicated.

NMF447	**MF177**	(–) violet & black	12·50	13·50

1967. No value indicated.

NMF488	**MF189**	(–) mult	2·50	2·75

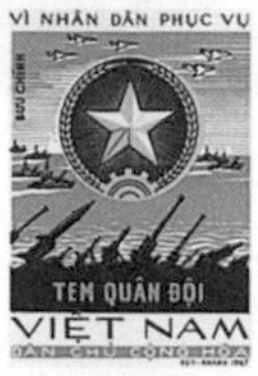
TEM QUÂN ĐỘI
VIỆT NAM

MF189 "Star" Badge of People's Army

1968. No value indicated.

NMF519		(–) brown and green	12·50	13·50

No. NMF519 is similar in design to No. NMF447, but shows more modern equipment and is dated "1967".

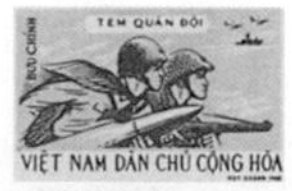
VIỆT NAM DÂN CHỦ CỘNG HÒA

MF204 Soldiers attacking

1968. No value indicated.

NMF547	**MF204**	(–) lilac	2·00	2·10

1969. Type **MF177**, but undated. No value indicated.

NMF579	**MF177**	(–) brown & green	25·00	

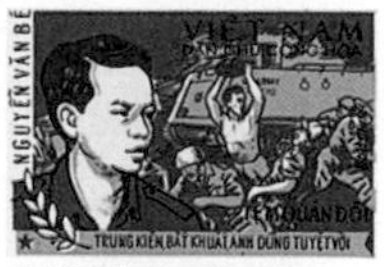
VIỆT NAM

MF231 Nguyen Van Be attacking Tank

1971. No value indicated.

NMF648	**MF231**	(–) blk, red & drab	1·90	2·00

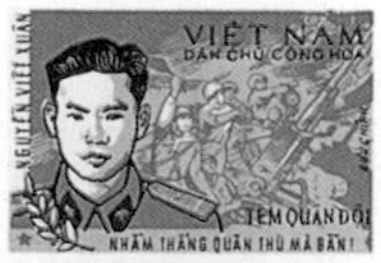
VIỆT NAM
DÂN CHỦ CỘNG HÒA
TEM QUÂN ĐỘI

MF242 Nguyen Viet Yuan and Anti-aircraft Gun

1971. No value indicated.

NMF677	**MF242**	(–) black, pink and buff	1·30	1·30
NMF678	**MF242**	(–) brown & green	1·30	1·30

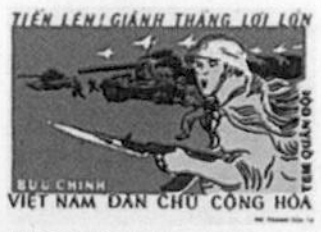
VIỆT NAM DÂN CHỦ CỘNG HÒA

MF265 Soldier with Bayonet advancing

1974. No value indicated.

NMF756	**MF265**	(–) black, yellow & blue	65	65
NMF757	-	(–) black, red and brown	65	65
NMF758	**MF265**	(–) black, flesh and red	1·30	1·30

DESIGN: No. NMF757, Soldier with sub-machine gun, and tanks. No. NMF757 is 40×24 mm; No. NMF758 31×21 mm.

OFFICIAL STAMPS

A. Tongking

The values on Official stamps issued 1952 to 1954 are in kilogrammes of rice, the basis of the State's economy.

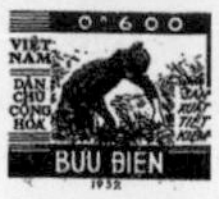
BUU DIEN

O6 Rice-harvester

1953. Production and Economy Campaign.

NO17	**O6**	0.600k. red	13·00	2·50
NO18	**O6**	1.000k. brown	13·50	5·25
NO19	**O6**	2.000k. orange	10·50	16·00
NO20	**O6**	5.000k. slate	16·00	21·00

B. Central Annam.

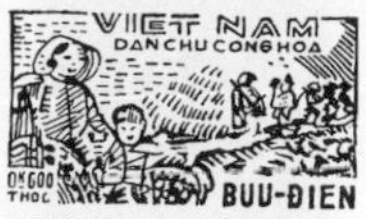
VIỆT NAM
DAN CHU CONG HOA
BUU-DIEN

NAO3 "Family Left Behind"

1952. Issue for Central Annam. Imperf.

NAO9	**NAO3**	0.050k. red	£250	
NAO10	**NAO3**	0.300k. red	£250	
NAO11	**NAO3**	0.300k. violet	£250	
NAO12	**NAO3**	0.600k. green	£250	
NAO13	**NAO3**	0.600k. blue	£500	
NAO14	**NAO3**	1000k. green	£500	

1954. No. NA5 surch **TEMSU VU 0.k300 THOC**.

NAO15	**NA1**	0.300k. on 30d. on 5d. green	£500	£425

1954. Nos. 56/7 of Vietnam Democratic Republic surch in Kg. No. NAO17 also optd **LKV** at top and **THOC** below value.

NAO16	**3**	0kg05 on 1h. green	£250	
NAO17	**3**	0kg050 on 3h. red	£250	

1954. Surch **TEMSU VU** and new value. (a) On unsurcharged stamps with coloured (NAO20) or white (others) figures.

NAO20	**NA1**	0,750k. on 10d. mauve		
NAO21	**NA1**	0,800k. on 1d. violet		
NAO22	**NA1**	0,900k. on 5d. green		

(b) On stamps with coloured figures, previously surcharged.

NAO23	0,030k. on 3d. on 35d. purple
NAO24	0,050k. on 35d. on 300d. blue
NAO25	0,350k. on 70d. on 100d. grey

C. General issues.

1954. Dien-Bien-Phu Victory. As T **9** but value in "KILO". Imperf.

NO24	0.600k. ochre and sepia	23·00	13·00

1955. Surch **0 k, 100 THOC**.

NO33	**2**	0.100k. on 2d. brown	£250	£180
NO34	**2**	0.100k. on 5d. red	£250	£180

1955. Land Reform. As T **13** but inscr "SU VU".

NO38	40d. blue	16·00	9·75
NO39	80d. red	23·00	11·00

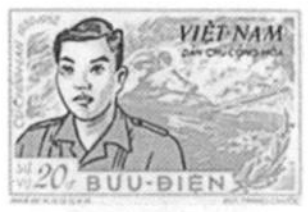
VIỆT-NAM
BUU-ĐIỆN

O17 Cu Chinh Lan (Tank Destroyer)

1956. Cu Chinh Lan Commemoration.

NO50	**O17**	20d. green & turquoise	5·00	5·50
NO51	**O17**	80d. mauve and red	5·75	6·00
NO52	**O17**	100d. sepia and drab	6·75	7·00
NO53	**O17**	500d. blue & light blue	19·00	20·00
NO54	**O17**	1000d. brown & orge	45·00	47·00
NO55	**O17**	2000d. purple & green	70·00	75·00
NO56	**O17**	3000d. lake and lilac	£120	£130

1957. Fourth World T.U. Conference, Leipzig. As T **24** but inscr "SU VU".

NO69	20d. green	3·50	3·25
NO70	40d. blue	4·50	4·25
NO71	80d. lake	5·75	5·50
NO72	100d. brown	11·50	11·00

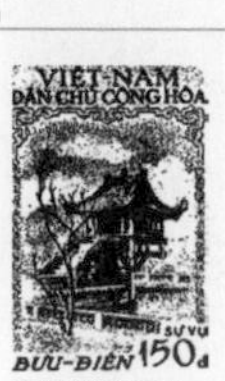
VIỆT-NAM
DÂN CHỦ CỘNG HÒA

O26 Mot Cot Pagoda, Hanoi

1957

NO75	**O26**	150d. brown and green	11·50	5·00
NO76	**O26**	150d. black and yellow	18·00	8·75

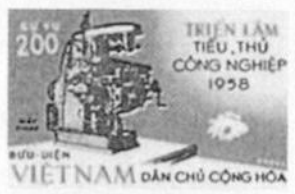

O30 Lathe

1958. Arts and Crafts Fair, Hanoi.

NO83	**O30**	150d. black and pink	4·00	2·75
NO84	**O30**	200d. blue and orange	5·00	3·75

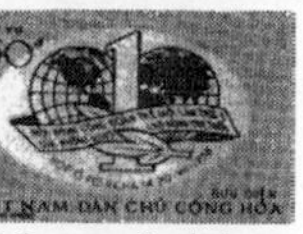

O31 Congress Symbol

1958. First World Congress of Young Workers, Prague.

NO85	**O31**	150d. red and green	4·00	2·20

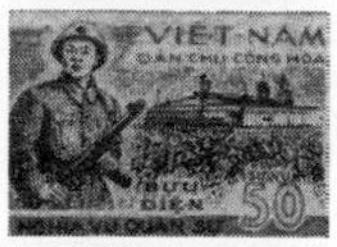

O34 Soldier, Factory and Crops

1958. Military Service.

NO91	**O34**	50d. blue and purple	3·00	1·10
NO92	**O34**	150d. brown and green	4·00	1·60
NO93	**O34**	200d. red and yellow	6·25	2·40

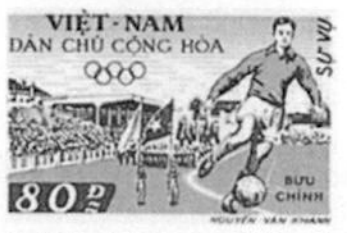

O40 Footballer and Hanoi Stadium

1958. Opening of New Hanoi Stadium.

NO102	**O40**	10d. lilac and blue	1·10	85
NO103	**O40**	20d. olive and salmon	1·80	1·10
NO104	**O40**	80d. brown and ochre	3·00	1·60
NO105	**O40**	150d. brown & turq	5·00	2·20

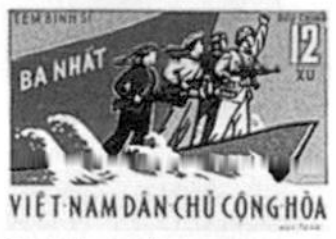

O97 Armed Forces on Boat

1962. Miltiary Service.

NO223	**O97**	12x. multicoloured	8·25	4·00

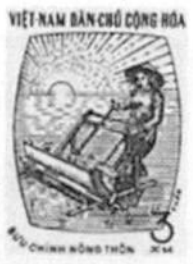

O100 Woman with Rice-planter

1962. Rural Service.

NO229	**O100**	3x. red	90	90
NO230	**O100**	6x. turquoise	1·30	1·30
NO231	**O100**	12x. olive	1·60	1·60

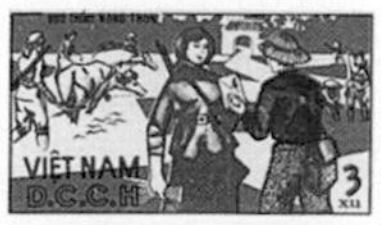

O176 Postman delivering Letter

1966. Rural Service.

NO445	**O176**	3x. purple, bistre and lilac	1·90	80
NO446	-	6x. purple, bistre and turquoise	2·50	1·10

DESIGN: 6x. As Type O **176** but design reversed.

POSTAGE DUE STAMPS

1952. Handstamped TT in diamond frame.

ND33	**3**	100d. green	85·00
ND34	**3**	100d. brown	85·00
ND35	**5**	100d. violet	85·00
ND36	**3**	200d. red	85·00

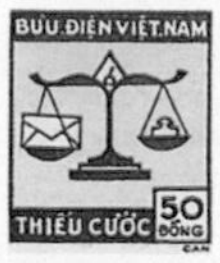

D13 Letter Scales

1955

ND40	**D13**	50d. brown and lemon	16·00	9·75

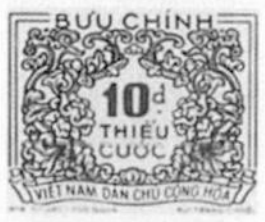

D39

1958

ND101	**D39**	10d. red and violet	1·20	1·10
ND102	**D39**	20d. green & orange	2·50	2·20
ND103	**D39**	100d. red and slate	5·25	4·25
ND104	**D39**	300d. red and olive	8·00	6·00

F. SOCIALIST REPUBLIC OF VIETNAM

Following elections in April 1976 a National Assembly representing the whole of Vietnam met in Hanoi on 24 June 1976 and on 2 July proclaimed the reunification of the country as the Socialist Republic of Vietnam, with Hanoi as capital.

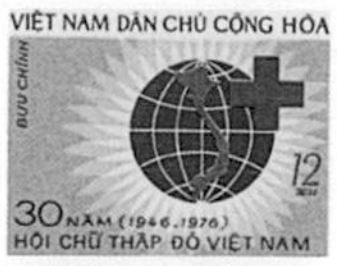

18 Red Cross and Vietnam Map on Globe

1976. 30th Anniv of Vietnamese Red Cross.

99	**18**	12x. red, blue and green	3·25	1·00

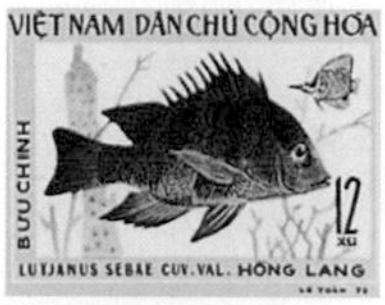

20 Emperor Snapper

1976. Marine Fish. Multicoloured.

102	12x. Type **20**	90	65
103	12x. Black-striped dottyback	90	65
104	20x. Tigerperch	1·10	70
105	30x. Two-striped anemonefish	1·40	75
106	40x. Stripe-tailed damselfish	1·50	80
107	50x. Pennant coralfish	1·80	90
108	60x. Large-mouthed anemonefish	1·90	95
109	1d. Sail-finned snapper	2·50	1·30

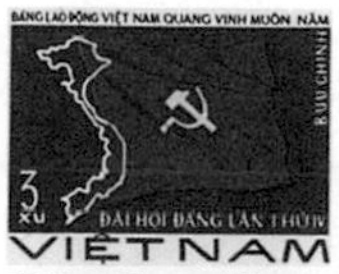

22 Party Flag and Map

1976. Fourth Congress of Vietnam Workers' Party (1st issue). Flag in yellow and red, background colours given below.

111	**22**	2x. blue	65	50
112	**22**	3x. purple	65	50
113	**22**	5x. green	65	50
114	**22**	10x. green	70	55
115	**22**	12x. green	75	65
116	**22**	20x. green	90	70

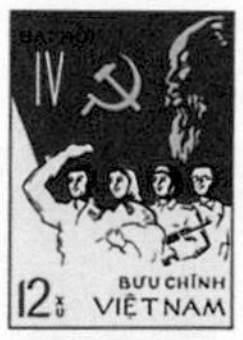

23 Workers and Flag

1976. Fourth Congress of Vietnam Workers' Party (2nd issue).

117	**23**	12x. black, red and yellow	1·30	65
118	-	12x. red, orange and black	1·30	65

DESIGN: No. 118, Industry and agriculture.

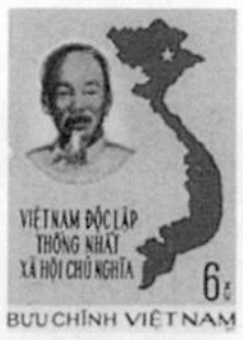

24 Ho Chi Minh and Map of Vietnam

1976. "Unification of Vietnam".

119	**24**	6x. multicoloured	1·50	70
120	**24**	12x. multicoloured	1·50	70

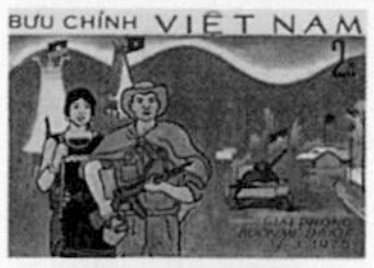

25 Soldiers seizing Buon Me Thuot

1976. Liberation of South Vietnam. Multicoloured.

121	2x. Type **25**	65	50
122	3x. Soldiers on Son Tra peninsula, Da Nang	65	50
123	6x. Soldiers attacking Presidential Palace, Saigon	65	50
124	50x. Type **25**	75	55
125	1d. As 3x.	1·30	70
126	2d. As 6x.	3·25	1·30

1976. As Nos. N848/9 but inscr "VIET NAM 1976" at foot and background colours changed.

126a	**289**	6x. yellow, green & orange	6·25	5·00
126b	**289**	12x. yellow, light green and green	6·25	5·00

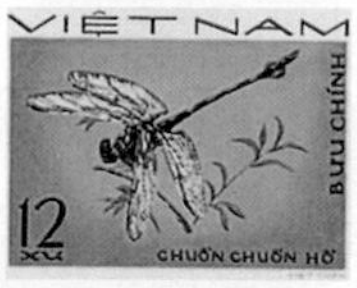

26 "Crocothemis servilia" (Ho)

1977. Dragonflies. Multicoloured.

127	12x. Type **26**	65	15
128	12x. "Ictinogomphus clavatus" (Bao)	65	15
129	20x. "Rhinocypha fenestrella"	65	15
130	30x. "Neurothemis tullia"	65	15
131	40x. "Neurobavis chinensis"	1·00	25
132	50x. "Neurothemis fulvia"	1·40	40
133	60x. "Rhyothemis variegata"	1·50	45
134	1d. "Rhyothemis fuliginosa"	2·00	65

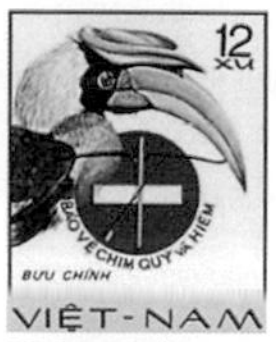

27 Great Indian Hornbill and Emblem of Protection

1977. Rare Birds. Multicoloured.

135	12x. Type **27**	65	25
136	12x. Tickell's hornbill	65	25
137	20x. Long-crested hornbill	75	30
138	30x. Wreathed hornbill	90	35
139	40x. Indian pied hornbill	1·30	40
140	50x. Black hornbill	1·50	50
141	60x. Great Indian hornbill	2·00	90
142	1d. Rufous-necked hornbill	2·40	1·10

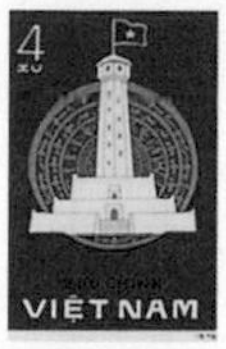

28 Thang Long Tower and Bronze Drum

1977. First Anniv of National Assembly General Election.

143	**28**	4x. multicoloured	65	50
144	-	5x. multicoloured	75	65
145	-	12x. bistre, black and green	1·30	90
146	-	50x. multicoloured	2·50	1·30

DESIGNS: 5x. Map of Vietnam and drum; 12x. Lotus flower and drum; 50x. Vietnamese flag and drum.

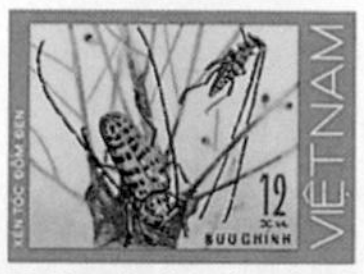

29 "Anoplophora bowringii"

1977. Beetles. Multicoloured.

147	12x. Type **29**	65	15
148	12x. "Anoplophora horsfieldi"	65	15
149	20x. "Aphrodisium griffithi"	75	20
150	30x. Musk beetle	90	25
151	40x. "Calloplophora tonkinea"	1·00	30
152	50x. "Thysia wallacei"	1·30	40
153	60x. "Aristobia approximator"	1·40	45
154	1d. "Batocera rubus"	2·30	90

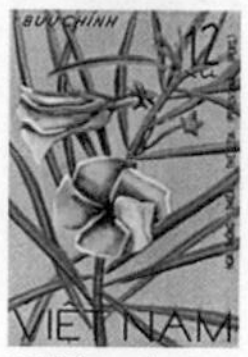

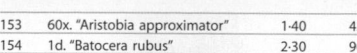

30 "Thevetia peruviana"

1977. Wild Flowers. Multicoloured.

155	12x. Type **30**	40	15
156	12x. "Broussonetia papyrifera"	40	15
157	20x. "Aleurites montana"	65	20
158	30x. "Cerbera manghes"	70	20
159	40x. "Cassia multijuga"	75	25
160	50x. "Cassia nodosa"	1·00	40
161	60x. "Hibiscus schizopetalus"	1·30	45
162	1d. "Lagerstroesnia speciosa"	1·90	90

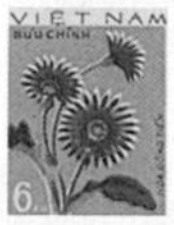

31 Pink Dahlias (Hoa Dong Tien)

1977. Cultivated Flowers (1st series). Multicoloured.

163	6x. Type **31**	1·10	25
164	6x. Orange cactus dahlias (Bong tien kep)	1·10	25
165	12x. Type **31**	1·50	40
166	12x. As No. 164	1·50	40

See also Nos. 192/5.

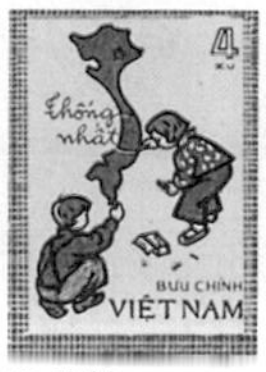

32 Children drawing Map of Vietnam

1977. Unification of Vietnam.

167	**32**	4x. multicoloured	65	40
168	**32**	5x. multicoloured	65	40
169	**32**	10x. multicoloured	1·30	65
170	**32**	12x. multicoloured	1·40	70
171	**32**	30x. multicoloured	1·90	90

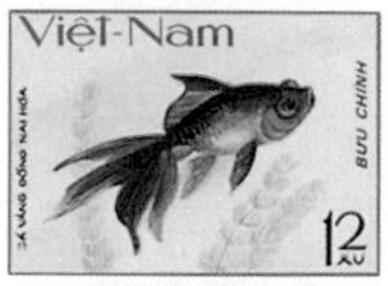

33 Goldfish (Dong Nai Hoa)

1977. Veil-tailed Goldfish. Multicoloured.

172	12x. Type **33**	50	15
173	12x. Hoa nhung	50	15
174	20x. Tau xanh	65	20
175	30x. Mat rong	75	25
176	40x. Cam trang	1·10	40
177	50x. Ngu sac	1·30	45
178	60x. Dong nai	1·50	50
179	1d. Thap cam	2·50	1·00

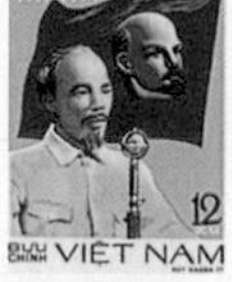

34 Ho Chi Minh and Lenin Banner

1977. 60th Anniv of Russian Revolution. Multicoloured.

180	12x. Type **34** (blue background)	65	50
181	12x. Type **34** (bistre background)	65	50
182	50x. Mother holding child with flag	90	65
183	1d. Workers, banner, Moscow Kremlin and battleship "Aurora"	1·90	1·00

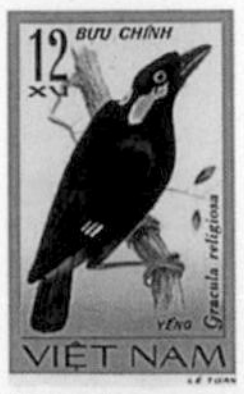
35 Southern Grackle

1978. Songbirds. Multicoloured.

184	12x. Type **35**	25	15
185	20x. Spotted-neck dove	40	20
186	20x. Melodious laughing thrush	40	20
187	30x. Black-headed shrike	65	25
188	40x. Crimson-winged laughing thrush	1·00	40
189	50x. Black-throated laughing thrush	1·30	65
190	60x. Chinese jungle mynah	1·90	90
191	1d. Yersin's laughing thrush	3·25	1·30

1978. Cultivated Flowers (2nd series). As T **31**. Multicoloured.

192	5x. Sunflower	1·30	25
193	6x. Marguerites	1·30	25
194	10x. As 5x.	1·50	45
195	12x. As 6x.	1·90	65

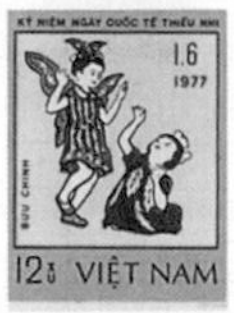
36 Vietnamese Children

1978. International Children's Day.

196	**36**	12x. multicoloured	2·50	75

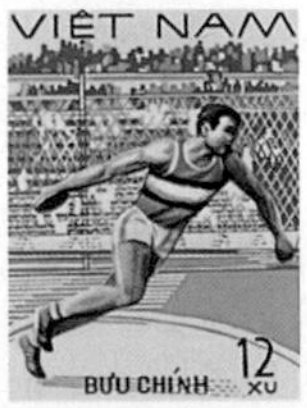
37 Throwing the Discus

1978. Athletics. Multicoloured.

197	12x. Type **37**	40	15
198	12x. Long jumping	40	15
199	20x. Hurdling	50	20
200	30x. Throwing the hammer	65	25
201	40x. Putting the shot	75	30
202	50x. Throwing the javelin	90	40
203	60x. Sprinting	1·30	65
204	1d. High jumping	1·50	90

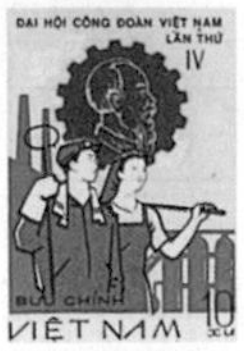
38 Ho Chi Minh and Workers

1978. Fourth Vietnamese Trade Union Congress. Multicoloured.

205	10x. Trade Union Emblem	1·50	25
206	10x. Type **38**	1·50	65

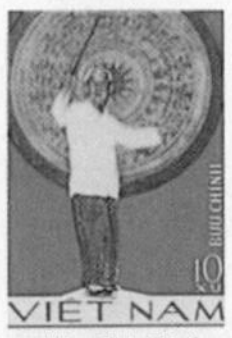
39 Ho Chi Minh

1978. 88th Birth Anniv of Ho Chi Minh. Multicoloured.

207	10x. Type **39**	1·50	65
208	12x. Ho Chi Minh Monument (38×22 mm)	1·60	75

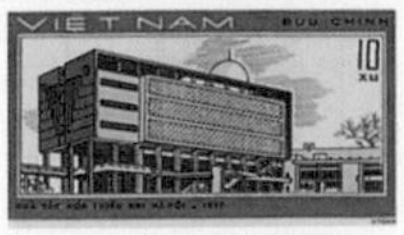
40 Young Pioneers' Cultural House, Hanoi

1978. International Children's Day.

209	**40**	10x. black, flesh and red	2·00	90

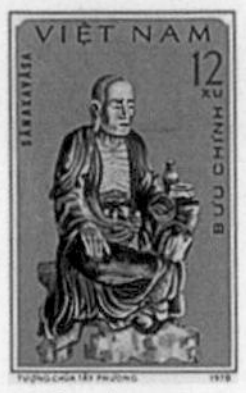
41 Sanakavasa

1978. Sculptures from Tay Phuong Pagoda. Multicoloured.

210	12x. Type **41**	65	15
211	12x. Parsva	65	15
212	12x. Punyasas	65	15
213	20x. Kumarata	75	20
214	20x. Nagarjuna	75	20
215	30x. Yayata	90	25
216	40x. Cadiep	1·10	30
217	50x. Ananda	1·30	40
218	60x. Buddhamitra	1·90	65
219	1d. Asvaghosa	3·25	90

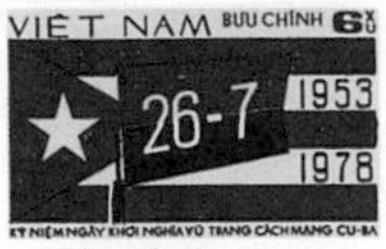
42 Cuban Flag

1978. 25th Anniv of Cuban Revolution.

220	**42**	6x. red, black and blue	1·50	65
221	**42**	12x. red, black and blue	1·60	75

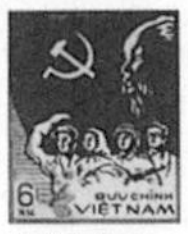
43 Worker, Peasant, Soldier and Intellectual

1978. 33rd Anniv of Proclamation of Vietnam Democratic Republic.

222	**43**	6x. red, yellow and mauve	1·00	65
223	-	6x. turquoise, green & blue	1·00	65
224	**43**	12x. red, yellow and mauve	1·50	1·30
225	-	12x. red and pink	1·50	1·30

DESIGN: Nos. 223 and 225, Industrial complex and tractor on field.

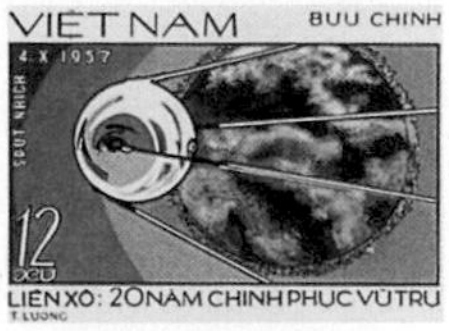
44 "Sputnik"

1978. 20 Years of Russian Space Exploration. Multicoloured.

226	12x. Type **44**	50	15
227	12x. "Venus 1"	50	15
228	30x. Space capsules docking	65	20
229	40x. "Molniya 1" satellite	1·00	25
230	60x. "Soyuz"	1·30	40
231	2d. A. Gubarev and G. Grechko	2·50	1·30

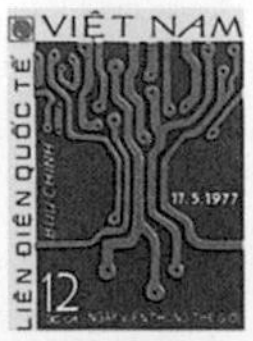
45 Printed Circuit

1978. World Telecommunications Day.

232	**45**	12x. orange and brown	1·50	65
233	-	12x. brown and orange	1·50	65

DESIGN: No. 233, I.T.U. emblem.

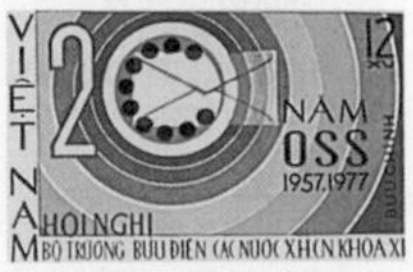
46 Telephone Dial and Letter

1978. 20th Congress of Socialist Countries' Postal Ministers.

234	**46**	12x. multicoloured	1·90	65

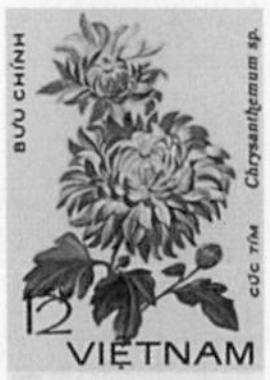
47 Chrysanthemum "Cuc Tim"

1978. Chrysanthemums. Multicoloured.

235	12x. Type **47**	65	15
236	12x. "Cuc kim tien"	65	15
237	20x. "Cuc hong"	75	20
238	30x. "Cuc van tho"	90	25
239	40x. "Cuc vang"	1·00	30
240	50x. "Cuc thuy tim"	1·10	40
241	60x. "Cuc vang mo"	1·30	45
242	1d. "Cuc nau do"	2·00	75

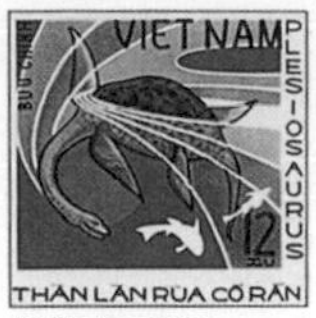
48 Plesiosaurus

1979. Prehistoric Animals. Multicoloured.

243	12x. Type **48**	75	15
244	12x. Brontosaurus	75	15
245	20x. Iguanodon	1·00	20
246	30x. Tyrannosaurus	1·30	25
247	40x. Stegosaurus	1·50	30
248	50x. Mozasaurus	1·90	40
249	60x. Triceratop	2·30	50
250	1d. Pteranodon	3·25	90

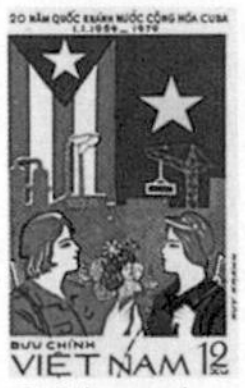
49 Cuban and Vietnamese Flags and Militiawomen

1979. 20th Anniv of Socialist Republic of Cuba.

251	**49**	12x. multicoloured	1·90	65

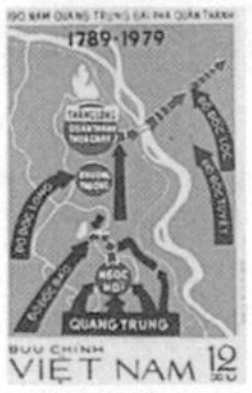
50 Battle Plan

1979. 190th Anniv of Quang Trung's Victory over the Thanh.

252	**50**	12x. green, red and blue	1·50	65
253	-	12x. multicoloured	1·50	65

DESIGN: No. 253, Quang Trung.

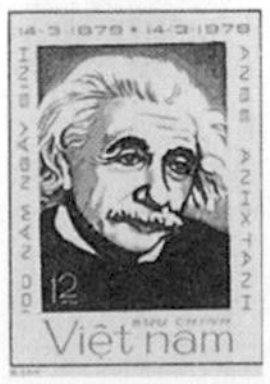
51 Einstein

1979. Birth Cent of Albert Einstein (physicist).

254	**51**	12x. black, brown and blue	1·90	65
255	-	60x. multicoloured	3·25	1·00

DESIGN: 60x. Equation, sun and planets.

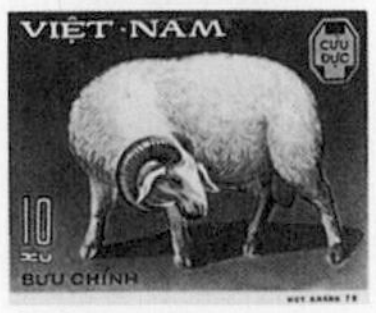
52 Ram

1979. Domestic Animals. Multicoloured.

256	10x. Type **52**	50	15
257	12x. Ox	50	15
258	20x. Ewe and lamb	65	20
259	30x. White buffalo (vert)	70	20
260	40x. Cow	75	25
261	50x. Goat	1·30	40
262	60x. Buffalo and calf	1·40	45
263	1d. Young goat (vert)	1·50	65

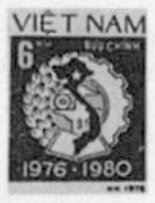
53 Emblem

1979. Five Year Plan.

264	**53**	6x. mauve and light mauve	1·00	50
265	-	6x. green and buff	1·00	50
266	-	6x. green and purple	1·00	50
267	-	6x. orange and green	1·00	50
268	-	6x. blue and yellow	1·00	50
269	**53**	12x. red and pink	1·30	65
270	-	12x. brown and pink	1·30	65
271	-	12x. green and yellow	1·30	65
272	-	12x. blue and brown	1·30	65
273	-	12x. purple and blue	1·30	65

DESIGNS: Nos. 265, 270, Worker; 266, 271, Peasant and tractor; 267, 272, Soldier; 268, 273, Intellectual.

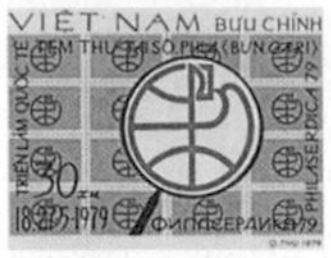
54 "Philaserdica '79" Emblem

1979. "Philaserdica '79" International Stamp Exhibition, Sofia, Bulgaria.

274	**54**	12x. blue, brown & orange	1·50	65
275	**54**	30x. blue, brown and pink	1·60	75

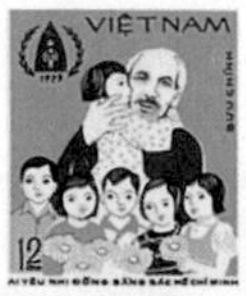
55 Ho Chi Minh and Children

1979. International Children's Day. Multicoloured.

276	12x. Type **55**	65	50
277	20x. Nurse, mother and child	1·00	65
278	50x. Children with painting materials and model glider	1·50	75
279	1d. Children of different races	2·50	1·00

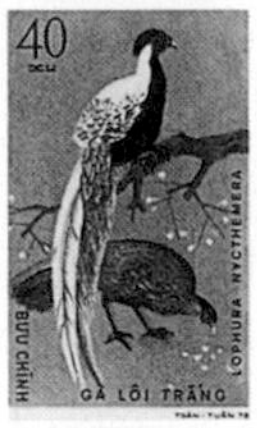
56 Silver Pheasant

1979. Ornamental Birds. Multicoloured.

280	12x. Siamese fireback pheasant ("Lophura diardi") (horiz)	65	25
281	12x. Temminck's tragopan ("Tragopan temminckii") (horiz)	65	25
282	20x. Common pheasant (horiz)	70	30
283	30x. Edwards's pheasant (horiz)	75	35
284	40x. Type **56**	80	40
285	50x. Germain's peacock-pheasant	1·30	45
286	60x. Great argus pheasant	1·40	50
287	1d. Green peafowl	2·50	1·00

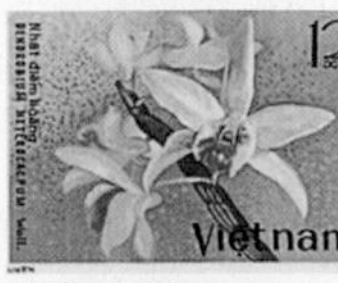
57 "Dendrobium heterocacpum"

1979. Orchids. Multicoloured.

288	12x. Type **57**	65	25
289	12x. "Cymbidium hybridum"	65	25
290	20x. "Rhynchostylis gigantea"	70	30
291	30x. "Dendrobium nobile"	75	35
292	40x. "Aerides falcatum"	80	40
293	50x. "Paphiopedilum callosum"	1·30	45
294	60x. "Vanda teres"	1·40	50
295	1d. "Dendrobium phalaenopsis"	2·50	1·00

58 Cat (Meo Muop)

1979. Cats. Multicoloured.

296		12x. Type **58**	65	50
297		12x. Meo Tam The (horiz)	65	50
298		20x. Meo Khoang	70	55
299		30x. Meo Dom Van (horiz)	75	65
300		40x. Meo Muop Dom	80	70
301		50x. Meo Vang	1·00	75
302		60x. Meo Xiem (horiz)	1·50	1·00
303		1d. Meo Van Am (horiz)	2·30	1·30

60 Citizens greeting Soldiers

1979. 35th Anniv of Vietnam People's Army.

306	**60**	12x. brown and green	75	65
307	-	12x. brown and green	75	65

DESIGN: No. 307, Soldiers in action.

62 Red and Pink Roses

1980. Roses. Multicoloured.

311		1x. Type **62**	1·30	65
312		2x. Single pink rose	1·30	65
313		12x. Type **62**	1·60	75
314		12x. As No. 312	1·60	75

63 "Nelumbium nuciferum"

1980. Water Flowers. Multicoloured.

315		12x. Type **63**	65	15
316		12x. "Nymphala stellata"	65	15
317		20x. "Ipomola reptans"	75	20
318		30x. "Nymphoides indicum"	80	25
319		40x. "Jussiala repens"	90	30
320		50x. "Eichhornia crassipes"	1·40	45
321		60x. "Monochoria voginalis"	1·50	50
322		1d. "Nelumbo nucifera"	2·50	90

64 Peasants with Banner and Implements as Weapons

1980. 50th Anniv of Vietnamese Communist Party. Multicoloured.

323		12x. Type **64**	65	50
324		12x. Ho Chi Minh proclaiming independence	65	50
325		20x. Soldiers with flag at Dien Bien Phu	75	65
326		20x. Map of Vietnam and soldiers and tanks storming Palace (Unification of Vietnam)	75	65
327		2d. Ho Chi Minh, soldier and workers and industrial and agricultural scene	3·25	1·30

65 Lenin

1980. 110th Birth Anniv of Lenin.

328	**65**	6x. flesh and green	75	65
329	**65**	12x. flesh and purple	90	65
330	**65**	1d. flesh and blue	2·10	1·90

66 Running

1980. Olympic Games, Moscow. Multicoloured.

331		12x. Type **66**	65	15
332		12x. Hurdles	65	15
333		20x. Basketball	75	20
334		30x. Football	80	25
335		40x. Wrestling	90	30
336		50x. Gymnastics (horiz)	1·30	40
337		60x. Swimming (horiz)	1·40	45
338		1d. Sailing (horiz)	2·50	90

67 Ho Chi Minh in 1924

1980. President Ho Chi Minh's 90th Birthday.

339		12x. Type **67**	75	65
340		40x. Ho Chi Minh as President	1·80	1·30

68 Children dancing around Globe

1980. International Children's Day.

341	**68**	5x. multicoloured	1·50	65

69 Soviet and Vietnamese Cosmonauts

1980. Soviet–Vietnamese Space Flight. Multicoloured.

342		12x. Type **69**	65	15
343		12x. Launch of rocket	65	15
344		20x. "Soyuz 37"	75	20
345		40x. "Soyuz–Salyut" space complex	1·30	25
346		1d. "Soyuz" re-entering Earth's atmosphere	2·50	50
347		2d. Parachute landing	5·25	1·30
MS348	111×91 mm. 3d. Cosmonauts and "Soyuz—Salyut"		7·50	7·50

70 Whale Shark

1980. Marine Fauna. Multicoloured.

349		12x. Type **70**	50	25
350		12x. Tiger shark	50	25
351		20x. Bearded shark	65	30
352		30x. Zebra horn shark	70	40
353		40x. Coachwhip stingray	75	45
354		50x. Wide sawfish	90	50
355		60x. Scalloped hammerhead	1·30	65
356		1d. Tobij-ei eagle ray	2·50	1·00

71 Ho Chi Minh telephoning

1980. Posts and Telecommunications Day. Multicoloured.

357		12x. Ho Chi Minh reading newspaper "Nhan Dan"	75	45
358		12x. Type **71**	90	50
359		50x. Kim Dong, "the heroic postman", carrying magpie robin in cage	1·30	65
360		1d. Dish aerial	2·50	90

72 Pink Rose (Hong Bach)

1980. Flowers.

361	**72**	12x. pink and green	1·30	65
362	-	12x. red and green	1·30	65
363	-	12x. mauve and green	1·30	65

DESIGNS—As Type **72**: No. 362, Red roses (Hong nhung). 15×20 mm: No. 363, Camellia.

73 Telephone Switchboard Operator

1980. National Telecommunications Day.

364		12x. Type **73**	1·50	70
365		12x. Diesel train and railway route map	1·50	70

74 Ho Chi Minh

1980. 35th Anniv of Democratic Republic of Vietnam. Multicoloured.

366		12x. Type **74**	65	50
367		12x. Arms of Vietnam (29×40 mm)	65	50
368		40x. Pac Bo cave (29×40 mm)	1·30	65
369		1d. Source of Lenine (40×29 mm)	3·25	1·30

75 Vietnamese Arms

1980. National Emblems.

370	**75**	6x. multicoloured	1·90	65
371	-	12x. yellow, red and black	1·90	65
372	-	12x. black, orange & yellow	1·90	65

DESIGNS—VERT: No. 372, National Anthem. HORIZ: No. 371, National flag.

76 Nguyen Trai

1980. 600th Birth Anniv of Nguyen Trai (national hero).

373	**76**	12x. yellow and black	65	50
374	-	50x. black and blue	2·50	75
375	-	1d. black and brown	3·75	1·30

DESIGNS—HORIZ: 50x. Three books by Nguyen Trai. VERT: 1d. Ho Chi Minh reading commem- orative stele in Con Son Pagoda.

77 Ho Chi Minh with Women

1980. 50th Anniv of Vietnamese Women's Union.

376	**77**	12x. green, blue and lilac	1·00	65
377	-	12x. blue and lilac	1·00	65

DESIGN: No. 377, Group of women.

78 "Biguoniaceae venusta"

1980. Flowers. Multicoloured.

378		12x. Type **78**	65	15
379		12x. "Ipomoea pulchella"	65	15
380		20x. "Petunia hybrida"	75	20
381		30x. "Trapaeolum majus"	80	25
382		40x. "Thunbergia grandiflora"	90	30
383		50x. "Anlamanda cathartica"	1·30	40
384		60x. "Campsis radicans"	1·40	45
385		1d. "Bougainvillaea spectabilis"	2·50	75

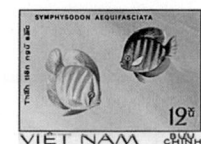

79 Blue Discus

1981. Ornamental Fish. Multicoloured.

386		12x. Type **79**	65	50
387		12x. Siamese fighting fish	65	50
388		20x. Platy	75	65
389		30x. Guppy	80	70
390		40x. Tiger barb	90	75
391		50x. Freshwater angelfish	1·30	80
392		60x. Swordtail	1·40	90
393		1d. Pearl gourami	2·50	1·30

80 Rocket, Flowers and Flag

1981. 26th U.S.S.R. Communist Party Congress. Multicoloured.

394		20x. Type **80**	65	50
395		50x. Young citizens with flag	2·50	1·10

81 Bear Macaque

1981. Animals of Cue Phuong Forest. Multicoloured.

396		12x. Type **81**	65	25
397		12x. Crested gibbons	65	25
398		20x. Asiatic black bears	75	30
399		30x. Dhole	90	40
400		40x. Wild boar	1·30	45
401		50x. Sambars	1·40	50
402		60x. Leopard	1·50	55
403		1d. Tiger	2·50	90

82 Green Imperial Pigeon

1981. Turtle Doves. Multicoloured.
404		12x. Type **82**	65	50
405		12x. Japanese green pigeon (horiz)	65	50
406		20x. Red-collared dove	70	55
407		30x. Bar-tailed cuckoo dove	75	65
408		40x. Mountain imperial pigeon	80	70
409		50x. Pin-tailed green pigeon (horiz)	90	75
410		60x. Emerald dove (horiz)	1·40	1·00
411		1d. Yellow-vented pin-tailed green pigeon (horiz)	2·50	1·30

83 Yellow-backed Sunbird

1981. Nectar-sucking Birds. Multicoloured.
412		20x. Type **83**	50	25
413		20x. Ruby-cheeked sunbird	50	25
414		30x. Black-throated sunbird	55	30
415		40x. Mrs. Gould's sunbird	65	40
416		50x. Macklot's sunbird	1·00	45
417		50x. Blue-naped sunbird	1·10	50
418		60x. Van Hasselt's sunbird	1·40	65
419		1d. Green-tailed sunbird	2·10	90

85 "Elaeagnus latifolia"

1981. Fruit. Multicoloured.
422		20x. Type **85**	50	15
423		20x. "Fortunella japonica"	50	15
424		30x. "Nephelium lappaceum"	65	20
425		40x. "Averrhoa bilimbi"	70	25
426		50x. "Ziziphus mauritiana"	90	30
427		50x. Strawberries ("Fragaria vesca")	90	30
428		60x. "Bouea oppositifolia"	1·00	40
429		1d. "Syzygium aqueum"	1·90	90

86 Girl with Rice Sheaf

1981. World Food Day.
430	**86**	30x. green	75	50
431	**86**	50x. green	1·00	65
432	-	2d. orange	3·25	1·30
DESIGN: 2d. F.A.O. emblem and rice.

87 Ho Chi Minh planting Tree

1981. Tree Planting Festival.
433	**87**	30x. orange and blue	1·30	40
434	-	30x. pink and blue	1·30	40
DESIGN: No. 434, Family planting tree.

88 European Bison

1981. Animals. Multicoloured.
435		30x. Type **88**	65	15
436		30x. Orang-utan	65	15
437		40x. Hippopotamus	75	25
438		40x. Red kangaroo	75	25
439		50x. Giraffe	1·00	40
440		50x. Javan rhinoceros	1·00	40
441		60x. Common zebra	1·30	50
442		1d. Lion	1·50	75

89 Congress Emblem

1982. Tenth World Trade Unions Congress, Havana, Cuba.
443	**89**	50x. multicoloured	1·30	65
444	**89**	5d. multicoloured	5·00	2·50

90 Ho Chi Minh and Party Flag

1982. Fifth Vietnamese Communist Party Congress (1st issue). Multicoloured.
445		30x. Type **90**	1·30	65
446		30x. Hammer, sickle and rose	1·30	65
See also Nos. 455/6.

91 "Thyreus decorus" (carpenter bee)

1982. Bees and Wasps. Multicoloured.
447		20x. Type **91**	50	15
448		20x. "Vespa affinis" (wasp)	50	15
449		30x. "Eumenes esuriens" (mason wasp)	65	20
450		40x. "Polistes sp." (wasp)	75	25
451		50x. "Sphex sp." (wasp)	1·00	40
452		50x. "Chlorion lobatum" (wasp)	1·00	40
453		60x. "Xylocopa sp." (carpenter bee)	1·40	65
454		1d. Honey bee	1·50	75

92 Electricity Worker and Pylon

1982. Fifth Vietnamese Communist Party Congress (2nd issue).
455	**92**	30x. stone, black and mauve	1·30	65
456	-	50x. multicoloured	1·90	90
DESIGN: 50x. Women harvesting rice.

93 Football

1982. Football Training Movement.
457	**93**	30x. multicoloured	50	15
458	-	30x. multicoloured (Two players)	50	15
459	-	40x. multicoloured	65	20
460	-	40x. multicoloured (diag striped background)	65	20
461	-	50x. multicoloured (vert striped background)	90	25
462	-	50x. multicoloured (horiz striped background)	90	25

463	-	60x. multicoloured	1·00	40
464	-	1d. multicoloured	1·90	65
DESIGNS: Nos. 458/64, Various football scenes.

94 Militiawoman

1982
465	**94**	30x. multicoloured	1·90	1·30
See also Nos. MF466/7.

95 Arms of Bulgaria

1982. 1300th Anniv of Bulgarian State.
468	**95**	30x. pink and red	75	50
469	**95**	50x. stone and red	1·50	90
470	**95**	2d. orange and red	4·00	1·60

96 Map of Vietnam and Red Cross

1982. 35th Anniv of Vietnamese Red Cross.
471	**96**	30x. red, blue and black	90	65
472	-	1d. red, green and black	3·25	1·30
DESIGN: 1d. Red Cross.

97 Georgi Dimitrov

1982. Birth Centenary of Georgi Dimitrov (Bulgarian statesman).
473	**97**	30x. orange and black	65	50
474	**97**	3d. brown and black	5·00	2·50

98 Rejoicing Women

1982. Fifth National Women's Congress. Multicoloured.
475	**98**	12x. Type **98**	1·30	65
476		12x. Congress emblem and three women	1·30	65

99 Common Kestrel

1982. Birds of Prey. Multicoloured.
477		30x. Type **99**	65	15
478		30x. Pied falconet	65	15
479		40x. Black baza	75	20
480		50x. Black kite	1·00	25
481		50x. Lesser fishing eagle	1·00	25
482		60x. White-rumped pygmy falcon (horiz)	1·30	40
483		1d. Black-shouldered kite (horiz)	2·50	90
484		1d. Short-toed eagle	2·50	90

100 Red Dahlia

1982. Dahlias. Multicoloured.
485		30x. Type **100**	65	15
486		30x. Orange dahlia	65	15
487		40x. Rose dahlia	75	20
488		50x. Red decorative dahlia	1·00	25
489		50x. Yellow dahlia	1·00	25
490		60x. Red single dahlia	1·30	40
491		1d. White dahlia	2·10	90
492		1d. Pink dahlia	2·10	90

101 Dribble

1982. World Cup Football Championship, Spain. Multicoloured.
493		50x. Type **101**	1·00	50
494		50x. Tackle	1·00	50
495		50x. Passing ball	1·00	50
496		1d. Heading ball	1·50	65
497		1d. Goalkeeper saving ball	1·50	65
498		2d. Shooting	4·00	1·60

102 Cuban Flag

1982. 20th Anniv of Cuban Victory at Giron.
499	**102**	30x. multicoloured	1·90	65

103 Ho Chi Minh and Children planting Tree

1982. World Environment Day.
500	**103**	30x. green and black	1·50	65
501	-	30x. green and black	1·50	65
DESIGN: No. 501, U.N. environment emblem and plants.

104 Rabindranath Tagore

1982. 120th Birth Anniv (1981) of Rabindranath Tagore (Indian poet).
502	**104**	30x. orange, brown and black	2·30	75

105 "Sycanus falleni" (soldier bug)

1982. Harmful Insects. Multicoloured.
503		30x. Type **105**	50	15
504		30x. "Catacanthus incarnatus" (shieldbug)	50	15

505	40x. "Nezara viridula" (shield-bug)	65	20
506	50x. "Helcomeria spinosa" (squashbug)	90	25
507	50c. "Lohita grandis" (fire bug)	90	25
508	60x. "Chrysocoris stolli" (shieldbug)	1·00	40
509	1d. "Tiarodes ostentans" (soldier bug)	2·30	1·00
510	1d. "Pterygamia grayi" (squashbug)	2·30	1·00

106 Lenin and Cruiser "Aurora"

1982. 65th Anniv of Russian Revolution.
| 511 | **106** | 30x. red and black | 1·30 | 65 |
| 512 | - | 30x. red and black | 1·30 | 65 |

DESIGN: No. 512, Russian man and woman, Lenin and space station.

108 Swimming

1982. Ninth South East Asian Games, New Delhi.
514	**108**	30x. blue and lilac	1·30	65
515	-	30x. blue and mauve	1·30	65
516	-	1d. orange and blue	1·90	90
517	-	2d. green and brown	2·50	1·10

DESIGNS: 30x. (No. 515) Table tennis; 1d. Wrestling; 2d. Rifle shooting.

109 Gray's Crested Flounder

1982. Fish. Soles. Multicoloured.
518	30x. Type **109**	65	15
519	30x. Chinese flounder	65	15
520	40x. Queensland halibut ("Psettodes erumei")	75	20
521	40x. Zebra sole ("Zebrias zebra")	75	20
522	50x. Peacock sole ("Pardachirus pavoninus")	1·00	25
523	50x. Spotted tonguesole ("Cynoglossus puncticeps")	1·00	25
524	60x. Oriental sole	1·30	50
525	1d. Iijima lefteye flounder	1·50	75

110 Foundry and Textile Workers

1982. "All for the Socialist Fatherland, All for Happiness of the People".
526	**110**	30x. light blue and blue	1·00	65
527	-	30x. brown and yellow	1·00	65
528	-	1d. brown and green	1·90	1·00
529	-	2d. pink and purple	3·75	1·50

DESIGNS: 30x. Women holding sheaf of wheat and basket of grain; 1d. Soldiers; 2d. Nurse with children holding books.

111 Lenin on Map

1982. 60th Anniv of U.S.S.R.
| 530 | **111** | 30x. multicoloured | 3·75 | 1·00 |

112 Sampan

1983. Boats. Multicoloured.
531	30x. Type **112**	65	15
532	50x. Junk with striped sails	75	20
533	1d. Houseboats	90	25
534	3d. Junk	1·50	40
535	5d. Sampan with patched sails	2·50	65
536	10d. Sampan (horiz)	3·75	1·60

113 Type 231-300

1983. Steam Railway Locomotives. Multicoloured.
537	30x. Type **113**	40	15
538	50x. Type 230-000	65	25
539	1d. Type 140-601	75	30
540	2d. Type 241-000	1·30	50
541	3d. Type 141-500	1·90	65
542	5d. Type 150-000	2·50	90
543	8d. Type 40-300	3·25	1·40

114 Montgolfier Balloon, 1783

1983. Bicentenary of Manned Flight. Multicoloured.
544	30x. Type **114**	40	15
545	50x. Charles's hydrogen balloon, 1783	65	20
546	1d. Parseval Sigsfeld kite-type observation balloon, 1898	90	25
547	2d. Eugene Godard's balloon "L'Aigle", 1864	1·60	40
548	3d. Blanchard and Jeffries' balloon, 1785	2·00	50
549	5d. Nadar's balloon "Le Geant", 1863	2·75	75
550	8d. Balloon	4·25	1·40
MS551	70×80 mm. 10d. Montgolfier balloon (different) (31×31 mm)	7·50	2·50

115 Flags and Dove

1983. Laos–Kampuchea–Vietnam Summit Conf.
| 552 | **115** | 50x. red, yellow and blue | 65 | 50 |
| 553 | **115** | 5d. red, blue and yellow | 3·75 | 1·30 |

116 Robert Koch

1983. Centenary of Discovery of Tubercle Bacillus.
| 554 | **116** | 5d. black, blue and red | 3·75 | 1·30 |

117 "Teratolepis fasciata"

1983. Reptiles. Multicoloured.
555	30x. Type **117**	65	40
556	30x. Jackson's chameleon	65	40
557	50x. Spiny-tailed agamid	75	50

558	80x. "Heloderma suspectum"	90	65
559	1d. "Chamaeleo meileri"	1·00	75
560	2d. "Amphibolurus barbatus"	1·90	1·00
561	5d. "Chlamydosaurus kingi"	2·50	1·10
562	10d. "Phrynosoma coronatum"	4·50	1·60

118 A. Gubarev and V. Remek

1983. Cosmonauts. Multicoloured.
563	30x. Type **118**	40	15
564	50x. P. Klimuk and Miroslaw Hermaszewski	50	20
565	50x. V. Bykovsky and Sigmund Jahn	50	20
566	1d. Nikolai Rukavishnikov and Georgi Ivanov	65	25
567	1d. Bertalan Farkas and V. Kubasov	65	25
568	2d. V. Gorbatko and Pham Tuan	1·30	40
569	2d. Arnaldo Tamayo Mendez and I. Romanenko	1·30	40
570	5d. V. Dzhanibekov and Gur-ragcha	2·50	65
571	8d. L. Popov and D. Prunariu	3·25	1·00
MS572	80×80 mm. 10d. Yuri Gagarin (first man in space) (36×28 mm)	6·25	2·50

119 "Madonna of the Chair"

1983. 500th Birth Anniv of Raphael (artist). Multicoloured.
573	30x. Type **119**	40	15
574	50x. "Madonna of the Grand Duke"	65	20
575	1d. "Sistine Madonna"	90	25
576	2d. "The Marriage of Mary"	1·30	40
577	3d. "The Beautiful Gardener"	1·90	50
578	5d. "Woman with Veil"	2·50	75
579	8d. "Self-portrait"	3·25	1·10
MS580	93×71 mm. 10d. Close-up of "Self-portrait"	8·25	2·50

121 Burmese King and Rook

1983. Chess Pieces. Multicoloured.
582	30x. Type **121**	40	15
583	50x. 18th-century Delhi king (elephant)	50	20
584	1d. Lewis knight and bishop	75	25
585	2d. 8th/9th-century Arabian king (elephant)	1·30	40
586	3d. 12th-century European knight	1·90	50
587	5d. 16th-century Russian rook (sailing boat)	2·50	75
588	8d. European Chinese-puzzle bishop and rook (fool and elephant)	3·25	1·10
MS589	77×79 mm. 10d. Abstract king and queen (28×36 mm)	10·00	3·00

122 Coach and Horse

1983. "Tembal '83" International Stamp Exhibition, Basel. Sheet 90×70 mm.
| MS590 | 10d. multicoloured | 7·50 | 2·50 |

123 Long Jumping

1983. Olympic Games, Los Angeles (1984). Multicoloured.
591	30x. Type **123**	40	15
592	50x. Running	50	20
593	1d. Javelin throwing	65	25
594	2d. High jumping (horiz)	1·30	40
595	5d. Hurdling (horiz)	1·90	50
596	5d. Putting the shot	2·50	75
597	8d. Pole vaulting	3·25	1·10
MS598	82×71 mm. 10d. Throwing the discus (31×39 mm)	8·75	6·25

124 Toco Toucan

1983. "Brasiliana '83" International Stamp Exhibition, Rio de Janeiro. Sheet 69×95 mm.
| MS599 | 10d. multicoloured | 23·00 | 3·75 |

125 Common Grass Yellow

1983. Butterflies. Multicoloured.
600	30x. Type **125**	75	50
601	30x. Green dragontail ("Leptocircus meges")	75	50
602	40x. "Nyctalemon patroclus"	1·00	65
603	40x. Tailed jay ("Zetides agamemnon")	1·00	65
604	50x. Peacock ("Precis almana")	1·30	75
605	50x. "Papilio chaon"	1·30	75
606	60x. Tufted jungle king	1·50	90
607	1d. Leaf buttefly	2·50	1·50

127 Steam Car

1983. "Bangkok 1983" International Stamp Exhibition. Sheet 102×67 mm.
| MS616 | 10d. multicoloured | 15·00 | 4·50 |

128 Karl Marx

1983. Death Centenary of Karl Marx.
| 617 | **128** | 50x. black and red | 1·90 | 65 |
| 618 | **128** | 10d. black and purple | 5·00 | 1·30 |

129 Postman

1983. World Communications Year. Multicoloured.
619	50x. Type **129**	40	25
620	2d. Mail sorting office	1·30	65
621	8d. Telephonists	2·75	90
622	10d. Wireless operator and dish aerial	3·75	1·30
MS623	77×64 mm. 10d. Telephone, air mail envelope, dish aerial, truck and boat	6·25	2·50

130 Running, Stadium and Sports Pictograms

1983. National Youth Sports Festival.
624	**130**	30x. blue and turquoise	65	50
625	**130**	1d. brown and orange	2·50	90

131 Oyster Fungus ("Pleurotus ostreatus")

1983. Fungi. Multicoloured.
626	**50x.** Type **131**		65	50
627	50x. Common ink cap ("Coprinus atramentarius")		65	50
628	50x. Golden mushroom ("Flammulina velutipes")		65	50
629	50x. Chanterelle ("Cantharellus cibarius")		65	50
630	1d. Chinese mushroom		1·30	65
631	2d. Red-staining mushroom		1·90	75
632	5d. Common morel		3·75	1·10
633	10d. Caesar's mushroom		6·25	1·60

132 Child with Fish

1983. World Food Day. Multicoloured.
634	50x. Type **132**		65	50
635	4d. Family		2·50	1·10

133 Envelope with I.T.U. Emblem

1983. World Telecommunications Year.
636	**133**	50x.+10x. blue, green & red	2·00	75
637	-	50x.+10x. red, buff and brown	2·00	75

DESIGN: No. 637, W.C.Y. emblem and dish aerial.

134 Building Dam

1983. Fifth Anniv of U.S.S.R.–Vietnam Co-operation Treaty.
638		20x. green and yellow	3·25	1·90
639		50x. chestnut and brown	4·50	2·50
640	**134**	4d. grey and black	15·00	3·25
641	**134**	20d. pink and brown	46·00	6·25

DESIGNS: 20x. Building Cultural Palace; 50x. Building road/rail bridge.

135 Girl with Flowers

1983. Fifth Trade Unions Congress.
642	**135**	50x. blue, orange and black	65	50
643	-	2d. black, blue and brown	1·30	65
644	-	30d. black, blue and pink	7·50	1·30

DESIGNS: 2, 30d. Worker and industrial complex.

136 Grey Herons

1983. Birds. Multicoloured.
645	50x. Type **136**	65	50
646	50x. Painted storks ("Ibis leucocephalus")	65	50
647	50x. Black storks ("Ciconia nigra")	65	50
648	50x. Purple herons ("Ardea purpurea")	65	50
649	1d. Common cranes	90	65
650	2d. Black-faced spoonbills	1·30	75
651	5d. Black-crowned night herons	3·25	1·30
652	10d. Asian open-bill storks	4·50	1·60

137 Conference Emblem and Hands

1983. World Peace Conference, Prague.
653	-	50x. blue, red and yellow	25	15
654	**137**	3d. green, red and yellow	1·90	65
655	**137**	5d. lilac, red and yellow	3·75	1·30
656	**137**	20d. blue, red and yellow	7·50	1·90

DESIGN: 50x. Conference emblem and women.

138 Biathlon

1984. Winter Olympic Games, Sarajevo. Multicoloured.
657	50x. Type **138**	25	15
658	50x. Cross-country skiing	65	15
659	1d. Speed skating	75	25
660	2d. Bobsleighing	1·30	40
661	3d. Ice hockey (horiz)	1·90	65
662	5d. Ski jumping (horiz)	2·50	1·10
663	6d. Slalom (horiz)	3·25	1·30
MS664	72×88 mm. 10d. Ice skating (39×31 mm)	6·25	2·50

139 Marbled Cat

1984. Protected Animals. Multicoloured.
665	50x. Type **139**	65	15
666	50x. Leopard	65	15
667	50x. Tiger	65	15
668	1d. Common gibbon	1·30	25
669	1d. Slow loris	1·30	25
670	2d. Indian elephant	2·50	65
671	2d. Gaur	2·50	65

140 Orchid Tree

1984. Flowers. Multicoloured.
672	50x. Type **140**	65	15
673	50x. "Caesalpinia pulcherrima"	65	15
674	1d. Golden shower	90	20
675	2d. Flamboyant	1·30	25
676	3d. "Artabotrys uncinatus"	1·90	75
677	5d. "Corchorus olitorius"	2·50	1·10

678	8d. "Bauhinia grandiflora"	3·25	1·50
MS679	70×106 mm. 10d. As No. 675 but with inscriptions rearranged	6·25	2·50

141 "Brasse cattleya"

1984. Orchids. Multicoloured.
680	50x. Type **141**	40	15
681	50x. "Cymbidium sp."	40	15
682	1d. "Cattleya dianx" var. "alba"	65	20
683	2d. "Cymbidium sp." (different)	1·30	40
684	3d. "Cymbidium hybridum"	1·80	50
685	5d. Phoenix-winged orchids	2·50	75
686	8d. Yellow queen orchids	3·25	1·10

1984. Nos. 362 and 373 surch **50xu.**
687	-	50x. on 12x. red and green	2·50	1·90
688	**76**	50x. on 12x. yellow and black	2·50	1·90

143 Flyingfish

1984. Deep Sea Fish. Multicoloured.
688a	30x. Type **143**	40	25
688b	30x. Long-horned cowfish	40	25
688c	50x. Porcupinefish	65	50
688d	80x. Copper-banded butterflyfish	75	65
688e	1d. Bearded anglerfish	80	70
688f	2d. Plane-tailed lionfish	1·30	90
688g	5d. Oceanic sunfish	2·50	1·10
688h	10d. Lionfish	3·75	1·60

144 White Storks

1984. "Espana 84" International Stamp Exhibition, Madrid. Sheet 81×80 mm.
MS689	10d. multicoloured	12·50	4·50

146 Ho Chi Minh discussing Battle Plan

1984. 30th Anniv of Battle of Dien Bien Phu. Multicoloured.
691	50x. Type **146**	50	15
692	50x. Vietnamese soldiers and truck	50	15
693	1d. Students carrying provisions	75	20
694	2d. Pulling field gun up hill	1·00	40
695	3d. Anti-aircraft gun and crashed airplane	1·30	50
696	5d. Fighting against tanks	2·00	75
697	8d. Vietnamese soldiers with flag on bunker	2·75	1·30
MS698	99×110 mm. 10d. Type **146** (36×26 mm)	6·25	3·25

147 Junkers Ju 52/3m

1984. Universal Postal Union, Congress, Hamburg and 50th Anniv of First South Atlantic Air Service. Sheet 68×60 mm.
MS699	10d. multicoloured	7·00	3·75

148 Three-spotted Gourami

1984. Fish. Multicoloured.
700	50x. Type **148**	30	15
701	50x. Zebra danio	30	15
702	1d. Paradise fish	65	25
703	2d. Black widow tetra	1·00	50
704	3d. Serpa tetra	1·30	75
705	5d. Red-tailed black shark	1·90	1·30
706	8d. Siamese fightingfish	3·25	2·10

149 Nguyen Duc Canh

1984. 55th Anniv of Vietnamese Trade Union Movement.
707	**149**	50x. red and black	30	20
708	-	50x. red and black	30	20
709	-	1d. multicoloured	75	25
710	-	2d. multicoloured	1·30	50
711	-	3d. multicoloured	1·90	75
712	-	5d. multicoloured	2·50	1·50
MS713	99×98 mm. 2d. multicoloured. Imperf	15·00	15·00

DESIGNS—VERT: No. 708, Founder's house. HORIZ: No. 709, Workers presenting demands to employer; 710, **MS**713, Ho Chi Minh with workers; 711, Factory; 712, Workers, procession and doves.

150 Hon Dua

1984. Coastal Scenes. Multicoloured.
714	50x. Type **150**	50	15
715	50x. Hang Con Gai	50	15
716	50x. Hang Bo Nau	50	15
717	50x. Nui Yen Ngua	50	15
718	1d. Hon Ga Choi	75	25
719	1d. Hon Coc	75	25
720	2d. Hon Dinh Huong	1·00	40
721	3d. Hon Su Tu	1·30	50
722	5d. Hon Am	2·00	90
723	8d. Nui Bai Tho	2·50	1·40

151 Styracosaurus

1984. Prehistoric Animals. Multicoloured.
724	50x. Type **151**	90	40
725	50x. Diplodocus	90	40
726	1d. Rhamphorhynchus	1·40	50
727	1d. Corythosaurus	1·40	50
728	2d. Seymouria	1·90	65
729	3d. Allosaurus	2·50	90
730	5d. Dimetrodon	3·75	1·30
731	8d. Brachiosaurus	6·25	1·90

153 Dove and Flags

1984. Laos–Kampuchea–Vietnam Co-operation.
733	**153**	50x. red, blue and yellow	40	25
734	**153**	10d. red, blue and yellow	6·00	1·50

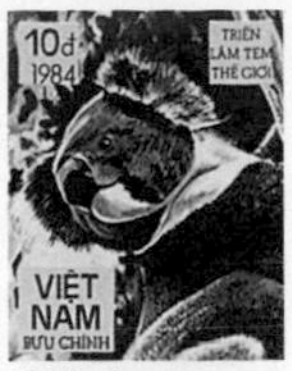

154 Koala

1984. Ausipex 84 International Stamp Exhibition, Melbourne.

MS735	**154**	10d. multicoloured	12·50	4·50

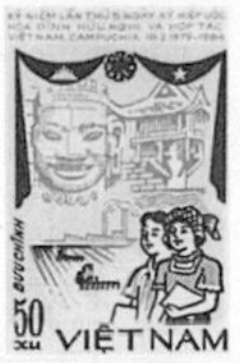

155 Students and Cultural and Industrial Motifs

1984. Fifth Anniv of Kampuchea–Vietnam Friendship Treaty. Multicoloured.

736	50x. Type **155**	40	25
737	3d. Type **155**	1·90	1·00
738	50d. Kampuchean and Vietnamese dancers	10·50	5·00

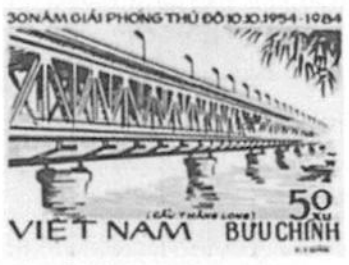

156 Bridge

1984. 30th Anniv of Liberation of Hanoi.

739	**156**	50x. green and yellow	1·30	40
740	-	1d. brown and red	1·90	65
741	-	2d. brown and mauve	3·25	1·30

DESIGNS: 1d. Gateway; 2d. Ho Chi Minh mausoleum.

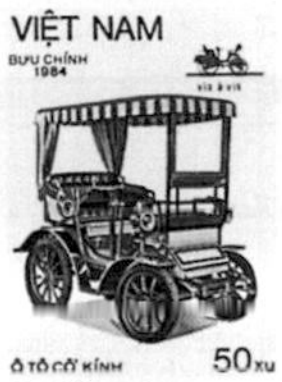

157 Vis-a-vis

1984. Motor Cars. Multicoloured.

743	50x. Type **157**	40	20
744	50x. Two-seater	40	20
745	1d. Tonneau	65	25
746	2d. Double phaeton	1·00	50
747	3d. Landaulet	1·30	75
748	5d. Torpedo	1·50	1·00
749	6d. Town coupe	2·40	1·10

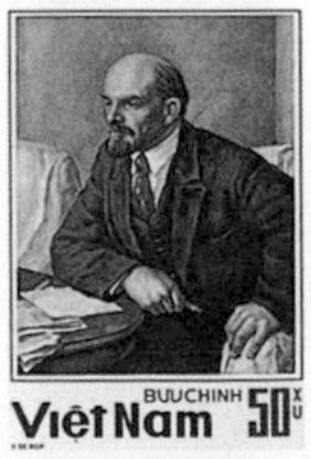

159 "Lenin" (V. A. Serov)

1984. 60th Death Anniv of Lenin. Multicoloured.

751	50x. Type **159**	50	25
752	1d. Painting by A. Plotnov of Lenin at meeting	75	40
753	3d. Painting by K. V. Filatov of Lenin at factory	1·50	75
754	5d. Painting by V. A. Serov of Lenin with three comrades	2·30	1·10

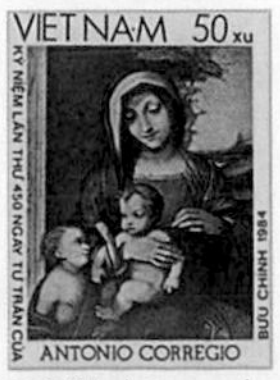

160 "Madonna and Child with St. John"

1984. 450th Death Anniv of Correggio (artist). "Madonna and Child" Paintings. Multicoloured.

755	50x. Type **160**	25	15
756	50x. Bolognini Madonna	25	15
757	1d. Campori Madonna	50	25
758	2d. "Virgin adoring the Child"	1·00	50
759	3d. "Madonna della Cesta"	1·30	75
760	5d. "Madonna della Scodella"	1·90	1·00
761	6d. "Madonna and Child with Angels"	2·50	1·30
MS762	59×73 mm. 10d. "Madonna and Child with St. Catherine" (31×39 mm)	7·50	3·75

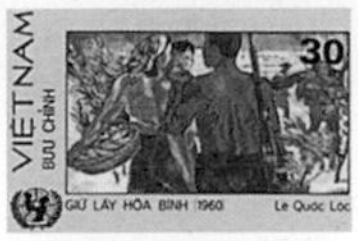

161 "Keep the Peace" (Le Quoc Loc)

1984. UNICEF. Multicoloured.

763	30x. Type **161**	25	15
764	50x. "Sunday" (Nguyen Tien Chung)	40	20
765	1d. "Baby of the Mining Region" (Tran Van Can)	50	25
766	3d. "Little Thuy" (Tran Van Can) (vert)	1·30	65
767	5d. "Children at Play" (Nguyen Phan Chanh)	1·90	1·10
768	10d. "After Guard Duty" (Nguyen Phan Chanh) (vert)	3·75	2·00

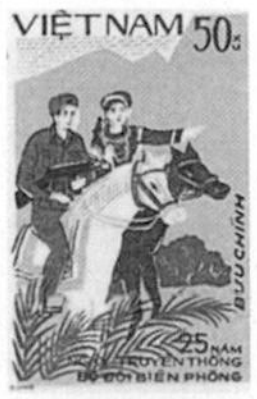

162 Mounted Frontier Guards

1984. 25th Anniv of Frontier Forces.

769	**162**	50x. black, blue and brown	40	25
770	**162**	30d. black, green & turq	14·00	5·00

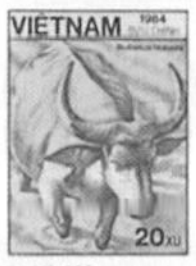

163 Water Buffalo

1984

771	**163**	20x. brown	15	10
772	-	30x. red	20	15
773	-	50x. green	25	20
774	-	50x. red	25	20
775	-	50x. mauve	25	20
776	-	50x. brown	25	20
777	-	1d. violet	65	25
778	-	1d. orange	65	25
779	-	1d. blue	65	25
780	-	1d. blue	65	25
781	-	2d. brown	1·40	65
782	-	2d. orange	1·40	65
783	-	2d. red	1·40	65
784	-	5d. mauve	3·75	1·50
785	-	10d. green	6·25	2·50

DESIGNS: No. 772, Marbled cat; 773, Siamese fighting fish; 774, Cabbage rose; 775, Hibiscus; 776, Lesser panda; 777, "Chrysanthemum sinense"; 778, Tiger; 779, Water lily; 780, Eastern white pelican; 781, Slow loris; 782, Dahlia; 783, Crab-eating macaque; 784, Tokay gecko; 785, Great Indian hornbill.

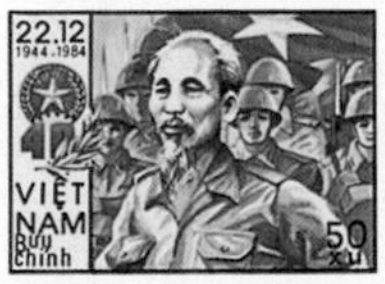

165 Ho Chi Minh and Troops

1984. 40th Anniv of Vietnamese People's Army. Multicoloured.

787	50x. Type **165**	40	20
788	50x. Oath-taking ceremony	40	20
789	1d. Soldier with flag and Boeing B-52 Stratofortress bomber on fire	65	30
790	2d. Civilians building gun emplacement	1·00	50
791	5d. Soldiers and tank breaking through gates	1·40	90
792	5d. Soldier instructing civilians	1·80	1·40
793	8d. Map and soldiers	2·50	1·90
MS794	78×58 mm. 10d. Flag and Vietnamese soldiers, sailor and airman	5·00	2·75

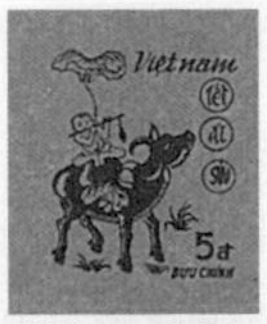

166 Boy on Buffalo

1985. New Year. Year of the Buffalo.

795	**166**	3d. purple and pink	1·60	75
796	**166**	5d. brown and orange	2·40	1·00

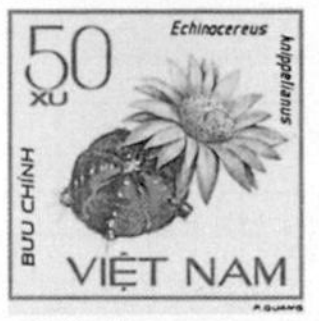

167 "Echinocereus knippelianus"

1985. Flowering Cacti. Multicoloured.

797	50x. Type **167**	40	25
798	50x. "Lemaireocereus thurberi"	40	25
799	1d. "Notocactus haselbergii"	75	50
800	2d. "Parodia chrysacanthion"	1·30	65
801	3d. "Pelecyphora pseudopectinata"	1·80	75
802	5d. "Rebutia frebrighii"	2·50	1·00
803	8d. "Lobivia aurea"	3·00	1·30

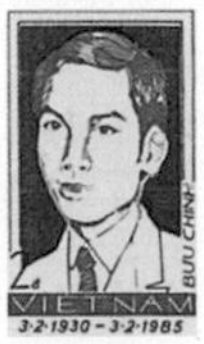

168 Nguyen Ai Quoc (Ho Chi Minh)

1985. 55th Anniv of Vietnam Communist Party.

804	**168**	2d. grey and red	1·50	75

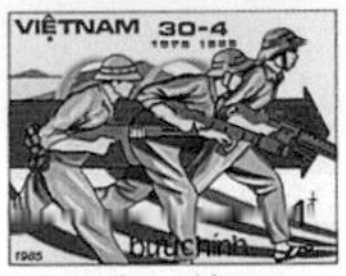

169 Soldiers with Weapons

1985. Tenth Anniv of Reunification of South Vietnam. Multicoloured.

805	1d. Type **169**	65	40
806	2d. Soldiers and tank	1·30	50
807	4d. Soldier and oil rig	1·90	65
808	5d. Map, flag and girls	2·50	1·00
MS809	65×90 mm. 10d. As No. 806	5·00	2·75

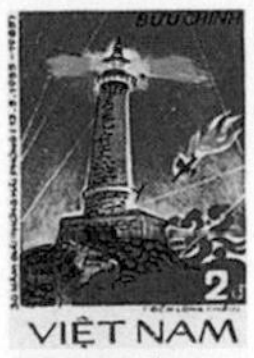

170 Long Chau Lighthouse

1985. 30th Anniv of Liberation of Haiphong.

810	**170**	2d. multicoloured	1·90	65
811	-	5d. multicoloured	4·50	1·50
MS812		110×75 mm. 10d. brown and green	4·50	2·50

DESIGN—HORIZ: 5d. An Duong bridge. VERT: 10d. To Hieu (Communist Party official in Haiphong).

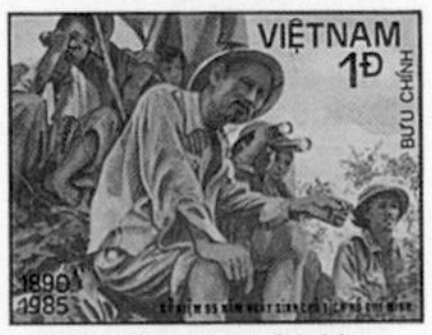

171 Ho Chi Minh and Soldiers

1985. 95th Birth Anniv of Ho Chi Minh (President). Multicoloured.

813	1d. Type **171**	65	25
814	2d. Ho Chi Minh reading in cave at Viet Bac	1·00	50
815	4d. Portrait (vert)	1·50	1·00
816	5d. Ho Chi Minh writing in garden of Presidential Palace	1·90	1·40
MS817	74×99 mm. 10d. As No. 815 but smaller (28×35 mm)	5·00	2·50

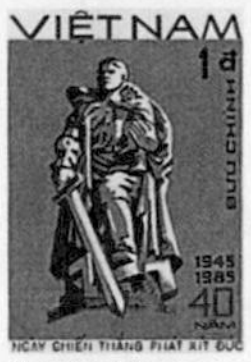

172 Soviet Memorial, Berlin-Treptow

1985. 40th Anniv of Victory in Europe Day. Multicoloured.

818	1d. Type **172**	65	25
819	2d. Soldier and fist breaking swastika	1·00	50
820	4d. Hand releasing dove and eagle falling	2·10	90
821	5d. Girl releasing doves	2·50	1·10
MS822	115×78 mm. 10d. Type **172**	5·00	2·50

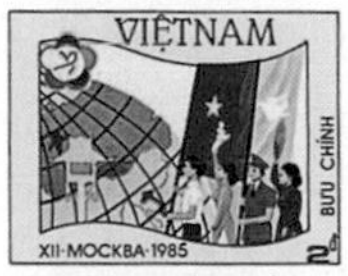

173 Globe and People carrying Flags

1985. 12th World Youth and Students' Festival, Moscow. Multicoloured.

823	2d. Type **173**	1·30	65
824	2d. Workers, pylons and dish aerial	1·30	65
825	4d. Coastguards and lighthouse	1·90	90
826	5d. Youths and balloons	2·50	1·10
MS827	82×100 mm. 10d. Main motif of Type **173** and plan of Moscow Kremlin (39×32 mm)	4·50	2·10

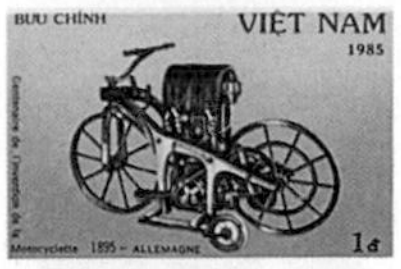

174 Daimler, 1885

1985. Centenary of Motor Cycle. Multicoloured.

828	1d. Type **174** (wrongly inscr "1895")	50	25
829	1d. Three-wheeled vehicle, France, 1898	50	25
830	2d. Harley Davidson, U.S.A., 1913	75	40
831	2d. Cleveland, U.S.A., 1918	75	40
832	3d. Simplex, U.S.A., 1935	1·30	65
833	4d. Minarelli, Italy, 1984	1·50	75
834	6d. Honda, Japan, 1984	2·30	1·30
MS835	82×48 mm. 10d. Honda, Japan, 1984 (31×39 mm)	5·00	2·50

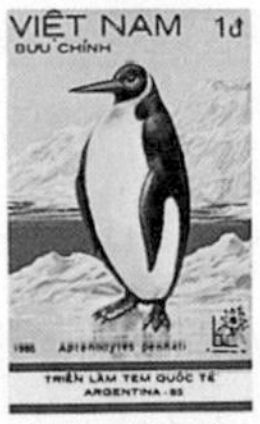

175 King Penguin

1985. "Argentina '85". International Stamp Exhibition, Buenos Aires. Multicoloured.

836	1d. Type **175**	75	25
837	1d. Patagonian cavy	75	25
838	2d. Capybara (horiz)	1·00	40
839	2d. Leopard (horiz)	1·00	40
840	3d. Lesser rhea	1·90	65
841	4d. Giant armadillo (horiz)	2·50	1·00
842	6d. Andean condor (horiz)	3·75	1·50
MS843	97×80 mm. 10d. Llama (39×31 mm)	6·25	3·25

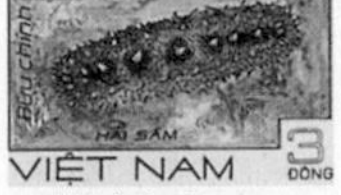

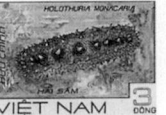

176 "Holothuria monacaria"

1985. Marine Life. Multicoloured.

844	3d. Type **176**	1·30	50
845	3d. "Stichopus chloronotus"	1·30	50
846	3d. "Luidia maculata"	1·30	50
847	3d. "Nadoa tuberculata"	1·30	50
848	4d. "Astropyga radiata"	1·90	75
849	4d. "Linckia laevigata"	1·90	75
850	4d. "Astropecten scoparius"	1·90	75

177 Flag and Sickle "40"

1985. 40th Anniv of Socialist Republic. Multicoloured.
851	2d. Type **177**	75	50
852	3d. Doves around globe as heart above handclasp	1·00	65
853	5d. Banner	1·80	75
854	10d. Ho Chi Minh, flag and laurel branch	2·75	1·30
MS855	70×100 mm. 10d. Similar to Type **177** (25×35 mm)	12·50	10·00

178 Globe, Transport and People around Postman

1985. 40th Anniv of Postal and Telecommunications Service. Multicoloured.
856	2d. Type **178**	75	40
857	2d. Telephonist and telegraph operator	75	40
858	4d. Wartime deliveries and postwoman Nguyen Thi Nghia	1·60	1·00
859	5d. Dish aerial	1·90	1·40

179 Profile of Ho Chi Minh and Policeman

1985. 40th Anniv of People's Police.
860	**179**	10d. red and black	5·75	1·30

180 Gymnasts

1985. First National Sports and Gymnastics Games. Multicoloured.
862	5d. Type **180**	1·90	65
863	10d. Badminton player, gymnast, athlete and swimmer	4·50	1·00

181 Locomotive "Beuth", 1843

1985. 150th Anniv of German Railways. Multicoloured.
864	1d. Type **181**	75	25
865	1d. German tank locomotive, 1900	75	25
866	2d. Locomotive "Saxonia", 1836, Saxony	1·50	40
867	2d. German passenger locomotive	1·50	40
868	3d. Prussian steam locomotive No. 2024, 1910	2·30	75
869	4d. Prussian tank locomotive, 1920	3·00	1·00
870	6d. Bavarian State steam locomotive No. 659, 1890	4·50	1·40
MS871	80×53 mm. 10d. Stephenson locomotive "Adler", 1985 (31×39 mm)	7·50	3·75

182 Off-shore Rig, Derrick and Helicopter

1985. 30th Anniv of Geological Service.
872	**182**	1d. blue and purple	1·40	65
873	–	1d. green and brown	1·40	65

DESIGN: No. 873, Airplane over coastline.

183 Alfa Romeo, 1922

1985. "Italia'85" International Stamp Exhibition, Rome. Motor Cars. Multicoloured.
874	1d. Type **183**	50	25
875	1d. Bianchi "Berlina", 1932	50	25
876	2d. Isotta Fraschini, 1928	75	40
877	2d. Bugatti, 1930	75	40
878	3d. Itala, 1912	1·30	50
879	4d. Lancia "Augusta", 1934	1·50	75
880	6d. Fiat, 1927	2·50	1·40
MS881	76×60 mm. 10d. Fiat (1927) (different) (39×31 mm)	5·00	2·50

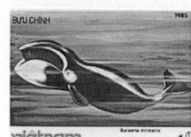

184 Sei Whale

1985. Marine Mammals. Multicoloured.
882	1d. Type **184**	50	25
883	1d. Blue whale	50	25
884	2d. Killer whale	75	40
885	2d. Common dolphin	75	40
886	4d. Humpback whale	1·30	50
887	4d. Fin whale	1·90	90
888	6d. Black right whale	3·75	1·60

185 Goalkeeper attempting to save Ball

1985. World Cup Football Championship, Mexico (1986) (1st issue). Multicoloured.
889	1d. Type **185**	50	25
890	1d. Scoring goal	50	25
891	2d. Goalkeeper diving for ball	75	40
892	2d. Goalkeeper holding ball (vert)	75	40
893	3d. Goalkeeper preparing to catch ball (vert)	1·30	50
894	4d. Punching ball away (vert)	1·50	75
895	6d. Goalkeeper catching ball (vert)	2·50	1·00
MS896	92×67 mm. 10d. Goalmouth scene (39×31 mm)	5·00	2·50

See also Nos. 920/**MS927**.

186 Laotian Girl and Dove

1985. Tenth Anniv of Laos People's Democratic Republic. Multicoloured.
897	1d. Type **186**	1·00	90
898	1d. Laotian girl and arms	1·00	90

187 Decorated Drum

1985. Traditional Musical Instruments. Multicoloured.
899	1d. Type **187**	50	25
900	1d. Xylophone	50	25
901	2d. Double-ended drum	75	40
902	2d. Flutes	75	40
903	3d. Single-stringed instrument	1·30	50
904	4d. Four-stringed instrument	1·50	75
905	6d. Double-stringed bowed instrument	2·50	1·00

188 Agriculture

1985. 40th Anniv of Independence.
906	10d. Type **188**	6·25	2·75
907	10d. Industry	12·50	6·25
908	20d. Health care	19·00	8·75
909	30d. Education	19·00	8·75

189 Hands, Emblem and Dove

1986. 40th Anniv of U.N.O.
910	**189**	1d. multicoloured	1·30	75

190 Ho Chi Minh, Map, Line of Voters and Ballot Box

1986. 40th Anniv of First Assembly Elections.
911	**190**	50x. mauve and black	65	40
912	**190**	1d. orange and black	1·30	65

191 Isaac Newton

1986. Appearance of Halley's Comet.
913	**191**	2d. Type **191**	65	40
914		2d. Edmond Halley	65	40
915		3d. Launch of "Vega" space probe and flags	1·30	65
916		5d. Comet and planet	2·50	1·00

192 Map of U.S.S.R. and Kremlin Buildings

1986. 27th Communist Party Congress, Moscow. Multicoloured.
917	**192**	50x. Type **192**	65	40
918		1d. Lenin on flag and transport, industrial and scientific motifs	1·30	65

193 Plan of Battle of Chi Lang

1986. 600th Birth Anniv (1985) of Le Loi (founder of Le Dynasty).
919	**193**	1d. multicoloured	1·40	70

194 Footballer

1986. World Cup Football Championship, Mexico (2nd issue). Multicoloured.
920	1d. Type **194**	40	25
921	1d. Two players	40	25
922	2d. Player heading ball	75	40
923	3d. Player tackling	1·30	65
924	3d. Two players chasing ball	1·30	65
925	5d. Footballer (different)	1·90	1·00
926	5d. Two players (different)	1·90	1·00
MS927	113×52 mm. 10d. Goalkeeper (39×31 mm)	5·00	2·50

195 Konstantin Tsiolkovski and "Sputnik 1"

1986. 25th Anniv of First Man in Space. Multicoloured.
928	1d. Type **195**	40	25
929	1d. Rocket on launch vehicle, Baikanur cosmodrome	40	25
930	2d. Yuri Gagarin and "Vostok 1"	75	40
931	3d. Valentina Tereshkova and "Vostok VI" on launch vehicle (vert)	1·30	65
932	3d. Cosmonaut Leonov and cosmonaut on space walk	1·30	65
933	5d. "Soyuz"–"Apollo" link and crews	1·90	1·00
934	5d. "Salyut"–"Soyuz" link and two cosmonauts	1·90	1·00
MS935	60×81 mm. 10d. Cosmonauts (31×39 mm)	5·00	2·50

196 Thalmann and Flag

1986. Birth Centenary of Ernst Thalmann (German Communist leader).
936	**196**	2d. red and black	1·60	75

197 Flag, Hammer and Globe in Sickle

1986. Centenary of May Day.
937	**197**	1d. red and blue	50	25
938	**197**	5d. red and brown	2·00	90

198 Hawker Hart

1986. "Expo '86" World's Fair, Vancouver. Historic Aircraft. Multicoloured.
939	1d. Type **198**	40	25
940	1d. Curtiss JN-4 "Jenny"	40	25
941	2d. PZL P-23 Karas	75	40
942	3d. Yakovlev Yak-11	1·30	65
943	3d. Fokker Dr-1 triplane	1·30	65
944	5d. Boeing P12, 1920	1·90	1·00
945	5d. Nieuport-Delage 29C1, 1929	1·90	1·00

199 Ho Chi Minh and People working on Barriers

1986. 40th Anniv of Committee for Protection of Flood Barriers.

946	**199**	1d. pink and brown	1·30	75

200 Black and White Cat

1986. Cats. Multicoloured.

947	1d. Type **200**	40	25
948	1d. Grey and white cat	40	25
949	2d. White cat	75	40
950	3d. Brown-faced cat	1·30	65
951	3d. Beige cat	1·30	65
952	5d. Black-faced cat (vert)	1·90	1·00
953	5d. Beige and cream cat	1·90	1·00

201 Thai Den House

1986. Traditional Architecture. Multicoloured.

954	1d. Type **201**	40	25
955	1d. Nung house	40	25
956	2d. Thai Trang house	75	40
957	3d. Tay house	1·30	65
958	3d. H'mong house	1·30	65
959	5d. Dao house	1·90	1·00
960	5d. Tay Nguyen house (vert)	1·90	1·00
MS961	100×70 mm. 10d. As No. 960	5·00	2·50

202 European Bee Eater

1986. "Stockholmia 86" International Stamp Exhibition. Birds. Multicoloured.

962	1d. Type **202**	40	25
963	1d. Green magpie	40	25
964	2d. Red-winged shrike babbler	75	40
965	3d. White-crested laughing thrush	1·30	65
966	3d. Long-tailed broadbill (horiz)	1·30	65
967	5d. Pied wagtail	1·90	1·00
968	5d. Azure-winged magpie (horiz)	1·90	1·00
MS969	95×65 mm. 10d. White-rumped shamas (31×39 mm)	6·25	3·00

203 Plymouth Rock Cock

1986. Domestic Fowl. Multicoloured.

970	1d. Type **203**	40	40
971	1d. Common turkey	40	40
972	2d. Rhode Island red cock	75	50
973	2d. White Plymouth rock cock	75	50
974	3d. Rhode Island (inscr "Islan") red hen	1·30	65
975	3d. White leghorn cock	1·30	65
976	3d. Rhode Island red cock (different)	1·30	65
977	5d. Barred Plymouth rock cock	1·90	1·00

204 Emblem

1986. 11th World Federation of Trades Unions Congress, Berlin.

978	**204**	1d. blue and red	1·30	65

206 Woman-shaped Sword Handle

1986. Historic Bronzes Excavated at Mt. Do. Multicoloured.

980	1d. Type **206**	40	45
981	1d. Seated figure with man on back	40	45
982	3d. Saddle pommel (horiz)	75	50
983	3d. Shoe-shaped hoe (horiz)	1·30	65
984	3d. Bowl (horiz)	1·30	65
985	5d. Vase (horiz)	1·90	90
986	5d. Pot with lid (horiz)	1·90	90
MS987	107×88 mm. 10d. As No. 981	5·00	2·50

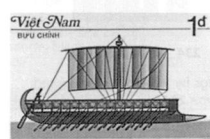

207 Greek Bireme

1986. Sailing Ships. Multicoloured.

988	1d. Type **207**	50	25
989	1d. Viking longship	50	25
990	2d. Medieval kogge (36×46 mm)	90	40
991	3d. Greek cargo galley	1·30	65
992	3d. Phoenician war galley with ram	1·30	65
993	5d. Ancient Mediterranean cargo ship	1·90	90
994	5d. Roman trireme	1·90	90

208 Hands cupping Red Cross in Flower

1986. 40th Anniv of Vietnamese Red Cross.

995	**208**	3d. mauve and blue	1·30	65

209 "Catopsilia scylla"

1986. Butterflies. Multicoloured.

996	1d. Type **209**	40	20
997	1d. "Euploea midamus"	40	20
998	2d. Orange albatross	75	40
999	3d. Common mormon ("Papilio polytes")	1·30	65
1000	3d. African monarch ("Danaus chrysippus")	1·30	65
1001	5d. Tawny rajah ("Charaxes polyxena")	1·90	90
1002	5d. Magpie crow ("Euploea diocletiana")	1·90	90

210 Red Flag and Symbols of Industry and Agriculture

1986. Sixth Vietnamese Communist Party Congress. Multicoloured.

1003	1d. Type **210**	75	50
1004	2d. Red flag and weapons	1·50	65
1005	4d. Red flag and Ho Chi Minh	2·50	1·00
1006	5d. Red flag and symbols of peace	2·75	1·30
MS1007	73×110 mm. 10d. Type **210**. Imperf	5·00	2·50

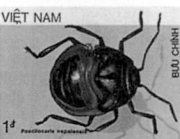

211 "Poecilocoris nepalensis" (shieldbug)

1986. Insects. Multicoloured.

1008	1d. Type **211**	50	40
1009	1d. "Bombus americanorum" (bee)	50	40
1010	2d. "Romalea microptera" (grasshopper)	1·00	50
1011	3d. "Chalcocoris rutilans" (shieldbug)	1·50	65
1012	3d. "Chrysocoris sellatus" (shieldbug)	1·50	65
1013	5d. "Crocisa crucifera" (wasp)	1·90	90
1014	5d. "Paranthrene palmi" (moth)	1·90	90
MS1015	78×78 mm. 10d. "Anabrus simplex" (31×39 mm)	5·00	2·50

212 Dove and Emblem

1986. International Peace Year.

1016	**212**	1d. green and black	75	65
1017	**212**	3d. pink and black	1·80	90

213 "Ficus glomerata"

1986. Bonsai. Multicoloured.

1018	1d. Type **213**	40	45
1019	1d. "Ficus benjamina"	40	45
1020	2d. "Ulmus tonkinensis"	75	50
1021	3d. "Persica vulgaris"	1·30	65
1022	3d. "Strebius asper"	1·30	65
1023	5d. "Podocarpus macrophyllus"	1·90	75
1024	5d. "Pinus khasya"	1·90	75
MS1025	86×66 mm. 10d. "Serissa foetida" (41×29 mm)	5·25	2·50

214 Basket

1986. Basketry and Wickerwork. Multicoloured.

1026	1d. Type **214**	40	45
1027	1d. Tall basket with lid and handles	40	45
1028	2d. Stool	75	50
1029	3d. Handbag	1·30	65
1030	3d. Dish	1·30	65
1031	5d. Tall basket for carrying on back	1·90	75
1032	5d. Square basket with star-shaped foot	1·90	75
MS1033	107×90 mm. 10d. Tall basket	5·00	2·50

215 Soldiers and Women

1986. 40th Anniv of National Resistance.

1034	**215**	2d. brown and green	1·60	75

216 "Fokienia hodginsii"

1986. Fruit of Conifers. Multicoloured.

1035	1d. Type **216**	40	45
1036	1d. "Amentotaxus yunnanensis"	40	45
1037	2d. "Pinus kwangtungensis"	75	50
1038	3d. "Cupressus torulosa"	1·30	65
1039	3d. "Taxus chinensis"	1·30	65
1040	5d. "Tsuga yunnanensis"	1·90	75
1041	5d. "Ducampopinus krempfii"	1·90	75
MS1042	67×85 mm. 10d. "Abies nukiangensis"	5·00	2·50

217 Mother and Calf

1986. Elephants.

1043	1d. Type **217**	65	25
1044	1d. Two elephants	65	25
1045	3d. Elephant (vert)	1·50	50
1046	3d. Elephant feeding	1·50	50
1047	5d. Working elephant (vert)	2·30	75
1048	5d. Elephants by water (68×27 mm)	2·30	75

218 Girl watering Tree

1987. New Year. Year of the Cat.

1049	**218**	3d. brown and mauve	1·50	75

219 My Chan

1987. "Son Tinh-Thuy Tinh" (folktale). Multicoloured.

1050	3d. Type **219**	1·30	65
1051	3d. Mountain Genius bearing gift and leading horse	1·30	65
1052	3d. Elephants carrying materials for flood barrier	1·30	65
1053	3d. Men working through the night against flood sent by Water Genius	1·30	65
1054	3d. Men felling trees	1·30	65
1055	3d. Pounding rice in preparation for festival after storms	1·30	65
1056	3d. Canoes bringing fruit and grain	1·30	65
1057	3d. Canoe	1·30	65

Nos. 1050/7 were issued together, se-tenant, forming a composite design.

220 "Nymphaea lotus"

1987. Water Lilies. Multicoloured.

1058	5d. Type **220**	25	20
1059	10d. "Nymphaea nouchali"	65	40
1060	10d. "Nymphaea pubescens"	65	40
1061	20d. "Nymphaea rubra"	90	50
1062	20d. "Nymphaea gigantea"	90	50
1063	30d. "Nymphaea laydekeri"	1·30	65
1064	50d. "Nymphaea capensis"	1·80	90

1988. Sea Shells. Multicoloured.

1258	10d. Type **266**	40	25
1259	10d. Silver conch ("Strombus lentiginosus")	40	25
1260	20d. Common frog shell ("Bursa rana")	75	50
1261	20d. Chambered nautilus ("Nautilus")	75	50
1262	30d. Red-mouth olive ("Oliva erythrostoma")	1·30	65
1263	30d.	1·30	65
1264	50d. Episcopal mitre	1·80	90
MS1265	90×65 mm. 80d. "Tonna tessellate"	5·00	2·50

The inscriptions on Nos. 1261 and 1263 have been transposed.

267 Class VL85 Diesel Locomotive, Russia

1988. Railway Locomotives. Multicoloured.

1266	20d. Type **267**	75	40
1267	20d. LRC high speed diesel, Canada	75	40
1268	20d. Monorail train, Japan	75	40
1269	20d. KiHA 80 diesel railcar, Japan	75	40
1270	30d. Class DR 1A diesel-electric, Russia	1·30	65
1271	30d. Class RC 1 electric, Sweden	1·30	65
1272	50d. Class TE-136 diesel-electric, Russia	1·80	1·30
MS1273	102×71 mm. 80d. "Z6400", France (36×26 mm)	5·00	2·50

268 Gourd

1988. Fruit. Multicoloured.

1274	10d. Type **268**	40	35
1275	10d. "Momordica charantia"	40	35
1276	20d. Pumpkin ("Cucurbita moschata")	1·00	50
1277	20d. Eggplant ("Solanum melongena")	1·00	50
1278	30d. "Benincasa hispida"	1·30	65
1279	30d. Luffa gourd	1·30	65
1280	50d. Tomatoes	1·80	90

269 Soldiers and Field Workers

1989. Tenth Anniv of People's Republic of Kampuchea. Multicoloured.

1281	100d. Type **269**	75	65
1282	500d. Crowd greeting soldier and mother with child	3·00	1·60

270 Junk from Quang Nam

1989. Regional Fishing Junks. Multicoloured.

1283	10d. Type **270**	65	30
1284	10d. Quang Tri	65	30
1285	20d. Thua Thien	90	45
1286	20d. Da Nang	90	45
1287	30d. Quang Tri (different)	1·00	50
1288	30d. Da Nang (different)	1·00	50
1289	50d. Hue	1·30	65

271 Caribbean Buckeye ("Junonia evarete")

1989. "India-89" International Stamp Exhibition, New Delhi (1st issue). Butterflies. Multicoloured.

1290	50d. Type **271**	50	40
1291	50d. "Anaea echemus"	50	40
1292	50d. Great southern white ("Ascia monuste")	50	40
1293	100d. Red-splashed sulphur ("Phoebis avellaneda")	75	65
1294	100d. Jamaican orange ("Eurema proterpia")	75	65
1295	200d. "Papilio palamedes"	1·50	75
1296	300d. Monarch ("Danaus plexippus")	1·80	90
MS1297	87×77 mm. 400d. "Parides gundlachiamus" (39×31 mm)	4·50	2·30

See also Nos. 1298/1301.

272 Flag and Telecommunications

1989. "India-89" International Stamp Exhibition, New Delhi (2nd issue).

1298	**272**	100d. multicoloured	65	40
1299	-	100d. multicoloured	65	40
1300	-	300d. multicoloured	1·40	65
1301	-	600d. brown, orge & green	3·00	1·10

DESIGNS: 100d. (No. 1299), Oil and electricity industries; 300d. Government Secretariat and Asokan capital; 600d. Jawaharlal Nehru (Indian statesman, birth centenary).

273 Festival

1989. Bicentenary of Battle of Dongda.

1302	**273**	100d. violet and green	65	40
1303	-	1000d. mauve and pink	3·75	2·10

DESIGN: 1000d. Battle scene.

274 Emblems on Banner

1989. Centenary of Interparliamentary Union.

1304	**274**	100d. multicoloured	75	40
1305	-	200d. gold, ultramarine and blue	1·80	90

DESIGN: 200d. "100" on banner.

275 Dachshunds

1989. Dogs. Multicoloured.

1306	50d. Type **275**	50	25
1307	50d. Basset hounds	50	25
1308	50d. Setter (vert)	50	25
1309	100d. Hunting dog (vert)	75	40
1310	100d. Basset hounds (66×25 mm)	75	40
1311	200d. Hound (vert)	1·50	75
1312	300d. Basset hound puppy	1·80	1·00

276 Footballers

1989. World Cup Football Championship, Italy (1st issue). Multicoloured.

1313	50d. Type **276**	50	25
1314	50d. Striker and goalkeeper	50	25
1315	50d. Goalkeeper	50	25
1316	100d. Player No. 5 tackling	75	40
1317	100d. Tackling (vert)	75	40
1318	200d. Player No. 3 (vert)	1·50	75
1319	300d. Players heading ball (vert)	1·80	1·00
MS1320	62×92 mm. 400d. Player (31×39 mm)	5·00	2·50

See also Nos. 1382/**MS**1389 and 1482/9.

277 Jug

1989. Pottery. Multicoloured.

1321	50d. Type **277**	50	25
1322	100d. Bowl with geometric pattern	75	40
1323	100d. Round pot with flower decoration	75	40
1324	200d. Tall pot with animal decoration	1·50	75
1325	300d. Vase	1·80	90

278 Baby Thanh Giong with Mother

1989. Legend of Thanh Giong. Multicoloured.

1326	50d. Type **278**	50	25
1327	100d. Thanh Giong with King's messenger	75	40
1328	100d. Thanh Giong at head of army	75	40
1329	200d. Thanh Giong beating out flames	1·50	75
1330	300d. Thanh Giong riding to heaven	1·80	90

279 "Fuchsia fulgens"

1989. Flowers. Multicoloured.

1331	50d. Type **279**	50	25
1332	50d. Bird-of-paradise flower ("Strelitzia reginae")	50	25
1333	100d. Glory lily ("Gloriosa superba")	75	40
1334	100d. Orange day lily ("Hemerocallis fulva")	75	40
1335	200d. "Paphiopedilum siamense"	1·50	75
1336	300d. "Iris sp."	1·80	90

On Nos. 1332 and 1335 the inscriptions have been transposed.

280 Bird carrying Envelope above Dish Aerial

1989. Communications.

1337	**280**	100d. brown	1·30	65

281 Birds

282 "Return from Varennes"

1989. Bicentenary of French Revolution and "Philexfrance 89" International Stamp Exhibition, Paris. (a) As T **281**. Multicoloured.

1338	100d. Type **281**	50	30
1339	500d. "Liberty guiding the People" (detail, Eugene Delacroix)	2·00	1·00

(b) As T **282**.

1340	50d. Type **282**	50	25
1341	50d. "Revolutionary Court"	50	25
1342	50d. "Oath of the Tennis Court" (Jacques-Louis David) (vert)	50	25
1343	100d. "Assassination of Marat" (David) (vert)	75	40
1344	100d. "Storming the Bastille" (vert)	75	40
1345	200d. Two children (Pierre-Paul Prud'hon) (vert)	1·50	75
1346	300d. "Slave Trade" (Jean-Leon Gerome)	2·40	1·40
MS1347	105×105 mm. 400d. "Liberty guiding the People" (Eugene Delacroix) (32×43 mm)	4·50	2·30

283 Man and Ox

1989. Rice Cultivation. Multicoloured.

1348	50d. Type **283**	50	25
1349	100d. Ploughing with ox	75	40
1350	100d. Flooding fields	75	40
1351	200d. Fertilizing	1·50	75
1352	300d. Harvesting crop	1·80	90

284 Appaloosa

1989. Horses. Multicoloured.

1353	50d. Type **284**	50	25
1354	50d. Tennessee walking horse	50	25
1355	50d. Tersky	50	25
1356	100d. Kladruber	75	40
1357	100d. Welsh cob	75	40
1358	200d. Pinto	1·50	75
1359	300d. Pony and bridle (68×27 mm)	1·80	1·00

285 Brandenburg Gate, Flag and Emblem

1989. 40th Anniv of German Democratic Republic.

1360	**285**	200d. yellow, black and mauve	1·50	75

286 Polio Oral Vaccination

1989. Immunization Campaign.

1361	**286**	100d. brown, black & red	75	50
1362	-	100d. pink, black & green	75	50
1363	-	100d. green, black and red	75	50

DESIGNS: No. 1362, Vaccinating pregnant woman; 1363, Health clinic.

287 Horse

1989. Paintings of Horses by Hsu Pei-Hung. Multicoloured.

1364	100d. Type **287**	25	15
1365	200d. Two horses galloping	40	20
1366	300d. Three horses grazing	65	25
1367	500d. Horse galloping (horiz)	90	30
1368	800d. Galloping horse	1·50	45
1369	1000d. Two horses under tree	2·00	65
1370	1500d. Galloping horse (different)	2·50	90
MS1371	117×72 mm. 2000d. Horses (43×32 mm)	7·50	3·00

288 "Nina", "Pinta" and "Santa Maria" and Mochica Ceramic Figure

1989. 500th Anniv (1992) of Discovery of America by Columbus (1st issue). Multicoloured.

1372	50d. Type **288**	40	25
1373	100d. Columbus and King Ferdinand the Catholic and Peruvian ceramic bottle	90	65
1374	100d. Columbus's arrival at Rabida and Mexican decorated vessel	90	65
1375	100d. Columbus offering gifts (18th-century engraving) and human-shaped jug	90	65
1376	200d. Early map and Peruvian ceramic	1·60	1·30
1377	200d. Portrait and arms of Columbus and Nazca ceramic	1·60	1·30
1378	300d. Chart by Toscanelli and Chimu vessel	1·90	1·50
MS1379	85×69 mm. 500d. Teotihuacana lidded vessel (36×30 mm)	4·50	3·75

See also Nos. 1545/**MS**1552 and 1664/**MS**1699.

289 Storming of Presidential Palace, Saigon, and Ho Chi Minh

1990. 60th Anniv of Vietnamese Communist Party. Multicoloured.

1380	100d. Type **289**	75	65
1381	500d. Industry, workers, hammer and sickle and flag	3·00	1·40

290 Players

1990. World Cup Football Championship, Italy (2nd issue). Multicoloured.

1382	100d. Type **290**	20	15
1383	200d. Argentina player with possession	20	15
1384	300d. Netherlands and Scotland players	25	20
1385	500d. Soviet Union player tackling	50	25
1386	1000d. Scotland and West Germany player	1·00	40
1387	2000d. Soviet Union player losing possession	1·50	65
1388	3000d. Goalkeeper	2·30	75
MS1389	90×67 mm. 3500d. Boy with ball behind goal net (30×37 mm)	3·75	2·00

291 Hybrids of Mallard and Local Species

1990. Ducks. Multicoloured.

1390	100d. Type **291**	25	15
1391	300d. European mallard	40	25
1392	500d. Mallards	65	30
1393	1000d. Red-billed pintails	1·30	45
1394	2000d. White duck preening	2·30	65
1395	3000d. African yellow-bills	3·00	90

292 Mack Truck and Trailer

1990. Trucks. Multicoloured.

1396	100d. Type **292**	15	15
1397	200d. Volvo "F89" tipper	25	15
1398	300d. Tatra "915 S1" tipper	30	20
1399	500d. Hino "KZ30000" lorry	50	25
1400	1000d. Italia Iveco	75	40
1401	2000d. Leyland-Daf "Super Comet" tipper	1·50	65
1402	3000d. Kamaz "53212" lorry	2·30	80

293 8th/9th-century Viking Longship

1990. Sailing Ships. Multicoloured.

1403	100d. Type **293**	15	15
1404	500d. 15th-century caravel	50	30
1405	1000d. 15th-century carrack (vert)	1·00	75
1406	1000d. 14th/15th-century carrack	1·00	75
1407	1000d. 17th-century frigate	1·00	75
1408	2000d. 16th-century galleons and pinnace (vert)	2·00	1·50
1409	3000d. 16th-century galleon	2·50	1·90
MS1410	60×53 mm. 4200d. Ancient Egyptian Nile galley (43×32 mm)	4·75	4·50

294 Bubble-eyed Goldfish

1990. Goldfish. Multicoloured.

1411	100d. Type **294**	20	15
1412	300d. Calico veil-tailed	25	15
1413	500d. Red-capped	50	25
1414	1000d. Veil-tailed (vert)	90	40
1415	2000d. Celestial (vert)	1·90	75
1416	3000d. Comet (vert)	2·50	1·00

295 Gate of Noble Mankind

1990. Hue Temples. Multicoloured.

1417	100d. Type **295**	65	25
1418	100d. Lotus pool at tomb of Emperor Tu Duc	65	25
1419	200d. Southern Gate	1·30	50
1420	300d. Thien Pagoda	1·90	1·30
MS1421	97×68 mm. 400d. Great Stairway, Khai-Dinh burial place	3·75	1·90

296 "Antonia Zarate" (Francisco de Goya)

1990. "Stamp World London 90" International Stamp Exhibition. Multicoloured.

1422	100d. Type **296**	15	10
1423	200d. "Girl with Paper Fan" (Auguste Renoir)	20	15
1424	300d. "Janet Grizel" (John Russell)	25	20
1425	500d. "Love unfasten's Beauty's Girdle" (Joshua Reynolds)	50	25
1426	1000d. "Portrait of a Lady" (George Romney) (wrongly inscr "Omney")	1·00	45
1427	2000d. "Mme. Ginoux" (Vincent van Gogh)	1·90	75
1428	3000d. "Lady in Green" (Thomas Gainsborough)	2·50	1·00
MS1429	90×70 mm. 3500d. "Girl sitting in a Wheat Field" (Vincent van Gogh) (26×38 mm)	5·00	2·50

297 Henry Giffard's Steam-powered Dirigible Airship

1990. "Helvetia 90" International Stamp Exhibition, Geneva. Airships. Mult. With or without gum.

1430	100d. Type **297**	15	10
1431	200d. Lebaudy-Juillot airship No. 1 "La Jaune"	20	15
1432	300d. "Graf Zeppelin'	25	20
1433	500d. R-101	50	40
1434	1000d. "Osoaviakhim"	1·00	75
1435	2000d. Tissandier Brothers' airship	2·00	2·30
1436	3000d. U.S. Navy "N" Class airship	3·00	2·50
MS1437	77×104 mm. 3500d. Zodiac (35×28 mm)	3·75	3·50

No. 1431 is wrongly inscr "Lebandy".

298 Silver Tabby and White Cat

1990. Cats. Multicoloured.

1438	100d. Type **298**	15	10
1439	200d. Black cat (vert)	20	15
1440	300d. Black and white cat	40	20
1441	500d. Brown tabby and white (vert)	65	25
1442	1000d. Silver tabby	1·10	40
1443	2000d. Tortoiseshell and white (vert)	1·50	65
1444	3000d. Tortoiseshell tabby and white (vert)	1·80	75
MS1445	67×95 mm. 3500d. Silver tabby (43×32 mm)	4·50	2·20

299 Ho Chi Minh, 1923

1990. Birth Centenary of Ho Chi Minh. Multicoloured.

1446	100d. Type **299**	15	10
1447	300d. Ho Chi Minh, 1945	25	20
1448	500d. Dove, hand holding rifle, and Ho Chi Minh	50	40
1449	1000d. Ho Chi Minh conducting	1·00	75
1450	2000d. Ho Chi Minh embracing child	1·50	1·00
1451	3000d. Globe and Ho Chi Minh	1·80	1·30
MS1452	86×94 mm. 3500d. Ho Chi Minh and star (29×42 mm)	3·50	3·25

300 King Charles Spaniel

1990. "New Zealand 90" International Stamp Exhibition, Auckland. Dogs. Multicoloured.

1453	100d. Type **300**	15	10
1454	200d. Spaniel	20	15
1455	300d. Saluki	40	20
1456	500d. Dachshund	65	25
1457	1000d. Dalmatian	1·10	40
1458	2000d. Highland terrier	1·50	65
1459	3000d. Boxer	1·80	75
MS1460	85×85 mm. 3500d. Rough collie and pups (32×43 mm)	4·50	2·30

301 Gorgosaurus

1990. Prehistoric Animals. Multicoloured.

1461	100d. Type **301**	15	10
1462	500d. Ceratosaurus	65	25
1463	1000d. Ankylosaurus	1·10	90
1464	2000d. Ankylosaurus (different)	2·75	2·00
1465	3000d. Edaphosaurus	3·25	2·50

302 High Jumping

1990. 11th Asian Games, Peking. Multicoloured.

1466	100d. Type **302**	15	10
1467	200d. Basketball	20	15
1468	300d. Table tennis	25	20
1469	500d. Volleyball	50	40
1470	1000d. Gymnastics	1·00	75
1471	2000d. Tennis	2·00	1·50
1472	3000d. Judo	3·00	2·40
MS1473	73×93 mm. 3500d. Steeplechase (32×43 mm)	3·50	3·25

1990. Tourism. Nos. 626/33 optd **DULICH'90** and emblem.

1474	50x. Type **131**	25	20
1475	50x. Common ink cap ("Coprinus atramentarius")	25	20
1476	50x. Golden mushroom ("Flammulina velutipes")	25	20
1477	50x. Chanterelle ("Cantharellus cibarius")	25	20
1478	1d. Chinese mushroom	50	40
1479	2d. Red-staining mushroom	1·00	90
1480	5d. Common morel	2·50	2·20
1481	10d. Caesar's mushroom	5·00	4·50

1990. World Cup Football Championship, Italy (3rd series). Nos. 457/64 optd **ITALIA'90** and ball.

1482	**90**	30x. multicoloured	50	40
1483	-	30x. mult (No. 458)	50	40
1484	-	40x. mult (No. 459)	65	50
1485	-	40x. mult (No. 460)	65	50
1486	-	50x. mult (No. 461)	90	75
1487	-	50x. mult (No. 462)	90	75
1488	-	60x. multicoloured	1·00	90
1489	-	1d. multicoloured	1·90	1·40

305 "Pyotr Yemtsov" (container ship)

1990. Ships. Multicoloured.

1490	100d. Type **305**	15	10
1491	300d. Mexican Lines container ship	25	20
1492	500d. Liner	50	40
1493	1000d. "Ben Nevis" (tanker)	1·00	80
1494	2000d. Roll-on roll-off ferry	2·00	1·90
1495	3000d. Sealink train ferry "Nord Pas de Calais"	3·00	2·75

306 Emblem, Globe and Dove

1990. 45th Anniv of Postal Service. Multicoloured.

1496	100d. Type **306**	40	15
1497	1000d. Emblem, dish aerial and globe	1·10	1·00

307 Red Flags and Symbols of Construction and Agriculture

1990. 45th Anniv of Independence. Multicoloured.

1498	100d. Type **307**	15	10
1499	500d. Map, storming of Government Palace (1945), siege of Dien Bien Phu and tank entering Presidential Palace, Saigon (1975)	50	40
1500	1000d. Satellite communications ship, dish aerial and "VI"	1·00	90
1501	3000d. Hammer and sickle, industrial symbols and couple	3·00	2·75
MS1502	69×105 mm. 3500d. State arms and Ho Chi Minh proclaiming independence (32×43 mm)	3·50	3·25

308 Thach Sanh collecting Wood

1990. Legend of Thach Sanh. Multicoloured.

1503	100d. Type **308**	15	10
1504	300d. Ly Thong	25	20
1505	500d. Thach Sanh fighting fire-breathing snake	50	40

1506	1000d. Thach Sanh shooting down bird	1·00	90
1507	2000d. Thach Sanh in prison	2·00	1·90
1508	3000d. Thach Sanh and wife	3·00	2·75

1990. World Cup Football Championship Results. Nos. 1382/MS1389 optd 1. GERMANY 2. ARGENTINA 3. ITALY.

1509	**290**	100d. multicoloured	15	10
1510	-	200d. multicoloured	20	15
1511	-	300d. multicoloured	25	20
1512	-	500d. multicoloured	50	40
1513	-	1000d. multicoloured	1·00	90
1514	-	2000d. multicoloured	2·00	1·90
1515	-	3000d. multicoloured	3·00	2·75

MS1516 90×67 mm. 3500d. multi-coloured — 5·00 4·50

1990. Red Cross. Nos. N598/605 optd with red cross and **FOR THE FUTURE GENERATION** in various languages (given in brackets).

1517	12x. multicoloured (Italian)	40	25
1518	12x. multicoloured (Chinese)	40	25
1519	20x. multicoloured (German)	65	50
1520	20x. mult (Vietnamese)	65	50
1521	30x. multicoloured (English)	1·00	90
1522	40x. multicoloured (Russian)	1·30	1·10
1523	50x. multicoloured (French)	1·50	1·40
1524	60x. multicoloured (Spanish)	1·80	1·60

311 Soldier

1990. 60th Anniv of Vietnamese Women's Union. Multicoloured.

1525	100d. Type **311**	25	15
1526	500d. Women in various occupations	50	40

312 Emblems

1990. 20th Anniv of Asian–Pacific Postal Training Centre, Bangkok.

1527	**312**	150d. multicoloured	75	65

313 Hands holding Forest and City

1990. Preservation of Forests. Multicoloured.

1528	200d. Type **313**	40	15
1529	1000d. Forest fire, "S.O.S." and river	1·40	50

314 Panther Cap

1991. Poisonous Fungi. Multicoloured.

1530	200d. Type **314**	15	10
1531	300d. Death cap	40	15
1532	1000d. Destroying angel	90	50
1533	1500d. Fly agaric	1·40	65
1534	2000d. "Russula emetica"	2·00	90
1535	3000d. Satan's mushroom	2·75	1·30

315 Yachting

1991. Olympic Games, Barcelona (1992). Multicoloured.

1536	200d. Type **315**	15	10
1537	300d. Boxing	30	15

1538	400d. Cycling	40	25
1539	1000d. High jumping	1·10	40
1540	2000d. Show jumping	1·80	65
1541	3000d. Judo	2·50	1·10
1542	3000d. Wrestling (horiz)	2·50	1·10

MS1543 80×92 mm. 5000d. Football (43×32 mm) — 4·50 2·30

See also Nos. 1679/MS1686.

316 Nguyen Binh Khiem

1991. 500th Birth Anniv of Nguyen Binh Khiem (poet).

1544	316	200d. black, brown and ochre	1·00	45

317 "Marisiliana"

1991. 500th Anniv (1992) of Discovery of America by Columbus (2nd issue). Multicoloured.

1545	200d. Type **317**	15	10
1546	400d. "Venitien"	40	25
1547	400d. "Cromster" (vert)	40	25
1548	2000d. "Pinta"	1·60	50
1549	2000d. "Nina"	1·60	50
1550	3000d. "Howker" (vert)	2·30	75
1551	5000d. "Santa Maria"	3·75	1·40

MS1552 98×74 mm. 6500d. Columbus (39×27 mm) — 4·50 2·30

318 Woman in Blue Tunic

1991. Golden Heart Charity.

1553	**318**	200d. multicoloured	15	10
1554	-	500d. multicoloured	25	20
1555	-	1000d. multicoloured	90	40
1556	-	5000d. multicoloured	4·50	1·60

DESIGNS: 500d. to 5000d. Traditional women's costumes.

319 Japanese White-naped Crane

1991. Birds. Multicoloured.

1557	200d. Type **319**	40	20
1558	300d. Sarus crane chick (vert)	50	25
1559	400d. Manchurian crane (vert)	65	30
1560	1000d. Sarus cranes (adults) (vert)	1·10	45
1561	2000d. Black-necked crane (vert)	2·10	1·00
1562	3000d. South African crowned cranes (vert)	3·25	1·30
1563	3000d. Great white crane	3·25	1·30

320 Black-finned Reef Shark

1991. Sharks. Multicoloured.

1564	200d. Type **320**	15	10
1565	300d. Grey reef shark	20	15
1566	400d. Leopard shark	40	25
1567	1000d. Great hammerhead	65	30
1568	2000d. White-tipped reef shark	1·40	65
1569	3000d. Sand tiger	2·50	95
1570	3000d. Bull shark	2·50	95

321 Lobster

1991. Shellfish. Multicoloured.

1571	200d. Type **321**	40	15
1572	300d. "Alpheus bellulus"	50	20
1573	400d. "Periclemenes brevi-carpalis"	65	25
1574	1000d. Lobster (different)	1·00	30
1575	2000d. Lobster (different)	1·90	65
1576	3000d. Lobster (different)	3·50	90
1577	3000d. "Astacus sp."	3·50	90

322 "Fusee", 1829

1991. Early Locomotives. Multicoloured.

1578	400d. Type **322**	25	20
1579	400d. Blenkinsop's rack locomotive (wrongly inscr "Puffing Billy")	25	20
1580	500d. John Stevens rack locomotive, 1825 (horiz)	40	25
1581	1000d. Crampton No 80 locomotive, 1852, France (horiz)	65	40
1582	2000d. "Locomotion", 1825 (horiz)	1·40	65
1583	3000d. "Saint-Lo", 1843 (horiz)	2·50	95
1584	3000d. "Coutances", 1855 (horiz)	2·50	95

MS1585 83×62 mm. 5000d. "Atlantic", 1843 (32×43 mm) — 4·50 2·30

323 Ho Chi Minh, "VII" and Buildings

1991. Seventh Vietnamese Communist Party Congress. Multicoloured.

1586	200d. Type **323**	40	25
1587	300d. Workers	65	40
1588	400d. Mother and children	90	50

324 Pioneers

1991. 50th Anniv of Vietnam Youth Pioneers (200d.) and United Nations Convention on Children's Rights (400d.). Multicoloured.

1589	200d. Type **324**	75	40
1590	400d. Child's face and U.N. emblem	1·30	65

325 Lada

1991. Rally Cars. Multicoloured.

1591	400d. Type **325**	25	20
1592	400d. Nissan	25	20
1593	500d. Ford Sierra RS Cosworth	40	25
1594	1000d. Suzuki	65	30
1595	2000d. Mazda "323"	1·40	65
1596	3000d. Peugeot	2·50	95
1597	3000d. Lancia	2·50	95

MS1598 85×75 mm. 5000d. Peugeot "405" (43×29 mm) — 5·75 2·75

326 Yellow-banded Poison-arrow Frog

1991. Frogs. Multicoloured.

1599	200d. Type **326**	40	20
1600	400d. Edible frog	50	25
1601	500d. Golden mantella	65	30
1602	1000d. Dyeing poison-arrow frog	1·00	40
1603	2000d. Tree frog	2·00	75
1604	3000d. Red-eyed tree frog ("Agalychnis calidryas")	3·25	1·30
1605	3000d. Golden tree frog ("Hyla aurea")	3·25	1·30

327 Ho Chi Minh and Party Emblem

1991. 60th Anniv (1990) of Vietnamese Communist Party.

1606	**327**	100d. red	1·90	1·60

328 Speed Skating

1991. Winter Olympic Games, Albertville (1992) (1st issue). Multicoloured.

1607	200d. Type **328**	25	15
1608	300d. Freestyle skiing	30	20
1609	400d. Four-man bobsleighing (horiz)	40	25
1610	1000d. Biathlon (rifle shooting) (horiz)	65	30
1611	2000d. Skiing (horiz)	1·40	65
1612	3000d. Cross-country skiing	2·75	1·10
1613	3000d. Ice skating	2·75	1·10

MS1614 93×106 mm. 5000d. Ice Hockey (32×43 mm) — 4·50 2·30

See also Nos. 1659/63.

329 "Arsinoitherium zitteli"

1991. Prehistoric Animals. Multicoloured.

1615	200d. Type **329**	25	20
1616	500d. "Elephas primigenius"	40	25
1617	1000d. "Baluchitherium"	65	40
1618	2000d. "Deinotherium gigan-teum"	2·00	65
1619	3000d. "Brontops"	2·75	1·10
1620	3000d. "Uintatherium"	2·75	1·10

330 Pawn

1991. Chess. Staunton Pieces.

1621	200d. Type **330**	25	20
1622	300d. Knight	40	25
1623	1000d. Rook	65	40
1624	2000d. Queen	1·60	65
1625	3000d. Bishop	2·50	1·00
1626	3000d. King	2·50	1·00

MS1627 92×70 mm. 5000d. Knight, pawn and king — 4·50 2·30

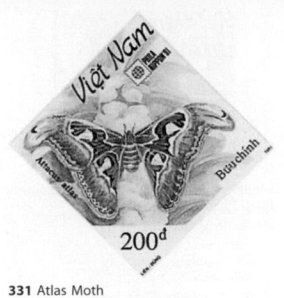

331 Atlas Moth

1991. "Phila Nippon '91" International Stamp Exhibition, Tokyo. Moths and Butterflies. Mult.

1628	200d. Type **331**	25	15
1629	400d. Blue morpho	40	20
1630	500d. Birdwing	50	25
1631	1000d. Red admiral	90	40
1632	1000d. "Papilio demetrius"	90	40
1633	3000d. "Papilio weiskei"	2·30	90
1634	5000d. Lesser purple emperor	3·25	1·40
MS1635 85×87 mm. 5500d. "Heliconius melpomene-aglaope" (43×32 mm)		4·50	2·30

332 Means of Communication

1991. 25th Anniv of Post and Telecommunications Research Institute. Multicoloured.

1636	200d. Type **332**	1·00	40
MS1637 90×73 mm. 3500d. Means of communication (different) (43×32 mm)		3·75	1·90

333 Eye and Clasped Hands

1991. Golden Heart Charity for Disabled People.

1638	**333** 200d. blue, lilac & orange	50	25
1639	– 3000d. violet, blue and turquoise	3·25	1·30

DESIGN: 3000d. Tennis player in wheelchair.

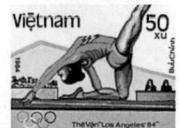

334 Gymnastics

1992. Olympic Games, Los Angeles (1984). Multicoloured.

1640	50x. Type **334**	25	15
1641	50x. Football (vert)	25	15
1642	1d. Wrestling	50	25
1643	2d. Volleyball (vert)	1·00	40
1644	3d. Hurdling	1·30	50
1645	5d. Basketball (vert)	1·50	90
1646	8d. Weightlifting	3·25	1·40
MS1647 80×100 mm. 10d. Running (31×39 mm)		6·25	3·50

1992. "Expo '92" World's Fair, Seville. Nos. 1372/8 optd **SEVILLA'92** and emblem.

1648	**288** 50d. multicoloured	65	25
1649	– 100d. mult (No. 1373)	1·10	40
1650	– 100d. mult (No. 1374)	1·10	40
1651	– 100d. mult (No. 1375)	1·10	40
1652	– 200d. mult (No. 1376)	2·00	65
1653	– 200d. mult (No. 1377)	2·00	65
1654	– 300d. multicoloured	3·25	1·60
MS1655 85×69 mm. 500d. multicoloured		7·00	3·00

336 Chu Van An teaching

1992. 700th Death Anniv of Chu Van An.

1656	**336** 200d. multicoloured	31·00	10·00

337 Atomic Symbol, Communications, Industry and Agriculture

1992. Resolutions of Seventh Communist Party Congress. Multicoloured.

1657	200d. Type **337**	50	25
1658	2000d. Hands clasped and map of Asia	3·25	2·50

338 Biathlon

1992. Winter Olympic Games, Albertville (2nd issue). Multicoloured.

1659	200d. Type **338**	40	25
1660	2000d. Ice hockey	1·00	40
1661	4000d. Skiing (slalom)	1·90	50
1662	5000d. Ice skating	2·30	90
1663	6000d. Skiing (downhill)	3·25	1·30

339 Columbus's Fleet

1992. 500th Anniv of Discovery of America by Columbus (3rd issue). Multicoloured.

1664	400d. Type **339**	40	25
1665	3000d. "Santa Maria"	1·30	40
1666	4000d. Columbus and flag on land	2·10	50
1667	6000d. Columbus offering gifts to Amerindians	2·75	90
1668	8000d. Ship returning home	3·25	1·30
MS1669 102×70 mm. 11000d. Columbus before King Ferdinand and Queen Isabella (vert)		6·25	3·00

340 Tupolev Tu-154M

1992. Aircraft. Multicoloured.

1670	400d. Type **340**	25	15
1671	500d. Concorde	30	20
1672	1000d. Airbus Industrie A-320	40	25
1673	3000d. Airbus Industrie A340-300	50	40
1674	4000d. De Havilland D.H.C.8 Dash Eight-400	1·90	65
1675	5000d. Boeing 747-200	2·50	1·00
1676	6000d. McDonnell Douglas MD-11CF	3·00	1·30

341 Weather System and Forecasting Equipment

1992. International Decade for Natural Disaster Reduction. Multicoloured.

1677	400d. Type **341**	50	25
1678	4000d. Man taking flood depth readings	2·00	90

342 Archery

1992. Olympic Games, Barcelona (2nd issue). Multicoloured.

1679	400d. Type **342**	40	20
1680	600d. Volleyball	50	25
1681	1000d. Wrestling	65	30
1682	3000d. Fencing	1·30	40
1683	4000d. Running	1·90	50
1684	5000d. Weightlifting	2·10	65
1685	6000d. Hockey	3·25	1·30
MS1686 94×74 mm. 10000d. Basketball (27×39 mm)		6·25	3·00

343 Suzuki "500 F"

1992. Racing Motor Cycles. Multicoloured.

1687	400d. Type **343**	40	20
1688	500d. Honda "CBR 600F"	50	25
1689	1000d. Honda "HRC 500F"	65	30
1690	3000d. Kawasaki "250F" (vert)	1·30	40
1691	4000d. Suzuki "RM 250 F" (vert)	1·90	50
1692	5000d. Suzuki "500F"	2·10	65
1693	6000d. BMW "1000F"	3·00	1·10
MS1694 103×78 mm. 10000d. Suzuki "RM 250 F" (different) (32×42 mm)		6·25	3·00

344 Shuttle Launch

1992. International Space Year. Multicoloured.

1695	400d. Type **344**	40	20
1696	500d. Launch of space shuttle "Columbia"	50	25
1697	3000d. "Columbia" in space (horiz)	1·30	40
1698	4000d. Projected shuttle "Hermes" docked at space station (horiz)	1·60	65
1699	5000d. "Hermes" in space with solar panel (horiz)	2·10	75
1700	6000d. Astronauts repairing Hubble space telescope	3·00	1·10

345 Main Entrance

1992. Centenary of Saigon Post Office. Multicoloured.

1701	200d. Type **345**	1·50	40
MS1702 84×69 mm. 10000d. Post Office		4·50	2·50

346 Footballer

1992. European Cup Football Championship. Multicoloured.

1703	200d. Type **346**	25	20
1704	2000d. Goalkeeper	65	25
1705	4000d. Two players with ball on ground	1·40	65
1706	5000d. Two players with ball in air	1·90	90
1707	6000d. Three players	2·75	1·10
MS1708 70×93 mm. 9000d. Players (42×30 mm)		5·75	3·00

347 "Portrait of a Girl" (Francisco de Zurbaran)

1992. "Expo '92" World's Fair, Seville. Paintings by Spanish Artists. Multicoloured.

1709	400d. Type **347**	40	20
1710	500d. "Woman with a Jug" (Bartolome Esteban Murillo)	50	25
1711	1000d. "Maria Aptrickaia" (Diego Velazquez)	75	30
1712	3000d. "Holy Family with St. Katharine" (Jose de Ribera)	1·30	40
1713	4000d. "Madonna and Child with Sts. Agnes and Thekla" (El Greco)	1·90	65
1714	5000d. "Woman with Jug" (Francisco Goya)	2·30	70
1715	6000d. "The Naked Maja" (Francisco Goya) (horiz)	3·25	1·10
MS1716 82×85 mm. 10000d. "Three Women" (Pablo Picasso) (43×32 mm)		6·25	3·00

348 Clean Water sustaining Life and Polluted Water

1992. 20th Anniv of United Nations Conference on Environmental Protection. Multicoloured.

1717	200d. Type **348**	40	25
1718	4000d. Graph comparing current world development and environmentally sound development	1·80	65

349 Cu Lao Xanh Lighthouse

1992. "Genova '92" International Thematic Stamp Exhibition. Lighthouses. Multicoloured.

1719	200d. Type **349**	40	25
1720	3000d. Can Gio	1·00	40
1721	4000d. Vung Tau	2·00	65
1722	6000d. Long Chau	3·25	1·00

350 "Citrus maxima"

1992. Flowers. Multicoloured.

1723	200d. Type **350**	40	20
1724	2000d. "Nerium indicum"	90	25
1725	4000d. "Ixora coccinea"	1·40	40
1726	5000d. "Cananga oborata"	1·80	45
1727	6000d. "Cassia surattensis"	2·75	90

351 Australian Pied Imperial Pigeons

1992. Pigeons and Doves. Multicoloured.

1728	200d. Type **351**	40	20
1729	2000d. Red-plumed pigeon	90	25
1730	4000d. Feral rock pigeon	1·50	40
1731	5000d. Top-knot pigeon	2·30	55
1732	6000d. Laughing doves (horiz)	2·50	90

352 Guinea Pig

1992. Rodents. Multicoloured.

1733	200d. Type **352**	40	20
1734	500d. Guinea pigs	50	25
1735	3000d. Indian crested por-cupine	1·30	40
1736	4000d. Lesser Egyptian gerbil (vert)	1·80	50
1737	5000d. Red giant flying squirrel (vert)	2·30	90
1738	6000d. Common rabbit (vert)	3·25	1·30

353 Memorials and "45"

1992. 45th Anniv of Disabled Soldiers' Day.

1739	**353**	200d. multicoloured	75	40

354 Stylized Sportsmen

1992. Third Phu Dong Games.

1740	**354**	200d. blue, ultramarine and light blue	75	40

355 Siamese Fighting Fish

1992. Siamese Fighting Fish.

1741	**355**	200d. multicoloured	40	20
1742	-	500d. multicoloured	50	25
1743	-	3000d. multicoloured	1·50	40
1744	-	4000d. multicoloured	1·80	45
1745	-	5000d. multicoloured	2·10	90
1746	-	6000d. multicoloured	3·25	1·20

DESIGNS: 500d. to 6000d. Different Siamese fighting fishes.

356 Members' Locations on Map

1992. 40th Anniv of International Planned Parenthood Federation. Multicoloured.

1747	200d. Type **356**	40	25
1748	4000d. Emblem on world map (horiz)	1·80	65

357 Trainee Doctors

1992. 90th Anniv of Hanoi Medical School. Multicoloured.

1749	200d. Type **357**	40	25
1750	5000d. Alexandre Yersin (bacte-riologist) and school	2·10	75

358 Adult protecting Child

1992. SOS Children's Villages. Multicoloured.

1751	200d. Type **358**	40	25
1752	5000d. Houses and woman with children	2·10	75

359 Kick Boxing

1993. 17th South-East Asian Games, Singapore.

1753	**359**	200d. multicoloured	90	40

360 Giant Bee

1993. Bees. Multicoloured.

1754	200d. Type **360**	40	20
1755	800d. "Apis koschevnikovi"	50	25
1756	1000d. "Apis laboriosa"	75	30
1757	2000d. "Apis cerana japonica"	1·30	40
1758	5000d. "Apis cerana cerana"	2·30	90
1759	10000d. Honey bee (vert)	4·25	1·50

361 Tam-Cam returning from the River

1993. Legend of Tam-Cam. Multicoloured.

1760	200d. Type **361**	40	20
1761	800d. Apparition of old man by goldfish basin	50	25
1762	1000d. Tam-Cam with unsold rice at the market	75	30
1763	3000d. Tam-Cam trying on slipper for Prince	1·10	40
1764	4000d. Tam-Cam rising from lotus	2·00	90
1765	10000d. The royal couple	3·75	1·40

362 Rooster with Family

1993. New Year. Year of the Cock. Multicoloured.

1766	200d. Type **362**	65	25
1767	5000d. Rooster with family (different)	2·10	65

363 "Atractylodes macrocephala"

1993. Medicinal Plants. Multicoloured.

1768	200d. Type **363**	40	20
1769	1000d. Rangoon creeper ("Quisqualis indica")	50	25
1770	1000d. Japanese honeysuckle ("Lonicera japonica")	50	25
1771	3000d. "Rehmannia glutinosa"	1·80	40
1772	12000d. "Gardenia jasminoides"	5·75	1·80

364 Communications Equipment

1993. "Communication in Service of Life". Multicoloured.

1773	200d. Type **364**	25	15
1774	2500d. Fibre-optic cable and map of Hong Kong–Sri Racha submarine cable route	1·00	40

365 Giant Panda

Gấu trúc *Ailuropoda melanoleuca*

1993. Mammals. Multicoloured.

1775	200d. Type **365**	25	15
1776	800d. Tiger	50	20
1777	1000d. Indian elephant	65	25
1778	3000d. Indian rhinoceros	1·50	40
1779	4000d. Family of gibbons	2·10	75
1780	10000d. Clouded leopard	3·75	1·60
MS1781	79×85 mm. 10000d. Kouprey ("Bos sauveli")	5·00	2·50

366 Players, Statue of Liberty and Emblem

1993. World Cup Football Championship, U.S.A. (1994) (1st issue).

1782	**366**	200d. multicoloured	25	15
1783	-	1500d. multicoloured	75	25
1784	-	7000d. multicoloured	2·75	75

DESIGNS: 1500, 7000d. Different match scenes.
See also Nos. 1865/**MS**1871.

367 Wheelbarrow

1993. Traditional Transport. Multicoloured.

1785	200d. Type **367**	25	15
1786	800d. Buffalo cart	50	20
1787	1000d. Rickshaw	65	25
1788	2000d. Rickshaw with passenger	1·30	40
1789	5000d. Rickshaw (different)	2·50	90
1790	10000d. Horse-drawn carriage	3·75	1·80

368 Pylon and Lightbulb

1993. 500 kV Electricity Lines.

1791	**368**	300d. black, orange and red	50	25
1792	**368**	400d. black, blue and orange	75	40

369 "Sunflowers" (Vincent van Gogh)

1993. "Polska'93" International Stamp Exhibition, Poznan. Paintings. Multicoloured.

1793	200d. Type **369**	25	15
1794	1000d. "Young Woman" (Amedeo Modigliani)	50	25
1795	1000d. "Couple in Forest" (Henri Rousseau)	50	25
1796	5000d. "Harlequin with Family" (Pablo Picasso)	2·30	40
1797	10000d. "Female Model" (Henri Matisse) (horiz)	4·75	1·30
MS1798	85×85 mm. 10000d. "Dr. Gachet" (Vincent van Gogh) (27×37 mm)	5·75	3·00

370 "Paphiopedilum hirsutissimum"

1993. Centenary of Da Lat. Orchids. Multicoloured.

1799	400d. Type **370**	25	15
1800	1000d. "Paphiopedilum gratrixianum"	50	25
1801	1000d. "Paphiopedilum malipoense"	50	25
1802	12000d. "Paphiopedilum hennisianum"	5·75	2·30

371 Wat Phra Sri Rattana Satsadaram, Thailand

1993. Historic Asian Architecture. Multicoloured.

1803	400d. Type **371**	25	15
1804	800d. Prambanan Temple, Indonesia	40	20
1805	1000d. City Hall, Singapore	50	25
1806	2000d. Angkor Vat, Cambodia (horiz)	90	40
1807	2000d. Ubudiah Mosque, Kuala Kangsar, Malaysia (horiz)	1·00	45
1808	6000d. That Luang, Laos (horiz)	2·30	75
1809	8000d. Omar Ali Saifuddin Mosque, Brunei (horiz)	3·25	1·00
MS1810	86×116 mm. 10000d. Chua Keo, Thai Binh, Vietnam (31×42 mm)	5·00	2·50

372 Industry and Communications

1993. Seventh Trade Unions Congress. Multicoloured.

1811	400d. Type **372**	25	15
1812	5000d. Doves, atomic symbol, hammer in hand and flowers	2·00	65

373 "Scylla serrata"

1993. Salt-water Crabs. Multicoloured.

1813	400d. Type **373**	15	10
1814	800d. "Portunus sanguinolentus"	25	15
1815	1000d. "Charybdis bimaculata"	40	20
1816	2000d. "Paralithodes brevipes"	75	25
1817	5000d. "Portunus pelagicus"	2·00	65
1818	10000d. "Lithodes turritus"	3·25	1·10

374 Stamps and Globe

1993. Stamp Day. Multicoloured.

1819	400d. Type **374**	25	15
1820	5000d. Airmail letter	2·00	65

375 Player

1994. Tennis.

1821	**375**	400d. multicoloured	25	15

1822	-	1000d. multicoloured (male player)	65	25
1823	-	1000d. multicoloured (female player)	65	25
1824	-	12000d. multicoloured	4·50	1·50

DESIGNS: Nos. 1822/4, Different players.

376 Lo Lo Costume

1993. "Bangkok 1993" International Stamp Exhibition.

1825	400d. Type **376**	25	15
1826	800d. Thai costume	40	20
1827	1000d. Dao Do costume	50	25
1828	2000d. H'mong costume	75	30
1829	5000d. Kho Mu costume	2·10	75
1830	10000d. Kinh costume	3·00	1·30
MS1831	78×108 mm. 10000d. Precious stones (42×31 mm)	5·75	3·00

377 Dog with Puppies

1994. New Year. Year of the Dog. Multicoloured.

1832	400d. Type **377**	65	25
1833	6000d. Dog	3·25	90

378 Peach

1994. Flowers of the Four Seasons. Multicoloured.

1834	400d. Type **378** (spring)	90	25
1835	400d. "Chrysanthemum morifolium" (autumn)	90	25
1836	400d. "Prunus mume" (winter)	90	25
1837	13000d. Delonix regia (summer)	6·25	2·10

379 Anatoly Karpov

1994. Chess. Multicoloured.

1838	400d. Type **379**	25	15
1839	1000d. Gary Kasparov	65	25
1840	2000d. Robert Fischer	1·00	40
1841	4000d. Emanuel Lasker	1·90	65
1842	10000d. Jose Raul Capablanca	3·75	1·30
MS1843	85×90 mm. 10000d. Chess piece (vert)	5·75	2·75

No. 1840 is wrongly inscribed "Robers".

380 Hoi Lim

1994. "Hong Kong '94" Stamp Exhibition. Traditional Festivals. Multicoloured.

1844	400d. Type **380**	25	15
1845	800d. Cham	50	20
1846	1000d. Tay Nguyen	75	25
1847	12000d. Nam Bo	4·75	1·50

381 Loi Nhuoc

1994. Operatic Masks. Multicoloured.

1848	400d. Type **381**	25	15

1849	500d. Dao Tax Xuan	40	20
1850	2000d. Ta Ngoc Lan	75	25
1851	3000d. Ly Khac Minh	1·30	40
1852	4000d. Ta On Dinh	1·90	65
1853	7000d. Khuong Linh Ta	3·25	1·30

382 Red Gladioli

1994. Gladioli. Multicoloured.

1854	400d. Type **382**	25	15
1855	2000d. Salmon gladioli	75	30
1856	5000d. White gladioli	2·10	65
1857	8000d. Magenta gladioli	3·25	1·30

383 Painting by Utamaro Kitagawa

1994. Paintings by Japanese Artists. Multicoloured.

1858	400d. Type **383** (wrongly inscr "Kigatawa")	25	15
1859	500d. Harunobu Suzuki	40	20
1860	1000d. Hokusai Katsushika	50	25
1861	2000d. Hiroshige	90	30
1862	3000d. Hokusai Katsushika (different)	1·10	40
1863	4000d. Utamaro Kitagawa (different)	1·50	50
1864	9000d. Choki Eishosai	3·50	1·40

384 Footballers

1994. World Cup Football Championship, U.S.A. (2nd issue). Multicoloured.

1865	400d. Type **384**	25	15
1866	600d. Running with ball	40	20
1867	1000d. Heading ball	50	25
1868	2000d. Goalkeeper	75	30
1869	3000d. Two players chasing ball	1·50	50
1870	11000d. Tackling	4·75	1·60
MS1871	102×77 mm. 10000d. Play at goalmouth (31×42 mm)	5·75	2·75

385 Hauling Piece of Equipment

1994. 40th Anniv of Victory at Dien Bien Phu.

1872	**385**	400d. brown, cinnamon and black	65	20
1873	-	3000d. ultramarine, blue and black	1·90	65

DESIGN: 3000d. Entertaining the troops.

386 Pioneers reading Newspaper

1994. 40th Anniv of "Young Pioneer" (newspaper).

1874	**386**	400d. red and black	90	25

387 Estuarine Crocodile

1994. Reptiles. Multicoloured.

1875	400d. Type **387**	25	15
1876	600d. Mississippi alligator	40	20

1877	2000d. Nile crocodile	75	25
1878	3000d. Chinese alligator	1·10	40
1879	4000d. Paraguay caiman	1·90	65
1880	9000d. Australian crocodile	3·75	1·30
MS1881	100×67 mm. 10000d. Spectacled caiman (42×31 mm)	5·75	2·75

388 Alexandre Yersin

1994. Centenary of Discovery of Plague Bacillus.

1882	**388**	400d. multicoloured	1·30	40

389 Pierre de Coubertin (founder)

1994. Cent of International Olympic Committee. Multicoloured.

1883	400d. Anniversary and National Committee emblems and sports pictograms	1·50	65
1884	6000d. Type **389**	3·00	90

390 "Cicindela aurulenta"

1994. Beetles. Multicoloured.

1885	400d. Type **390**	65	25
1886	1000d. "Harmonia octomaculata"	1·00	30
1887	6000d. "Cicindela tennipes"	2·30	65
1888	9000d. "Callipappa apa"	3·75	1·50

391 Anniversary Emblem

1994. 120th Anniv of U.P.U. Multicoloured.

1889	400d. Type **391**	40	15
1890	5000d. Envelopes forming world map	2·10	65
MS1891	100×80 mm. 10000d. UPU emblem (29×41 mm)	5·75	2·75

392 Curlew

1994. "Philakorea 1994" International Stamp Exhibition, Seoul. Sea Birds. Multicoloured.

1892	400d. Type **392**	25	15
1893	600d. Wilson's storm petrel	40	20
1894	1000d. Great frigate bird	50	25
1895	2000d. Cape gannet	75	30
1896	3000d. Tufted puffins	1·50	50
1897	11000d. Band-tailed gulls	4·75	1·50
MS1898	78×65 mm. 10000d. Greyrumped swiftlet (38×31 mm)	5·75	2·75

393 "Bambusa blumeana"

1994. "Singpex '94" Stamp Exhibition, Singapore. Bamboos. Multicoloured.

1899	400d. Type **393**	25	15
1900	1000d. "Phyllostachys aurea"	50	25

1901	2000d. "Bambusa vulgaris"	1·00	40
1902	4000d. "Tetragonocalamus quadrangularis"	1·60	50
1903	10000d. "Bambusa venticosa"	4·75	1·80

394 Log Bridge with Handrail

1994. Rudimentary Bridges. Multicoloured.

1904	400d. Type **394**	25	15
1905	900d. Interwoven bridge	90	50
1906	8000d. Log bridge on stilts	3·25	1·00

395 Girl in Wheelchair and Boy playing

1994. "For Our Children's Future". Multicoloured.

1907	400d.+100d. Type **395**	25	15
1908	2000d. Children dancing around emblem (vert)	1·00	50

396 Electric Tramcar No. 1

1994. Trams. Multicoloured.

1909	400d. Type **396**	25	15
1910	900d. Paris double-deck battery-powered tram	75	40
1911	8000d. Philadelphia U.S. Mail electric tram	3·50	1·10

397 Civilians greeting Soldiers

1994. 40th Anniv of Liberation of Hanoi. Multicoloured.

1912	400d. Type **397**	25	15
1913	2000d. Workers and students and symbols of development	1·00	50

398 Airplane in Air

1994. 50th Anniv of I.C.A.O. Multicoloured.

1914	400d. Type **398**	50	20
1915	3000d. Airplane on ground	1·80	70

399 Parade

1994. 50th Anniv of Vietnamese People's Army. Multicoloured.

1916	400d. Type **399**	25	15
1917	1000d. Plan of attacks on Saigon	50	25
1918	2000d. Veteran recounting the past to young girl	75	40
1919	4000d. Naval anti-aircraft gun crew	1·80	70

400 Sow with Piglets

1995. New Year. Year of the Pig. Multicoloured.

1920	400d. Type **400**	50	20
1921	8000d. Pig	3·25	1·30

401 Osprey ("Pandion haliaetus")

1995. Birds.
1922	**401**	400d. blue	25	15
1923	-	400d. green	25	15
1924	-	400d. purple	25	15
1925	-	400d. orange	25	15
1926	-	5000d. red	2·10	75

DESIGNS—HORIZ: No. 1923, Sociable weaver ("Philetarius socius"); 1924, Sharpbill ("Oxyruncus cristatus"); 1925, Golden plover ("Pluvialis apricaria"). VERT: No. 1926, Red-legged seriema ("Cariama cristata").

402 Girls with Bicycle

1995. Women's Costumes. Multicoloured.
1927	400d. Type **402**		25	15
1928	3000d. Girl with sheaf of flowers		1·00	40
1929	5000d. Girl with traditional hat		2·50	75

403 Statue and Building

1995. "Vietstampex '95" Stamp Exhibition. F.I.A.P. Executive Committee Meeting.
1930	**403**	5500d. multicoloured	2·10	90

404 Brown Fish Owl

1995. Owls. Multicoloured.
1931	400d. Type **404**		25	15
1932	1000d. Tawny owl		50	25
1933	2000d. Great grey owl		75	30
1934	5000d. Spotted wood owl		1·80	65
1935	10000d. White-faced scops owl		3·25	1·40
MS1936	64×81 mm. 12500d. Barn owl (31×42 mm)		5·75	2·75

405 Grey Angelfish

1995. Fish. Multicoloured.
1937	400d. Type **405**		25	15
1938	1000d. Rectangle triggerfish		50	25
1939	2000d. Regal angelfish		75	30
1940	4000d. Queen angelfish		1·10	45
1941	5000d. Queen triggerfish		1·90	65
1942	9000d. Clown triggerfish		3·00	1·10

406 Throwing the Hammer

1995. Olympic Games, Atlanta (1996) (1st issue). Multicoloured.
1943	400d. Type **406**		25	15
1944	3000d. Cycling		1·00	40
1945	4000d. Running		1·10	50
1946	10000d. Pole vaulting		3·25	1·30
MS1947	59×100 mm. 12500d. Handball		5·75	2·75

See also Nos. 2063/5.

407 Lenin

1995. 125th Birth Anniv of Lenin.
1948	**407**	400d. black and red	75	30

408 Adult and Young

1995. The Malayan Tapir. Multicoloured. (a) With World Wildlife Fund emblem.
1949	400d. Type **408**		1·00	40
1950	1000d. Standing		1·50	65
1951	2000d. Walking		1·90	75
1952	4000d. Calling		2·50	1·00

Nos. 1949/52 were issued together, se-tenant, forming a composite design.

(b) Without W.W.F. emblem.
1953	4000d. Standing by trees		1·50	65
1954	4000d. Eating		1·50	65
1955	5000d. Swimming		1·90	75
1956	6000d. In water		2·10	80

Nos. 1953/6 were issued together, se-tenant, forming a composite design.

409 Dove and "50"

1995. 50th Anniv of End of Second World War in Europe.
1957	**409**	400d. multicoloured	90	30

410 Montgolfier's Hot Air Balloon, 1783

1995. "Finlandia 95" International Stamp Exhibition, Helsinki. Balloons. Multicoloured.
1958	500d. Type **410**		25	15
1959	1000d. Jacques Charles and Marie-Noel Robert's balloon (first untethered flight by manned hydrogen balloon)		40	20
1960	2000d. Jean-Pierre Blanchard's oared balloon		75	25
1961	3000d. Jean-Francois Pilatre de Rozier and Jules Romain's balloon over English Channel, 1785		1·00	30
1962	4000d. Free balloon		1·10	40
1963	5000d. Captive balloon over Red Square, Moscow, 1890		1·50	50
1964	7000d. Auguste Piccard's balloon "F.N.R.S.", 1931		2·50	90

411 Parachutist

1995. Parachuting. Multicoloured.
1965	400d. Type **411**		40	20
1966	2000d. Two parachutists		75	25
1967	3000d. Landing		1·10	40

1968	4000d. Gathering in the parachute		2·75	1·10

Nos. 1965/8 were issued together, se-tenant, forming a composite design.

412 "Rhododendron fleuryi"

1995. Rhododendrons. Multicoloured.
1969	400d. Type **412**		25	15
1970	1000d. "Rhododendron sulphoreum"		50	25
1971	2000d. "Rhododendron sino-falconeri"		75	30
1972	3000d. "Rhododendron lyi"		1·00	40
1973	5000d. "Rhododendron ovatum"		1·80	65
1974	9000d. "Rhododendron tanastylum"		3·25	1·40

413 Tan and Lang pay Court to Lu's Daughter

1995. "Betel and Areca Nut" (fable). Multicoloured.
1975	400d. Type **413**		25	15
1976	1000d. Girl chooses Tan		50	25
1977	3000d. Lang changes into rock		1·00	40
1978	10000d. Girl changes into betel pepper plant and Tan into areca nut palm		3·25	1·10

Nos. 1975/8 were issued together, se-tenant, forming a composite design.

414 Statue of Mother and Child

1995. 65th Anniv of Women's Union (400d.) and World Conference on Women, Peking (3000d.). Multicoloured.
1979	400d. Type **414**		50	20
1980	3000d. Globe and women of different races (horiz)		1·00	50

415 Flags around Emblem

1995. Admission of Vietnam to Association of South East Asian Nations.
1981	**415**	400d. multicoloured	75	30

416 Ho Chi Minh, Dove and Crowd

1995. Anniversaries. Multicoloured.
1982	**416**	400d. Type **416** (65th anniv of Communist Party of Indo-China)	25	15
1983		400d. Ho Chi Minh embracing child (105th birth anniv)	25	15
1984		1000d. Civic building, road bridge, power lines and oil derrick (40th anniv of evacuation of French troops from North Vietnam)	50	25
1985		1000d. Ho Chi Minh saluting and building flying flags (20th anniv of end of Vietnam war)	50	25
1986		2000d. Soldiers and flag (50th anniv of National Liberation Army)	90	45

1987	2000d. Radio mast, dish aerial, motor cycle couriers and mail van (50th anniv of postal and telecommunications services)		90	45

417 Bust of Hill and Penny Black

1995. Birth Bicentenary of Sir Rowland Hill (instigator of postage stamp).
1988	**417**	4000d. multicoloured	1·50	50

418 Torch Carriers and Sports Pictograms

1995. National Sports Festival.
1989	**418**	400d. blue, red and lilac	75	30

419 "Paphiopedilum druryi"

1995. "Singapore '95" International Stamp Exhibition. Orchids. Multicoloured.
1990	400d. Type **419**		25	15
1991	2000d. "Dendrobium ochraceum"		75	30
1992	3000d. "Vanda sp."		1·00	40
1993	4000d. "Cattleya sp."		1·10	45
1994	5000d. "Paphiopedilum hirsutissimum"		1·90	65
1995	6000d. "Christenosia vietnamica"		2·50	1·00
MS1996	65×90 mm. 12500d. "Angraecum sesquipedale" (31×42 mm)		5·75	2·75

420 Palace, Hue

1995. Asian Cityscapes. Multicoloured.
1997	400d. Type **420**		25	15
1998	3000d. Park, Doanh Chau		1·00	40
1999	4000d. Temple, Macao		1·10	45
2000	5000d. Kowloon, Hong Kong		1·90	65
2001	6000d. Pagoda, Dai Loan		2·00	75

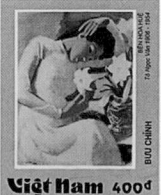

421 Dove and Anniversary Emblem

1995. 50th Anniv of U.N.O.
2002	**421**	2000d. multicoloured	90	40

422 Woman with Vase of Flowers (To Ngoc Van)

1995. Paintings. Multicoloured.
2003	400d. Type **422**		50	25
2004	2000d. Woman washing hair (Tran Van Can)		90	65
2005	6000d. Woman and vase of flowers (To Ngoc Van)		1·80	1·60

| 2006 | 8000d. Two women resting (Tran Van Can) | 2·50 | 2·30 |

423 Map and Eclipse

1995. Total Eclipse of the Sun.

| 2007 | **423** | 400d. multicoloured | 1·00 | 50 |

424 Rats carrying Canopy and on Horseback

1996. New Year. Year of the Rat. Multicoloured.

2008		400d. Type **424**	65	30
2009		8000d. Rats in and carrying sedan chair	3·75	2·00
MS2010	110×75 mm. 13000d. Rat carrying placard (31×42 mm)		5·00	4·50

425 Apricot

1996. Flowers.

2011	**425**	400d. brown	25	15
2012	-	400d. purple	25	15
2013	-	400d. red	25	15
2014	-	400d. blue	25	15
2015	-	5000d. red	1·80	1·30

DESIGNS—HORIZ: No. 2012, Chrysanthemums; 2013, Orchid; 2014, Orchids (different). VERT: No. 2015, Asters.

426 Communist Symbols and Ho Chi Minh

1996. Eighth Vietnamese Communist Party Congress. Multicoloured.

| 2016 | | 400d. Type **426** | 25 | 15 |
| 2017 | | 3000d. Symbols of communications, industry, Communism and agriculture within outline of dove | 1·00 | 90 |

427 Thanh Tru Tai

1996. Statues in Tay Phuong Pagoda, Thach That. Multicoloured.

2018		400d. Type **427**	25	15
2019		600d. Tich Doc Than	40	20
2020		1000d. Hoang Tuy Cau	50	25
2021		2000d. Bach Tinh Thuy	65	50
2022		3000d. Xich Thanh Hoa	90	75
2023		5000d. Dinh Tru Tai	1·30	1·10
2024		6000d. Tu Hien Than	1·50	1·40
2025		8000d. Dai Than Luc	2·30	2·00

428 Tsintaosaurus

1996. Prehistoric Animals. Multicoloured.

2026		400d. Type **428**	25	15
2027		1000d. Archaeopteryx	40	25
2028		2000d. Psittacosaurus	75	50
2029		3000d. Hypsilophodon	1·10	90
2030		13000d. Parasaurolophus	3·75	3·25

429 White-throated Kingfisher

1996. Kingfishers. Multicoloured.

2031		400d. Type **429**	25	15
2032		1000d. Belted kingfisher	40	25
2033		2000d. River kingfisher	65	50
2034		4000d. Ruddy kingfisher	1·10	1·00
2035		12000d. Lesser pied kingfisher	3·25	3·00

430 Temple of Literature, Hanoi

1996. Asian Temples. Multicoloured.

2036		400d. Type **430**	25	15
2037		2000d. Wat Mahathat, Sukhothai, Thailand	65	55
2038		3000d. Lingaraja Temple, Bhubaeshwar, India	90	80
2039		4000d. Kinkakuju Temple, Kyoto, Japan	1·40	1·20
2040		10000d. Borobudur Temple, Java, Indonesia	3·25	2·75

431 Dan Ty Ba

1996. "China '96" Ninth Asian International Stamp Exhibition, Peking. Stringed Musical Instruments. Multicoloured.

2041		400d. Type **431**	40	30
2042		3000d. Dan nhi	1·10	1·00
2043		4000d. Dan day	1·40	1·20
2044		9000d. Dan tranh	2·75	2·50

432 Ho Chi Minh

1996. 50th Anniv of Vietnamese Red Cross.

| 2045 | **432** | 3000d. multicoloured | 1·50 | 1·40 |

433 Children of Different Races

1996. 50th Anniv of UNICEF. Multicoloured.

| 2046 | | 400d. Type **433** | 50 | 45 |
| 2047 | | 7000d. Water droplets containing symbols and globe "plant" | 2·30 | 2·00 |

434 Tiger Beetle

1996. Beetles. Multicoloured.

2048		400d. Type **434**	25	15
2049		500d. "Calodema wallacei"	40	25
2050		1000d. Blister beetle	65	55
2051		4000d. "Chrysochroa buqueti"	1·30	1·10
2052		5000d. "Ophloniea nigrofasciata"	1·40	1·20
2053		12000d. Ground beetle	3·25	2·75

435 Emblem in Hand

1996. 50th Natural Disaster Reduction Day.

| 2054 | **435** | 400d. multicoloured | 75 | 70 |

436 Goalkeeper

1996. European Football Championship, England. Multicoloured.

| 2055 | | 400d. Type **436** | 50 | 25 |
| 2056 | | 8000d. Player | 2·50 | 2·30 |

Nos. 2055/6 were issued together, se-tenant, forming a composite design.

437 Airbus Industrie A320

1996. Aircraft. Multicoloured.

2057		400d. Type **437**	25	15
2058		1000d. Antonov An-72	40	25
2059		2000d. McDonnell Douglas MD-11F	75	70
2060		6000d. RJ-85	1·90	1·70
2061		10000d. Boeing 747-400F	3·25	2·75
MS2062	86×50 mm. 13000d. Space shuttle riding on Boeing 747 (42×31 mm)		4·50	4·00

438 Women's Football

1996. Olympic Games, Atlanta, U.S.A. (2nd issue). Multicoloured.

2063		2000d. Type **438**	75	70
2064		4000d. Yachting	1·50	1·40
2065		5000d. Hockey	2·10	1·90

439 1946 1h. Stamp

1996. Stamp Day. 50th Anniv of First Unoverprinted Vietnamese Stamp.

| 2066 | **439** | 400d. multicoloured | 75 | 70 |

440 Orange Peel Fungus

1996. Fungi. Multicoloured.

2067		400d. Type **440**	25	15
2068		500d. "Morchella conica"	40	25
2069		1000d. "Anthurus archeri"	65	55
2070		4000d. Chicken mushroom	1·10	1·00
2071		5000d. "Filoboletus manipularis"	1·50	1·40
2072		12000d. "Tremiscus helvelloides"	3·75	3·25

441 Pupils at Main Gate

1996. Centenary of Hue School. Multicoloured.

| 2073 | | 400d. Type **441** | 40 | 25 |
| 2074 | | 3000d. Main building | 1·00 | 90 |

442 Woman and Vase of Lotus Flowers

1996. Paintings by Nguyen Sang. Multicoloured.

| 2075 | | 400d. Type **442** | 75 | 55 |
| 2076 | | 8000d. Soldiers at Dien Bien Phu | 2·75 | 2·30 |

443 Variegated Langurs

1996. "Taipeh '96" International Stamp Exhibition, Taiwan. Endangered Animals. Multicoloured.

2077		400d. Type **443**	50	30
2078		2000d. Tigers	75	70
2079		4000d. Javan rhinoceroses	1·30	1·10
2080		10000d. South African crowned cranes	3·25	2·75

444 Tree of Children's Heads

1996. Campaign for Use of Iodized Salt.

| 2081 | **444** | 400d. multicoloured | 75 | 55 |

445 Armed Combatants, National Flag and Quote from Ho Chi Minh

1996. 50th Anniv of Formation of National Front for the Liberation of South Vietnam.

| 2082 | **445** | 400d. multicoloured | 75 | 55 |

446 Rambutan

1997. Fruit.

2083	**446**	400d. red and black	40	25
2084	-	400d. brown and black	40	25
2085	-	400d. green and black	40	25
2086	-	400d. violet and black	40	25
2087	-	400d. purple and black	40	25

DESIGNS: No. 2084, Durian; 2085, Avocado; 2086, Mangostela; 2087, Queen-of-the-night.

447 Ox and Calf

1997. New Year. Year of the Ox. Multicoloured.

| 2088 | | 400d. Type **447** | 50 | 30 |
| 2089 | | 8000d. Ox | 2·75 | 2·50 |

448 Flags and Symbols of Development

1997. Eighth Vietnamese Communist Party Congress.

| 2090 | **448** | 400d. multicoloured | 85 | 70 |

449 Red-capped Goldfish

1997. Goldfish. Multicoloured.

2091	400d. Type **449**	30	15
2092	1000d. Black and red and long-tailed red goldfish	45	35
2093	5000d. Goldfish with gaping mouth	1·70	1·40
2094	7000d. Black and yellow goldfish	2·50	2·00
2095	8000d. Red goldfish with black tail and fins	2·75	2·30
MS2096	110×80 mm. 14000d. Two red-capped goldfinches (42×31 mm)	6·50	5·00

450 Snake Design

1997. Ly Dynasty Sculptures. Multicoloured.

2097	400d. Type **450**	30	15
2098	1000d. Terracotta dragon's head	45	35
2099	3000d. Musicians in rectangular panel (horiz)	1·30	1·00
2100	5000d. Lion base (horiz)	2·30	1·80
2101	10000d. Vessel with dragon design (horiz)	3·50	2·75

451 Pagoda in Lake, Ha Tay

1997. Landscapes. Multicoloured.

2102	400d. Type **451**	30	15
2103	5000d. Bamboo suspension bridge, Lai Chau	1·80	1·50
2104	7000d. Mist-wreathed trees behind village, Lao Cai	2·40	1·90

452 Red Lily

1997. The Lily. Multicoloured.

2105	400d. Type **452**	30	15
2106	1000d. White lily	45	35
2107	5000d. Pink and white lily	2·10	1·70
2108	10000d. Red and cream lily	3·50	2·75

453 Huynh Thuc Khang

1997. 50th Death Anniv of Huynh Thuc Khang.

2109	**453** 400d. multicoloured	1·40	90

454 Tennis

1997. Sports for Disabled People. Multicoloured.

2110	1000d. Type **454**	45	35
2111	6000d. Rifle shooting	2·30	1·80

455 Owton's Palm Civet

1997. Cat Ba National Park. Multicoloured.

2112	400d. Type **455**	30	15
2113	3000d. European otter	1·10	90
2114	4000d. Palla's squirrel	1·70	1·40
2115	10000d. Leopard cat	3·50	2·75

456 Golden Gate Bridge, San Francisco

1997. "Pacific '97" International Stamp Exhibition, San Francisco. Suspension Bridges. Multicoloured.

2116	400d. Type **456**	30	15
2117	5000d. Raippaluoto Bridge, Finland	1·70	1·40
2118	10000d. Seto Great road and rail bridge, Japan	3·75	3·00

457 Women and Girl

1997. Eighth Vietnamese Women's Union Congress.

2119	**457** 400d. multicoloured	1·70	90

458 Umbrella protecting Children

1997. Children's Rights. Multicoloured.

2120	400d. Type **458** (United Nations Convention on Rights of the Child)	30	15
2121	5000d. Mother breast-feeding ("Breastmilk is Best")	1·80	1·50

459 Chua Lang, Hanoi, Vietnam

1997. Asian Temples. Multicoloured.

2122	400d. Type **459**	30	15
2123	1000d. Persepolis, Iran	45	35
2124	3000d. Statue, Denion, Iraq	1·00	80
2125	5000d. Kyaiktiyo Pagoda, Myanmar	1·70	1·40
2126	10000d. Sleeping Buddha, Polonnaruwa, Sri Lanka	3·75	3·00

460 San Chay

1997. Women's Costumes. Multicoloured.

2127	400d. Type **460**	45	35
2128	2000d. Daco	85	70
2129	5000d. Phu La	2·00	1·60
2130	10000d. Kho Me	3·75	3·00

461 Ringing Bell

1997. Anti-AIDS Campaign.

2131	**461** 400d. multicoloured	2·10	1·70

462 War Memorial, Cu Chi

1997. 50th Anniv of War Disabled Day.

2132	**462** 400d. multicoloured	1·40	1·10

463 "Hibiscus rosa-sinensis"

1997. Flowers. Multicoloured.

2133	1000d. Type **463**	55	45
2134	3000d. "Hibiscus schizopetalus"	1·10	90
2135	5000d. "Hibiscus syriacus" (pink)	2·10	1·70
2136	9000d. "Hibiscus syriacus" (yellow)	3·50	2·75

464 Flags of Member Nations

1997. 30th Anniv of Association of South East Asian Nations.

2137	**464** 400d. multicoloured	1·10	90

465 Statue and Women using Modern Technology

1997. 50th Anniv of Vietnamese Post and Telecommunications Union.

2138	**465** 400d. multicoloured	1·10	90

466 Seahorses

1997. Seahorses. Multicoloured.

2139	400d. Type **466**	30	15
2140	1000d. Seahorses	45	35
2141	3000d. Common seahorse	1·00	80
2142	5000d. "Hippocampus kelloggi"	1·70	1·40
2143	6000d. "Hippocampus japonicus"	2·10	1·70
2144	7000d. Short-snouted seahorse	2·50	2·00

467 Globe and Emblem

1997. Seventh Francophone Summit, Hanoi.

2145	**467** 5000d. multicoloured	4·25	3·50

468 Table Tennis Player

1997. 19th South East Asian Games, Djakarta.

2146	**468** 5000d. multicoloured	3·00	2·30

469 Elliot's Pheasant

1997. Pheasants. Multicoloured.

2147	400d. Type **469**	30	15
2148	3000d. Siamese fireback pheasant	1·00	80
2149	5000d. Common pheasant	1·80	1·50
2150	6000d. Lady Amherst's pheasant	2·30	1·80
2151	8000d. Germain's peacock-pheasant	3·00	2·50
MS2152	80×87 mm. 14000d. Imperial pheasants (42×30 mm)	5·75	4·50

470 Lamp

1998. Wickerwork.

2153	**470** 400d. brown, black and green	30	15
2154	- 400d. black, red and blue	30	15
2155	- 400d. stone, black and blue	30	15
2156	- 400d. lilac, brown and black	30	15
2157	- 2000d. grey, pink and black	1·30	1·00

DESIGNS: No. 2154, Dish and bowl; 2155, Swan-shaped basket; 2156, Deer-shaped basket; 2157, Basket with handle.

471 Mother Tiger with Cubs

1998. New Year. Year of the Tiger. Multicoloured.

2158	400d. Type **471**	55	45
2159	8000d. Tiger	3·50	2·75

472 Flag, Helmet and Rifle

1998. 30th Anniv of Tet Offensive.

2160	**472** 400d. multicoloured	1·40	1·10

473 Ca Na Beach, Ninh Thuan Province

1998. Central Vietnam Landscapes. Multicoloured.
2161	400d. Type **473**		30	15
2162	400d. Phong Nha Cave, Quang Binh Province		30	15
2163	10000d. Hoi An Town, Quang Nam Province		3·50	2·75

474 Karl Marx and Freidrich Engels (authors)

1998. 150th Anniv of "Communist Manifesto".
2164	**474**	400d. multicoloured	1·40	1·10

475 "Limonia acidissima"

1998. Bonsai Trees. Multicoloured.
2165	400d. Type **475**		30	15
2166	400d. "Deeringia polysperma"		30	15
2167	400d. "Pinus merkusii" (vert)		30	15
2168	4000d. "Barringtonia acutangula" (vert)		1·70	1·40
2169	6000d. India rubber-tree (vert)		2·10	1·70
2170	10000d. "Wrightia religiosa" (vert)		3·50	2·75
MS2171	75×99 mm. 14000d. Desert rose ("Adenium obesum")		5·75	4·50

476 Thi Kinh is falsely accused of killing Husband

1998. "Quan Am Thi Kinh" (opera). Multicoloured.
2172	400d. Type **476**		30	15
2173	1000d. Thi Kinh as Buddhist novice and Thi Mau (with fan)		45	35
2174	2000d. Thi Mau and servant with basket on head		55	45
2175	4000d. Me Dop (village chief) and Thi Mau		1·30	1·00
2176	6000d. Me Dop, Thi Mau and Thi Kinh		2·00	1·60
2177	9000d. Thi Kinh with Thi Mau's baby begging for alms		2·75	2·30

477 Pres. Ho Chi Minh and Nha Rong Wharf

1998. 300th Anniv of Ho Chi Minh City (formerly Saigon). Multicoloured.
2178	400d. Type **477**		70	55
2179	5000d. "Uncle Ho with Children" (sculpture, Diep Minh Chau)		2·40	1·90
MS2180	110×102 mm. 14000d. Statue of Nguyen Huu Canh (founder of Saigon)		5·75	4·50

478 Western Honey Buzzard

1998. Birds. Multicoloured.
2181	400d. Type **478**		30	15
2182	400d. Northern goshawk ("Accipiter gentilis")		30	15
2183	400d. Ornate hawk eagle ("Spizaetus ornatus")		30	15
2184	3000d. Common buzzard		1·10	90
2185	5000d. Pied harrier		1·70	1·40
2186	12000d. White-tailed sea eagle		4·25	3·50

479 "Paphiopedilum appletonianum"

1998. Orchids. Multicoloured.
2187	400d. Type **479**		45	35
2188	6000d. "Paphiopedilum helenae"		2·75	2·10

480 Children going to School (Nguyen Tram)

1998. Vietnamese Children's Fund. Winning Paintings in UNICEF Contest. Multicoloured.
2189	400d. Type **480**		55	45
2190	5000d. Children playing in park (Vu Thi Tuyet)		2·50	2·00

481 Players competing for Ball

1998. World Cup Football Championship, France. Multicoloured.
2191	400d. Type **481**		30	15
2192	5000d. Players chasing ball		1·80	1·50
2193	7000d. Tackle		2·75	2·30

482 Dragon, Boi Khe Pagoda

1998. Sculptures from Tran Dynasty. Multicoloured.
2194	400d. Type **482**		30	15
2195	400d. Birds with human heads, Thai Lac Pagoda		30	15
2196	1000d. Dragons' heads, ship's planks and waves (throne back), Thay Pagoda		70	55
2197	8000d. Fairy offering flower, Hang Pagoda		3·00	2·50
2198	9000d. Kneeling figure, Thai Lac Pagoda		3·50	2·75

483 Wushu

1998. 13th Asian Games, Bangkok.
2199	**483**	2000d. multicoloured	1·80	1·50

484 Underwater Scene

1998. International Year of the Ocean.
2200	**484**	400d. multicoloured	1·40	1·10

485 Alexander Graham Bell's Telephone, 1876

1998. Stamp Day. 35th Anniv of Posts and Telecommunications Department.
2201	**485**	400d. multicoloured	1·40	1·10

486 Ton Duc Thang

1998. 110th Birth Anniv of Ton Duc Thang (President 1969–80).
2202	**486**	400d. multicoloured	1·40	1·10

487 Moth

1998. Moths. Multicoloured.
2203	400d. Type **487**		45	35
2204	400d. Atlas moth ("Attacus atlas")		45	35
2205	4000d. Tailed comet moth (vert)		2·75	2·30
2206	10000d. "Argema maenas" (vert)		4·25	3·50

488 "Dragonfly and Lotus"

1998. 135th Birth Anniv of Qi Baishi (painter). Multicoloured.
2207	400d. Type **488**		30	15
2208	1000d. "Chickens and Chrysanthemum"		55	45
2209	2000d. "Shrimps"		85	70
2210	4000d. "School of Crabs"		1·40	1·10
2211	6000d. "Ducks and Lotus"		2·10	1·70
2212	9000d. "Shrimps" (different)		3·50	2·75

489 Milan Cathedral and Statue

1998. "Italia 98" International Stamp Exhibition, Milan. Sheet 100×62 mm.
MS2213	16000d. multicoloured		7·75	6·25

490 King Le Loi on Boat

1998. Legend of Restored Sword Lake, Hanoi. Multicoloured.
2214	400d. Type **490**		1·00	80
2215	400d. Jade Hill Temple and Huc Sunrise bridge		1·00	80

491 King Le Thang Tong (statue)

1998. 500th Death Anniv (1997) of King Le Thang Tong.
2216	**491**	400d. multicoloured	1·00	80

492 Emblem and Couple

1998. Eighth Trade Unions Congress.
2217	**492**	400d. multicoloured	1·00	80

493 King Quang Trung (statue) and Quy Nhon Port

1998. Centenary of Quy Nhon as Binh Dinh Provincial Capital.
2218	**493**	400d. multicoloured	1·00	80

494 Duong Quang Ham (first Vietnamese headmaster) and School

1998. 90th Anniv of Buoi Chu Van An Secondary School, Hanoi. Multicoloured.
2219	400d. Type **494**		45	15
2220	5000d. Ho Chi Minh and students		2·75	2·30

495 Doves around Emblem

1998. Sixth Association of South East Asian Nations Summit, Hanoi.
2221	**495**	1000d. multicoloured	1·40	1·10

496 Industrial Symbols, Revolutionary Memorial, Havana and Cuban Flag forming "40"

1998. 40th Anniv (1999) of Cuban Revolution.
2222	**496**	400d. multicoloured	1·10	90

497 Spring

1999. Four Seasons Paintings (1st series). Multicoloured.
2223	400d. Type **497**		45	35
2224	1000d. Summer		70	55

2225	3000d. Autumn	1·30	1·00
2226	12000d. Winter	4·00	3·25

See also Nos. 2391/3.

498 Cat going to Tet Flower Market

1999. New Year. Year of the Cat. Multicoloured.

2227	400d. Type **498**	45	35
2228	8000d. Cats fighting	3·00	2·50
MS2229	100×73 mm. 13000d. Kittens (31×42 mm)	5·75	4·50

499 Eagle Kite

1999. Kites. Multicoloured.

2230	400d. Type **499**	70	55
2231	5000d. Kite with bamboo flute	2·10	1·70
2232	7000d. Peacock	2·75	2·30

500 Ha Long Bay Net Boat

1999. "Australia '99" World Stamp Exhibition, Melbourne. Local Craft. Multicoloured.

2233	400d. Type **500**	30	15
2234	400d. Cua Lo bamboo junk	30	15
2235	7000d. Nha Trang bamboo junk	2·50	2·00
2236	9000d. Ne Cape junk	2·75	2·30

501 *Kaempferia galanga*

1999. Medicinal Herbs. Multicoloured.

2237	400d. Type **501**	30	15
2238	400d. *Tacca chantrieri* Andree (vert)	30	15
2239	400d. *Alpinia galanga* Willd (vert)	30	15
2240	6000d. *Typhonium trilobatum* Schott (vert)	2·10	1·70
2241	13000d. *Asarum maximum* Hemsl (vert)	4·00	3·25

502 Syringe, Fields, City and Family

1999. International Day Against Drugs.

2242	**502** 400d. multicoloured	1·10	90

503 Van Trong Mask

1999. Tuong Stage Masks. Multicoloured.

2243	400d. Type **503**	30	15
2244	1000d. Hoang Phi Ho	55	45
2245	2000d. Chau Thuong	1·00	80
2246	5000d. Tiet Cuong	1·40	1·10
2247	6000d. Mao At	1·80	1·50
2248	10000d. Tran Long	3·00	2·50

504 *Octopus gibertianus*

1999. "iBRA 99" International Stamp Exhibition, Nuremberg, Germany. Octopuses. Multicoloured.

2249	400d. Type **504**	30	15
2250	400d. *Philonexis catenulata*	30	15
2251	4000d. *Paroctopus yendoi*	1·80	1·50
2252	12000d. Common octopus	4·00	3·25

505 Cape, Ca Mau Province

1999. Southern Vietnam Landscapes. Multicoloured.

2253	400d. Type **505**	55	45
2254	400d. Father and Son Islet, Kien Giang Province	55	45
2255	12000d. Vinh Hung Tower, Bac Lieu Province	4·50	3·50

506 Emblem, Map and Satellite

1999. 20th Anniv of Asia-Pacific Telecommunity.

2256	**506** 400d. multicoloured	4·00	3·25

507 Greater flame-backed Woodpecker

1999. Woodpeckers. Multicoloured.

2257	400d. Type **507**	85	70
2258	1000d. Speckled piculet	1·00	80
2259	3000d. Red-collared wood-pecker	1·40	1·10
2260	13000d. Bay woodpecker	4·25	3·50

508 Large Hand and Child cowering

1999. Vietnamese Children's Fund.

2261	**508** 400d. lilac, green and black	70	55
2262	- 5000d. blue, grey and black	2·40	1·90

DESIGN: 5000d. Young man carrying buildings.

509 Northern Government Office, Hanoi

1999. Architecture. Multicoloured.

2263	400d. Type **509**	30	15
2264	400d. History Museum, Ho Chi Minh City	30	15
2265	12000d. Duc Ba Cathedral (vert)	4·00	3·25
MS2266	96×94 mm. 15000d. Big Theatre, Hanoi (42×31 mm)	6·50	5·00

510 Da Rang Bridge and Nhan Mountains

1999. Phu Yen Province.

2267	**510** 400d. multicoloured	1·40	1·10

511 Man fighting Tiger, Chay Communal House, Ha Nam Province

1999. Le Dynasty Sculptures. Multicoloured.

2268	1000d. Type **511**	70	55
2269	1000d. Phoenix, But Thap Pagoda, Bac Ninh Province	70	55
2270	3000d. Playing chess, Ngoc Canh Communal House, Vinh Phuc Province (vert)	2·10	1·70
2271	7000d. Oster, Quang Phuc Communal House, Ha Tay Province (vert)	4·25	3·50
2272	9000d. Stone dragon, Kinh Thien Temple, Hanoi	5·00	4·00

512 Globe and Family

1999. Birth of World's Six Billionth Inhabitant.

2273	**512** 400d. multicoloured	1·40	1·10

513 Van Tho Hill, Di Hoa Park, Peking

1999. Chinese Landscapes. Multicoloured.

2274	400d. Type **513**	45	35
2275	2000d. Hoang Mountain, An Huy	1·00	80
2276	3000d. Bong Lai Cap, Dong Hill	1·40	1·10
2277	10000d. Di Hoa Park, Peking	3·50	2·75
MS2278	93×88 mm. 14000d. Great Wall, China	6·50	5·00

514 Racing Boats, North Vietnam

1999. Traditional Boat Racing Festivals. Multicoloured.

2279	400d. Type **514**	45	35
2280	2000d. Three boats, Central Vietnam	1·00	80
2281	10000d. Two boats, South Vietnam	3·50	2·75

515 Buffaloes fighting

1999. Buffalo Festival. Multicoloured.

2282	400d. Type **515**	70	55
2283	5000d. Buffalo No. 2 goring fallen animal	2·40	1·90

516 Traditional Velvet Dress

1999. Women's Costumes. Multicoloured.

2284	400d. Type **516**	70	55
2285	400d. Magenta brocade dress	70	55
2286	12000d. Green dress	4·25	3·50

517 Ngo Quyen (statue) and Battle of Bach Dang, 938

1999. 1100th (1998) Birth Anniv of Ngo Quyen (ruler).

2287	**517** 400d. multicoloured	1·40	1·10

518 Van Sieu and The Tower of the Pen Brush, Ba Dinh

1999. Birth Bicentenary of Nguyen Van Sieu (scholar).

2288	**518** 400d. multicoloured	1·40	1·10

519 Tran Xan Soan

1999. 150th Birth Anniv of Tran Xuan Soan (revolutionary).

2289	**519** 400d. multicoloured	1·40	1·10

520 Fisherwoman, Farmer and Woman carrying Child

1999. United Nations Development Programme. Fight Against Poverty. Multicoloured.

2290	400d. Type **520**	1·40	1·10
2291	8000d. Buildings and villagers' meeting	2·75	2·30

521 Hammer and Sickle above Workers (forming of Vietnamese Communist Party, 1930)

2000. The Twentieth Century. Multicoloured.

2292	400d. Type **521**	30	15
2293	400d. Pres. Ho Chi Minh making Independence speech (formation of Democratic Republic, 1945)	30	15
2294	1000d. Flag, tank and people celebrating (liberation of South Vietnam, 1975)	70	55
2295	1000d. Symbols of agriculture and industry (Communist Party's ten year renovation plan)	70	55
2296	8000d. Symbols of industry and communications (industrialization)	2·75	2·30

2297	12000d. Emblems (integration into international community)	5·00	4·00
MS2298	194×124 mm. Nos. 2292/7	13·00	10·00

522 Dragon

2000. New Year. Year of the Dragon. Multicoloured.

2299	400d. Type **522**	1·00	80
2300	8000d. Dragon and One Pillar Pagoda, Hanoi	4·00	3·25

523 Globe and UNESCO "City for Peace" Prize (Hanoi, 1999)

2000. International Year of Culture and Peace.

2301	**523**	400d. multicoloured	1·40	1·10

524 Pres. Ho Chi Minh (founder)

2000. 70th Anniv of Communist Party. Multicoloured.

2302	400d. Type **524**	70	55
2303	400d. Tran Phu (first General Secretary, 1930–31)	70	55
2304	400d. Le Hong Phong (General Secretary, 1935–36)	70	55
2305	400d. Ha Huy Tap (General Secretary, 1936–38)	70	55
2306	400d. Nguyen Van Cu (General Secretary, 1938–41)	70	55
2307	400d. Truong Chinh (General Secretary, 1941–56 and 1986)	70	55
2308	400d. Le Duan (General Secretary, 1960–86)	70	55
2309	400d. Nguyen Van Linh (General Secretary, 1986–91)	70	55

525 Cocks fighting (Double Cock's Kick)

2000. Cock Fighting. Showing cocks fighting. Multicoloured.

2310	400d. Type **525**	30	15
2311	400d. "Long vu da dao" posture	30	15
2312	7000d. "Song long phuing hoang" posture	2·75	2·30
2313	9000d. "Nhan o giap chien" posture	3·75	3·00

526 Fringed Palanquin

2000. "Bangkok 2000" International Stamp Exhibition. Processional Litters. Multicoloured.

2314	400d. Type **526**	30	15
2315	7000d. Throne-shaped litter	2·75	2·30
2316	8000d. Palanquin with pagoda-style roof	3·25	2·50
MS2317	95×65 mm. 15000d. Palanquin being carried	6·50	5·00

527 Marriage of Lac Long Quan and Au Co

2000. Legend of Lac Long Quan and Au Co. Multicoloured.

2318	400d. Type **527**	30	15
2319	400d. Au Co surrounded by sons	30	15
2320	500d. Au Co and children riding elephants	45	35
2321	3000d. Lac Long Quan and sons by the sea	1·70	1·40
2322	4000d. Eldest son Hung Vuong	2·30	1·80
2323	11000d. Vietnamese ethnic groups	4·25	3·50

528 Iveco Magirus Fire Engine, Germany

2000. Fire Engines. Sheet 104×89 mm. containing T **528** and similar horiz designs. Multicoloured.

MS2324	400d. Type **528**; 1000d. Hino, Japan; 5000d. ZIL 130E, Russia; 12000d. FPS.32 Camiva, France	7·75	6·25

529 Sao La

2000. Endangered Species. Sao La. Multicoloured.

2325	400d. Type **529**	30	15
2326	400d. Juvenile in grass	30	15
2327	5000d. Beside lake	2·30	1·80
2328	10000d. Head of adult	4·25	3·50

530 Ho Chi Minh and Birthplace

2000. 110th Birth Anniv of President Ho Chi Minh.

2329	**530**	400d. multicoloured	1·40	1·10

531 Buffon Teu

2000. "World Stamp Expo 2000", Anaheim, California. Water Puppetry. Showing traditional puppets. Multicoloured.

2330	400d. Type **531**	30	15
2331	400d. Fairy and phoenix	30	15
2332	400d. Ploughman	30	15
2333	3000d. Peasant woman	1·40	1·10
2334	9000d. Drummer	2·75	2·30
2335	11000d. Fisherman	4·25	3·50

532 Young Girl waving Flag

2000. 50th Anniv of Youth Volunteers.

2336	**532**	400d. multicoloured	1·40	1·10

533 Swimmers and Emblem

2000. Fifth National Youth Sports Festival, Dong Thap.

2337	**533**	400d. multicoloured	1·40	1·10

534 Coral Hind

2000. Coral Reef Fish. Multicoloured.

2338	400d. Type **534**	30	15
2339	400d. Emperor angelfish (*Pomacanthus imperator*)	30	15
2340	400d. Honeycomb grouper (*Epinephelus merra*)	30	15
2341	4000d. Moorish idol (*Zanclus cornutus*) (vert)	1·00	80
2342	6000d. Saddle butterflyfish (vert)	2·10	1·70
2343	12000d. Pennant coralfish (vert)	4·50	3·50
MS2344	74×99 mm. 15000d. Racoon butterflyfish	5·75	4·50

535 Postal Workers and Means of Communications

2000. 55th Anniv of Vietnam Posts and Telecommunications Service.

2345	**535**	400d. multicoloured	1·30	1·00

536 Ho Chi Minh with Policemen

2000. 55th Anniv of National Police Force. Multicoloured.

2346	400d. Type **536**	55	45
2347	2000d. Police personnel (vert)	1·10	90

537 Statue of Nguyen Tri Phuong, Da Nang

2000. Birth Bicentenary of Nguyen Tri Phuong (provincial Governor).

2348	**537**	400d. multicoloured	1·40	1·10

538 Children and Emblem

2000. Tenth Anniv of United Nations Convention on Children's Rights. Multicoloured.

2349	400d. Type **538**	70	55
2350	5000d. Children's faces around emblem (vert)	2·40	1·90

539 Running

2000. Olympic Games, Sydney. Multicoloured.

2351	400d. Type **539**	30	15
2352	6000d. Shooting	2·00	1·60
2353	7000d. Taekwondo (vert)	2·75	2·10

540 Tran Hung Dao Monument, An Phu

2000. 700th Death Anniv of General Tran Hung Dao.

2354	**540**	400d. multicoloured	1·40	1·10

541 Silver-eared Mesia

2000. Birds. Multicoloured.

2355	400d. Type **541**	30	15
2356	400d. Eliott's pitta (*Pitta ellioti*)	30	15
2357	400d. Coral-billed scimitar babbler (*Pomatorhinus ferruginosus*) (inscr "Pomatorinus")	30	15
2358	5000d. Greater racquet-tailed drongo (vert)	2·10	1·70
2359	7000d. Sultan tit (vert)	2·75	2·10
2360	10000d. Spot-necked tree babbler (vert)	3·50	2·75
MS2361	106×81 mm. 15000d. Blue-backed fairy bluebird (42×31 mm)	6·50	5·00

542 North Vietnam 1976 12x. Stamp, Magnifying Glass and Emblem

2000. 40th Anniv of Vietnamese Philatelic Association.

2362	**542**	400d. multicoloured	1·40	1·10

543 Pigs feeding and Agricultural Workers

2000. 70th Anniv of Vietnamese Farmers' Association.

2363	**543**	400d. multicoloured	1·40	1·10

544 Dien Huu Pagoda and King Ly Thai To

2000. 990th Anniv of Hanoi. Multicoloured.

2364	400d. Type **544**	30	15
2365	3000d. Van Mieu-Quoc Tu Giam (Confucian temple) and university	1·30	1·00
2366	10000d. Hanoi city scene	3·50	2·75
MS2367	97×90 mm. 15000d. Women releasing doves (42×31 mm)	6·50	5·00

545 Harlequin Bat (*Scotomanes ornatus*)

2000. Bats. Multicoloured.

2368	400d. Type **545**	30	15
2369	400d. *Pteropus lylei*	30	15
2370	2000d. *Rhinolophus paradoxolophus*	85	70
2371	6000d. Cave fruit bat (*Eonycteris spelaea*)	2·10	1·70
2372	11000d. Short-nosed fruit bat (*Cynopterus sphinx*)	3·50	2·75

546 "70" and Dove

2000. 70th Anniv of Vietnamese Women's Union.

2373	**546**	400d. multicoloured	1·10	90

547 Workers

2000. Sixth National "Heroes of Labour" Congress. Multicoloured.

2374	400d. Type **547**	45	35
2375	3000d. Flower and industrial symbols (vert)	1·30	1·00

548 Oxyspora sp.

2000. Cornflowers. Multicoloured.

2376	400d. Type **548**	55	45
2377	5000d. Melastoma villosa	2·50	2·00

549 Ho Chi Minh and Crowd

2000. 70th Anniv of Vietnam Fatherland Front.

2378	**549**	400d. multicoloured	1·30	1·00

550 Hon Khoai Island and Statue

2000. 60th Anniv of Hon Khoai Uprising.

2379	**550**	400d. multicoloured	1·30	1·00

551 Banners and Satellite

2001. New Millennium.

2380	**551**	400d. multicoloured	1·30	1·00

552 Snake

2001. New Year. Year of the Snake. Multicoloured.

2381	400d. Type **552**	45	35
2382	8000d. Green snake	3·00	2·50

553 Archerfish (Toxotes macrolepis)

2001. "HONG KONG 2001" International Stamp Exhibition. Freshwater Fish. Multicoloured.

2383	400d. Type **553**	30	15
2384	800d. Carp (Cosmochilus harmandi) (wrongly inscr "Cosmocheilus")	55	45
2385	2000d. Indian short-finned eel (Anguilla bicolor pacifica)	1·00	80
2386	3000d. Chitala ornata	1·30	1·00
2387	7000d. Indo-Pacific tarpon (Megalops cyprinoides)	2·10	1·70
2388	8000d. Esok (Probarbus jullieni)	2·50	2·00

555 Spring

2001. Centenary of Nobel Prizes.

2389	**554**	400d. blue, yellow and black	1·10	90

554 Alfred Nobel (founder)

2001. Four Seasons Paintings (2nd series). Multicoloured.

2390	400d. Type **555**	45	35
2391	800d. Summer	85	70
2392	4000d. Autumn	1·70	1·40
2393	10000d. Winter	4·00	3·25

556 Rubus cochinchinensis

2001. Forest Fruit. Multicoloured.

2394	400d. Type **556**	45	35
2395	400d. Rhizophora mucronata	45	35
2396	400d. Podocarpus neriifolius	45	35
2397	400d. Magnolia pumila	45	35
2398	15000d. Taxus chinensis	5·00	4·00

557 Co Tien Mountains, Ha Giang Province

2001. Northern Vietnam Landscapes. Multicoloured.

2399	400d. Type **557**	45	35
2400	400d. Dong Pagoda, Yen Tu, Quang Ninh Province	45	35
2401	10000d. King Dinh Temple, Ninh Binh Province	5·00	4·00

558 Medals and Mastheads on "50"

2001. 50th Anniv of Nhan Dan (Communist Party newspaper).

2402	**558**	400d. multicoloured	1·10	90

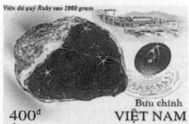

559 Starlight Ruby

2001. Rubies. Design showing named rubies before and after cutting. Multicoloured.

2403	400d. Type **559**	70	55
2404	6000d. Vietnam Star	3·50	2·75

560 Youths and Emblem

2001. 70th Anniv of Ho Chi Minh Youth Union.

2405	**560**	400d. multicoloured	1·10	90

561 David's Tree Partridge (Arborophila davidi)

2001. Animals in Cat Tien National Park. Multicoloured.

2406	400d. Type **561**	45	35
2407	800d. Jungle queen butterfly (Stichophthalma uemurai)	70	55
2408	3000d. Vietnamese Javan rhino (Rhinoceros sondaicus annamiticus)	1·80	1·50
2409	5000d. Siamese crocodile (Crocodylus siamensis)	2·50	2·00

562 Ho Chi Minh, Flag and Map of Vietnam

2001. Ninth Vietnamese Communist Party Congress. Multicoloured.

2410	400d. Type **562**	30	15
2411	3000d. Hammer, sickle and Ngoc Lu drum head (vert)	1·30	1·00

563 Veiled Stinkhorn (Phallus indusiatus)

2001. Fungi. Multicoloured.

2412	400d. Type **563**	30	15
2413	400d. Aseroe arachnoidea	30	15
2414	400d. Phallus tenuis	30	15
2415	2000d. Phallus impudicus	1·30	1·00
2416	5000d. Phallus rugulosus	2·00	1·60
2417	6000d. Simblum periphragmoides	2·30	1·80
2418	7000d. Mutinus bambusinus	2·75	2·30

MS2419 86×86 mm. 13000d. Pseudocolus schellenbergiae (42×31 mm) — 7·00 — 5·75

564 Ho Chi Minh, Girl and Flowers

2001. 60th Anniv of Vietnam Youth Pioneers.

2420	**564**	400d. multicoloured	1·10	90

565 Ho Chi Minh, Crowd and Flag

2001. 60th Anniv of Vietnam Independence League.

2421	**565**	400d. multicoloured	1·10	90

566 Cigarette and Flower

2001. World No-Smoking Day.

2422	**566**	800d. multicoloured	1·40	1·10

567 Children wearing Protective Clothing

2001. United Nations Children's Fund (400d.) and United Nations General Assembly Special Session on Children (5000d.). Multicoloured.

2423	400d. Type **567**	70	55
2424	5000d. Children of different races and emblem	2·40	1·90

568 Locomotive D18E

2001. Diesel Locomotives. Multicoloured.

2425	400d. Type **568**	30	15
2426	400d. Locomotive D4H	30	15
2427	800d. Locomotive D11H in station	55	45
2428	2000d. Locomotive D5H	1·30	1·00
2429	6000d. Locomotive D9E	2·50	2·00
2430	7000d. Locomotive D12E	2·75	2·30

MS2431 96×66 mm. 13000d. Locomotive D11H on lakeside track (42×31 mm) — 6·50 — 5·00

569 Vanda sp.

2001. Orchids. Multicoloured.

2432	800d. Type **569**	45	35
2433	800d. Dendrobium lowianum	45	35
2434	800d. Phajus wallachii	45	35
2435	800d. Habenaria medioflexa	45	35
2436	800d. Arundina graminifolia (vert)	45	35
2437	12000d. Calanthe clavata (vert)	5·00	4·00

570 Golden Birdwing (Troides aeacus)

2001. "PHILA NIPPON '01" International Stamp Exhibition, Tokyo. Butterflies. Multicoloured.

2438	800d. Type **570**	45	35
2439	800d. Peacock (Inachis io)	45	35
2440	800d. Ancyluris formosissima	45	35
2441	5000d. Red glider (Cymothoe sangaris) (wrongly inscr "sanguris")	1·40	1·10
2442	7000d. Taenaris selene	2·50	2·00
2443	10000d. Raja Brooke's birdwing (Trogonoptera brookiana)	4·00	3·25

MS2444 94×69 mm. 13000d. Atrophaneura horishanus (31×42 mm) — 7·00 — 5·75

571 Footballer

2001. World Cup Football Championship, Japan and South Korea. Multicoloured.

2445	800d. Type **571**	1·40	1·10
2446	3000d. Footballer and map including Americas	2·75	2·30

Nos. 2445/6 were issued together, se-tenant, forming a composite design.

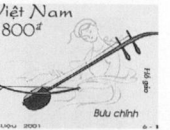

572 Ho Gao

2001. Traditional Musical Instruments. Multicoloured.

2447	800d. Type **572**	45	35
2448	800d. Kenh (pan-pipes)	45	35

2449	800d. Dan Tu (stringed instrument) (vert)	45	35
2450	2000d. Dan T'rung (vert)	1·00	80
2451	6000d. Trong Kinang (drum) (vert)	2·00	1·60
2452	9000d. Tinh Tau (stringed instrument) (vert)	3·50	2·75

573 Children encircling Globe

2001. United Nations Year of Dialogue among Civilizations.

2453	573	800d. multicoloured	1·80	1·50

574 Tran Huy Lieu and Books

2001. Birth Centenary of Tran Huy Lieu (writer and revolutionary).

2454	574	800d. multicoloured	1·40	1·10

575 Nam Cao and Titles of his Works

2001. 50th Death Anniv of Nam Cao (Tran Huu Tri) (writer).

2455	575	800d. multicoloured	1·40	1·10

576 Leaves around Globe

2001. Environment Protection. Multicoloured.

2456		800d. Type 576	55	45
2457		3000d. Globe in tree with nesting peace dove	1·80	1·50

577 "To He" Horse

2002. New Year. Year of the Horse. Multicoloured.

2458		800d. Type 577	1·10	90
2459		8000d. Horse with parasol	3·00	2·50
MS2460	76×66 mm. 14000d. Flying horse (42×31 mm)		6·50	5·00

578 Giap Tuong Nam

2002. Tuong (classical opera) Costumes. Costumes. Multicoloured.

2461		1000d. Type 578	55	45
2462		1000d. Giap Tuong Nu	55	45
2463		2000d. Giap Tuong Phan Dien	1·10	90
2464		3000d. Long Chan	1·70	1·40
2465		5000d. Giap Tuong Phien	2·10	1·70
2466		9000d. Lung Xiem Quan Giap	3·00	2·50

579 Vo Thi Sau

2002. 50th Death Anniv of Vo Thi Sau (resistance fighter).

2467	579	1000d. multicoloured	1·40	1·10

580 Symbols of Industry and Communications

2002. Ninth Communist Party Congress Resolutions. Multicoloured.

2468		800d. Type 580	70	55
2469		3000d. Thang Long Citadel gate, flag and people	1·70	1·40

581 Echinocereus Ibatus

2002. Cacti. Multicoloured.

2470		1000d. Type 581	45	35
2471		1000d. Echinocereus delaetii	45	35
2472		1000d. Cylindropuntia bigelowii	45	35
2473		5000d. Echinocereus triglochidatus	1·70	1·40
2474		10000d. Epiphyllum truncatum	3·50	2·75

582 Emblem and Woman's Face

2002. Ninth National Women's Congress.

2475	582	800d. multicoloured	1·40	1·10

583 Hugo and "Liberty Guiding the People" (painting, Eugene Delacroix)

2002. Birth Bicentenary of Victor Hugo (writer).

2476	583	1000d. multicoloured	1·70	1·40

584 Black-crowned Barwing (Actinodura sodangorum)

2002. Birds. Multicoloured.

2477		600d. Type 584	30	15
2478		800d. Golden-winged laughing thrush (Garrulax ngoclinhensis)	45	35
2479		800d. Long-billed scimitar babbler (Pomatorhinus hypoleucos)	45	35
2480		800d. Greater necklaced laughing thrush (Garrulax pectoralis)	45	35
2481		5000d. Red-tailed minla (Minla ignotincta)	2·10	1·70
2482		8000d. Blue-winged minla (Minla cynouroptera)	3·50	2·75

585 Ganh Son Coast, Binh Thuan Province

2002. Central Vietnam Landscapes. Multicoloured.

2483		800d. Type 585	70	55
2484		800d. Tung Estuary, Quang Tri Province	70	55
2485		10000d. Sa Huynh Harbour, Quang Ngai Province	4·25	3·50

586 Golden-headed Langur (Trachypithecus poliocephalus)

2002. Primates. Multicoloured.

2486		600d. Type 586	30	15
2487		800d. Delacour's langur (Trachypithecus delacouri)	45	35
2488		1000d. Tonkin snub-nosed monkey (Rhinopithecus avunculus)	55	45
2489		2000d. Grey-shanked douc langur (Pygathrix cinerea)	85	70
2490		4000d. Black crested gibbon (Nomascus concolor)	1·00	80
2491		5000d. Ha Tinh langur (Trachypithecus laotum hatinhensis)	1·40	1·10
2492		7000d. Phayre's langur (Trachypithecus phayrei)	2·00	1·60
2493		9000d. Red-shanked douc langur (Pygathrix nemaeus nemaeus)	2·50	2·00
MS2494	179×141 mm. Nos. 2486/93 plus label		10·50	8·50

587 Bui Thi Xuan riding Elephant

2002. Death Bicentenary of Commander-in-Chief Bui Thi Xuan.

2495	587	1000d. multicoloured	1·40	1·10

588 Footballer

2002. World Cup Football Championship, Japan and South Korea. Sheet 112×100 mm containing T 588 and similar vert designs. Multicoloured.

MS2496	1000d. Type 588; 2000d. Two players; 5000d. Player with ball; 7000d. Goalkeeper		5·75	4·50

589 Yellow Slipper Orchid (Paphiopedilum concolor)

2002. Flowers of Ha Long Bay. Multicoloured.

2497		600d. Type 589	30	15
2498		800d. Velvet-pod tree (Sterculia lanceolata)	45	35
2499		1000d. Ha Long schefflera (Schefflera alongensis)	55	45
2500		2000d. Sea hibiscus (Hibiscus tiliaceus)	70	55

2501	3000d. White butterfly tree (Mussaenda glabra)	1·10	90
2502	5000d. Puff-fruit tree (Bonionedron parviflorum)	1·70	1·40
2503	9000d. Fragrant bauhinia (Bauhinia ornate)	2·50	2·00

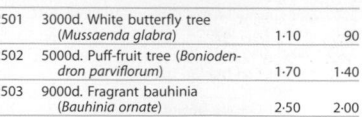

590 Chau Van Liem

2002. Birth Centenary of Chau Van Liem (revolutionary).

2504	590	800d. multicoloured	1·40	1·10

591 Winged Envelopes and Globe

2002. Stamp Day. 25th Anniv of Vietnam Stamp Company.

2505	591	800d. multicoloured	1·60	1·20

592 Victory Statue, People and Nup (revolutionary)

2002. Tay Nguyen (Western highlands).

2506	592	800d. multicoloured	1·40	1·10

593 Asian Giant Soft-shelled Turtle (Pelochelys bibroni)

2002. Soft-shelled Turtles. Showing soft-shelled turtles. Multicoloured.

2507		800d. Type 593	45	35
2508		2000d. Chinese turtle (Pelodiscus sinensis)	1·00	80
2509		5000d. Wattle-necked turtle (Palea steindachneri)	1·80	1·50
2510		9000d. Black-rayed turtle (Trionyx cartilaginous)	3·75	3·00
MS2511	173×100 mm. Nos. 2507/10, each ×2		14·00	11·50

594 Khue Van Pavilion, Vietnam and That Luang, Laos

2002. 25th Anniv of Friendship and Co-operation Treaty. 40th Anniv of Vietnam–Laos Diplomatic Relations.

2512	594	800d. multicoloured	1·40	1·10

595 Beech 200 Super King Air

2002. Civilian Aircraft. Multicoloured.

2513		800d. Type 595	45	35
2514		2000d. Fokker 70 twin-engine jet airliner	85	70
2515		3000d. ATR72-202 twin-turboprop engine aircraft	1·30	1·00
2516		8000d. Boeing 767-300 ER	3·50	2·75
MS2517	90×60 mm. 14000d. Beech 200 Super King Air (different)		6·00	4·75

596 Ong Sao Lantern

2002. Mid-Autumn Festival Lanterns. Multicoloured.

2518	800d. Type **596**	45	35
2519	800d. Ong Su lantern	45	35
2520	2000d. Con Tho Om Trang lantern	1·00	80
2521	7000d. Chinese lantern	2·75	2·30

597 Statue, Computer Operators and Satellite

2002. 55th Anniv of Posts and Telecommunication Worker's Trade Union.

2522	**597**	800d. multicoloured	1·40	1·10

598 Long Bien Bridge

2002. Bridges. Multicoloured.

2523	800d. Type **598**	45	35
2524	800d. Song Han bridge	45	35
2525	2000d. Truong Tien bridge	1·00	80
2526	10000d. My Thuan bridge	3·50	2·75

599 Open Book and Flowers

2002. 72nd Anniv of Ideology and Culture Commission.

2527	**599**	800d. multicoloured	1·40	1·10

600 Ho Hac Di (first principal) and College Building

2002. Centenary of Hanoi Medical University.

2528	**600**	800d. multicoloured	1·40	1·10

601 Teacher and Pupil

2002. 20th Anniv of Teachers' Day.

2529	**601**	800d. multicoloured	1·40	1·10

602 Goat

2002. New Year. Year of the Goat. Multicoloured.

2530	800d. Type **602**	55	45
2531	8000d. Goat (different)	3·00	2·40

603 One Pillar Pagoda, Hanoi

2002. Tenth Anniv of Vietnam–North Korea Diplomatic Relations. Multicoloured.

2532	800d. Type **603**	85	70

2533	800d. Dabotap Pagoda, Bulguk-sa Temple, North Korea	85	70

604 Rubber Forest, Phuoc Long

2003. Southern Vietnam Landscapes. Multicoloured.

2534	800d. Type **604**	55	45
2535	3000d. Ba Om pond, Tra Vinh	1·10	90
2536	7000d. Rach Gam–Xoai Mut river	2·30	1·80

605 Emblem

2003. 60th Anniv of Vietnam Cultural Programme.

2537	**605**	800d. multicoloured	1·10	90

606 Phi Nga (actress) and Scene from "Sharing a River of Love"

2003. 50th Anniv of Vietnamese Revolutionary Cinema.

2538	**606**	1000d. multicoloured	1·10	90

607 Dien Khanh Citadel

2003. 350th Anniv of Khanh Hoa Province.

2539	**607**	800d. multicoloured	1·10	90

608 Quan Chuong Gate and Cyclo, Hanoi

2003. Cyclo (cycle rickshaw). Multicoloured.

2540	800d. Type **608**	70	55
2541	3000d. Notre Dame Cathedral and cyclo, Ho Chi Minh City	1·10	90
2542	8000d. Post Office and cyclo, Hai Phong	2·40	1·90

609 Mother Cricket and Young

2003. "A Cricket's Adventures" by To Hoai. Multicoloured.

2543	800d. Type **609**	30	15
2544	1000d. Cricket as adult	45	35
2545	2000d. Cricket lamenting his faults	55	45
2546	3000d. Cricket and Mole	85	70
2547	5000d. Crickets helping one another	1·60	1·20
2548	8000d. Animals united	2·50	2·00

Nos. 2543/8 were issued together, *se-tenant*, forming a composite design.

610 Pangolin (*Manis pentadactyla*)

2003. Fauna. Multicoloured.

2549	800d. Type **610**	45	35
2550	800d. Giant flying squirrel (*Petaurista petaurista*)	45	35
2551	5000d. Asiatic black bear (*Selenarctos thibetanus*)	1·70	1·40
2552	10000d. Serow (*Capricornis sumatraensis*)	3·50	2·75

611 Football

2003. 22nd South East Asian Games, Vietnam. Multicoloured.

2553	800d. Type **611**	55	45
2554	2000d. Hurdling	1·00	80
2555	3000d. Canoeing	1·40	1·10
2556	7000d. Wrestling	2·10	1·70
MS2557	96×73 mm. 10000d. Emblem (horiz)	5·75	4·50

612 Hands holding Nine Roses enclosing Emblem

2003. Ninth Trade Unions Federation Congress.

2558	**612**	800d. multicoloured	1·10	90

613 *Camellia petelotii*

2003. Camellias. Multicoloured.

2559	800d. Type **613**	45	35
2560	1000d. *Camellia rubriflora*	55	45
2561	5000d. *Camellia vietnamensis*	1·40	1·10
2562	6000d. *Camellia gilberti*	1·80	1·50

614 Young Elephant

2003. Endangered Species. Asian Elephant (*Elephas maximus*). Multicoloured.

2563	800d. Type **614**	45	35
2564	1000d. Elephants and riders	55	45
2565	2000d. Adult	1·10	90
2566	8000d. Mother and calf	3·50	2·75
MS2567	170×126 mm. Nos. 2563/6, each×2	11·50	9·00

615 *Paphiopedilum dianthum*

2003. Orchids. Multicoloured.

2568	800d. Type **615**	85	70
2569	8000d. *Pleione bulbocodioides*	3·75	3·00

616 Ruins

2003. UNESCO World Heritage Sites. My Son. Multicoloured.

2570	800d. Type **616**	55	45
2571	3000d. Ruins (different)	1·70	1·40
2571a	8000d. Ruins (different)	4·25	3·50
MS2572	125×65 mm. 10000d. Temple (43×32 mm)	5·00	4·00

617 Monkeys

2003. New Year. Year of the Monkey. Multicoloured.

2573	800d. Type **617**	55	45
2574	8000d. Mother and baby holding leaf	2·30	1·80

618 Ngo Gia Tu

2003. 95th Birth Anniv of Ngo Gia Tu (revolutionary).

2575	**618**	800d. vermilion, black and lemon	1·10	90

619 Flowers

2004. Greetings Stamps. Multicoloured.

2576	800d. Type **619**	70	55
2577	8000d. Dove	2·40	1·90

620 *Murex troscheli* (inscr "trocheli")

2004. Molluscs. Multicoloured.

2578	800d. Type **620**	55	45
2579	3000d. *Murex haustellum*	1·70	1·40
2580	8000d. *Chicoreus ramosus*	3·50	2·75

621 Bamboo Lantern

2003. Bamboo Lanterns. Multicoloured.

2581	400d. Type **621**	30	15
2582	1000d. Square lantern	55	45
2583	7000d. Branched holder and lanterns	3·00	2·50

622 Phu Van Lau

2004. UNESCO World Heritage Sites. Hue (ancient capital). Multicoloured.

2584	800d. Type **622**	45	35
2585	4000d. Ngo Mon	1·10	90
2586	8000d. Hien Lam Cac	2·10	1·70
MS2587	64×88 mm. 8000d. Dien Thai Hoa (43×32 mm)	4·25	3·50

623 Building Facade and Tran Phu

2004. Birth Centenary of Tran Phu (revolutionary).

| 2588 | 623 | 800d. multicoloured | 1·10 | 90 |

624 Resistance Fighter

2004. 50th Anniv of Dien Bien Phu Victory. Multicoloured.

2589	800d. Type **624**		85	70
2590	5000d. Dancer and symbols of industry		2·40	1·90
MS2591 96×76 mm. 8000d. Dancers			4·25	3·50

625 Anniversary Emblem

2004. Centenary of FIFA (Federation Internationale de Football Association).

| 2592 | 625 | 800d. multicoloured | 1·10 | 90 |

626 "50" and Bamboo Sprout

2004. 50th Anniv of "Young Pioneer" Newspaper.

| 2593 | 626 | 800d. multicoloured | 1·10 | 90 |

627 Ficus microcarpa

2004. Bonsai Trees. Multicoloured.

2594	800d. Type **627**		55	45
2595	2000d. Premna serratifolia		1·10	90
2596	3000d. Ficus pilosa		1·40	1·10
2597	8000d. Ficus religiosa		3·50	2·75

628 Hurdling

2004. Olympic Games, Athens. Multicoloured.

2598	800d. Type **628**		55	45
2599	1000d. Swimming (horiz)		70	55
2600	6000d. Shooting (horiz)		2·00	1·60
2601	7000d. Taekwondo		2·50	2·00

629 Citadel, Hue

2004. Bicentenary of Vietnam (as country name). Multicoloured.

| 2602 | 800d. Type **629** | | 55 | 45 |
| 2603 | 5000d. Ho Chi Minh and flag | | 2·30 | 1·80 |

630 World Map and Binary Code

2004. World Summits on the Information Society, Geneva (2003) and Tunis (2005).

| 2604 | 630 | 1000d. multicoloured | 1·10 | 90 |

631 Symbols of Industry, People and Dove

2004. 50th Anniv of the Liberation of Hanoi.

| 2605 | 631 | 800d. multicoloured | 1·10 | 90 |

632 Weaver, Waterfall and Elephant Riders

2004. Centenary of Daklak Province.

| 2606 | 632 | 800d. multicoloured | 1·10 | 90 |

633 Bridge

2004. UNESCO World Heritage Sites. Hoi An. Multicoloured.

| 2607 | 800d. Type **633** | | 1·60 | 1·40 |
| MS2608 100×74 mm. 8000d. Temple entrance (43×32 mm) | | | 4·25 | 3·50 |

634 Rooster

2004. New Year. Year of the Rooster. Multicoloured.

2609	800d. Type **634**		55	45
2610	8000d. Hen and chicks		3·50	2·75
MS2611 120×85 mm. Nos. 2609/10			4·25	3·50

635 Ho Chi Minh and Oil Platform

2005. 75th Anniv of Communist Party.

| 2612 | 635 | 800d. multicoloured | 1·10 | 90 |

636 Gia Lai Province

2005. Landscapes.

| 2613 | 636 | 800d. multicoloured | 1·10 | 90 |

637 Boat and Coastline

2005. Nha Trang Bay. Multicoloured.

| 2614 | 800d. Type **637** | | 85 | 70 |
| 2615 | 8000d. Coast road and surf | | 2·30 | 1·80 |

638 Civet

2005. Endangered Species. Owston's Palm Civet (Chrotogale owstoni). Multicoloured.

2616	800d. Type **638**		45	35
2617	3000d. With outstretched tail		1·00	80
2618	5000d. Sniffing		1·70	1·40
2619	8000d. Two civets		2·50	2·00
MS2620 102×74 mm. Nos. 2616/19			5·75	4·50

639 Battle Scenes

2005. 50th Anniv of Liberation of Hai Phong. Multicoloured.

| 2621 | 800d. Type **639** | | 55 | 45 |
| 2622 | 5000d. Ships in dock | | 2·30 | 1·80 |

640 Ho Chi Minh (statue) and Soldiers

2005. 60th Anniv of Public Security Force. Multicoloured.

| 2623 | 800d. Type **640** | | 55 | 45 |
| 2624 | 10000d. Modern police and people | | 2·50 | 2·00 |

641 Symbols of Communication

2005. 60th Anniv of Posts and Telecommunications. Multicoloured.

| 2625 | 800d. Type **641** | | 1·10 | 90 |
| MS2626 70×80 mm. 8000d. As No. 2625 | | | 3·50 | 2·75 |

642 Crowd (meeting, Opera House, Hanoi)

2005. 60th Anniv of Revolution. Multicoloured.

2627	1000d. Type **642**		45	35
2628	2000d. Crowd on terrace (meeting, Hue)		85	70
2629	4000d. Procession (meeting, Saigon)		1·70	1·40
MS2630 141×86 mm. Nos. 2627/9			3·00	2·50

643 Ba-na

2005. Ethnic Groups. Designs showing couples. Multicoloured.

2631	800d. Type **643**	30	15
2632	800d. Bo Y	30	15
2633	800d. Brau	30	15
2634	800d. Bru-Van Kieu	30	15
2635	800d. Cham	30	15
2636	800d. Cho-ro	30	15
2637	800d. Chu-ru	30	15
2638	800d. Chut	30	15
2639	800d. Co	30	15
2640	800d. Cong	30	15
2641	800d. Co-ho	30	15
2642	800d. Co Lao	30	15
2643	800d. Co-tu	30	15
2644	800d. Dao	30	15
2645	800d. E-de	30	15
2646	800d. Gia-rai	30	15
2647	800d. Giay	30	15
2648	800d. Gie-Trieng	30	15
2649	800d. Ha Nhi	30	15
2650	800d. Hoa	30	15
2651	800d. Hre	30	15
2652	800d. Khang	30	15
2653	800d. Khmer	30	15
2654	800d. Kho-mu	30	15
2655	800d. Kinh	30	15
2656	800d. La Chi	30	15
2657	800d. La Ha	30	15
2658	800d. La Hu	30	15
2659	800d. Lao	30	15
2660	800d. Lo Lo	30	15
2661	800d. Lu	30	15
2662	800d. Ma	30	15
2663	800d. Mang	30	15
2664	800d. Mnong	30	15
2665	800d. Mong	30	15
2666	800d. Muong	30	15
2667	800d. Ngai	30	15
2668	800d. Nung	30	15
2669	800d. O Du	30	15
2670	800d. Pa Then	30	15
2671	800d. Phu La	30	15
2672	800d. Pu Peo	30	15
2673	800d. Ra-glai	30	15
2674	800d. Ro-mam	30	15
2675	800d. San Chay	30	15
2676	800d. San Diu	30	15
2677	800d. Si La	30	15
2678	800d. Ta-oi	30	15
2679	800d. Tay	30	15
2680	800d. Thai	30	15
2681	800d. Tho	30	15
2682	800d. Xinh-mun	30	15
2683	800d. Xo-dang	30	15
2684	800d. Xtieng	30	15

644 Statue, Musicians, Elephants and Early Soldiers

2005. 1000th (2010) Anniv of Thang Long—Hanoi. Multicoloured.

2685	800d. Type **644**		45	35
2686	5000d. Statue and anti-colonial fighters		1·40	1·10
2687	8000d. Statue and anti-USA fighters		2·40	1·90
MS2688 86×93 mm. 8000d. Dignitaries			3·00	2·50

645 Dog and Puppies

2005. New Year. Year of the Dog. Multicoloured.

2689	800d. Type **645**		55	45
2690	8000d. Dog		2·50	2·00
MS2691 120×85 mm. Nos. 2609/90			3·25	2·50

646 National Emblem

2006. 50th Anniv of National Emblem.

| 2692 | 646 | 1000d. multicoloured | 1·40 | 1·10 |

647 Ho Chi Minh

2006. Tenth Communist Party Congress.

| 2693 | 647 | 800d. yellow, vermilion and black | 1·10 | 90 |

648 Pham Van Dong

2006. Birth Centenary of Pham Van Dong (revolutionary and politician).

| 2694 | 648 | 800d. multicoloured | 1·10 | 90 |

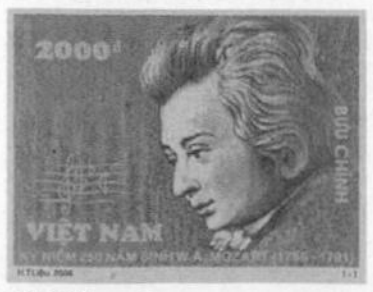

649 Mozart

2006. 250th Birth Anniv of Wolfgang Amadeus Mozart (composer and musician).

2695	**649**	2000d. multicoloured	1·80	1·50

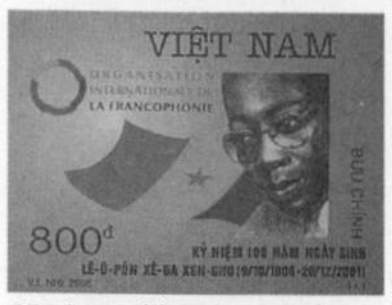

650 Leopold Sedar Senghor

2006. Birth Centenary of Leopold Sedar Senghor (writer and politician).

2696	**650**	800d. multicoloured	1·10	90

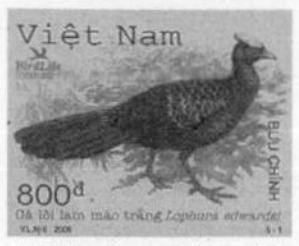

651 *Lophura edwardsi*

2006. Birds. Multicoloured.

2697	800d. Type **651**	45	35
2698	2000d. *Arborophila davidi*	1·00	80
2699	3000d. *Lophura hatinhensis*	1·40	1·10
2700	5000d. *Polyplectron germaini* (49×23 mm)	2·10	1·70
2701	8000d. *Rheinardia ocellata* (49×23 mm)	3·50	2·75
MS2702	126×85 mm. Nos. 2697/701	8·50	6·75

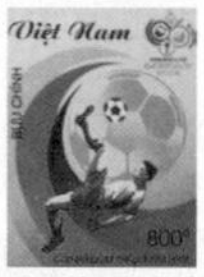

652 Player and Ball

2006. World Cup Football Championship, Germany. Multicoloured.

2703	800d. Type **652**	45	35
2704	10000d. Two players	4·75	3·75

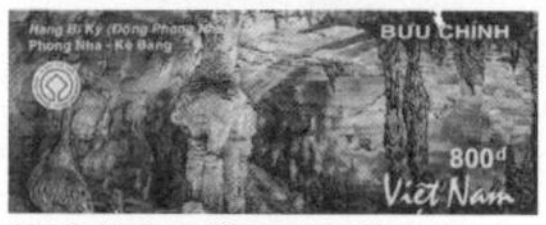

653 Bi Ky Cave (Phong Nha Cavern)

2006. World Heritage Sites. Multicoloured.

2705	800d. Type **653**	55	45
2706	4000d. Xuyen Son cavern	1·70	1·40
2707	8000d. Nuoc Moc stream	3·50	2·75
MS2708	88×80 mm. 12000d. Tien Cave (Phong Nha cavern) (32×44 mm)	6·50	5·00

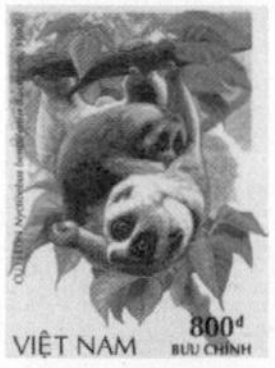

654 *Nycticebus begalensis*

2006. Animals of Ben En National Park. Multicoloured.

2709	800d. Type **654**	30	25
2710	1000d. *Neofelis nebulosa* (horiz)	45	35
2711	7000d. *Cuon alpinus* (horiz)	2·40	1·90
2712	10000d. *Nomascus leucogenys*	3·50	2·75
MS2713	88×80 mm. 12000d. *Physignathus cocincinus* (horiz)	5·00	4·00

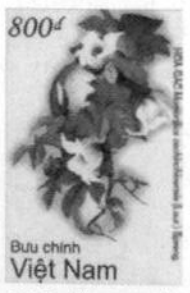

655 *Momordica cochinchinensis*

2006. Flowering Vines. Multicoloured.

2714	800d. Type **655**	30	25
2715	3000d. *Telosma cordata*	1·10	90
2716	5000d. *Mormordica charantia*	1·70	1·40
2717	8000d. *Luffa cylindrical*	2·75	2·30

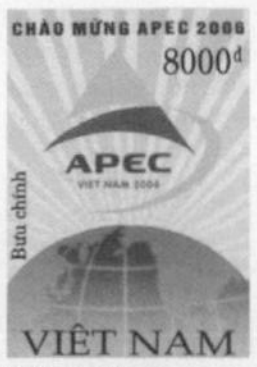

656 Emblem

2006. 14th APEC Economic Leaders' Meeting, Hanoi.

2718	**656**	8000d. multicoloured	2·75	2·30

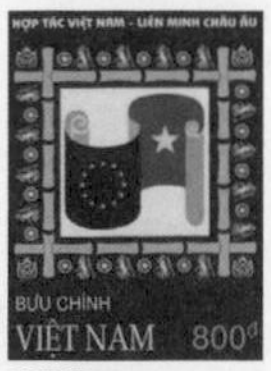

657 Flags

2006. Vietnam—European Union Co-operation.

2719	**657**	800d. multicoloured	70	55

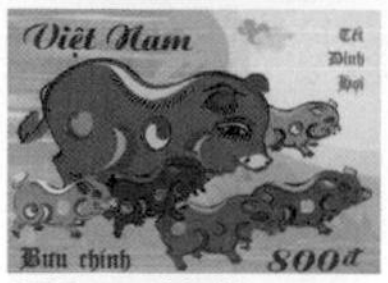

658 Sow and Piglets

2006. New Year. Year of the Pig. Multicoloured.

2720	800d. Type **658**	30	25
2721	8000d. Pig	2·75	2·30

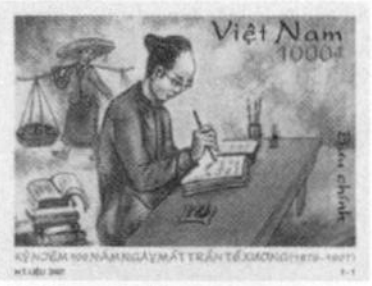

659 Tran Te Xuong

2007. Death Centenary of Tran Te Xuong (writer).

2722	**659**	1000d. multicoloured	1·40	1·10

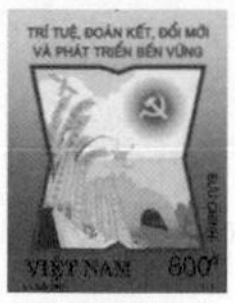

660 Symbols of Prosperity

2007. Tenth National Communist Party Congress.

2723	**660**	800d. multicoloured	1·10	90

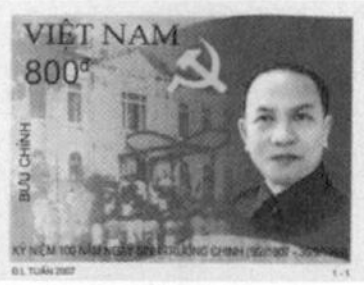

661 Truong Chinh

2007. Birth Centenary of Truong Chinh (National Communist Party General Secretary).

2724	**661**	800d. multicoloured	1·10	90

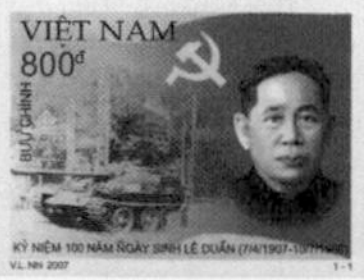

662 Le Duan

2007. Birth Centenary of Le Duan (founder of Indo-Chinese Communist Party).

2725	**662**	800d. multicoloured	1·10	90

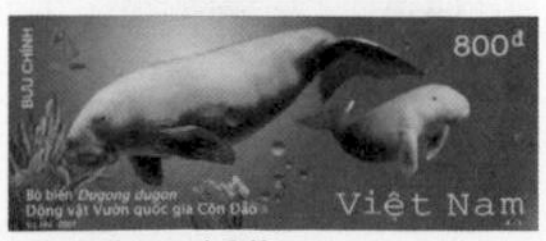

663 Mother and Calf

2007. Con Dao National Park Animals. Dugong (Dugong dugon). Multicoloured.

2726	800d. Type **663**	45	35
2727	1000d. Mother and two calves	55	45
2728	7000d. Mother and larger calf	2·00	1·60
2729	9000d. Mother and calf (different)	2·40	1·90

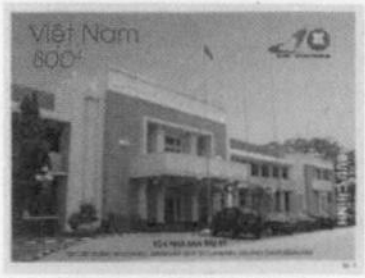

664 Secretariat Building, Bandar Seri Begawan, Brunei Darussalam

2007. Architecture. 40th Anniv of ASEAN (Association of South-East Asian Nations). Multicoloured.

2730	800d. Type **664**	45	35
2731	800d. National Museum, Cambodia	45	35
2732	800d. Fatahillah Museum, Jakarta	45	35
2733	800d. Traditional house, Laos	45	35
2734	800d. Railway Headquarters Building, Malaysia	45	35
2735	800d. Yangon Post Office, Union of Myanmar	45	35
2736	800d. Malacanang Palace, Manila	45	35
2737	800d. National Museum, Singapore	45	35
2738	800d. Vimanmek Mansion, Bangkok, Thailand	45	35
2739	800d. Presidential Palace, Hanoi, Vietnam	45	35

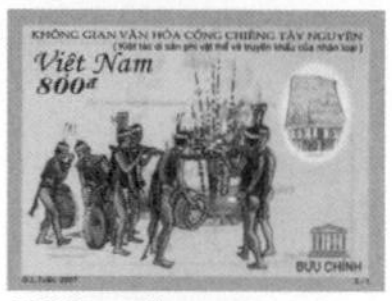

665 Gong Players

2007. Gongs of Tay Nguyen Region–UNESCO Intangible Cultural Heritage. Multicoloured.

2740	800d. Type **665**	45	35
2741	5000d. In procession	1·10	90
2742	8000d. Players seated, standing with gongs and dancers	2·10	1·70
MS2743	90×63 mm. 12000d. Player with large hand gong	4·25	3·50

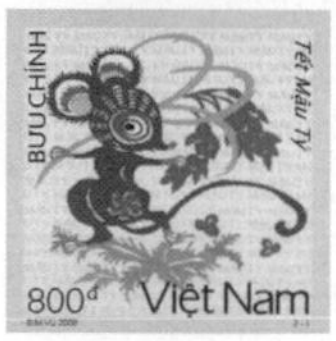

666 Rat

2007. New Year. Year of the Rat.

2744	800d. Type **666**	70	55
2745	8000d. Rat facing left	2·10	1·70

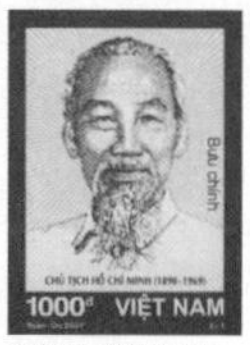

667 Ho Chi Minh

2007

2746	**667**	1000d. carmine	55	45
2747	**667**	3000d. green	85	70
2748	**667**	4000d. ultramarine	1·40	1·10

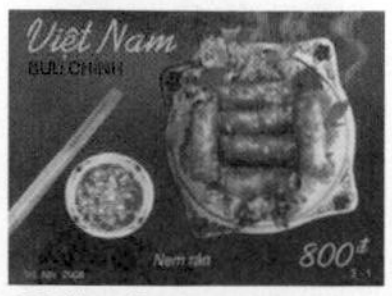

668 Nem Ran

2008. Traditional Foods. Multicoloured.

2749	800d. Type **668**	45	35
2750	9000d. Pho bo	2·40	1·90

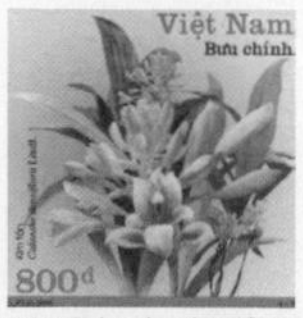

669 *Calanthe densiflora*

2008. Orchids. Multicoloured.

2751	800d. Type **669**	45	35
2752	2000d. *Ludisia discolor*	55	45
2753	6000d. *Spathoglottis affinis*	1·40	1·10
2754	8000d. *Calanthe argenteo-striata*	1·80	1·50

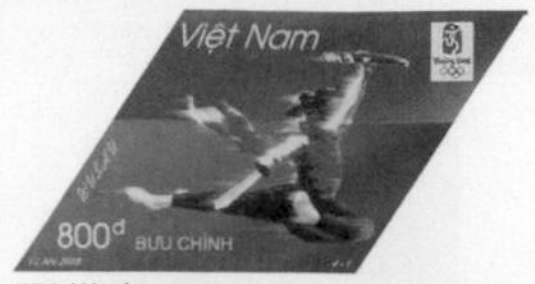

670 Wushu

2008. Beijing 2008 Wushu Tournament (2755) and Olympic Games, Beijing (2756/8). Multicoloured.

2755	800d. Type **670**	45	35
2756	3000d. Swimming	70	55
2757	5000d. Taekwando	1·10	90
2758	9000d. Canoeing	2·00	1·60

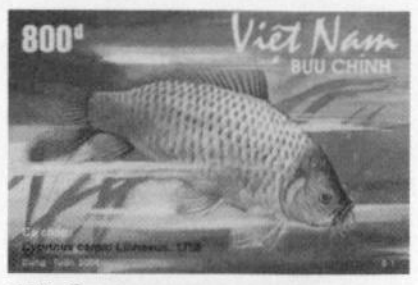

671 Carp

2008. Common Carp Cyprinus carpio. Multicoloured.

2759	800d. Type **671**	45	35
2760	6000d. Swimming left	1·40	1·10
2761	8000d. Two carp	2·40	1·90

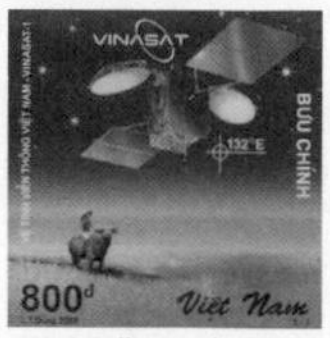

672 Satellite and Water Buffalo Rider

2008. Vietnam Communication Satellite VINASAT-1.

2762	**672**	800d. multicoloured	1·00	80

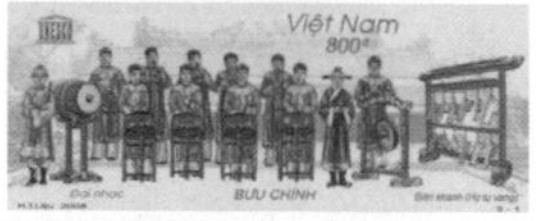

673 Drummers

2008. Hue's Court Music—UNESCO Intangible Cultural Heritage.Multicoloured.

2763	800d. Type **673**	70	55
2764	4000d. Musicians	1·40	1·10
2765	8000d. Dancers	2·10	1·70
MS2766	102×66 mm. 9000d. Choir (40×28 mm)	3·00	2·50

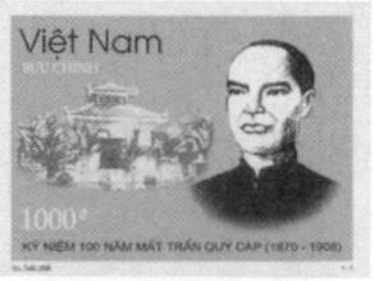

674 Tran Quy Cap

2008. Death Centenary of Tran Quy Cap (writer).

2767	**674**	1000d. multicoloured	85	70

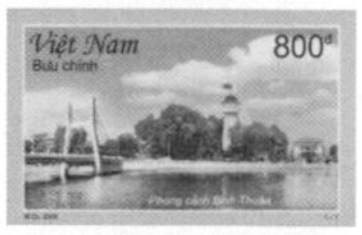

675 Landscape, Binh Thuan Province

2008. Provinces.

2768	**675**	800d. multicoloured	85	70

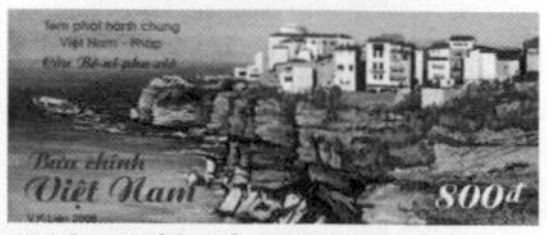

676 Strait of Bonifacio, France

2008. Vietnam—France Relations.. Multicoloured.

2769	800d. Type **676**	70	55
2770	14000d. Ha Long Bay, Vietnam	3·50	2·75

Stamps of a similar design were issued by France.

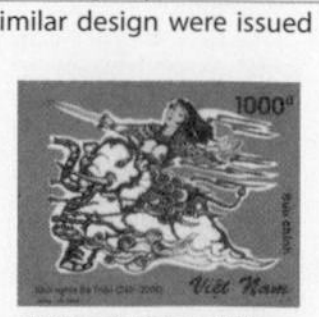

677 Lady Trieu riding Elephant into Battle

2008. 1760th Anniv of Lady Trieu's Rebellion against Chinese.

2771	**677**	1000d. multicoloured	85	70

678 *Ceiba chodatii*

2008. Flowers. Multicoloured.
| 2772 | 800d. Type **678** | 55 | 45 |
| 2773 | 10000d. *Nelumbo nucifera* | 2·50 | 2·00 |

679 *Durio zibethinus* (durian)

2008. Fruit. Multicoloured.
| 2774 | 2000d. Type **679** | 55 | 45 |
| 2775 | 8000d. *Hylocereus undatus* (dragon fruit) | 2·30 | 1·80 |

Stamps of similar designs were issued by Singapore.

680 Ox

2008. Chinese New Year. Year of the Ox. Multicoloured.
2776	2000d. Type **680**	70	55
2777	9000d. Cow and calf	2·10	1·70
MS2778	105×75 mm. 2000d. As Type **680**; 9000d. As No. 2777	3·50	2·75

681 Nguyen Khuyen

2009. Death Centenary of Nguyen Khuyen (writer).
| 2779 | **681** | 2000d. multicoloured | 1·10 | 90 |

682 Charles Darwin

2009. Birth Bicentenary of Charles Robert Darwin (evolutionary theorist).
| 2780 | **682** | 2000d. multicoloured | 1·10 | 90 |

683 Service Personnel

2009. 50th Anniv of Day of Vietnamese People's Border and Coast Guard and 20th Anniv Frontier Guard Day.
| 2781 | **683** | 2000d. multicoloured | 1·10 | 90 |

684 Lampshade

2009. Bamboo Lamps and Lantern. Multicoloured.
2782	1200d Type **684**	30	20
2783	2000d. As Type **684**	50	35
2784	2500d. As Type **684**	65	50
2785	4500d. As Type **684**	95	75
2786	5000d. Square lantern	1·10	85
2787	6500d. As No. 2786	1·40	1·10

2788	9500d. As No. 2786	2·10	1·60
2789	10500d. As No. 2786	2·40	1·80
2790	13500d. Upright lamp with three lampshades	3·00	2·30
2791	14500d. As No. 2790	3·25	2·50
2792	17500d. As No. 2790	3·75	3·00
2793	18500d. As No. 2790	4·00	3·25

685 Soldiers

2009. 50th Anniv of Ho Chi Minh Trail and Day of Truong Son Soldiers.
| 2794 | **685** | 2000d. multicoloured | 1·10 | 85 |

686 *Mantis religiosa*

2009. Mantises. Multicoloured.
| 2795 | 1500d. Type **686** | 50 | 35 |
| 2796 | 12500d. *Tenodera aridiflora* (dragon fruit) | 3·50 | 2·75 |

687 *Rhododendron fortunei*

2009. Ericaceous Shrubs. Multicoloured.
2797	500d. Type **687**	15	10
2798	1200d. *Rhododendron simsii*	30	25
2799	4500d. *Rhododendron*	1·10	85
2800	14500d. *Enkianthus quinqueflorus*	4·00	3·00

688 *Bota macracanthus*

2009. Fish. Multicoloured.
2801	2000d. Type **688**	50	35
2802	3000d. *Trichopsis pumila*	65	50
2803	6500d. *Cynolebias elongatus*	1·40	1·10
2804	10500d. *Centropyge flavissima*	2·40	1·80
MS2805	85×60 mm. 14500d. *Scleropages formosus*	3·25	2·50

689 Tiger

2009. Chinese New Year. Year of the Tiger. Multicoloured.
| 2806 | 2000d. Type **689** | 50 | 35 |
| 2807 | 8500d. Tiger, seated | 1·90 | 1·50 |

690 Anniversary Emblem

2010. 80th Anniv of National Communist Party
| 2808 | **690** | 2000d. multicoloured | 80 | 60 |

691 Chopin, Keyboard and Score

2010. Birth Bicentenary of Frédéric François Chopin (Fryderyk Franciszek Chopin) (composer)
| 2809 | **691** | 2000d. multicoloured | 80 | 60 |

692 Woman

2010. Centenary of International Women's Day
| 2810 | **692** | 3000d. multicoloured | 1·30 | 95 |

693 President Ho Chi Minh

2010. 120th Birth Anniv of Ho Chi Minh
| 2811 | **693** | 2000d. multicoloured | 80 | 60 |

694 *Tringa guttifer* (Nordmann's greenshank)

2010. Coastal Birds. Multicoloured.
2812	2000d. Type **694**	80	60
2813	6500d. *Calidris pygmeus* (Spoon-billed sandpiper)	1·60	1·20
2814	8500d. *Larus saundersi* (Saunders's gull)	2·40	1·80
MS2815	80×60 mm. 14500d. *Rynchops albicollis* (Indian skimmer)	3·25	2·50

695 Nguyễn Hữu Thọ

2010. Birth centebnary of Nguyễn Hữu Thọ (lawyer and politician)
| 2816 | **695** | 2000d. multicoloured | 80 | 60 |

696 Tạ Quang Bửu

2010. Birth Centenary of Tạ Quang Bửu (Headmaster of Hanoi University of Technology (1956-1961) and first Minister of Ministry of Higher and Secondary Professional Education (1965-1976))
| 2817 | **696** | 2000d. multicoloured | 80 | 60 |

697 *Zephyranthes carinata*

2010. Fairy Lilies. Multicoloured.
| 2818 | 3500d. Type **697** | 1·30 | 95 |
| 2819 | 10500d. *Zephyranthes ajax* | 3·50 | 2·75 |

698 *Prionallurus viverrinus* (Fishing cat)

2010. Fishing Cat (*Prionallurus viverrinus*). Multicoloured.
2820	2000d. Type **694**	80	60
2821	2500d. With fish in mouth	95	75
2822	4500d. In stream facing left	1·60	1·20
2823	10500d. Crouched by water's edge	3·50	2·75

699 Royal Proclamation and Outline of Hanoi Flag Tower

2010. Millenary of Hanoi. Multicoloured.
2824	2000d. Type **699**	80	60
2825	2500d. Quan Chưởng City Gate and outline National Conference Centre	95	75
2826	4500d. Long Biên and Nhật Tân bridges	1·60	1·20
2827	6500d. Hanoi Station and outline of Nội Bài Airport	2·40	1·80
MS2828	93×86 mm. 14000d. Teacher and students (vert)	5·00	3·75

700 Flags of Members

2010. Vietnam in ASEAN
| 2829 | **700** | 8500d. multicoloured | 3·25 | 2·40 |

701 Cat

2010. Chinese New Year. Year of the Cat (Year of the Tiger). Multicoloured.
| 2830 | 2000d. Type **701** | 95 | 65 |
| 2831 | 10500d. Blue cat facing left | 4·25 | 3·00 |

702 '50' and Flags of Vietnam and Cuba

2010. 50th Anniv of Vietnamese - Cuba Diplomatic Relations
| 2832 | **702** | 2000d. multicoloured | 1·00 | 70 |

703 Ho Chi Minh

2011. 11th Communist Party Congress
| 2833 | **703** | 2000d. multicoloured | 1·00 | 70 |

704 Four Singers

2011. Cultural Heritage. UNESCO Intangible Representation of Humanity. Quan họ Bắc Ninh (folk songs of Northern delta of Vietnam). Multicoloured.
2834	3000d. Type **704**	65	45
2835	4500d. Four singers (two men, two women) seated (horiz)	1·00	70
2836	10500d. Two male singers in boat, two female singers on shore	2·30	1·60
MS2837	90×60 mm. 12500d. Six singers in boat (horiz)	2·75	1·80

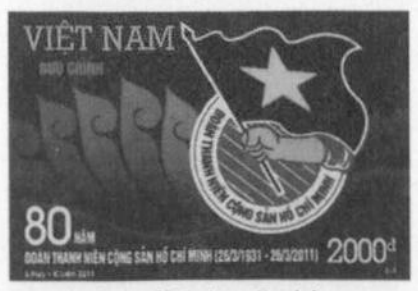

705 '80' and Union Emblem

2011. 80th Anniv of Ho Chi Minh Communist Youth Union

2838 **705** 2000d. multicoloured 1·00 70

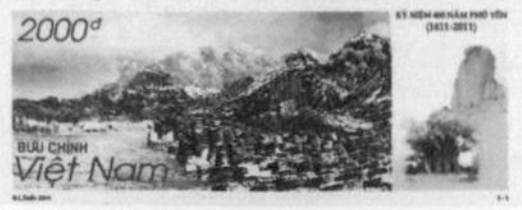

706 Phú Yên Landscape

2011. 400th Anniv of Phú Yên (southern central coastal province)

2839 **706** 2000d. multicoloured 1·00 70

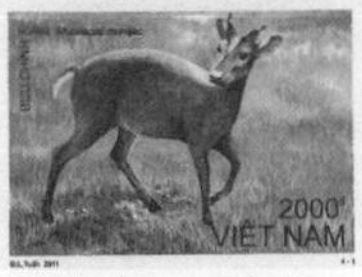

707 *Muntiacus muntjak* (insc 'Muntiacus muntjac') (muntjac deer)

2011. Ba Bể National Park. Fauna. Multicoloured.

2840 2000d. Type **707** 65 45

2841 2500d. *Gorsachius magnificus* (white-eared night heron) 1·00 70

2842 4500d. *Acanthosaura lepidogaster* (mountain horned dragon) 1·90 1·30

2843 6500d. *Pyxidea mouhoti* (keeled box turtle) 2·75 1·80

MS2844 90×60 mm. 14500d. *Catopuma temminckii* (Asian golden cat) (43×32 mm) 4·25 2·75

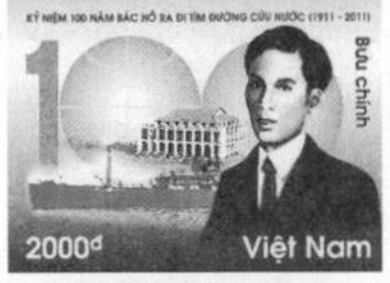

708 Ho Chi Minh as Young Man

2011. Centenary of Ho Chi Minh's departure to France

2845 **708** 2000d. multicoloured 1·00 70

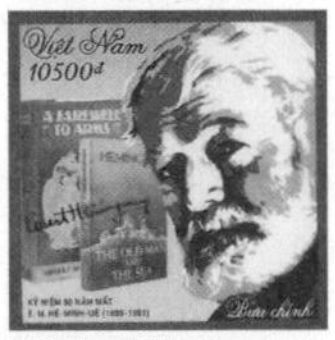

709 Ernest Hemingway, *The Old Man and the Sea* and *A Farewell to Arms*

2011. 50th Death Anniv of Ernest Miller Hemingway (novelist, short story writer and journalist)

2846 **709** 10500d. multicoloured 3·25 2·30

Nos. 2847/50, T **710** have been left for stamps not received.

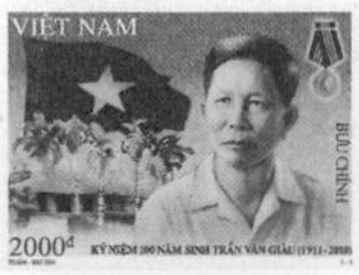

711 Tran Van Giau

2011. Birth Centenary Tran Van Giau (educator, historian, philosopher and Party Secretary of South Vietnam)

2851 **711** 2000d. multicoloured 1·00 70

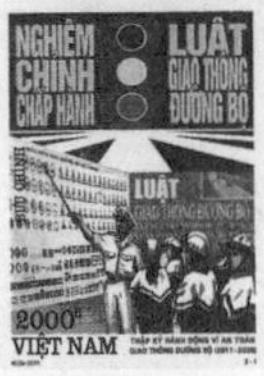

712 Traffic Lights, Teacher and Students

2011. Decade of Action for Road Safety. Multicoloured.

2852 2000d. Type **712** 1·00 70

2853 6500d. Using Zebra Crossing to cross road 3·25 2·10

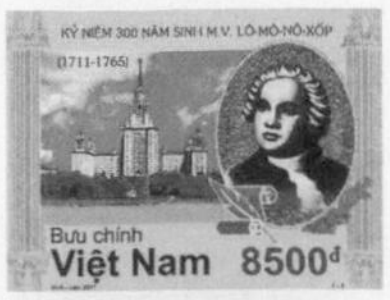

713 Mikhail Lomonosov

2011. 300th Birth Anniv of Mikhail Vasilyevich Lomonosov (Russian scientist)

2854 **713** 8500d. multicoloured 4·25 2·75

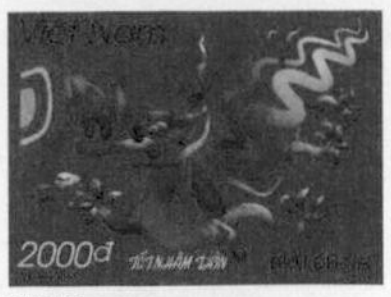

714 Dragon

2011. Chinese New Year. Year of the Dragon. Multicoloured.

2855 2000d. Type **714** 1·00 70

2856 10500d. Dragon, green background 3·25 2·30

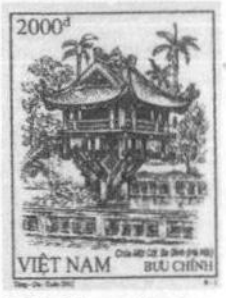

715 Chua Mot Cot

2012. Architecture

2857 2000d. brown-red 1·00 70

2858 3000d. yellowish green 1·30 85

2859 3500d. reddish orange 1·40 90

2860 4500d. bright purple 1·50 1·00

2861 6500d. new blue (horiz) 2·10 1·40

2862 10500d. bright rose-red (horiz) 3·25 2·30

Designs: 2000d. Type **715**; 3000d. As Type **715**; 3500d. Chua Keo; 4500d. As No. 2857; 6500d. Chua Cau; As No. 2859

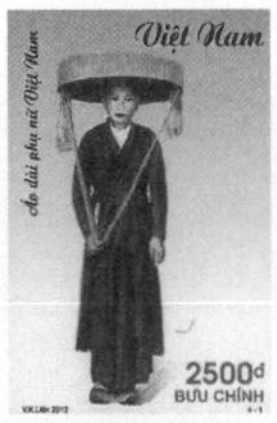

716 Early Ao dai

2012. Evolution of Ao dai (Women's National Costume). Multicoloured.

2863 2000d. Type **716** 1·00 70

2864 3000d. Two women wearing loose Ao dai and turbans 1·30 85

2865 6000d. Two women wearing modern Ao dai, one carrying hat 2·10 1·40

2866 10500d. Two women wearing decorated modern Ao dai, one seated 3·25 2·30

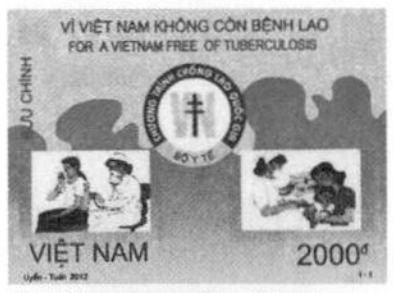

717 Nurse treating Woman, Nurse inoculating Child and Emblem

2012. For a Vietnam Free of Tuberculosis. World TB Day

2867 **717** 2000d. multicoloured 1·00 70

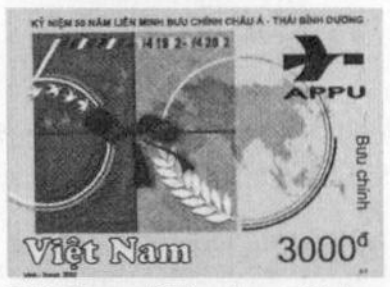

718 Flags of Members, Globe and Emblem

2012. 50th Anniv of Asian Pacific Postal Union

2868 **718** 3000d. multicoloured 1·30 85

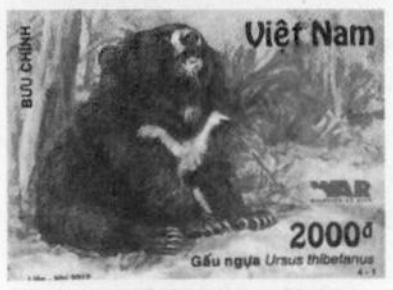

719 *Ursus thibetanus* (Asian Black Bear)

2012. Bears of Vietnam. 'Say No to all Bear Products'. Multicoloured.

2869 2000d. Type **719** 1·00 70

2870 4500d. *Ursus malayanus* (Sun Bear) 1·50 1·00

2871 8500d. Sun Bear standing 1·70 1·10

2872 10500d. Asian Black Bear facing left 3·25 2·30

MS2873 86×65 mm. 14500d. Asian Black Bear in tree 4·25 2·75

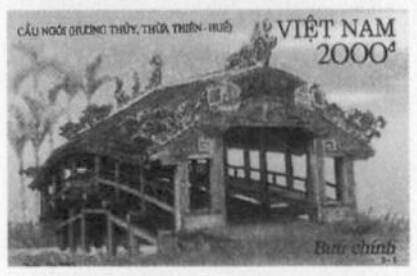

720 Bridge, Huong Thuy, Thua Thien-Hue

2012. Tiled Roof Bridges. Multicoloured.

2874 2000d. Type **720** 1·00 70

2875 3000d. Narrow, red-roofed bridge, Kim Son, Ninh Binh 1·30 85

2876 12000d. Curved roof bridge with arched pediment, Hai Hau, Nam Dinh 3·75 2·50

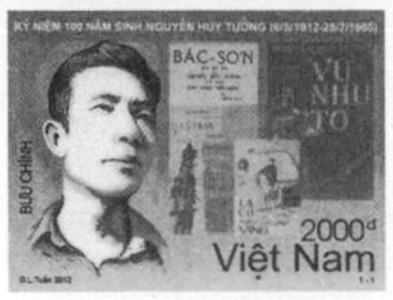

721 Nguyen Huy Tuong

2012. Birth Centenary of Nguyen Huy Tuong (writer and revolutionary)

2877 **721** 2000d. multicoloured 1·00 70

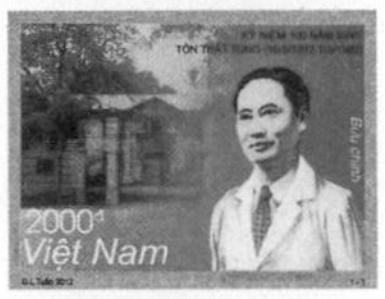

722 Ton That Tung

2012. Birth Centenary of Ton That Tung (Doctor, Surgeon and Teacher)

2878 **722** 2000d. multicoloured 1·00 70

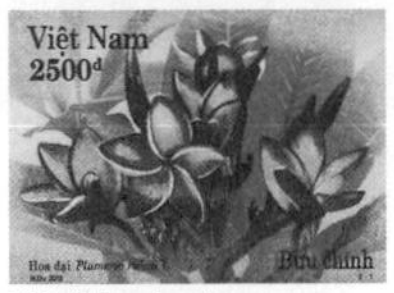

723 *Pulmeria rubra*

2012. Flora. Multicoloured.

2879 2500d. Type **723** 1·10 80

2880 8500d. *Pulmeria alba* 1·70 1·10

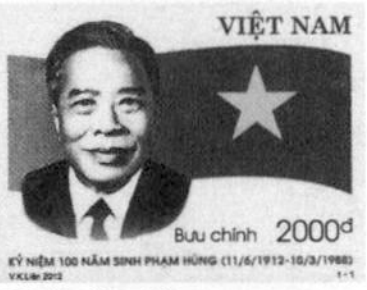

724 Vu Kim Lien

2012. Birth Centenary of Pham Hung

2881 **724** 2000d. multicoloured 1·00 70

FRANK STAMPS

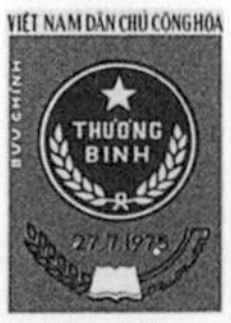

F19 Invalid's Badge

1976. For use by disabled veterans. Dated "27.7.75". No value indicated.

F100 **F19** (-) red and blue 1·30 1·30

F101 - (-) green, light green and brown 1·30 1·30

DESIGN: No. F101, Disabled veteran in factory.

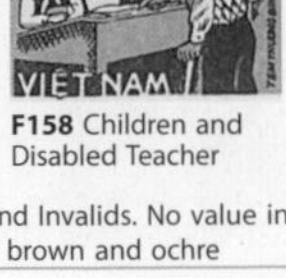

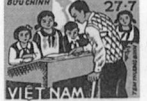

F158 Children and Disabled Teacher

1984. Disabled and Invalids. No value indicated.

F750 **F158** (-) brown and ochre 1·00 75

1985. No value indicated. As T **179**.

F861 (-) red and black (Policeman and militia members) 90 90

MILITARY FRANK STAMPS

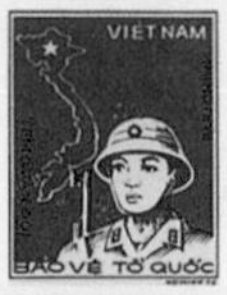

MF21 Soldier and Map of Vietnam

1976. No value indicated.

MF110 **MF21** (-) black and red 1·30 1·30

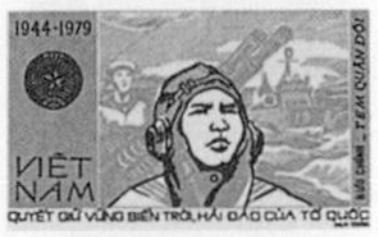

MF59 Pilot

1979. 35th Anniv of Vietnam People's Army. No value indicated.

MF304 **MF59** (-) purple and pink 1·90 1·90

MF305 - (-) purple and pink 1·90 1·90

DESIGN: No. MF305, Badge of People's Army.

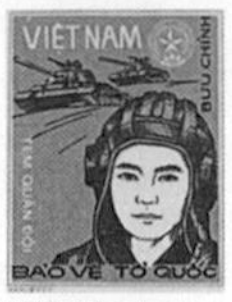

MF61 Tank Driver and Tanks

1979. No value indicated.

MF308 **MF61** (-) black and mauve 1·90 1·00

MF309 - (-) violet and green 1·90 1·00

MF310 - (-) black and red 1·90 1·00

DESIGNS: No. MF309, Sailor and ship; MF310, Pilot and jet fighters.

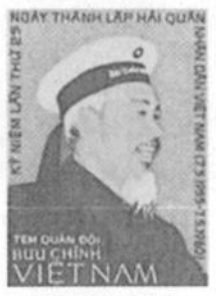

MF84 Ho Chi Minh in Naval Uniform

1981. No value indicated.

MF420 **MF84** (-) pink and blue 1·30 1·30

MF421 - (-) multicoloured 1·30 1·30

DESIGN—13×17 mm: No. MF421, Factory militiawoman.

1982. Multicoloured. No value indicated.

MF466 (-) Soldier and militiawoman 1·30 1·30

MF467 (-) Type **94** 75 50

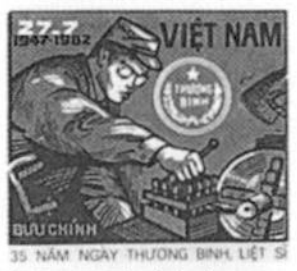

MF107 Disabled Soldier

1982. 35th Anniv of Disabled Soldiers' Day. No value indicated.

MF513 **MF107** (-) mauve and green 90 75

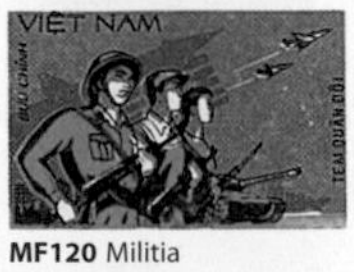

MF120 Militia

1983. No value indicated.

MF581 **MF120** (-) multicoloured 1·30 1·30

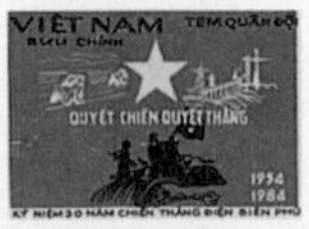

MF145 Star and Soldiers on Bunker

1984. 30th Anniv of Battle of Dien Bien Phu. No value indicated.

MF690 **MF145** (-) yellow, orange & brn 1·00 75

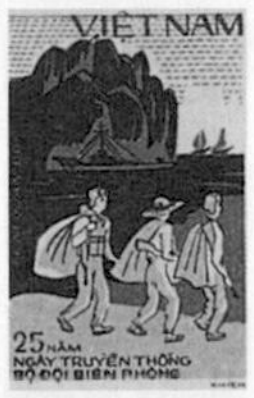

MF152 Coastal Militia

1984. No value indicated.

MF732	**MF152**	(–) brown, orange & yellow	1·30	75

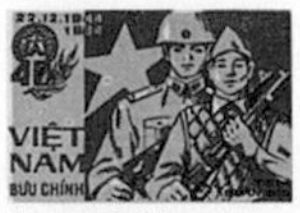

MF164 Soldiers and Emblem

1984. No value indicated.

MF786	**MF164**	(–) orange, red and black	90	75

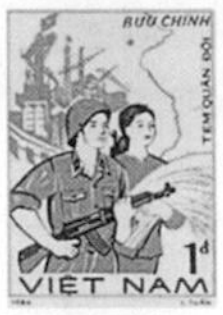

MF205 Soldier and Woman holding Sheaf of Rice

1986

MF979	**MF205**	1d. brown and black	1·10	1·10

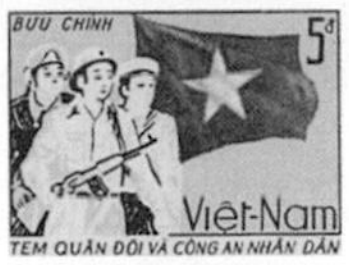

MF232 Armed Forces Personnel and Flag

1987

MF1119	**MF232**	5d. red & brown	1·50	1·50

Pt. 1

WADHWAN

A state of Kathiawar, India. Now uses Indian stamps.

4 pice = 1 anna.

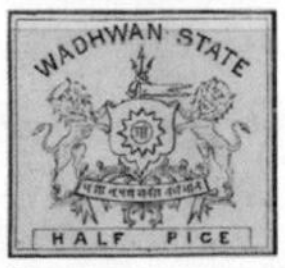

1

1888

5	**1**	½pice black	13·00	14·00

Pt. 6

WALLIS & FUTUNA ISLANDS

A group of French islands in the Pacific Ocean north-east of Fiji. Attached to New Caledonia for administrative purposes in 1888. In 1961 they became a French Overseas Territory.

100 centimes = 1 franc.

1920. Stamps of New Caledonia optd **ILES WALLIS et FUTUNA.**

1	**15**	1c. black on green	20	3·00
2	**15**	2c. brown	35	5·75
3	**15**	4c. blue on orange	75	5·75
4	**15**	5c. green	55	7·75
18	**15**	5c. blue	45	8·00
5	**15**	10c. red	1·30	4·25
19	**15**	10c. green	1·10	8·25
6	**15**	15c. lilac	2·50	7·75
7	**16**	20c. brown	1·20	8·00
8	**16**	25c. blue on green	2·50	8·00
21	**16**	25c. red on yellow	1·70	7·25
9	**16**	30c. brown on orange	3·00	8·75
22	**16**	30c. red	2·00	8·00
24	**16**	30c. green	1·40	10·50
10	**16**	35c. black on yellow	1·30	8·00
11	**16**	40c. red on green	2·30	8·00
12	**16**	45c. purple	1·80	8·25
13	**16**	50c. red on orange	2·75	4·75
25	**16**	50c. blue	1·40	8·50
26	**16**	50c. grey	3·00	9·50
27	**16**	65c. blue	6·00	14·00
14	**16**	75c. green	2·30	10·50
15	**17**	1f. blue on green	4·50	13·00
28	**17**	1f.10 brown	2·50	8·50
16	**17**	2f. red on blue	7·75	20·00
17	**17**	5f. black on orange	12·00	34·00

1922. As last surch.

29	**15**	0,01 on 15c. lilac	55	8·00
30	**15**	0,02 on 15c. lilac	70	8·00
31	**15**	0,04 on 15c. lilac	55	8·00
32	**15**	0,05 on 15c. lilac	1·60	8·00
33	**17**	25c. on 2f. red on blue	1·40	8·25
34	**17**	25c. on 5f. black on orange	1·50	8·25
35	**16**	65 on 40c. red on green	1·80	7·75
36	**16**	85 on 75c. green	1·80	8·00
37	**16**	90 on 75c. red	2·00	9·00
38	**17**	1f.25 on 1fr. blue	2·30	7·50
39	**17**	1f.50 on 1fr. blue on blue	5·00	11·50
40	**17**	3f. on 5f. mauve	10·50	23·00
41	**17**	10f. on 5f. green on mauve	21·00	65·00
42	**17**	20f. on 5f. red on yellow	37·00	80·00

1930. Stamps of New Caledonia, some with colours changed, optd **ILES WALLIS et FUTUNA.**

43	**22**	1c. blue and purple	35	6·75
44	**22**	2c. green and brown	20	6·75
45	**22**	3c. blue and red	50	6·75
46	**22**	4c. green and red	35	7·00
47	**22**	5c. brown and blue	35	6·00
48	**22**	10c. brown and lilac	35	7·75
49	**22**	15c. blue and brown	30	4·50
50	**22**	20c. brown and red	40	7·75
51	**22**	25c. brown and green	2·50	8·25
52	**23**	30c. turquoise and green	45	8·00
53	**23**	35c. green and deep green	2·00	8·50
54	**23**	40c. green and red	30	7·75
55	**23**	45c. red and blue	3·75	8·25
56	**23**	45c. green and turquoise	3·25	8·25
57	**23**	50c. brown and mauve	60	8·00
58	**23**	55c. red and blue	2·30	10·50
59	**23**	60c. red and blue	55	8·00
60	**23**	65c. blue and brown	4·25	9·00
61	**23**	70c. brown and mauve	2·30	8·50
62	**23**	75c. drab and blue	5·00	10·50
63	**23**	80c. green and purple	2·30	8·00
64	**23**	85c. brown and green	3·75	13·00
65	**23**	90c. carmine and red	2·75	10·00
66	**23**	90c. red and brown	3·25	8·25
67	**24**	1f. red and drab	7·75	13·00
68	**24**	1f. carmine and red	6·00	8·50
69	**24**	1f. green and red	75	8·25
70	**24**	1f.10 brown and green	36·00	70·00
71	**24**	1f.25 green and brown	5·25	10·50
72	**24**	1f.25 carmine and red	3·75	8·25
73	**24**	1f.40 red and blue	3·75	8·50
74	**24**	1f.50 blue and ultra-marine	2·30	8·00
75	**24**	1f.60 brown and green	4·75	8·50
76	**24**	1f.75 red and blue	34·00	40·00
77	**24**	1f.75 blue	6·50	10·50
78	**24**	2f. brown and orange	1·80	9·00
79	**24**	2f.25 blue and ultra-marine	3·75	8·50
80	**24**	2f.50 brown	3·75	8·50
81	**24**	3f. brown and purple	1·60	9·00
82	**24**	5f. brown and blue	2·50	9·00
83	**24**	10f. brown & mauve on pink	1·40	11·50
84	**24**	20f. brown and red on yellow	1·60	14·50

1931. "Colonial Exhibition" key-types.

85	**E**	40c. green and black	5·50	16·00
86	**F**	50c. mauve and black	5·50	16·00
87	**G**	90c. red and black	5·50	16·00
88	**H**	1f.50 blue and black	7·00	17·00

1939. New York World's Fair. As T **41** of St. Pierre et Miquelon.

89	1f.25 red	2·75	10·00
90	2f.25 blue	3·75	10·00

1939. 150th Anniv of French Revolution. As T **42** of St. Pierre et Miquelon.

91	45c.+25c. green and black	20·00	48·00
92	70c.+30c. brown and black	20·00	48·00
93	90c.+35c. orange and black	20·00	48·00
94	1f.25c.+1f. red and black	20·00	48·00
95	2f.25c.+2f. blue and black	20·00	48·00

1941. Adherence to General de Gaulle. Stamps of 1930 optd **France Libre.**

96	**22**	1c. blue and purple	1·80	8·75
97	**22**	2c. green and brown	2·75	8·75
97a	**22**	3c. blue and red	£130	£130
98	**22**	4c. green and orange	1·30	8·75
99	**22**	5c. brown and blue	1·30	8·75
100	**22**	10c. brown and lilac	1·80	8·75
101	**22**	15c. blue and brown	5·00	8·75
102	**22**	20c. brown and red	7·25	11·00
103	**22**	25c. brown and green	7·25	11·00
104	**23**	30c. green	6·00	11·00
105	**23**	35c. green	3·50	8·75
106	**23**	40c. green and red	4·00	11·00
107	**23**	45c. red and blue	4·00	11·00
107a	**23**	45c. green and turquoise	£110	£130
108	**23**	50c. brown and mauve	3·75	8·75
109	**23**	55c. red and blue	3·75	8·75
109a	**23**	60c. red and blue	£130	£130
110	**23**	65c. blue and brown	3·00	8·75
111	**23**	70c. brown and mauve	4·00	8·75
112	**23**	75c. drab and blue	4·50	8·75
113	**23**	80c. green and purple	3·00	8·75
114	**23**	85c. brown and green	4·00	11·00
115	**23**	90c. carmine and red	4·25	8·75
116	**24**	1f. carmine and red	5·50	11·00
117	**24**	1f.25 green and brown	5·25	11·00
118	**24**	1f.50 blue and deep blue	5·00	8·75
119	**24**	1f.75 blue	5·00	8·75
120	**24**	2f. brown and orange	5·25	11·00
121	**24**	2f.50 brown	£140	£160
122	**24**	3f. brown and purple	3·75	8·75
123	**24**	5f. brown and blue	9·75	18·00
124	**24**	10f. brown and mauve on pink	55·00	£100
125	**24**	20f. brown & red on yell	60·00	£130

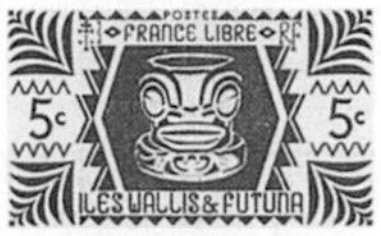

5 Native Ivory Head

1944. Free French Administration.

126	**5**	5c. brown	10	7·00
127	**5**	10c. blue	35	6·50
128	**5**	25c. green	10	7·00
129	**5**	30c. orange	55	7·00
130	**5**	40c. green	1·00	5·25
131	**5**	80c. purple	90	7·25
132	**5**	1f. purple	1·10	7·25
133	**5**	1f.50 red	90	7·00
134	**5**	2f. black	1·00	6·75
135	**5**	2f.50 blue	1·60	7·50
136	**5**	4f. violet	1·40	7·50
137	**5**	5f. yellow	1·00	7·25
138	**5**	10f. brown	2·20	8·75
139	**5**	20f. green	2·75	7·25

1944. Mutual Aid and Red Cross Funds. As T **49** of St. Pierre et Miquelon.

140	5f.+20f. orange	90	9·50

1945. Surch.

141	50c. on 5c. brown	75	5·50
142	60c. on 5c. brown	60	6·00
143	70c. on 5c. brown	60	6·25
144	1f.20 on 5c. brown	90	8·00
145	2f.40 on 35c. green	85	6·25
146	3f. on 25c. green	85	6·75
147	4f.50 on 25c. green	1·80	8·25
148	15f. on 2f.50 blue	1·80	7·50

1946. Air. Victory. As T **52** of St. Pierre et Miquelon.

149	8f. violet	45	6·25

1946. Air. From Chad to the Rhine. As T **53** of St. Pierre et Miquelon.

150	5f. violet	1·70	9·50
151	10f. green	1·70	9·50
152	15f. brown	1·70	9·50
153	20f. blue	2·00	10·50
154	25f. orange	2·00	11·50
155	50f. red	2·75	13·00

1949. Air. 75th Anniv of Universal Postal Union. As T **58** of St. Pierre et Miquelon.

156	10f. multicoloured	4·50	20·00

1949. Air. Nos. 325/6 of New Caledonia, with colours changed, optd **WALLIS ET FUTUNA.**

157	**37**	50f. red and yellow	10·50	32·00
158	-	100f. brown and yellow	11·00	44·00

1952. Centenary of Military Medal. As T **60** of St. Pierre et Miquelon.

159	2f. turquoise, yellow and green	4·75	11·00

1954. Air. Tenth Anniv of Liberation. As T **61** of St. Pierre et Miquelon.

160	3f. brown and deep brown	5·75	23·00

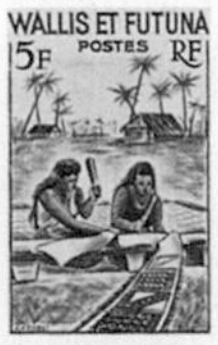

7 Making Tapa (cloth)

1955. (a) Postage, as T **7**.

161	-	3f. purple, mauve and lilac	1·60	8·50
162	**7**	5f. chocolate, brown & grn	6·00	5·50
163	-	7f. brown and turquoise	6·25	4·00
164	-	9f. deep purple, purple and blue	1·50	11·50
165	-	17f. multicoloured	8·25	12·00
166	-	19f. green and red	11·50	13·50

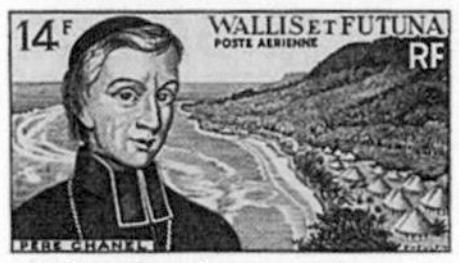

8 Father Chanel

(b) Air, as T **8**.

167	**8**	14f. blue, green and indigo	2·50	9·75
168	-	21f. green, brown and blue	6·00	16·00
168a	-	27f. green, blue and brown	11·50	9·75
169	-	33f. brown, blue & turq	7·25	32·00

DESIGNS—HORIZ: 9f. Wallisian and island view; 7f. Preparing kava; 17f. Dancers; 21f. View of Mata-Utu, Queen Amelia and Mgr. Bataillon; 27f. Wharf, Mata-Utu; 33f. Map of Wallis and Futuna Islands and "Stella Matutina" (full-rigged ship). VERT: 19f. Paddle dance.

1958. Tropical Flora. As T **67** of St. Pierre et Miquelon.

170	5f. multicoloured	1·80	9·00

DESIGN—HORIZ: 5f. "Montrouziera".

1958. Tenth Anniv of Declaration of Human Rights. As T **66** of St. Pierre et Miquelon.

171	17f. blue and ultramarine	2·30	16·00

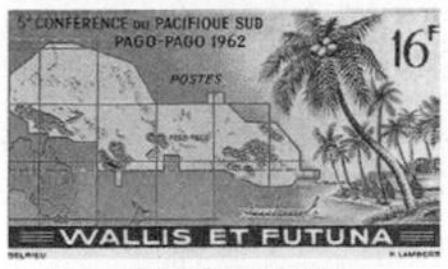

8a Map of Pacific and Palms

1962. Fifth South Pacific Conference, Pago Pago.

172	**8a**	16f. multicoloured	3·00	9·75

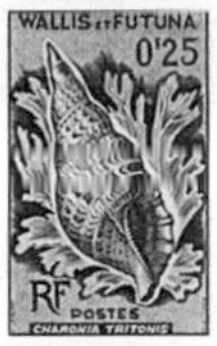

9 Trumpet Triton

1962. Marine Fauna.

173	**9**	25c. brown and green (postage)	55	6·00
174	-	1f. red and green	1·20	2·75
175	-	2f. brown and blue	2·30	3·50
176	-	4f. brown and blue	2·50	3·75
177	-	10f. multicoloured	6·00	16·00
178	-	20f. brown and blue	11·50	29·00
179	-	50f. brown, blue & pur (air)	5·50	23·00
180	-	100f. black, green & purple	14·00	50·00

DESIGNS—As T **9**: 1f. Episcopal mitre; 2f. Bull-mouth helmet; 4f. Venus comb murex; 10f. Red-mouth olive; 20f. Tiger cowrie. 26½×48 mm: 50f. Ventral harp. 48×26½ mm: 100f. Fishing underwater for commercial trochus shells.

1962. Air. First Trans-Atlantic TV Satellite Link. As T **71** of St. Pierre et Miquelon.

181	12f. blue, purple and violet	1·20	11·50

1963. Red Cross Centenary. As T **75** of St. Pierre et Miquelon.

182	12f. red, grey and purple	2·75	8·50

1963. 15th Anniv of Declaration of Human Rights. As T **76** of St. Pierre et Miquelon.

183	29f. ochre and red	6·50	20·00

1964. "PHILATEC 1964" Int Stamp Exn, Paris. As T **77** of St. Pierre et Miquelon.

184	9f. red, green and deep green	2·30	9·00

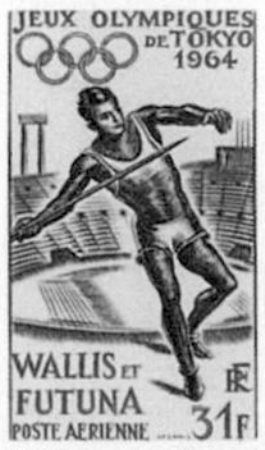

10 Throwing the Javelin

1964. Air. Olympic Games. Tokyo.
185 **10** 31f. purple, red and
green 9·25 46·00

11 Inter-island Ferry
"Reine Amelia"

1965
186 **11** 11f. multicoloured 11·50 9·50

1965. Air. Centenary of I.T.U. As T **80** of St. Pierre et Miquelon.
187 50f. brown, purple and red 9·25 50·00

1966. Air. Launching of First French Satellite. As T **82** of St. Pierre et Miquelon.
188 7f. red, claret and vermilion 2·75 10·00
189 10f. red, claret and vermilion 3·75 14·50

1966. Air. Launching of Satellite "D1". As T **82** of St. Pierre et Miquelon.
190 10f. red, lake and green 1·80 11·50

12 W.H.O. Building

1966. Air. Inauguration of W.H.O. Headquarters, Geneva.
191 **12** 30f. red, yellow and blue 2·75 7·00

13 Art Students

1966. Air. 20th Anniv of UNESCO.
192 **13** 50f. brown, green &
orange 3·25 8·25

14 Athlete and Decorative
Pattern

1966. Air. South Pacific Games, Noumea.
193 **14** 32f. multicoloured 4·50 11·50
194 - 38f. green and mauve 6·00 13·50
DESIGN: 38f. Woman with ball, and decorative pattern.

15 Samuel Wallis's Frigate H.M.S.
"Dolphin" at Uvea

1967. Air. Bicentenary of Discovery of Wallis Island.
195 **15** 12f. multicoloured 8·25 10·50

1968. 20th Anniv of W.H.O. As T **90** of St. Pierre et Miquelon.
196 17f. purple, orange and green 3·25 11·50

1968. Human Rights Year. As T **92** of St. Pierre et Miquelon.
197 19f. brown, mauve and purple 3·25 11·50

1969. Air. First Flight of Concorde. As T **94** of St. Pierre et Miquelon.
198 20f. black and purple 10·00 30·00

16 Gathering Coconuts

1969. Scenes of Everyday Life. Multicoloured.
199 1f. Launching outrigger canoe
(35×22 mm) (postage) 4·75 6·25
200 20f. Type **16** (air) 3·75 7·00
201 32f. Horse-riding 5·50 8·00
202 38f. Wood-carving 4·50 9·00
203 50f. Fishing 10·50 16·00
204 100f. Marketing fruit 12·00 25·00

1969. 50th Anniv of Int Labour Organization. As T **100** of St. Pierre et Miquelon.
205 · 9f. blue, brown and salmon 4·00 5·00

1970. Inauguration of New U.P.U. Headquarters Building, Berne As T **101** of St. Pierre et Miquelon.
206 21f. brown, blue and purple 8·00 11·50

1971. Surch.
207 12f. on 19f. (No. 166) (postage) 3·75 7·25
208 21f. on 33f. (No. 169) (air) 7·75 12·50

18 Weightlifting

1971. Fourth South Pacific Games, Papeete, Tahiti.
209 **18** 24f. brown, blue and
green (postage) 4·75 10·50
210 - 36f. blue, olive and red 5·75 12·50
211 - 48f. brown, green and
lilac (air) 6·00 10·50
212 - 54f. red, purple and blue 6·50 16·00
DESIGNS—As T **18**: 36f. Basketball. 47×27 mm: 48f. Pole-vaulting; 54f. Archery.

1971. First Death Anniv of General Charles de Gaulle. As T **110** of St. Pierre et Miquelon.
213 30f. black and blue 5·50 9·75
214 70f. black and blue 9·25 25·00

19 Commission Headquarters,
Noumea

1972. Air. 25th Anniv of South Pacific Commission.
215 **19** 44f. multicoloured 11·50 12·50

20 Pacific Island
Dwelling

1972. Air. South Pacific Arts Festival, Fiji.
216 **20** 60f. violet, green and red 8·75 16·00

21 Model Pirogue

1972. Sailing Pirogues. Multicoloured.
217 14f. Type **21** (postage) 8·50 10·50
218 16f. Children with model
pirogues 8·50 10·50
219 18f. Racing pirogue 9·25 16·00
220 200f. Pirogue race (47×27
mm) (air) 20·00 55·00

22 La Perouse and "La Boussole"

1973. Air. Explorers of the Pacific.
221 **22** 22f. brown, grey and red 10·00 8·50
222 - 28f. green and blue 12·00 10·50
223 - 40f. brown, blue &
lt blue 16·00 16·00
224 - 72f. brown, blue and
violet 27·00 21·00
DESIGNS: 28f. Samuel Wallis and H.M.S. "Dolphin"; 40f. Dumont d'Urville and "L'Astrolabe"; 72f. Bougainville and "La Boudeuse".

23 General De Gaulle

1973. Air. Third Death Anniv of General Charles de Gaulle.
225 **23** 107f. purple and brown 11·00 28·00

24 "Plumeria rubra"

1973. Air. Flora of Wallis Islands. Multicoloured.
226 12f. Type **24** 2·20 4·25
227 17f. "Hibiscus tiliaceus" 2·30 6·75
228 19f. "Phaeomeria magnifica" 2·50 7·00
229 21f. "Hibiscus rosa sinensis" 2·75 7·00
230 23f. "Allamanda cathartica" 3·25 8·25
231 27f. "Barringtonia asiatica" 3·25 9·75
232 39f. Bouquet in vase 7·25 16·00

25 Rhinoceros Beetle

1974. Insects Multicoloured.
233 15f. Type **25** 5·00 6·75
234 25f. "Cosmopolites sordidus"
(weevil) 6·00 8·00
235 35f. Tropical fruit-piercer 7·75 8·50
236 45f. "Pantala flavescens" (darter) 11·50 12·50

26 "Flower Hand"
holding Letter

1974. Air. Centenary of Universal Postal Union.
237 **26** 51f. purple, brown &
green 6·00 12·50

27 "Holy Family"
(Kamalielf-Filimoehala)

1974. Air. Christmas.
238 **27** 150f. multicoloured 9·25 25·00

28 Tapa Pattern

1975. Air. Tapa Mats. Each brown, gold and yellow.
239 3f. Type **28** 2·00 5·75
240 24f. "Villagers" 3·00 7·00
241 36f. "Fishes" 4·00 9·00
242 80f. "Fishes and Dancers" 7·75 19·00

29 Boeing 707 in
Flight

1975. Air. First Regular Air Service to New Caledonia.
243 **29** 100f. multicoloured 18·00 19·00

30 Volleyball

1975. Air. Fifth South Pacific Games, Guam. Multicoloured.
244 26f. Type **30** 4·75 6·50
245 44f. Football 3·75 7·50
246 56f. Throwing the javelin 4·50 9·75
247 105f. Skin diving 11·50 21·00

1976. Pres. Pompidou Commemoration. As T **131** of St. Pierre et Miquelon.
248 50f. grey and blue 6·50 11·50

31 Lalolalo Lake, Wallis

1976. Landscapes. Multicoloured.
249 10f. Type **31** (postage) 4·25 5·25
250 29f. Vasavasa, Futuna (air) 5·25 7·00
251 41f. Sigave Bay, Futuna 6·50 8·25
252 68f. Gahi Bay, Wallis 9·50 11·50

32 Concorde

1976. Air. First Commercial Flight of Concorde.
253 **32** 250f. multicoloured 48·00 50·00

33 Washington and Battle of
Yorktown

1976. Bicentenary of American Revolution.
254 **33** 19f. green, blue and red 3·25 4·50
255 - 47f. purple, red and blue 6·50 14·50
DESIGN: 47f. Lafayette and Battle of Virginia Capes.

34 Throwing the Hammer

1976. Air. Olympic Games, Montreal.
256 **34** 31f. purple, blue and red 4·00 8·25
257 - 39f. mauve, red and
purple 5·50 9·75
DESIGN: 39f. High-diving.

35 Admiral Cone

1976. Sea Shells. Multicoloured.
258 20f. Type **35** 5·25 7·50
259 23f. Banded cowrie 5·25 6·50
260 43f. Tapestry turban 9·00 11·50
261 61f. Papal mitre 14·00 19·00

36 Father Chanel and Sanctuary
Church, Poi

1977. Father Chanel Memorial. Multicoloured.
262 22f. Type **36** 3·25 6·50
263 32f. Father Chanel and map 5·00 7·00

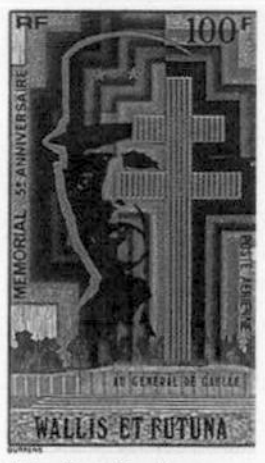

36a De Gaulle Memorial

1977. Fifth Anniv of General de Gaulle Memorial.

264	**36a**	100f. multicoloured	9·25	21·00

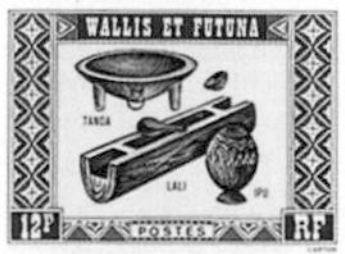

37 Tanoa (bowl), Lali (mortar trough) and Ipu (coconut shell)

1977. Handicrafts. Multicoloured.

265	12f. Type **37**	4·75	5·50
266	25f. Wallis and Futuna kumetes (bowls) and tuluma (box)	4·50	6·00
267	33f. Milamila (comb), ike (club) and tutua (model outrigger)	6·00	6·50
268	45f. Kolo (Futuna clubs)	5·50	7·50
269	69f. Kailao (Wallis and Futuna lances)	8·50	9·75

1977. Air. First Commercial Flight of Concorde, Paris–New York. Optd **PARIS NEW-YORK 22.11.77 Ier VOL COMMERCIAL**.

270	**32**	250f. multicoloured	28·00	46·00

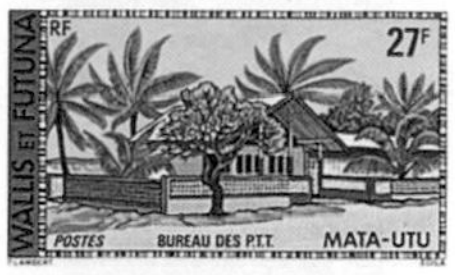

39 Post Office, Mata-Utu

1977. Building and Monuments. Multicoloured.

271	27f. Type **39**	3·00	6·50
272	50f. Sia Hospital, Mata Utu	3·25	7·50
273	57f. Government Buildings, [illegible]	[illegible]	[illegible]
274	83f. St Joseph's Church, Sigave	4·75	9·75
275	120f. Royal Palace, Mata-Utu	5·75	14·00

1977. Bicentenary of Captain Cook's Discovery of Hawaii. Nos. 254/5 optd **JAMES COOK Bicentenaire de la decouverte des Iles Hawaii 1778–1978.**

276	**33**	19f. green, blue and red	2·30	8·50
277	-	47f. purple, red and blue	4·50	12·50

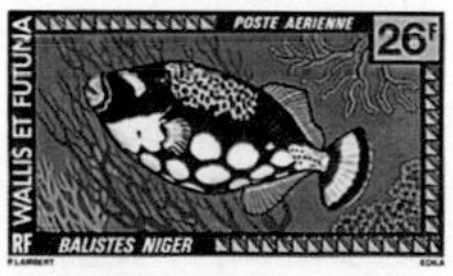

41 Clown Triggerfish

1977. Air. Fish. Multicoloured.

278	26f. Type **41**	3·75	5·25
279	35f. Barrier Reef anemonefish	4·25	9·00
280	49f. Emperor angelfish	5·25	9·00
281	51f. Moorish idol	7·50	9·75

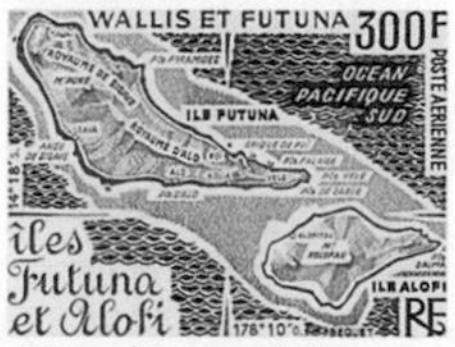

42 Map of Futuna and Alofi

1978. Maps of Wallis and Futuna Islands.

282	**42**	300f. turquoise, blue and ultramarine	22·00	44·00
283	-	500f. brown, blue and ultramarine	29·00	55·00

DESIGN—VERT: 500f. Map of Wallis Island.

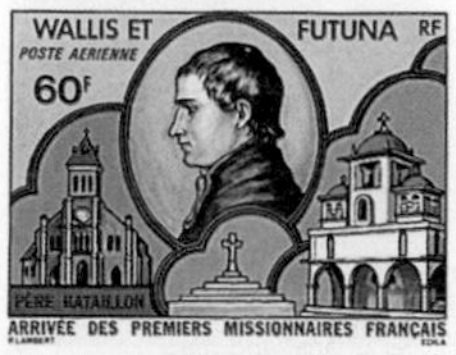

43 Father Bataillon and Churches

1978. Air. Arrival of First French Missionaries. Multicoloured.

284	60f. Type **43**	5·50	8·25
285	72f. Monsgr. Pompallier and map	5·00	9·75

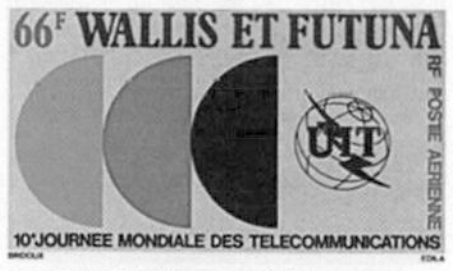

44 I.T.U. Emblem and Antennae

1978. Air. World Telecommunications Day.

286	**44**	66f. multicoloured	3·25	8·50

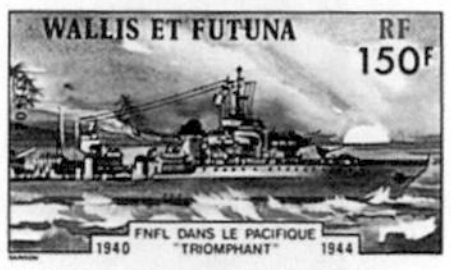

45 "Triomphant" (destroyer)

1978. Free French Pacific Naval Force, 1940–44. Multicoloured.

287	150f. Type **45**	10·50	23·00
288	200f. "Cap des Palmes" and "Chevreuil" (patrol boats)	11·00	30·00
289	280f. "Savorgnan de Brazza" (destroyer)	13·00	46·00

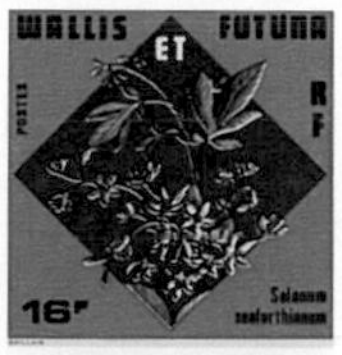

46 "Solanum seaforthianum"

1978. Tropical Flowers. Multicoloured.

290	16f. Type **46**	3·25	5·50
291	24f. "Cassia alata"	3·25	5·75
292	29f. "Gloriosa superba"	4·00	6·25
293	36f. "Hymenocallis littoralis"	4·75	7·00

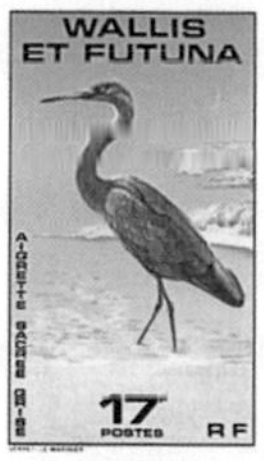

47 Reef Heron

1978. Ocean Birds. Multicoloured.

294	17f. Type **47**	4·50	5·75
295	18f. Red-footed booby	4·50	5·75
296	28f. Brown booby	5·50	6·50
297	35f. White tern	6·75	7·50

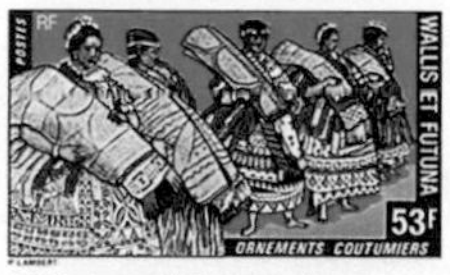

48 Costumed Carpet-sellers

1978. Costumes and Traditions. Multicoloured.

298	53f. Type **48**	4·00	7·25
299	55f. "Festival of God" procession	4·00	8·25
300	59f. Guards of honour	4·50	8·25

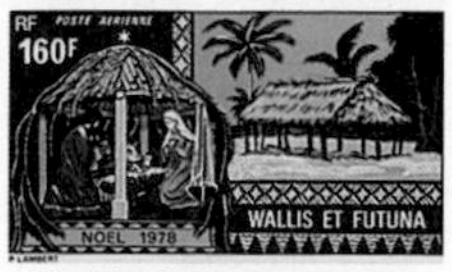

49 Nativity Scene

1978. Air. Christmas.

301	**49**	160f. multicoloured	7·25	16·00

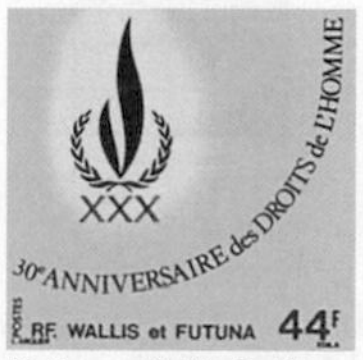

50 Human Rights Emblem

1978. 30th Anniv of Declaration of Human Rights.

302	**50**	44f. multicoloured	2·30	7·00
303	**50**	56f. multicoloured	2·75	8·25

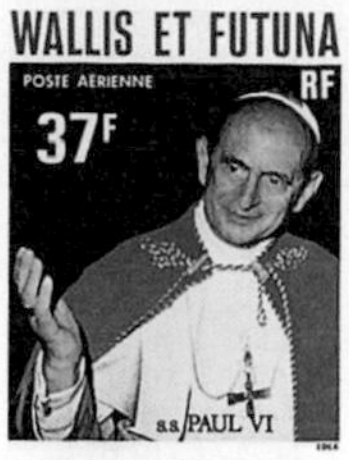

51 Pope Paul VI

1979. Air. Popes. Multicoloured.

304	37f. Type **51**	2·50	7·00
305	41f. Pope John-Paul I	3·00	7·75
306	105f. St. Peter's, Rome, and Popes Paul VI and John-Paul I (horiz)	4·75	11·50

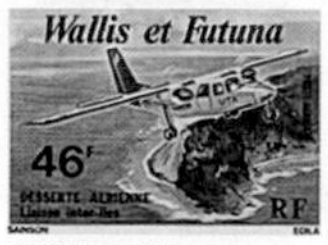

52 Britten Norman Islander

1979. Air. Inter-Island Communications (1st series). Multicoloured.

307	46f. Type **52**	2·00	6·75
308	68f. Freighter "Moana II"	1·30	8·00
309	80f. Hihifo Airport	2·75	8·50

See also Nos. 349/51.

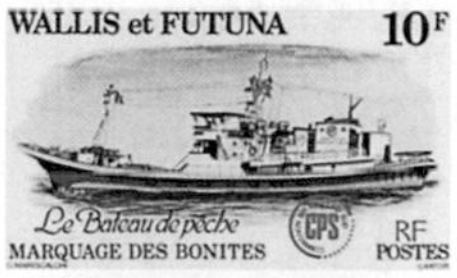

53 Fishing Boat

1979. Tagging Skipjack Tuna. Multicoloured.

310	10f. Type **53**	2·75	5·50
311	30f. Weighing skipjack tuna	3·75	6·00
312	34f. Young skipjack tuna	3·75	6·50
313	38f. Tagging skipjack tuna	2·50	6·50
314	40f. Angling for skipjack tuna	2·50	7·25
315	48f. Skipjack tuna	3·50	8·50
MS316	174×100 mm. Nos. 310/5 plus 3 labels	24·00	28·00

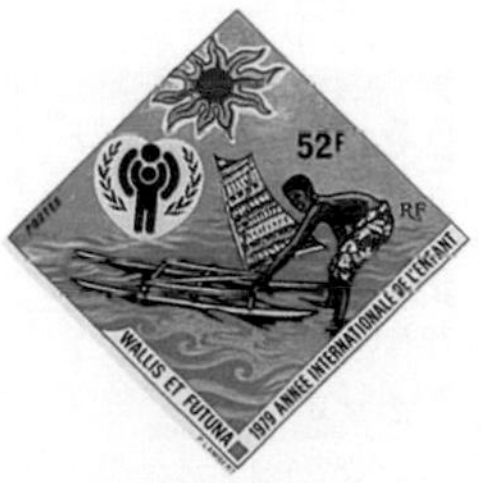

54 Boy with Model Outrigger Canoe

1979. International Year of the Child. Multicoloured.

317	52f. Type **54**	2·75	6·75
318	58f. Girl on horseback	3·00	7·00

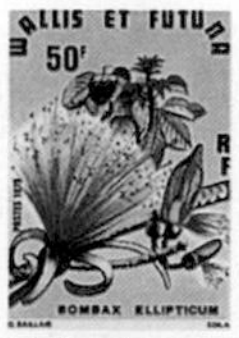

55 "Bombax ellipticum"

1979. Flowering and Fruiting Trees. Multicoloured.

319	50f. Type **55**	2·30	6·75
320	64f. "Callophyllum inophyllum"	2·75	7·25
321	76f. "Pandanus odoratissimus"	3·25	9·00

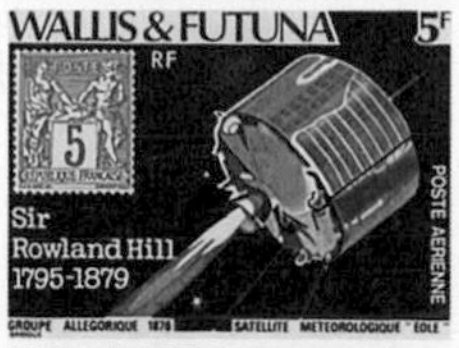

56 French 1876 5c. Stamp and "Eole" Meteorological Satellite

1979. Air. Death Centenary of Sir Rowland Hill.

322	**56**	5f. multicoloured	35	5·50
323	-	70f. multicoloured	2·30	7·25
324	-	90f. black and red	2·50	8·25
325	-	100f. brown, yellow & blue	2·75	9·75

DESIGNS—VERT: 70f. Hibiscus and Wallis and Futuna 1920 1f. stamp. HORIZ: 90f. Sir Rowland Hill and Great Britain Penny Black; 100f. "Birds" (Kano School) and Japan 1872 ½s. stamp.

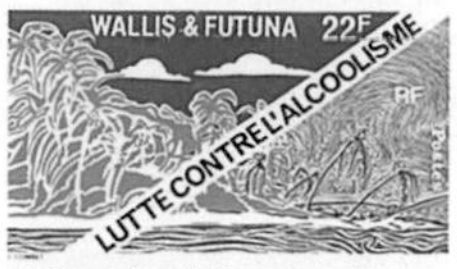

57 Normal and Distorted Landscapes

1979. Anti-alcoholism Campaign.

326	**57**	22f. multicoloured	2·75	6·75

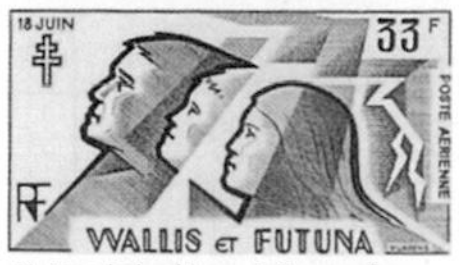

58 Heads looking at Cross of Lorraine

1979. Air. 39th Anniv of 18 June Appeal by General de Gaulle.

327	**58**	33f. red, blue and grey	3·50	7·00

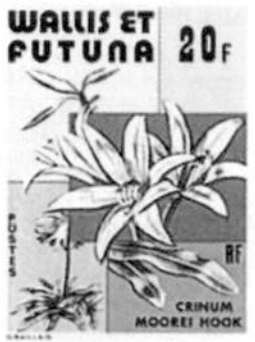

59 "Crinum moorei"

1979. Flowers (1st series). Multicoloured.

328	20f. Type **59**	2·75	5·50
329	42f. Passion flower	4·00	6·75
330	62f. "Canna indica"	4·25	8·00

See also Nos. 392/4.

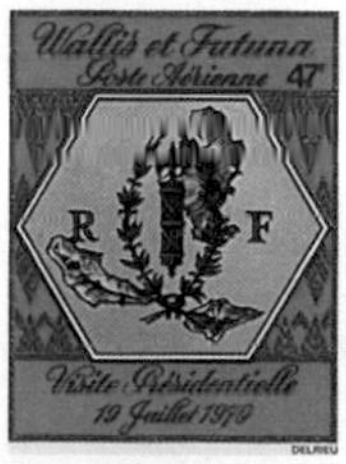

60 Map of Islands and French Arms

1979. Air. Presidential Visit.

331	**60**	47f. multicoloured	3·00	7·25

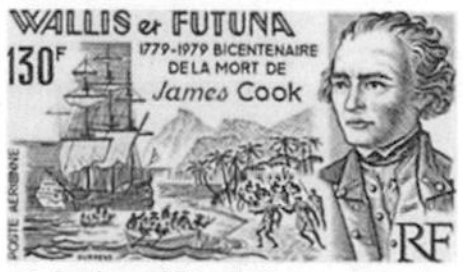

61 Cook and Death Scene, Hawaii

1979. Air. Death Bicentenary of Captain Cook.

332	**61**	130f. grey, blue and brown	11·00	12·50

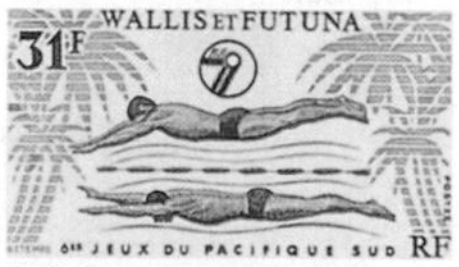

62 Swimmers

1979. Sixth South Pacific Games, Fiji.

333	**62**	31f. olive, red and green	4·50	6·50
334	-	39f. brown, turquoise & green	6·25	7·00

DESIGN: 39f. High-jumper.

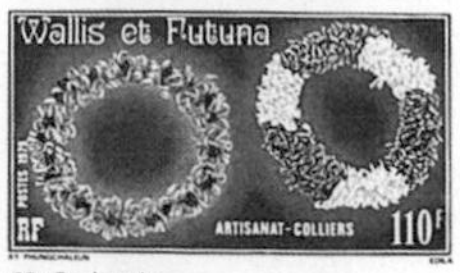

63 Garlands

1979. Necklaces. Multicoloured.

335	110f. Type **63**	2·50	9·75
336	140f. Coral necklaces	3·50	11·50

64 Satellite and Dish Aerial

1979. Air. Third World Telecommunications Exhibition, Geneva.
337   **64**   120f. multicoloured   4·75   11·50

65 Detail of Painting by Mme. Sutita

1979. Works of Local Artists. Multicoloured.
338   27f. Painting by Mme Sutita
        (detail) (different)   1·60   6·75
339   65f. Painting by M. A. Pilioko
        (detail) (vert)   2·20   8·00
340   **65**   78f. Type **65**   2·75   9·00

66 Squilla

1979. South Pacific Fauna. Multicoloured.
341   **66**   15f. Type **66**   2·50   5·50
342   25f. Spanish dancer   2·50   5·75
343   25f. Cat's-tongue thorny oyster   3·00   6·25
344   43f. Sea fan   3·25   6·25
345   45f. Starfish   3·25   6·50
346   63f. Fluted giant clam   4·00   9·00

67 "Virgin of the Crescent Moon" (detail, Durer)

1979. Air. Christmas.
347   **67**   180f. black and red   8·75   18·00
    See also No. 554.

68 Concorde, Map and Rotary Emblem

1980. Air. 75th Anniv of Rotary International.
348   **68**   86f. multicoloured   5·75   11·50

1980. Inter-Island Communications (2nd series). As Nos. 307/9.
349   1f. Type **52**   65   4·00
350   3f. As No. 308   45   4·00
351   5f. As No. 309   75   4·00

69 Radio Station

1980. First Anniv of Radio Station FR3.
352   **69**   47f. multicoloured   3·00   6·00

70 "Jesus laid in the Tomb" (Maurice Denis)

1980. Easter.
353   **70**   25f. multicoloured   1·90   5·00

71 Rochambeau and Soldiers

1980. Air. Bicentenary of Rochambeau's Landing at Newport, Rhode Island.
354   **71**   102f. sepia, blue and
        brown   5·50   13·00

72 Flags and Island

1980. Air. National Day.
355   **72**   71f. multicoloured   2·75   6·00

73 Mozambique Emperor

1980. Fish. Multicoloured.
356   **73**   23f. Type **73**   2·30   4·50
357   27f. Crimson jobfish   2·50   4·75
358   32f. Ruby snapper   2·50   5·75
359   51f. Golden hind   3·25   6·75
360   59f. Rusty jobfish   4·50   9·50

74 Mermoz and "Arc en Ciel"

1980. Air. 50th Anniv of 1st South Atlantic Airmail Flight.
361   **74**   122f. blue, deep blue
        & red   10·50   11·50

1980. "Sydpex 80" International Stamp Exhibition, Sydney. No. 315 surch **50F SYDPEX 80 29 Septembre**.
362   50f. on 48f. multicoloured   4·50   6·00

76 Fleming and Penicillin Slide

1980. Air. 25th Death Anniv of Alexander Fleming (discoverer of penicillin).
363   **76**   101f. blue, brown
        and red   5·50   8·25

77 Charles de Gaulle

1980. Air. Tenth Death Anniv of Charles de Gaulle (French statesman).
364   **77**   200f. green and brown   9·25   19·00

78 "The Virgin, Child and St. Catherine" (Lorenzo Lotto)

1980. Air. Christmas.
365   **78**   150f. multicoloured   5·50   11·50

79 Alan Shepard and "Freedom 7"

1981. Air. 20th Anniv of First Men in Space. Multicoloured.
366   **79**   37f. Type **79**   1·50   5·00
367   44f. Yuri Gagarin and "Vostok 1"   2·75   5·75

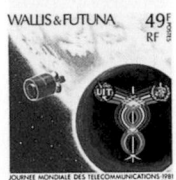

80 Ribbons and I.T.U. and W.H.O. Emblems forming Caduceus and Satellite

1981. World Telecommunications Day.
368   **80**   49f. multicoloured   2·30   5·75

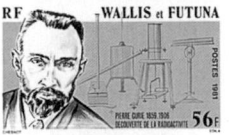

81 Curie and Laboratory Equipment

1981. 75th Death Anniv of Pierre Curie (physicist and discoverer of radium).
369   **81**   56f. multicoloured   3·50   6·00

82 Coral

1981. Undersea Fauna. Multicoloured.
370   **82**   28f. Type **82**   90   5·00
371   30f. Blue-green algae   90   5·00
372   31f. "Ceratium vultur" (dino-
        flagellate)   90   5·00
373   35f. Tomato anemonefish   1·40   5·25
374   40f. Textile cone   1·70   5·75
375   55f. Feather-star (echinoderm)   1·80   6·00

83 Doctor inoculating Child

1981. 60th Anniv of 1st B.C.G. Anti-tuberculosis Inoculation.
376   **83**   27f. multicoloured   1·80   4·75

84 Section of Globe

1981. International Year of Disabled Persons.
377   **84**   42f. multicoloured   2·50   5·25

85 Edison and Phonograph

1981. 50th Death Anniv of Thomas Edison (inventor).
378   **85**   59f. black, blue and red   3·00   6·00

1981. No. 341 surch **5F**.
379   5f. on 15f. multicoloured   1·80   4·00

87 Battle Scene

1981. Bicentenary of Battle of Virginia Capes.
380   –   66f. purple, blue and
        slate   3·00   5·50
381   **87**   74f. green, violet and
        light green   3·50   6·00
DESIGN: 66f. Admiral Francois de Grasse and battle scene.

88 "Vase of Flowers" (Cezanne)

1981. Air. 75th Death Anniv of Paul Cezanne and Birth Centenary of Pablo Picasso (artists).
382   **88**   53f. Type **88**   1·80   6·00
383   135f. "Harlequin leaning"
        (Picasso)   4·25   10·50

89 Football

1981. Air. World Cup Football Championship, Spain (1982).
384   **89**   120f. brown, black &
        green   4·50   9·50
385   **89**   120f. brown, mauve and
        green   4·50   9·50

90 Patrol Boat "La Dieppoise"

1981. Surveillance of 200-mile Zone. Multicoloured.
386   **90**   60f. Type **90**   1·70   6·00
387   85f. Frigate "Protet"   2·50   7·50

91 Crib

1981. Air. Christmas.
388   **91**   180f. multicoloured   7·00   9·25

92 "Pilioko Aloi" (tapestry)

1982. Air.
389	**92**	100f. multicoloured	3·75	8·25

93 Dr. R. Koch
at Microscope

1982. Centenary of Discovery of Tubercle Bacillus.
390	**93**	45f. multicoloured	3·25	5·75

94 "Fishing Boats at
Collioure"

1982. Air. Death Cent of Georges Braque (painter).
391	**94**	300f. multicoloured	12·00	20·00

1982. Flowers (2nd series). Multicoloured.
392		1f. As Type **59**	1·40	3·50
393		2f. As No. 329	1·60	3·75
394		3f. As No. 330	1·80	4·00

95 1930 Stamp

1982. "Philexfrance" International Stamp Exhibition, Paris.
395	**95**	140f. violet, blue and red	4·75	8·25

96 "Acanthe phippium"

1982. Orchids. Multicoloured.
396		34f. Type **96**	1·00	4·25
397		68f. "Acanthe phippium" (different)	2·00	5·75
398		70f. "Spathoglottis pacifica"	2·30	5·75
399		83f. "Mussaenda raiateensis"	2·75	7·25

97 Lord Baden-Powell

1982. 125th Birth Anniv of Lord Baden-Powell (founder of Boy Scout Movement).
400	**97**	80f. multicoloured	4·00	6·75

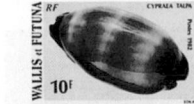

98 Mole Cowrie

1982. Sea Shells (1st series). Multicoloured.
401		10f. Type **98**	1·20	4·00
402		15f. Pacific deer cowrie	1·40	4·00
403		25f. Eyed cowrie	1·60	4·25
404		27f. Closely-related carnelian cowrie	1·70	4·50
405		40f. All-red map cowrie	1·80	4·75

406		50f. Tiger cowrie	2·30	5·50

See also Nos. 428/33, 440/5, 459/64, 481/6 and 510/15.

99 Santos-Dumont, Airship "Ballon No. 14" and Biplane "14 bis"

1982. Air. 50th Death Anniv of Alberto Santos-Dumont (aviation pioneer).
407	**99**	95f. brown, green and blue	5·50	7·00

1982. Air. World Cup Football Championship Result. No. 384 optd **ITALIE VAINQUEUR 1982**.
408	**89**	120f. brown, black and green	5·50	9·50

101 Beach

1982. Air. Overseas Week.
409	**101**	105f. multicoloured	3·75	8·25

102 Coral

1982. Marine Life. Multicoloured.
410		32f. Type **102**	2·50	4·50
411		35f. Starfish	2·75	4·50
412		46f. Spanish dancer	3·00	5·00
413		63f. Cat's-tongue thorny oyster	3·75	6·00

103 Hands
reaching towards
Eye

1982. Air. Blind Day.
414	**103**	130f. blue, scarlet and red	5·50	9·50

104 St. Theresa of Avila

1982. 400th Death Anniv of St. Theresa of Avila.
415	**104**	31f. brown, green and deep brown	2·50	4·75

See also No. 447.

105 "Adoration of the Virgin" (Correggio)

1982. Air. Christmas.
416	**105**	170f. multicoloured	5·50	11·50

106 Wallis Meeting House

1983.
417	**106**	19f. multicoloured	1·00	4·25

107 Eiffel and Eiffel Tower under Construction

1983. 60th Death Anniv of Gustave Eiffel (engineer).
418	**107**	97f. purple, red and green	4·75	7·75

108 Windsurfing

1983. Air.
419	**108**	270f. multicoloured	13·00	14·50

109 Island Scene and U.P.U. Emblem

1983. Air. World U.P.U. Day.
420	**109**	100f. multicoloured	4·50	7·00

110 Vincenzo Lunardi's Balloon, 1784

1983. Air. Bicentenary of Manned Flight.
421	**110**	205f. multicoloured	12·00	13·00

111 "Cat"

1983. Air. 15th Death Anniv of Foujita (painter).
422	**111**	102f. multicoloured	6·75	7·00

112 Thai Goddess

1983. "Bangkok 1983" International Stamp Exn.
423	**112**	92f. red, black and blue	3·75	6·00

113 Javelin-thrower

1983. Air. Olympic Games, Los Angeles (1984) (1st issue).
424	**113**	250f. brown, green & yellow	10·00	10·00

See also No. 438.

114 Nobel

1983. Air. 150th Birth Anniv of Alfred Nobel (inventor of dynamite and founder of Nobel Prizes).
425	**114**	150f. red and green	6·00	9·50

115 Satellite,
Dish Aerial and
W.C.Y. Emblem

1983. World Communications Year.
426	**115**	20f. multicoloured	1·00	4·25

116 Niepce and Early Photograph

1983. Air. Death Centenary of Nicephore Niepce (pioneer of photography).
427	**116**	75f. purple and green	4·00	6·00

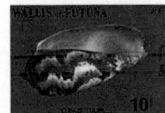

117 Tulip Cone

1983. Sea Shells (2nd series). Multicoloured.
428		10f. Type **117**	60	3·50
429		17f. Captain cone	65	3·50
430		21f. Virgin cone	70	3·50
431		39f. Calf cone	1·00	3·50
432		52f. Marble cone	1·20	4·75
433		65f. Leopard cone	1·80	5·00

118 "Triumph of Galatea"

1983. Air. 500th Birth Anniv of Raphael (artist).
434	**118**	167f. multicoloured	5·75	11·50

119 Pandanus Tree

1983. Air.
435	**119**	137f. multicoloured	5·50	8·25

120 "Madonna and Pope
Sixtus" (Raphael)

1983. Air. Christmas.
436   **120**   200f. multicoloured   6·50   13·00

121 Frigate "Commandant Bory"

1984. Air.
437   **121**   67f. multicoloured   3·00   6·00

122 Weightlifting

1984. Air. Olympic Games, Los Angeles (2nd issue).
438   **122**   85f. multicoloured   3·25   7·00

123 Frangipani

1984. Air.
439   **123**   130f. multicoloured   4·50   6·50

1984. Sea Shells (3rd series). As T **117**. Multicoloured.
440   **117**   22f. Silver conch   70   3·75
441   **117**   25f. Chiragra spider conch   70   3·75
442   **117**   35f. Samar conch   90   4·00
443   **117**   43f. Scorpion conch   1·10   4·25
444   **117**   49f. Diana conch   1·30   4·75
445   **117**   76f. Orange spider conch   1·80   6·25

124 "Deposition of
Christ" (Alele Chapel)

1984. Air. Easter.
446   **124**   190f. multicoloured   6·50   8·25

1984. "Espana 84" International Stamp Exhibition, Madrid.
As T **104** but with "Espana 84" emblem.
447   **104**   70f. sepia, green and brown   2·75   6·00

125 Diderot and
Title Page of
Encyclopedia

1984. Death Bicentenary of Denis Diderot (encyclopedist).
448   **125**   100f. brown and blue   3·75   7·00

126 Killer Whale

1984. Nature Protection.
449   **126**   90f. multicoloured   4·50   7·00

127 Painting

1984. Air. 95th Birth Anniv of Jean Cocteau (artist).
450   **127**   150f. multicoloured   3·75   10·50

128 Tiki

1984. Air. Soane Hoatau Sculpture.
451   **128**   175f. multicoloured   5·00   11·50

129 "Alice"

1984. Air. Birth Centenary of Amedeo Modigliani
(painter).
452   **129**   140f. multicoloured   3·00   3·75

130 "Pilioko Aloi"
(tapestry)

1984. Air. "Ausipex 84" International Stamp Exhibition,
Melbourne.
453   **130**   180f. multicoloured   6·50   7·25

131 "Local Dances" (Jean Michon)

1984. Air.
454   **131**   110f. multicoloured   4·50   8·25

132 Altar, Mount Lulu
Chapel

1984. Air.
455   **132**   52f. multicoloured   1·80   3·00

133 Islanders wearing Leis

1985. Fourth Pacific Arts Festival.
456   **133**   160f. multicoloured   4·50   10·50

134 Common Spider Conch and
Virgin and Child

1984. Air. Christmas.
457   **134**   260f. multicoloured   9·25   13·00

135 Lapita Pottery

1985. Archaeological Expedition, 1983.
458   **135**   53f. multicoloured   2·20   4·75

1985. Sea Shells (4th series). As T **117**. Multicoloured.
459   **117**   2f. Chambered nautilus   35   4·00
460   **117**   3f. Adusta murex   65   4·00
461   **117**   41f. Vibex bonnet   1·40   4·50
462   **117**   47f. Flag cone   1·70   5·00
463   **117**   56f. True harp   2·00   5·25
464   **117**   71f. Ramose murex   2·30   6·00

136 Victor Hugo

1985. Death Centenary of Victor Hugo (writer).
465   **136**   89f. deep blue, blue
and red   4·00   6·75

137 "Pilioko Aloi" (tapestry)

1985. Air.
466   **137**   500f. multicoloured   10·00   10·50

138 Flying Fox

1985
467   **138**   38f. multicoloured   2·30   4·75

139 Children

1985. International Youth Year.
468   **139**   64f. multicoloured   2·20   5·50

140 "The Post Office"

1985. Air. 30th Death Anniv of Maurice Utrillo (artist).
469   **140**   200f. multicoloured   5·50   7·25

141 Hands and U.N. Emblem

1985. 40th Anniv of U.N.O.
470   **141**   49f. green, blue and red   2·20   5·00

142 Sailing Canoe

1985. Air.
471   **142**   350f. multicoloured   9·25   15·00

143 Ronsard, Organist and Muse
of Poetry

1985. 400th Death Anniv of Pierre de Ronsard (poet).
472   **143**   170f. brown, deep brown
and blue   6·00   10·50

144 Landing Ship
"Jacques Cartier"

1985. Air.
473   **144**   51f. deep blue, blue and
turquoise   1·40   4·00

145 "Portrait of Young
Woman" (Patrice Nielly)

1985. Air.
474   **145**   245f. multicoloured   7·00   8·00

146 Schweitzer, African Boy and
Cathedral Organ

1985. 20th Death Anniv of Dr. Albert Schweitzer
(missionary).
475   **146**   50f. black, purple &
brown   2·20   5·00

147 "Virgin and Child"
(Jean Michon)

1985. Air. Christmas.
476 **147** 330f. multicoloured 9·25 19·00

148 Bread-fruit

1986. Food and Agriculture Organization.
477 **148** 39f. multicoloured 1·80 4·75

149 Flamboyant Flower

1986
478 **149** 38f. multicoloured 1·60 4·75

150 Comet and "Giotto" Space
Probe

1986. Air. Appearance of Halley's Comet.
479 **150** 100f. multicoloured 2·75 3·25

151 Vianney
praying

1986. Air. Birth Bicentenary of Cure d'Ars.
480 **151** 200f. light brown, brown
and black 5·50 4·75

1986. Sea Shells (5th series). As T **117**. Multicoloured.
481 4f. Giant spider conch 40 4·00
482 5f. Trumpet triton 35 4·00
483 10f. Red-mouth olive 50 4·00
484 18f. Common distorsio 1·50 4·25
485 25f. Episcopal mitre 1·60 4·25
486 107f. Distant cone 2·30 7·00

152 Players and Boy with Football

1986. World Cup Football Championship, Mexico.
487 **152** 95f. multicoloured 2·75 6·75

153 Willem Schouten and
"Eendracht"

1986. 370th Anniv of Discovery of Horn Islands. Each
purple, green and blue.
488 8f. Type **153** 2·40 3·25
489 9f. Jacob le Maire and "Hoorn" 2·40 3·25
490 155f. Map of Futuna and Alofi
Islands 8·25 8·25

154 Watt and Steam Engine

1986. 250th Birth Anniv of James Watt (inventor).
491 **154** 74f. red and black 3·25 6·00

155 Queen Amelia

1986. Air. Centenary of Request for Protectorate and
25th Anniv of French Overseas Territory Status. Each
purple, red and blue.
492 90f. Type **155** 4·25 7·50
493 137f. Law of 1961 bestowing
Overseas Territory status 4·50 10·50

156 Patrol Boat "La Lorientaise"

1986. Naval Ships.
494 **156** 6f. red, purple and blue 1·40 4·00
495 – 7f. violet, orange and red 1·40 4·00
496 – 120f. turquoise, red
& blue 4·25 7·75
DESIGNS: 7f. Frigate "Commandant Blaison"; 120f. Frigate
"Balny".

157 Oleander

1986
497 **157** 97f. multicoloured 3·00 7·00

158 U.P.U. Emblem and Dove
carrying Envelope

1986. Air. World Post Day.
498 **158** 270f. multicoloured 7·25 17·00

159 New York,
Statue and Paris

1986. Air. Centenary of Statue of Liberty.
499 **159** 205f. multicoloured 4·50 11·50

160 "Virgin and Child"
(Botticelli)

1986. Christmas.
500 **160** 250f. multicoloured 6·00 14·00

161 "Papilio
montrouzieri"

1987. Butterflies. Multicoloured.
501 2f. Type **161** 1·50 4·00
502 42f. Caper white 1·70 4·50
503 46f. "Delias ellipsis" 1·80 4·75
504 50f. "Danaus pumila" 2·50 5·00
505 52f. "Lutbrodes cleotas" 2·50 5·00
506 59f. Meadow argus 3·00 5·75

162 Father Chanel
and Basilica

1987. Air. First Anniv of Poi Basilica.
507 **162** 230f. multicoloured 5·50 11·50

163 "Telstar", Globe and
Pleumeur-Bodou

1987. Air. World Communications Day. 25th Anniv of
Launch of "Telstar" Communications Satellite.
508 **163** 200f. blue, black and red 6·00 9·50

164 Wrestlers

1987. World Wrestling Championships, Clermont-Ferrand.
509 **164** 97f. multicoloured 3·75 6·75

1987. Sea Shells (6th series). As T **117**. Multicoloured.
510 3f. Common hairy triton 30 4·00
511 4f. Textile cone 35 4·00
512 28f. Humpback cowrie 90 4·25
513 44f. Giant frog shell 1·20 4·75
514 48f. Turtle cowrie 1·40 5·00
515 78f. Bull-mouth helmet 1·80 6·00

165 Piccard,
Stratosphere
Balloon "F.N.R.S."
and Bathyscaphe

1987. Air. 25th Death Anniv of Auguste Piccard
(physicist).
516 **165** 135f. deep blue, blue
and green 5·50 7·75

1987. "Olymphilex 87" Olympic Stamps Exhibition, Rome.
No 509 optd **OLYMPHILEX '87 ROME** and Olympic
rings.
517 **164** 97f. multicoloured 3·75 6·75

167 Bust of Girl

1987. 70th Death Anniv of Auguste Rodin (sculptor).
518 **167** 150f. purple 3·75 8·25
See also No. 557.

168 Letters between Globes and
Postbird

1987. World Post Day.
519 **168** 116f. blue, deep blue
and yellow 4·25 7·00

169 Pacific Black
Duck

1987. Birds. Multicoloured.
520 6f. Type **169** 65 4·00
521 19f. Pacific golden plover 75 4·25
522 47f. Friendly quail dove 1·70 4·75
523 56f. Ruddy turnstone 2·10 5·00
524 64f. Buff-banded rail 2·50 5·25
525 68f. Bar-tailed godwit 2·75 5·75

170 Mgr. Bataillon, French Frigate
and Islands

1987. Air. 150th Anniv of Arrival of First Missionaries.
526 **170** 260f. turquoise, blue and
brown 8·25 14·00

171 Nativity Scene

1987. Air. Christmas.
527 **171** 300f. multicoloured 5·50 17·00

172 Carco and Parisian Scenes

1988. 30th Death Anniv of Francis Carco (writer).
528 **172** 40f. multicoloured 2·00 4·50

173 Morane Saulnier Type I and
Garros

1988. Air. 70th Death Anniv of Roland Garros (aviator).
529 **173** 600f. deep blue, brown
and blue 18·00 32·00

174 La Perouse, "L'Astrolabe" and "La Boussole"

1988. Bicentenary of Disappearance of La Perouse's Expedition.
530   174   70f. green, blue and brown   5·50   5·75

175 "Self-portrait wearing Lace Jabot"

1988. Air. Death Bicentenary of Maurice Quentin de la Tour (painter).
531   175   500f. multicoloured   9·25   28·00

176 Arrows and Dish Aerial

1988. Air. World Telecommunications Day.
532   176   100f. multicoloured   1·70   6·75

177 Map and Bishop with Crosier

1988. Air. South Pacific Episcopal Conference.
533   177   90f. multicoloured   1·60   6·00

178 Nurse, Child and Anniversary Emblem

1988. 125th Anniv of International Red Cross.
534   178   30f. black, green and red   1·10   4·50

179 Throwing the Javelin

1988. Olympic Games, Seoul. Each brown, red and blue.
535   11f. Type **179**   1·10   4·00
536   20f. Volleyball   1·40   4·25
537   60f. Windsurfing   2·50   6·00
538   80f. Sailing   2·75   7·00

180 Envelopes forming Map

1988. World Post Day.
539   180   17f. yellow, blue and black   1·50   4·00

181 Becquerel

1988. Birth Bicent of Antoine Cesar Becquerel (physicist).
540   181   18f. black and blue   1·60   4·00

182 Nativity Scene

1988. Air. Christmas.
541   182   400f. multicoloured   11·00   21·00

183 "Amiral Charner" (frigate)

1989. International Maritime Organization.
542   183   26f. multicoloured   1·80   4·50

184 Renior and Scene from "The Great Illusion"

1989. Tenth Death Anniv of Jean Renoir (film director).
543   184   24f. brown, mauve & orange   1·80   4·25

185 Royal Throne (Aselo Kulimoetoke)

1989. Air.
544   185   700f. multicoloured   12·00   34·00

186 Map

1989. Futuna Hydro-electric Power Station.
545   186   25f. multicoloured   1·60   4·75

188 Satellite above Earth

1989. International Telecommunications Day.
546   188   21f. multicoloured   90   4·75

189 Mural (H. Tailhade)

1989
547   189   22f. multicoloured   1·80   4·75

190 Globe and Emblem

1989. "Philexfrance '89" International Stamp Exhibition, Paris (548) and Bicentenary of Declaration of Rights of Man and South Pacific Youth Meeting (549). Multicoloured.
548   29f. Type **190** (postage)   2·00   4·75
549   900f. Sportsmen (air)   17·00   27·00
MS550 200×90 mm. Nos. 548/9 (sold at 1000f.)   23·00   65·00

191 Cyclists

1989. World Cycling Championships, France.
551   191   10f. black, brown & green   1·60   4·00

192 Envelopes around Globe of Flags

1989. World Post Day.
552   192   27f. multicoloured   2·00   4·25

193 Landscape

1989
553   193   23f. multicoloured   2·75   5·00

1989. Air. Christmas. As No. 347 but date, value and colour changed.
554   67   800f. mauve   22·00   40·00

194 "Star of Bethlehem"

1990
555   194   44f. multicoloured   1·80   4·75

195 Tortoise Fossil

1990
556   195   48f. multicoloured   2·00   4·75

1990. 150th Birth Anniv of Auguste Rodin (sculptor). As No. 518 but value and colour changed.
557   167   200f. blue   5·00   10·50

197 Footballers

1990. World Cup Football Championship, Italy.
558   197   59f. multicoloured   2·20   5·50

198 Orchids

1990. Mothers' Day.
559   198   78f. multicoloured   3·25   6·00

199 "Avion III", Airbus Industrie A310 and Clement Ader

1990. Air. Cent of First Heavier-than-Air Flight and 1st Anniv of Wallis–Tahiti Air Link.
560   199   56f. brown, mauve and red   2·00   5·00

200 Red-tailed Tropic Bird

1990. Multicoloured.
561   300f. Type **200**   8·25   14·50
562   600f. South Pacific islet   16·00   32·00

201 "Moana II" (inter-island freighter)

1990. Ships.
563   201   40f. brown, green and blue   3·50   5·00
564   -   50f. brown, blue and green   3·75   5·50
DESIGN: 50f. "Moana III" (container ship) at jetty.

202 Traditional Dwellings

1990
565   202   28f. multicoloured   1·80   4·25

203 Doves and Globe

1990. Stamp Day.
566   203   97f. multicoloured   4·50   7·00

204 Outrigger Canoe

1990
567   204   46f. multicoloured   2·00   5·00

205 De Gaulle

1990. Air. Birth Centenary of Charles de Gaulle (French statesman).
568   205   1000f. multicoloured   27·00   46·00

206 Palm Trees

1990. "Best Wishes".
569   **206**   100f. multicoloured   4·50   7·00

207 Patrol Boat "La Glorieuse"

1991
570   **207**   52f. blue, green and red   6·25   5·50
See also No. 578.

208 Warrior

1991. Tradition. Multicoloured.
571   7f. Breadfruit gatherer   1·50   4·00
572   54f. Taro planter   1·70   4·75
573   62f. Spear fisherman   1·80   5·00
574   72f. Type **208**   2·10   5·00
575   90f. Kailao dancer   2·75   5·50
MS576 185×104 mm. Nos. 571/5 (sold
    at 300f.)   13·00   26·00

209 Aspects of Health
Care

1991. 20th Anniv of Medecins sans Frontieres (medical
    charity).
577   **209**   55f. multicoloured   2·75   5·00

1991. Patrol Boat "La Moqueuse". As T **207**.
578   42f. black, blue and red   5·50   5·00

210 Chanel and Reliquary

1991. Air. 150th Death Anniv of Father Chanel
    (missionary).
579   **210**   235f. multicoloured   7·50   13·00

211 Players through the Ages

1991. Air. Centenary of French Open Tennis
    Championships.
580   **211**   250f. black, orange and
        green   8·00   13·00

212 Map and Microlight

1991. Microlight Aircraft Flying in Wallis and Futuna.
581   **212**   85f. multicoloured   4·75   6·00

213 "Portrait of Jean"

1991. 150th Birth Anniv of Pierre Auguste Renior
    (painter). Perf or imperf (self-adhesive).
582   **213**   400f. multicoloured   12·00   19·00

214 Map

1991. 30th Anniv of French Overseas Territory Status.
584   **214**   102f. multicoloured   3·50   6·00

215 Islanders in Festive Dress and
Angel

1991. Feast of the Assumption.
585   **215**   30f. multicoloured   2·30   4·25

216 Mozart and Scene
from "The Marriage of
Figaro"

1991. Air. Death Bicentenary of Wolfgang Amadeus
    Mozart (composer).
586   **216**   500f. blue, lilac and red   8·25   21·00

217 Imprisoned Figure

1991. 30th Anniv of Amnesty International.
587   **217**   140f. yellow, violet
        & blue   2·75   7·00

218 House and Generator

1991. 50th Anniv of Central Economic Co-operation
    Bank.
588   **218**   10f. multicoloured   2·00   4·00

219 "Allamanda
cathartica"

1991. Flowers. Multicoloured.
589   1f. Type **219**   85   4·00
590   4f. "Hibiscus rosa sinensis" (vert)   1·00   4·00
591   80f. Water lily   3·00   5·75

220 Santa Claus on Beach

1991. Christmas.
592   **220**   60f. multicoloured   2·50   4·75

221 Ski Jumping

1992. Winter Olympic Games, Albertville.
593   **221**   150f. multicoloured   5·50   7·75

222 Map, Plants and Dassault
Breguet Mystere Falcon 20

1992. "Escadrille 9S" Maritime Surveillance Service.
594   **222**   48f. multicoloured   1·60   4·50

223 Canadian 1938 $1 and Wallis and Futuna 1920 2f.
Stamps

1992. "Canada 92" International Youth Philatelic
    Exhibition, Montreal.
595   **223**   35f. black, red and violet   3·75   4·25

224 Throwing the Javelin

1992. Olympic Games, Barcelona.
596   **224**   106f. indigo, blue &
        green   6·50   5·75

225 Spanish 1975 4p. Stamp and Wallis
Post Office

1992. "Granada 92" International Stamp Exhibition.
597   **225**   100f. black, blue &
        purple   4·25   5·50

226 Columbus's Fleet, Pavilion and
Seville

1992. "Expo 92" World's Fair, Seville.
598   **226**   200f. green, blue &
        orange   7·25   10·00

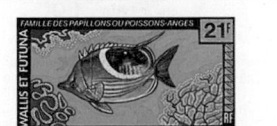

227 Saddle Butterflyfish

1992. Butterfly and Angel Fish. Multicoloured.
599   21f. Type **227**   2·00   4·00
600   22f. Thread-finned butterflyfish   2·00   4·00
601   23f. Masked bannerfish   2·00   4·00
602   24f. Regal angelfish   2·00   4·00
603   25f. Conspicuous angelfish   2·00   4·00
604   26f. Teardrop butterflyfish   2·00   4·00

228 Columbus and Map

1992. Air. "World Columbian Stamp Expo 92", Chicago.
605   **228**   100f. multicoloured   4·75   5·50
See also No. 612.

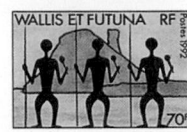

229 Three Spearmen

1992. Wallis Islands. Multicoloured.
606   70f. Type **229**   2·75   4·75
607   70f. Two spearmen and palm
        trees   2·75   4·75
608   70f. Pirogues   2·75   4·75
609   70f. Two fishermen and palm
        trees   2·75   4·75
610   70f. Three fishermen and palm
        trees   2·75   4·75
MS611 210×92 mm. Nos. 606/10 (sold
    at 450f.)   14·50   27·00
    Nos. 606/10 were issued together, se-tenant, forming a
composite design.

1992. Air. "Genova '92" International Thematic Stamp
    Exhibition. As T **228** but with different Exhibition
    emblem.
612   800f. multicoloured   20·00   28·00

230 Victorious Marianne

1992. Air. Bicentenary of Year One of First French
    Republic.
613   **230**   350f. black, blue and red   6·00   13·00

231 "La Garonne" (supply
vessel)

1992
614   **231**   20f. multicoloured   2·10   4·00

232 "L'Idylle
d'Ixelles"

1992. 75th Death Anniv of Auguste Rodin (sculptor).
615   **232**   300f. black and mauve   10·00   11·00

233 "Mirabilis jalapa"

1992
616   **233**   200f. multicoloured   5·00   7·75

234 Dassault Breguet Gardian,
Frigate and Native Canoes

1993. French Naval Forces in the Pacific.
617   **234**   130f. multicoloured   4·25   6·75

235 Abstract (J. E. Korda)

1993. School Art.
618   **235**   56f. multicoloured   3·00   6·00
See also Nos. 635/6.

236 Buff-banded Rail

1993. Birds. Multicoloured.
619   50f. Type **236**   2·00   4·50
620   60f. Purple swamphen   2·30   4·75
621   110f. Grey's fruit dove   3·25   5·50

237 Building Facade

1993. Air. Bicentenary of the Louvre, Paris.
622   **237**   315f. ultramarine, red
            and blue   7·75   11·50

238 Copernicus and Planetary
        Model

1993. Air. "Polska 93" International Stamp Exhibition,
Poznan. 450th Death Anniv of Nicolas Copernicus
(astronomer).
623   **238**   600f. red, brown and
            crimson   17·00   22·00

239 Hibiscus

1993. Mothers' Day. Multicoloured.
624   95f. Type **239**   3·25   5·25
625   120f. Bouquet of stephanotis   3·75   5·75

240 Sail-finned Tang

1993. Fish. Multicoloured.
626   27f. Spotted rabbitfish   1·60   3·50
627   35f. Type **240**   2·00   4·25
628   45f. Palette surgeonfish   2·30   4·50
629   53f. Fox-faced rabbitfish   2·50   4·75

241 D'Entrecasteaux and Flagship

1993. Death Bicentenary of Bruni d'Entrecasteaux
(explorer).
630   **241**   170f. red, blue and black   6·50   7·00

242 Symbols of Taiwan

1993. "Taipei '93" International Stamp Exhibition.
631   **242**   435f. multicoloured   8·25   13·50

243 Tepa Church, Wallis Island

1993. Churches. Multicoloured.
632   30f. Type **243**   1·40   2·00
633   30f. Vilamalia Church, Futuna
            Island   1·40   2·00

244 "La Marseillaise"

1993. Air. Bicentenary of Year Two of First French
Republic.
634   **244**   400f. red, blue and black   7·50   12·50

1993. School Art. As T **235**.
635   28f. blue, black and grey   1·00   2·75
636   52f. multicoloured   1·50   3·00
DESIGNS—HORIZ: 28f. Palm trees (T. Tuhimutu). VERT: 52f.
People (M. Hakula).

245 Nativity

1993. Christmas.
637   **245**   80f. multicoloured   1·80   3·50

246 "Wallis Landscape" (P. Legris)

1994. Air.
638   **246**   400f. multicoloured   12·00   12·50

247 Landscape and Emblem

1994. Air. "Hong Kong '94" International Stamp Exhibition.
639   **247**   700f. multicoloured   21·00   18·00

248 Emblem

1994. Traditional Crafts Show, Wallis and Futuna.
640   **248**   80f. multicoloured   2·50   3·75

249 Manning the Barricades

1994. 50th Anniv of Liberation of Paris.
641   **249**   110f. black, red and blue   3·00   4·00

250 Pacific Islands on Globe

1994. Air. South Pacific Geographical Days.
642   **250**   85f. multicoloured   2·50   4·00

251 Earth Station

1994. Satellite Communications.
643   **251**   10f. multicoloured   1·30   2·75

252 Goalkeeper saving Ball

1994. World Cup Football Championship, U.S.A.
644   **252**   105f. multicoloured   3·75   3·50

253 Uvean
        Princesses, 1903

1994.
645   **253**   90f. black, red and blue   2·50   3·75

254 Seaplane

1994. Microlight Aircraft.
646   **254**   5f. multicoloured   1·00   2·75

255 Four Suits

1994. Bridge.
647   **255**   40f. multicoloured   2·00   3·00

256 Dahlia

1994. Air. First European Stamp Salon, Flower Gardens,
Paris.
648   **256**   300f. multicoloured   12·00   7·75

257 Trees and
        Coconuts

1994. The Coconut.
649   **257**   36f. multicoloured   1·60   3·00

258 Saint-Exupery and Aircraft

1994. Air. 50th Death Anniv of Antoine de Saint-Exupery
(author and pilot).
650   **258**   800f. olive, green and
            blue   27·00   21·00

259 Blue-crowned Lories

1994. Parrots of Futuna.
651   **259**   62f. multicoloured   2·50   3·50

260 Lodge Emblem and Symbols
        of Freemasonry

1994. Centenary of Grand Lodge of France.
652   **260**   250f. brown, turquoise
            and blue   6·00   7·75

261 Polynesian Baby

1994. Air. Christmas.
653   **261**   150f. multicoloured   6·25   4·75

262 Preparing Traditional Meal
        (after P. Legris)

1995.
654   **262**   80f. multicoloured   2·50   3·50

263 Nukulaelae

1995. Aerial Views of Lagoon Islets. Multicoloured.
655   85f. Type **263**   2·30   3·25
656   90f. Nukufetau (vert)   2·30   3·50
657   100f. Nukufotu and Nukuloa   2·50   4·00

264 Pasteur

1995. Air. Death Cent of Louis Pasteur (chemist).
658   **264**   350f. multicoloured   7·25   7·75

265 Outrigger Canoes (emblem of district)

1995. Mua District.
| 659 | **265** | 35f. multicoloured | 1·70 | 3·00 |

266 Emblem

1995. University of the Pacific Teacher Training Institute.
| 660 | **266** | 115f. multicoloured | 2·75 | 4·00 |

267 Coconuts

1995. Air.
| 661 | **267** | 200f. multicoloured | 5·00 | 5·25 |

268 U.N. Helmet and Blitzed and Rebuilt Cities

1995. 50th Anniv of Signing of U.N. Charter.
| 662 | **268** | 55f. multicoloured | 2·00 | 3·00 |

269 Young People

1995. Air. Tenth Anniv of International Youth Year.
| 663 | **269** | 450f. multicoloured | 11·00 | 10·00 |

270 Javelin Thrower

1995. Tenth South Pacific Games, Tahiti.
| 664 | **270** | 70f. multicoloured | 2·30 | 3·50 |

271 City Skyline

1995. Air. "Singapore'95" Int Stamp Exn.
| 665 | **271** | 500f. multicoloured | 14·00 | 12·50 |

272 Lumiere Brothers and Film

1995. Air. Centenary of Motion Pictures.
| 666 | **272** | 600f. multicoloured | 16·00 | 13·00 |

273 Breadfruit

1995. Shrubs. Multicoloured.
667	20f. Type **273**		2·75	3·00
668	60f. Tarot		3·50	3·25
669	65f. Kava		3·75	3·50
See also Nos. 675/6.

274 De Gaulle

1995. Air. 25th Death Anniv of Charles de Gaulle (French statesman).
| 670 | **274** | 315f. black, red and blue | 5·50 | 9·00 |

275 Human Activities

1995. Tapa (bark of paper-mulberry tree) Designs. Multicoloured.
| 671 | 25f. Type **275** | | 90 | 3·00 |
| 672 | 26f. Marine life (horiz) | | 90 | 3·00 |

276 Three Generations

1995. Island Mothers.
| 673 | **276** | 80f. multicoloured | 2·20 | 3·50 |

277 Golf Course

1995. Golfing on Wallis.
| 674 | **277** | 95f. multicoloured | 3·00 | 3·75 |

1996. Tuberous Plants. As T **273**. Multicoloured.
| 675 | 28f. Taro ("Mahoaa") | | 85 | 3·00 |
| 676 | 52f. Yam ("Ufi") | | 1·70 | 3·25 |

278 Pirogue

1996. Air. World Polynesian Pirogue Championships, Noumea.
| 677 | **278** | 240f. multicoloured | 6·00 | 6·75 |

279 Emblems

1996. Air. Sisia College, Futuna.
| 678 | **279** | 235f. multicoloured | 5·50 | 6·75 |

280 "Cananga odorata"

1996. Flowers. Multicoloured.
| 679 | 27f. Type **280** | | 1·50 | 2·75 |
| 680 | 45f. Hibiscus | | 1·80 | 3·00 |

281 Trees reflected in Water

1996. Swamplands.
| 681 | **281** | 53f. multicoloured | 1·80 | 3·25 |

282 Chessmen and Board

1996. Chess in Wallis and Futuna.
| 682 | **282** | 110f. multicoloured | 3·00 | 4·00 |

283 Guglielmo Marconi (inventor) and Radio Equipment

1996. Air. Centenary of Radio-telegraphy.
| 683 | **283** | 550f. brown, blue and orange | 13·00 | 14·50 |

284 Stadium and Sportsmen

1996. Air. Centenary of Modern Olympic Games.
| 684 | **284** | 1000f. blue | 20·00 | 29·00 |

285 Caladium

1996. Flowers. Multicoloured.
| 685 | 30f. Type **285** | | 1·40 | 2·75 |
| 686 | 48f. Caladium (different) | | 1·60 | 3·00 |

286 Woman with Stamps in Hair

1996. Air. 50th Autumn Stamp Fair.
| 687 | **286** | 175f. multicoloured | 3·75 | 5·25 |

287 Map and Perroton

1996. Francoise Perroton (first woman missionary to Wallis) Commemoration.
| 688 | **287** | 50f. multicoloured | 1·80 | 3·25 |

288 Distressed Woman with Children and Drunken Man

1996. Air. Campaign against Alcohol Abuse.
| 689 | **288** | 260f. multicoloured | 6·50 | 6·75 |

289 Children and Emblem

1996. 50th Anniv of UNICEF.
| 690 | **289** | 25f. multicoloured | 1·40 | 3·00 |

290 Emblem

1997. 50th Anniv of South Pacific Commission.
| 691 | **290** | 7f. multicoloured | 30 | 2·75 |

291 King Lavelua of Uvea (Wallis)

1997. Royal Standards.
692	**291**	56f. red, black and blue	1·40	2·75
693	-	60f. multicoloured	1·50	2·75
694	-	70f. multicoloured	1·70	2·75
DESIGNS: 60f. King Tuiagaifo of Alo (Futuna); 70f. King Tuisigave of Sigave (Futuna).

292 Lapita Pot (1000 B.C.)

1997. Air. National Centre for Scientific Research.
| 695 | **292** | 400f. multicoloured | 7·25 | 9·00 |

293 Kava Brewer

1997
| 696 | **293** | 170f. multicoloured | 3·75 | 4·75 |

294 Story-telling

1997. Scenes of Island Life. Multicoloured.
697		10f. Type **294**	30	2·75
698		36f. Hand-weaving mat (vert)	85	3·00
699		40f. Feasting	1·00	3·00

295 Turtle on Beach

1997. The Green Turtle. Multicoloured.
700		62f. Type **295**	1·80	2·75
701		80f. Turtle swimming	2·30	3·25

296 Airplane approaching Airport

1997. Air. Inauguration of Hihifo Airport.
702	**296**	130f. multicoloured	3·25	4·00

297 Treble Clef, Dancers, Theatre Masks and Fireworks over Papal Palace

1997. 50th Anniv of Avignon Festival.
703	**297**	160f. multicoloured	3·00	4·25

298 Medals and Shot Putter

1997. "Handisport" Sporting Event, Berlin.
704	**298**	35f. multicoloured	1·20	3·00

299 Sunset over Lagoon (after Rebecca Hoatau)

1997. Air.
705	**299**	300f. multicoloured	5·50	6·75

300 Club Emblem

1997. Uvea Karate Club, Wallis.
706	**300**	24f. multicoloured	1·30	2·75

301 Stamps on Globe

1997. Air. Fourth Stamp World Cup and 51st Autumn stamp Show. Multicoloured.
707		350f. Type **301**	6·50	7·75

MS708 150×85 mm. 100f. Two views of Earth encircled by stamps. Imperf   20·00   27·00

302 Notre Dame Cathedral, Tanks and Leclerc

1997. Air. 50th Death Anniv of Marshal Leclerc.
709	**302**	800f. multicoloured	11·00	18·00

303 Couple

1997. Anti-AIDS Campaign.
710	**303**	5f. multicoloured	65	2·75

304 Daudet, Windmill, Foxgloves and Goat

1997. Air. Death Centenary of Alphonse Daudet (writer).
711	**304**	710f. multicoloured	12·00	16·00

305 Nativity

1997. Christmas.
712	**305**	85f. multicoloured	2·00	3·50

306 "Preparation of Umu" (Christiane Pierret)

1998
713	**306**	800f. multicoloured	13·00	14·50

307 "Vanda T.M.A."

1998. Orchids. Multicoloured.
714		70f. Type **307**	1·80	3·00
715		85f. "Cattleya Bow Bells" (horiz)	2·30	3·25
716		90f. "Arachnis"	2·30	3·25
717		105f. "Cattleya" (horiz)	2·50	3·25

308 Modern Technology

1998. Telecom 2000.
718	**308**	7f. multicoloured	90	2·75

309 Alofi Beach

1998. Air.
719	**309**	315f. multicoloured	5·50	6·75

310 Fisherman casting Net

1998. Lagoon Fishing. Multicoloured.
720		50f. Type **310**	2·50	3·00
721		52f. Fisherman with catch	2·50	3·00

311 Footballers

1998. World Cup Football Championship, France.
722	**311**	80f. multicoloured	1·70	3·00

312 Darter

1998. Insects. Multicoloured.
723		36f. Type **312**	90	2·75
724		40f. Cicada	1·00	2·75

313 Coral

1998. Corals.
725	**313**	4f. multicoloured	90	2·75
726	-	5f. multicoloured	90	2·75
727	-	10f. multicoloured	90	2·75
728	-	15f. multicoloured	90	2·75
DESIGNS: 5f. to 15f. Different corals.

314 Cricketer

1998. Air. Cricket.
729	**314**	106f. multicoloured	2·20	3·25

315 Gauguin and View of Island

1998. Air. 150th Birth Anniv of Paul Gauguin (artist).
730	**315**	700f. multicoloured	11·00	13·00

316 Coral, Sail Canoe and Fishes

1998. 52nd Autumn Stamp Show, Paris.
731	**316**	175f. multicoloured	3·25	4·50

317 "The Garden of Happiness"

1998. Air.
732	**317**	460f. multicoloured	8·25	8·25

318 Jigsaw Pieces

1998. World Anti-AIDS Day.
733	**318**	62f. multicoloured	1·30	3·00

319 Polynesian Dancer

1998. Air.
734	**319**	250f. multicoloured	5·50	5·00

320 Carrying Kava

1999. Air.
735	**320**	600f. multicoloured	12·50	11·50

321 Precious Wentletrap

1999. Air. Shells. Multicoloured.
736		95f. Type **321**	2·75	3·25
737		100f. Horned helmet	2·75	3·25
738		110f. Trumpet triton (horiz)	3·25	3·25
739		115f. Common spider conch (horiz)	3·25	3·25

322 Rock Formation

1999. Islet of Nuku Taakimoa.
740	**322**	130f. multicoloured	3·25	3·50

323x 323 "Finemui"

1999. Air.
741	**323**	900f. multicoloured	18·00	17·00

324 Marine Life

1999. Marine Life. Sheet 170×86 mm containing T **324** and similar square designs. Multicoloured.
MS742 20f. Type **324**; 855f. Flying fish and diver ... 23·00 23·00

325 Little Egrets

1999. Air. Birds of Nuku Fotu. Multicoloured.
743 | **325** | 10f. Type **325** | 1·50 | 1·40
744 | | 20f. Audubon's shearwaters | 1·60 | 1·50
745 | | 26f. Ascension frigate bird ("Christmas Island Frigate Birds") | 1·70 | 1·70
746 | | 54f. Red-tailed tropic bird | 2·10 | 2·75

326 Emblem and Hibiscus

1999. "Philexfrance 99" International Stamp Exhibition, Paris.
747 | **326** | 200f. multicoloured | 4·50 | 4·75

327 Senate and Marianne

1999. Bicentenary of French Senate.
748 | **327** | 125f. blue and red | 3·50 | 3·25

328 Assembly Building

1999. Territorial Assembly.
749 | **328** | 17f. multicoloured | 1·10 | 2·40

329 Pandanus Tree

1999
750 | **329** | 25f. multicoloured | 2·30 | 2·75

330 Carving Pirogue

1999
751 | **330** | 55f. multicoloured | 1·50 | 1·60

331 "Wind Song" (modern tourist ship)

1999. Air.
752 | **331** | 325f. blue, green & ultramarine | 8·25 | 7·25

332 1931 50c. International Colonial Exhibition Stamp

1999. 150th Anniv of First French Postage Stamp.
753 | **332** | 65f. multicoloured | 2·10 | 2·20

333 Sunrise over Lagoon

1999. Air.
754 | **333** | 500f. multicoloured | 12·50 | 8·75

334 Firework and Globe

2000. New Millennium.
755 | **334** | 350f. multicoloured | 8·25 | 7·25

335 Mata'Utu Cathedral

2000
756 | **335** | 300f. multicoloured | 7·00 | 5·75

336 La Glorieuse (patrol boat)

2000
757 | **336** | 155f. black, blue and green | 4·50 | 4·75

337 Makape

2000. Second Death Anniv of Sosefo Papilio Makape (President of General Council, 1962–77).
758 | **337** | 115f. red and blue | 3·50 | 3·75

338 Institute Building

2000. French Overseas Monetary Institute.
759 | **338** | 200f. multicoloured | 5·50 | 5·75

339 Crops

2000
760 | **339** | 275f. multicoloured | 7·00 | 7·25

340 Airport and Aircraft

2000. Air. 30th Anniv of Air Transport on Futuna Island.
761 | **340** | 350f. multicoloured | 9·75 | 10·50

341 Man throwing Spear

2000. Olympic Games, Sydney. Traditional Sports of Wallis and Futuna. Multicoloured.
762 | **341** | 85f. Type **341** | 2·50 | 2·75
763 | | 85f. Racing outrigger canoes | 2·50 | 2·75
764 | | 85f. Kayak racing | 2·50 | 2·75
765 | | 85f. Volleyball | 2·50 | 2·75

342 Tattooed Profiles

2000. Eighth Pacific Arts Festival, Kanaky, New Caledonia.
766 | **342** | 330f. multicoloured | 9·75 | 10·50

343 Dolphinfish (mahi-mahi)

2000. Fish. Multicoloured.
767 | **343** | 115f. Type **343** | 3·50 | 3·75
768 | | 115f. Blue-finned trevally (Caranx melampygus) (inscr "melanpygus") | 3·50 | 3·75
769 | | 115f. Yellow-finned tuna (Thunnus albacares) | 3·50 | 3·75

344 Champagnat

2000. Holy Year 2000. First Anniversary of Canonization of Marcellin Champagnat (educationalist and founder of Marist Order).
770 | **344** | 380f. multicoloured | 10·50 | 11·00

345 Talietumu

2000. Archaeology.
771 | **345** | 205f. multicoloured | 5·75 | 6·25

346 Mother and Child

2000. Christmas.
772 | **346** | 225f. multicoloured | 6·50 | 7·00

347 Jacques Cartier (landing ship)

2001
773 | **347** | 225f. black, blue and green | 6·50 | 7·00

348 Bottle and Cans

2001. Campaign against Alcoholism.
774 | **348** | 75f. multicoloured | 2·20 | 2·30

349 Design including Shells

2001. Tapas (bark of paper-mulberry tree). Multicoloured.
775 | **349** | 90f. Type **349** | 2·50 | 2·75
776 | | 90f. Design including leaves, diamonds and triangles | 2·50 | 2·75
777 | | 90f. Scenes of island life | 2·50 | 2·75
778 | | 90f. Design including overlapping ovals | 2·50 | 2·75

350 Mixed Flowers (M. Uhilamoafa)

2001. Children's Flower Paintings. Multicoloured.
779 | **350** | 50f. Type **350** | 2·20 | 2·30
780 | | 55f. Stem of flowers | 2·30 | 2·50
781 | | 95f. Vase of red and yellow flowers | 3·00 | 3·25
782 | | 100f. Pink orchid | 3·00 | 3·25

351 Man with Arm Raised

2001. 40th Anniv of French Overseas Territory Status.
783 | **351** | 165f. multicoloured | 4·50 | 4·75

352 Apple Canelle (T. Taika)

2001. Children's Fruit Paintings. Multicoloured.
784 | **352** | 65f. Type **352** | 1·90 | 2·10
785 | | 65f. Breadfruit (E. Mougatoga) | 1·90 | 2·10
786 | | 65f. Pineapple (E. Hamaivao) | 1·90 | 2·10
787 | | 65f. Mango (I. Mougatoga) | 1·90 | 2·10

353 Emblem

2001. First Anniv of Installation of Delegate of Mediator of the Republic.
788 **353** 800f. multicoloured 15·00 14·00

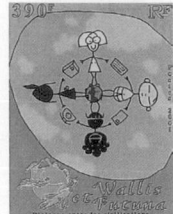

354 Children encircling Globe

2001. United Nations Year of Dialogue among Civilizations.
789 **354** 390f. multicoloured 10·50 11·00

355 Pacific Pigeon (*Ducula pacifica*)

2001. 55th Autumn Stamp Show. Birds. Multicoloured.
790 **355** 150f. Type **355** (inscr "Dacula") 3·75 4·25
791 150f. Blue-crowned lory (*Vini australis*) 3·75 4·25
792 150f. Barn owl (*Tyto alba*) 3·75 4·25

356 Grave

2001. Grave of Fakavelikele (first king of Wallis and Futuna).
793 **356** 325f. multicoloured 9·00 9·75

357 Building

2002. Inauguration of Finemui College, Teesi (French college).
794 **357** 115f. multicoloured 3·25 3·50

358 Queen Aloisia

2002. International Women's Day.
795 **358** 800f. brown 15·00 17·00

359 Arms

2002. Monseigneur Pompallier (first bishop of Western Oceanie).
796 **359** 500f. buff, green and red 10·50 11·00

360 Emblem

2002. Fire Service of Uvea Island.
797 **360** 85f. multicoloured 2·50 2·75

361 Stylized Footballer

2002. World Cup Football Championship, Japan and South Korea.
798 **361** 65f. multicoloured 1·90 2·10

362 Tree, Bird, Turtle and Sea

2002. World Environment Day.
799 **362** 330f. multicoloured 9·00 9·75

363 House with Veranda

2002. Traditional Thatched Houses (fale). Houses. Multicoloured.
800 **363** 50f. Type **363** 1·50 1·70
801 50f. Without walls (vert) 1·50 1·70
802 55f. With window shutters 1·70 1·80
803 55f. Amongst tall trees (vert) 1·70 1·80

364 Jacob Lemaire

2002. Discovery of Futuna.
804 **364** 125f. Type **364** (joint finder) 3·50 3·75
805 125f. Futuna and Aloti islands 3·50 3·75
806 125f. William Schouten (joint finder) 3·50 3·75
MS807 175×100 mm (oval). Nos. 804/6 5·00 5·00

365 Utua Bay

2002. Landscapes. Multicoloured.
807 95f. Type **365** 2·75 3·00
808 100f. Liku Bay 2·75 3·00
809 105f. Kingfisher and Vele Point 3·00 3·25
810 135f. Aka Aka Bay 3·25 3·50

366 *Enygrus bibroni* (snake)

2002
811 **366** 75f. multicoloured 2·30 2·50

367 Fu Manchu Lion Fish (*Dendrochirus biocellatus*)

2002. 56th Autumn Stamp Show. Fish. Multicoloured.
812 **367** 110f. Type **367** 3·25 3·50
813 110f. Spikefin goby (*Discordipina griessingeri*) 3·25 3·50
814 110f. Spotfin frogfish (*Antennarius nummifer*) (inscr "Antennacius") 3·25 3·50
815 110f. Dragon wrasse (*Novaculichthys taeniourus*) 3·25 3·50

368 Yacht, Sea Cliffs and Beach

2002. Christmas.
816 **368** 140f. multicoloured 3·75 4·25

369 Avro Type 683 Lancaster WU 21 and Insignia of Escadrille 9S

2003. 40th Anniv of Last Flight of Escadrille 9S Lancaster WU 21 (26 January 1963).
817 **369** 135f. multicoloured 3·75 4·25

370 Sailing Canoe Enclosed in Heart-shape

2003. St. Valentine's Day.
818 **370** 85f. multicoloured 2·50 2·75

371 Euro Coin

2003. First Anniv of Introduction of Euro.
819 **371** 125f. multicoloured 3·75 4·25

372 Alain Gerbault aboard *Firecrest*

2003. Alain Gerbault (sailor) Commemoration.
820 **372** 600f. sepia and green 14·00 15·00

373 Bottle

2003. Art. Multicoloured.
821 **373** 5f. Type **373** 25 30
822 10f. Globe, hand, yacht and island 30 35
823 15f. Flower 40 40
824 20f. Fish 65 70
825 40f. Islands 1·20 1·20

374 Coral

2003. Coral Landscapes Multicoloured.
826 **374** 95f. Type **374** 2·75 3·00
827 105f. Flat coral 3·00 3·25
828 110f. Spiny coral 3·25 3·50
829 115f. Underwater valley 3·50 3·75

375 Pierre Chanel

2003. Birth Bicentenary of Pierre-Louis-Marie Chanel (martyred missionary).
830 **375** 130f. violet and brown 4·00 4·25

376 Emblem

2003. Census.
831 **376** 55f. multicoloured 1·70 1·80

377 Eel

2003. Legends of the Pacific. "How the Eel gave Birth to a Coconut". Multicoloured.
832 **377** 30f. Type **377** 95 95
833 50f. Coconut tree 1·60 1·70
834 60f. Coconuts 1·90 1·90
835 70f. Palm trees 2·30 2·30
MS836 168×112 mm. Nos. 832/5 6·75 6·75

378 "Still-life with Maori Statue"

2003. Death Centenary of Paul Gauguin (artist).
837 100f. Type **378** 3·25 3·25
MS838 130×90 mm. 100f.×2, Sketches of Tahitian Heads 6·50 6·50
Stamps of a similar design were issued by New Caledonia.

379 Waterfall

2003

839	379	115f. multicoloured	3·75	3·75

380 Le Nivose (frigate)

2003

840	380	325f. blue, light blue and magenta	10·50	11·00

381 Alexandre Poncet

2003. 30th Death Anniv of Bishop Alexandre Poncet.

841	381	205f. light blue and blue	6·75	7·00

382 Arms

2003. Monseigneur Bataillon (first Bishop of Central Oceania).

842	382	500f. multicoloured	16·00	17·00

383 Emblem

2003. Rugby World Cup Championships, Sydney.

843	383	65f. multicoloured	2·00	2·10

384 Parinari insularum

2003. 57th Autumn Stamp Show. Fruit.

844	384	250f. multicoloured	8·00	8·25

385 Havea Hikule'O

2004

845	385	85f. multicoloured	2·75	2·75

386 Canoe

2004. Departure of Kumete.

846	386	75f. multicoloured	2·40	2·50

387 Face and Mosquito

2004. Control of Dengue Fever Awareness Campaign. Sheet 130×105 mm containing T **387** and similar vert designs.

MS847 5f. Type **38**; 10f. Bandaged figure and mosquitoes; 20f. Mosquitoes and rubbish; 30f. Sleeping under mosquito net — 2·00 / 2·10

388 Shuttlecock, Racquet and Island

2004. Badminton.

848	388	55f. multicoloured	1·70	1·80

389 Men seated around Table

2004. Kava (alcoholic drink).

849	389	205f. multicoloured	6·75	7·00

390 Inscr "Tarot"

2004. Fruit. Multicoloured.

850	390	15f. Type **390**	55	55
851		25f. Papaya	80	85
852		35f. Breadfruit	1·20	1·20
853		40f. Yam	1·30	1·40

391 Savorgnan de Brazza (sloop)

2004. First Flight over Wallis et Futuna.

854	391	300f. blue, indigo and plum	9·25	9·75
855	—	380f. blue, sepia and violet	12·00	12·50

MS856 100×81 mm. Nos. 854/5 — 21·00 / 21·00

DESIGNS: 300f. Type **391**; 380f. Gourdou-Leseurre GL 832.

392 Ylang-ylang (Canaga odorata)

2004. Le Salon de Timbres International Stamp Exhibition, Paris (1st issue) Flowers. Sheet 121×115 mm containing T **392** and similar heart-shaped designs. Multicoloured. Self-adhesive.

MS857 85f., Type **392**; 85f., Frangipani (Plumeria rubra); 85f., Hibiscus; 115f., Gardenia taitensis; Ipomea pes-caprae — 13·50 / 13·50

See also No. MS858.

393 Turbinaria ornate

2004. Le Salon de Timbres International Stamp Exhibition, Paris (2nd issue) Algae. Sheet 126×104 mm containing T **393** and similar vert designs. Multicoloured.

MS858 105f.×2, Type **393**; 155f.×2, Padina melemele; 175f.×2, iTurbinaria concoides — 28·00 / 28·00

394 Emblem

2004. Ninth Pacific Arts Festival, Palau.

859	394	200f. multicoloured	6·25	6·50

395 Le Pili'Uli (lizard)

2004

860	395	100f. multicoloured	3·25	3·25

396 Arms

2004. Monseigneur Louis Elloy (missionary).

861	396	500f. multicoloured	16·00	17·00

2004. No. 740 surch 115f.

862		115f. on 130f. multicoloured	3·75	3·75

398 House and Palm tree

2004. 58th Autumn Stamp Show. Traditional Thatched Houses (fale). Sheet 150×132 mm containing T **398** and similar design.

MS863 95f.×4 Type **398**; 130f.×4 House enclosed by trees (26×36 mm) — 29·00 / 29·00

399 Conus eburneus

2005. Shells. Sheet 95×80 mm containing T **399** and similar horiz designs. Multicoloured.

MS864 55f.×4, Type **399**; Conus imperialis; Conus generalis; Gastridium textile (inscr "texile") — 6·75 / 6·75

400 Starfish, Bird, Eel, Turtle and Whale

2005. Legends. Sheet 130×100 mm containing T **400** and similar horiz designs.

MS865 65f. Type **400**; 65f. Fish, eels and butterfly; 75f. Clef, notes and waves; 75f. Butterflies, waves and notes — 8·75 / 8·75

401 Traditional Pirogue

2005

866	401	330f. multicoloured	10·00	10·50

402 People from Many Nations

2005. French-speaking Culture.

867	402	135f. multicoloured	4·25	4·50

A stamp of similar design was issued New Caledonia.

403 Emblem

2005. Family Budget Census.

868	403	205f. multicoloured	6·25	6·50

404 Warriors

2005. Rock Paintings.

869	369	5f. multicoloured	15	15
870	369	10f. multicoloured	30	30
871	369	20f. multicoloured	60	60
872	369	30f. multicoloured	90	95
873	369	50f. multicoloured	1·60	1·70

405 Player

2005. Kilikiti (cricket).

874	405	190f. multicoloured	6·00	6·50

406 Papilio montrouzieri

2005. Butterflies. Multicoloured.

875	406	40f. Type **406**	1·20	1·20
876		60f. Danaus pumila	1·90	2·00

Nos. 875/6 were issued together, se-tenant, forming a composite design.

407 Ulutoa Thrower

2005. Self-Adhesive.

877	407	115f. multicoloured	3·75	4·00

408 Early Village

2005. National Stamp Exhibition. Early Photographs. Each brown.

878		155f. Type **408**	4·75	5·00
879		175f. Seated women	5·50	6·00

409 Adult

2005. Green Turtle (Chelonia mydas (inscr "Chelomia")). Sheet 125×145 mm containing T **409** and similar horiz designs. Multicoloured.
MS880 85f.×4 Type **409**; Young; Head of adult; Adult swimming   10·50   10·50
The stamps and margins of **MS**880 form a composite design.

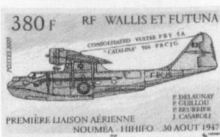
410 Consolidated Vultee PBY 5A Catalina

2005. 58th Anniv of First Flight between Noumea and Hihifo.
881   **410**   380f. multicoloured   11·00   11·50

411 Arms

2005. Bishop Jean Armand Lamaze (Titular Bishop of Olympe and Apostolic Vicar of Central Oceania).
882   **411**   500f. multicoloured   18·00   19·00

412 Inscr "Spattoglottis cinguiculata"

2005. Orchid.
883   **412**   100f. multicoloured   3·50   3·75

2005. 59th Autumn Stamp Show. No. 4 surch **ILES WALLIS et FUTUNA 150f.** and No. 87 surch **150F. WALLIS ET FUTUNA.**
884   150f. on 5c. green (No. 4)   4·50   4·75
885   150f. on 90c. vermilion and black (No. 87)   4·50   4·75

415 Island Child

2006
886   **415**   75f. multicoloured   2·75   2·75

416 Royal Flag of Sigave Kingdom

2006. Flags. Self-adhesive. Multicoloured.
887   65f. Type **416**   2·10   2·20
888   85f. Royal flag of Alo Kingdom   3·00   3·00

417 Haka Mai

2006
889   **417**   190f. multicoloured   6·00   6·50

418 The Crucifixion

2006. 80th Birth Anniv of Jean Soane Michon (artist).
890   **418**   400f. multicoloured   12·50   13·50

419 Player

2006. World Cup Football Championship, Germany.
891   **419**   100f. multicoloured   3·25   3·50

2006. Flags. Self-adhesive. As T **416**. Vermilion, scarlet and ultramarine.
892   55f. Royal flag of Uvea Kingdom   1·90   2·00

420 Mata vai

2006. Salon du Timbre et de l'Ecrit. Multicoloured.
893   140f. Type **420**   4·50   4·75
894   200f. Mata tai   6·25   6·50

421 Young Girls' Dance

2006. Wallis et Futuna in the Past. Each chocolate.
895   330f. Type **421**   10·50   11·00
896   380f. Mua Church   12·50   13·50

422 Faces

2006. Colours of Oceania.
897   **422**   130f. multicoloured   4·75   5·00

423 Ville de Paris

2006. 20th Anniv of DeHavilland Twin Otter Ville de Paris.
898   **423**   30f. multicoloured   1·10   1·20

424 Emblem

2006. French Rugby Federation.
899   **424**   10f. multicoloured   45   45

425 Uhilamoafa Grave

2006
900   **425**   290f. multicoloured   9·00   9·75

426 Arms

2006. Bishop Joseph Felix Blanc (Titular Bishop of Dibon and Vicar Apostolic of Central Oceania).
901   **426**   500f. multicoloured   14·00   15·00

427 Tapestry

2006. Cultural Heritage. Tapestry. Each grey and brown.
902   85f. Type **427**   2·50   2·75
903   85f. Women (Maka a Ono)   2·50   2·75
904   85f. Musicians (Tausu a Leava)   2·50   2·75
905   85f. Tapestry (different)   2·50   2·75

428 Tagaloa

2006. Kiwipex 2006 Stamp Exhibition.
906   **428**   150f. multicoloured   4·75   5·00

429 The Nativity

2006. Christmas. Sheet 85×55 mm.
MS907   **429**   225f. multicoloured   7·00   7·00
The stamp and margin of **MS**907 form a composite design.

430 Pio Taofinu'u

2007. First Death Anniv of Pio Taofinu'u (first Oceania Cardinal).
908   **430**   800f. multicoloured   19·00   21·00

431 Hands enclosing Symbols of Medicine and Communication

2007. Telemedicine Network.
909   **431**   5f. multicoloured   25   30

432 Building Facade

2007. Bicentenary of Court of Auditors.
910   **432**   105f. blue and vermilion   3·50   3·75

433 Woman, Fruit and Pot

2007. Scenes from Daily Life.
911   **433**   75f. multicoloured   2·50   2·75

434 Douglas DC3 Dakota F BGXN

2007. 50th Anniv of Noumea–Hihifo Regular Air Flights.
912   **434**   290f. multicoloured   9·25   10·00

435 Eviota sigillata

2007. Coral Fish. Multicoloured.
913   40f. Type **435**   1·50   1·70
914   50f. Trimma   1·50   1·70

436 Emblem

2007. 60th Anniv of Secretariat of the Pacific Community.
915   **436**   155f. multicoloured   5·00   5·25

437 Lolesio Tuita

2007. Tuita (Pacific Games Champion and French Champion javelin thrower).
916   **437**   330f. violet and vermilion   11·00   11·50

2007. Wallis et Futuna in the Past. As T **421**. Each chocolate.
917   190f. House, Tamana Village   6·00   6·50
918   200f. Pierre Chanel's house   6·50   7·00

438 Togatapu Island, Figures and Canoe

2007. Legends of Lomipeau. Multicoloured.
919   20f. Type **438**   75   80
920   30f. Canoe, figures and Uvea Island   1·00   1·10

439 Samuel Wallis

2007. 240th Anniv of Discovery of Uvea Island.
921   **439**   225f. multicoloured   7·50   8·00
MS922 100×119 mm. **439** 225f. multicoloured   8·00   8·00

440 Emblem of Wallis-et-Futuna Handisport League

2007
923   **440**   10f. multicoloured   30   30

441 Players

2007. Rugby World Cup Championship, France.
924   **441**   205f. multicoloured   6·25   6·75

442 Arms

2007. Bishop Armand Olier (Vicar Apostolic of Central Oceania from 1906–1911).

| 925 | **442** | 500f. lemon, green and black | 16·00 | 17·00 |

443 'Mio'

2007. Autumn Stamp Show. Traditional Dances. Multicoloured.

| 926 | 100f. Type **443** | 3·50 | 3·75 |
| 927 | 100f. 'Kailao Tokotoko' | 3·50 | 3·75 |

444 Woman and @

2008. Tenth Anniv of Internet Connection.

| 928 | **444** | 55f. multicoloured | 2·40 | 2·50 |

445 Women and Yellow Hibiscus

2008

| 929 | **445** | 65f. multicoloured | 2·75 | 3·00 |

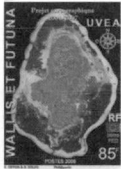

446 Uvea

2008. Cartography. Multicoloured.

| 930 | 85f. Type **446** | 3·25 | 3·50 |
| 931 | 85f. Futuna and Alofi (horiz.) | 3·25 | 3·50 |

447 Diving

2008

| 932 | **446** | 95f. multicoloured | 3·75 | 3·75 |

448 Kayaking

2008. Olympic Games, Beijing.

| 933 | **448** | 75f. multicoloured | 3·25 | 3·50 |

449 Sea Fauna

2008. Year of Planet Earth.

| 934 | **449** | 190f. multicoloured | 8·25 | 8·75 |
| MS935 | 128×90 mm. 200f. As Type **449** | 8·75 | 8·75 |

450 Lavelua Kulimoetoke

2008. Tomasi Kulimoetoke (50th lavelua (king)) Commemoration.

| 936 | **450** | 380f. brown | 15·00 | 16·00 |

451 Aglaia psilopetala

2008. Flora.

| 937 | **451** | 105f. multicoloured | 4·25 | 4·50 |

452 Weaving

2008. Wallis et Futuna in the Past. Each chocolate.

| 938 | 110f. Type **452** | 4·50 | 4·75 |
| 939 | 155f. Returning to Island | 6·00 | 6·50 |

Nos. 938/9 were printed, *se-tenant*, in horizontal strips of two stamps surrounding a central stamp size label

453 Saint Therese

2008. Stained Glass Windows of Lano Church. Multicoloured.

| 940 | 100f. Type **453** | 4·25 | 4·50 |
| 941 | 140f. Saint Pierre Chanel | 5·50 | 6·00 |

454 Blue and White Hull

2008. Hulls of Traditional Canoes. Designs showing hulls. Multicoloured.

942	5f. Type **454**	30	30
943	20f. Red, blue, black and yellow	1·10	1·10
944	40f. Mottled green blue and black	2·00	2·10
945	50f. Blue and red	2·30	2·40

455 Lolesio Tuita Stadium

2008

| 946 | **455** | 55f. multicoloured | 2·50 | 2·75 |

456 Arms

2008. Bishop Alexandre Poncet.

| 947 | **456** | 500f. multicoloured | 20·00 | 21·00 |

457 Emblem

2008. World Youth Day—Sydney 2008.

| 948 | **457** | 10f. multicoloured | 60 | 65 |

458 Young Pig

2008. Autumn Stamp Show. 'Puaka' the Pig. Multicoloured.

| 949 | 115f. Type **458** | 5·00 | 5·25 |
| 950 | 115sf. Large pig | 5·00 | 5·25 |

Nos. 949/50 were issued in *se-tenant* forming a composite design.

459 Constitution and General de Gaulle (statue)

2008. 50th Anniv of Constitution of Fifth Republic.

| 951 | **459** | 225f. multicoloured | 7·50 | 8·00 |

460 Louis Braille

2009. Birth Bicentenary of Louis Braille (inventor of Braille writing for the blind).

| 952 | **460** | 330f. multicoloured | 14·00 | 15·00 |

461 Bougainvillea

2009. Bougainvillea spectabilis. Multicoloured.

953	55f. Type **461**	2·50	2·75
954	55f. Lilac with variegated leaves	2·50	2·75
955	55f. Pink and white with red background	2·50	2·75
956	55f. Cluster of white edged with pink against brown background	2·50	2·75

462 Akihito futuna

2009. New Species of Freshwater Gobi from Futuna Islands. Multicoloured.

| 957 | 65f. Type **462** | 2·75 | 3·00 |
| 958 | 65f. Stiphodon rubromaculatus | 2·75 | 3·00 |

463 Nun

2009. St. Theresa Carmel Convent.

| 959 | **463** | 140f. multicoloured | 6·25 | 6·75 |

464 Ox

2009. Chinese New Year. Year of the Ox.

| 960 | **464** | 95f. multicoloured | 4·50 | 4·75 |

465 Player

2009. Petanque.

| 961 | **465** | 105f. multicoloured | 4·75 | 5·25 |

466 Arms

2009. Bishop Michel Maurice Augustin Marie Darmancier.

| 962 | **466** | 500f. multicoloured | 20·00 | 21·00 |

467 French Residency

2009. Wallis et Futuna in the Past. Campagne de Kersaint. Each chocolate.

| 963 | 190f. Type **467** | 9·00 | 9·75 |
| 964 | 190f. Returning to Island | 9·00 | 9·75 |

468 Brewing Kava

2009. Traditional Foods.

| 965 | **468** | 115f. multicoloured | 5·00 | 5·25 |

469 Map as Ballot Box

2009. 50th Anniv of Territory.

| 966 | **469** | 205f. multicoloured | 8·50 | 9·00 |

470 La Tour Eiffel en Tapas (Ecole de Liku)

2009. Art.

| 967 | **470** | 85f. black and brown | 3·50 | 3·75 |

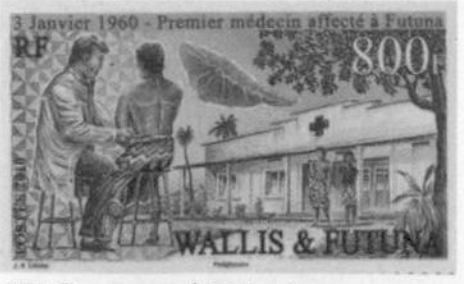

471 Doctor and Patient

2010. 50th Anniv of Arrival of First Medical Assistance on Futuna

968	**471**	800f. multicoloured	32·00	32·00

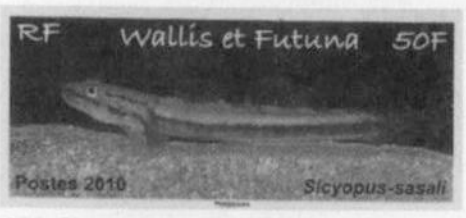

472 Sicyopus sasali

2010. Gobies. Multicoloured.

969	50f. Type **472**	2·20	2·20
970	65f. *Stenogobius keletaona*	3·00	3·00

Nos. 969/70 were printed, *se-tenant*, in horizontal pairs within the sheet

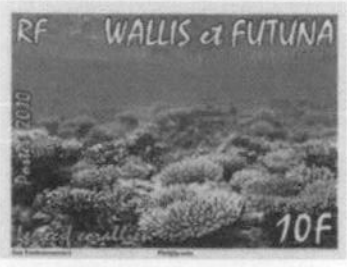

473 Coral

2010. Coral. Multicoloured.

971	10f. Type **473**	55	55
972	20f. Purple coral	1·10	1·10
973	30f. Purple twig-like coral	1·50	1·50
974	40f. Flat orange and yellow coral	2·20	2·20

Nos. 971/4 were printed, *se-tenant*, in horizontal strips of four stamps within the sheet

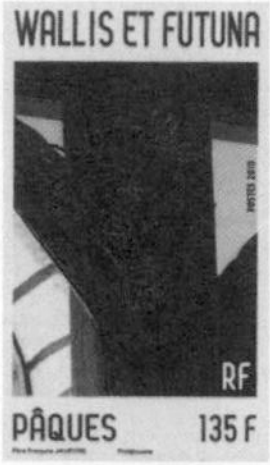

474 Christ Crucified

2010. Easter

975	**474**	135f. multicoloured	6·00	6·00

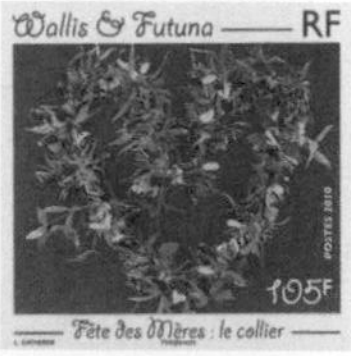

475 Wreath

2010. Mothers' Day

976	**475**	105f. multicoloured	4·75	4·75

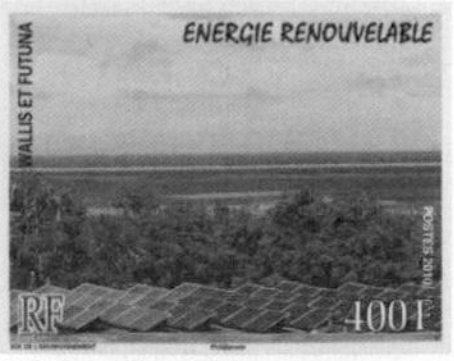

476 Solar Panel Array

2010. Renewable Energy. Multicoloured.

977	400f. Type **476**	17·00	17·00
978	400f. Solar panels on roof	17·00	17·00

Nos. 977/8 were printed, *se-tenant*, in horizontal strips of two stamps surrounding a central stamp size label

POSTAGE DUE STAMPS

1920. Postage Due Stamps of New Caledonia optd **ILES WALLIS et FUTUNA**.

D18	**D18**	5c. blue	30	8·50
D19	**D18**	10c. brown on buff	30	8·50
D20	**D18**	15c. green	1·60	8·50
D21	**D18**	20c. black on yellow	75	8·75
D22	**D18**	30c. red	90	9·00
D23	**D18**	50c. blue on cream	2·50	10·50
D24	**D18**	60c. green on blue	2·30	9·75
D25	**D18**	1f. green on cream	3·00	12·00

1927. As Postage Due stamp of New Caledonia, but colour changed, surch.

D43	2f. on 1f. mauve	5·50	34·00
D44	3f. on 1f. brown	7·00	44·00

1930. Postage Due stamps of New Caledonia optd **ILES WALLIS et FUTUNA.**

D85	**D25**	2c. brown and blue	35	7·25
D86	**D25**	4c. green and red	35	7·50
D87	**D25**	5c. blue and red	45	6·75
D88	**D25**	10c. blue and purple	45	7·50
D89	**D25**	15c. red and green	80	7·75
D90	**D25**	20c. brown and purple	65	7·75
D91	**D25**	25c. blue and brown	65	7·75
D92	**D25**	30c. brown and green	1·00	8·75
D93	**D25**	50c. red and brown	90	8·00
D94	**D25**	60c. red and mauve	1·60	10·50
D95	**D25**	1f. green and blue	1·40	9·25
D96	**D25**	2f. brown and red	1·40	9·50
D97	**D25**	3f. brown and mauve	1·80	9·50

1943. Nos. D85/97 optd **FRANCE LIBRE**.

D126	2c. brown and blue	42·00	75·00
D127	4c. green and red	42·00	75·00
D128	5c. blue and red	42·00	75·00
D129	10c. blue and purple	42·00	75·00
D130	15c. red and green	42·00	75·00
D131	20c. brown and purple	42·00	75·00
D132	25c. blue and brown	42·00	75·00
D133	30c. brown and green	42·00	75·00
D134	50c. red and brown	42·00	75·00
D135	60c. red and mauve	42·00	75·00
D136	1f. green and blue	46·00	85·00
D137	2f. brown and red	46·00	85·00
D138	3f. brown and mauve	46·00	85·00

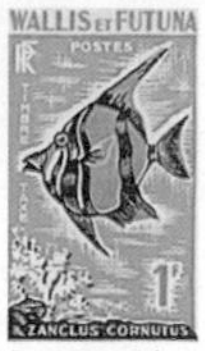

D10 Moorish Idol

1963. Fish.

D182	**D10**	1f. black, yellow & bl	2·75	4·50
D183	-	3f. red, green and blue	3·25	5·50
D184	-	5f. orange, black & bl	3·75	6·50

DESIGNS—HORIZ: 3f. Moon wrasse; 5f. Orange clownfish.

Pt. 10

WENDEN

Formerly part of W. Russia but later became part of Latvia. Issued stamps for use within the district until 1903.

100 kopeks = 1 rouble.

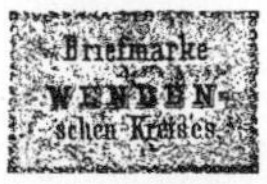

2

1863. Inscr "Briefmarke des WENDEN-schen Kreises". Imperf.

1	**2**	2k. black and red	£450	£650

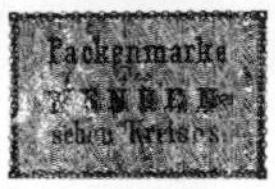

3

1863. Inscr "Packenmarke des WENDEN-schen Kreises". Imperf.

2	**3**	4k. black and green	£325	£650

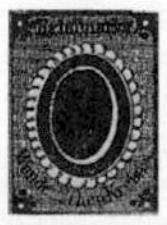

6

1863. Imperf.

6	**6**	2k. green and red	46·00	46·00

1864. As T **6**, but with horse in central oval. Imperf.

5	2k. green and red	£130	£325

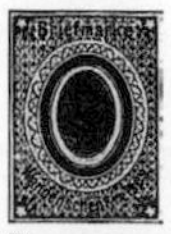

7

1871. Imperf.

7	**7**	2k. green and red	46·00	46·00

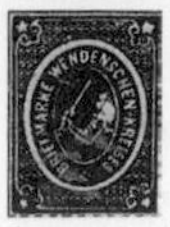

8

1872. Perf.

8	**8**	2k. red and green	46·00	65·00

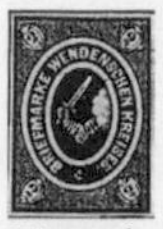

9 Arms of Wenden

1875

9	**9**	2k. green and red	13·00	20·00

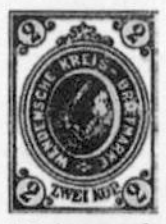

10 Arms of Wenden

1878

10	**10**	2k. green and red	13·00	33·00
11	**10**	2k. red, brown and green	13·00	33·00
13	**10**	2k. green, black and red	16·00	65·00

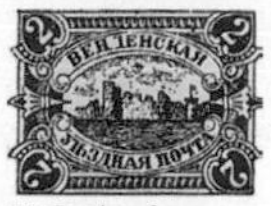

11 Castle of Wenden

1901

14	**11**	2k. brown and green	9·75	33·00
15	**11**	2k. red and green	9·75	33·00
16	**11**	2k. purple and green	9·75	33·00

Pt. 21

WEST IRIAN

The following stamps superseded Nos. 1-19 of West New Guinea, after the former Dutch territory became part of Indonesia. From 1971 Indonesian stamps have been used.

100 cents or sen = 1 rupiah.

1963. Stamps of Indonesia optd **IRIAN BARAT** or surch also.

1	-	1s. on 70s. red (No. 724)	10	45
2	-	2s. on 90s. green (No. 727)	10	45
3	-	5s. grey (No. 830)	10	45
4	-	6s. on 20s. bistre (No. 833)	10	45
5	-	7s. on 50s. blue (No. 835)	10	45
6	-	10s. brown (No. 831)	10	45
7	-	15s. purple (No. 832)	10	45
8	**134**	25s. green	20	65
9	-	30s. on 75s. red (No. 836)	20	65
10	-	40s. on 1r.15 red (No. 837)	35	75
11	**99**	1r. mauve	85	1·40
12	**99**	2r. green	1·60	2·40
13	**99**	3r. blue	2·75	4·00
14	**99**	5r. brown	4·50	8·25

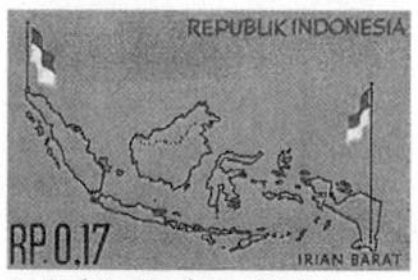

1a Indonesia, from Atjeh to Merauke

1963. Acquisition of West Irian.

21	**1a**	12s. orange, red and black	10	35
22	**1a**	17s. orange, red and black	10	45
23	-	20s. blue, green and purple	25	65
24	-	50s. blue, green and purple	35	1·10
25	-	60s. brown, yellow and green	75	1·20
26	-	75s. brown, yellow and green	1·00	2·20

DESIGNS: 20, 50s. Parachutist; 60, 75s. Greater bird of paradise.

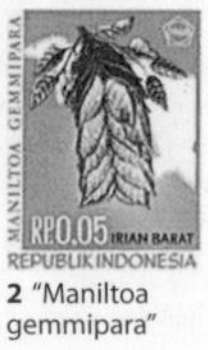

2 "Maniltoa gemmipara"

1968. Flora and Fauna.

27	**2**	5s. purple and green	75	1·30
28	-	15s. violet and green	1·10	2·20
29	-	30s. green and orange	1·80	3·50
30	-	40s. violet and yellow	2·20	4·00
31	-	50s. black and purple	3·25	5·00
32	-	75s. black and blue	4·00	6·50
33	-	1r. black and brown	5·00	9·75
34	-	3r. black and green	8·75	13·00
35	-	5r. multicoloured	2·00	5·50
36	-	10r. multicoloured	2·40	9·25

DESIGNS: 15s. "Dendrobium lancifolium"; 30s. "Gardenia gjellerupii"; 40s. "Maniltoa gemmipara" (blossom); 50s. Common phalanger; 75s. One-wattled cassowary; 1r. Common forest wallaby; 3r. Blue crowned pigeons; 5r. Black-capped lory; 10r. Greater bird of paradise.

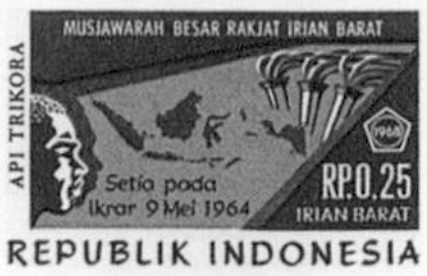

3 Map of Indonesia

1968. West Irian People's Pledge of 9 May 1964.

43	**3**	10s. gold and blue	3·75	2·00
44	**3**	25s. gold and red	6·50	3·50

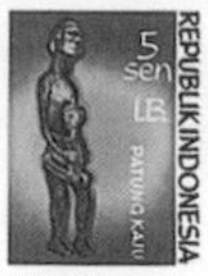

4 Mother and Child Figurine

1970. West Irian Woodcarvings. Multicoloured.

45	5s. Type **4**	45	75
46	6s. Carved shield	45	75
47	7s. Man and serpents	75	2·20
48	10s. Drum	75	2·20
49	25s. Seated warrior	75	75
50	30s. "Female" drum	85	1·10
51	50s. Bamboo vessel	1·00	1·10
52	75s. Seated man and tree	1·10	1·30
53	1r. Decorated shield	1·20	1·60
54	2r. Seated figure	1·40	1·80

Nos. 45/54 are inscr "I.B." ("Irian Barat").

POSTAGE DUE STAMPS

1963. Postage Due Stamps as Type **D100** of Indonesia optd **IRIAN BARAT**.

D15	1s. slate	10	55
D16	5s. olive	10	65
D17	10s. turquoise	20	75
D18	25s. slate	35	1·20
D19	40s. orange	55	1·80
D20	100s. brown	1·40	3·50

1968. As Type **D100** of Indonesia, but with coloured network background incorporating "1968", optd IRIAN BARAT.

D37	1s. blue and green	20	75
D38	5s. green and pink	20	85
D39	10s. red and grey	20	85
D40	25s. green and yellow	35	1·40
D41	40s. purple and green	65	2·20
D42	100s. red and olive	1·50	4·25

Scan the QR code below to get your FREE APPS from Stanley Gibbons

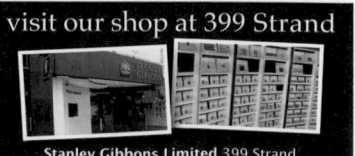

visit our shop at 399 Strand

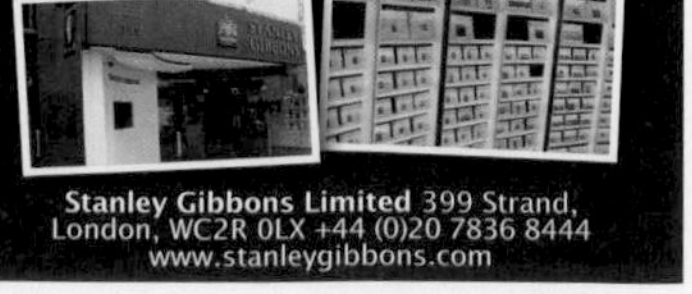

Stanley Gibbons Limited 399 Strand, London, WC2R 0LX +44 (0)20 7836 8444
www.stanleygibbons.com

WEST NEW GUINEA

Pt. 4

U.N. Administration of former Netherlands New Guinea from 1 October 1962 to 30 April 1963, when it became known as West Irian and became part of Indonesia.

100 cents = 1 gulden.

1962. "United Nations Temporary Executive Authority" Stamps of Netherlands New Guinea optd **UNTEA**.

1	5	1c. yellow and red	60	60
21	-	2c. orange	60	1·70
3	5	5c. yellow and brown	60	1·70
4	-	7c. purple, bl & brn (No. 60)	1·20	1·70
5	-	10c. brown and blue (No. 27)	80	1·70
6	-	12c. pur, bl & grn (No. 61)	1·20	1·70
7	-	15c. brown & yell (No. 28)	1·20	1·70
8	-	17c. pur, bl & blk (No. 62)	1·70	1·70
9	-	20c. brown & green (No. 29)	1·70	1·20
10	6	25c. red	2·00	3·00
11	6	30c. blue	2·00	3·00
12	6	40c. orange	2·00	3·00
13	6	45c. green	4·00	3·50
14	6	55c. turquoise	2·50	3·50
34	6	80c. grey	11·50	14·00
35	6	85c. brown	7·00	8·75
36	6	1g. purple	7·00	8·75
37	-	2g. brown (No. 20)	17·00	23·00
19	-	5g. green (No. 21)	17·00	17·00

For later issues see **WEST IRIAN**

WEST UKRAINE

Pt. 10

Before the 1914/18 War this district, known as E. Galicia was part of Austria. It achieved temporary independence after the war when stamps were issued. In June 1919 it became part of Poland but was transferred to the Ukraine in 1945.

100 heller = 1 krone.

(5)

1919. Stamps of Austria 1916 optd with T **5**.

70	49	3h. violet	65	1·40
71	49	5h. green	65	1·40
72	49	6h. orange	65	1·40
73	49	10h. red	65	1·40
74	49	12h. blue	65	1·40
75	60	15h. red	65	1·40
76	60	20h. green	65	1·40
77	60	25h. blue	65	1·40
78	60	30h. violet	65	1·40
79	51	40h. olive	80	1·80
80	51	50h. green	80	1·80
81	51	60h. blue	80	1·80
82	51	80h. brown	90	2·00
83	51	90h. purple	90	2·40
84	51	1k. red on yellow	1·30	6·00
85	52	2k. blue	2·50	9·00
86	52	3k. red	3·25	9·00
87	52	4k. green	26·00	33·00
88	52	10k. violet	39·00	£110

For other issues, which were mainly of a local character, see Part 10 (Russia) of the standard catalogue.

WESTERN AUSTRALIA

Pt. 1

The western state of the Australian Commonwealth, whose stamps it now uses.

12 pence = 1 shilling; 20 shillings = 1 pound.

1   2   3

1854. Imperf or roul.

1	1	1d. black	£1300	£275
25	1	2d. orange	£130	80·00
3	2	4d. blue	£375	£200
26	1	4d. blue	£300	£1800
28	1	6d. green	£2500	£400
4c	3	1s. brown	£475	£325

5

1857. Imperf or roul

15	5	2d. brown on red	£5500	£550
18	5	6d. bronze to black	£7000	£650

1861. Perf.

76	1	1d. yellow	28·00	2·00
103	1	1d. red	29·00	3·50
41	1	2d. blue	£100	24·00
77	1	2d. yellow	42·00	2·00
104	1	2d. grey	80·00	1·25
56	1	4d. red	£130	7·00
105	1	4d. brown	80·00	29·00
42	1	6d. brown	£500	50·00
79	1	6d. lilac	£120	3·00
61	1	1s. green	£225	19·00

7

1871

87	7	3d. brown	10·00	3·75

1874. Surch **ONE PENNY**.

67	1	1d. on 2d. yellow	£650	55·00

1884. Surch in figures.

90		½d. on 1d. yellow	16·00	27·00
91a	7	1d. on 3d. brown	80·00	27·00

12   13   14

15

1885

94a	12	½d. green	4·00	70
112	13	1d. red	8·00	30
96a	14	2d. grey	28·00	3·25
113	14	2d. yellow	27·00	2·75
97a	14	2½d. blue	22·00	2·25
98	14	4d. brown	13·00	2·50
99	14	5d. yellow	16·00	4·25
100	15	6d. violet	18·00	2·00
102	15	1s. green	28·00	5·00

1893. Surch in words

107	7	1d. on 3d. brown	14·00	8·00
110a	7	½d. on 3d. brown	10·00	35·00

19   23   21

28   29   30

31   32   24

1901

140	23	2d. yellow	7·00	2·00
114	19	2½d. blue	15·00	1·25
142b	24	4d. brown	18·00	3·75
143	15	5d. olive	29·00	2·00
168	19	6d. violet	15·00	24·00
121	12	8d. green	19·00	4·25
145	24	9d. orange	32·00	6·00
123	19	10d. red	32·00	9·50
116	21	1s. green	45·00	6·00
124b	28	2s. red on yellow	50·00	12·00
125	29	2s.6d. blue on red	55·00	19·00
126	30	5s. green	80·00	48·00
127	31	10s. mauve	£170	£100
128	32	£1 orange	£400	£180

WURTTEMBERG

Pt. 7

Formerly an independent kingdom, Wurttemberg became part of the German Empire in 1902.

1851 60 kreuzer = 1 gulden.
1875. 100 pfennige = 1 mark.

1

1851. Imperf.

1	1	1k. black on buff	£1600	£140
3	1	3k. black on yellow	£425	11·50
5	1	6k. black on green	£2000	47·00
7	1	9k. black on pink	£6500	47·00
9	1	18k. black on lilac	£2250	£1100

2

1857. Imperf.

10	2	1k. brown	£1100	£120
24	2	3k. orange	£550	35·00
15	2	6k. green	£1100	95·00
17	2	9k. red	£2750	£110
19	2	18k. blue	£5500	£2500
85	2	70k. violet	£2500	£6000

1859. Perf.

45		1k. brown	£900	£650
40		3k. yellow	£275	95·00
41		6k. green	£550	£160
42		9k. red	£1800	£450
43		9k. purple	£2000	£550
44		18k. blue	£4250	£3250

1863. Perf or roul.

60		1k. green	60·00	18·00
49		3k. pink	80·00	4·75
54		6k. blue	£225	80·00
66		7k. blue	£1300	£190
57		9k. brown	£350	75·00
59		18k. orange	£1700	£600

3

1869. Roul or perf (1k.); perf (others).

72	3	1k. green	£325	£140
74	3	2k. orange	£250	£200
77	3	3k. pink	22·00	2·30
78	3	7k. blue	95·00	26·00
80	3	9k. bistre	£110	60·00
82	3	14k. yellow	£120	70·00

4

1875. New Currency.

123	4	2pf. grey	2·75	1·40
89	4	3pf. green	28·00	2·30
124	4	3pf. brown	1·10	80
91	4	5pf. mauve	13·50	1·20
127	4	5pf. green	2·20	80
93	4	10pf. red	1·70	1·20
95	4	20pf. blue	1·70	1·60
97	4	25pf. brown	£180	14·00
130	4	25pf. orange	4·00	2·30
151	4	30pf. black and orange	5·50	7·00
152	4	40pf. black and red	6·00	8·25
99	4	50pf. grey	£1000	60·00
101	4	50pf. green	90·00	9·25
132	4	50pf. brown	4·50	1·40
102	4	2m. yellow	£1100	£375
103	4	2m. red on orange	£4000	£190
121	4	2m. black and orange	11·00	14·00
122	4	5m. black and blue	60·00	£225

For issues of 1947-49 see Germany (French Zone).

1906. Surch **ONE PENNY**.

172	23	1d. on 2d. yellow	2·25	2·75

MUNICIPAL SERVICE STAMPS

M5

1875

M147	M5	2pf. grey	3·25	2·30
M169	M5	2½pf. grey	1·10	60
M170	M5	3pf. brown	1·30	60
M104	M5	5pf. mauve	60·00	3·50
M171	M5	5pf. green	1·10	60
M172	M5	7½pf. orange	1·10	60
M173	M5	10pf. red	1·10	60
M261	M5	10pf. orange	45	45
M174	M5	15pf. brown	2·75	60
M262	M5	15pf. violet	45	45
M176	M5	20pf. blue	2·20	60
M263	M5	20pf. green	45	45
M177	M5	25pf. orange	1·30	60
M178	M5	25pf. black and brown	1·70	60
M179	M5	35pf. brown	2·20	1·40
M264	M5	40pf. red	45	45
M265	M5	50pf. purple	45	45
M266	M5	60pf. green	65	45
M267	M5	1m.25 green	45	45
M268	M5	2m. grey	45	45
M269	M5	3m. brown	65	45

1906. Centenary of Establishment of Kingdom. Optd **1806–1906** under crown.

M153		2pf. grey	60·00	21·00
M154		3pf. brown	19·00	15·00
M155		5pf. green	6·75	6·25
M156		10pf. pink	6·75	5·50
M157		25pf. orange	65·00	18·00

1916. Surch **25Pf.**

M199		25pf. on 25pf. orange	5·50	1·40

M9

1916. Jubilee of King Wilhelm II.

M202	M9	2½pf. grey	2·20	2·10
M203	M9	7½pf. red	1·80	2·10
M204	M9	10pf. red	1·80	2·10
M205	M9	15pf. bistro	1·00	£10
M206	M9	20pf. blue	1·80	2·10
M207	M9	25pf. grey	5·50	2·10
M208	M9	50pf. brown	11·00	2·10

1919. Surch **2.**

M219	M5	2 on 2½pf. grey	1·10	70

1919. Optd **Volksstaat Wurttemberg**.

M222		2½pf. grey	55	80
M223		3pf. brown	17·00	80
M224		5pf. green	45	80
M225		7½pf. orange	1·40	80
M226		10pf. pink	45	80
M227		15pf. purple	45	80
M228		20pf. blue	55	80
M229		25pf. black and brown	55	80
M230		35pf. brown	5·50	80
M231		50pf. purple	7·75	80

MUNICIPAL SERVICE STAMPS

M14

1920

M245	M14	10pf. purple	2·00	2·30
M246	M14	15pf. brown	2·00	2·30
M247	M14	20pf. blue	2·00	2·30
M248	M14	30pf. green	2·00	2·30
M249	M14	50pf. yellow	2·20	2·30
M250	M14	75pf. bistre	4·50	2·30

1922. Surch in Marks.

M270	M5	5m. on 10pf. orange	35	80
M271	M5	10m. on 15pf. violet	35	80
M272	M5	12m. on 40pf. red	35	80
M273	M5	20m. on 10pf. orange	35	80
M274	M5	25m. on 20pf. green	35	80
M275	M5	40m. on 20pf. green	35	80
M276	M5	50m. on 60pf. green	35	80
M277	M5	60m. on 1m.25 green	35	80
M278	M5	100m. on 40pf. red	35	80
M279	M5	200m. on 2m. grey	35	80
M280	M5	300m. on 50pf. purple	35	80
M281	M5	400m. on 3m. brown	35	80

M282	M5	1000m. on 60pf. green	35	80
M283	M5	2000m. on 1m.25 grn	35	80

1923. Surch with new value (T=Tausend (thousand); M = Million; Md = Milliard).

M284	5T. on 10pf. orange	35	70
M285	20T. on 40pf. red	35	70
M286	50T. on 15pf. violet	1·10	70
M287	75T. on 2m. grey	2·20	70
M288	100T. on 20pf. green	35	70
M289	250T. on 3m. brown	35	70
M290	1M. on 60pf. green	1·70	70
M291	2M. on 50pf. purple	35	70
M292	5M. on 1m.25 green	35	70
M293	4Md. on 50pf. purple	5·50	70
M294	10Md. on 3m. brown	4·50	70

1923. Surch in figures only, representing gold pfennige.

M295	3pf. on 25pf. orange	60	45
M296	5pf. on 25pf. orange	60	45
M297	10pf. on 25pf. orange	60	45
M298	20pf. on 25pf. orange	60	45
M299	50pf. on 25pf. orange	80	45

OFFICIAL STAMPS

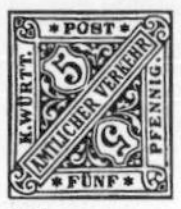
O5

1881

O181	O5	2pf. grey	65	45
O182	O5	2½pf. grey	80	70
O108	O5	3pf. green	33·00	6·50
O183	O5	3pf. brown	65	45
O112	O5	5pf. mauve	11·00	2·75
O184	O5	5pf. green	65	45
O185	O5	7½pf. orange	80	70
O186	O5	10pf. pink	65	45
O187	O5	15pf. brown	80	70
O188	O5	15pf. purple	1·70	60
O189	O5	20pf. blue	90	45
O117	O5	25pf. brown	50·00	9·25
O191	O5	25pf. orange	65	45
O192	O5	25pf. black and brown	55	55
O193	O5	30pf. black and orange	65	45
O194	O5	35pf. brown	2·20	4·75
O195	O5	40pf. black and red	65	45
O119	O5	50pf. green	9·00	13·00
O141	O5	50pf. brown	£325	£2500
O196	O5	50pf. purple	90	45
O120	O5	1m. yellow	£100	£275
O197	O5	1m. violet	3·25	60
O198	O5	1m. black and grey	3·25	1·20

1906. Centenary of Establishment of Kingdom. Optd **1806–1906** under crown.

O158	2pf. grey	39·00	29·00
O159	3pf. brown	7·75	80
O160	5pf. green	6·75	80
O161	10pf. pink	6·25	80
O162	20pf. blue	6·75	80
O163	25pf. orange	16·00	15·00
O164	30pf. black and orange	13·50	14·00
O165	40pf. black and red	50·00	20·00
O166	50pf. purple	45·00	20·00
O167	1m. violet	90·00	21·00

1916. Surch.

O200	25pf. on 25pf. orange	4·00	1·20
O201	50pf. on 50pf. purple	2·20	1·60

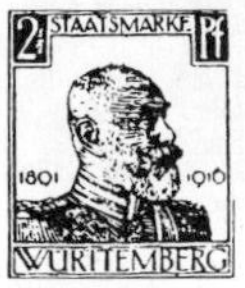
O10 King Wilhelm II

1916. Jubilee of King Wilhelm II.

O209	O10	2½pf. grey	1·10	1·30
O210	O10	7½pf. red	1·10	1·30
O211	O10	10pf. red	1·10	1·30
O212	O10	15pf. bistre	1·10	1·30
O213	O10	20pf. blue	1·10	1·30
O214	O10	25pf. grey	2·20	1·30
O215	O10	30pf. green	2·20	1·30
O216	O10	40pf. purple	3·25	1·30
O217	O10	50pf. brown	4·50	1·30
O218	O10	1m. mauve	4·50	1·30

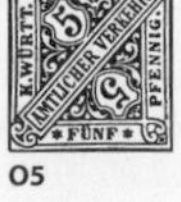
O5

1919. Surch in figures only.

O220	O5	2 on 2½pf. grey	2·20	2·10
O245	O5	75 on 3pf. brown (O183)	1·70	1·70

1919. Optd **Volksstaat Wurttemberg**.

O232	2½pf. grey	80	60
O233	3pf. brown	10·00	1·20
O234	5pf. green	55	55
O235	7½pf. orange	55	55
O236	10pf. pink	55	55
O237	15pf. purple	55	55
O238	20pf. blue	55	55
O239	25pf. black and brown	55	55
O240	30pf. black and orange	1·10	55
O241	35pf. brown	80	55
O242	40pf. black and red	80	55
O243	50pf. purple	1·10	95
O244	1m. black and green	1·10	1·10

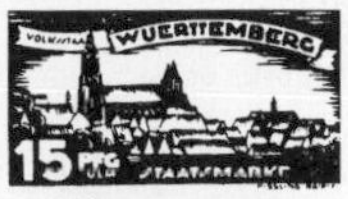
O16 Ulm

1920

O251	-	10pf. purple	80	1·80
O252	O16	15pf. brown	80	1·80
O253	-	20pf. blue	80	1·80
O254	-	30pf. green	80	1·80
O255	-	50pf. yellow	80	1·80
O256	O16	75pf. bistre	80	1·80
O257	-	1m. red	1·10	1·80
O258	-	1m.25 violet	1·10	1·80
O259	-	2m.50 blue	2·75	1·80
O260	-	3m. green	3·25	1·80

VIEWS: 10, 50pf., 2m.50, 3m. Stuttgart; 20pf., 1m. Tubingen; 30pf., 1m.25, Ellwangen.

Pt. 19

YEMEN

A Republic in S.W. Arabia, ruled as a kingdom and imamate until 1962. From 1962 stamps were issued concurrently by the Republican Government and the Royalists. The latter are listed after the Republican issues.

In 1990 the Yemen Arab Republic and Yemen People's Democratic Republic united (see YEMEN REPUBLIC (combined)).

1926. 40 bogaches = 1 imadi.
1964. 40 bogaches = 1 rial.
1975. 100 fils = 1 riyal.

KINGDOM

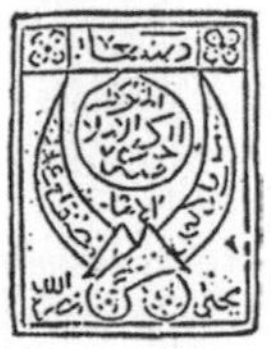
1 (2½b.)

1926. Imperf or perf.

1	1	2½b. black on white	90·00	90·00
2	1	2½b. black on orange	90·00	90·00
3	1	5b. black on white	90·00	90·00

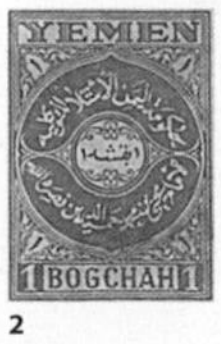
2

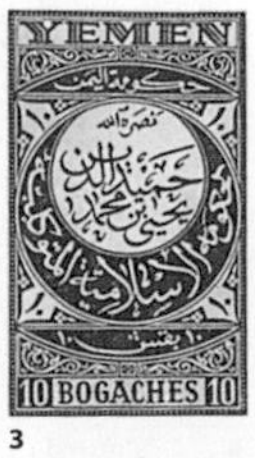
3

1930

10	2	½b. yellow	55	45
11	2	1b. green	60	50
5	2	2b. green	1·50	90
12	2	2b. brown	90	80
13	2	3b. lilac	1·10	90
14	2	4b. red	1·70	1·30
15	2	5b. grey	2·00	1·50
16	3	6b. blue	2·75	2·00
17	3	8b. purple	3·25	2·20
18	3	10b. brown	4·50	2·75
19	3	20b. green	13·50	11·00
9	3	1i. blue and brown	39·00	22·00
20	3	1i. green and purple	33·00	22·00

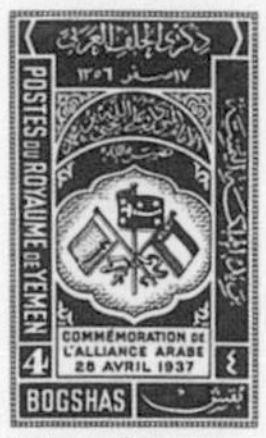
4 Flags of Saudi Arabia, Yemen and Iraq

1939. Second Anniv of Arab Alliance.

21	4	4b. blue and red	2·00	1·30
22	4	6b. ultramarine and blue	2·50	1·70
23	4	10b. blue and brown	3·25	2·75
24	4	14b. blue and green	5·50	5·25
25	4	20b. blue and green	7·75	6·75
26	4	1i. blue and purple	17·00	16·00

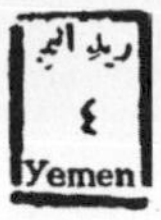
(6)

1939. Surch with T **6**.

27	2	4b. on ½b. yellow	22·00	22·00
65	2	4b. on 1b. green	4·00	1·70
66	2	4b. on 2b. brown	25·00	12·50
67	2	4b. on 3b. lilac	4·00	2·20
68	2	4b. on 5b. grey	4·00	2·20

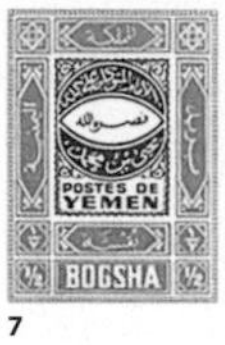
7

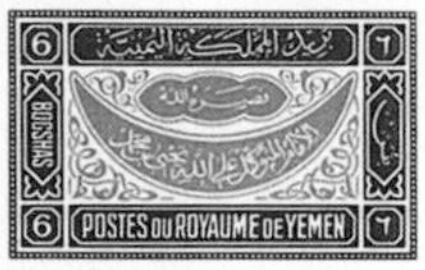
8

1940

28	7	½b. blue and orange	80	55
29	7	1b. red and green	85	55
30	7	2b. violet and bistre	90	55
31	7	3b. blue and mauve	95	55
32	7	4b. green and red	1·00	55
33	7	5b. bistre and green	1·10	65
34	8	6b. orange and blue	1·30	75
35	8	8b. blue and purple	1·70	1·10
36	8	10b. green and orange	2·00	1·30
37	8	14b. violet and green	2·50	1·70
38	8	18b. black and green	3·25	2·75
39	8	20b. purple and green	5·00	4·00
40	8	1i. red, green and purple	12·50	7·75

The 5b. (for which there had originally been no postal use) was released in 1957 to serve as 4b., without surcharge.

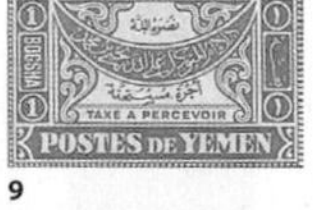
9

1942

41	9	1b. green and orange	55	35
42	9	2b. green and orange	85	45
43	9	4b. green and orange	1·00	80
44	9	6b. blue and orange	1·50	90
45	9	8b. blue and orange	2·00	1·30
46	9	10b. blue and orange	2·75	2·00
47	9	12b. blue and orange	2·50	2·50
48	9	20b. blue and orange	5·00	5·00

Although inscribed "TAXE A PERCEVOIR" these stamps were only used for ordinary postage purposes as there was no postage due system in Yemen.

1945. Surch with T **6**.

49a	7	4b. on ½b. blue and orange	3·75	1·50
50	7	4b. on 1b. red and green	6·75	7·75
51a	7	4b. on 2b. violet and bistre	3·75	3·75
52a	7	4b. on 3b. blue and mauve	3·75	3·75
53	7	4b. on 5b. bistre and green	7·75	9·00

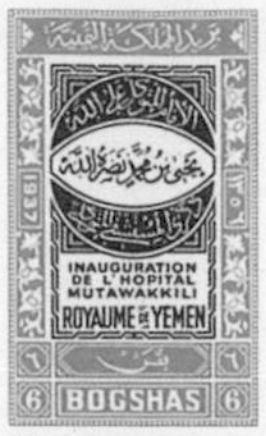
10

1949. Inauguration of Yemeni Hospital.

54	10	4b. black and green	2·50	2·00
55	10	6b. pink and green	4·25	3·50
56	10	10b. blue and green	5·50	4·50
57	10	14b. olive and green	10·00	7·75

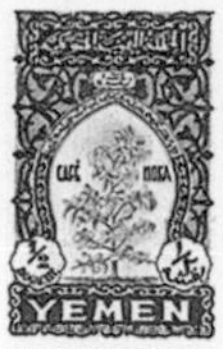
11 Coffee Plant

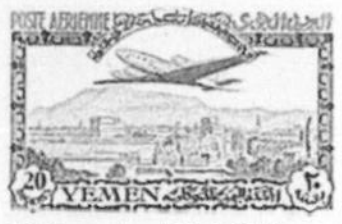
12 Douglas DC-4 Airliner over Sana'a

1947

58	11	½b. brown (postage)	55	45
59	11	1b. purple	1·10	90
60	11	2b. violet	2·20	1·70
61	-	4b. red	3·25	2·20
62	-	5b. blue	4·00	2·75
62a	11	6b. green	5·50	3·25
63	12	10b. blue (air)	11·00	5·50
64	12	20b. green	17·00	11·00

DESIGN—VERT: 4b., 5b. Palace, Sana'a.

The 5b. was put on sale in 1957 to serve as 4b., without surcharge.

1949. Surch as T **6** (size varies).

68a	11	4b. on ½b. brown	5·50	4·50
69a	11	4b. on 1b. purple	6·75	5·50
70b	11	4b. on 2b. blue	9·00	6·75

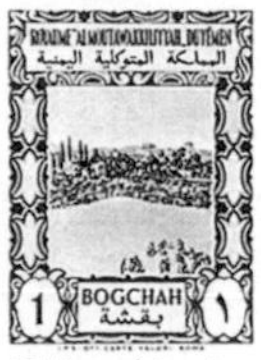
13 View of Sana'a Parade Ground

1951. (a) Postage.

71	13	1b. brown	65	35
72	13	2b. brown	1·30	65
73	13	3b. mauve	1·70	1·10
74	-	5b. red and blue	2·75	1·70
75	-	6b. red and purple	3·25	2·00
76	-	8b. green and blue	3·25	2·20
77	-	10b. purple	4·00	2·75
78	-	14b. green	5·00	4·00
79	-	20b. red	7·25	5·50
80	-	1i. violet	17·00	11·00

DESIGNS—HORIZ: 5b. Yemeni flag; 10b. Mosque, Sana'a; 14b. Walled city of Sana'a; 20b., 1i. Taiz and citadel. VERT: 6b. Eagle and Yemeni flag; 8b. Coffee plant.

(b) Air. With airplane.

81	6b. blue	2·20	1·70
82	8b. brown	2·75	2·20
83	10b. green	3·25	2·75
84	12b. blue	4·00	3·25
85	16b. purple	5·00	4·00
86	20b. orange	6·25	4·50
87	1i. red	16·00	9·00

DESIGNS—HORIZ: 6b., 8b. Sana'a; 10b. Trees; 16b. Taiz Palace. VERT: 12b. Palace of the Rock, Wadi Dhahr; 20b. Crowd of people; 1i. Land-scape.

The 5b. postage stamp was released in 1956 to serve as 4b. without surcharge and it was again put on sale as 8b. in 1957. The 6b. and 8b. air stamps were released in 1957 to serve as ordinary postage stamps.

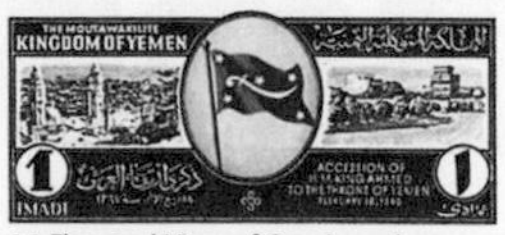
14 Flag and View of Sana'a and Hodeida

1952. Fourth Anniv of Accession of King Ahmed. Flag in red. Perf or imperf.

88	14	1i. black and lake (postage)	22·00	17·00
89	14	1i. blue and brown (air)	22·00	17·00

1952. Fourth Anniv of Victory. As T **14** but inscr **"COMMEMORATION OF VICTORY"**. Flag in red. Perf or imperf.

90	30b. green and red (postage)	17·00	13·50
91	30b. blue and green (air)	17·00	13·50

1952. Surch as T **6**.

91a	**13**	4b. on 1b. brown	17·00	11·00
92	**13**	4b. on 2b. brown	17·00	14·50
93	**13**	4b. on 3b. mauve	19·00	22·00

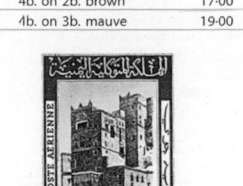

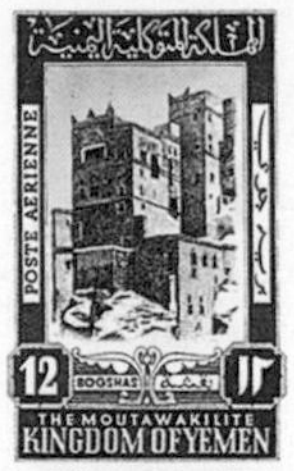
POSTE AERIENNE
12
THE MOUTAWAKILITE
KINGDOM OF YEMEN
15 Palace of the Rock, Wadi Dhahr

1952. Sky in blue. Perf or imperf.

94	**15**	12b. green & brn (postage)	11·00	9·00
95	-	20b. brown and red	16·00	13·50
96	**15**	12b. brown and green (air)	13·50	11·00
97	-	20b. brown and blue	13·50	11·00

DESIGN: 20b. (2), Walls of Ibb.

1953. Surch as T **6**.

98	**9**	4b. on 1b. green and orange	17·00	13·50
99	**9**	4b. on 2b. green and orange	17·00	13·50

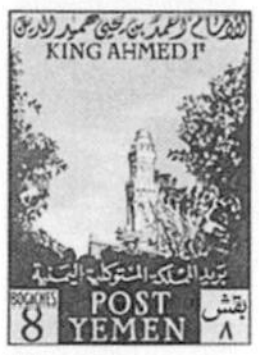
KING AHMED I
POST
YEMEN
8
16

1953

100	**16**	4b. orange (postage)	2·20	1·70
101	**16**	6b. blue	3·25	2·20
102	**16**	8b. green	4·50	2·75
103	**16**	[illegible] (air)	[illegible]	3·25
104	**16**	12b. blue	6·75	4·50
105	**16**	20b. brown	11·00	5·50

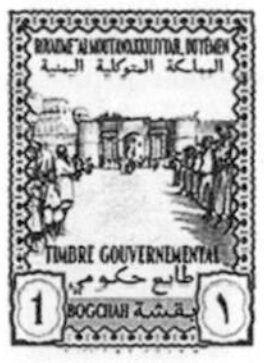
TIMBRE GOUVERNEMENTAL
BOGCHAH
16a Bab al-Yemen Gate, Sana'a

1956. Unissued official stamps issued for ordinary postal use without surch.

105a	**16a**	1b. brown	1·70	6·75
105b	**16a**	5b. blue	2·00	5·50
105c	**16a**	10b. blue	2·50	5·75

The 1 and 5b. were each sold for use as 4b. and the 10b. as 10b. for inland registered post.

1957. Arab Postal Union. As T **96a** of Syria but inscr "YEMEN" at top and inscriptions in English.

106	4b. brown	3·25	2·20
107	6b. green	4·00	2·75
108	16b. violet	7·25	6·25

1959. First Anniv of Proclamation of United Arab States (U.A.R. and Yemen). As T **139a** of Syria.

109	1b. black and red (postage)	55	45
110	2b. black and green	80	55
111	4b. red and green	1·10	90
112	6b. black and orange (air)	1·70	1·10
113	10b. black and red	2·75	2·20
114	16b. red and violet	4·50	3·25

1959. Arab Telecommunications Union. As T **138a** of Syria.

115	4b. red	2·75	1·80

1959. Inauguration of Automatic Telephone, Sana'a. Optd **AUTOMATIC TELEPHONE INAUGURATION SANAA MARCH 1959** in English and Arabic.

116	**3**	6b. blue	1·80	1·30
117	**3**	8b. red	2·20	1·70
118	**3**	10b. brown	3·25	2·75
119	**3**	20b. green	6·75	4·50
120	**3**	1i. green and red	9·00	6·75

1960. Air. Optd with Douglas DC-4 airliner and **AIR MAIL 1959** in English and Arabic.

121	6b. blue	2·75	2·20
122	10b. brown	4·50	3·25

1960. Inaug of Arab League Centre, Cairo. As T **154a** of Syria but with different arms.

123	4b. black and green	1·50	1·50

IMPERF STAMPS. From this point many issues also exist imperf. This applies also to Republican and Royalist issues.

1960. World Refugee Year. As T **155a** of Syria.

124	4b. brown	1·80	1·80
125	6b. green	3·00	3·00
MS125a 103×85 mm. Nos. 124/5 in new colours. Imperf		65·00	65·00

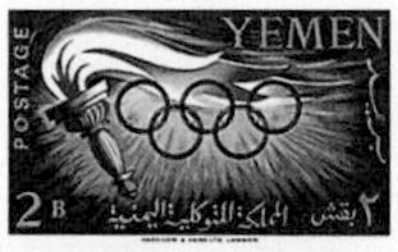
YEMEN
POSTAGE
2B
19 Olympic Torch

1960. Olympic Games, Rome.

126	**19**	2b. red and black	90	90
127	**19**	4b. yellow and black	1·30	1·30
128	**19**	6b. orange and black	1·90	1·90
129	**19**	8b. green and brown	3·25	3·25
130	**19**	20b. orange and violet	7·75	7·75
MS130a 100×60 mm. No. 127. Imperf			£130	£130

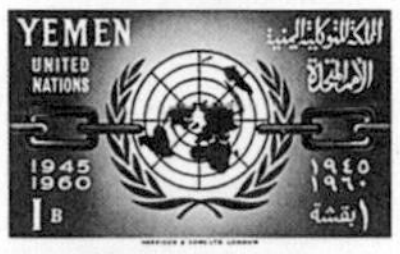
YEMEN
UNITED NATIONS
1945
1960
1B
20 U.N. Emblem

1961. 15th Anniv of U.N.O.

131	**20**	1b. violet	55	45
132	**20**	2b. green	65	55
133	**20**	3b. blue	80	65
134	**20**	4b. blue	90	80
135	**20**	6b. purple	1·10	90
136	**20**	14b. red	1·70	1·30
137	**20**	20b. brown	2·75	2·20
MS137a 100×60 mm. No. 134. Imperf			33·00	39·00

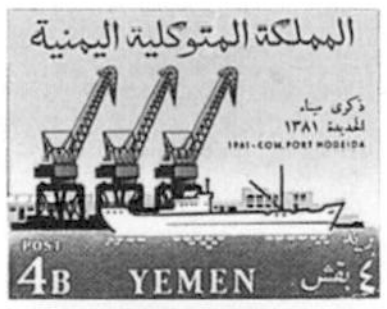
المملكة المتوكلية اليمنية
4B
YEMEN
21 Hodeida Port and Freighter

1961. Inauguration of Hodeida Port.

138	**21**	4b. multicoloured	1·30	1·10
139	**21**	6b. multicoloured	2·20	1·80
140	**21**	16b. multicoloured	4·50	4·50
MS140a 160×130 mm. Nos. 138/40. Imperf			9·00	9·00

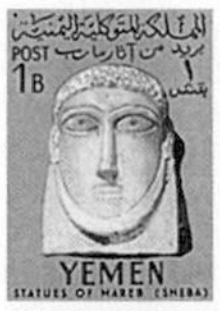
POST
1B
YEMEN
STATUES OF MAREB
22 Alabaster Death-mask

1961. Statues of Marib.

141	1b. black and orange (postage)	55	35
142	2b. black and violet	90	45
143	4b. black and brown	1·20	55
144	8b. black and mauve	1·50	90
145	10b. black and yellow	2·50	1·10
146	12b. black and blue	3·00	1·30
147	20b. black and grey	3·50	2·20
148	1i. black and green	7·25	2·75
149	6b. black and green (air)	1·50	65
150	16b. black and blue	4·00	2·00

DESIGNS: 1b. Type **22**; 2b. Horned head (8th- century B.C. frieze, Temple of the Moon God); 4b. Bronze head of Himyaritic emperor of 1st or 2nd century; 6b. "Throne of Bilqis" (8th-century B.C. limestone columns, Moon God Temple); 8b. Bronze figure of Himyaritic Emperor Dhamar Ali, 2nd or 3rd century; 10b. Alabaster statuette of 2nd or 3rd-century child; 12b. Entrance to Moon God Temple; 16b. Control tower and spillway, Marib dam; 20b. 1st-century alabaster relief of boy with dagger riding legendary monster, Moon God Temple; 1i. 1st-century alabaster relief of woman with grapes, Moon God Temple.

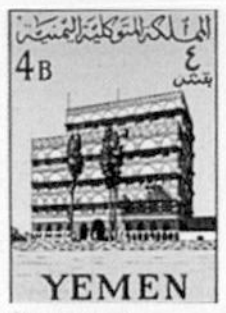
4B
YEMEN
23 Imam's Palace, Sana'a

1961. Yemeni Buildings.

151	4b. black, grn & turq (postage)	55	55
152	8b. black, green and mauve	1·10	1·10
153	10b. black, green and orange	1·30	1·30
154	6b. black, green and blue (air)	90	90
155	16b. black, green and pink	2·20	2·20

DESIGNS—VERT: 4b. Type **23**; 10b. Palace of the Rock, Wadi Dhahr; 16b. Palace of the Rock (different view). HORIZ: 6b. Bab al-Yemen Gate, Sana'a; 8b. Imam's Palace, Sana'a (different view).

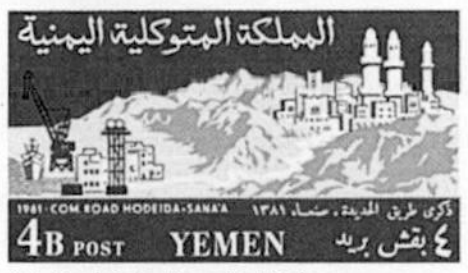
المملكة المتوكلية اليمنية
4B POST YEMEN
24 Hodeida–Sana'a Highway

1961. Inaug of Hodeida–Sana'a Highway.

156	**24**	4b. multicoloured	1·20	90
157	**24**	6b. multicoloured	1·60	1·50
158	**24**	10b. multicoloured	2·50	1·70
MS158a 160×130 mm. Nos. 156/8. Imperf			11·00	11·00

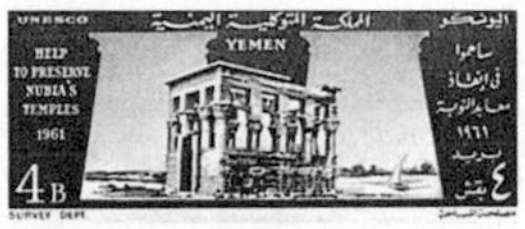
UNESCO
YEMEN
HELP TO PRESERVE NUBIA'S TEMPLES
1961
4B
25 Nubian Temple

1962. UNESCO. Campaign for Preservation of Nubian Monuments.

159	**25**	4b. brown	5·50	4·50
160	**25**	6b. green	10·00	5·50
MS160a 111×90 mm. Nos. 159/60. Imperf			20·00	20·00

1962. Arab League Week. As T **178** of Syria.

161	4b. green	1·10	90
162	6b. blue	1·30	1·10
MS162a 95×80 mm. Nos. 161/2. Imperf		5·50	5·50

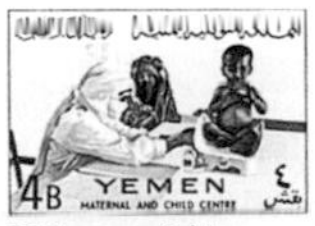
4B
YEMEN
26 Nurse weighing Child

1962. Maternity and Child Centre. Multicoloured.

163	2b. Putting child to bed	1·00	80
164	4b. Type **26**	1·30	1·00
165	6b. Taking child's temperature	1·70	1·20
166	10b. Weighing baby	2·75	1·70

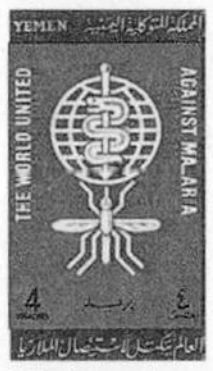
YEMEN
THE WORLD UNITED
AGAINST MALARIA
4
26a Campaign Emblem

1962. Malaria Eradication.

167	**26a**	4b. orange and black	1·10	1·10
168	-	6b. green and brown	1·70	1·70
MS168a 95×80 mm. Nos. 167/8. Imperf			22·00	22·00

DESIGN: 6b. As T **26a** but with laurel and inscription around emblem.

1962. 17th Anniv of U.N.O. Nos. 131/7 optd **1945-1962** in English and Arabic with bars over old dates.

169	**20**	1b. violet	2·20	2·20
170	**20**	2b. green	2·20	2·20
171	**20**	3b. blue	2·20	2·20
172	**20**	4b. blue	2·20	2·20
173	**20**	6b. purple	2·20	2·20
174	**20**	14b. red	2·20	2·20
175	**20**	20b. brown	2·20	2·20

REPUBLIC

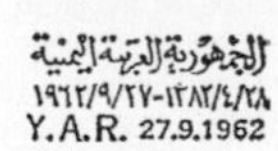
الجمهورية العربية اليمنية
١٩٦٢/٩/٢٧-١٣٨٢/٤/٢٨
Y.A.R. 27.9.1962
(28)

1963. Various issues optd as T **28**. (a) Nos. 141/50.

176	1b. black and orange (postage)	20	20
177	2b. black and violet	35	35
178	4b. black and brown	65	65
179	8b. black and mauve	90	90
180	10b. black and yellow	1·10	1·10
181	12b. black and blue	1·70	1·70
182	20b. black and grey	2·20	2·20
183	1i. black and green	3·00	3·00
184	6b. black and turquoise (air)	3·25	3·25
185	16b. black and blue	9·00	9·00

(b) Nos. 151/5.

186	4b. black, grn & turq (postage)	90	90
187	8b. black, green and mauve	1·70	1·70
188	10b. black, green and orange	2·75	2·75
189	6b. black, green and blue (air)	1·30	1·30
190	16b. black, green and pink	4·50	4·50

(c) Nos. 163/6.

191	2b. multicoloured	65	65
192	4b. multicoloured	90	90
193	6b. multicoloured	1·10	1·10
194	10b. multicoloured	2·75	2·75

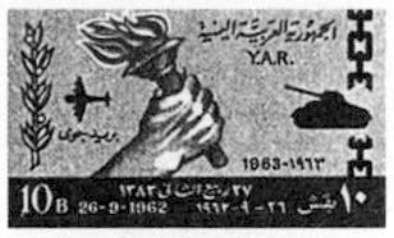
Y.A.R.
1963-1913
10B 26-9-1962
29 "Torch of Freedom"

1963. "Proclamation of Republic".

195	-	4b. brown & mauve (postage)	90	90
196	-	6b. red and blue	1·30	1·30
197	-	8b. black and purple (air)	2·20	2·20
198	**29**	10b. red and violet	3·25	3·25
199	-	16b. red and green	4·50	4·50
MS199a Two sheets each 165×140 mm. Nos. 195/6 and 199 in new colours. Imperf			25·00	25·00

DESIGNS—VERT: 4b. Soldier with flag; 6b. Tank and flag; 8b. Bayonet and torch. HORIZ: 16b. Flag and torch.

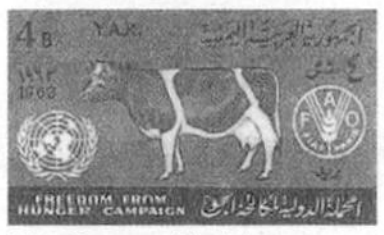
Y.A.R.
FREEDOM FROM HUNGER CAMPAIGN
29a Cow and Emblem

1963. Freedom from Hunger.

200	**29a**	[illegible]	[illegible]	1·10
201	-	6b. yellow and violet	1·50	1·30
MS201a 110×120 mm. Nos. 200/1. Imperf			22·00	22·00

DESIGN: 6b. Corn-cob and ear of wheat.

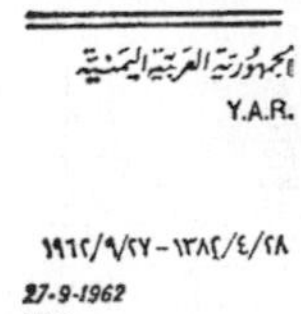
Y.A.R.
١٩٦٢/٩/٢٧-١٣٨٢/٤/٢٨
27-9-1962
(30)

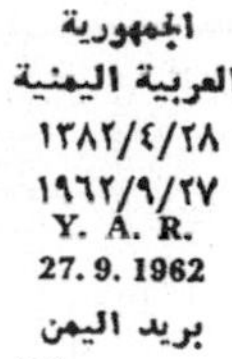
الجمهورية
العربية اليمنية
١٣٨٢/٤/٢٨
١٩٦٢/٩/٢٧
Y. A. R.
27. 9. 1962
بريد اليمن
(31)

1963. Various issues optd. (a) With T **30**. On Nos. 161/2.

202	4b. green	11·00	11·00
203	6b. blue	11·00	11·00

(b) With T **31**.

207	**2**	5b. grey	2·20	2·20
204	**3**	6b. blue	2·75	2·75
208	**3**	8b. purple	3·25	3·25
205	**3**	10b. brown	4·00	4·00
210	**3**	20b. green	4·50	4·50
206	**3**	1i. blue and brown	11·00	11·00
211	**3**	1i. green and purple	8·25	8·25

(c) As T **31** but with lowest line of inscription at top.

212	**10**	6b. pink and green	2·75	2·75
213	**10**	10b. blue and green	4·00	4·00
214	**10**	14b. olive and green	11·00	11·00

(d) As T **31** but with lowest line of inscription omitted and bar at top. On Nos. 167/8.

215	4b. orange and black	4·50	4·50
216	6b. green and brown	6·75	6·75

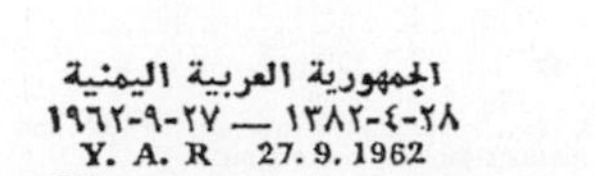
الجمهورية العربية اليمنية
١٩٦٢-٩-٢٧ — ١٣٨٢-٤-٢٨
Y. A. R 27. 9. 1962
(32)

(e) With T **32**. (i) On Nos. 139/40.

217	**21**	6b. multicoloured	2·75	2·75
218	**21**	16b. multicoloured	4·00	4·00
MS218a Sheet No. **MS**140a optd on each stamp			22·00	22·00

(ii) On Nos. 157/8.

219	24	6b. multicoloured	2·75	2·75
220	24	10b. multicoloured	4·00	4·00

(f) As T **32** but with only one bar over old inscription.

(i) Nos. 126/8.

221	19	2b. red and black	7·75	7·75
222	19	4b. yellow and black	7·75	7·75
223	19	6b. orange and black	7·75	7·75

(ii) Nos. 159/60.

224	25	4b. brown	9·00	9·00
225	25	6b. green	13·50	13·50

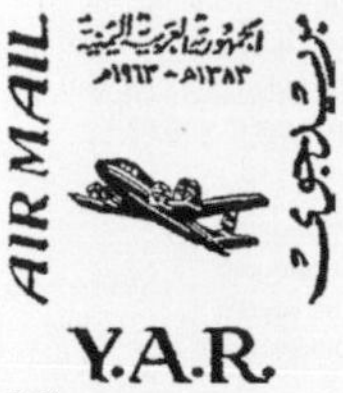

(34)

(g) Air. With T **34**.

226	4	6b. ultramarine and blue	2·20	2·20
227	4	10b. blue and brown	2·75	2·75
228	4	14b. blue and green	3·25	3·25
229	4	20b. blue and green	4·50	4·50
230	4	1i. blue and purple	9·50	9·50

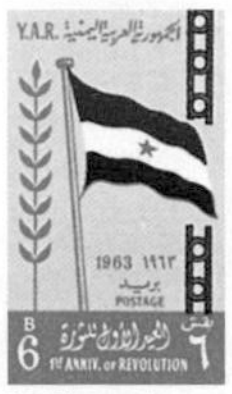

35 Flag and Laurel Sprig

1963. First Anniv of Revolution.

231	-	2b. red, green and black	55	45
232	-	4b. red, black and green	90	65
233	35	6b. red, black and green	1·50	1·10
MS233a 150×90 mm. Nos. 231/3. Imperf			7·75	7·75

DESIGNS—HORIZ: 4b. Flag, torch and broken chain. VERT: 2b. Flag, torch and candle.

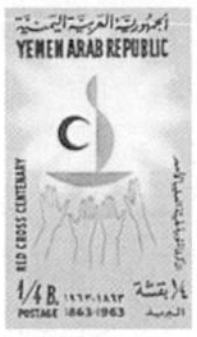

36 Hands reaching for Centenary Emblem

1963. Red Cross Centenary. Crescent red; inscription black.

234	36	¼b. blue	65	65
235	36	½b. brown	75	75
236	36	½b. grey	90	90
237	-	4b. lilac	1·10	1·10
238	-	8b. stone	2·20	2·20
239	-	20b. green	5·50	5·50
MS239a 100×75 mm. Nos. 237/8. Imperf			17·00	17·00

DESIGN: 4b. to 20b. Centenary emblem.

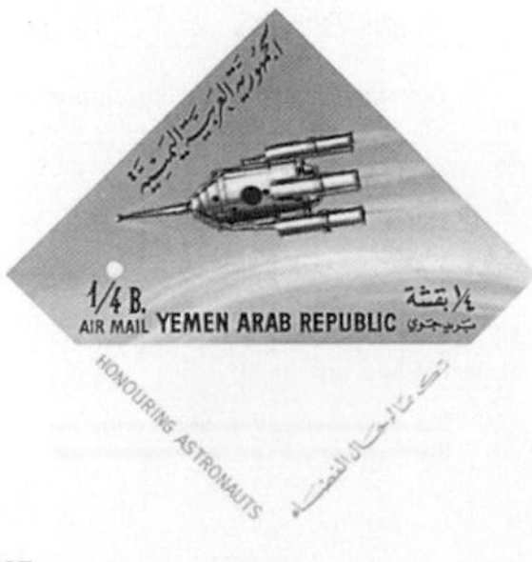

37

1963. Air. "Honouring Astronauts". T **37** and similar designs showing rockets, etc.

240	37	¼b. multicoloured	1·30	1·10
241	-	½b. multicoloured	1·30	1·10
242	-	½b. multicoloured	1·30	1·10
243	-	4b. multicoloured	2·75	2·20
244	-	20b. multicoloured	10·00	9·00
MS244a 90×100 mm. No. 244. Imperf			13·50	13·50

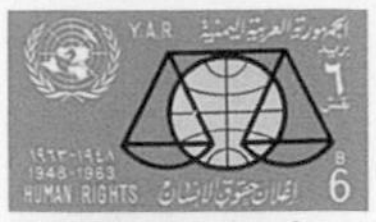

38 Globe and Scales of Justice

1963. 15th Anniv of Declaration of Human Rights.

245		4b. black, orange and lilac	90	90
246	38	6b. black, green & turquoise	1·10	1·10
MS246a 78×93 mm. Nos. 245/6. Imperf			17·00	17·00

DESIGN: 4b. As Type **38** but differently arranged.

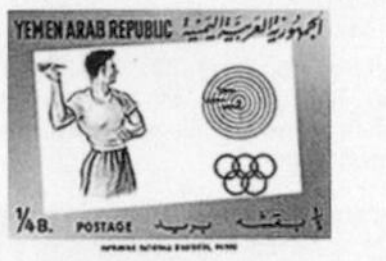

39 Darts

1964. Olympic Games, Tokyo (1st issue).

247		¼b. green, brown and orange (postage)	20	20
248		½b. brown, blue and violet	20	20
249		½b. brown, blue and mauve	20	20
250		1b. brown, green and blue	90	55
251		1½b. red, brown and grey	1·10	55
252		4b. brown, black and blue (air)	1·10	80
253		20b. blue, deep blue and brown	3·25	2·75
254		1r. red, brown and green	10·00	7·75
MS254a Two sheets each 90×70 mm. Nos. 252 and 253. Imperf			18·00	18·00

DESIGNS—HORIZ: ¼b. Type **39**;½b. Table tennis; 4b. Horse-racing; 20b. Pole vaulting. VERT: ½b. Running; 1b. Volleyball; 1½b. Football; 1r. Basketball. All designs include the Olympic "Rings" symbol.

See also Nos. 272/**MS**280a.

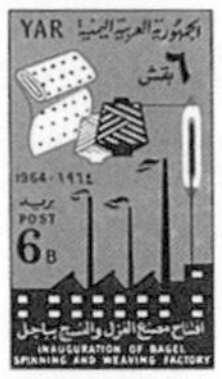

40 Factory, Bobbins and Cloth

1964. Inauguration of Bagel Spinning and Weaving Factory.

255	-	2b. blue & yellow (postage)	45	20
256	-	4b. blue and yellow	65	45
257	40	6b. green and brown	90	55
258	-	16b. orange, blue and grey (air)	2·50	2·20
MS258a 76×61 mm. No. 258. Imperf			6·75	6·75

DESIGNS—VERT: 2b. Factory, bobbins and cloth (different); 4b. Loom. HORIZ: 16b. Factory and lengths of cloth.

1964. Air. President Kennedy Memorial Issue. Nos. 240/2 optd **JOHN F. KENNEDY 1917 1963** in English and Arabic and with portrait and laurel.

259	37	¼b. multicoloured	2·20	2·20
260	-	½b. multicoloured	2·20	2·20
261	-	½b. multicoloured	2·20	2·20
MS261a Sheet No. **MS**244a optd			65·00	65·00

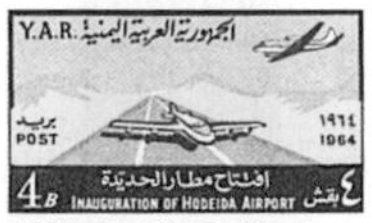

42 Boeing 707 on Runway

1964. Inauguration of Hodeida Airport.

262	42	4b. yellow and blue	65	55
263	-	6b. green and blue	90	80
264	-	10b. blue, yellow & dp blue	1·20	90
MS264a 72×62 mm. No. 264. Imperf			5·50	5·50

DESIGNS: 6b. Control tower and Boeing 707 on runway; 10b. Control tower, Boeing 707 and ship.

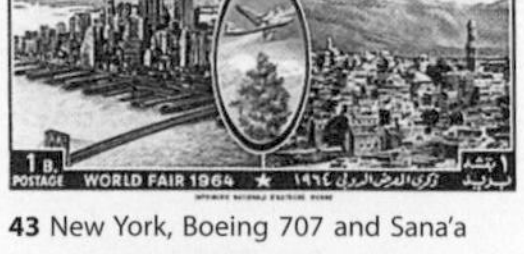

43 New York, Boeing 707 and Sana'a

1964. New York World's Fair.

265	43	¼b. brn, bl & grn (postage)	45	20
266	-	½b. black, red and green	65	20
267	-	½b. green, red and blue	90	45
268	43	1b. indigo, blue and green	1·10	55
269	-	4b. blue, red and green	2·00	1·30
270	-	16b. brown, red & blue (air)	4·50	3·00
271	43	20b. purple, blue and green	5·50	4·00
MS271a 100×70 mm. No. 271. Imperf			9·00	9·00

DESIGNS:½b., 4b. Flag, Empire State Building, New York, and Mosque, Sana'a; ½b., 16b. Statue of Liberty, New York, liner and Harbour, Hodeida.

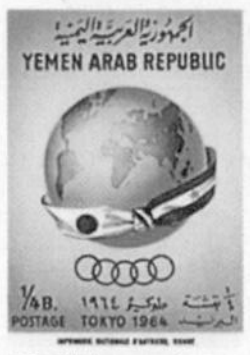

44 Globe and Flags

1964. Olympic Games, Tokyo (2nd issue). Multicoloured.

272		¼b. Type **44** (postage)	20	20
273		½b. Olympic Torch	35	30
274		½b. Discus-thrower	45	35
275		1b. Yemeni flag	55	35
276		1½b. Swimming (horiz)	65	40
277		4b. Swimming (horiz) (air)	1·10	55
278		6b. Olympic Torch	1·70	65
279		12b. Type **44**	3·25	1·10
280		20b. Discus-thrower	5·50	2·20
MS280a 70×90 mm. No. 280. Imperf			13·50	13·50

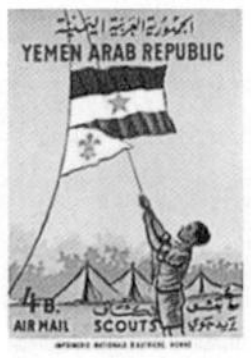

45 Scout hoisting Flag

1964. Yemeni Scouts. Multicoloured.

281		¼b. Type **45** (postage)	20	20
282		½b. Scout badge and scouts guarding camp	20	20
283		½b. Bugler	20	20
284		1b. As No. 282	45	35
285		1½b. Scouts by camp-fire	65	45
286		4b. Type **45** (air)	80	50
287		6b. As No. 282	90	55
288		16b. Bugler	1·60	1·10
289		20b. Scouts by camp-fire	3·00	2·20
MS289a Two sheets each 70×90 mm. Nos. 288/9. Perf or imperf			14·50	14·50

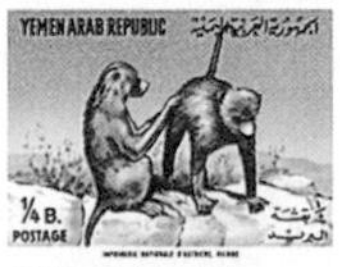

46 Hamadryas Baboons

1964. Animals.

290	46	¼b. brown & lilac (postage)	20	20
291	-	½b. brown and blue	20	20
292	-	½b. brown and orange	35	30
293	-	1b. brown and blue	45	35
294	-	1½b. brown and blue	55	40
295	-	4b. red and green (air)	1·10	55
296	-	12b. brown and buff	2·75	1·70
297	-	20b. brown and blue	5·50	2·20

ANIMALS:½b. Arab horses; ½, 12b. Bullock; 1, 20b. Lion and lioness; 1½, 4b. Mountain gazelles.

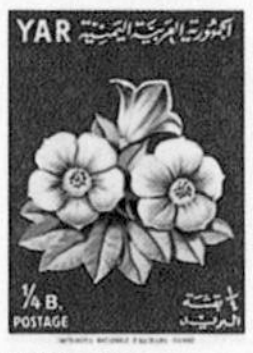

47 Gentian

1964. Flowers. Multicoloured.

298		¼b. Type **47** (postage)	20	20
299		½b. Lily	20	20
300		½b. Poinsettia	35	30
301		1b. Rose	55	35
302		1½b. Viburnum	80	45
303		4b. Rose (air)	1·10	55
304		12b. Poinsettia	2·75	1·10
305		20b. Viburnum	5·50	2·75

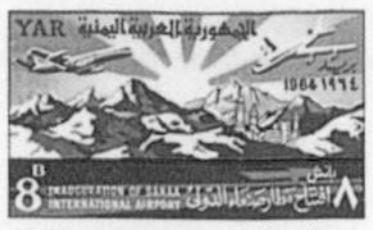

48 Boeing 707 and Hawker Siddeley Comet 4 Airliners over Mountains

1964. Inauguration of Sana'a Int Airport.

306	48	1b. brown & blue (postage)	55	55
307	-	2b. brown and blue	55	55
308	-	4b. brown and blue	55	55
309	48	8b. brown and blue	1·10	1·10
310	-	6b. brown and blue (air)	1·10	1·10
MS310a 120×70 mm. Nos. 308 and 310. Imperf			6·75	6·75

DESIGNS: 2b., 4b. Boeing 707 and Vickers Viscount 800 airliners over runway; 6b. Hawker Siddeley Comet 4 airliners in flight and on ground.

49 A.P.U. Emblem

1964. Tenth Anniv of Arab Postal Union's Permanent Office, Cairo.

311	49	4b. black, red and orange (postage)	1·20	1·00
312	49	6b. black, green and turquoise (air)	1·60	1·20
MS312a 77×97 mm. No. 312. Imperf			4·50	4·50

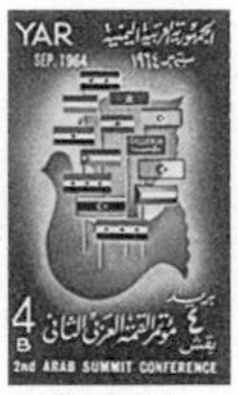

50 Flags and Dove

1964. Second Arab Summit Conference.

313	50	4b. green	1·20	1·00
314	-	6b. brown	1·60	1·20
MS314a 80×130 mm. No. 313/14. Imperf			4·50	4·50

DESIGN: 6b. Arms within conference emblem and map.

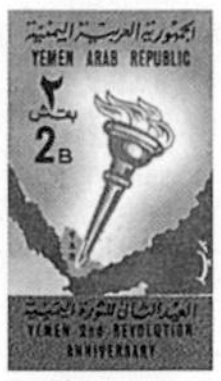

51 Flaming Torch

1964. Second Anniv of Revolution.

315	51	2b. brown and blue	55	45
316	-	4b. green and yellow	1·10	80
317	-	6b. pink, red and green	1·10	80
MS317a 102×80 mm. No. 317. Imperf			4·50	4·50

DESIGNS: 4b. Yemeni soldier; 6b. Candles on map.

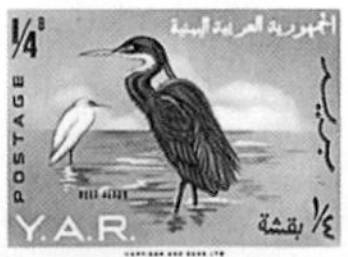

52 Western Reef Heron ("Reef Heron") and Little Egret

1965. Birds. Multicoloured.

318		¼b. Type **52** (postage)	45	20
319		½b. Arabian chukar (inscr "Arabian red-legged partridge")	55	20
320		¾b. Desert eagle owl ("Eagle Owl") (vert)	60	30
321		1b. Hammerkop	90	35
322		1½b. Yemeni linnets	1·10	55
323		4b. Hoopoes	2·20	1·10
324		6b. Violet starlings (air)	2·75	1·30
325		8b. Waldrapp (inscr "Bald ibis") (vert)	3·25	1·70
326		12b. Arabian woodpecker (vert)	4·50	2·20
327		20b. Bateleur (vert)	7·75	3·25
328		1r. Yellow-bellied ("Bruce's") green pigeon	16·00	5·50
MS328a 76×60 mm. 20b. in design of 1½b. Imperf			39·00	28·00

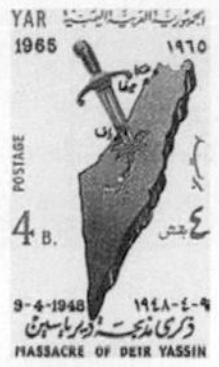
YAR
1965
POSTAGE
MASSACRE OF DEIR YASSIN
52a Dagger on Deir Yassin, Palestine

1965. Deir Yassin Massacre.

329	**52a**	4b. purple and blue (postage)	1·20	65
330	**52a**	6b. red and orange (air)	1·60	90

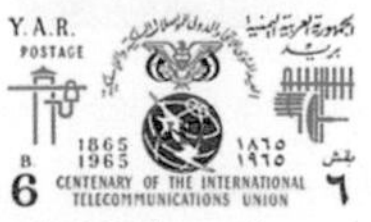
Y.A.R.
POSTAGE
CENTENARY OF THE INTERNATIONAL TELECOMMUNICATIONS UNION
53 I.T.U. Emblem and Symbols

1965. I.T.U. Centenary.

331	-	4b. red and blue	1·10	80
332	**53**	6b. green and red	1·30	90
MS332a 106×67 mm. No. 332			6·75	5·50

DESIGN—VERT: 4b. As Type **53** but rearranged.

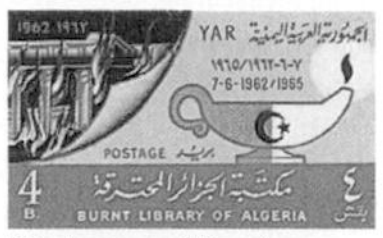
POSTAGE
BURNT LIBRARY OF ALGERIA
53a Lamp and Burning Library

1965. Burning of Algiers Library.

333	**53a**	4b. green, red and black (postage)	1·10	80
334	**53a**	6b. blue, red and deep red (air)	1·30	90
MS334a 75×65 mm. No. 334			4·00	2·75

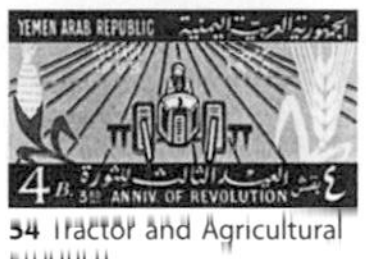
YEMEN ARAB REPUBLIC
3rd ANNIV. OF REVOLUTION
54 Tractor and Agricultural Produce

1965. Third Anniv of Revolution.

335	**54**	4b. blue and yellow	1·10	80
336	-	6b. blue and yellow	1·30	90
MS336a 81×72 mm. No. 336. Imperf			4·50	4·00

DESIGN: 6b. Tractor and landscape.

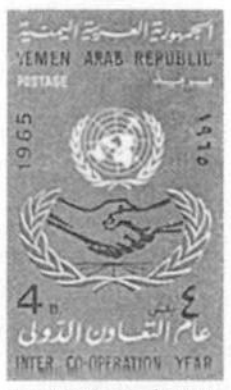
YEMEN ARAB REPUBLIC
INTER. CO-OPERATION YEAR
55 I.C.Y. and U.N. Emblems

1965. International Co-operation Year.

337	**55**	4b. green and orange	1·20	90
338	-	6b. brown and blue	1·70	1·00
MS338a 71×80 mm. No. 338. Imperf			5·50	4·50

DESIGN: 6b. U.N. Headquarters and General Assembly Building, New York.

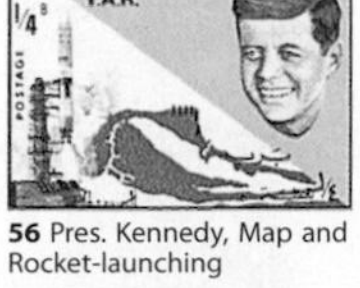
Y.A.R.
56 Pres. Kennedy, Map and Rocket-launching

1965. Pres. Kennedy Commem. Designs each include portrait of Pres. Kennedy. Multicoloured.

339	¼b. Type **56** (postage)	45	20
340	¼b. Rocket gantries	45	20
341	¼b. Rocket	45	20
342	⅓b. Type **56**	45	20
343	½b. Rocket	45	20
344	4b. Capsule and U.S. flag	1·20	1·00
345	8b. Capsule in ocean (air)	2·75	2·00
346	12b. Rocket gantries	5·25	3·25
MS346a Two sheets each 90×80 mm. Nos. 344 and 345. Imperf		17·00	17·00

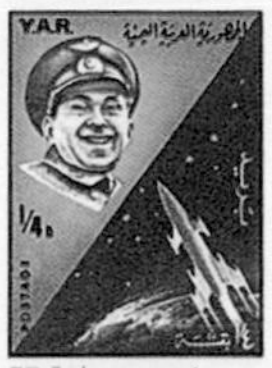
Y.A.R.
57 Belyaev and Rocket

1965. Space Achievements. Multicoloured.

347	¼b. Type **57** (postage)	20	10
348	¼b. Leonov and rocket	20	10
349	¼b. Scott and capsule	20	10
350	⅓b. Carpenter and rocket gantry	20	10
351	½b. Scott and capsule	20	10
352	4b. Leonov and rocket (air)	1·60	1·10
353	8b. Type **57**	3·00	2·20
354	16b. Carpenter and rocket gantry	5·50	4·50
MS355 90×80 mm. 16b. black, cobalt and blue (Scott and Carpenter, and astronaut filming in space). Imperf		17·00	13·50

1966. Anti T.B. Campaign. Nos. 200/1 optd **Tuberculous Campaign 1965** in English and Arabic.

356	4b. brown and red	1·70	1·10
357	6b. yellow and violet	2·75	1·70
MS358 110×120 mm. No. 356/7. Imperf		17·00	17·00

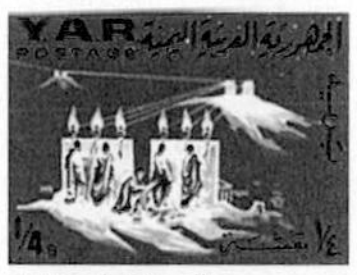
YAR
POSTAGE
59 Torch Signalling

1966. Telecommunications.

359	**59**	¼b. black and red (postage)	35	20
360	-	¼b. black and blue	35	20
361	-	¼b. black and brown	35	20
362	-	⅓b. black and red	35	20
363	-	½b. black and blue	35	20
364	-	4b. black and green (air)	1·00	55
365	-	6b. black and brown	1·60	1·10
366	-	20b. black and blue	5·00	4·50
MS367 90×70 mm. No. 366. Imperf			11·00	5·50

DESIGNS: No. 360, Morse telegraphy; 361, Early telephone; 362, Wireless telegraphy; 363, Television; 364, Radar; 365, Telex; 366, "Early Bird" Satellite.

1966. Prevention of Cruelty to Animals. Nos. 318/20 optd **Prevention of Cruelty to Animals** in English and Arabic.

368	**52**	¼b. multicoloured	90	55
369	-	½b. multicoloured	80	65
370	-	¾b. multicoloured	2·10	1·00
MS370a 76×60 mm. 20b. multicoloured. Imperf			13·50	11·00

1966. Third Arab Summit Conference Nos. 313/14 optd **3rd. Arab Summit Conference 1965** in English and Arabic.

371	**50**	4b. green	1·10	80
372	-	6b. brown	1·30	90
MS373 Sheet No. **MS**314a optd on each stamp			6·75	6·75

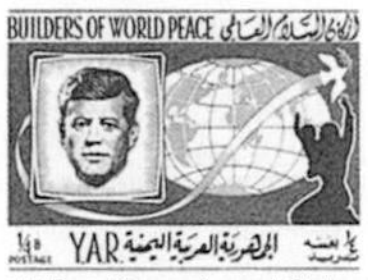
BUILDERS OF WORLD PEACE
YAR
62 Pres. Kennedy and Globe

1966. "Builders of World Peace". (a) Postage. Size 39×28½ mm.

374	**62**	¼b. brown	20	20
375	-	¼b. green	20	20
376	-	¼b. blue	20	20
377	-	⅓b. brown	35	20
378	-	½b. purple	35	20
379	**62**	4b. purple	1·10	55
MS380 90×70 mm. 4b. purple (portraits only as in Nos. 374/6). Imperf			5·50	4·50

(b) Air. Size 51×38 mm.

381	6b. brown and green	1·30	90
382	10b. brown and blue	1·80	1·10
383	12b. brown and mauve	2·20	1·70
MS384 90×70 mm. 8b. brown and blue (portraits only as in Nos. 381/3). Imperf		11·00	9·00

PORTRAITS: Nos. 375, 377, Dag Hammarskjold; 376, 378, Nehru; 381, Mohammed Abdul Chalek Hassuna; 382, U. Thant; 383, Pope Paul VI.

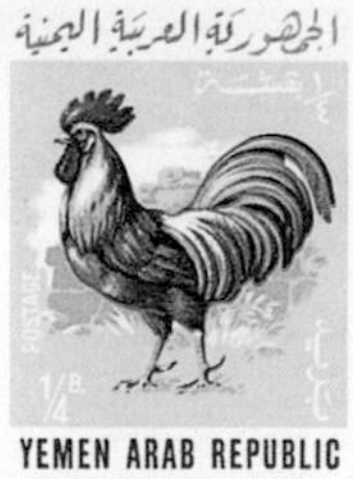
YEMEN ARAB REPUBLIC
63 Red Junglefowl

1986. Animals and Insects. Multicoloured. (a) Postage.

385	¼b. Type **63**	35	20
386	¼b. Brown hare	35	20
387	¼b. Pony	35	20
388	⅓b. Cat	35	20
389	½b. Sheep and lamb	35	20
390	4b. Dromedary	1·50	1·10

(b) Air. Butterflies.

391	6b. Red admiral	4·50	1·70
392	8b. Swallowtail	5·50	1·90
393	10b. Garden tiger moth	6·75	2·20
394	16b. Mocker swallowtail	10·00	3·25
MS395 90×70 mm. 22b. multicoloured (Farmyard scene). Imperf		7·25	5·50

1966. Space Flight of "Luna 9". Nos. 347/54 optd **LUNA IX 3 February 1966** in English and Arabic and spacecraft.

396	**57**	¼b. multicoloured (postage)	35	20
397	-	¼b. multicoloured	35	20
398	-	¼b. multicoloured	35	20
399	-	⅓b. multicoloured	35	20
400	-	½b. multicoloured	35	20
401	-	4b. multicoloured (air)	65	45
402	**57**	8b. multicoloured	1·60	1·10
403	-	16b. multicoloured	2·20	1·80
MS404 90×80 mm. 16b. (No.**MS**355 optd)			13·50	13·50

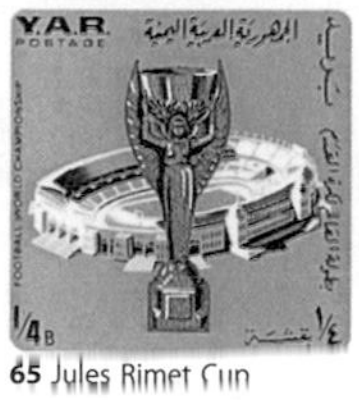
Y.A.R.
POSTAGE
65 Jules Rimet Cup

1966. World Cup Football Championships, England.

405	**65**	¼b. multicoloured (postage)	20	20
406	-	¼b. multicoloured	20	20
407	-	¼b. multicoloured	20	20
408	-	⅓b. multicoloured	20	20
409	-	½b. multicoloured	20	20
410	-	4b. multicoloured (air)	90	80
411	-	5b. multicoloured	1·60	1·30
412	-	20b. multicoloured	3·25	3·00
MS413 70×90 mm. No. 412. Imperf			10·00	6·75

DESIGNS: No. 406/11, Footballers in play (all different); 412, World Cup emblem.

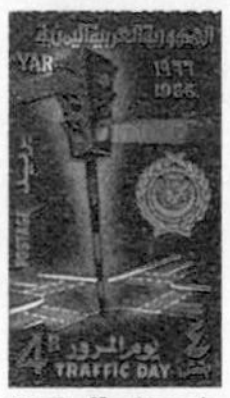
TRAFFIC DAY
66 Traffic Signals

1966. Traffic Day.

414	**66**	4b. red, emerald and green	1·10	80
415	**66**	6b. red, emerald and green	1·30	90
MS416 84×75 mm. No. 415. Imperf			6·25	5·50

1966. Space Flight of "Surveyor 1". Nos. 347/51 surch with spacecraft, **SURVEYOR 1 2 June 1966** and new value in English and Arabic.

417	**57**	1b. on ¼b. multicoloured	1·10	90
418	-	1b. on ¼b. multicoloured	1·10	90
419	-	1b. on ¼b. multicoloured	1·10	90
420	-	3b. on⅓b. multicoloured	1·70	1·20
421	-	4b. on ½b. multicoloured	2·75	2·20

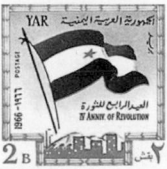

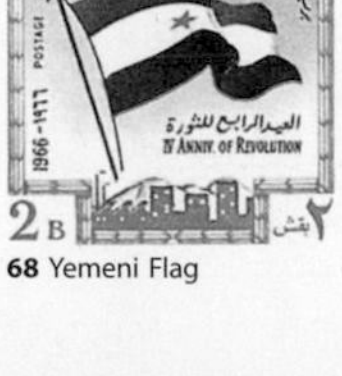
YAR
POSTAGE
4th ANNIV. OF REVOLUTION
68 Yemeni Flag

1966. Fourth Anniv of Revolution.

422	**68**	2b. black, red and green	45	35
423	-	4b. multicoloured	90	55
424	-	6b. multicoloured	1·50	80
MS424a 82×102 mm. Nos. 423/4. Imperf			5·50	4·50

DESIGNS—VERT (25×42 mm): 4b. Automatic weapon; 6b. "Agriculture and Industry".

1966. "World Fair, Sana'a, 1965". Nos. 265/71 optd **1965 SANA'A** in English and Arabic.

425	**43**	¼b. brn, bl & grn (postage)	35	20
426	-	⅓b. black, red and green	35	20
427	-	½b. green, red and blue	35	20
428	**43**	1b. indigo, blue and green	55	35
429	-	4b. blue, red and green	1·30	1·10
430	-	16b. brown, red & blue (air)	4·50	4·00
431	**43**	20b. purple, blue and green	6·25	5·00
MS432 100×70 mm. No. 431. Imperf			13·50	11·00

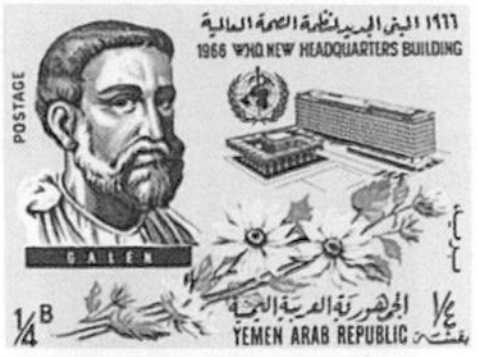
1966 WHO NEW HEADQUARTERS BUILDING
POSTAGE
GALEN
YEMEN ARAB REPUBLIC
70 Galen, Helianthus and W.H.O. Building

1966. Inauguration of W.H.O. Headquarters, Geneva. Designs incorporating W.H.O. Building. Multicoloured.

433	¼b. Type **70** (postage)	45	35
434	¼b. Hippocrates and ipomoeas	45	35
435	¼b. Ibn Sina (Avicenna) and peonies	45	35
436	4b. Type **70** (air)	1·10	55
437	8b. As No. 434	2·20	1·10
438	16b. As No. 435	4·50	3·00
MS439 130×100 mm. No. 438. Imperf		13·50	9·00

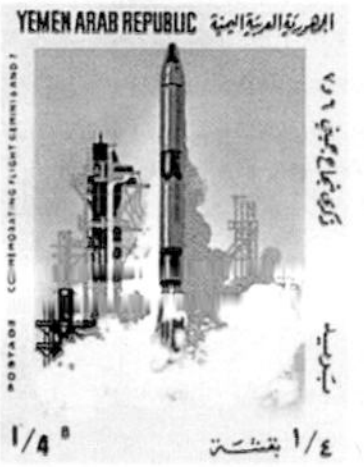
YEMEN ARAB REPUBLIC
POSTAGE
71 Spacecraft Launching

1966. Space Flight of "Gemini 6" and "7". Multicoloured.

440	¼b. Type **71** (postage)	35	20
441	¼b. Astronauts	35	20
442	¼b. "Gemini" spacecraft (horiz)	35	20
443	⅓b. "Gemini 6" and "7" (horiz)	35	20
444	½b. Recovery operations at sea	35	20
445	2b. As⅓b.	65	45
446	8b. As ½b. (air)	1·90	1·60
447	12b. "Gemini 6" and "7" link (horiz)	2·75	1·90
MS448 105×78 mm. No. 447. Imperf		13·50	9·00

1966. Space Flight of "Gemini 9". Nos. 440/7 optd **GEMINI IX CERNAN - STAFFORD JUNE 3-1966** in English and Arabic.

449	**71**	¼b. multicoloured (postage)	35	20
450	-	¼b. multicoloured	35	20
451	-	¼b. multicoloured	35	20
452	-	⅓b. multicoloured	35	20
453	-	½b. multicoloured	35	20
454	-	2b. multicoloured	65	45
455	-	8b. multicoloured (air)	2·50	1·80
456	-	12b. multicoloured	3·25	2·20
MS457 105×78 mm. No. 456. Imperf			13·50	9·00

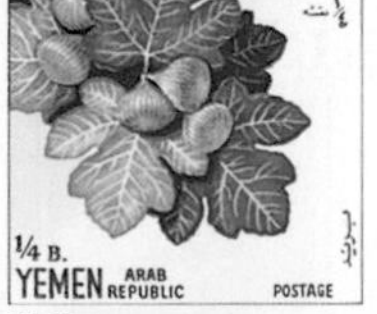
YEMEN ARAB REPUBLIC
POSTAGE
73 Figs

1967. Fruit. Multicoloured.

458	¼b. Type **73** (postage)	20	10
459	¼b. Quinces	20	10
460	¼b. Grapes	20	10
461	⅓b. Dates	20	10
462	½b. Apricots	20	10
463	2b. Quinces	55	20
464	4b. Oranges	1·10	55

465		6b. Bananas (air)	1·70	80
466		8b. Type 73	2·20	1·10
467		10b. Grapes	2·75	1·30

1967. Arab League Day. As No. 908 of Egypt.

471		4b. brown and violet	90	80
472		6b. brown and violet	1·90	1·50
473		8b. brown and violet	2·75	2·20
474		20b. brown and green	4·00	2·75
475		40b. black and green	9·50	7·75

73a Women in Factory

1967. Labour Day.

475a	73a	2b. blue and violet	80	65
475b	73a	4b. green and red	1·50	1·30
475c	73a	6b. purple and green	2·20	1·70
475d	73a	8b. green and blue	2·75	1·80
MS475e	78×70 mm. **73a** 10b. emerald and vermilion		13·50	13·50

74 Ploughing and Sunset

1967

476	74	1b. multicoloured	20	10
477	74	2b. multicoloured	35	20
478	74	4b. multicoloured	55	35
479	74	6b. multicoloured	90	55
480	74	8b. multicoloured	1·30	90
481	74	10b. multicoloured	1·70	1·20
482	74	12b. multicoloured	2·20	1·70
483	74	16b. multicoloured	2·75	2·20
484	74	20b. multicoloured	4·00	2·75
485	74	40b. multicoloured	8·25	3·25

75 Pres. Al-Salal and Soldiers

1968. Sixth Anniv of Revolution. Multicoloured.

486	75	2b. Type 75	45	45
487		4b. Yemen Arab Republic flag	90	90
488		6b. Pres. Abdullah al-Salal (vert)	1·30	1·30
MS489	80×98 mm. No. 488. Imperf		4·00	4·00

76 Map of Yemen and Dove

1969. Seventh Anniv of Revolution. Multicoloured.

490	76	2b. Type 76	35	35
491		4b. Government building (horiz)	65	65
492		6b. Yemeni workers (horiz)	1·50	1·50
MS493	80×100 mm. No. 492. Imperf		11·00	11·00

77 "Lenin addressing Crowd"

1970. Air. Birth Centenary of Lenin. Multicoloured.

| 494 | 77 | 6b. Type 77 | 2·20 | 1·70 |
| 495 | | 10b. "Lenin with Arab Delegates" | 4·50 | 2·75 |

78 Arab League Flag, Arms and Map

1970. 25th Anniv of Arab League.

496	78	5b. purple, green and orange	55	55
497	78	7b. brown, green and blue	1·20	1·20
498	78	16b. blue, green and olive	3·00	3·00
MS499	84×76 mm. No. 498		5·00	5·00

1971. Various 1968 issues listed in Appendix surch.

499a		40b. on 10b. black, red and green on gold foil (Yemen Red Crescent issue)	9·50	9·50
499b		60b. on 15b. multicoloured on gold foil (Olympics—Chariot Racing issue)	12·50	12·50
499c		80b. on 10b. multicoloured on gold foil (Int Human Rights and U Thant issue)	17·00	17·00

79 Yemeni Castle

1971. Eighth Anniv (1970) of Revolution. Multicoloured.

500	79	5b. Type 79 (postage)	1·10	1·10
501		7b. Yemeni workers and soldier (air)	1·70	1·70
502		16b. Clasped hands, flag and torch	2·20	2·20
MS503	100×78 mm. No. 502		7·75	7·75

1971. Air. Proclamation of first Permanent Constitution. No. 502 optd **PROCLAMATION OF THE INSTITUTION** 1/11/1390 H. 28/12/1970 C. in English and Arabic.

| 504 | | 16b. multicoloured | 11·00 | 11·00 |

81 U.N. Emblems and Globe

1971. 25th Anniv (1970) of U.N.O.

505	81	5b. purple, green and olive	90	65
506	81	7b. indigo, green and blue	1·50	1·10
MS507	83×73 mm. **81** 16b. chocolate, emerald and salmon. Imperf		3·25	2·20

82 View of Sana'a

1972. Ninth Anniv (1971) of Revolution.

508	82	7b. Type 82	1·70	1·70
509		18b. Military parade	2·75	2·75
510		24b. Mosque, Sana'a	4·50	4·50
MS511	97×77 mm. No. 510. Imperf		5·50	5·50

83 A.P.U. Emblem and Flags

1972. 25th Anniv (1971) of Founding of Arab Postal Union at Sofar Conference.

512	83	5b. multicoloured	55	55
513	83	7b. multicoloured	1·10	1·10
514	83	10b. multicoloured	2·20	2·20
MS515	77×97 mm. **83** 16b. multicoloured		3·25	3·25

84 Arms and Flags

1972. Tenth Anniv of Revolution.

516	84	7b. multicoloured (postage)	1·50	1·50
517	84	10b. multicoloured	2·10	2·10
518	84	21b. multicoloured (air)	6·25	6·25

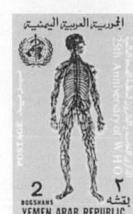

85 Skeleton and Emblem

1972. 25th Anniv of W.H.O.

519	85	2b. multicoloured	55	45
520	85	21b. multicoloured	4·00	3·00
521	85	37b. multicoloured	7·25	6·25

86 Dome of the Rock, Jerusalem

1973. Second Anniv of Burning of Al-Aqsa Mosque, Jerusalem.

522	86	7b. multicoloured (postage)	1·70	1·10
523	86	18b. multicoloured	4·00	2·75
524	86	24b. multicoloured (air)	5·50	4·50
MS525	83×73 mm. No. 524. Imperf		5·50	5·50

87 Arab Child with Book

1973. 25th Anniv (1971) of UNICEF.

526	87	7b. multicoloured (postage)	1·30	90
527	87	10b. multicoloured	2·50	1·70
528	87	18b. multicoloured (air)	3·00	2·50
MS529	83×73 mm. No. 528. Imperf		5·00	4·00

88 Modern Office Building

1973. Air. 11th Anniv of Revolution.

530	88	7b. red and green	80	55
531	-	10b. orange and green	1·00	90
532	-	18b. violet and green	2·50	1·90

DESIGNS: 10b. Factory; 18b. Flats.

89 U.P.U. Emblem

1974. Centenary of U.P.U.

533	89	10b. red, black and blue	80	55
534	89	30b. red, black and green	1·90	1·70
535	89	40b. red, black and stone	2·50	2·20

90 Yemeni Town and Emblem

1975. Tenth Anniv of F.A.O. World Food Programme.

536	90	10b. multicoloured	90	55
537	90	30b. multicoloured	2·75	2·20
538	90	63b. multicoloured	5·50	4·50

91 Janad Mosque

1975. 12th Anniv (1974) of Revolution. Multicoloured.

| 539 | 91 | 25f. Type 91 | 1·10 | 80 |
| 540 | | 75f. Althawra Hospital | 3·50 | 2·75 |

1975. Various stamps surch.

541	84	75f. on 7b. mult (postage)	4·00	4·00
542	86	75f. on 7b. multicoloured	4·00	4·00
542b	85	75f. on 21b. mult	4·00	4·00
542c	89	160f. on 40b. red, black and stone	8·25	8·25
543	86	278f. on 7b. mult	13·50	13·50
544	87	75f. on 18b. mult (air)	4·00	4·00
544a	84	75f. on 21b. mult	3·50	3·50
545	88	90f. on 7b. red and green	9·00	4·50
546	-	120f. on 18b. violet and green (No. 532)	6·75	6·75

93 Early and Modern Telephones

1976. Telephone Centenary.

547	93	25f. black and purple	80	80
548	93	75f. black and green	2·50	2·50
549	93	160f. black and brown	4·00	4·00
MS550	92×100 mm. No. 548. Perf or imperf		5·00	5·00

94 Coffee Beans

1976

551	94	1f. multicoloured	10	10
552	94	3f. multicoloured	10	10
553	94	5f. multicoloured	10	10
554	94	10f. multicoloured	20	20
555	94	25f. multicoloured	45	45
556	94	50f. multicoloured	1·10	1·10
557	94	75f. multicoloured	2·00	1·50
558	94	1r. multicoloured	2·75	2·00
559	94	1r.50 multicoloured	5·00	4·00
560	94	2r. multicoloured	7·75	5·00
561	94	5r. multicoloured	18·00	12·50

Nos. 558/61 are larger, 22×30 mm.

95 Industrial Scaffolding

1976. Second Anniv of Reformation Movement. Multicoloured.

562	95	75f. Type 95	2·50	2·50
563		135f. Hand holding pick	4·00	4·00
MS564	99×105 mm. 135f. As No. 563 but size 32×47 mm		6·75	6·75

96 Emblem of
National Institute
of Public
Administration

1976. 14th Anniv of Revolution. Multicoloured.
565		25f. Type **96**	90	90
566		75f. Yemeni family (Housing and population census)	2·50	2·50
567		160f. Shield emblem (Sana'a University)	4·50	4·50
MS568 98×106 mm. 160f. As No. 567 but size 33×49 mm			7·75	7·75

97 President
Ibrahim M.
al-Hamdi

1977. First Anniv of Assassination of Pres. Ibrahim al-Hamdi.
569	**97**	25f. green and black	55	55
570	**97**	75f. brown and black	1·90	1·70
571	**97**	160f. blue and black	4·00	2·75
MS572 82×85 mm. 160f. No. 571			7·75	6·75

98 Sa'ada and Sana'a

1978. 15th Anniv (1977) of Revolution. Multicoloured.
573		25f. Type **98**	65	55
574		75f. Television and transmitter	1·80	1·20
575		160f. Type **98**	4·00	3·00
MS576 101×75 mm. No. 575			7·75	6·75

99 A.P.U.
Emblem

1978. 25th Anniv of Arab Postal Union.
577	**99**	25f. multicoloured	1·30	1·10
578	**99**	60f. multicoloured	3·25	2·50
MS579 73×78 mm. No. 578			7·75	6·75

100 Dish Aerial

1978. Third Anniv of Correction Movement. Multicoloured.
580		25f. Type **100**	65	45
581		75f. Operating a computer	1·80	1·00
MS582 82×95 mm. No. 581			6·25	5·50

101 View of Sana'a

1979. 30th Anniv (1977) of I.C.A.O.
583	**101**	75f. multicoloured	2·75	1·50
584	**101**	135f. multicoloured	4·50	2·50
MS585 80×70 mm. No. 584			7·75	6·75

102 Koran on Map of World

1979. The Arabs.
586	**102**	25f. multicoloured	90	55
587	**102**	75f. multicoloured	2·20	1·50
MS588 99×75 mm. No. 587			5·50	5·00

103 Viewers and
Video-screen

1980. World Telecommunications Day (1979). Multicoloured.
589		75f. Type **103**	2·75	1·50
590		135f. As No. 589 (horiz)	4·00	2·50
MS591 67×75 mm. No. 590			7·75	6·75

104 Dome of
the Rock,
Jerusalem

1980. Palestinian Welfare.
592	**104**	5f. multicoloured	65	10
593	**104**	10f. multicoloured	90	20

105 Girl and Chaffinch

1980. Int Year of the Child (1979). Multicoloured.
594		25f. Type **105** (postage)	2·50	55
595		50f. Girl and great tit	3·25	1·20
596		75f. Child and butterfly	3·50	1·90
597		80f. Girl and northern bullfinch (air)	4·75	1·90
598		100f. Child and butterfly	5·00	2·00
599		150f. Child and butterfly	6·75	2·75

Each stamp shows a different variety of bird or butterfly.

106 Scoring a Goal (Austria v. Spain)

1980. World Cup Football Championship, Argentina (1978). Multicoloured.
601	**106**	25f. Type **106** (postage)	90	90
602		30f. Tunisia v. Mexico	1·00	95
603		35f. Netherlands v. Iran	1·30	1·00
604		50f. Brazil v. Sweden	1·90	1·30
605		60f. Peru v. Scotland (air)	2·50	1·50
606		75f. Italy v. France	3·25	1·70
607		80f. Argentina v. Hungary	3·50	1·90
608		100f. West Germany v. Poland	5·50	2·75

107 Scout Fishing

1980. World Scout Jamboree. Multicoloured.
610		25f. Type **107** (postage)	90	45
611		35f. Scouts and Concorde Supersonic airliner	2·00	80
612		40f. Parade and scout on horseback	1·80	75
613		50f. Scouts with telescope	2·20	1·00
614		60f. Parade and cyclist (air)	3·00	1·20
615		75f. Poppy and fencer	3·50	1·70
616		120f. Scouts catching butterflies	5·50	2·20

108 Match Scene and Flag of Poland

1980. World Cup Football Championship Quarter Finalists. Match Scenes and Flags. Multicoloured.
617		25f. Type **108** (postage)	90	45
618		30f. Peru	1·10	55
619		35f. Brazil	1·20	65
620		50f. Austria	1·80	1·20
621		60f. Italy (air)	1·90	1·30
622		75f. Netherlands	2·75	1·50
623		80f. West Germany	3·25	1·70
624		100f. Argentina (winners)	4·00	2·20

109 Kaaba, Mecca

1980. Pilgrimage to Mecca. Multicoloured.
625		25f. Type **109**	20	20
626		75f. Type **109**	65	45
627		160f. Pilgrims around the Kaaba	1·30	80
MS628 89×76 mm. No. 627			5·50	5·50

110 Government Buildings,
Sana'a

1980. 18th Anniv of Revolution. Multicoloured.
629		25f. Arm and cogwheel encircling flower and factories (vert)	35	20
630		75f. Type **110**	1·10	90
MS631 88×77 mm. 100f. Emblem (as No. 629) and Government buildings			3·25	2·75

111 Al-Rawdha Mosque

1980. 1400th Anniv of Hegira. Multicoloured.
632	**111**	25f. Type **111**	45	20
633		75f. Al-Aqsa Mosque	1·60	90
634		100f. Al-Nabawi Mosque	4·00	1·70
635		160f. Al-Haram Mosque	4·75	3·25
MS636 139×75 mm. 160f. Al-Nabawi, Al-Haram and Al-Aqsa Mosques (110×47 mm)			8·25	7·75

112 Figure clothed
in Palestinian Flag

1980. Int Day of Solidarity with Palestinian People.
637	**112**	25f. multicoloured	35	20
638	**112**	75f. multicoloured	1·10	80

113 Al-Aamiriya Mosque

1981. Ninth Arab Archaeological Conf. Multicoloured.
639		75f. Type **113**	1·30	65
640		125f. Al-Hadi Mosque	1·80	90
MS641 82×117 mm. Nos. 639/40			3·25	2·75

114 Tower and
Ramparts

1981. World Tourism Conf, Manila. Multicoloured.
642		25f. Type **114**	20	20
643		75f. Mosque and houses	80	45
644		100f. Columns (horiz)	90	55
645		135f. Bridge	1·10	65
646		160f. View of Sana'a (horiz)	1·70	90
MS647 88×79 mm. No. 646			5·50	5·00

115 Hill and U.P.U. Emblem

1981. Sir Roland Hill Commemoration. Multicoloured.
648		25f. Type **115** (postage)	1·70	80
649		30f. U.P.U. and A.P.U. emblems and Y.A.R. 4b. stamp of 1963	1·90	1·10
650		50f. Hill, magnifying glass and stamps	2·75	1·70
651		75f. Hill and jet airliner circling globe (air)	4·50	2·75
652		100f. Hill, album and hand holding stamp with tweezers	6·25	3·25
653		150f. Air letter, jet airliner and Y.A.R. 160f. stamp of 1976	11·00	5·00

1981. Nos. 551/5 surch.
654	**94**	125f. on 1f. multicoloured	3·00	1·60
655	**94**	150f. on 3f. multicoloured	3·25	1·90
656	**94**	325f. on 5f. multicoloured	7·75	4·50
657	**94**	350f. on 10f. multicoloured	9·00	4·75
658	**94**	375f. on 25f. multicoloured	9·50	5·50

117 Map of Yemen

1982. Air. 19th Anniv (1981) of Revolution. Multicoloured.
659		75f. Type **117**	1·30	65
660		125f. Yemenis looking towards map within sun	2·00	1·10
661		325f. Sun, fist, dove with flags for wings and industrial scene	6·25	4·00
662		400f. Air display	7·75	4·75
MS663 95×120 mm. No. 661			16·00	14·50

118 Al-Hasan ibn Ahmed
al-Hamadani

1982. Air. Birth Millenary of Al-Hasan ibn Ahmed al-Hamadani (philosopher).
664	**118**	125f. multicoloured	2·20	1·20

665	**118**	325f. multicoloured	6·25	3·00
MS666		111×90 mm. 375f. multicoloured	18·00	17·00

DESIGN—VERT: Portrait as in centre of T **118**.

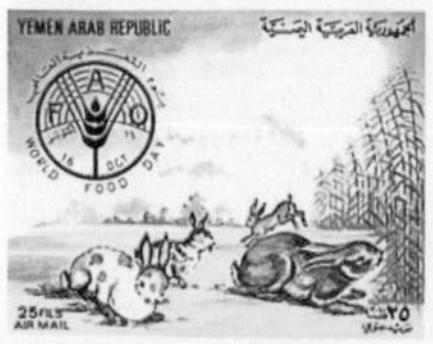

119 Common Rabbits

1982. World Food Day. Multicoloured.

667	25f. Type **119**	1·80	80
668	50f. Cock and hens	3·50	1·70
669	60f. Common turkeys	4·00	2·00
670	75f. Sheep	5·00	2·50
671	100f. Cow and calf	6·75	3·00
672	125f. Red deer	7·25	3·50
MS673	Two sheets, each 138×118 mm. (a) 100f. Aubergines; 100f. Tomatoes; 100f. Beetroot and runner beans; 100f. Carrots and cauliflower. (b) 125f. Birds in garden; 125f. Pelicans by lake; 125f. Fish in basket by shore; 125f. Swans on lake	38·00	38·00

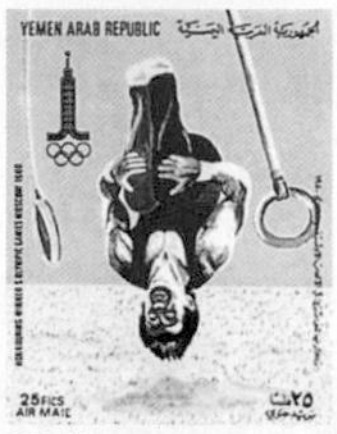

120 Gymnast

1982. Air. Olympic Games, Moscow (1980). Multicoloured.

674	25f. Type **120**	1·80	80
675	50f. Pole vault	3·50	1·70
676	60f. Throwing the javelin	4·00	2·00
677	75f. Runner	5·00	2·50
678	100f. Basketball	6·75	3·00
679	125f. Football	7·25	3·50
MS680	Two sheets, each 139×118 mm. (a) 100f. Boxing; 100f. Wrestling; 100f. Canoeing; 100f. Swimming. (b) 125f. Weightlifting; 125f. Discus throwing; 125f. Long jumping; 125f. Fencing	25·00	25·00

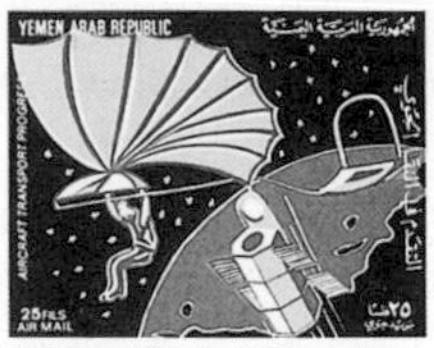

121 Otto Lilienthal's Monoplane Glider and Satellite

1982. Air. Progress in Air Transport. Multicoloured.

681	25f. Type **121**	1·90	65
682	50f. Alberto Santos-Dumonts biplane "14 bis"	2·75	1·00
683	60f. Biplane and satellite	3·50	1·10
684	75f. Early airplane and satellite	4·00	1·30
685	100f. De Havilland D.H.60G Gipsy Moth biplane and satellite	4·75	2·00
686	125f. Fokker F.VIIa/3m airplane and satellite	6·75	2·75
MS687	Two sheets, each 138×117 mm. (a) 100f. Airplane and cylinder satellite; 100f. Early glider; 100f. Airship; 100f. Airplane and round satellite. (b) 125f. Airplane; 125f. Concorde and satellite with four "arms"; 125f. Concorde; 125f. Helicopter	25·00	25·00

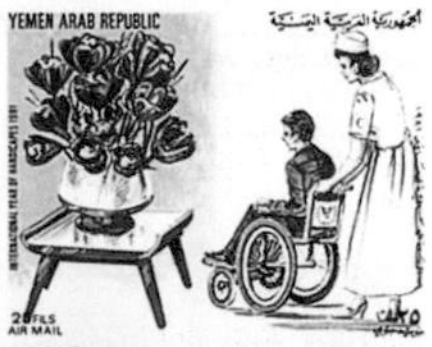

122 Crocuses and Nurse pushing Wheelchair

1982. Air. International Year of Disabled Persons (1981). Multicoloured.

688	25f. Type **122**	1·90	65
689	50f. Bowl of roses and nurse pushing wheelchair	2·20	1·20
690	60f. Bowl of pasque flowers and nurse pushing wheelchair	2·75	1·70
691	75f. Mixed flower arrangement and nurse pushing wheelchair	4·75	2·50
692	100f. Bowl of lilies and nurse pushing wheelchair	6·25	3·25
693	125f. Bowl of gladioli and nurse pushing wheelchair	7·25	3·50
MS694	Two sheets, each 139×117 mm. (a) 100f. IYDP emblem and carnation; 100f. IYDP emblem on globe; 100f. IYDP, World Health Organization and United Nations emblems and Yemeni flags; 100f. Nurse pushing trolley of presents. (b) 125f. Nurse and globe pierced with flags; 125f. UN and WHO emblems and lily; 125f. Wheelchair user and IYDP emblem; 125f. Nurse pushing trolley of presents	45·00	45·00

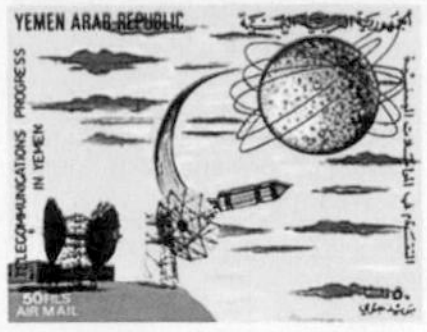

123 Aerials and Satellite circling Globe

1982. Air. Telecommunications Progress. Multicoloured.

695	25f. Modern radio communications	90	55
696	50f. Type **123**	1·30	65
697	60f. Radio masts, watch and dish aerials	1·70	1·10
698	75f. Dish aerials and landscape	2·00	1·30
699	100f. Dish aerials, satellites and morse transmitter	2·50	1·70
700	125f. Aerials, jet airliner and globe	3·25	2·50
MS701	Two sheets, each 139×120 mm. (a) 100f. Dish aerials and satellite orbit; 100f. Cameraman, satellite orbit and television screen; 100f. Satellite orbit and telex operator; 100f. Urban building, telephone and satellite orbit. (b) 125f. Dish aerials, satellite and ship; 125f. Switchboard and dish aerials; 125f. Dish aerials and modes of transport; 125f. Radar operator and dish aerials	25·00	25·00

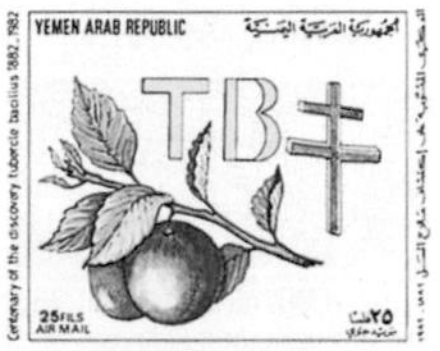

124 Oranges, "TB" and Cross of Lorraine

1982. Air. Centenary of Discovery of Tubercle Bacillus. Multicoloured.

702	25f. Type **124**	1·20	45
703	50f. Blossom, pears, cross of Lorraine and Robert Koch	1·90	90
704	60f. Pomegranates, flowers and cross of Lorraine	2·20	90
705	75f. Roses, grapes and bacillus	2·75	1·20
706	100f. Cherries, blossom and microscope	3·50	1·50
707	125f. Lemons, cross of Lorraine and microscope	4·50	2·00
MS708	Two sheets, each 139×119 mm. (a) 100f. Strawberries and Robert Koch with microscope; 100f. Plums and Robert Koch with microscope; 100f. Apples and Robert Koch with microscope; 100f. Apricots and Robert Koch with microscope. (b) 125f. Roses, cross of Lorraine and Robert Koch; 125f. Dandelions, cross of Lorraine and Robert Koch; 125f. Blossom, cross of Lorraine and Robert Koch; 125f. Mimosa, cross of Lorraine and Robert Koch	33·00	33·00

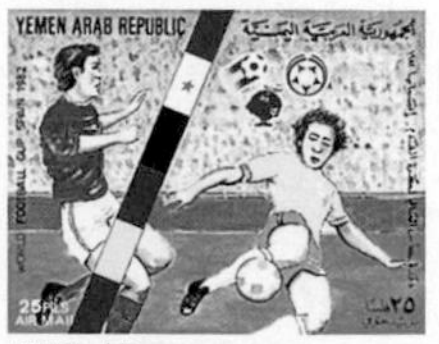

125 Tackling

1982. Air. World Cup Football Championship, Spain. Multicoloured.

709	25f. Type **125**	80	35
710	50f. Marking the opposition	1·20	45
711	60f. Players with ball	1·80	80
712	75f. Scoring a goal	2·00	1·00
713	100f. Dribbling	2·50	1·30
714	125f. Intercepting the ball	3·00	1·70
MS715	Two sheets, each 139×118 mm. (a) 75f. Marking the opposition; 75f. Players with goalkeeper; 75f. Dribbling; 75f. Tackling. (b) 75f. Tackling; 75f. Preparing to score; 75f. Intercepting the ball; 75f. Scoring a goal	22·00	22·00

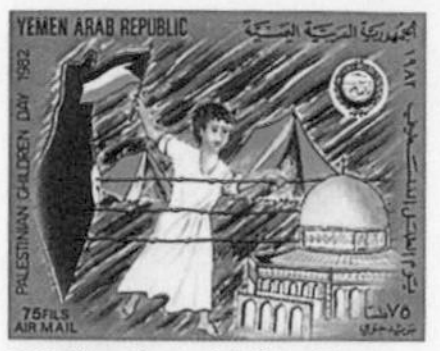

126 Map, Boy with Flag, Tents and Dome of the Rock

1982. Air. Palestinian Children's Day. Multicoloured.

716	75f. Type **126**	2·50	1·20
717	125f. As Type **126** but girl with flag	4·00	2·50
718	325f. As Type **126** but boy and girl	9·00	4·75
MS719	120×90 mm. No. 718	13·50	7·75

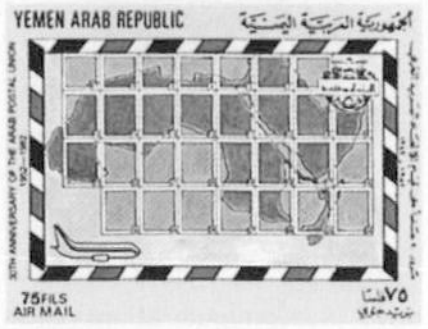

127 Map under Grid and Airplane

1982. Air. 30th Anniv of Arab Postal Union. Multicoloured.

720	75f. Type **127**	1·70	90
721	125f. Map under grid and ship	2·75	1·30
722	325f. Map under grid and emblem	7·25	3·00
MS723	120×90 mm. No. 722	14·50	5·50

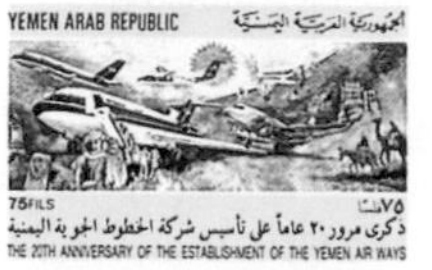

128 Passengers and Airliners

1983. 20th Anniv of Yemen Airways.

724	**128**	75f. multicoloured	1·90	1·10
725	**128**	125f. multicoloured	3·25	1·80
726	**128**	325f. multicoloured	7·25	4·00

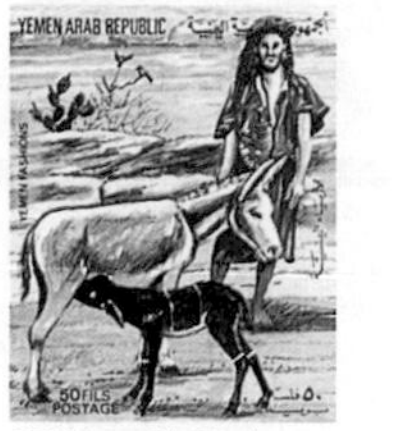

129 Man with Donkey and Foal

1983. Traditional Costumes. Multicoloured.

727	50f. Type **129** (postage)	3·25	1·80
728	50f. Woman in embroidered veil carrying jug on head	3·25	1·80
729	50f. Shepherds in country	3·25	1·80
730	50f. Man walking through city and shepherds	3·25	1·80
731	75f. Women at well (horiz) (air)	5·00	2·75
732	75f. Woman sitting by shore (horiz)	5·00	2·75
733	75f. Man ploughing with camel (horiz)	5·00	2·75
734	75f. Man reading (horiz)	5·00	2·75
MS735	Two sheets, each 119×93 mm. (a) 200f. Woman wearing silver jewellery (perf); 200f. Three-quarter length portrait of man (imperf)	27·00	27·00

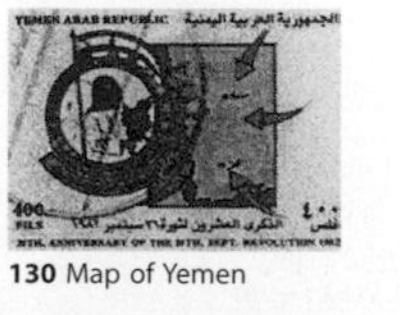

130 Map of Yemen

1983. 20th Anniv (1982) of Revolution. Multicoloured.

736	100f. Houses, airliner, telephone and dish aerial	2·50	1·30
737	150f. Literacy campaign emblem	3·25	2·00
738	325f. Tree and houses	7·75	4·50
739	400f. Type **130**	11·00	5·50

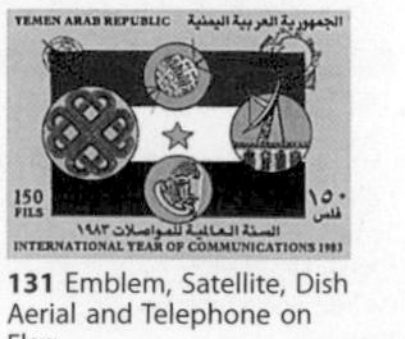

131 Emblem, Satellite, Dish Aerial and Telephone on Flag

1983. World Communications Year.

741	**131**	150f. multicoloured	4·00	2·20
742	**131**	325f. multicoloured	8·25	5·00
MS743		120×80 mm. No. 742	14·50	8·25

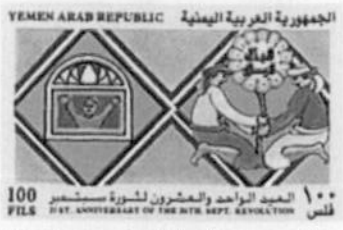

132 Man at Window and Men planting Tree

1984. 21st Anniv (1983) of Revolution. Multicoloured.

744	100f. Type **132**	3·25	1·60
745	150f. Fist and bust	3·50	2·20
746	325f. Sun, tank and open gates	7·75	4·00
MS747	120×90 mm. No. 746	16·00	8·25

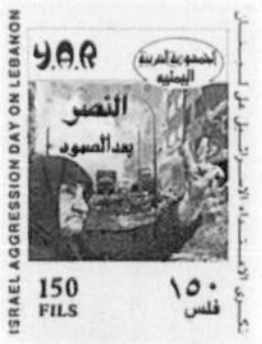

133 Woman in Bombed Street

1984. "Israeli Aggression against Lebanon".

748	**133**	150f. multicoloured	3·25	1·70
749	**133**	325f. multicoloured	9·00	5·00
MS750		90×120 mm. As No. 749 but larger. Imperf	16·00	9·50

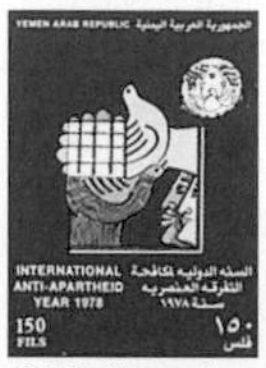

134 Profiles and Clasped Hands as Doves

1985. International Anti-apartheid Year (1978).

751	**134**	150f. multicoloured	3·25	1·70
752	**134**	325f. multicoloured	7·75	4·50
MS753		79×120 mm. No. 752	16·00	7·75

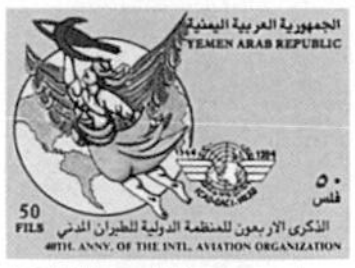

135 Winged Figure and Globe

1985. 40th Anniv of I.C.A.O.

754	**135**	25f. multicoloured	55	20
755	**135**	50f. multicoloured	1·10	45
756	**135**	150f. multicoloured	2·75	1·30
757	**135**	325f. multicoloured	6·75	3·00
MS758		120×90 mm. No. 757	16·00	7·75

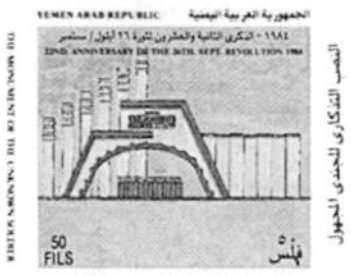

136 Monument of Unknown Soldier

1985. 22nd Anniv (1984) of Revolution. Multicoloured.

759	50f. Type **136**	1·50	65
760	150f. Reconstruction of Marem Dam	4·00	2·50
761	325f. Althawrah Sports Stadium	8·25	4·75
MS762	120×90 mm. No. 761	16·00	7·75

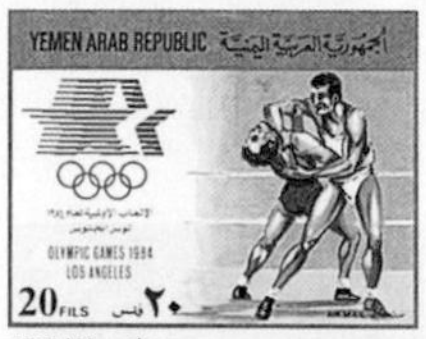

137 Wrestling

1985. Air. Olympic Games, Los Angeles (1984). Multicoloured.

763	20f. Type **137**	55	35
764	30f. Boxing	65	45
765	40f. Running	90	65
766	60f. Hurdling	1·10	90
767	150f. Pole vaulting	2·50	1·60
768	325f. Throwing the javelin	5·50	3·25

MS769 Two sheets, each 140×130 mm. (a) 75f. Gymnastics; 75f. Weightlifting; 75f. Putting the shot; 75f. Throwing the discus. (b) 75f. Diving; 75f. Swimming; 75f. Rowing; 75f. Canoeing	38·00	38·00

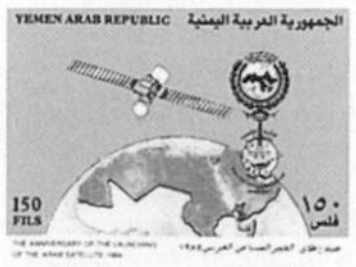

138 Emblem and Satellite over Globe

1986. First Anniv of "Arabsat" Communications Satellite.

770	**138**	150f. multicoloured	4·50	2·20
771	**138**	325f. multicoloured	9·00	4·50
MS772		120×90 mm. No. 771	12·50	7·25

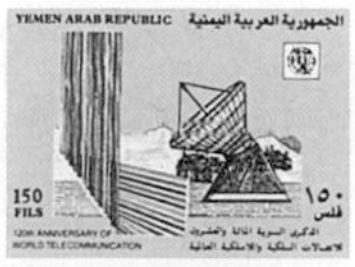

139 Dish Aerial and Cables

1986. 120th Anniv of World Telecommunications.

773	**139**	150f. multicoloured	4·50	2·20
774	**139**	325f. multicoloured	9·00	4·50
MS775		120×90 mm. No. 774	10·50	7·25

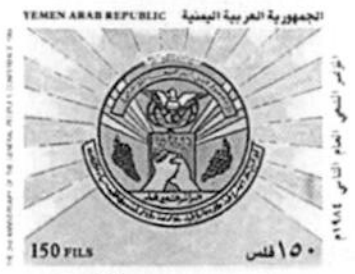

140 Emblem

1986. Second Anniv of General People's Conference.

776	**140**	150f. multicoloured	4·00	2·20
777	**140**	325f. multicoloured	7·25	4·50
MS778		120×90 mm. No. 777	9·00	7·25

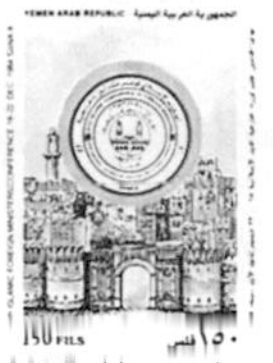

141 Emblem and Sana'a

1986. 15th Islamic Foreign Ministers Conference, Sana'a (1984).

779	**141**	150f. multicoloured	4·00	2·20
780	**141**	325f. multicoloured	7·25	4·50
MS781		90×120 mm. No. 783	9·00	7·25

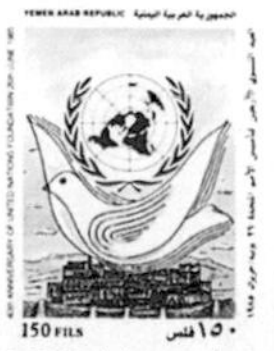

142 Emblem and Dove

1986. 40th Anniv of U.N.O.

782	**142**	150f. multicoloured	4·00	2·20
783	**142**	325f. multicoloured	7·25	4·50
MS784		90×120 mm. No. 783	9·00	7·25

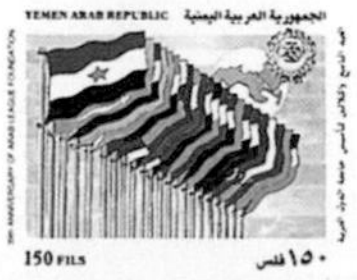

143 Members' Flags, Map and Emblem

1986. 39th Anniv (1984) of Arab League.

785	**143**	150f. multicoloured	4·00	2·20
786	**143**	325f. multicoloured	7·25	4·50

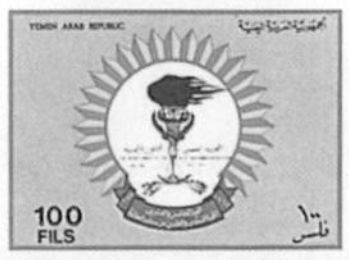

144 Anniversary Emblem

1987. 25th Anniv of Revolution.

787	**144**	100f. multicoloured	1·30	45
788	**144**	150f. multicoloured	1·90	1·00
789	**144**	425f. multicoloured	5·50	3·50
790	**144**	450f. multicoloured	6·25	3·50
MS791		90×70 mm. No. 789	6·25	5·50

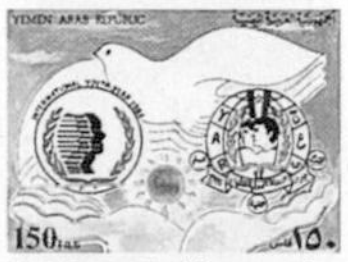

145 Dove, Emblems and Open Hands

1987. International Youth Year (1985).

792	**145**	150f. multicoloured	4·00	1·70
793	**145**	425f. multicoloured	7·25	4·00
MS794		90×70 mm. No. 793	9·00	6·75

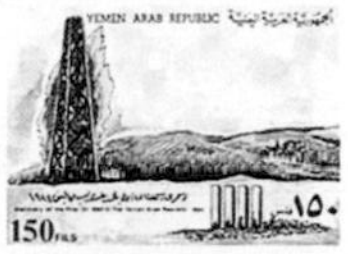

146 Burning Oil

1987. Third Anniv of Discovery of Oil in Yemen Arab Republic. Multicoloured.

795	150f. Type **146**	4·00	1·70
796	425f. Oil derrick and refinery	7·25	4·00
MS797	90×70 mm. 425f. No. 796	9·00	6·75

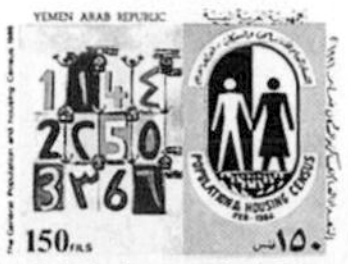

147 Numbers and Emblem

1987. General Population and Housing Census (1986).

798	**147**	150f. multicoloured	4·00	1·70
799	**147**	425f. multicoloured	7·25	4·00
MS800		90×70 mm. No. 799	9·00	6·75

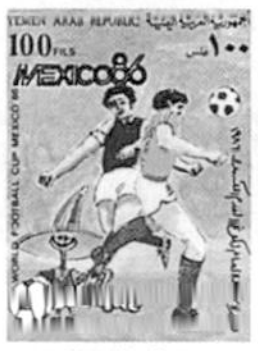

148 Footballers and Pique (mascot)

1988. World Cup Football Championship, Mexico (1986). Multicoloured.

801	100f. Type **148**	1·70	80
802	150f. Goalkeeper saving ball	2·75	1·50
803	425f. Players and Pique (horiz)	6·75	3·25
MS804	90×70 mm. No. 803	11·00	6·75

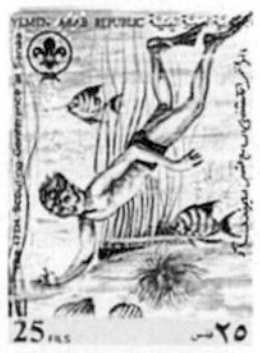

149 Skin Diving

1988. 17th Scout Conference, Sana'a. Scout Activities. Multicoloured.

805	25f. Type **149**	45	20
806	30f. Table tennis	65	30
807	40f. Tennis	80	35
808	50f. Game with flag	1·00	45
809	60f. Volleyball	1·20	55
810	100f. Tug-of-war	2·00	90
811	150f. Basketball	2·75	1·30
812	425f. Archery	7·75	4·00
MS813	90×70 mm. 425f. Scout, emblem and salute (horiz)	9·00	6·75

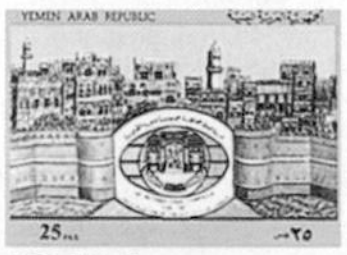

150 Old City

1988. Int Campaign for Preservation of Old Sana'a.

814	**150**	25f. multicoloured	45	20
815	**150**	50f. multicoloured	90	45
816	**150**	100f. multicoloured	1·90	90
817	**150**	150f. multicoloured	2·75	1·30
818	**150**	425f. multicoloured	7·75	4·00
MS819		90×70 mm. No. 818	8·25	6·75

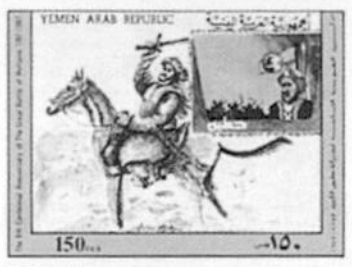

151 Horseman

1988. 800th Anniv (1987) of Battle of Hattin.

820	**151**	150f. multicoloured	3·25	2·20
821	**151**	425f. multicoloured	12·50	5·50
MS822		90×70 mm. No. 821	16·00	11·00

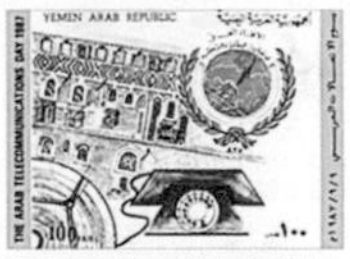

152 Building, Dish Aerial, Telephone and Emblem

1988. Arab Telecommunications Day (1987).

823	**152**	100f. multicoloured	2·20	1·00
824	**152**	150f. multicoloured	3·50	1·80
825	**152**	425f. multicoloured	10·00	4·75
MS826		90×70 mm. No. 825	13·50	11·00

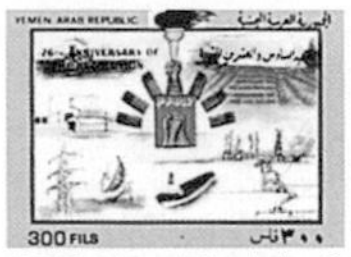

153 Torch and Symbols of Development

1989. 26th Anniv (1988) of Revolution. Multicoloured.

827	300f. Type **153**	2·20	90
828	375f. Type **153**	3·25	1·20
829	850f. Flag, Koran and symbols of agriculture and industry (vert)	6·75	2·50
830	900f. As No. 829	7·00	2·75

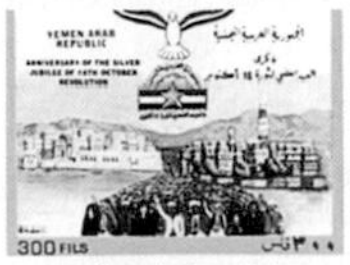

154 Old and New Cities and Crowd

[illegible] Anniv of 14th October Revolution. Multicoloured.

831	300f. Type **154**	2·20	90
832	375f. Type **154**	3·25	1·20
833	850f. City street and crowd (vert)	6·75	2·50
834	900f. As No. 833 (vert)	7·00	2·75

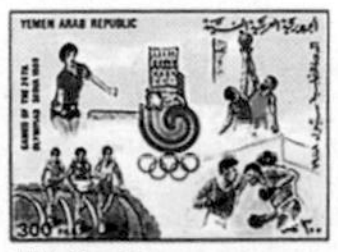

155 Sports

1989. Olympic Games, Seoul (1988). Multicoloured.

835	300f. Type **155**	2·50	90
836	375f. Football	3·25	1·20
837	850f. Football and judo (vert)	7·75	2·50
838	900f. Emblem and torch bearer	8·00	2·75
MS839	90×70 mm. As No. 836 but 37×27 mm	18·00	12·50

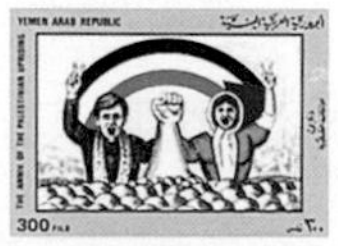

156 Flag, Couple and Fist

1989. Palestinian "Intifida" Movement. Multicoloured.

840	300f. Type **156**	2·20	90
841	375f. Soldier raising flag (vert)	3·25	1·20
842	850f. Dome of the Rock, youths and burning tyres	6·75	2·50
843	900f. Crowd of youths (vert)	7·00	2·75
MS844	70×90 mm. As No. 841 but 31×40 mm	18·00	12·50

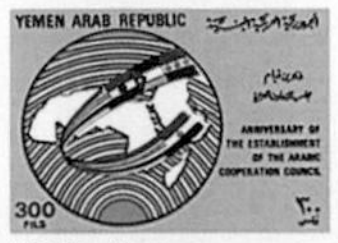

157 Emblem

1990. First Anniv of Arab Co-operation Council.

845	**157**	300f. multicoloured	2·20	90
846	**157**	375f. multicoloured	3·25	1·20
847	**157**	850f. multicoloured	6·75	2·50
848	**157**	900f. multicoloured	7·00	2·75
MS849		90×70 mm. As No. 846 but 36×27 mm	18·00	12·50

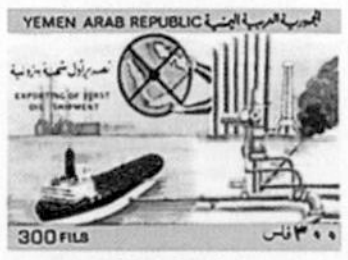

158 Loading Tanker

1990. First Shipment of Oil. Multicoloured.

850	300f. Type **158**	2·20	90
851	375f. Type **158**	3·25	1·20
852	850f. Pipeline around globe and tanker	6·75	2·50
853	900f. As No. 852	7·00	2·75
MS854	90×67 mm. No. 851	18·00	12·50

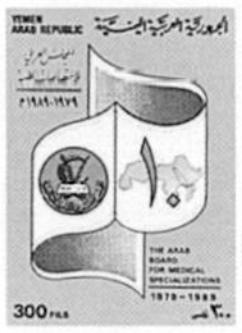

159 Emblem

1990. Tenth Anniv (1989) of Arab Board for Medical Specializations.

855	**159**	300f. multicoloured	1·80	90
856	**159**	375f. multicoloured	2·20	1·10
857	**159**	850f. multicoloured	4·75	2·20
858	**159**	900f. multicoloured	5·25	2·50
MS859		70×90 mm. No. 856	5·50	2·75

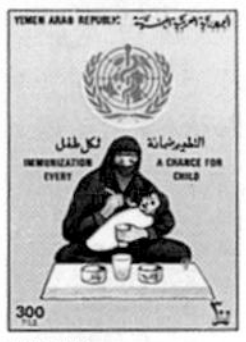

160 Woman feeding Baby

1990. Immunization Campaign. Multicoloured.

860	300f. Type **160**	2·20	90
861	375f. Type **160**	3·25	1·20
862	850f. Nurse weighing baby (horiz)	[illegible]	[illegible]
863	900f. As No. [illegible]	7·00	2·75
MS864	70×90 mm. As No. 861 but 26×37 mm	18·00	12·50

For further issues see **YEMEN REPUBLIC (combined)**.

POSTAGE DUE STAMPS

1964. Designs as Nos. 291, 295/6 (Animals), but inscr "POSTAGE DUE".

D298	4b. brown and green	3·25	1·10
D299	12b. brown and orange	6·75	3·25
D300	20b. black and violet	12·50	4·50

DESIGNS: 4b. Mountain gazelles; 12b. Bullock; 20b. Arab horses.

1964. Designs as Nos. 303/5, but inscr "POSTAGE DUE". Multicoloured.

D306	4b. Roses	3·25	1·10
D307	12b. Poinsettia	6·75	2·20
D308	20b. Viburnum	12·50	4·75

1966. Nos. 324/8 optd **POSTAGE DUE** in English and Arabic.

D371	6b. multicoloured	6·75	4·50
D372	8b. multicoloured	7·25	5·50
D373	12b. multicoloured	10·00	6·75
D374	20b. multicoloured	17·00	12·50
D375	1r. multicoloured	36·00	25·00

1966. Designs as Nos. 410/12 (Football), but inscr "POSTAGE DUE".

D414	4b. multicoloured	3·25	1·70
D415	5b. multicoloured	5·50	4·00
D416	20b. multicoloured	11·00	7·75

1967. Designs as Nos. 465/7, but inscr "POSTAGE DUE" instead of "AIR MAIL". Multicoloured.

D468	-	6b. Bananas	2·20	1·10
D469	**73**	8b. Figs	4·50	2·20
D470	-	10b. Grapes	6·75	3·25

ROYALIST CIVIL WAR ISSUES

Fighting continued between the Royalists and Republicans until 1970. In 1970 Saudi Arabia recognised the Republican government as the rulers of Yemen, and the royalist position crumbled.

1962. Various issues optd. (i) Optd **FREE YEMEN FIGHTS FOR GOD, IMAM, COUNTRY** in English and Arabic.

R1	**19**	2b. red and black	5·50	2·75
R3	**19**	4b. yellow and black	5·50	2·75

(ii) Optd **FREE YEMEN FIGHTS FOR GOD, IMAM & COUNTRY** in English and Arabic. (a) Nos. 156/8.

R5	**24**	4b. multicoloured	11·00	9·00

R6	24	6b. multicoloured	11·00	9·00
R7	24	10b. multicoloured	13·50	11·00

(b) Nos. 159/60.

R8	25	4b. brown	39·00	33·00
R9	25	6b. green	39·00	33·00

(c) Nos. 161/2.

R10	4b. green	11·00	9·00
R11	6b. blue	11·00	9·00

(d) Nos. 167/8.

R12	4b. orange and black	4·50	4·50
R13	6b. green and brown	6·75	6·75

(e) Nos. 126/30.

R14	19	2b. red and black		
R15	19	4b. yellow and black		
R16	19	6b. orange and black		
R17	19	8b. green and brown		
R18	19	20b. orange and violet Set of 5	£130	£100

(f) Nos. 169/75.

R19	20	1b. violet	4·50	4·00
R20	20	2b. green	4·50	4·00
R21	20	3b. blue	9·00	6·75
R22	20	4b. blue	10·50	9·50
R23	20	6b. purple	18·00	14·00
R24	20	14b. red	22·00	20·00
R25	20	20b. brown	33·00	32·00

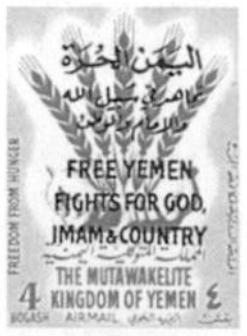
R6 Five Ears of Wheat

1963. Air. Freedom from Hunger.

R26	R6	4b. red, green and stone	2·20	2·20
R27	R6	6b. red, green and blue	3·25	3·25

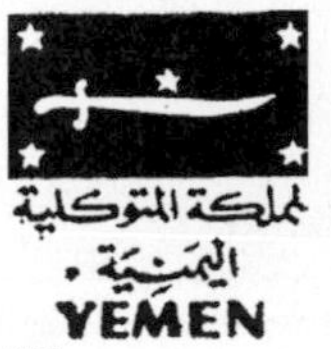

(R7)

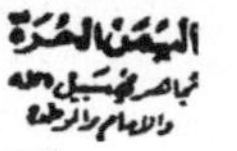
(R8)

1963. Captured Y.A.R. stamps variously optd. (a) No. 195 optd with Type **R7**.

R28	4b. brown and mauve	95·00	90·00

(b) No. 196 optd with Type **R7** plus first line of Arabic inscr repeated at foot.

R29	6b. red and blue	95·00	90·00

(c) No. 196 optd with Types **R7** and **R8**.

R30	6b. red and blue	£110	£100

1963. Surch in figures with stars over old value, for use on circulars.

R31	1b. on 4b. red, green and stone	4·50	4·50
R32	2b. on 6b. red, green and blue	4·50	4·50

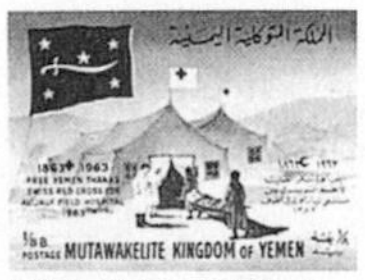
R10 Red Cross Field Post

1963. Red Cross Cent. Flags in red; inscr in black.

R33	R10	⅛b. violet (postage)	1·10	90
R34	R10	¼b. mauve	1·10	90
R35	R10	½b. brown	1·10	90
R36	R10	4b. green	1·70	1·60
R37	R10	6b. blue (air)	2·75	2·50
MSR37a 110×80 mm. Nos. R36/7. Imperf			20·00	20·00

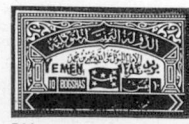

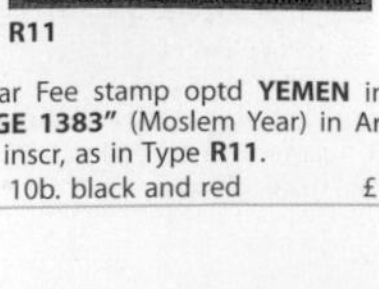
R11

1963. Consular Fee stamp optd **YEMEN** in English and **"POSTAGE 1383"** (Moslem Year) in Arabic with bar over old inscr, as in Type **R11**.

R38	R11	10b. black and red	£1100	£1100

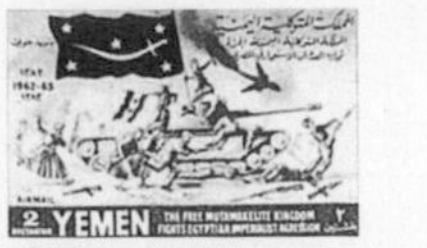

R12 Troops in Action

1964. Air. "The Patriotic War". Flags and emblem in red.

R39	R12	⅛b. green	1·30	1·10
R40	R12	1b. black	1·30	1·10
R41	R12	2b. purple	1·50	1·30
R42	R12	4b. green	1·50	1·30
R43	R12	6b. blue	3·00	1·80
MSR43a 112×90 mm. R 12 24b. blue (57×37 mm). Imperf			22·00	17·00

1964. Air. Surch **AIR MAIL**, red cross, **1963–64 HONOURING BRITISH RED CROSS SURGICAL TEAM** and value and Arabic equivalent.

R44	10b. on 4b. green	9·00	7·75
R45	18b. on ½b. green	13·50	12·50

1964. Air. Surch **AIR MAIL** and value in English and Arabic and airplane motif.

R46	R10	10b. on⅛b. violet	5·50	4·50
R47	R10	18b. on ¼b. mauve	9·00	7·75
R48	R10	28b. on ½b. brown	14·50	13·50

1964. Air. Surch **4 REVALUED** in English and Arabic with dotted frameline around stamp.

R49	R12	4b. on ⅛b. green	13·50	11·00
R50	R12	4b. on 1b. black	13·50	11·00
R51	R12	4b. on 2b. purple	13·50	11·00

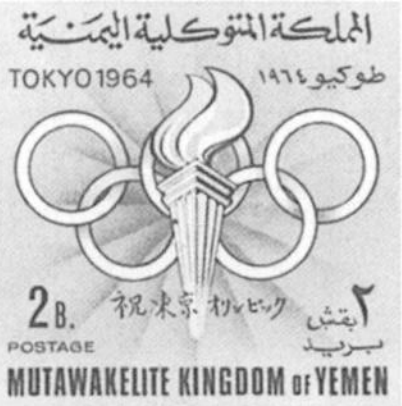

R16 Olympic Flame and "Rings"

1964. Olympic Games, Tokyo.

R52	R16	2b. blue (postage)	2·20	1·10
R53	R16	4b. violet	4·00	3·25
R54	R16	6b. brown (air)	5·00	4·50
MSR54a 102×80 mm. R 16 4b. ultramarine (38×38 mm). Imperf			22·00	17·00

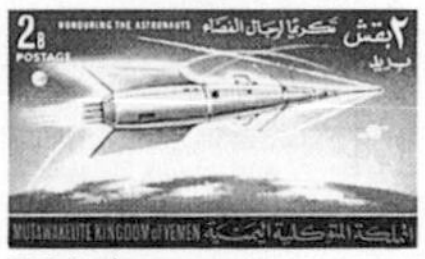
R17 Rocket

1964. Astronauts.

R55	R17	2b. orange, violet and black (postage)	3·25	3·25
R56	R17	4b. brown, blue and black	4·50	4·50
R57	R17	6b. yellow & black (air)	5·50	5·50
MSR57a 89×63 mm. R 17 6b. blue and sepia (48×38 mm). Imperf			20·00	20·00

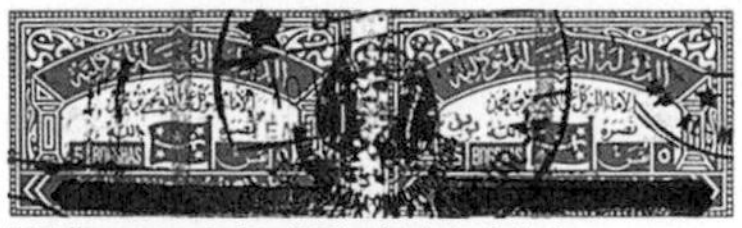
R18 (image scaled to 54% of original size)

1964. Consular Fee stamps optd across a pair as in Type **R18**.

R58	R18	10b. (5b.+5b.) purple	£1500	£1500

Owing to a shortage of 10b. postage stamps, 5b. Consular Fee stamps were optd across pairs with **YEMEN** in English and "POSTAGE 1383" (Moslem Year) in Arabic, in frame, together with the Ministry of Communications' Royal Arms seal and a bar over old inscription at foot.

1965. Air. British Yemen Relief Committee. Nos. R46/8 additionally optd **HONOURING BRITISH YEMEN RELIEF COMMITTEE 1963 1965** in English and Arabic.

R59	R10	10b. on ½b. violet	5·50	5·50
R60	R10	18b. on ¼b. mauve	11·00	11·00
R61	R10	28b. on ½b. brown	13·50	13·50

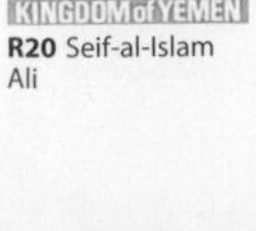

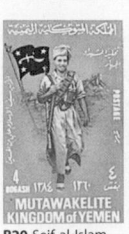

R20 Seif-al-Islam Ali

1965. Prince Seif-al-Islam Ali Commemoration.

R62	R20	4b. grey and red	11·00	11·00

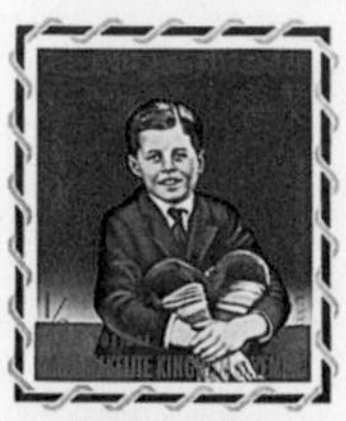
R21 Kennedy as Young Man

1965. Pres. Kennedy Commemoration.

R63	R21	⅛b. black, mauve and gold (postage)	80	80
R64	-	¼b. violet, turq & gold	90	90
R65	-	½b. brown, blue and gold	1·10	1·10
R66	-	4b. brown, yell & gold	3·25	3·25
R67	-	6b. black, green and gold (air)	5·00	5·00
MSR67a 134×102 mm. 4b. multicoloured (Kennedy with family). Imperf			29·00	29·00

DESIGNS (Kennedy): ¼b. As naval officer; ½b. Sailing with Mrs. Kennedy; 4b. In rocking-chair; 6b. Full face portrait.

1965. Churchill Commemoration (1st issue). No. R62, with colours changed, optd **IN MEMORY OF SIR WINSTON CHURCHILL 1874-1965** in English and Arabic.

R68	R20	4b. blue and red	17·00	17·00

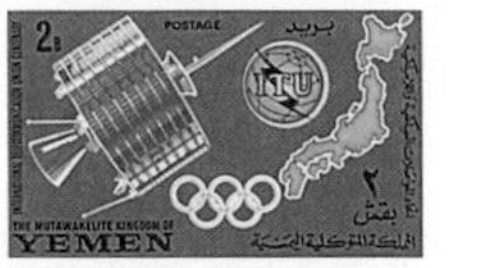

R23 Satellite and Emblems

1965. I.T.U. Centenary.

R69	R23	2b. yellow, violet and black (postage)	3·25	3·25
R70	R23	4b. red, blue and black	5·00	5·00
R71	R23	6b. green, violet and black (air)	7·25	7·25
MSR71a 90×65 mm. No. R70. Imperf			20·00	20·00

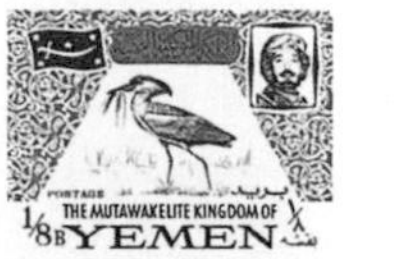

R24 Hammerkop

1965. Birds. Multicoloured.

R72	⅛b. Type R **24** (postage)	1·70	20
R73	¼b. Yemeni linnet	2·00	30
R74	½b. Hoopoe	2·75	35
R75	4b. Arabian woodpecker	4·75	1·30
R76	6b. Violet starling (air)	11·00	2·00
MSR76a 89×65 mm. No. R75. Imperf		33·00	28·00

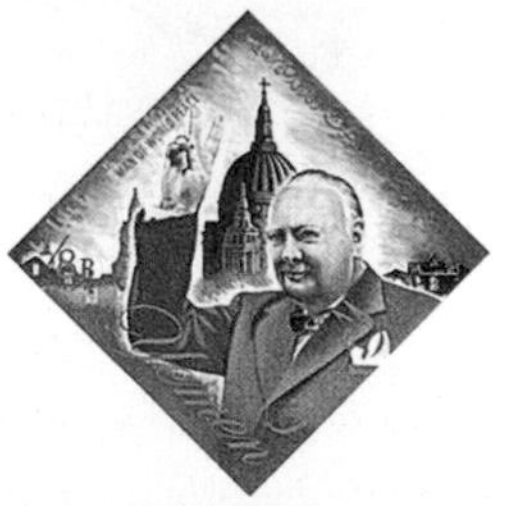
R25 Sir Winston Churchill and St. Paul's Cathedral

1965. Churchill Commem (2nd issue). Multicoloured.

R77	⅛b. Type R **25**	45	20
R78	¼b. Churchill and Houses of Parliament	45	20
R79	½b. Full-face portrait	55	30
R80	1b. Type R **25**	1·30	45
R81	2b. Churchill and Houses of Parliament	2·20	55
R82	4b. Full-face portrait	4·00	1·10
MSR82a 109×85 mm. 4b. red, blue and gold (Churchill seated and flags). Imperf		17·00	17·00

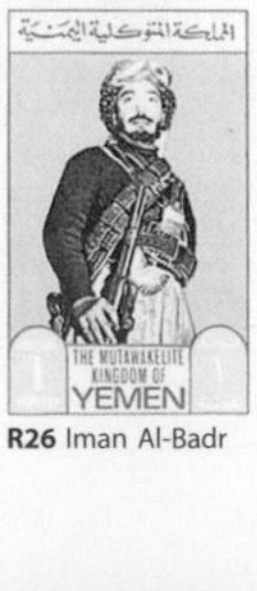

R26 Iman Al-Badr

1965

R83	R26	1b. black & bl (postage)	65	55
R83a	R26	1½b. black and green	28·00	55·00
R84	-	2b. red and green	1·70	1·10
R85	R26	4b. black and purple	2·20	1·70
R86	-	6b. red and violet (air)	3·00	2·20
R87	-	18b. red and brown	8·25	4·00
R88	-	24b. red and blue	13·50	5·50

DESIGNS—VERT: 2b., 18b. Royal arms. HORIZ: 6b., 24b. Flag.

1965. Space Flight of "Mariner 4". Nos. R55/7 optd **MARINER 4** in English and Arabic.

R89	R17	2b. orange, violet and black (postage)	4·50	4·50
R90	R17	4b. brown, blue & black	9·00	9·00
R91	R17	6b. yellow & black (air)	13·50	13·50
MSR91a Sheet No. **MS**R57a optd as Nos. R89/91			25·00	25·00

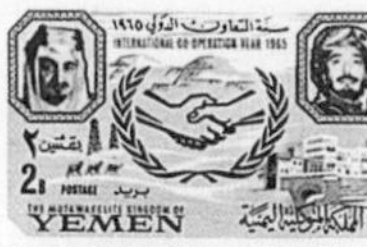

R28 I.C.Y. Emblem, King Faisal of Saudi Arabia and Iman Al-Badr

1965. International Co-operation Year.

R92	R28	2b. blue and brown (postage)	1·70	1·70
R93	R28	4b. red and green	2·75	2·75
R94	R28	6b. brown and blue (air)	4·00	4·00
MSR94a 101×76 mm. No. R93 in new colours. Imperf			13·50	11·00

1965. Space Flight of "Gemini 5". Nos. R69/71 optd **'GEMINI-V' GORDON COOPER & CHARLES CONRAD AUGUST 21-29, 1965** and space capsule.

R95	R23	2b. yellow, violet and black (postage)	4·50	4·50
R96	R23	4b. red, blue and black	9·00	9·00
R97	R23	6b. green, violet and black (air)	14·50	14·50
MSR98 Sheet No. **MS**R71a optd as Nos. R95/7			85·00	£170

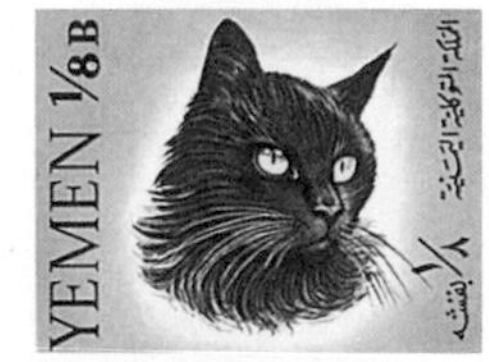

R30 Black Persian

1965. Cats. Multicoloured.

R99	⅛b. Type R **30**	55	55
R100	¼b. Tortoiseshell	55	55
R101	½b. Sealpoint Siamese	90	90
R102	1b. Silver tabby Persian	1·50	1·50
R103	2b. Cream Persian	2·75	2·75
R104	4b. Red tabby	5·00	5·00
MSR105 120×90 mm. 4b. multicoloured incorporating designs of Nos. R99/104. Imperf		20·00	20·00

Nos R102/4 are vert.

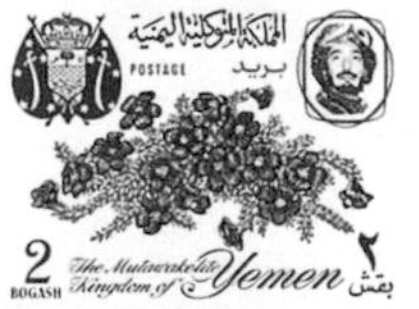

R31 Red Saxifrage

1965. Flowers. Multicoloured.

R106	⅛b. Verbena (vert)	45	10
R107	¼b. Dianthus (vert)	55	20
R108	½b. Dahlia (vert)	65	35
R109	1b. Nasturtium	1·30	65
R110	2b. Type R **31**	2·75	90
R111	4b. Wild rose	5·50	1·10
MSR112 102×76 mm. No. R111. Imperf		25·00	25·00

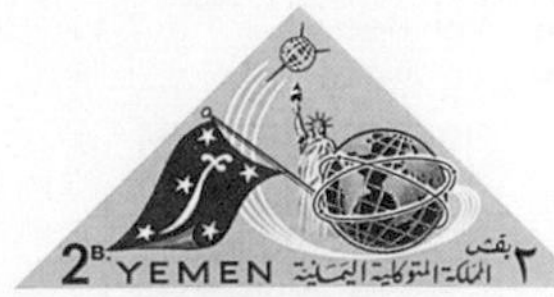

R32 Flag and Globe

1965. Pope Paul's Visit to U.N. Organization.

R113	R32	2b. red, black and green	2·75	2·20
R114	R32	4b. red, black and violet	4·50	4·00
R115	R32	6b. red, black and blue	5·00	4·50
MSR116 177×127 mm. Nos. R113/15. Imperf			17·00	17·00

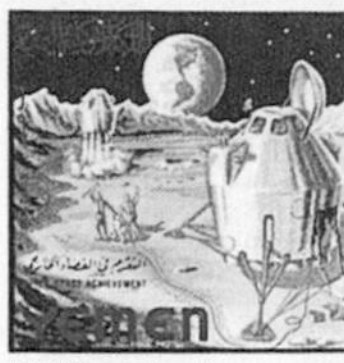

R33 Moon Landing

1965. Space Achievements. Multicoloured. (a) Postage. (i) Size as Type **R33**.

R117	⅛b. Type R **33**	45	20
R118	¼b. Astronauts on Moon	55	20
R119	½b. Pres. Kennedy and Cape Kennedy (vert)	65	25

(ii) Size 48×28 mm.

R120	4b. Belyaev and Leonov in space	4·50	90

(b) Air. Size 48×28 mm.

R121	6b. White and Mcdivitt in space	7·25	1·30
MSR122	114×84 mm. 4b. multicoloured incorporating designs of Nos. R119/21. Imperf	28·00	28·00

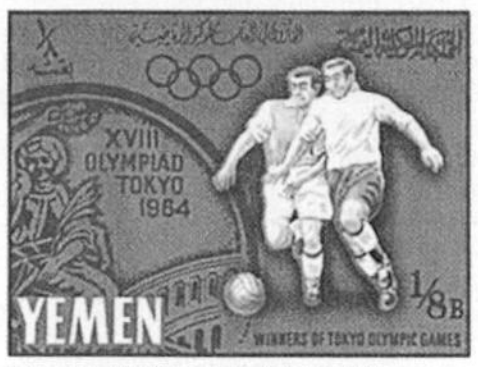

R34 Football and Gold Medal

1965. Winners of Olympic Games, Tokyo (1964). Each design showing a sport with a gold medal. Multicoloured.

R123	⅛b. Type R **34** (postage)	45	20
R124	¼b. Running	55	20
R125	½b. Throwing the discus	65	25
R126	2b. Judo	2·75	45
R127	4b. Wrestling	4·00	90
R128	6b. Horse-jumping (air)	5·00	1·30
MSR129	101×77 mm. 4b. multicoloured (design adapted from No. R128). Imperf	16·00	16·00

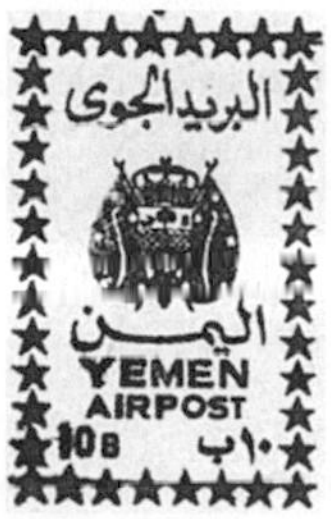

R35 Arms

1966. Air. Size varies. Imperf.

R130	**R35**	10b. red on white	
R131	**R35**	10b. violet on white	
R132	**R35**	10b. red on yellow	
R133	**R35**	10b. violet on orange	
R134	**R35**	10b. violet on mauve	

These handstamps were also applied directly to envelopes and aerogrammes.

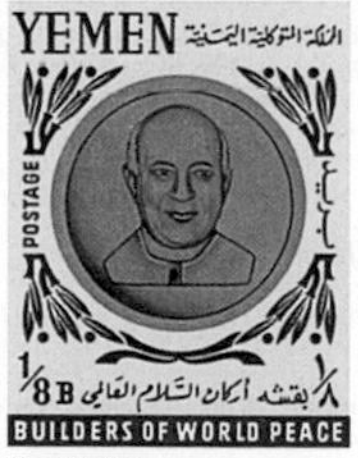

R36 Nehru

1966. Builders of World Peace (1st series). Portraits in gold and black; inscr in black.

R136	**R36**	⅛b. green	45	20
R137	-	¼b. brown	45	20
R138	-	½b. grey	45	20
R139	-	1b. blue	2·00	80
R140	-	4b. green	3·25	1·30
MSR141		120×100 mm. 4b. black, gold and grey (incorporating portraits of Nos. R136/40). Imperf	17·00	17·00

DESIGNS: ¼b. Dag Hammarskjold; ½b. Pope John XXIII; 1b. Sir Winston Churchill; 4b. Pres. Kennedy.

See also Nos. R146/51.

1966. Nos. R63/5 and R67 surch with new values in English and Arabic.

R142	**R21**	4b. on⅛b. black, mauve and gold (postage)	1·10	1·10
R143	-	8b. on ¼b. violet, turquoise and gold	2·20	2·20
R144	-	10b. on ½b. brown, blue and gold	3·25	3·25
R145	-	1r. on 6b. black, green and gold (air)	10·00	10·00

1966. Builders of World Peace (2nd series). As Type **R36**. Portraits in black and gold; inscr in black.

R146	⅛b. yellow	20	10
R147	¼b. pink	20	10
R148	½b. mauve	20	20
R149	1b. blue	1·70	65
R150	1b. green	1·70	65
R151	4b. green	4·50	1·70
MSR152	120×100 mm. 4b. black, gold and buff (incorporating portraits of Nos. R146/9 and R151). Imperf	13·50	13·50

PORTRAITS: ⅛b. Pres. Lubke; ¼b. Pres. De Gaulle; ½b. Pope Paul VI; 1b. (R149) Pres. Johnson; 1b. (R150) King Faisal of Saudi Arabia; 4b. U Thant.

1966. Newspaper Stamps. Optd **PERIODICALS** in English and Arabic in frame. (a) Similar to Nos. R26/7, but imperf.

R153	**R6**	4b. red, green and stone	22·00	28·00
R154	**R6**	6b. red, green and blue	22·00	28·00

(b) Unissued 1963 Red Cross Centenary issue (Nos. R26/7 surch).

R155	1b. on 4b. red, green and stone	28·00	33·00
R156	2b. on 6b. red, green and blue	45·00	50·00

(c) Miniature Sheet. Unissued 1963 Red Cross issue No. **MS**27a optd as Nos. R154/4, but larger 36×15 mm in Arabic only on 4b. and in English only on 6b.

MSR157	107×80 mm. Imperf	80·00	£110

The overprint on **MS**R157 reads "**RED GRESCENT**" instead of "**RED CRESCENT**" and for this reason it was not issued originally in 1963.

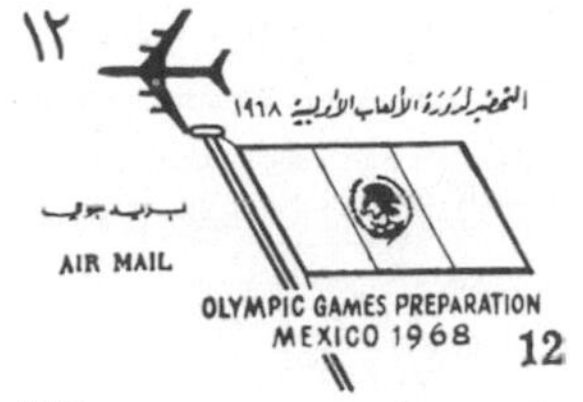

(R39)

1966. Air. Olympic Games Preparation, Mexico (1968). Nos. R123/5 in new colours and **MS**R129 surch as Type **R39**.

R158	12b. on⅛b. multicoloured	6·75	9·50
R159	28b. on ¼b. multicoloured	10·00	10·00
R160	34b. on ½b. multicoloured	11·00	11·00
MSR161	101×77 mm. No. **MS**R129 optd as Type R **39** but without surch or "AIR MAIL" etc	20·00	20·00

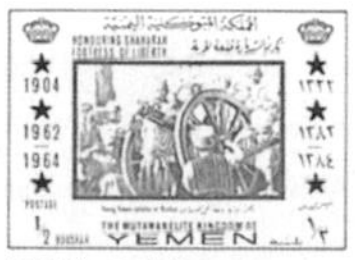

R40 Yemeni Cannon

1966. Shaharah Fortress. Frame and stars in red.

R162	**R40**	½b. bistre (postage)	55	55
R163	-	1b. grey	1·10	1·10
R164	-	1½b. blue	1·70	1·70
R165	-	2b. brown	2·20	2·20
R166	-	4b. green	2·75	2·75
R167	-	6b. violet (air)	3·25	3·25
R168	-	10b. black	5·00	5·00
MSR169		114×88 mm. 10b. green. Imperf	13·50	13·50

DESIGNS—VERT: 1b. Bombed Mosque; 2b. Victory Gate; 4b. Yemeni cannon (different); 10b. Bombed houses. HORIZ: 1½b. Shaharah Fortress; 6b. Yemeni cannon (different); 10b. (**MS**R169), Type R**40**.

1966. Nos. R33/5 surch **4B REVALUED** in English and Arabic within border of stars. Flags red; inscr in black.

R170	**R10**	4b. on⅛b. violet	£110	£110
R171	**R10**	4b. on ¼b. mauve	£110	£110
R172	**R10**	4b. on ½b. brown	£110	£110

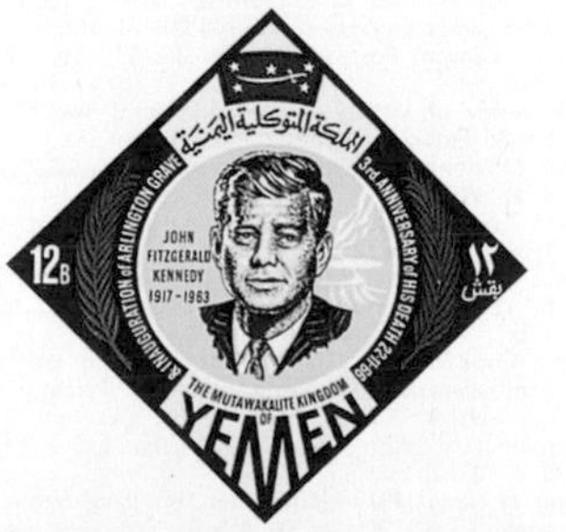

R42 President Kennedy

1967. Third Anniv of Pres. Kennedy's Death and Inauguration of Arlington Grave.

R173	**R42**	12b. multicoloured	1·70	55
R174	**R42**	28b. multicoloured	4·00	90
R175	**R42**	34b. multicoloured	5·50	1·30
MSR176		115×77 mm. 24b. multicoloured (Arlington Grave and scrolls). Imperf	8·25	8·25

1967. England's Victory in World Cup Football Championship (1966). Nos. R123/8 optd **WORLD CHAMPIONSHIP-CUP ENGLAND 1966** in English and Arabic, **ENGLAND WINNER** in English only and World Cup emblem.

R177	**R34**	⅛b. mult (postage)	65	65
R178	-	¼b. multicoloured	45	45
R179	-	½b. multicoloured	65	65
R180	-	2b. multicoloured	2·20	2·20
R181	-	4b. multicoloured	4·00	4·00
R182	-	6b. multicoloured (air)	5·50	5·50

1967. Surch **4B REVALUED** in English and Arabic within border of stars. (a) Nos. R123/5.

R183	**R34**	4b. on⅛b. mult		
R184	-	4b. on ¼b. mult		
R185	-	4b. on ½b. mult		

(b) Nos. R177/9.

R186	**R34**	4b. on⅛b. mult		
R187	-	4b. on ¼b. mult		
R188	-	4b. on ½b. mult		

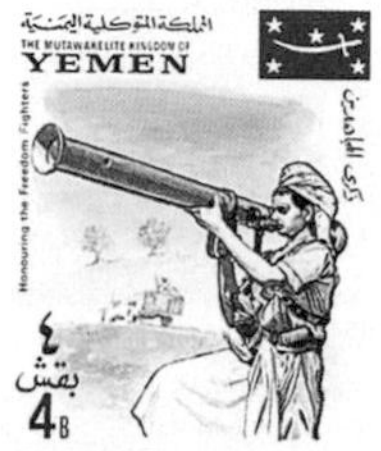

R44 Bazooka

1967. Freedom Fighters. Designs showing Freedom Fighters with various weapons. Multicoloured.

R189	4b. Type R **44**	1·70	55
R190	4b. Fighter in fez with rifle	1·70	55
R191	4b. Bare-headed man with rifle	1·70	55
R192	4b. Fighters holding bazooka and round	1·70	55
R193	4b. Anti-aircraft gun	1·70	55
R194	4b. Heavy machine-gun	1·70	55
R195	4b. Light machine-gun	1·70	55
R196	4b. Fighter with bazooka on mount and rifle	1·70	55
MSR197	114×77 mm. No. R196 (sold at 10b.)	8·25	5·50

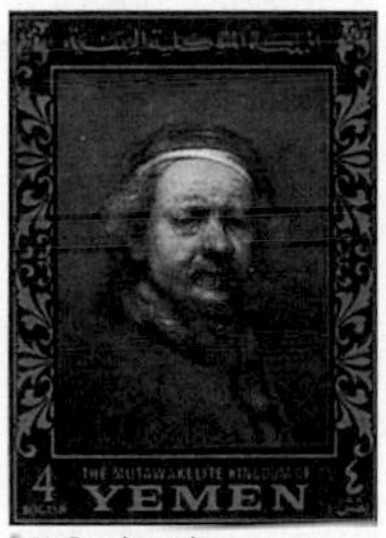

R45 Rembrandt—Self-portrait

1967. "AMPHILEX" Stamp Exhibition, Amsterdam. Rembrandt Paintings. Multicoloured. (a) Borders in gold.

R198	2b. "An Elderly Man as St. Paul"	35	20
R199	4b. Type R **45**	45	20
R200	6b. "Portrait of Jacob Trip"	65	25
R201	10b. "An Old Man in an Armchair"	90	45
R202	12b. Self-portrait (different)	1·30	55
R203	20b. "A Woman Bathing"	2·00	60
MSR204	177×150 mm. Nos. R198/203	10·00	4·00

(b) Borders in silver.

R205	2b. As No. R198	45	20
R206	4b. Type R **45**	65	20
R207	6b. As No. R200	90	30
R208	10b. As No. R201	1·10	45
R209	12b. As No. R202	2·00	55
R210	20b. As No. R203	3·25	65
MSR211	177×150 mm. Nos. R205/10	10·00	4·00

1967. Pres. Kennedy's 50th Birth Anniv. Nos. R173/5 optd **50th. ann. 29 MAY** in English only.

R212	**R42**	12b. multicoloured	1·70	55
R213	**R42**	28b. multicoloured	4·00	90
R214	**R42**	34b. multicoloured	5·50	1·30
MSR215		115×77 mm. 24b. multicoloured. Imperf	8·25	8·25

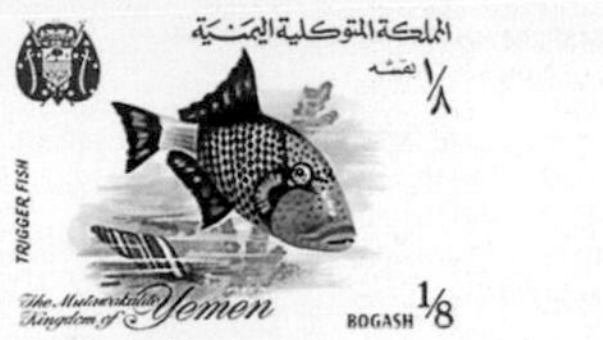

R47 Triggerfish

1967. Red Sea Fish. Multicoloured.

R216	⅛b. Type R **47** (postage)	1·60	45
R217	¼b. Striped rudderfish	1·60	45
R218	½b. Hooded butterflyfish	1·60	45
R219	1b. Spotted coral grouper	1·30	45
R220	4b. Lionfish	1·70	45
R221	6b. Brown anemonefish	2·20	45
R222	10b. Violet-hued berycid	3·25	45
R224	12b. As No. R222 (air)	1·10	10
R225	14b. Cuckoo wrasse	1·30	10
R226	16b. Japanese bonyhead	1·60	20
R227	18b. As No. R221	1·80	35
R228	24b. As No. R220	2·00	45
R229	34b. As No. R219	2·50	65
MSR223	147×109 mm. 10b. Butterflyfish	7·25	5·50

Nos. R216/22 are Type R **47**; Nos. R224/9 are larger, size 58×42 mm.

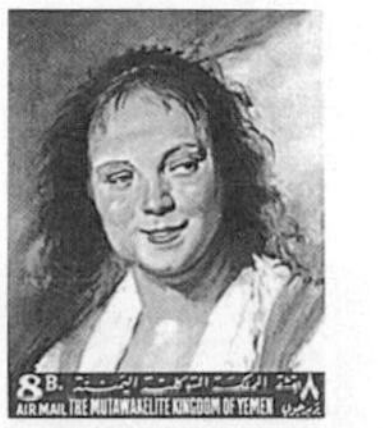

R48 "The Gipsy Girl" (Frans Hals)

1967. Air. Famous Paintings. Multicoloured.

R230	8b. Type R **48**	55	20
R231	10b. "The Zouave" (Van Gogh)	80	20
R232	12b. Self-portrait (Rubens)	1·00	35
R233	14b. "Buys Eating Melon" (Murilio)	1·20	35
R234	16b. "The Knight's Dream" (Raphael)	1·60	40
R235	20b. "St. George and the Dragon" (Ucello) (horiz)	1·70	45

1967. "For Poison Gas Victims". Surch **FOR POISON GAS VICTIMS** and surcharge in English and Arabic with skull and crossbones within frame.

R236	**R40**	½b.+1b. (No. R162) (postage)		
R237	-	1b.+1b. (R163)		
R238	-	1½b.+1b. (R164)		
R239	-	2b.+1b. (R84)		
R240	-	2b.+1b. (R126)		
R241	-	2b.+1b. (R165)		
R242	**R20**	4b.+2b. (R62)		
R243	-	4b.+2b. (R66)		
R244	**R20**	4b.+2b. (R68)		
R245	**R26**	4b.+2b. (R85)		
R246	**R34**	4b.+2b. (R93)		
R247	-	4b.+2b. (R127)		
R248	-	4b.+2b. (R166)		
R249	-	6b.+3b. (R86) (air)		
R250	-	6b.+3b. (R128)		
R251	-	6b.+3b. (R167)		
R252	**R35**	10b.+5b. (R130)		
R253	-	10b.+5b. (R168)		
R254	**R32**	12b.+6b. (R158)		
R255	-	18b.+9b. (R87)		
R256	**R12**	24b.+12b. red and blue (imperf, size 57×36 mm)		
R257	-	24b.+12b. (R88)		
R258	-	28b.+14b. (R159)		
R259	-	34b.+17b. (R160)		
MSR260		24b.+12b. (**MS**R43a)	31·00	31·00

The amount of surcharge was 50 per cent of the face value of each stamp (except Nos. R236/8 where the surcharge was 1b. each). Some higher values have two handstamps, which, when added together, make up the 50 per cent.

1967. Jordan Relief Fund. Surch **JORDAN RELIEF FUND** and value in English and Arabic with Crown. (a) No. R66 (Kennedy).

R261	4b.+2b. brown, yellow and gold	9·00	9·00

(b) Nos. R75/6 and **MS**R76a (Birds).

R262	4b.+2b. mult (postage)	4·50	4·50
R263	6b.+3b. mult (air)	6·75	6·75
MSR264	4b.+2b. multicoloured	11·00	11·00

(c) Nos. R92/4 and **MS**R94a (I.C.Y.).

R265	**R34**	2b.+1b. blue and brown (postage)	1·10	1·10
R266	**R34**	4b.+2b. red and green	1·70	1·70
R267	**R34**	6b.+3b. brown and blue (air)	2·20	2·20

MSR268		4b.+2b. As no. R93 in new colours.	11·00	11·00

(d) Nos. R102/4 and MSR105 (Cats).

R269		1b.+1b. multicoloured	1·70	1·70
R270		2b.+1b. multicoloured	2·20	2·20
R271		4b.+2b. multicoloured	4·00	4·00
MSR272		4b.+2b. mult	11·00	11·00

(e) R109/11 and MSR112 (Flowers).

R273	-	1b.+1b. multicoloured	1·70	1·70
R274	R30	2b.+1b. multicoloured	2·20	2·20
R275	-	4b.+2b. multicoloured	2·75	2·75
MSR276		4b.+2b. multicoloured	13·50	13·50

(f) Nos. R136/40 and MSR141 (Builders of World Peace).

R277	R36	⅛b.+1b. gold, black and green	1·10	1·10
R278	-	¼b.+1b. gold, black and brown	1·70	1·70
R279	-	½b.+1b. gold, black and grey	1·70	1·70
R280	-	1b.+1b. gold, black and blue	1·80	1·80
R281	-	4b.+2b. gold, black and green	3·25	3·25
MSR282		4b.+2b. black, gold and grey	45·00	

(g) Nos. R146/51 and MSR152 (Builders of World Peace).

R283	⅛b.+1b. gold, black and yellow	1·10	1·10
R284	¼b.+1b. gold, black and pink	1·10	1·10
R285	½b.+1b. gold, black and mauve	1·10	1·10
R286	1b.+1b. gold, black and blue	2·20	2·20
R287	1b.+1b. gold, black and green	1·10	1·10
R288	4b.+2b. gold, black and green	5·50	5·50
MSR289	4b.+2b. black, gold and buff	22·00	22·00

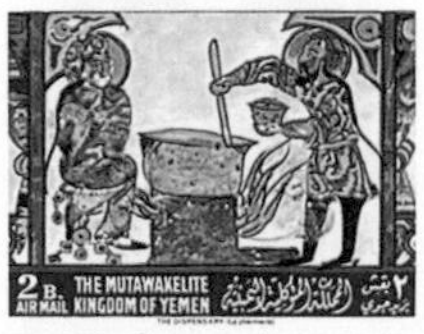

R51 "The Pharmacy"

1967. Air. Paintings. Multicoloured. (a) Asiatic Paintings.

R290	⅛b. "Mountains and Forests" (Wang Hwei)	20	20
R291	¼b. "Tiger" (Sim Sajoug)	30	30
R292	½b. "Mountain Views" (Tong K'itch'ang)	35	35
R293	¾b. "Rama Lakshama and Shiva" (Indian 16th century)	40	40
R294	1b. "Ladies" (T. Kiyomitsu)	45	45

(b) Arab Paintings.

R295	1½b. "Bayad plays the Oud and sings"	55	55
R296	2b. Type R **51**	65	65
R297	3b. "Dioscorides and a Student"	80	80
R298	4b. "The Scribe"	1·10	1·10
R299	6b. "Abu Zayd asks to be taken over by boat"	1·70	1·70
MSR300	90×72 mm. No. R299. Imperf	6·75	6·75

The⅛, 1½, 2 and 6b. are horiz and the remainder vert.

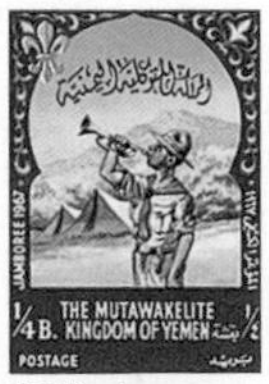

R52 Bugler

1967. World Scout Jamboree, Idaho. Multicoloured.

R301	¼b. Type R **52** (postage)	10	10
R302	½b. Campfire	10	10
R303	4b. Type R **52**	65	65
R304	6b. As ½b.	1·10	1·10
R305	⅛b. Scout badge and Yemeni flag (air)	20	20
R306	10b. As⅛b.	1·70	1·70
R307	20b. Scout and satellite	3·25	3·25
MSR308	72×99 mm. No. R307 but larger. Imperf	6·75	6·75

1967. Jordan Refugees Relief Fund. Surch **JORDAN REFUGEES RELIEF FUND** and value in English and Arabic, and Refugee Emblem. (a) Nos. R52/4 and **MS**R54a (Olympic Games).

R309	R16	2b.+2b. bl (postage)	1·10	1·10
R310	R16	4b.+4b. violet	2·20	2·20
R311	R16	6d.+6d. brown (air)	3·25	3·25
MSR312		4b.+2b. ultramarine	13·50	13·50

(b) Nos. R55/7 and MSR57a (Astronauts).

R313	R17	2b.+2b. brown, violet and black (postage)	1·10	1·10
R314	R17	4b.+4b. brown, blue and black	2·20	2·20
R315	R17	6b.+6b. yellow and black (air)	3·25	3·25
MSR316		6b.+6b. blue and sepia	13·50	13·50

(c) Nos. R63/7 and MSR67a (Kennedy).

R317	R21	⅛b.+⅛b. black, mauve and gold (postage)	20	20
R318	-	¼b.+¼b. violet, turquoise and gold	45	45
R319	-	½b.+½b. brown, blue and gold	90	90
R320	-	4b.+4b. brown, yellow and gold	4·50	4·50
R321	-	6b.+6b. black, green and gold (air)	7·75	7·75
MSR322		4b.+4b. black, green and gold	17·00	17·00

(d) No. R68 (Churchill opt).

R323	R20	4b.+4b. blue and red	17·00	17·00

(e) R69/71 and MSR71a (I.T.U.).

R324	R23	2b.+2b. yellow, violet and black (postage)	1·10	2·50
R325	R23	4b.+4b. red, blue and black	2·20	4·50
R326	R23	6b.+6b. green, violet and black (air)	3·25	9·50
MSR327		4b.+4b. red, blue and black	29·00	29·00

(f) R77/82 and MSR72a (Churchill).

R328	R25	⅛b.+⅛b. multicoloured	10	10
R329	-	¼b.+¼b. multicoloured	45	45
R330	-	½b.+½b. multicoloured	65	65
R331	R25	1b.+1b. multicoloured	1·10	1·10
R332	-	2b.+2b. multicoloured	2·20	2·20
R333	-	4b.+4b. multicoloured	4·00	4·00
MSR334		4b.+4b. multicoloured	17·00	17·00

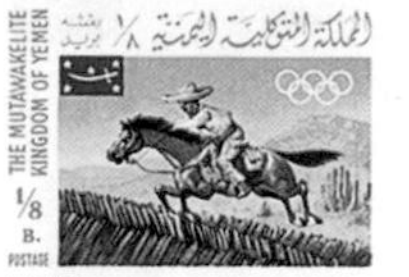

R54 Vaquero

1967. Olympic Games, Mexico (1968). Multicoloured.

R335	⅛b. Type R **54** (postage)	10	10
R336	¼b. Fishermen on Lake Patzcuaro	10	10
R337	½b. Football (vert)	10	10
R338	4b. Avenida de la Reforma, Mexico City	55	55
R339	8b. Fine Arts Theatre, Mexico City	90	90
R340	12b. Mayan ruins (air)	1·10	1·10
R341	16b. Type R **54**	1·70	1·70
R342	20b. As ¼b.	2·20	2·20
MSR343	97×70 mm. 16b. As Type R **54**, but larger and without flag. Imperf	9·00	9·00

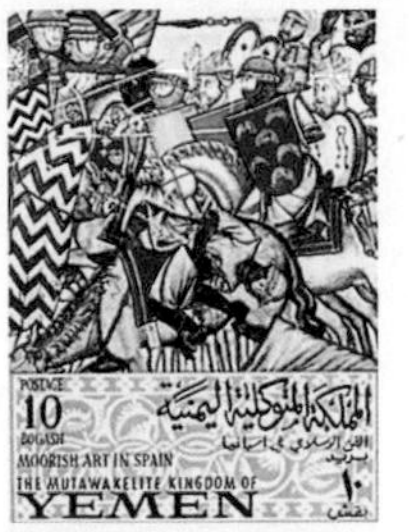

R55 Battle Scene

1967. Moorish Art in Spain. Multicoloured.

R344	2b. Moor slaying knight (horiz) (postage)	20	20
R345	4b. Arab kings of Granada (horiz)	45	45
R346	6b. Diagram of chess game (from King Alfonso X's "Book of Chess, Dice and Tablings") (horiz)	65	65
R347	10b. Type R **55**	1·10	1·10
R348	12b. Moors with prisoners	1·30	1·30
R349	20b. Meeting of Moor and Christian (air)	1·80	1·80
R350	22b. Bullfight	2·20	2·20
R351	24b. Lute players	2·50	2·50
MSR352	106×80 mm. 28b. black, red and light blue (interior of Alhambra, Granada and treasures). Imperf	6·75	2·75

APPENDIX

The following stamps have either been issued in excess of postal needs or have not been available to the public in reasonable quantities at face calue. Such stamps may later be given full listing if there is evidence of regular postal needs.

REPUBLIC

1967

5th Anniv of Revolution Nos. 476/81 optd in Arabic 1, 2, 4, 6, 8, 10b.
Paintings by Flemish Masters. Postage ¼,⅓, ½b.; Air 3, 6b.
Paintings by Florentine Masters. Postage ¼,⅓, ½b.; Air 3, 6b.
Paintings by Spanish Masters. Postage ¼,⅓, ½b.; Air 3, 6b.
Winter Olympic Games, Grenoble (1968) (1st issue). Embossed on gold foil. Air 5, 10, 15, 50b.
Winter Olympic Games, Grenoble (1968) (2nd issue). Sports ¼,⅓, ½, 3, 6b.
Chancellor Adenauer Commemoration (1st issue). Embossed on gold foil. Air 50b.

1968

Yemen Red Crescent. Embossed on gold foil. Air 5, 10, 15, 50b.
Paintings by Gauguin. Postage ¼, ¼,⅓,⅓, ½, ½b.; Air 3, 3, 6, 6b.
Paintings by Van Gogh. Postage ¼, ¼,⅓,⅓, ½, ½b.; Air 3, 3, 6, 6b.
Paintings by Rubens. Postage ¼, ¼,⅓,⅓, ½, ½b.; Air 3, 3, 6, 6b.
Provisionals. Various 1930/31 values optd "Y.A.R." and date in English and Arabic. ½, 1, 1, 2, 2, 3, 4, 4, 5, 6, 6, 10, 10, 20b., 1, 1i.
Gold Medal Winners. Winter Olympic Games, Grenoble (1st issue). 1967 Winter Olympic Games (1st issue) optd with names of winners. Air 50b.×4.
1st Death Anniv of Vladimir Komarov (Russian cosmonaut). Air 5, 10, 15, 50b.
International Human Rights Year and U Thant Commemoration. Embossed on gold foil. Air 5, 10, 15, 50b.
Chancellor Adenauer Commemoration (2nd issue). Air 5, 10, 15b.
Refugee Relief. Adenauer (2nd issue) optd in Arabic only. Air 5, 10, 15, 50b.
Olympic Games, Mexico (1st issue). Chariot-racing. Embossed on gold foil. Air 5, 10, 15, 50b.
Paintings of Horses. Postage ¼,⅓, ½b.; Air 3, 6b.
Paintings by Raphael. Postage ¼,⅓, ½b.; Air 3, 6b.
Paintings by Rembrandt. Postage ¼,⅓, ½b.; Air 3, 6b.
Dr. Martin Luther King Commemoration (1st issue). Human Rights issue optd. Air 50b.
Gold Medal Winners. Winter Olympic Games, Grenoble (2nd Issue). Postage ¼,⅓, ½, 2b.; Air 3, 4b.
Olympic Games, Mexico (2nd issue). Greek and Mexican Folklore. Postage ¼,⅓, ½, 2b.; Air 3, 4b.
Gold Medal Winners, Olympic Games, Mexico (1st issue). Mexico Olympics (1st issue) optd with names of various winners. Air 50b.×4.
Gold Medal Winners Olympic Games, Mexico (2nd issue). Postage ¼,⅓, ½, 2b.; Air 3, 4b.
Dr. Martin Luther King Commemoration (2nd issue). Embossed on gold foil. 16b.
Emblems of Winter Olympic Games. Postage ¼,⅓, ½, 2b.; Air 3, 4b.
Emblems of Olympic Games. Postage ¼,⅓, ½, 2b.; Air 3, 4b.
Dag Hammarskjold and Kennedy Brothers Commemoration. ½, 2, 6, 14b.
Dr. Christian Barnard's Heart Transplant Operations. ¼, ¾, 8, 10b.
Dr. Martin Luther King Commemoration (3rd issue). 1, 4, 12, 16b.
John and Robert Kennedy Commemoration. Embossed on gold foil. 10b.

1969

Paintings from the Louvre, Paris. Postage ¼,⅓, ½, 2b.; Air 3, 4b.
1st Death Anniv of Yurstet Gagarin (Russian cosmonaut). Optd on 1968 Komarov issue. Air 50b.
Paintings from the Uffizi Gallery, Florence. Postage ¼,⅓, ½, 2b.; Air 3, 4b.
Paintings from the Prado, Madrid. Postage ¼,⅓, ½, 2b.; Air 3b, 4b.
Birth Bicentenary of Napoleon (1st issue). Embossed on gold foil. Air 4b.
Space Exploration (1st series). Inscr "DISCOVERIES OF UNIVERSE". Postage ¼, ¼,⅓,⅓b.; Air 3, 6, 10b.
Space Exploration (2nd series). Inscr "FLIGHTS TO THE PLANETS". Postage ¼, ¼,⅓,⅓b.; Air 2, 4, 22b.
First Man on the Moon. Embossed on gold foil. Air 10b.
50th Anniv of International Labour Organization. Postage 1, 2, 3, 4b.; Air 6, 8, 10b.
Space Exploration (3rd series). Inscr "MAN IN SPACE". Postage ¼, ¼,⅓,⅓b.; Air 3, 6, 10b.
Birth Bicentenary of Napoleon (2nd issue). Postage ¼,⅓, ½, ¾b.; Air 4, 8, 10b.
Space Exploration (4th series). "Apollo" Moon Flights. Postage ¼, ¼,⅓,⅓b.; Air 2, 4, 22b.
Winter Olympic Games, Sapporo (1972) Preparation. Optd on 1967 Grenoble Winter Olympics issue. Air 50b.
Olympic Games, Munich (1972) Preparation. Optd on 1968 Mexico Olympics issue. Air 50b.
Paintings from the National Gallery, Washington. Postage ¼,⅓, ½, 2b.; Air 3, 4b.
Paintings from the National Gallery, London. Postage ¼,⅓, ½, 2b.; Air 3, 4b.
French Monarchs and Statesmen. Postage 1¾, 2, 2¼, 2½b.; Air 3½, 5, 6b.

1970

Tutankhamun Exhibition, Paris. Postage ¼,⅓, ½, 2b.; Air 3, 4b.
Siamese Sculptures. Postage ¼,⅓, ½, 2b.; Air 3, 4b.
"EXPO 70" World Fair, Osaka, Japan (1st issue). Japanese Paintings. Postage ¼,⅓, ½, 2b.; Air 3, 4b.
EXPO 70" World Fair, Osaka, Japan (2nd issue). Japanese Puppets. Postage ¼,⅓, ½, 2b.; Air 3, 4b.
World Cup Football Championship, Mexico (1st issue). Views and Maps. Postage 1¾, 2, 2¼, 2½b.; Air 3½, 5, 6, 7, 8b.
World Cup Football Championship, Mexico (2nd issue). Jules Rimet. Embossed on gold foil. Air 10b.
"United Europe". Postage 1⅓, 1¾, 2¼, 2½, 5b.; Air 7, 8, 10b.
25th Anniv of Victory in Second World War. Gen. de Gaulle. Embossed on gold foil. Air 6b.
Moon Mission of "Apollo 12". Postage 1, 1¼, 1⅓, 1½b.; Air 4, 4½, 7b.
World Cup Football Championship, Mexico (3rd issue). Teams. Postage ¼,⅓, ½, ¾b.; Air 4, 4½b.
World Cup Football Championship, Mexico (4th issue). Beckenbauer and Pele. Embossed on gold foil. Air 10b.
World Cup Football Championship, Mexico (5th issue). Footballers and Mexican Antiquities. Postage 1, 1¼, 1⅓, 1½b.; Air 3, 10b.
Interplanetary Space Travel. Postage 1¾, 2, 2¼, 2½b.; Air 5, 8, 10, 22b.
Inaug of New U.P.U. Headquarters Building, Berne. Postage⅓, 1¼, 1½, 2b.; Air 3½, 4½, 6b.
"Philympia 70" Stamp Exhibition, London. Postage ¼, ½, 1, 3b.; Air 4b.
8th Anniv of Revolution. Flowers. ¼b.×5.
Olympic Games, Munich (1972) (1st issue). Buildings. Postage 1, 1¾, 2½, 3, 3½b.; Air 8, 10b.
Olympic Games, Munich (2nd issue). Statue. Embossed on gold foil. Air 6b.
25th Anniv of United Nations. Human Rights Year issue of 1968 optd. Air 50b.
Winter Olympic Games, Sapporo (1st issue). Buildings and Emblem. Postage 1½, 2½, 4½, 5, 7b.; Air 8, 10b.
Winter Olympic Games, Sapporo (2nd issue). Snow Sculpture. Embossed on gold foil. Air 40b.
General Charles de Gaulle Commemoration. 1970 25th Anniv of Victory issue optd. Air 6b.
German Gold Medal Winners in Olympic Games. Postage ¼, ¼,⅓,⅓b. Air 6b.

1971

Pres. Gamal Nasser of Egypt Commemoration. Postage ⅛b.×4, ½b.×2; Air 1, 2, 5, 7, 10, 16b.
International Sporting Events. Postage ¼,⅓, ½, 2b.; Air 3, 4b.
Olympic Games, Munich (3rd issue). Theatre Productions. Postage ½, 1¼, 1¾, 2¼, 4½b.; Air 5, 6b.
Moon Mission of "Apollo 14" 1969 Moon Landing issue optd. Air 10b.
Olympic Games, Munich (4th issue). Paintings from the Pinakothek. Postage ¼,⅓, ¾, 1½, 2b.; Air 4, 7b.
Chinese Paintings. Postage ¼,⅓, ½, 2b.; Air 3, 4b.
Winter Olympic Games, Sapporo (3rd issue). Winter Sports and Japanese Works of Art. Postage ¼, ½, 1, 1⅓, 2b.; Air 3, 4b.
Winter Olympic Games, Sapporo (4th issue). Japanese Skier. Embossed on gold foil. Air 8b.
Launching of Soviet "Salyut" Space Station. Interplanetary issue of 1970 optd. Air 22b.
Olympic Games, Munich (5th issue). Sports and Sculptures. Postage⅛, 1, 1⅓, 1¾, 2¼b.; Air 4½, 7, 10b.
Olympic Games, Munich (6th issue). Gold Medals. Embossed on gold foil. Air 8b.
Exploration of Outer Space. Postage ¼,⅓, ½, ¾b.; Air 3, 3½, 6b.
Birth Bicentenary of Beethoven. Postage ¼×4, ½b.×2; Air 1, 2, 5, 7, 10b.
Indian Paintings. Postage ¼,⅓, ½, 2b.; Air 3, 4b.
Olympic Games, Munich (7th issue). Sailing Events at Kiel. Postage ¼, ½, 1¼, 2, 3b.; Air 4b.
Winter Olympic Games, Sapporo (5th issue). Sports. Postage⅓, ¾, 1¼, 1¾, 2¼b.; Air 3½, 6b.
Winter Olympic Games, Sapporo (6th issue). Slalom Skier. Embossed on gold foil. Air 10b.
Persian Miniatures. Postage ¼,⅓, ½, 2b.; Air 3, 4b.
Olympic Games, Munich (8th issue). Sports. Postage 1½, 2½, 3½, 5b.; Air 6, 8b.
Olympic Games, Munich (9th issue). Discus-thrower. Embossed on gold foil. Air 10b.
Italian Gold Medal Winners in Olympic Games. Postage ¼b.×2,⅓b.×2; Air 22b.

1972

French Gold Medal Winners in Olympic Games. Postage 2, 3b.; Air 4, 10b.
Works of Art. Postage 1, 1¼, 1⅓, 1½b.; Air 3, 4½, 7b.

ROYALIST ISSUES

1967

Visit of Queen of Sheba to Solomon.⅛, ¼, ½, 4, 6, 20, 24b.
Arab Horses.⅛, ¼, ½, 4, 10b.

1968

Winter Olympic Games, Grenoble (1st issue). Nos. R216/29 optd. Postage⅛, ¼, ½, 1, 4, 6, 10b.; Air 12, 14, 16, 24, 34b.
Butterflies. Air 16, 20, 40b.
Postage Due. Butterflies and Horse. 4, 16, 20b.
Winter Olympic Games, Grenoble (2nd issue). Sports. Postage 1, 2, 3, 4, 6b.; Air 10, 12, 18, 24, 28b.
Gold Medal Winners, Grenoble Winter Olympics. Winter Olympic Games, Grenoble (2nd issue) optd with names of various medal winners. Postage 1, 2, 3, 4, 6b.; Air 10, 12, 18, 24, 28b.
20th Anniv of UNESCO. ½, 1, 1½, 2, 3, 4, 6, 10b.
Mothers' Day. Paintings. Postage 2, 4, 6b.; Air 24, 28, 34b.
Olympic Games, Mexico (1st issue). Sports. Postage 1, 2, 3, 4, 6b.; Air 10, 12, 18, 24, 28b.
UNESCO. "Save Florence" Campaign. Paintings. Postage 2, 4, 6b.; Air 10, 12, 18b.
UNESCO. "Save Venice" Campaign. Paintings. ½, 1, 1½, 24b.; Air 28, 34b.
Olympic Games, Mexico (2nd issue). Athletes and Flags. 4b.×11.
Winter Olympic Games since 1924. Competitors and Flags. Postage. 1, 2, 3, 4, 6b.; Air 10, 12, 18, 24, 28b.
International Human Rights Year. 2b.×4, 4b.×4, 6b.×4.
Paintings by European and American Artists. Postage 1, 2, 3, 4, 6, 10b.; Air 12, 18, 24, 28b.
Coronation of Shah of Iran. Postage 1, 2, 3, 4b.; Air 24, 28b.
International Philately. Postage 1, 2, 3, 4, 6b.; Air 10, 12, 18, 24, 28b.
World Racial Peace. Postage 4, 6, 18b.; Air 10b.
Children's Day. Paintings. Postage 1, 2, 3, 4b.; Air 6, 10, 12, 18, 24, 28b.
Gold Medal Winners, Mexico Olympic Games (1st issue). Mexico Olympics (1st issue) optd with names of various medal winners. Postage 1, 2, 3, 4, 6b.; Air 10, 12, 18, 24, 28b.
Gold Medal Winners, Mexico Olympics (2nd issue). Athletes and Medals. Air 12, 18, 24, 28, 34b.
Gold Medal Winners, Mexico Olympics (3rd issue). Embossed on gold foil. 28b.
"EFIMEX 68" Stamp Exhibition, Mexico City. Air 12, 18, 24, 28, 34b.

1969

Motor-racing Drivers. Postage 1, 2, 3, 4, 6b.; Air 10, 12, 18, 24, 28b.
Space Flight of "Apollo 7". 4, 8, 12, 24, 28b.
Space Flight of "Apollo 8" (1st issue). 4, 6, 10, 18, 34b.
Space Flight of "Apollo 8" (2nd issue). Embossed on gold foil. 28b.
5th Anniv of Imam's Meeting with Pope Paul VI at Jerusalem (1st issue). Scenes from Pope's Visit.⅛, ¼, ¼, 1, 1½, 2, 3, 4, 5, 6b.
5th Anniv of Imam's Meeting with Pope Paul VI at Jerusalem (2nd issue). Paintings of the Life of Christ. Postage 1, 2, 3, 4, 5, 6, 7, 8, 9, 10b.; Air 11, 12, 13, 14, 15, 16, 17, 18, 19, 20, 21, 22, 23, 24, 25, 26, 27, 28, 29, 30b.

5th Anniv of Imam's Meeting with Pope Paul VI at Jerusalem (3rd issue). Abraham's Tomb, Hebron. 4b.
Paintings by Rembrandt (1st series). Postage 1, 2, 4b.; Air 6, 12b., 1i.
Paintings by Rembrandt (2nd series). Embossed on gold foil. 20b.
Paintings by European Artists. Postage ½, 1½, 3, 5b.; Air 10, 18, 24, 28, 34b.
"Apollo" Moon Programme. Postage 1, 2, 3, 4, 5b.; Air 6, 7, 8, 9, 10, 11, 12, 13, 14, 15b.
Moon Flight of "Apollo 10". Postage 2, 4, 6b.; Air 8, 10, 12, 18, 24, 28, 34b.
Olympic Games, Munich (1972). Athletes and Olympic Rings. Postage 1, 2, 4, 5, 6b.; Air 10, 12, 18, 24, 34b.
World Wildlife Conservation. Postage ½b.×2 1b.×2, 2b.×2, 4b.×2, 6b.×2; Air 8b.×2, 10b.×2, 18b.×2.
First Man on the Moon (1st issue). Air 6, 10, 12, 18b.
First Man on the Moon (2nd issue). Air 6, 10, 12, 18, 24b.
First Man on the Moon (3rd issue). Embossed on gold foil. 24b.×2.
First Man on the Moon (4th issue). Embossed on gold foil. 28b.
First Man on the Moon (5th issue). Air 10, 12 18, 24b.
Palestine Holy Places. Postage 4b.×4, 6b.×10; Air 12b.×8.
Famous Men. Postage 4b.×4, 6b.×10; Air 12b.×2.
History of Space Exploration. Air 6b.×27.
Olympic Sports. Postage 1, 2, 4, 5, 6b.; Air 10, 12, 18, 24, 34b.
World Cup Football Championship, Mexico. Air 12b.×8.
Christmas. Ikons. Postage ½, 1, 1½, 2, 4, 5, 6b.; Air 10, 12, 18, 24, 28, 34b.
Burning of Al-Aqsa Mosque, Jerusalem. Postage 4b.+2b., 6b.+3b.; Air 10b.+5b.

1970

Brazil's Victory in World Cup Football Championship, Mexico. 1969 World Cup issue optd. Air 12b.×3.
Dogs. Postage 2, 4, 6b.; Air 8, 12b.
Paintings of Horses. Postage 2, 4, 6b.; Air 8, 12b.

We close the Appendix with stamps believed to have been issued prior to July 1970, when first Saudi Arabia and then the United Kingdom recognised the Republican government in Yemen.

Pt. 19

YEMEN PEOPLE'S DEMOCRATIC REPUBLIC

The former People's Republic of Southern Yemen was known by the above title from 30 November 1970. In 1990 it united with Yemen Arab Republic (see YEMEN REPUBLIC (combined)).

1000 fils = 1 dinar.

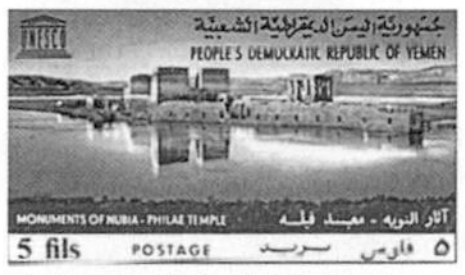

22 Temple of Isis, Philae, Egypt

1971. Preservation of Philae Temples Campaign.

65	**22**	5f. multicoloured	20	20
66	**22**	35f. multicoloured	85	55
67	**22**	65f. multicoloured	2·10	1·40

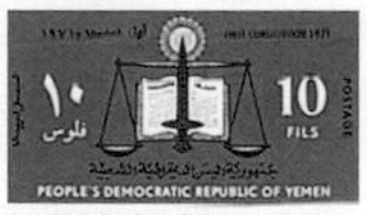

23 Symbols of Constitution

1971. Introduction of First Constitution.

68	**23**	10f. multicoloured	20	20
69	**23**	15f. multicoloured	45	30
70	**23**	35f. multicoloured	85	65
71	**23**	50f. multicoloured	1·20	95

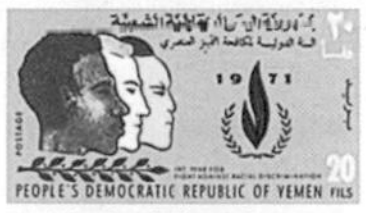

24 Heads of Three Races and Flame

1971. Racial Equality Year.

72	**24**	20f. multicoloured	30	30
73	**24**	35f. multicoloured	75	75
74	**24**	75f. multicoloured	1·60	1·30

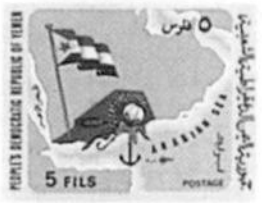

25 Map, Flag and Products

1971

75	**25**	5f. multicoloured	10	10
76	**25**	10f. multicoloured	10	10
77	**25**	15f. multicoloured	20	10
78	**25**	20f. multicoloured	20	20
79	**25**	25f. multicoloured	30	20
80	**25**	35f. multicoloured	45	20
81	**25**	40f. multicoloured	65	20
82	**25**	50f. multicoloured	85	65
82a	**25**	60f. multicoloured	1·80	75
83	**25**	65f. multicoloured	1·20	75
84	**25**	80f. multicoloured	1·40	1·10
84a	**25**	90f. multicoloured	1·90	85
84b	-	110f. multicoloured	2·75	1·20
85	-	125f. multicoloured	2·10	1·90
86	-	250f. multicoloured	3·75	2·75
87	-	500f. multicoloured	8·00	5·25
88	-	1d. multicoloured	18·00	10·50

DESIGN—42×25 mm: Nos. 84b/8, "Dam-al-Khawain" tree, Socotra.

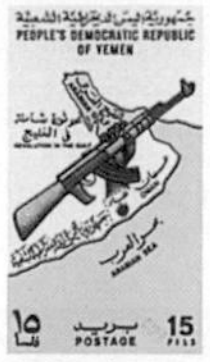

26 Hand holding Sub-machine Gun, and Map

1971. Sixth Anniv of Revolutionary Activity in Arabian Gulf Area. Multicoloured.

89	15f. Type **26**	30	20
90	45f. Girl guerrilla and emblem (horiz)	85	75
91	50f. Guerrilla on the march	1·50	95

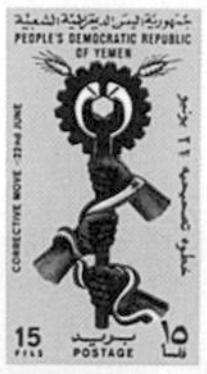

27 Hands supporting Cogwheel

1971. Second Anniv of "Corrective Move" in Revolutionary Government. Multicoloured.

92	15f. Type **27**	20	20
93	25f. Torch and revolutionary emblems	75	65
94	65f. Salt-works and windmill	1·60	95

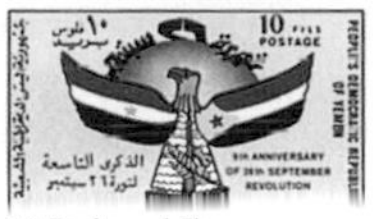

28 Eagle and Flags

1971. Ninth Anniv of 26 September Revolution. Multicoloured.

95	10f. Type **28**	30	20
96	40f. Flag on "United Jemen"	95	75

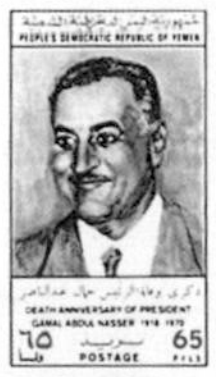

29 Gamal Nasser

1971. First Death Anniv of Gamal Nasser (Egyptian statesman).

97	**29**	65f. multicoloured	1·80	85

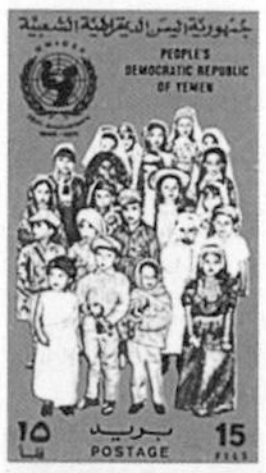

30 "Children of the World"

1971. 25th Anniv of UNICEF.

98	**30**	15f. black, red and orange	20	20
99	**30**	40f. black, purple and blue	65	55
100	**30**	50f. black, red and green	85	75

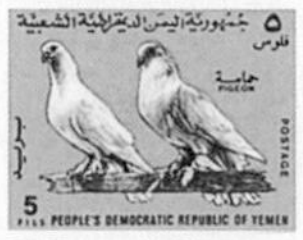

31 Domestic Pigeons

1971. Birds.

101	**31**	5f. black, purple and blue	30	20
102	-	40f. multicoloured	1·60	85
103	-	65f. black, red and green	3·75	1·40
104	-	100f. multicoloured	6·50	2·50

DESIGNS: 40f. Arabian chukar (inscr "Partridge"); 65f. Helmeted guineafowl and Arabian chukar (inscr "Partridge"); 100f. Black kite (inscr "Glede").

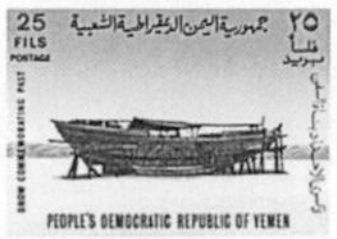

32 Dhow-building

1972. Dhow-building in Aden. Multicoloured.

105	25f. Type **32**	95	55
106	80f. Dhow at sea (vert)	2·75	2·00

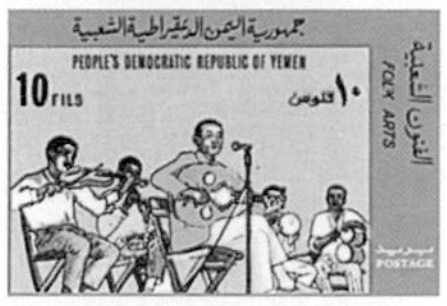

33 Singer with Oud (lute), and Band

1972. Folk Dances. Multicoloured.

107	10f. Type **33**	10	10
108	25f. Yemeni girls dancing	45	30
109	40f. Dancing teams	1·10	65
110	80f. Festival dance	2·10	1·30

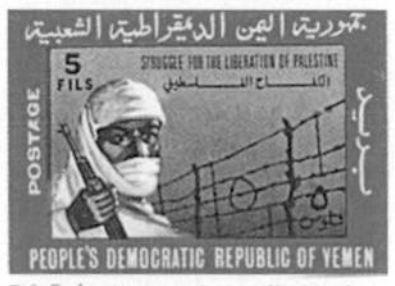

34 Palestinian Guerrilla and Barbed-wire

1972. Palestine Day.

111	**34**	5f. multicoloured	20	10
112	**34**	20f. multicoloured	65	30
113	**34**	65f. multicoloured	2·10	1·50

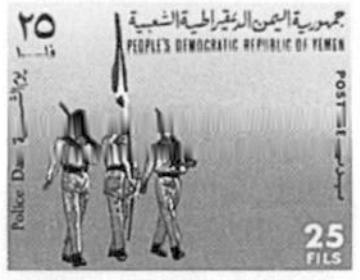

35 Police Colour Party

1972. Police Day. Multicoloured.

114	25f. Type **35**	75	20
115	80f. Girls of People's Militia on parade	2·75	1·60
MS116	122×74 mm. Nos. 114/15 (sold at 150f.)	12·00	12·00

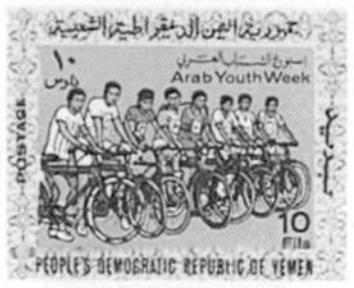

36 Start of Cycle Race

1972. Arab Youth Week. Multicoloured.

117	10f. Type **36**	55	10
118	15f. Girls on parade	75	20
119	40f. Guides and scouts	1·40	75
120	80f. Acrobatic team (vert)	2·10	1·50

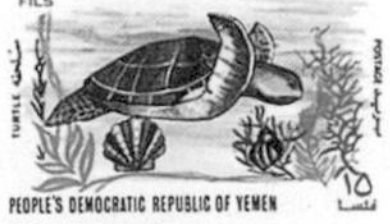

37 Turtle

1972. Marine Life. Multicoloured.

121	15f. Type **37**	95	45
122	40f. Sailfish	1·30	85
123	65f. Narrow-barred Spanish mackerel and John Dory	1·90	1·40
124	125f. Lobster	3·75	2·75

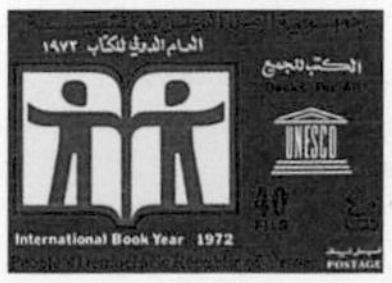

38 Book Year Emblem

1972. International Book Year.

125	**38**	40f. multicoloured	85	75
126	**38**	65f. multicoloured	1·50	1·10

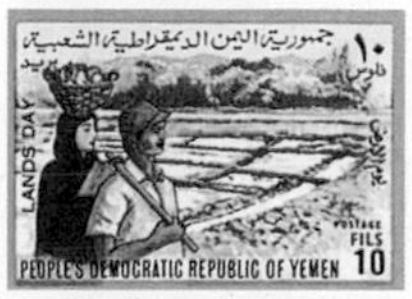

39 Farmworkers and Field

1972. Agriculture Day.

127	**39**	10f. multicoloured	20	20
128	**39**	25f. multicoloured	95	65
129	**39**	40f. multicoloured	1·80	1·10

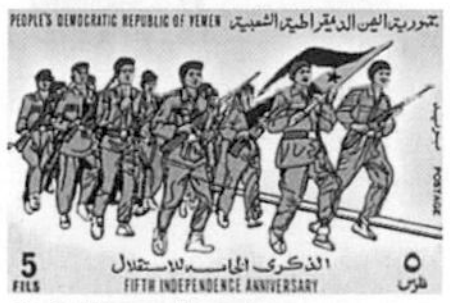

40 Soldiers advancing

1972. Fifth Anniv of Independence. Multicoloured.

130	5f. Type **40**	20	10
131	20f. Soldier and town	65	45
132	65f. Vignettes of Yemeni life (vert)	1·50	1·10
MS133	134×142 mm. Nos. 130/2 (sold at 125f.)	5·25	4·25

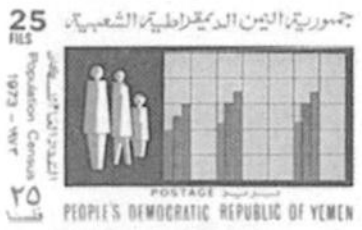

41 Population Graph

1973. Population Census.

134	**41**	25f. emerald, red and green	65	30
135	**41**	40f. lt blue, mauve and blue	1·10	75

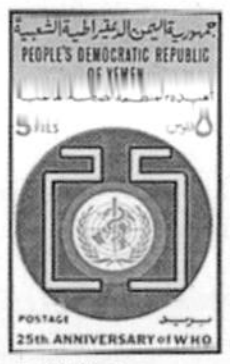

42 W.H.O. Emblem within "25"

1973. 25th Anniv of W.H.O. Multicoloured.

136	5f. Type **42**	20	20
137	25f. W.H.O. emblem on globe (horiz)	65	45
138	125f. "25" and W.H.O. emblem (horiz)	2·50	2·10

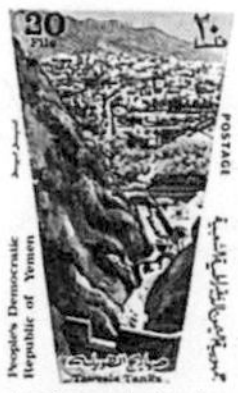

43 Taweela Tanks, Aden

1973. Tourism. Multicoloured.

139	20f. Type **43**	45	20
140	25f. Shibam Town (horiz)	65	45
141	40f. Elephant Bay, Aden (horiz)	1·40	85
142	100f. Al-Mohdar Mosque, Tarim (horiz)	2·40	1·60

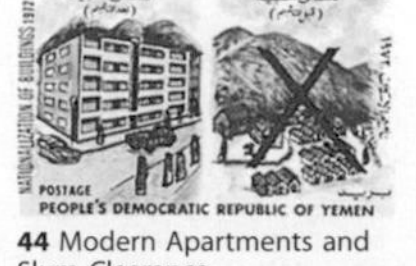

44 Modern Apartments and Slum Clearance

1973. Nationalization of Buildings (1972). Multicoloured.

143	20f. Type **44**	65	20
144	80f. Street scene (vert)	2·10	1·40

45 Women's Corps on Parade

1973. People's Army. Multicoloured.
145	10f. Type **45**		20	10
146	20f. Soldiers marching		45	20
147	40f. Naval contingent		1·30	85
148	80f. Column of tanks		2·10	1·50

46 Quayside Crane

1973. Tenth Anniv of World Food Programme. Multicoloured.
149	20f. Type **46**		45	20
150	80f. Granary workers		1·90	1·30

47 "U.P.U. Letter"

1974. Centenary of U.P.U. Multicoloured.
151	5f. Type **47**		10	10
152	20f. "100" formed of people and U.P.U. emblems		55	30
153	40f. U.P.U. emblem and Yemeni flag (vert)		85	65
154	125f. Map of People's Republic (vert)		1·70	1·50

48 Irrigation Canal

1974. Agricultural Progress. Multicoloured.
155	10f. Type **48**		20	20
156	20f. Bulldozers clearing land		65	20
157	100f. Tractors with harrows		1·80	1·30

49 Lathe Operator

1975. Industrial Progress. Multicoloured.
158	10f. Type **49**		20	10
159	40f. Workers in clothing factory		85	65
160	80f. Women textile workers (horiz)		1·60	1·20

50

1975. Women's Costumes.
161	**50**	5f. brown and black	10	10
162	-	10f. violet and black	20	10
163	-	15f. green and black	30	20
164	-	25f. purple and black	65	55
165	-	40f. blue and black	95	85
166	-	50f. brown and black	1·70	1·60
DESIGNS: Nos. 162/6 show different costumes.

51 Women in Factory

1975. International Women's Year.
167	**51**	40f. black and brown	85	55
168	**51**	50f. black and green	1·10	75

52

1976. Yemeni Football.
169	**52**	5f. multicoloured	10	10
170	-	40f. multicoloured	85	65
171	-	80f. multicoloured	1·70	1·40
DESIGNS: Nos. 170/1 show footballers in different positions.

53 Lunar Launch

1976. Russian Space Exploration. Multicoloured.
172	10f. Type **53**		10	10
173	15f. V. A. Shatalov (cosmonaut)		30	20
174	40f. Luna vehicle (horiz)		1·30	75
175	65f. Valentina Tereshkova and rocket		1·90	1·10

54 Members of Presidential Council

1977. First Anniv of Unification Congress. Multicoloured.
176	25f. Type **54**		45	30
177	35f. Text of document		75	65
178	65f. Girls of People's Militia		1·10	95
179	95f. Aerial view of textile factory		1·40	1·30

55 Traffic Policeman and Woman Trainee

1977. Traffic Change to Right.
180	**55**	25f. black and red	55	30
181	**55**	60f. black and yellow	1·30	1·10
182	**55**	75f. black and green	1·90	1·60
183	**55**	110f. black and blue	3·25	2·10

56 A.P.U. Emblem within Flags of Member States

1977. 25th Anniv of Arab Postal Union.
184	**56**	20f. multicoloured	45	20
185	**56**	60f. multicoloured	95	75
186	**56**	70f. multicoloured	1·30	1·10
187	**56**	110f. multicoloured	1·50	1·20

57 Festive Volute

1977. Cowries. Multicoloured.
188	60f. Type **57**		1·90	85
189	90f. Pringle's marginella (horiz)		3·00	1·30
190	110f. Clay cone (horiz)		3·75	1·60
191	180f. Broderip's cowrie (horiz)		6·50	3·75

58 Dove of Peace and Flag

1977. Tenth Anniv of Independence. Multicoloured.
192	5f. Type **58**		10	10
193	20f. Man with broken manacle		30	10
194	90f. Oil pipeline		65	65
195	110f. "Pillar of Freedom"		1·30	75

59 Dome of the Rock, Jerusalem

1978. Palestinian Welfare.
196	**59**	5f. multicoloured	85	45
For smaller design with value at top right, see No. 264.

60 Almarfaa (drum)

1978. Musical Instruments. Multicoloured.
197	35f. Type **60**		45	20
198	60f. Almizmar (pipes)		95	45
199	90f. Alqnboos (fiddle)		1·70	65
200	110f. Simsimiya (lyre)		2·10	85

61 Almotl (armbands)

1978. Silver Ornaments. Multicoloured.
201	10f. Type **61**		10	10
202	15f. Aloodhad (ring)		30	20
203	20f. Al Hizam (necklace)		45	30
204	60f. Alhoogaalah (bangle)		85	45
205	90f. Al Muk-Hala (perfume flask)		1·30	65
206	110f. Al Janbiya (dagger)		1·70	85

62 Palm Tree Emblem

1978. 11th World Youth Festival, Cuba. Multicoloured.
207	5f. Type **62**		10	10
208	60f. Global emblem		75	45
209	90f. Flower emblem		1·10	65
210	110f. Girl, youth and emblems		1·50	95

63 "V" for Vanguard and Cogwheel

1978. First Conference of Vanguard Party.
211	**63**	5f. multicoloured	10	10
212	**63**	20f. multicoloured	20	10
213	**63**	60f. multicoloured	45	30
214	**63**	180f. multicoloured	1·60	1·10

64 Calligraphic Emblem, Symbols of Peace and Freedom

1978. 15th Anniv of 14 October Revolution. Multicoloured.
215	10f. Type **64**		10	10
216	35f. Emblems of growth (vert)		30	20
217	60f. Candle and figure "15" (vert)		65	30
218	110f. Revolutionaries and figure "15" (vert)		85	65

65 Map of Yemen, Child with Olive-branch and Dove

1979. International Year of the Child.
219	**65**	15f. multicoloured	20	10
220	**65**	20f. multicoloured	30	10
221	**65**	60f. multicoloured	65	30
222	**65**	90f. multicoloured	1·20	75

66 "Agricultural Progress"

1979. Tenth Anniv of "Corrective Move" in Revolutionary Government. Multicoloured.
223	20f. Type **66**		10	10
224	35f. "Industrial Progress"		30	20
225	60f. Students		65	30
226	90f. Woman with star and doves		85	65

67 Sir Rowland Hill and Yemeni Costume Stamp of 1970

1979. Death Cent of Sir Rowland Hill. Multicoloured.
227	90f. Type **67**		85	65
228	110f. Yemeni camel stamp of 1970		95	85
MS229	125×90 mm. 250f. Aden dhow stamp of 1937		3·00	2·75

68 World Map, Koran and Symbols of Arab Achievements

1979. The Arabs.
230	**68**	60f. multicoloured	95	55

69 Emblem of Yemeni Socialist Party

1979. First Anniv of Yemeni Socialist Party.
231	**69**	60f. multicoloured	95	65

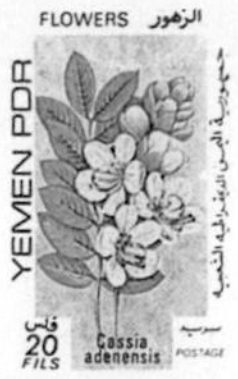

70 "Cassia adenensis"

1979. Flowers (1st series). Multicoloured.

232	20f. Type **70**	20	10
233	90f. "Nerium oleander"	85	75
234	110f. "Calligonum comosum"	1·70	85
235	180f. "Adenium obesum"	2·40	1·30

See also Nos. 265/8.

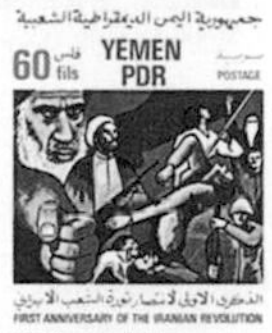

71 Ayatollah Khomeini and Crowd

1980. First Anniv of Iranian Revolution.

236	**71**	60f. multicoloured	1·60	1·30

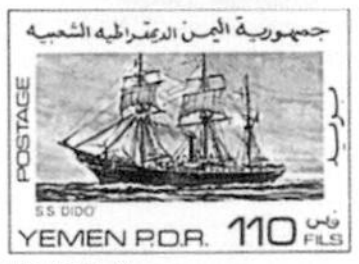

72 "Dido"

1980. Screw Steamers. Multicoloured.

237	110f. Type **72**	1·30	95
238	180f. "Anglia"	1·90	1·70
239	250f. "India"	2·50	2·10

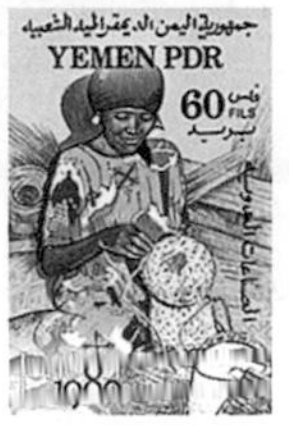

73 Woman Basket-making

1980. "London 1980". Handicrafts. Multicoloured.

240	60f. Type **73**	55	30
241	90f. Making a hubble-bubble pipe	85	55
242	110f. Man at loom	1·30	85
243	250f. Boy making clay pot	2·10	1·60

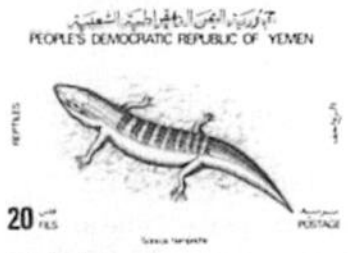

74 Skink

1980. Reptiles. Multicoloured.

244	20f. Type **74**	55	20
245	35f. Mole viper	75	45
246	110f. Gecko	2·00	85
247	180f. Cobra	3·50	1·40

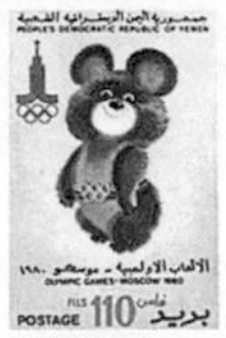

75 Misha the Bear (Olympic Mascot)

1980. Olympic Games, Moscow.

248	**75**	110f. multicoloured	1·40	75

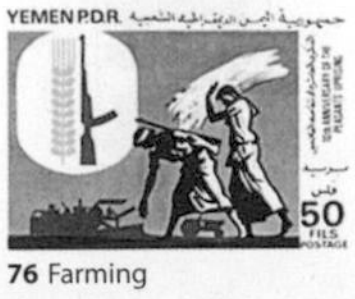

76 Farming

1980. Tenth Anniv of Peasants' Uprising. Multicoloured.

249	50f. Type **76**	55	20
250	90f. Peasants	85	55
251	110f. Corn sickle and fist	1·30	65

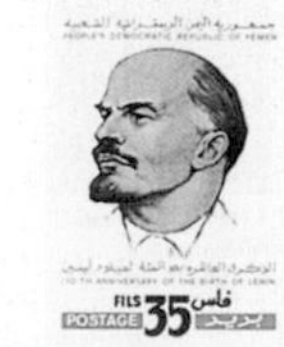

77 Lenin

1980. 110th Birth Anniv of Lenin.

252	**77**	35f. multicoloured	65	30

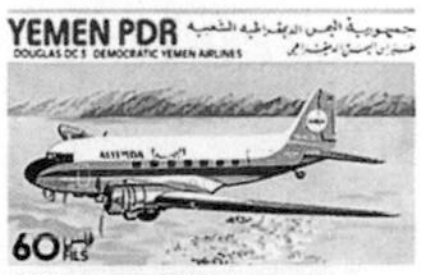

78 Douglas DC-3

1981. Democratic Yemen Airlines. Multicoloured.

253	60f. Type **78**	1·10	75
254	90f. Boeing 707	2·10	1·20
255	250f. De Havilland D.H.C.7 Dash Seven	4·75	2·75

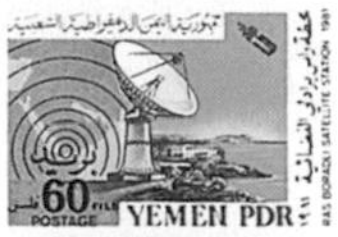

79 Map, Dish Aerial and Satellite

1981. Ras Boradli Satellite Station.

256	**79**	60f. multicoloured	1·20	75

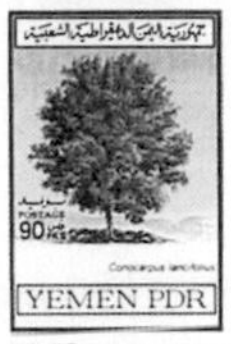

80 "Conocarpus lancifolius"

1981. Trees. Multicoloured.

257	90f. Type **80**	1·40	65
258	180f. "Ficus vasta"	2·75	1·40
259	250f. "Maerua crassifolia"	4·00	2·10

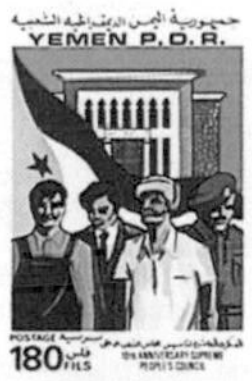

81 Council Building, Citizens and Flag

1981. Tenth Anniv of Supreme People's Council.

260	**81**	180f. multicoloured	2·20	1·70

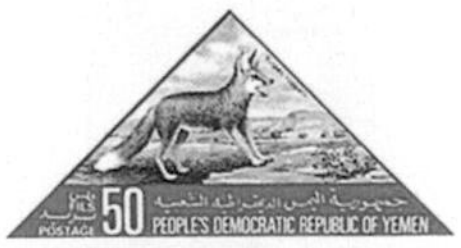

82 Sand Fox

1981. Wildlife Conservation. Multicoloured.

261	50f. Type **82**	90	45
262	90f. Leopard	1·80	1·30
263	250f. Ibex	4·00	3·00

1981. Palestinian Welfare. As T **59**, but smaller, 25×27 mm, and value at top right.

264	5f. multicoloured	65	20

1981. Flowers (2nd series). As T **70**. Multicoloured.

265	50f. "Tephrosia apollinea"	80	45
266	90f. "Citrullus colocynthis"	1·50	80
267	110f. "Aloe squarrosa"	2·20	80
268	250f. "Lawsonia inermis"	4·50	2·50

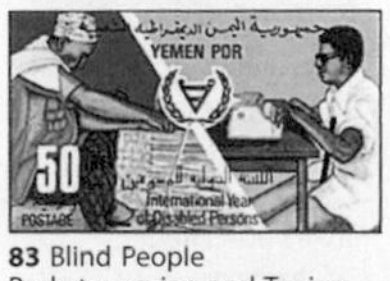

83 Blind People Basket-weaving and Typing

1982. International Year of Disabled Persons.

269	**83**	50f. multicoloured	65	45
270	**83**	100f. multicoloured	1·50	90
271	**83**	150f. multicoloured	2·20	1·20

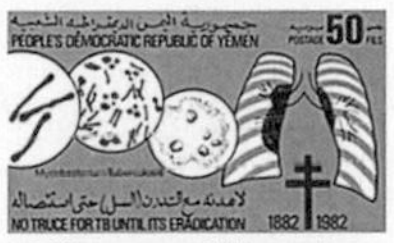

84 Microscope Slides and Lungs

1982. Centenary of Discovery of Tubercle Bacillus.

272	**84**	50f. black, orange and red	1·30	55

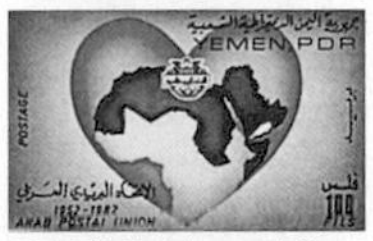

85 A.P.U. Emblem and Map within Heart

1982. 30th Anniv of Arab Postal Union.

273	**85**	100f. red, black and blue	1·80	90

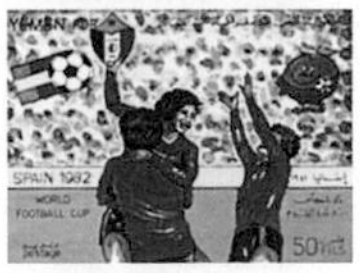

86 Footballers

1982. World Cup Football Championship, Spain. Multicoloured.

274	50f. Type **86**	90	55
275	100f. Match scene	1·70	90
276	150f. Players and shield	2·75	1·70
277	200f. Player and flags	3·50	2·00
MS278	114×94 mm. Nos. 274/7	10·00	6·25

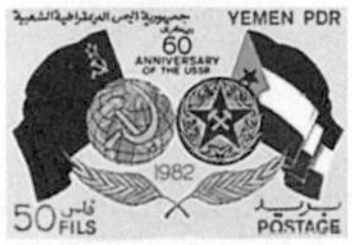

87 Emblems and Flags of Russia and Yemen

1982. 60th Anniv of U.S.S.R.

279	**87**	50f. multicoloured	90	55

1982. World Cup Football Championship Result. Nos. 274/7 optd **WORLD CUP WINNERS 1982 1st ITALY 2nd W-GERMANY 3rd POLAND 4th FRANCE** and player holding trophy.

280	50f. Type **86**	90	55
281	100f. Match scene	1·70	90
282	150f. Players and shield	2·75	1·70
283	200f. Player and flags	3·50	2·00
MS284	114×94 mm. Nos. 280/3	10·00	6·25

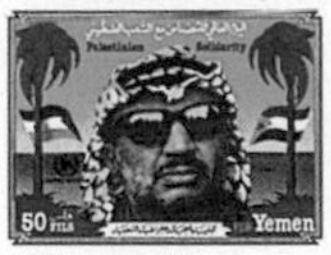

89 Yasser Arafat

1983. Palestinian Solidarity. Multicoloured.

285	50f. Type **89**	1·30	1·00
286	100f. Yasser Arafat and Dome of the Rock	3·25	1·20
MS287	100×80 mm. No. 286. Imperf	4·50	3·75

1983. "Tembal 83" Stamp Exhibition, Basel. No. 248 optd **TEMBAL 83 MAY 21st-29th, 1983** and emblem.

288	**75**	110f. multicoloured	6·75	2·75

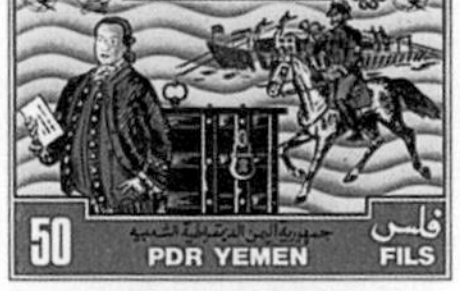

91 Man with Letter, Postal Barge and Postman

1983. World Communications Year.

289	**91**	50f. black and blue	90	65
290	-	100f. black and red	1·90	1·00
291	-	150f. black, green and olive	3·00	1·50
292	-	200f. multicoloured	3·50	1·60
MS293		120×91 mm. 150f. multicoloured	4·50	3·75

DESIGNS: 100f. Postman, stage coach and morse code equipment; 150f. Motor coach and telephones; 150f. (**MS**293), Amalgam of motifs from Nos. 289/92; 200f. Transmitter, airplane, satellite, television, envelope and dish aerial.

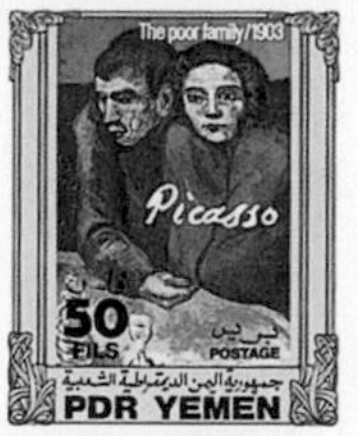

92 "The Poor Family"

1983. Tenth Death Anniv of Picasso (artist). Multicoloured.

294	50f. Type **92**	1·20	45
295	100f. "Woman with Crow"	2·00	1·00
MS296	Two sheets. (a) 130×75 mm. 50f. "Le Gourmet"; 100f. "Woman with Child on Beach"; 150f. "Sitting Beggar"; (b) 120×91 mm. 150f. "The Solar Family" (49×39 mm)	24·00	24·00

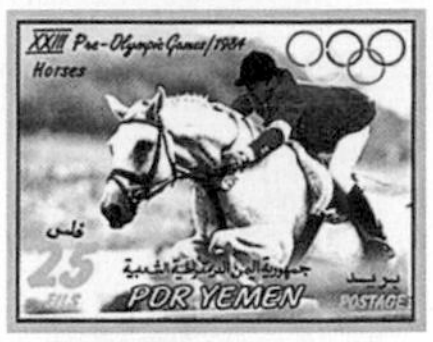

93 Show Jumping

1983. Olympic Games, Los Angeles (1st issue). Equestrian Events. Multicoloured.

297	25f. Type **93**	1·30	45
298	50f. Show jumping (different)	1·90	90
299	100f. Horse crossing water (Three-day event)	3·00	1·80
MS300	Two sheets. (a) 130×75 mm. 20f. Head of bay (*vert*), 40f. Head of grey (*vert*), 60f. Bay (*vert*), 80f. Arabian (*vert*); (b) 121×150 mm. 200f. Show jumping (*vert*)	29·00	29·00

See also Nos. 316/**MS**319.

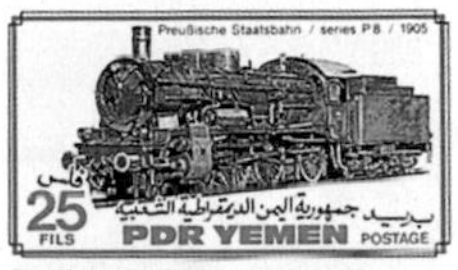

94 Class P8 Steam Locomotive, 1905, Prussia

1983. Railway Locomotives. Multicoloured.

301	25f. Type **94**	2·00	80
302	50f. Class 880 steam locomotive, 1915, Italy	3·50	1·50
303	100f. Class Gt2 steam locomotive, 1923, Bavaria	5·50	2·75
MS304	Two sheets. (a) 118×121 mm. 40f. Class D51 steam locomotive, 1936, 60f. Series 45 locomotive, 1937, 100f. Class Pt47 locomotive, 1948; (b) 92×94 mm. 200f. Class P36 locomotive, 1950	55·00	49·00

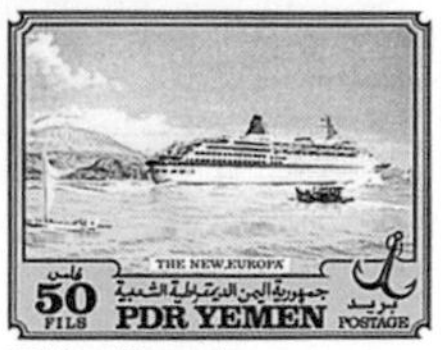

95 Liner "Europa"

1983. Ships. Multicoloured.

305	50f. Type **95**	2·00	1·00
306	100f. Liner "World Discoverer"	3·75	2·10
MS307	Two sheets. (a) 174×130 mm. 20f. "Kruzenshtern" (Russian cadet barque), 40f. "Grossherzogin Elisabeth" (German cadet schooner), 60f. "Sedov" (Russian cadet barque), 80f. "Dar Pomorza" (Polish cadet full-rigged ship); (b) 120×91 mm. 200f. "Gorch Fock" (German cadet barque)	45·00	41·00

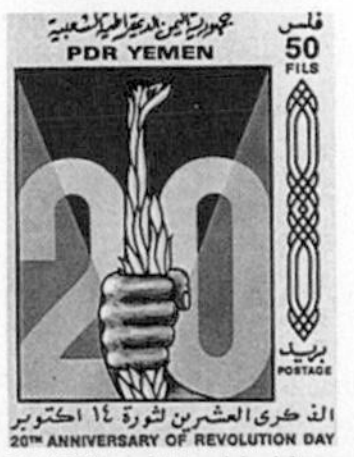

96 "20" and Hand holding Sheaf of Corn

1983. 20th Anniv of Revolution. Multicoloured.

308	50f. Type **96**	1·20	65
309	100f. Flag, man with gun and "XX"	2·75	1·20

97 Pierre Testu-Brissy's Balloon, 1798

1983. Bicentenary of Manned Flight. Multicoloured.

310	50f. Type **97**	1·10	55
311	100f. Unmanned Montgolfier balloon, 1783	2·20	1·10

MS312 Two sheets. (a) 130×175 mm. 20f. Vincenzo Lunardi's balloon (1785), 40f. Charles's hydrogen balloon (1783), 60f. John Wise's balloon *Atlantic* (1859), 80f. Blanchard and Jefferies balloon (1785); (b) 90×120 mm. 200f. Eugene Godard's quintuple acrobatic balloon (1850) — 36·00 30·00

98 Skiing

1983. Winter Olympic Games, Sarajevo. Multicoloured.

313	50f. Type **98**	1·10	55
314	100f. Bobsleigh	2·20	1·10

MS315 Two sheets. (a) 130×175 mm. 40f. Ski jumping, 60f. Figure skating (pairs), 100f. No. 314; (b) 90×120 mm. 200f. Ice hockey — 27·00 22·00

99 Fencing

1984. Olympic Games, Los Angeles (2nd issue). Multicoloured.

316	25f. Type **99**	55	20
317	50f. Fencing (different)	1·10	55
318	100f. Fencing (different)	1·70	90

MS319 Two sheets. (a) 130×175 mm. 20f. Gymnastics, 40f. Water polo, 80f. Show jumping, 60f. Wrestling; (b) 120×90 mm. 200f. Show jumping (different) — 27·00 22·00

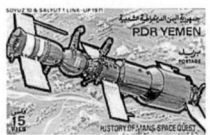

100 "Soyuz 10"–"Salyut 1" Link-up, 1971

1984. Space. Multicoloured.

320	15f. Type **100**	20	20
321	20f. "Apollo 8" and Moon, 1968	45	20
322	50f. "Apollo 11" and first man on Moon, 1969	1·00	65
323	100f. "Soyuz"–"Apollo" link-up, 1975	2·00	1·50

MS324 118×88 mm. 200f. "Columbia" (space shuttle) returning to Earth's atmosphere — 9·00 7·25

1984. Nos. 83 and 84b surch.

325	**25** 50f. on 65f. multicoloured	1·20	80
326	— 100f. on 110f. mult	2·75	1·20

102 Starry Triggerfish

1984. Fish. Multicoloured.

327	10f. Type **102**	10	10
328	15f. Golden trevally	10	10
329	20f. Saddled grunt	20	15
330	35f. Diagonal butterflyfish	35	20
331	35f. Emperor angelfish	45	30
332	50f. Indian mackerel	65	35
333	100f. Kawakawa	1·30	45

334	150f. Pennant coralfish	2·10	1·10
335	200f. Yellow-banded angelfish	3·00	1·30
336	250f. Plane-tailed lionfish	4·00	2·10
337	400f. Long-spined seabream	6·25	3·00
338	500f. Coachwhip stingray	7·75	4·00
339	1d. Brown-spotted grouper	17·00	9·50
340	2d. Long-finned drepane	36·00	18·00

1984. Olympic Winners, Sarajevo. No. 314 optd **WINNERS B.Lehmann–B. Musiol (DDR)**.

341	100f. multicoloured	10·50	9·50

MS342 130×175 mm. 40f. As No. 341 60f. "WINNERS J. Torvill–C. Dean (GB)"; 100f. "WINNERS W. Hoppe–D. Schauerhammer (DDR)" — 22·00 19·00

104 Women writing

1985. National Literacy Campaign. Multicoloured.

343	50f. Type **104**	1·80	90
344	100f. Pen held in manacled fist	3·50	1·50

105 Victory Parade, Red Square

1985. 40th Anniv of End of Second World War.

345	**105** 100f. multicoloured	2·00	90

106 Flag within Emblem

1985. 12th World Youth and Students' Festival, Moscow. Multicoloured.

346	50f. Type **106**	1·90	90
347	100f. Hand holding emblem as placard	3·75	1·60

107 Modern Buildings

1985. UNESCO World Heritage Site. Shibam City. Multicoloured.

348	50f. Type **107**	1·10	65
349	50f. View of city	1·10	65
350	100f. Screen	2·20	1·60
351	100f. Gate (vert)	2·20	1·60

108 Industrial Symbols

1985. Third Yemeni Socialist Party General Congress. Multicoloured.

352	25f. Type **108**	90	55
353	50f. Crane loading ship	1·60	80
354	100f. Combine harvesters	3·00	1·30

109 Mother feeding Child

1985. UNICEF Child Survival Campaign. Multicoloured.

355	50f. Type **109**	1·20	95
356	50f. Immunization	1·20	95
357	100f. Breastfeeding	2·30	1·60
358	100f. Oral rehydration therapy	2·30	1·60

110 Wheat and Al-Mohdar Mosque, Tarim

1986. World Food Day. 40th Anniv (1985) of F.A.O. Multicoloured.

359	20f. Type **110**	1·20	35
360	180f. Palm trees	4·75	2·20

111 Lenin addressing Crowd in Red Square

1986. 27th Russian Communist Party Congress. Multicoloured.

361	**111** 75f. multicoloured	2·30	95
362	**111** 250f. multicoloured	4·75	2·50

112 Bride in Yashmak

1986. Brides and Bridegrooms of Yemen. Multicoloured.

363	50f. Type **112**	1·00	70
364	50f. Bride with striped shawl	1·00	70
365	50f. Bride with long dressed hair	1·00	70
366	100f. Bridegroom in modern jacket with knife	2·10	1·60
367	100f. Bridegroom in traditional clothes with gun	2·10	1·60
368	100f. Bride in modern dress	2·10	1·60

113 Ali Ahmed N. Antar

1986. "Party and Homeland Martyrs". Multicoloured.

369	75f. Type **113**	1·40	95
370	75f. Saleh Musleh Kasim	1·40	95
371	75f. Ali Shayaa Hadi	1·40	95
372	75f. Abdul Fattah Ismail	1·40	95

114 Immunizing Pregnant Woman against Tetanus

1987. UNICEF Immunization Campaign. Multicoloured.

373	20f. Type **114**	45	25
374	75f. Immunizing baby	1·50	95
375	140f. Nurse giving oral poliomy- elitis vaccine to baby	3·00	1·40
376	150f. Pregnant woman and children carrying syringes	3·00	1·60

115 Party Emblem and Worker

1987. Yemeni Socialist Party General Conference.

377	**115** 75f. multicoloured	1·40	60
378	**115** 150f. multicoloured	2·75	1·30

116 Lenin and Soldier

1987. 70th Anniv of Russian October Revolution.

379	**116** 250f. multicoloured	5·75	3·00

117 Steps to King's Court

1987. Shabwa Remains. Multicoloured.

380	25f. Type **117**	60	35
381	75f. Royal Palace	1·40	70
382	140f. Winged lion, King's Court (vert)	2·50	1·40
383	150f. Inscribed bronze plaque (vert)	3·00	1·60

118 Students and College Buildings

1987. 20th Anniv of Independence. Multicoloured.

384	25f. Type **118**	45	25
385	75f. Family and housing	1·30	60
386	140f. Workers, oil derrick and power station	2·50	1·20
387	150f. Party headquarters and members	2·75	1·30

119 Tank and Liberty Monument, Sana'a

1988. 25th Anniv (1987) of 26th September Revolution in Yemen.

388	**119** 75f. multicoloured	1·40	60

120 Tap, Boy and Rainbow (safe water)

1988. World Health Day. 40th Anniv of W.H.O. Multicoloured.

389	40f. Type **120**	45	35
390	75f. Child with globe as head breaking cigarette (No Smoking day)	1·30	45
391	140f. Nurse immunizing baby (immunization campaign)	2·30	95
392	250f. Red Crescent worker instructing group (Health for all)	3·50	1·70

121 Weightlifting

1988. Olympic Games, Seoul. Multicoloured.

393	40f. Type **121**	60	35
394	75f. Running	1·30	60
395	140f. Boxing	2·50	1·40
396	150f. Football	2·75	1·70

122 Crowd and Flag

1988. 25th Anniv of 14 October Revolution.

397	**122** 25f. black and red	45	25

398	-	75f. multicoloured	1·30	45
399	-	300f. multicoloured	5·25	2·30

DESIGNS—HORIZ: 75f. Radfan mountains and revolutionary. VERT: 300f. Anniversary emblem.

123 Yellow-bellied Green Pigeon

1988. Birds. Multicoloured.

400		40f. Type **123**	70	35
401		50f. Lilac-breasted roller (vert)	1·00	70
402		75f. Hoopoe (vert)	1·70	1·00
403		250f. Houbara bustard	4·75	2·50

124 Incense Burner

1988. Traditional Crafts. Multicoloured.

404		25f. Type **124**	35	35
405		70f. Mashjub (rack used when impregnating dresses with incense)	1·30	60
406		150f. Cosmetic basket made of palm fibre with cowrie shell decoration	2·30	1·40
407		250f. Woman making palm fibre basket	4·25	2·30

125 Shipping entering Old Harbour

1988. Centenary of Port of Aden. Multicoloured.

408		75f. Type **125**	2·00	70
409		300f. Section of new harbour project	5·75	2·75

126 Old City

1988. International Campaign for Preservation of Old Sana'a. Multicoloured.

410		75f. Type **126**	1·30	95
411		250f. City (different)	5·00	2·20

127 Sand Cat Kitten

1989. Endangered Animals. Multicoloured.

412		20f. Type **127**	1·70	25
413		25f. Adult sand cat	1·90	35
414		50f. Fennec fox cub	3·50	60
415		75f. Adult fennec fox	4·75	95

128 Symbols of War in Star

1989. 20th Anniv of "Corrective Move" in Revolutionary Government. Multicoloured.

416		25f. Type **128**	45	25
417		35f. Industrial symbols in hook	60	30
418		40f. Agricultural symbols	70	35

129 Ismail

1989. 50th Birth Anniv of Adbul Fattah Ismail (founder of People's Socialist Party).

419	**129**	75f. multicoloured	95	70
420	**129**	150f. multicoloured	2·00	1·90

130 "Children at Play" (Abeer Anwer)

1989. 15th Anniv of Ali Anter Pioneer Organization. Multicoloured.

421		10f. Type **130**	25	20
422		25f. Girl pioneer	45	25
423		75f. Pioneers parading at Khormaksar (horiz)	1·20	70

131 Sana'a and Fighters

1989. 22nd Anniv of Siege of Sana'a.

424	**131**	150f. multicoloured	2·50	1·30

132 Taj Mahal and Nehru

1989. Birth Centenary of Jawaharal Nehru (Indian statesman).

425	**132**	250f. black and brown	3·75	1·70

133 Coffee Plant

1989. Centenary of Interparliamentary Union.

426	**133**	300f. multicoloured	5·75	3·00

134 Seera Rock, Aden, Birds and Arc de Triomphe, Paris

1989. Bicentenary of French Revolution.

427	**134**	250f. multicoloured	5·00	3·00

135 U.S.A. v Belgium (Uruguay, 1930)

1990. World Cup Football Championship, Italy. Matches from previous championships. Multicoloured.

428		5f. Type **135**	10	10
429		10f. Switzerland v Netherlands (Italy, 1934)	10	10
430		20f. Italy v France (France, 1938)	10	10
431		35f. Sweden v Spain (Brazil, 1950)	35	35
432		50f. West Germany v Austria (Switzerland, 1954)	45	45
433		60f. Brazil v England (Sweden, 1958)	60	60
434		500f. U.S.S.R. v Uruguay (Chile, 1962)	5·25	1·20
MS435		90×61 mm. 340f. Footballers	4·75	2·30

Pt. 19

YEMEN REPUBLIC (COMBINED)

A draft joint constitution was ratified by the parliaments of Yemen Arab Republic and the Yemen People's Democratic Republic on 21 May 1990 and the unification of the two countries was declared the following day.

The currencies of both the previous republics have legal validity throughout Yemen.

100 fils = 1 rial (North Yemen).
1000 fils = 1 dinar (South Yemen).

1 Scouts supporting Globe

1990. 75th Anniv of Arab Scout Movement. Multicoloured.

1	300f. Type **1**	2·40	1·20
2	375f. Type **1**	3·00	1·60
3	850f. Oil derrick, scouts with flag, anniversary emblem and tower	6·00	3·00
4	900f. As No. 3	7·25	3·50
MS5	90×70 mm. As No. 2 but 37×27 mm	11·50	6·00

Nos. 1/**MS**5 are inscribed "YEMEN ARAB REPUBLIC".

2 Pintail

1990. Ducks. Multicoloured.

6	10f. Type **2**	10	10
7	20f. European wigeon	25	25
8	25f. Ruddy shelduck	35	25
9	40f. Gadwall	50	35
10	75f. Common shelduck	85	60
11	150f. Common shoveler pair	1·90	85
12	600f. Green-winged teal	7·75	1·80
MS13	89×67 mm. 460f. Pintail flying	16·00	3·75

3 City Rooftops

1990. 40th Anniv of U.N. Development Programme.

14	**3**	150f. multicoloured	2·10	1·60

4 "Dirphia multicolor"

1990. Moths and Butterflies. Multicoloured.

15	5f. Type **4**	10	10
16	20f. "Automeris io"	20	10
17	25f. Swallowtail	25	20
18	40f. Bhutan glory	35	25
19	55f. Silver king shoemaker	50	35
20	75f. Tiger moth	60	50
21	700f. "Attacus edwardsii" (moth)	6·75	1·70
MS22	65×90 mm. 460f. Oleander hawk moth (vert)	16·00	3·75

5 Protembolotherium

1990. Prehistoric Animals. Multicoloured.

23	5f. Type **5**	10	10
24	10f. Diatryma	20	20
25	35f. Mammoth (horiz)	20	20
26	40f. Edaphosaurus (horiz)	25	25
27	55f. Dimorphodon (horiz)	50	35
28	75f. Phororhacos (horiz)	60	50
29	700f. Ichthyosaurus (wrongly inscr "Ichtyosaurus")	7·25	1·80
MS30	62×90 mm. 460f. Tyrannosaurus rex. Imperf	8·50	3·75

6 Abyssinian Kitten

1990. Cats. Multicoloured.

31	5f. Type **6**	10	10
32	15f. Blue longhair	20	20
33	35f. Siamese	25	25
34	55f. Burmese	50	35
35	60f. Sealpoint colourpoint	55	40
36	150f. Red British shorthair	1·40	60
37	600f. Leopard cat	5·50	1·20
MS38	70×90 mm. 460f. Black-smoke longhair kitten. Imperf	16·00	3·75

7 "Boletus aestivalis"

1991. Fungi. Multicoloured.

39	50f. Type **7**	50	25
40	60f. Butter mushroom	60	35
41	80f. Beefsteak morel	85	50
42	100f. Brown birch bolete	1·10	60
43	130f. Fly agaric	1·40	70
44	200f. Flaky-stemmed witches' mushroom	2·40	85
45	300f. Red cap	3·50	95
MS46	70×90 mm. 460f. Verdigris agaric. Imperf	7·75	3·75

8 State Arms

1991. First Anniv of Yemen Republic. Multicoloured.

47	300f. Type **8**	1·30	60
48	375f. Type **8**	1·70	95
49	850f. Hand holding flag, map and sun	4·00	1·20
50	900f. As No. 49	4·25	1·60
MS51	90×70 mm. As No. 48 but 36×27 mm	3·75	2·30

9 Shaking Hands

1991. Signing of Unity Agreement (in November 1989) Commemoration. Multicoloured.

52	225f. Type **9**	70	35
53	300f. Hand holding flag over map	1·20	60
54	375f. As No. 53	1·60	85
55	650f. Type **9**	2·40	1·10
56	850f. As No. 53	3·25	1·40
MS57	70×90 mm. As No. 54 but 27×36 mm	3·75	2·30

10 Cigarettes and Skull on Globe

1991. World Anti-smoking Day. Multicoloured.

58	225f. Type **10**	70	35
59	300f. Skull smoking and man	1·20	60
60	375f. As No. 59	1·70	70
61	650f. Type **10**	2·75	1·20
62	850f. As No. 59	3·50	1·40
MS63	90×70 mm. As No. 60 but 36×26 mm	4·50	2·30

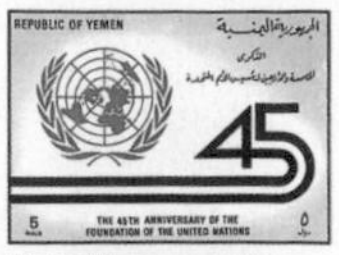

11 Emblem

1991. 45th Anniv of U.N.O.

64	11	5r. multicoloured	2·40	95
65	11	8r. multicoloured	3·00	1·40
66	11	10r. multicoloured	4·25	1·80
67	11	12r. multicoloured	4·75	3·00
MS68		90×70 mm. **11** 6r. multicoloured (37×27 mm)	3·75	2·40

1993. Various stamps surch. (a) Stamps of Yemen Arab Republic. (i) Postage.

69	**94**	5r. on 75f. multicoloured	5·50	5·50
70	**144**	8r. on 425f. multicoloured	6·75	6·75
71	**150**	8r. on 425f. multicoloured	6·75	6·75
72	-	10r. on 900f. mult (No. 830)	7·25	7·25
73	-	10r. on 900f. mult (No. 834)	7·25	7·25
74	-	10r. on 900f. mult (No. 838)	7·25	7·25
75	-	10r. on 900f. mult (No. 843)	7·25	7·25
76	**157**	10r. on 900f. multicoloured	7·25	7·25
77	-	10r. on 900f. mult (No. 853)	7·25	7·25
78	**159**	10r. on 900f. multicoloured	7·25	7·25
79	-	10r. on 900f. mult (No. 863)	7·25	7·25
80	-	12r. on 850f. mult (No. 829)	9·75	9·75
81	-	12r. on 850f. mult (No. 833)	9·75	9·75
82	-	12r. on 850f. mult (No. 837)	9·75	9·75
83	-	12r. on 850f. mult (No. 842)	9·75	9·75
84	**157**	12r. on 850f. multicoloured	9·75	9·75
85	-	12r. on 850f. mult (No. 852)	9·75	9·75
86	**159**	12r. on 850f. multicoloured	9·75	9·75

(ii) Air. Additionally optd **AIR MAIL** (except for No. 87).

87	**118**	3r. on 125f. multicoloured	3·00	3·00
88	-	3r. on 125f. mult (No. 672)	3·00	3·00
89	-	3r. on 125f. mult (No. 679)	3·00	3·00
90	-	3r. on 125f. mult (No. 686)	3·00	3·00
91	-	3r. on 125f. mult (No. 700)	3·00	3·00
92	-	3r. on 125f. mult (No. 707)	3·00	3·00
93	-	5r. on 75f. mult (No. 670)	4·75	4·75
94	-	5r. on 75f. mult (No. 677)	4·75	4·75
95	-	5r. on 75f. mult (No. 684)	4·75	4·75
96	-	5r. on 75f. mult (No. 691)	4·75	4·75
97	-	5r. on 75f. mult (No. 698)	4·75	4·75
98	-	5r. on 75f. mult (No. 705)	4·75	4·75
99	**145**	8r. on 425f. multicoloured	7·25	7·25
100	-	8r. on 425f. mult (No. 796)	7·25	7·25
101	**147**	8r. on 425f. multicoloured	7·25	7·25
102	-	8r. on 425f. mult (No. 803)	7·25	7·25
103	-	8r. on 425f. mult (No. 812)	7·25	7·25
104	**151**	8r. on 425f. multicoloured	7·25	7·25
105	**152**	8r. on 425f. multicoloured	7·25	7·25
106	-	12r. on 850f. mult (No. 862)	13·50	13·50

(b) Stamps of Yemen Republic (combined).

107		10r. on 900f. mult (No. 4)	7·75	7·75
108		10r. on 900f. mult (No. 50)	7·75	7·75
109		12r. on 850f. mult (No. 3)	7·25	7·25
110		12r. on 850f. mult (No. 49)	7·25	7·25
111		12r. on 850f. mult (No. 56)	7·25	7·25
112		12r. on 850f. mult (No. 62)	7·25	7·25
113		50r. on 150f. mult (No. 11)	39·00	24·00
114	**3**	50r. on 150f. multicoloured	39·00	24·00
115	**10**	50r. on 225f. multicoloured	£250	
116	**8**	50r. on 375f. multicoloured	39·00	24·00
117	-	50r. on 375f. mult (No. 54)	39·00	24·00
118	-	50r. on 375f. mult (No. 60)	39·00	24·00
119	**8**	100r. on 300f. mult	70·00	42·00
120	-	100r. on 300f. mult (No. 53)	£250	
121	-	100r. on 300f. mult (No. 59)	£475	

(c) Stamps of Yemen People's Democratic Republic. (i) In Western and Arabic figures.

122		8r. on 110f. mult (No. 84b)	5·50	3·50
123		8r. on 110f. mult (No. 200)	5·50	3·50
124		8r. on 110f. mult (No. 206)	5·50	3·50
125		8r. on 110f. mult (No. 218)	5·50	3·50
126		8r. on 110f. mult (No. 234)	5·50	3·50
127	**72**	8r. on 110f. multicoloured	5·50	3·50
128	-	8r. on 110f. mult (No. 246)	5·50	3·50
129	-	8r. on 110f. mult (No. 267)	5·50	3·50
130	-	50r. on 500f. mult (No. 434)	£120	
131	**133**	100r. on 300f. mult	65·00	42·00
132	-	100r. on 2d. mult (No. 340)	65·00	42·00
133	**25**	200r. on 5f. multicoloured	£130	80·00
134	**135**	200r. on 5f. multicoloured	£130	80·00
135	**127**	200r. on 20f. multicoloured	£130	80·00
136	-	200r. on 20f. mult (No. 430)	£130	80·00
137	-	200r. on 75f. mult (No. 423)	£130	80·00
138	**132**	200r. on 250f. black & brn	£130	80·00

(ii) Surch **R.** and Arabic figures.

139	**100**	200r. on 15f. multicoloured	£130	80·00
140	-	200r. on 15f. mult (No. 328)	£130	80·00
141	-	200r. on 20f. mult (No. 321)	£130	80·00
142	-	200r. on 20f. mult (No. 329)	£130	80·00

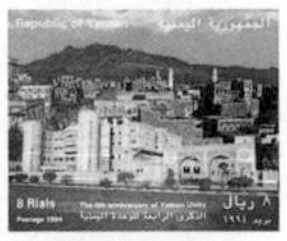

15 Sana'a

1994. Fourth Anniv of Yemen Republic.

143		3r. multicoloured	1·00	50
144		5r. multicoloured	1·90	90
145	**15**	8r. multicoloured	2·75	1·40
146	-	20r. multicoloured	7·00	3·75
MS147		70×60 mm. 20r. multicoloured	9·00	4·25

DESIGNS: Nos. 143/4, 146, **MS**147. Different views of the principal building Type **15**.

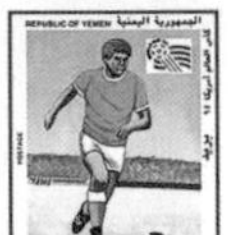

16 Player dribbling Ball

1994. World Cup Football Championship, U.S.A. Multicoloured.

148	2r. Type **16**	80	40
149	6r. Dribbling (different)	2·10	1·00
150	10r. Goalkeeper catching ball (horiz)	3·25	1·70
151	12r. Player heading ball	4·25	2·10
MS152	70×60 mm. 12r. Tackling (horiz)	5·75	4·25

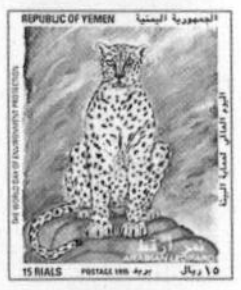

17 Arabian Leopard

1995. World Environmental Protection Day. Multicoloured.

153	15r. Type **17**	2·10	1·30
154	20r. Caracal lynx	2·30	1·40
155	30r. Helmeted guineafowl (horiz)	3·25	1·80
MS156	70×60 mm. 50r. Partridge (horiz)	7·75	5·75

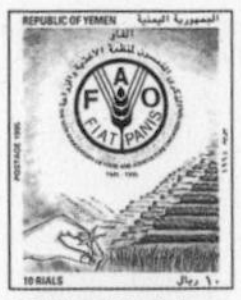

18 Hand holding Seedling

1995. 50th Anniv of F.A.O. Multicoloured.

157	10r. Type **18**	1·40	1·00
158	25r. Hand holding seeds	3·25	1·80
159	30r. Hand holding fish	4·50	2·20
MS160	70×60 mm. 50r. Hand holding plant	7·00	5·00

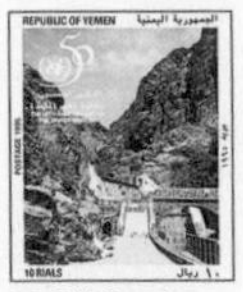

19 Old Sana'a

1995. 50th Anniv of U.N.O. Multicoloured.

161	10r. Type **19**	1·40	1·00
162	20r. Different viewpoint of scene on 10r	3·25	1·80
163	25r. Rampart walk (horiz)	4·50	2·20
MS164	70×60 mm. 50r. Aden reservoir (horiz)	7·00	5·00

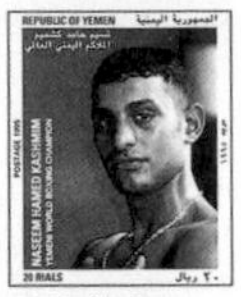

20 Kashmim

1995. Naseem Hamed Kashmim (boxer). Multicoloured.

165	10r. Kashmim with Lonsdale Belt	1·20	65
166	20r. Type **20**	2·30	1·00
167	25r. Scene from boxing match (horiz)	2·75	1·30
168	30r. Kashmim raising arm in triumph	3·25	1·60
MS169	70×60 mm. 50r. Scene from boxing match (different) (horiz)	7·00	5·00

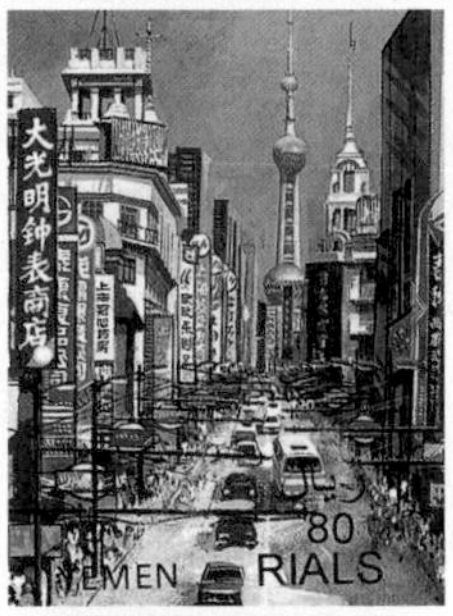

21 Shanghai

1996. "China '96" International Stamp Exhibition, Peking. Sheet 100×140 mm.

MS170	80r. multicoloured	11·00	7·00

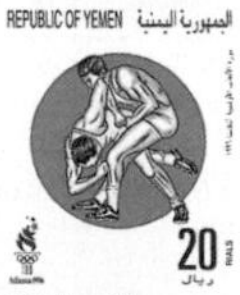

22 Wrestling

1996. Olympic Games, Atlanta, U.S.A. Multicoloured.

171	20r. Type **22**	1·20	65
172	50r. High jumping (horiz)	3·00	1·90
173	60r. Running	3·75	2·30
174	70r. Gymnastics	4·25	2·75
175	100r. Judo	6·25	3·25
MS176	70×60 mm. 150r. Throwing the javelin	16·00	8·50

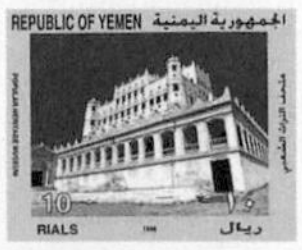

23 Popular Heritage Museum, Seiyoan

1996. Heritage Sites. Multicoloured.

177	10r. Type **23**	40	15
178	15r. Rock Palace, Wadi Dhahr (vert)	65	25
179	20r. Old Sana'a city	90	40
180	30r. Al-Mohdhar minaret, Tarim (vert)	1·40	50
181	40r. As 15r.	1·70	80
182	50r. As 30r.	2·20	1·00
183	60r. As 15r.	2·75	1·30
184	70r. As 10r.	3·25	1·60
185	100r. As 20r.	4·75	1·90
186	150r. As 30r.	6·50	2·50
187	200r. As 20r.	9·00	3·25
188	250r. As 10r.	11·50	4·00
189	300r. As 30r.	16·00	4·50
190	500r. As 15r.	23·00	6·50

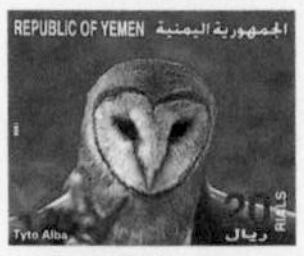

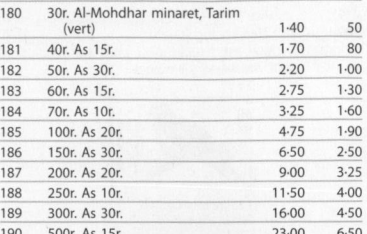

24 Barn Owl

1996. Birds. Multicoloured.

191	20r. Type **24**	1·00	65
192	50r. Philby's rock partridge	2·50	1·30
193	60r. Lammergeier	3·25	1·60
194	70r. Arabian chukar	3·75	2·30
195	100r. Houbara bustard	5·00	3·25
MS196	60×70 mm. 150r. Little bittern (vert)	12·50	7·00

See also Nos. 220/**MS**225.

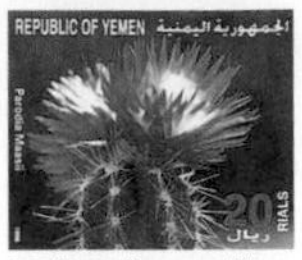

25 "Parodia maasii"

1996. Multicoloured. (a) Rare Plants.

197	20r. Type **25**	1·00	65
198	50r. "Notocatus cristata"	2·30	1·30
199	60r. "Adenium obesum socotranum"	2·75	1·60
200	70r. Dragon's blood tree	3·25	2·30
201	100r. "Mammillaria erythrosperma"	4·75	3·25
MS202	70×60 mm. 150r. "Parodia maasii" (different)	11·00	7·00

(b) Fishes.

203	20r. Moorish idol	1·20	80
204	50r. Hump-headed wrasse	2·50	1·70
205	60r. Purple tang	3·75	2·10
206	70r. Emperor angelfish	4·50	2·75
207	100r. Yellow-faced angelfish	6·00	4·25
MS208	60×70 mm. 150r. As No. 204	12·50	7·00

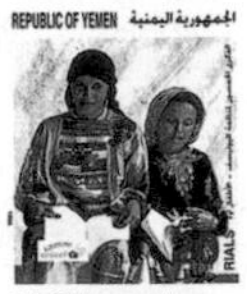

26 Girls reading

1996. 50th Anniv of UNICEF. Multicoloured.

209	20r. Type **26**	1·20	65
210	50r. Girls playing	2·30	1·30
211	60r. Mother and child	2·75	1·60
212	70r. Mother with three children	3·25	2·30
MS213	70×60 mm. 150r. Girl making jewellery (horiz)	11·50	7·00

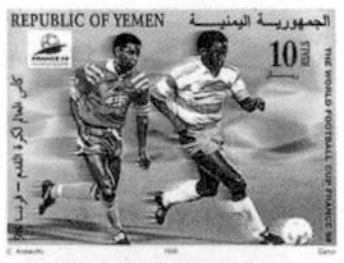

27 Players chasing Ball

1998. World Cup Football Championship, France. Multicoloured.

214	10r. Type **27**	65	40
215	15r. Heading ball	1·00	50
216	35r. Tackle	2·20	1·00
217	65r. Tackle (different)	3·75	1·80
218	75r. Kicking high ball	4·25	2·10
MS219	200×100 mm. Nos. 214/18	16·00	8·50

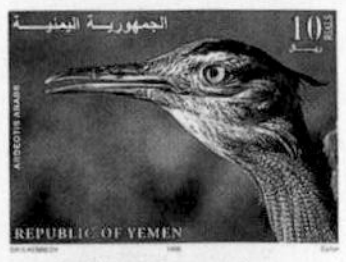

28 Arabian Bustard

1998. Birds. Multicoloured.

220	10r. Type **28**	80	40
221	15r. Egyptian vulture	1·00	50
222	35r. Abyssinian roller	2·10	1·00
223	65r. Violet starling	3·75	1·80

224	75r. Dark chanting goshawk	4·25	2·10
MS225	200×100 mm. Nos. 220/4	16·00	8·50

29 Upraised Hands and Anniversary Emblem

1998. 50th Anniv of Universal Declaration of Human Rights. Multicoloured.

226	15r. Type **29**	1·40	80
227	35r. Handshakes	2·75	1·40
228	100r. Outspread hands reaching to emblem	7·00	3·25
MS229	205×105 mm. Nos. 226/8	11·00	6·50

30 Dhows and Emblem

2000. First General Conference of Yemeni Immigrants, Sana'a. Multicoloured.

230	60r. Type **30**	3·00	1·70
231	90r. Wadi Dhahr and emblem	4·50	3·25
MS232	97×69 mm. Nos. 230/1	7·75	6·00

31 Emblem

2000. Tenth Anniv of Unification. National Day.

233	**31** 30r. multicoloured	1·40	1·20
234	**31** 50r. multicoloured	2·75	1·80
235	**31** 70r. multicoloured	3·75	2·75
MS236	69×109 mm. **31** 150r. multicoloured	8·50	6·00

32 Euphorbia abdalkuri

2000. Plants of Socotra Archipelago. Multicoloured.

237	30r. Type **32**	1·20	80
238	70r. Dendrosicyos socotranus	2·75	1·80
239	80r. Caralluma socotrana	3·25	2·30
240	120r. Dracaena cinnabari	5·00	2·75
MS241	97×69 mm. "Exacum affine"	17·00	11·50

33 Emblem

2000. Olympic Games, Sydney. Showing sports pictograms. Multicoloured.

242	50r. Type **33**	2·30	1·60
243	70r. Running	3·00	1·80
244	80r. Hurdling	3·25	2·10
245	100r. Rifle shooting	4·25	2·30
MS246	69×109 mm. 300r. Tennis	17·00	11·50

34 Mohammed Al Durra

2002. Intifada. Multicoloured.

247	30r. Type **34**	1·00	1·00
248	60r. Eiman Hajjo	2·10	2·10
MS249	112×78 mm. 90r. Mosque. Imperf	2·75	2·75

35 Scout leading Elderly Man across Road

2002. 75th Anniv of Yemen Boy Scouts. Multicoloured.

250	30r. Type **35**	1·00	1·00
251	60r. Planting	2·10	2·10
252	70r. In rowing boat	2·30	2·30
MS253	77×112 mm. 160r. Saluting (20×30 mm)	5·50	5·50

36 Player and Football

2002. World Cup Football Championship, Japan and South Korea. Multicoloured.

254	30r. Type **36**	1·00	1·00
255	70r. Two players (horiz)	2·40	2·40
256	100r. Player running	3·50	3·50
257	120r. Player preparing to kick ball	4·00	4·00
MS258	116×16 mm. Circular:—160r. ×2 Leg and ball (33×33 mm); Championship trophy (33×33 mm)	14·50	14·50

37 Stone Idols (3000 BC)

2002. Antiquities. (1st series). Multicoloured.

259	30r. Type **37**	1·00	1·00
260	70r. Ma'adi Karib (statue, 800 BC)	2·10	2·40
261	100r. Horned griffin (plaque, 300 AD)	3·50	3·50
262	120r. Awsan Yasduq Eil (statue, 100 BC)	4·00	4·00
MS263	111×78 mm. 320r. Stele with bull's head (100 BC). Imperf	14·50	14·50

See also Nos. 272/**MS**275.

38 Abdullah Al Baradony

2002. Poets. Multicoloured.

264	30r. Type **38**	1·40	1·40
265	30r. Hussein Al-Muhdhar wearing turban	1·40	1·40
266	60r. Abdullah Al Baradony facing left	2·75	2·75
267	60r. Hussein Al-Muhdhar wearing fez	2·75	2·75
MS268	112×78 mm. 70c. ×2 Hussein Al-Muhdhar (20×30 mm); Abdullah Al Baradony (20×30 mm)	6·50	6·50

39 Anniversary Emblem

2002. 40th Anniv of Revolution. Multicoloured.

269	**39** 30r. multicoloured	1·40	1·40
270	**39** 60r. multicoloured	2·75	2·75
MS271	111×77 mm. 90r. emblem. Imperf	3·75	3·75

40 Two Players and Ball

2003. Yemen Under 17 Qualifying Team FIFA World Championship Final 2003. Showing two players with football.

272	30r. Type **40**	1·00	1·00
273	50r. Player wearing white	1·70	1·70
274	70r. Player wearing red	2·40	2·40
275	100r. Player wearing green and white	3·50	3·50
MS276	109×75 mm. 250r. Team members. Imperf	8·50	8·50

41 Stone Statue

2003. Antiquities (2nd series). Multicoloured.

277	20r. Type **41**	1·00	1·00
278	40r. Carved pillar	1·40	1·40
279	50r. Bearded man (statue)	1·70	1·70
280	150r. Man wearing kilt (plaque)	5·00	5·00
MS281	111×76 mm. 260r. Musician (plaque) (horiz)	8·50	8·50

42 Woman wearing Striped Headdress

2003. Traditional Women's Costumes. Multicoloured.

282	30r. Type **42**	1·00	1·00
283	60r. Wearing striped dress with bodice	2·00	2·00
284	70r. Older woman wearing hat	2·40	2·40
285	100r. Wearing transparent face covering	3·50	3·50
286	150r. Wearing black and white dress	5·00	5·00
MS287	111×76 mm. Wearing turban (horiz)	13·50	13·50

43 Girl on Globe

2003. Winning Designs in Children's Painting Competition. Multicoloured.

288	20r. Type **43**	70	70
289	30r. Dove above ruins	1·00	1·00
290	40r. Dove carrying children	1·40	1·40
291	50r. Houses, road, children and tree (horiz)	1·70	1·70
292	60r. Trees, animals and river (horiz)	2·00	2·00
293	70r. Park and houses (horiz)	2·40	2·40

44 Old City, Sana'a

2003. Sana'a, Arab City of Culture, 2004. Multicoloured.

294	30r. Type **44**	1·00	1·00
295	50r. al-Aqil minaret	1·70	1·70
296	70r. Five-storied building	2·40	2·40
297	100r. Street market	3·50	3·50
298	150r. al-Milh souk	5·00	5·00
MS299	111×76 mm. 400r. Buildings with takhrim windows (horiz)	13·50	13·50

45 Map as Footballer

2004. Centenary of FIFA (Federation Internationale de Football).

300	**45** 100r. multicoloured	2·75	2·75

46 Running

2004. Olympic Games, Athens. Multicoloured.

301	70r. Type **46**	2·00	2·00
302	80r. Rifle shooting	2·20	2·20
303	100r. Swimming	2·75	2·75
MS304	114×78 mm. 250r. Showjumping	6·75	6·75

47 Emblem

2004. Telecommunications. Multicoloured.

305	60r. Type **47**	1·70	1·70
306	70r. Computer and figures (vert)	2·00	2·00
307	100r. "Yemen Mobile" (vert)	2·75	2·75
MS308	135×98 mm. 400r. As No. 306 (vert)	11·00	11·00

48 Habrocestum albopunctatum

2004. Multicoloured. Multicoloured.

309	50r. Type **48**	1·40	1·40
310	50r. Rafalus insignipalpis	1·40	1·40
311	50r. Latrodectus hystrix	1·40	1·40
312	50r. Atrophothele socotrana	1·40	1·40
313	50r. Tidarren argo	1·40	1·40
314	50r. Scelidomachus socotranus	1·40	1·40
MS315	114×80 mm. 300r. As No. 314	8·25	8·25

49 Traditional Costume

2004. Traditional Men's Costume. Multicoloured.

316	50r. Type **49**	1·40	1·40
317	60r. Man holding stick	1·70	1·70
318	70r. Holding sword	2·00	2·00
319	100r. Wearing white shift	2·75	2·75
MS320	112×77 mm. 360r. As No. 318	9·25	9·25

50 Craftsman

2004. Crafts. Multicoloured.

321	70r. Type **50**	2·00	2·00
322	70r. Jewellery maker	2·00	2·00
323	70r. Weaver	2·00	2·00
324	70r. Metal worker	2·00	2·00
MS325	115×79 mm. 300r. As No. 324	8·25	8·25

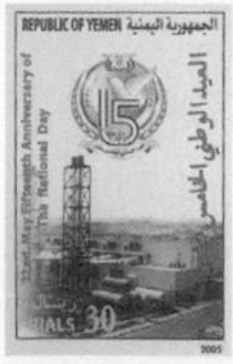

51 Emblem

2005. 15th Anniv of Unification. Multicoloured.

326	30r. Type **51**	85	85
327	60r. Emblem and river	1·70	1·70
328	70r. Man holding national flag	2·00	2·00
MS329	111×77 mm. 90r. Emblem and city	2·50	2·50

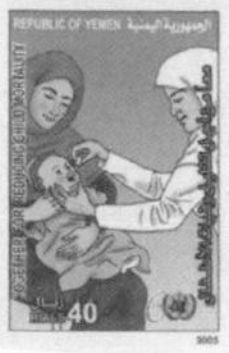

52 Immunizing Baby (Reducing Infant Mortality)

2005. 60th Anniv of United Nations. Development Aims. Multicoloured.

330	40r. Type **52**	1·00	1·00
331	40r. Taking blood pressure (Improving Maternal Health)	1·00	1·00
332	40r. Recyling (Clean and Sustainable Environment)	1·00	1·00
333	40r. Woman reading (Universal Primary Education)	1·00	1·00
334	40r. Mosquito, anti-viral drugs and AIDS ribbon (Combating AIDS, TB and Malaria)	1·00	1·00
335	80r. Woman and child (Halving Extreme Poverty and Hunger)	2·00	2·00
336	100r. Scales (Gender Equality and Women Empowerment)	2·50	2·50
337	120r. Shaking hands (Global Partnership and Development)	3·00	3·00
MS338	111×83 mm. 130r. United Nations emblem	3·25	3·25

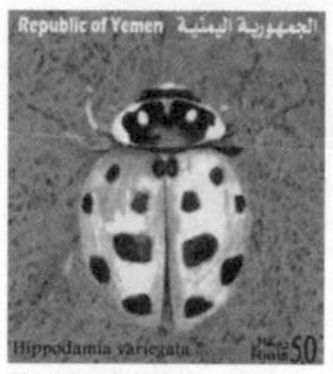

53 *Hippodamia variegata*

2007. Insects. Multicoloured.

339	50r. Type **53**	1·40	1·40
340	50r. *Cheilomenes propinqua vicina*	1·40	1·40
341	50r. *Cheilomenes lunata yemenensis*	1·40	1·40
342	50r. Inscr 'Pharoscymnus luteus'	1·40	1·40
343	50r. *Serangium buettikeri*	1·40	1·40
344	50r. *Brumoides nigrifrons*	1·40	1·40
MS345	150×140 mm. 250r. Inscr 'Pharoscymnus luteus'	6·75	6·75

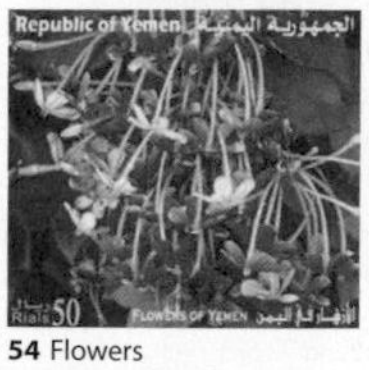

54 Flowers

2007. Flowers of Yemen. Multicoloured.

346	50r. Type **54**	1·40	1·40
347	80r. Pink flowers on bare stems	2·00	2·00
348	110r. Yellow flowers	2·75	2·75
349	130r. Orange flowers with long stamens	3·25	3·25
350	140r. Yellow flowers with long stamens	3·50	3·50
351	150r. Pale pink flowers	3·75	3·75
MS352	150×140 mm. 300r. Dahlia	8·25	8·25

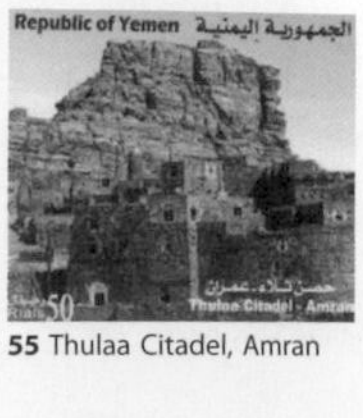

55 Thulaa Citadel, Amran

2007. Castles and Citadels. Multicoloured.

353	50r. Type **55**	1·40	1·40
354	80r. Al-Tawama Citadel, Hadramout	2·00	2·00
355	100r. Sarah Castle, Aden	2·50	2·50
356	110r. Sumarah Castle, Ibb	2·75	2·75
357	120r. Al-Qahira Castle, Taiz	3·00	3·00
MS358	150×140 mm. 300r. Hill top castle	8·25	8·25

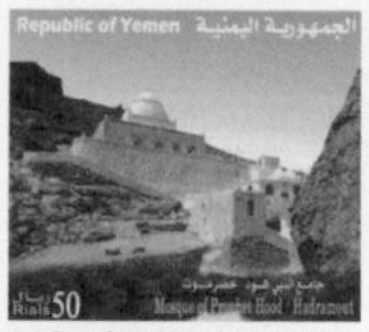

56 Prophet Hood Mosque, Hadramout

2007. Mosques. Multicoloured.

359	50r. Type **56**	1·40	1·40
360	80r. Al-Ameria Mosque, Radaa	2·00	2·00
361	100r. Queen Arwa Mosque, Jebla	2·50	2·50
362	110r. Al-Ashrafiah Mosque, Taiz	2·75	2·75
363	130r. Al-Aidarous Mosque, Aden	3·25	3·25
364	200r. Al-Bukiriah Mosque, Sana'a	5·00	5·00
MS365	150×140 mm. 300r. Mosque	8·25	8·25

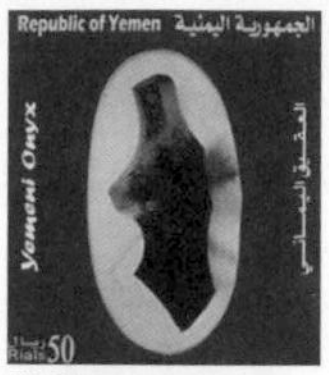

57 Onyx

2007. Onyx. Designs showing onyx. Multicoloured.

366	50r. Type **57**	1·40	1·40
367	80r. With irregular vertical striations	2·00	2·00
368	100r. Amber coloured with flame shaped striation	2·50	2·50
369	110r. Pendant	2·75	2·75
370	120r. With falcon shaped markings	3·00	3·00
371	130r. With horizontal markings	3·25	3·25
372	140r. With leaves	3·50	3·50
373	160r. With vertical striations swirling to the right	3·75	3·75
MS374	150×140 mm. 250r. As No. 369	7·75	7·75

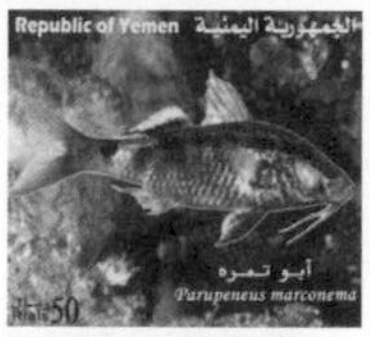

58 *Parupeneus marconema*

2007. Marine Life. Multicoloured.

375	50r. Type **58**	1·40	1·40
376	80r. *Sarda orientalis*	2·00	2·00
377	100r. *Carcharhinus melanopterus*	2·50	2·50
378	110r. *Plectorhinchus schotaf*	2·75	2·75
379	130r. *Panulirus homarus*	3·25	3·25
380	160r. *Seriola rivoliana*	3·75	3·75
MS381	150×140 mm. 300r. As No. 379	8·25	8·25

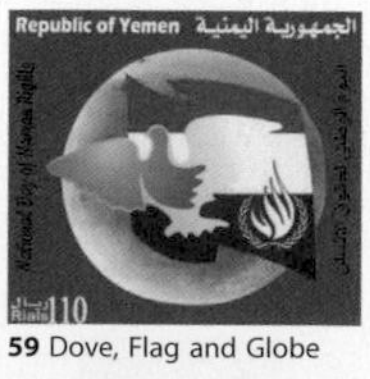

59 Dove, Flag and Globe

2007. National Human Rights Day. Multicoloured.

382	110r. Type **59**	2·75	2·75
383	130r. As Type **59**	3·25	3·25
MS384	150×140 mm. 250r. Dove (vert)	7·75	7·75

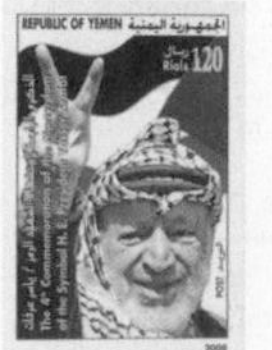

60 Yasser Arafat

2008. Yasser Arafat Commemoration.

385	120r. Type **60**	8·00	8·00
MS386	110×70 mm. 300r. Yasser Arafat and flag. Imperf	8·00	8·00

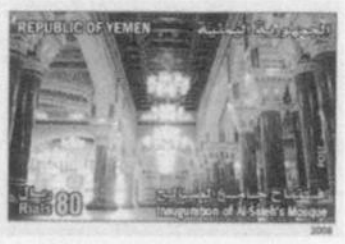

61 Interior

2008. Inauguration of Al-Saleh's Mosque. Multicoloured.

387	80r. Type **61**	2·20	2·20
388	100r. Doorways	2·75	2·75
389	120r. Minarets and exterior façade	3·00	3·00
MS390	110×70 mm. 300r. Entrance and exterior façade. Imperf	8·00	8·00

Pt. 3

YUGOSLAVIA

The kingdom of the Serbs, Croats and Slovenes, in S.E. Europe, established after the 1914–18 war and comprising Serbia, Montenegro, Bosnia, Herzegovina and parts of pre-war Hungary.

From 1945 it was a Federal Republic comprising six republics. In 1991 four of these republics seceded, from when the Federation consisted of the Republics of Montenegro and Serbia and the two autonomous provinces of Kosovo and Vojvodina.

A. KINGDOM OF THE SERBS, CROATS AND SLOVENES
I. Issues for Bosnia and Herzegovina
100 heller = 1 kruna.

II. Issues for Croatia
100 filir (heller) = 1 kruna (krone).

III. Issues for Slovenia
1919. 100 vinar (heller) = 1 kruna (krone).
1920. 100 paras = 1 dinar.

IV. Issues for the Whole Kingdom
100 paras = 1 dinar.

B. KINGDOM OF YUGOSLAVIA
100 paras = 1 dinar.

C. DEMOCRATIC FEDERATION OF YUGOSLAVIA
I. Regional Issues
Bosnia and Herzegovina
Currency: Croatian Kunas.

Croatia
Currency: Kunas.

Montenegro
Currency: Italian Lire.

Serbia
Currency:Hungarian Filler.

Slovenia
Currencies: Italian (Ljubljana); German (Maribor); Hungarian (Murska Sobota).

II. General Issues
100 paras = 1 dinar.

D. FEDERAL PEOPLE'S REPUBLIC
100 paras = 1 dinar.

A. KINGDOM OF THE SERBS, CROATS AND SLOVENES

I. ISSUES FOR BOSNIA AND HERZEGOVINA

1918. 1910 commem stamps of Bosnia (with date labels) optd **DRZAVA S.H.S. 1918 1918 Bosna i Hercegovina** or the same in Cyrillic characters or surch also.

1	3h. olive (No. 345)	50	1·00
2	5h. green	50	50
3	10h. red	50	50
4	20h. sepia	50	50
5	25h. blue	50	50
6	30h. green	50	50
7	40h. orange	50	50
8	45h. red	50	50
9	50h. purple	75	1·00
10	60h. on 50h. purple	50	50
11	80h. on 6h. brown	50	50
12	90h. on 35h. green	50	50
13	2k. green	50	50
14	3k. on 3h. olive	2·50	3·75
15	4k. on 1k. lake	5·25	6·25
16	10k. on 2h. violet	7·75	9·00

1918. Newspaper Express stamps of Bosnia. 5h. optd as last and **HELERA** and 2h. the same but in Cyrillic.

17	**N35**	2h. red	7·75	7·75
18	**N35**	5h. green	4·25	4·25

These were issued for use as ordinary postage stamps.

1918. Bosnian War Invalids Fund stamps optd **DRAVA S.H.S. Bosna Hercegovina** or the same in Cyrillic characters.

19	**31**	5h. (+2h.) green	£225	£250
20	-	10h. (+2h.) red	£140	£150
21	-	10h. (+2h.) blue	1·00	1·10
22	**31**	15h. (+2h.) brown	2·50	2·75

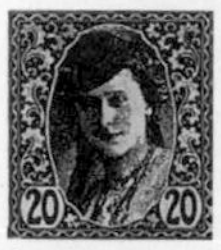

6a

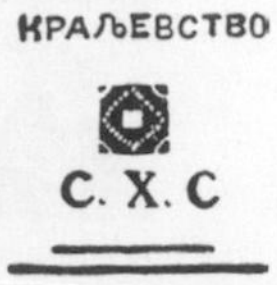

(7)

1918. Newspaper stamps of Bosnia of 1913 (as T **6a**) surch. Imperf.

50	**6a**	2 on 6h. mauve	£200	£225
51	**6a**	2 on 10h. red	50·00	55·00
52	**6a**	2 on 20h. green	10·50	11·00
23	**6a**	3 on 2h. blue	50	55
24	**6a**	5 on 6h. mauve	50	55

Most of these were used for ordinary postage purposes.

1919. Perf.

25	2h. blue	50	55
26	6h. mauve	2·50	3·25
27	10h. red	1·00	1·70
28	20h. green	50	55

The above were issued for use as ordinary postage stamps.

These stamps imperforate were issued as Newspaper stamps for Bosnia q.v.

1919. Types of Bosnia optd with T **7** or similar type with wording **KRALJEVSTVO S.H.S.**, or surch also.

29	**25**	3h. lake	50	1·10
30	**25**	5h. green	50	55
31	**25**	10 on 6h. black	50	55
32	**26**	20 on 35h. green	50	55
33	**25**	25h. blue	50	55
34	**25**	30h. red	50	55
35	**26**	45h. brown	50	55
36	**33**	45 on 80h. brown	50	55
37	**26**	50h. blue	£100	£130
38	**26**	50h. on 72h. blue	50	55
39	**26**	60h. purple	50	55
40	**33**	80h. brown	50	55
41	**33**	90h. purple	50	55
42	-	2k. green (No. 200)	50	55
43	**26**	3k. red on green	50	80
44	**34**	4k. red on green	2·10	2·75
45	**26**	5k. lilac on grey	2·10	3·25
46	**34**	10k. violet on grey	4·25	5·50

1919. War Victims' Fund. Stamps of Bosnia of 1906 surch **KRALJEVSTVO Srba. Hrvata i Slovenaca** or same in Cyrillic characters and new value.

47	-	10x.+10x. on 40h. orange (No. 196)	1·60	2·75
48	-	20x.+10x. on 20h. sepia (No. 192)	75	2·50
49	**5**	45x.+15x. on 1k. lake	6·25	9·00

II. ISSUES FOR CROATIA

The provisional issues on Hungarian stamps were sold in Yugoslavia "heller" and "krone" currency, but as this is not expressed on the stamps (except for Nos. 69/73) we have retained the Hungarian descriptions to facilitate reference to the original stamps.

1918. Various issues of Hungary optd **HRVATSKA SHS** and bar or wheel. "Turul" issue of 1900.

53	**7**	6f. olive	1·00	2·20
54	**7**	50f. lake on blue	1·60	2·75

"Harvesters" and "Parliament" issues of 1916.

55	**18**	2f. brown	50	55
56	**18**	3f. red	50	55
57	**18**	5f. green	50	55
58	**18**	6f. green	50	55
59	**18**	10f. red	10·50	11·00
60	**18**	15f. violet (No. 244)	£100	£170
61	**18**	15f. violet (No. 251)	50	55
62	**18**	20f. brown	50	55
63	**18**	25f. blue	50	55
64	**18**	35f. brown	50	55
65	**18**	40f. green	50	1·10
66	**19**	50f. purple	50	55
67	**19**	75f. blue	50	55
68	**19**	80f. green	50	55
69	**19**	1k. red	50	55
70	**19**	2k. brown	50	55
71	**19**	3k. grey and violet	50	55
72	**19**	5k. light brown and brown	3·25	4·00
73	**19**	10k. mauve and brown	16·00	19·00

The kroner values are overprinted **KRUNA** or **KRUNE** also.

"Charles" and "Zita" issue of 1918.

74	**27**	10f. red	50	55
75	**27**	20f. brown	50	55
76	**27**	25f. blue	50	1·10
77	**28**	40f. olive	50	55

1918. Stamps of Hungary optd **HRVATSKA SHS ZF ZA NAROD VIJECE.** War Charity issue of 1916.

78	**20**	10+2f. red	50	65
79	-	15+2f. violet	50	55
80	**22**	40+2f. lake	50	55

Coronation issue of 1916.

81	**23**	10f. mauve	£100	£170
82	-	15f. red	£100	£170

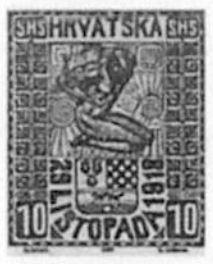

20 "Freedom of Croatia"

1918. Freeing of the Yugoslavs.

83	**20**	10h. red	3·25	3·25
84	**20**	20h. violet	3·25	3·25
85	**20**	25h. blue	6·75	9·00
86	**20**	45h. grey	65·00	75·00

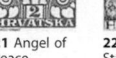

21 Angel of Peace

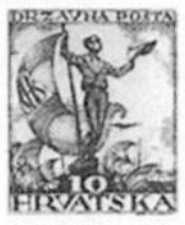

22 Sailor with Standard and Falcon

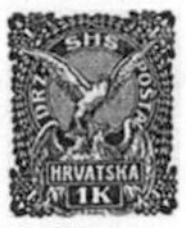

23 Falcon ("Liberty")

1919

87	**21**	2h. brown	10	55
88	**21**	3h. mauve	10	65
89	**21**	5h. green	10	10
90	**22**	10h. red	10	10
91	**22**	20h. brown	10	10
92	**22**	25h. blue	10	10
93	**22**	45h. olive	20	20
94	**23**	1k. red	30	35
95	-	3k. purple	1·00	1·30
96	-	5k. brown	1·60	1·10

DESIGN: 3, 5k. as Type **5** but light background behind falcon.

III. ISSUES FOR SLOVENIA

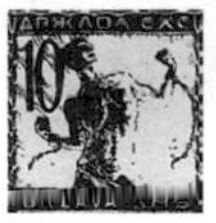

25 Chainbreaker

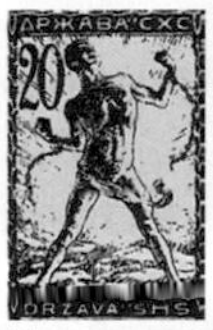

26 Chainbreaker

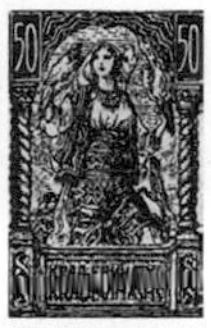

27 "Yugoslavia" with Three Falcons

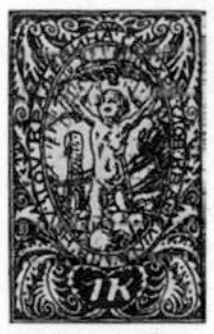

28 Angel of Peace

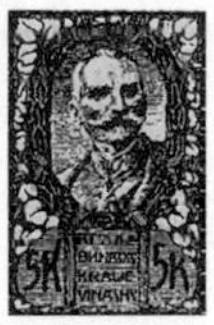

29 King Petar I

1919. Perf or rouletted.

97a	**25**	3v. violet	30	20
107	**25**	5v. green	20	10
108	**25**	10v. red	20	10
100	**25**	15v. blue	30	20
101	**26**	20v. brown	85	20
102	**26**	25v. blue	40	20
103	**26**	30v. pink	40	20
111	**26**	30v. red	40	20
104a	**26**	40v. yellow	45	20
122	**27**	50v. green	50	10
135	**27**	60v. violet	1·20	60
136	**28**	1k. red	95	35
120	**28**	2k. blue	90	20
126	**29**	5k. red	85	30
139	**29**	10k. blue	4·75	1·10
105	**29**	15k. green	16·00	20·00
106	**29**	20k. purple	3·25	4·00

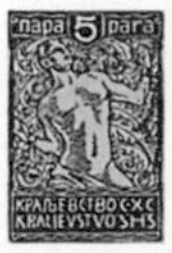

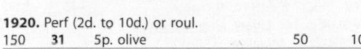

31 Chainbreaker

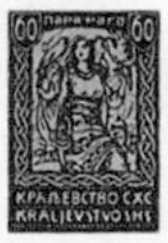

32 "Yugoslavia" with Three Falcons

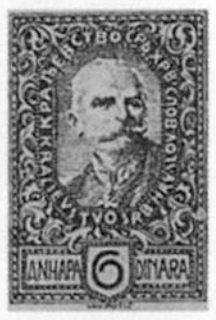

34 King Petar I

1920. Perf (2d. to 10d.) or roul.

150	**31**	5p. olive	50	10
151	**31**	10p. green	20	10
152	**31**	15p. brown	20	10
153	**31**	20p. red	1·00	55
154	**31**	25p. brown	1·00	10
155	**32**	40p. violet	20	20
156	**32**	45p. yellow	20	20
157	**32**	50p. blue	20	10
158	**32**	60p. brown	20	10
159	**34**	1d. brown	20	10
160	-	2d. black	20	10
161	**34**	4d. slate	85	45
162	-	6d. olive	50	1·30
163	-	10d. brown	85	1·10

The 2, 6 and 10d. are as Type **34** but larger.

1920. Carinthian Plebiscite. Newspaper stamps of Yugoslavia of 1919 surch **1920KGCA** and new value. Imperf.

163a	**N30**	5p. on 4v. grey	10	35
163b	**N30**	15p. on 4v. grey	10	35
163c	**N30**	25p. on 4v. grey	20	80
163d	**N30**	45p. on 2v. grey	20	1·70
163e	**N30**	50p. on 2v. grey	30	1·90
163f	**N30**	2d. on 2v. grey	2·50	8·50

These stamps were sold at three times face value on aid of the Plebiscite Propaganda Fund.

IV. ISSUES FOR THE WHOLE KINGDOM

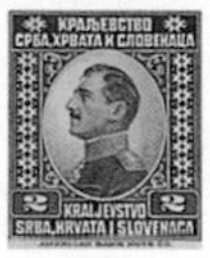

35 King Alexander when Prince

1921. Inscr "KRALJEVSTVO" at foot.

164	**35**	2p. brown	10	10
165	**35**	5p. green	10	10
166	**35**	10p. red	10	10
167	**35**	15p. purple	10	10
168	**35**	20p. black	10	10
169	**35**	25p. blue	10	10
170	**35**	50p. olive	10	10
171	**35**	60p. red	20	10
172	**35**	75p. violet	10	10
173	-	1d. orange	50	10
174	-	2d. olive	75	10
175	-	4d. green	1·60	10
176	-	5d. red	5·25	10
177	-	10d. brown	16·00	55

DESIGN: 1d. to 10d. as Type **35**, but portrait of King Petar I.

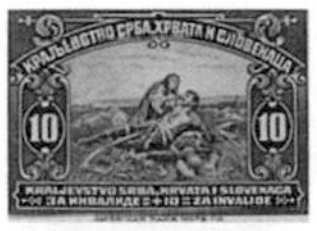

37 Kosovo Maiden, 1389

1921. Disabled Soldiers' Fund.

178	**37**	10+10p. red	10	10
179	-	15+15p. brown	10	10
180	-	25+25p. blue	10	10

DESIGN: 15p. Wounded soldier typifying retreat through Albania, 1915; 25p. Symbol of national unity.

1922. Nos. 178/180 surch.

181	1d. on 10p. red	10	10
183	1d. on 15p. brown	10	10
182	1d. on 25p. blue	10	10
184	3d. on 15p. brown	3·25	1·70
186	8d. on 15p. brown	3·75	20
187	20d. on 15p. brown	21·00	1·10
188	30d. on 15p. brown	33·00	2·20

1923. As T **35**, but inscr "KRALJEVINA" at foot.

189	**35**	1d. brown	5·25	20
190	**35**	5d. red	10·50	20
191	**35**	8d. purple	21·00	35
192	**35**	20d. green	50·00	1·10
193	**35**	30d. orange	£180	3·75

1924. Nos. 171 and 191 surch.

195	20p. on 60p. red	75	10
196	5d. on 8d. purple	23·00	1·00

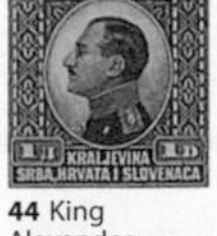

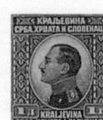

44 King Alexander

1924

197	**44**	20p. black	10	10
198	**44**	50p. brown	10	10
199	**44**	1d. red	10	10
200	**44**	2d. green	50	10
201	**44**	3d. blue	50	10
202	**44**	5d. brown	3·75	10
203	-	10d. violet	31·00	10
204	-	15d. green	21·00	20
205	-	20d. orange	21·00	20
206	-	30d. green	16·00	1·50

The 10d. to 30d. have the head in a square panel.

1925. Surch.

207	**44**	25p. on 3d. blue	50	10
208	**44**	50p. on 3d. blue	50	10

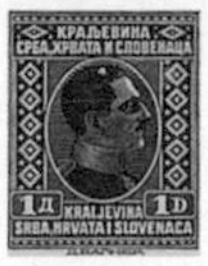

46 King Alexander

1926

209	**46**	25p. green	10	10
210	**46**	50p. brown	10	10
211	**46**	1d. red	50	10
212	**46**	2d. black	50	10
213	**46**	3d. blue	75	10
214	**46**	4d. red	1·30	10
215	**46**	5d. violet	2·10	10
216	**46**	8d. brown	10·50	10
217	**46**	10d. green	5·25	10
218	**46**	15d. brown	31·00	10
219	**46**	20d. violet	42·00	35
220	**46**	30d. orange	£160	55

1926. Danube Flood Fund. Surch.

221	**46**	25p.+0.25 green	10	10
222	**46**	50p.+0.50 brown	10	10
223	**46**	1d.+0.50 red	10	10
224	**46**	2d.+0.50 black	50	10
225	**46**	3d.+0.50 blue	50	10
226	**46**	4d.+0.50 red	75	10
227	**46**	5d.+0.50 violet	1·30	10
228	**46**	8d.+0.50 brown	2·50	55
229	**46**	10d.+1.00 green	5·25	10
230	**46**	15d.+1.00 brown	16·00	1·10
231	**46**	20d.+1.00 violet	21·00	80
232	**46**	30d.+1.00 orange	60·00	4·50

1928. Nos. 223/32 optd **XXXX** over previous surch.

233	**46**	1d. red	50	20
234	**46**	2d. black	1·60	20
235	**46**	3d. blue	2·50	45
236	**46**	4d. red	6·25	65
237	**46**	5d. violet	5·25	20
238	**46**	8d. brown	21·00	1·10
239	**46**	10d. green	42·00	20
240	**46**	15d. brown	£250	3·25
241	**46**	20d. violet	£160	3·25
242	**46**	30d. orange	£350	13·50

B. KINGDOM OF YUGOSLAVIA

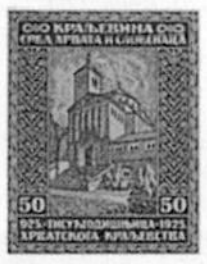

49 Duvno Cathedral

1929. Millenary of Croatian Kingdom (1925).

243	**49**	50p.+50p. olive	50	20
244	-	1d.+50p. red	1·60	55
245	-	3d.+1d. blue	4·25	1·50

DESIGNS—As Type **49**: 3d. King Tomislav. Horiz (34×23 mm): Kings Tomislav and Alexander I.

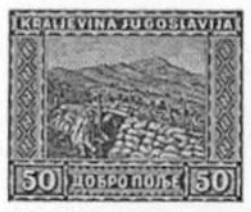

52 Dobropolje

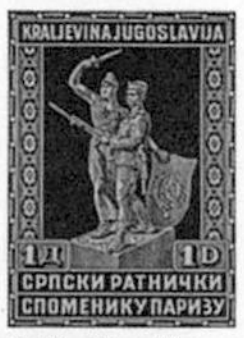

53 Serbian War Memorial, Paris

1931. Serbian War Memorial (Paris) Fund.

246	**52**	50p.+50p. green	10	10
247	**53**	1d.+50p. red	10	10
248	-	3d.+1d. blue	20	20

DESIGN—As Type **52**: 3d. Kajmakcalan.

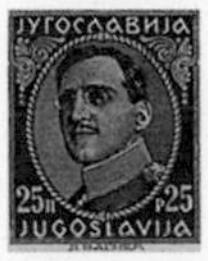

55 King Alexander

1931

249	**55**	25p. black	10	10
250	**55**	50p. green	10	10
251	**55**	1d. red	15	10
252	**55**	3d. blue	1·00	10
253	**55**	4d. orange	7·75	10
254	**55**	5d. violet	7·75	10
255	**55**	10d. olive	26·00	10
256	**55**	15d. brown	26·00	10
257	**55**	20d. purple	50·00	10
258	**55**	30d. red	27·00	65
262	**55**	75p. green	75	10
263	**55**	1d.50 red	1·90	10
263b	**55**	1d.75 red	3·25	45
263c	**55**	3d.50 blue	4·25	45

1931. Optd **KRALJEVINA JUGOSLAVIJA** and also in Cyrillic characters.

259	**49**	50p.+50p. olive	10	10
260	-	1d.+50p. red	10	10
261	-	3d.+1d. blue	75	90

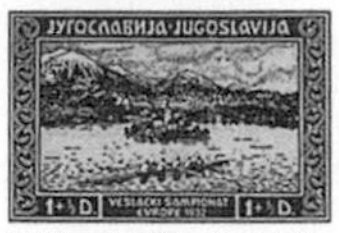

57 Rowing "four" on Lake Bled

1932. European Rowing Championship. Inscr ending "EUROPE 1932".

264		75p.+50p. green	85	1·30
265	**57**	1d.+½d. red	85	1·30
266	-	1½d.+½d. red	1·50	1·90
267	-	3d.+1d. blue	2·50	3·25
268	-	4d.+1d. blue and orange	10·50	22·00
269	-	5d.+1d. lilac and violet	10·50	17·00

DESIGNS—HORIZ: 75p. Single sculler on Danube at Smederevo; 1½d. Rowing "eight" on Danube at Belgrade; 3d. Rowing "pair" at Split harbour. VERT: 4d. Rowing "pair" on river and Zagreb Cathedral; 5d. Prince Peter.

1933. 11th International PEN Club Congress, Dubrovnik. As T **55** with additional value and "XI. int. kongres Pen-Klubova u Dubrovniku 1933" inscr below in Roman or Cyrillic characters.

270	**55**	50p.+25p. black	10·50	13·50
271	**55**	75p.+25p. green	10·50	13·50
272	**55**	1d.50+50p. red	10·50	13·50
273	**55**	3d.+1d. blue	10·50	13·50
274	**55**	4d.+1d. green	10·50	13·50
275	**55**	5d.+1d. yellow	10·50	13·50

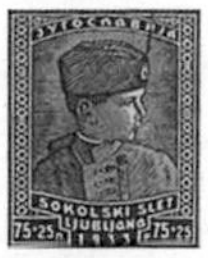

60 Crown Prince Petar in "Sokol" Uniform

1933. "Sokol" Meeting, Ljubjana.

276	**60**	75p.+25p. green	50	35
277	**60**	1½d.+½d. red	50	35

1933. Optd **JUGOSLAVIJA** in Roman and Cyrillic characters. (a) Postage.

278	**46**	25p. green	10	10
279	**46**	50p. brown	10	10
280	**46**	1d. red	1·00	10
281	**46**	2d. black	1·60	10
282	**46**	3d. blue	5·25	10
283	**46**	4d. red	2·50	10
284	**46**	5d. violet	5·25	10
285	**46**	8d. brown	16·00	1·90
286	**46**	10d. olive	31·00	20
287	**46**	15d. brown	50·00	2·50
288	**46**	20d. violet	75·00	1·10
289	**46**	30d. orange	70·00	1·10

(b) Charity stamps. Nos. 221/3.

290	25p.+0.25 green	1·30	20
291	50p.+0.50 brown	1·30	20
292	1d.+0.50 red	3·75	65

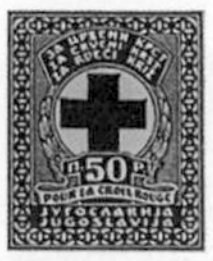

62

1933. Obligatory Tax. Red Cross.

293	**62**	50p. red and blue	30	20

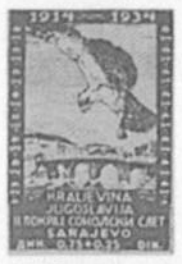
63 Osprey over R. Bosna

1934. 20th Anniv of "Sokol" Games, Sarajevo.

294	**63**	75p.+25p. green	10·50	12·50
295	**63**	1d.50+50p. red	16·00	13·50
296	**63**	1d.75+25p. brown	26·00	13·50

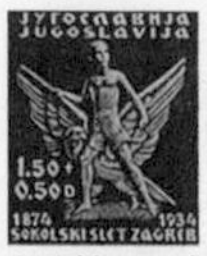
64 Athlete and Falcon (from sculpture by Krsinic)

1934. 60th Anniv of Croat "Sokol" Games, Zagreb.

297	**64**	75p.+25p. green	5·25	4·50
298	**64**	1d.50+50p. red	5·25	6·75
299	**64**	1d.75+25p. brown	12·50	17·00

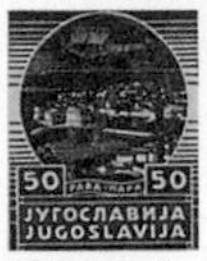
65 Dubrovnik

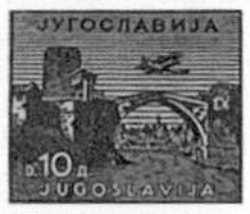
69 Mostar Bridge

1934. Air.

300	**65**	50p. purple	10	20
301	-	1d. green	20	20
302	-	2d. red	75	55
303	-	3d. blue	2·30	80
304	**69**	10d. orange	5·25	5·25

DESIGNS: 1d. Lake of Bled; 2d. Waterfall at Jajce; 3d. Oplenac.

1934. King Alexander Mourning issue. With black margins.

305	**55**	25p. black (postage)	10	10
306	**55**	50p. green	10	10
307	**55**	75p. green	10	10
308	**55**	1d. red	10	10
309	**55**	1d.50 red	10	10
310	**55**	1d.75 red	10	10
311	**55**	3d. blue	10	10
312	**55**	3d.50 blue	50	10
313	**55**	4d. orange	50	10
314	**55**	5d. violet	1·30	10
315	**55**	10d. olive	3·75	10
316	**55**	15d. brown	7·75	35
317	**55**	20d. purple	16·00	35
318	**55**	30d. red	10·50	55
319	-	3d. blue (No. 303) (air)	6·25	5·50

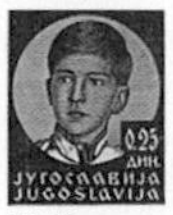
70 King Petar II

1935

320	**70**	25p. black	10	10
321	**70**	50p. orange	10	10
322	**70**	75p. green	20	10
323	**70**	1d. brown	20	10
324	**70**	1d.50 red	30	10
325	**70**	1d.75 red	50	10
325a	**70**	2d. red	30	10
326	**70**	3d. orange	30	10
327	**70**	3d.50 blue	75	10
328	**70**	4d. green	2·50	10
329	**70**	4d. blue	50	10
330	**70**	10d. violet	2·50	10
331	**70**	15d. brown	2·75	10
332	**70**	20d. blue	10·50	35
333	**70**	30d. pink	5·25	35

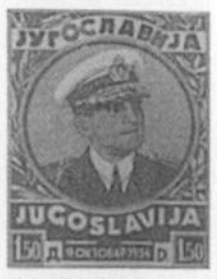
71 King Alexander

1935. First Anniv of King Alexander's Assassination.

334	**71**	75p. green	50	55
335	**71**	1d.50 red	50	55
336	**71**	1d.75 brown	75	1·10
337	**71**	3d.50 blue	4·25	4·50
338	**71**	7d.50 red	2·50	2·75

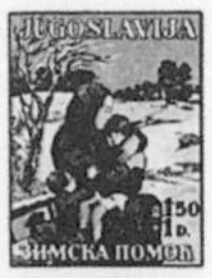
72

1935. Winter Relief Fund.

339	**72**	1d.50+1d. brown	3·25	1·70
340	**72**	3d.50+1d.50 blue	5·25	4·00

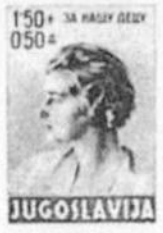
73 Queen Marie

1936. Child Welfare.

341	**73**	75p.+25p. green	50	55
342	**73**	1d.50+50p. red	50	55
343	**73**	1d.75+75p. brown	3·25	3·25
344	**73**	3d.50+1d. blue	4·25	4·50

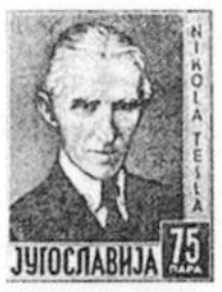
74 Nicola Tesla

1936. 80th Birthday of Dr. Tesla (physicist).

345	**74**	75p. brown and green	40	35
346	**74**	1d.75 grey and blue	65	40

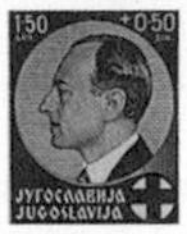
75 Prince Paul

1936. Red Cross Fund.

347	**75**	75p.+50p. green	40	45
348	**75**	1d.50+50p. red	40	45

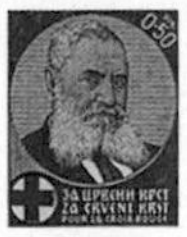
76 Dr. Vladan Djordjevic (founder)

1936. Obligatory Tax. Jubilee of Serbian Red Cross.

349	**76**	50p. brown	50	35

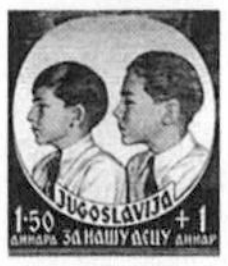
77 Princess Tomislav and Andrej

1937. Child Welfare. T **77** and similar horiz portrait.

350	-	25p.+25p. brown	30	35
351	-	75p.+75p. orange	50	55
352	**77**	1d.50+1d. orange	85	90
353	**77**	2d.+1d. mauve	1·60	1·70

78 Oplenac

1937. Little Entente.

354	**78**	3d. green	2·50	80
355	**78**	4d. blue	2·50	1·70

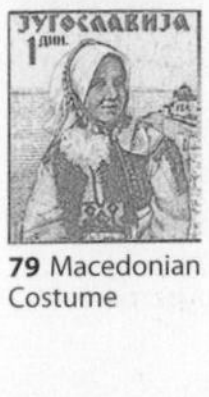
79 Macedonian Costume

1937. First Yugoslav Philatelic Exhibition, Belgrade (ZEFIB). Sheet 109×150 mm, comprising T **79** and similar designs showing girls in national costumes.

MS356 1d. green (T **79**); 1d.50 purple (Bosnia); 2d. scarlet (Slovenia); 4d. blue (Croatia) Sold at the Exhibition P.O. at 15d.	13·50	13·50

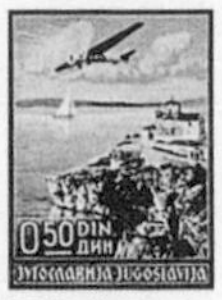
80 St. Naum Convent, Lake Ohrid

1937. Air.

360	**80**	50p. brown	10	10
361	-	1d. green	15	10
362	-	2d. blue	20	15
363	-	2d.50 red	30	20
364	**80**	5d. violet	50	35
365a	-	10d. red	1·30	35
366	-	20d. green	2·00	2·00
367	-	30d. blue	2·50	2·50

DESIGNS VERT: 1, 10d. Rab (Arbe) Harbour. HORIZ: 2, 20d. Sarajevo; 2d.50, 30d. Laibach (Ljubljana).

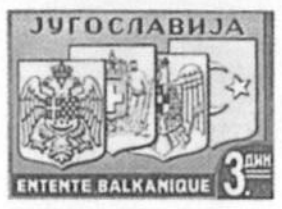
83 Arms of Yugoslavia, Greece, Rumania and Turkey

1937. Balkan Entente.

368	**83**	3d. green	2·50	55
369	**83**	4d. blue	3·25	1·30

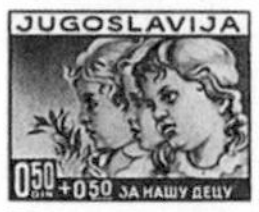
84

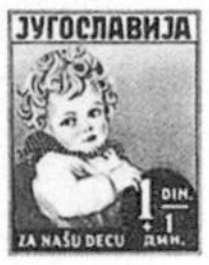
85

1938. Child Welfare.

370	**84**	50p.+50p. brown	30	20
371	**85**	1d.+1d. green	50	45
372	**84**	1d.50+1d.50 red	1·30	1·10
373	**85**	2d.+2d. mauve	3·25	2·75

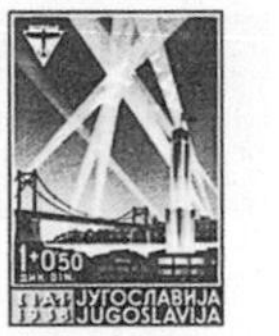
86 Searchlight Display and Parachute Tower

1938. Int Aeronautical Exhibition, Belgrade, and Yugoslav Air Club Fund.

374	**86**	1d.+50p. green	1·00	1·10
375	**86**	1d.50+1d. red	1·60	1·70
376	**86**	2d.+1d. mauve	3·25	3·25
377	**86**	3d.+1d. blue	5·25	5·50

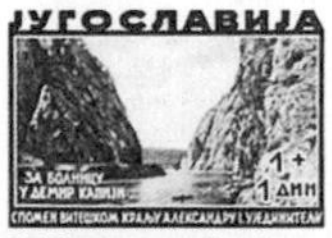
87 Entrance to Demir Kapija Cliff

1938. Railway Employees' Hospital Fund.

378	**87**	1d.+1d. green	1·00	55
379	-	1d.50+1d.50 red	1·80	80
380	-	2d.+2d. mauve	4·50	4·50
381	-	3d.+3d. blue	4·75	4·50

DESIGNS—HORIZ: 1d.50, Demir Kapija Hospital. VERT: 2d. Runner carrying torch; 3d. King Alexander.

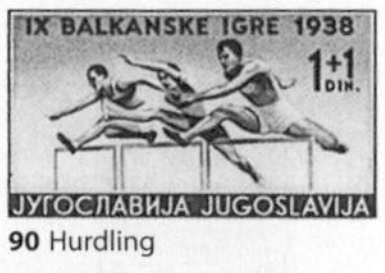

90 Hurdling

1938. Ninth Balkan Games.

382		50p.+50p. orange	3·25	3·25
383	**90**	1d.+1d. green	3·25	3·25
384	-	1d.50+1d.50 mauve	3·25	3·25
385	-	2d.+2d. blue	6·25	6·75

DESIGNS—HORIZ: 1d.50, Pole vaulting. VERT: 50p. Breasting the tape; 2d. Putting the shot.

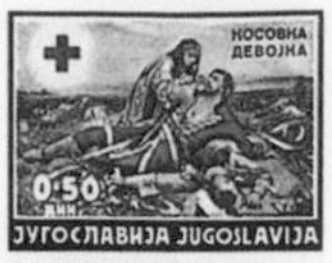
91 Maiden of Kosovo (after P. Jovanovic)

1938. Obligatory Tax. Red Cross.

386	**91**	50p. multicoloured	50	35
386a	**91**	50p. red and blue	75	55

1938. Child Welfare. Optd **SALVATE PARVULOS.**

387	**84**	50p.+50p. brown	1·00	80
388	**85**	1d.+1d. green	1·00	1·10
389	**84**	1d.50+1d.50 red	1·60	1·70
390	**85**	2d.+2d. mauve	3·25	3·25

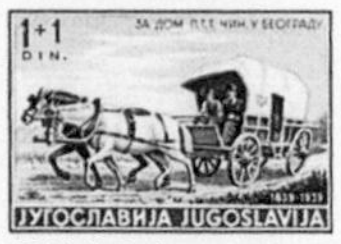
93 Mail Carrier

1939. Postal Centenary and Railway Benevolent Association Fund.

391	-	50p.+50p. orange and brown	75	80
392	**93**	1d.+1d. green and black	75	80
393	-	1d.50+1d.50 red	4·25	2·75
394	-	2d.+2d. purple and violet	4·25	4·00
395	-	4d.+4d. blue and light blue	5·25	5·50

DESIGNS: 50p. Mounted postmen; 1d.50, Steam mail train; 2d. Mail coach; 4d. Lockheed 10 Electra mail plane.

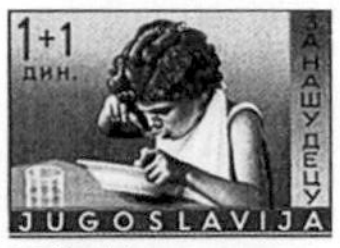
94 Meal-time

1939. Child Welfare.

396	**94**	1d.+1d. green	1·30	1·30
397	-	1d.50+1d.50 red & brown	5·25	4·50
398	-	2d.+2d. mauve & brown	3·75	4·00
399	-	4d.+4d. light blue & blue	3·75	4·25

DESIGNS—HORIZ: 2d. Young carpenter. VERT: 1d.50, Children playing on sands; 4d. Children whispering.

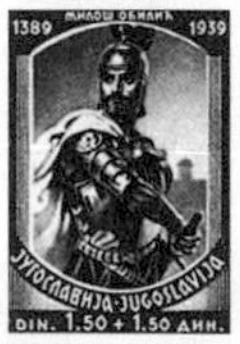
95 Milos Obilic

1939. 550th Anniv of Battle of Kosovo.

400		1d.+1d. green and olive	4·25	2·20
401	**95**	1d.50+1d.50 red and carmine	4·25	2·20

DESIGN: 1d. Prince Lazar.

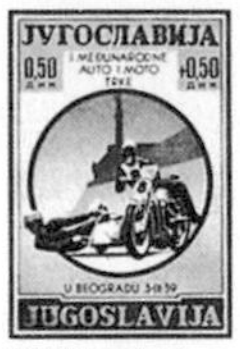
96 Motor Cycle and Sidecar

1939. First International Motor Races, Belgrade.

402	**96**	50p.+50p. orange and brown	1·30	1·10
403	-	1d.+1d. green and black	2·50	2·20
404	-	1d.50+1d.50 carmine and red	3·75	3·25
405	-	2d.+2d. blue and indigo	6·25	5·50

DESIGNS—HORIZ: 1, 2d. Racing cars. VERT: 1d.50, Motor cycle.

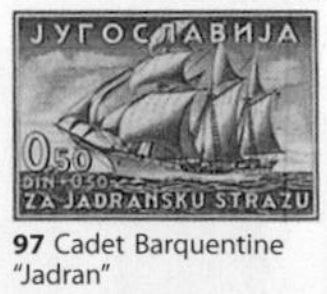
97 Cadet Barquentine "Jadran"

1939. King Petar's Birthday and Adriatic Guard Fund.

406	**97**	50p.+50p. red	1·00	1·10
407	-	1d.+50p. green	2·10	2·20
408	-	1d.50+1d. red	3·25	3·25
409	-	2d.+1d.50 blue	5·25	5·50

DESIGNS: 1d. Liner "King Alexander"; 1d.50, Freighter "Triglav"; 2d. Destroyer "Dubrovnik".

98 Unknown Warrior's
Tomb, Avala

1939. Fifth Death Anniv of King Alexander. War Invalids' Fund.

410	98	1d.+50p. green	2·50	2·20
411	98	1d.50+1d. red	2·50	2·20
412	98	2d.+1d.50 purple	3·25	3·25
413	98	3d.+2d. blue	6·25	5·50

99 King Petar II

1939

414	99	25p. black	30	10
415	99	50p. orange	30	10
416	99	1d. green	30	10
417	99	1d.50 red	30	10
418	99	2d. pink	30	10
419	99	3d. brown	50	10
420	99	4d. blue	50	10
420a	99	5d. blue	50	20
420b	99	5d.50 violet	1·30	20
421	99	6d. blue	2·50	20
422	99	8d. brown	3·25	20
423	99	12d. violet	4·75	20
424	99	16d. purple	6·25	35
425	99	20d. blue	6·25	35
426	99	30d. pink	14·50	80

100 Postman
delivering Letters

1940. Belgrade Postal Employees' Fund. Inscr "ZA DOM P.T.T. ZVAN. I SLUZ".

427	100	50p.+50p. orange & brn	1·10	1·70
428	-	1d.+1d. green and black	1·40	1·70
429	-	1d.50+1d.50 red & brown	2·50	3·25
430	-	2d.+2d. mauve & purple	3·25	3·25
431	-	4d.+4d. blue and grey	10·50	9·00

DESIGNS: 1d. Postman collecting letters; 4d. Telegraph linesman. HORIZ: 1d.50, Mail-van; 2d. Loading mail train.

101 Arrival of Thorval

1940. Zagreb Postal Employees' Fund. Inscr "ZA DOM P.T.T. CINOV U ZAGREBU".

432	101	50p.+50p. orange & brown	75	80
433	-	1d.+1d. green	75	80
434	-	1d.50+1d.50 red	1·30	80
435	-	2d.+2d. red	3·25	3·25
436	-	4d.+2d. blue	3·75	4·00

DESIGNS—25½×35½ mm: 1d. King Tomislav enthroned; 1d.50, Death of Matija Gubec. 37×27 mm: 2d. Radic Brothers. 34×25 mm: 4d. Divisional map of Yugoslavia.

102 Winter Games

1940. Child Welfare. Inscr "ZA NASU DECU".

437	102	50p.+50p. orange and red	50	55
438	-	1d.+1d. green and olive (20×26 mm)	50	55
439	102	1d.50+1d.50 red and brown	1·60	1·10
440	-	2d.+2d. mauve and violet (20×26 mm)	2·75	2·20

DESIGN—VERT: 1, 2d. Children at seaside (Summer Games).

103 Arms of
Yugoslavia,
Greece, Rumania
and Turkey

1940. Balkan Entente. Inscr "JUGOSLAVIJA" alternately at top in Cyrillic (A) or Roman (B) thoughout the sheet.

A.

441A	103	3d. blue	2·10	65
442A	103	4d. blue	2·10	65

B.

441B		3d. blue	2·10	65
442B		4d. blue	2·10	65

104 Zagreb Cathedral
and Junkers Ju 86

1940. Air.

443	104	40d. green	6·75	2·75
444	-	50d. blue	9·00	5·00

DESIGN: 50d. Suspension Bridge at Belgrade and Fokker F.VIIa/3m.

105 Obod, Scene of early
Press, 1493

1940. 500th Anniv of Invention of Printing Press by Johannes Gutenberg.

445	105	5d.50 deep green and green	4·75	4·50

1940. Anti-T.B. Fund. Nos. 364/7 surch.

446	80	50p.+50p. on 5d. violet	30	35
447	-	1d.+1d. on 10d. red	50	55
448	-	1d.50+1d.50 on 20d. green	2·10	1·90
449	-	2d.+2d. on 30d. blue	2·30	2·50

107 St. Peter's Cemetery,
Ljubljana

1941. Ljubljana War Veterans' Fund.

450	107	50p.+50p. green	50	55
451	-	1d.+1d. red	50	55
452	-	1d.50+1d.50 green	1·60	1·70
453	-	2d.+2d. lilac and blue	2·50	2·75

DESIGNS—HORIZ: 2d. War Memorial, Brezje. VERT: 1d. National costumes; 1d.50, Memorial Chapel, Kajmakcalan.

109 Kamenita
Gate, Zagreb

1941. Philatelic Exhibitions. (a) Second Croatian Philatelic Exhibition, Zagreb.

454	109	1d.50+1d.50 brown	1·60	1·70
455	-	4d.+3d. black	1·60	1·70

(b) First Philatelic Exhibition, Slav Brod.

456	109	1d.50+1d.50 black	23·00	28·00
457	-	4d.+3d. brown	23·00	28·00

DESIGN: 4d. (2) Old Cathedral, Zagreb.

NOTE. From 1941 until 1945 Yugoslavia ceased to exist as a stamp-issuing entity, except for the following series, Nos 468/81, which were issued by the exiled government for the use of the Yugoslav Merchant Navy working with the Allies.

110 King Petar II

1943. Second Anniv of Overthrow of Regency and King Petar's Assumption of Power.

468	110	2d. blue	40	1·10
469	110	3d. grey	40	1·10
470	110	5d. red	40	1·70
471	110	10d. black	85	2·20

1943. Red Cross Fund. Surch **CRVENI KRST+ 12.50.**

472		2d.+12d.50 blue	2·10	5·50
473		3d.+12d.50 grey	2·10	5·50
474		5d.+12d.50 red	2·10	5·50
475		10d.+12d.50 black	2·10	5·50

112 V. Vodnik
(poet)

1943. 25th Anniv of Formation of Yugoslavia.

476	112	1d. black and red	50	
477	-	2d. black and green	85	
478	-	3d. blue and blue	85	
479	-	4d. brown and violet	1·60	
480	-	5d. brown and purple	1·60	
481	-	10d. deep brown and brown	5·25	
MS481a	127×185 mm. Nos. 476/81		75·00	

DESIGNS: 2d. Petar Njegos (poet); 3d. Ljudevit Gaj (writer); 4d. Vuk Karadzic (poet); 5d. Bishop Josip Strosmajer (politician); 10d. Djordje Petrovic (Karageorge).

C. DEMOCRATIC FEDERATION OF YUGOSLAVIA
I. REGIONAL ISSUES
Bosnia and Herzegovina

1945. Mostar Issue. Stamps of Croatia surch **Demokratska Federativna Jugoslavija** and value. (a) Pictorial Stamps of 1941–43.

R1		10k. on 25b. red	1·00	1·00
R2		10k. on 50b. green	1·00	1·00
R3		10k. on 2k. red	1·00	1·00
R4		10k. on 3k.50 brown	1·00	1·00
R5		40k. on 1k. green	1·00	1·00
R6		50k. on 4k. blue	5·25	5·25
R7		50k. on 5k. blue	26·00	26·00
R8		50k. on 6k. green	5·25	5·25
R9		50k. on 7k. red	£100	£100
R10		50k. on 8k. brown	£130	£130
R11		50k. on 10k. violet	1·00	1·00

(b) Famous Croats issue of 1943.

R12		20k. on 1k. blue	1·00	1·00
R13		30k. on 12k.50 purple	1·00	1·00

(c) Boskovic issue of 1943.

R14	28	30k. on 3k.50 blue	1·00	1·00
R15	28	30k. on 12k.50 purple	2·50	2·50

(d) War Victims Charity Tax stamps of 1944.

R16	34	20k. on 1k. green	1·00	1·00
R17	35	20k. on 2k. red	1·00	1·00
R18	35	20k. on 5k. green	1·00	1·00
R19	35	20k. on 10k. blue	1·00	1·00
R20	35	20k. on 20k. brown	1·00	1·00

Croatia

DEMOKRATSKA FEDERATIVNA
 20 KUNA
JUGOSLAVIJA

(R2)

1945. Split issue. Stamps of Croatia 1941–43 surch as Type **R2**.

R21		10k. on 25b. red	50	50
R22		10k. on 50b. green	50	50
R23		10k. on 75b. green	50	50
R24		10k. on 1k. green	50	50
R25		20k. on 2k. red	50	50
R26		20k. on 3k. brown	50	50
R27		20k. on 3k.50 brown	50	50
R28		20k. on 4k. blue	50	50
R29		20k. on 5k. blue	50	50
R30		20k. on 6k. green	16·00	16·00
R31		30k. on 7k. red	50	50
R32		30k. on 8k. brown	19·00	19·00
R33		30k. on 10k. violet	50	50
R34		30k. on 12k.50 black	50	50
R35		40k. on 20k. brown	50	50
R36		40k. on 30k. brown	50	50
R37		50k. on 50k. green	50	50

1945. Zagreb issue. Stamps of Croatia, 1941–43, surch **DEMOKRATISKA FEDERATIVNA JUGOSLAVIJA**, value and star.

R38		20k. on 5k. blue	30	30
R39		40k. on 1k. green	30	30
R40		60k. on 3k.50 brown	30	30
R41		80k. on 2k. red	30	30
R42		160k. on 50b. brown	30	30

R43		200k. on 12k.50 black	30	30
R44		400k. on 25b. red	30	30

Montenegro

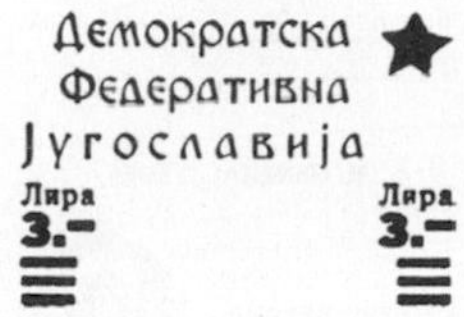

(R4)

1945. Cetinje issue. Stamps of Italian Occupation surch with Type **R4**. (a) National Poem Issue of 1943.

R50		1l. on 10c. green	2·10	2·10
R51		2l. on 25c. green	1·00	1·00
R52		3l. on 50c. mauve	1·00	1·00
R53		5l. on 1l.25 blue	1·00	1·00
R54		10l. on 15c. brown	2·10	2·10
R55		15l. on 20c. orange	2·10	2·10
R56		20l. on 2l. green	2·10	2·10

(b) Air stamps of 1943, for use as ordinary postage stamps.

R57		3l. on 50c. brown	5·25	5·25
R58		6l. on 1l. blue	5·25	5·25
R59		10l. on 2l. red	5·25	5·25
R60		20l. on 5l. green	5·25	5·25

Serbia

1944. Senta issue. Various stamps of Hungary optd with a large star, **8.X.1944** and **"Yugoslavia"** in Cyrillic characters.

R63		1f. grey	8·25	8·25
R64		2f. red	8·25	8·25
R65		3f. blue	8·25	8·25
R66		4f. brown	8·25	8·25
R67		5f. red	8·25	8·25
R68		8f. green	8·25	8·25
R69		10f. brown	£190	£190
R70		24f. brown	£325	£325
R71		24f. purple	10·50	10·50
R72		30f. red	£190	£190

Slovenia

(R5)

1945. Ljubljana issue. Pictorial stamps of German Occupation, 1945, optd as Type **R5**.

R74		5c. brown	30	30
R75		10c. orange	30	30
R76		20c. brown	30	30
R77		25c. green	30	30
R78		50c. violet	30	30
R79		75c. red	30	30
R80		1l. green	30	30
R81		1l.25 blue	30	30
R82		1l.50 green	30	30
R83		2l. blue	30	30
R84		2l.50 brown	30	30
R85		3l. mauve	50	50
R86		5l. brown	75	75
R87		10l. green	50	50
R88		20l. blue	4·25	4·25
R89		30l. red	26·00	26·00

1945. Maribor issue. Hitler stamps of Germany, 1941–44, optd **SLOVENIJA 9.5. 1945 JUGOSLAVIJA** and star.

R90	173	1pf. grey	5·25	5·25
R91	173	3pf. brown	50	50
R92	173	4pf. grey	4·25	4·25
R93	173	5pf. green	3·25	3·25
R94	173	6pf. violet	50	50
R95	173	8pf. red	75	75
R96	173	10pf. brown (No. 775)	3·25	3·25
R97	173	12pf. red (No. 776)	35	35
R98	173	15pf. brown	6·25	6·25
R99	173	20pf. blue	4·00	4·00
R100	173	24pf. brown	4·25	4·25
R101	173	25pf. blue	10·50	10·50
R102	173	30pf. green	1·00	1·00
R103	173	40pf. mauve	1·00	1·00
R104	225	42pf. green	1·00	1·00
R105	173	50pf. green	3·75	3·75
R106	173	60pf. brown	1·00	1·00
R107	173	80pf. blue	2·50	2·50

1945. Murska Sobota issue. Various stamps of Hungary optd as Nos. R90/107.

R108		1f. grey	6·25	6·25
R109		4f. brown	50	50
R110		5f. red	6·25	6·25
R111		10f. brown	50	50
R112		18f. black	50	50
R113		20f. brown	50	50

R114		30f. red	50	50
R115		30f. red	50	50
R116		50f. blue	10·50	10·50
R117		70f. brown	10·50	10·50
R118		80f. brown	50·00	50·00
R119		1p. green	7·75	7·75

II. GENERAL ISSUES

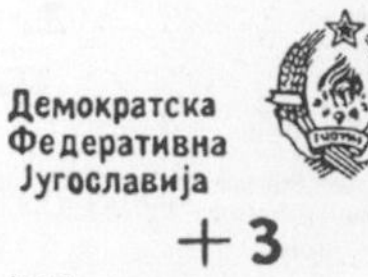
Демократска
Федеративна
Југославија
+3
(113)

1944. Monasteries. Stamps of German Occupation of Serbia, 1942, surch as T **113**.

482		3d.+2d. pink (No. 64)	20	20
485		4d.+21d. blue (No. 65)	20	20
483		7d.+3d. green (No. 66)	20	20

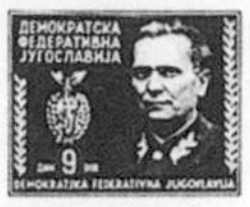
114 Marshal Tito

1945

491	**114**	25p. green	30	10
492	**114**	50p. green	30	10
493	**114**	1d. red	3·25	40
494	**114**	2d. red	30	10
495	**114**	4d. blue	40	10
487	**114**	5d. green	10	10
496	**114**	6d. violet	50	10
497	**114**	9d. brown	1·00	20
488	**114**	10d. red	10	10
498	**114**	20d. yellow	4·75	2·10
489	**114**	25d. violet	20	15
490	**114**	30d. blue	25	15

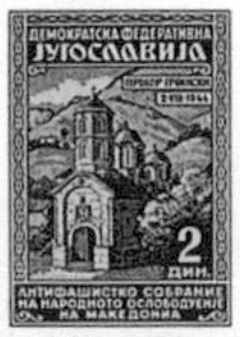
115 Chapel at Prohor Pcinjski

1945. First Anniv of Anti-Fascist Chamber of Deputies, Macedonia.

499	**115**	2d. red	5·25	2·50

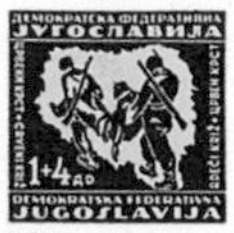
116 Partisans

1945. Red Cross Fund.

500	**116**	1d.+4d. blue	1·30	1·00
501	-	2d.+6d. red	1·30	1·00

DESIGN—VERT: 2d.+6d. Child's head.

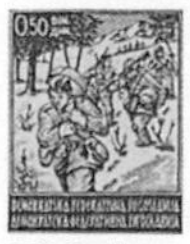
119 Partisans

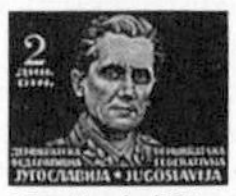
120 Marshal Tito

1945. Partisans.

502	**119**	50p. brown	30	10
503	**119**	1d. green	30	10
504	-	1d.50 brown	30	10
505	**120**	2d. red	30	10
506	-	2d.50 red	85	10
507	-	3d. brown	4·75	10
508	-	3d. red	1·30	10
509	**120**	4d. blue	85	10
510	-	5d. green	2·75	10
511	-	5d. blue	3·75	10
512	-	6d. black	1·30	10
513	-	8d. orange	2·10	10
514	-	9d. purple	1·00	10
515	-	12d. blue	2·30	10
516	**119**	16d. blue	2·30	10
517	-	20d. red	4·25	50

DESIGNS—As Type **119**: 1d.50, 12, 20d. Riflemen. VERT: 3, 5d. Town of Jajce inscr "29-XI-1943". HORIZ: 2d.50, 6, 8, 9d. Girl with flag.

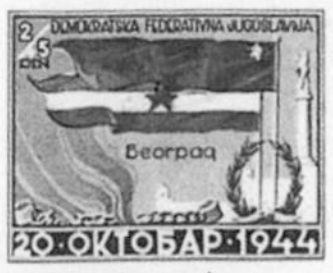
Београд
20-ОКТОБАР-1944
122 Russian and Yugoslav Flags

1945. First Anniv of Liberation of Belgrade.

518	**122**	2d.+5d. multicoloured	2·10	2·10

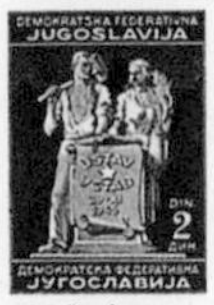
124 "Industry and Agriculture"

1945. Meeting of the Constituent Assembly. Inscr in Cyrillic at top and Roman characters at foot (A) or vice-versa (B).

519	**124**	2d. red (A)	4·25	4·25
519b	**124**	2d. red (B)	4·25	4·25
520	**124**	4d. blue (A)	4·25	4·25
520b	**124**	4d. blue (B)	4·25	4·25
521	**124**	6d. green (A)	4·25	4·25
521b	**124**	6d. green (B)	4·25	4·25
522	**124**	9d. red (A)	4·25	4·25
522b	**124**	9d. red (B)	4·25	4·25
523	**124**	16d. blue (A)	4·25	4·25
523b	**124**	16d. blue (B)	4·25	4·25
524	**124**	20d. brown (A)	4·25	4·25
524b	**124**	20d. brown (B)	4·25	4·25
MS524c 150×110 mm. Nos. 522 and 524 (A)			31·00	31·00
MS524d Nos. 522b and 524b (B)			31·00	31·00

D. FEDERAL PEOPLE'S REPUBLIC

1946. Type of 1945 (Girl with flag), surch.

525		2d.50 on 6d. red	1·00	30
526		8d. on 9d. orange	1·30	30

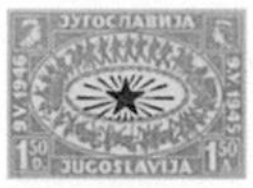
126

1946. First Anniv of Victory over Fascism. Star in red.

527	**126**	1d.50 yellow	1·00	75
528	**126**	2d.50 red	2·10	1·00
529	**126**	5d. blue	7·25	2·10

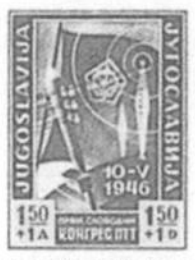
127 Symbolic of Communications

1946. Postal Congress.

530	**127**	1d.50+1d. green	5·25	4·25
531	**127**	2d.50+1d.50 red	5·25	4·25
532	**127**	5d.+2d. blue	5·25	4·25
533	**127**	8d.+3d.50 brown	5·25	4·25

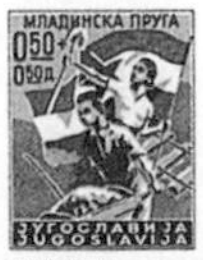
128 Railway Construction

1946. Volunteer Workers' Railway Reconstruction Fund.

534	**128**	50p.+50p. brown, blue and red	3·75	2·10
535	**128**	1d.50+1d. green, blue and red	3·75	2·10
536	**128**	2d.50+2d. lilac, blue and red	3·75	2·10
537	**128**	5d.+3d. grey, blue & red	3·75	2·10

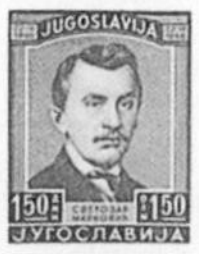
129 Svetozar Markovic

1946. Birth Centenary of S. Markovic (socialist writer).

538	**129**	1d.50 green	1·70	50
539	**129**	2d.50 purple	1·70	75

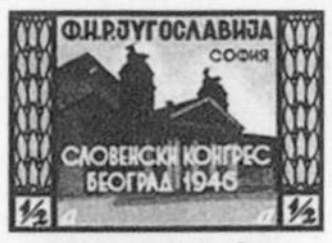
ФНРЈУГОСЛАВИЈА
СЛОВЕНСКИ КОНГРЕС
БЕОГРАД 1946
130 Theatre in Sofia

1946. Slav Congress.

540	**130**	½d. brown and buff	3·25	3·00
541	-	1d. green and light green	3·25	3·00
542	-	1½d. red and pink	3·25	3·00
543	-	2½d. orange and buff	3·25	3·00
544	-	5d. blue and light blue	3·25	3·00

DESIGNS—HORIZ: 1d. Charles Bridge and Hradcany, Prague. VERT: 1½d. Sigismund Monument, Warsaw; 2½d. Victory Monument, Belgrade; 5d. Kremlin Tower, Moscow.

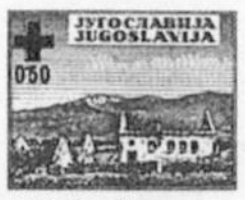
131 Roofless Houses

1947. Obligatory Tax. Red Cross.

545	**131**	50p. brown	35	10

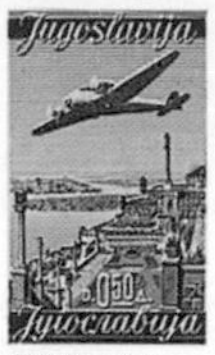
Jugoslavija
Југославија
132 Ilyushin Il-4 DB-3 Bomber over Kalimegdan Terrace, Belgrade

1947. Air. Inscr in Cyrillic at top and Roman characters at foot (A) or vice versa (B).

546	**132**	50p. green and brown (A)	20	20
546b	**132**	50p. green and brown (B)	20	20
547	-	1d. green and red (A)	30	20
547b	-	1d. green and red (B)	30	20
548	**132**	2d. blue and black (A)	45	20
548b	**132**	2d. blue and black (B)	45	20
549	-	5d. drab and green (A)	55	30
549b	-	5d. drab and green (B)	55	30
550	-	10d. brown and sepia (A)	65	40
550b	-	10d. brown and sepia (B)	65	40
551	**132**	20d. green and blue (A)	1·30	1·00
551b	**132**	20d. green and blue (B)	1·30	1·00

DESIGN: 1, 5, 20d. Ilyushin Il-4 DB-3 over Dubrovnik.

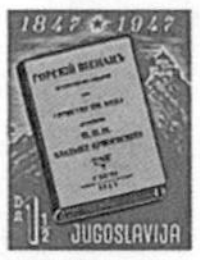
133 "Wreath of Mountains"

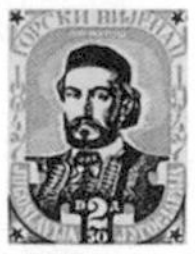
134 Petar Njegos (author)

1947. Centenary of Publication of "Wreath of Mountains".

552	**133**	1½d. black and green	75	60
553	**134**	2d.50 red and buff	75	60
554	**133**	5d. black and blue	75	60

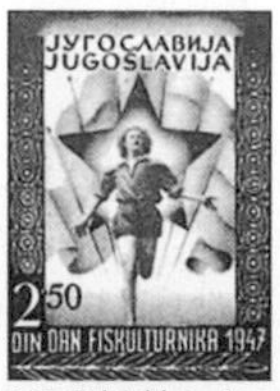
ЈУГОСЛАВИЈА
JUGOSLAVIJA
DIN DAN FISKULTURNIKA 1947
135 Girl Athlete, Star and Flags

1947. Federal Sports Meeting.

555	-	1d.50 brown	1·50	70
556	**135**	2d.50 red	1·50	70
557	-	4d. blue	1·60	75

DESIGNS—VERT: 1d.50, Physical training groups. HORIZ: 4d. Parade of athletes.

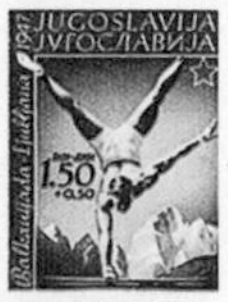
JUGOSLAVIJA
ЈУГОСЛАВИЈА
137 Gymnast

1947. Balkan Games.

558	**137**	1d.50+0.50 green	3·50	3·25
559	**137**	2d.50+0.50 red	3·50	3·25
560	**137**	4d.+0.50 blue	3·50	3·25

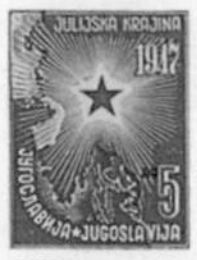
138 Star and Map of Julian Province

1947. Annexation of Julian Province to Yugoslavia.

561	**138**	2d.50 red and blue	65	60
562	**138**	5d. brown and green	65	60

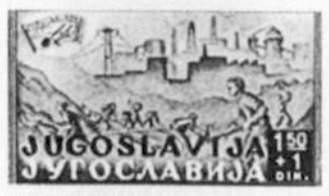
139 Railway Construction

1947. Juvenile Labour Organizations' Relief Fund.

563	**139**	1d.+0.50 orange	95	85
564	**139**	1d.50+1d. green	95	85
565	**139**	2d.50+1d.50 red	95	85
566	**139**	5d.+2d. blue	95	85

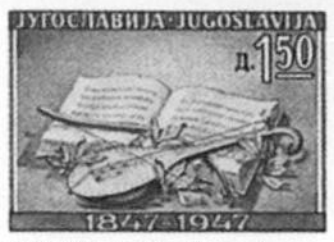
140 Music Book and Fiddle

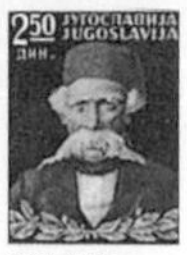
141 Vuk Karadzic (poet)

1947. Centenary of Serbian Literature.

567	**140**	1d.50 green	65	60
568	**141**	2d.50 red	65	60
569	**140**	5d. blue	65	60

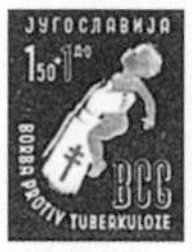
142 "B.C.G. Vaccine defeating Tuberculosis"

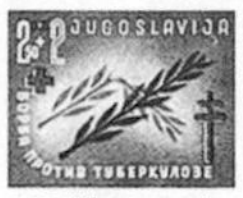
143 "Illness and Recovery"

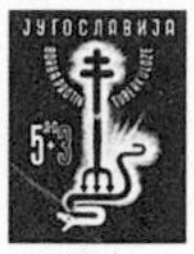
144 "Fight against Tuberculosis"

1948. Anti-T.B. Fund.

570	**142**	1d.50+1d. green and red	75	70
571	**143**	2d.50+2d. green and red	75	70
572	**144**	5d.+3d. blue and red	75	70

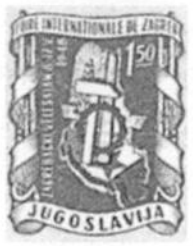
145 Map of Yugoslavia and Symbols of Industry and Agriculture

1948. International Fair, Zagreb.

573	**145**	1d.50 green, blue and red	2·00	1·40
574	**145**	2d.50 purple, blue and red	2·00	1·40
575	**145**	5d. indigo, blue and red	2·00	1·40

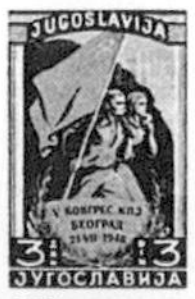
146 Flag-bearers

1948. Fifth Yugoslav Communist Party Congress, Belgrade.

576	**146**	2d. green and deep green	65	35
577b	**146**	3d. purple and red	1·00	60
578a	**146**	10d. ultramarine and blue	1·00	60

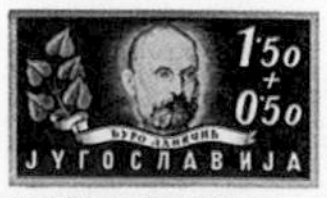
ЈУГОСЛАВИЈА
147 Djura Danicic

1948. 80th Anniv of Yugoslav Academy.

579	**147**	1d.50+0.50 green	75	70
580	-	2d.50+1d. red	75	70
581	-	4d.+2d. blue	75	70

PORTRAITS: 2d.50, Franjo Racki; 4d. Bishop Josip Strosmajer (inscr "Strossmayer").

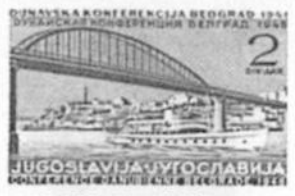

148 "Krajina" (former royal yacht) passing under Danube Railway Bridge

1948. Danube Conference.

582	**148**	2d. green	3·75	3·50
583	**148**	3d. red	3·75	3·50
584	**148**	5d. blue	3·75	3·50
585	**148**	10d. brown	3·75	3·50

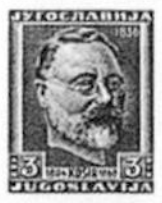

149 Lovrenz Kosir

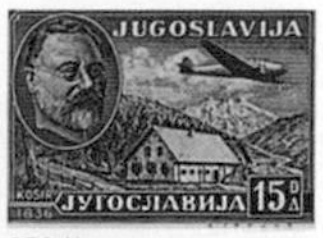

150 Kosir and his Birthplace

1948. 80th Death Anniv of Kosir ("idealogical creator of first postage stamp").

586	**149**	3d. purple (postage)	65	35
587	**149**	5d. blue	65	35
588	**149**	10d. orange	65	35
589	**149**	12d. green	65	35
590	**150**	15d. mauve (air)	1·30	1·10

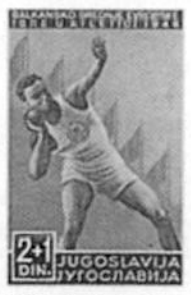

151 Putting the Shot

1948. Projected Balkan Games.

591	**151**	2d.+1d. green	75	70
592	-	3d.+1d. red	75	70
593	-	5d.+2d. blue	1·80	1·20

DESIGNS: 3d. Girl hurdler; 5d. Pole vaulting.

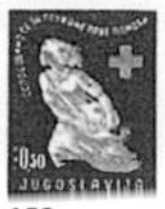

152

1948. Obligatory Tax. Red Cross.

594	**152**	50p. red and blue	35	20

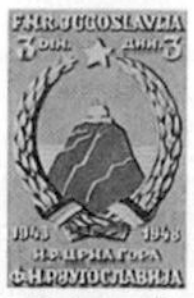

153 Arms of Montenegro

1948. Fifth Anniv of Republic.

595	-	3d. blue (Serbia)	70	65
596	-	3d. red (Croatia)	70	65
597	-	3d. orange (Slovenia)	70	65
598	-	3d. green (Bosnia and Herzegovina)	70	65
599	-	3d. mauve (Macedonia)	70	65
600	**153**	3d. black	70	65
601	-	10d. red (Yugoslavia)	1·70	1·60

No. 601 is larger, 24½×34½ mm.

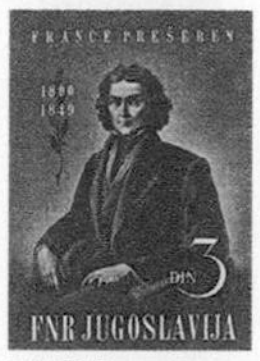

154 F. Preseren

1949. Death Centenary of Franc Preseren (author).

602	**154**	3d. blue	55	20
603	**154**	5d. orange	55	30
604	**154**	10d. sepia	2·75	1·00

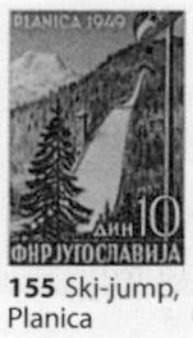

155 Ski-jump, Planica

1949. Ski Jumping Competition, Planica.

605	**155**	3d. red	1·10	85
606	-	12d. blue (Ski jumper)	2·20	95

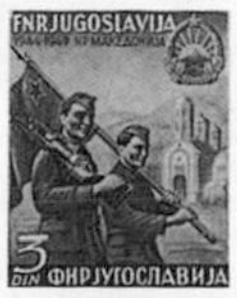

156 Soldiers

1949. Fifth Anniv of Liberation of Macedonia. (a) Postage.

607	**156**	3d. red	90	85
608	-	5d. blue	1·10	1·00
608a	-	12d. brown	3·50	3·25

DESIGNS: 5d. Industrial and agricultural workers; 12d. Arms and flags of Yugoslavia and Macedonia.

(b) Air. Optd with Lisunov Li-2 airplane and **AVIONSKA POSTA**.

609	**156**	3d. red	10·00	9·25
610	-	5d. blue (No. 608)	10·00	9·25
610a	-	12d. brown (No. 608a)	10·00	9·25

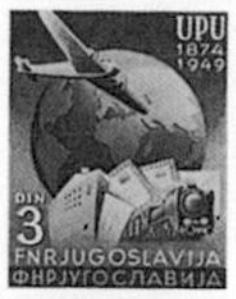

158 Globe, Letters and Forms of Transport

1949. 75th Anniv of U.P.U.

611	**158**	3d. red	4·00	3·75
612	-	5d. blue	80	75
613	**158**	12d. brown	80	75

DESIGN—HORIZ: 5d. Airplane, train and mail coach.

1949. Surch with bold figures and bars.

614	**O130**	3d. on 8d. brown	1·30	50
615	**O130**	3d. on 12d. violet	1·30	50

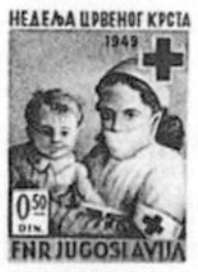

160 Nurse and Child

1949. Obligatory Tax. Red Cross.

616	**160**	50p. brown and red	35	20

ФНР ЈУГОСЛАВИЈА

D3

FNR JUGOSLAVIJA (161)

F N R D10 JUGOSLAVIJA (162)

1949. Surch with T **161** or **162**.

617	3d. on 8d. yellow (No. 513)	1·10	20
618	10d. on 20d. red (No. 517)	1·20	20

ФНР

FNR JUGOSLAVIJA (163)

F N R (164)

F N R JUGOSLAVIJA (165)

1949. Optd with T **163** on 2d., **164** on 3d. and 5d., or **165** on others.

619	**119**	50p. olive	55	10
620	**119**	1d. green	55	10
621	**119**	1d. orange	1·10	20
622	**120**	2d. red	55	10
623	**120**	2d. green	1·10	20
624	-	3d. red (No. 508)	55	10
625	-	3d. pink	1·70	30
626	-	5d. blue (No. 511)	55	20
627	-	5d. blue	1·70	30
628	-	12d. violet (No. 515)	55	10
629	**119**	16d. blue	1·50	75
630	**119**	20d. red	1·10	30

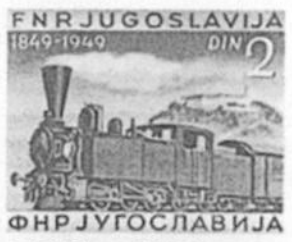

166 Class 151 Steam Locomotive, 1885

1949. Centenary of National Railways.

631	**166**	2d. green	2·75	2·50
632	-	3d. red	2·75	2·50
633	-	5d. blue	2·75	2·50
633a	-	10d. orange	50·00	31·00

As No. 633a but colour, sheet 49×70 mm. Perf and Imperf.

MS633b 10d. purple	£225	£140

DESIGNS: 3d. Class 389 steam locomotive, 1930; 5d. Diesel locomotive, 1937, France; 10d. Electric train on bridge over River Vintgar.

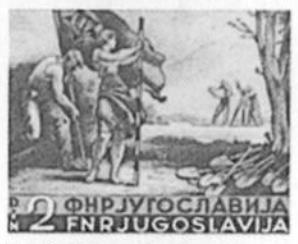

167 Surveying

1950. Completion of Belgrade–Zagreb Road.

634	**167**	2d. green	95	70
635	-	3d. purple	95	70
636	-	5d. blue	1·50	1·20

DESIGNS: 3d. Map, road and car; 5d.Youth, road and flag.

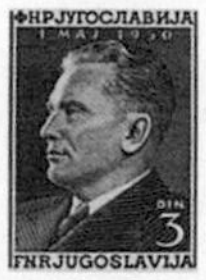

168 Marshal Tito

1950. May Day.

637	**168**	3d. red	2·75	1·00
638	**168**	5d. blue	2·75	1·00
639	**168**	10d. brown	36·00	26·00
640	**168**	12d. black	2·75	2·75

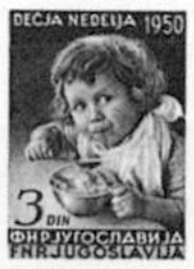

169 Child Eating

1950. Child Welfare.

641	**169**	3d. red	2·20	65

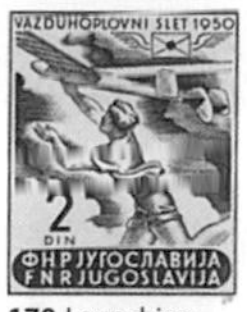

170 Launching Model Glider

1950. Third Aeronautical Meeting.

642	**170**	2d. green	4·50	4·25
643	-	3d. red	4·50	4·25
644	-	5d. violet	4·50	4·25
645	-	10d. brown	4·50	4·25
646	-	20d. blue	35·00	35·00

DESIGNS—VERT: 3d. Glider in flight; 5d. Parachutists landing; 10d. Woman pilot; 20d. Glider on water.

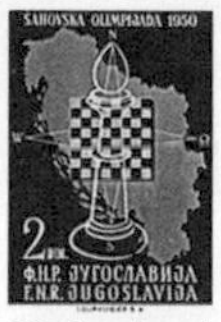

171 Chessboard and Bishop

1950. Ninth Chess Olympiad, Dubrovnik.

647	**171**	2d. brown	1·30	1·00
648	-	3d. bistre, brown and drab	1·30	1·00
649	-	5d. blue, yellow and green	2·75	1·00
650	-	10d. yellow, purple and blue	2·75	2·50
651	-	20d. yellow and blue	60·00	29·00

DESIGNS—VERT: 3d. Rook and flags; 5d. Globe and chessboard showing 1924 Capablanca v. Lasker game; 10d. Chequered globe, map and players; 20d. Knights and flags.

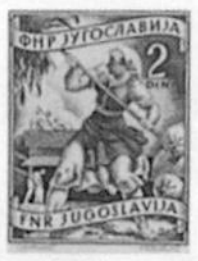

172 Girl Harvester

1950

652		50p. brown	20	10
653		1d. green	20	10
705	-	1d. grey	20	10
654	**172**	2d. orange	20	10
706	**172**	2d. red	55	10
655	-	3d. red	20	10
656	-	5d. blue	1·70	10
719	-	5d. orange	8·50	10
657	-	7d. grey	1·70	10
720	-	8d. blue	5·50	20
658	-	10d. brown	1·70	10
721	-	10d. green	11·00	10
659	-	12d. brown	5·50	10
723	-	15d. red	22·00	10
660	-	16d. blue	4·50	30
723a	-	17d. purple	5·50	20
661	-	20d. olive	4·50	40
710	-	20d. purple	5·50	10
711a	**172**	25d. bistre	22·00	10
662	-	30d. brown	11·00	75
712	-	30d. blue	2·75	10
713	-	35d. brown	4·00	20
662a	-	50d. violet	50·00	31·00
714	-	50d. green	2·75	10
715	-	75d. violet	5·50	20
716	-	100d. sepia	11·00	20

DESIGNS—VERT: 50, 100d. Metallurgy; 1d. Electrical supply engineer; 3, 35d. Man and woman with wheelbarrow; 5d. Fishing; 7, 8d. Mining; 10d. Apple-picking; 12, 75d. Lumbering; 14, 15, 16d. Picking sunflowers; 17, 20d. Woman and farm animals; 30d. Girl printer; 50d. Dockers unloading cargo.

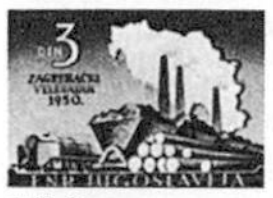

173 Steam Locomotive and Map

1950. Zagreb Exhibition.

663	**173**	3d. red	2·20	50

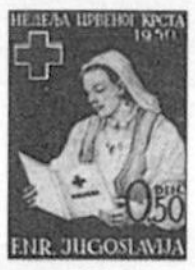

174 Girl in National Costume

1950. Obligatory Tax. Red Cross.

664	**174**	50p. green and red	35	20

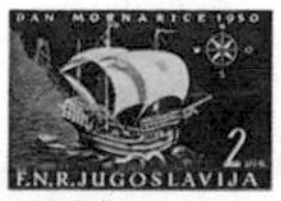

175 Galleon

1950. Navy Day.

665	**175**	2d. purple	55	20
666	-	3d. brown	55	20
667	-	5d. green	55	20
668	-	10d. blue	55	20
669	-	12d. grey	2·20	65
670	-	20d. red	25·00	3·75

DESIGNS: 3d. Partisan patrol boat; 5d. Freighter discharging cargo; 10d. "Zagreb" (freighter) and globe; 12d. Yachts; 20d. Sailor, gun and "Golesnica" (torpedo boat).

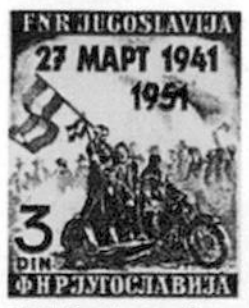

176 Patriots of 1941

1951. Tenth Anniv of Revolt against Pact with Axis.

671	**176**	3d. lake and red	10·00	4·75

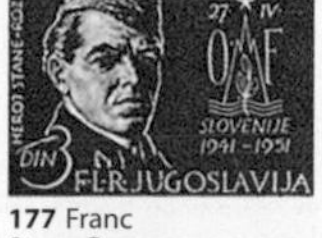

177 Franc Stane-Rozman

1951. Tenth Anniv of Partisan Rising in Slovenia.

672	**177**	3d. brown	65	50
673	-	5d. blue (Boy courier)	1·30	85

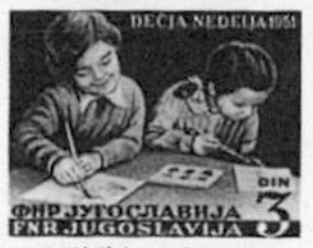

178 Children Painting

1951. International Children's Day.

674	**178**	3d. red	2·20	30

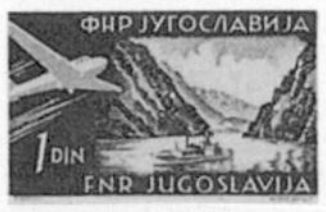

179 "Iron Gates", Danube

1951. Air.

675	**179**	1d. orange	20	10
676	-	2d. green	20	10
677	-	3d. red	55	10
677a	-	5d. brown	55	10
678	-	6d. blue	5·50	5·25
679	-	10d. brown	55	10
680	-	20d. grey	1·10	10
681	-	30d. red	2·75	10
682	-	50d. violet	4·00	10
683	-	100d. grey	80·00	11·50
683a	-	100d. green	2·20	20
683b	-	200d. red	3·25	30
683c	-	500d. blue	11·00	50

DESIGNS: (all show airplane)—As T **179**: 2, 5d. Plitvice Cascades; 3, 100d. (green) Gozd-Martuljak (mountain village); 6, 200d. Old Bridge, Mostar; 10d. Ohrid; 20d. Kotor Bay; 30d. Dubrovnik; 50d. Bled. 40×27 mm: 100d. (grey), 500d. Belgrade.

1951. Air. Zagreb Philatelic Exhibition. No. 678 in new colour optd **ZEFIZ 1951**.

684	6d. green	11·00	4·75

As No 683, but colour changed, sheet 70×70 mm. Imperf.

MS684a 100d. brown	£250	£225

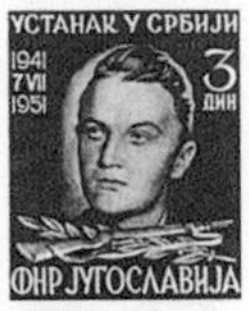

181 Zivorad Jovanovic

1951. Tenth Anniv of Serbian Insurrection.

685	**181**	3d. brown	80	65
686	-	5d. blue	1·50	1·20

DESIGN—HORIZ: 5d. Armed insurgents.

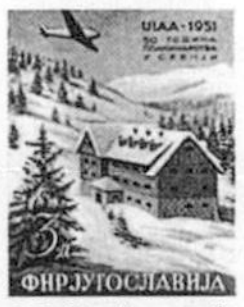

183 Mt. Kopaonik

1951. Air. International Mountaineering Assn Meeting, Bled. Inscr "UIAA-1951".

687	**183**	3d. mauve	3·25	3·00
688	-	5d. blue	3·25	3·00
689	-	20d. green	95·00	65·00

DESIGNS: 5d. Mt. Triglav, Slovenia; 20d. Mt. Kalnik, Croatia.

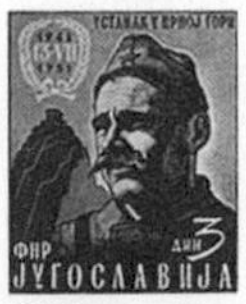

184 Sava Kovacevic

1951. Tenth Anniv of Montenegrin Insurrection.

690	**184**	3d. red	1·10	65
691	-	5d. blue	2·50	1·50

DESIGN—HORIZ: 5d. Partisan and mountains.

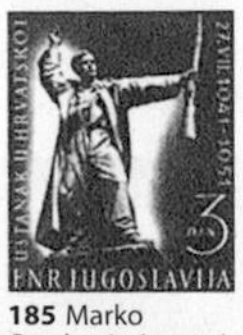

185 Marko Oreskovic (statue)

1951. Tenth Anniv of Croatian Insurrection.

692	**185**	3d. red	1·10	65
693	-	5d. green	1·70	1·20

DESIGN: 5d. "Transport of a Wounded Man" (sculpture, A. Augustincic).

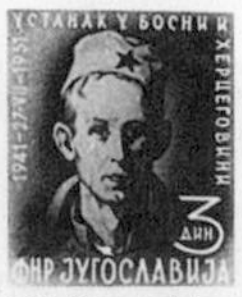

186 Simo Solaja

1951. Tenth Anniv of Insurrection of Bosnia and Herzegovina.

694	**186**	3d. red	1·10	65
695	-	5d. blue	1·70	1·20

DESIGN—VERT: 5d. Group of insurgents.

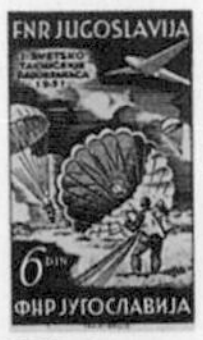

187 Parachutists Landing

1951. Air. First World Parachute Jumping Championship, Bled.

696	**187**	6d. lake	5·50	2·50

As No. 682 in new colour optd **I SVETSKO TAKMICENJE PADOBRANACA 1951**.

697	50d. blue	90·00	50·00

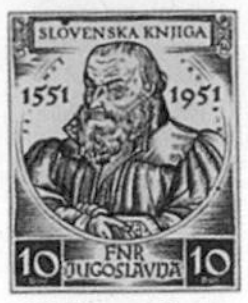

189 Primoz Trubar (writer)

1951. Cultural Anniversaries.

698	**189**	10d. black	5·75	5·25
699	-	12d. red	5·75	5·25
700	-	20d. lilac	18·00	17·00

DESIGNS: 12d. Marko Marulic (Croatian writer, 500th birth anniv (1950)); 20d. Tsar Stepan Dusan (600th anniv (1949) of "Tsar Dusan's Book of Laws").

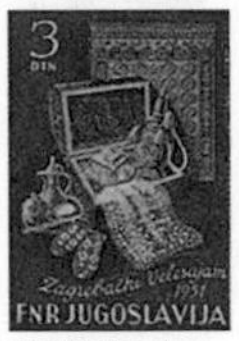

190 National Products

1951. Zagreb International Fair.

701	**190**	3p. yellow, red and blue	3·25	1·60

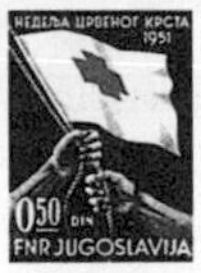

191 Hoisting the Flag

1951. Obligatory Tax. Red Cross.

702	**191**	50p. blue and red	35	20

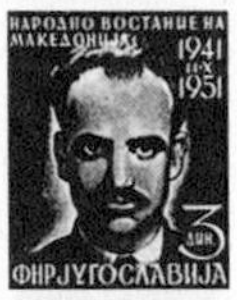

192 Mirce Acev

1951. Tenth Anniv of Macedonian Insurrection.

703	**192**	3d. mauve	1·10	85
704	-	5d. violet	2·20	1·60

DESIGN—HORIZ: 5d. War Victims' Monument, Skopje.

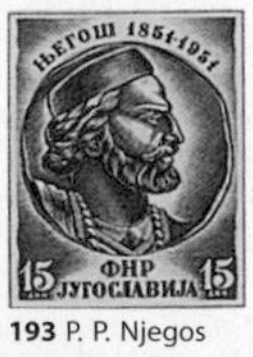

193 P. P. Njegos

1951. Death Centenary of Petar Njegos (poet).

724	**193**	15d. purple	4·50	1·00

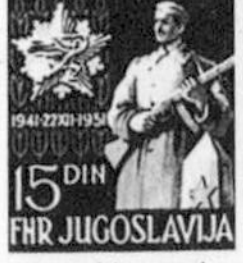

194 Soldier and Badge

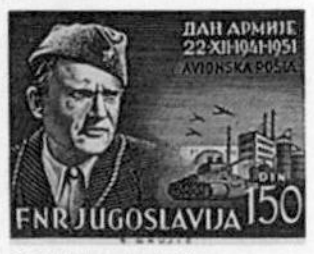

195 Marshal Tito

1951. Army Day.

725	**194**	15d. red (postage)	65	10
726	**195**	150d. blue (air)	13·50	10·50

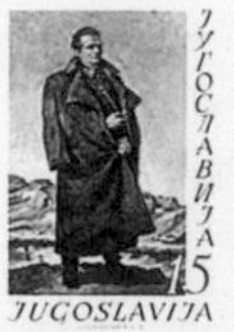

196 Marshal Tito

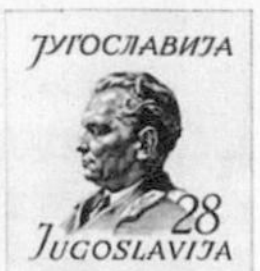

197 Marshal Tito

1952. Marshal Tito's 60th Birthday.

727	**196**	15d. brown	1·10	1·00
728	**197**	28d. lake	2·00	1·80
729	-	50d. green	55·00	40·00

DESIGN—As T **196**: 50d. Statue of Marshal Tito.

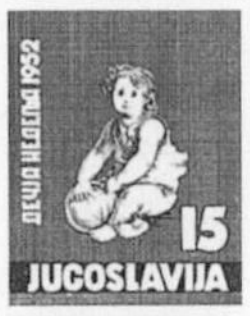

198

1952. Children's Week.

730	**198**	15d. red	8·50	3·75

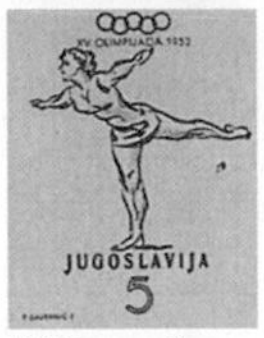

199 Gymnastics

1952. 15th Olympic Games, Helsinki. Inscr "XV OLIMPIJADA 1952".

731	**199**	5d. brown on buff	1·10	25
732	-	10d. brown on yellow	1·70	25
733	-	15d. blue on pink	1·70	50
734	-	28d. brown on flesh	4·00	1·00
735	-	50d. green on cream	6·75	5·75
736	-	100d. brown on mauve	65·00	36·00

DESIGNS: 10d. Running; 15d. Swimming; 28d. Boxing; 50d. Basketball; 100d. Football.

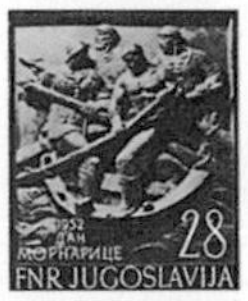

200 "Fishing Boat" (from relief by Krsinic)

1952. Navy Day. Views. Inscr "1952".

737		15d. purple	1·10	1·00
738	**200**	28d. brown	2·20	2·10
739	-	50d. black	25·00	19·00

DESIGNS: 15d. Split, Dalmatia; 50d. Sveti Stefan, Montenegro.

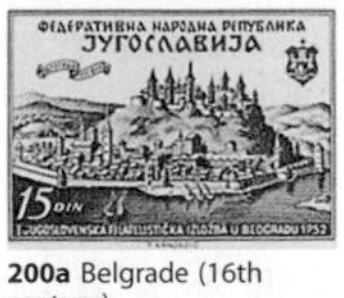

200a Belgrade (16th century)

1952. Philatelic Exhibition, Belgrade.

739a	**200a**	15d. purple	13·50	13·50

No. 739a was only sold at the Exhibition at 35d. (20d. entrance fee).

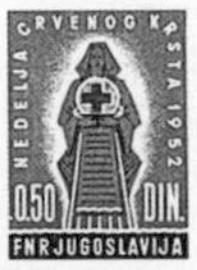

201

1952. Obligatory Tax. Red Cross.

740	**201**	50p. red, grey and black	35	20

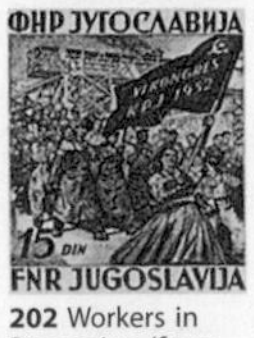

202 Workers in Procession (from fresco by Slavko Pengov)

1952. Sixth Yugoslavia Communist Party Congress.

741	**202**	15d. brown	1·70	1·60
742	**202**	15d. turquoise	1·70	1·60
743	**202**	15d. brown	1·70	1·60
744	**202**	15d. blue	1·70	1·60

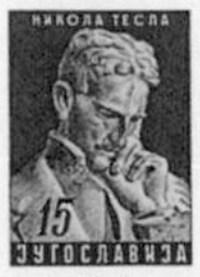

203 Nikola Tesla

1953. Tenth Death Anniv of Tesla (inventor).

745	**203**	15d. lake	1·10	20
746	**203**	30d. blue	4·50	85

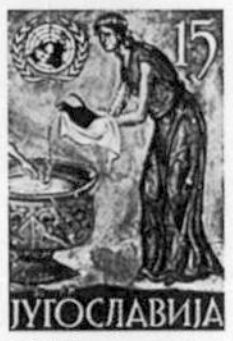

204 Fresco, Sopocani Monastery

1953. United Nations Commemoration.

747	**204**	15d. green	1·10	85
748	-	30d. blue	2·20	85
749	-	50d. lake	25·00	5·75

DESIGNS—VERT: 30d. Fresco, St. Panteleimon Church, Nerezim, Skopje; 50d. Fresco, St. Dimitri Church, Pec.

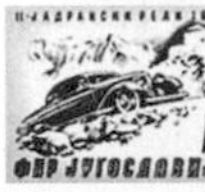

205

1953. Adriatic Car and Motor Cycle Rally.

750	**205**	15d. mauve and orange	55	30
751	-	30d. deep blue and blue	90	30
752	-	50d. brown and yellow	1·70	50
753	-	70d. green and emerald	43·00	6·25

DESIGNS—HORIZ: 30d. Motor cyclist and coastline; 50d. Racing car and flags; 70d. Saloon car descending mountain roadway.

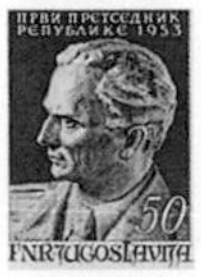

206 Marshal Tito

1953. Marshal Tito Commemoration.

754	**206**	50d. violet	17·00	10·50

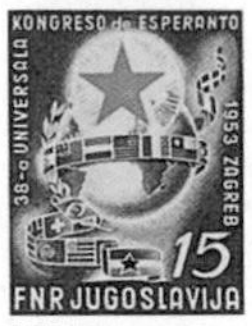

207

1953. 38th Esperanto Congress, Zagreb.

755	**207**	15d. green & black (postage)	4·00	3·25
756	**207**	300d. green and blue (air)	£250	£225

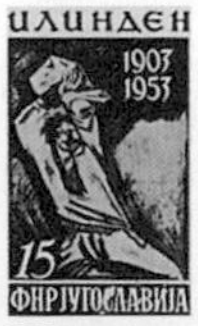

208 "Insurrection" (Borko Lazevski)

1953. 50th Anniv of Macedonian Insurrection.

757	**208**	15d. purple	90	85
758	-	30d. green	4·75	4·25

DESIGN: 30d. Nikola Karev (revolutionary).

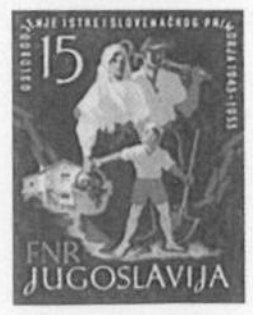

209

1953. Tenth Anniv of Liberation of Istria and Slovene Coast.

759	**209**	15d. green	£225	75·00

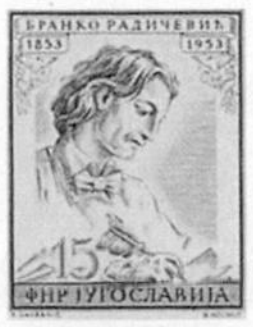

210 B. Radicevic

1953. Death Centenary of Branko Radicevic (poet).

760	**210**	15d. purple	6·75	2·50

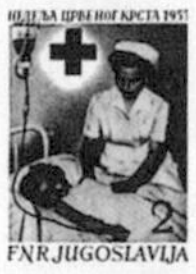

211 Blood-transfusion

1953. Obligatory Tax. Red Cross.

761	**211**	2d. red and purple	55	20

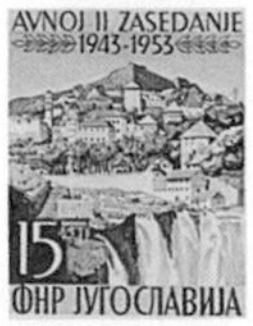

212 Jajce

1953. Tenth Anniv of First Republican Legislative Assembly.

762	**212**	15d. green	1·20	1·00
763	-	30d. red	1·70	1·60
764	-	50d. sepia	11·50	10·50

DESIGNS: 30d. Assembly Building; 50d. Marshal Tito addressing assembly.

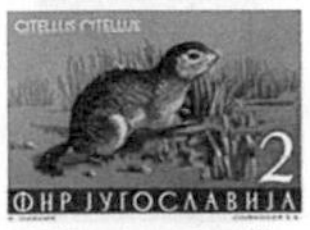

213 European Souslik

1954. Animals.

765	**213**	2d. grey, buff and green	35	20
766	-	5d. brown, buff and green	60	20
767	-	10d. brown and black	1·20	20
768	-	15d. brown and blue	1·40	20
769	-	17d. brown and purple	2·30	20
770	-	25d. yellow, blue and violet	3·50	50
771	-	30d. brown and blue	4·00	50
772	-	35d. black and brown	4·75	75
773	-	50d. brown and green	15·00	2·50
774	-	65d. black and red	26·00	13·50
775	-	70d. brown and green	23·00	13·50
776	-	100d. black and blue	95·00	42·00

DESIGNS—HORIZ: 5d. Lynx; 10d. Red deer; 15d. Brown bear; 17d. Chamois; 25d. Eastern white pelican. VERT: 30d. Lammergeier; 35d. "Procerus gigas" (ground beetle); 50d. "Callimenius pancici" (cricket); 65d. Black Dalmatian lizard; 70d. Blind cave-dwelling salamander; 100d. Brown trout.

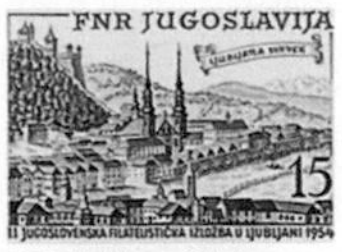

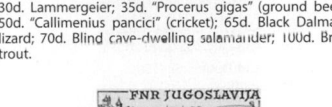

214 Ljubljana (17th century)

1954. Philatelic Exhibition, Ljubljana.

777	**214**	15d. brown, green & black	14·00	12·50

No. 777 was only sold at the Exhibition at 35d. (20d. entrance fee).

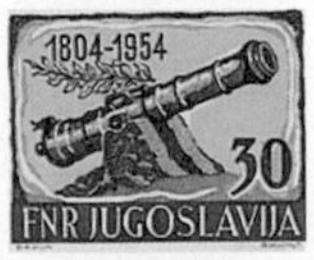

215 Cannon, 1804

1954. 150th Anniv of Serbian Insurrection. Multicoloured.

778	15d. Serbian flag	1·20	30
779	30d. Type **215**	1·70	75
780	50d. Seal of insurgents' council	5·75	3·25
781	70d. Karageorge	44·00	27·00

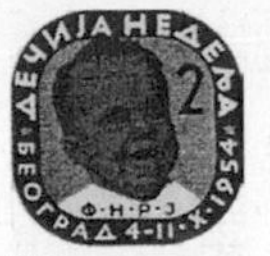

215a

1954. Children's Week.

781a	**215a**	2d. red	1·70	85

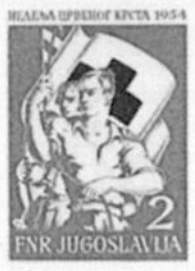

216

1954. Obligatory Tax. Red Cross.

782	**216**	2d. red and green	60	40

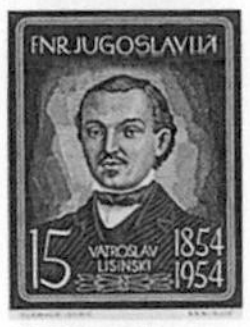

217 Vatroslav Lisinski (composer)

1954. Cultural Anniversaries.

783	**217**	15d. green	3·00	2·50
784	-	30d. brown	3·00	2·50
785	-	50d. purple	3·00	2·50
786	-	70d. blue	8·75	7·75
787	-	100d. violet	29·00	21·00

PORTRAITS: 15d. Type **217** (death centenary); 30d. Andrija Kacic-Miosic (writer, 250th birth anniv); 50d. Jury Vega (mathematician, birth bicentenary); 70d. Jovan Jovanovic-Zmaj (poet, 50th death anniv); 100d. Filip Visnjic (poet and musician, 120th death anniv).

See also Nos. 975/80.

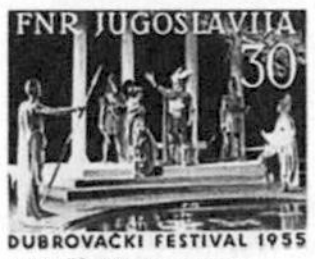

218 "A Midsummer Night's Dream" (Shakespeare)

1955. Dubrovnik Festival.

788	-	15d. blue	1·20	50
789	**218**	30d. blue	4·75	2·50

DESIGN—VERT: 15d. Scene from "Robinja" by Hanibal Lucic.

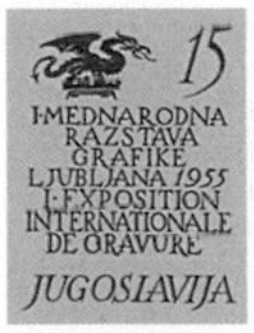

219

1955. First Int Exn of Engraving, Ljubljana.

790	**219**	15d. brown and green on stone	8·75	5·25

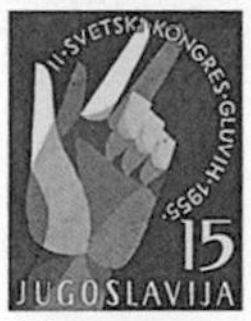

220

1955. Second World Congress of the Deaf and Dumb.

791	**220**	15d. red	3·00	65

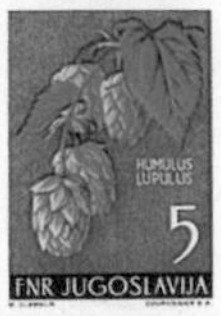

221 Hops

1955. Floral Designs.

792	**221**	5d. green and brown	25	10
793	-	10d. purple, green and buff	25	10
794	-	15d. multicoloured	25	10
795	-	17d. buff, green and lake	25	10
796	-	25d. yellow, green and blue	35	15
797	-	30d. multicoloured	70	30
798	-	50d. red, green and brown	3·50	2·10
799	-	70d. orange, green and brown	5·75	3·75
800	-	100d. multicoloured	30·00	19·00

FLOWERS: 10d. Tobacco; 15d. Opium poppy; 17d. Small-leaved lime; 25d. False chamomile; 30d. Sage; 50d. Dog rose; 70d. Great yellow gentian; 100d. Yellow pheasant's-eye.

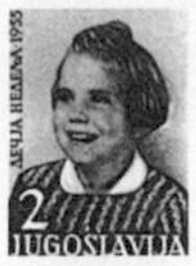

222 Laughing Girl

1955. Obligatory Tax. Children's Week.

801	**222**	2d. red and cream	60	30

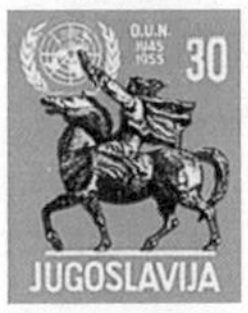

223 Peace Monument, U.N. Building, New York (A. Augustincic)

1955. Tenth Anniv of United Nations.

802	**223**	30d. black and blue	1·20	1·00

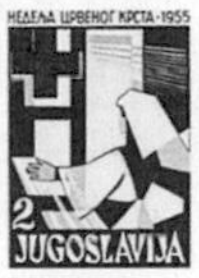

224 Red Cross Nurse

1955. Obligatory Tax. Red Cross.

803	**224**	2d. black, grey and red	35	20

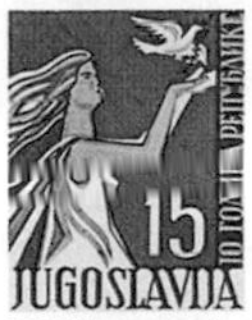

225 Woman and Dove

1955. Tenth Anniv of Republic.

804	**225**	15d. violet	1·20	75

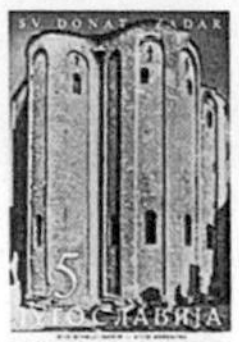

226 St. Donat's Church, Zadar

1956. Yugoslav Art.

805	**226**	5d. grey	60	20
806	-	10d. green	60	20
807	-	15d. brown	60	20
808	-	20d. brown	60	20
809	-	25d. sepia	60	20
810	-	30d. purple	60	20
811	-	35d. green	1·70	50
812	-	40d. brown	3·00	75
813	-	50d. brown	3·50	1·00
814	-	70d. green	11·50	10·50
815	-	100d. purple	41·00	26·00
816	-	200d. blue	£100	42·00

DESIGNS—VERT: 10d. Bas-relief of Croat King, Diocletian Palace, Split; 15d. Church portal, Studenica, Serbia; 20d. Master Radovan's portal, Trogir Cathedral; 25d. Fresco, Sopocani, Serbia; 30d. Monument, Radimije, Herzegovina; 50d. Detail from Bozidarevic Triptych, Dubrovnik; 70d. Carved figure, Belec Church, Croatia; 100d. Self-portrait of Rikard Jakopic; 200d. Peace Monument by A. Augustinic, New York. HORIZ: 35d. Heads from Cathedral cornice, Sibenik, Dalmatia; 40d. Frieze, Kotor Cathedral, Montenegro.

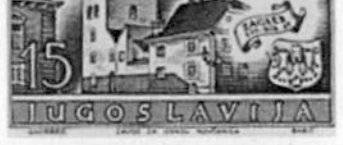

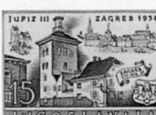

227 Zagreb through the Centuries

1956. Yugoslav Int Philatelic Exn, Zagreb.

817	**227**	15d. deep brown, brown and black (postage)	1·20	20
818	**227**	30d. blue, red and black (air)	4·75	1·80

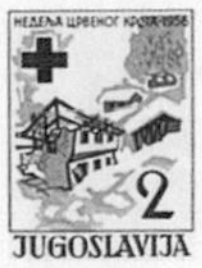

228 Houses ruined by Avalanche

1956. Obligatory Tax. Red Cross.

819	**228**	2d. sepia, brown and red	45	30

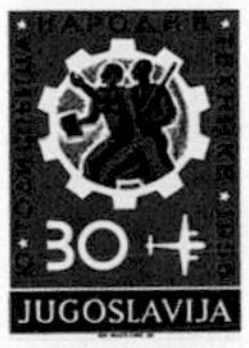

229 "Technical Education"

1956. Air. Tenth Anniv of Technical Education.

820	**229**	30d. black and red	2·00	1·80

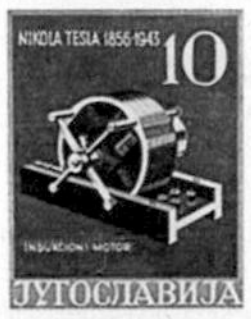

230 Induction Motor

1956. Birth Centenary of Nikola Tesla (inventor).

821	**230**	10d. olive	60	30
822	-	15d. brown	60	30
823	-	30d. blue	3·00	1·60
824	-	50d. purple	7·50	3·75

DESIGNS: 15d. Transformer; 30d. "Telekomanda" (invention); 50d. Portrait of Tesla.

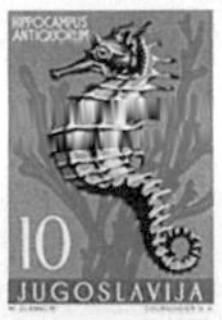

231 Short-snouted Seahorse

1956. Adriatic Sea Creatures.

825	**231**	10d. brown, purple & green	60	30
826	-	15d. black, pink and blue	60	30
827	-	20d. multicoloured	60	30
828	-	25d. multicoloured	1·20	30
829	-	30d. multicoloured	1·20	30
830	-	35d. mauve, yellow & blue	2·30	75
831	-	50d. red, yellow and blue	5·75	3·25
832	-	70d. multicoloured	11·50	5·25
833	-	100d. multicoloured	47·00	26·00

DESIGNS: 15d. Common paper nautilus; 20d. Rock lobster; 25d. Rainbow wrasse; 30d. Painted comber; 35d. Striped red mullet; 50d. Red scorpionfish; 70d. Cuckoo wrasse; 100d. John Dory.

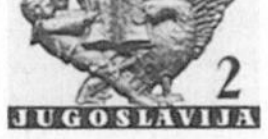

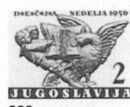

232

1956. Obligatory Tax. Children's Week.

834	**232**	2d. green	60	30

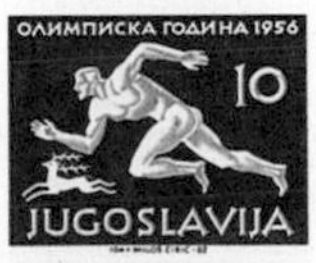

233 Running

1956. Olympic Games. Figures, values and country name in ochre.

835	**233**	10d. red	1·20	50
836	-	15d. blue (Canoeing)	1·20	50
837	-	20d. blue (Skiing)	2·30	1·00
838	-	30d. green (Swimming)	2·30	1·00
839	-	35d. sepia (Football)	2·30	1·00
840	-	50d. green (Water polo)	2·30	1·00

841	-	70d. purple (Table tennis)	£120	29·00
842	-	100d. red (Shooting)	£120	29·00

234

1957. Obligatory Tax. Red Cross.

843	**234**	2d. red, black and blue	45	30

235 Common Centaury

1957. Flowers. Multicoloured.

844	10d. Type **235**	10	10
845	15d. Deadly nightshade	15	10
846	20d. Saffron crocus	25	10
847	25d. Marsh mallow	25	10
848	30d. Common valerian	35	20
849	35d. Woolly foxglove	80	20
850	50d. Male fern	1·70	65
851	70d. Green-winged orchid	3·00	1·60
852	100d. Pyrethrum	20·00	9·00

236 Factory in Worker's Hand

1957. First Congress of Workers' Councils, Belgrade.

853	**236**	15d. lake	60	30
854	**236**	30d. blue	1·70	1·00

237 Gymnastics

1957. Second Gymnastics Festival, Zagreb. Vert designs as T **237**.

855	**237**	10d. olive and black	35	20
856	-	15d. brown and black	35	20
857	-	30d. blue and black	1·20	20
858	-	50d. brown and black	5·25	1·60

239 Musician and Dancers of Slovenia

1957. Yugoslav Costumes (1st series).

860		10d. multicoloured	25	10
861		15d. multicoloured	35	10
862		30d. multicoloured	45	20
863		50d. green, brown and buff	60	30
864		70d. black, brown and buff	80	50
865	**239**	100d. multicoloured	11·50	4·50

DESIGNS—HORIZ: 10d. Montenegrin musician, man and woman; 15d. Macedonian dancers; 30d. Croatian shepherdess and shepherd boys. VERT: 50d. Serbian peasants; 70d. Bosnian villagers.

See also Nos. 1020/5.

240 Children

1957. Obligatory Tax. Children's Week.

866	**240**	2d. slate and red	45	30

241 Revolutionaries

1957. 40th Anniv of Russian Revolution.

867	**241**	15d. red and ochre	95	65

242 Simon Gregorcic (poet)

1957. Cultural Anniversaries.

868	**242**	15d. sepia	60	30
869	-	30d. blue	60	30
870	-	50d. brown	1·20	50
871	-	70d. violet	9·25	6·25
872	-	100d. green	14·00	10·50

PORTRAITS: 15d. Type **242** (50th death anniv (1956)); 30d. Anton Linhart (dramatist, birth bicentary (1956)); 50d. Oton Kucera (physicist, birth centenary); 70d. Stevan Mokranjac (composer, birth centenary (1956)); 100d. Jovan Popovic (writer, death centenary (1956)).

244

1958. Seventh Yugoslav Communist Party Congress.

877	**244**	15d. purple	1·20	20

245 Fresco of Sopocani Monastery

1958. Obligatory Tax. Red Cross.

878	**245**	2d. multicoloured	60	30

246 Mallard

1958. Yugoslav Game Birds. Birds in natural colours. Background colours given below.

879	**246**	10d. brown	10	10
880	-	15d. mauve	15	10
881	-	20d. blue	35	15
882	-	25d. green	60	20
883	-	30d. turquoise	80	25
884	-	35d. bistre	1·70	30
885	-	50d. purple	4·00	2·10
886	-	70d. blue	7·00	3·25
887	-	100d. brown	30·00	21·00

DESIGNS—HORIZ: 15d. Western capercaillie; 20d. Common pheasant; 35d. Water rail; 70d. Eurasian woodcock. VERT: 25d. Black coot; 30d. Water rail; 50d. Rock partridge; 100d. Common crane.

247 Pigeon

1958. Opening of Postal Museum, Belgrade.

888	**247**	15d. black	1·20	20

248 Battle Flag

1958. 15th Anniv of Battle of Sutjeska River.

889	**248**	15d. lake	70	40

249 Pomet (hero of Drzic's comedy "Dundo Maroje") and Ancient Fountain at Dubrovnik

1958. 450th Birth Anniv of Marin Drzic (writer).

890	**249**	15d. brown and black	2·30	20

243 Steel Plant, Sisak

1958

891	-	2d. green	10	10
892	-	5d. red	25	10
983	-	5d. orange	30	10
893	-	8d. purple	25	10
984	-	8d. violet	25	10
894	**243**	10d. green	35	10
985	**243**	10d. brown	25	10
896	-	15d. red	60	10
986	-	15d. green	35	10
898	-	17d. purple	60	10
899	-	20d. red	60	10
987	-	20d. blue	80	10
987a	-	20d. green	45	10
900	-	25d. grey	60	10
988	-	25d. red	30	10
901	-	30d. blue	60	10
989	-	30d. brown	8·75	10
989a	-	30d. red	80	10
902	-	35d. red	60	10
903	-	40d. red	60	10
904	-	40d. blue	8·25	10
990	-	40d. purple	25	10
905	-	50d. blue	60	10
991	-	50d. blue	2·30	10
906	-	55d. red	9·25	10
992	-	65d. green	25	10
907	-	70d. red	1·70	10
908	-	80d. red	21·00	10
909	-	100d. green	9·25	10
993	-	100d. green	3·50	10
994	-	150d. red	1·20	10
910	-	200d. brown	4·00	10
995	-	200d. blue	80	10
996	-	300d. green	2·20	10
911	-	500d. blue	9·25	10
997	-	500d. violet	1·40	10
998	-	1000d. brown	3·00	10
999	-	2000d. purple	8·75	50

DESIGNS—VERT: 2, 100d. (993) Oil derricks, Nafta; 5d. Shipbuilding; 8, 17d. Timber industry, cable railway; 15 (896), 20d. Jablanica Dam; 15 (986), 25d. (900) Ljubljana–Zagreb motor road; 25d. (988) Cable industry; 30d. "Litostroj" turbine factory, Ljubljana; 35, 40d. (990) Coke plant, Lukavac; 50d. (991) Iron foundry, Zenica; 65d. Furnace, Sovojno. HORIZ: 40 (903/4), 150d. Hotel Titograd; 50 (905), 55, 200d. (995) Skopje; 70, 80, 300d. Sarajevo railway station and obelisk; 100 (909), 500d. (997) Bridge, Ljubljana; 200 (910), 1000d. Theatre, Zagreb; 500 (911), 2000d. Parliament House, Belgrade.

See also Nos. 1194/1204.

250 Children at Play

1958. Obligatory Tax. Children's Week.

912	**250**	2d. black, olive and yellow	35	20

251 Ship with Oceanographic Equipment

1958. International Geophysical Year.

913	**251**	15d. purple (postage)	60	30
914	-	300d. blue (air)	10·50	4·00

DESIGN: 300d. Moon and Earth with orbital tracks of artificial satellites.

252 "Human Rights"

1958. Tenth Anniv of Declaration of Human Rights.

915	**252**	30d. green	1·30	1·00

253 Old City, Dubrovnik

1959. Tourist Publicity (1st series). Views.

916	**253**	10d. yellow and red	10	10
917	-	10d. blue and green	10	10
918	-	15d. violet and blue	10	10
919	-	15d. green and blue	10	10
920	-	20d. green and brown	15	10
921	-	20d. green and blue	15	10
922	-	30d. violet and orange	1·20	10
923	-	30d. green and blue	1·20	10
924	-	70d. black and blue	6·50	4·25

DESIGNS: No. 917, Bled; 918, Postojna grottoes; 919, Ohrid; 920, Plitvice Lakes; 921, Opatija; 922, Split; 923, Sveti Stefan; 924, Belgrade.

See also Nos. 1033/41, 1080/5 and 1165/70.

254 Communist Party Emblem and Red Flags

1959. 40th Anniv of Yugoslav Communist Party.

925	**254**	20d. multicoloured	1·70	20

255 "Family Assistance"

1959. Obligatory Tax. Red Cross.

926	**255**	2d. blue and red	45	20

256 Dubrovnik (15th century)

1959. Philatelic Exhibition, Dubrovnik ("JUFIZ IV").

927	**256**	20d. myrtle, green and blue	10·50	4·75

257 Dutch Lavender

1959. Medicinal Plants.

928	**257**	10d. violet, green and blue	10	10
929	-	15d. multicoloured	10	10
930	-	20d. multicoloured	10	10
931	**257**	25d. lilac, green and olive	20	10
932	-	30d. green, blue and pink	35	15
933	-	35d. blue, green and brown	60	30
934	-	50d. yellow, green & brn	3·00	50
935	-	70d. multicoloured	3·50	1·30

936	-	100d. grey, green & brown	16·00	7·75

FLOWERS: 15d. Alder blackthorn; 20d. Scopolia; 25d. Monkshood; 30d. Bilberry; 35d. Common juniper; 50d. Cowslip; 70d. Pomegranate; 100d. Thorn-apple.

258 Tug-of-War

1959. "Partisan" Physical Culture Festival, Belgrade.

937	258	10d. black and ochre	10	10
938	-	15d. blue and sepia	10	10
939	-	20d. violet and brown	10	10
940	-	35d. purple and grey	25	10
941	-	40d. violet and grey	35	10
942	-	55d. green and brown	70	10
943	-	80d. olive and slate	1·20	65
944	-	100d. violet and ochre	8·75	4·50

DESIGNS—HORIZ: 15d. High jumping and running; 20d. Gymnastics; 35d. Female exercises with hoops; 40d. Sailors' exercises; 55d. Handball and basketball; 80d. Swimming and diving. VERT: 100d. "Partisan" Association insignia.

259 Fair Emblem

1959. Zagreb International Fair.

945	259	20d. black and blue	3·00	1·60

260

1959. Obligatory Tax. Children's Week.

946	260	2d. slate and yellow	45	20

261 Athletes

1960. Olympic Games.

947	261	15d. yellow, buff and violet	60	50
948	-	20d. drab, lavender & blue	60	50
949	-	30d. blue, stone & ultram	60	50
950	-	35d. grey, brown & purple	60	50
951	-	40d. drab, green and bronze	60	50
952	-	55d. blue, drab and green	60	50
953	-	80d. ochre, grey and red	10·50	5·25
954	-	100d. ochre, drab and violet	10·50	5·25

DESIGNS: 20d. Swimming; 30d. Skiing; 35d. Graeco-Roman wrestling; 40d. Cycling; 55d. Yachting; 80d. Equestrian; 100d. Fencing.

Nos. 948, 950, 952 and 954 are inscr in Cyrillic characters.

262 "Reconstruction" (sculpture by L. Dolinar)

1960. Obligatory Tax. Red Cross.

955	262	2d. blue and red	45	20

1960. Yugoslav Forest Mammals. As T **213**. Animals in natural colours. Background colours given.

956		15d. blue (West European hedgehog)	25	20
957		20d. olive (Eurasian red squirrel)	35	30
958		25d. turquoise (Pine marten)	45	40
959		30d. olive (Brown hare)	60	50
960		35d. brown (Red fox)	70	65

961		40d. lake (Eurasian badger)	80	75
962		55d. blue (Wolf)	1·50	1·40
963		80d. violet (Roe deer)	1·70	1·60
964		100d. red (Wild boar)	4·75	4·25

263 Lenin

1960. 90th Birth Anniv of Lenin.

965	263	20d. grey and green	25	10

264 Accelerator

1960. Nuclear Energy Exhibition, Belgrade.

966	264	15d. green	11·50	10·50
967	-	20d. red	11·50	10·50
968	-	40d. blue	11·50	10·50

DESIGNS: 20d. Neutron generator; 40d. Nuclear reactor.

265 Young Girl

1960. Obligatory Tax. Children's Week.

969	265	2d. red	35	20

266 National Theatre. Novi Sad (Centenary)

1960. Anniversaries.

970	266	15d. black	70	65
971	-	20d. sepia	80	75
972	-	40d. blue	1·00	95
973	-	55d. purple	1·20	1·00
974	-	80d. green	1·40	1·30

DESIGNS: 20d. Detail of "Illyrian Renaissance", V. Bukovac (cent of Croat National Theatre, Zagreb); 40d. Edvard Rusijan and Bleriot XI airplane (50th anniv of 1st flight in Yugoslavia); 55d. Symbolic hand holding fruit (15th anniv of Republic); 80d. Symbol of nuclear energy (15th anniv of U.N.O.).

1960. Portraits as T **217**.

975		15d. green	60	40
976		20d. brown	60	40
977		40d. brown	60	40
978		55d. red	60	40
979		80d. blue	60	40
980		100d. blue	60	40

PORTRAITS: 15d. Ivan Cankar (writer); 20d. Silvije Kranjcevic (poet); 40d. Paja Jovanovic (painter); 55d. Djura Jaksic (writer); 80d. Mihajlo Pupin (physicist); 100d. Rudjer Boskovic (astronomer).

268 "Blood Transfusion"

1961. Obligatory Tax. Red Cross. Perf or imperf.

981	268	2d. multicoloured	45	20

269 "Atomic Energy"

1961. Int Nuclear Electronic Conference, Belgrade.

982	269	25d. multicoloured	1·20	20

1961. Medicinal Plants. As T **257**. Multicoloured.

1000		10d. Yellow foxglove	45	20
1001		15d. Marjoram	45	20
1002		20d. Hyssop	45	20
1003		25d. Hawthorn	45	20
1004		40d. Hollyhock	45	20
1005		50d. Soapwort	45	20
1006		60d. Clary	45	20
1007		80d. Blackthorn	90	20
1008		100d. Pot marigold	13·00	6·75

See also Nos. 1074/9.

271 Stevan Filipovic (statue by V. Bakic)

1961. 20th Anniv of Yugoslav Insurrection. Inscriptions in gold.

1009	271	15d. brown and red	25	10
1010	-	20d. yellow and sepia	25	10
1011	-	25d. green and turquoise	25	10
1012	-	60d. violet and blue	25	10
1013	-	100d. indigo and blue	35	20
MS1013a		64×82 mm. 500d. indigo, blue and gold. Imperf	£170	£170

DESIGNS: 20d. Insurrection Monument, Bosansko Grahovo (relief by S. Stojanivic); 25d. Executed Inhabitants Monument, Kagujevav (by A. Grzetic); 60d. Nova Gradisks Victory Monument (A. Augustincic); 100, 500d, Marshal Tito (Revolution Monument, Titovo Uzice, (statue by F. Krsinic).

272

1961. Non-Aligned Countries Conf, Belgrade.

1014	272	250d. sepia (postage)	10	10
1015	-	50d. green	25	10
MS1015a		72×65 mm. 1000d. purple (T **272**). Imperf	23·00	23·00

| 1016 | 272 | 250d. purple (air) | 1·30 | 75 |
| 1017 | - | 500d. blue | 2·50 | 1·60 |

DESIGN: 50, 500d. National Assembly Building, Belgrade.

273 St. Clement (14th-century wood-carving)

1961. 12th International Congress of Byzantine Studies, Ohrid.

1018	273	25d. sepia and olive	3·75	85

274 Bird with Flower in Beak

1961. Obligatory Tax. Children's Week.

1019	274	2d. orange and violet	35	20

1961. Yugoslav Costumes (2nd series). As T **239**. Inscr "1941–1961".

1020		15d. multicoloured	25	10
1021		25d. black, red and brown	25	10
1022		30d. sepia, red and brown	25	10
1023		50d. multicoloured	25	10
1024		65d. multicoloured	50	15
1025		100d. multicoloured	2·30	1·00

DESIGNS—HORIZ: Costumes of: 15d. Serbia; 25d. Montenegro; 30d. Bosnia and Herzegovina; 50d. Macedonia; 65d. Croatia; 100d. Slovenia.

275 Luka Vukalovic (revolutionary leader)

1961. Centenary of Herzegovina Insurrection.

1026	275	25d. black	25	10

276 Hands holding Flower and Rifle

1961. 20th Anniv of Yugoslav Partisan Army.

1027	276	25d. blue and red	25	10

277 Dimitur and Konstantin Miladinov

1961. Centenary of Publication of Macedonian National Songs by Miladinov Brothers.

1028	277	25d. purple and buff	25	10

(after P. Krsinic)

1962. 15th Anniv of UNICEF.

1029	278	50d. black on drab	25	10

279 Mosquito

1962. Malaria Eradication.

1030	279	50d. black on blue	25	10

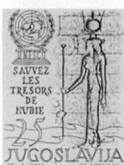

280 Goddess Isis (from Temple at Kalabscha)

1962. 15th Anniv of UNESCO. Save Nubian Monuments.

| 1031 | 280 | 25d. green on stone | 10 | 10 |
| 1032 | - | 50d. brown on drab | 25 | 10 |

DESIGN: 50d. Rameses II (from temple, Abu Simbel).

1962. Tourist Publicity (2nd series). Views as T **253**. Inscr "1941–1961".

1033		15d. brown and blue	35	10
1034		15d. bistre and turquoise	35	10
1035		25d. brown and blue	35	10
1036		25d. blue and light blue	35	10
1037		30d. blue and brown	35	10
1038		30d. blue and purple	45	10
1039		50d. turquoise and bistre	1·20	10
1040		50d. blue and bistre	1·20	10
1041		100d. grey and green	10·50	4·25

VIEWS: No. 1033, Portoroz; 1034, Jajce; 1035, Zadar; 1036, Popova Sapka; 1037, Hvar; 1038, Kotor Bay; 1039, Djerdap; 1040, Rab; 1041, Zagreb.

281 Bandages and Symbols

1962. Obligatory Tax. Red Cross.

1042	**281**	5d. red, brown and grey	35	20

282 Marshal Tito (after sculpture by A. Augustincic)

1962. Marshal Tito's 70th Birthday.

1043	**282**	25d. green	10	10
1044	-	50d. brown	35	10
1045	**282**	100d. blue	1·20	20
1046	-	200d. green and brown	2·30	1·00

MS1046a 76×104 mm. Nos. 1043/6. Imperf (sold at 400d.) 47·00 47·00

DESIGNS: 50, 200d. As T **282** but profile view of bust.

1962. Amphibians and Reptiles. As T **213**.

1047	15d. brown, red and green	60	40
1048	20d. black, yellow and violet	60	40
1049	25d. multicoloured	60	40
1050	30d. brown, green and blue	60	40
1051	50d. brown, yellow and red	60	40
1052	65d. black, stone and green	60	40
1053	100d. green, brown and black	1·60	1·50
1054	150d. red, black and brown	2·40	2·20
1055	200d. black, drab and red	13·50	7·50

DESIGNS: 15d. Crested newt; 20d. Spotted salamander; 25d. Yellow-bellied toad; 30d. Marsh frog; 50d. European pond turtle, 100d. Green lizard; 200d. Adder.

283 Pole Vaulting

1962. Seventh European Athletic Championships, Belgrade. Sportsmen in black.

1056	**283**	15d. blue	45	20
1057	-	25d. purple	45	20
1058	-	30d. green	45	20
1059	-	50d. red	45	20
1060	-	65d. blue	45	20
1061	-	100d. turquoise	1·00	20
1062	-	150d. orange	4·25	40
1063	-	200d. brown	10·50	80

MS1063a 57×71 mm. 600d. black and violet. Imperf 17·00 17·00

DESIGNS—HORIZ: 25d. Throwing the discus; 50d. Throwing the javelin; 100d. Start of sprint; 200d. High jumping. VERT: 30d. Running; 65d. Putting the shot; 150d. Hurdling; 600d. Army Stadium, Belgrade.

284 "Physical Culture"

1962. Children's Week.

1064	**284**	25d. black and red	25	10

285 "Bathing the Newborn Child" (Decani Monastery)

962. Yugoslav Art. Multicoloured.

1065	25d. Situla of Vace (detail from bronze vessel) (horiz)	25	25
1066	30d. Golden Mask of Trebiniste (5th-cent burial mask) (horiz)	25	25
1067	50d. The God Kairos (Trogir Monastery)	25	25
1068	65d. Pigeons of Nerezi (detail from series of frescoes, "The Visitation", Nerezi Church, Skopje)	25	25
1069	100d. Type **285**	40	40
1070	150d. Icon of Ohrid (detail from 14th-cent icon, "The Annunciation") (horiz)	1·60	85

See also Nos. 1098/1103.

286 Ear of Wheat and Parched Earth

1963. Freedom from Hunger.

1071	**286**	50d. purple on stone	25	10

287 Andrija Mohorovicic (meteorologist)

1963. World Meteorological Day.

1072	**287**	50d. blue on grey	25	10

288 Centenary Emblem

1963. Obligatory Tax. Red Cross Centenary and Red Cross Week.

1073	**288**	5d. red, grey and ochre	45	20

1963. Medicinal Plants. As T **257**.

1074	15d. black, green & lt green	35	30
1075	25d. multicoloured	35	30
1076	30d. multicoloured	35	30
1077	50d. multicoloured	35	30
1078	65d. multicoloured	75	65
1079	100d. drab, green and black	4·00	2·75

FLOWERS: 15d. Lily of the valley; 25d. Iris; 30d. Bistort; 50d. Henbane; 65d. Perforate St. John's wort; 100d. Caraway.

1963. Tourist Publicity (3rd series). Views as T **253**. Inscr "1963". Multicoloured.

1080	15d. Pula	10	10
1081	25d. Vrnjacka Banja	10	10
1082	30d. Crikvenica	10	10
1083	50d. Korcula	25	10
1084	65d. Durmitor	25	15
1085	100d. Ljubljana	2·10	65

289 Partisans in File

1963. 20th Anniv of Battle of Sutjeska River.

1086	**289**	15d. green and drab	10	10
1087	-	25d. green	10	10
1088	-	50d. violet and brown	20	10

DESIGNS—VERT: 25d. Sutjeska Gorge. HORIZ: 50d. Partisans in battle.

See also No. 1125.

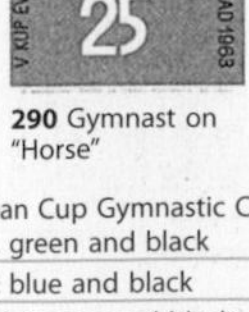

290 Gymnast on "Horse"

1963. Fifth European Cup Gymnastic Championships.

1089	**290**	25d. green and black	60	20
1090	-	50d. blue and black	1·20	35
1091	-	100d. brown and black	1·70	50

DESIGNS—Gymnast: 50d. on parallel bars; 100d. exercising with rings.

291 "Mother"

1963. Sculptures by Ivan Mestrovic.

1092	**291**	25d. bistre on brown	10	10
1093	-	50d. olive on green	25	10
1094	-	65d. green on blue	80	30
1095	-	100d. black on grey	1·20	65

SCULPTURES: 50d. "Reminiscence" (nude female figure); 65d. "Kraljevic Marko" (head); 100d. "Indian on horseback".

292 Children with Toys

1963. Children's Week.

1096	**292**	25d. multicoloured	45	20

293 Soldier and Emblem

1963. 20th Anniv of Yugoslav Democratic Federation.

1097	**293**	25d. red, green and drab	25	10

1963. Yugoslav Art. As T **285**. Inscr "1963". Multicoloured.

1098	25d. "Man", relief on Radimlje tombstone (13th–15th century)	25	10
1099	30d. Detail of relief on door of Split Cathedral (Andrija Buvina) (13th century) (horiz)	25	10
1100	50d. Detail of fresco in Beram Church (15th cent) (horiz)	25	10
1101	65d. Archangel Michael from plaque in Dominican Monastery, Dubrovnik (15th cent)	25	10
1102	100d. Figure of man on Baroque fountain, by Francesco Robba, Ljubljana (18th cent)	25	10
1103	150d. Archbishop Eufraise, detail of mosaic in Porec Basilica (6th cent)	1·10	70

294 Dositej Obradovic (writer)

1963. Cultural Celebrities.

1104	**294**	25d. black on buff	25	10
1105	-	30d. black on blue	25	10
1106	-	50d. black on cream	25	10
1107	-	65d. black on lilac	1·00	10
1108	-	100d. black on pink	1·30	65

PORTRAITS: 30d. Vuk Karadzic (language reformer); 50d. Franc Miklosic (philologist); 65d. Ljudevit Gaj (writer); 100d. Petar Njegos (poet).

See also Nos. 1174/9.

295 Parachute

1964. Obligatory Tax. Red Cross Week and 20th Anniv of Yugoslav Red Cross.

1109	**295**	5d. red, purple and blue	35	20

296 Peacock

1964. Butterflies. Multicoloured.

1110	25d. Type **296**	45	40
1111	30d. Camberwell beauty	45	40
1112	40d. Oleander hawk moth	45	40
1113	50d. Apollo	45	40
1114	150d. Viennese emperor moth	4·75	4·25
1115	200d. Swallowtail	4·75	4·25

297 Fireman saving Child

1964. Centenary of Voluntary Fire Brigade.

1116	**297**	25d. sepia and red	25	10

298 Running

1964. Olympic Games, Tokyo.

1117	**298**	25d. yellow, black & grey	35	20
1118	-	30d. violet, black and grey	35	20
1119	-	40d. green, black and grey	35	20
1120	-	50d. multicoloured	35	20
1121	-	150d. multicoloured	5·50	1·20
1122	-	200d. blue, black and grey	5·50	1·20

DESIGNS: 30d. Boxing; 40d. Rowing; 50d. Basketball; 150d. Football; 200d. Water polo.

299 "Reconstruction"

1964. First Anniv of Skopje Earthquake.

1123	**299**	25d. brown	25	10
1124	-	50d. blue	25	10

DESIGN: 50d. "International Aid" (U.N. flag over town).

1964. 20th Anniv of Occupation of Vis Island. As T **289** but inscr "VIS 1944–1964" at foot.

1125	25d. red and grey	25	10

300 Costumes of Kosovo-Metohija (Serbia)

1964. Yugoslav Costumes (3rd series). As T **300**. Multicoloured.

1126	25d. Type **300**	60	55
1127	30d. Slovenia	60	55
1128	40d. Bosnia and Herzegovina	60	55
1129	50d. Hrvatska (Croatia)	60	55
1130	150d. Macedonia	3·00	2·50
1131	200d. Crna Gora (Montenegro)	3·00	2·50

301 Friedrich Engels

1964. Centenary of "First International".

1132	**301**	25d. black on cream	25	10
1133	-	50d. black on lilac	25	10

DESIGN: 50d. Karl Marx.

302 Children on Scooter

1964. Children's Week.

1134	302	25d. green, black and red	25	10

303 "Victor" (after Ivan Mestrovic)

1964. 20th Anniv of Liberation of Belgrade.

1135	303	25d. black and green on pink	25	10

304 Initial of Hilander's Gospel (13th cent)

1964. Yugoslav Art. Inscr "1964". Multicoloured.

1136		25d. Type 304	25	10
1137		30d. Initial of Miroslav's gospel (12th cent)	25	10
1138		40d. Detail from Cetinje octateuch (15th cent)	25	10
1139		50d. Miniature from Trogir's gospel (15th cent)	25	10
1140		150d. Miniature from Hrvoe's missal (15th cent)	40	10
1141		200d. Miniature from Herman Priory, Ristrica (14th cent) (horiz)	80	40

305 "Hand of Equality"

1964. Eighth Yugoslav Communist League Congress. Multicoloured.

1142		25d. Type 305	10	10
1143		50d. Dove and factory ("Peace and Socialism")	25	10
1144		100d. Industrial plant ("Socialism")	45	20

306 Player

1965. World Table Tennis Championships, Ljubljana.

1145	306	50d. multicoloured	4·75	4·25
1146	-	150d. multicoloured	4·75	4·25

DESIGN: 150d. As Type 306 but design arranged in reverse.

307 Children around Red Cross

1965. Obligatory Tax. Red Cross Week.

1147	307	5d. red and brown	25	10

308 Titograd

1965. 20th Anniv of Liberation. Yugoslav Capitals.

1148	308	25d. purple	25	10
1149	-	30d. brown	25	10
1150	-	40d. violet	25	10
1151	-	50d. green	70	65
1152	-	150d. violet	70	65
1153	-	200d. blue	95	85

CAPITALS: 30d. Skopje; 40d. Sarajevo; 50d. Ljubljana; 150d. Zagreb; 200d. Belgrade.

309 Young Partisan (after D. Andrejevic-Kun)

1965. "Twenty Years of Freedom" Pioneer Games.

1154	309	25d. black & brown on buff	25	10

310 T.V. Tower, Avala (Belgrade)

1965. Centenary of I.T.U.

1155	310	50d. blue	25	10

1965. Inauguration of Djerdap Hydro-electric Project. As Nos. 3271/2 of Rumania.

1156		25d. (30b.) green and grey	25	10
1157		50d. (55b.) red and grey	60	20
MS1157a		103×80 mm. 80b., 11.20, 100,150d. multicoloured (sold at 500d. or 4l.)	5·75	5·75

DESIGN: 25d. Djerdap Gorge; 50d. Djerdap Dam. Nos. 1156/7 were issued simultaneously in Rumania.

311 Yarrow

1965. Medicinal Plants. Multicoloured.

1158		25d. Type 311	45	40
1159		30d. Rosemary	45	40
1160		40d. Elecampane	45	40
1161		50d. Deadly nightshade	45	40
1162		150d. Peppermint	45	40
1163		200d. Rusty foxglove	3·00	2·50

312 I.C.Y. Emblem

1965. International Co-operation Year.

1164	312	50d. violet, indigo and blue	25	10

313 Sibenik

1965. Tourist Publicity (4th series). Multicoloured.

1165		25d. Rogaska Slatina	60	50
1166		30d. Type 313	60	50
1167		40d. Prespa Lake	60	50
1168		50d. Prizren	60	50
1169		150d. Skadar Lake	1·70	1·60
1170		200d. Sarajevo	3·00	2·50

314 Cat

1965. Children's Week.

1171	314	30d. lake and yellow	35	10

1965. Nos. 984 and 988 surch.

1172		5d. on 8d. violet	45	10
1173		50d. on 25d. red	70	10

1965. Cultural Celebrities. Portraits as T 294.

1174		30d. red on pink	35	30
1175		50d. slate on blue	35	30
1176		60d. sepia on brown	35	30
1177		85d. indigo on blue	35	30
1178		200d. olive on olive	35	30
1179		500d. mauve on purple	60	50

PORTRAITS: 30d. Branislav Nusic (author and dramatist); 50d. Antun Matos (poet); 60d. Ivan Mazuranic (author); 85d. Fran Levstik (writer); 200d. Josif Pancic (botanist); 500d. Dimitrije Tucovic (politician).

316 Marshal Tito

1966

1180	316	20p. green	25	10
1181	316	30p. red	25	10

317 Long Jumping (Balkan Games, Sarajevo)

1966. Sports Events.

1182	317	30p. red	25	10
1183	-	50p. violet	25	10
1184	-	1d. green	25	10
1185	-	3d. brown	1·60	1·40
1186	-	5d. blue	1·60	1·40

DESIGNS AND EVENTS: 50p. Ice hockey and 3d. Ice hockey sticks and puck (World Ice Hockey Championships, Jesenice, Ljubljana and Zagreb); 1d. Rowing and 5d. Oars (World Rowing Championships, Bled).

318 "T", 15th-cent Psalter

1966. Yugoslav Art. Manuscript initials. Multicoloured.

1187	318	30p. Type 318	10	10
1188		50p. "V", 14th-cent Divos gospel	10	10
1189		60p. "R", 12th-cent Libri moralium of Gregory I	10	10
1190		85p. "P", 12th-cent Miroslav gospel	10	10
1191		2d. "B", 13th-cent Radomir gospel	25	10
1192		5d. "F", 11th-cent passional	60	50

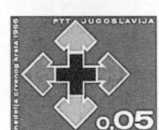

319 Red Cross Emblem

1966. Obligatory Tax. Red Cross Week.

1193	319	5p. multicoloured	25	10

1966. As Nos. 983, etc, but values expressed "0.05" etc, colours changed and new values.

1194		5p. orange	40	30
1195		10p. brown	40	30
1196		15p. blue	40	30
1197		20p. green	65	30
1198		30p. red	1·00	30
1199		40p. purple	40	30
1200		50p. blue	50	30
1201		60p. brown	50	30
1202		65p. green	75	30
1203		85p. purple	1·20	30
1204		1d. olive	1·70	30

NEW VALUES: 60p. as No. 988, 85p. as No. 984.

320 Beam Aerial on Globe

1966. International Amateur Radio Union Regional Conference, Opatija.

1205	320	85p. blue	1·90	85

321 Stag Beetle

1966. Insects. Multicoloured.

1206		30p. Type 321	35	20
1207		50p. Rose chafer	35	20
1208		60p. "Meloe violaceus" (oil beetle)	35	20
1209		85p. Seven-spotted ladybird	35	20
1210		2d. Alpine longhorn beetle	35	20
1211		5d. Great diving beetle	60	30

322 Serbian 1 para Stamp of 1866

1966. Serbian Stamp Centenary.

1212	322	30p. green, lake & brown	25	10
1213	-	50p. lake, bistre and ochre	25	10
1214	-	60p. orange and green	25	10
1215	-	85p. red and blue	25	10
1216	-	2d. blue, deep green & green	60	30
MS1217		62½×73½ mm. 10d. multicoloured. Imperf	2·30	2·30

DESIGNS—(Serbian Stamps of 1866): 50p.—2p.; 60p.—10p.; 85p.—20p.; 2d.—40p.; 10d. —1p.

323 Rebels on Shield

1966. 25th Anniv of Yugoslav Insurrection.

1218	323	20p. brown, gold & green	10	10
1219	323	30p. mauve, gold & buff	10	10
1220	323	85p. blue, gold and stone	10	10
1221	323	2d. violet, gold and blue	15	15

324 Josip Strossmayer and Racki (founders)

1966. Centenary of Yugoslav Academy, Zagreb.

1222	324	30p. black, stone and drab	25	10

325 Old Bridge, Mostar

1966. 400th Anniv of Old Bridge, Mostar.

1223	325	30p. purple	3·75	1·20

325a Medieval View of Sibenik

1966. 900th Anniv of Sibenik.

1224	325a	30p. purple	25	10

326 "The Girl in Pigtails"

1966. Children's Week.
| 1225 | 326 | 30p. multicoloured | 1·80 | 1·60 |

327 UNESCO Emblem

1966. 20th Anniv of UNESCO.
| 1226 | 327 | 85p. blue | 25 | 10 |

328 Stylized Winter Landscape

1966. Christmas.
1227	328	15p. yellow and blue	45	20
1228	-	20p. yellow and violet	45	20
1229	-	30p. yellow and green	45	20

DESIGNS: 20p. Father Christmas; 30p. Stylized Christmas tree.
See also Nos. 1236/8.

329 Dinar of Durad I Balsic

1966. Yugoslav Art. Designs showing different coins.
1230	329	30p. multicoloured	10	10
1231	-	50p. multicoloured	10	10
1232	-	60p. multicoloured	10	10
1233	-	85p. multicoloured	10	10
1234	-	2d. multicoloured	25	10
1235	-	5d. multicoloured	60	20

MEDIEVAL COINS (Dinars of): 50p. King Stefan Tomasevic; 60p. Djurad Brankovic; 85p. Ljubljana; 2d. Split; 5d. Emperor Stefan Dusan.

1966. New Year. As Nos. 1227/9 but colours changed.
1236		15p. gold, blue and indigo	25	15
1237		20p. gold, red and pink	25	15
1238		30p. gold, myrtle and green	25	15

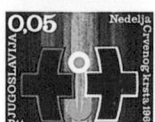

330 Flower between Red Crosses

1967. Obligatory Tax. Red Cross Week.
| 1239 | 330 | 5p. red, green and blue | 25 | 10 |

331 Arnica

1967. Medicinal Plants. Multicoloured.
1240	331	30p. Type 331	25	10
1241		50p. Common flax	25	10
1242		85p. Oleander	25	10
1243		1d.20 Gentian	25	10
1244		3d. Laurel	35	10
1245		5d. African rue	1·20	85

332 President Tito

1967. Pres. Tito's 75th Birthday. (a) Size 20×27 mm.
1246	332	5p. orange	10	10
1247	332	10p. brown	10	10
1248	332	15p. violet	10	10
1249	332	20p. green	10	10
1260	332	20p. blue	1·70	10
1261	332	25p. purple	25	10
1250	332	30p. red	10	10
1263	332	30p. myrtle	35	10
1251	332	40p. black	10	10
1252	332	50p. turquoise	10	10
1266a	332	50p. red	35	10
1253	332	60p. lilac	15	10
1268	332	70p. sepia	45	10
1269	332	75p. green	60	10
1270	332	80p. brown	3·00	10
1270a	332	80p. red	60	10
1254	332	85p. blue	20	10
1272	332	90p. brown	35	10
1273	332	1d. red	25	10
1274	332	1d.20 blue	70	10
1274a	332	1d.20 green	70	10
1275	332	1d.25 blue	45	10
1276	332	1d.50 green	60	10

(b) Size 20×30 mm.
1277		2d. sepia	3·00	10
1278		2d.50 green	1·70	10
1279		5d. purple	1·20	20
1280		10d. purple	3·00	50
1281		20d. green	2·75	30

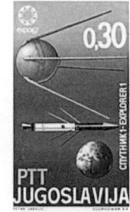

333 "Sputnik I" and "Explorer I"

1967. World Fair, Montreal. Space Achievements. Multicoloured.
1282		30p. Type 333	10	10
1283		50p. "Tiros", "Telstar" and "Molyna"	10	10
1284		85p. "Luna 9" and lunar orbiter	10	10
1285		1d.20 "Mariner 4" and "Venus 3"	10	10
1286		3d. "Vostok I" and Gemini-Agena space vehicle	45	20
1287		5d. Leonov in space	4·00	3·75

334 St. Tripun's Church, Kotor

1967. International Tourist Year.
1288	334	30p. green and blue	10	10
1289	-	50p. violet and brown	10	10
1290	-	85p. purple and blue	10	10
1291	-	1d.20 brown and purple	20	10
1292	-	3d. olive and brown	25	10
1293	-	5d. brown and olive	2·50	50

DESIGNS: 50p. Town Hall, Maribor; 85p. Trogir Cathedral; 1d.20, Fortress gate, Nis; 3d. Bridge, Visegrad; 5d. Ancient bath, Skopje.

335 Northern Bobwhite

1967. International Hunting and Fishing Exhibition and Fair, Novi Sad. Multicoloured.
1294		30p. Type 335	50	30
1295		50p. Northern pike	50	30
1296		1d.20 Red deer	70	45
1297		5d. Peregrine falcon	2·00	1·20

336 Congress Emblem

1967. Int Astronautical Federation Congress, Belgrade.
| 1298 | 336 | 85p. gold, light blue and blue | 25 | 10 |

337 Old Theatre Building

1967. Centenary of Slovene National Theatre, Ljubljana.
| 1299 | 337 | 30p. brown and green | 25 | 10 |

338 "Winter Landscape" (A. Becirovic)

1967. Children's Week.
| 1300 | 338 | 30p. multicoloured | 70 | 10 |

339 "Lenin" (from bust by Ivan Mestrovic)

1967. 50th Anniv of October Revolution.
1301	339	30p. violet	10	10
1302	339	85p. brown	25	10
MS1303		58×77 mm. 339 10d. lake. Imperf	9·50	9·50

340 Four-leaved Clover

1967. New Year. Inscr "1968".
1304	340	20p. gold, blue and green	10	10
1305	-	30p. gold, violet and yellow	10	10
1306	-	50p. gold, red and lilac	10	10

DESIGNS: 30p. Sweep with ladder; 50p. Horseshoe and flower.
See also Nos. 1347/9.

341 "The Young Sultana" (Vlaho Bukovac)

1967. Yugoslav Paintings. Multicoloured.
1307		85p. "The Watchtower" (Djura Jaksic) (vert)	1·90	40
1308		1d. Type 341	1·90	40
1309		2d. "At Home" (Josip Petkovsek)	1·90	40
1310		3d. "The Cock-fight" (Paja Jovanovic)	1·90	40
1311		5d. "Summer" (Ivana Kobilca) (vert)	6·50	3·00

See also Nos. 1337/41, 1399/1404. 1438/43, 1495/1500, 1535/40, 1570/5, 1616/19, 1750/5 and 1793/8.

342 Ski Jumping

1968. Winter Olympic Games, Grenoble.
1312	342	50p. purple and blue	45	15
1313	-	1d. olive and brown	45	15
1314	-	2d. lake and black	95	45
1315	-	5d. blue and olive	6·50	2·75

DESIGNS: 1d. Figure skating (pairs); 2d. Downhill skiing; 5d. Ice hockey.

343 "The Madonna and Child" (St. George's Church, Prizren)

1968. Medieval Icons. Multicoloured.
1316		50p. Type 343	10	10
1317		1d. "The Annunciation" (Ohrid Museum)	15	10
1318		1d.50 "St. Sava and St. Simeon" (Belgrade Museum)	20	10
1319		2d. "The Descent" (Ohrid Museum)	30	15
1320		3d. "The Crucifixion" (St. Clement's Church, Ohrid)	45	40
1321		5d. "The Madonna and Child" (Gospe od zvonika Church, Split)	75	60

344 Honeycomb on Red Cross

1968. Obligatory Tax. Red Cross Week.
| 1322 | 344 | 5p. multicoloured | 25 | 10 |

345 Northern Bullfinch

1968. Song Birds. Multicoloured.
1323		50p. Type 345	45	40
1324		1d. Eurasian goldfinch	45	40
1325		1d.50 Chaffinch	45	40
1326		2d. Western greenfinch	45	40
1327		3d. Red crossbill	45	40
1328		5d. Hawfinch	5·50	3·00

346 Running (Women's 800 m)

1968. Olympic Games, Mexico.
1329	346	50p. pur & brn on cream	45	40
1330	-	1d. olive & turq on grn	45	40
1331	-	1d.50 sepia & bl on flesh	45	40
1332	-	2d. green & bis on cream	1·90	40
1333	-	3d. indigo & violet on blue	1·90	40
1334	-	5d. purple & green on mauve	21·00	5·00

DESIGNS: 1d. Basketball; 1d.50, Gymnastics; 2d. Sculling; 3d. Water polo; 5d. Wrestling.

347 Rebel Cannon

1968. 65th Anniv of Ilinden Uprising.
| 1335 | 347 | 50p. brown and gold | 25 | 10 |

348 "Mother and Children" (fresco in Hrastovlje Church, Slovenia)

1968. 25th Anniv of Partisan Occupation of Istria and Slovenian Littoral.

| 1336 | **348** | 50p. multicoloured | 25 | 10 |

349 "Lake of Klansko" (Marko Pernhart)

1968. Yugoslav Paintings. 19th-cent Landscapes. Multicoloured.

1337	1d. Type **349**		20	10
1338	1d.50 "Bavarian Landscape" (Milan Popovic)		20	10
1339	2d. "Gateway, Zadar" (Ferdo Quiquerez)		20	10
1340	3d. "Triglav from Bohinj" (Anton Karinger)		35	25
1341	5d. "Studenica Monastery" (Djordje Krstic)		2·00	80

350 A. Santic

1968. Birth Centenary of Aleksa Santic (poet).

| 1342 | **350** | 50p. blue | 25 | 10 |

351 "Promenade" (Marina Cudov)

1968. Children's Week.

| 1343 | **351** | 50p. multicoloured | 25 | 10 |

352 Karl Marx (after sculpture by N. Mitric)

1968. 150th Birth Anniv of Karl Marx.

| 1344 | **352** | 50p. red | 25 | 10 |

353 Aztec Emblem and Olympic Rings

1968. Obligatory Tax. Olympic Games Fund.

| 1345 | **353** | 10p. multicoloured | 25 | 10 |

354 Old Theatre and View of Kalemegdan

1968. Centenary of Serbian National Theatre, Belgrade.

| 1346 | **354** | 50p. brown and green | 25 | 10 |

1968. New Year. Designs as Nos. 1304/6 but colours changed and inscr "1969".

1347	20p. gold, blue and lilac	35	15
1348	30p. gold, violet and green	35	15
1349	50p. gold, red and yellow	35	15

355 Hassan Brkic

1968. Yugoslav National Heroes.

1350	**355**	50p. violet	20	10
1351	-	75p. black	20	10
1352	-	1d.25 brown	20	10
1353	-	2d. blue	20	10
1354	-	2d.50 green	30	15
1355	-	5d. lake	1·40	80

MS1356 Two sheets each 156×108 mm. (a) 2× Nos. 1350/2 (b) 2× 1353/5 Pair   28·00 28·00

PORTRAITS: 75p. Ivan Milutinovic; 1d.25, Rade Koncar; 2d. Kuzman Josifovski; 2d.50, Tone Tomsic; 5d. Mosa Pijade.

356 "Family" (sculpture by J. Soldatovic) and Human Rights Emblem

1968. Human Rights Year.

| 1357 | **356** | 1d.25 blue | 30 | 15 |

357 I.L.O. Emblem

1969. 50th Anniv of I.L.O.

| 1358 | **357** | 1d.25 black and red | 30 | 15 |

358 Dove on Hammer and Sickle Emblem

1969. 50th Anniv of Yugoslav Communist Party.

1359	**358**	50p. red and black	10	10
1360	-	75p. black and ochre	10	10
1361	-	1d.25 black and red	15	10

MS1362 118×140 mm. Nos. 1359 (4), 1360 (2), 1361 (2) and 10d. chocolate   7·50 7·50

DESIGNS: 75p. "Tito" and star (wall graffiti); 1d.25 Five-pointed crystal formation; 10d. President Tito.

359 "St. Nikita" (Manasija Monastery)

1969. Medieval Frescoes in Yugoslav Monasteries. Multicoloured.

1363	**359**	50p. Type **359**	20	10
1364		75p. "Jesus and the Apostles" (Sopocani)	20	10
1365		1d.25 "The Crucifixion" (Studenica)	20	10
1366		2d. "Cana Wedding Feast" (Kalenic)	20	10
1367		3d. "Angel guarding Tomb" (Mileseva)	35	10
1368		5d. "Mourning over Christ" (Nerezi)	2·75	70

360 Roman Memorial and View of Ptuj

1969. 1900th Anniv of Ptuj (Poetovio) (Slovene town).

| 1369 | **360** | 50p. brown | 20 | 10 |

361 Vasil Glavinov

1969. Birth Centenary of Vasil Glavinov (Macedonian revolutionary).

| 1370 | **361** | 50p. purple and brown | 20 | 10 |

362 Globe between Hands

1969. Obligatory Tax. Red Cross Week.

| 1371 | **362** | 20p. black, red and deep red | 20 | 10 |

363 Thin-leafed Peony

1969. Flowers. Multicoloured.

1372	50p. Type **363**	20	10
1373	75p. Coltsfoot	20	10
1374	1d.25 Primrose	20	10
1375	2d. Hellebore	20	10
1376	2d.50 Sweet violet	20	10
1377	5d. Pasque flower	3·25	3·25

364 "Eber" (V. Ivankovic)

1969. Dubrovnik Summer Festival. Sailing Ships. Multicoloured.

1378	50p. Type **364**	20	10
1379	1d.25 "Tare in Storm" (Fra nasovic)	20	10
1380	1d.50 "Brigantine Sela" (Ivankovic)	25	10
1381	2d.50 "16th-century Dubrovnik Galleon"	35	20
1382	3d.25 "Frigate Madre Mimbelli" (A. Roux)	60	35
1383	5d. "Shipwreck" (16th-century icon)	1·40	1·10

365 Games' Emblem

1969. Ninth World Deaf and Dumb Games, Belgrade.

| 1384 | **365** | 1d.25 lilac and red | 20 | 10 |

366 Bosnian Mountain Horse

1969. 50th Anniv of Veterinary Faculty, Zagreb. Multicoloured.

1385	75p. Type **366**	30	15
1386	1d.25 Lipizzaner horse	30	15
1387	3d.25 Ljutomer trotter	35	15
1388	5d. Yugoslav half-breed	3·75	1·00

367 Children and Chicks

1969. Children's Week.

| 1389 | **367** | 50p. multicoloured | 20 | 10 |

368 Arms of Belgrade

1969. 25th Anniv of Yugoslav Liberation. Arms of Regional Capitals. Multicoloured.

1390	50p. Type **368**	20	10
1391	50p. Skopje	20	10
1392	50p. Titograd (Podgorica)	20	10
1393	50p. Sarajevo	20	10
1394	50p. Zagreb	20	10
1395	50p. Ljubljana	20	10

MS1396 89×106 mm. Nos. 1390/5 and 12d. gold, red and black (Yugoslav Arms) with two stamp-size labels. Size of individual designs reduced to 21½×27½ mm.   16·00 16·00

369 Dr. Josip Smodlaka

1969. Birth Centenary of Dr. Josip Smodlaka (politician).

| 1397 | **369** | 50p. blue | 20 | 10 |

370 Torch, Globe and Olympic Rings

1969. Obligatory Tax. Olympic Games Fund.

| 1398 | **370** | 10p. multicoloured | 45 | 15 |

371 "Gipsy Girl" (Nikola Martinoski)

1969. Yugoslav Nude Paintings. Multicoloured.

1399	50p. Type **371**	20	10
1400	1d.25 "Girl in Red Armchair" (Sava Sumanovic)	20	10
1401	1d.50 "Girl Brushing Hair" (Marin Tartaglia)	20	10
1402	2d.50 "Olympia" (Miroslav Kraljevic) (horiz)	45	30
1403	3d.25 "The Bather" (Jovan Bijelic)	75	40
1404	5d. "Woman on a Couch" (Matej Sternen) (horiz)	1·90	1·50

372 University Building

1969. 50th Anniv of Ljubljana University.

| 1405 | **372** | 50p. green | 20 | 10 |

373 University
Seal

1969. 300th Anniv of Zagreb University.
| 1406 | 373 | 50p. gold, purple and blue | 20 | 10 |

374 Colonnade

1969. Europa.
| 1407 | 374 | 1d.25 brown, light brown and green | 1·60 | 1·60 |
| 1408 | 374 | 3d.25 blue, grey & purple | 6·25 | 6·25 |

375 Jovan Cvijic
(geographer)

1970. Famous Yugoslavs.
1409	375	50p. purple	10	10
1410	-	1d.25 black	10	10
1411	-	1d.50 purple	15	10
1412	-	2d.50 olive	15	10
1413	-	3d.25 brown	25	10
1414	-	5d. blue	30	25

CELEBRITIES: 1d.25, Dr. Andrija Stampar (hygienist); 1d.50, Joakim Krcovski (author); 2d.50, Marko Miljanov (soldier); 3d.25, Vasa Pelagic (socialist revolutionary); 5d. Oton Zupancic (poet).

376 "Punishment
of Dirka" (4th-cent
mosaic)

1970. Mosaics. Multicoloured.
1415	50p. Type **376**		30	15
1416	1d.25 "Cerberus" (5th-cent) (horiz)		30	15
1417	1d.50 "Angel of Annunciation" (6th-cent)		30	15
1418	2d.50 "Hunters" (4th-cent)		30	15
1419	3d.25 "Bull beside Cherries" (5th-cent) (horiz)		60	15
1420	5d. "Virgin and Child Enthroned" (6th-cent)		1·60	1·20

377 Lenin (after
sculpture by S.
Stojanovic)

1970. Birth Centenary of Lenin.
| 1421 | 377 | 50p. lake | 20 | 10 |
| 1422 | - | 1d.25 blue | 20 | 10 |

DESIGN: 1d.25, As Type **377**, but showing left side of Lenin's bust.

378 Trying for
Goal

1970. Sixth World Basketball Championships.
| 1423 | 378 | 1d.25 red | 20 | 10 |

379 Red Cross Trefoil

1970. Obligatory Tax. Red Cross Week.
| 1424 | 379 | 20p. multicoloured | 20 | 10 |

380 "Flaming Sun"

1970. Europa.
| 1425 | 380 | 1d.25 deep blue, turquoise and blue | 20 | 10 |
| 1426 | 380 | 3d.25 brown, vio & pur | 50 | 40 |

381 Istrian Short-haired
Hound

1970. Yugoslav Dogs. Multicoloured.
1427	50p. Type **381**		10	10
1428	1d.25 Yugoslav tricolour hound		10	10
1429	1d.50 Istrian hard-haired hound		10	10
1430	2d.50 Balkan hound		10	10
1431	3d.25 Dalmatian		10	10
1432	5d. Shara mountain dog		3·00	2·30

382 Olympic Flag

1970. Obligatory Tax. Olympic Games Fund.
| 1433 | 382 | 10p. multicoloured | 20 | 10 |

383 Telegraph Key

1970. Centenary of Montenegro Telegraph Service.
| 1434 | 383 | 50p. gold, black & brown | 20 | 10 |

384 "Bird in Meadow"
(Lidija Dobronjovska)

1970. Children's Week.
| 1435 | 384 | 50p. multicoloured | 20 | 10 |

385 "Gymnast"

1970. 17th World Gymnastics Championships, Ljubljana.
| 1436 | 385 | 1d.25 blue and purple | 20 | 10 |

386 "Hand Holding
Dove" (Makoto)

1970. 25th Anniv of United Nations.
| 1437 | 386 | 1d.25 multicoloured | 20 | 10 |

1970. Yugoslav Paintings. Baroque Period. Designs as T **341** but vert. Multicoloured.
1438	50p. "The Ascension" (Teodor Kracun)		20	10
1439	75p. "Abraham's Sacrifice" (Federiko Benkovic)		20	10
1440	1d.25 "The Holy Family" (Francisek Jelovsek)		20	10
1441	2d.50 "Jacob's Dream" (Hristofor Zefarovic)		20	10
1442	3d.25 "Christ's Baptism" (Serbian village artist)		30	10
1443	5d.75 "Coronation of the Virgin" (Tripo Kokolja)		80	60

388 Rusty-leaved
Alpenrose

1970. Nature Conservation Year. Multicoloured.
| 1444 | 1d.25 Type **388** | | 1·70 | 1·20 |
| 1445 | 3d.25 Lammergeier | | 16·00 | 7·75 |

389 Frano Supilo

1971. Birth Cent of Frano Supilo (politician).
| 1446 | 389 | 50p. brown and buff | 20 | 10 |

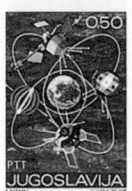

390 Different
Nations' Satellites
("International
Co-operation")

1971. Space Exploration. Multicoloured.
1447	50p. Type **390**		20	10
1448	75p. Telecommunications satellite		20	10
1449	1d.25 Unmanned Moon flights		20	10
1450	2d.50 Exploration of Mars and Venus (horiz)		55	25
1451	3d.25 Space-station (horiz)		70	50
1452	5d.75 Astronauts on the Moon (horiz)		1·70	1·30

391 "Proclamation of the
Commune" (A. Daudenarde,
after A. Lamy)

1971. Centenary of Paris Commune.
| 1453 | 391 | 1d.25 brown and orange | 20 | 10 |

392 Red Cross Ribbon

1971. Obligatory Tax. Red Cross Week.
| 1454 | 392 | 20p. multicoloured | 20 | 10 |

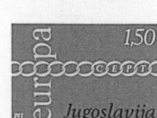

393 Europa Chain

1971. Europa.
| 1455 | 393 | 1d.50 multicoloured | 20 | 15 |
| 1456 | 393 | 4d. pink, purple & mauve | 65 | 55 |

394 Congress
Emblem (A.
Pajvancic)

1971. 20th Anniv of Yugoslav "Self-Managers" Movement.
| 1457 | 394 | 50p. red, black and gold | 75 | 55 |
| 1458 | - | 1d.25 red, black and gold | 1·90 | 1·40 |

DESIGN: 1d.25, "Self-Managers" emblem (designed by M. Miodragovic).

395 Common
Mallow

1971. Flowers. Multicoloured.
1459	50p. Type **395**		30	15
1460	1d.50 Buckthorn		30	15
1461	2d. White water-lily		30	15
1462	2d.50 Common poppy		40	15
1463	4d. Chicory		85	60
1464	6d. Chinese lantern		4·50	3·25

396 Olympic
"Spiral" and Rings

1971. Obligatory Tax. Olympic Games Fund.
| 1465 | 396 | 10p. black, purple & blue | 20 | 10 |

397 Krk,
Dalmatia

1971. Tourism.
1478	-	1d. red	2·50	30
1641	-	5p. orange	60	20
1642	-	10p. brown	60	30
1468	-	20p. lilac	20	10
1644	-	25p. red	1·70	20
1469	397	30p. green	60	10
1645	397	30p. olive	60	20
1646	-	35p. red	1·20	75
1647	-	40p. olive	60	20
1473	-	50p. red	1·00	15
1474	-	50p. green	20	10
1650	-	60p. purple	60	20
1652	-	75p. purple	1·20	20
1476	-	75p. green	50	10
1477	-	80p. red	1·20	15
1656	-	1d. lilac	25	10
1657	-	1d. green	60	10
1479	-	1d.20 green	1·50	15
1480	-	1d.25 blue	70	15
1481	-	1d.50 blue	30	10
1660	-	1d.50 red	1·70	20
1482	-	2d. turquoise	65	10
1661	-	2d.10 green	25	10
1483	-	2d.50 violet	65	10
1662a	-	2d.50 red	1·20	10
1663	-	2d.50 blue	25	10
1664a	-	3d. grey	35	10
1665	-	3d.20 blue	25	10
1666	-	3d.40 green	1·20	10
1667	-	3d.50 red	25	10
1668a	-	4d. red	35	10
1669	-	4d.90 blue	4·00	20
1670	-	5d. green	60	20
1671	-	5d.60 olive	25	10
1672	-	6d. brown	60	10
1673a	-	6d.10 green	60	20
1674	-	8d. grey	35	10
1675a	-	8d.80 grey	60	20
1676	-	10d. purple	60	10
1677	-	16d.50 blue	35	10
1678	-	26d. blue	35	10
1679	-	38d. mauve	60	10

1680	-	70d. blue	80	65

DESIGNS: 5p. Krusevo, Macedonia; 10p. Gradacac; 20p., 75p. Bohinj, Slovenia; 25p. Budva; 35p. Omis, Dalmatia; 40p. Pec; 50p. (1473/4), Krusevac, Serbia; 60p. Logarska valley; 75p. (1652), Rijeka; 80p. Piran; 1d. (1478), Bitola, Macedonia; 1d. (1656/7), 16d.50, Ohrid; 1d.20, 4d. Pocitelj; 1d.25, 1d.50 (1481), 8d.80, Herceg Novi; 1d.50 (1660), Bihac; 2d. Novi Sad; 2d.10, 6d.10, Hvar; 2d.50 (1483), Rijeka Crnojevica, Montenegro; 2d.50 (1662a/3), Kragujevac; 3d., 3d.20, Skofja Loka; 3d.40; Vranje; 3d.50, Vrsac; 4d.90, Perast; 5d. Osijek; 5d.60, Travnik; 6d. Kikinda; 8d. Dubrovnik; 10d. Sarajevo; 26d. Korcula; 38d. Maribor; 70d. Zagreb.

398 "Prince Lazar Hrebeljanovic" (from fresco, Lazarica Church)

1971. 600th Anniv of City of Krusevac.

1487	**398**	50p. multicoloured	20	10

399 "Satyr"

1971. Bronze Archaeological Discoveries. Multicoloured.

1488		50p. Head of Emperor Constantine	10	10
1489		1d.50 "Boy with Fish" (statuette)	10	10
1490		2d. "Hercules" (statuette)	10	10
1491		2d.50 Type **399**	10	10
1492		4d. "Goddess Aphrodite" (head)	30	15
1493		6d. "Citizen of Emona" (statue)	65	45

400 "Children in Balloon"

1971. Children's Week and 25th Anniv of UNICEF.

1494	**400**	50p. multicoloured	20	10

1971. Yugoslav Portraits. As T **371**. Multicoloured.

1495		50p. "Girl in Serbian Dress" (Katarina Ivanovic)	10	10
1496		1d.50 "Ivanisevic the Merchant" (Anastas Bocaric)	10	10
1497		2d. "Anne Kresic" (Vjekoslav Karas)	10	10
1498		2d.50 "Pavla Jagodica" (Konstantin Danil)	20	10
1499		4d. "Louise Pasjakova" (Mihael Stroj)	30	15
1500		6d. "Old Man at Ljubljana" (Matevz Langus)	1·00	80

402 "Postal Codes"

1971. Introduction of Postal Codes.

1501	**402**	450p. multicoloured	20	10

403 Dame Gruev

1971. Birth Cent of Dame Gruev (Macedonian revolutionary).

1502	**403**	50p. blue	20	15

404 Speed Skating

1972. Winter Olympic Games, Sapporo, Japan. Multicoloured.

1503		1d.25 Type **404**	60	45
1504		6d. Skiing	2·50	1·90

405 First Page of Statute

1972. 700th Anniv of Dubrovnik Law Statutes.

1505	**405**	1d.25 multicoloured	20	10

406 Ski-jump, Planica

1972. First World Ski-jumping Championships, Planica.

1506	**406**	1d.25 multicoloured	20	10

407 Water-polo

1972. Olympic Games, Munich. Multicoloured.

1507		50p. Type **407**	10	10
1508		1d.25 Basketball	10	10
1509		2d.50 Swimming	15	10
1510		3d.25 Boxing	30	10
1511		5d. Running	50	15
1512		6d.50 Sailing	1·00	65

408 Red Cross and Hemispheres

1972. Obligatory Tax. Red Cross Week.

1513	**408**	20p. multicoloured	20	10

409 "Communications"

1972. Europa.

1514	**409**	1d.50 multicoloured	50	40
1515	**409**	5d. multicoloured	1·00	80

410 Wallcreeper

1972. Birds. Multicoloured.

1516		50p. Type **410**	30	15
1517		1d.25 Little bustard	30	15
1518		2d.50 Red-billed chough	35	15
1519		3d.25 White spoonbill	90	15
1520		5d. Eagle owl	1·60	60
1521		6d.50 Rock ptarmigan	3·75	2·30

411 President Tito

1972. President Tito's 80th Birthday.

1522	**411**	50d. brown and buff	20	10
1523	**411**	1d.25 blue and grey	50	20
MS1524	61×76 mm. **411** 10d. brown and drab. Imperf		3·00	3·00

412 Communications Tower, Olympic Rings and 1972 Games' Emblem

1972. Obligatory Tax. Olympic Games Fund.

1525	**412**	10p. multicoloured	20	10

413 Locomotive No. 1 "King of Serbia", 1882

1972. 50th Anniv of International Railway Union. Multicoloured.

1526		1d.50 Type **413**	30	10
1527		5d. Electric locomotive No. 441.013, 1967	1·00	55

414 Glider in Flight

1972. 13th World Gliding Championships, Vrsac.

1528	**414**	2d. black, blue and gold	20	15

415 Pawn

1972. 20th Chess Olympiad, Skopje.

1529	**415**	1d.50 brown, vio & pur	30	10
1530	-	6d. black, blue & dp blue	1·60	1·00

DESIGN: 6d. Chessboard, king and queen.

416 "Child on Horse" (B. Zlatec)

1972. Children's Week.

1531	**416**	80p. multicoloured	20	10

417 G. Delcev

1972. Birth Cent of Goce Delcev (Macedonian revolutionary).

1532	**417**	80p. black and green	20	10

418 Father Martic (sculpture, Ivan Mestrovic)

1972. 150th Birth Anniv of Father Grge Martic (politician).

1533	**418**	80p. black, green and red	20	10

419 National Library

1972. 140th Anniv of and Re-opening of National Library, Belgrade.

1534	**419**	50p. brown	20	10

420 "Fruit Dish and Broken Majolica Vase" (Milos Tenkovic)

1972. Yugoslav Art. Still Life. Multicoloured.

1535		50p. Type **420**	10	10
1536		1d.25 "Mandoline and Book" (Jozef Petkovsec) (vert)	10	10
1537		2d.50 "Basket with Grapes" (Katarina Jovanovic)	20	10
1538		3d.25 "Water-melon" (Konstantin Danil)	30	15
1539		5d. "In a Stable" (Nikola Masic) (vert)	50	20
1540		6d.50 "Scrap-books" (Celestin Medovic)	75	65

421 Battle of Stubica

1973. 500th Anniv of Slovenian Peasant Risings and 400th Anniv of Croatian–Slovenian Rebellion. Multicoloured.

1541		2d. Type **421**	30	10
1542		6d. Battle of Krsko	1·00	75

422 R. Domanovic

1973. Birth Centenary of Radoje Domanovic (Serbian satirist).

1543	**422**	80p. brown and drab	40	10

423 Skofja Loka

1973. Millenary of Skofja Loka.

1544	**423**	80p. brown and buff	30	10

424 "Novi Sad" (Petar Demetrovic)

1973. Old Engravings of Yugoslav Towns. Each black and gold.

1545		50p. Type **424**	10	10
1546		1d.25 "Zagreb" (Josef Szeman)	10	10
1547		2d.50 "Kotor" (Pierre Montier)	15	10
1548		3d.25 "Belgrade" (Mancini)	15	10
1549		5d. "Split" (Louis Cassas)	30	15
1550		6d.50 "Kranj" (Matthaus Merian)	65	50

425 Table Tennis Bat and Ball

1973. 32nd World Table Tennis Championships, Sarajevo.

1551	**425**	2d. multicoloured	35	10

426 Red Cross Emblem

1973. Obligatory Tax. Red Cross Week.

1552	**426**	20p. multicoloured	20	10

427 Europa "Posthorn"

1973. Europa.

1553	**427**	2d. lilac, green and blue	35	30
1554	**427**	5d.50 pink, green & purple	1·50	1·30

428 Birthwort

1973. Medicinal Plants. Multicoloured.

1555		80p. Type **428**	20	10
1556		2d. Globe thistle	20	10
1557		3d. Olive	30	10
1558		4d. "Corydalis cava"	50	10
1559		5d. Mistletoe	75	50
1560		6d. Comfrey	2·30	2·00

429 Globe and Olympic Rings

1973. Obligatory Tax. Olympic Games Fund.

1561	**429**	10p. multicoloured	20	10

430 A. Jansa and Bee

1973. Death Bicent of Anton Jansa (apiculturist).

1562	**430**	80p. black	40	10

431 Aquatic Symbol

1973. First World Aquatic Championships, Belgrade.

1563	**431**	2d. multicoloured	30	10

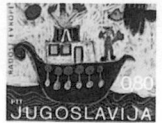

432 "Children on Boat" (Ivan Vukovic)

1973. Children's Week.

1564	**432**	80p. multicoloured	1·60	1·00

433 Posthorn

1973

1565	**433**	30p. brown	20	10
1565a	**433**	50p. blue	20	10
1566	**433**	80p. red	20	10

1566a	**433**	1d. green	20	10
1567	**433**	1d.20 red	20	10
1567a	**433**	1d.50 red	20	10

434 Dalmatinac (after sculpture by Ivan Mestrovic)

1973. 500th Death Anniv of Juraj Dalmatinac (sculptor and architect).

1568	**434**	80p. green and grey	25	10

435 "Self-portrait"

1973. Birth Cent of Nadezda Petrovic (painter).

1569	**435**	2d. multicoloured	30	20

436 "The Plaster Head" (Marko Celebonovic)

1973. Yugoslav Art. Interiors. Multicoloured.

1570		80p. Type **436**	10	10
1571		2d. "St. Duja Church" (Emanuel Vidovic)	10	10
1572		3d. "Slovenian Housewife" (Marino Tartaglia)	10	10
1573		4d. "Dedicated to Karas" (Miljenko Stancic)	15	10
1574		5d. "My Studio" (Milan Konjovic)	25	20
1575		6d. "Tavern in Stara Loka" (France Slana)	65	50

437 Dragojlo Dudic

1973. National Heroes. (a) Each black.

1576		80p. Type **437**	10	10
1577		80p. Strahil Pindzur	10	10
1578		80p. Boris Kidric	10	10
1579		80p. Radoje Dakic	10	10

(b) Each red.

1580		2d. Josip Mazar-Sosa	20	20
1581		2d. Zarko Zrenjanin	20	20
1582		2d. Emin Duraku	20	20
1583		2d. Ivan Lola Ribar	20	20

438 "M" for "Metrication"

1974. Centenary of Introduction of Metric System in Yugoslavia.

1584	**438**	80p. multicoloured	25	10

439 Skater

1974. European Figure Skating Championships, Zagreb.

1585	**439**	2d. multicoloured	60	30

440 Satjeska Monument

1974. Monuments.

1586	-	3d. green	95	20
1587	-	4d.50 brown	1·40	20
1588	-	5d. violet	1·40	20
1589	**440**	10d. green	2·30	30
1590	-	20d. purple	2·50	30
1828	-	50d. blue	3·75	1·70

DESIGNS—VERT: 3d. Ljubljana; 4d.50, Kozara; 5d. Belcista. HORIZ: 20d. Podgaric; 50d. Kragujevac.

441 Mailcoach

1974. Centenary of Universal Postal Union.

1592	**441**	80p. black, yellow and buff	10	10
1593	-	2d. black, red and rose	10	10
1594	-	8d. black, blue and pale blue	65	55

DESIGNS: 2d. U.P.U. H.Q. Building; 8d. Boeing 707 jetliner.

442 Montenegrin 25n. Stamp of 1874

1974. Montenegro Stamp Centenary.

1595		80p. bistre, gold and green	25	10
1596	**442**	6d. purple, gold and claret	45	40

DESIGN: 80p. Montenegrin 2n. stamp of 1874.

443 President Tito

1974

1597	**443**	50p. green	10	10
1598	**443**	80p. red	25	10
1599	**443**	1d.20 green	25	10
1600	**443**	2d. blue	30	10

444 Lenin

1974. 50th Death Anniv of Lenin.

1601	**444**	2d. black and silver	30	10

445 Red Cross Emblems

1974. Obligatory Tax. Red Cross Week.

1602	**445**	20p. multicoloured	25	10

446 "Dwarf" (Lepenski settlement, c. 4950 B.C.)

1974. Europa. Sculptures. Multicoloured.

1603		2d. Type **446**	35	30
1604		6d. "Widow and Child" (Ivan Mestrovic)	1·30	1·30

447 Great Tit

1974. Youth Day. Multicoloured.

1605		80p. Type **447**	25	10
1606		2d. Roses	65	20
1607		6d. Cabbage white (butterfly)	1·60	1·20

448 Congress Poster

1974. Tenth Yugoslav League of Communists' Congress, Belgrade.

1608	**448**	80p. multicoloured	10	10
1609	**448**	2d. multicoloured	25	10
1610	**448**	6d. multicoloured	60	40

449 Olympic Rings and Stadium

1974. Obligatory Tax. Olympic Games Fund.

1611	**449**	10p. multicoloured	25	10

450 Dish Aerial, Ivanjica

1974. Inauguration of Satellite Communications Station, Ivanjica.

1612	**450**	80p. blue	25	10
1613	-	6d. lilac	1·00	65

DESIGN: 6d. "Intelstat 4" in orbit.

451 World Cup

1974. World Cup Football Championship, West Germany.

1614	**451**	4d.50 multicoloured	1·10	70

452 Edelweiss and Klek Mountain

1974. Centenary of Croatian Mountaineers' Society.

1615	**452**	2d. multicoloured	30	10

453 "Children's Dance" (Jano Knjazovic)

1974. Paintings. Multicoloured.

1616		80p. Type **453**	25	10
1617		2d. "Crucified Rooster" (Ivan Generalic) (vert)	25	10
1618		5d. "Laundresses" (Ivan Lackovic) (vert)	50	35
1619		8d. "Dance" (Janko Brasic)	1·30	1·10

454 "Rooster and Flower" (Kaca Milinojsin)

1974. Children's Week and Sixth "Joy of Europe" Meeting, Belgrade. Children's Paintings. Multicoloured.

1620	1d.20 Type **454**	10	10
1621	3d.20 "Girl and Boy" (Eva Medrzecka) (vert)	25	10
1622	5d. "Cat and Kitten" (Jelena Anastasijevic)	60	30

455 Interior of Library

1974. Bicent of National and University Library.

1623	**455**	1d.20 black	25	10

456 "White Peonies" (Petar Dobrovic)

1974. Floral Paintings. Multicoloured.

1624	80p. Type **456**	10	10
1625	2d. "Carnations" (Vilko Gecan)	10	10
1626	3d. "Flowers" (Milan Konjovic)	10	10
1627	4d. "White Vase" (Sava Sumanovic)	25	15
1628	5d. "Branching Larkspurs" (Stane Kregar)	45	20
1629	8d. "Roses" (Petar Lubarda)	1 00	50

457 Title Page of Volume I

1975. 150th Anniv of "Matica Srpska" Annals.

1630	**457**	1d.20 black, olive and green	25	10

458 Dove and Map of Europe

1975. Second European Security and Co-operation Conference, Belgrade.

1631	**458**	3d.20 multicoloured	45	20
1632	**458**	8d. multicoloured	1·50	80

459 Gold-plated Bronze Ear-ring (14th–15th century), Alisici, Bosnia

1975. Archaeological Discoveries. Multicoloured.

1633	1d.20 Type **459**	10	10
1634	2d.10 Silver bracelet (19th-century), Kosovo	10	10
1635	3d.20 Gold-plated silver buckle (18th-century), Bitola	15	10
1636	5d. Gold-plated ring (14th-century), Novi Sad	25	10
1637	6d. Silver necklace (17th-century), Kosovo	55	30
1638	8d. Gold-plated bronze bracelet (18th-century), Bitola	65	55

460 "Svetozar Markovic" (sculpture by S. Bodnarov)

1975. Death Centenary of Svetozar Markovic (writer and statesman).

1639	**460**	1d.20 blue	40	10

461 "Fettered" (sculpture by F. Krsinic)

1975. International Women's Year.

1640	**461**	3d.20 brown and gold	25	20

462 Red Cross and Hands

1975. Obligatory Tax. Red Cross Week.

1681	**462**	20p. multicoloured	25	10

463 "Still Life with Eggs" (Mosa Pijade)

1975. Europa. Paintings. Multicoloured.

1682	3d.20 Type **463**	25	20
1683	8d. "The Three Graces" (Ivan Radovic)	70	65

464 "Liberation Monument" (Dzamonja)

1975. 30th Anniv of Liberation.

1684	**464**	3d.20 multicoloured	25	10

465 Garland Flower

1975. National Youth Day. Flowers. Multicoloured.

1685	1d.20 Type **465**	10	10
1686	2d.10 Touch-me-not balsam	10	10
1687	3d.20 Rose-mallow	10	10
1688	5d. Dusty cranesbill	25	15
1689	6d. Crocus	35	20
1690	8d. Rosebay willowherb	1·40	1·30

466 Games Emblem

1975. Obligatory Tax. Olympic Games Fund.

1691	**466**	10p. multicoloured	25	10

467 Canoeing

1975. World Canoeing Championships, Macedonia.

1692	**467**	3d.20 multicoloured	25	10

468 "Herzegovinian Insurgents in Ambush"

1975. Cent of Bosnian-Herzegovinian Uprising.

1693	**468**	1d.20 multicoloured	25	10

469 "Skopje Earthquake"

1975. Obligatory Tax. Solidarity Week.

1694	**469**	30p. black, grey and blue	25	10

See also Nos. 1885 and 1933.

470 Stjepan Mitrov Ljubisa

1975. Writers.

1695	**470**	1d.20 black and red	10	10
1696	-	2d.10 black and green	10	10
1697	-	3d.20 black and bistre	10	10
1698	-	5d. black and orange	15	10
1699	-	6d. black and green	25	10
1700	-	8d. black and blue	60	40

PORTRAITS: 2d.10, Ivan Prijatelj; 3d.20, Jakov Ignjatovic; 5d. Dragojla Jarnevic, 6d. Svetozar Corivic; 8d. Ivana Brlic Mazuranic.

471 "Young Lion" (A. Savic)

1975. Children's Week and Seventh "Joy of Europa" Meeting, Belgrade. Children's Paintings. Multicoloured.

1701	3d.20 Type **471**	35	10
1702	6d. "Baby in Pram"	1 30	55

472 Peace Dove within "EUROPA"

1975. European Security and Co-operation Conference, Helsinki.

1703	**472**	3d.20 multicoloured	15	10
1704	**472**	8d. multicoloured	65	40

473 Red Cross and Map within "100"

1975. Centenary of Red Cross. Multicoloured.

1705	1d.20 Type **473**	15	10
1706	8d. Red Cross and people	60	30

474 "Folk Kitchen" (Djordje Andrejevic-Kun)

1975. Republic Day. Paintings. Multicoloured.

1707	1d.20 Type **474**	10	10
1708	2d.10 "On the Doorstep" (Vinko Grdan)	10	10
1709	3d.20 "The Drunken Coach-load" (Marijan Detoni) (horiz)	10	10
1710	5d. "Lunch" (Tone Kralj) (horiz)	20	10
1711	6d. "Waterwheel" (Lazar Licenoski)	35	10
1712	8d. "Justice" (Krsto Hegedusic)	65	50

475 Diocletian's Palace, Split (3rd-century)

1975. European Architectural Heritage Year.

1713	**475**	1d.20 brown	10	10
1714	-	3d.20 black	10	10
1715	-	8d. blue	65	40

DESIGNS—VERT: 3d.20, House in Ohrid (19th century). HORIZ: 8d. Gracanica Monastery, Kosovo (14th century).

476 Ski Jumping

1976. Winter Olympic Games, Innsbruck.

1716	**476**	3d.20 blue	25	10
1717	-	8d. lake	80	50

DESIGN: 8d. Figure skating.

477 Red Flag

1976. Centenary of "Red Flag" Insurrection (workers' demonstration), Kragujevac.

1718	**477**	1d.20 multicoloured	25	10

478 Svetozar Miletic

1976. 150th Birth Anniv of Svetozar Miletic (politician).

1719	**478**	1d.20 green and grey	25	10

479 Bora Stankovic

1976. Birth Cent of Bora Stankovic (writer).

1720	**479**	1d.20 red, brown and yellow	25	10

480 "King Matthias" (sculpture, J. Pogorelec)

1976. Europa. Handicrafts. Multicoloured.

1721	3d.20 Type **480**	25	10
1722	8d. Base of beaker	45	40

481 Ivan Cankar

1976. Birth Centenary of Ivan Cankar (Slovenian writer).

1723	**481**	1d.20 purple, brown and pink	25	10

482 Stylized Figure

1976. Obligatory Tax. Red Cross Week.

1724	**482**	20p. multicoloured	1·20	75

483 Electric Train
crossing Viaduct

1976. Inauguration of Belgrade–Bar Railway.

1725	**483**	3d.20 brown	35	20
1726	–	8d. blue	1·00	50

DESIGN: 8d. Electric train crossing bridge.

484 Emperor Dragonfly

1976. Youth Day. Freshwater Fauna. Multicoloured.

1727	1d.20 Type **484**	35	30
1728	2d.10 River snail	35	30
1729	3d.20 Rudd	35	30
1730	5d. Common frog	1·20	1·00
1731	6d. Ferruginous duck	1·20	1·00
1732	8d. Muskrat	3·50	3·25

485 Vladimir
Nazor

1976. Birth Centenary of Vladimir Nazor (writer).

1733	**485**	1d.20 blue and lilac	25	15

486 "Battle of Vucji Dol" (from
"Eagle" journal of 1876)

1976. Centenary of Montenegrin Liberation Wars.

1734	**486**	1d.20 brown, yellow and gold	25	15

487 Jug, Aleksandrovac,
Serbia

1976. Ancient Pottery. Multicoloured.

1735	1d.20 Type **487**	10	10
1736	2d.10 Pitcher, Ptuj, Slovenia	10	10
1737	3d.20 Coffee-pot, Visnjica, Sarajevo	10	10
1738	5d. Pitcher, Backi Breg, Vojvodina	20	10
1739	6d. Goblet, Vranestica, Macedonia	30	15
1740	8d. Jug, Prizren, Kosovo	75	40

488 Nikola Tesla
Monument and Niagara
Falls

1976. 120th Birth Anniv of Nikola Tesla (scientist).

1741	**488**	5d. blue and green	60	40

489 Long Jumping

1976. Olympic Games, Montreal.

1742	**489**	1d.20 purple	25	10
1743	–	3d.20 green	25	10
1744	–	5d. brown	25	10
1745	–	8d. blue	1·80	1·20

DESIGNS: 3d.20, Handball; 5d. Shooting; 8d. Rowing.

490 Stadium and
Olympic Rings

1976. Obligatory Tax. Olympic Games Fund.

1746	**490**	10p. blue	25	10

491 Globe

1976. Fifth Non-aligned Nations' Summit Conf, Colombo.

1747	**491**	4d.90 multicoloured	35	10

492 "Navy Day" (Nikola
Mitar)

1976. Children's Week and Eighth "Joy of Europe"
Meeting, Belgrade. Children's Paintings.
Multicoloured.

1748	4d.90 Type **492**	30	10
1749	8d. "Children's Trains" (Wiggo Gulbrandsen)	75	50

493 "Battle of
Montenegrins" (Djura
Jaksic)

1976. Paintings. Historical Events. Multicoloured.

1750	1d.20 Type **493**	10	10
1751	2d.10 "Nikola Subic Zrinjski at Siget" (Oton Ivekovic)	10	10
1752	3d.20 "Herzegovinian Fugitives" (Uros Predic) (horiz)	15	10
1753	5d. "The Razlovic Uprising" (Borko Lazeski) (horiz)	25	10
1754	6d. "Enthronement of the Slovenian Duke, Gosposvetsko Field" (Anton Gojmir Kos) (horiz)	45	20
1755	8d. "Breach of the Solun Front" (Veljko Stanojevic) (horiz)	1·20	1·00

1976. No. 1203 surch.

1756	1d. on 85p. purple	60	20

495 Nenadovic
(after Uros
Knezevic)

1977. Birth Bicentenary of Prota Mateja Nenadovic
(soldier and diplomat).

1757	**495**	4d.90 multicoloured	35	20

496 Rajko
Zinzifov

1977. Death Centenary of Rajko Zinzifov (writer).

1758	**496**	1d.50 brown and sepia	25	10

497 Phlox

1977. Flowers. Multicoloured.

1759	1d.50 Type **497**	10	10
1760	3d.40 Tiger lily	15	10
1761	4d.90 Bleeding heart	25	10
1762	6d. Zinnia	35	10
1763	8d. French marigold	45	20
1764	10d. Geranium	1·50	1·00

498 Institute Building

1977. 150th Anniv of Croatian Music Institute.

1765	**498**	4d.90 brown and black	35	20

499 Alojz Kraigher

1977. Birth Centenary of Alojz Kraigher (author).

1766	**499**	1d.50 brown and black	25	10

500 "Kotor Bay" (Milo
Milunovic)

1977. Europa. Landscapes. Multicoloured.

1767	4d.90 Type **500**	25	10
1768	10d. "Zagorje in November" (Ljubo Babic)	60	50

501 Figure and
Emblems

1977. Obligatory Tax. Red Cross Week.

1769	**501**	20p. red and brown	3·50	1·00
1770	**501**	50p. red and green	3·00	85
1771	**501**	1d. red and blue	2·30	50

502 "President Tito"
(Omer Mujadzic)

1977. 85th Birthday of President Tito.

1772	**502**	1d.50 brown, olive and gold	25	10
1773	**502**	4d.90 brown, pink and gold	35	20
1774	**502**	8d. brown, olive and gold	70	50

503 Alpine Scene

1977. International Environment Protection Day.
Multicoloured.

1775	4d.90 Type **503**	35	10
1776	10d. Plitvice waterfall and red-breasted flycatcher	80	50

504 Petar Kocic

1977. Birth Centenary of Petar Kocic (writer).

1777	**504**	1d.50 mauve and green	25	10

505 Dove and Map of
Europe

1977. European Security and Co-operation Conf,
Belgrade.

1778	**505**	4d.90 multicoloured	35	20
1779	**505**	10d. multicoloured	1·90	1·70

506 Tree

1977. Obligatory Tax. Anti-tuberculosis Week.

1780	**506**	50p. multicoloured	17·00	17·00
1781	**506**	1d. multicoloured	1·20	1·00

507 "Bather" (Mrak
Franci)

1977. Children's Week and Ninth "Joy of Europe" Meeting,
Belgrade. Children's Paintings. Multicoloured.

1782	4d.90 Type **507**	35	10
1783	10d. "One Fruit into Pail — the other into Mouth" (Tanja Ilinskaja)	80	55

508 Congress Building,
Belgrade

1977. European Security and Co-operation Conf,
Belgrade.

1784	**508**	4d.90 grey, blue and gold	35	20
1785	**508**	10d. red, rose and gold	2·20	2·00

509 Exhibition
Emblem

1977. "Balkanphila 6" Stamp Exhibition, Belgrade.

1786	**509**	4d.90 multicoloured	25	10

510 Double Flute

1977. Musical Instruments in Ethnographical Museum,
Belgrade.

1787	**510**	1d.50 brown and yellow	10	10
1788	–	3d.40 brown and green	10	10
1789	–	4d.90 yellow and brown	15	10
1790	–	6d. brown and blue	25	10
1791	–	8d. brown and orange	35	20
1792	–	10d. brown and green	80	65

DESIGN: 3d.40, Tambura (string instrument); 4d.90, Gusle
(string instrument); 6d. Lijerica (string insrtument); 8d.
Bagpipe; 10d. Pan's flute.

511 Ivan Vavpotic

1977. Self-portraits. Multicoloured.

1793	1d.50 Type **511**	10	10
1794	3d.40 Mihailo Vukotic	15	10
1795	4d.90 Kosta Hakman	20	10

1796	6d. Miroslav Kraljevic	25	15
1797	8d. Nikola Martinovski	35	20
1798	10d. Milena Paviovic-Barili	75	65

512 Globe and Olympic Rings

1977. Obligatory Tax. Olympic Games Fund.

1799	**512**	10p. yellow, turq & bl	25	10

513 "Ceremony of Testaccio" (miniature from Officum Virginis)

1978. 400th Death Anniv of Julije Klovic (Croat miniaturist). Multicoloured.

1800		4d.90 Type **513**	20	10
1801		10d. "Portrait of Klovic" (El Greco)	50	35

514 Pre-stamp Letter (Bavaniste-Kubin)

1978. Post Office Museum Exhibits. Multicoloured.

1802		1d.50 Type **514**	10	10
1803		3d.40 19th-century mail box	10	10
1804		4d.90 Ericsson Induction table telephone	15	10
1805		10d. Morse's first electro-magnetic telegraph set	45	40

515 Battle of Pirot

1978. Centenary of Serbo-Turkish War.

1806	**515**	1d.50 multicoloured	2·50	2·20

516 S-49A Trainer, 1949

1978. Aeronautical Day.

1807	**516**	1d.50 pink, brown and orange	10	10
1808	-	3d.40 blue, black and slate	20	10
1809	-	4d.90 black and brown	30	10
1810	-	10d. yellow, brown & grn	85	65

DESIGNS: 3d.40, SOKO Gabeb 3 jet trainer; 4d.90, UTVA 75 elementary trainer; 10d. Jurom Orao jet fighter.

517 Golubac

1978. Europa. Multicoloured.

1811		4d.90 Type **517**	25	20
1812		10d. St. Naum Monastery	1·20	1·10

518 Boxing Glove on Glove

1978. Second World Amateur Boxing Championship, Belgrade.

1813	**518**	4d.90 brown, blue and deep blue	35	10

519 Symbols of Red Crescent, Red Cross and Red Lion

1978. Obligatory Tax. Red Cross Week. No. 1814 surch.

1814	**519**	20p. on 1d. blue and red	75	35
1815	**519**	1d. blue and red	35	20

520 Honey Bee

1978. Bees. Multicoloured.

1816		1d.50 Type **520**	10	10
1817		3d.40 "Halictus scabiosae" (mining bee)	25	15
1818		4d.90 Blue carpenter bee	50	20
1819		10d. Buff-tailed bumble bee	1·40	1·20

521 Filip Filipovic and Radovan Dragovic

1978. Birth Centenaries of F. Filipovic and R. Dragovic (socialist movement leaders).

1820	**521**	1d.50 green and red	25	10

522 President Tito (poster)

1978. 11th Communist League Congress. Multicoloured.

1821		2d. Type **522**	25	10
1822		4d.90 Hammer and sickle (poster)	50	35
MS1823	70×93 mm. 15d. As No. 1821. Imperf		3·25	3·00

1978. Various stamps surch.

1829	-	35p. on 10p. brown (No. 1642)	1·50	30
1830	332	60p. on 85p. blue (No. 1271)	1·50	30
1831	443	80p. on 1d.20 green (No. 1599)	1·50	30
1832	-	2d. on 1d. green (No. 1657)	6·50	20
1833	-	3d.40 on 2d.10 green (No. 1662)	60	20

524 Conference Emblem over Belgrade

1978. Conference of Foreign Ministers of Non-aligned Countries.

1834	**524**	4d.90 blue and light blue	25	10

525 Championship Emblem

1978. 14th Kayak and Canoe "Still Water" World Championships, Belgrade.

1835	**525**	4d.90 black, blue and light blue	25	10

526 North Face, Mount Triglav

1978. Bicent of First Ascent of Mount Triglav.

1836	**526**	2d. multicoloured	25	10

527 Hand holding Flame

1978. Obligatory Tax. Anti-tuberculosis Week.

1837	**527**	1d. multicoloured	1·00	55

528 Black Lake, Durmitor

1978. Protection of the Environment. Multicoloured.

1838		4d.90 Type **528**	25	10
1839		10d. River Tara	75	55

529 Olympic Rings on Map of World

1978. Obligatory Tax. Olympic Games Fund.

1840	**529**	30p. multicoloured	50	20

530 Star Map

1978. 29th International Astronautical Federation Congress, Dubrovnik.

1841	**530**	4d.90 multicoloured	25	10

531 "People in Forest" (Ivana Balen)

1978. Children's Week and Tenth "Joy of Europe" Meeting, Belgrade. Multicoloured.

1842		4d.90 Type **531**	25	10
1843		10d. "Family round a Pond" (Vincent Christel)	70	50

532 Seal

1978. Centenary of Kresna Uprising.

1844	**532**	2d. black, brown and gold	25	10

533 Old College Building

1978. Bicentenary of Teachers' Training College, Sombor.

1845	**533**	2d. brown, yellow & gold	25	10

534 Red Cross

1978. Centenary of Croatian Red Cross.

1846	**534**	2d. red, blue and black	25	10

535 Metallic Sculpture "XXII" (Dusan Dzamonja)

1978. Modern Sculpture.

1847	**535**	2d. black, brown & silver	10	10
1848	-	3d.40 blue, grey and silver	20	10
1849	-	4d.90 olive, brown and silver	20	10
1850	-	10d. brown, buff and silver	80	55

DESIGNS—VERT: 3d.40, "Circulation in Space I" (Vojin Bakic); 4d.90, "Tectonic Octopod" (Olga Jevric). HORIZ: 10d. "The Tree of Life" (Drago Trsar).

536 "Crossing the Neretva" (Ismet Mujezinovic)

1978. 35th Anniv of Battle of Neretva.

1851	**536**	2d. multicoloured	25	10

537 "People from the Seine" (Marijan Detoni)

1978. Republic Day. Graphic Art.

1852	**537**	2d. black, stone and gold	10	10
1853	-	3d.40 black, grey and gold	10	10
1854	-	4d.90 black, yellow and gold	25	10
1855	-	6d. black, flesh and gold	35	20
1856	-	10d. black, flesh and gold	1·00	90

DESIGNS—3d.40, "Labourers" (Maksim Sedej); 4d.90, "Felling of Trees" (Daniel Ozmo); 6d. "At a Meal" (Pivo Karamatijevic); 10d. "They are not afraid, even at a most loathsome crime" (Djordje Andrejevic Kun).

538 Eurasian Red Squirrel

1978. New Year. Multicoloured.

1857		1d.50 Type **538**	25	10
1858		1d.50 Larch	25	10
1859		2d. Red deer	25	10
1860		2d. Sycamore	25	10
1861		3d.40 Rock partridge (pink background)	50	20
1861a		3d.40 Rock partridge (green background)	50	20
1862		3d.40 Alder (pink background)	50	20
1862a		3d.40 Alder (green background)	50	20
1863		4d.90 Western capercaillie (green background)	60	20
1863a		4d.90 Western capercaillie (yellow background)	60	20
1864		4d.90 Oak (green background)	60	20
1864a		4d.90 Oak (yellow background)	60	20

539 Masthead

1979. 75th Anniv of "Politika" Newspaper.

1865	**539**	2d. black and gold	25	10

540 Flags

1979. Tenth Anniv of Self-Managers' Meeting.
1866 **540** 2d. multicoloured 25 10

541 Games Mascot

1979. Obligatory Tax. Mediterranean Games Fund.
1867 **541** 1d. blue and deep blue 35 20
See also No. 1886.

542 Child

1979. International Year of the Child.
1868 **542** 4d.90 blue and gold 55 35

543 Sabre, Mace and Enamluk (box holding Koranic texts)

1979. Ancient Weapons from Ethnographic Museum, Belgrade. Multicoloured.
1869 2d. Type **543** 10 10
1870 3d.40 Pistol and ammunition stick 10 10
1871 4d.90 Carbine and powder-horn 25 10
1872 10d. Rifle and cartridge-pouch 75 65

544 Hammer and Sickle on Star

1979. 60th Anniv of Yugoslav Communist Party and League for Communist Youth.
1873 **544** 2d. multicoloured 10 10
1874 **544** 4d.90 multicoloured 25 10

545 University

1979. 30th Anniv of Cyril and Methodius University, Skopje.
1875 **545** 2d. brown, buff and pink 25 10

546 "Panorama of Belgrade" (Carl Goebel)

1979. Europa. Multicoloured.
1876 4d.90 Type **546** 60 55
1877 10d. Postilion and view of Ljubljana (after Jan van der Heyden) 75 65

547 Stylized Bird

1979. Obligatory Tax. Red Cross Week.
1878 **547** 1d. turquoise, blue & red 25 10

548 Alpine Sow-thistle

1979. Alpine Flowers. Multicoloured.
1879 2d. Type **548** 10 10
1880 3d.40 "Anemone narcissiflora" 10 10
1881 4d.90 Milk-vetch 25 10
1882 10d. Alpine clover 1·10 1·00

549 Milutin Milankovic (after Paja Jovanovic)

1979. Birth Centenary of Milutin Milankovic (scientist).
1883 **549** 4d.90 multicoloured 35 10

550 Kosta Abrasevic

1979. Birth Centenary of Kosta Abrasevic (poet).
1884 **550** 2d. grey, pink and black 25 10

1979. Obligatory Tax. Solidarity Week. As T **469** but inscribed "1.-7.VI".
1885 30p. black, grey and blue 50 30
See also Nos. 1933 and 2218/19.

1979. Obligatory Tax. Mediterranean Games Fund. As No. 1867 but colour changed.
1886 **541** 1d. blue and deep blue 25 10

551 Rowing Crew

1979. Ninth World Rowing Championships. Bled.
1887 **551** 4d.90 multicoloured 50 10

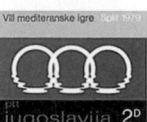
552 Games Emblem

1979. Eighth Mediterranean Games. Multicoloured.
1888 2d. Type **552** 10 10
1889 4d.90 Mascot and emblem 20 10
1890 10d. Map and flags of participating countries 55 35

553 Girl playing Hopscotch

1979. Obligatory Tax. Anti-tuberculosis Week.
1891 **553** 1d. multicoloured 50 20

554 Arms of Zagreb, 1499

1979. 450th Anniv of Zagreb Postal Service.
1892 **554** 2d. grey and red 25 10

555 Lake Palic

1979. Environmental Protection. Multicoloured.
1893 4d.90 Type **555** 25 10
1894 10d. Lake in Prokletije range 60 55

556 Emblems

1979. Meeting of International Bank for Reconstruction and Development and of International Monetary Fund.
1895 **556** 4d.90 multicoloured 25 10
1896 **556** 10d. multicoloured 60 45

557 Street in Winter (Mirjana Markovic)

1979. 11th "Joy of Europe" Meeting, Belgrade. Children's Paintings. Multicoloured.
1897 4d.90 Type **557** 30 10
1898 10d. House and garden (Jacques An) 75 65

558 Milhailo Pupin

1979. 125th Birth Anniv of Milhailo Pupin (scientist).
1899 **558** 4d.90 brown, light blue and blue 30 10

559 Olympic Rings

1979. Obligatory Tax. Olympic Games Fund.
1900 **559** 30p. red and blue 25 10
MS1900 60×83 mm. 30d. brown, gold and silver. Imperf 1·25 1·25
DESIGN: 30d. Lenin Monument and Star of Order.

560 Marko Cepenkov

1979. 150th Anniv of Marko Cepenkov (author and folklorist).
1901 **560** 2d. brown, green and olive 25 10

561 Pristina University

1979. Tenth Anniv of Pristina University.
1902 **561** 2d. multicoloured 25 10

562 Lion on Column (Trogir Cathedral)

1979. Romanesque Sculpture. Multicoloured.
1903 2d. Type **562** 10 10
1904 3d.40 Apostle (detail of choir stall, Split Cathedral) 20 10
1905 4d.90 Window (Church of the Ascension, Decani) 25 10
1906 6d. Detail of Buvina door (Split Cathedral) 35 10
1907 10d. Virgin and Child (West door, Church of the Virgin, Studenica) 55 45

563 Sarajevo University

1979. 30th Anniv of Sarajevo University.
1908 **563** 2d. black, brown and grey 25 10

564 Djakovic and Hecimovic

1979. 50th Death Anniv of Djuro Djakovic and Nikola Hecimovic (leaders of socialist movement).
1909 **564** 2d. multicoloured 25 10

565 Paddle-steamer "Srbija"

1979. Danube Conference. Multicoloured.
1910 4d.90 Paddle-steamer "Deligrad" 75 65
1911 10d. Type **565** 1·60 1·40

566 Milton Manaki

1980. Birth Centenary of Milton Manaki (first Balkan film maker).
1912 **566** 2d. purple, yellow and brown 25 10

567 Edvard Kardelj

1980. 70th Birth Anniv of Edvard Kardelj (revolutionary).
1913 **567** 2d. multicoloured 25 10

1980. Renaming of Ploce as Kardeljevo. No. 1913 optd **PLOCE-1980-KARDELJEVO**.
1914 2d. multicoloured 25 10

569 Speed Skating

1980. Winter Olympic Games, Lake Placid. Multicoloured.
1915 4d.90 Type **569** 35 20
1916 10d. Skiing 2·20 2·00

570 Belgrade University

1980. 75th Anniv of Belgrade University.
1917 **570** 2d. multicoloured 25 10

571 Fencing

1980. Olympic Games, Moscow. Multicoloured.
1918 2d. Type **571** 10 10
1919 3d.40 Cycling 20 10
1920 4d.90 Hockey 25 15
1921 10d. Archery 75 65

572 President Tito
(relief by Antun
Augustincic)

1980. Europa. Multicoloured.
| 1922 | 4d.90 Type **572** | 30 | 30 |
| 1923 | 13d. Portrait of Tito by Djordje Prudnikov | 1·60 | 1·40 |

573 Pres. Tito

1980. Death of President Tito. Portraits by Bozidar Jakac.
| 1924 | **573** | 2d.50 purple | 35 | 10 |
| 1925 | - | 4d.90 black | 1·00 | 1·00 |

DESIGN: 4d.90, Different portrait of President Tito.

574 Sculpture of
S. Kovacevic

1980. Obligatory Tax. Red Cross Week.
| 1926 | **574** | 1d. multicoloured | 50 | 20 |

575 Šava Kovacevic

1980. 75th Birth Anniv of Šava Kovacevic (partisan).
| 1927 | **575** | 2d. brown, orange & yell | 25 | 10 |

576 Estafette and Letter
from Youth of Belgrade,
1945

1980. 35th Anniv of Tito's 1st Estafette (youth celebration
of Tito's birthday).
| 1928 | **576** | 2d. multicoloured | 25 | 10 |

577 Flying
Gurnard

1980. Adriatic Sea Fauna. Multicoloured.
1929	2d. Type **577**	20	10
1930	3d.40 Turtle	30	15
1931	4d.90 Little tern	45	20
1932	10d. Common dolphin	2·20	2·00

1980. Obligatory Tax. Solidarity Week. As No. 1885.
| 1933 | **469** | 1d. black, grey and blue | 50 | 35 |

578 Decius
Trajan (249–51)

1980. Roman Emperors on Coins. Multicoloured.
1934	2d. Type **578**	10	10
1935	3d.40 Aurelian (270–75)	20	10
1936	4d.90 Probus (276–82)	35	10
1937	10d. Diocletian (284–305)	75	45

1980. Nos. 1660 and 1652 surch.
| 1938 | 2d.50 on 1d.50 red | 60 | 10 |
| 1939 | 5d. on 75p. purple | 2·20 | 20 |

See also Nos. 1992/3.

580 Lipica Horses

1980. 400th Anniv of Lipica Stud Farm.
| 1940 | **580** | 2d.50 black | 25 | 10 |

581 Tito

1980. 30th Anniv of Self-Management Law.
| 1941 | **581** | 2d. deep red and red | 25 | 10 |

582 Novi Sad University

1980. 20th Anniv Novi Sad University.
| 1942 | **582** | 2d.50 green | 25 | 10 |

583 Mljet

1980. Protection of the Environment. National Parks.
Multicoloured.
| 1943 | 4d.90 Type **583** | 35 | 15 |
| 1944 | 13d. Galicica, Ohrid | 80 | 55 |

584 Pyrrhotine

1980. Crystals. Multicoloured.
1945	2d.50 Type **584**	10	10
1946	3d.40 Dolomite	20	10
1947	4d.90 Sphalerite	30	20
1948	13d. Wulfenite	75	65

585 Lake

1980. Obligatory Tax. Anti-tuberculosis Week.
| 1949 | **585** | 1d. multicoloured | 35 | 10 |

586 Kotor

1980. 21st Session of UNESCO General Conference,
Belgrade.
| 1950 | **586** | 4d.90 blue, gold, and deep blue | 35 | 10 |

587 "Children with
Balloons" (Gabrijela
Radojevic)

1980. 12th "Joy of Europe" Meeting, Belgrade. Children's
Drawings. Multicoloured.
| 1951 | 4d.90 Type **587** | 30 | 15 |
| 1952 | 13d. "Face" (Renata Pisarcikova) | 80 | 55 |

588 Olympic Flag
and Globe

1980. Obligatory Tax. Olympic Games Fund.
| 1953 | **588** | 50p. multicoloured | 25 | 10 |

589 Dove and Madrid

1980. European Security and Co-operation Conference,
Madrid.
| 1954 | **589** | 4d.90 green and deep green | 25 | 10 |
| 1955 | **589** | 13d. bistre and brown | 65 | 55 |

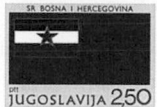

590 Flag of Bosnia and
Herzegovina Socialist
Republic

1980. Flags of Yugoslav Socialist Republics and of Federal
Republic.
1956	**590**	2d.50 multicoloured	20	10
1957	-	2d.50 multicoloured	20	10
1958	-	2d.50 multicoloured	20	10
1959	-	2d.50 multicoloured	20	10
1960	-	2d.50 multicoloured	20	10
1961	-	2d.50 red, gold and grey	20	10
1962	-	2d.50 multicoloured	20	10
1963	-	2d.50 multicoloured	20	10

DESIGNS: No. 1957, Montenegro; 1958, Croatia; 1959, Yugoslavia (inscr in Roman alphabet); 1960, Yugoslavia (inscr in Cyrillic alphabet); 1961, Macedonia; 1962, Slovenia; 1963, Serbia.

591 "Complaint" (Milos
Vuskovic)

1980. Paintings. Multicoloured.
1964	2d.50 "Woman in a Straw Hat" (Stojan Aralica) (horiz)	10	10
1965	3d.40 "Atelier No. 1" (Gabrijel Stupica) (horiz)	10	10
1966	4d.90 "To the Glory of Sutjeska Fighters" (detail Ismet Mujezinovic) (horiz)	15	10
1967	8d. "Serenity" (Marino Tartaglia)	25	10
1968	13d. Type **591**	1·20	1·10

592 Sports Complex,
Novi Sad

1980. Obligatory Tax. World Table Tennis Championships,
Novi Sad.
| 1969 | **592** | 1d. green, yellow and blue | 25 | 10 |

593 Ivan Ribar

1981. Birth Centenary of Ivan Ribar (politician).
| 1970 | **593** | 2d.50 black and red | 25 | 10 |

594 "Cementusa" Hand
Bomb

1981. Partisan Arms in Belgrade Military Museum.
1971	**594**	3d.50 black and red	10	10
1972	-	5d.60 black and green	20	10
1973	-	8d. black and brown	25	15
1974	-	13d. black and purple	75	65

DESIGNS: 5d.60, "Partizanka" rifle; 8d. Cannon; 13d. Tank.

595 Virgin of Eleousa
Monastery

1981. 900th Anniv of Virgin of Eleousa Monastery,
Veljusa, Macedonia.
| 1975 | **595** | 3d.50 grey, brown and blue | 1·00 | 90 |

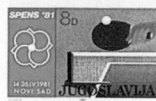

596 Table Tennis

1981. "SPENS '81" World Table Tennis Championships,
Novi Sad.
| 1976 | **596** | 8d. multicoloured | 45 | 20 |

597 "Lamp"

1981. Obligatory Tax. Red Cross Week.
| 1977 | **597** | 1d. multicoloured | 25 | 10 |

598 "Herzegovinian
Wedding" (detail)

1981. Europa. Paintings by Nikola Arsenovic.
Multicoloured.
| 1978 | 8d. Type **598** | 50 | 20 |
| 1979 | 13d. "Witnesses at a Wedding" | 60 | 40 |

599 Tucovic and
Dimitrije Tucovic Square

1981. Birth Centenary of Dimitrije Tucovic (socialist
leader).
| 1980 | **599** | 3d.50 blue and red | 25 | 10 |

600 Tito (after
Milivoje Unkovic)

1981. 89th Birth Anniv of Tito.
| 1981 | **600** | 3d.50 multicoloured | 50 | 20 |

601 Sunflower

1981. Cultivated Plants. Multicoloured.
1982	3d.50 Type **601**	15	10
1983	5d.60 Hop	20	10
1984	8d. Corn	35	20
1985	13d. Wheat	70	55

602 Congress
Emblem

1981. Third Congress of Self-managers.
1986 **602** 3d.50 multicoloured 25 10

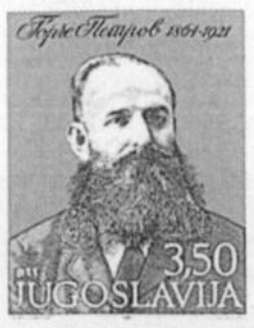

603 Djordje Petrov

1981. 60th Death Anniv of Djordje Petrov (politician).
1987 **603** 3d.50 yellow and red 25 10

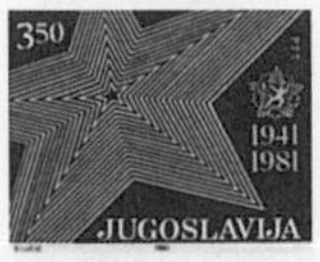

604 Star

1981. 40th Anniv of Yugoslav Insurrection.
1988 **604** 3d.50 yellow and red 25 10
1989 **604** 8d. orange and red 45 20
MS1990 60×83 mm. 30d. brown, gold and silver. Imperf 1·90 1·90
DESIGN: 30d. Lenin Monument and Star of Order.

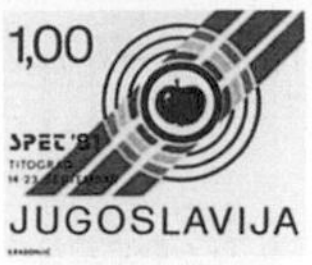

605 Apple and Target

1981. Obligatory Tax. "Spet 81" European Shooting Championships, Titograd.
1991 **605** 1d. blue, red and orange 9·00 9·00

1981. Nos. 1666 and 1669 surch.
1992 3d.50 on 3d.40 green 60 20
1993 5d. on 4d.90 blue 1·20 20

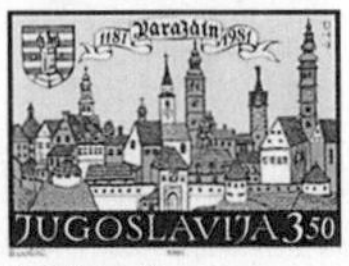

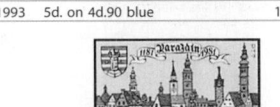

606 Varazdin (18th-century illustration)

1981. 800th Anniv of Varazdin.
1994 **606** 3d.50 yellow and blue 25 10

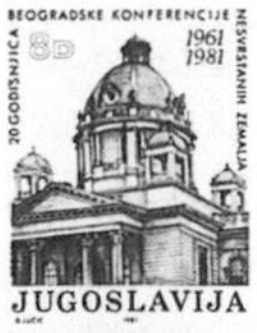

607 Parliament Building, Belgrade

1981. 20th Anniv of 1st Non-aligned Countries Conference, Belgrade.
1995 **607** 8d. blue and red 25 10

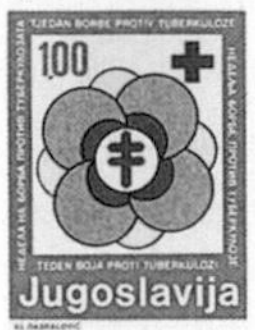

608 "Flower"

1981. Obligatory Tax. Anti-tuberculosis Week.
1996 **608** 1d. red, yellow and blue 25 10

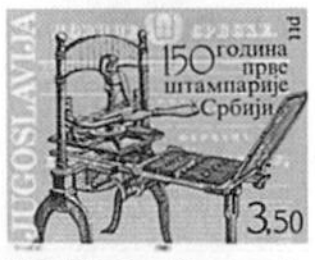

609 Printing Press and Serbian Newspaper

1981. 150th Anniv of First Serbian Printing House.
1997 **609** 3d.50 pink and blue 25 10

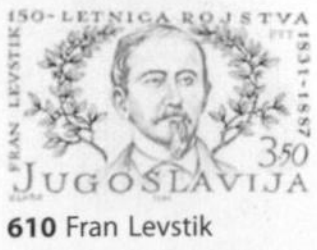

610 Fran Levstik

1981. 150th Birth Anniv of Fran Levstik (writer).
1998 **610** 3d.50 grey and red 25 10

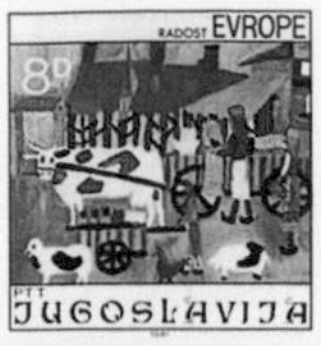

611 "Village Scene" (Saso Arsovski)

1981. 13th "Joy of Europe" Meeting, Belgrade. Children's Drawings. Multicoloured.
1999 8d. Type **611** 25 10
2000 13d. "Skiers" (Aino Jokinen) 55 45

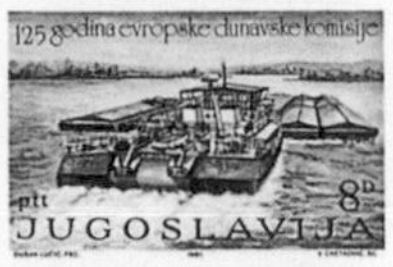

612 Tug "Karlovac" pushing Barges

1981. 125th Anniv of European Danube Commission. Multicoloured.
2001 8d. Type **612** 35 35
2002 13d. Paddle-steamer towed by steam railway locomotive on Sip Canal 85 80

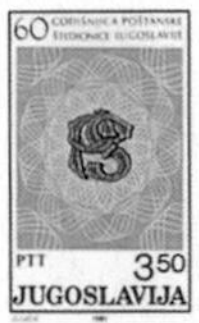

613 Postal Savings Bank Emblem

1981. 60th Anniv of Postal Savings Bank.
2003 **613** 3d.50 red and yellow 25 10

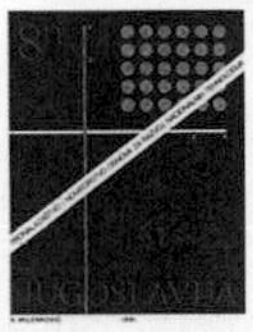

614 Emblem

1982. World Intellectual Property Organization Conference.
2004 **614** 8d. red and gold 35 20

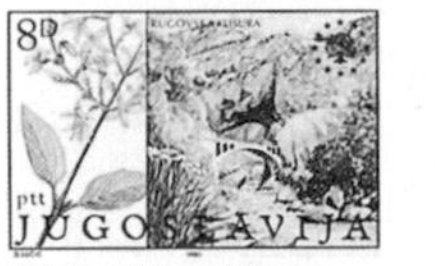

615 Forsythia and Rugovo Ravine

1981. Protection of Nature. Multicoloured.
2005 8d. Type **615** 35 20
2006 13d. Lynx and Prokletije 1·10 1·00

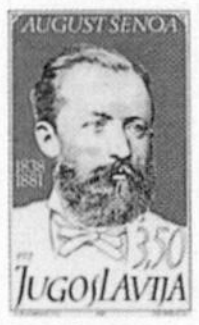

616 August Senoa

1981. Death Centenary of August Senoa (writer).
2007 **616** 3d.50 purple and brown 25 10

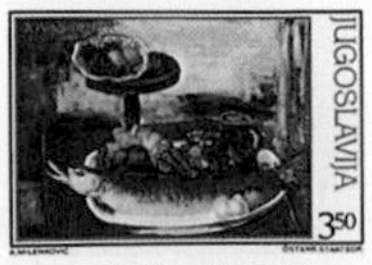

617 "Still Life with Fish" (Jovan Bijelic)

1981. Paintings of Animals. Multicoloured.
2008 3d.50 Type **617** 25 10
2009 5d.60 "Raven" (Milo Milunovic) 25 10
2010 8d. "Bird on Blue Background" (Marko Celebonovic) 25 10
2011 10d. "Horses" (Peter Lubarda) 45 20
2012 13d. "Sheep" (Nikola Masic) 85 80

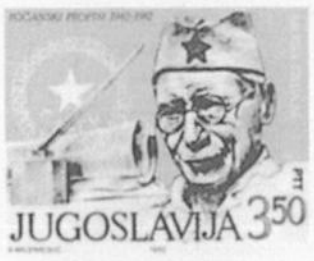

618 Mosa Pijade (politician)

1982. 40th Anniv of Foca Regulations.
2013 **618** 3d.50 blue and mauve 25 10

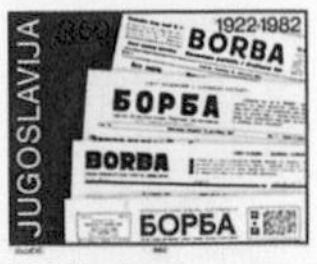

619 Mastheads

1982. 60th Anniv of "Borba" (newspaper).
2014 **619** 3d.50 black and red 25 10

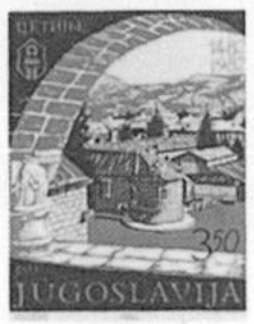

620 Cetinje

1982. 500th Anniv of City of Cetinje.
2015 **620** 3d.50 brown and black 25 10

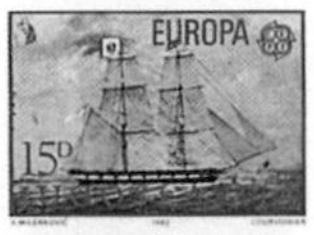

621 Visin's Ship "Splendido"

1982. Europa. Multicoloured.
2016 8d. Capt. Ivo Visin (first Yugoslav to sail round world) and naval chart 35 20
2017 15d. Type **621** 60 55

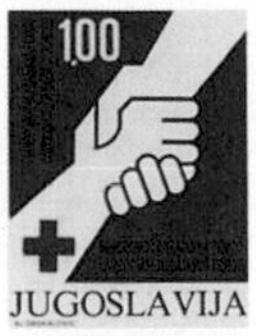

622 Clasped Hands

1982. Obligatory Tax. Red Cross Week.
2018 **622** 1d. black and red 25 10

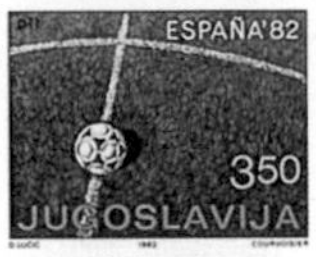

623 Ball placed for Kick-off

1982. World Cup Football Championship, Spain. Sheet 97×84 mm containing T **623** and similar horiz designs. Multicoloured.
MS2019 3d.50 Type **623**; 5d.60, Ball placed for corner kick; 8d. Ball in top of net; 15d. Player carrying ball under arm 2·50 2·50

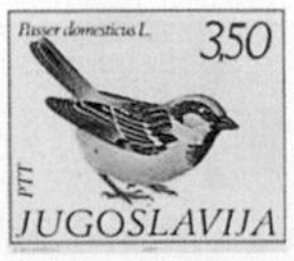

624 House Sparrow (male)

1982. Multicoloured.
2020 3d.50 Type **624** 25 10
2021 5d.60 House sparrow (female) 30 20
2022 8d. Spanish sparrow (female) 50 45
2023 15d. Eurasian tree sparrow (male) 1·70 1·60

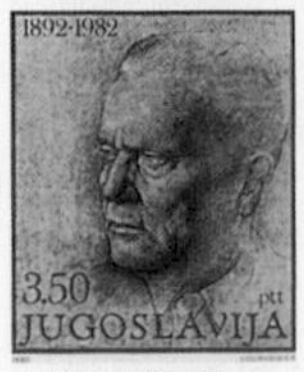

625 Tito (after Dragan Dosen)

1982. 90th Birth Anniv of Tito.
2024 **625** 3d.50 multicoloured 25 10

626 Poster (Dobrilo Nikolic)

1982. 12th Communist League Congress, Belgrade.
2025 **626** 3d.50 brown, orge & red 25 10
2026 **626** 8d. light grey, grey and red 35 20
MS2027 70×95 mm. **626** 10d. orange and scarlet; 20d. grey, olive and scarlet 1·60 1·40

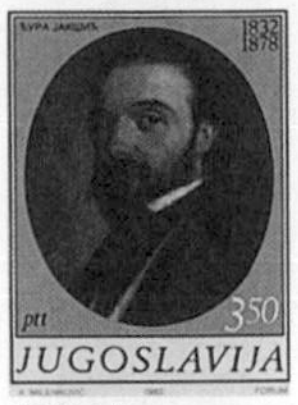

627 Jaksic (self-portrait)

1982. 150th Birth Anniv of Dura Jaksic (writer and painter).
2028 **627** 3d.50 multicoloured 25 10

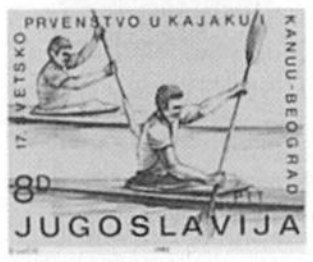

628 Kayaks

1982. Sports Championships.
2029 **628** 8d. light blue and blue 75 35
2030 - 8d. light green and green 75 35
2031 - 8d. pink and red 75 35
DESIGNS AND EVENTS: No. 2029, Type **628** (17th World Kayak and Canoe Still Water Championships, Belgrade); 2030, Weightlifting(36th World Weightlifting Championships, Ljubljana); 2031, Gymnastics (6th World Gymnastics Cup, Zagreb).

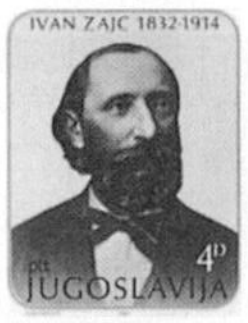

629 Ivan Zajc

1982. 150th Birth Anniv of Ivan Zajc (composer).
2032 **629** 4d. orange and brown 25 10

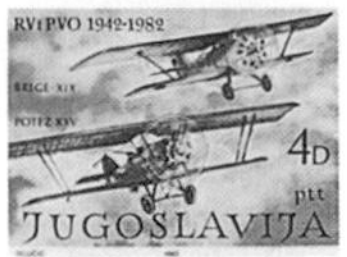

630 Breguet 19 and Potez 25 Biplanes

1982. 40th Anniv of Air Force, Anti-aircraft Defence and Navy.
2033 **630** 4d. black and blue 25 10
2034 - 6d.10 multicoloured 30 10
2035 - 8d.80 black and green 45 20
2036 - 15d. multicoloured 75 65
DESIGNS: 6d.10, SOKO G-4 Super Galeb jet trainer; 8d.80, National Liberation Army armed tug; 15d. "Rade Koncar" (missile gunboat).

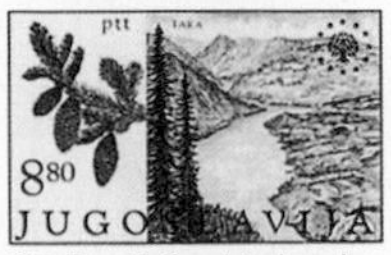

631 Tara National Park and Pine Cones

1982. Nature Protection. Multicoloured.
2037 8d.80 Type **631** 50 20
2038 15d. Kornati National Park and Mediterranean monk seal 85 80

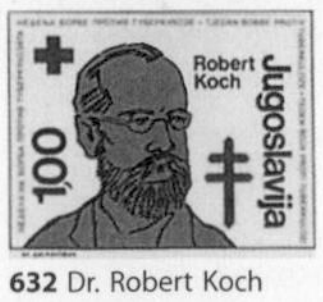

632 Dr. Robert Koch

1982. Obligatory Tax. Anti-tuberculosis Week.

| 2039 | 632 | 1d. orange, black and black | 35 | 15 |

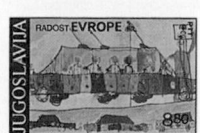

633 "Traffic" (Tibo Bozo)

1982. 14th "Joy of Europe" Meeting, Belgrade. Children's Drawings. Multicoloured.

| 2040 | | 8d.80 Type **633** | 35 | 20 |
| 2041 | | 15d. "In the Bath" (Heiko Jakel) | 75 | 65 |

634 Small Onofrio Fountain, Dubrovnik

1982. 16th World Federation of Travel Agents' Associations Congress, Dubrovnik.

| 2042 | 634 | 8d.80 multicoloured | 25 | 15 |

635 Herceg Novi (from old engraving)

1982. 600th Anniv of Herceg Novi.

| 2043 | 635 | 4d. multicoloured | 65 | 55 |

636 Bridge, Miljacka

1982. Winter Olympic Games, Sarajevo. Each black, light blue and blue.

2044		1d. Type **636**	25	20
2045		6d.10 Mosque tower and cable cars, Sarajevo	35	25
2046		8d.80 Evangelical Church, Sarajevo	65	55
2047		15d. Old Street, Sarajevo	1·70	1·50

637 Bihac

1982. 40th Anniv of Avnoj-a (anti-fascist council) Session, Bihac.

| 2048 | 637 | 4d. brown and orange | 25 | 10 |

638 "Prophet on Golden Background" (Joze Ciuha)

1982. Modern Art. Multicoloured.

2049		4d. Type **638**	25	10
2050		6d.10 "Journey to the West" (Andrej Jemec)	25	10
2051		8d.80 "Black Comb with Red Band" (Riko Debenjak)	25	10
2052		10d. "Manuscript" (Janez Bernik) (horiz)	25	10
2053		15d. "Display Case" (Adriana Maraz) (horiz)	90	80

639 Predic (self-portrait)

1982. 125th Birth Anniv of Uros Predic (painter).

| 2054 | 639 | 4d. orange and brown | 25 | 10 |

641 Pioneer Badge

1982. 40th Anniv of Pioneer League.

| 2056 | 641 | 4d. brown, silver and red | 25 | 10 |

1983. Nos. 1663 and 1667 surch.

2057		30p. on 2d.50 blue	1·30	20
2055a		50p. on 2d.50 blue	2·00	35
2058		60p. on 2d.50 blue	25	20
2059a		1d. on 3d.50 red	25	20
2060		2d. on 2d.50 red	2·75	20

644 Lead Pitcher (16th century)

1983. Museum Exhibits.

2061	644	4d. black, bistre and silver	25	10
2062	-	6d.10 black, brown and silver	25	10
2063	-	8d.80 gold, purple and grey	25	10
2064	-	15d. gold, purple and grey	55	45

DESIGNS: 6d.10, Silver-plated tin jar (18th century); 8d.80, Silver-gilt dish (16th century); 15d. Bronze mortar (15th century).

645 Jalover Mountain Peak and Edelweiss

1983. 90th Anniv of Slovenian Mountaineering Society.

| 2065 | 645 | 4d. blue, light blue and deep blue | 25 | 10 |

646 Ericsson Wall Telephone and War Ministry, Belgrade

1983. Centenary of Telephone in Serbia.

| 2066 | 646 | 3d. brown and blue | 25 | 10 |

647 I.M.O. Emblem and Freighters

1983. 25th Anniv of International Maritime Organization.

| 2067 | 647 | 8d.80 multicoloured | 25 | 10 |

648 Field Mushroom

1983. Edible Mushrooms. Multicoloured.

2068		4d. Type **648**	40	35
2069		6d.10 Common morel	40	35
2070		8d.80 Cep	40	35
2071		15d. Chanterelle	1·10	90

649 Series 401 Steam Locomotive

1983. 110th Anniv of Rijeka Railway.

| 2072 | 649 | 4d. grey and red | 35 | 30 |
| 2073 | - | 23d.70 on 8d.80 grey and red | 70 | 55 |

DESIGN: 23d.70, Series 442 electric locomotive. No. 2073 was only issued surcharged.

650 Monument, Landovica

1983. 40th Death Anniv of Boro Vukmirivic and Ramiz Sadiku (revolutionaries).

| 2074 | 650 | 4d. grey and violet | 30 | 10 |

651 Nobel Prize Medal and Manuscript of "Travnik Chronicle" by Andric

1983. Europa. Multicoloured.

| 2075 | | 8d.80 Type **651** | 30 | 15 |
| 2076 | | 20d. Ivo Andric (author and Nobel Prize winner) and bridge over the Drina | 55 | 45 |

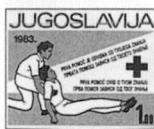

652 First Aid

1983. Obligatory Tax. Red Cross Week.

| 2077 | 652 | 1d. deep brown, brown and red | 30 | 10 |
| 2078 | 652 | 2d. deep brown, brown and red | 30 | 10 |

653 Combine Harvester

1983. 50th International Agriculture Fair, Novi Sad.

| 2079 | 653 | 4d. green and purple | 30 | 10 |

654 "Assault" (Pivo Karamatijevic)

1983. 40th Anniv of Battle of Sutjeska.

| 2080 | 654 | 3d. pink and brown | 30 | 10 |

655 Tito (after Bozidar Jakac) and Parliament Building

1983. 30th Anniv of Tito's Election to Presidency.

| 2081 | 655 | 4d. brown and green | 30 | 10 |

656 Delahaye Postbus, 1903

1983. 80th Anniv of Postbus Service in Montenegro.

| 2082 | 656 | 4d. black and brown | 30 | 10 |
| 2083 | - | 16d.50 black and brown | 55 | 35 |

DESIGN: 16d.50, Road used by first postbus.

657 Statue by V. Bakic, Valjevo

1983. Monuments.

| 2084 | 657 | 100d. orange and blue | 4·25 | 55 |
| 2085 | | 200d. orange and green | 3·75 | 1·30 |

DESIGN—HORIZ: 200d. Triumphal Arch, Titograd.

658 Graph

1983. Sixth U.N. Conference for Trade and Development Session, Belgrade.

| 2086 | 658 | 23d.70 multicoloured | 1·00 | 40 |

659 Pazin (after engraving by Valvasor)

1983. Millenary of Pazin.

| 2087 | 659 | 4d. brown and green | 30 | 10 |

660 Skopje

1983. 20th Anniv of Skopje Earthquake.

| 2088 | 660 | 23d.70 red | 70 | 30 |

661 "The Victor"

1983. Birth Cent of Ivan Mestrovic (sculptor).

| 2089 | 661 | 6d. deep brown, brown and blue | 30 | 10 |

662 Gentian and Kupaonik National Park

1983. Nature Protection. Multicoloured.

| 2090 | | 16d.50 Type **662** | 55 | 45 |
| 2091 | | 23d.70 Chamois and Sutjeska National Park | 1·10 | 90 |

663 Apple

1983. Obligatory Tax. Anti-tuberculosis Week.

| 2092 | 663 | 1d. red, black & turquoise | 30 | 10 |
| 2093 | 663 | 2d. red, black & turquoise | 30 | 10 |

664 "Newly Weds" (Vesna Paunkovic)

1983. 15th "Joy of Europe" Meeting, Belgrade. Children's Drawings.

| 2094 | 664 | 16d.50 yellow, black and red | 30 | 20 |
| 2095 | - | 23d.70 multicoloured | 70 | 55 |

DESIGN: 23d.70, "Andres and his Mother" (Marta Lopez-Ibor).

665 School and Seal

1983. 150th Anniv of Kragujevac Grammar School.

| 2096 | 665 | 5d. brown and blue | 30 | 10 |

666
Monument by
Antun
Augustincic

1983. Centenary of Timocka Buna Uprising.
| 2097 | **666** | 5d. blue and purple | 30 | 10 |

667 Skier and
Games Emblem

1983. Obligatory Tax. Winter Olympic Games, Sarajevo.
| 2098 | **667** | 2d. blue and deep blue | 30 | 10 |

668 Zmaj and "Neven"
Periodical

1983. 150th Birth Anniv of Jovan Jovanovic Zmaj (poet and editor).
| 2099 | **668** | 5d. red and green | 30 | 10 |

669 Ski Jump, Malo Polje,
Mt. Igman

1983. Winter Olympic Games, Sarajevo (1st issue).
2100	**669**	4d. black, green & brown	20	10
2101	-	4d. dp blue, blue & brown	20	10
2102	-	16d.50 lilac, deep brown and brown	60	20
2103	-	16d.50 green, blue & brn	60	20
2104	-	23d.70 deep brown, green and brown	90	55
2105	-	23d.70 black, green and brown	90	55
MS2106	60×74 mm. 50d. ultramarine and magenta. Imperf		2·40	2·40

DESIGNS: No. 2101, Women's slalom run, Mt. Jahorina, 2102, Bob-sleigh and luge run, Mt. Trebevic; 2103, Men's alpine downhill ski run. Mt. Bjelasnice; 2104, Olympic Hall (for ice hockey and figure skating), Zetra; 2105 Speed skating rink, Zetra. 26×33 mm 50d. Games emblem.

670 "The Peasant
Wedding" (Brueghel
the Younger)

1983. Paintings. Multicoloured.
2107	**670**	4d. Type **670**	30	10
2108		16d.50 "Susanna and the Elders" (Master of "The Prodigal Son")	40	20
2109		16d.50 "The Allegory of Wisdom and Strength" (Paolo Veronese)	40	20
2110		23d.70 "The Virgin Mary from Salamanca" (Robert Campin)	1·00	55
2111		23d.70 "St. Anne with the Madonna and Jesus" (Albrecht Durer)	1·00	55

671 Jajce

1983. 40th Anniv of Second Avnoj-a (anti-fascist council) Session, Jajce.
| 2112 | **671** | 5d. red and blue | 30 | 10 |
| MS2113 | 59×74 mm. 30d. red, grey and gold (Tito). Imperf | | 1·70 | 1·70 |

672 Drawing by
Hasukic Sabina

1983. World Communications Year.
| 2114 | **672** | 23d.70 multicoloured | 50 | 25 |

673 Koco
Racin

1983. 75th Birth Anniv of Koco Racin (writer).
| 2115 | **673** | 5d. blue and brown | 30 | 10 |

674 First Issue of
"Politika"

1984. 80th Anniv of "Politika" (daily newspaper).
| 2116 | **674** | 5d. black and red | 30 | 10 |

675 Veljko Petrovic

1984. Birth Centenary of Veljko Petrovic (writer).
| 2117 | **675** | 5d. brown, orange and grey | 30 | 10 |

676 Giant Slalom

1984. Winter Olympic Games, Sarajevo (2nd issue).
2118	**676**	4d. multicoloured	30	20
2119	-	4d. multicoloured	30	20
2120	-	5d. multicoloured	30	20
2121	-	5d. multicoloured	30	20
2122	-	16d.50 multicoloured	40	20
2123	-	16d.50 multicoloured	40	20
2124	-	23d.70 multicoloured	70	35
2125	-	23d.70 multicoloured	70	35
MS2126	Two sheets, each 60×74 mm. Imperf (a) 50d. blue, magenta and silver; (b) 100d. magenta, gold and blue		7·00	7·00

DESIGNS: No. 2119, Biathlon; 2120, slalom; 2121, Bob-sleigh; 2122, Speed skating; 2123, Ice hockey; 2124, Ski jumping; 2125, Downhill skiing. 26×33 mm—50d. Olympic flame; 100d. Flame and map of Yugoslavia.

677 Marija Bursac

1984. Women's Day. National Heroines. Each grey, blue and black.
2127	**677**	5d. Type **677**	30	10
2128		5d. Jelena Cetkovic	30	10
2129		5d. Nada Dimic	30	10
2130		5d. Elpida Karamandi	30	10
2131		5d. Toncka Cec Olga	30	10
2132		5d. Spasenija Babovic Cana	30	10
2133		5d. Jovanka Radivojevic Kica	30	10
2134		5d. Sonja Marinkovic	30	10

678 Bond and
Banknote

1984. 40th Anniv of Slovenian Monetary Institute.
| 2135 | **678** | 5d. blue and red | 30 | 10 |

679 Belgrade Central
Station and Steam Mail
Train, 1884

1984. Centenary of Serbian Railway.
| 2136 | **679** | 5d. brown and deep brown | 70 | 20 |

680 Jure Franko
and Silver Medal

1984. First Yugoslav Winter Olympics Medal.
| 2137 | **680** | 23d.70 multicoloured | 1·40 | 1·10 |

681 Bridge

1984. Europa. 25th Anniv of European Post and Telecommunications Conference.
| 2138 | **681** | 23d.70 multicoloured | 40 | 35 |
| 2139 | **681** | 50d. multicoloured | 1·10 | 90 |

682 Globe as
Jigsaw Pieces

1984. Obligatory Tax. Red Cross Week.
2140	**682**	1d. multicoloured	15	10
2141	**682**	2d. multicoloured	30	20
2142	**682**	4d. multicoloured	40	35
2143	**682**	5d. multicoloured	85	65

683 Basketball

1984. Olympic Games, Los Angeles. Multicoloured.
2144		5d. Type **683**	30	10
2145		16d.50 Diving	40	20
2146		23d.70 Equestrian	1·00	80
2147		50d. Running	3·50	2·75

684 Tito (after Bozidar
Jakac)

1984. 40th Anniv of Failure of German Attack on National Liberation Movement's Headquarters at Drvar.
| 2148 | **684** | 5d. brown and light brown | 30 | 10 |

685 "Skopje
Earthquake"

1984. Obligatory Tax. Solidarity Week. Self-adhesive. Imperf.
| 2149 | **685** | 1d.50 blue and red | 1·00 | 55 |

686 Mt. Biokovo Natural Park
and "Centaurea gloriosa"

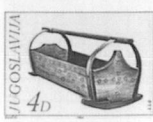

1984. Nature Protection. Multicoloured.
| 2150 | | 26d. Type **686** | 70 | 55 |
| 2151 | | 40d. Pekel Cave and "Anophthalmus schmidti" (Longhorn beetle) | 1·10 | 90 |

687 Great
Black-backed Gull

1984. Birds. Multicoloured.
2152		4d. Type **687**	70	45
2153		5d. Black-headed gull	70	45
2154		16d.50 Herring gull	70	45
2155		40d. Common tern	4·50	2·00

688 Cradle from Bihac,
Bosnia and Herzegovina

1984. Museum Exhibits. Cradles.
2156	**688**	4d. green	15	10
2157	-	5d. purple and red	30	20
2158	-	26d. light brown and brown	70	55
2159	-	40d. ochre and orange	1·10	90

DESIGNS: Cradles from—5d. Montenegro; 26d. Macedonia; 40d. Rasina, Serbia.

689 Red Cross and
Leaves

1984. Obligatory Tax. Anti-tuberculosis Week.
2160	**689**	1d. multicoloured	30	10
2161	**689**	2d. multicoloured	30	10
2162	**689**	2d.50 multicoloured	30	10
2163	**689**	4d. multicoloured	30	20
2164	**689**	5d. multicoloured	40	35

690 Olive Trees,
Mirovica

1984
| 2165 | **690** | 5d. multicoloured | 30 | 10 |

691 "National
Costume" (Erika
Sarcevic)

1984. 16th "Joy of Europe" Meeting, Belgrade. Children's Paintings. Multicoloured.
| 2166 | | 26d. Type **691** | 55 | 45 |
| 2167 | | 40d. "Girl pushing bear in buggy" (Eva Gug) | 1·50 | 1·20 |

692 Virovitica
(17th-century engraving)

1984. 750th Anniv of Virovitica.
| 2168 | **692** | 5d. orange and black | 30 | 10 |

693 Map and
Radio Waves

1984. 80th Anniv of Radio-Telegraphic Service in Montenegro.
2169 693 6d. blue and green 30 10

694 "Flower"

1984. Veterans' Conference on Security, Disarmament and Co-operation in Europe, Belgrade.
2170 694 26d. pink, black and violet 1·50 1·20
2171 694 40d. green, black and blue 2·10 1·70

695 City Arms and "40"

1984. 40th Anniv of Liberation of Belgrade.
2172 695 6d. red, silver and blue 30 10

696 Milojevic and Music Score

1984. Birth Centenary of Miloje Milojevic (composer).
2173 696 6d. lilac and green 30 10

697 Issues of 1944 and 1984

1984. 40th Anniv of "Nova Makedoniya" (newspaper).
2174 697 6d. blue and red 30 10

698 Boxing

1984. Yugoslav Olympic Games Medal Winners. Each blue and red.
2175 26d. Type. 698 40 35
2176 26d. Wrestling 40 35
2177 26d. Canoeing 40 35
2178 26d. Handball 40 35
2179 26d. Football 40 35
2180 26d. Basketball 40 35
2181 26d. Water polo 40 35
2182 26d. Rowing 40 35

699 "Madame Tatichek" (Ferdinand Waldmuller)

1984. Paintings. Multicoloured.
2183 6d. Type 699 30 20
2184 26d. "The Bathers" (Pierre-Auguste Renoir) 40 35
2185 26d. "At the Window" (Henri Matisse) 40 35
2186 38d. "The Tahitians" (Paul Gauguin) (horiz) 70 55
2187 40d. "The Ballerinas" (Edgar Degas) (horiz) 85 65

1984. Nos. 1675a, 1668a and 2088 surch.
2188a 2d. on 8d.80 grey 70 20
2189 6d. on 4d. red 70 20
2190 20d. on 23d.70 red 70 35

701 "Aturia aturi" (cephalopod)

1985. Museum Exhibits. Fossils.
2191 701 5d. purple and blue 15 10
2192 - 6d. brown and light brown 30 20
2193 - 33d. brown and yellow 70 55
2194 - 60d. brown and orange 1·50 1·20
DESIGNS: 6d. "Pachyophis woodwardi" (snake); 33d. Hoefer's butterflyfish; 60d. Skull of Neanderthal man.

702 Hopovo Church

1985. 40th Anniv of Organized Protection of Yugoslav Cultural Monuments.
2195 702 6d. red, yellow and green 40 20

703 Three Herons in Flight

1985. 50th Anniv of Planica Ski-jump.
2196 703 6d. multicoloured 6·00 2·00

704 Lammergeier and Douglas DC-10 Jetliner over Mountains

1985. Air. Multicoloured.
2197 500d. Type 704 6·25 2·20
2199 1000d. Red-rumped swallow and airplane at airport 2·50 1·25

705 Osprey

1985. Nature Protection. Birds. Multicoloured.
2202 42d. Type 705 2·10 1·10
2203 60d. Hoopoe 4·25 1·70

706 Three Herons in Flight

1985. Obligatory Tax. 50th Anniv of Planica Ski-jump.
2204 706 2d. blue and green 30 10

707 "St. Methodius" (detail "Seven Slav Saints", St. Naum's Church Ohrid)

1985. 1100th Death Anniv of Saint Methodius, Archbishop of Moravia.
2205 707 10d. multicoloured 2·10 1·10

708 Handshake

1985. Tenth Anniv of Osimo Agreements between Yugoslavia and Italy.
2206 708 6d. blue and deep blue 30 10

709 Flute, Darabukka and Josip Slavenski (composer)

1985. Europa. Multicoloured.
2207 60d. Type 709 85 65
2208 80d. Score of "Balkanophonia" (Slavenski) 85 65

710 Red Cross and Faces

1985. Obligatory Tax. Red Cross Week.
2209 710 1d. violet and red 20 10
2210 710 2d. violet and red 20 10
2211 710 3d. violet and red 20 10
2212 710 4d. violet and red 20 10

711 Vujic (after Dimitrije Auramovic)

1985. 150th Anniv of Joakim Vujic Theatre, Kragujevac.
2213 711 10d. multicoloured 30 10

712 Order of Liberty

1985. 40th Anniv of V.E. (Victory in Europe) Day. Multicoloured.
2214 10d. Type 712 30 10
2215 10d. Order of National Liberation 30 10

713 Franjo Kluz and Rudi Cajavec (pilots) and Potez 25 Biplane

1985. Air Force Day.
2216 713 10d. blue, purple & brown 40 20

714 Tito (after Bozidar Jakac)

1985. 93rd Birth Anniv of Tito.
2217 714 10d. multicoloured 70 35

715 Red Cross and "Skopje Earthquake"

1985. Obligatory Tax. Solidarity Week. (a) As Nos. 1885 and 1933.
2218 2d.50 black, grey and blue 70 55
2219 3d. black, grey and blue 85 55

(b) Type 715.
2220 715 3d. blue and red 2·10 1·70
See also Nos. 23215/16, 2460, 2532, 2636 and 2716.

716 Villa, Map of Islands and Arms

1985. Centenary of Tourism in Cres-Losinj Region.
2221 716 10d. multicoloured 1·10 90

717 U.N. Emblem and Rainbow

1985. 40th Anniv of U.N.O.
2222 717 70d. multicoloured 70 35

718 Regatta Emblem

1985. 30th Anniv of International European Danubian Regatta.
2223 718 70d. multicoloured 70 55
MS2224 95×79 mm. 100d. silver, blue and deep blue (regatta course) (34×28 mm) 2·20 2·20

719 Aerial View of Yacht

1985. Nautical Tourism. Multicoloured.
2225 8d. Type 719 40 35
2226 10d. Windsurfing 70 55
2227 50d. Yacht in sunset 1·40 1·10
2228 70d. Yacht by coastline 4·25 3·25

720 Model Airplane

1985. World Free Flight Aeromodels Championships, Livno.
2229 720 70d. multicoloured 1·00 80

721 Emblem and Text

1985. Obligatory Tax. 20th European Shooting Championships, Osijek.
2230 721 3d. blue 40 20

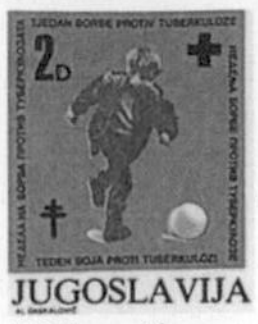

722 Boy with Football

1985. Obligatory Tax. Anti-tuberculosis Week.

2231	**722**	2d. black, orange and red	15	10
2232	**722**	3d. black, orange and red	15	10
2233	**722**	4d. black, orange and red	20	10
2234	**722**	5d. black, orange and red	55	45

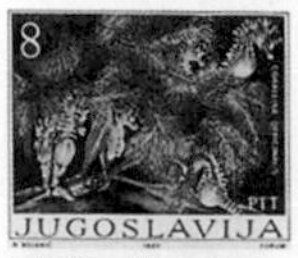

723 "Corallina officinalis" and Seahorses

1985. Marine Flora. Multicoloured.

2235		8d. Type **723**	15	10
2236		10d. "Desmarestia viridis"	30	20
2237		50d. Bladder wrack seaweed	40	35
2238		70d. "Padina pavonia"	2·50	2·00

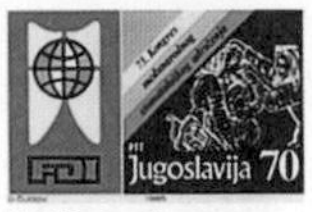

724 Federation Emblem

1985. 73rd International Stomatologists Federation Congress, Belgrade.

2239	**724**	70d. multicoloured	70	55

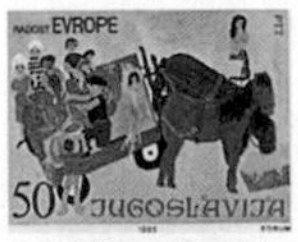

725 Selling Vegetables from Cart (Branka Lukic)

1985. 17th "Joy of Europe" Meeting, Belgrade. Children's Paintings. Multicoloured.

2240		50d. Type **725**	70	55
2241		70d. "Children playing" (Suzanne Straathof)	2·10	1·70

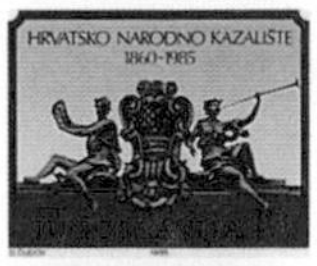

726 Detail of Theatre Facade

1985. 125th Anniv of Croatian National Theatre, Zagreb.

2242	**726**	10d. multicoloured	40	35

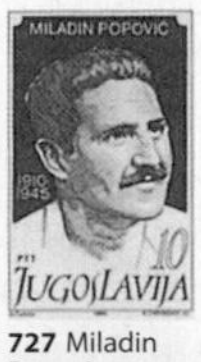

727 Miladin Popovic

1985. 75th Birth Anniv and 40th Death Anniv of Miladin Popovic (Communist Party worker).

2243	**727**	10d. brown and orange	30	10

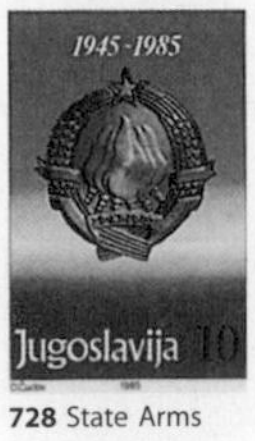

728 State Arms

1985. 40th Anniv of Federal Republic.

2244	**728**	10d. multicoloured	30	10
MS2245		62×75 mm. **728** 100d. multicoloured (15×25 mm). Imperf	1·70	1·70

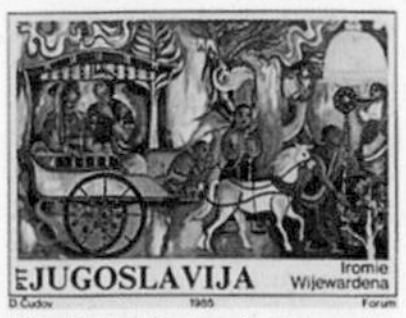

729 "Royal Procession" (Iromie Wijewardena)

1985. Paintings. Multicoloured.

2246		8d. Type **729**	20	10
2247		10d. "Return from Hunting" (Mama Cangare)	30	20
2248		50d. "Drum of Coca" (Agnes Ovando Sanz de Franck)	50	35
2249		50d. "The Cock" (Mariano Rodriguez) (vert)	50	35
2250		70d. "Three Women" (Quamrul Hassan) (vert)	2·40	1·90

1985. Nos. 1641, 1644, 1646, 1671, 1672 and 1677/9 surch.

2251		1d. on 25p. red	1·40	10
2252		2d. on 5p. orange	70	10
2253		3d. on 35p. red	40	10
2254		4d. on 5d.60 olive	40	10
2255		8d. on 6d. brown	40	10
2256		20d. on 26d. blue	40	20
2257		50d. on 16d.50 blue	1·40	35
2258		70d. on 38d. mauve	1·70	55

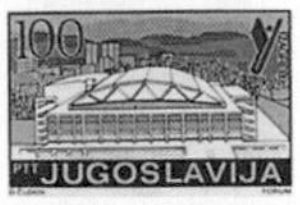

731 Zagreb Exhibition Hall

1986

2259	**731**	100d. violet and yellow	85	35

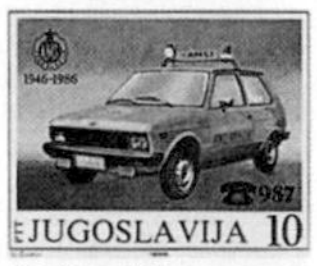

732 Patrol Car

1986. 40th Anniv of Yugoslav Automobile Association. Multicoloured.

2260		10d. Type **732**	30	10
2261		70d. Red Cross helicopter	1·40	1·10

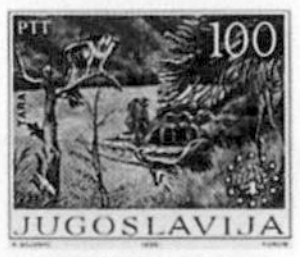

733 Wildlife on River Bank

1986. Nature Protection. River Tara. Multicoloured.

2262		100d. Type **733**	70	55
2263		150d. Bridge over river	1·40	1·10

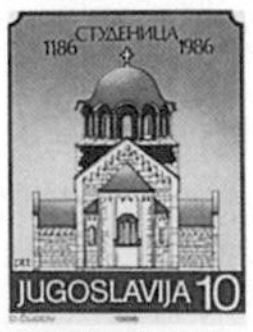

734 Church of the Virgin

1986. 800th Anniv of Studenica Monastery.

2264	**734**	10d. red, green and blue	1·00	55

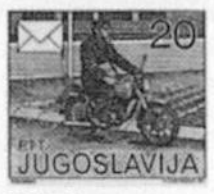

735 Postman on Motor Cycle

1986. Postal Services.

2265a	**735**	20d. purple	70	20
2266a	-	30d. brown	1·40	20
2267	-	40d. red	70	20
2268	-	50d. violet	70	20
2269	-	60d. green	70	20
2270	-	93d. blue	70	20
2271	-	100d. purple	1·40	20
2272	-	106d. red	70	20
2272a	-	106d. brown	70	20
2273	-	120d. green	30	10
2274	-	140d. red	30	10
2275	-	170d. green	70	20
2276	-	200d. blue	1·50	55
2277	-	220d. brown	70	20
2278	-	300d. red	70	20
2279	-	500d. blue and orange	2·75	55
2279a	-	500d. blue and yellow	70	55
2280	**735**	800d. blue	30	20
2281	-	1000d. violet and green	1·00	65
2282	-	2000d. green and orange	40	20
2283	-	5000d. blue and red	1·40	55
2284a	-	10000d. violet & orange	30	20
2285a	-	20000d. brown and green	30	20

DESIGNS—As T **735**. HORIZ: 40d. Forklift truck; 50, 20000d. Electric train; 200d. Freighter. VERT: 30, 10000d. Postman giving letters to man; 60d. Posting letters; 93d. Envelope and leaflet; 106d. (2272), Woman working at computer and woman filling envelopes; 106 (2272a), 140d. Woman working at computer; 120d. Woman with Valentine card; 170, 300d. Flower and post box; 220d. Mail coach and cover; 500d. (both) Postal sorter; 1000d. Woman using public telephone; 2000d. Telephone card, tokens and handset; 5000d. Posthorn, globe and bird with stamp. 20×18 mm: 100d. Postman and van.

See also Nos. 2587/98.

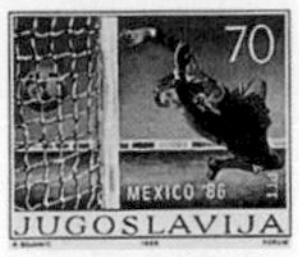

736 Player and Ball in Goal

1986. World Cup Football Championship, Mexico. Multicoloured.

2286		70d. Type **736**	1·10	90
2287		150d. Players and ball in goal	1·40	1·10

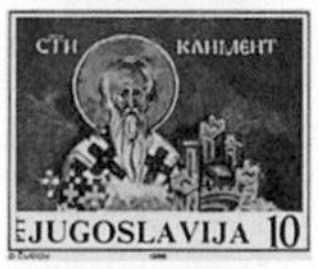

737 St. Clement and Model of Ohrid (fresco, Church of St. Spas)

1986. 1100th Anniv of Arrival of St. Clement of Ohrid in Macedonia.

2288	**737**	10d. multicoloured	8·25	6·75

1986. No. 1674 surch.

2289		5d. on 8d. grey	70	20

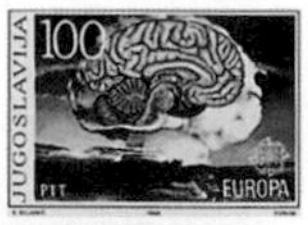

739 Human Brain as Nuclear Cloud

1986. Europa. Multicoloured.

2290		100d. Type **739**	70	55
2291		200d. Injured deer on road	2·10	1·10

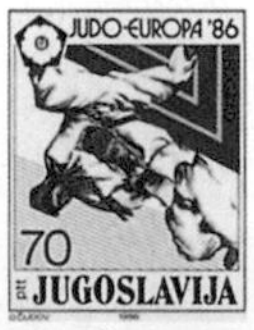

740 Judo

1988. European Men's Judo Championships, Belgrade.

2292	**740**	70d. brown, pink and blue	85	55

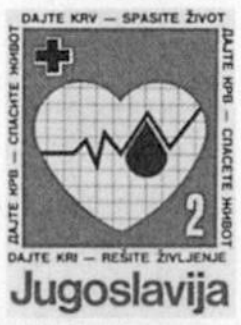

741 Graph and Blood Drop within Heart

1986. Obligatory Tax. Red Cross Week.

2293	**741**	2d. black, blue and red	15	10
2294	**741**	3d. black, blue and red	15	10
2295	**741**	4d. black, blue and red	30	20
2296	**741**	5d. black, blue and red	30	20
2297	**741**	11d. black, blue and red	30	20
2298	**741**	20d. black, blue and red	1·00	80

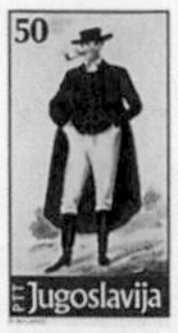

742 Costume of Slovenia

1986. Yugoslav Costumes. Multicoloured.

2299		50d. Type **742**	70	55
2300		50d. Vojvodina (woman with red apron)	70	55
2301		50d. Croatia (man in embroidered trousers)	70	55
2302		50d. Macedonia (woman hand spinning)	70	55
2303		50d. Serbia (woman in bolero)	70	55
2304		50d. Montenegro (man with rifle)	70	55
2305		50d. Kosovo (woman carrying basket)	70	55
2306		50d. Bosnia and Herzegovina (man carrying bag on back)	70	55

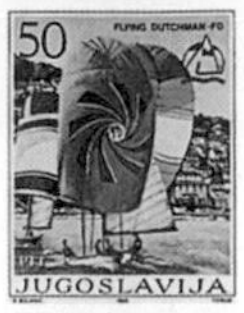

743 Yachts

1986. "Flying Dutchman" Class European Sailing Championships, Moscenicka Draga. Mult.

2307		50d. Type **743**	40	20
2308		80d. Yachts (different)	70	55
MS2309		66×85 mm. 100d. Yachts (different). Imperf	5·50	5·50

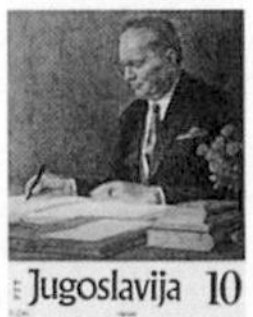

744 Tito (after Safet Zec)

1986. 94th Birth Anniv of Tito.

2310	**744**	10d. multicoloured	30	10

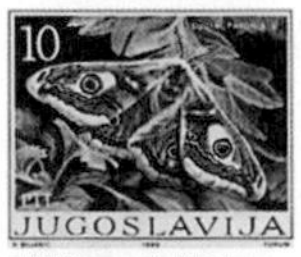

745 Peacock Moth

1986. Butterflies and Moths. Multicoloured.

2311		10d. Type **745**	40	35
2312		20d. Peacock	70	55
2313		50d. Apollo	1·40	1·10
2314		100d. Purple emperor	2·75	2·20

1986. Obligatory Tax. Solidarity Week. (a) As No. 2200.

2315	**715**	10d. blue and red	1·40	80

(b) As Type **715** but inscr "Solidarity Week" in four languages.

2316		10d. blue and red	1·40	80

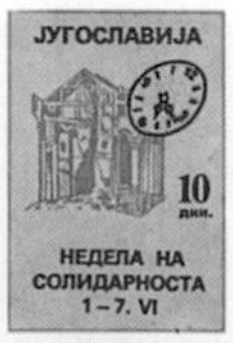

746 "Skopje Earthquake"

(c) Type **746**.

2317	**746**	10d. lilac and red	1·40	80

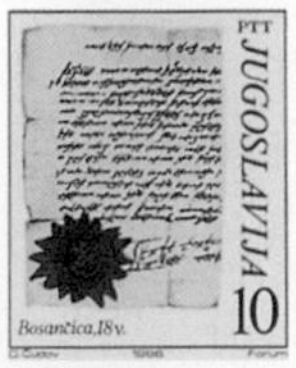

747 Bosancica Manuscript

1986. Museum Exhibits. Ancient Manuscripts. Multicoloured.

2319		10d. Type **747**	15	10

2320	20d. Leontije's Gospel	30	20
2321	50d. Astrological writing, Mesopotamia	70	55
2322	100d. Hagada (ritual book), Spain	1·10	90

748 Congress Poster (Branislav Dobanovacki)

1986. 13th Communist League Conference, Belgrade.

2323	**748**	10d. black and red	30	10
2324	-	20d. black and red	30	10
MS2325		60×75 mm. 100d. black and vermilion. Imperf	1·40	1·40

DESIGN: 20, 100d. Showing parts of Congress advertising poster.

749 Trubar and Title Page of "Abecedari"

1986. 400th Death Anniv of Primoz Trubar (founder of Slovenian literary language and religious reformer).

2326	**749**	20d. multicoloured	1·00	55

750 Emblem

1986. 125th Anniv of Serbian National Theatre, Novi Sad.

2327	**750**	40d. multicoloured	30	10

751 Dancers

1986. Rugovo Dance.

2328	**751**	40d. multicoloured	30	10

753 Crosses forming Earth and Sky

1986. Obligatory Tax. Anti-tuberculosis Week.

2330	**753**	2d. multicoloured	30	10
2331	**753**	5d. multicoloured	30	10
2332	**753**	6d. multicoloured	30	10
2333	**753**	7d. multicoloured	30	10
2334	**753**	8d. multicoloured	30	10
2335	**753**	10d. multicoloured	30	10
2336	**753**	11d. multicoloured	40	35
2337	**753**	14d. multicoloured	40	35
2338	**753**	20d. multicoloured	40	35

754 Volleyball

1986. "Universiade '87" University Games, Zagreb. Zagi (games mascot). Multicoloured.

2339	30d. Type **754**	40	35
2340	40d. Canoeing	55	45
2341	100d. Gymnastics	1·00	80
2342	150d. Fencing	1·40	1·10

755 "Bird and Child running on Globe" (Tanja Faletic)

1986. 18th "Joy of Europe" Meeting, Belgrade. Children's Paintings. Multicoloured.

2343	100d. Type **755**	1·00	80
2344	150d. "City of the Future" (Johanna Kraus)	1·40	1·10

756 Diagram of Rotary Selector and Bled

1986. 50th Anniv of Automatic Telephone Exchange Network.

2345	**756**	40d. multicoloured	30	10

757 Criminal in Stocking Mask

1986. 55th Interpol General Assembly Session, Belgrade.

2346	**757**	150d. multicoloured	70	55

758 Brigade Member addressing Crowd (after Djordje Andrejevic-Kun)

1986. 50th Anniv of Formation of International Brigades in Spain.

2347	**758**	40d. brown, gold and orange	30	10

759 Academy

1986. Centenary of Serbian Academy of Arts and Sciences.

2348	**759**	40d. multicoloured	30	10

760 People riding on Doves (Branislav Barnak)

1986. International Peace Year.

2349	**760**	150d. multicoloured	85	65

761 "Portrait" (Bernard Buffet)

1986. Paintings in Museum of Contemporary Arts, Skopje. Multicoloured.

2350	30d. "Still Life" (Frantisek Muzika)	15	10
2351	40d. "Disturbance" (detail, Rafael Canogar)(horiz)	30	20
2352	100d. Type **761**	70	55
2353	100d. "IOL" (Victor Vasarely)	70	55

2354	150d. "Woman's Head" (Pablo Picasso)	1·10	90

762 European Otter

1987. Protected Animals. Multicoloured.

2355	30d. Type **762**	1·10	90
2356	40d. Argali	1·10	90
2357	100d. Red deer	1·10	90
2358	150d. Brown bear	1·10	90

763 Boskovic, Brera Observatory and Solar Eclipse

1987. Death Bicentenary of Ruder Boskovic (astronomer).

2359	**763**	150d. multicoloured	85	55

764 Mountains, Woodlands and Animal Feeder

1987. Nature Protection. Triglav National Park. Multicoloured.

2360	150d. Type **764**	1·70	1·30
2361	400d. Mountains, woodland and glacial lake	2·50	2·00

765 Potez 29-4 Biplane

1987. 60th Anniv of Civil Aviation in Yugoslavia. Multicoloured.

2362	150d. Type **765**	1·00	80
2363	400d. Douglas DC-10 jetliner	2·10	1·70

766 Mateja Svet

1987. Yugoslav Medals at World Alpine Skiing Championships, Crans Montana.

2364	**766**	200d. multicoloured	4·25	3·25

767 Kole Nedelkovski

1987. 75th Birth Anniv of Kole Nedelkovski (poet and revolutionary).

2365	**767**	40d. multicoloured	30	10

768 Gusle and Battle Flags of Vucji Do and Grahovo

1987. 125th Anniv of Liberation Wars of Montenegro.

2366	**768**	40d. multicoloured	30	10

769 "Founding the Party at Cebine, 1937" (Anton Gojmir Kos)

1987. 50th Anniv of Slovenian Communist Party.

2367	**769**	40d. multicoloured	30	10

770 Tito Bridge (Ilija Stojadinovic)

1987. Europa. Architecture. Multicoloured.

2368	200d. Type **770**	1·00	80
2369	400d. Bridges over River Ljubljanica (Joze Plecnik)	1·40	1·10

771 Children of Different Races in Flower

1987. Obligatory Tax. Red Cross Week.

2370	**771**	2d. multicoloured	40	35
2371	**771**	4d. multicoloured	40	35
2372	**771**	5d. multicoloured	40	35
2373	**771**	6d. multicoloured	40	35
2374	**771**	7d. multicoloured	40	35
2375	**771**	8d. multicoloured	40	35
2376	**771**	10d. multicoloured	40	35
2377	**771**	11d. multicoloured	40	35
2378	**771**	12d. multicoloured	40	35
2379	**771**	14d. multicoloured	40	35
2380	**771**	17d. multicoloured	40	35
2381	**771**	20d. multicoloured	40	35

772 Almonds

1987. Fruit. Multicoloured.

2382	60d. Type **772**	30	20
2383	150d. Pear	1·00	80
2384	200d. Apple	1·40	1·10
2385	400d. Plum	2·20	1·80

773 Tito (after Mosa Pijade)

1987. 95th Birth Anniv of Josip Broz Tito.

2386	**773**	60d. multicoloured	40	35

774 "Skopje Earthquake"

1987. Obligatory Tax. Solidarity Week.

2387	**774**	30d. multicoloured	70	35

775 Bust of Karadzic (Petar Ubavkic), Trsic (birthplace) and Vienna

1987. Birth Bicentenary of Vuk Stefanovic Karadzic (linguist and historian). Multicoloured.

2388		60d. Type **775**	30	10
2389		200d. Serbian alphabet and Karadzic (portrait by Uros Knezevic)	70	55

776 Mail Coach in Zrenjanin

1987. 250th Anniv of Postal Services in Zrenjanin.

2390	**776**	60d. multicoloured	30	10

777 Emblem and Mascot

1987. Obligatory Tax. "Universiade '87" University Games, Zagreb.

2391	**777**	20d. blue and green	70	35

778 Hurdling

1987. "Universiade '87" University Games, Zagreb. Multicoloured.

2392		60d. Type **778**	40	35
2393		150d. Basketball	70	55
2394		200d. Gymnastics	1·00	80
2395		400d. Swimming	2·10	1·70

779 Canadair CL-215 Amphibian spraying Forest Fire

1987. Fire Fighting. Multicoloured.

2396		60d. Type **779**	30	20
2397		200d. Fire-fighting tug	65	20

780 Monument, Anindol Park

1987. 50th Anniv of Croatian Communist Party.

2398	**780**	60d. multicoloured	30	10

781 School and Foundation Document

1987. 150th Anniv of Sabac High School.

2399	**781**	80d. brown, orange and blue	30	10

782 Crosses and Children's Head

1987. Obligatory Tax. Anti-tuberculosis Week.

2400	**782**	2d. multicoloured	30	10
2401	**782**	4d. multicoloured	30	10
2402	**782**	6d. multicoloured	30	10
2403	**782**	8d. multicoloured	30	10
2404	**782**	10d. multicoloured	30	10
2405	**782**	12d. multicoloured	30	10
2406	**782**	14d. multicoloured	30	10
2407	**782**	20d. multicoloured	30	10
2408	**782**	25d. multicoloured	30	10
2409	**782**	40d. multicoloured	30	10

783 Emblem, Map and Flowers

1987. "Balkanphila XI" Balkans Stamp Exhibition, Novi Sad. Multicoloured.

2410		250d. Type **783**	70	55
MS2411		60x75 mm. 400d. Novi Sad behind Petrovaradin Fortress (22x32 mm). Imperf	2·10	2·10

1987. No. 2269 surch **80.**

2412		80d. on 60d. green	70	20

785 "Children playing amongst Trees" (Bedic Aranka)

1987. 19th "Joy of Europe" Meeting. Multicoloured.

2413		250d. Type **785**	1·10	90
2414		400d. "Child and scarecrow in orchard" (Ingeborg Schaffer)	1·40	1·10

786 SPRAM Emblem

1987. Obligatory Tax. Model Airplane Championships, Belgrade.

2415	**786**	20d. blue	30	10

787 Arslanagica Bridge, Trebinje

1987. Bridges. Multicoloured.

2416		80d. Type **787**	40	35
2417		250d. Terzija Bridge, Djakovica	70	55

788 Tug in Canal

1987. 600th Anniv of Titov Vrbas.

2418	**788**	80d. multicoloured	30	10

789 Eclipse, First Telescope and Old Observatory Building

1987. Cent of Astronomical and Meteorological Observatory, Belgrade.

2419	**789**	80d. multicoloured	30	10

790 "St. Luke the Evangelist" (Raphael)

1987. Paintings in Mimara Museum, Zagreb. Multicoloured.

2420		80d. Type **790**	30	20
2421		200d. "Infanta Maria Theresa" (Diego Velazquez)	70	55
2422		250d. "Nicolaus Rubens" (Peter Paul Rubens)	75	60
2423		400d. "Louise Laure Sennegon" (Camille Corot)	1·80	1·50

791 Bull Fighting (Grmec)

1987. Museum Exhibits. Folk Games. Multicoloured.

2424		80d. Type **791**	30	20
2425		200d. Sword used in Ljuvicevo Horse Games	70	55
2426		250d. Crown worn at Moresca Games (Korcula)	75	60
2427		400d. Sinj Iron Ring	2·50	2·00

792 Codex and Novi Vinodol

1988. 700th Anniv of Vinodol Law Codex.

2428	**792**	100d. multicoloured	30	10

793 Skier

1988. 25th Anniv of Golden Fox Skiing Competition, Maribor.

2429	**793**	350d. multicoloured	30	10

794 Cub

1988. Protected Wildlife. The Brown Bear. Multicoloured.

2430		70d. Type **794**	3·00	2·20
2431		80d. Bears among branches	3·00	2·20
2432		200d. Adult bear	3·25	2·20
2433		350d. Adult stalking prey	10·00	6·75

795 Skier

1988. Winter Olympic Games, Calgary. Multicoloured.

2434		350d. Type **795**	1·40	1·10
2435		1200d. Ice hockey	2·10	1·70

796 Map of Europe

1988. Balkan Countries' Foreign Affairs Ministers Meeting, Belgrade. Sheet 69x75 mm.

MS2436		1500d. multicoloured	3·00	3·00

797 Basketball

1988. Olympic Games, Seoul. Multicoloured.

2437		106d. Type **797**	70	55
2438		450d. High jumping	90	75
2439		500d. Gymnastics	1·00	80
2440		1200d. Boxing	2·40	2·00
MS2441		62x77 mm. 1500d. Korean landscape. Imperf	3·50	3·50

798 White Carnations

1988. Obligatory Tax. Anti-cancer Campaign. Multicoloured.

2442		4d. Type **798**	30	10
2443		8d. Red flowers	30	10
2444		12d. Red roses	30	10

799 "INTELSAT V-A", Globe and Dish Aerials, Ivanjica

1988. Europa. Transport and Communications. Multicoloured.

2445		450d. Type **799**	70	55
2446		1200d. Woman using mobile telephone and methods of transport	1·40	1·10

800 Anniversary Emblem

1988. Obligatory Tax. 125th Anniv of Red Cross.

2447	**800**	4d. blue, red and grey	40	20
2448	**800**	8d. blue, red and grey	40	20
2449	**800**	10d. blue, red and grey	40	20
2450	**800**	12d. blue, red and grey	40	20
2451	**800**	20d. blue, red and grey	40	20
2452	**800**	30d. blue, red and grey	40	20
2453	**800**	50d. blue, red and grey	40	20

801 Great Top Shell

1988. Molluscs. Multicoloured.

2454		106d. Type **801**	70	55
2455		550d. St. James's scallop	1·10	90
2456		600d. Giant tun	1·40	1·10
2457		1000d. "Argonauta cygnus" (wrongly inscr "argo")	1·70	1·30

802 Tito

1988. 60th Anniv of Trial of Josip Broz Tito.

2458	**802**	106d. brown and black	30	10

803 "Skopje Earthquake"

1988. Obligatory Tax. Solidarity Week. (a) Type 803.

2459	**803**	50d. grey, brown and red	70	20

(b) As No. 2220 but value changed.

2460	**715**	50d. blue and red	70	20

(c) No. 2387 surch **50** and emblem.

2461	**774**	50d. on 30d. mult	70	20

805 First Lyceum
Building

1988. 150th Anniv of Belgrade University.
2462 **805** 106d. multicoloured 30 10

806 Krleza

1988. Obligatory Tax. Culture Fund. 95th Birth Anniv of
Miroslav Krleza (writer).
2463 **806** 30d. brown and orange 30 10

1988. Nos. 2270 and 2272a surch.
2464 120d. on 93d. blue 30 10
2465 140d. on 106d. brown 30 10

808 "Phelypaea
boissieri"

1988. Nature Protection Macedonian Plants.
Multicoloured.
2466 600d. Type **808** 1·10 90
2467 1000d. "Campanula formane-
kiana" 1·40 1·10

809 Globe and
Flags

1988. Centenary of Esperanto (invented language).
2468 **809** 600d. blue and green 1·40 80

810 Shipping on
the Danube

1988. 40th Anniv of Danube Conference. Multicoloured.
2469 1000d. Type **810** 85 65
MS2470 84×68 mm. 2000d. Map of
Danube. Imperf 5·50 5·50

811 Globe as Ball
in Basket

1988. 13th European Junior Basketball Championships,
Tito Vrbas and Srbobran.
2471 **811** 600d. multicoloured 70 55

812 Horse Racing

1988. 125th Anniv of Belgrade Horse Races.
Multicoloured.
2472 140d. Type **812** 40 35
2473 600d. Show jumping 1·00 80
2474 1000d. Trotting race 1·40 1·10

813 Douglas DC-10
Jetliner and Globe

1988. Air.
2475 **813** 2000d. multicoloured 1·70 65

814 Museum and
Bosnian Bellflower

1988. Centenary of Bosnia amd Herzegovina Museum,
Sarajevo.
2476 **814** 140d. multicoloured 30 10

Jugoslavija

815 Flame
and Hand

1988. Obligatory Tax. Anti-tuberculosis Week. (a) Type
815.
2477 **815** 4d. multicoloured 30 20
2478 **815** 8d. multicoloured 30 20
2479 **815** 12d. multicoloured 30 20
2480 **815** 20d. multicoloured 30 20
2481 **815** 50d. multicoloured 30 20
2482 **815** 70d. multicoloured 30 20

(b) No. 2039 surch **1988** 12.
2483 632 12d. on 1d. orange,
black and red 7·75 7·75

817 Arm and Crab's
Claw (anti-cancer)

1988. Health Campaigns. Multicoloured.
2484 140d. Type **817** 30 10
2485 1000d. Screaming mouth in
splash of blood (anti-AIDS) 1·10 90

818 "Daughter of
the Artist" (Peter
Ranosovic)

1988. 20th "Joy of Europe" Meeting. Multicoloured.
2486 1000d. Type **818** 1·10 90
2487 1100d. "Girl wuth Straw Hat"
(Pierre-Auguste Renoir) 1·40 1·10

819 1701 Arms and Present
Emblem

1988. 50th Anniv of Slovenian Academy of Arts and
Sciences.
2488 **819** 200d. multicoloured 30 10

820 Galicnik Wedding

1988. Museum Exhibits. Traditional Crafts and Customs.
Multicoloured.
2489 200d. Type **820** 30 20
2490 1000d. Weapons from Bay
of Kotor 1·00 85

2491 1000d. Vojvodina embroidery
(horiz) 1·00 85
2492 1100d. Masks from Ptuj (horiz) 1·10 90

821 Title Page of "Gorski
Vijenac" and Petar II (after
J. Boss)

1988. 175th Birth Anniv of Prince-Bishop Petar II of
Montenegro. Multicoloured.
2493 200d. Type **821** 40 35
2494 1000d. Njegos Mausoleum, Lov-
cen and Petar II in bishop's
robes (after Josip Tominc) 1·00 80

822 "Girl with Lyre"

1988. Greek Terracotta Figures from Josip Broz Tito
Memorial Centre Collection. Multicoloured.
2495 200d. Type **822** 30 20
2496 1000d. "Girl on a stone" 85 65
2497 1000d. "Eros and Psyche" 85 65
2498 1100d. "Girl by Stele" 1·00 85

823 Krsmanovic House,
Belgrade

1988. 70th Anniv of Yugoslavian State.
2499 **823** 200d. multicoloured 30 10

1988. Nos. 2273/4 surch.
2500 170d. on 120d. green 1·40 35
2501 220d. on 140d. red 1·40 35

825 Pistol shooting

1988. Yugoslavian Medals at Olympic Games.
Multicoloured.
2502 500d. Type **825** (2 gold, 1
bronze) 55 45
2503 500d. Handball (bronze) 55 45
2504 500d. Table tennis (silver and
bronze) 55 45
2505 500d. Wrestling (silver) 55 45
2506 500d. Rowing (bronze) 55 45
2507 500d. Basketball (2 silver) 55 45
2508 500d. Water polo (gold) 55 45
2509 500d. Boxing (bronze) 55 45

826 Gundulic and
Dubrovnik

1989. 400th Birth Anniv of Ivan Gundulic (poet).
2510 **826** 220d. multicoloured 70 45

827 Mallards

1989. Wild Ducks. Multicoloured.
2511 300d. Type **827** 1·30 90
2512 2100d. Green-winged teal 2·50 1·40
2513 2200d. Pintail 2·50 1·40
2514 2200d. Common shoveler 2·50 1·40

827a Emblem

1989. Obligatory Tax. Anti-cancer Week. (a) Type **827a**.
2514a **827a** 110d. multicoloured 40 20

(b) Inscr **"YUGOSLAVIJA MAKEDONIJA".** Surch 1989
and value.
2514b 110d. on 20d. black, red and
gold 40 20
DESIGN: No. 2514b, Sword emblem with blade doubling
as Aesculapius rod enclosing crab against background of
"flower".

828 Valvasor and
Wagensperg Castle

1989. 300th Anniv of Publishing of "The Glory of the
Duchy of Kranjska" by Johann Weickhard Valvasor.
2515 **828** 300d. multicoloured 30 10

829 "Bulbocodium
vernum"

1989. Flowers. Multicoloured.
2516 300d. Type **829** 95 75
2517 2100d. White water-lily 1·40 90
2518 2200d. "Fritillaria degeniana"
(vert) 1·50 90
2519 3000d. "Orchis simia" (vert) 1·70 1·00

830 Envelopes and
Dish Aerial

1989. Air.
2520 **830** 10000d. blue, mauve
and yellow 2·10 1·00
2521 - 20000d. orange, violet
and red 1·40 90
DESIGN: 20000d. Europe on globe and satellite.

1989. No. 1657 surch **100**.
2522 100d. on 1d. green 1·40 20

832 Competitor

1989. Sixth World Air Gun Championships, Sarajevo.
2523 **832** 3000d. multicoloured 85 65

833 Girl looking
through Magic Cube

1989. Europa. Children's Games and Toys. Multicoloured.
2524 3000d. Type **833** 1·40 1·10
2525 6000d. Boy playing with marbles and paper boats 1·80 1·40

834
Anniversary
Emblem

1989. Obligatory Tax. 125th Anniv (1988) of International
Red Cross.
2526 **834** 20d. blue, silver and red 30 20

2527	834	80d. blue, silver and red	30	20
2528	834	150d. blue, silver and red	30	20
2529	834	160d. blue, silver and red	30	20

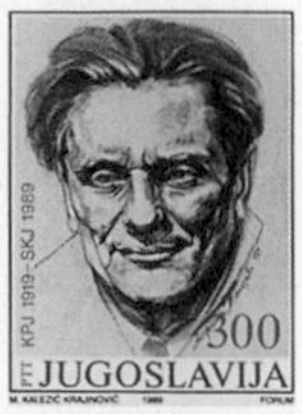

835 Josip Broz Tito

1989. 70th Anniv of Yugoslavian Communist Party.

2530	835	300d. multicoloured	30	10

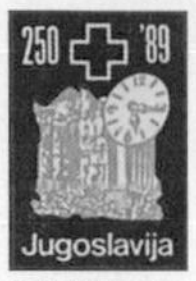

836 "Skopje Earthquake"

1989. Obligatory Tax. Solidarity Week. (a) Perf.

2531	836	250d. silver and red	1·00	55

(b) Rouletted.

2532	715	400d. blue and red	1·80	65

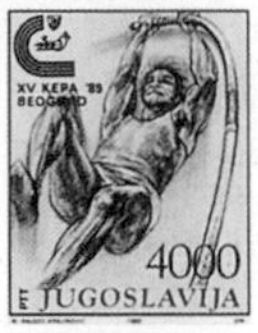

837 Pole Vaulting

1989. 15th European Trophy Athletic Clubs Championship, Belgrade.

2533	837	4000d. multicoloured	1·40	1·10

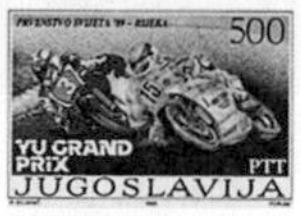

838 Racers

1989. Motor Cycle Grand Prix, Rijeka. Multicoloured.

2534		500d. Type **838**	30	20
2535		4000d. Racers (different)	70	55
MS2536		85×65 mm. 6000d. Race participants numbers 18 and 6 (53×34 mm)	2·50	2·50

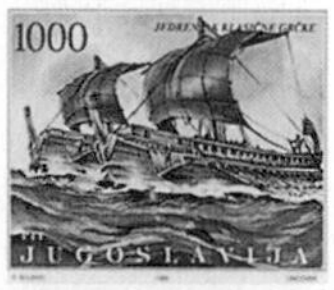

839 Ancient Greek Galleys

1989. Sailing Ships. Multicoloured.

2537		1000d. Type **839**	55	35
2538		1000d. Roman warships	55	35
2539		1000d. 13th-century Crusader nefs	55	35
2540		1000d. 16th-century Dubrovnik navas	55	35
2541		1000d. 17th-century French warships	55	35
2542		1000d. 18th-century ships of the line	55	35
MS2543		115×85 mm. 3000d. Engraving of Dubrovnik (74×32 mm)	1·10	1·10

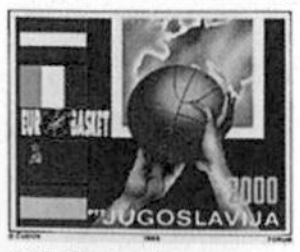

840 Flags of Netherlands, Italy, U.S.S.R. and Spain and Ball

1989. 26th European Men's Basketball Championship, Zagreb. Multicoloured.

2544		2000d. Type **840** (Group A)	30	10
2545		2000d. Flags of France, Yugoslavia, Greece and Bulgaria and ball (Group B)	30	10

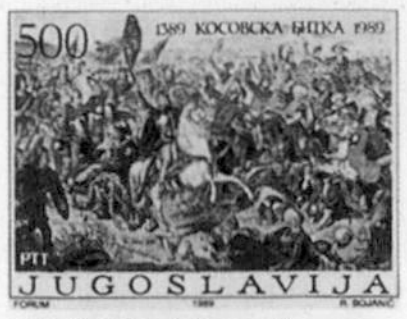

841 "Battle of Kosovo" (lithograph, Adam Stefanovic)

1989. 600th Anniv of Battle of Kosovo.

2546	841	500d. multicoloured	30	10

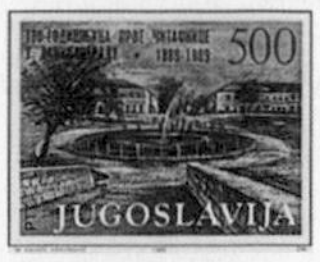

842 Danilovgrad

1989. Centenary of First Reading Room at Danilovgrad.

2547	842	500d. multicoloured	30	10

1989. No. 2277 surch **700**.

2548		700d. on 220d. brown	1·40	20

1989. Nos. 2266 and 2275 surch.

2549		400d. on 30d. brown	1·40	20
2550		700d. on 170d. green	1·40	20

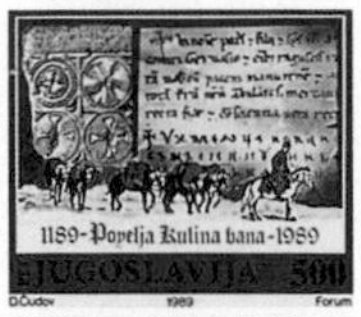

845 Stone Tablet, Detail of Charter and Mule Train

1989. 800th Anniv of Kulin Ban Charter (granting free trade to Dubrovnik).

2551	845	500d. multicoloured	30	10

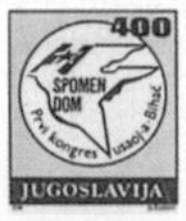

846 Emblem

1989. Obligatory Tax. Construction of Youth House.

2552	846	400d. blue and red	30	10

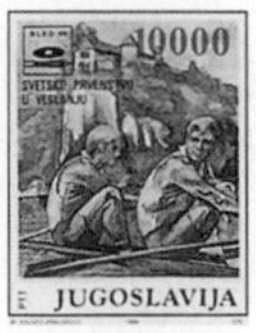

847 Rowers of Bled Lake

1989. World Rowing Championship, Bled.

2553	847	10000d. multicoloured	85	65

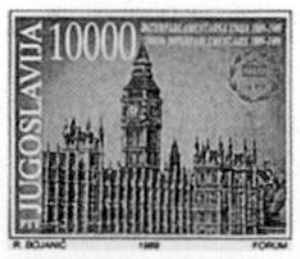

848 Houses of Parliament, London

1989. Centenary of Interparliamentary Union.

2554		10000d. Type **848**	70	55
2555		10000d. Notre Dame Cathedral, Paris	70	55

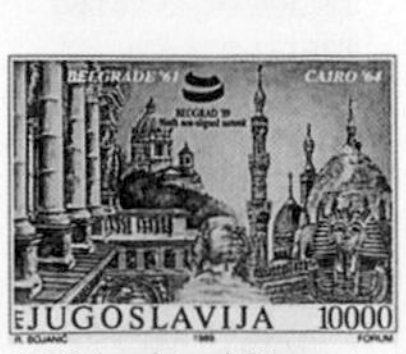

849 Belgrade and Cairo

1989. Ninth Heads of Non-aligned Countries Conference, Belgrade. Previous Host Cities. Multicoloured.

2556		10000d. Type **849**	70	55
2557		10000d. Lusaka and Algiers	70	55
2558		10000d. Colombo and Havana	70	55
2559		10000d. New Delhi and Harare	70	55
MS2560		64×85 mm. 20000d. View of Belgrade and maps showing member states in 1961 and 1989	2·20	2·20

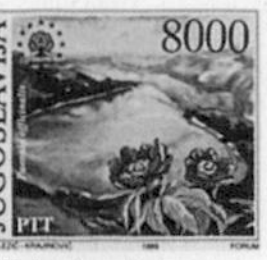

850 Jazinac Lake, Brezovica, and "Paeonia officinalis"

1989. Nature Protection. Kosovo. Multicoloured.

2561		8000d. Type **850**	70	55
2562		10000d. Mirusa Canyon and "Paeonia corallina"	85	65

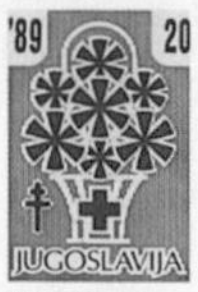

851 Crosses as Basket of Flowers

1989. Obligatory Tax. Anti-tuberculosis Week.

2563	851	20d. red and black	30	20
2564	851	200d. red and black	30	20
2565	851	250d. red and black	30	20
2566	851	400d. red and black	30	20
2567	851	650d. red and black	30	20

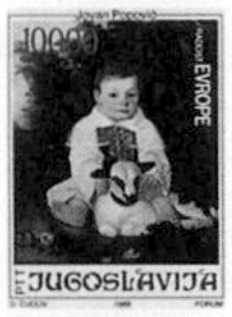

852 "Child with Lamb" (Jovan Popovic)

1989. 21st "Joy of Europe" Meeting. Multicoloured.

2568		10000d. Type **852**	85	65
2569		10000d. "Girl feeding Dog" (Aelbert Cuyp)	85	65

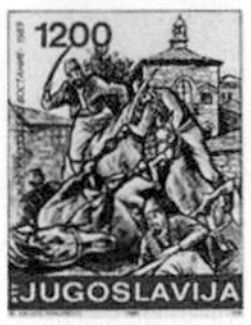

853 Men Fighting

1989. 300th Anniv of Karpos Insurrection.

2570	853	1200d. multicoloured	30	10

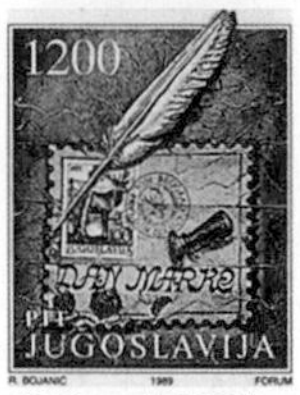

854 Cancelled 100d. Stamp, Quill and Seal

1989. Stamp Day.

2571	854	1200d. multicoloured	30	10

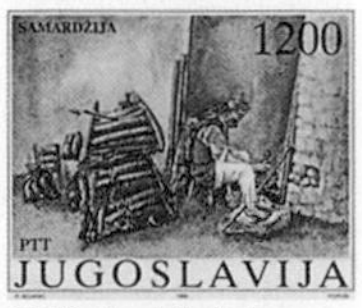

855 Packsaddle Maker

1989. Museum Exhibits. Traditional Crafts. Multicoloured.

2572		1200d. Type **855**	30	10
2573		14000d. Cooper	1·00	80
2574		15000d. Wine maker	1·40	1·10
2575		30000d. Weaver	2·20	1·80

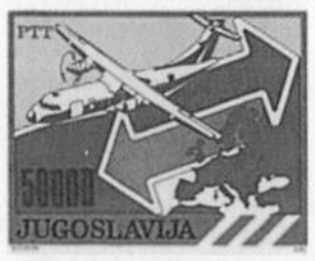

856 Aerospatiale/Aeritalia ATR 42 Airliner, Arrows and Map

1989. Air.

2576	856	50000d. blue and orange	1·70	1·30

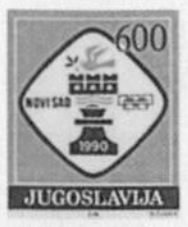

856a Emblem

1989. Obligatory Tax. 29th Chess Olympiad, Novi Sad.

2577	856a	600d. black and blue	40	20

See also No. 2660.

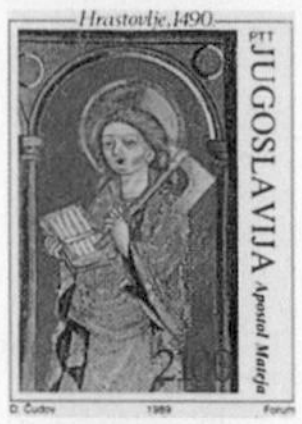

857 "Apostle Matthias"

1989. Frescoes by Iohannes de Kastua from Holy Trinity Church, Hrastovlje, Slovenia. Multicoloured.

2578		2100d. Type **857**	30	10
2579		21000d. "St. Barbara"	70	55
2580		30000d. "Creation of the Universe, the Fourth Day" (horiz)	1·40	1·10
2581		50000d. "Creation of the Universe, the Fifth Day" (horiz)	2·10	1·70

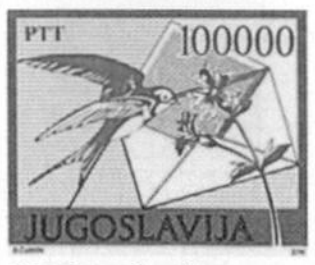

858 Barn Swallow, Envelope and Flower

1989

2582	858	100000d. green & orange	2·10	1·50

1989. No. 1680 surch **700**.

2583		700d. on 70d. blue	70	20

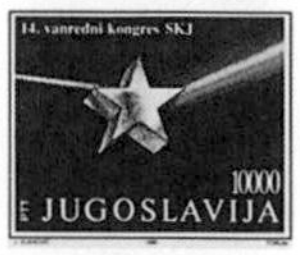

860 Colour Spectrum entering Star

1990. 14th Extraordinary Congress of League of Communists of Yugoslavia, Belgrade.

2584	860	10000d. multicoloured	40	35
2585	-	50000d. multicoloured	1·00	80
MS2586		66×86 mm. 100000d. red, ultramarine and silver. Imperf	2·20	2·20

DESIGNS—HORIZ: 50000d. Hammer and sickle on computer screen. VERT: 100000d. Congress poster (Ivan Dorogi).

1990. Postal Services. As T **735** but in revised currency.

2587		10p. violet and green	30	10
2588		20p. red and yellow	30	10
2589		30p. green and orange	30	10
2590		40p. green and purple	30	10
2591		50p. green and violet	40	10
2592		60p. mauve and red	40	10
2593		1d. blue and purple	70	20
2594		2d. blue and red	1·40	20
2595		3d. blue and red	1·40	35
2596		5d. ultramarine and blue	1·40	55
2597		10d. blue and red	2·75	1·70
2598		20d. red and orange	70	35

DESIGNS—VERT: 10p. Man posting letters; 20p. Postal sorter; 30p. Postman giving letters to man; 40p., 20d. Woman telephoning; 50p. Posthorn, globe and bird; 60p. Telephone card, tokens and handset; 3d. Post-box; 5d. Airplane, letters and map; 10d. Barn swallow, flower and envelope. HORIZ: 1d. Electric train; 2d. Freighter.

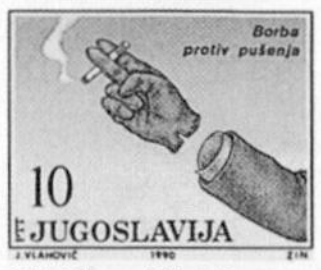

861 Gloved Hand holding Lighted Cigarette

1990. Anti-smoking Campaign.

2605	861	10d. multicoloured	1·80	1·10

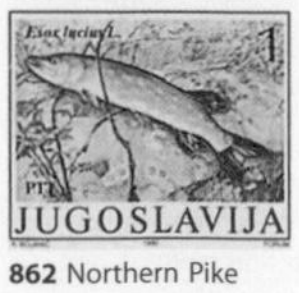

862 Northern Pike

1990. Endangered Fish. Multicoloured.

2606	1d. Type **862**	1·20	90
2607	5d. Wels	1·60	1·10
2608	10d. Burbot	2·10	1·30
2609	15d. Eurasian perch	2·75	1·60

862a Pink
Flowers

1990. Obligatory Tax. Anti-cancer Week. Multicoloured.

| 2610 | 30p. Type **862a** | 40 | 10 |
| 2611 | 30p. Yellow flowers | 40 | 10 |

863 Zabljak Fortress,
Printed Page from 1494
and Arms

1990. 500th Anniv of Enthronement of Djuradj Crnojevic of Montenegro.

| 2612 | **863** | 50p. multicoloured | 1·80 | 1·50 |

864 Telegraphist and V.D.U.
Screen

1990. 125th Anniv of I.T.U.

| 2613 | **864** | 6d.50 multicoloured | 1·40 | 1·10 |

865 Footballers

1990. World Cup Football Championship, Italy.

| 2614 | - | 6d.50 multicoloured | 2·10 | 1·70 |
| 2615 | **865** | 10d. multicoloured | 2·50 | 2·00 |

DESIGN: 6d.50, Footballers (different)

866 Skopje Posts and
Telecommunications
Centre

1990. Europa. Post Office Buildings. Multicoloured.

| 2616 | 6d.50 Type **866** | 2·10 | 1·70 |
| 2617 | 10d. Belgrade Telephone Exchange | 2·50 | 2·00 |

867 Chicago Water
Tower and
Carnation

1990. Centenary of Labour Day.

| 2618 | **867** | 6d.50 multicoloured | 1·50 | 1·20 |

868 Record, Notes
and Pen

1990. Eurovision Song Contest, Zagreb. Multicoloured.

| 2619 | 6d.50 Type **868** | 1·70 | 1·30 |

| 2620 | 10d. Conductor and score of "Te Deum" by Marc-Antoine Charpentier (theme tune of contest) | 2·10 | 1·70 |

869 Cross and
Leaves

1990. Obligatory Tax. (a) Red Cross Week.

2621	**869**	10p. red and green	30	20
2622	**869**	20p. red and green	30	20
2623	**869**	30p. red and green	30	20

870 Large Yellow
Flowers

(b) 45th Anniv of Macedonian Red Cross. Flower Paintings by Zivko Popovski. Multicoloured.

2624	20p. Type **870**	30	20
2625	20p. Arrangement of small yellow flowers	30	20
2626	20p. Anniversary emblem	30	20

See also Nos. 2633/4.

871 Server

1990. Yugoslav Open Tennis Championship, Umag. Multicoloured.

| 2627 | 6d.50 Type **871** | 2·10 | 1·70 |
| 2628 | 10d. Receiver | 2·40 | 1·90 |

1990. No. 2282 surch **0,50**.

| 2629 | **735** | 50p. on 800d. blue | 70 | 20 |

873 Tito (bronze,
Antun Augustincic)

1990. 98th Birth Anniv of Josip Broz Tito.

| 2630 | **873** | 50p. multicoloured | 40 | 35 |

874 "Tartar Post Riders" (Carl
Goebel)

1990. 150th Anniv of Public Postal Service in Serbia.

| 2631 | **874** | 50p. multicoloured | 3·50 | 1·90 |

875 "Skopje
Earthquake"   **876** "Skopje
Earthquake"

1990. Obligatory Tax. Solidarity Week.

2632	**875**	20p. brown, silver and red	1·00	55
2633	-	20p. multicoloured	30	10
2634	-	20p. multicoloured	30	10
2635	**876**	20p. blue and red	70	55
2636	**715**	30p. blue and red	55	35

DESIGNS—As T **875**: No. 2633, Mauve flowers; 2634, Red and yellow flowers.
See also No. 2711.

877 Fantail

1990. Pigeons. Multicoloured.

2637	50p. Type **877**	85	65
2638	5d. Serbian high flier	1·40	1·10
2639	6d.50 Carrier pigeon (vert)	1·70	1·30
2640	10d. Pouter (vert)	4·25	3·25

878 Idrija Town

1990. 500th Anniversaries of Idrija Town (2641) and Mercury Mine (2642). Multicoloured.

| 2641 | 50p. Type **878** | 30 | 10 |
| 2642 | 6d.50 Mine | 1·50 | 1·20 |

879 Newspaper
Offices, Museum
and Mastheads

1990. 50th Anniv of "Vjesnik" (newspaper).

| 2643 | **879** | 60p. multicoloured | 1·10 | 90 |

1990. Nos. 2588/9 surch.

| 2644 | 50p. on 20p. red and yellow | 70 | 20 |
| 2645 | 1d. on 30p. green and orange | 70 | 20 |

881 Runners leaving
Blocks

1990. European Athletics Championships, Split. Multicoloured.

2646	1d. Type **881**	1·00	80
2647	6d.50 Runners' feet	1·40	1·10
MS2648	85×65 mm. 10d. Runners and their reflections (52×34 mm)	3·50	3·50

881a
Emblem

1990. Obligatory Tax. European Athletics Championships, Split.

| 2649 | **881a** | 50p. blue and red | 40 | 20 |

882 Nurse
and Sun   **883** Flowers
in Vase and
Birds

1990. Obligatory Tax. Anti-tuberculosis Week.

2650	**882**	20p. yellow, blue and red	30	10
2651	**882**	25p. yellow, blue and red	30	10
2652	**882**	50p. yellow, blue and red	40	20
2653	**883**	50p. brown, red and grey	40	20

884 "Pec Patriachate" (Dimitrije
Cudov)

1990. 300th Anniv of Great Migration of Serbs. Multicoloured.

| 2654 | 1d. Type **884** | 30 | 10 |
| 2655 | 6d.50 "Migration of Serbs" (Paja Jovanovic) | 1·40 | 1·10 |

1990. No. 2590 surch **2**.

| 2656 | 2d. on 40p. green and purple | 1·40 | 55 |

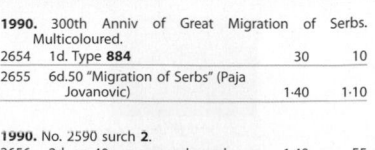

887 "Little Sisters"
(Ivana Kobilca)

1990. 22nd "Joy of Europe" Meeting. Multicoloured.

| 2658 | 6d.50 Type **887** | 1·80 | 1·50 |
| 2659 | 10d. "Willem III of Orange as a child" (Adriaen Hanneman) (vert) | 2·40 | 1·90 |

1990. Obligatory Tax. 29th Chess Olympiad, Novi Sad. As No. 2577 but value in reformed currency.

| 2660 | **856a** | 1d. black and blue | 40 | 20 |

888 Chess Pieces

1990. 29th Chess Olympiad, Novi Sad. Multicoloured.

2661	1d. Type **888**	35	20
2662	5d. Rook, bishop, knight and chessboard	1·70	1·40
2663	6d.50 Knights, queen, king, pawn and chessboard	2·00	1·60
2664	10d. Chess pieces and symbols	2·75	2·20
MS2665	84×97 mm. As Nos. 2661/4 but with emblem in gold (instead of silver). Imperf	12·50	12·50

888a
Dubrovnik

1990. Obligatory Tax. European Judo Championships, Dubrovnik.

| 2666 | **888a** | 1d. violet and blue | 40 | 20 |

889 "St. Vlaho and Ragusa"
(detail of triptych, Nikola
Bozidarevic) and Penny Black

1990. Stamp Day.

| 2667 | **889** | 2d. multicoloured | 1·00 | 65 |

890 Vransko Lake

1990. Nature Protection. Multicoloured.

| 2668 | 6d.50 Type **890** | 1·80 | 1·50 |
| 2669 | 10d. Griffon vulture | 2·40 | 1·90 |

891 "King Milutin" and
Monastery of our Lady,
Ljeviska

1990. Monastery Frescoes. Multicoloured.

2670	2d. Type **891**	70	55
2671	5d. "St. Sava" and Mileseva Monastery	1·40	1·10
2672	6d.50 "St. Elias" and Moraca Monastery	1·70	1·30
2673	10d. "Jesus Christ" and Sopocani Monastery	2·10	1·70

892 Milanovic and
Kringa (birthplace)

1990. Birth Centenary of Dr. Bozo Milanovic (politician).
2674　**892**　2d. multicoloured　　40　　35

893 "Arrival of Mary
in the Temple"

1990. Museum Exhibits. Icon Screens of St. Jovan
Bigorski Monastery, Bistra. Multicoloured.
2675　　2d. Type **893**　　　70　　55
2676　　5d. "Nativity"　　　1·10　　90
2677　　6d. "Flight into Egypt" (horiz)　1·40　1·10
2678　　10d. "Entry into Jerusalem"
　　　(horiz)　　　1·70　1·30

894 Northern
Lapwing

1991. Protected Birds. Multicoloured.
2679　　2d. Type **894**　　35　　30
2680　　5d. Woodchat shrike　　95　　75
2681　　6d.50 Common crane　　1·30　1·00
2682　　10d. Goosander　　1·90　1·50

895 "Crocus
kosaninii"

1991. Crocuses. Multicoloured.
2683　　2d. Type **895**　　70　　55
2684　　6d. "Crocus scardicus"　85　　65
2685　　7d.50 "Crocus rujanensis"　1·00　　80
2686　　15d. "Crocus adamii"　　3·00　2·50

895a Hands
and Flower

895b Emblem

1991. Obligatory Tax. Anti-cancer Week.
2687　**895a**　1d. blue and orange　40　　20
2688　**895b**　1d.20 multicoloured　40　　20
2689　-　1d.20 multicoloured　40　　20
2690　-　1d.20 multicoloured　40　　20
2691　-　1d.20 multicoloured　40　　20
DESIGNS: As T **895b**: No 2689, Butterfly; 2690, Sunbathers
on rocky beach; 2691, Street in town.

896 Bishop Josip Juraj
Strossmayer (founder)
(after Vlaho Bukovac)

1991. 125th Anniv of Yugoslav Academy of Arts and
Sciences.
2692　**896**　2d. multicoloured　　1·40　　65

897 Mozart (after P.
Lorenzoni)

1991. Death Bicentenary of Wolfgang Amadeus Mozart
(composer).
2693　**897**　7d.50 multicoloured　1·70　1·30

898 Edvard Rusijan
(Slovenian pioneer)
and Bleriot XI

1991. Centenary of First Heavier-than-air Flight by
Lilienthal. Multicoloured.
2694　　7d.50 Type **898**　　1·70　1·30
2695　　15d. Otto Lilienthal and
　　　Lilienthal biplane glider　2·10　1·70

899 Route of Climb and
Cesen

1991. First Anniv of Tomo Cesen's Ascent of South Face
of Lhotse Peak.
2696　**899**　7d.50 multicoloured　1·70　1·30

900 Satellite and
Earth

1991. Europa. Europe in Space. Multicoloured.
2697　　7d.50 Type **900**　　1·70　1·30
2698　　15d. Dish aerial reflecting rays
　　　from satellite to telephone　2·75　2·20

901 Figures
902 Red Cross
and Rays

1991. Obligatory Tax. Red Cross Week.
2699　**901**　60p. multicoloured　15　　10
2700　**901**　1d.20 multicoloured　30　　20
2701　-　2d.50 multicoloured　55　　45
2702　-　1d.70 multicoloured　30　　20
2703　**902**　1d.70 multicoloured　30　　20
2704　-　1d.70 multicoloured　30　　20
2705　-　1d.70 multicoloured　30　　20
2706　-　1d.70 multicoloured　30　　20
DESIGNS—29×24 mm: No. 2702, Similar to T **901** but differently inscribed. As T **902**: No. 2704, Pink flowers; 2705,
Children on globe; 2706, Yellow flowers.

903 Miraculous Icon
of St. Mary of Trsat
(14th century)

1991. 700th Anniv of Franciscan Monastery, Rijeka.
2707　**903**　3d.50 multicoloured　1·30　　65

904 Danube River
Steamer

1991. Community of Danubian Regions Conference,
Belgrade. Multicoloured.
2708　　7d.50 Type **904**　　1·40　1·10
2709　　15d. Steamer on river at sunset　2·10　1·70
MS2710 85×65 mm. 20d. Map of
　　Danube (54×34 mm)　　9·75　9·75

905 Woman with
Horse

1991. Obligatory Tax. Solidarity Week.
2711　**876**　2d. green and orange　40　　35
2712　-　2d. brown, red and gold　40　　35
2713　**905**　2d. brown, red and gold　40　　35
2714　-　2d. brown, red and gold　40　　35
2715　-　2d. brown, red and gold　40　　35
2716　**715**　2d.20 blue and red　65　　45
DESIGNS—As T **905**: No. 2712, "Skopje Earthquake"; 2714,
Woman and tree; 2715, Woman holding cockerel.

906 "Karavanke Pass"
(17th-century engraving,
Johann Valvasor)

1991. Opening of Karavanke Road Tunnel. Multicoloured.
2717　　4d.50 Type **906**　　1·00　　80
2718　　11d. Tunnel entrance　　1·40　1·10

907 Balls and Baskets

1991. Centenary of Basketball. Multicoloured.
2719　　11d. Type **907**　　1·70　1·30
2720　　15d. Aerial view of baskets　2·20　1·80

907a
Exhibitor
carrying
Painting

1991. Obligatory Tax. Cetinje Biennale.
2721　**907a**　2d. red and blue　　40　　20

908 Order of
the Partisan
Star

1991. 50th Anniversaries of Yugoslav Insurrection and
National Army. Multicoloured.
2722　　4d.50 Type **908**　　55　　45
2723　　11d. Order for Bravery　　1·10　　90

909 Ujevic

1991. Birth Centenary of Tin Ujevic (writer).
2724　**909**　4d.50 multicoloured　1·00　　55

910 Score and Gallus

1991. 400th Death Anniv of Jacobus Gallus (composer).
2725　**910**　11d. multicoloured　1·10　　90

911 Savudrija, 1818

1991. Lighthouses of the Adriatic and the Danube.
Multicoloured.
2726　　10d. Type **911**　　1·40　1·10
2727　　10d. Sveti Ivan na Pucini, 1853　1·40　1·10
2728　　10d. Porer, 1833　　1·40　1·10
2729　　10d. Stoncica, 1865　　1·40　1·10
2730　　10d. Olipa, 1842　　1·40　1·10
2731　　10d. Glavat, 1884　　1·40　1·10
2732　　10d. Veli Rat, 1849　　1·40　1·10
2733　　10d. Vir, 1881　　1·40　1·10
2734　　10d. Tajerske Sestrice, 1876　1·40　1·10
2735　　10d. Razanj, 1875　　1·40　1·10
2736　　10d. Derdap, Danube　　1·40　1·10
2737　　10d. Tamis, Danube　　1·40　1·10

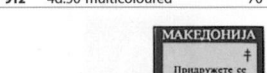

912 "Sremski Karlovci School"
(Ljubica Sokic)

1991. Bicent of Sremski Karlovci High School.
2738　**912**　4d.50 multicoloured　70　　35

913 Girl
914 Inscription

1991. Obligatory Tax. Anti-tuberculosis Week.
2739　**913**　1d.20 blue, red & yellow　20　　10
2740　**913**　2d.50 blue, red & yellow　30　　20
2741　**914**　2d.50 black, yell & mve　30　　20
2742　-　2d.50 multicoloured　30　　20
2743　-　2d.50 multicoloured　30　　20
2744　-　2d.50 black, yell & mve　30　　20
DESIGNS—As T **914**: No. 2742, Doctor and patient; 2743,
Children on path; 2744, Girl with birds and flowers.

915 Mayfly

1991. Nature Protection. Multicoloured.
2745　　11d. Type **915**　　1·50　1·20
2746　　15d. Pygmy cormorants　2·00　1·60

916 Town Hall
(stained glass)

1991. 600th Anniv of Subotica.
2747　**916**　4d.50 multicoloured　70　　55

917 Honey Bees and
Congress Emblem

1991. "Apimondia" 33rd International Bee Keeping Congress, Split.
| 2748 | **917** | 11d. multicoloured | 1·70 | 1·20 |

918 "Little Dubravka" (Jovan Bijelic)

1991. 23rd "Joy of Europe" Meeting. Multicoloured.
| 2749 | | 5d. Type **918** | 1·10 | 90 |
| 2750 | | 30d. "Little Girl with a Cat" (Mary Cassatt) | 1·70 | 1·30 |

919 Statue of Prince Michael Obrenovic and Serbian 1866 1p. Newspaper Stamp

1991. Stamp Day.
| 2751 | **919** | 4d.50 multicoloured | 1·00 | 80 |

919a Protecting Refugee

1991. Obligatory Tax. Serbian Refugee Fund.
| 2752 | **919a** | 2d. mauve and blue | 45 | 20 |

920 Battle of Vucji. Flag and Medal for Military Valour

1991. Cetinje Museum Exhibits, Montenegrin Flags and Medals. Multicoloured.
2753		20d. Type **920**	45	35
2754		30d. Battle of Grahovo flag and medal	70	55
2755		40d. State flag and Medal for bravery	1·00	80
2756		50d. Court flag and Petrovic dynasty commemorative medal	1·70	1·30

921 Angel carrying Sun (Andrija Raicevic) (17th century)

1991. Illustrations from Ancient Manuscripts. Multicoloured.
2757		20d. Type **921**	45	35
2758		30d. "April" (Celnica Gospel) (14th century)	70	55
2759		40d. "Annunciation" (Trogir Evangeliarum) (13th century)	1·00	80
2760		50d. Mary Magdalene in initial V (Miroslav Gospel) (12th century)	1·70	1·30

1991. Nos. 2592 and 2587 surch.
| 2761 | | 5d. on 60p. mauve and red | 70 | 20 |
| 2762 | | 10d. on 10p. violet and green | 70 | 35 |

923 Delcev

1992. 120th Birth Anniv of Goce Delcev (Macedonian revolutionary).
| 2763 | **923** | 5d. multicoloured | 3·25 | 2·50 |

924 Trophies and Club Emblem

1992. Victories of Red Star Club, Belgrade, in European and World Football Championships.
| 2764 | **924** | 17d. multicoloured | 3·50 | 2·75 |

925 Luge

1992. Winter Olympic Games, Albertville, France. Multicoloured.
| 2765 | | 80d. Type **925** | 2·30 | 1·80 |
| 2766 | | 100d. Acrobatic skiing | 2·75 | 2·20 |

926 European Hare

1992. Protected Animals. Multicoloured.
2767		50d. Type **926**	1·40	1·10
2768		60d. Siberian flying squirrels	1·60	1·20
2769		80d. Forest dormouse	1·90	1·50
2770		100d. Common hamsters	2·30	1·80

927 "Mary feeding Jesus" (fresco, Pec Patriarchate)

1992. United Nations Children's Fund Breastfeeding Campaign.
| 2771 | **927** | 80d. multicoloured | 1·70 | 1·30 |

928 Skier

1992. Centenary of Skiing in Montenegro.
| 2772 | **928** | 8d. multicoloured | 5·50 | 4·25 |

929 Fountain, Belgrade

1992
| 2773 | **929** | 50d. violet and lilac | 70 | 55 |
| 2774 | - | 100d. deep green and green | 45 | 20 |

DESIGN: 100d. Fisherman Fountain, Kalemgdan Fortress, Belgrade.
See also Nos. 2825/32 and 2889/90.

930 "Titanic"

1992. 80th Anniv of Sinking of Liner "Titanic".
| 2783 | **930** | 150d. multicoloured | 1·60 | 1·10 |

931 La Barqueta Bridge and Seville (engraving)

1992. "Expo '92" World's Fair, Seville.
| 2784 | **931** | 150d. multicoloured | 1·60 | 1·10 |

932 Christopher Columbus

1992. Europa. 500th Anniv of Discovery of America by Columbus. Multicoloured.
2785		300d. Type **932**	4·50	3·50
2786		500d. Columbus's fleet	5·25	4·25
MS2787		85×65 mm. 1200d. "Lisbon Harbour" (engraving) (52×34 mm)	14·50	14·50

934 Water Polo

1992. Olympic Games, Barcelona. Multicoloured.
2791		500d. Type **934**	1·40	1·10
2792		500d. Shooting	1·40	1·10
2793		500d. Tennis	1·40	1·10
2794		500d. Handball	1·40	1·10

935 Players' Legs

1992. European Football Championship, Sweden. Multicoloured.
| 2795 | | 1000d. Type **935** | 2·50 | 2·00 |
| 2796 | | 1000d. Players | 2·50 | 2·00 |

936 Red Tabby

1992. Domestic Cats. Multicoloured.
2797		1000d. Type **936**	2·50	2·00
2798		1000d. White Persian	2·50	2·00
2799		1000d. Blue and white British shorthair	2·50	2·00
2800		1000d. Red-point colourpoint longhair	2·50	2·00

937 Class 162, 1880

1992. Steam Railway Locomotives. Multicoloured.
2801		1000d. Type **937**	3·25	2·50
2802		1000d. Class 151, 1885	3·25	2·50
2803		1000d. Class 73, 1913	3·25	2·50
2804		1000d. Class 83, 1929	3·25	2·50
2805		1000d. Class 16 locomotive "Sava", 1936	3·25	2·50
2806		1000d. Prince Nicholas's steam railcar, 1909	3·25	2·50

1992. Various stamps surch.
2807		2d. on 30p. green and orange (No. 2589)	2·75	55
2808		5d. on 20p. red and yellow (No. 2588)	2·75	55
2809		5d. on 40p. green and purple (No. 2590)	2·75	55
2810		10d. on 50p. green and violet (No. 2591)	2·75	55
2811		10d. on 5d. ultramarine and blue (No. 2596)	2·75	55
2812		20d. on 1d. blue and purple (No. 2593)	4·25	1·10
2813		20d. on 5d. blue, green and yellow (as No. 2596)	2·75	55
2814		50d. on 2d. blue and red (No. 2594)	2·75	55
2815		100d. on 3d. blue and red (No. 2595)	5·75	1·10

No. 2813 was not issued without surcharge.

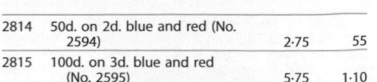

939 Fischer (champion, 1972–75)

1992. Unofficial Chess Re-match between Former World Champions Robert Fischer and Boris Spassky. Multicoloured.
| 2816 | | 500d. Type **939** | 2·75 | 2·10 |
| 2817 | | 500d. Spassky (1969–72) | 2·75 | 2·10 |

940 Old Telephone and Buildings in Novi Sad, Subotica and Zrenjanin

1992. Centenary of Telephone Service in Vojvodina.
| 2818 | **940** | 10d. multicoloured | 2·20 | 1·70 |

941 "Ballerina" (Edgar Degas)

1992. 24th "Joy of Europe" Meeting. Paintings. Multicoloured.
| 2819 | | 500d. Type **941** | 2·20 | 1·70 |
| 2820 | | 500d. Youth (V. Knezevic) | 2·20 | 1·70 |

942 Montenegro 1874 25n. Stamp and Musician

1992. Stamp Day.
| 2821 | **942** | 50d. multicoloured | 1·70 | 1·30 |

943 Western Capercaillie, Durmitor Mountains

1992. Nature Protection. Multicoloured.
| 2822 | | 500d. Type **943** | 5·75 | 4·50 |
| 2823 | | 500d. Eastern white pelican ("Pelecanus onocrotalus"), Skadar Sea | 5·75 | 4·50 |

944 Book and Emblem

1992. Centenary of Serbian Literary Association.
| 2824 | **944** | 100d. multicoloured | 1·40 | 1·10 |

1992. As T **929**.
2825		5d. brown and green	1·40	20
2826		50d. blue and azure	70	20
2827		100d. lilac and pink	70	20
2828		300d. brown and chestnut	70	20
2829		500d. green and flesh	1·40	20
2830		3000d. orange	70	20
2831		5000d. purple and yellow	70	20
2832		500000d. violet and blue	85	35

DESIGNS: 5d. 14th-century relief; 50d. As No. 2774; 100d. Type **929**; 300d. Fountain, Kalemegdan Fortress, Belgrade; 500d. Fountain, Sremski Korlovci; 3000d. Fountain, Studenica; 5000d. Fountain, Oplentsu; 500000d. Thermal baths, Vrnjacka Banja.

945 Brvnara Summer Pasture Hut, Zlatibor

1992. Museum Exhibits. Traditional Houses. Multicoloured.

2833	500d. Type **945**	1·40	1·10
2834	500d. House, Morava	1·40	1·10
2835	500d. House, Metokhija	1·40	1·10
2836	500d. Farmhouse, Vojvodina	1·40	1·10

946 Sun over Able-bodied and Disabled People

1992. Obligatory Tax. Disabled Persons' Week.

2837	**946** 13d. yellow and blue	45	20

947 St. Simeon Nemanja with Model of Church of the Blessed Virgin, Studenica (mosaic, Oplenac)

1992. Mosaics and Icons. Multicoloured.

2838	500d. Type **947**	1·40	1·10
2839	500d. Prince Lazarevic with model of Ravanica Monastery (mosaic),Oplenac	1·40	1·10
2840	500d. St. Petka (icon) and St. Petka's Church, Belgrade (horiz)	1·40	1·10
2841	500d. St. Vasilii Ostronoski (icon) and Monastery, Montenegro (horiz)	1·40	1·10

948 Bleriot XI (monoplane)

1992. 80th Anniv of Aviation in Yugoslavia.

2842	**948** 500d. multicoloured	1·90	1·50

949 Detail of Fresco, Sirmium

1993. 1700th Anniv of Formation of the Tetrarchy (Diocletian's reform of government of Roman Empire).

2843	**949** 1500d. multicoloured	1·70	1·30

950 Museum and Medal

1993. Centenary of Cetinje State Museum.

2844	**950** 2500d. multicoloured	1·70	1·30

1993. Obligatory Tax. Anti-cancer Week. No. 2687 surch **1500 d.**

2844a	**895a** 1500d. on 1d. blue and orange	1·70	1·30

952 Common Sturgeon

1993. Marine Animals. Multicoloured.

2845	10000d. Type **952**	2·20	1·70
2846	10000d. Red scorpionfish	2·20	1·70
2847	10000d. Swordfish	2·20	1·70
2848	10000d. Bottle-nosed dolphin	2·20	1·70

953 Charter and 1868 10p. Coin

1993. 125th Anniv of Reintroduction of Serbian Coins (2849) and 120th Anniv of the Dinar (2850). Multicoloured.

2849	10000d. Type **953**	2·20	1·70
2850	10000d. 5d. banknote and 1879 5d. coin	2·20	1·70

954 Milos Crnjanski (writer)

1993. Anniversaries. Multicoloured.

2851	40000d. Type **954** (birth centenary)	2·30	1·80
2852	40000d. Nikola Tesla (physicist, 50th death anniv)	2·30	1·80
2853	40000d. Mihailo Petrovic (mathematician, 50th death anniv)	2·30	1·80
2854	40000d. Aleksa Santic (poet, 125th birth anniv)	2·30	1·80

955 Girl holding Flowers, and Bird (M. Markovski)

1993. Children for Peace. Multicoloured.

2855	50000d. Type **955**	2·40	1·90
2856	50000d. Birds flying above children (J. Rugovac)	2·40	1·90

956 Illuminated Letter from Miroslav Gospel

1993. No value expressed.

2857	**956** A (3000d.) red (18×22 mm)	2·75	55

See also No. 3100.

957 "Nude with Mirror" (M. Milunovic)

1993. Europa. Contemporary Art. Multicoloured.

2858	95000d. Type **957**	4·25	3·25
2859	95000d. "Composition" (Milena Barili)	4·25	3·25

958

1993. Obligatory Tax. Red Cross Week.

2860	**958** 350d. black and red	45	20
2861	**958** 1000d. black and red	70	35

No. 2860 was for use in Montenegro and No. 2861 for Serbia.

959 Map of Europe and Envelopes

1993

2862	**959** 50000d. silver and blue	70	20
2863	– 100000d. blue and red	1 40	55

DESIGN: 100000d. Airplane.

961 Sutorina

1993. Fortresses. Multicoloured.

2865	900000d. Type **961**	1·70	1·30
2866	900000d. Kalemegdan, Belgrade	1·70	1·30
2867	900000d. Medun	1·70	1·30
2868	900000d. Petrovaradin	1·70	1·30
2869	900000d. Bar	1·70	1·30
2870	900000d. Golubac	1·70	1·30

962 Marguerites and Roses

1993. Flower Arrangements. Multicoloured.

2871	1000000d. Type **962**	2·20	1·70
2872	1000000d. Roses and gerbera	2·20	1·70
2873	1000000d. Roses and lilies	2·20	1·70
2874	1000000d. Rose, carnations and stephanotis	2·20	1·70

963 Generating Plant, Street Lamp and Town

1993. Centenary of Electrification of Serbia.

2875	**963** 2500000d. mult	1·20	90

964 Jays

1993. Nature Protection. Fruska Highlands. Multicoloured.

2876	300,000,000d. Type **964**	10·50	7·75
2877	300,000,000d. Golden oriole	10·50	7·75

1993. Various stamps surch.

2878	10d. on 100000d. blue and red (No. 2863)	1·50	35
2879	50d. on 5d. brown and green (No. 2825)	1·50	35
2880	100d. on 5000d. purple and yellow (No. 2831)	1·50	35
2881	500d. on 50d. blue and azure (No. 2826)	1·50	35
2882	1000d. on 3000d. orange (No. 2830)	1·50	35
2883	10000d. on 300d. brown and chestnut (No. 2828)	1·50	35
2884	50000d. stone, brown and green (No. 2825)	1·50	35

966 River Freighters

1993. The Danube, "River of Co-operation". Multicoloured.

2885	15000d. Type **966**	2·30	1·70
2886	15000d. Passenger ferry	2·30	1·70
MS2887	87×57 mm. 20000d. Course of River Danube on map (34×29 mm)	4·50	4·50

967 Jagodina Cancellation and Market

1993. Stamp Day. 150th Anniv of Jagodina Postal Service.

2888	**967** 12000d. multicoloured	2·00	1·50

1993. Thermal Baths. As T **929**.

2889	10000d. blue and violet	1·50	20
2890	100000d. brown and red	1·50	20

DESIGNS: 10000d. As No. 2832; 100000d. Bukovicka Banja.

968 "Boy with Cat" (Sava Sumanovic)

1993. 25th "Joy of Europe" Meeting. Multicoloured.

2891	2000000d. Type **968**	2·30	1·70
2892	2000000d. "Circus Rider" (Georges Rouault)	2·30	1·70

969 "Madonna and Child" (from Bogorodica Ljeviska)

1993. Icons. Multicoloured.

2893	400,000,000d. Type **969**	1·50	1·10
2894	400,000,000d. "Christ entering Jerusalem" (from Oplenac)	1·50	1·10
2895	400,000,000d. "Birth of Christ" (from Studenica)	1·50	1·10
2896	400,000,000d. "The Annunciation" (from Mileseva)	1·50	1·10

970 Summer Pasture Hut, Savardak

1993. Museum Exhibits. Traditional Buildings. Multicoloured.

2897	50d. Type **970**	1·50	1·10
2898	50d. "Crmnicka" house, Bar	1·50	1·10
2899	50d. Watchtower, Chardak (vert)	1·50	1·10
2900	50d. Coast house, Primorsten (vert)	1·50	1·10

971 Illuminated Page

1994. 500th Anniv of Printing of "Oktoukh" (book). Multicoloured.

2901	1000d. Type **971**	1·20	90
2902	1000d. Illustration of church and saints	1·20	90

972 Egyptian Vultures

1994. Birds. Multicoloured.

2903	80p. Type **972**	3·25	2·50
2904	80p. Saker falcons ("Falco cherrug")	3·25	2·50
2905	80p. Long-legged buzzards ("Buteo rufinus")	3·25	2·50
2906	80p. Lesser kestrels ("Falco naumanni")	3·25	2·50

973 Mimosa

1994. International Mimosa Festival, Herceg Novi.

2907	**973** 80p. multicoloured	2·30	1·70

974 Illumination from Miroslav Gospel and Museum

1994. 150th Anniv of National Museum (2908) and 125th Anniv of National Theatre (2909), Belgrade. Multicoloured.

2908	80p. Type **974**	2·30	1·70
2909	80p. Prince Milos Obrenovic and theatre	2·30	1·70

975 Speed Skating

1994. Winter Olympic Games, Lillehammer, Norway. Multicoloured.

2910	60p. Type **975**	1·70	1·20
2911	60p. Olympic rings and flame	1·70	1·20
2912	60p. Skiing	1·70	1·20

976 Caudron C-61 and Route Map

1994. Europa. 71st Anniv of First Paris–Belgrade–Bucharest–Istanbul Regular Night Flight. Multicoloured.

2913	60p. Type **976**	3·00	2·20
2914	1d.80 Caudron C-61, Belgrade and route map	3·75	2·75

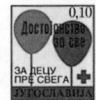

977 Balloons

1994. Obligatory Tax. Red Cross Week.

2915	**977** 10p. red, black and blue	75	55

978 "The Burning of St. Sava"

1994. 400th Anniv of Burning of St. Sava's Relics.

2916	**978** 60p. multicoloured	3·00	2·20

979 Jubilant Players

1994. World Cup Football Championship, U.S.A. Multicoloured.

2917	60p. Type **979**	2·30	1·70
2918	1d. Goalkeeper and players on ground	2·30	1·70

980 Basset Hound

1994. Dogs. Multicoloured.

2919	60p. Type **980**	2·30	1·70
2920	60p. Maltese terrier	2·30	1·70
2921	60p. Welsh terrier	2·30	1·70
2922	1d. Husky	2·30	1·70

1994. Nos. 2888/9 surch.

2923	10p. on 100000d. brn & red	75	55
2924	50p. on 10000d. blue & violet	1·50	80

982 Bell and Globe

1994. Assembly of Eastern Orthodox Nations.

2925	**982** 60p. multicoloured	2·30	1·70

983 River Valley

1994. Protection of Environment in Montenegro.

2926	**983** 50p. multicoloured	2·30	1·70

984 Moraca

1994. Churches.

2927	**984** 1p. violet and bistre	2·30	20
2928	- 5p. blue and orange	2·30	20
2929	- 10p. green and red	90	20
2930	- 20p. purple and lilac	1·50	20
2931	- 20p. black and red	30·00	20
2932	- 50p. purple and violet	90	20
2933	- 1d. red and blue	2·30	55
2935	- 5d. violet and blue	3·00	1·70
2936	- 10d. red and orange	6·00	3·25
2938	- 20d. turquoise and blue	12·00	6·75

DESIGNS: 5p. Gracanica; 10p. Ostrog Monastery; 20p. (2930/1) Lazarica; 50p. Studenica; 1d. Sopocani; 5d. Ljeviska; 10d. Zica Monastery; 20d. Decani Monastery.

985 St. Arsenius and Sremski

1994. Bicentenary of St. Arsenius Seminary, Sremski Karlovci.

2940	**985** 50p. multicoloured	1·50	1·10

986 Syringe

1994. Obligatory Tax. Anti-tuberculosis Week.

2941	**986** 10p. black, yellow and red	75	55

987 River Bojana

1994. Nature Protection. Multicoloured.

2942	1d. Type **987**	4·50	3·00
2943	1d.50 Lake Biograd	5·00	3·25

988 Painting by U. Knezevic

1994. 26th "Joy of Europe" Meeting.

2944	**988** 1d. multicoloured	3·25	2·20

989 "Revenge" (English galleon)

1994. Ships in Bottles. Multicoloured.

2945	50p. Type **989**	1·50	1·10
2946	50p. 17th-century yacht	1·50	1·10
2947	50p. "Santa Maria" (Columbus's flagship)	1·50	1·10
2948	50p. 15th-century nau	1·50	1·10
2949	50p. "Mayflower" (Pilgrim Fathers' ship)	1·50	1·10
2950	50p. 14th-century caravel	1·50	1·10

990 Aerospatiale ATR 42 Mail Plane, Mail Coach and Letter

1994. Stamp Day.

2951	**990** 50p. multicoloured	6·00	4·50

991 Tombstone

1994. Museum Exhibits. Illustrated Tombstones. Multicoloured.

2952	50p. Type **991**	1·40	1·00
2953	50p. Double stone and railing	1·40	1·00
2954	50p. Two stones	1·40	1·00
2955	50p. Cemetery	1·40	1·00

992 "Madonna and Child" (T. Cesljar)

1994. Paintings. Multicoloured.

2956	60p. Type **992**	1·50	1·10
2957	60p. "Adoration of the Three Wise Men" (N. Neshkovic)	1·50	1·10
2958	60p. "The Annunciation" (D. Bacevic)	1·50	1·10
2959	60p. "St. John baptizing Christ" (T. Kracun)	1·50	1·10

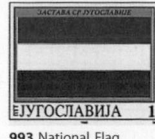

993 National Flag

994 Wilhelm Steinitz (1886–94)

1995. Multicoloured

2960	1d. Type **993**	2·30	1·70
2961	1d. National arms	2·30	1·70

1995. Chess (1st series). Chessmen or World Champions. Multicoloured.

2962	60p. Type **994**	1·80	1·30
2963	60p. Pieces	1·80	1·30
2964	60p. Emanuel Lasker (1894–1921)	1·80	1·30
2965	60p. Black knight	1·80	1·30
2966	60p. Pawns, king and knight	1·80	1·30
2967	60p. Jose Raul Capablanca (1921–27)	1·80	1·30
2968	60p. Rook, bishop, queen and pawns	1·80	1·30
2969	60p. Aleksandr Alekhine (1927–35 and 1937–46)	1·80	1·30

See also Nos. 2988/95 and 3021/9.

995 Emblem

1995. 50th Anniv of Red Star Sports Club, Belgrade.

2970	**995** 60p. red, blue and gold	2·50	1·90

996 Fire Salamander

1995. Amphibians. Multicoloured.

2971	60p. Type **996**	2·00	1·50
2972	60p. Alpine newt ("Triturus alpestris")	2·00	1·50
2973	60p. Stream frog ("Rana graeca")	2·00	1·50
2974	60p. Eastern spadefoot ("Pelobates syriacus balcanicus")	2·00	1·50

997 Sportsman and Emblem

1995. 75th Anniv of Radnicki Sports Club, Belgrade.

2975	**997** 60p. multicoloured	2·30	1·70

998 Lammergeier over Mountainside

1995. Europa. Peace and Freedom. Multicoloured.

2976	60p. Type **998**	4·50	2·75
2977	1d.90 Child with tricycle and elderly couple on park bench (horiz)	4·50	2·75

999 Globes

1995. Obligatory Tax. Red Cross Week.

2978	**999** 10p. yellow, blue and red	75	55

1000 Dove with Black Bird in Beak

1995. 50th Anniv of End of Second World War.
2979 **1000** 60p. multicoloured 2·30 1·70

1001 Station Concourse and Train

1995. Opening of Vukov Monument Underground Railway Station, Belgrade.
2980 **1001** 60p. multicoloured 3·00 2·20

1002 Leaves and Flowers

1995. The Whitlow-grass. Multicoloured.
2981 60p. Type **1002** 2·30 1·70
2982 60p. Clumps of leaves and flowers 2·30 1·70
2983 60p. Plant growing on mountainside 2·30 1·70
2984 60p. Plant and tree branch 2·30 1·70

1003 Shore Lark, Rtanj

1995. Nature Protection. Multicoloured.
2985 60p. Type **1003** 3·00 2·20
2986 1d.90 Blasius's horseshoe bat, Lazareva Reka Canyon 3·75 2·75

1004 "Slovakian Village Gathering" (Zuzka Medvedova)

1995
2987 **1004** 60p. multicoloured 1·80 1·30

1995. Chess (2nd series). Chessmen or World Champions. As T **994**. Multicoloured.
2988 60p. Max Euwe (1935–37) 1·20 90
2989 60p. Pawn and chessboard and pieces 1·20 90
2990 60p. Mikhail Botvinnik (1948–57, 1958–60 and 1961–63) 1·20 90
2991 60p. Queen and chessboard and pieces 1·20 90
2992 60p. Board and white bishop and knight 1·20 90
2993 60p. Vasily Smyslov (1957–58) 1·20 90
2994 60p. Rook, knight, queen and board 1·20 90
2995 60p. Mikhail Tal (1960–61) 1·20 90

1005 Wilhelm Rontgen (discoverer of X-rays)

1995. Obligatory Tax. Anti-tuberculosis Week.
2996 **1005** 10p. red and blue 75 55

1006 Player on Globe

1995. Centenary of Volleyball.
2997 **1006** 90p. multicoloured 1·80 1·30

1007 Church

1995. 800th Anniv of St. Luke's Church, Kotor.
2998 **1007** 80p. multicoloured 1·80 1·30

1008 Coronation of King Petar II

1995. Centenary of Motion Pictures. Each brown and orange.
2999 1d.10 Type **1008** 2·00 1·50
3000 2d.20 Auguste and Louis Lumiere (cine camera pioneers) 3·00 1·70

1009 Club Emblem

1995. 50th Anniv of Partizan Army Sports Club.
3001 **1009** 80p. multicoloured 1·80 1·30

1010 "Flower Seller" (Milos Tenkovic)

1995. 27th "Joy of Europe" Meeting. Multicoloured.
3002 1d.10 Type **1010** 2·00 1·50
3003 2d.20 "Child at Table" (Pierre Bonnard) 3·00 1·70

1011 Golden Gate Bridge, San Francisco

1995. 50th Anniv of U.N.O.
3004 **1011** 1d.10 multicoloured 1·80 1·30
San Francisco was where the Charter was signed.

1012 Post Office, Seal and Letter

1995. Stamp Day.
3005 **1012** 1d.10 multicoloured 1·80 1·30

1013 Montenegro 1898 10n. and Serbia 1866 40p. Stamps

1995. "Jufia VIII" National Stamp Exhibition, Budva. Sheet 71×95 mm.
MS3006 2d.50 multicoloured 3·25 3·25

1014 Saric No. 1

1995. Museum Exhibits. Aircraft. Multicoloured.
3007 1d.10 Type **1014** 75 55
3008 1d.10 Douglas DC-3 75 55
3009 2d.20 Fizir FN biplane 1·50 1·10
3010 2d.20 Sud Aviation Caravelle jetliner 1·50 1·10

1015 "Birth of Christ" (D. Milojevic)

1995. Paintings. Multicoloured.
3011 1d.10 Type **1015** 75 55
3012 1d.10 "Flight into Egypt" (Z. Halupova) (horiz) 75 55
3013 2d.20 "Sunday" (M. Rasic) 1·50 1·10
3014 2d.20 "Traditional Christmas Festival" (J. Brasic) (horiz) 1·50 1·10

1016 Battle Scene

1996. 70th Anniv of Battle of Mojkovac.
3015 **1016** 1d.10 multicoloured 75 55

1017 Painting

1996. Birth Centenary of Save Sumanovic (painter).
3016 **1017** 1d.10 multicoloured 75 55

1018 "Pyrgomorphela serbica"

1996. Protected Insects. Multicoloured.
3017 1d.10 Type **1018** 75 55
3018 1d.10 Red wood ant ("Formica rufa") 75 55
3019 2d.20 Searcher ("Calosoma sycophanta") 1·50 1·10
3020 2d.20 Owl-fly ("Ascalaphus macaronius") 1·50 1·10

1996. Chess (3rd series). Chessmen and Timepieces or World Champions. As T **994**. Multicoloured.
3021 1d.50 Tigran Vartanovich Petrosyan (1963–69) 75 55
3022 1d.50 Queen, knight and portable sundial 75 55
3023 1d.50 Boris Vasilevich Spassky (1969–72) 75 55
3024 1d.50 Competition clock, chessboard and pieces 75 55
3025 1d.50 Garry Kimovich Kasparov (1985–93) 75 55
3026 1d.50 Chessboard, pieces and hourglass 75 55
3027 1d.50 Robert Fischer (1972–75) 75 55

3028 1d.50 Chess pieces, clocks and chessboard 75 55
3029 1d.50 Anatoly Yevgenievich Karpov (1975–85 and 1993–) 75 55

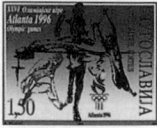

1019 Discus Throwers

1996. Centenary of Modern Olympic Games. Multicoloured.
3030 1d.50 Type **1019** 1·10 80
3031 2d.50 Ancient Greek and modern athletes 2·00 1·50

1020 Athletics

1996. Olympic Games, Atlanta. Multicoloured.
3032 1d.50 Type **1020** 2·30 1·70
3033 1d.50 Basketball 2·30 1·70
3034 1d.50 Handball 2·30 1·70
3035 1d.50 Shooting 2·30 1·70
3036 1d.50 Volleyball 2·30 1·70
3037 1d.50 Water polo 2·30 1·70
MS3038 107×60 mm. 5d. Tara (house from "Gone with the Wind") 3·25 3·25

1021 Postman, Railway Mail Van and Arms of Royal Serbian Post

1996. Stamp Day.
3039 **1021** 1d.50 multicoloured 90 65

1022 Isidora Sekulic

1996. Europa. Famous Women Writers. Multicoloured.
3040 2d.50 Type **1022** 3·00 2·20
3041 5d. Desanka Maksimovic 4·00 3·00

1023 Dr. Vladan Djordjevic (founder)

1996. 120th Anniv of Serbian Red Cross.
3042 **1023** 1d.50 multicoloured 90 65

1024 Child and Cross

1996. Obligatory Tax. Red Cross Week.
3043 **1024** 15p. blue, brown and red 60 45

1025 Columns, Caryatid and Diagrams of Proportion

1996. 150th Anniv of Architecture Education in Serbia.
3044 **1025** 1d.50 light blue, deep blue and blue 90 65

1026 White Spoonbill

1996. Nature Protection. Multicoloured.
3045	2d.50 Type **1026**	1·50	1·10
3046	5d. Glossy ibis	3·00	2·20

1027 Prince Petar I
Petrovic (Battle of
Martinici)

1996. Battle Bicentenaries. Multicoloured.
3047	1d.50 Type **1027**	75	55
3048	2d.50 "Prince's Guard" (Theodore Valerio) (Battle of Kruse) (vert)	1·50	1·10

1028 Waiting for the
Off

1996. Ljubicevo Race Meeting. Multicoloured.
3049	1d.50 Type **1028**	75	55
3050	2d.50 Horses racing	1·50	1·10

1029 Palm Cockatoo

1996. 60th Anniv of Belgrade Zoo. Multicoloured.
3051	1d.50 Type **1029**	75	55
3052	1d.50 Common zebra	75	55
3053	2d.50 Maroon-breasted crowned pigeon	1·50	1·10
3054	2d.50 Tiger	1·50	1·10

1030
Landscape
on Leaf

1996. Obligatory Tax. Anti-tuberculosis Week.
3055	**1030** 20p. multicoloured	60	45

1031 Fantasy Scene

1996. 28th "Joy of Europe" Meeting. Multicoloured.
3056	1d.50 Type **1031**	75	55
3057	2d.50 Toucan	1·50	1·10

1032 Basketball (silver)

1996. Olympic Games Medal Winners. Multicoloured.
3058	2d.50 Type **1032**	1·80	1·30
3059	2d.50 Small-bore rifle shooting (gold)	1·80	1·30
3060	2d.50 Air-rifle shooting (bronze)	1·80	1·30
3061	2d.50 Volleyball (bronze)	1·80	1·30

1033 Coins,
Banknotes and
Credit Card

1996. 75th Anniv of Post Office Savings Bank.
3062	**1033** 1d.50 multicoloured	1·10	80

1034 Footballer

1996. Centenary of Football in Serbia.
3063	**1034** 1d.50 multicoloured	1·10	80

1035 Mother and
Child (statuette)

1996. Museum Exhibits. Archaeological Finds. Multicoloured.
3064	1d.50 Type **1035**	1·10	80
3065	1d.50 Tombstone depicting Genius, god of autumn (Komani, nr. Pljevlja)	1·10	80
3066	2d.50 Marble head of woman (from Podgorica)	1·50	1·10
3067	2d.50 Statuette of red-headed goddess	1·50	1·10

1036 "The
Annunciation"
(Nikola Neskovic)

1996. Icons from Serbian Orthodox Church Museum, Belgrade. Multicoloured.
3068	1d.50 Type **1036**	1·10	80
3069	1d.50 "Madonna and Child"	1·10	80
3070	2d.50 "Nativity"	1·50	1·10
3071	2d.50 "Entry of Christ into Jerusalem" (Stanoje Popovic)	1·50	1·10

1037 Putnik in
Dress Uniform

1997. 150th Birth Anniv of Radomir Putnik (army Commander in Chief).
3072	**1037** 1d.50 multicoloured	90	65

1038 Film Frames

1997. 25th International Film Festival, Belgrade.
3073	**1038** 1d.50 multicoloured	90	65

1039 Great
Spotted
Woodpecker

1997. Nature Protection. Woodland Birds. Multicoloured.
3074	1d.50 Type **1039**	90	65
3075	1d.50 Crested tit ("Parus cristatus")	90	65
3076	2d.50 Spotted nutcracker ("Nucifraga caryocatactes")	1·40	1·00
3077	2d.50 European robin ("Erithacus rubecula")	1·40	1·00

1040 Christ and
King Dragutin
holding Model of
Church (fresco)

1997. 700th Anniv of St. Ahilije's Church, Arilje.
3078	**1040** 1d.50 multicoloured	1·50	1·10

1041 St. Petar

1997. 250th Birth Anniv of Prince-Bishop Petar I of Montenegro (St. Petar of Cetinje).
3079	**1041** 1d.50 multicoloured	1·50	1·10

1042 Belgrade and
Emblem

1997. Tenth Belgrade Marathon.
3080	**1042** 2d.50 multicoloured	2·00	1·50

1043 Ambulance,
1876, and
Association
Building

1997. 125th Anniv of Serbian Medical Association.
3081	**1043** 2d.50 multicoloured	2·00	1·50

1044 Loading Air Mail
at Night

1997. Stamp Day.
3082	**1044** 2d.50 multicoloured	2·00	1·50

1045 "1997" and Cross

1997. Obligatory Tax. Red Cross Week.
3083	**1045** 20p. red and blue	60	45

1046 Belgrade

1997. Tennis Championships in Yugoslavia. Design showing player and Town Arms. Multicoloured.
3084	2d.50 Type **1046**	2·00	1·50
3085	2d.50 Budva	2·00	1·50
3086	2d.50 Novi Sad	2·00	1·50

1047 Bas Celik shackled
before King

1997. Europa. Myths and Legends. Multicoloured.
3087	2d.50 Type **1047**	2·00	1·50
3088	6d. Prince on horseback fighting chained Bas Celik	3·00	2·30

1048 "Cerambyx cerdo"
(longhorn beetle)

1997. Nature Protection. Multicoloured.
3089	2d.50 Type **1048**	1·60	1·20
3090	6d. Pedunculate oak	3·00	2·30

1049 Prince Bishop
Peter Njegos, Village
and Printing Press

1997. 150th Anniv of Publication of "Gorski Vijenc".
3091	**1049** 2d.50 multicoloured	1·60	1·20

1050 Binicki

1997. 125th Birth Anniv of Stanislav Binicki (composer).
3092	**1050** 2d.50 multicoloured	1·60	1·20

1051 "Pelargonium
grandiflorum"

1997. Flowers. Multicoloured.
3093	1d.50 Type **1051**	80	60
3094	1d.50 "Hydrangea x macrophylla"	80	60
3095	2d.50 African violet ("Saintpaulia ionantha")	1·60	1·20
3096	2d.50 "Oncidium varicosum"	1·60	1·20

1052 Statue by Dragomir
Arambasic before Cvijeta Zuzoric
Art Gallery (venue)

1997. "Jufiz IX" National Stamp Exhibition, Belgrade. Sheet 96×75 mm.
MS3097 **3097** 5d. multicoloured		4·00	4·00

1053 Dr.
Milutin
Rankovic

1997. Obligatory Tax. Anti-tuberculosis Week.
3098	**1053** 20p. brown, ochre and red	60	45

1054 Society Emblem

1997. Centenary of Serbian Chemical Association.
3099	**1054** 2d.50 multicoloured	1·60	1·20

1997. No value expressed. As No. 2857 but 18×20 mm.
3100	**956** A red	1·60	25

1055 Collage
(Milan Ugrisic)

1997. 29th "Joy of Europe" Meeting. Multicoloured.
3101	2d.50 Type **1055**	1·60	1·20
3102	5d. Collage (Stanislava Antic)	3·00	2·30

1056 "May Assembly, Sremski
Karlovci, 1848" (Pavle Simic)

1997. 150th Anniv of Matica Srpska Art Gallery.
3103	**1056**	2d.50 multicoloured	1·60	1·20

1057 Helmet from
Srem (4th century)

1997. Archaeological Finds in Vojvodina Museum.
Multicoloured.
3104	1d.50 Type **1057**	80	60
3105	1d.50 Two-headed terracotta figure from Srem	80	60
3106	2d.50 Teracotta figure from Backa	1·60	1·20
3107	2d.50 "Madonna and Child" (relief from Srem, 12th century)	1·60	1·20

1058 "Christ
Pantocrator"

1997. Icons from Chelandari Serbian Monastery, Mount Athos. Multicoloured.
3108	1d.50 Type **1058**	80	60
3109	1d.50 "Madonna and Child"	80	60
3110	2d.50 "Madonna and Child" (different)	1·60	1·20
3111	2d.50 "Three-handed Madonna with Child"	1·60	1·20

1059 Savina

1998. Monasteries in Montenegro. Multicoloured.
3112	1d.50 Type **1059**	95	70
3113	2d.50 Donji Brceli	1·60	1·20

1060 Ice Skater

1998. Winter Olympic Games, Nagano, Japan. Multicoloured.
3114	2d.50 Type **1060**	1·60	1·20
3115	6d. Skier	3·50	2·50

1061 Mare and Foal

1998. Horses. Multicoloured.
3116	1d.50 Type **1061**	1·60	1·20
3117	1d.50 Stallion	1·60	1·20
3118	2d.50 Head of grey	2·30	1·70
3119	2d.50 Racehorse	2·30	1·70

1062 Women and Flowers

1998. International Women's Day.
3120	**1062**	2d.50 multicoloured	1·60	1·20

1063 Glider and
Emblems

1998. 50th Anniv of Yugoslav Aeronautics Association.
3121	**1063**	2d.50 multicoloured	1·60	1·20

1064 "The Adornment of the
Bride" (Paja Jovanovic)

1998. Europa. National Festivals. Multicoloured.
3122	6d. Type **1064**	4·75	3·50
3123	9d. "The Prince-Bishop celebrates Victory" (Pero Pocek)	4·75	3·50

1065
Metropolitan
Mihailo
Jovanovic

1998. Obligatory Tax. Red Cross Week.
3124	**1065**	20p. multicoloured	60	45

1066 Player
evading Tackle

1998. World Cup Football Championship, France. Multicoloured.
3125	6d. Type **1066**	2·75	2·10
3126	9d. Goalkeeper and players	4·25	3·25

1067 Map of Europe

1998. 50th Anniv of Danube Commission. Sheet 88×65 mm.
MS3127	9d. multicoloured	6·25	6·00

1068 "Hieracium
blecicii"

1998. Nature Protection. Multicoloured.
3128	6d. Type **1068**	2·00	1·50
3129	9d. Oceanic sunfish	2·75	2·00

1069 Djura Jaksic
(poet and painter)

1998. Anniversaries. Each brown, black and ochre.
3130	1d.50 Type **1069** (120th death anniv)	60	45
3131	1d.50 Nadezda Petrovic (painter, 125th birth anniv)	60	45
3132	1d.50 Radoje Domanovic (satirist, 125th birth anniv)	60	45
3133	1d.50 Vasilije Mokranjac (composer, 75th birth anniv)	60	45
3134	1d.50 Sreten Stojanovic (sculptor, birth centenary)	60	45
3135	1d.50 Milan Konjovic (painter, birth centenary)	60	45
3136	1d.50 Desanka Maksimovic (writer, birth centenary)	60	45
3137	1d.50 Ivan Tabakovic (painter, birth centenary)	60	45

1070 Trophy

1998. Victory of Yugoslavia in World Basketball Championship, Athens. Sheet 80×98 mm.
MS3138	10d. multicoloured	9·25	9·25

1071 Pine Marten

1998. 50th Anniv of Serbian Nature Protection Institute. Multicoloured.
3139	2d. Type **1071**	1·20	95
3140	2d. Demoiselle crane ("Anthropoides virgo")	1·20	95
3141	5d. Lynx ("Lynx lynx")	2·30	1·70
3142	5d. Red crossbill ("Loxia curvirostra")	2·30	1·70

1072 Machine-gunners

1998. 80th Anniv of Thessalonica Front.
3143	**1072**	5d. grey and brown	2·75	2·10
3144	–	5d. brown and sepia	2·75	2·10
DESIGN: No. 3144, Field gun.			

1073 "50 Years" on
Stamp

1998. Stamp Day. 50th Anniv of Serbian Philatelic Society.
3145	**1073**	6d. blue	2·20	1·60

1074 "Sea Life" (Bojan
Dakic)

1998. 30th "Joy of Europe" Meeting. Multicoloured.
3146	6d. Type **1074**	2·30	1·70
3147	9d. "Sea Life" (collage by Ana Rockov)	3·00	2·30

1075 Steam
Locomotive, 1847

1998. Locomotives. Multicoloured.
3148	2d.50 Type **1075**	2·30	1·70
3149	2d.50 Steam locomotive, 1900	2·30	1·70
3150	2d.50 Steam locomotive, 1920	2·30	1·70
3151	2d.50 Steam locomotive, 1930	2·30	1·70
3152	2d.50 Diesel locomotive "Kennedy"	2·30	1·70
3153	2d.50 High speed train, 1990	2·30	1·70

1076 Pjerino (brig), 1883

1998. Museum Exhibits. Ship Paintings by Vasilije Ivankovic. Multicoloured.
3154	2d. Type **1076**	80	60
3155	2d. Vera Cruz (steamer), 1873	80	60
3156	5d. Vizin-Florio (full-rigged ship)	2·30	1·70
3157	5d. Draghetto (barque), 1865	2·30	1·70

1077 Hilandar Monastery

1998. 800th Anniv of Hilandar Monastery. Paintings by Milutin Dedic. Multicoloured.
3158	2d. Type **1077**	80	60
3159	2d. Monastery facade	80	60
3160	5d. Hills behind Monastery buildings	2·30	1·70
3161	5d. Aerial view of Monastery	2·30	1·70

1078 Flags around
Envelope on Map

1998. South-East European Postal Ministers Congress.
3162	**1078**	5d. multicoloured	4·75	3·50

1079 Volleyball

1998. Yugoslavia. Silver Medal Winners in World Volleyball Championship, Japan. Sheet 70×78 mm.
MS3163	**1079**	10d. multicoloured	60·00	60·00

1080 Postal
Messenger arriving
in Belgrade

1998. 75th Anniv of Post and Telecommunications Museum.
3164	**1080**	5d. brown and green	1·60	1·20
3165	**1080**	5d. red and brown	1·60	1·20

1081 Visoki Decani Monastery

1999. Serbian Monasteries. Paintings by Milutin Dedic. Multicoloured.
3166	2d. Type **1081**		95	70
3167	5d. Gracanica Monastery		2·50	1·90

1082 Woolly Pig

1999. Animals. Multicoloured.
3168	2d. Type **1082**		80	60
3169	2d. Cattle		80	60
3170	6d. Balkan goat		2·00	1·50
3171	6d. Hungarian sheep		2·00	1·50

1083 Scouts making Campfire and Emblem

1999. Scouts.
3172	**1083**	6d. multicoloured	3·00	2·30

1084 Emblem, Goddess Justitia and Globe

1999. 70th Anniv of Bar Association.
3173	**1084**	6d. brown and buff	2·20	1·60

1085 Target

1999. No value expressed.
3174	**1085**	A black	4·75	3·50
3175	-	A black and red	4·75	3·50
DESIGN: No. 3175, Target with heart at centre.

1086 Emblem and Player

1999. World Table Tennis Championships, Belgrade. Multicoloured.
3176	6d. Type **1086**		3·00	2·30
3177	6d. Player facing left		3·00	2·30

1087 Kopaonik National Park

1999. Europa. Parks and Gardens. Multicoloured.
3178	6d. Type **1087**		4·75	3·50
3179	15d. Lovcen National Park		7·75	5·75

1088 Red Cross Volunteers

1999. Obligatory Tax Red Cross Week.
3180	**1088**	1d. multicoloured	60	45

1089 Emblem, Cobweb and Spade

1999. Nature Protection. Multicoloured.
3181	6d. Type **1089**		4·00	3·00
3182	15d. Thumb squeezing water droplet from Earth		4·25	3·25

1090 Destroying Angel (*Amanita virosa*)

1999. Fungi. Multicoloured.
3183	6d. Type **1090**		2·30	1·70
3184	6d. False blusher (*Amanita pantherina*)		2·30	1·70
3185	6d. Clustered woodlover (*Hypholoma fasciculare*)		2·30	1·70
3186	6d. *Ramaria pallida*		2·30	1·70

1091 Stjepan Mitrov Ljubisa (author)

1999. Personalities. Each brown, yellow and black.
3187	2d. Type **1091**		60	45
3188	2d. Marko Miljanov (author)		60	45
3189	2d. Pero Pocek (painter)		60	45
3190	2d. Risto Stijovic (sculptor)		60	45
3191	2d. Milo Milunovic (painter)		60	45
3192	2d. Petar Lubarda (painter)		60	45
3193	2d. Vuko Radovic (painter)		60	45
3194	2d. Mihailo Lalic (author)		60	45

1092 Thistle

1999. Obligatory Tax. Anti-tuberculosis Week.
3195	**1092**	1d. multicoloured	1·10	80

1093 World Map and Emblem

1999. 125th Anniv of Universal Postal Union. Multicoloured.
3196	6d. Type **1093**		1·60	1·20
3197	12d. Envelopes encircling globe		3·00	2·30

1094 Lion (Luka Minic)

1999. 31st "Joy in Europe" Meeting. Winning Designs in Children's Painting Competition. Multicoloured.
3198	6d. Type **1094**		1·60	1·20
3199	15d. Girl with doll (Andreas Kaparis) (vert)		4·00	3·00

1095 Chopin and Music Score

1999. 150th Death Anniv of Frederic Chopin (composer).
3200	**1095**	10d. multicoloured	3·50	2·50

1096 Mastheads

1999. Stamp Day. 50th Anniv of Philatelist (magazine).
3201	**1096**	10d. multicoloured	2·30	1·70

1097 Murino Bridge

1999. Bombed Bridges. Multicoloured.
3202	2d. Type **1097**		80	60
3203	2d. Varadinski Most		80	60
3204	2d. Ostruznica		80	60
3205	6d. Bistrica		1·60	1·20
3206	6d. Grdelica		1·60	1·20
3207	6d. Zezeljev Most		1·60	1·20

1098 Fragments of Roman Relief Depicting Mithurica and Jupiter (statue), Sabac

1999. Year 2000. Multicoloured.
3208	6d. Type **1098**		1·60	1·20
3209	6d. Mosaic depicting Emperor Trajan with army leaders, Sirmium, lamp and lead mirror		1·60	1·20
3210	6d. Mosaic of Dionysus and painting of Belgrade		1·60	1·20
3211	6d. Haghia Sophia, mosaic and bust of Emperor Constantin		1·60	1·20
3212	6d. Gold artefacts, pot and lamp		1·60	1·20
3213	6d. St. Peter's Church and title page of *Temnic*		1·60	1·20
MS3214	138×88 mm. 15d. Birth and crucifixion of Christ, ships and scenes of everyday life (105×54 mm)		2·30	2·30

1099 Fireman dousing Flames

1999. Bombed Buildings. Multicoloured.
3215	2d. Type **1099**		80	60
3216	2d. Oil refinery		80	60
3217	2d. Dish aerials		80	60
3218	6d. Hospital		1·60	1·20
3219	6d. Radio and television station		1·60	1·20
3220	6d. Television tower, Mt. Avala		1·60	1·20

1100 Saints

1999. 500th Anniv of Poganovo Monastery Frescoes. Multicoloured.
3221	6d. Type **1100**		1·20	95
3222	6d. Four saints with long beards		1·20	95
3223	6d. Four saints, one holding a scroll and one an open book		1·20	95
3224	6d. Four saints, three holding scrolls and one with a stick		1·20	95

1101 Couple washing for Gold

1999. Museum Exhibits. Gold Washing on the River Pek. Multicoloured.
3225	6d. Type **1101**		1·20	95
3226	6d. Man and two youths panning for gold		1·20	95
3227	6d. Women digging gravel panning for gold		1·20	95
3228	6d. Man holding spade and pan with two boys		1·20	95

1102 Krushedol Monastery

2000. Monasteries. Multicoloured.
3229	10d. Type **1102**		2·30	1·70
3230	10d. Rakovac Monastery		2·30	1·70

1103 Building and Emblem

2000. 50th Anniv of National Archives.
3231	**1103**	10d. lilac and blue	35·00	35·00

1104 Large Tortoiseshell (*Nymphalis polychloros*)

2000. Butterflies. Multicoloured.
3232	10d. Type **1104**		4·00	3·00
3233	10d. Southern festoon (*Parnalius polyxena*)		4·00	3·00
3234	10d. Poplar admiral (*Limenitis populi*)		4·00	3·00
3235	10d. Marbled white (*Melanargia galathea*)		4·00	3·00

1105 Grey Partridges (*Perdix perdix*)

2000. Endangered Species. Partridges. Multicoloured.
3236	10d. Type **1105**		4·00	3·00
3237	10d. Grey partridge (different)		4·00	3·00
3238	10d. Rock partridge (*Alectoris graeca*) on nest		4·00	3·00
3239	10d. Two rock partridges		4·00	3·00

1106 General Staff Building, Belgrade

2000. Bombed Buildings.
3240	**1106**	10d. blue	4·00	3·00
3241	-	20d. brown	4·25	3·25
DESIGN: No. 3241, Air Force and Air Defence Command, Zemun.

1107 Exhibition
Medal (P90)

2000. "Jufiz X" National Stamp Exhibition, Belgrade. Sheet
68×75 mm.
MS3242 15d. multicoloured — 75·00 — 75·00

1108 Tree and
World Map

2000. Environment Protection. Multicoloured.
3243 30d. Type **1108** — 3·00 — 2·30
3244 30d. Barn swallows in nest — 3·00 — 2·30

1109 "2000" and
View of Bethlehem

2000. Europa. Multicoloured.
3245 30d. Type **1109** — 6·25 — 4·75
3246 30d. "2000" and astronaut on
Moon — 6·25 — 4·75

1110 Players
chasing Ball

2000. European Football Championship, Belgium and The
Netherlands. Multicoloured.
3247 30d. Type **1110** — 4·75 — 3·50
3248 30d. Players heading ball — 4·75 — 3·50

1111 Post Office
Building, Post Van,
Post Box, Letter,
Envelope and Quill

2000. 160th Anniv of Postal Service in Serbia.
3249 **1111** 10d. multicoloured — 3·00 — 2·30

1112 Map of
Australia and
Kangaroo

2000. Olympic Games, Sydney. Showing map of Australia
and animal or bird. Multicoloured.
3250 6d. Type **1112** — 80 — 60
3251 12d. Emu — 1·20 — 95
3252 24d. Koala — 2·30 — 1·70
3253 30d. Cockatoo — 3·00 — 2·30

1113 Airship LZ-127
"Graf Zeppelin" (1928)
and Cover

2000. Stamp Day. Centenary of First Zeppelin Flight.
3254 **1113** 10d. multicoloured — 7·00 — 5·25

1114 Goats

2000. 32nd "Joy in Europe" Meeting. Winning Designs in
Children's Painting Competition. Multicoloured.
3255 30d. Type **1114** — 2·50 — 1·90
3256 40d. Storks (vert) — 3·00 — 2·30

1115 Hand holding Pen

2000. UNESCO. World Teachers' Day.
3257 **1115** 10d. multicoloured — 30·00 — 30·00

1116 Bee on Flower

2000. 13th Apislavia (Slavonic bee-keeping association)
Congress.
3258 **1116** 10d. multicoloured — 7·75 — 7·75

1117 Water Polo
(bronze)

2000. Yugoslav Medals at Olympic Games. Multicoloured.
3259 20d. Type **1117** — 2·30 — 1·70
3260 20d. Air pistol (silver) — 2·30 — 1·70
MS3261 70×83 mm. 30d. Volleyball
(gold) (34×46 mm) — 30·00 — 30·00

1118 Sailing Ships

2000. New Millennium. Multicoloured.
3262 12d. Type **1118** — 95 — 70
3263 12d. Parchment production — 95 — 70
3264 12d. Man and instruments (first
accurate maps and optical
instruments) — 95 — 70
3265 12d. G. and R. Stephenson's
Rocket (1829) and *Clermont*
(first commercial paddle-
steamer) — 95 — 70
3266 12d. Nikola Tesla (Yugoslav
scientist), telegraph and
telephone — 95 — 70
3267 12d. Futuristic settlement,
astronaut and satellite — 95 — 70
MS3268 138×86 mm. 40d. Horses on
river bank, ship in full sail and ice-
bound ship (104×54 mm) — 3·75 — 3·75

1119 Christ
bathing
(fresco,
Monastery,
Pec)

2000. No value expressed.
3269 **1119** A multicoloured — 5·50 — 60

1120 Waistcoat
(Jagodina)

2000. Museum Exhibits. 19th-century Serbian Costumes.
Multicoloured.
3270 6d. Type **1120** — 45 — 35
3271 12d. Dress (Metohija) — 80 — 60

3272 24d. Blouse (Pec) — 1·60 — 1·20
3273 30d. Waistcoat (Kupres) — 1·90 — 1·40

1121 Mary and Jesus
(icon, Piva Monastery)

2000. Art. Icons and Frescoes of Montenegro.
Multicoloured.
3274 6d. Type **1121** — 45 — 35
3275 12d. Nativity (fresco, Holy Cross
Church) — 80 — 60
3276 24d. St. Luke painting an icon
(fresco, Moraca Monastery) — 1·60 — 1·20
3277 30d. Mary and Jesus, St. John
and St. Stephen (fresco, Mary
of the Ascension Church,
Moraca) — 1·90 — 1·40

1122 Map of Europe
and Emblem

2000. Yugoslavia's Resumption of Membership of the
Organization for Security and Co-operation in
Europe (3278) and the United Nations (3279).
Multicoloured.
3278 6d. Type **1122** — 80 — 60
3279 12d. Emblem (vert) — 95 — 70

1123 Vatoped
Monastery

2001. Monasteries on Mount Athos. Multicoloured.
3280 10d. Type **1123** — 80 — 60
3281 27d. Esfigmen monastery — 2·30 — 1·70

1124 Association
Building

2001. 175th Anniv of "Matice Srpske" (Serbian literary
association).
3282 **1124** 15d. multicoloured — 1·60 — 1·20

1125 Lions

2001. 50th Anniv of Zoo Palic, Subotica. Endangered
Species. Multicoloured.
3283 6d. Type **1125** (*Panthera leo*)
(inscr "Felis leo") — 60 — 45
3284 12d. Polar bear and cub (*Ursus
maritimus*) — 1·20 — 95
3285 24d. Japanese macaques
(*Macaca fuscata*) — 1·60 — 1·20
3286 30d. Humboldt penguins
(*Spheniscus humboldti*) — 2·00 — 1·50

1126 Vera
Mencikova

2001. Women World Chess Champions. Multicoloured.
3287 10d. Type **1126** — 60 — 45
3288 10d. Lyudmila Vladimirovna
Rudenko — 60 — 45
3289 10d. Elizaveta Ivanovna Bykova — 60 — 45
3290 10d. Olga Nikelaevna Rubtsova — 60 — 45
3291 10d. Nona Terentievna Gaprin-
dashvili — 60 — 45

3292 10d. Maia Grigorevna Chiburda-
nidze — 60 — 45
3293 10d. Zsusza Polgar — 60 — 45
3294 10d. Jun Xie — 60 — 45

1127 Stevan
Stojanovic
Mokranjac
(portrait, Uros
Predic)

2001. Personalities. Multicoloured.
3295 50d. Type **1127** (composer) — 3·50 — 2·50
3296 100d. Nikola Tesla (inventor) — 6·75 — 5·00

1128 Rose-of-Sharon
(*Hibiscus syriacus*)

2001. Flora. Multicoloured.
3297 6d. Type **1128** — 45 — 35
3298 12d. Oleander (*Nerium oleander*) — 80 — 60
3299 24d. Chilean bellflower (*Lapa-
geria rosea*) — 1·40 — 1·00
3300 30d. Rowan (*Sorbus aucuparia*) — 2·00 — 1·50

1129 River Vratna,
Eastern Serbia

2001. Europa. Water Resources. Multicoloured.
3301 30d. Type **1129** — 4·00 — 3·00
3302 45d. Jerme Gorge, Dimitrovgrad — 4·25 — 3·25

1130 Mountains,
Emblem and Climbers

2001. Centenary of Serbian Mountaineering Association.
3303 **1130** 15d. multicoloured — 1·90 — 1·40

1131 Lake Ludasko and
Heron

2001. Nature Protection. Lakes. Multicoloured.
3304 30d. Type **1131** — 2·30 — 1·70
3305 45d. Lake and stork in flight,
Carska Bara Special Nature
Reserve — 3·00 — 2·30

1132 Illuminated
Letter

2001. No value expressed.
3306 **1132** E multicoloured — 2·30 — 1·70

1133 Players and Ball

2001. European Water Polo Champions. Sheet 86×67
mm.
MS3307 **1133** 30d. multicoloured — 9·25 — 9·25

1134 Seated Figure

2001. 50th Anniv of Serbian Stamps. "SRBIJAFILA 12" National Stamp Exhibition. Sheet 97×85 mm.
MS3308 **1134** 30d. multicoloured   4·00   4·00

1135 Sun and Emblems

2001. Energy Conservation. Solar Power.
3309 **1135** 15d. multicoloured   1·60   1·20

1136 Hands holding Bridge

2001. Danube Commission. Cleaning the Danube. Multicoloured.
3310   30d. Type **1136**   3·00   2·30
3311   45d. Hand, clock and ship   4·00   3·00

1137 "The Child" (Marko Celbonovic)

2001. 33rd "Joy in Europe" Meeting. Children's Day. Paintings. Multicoloured.
3312   30d. Type **1137**   3·00   2·30
3313   45d. "Girl in Orchard" (Beta Vukanovic)   4·00   3·00

1138 Ball and Outstretched Arms

2001. Yugoslavia, European Basketball (No. 3314) and Volleyball (3315) Champions. Multicoloured.
3314   30d. Type **1138**   23·00   23·00
3315   30d. Players, ball and net   23·00   23·00

1139 Stamps and Society Emblem

2001. Stamp Day. 75th Anniv of Federation Internationale de Philatelie (the International Philatelic Federation or FIP).
3316 **1139** 15d. multicoloured   2·30   1·70

1140 Antimonite

2001. Museum Exhibits. Minerals. Multicoloured.
3317   7d. Type **1140**   45   35
3318   14d. Calcite   80   60
3319   26d.20 Quartz   1·40   1·00
3320   28d.70 Calcite and Galenite   1·60   1·20
   Nos. 3317/20 were issued together, se-tenant, forming a composite design of a cave within the sheet.

1141 School Building

2001. Centenary of Tanasije Pejanovic Secondary School, Pljevlja.
3321 **1141** 15d. multicoloured   3·00   2·30

1142 Telephone Box and Man using "Candlestick" Telephone

2001. Centenary of First Serbian Telephone Box.
3322 **1142** 15d. multicoloured   2·30   1·70

1143 The Nativity (14th-century fresco)

2001. Christmas. Showing paintings of the Nativity. Multicoloured.
3323   7d. Type **1143**   80   60
3324   14d. Nativity, Lesnovo Monastery   1·60   1·20
3325   26d.20 Nativity (different)   1·90   1·40
3326   28d.70 Nativity, Sveta Trojica   2·00   1·50

1144 Players

2002. Junior World Ice Hockey Championship, Czech Republic.
3327 **1144** 14d. multicoloured   14·00   10·50

1145 Skier

2002. Winter Olympic Games, Salt Lake City. Multicoloured.
3328   28d.70 Type **1145**   16·00   11·50
3329   50d. Bobsleigh (vert)   19·00   14·00

1146 Jovan Karamata

2002. Birth Centenary of Jovan Karamata (mathematician).
3330 **1146** 14d. multicoloured   16·00   11·50

1147 Stonechat (Saxicola torquata)

2002. Songbirds. Multicoloured.
3331   7d. Type **1147**   2·30   1·70
3332   14d. Whinchat (Saxicola rubetra)   4·00   3·00
3333   26d.20 Blue tit (Parus caeruleus)   7·75   5·75
3334   28d.70 Song thrush (Turdus philomelos)   7·75   5·75

1148 Crucified Christ (1208)

2002. Easter. Multicoloured.
3335   7d. Type **1148**   2·30   1·70
3336   14d. Christ surrounded by angels (1300)   4·00   3·00
3337   26d.20 Resurrection (1540)   7·75   5·75
3338   28d.70 Churches and acorn (painting) (1980)   7·75   5·75

1149 Woman wearing Blouse and Skirt with Sash (Bunjevac)

2002. National Costumes. Multicoloured.
3339   7d. Type **1149**   3·00   2·30
3340   28d.70 Woman wearing dress and bonnet carrying scarf (Bunjevac)   4·00   3·00

1150 Zarko Tomic-Sremac

2002. Zarko Tomic-Sremac (folk hero). Commemoration.
3341   **1150** 14d. multicoloured   17·00   10·00

1151 Roach (Rutilus rutilus)

2002. Fish. Multicoloured.
3342   7d. Type **1151**   2·30   1·70
3343   14d. Sterlet (Acipenser ruthenus)   4·00   3·00
3344   26d.20 Beluga (Huso huso)   7·75   5·75
3345   28d.70 Zander (Stizostedion lucioperca)   7·75   5·75

1152 Trapeze Artistes

2002. Europa. Circus. Multicoloured.
3346   28d.70 Type **1152**   7·75   5·75
3347   50d. Tigers   9·25   7·00
MS3348 85×74 mm. 45d. Circus ring (47×35 mm)   80·00   80·00

1153 Potez 29 Bi-plane

2002. 75th Anniv of Civil Aviation. Multicoloured.
3349   7d. Type **1153**   20·00   15·00
3350   28d.70 Boeing 737   26·00   20·00

1154 Valley, Tara National Park

2002. Nature Protection. National Parks. Multicoloured.
3351   28d.70 Type **1154**   4·75   3·50
3352   50d. Flower and hills, Golija   8·50   6·50

1155 Windmill, Melenci

2002. Mills. Multicoloured.
3353   7d. Type **1155**   6·25   4·75
3354   28d.70 Watermill, Ljuberadja   7·75   5·75

1156 City Museum, Niksic

2002. 125th Anniv of Liberation of Niksic.
3355 **1156** 14d. multicoloured   31·00   10·50

1157 Hand and Globe

2002. Yugoslavia—World Basketball Champions, Indianapolis (2002). Sheet 84×73 mm.
MS3356 **1157** 30d. multicoloured   17·00   17·00

1158 Buildings, Belgrade

2002. Jufiz XI, Yugoslav Philatelic Exhibition, Belgrade. Sheet 84×65 mm.
MS3357 30d. multicoloured   14·00   14·00

1159 Houseboat (Jana Misurovic)

2002. 34th "Joy in Europe" Meeting. Children's Day. Multicoloured.
3358   28d.70 Type **1159**   4·75   3·50
3359   50d. Bird (Manja Pavicevic)   8·50   6·50

1160 John the Baptist and Monastery

2002. 750th Anniv of Maraca Monastery.
3360 **1160** 16d. multicoloured   19·00   14·00

2002. No. 2928 surch **0.50**.
3361   50p. on 5p. blue and orange   4·00   3·00

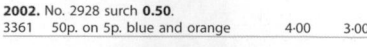

1162 World Map and Mercury

2002. Stamp Day. 50th Anniv of ifsda (International Federation of Stamp Dealers Association).
3362 **1162** 16d. multicoloured   11·50   8·75

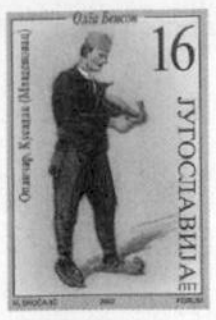

1163 Man's Costume, Kusadak

2002. Museum Exhibits. Serbian Folk Costumes. Multicoloured.

3363	16d. Type **1163**	1·60	1·20
3364	24d. Woman's costume, Komodraz	2·50	1·90
3365	26d.20 Man's costume, Novo Selo	2·75	2·10
3366	28d.70 Woman and child, Kumodraz	3·00	2·30

2002. No. 2889 surch **10**.

3367	10d. on 10000d. blue and violet	9·25	7·00

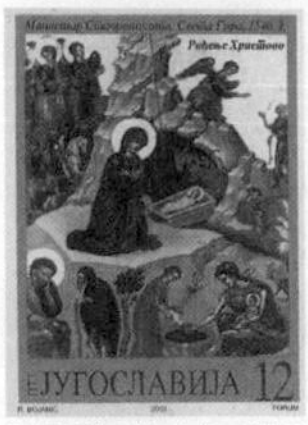

1165 The Nativity, 1546

2002. Christmas. Art. Multicoloured.

3368	12d. Type **1165**	1·60	1·20
3369	16d. Nativity, 1618	2·30	1·70
3370	26d.20 Nativity (15th-century)	4·00	3·00
3371	28d.70 Nativity (Sandro Botticelli)	4·25	3·25

2002. No. 2927 surch **12**.

3372	12d. on 1p. violet and bistre	8·50	6·50

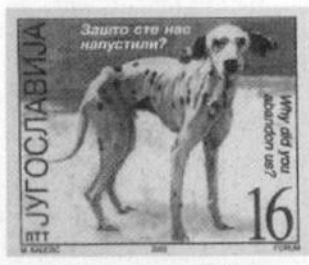

1167 Emaciated Dog

2003. Prevention of Abandoned Dogs Campaign. Multicoloured.

3373	16d. Type **1167**	2·30	1·70
3374	24d. Caged dog	3·00	2·30
3375	26d.20 Two dogs	4·00	3·00
3376	28d.70 Puppy	4·25	3·25

On 4 February 2003 Serbia became Serbia and Montenegro. See Serbia and Montenegro for subsequent listings.

EXPRESS LETTER STAMP

CROATIA

1918. Express Letter stamp of Hungary optd **HRVATSKA SHS ZURNO**.

E84	**E18**	2f. olive and red	50	55

NEWSPAPER STAMPS

CROATIA

1918. Newspaper stamp of Hungary optd **HRVATSKA SHS**.

N83	**N9**	2f. orange	50	55

SLOVENIA

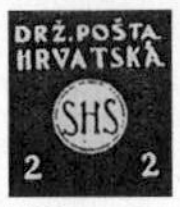

N25

1919. Imperf.

N97	**N25**	2h. yellow	20	1·70

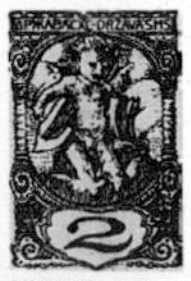

N30 Cherub with Newspapers

1919. Imperf.

N150	**N30**	2v. grey	10	15
N155	**N30**	2v. blue	10	10
N151	**N30**	4v. grey	20	55
N156	**N30**	4v. blue	10	15
N152	**N30**	6v. grey	4·75	5·50
N157	**N30**	6v. blue	4·00	5·00
N153	**N30**	10v. grey	10	20
N158	**N30**	10v. blue	10	10
N154	**N30**	30v. grey	10	55

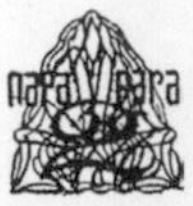

(N35)

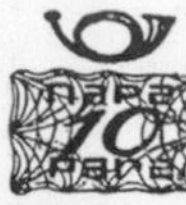

(N36)

1920. Surch as Type **N35** (2 to 6p.) or Type **N36** (10p. and 30p.).

N164		2p. on 2v. grey	75	1·30
N169		2p. on 2v. blue	10	55
N165		4p. on 2v. grey	75	1·30
N170		4p. on 2v. blue	10	55
N166		6p. on 2v. grey	1·00	1·30
N171		6p. on 2v. blue	10	55
N167		10p. on 2v. grey	1·30	1·70
N172		10p. on 2v. blue	30	80
N168		30p. on 2v. grey	1·30	1·70
N173		30p. on 2v. blue	50	1·10

OBLIGATORY TAX STAMPS

SERBIA

The following obligatory tax stamps were for use in Serbia only. Except for the Children's Week issues they are all inscribed "SRBIJA".

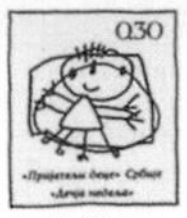

S1 Child

1990. Children's Week.

S1	**S1**	30p. red	40	10

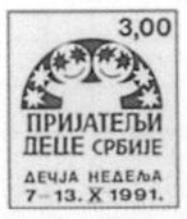

S2 Children

1991. Children's Week.

S2	**S2**	3d. blue	55	20

S3 Hands and Flower

1992. Anti-cancer Week.

S3	**S3**	3d. violet and orange	55	10

1993. Anti-cancer Week. No. S3 surch **1500**.

S4		1500d. on 3d. violet and orange	2·10	1·10

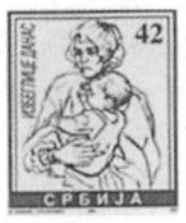

S4 Mother and Child

1993. Serbian Refugee Fund.

S5	**S4**	42d. green and yellow	40	10
S6	**S4**	75d. blue and light blue	40	15
S7	**S4**	150d. violet and lilac	70	20

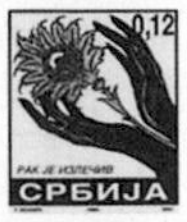

S5 Hands and Flower

1994. Anti-cancer Week.

S8	**S5**	12p. violet	55	20

See also No. S11.

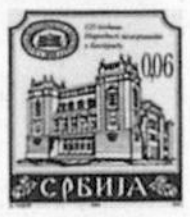

S6

1994

S9	**S6**	6p. purple	40	10

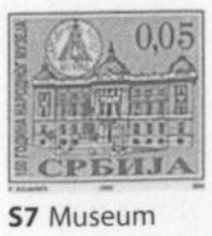

S7 Museum

1994. 150th Anniv of National Museum, Belgrade.

S10	**S7**	5p. blue	40	10

1995. Anti-cancer Week.

S11	**S5**	6p. mauve	40	10

1996. Anti-Cancer Week. As Type **S5**.

S12		10p. reddish brown	10	10

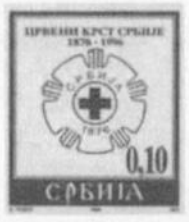

S8 Emblem

1996. 120th Anniv of Red Cross.

S13	**S8**	10p. vermilion	10	10

1997. Anti-Cancer Week. As Type **S5**.

S14	**S**	15p. turquoise	10	10

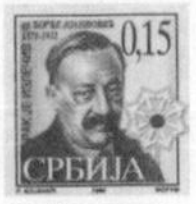

S9 Dr. Jovanovich

1998. Dr. Jovanovich Commemoration. Anti-Cancer Week.

S15	**S9**	15p. multicoloured	15	10

S10 Hilander Monastery

1998. 800th Anniv of Hilander Monastery.

S16	75p. yellow, reddish brown and bistre-yellow	55	15
S17	1d. pink and reddish brown (horiz)	65	25

DESIGNS: 75p. Type S **10**; 1d. Monastery from left.

═ 1,00

(S11)

1999. 800th (1998) Anniv of Hilander Monastery. No. S16 Surch as Type **S11**.

S18	1d. on 75p. yellow, reddish brown and bistre-yellow	65	25

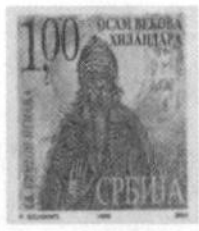

S12 St. Simeon (Stefan Nemanja)

1999. 800th (1998) Anniv of Hilander Monastery.

S19	1d. multicoloured	65	25
S20	1d. turquoise-green and indigo	65	25

DESIGNS: 75p. Type S **12**; 1d. Hilander Monastery.

S13 Hearts enclosed in Safety Pin and Male and Female Symbols

1999. AIDS Awareness Campaign.

S21	**S 13**	1d. multicoloured	65	25

OFFICIAL STAMPS

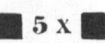

O130

1946

O540	**O130**	50p. orange	20	10
O541	**O130**	1d. green	20	10
O542	**O130**	1d.50 olive	35	10
O543	**O130**	2d.50 red	35	10
O544	**O130**	4d. brown	1·10	10
O545	**O130**	5d. blue	1·70	10
O546	**O130**	8d. brown	3·25	20
O547	**O130**	12d. violet	4·00	30

POSTAGE DUE STAMPS

BOSNIA AND HERZEGOVINA

ДРЖАВА С.Х.С.
БОСНА И
ХЕРЦЕГОВИНА

хелера

(D5)

1918. Postage Due Stamps of Bosnia optd as Type **D5** or **DRZAVA S.H.S. BOSNA I HERCEGOVINA HELERA**.

D19	**D35**	2h. red	10	10
D20	**D35**	4h. red	75	80
D21	**D35**	5h. red	10	10
D22	**D35**	6h. red	1·20	1·20
D23	**D35**	10h. red	10	10
D24	**D35**	15h. red	9·00	9·50
D25	**D35**	20h. red	10	10
D26	**D35**	25h. red	75	80
D27	**D35**	30h. red	75	80
D28	**D35**	40h. red	20	20
D29	**D35**	50h. red	1·60	1·70
D30	**D35**	1k. blue	75	80
D31	**D35**	3k. blue	50	55

КРАЉЕВСТВО
СРБА, ХРВАТА
И СЛОВЕНАЦА

ПОРТО

5 X

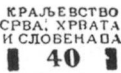

(D13)

1919. "Eagle" type of Bosnia surch as Type **D13** or **KRALJEVSTVO SRBA, HRVATA I SLOVENACA PORTO** and value.

D50	**2**	2h. on 35h. blue and black	75	1·10
D51	**2**	5h. on 45h. blue and black	1·30	1·70
D52	**2**	10h. on 10h. red	10	10
D53	**2**	15h. on 40h. orange and black	50	65
D54	**2**	20h. on 5h. green	10	15
D55	**2**	25h. on 20h. pink and black	50	80
D56	**2**	30h. on 30h. bistre and black	50	80
D57	**2**	1k. on 50h. purple	20	80
D58	**2**	3k. on 25h. blue	65	80

КРАЉЕВСТВО
СРБА, ХРВАТА
И СЛОВЕНАЦА
40

40 хелера 40

(D14)

1919. Postage Due stamps of Bosnia with surch or optd as Type **D14** or **KRALJEVSTVO SRBA, HRVATA SLOVENACA,** and value.

D59	**D4**	40h. on 6h. black, red and yellow	10	10
D60	**D4**	50h. on 8h. black, red and yellow	10	10
D61	**D4**	200h. black, red & green	10·50	9·50
D62	**D4**	4k. on 7h. black, red and yellow	50	80

CROATIA

1919. Postage Due stamps of Hungary, with figures in red (except 50f. in black), optd HRVATSKA SHS.

D85	**D9**	1f. green (No. D190)	37·00	50·00
D86	**D9**	2f. green	1·80	1·90
D87	**D9**	10f. green	1·30	1·30
D88	**D9**	12f. green	£100	£120
D89	**D9**	15f. green	1·00	1·10
D90	**D9**	20f. green	1·00	1·10
D91	**D9**	30f. green	2·50	2·75
D92	**D9**	50f. green (No. D177)	42·00	55·00

SLOVENIA

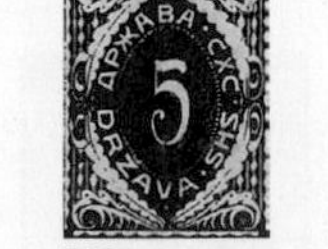

D30

1919

D150	**D30**	5v. red	10	10
D151	**D30**	10v. red	10	10
D152	**D30**	20v. red	10	10
D153	**D30**	50v. red	20	10
D154	**D30**	1k. blue	30	30
D155	**D30**	5k. blue	75	30
D156	**D30**	10k. blue	1·70	90

(D35)

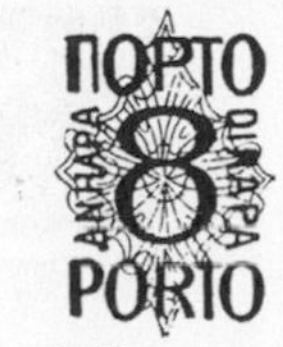
(D36)

1920. Stamps of 1919 issue surch as Types **D35** or **D36**.

D164	**25**	5p. on 15v. blue	10	10
D165	**25**	10p. on 15v. blue	1·60	1·60
D166	**25**	20p. on 15v. blue	20	10
D167	**25**	50p. on 15v. blue	10	10
D168	**26**	1d. on 30v. pink (or red)	30	20
D169	**26**	3d. on 30v. pink (or red)	50	20
D170	**26**	8d. on 30v. pink (or red)	4·25	1·10

GENERAL ISSUES

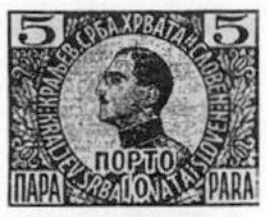
D39 King Alexander I when Prince

1921

D182	**D39**	10 on 5p. green	30	10
D183	**D39**	30 on 5p. green	50	10

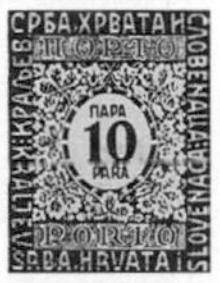
D40

1921

D184	**D40**	10p. red	10	10
D185	**D40**	30p. green	50	10
D197	**D40**	50p. violet	10	10
D198	**D40**	1d. brown	50	10
D188	**D40**	2d. blue	1·00	10
D200	**D40**	5d. orange	4·25	10
D190	**D40**	10d. brown	16·00	55
D191	**D40**	25d. pink	90·00	2·20
D192	**D40**	50d. green	80·00	2·50

There are two issues in this type, differing in the lettering, etc.

1928. Surcharged **10**.

D233	10 on 25d. pink	8·25	55
D234	10 on 50d. green	8·25	55

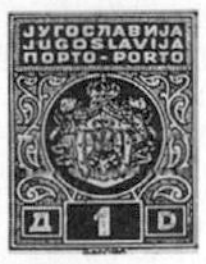
D56

1931

D259	**D56**	50p. violet	10	10
D260	**D56**	1d. red	10	10
D261	**D56**	2d. blue	10	10
D262	**D56**	5d. orange	10	10
D263	**D56**	10d. brown	20	15

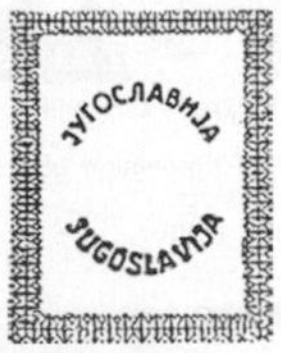
(D62)

1933. Optd with Type **D62**.

D293a	**D40**	50p. violet	20	10
D294a	**D40**	1d. brown	30	10
D295a	**D40**	2d. blue	65	10
D296b	**D40**	5d. orange	2·10	10
D297a	**D40**	10d. brown	10·50	10

1933. Red Cross. As T **62** but inscr "PORTO" in Latin and Cyrillic characters.

D298	**62**	50p. red and green	85	35

DEMOCRATIC FEDERATION OF YUGOSLAVIA

(a) REGIONAL ISSUES

CROATIA

1945. Zagreb issue. Croatian Postage Due stamps of 1942 surch **DEMOKRATSKA FEDERATIVNA JUGOSLAVIJA**, value and star.

RD45	**D15**	40k. on 50b. brown and blue	30	30
RD46	**D15**	60k. on 1k. brown and blue	30	30
RD47	**D15**	80k. on 2k. brown and blue	30	30
RD48	**D15**	100k. on 5k. brown and blue	30	30
RD49	**D15**	200k. on 6k. brown and blue	30	30

MONTENEGRO

1945. Cetinje issue. National Poem issue of Italian Occupation surch as Type **R4**, with **"PORTO"** in addition.

RD61	10l. on 5c. violet	£325	£325
RD62	20l. on 5l. red on buff	£160	£160

SERBIA

1944. Senta issue. No. D684 of Hungary optd with a large star, **8.X.1944** and **"Yugoslavia"** in Cyrillic characters and surch in addition.

RD73	**D115**	10(f.) on 2f. brown	50·00	50·00

(b) GENERAL ISSUES

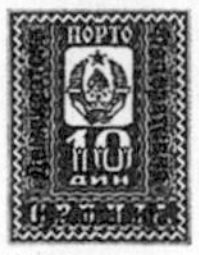
D114

1944. Postage Due stamps of Serbia optd in Cyrillic characters, as Type **D114**.

D487	10d. red	1·60	75
D488	20d. blue	1·60	75

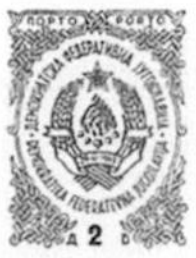
D115

1945. (a) Value in black.

D489	2d. brown	40	10
D490	3d. violet	40	10
D491	5d. green	40	10
D492	7d. brown	40	10
D493	10d. lilac	40	10
D494	20d. blue	40	10
D495	30d. green	1·00	40
D496	[illegible]	1·00	30

(b) Value in colour.

D497	1d. green	30	10
D498	1d.50 blue	30	10
D499	2d. red	1·00	10
D500	3d. brown	1·00	10
D501	4d. violet	1·60	20

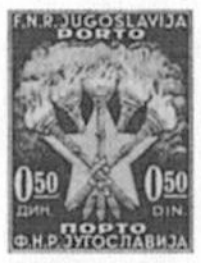
D126

1946

D527	**D126**	50p. orange	20	10
D528	**D126**	1d. orange	20	10
D724	**D126**	1d. brown	55	10
D529	**D126**	2d. blue	20	10
D725	**D126**	2d. green	55	10
D530	**D126**	3d. green	20	10
D531	**D126**	5d. violet	20	10
D726	**D126**	5d. blue	80	10
D532	**D126**	7d. red	1·80	10
D533	**D126**	10d. pink	2·10	30
D727	**D126**	10d. red	2·75	10
D534	**D126**	20d. lake	5·25	75
D1030	**D126**	20d. violet	4·75	20
D1031	**D126**	30d. orange	10·00	20
D1032	**D126**	50d. blue	47·00	1·00
D1033	**D126**	100d. purple	29·00	1·60

1947. Red Cross. As No. 545, but with "PORTO" added. Colour changed.

D546	**131**	50p. green and red	65	30

1948. Red Cross. As No. 594, but inscr "PORTO".

D595	**152**	50p. red and green	55	20

1949. Red Cross. As T **160** but inscr "PORTO".

D617	**160**	50p. purple and red	80	30

ФНРЈУГОСЛАВИЈА

FNR JUGOSLAVIJA
(D168)

1950. Optd with Type **D168**.

D637	**D115**	1d.50 blue	55	10
D638	**D115**	3d. brown	55	10
D639	**D115**	4d. violet	55	20

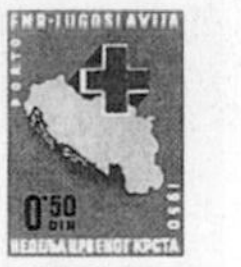
D175 Map

1950. Red Cross.

D665	**D175**	50p. brown and red	55	30

1951. Red Cross. Inscr "PORTO".

D703	**191**	50p. green and red	55	30

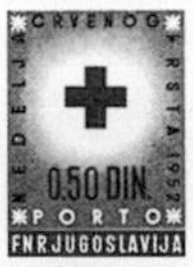
D202

1952. Red Cross.

D741	**D202**	50p. red and grey	65	30

1953. Red Cross. Inscr "PORTO".

D762	**211**	2d. red and brown	1·10	50

1954. Red Cross. Inscr "PORTO".

D783	**216**	2d. red and lilac	1·00	40

1955. Children's Week. Inscr "PORTO".

D802	**222**	2d. green and light green	80	30

1955. Red Cross. Inscr "PORTO".

D804	**224**	2d. brown, choc & red	1·20	30

1956. Red Cross. Inscr "PORTO".

D820	**228**	2d. green, turq & red	80	30

1956. Children's Week. Inscr "PORTO".

D835	**232**	2d. chocolate & lt brn	80	30

1957. Red Cross. Inscr "PORTO".

D844	**234**	2d. red, black and grey	80	30

1957. Children's Week. Inscr "PORTO".

D867	**240**	2d. brown and blue	80	20

1958. Red Cross. Inscr "PORTO".

D879	**245**	2d. multicoloured	1·20	50

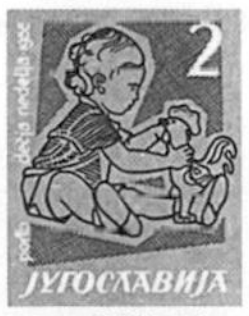
D251 Child with Toy

1958. Children's Week.

D913	**D251**	2d. black and blue	80	30

1959. Red Cross. Inscr "PORTO".

D927	**255**	2d. orange and red	80	30

1959. Children's Week. As T **260**. Inscr "PORTO".

D947	2d. purple and yellow	60	20

DESIGN: Tree, cockerel and ears of wheat.

1960. Red Cross. Inscr "PORTO".

D956	**262**	2d. purple and red	70	30

1960. Children's Week. As T **265**. Inscr "PORTO".

D970	2d. blue (Young boy)	45	20

1961. Red Cross. Inscr "PORTO". Perf or imperf.

D982	**268**	2d. multicoloured	60	20

1961. Children's Week. Inscr "PORTO".

D1020	**274**	2d. green and sepia	45	20

1962. Red Cross. Inscr "PORTO".

D1043	**281**	5d. red, brown and blue	45	20

1963. Red Cross Cent. and Week. Inscr "PORTO".

D1074	**288**	5d. red, purple & orge	70	30

REGISTERED LETTER STAMPS

R960 Hands holding Envelope

1993. No value expressed.

R2864	**R960**	R (11000d.) blue	55	15

Pt. 17

YUNNANFU

Yunnanfu (formerly Yunnansen), the chief city of the Chinese Province of Yunnan, had an Indo-Chinese Post Office from 1900 to 1922.

1901. 100 centimes = 1 franc.
1918. 100 cents = 1 piastre.

Stamps of Indo-China surcharged.

1903. "Tablet" key-type surch with value in Chinese and YUNNANSEN.

1	**D**	1c. black and red on blue	11·00	23·00
2	**D**	2c. brown and blue on buff	19·00	21·00
3	**D**	4c. brown and blue on grey	14·00	22·00
4	**D**	5c. green and red	9·00	20·00
5	**D**	10c. red and blue	9·00	16·00
6	**D**	15c. grey and red	9·50	11·00
7	**D**	20c. red and blue on green	8·50	24·00
8	**D**	25c. blue and red	9·50	20·00
9	**D**	30c. brown and blue on drab	12·00	24·00
10	**D**	40c. red and blue on yellow	£110	90·00
11	**D**	50c. red and blue on pink	£475	£450
12	**D**	50c. brown and red on blue	£200	£225
13	**D**	75c. brown and red on orange	£110	£100
14	**D**	1f. green and red	90·00	£110
15	**D**	5f. mauve and blue on lilac	£160	£160

1906. Surch **Yunnan-Fou** and value in Chinese.

16	**8**	1c. green	3·25	6·25
17	**8**	2c. purple on yellow	4·25	7·50
18	**8**	4c. mauve on blue	4·25	5·75
19	**8**	5c. green	6·50	7·75
20	**8**	10c. pink	7·50	11·50
21	**8**	15c. brown on blue	16·00	25·00
22	**8**	20c. red on green	7·25	15·00
23	**8**	25c. blue	7·25	12·50
24	**8**	30c. brown on cream	8·00	12·00
25	**8**	35c. black on yellow	13·00	26·00
26	**8**	40c. black on grey	11·00	12·50
27	**8**	50c. brown on cream	10·00	24·00
28	**D**	75c. brown on orange	[illegible]	£100
29	**8**	1f. green	36·00	70·00
30	**8**	2f. brown on yellow	38·00	70·00
31	**D**	5f. mauve on lilac	£120	£140
32	**8**	10f. red on green	£110	£150

1908. Native types surch **YUNNANFOU** and value in Chinese.

33	**10**	1c. black and brown	1·30	1·20
34	**10**	2c. black and brown	1·40	1·60
35	**10**	4c. black and blue	2·75	2·10
36	**10**	5c. black and green	3·00	2·00
37	**10**	10c. black and red	3·25	1·70
38	**10**	15c. black and violet	7·75	8·75
39	**11**	20c. black and violet	7·75	14·00
40	**11**	25c. black and blue	11·00	9·75
41	**11**	30c. black and brown	10·00	20·00
42	**11**	35c. black and green	7·25	20·00
43	**11**	40c. black and brown	20·00	30·00
44	**11**	50c. black and red	11·00	30·00
45	**12**	75c. black and orange	13·00	29·00
46	**12**	1f. black and red	22·00	44·00
47	**12**	2f. black and green	60·00	75·00
48	**12**	5f. black and blue	80·00	£100
49	**12**	10f. black and violet	£160	£150

1919. As last, surch in addition with value in figures and words.

50	**10**	⅖c. on 1c. black and brown	1·20	2·50
51	**10**	⅘c. on 2c. black and brown	1·60	6·25
52	**10**	1⅗c. on 4c. black and blue	2·75	9·25
53	**10**	2c. on 5c. black and green	4·50	2·30
54	**10**	4c. on 10c. black and red	4·25	2·10
55	**10**	6c. on 15c. black and violet	3·00	1·70
56	**11**	8c. on 20c. black and violet	7·25	9·50
57	**11**	10c. on 25c. black and blue	10·00	10·00
58	**11**	12c. on 30c. black & brown	6·00	10·50
59	**11**	14c. on 35c. black and green	12·00	14·00
60	**11**	16c. on 40c. black & brown	12·50	12·50
61	**11**	20c. on 50c. black and red	6·50	3·75
62	**12**	30c. on 75c. black & orange	10·00	14·50
63	**12**	40c. on 1f. black and red	10·50	17·00

64	12	80c. on 2f. black and green	20·00	23·00
65	12	2p. on 5f. black and blue	70·00	85·00
66	12	4p. on 10f. black and violet	30·00	55·00

Pt. 14

ZAIRE

In 1971 the Congo Republic (Kinshasa), formerly Belgian Congo, changed its name to Zaire.

100 sengi = 1 (li)kuta; 100 (ma)kuta = 1 zaire.

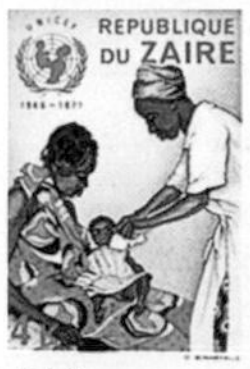

176 Nurse tending Child

1971. 25th Anniv of UNICEF. Multicoloured.

788		4k. Type **176**	30	20
789		14k. Zaire Republic on map of Africa	85	55
790		17k. Child in African village	1·10	90

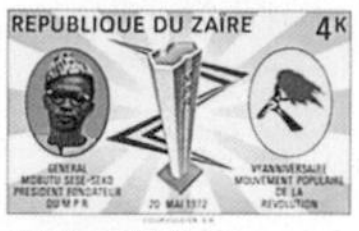

177 Pres. Mobutu, Memorial and Emblem

1972. Fifth Anniv of Revolution.

791	**177**	4k. multicoloured	3·25	2·75
792	**177**	14k. multicoloured	3·25	2·75
793	**177**	22k. multicoloured	4·50	3·25

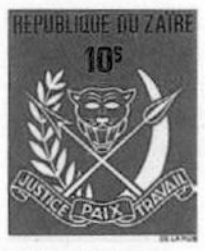

177a Arms

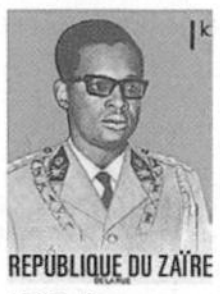

177b Pres. Mobutu

1972

794	**177a**	10s. orange and black	10	10
795	**177a**	40s. blue and black	10	10
796	**177a**	50s. yellow and black	10	10
797	**177b**	1k. multicoloured	10	10
798	**177b**	2k. multicoloured	10	10
799	**177b**	3k. multicoloured	10	10
800	**177b**	4k. multicoloured	10	10
801	**177b**	5k. multicoloured	15	10
802	**177b**	6k. multicoloured	15	10
803	**177b**	8k. multicoloured	20	15
804	**177b**	9k. multicoloured	30	15
805	**177b**	10k. multicoloured	35	15
806	**177b**	14k. multicoloured	45	20
807	**177b**	17k. multicoloured	50	35
808	**177b**	20k. multicoloured	65	40
809	**177b**	50k. multicoloured	1·75	85
810	**177b**	100k. multicoloured	3·50	2·00

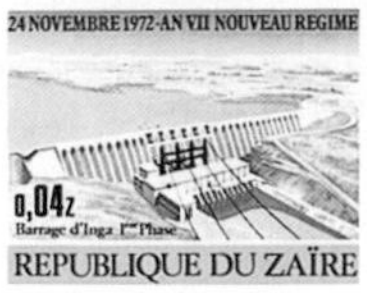

178 Inga Dam

1973. Inga Dam. Completion of First Stage.

811	**178**	0.04z. multicoloured	10	10
812	**178**	0.14z. multicoloured	45	35
813	**178**	0.18z. multicoloured	80	45

1973. As T **177b**, but face values in Zaires.

814		0.01z. multicoloured	10	10
815		0.02z. multicoloured	10	10
816		0.03z. multicoloured	10	10
817		0.04z. multicoloured	10	10
818		0.10z. multicoloured	45	20
819		0.14z. multicoloured	80	35

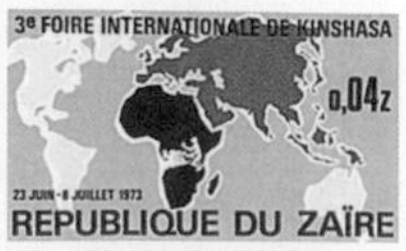

179 Africa on World Map

1973. Third International Fair, Kinshasa.

820	**179**	0.04z. multicoloured	15	10
821	**179**	0.07z. multicoloured	30	15
822	**179**	0.18z. multicoloured	80	45

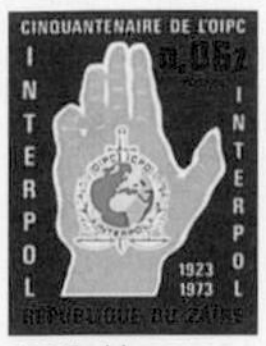

180 Emblem on Hand

1973. 50th Anniv of Criminal Police Organization (Interpol).

823	**180**	0.06z. multicoloured	35	20
824	**180**	0.14z. multicoloured	80	35

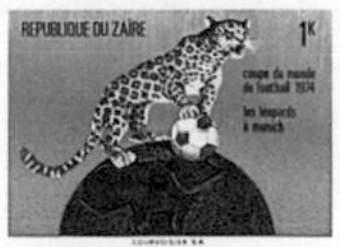

181 Leopard with Football on Globe

1974. World Cup Football Championship, Munich.

825	**181**	1k. multicoloured	10	10
826	**181**	2k. multicoloured	10	10
827	**181**	3k. multicoloured	15	10
828	**181**	4k. multicoloured	20	10
829	**181**	5k. multicoloured	30	10
830	**181**	14k. multicoloured	1·40	55

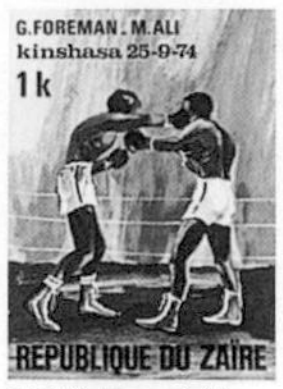

182 Muhamed Ali and George Foreman

1974. World Heavyweight Boxing Title Fight, Kinshasa.

831	**182**	1k. multicoloured	10	10
832	**182**	4k. multicoloured	15	10
833	**182**	6k. multicoloured	20	10
834	**182**	14k. multicoloured	55	30
835	**182**	20k. multicoloured	90	40

1975. World Heavyweight Boxing Title Fight, Kinshasa. As T **182** optd with amended date **25-9-74**.

836	**182**	0.01z. multicoloured	10	10
837	**182**	0.04z. multicoloured	10	10
838	**182**	0.06z. multicoloured	20	10
839	**182**	0.14z. multicoloured	45	15
840	**182**	0.20z. multicoloured	80	30

Nos. 836/40 differ from Type **182** by having the face values expressed as decimals of the zaire. Both dates are in fact incorrect as the fight was held on 30 October 1974.

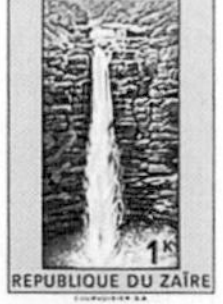

185 Waterfall

1975. 12th General Assembly of International Union for Conservation of National Resources, Kinshasa.

858	**185**	1k. multicoloured	15	15
859	**185**	2k. multicoloured	15	15
860	**185**	3k. multicoloured	30	15
861	**185**	4k. multicoloured	45	15
862	**185**	5k. multicoloured	60	15

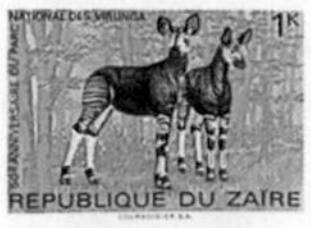

186 Okapis

1975. 50th Anniv of Virunga National Park.

863	**186**	1k. multicoloured	20	20
864	**186**	2k. multicoloured	40	20
865	**186**	3k. multicoloured	65	20
866	**186**	4k. multicoloured	85	20
867	**186**	5k. multicoloured	1·10	20

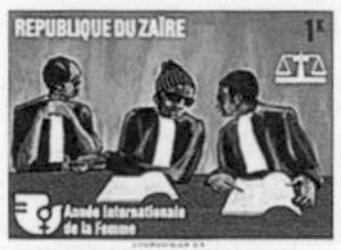

187 Woman Judge with Barristers

1975. International Women's Year.

868	**187**	1k. multicoloured	10	10
869	**187**	2k. multicoloured	10	10
870	**187**	4k. multicoloured	20	10
871	**187**	14k. multicoloured	65	20

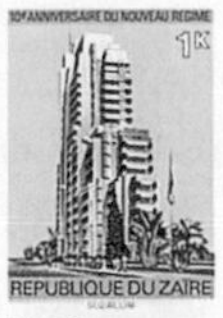

188 Sozacom Building

1976. Tenth Anniv of "New Regime". Multicoloured.

872		1k. Type **188**	10	10
873		2k. Siderna Maluku Industrial Complex (horiz)	10	10
874		3k. Flour mill, Matadi	10	10
875		4k. Women parachutists (horiz)	20	10
876		8k. Pres. Mobutu with Mao Tse-Tung	35	10
877		10k. Soldiers clearing vegetation along the Salongo (horiz)	45	20
878		14k. Pres. Mobutu addressing U.N. General Assembly, 4 October 1973 (horiz)	65	30
879		15k. Rejoicing crowd (horiz)	80	20

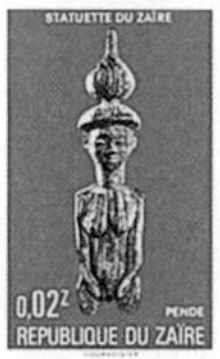

189 Pende Statuette

1977. Masks and Statuettes. Multicoloured.

880		2z. Type **189**	10	10
881		4z. Type **189**	10	10
882		5z. Tshokwe mask	10	10
883		7z. As 5k.	15	10
884		10z. Suku mask	20	10
885		14z. As 10k.	35	15
886		15z. Kongo statuette	40	15
887		18z. As 15k.	45	30
888		20z. Kuba mask	65	35
889		25z. As 20k.	80	45

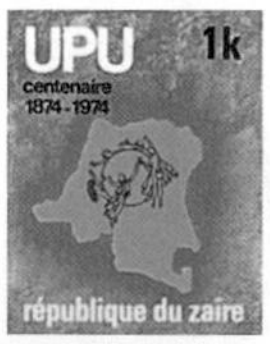

190 U.P.U. Emblem on Map

1977. Centenary of Universal Postal Union.

890	**190**	1k. multicoloured	10	10
891	**190**	4k. multicoloured	20	10
892	**190**	7k. multicoloured	50	35
893	**190**	50k. multicoloured	4·25	2·25

1977. Various stamps of Congo (Kinshasa) and Zaire, surch **REPUBLIQUE DU ZAIRE** or with new value only (No. 904).

894	**158**	1k. on 10s. red and black	10	10
895	**152**	2k. on 9.6k. black on red	10	10
896	**158**	5k. on 30s. green & black	10	10
897	**173**	10k. on 10s. mult	40	10
898	**158**	10k. on 15s. blue & black	15	10
899	-	20k. on 9.6k. mult (No. 673)	40	10
900	**167**	25k. on 10s. mult	75	20
901	**174**	30k. on 12s. mult	75	20
902	**159**	40k. on 9.6k. mult	1·10	30
903	**168**	48k. on 10s. mult	1·25	35
904	**158**	100k. on 40s. blue & black	2·75	60

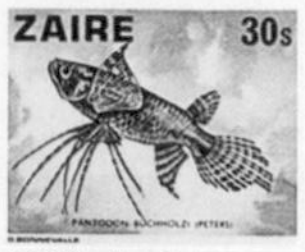

192 Freshwater Butterflyfish

1978. Fish. Multicoloured.

905		30s. Type **192**	10	15
906		70s. Striped killifish	10	15
907		5k. Banded ctenopoma	15	15
908		8k. Electric catfish	25	15
909		10k. Jewel cichlid	45	20
910		30k. Isidor's elephantfish	70	60
911		40k. Blotched upsidedown catfish	1·10	65
912		48k. Golden Julie	1·40	80
913		100k. Brien's notho	3·50	1·75
MS914		80×74 mm. 250k. Congo Tetra "Micralestes interruptus" (46×35 mm)	8·00	2·50

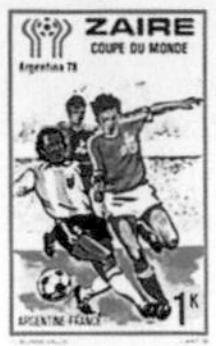

193 Argentina v. France

1978. World Cup Football Championship, Argentina. Multicoloured.

915		1k. Type **193**	10	10
916		3k. Austria v. Brazil	10	10
917		7k. Scotland v. Iran	10	10
918		9k. Netherlands v. Peru	10	10
919		10k. Hungary v. Italy	15	10
920		20k. West Germany v. Mexico	35	20
921		50k. Tunisia v. Poland	85	45
922		100k. Spain v. Sweden	1·90	1·00
MS923		Two sheets each 114×79 mm each containing 500k. World Cup, flags and emblems (47×35 mm). (a) Green margin, inscr "Argentina 78/ COUPE DE MONDE"; (b) Blue margin inscr "Finalists Coupe du Monde 78/ ARGENTINE 3—HOLLANDE 1"	9·50	5·00

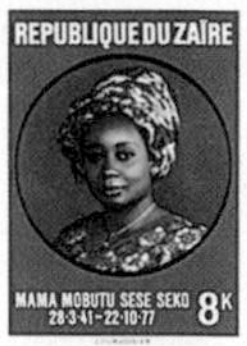

194 Mama Mobutu

1978. First Death Anniv of Mama Mobutu Sese Seko (wife of President).

924	**194**	8k. multicoloured	20	10

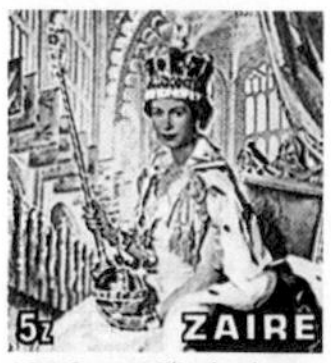

195 Queen Elizabeth II

1978. 25th Anniv of Coronation of Queen Elizabeth II. Sheet 71×92 mm.

MS925	**195**	5z. multicoloured	1·50	85

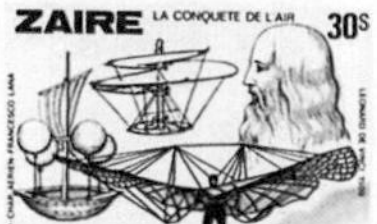

197 Da Vinci, Lilienthal and Flying Machines

1978. History of Aviation. Multicoloured.

927		30s. Type **197**	15	10
928		70s. Wright Type A and Santos-Dumont's "14 bis"	15	10
929		1k. Farman F 60 Goliath and Bleriot XI	15	10
930		5k. Junkers G.38ce "Deutschland" and "Spirit of St. Louis"	15	10
931		8k. Macchi Castoldi MC-72 seaplane and Sikorsky S-42B flying boat	25	15
932		10k. Boeing 707 and Fokker F.VIIb/3m	45	20
933		50k. "Apollo XI" space capsule and Concorde	1·75	55

934	75k. Sikorsky S-61N helicopter and Douglas DC10	2·10	90
MS935	89×125 mm. 5z. Giffard's steam-powered dirigible airship and Zeppelin	1·50	85

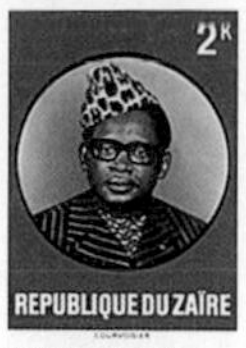

198 President Mobutu

1978

936	**198**	2k. multicoloured	10	10
937	**198**	5k. multicoloured	10	10
938	**198**	6k. multicoloured	10	10
939	**198**	8k. multicoloured	10	10
940	**198**	10k. multicoloured	10	10
941	**198**	25k. multicoloured	10	10
942	**198**	48k. multicoloured	35	15
942a	**198**	50k. multicoloured	20	10
943	**198**	1z. multicoloured	80	30
943a	**198**	2z. multicoloured	65	35
943b	**198**	5z. multicoloured	1·50	85

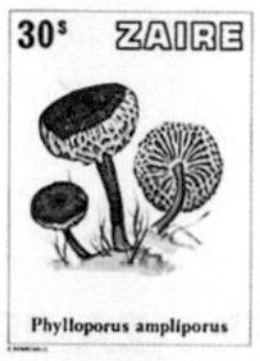

199 "Phyllophorus ampliporus"

1979. Mushrooms. Multicoloured.

944	30s. Type **199**	10	30
945	5k. "Englerornyces goetzei"	15	30
946	8k. "Scutellinia virungae"	30	30
947	10k. "Pycnoporus sanguineus"	35	30
948	30k. "Cantharellus miniatescens"	1·00	75
949	40k. "Lactarius phlebonemus"	1·60	90
950	48k. "Phallus indusiatus"	2·50	1·10
951	100k. "Ramaria moelleriana"	4·00	2·40

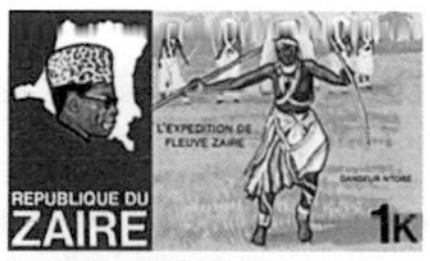

200 Ntore Dancer

1979. Zaire River Expedition. Multicoloured.

952	1k. Type **200**	10	10
953	3k. Regal sunbird	1·50	25
954	4k. African elephant	10	10
955	10k. Diamond, cotton boll and tobacco	10	10
956	14k. Hand holding flaming torch	15	10
957	17k. Lion and water lily	20	15
958	25k. Inzia Falls	30	15
959	50k. Wagenia fisherman	55	35
MS960	Two sheets each 132×100 mm. (a) Nos. 952/5; (b) Nos. 956/9	2·75	1·25

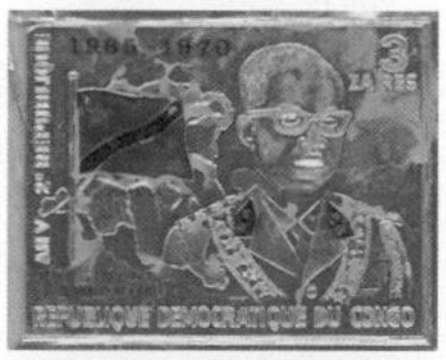

201 President Mobutu and Flag

1979. Fifth Anniv (1970) of 2nd Republic.

961	**201**	3z. gold, red and blue	26·00	

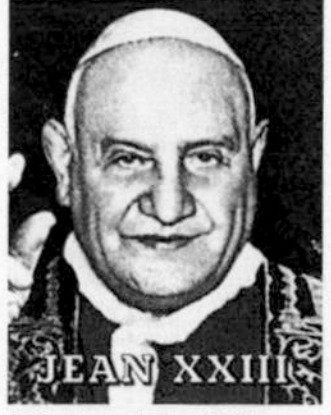

202 Pope John XXIII

1979. Popes. Three sheets each 96×130 mm containing T **202** or similar vert design. Multicoloured.

MS962	Three sheets (a) 250k. Type **202**; (b) 250k. Pope Paul IV; (c) 250k. Pope John-Paul I	7·00	3·25

See also **MS**1011.

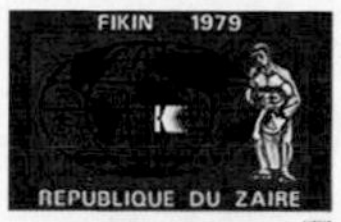

203 Globe and Drummer

1979. Sixth International Fair, Kinshasa.

963	**203**	1k. multicoloured	10	10
964	**203**	9k. multicoloured	10	10
965	**203**	90k. multicoloured	65	30
966	**203**	100k. multicoloured	80	35
MS967		104×61 mm. **203** 500k. blue (48×26 mm)	3·75	1·75

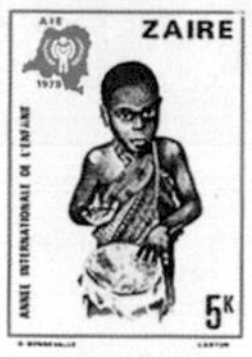

204 Boy with Drum

1979. International Year of the Child. Multicoloured.

968	5k. Type **204**	10	10
969	10k. Girl	10	10
970	20k. Boy	20	10
971	50k. Laughing boy	40	20
972	100k. Two children	85	35
973	300k. Mother and child	3·00	1·60
MS974	80×60 mm. 10z. Mother with two children (horiz)	3·00	1·75

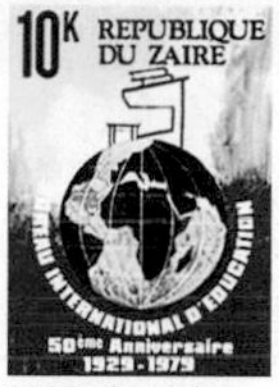

205 Desk standing on Globe

1979. 50th Anniv of International Bureau of Education.

975	**205**	10k. multicoloured	10	10

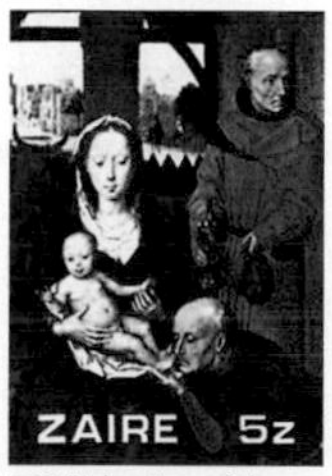

206 "Adoration of the Magi" (Hans Memling)

1979. Christmas. Sheet 94×74 mm.

MS976	**206** 5z. multicoloured	3·00	3·75

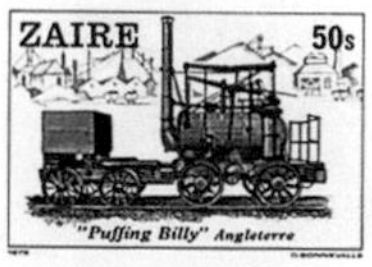

207 "Puffing Billy", 1813–14, Great Britain

1980. Locomotives. Multicoloured.

977	50s. Type **207**	10	10
978	1k.50 Buddicom No. 33, 1844, France	10	10
979	5k. "Elephant", 1835, Belgium	10	10
980	8k. No. 601, Zaire	10	10
981	50k. No. 171 "Slieve Gullion", 1913, Ireland	70	70
982	75k. "Black Elephant", Prussia	1·00	1·00
983	2z. Type 1-15, Zaire	2·75	2·75
984	5z. "Golden State Limited" express, U.S.A.	7·00	7·00
MS985	78×58 mm. 10z. Type "E.D.75" electric locomotive, Zaire	13·00	13·00

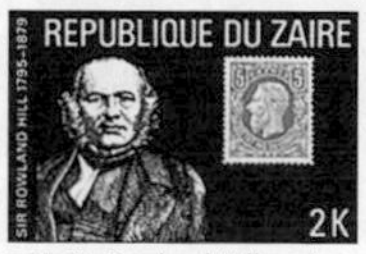

208 Sir Rowland Hill and Congo 5f. Stamp, 1886

1980. Death Cent of Sir Rowland Hill. Multicoloured.

986	2k. Type **208**	10	10
987	4k. Congo 10f. stamp, 1887	10	10
988	10k. Congo 1f. African elephant stamp, 1884	10	10
989	20k. Belgian Congo overprinted 3f.50 stamp, 1909	15	10
990	40k. Belgian Congo 10f. African Elephant stamp, 1925	20	10
991	150k. Belgian Congo 1f.50+1f.50 Chimpanzees stamp, 1939	85	40
992	200k. Belgian Congo 1f.75 Leopard stamp, 1942	1·25	60
993	250k. Belgian Congo 2f.50 Railway stamp, 1948	3·00	2·50
MS994	84×58 mm. 10z. as No. 992	3·75	3·75

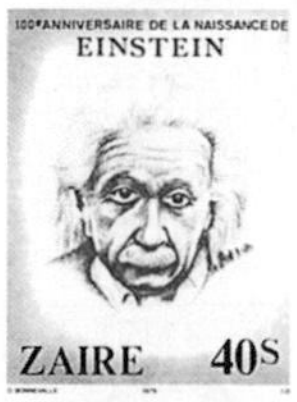

209 Einstein

1980. Birth Cent of Albert Einstein (physicist).

995	**209**	40s. brown, black & mve	10	10
996	**209**	2k. brown, black & green	10	10
997	**209**	4k. brown, black & yell	10	10
998	**209**	15k. brown, black & blue	15	10
999	**209**	50k. brown, black and red	35	20
1000	**209**	300k. brown, blk & lilac	2·00	1·00
MS1001		79×67 mm. 5z. multicoloured	3·75	3·75

DESIGN: 34×50 mm. 5z. Three-quarter face portrait of Einstein.

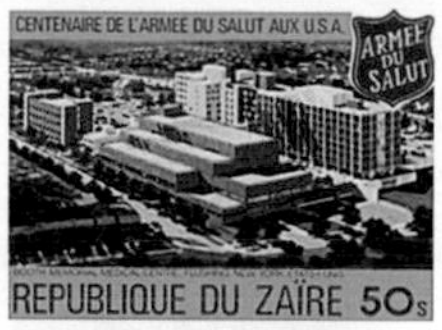

210 Booth Memorial Medical Centre, Flushing, New York

1980. Centenary of Salvation Army in the United States. Multicoloured.

1002	50s. Type **210**	10	10
1003	4k.50 Arrival of Railton in America	10	10
1004	10k. Mobile dispensary, Musina, Zaire	10	10
1005	20k. General Evangeline Booth and salvationist holding child (vert)	10	10
1006	40k. Army band	20	15
1007	75k. Mobile clinic in bush, Zaire	45	20
1008	1z.50 Canteen serving firefighters	90	40
1009	2z. American unit marching with flags (vert)	1·40	55
MS1010	150×81 mm. 10z. General and Mrs. Arthur Brown (51×37 mm)	3·75	3·75

1980. Papal Visit (1st issue). Sheet 96×130 mm containing vert design as T **202**. Multicoloured.

MS1011	10z. John-Paul II	3·75	3·75

See also Nos. 1061/6.

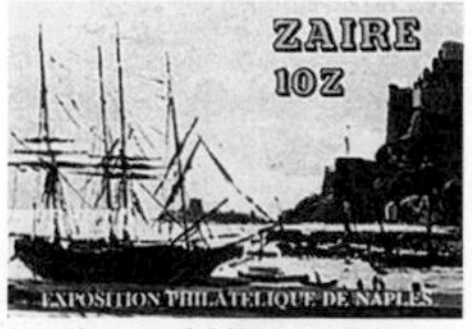

211 "Baia Castle" (Antonio Pitloo)

1980. Naples International Stamp Exhibition. Sheet 145×115 mm.

MS1012	**211** 10z. multicoloured	3·75	3·75

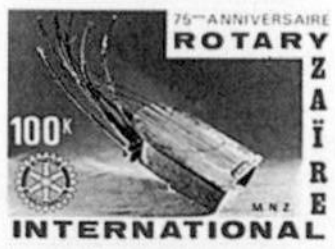

212 Musical Instrument

1980. 75th Anniv of Rotary International. Multicoloured.

1013	50k. Drawing of mother and child (Kamba)	30	15
1014	100k. Type **212**	55	30
1015	500k. Statuette (Liyolo) (vert)	2·00	1·40
MS1016	199×130 mm. As Nos. 1013/15 but larger (56×35 or 35×56 mm). Perf or imperf	2·75	2·75

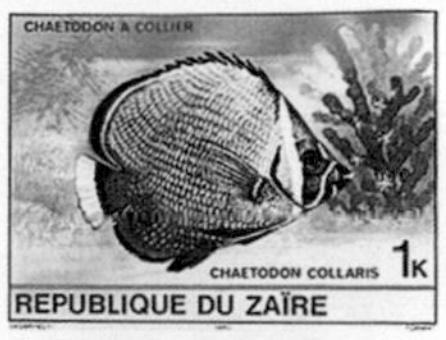

213 Red-tailed butterflyfish

1980. Tropical Fish. Multicoloured.

1017	1k. Type **213**	10	10
1018	5k. Sail-finned tang	10	10
1019	10k. Yellow-faced angelfish	10	10
1020	20k. Blue-ringed angelfish	20	10
1021	50k. Flame angelfish	45	20
1022	150k. Harlequin filefish	1·25	55
1023	200k. Black triggerfish	1·75	90
1024	250k. Picasso triggerfish	2·25	1·10
MS1025	118×80 mm. 5z. Undulate triggerfish "Balistapus undulates"	2·00	2·00

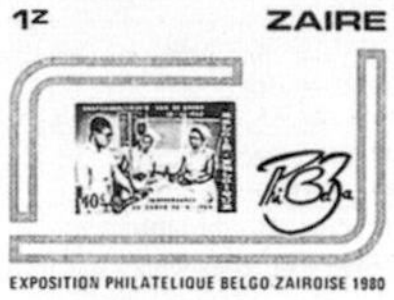

214 Belgium 40c. Congo Independence Stamp, 1960 and "Phibelza"

1980. "Phibelza" Belgian–Zaire Stamp Exhibition, Kinshasa. Multicoloured.

1026	1z. Type **214**	40	30
1027	1z. Congo 20f. Independence stamp, 1960	40	30
1028	2z. Belgium 10f.+5f. Zoo stamp, 1968	80	20
1029	2z. Congo 40c. Birds stamp, 1963	85	40
1030	3z. Belgium 10f.+5f. Brussels stamp, 1971	1·25	85
1031	3z. Zaire 22k. stamp, 1972	1·25	85
1032	4z. Belgium 25f.+10f. stamp, 1980	1·60	1·10
1033	4z. Congo 24f. stamp, 1966	1·60	1·10

Nos. 1026/33 exist in two versions with the exhibition logo either at the right or the left of the design. Prices are the same for either version.

1980. 20th Anniv of Independence. Various stamps optd **20e Anniversaire - Indépendance - 1960-1980.**

1034	**207**	50s. "Puffing Billy"	25	25
1035	-	1k.50 Buddicom locomotive No. 33 (No. 978)	40	40
1036	-	10k. Boeing 707 and Fokker F.VIIb/3m (No. 932)	50	50
1037	-	50k. "Slieve Gullion" (No. 981)	60	60
1038	-	75k. Sikorsky S-61N helicopter and Douglas DC-10 (No. 934)	70	70
1039	**203**	100k. Globe and drummer	45	25
1040	-	1z. on 5z. on 100k. Two children (No. 972)	45	25
1041	-	250k. Rowland Hill and railway stamp of 1948 (No. 993)	3·50	3·50
1042	-	5z. on 100k. Two children (No. 972)	2·75	1·25

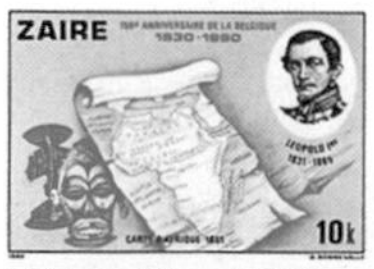

216 Leopold I and 1851 Map of Africa

1980. 150th Anniv of Belgian Independence.

1043	**216**	10k. green and blue	10	10
1044	-	75k. brown and blue	45	20
1045	-	100k. violet and blue	45	20
1046	-	145k. blue and deep blue	1·60	50
1047	-	270k. red and blue	1·60	85

DESIGNS: 75k. Leopold II and Stanley's expedition; 100k. Albert I and colonial troops of 1914–18 war; 145k. Leopold III and African animals; 270k. Baudouin I and visit to Zaire of King Baudouin and Queen Fabiola.

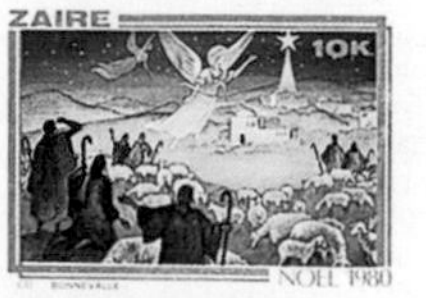

217 Angels appearing to Shepherds

1980. Christmas. Multicoloured.

1048	10k. Type **217**	10	10
1049	75k. Flight into Egypt	35	20

1050	80k. Three Kings	45	20
1051	145k. In the stable	80	45
MS1052	113×77 mm. 10z. Kings presenting crowns to infant	3·75	3·75

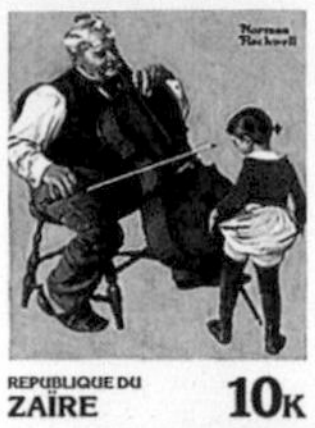
Norman Rockwell
REPUBLIQUE DU ZAIRE
10K
218 Girl dancing to Cello

1981. Norman Rockwell Paintings. Multicoloured.

1053	10k. Type **218**	10	10
1054	20k. Couple with saluting boy scout	10	10
1055	50k. Sorter reading mail	20	10
1056	80k. Cupid whispering in youth's ear	35	15
1057	100k. Signing Declaration of Independence	50	20
1058	125k. Boy looking through telescope held by sailor	80	25
1059	175k. Boy in armchair playing trumpet	1·10	55
1060	200k. Weakling exercising with dumb bells	1·10	50

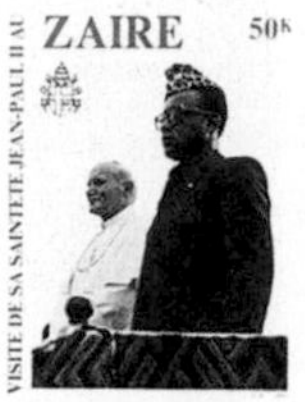
ZAIRE 50K
VISITE DE SA SAINTETE JEAN-PAUL II AU
219 Pope John-Paul II and Pres. Mobutu

1981. Papal Visit. Multicoloured.

1061	5k. Pope kneeling at shrine (horiz)	10	10
1062	10k. Pres. Mobutu greeting Pope (horiz)	10	10
1063	50k. Type **219**	20	10
1064	100k. Pope talking to child (horiz)	65	35
1065	500k. Pope leading prayers	2·75	1·25
1066	800k. Pope making speech (horiz)	4·00	2·00

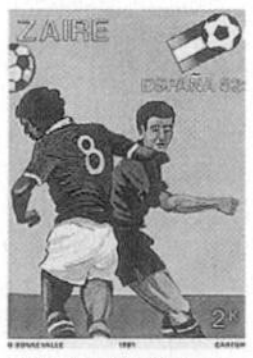
ZAIRE
ESPAÑA 82
2K
220 Footballers

1981. World Cup Football Championship, Spain (1982).

1067	**220**	2k. multicoloured	10	10
1068	-	10k. multicoloured	10	10
1069	-	25k. multicoloured	10	10
1070	-	90k. multicoloured	35	15
1071	-	2z. multicoloured	65	35
1072	-	3z. multicoloured	1·25	55
1073	-	6z. multicoloured	2·40	1·10
1074	-	8z. multicoloured	3·25	1·60
MS1075		104×79 mm. 5z. Type **220**; 5z. As No. 1073	3·75	3·75

DESIGN: Nos. 1068/**MS**1075. Similar footballing scenes.

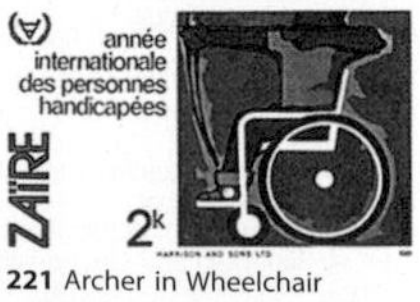
année internationale des personnes handicapées
ZAÏRE
2K
221 Archer in Wheelchair

1981. International Year of Disabled People. Multicoloured.

1076	2k. Type **221**	10	10
1077	5k. Ear and sound wave	10	10
1078	10k. One-legged person with crutch	10	10
1079	18k. Glasses, Braille and white cane	10	10
1080	50k. Crippled legs	20	10
1081	150k. Sign language	45	20
1082	500k. Hand and model showing joints	1·60	90
1083	800k. Dove shedding feathers	2·50	1·60

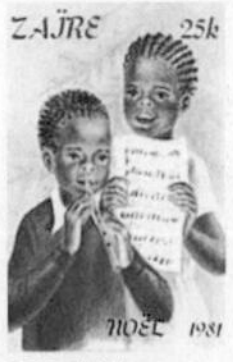
ZAÏRE 25k
NOEL 1981
222 Children performing Carols

1981. Christmas. Multicoloured.

1084	25k. Type **222**	10	10
1085	1z. Boy lighting candle	35	15
1086	1z.50 Boy praying	45	20
1087	3z. Girl with presents	95	45
1088	5z. Children admiring baby	1·75	85
MS1089	92×64 mm. 10z. Nativity (horiz)	3·50	3·50

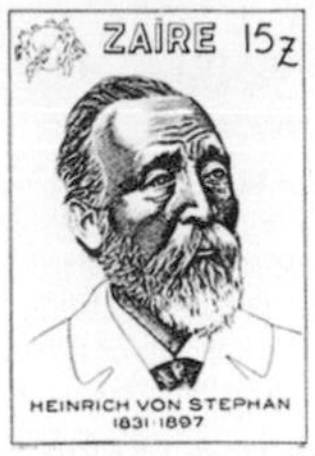
ZAÏRE 15Z
HEINRICH VON STEPHAN
1831-1897
223 Heinrich von Stephan

1981. 150th Birth Anniv of Heinrich von Stephan (founder of UPU). Sheet 65×85 mm.

MS1090	**223** 15z. violet	5·00	5·00

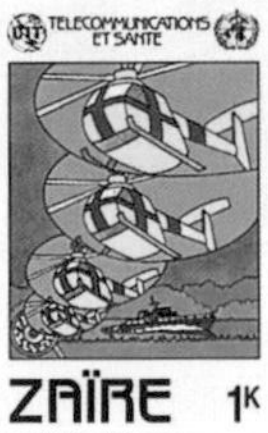
TELECOMMUNICATIONS ET SANTE
ZAÏRE 1K
224 Red Cross Helicopters

1982. Telecommunications and Health. Multicoloured.

1091	1k. Type **224**	10	10
1092	25k. Doctor and telephone	10	10
1093	90k. Antenna and map	20	15
1094	1z. Patient	35	15
1095	1z.70 Teleprinter	45	20
1096	3z. Nurse and television	90	35
1097	4z.50 Tape recorder	1·60	85
1098	5z. Babies and walkie-talkie	1·75	85

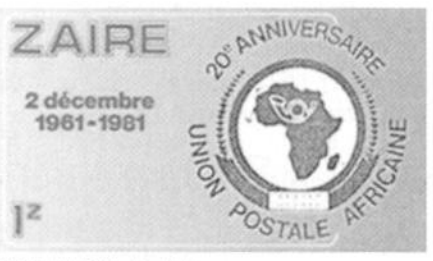
ZAIRE
2 décembre 1961-1981
20e ANNIVERSAIRE
UNION POSTALE AFRICAINE
1Z
225 U.P.U. Emblem

1982. 20th Anniv (1981) of African Postal Union.

1099	**225**	1z. green and gold	45	20

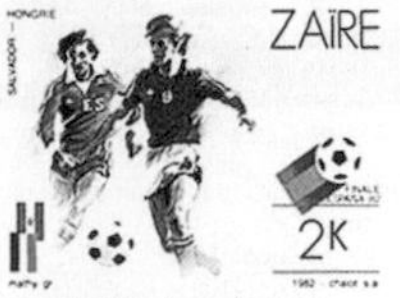
ZAIRE
2K
226 El Salvador v. Hungary

1982. World Cup Football Championship, Spain. Multicoloured.

1100	2k. Type **226**	10	10
1101	8k. Cameroun v. Peru	10	10
1102	25k. Brazil v. Russia	10	10
1103	50k. Kuwait v. Czechoslovakia	10	10
1104	90k. Yugoslavia v. Northern Ireland	30	15
1105	1z. Austria v. Chile	35	15
1106	1z.45 France v. England	45	15
1107	1z.70 West Germany v. Algeria	55	35
1108	3z. Spain v. Honduras	1·00	50
1109	3z.50 Belgium v. Argentina	1·10	60
1110	5z. Scotland v. New Zealand	1·60	85
1111	6z. Italy v. Poland	2·00	95

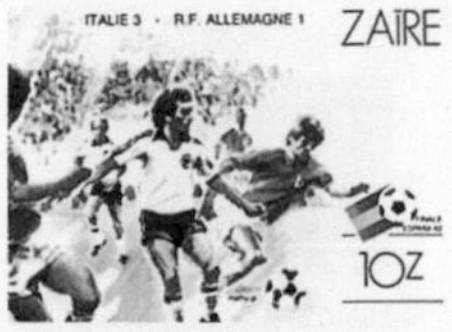
ITALIE 3 - R.F. ALLEMAGNE 1
ZAIRE
10Z
227 Italy v. West Germany

1982. World Cup Football Championship Results. Sheet 111×86 mm.

MS1112	**227** 10z. multicoloured	3·00	3·00

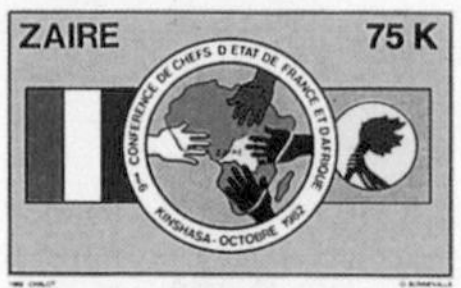
ZAIRE
75 K
228 Hands reaching towards Zaire

1982. Ninth French and African Heads of State Conference, Kinshasa.

1113	**228**	75k. multicoloured	20	10
1114	**228**	90k. multicoloured	30	15
1115	**228**	1z. multicoloured	35	15
1116	**228**	1z.50 multicoloured	45	20
1117	**228**	3z. multicoloured	95	50
1118	**228**	5z. multicoloured	1·60	85
1119	**228**	8z. multicoloured	2·50	1·10

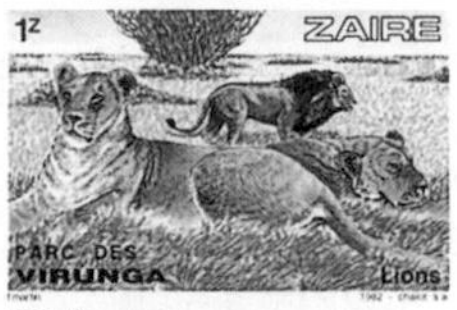
1Z
ZAIRE
PARC DES VIRUNGA
Lions
229 Lions

1982. Virunga National Park. Multicoloured.

1120	1z. Type **229**	40	25
1121	1z.70 African buffalo	65	50
1122	3z.50 African elephant	1·25	90
1123	6z.50 Topi	2·25	1·40
1124	8z. Hippopotamus	3·25	1·90
1125	10z. Savanna monkey	4·50	2·25
1126	10z. Leopard	4·50	2·25

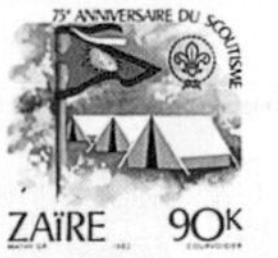
75e ANNIVERSAIRE DU SCOUTISME
ZAÏRE 90K
230 Scout Camp

1982. 75th Anniv of Boy Scout Movement. Multicoloured.

1127	90k. Type **230**	30	15
1128	1z.70 Camp-fire	55	25
1129	3z. Scout	95	45
1130	5z. Scout carrying injured person	1·75	85
1131	8z. Scout signalling with flags	2·75	1·10
MS1132	87×64 mm. 10z. Lord Baden-Powell	3·50	3·50

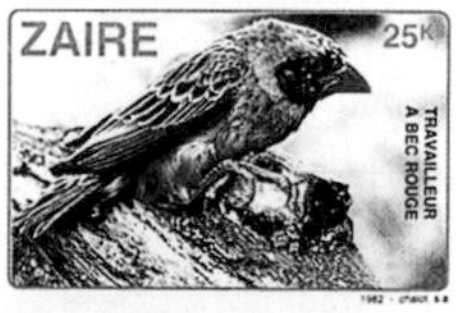
ZAIRE
25K
TRAVAILLEUR A BEC ROUGE
231 Red-billed Quelea

1982. Birds. Multicoloured.

1133	25k. Type **231**	10	10
1134	50k. African pygmy kingfisher	15	10
1135	90k. Green turaco	35	15
1136	1z.50 Three-banded plover	45	25
1137	1z.70 Temminck's courser	55	30
1138	2z. Bennett's woodpecker	65	45
1139	3z. Little grebe	80	60
1140	3z.50 Lizard buzzard (vert)	1·00	80
1141	5z. African black crake	2·00	90
1142	8z. White-headed vulture (vert)	3·25	1·75

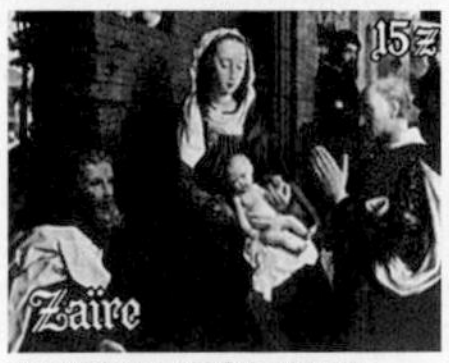
15Z
Zaïre
232 "Adoration of the Magi" (Hugo Van Der Goes)

1982. Christmas. Sheet 103×65 mm.

MS1143	**232** 15z. multicoloured	3·50	3·50

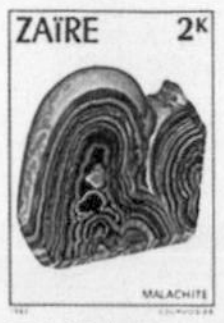
ZAÏRE 2K
MALACHITE
233 Malachite

1983. Minerals. Multicoloured.

1144	2k. Type **233**	10	10
1145	45k. Quartz (horiz)	20	10
1146	75k. Gold (horiz)	35	10
1147	1z. Uranium and pitchblende (horiz)	45	15
1148	1z.50 Bournonite	55	30
1149	3z. Cassiterite (horiz)	1·10	50
1150	6z. Dioptase	2·25	95
1151	8z. Cuprite	3·25	1·40
MS1152	72×52 mm. 10z. Diamond (horiz)	4·00	4·00

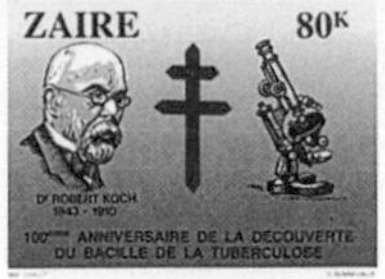
ZAIRE
80K
Dr ROBERT KOCH
1843-1910
100ème ANNIVERSAIRE DE LA DECOUVERTE DU BACILLE DE LA TUBERCULOSE
234 Dr. Koch and Microscope

1983. Centenary (1982) of Discovery of Tubercle Bacillus.

1153	**234**	80k. multicoloured	20	15
1154	**234**	1z.20 multicoloured	35	20
1155	**234**	3z.60 multicoloured	1·10	55
1156	**234**	9z.60 multicoloured	2·75	1·40

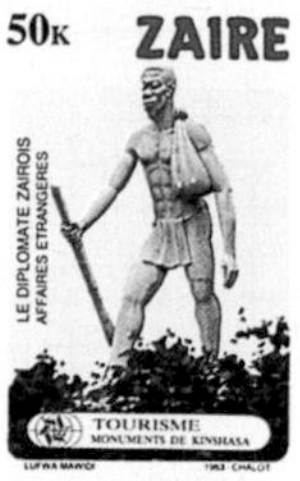
50K ZAIRE
LE DIPLOMATE ZAIROIS AFFAIRES ETRANGERES
TOURISME
MONUMENTS DE KINSHASA
235 "Zaire Diplomat" (Lufwa Mawidi)

1983. Kinshasa Monuments. Multicoloured.

1157	50k. Type **235**	15	10
1158	1z. "Echo of Zaire" (Lufwa Mawidi) (horiz)	25	15
1159	1z.50 "Messengers" (Liyolo Limbe Mpuanga)	40	20
1160	3z. "Shield of Revolution" (Liyolo Limbe Mpuanga)	85	20
1161	5z. "Weeping Woman" (Wuma Mbambila) (horiz)	1·40	85
1162	10z. "The Militant" (Liyolo Limbe Mpuanaga)	2·50	1·25

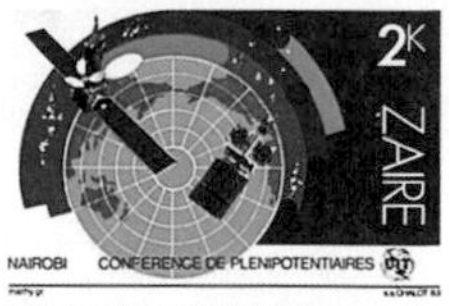
2K
ZAIRE
NAIROBI CONFERENCE DE PLENIPOTENTIAIRES
236 Satellite over Globe

1983. I.T.U. Delegates' Conference, Nairobi. Multicoloured.

1163	2k. Type **236**	10	10
1164	4k. Dish aerial	10	10
1165	25k. Dish aerial (different)	10	10
1166	1z.20 Satellite and microwave antenna	45	15
1167	2z.05 Satellite	65	30
1168	3z.60 Satellite and microwave antenna (different)	1·10	45
1169	6z. Map of Zaire	1·60	70
1170	8z. Satellite (different)	2·40	1·40

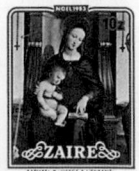

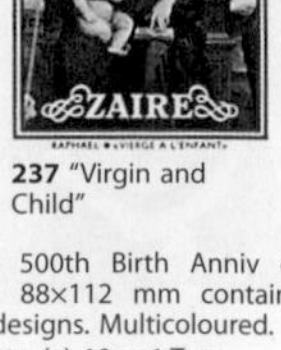
ZAIRE
237 "Virgin and Child"

1983. Christmas. 500th Birth Anniv of Raphael. Two sheets each 88×112 mm containing T **237** and similar vert designs. Multicoloured.

MS1171	Two sheets. (a) 10z.×4 Type **237**; "The Holy Family"; "Esterhazy Madonna"; "Sistine Madonna". (b) 15z.×4 "La Belle Jardiniere"; "Virgin of Alba"; "The Holy Family"; "Virgin and Child"	15·00	15·00

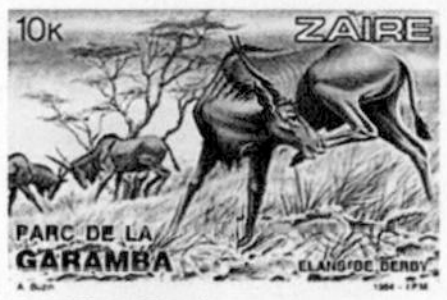

238 Giant Eland

1984. Garamba National Park. Multicoloured.

1172	10k. Type **238**	10	10
1173	15k. Tawny eagles	1·00	30
1174	3z. Servals	25	10
1175	10z. White rhinoceros	90	35
1176	15z. Lions	1·10	55
1177	37z.50 Warthogs	3·00	1·10
1178	40z. Kori bustards	5·75	2·00
1179	40z. South African crowned cranes and game lodge	5·75	2·00

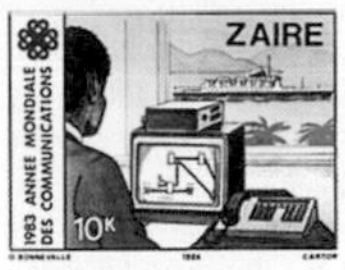

239 Visual Display Unit and Ferry

1984. World Communications Year. Multicoloured.

1180	10k. Type **239**	10	10
1181	15k. Communications satellite	10	10
1182	8z.50 Radio telephone	1·50	75
1183	10z. Satellite and aerial	55	35
1184	15z. Video camera	95	80
1185	37z.50 Satellite and dish antenna	2·75	1·25
1186	80z. Switchboard operator	5·50	2·75

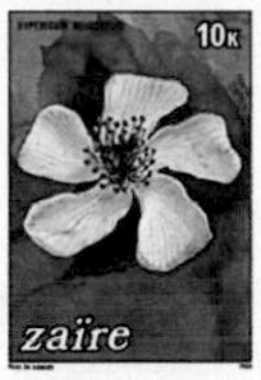

240 "Hypericum revolutum"

1984. Flowers. Multicoloured.

1187	10k. Type **240**	10	15
1188	15k. "Borreria dibrachiata"	10	15
1189	3z. "Disa erubescens"	15	15
1190	8z.50 "Scaevola plumieri"	40	50
1191	10z. "Clerodendron thompsonii"	60	50
1192	15z. "Thumbergia erecta"	85	95
1193	37z.50 "Impatiens niamniamesis"	2·10	2·25
1194	100z. "Canarina eminii"	6·00	4·75

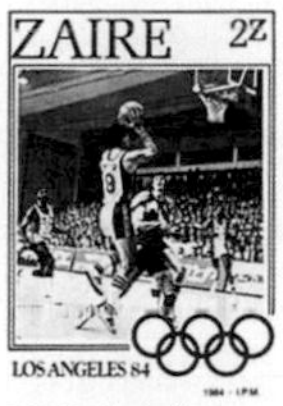

241 Basketball

1984. Olympic Games, Los Angeles. Multicoloured.

1195	2z. Type **241**	15	10
1196	3z. Equestrian	20	10
1197	10z. Running	70	35
1198	15z. Long jump	1·10	55
1199	20z. Football	1·60	80
MS1200	115×95 mm. 50z. Canoeing (31×48 mm)	3·75	3·75

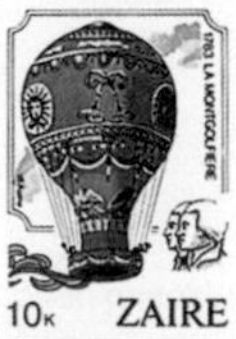

242 Montgolfier Balloon, 1783

1984. Bicentenary of Manned Flight. Multicoloured.

1201	10k. Type **242**	10	10
1202	15k. Charles's hydrogen balloon, 1783	10	10
1203	3z. Montgolfier balloon "Le Gustave", 1784	15	10
1204	5z. Santos-Dumont's airship "Ballon No. 3", 1899	30	15
1205	10z. Piccard's stratosphere balloon "F.N.R.S.", 1931	70	40
1206	15z. Airship "Hindenburg"	1·10	60
1207	37z.50 Balloon "Double Eagle II", 1978	2·50	1·40
1208	80z. Hot-air balloons	6·00	3·00

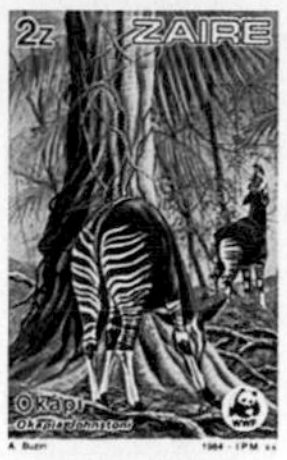

243 Okapi feeding

1984. Wildlife Protection. Okapi. Multicoloured.

1209	2z. Type **243**	40	50
1210	3z. Okapi resting	85	50
1211	8z. Okapi and foal	1·75	2·00
1212	10z. Okapi crossing stream	2·40	2·00
MS1213	75×100 mm. 50z. As No. 1212 (35×51 mm)	3·75	3·75

1985. 50th Anniv of SABENA Brussels–Kinshasa Air Service. Nos. 927/34 surch **SABENA/1935-1985** and new value.

1214	2z.50 on 30s. multicoloured	15	10
1215	5z. on 5k. multicoloured	40	20
1216	6z. on 70s. multicoloured	45	30
1217	7z.50 on 1k. multicoloured	55	35
1218	8z.50 on 1k. multicoloured	65	40
1219	10z. on 8k. multicoloured	80	45
1220	12z.50 on 75k. multicoloured	90	60
1221	30z. on 50k. multicoloured	2·25	1·25
MS1222	89×125 mm. 50z. on 5z. multicoloured	4·00	4·00

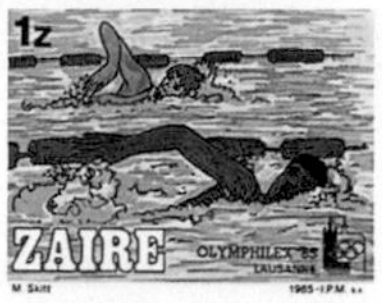

245 Swimming

1985. "Olymphilex '85" Olympic Stamps Exhibition, Lausanne. Multicoloured.

1223	1z. Type **245**	10	10
1224	2z. Football (vert)	15	10
1225	3z. Boxing	20	10
1226	4z. Basketball (vert)	30	15
1227	5z. Show jumping	35	20
1228	10z. Volleyball (vert)	70	45
1229	15z. Running	1·00	65
1230	30z. Cycling (vert)	2·25	1·25

1985. Second Papal Visit. Nos. 1061/5 surch **AOUT 1985.**

1231	2z. on 5k. multicoloured	15	10
1232	3z. on 10k. multicoloured	20	15
1233	5z.50 multicoloured	45	20
1234	10z. on 100k. multicoloured	90	50
1235	15z. on 500k. multicoloured	1·40	65
1236	40z. on 800k. multicoloured	3·00	1·40
MS1237	96×130 mm. 50z. on 10z. multicoloured	4·00	4·00

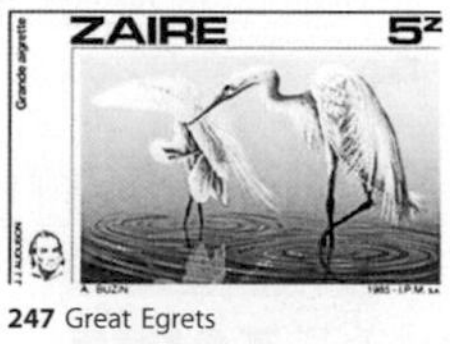

247 Great Egrets

1985. Birth Bicentenary of John J. Audubon (ornithologist). Multicoloured.

1238	5z. Type **247**	60	30
1239	10z. Black scoter	1·25	60
1240	15z. Black-crowned night heron	2·10	95
1241	25z. Surf scoter	4·25	2·00

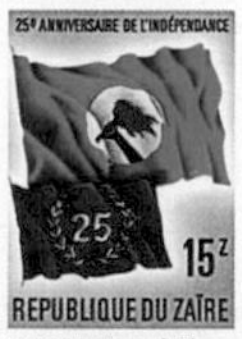

248 National Flag and "25" on Flag

1985. 25th Anniv of Independence.

1242	**248**	5z. multicoloured	20	10
1243	**248**	10z. multicoloured	45	20
1244	**248**	15z. multicoloured	65	35
1245	**248**	20z. multicoloured	90	40
MS1246		56×82 mm. 50z. multicoloured (president Mobutu, laurel wreath and emblem) (25×38 mm)	2·25	2·25

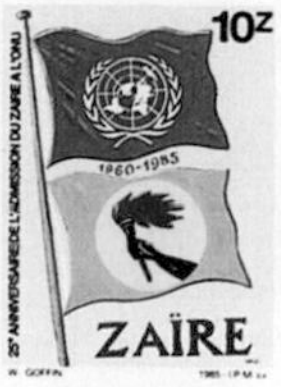

249 U.N. and Zaire Flags

1985. 40th Anniv of U.N.O. and 25th Anniv of Zaire Membership. Multicoloured.

1247	10z. Type **249**	45	30
1248	50z. U.N. building and emblem	2·25	1·10

1985. International Youth Year. Nos. 1127/31 optd **1985** and I.Y.Y. emblem and surch also.

1249	3z. on 3z. multicoloured	10	10
1250	5z. on 5z. multicoloured	20	10
1251	7z. on 90k. multicoloured	35	15
1252	10z. on 90k. multicoloured	45	15
1253	15z. on 1z.70 multicoloured	55	25
1254	20z. on 8z. multicoloured	1·10	45
1255	50z. on 90k. multicoloured	2·75	1·00
MS1256	87×64 mm. 50z. on 10z. multicoloured	2·75	2·75

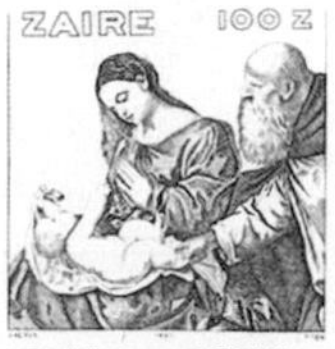

251 "Virgin and Child" (Titian)

1985. Christmas. Sheet 72×85 mm.

MS1257	**251** 100z. brown	4·50	4·50

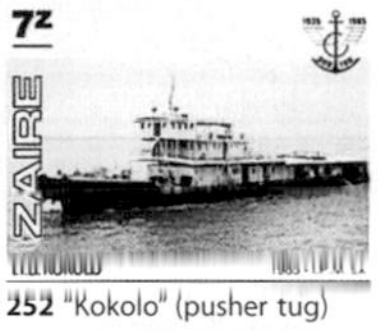

252 "Kokolo" (pusher tug)

1985. 50th Anniv of National Transport Office.

1258	7z. Type **252**	50	20
1259	10z. Early steam locomotive	75	40
1260	15z. "Luebo" (pusher tug)	75	35
1261	50z. Modern diesel locomotive	2·25	1·10

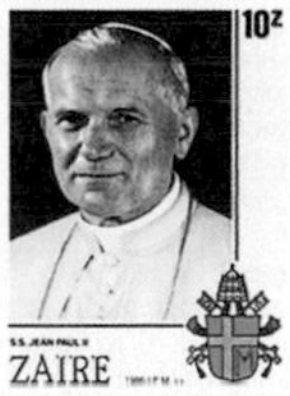

253 Pope John Paul II

1985. Beatification of Sister Anuarite Nengapeta. Multicoloured.

1262	10z. Type **253**	45	20
1263	15z. Sister Anuarite	65	35
1264	25z. Pope and Sister Anuarite (horiz)	1·10	55
MS1265	105×75 mm. 100z. Pope and Sister Anuarite (different). Imperf	4·50	4·50

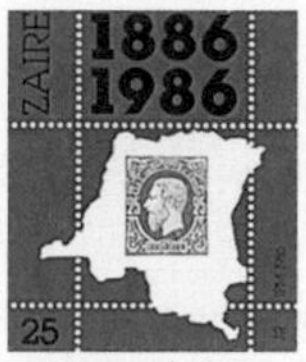

254 Map and 1886 25c. Stamp

1988. Centenary of First Congo Free State Stamp.

1266	**254**	25z. blue, grey and deep blue	1·10	55

255 Congo Free State 1898 10f. stamp

1988. "Cenzapost" Stamp Centenary Exhibition. Multicoloured.

1267	7z. Type **255**	30	10
1268	15z. Belgian Congo 1939 1f.25+1f.25 stamp	55	30
1269	20z. Belgian Congo 1942 50f. stamp (vert)	65	30
1270	25z. Zaire 1982 8k. stamp	80	35
1271	40z. Zaire 1984 37z.50 stamp (vert)	1·40	65
MS1272	121×76 mm. 50z. Zaire 1978 2k. stamp and Belgium 1984 20f. King Baudouin stamp (47×32 mm)	2·25	2·25

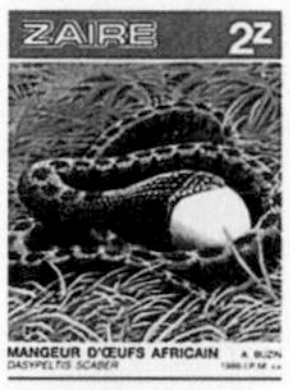

256 African Egg Eater

1987. Reptiles. Multicoloured.

1273	2z. Type **256**	15	20
1274	5z. Rainbow lizard	15	20
1275	10z. Royal python	25	20
1276	15z. Cape chameleon	60	30
1277	25z. Green mamba	1·00	60
1278	50z. Black-necked cobra	1·60	1·10

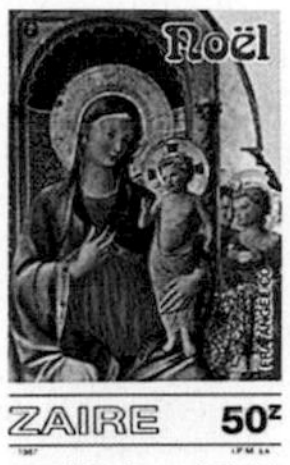

257 "Virgin and Child with Angels" (from Cortone triptych)

1987. Christmas. Paintings by Fr. Angelico. Multicoloured.

1279	50z. Type **257**	65	35
1280	100z. "St. Catherine and St. Peter adoring the Child"	1·40	65
1281	120z. "Virgin and Child of the Angels and Four Saints" (detail, Fiesole Retable)	1·60	80
1282	180z. "Virgin and Child and Six Saints" (detail, Annalena Retable)	2·50	1·10

1990. Various stamps surch.

1283	-	20z. on 20k. mult (No. 920)	15	20
1284	236	40z. on 2k. mult	30	55
1285	-	40z. on 4k. mult (1164)	30	55
1286	218	40z. on 10k. mult	30	55
1287	231	40z. on 25k. mult	30	55
1288	-	40z. on 25k. mult (1165)	30	40
1289	-	40z. on 50k. mult (1055)	30	55
1290	-	40z. on 50k. mult (1134)	30	35
1291	235	40z. on 50k. mult	30	55
1292	228	40z. on 75k. mult	30	55
1293	-	40z. on 80k. mult (1056)	30	40
1294	-	40z. on 90k. mult (1093)	30	55
1295	228	40z. on 90k. mult	30	35
1296	-	40z. on 90k. mult (1135)	30	40
1297	236	80z. on 2k. mult	55	60
1298	-	80z. on 4k. mult (1164)	60	65
1299	218	80z. on 10k. mult	60	65
1300	231	80z. on 25k. mult	55	60
1301	-	80z. on 25k. mult (1165)	55	70
1302	-	80z. on 50k. mult (1134)	60	65
1303	235	80z. on 50k. mult	55	60
1304	228	80z. on 75k. mult	55	60
1305	-	80z. on 80k. mult (1056)	55	45
1306	-	80z. on 90k. mult (1093)	55	60
1307	228	80z. on 90k. mult	60	65
1308	-	80z. on 90k. mult (1135)	55	70
1309	209	100z. on 40s. brown, black and mauve	70	80
1311	220	100z. on 2k. mult	70	80
1312	221	100z. on 2k. mult	70	80
1313	226	100z. on 2k. mult	70	80
1314	209	100z. on 4k. brown, black and yellow	70	65
1315	-	100z. on 5k. mult (930)	70	80
1316	-	100z. on 5k. mult (1061)	70	80
1317	-	100z. on 5k. mult (1077)	70	65
1318	-	100z. on 8k. mult (908)	95	55
1319	-	100z. on 8k. mult (931)	75	65
1320	-	100z. on 8k. mult (946)	70	80
1322	-	100z. on 10k. mult (947)	70	65
1323	-	100z. on 10k. mult (969)	70	80
1324	-	100z. on 10k. mult (1036)	65	70

1325	217	100z. on 10k. mult	65	70
1326	-	100z. on 10k. mult (1062)	70	65
1327	-	100z. on 10k. mult (1068)	70	65
1328	209	100z. on 15k. brown, black and blue	65	70
1329	-	100z. on 18k. mult (1079)	65	70
1330	-	100z. on 20k. mult (970)	70	65
1331	-	100z. on 20k. mult (1020)	95	80
1332	177	100z. on 22k. mult	70	80
1333	-	100z. on 25k. mult (1069)	65	70
1335	-	100z. on 48k. mult (912)	70	65
1336	-	100z. on 48k. mult (950)	65	70
1337	-	100z. on 50k. mult (1013)	70	80
1338	-	100z. on 50k. mult (1080)	85	90
1339	-	100z. on 50k. mult (1103)	65	70
1340	-	100z. on 75k. mult (1038)	70	80
1341	-	100z. on 75k. mult (1049)	70	80
1342	203	100z. on 90k. mult	70	80
1343	-	100z. on 80k. mult (1050)	70	70
1344	234	100z. on 80k. mult	70	80
1345	-	100z. on 90k. mult (1070)	85	90
1346	-	100z. on 90k. mult (1104)	70	65
1348	233	300z. on 2k. mult	2·25	3·00
1349	-	300z. on 8k. mult (980)	3·25	5·50
1350	216	300z. on 10k. green & bl	2·25	3·00
1351	-	300z. on 14k. mult (789)	2·25	3·00
1352	159	300z. on 17k. mult (807)	2·25	3·00
1353	-	300z. on 20k. mult (989)	2·25	3·00
1354	-	300z. on 45k. mult (1145)	2·25	2·00
1355	-	300z. on 75k. brown and blue (1044)	2·25	2·00
1356	-	300z. on 75k. mult (1146)	2·10	2·50
1357	198	500z. on 8k. mult	4·75	5·50
1358	198	500z. on 10k. mult	3·75	3·50
1359	198	500z. on 25k. mult	4·00	5·00
1360	198	500z. on 48k. mult	4·00	3·50

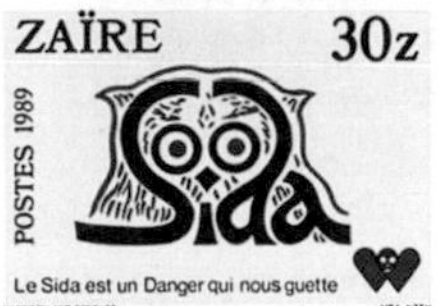

259 "Sida" forming Owl's Face

1990. Anti-AIDS Campaign. Multicoloured.

1361	30z. Type **259**	50	20
1362	40z. Skeleton firing arrow through "SIDA"	60	35
1363	80z. Leopard	1·10	80
MS1364	85×65 mm. 150z. Map showing spread of AIDS (50×36 mm)	2·25	2·25

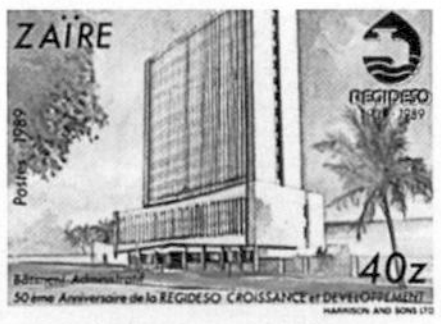

260 Administration Building

1990. 50th Anniv of Regideso (development organization). Multicoloured.

1365	40z. Type **260**	55	35
1366	50z. Modern factory	65	45
1367	75z. Old water treatment plant	1·00	65
1368	120z. Communal water tap	1·40	80

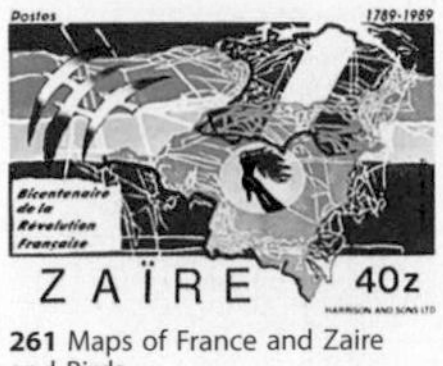

261 Maps of France and Zaire and Birds

1990. Bicentenary of French Revolution. Multicoloured.

1369	40z. Type **261**	55	35
1370	50z. Article 1 of Declaration of Rights of Man and the Citizen within outline of person	65	45
1371	100z. Crowd	1·25	65
1372	120z. Globe	1·40	80

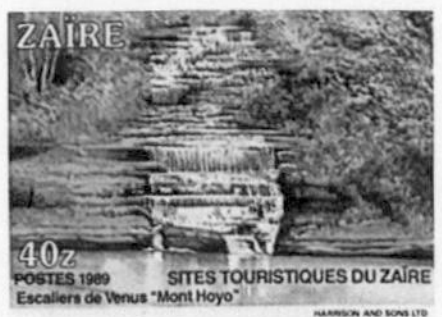

262 Stairs of Venus, Mount Hoyo

1990. Tourist Sites. Multicoloured.

1373	40z. Type **262**	45	20
1374	60z. Scenic road to village	65	35
1375	100z. Lake Kivu	1·25	55
1376	120z. Niyara Gongo volcano	1·60	25
MS1377	70×90 mm. 300z. Kisantu botanical garden (vert)	3·75	3·75

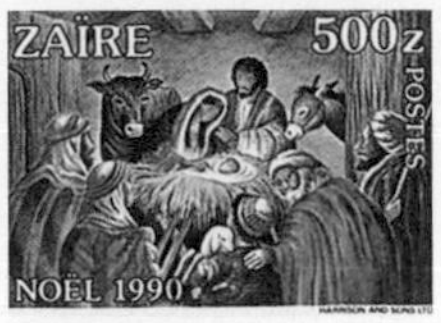

263 Nativity

1991. Christmas. Sheet 89×69 mm.

MS1378	**263**	500z. multicoloured	1·25	1·25

1991. Various stamps surch.

1379	-	1000z. on 100k. mult (1064)	25	25
1380	-	1000z. on 1z. mult (1105)	25	25
1381	214	1000z. on 1z. mult (1026)	25	25
1383	-	1000z. on 1z. mult (1027)	25	25
1385	-	2000z. on 100k. violet and blue (1045)	50	50
1386	-	2000z. on 1z. mult (1147)	50	50
1387	228	2500z. on 1z. mult	65	65
1388	225	3000z. on 1z. green and gold	75	75
1389	-	4000z. on 1z. mult (1158)	1·00	1·00
1390	-	5000z. on 1z. mult (1158)	1·25	1·25
1391	228	10000z. on 1z. mult	2·50	2·50
1392	225	15000z. on 1z. green and gold	3·75	3·75

Nos. 1381 and 1383 exist in two versions with the exhibition logo either at the right or left of the design.

1992. Various stamps surch.

1393	-	50,000z. on 125k. multicoloured (1058)	55	70
1394	-	100,000z. on 1z.20 multicoloured (1166)	55	70
1395	234	150,000z. on 1z.20 multicoloured	55	70
1396	-	200,000z. on 145k. blue and indigo (1046)	80	70
1397	234	250,000z. on 1z.20 multicoloured	1·10	1·00
1398	-	300,000z. on 1z.20 multicoloured (1166)	1·40	1·40
1399	234	500,000z. on 1z.20 multicoloured	1·90	1·75

1993. Various stamps surch. (a) Nos. 944/51.

1400	199	500,000z. on 30s. multicoloured	30	50
1401	-	500,000z. on 5k. multicoloured	30	50
1402	-	750,000z. on 8k. multicoloured	45	50
1403	-	750,000z. on 10k. multicoloured	45	50
1404	-	1,000,000z. on 30k. multicoloured	60	70
1405	-	1,000,000z. on 40k. multicoloured	60	70
1406	-	5,000,000z. on 48k. multicoloured	3·00	2·75
1407	-	10,000,000z. on 100k. multicoloured	5·75	5·25

(b) Nos. 1262/4.

1408	253	3,000,000z. on 10z. multicoloured	1·25	1·50
1409	-	5,000,000z. on 15z. multicoloured	2·50	2·50
1410	-	10,000,000z. on 25z. multicoloured	5·00	4·75
MS1411		105×75 mm. 10,000,000z. on 100z. multicoloured	5·75	5·75

BOGUS SURCHARGES. Surcharges with commemorative inscriptions on Nos. 1365/8 for the inauguration of a pumping station and on Nos. 1373/6 for the sixth anniversary of the National Tourism Office are bogus.

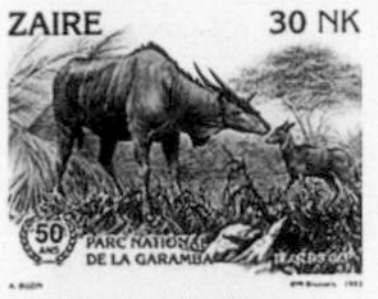

268 Eland and Calf

1993. 50th Anniv of Garamba National Park. Multicoloured.

1412	30k. Type **268**	30	30
1413	50k. African elephants	30	30
1414	1z.50 Giant elands	60	30
1415	3z.50 Two white rhinoceros	90	75
1416	5z. Bongo	1·75	1·40

1993. Various stamps surch. (a) Nos. 1201/8.

1417	242	30k. on 10k. mult	30	35
1418	-	50k. on 15k. mult	65	65
1419	-	1z.50 on 3z. mult	1·25	1·25
1420	-	2z.50 on 5z. mult	1·75	1·75
1421	-	3z.50 on 10z. mult	2·40	2·40
1422	-	5z. on 15z. mult	3·50	3·50
1423	-	7z.50 on 37z.50 mult	4·75	4·75
1424	-	10z. on 80z. mult	6·75	6·75

(b) Nos. 1043/7.

1425	216	30k. on 10k. green and blue	40	15
1426	-	50k. on 75k. brown and blue	60	20
1427	-	1z.50 on 100k. violet and blue	1·90	60
1428	-	3k.50 on 145k. blue and deep blue	2·75	90
1429	-	5z. on 270k. red and blue	3·00	1·00

(c) Nos. 1238/41.

1430	247	50k. on 5z. mult	60	80
1431	-	1z.50 on 10z. mult	1·90	2·40
1432	-	3z.50 on 15z. mult	2·75	3·50
1433	-	5z. on 25z. mult	3·00	4·00

1994. Various stamps surch.

1434		20z. on 3z. mult (No. 1139)	10	15
1435		40z. on 270k. red and blue (No. 1047)	10	15
1436		50z. on 3z. mult (No. 1174)	15	15
1437		75z. on 3z. mult (No. 1196)	20	15
1438		100z. on 2z.05 mult (No. 1167)	35	30
1439		150z. on 1z.70 mult (No. 1121)	40	35
1440		200z. on 50k. mult (No. 1413)	50	40
1441		250z. on 1z.50 mult (No. 1136)	55	60
1442	234	300z. on 3z.60 mult	65	65
1443	-	500z. on 3z.60 mult (No. 1168)	90	90

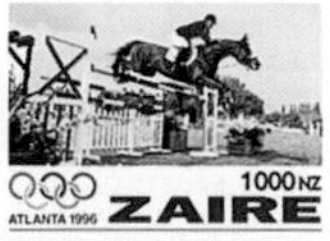

271 Show Jumping

1996. Olympic Games, Atlanta, U.S.A. Multicoloured.

1444	1000z. Type **271**	10	10
1445	12500z. Boxing	65	40
1446	25000z. Table tennis	1·25	75
1447	35000z. Basketball (vert)	1·75	1·10
1448	50000z. Tennis	2·50	1·50

1996. Various stamps. Surch.

1449	-	100z. on 3z.50 mult (No. 1109)	10	15
1450	234	500z. on 3z.60 mult	10	15
1451	-	1000z. on 2z.05 mult (No. 1167)	20	20
1452	-	2500z. on 1z.50 multicoloured (No. 1136)	35	35
1453	-	5000z. on 3z.60 multicoloured (No. 1168)	75	75
1454	-	6000z. on 1z.50 multicoloured (No. 1136)	80	80
1455	234	15000z. on 3z.60 multicoloured	1·10	1·10
1456	-	25000z. on 3z.60 multicoloured (No. 1168)	1·40	1·50

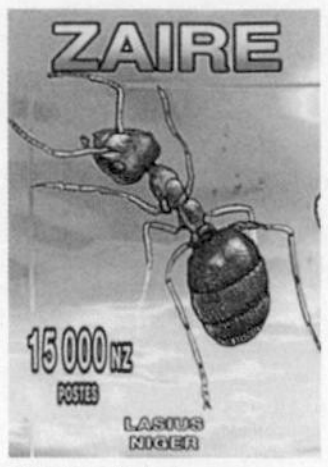

272 Black Ant

1996. Fauna, Flora and Minerals. Multicoloured.

1457	15000z. Type **272**	1·25	1·25
1458	15000z. Calopterygides	1·25	1·25
1459	15000z. Green lynx spider (Peucetia)	1·25	1·25
1460	15000z. Sphecides	1·25	1·25
1461	20000z. Scutellosaurus	1·40	1·40
1462	20000z. Compsognathus	1·40	1·40
1463	20000z. Dryosaurus	1·40	1·40
1464	20000z. Velociraptor	1·40	1·40
1465	25000z. Panda eating (face value at left)	2·40	2·40
1466	25000z. Panda eating (face value at right)	2·40	2·40
1467	25000z. Sitting	2·40	2·40
1468	25000z. Walking	2·40	2·40
1469	25000z. *Eulophia streptopetala*	1·60	1·60
1470	25000z. *Oeceoclades saundersiana*	1·60	1·60
1471	25000z. *Eulophia gracilis*	1·60	1·60
1472	25000z. *Bulbophyllum falcatum*	1·60	1·60
1473	35000z. *Termitomyces aurantiacus*	2·10	2·10
1474	35000z. *Tricholoma lobayensis*	2·10	2·10
1475	35000z. *Lepiota esculenta*	2·10	2·10
1476	35000z. *Phlebopus sudanicus*	2·10	2·10
1477	40000z. Uraninite	1·75	1·75
1478	40000z. Malachite	1·75	1·75
1479	40000z. Ruby	1·75	1·75
1480	40000z. Diamond	1·75	1·75
1481	50000z. Congo serpent eagle	3·00	3·00
1482	50000z. Crowned eagle ("Aigle Couronne")	3·00	3·00
1483	50000z. Dark chanting goshawk (*Melierax metabates*)	3·00	3·00
1484	50000z. African long-tailed hawk (*Urotriorchis macrourus*)	3·00	3·00
1485	70000z. Red glider (*Cymthoe sangaris*)	3·50	3·50
1486	70000z. Purple-tip (*Colotis zoe*)	3·50	3·50
1487	70000z. Physcaeneura leda	3·50	3·50
1488	70000z. Green-veined charaxes (*Charaxes candiope*)	3·50	3·50
1489	100000z. Diamond	5·75	5·75
1490	100000z. Dioptase	5·75	5·75
1491	100000z. Cuprite	5·75	5·75
1492	100000z. Chrysocolle	5·75	5·75
MS1493	Two sheets (a) 120×90 mm. 105000z. Tyrannosaurus rex (horiz); (b) 140×110 mm. 105000z. Uranotile and Cuprosklodowskite (horiz)	11·00	11·00

Nos. 1457/60 (insects), 1461/4 and **MS**1493 (dinosaurs), 1465/8 (pandas), 1469/72 (orchids), 1473/6 (fungi), 1477/80, 1489/92 (minerals), 1481/4 (birds) and 1485/8 (butterflies) respectively were issued together, se-tenant, with the backgrounds forming a composite design.

OFFICIAL STAMPS

1975. Optd **SP**.

O841	172	10s. orange and black	10	10
O842	172	40s. blue and black	10	10
O843	172	50s. yellow and black	10	10
O844	177b	1k. multicoloured	10	10
O845	177b	2k. multicoloured	10	10
O846	177b	3k. multicoloured	10	10
O847	177b	4k. multicoloured	15	10
O848	177b	5k. multicoloured	20	10
O849	177b	6k. multicoloured	20	10
O850	177b	8k. multicoloured	35	15
O851	177b	9k. multicoloured	35	20
O852	177b	10k. multicoloured	45	20
O853	177b	14k. multicoloured	55	25
O854	177b	17k. multicoloured	80	45
O855	177b	20k. multicoloured	1·00	50
O856	177b	50k. multicoloured	2·50	1·00
O857	177b	100k. multicoloured	6·75	2·75

For later issues see **CONGO DEMOCRATIC REPUBLIC**.

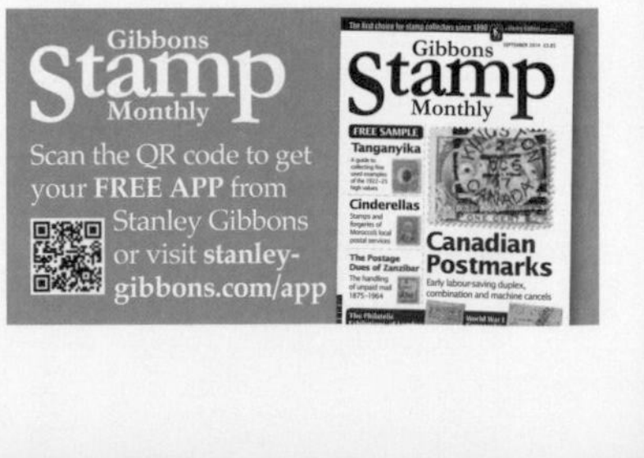

Pt. 9

ZAMBEZIA

Formerly administered by the Zambezia Co. This district of Portuguese E. Africa was later known as Quelimane and is now part of Mozambique.

1000 reis = 1 milreis.

1894. "Figures" key-type inscr "ZAMBEZIA".

1	**R**	5r. orange	60	50
2	**R**	10r. mauve	95	85
3	**R**	15r. brown	1·80	1·30
4	**R**	20r. lilac	1·80	1·30
12	**R**	25r. green	3·25	2·30
13	**R**	50r. blue	3·25	2·30
14	**R**	75r. pink	7·50	6·50
15	**R**	80r. green	6·00	5·00
8	**R**	100r. brown on buff	4·50	3·50
16	**R**	150r. red on pink	7·50	5·50
17	**R**	200r. blue on blue	7·50	5·50
18	**R**	300r. blue on brown	11·50	8·50

1898. "King Carlos" key-type inscr "ZAMBEZIA". Name and value in red (500r.) or black (others).

20	**S**	2½r. grey	75	65
21	**S**	5r. red	75	65
22	**S**	10r. green	1·20	65
23	**S**	15r. brown	2·10	1·50
55	**S**	15r. green	2·30	2·00
24	**S**	20r. lilac	2·10	1·50
25	**S**	25r. green	2·10	1·50
56	**S**	25r. red	2·00	1·20
26	**S**	50r. blue	2·10	1·50
57	**S**	50r. brown	4·00	3·50
58	**S**	65r. blue	12·50	10·00
27	**S**	75r. pink	15·00	8·00
59	**S**	75r. purple	5·50	3·50
28	**S**	80r. mauve	8·75	4·75
29	**S**	100r. blue on blue	3·25	2·50
60	**S**	115r. brown on pink	14·00	9·00
61	**S**	130r. brown on yellow	14·00	9·00
30	**S**	150r. brown on yellow	9·25	5·50
31	**S**	200r. purple on pink	9·75	5·25
32	**S**	300r. blue on pink	10·50	5·25
62	**S**	400r. blue on cream	18·00	13·50
33	**S**	500r. black on blue	18·00	9·75
34	**S**	700r. mauve on yellow	22·00	12·50

1902. Surch.

[illegible]	**S**	50r. on 65r. blue	3·00	3·00
35	**R**	65r. on 10r. mauve	14·00	10·50
36	**R**	65r. on 15r. brown	14·00	10·50
37	**R**	65r. on 20r. lilac	14·00	10·50
38	**R**	65r. on 300r. blue on brown	14·00	10·50
40	**R**	115r. on 5r. orange	14·00	10·50
41	**R**	115r. on 25r. green	14·00	10·50
42	**R**	115r. on 80r. green	14·00	10·50
46	**V**	130r. on 2½r. brown	14·00	10·50
43	**R**	130r. on 75r. pink	10·50	7·00
45	**R**	130r. on 150r. red on pink	8·25	7·50
47	**R**	400r. on 50r. blue	3·25	3·00
49	**R**	400r. on 100r. brown on buff	3·25	3·00
50	**R**	400r. on 200r. blue on blue	2·75	2·75

1902. 1898 issue optd **PROVISORIO**.

51	15r. brown	3·00	1·90
52	25r. green	3·00	1·90
53	50r. blue	3·00	1·90
54	75r. pink	8·75	4·50

1911. 1898 issue optd **REPUBLICA**.

64	2½r. grey	55	35
65	5r. red	55	35
66	10r. green	60	50
67	15r. green	60	50
68	20r. lilac	80	55
69	25r. red	2·30	1·40
108	25r. green	18·00	14·50
70	50r. brown	60	55
71	75r. purple	1·80	1·20
72	100r. blue on blue	1·80	1·20
73	115r. brown on pink	1·80	1·20
74	130r. brown on yellow	1·80	1·20
75	200r. purple on pink	1·80	1·20
76	400r. blue on cream	3·25	1·70
77	500r. black on blue	3·25	1·70
78	700r. mauve on yellow	3·25	2·50

1914. Provisionals of 1902 optd **REPUBLICA**.

94	**S**	50r. blue (No. 53)	1·10	85
95	**S**	50r. on 65r. blue	4·50	2·75
81		75r. pink (No. 54)	2·20	1·80
96	**R**	115r. on 5r. orange	1·10	80
97	**R**	115r. on 25r. green	1·10	80
98	**R**	115r. on 80r. green	1·10	80
99	**V**	130r. on 2½r. brown	1·10	80
100	**R**	130r. on 75r. pink	1·10	80
102	**R**	130r. on 150r. red on pink	1·10	85
90	**R**	400r. on 50r. blue	3·25	2·50
92	**R**	400r. on 100r. brn on buff	3·75	3·00
93	**R**	400r. on 200r. blue on blue	3·75	3·00

NEWSPAPER STAMP

1893. "Newspaper" key-type inscr "ZAMBEZIA".

N1	**V**	2½r. brown	75	70

Pt. 1

ZAMBIA

Formerly Northern Rhodesia, attained independence on 24 October 1964 and changed its name to Zambia.

1964. 12 pence = 1 shilling; 20 shillings = 1 pound.
1968. 100 ngwee = 1 kwacha.

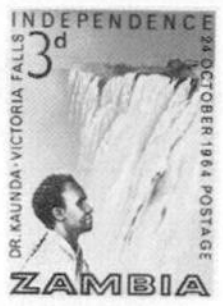
11 Pres. Kaunda and Victoria Falls

1964. Independence.

91	**11**	3d. sepia, green and blue	10	10
92	-	6d. violet and yellow	15	20
93	-	1s.3d. multicoloured	20	25

DESIGNS—HORIZ: 6d. College of Further Education, Lusaka. VERT: 1s.3d. Barotse dancer.

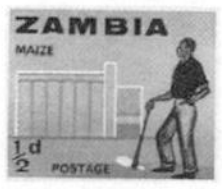
14 Maize – Farmer and Silo

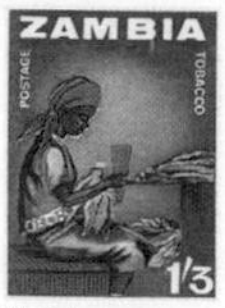
22 Tobacco Worker

1964

94	**14**	½d. red, black and green	10	1·50
95	-	1d. brown, black and blue	10	10
96	-	2d. red, brown and orange	10	10
97	-	3d. black and red	10	10
98	-	4d. black, brown and orange	15	10
99	-	6d. orange, brown and turquoise	30	10
100	-	9d. red, black and blue	15	10
101	-	1s. black, bistre and blue	15	10
102	**22**	1s.3d. multicoloured	20	10
103	-	2s. multicoloured	25	30
104	-	2s.6d. black and yellow	1·00	35
105	-	5s. black, yellow and green	1·00	1·00
106	-	10s. black and orange	4·50	4·50
107	-	£1 multicoloured	2·00	6·50

DESIGNS—VERT (as Type **14**): 1d. Health – radiographer; 2d. Chinyau dancer; 3d. Cotton- picking. (As Type **22**): 2s. Tonga basket-making; £1 Makishi dancer. HORIZ (as Type **14**): 4d. Angoni bull. (As Type **22**): 6d. Communications, old and new; 9d. Zambezi sawmills and redwood flower; 1s. Fishing at Mpulungu; 2s.6d. Luangwa Game Reserve; 5s. Education – student; 10s. Copper mining.

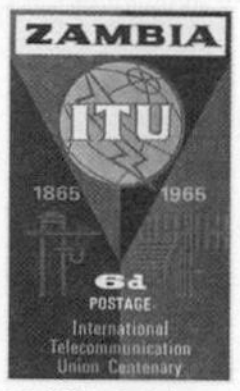
28 I.T.U. Emblem and Symbols

1965. Centenary of I.T.U.

108	**28**	6d. violet and gold	15	10
109	**28**	2s.6d. grey and gold	85	1·50

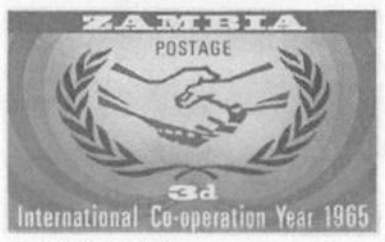
29 I.C.Y. Emblem

1965. International Co-operation Year.

110	**29**	3d. turquoise and gold	15	10
111	**29**	1s.3d. blue and gold	45	45

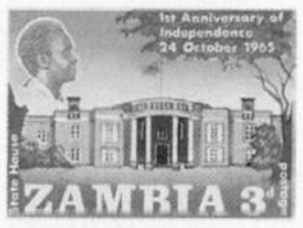
30 State House, Lusaka

1965. First Anniv of Independence. Multicoloured.

112	3d. Type **30**	10	10
113	6d. Fireworks, Independence Stadium	10	10
114	1s.3d. Clematopsis (vert)	15	10
115	2s.6d. "Tithonia diversifolia" (vert)	30	1·25

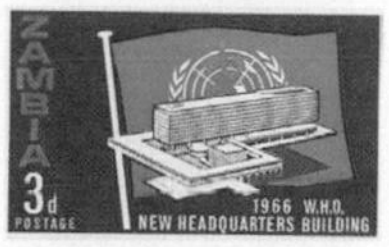
34 W.H.O. Building and U.N. Flag

1966. Inaug of W.H.O. Headquarters, Geneva.

116	**34**	3d. brown, gold and blue	40	10
117	**34**	1s.3d. violet, gold and blue	1·40	95

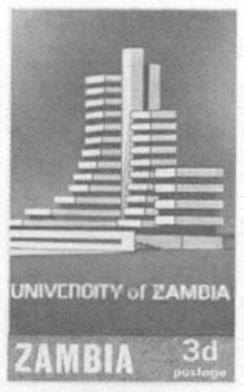
35 University Building

1966. Opening of Zambia University.

118	**35**	3d. green and bronze	10	10
119	**35**	1s.3d. violet and bronze	20	10

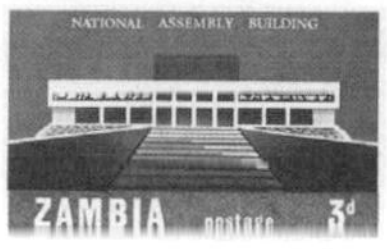
36 National Assembly Building

1967. Inaug of National Assembly Building.

120	**36**	3d. black and gold	10	10
121	**36**	6d. green and gold	10	10

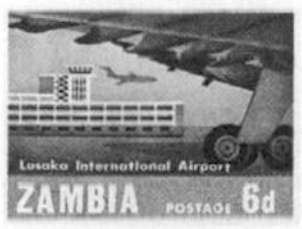
37 Airport Scene

1967. Opening of Lusaka International Airport.

122	**37**	6d. blue and bronze	15	10
123	**37**	2s.6d. brown and bronze	60	1·00

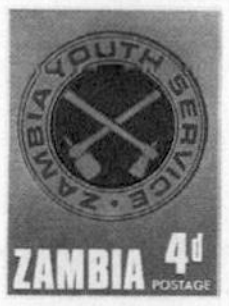
38 Youth Service Badge

1967. National Development.

124	**38**	4d. black, red and gold	10	10
125	-	6d. black, gold and blue	10	10
126	-	9d. black, blue and silver	15	50
127	-	1s. multicoloured	50	10
128	-	1s.6d. multicoloured	70	2·25

DESIGNS—HORIZ: 6d. "Co-operative Farming"; 1s.6d. Road link with Tanzania. VERT: 9d. "Communications"; 1s. Coal-fields.

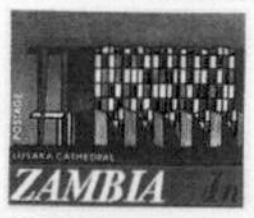
43 Lusaka Cathedral

1968. Decimal Currency.

129	**43**	1n. multicoloured	10	10
130	-	2n. multicoloured	10	10
131	-	3n. multicoloured	10	10
132	-	5n. brown and bronze	10	10
133	-	8n. multicoloured	15	10
134	-	10n. multicoloured	35	10
135	-	15n. multicoloured	2·75	10
136	-	20n. multicoloured	4·75	10
137	-	25n. multicoloured	25	10
138	-	50n. brown, orange and bronze	30	15
139	-	1k. blue and bronze	7·00	20
140	-	2k. black and bronze	1·75	1·25

DESIGNS—VERT (as Type **43**): 2n. Baobab tree; 5n. National Museum, Livingstone; 8n. Vimbuza dancer; 10n. Tobacco picking. (26×32 mm): 20n. South African crowned cranes; 25n. Angoni warrior; 50n. Chokwe dancer. HORIZ (as Type **43**): 3n. Zambia Airways Vickers VC-10 jetliner. (32×26 mm): 15n. "Imbrasia zambesina" (moth); 1k. Kafue Railway Bridge; 2k. Eland.

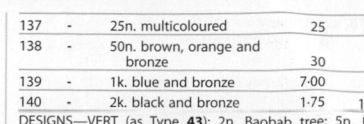

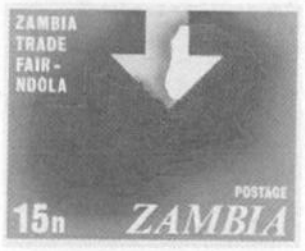
55 Ndola on Outline of Zambia

1968. Trade Fair, Ndola.

141	**55**	15n. green and gold	10	10

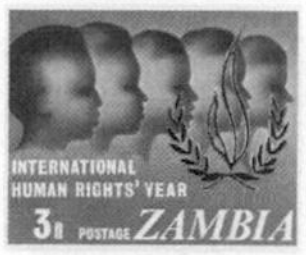
56 Human Rights Emblem and Heads

1968. Human Rights Year.

142	**56**	3n. blue, violet and gold	10	10

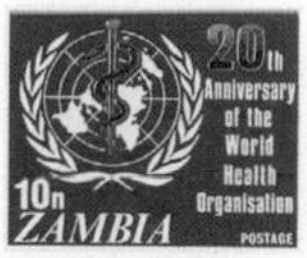
57 W.H.O. Emblem

1968. 20th Anniv of World Health Organization.

143	**57**	10n. gold and violet	10	10

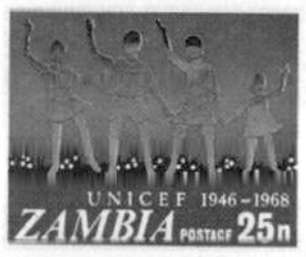
58 Group of Children

1968. 22nd Anniv of UNICEF.

144	**58**	25n. black, gold and blue	15	70

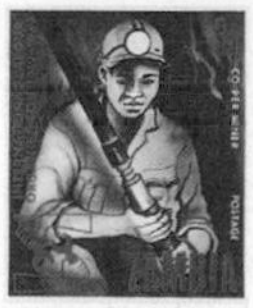
59 Copper Miner

1969. 50th Anniv of Int Labour Organization.

145	**59**	3n. copper and violet	25	10
146	-	25n. yellow, copper & brown	1·00	1·00

DESIGN—HORIZ: 25n. Poling a furnace.

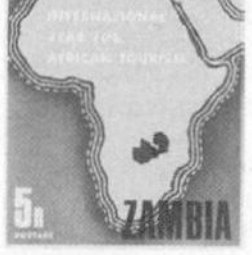
61 Zambia outlined on Map of Africa

1969. International African Tourist Year. Multicoloured.

147	5n. Type **61**	10	10
148	10n. Waterbuck (horiz)	15	10
149	15n. Kasaba Bay golden perch (horiz)	35	40
150	25n. Carmine bee eater	1·00	1·75

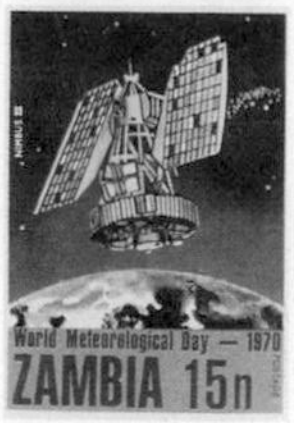
65 Satellite "Nimbus 3" orbiting the Earth

1970. World Meteorological Day.

151	**65**	15n. multicoloured	20	50

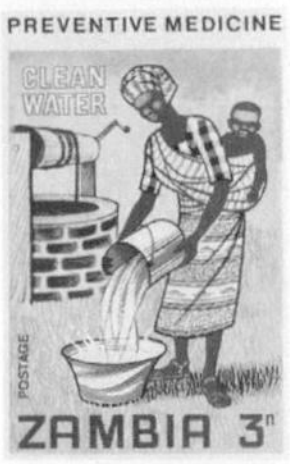

66 Woman collecting Water from Well

1970. Preventive Medicine.

152	**66**	3n. multicoloured	15	10
153	-	15n. multicoloured	30	30
154	-	25n. blue, red and sepia	65	70

DESIGNS: 15n. Child on scales; 25n. Child being immunized.

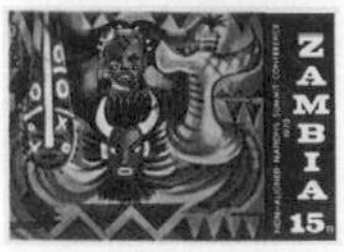

67 "Masks" (mural by Gabriel Ellison)

1970. Conference of Non-Aligned Nations.

155	**67**	15n. multicoloured	30	30

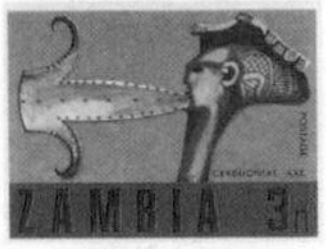

68 Ceremonial Axe

1970. Traditional Crafts. Multicoloured.

156	3n. Type **68**	10	10
157	5n. Clay smoking-pipe bowl	10	10
158	15n. Makishi mask	35	30
159	25n. Kuomboka Ceremony	55	1·00
MS160	133×83 mm. Nos. 156/9. Imperf	6·00	13·00

SIZES—HORIZ: 5n. as T **68**; 25n. 72×19 mm. VERT: 15n. 30×47 mm.

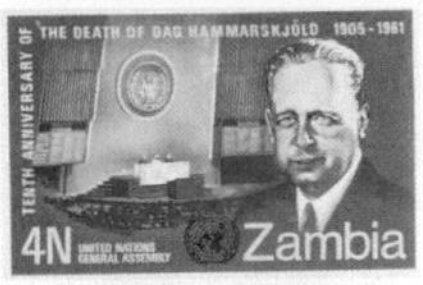

69 Dag Hammarskjold and U.N. General Assembly

1971. Tenth Death Anniv of Dag Hammarskjold. Multicoloured.

161	4n. Type **69**	10	10
162	10n. Tail of aircraft	15	10
163	15n. Dove of Peace	15	25
164	25n. Memorial tablet	30	1·75

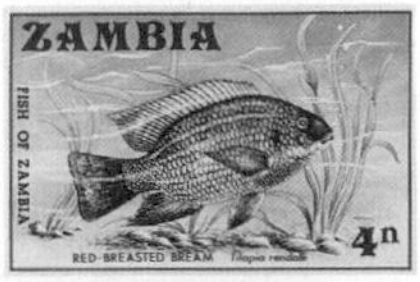

70 Red-breasted Tilapia

1971. Fish. Multicoloured.

165	4n. Type **70**	30	10
166	10n. Long-finned tilapia ("Green-headed bream")	50	40
167	15n. Tigerfish	60	2·50

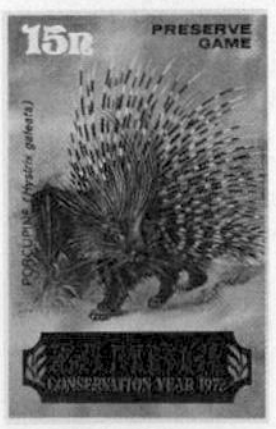

71 North African Crested Porcupine

1972. Conservation Year (1st issue). Multicoloured.

168	4n. Cheetah (horiz)	15	25
169	10n. Lechwe (horiz)	20	60
170	15n. Type **71**	25	85
171	25n. African elephant	1·25	3·00

Nos. 168/9 are size 58×21 mm.

1972. Conservation Year (2nd issue). As T **71**. Multicoloured.

172	4n. Soil conservation	15	20
173	10n. Forestry	15	30
174	15n. Water	20	80
175	25n. Maize	45	1·60

Nos. 174/5 are size 58×21 mm.

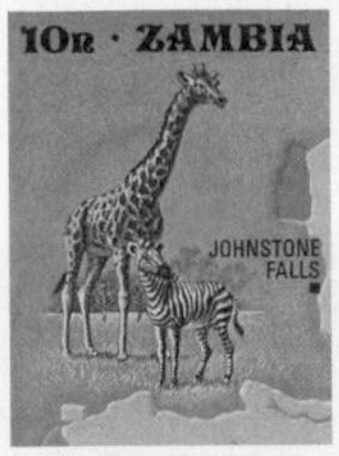

72 Giraffe and Common Zebra

1972. National Parks. Sheet 114×140 mm, containing T **72** and similar vert designs. Multicoloured.

MS176	10n. (×4) Type **72**; Black rhinoceros; hippopotamus and common panther, lion	6·50	12·00

Each design includes part of a map showing Zambian National Parks, the four forming a composite design.

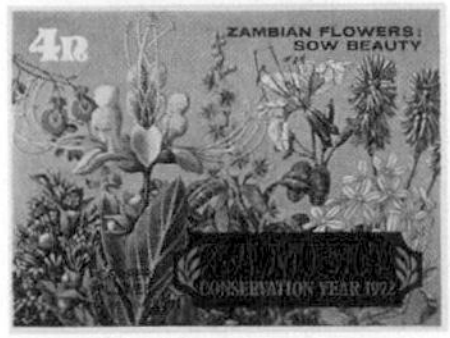

73 Zambian Flowers

1972. Conservation Year (3rd issue). Multicoloured.

177	4n. Type **73**	30	30
178	10n. "Papilio demodocus" (butterfly)	80	80
179	15n. "Apis mellifera" (bees)	85	1·40
180	25n. "Nomadacris septemfasciata" (locusts)	1·25	2·25

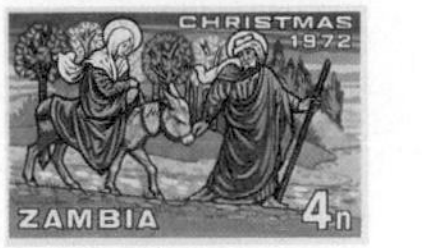

74 Mary and Joseph

1972. Christmas. Multicoloured.

181	4n. Type **74**	10	10
182	9n. Mary, Joseph and Jesus	10	10
183	15n. Mary, Jesus and the shepherds	10	10
184	25n. The Three Wise Men	20	40

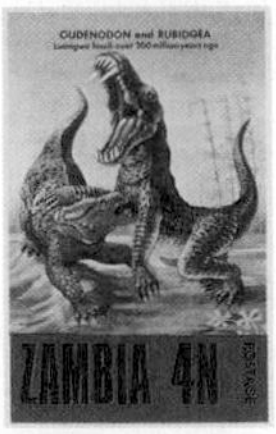

75 Oudenodon and Rubidgea

1973. Zambian Prehistoric Animals. Multicoloured.

185	4n. Type **75**	85	85
186	9n. Broken Hill Man	90	90
187	10n. Zambiasaurus	1·00	1·50
188	15n. "Luangwa drysdalli"	1·10	2·00
189	25n. Glossopteris	1·25	3·00

Nos. 186/9 are smaller, 38×21 mm.

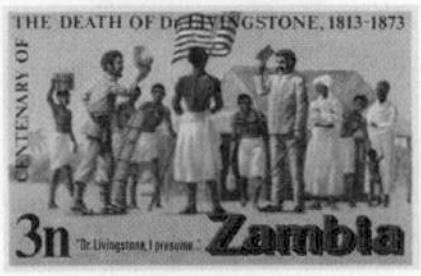

76 "Dr. Livingstone, I Presume"

1973. Death Cent of Dr. Livingstone. Multicoloured.

190	3n. Type **76**	15	15
191	4n. Scripture lesson	15	15
192	9n. Victoria Falls	30	40
193	10n. Scattering slavers	20	45
194	15n. Healing the sick	30	1·60
195	25n. Burial place of Livingstone's heart	30	2·75

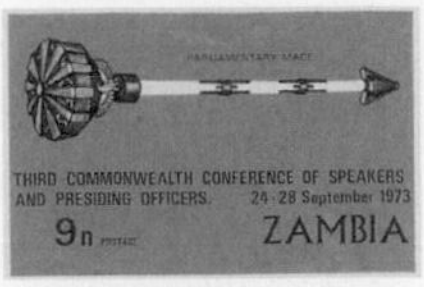

77 Parliamentary Mace

1973. Third Commonwealth Conference of Speakers and Presiding Officers, Lusaka.

196	**77**	9n. multicoloured	35	55
197	**77**	15n. multicoloured	40	1·10
198	**77**	25n. multicoloured	50	1·50

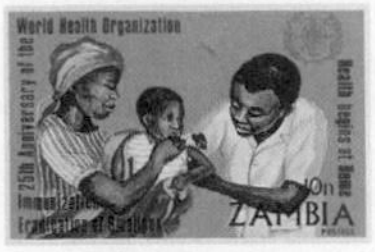

78 Inoculation

1973. 25th Anniv of W.H.O. Multicoloured.

199	4n. Mother washing baby (vert)	42·00	23·00
200	9n. Nurse weighing baby (vert)	45	2·25
201	10n. Type **78**	50	3·00
202	15n. Child eating meal	90	5·00

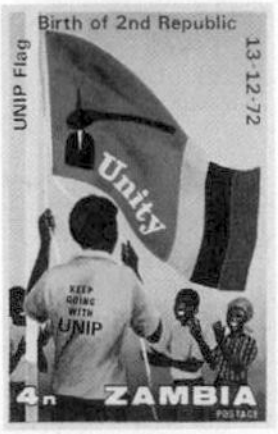

79 U.N.I.P. Flag

1974. First Anniv of Second Republic. Multicoloured.

203	4n. Type **79**	7·00	7·00
204	9n. Freedom House	30	1·50
205	10n. Army band	30	2·00
206	15n. "Celebrations" (dancers)	50	3·25
207	25n. Presidential chair	75	5·00

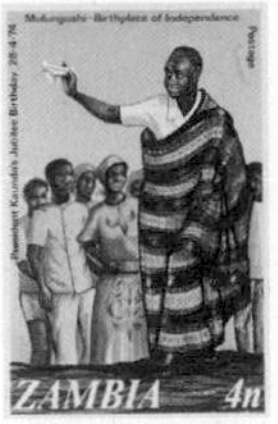

80 President Kaunda at Mulungushi

1974. 50th Birthday of President Kaunda. Multicoloured.

208	4n. Type **80**	40	40
209	9n. President's former residence	20	20
210	15n. President holding Independence flame	50	1·25

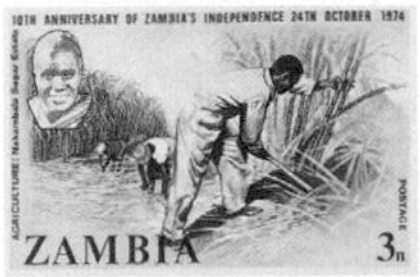

81 Nakambala Sugar Estate

1974. Tenth Anniv of Independence. Multicoloured.

211	3n. Type **81**	15	10
212	4n. Local market	15	10
213	9n. Kapiri glass factory	20	10
214	10n. Kafue hydro-electric scheme	25	10
215	15n. Kafue Railway Bridge	50	95
216	25n. Non-aligned Conference, Lusaka, 1970	60	1·25
MS217	141×105 mm. 15n. (×4) Academic Education; Teacher Training College; Technical Education; Zambia University	5·00	8·50

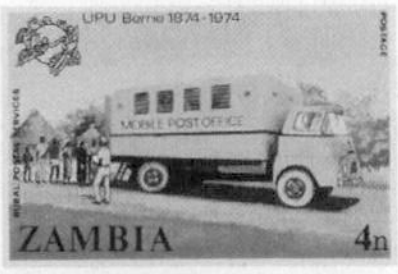

82 Mobile Post-van

1974. Centenary of U.P.U. Multicoloured.

218	4n. Type **82**	20	15
219	9n. Hawker Siddeley H.S.748 airplane on tarmac	30	30
220	10n. Chipata Post Office	30	40
221	15n. Modern training centre	45	1·75

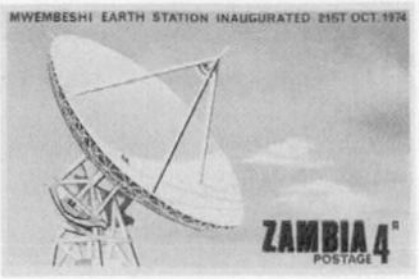

83 Dish Aerial

1974. Opening of Mwembeshi Earth Station. Multicoloured.

222	4n. Type **83**	25	20
223	9n. View at dawn	35	30
224	15n. View at dusk	40	70
225	25n. Aerial view	50	1·50

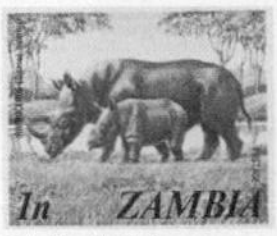

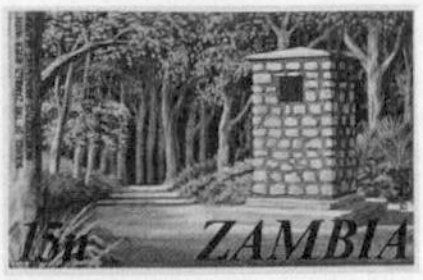

84 Black Rhinoceros and Calf

85 Independence Monument

1975. Black Rhinoceros and Calf. Multicoloured

226	1n. Type **84**	75	1·00
227	2n. Helmeted guineafowl	75	1·00
228	3n. National Dancing Troupe	15	1·00
229	4n. African fish eagle	1·00	10
230	5n. Knife-edge Bridge	1·00	1·00
231	8n. Sitatunga (antelope)	1·00	75
232	9n. African elephant, Kasaba Bay	1·25	70
233	10n. Temminck's ground pangolin	20	10
234	15n. Type **85**	30	10
235	20n. Harvesting groundnuts	85	1·25
236	25n. Tobacco growing	1·25	1·50
237	50n. Flying Doctor service	3·25	2·50
238	1k. Lady Ross's turaco	4·50	1·75
239	2k. Village scene	3·00	6·00

Nos. 234/9 are as Type **85**.

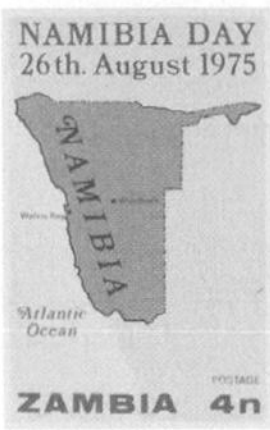

86 Map of Namibia

1975. Namibia Day.

240	**86**	4n. green and yellow	15	20
241	**86**	9n. blue and green	20	30
242	**86**	15n. orange and yellow	30	75
243	**86**	25n. red and orange	45	1·50

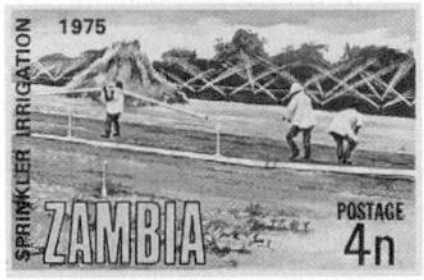

87 Erection of Sprinkler Irrigation

1975. Silver Jubilee of International Commission on Irrigation and Drainage. Multicoloured.

244	4n. Type **87**	15	20
245	9n. Sprinkler irrigation	30	50
246	15n. Furrow irrigation	65	1·50

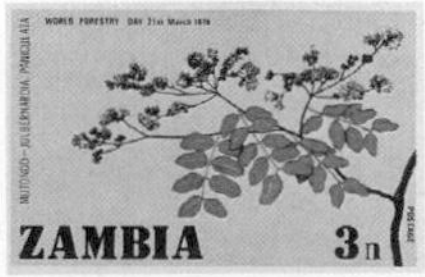

88 Mutondo

1976. World Forestry Day. Multicoloured.

247	3n. Type **88**	15	10
248	4n. Mukunyu	15	10
249	9n. Mukusi	25	25
250	10n. Mopane	25	25
251	15n. Musuku	45	1·40
252	25n. Mukwa	55	2·00

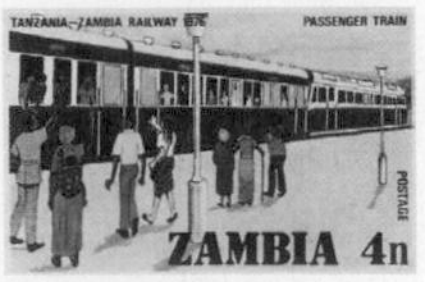

89 Passenger Train

1976. Opening of Tanzania–Zambia Railway. Multicoloured.

253	4n. Type **89**	30	30
254	9n. Copper exports	45	55
255	15n. Machinery imports	70	95
256	25n. Goods train	1·10	1·75
MS257	140×106 mm. 10n. Clearing bush; 15n. Laying track; 20n. Railway workers; 25n. Completed track	3·00	4·00

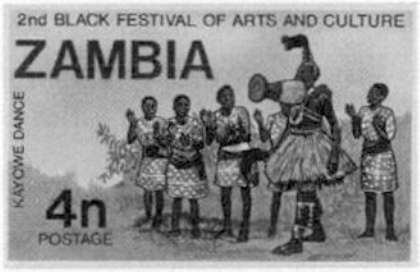

90 Kayowe Dance

1977. Second World Black and African Festival of Arts and Culture, Nigeria. Multicoloured.

258	4n. Type **90**	15	10
259	9n. Lilombola dance	15	15
260	15n. Initiation ceremony	30	40
261	25n. Munkhwele dance	55	1·00

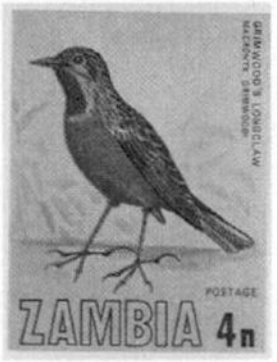

91 Grimwood's Longclaw

1977. Birds of Zambia. Multicoloured.

262	4n. Type **91**	40	10
263	9n. Shelley's sunbird	55	50
264	10n. Black-cheeked lovebird	55	50
265	15n. Locust finch	1·00	1·75
266	20n. White-chested tinkerbird	1·10	2·25
267	25n. Chaplin's barbet	1·10	2·75

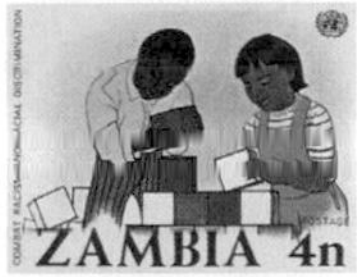

92 Girls with Building Blocks

1977. Decade for Action to Combat Racism and Racial Discrimination. Multicoloured.

268	4n. Type **92**	15	10
269	9n. Women dancing	20	20
270	15n. Girls with dove	30	1·00

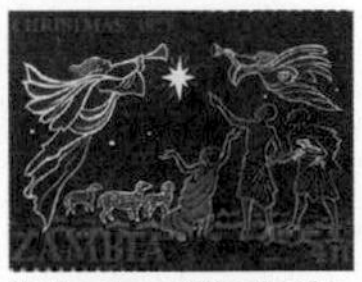

93 Angels and Shepherds

1977. Christmas. Multicoloured.

271	4n. Type **93**	10	10
272	9n. The Holy Family	10	10
273	10n. The Magi	10	15
274	15n. Jesus presented to Simeon	20	1·00

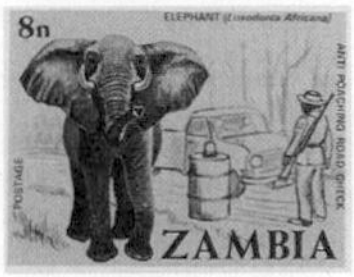

94 African Elephant and Road Check

1978. Anti-poaching Campaign. Multicoloured.

275	8n. Type **94**	45	20
276	18n. Lechwe and canoe patrol	30	65
277	28n. Warthog and Bell 206 JetRanger helicopter	75	1·10
278	32n. Cheetah and game guard patrol	75	1·50

1979. Various stamps surch.

279	-	8n. on 9n. multicoloured (No. 232)	70	10
280	-	10n. on 3n. multicoloured (No. 228)	10	10
281	-	18n. on 25n. mult (No. 236)	15	15
282	**85**	28n. on 15n. mult	20	25

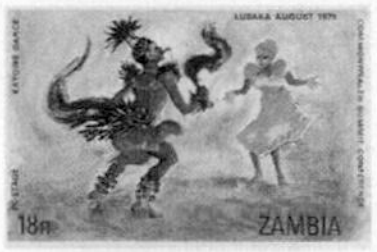

96 Kayowe Dance

1979. Commonwealth Summit Conference, Lusaka. Multicoloured.

283	18n. Type **96**	15	25
284	32n. Kutambala dance	20	40
285	42n. Chitwansombo drummers	20	60
286	58n. Lilombola dance	25	80

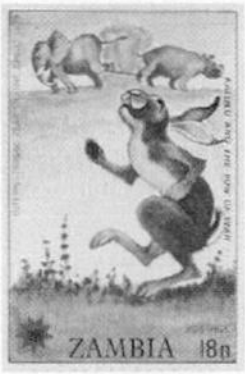

97 "Kalulu and the Tug of War"

1979. International Year of the Child. Multicoloured.

287	18n. Type **97**	25	30
288	32n. "Why the Zebra has no Horns"	30	55
289	42n. "How the Tortoise got his Shell"	35	85
290	58n. "Kalulu and the Lion"	45	1·00
MS291	90×120 mm. Nos. 287/91	1·25	2·25

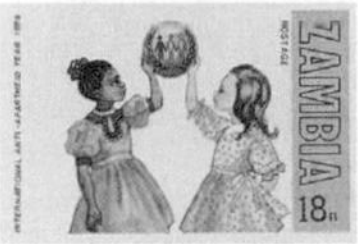

98 Children of Different Races holding Anti-Apartheid Emblem

1979. International Anti-Apartheid Year. Multicoloured.

292	18n. Type **98**	15	25
293	32n. Children with toy car	25	40
294	42n. Young children with butterfly	35	70
295	58n. Children with microscope	50	1·00

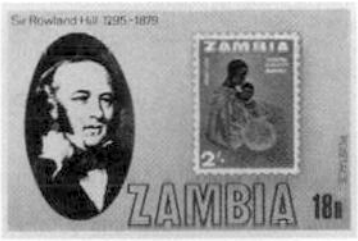

99 Sir Rowland Hill and 2s. Definitive Stamp of 1964

1979. Death Cent of Sir Rowland Hill. Multicoloured.

296	18n. Type **99**	15	25
297	32n. Sir Rowland Hill and mailman	20	55
298	42n. Sir Rowland Hill and Northern Rhodesia 1963 ½d. definitive stamp	20	70
299	58n. Sir Rowland Hill and mail-carrying oxwaggon	20	1·10
MS300	112×89 mm. Nos. 296/9	1·00	2·50

1980. "London 1980" International Stamp Exhibition. Nos. 296/9 optd **LONDON 1980.**

301	**99**	18n. multicoloured	25	40
302	-	32n. multicoloured	30	60
303	-	42n. multicoloured	40	75
304	-	58n. multicoloured	60	90
MS305		112×89 mm. Nos. 301/4	2·50	3·75

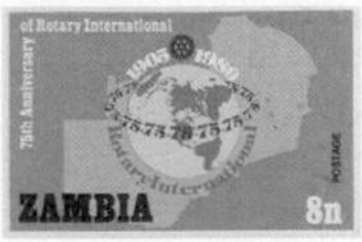

101 Rotary Anniversary Emblem

1980. 75th Anniv of Rotary International.

306	**101**	8n. multicoloured	10	10
307	**101**	32n. multicoloured	30	40
308	**101**	42n. multicoloured	35	50
309	**101**	58n. multicoloured	45	80
MS310		115×89 mm. Nos. 306/9	1·50	2·25

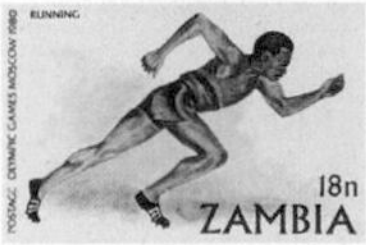

102 Running

1980. Olympic Games, Moscow. Multicoloured.

311	18n. Type **102**	20	25
312	32n. Boxing	30	45
313	42n. Football	40	80
314	58n. Swimming	50	1·25
MS315	142×144 mm. Nos. 311/14	2·50	3·25

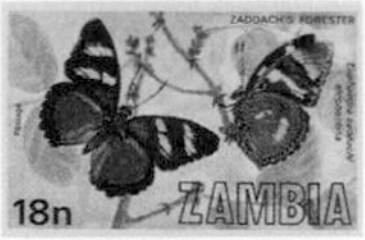

103 "Euphaedra zaddachi"

1980. Butterflies. Multicoloured.

316	18n. Type **103**	15	15
317	32n. "Aphnaeus questiauxi"	25	40
318	42n. "Abantis zambesiaca"	40	90
319	58n. "Spindasis modesta"	60	1·75
MS320	114×86 mm. Nos. 316/19	4·25	3·25

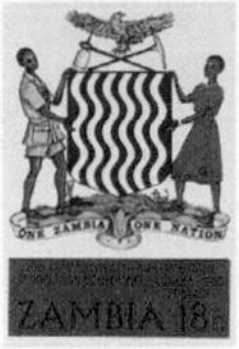

104 Zambia Coat of Arms

1980. 26th Commonwealth Parliamentary Association Conference, Lusaka.

321	**104**	18n. multicoloured	15	25
322	**104**	32n. multicoloured	25	45
323	**104**	42n. multicoloured	30	75
324	**104**	58n. multicoloured	40	1·50

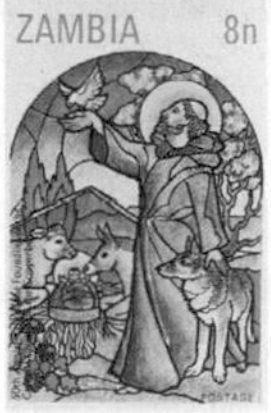

105 Nativity and St. Francis of Assisi (stained glass window, Ndola Church)

1980. 50th Anniv of Catholic Church on the Copperbelt.

325	**105**	8n. multicoloured	10	10
326	**105**	28n. multicoloured	30	70
327	**105**	32n. multicoloured	30	70
328	**105**	42n. multicoloured	45	1·50

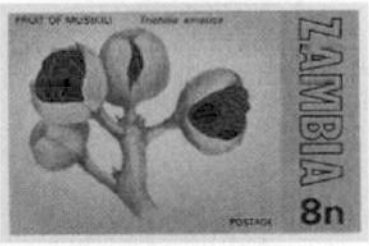

106 Musikili

1981. World Forestry Day. Seedpods. Multicoloured.

329	8n. Type **106**	10	10
330	18n. Mupapa	20	45
331	28n. Mulunguti	25	90
332	32n. Mulama	25	1·40

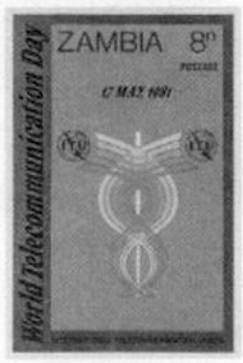

107 I.T.U. Emblem

1981. World Telecommunications and Health Day. Multicoloured.

333	8n. Type **107**	20	10
334	18n. W.H.O. emblems	25	35
335	28n. Type **107**	30	70
336	32n. As 18n.	35	85

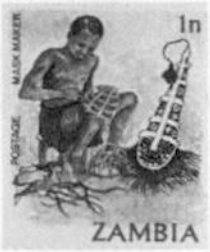

108 Mask Maker

1981. Native Crafts. Multicoloured.

337	1n. Type **108**	10	10
338	2n. Blacksmith	10	10
339	5n. Pottery making	10	10
340	8n. Straw-basket fishing	10	10
341	10n. Thatching	10	10
342	12n. Mushroom picking	3·00	1·75
343	18n. Millet grinding on stone	30	10
344	28n. Royal Barge paddler	75	10
345	30n. Makishi tightrope dancer	50	10
346	35n. Tonga Ila granary and house	55	10
347	42n. Cattle herding	55	1·75
348	50n. Traditional healer (38×26 mm)	75	10
349	75n. Women carrying water (38×26 mm)	55	60
350	1k. Pounding maize (38×26 mm)	55	60
351	2k. Pipe smoking, Gwembe Valley belle (38×26 mm)	55	60

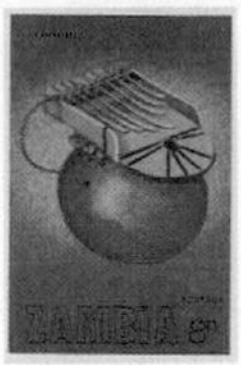

109 Kankobele

1981. Traditional Musical Instruments. Multicoloured.

356	8n. Type **109**	20	10
357	18n. Inshingili	25	55
358	28n. Ilimba	30	1·50
359	32n. Bango	35	1·75

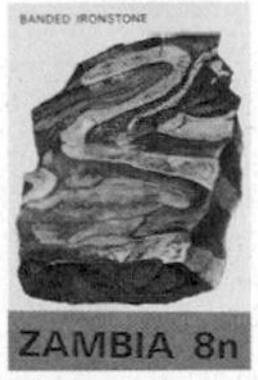

110 Banded Ironstone

1982. Minerals (1st series). Multicoloured.

360	8n. Type **110**	1·00	10
361	18n. Cobaltocalcite	2·00	80
362	28n. Amazonite	2·75	1·25
363	32n. Tourmaline	3·00	2·75
364	42n. Uranium ore	3·25	4·00

See also Nos. 370/4.

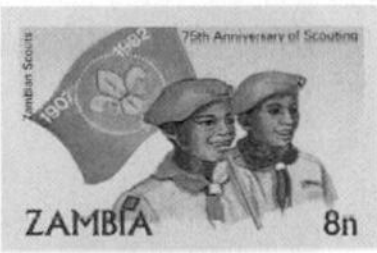

111 Zambian Scouts

1982. 75th Anniv of Boy Scout Movement. Multicoloured.

365	8n. Type **111**	20	10
366	18n. Lord Baden-Powell and Victoria Falls	60	40
367	28n. African buffalo and Zambian scout patrol pennant	60	50
368	1k. African fish eagle and Zambian conservation badge	1·40	4·50
MS369	105×78 mm. Nos. 365/8	2·50	5·00

1982. Minerals (2nd series). As T **110**. Multicoloured.

370	8n. Bornite	95	10
371	18n. Chalcopyrite	2·25	90
372	28n. Malachite	2·75	3·00
373	32n. Azurite	2·75	3·00
374	42n. Vanadinite	3·25	4·25

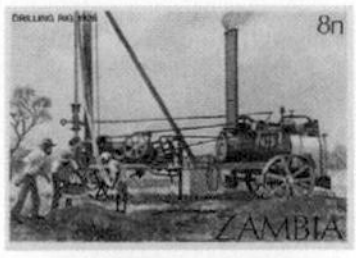

112 Drilling Rig, 1926

1983. Early Steam Engines. Multicoloured.

375	8n. Type **112**	45	20
376	18n. Fowler road locomotive, 1900	55	80
377	28n. Borsig ploughing engine, 1925	1·00	2·50
378	32n. Rhodesian Railways 7th Class steam locomotive, 1900	1·25	2·75

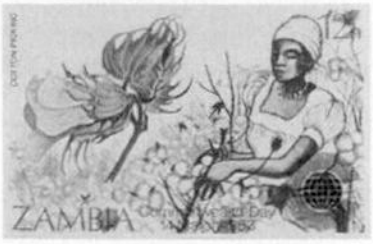

113 Cotton Picking

1983. Commonwealth Day. Multicoloured.

379	12n. Type **113**	20	10
380	18n. Mining	40	30
381	28n. Ritual pot and traditional dances	30	50
382	1k. Violet-crested turaco and Victoria Falls	2·75	5·50

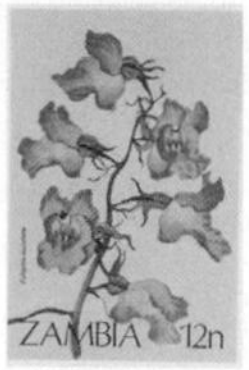

114 "Eulophia cucullata"

1983. Wild Flowers. Multicoloured.

383	12n. Type **114**	20	10
384	28n. "Kigelia africana"	25	40
385	35n. "Protea gaguedi"	30	80
386	50n. "Leonotis nepetifolia"	50	2·25
MS387	141×71 mm. Nos. 383/6	1·00	3·50

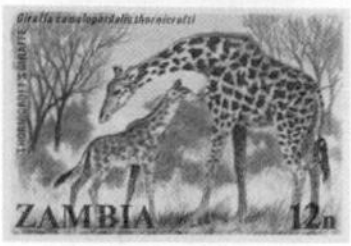

115 Giraffe

1983. Wildlife of Zambia. Multicoloured.

388	12n. Type **115**	70	10
389	28n. Blue wildebeest	75	70
390	35n. Lechwe	80	90
391	1k. Yellow-backed duiker	1·25	4·25

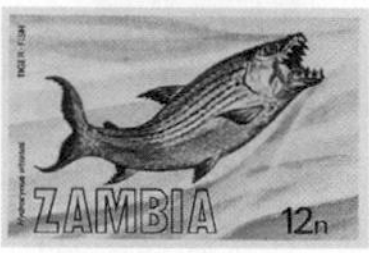

116 Tigerfish

1983. Fish of Zambia. Multicoloured.

392	12n. Type **116**	35	15
393	28n. Silver catfish	50	70
394	35n. Large-spotted squeaker	60	1·75
395	38n. Red-breasted tilapia	60	1·75

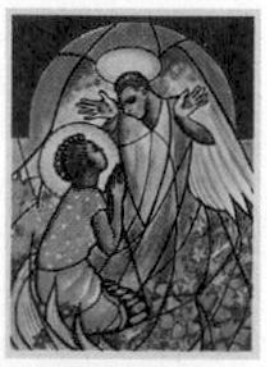

117 The Annunciation

1983. Christmas. Multicoloured.

396	12n. Type **117**	15	10
397	28n. The Shepherds	30	40
398	35n. Three Kings	40	1·25
399	38n. Flight into Egypt	45	1·75

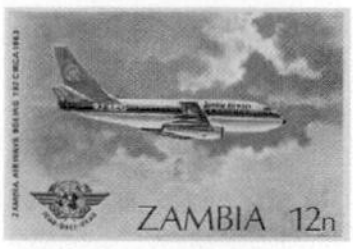

118 Boeing 737

1984. Air Transport. Multicoloured.

400	12n. Type **118**	25	10
401	28n. De Havilland D.H.C.2 Beaver	45	40
402	35n. Short S-45A Solent 3 flying boat	55	70
403	1k. De Havilland D.H.66 Hercules "City of Basra"	1·00	3·25

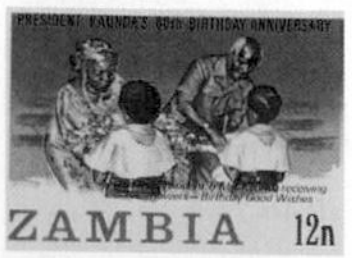

119 Receiving Flowers

1984. 60th Birthday of President Kaunda. Multicoloured.

404	12n. Type **119**	20	10
405	28n. Swearing-in ceremony (vert)	25	40
406	60n. Planting cherry tree	50	2·25
407	1k. Opening of 5th National Assembly (vert)	65	3·25

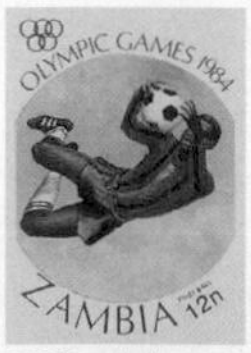

120 Football

1984. Olympic Games, Los Angeles. Multicoloured.

408	12n. Type **120**	25	10
409	28n. Running	30	50
410	35n. Hurdling	40	80
411	60n. Boxing	45	1·75

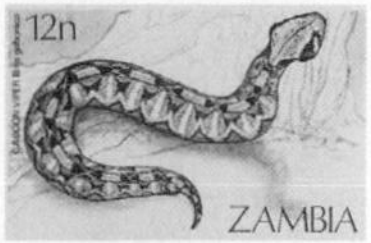

121 Gaboon Viper

1984. Reptiles. Multicoloured.

412	12n. Type **121**	20	10
413	28n. Chameleon	40	50
414	35n. Nile crocodile	50	70
415	1k. Blue-headed agama	1·00	2·75
MS416	120×101 mm. Nos. 412/15	2·00	4·00

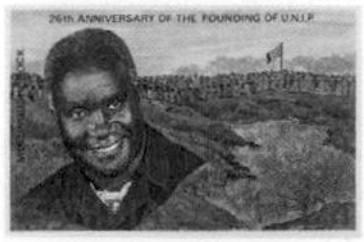

122 Pres. Kaunda and Mulungushi Rock

1984. 26th Anniv of United National Independence Party and 20th Anniv of Independence (1st issue). Multicoloured.

417	12n. Type **122**	20	10
418	28n. Freedom Statue	30	50
419	1k. Pres. Kaunda and agricultural produce ("Lima Programme")	75	3·00

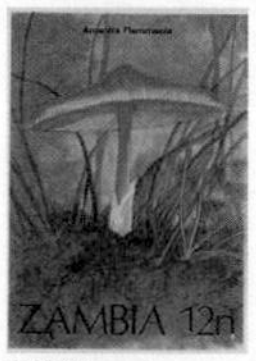

123 "Amanita flammeola"

1984. Fungi. Multicoloured.

420	12n. Type **123**	60	30
421	28n. "Amanita zambiana"	75	90
422	32n. "Termitomyces letestui"	75	1·50
423	75n. "Cantharellus miniatescens"	1·00	1·00

1985. No. 237 surch **K5**.

424	5k. on 50n. Flying Doctor service	1·75	3·50

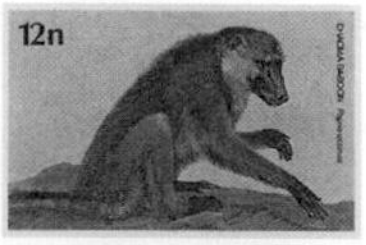

125 Chacma Baboon

1985. Zambian Primates. Multicoloured.

425	12n. Type **125**	45	10
426	20n. Diademed monkey	60	40
427	45n. Diademed monkey (different)	90	1·25
428	1k. Savanna monkey	1·50	4·50

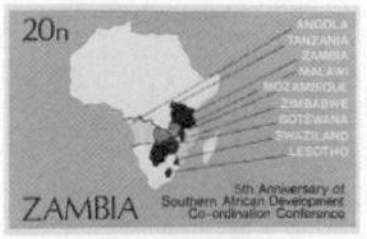

126 Map showing S.A.D.C.C. Member States

1985. Fifth Anniv of Southern African Development Co-ordination Conference.

429	**126**	20n. multicoloured	75	15
430	-	45n. black, blue and light blue	1·75	1·10
431	-	1k. multicoloured	2·00	3·75

DESIGNS: 45n. Mining; 1k. Flags of member states and Mulungushi Hall.

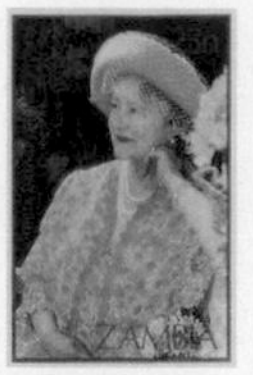

127 The Queen Mother in 1980

1985. Life and Times of Queen Elizabeth the Queen Mother.

432	**127**	25n. multicoloured	10	10
433	-	45n. blue and gold	10	15
434	-	55n. blue and gold	15	25
435	-	5k. multicoloured	1·25	2·75

DESIGNS—VERT: 45n. The Queen Mother at Clarence House, 1963. HORIZ: 55n. With the Queen and Princess Margaret, 1980; 5k. At Prince Henry's Christening, 1984.

1985. Nos. 340 and 342 surch.

436	20n. on 12n. Mushroom picking	2·75	1·00
437	25n. on 8n. Straw-basket fishing	1·00	65

1985. 26th Anniv of United National Independence Party (No. 438) and 20th Anniv of Independence (others) (2nd issue). As Nos. 417/19 but larger, 55×34 mm. On gold foil.

438	5k. As Type **122**	1·25	2·25
439	5k. Freedom Statue	1·25	2·25
440	5k. Pres. Kaunda and agricultural produce ("Lima Programme")	1·25	2·25

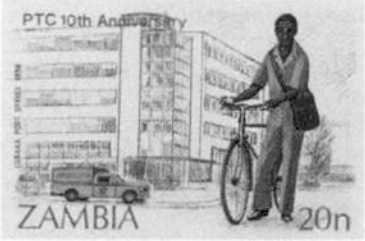

129 Postman and Lusaka Post Office, 1958

1985. Tenth Anniv of Posts and Telecommunication Corporation. Multicoloured.

441	20n. Type **129**	40	10
442	45n. Postman and Livingstone Post Office, 1950	65	25
443	55n. Postman and Kalomo Post Office, 1902	75	70
444	5k. Africa Trans-Continental Telegraph Line under construction, 1900	2·00	6·00

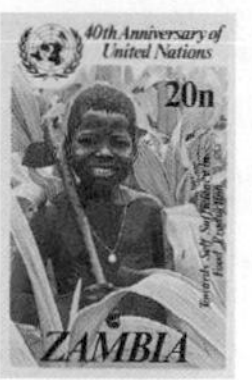

130 Boy in Maize Field

1985. 40th Anniv of United Nations Organization.

445	**130**	20n. multicoloured	25	10
446	-	45n. black, blue and brown	40	20
447	-	1k. multicoloured	75	2·00
448	-	2k. multicoloured	1·10	3·00

DESIGNS: 45n. Logo and "40"; 1k. President Kaunda addressing U.N. General Assembly, 1970; 2k. Signing of U.N. Charter, San Francisco, 1945.

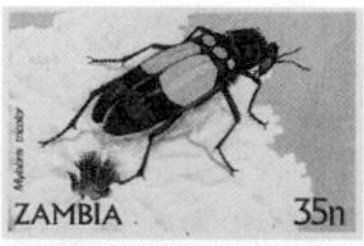

131 "Mylabris tricolor"

1986. Beetles. Multicoloured.

449	35n. Type **131**	15	10
450	1k. "Phasgonocnema melanianthe"	20	20
451	1k.70 "Amaurodes passerinii"	30	50
452	5k. "Ranzania petersiana"	85	2·00

1986. 60th Birthday of Queen Elizabeth II. As T **145a** of St. Helena. Multicoloured.

453	35n. Princess Elizabeth at Flower Ball, Savoy Hotel, 1951	10	10
454	1k.25 With Prince Andrew, Lusaka Airport, 1979	15	20
455	1k.70 With President Kaunda	15	25
456	1k.95 In Luxembourg, 1976	15	30
457	5k. At Crown Agents Head Office, London, 1983	25	85

1986. Royal Wedding. As T **146a** of St. Helena. Multicoloured.

458	1k.70 Prince Andrew and Miss Sarah Ferguson	30	35
459	5k. Prince Andrew in Zambia, 1979	80	1·40

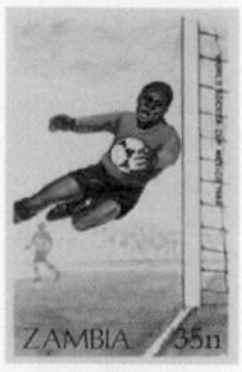

132 Goalkeeper saving Goal

1986. World Cup Football Championship, Mexico. Multicoloured.

460	35n. Type **132**	85	15
461	1k.25 Player kicking ball	2·00	1·40
462	1k.70 Two players competing for ball	2·25	1·90
463	5k. Player scoring goal	3·25	6·00

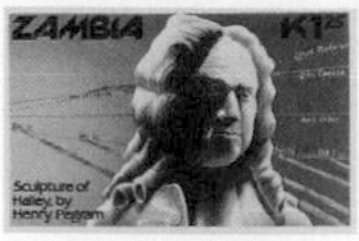

133 Sculpture of Edmond Halley by Henry Pegram

1986. Appearance of Halley's Comet.

464	**133**	1k.25 multicoloured	1·00	55
465	-	1k.70 multicoloured	1·25	85
466	-	2k. multicoloured	1·75	1·75
467	-	5k. blue and black	3·50	6·50

DESIGNS: 1k.70, "Giotto" spacecraft approaching nucleus of Comet; 2k. Studying Halley's Comet in 1682 and 1986; 5k. Part of Halley's chart of southern sky.

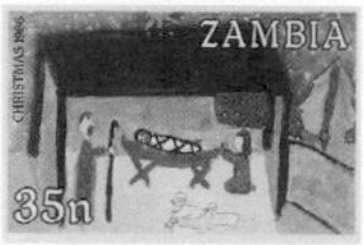

134 The Nativity

1986. Christmas. Children's Paintings. Multicoloured.

468	35n. Type **134**	50	10
469	1k.25 Visit of the Three Kings	1·75	75
470	1k.60 The Holy Family with Shepherd and King	1·90	1·50
471	5k. Angel and Christmas tree	4·00	7·50

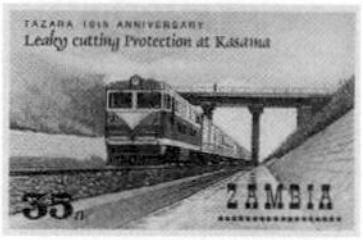

135 Diesel Train in Kasama Cutting

1986. Tenth Anniv of Tanzania–Zambia Railway. Multicoloured.

472	35n. Type **135**	25	10
473	1k.25 Passenger train leaving Tunnel No. 21	35	50
474	1k.70 Train between Tunnels Nos. 6 and 7	35	70
475	5k. Trains near Mpika Station	70	3·00

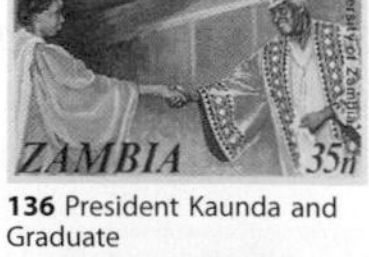

136 President Kaunda and Graduate

1987. 20th Anniv of University of Zambia. Multicoloured.

476	35n. Type **136**	25	10
477	1k.25 University badge (vert)	55	60
478	1k.60 University statue	60	1·00
479	5k. President Kaunda laying foundation stone (vert)	2·00	6·50

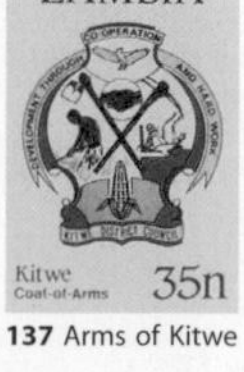

137 Arms of Kitwe

1987. Arms of Zambian Towns. Multicoloured.

480	35n. Type **137**	10	10
481	1k.25 Ndola	15	20
482	1k.70 Lusaka	20	25
483	20k. Livingstone	3·50	7·50

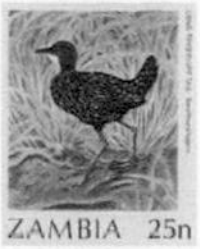

138 African Chestnut-headed Crake

1987. Birds (1st series). Multicoloured.

484	5n. Cloud-scraping cisticola	10	10
485	10n. White-winged starling	10	10
486a	20n. on 1n. Yellow swamp warbler	20	20
487	25n. Type **138**	2·50	1·00
488	30n. Miombo pied barbet	20	10
489	35n. Black and rufous swallow	2·50	2·25
490	40n. Wattled crane	20	10
491	50n. Slaty egret	20	10
492	75n. on 2n. Olive-flanked robin chat	30	1·40
493	1k. Bradfield's hornbill	2·75	40
494	1k.25 Boulton's puff-back fly-catcher ("Margaret's Batis")	2·50	3·00
495	1k.60 Anchieta's sunbird	2·50	1·50
496	1k.65 on 30n. Miombo pied barbet	30	1·75
497	1k.70 Boehm's bee eater	2·50	3·00
498	1k.95 Perrin's bush shrike	2·50	2·25
499	2k. Whale-headed stork ("Shoebill")	35	35
500	5k. Taita falcon	3·00	80
501	10k. on 50n. Slaty egret	1·10	2·50
502	20k. on 2k. Whale-headed stork	1·25	3·75

Nos. 491, 493/5 and 497/502 are larger, size 24×39 mm.

No. 502 is surcharged "K20". For No. 499 surcharged "K20.00" see No. 594.

See also Nos. 587/95 and 625/38.

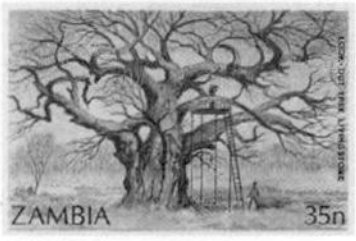

139 Look-out Tree, Livingstone

1987. Tourism. Multicoloured.

503	35n. Type **139**	30	15
504	1k.25 Rafting on Zambezi	45	25
505	1k.70 Tourists photographing lions, Luangwa Valley	1·75	90
506	10k. Eastern white pelicans ("White Pelican")	8·50	11·00

1987. Various stamps surch. (a) Nos. 432/5.

507	**127**	3k. on 25n. mult	1·00	1·00
508	-	6k. on 45n. blue and gold	2·00	2·00
509	-	10k. on 55n. blue and gold	2·50	2·75
510	-	20k. on 5k. mult	5·00	7·50

(b) Nos. 453/7.

511	3k. on 35n. Princess Elizabeth at Flower Ball, Savoy Hotel, 1951	55	65
512	4k. on 1k.25 With Prince Andrew, Lusaka Airport, 1979	65	75
513	6k. on 1k.70 With President Kaunda	1·00	1·25
514	10k. on 1k.95 In Luxembourg, 1976	1·60	2·25
515	20k. on 5k. At Crown Agents Head Office, London, 1983	4·00	5·50

(c) Nos. 460/3.

516	3k. on 35n. Type **132**	1·00	1·00
517	6k. on 1k.25 Player kicking ball	2·00	2·00
518	10k. on 1k.70 Two players competing for ball	2·50	2·75
519	20k. on 5k. Player scoring goal	5·00	7·50

(d) Nos. 464/7.

520	**133**	3k. on 1k.25 mult	2·00	1·25
521	-	6k. on 1k.70 mult	2·75	2·25
522	-	10k. on 2k. mult	4·00	5·00
523	-	20k. on 5k. blue and black	7·50	10·00

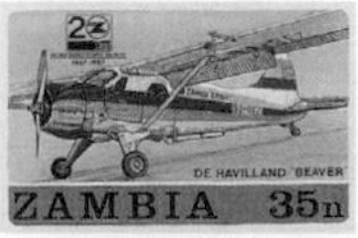

141 De Havilland D.H.C.2 Beaver

1987. 20th Anniv of Zambia Airways. Aircraft. Multicoloured.

524	35n. Type **141**	85	10
525	1k.70 Douglas DC-10	2·00	70
526	5k. Douglas DC-3	4·25	3·75
527	10k. Boeing 707	6·50	8·00

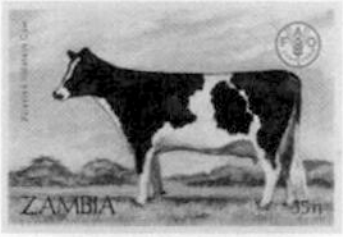

142 Friesian/Holstein Cow

1987. 40th Anniv of F.A.O. Multicoloured.

528	35n. Type **142**	15	10
529	1k.25 Simmental bull	30	25
530	1k.70 Sussex bull	30	30
531	20k. Brahman bull	1·25	3·25

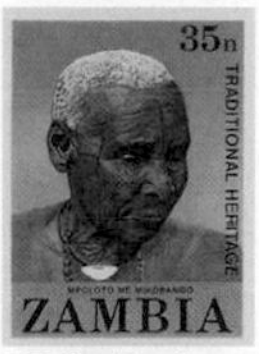

143 Mpoloto Ne Mikobango

1987. People of Zambia. Multicoloured.

532	35n. Type **143**	15	10
533	1k.25 Zintaka	25	25
534	1k.70 Mufuluhi	30	30
535	10k. Ntebwe	80	1·75
536	20k. Kubangwa Aa Mbulunga	1·25	3·50

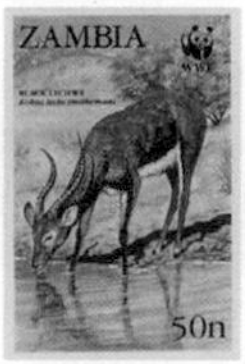

144 Black Lechwe at Waterhole

1987. Black Lechwe. Multicoloured.

537	50n. Type **144**	75	10
538	2k. Black lechwe resting by pool (horiz)	2·00	40
539	2k.50 Running through water (horiz)	2·00	80
540	10k. Watching for danger	5·00	7·00
MS541	Two sheets, each 103×74 mm. (a) 20k. Caracal (predator). (b) 20k. Cheetah (predator) Set of 2 sheets	15·00	13·00

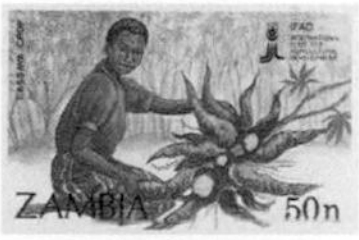

145 Cassava Roots

1988. International Fund for Agricultural Development. Multicoloured.

542	50n. Type **145**	15	10
543	2k.50 Fishing	70	50
544	2k.85 Farmer and cattle	75	55
545	10k. Picking coffee beans	1·50	2·50

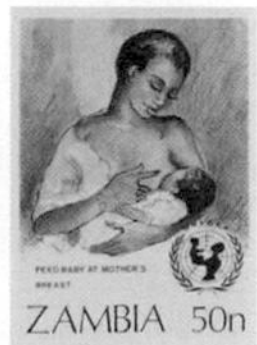

146 Breast-feeding

1988. UNICEF Child Survival Campaign. Multicoloured.

546	50n. Type **146**	20	10
547	2k. Growth monitoring	60	30
548	2k.85 Immunization	70	70
549	10k. Oral rehydration	1·40	3·25

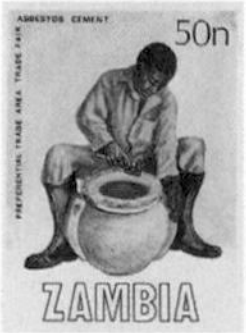

147 Asbestos Cement

1988. Preferential Trade Area Fair. Multicoloured.

550	50n. Type **147**	15	10
551	2k.35 Textiles	25	30
552	2k.50 Tea	25	40
553	10k. Poultry	90	3·00

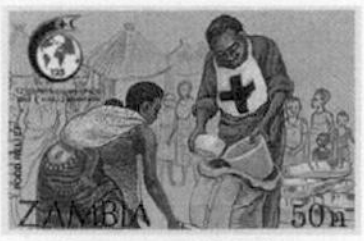

148 Emergency Food Distribution

1988. 125th Anniv of Int Red Cross. Multicoloured.

554	50n. Type **148**	25	10
555	2k.50 Giving first aid	60	60
556	2k.85 Practising bandaging	65	85
557	10k. Henri Dunant (founder)	1·75	4·00

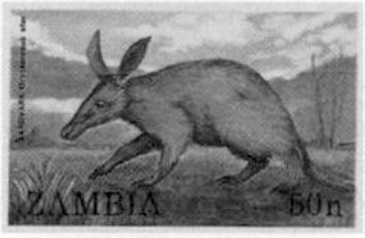

149 Aardvark

1988. Endangered Species of Zambia. Multicoloured.

558	50n. Type **149**	25	10
559	2k. Temminck's ground pangolin	50	40
560	2k.85 Hunting dog	70	75
561	20k. Black rhinoceros and calf	8·00	7·75

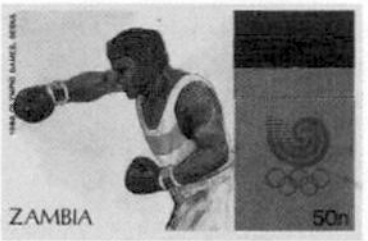

150 Boxing

1988. Olympic Games, Seoul. Multicoloured.

562	50n. Type **150**	15	10
563	2k. Athletics	35	40
564	2k.50 Hurdling	40	70
565	20k. Football	3·25	6·50
MS566	Two sheets, each 97×72 mm. (a) 30k. Tennis. (b) 30k. Karate Set of 2 sheets	8·00	11·00

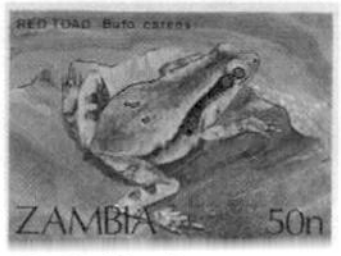

151 Red Toad

1989. Frogs and Toads. Multicoloured.

567	50n. Type **151**	15	10
568	2k.50 Puddle frog	50	50
569	2k.85 Marbled reed frog	55	75
570	10k. Young reed frogs	1·60	3·75

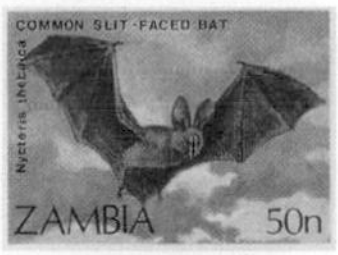

152 Common Slit-faced Bat

1989. Bats. Multicoloured.

571	50n. Type **152**	20	10
572	2k.50 Little free-tailed bat	55	55
573	2k.85 Hildebrandt's horseshoe bat	65	75
574	10k. Peters' epauletted fruit bat	1·75	4·00

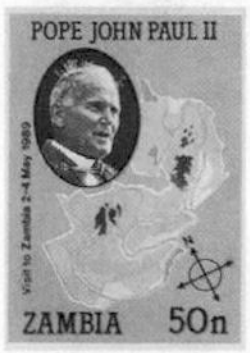

153 Pope John Paul II and Map of Zambia

1989. Visit of Pope John Paul II. Designs each with inset portrait. Multicoloured.

575	50n. Type **153**	1·00	35
576	6k.85 Peace dove with olive branch	3·00	3·00
577	7k.85 Papal arms	3·50	3·50
578	10k. Victoria Falls	6·00	4·75

1989. Various stamp surch. (a) On Nos. 339, 341/3, 345/6, 349 and 351.

579	1k.20 on 35n. Tonga Ila granary and house	20	15
580	3k.75 on 5n. Pottery making	30	20
581	8k.11 on 10n. Thatching	50	50
582	9k. on 30n. Makishi tightrope dancer	50	50
583	10k. on 75n. Women carrying water (38×26 mm)	50	50
584	18k.50 on 2k. Pipe-smoking Gwembe Valley belle (38×26 mm)	1·00	1·75
585	19k.50 on 12n. Mushroom picking	3·50	3·25
586	20k.50 on 18n. Millet grinding on stone	1·25	2·50

(b) On Nos. 484, 489, 493/5 and 497/500.

587	70n. on 35n. Black and rufous swallow	1·00	15
588	3k. on 5n. Cloud-scraping cisticola	1·00	30
589	8k. on 1k.25 Boulton's puff-back flycatcher	1·25	60
590	9k.90 on 1k.70 Boehm's bee eater	1·75	80
591	10k.40 on 1k.60 Anchieta's sunbird	1·75	90
592	12k.50 on 1k. Bradfield's hornbill	1·25	1·25
593	15k. on 1k.95 Perrin's bush strike	1·25	2·00
594	20k. on 2k. Whale-headed stork	1·75	2·75
595	20k.35 on 5k. Taita falcon	2·25	2·75

No. 594 shows the surcharge as "K20.00". The previously listed 20k. on 2k., No. 499, is surcharged "K20" only.

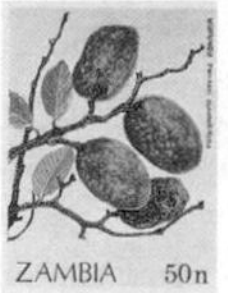

156 "Parinari curatellifolia"

1989. Edible Fruit. Multicoloured.

596	50n. Type **156**	15	10
597	6k.50 "Uapaca kirkiana"	1·25	1·50
598	6k.85 Wild fig	1·25	2·00
599	10k. Bottle palm	2·25	3·25

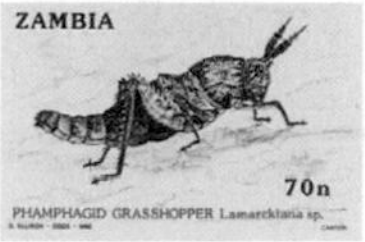

157 "Lamarckiana sp."

1989. Grasshoppers. Multicoloured.

600	70n. Type **157**	20	10
601	10k.40 "Dictyophorus sp."	1·75	1·75
602	12k.50 "Cymatomera sp."	2·00	2·50
603	15k. "Phymateus iris"	2·50	4·50

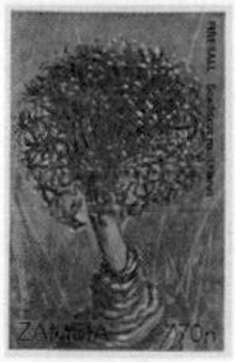
158 Fireball

1989. Christmas. Flowers. Multicoloured.

604	70n. Type **158**	15	10
605	10k.40 Flame lily	1·25	1·25
606	12k.50 Foxglove lily	1·75	1·75
607	20k. Vlei lily	2·75	4·75

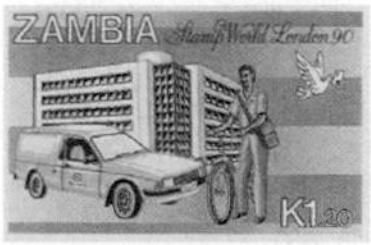

159 Postvan, Postman on Bicycle and Main Post Office, Lusaka

1990. "Stamp World London 90" International Stamp Exhibition. Multicoloured.

608	1k.20 Type **159**	30	10
609	19k.50 Zambia 1980 18n. butterflies stamp	2·75	2·75
610	20k.50 Rhodesia and Nyasaland 1962 9d. and Northern Rhodesia 1925 ½d. stamps	2·75	2·75
611	50k. 1840 Penny Black and Maltese Cross cancellation	5·00	7·00

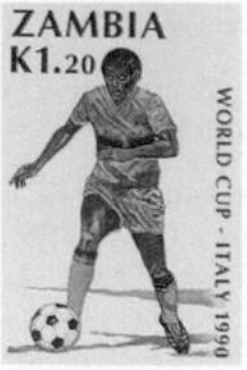

160 Footballer and Ball

1990. World Cup Football Championship, Italy.

612	**160**	1k.20 multicoloured	10	10
613	-	18k.50 multicoloured	2·00	2·50
614	-	19k.50 multicoloured	2·00	2·50
615	-	20k.50 multicoloured	2·00	2·50
MS616		100×73 mm. 50k. multicoloured	10·00	12·00

DESIGNS: 18k.50 to 50k, Different football scenes.

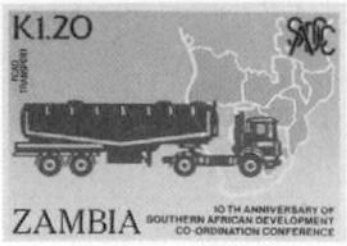

161 Road Tanker

1990. Tenth Anniv of Southern African Development Co-ordination Conference. Each showing map of Southern Africa. Multicoloured.

617	1k.20 Type **161**	30	10
618	19k.50 Telecommunications	2·00	2·50
619	20k.50 "Regional Co-operation"	2·00	2·50
620	50k. Transporting coal by cable	8·00	9·50

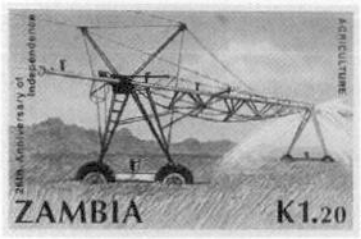

162 Irrigation

1990. 26th Anniv of Independence. Multicoloured.

621	1k.20 Type **162**	10	10
622	19k.50 Shoe factory	1·10	1·40
623	20k.50 Mwembeshi II satellite earth station	1·25	1·60
624	50k. "Mother and Child" (statue)	2·50	4·25

1990. Birds (2nd series). As T **138**. Multicoloured.

625	10n. Livingstone's flycatcher	1·25	1·00
626	15n. Bar-winged weaver	1·25	1·00
627	30n. Purple-throated cuckoo shrike	1·25	1·00
628	50n. Retz's red-billed helmet shrike	1·25	1·25
629	50n. As 10n.	1·75	1·25
630	1k. As 15n.	1·40	1·00
631	1k.20 Bronze-naped pigeon ("Western Bronze-naped Pigeon")	1·25	20
632	2k. As 30n.	1·40	70
633	3k. As 50n.	1·40	70
634	5k. As 1k.20	3·00	70
635	15k. Corn crake	1·25	40
636	20k. Dickinson's kestrel	2·25	1·50
637	20k.50 As 20k.	1·25	1·25
638	50k. Denham's bustard	1·25	1·50

Nos. 635/8 are larger, size 23×39 mm.

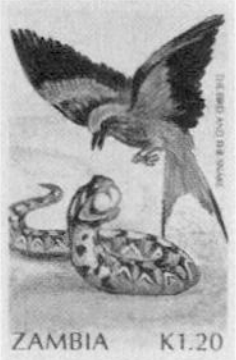

163 The Bird and the Snake

1991. Int Literacy Year. Folklore. Multicoloured.

639	1k.20 Type **163**	50	20
640	18k.50 Kalulu and the Leopard	2·75	3·25
641	19k.50 The Mouse and the Lion	2·75	3·25
642	20k.50 Kalulu and the Hippopotamus	3·25	3·25

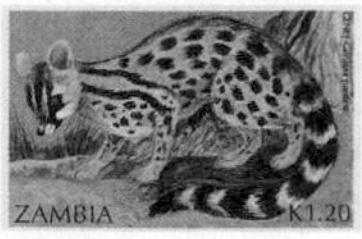

164 Genet

1991. Small Carnivores. Multicoloured.

643	1k.20 Type **164**	50	15
644	18k.50 Civet	3·25	3·75
645	19k.50 Serval	3·25	3·75
646	20k.50 African wild cat	3·25	3·75

1991. Nos. 441/4 surch **K2**.

647	2k. on 20n. Type **129**	12·00	5·50
648	2k. on 45n. Postman and Livingstone Post Office, 1950	12·00	5·50
649	2k. on 55n. Postman and Kalomo Post Office, 1902	12·00	5·50
650	2k. on 5k. African Trans-Continental Telegraph Line under construction, 1900	12·00	5·50

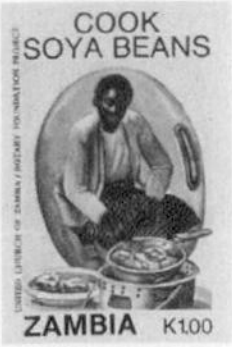

166 Woman cooking

1991. Soya Promotion Campaign. Multicoloured.

651	1k. Type **166**	10	10
652	2k. Soya bean and field	10	10
653	5k. Mother feeding child	30	15
654	20k. Healthy and malnourished children	1·50	2·00
655	50k. President Kaunda holding child	2·50	3·50

1991. Various stamps surch **K2**.

656	**130**	2k. on 20n. mult	32·00	5·00
657	**127**	2k. on 25n. mult	90·00	5·00
658	-	2k. on 28n. mult (No. 344)	35·00	5·00
659	-	2k. on 28n. mult (No. 393)	45·00	5·00
660	-	2k. on 28n. mult (No. 401)	£250	5·00
661	-	2k. on 28n. mult (No. 418)		5·00
662	-	2k. on 32n. mult (No. 422)	27·00	5·00
663	-	2k. on 35n. mult (No. 453)		5·00
664	**134**	2k. on 35n. mult	75·00	5·00
665	**137**	2k. on 35n. mult	42·00	5·00
666	-	2k. on 45n. mult (No. 427)	42·00	5·00
667	-	2k. on 45n. black, blue and light blue (No. 430)	60·00	5·00
668	-	2k. on 45n. blue and gold (No. 433)	90·00	5·00
669	-	2k. on 45n. black, blue and brown (No. 446)	45·00	5·00
670	-	2k. on 1k.60 mult (No. 470)	75·00	5·00
671	-	2k. on 1k.70 mult (No. 451)	45·00	5·00
672	-	2k. on 1k.70 mult (No. 482)		5·00
673	-	2k. on 5k. mult (No. 435)	15·00	5·00
674	-	2k. on 5k. mult (No. 452)	15·00	5·00
675	-	2k. on 6k.50 mult (No. 597)	42·00	5·00
676	-	2k. on 6k.85 mult (No. 576)	60·00	5·00
677	-	2k. on 6k.85 mult (No. 598)	16·00	5·00
678	-	2k. on 7k.85 mult (No. 577)	£100	5·00

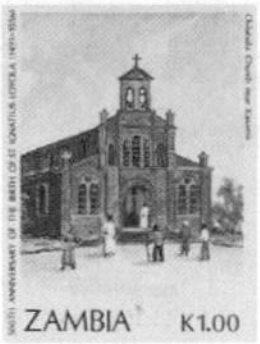

167 Chilubula Church near Kasama

1991. 500th Birth Anniv of St. Ignatius Loyola. Multicoloured.

679	1k. Type **167**	10	10
680	2k. Chikuni Church near Monze	15	15
681	20k. Bishop Joseph du Pont	2·75	2·75
682	50k. Saint Ignatius Loyola	4·50	6·50

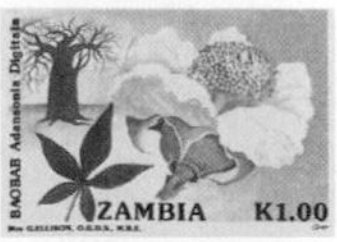

168 "Adansonia digitata"

1991. Flowering Trees. Multicoloured.

683	1k. Type **168**	20	10
684	2k. "Dichrostachys cinerea"	30	15
685	10k. "Stereospermum kunthianum"	1·75	1·40
686	30k. "Azana garckeana"	3·25	4·50

No. 685 is inscribed "Sterospermum" in error.

1992. 40th Anniv of Queen Elizabeth II's Accession. As T **168a** of St. Helena. Multicoloured.

687	4k. Queen's House	10	10
688	32k. Traditional village	1·00	70
689	35k. Fisherman hauling nets	1·00	90
690	38k. Three portraits of Queen Elizabeth	1·25	1·25
691	50k. Queen Elizabeth II	1·60	2·75

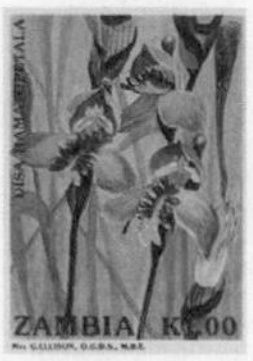

169 "Disa hamatopetala"

1992. Orchids. Multicoloured.

692	1k. Type **169**	50	15
693	2k. "Eulophia paivaeana"	50	20
694	5k. "Eulophia quartiniana"	85	40
695	20k. "Aerangis verdickii"	3·50	5·00

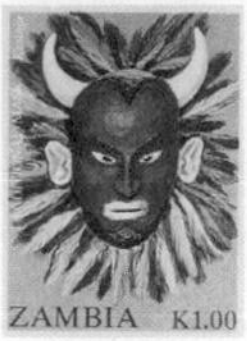

170 Kasinja Mask

1992. Tribal Masks. Multicoloured.

696	1k. Type **170**	25	30
697	2k. Chizaluke	30	30
698	10k. Mwanapweu	1·25	70
699	30k. Maliya	3·00	4·75

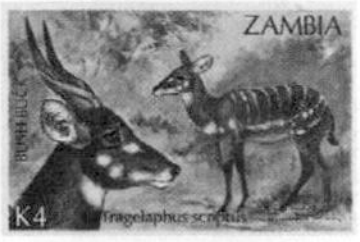

171 Bushbuck

1992. Antelopes. Multicoloured.

700	4k. Type **171**	25	60
701	40k. Eland	1·25	60
702	45k. Roan antelope	1·25	60
703	100k. Sable antelope	2·25	5·50

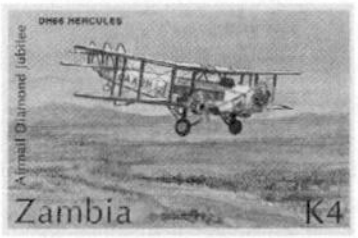

172 De Havilland D.H.66 Hercules "City of Basra"

1992. 60th Anniv of Airmail Service. Multicoloured.

704	4k. Type **172**	50	50
705	40k. Vickers Super VC-10	2·25	1·00
706	45k. Short S.45A Solent 3 flying boat "Severn"	2·25	1·00
707	100k. Douglas DC-10	3·75	6·50

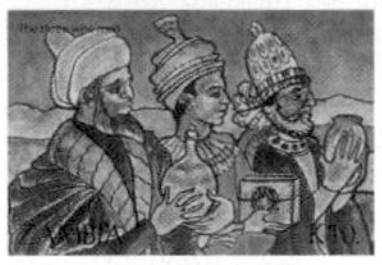
173 Wise Men with Gifts

1992. Christmas. Multicoloured.

708	10k. Type **173**	30	10
709	80k. Nativity	2·00	2·00
710	90k. Angelic choir	2·25	2·50
711	100k. Angel and shepherds	2·25	3·00
MS712	209×57 mm. Nos. 708/11	10·00	12·00

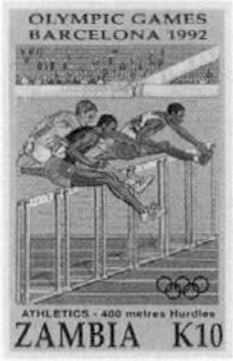

174 Hurdling

1992. Olympic Games, Barcelona. Multicoloured.

713	10k. Type **174**	25	10
714	40k. Boxing	65	40
715	80k. Judo	1·40	2·25
716	100k. Cycling	3·75	4·00

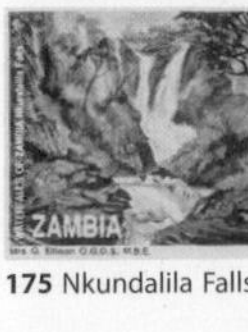

175 Nkundalila Falls

1993. Waterfalls. Multicoloured.

717	50k. Type **175**	60	20
718	200k. Chishimba Falls	1·50	1·50
719	250k. Chipoma Falls	1·75	1·90
720	300k. Lumangwe Falls	1·90	2·25

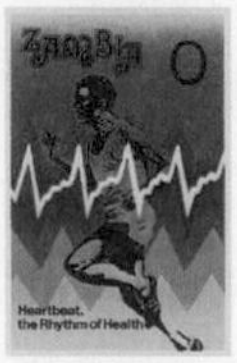

176 Athlete and Cardiograph

1993. Heartbeat Campaign. Multicoloured.

721	(O) Type **176**	1·00	55
722	(P) Heart and cardiograph	1·00	55

These stamps were initially sold at 50k. (No. 721) for ordinary post and 80k. (No. 722) for priority mail. These face values were increased to reflect postage rate increases.

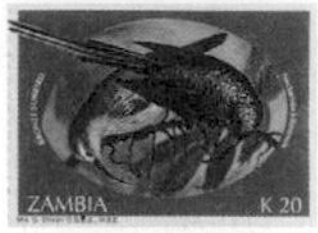

177 Bronze Sunbird

1994. Sunbirds. Multicoloured. (a) Face values as T **177**.

723	20k. Type **177**	45	1·00
724	50k. Violet-backed sunbird	55	50
725	100k. Scarlet-chested sunbird	80	10
726	150k. Bannerman's sunbird	1·00	10
727	200k. Oustalet's white-bellied sunbird	1·00	10
728	250k. Anchieta's sunbird ("Red and blue sunbird")	1·00	20
729	300k. Olive sunbird	1·25	40
730	350k. Green-headed sunbird	1·25	40
731	400k. Red-tufted malachite sunbird	1·25	50
732	500k. Variable sunbird	1·25	50
733	800k. Coppery sunbird	1·50	1·75
734	1000k. Southern orange-tufted sunbird ("Orange-tufted Sunbird")	1·75	2·00
735	1500k. Amethyst sunbird ("Black Sunbird")	2·00	3·00
736	2000k. Green-throated sunbird	2·25	3·50

(b) Face values shown as capital letters.

737	(O) Mariqua sunbird ("Marico Sunbird")	1·25	55
738	(P) Eastern double-collared sunbird	1·25	55

Nos. 737/8 were initially sold at 50k. for ordinary post (No. 737) and 80k. for priority mail (No. 738). These rates were increased to 100k. for ordinary post and 150k. for priority mail on 20th June 1994. On 1 March 1995 the difference between the two rates was abolished and both "O" and "P" stamps were sold at 500k. This was reduced to 400k. each on 1 April 1995, but the rate reverted to 500k. on 8 February 1996.

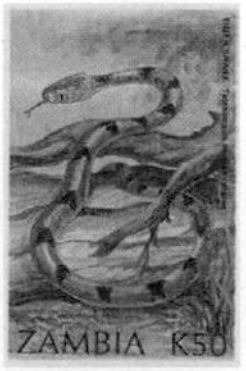

178 Tiger Snake

1994. Snakes. Multicoloured.

739	50k. Type **178**	60	10
740	200k. Egyptian cobra	1·75	65
741	300k. African python	2·00	1·75
742	500k. Green mamba	2·50	4·00

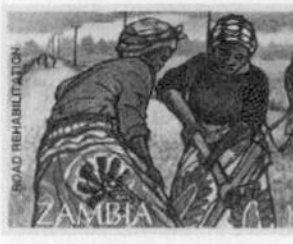

179 Women working on Road

1995. 75th Anniv of I.L.O. Multicoloured.

743	100k. Type **179**	50	20
744	450k. Women making cement blocks	2·00	2·75

180 Angel playing Kalimba and Flowers

1995. Christmas (1994). Multicoloured.

745	100k. Type **180**	45	15
746	300k. Angel at prayer and animals	1·00	60
747	450k. Angel with flute and birds	1·60	2·00
748	500k. Angel with drum and Baobab trees	1·75	2·25

181 Anniversary Emblem, Rainbow and Map

1995. 50th Anniv of United Nations.

749	**181**	700k. multicoloured	2·25	3·25

182 David Livingstone (missionary) and Memorial

1995. Monuments. Multicoloured.

750	100k. Type **182**	30	10
751	300k. Mbereshi Mission	80	60
752	450k. Von Lettow-Vorbeck Monument	1·40	2·00
753	500k. Niamkolo Church	1·50	2·00

183 Saddle-bill Stork

1996. Endangered Species. Birds. Multicoloured.

754	200k. Type **183**	40	20
755	300k. Black-cheeked lovebird	55	35
756	500k. Pair of black-cheeked lovebirds	75	85
757	900k. Saddle-bill stork and chicks	1·00	2·00
MS758	120×90 mm. Nos. 754/7	75·00	75·00

1996. Christmas. Nos. 709/10 surch.

759	(O) on 90k. Angelic choir	50	15
760	900k. on 80k. Nativity	2·50	3·50

No. 759 was sold at 500k., which was the minimum local postage rate for ordinary post.

185 "Precis octavia sesamus"

1997. Butterflies and Moths. Multicoloured.

761	300k. Type **185**	1·50	30
762	500k. "Argema mimosae"	1·75	40
763	700k. "Imbrasia dione"	2·50	2·75
764	900k. "Papilio ophidicephalus cotterell"	4·00	4·50
MS765	85×120 mm. As Nos. 761/4, but each with face value of 900k.	15·00	16·00

1997. Nos. 688/90 surch.

766	(O) on 32k. Traditional village	2·50	55
767	500k. on 35k. Fishermen hauling nets	2·50	70
768	900k. on 38k. Three portraits of Queen Elizabeth	5·00	5·50

No. 766 was sold at 500k. which was the minimum local postage rate for ordinary post.

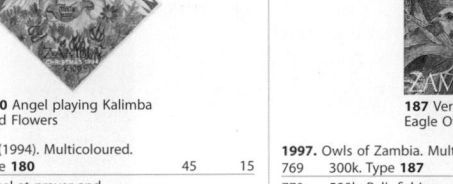

187 Verreaux's Eagle Owl

1997. Owls of Zambia. Multicoloured.

769	300k. Type **187**	1·25	50
770	500k. Pel's fishing owl	2·25	60
771	700k. Barn owl	3·00	2·75
772	900k. Spotted eagle owl	4·00	4·50
MS773	128×85 mm. As Nos. 769/72, but each with face value of 900k.	10·00	11·00

188 Gandhi as Law Student, London, 1888

1998. 50th Death Anniv of Mahatma Gandhi. Multicoloured.

774	250k. Type **188**	1·50	80
775	(O) Gandhi at Red Fort, Delhi	2·50	1·50
776	500k. Gandhi with Nehru, 1946 (horiz)	2·50	1·50
777	900k. Gandhi at prayer	4·00	4·50
MS778	70×100 mm. 2000k. At Second Round Table Conference, London, 1931	7·00	8·00

No. 775 was sold at 500k. which was the minimum local postage rate for ordinary post.

189 Map of Zambia

1998. 18th Anniv of Pan African Postal Union.

779	**189**	(O) multicoloured	1·50	55
780	-	500k multicoloured	1·50	55
781	-	900k. black, red and orange	2·00	2·75

DESIGNS: 500k. Lechwe at Kafue Flats; 900k. Dove with "18th" note in beak.

No. 779 was sold at 500k. which was the minimum local postage rate for ordinary post.

190 Traveller and Dog ("Luchele nganga")

1998. Christmas. Traditional Stories. Multicoloured.

782	300k. Type **190**	1·25	30
783	500k. Man feeding crocodile ("Kasuli")	1·50	70
MS784	111×70 mm. 2000k. Type **190**; 2000k. As 500k.	7·00	8·00

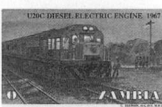

191 "U20C" Diesel-electric Locomotive, 1967

1999. Trains. Multicoloured.

785	(O) Type **191**	60	30
786	800k. Beyer-Garratt Class 15A No. 401 steam locomotive, 1950	1·50	1·75
787	800k. Class 7 No. 70 steam locomotive, 1900	1·50	1·75
788	900k. Class 20 No. 708 steam locomotive, 1954	1·50	1·75
789	900 k . H.P. diesel-electric railcar, 1966	1·50	1·75
MS790	112×85 mm. 1000k. Class 7 No. 955 steam locomotive, 1892	2·00	3·00

1999. No. 743 surch **K500**.

791	500k. on 100k. Type **179**	4·00	1·25

193 Conference Emblem and Dam

1999. 11th International Conference on AIDS and STDs in Africa, Lusaka. Multicoloured.

792	500k. Type **193**	1·75	50
793	900k. Conference emblem and Victoria Falls	2·50	2·75

194 Blacksmith Plover

1999. Water Birds. Multicoloured.

794	50k. Type **194**	15	30
795	100k. Sacred ibis	25	30
796	200k. Purple swamphen ("Purple Gallinule")	35	35
797	250k. Purple heron	40	40
798	300k. Glossy ibis	40	40
799	400k. Marabou stork	50	50
800	450k. African spoonbill	50	50
801	500k. Peter's finfoot ("African Finfoot")	50	20
802	(O) Comb duck ("Knob-billed Duck")	50	20
803	600k. African darter	50	20
804	700k. African skimmer	3·00	65
805	800k. Spur-winged goose	50	35
806	900k. Hammerkop	50	35
807	1000k. Eastern white pelican	3·00	2·00
808	1500k. Black-winged stilt	4·00	3·25
809	2000k. Black-crowned night heron	1·00	1·25

No. 802 was sold at 500k. which was the minimum local postage rate for ordinary post.

No. 794 is inscribed "Sarkidiomis melamotos" and No. 805 "Plectroterus gambensis", both in error.

2000. No. 750 surch **K700**.

813	700k. on 100k. Type **182**	5·00	1·75

2000. Nos. 774 and 776 surch **K1,200**.

814	1200k. on 250k. Type **188**	6·00	4·00
815	1500k. on 500k. Gandhi with Nehru 1946 (horiz)	6·00	4·50

No. 775 was re-issued with Nos. 814/15 and sold at 700k.

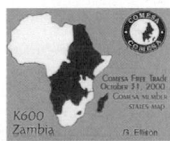

197 Map of Africa showing COMESA Member States

2000. Common Market for Eastern and Southern Africa (COMESA). Multicoloured.

816	600k. Type **197**	1·25	45
817	700k. Truck crossing free trade border	1·50	80
818	1000k. Exchange of money and sale of goods at border	1·75	2·00

198 "Creation in Clay"

2000. African Legends of Creation. Multicoloured.

819	600k. Type **198**	75	25
820	1000k. "The Chameleon and the Lizard"	1·25	1·00
821	1400k. "Why the Stones do not Die"	1·50	2·00
MS822	128×125 mm. As Nos. 819/21, but with brown borders, each ×3	6·50	8·00
MS823	90×70 mm. 3500k. "The Rooster in the Sky"	4·50	5·50

199 Feeding Refugee Children

2001. 50th Anniv of United Nations High Commissioner for Refugees. Multicoloured.

824	700k. Type **199**	65	40
825	1500k. Refugees fleeing from conflict	1·25	2·00

200 African Buffalo

2001. Animals of Africa. Multicoloured.

826	500k. Type **200**	45	15
827	1000k. Cheetah (vert)	70	65
828	2000k. African elephant	2·25	2·00
829	3200k. Ruffed lemur (vert)	2·25	2·75
MS830	145×78 mm. 2000k. Cheetah; 2000k. Three adult and one young Impala; 2000k. Four adult impala; 2000k. Warthog; 2000k. Two lionesses; 2000k. Four lionesses	5·50	6·50
MS831	74×165 mm. 2000k. Crimson-breasted shrike; 2000k. European bee eater ("Common Bee Eater"); 2000k. Blue monkey; 2000k. Chimpanzee; 2000k. Lesser bushbaby; 2000k. Small-spotted genet (all vert)	5·50	6·50
MS832	145×78 mm. 2000k. Defussa waterbuck; 2000k. Crowned crane; 2000k. Hartebeest; 2000k. Pygmy hippopotamus; 2000k. White rhinoceros; 2000k. Giant forest hog	5·50	6·50
MS833	Three sheets, each 85×62 mm. (a) 6000k. African elephant. (b) 6000k. Grevy's zebra. (c) 6000k. Black rhinoceros Set of 3 sheets	7·50	8·50

201 Woman watching Eclipse

2001. Solar Eclipse of 21 June 2001. Multicoloured.

834	1000k. Type **201**	60	30
835	1500k. Stylized bird	80	70
836	1700k. Chameleon watching eclipse	80	1·10
837	1800k. Hand holding spear and elephant	90	1·40
838	2200k. Man with spear watching eclipse	1·10	1·75

202 "Sanjo Kantaro II and Ichikawa Monnosuke I, 1720s" (Okumura Masanobu)

2001. "Philanippon '01" International Stamp Exhibition, Tokyo. Japanese Art. Multicoloured (except No. 841).

839	500k. Type **202**	30	35
840	500k. "Nakamura Senya as Toknatsu" (Torii Kiyomasu I)	30	35
841	1000k. "Standing Figure of a Woman" (Torii Kiyomasu I) (black, green and brown)	55	80
842	1000k. "Sanjo Kantaro and Ichikawa Monosuke, c. 1730" (Masanobu)	55	80
843	1500k. "Ono no Komachii?" (Masanobu)	80	1·10
844	1800k. "Dog bringing a Love Letter" (Shigenaga)	90	1·40
MS845	140×94 mm. 3200k. "Nakamura Kumetaro I" (Shunsho); 3200k. "Actor in Female Role" (Kiyomasu I); 3200k. "Segawa Kikunojo leaning on Sugoroku Board" (Kiyomasu I); 3200k. "Ichikawa Gennosuke as a Wakashu" (Kiyomasu I)	4·50	5·50
MS846	140×94 mm. 3200k. "Nakamura Matsue as a Cat Woman" (Shunsho); 3200k. "Sanjo Kantaro with Branch of Bamboo" (Kiyomasu I); 3200k. "Yamashika Kinsaku I as Peddler" (Torii Kiyomasu I); 3200k. "Portrait of an Actor" (Shunsho)	4·50	5·50
MS847	Two sheets. (a) 6000k. "Akashi of the Tamaya" (Hishikawa Ryukoku). (b) 6000k. "Events of Year in the Floating World" (Moroshige) (horiz) Set of 2 sheets	4·50	5·50

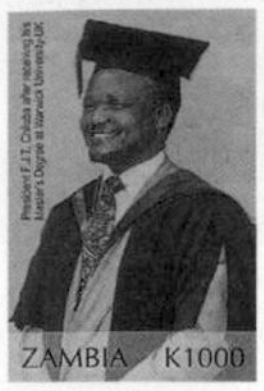

203 President Chiluba receiving Master's Degree, Warwick University

2001. Frederick Chiluba (President of Zambia, 1991–2002). Multicoloured.

848	1000k. Type **203**	60	30
849	1500k. President Chiluba signing affidavit for second term of office, 1996	85	85
850	1700k. President after PHI Housing Empowerment of the people (horiz)	1·25	1·50
MS851	73×98 mm. 6000k. President receiving Master's Degree	3·00	4·00

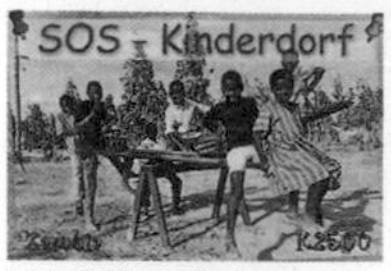

204 Children playing

2001. SOS Children's Villages (Kinderdorf International).

852	**204**	2500k. multicoloured	1·50	2·00

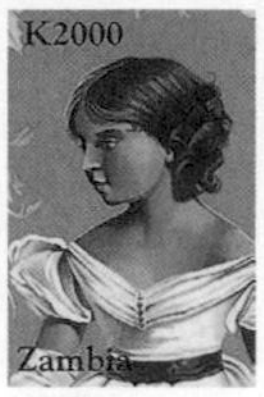

205 Princess Victoria as Young Girl

2001. Death Centenary of Queen Victoria. T **205** and similar vert designs. Multicoloured.

MS853	2000k. Type **205**; 2000k. Queen Victoria as widow; 2000k. With baby daughter; 2000k. With Prince Albert; 2000k. After being crowned Empress of India, 1876; 2000k. Princess Victoria as teenager	2·75	3·25
MS854	93×126 mm. 7000k. Young Queen Victoria	1·90	2·00

2001. 25th Death Anniv of Mao Tse-tung (Chinese leader). As T **102** of St. Kitts. Multicoloured.

MS855	177×183 mm. 3200k. As student, 1918; 3200k. Mao in 1945; 3200k. As guerrilla leader, 1937	2·75	3·25
MS856	132×128 mm. 4000k. Writing	1·00	1·50

2001. 75th Death Anniv of Claude-Oscar Monet (French artist). As T **103** of St. Kitts. Multicoloured.

MS857	136×177 mm. 1500k. "The Promenade at Argenteuil"; 1500k. "View of the Argenteuil Plain from the Sannois Hills"; 1500k. "The Seine at Argenteuil"; 1500k. "The Basin at Argenteuil"	2·00	2·50
MS858	137×110 mm. 6000k. "Rouen Cathedral, Portal, Overcast Weather" (vert)	2·00	2·50

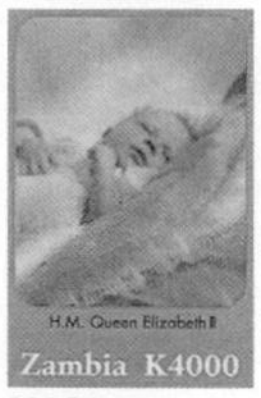

206 Princess Elizabeth as Baby

2001. 75th Birthday of Queen Elizabeth II. Multicoloured.

MS859	157×175 mm. 4000k. Type **206**; 4000k. Princess Elizabeth as schoolgirl; 4000k. As young girl in garden; 4000k. In Women's Army Auxilliary Unit uniform, c. 1942	3·50	4·00
MS860	79×109 mm. 8000k. Queen Elizabeth II as young woman (42×56 mm)	2·25	2·50

2001. Death Centenary of Giuseppe Verdi (Italian composer). As T **105** of St. Kitts showing scenes from Falstaff (opera). Multicoloured.

MS861	160×180 mm. 4000k. Benjamin Luxon as Falstaff (in white shirt); 4000k. Benjamin Luxon as Falstaff (in red and gold); 4000k. Paul Plishka as Falstaff; 4000k. Anne Collin as Mistress Quickly	6·00	6·00
MS862	79×109 mm. 8000k. 19th-century poster for Falstaff	3·00	3·00

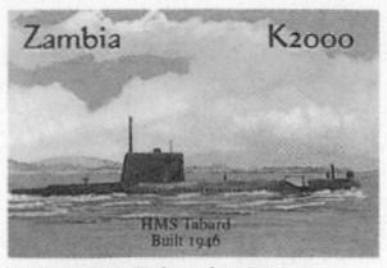

207 HMS *Tabard*, 1946

2001. Centenary of Royal Navy Submarine Service. Submarines. Multicoloured.

MS863	2000k. Type **207**; 2000k. HMS *Opossum*, 1963; 2000k. HMS *Unicorn*, 1992; 2000k. HMS *Churchill*, 1968; 2000k. HMS *Victorious*, 1992; 2000k. HMS *Triumph*, 1982	6·00	7·00
MS864	101×78 mm. 6000k. Lieut-Commander Wanklyn (VC) and crew of HMS *Upholder*, 1941 (vert)	3·25	3·50

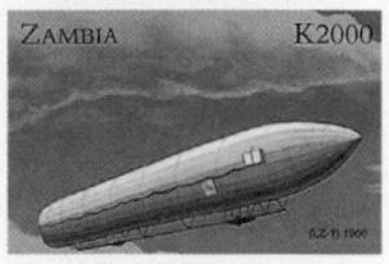

208 LZ-1, 1900

2001. Zeppelins. Multicoloured.

MS865	145×132 mm. 2000k. Type **208**; 2000k. Parseval PL25, 1915; 2000k. LZ-3, 1906; 2000k. Baldwin, 1908; 2000k. LZ-129 *Hindenburg*, 1936; 2000k. *Norge*, 1926	4·50	5·50

2002. "United We Stand". Support for Victims of 11 September 2001 Terrorist Attacks. As T **445** of St. Vincent. Multicoloured.

866	3200k. U.S. flag around Statue of Liberty and Zambian flag	1·00	1·50

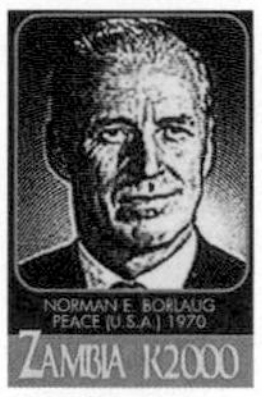

209 Norman Borlaug (USA, 1970)

2002. Centenary of Nobel Prizes. Multicoloured.

MS867	146×210 mm. 2000k. Type **209**; 2000k. Lester B. Pearson (Canada, 1957); 2000k. International Red Cross (1944); 2000k. Anwar Sadat (Egypt, 1978); 2000k. Georges Pire (Belgium, 1958); 2000k. Linus Pauling (USA, 1962)	4·00	5·00
MS868	146×210 mm. 2000k. Seamus Heaney (Ireland, 1995); 2000k. Toni Morrison (USA, 1993); 2000k. Gunter Grass (Germany, 1999); 2000k. Wislawa Szymborska (Poland, 1996); 2000k. Dario Fo (Italy, 1997); 2000k. Jose Saramango (Portugal, 1998)	4·00	5·00
MS869	146×210 mm. 2000k. Isaac Bashevis Singer (USA, 1978); 2000k. Gao Xingjian (China, 2000); 2000k. Claude Simon (France, 1985); 2000k. Naguib Mahfouz (Egypt, 1988); 2000k. Camilo Jose Cela (Spain, 1989); 2000k. Czeslaw Milosz (USA, 1980)	4·00	5·00
MS870	Three sheets, each 106×128 mm. (a) 6000k. George Marshall (Peace, USA, 1953). (b) 6000k. Gerard Debreu (Economics, USA, 1983). (c) 6000k. Robert Fogel (Economics, USA, 1993) Set of 3 sheets	5·00	6·00

No. **MS**868 shows recipients of Nobel Peace Prizes and Nos. **MS**869/70 Literature Prize winners.

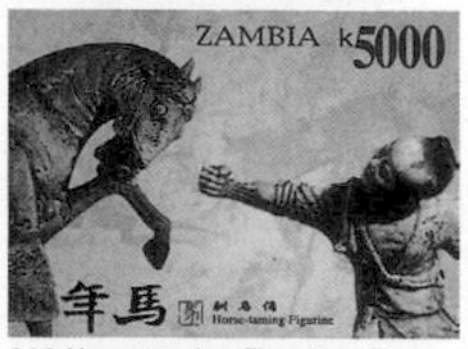

210 Horse-taming Figurines, Tang Dynasty

2002. Chinese New Year ("Year of the Horse"). Sheet 108×76 mm.

MS871	**210** 5000k. multicoloured	1·40	1·75

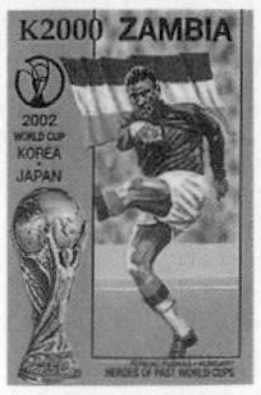

211 Ferenc Puskas (Hungary)

2002. World Cup Football Championship, Japan and Korea (2002). Multicoloured.

MS872	142×164 mm. 2000k. Type **211**; 2000k. Official poster of 1962 World Cup, Chile; 2000k. Spanish player; 2000k. England player; 2000k. Player and Jeonju World Cup Stadium, Korea (57×42 mm)	2·00	2·75
MS873	142×164 mm. 2000k. Official poster of 1954 World Cup, Switzerland; 2000k. Stanley Matthews (England); 2000k. Scotland player; 2000k. Belgian player; 2000k. Player and Daejeon World Cup Stadium, Korea (57×42 mm)	3·00	3·75
MS874	Two sheets, each 70×100 mm. (a) 8000k. Bryan Robson (England) scoring goal against France, 1982 (42×57 mm). (b) 8000k. Salenko (Russia) scoring goal against Cameroon, 1994 (57×42 mm) Set of 2 sheets	4·50	5·50

2002. Nos. 724, 739, 743 and 745 surch.

875	250k. on 50k. Type **178**	40	20
876	300k. on 50k. Violet-backed Sunbird	50	20
877	500k. on 100k. Type **179**	65	20
878	1000k. on 100k. Type **180**	1·25	60

2002. Golden Jubilee. As T **110** of St. Kitts. Multicoloured.

MS879	132×100 mm. 3200k. Queen Elizabeth II disembarking from plane; 3200k. Wearing pink blouse; 3200k. With Prince Edward; 3200k. Wearing tiara	4·00	5·00
MS880	76×108 mm. 7500k. With Duke of Edinburgh in library	2·50	3·00

2002. Winter Olympic Games, Salt Lake City. As T **111** of St. Kitts. Multicoloured.

881	1000k. Ice hockey	1·00	55
882	3200k. Cross-country skier	1·75	2·00

2002. 20th World Scout Jamboree, Thailand. As T **116** of St. Kitts. Multicoloured.

MS883	153×115 mm. 3200k. Troop hiking; 3200k. Knot tying; 3200k. Archery; 3200k. Fire-making	4·00	5·00
MS884	58×76 mm. 8000k. Scout by campfire (vert)	2·75	3·25

2002. International Year of Mountains. As T **115** of St. Kitts. Multicoloured.

MS885	151×109 mm. 1500k. Mount Whitney, USA; 1500k. Aconcagua, Argentina/Chile border; 1500k. Mönch, Switzerland; 1500k. Mount Ararat, Turkey	2·50	3·00
MS886	74×56 mm. 9000k. Mount Everest, Nepal/China border	3·50	4·00

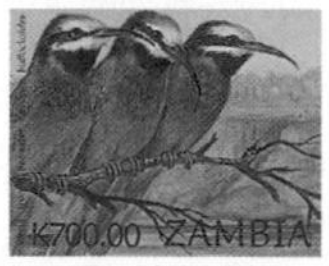

213 White-fronted Bee Eater

2002. Birds of Zambia. Multicoloured. (a) Size 35×28 mm.

887	700k. Type **213**	45	30
888	1200k. Blue-cheeked bee eater	1·50	1·25
889	1400k. Boehm's bee eater	1·50	1·50
890	1500k. Little bee eater	1·60	1·60

(b) Size 25×21 mm.

891	1000k. Type **213**	1·25	65
892	1200k. Little bee eater	1·50	1·25
893	1500k. Blue-cheeked bee eater	1·50	1·50
894	1800k. Boehm's bee eater	1·75	2·00

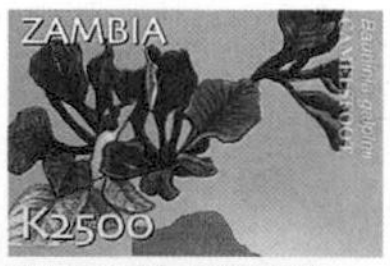

214 Camelsfoot (*Bauhinia galpinii*)

2002. Flowers, Butterflies and Mushrooms of Zambia. Multicoloured.

MS895	120×120 mm. 2500k. Type **214**; 2500k. Christmas bells (*Sandersonia aurantiaca*); 2500k. Impala lily (*Adenium obesum*); 2500k. Everlasting (*Helichrysum ecklonis*); 2500k. *Anomatheca grandiflora*; 2500k. Soldier Lily (*Cyrtanthus obliquus*)	5·00	6·00
MS896	120×120 mm. 2500k. False monarch (*Mimicraea marshalli*); 2500k. Golden piper (*Eurytera dryope*); 2500k. Blue pansy (*Junonia orithya*); 2500k. Christmas treeacraea (*Acraea anemosa*); 2500k. Grass yellow (*Eurema brigitta*); 2500k. Gold-spotted sylph (*Metisella metis*)	5·00	6·00
MS897	120×120 mm. 2500k. Copper trumpet (*Clitocybe olearia*); 2500k. King bolete (*Boletus edulis*); 2500k. Death cap (*Amanita phalloides*); 2500k. Fly agaric (*Amanita muscaria*); 2500k. Chantarelle (*Cantharellus cibarius*); 2500k. Deadly fiber cap (*Inocybe erubescens*)	5·00	6·00
MS898	Three sheets, each 100×70 mm. (a) 8000k. Arum lily (*Zantedeschia aethiopica*). (b) 8000k. African monarch (*Danaus chrysippus*). (c) 8000k. Stump brittle-head (*Psathyrella piluliformis*) Set of 3 sheets	8·50	9·50

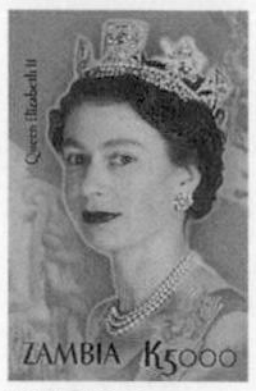

215 Queen Elizabeth II

2003. 50th Anniv of Coronation. Multicoloured.

MS899	156×93 mm. 5000k. Type **215**; 5000k. Wearing tiara and smiling; 5000k.Wearing fuchsia hat and outfit	3·50	4·00
MS900	76×106 mm. 10000k. Wearing floral hat and outfit	3·00	4·00

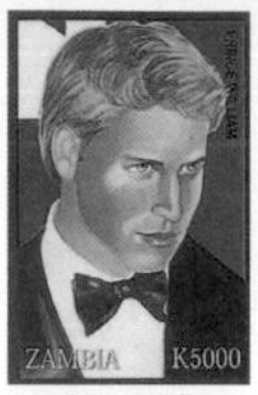

216 Prince William

2003. 21st Birthday of Prince William. Multicoloured.

MS901	157×104 mm. 5000k. Type **216**; 5000k. As young boy; 5000k. Wearing yellow polo neck shirt	3·50	4·00
MS902	68×98 mm. 10000k. Wearing cream round neck jumper and laughing	3·00	4·00

2003. Nos. 754/7 surch **1000k.**

903	1000k. on 200k. Type **183**	7·00	4·00
904	1000k. on 300k. Black-cheeked lovebird	7·00	4·00
905	1000k. on 500k. Pair of black-cheeked lovebirds	7·00	4·00
906	1000k. on 900k. Saddle-bill stork and chicks	7·00	4·00

2003. Nos. 739/42 surch **1700k.**

907	1700k. on 50k. Type **178**	2·25	2·50
908	1700k. on 200k. Egyptian cobra	2·25	2·50
909	1700k. on 300k. African python	2·25	2·50
910	1700k. on 500k. Green mamba	2·25	2·50

2003. Nos. 717/20 surch as **1800k.**

911	1800k. on 50k. Type **175**	2·25	2·50
912	1800k. on 200k. Chishimba Falls	2·25	2·50
913	1800k. on 250k. Chipoma Falls	2·25	2·50
914	1800k. on 300k. Lumangwe Falls	2·25	2·50

2003. Nos. 750/3 surch as **2200k.**

915	2200k. on 100k. Type **182**	2·50	2·75
916	2200k. on 300k. Mbereshi Mission	2·50	2·75
918	2200k. on 500k. Niamkolo Church	2·50	2·75

2003. Nos. 779/81 surch as **2500k.**

919	2500k. on (O) Type **189**	2·75	3·00
920	2500k. on 500k. Lechwe at Kafue Flats	2·75	3·00
921	2500k. on 900k. Dove with "18th" note in beak	2·75	3·00

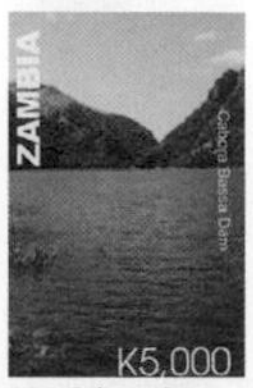

224 Cabora Bassa Dam

2003. United Nations International Year of Freshwater. Multicoloured.

MS922	(a) 147×85 mm. 5000k.×3, Type **224**; Lake Kariba; Mana Pools National Park. (b) 97×67 mm. 10000k. Victoria Falls	7·00	8·00

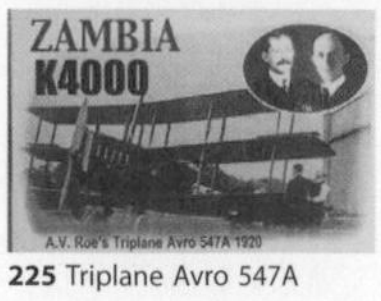

225 Triplane Avro 547A

2003. Centenary of Powered Flight. Planes of A. V. Roe. Multicoloured.

923	4000k. Type **225**	1·90	2·25
924	4000k.50 40 with floats	1·90	2·25
925	4000k. Avro 584 Avrocet	1·90	2·25
926	4000k. Avro 504M	1·90	2·25
MS927	106×76 mm. 9000k. Avro No. 621 Tutor Replica	4·75	5·50

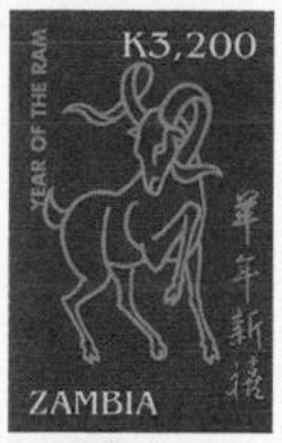

226 Stylised Ram

2003. Chinese New Year ("Year of the Ram").

928	**226**	3200k. green, orange and deep green; mauve, orange and ultramarine; orange and lake; violet; rose and orange	5·50	6·50

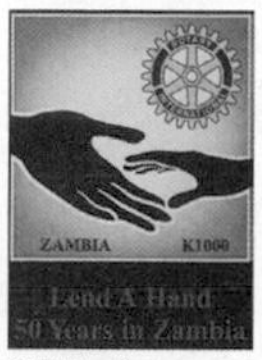

227 Hands

2003. 50th Anniv of Rotary International (humanitarian organisation).

932	**227**	1000k. multicoloured	1·25	1·00
933	-	1200k. red; lemon and ultramarine	1·50	1·50

DESIGNS: No. 932, Type **227**; 933, Rotary International emblem.

2004. First Joint Issue of Southern Africa Postal Operators Association Members. Sheet 170×95 mm containing hexagonal designs as T **470a** of South Africa showing national birds of Association members. Multicoloured.

MS934	500k. Two African fish eagles perched (Zimbabwe); 750k. Cattle egret (Botswana); 1000k. Two African fish eagles in flight (Zambia); 1100k. Peregrine falcon (Angola); 1500k. Bar-tailed trogon (Malawi) (inscribed "apaloderma vittatum"); 1700k. African fish eagle (Namibia); 1800k. Purple-crested turaco ("Lourie") (Swaziland); 2200k. Stanley ("Blue") crane (South Africa)	8·00	9·00

The stamp depicting the Bar-tailed Trogon is not inscribed with the country of which the bird is a national symbol. Miniature sheets of similar designs were also issued by Namibia, Zimbabwe, Angola, Botswana, Swaziland, Malawi and South Africa.

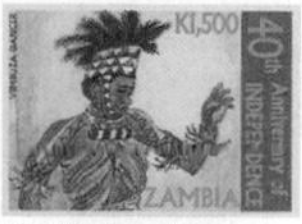

228 Vimbuza Dancer

2004. 40th Anniv of Independence. Multicoloured.

935	1500k. Type **228**	85	50
936	1800k. Kayowe dancer	90	60
937	2700k. Ngoma dancer	1·40	1·75
938	3300k. Ukishi Dancer	1·75	2·25

2004. No. 749 surch **1000k**.

939	1000k. on 700k. Type **181**	1·75	70

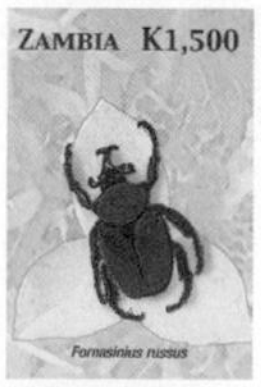

230 *Fornasinius russus*

2005. Beetles. Multicoloured.

940	1500k. Type **230**	75	50
941	2250k. *Macrorhina*	1·40	1·75
942	2250k. *Goliathus giganteus*	1·40	1·75
943	2700k. *Chelorrhina polyphemus*	1·75	2·25
MS944	145×125 mm. 3300k.×4, *Sternotomis virescens* and *Sternotomis cava*; *Cicindela regalis*; *Goliathus meleagris*; *Mecosasms explanta*	8·50	10·00
MS945	66×98 mm. 10000k. *Meloid*	6·50	8·00

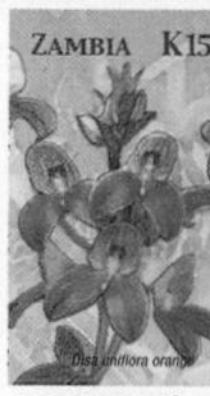

231 *Disa Uniflora* orange

2005. Orchids. Multicoloured.

946	1500k. Type **231**	1·50	1·50
947	1500k. *Disa draconis*	1·50	1·50
948	1500k. *Disa uniflora*(red petals)	1·50	1·50
949	2700k. *Phalaenopsis penetrate*	2·75	3·25
MS950	145×125 mm. 3300k.×4, *Ansellia Africana* (yellow petals); *Ansellia africana* (speckled petals); *Cattelya lueddemanniana*; *Laelia tenebrosa*	8·50	9·50
MS951	72×102 mm. 10000k. *Cymbidium*	7·50	8·50

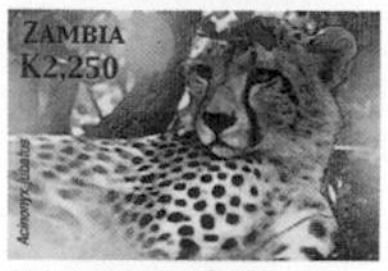

232 *Acinonyx Jubatus*

2005. Mammals. Multicoloured.

952	2250k. Type **232**	2·00	2·25
953	2250k. *Giraffa camelopardalis*	2·00	2·25
954	2250k. *Phacochoerus aethiopicus*	2·00	2·25
955	2700k. *Syncerus caffer*	2·25	2·50
MS956	145×125 mm. 3300k.×4, *Panthera pardus* (vert); *Pan troglodytes* (vert); *Lycaon pictus* (vert); *Equus burchelli* (vert)	8·00	9·00
MS957	67×96 mm. 10000k. *Diceros bicornis* (vert)	9·00	9·50

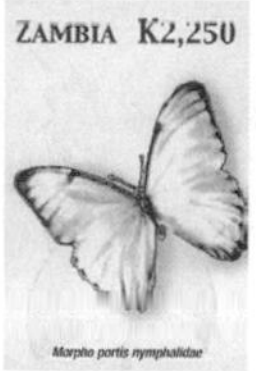

233 *Morpho Portis Nymphalidae*

2005. Butterflies and Moths. Multicoloured.

958	2250k. Type **233**	2·00	2·00
959	2250k. *Ropalo ceres*	2·00	2·00
960	2250k. *Phyllocnistis citrella*	2·00	2·00
961	2700k. *H. misippus*	2·50	2·50
MS962	144×125 mm. 3300k.×4, *Colotis evippe*; *Papilio lormieri*; *Papilio dardanus*; *Papilio zalmoxis*	9·00	10·00
MS963	72×106 mm. 10000k. *Epiphora albida druce*	8·00	9·00

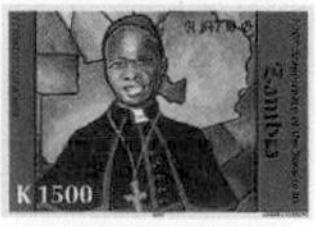

234 Bishop Paul Lungu

2005. Centenary of the Jesuits in Zambia. Multicoloured.

964	1500k. Type **234**	1·60	1·10
965	2550k. Father Torrend, Kasisi Church	2·25	2·75
966	2700k. Father Moreau, Chikuni Church	2·75	3·25
967	3300k. Saint Ignatius Loyola	3·00	3·50
MS968	102×75 mm. Nos. 964/7	8·75	10·00

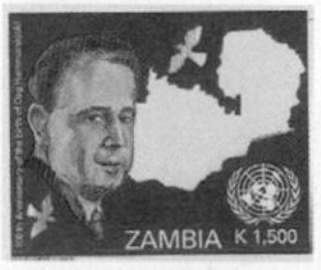

235 Dag Hammarskjold

2005. Birth Centenary of Dag Hammarskjold (Swedish diplomat, Secretary of UN and winner of Nobel Peace Prize, 1961). Background colours given.

969	**235**	1500k. ultramarine	1·60	1·10
970	**235**	2700k. green	2·75	3·50
MS971		108×80 mm. Nos. 969/70	2·40	2·50

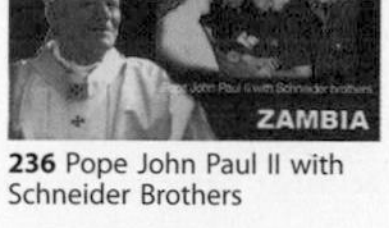

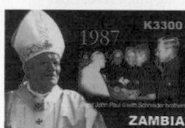

236 Pope John Paul II with Schneider Brothers

2005. Pope John Paul II Commemoration. Multicoloured.

972	3300k. With Sri Chinmoy	4·00	4·00
973	3300k. With boy and dove	4·00	4·00
974	3300k. Type **236**	4·00	4·00
975	3300k. Visiting Ukraine	4·00	4·00
976	7000k. With Jimmy Carter	9·00	9·00

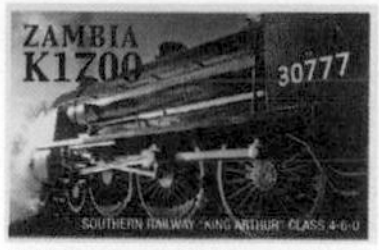

237 Southern Railways "King Arthur" Class

2005. Bicentenary of Steam Locomotives. Multicoloured.

977	1700k. Type **237**; Berkshire at Kaiman's Bridge; Indian Railways WT Class suburban tank steam locomotive; Steel cylinder ("railway builders"); Railway carriage under construction; New locomotive in factory; New train in factory; New railway carriage in factory; New steam locomotive in factory	12·00	14·00
986	1700k. Great Western Railway Hall Class; Argentinian 15B class; Mallet metre gauge steam locomotive, East Germany; Track repairs; Overhead cable repairs; Maintaining signals from mobile crane; Ground crew, two overhead crews and vehicle; Maintainance crew; Working on tracks	12·00	14·00
995	1700k. British Rail Class 4MT; South African Railways Class 12A; Cuban sugar plantation steam locomotive; LNER A4 Pacific (in wooded cutting); LNER A4 Pacific (in city); GWR City of Truro; British Railways HST Intercity 125; Eurostar; LNER A3 *Flying Scotsman*	12·00	14·00
1004	4200k. Chinese Class KF; Indian Class WP; Irish 800 Class; French 241A Class	12·00	14·00
MS1008	Four sheets, each 100×70 mm. (a) 8000k. Finnish Class Hv2. (b) 8000k. Interior of *Orient Express*. (c) 8000k. Edinburgh to London Intercity train. (d) 8000k. Bernina [illegible]	20·00	20·00

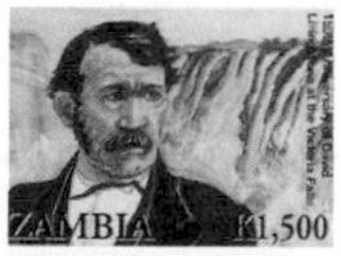

238 David Livingstone and Victoria Falls

2006. 150th Anniv of Discovery of Victoria Falls by David Livingstone (explorer). Multicoloured.

1009	1500k. Type **238**	2·00	1·10
1010	2700k. David Livingstone and steam train on Rail Bridge	4·00	4·50

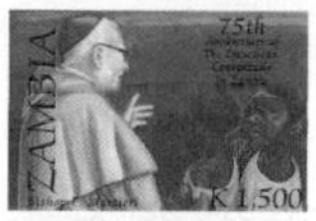

239 Bishop Mazzieri with Boys

2006. 75th Anniv of the Franciscan Conventuals in Zambia. Multicoloured.

1011	1500k. Type **239**	1·60	1·10
1012	2250k. "Sister Moon"	2·25	2·50
1013	2700k. "Brother Sun"	2·75	3·25
1014	3300k. "Sister Water"	3·00	3·75

2006. 80th Birthday of Queen Elizabeth II. As T **159** of St. Kitts. Multicoloured.

1015	3200k. Wearing diadem, c. 1955	4·00	4·00
1016	3200k. Queen Elizabeth, c. 1955	4·00	4·00
1017	3200k. Princess Elizabeth	4·00	4·00
1018	3200k. With baby Princess Anne	4·00	4·00
MS1019	120×120 mm. 6500k. Wearing green hat and coat, c. 2000	8·00	8·50

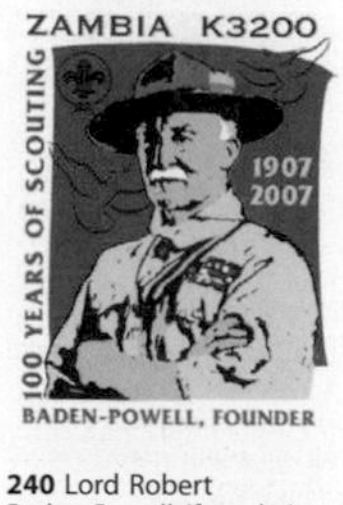

240 Lord Robert Baden-Powell (founder)

2006. Centenary (2007) of World Scouting. Multicoloured.

1020	3200k. Type **240**	4·00	4·00
1021	3200k. As Type **240** (orange and lemon background)	4·00	4·00
1022	3200k. As Type **240** (light blue and blue background)	4·00	4·00
1023	3200k. As Type **240** (green and light green background)	4·00	4·00
MS1024	110×80 mm. 6500k. Lord Baden-Powell and scout emblem (horiz)	8·00	8·50

2007. Nos. 889 and 892 surch.

1025	1500k. on 1200k. Little bee-eater (No. 892)	3·00	1·60
1026	3300k. on 1400k. Boehm's bee-eater (No. 889)	6·00	3·75

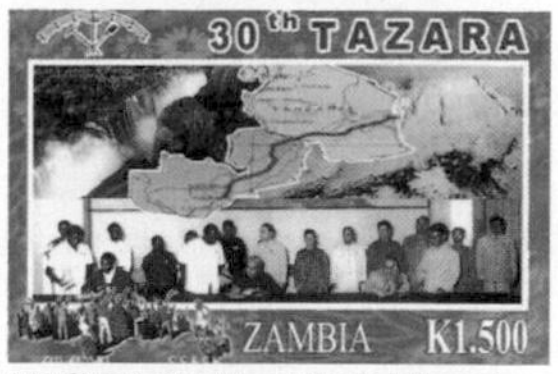

243 Signatories, Map, Victoria Falls and Mount Kilimanjaro

2007. 30th Anniv of TAZARA Railways (2006). Multicoloured.

1027	1500k. Type **243**	2·25	2·25
1028	1500k. Kenneth Kaunda (Zambian President) and Julius Nyerere (Tanzanian Prime Minister) at inauguration, 1975	2·25	2·25
1029	1500k. TAZARA Headquarters, Dar-es-Salaam, Tanzania	2·25	2·25
1030	1500k. New Kapiri Mposhi railway station	2·25	2·25
1031	1500k. Train on viaduct	2·25	2·25
1032	1500k. Train on river bridge	2·25	2·25

Stamps in similar designs were issued by Tanzania.

2007. No. 723 surch.

1033	1850k. on 20k. Type **177**	3·50	4·00

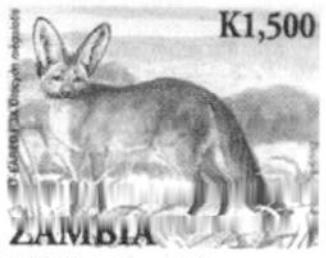

245 Bat-eared Fox

2007. Animals of Zambia. Multicoloured.

1034	1500k. Type **245**	1·75	1·00
1035	2250k. Spotted hyaena	2·75	2·75
1036	2700k. Aardwolf	3·25	3·50
1037	3300k. Side-striped jackal	4·25	4·75
MS1038	143×110 mm. Nos. 1034/7	11·00	12·00

2007. Second Joint Issue of Southern Africa Postal Operators Association Members. Designs as T **236** of Zimbabwe showing national mammals of association members. Multicoloured.

1039	1500k. Buffalo (Zambia)	1·75	1·00
1040	1800k. Nyala (Malawi)	2·00	2·00
1041	2250k. Nyala (Zimbabwe)	2·75	2·75
1042	2700k. Burchell's zebra (Botswana)	3·25	3·50
1043	3300k. Oryx (Namibia)	4·25	4·75
MS1044	135×170 mm. Nos. 1039/43	13·00	14·00

Miniature sheets of similar designs were also issued by Botswana, Malawi, Nambia and Zimbabwe. Botswana also issued sheet stamps.

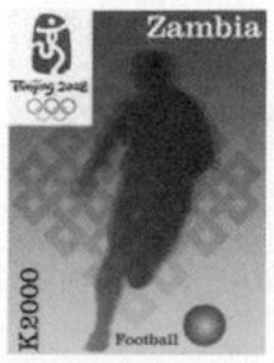

246 Football

2008. Olympic Games, Beijing. Multicoloured.

1045	2000k. Type **246**	2·10	2·25
1046	2000k. Hurdles	2·10	2·25
1047	2000k. Boxing	2·10	2·25
1048	2000k. Swimming	2·10	2·25

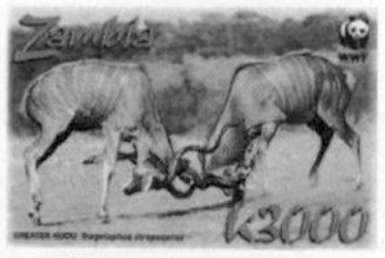

247 Greater Kudu Males fighting

2008. Endangered Species. Greater Kudu (Tragelaphus strepsiceros). Multicoloured.

1049	3000k. Type **247**	3·00	3·25
1050	3000k. Female with suckling calf	3·00	3·25

1051	3000k. Male drinking	3·00	3·25
1052	3000k. Head of female	3·00	3·25
MS1053	115×168 mm. Nos. 1049/52, each ×2	17·00	19·00

2008. No. 821 surch.

1054	1500k. on 1400k. Why the Stones do not Die	4·00	3·50

2009. No. 933 surch.

1055	1500k. on 1200k. orange-red, lemon and ultramarine	1·75	1·75

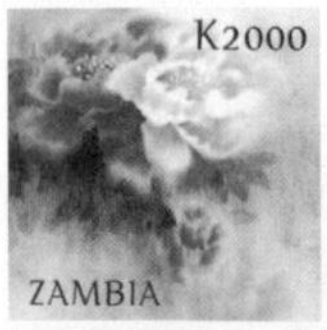

250 Peonies

2009. China 2009 World Stamp Exhibition, Luoyang.

1056	**250**	2000k. multicoloured	2·25	2·50

2009. Nos. 894 and 1035 surch.

1057	1500k. on 1800k. Boehm's bee-eater	2·25	1·75
1058	3300k. on 2250k. Spotted hyaena	3·75	4·00

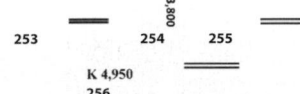

K 3,500 **253**

K3,800 **254**

K 4,050 **255**

K 4,950 **256**

2009. Nos. 937, 969, 1010 and 1036 surch with T **253/6**

1059	3500k. on 2700k. Type **235**	2·50	2·50
1060	3800k. on 2700k. Ngoma dancer	2·50	2·50
1061	4050k. on 2700k. David Livingstone and steam train on Rail Bridge	2·50	2·50
1062	4950k. on 2700k. Aardwolf	2·50	2·50

2010. Third Joint Issue of Southern Africa Postal Operators Association Members. Multicoloured.

1063	2500k. Zambia	1·40	1·50
1064	4050k. Namibia	2·00	2·25
1065	4950k. South Africa	2·40	2·50
MS1066	188×167 mm. 900k. Lesotho; 1000k. Mauritius; 2050k. Botswana; 2250k. Zimbabwe; 2500k. As No. 1063; 3500k. Malawi; 3800k. Swaziland; 4050k. As No. 1064; 4950k. As No. 1065	6·75	6·75

Similar miniature sheets were issued by Botswana, Lesotho, Malawi, Mauritius, Namibia, South Africa, Swaziland and Zimbabwe.

K2.500 B

257

2010. No. 811B surch with T **257**. Multicoloured.

1067	2500k. (B)on Sacred ibis	3·25	3·25

POSTAGE DUE STAMPS

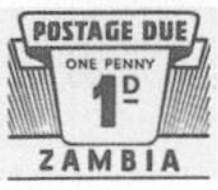

D3

1964

D11	**D3**	1d. orange	35	2·50
D12	**D3**	2d. blue	35	2·50
D13	**D3**	3d. lake	45	1·75
D14	**D3**	4d. blue	45	2·25
D15	**D3**	6d. purple	45	2·25
D16	**D3**	1s. green	55	4·25

APPENDIX

The following stamps have either been issued in excess of postal needs, or have not been made available to the public in reasonable quantities at face value.

1984

Olympic Games, Los Angeles. 90n.×5, each embossed on gold foil.

1987

Classic Cars 1k.50×25, each embossed on gold foil.

The following issues are reported by the Zambia Postal Services Corporation as being available from Philatelic Counters only.

1997

Disney's Chinese New Year. 250, 400, 500k.×7, 600, 750, 1000k.
Endangered Species. 500k.×6, 1000k.×6
Trains of the World. 200, 300, 500k.×7, 900, 1000, 1500k.
Golden Wedding of Queen Elizabeth II and Prince Philip. 500k.×6.
50th Death Anniv of Paul P. Harris (founder of Rotary International). 1000k.
"Pacific '97" International Stamp Exhibition, San Francisco. Death Centenary of Heinrich von Stephan (founder of the U.P.U.). 1000k.×3.
Christmas. Religious Paintings. 50k.×2, 100k.×2, 500, 1000k.

1998

Diana, Princess of Wales Commemoration. 500k.×6, 700k.×6.
Flowers. 500k.×13.
Chinese New Year ("Year of the Tiger"). 700k.×4.
Indian landmarks. 900k.×3.
Indian art. 700k.×4.
World Cup Football Championship, France. 450k.×8, 500k.×16.
Muhamed Ali. 500k.×6.
Parrots, Lories and Cockatoos. 500k.×6, 1000k.×6.
Mushrooms. 250k.×2, 450k.×2, 500k.×2, 900k.×14, 1000k.×2.
Cars. 300k., 500, 900k.×13, 1000k.

1999

Lunar New Year ("Year of the Rabbit"). 700k.×4.
Orchids. 100k.×2, 500k.×2, 900k.×18, 1000k.×2.
China '99 International Stamp Exhibition, Beijing. Hang Daqian Paintings. 500k.×10.
"Queen Elizabeth the Queen Mother's Century". 2000k.×4.
Prehistoric Animals. 50, 100, 500, 900k.×19, 1000, 1800k.
Fauna and Flora. 50, 100, 500k.×5, 700k.×36, 900k., 1000, 1800k.
250th Birth Anniv of Johann von Goethe (German writer). 2000k.×3.
Royal Wedding. 500k., 900k., 1000k.
"iBra '99" International Stamp Exhibition, Nuremberg. 1000, 3200k.
Cats and Dogs. 50, 100k.×2, 500k.×2, 900k.×2, 1000k.×25.
Princess Diana Photomosaic. 1000k.×8.
New Millennium. Events of Second Half of 20th Century. 500k.×18.

2000

"The Stamp Show 2000" International Stamp Exhibition, London. Orchids. 1500k.×22.
Popes of the Millennium. 1500k.×12.
Birds of the World. 400, 500, 600, 700, 800, 100k.×10, 1200k.×9, 1400k.×9, 1500k.×25, 2000, 3000k.

Pt. 1

ZANZIBAR

A Br. Protectorate consisting of several islands off the coast of Tanganyika, E. Africa. Independent in 1963 and a republic within the Br. Commonwealth in 1964. The "United Republic of Tanganyika and Zanzibar" was proclaimed in July 1964, and the country was later renamed Tanzania. Separate issues for Zanzibar ceased on 1 January 1968 and Tanzania stamps became valid for the whole country.

1895. 16 annas = 1 rupee.
1908. 100 cents = 1 rupee.
1936. 100 cents = 1 shilling.

1895. Stamps of India (Queen Victoria) optd **Zanzibar**

3	**23**	½a. turquoise	4·50	4·75
4	**23**	1a. purple	4·75	3·75
5	**23**	1½a. brown	5·00	4·75
6	-	2a. blue	9·00	8·00
8	-	2½a. green	9·00	8·00
10	-	3a. orange	12·00	16·00
12	-	4a. green (No. 96)	21·00	23·00
13	-	6a. brown (No. 80)	20·00	11·00
15	-	8a. mauve	24·00	29·00
16	-	12a. purple on red	18·00	10·00
17	-	1r. grey	£120	90·00
18	**37**	1r. green and red	21·00	38·00
19	**38**	2r. red and orange	£110	£120
20	**38**	3r. brown and green	90·00	£100
21	**38**	5r. blue and violet	95·00	£130

1895. Nos. 4/6 surch **2½**.

23	**23**	2½ on 1a. purple	£180	£100
22	**23**	2½ on 1½a. brown	75·00	55·00
26	-	2½ on 2a. blue	70·00	42·00

1896. Stamps of British East Africa (Queen Victoria) optd **Zanzibar**.

41	**11**	½a. green	42·00	24·00
42	**11**	1a. red	42·00	17·00
43	**11**	2½a. blue	90·00	48·00
44	**11**	4½a. yellow	50·00	60·00
45	**11**	5a. brown	65·00	40·00
46	**11**	7½a. mauve	55·00	65·00

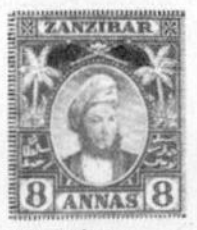

13 Sultan Seyyid Hamed-bin-Thwain

1896. The Rupee values are larger.

178	**13**	½a. green and red	1·50	35
179	**13**	1a. blue and red	5·50	1·25
159	**13**	2a. brown and red	3·75	75
181	**13**	2½a. blue and red	5·00	30
182	**13**	3a. grey and red	7·50	75
183	**13**	4a. green and red	3·75	1·25
184	**13**	4½a. orange and red	15·00	1·00
166	**13**	5a. brown and red	9·00	4·25
167	**13**	7½a. mauve and red	6·50	6·50
187	**13**	8a. olive and red	21·00	2·50
169	-	1r. blue and red	25·00	9·00
171	-	2r. green and red	30·00	9·50
172	-	3r. purple and red	32·00	9·50
173	-	4r. lake and red	25·00	13·00
174	-	5r. brown and red	32·00	13·00

1896. Surch **2½**.

175	2½ on 4a. green and red	90·00	50·00

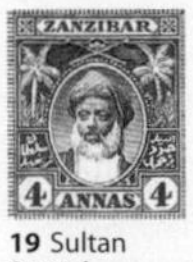

19 Sultan Seyyid Hamoud-bin-Mahommed bin Said

1899. The Rupee values are larger.

188	**19**	½a. green and red	2·75	60
189	**19**	1a. blue and red	4·50	20
190	**19**	1a. red	3·75	20
191	**19**	2a. brown and red	4·50	1·25
192	**19**	2½a. blue and red	4·50	90
193	**19**	3a. grey and red	6·50	3·00
194	**19**	4a. green and red	6·50	3·25
195	**19**	4½a. orange and red	18·00	9·00
196	**19**	4½a. black and red	20·00	14·00
197	**19**	5a. brown and red	6·50	2·75
198	**19**	7½a. mauve and red	6·50	7·00
199	**19**	8a. olive and red	6·50	5·50
200	-	1r. blue and red	23·00	15·00
201	-	2r. green and red	26·00	23·00
202	-	3r. purple and red	45·00	50·00
203	-	4r. lake and red	55·00	70·00
204	-	5r. brown and red	75·00	95·00

1904. Surch in words.

205	**19**	1 on 4½a. orange and red	4·00	6·00
206	**19**	1 on 4½a. black and red	6·00	18·00
207	**19**	2 on 4a. green and red	14·00	18·00
208	**19**	2½ on 7½a. mauve and red	17·00	24·00
209	**19**	2½ on 8a. olive and red	30·00	40·00

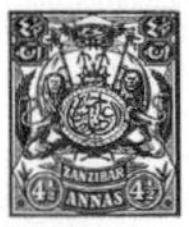

23 Monogram of Sultan Seyyid Ali bin Hamoud bin Naherud

1904. The Rupee values are larger.

210	**23**	½a. green	2·75	50
211	**23**	1a. red	2·75	10
212	**23**	2a. brown	4·75	45
213	**23**	2½a. blue	4·75	35
214	**23**	3a. grey	6·00	2·25
215	**23**	4a. green	4·25	1·60
216	**23**	4½a. black	5·00	2·50
217	**23**	5a. brown	7·00	2·25
218	**23**	7½a. mauve	8·50	8·00
219	**23**	8a. olive	6·00	5·50
220	-	1r. blue and red	38·00	26·00
221	-	2r. green and red	42·00	50·00
222	-	3r. violet and red	60·00	90·00
223	-	4r. deep red and red	65·00	£100
224	-	5r. brown and red	65·00	£100

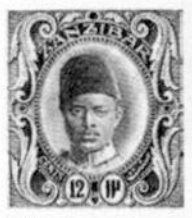

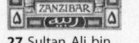

25

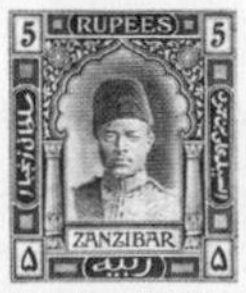

27 Sultan Ali bin Hamoud

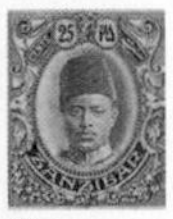

26

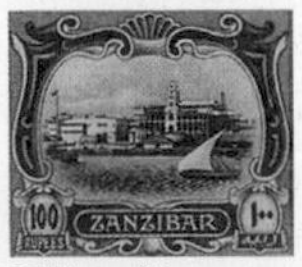

28 View of Port

1908

225	**25**	1c. grey	2·25	30
226	**25**	3c. green	14·00	10
227	**25**	6c. red	11·00	10
228	**25**	10c. brown	7·00	2·25
229a	**25**	12c. violet	15·00	1·25
230	**26**	15c. blue	21·00	40
231	**26**	25c. brown	8·50	1·00
232	**26**	50c. green	11·00	7·50
233	**26**	75c. black	16·00	18·00
234	**27**	1r. green	45·00	12·00
235	**27**	2r. violet	20·00	16·00
236	**27**	3r. bistre	38·00	50·00
237	**27**	4r. red	65·00	95·00
238	**27**	5r. blue	70·00	70·00
239	**28**	10r. green and brown	£200	£350
240	**28**	20r. black and green	£600	£800
241	**28**	30r. black and brown	£700	£1000
242	**28**	40r. black and orange	£900	
243	**28**	50r. black and mauve	£800	
244	**28**	100r. black and blue	£1200	
245	**28**	200r. brown and black	£1600	

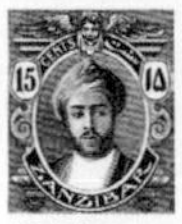

29 Sultan Kalif bin Harub

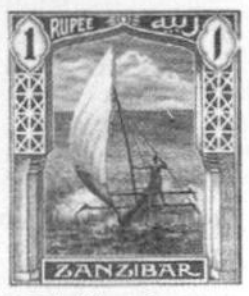

30 Sailing Canoe

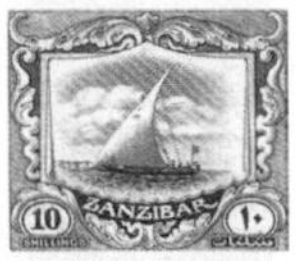

31 Dhow

1913

246	**29**	1c. grey	40	75
247	**29**	3c. green	1·50	75
278	**29**	3c. yellow	40	10
279	**29**	4c. green	60	2·50
280	**29**	6c. red	40	50
281	**29**	6c. purple on blue	45	10
264	**29**	8c. purple on yellow	1·00	7·00
249	**29**	10c. brown	1·25	3·50
265	**29**	10c. green on yellow	85	30
283	**29**	12c. violet	50	30
284	**29**	12c. red	50	40
251	**29**	15c. blue	3·25	50
286	**29**	20c. blue	1·00	30
252	**29**	25c. brown	1·50	2·75
288	**29**	50c. green	3·00	7·00
254	**29**	75c. black	2·75	6·00
270	**30**	1r. green	5·50	3·50
291	**30**	2r. violet	3·50	16·00
292	**30**	3r. bistre	5·00	7·50
293	**30**	4r. red	12·00	48·00
259	**30**	5r. blue	55·00	55·00
260	**31**	10r. green and brown	£200	£400
260b	**31**	20r. black and green	£350	£650
260c	**31**	30r. black and brown	£375	£800
260d	**31**	40r. black and orange	£600	£1000
260e	**31**	50r. black and purple	£600	£1100
260f	**31**	100r. black and blue	£750	
260g	**31**	200r. brown and black	£1100	

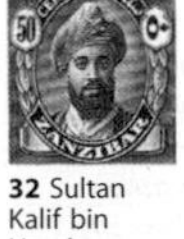

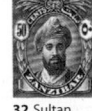

32 Sultan Kalif bin Harub

1926

299	**32**	1c. brown	1·00	10
300	**32**	3c. orange	30	15
301	**32**	4c. green	30	50
302	**32**	6c. violet	30	10
303	**32**	8c. grey	1·00	4·50
304	**32**	10c. olive	1·00	40
305	**32**	12c. red	3·00	10
306	**32**	20c. blue	60	30
307	**32**	25c. purple on yellow	13·00	2·50
308	**32**	50c. red	4·75	35
309	**32**	75c. sepia	32·00	42·00

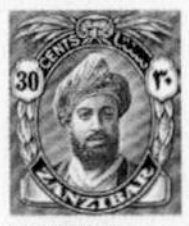

33 Sultan Kalif bin Harub

1936

310	**33**	5c. green	10	10
311	**33**	10c. black	10	10

312	**33**	15c. red	15	1·25
313	**33**	20c. orange	15	10
314	**33**	25c. purple on yellow	15	10
315	**33**	30c. blue	15	10
316	**33**	40c. brown	15	10
317	**33**	50c. red	30	10
318	**30**	1s. green	75	10
319	**30**	2s. violet	3·25	1·75
320	**30**	5s. red	25·00	6·50
321	**30**	7s.50c. blue	42·00	38·00
322	**31**	10s. green and brown	42·00	32·00

In Type **33** the letters of the word "CENTS" are without serifs. In Type **32** they have serifs.

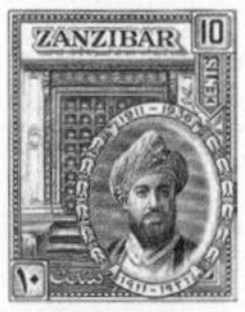

36 Sultan Kalif bin Harub

1936. Silver Jubilee of Sultan.

323	**36**	10c. black and olive	3·25	30
324	**36**	20c. black and purple	4·50	2·75
325	**36**	30c. black and blue	15·00	35
326	**36**	50c. black and orange	15·00	6·50

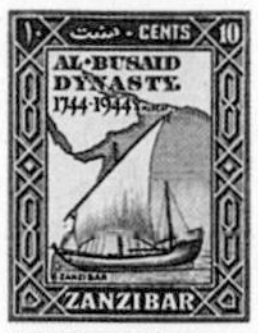

37 "Sham Alam" (Sultan's dhow)

1944. Bicentenary of Al Busaid Dynasty.

327	**37**	10c. blue	1·00	5·50
328	**37**	20c. red	1·50	3·75
329	**37**	50c. green	1·50	30
330	**37**	1s. purple	1·50	1·00

1946. Victory. Optd **VICTORY ISSUE 8TH JUNE 1946**.

331	**33**	10c. black	20	50
332	**33**	30c. blue	30	50

1948. Silver Wedding. As T **33b/c** of St. Helena.

333	20c. orange	30	1·50
334	10s. brown	25·00	40·00

1949. 75th Anniv of U.P.U. As T **33d/g** of St. Helena.

335	20c. orange	30	4·00
336	30c. blue	1·75	2·00
337	50c. mauve	1·00	3·25
338	1s. green	1·00	4·50

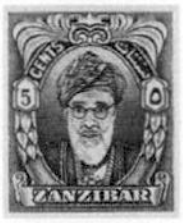

39 Sultan Kalif bin Harub

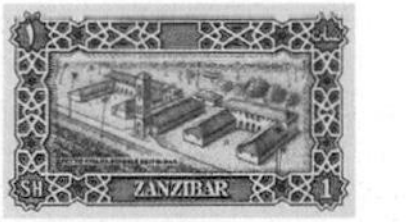

40 Seyyid Khalifa Schools, Beit-el-Ras

1952

339	**39**	5c. black	10	10
340	**39**	10c. orange	10	10
341	**39**	15c. green	2·25	3·25
342	**39**	20c. red	75	70
343	**39**	25c. purple	1·00	10
344	**39**	30c. green	1·00	10
345	**39**	35c. blue	1·00	3·50
346	**39**	40c. brown	1·00	1·25
347	**39**	50c. violet	3·25	10
348	**40**	1s. green and brown	60	10
349	**40**	2s. blue and purple	3·00	2·50
350	**40**	5s. black and red	3·50	7·00
351	**40**	7s.50 black and green	28·00	24·00
352	**40**	10s. red and black	10·00	16·00

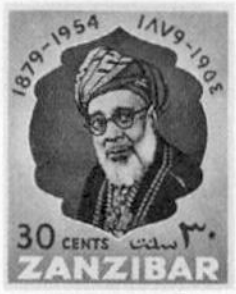

41 Sultan Kalif bin Harub

1954. 75th Birthday of Sultan.

353	**41**	15c. green	10	10
354	**41**	20c. red	10	10
355	**41**	30c. blue	10	10
356	**41**	50c. purple	20	10
357	**41**	1s.25 red	20	75

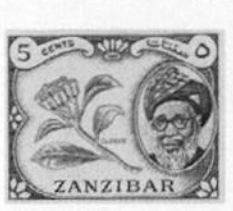

42 Cloves

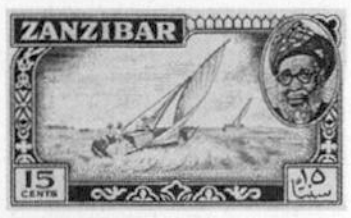

43 "Ummoja Wema" (dhow)

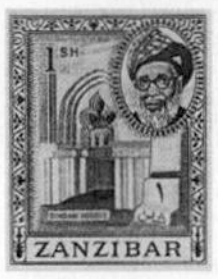

47 Dimbani Mosque

1957

358	**42**	5c. orange and green	10	40
359	**42**	10c. green and red	10	10
360	**43**	15c. green and sepia	30	2·75
361	-	20c. blue	15	10
362	-	25c. brown and black	45	1·25
363	**43**	30c. red and black	20	1·25
364	-	35c. slate and green	45	20
365	-	40c. brown and black	15	10
366	-	50c. blue and myrtle	60	30
367	**47**	1s. red and black	20	30
368	**43**	1s.25 slate and red	3·50	20
369	**47**	2s. orange and green	3·50	2·25
370	-	5s. blue	5·00	2·00
371	-	7s.50 green	16·00	4·00
372	-	10s. red	16·00	6·00

DESIGNS—HORIZ (as Type **47**): 20c. Sultan's Barge; 25, 35, 50c. Map of East African coast. VERT (as Type **47**): 40c. Minaret Mosque. (As Type **43**) 5, 7s.50c., 10s. Kibweni Palace.

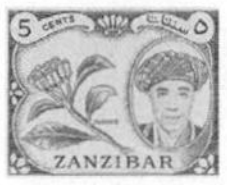

49 Sultan Seyyid Sir Abdulla bin Khalifa

1961. As 1957 issue but with portrait of Sultan Sir Abdulla as in T **49**.

373	5c. orange and green	40	1·25
374	10c. green and red	40	10
375	15c. green and sepia	75	3·75
376	20c. blue	40	30
377	[illegible] and black	[illegible]	[illegible]
378	30c. red and black	3·00	3·00
379	35c. slate and green	3·50	5·50
380	40c. brown and black	40	20
381	50c. blue and myrtle	3·75	10
382	1s. red and black	50	1·50
383	1s.25 slate and red	3·50	7·00
384	2s. orange and green	1·00	3·50
385	5s. blue	3·50	11·00
386	7s.50 green	3·50	20·00
387	10s. red	4·00	12·00
388	20s. sepia (Kibweni Palace)	17·00	28·00

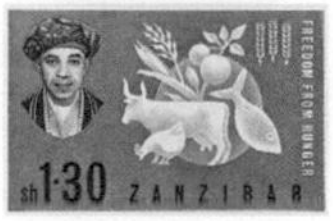

50 "Protein Foods"

1963. Freedom from Hunger.

389	**50**	1s.30 sepia	1·25	75

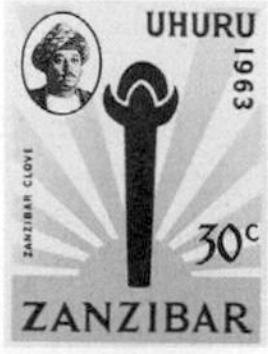

51 Zanzibar Clove

1963. Independence. Inscr "UHURU 1963". Multicoloured.

390	30c. Type **51**	25	1·00
391	50c. "To Prosperity" (Zanzibar doorway)	25	30
392	1s.30 "Religious Tolerance" (mosques and churches)	25	4·00
393	2s.50 "Towards the Light" (Mangapwani Cave)	35	4·75

No. 392 is horiz.

1964. Optd **JAMHURI 1964**. Nos. 373/88.

414	5c. orange and green	10	10
415	10c. green and red	10	10
416	15c. green and sepia	20	10
417	20c. blue	10	10
418	25c. brown and black	30	10
419	30c. red and black	20	10
420	35c. slate and green	30	10
421	40c. brown and black	10	10
422	50c. blue and myrtle	30	10
423	1s. red and black	10	10
424	1s.25 slate and red	2·00	1·75
425	2s. orange and green	50	40
426	5s. blue	50	35
407	7s.50 green	2·00	1·75
408	10s. red	2·00	1·75
429	20s. sepia	2·25	8·00

1964. Optd **JAMHURI 1964**. Nos. 373/88

430	30c. multicoloured	10	10
431	50c. multicoloured	10	10
432	1s.30 multicoloured	10	10
433	2s.50 multicoloured	15	65

NOTE. For the set inscribed "UNITED REPUBLIC OF TANGANYIKA & ZANZIBAR" see Nos. 124/7 of Tanganyika.

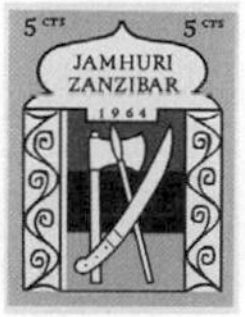

58 Axe, Spear and Dagger

1964. Multicoloured

434	5c. Type **58**	20	10
435	10c. Bow and arrow breaking chains	30	10
436	15c. Type **58**	30	10
437	20c. As 10c.	50	10
438	25c. Zanzibari with rifle	50	10
439	30c. Zanzibari breaking manacles	30	10
440	40c. As 25c.	50	10
441	50c. As 30c.	30	10
442	1s. Zanzibari, flag and sun	30	10
443	1s.30 Hands breaking chains (horiz)	30	1·25
444	2s. Hand waving flag (horiz)	30	30
445	5s. Map of Zanzibar and Pemba on flag (horiz)	1·00	5·00
446	10s. Flag on map	4·75	7·00
447	20s. National flag (horiz)	4·50	25·00

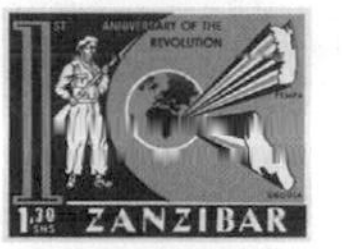

68 Soldier and Maps

1965. First Anniv of Revolution.

448	**68**	20c. light green and green	10	10
449	-	30c. brown and orange	10	10
450	**68**	1s.30 blue and deep blue	10	15
451	-	2s.50 violet and red	10	25

DESIGN—VERT: 30c., 2s.50, Building construction.

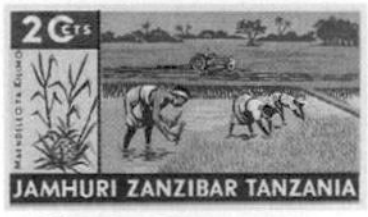

70 Planting Rice

1965. Agricultural Development.

452	**70**	20c. sepia and blue	10	1·00
453	-	30c. sepia and mauve	10	1·00
454	-	1s.30 sepia and orange	20	2·00
455	**70**	2s.50 sepia and green	30	7·00

DESIGN: 30 c, 1s.30, Hands holding rice.

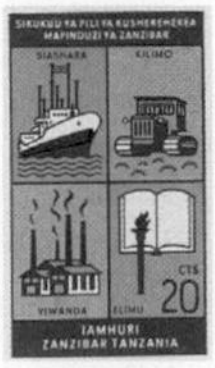

72 Freighter, Tractor, Factory and Open Book and Torch

1966. Second Anniv of Revolution. Multicoloured.

456	20c. Type **72**	20	20
457	50c. Soldier	15	30
458	1s.30 Type **72**	25	30
459	2s.50 As 50c.	25	1·75

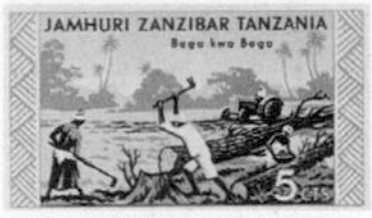

74 Tree-felling

1966

460	**74**	5c. purple and olive	70	80
461	-	10c. purple and green	70	80
462	-	15c. purple and blue	70	80
463	-	20c. blue and orange	40	20
464	-	25c. purple and yellow	40	30
465	-	30c. purple and yellow	70	20
466	-	40c. brown and red	80	20
467	-	50c. green and yellow	80	20
468	-	1s. purple and blue	80	20
469	-	1s.30 purple and turquoise	80	3·00
470	-	2s. purple and green	80	40
471	-	5s. red and blue	1·25	5·50
472	-	10s. red and yellow	2·25	18·00
473	**74**	20s. brown and mauve	5·00	42·00

DESIGNS—HORIZ: 10c., 1s. Clove cultivation; 15c., 40c. Chair-making; 20c., 5s. Lumumba College; 25c., 1s.30, Agriculture; 30c., 2s. Agricultural workers. VERT: 50c., 10s. Zanzibar street.

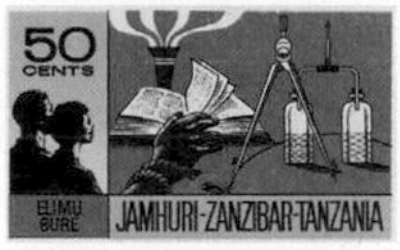

81 "Education"

1966. Introduction of Free Education.

474	**81**	50c. black, blue and orange	10	1·00
475	**81**	1s.30 black, blue and green	15	1·75
476	**81**	2s.50 black, blue and pink	55	4·50

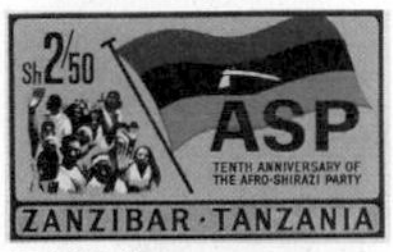

82 A.S.P. Flag

1967. Tenth Anniv of Afro-Shirazi Party.

477	**82**	30c. multicoloured	20	1·25
478	-	50c. multicoloured	20	1·00
479	-	1s.30 multicoloured	20	2·25
480	**82**	2s.50 multicoloured	50	3·75

[illegible] Vice President M. A. Karume of Tanzania, flag and crowd.

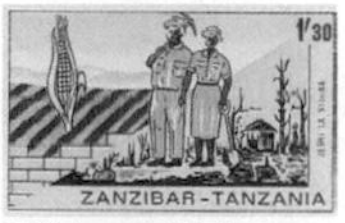

84 Voluntary Workers

1967. Voluntary Workers Brigade.

481	**84**	1s.30 multicoloured	20	2·25
482	**84**	2s.50 multicoloured	55	5·50

POSTAGE DUE STAMPS

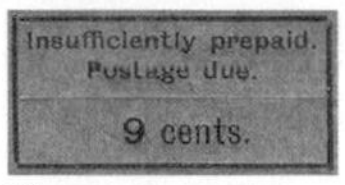

D1

1930. Roul or roul×imperf.

D1	**D 1**	1c. black on orange	11·00	£150
D18	**D 1**	2c. black on orange	27·00	40·00
D3	**D 1**	3c. black on orange	5·00	65·00
D19	**D 1**	3c. black on red	3·50	65·00
D21	**D 1**	6c. black on yellow	3·25	38·00
D5	**D 1**	9c. black on orange	2·75	40·00
D6	**D 1**	12c. black on orange	£15000	£12000
D7	**D 1**	12c. black on green	£1500	£600
D22	**D 1**	12c. black on blue	4·50	30·00
D8	**D 1**	15c. black on orange	2·75	42·00
D9	**D 1**	18c. black on orange	5·50	55·00
D11	**D 1**	20c. black on orange	4·50	80·00
D12	**D 1**	21c. black on orange	3·50	50·00
D13	**D 1**	25c. black on purple	£2750	£1300
D14	**D 1**	25c. black on orange	£19000	£17000
D23	**D 1**	25c. black on red	10·00	£140
D24	**D 1**	25c. black on lilac	26·00	85·00
D15	**D 1**	31c. black on orange	9·50	£110
D16	**D 1**	50c. black on orange	21·00	£250
D17	**D 1**	75c. black on orange	80·00	£600

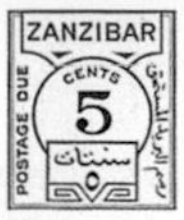

D3

1936

D25	**D3**	5c. violet	8·50	14·00
D26	**D3**	10c. red	7·00	2·75
D27	**D3**	20c. green	2·50	7·00
D28a	**D3**	30c. brown	35	14·00
D29a	**D3**	40c. blue	75	50·00
D30a	**D3**	1s. grey	1·00	25·00

Pt. 1

ZIL ELWANNYEN SESEL

Beginning in June 1980 stamps were issued for use in Zil Elwannyen Sesel (Seychelles Outer Islands), including Aldabra, Coetivy, Farquhar and the Amirante Islands.

100 cents = 1 rupee.

A. Inscr "ZIL ELOIGNE SESEL"

1980. As Nos. 404/19 of Seychelles but inscr "ZIL ELOIGNE SESEL".

1	-	5c. multicoloured	15	75
2	-	10c. multicoloured	15	75
3	-	15c. multicoloured	15	75
4	-	20c. multicoloured	20	75
5	-	25c. multicoloured	1·00	75
6	**103**	40c. multicoloured	30	75
7	-	50c. multicoloured	30	60
8	-	75c. multicoloured	35	60
9	-	1r. multicoloured	1·25	1·00
10	-	1r.10 multicoloured	40	1·00
11	-	1r.25 multicoloured	1·50	70
12	-	1r.50 multicoloured	45	70
13	-	5r. multicoloured	70	1·00
14	-	10r. multicoloured	80	1·50
15	-	15r. multicoloured	80	3·00
16	-	20r. multicoloured	80	3·25

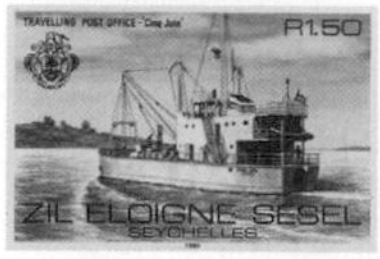

2 "Cinq Juin"

1980. Establishment of Travelling Post Office. Multicoloured.

17	1r.50 Type **2**	20	20
18	2r.10 Hand-stamping covers	25	25
19	5r. Map of Zil Eloigne Sesel	40	40

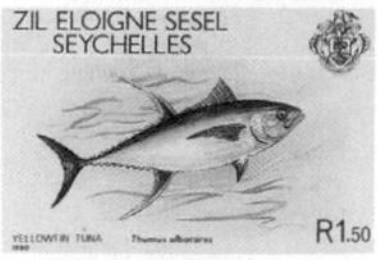

3 Yellow-finned Tuna

1980. Marine Life. Multicoloured.

20	1r.50 Type **3**	15	20
21	2r.10 Blue marlin	20	35
22	5r. Sperm whale	50	70

1981. Royal Wedding. As T **14a/b** of St. Kitts. Multicoloured.

23	40c. "Royal Escape"	10	10
24	40c. Prince Charles and Lady Diana Spencer	40	55
25	5r. "Victoria and Albert"	35	40
27	10r. "Britannia"	60	85
28	10r. As No. 24	1·50	3·25
MS29	120×109 mm. 7r.50 As No. 24	1·40	1·75
31	5r. As No. 24	1·00	1·75

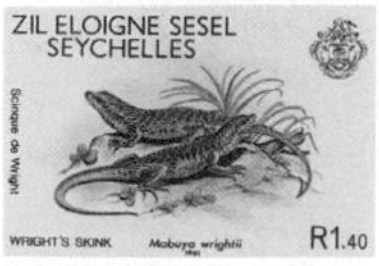

4 Wright's Skink

1981. Wildlife. (1st series). Multicoloured.

32	1r.40 Type **4**	15	15
33	2r.25 Tree frog	20	20
34	5r. Robber crab	40	40

See also Nos. 45/7.

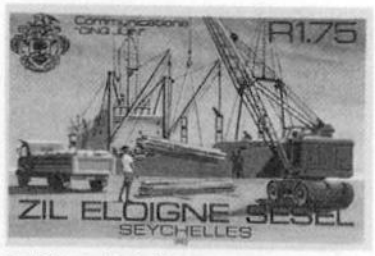

5 "Cinq Juin" ("Communications")

1982. Island Development. Ships.

35	**5**	1r.75 black and orange	35	30
36	-	2r.10 black and blue	40	45
37	-	5r. black and red	50	60

DESIGNS: 2r.10, "Junon" (fisheries protection); 5r. "Diamond M. Dragon" (drilling ship).

B. Inscr "ZIL ELWAGNE SESEL"

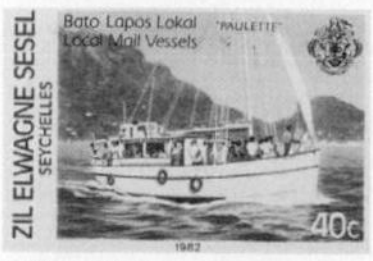

6 "Paulette"

1982. Local Mail Vessels. Multicoloured.

38	40c. Type **6**	35	45
39	1r.75 "Janette"	40	80
40	2r.75 "Lady Esme"	50	95
41	3r.50 "Cinq Juin"	50	1·00

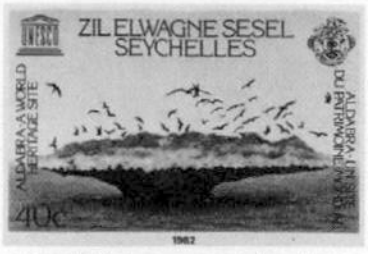

7 Birds flying over Island

1982. Aldabra, World Heritage Site. Multicoloured.

42	40c. Type **7**	30	15
43	2r.75 Map of the atoll	45	35
44	7r. Giant tortoises	50	75

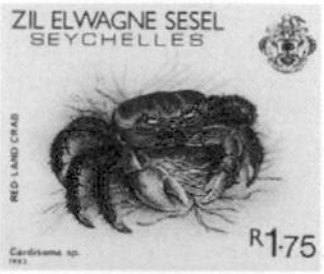

8 Red Land Crab

1983. Wildlife (2nd series). Multicoloured.

45	1r.75 Type **8**	35	40
46	2r.75 Black terrapin	45	55
47	7r. Madagascar green gecko	90	1·25

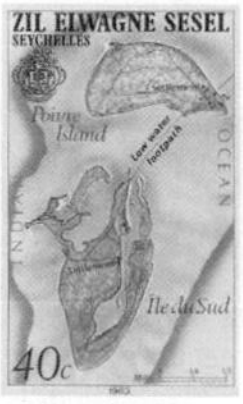

9 Map of Poivre Island and Ile du Sud

1983. Island Maps. Multicoloured.

48	40c. Type **9**	20	40
49	1r.50 Ile des Roches	30	55
50	2r.75 Astove Island	40	80
51	7r. Coetivy Island	50	1·60
MS52	93×129 mm. Nos. 48/51	1·75	3·00

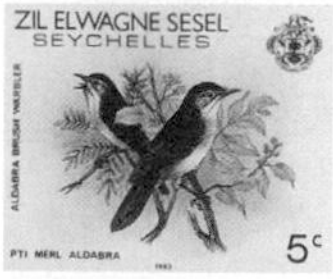

10 Aldabra Warbler

1983. Birds. Multicoloured.

53	5c. Type **10**	40	60
54	10c. Zebra dove ("Barred Ground Dove")	1·00	60
55	15c. Indian nightjar	30	40
56	20c. Madagascar cisticola ("Malagasy Grass Warbler")	30	40
57	25c. Madagascar white-eye	60	60
58	40c. Mascarene fody	30	40
59	50c. White-throated rail	5·00	60
60	75c. Black bulbul	40	60
61	2r. Western reef heron ("Dimorphic little egret")	2·00	1·25
62	2r.10 Souimanga sunbird	50	1·00
63	2r.50 Madagascar turtle dove	1·00	65
64	2r.75 Sacred ibis	70	75
65	3r.50 Black coucal (vert)	1·00	1·10
66	7r. Seychelles kestrel (vert)	3·00	1·90
67	15r. Comoro blue pigeon (vert)	3·00	5·00
68	20r. Greater flamingo (vert)	3·50	5·50

See also Nos. 165 etc. (1985).

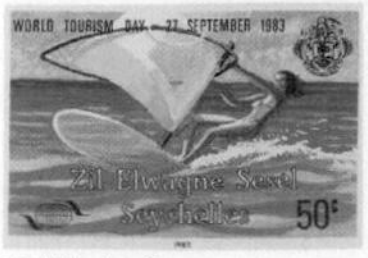

11 Windsurfing

1983. Tourism. Multicoloured.

69	50c. Type **11**	10	10
70	2r. Hotel	25	25
71	3r. View of beach	30	35
72	10r. Islands at sunset	75	1·75

1983. Nos. 23/8 surch.

73	30c. on 40c. "Royal Escape"	25	25
74	30c. on 40c. Prince Charles and Lady Diana Spencer	50	60
75	2r. on 5r. "Victoria and Albert II"	70	70
76	2r. on 5r. As No. 74	1·25	1·75
77	3r. on 10r. "Britannia"	85	85
78	3r. on 10r. As No. 74	1·60	2·50

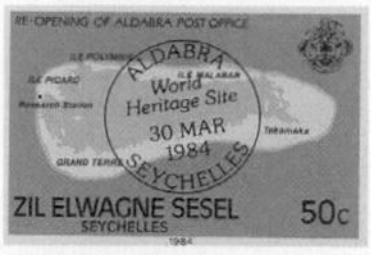

12 Map of Aldabra and Commemorative Postmark

1984. Re-opening of Aldabra Post Office. Multicoloured.

79	50c. Type **12**	15	30
80	2r.75 White-throated rail	60	1·10
81	3r. Giant tortoise	60	1·25
82	10r. Red-footed booby	2·25	3·50

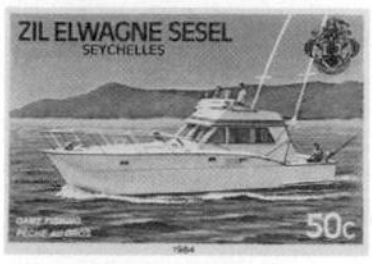

13 Fishing from Launch

1984. Game Fishing. Multicoloured.

83	50c. Type **13**	15	30
84	2r. Hooked fish (vert)	45	75
85	3r. Weighing catch (vert)	60	1·00
86	10r. Fishing from boat (different)	2·00	3·00

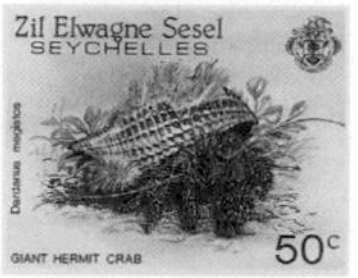

14 Giant Hermit Crab

1984. Crabs. Multicoloured.

87	50c. Type **14**	25	40
88	2r. Fiddler crabs	55	1·10
89	3r. Sand crab	65	1·50
90	10r. Spotted pebble crab	1·40	4·25

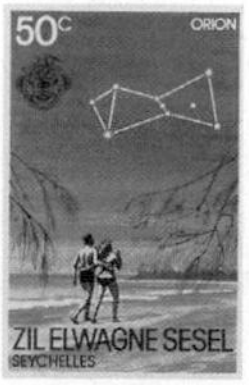

15 Constellation of "Orion"

1984. The Night Sky. Multicoloured.

91	50c. Type **15**	25	15
92	2r. "Cygnus"	50	55
93	3r. "Virgo"	60	80
94	10r. "Scorpio"	1·40	2·25

C. Inscr "ZIL ELWANNYEN SESEL"

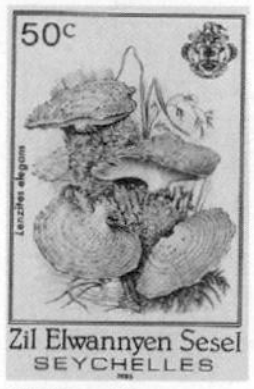

16 "Lenzites elegans"

1985. Fungi. Multicoloured.

95	50c. Type **16**	60	85
96	2r. "Xylaria telfairei"	1·50	2·00
97	3r. "Lentinus sajor-caju"	1·50	2·00
98	10r. "Hexagonia tenuis"	2·75	3·50

1985. As Nos. 53/4, 57 and 61 but inscr "Zil Elwannyen Sesel".

103	25c. Madagascar white eye	3·50	1·50
105	50c. White-throated rail	4·00	1·60
165	5c. Type **10**	2·50	2·25
166	10c. Zebra dove ("Barred Ground Dove")	2·50	2·25
226	2r. Western reef heron ("Dimorphic Little Egret")	3·50	3·25

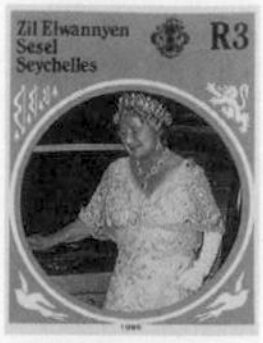

17 The Queen Mother attending Royal Opera House, Covent Garden

1985. Life and Times of Queen Elizabeth the Queen Mother. Multicoloured.

115	1r. The Queen Mother, 1936 (from photo by Dorothy Wilding)	20	25
116	2r. With Princess Anne at Ascot, 1974	35	50
117	3r. Type **17**	45	70
118	5r. With Prince Henry at his christening (from photo by Lord Snowdon)	60	1·25
MS119	91×73 mm. 10r. In a launch, Venice, 1985	1·50	2·75

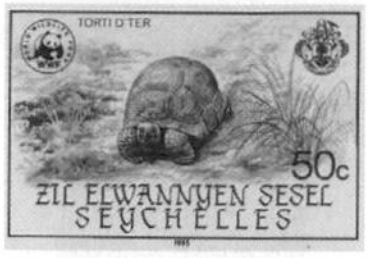

18 Giant Tortoise

1985. Giant Tortoises of Aldabra (1st series). Multicoloured.

120	50c. Type **18**	3·25	1·25
121	75c. Giant tortoises at stream	3·50	1·40
122	1r. Giant tortoises on grassland	3·75	1·60
123	2r. Giant tortoise (side view)	4·75	2·25
MS124	70×60 mm. 10r. Two tortoises	16·00	15·00

For stamps as Nos. 120/3 but without circular inscription around W.W.F. emblem see Nos. 153/6.

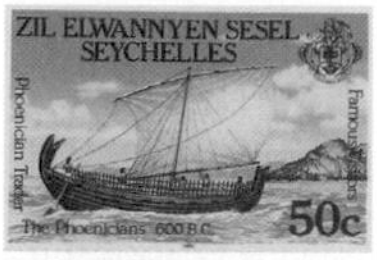

19 Phoenician Trading Ship (600 B.C.)

1985. Famous Visitors. Multicoloured.

125	50c. Type **19**	80	80
126	2r. Sir Hugh Scott and H.M.S. "Sealark", 1908	1·50	2·00
127	10r. Vasco da Gama and "Sao Gabriel", 1502	2·50	4·50

1986. 60th Birthday of Queen Elizabeth II. As T **145a** of St. Helena. Multicoloured.

128	75c. Princess Elizabeth at Chester, 1951	15	25
129	1r. Queen and Duke of Edinburgh at Falklands Service, St. Paul's Cathedral, 1985	15	25
130	1r.50 At Order of St. Michael and St. George service, St. Paul's Cathedral, 1968	25	40
131	3r.75 In Mexico, 1975	40	90
132	5r. At Crown Agents Head Office, London, 1983	45	1·25

1986. Royal Wedding. As T **146a** of St. Helena. Multicoloured.

133	3r. Prince Andrew and Miss Sarah Ferguson on Buckingham Palace balcony	45	75
134	7r. Prince Andrew in naval uniform	65	1·75

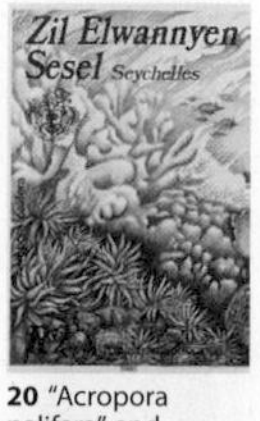

20 "Acropora palifera" and "Tubastraea coccinea"

1986. Coral Formations. Multicoloured.

135	2r. Type **20**	1·75	1·75
136	2r. "Echinopora lamellosa" and "Favia pallida"	1·75	1·75
137	2r. "Sarcophyton sp." and "Porites lutea"	1·75	1·75
138	2r. "Goniopora sp." and "Goniastrea retiformis"	1·75	1·75
139	2r. "Tubipora musica" and "Fungia fungites"	1·75	1·75

Nos. 135/9 were printed together, se-tenant, forming a composite design.

21 "Hibiscus tiliaceus"

1986. Flora. Multicoloured.
140	50c. Type **21**	35	30
141	2r. "Crinum angustum"	1·60	1·50
142	3r. "Phaius tetragonus"	2·25	2·00
143	10r. "Kothmannia annae"	3·75	4·00

22 Teardrop Butterflyfish and Lined Butterflyfish

1987. Coral Reef Fish. Multicoloured.
144	2r. Type **22**	1·10	1·40
145	2r. Knifejaw	1·10	1·40
146	2r. Narrow-banded batfish	1·10	1·40
147	2r. Ringed-sergeant	1·10	1·40
148	2r. Lined butterflyfish and Meyer's butterflyfish	1·10	1·40

Nos. 144/8 were printed together, se-tenant, forming a composite design.

23 Coconut

1987. Trees. Multicoloured.
149	1r. Type **23**	80	85
150	2r. Mangrove	1·40	1·75
151	3r. Pandanus palm	2·00	2·50
152	5r. Indian almond	3·00	3·75

1987. Giant Tortoises of Aldabra (2nd series). Designs as Nos. 120/3 but without circular inscr around W.W.F. emblem. Multicoloured.
153	50c. As Type **18**	3·00	2·00
154	75c. Giant tortoises at pool	4·00	2·75
155	1r. Giant tortoises on grassland	4·50	3·75
156	2r. Giant tortoise (side view)	5·50	5·00

1987. Royal Ruby Wedding. Nos. 128/32 optd **40TH WEDDING ANNIVERSARY**.
157	75c. Princess Elizabeth at Chester, 1951	25	20
158	1r. Queen and Duke of Edinburgh at Falklands Service, St. Paul's Cathedral, 1985	30	25
159	1r.50 At Order of St. Michael and St. George service, St. Paul's Cathedral, 1968	40	40
160	3r.75 In Mexico, 1975	60	90
161	5r. At Crown Agents Head Office, London, 1983	70	1·25

24 "Vallee de Mai" (Christine Harter)

1987. Tourism. Multicoloured.
162	3r. Type **24**	3·25	3·25
163	3r. Ferns	3·25	3·25
164	3r. Bamboo	3·25	3·25

Nos. 162/4 were printed together, se-tenant, forming a composite picture.

25 "Yanga seychellensis" (beetle)

1988. Insects. Multicoloured.
180	1r. Type **25**	1·25	1·00
181	2r. "Belenois aldabraensis" (butterfly)	2·00	1·60
182	3r. "Polyspilota seychelliana" (mantid)	2·25	2·25
183	5r. "Polposipus herculeanus" (beetle)	2·75	3·00

26 Olympic Rings

1988. Olympic Games, Seoul. Sheet 99×73 mm.
| MS184 **26** 10r. multicoloured | 4·00 | 2·75 |

1988. 300th Anniv of Lloyd's of London. As T **152a** of St. Helena. Multicoloured.
185	1r. Modern Lloyd's Building, London	70	65
186	2r. "Retriever" (cable ship) (horiz)	1·50	1·10
187	3r. "Chantel" (fishing boat) (horiz)	2·00	1·50
188	5r. Wreck of "Torrey Canyon" (tanker), Cornwall, 1967	2·75	1·75

27 "Father Christmas landing with Presents" (Jean-Claude Boniface)

1988. Christmas. Children's Paintings. Multicoloured.
189	1r. Type **27**	55	40
190	2r. "Church" (Francois Barra) (vert)	60	80
191	3r. "Father Christmas flying on Bird" (Wizy Ernesta) (vert)	85	1·25
192	5r. "Father Christmas in Sleigh over Island" (Federic Lang)	1·40	2·00

1989. 20th Anniv of First Manned Landing on Moon. As T **50a** of St. Kitts. Multicoloured.
193	1r. Firing Room, Launch Control Centre	2·00	1·50
194	2r. Crews of "Apollo–Soyuz" mission (30×30 mm)	2·50	2·25
195	3r. "Apollo–Soyuz" emblem (30×30 mm)	2·75	3·00
196	5r. "Apollo" and "Soyuz" docking in space	3·75	4·50
MS197 82×100 mm. 10r. Recovery of "Apollo 11"	11·00	13·00

28 Dumb Cane

1989. Poisonous Plants (1st series). Multicoloured.
198	1r. Type **28**	2·50	1·75
199	2r. Star of Bethlehem	3·00	2·75
200	3r. Indian liquorice	3·25	3·25
201	5r. Black nightshade	4·25	4·75

See also Nos. 214/17.

29 Tec-Tec Broth

1989. Creole Cooking. Multicoloured.
202	1r. Type **29**	1·50	1·50
203	2r. Pilaff a la Seychelloise	2·00	2·25
204	3r. Mullet grilled in banana leaves	2·25	2·50
205	5r. Daube	3·25	3·75
MS206 125×80 mm. Nos. 202/5	11·00	13·00

30 1980 Marine Life 5r. Stamp

1990. "Stamp World London 90" International Stamp Exhibition. Showing stamps. Multicoloured.
207	1r. Type **30**	2·25	1·75
208	2r. 1980 5r. definitive	2·75	2·50
209	3r. 1983 2r.75 definitive	3·00	3·00
210	5r. 1981 Wildlife 5r.	4·00	4·50
MS211 124×84 mm. Nos. 207/10	12·00	13·00

1990. 90th Birthday of Queen Elizabeth the Queen Mother. As T **116a** of St. Helena.
| 212 | 2r. multicoloured | 1·75 | 1·75 |
| 213 | 10r. black and brown | 3·75 | 5·50 |

DESIGNS—21×36 mm: 2r. Duchess of York with baby Princess Elizabeth, 1926. 29×37 mm: 10r. King George VI and Queen Elizabeth visiting bombed district, London, 1940.

1990. Poisonous Plants (2nd series). As T **28**. Multicoloured.
214	1r. Ordeal plant	1·75	1·75
215	2r. Thorn apple	2·25	2·50
216	3r. Strychnine tree	2·50	2·75
217	5r. Bwa zasmen	3·50	4·00

1991. 65th Birthday of Queen Elizabeth II and 70th Birthday of Prince Philip. As T **165a** of St. Helena. Multicoloured.
| 234 | 4r. Queen Elizabeth II | 1·90 | 2·25 |
| 235 | 4r. Prince Philip | 1·90 | 2·25 |

31 "St. Abbs" (full-rigged ship), 1860

1991. Shipwrecks. Multicoloured.
236	1r.50 Type **31**	2·50	2·00
237	3r. "Norden" (barque), 1862	3·00	2·50
238	3r.50 "Clan Mackay" (freighter), 1894	3·25	2·75
239	10r. "Glenlyon" (freighter), 1905	7·00	7·50

1992. 40th Anniv of Queen Elizabeth II's Accession. As T **168a** of St. Helena. Multicoloured.
240	1r. Beach	75	75
241	1r.50 Aerial view of Desroches	1·10	1·25
242	3r. Tree-covered coastline	1·50	1·75
243	3r.50 Three portraits of Queen Elizabeth II	1·60	1·90
244	5r. Queen Elizabeth II	1·75	2·25

32 "Lomatopyllum aldabrense" (plant)

1992. Tenth Anniv of Aldabra as a World Heritage Site. Multicoloured.
245	1r.50 Type **32**	1·75	1·75
246	3r. White-throated rail	5·00	3·50
247	3r.50 Robber crab	2·75	3·50
248	10r. Aldabra drongo	9·50	11·00

Pt. 1

ZIMBABWE

Rhodesia became independent on 18 April 1980 and was renamed Zimbabwe.

100 cents = 1 dollar.

113 Morganite

1980. As Nos. 555/69 of Rhodesia and new value inscr "ZIMBABWE".
576	1c. Type **113**	10	30
577	3c. Amethyst	15	30
578	4c. Garnet	15	10
579	5c. Citrine	15	10
580	7c. Blue topaz	15	10
581	9c. White rhinoceros	15	10
582	11c. Lion	15	15
583	13c. Warthog	15	15
584	15c. Giraffe	15	20
585	17c. Common zebra	15	20
586	21c. Odzani Falls	15	25
587	25c. Goba Falls	15	30
588	30c. Inyangombi Falls	15	50
588a	40c. Bundi Falls	2·50	4·00
589	$1 Bridal Veil Falls	20	1·50
590	$2 Victoria Falls	35	3·00

114 Rotary Anniversary Emblem

1980. 75th Anniv of Rotary International.
591	**114**	4c. multicoloured	10	10
592	**114**	13c. multicoloured	15	20
593	**114**	21c. multicoloured	20	35
594	**114**	25c. multicoloured	20	60
MS595 140×84 mm. Nos. 591/4		75	1·60

115 Olympic Rings

1980. Olympic Games, Moscow.
| 596 | **115** | 17c. multicoloured | 30 | 40 |

116 Gatooma Post Office, 1912

1980. 75th Anniv of Post Office Savings Bank.
597	**116**	5c. black and brown	10	10
598	-	7c. black and orange	10	10
599	-	9c. black and yellow	10	10
600	-	17c. black and light blue	75	25
MS601 125×84 mm. Nos. 597/600		55	1·25

DESIGNS: 7c. Salisbury Post Office, 1912; 9c. Umtali Post Office, 1901; 17c. Bulawayo Post Office, 1895.

117 Stylized Blind Person

1981. Int Year of Disabled Persons. Multicoloured.
602	5c. Type **117**	10	10
603	7c. Deaf person	10	10
604	11c. Person with one leg	15	10
605	17c. Person with one arm	20	25

118 Msasa

1981. National Tree Day. Multicoloured.
606	5c. Type **118**	10	10
607	7c. Mopane	10	10
608	21c. Flat-crowned acacia	20	25
609	30c. Pod mahogany	25	45

119 Painting from Gwamgwadza Cave, Mtoko Area

1982. Rock Paintings. Multicoloured.
610	9c. Type **119**	15	10
611	11c. Epworth Mission, near Harare	15	10
612	17c. Diana's Vow, near Harare	20	15

613	21c. Gwamgwadza Cave, Mtoko Area (different)	25	15
614	25c. Mucheka Cave, Msana Communal Land	35	50
615	30c. Chinzwini Shelter, Chiredzi Area	25	70

120 Scout Emblem

1982. 75th Anniv of Boy Scout Movement. Multicoloured.

616	9c. Type **120**	15	10
617	11c. Scouts around campfire	15	10
618	21c. Scouts map-reading	20	35
619	30c. Lord Baden-Powell	25	65

121 Dr. Robert Koch

1982. Centenary of Dr. Robert Koch's Discovery of Tubercle Bacillus.

| 620 | **121** | 11c. orange, black and grey | 40 | 10 |
| 621 | – | 30c. multicoloured | 60 | 1·50 |

DESIGN: 30c. Man looking through microscope.

122 "Wing Woman" (Henry Mudzengerere)

1983. Commonwealth Day. Sculptures. Multicoloured.

622	9c. Type **122**	10	10
623	11c. "Telling Secrets" (Joseph Ndandarika) (horiz)	10	10
624	30c. "Hornbill Man" (John Takawira) (horiz)	15	15
625	$1 "The Child" (Nicholas Mukomberanwa)	40	1·25

123 Traditional Ploughing Team (moving right)

1983. World Ploughing Contest. Multicoloured.

626	21c. Type **123**	15	25
627	21c. Traditional ploughing team (moving left)	15	25
628	30c. Tractor ploughing	20	35
629	30c. Modern plough	20	35

The two designs of each value were issued in horizontal se-tenant pairs, forming composite designs.

124 Postman on Cycle

1983. World Communications Year. Multicoloured.

630	9c. Type **124**	20	10
631	11c. Aircraft controller directing airliner	20	10
632	15c. Switchboard operator	20	20
633	17c. Printing works	20	20
634	21c. Road transport (horiz)	35	40
635	30c. Rail transport (horiz)	45	1·00

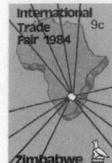

125 Map of Africa showing Zimbabwe

1984. Zimbabwe Int Trade Fair, 1984. Multicoloured.

636	9c. Type **125**	10	10
637	11c. Globe	15	10
638	30c. Zimbabwe flag and Trade Fair logo	45	50

126 Cycling

1984. Olympic Games, Los Angeles. Children's Pictures. Multicoloured.

639	11c. Type **126**	40	15
640	21c. Swimming	20	20
641	30c. Running	25	55
642	40c. Hurdling	25	1·10

127 Liberation Heroes

1984. Heroes' Day. Multicoloured.

643	9c. Type **127**	15	10
644	11c. Symbolic tower and flame (vert)	15	10
645	17c. Bronze sculpture (vert)	20	30
646	30c. Section of bronze mural	30	70

DESIGNS: 9c. to 30c. Various aspects of Heroes' Acre.

128 African Fish Eagle ("Fish Eagle")

1984. Birds of Prey. Multicoloured.

647	9c. Type **128**	25	15
648	11c. Long-crested eagle	25	15
649	13c. Bateleur	30	30
650	17c. Verreaux's eagle ("Black Eagle")	35	20
651	21c. Martial eagle	45	35
652	30c. African hawk eagle	65	1·00

129 9th Class Locomotive No. 86

1985. "Zimbabwe Steam Safaris". Railway Locomotives. Multicoloured.

653	9c. Type **129**	30	15
654	11c. 12th Class locomotive No. 190	30	15
655	17c. 15th Class Beyer-Garratt locomotive No. 424 "Isilwane"	45	20
656	30c. 20th Class Garratt locomotive No. 726 "Gwaai"	90	1·25

130 "Intelsat V" Telecommunications Satellite

1985. Earth Satellite Station. Mazowe. Multicoloured.

| 657 | 26c. Type **130** | 40 | 25 |
| 658 | 57c. Earth Satellite Station, Mazowe (65×25 mm) | 1·00 | 2·50 |

131 Tobacco

1985. National Infrastructure. Multicoloured.

659	1c. Type **131**	10	10
660	3c. Maize	10	10
661	4c. Cotton	15	10
662	5c. Tea	50	10
663	10c. Cattle	30	10
664	11c. Birchenough Bridge	75	10
665	12c. Ore stamp mill	1·25	10
666	13c. Gold pouring	2·75	15
667	15c. Dragline coal mining	2·25	15
668	17c. Uncut amethyst	2·75	1·25
669	18c. Electric locomotive	2·25	2·75
670	20c. Kariba Dam	1·50	30
671	23c. Elephants at water hole	4·25	45
672	25c. Sunset over Zambezi	65	30
673	26c. Baobab tree	65	20
674	30c. Ruins of Great Zimbabwe	75	70
675	35c. Traditional dancing	60	30
676	45c. Village women crushing maize	1·00	40
677	57c. Woodcarving	75	70
678	$1 Playing Mbira (musical instrument)	1·25	90
679	$2 Mule-drawn Scotch cart	2·00	3·00
680	$5 Zimbabwe coat-of-arms	2·25	4·50

132 Chief Mutapa Gatsi Rusere and 17th-century Seal

1985. 50th Anniv of National Archives. Multicoloured.

681	12c. Type **132**	20	15
682	18c. Chief Lobengula, seal and 1888 Treaty	25	40
683	26c. Exhibition gallery	35	45
684	35c. National Archives building	45	75

133 Computer Operator

1985. U.N. Decade for Women. Multicoloured.

685	10c. Type **133**	20	10
686	17c. Nurse giving injection	30	20
687	26c. Woman student	60	1·40

134 Harare Conference Centre

1986. Harare Int Conference Centre. Multicoloured.

| 688 | 26c. Type **134** | 40 | 20 |
| 689 | 35c. Interior of conference hall | 70 | 90 |

135 Grain Storage Silo

1986. Sixth Anniv of Southern African Development Co-ordination Conference. Multicoloured.

690	12c. Type **135**	55	20
691	18c. Rhinoceros and hawk at sunset	2·50	1·25
692	26c. Map showing S.A.D.C.C. member states and Boeing 737	2·50	1·50
693	35c. Map and national flags of S.A.D.C.C. members	2·75	2·00

136 "Bunaeopsis jacksoni"

1986. Moths of Zimbabwe. Multicoloured.

694	12c. Type **136**	35	20
695	18c. "Deilephila nerii"	50	45
696	26c. "Bunaeopsis zaddachi"	55	60
697	35c. "Heniocha apollonia"	80	2·75

137 Victoria Falls

1986. Eighth Non-Aligned Summit Conference. Multicoloured.

| 698 | 26c. Type **137** | 75 | 30 |
| 699 | $1 Ruins of Great Zimbabwe (62×24 mm) | 1·50 | 4·50 |

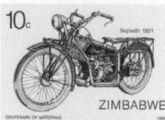

138 Sopwith Motorcycle (1921)

1986. Centenary of Motoring. Multicoloured.

700	10c. Type **138**	20	10
701	12c. Gladiator motor car (1902)	20	10
702	17c. Douglas motorcycle (1920)	30	10
703	26c. Ford "Model A" (1930)	40	15
704	35c. Schacht motor car (1909)	55	1·00
705	40c. Benz three-wheeled car (1886)	80	1·50

139 Growth Monitoring

1987. Child Survival Campaign. Multicoloured.

706	12c. Type **139**	75	1·25
707	12c. Breast-feeding	75	1·25
708	12c. Oral rehydration therapy	75	1·25
709	12c. Immunization	75	1·25

140 African Barred Owlet ("Barred Owl")

1987. Owls (1st series). Multicoloured.

710	12c. Type **140**	2·00	30
711	18c. Pearl-spotted owlet ("Pearl Spotted Owl")	2·50	70
712	26c. White-faced scops owl ("White Faced Owl")	3·00	70
713	35c. African scops owl ("Scops Owl")	4·00	2·50

See also Nos. 850/3 and 988/91.

141 Brownie, Guide and Ranger saluting ("Commitment")

1987. 75th Anniv of Girl Guides Association of Zimbabwe. Multicoloured.

714	15c. Type **141**	40	15
715	23c. Guides preparing meal over campfire ("Adventure")	55	20
716	35c. Guide teaching villagers to read ("Service")	70	30
717	$1 Handshake and globe ("International Friendship")	1·50	2·50

142 Common Grey Duiker

1987. Duikers of Africa Survey. Multicoloured.

718	15c. Type **142**	45	15
719	23c. Zebra duiker	55	20
720	25c. Yellow-backed duiker	55	70
721	30c. Blue duiker	60	90

722	35c. Jentink's duiker	60	1·00
723	38c. Red duiker	75	1·50

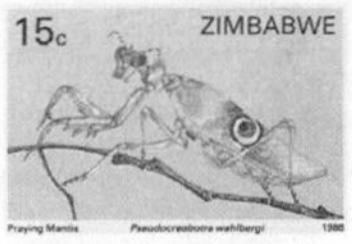
143 "Pseudocreobotra wahlberghi" (mantid)

1988. Insects. Multicoloured.

724	15c. Type **143**	70	15
725	23c. "Dicranorrhia derbyana" (beetle)	85	30
726	35c. "Dictyophorus spumans" (grasshopper)	1·10	85
727	45c. "Chalcocoris rutilus" (bug)	1·40	2·00

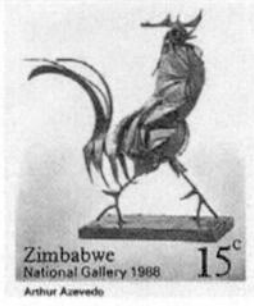
144 "Cockerel" (Arthur Azevedo)

1988. 30th Anniv of National Gallery of Zimbabwe. Designs showing painting (38c.) or sculptures (others). Multicoloured.

728	15c. Type **144**	20	10
729	23c. "Man into Hippo" (Bernard Matemera)	30	20
730	30c. "Spirit Python" (Henry Munyaradzi)	35	30
731	35c. "Spirit Bird carrying People" (Thomas Mukarobgwa) (horiz)	35	30
732	38c. "The Song of the Herd Boy" (George Nene) (horiz)	35	40
733	45c. "War Victim" (Joseph Muzondo) (horiz)	40	50

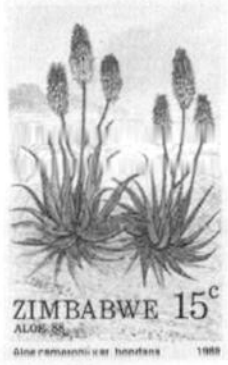
145 "Aloe cameronii var. bondana"

1988. Aloes. Multicoloured.

734	15c. Type **145**	30	10
735	23c. "Orbeopsis caudata"	45	20
736	25c. "Euphorbia wildii"	45	35
737	30c. "Euphorbia fortissima"	50	45
738	35c. "Aloe aculeata"	50	55
739	38c. "Huernia zebrina"	60	70

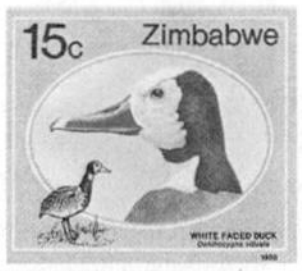
146 White-faced Whistling Duck ("White-faced Duck")

1988. Wild Ducks and Geese of Zimbabwe. Multicoloured.

740	15c. Type **146**	75	20
741	23c. African pygmy goose ("Pygmy Goose")	85	20
742	30c. Hottentot teal	95	85
743	35c. Comb duck ("Knob-billed duck")	1·10	1·25
744	38c. White-backed duck	1·10	1·50
745	45c. Maccoa duck	1·60	2·75

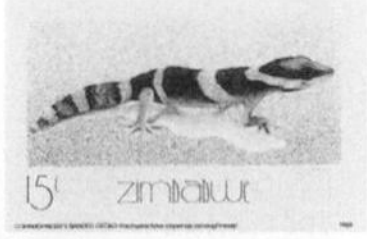
147 O'Shaughnessy's Banded Gecko

1989. Geckos. Multicoloured.

746	15c. Type **147**	80	15
747	23c. Tiger rock gecko	95	40
748	35c. Tasman's gecko	1·50	1·25
749	45c. Bibron's gecko	1·75	2·00

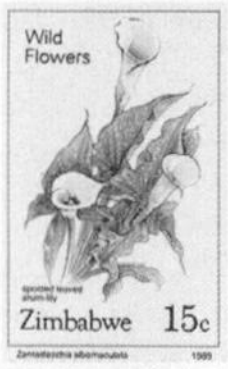
148 Spotted Leaved Arum-Lily

1989. Wild Flowers (1st series). Multicoloured.

750	15c. Type **148**	50	10
751	23c. Grassland vlei-lily	60	25
752	30c. Manica protea	65	40
753	35c. Flame lily	75	40
754	38c. Poppy hibiscus	80	55
755	45c. Blue sesbania	90	65

See also Nos. 1093/99.

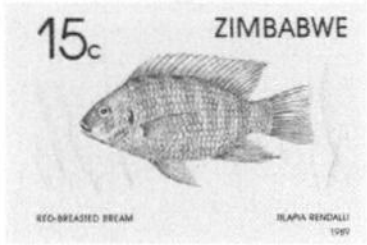
149 Red-breasted Tilapia

1989. Fish (1st series). Multicoloured.

756	15c. Type **149**	50	15
757	25c. Chessa	70	25
758	30c. Eastern bottlenose	75	50
759	35c. Vundu	75	50
760	38c. Large-mouthed black bass	80	80
761	45c. Lesser tigerfish	1·00	1·50

See also Nos. 864/9.

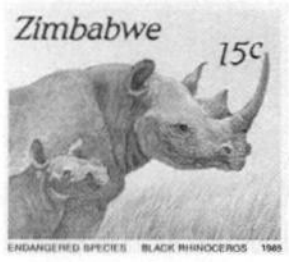
150 Black Rhinoceros

1989. Endangered Species. Multicoloured.

762	15c. Type **150**	1·25	40
763	25c. Cheetah	1·25	45
764	30c. Wild dog	1·40	90
765	35c. Pangolin	1·40	1·25
766	38c. Brown hyena	1·50	2·00
767	45c. Roan antelope	1·60	2·25

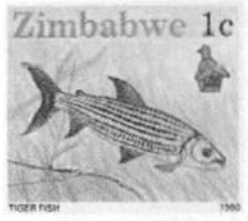
151 Giant Tigerfish

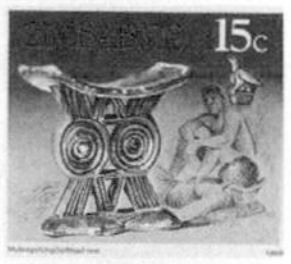
152 Headrest

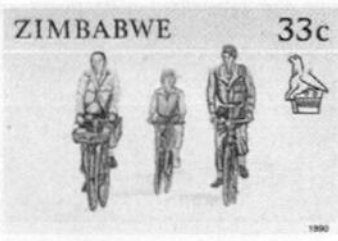
153 Bicycles

1990. Multicoloured. (a) Wildlife. As T **151**.

768	1c. Type **151**	30	20
769	2c. Helmeted guineafowl	1·00	20
770	3c. Scrub hare	20	20
771	4c. Temminck's ground pangolin	40	20
772	5c. Greater kudu	40	20
773	9c. Black rhinoceros	1·75	30

(b) Cultural Artifacts. As T **152**.

774	15c. Type **152**	40	20
775	20c. Hand axe and adze	20	20
776	23c. Gourd and water pot	20	20
777	25c. Snuff container	20	20
778	26c. Winnowing tray and basket	70	30
779	30c. Grinding stone	30	30

(c) Transport. As T **153**.

780	33c. Type **153**	1·75	30
781	35c. Buses	2·00	40
782	38c. Diesel train	2·50	40
783	45c. Mail motorcycle and trailer	1·75	40
784	$1 Air Zimbabwe Boeing 737 airliner	2·75	90
785	$2 Lorry	2·00	1·60

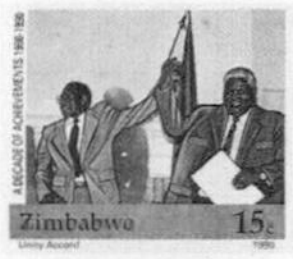
154 Pres. Mugabe and Joshua Nkomo at Signing of Unity Accord, 1987

1990. Tenth Anniv of Independence. Multicoloured.

786	15c. Type **154**	45	10
787	23c. Conference Centre, Harare	50	20
788	30c. Children in class	55	40
789	35c. Intelsat aerial, Mazowe Earth Satellite Station	65	70
790	38c. National Sports Stadium	65	80
791	45c. Maize field	1·00	1·40

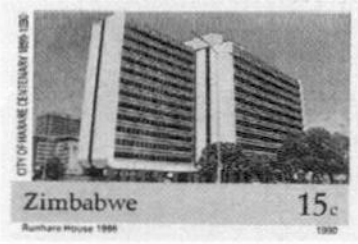
155 Runhare House, 1986

1990. Cent of the City of Harare. Multicoloured.

792	15c. Type **155**	30	10
793	23c. Market Hall, 1894	50	20
794	30c. Charter House, 1959	55	35
795	35c. Supreme Court, 1927	60	80
796	38c. Standard Chartered Bank, 1911	60	90
797	45c. The Town House, 1933	80	1·40

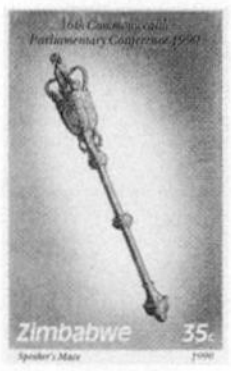
156 Speaker's Mace

1990. 36th Commonwealth Parliamentary Conference, Harare. Multicoloured.

798	35c. Type **156**	50	25
799	$1 Speaker's chair	1·25	2·00

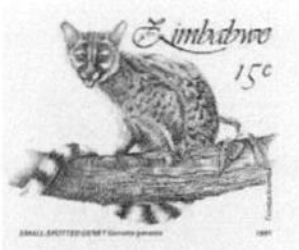
157 Small-spotted Genet

1991. Small Mammals. Multicoloured.

800	15c. Type **157**	1·00	20
801	23c. Red squirrel	1·10	30
802	35c. Night-ape	1·60	1·25
803	45c. Bat-eared fox	2·25	2·25

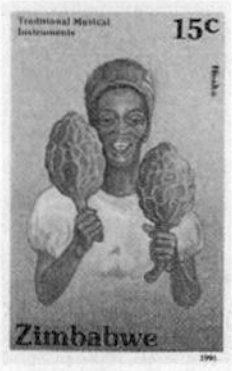
158 Hosho (rattles)

1991. Traditional Musical Instruments. Multicoloured.

804	15c. Type **158**	50	10
805	23c. Mbira (thumb piano)	55	15
806	30c. Ngororombe (pan pipes)	60	40
807	35c. Chipendani (mouth bow)	70	70
808	38c. Marimba (xylophone)	70	80
809	45c. Ngoma (drum)	80	1·10

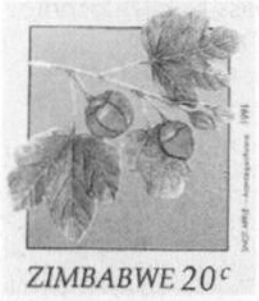
159 Snot-apple

1991. Wild Fruit (1st series). Multicoloured.

810	20c. Type **159**	55	10
811	39c. Marula	55	30
812	51c. Mobola plum	65	80
813	60c. Water berry	75	85
814	65c. Northern dwaba berry	80	85
815	77c. Mahobohobo	90	1·10

See also Nos. 1038/43.

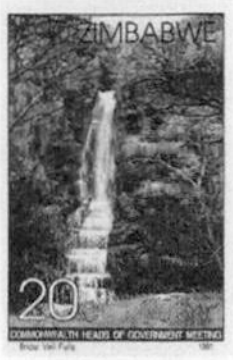
160 Bridal Veil Falls

1991. Commonwealth Heads of Government Meeting, Harare. Multicoloured.

816	20c. Type **160**	80	15
817	39c. Meeting logo	65	35
818	51c. Chinhoyi Caves	1·50	75
819	60c. Kariba Dam	1·50	1·00
820	65c. Victoria Falls	1·75	1·25
821	77c. Balancing rocks	2·00	1·50

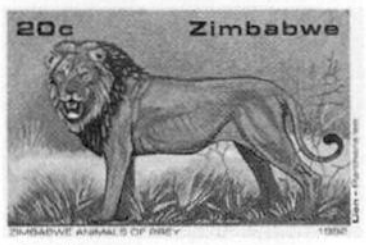
161 Lion

1992. Wildlife Conservation. Big Cats. Multicoloured.

822	20c. Type **161**	90	15
823	39c. Leopard	1·60	40
824	60c. Cheetah	2·25	1·75
825	77c. Serval	2·50	2·00

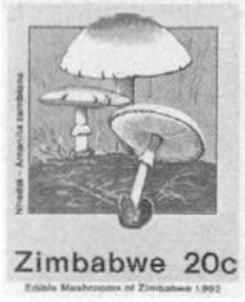
162 "Amanita zambiana"

1992. Edible Mushrooms. Multicoloured.

826	20c. Type **162**	40	15
827	39c. "Boletus edulis	55	30
828	51c. "Termitomyces sp."	60	60
829	60c. "Cantharellus densifolius"	70	80
830	65c. "Cantharellus longisporus"	75	95
831	77c. "Cantharellus cibarius"	1·00	1·50

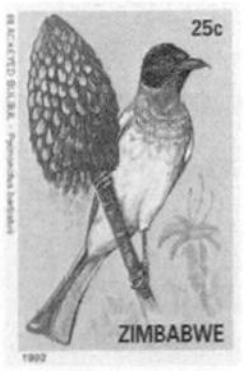
163 Garden Bulbul ("Blackeyed Bulbul")

1992. Birds. Multicoloured.

832	25c. Type **163**	80	15
833	59c. Fiscal shrike	1·10	45
834	77c. Forktailed drongo	1·25	80
835	90c. Cardinal woodpecker	1·40	95
836	98c. Southern yellow-billed hornbill ("Yellowbilled Hornbill")	1·40	95
837	$1.16 Crested francolin	1·50	1·40

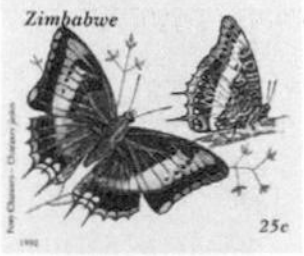
164 "Charaxes jasius"

1992. Butterflies. Multicoloured.

838	25c. Type **164**	1·10	20
839	59c. "Eronia leda"	1·75	75
840	77c. "Princeps ophidicephalus"	1·90	1·25
841	90c. "Junonia oenone"	2·50	1·75
842	98c. "Danaus chrysippus"	2·50	1·90
843	$1.16 "Junonia octavia"	2·75	2·25

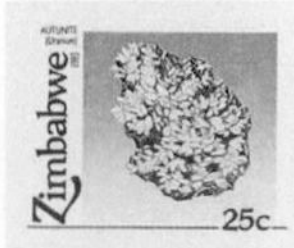
165 Uranium

1993. Minerals. Multicoloured.

844	25c. Type **165**	1·60	20
845	59c. Chrome	2·25	55

846	77c. Copper	2·75	1·00
847	90c. Coal	3·00	1·50
848	98c. Gold	3·00	1·75
849	$1.16 Emerald	3·25	2·25

1993. Owls (2nd series). As T **140**. Multicoloured.

850	25c. African wood owl ("Wood Owl")	2·75	50
851	59c. Pel's fishing owl	3·75	1·10
852	90c. Spotted eagle owl	4·75	4·50
853	$1.16 Verreaux's eagle owl ("Giant Eagle Owl")	5·50	6·50

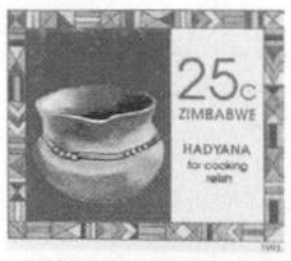

166 Hadyana (relish pot)

1993. Household Pottery. Multicoloured.

854	25c. Type **166**	65	10
855	59c. Chirongo (water jar)	80	30
856	77c. Mbiya (relish bowl)	90	60
857	90c. Pfuko (water jar)	1·00	85
858	98c. Tsaya (cooking pot)	1·10	85
859	$1.16 Gate (beer pot)	1·25	1·00

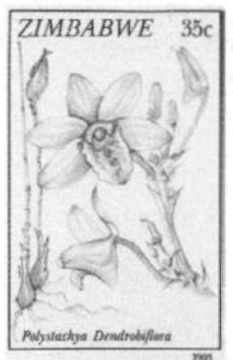

167 "Polystachya dendrobiflora"

1993. Orchids. Multicoloured.

860	35c. Type **167**	1·25	20
861	$1 "Diaphananthe subsimplex"	2·25	75
862	$1.50 "Ansellia gigantea"	3·00	1·90
863	$1.95 "Vanilla polyepis"	3·25	2·50

1994. Fish (2nd series). As T 149. Multicoloured.

864	35c. Manyame labeo ("Hunyani salmon")	50	10
865	$1 Sharp-toothed catfish ("Barbel")	80	30
866	$1.30 Rainbow trout	90	65
867	$1.50 African mottled eel	95	70
868	$1.65 Common carp	1·00	85
869	$1.95 Nembwe ("Robustus bream")	1·10	1·00

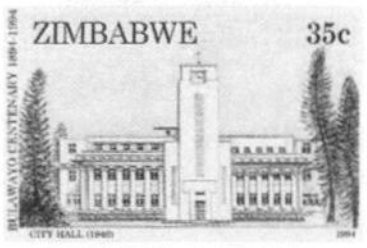

168 City Hall, 1940

1994. Centenary of Bulawayo. Multicoloured.

870	35c. Type **168**	15	10
871	80c. Cresta Churchill Hotel, 1974	30	20
872	$1.15 High Court, 1938	40	40
873	$1.75 Douslin House, 1902	50	70
874	$1.95 Goldfields Building, 1895	60	90
875	$2.30 Parkade Centre, 1975	85	1·25

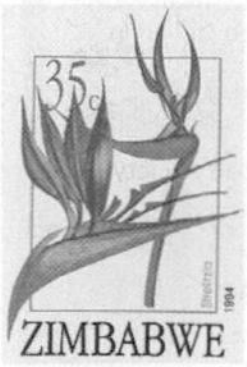

169 Strelitzia

1994. Export Flowers. Multicoloured.

876	35c. Type **169**	40	10
877	80c. Protea	70	25
878	$1.15 Phlox	85	60
879	$1.75 Chrysanthemum	95	1·40
880	$1.95 Ullum	1·25	2·25
881	$2.30 Rose	1·50	2·75

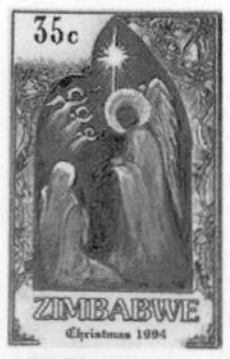

170 The Annunciation

1994. Christmas. Multicoloured.

882	35c. Type **170**	30	10
883	80c. Journey to Bethlehem	55	15
884	$1.15 The Nativity	70	40
885	$1.75 Shepherds	1·00	1·50
886	$1.95 Wise Men	1·10	1·90
887	$2.30 Mary and Jesus	2·50	2·50

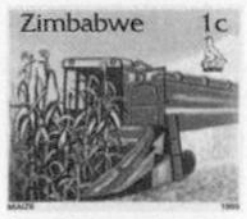

171 Harvesting Maize

1995. Zimbabwe Culture. Multicoloured.

888	1c. Type **171**	10	60
889	2c. Loading sugar cane	10	60
890	3c. Sunflowers	10	60
891	4c. Sorghum	10	60
892	5c. Miners	1·25	45
893	10c. Drilling for gold	1·75	50
894	20c. Opencast coal mining, Wankie	2·00	50
895	30c. Chrome smelting, Kwekwe	2·00	30
896	40c. Opencast iron extraction, Redcliff	2·00	20
896a	45c. Underground mining team	2·00	20
897	50c. Gold smelting	2·00	20
898	70c. Bogie Clock Tower, Gweru	30	20
899	80c. Masvingo Watchtower	30	20
900	$1 Hanging Tree, Harare	30	25
901	$2 Cecil House, Harare	40	55
902	$5 The Toposcope, Harare	50	1·00
903	$10 Paper House, Kwekwe	70	1·50

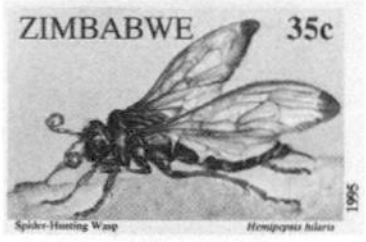

172 Spider-hunting Wasp

1995. Insects. Multicoloured.

904	35c. Type **172**	60	10
905	$1.15 European dragonfly	1·40	55
906	$1.75 Foxy charaxes (butterfly)	2·25	2·75
907	$2.30 Antlion	2·75	3·50

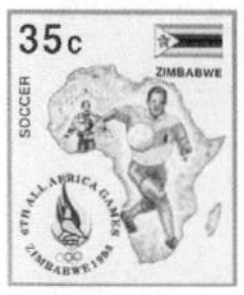

173 Football

1995. Sixth All-Africa Games, Harare. Each showing sport within map of Africa. Multicoloured.

908	35c. Type **173**	40	10
909	80c. Running	50	20
910	$1.15 Boxing	55	30
911	$1.75 Swimming	80	1·00
912	$1.95 Hockey	3·50	3·25
913	$2.30 Volleyball	1·75	3·25

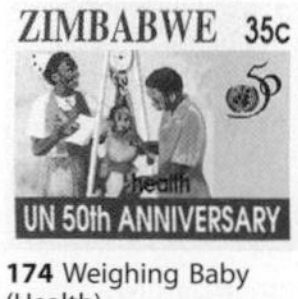

174 Weighing Baby (Health)

1995. 50th Anniv of United Nations. Multicoloured.

914	35c. Type **174**	15	10
915	$1.15 Women at pump (Environment)	30	35
916	$1.75 Workers on lorry (Food distribution)	50	80
917	$2.30 Teacher and children (Education)	60	1·60

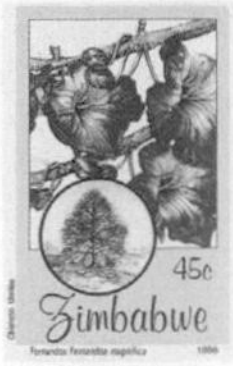

175 Fernandoa Tree

1996. Indigenous Flowering Trees. Multicoloured.

918	45c. Type **175**	30	10
919	$1 Round leaf mukwa	50	20
920	$1.50 Luckybean ree	70	60
921	$2.20 Winter cassia	85	1·00
922	$2.50 Sausage tree	90	1·40
923	$3 Sweet thorn	1·00	1·75

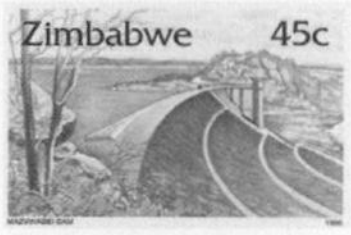

176 Mazvikadei Dam

1996. Dams of Zimbabwe. Multicoloured.

924	45c. Type **176**	15	10
925	$1.50 Mutirikwi Dam	45	40
926	$2.20 Ncema Dam	65	90
927	$3 Odzani Dam	75	1·40

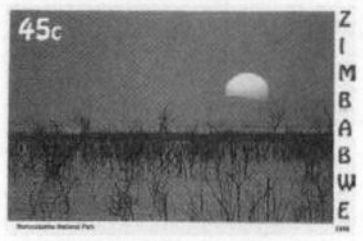

177 Matusadonha National Park at Sunset

1996. Scenic Views. Multicoloured.

928	45c. Type **177**	15	10
929	$1.50 Juliasdale rocky outcrop	45	40
930	$2.20 Honde Valley	75	1·00
931	$3 Finger Rocks at Morgenster Mission	85	1·60

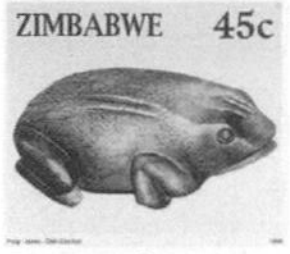

178 Carved Frog

1996. Animal Wood Carvings. Multicoloured.

932	45c. Type **178**	15	10
933	$1.50 Tortoise	30	20
934	$1.70 Kudu	35	40
935	$2.20 Chimpanzee	50	80
936	$2.50 Porcupine	55	90
937	$3 Rhinoceros	60	1·10

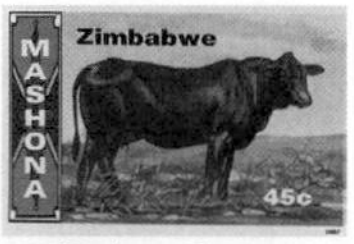

179 Mashona Cow

1997. Cattle Breeds. Multicoloured.

938	45c. Type **179**	35	10
939	$1.50 Tuli cow	65	25
940	$2.20 Nkoni bull	85	1·00
941	$3 Brahman bull	1·25	1·75

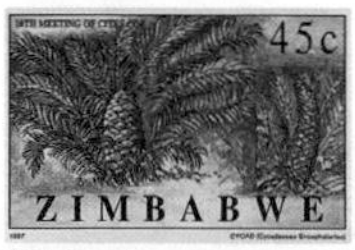

180 Cycad

1997. Tenth Meeting of Convention on International Trade in Endangered Species Members, Harare. Multicoloured.

942	45c. Type **180**	10	10
943	$1.50 Peregrine falcon	1·25	65
944	$1.70 Temminck's ground pangolin	30	60
945	$2.20 Black rhinoceros	1·25	1·50
946	$2.50 African elephant	1·25	1·50
947	$3 Python	70	1·60

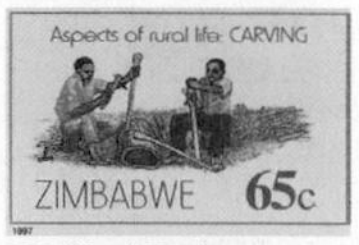

181 Wood Carving

1997. Rural Life. Multicoloured.

948	65c. Type **181**	15	10
949	$1 Winnowing	15	10
950	$2.40 Dancing	25	35
951	$2.50 Ploughing	25	35
952	$3.10 Stamping cereals	30	50
953	$4.20 Fetching water	45	70

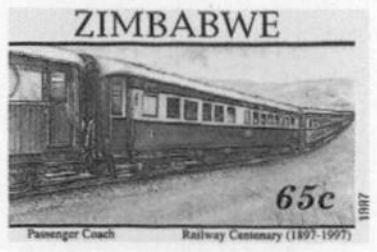

182 Passenger Coach No. 1826

1997. Centenary of Zimbabwe Railways. Multicoloured.

954	65c. Type **182**	20	15
955	$1 Class 12 steam locomotive No. 257	20	15
956	$2.40 Class 16A steam locomotive No. 605	25	35
957	$2.50 Class EL 1 electric locomotive No. 4107	25	35
958	$3.10 Steam locomotive No. 7 "Jack Tar"	30	50
959	$4.20 Class DE 2 diesel-electric locomotive No. 1211	40	70

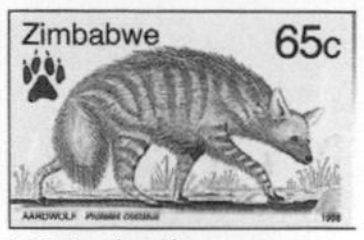

183 Aardwolf

1998. Lesser Known Animals of Zimbabwe. Multicoloured.

960	65c. Type **183**	20	10
961	$2.40 Large grey mongoose	25	30
962	$3.10 Clawless otter	30	55
963	$4.20 Antbear	35	80

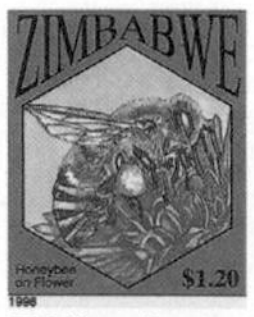

184 Honeybee on Flower

1998. Bees and Bee-keeping. Multicoloured.

964	$1.20 Type **184**	30	10
965	$4.10 Queen, worker and drone	35	35
966	$4.70 Queen and retinue	35	35
967	$5.60 Rural bee-keeper	45	50
968	$7.40 Commercial bee-keepers	65	80
969	$9.90 Products of the hive	85	1·10

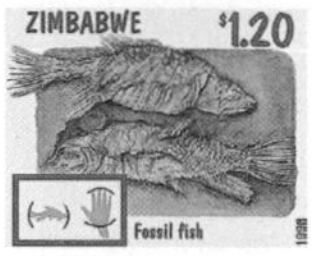

185 Fossil Fish

1998. Fossils. Multicoloured.

970	$1.20 Type **185**	80	10
971	$5.60 Allosaurus footprints	1·10	70
972	$7.40 Left foot of Massospondylus	1·25	1·10
973	$9.90 Fossil wood	1·50	1·75

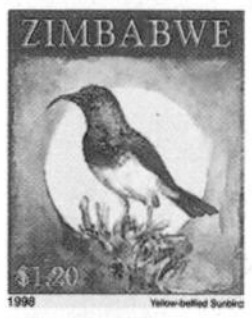

186 Variable Sunbird ("Yellow-bellied Sunbird")

1998. Birds. Multicoloured.

974	$1.20 Type **186**	50	15
975	$4.10 Lesser blue-eared glossy starling ("Lesser Blue-eared Starling")	70	35
976	$4.70 Grey-headed kingfisher ("Grey-hooded Kingfisher")	70	45
977	$5.60 Miombo grey tit	75	75
978	$7.40 Chirinda apalis	85	1·00
979	$9.90 Swynnerton's robin	95	1·40

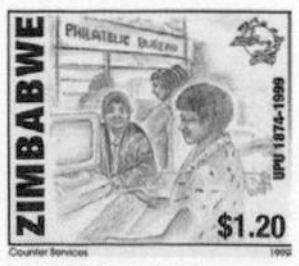

187 Philatelic Counter

1999. 125th Anniv of U.P.U. Multicoloured.

980	$1.20 Type **187**	20	10
981	$5.60 Postman delivering letters	55	25
982	$7.40 19th-century runner, motorcycle and truck	1·75	70
983	$9.90 Harare Central Sorting Office	60	80

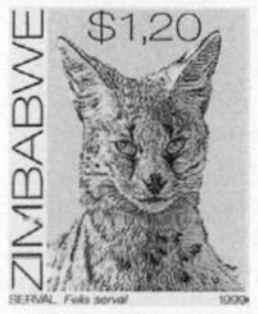

188 Serval

1999. Cats. Multicoloured.

984	$1.20 Type **188**	30	10
985	$5.60 Cheetah	65	45
986	$7.40 Caracal	80	90
987	$9.90 Leopard	1·25	1·60

1999. Owls (3rd series). As T **140**. Multicoloured.

988	$1.20 Cape eagle owl	1·10	35
989	$5.60 Grass owl	1·75	90
990	$7.40 Barn owl	2·25	2·25
991	$9.90 African marsh owl ("Marsh Owl")	2·50	2·75

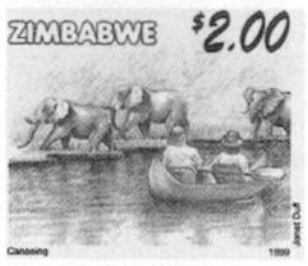

189 Canoe Safari

1999. Tourism in Zimbabwe. Multicoloured.

992	$2 Type **189**	15	15
993	$6.70 Rock climbing	50	40
994	$7.70 Flying microlight	55	50
995	$9.10 White water rafting	70	70
996	$12.00 Mountain scenery	80	1·10
997	$16.00 Game watching	1·10	1·75

No. 997 is inscribed "Game Veiwing" in error.

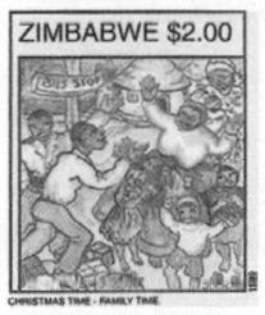

190 Family Reunion

1999. Christmas. Multicoloured.

998	$2 Type **190**	20	10
999	$6.70 Elephants around Christmas tree	30	25
1000	$7.70 Children and dog with balloons	30	25
1001	$9.10 Flame Lily	40	35
1002	$12 Madonna and Child	55	85
1003	$16 The Nativity	65	1·10

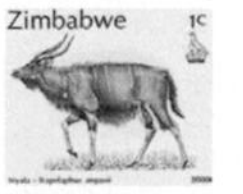

191 Nyala

2000. Fauna, Industry and Development. Multicoloured.

1004	1c. Type **191**	10	20
1005	10c. Building development	10	20
1006	30c. Timber yard	10	20
1007	50c. Tobacco auction	10	20
1008	70c. Central Sorting Office, Harare	10	30
1009	80c. Harare New International Airport	50	30
1010	$1 Westgate shopping complex	10	20
1011	$2 Nile Crocodile	50	30
1012	$3 Pungwe river water project	20	30
1013	$4 Zebra	50	30
1014	$5 Mining	65	35
1015	$7 National University of Science and Technology	20	35
1016	$10 Ostrich	1·00	40
1017	$15 Brown-necked parrot ("Cape Parrot")	1·00	60
1018	$20 Leather products	60	80
1019	$30 Lilac-breasted roller	1·50	1·00
1020	$50 Victoria Falls	1·60	1·60
1021	$100 Mukorsi Dam, Tokwe River	2·25	3·00
1021a	(–) Bateleur	50	30
1021b	$500 Goliath heron	1·00	75
1021c	$1000 White rhinoceros	2·50	1·75
1021d	$5000 Cheetah	1·50	2·00

No. 1021a is inscribed "Standard postage" and was initially sold at $100.

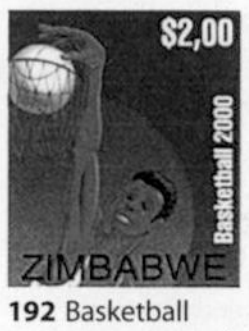

192 Basketball

2000. Sporting Activities. Multicoloured.

1022	$2 Type **192**	15	10
1023	$6.70 Tennis	40	35
1024	$7.70 Netball	40	45
1025	$9.10 Weightlifting	40	50
1026	$12 Taekwondo	55	65
1027	$16 Diving	65	75

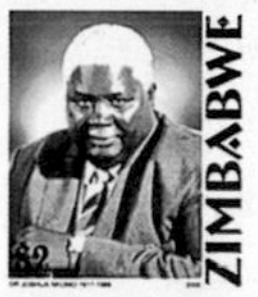

193 Dr. Joshua Nkomo

2000. First Death Anniv of Dr. Joshua Nkomo (nationalist leader). Multicoloured.

1028	$2 Type **193**	15	10
1029	$9.10 Nkomo in traditional costume	40	50
1030	$12 Type **193**	55	65
1031	$16 As $9.10	65	90

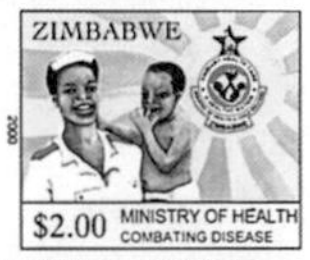

194 Nurse with Baby and Ministry of Health Logo

2000. Health Promotion Campaign. Multicoloured.

1032	$2 Type **194**	15	10
1033	$6.70 Boy with football and anti-tuberculosis emblem	30	30
1034	$7.70 Couple with baby and "New Start" logo	35	30
1035	$9.10 Health technician on motorcycle and Riders for Health badge	60	50
1036	$12 Ribbon emblem on map and Ministry of Health logo	65	70
1037	$16 Fisherman and Rotary International emblem	70	80

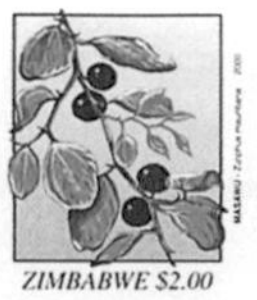

195 Masawu Fruit

2000. Wild Fruit (2nd series). Multicoloured.

1038	$2 Type **195**	15	10
1039	$6.70 Spiny monkey orange	30	30
1040	$7.70 Bird plum	30	35
1041	$9.10 Shakama plum	40	45
1042	$12 Wild medlar	60	65
1043	$16 Wild custard apple	65	75

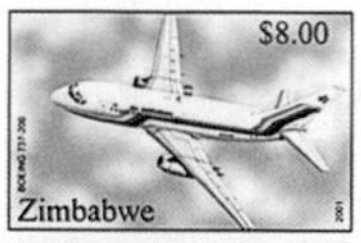

196 Boeing 737-200

2001. Aircraft. Multicoloured.

1044	$8 Type **196**	50	25
1045	$12 BAe Hawk MK 60	65	70
1046	$14 Hawker Hunter FGA-9	75	85
1047	$16 Cessna/Reims F-337	85	70
1048	$21 Aerospatiale Alouette III helicopter	95	1·10
1049	$28 Boeing 767-200ER	1·40	1·75

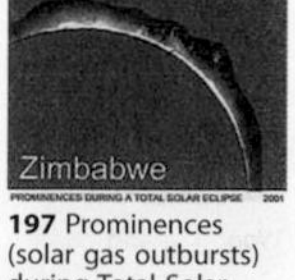

197 Prominences (solar gas outbursts) during Total Solar Eclipse

2001. Total Solar Eclipse, 21 June 2001. Multicoloured.

1050	$8 Type **197**	55	25
1051	$21 Path of eclipse over Southern Africa	1·25	1·40
1052	$28 Phases of total solar eclipse (62×22 mm)	1·40	1·75

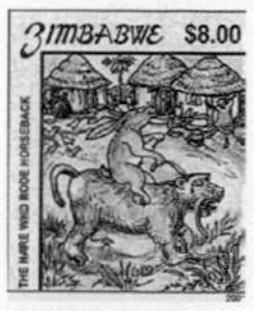

198 "The Hare who rode Horseback"

2001. African Folk Tales. Multicoloured.

1053	$8 Type **198**	35	25
1054	$12 "The Hippo who lost his Hair"	45	35
1055	$13 "The Lion who was saved by a Mouse"	45	40
1056	$16 "The Bush Fowl who wakes the Sun"	60	50
1057	$21 "The Chameleon who came too Late"	85	90
1058	$28 "The Tortoise who collected Wisdom"	1·10	1·40
MS1059	126×105 mm. Nos. 1053/8	3·50	3·50

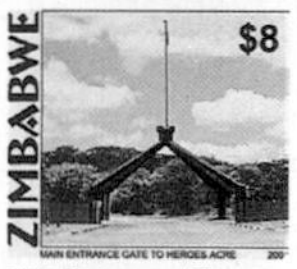

199 Entrance, Heroes Acre Memorial, Harare

2001. 21st Anniv of Independence. Heroes Acre Memorial, Harare. Multicoloured.

1060	$8 Type **199**	40	25
1061	$16 Statue of Unknown Soldier	60	45
1062	$21 Obelisk	80	1·00
1063	$28 Aerial view	1·10	1·40

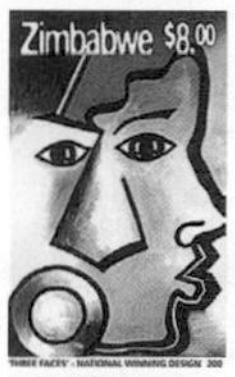

200 "Three Faces" (N. Mguni) (national winner)

2001. U.N. Dialogue Among Civilizations. Multicoloured.

1064	$8 Type **200**	75	25
1065	$21 "Children encircling globe" (Urska Golob) (international winner)	1·75	2·00

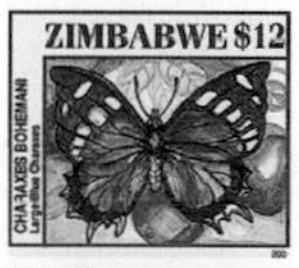

201 *Charaxes bohemani* (butterfly)

2001. Butterflies (2nd series). Multicoloured.

1066	$12 Type **201**	75	35
1067	$20 *Vanessa cardui*	1·00	70
1068	$25 *Precis oenone cebrene*	1·25	90
1069	$30 *Euphaedra neophron*	1·40	1·40
1070	$35 *Iolaus silas* (female)	1·60	1·60
1071	$45 *Acrea aglanice*	1·90	2·25
MS1072	140×95 mm. Nos. 1066/71	7·25	8·00

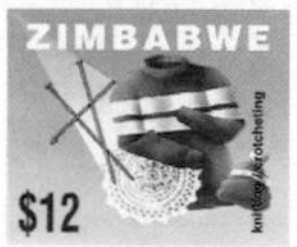

202 Knitting and Crotchet Work

2002. Local Crafts. Multicoloured.

1073	$12 Type **202**	45	35
1074	$20 Art and design	60	55
1075	$25 Baskets	70	70
1076	$30 Pottery	80	90
1077	$35 Woodcarving	90	1·10
1078	$45 Sculpture	1·25	1·40

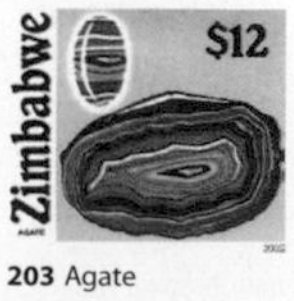

203 Agate

2002. Gemstones. Multicoloured.

1079	$12 Type **203**	1·00	35
1080	$25 Aquamarine	1·50	1·00
1081	$35 Diamond	1·90	1·90
1082	$45 Emerald	2·25	2·50

204 "Two Girls arm-in-arm" (Tazivei Makwavarara)

2002. Fifth Anniv of Childline in Zimbabwe. Multicoloured.

1083	$12 Type **204**	75	35
1084	$25 "Girl using telephone" (Ashley Elkington)	1·25	90
1085	$35 "Teddy bear" (Goldine Hobbs)	1·60	1·75
1086	$45 "Hand holding telephone" (Admire Kacheche)	2·00	2·50

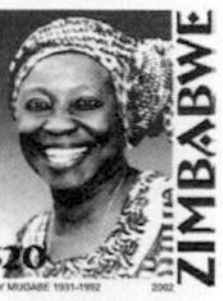

205 Sally Mugabe

2002. Tenth Death Anniv of Sally Mugabe (wife of President). Multicoloured.

1087	$20 Type **205**	70	55
1088	$50 Mrs. Mugabe in black and white dress	1·50	1·75
1089	$70 Type **205**	1·90	2·25
1090	$90 As $50	2·50	3·00

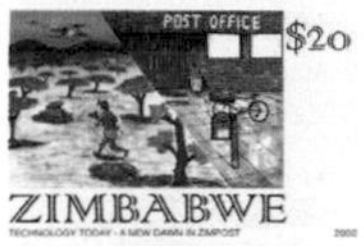

206 "Mail Runner and Local Post Office" (Agreement Ngwenya)

2002. "Technology Today" School Design Competition Winners. Multicoloured.

1091	$20 Type **206**	1·00	55
1092	$70 "Mail runner and Airliner" (Kudzai Chikomo)	3·25	3·50

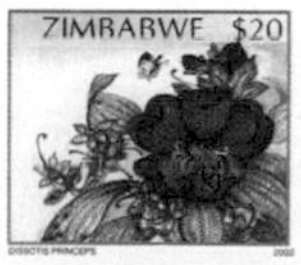

207 *Dissotis princeps*

2002. Wild Flowers (2nd series). Multicoloured.

1093	$20 Type **207**	80	55
1094	$35 *Leonotis nepetifolia*	1·25	90
1095	$40 *Hibiscus vitifolius*	1·40	1·25
1096	$50 *Boophane disticha*	1·60	1·60
1097	$70 *Pycnostachys urticifolia*	2·00	2·50
1098	$90 *Gloriosa superba*	2·75	4·25
MS1099	120×105 mm. Nos. 1093/8	9·00	10·00

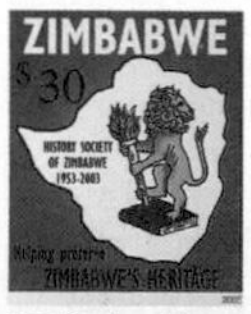

208 Society Logo

2003. 50th Anniv of History Society of Zimbabwe. Multicoloured.

1100	$30 Type **208**	60	15
1101	$80 Books and scroll (Historical Evidence)	1·50	90
1102	$110 Oral traditions	1·75	2·25
1103	$140 Old buildings	2·00	2·75

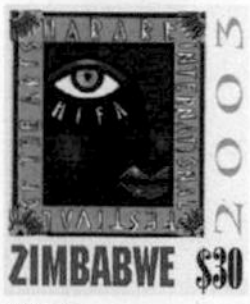

209 Logo

2003. Harare International Festival of the Arts. Multicoloured.

1104	$30 Type **209**	25	10
1105	$80 Green logo and pink daisy	65	45
1106	$110 Eye logo and three pink daisies	85	85
1107	$140 Pink logo with pink and orange daisies	1·10	1·40

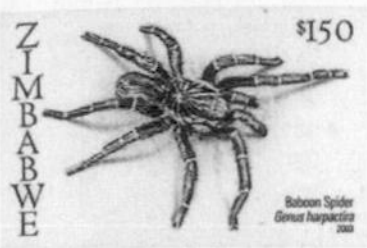

210 Baboon Spider (*Genus harpactira*)

2003. Spiders of Zimbabwe. Multicoloured.

1108	$150 Type **210**	30	15
1109	$200 Rain spider (*Genus palystes*)	30	15
1110	$600 Black button (Widow) spider (*Latrodectus renivulvatus*)	75	30
1111	$900 Wolf spider (*Lycosidae*)	1·10	1·10
1112	$1250 Violin spider (*Loxoscelidae*)	1·25	1·60
1113	$1600 Wall spider (*Selenopidae*)	1·50	2·00
MS1114	159×98 mm. Nos. 1108/13	4·75	5·50

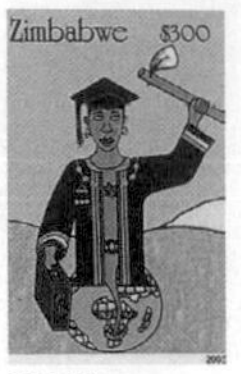

211 Woman Graduate with Briefcase and Hoe (Tamuka Makuluni)

2003. Empowerment of Women. Winning entries from national stamp design competition. Multicoloured.

1115	$300 Type **211**	50	15
1116	$2100 Woman graduate with friend (Chloe Edwards)	2·25	2·50

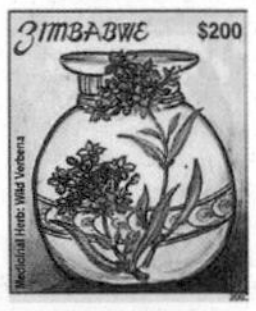

212 Wild Verbena

2003. Endangered Medicinal Herbs of Zimbabwe. Multicoloured.

1117	$200 Type **212**	30	10
1118	$500 Pimpernel	70	20
1119	$1000 African arrowroot	1·25	70
1120	$3000 Bird pepper	2·50	2·75
1121	$4200 Wild garlic	3·00	3·50
1122	$5400 Cleome	3·50	4·25
MS1123	116×116 mm. Nos. 1117/22	10·00	11·00

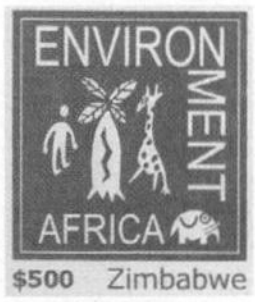

213 Environment Africa Emblem

2004. Environment Africa.

1124	**213**	$500 green	70	20
1125	-	$3000 multicoloured	2·50	2·25
1126	-	$4200 blue, cobalt and black	3·00	3·25
1127	-	$5400 black, yellow and emerald	3·50	4·25

DESIGNS: $3000 Sondela emblem; $4200 Water Africa emblem; $5400 Tree Africa emblem.

Due to the collapse of the Zimbabwe dollar, we are unable to price the following new issues.

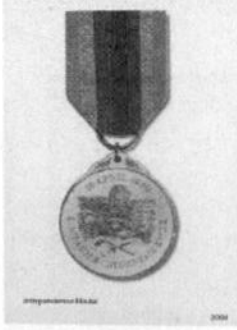

214 Independence Medal

2004. Medals. Multicoloured.

1128	$15000 Type **214**	35	10
1129	$90000 Bronze Cross of Zimbabwe	2·20	2·20
1130	$130000 Silver Cross of Zimbabwe	3·25	3·50
1131	$165000 Gold Cross of Zimbabwe	4·00	4·25

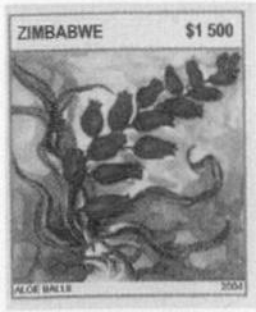

215 *Aloe Ballii*

2004. Aloes. Multicoloured.

1132	$15000 Type **215**	35	10
1133	$30000 *Aloe Rhodesiana*	75	20
1134	$90000 *Aloe Greatheadii*	2·20	2·10
1135	$100000 *Aloe Ortholopha*	2·50	2·75
1136	$130000 *Aloe Inyangensis*	3·25	3·75
1137	$165000 *Aloe Arborescens*	4·00	4·75
MS1138	120×106 mm. Nos. 1132/7	13·00	13·00

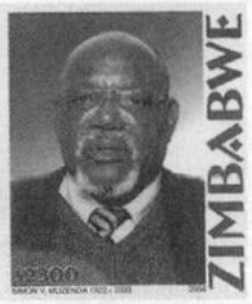

216 Simon Vengai Muzenda

2004. First Death Anniv of Simon Vengai Muzenda (Co-Vice Pres.). Multicoloured.

1139	**216**	$23000 red background	65	30
1140	**216**	$120000 yellow background	2·00	2·00
1141	**216**	$170000 green background	2·50	2·50
1142	**216**	$220000 grey background	3·75	4·50

2004. First Joint Issue of Southern Africa Postal Operators Association Members. Sheet 170×95 mm containing hexagonal designs as T **227a** of Zambia showing national birds of Association members. Multicoloured.

MS1143 $500 African fish eagles in flight (Zimbabwe); $1000 Purple-crested turaco ('lourie') (Swaziland); $2300 African fish eagles perched on tree (Zimbabwe); $3000 Stanley ('Blue') crane (South Africa); $5000 Cattle egret (Botswana); $9000 Peregrine falcon (Angola); $12000 Bar-tailed trogon (Malawi) (inscr 'apaloderma vittatum'); $17000 African fish eagles perched and in flight (Namibia) 35·00 35·00

The stamp depicting the bar-tailed trogon is not inscribed with the country of which the bird is a national symbol.

Miniature sheets of similar designs were also issued by Angola, Botswana, Malawi, Namibia, South Africa, Swaziland and Zambia.

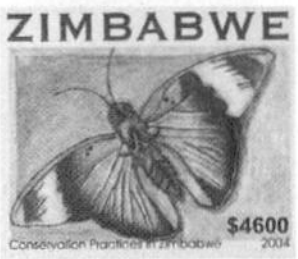

217 Butterfly (*Kingston Chigidhani*)

2004. "Conservation Practices in Zimbabwe" Stamp Design Competition. Winning Stamps from the Junior and Open Categories. Multicoloured.

1144	$46000 Type **217**	1·90	2·00
1145	$335000 Hands "protecting" wildlife (Kudzai Chikomo)	3·50	4·50

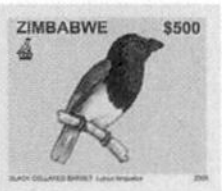

218 Black-collared Barbet

2005. Birds of Zimbabwe (1st series). Multicoloured.

1146	$5000 Type **218**	50	75
1147	$50000 Grey-headed bush shrike	1·00	50
1148	(Z) Red-headed weaver	1·25	55
1149	$100000 Golden-breasted bunting	1·25	70
1150	$200000 Cut-throat weaver ("cut-throat finch")	1·75	1·25
1151	(A) Cabanis's yellow bunting ("Cabanis's bunting")	2·00	1·50
1152	(E) Miombo double-collared sunbird	2·00	1·50
1153	(R) Levaillant's barbet ("Crested barbet")	2·50	2·75
1154	$500000 White-browed robin chat ("Heuglin's robin")	5·00	6·00
1155	$1000000 Giant kingfisher	8·00	9·00

Nos. 1148 and 1151/3 were all inscribed "STANDARD POSTAGE" and were initially sold for $6900, $30000, $400000 or $500000 respectively.

See also Nos. 1215/**MS**1225 and 1234/9.

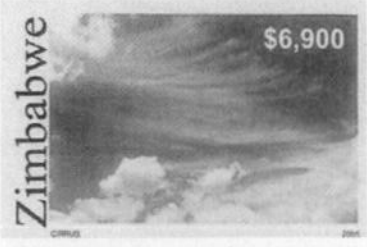

219 Cirrus

2005. Cloud Formations. Multicoloured.

1156	$69000 Type **219**	85	40
1157	$138000 Nimbo-stratus	1·75	80
1158	$300000 Alto cumulus	3·75	4·50
1159	$400000 Cumulo-nimbus	4·75	5·50

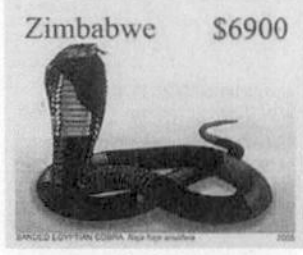

220 Banded Egyptian Cobra

2005. Snakes of Zimbabwe. Multicoloured.

1160	$69000 Type **220**	1·00	40
1161	$138000 Puff adder	1·50	70
1162	$200000 Boomslang	2·00	1·50
1163	$250000 Mocambique spitting cobra	2·50	2·50
1164	$300000 Gaboon viper	2·50	3·50
1165	$400000 Black mamba	3·50	4·50
MS1166	140×102 mm. Nos. 1160/5	12·00	13·00

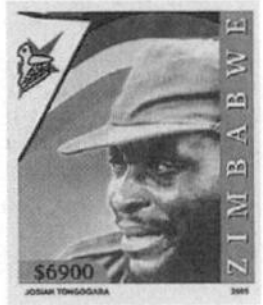

221 Josiah Tongogara (nationalist)

2005. Commemorations (1st series). Multicoloured.

1167	$69000 Type **221**	70	40
1168	$138000 Herbert Chitepo (nationalist)	1·00	70
1169	$300000 Bernard Chidzero (former Chief Minister)	2·00	2·25
1170	$500000 Moven Mahachi (Minister of Defence 1990–2001)	3·00	3·25

See also Nos. 1230/3.

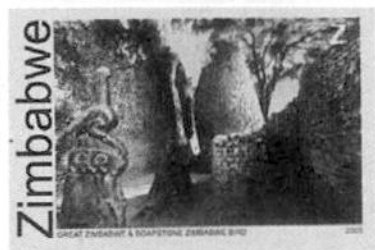

222 Great Zimbabwe and Soapstone Bird Sculpture

2005. World Heritage Sites of Zimbabwe. Multicoloured.

1171	(Z) Type **222**	60	30
1172	$155000 Wall patterns, Khami ruins	1·00	65
1173	$520000 Elephant eating apple ring acacia, Mana Pools National Park	6·00	6·00
1174	$620000 Victoria Falls	6·00	6·50
MS1175	118×101 mm. Nos. 1171/4	12·00	13·00

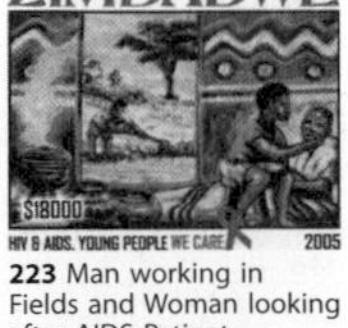

223 Man working in Fields and Woman looking after AIDS Patient

2005. Anti-HIV and AIDS Campaign. Design showing winning entries in stamp design competition. Multicoloured.

1176	$18000 Type **223**	1·50	1·00
1177	$80000 Children looking after AIDS patient and boy teaching	5·50	6·00

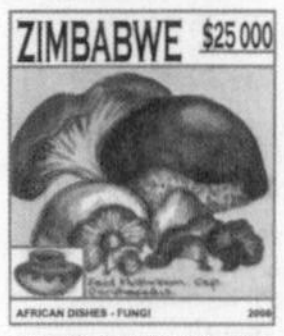

224 Field Mushroom, Cep, *Cantharellus longisporus* and *Cantharellus miniatescens*

2006. African Dishes. Multicoloured.

1178	$25000 Type **224**	1·25	50
1179	$35000 Rapoko, maize and sorghum (grains)	75	50
1180	$50000 Pumpkin, watermelon and spiny cucumber	90	65
1181	$150000 Jackal berry, wild loquat, marula, numnum, kei apple and bush orange (wild fruits)	2·25	2·25
1182	$250000 Bramble, okra, bird peppers, wild hibiscus, rosella (herbs) and mopane worms (caterpillars)	4·00	4·50
1183	$300000 Sweet potato, cassava and ground nuts	4·00	4·50
MS1184	114×104 mm. Nos. 1177/82	12·00	13·00

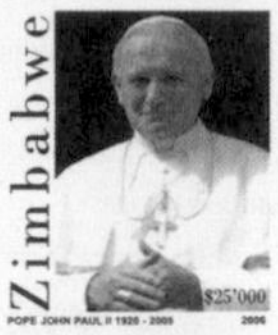

225 Pope John Paul II

2006. Pope John Paul II Commemoration. Multicoloured.

1185	$25000 Type **225**	2·00	75
1186	$250000 Pope with crozier and mitre	8·00	9·00
MS1187	101×77 mm. Nos. 1184/5	10·00	10·00

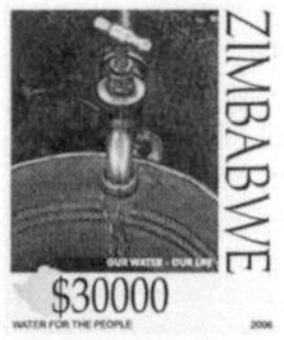

226 Water Tap

2006. Water Conservation and Useage in Zimbabwe. Multicoloured.

1188	$30000 Type **226**	50	25
1189	$225000 Irrigation channel and crops	2·25	1·50
1190	$375000 Lionesses drinking	3·00	3·50
1191	$450000 Sluice gates at Kariba Dam	3·25	3·75

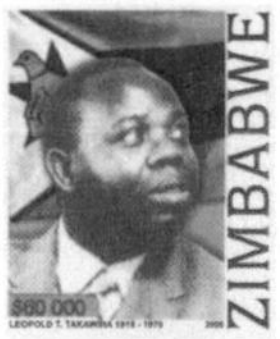

227 Leopold Takawira (nationalist)

2006. Commemorations. Multicoloured.

1192	$60000 Type **227**	60	35
1193	$350000 Simon Mazorodze (Deputy Minister of Health, 1980–1)	1·50	1·50
1194	$500000 Herbert Ushewokunze (Transport Minister, 1984–8)	2·00	2·50
1195	$650000 Tichafa Parirenyatwa (nationalist)	2·50	3·00

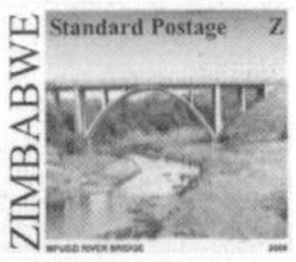

228 Mpudzi River Bridge

2006. Bridges of Zimbabwe. Multicoloured.

1196	Z Type **228**	70	35
1197	$450 Victoria Falls Bridge over Zambezi River seen from No. 2 Gorge	1·60	55
1198	$600 Limpopo River Railway Bridge, Beitbridge	2·25	1·75
1199	$750 Otto Beit Suspension Bridge over Zambezi River, Chirundu	2·75	3·00
1200	$800 Lake Kariba Barrage Road Bridge	2·75	3·00
1201	$1000 Birchenough Save River Bridge	3·25	4·50
MS1202	140×103 mm. Nos. 1196/1201	12·00	13·00

No. 1196 is inscribed "Standard Postage" and was originally sold for $100.

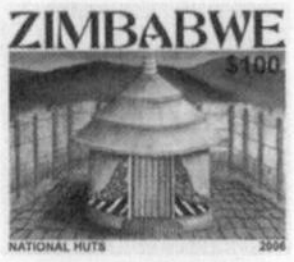

229 Ancient Hut (Freddy Tembo)

2006. National Huts. Design showing winning entries in postage stamp design competition. Multicoloured.

1203	$100 Type **229**	50	25
1204	$800 Ancient, modern and future huts (Elisha Homera)	4·50	4·75
MS1205	104×74 mm. Nos. 1203/4	5·00	6·00

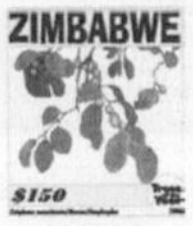

230 *Ziziphuus Mauritania*

2006. Trees of the Year. Multicoloured.

1206	$150 Type **230**	60	35
1207	$600 *Schlerochra birrea* (marula)	2·00	1·50
1208	$750 *Jatropha carcus*	2·75	3·00
1209	$1000 *Uaparca kirkiana*	3·25	4·00
MS1210	103×110 mm. Nos. 1206/9	7·75	8·50

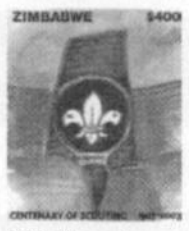

231 Scout Badge on Ruins of Great Zimbabwe

2007. Centenary of Scouting. Multicoloured.

1211	$400 Type **231**	70	35
1212	$1500 Scout badge on Zimbabwe flag	2·50	1·50
1213	$2000 Peace doves and bird sculpture from Great Zimbabwe	3·50	3·75
1214	$2500 Scout badge on map of Africa	4·50	5·50

2007. Birds of Zimbabwe (2nd series). As T **218**. Multicoloured.

1215	$50 Hoopoe	25	40
1216	$100 Cattle egret	30	40
1217	$500 Malachite Kingfisher	40	20
1218	$1000 Little bee-eater	50	30
1219	$2000 Purplecrested lourie	70	40
1220	$5000 Purple gallinule	1·00	70
1221	$10000 African jacana	2·00	1·25
1222	$20000 Ground hornbill	4·00	3·00
1223	$50000 Gorgeous bush shrike	[illegible]	[illegible]
1224	$100000 Secretary bird	11·00	12·00
MS1225	154×87 mm. Nos. 1215/24	25·00	26·00

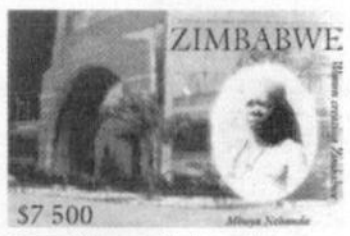

232 Mbuya Nehanda (resistance leader) and Reserve Bank of Zimbabwe

2007. 'Women creating Zimbabwe'. Multicoloured.

1226	$7500 Type **232**	70	50
1227	$29000 Lozikeyi (senior wife) and Lobengula's court	2·00	2·00
1228	$35000 Mother Patrick (missionary)	2·25	2·75
1229	$45000 Amai Sally Mugabe and Chinyaradzo Children's Home, Harare	2·75	3·25

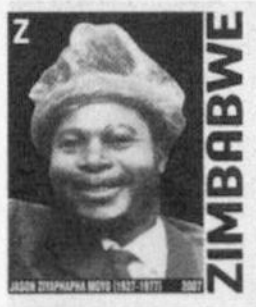

233 Jason Ziyaphapha Moyo

2007. Commemorations (2nd series). Multicoloured.

1230	(Z) Type **233**	60	20
1231	(A) Maurice Nyagumbo	1·25	70
1232	(E) Guy Clutton-Brock	2·00	2·00
1233	(R) Chief Rekayi Tangwena	3·25	3·75

No. 1230 (Z) was for domestic postage of letters weighing up to 20 grams. Nos. 1231/3 were for letters weighing up to 10 grams to Africa (A), Europe (E) and rest of the World (R).

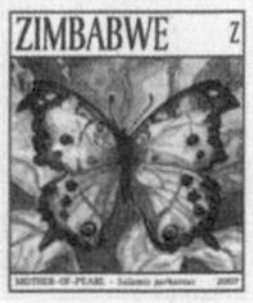

234 *Salamis parhassus* (mother-of-pearl)

2007. Butterflies (3rd series). Multicoloured.

1234	(Z) Type **234**	75	35
1235	(A) *Papilio demodocus* (citrus swallowtail)	1·25	70
1236	(E) *Anthocharis cardamines* (orange tip)	1·75	1·75
1237	(R) *Charaxes bohemani* (blue charaxes)	2·50	2·75
1238	$50000 *Colotis danae* (crimson tip)	3·50	3·75
1239	$100000 *Cynthia cardui* (painted lady)	6·00	6·50

No. **MS**1240 is left for a miniature sheet, not yet received.

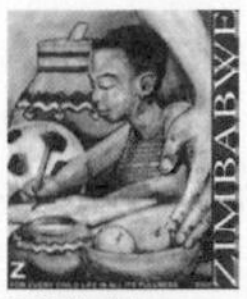

235 Healthy Young Boy studying (John Ndhlovu)

2007. 'For Every Child Life in All its Fullness'. Showing winning entries in postage stamp design competition. Multicoloured.

1241	(Z) Type **235**	75	30
1242	$100000 Mother feeding baby (Fungai Madzima)	4·75	5·50
MS1243	90×75 mm. Nos. 1241/2	5·50	6·00

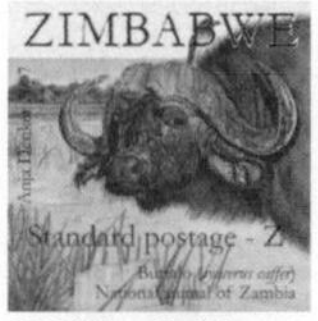

236 African Buffalo (Zambia)

2007. Second Joint Issue of Southern Africa Postal Operators Association Members. Designs showing national animals of Association Members. Multicoloured.

1244	Z Type **236**	75	35
1245	A Nyala (pair) (Malawi)	1·50	75
1246	$100000 Nyala (Zimbabwe)	2·25	2·25
1247	E Burchell's zebra (Botswana)	2·25	2·50
1248	R Oryx (Namibia)	2·75	3·25

No. **MS**1249 is left for miniature sheet not yet received.

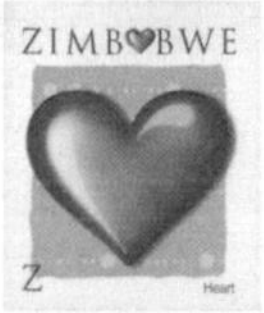

237 Heart

2008. Valentine's Day. Multicoloured.

1250	Z Type **237**	75	35
1251	A Cupid	1·25	75
1252	E Heart-shaped valentine cards	1·50	1·75
1253	R Red rose	2·00	2·50
MS1254	89×114 mm. Nos. 1250/3	5·00	5·50

No. 1250, initially sold at $25000, was for domestic postage of letters weighing up to 20 grams.

Nos. 1251/3 were initially sold at $100000 (A), $170000 (E) and $240000 (R). They were for letters weighing up to 10 grams to Africa, Europe and rest of the world.

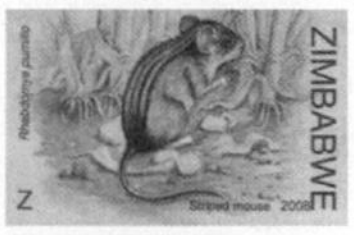

238 Striped Mouse (*Rhabdomys pumilio*)

2008. Rats and Mice of Zimbabwe. Multicoloured.

1255	Z Type **238**	70	35
1256	A Water rat (*Dasymys incomtus*)	1·00	70
1257	E Angoni vlei rat (*Otomys angoniensis*)	1·50	1·50
1258	R Woodland dormouse (*Graphiurus (claviglis) murinus*)	2·50	2·50
1259	$5000000 Bushveld gerbil (*Tatera leucogaster*)	3·00	3·25
1260	$10000000 Namaqua rock mouse (*Aethomys namaquensis*)	5·00	5·50
MS1261	125×125 mm. Nos. 1255/60	12·00	13·00

No. 1255, initially sold at $550,000, was for domestic postage of letters weighing up to 20 grams.

Nos. 1256/8 were initially sold at $1,900,000 (A), $3,150,000 (E) and $4,600,000 (R). They were for letters weighing up to 10 grams to Africa, Europe and rest of the world.

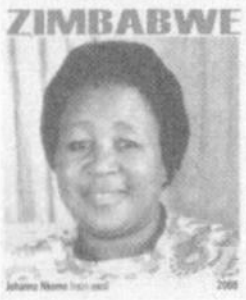

239 Johanna Nkomo

2008. Commemorations (3rd series). Multicoloured.

1262	Z Type **239**	75	35
1263	A Ruth Lottie Nomonde Chinamano	1·25	75
1264	E Swithun Tachiona Mombeshora	1·50	1·75
1265	R Willie Dzawanda Musarurwa	2·00	2·75

No. 1261, initially sold at $250m, was for domestic postage of letters weighing up to 20 grams.

Nos. 1262/4 were initially sold at $50bn (A), $90bn (E) or $110bn (R). They were for letters weighing up to 10 grams to Africa, Europe and rest of the world.

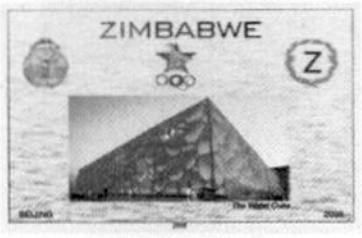

240 The Water Cube

2009. Olympic Games, Beijing. Multicoloured.

1266	(Z) Type **240**	1·00	60
1267	(A) Bird's Nest Stadium	1·75	1·50
1268	(E) The Olympic Pool	2·75	2·75
1269	(R) Zimbabwe flag	3·00	3·25

No. 1266 (Z) was for domestic postage. Nos. 1267/9 were for letters to Africa (A), Europe (E) and the rest of the world (R).

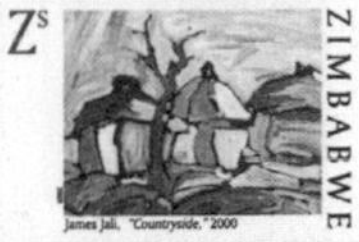

241 *Countryside* (James Jali), 2000

2009. Contemporary Paintings by Zimbabwean Artists. Multicoloured.

1270	(Zs) Type **241**	85	50
1271	(Zb) Gardener Scopo (Cosmos Shiridzinomwa), 2008	85	50
1272	(A) *Mountains* (George Churu), 1996	1·50	1·50
1273	(A) *Barn* (Hilary Kashiri), 1998	1·50	1·50
1274	(E) *Backyard 1* (Freddy Tauro), 2007	1·75	2·00
1275	(R) *X in the Land* (Admire Kamudzengere), 2008	2·25	2·75

No. **MS**1276 is left for a miniature sheet not yet received.

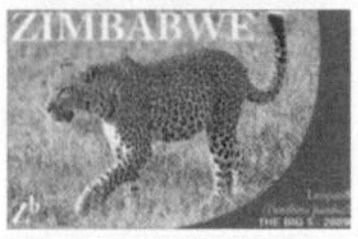

242 Leopard (*Panthera pardus*)

2009. 'The Big Five'. Multicoloured.

1277	(Zb) Type **242**	1·00	60
1278	(Zs) Black rhinoceros (*Diceros bicornis*)	1·50	1·00
1279	(A) African buffalo (*Synceros caffer*)	1·75	1·50
1280	(A) Lion (*Panthera leo*)	1·75	1·50
1281	(E) African elephant (*Loxodonta africana*)	2·75	2·75
1282	(R) 'The Big Five'	3·00	3·25

No. **MS**1283 is left for a miniature sheet not yet received.

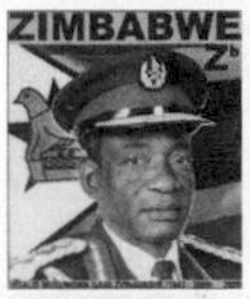

243 Vitalis Musungwa Gava Zvinavashe

2009. Commemorations (4th series). Multicoloured.

1284	(Zb) Type **243**	60	35
1285	(Zs) Garikayi Hlomayi Settled Magadzire	75	60
1286	(A) George Bodzo Nyandoro	1·00	1·00
1287	(E) Border Madzibaba Gezi	1·50	1·50
1288	(R) Seugeant Masotsha Ndlovu	1·75	2·00

Nos. 1284/5 were for domestic postage.

Nos. 1286/8 were for letters weighing up to 10 grams to Africa, Europe and rest of the world.

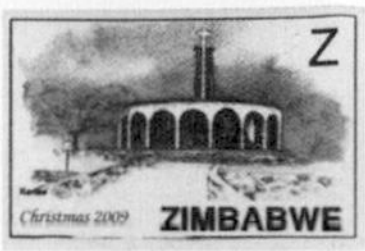

244 Santa Barbara's Catholic Church, Kariba Heights

2009. Christmas. Contemporary Rural Churches in Zimbabwe. Multicoloured.

1289	(Z) Type **244**	75	20
1290	(A) Catholic Church, Regina Coeli	1·25	80
1291	(E) Elim Evangelical Church, Katerere	1·50	1·50
1292	(R) Free Presbyterian Church, Mbuma	2·00	2·50

No. 1289 was for domestic postage.

Nos. 1290/2 were for letters weighing up to 10 grams to Africa, Europe and rest of the world. .

No. **MS**1293 was left for miniature sheet not yet received.

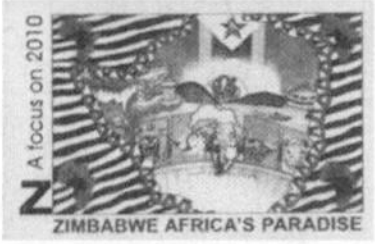

245 Map of Zimbabwe enclosing National Flag, Animals and Kariba Dam (Fredy Tembo)

2010. 'Zimbabwe Africa's Paradise'. Designs showing winning entries in postage stamp design competition. Multicoloured.

1294	(Z) Type **245**	1·25	60
1295	(A) Torch illuminating boatman, elephant and rhino (Munashe M. Patsanza)	2·00	1·50
1296	(E) Map of Africa and footballs enclosing Zimbabwe scenes (Methembe Dhlamini)	2·25	2·50
1297	(R) Victoria Falls, lion, walls of Great Zimbabwe, Zimbabwe bird and flower (Kudzai Chikomo)	2·75	3·00

No. 1294 was for domestic postage.

Nos. 1295/7 were for letters weighing up to 10 grams to Africa, Europe and rest of the world. .

No. **MS**1298 was left for miniature sheet not yet received.

2010. Third Joint Issue of Southern Africa Postal Operators Association Members. World Cup Football Championship, South Africa. Multicoloured.

1299	10c. Namibia	15	15
1300	15c. South Africa	20	20
1301	25c. Zimbabwe	40	30
1302	(Z) Botswana	40	30
1303	50c. Malawi	75	75
1304	(A) Mauritius	1·10	1·10
1305	75c. Swaziland	1·10	1·10
1306	(E) Lesotho	1·10	1·10
1307	(R) Zambia	1·50	2·00
MS1308	189×167 mm. As Nos. 1299/307 but gold foil background	9·00	9·00

Nos. 1299/301, 1303 and 1305 were donominated in US dollars.

Nos. 1302, 1304 and 1306/7 were originally sold at 25c. (Z), 50c. (A), 75c. (E) and $1 (R). No. 1302 was for domestic postage of letters weighing up to 20 grams. Nos. 1304 and 1306/7 were for letters weighing up to 10 grams to Africa, Europe and rest of the world.

Similar designs were issued by Botswana, Lesotho, Malawi, Mauritius, Namibia, South Africa, Swaziland and Zambia.

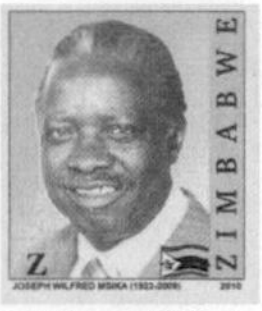

246 Joseph Wilfred Msika

2010. First Death Anniv of Joseph Wilfred Msika (Vice President 1999–2009). Multicoloured.

1309	(Z) Type **246**	90	45
1310	(A) As Type **246** (grey background)	1·40	1·10
1311	(E) Joseph Msika (wearing hat) (red background)	1·40	1·40
1312	(R) As No. 1311 (green background)	1·75	2·00

Nos. 1309/12 were originally sold at 25c. (Z), 50c. (A), 75c. (E) and $1 (R). No. 1309 was for domestic postage of letters weighing up to 20 grams. Nos. 1310/12 were for letters weighing up to 10 grams to Africa, Europe and rest of the world.

247 Map of Africa showing PAPU Countries

2010. 30th Anniv of the Pan-African Postal Union
1313	**247**	(Z) multicoloured	1·00	55

No. 1313 was inscr 'Z' and was originally valid for 25c. It was for domestic postage of letters weighing up to 20 grams.

248 Harare Railway Station

2011. Railway Stations of Zimbabwe. Multicoloured.
1314	25c. Type **248**	1·00	75
1315	30c. Kadoma	1·00	75
1316	85c. Bulawayo	2·25	2·50
1317	$1 Mutare	2·25	2·50

249 Tarcissius Malan George Silundika

2011. Commemorations (5th series). Multicoloured.
1318	25c. Type **249**	1·00	75
1319	30c. Julia Zvobgo	1·00	75
1320	85c. Ariston Maguranyanga Chambati	2·25	2·50
1321	$1 Joseph Luke Culverwell	2·25	2·50

250 Shona Hut

2011. Culture (Huts). Multicoloured.
1322	25c. Type **250**	1·00	75
1323	30c. Ndebele huts	1·00	75
1324	85c. Manyika huts	2·25	2·50
1325	$1 Tonga hut	2·25	2·50
MS1326	106×106 mm. Nos. 1322/5	6·50	6·50

251 Tobacco Wither (Henry Munyaradzi)

2012. Sculptures of Zimbabwe. Multicoloured.
1327	5c. Type **251**	20	15
1328	25c. Family (Bernard Matemera)	1·00	75
1329	30c. Mother and Daughters (Victor Mutongwizo)	1·00	75
1330	50c. As 5c.	1·50	1·00
1331	75c. Bird carrying Spirit People (Thomas Mukarobgwa) (35×30 mm)	2·00	2·25
1332	85c. Wounded Kudu (Bakali Manzi) (35×30 mm)	2·25	2·50
1333	$1 Witch and her Mate (Sylvester Mubayi) (35×30 mm)	2·25	2·50
1334	$1.50 As 75c. (35×30 mm)	3·75	4·00
MS1335	90×130 mm. Nos. 1327/30		
MS1336	105×106 mm. Nos. 1331/4		

252 Solomon Tapfumaneyi Ruzambo Mujuru (1945-2011)

2012. Commemorations. Multicoloured.
1337	30c. Type **252**	1·00	75
1338	75c. Eddison Jonas Mudadirwa Zvobgo (1935-2004)	2·00	2·25
1339	85c. Welshman Mabhena (1924-2010)	2·25	2·50
1340	$1 Robson Dayford Manyika (1936-85)	2·25	2·50

253 'Light up 5.30pm'

2012. Life Awareness Road Safety. Multicoloured.
1341	30c. Type **253**	1·00	75
1342	75c. Pickup truck with drunk driver and passengers ('Speed/drunk driving')	2·00	2·25
1343	85c. School child on pedestrian crossing ('Obey the code')	2·25	2·50
1344	$1 Street vendors in road wearing reflective vests ('Visibility')	2·25	2·50

254 Honeydew Ant

2012. Life of Ants and Termites. Multicoloured.
1345	5c. Type **254**	20	15
1346	30c. Philidris ant	1·00	75
1347	30c. Leaf cutter ant	1·00	75
1348	75c. Termite and Matebele soldier ant	2·00	2·25
1349	85c. Carpenter ant	2·25	2·50
1350	$1 Termite habitat	2·25	2·50

No. **MS**1351 is left for miniature sheet not yet received.

255 Rainbow (Ricardo Ribeiro)

2013. 'Eradicating Extreme Poverty and Hunger'. Winning Entries from Stamp Design Competition. Multicoloured.
1352	30c. Type **255**	1·00	75
1353	$1 Hungry child, bowl, maize and pestle and mortar (Russell Easterbrook)	2·25	2·50

256 Landa John Nkomo

2013. Landa John Nkomo (1934-2013, Co-Vice President) Commemoration. Multicoloured.
1354	30c. Type **256**	1·00	75
1355	75c. As older man	2·00	2·25
1356	85c. Type **256**	2·25	2·50
1357	$1 As 75c.	2·25	2·50

POSTAGE DUE STAMPS

D4 Zimbabwe Bird (soapstone sculpture)

1980
D23	**D4**	1c. green	20	1·25
D24	**D4**	2c. blue	20	1·25
D25	**D4**	5c. violet	25	1·25
D26	**D4**	6c. yellow	30	2·00
D27	**D4**	10c. red	40	2·50

D5

1985
D28	**D5**	1c. orange	35	1·25
D29	**D5**	2c. mauve	35	1·25
D30	**D5**	6c. green	70	1·50
D31	**D5**	10c. brown	80	1·50
D32	**D5**	13c. blue	80	1·50

1990. No. D27 surch **25**.
D33	**D4**	25c. on 10c. red	3·00	3·00

D7

1995
D34	**D7**	1c. yellow	10	80
D35	**D7**	2c. orange	10	80
D36	**D7**	5c. mauve	10	80
D37	**D7**	10c. blue	15	80
D38	**D7**	25c. violet	20	60
D39	**D7**	40c. green	30	70
D40	**D7**	60c. orange	45	80
D41	**D7**	$1 brown	55	1·00

D8 Bird Carving

2000
D42	**D8**	1c. black and green	10	65
D43	**D8**	10c. black and blue	10	65
D44	**D8**	50c. black and brown	15	65
D45	**D8**	$1 black and red	20	65
D46	**D8**	$2 black and yellow	30	70
D47	**D8**	$5 black and mauve	50	80
D48	**D8**	$10 black and red	90	1·25

Pt. 1

ZULULAND

A territory of south-eastern Africa, annexed by Great Britain in 1887, and incorporated in Natal in 1897.

12 pence = 1 shilling; 20 shilling = 1 pound.

1888. Stamps of Gt. Britain (Queen Victoria) optd **ZULULAND**.
1	**71**	½d. red	7·50	2·75
2	**57**	1d. lilac	28·00	6·50
3	**73**	2d. green and red	27·00	50·00
4	**74**	2½d. purple on blue	40·00	22·00
5	**75**	3d. purple on yellow	30·00	22·00
6	**76**	4d. green and brown	60·00	75·00
7	**78**	5d. purple and blue	£100	£120
8	**79**	6d. purple on red	21·00	17·00
9	**80**	9d. purple and blue	£120	£130
10	**82**	1s. green	£150	£170
11	-	5s. red (No. 181)	£700	£800

1888. Natal stamps optd **ZULULAND**.
13	**23**	½d. green	28·00	48·00
16	-	6d. lilac (No. 103)	65·00	55·00

3

1894
20	**3**	½d. mauve and green	6·50	6·00
21	**3**	1d. mauve and red	6·00	2·75
22	**3**	2½d. mauve and blue	14·00	9·00
23	**3**	3d. mauve and brown	8·00	3·00
24	**3**	6d. mauve and black	20·00	20·00
25	**3**	1s. green	50·00	38·00
26	**3**	2s.6d. green and black	90·00	£110
27	**3**	4s. green and red	£150	£225
28	**3**	£1 purple on red	£600	£650
29	**3**	£5 purple and black on red	£5500	£1600

visit our shop at 399 Strand

Stanley Gibbons Limited 399 Strand, London, WC2R 0LX +44 (0)20 7836 8444 www.stanleygibbons.com

Scan the QR code to get your FREE APP from Stanley Gibbons or visit stanley-gibbons.com/app

LOOKING FOR THAT ELUSIVE STAMP?

?

Send a copy of your wants list or call:
Andrew Mansi
on 020 7557 4455
email
amansi@stanleygibbons.com

Est 1856

STANLEY GIBBONS

Stanley Gibbons Limited
399 Strand, London,
WC2R 0LX
+44 (0)20 7836 8444
www.stanleygibbons.com

Index

Stanley Gibbons
Commonwealth Department

BY APPOINTMENT TO HER
MAJESTY THE QUEEN
PHILATELISTS
STANLEY GIBBONS LTD
LONDON

LOOKING FOR THAT ELUSIVE STAMP?

Send a copy of your wants list or call: Andrew Mansi on 020 7557 4455 email amansi@stanleygibbons.com
or Brian Lucas on 020 7557 4418 email blucas@stanleygibbons.com

Est 1856
STANLEY GIBBONS

Stanley Gibbons Limited
399 Strand, London, WC2R 0LX
+44 (0)20 7836 8444
www.stanleygibbons.com

Stanley Gibbons
Stamp Catalogues

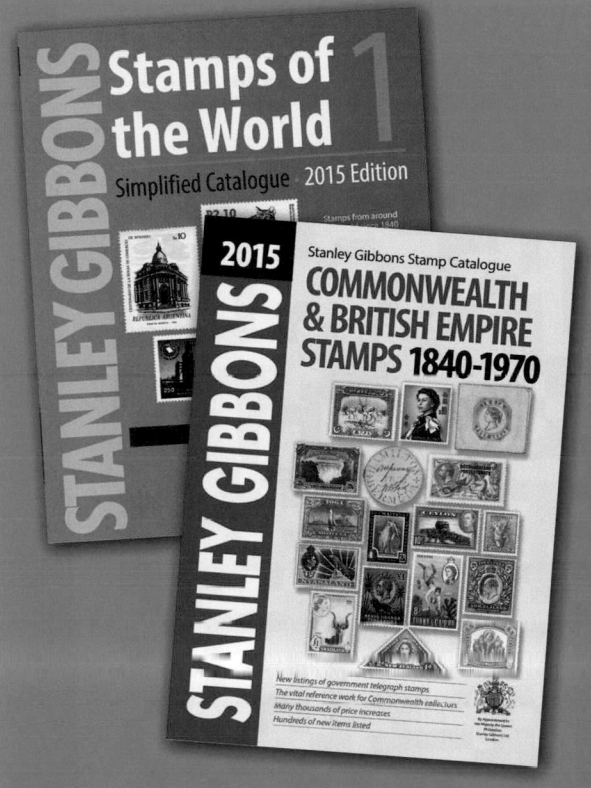

1 Commonwealth & British Empire Stamps 1840–1970 (117th edition, 2015)

Commonwealth Country Catalogues

Australia & Dependencies (9th Edition, 2014)
Bangladesh, Pakistan & Sri Lanka (2nd edition, 2010)
Belize, Guyana, Trinidad & Tobago (2nd edition, 2013)
Brunei, Malaysia & Singapore (4th edition, 2013)
Canada (5th edition, 2014)
Central Africa (2nd edition, 2008)
Cyprus, Gibraltar & Malta (3rd edition, 2011)
East Africa with Egypt & Sudan (3rd edition, 2014)
Eastern Pacific (2nd edition, 2011)
Falkland Islands (6th edition, 2013)
Hong Kong (4th edition, 2013)
India (including Convention & Feudatory States) (4th edition, 2013)
Indian Ocean (2nd edition, 2012)
Ireland (4th edition, 2011)
Leeward Islands (2nd edition, 2012)
New Zealand (5th edition, 2014)
Northern Caribbean, Bahamas & Bermuda (3rd edition, 2013)
St. Helena & Dependencies (5th edition, 2014)
Southern Africa (2nd edition, 2008)
Southern & Central Africa (1st edition, 2011)
West Africa (2nd edition, 2012)
Western Pacific (3rd edition, 2014)
Windward Islands & Barbados (2nd edition, 2012)

Stamps of the World 2015

Volume 1 Abu Dhabi – Charkhari
Volume 2 Chile – Georgia
Volume 3 German Commands – Jasdan
Volume 4 Jersey – New Republic
Volume 5 New South Wales – Singapore
Volume 6 Sirmoor – Zululand

We also produce a range of thematic catalogues for use with Stamps of the World.

Great Britain Catalogues

Collect British Stamps (65th edition, 2014)
Collect Channel Islands & Isle of Man (29th edition, 2014)
Great Britain Concise Stamp Catalogue (29th edition, 2014)

Great Britain Specialised

Volume 1 *Queen Victoria* (16th edition, 2012)
Volume 2 *King Edward VII to King George VI* (13th edition, 2009)
Volume 3 *Queen Elizabeth II Pre-decimal issues* (12th edition, 2011)
Volume 4 *Queen Elizabeth II Decimal Definitive Issues – Part 1* (10th edition, 2008)
Queen Elizabeth II Decimal Definitive Issues – Part 2 (10th edition, 2010)

Foreign Countries

2 *Austria & Hungary* (7th edition, 2009)
3 *Balkans* (5th edition, 2009)
4 *Benelux* (6th edition, 2010)
5 *Czech Republic, Slovakia & Poland* (7th edition, 2012)
6 *France* (7th edition, 2010)
7 *Germany* (10th edition, 2012)
8 *Italy & Switzerland* (8th edition, 2013)
9 *Portugal & Spain* (6th edition, 2011)
10 *Russia* (7th edition, 2014)
11 *Scandinavia* (7th edition, 2013)
15 *Central America* (3rd edition, 2007)
16 *Central Asia* (4th edition, 2006)
17 *China* (10th edition, 2014)
18 *Japan & Korea* (5th edition, 2008)
19 *Middle East* (7th edition, 2009)
20 *South America* (4th edition, 2008)
21 *South-East Asia* (5th edition, 2012)
22 *United States of America* (7th edition, 2010)

We have catalogues to suit every aspect of stamp collecting

Our catalogues cover stamps issued from across the globe - from the Penny Black to the latest issues. Whether you're a specialist in a certain reign or a thematic collector, we should have something to suit your needs. All catalogues include the famous SG numbering system, making it as easy as possible to find the stamp you're looking for.

To order, call 01425 472 363 or for our full range of catalogues, visit www.stanleygibbons.com

Est 1856
STANLEY GIBBONS

Stanley Gibbons Limited
7 Parkside, Christchurch Road, Ringwood, Hants, BH24 3SH
+44 (0)1425 472 363
www.stanleygibbons.com

Stanley Gibbons Goes Mobile

Scan the QR code below to get your **FREE APPS** from Stanley Gibbons

The Stanley Gibbons and Gibbons Stamp Monthly Apps are available now for Apple devices and are completely free to download, giving you the platform to buy 'virtual' editions of our catalogues and the UK's bestselling stamp magazine.

Find out more by visiting **www.stanleygibbons.com/app** or by scanning the QR code with your mobile device.

Est 1856
STANLEY GIBBONS

Stanley Gibbons Limited
7 Parkside, Christchurch Road, Ringwood, Hants, BH24 3SH
+44 (0)1425 472 363
www.stanleygibbons.com

Stanley Gibbons

www.stanleygibbons.com

BY APPOINTMENT TO HER
MAJESTY THE QUEEN
PHILATELISTS
STANLEY GIBBONS LTD
LONDON

Stanley Gibbons - the home of stamp collecting since 1856 and today's market leader for all your philatelic needs.

For the best quality in stamps, catalogues, albums and all other accessories log on to our website today and explore our unrivalled range of products all available at the touch of a button.

visit **www.stanleygibbons.com**

Est 1856
STANLEY
GIBBONS

Stanley Gibbons Limited
399 Strand, London, WC2R 0LX
+44 (0)20 7836 8444
www.stanleygibbons.com

Britannia Albums

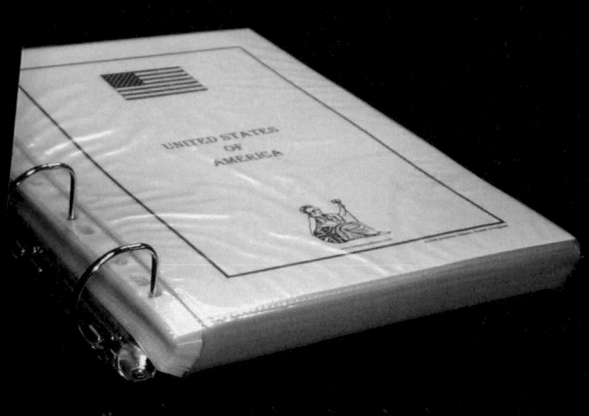

The perfect solution for housing stamps from any country

From Afghanistan to Zimbabwe...

Whichever country you collect, the Britannia range of albums contains something suitable for you. The binders are made from the best quality vinyl and come with polypropylene pockets, complete with 160gsm white acid free paper used are top quality products.

Each A4 (210mm x 297mm) page is specifically designed, having a space for each stamp with the date, title, and value of the stamp shown. These albums are compiled using the Scott (rather than SG) numbering system. Binders are available in blue or maroon.

There are over 900 volumes available including single countries, states, used abroad and omnibus issues. If you are looking for something in particular or would like a full list of Britannia albums, please contact us on the details at the bottom of the page and we will do all we can to help.

Please note: Delivery of these items will take a minimum of 21 days and are only printed to order. If you are unsure about the content of these albums, please contact us prior to ordering.

For a list of Britannia albums, visit **www.stanleygibbons.com/britannia**

Est 1856
STANLEY GIBBONS

Stanley Gibbons Limited
7 Parkside, Christchurch Road, Ringwood, Hants, BH24 3SH
+44 (0)1425 472 363
www.stanleygibbons.com

Stanley Gibbons
Country Albums

- *Stanley Gibbons Standard and Luxury Country Albums*

- *Perfect for storing and protecting your collection*

- *Prices start from £62.75 for the standard range*

For our full range check the website stanleygibbons.com

To order, call **0800 611 622** or for our full range of albums, **visit www.stanleygibbons.com**

Est 1856
STANLEY GIBBONS

Stanley Gibbons Limited
7 Parkside, Christchurch Road, Ringwood, Hants, BH24 3SH
+44 (0)1425 472 363
www.stanleygibbons.com

Gibbons Stamp Monthly

The first choice for stamp collectors since 1890

Subscribe TODAY!

" The premier philatelic magazine available anywhere – it's difficult to improve on perfection "

– Everett L. Parker, Global Stamp News

Gibbons Stamp Monthly offers you:

- Great value, usually 20-30% more pages than other stamp magazines
- More news
- More articles
- More on Great Britain and Commonwealth
- A magazine written by stamp collectors for stamp collectors
- Comprehensive catalogue supplement every month

The UK's **No.1** stamp magazine

By subscribing you will also receive:

- Monthly subscriber letters offering big discounts off Stanley Gibbons products
- Savings on the latest Stanley Gibbons catalogues
- Free access to GSM online with postal subscription

3 easy ways to subscribe

 Subscription Hotline **0800 611 622** (UK)
+44 1425 472 363 (Overseas)

 subscriptions@ stanleygibbons.com

 Complete the form facing this page and return to:
Gibbons Stamp Monthly, Stanley Gibbons Publications,
FREEPOST (BH252), Ringwood, Hampshire, BH24 3BR, UK

www.stanleygibbons.com

 Est 1856 **STANLEY GIBBONS**
A Stanley Gibbons Publication